S0-BSL-870

Precept Ministries
P.O. Box 182218
Chattanooga, TN 37422

Inductive study material in *The International Inductive Study Bible* compiled by K. Arthur and the staff of Precept Ministries.

Precept Ministries exists to serve the body of Jesus Christ by providing inductive Bible studies for individuals, churches, home study groups, and mission organizations.

over, interior design, and typesetting by Koechel Peterson and Associates, Inc.
bernacle and Temple illustrations by Stanley C. Stein

THE INTERNATIONAL INDUCTIVE STUDY BIBLE
© 1995 Precept Ministries
Published by Harvest House Publishers
075 Arrowsmith
ugene, Oregon 97402

taloging-in-Publication Data
ational. 1995.
nal inductive study bible : IISB, New International Version
m.
8-7 (hardcover)
-9 (leather : alk. paper)
5 (bonded)
(hardcover indexed)
(bonded indexed)
leather indexed)

95-1098
CIP

/ 01 00 99 98 97 96 95

THE INTERNATIONAL INDUCTIVE STUDY BIBLE

IISB

NEW INTERNATIONAL VERSION

HARVEST HOUSE PUBLISHERS
EUGENE, OREGON

DEDICATED

to the church of the
living God…to those
whose passion is to be
"*the pillar and foundation
of the truth.*"
1 TIMOTHY 3:15

THE INTERNATIONAL INDUCTIVE STUDY BIBLE

IISB

NEW INTERNATIONAL VERSION

HARVEST HOUSE PUBLISHERS
EUGENE, OREGON

DEDICATED

to the church of the
living God…to those
whose passion is to be
*"the pillar and foundation
of the truth."*
1 Timothy 3:15

Precept Ministries
P.O. Box 182218
Chattanooga, TN 37422

Inductive study material in *The International Inductive Study Bible* compiled by K. Arthur and the staff of Precept Ministries.

Precept Ministries exists to serve the body of Jesus Christ by providing inductive Bible studies for individuals, churches, home study groups, and mission organizations.

Cover, interior design, and typesetting by Koechel Peterson and Associates, Inc.
Tabernacle and Temple illustrations by Stanley C. Stein

THE INTERNATIONAL INDUCTIVE STUDY BIBLE
© 1995 Precept Ministries
Published by Harvest House Publishers
1075 Arrowsmith
Eugene, Oregon 97402

Library of Congress Cataloging-in-Publication Data
Bible. English. New International. 1995.
The international inductive study bible : IISB, New International Version
p. cm.
ISBN 1-56507-298-7 (hardcover)
ISBN 1-56507-350-9 (leather : alk. paper)
ISBN 1-56507-349-5 (bonded)
ISBN 1-56507-359-2 (hardcover indexed)
ISBN 1-56507-360-6 (bonded indexed)
ISBN 1-56507-361-4 (leather indexed)
I. Title.
BS195.N37 1995 95-1098
220.5'208—dc20 CIP

2 3 4 5 6 7 8 9 / 01 00 99 98 97 96 95

Printed in the United States of America.

PREFACE

THE NEW INTERNATIONAL VERSION is a completely new translation of the Holy Bible made by over a hundred scholars working directly from the best available Hebrew, Aramaic and Greek texts. It had its beginning in 1965 when, after several years of exploratory study by committees from the Christian Reformed Church and the National Association of Evangelicals, a group of scholars met at Palos Heights, Illinois, and concurred in the need for a new translation of the Bible in contemporary English. This group, though not made up of official church representatives, was transdenominational. Its conclusion was endorsed by a large number of leaders from many denominations who met in Chicago in 1966.

Responsibility for the new version was delegated by the Palos Heights group to a self-governing body of fifteen, the Committee on Bible Translation, composed for the most part of biblical scholars from colleges, universities and seminaries. In 1967 the New York Bible Society (now the International Bible Society) generously undertook the financial sponsorship of the project—a sponsorship that made it possible to enlist the help of many distinguished scholars. The fact that participants from the United States, Great Britain, Canada, Australia and New Zealand worked together gave the project its international scope. That they were from many denominations— including Anglican, Assemblies of God, Baptist, Brethren, Christian Reformed, Church of Christ, Evangelical Free, Lutheran, Mennonite, Methodist, Nazarene, Presbyterian, Wesleyan and other churches—helped to safeguard the translation from sectarian bias.

How it was made helps to give the New International Version its distinctiveness. The translation of each book was assigned to a team of scholars. Next, one of the Intermediate Editorial Committees revised the initial translation, with constant reference to the Hebrew, Aramaic or Greek. Their work then went to one of the General Editorial Committees, which checked it in detail and made another thorough revision. This revision in turn was carefully reviewed by the Committee on Bible Translation, which made further changes and then released the final version for publication. In this way the entire Bible underwent three revisions, during each of which the translation was examined for its faithfulness to the original languages and for its English style. All this involved many thousands of hours of research and discussion regarding the meaning of the texts and the precise way of putting them into English. It may well be that no other translation has been made by a more thorough process of review and revision from committee to committee than this one.

From the beginning of the project, the Committee on Bible Translation held to certain goals for the New International Version: that it would be an accurate translation and one that would have clarity and literary quality and so prove suitable for public and private reading, teaching, preaching, memorizing and liturgical use. The Committee also sought to preserve some measure of continuity with the long tradition of translating the Scriptures into English.

In working toward these goals, the translators were united in their commitment to the authority and infallibility of the Bible as God's Word in written form. They believe that it contains the divine answer to the deepest needs of humanity, that it sheds unique light on our path in a dark world, and that it sets forth the way to our eternal well-being.

The first concern of the translators has been the accuracy of the translation and its fidelity to the thought of the biblical writers. They have weighed the significance of the lexical and grammatical details of the Hebrew, Aramaic and Greek texts. At the same time, they have striven for more than a word-for-word translation. Because thought patterns and syntax differ from language to language, faithful communication of the meaning of the writers of the Bible demands frequent modifications in sentence structure and constant regard for the contextual meanings of words.

A sensitive feeling for style does not always accompany scholarship. Accordingly the Committee on Bible Translation submitted the developing version to a number of stylistic consultants. Two of them read every book of both Old and New Testaments twice—once before and once after the last major revision—and made invaluable suggestions. Samples of the translation were tested for clarity and ease of reading by various kinds of people—young and old, highly educated and less well educated, ministers and laymen.

Concern for clear and natural English—that the New International Version should be idiomatic but not idiosyncratic, contemporary but not dated—motivated the translators and consultants. At the same time, they tried to reflect the differing styles of the biblical writers. In view of the international use of English, the translators sought to avoid obvious Americanisms on the one hand and obvious Anglicisms on the other. A British edition reflects the comparatively few differences of significant idiom and of spelling.

As for the traditional pronouns "thou," "thee" and "thine" in reference to the Deity, the translators judged that to use these archaisms (along with the old verb forms such as "doest," "wouldest" and "hadst") would violate accuracy in translation. Neither Hebrew, Aramaic nor Greek uses special pronouns for the persons of the Godhead. A present-day translation is not enhanced by forms that in the time of the King James Version were used in everyday speech, whether referring to God or man.

For the Old Testament the standard Hebrew text, the Masoretic Text as published in the latest editions of *Biblia Hebraica*, was used throughout. The Dead Sea Scrolls contain material bearing on an earlier stage of the Hebrew text. They were consulted, as were the Samaritan Pentateuch and the ancient scribal traditions relating to textual changes. Sometimes a variant Hebrew reading in the margin of the Masoretic Text was followed instead of the text itself. Such instances, being variants within the Masoretic tradition, are not specified by footnotes. In rare cases, words in the consonantal text were divided differently from the way they appear in the Masoretic Text. Footnotes indicate this. The translators also consulted the more important early versions—the Septuagint; Aquila, Symmachus and Theodotion; the Vulgate; the Syriac Peshitta; the Targums; and for the Psalms the *Juxta Hebraica* of Jerome. Readings from these versions were occasionally followed where the Masoretic Text seemed doubtful and where accepted principles of textual criticism showed that one or more of these textual witnesses appeared to provide the correct reading. Such instances are footnoted. Sometimes vowel letters and vowel signs did not, in the judgment of the translators, represent the correct vowels for the original consonantal text. Accordingly some words were read with a different set of vowels. These instances are usually not indicated by footnotes.

The Greek text used in translating the New Testament was an eclectic one. No other piece of ancient literature has such an abundance of manuscript witnesses as does the New Testament. Where existing manuscripts differ, the translators made their choice of readings according to accepted principles of New Testament textual criticism. Footnotes call attention to places where there was uncertainty about what the original text was. The best current printed texts of the Greek New Testament were used.

There is a sense in which the work of translation is never wholly finished. This applies to all great literature and uniquely so to the Bible. In 1973 the New Testament in the New International Version was published. Since then, suggestions for corrections and revisions have been received from various sources. The Committee on Bible Translation carefully considered the suggestions and adopted a number of them. These were incorporated in the first printing of the entire Bible in 1978. Additional revisions were made by the Committee on Bible Translation in 1983 and appear in printings after that date.

As in other ancient documents, the precise meaning of the biblical texts is sometimes uncertain. This is more often the case with the Hebrew and Aramaic texts than with the Greek text. Although archaeological and linguistic discoveries in this century aid in understanding difficult passages, some uncertainties remain. The more significant of these have been called to the reader's attention in the footnotes.

In regard to the divine name *YHWH*, commonly referred to as the *Tetragrammaton*, the translators adopted the device used in most English versions of rendering that name as "LORD" in capital letters to distinguish it from *Adonai*, another Hebrew word rendered "Lord," for which small letters are used. Wherever the two names stand together in the Old Testament as a compound name of God, they are rendered "Sovereign LORD."

Because for most readers today the phrases "the LORD of hosts" and "God of hosts" have little meaning, this version renders them "the LORD Almighty" and "God Almighty." These renderings convey the sense of the Hebrew, namely, "he who is sovereign over all the 'hosts' (powers) in heaven and on earth, especially over the 'hosts' (armies) of Israel." For readers unacquainted with Hebrew this does not make clear the distinction between *Sabaoth* ("hosts" or "Almighty") and *Shaddai* (which can also be translated "Almighty"), but the latter occurs infrequently and is always footnoted. When *Adonai* and *YHWH Sabaoth* occur together, they are rendered "the Lord, the LORD Almighty."

As for other proper nouns, the familiar spellings of the King James Version are generally retained. Names traditionally spelled with "ch," except where it is final, are usually spelled in this translation with "k" or "c," since the biblical languages do not have the sound that "ch" frequently indicates in English—for example, in *chant*. For well-known names such as Zechariah, however, the traditional spelling has been retained. Variation in the spelling of names in the original languages has usually not been indicated. Where a person or place has two or more different names in the Hebrew, Aramaic or Greek texts, the more familiar one has generally been used, with footnotes where needed.

To achieve clarity the translators sometimes supplied words not in the original texts but required by the context. If there was uncertainty about such material, it is enclosed in brackets. Also for the sake of clarity or style, nouns, including some proper nouns, are sometimes substituted for pronouns, and vice versa. And though the Hebrew writers often shifted back and forth between first, second and third personal pronouns without change of antecedent, this translation often makes them uniform, in accordance with English style and without the use of footnotes.

Poetical passages are printed as poetry, that is, with indentation of lines and with separate stanzas. These are generally designed to reflect the structure of Hebrew poetry. This poetry is normally characterized by parallelism in balanced lines. Most of the poetry in the Bible is in the Old Testament, and scholars differ regarding the scansion of Hebrew lines. The translators determined the stanza divisions for the most part by analysis of the subject matter. The stanzas therefore serve as poetic paragraphs.

As an aid to the reader, italicized sectional headings are inserted in most of the books. They are not to be regarded as part of the NIV text, are not for oral reading, and are not intended to dictate the interpretation of the sections they head.

The footnotes in this version are of several kinds, most of which need no explanation. Those giving alternative translations begin with "Or" and generally introduce the alternative with the last word preceding it in the text, except when it is a single-word alternative; in poetry quoted in a footnote a slant mark indicates a line division. Footnotes introduced by "Or" do not have uniform significance. In some cases two possible translations were considered to have about equal validity. In other cases, though the translators were convinced that the translation in the text was correct, they judged that another interpretation was possible and of sufficient importance to be represented in a footnote.

In the New Testament, footnotes that refer to uncertainty regarding the original text are introduced by "Some manuscripts" or similar expressions. In the Old Testament, evidence for the reading chosen is given first and evidence for the alternative is added after a semicolon (for example: Septuagint; Hebrew *father*). In such notes the term "Hebrew" refers to the Masoretic Text.

It should be noted that minerals, flora and fauna, architectural details, articles of clothing and jewelry, musical instruments and other articles cannot always be identified with precision. Also measures of capacity in the biblical period are particularly uncertain (see the table of weights and measures following the text).

Like all translations of the Bible, made as they are by imperfect man, this one undoubtedly falls short of its goals. Yet we are grateful to God for the extent to which he has enabled us to realize these goals and for the strength he has given us and our colleagues to complete our task. We offer this version of the Bible to him in whose name and for whose glory it has been made. We pray that it will lead many into a better understanding of the Holy Scriptures and a fuller knowledge of Jesus Christ the incarnate Word, of whom the Scriptures so faithfully testify.

The Committee on Bible Translation

June 1978
(Revised August 1983)

Names of the translators and editors may be secured from the International Bible Society, translation sponsors of the New International Version, P.O. Box 62970, Colorado Springs, Colorado, 80962-2970 U.S.A.

Welcome to The International Inductive Study Bible

Do you long to know God? Do you yearn for a deep and abiding relationship with him? Do you want to live the Christian life faithfully—and to know what He requires of you? If so, *The International Inductive Study Bible* is designed for you.

God reveals himself through his Word. Through it, he shows us how to live. Jesus made it clear: "Man does not live on bread alone, but on every word that comes from the mouth of God" (Matthew 4:4). And where do we find this divine bread? In the Scriptures.

As you study this Bible with the help of the Holy Spirit, and live out the truths that God reveals to you, you will discover new stability, strength, and confidence. You will be able to say with the prophet Jeremiah: "When your words came I ate them; they were my joy and heart's delight" (Jeremiah 15:16).

Today, many people are convinced they cannot know truth for themselves. A babble of voices surrounds us claiming to know and interpret God's truth for us. Which voices are right? Which are wrong? How can you discern the true from the counterfeit unless you spend time with God and his Word?

Most Christians have been encouraged to study the Word of God, yet many have never been shown how. Others even feel inadequate to do so because they are not ministers or seminary students or scholars. Nothing could be further from the truth.

In fact, if you want to satisfy your hunger and thirst to know God and his Word in a deeper way, you must do more than merely read Scripture and study what someone else has said about it. Just as no one else can eat and digest your food for you, so no one else can feed on God's Word for you. You must interact with the text yourself, absorbing its truths and letting God engrave his truth on your heart and mind and life.

That is the very heart of inductive study: seeing truth for yourself, discerning what it means, and applying that truth to your life. In his inspired Word, God has given us everything we need to know about life and godliness. But he doesn't stop there. He gives every believer a resident teacher—the Holy Spirit—who guides us into his truth.

The Bible is unlike any other book. It is supernatural. It is complete in itself. The Bible needs no other books or truths to supplement it. In inductive study the Bible becomes its own commentary, and it can be understood by any believer.

Anyone who will take the time can see and understand what God has given us in his Word and how it applies to us today.

CONTENTS

The Old Testament

The New Testament

Bible Study Helps

HOW TO USE THE INTERNATIONAL INDUCTIVE STUDY BIBLE

IISB

HOW TO USE THE INDUCTIVE STUDY APPROACH

If you know there is more to the Word of God than you have discovered so far...

- If you sense there must be concrete answers to the complexities of life...
- If you want a bedrock faith that keeps you from being tossed around by conflicting philosophies in the world and the church...
- If you want to be able to face the uncertainties of the future without fear...

...then *The International Inductive Study Bible* is designed for you.

God's eternal, infallible Word is your guidebook for all of life, and inductive study gives you the key to understanding that guide.

Inductive study, a method anyone can use, involves three skills: *observation, interpretation,* and *application.*

OBSERVATION — Discover What It Says!

Observation teaches you to see precisely what the passage says. It is the basis for accurate interpretation and correct application. Observation answers the question: What does the passage say?

INTERPRETATION — Discover What It Means!

Interpretation answers the question: What does the passage mean?

APPLICATION — Discover How It Works!

Application answers the question: What does it mean to me personally? What truths can I put into practice? What changes should I make in my life?

When you know what God says, what he means, and how to put his truths into practice, you will be equipped for every circumstance of life. Ultimately, the goal of personal Bible study is a transformed life and a deep and abiding relationship with Jesus Christ.

The following ten steps provide the basis for inductive study. As you take these steps, observation, interpretation, and application will sometimes happen simultaneously. God can give you insight at any point in your study, so be sensitive to his leading. When words or passages make an impression on you, stop for a moment and meditate on what God has shown you. Record your personal notes and insights in the margin so that you can remember what you've learned.

One of the most valuable aspects of the *IISB* is its wide-margin format, which has been specifically designed to enable you to easily keep a record of what God personally reveals to you from his Word. Some people are hesitant to mark in their Bibles, but this interactive Bible has been designed with marking in mind.

As you study the Bible chapter by chapter and book by book, you will grow in your ability to comprehend the whole counsel of God. In the future, you will be able to refer to your notes again and again as you study portions of Scripture and grow in your knowledge of him.

OBSERVATION

Discover What It Says!

STEP ONE

BEGIN WITH PRAYER

Prayer is often the missing element in Bible study. You are about to learn the most effective method of Bible study there is. Yet apart from the work of the Holy Spirit, that's all it will be—a method. It is the indwelling Holy Spirit who guides us into all truth, who takes the things of God and reveals them to us. Always ask God to teach you as you open the Scriptures.

STEP TWO

ASK THE "5 W'S AND AN H"

As you study any passage of Scripture, any book of the Bible, train yourself to constantly ask: *Who? What? When? Where? Why? How?* These questions are the building blocks of precise observation, which is essential for accurate interpretation. Many times Scripture is misinterpreted because the context isn't carefully observed.

When we rush into interpretation without laying the vital foundation of observation, our understanding becomes colored by our presuppositions—what we think, what we feel, or what other people have said. We must be careful not to distort the Scriptures to our own destruction (2 Peter 3:16).

Accurate answers to the following questions will help assure correct interpretation.

Who *is speaking? Who is this about? Who are the main characters?* For example, look at the sample passage from 1 Peter 5 (see page IISB-19). In this chapter, "I" is speaking. Verse 1 tells us that "I" is a fellow elder, a witness of the sufferings of Christ, and one who will share in the glory to follow. From reading this and previous chapters (the context), you recognize that the "I" is Peter, the author of this epistle.

And, ***to whom*** *is he speaking?* Verse 1 refers to "the elders," verse 5 to "young men," and verse 6 to "yourselves" (the recipients of the epistle).

What *is the subject or event covered in the chapter? What do you learn about the people, the event, or the teaching from the text? What instructions are given?* In 1 Peter 5:2, Peter instructs the elders to be shepherds of God's flock and serve as overseers.

When *do or will the events occur? When did or will something happen to a particular person, people, or nation? When* is a key question in determining the progression of events. In 1 Peter 5:4, we learn that "when the Chief Shepherd appears," the elders will receive their "crown of glory that will never fade away."

Where *did or will this happen? Where was it said?* In 1 Peter 5, the only reference to a place is in verse 13, where there is a greeting from "she who is in Babylon."

Why *is something being said or mentioned? Why would or will this happen? Why at this time? Why this person?* First Peter 5:12 explains why and how Peter wrote this epistle, establishing the book's purpose: to encourage and testify that this is the true grace of God, that they may stand fast (or firm) in it.

***How** will it happen? How is it to be done? How is it illustrated?* In 1 Peter 5:2, note *how* the elders are to exercise oversight: voluntarily and eagerly, according to the will of God.

Every time you study a passage of the Bible, you should keep the "5 W's and an H" in mind. Don't be concerned if you can't find the answer to each question every time. Remember, there are many types of literature in the Bible and not all the questions will apply. As you ask *what, when, who, where, why,* and *how,* make notes in the margin of your Bible. Meditate on the truths God reveals to you. Think how they apply to you. This will keep your study from becoming an intellectual pursuit of knowledge for its own sake.

STEP *T*HREE

MARK KEY WORDS AND PHRASES

A key word is one that is essential to the text. It might be a noun, a descriptive word, or an action that plays a part in conveying the author's message. A key word or phrase is one which, when removed, leaves the passage devoid of meaning. Often key words and phrases are repeated in order to convey the author's point or purpose for writing. They may be repeated throughout a chapter, a segment of a book, or the book as a whole. For example, notice that some form of the word *suffering* is used three times in 1 Peter 5.

As you mark key words, ask the same *who, what, when, where, why,* and *how* questions of them as you did of the passage as a whole. For example, *who* suffers?, *what* caused the suffering?, etc.

Key words can be marked in several ways:

~ *Through the use of symbols.*

~ *Through the use of colors.* Colored pencils and multicolored ballpoint pens with fine tips work best.

FAITH HUMILITY GRACE

~ *Through a combination of colors and symbols.*

CHRIST SUFFERING

The value of a distinctive marking system cannot be overestimated. Whichever system you choose, mark each key word the same way every time you observe it. Then, in future study, the visual impact of your marks will help you track key subjects and quickly identify significant truths throughout Scripture. To be sure that you are consistent, list key words, symbols, and color codes on an index card and use it as a bookmark in your Bible.

Be sure to mark pronouns (*I, you, he, she, it, we, our,* and so on) and synonyms (words that have the same meaning in the context) the same way you mark the words to which they refer. For example, a synonym for the devil in 1 Peter 5:8 is "adversary." The pronoun "him" in verse 9 also refers to the devil. Notice how marking the synonym "adversary" for the devil gives additional insight into his nature.

STEP *F*OUR

LOOK FOR LISTS

Making lists can be one of the most enlightening things you do as you study a section of Scripture. Lists reveal truths and highlight

THE IISB MARKING APPROACH

1 PETER 5 ~ SAMPLE A

DEVELOP CHAPTER THEMES

IDENTIFY SIMPLE LISTS

MARK KEY WORDS AND PHRASES

Chapter 5 Theme Be Humble & Self-Controlled; Resist & Stand Fast

5 To the elders among you, I appeal as a fellow elder,[j] a witness[k] of
Christ's sufferings and one who also will share in the glory to be
revealed:[l] 2 Be shepherds of God's flock[m] that is under your care, serving
as overseers—not because you must, but because you are willing, as God
wants you to be; not greedy for money,[n] but eager to serve; 3 not lording it
over[o] those entrusted to you, but being examples[p] to the flock. 4 And when
the Chief Shepherd appears, you will receive the crown of glory[q] that will
never fade away.

5 Young men, in the same way be submissive[r] to those who are older.
All of you, clothe yourselves with humility toward one another, because,

"God opposes the proud
but gives grace to the humble."[bs]

6 Humble yourselves, therefore, under God's mighty hand, that he may
lift you up in due time.[t] 7 Cast all your anxiety on him[u] because he cares
for you.[v]

8 Be self-controlled and alert. Your enemy the devil prowls around[w]
like a roaring lion looking for someone to devour. 9 Resist him,[x] standing firm in the faith,[y] because you know that your brothers throughout
the world are undergoing the same kind of sufferings.[a]

10 And the God of all grace, who called you to his eternal glory[b] in
Christ, after you have suffered a little while, will himself restore you and
make you strong,[c] firm and steadfast. 11 To him be the power for ever
and ever. Amen.[d]

12 With the help of Silas,[ae] whom I regard as a faithful brother, I have
written to you briefly,[f] encouraging you and testifying that this is the
true grace of God. Stand fast in it.

13 She who is in Babylon, chosen together with you, sends you her
greetings, and so does my son Mark.[g] 14 Greet one another with a kiss
of love.[h]

Peace[i] to all of you who are in Christ.

Suffering:
1. Christ suffered.
2. Brothers are suffering.
3. You will suffer.
4. But God will restore, make you strong, firm, and steadfast after you have suffered!

MAKE TOPICAL LISTS FROM KEY WORDS—COMPILE IN THE MARGIN

important concepts. The best way to discover lists in the text is to observe how a key word is described, note what is said about someone or something, or group related thoughts or instructions together. (You may want to develop your lists on a worksheet before transferring them to your Bible.)

1 Peter 5:2, 3, for example, contains a *simple list* instructing the elders how to shepherd their flock. You can number simple lists within the text for easy reference.

Topical lists capture a truth, quality, or characteristic of a specific subject throughout a passage. One way to discover a topical list is to follow a key word through a chapter and note what the text says about the word each time it is used. (You may want to develop your lists on a worksheet before transferring them to the margin of your *IISB*.) See sample A for how a list could be made for the key word "suffering."

As you write your observations on suffering, you will begin to have a better and broader understanding of God's thoughts on this subject. You will learn that:

- Christ suffered
- the brothers in the world are suffering
- the recipients of the letter may also endure suffering

You will also discover that God:

- restores
- makes strong
- makes firm
- makes steadfast those who suffer

The application value of lists such as these is immeasurable. The next time you endure suffering, you will be able to recall more quickly that:

- Christ suffered
- others are suffering
- ultimately God will use suffering to strengthen your own life

Discovering truths that apply to your daily life is what makes lists such an important part of the inductive method.

STEP FIVE

WATCH FOR CONTRASTS AND COMPARISONS

Contrasts and comparisons use highly descriptive language to drive home significant truths and vital lessons. The word pictures they paint make it easier to remember what you've learned.

A *contrast* is a comparison of things that are different or opposite, such as light/darkness or proud/humble. The word "but" often signifies that a contrast is being made. Note contrasts in the text or in the margin of your Bible.

A *comparison* points out similarities and is often indicated by the use of words such as "like," "as," and "as it were." For example, Peter says in 1 Peter 5:8: "Your enemy the devil prowls around *like* a roaring lion." Highlight comparisons in a distinctive way in the text so that you will recognize them immediately when you return to the passage in the future.

STEP SIX

NOTE EXPRESSIONS OF TIME

The relationship of events in time often sheds light on the true meaning of the text. The timing of something can be observed in exact statements such as "on the tenth day of the eleventh month" or "at the feast of Booths." These phrases can be indicated in the margin by drawing a simple clock face (clock symbol) or a similar symbol.

Time is also indicated by words such as *until, then, when,* and *after*. These words show the relationship of one statement or event to another. Marking them will help you see the

THE IISB MARKING APPROACH

1 PETER 5 ~ SAMPLE B

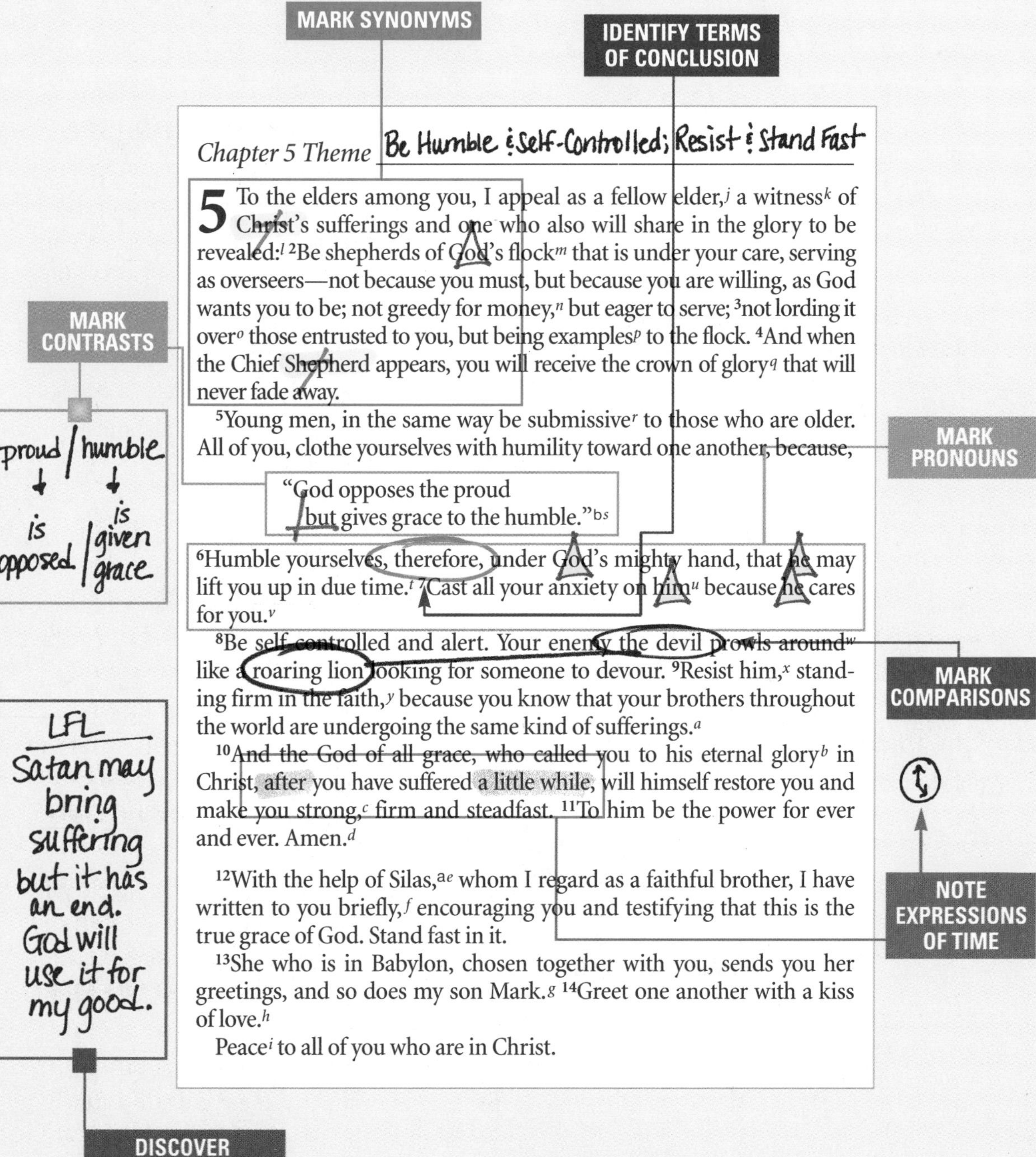

MARK SYNONYMS
IDENTIFY TERMS OF CONCLUSION
Chapter 5 Theme Be Humble & Self-Controlled; Resist & Stand Fast
5 To the elders among you, I appeal as a fellow elder,[j] a witness[k] of
Christ's sufferings and one who also will share in the glory to be
revealed:[l] 2Be shepherds of God's flock[m] that is under your care, serving
as overseers—not because you must, but because you are willing, as God
wants you to be; not greedy for money,[n] but eager to serve; 3not lording it
over[o] those entrusted to you, but being examples[p] to the flock. 4And when
the Chief Shepherd appears, you will receive the crown of glory[q] that will
never fade away.
5Young men, in the same way be submissive[r] to those who are older.
All of you, clothe yourselves with humility toward one another, because,
"God opposes the proud
but gives grace to the humble."[bs]
6Humble yourselves, therefore, under God's mighty hand, that he may
lift you up in due time.[t] 7Cast all your anxiety on him[u] because he cares
for you.[v]
8Be self-controlled and alert. Your enemy the devil prowls around[w]
like a roaring lion looking for someone to devour. 9Resist him,[x] standing firm in the faith,[y] because you know that your brothers throughout
the world are undergoing the same kind of sufferings.[a]
10And the God of all grace, who called you to his eternal glory[b] in
Christ, after you have suffered a little while, will himself restore you and
make you strong,[c] firm and steadfast. 11To him be the power for ever
and ever. Amen.[d]
12With the help of Silas,[ae] whom I regard as a faithful brother, I have
written to you briefly,[f] encouraging you and testifying that this is the
true grace of God. Stand fast in it.
13She who is in Babylon, chosen together with you, sends you her
greetings, and so does my son Mark.[g] 14Greet one another with a kiss
of love.[h]
Peace[i] to all of you who are in Christ.
MARK CONTRASTS
proud / humble
is opposed / is given grace
MARK PRONOUNS
MARK COMPARISONS
NOTE EXPRESSIONS OF TIME
LFL
Satan may bring suffering but it has an end. God will use it for my good.
DISCOVER LESSONS FOR LIFE

sequence of events and lead to accurate interpretation of Scripture.

STEP SEVEN

IDENTIFY TERMS OF CONCLUSION

Terms of conclusion usually follow an important sequence of thought and include words such as *therefore, for this reason,* and *finally.* As the saying goes, when you see a "therefore" (or any term of conclusion), note what it is there for. You should be able to look through the preceding verses and summarize the message. For example, 1 Peter 5:6 says, "Humble yourselves, *therefore*. . . ." If you will look, you will discover that you should humble yourself under the hand of God because God "opposes the proud but gives grace to the humble."

STEP EIGHT

DEVELOP CHAPTER THEMES

The theme of a chapter will center on the main person, event, teaching, or subject of that section of Scripture. Themes are often revealed by reviewing the key words and lists you developed. Try to express the theme as briefly as possible, using words found in the text.

Chapter 5 Theme Be Humble & Self-Controlle

5 To the elders among you, I appeal as a fello
Christ's sufferings and one who also will sl
revealed:[l] 2Be shepherds of God's flock[m] that is u
as overseers—not because you must, but because

For example, possible themes for 1 Peter 5 might be *Appeals to Elders, Young Men, and the Suffering,* or *God Gives Grace to the Humble.* The point of observation is to answer the question: What does the passage say? The theme summarizes the answer. If needed, you can adjust your themes as your study deepens.

STEP NINE

DISCOVER LESSONS FOR LIFE

In the process of observing the text and seeing how God instructed people and dealt with various individuals, the Holy Spirit will bring to your attention truths that God wants you to be aware of and live by in your own life. These "Lessons for Life" can be noted in the margin under the abbreviation "LFL," or you may wish to create a distinctive symbol to mark your Lessons for Life throughout your *IISB*.

STEP TEN

COMPLETE THE AT A GLANCE CHART

The AT A GLANCE chart, found at the end of every book in the *IISB*, provides a compact visual summary of the book that you can return to again and again for easy reference. See the sample AT A GLANCE charts on the following pages.

Record the author of the book. If the author is not mentioned by name, read the introduction for that book. If the author is not mentioned in either place, leave this space blank.

Record the date the book was written. If the date of writing is known, it will be mentioned in the introduction that precedes each book.

Record the key words. If the key words are not already listed on the AT A GLANCE

THE IISB AT A GLANCE CHARTS

1 PETER ~ SAMPLE C

1 PETER AT A GLANCE

Theme of 1 Peter: Suffering and Glory

SEGMENT DIVISIONS		CHAPTER THEMES
	1	Trials Prove Your Faith - Be Holy
	2	You're Chosen: Follow Christ's Example - Submit
	3	
	4	
	5	

Author: Peter

Date: 63 or 64 A.D.

Purpose: To encourage them to stand firm in true grace

Key Words:

- suffering (and all its synonyms)
- grace, gracious gift
- glory, glorious, glorify
- salvation
- Jesus Christ
- God
- Holy Spirit
- called
- chosen, elect
- holy

Complete the AT A GLANCE charts throughout the Bible as you discover book and chapter themes

chart, you will find them listed in the THINGS TO DO section at the beginning of each book.

In order to notice subjects which run throughout the entire Bible, there are some key words or phrases you will want to consistently mark in a distinctive manner. Write these on a card, color code them in the way you intend to mark them throughout your Bible, and use the card as a bookmark.

Some of the key words you will want to mark are listed below:

sin (wickedness, evil, iniquity)
covenant
death (die)
life (live)
repent
love
law
grace
believe (faith)
righteousness (righteous)
holy (holiness)
cry (cries, cried)
Babylon
nations
day of the Lord (that day)
Satan (any reference to the devil,
  spirits, demons, mediums)
any reference to:
  Jesus' first coming
  Jesus' second coming

Copy the chapter themes that you recorded at the beginning of each chapter. Because chapter divisions were added much later than the Bible was originally written, they do not always fall naturally in the text. Occasionally you will find a chapter with more than one theme. If this is true, record both themes.

Look for and record segment divisions. See if any of the chapters can be grouped under a common theme or a common event. This is called a *segment division.* Segment divisions help you see the framework of a book.

The number and types of segment divisions will vary. A book might be divided according to dates, geographical locations, reigns of kings, major characters or events, topics, or doctrines.

When you gain a broad view of a book through its segment divisions, it is easier to understand its content and purpose. The AT A GLANCE chart for the book of John (sample D) shows a number of ways this book could be divided. For example, on the last line under "Segment Divisions," you will notice "Structure of Book." This shows you how John presents his material to achieve his purpose for writing this gospel.

Record the purpose of the book. Discerning the author's purpose for writing and then keeping this purpose in mind while you study the text will help you handle the Word of God accurately. Unless the author specifically states his purpose for writing, as in 1 Peter 5:12 and John 20:31, you will have to discover it by other means:

1. Look for the main subjects covered in the book. These can often be recognized as you study the key repeated words.
2. Watch for any problems that are addressed. It may be that the author's purpose in writing was to deal with these problems.
3. Note exhortations and warnings that are given. These may be the reason for the book.
4. Observe what the author did *not* cover in his writing. When you know what the author covered and what was left unsaid, you are better able to narrow down the real purpose of the book.

Generally the instructions at the beginning of each book in your *IISB* will help you understand how that book might be divided.

The IISB At A Glance Charts

Gospel of John ~ Sample D

John at a Glance

Theme of John: Eternal life through Jesus Christ, Son of God

Segment Divisions: Structure of Book	Portrayals of Jesus Christ	Signs and Miracles	Ministry	Chapter	Chapter Themes
Introduces Jesus as Christ, Son of God	That you may believe Jesus is the Christ, Son of God	Water to wine	To Israel	1	Prologue-The Word / John the Baptist / calling disciples
				2	wedding Cana / cleansing temple
Gives signs that prove Jesus is Christ, Son of God				3	born again
		Heals official's son		4	woman at well / royal official
		Heals lame man		5	father / son
		Feeds 5,000 walks on water		6	bread / feeding 5,000
				7	feast of tabernacles / thirst-drink
				8	adulterous woman / truth sets free
		Heals blind man		9	blind man
				10	sheep / shepherd
		Raises Lazarus from dead		11	raising Lazarus
Decision time	Hour has come		To Disciples	12	dinner at Bethany / King on donkey
Life that belongs to those who believe God	That you may have life			13	last supper / washing-disciples
				14	Father's house / hearts be troubled
				15	remain / vine and branches
				16	Holy Spirit / another helper
				17	Lord's prayer / high-priestly prayer
Obtaining of that life—by death and resurrection			To All Mankind	18	arrest and trial
				19	crucifixion
		Resurrection appearances		20	resurrection
Purpose of life: love and follow			To Disciples	21	do you love me?

Author: John

Date: about A.D. 85

Purpose: that his readers would believe that Jesus is the Christ, God's Son, and thus have eternal life

Key Words:
signs/miracles
believe (believed, faith, trust)
life, live
judge, judging
judgment
condemn, verdict,
condemned, decision
witness, testify
testifying, testimony
true, truth,
truthful, real,
valid, right,
reliable, truly,
surely
king
kingdom
love, loved
works, work
command
fruit, fruitful
remain
ask, pray
prayer, praying

Record the main theme of the book. Once you have listed the theme for each chapter, evaluated the author's purpose for writing, and observed the content of the book chapter by chapter and segment by segment, you will be prepared to determine the theme of the book. What one statement best describes the book as a whole?

Once you have completed the ten steps of observation, you are ready to move into interpretation and application.

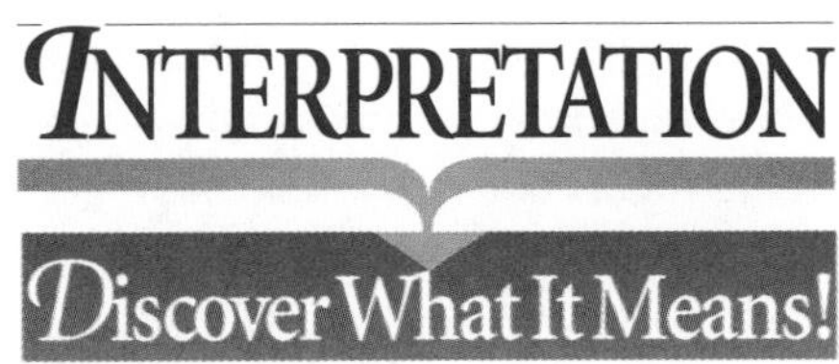
INTERPRETATION
Discover What It Means!

While observation leads to an accurate understanding of what the Word of God *says*, interpretation goes a step further and helps you understand what it *means*. When you accurately interpret the Word of God, you will be able to confidently put its truths into practice in your daily life.

Like many other people, you may have been taught a system of belief before you ever studied God's Word for yourself. Or you may have formed opinions of what the Bible teaches before you carefully examined the Scriptures. As you learn to handle God's Word accurately, you will be able to discern if what you believe is in agreement with Scripture. If this is your desire and you come to the Word of God with a teachable spirit, God will lead you and guide you into all truth.

As you seek to interpret the Bible accurately, the following guidelines will be helpful.

1. **Remember that context rules.**

The word *context* means "that which goes with the text." To understand the context you must be familiar with the Word of God. If you lay the solid foundation of observation, you will be prepared to consider each verse in the light of:

- the surrounding verses
- the book in which it is found
- the entire Word of God

As you study, ask yourself: Is my interpretation of a particular section of Scripture consistent with the theme, purpose, and structure of the book in which it is found? Is it consistent with other Scripture about the same subject, or is there a glaring difference? Am I considering the historic and cultural context of what is being said? Never take a Scripture out of its context to make it say what you want it to say. Discover what the author is saying; don't add to his meaning.

2. **Always seek the full counsel of the Word of God.**

When you know God's Word thoroughly, you will not accept a teaching simply because someone has used one or two isolated verses to support it. Those verses may have been taken out of context, or other important passages might have been overlooked or ignored that would have led to a different understanding. As you read the Bible regularly and extensively, and as you become more familiar with the whole counsel of God's Word, you will be able to discern whether a teaching is biblical or not.

Saturate yourself in the Word of God; it is your safeguard against wrong doctrine.

3. **Remember that Scripture will never contradict Scripture.**

The best interpretation of Scripture is Scripture. Remember, all Scripture is inspired by God; it is God-breathed. Therefore, Scripture will never contradict itself.

The Bible contains all the truth you

will ever need for any situation in life. Sometimes, however, you may find it difficult to reconcile two seemingly contradictory truths taught in Scripture. An example of this would be the sovereignty of God and the responsibility of man. When two or more truths that are clearly taught in the Word seem to be in conflict, remember that we as humans have finite minds. Don't take a teaching to an extreme that God doesn't. Simply humble your heart in faith and believe what God says, even if you can't fully understand or reconcile it at the moment.

4. **Don't base your convictions on an obscure passage of Scripture.**

An obscure passage is one in which the meaning is not easily understood. Because these passages are difficult to understand even when proper principles of interpretation are used, they should not be used as a basis for establishing doctrine.

5. **Interpret Scripture literally.**

The Bible is not a book of mysticism. God spoke to us that we might know truth. Therefore, take the Word of God at face value—in its natural, normal sense. Look for the clear teaching of Scripture, not a hidden meaning. Understand and recognize figures of speech and interpret them accordingly (see Bible Study Helps, page. 2205).

Consider what is being said in the light of its literary style. For example, you will find more similes and metaphors in poetical and prophetic literature than in historical or biographical books. Interpret portions of Scripture according to their literary style.

Some literary styles in the Bible are:

- Historical—Acts
- Prophetic—Revelation
- Biographical—Luke
- Didactic (teaching)—Romans
- Poetic—Psalms
- Epistle (letter)—2 Timothy
- Proverbial—Proverbs

6. **Look for the single meaning of the passage.**

Always try to understand what the author had in mind when you interpret a portion of the Bible. Don't twist verses to support a meaning that is not clearly taught. Unless the author of a particular book indicates that there is another meaning to what he says, let the passage speak for itself.

APPLICATION

Discover How It Works!

No matter how much you know *about* God's Word, if you don't apply what you learn, Scripture will never benefit your life. To be a hearer of the Word and not a doer is to deceive yourself (James 1:22-25). This is why application is so vital. Observation and interpretation are the "hearing" of God's Word. With *application*, you will be transformed into Christ's image. Application is the embracing of the truth, the "doing" of God's Word. It is this process which allows God to work in your life.

Second Timothy 3:16, 17 says: "All Scripture is God-breathed and is useful for teaching, rebuking, correcting and training in righteousness, so that the man of God may be thoroughly equipped for every good work." Here is the key to application: Apply Scripture in the light of its teaching, rebuking, correcting, and instructions on life.

Teaching (doctrine) is what the Word of God says on any particular subject. That teaching, whatever the subject, is always true. Therefore, everything that God says in his Bible about any given subject is absolute truth.

The first step in application is to find out what the Word of God says on any particular subject through accurate observation and correct interpretation of the text. Once you understand what the Word of God teaches, you are then obligated before God to accept that truth and to live by it. When you have adjusted any false concepts or teaching you may have believed, and embraced the truth revealed in God's Word, then you have *applied* what you have learned.

Rebuking exposes areas in your thinking and behavior that do not align with God's Word. Rebuking is finding out where you have thought wrongly or have not been doing what God says is right. The application of rebuking is to accept it and agree with God, acknowledging where you are wrong in thought or in behavior. This is how you are set free from unbelief, from sin.

Correcting is the next step in application, and often the most difficult. Many times we can see what is wrong, but we are reluctant to take the necessary steps to correct it. God has not left you without help or without answers in this step of correcting what is wrong. Sometimes the answers are difficult to find, but they are always there, and any child of God who wants to please his or her Father will be shown by the Spirit of God how to do so.

Many times correction comes by simply confessing and forsaking what is wrong. Other times, God gives very definite steps to take. An example of this is in Matthew 18:15-17, in which God tells us how to approach a brother when he sins. When you apply correction to your actions and attitudes, God will work in you to do his good purpose (Philippians 2:13). Joy will follow obedience.

Training in righteousness: Although God's Word is profitable for rebuking and correcting, the Bible was also given to us as a handbook for living. As we spend time studying his Word, God equips us through:

- teachings
- commands
- promises
- encouragements
- warnings
- and the lives of biblical characters and God's dealings with man

Scripture has everything you need to meet any and all situations of life, so that you "may be thoroughly equipped for every good work." The most effective application takes place as you go before the Lord and talk with him about those things that you have read, studied, seen, and heard.

INSIGHTS ON APPLYING SCRIPTURE

In applying Scripture to your life, the following questions may be helpful:

1. **What does the passage teach?** Is it general or specific? Does it apply only to specific people? To a cultural problem of the day? To a certain time in history? Has it been superseded by a broader teaching? For example, in the Old Testament, Jews were not allowed to eat certain foods or to wear a certain combination of materials. Are those prohibitions applicable to Christians today?

2. **Does this section of Scripture expose any error in my beliefs or in my behavior?** Are there any commandments that I have not obeyed? Are there any wrong attitudes or motives in my life that the Scriptures bring to light?

3. **What is God's instruction to me as his child?** Are there any new truths to be believed? Are there any new commandments to be acted upon? Are there any new insights I am to pursue? Are there any promises I am to embrace?

4. **When applying Scripture, beware of the following:**

- Applying cultural standards rather than biblical standards
- Attempting to strengthen a legitimate truth by using a Scripture incorrectly
- Applying Scripture out of prejudice from past training or teaching

One of the apostle Paul's concerns for Timothy, his son in the faith, was that Timothy learn to handle God's Word in a way that would please the Lord (2 Timothy 2:15). Someday we too will want to give a good account of our stewardship of God's Word. Did we handle it accurately? Were we gentle and reasonable about our faith, giving honor to those whom God has called to lead us, while at the same time searching Scripture ourselves to understand its truths? Did we allow God's living and active Word to change our lives?

Observation, interpretation, and application lead to *transformation*. This is the goal of our study of the Word of God. Through it we are changed from glory to glory into the image of Jesus.

GETTING STARTED

With this basic understanding of the inductive process, you are ready to begin a lifetime of personal Bible study. Prayerfully choose one of the Bible's 66 books, and then begin your study.

As you begin, quickly read through the THINGS TO DO section for an overview, but don't let the instructions overwhelm you. Taken one by one, chapter by chapter, and book by book, they become very manageable.

The THINGS TO THINK ABOUT section encourages you to get alone with God to consider how the truths of the book apply to you.

Old Testament historical and prophetic books have a HISTORICAL CHART usually located just before the first chapter to help you see where the book fits historically and chronologically. And many of the books in the New Testament contain an OBSERVATIONS CHART on which to record information you are instructed to look for in the THINGS TO DO section.

Finally, each book of the Bible ends with an AT A GLANCE chart, as discussed earlier.

For added insights on particular topics relevant to your personal Bible study, you will find a BIBLE STUDY HELPS section at the end of the Bible. This section also includes an overview of major events in Israel's history, a concordance, and color maps to provide a geographical frame of reference for your study of God's Word.

As you study the Bible inductively, you will get to know God in a deep, exciting, and enlightening way.

THE SPIRITUAL LIFE OF ISRAEL

COMPARATIVE TIMETABLE OF HISTORY

ITSB

The Tabernacle

and the High Priest in his priestly garments

The tabernacle was a sanctuary, built for God according to the pattern of his throne in heaven, where he chose to dwell among his people. It was the focal point of Israel's national life from the time God brought them out of the land of Egypt under Moses until they settled in the land of Canaan. For more than four centuries this elect nation would worship God in the tabernacle—yet from a distance, separated by the curtain from the presence of his glory, which hovered over the atonement cover on the ark of the covenant. Only the high priest in his priestly garments could enter, and that only once a year on the Day of Atonement.

SOLOMON'S TEMPLE

~ King David was grieved because he lived in Jerusalem in a house of cedar while the ark of the Lord was covered by curtains in the tabernacle. However, because David was a man of war, God gave the privilege of building the temple to David's son Solomon, who was a man of peace. ~ Solomon's magnificent work was overshadowed only when God's glory itself filled his temple. God's presence remained there for more than 350 years, until the days of Ezekiel the prophet. Then because of Judah's sin and God's impending judgment, the glory of the Lord departed. ~ In 586 B.C. the temple lay in ruins, destroyed by the Babylonians.

Herod's Temple

at the Time of Jesus During the Feast of Tabernacles

When the remnant of Israel returned after the Babylonian captivity, the task of rebuilding the temple was overwhelming. The work began in 536 B.C. but stopped two years later. The people found it easier to rebuild their own houses rather than the house of God. Then the Lord spoke through the prophet Haggai. Convicted, the people completed the temple. Although this temple, built under Zerubbabel's leadership, could not compare with Solomon's temple, and although God did not fill this temple with his glory, he honored the people's obedience. When Herod became king of Judea, he aspired to make this second temple more glorious than Solomon's. Magnificent as it was, the temple remained void of God's glory until Joseph and his wife, Mary, took their son, Jesus, there to present him to the Lord. The glory of God in the person of Jesus Christ (John 1:14) would frequent Herod's Temple until the day he walked out for the last time, leaving the temple desolate. The day they crucified him, the curtain in the temple was torn in two, for a new covenant had begun. In A.D. 70 Herod's Temple was destroyed, as Jesus prophesied it would be, by the Roman general Titus.

The Temple Mount

During the Second Temple Period

1. Second Temple (Herod's)
2. Western Wall
3. Wilson's Arch*
4. Barclay's Gate*
5. Small Shops
6. Main N-S Street
7. Robinson's Arch*
8. Upper City
9. Royal Porch
10. Pilasters
11. Double Gate
12. Triple Gate
13. Plaza
14. Ritual Bathhouse
15. Council House
16. Herodian Tower
17. Largest Ashlars
18. Antonia Fortress
19. Warren's Gate*
20. Court of the Gentiles
21. Eastern Gate

**Named after nineteenth-century explorers*

Note: See page 1723 for a floor plan of Herod's Temple

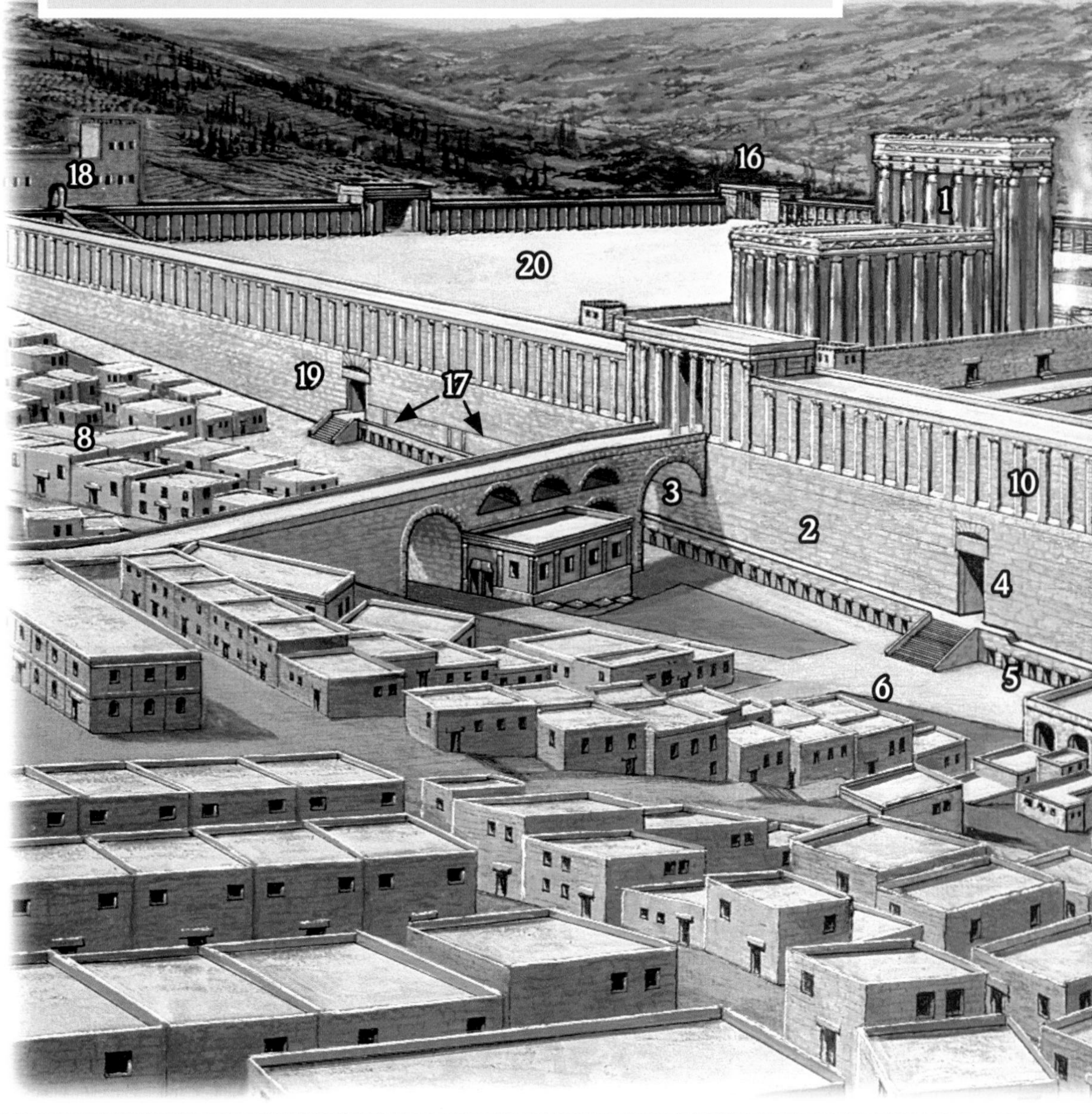

21
9
20
12
11
14
15
7
13

THE HISTORY OF ISRAEL—ADAM TO SOLOMON

To truly appreciate and fully comprehend the totality of God's revelation to man in the Word of God, one needs a clear understanding of the whole counsel of God. Keeping events, revelations, truths, and peoples in perspective is essential. This easy-to-understand guide to Israel's history from the beginning to modern times is designed to help you place Scripture in its proper historical and chronological context. It is a tool which will make your inductive study even more rewarding and enlightening.

(For a written history of this timeline, see pages 2189-2201.)

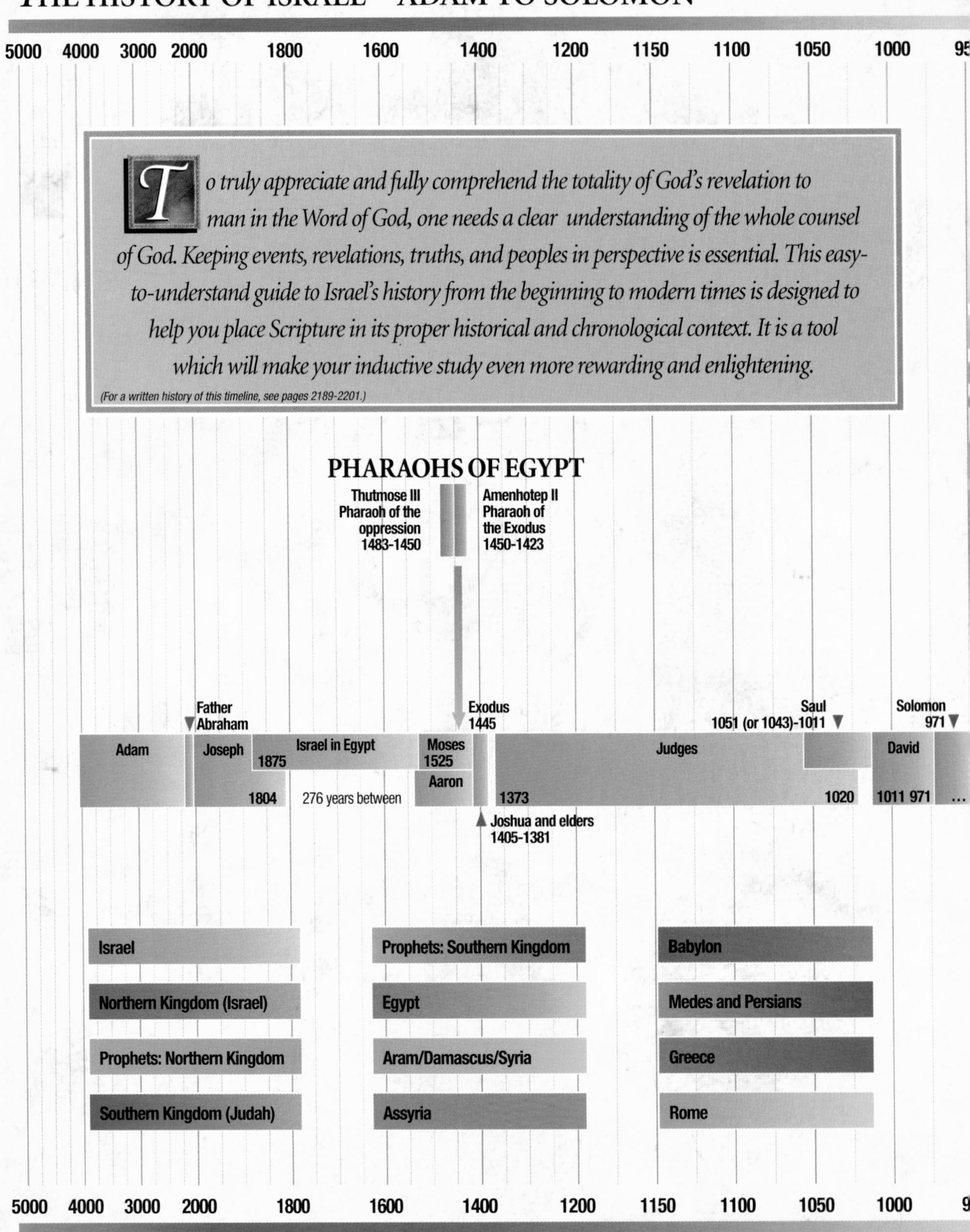

Scholars vary in the dating systems they use. The IISB generally follows John Whitcomb's system throughout for the sake of consistency.

THE HISTORY OF ISRAEL—THE DIVIDED KINGDOM

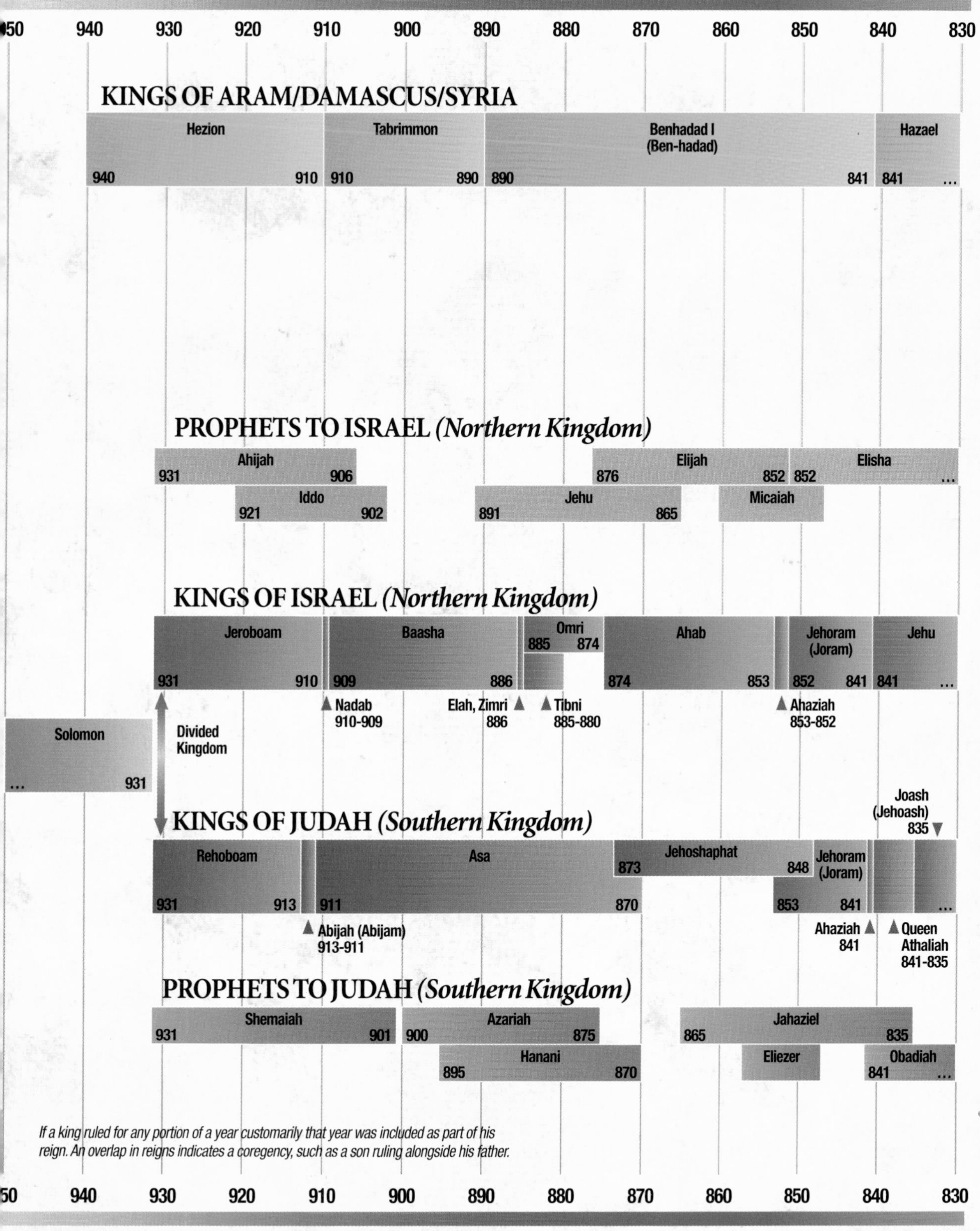

If a king ruled for any portion of a year customarily that year was included as part of his reign. An overlap in reigns indicates a coregency, such as a son ruling alongside his father.

THE HISTORY OF ISRAEL—THE ASSYRIAN CAPTIVITY

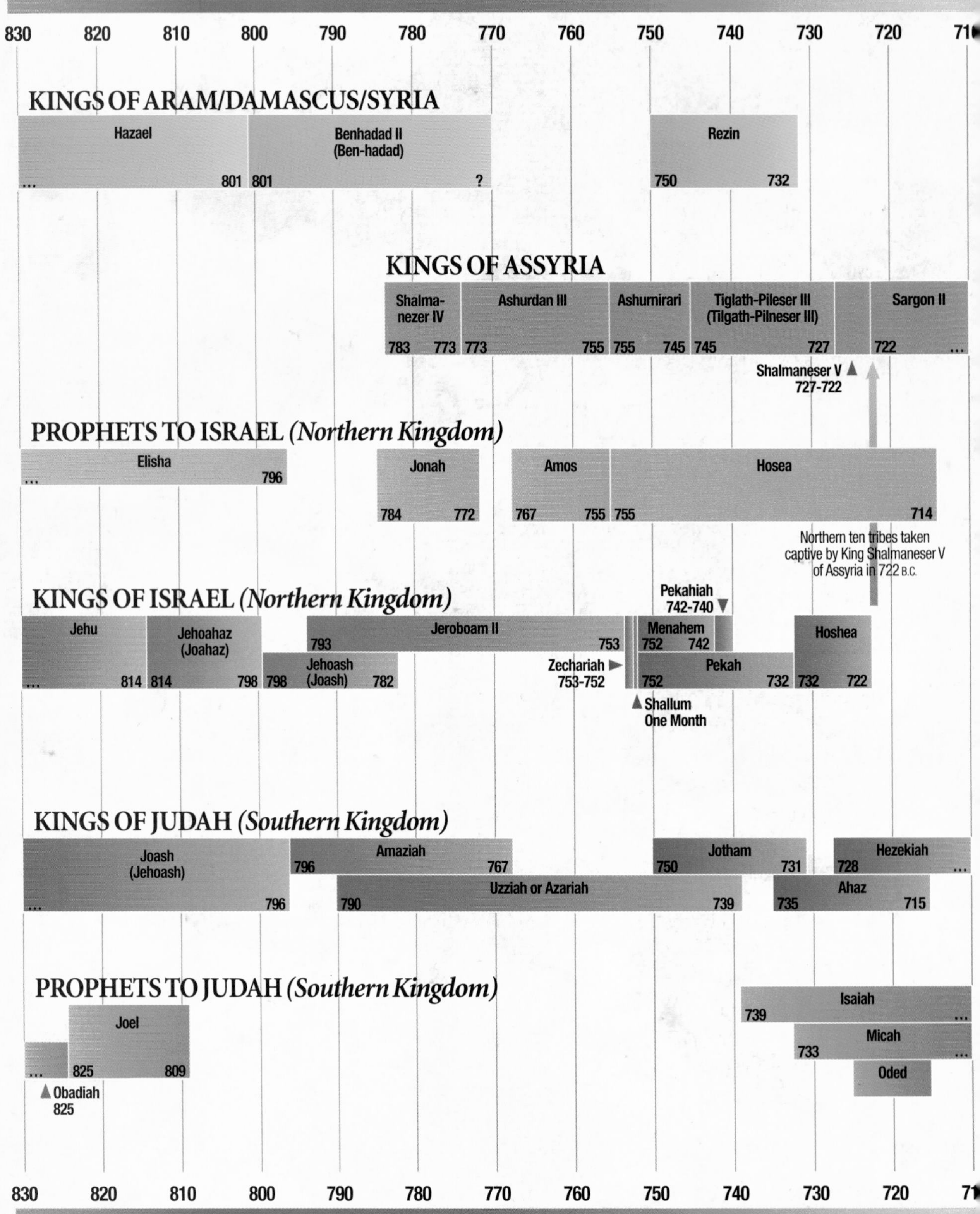

THE HISTORY OF ISRAEL—THE BABYLONIAN CAPTIVITY

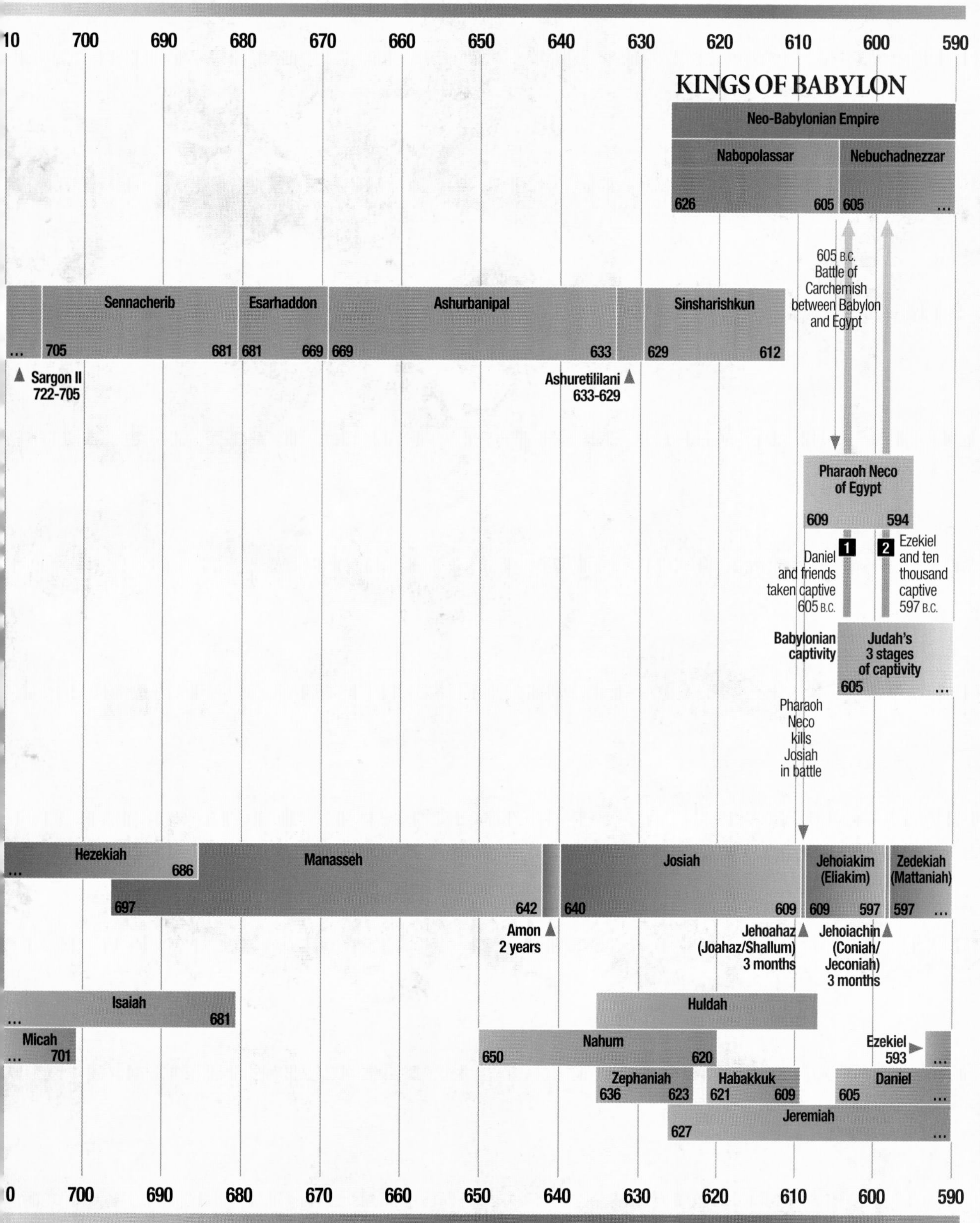

THE HISTORY OF ISRAEL—THE REBUILDING OF THE TEMPLE

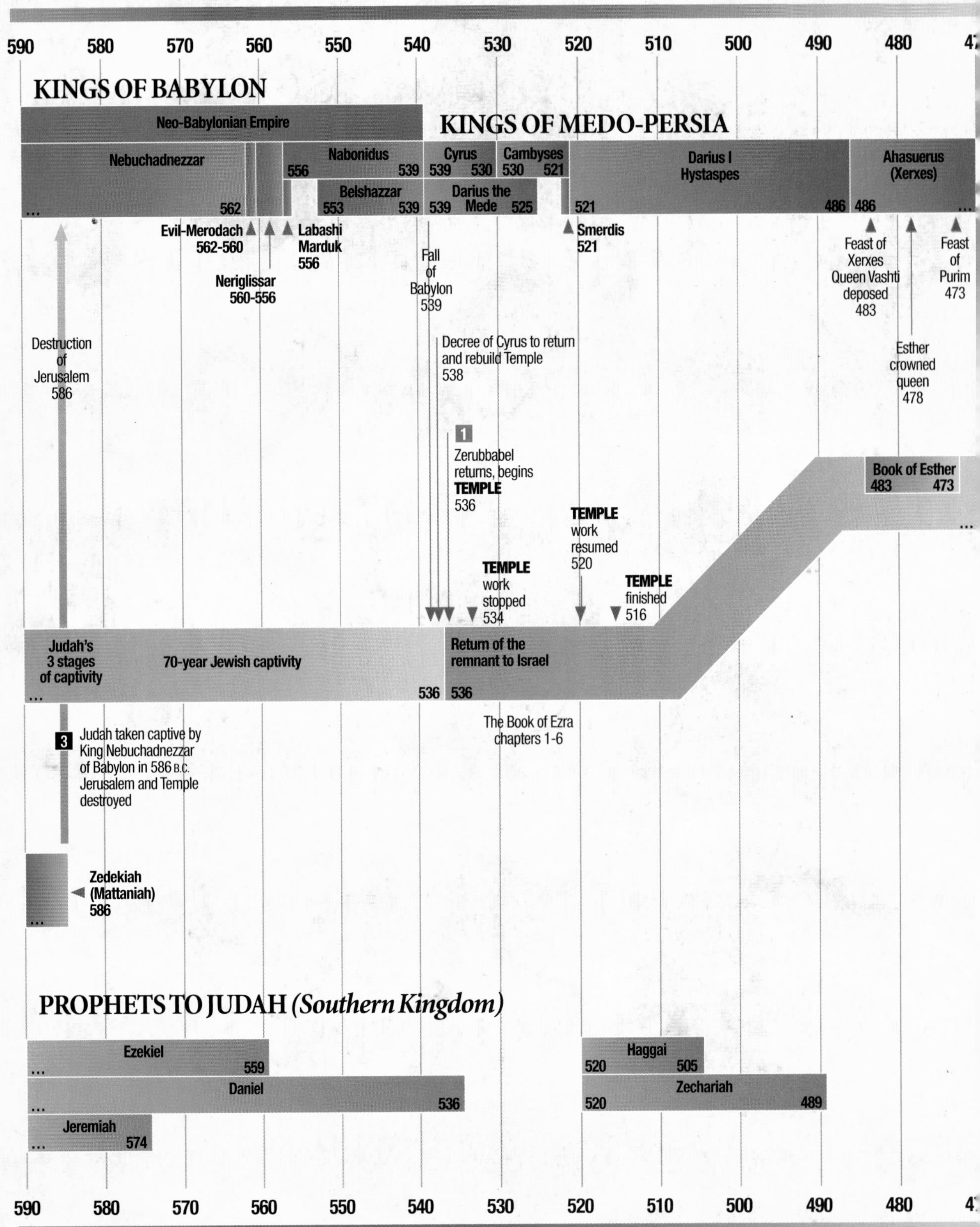

590 580 570 560 550 540 530 520 510 500 490 480
KINGS OF BABYLON
Neo-Babylonian Empire
KINGS OF MEDO-PERSIA
Nebuchadnezzar … 562
Nabonidus 556 539
Cyrus 539 530
Cambyses 530 521
Darius I Hystaspes 521 486
Ahasuerus (Xerxes) 486 …
Belshazzar 553 539
Darius the Mede 539 525
Evil-Merodach 562-560
Neriglissar 560-556
Labashi Marduk 556
Smerdis 521
Fall of Babylon 539
Feast of Xerxes Queen Vashti deposed 483
Feast of Purim 473
Esther crowned queen 478
Destruction of Jerusalem 586
Decree of Cyrus to return and rebuild Temple 538
1 Zerubbabel returns, begins TEMPLE 536
TEMPLE work resumed 520
TEMPLE work stopped 534
TEMPLE finished 516
Book of Esther 483 473
Judah's 3 stages of captivity …
70-year Jewish captivity 536
Return of the remnant to Israel 536
The Book of Ezra chapters 1-6
3 Judah taken captive by King Nebuchadnezzar of Babylon in 586 B.C. Jerusalem and Temple destroyed
Zedekiah (Mattaniah) 586
PROPHETS TO JUDAH (Southern Kingdom)
Ezekiel … 559
Daniel … 536
Jeremiah … 574
Haggai 520 505
Zechariah 520 489
590 580 570 560 550 540 530 520 510 500 490 480

THE HISTORY OF ISRAEL—THE GREEK AND ROMAN PERIODS

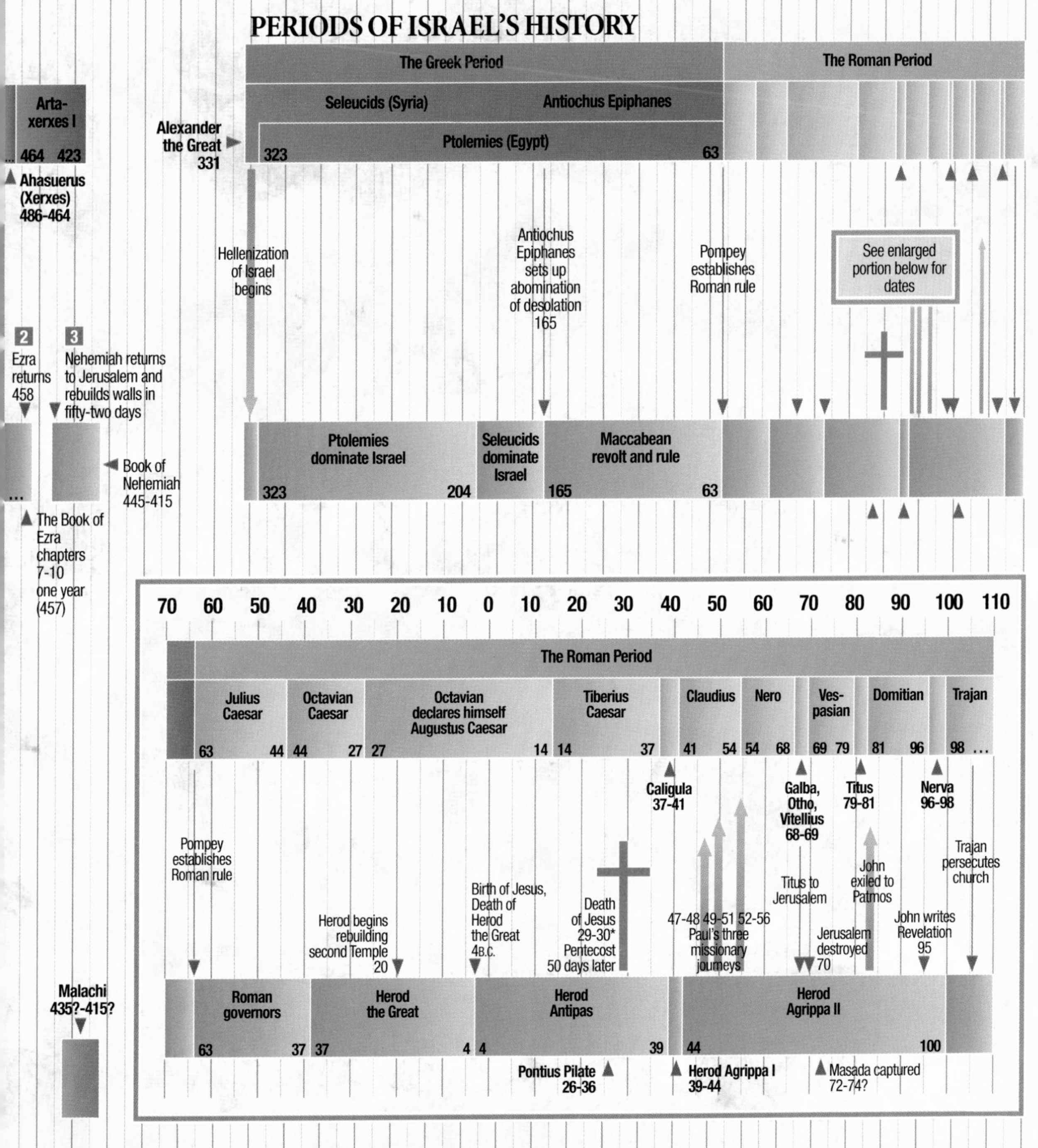

*Some scholars say 33 A.D.

THE HISTORY OF ISRAEL—110 A.D. TO MODERN TIMES

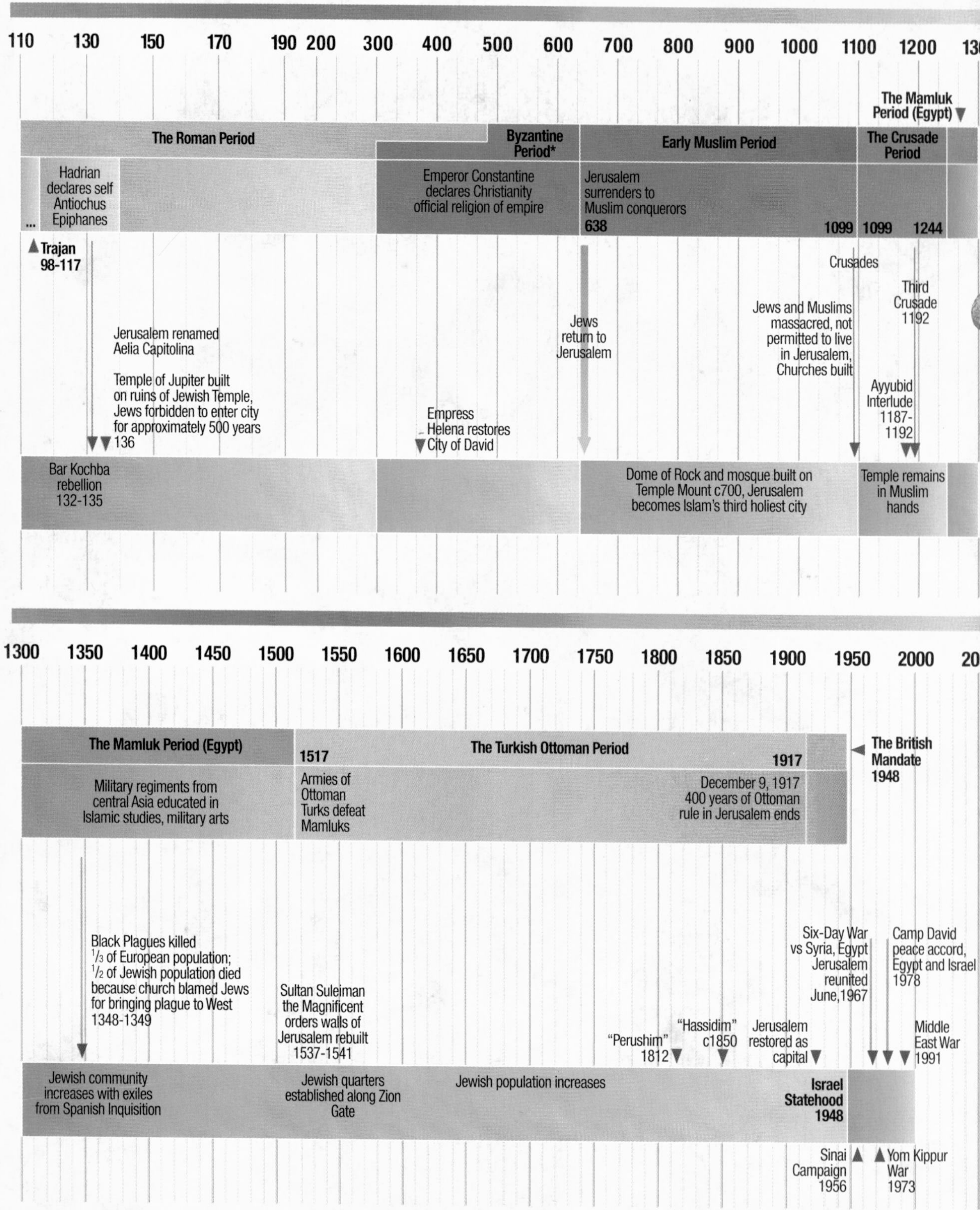

110
130
150
170
190
200
300
400
500
600
700
800
900
1000
1100
1200
The Mamluk Period (Egypt)
The Roman Period
Byzantine Period*
Early Muslim Period
The Crusade Period
Hadrian declares self Antiochus Epiphanes
Emperor Constantine declares Christianity official religion of empire
Jerusalem surrenders to Muslim conquerors 638
1099
1099
1244
Trajan 98-117
Crusades
Third Crusade 1192
Jews and Muslims massacred, not permitted to live in Jerusalem, Churches built
Jews return to Jerusalem
Jerusalem renamed Aelia Capitolina
Temple of Jupiter built on ruins of Jewish Temple, Jews forbidden to enter city for approximately 500 years 136
Ayyubid Interlude 1187-1192
Empress Helena restores City of David
Bar Kochba rebellion 132-135
Dome of Rock and mosque built on Temple Mount c700, Jerusalem becomes Islam's third holiest city
Temple remains in Muslim hands
1300
1350
1400
1450
1500
1550
1600
1650
1700
1750
1800
1850
1900
1950
2000
The Mamluk Period (Egypt)
1517
The Turkish Ottoman Period
1917
The British Mandate 1948
Military regiments from central Asia educated in Islamic studies, military arts
Armies of Ottoman Turks defeat Mamluks
December 9, 1917 400 years of Ottoman rule in Jerusalem ends
Black Plagues killed 1/3 of European population; 1/2 of Jewish population died because church blamed Jews for bringing plague to West 1348-1349
Sultan Suleiman the Magnificent orders walls of Jerusalem rebuilt 1537-1541
"Perushim" 1812
"Hassidim" c1850
Jerusalem restored as capital
Six-Day War vs Syria, Egypt Jerusalem reunited June, 1967
Camp David peace accord, Egypt and Israel 1978
Middle East War 1991
Jewish community increases with exiles from Spanish Inquisition
Jewish quarters established along Zion Gate
Jewish population increases
Israel Statehood 1948
Sinai Campaign 1956
Yom Kippur War 1973

* *The dates from the Byzantine Period are taken from **The Tower of David**, Museum of the History of Jerusalem.*

THE OLD TESTAMENT

ITSB

GENESIS

When there was nothing, there was God. Then God spoke.

THINGS TO DO

General Instructions

Genesis falls into two segments. The first, chapters 1 through 11, covers four major events. The second segment, chapters 12 through 50, covers the lives of four major characters. The instructions on how to study this book will be divided according to these two segments.

1. As you read chapter by chapter train yourself to ask the five W's and an H about the text: Who? What? When? Where? Why? and How? Ask questions such as: Who is speaking? What is happening? When is it happening? Where will it happen? Why was this said or done and what were the consequences? How did it happen? How was it to be done? etc.
2. Mark in a distinctive way any repeated words or phrases which are key to understanding the content of the chapter. There are several key words you should look for throughout the book of Genesis. These are listed on the GENESIS AT A GLANCE chart on page 90. Write these on an index card and use it as a bookmark while you study Genesis. (Instructions on how to mark key words and observe the text are in the introduction of this Bible. If you haven't read them, do so before you proceed any further.)
3. The timing of events can be very important. When you see a time phrase, draw in the margin an appropriate symbol in a color of your choice so you will be able to see it immediately.
4. In the margin, summarize the main things which occur in the chapter. List them in the order in which they occur. You may want to number them. For example, in Genesis 1 you could summarize what happens on each of the six days of creation.
5. As you study you will gain insights into God's character and ways. As you read each chapter, in the margin note what you learn about God. You may want to put a distinguishing mark such as this △ in the margin and then color it yellow so you can easily recognize it. Then list your insights under this symbol for God.
6. Look for the theme (subject) of each chapter. Record it on GENESIS AT A GLANCE. Also record the theme on the line next to the chapter number in the text.
7. Genesis is often referred to as the book of beginnings; it is the seedbed of truth. This is because the Word of God is a progressive revelation. *Progressive revelation* means that truth is unveiled over a period of time throughout various books of the Bible. God doesn't say everything he has to say about a particular subject at one time or in one place. Rather he will introduce a truth and then progressively reveal more and more about it.

Since Genesis is the book of beginnings, when you come to the "first" of anything, record it in the chapter margin in a special way or color so you can spot it easily. For example, next to Genesis 1:26, 27 you could write: "First man and woman."

Chapters 1-11

1. Genesis 1, 2
   a. In the margin note what is created on each day.
   b. Notice when a day begins and ends.

c. Chapter 2 gives a more detailed explanation of the creation of man: male and female. Note the order of events and the man's relationship and responsibilities to God and to the woman.

2. Genesis 3-5

a. In the margin of chapter 3 list all you learn about the serpent and his tactics: how he tempts Eve, what he says. Then note what happens to Satan because he deceives Eve.

b. Note Eve's progression into sin. List what happens before and after she sins.

c. Watch what happens to Adam and Eve's relationship with God. Note the consequence of Adam's disobedience.

d. In chapters 3 through 5 note the consequences of sin's entrance into the world. Record your insights in the chapter margins.

3. Genesis 6-9

a. As you study these chapters observe the reasons for the flood, how and when it came, who was affected and how.

b. Watch the timing of events. Mark time phrases with an appropriate symbol or record these in the margin; e.g., "Rains forty days and nights."

c. Mark the word *covenant* and list all you learn from the text about covenant.

4. Genesis 10, 11

a. Observe who was separated and why, how they were separated, when and where this occurred, and what happened as a result. Look at THE SETTLEMENT OF THE DESCENDANTS OF SHEM, HAM, AND JAPHETH on page 2306.

b. Babylon plays an intermittently prominent role throughout the Bible, and of course its roots are in Genesis. Therefore whenever you come to any mention of Babel or Babylon you need to record what you learn on WHAT THE BIBLE TEACHES ABOUT BABYLON, a chart beginning on page 2176. When you record your observations on Babylon note the book, chapter, and verse for future reference.

5. When you finish reading Genesis 11, look at GENESIS AT A GLANCE. Next to "Chapter Themes" you will find a place for segment divisions. Fill in the four main events covered in Genesis 1 through 11. The chapter divisions are noted on the chart.

Chapters 12-50

1. Genesis 12 through 50 covers the biographical segment of Genesis, which focuses on the lives of four main characters: Abraham, Isaac, Jacob (also called Israel), and Joseph. When you read:

a. Follow the "General Instructions" for studying each chapter (see page 1).

b. Watch for and mark every reference to time in the life of each of the major characters (including their wives and children) in these chapters. God will often tell how old the person was when certain events occurred in his or her life.

c. The word *covenant (treaty)* is more prominent in this last segment. Mark each occurrence of the word and then in the margin list everything you learn about covenant (treaty) from observing the text.

d. In the chapter margins note any insights or lessons you learned from the way these people lived. Note how and why God deals with these men, their families, and their associates, and what happens as a result.

2. Watch when the focus of a chapter moves from Abraham to Isaac, then to Jacob, and then to Joseph. Then on GENESIS AT A GLANCE, on the line where you recorded the four major events

of Genesis 1 through 11, divide the chapters into segments that cover the lives of Abraham, Isaac, Jacob, and Joseph. Look at the chapter themes to see where the focus moves from one of these men to the other.

3. When you finish reading Genesis 50, record on GENESIS AT A GLANCE the theme of Genesis. Under Segment Divisions, record the "firsts" that you marked throughout Genesis. (There is a blank line for any other segment divisions you might want to note.)

Things to Think About

1. What have you learned from the lives of those mentioned in Genesis—from Adam and Eve through Joseph? Remember that the things which were written in the Old Testament were written to teach us, that through endurance and the encouragement of Scripture we might have hope (Romans 15:4). What are the blessings of obedience and the consequences of disobedience?

2. What have you learned about God—his character, his attributes, and the ways he moves in the lives of men and nations? Since God never changes, can you trust him? Can you rely on what the Word of God reveals about him even though you may not fully understand his ways?

3. Jesus took the book of Genesis at face value. As you study the Gospels you will see that Jesus referred to the creation of Adam and Eve, to the flood, and to the destruction of Sodom and Gomorrah. He even referred to Satan as a murderer from the beginning. Jesus never contradicted the teachings of Genesis; he only affirmed them. Are you going to take God's Word at face value and believe as Jesus did, or are you going to listen to the philosophies of men? Are you going to follow men with finite minds who critique God and his Word, or are you going to accept the Bible as the Word of God and then think and live accordingly?

Chapter 1 Theme ____________________

1

In the beginning[a] God created the heavens and the earth.[b]
2Now the earth was[a] formless and empty,[c] darkness was over
the surface of the deep, and the Spirit of God[d] was hovering
over the waters.

3And God said,[e] "Let there be light," and there was light.[f] 4God
saw that the light was good, and he separated the light from
the darkness. 5God called the light "day," and the darkness
he called "night."[g] And there was evening, and there was
morning—the first day.
6And God said, "Let there be an expanse[h] between the waters to
separate water from water." 7So God made the expanse and
separated the water under the expanse from the water above
it.[i] And it was so. 8God called the expanse "sky." And there
was evening, and there was morning—the second day.
9And God said, "Let the water under the sky be gathered to one
place,[j] and let dry ground appear." And it was so. 10God
called the dry ground "land," and the gathered waters he
called "seas." And God saw that it was good.

1:1 [a]Jn 1:1-2 [b]Ps 90:2; Isa 42:5; Ac 17:24; Heb 11:3; Rev 4:11
1:2 [c]Jer 4:23 [d]Ps 104:30
1:3 [e]Ps 33:6,9 [f]2Co 4:6*
1:5 [g]Ps 74:16
1:6 [h]Jer 10:12
1:7 [i]Job 38:8-11,16; Ps 148:4
1:9 [j]Job 38:8-11; Ps 104:6-9; Pr 8:29; Jer 5:22; 2Pe 3:5

a2 Or possibly *became*

INSIGHT

The first five books of the Bible—Genesis, Exodus, Leviticus, Numbers, and Deuteronomy—are referred to as the ***Torah*** or the ***Pentateuch***. ***Torah***, a term used by the Jews, refers to the law or the teaching. ***Pentateuch***, a word coined about A.D. 200, means "the five scrolls" or the "five-volume book."

11Then God said, "Let the land produce vegetation:[a] seed-
bearing plants and trees on the land that bear fruit with seed
in it, according to their various kinds." And it was so. 12The
land produced vegetation: plants bearing seed according to
their kinds and trees bearing fruit with seed in it according
to their kinds. And God saw that it was good. 13And there
was evening, and there was morning—the third day.
14And God said, "Let there be lights[b] in the expanse of the sky to
separate the day from the night, and let them serve as signs[c]
to mark seasons[d] and days and years, 15and let them be lights
in the expanse of the sky to give light on the earth." And it
was so. 16God made two great lights—the greater light to
govern[e] the day and the lesser light to govern[f] the night. He
also made the stars.[g] 17God set them in the expanse of the sky
to give light on the earth, 18to govern the day and the night,[h]
and to separate light from darkness. And God saw that it was
good. 19And there was evening, and there was morning—
the fourth day.
20And God said, "Let the water teem with living creatures, and
let birds fly above the earth across the expanse of the sky."
21So God created the great creatures of the sea and every living and moving thing with which the water teems,[i] according
to their kinds, and every winged bird according to its kind.
And God saw that it was good. 22God blessed them and said,
"Be fruitful and increase in number and fill the water in the
seas, and let the birds increase on the earth."[j] 23And there
was evening, and there was morning—the fifth day.
24And God said, "Let the land produce living creatures according to their kinds: livestock, creatures that move along the
ground, and wild animals, each according to its kind." And
it was so. 25God made the wild animals[k] according to their
kinds, the livestock according to their kinds, and all the
creatures that move along the ground according to their
kinds. And God saw that it was good.

26Then God said, "Let us[l] make man in our image,[m] in our
likeness, and let them rule[n] over the fish of the sea and the
birds of the air, over the livestock, over all the earth,[a] and
over all the creatures that move along the ground."

27So God created man in his own image,[o]
in the image of God he created him;
male and female[p] he created them.

28God blessed them and said to them, "Be fruitful and
increase in number; fill the earth[q] and subdue it. Rule over

1:11 [a]Ps 65:9-13; 104:14
1:14 [b]Ps 74:16 [c]Jer 10:2 [d]Ps 104:19
1:16 [e]Ps 136:8 [f]Ps 136:9 [g]Job 38:7, 31-32; Ps 8:3; Isa 40:26
1:18 [h]Jer 33:20,25
1:21 [i]Ps 104:25-26
1:22 [j]ver 28; Ge 8:17
1:25 [k]Jer 27:5
1:26 [l]Ps 100:3 [m]Ge 9:6; Jas 3:9 [n]Ps 8:6-8
1:27 [o]1Co 11:7 [p]Ge 5:2; Mt 19:4*; Mk 10:6*
1:28 [q]Ge 9:1,7; Lev 26:9

a *26* Hebrew; Syriac *all the wild animals*

1:29 [a]Ps 104:14

the fish of the sea and the birds of the air and over every living creature that moves on the ground."

29 Then God said, "I give you every seed-bearing plant on the face of the whole earth and every tree that has fruit with seed in it. They will be yours for food.[a] 30 And to all the beasts of the earth and all the birds of the air and all the creatures that move on the ground—everything that has the breath of life in it—I give every green plant for food.[b]" And it was so.

1:30 [b]Ps 104:14,27; 145:15

31 God saw all that he had made,[c] and it was very good.[d] And there was evening, and there was morning—the sixth day.

Chapter 2 Theme ______________________

2 Thus the heavens and the earth were completed in all their vast array.

2 By the seventh day God had finished the work he had been doing; so on the seventh day he rested[a] from all his work.[e] 3 And God blessed the seventh day and made it holy,[f] because on it he rested from all the work of creating that he had done.

1:31 [c]Ps 104:24 [d]1Ti 4:4

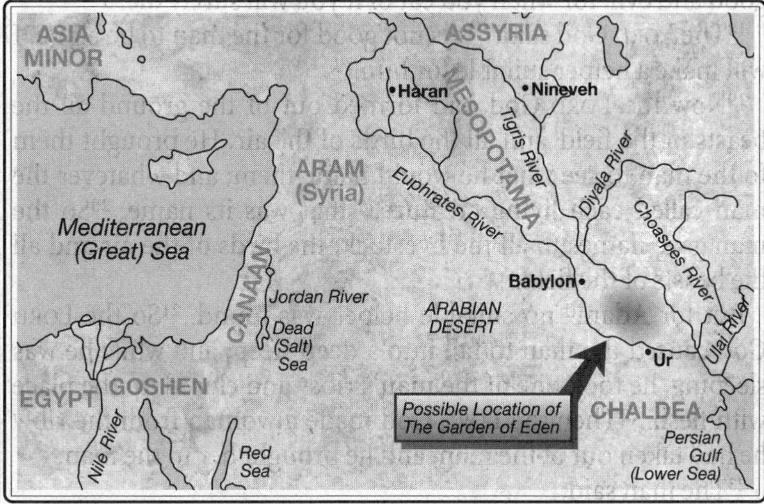

The Garden of Eden

2:2 [e]Ex 20:11; 31:17; Heb 4:4*

2:3 [f]Lev 23:3; Isa 58:13

4 This is the account of the heavens and the earth when they were created.

When the LORD God made the earth and the heavens— 5 and no shrub of the field had yet appeared on the earth[b] and no plant of the field had yet sprung up,[g] for the LORD God had not sent rain on the earth[b][h] and there was no man to work the ground, 6 but streams[c] came up from the earth and watered the

2:5 [g]Ge 1:11 [h]Ps 65:9-10

[a]2 Or *ceased*; also in verse 3 [b]5 Or *land*; also in verse 6 [c]6 Or *mist*

whole surface of the ground— 7the LORD God formed the man[a]
from the dust[a] of the ground[b] and breathed into his nostrils the
breath[c] of life,[d] and the man became a living being.[e]
8Now the LORD God had planted a garden in the east, in Eden;[f]
and there he put the man he had formed. 9And the LORD God made
all kinds of trees grow out of the ground—trees that were pleasing
to the eye and good for food. In the middle of the garden were
the tree of life[g] and the tree of the knowledge of good and evil.[h]
10A river watering the garden flowed from Eden; from there it
was separated into four headwaters. 11The name of the first is
the Pishon; it winds through the entire land of Havilah, where
there is gold. 12(The gold of that land is good; aromatic resin[b]
and onyx are also there.) 13The name of the second river is the
Gihon; it winds through the entire land of Cush.[c] 14The name of
the third river is the Tigris;[i] it runs along the east side of Asshur.
And the fourth river is the Euphrates.
15The LORD God took the man and put him in the Garden of
Eden to work it and take care of it. 16And the LORD God commanded the man, "You are free to eat from any tree in the garden; 17but you must not eat from the tree of the knowledge of
good and evil, for when you eat of it you will surely die."[j]
18The LORD God said, "It is not good for the man to be alone. I
will make a helper suitable for him."[k]
19Now the LORD God had formed out of the ground all the
beasts of the field[l] and all the birds of the air. He brought them
to the man to see what he would name them; and whatever the
man called each living creature,[m] that was its name. 20So the
man gave names to all the livestock, the birds of the air and all
the beasts of the field.
But for Adam[d] no suitable helper was found. 21So the LORD
God caused the man to fall into a deep sleep; and while he was
sleeping, he took one of the man's ribs[e] and closed up the place
with flesh. 22Then the LORD God made a woman from the rib[f][n]
he had taken out of the man, and he brought her to the man.
23The man said,

"This is now bone of my bones
  and flesh of my flesh;[o]
she shall be called 'woman,[g]'
  for she was taken out of man."

24For this reason a man will leave his father and mother and be
united[p] to his wife, and they will become one flesh.[q]

2:7 [a]Ge 3:19 [b]Ps 103:14 [c]Job 33:4 [d]Ac 17:25 [e]1Co 15:45*
2:8 [f]Ge 3:23,24; Isa 51:3
2:9 [g]Ge 3:22,24; Rev 2:7; 22:2,14,19 [h]Eze 47:12
2:14 [i]Da 10:4
2:17 [j]Dt 30:15,19; Ro 5:12; 6:23; Jas 1:15
2:18 [k]1Co 11:9
2:19 [l]Ps 8:7 [m]Ge 1:24
2:22 [n]1Co 11:8,9,12
2:23 [o]Ge 29:14; Eph 5:28-30
2:24 [p]Mal 2:15 [q]Mt 19:5*; Mk 10:7-8*; 1Co 6:16*; Eph 5:31*

[a]7 The Hebrew for *man (adam)* sounds like and may be related to the Hebrew for *ground (adamah)*; it is also the name *Adam* (see Gen. 2:20). [b]12 Or *good; pearls* [c]13 Possibly southeast Mesopotamia [d]20 Or *the man* [e]21 Or *took part of the man's side* [f]22 Or *part* [g]23 The Hebrew for *woman* sounds like the Hebrew for *man.*

25The man and his wife were both naked,[a] and they felt no
shame.

Chapter 3 Theme ________________________________

3 Now the serpent[b] was more crafty than any of the wild animals the LORD God had made. He said to the woman, "Did
God really say, 'You must not eat from any tree in the garden'?"
2The woman said to the serpent, "We may eat fruit from the
trees in the garden, 3but God did say, 'You must not eat fruit
from the tree that is in the middle of the garden, and you must
not touch it, or you will die.'"
4"You will not surely die," the serpent said to the woman.[c]
5"For God knows that when you eat of it your eyes will be
opened, and you will be like God,[d] knowing good and evil."
6When the woman saw that the fruit of the tree was good for
food and pleasing to the eye, and also desirable[e] for gaining wisdom, she took some and ate it. She also gave some to her husband, who was with her, and he ate it.[f] 7Then the eyes of both of
them were opened, and they realized they were naked; so they
sewed fig leaves together and made coverings for themselves.
8Then the man and his wife heard the sound of the LORD God
as he was walking[g] in the garden in the cool of the day, and they
hid[h] from the LORD God among the trees of the garden. 9But the
LORD God called to the man, "Where are you?"
10He answered, "I heard you in the garden, and I was afraid
because I was naked; so I hid."
11And he said, "Who told you that you were naked? Have you
eaten from the tree that I commanded you not to eat from?"
12The man said, "The woman you put here with me—she
gave me some fruit from the tree, and I ate it."
13Then the LORD God said to the woman, "What is this you
have done?"
The woman said, "The serpent deceived me,[i] and I ate."
14So the LORD God said to the serpent, "Because you have
done this,

"Cursed[j] are you above all the livestock
 and all the wild animals!
You will crawl on your belly
 and you will eat dust[k]
 all the days of your life.
15And I will put enmity
 between you and the woman,
 and between your offspring[a][l] and hers;[m]

2:25 [a]Ge 3:7,10-11
3:1 [b]2Co 11:3; Rev 12:9; 20:2
3:4 [c]Jn 8:44; 2Co 11:3
3:5 [d]Isa 14:14; Eze 28:2
3:6 [e]Jas 1:14-15; 1Jn 2:16 [f]1Ti 2:14
3:8 [g]Dt 23:14 [h]Job 31:33; Ps 139:7-12; Jer 23:24
3:13 [i]2Co 11:3; 1Ti 2:14
3:14 [j]Dt 28:15-20 [k]Isa 65:25; Mic 7:17
3:15 [l]Jn 8:44; Ac 13:10; 1Jn 3:8 [m]Isa 7:14; Mt 1:23; Rev 12:17

a *15* Or *seed*

he will crush[a] your head,[a]
and you will strike his heel."

16To the woman he said,

"I will greatly increase your pains in childbearing;
with pain you will give birth to children.
Your desire will be for your husband,
and he will rule over you.[b]"

17To Adam he said, "Because you listened to your wife and ate
from the tree about which I commanded you, 'You must not eat
of it,'

"Cursed[c] is the ground because of you;
through painful toil you will eat of it
all the days of your life.[d]
18It will produce thorns and thistles for you,
and you will eat the plants of the field.[e]
19By the sweat of your brow
you will eat your food[f]
until you return to the ground,
since from it you were taken;
for dust you are
and to dust you will return."[g]

20Adam[b] named his wife Eve,[c] because she would become the
mother of all the living.
21The LORD God made garments of skin for Adam and his wife
and clothed them. 22And the LORD God said, "The man has now
become like one of us, knowing good and evil. He must not be
allowed to reach out his hand and take also from the tree of life[h]
and eat, and live forever." 23So the LORD God banished him from
the Garden of Eden[i] to work the ground[j] from which he had
been taken. 24After he drove the man out, he placed on the east
side[d] of the Garden of Eden cherubim[k] and a flaming sword[l]
flashing back and forth to guard the way to the tree of life.[m]

Chapter 4 Theme ______________________________

4 Adam[b] lay with his wife Eve, and she became pregnant and
gave birth to Cain.[e] She said, "With the help of the LORD I have
brought forth[f] a man." 2Later she gave birth to his brother Abel.[n]
Now Abel kept flocks, and Cain worked the soil. 3In the course
of time Cain brought some of the fruits of the soil as an offering
to the LORD.[o] 4But Abel brought fat portions[p] from some of the

a15 Or *strike* b20, 1 Or *The man* c20 *Eve* probably means *living.* d24 Or *placed in front* e1 *Cain* sounds like the Hebrew for *brought forth* or *acquired.* f1 Or *have acquired*

3:15
[a]Ro 16:20; Heb 2:14
3:16
[b]1Co 11:3; Eph 5:22
3:17
[c]Ge 5:29; Ro 8:20-22
[d]Job 5:7; 14:1; Ecc 2:23
3:18
[e]Ps 104:14
3:19
[f]2Th 3:10
[g]Ge 2:7; Ps 90:3; 104:29; Ecc 12:7
3:22
[h]Rev 22:14
3:23
[i]Ge 2:8
[j]Ge 4:2
3:24
[k]Ex 25:18-22
[l]Ps 104:4
[m]Ge 2:9
4:2
[n]Lk 11:51
4:3
[o]Nu 18:12
4:4
[p]Lev 3:16

firstborn of his flock.[a] The LORD looked with favor on Abel and his offering,[b] 5but on Cain and his offering he did not look with favor. So Cain was very angry, and his face was downcast.

6Then the LORD said to Cain, "Why are you angry? Why is your face downcast? 7If you do what is right, will you not be accepted? But if you do not do what is right, sin is crouching at your door;[c] it desires to have you, but you must master it.[d]"

8Now Cain said to his brother Abel, "Let's go out to the field."[a] And while they were in the field, Cain attacked his brother Abel and killed him.[e]

9Then the LORD said to Cain, "Where is your brother Abel?"

"I don't know," he replied. "Am I my brother's keeper?"

10The LORD said, "What have you done? Listen! Your brother's blood cries out to me from the ground.[f] 11Now you are under a curse and driven from the ground, which opened its mouth to receive your brother's blood from your hand. 12When you work the ground, it will no longer yield its crops for you. You will be a restless wanderer on the earth."

13Cain said to the LORD, "My punishment is more than I can bear. 14Today you are driving me from the land, and I will be hidden from your presence;[g] I will be a restless wanderer on the earth, and whoever finds me will kill me."[h]

15But the LORD said to him, "Not so[b]; if anyone kills Cain[i], he will suffer vengeance seven times over.[j]" Then the LORD put a mark on Cain so that no one who found him would kill him. 16So Cain went out from the LORD's presence and lived in the land of Nod,[c] east of Eden.[k]

17Cain lay with his wife, and she became pregnant and gave birth to Enoch. Cain was then building a city, and he named it after his son[l] Enoch. 18To Enoch was born Irad, and Irad was the father of Mehujael, and Mehujael was the father of Methushael, and Methushael was the father of Lamech.

19Lamech married two women, one named Adah and the other Zillah. 20Adah gave birth to Jabal; he was the father of those who live in tents and raise livestock. 21His brother's name was Jubal; he was the father of all who play the harp and flute. 22Zillah also had a son, Tubal-Cain, who forged all kinds of tools out of[d] bronze and iron. Tubal-Cain's sister was Naamah.

23Lamech said to his wives,

> "Adah and Zillah, listen to me;
> wives of Lamech, hear my words.

4:4 [a]Ex 13:2,12 [b]Heb 11:4
4:7 [c]Nu 32:23 [d]Ro 6:16
4:8 [e]Mt 23:35; 1Jn 3:12
4:10 [f]Ge 9:5; Nu 35:33; Heb 12:24; Rev 6:9-10
4:14 [g]2Ki 17:18; Ps 51:11; 139:7-12; Jer 7:15; 52:3 [h]Ge 9:6; Nu 35:19, 21,27,33
4:15 [i]Eze 9:4,6 [j]ver 24; Ps 79:12
4:16 [k]Ge 2:8
4:17 [l]Ps 49:11

[a] *8* Samaritan Pentateuch, Septuagint, Vulgate and Syriac; Masoretic Text does not have *"Let's go out to the field."* [b] *15* Septuagint, Vulgate and Syriac; Hebrew *Very well* [c] *16* *Nod* means *wandering* (see verses 12 and 14). [d] *22* Or *who instructed all who work in*

I have killed[a][a] a man for wounding me,
 a young man for injuring me.
[24]If Cain is avenged[b] seven times,[c]
 then Lamech seventy-seven times."

[25]Adam lay with his wife again, and she gave birth to a son and named him Seth,[b][d] saying, "God has granted me another child in place of Abel, since Cain killed him."[e] [26]Seth also had a son, and he named him Enosh.

At that time men began to call on[c] the name of the LORD.[f]

Chapter 5 Theme

5

This is the written account of Adam's line.

When God created man, he made him in the likeness of God.[g] [2]He created them male and female[h] and blessed them. And when they were created, he called them "man.[d]"

[3]When Adam had lived 130 years, he had a son in his own likeness, in his own image;[i] and he named him Seth. [4]After Seth was born, Adam lived 800 years and had other sons and daughters. [5]Altogether, Adam lived 930 years, and then he died.[j]

[6]When Seth had lived 105 years, he became the father[e] of Enosh. [7]And after he became the father of Enosh, Seth lived 807 years and had other sons and daughters. [8]Altogether, Seth lived 912 years, and then he died.

[9]When Enosh had lived 90 years, he became the father of Kenan. [10]And after he became the father of Kenan, Enosh lived 815 years and had other sons and daughters. [11]Altogether, Enosh lived 905 years, and then he died.

[12]When Kenan had lived 70 years, he became the father of Mahalalel. [13]And after he became the father of Mahalalel, Kenan lived 840 years and had other sons and daughters. [14]Altogether, Kenan lived 910 years, and then he died.

[15]When Mahalalel had lived 65 years, he became the father of Jared. [16]And after he became the father of Jared, Mahalalel lived 830 years and had other sons and daughters. [17]Altogether, Mahalalel lived 895 years, and then he died.

[18]When Jared had lived 162 years, he became the father of Enoch.[k] [19]And after he became the father of Enoch, Jared lived 800 years and had other sons and daughters. [20]Altogether, Jared lived 962 years, and then he died.

[21]When Enoch had lived 65 years, he became the father of Methuselah. [22]And after he became the father of Methuselah, Enoch walked with God[l] 300 years and had other sons and

[a]23 Or *I will kill* [b]25 *Seth* probably means *granted.* [c]26 Or *to proclaim* [d]2 Hebrew *adam* [e]6 *Father* may mean *ancestor;* also in verses 7-26.

4:23 [a]Ex 20:13; Lev 19:18
4:24 [b]Dt 32:35 [c]ver 15
4:25 [d]Ge 5:3 [e]ver 8
4:26 [f]Ge 12:8; 1Ki 18:24; Ps 116:17; Joel 2:32; Zep 3:9; Ac 2:21; 1Co 1:2
5:1 [g]Ge 1:27; Eph 4:24; Col 3:10
5:2 [h]Ge 1:27; Mt 19:4; Mk 10:6; Gal 3:28
5:3 [i]Ge 1:26; 1Co 15:49
5:5 [j]Ge 3:19
5:18 [k]Jude 14
5:22 [l]ver 24; Ge 6:9; 17:1; 48:15; Mic 6:8; Mal 2:6

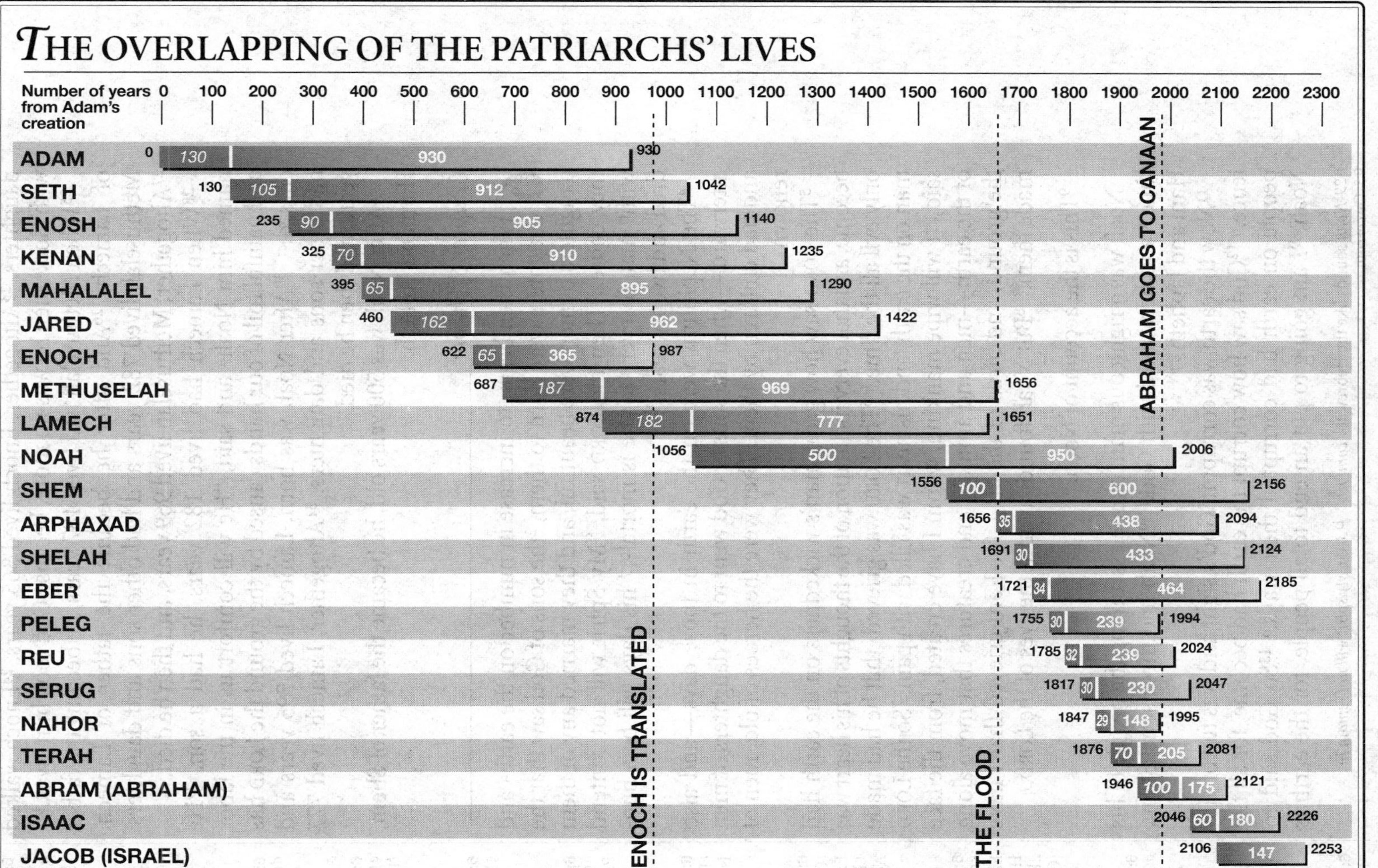

KEY: The first number inside the block is the man's age when his son (whose name is in the next line below) was born. The second number in the block is the number of years the man lived. The numbers preceding and following each block are the number of years from Adam's creation. The years on this chart begin with Adam's creation and are *not* calendar years.

daughters. 23 Altogether, Enoch lived 365 years. 24 Enoch walked with God;[a] then he was no more, because God took him away.[b]

25 When Methuselah had lived 187 years, he became the father of Lamech. 26 And after he became the father of Lamech, Methuselah lived 782 years and had other sons and daughters. 27 Altogether, Methuselah lived 969 years, and then he died.

28 When Lamech had lived 182 years, he had a son. 29 He named him Noah[a] and said, "He will comfort us in the labor and painful toil of our hands caused by the ground the LORD has cursed.[c]" 30 After Noah was born, Lamech lived 595 years and had other sons and daughters. 31 Altogether, Lamech lived 777 years, and then he died.

32 After Noah was 500 years old, he became the father of Shem, Ham and Japheth.

Chapter 6 Theme ______________________________

6 When men began to increase in number on the earth[d] and daughters were born to them, 2 the sons of God saw that the daughters of men were beautiful, and they married any of them they chose. 3 Then the LORD said, "My Spirit will not contend with[b] man forever,[e] for he is mortal[c];[f] his days will be a hundred and twenty years."

4 The Nephilim[g] were on the earth in those days—and also afterward—when the sons of God went to the daughters of men and had children by them. They were the heroes of old, men of renown.

5 The LORD saw how great man's wickedness on the earth had become, and that every inclination of the thoughts of his heart was only evil all the time.[h] 6 The LORD was grieved[i] that he had made man on the earth, and his heart was filled with pain. 7 So the LORD said, "I will wipe mankind, whom I have created, from the face of the earth—men and animals, and creatures that move along the ground, and birds of the air—for I am grieved that I have made them." 8 But Noah found favor in the eyes of the LORD.[j]

9 This is the account of Noah.

Noah was a righteous man, blameless among the people of his time,[k] and he walked with God.[l] 10 Noah had three sons: Shem, Ham and Japheth.[m]

11 Now the earth was corrupt in God's sight and was full of violence.[n] 12 God saw how corrupt the earth had become, for all the people on earth had corrupted their ways.[o] 13 So God said to Noah, "I am going to put an end to all people, for the earth is

a 29 *Noah* sounds like the Hebrew for *comfort.* b 3 Or *My spirit will not remain in*
c 3 Or *corrupt*

5:24 [a] ver 22 [b] 2Ki 2:1,11; Heb 11:5

5:29 [c] Ge 3:17; Ro 8:20

6:1 [d] Ge 1:28

6:3 [e] Isa 57:16 [f] Ps 78:39

6:4 [g] Nu 13:33

6:5 [h] Ge 8:21; Ps 14:1-3

6:6 [i] 1Sa 15:11,35; Isa 63:10

6:8 [j] Ge 19:19; Ex 33:12,13,17; Lk 1:30; Ac 7:46

6:9 [k] Ge 7:1; Eze 14:14,20; Heb 11:7; 2Pe 2:5 [l] Ge 5:22

6:10 [m] Ge 5:32

6:11 [n] Eze 7:23; 8:17

6:12 [o] Ps 14:1-3

filled with violence because of them. I am surely going to
destroy both them and the earth.[a] 14So make yourself an ark of
cypress[a] wood;[b] make rooms in it and coat it with pitch[c] inside
and out. 15This is how you are to build it: The ark is to be 450
feet long, 75 feet wide and 45 feet high.[b] 16Make a roof for it and
finish[c] the ark to within 18 inches[d] of the top. Put a door in the
side of the ark and make lower, middle and upper decks. 17I am
going to bring floodwaters on the earth to destroy all life under
the heavens, every creature that has the breath of life in it.
Everything on earth will perish.[d] 18But I will establish my covenant
with you,[e] and you will enter the ark[f]—you and your sons and
your wife and your sons' wives with you. 19You are to bring into
the ark two of all living creatures, male and female, to keep
them alive with you. 20Two[g] of every kind of bird, of every kind
of animal and of every kind of creature that moves along the
ground will come to you to be kept alive. 21You are to take every
kind of food that is to be eaten and store it away as food for you
and for them."

22Noah did everything just as God commanded him.[h]

Chapter 7 Theme

7 The Lord then said to Noah, "Go into the ark, you and your
whole family,[i] because I have found you righteous[j] in this
generation. 2Take with you seven[k] of every kind of clean[e] animal, a male and its mate, and two of every kind of unclean animal, a male and its mate, 3and also seven of every kind of bird,
male and female, to keep their various kinds alive throughout
the earth. 4Seven days from now I will send rain on the earth
for forty days and forty nights, and I will wipe from the face of
the earth every living creature I have made."

5And Noah did all that the LORD commanded him.[l]

6Noah was six hundred years old when the floodwaters came
on the earth. 7And Noah and his sons and his wife and his sons'
wives entered the ark to escape the waters of the flood. 8Pairs of
clean and unclean animals, of birds and of all creatures that
move along the ground, 9male and female, came to Noah and
entered the ark, as God had commanded Noah. 10And after the
seven days the floodwaters came on the earth.

11In the six hundredth year of Noah's life, on the seventeenth
day of the second month—on that day all the springs of the
great deep[m] burst forth, and the floodgates of the heavens[n] were
opened. 12And rain fell on the earth forty days and forty nights.[o]

6:13 [a] ver 17; Eze 7:2-3
6:14 [b] Heb 11:7; 1Pe 3:20 [c] Ex 2:3
6:17 [d] Ge 7:4,21-23; 2Pe 2:5
6:18 [e] Ge 9:9-16 [f] Ge 7:1,7,13
6:20 [g] Ge 7:15
6:22 [h] Ge 7:5,9,16
7:1 [i] Mt 24:38 [j] Ge 6:9; Eze 14:14
7:2 [k] ver 8; Ge 8:20; Lev 10:10; 11:1-47
7:5 [l] Ge 6:22
7:11 [m] Eze 26:19 [n] Ge 8:2
7:12 [o] ver 4

[a] *14* The meaning of the Hebrew for this word is uncertain. [b] *15* Hebrew *300 cubits long, 50 cubits wide and 30 cubits high* (about 140 meters long, 23 meters wide and 13.5 meters high) [c] *16* Or *Make an opening for light by finishing* [d] *16* Hebrew *a cubit* (about 0.5 meter) [e] *2* Or *seven pairs*; also in verse 3

13 On that very day Noah and his sons, Shem, Ham and Japheth,
together with his wife and the wives of his three sons, entered
the ark. 14 They had with them every wild animal according to its
kind, all livestock according to their kinds, every creature that
moves along the ground according to its kind and every bird
according to its kind, everything with wings. 15 Pairs of all creatures that have the breath of life in them came to Noah and
entered the ark.[a] 16 The animals going in were male and female
of every living thing, as God had commanded Noah. Then the
LORD shut him in.

17 For forty days[b] the flood kept coming on the earth, and as
the waters increased they lifted the ark high above the earth.
18 The waters rose and increased greatly on the earth, and the
ark floated on the surface of the water. 19 They rose greatly on
the earth, and all the high mountains under the entire heavens
were covered.[c] 20 The waters rose and covered the mountains to
a depth of more than twenty feet.[a,b] 21 Every living thing that
moved on the earth perished—birds, livestock, wild animals, all
the creatures that swarm over the earth, and all mankind.[d]
22 Everything on dry land that had the breath of life[e] in its nostrils died. 23 Every living thing on the face of the earth was wiped
out; men and animals and the creatures that move along the
ground and the birds of the air were wiped from the earth.[f]
Only Noah was left, and those with him in the ark.[g]

24 The waters flooded the earth for a hundred and fifty days.[h]

Chapter 8 Theme

8 But God remembered[i] Noah and all the wild animals and
the livestock that were with him in the ark, and he sent a
wind over the earth,[j] and the waters receded. 2 Now the springs of
the deep and the floodgates of the heavens[k] had been closed, and
the rain had stopped falling from the sky. 3 The water receded
steadily from the earth. At the end of the hundred and fifty days
the water had gone down, 4 and on the seventeenth day of the seventh month the ark came to rest on the mountains of Ararat. 5 The
waters continued to recede until the tenth month, and on the first
day of the tenth month the tops of the mountains became visible.

6 After forty days Noah opened the window he had made in
the ark 7 and sent out a raven, and it kept flying back and forth
until the water had dried up from the earth. 8 Then he sent out a
dove to see if the water had receded from the surface of the
ground. 9 But the dove could find no place to set its feet because
there was water over all the surface of the earth; so it returned to

a *20* Hebrew *fifteen cubits* (about 6.9 meters) b *20* Or *rose more than twenty feet, and the mountains were covered*

7:15 [a] Ge 6:19
7:17 [b] ver 4
7:19 [c] Ps 104:6
7:21 [d] Ge 6:7,13
7:22 [e] Ge 1:30
7:23 [f] Mt 24:39; Lk 17:27; 1Pe 3:20; 2Pe 2:5 [g] Heb 11:7
7:24 [h] Ge 8:3
8:1 [i] Ge 9:15; 19:29; Ex 2:24; 1Sa 1:11,19 [j] Ex 14:21
8:2 [k] Ge 7:11

Noah in the ark. He reached out his hand and took the dove and
brought it back to himself in the ark. 10 He waited seven more
days and again sent out the dove from the ark. 11 When the dove
returned to him in the evening, there in its beak was a freshly
plucked olive leaf! Then Noah knew that the water had receded
from the earth. 12 He waited seven more days and sent the dove
out again, but this time it did not return to him.

13 By the first day of the first month of Noah's six hundred and
first year, the water had dried up from the earth. Noah then
removed the covering from the ark and saw that the surface of
the ground was dry. 14 By the twenty-seventh day of the second
month the earth was completely dry.

15 Then God said to Noah, 16 "Come out of the ark, you and
your wife and your sons and their wives.[a] 17 Bring out every kind
of living creature that is with you—the birds, the animals, and
all the creatures that move along the ground—so they can multiply on the earth and be fruitful and increase in number
upon it."[b]

18 So Noah came out, together with his sons and his wife and
his sons' wives. 19 All the animals and all the creatures that move
along the ground and all the birds—everything that moves on
the earth—came out of the ark, one kind after another.

20 Then Noah built an altar to the LORD[c] and, taking some of all
the clean animals and clean[d] birds, he sacrificed burnt offerings[e]
on it. 21 The LORD smelled the pleasing aroma[f] and said in his
heart: "Never again will I curse the ground[g] because of man, even
though[a] every inclination of his heart is evil from childhood.[h]
And never again will I destroy all living creatures,[i] as I have done.

> 22 "As long as the earth endures,
> seedtime and harvest,
> cold and heat,
> summer and winter,
> day and night
> will never cease."[j]

Chapter 9 Theme ____________________

9 Then God blessed Noah and his sons, saying to them, "Be
fruitful and increase in number and fill the earth.[k] 2 The fear
and dread of you will fall upon all the beasts of the earth and all
the birds of the air, upon every creature that moves along the
ground, and upon all the fish of the sea; they are given into your
hands. 3 Everything that lives and moves will be food for you.[l]
Just as I gave you the green plants, I now give you everything.

8:16 [a] Ge 7:13
8:17 [b] Ge 1:22
8:20 [c] Ge 12:7-8; 13:18; 22:9 [d] Ge 7:8; Lev 11:1-47 [e] Ge 22:2,13; Ex 10:25
8:21 [f] Lev 1:9,13; 2Co 2:15 [g] Ge 3:17 [h] Ge 6:5; Ps 51:5; Jer 17:9 [i] Ge 9:11,15; Isa 54:9
8:22 [j] Ge 1:14; Jer 33:20,25
9:1 [k] Ge 1:22
9:3 [l] Ge 1:29

[a] 21 Or *man, for*

4“But you must not eat meat that has its lifeblood still in it.[a]
5And for your lifeblood I will surely demand an accounting. I will
demand an accounting from every animal.[b] And from each man,
too, I will demand an accounting for the life of his fellow man.[c]

> 6“Whoever sheds the blood of man,
>   by man shall his blood be shed;[d]
> for in the image of God[e]
>   has God made man.

7As for you, be fruitful and increase in number; multiply on the
earth and increase upon it.”[f]
8Then God said to Noah and to his sons with him: 9“I now
establish my covenant with you[g] and with your descendants
after you 10and with every living creature that was with you—
the birds, the livestock and all the wild animals, all those that
came out of the ark with you—every living creature on earth.
11I establish my covenant[h] with you: Never again will all life be
cut off by the waters of a flood; never again will there be a flood
to destroy the earth.[i]”
12And God said, “This is the sign of the covenant[j] I am making between me and you and every living creature with you, a
covenant for all generations to come: 13I have set my rainbow in
the clouds, and it will be the sign of the covenant between me
and the earth. 14Whenever I bring clouds over the earth and the
rainbow appears in the clouds, 15I will remember my covenant[k]
between me and you and all living creatures of every kind. Never again will the waters become a flood to destroy all life.
16Whenever the rainbow appears in the clouds, I will see it and
remember the everlasting covenant[l] between God and all living
creatures of every kind on the earth.”
17So God said to Noah, “This is the sign of the covenant[m] I have
established between me and all life on the earth.”
18The sons of Noah who came out of the ark were Shem, Ham
and Japheth. (Ham was the father of Canaan.)[n] 19These were
the three sons of Noah, and from them came the people who
were scattered over the earth.[o]
20Noah, a man of the soil, proceeded[a] to plant a vineyard.
21When he drank some of its wine, he became drunk and lay
uncovered inside his tent. 22Ham, the father of Canaan, saw his
father’s nakedness and told his two brothers outside. 23But Shem
and Japheth took a garment and laid it across their shoulders;
then they walked in backward and covered their father’s nakedness. Their faces were turned the other way so that they would
not see their father’s nakedness.

a *20* Or *soil, was the first*

9:4 [a]Lev 3:17; 17:10-14; Dt 12:16, 23-25; 1Sa 14:33

9:5 [b]Ex 21:28-32 [c]Ge 4:10

9:6 [d]Ge 4:14; Ex 21:12,14; Lev 24:17; Mt 26:52 [e]Ge 1:26

9:7 [f]Ge 1:22

9:9 [g]Ge 6:18

9:11 [h]ver 16; Isa 24:5 [i]Ge 8:21; Isa 54:9

9:12 [j]ver 17; Ge 17:11

9:15 [k]Ex 2:24; Lev 26:42,45; Dt 7:9; Eze 16:60

9:16 [l]ver 11; Ge 17:7,13,19; 2Sa 7:13; 23:5

9:17 [m]ver 12; Ge 17:11

9:18 [n]ver 25-27; Ge 10:6,15

9:19 [o]Ge 10:32

9:25 [24]When Noah awoke from his wine and found out what his
youngest son had done to him, [25]he said,

> "Cursed be Canaan![a]
> The lowest of slaves
> will he be to his brothers.[b]"

[26]He also said,

> "Blessed be the LORD, the God of Shem!
> May Canaan be the slave of Shem.[a]
> [27]May God extend the territory of Japheth[b];
> may Japheth live in the tents of Shem,
> and may Canaan be his[c] slave."

[28]After the flood Noah lived 350 years. [29]Altogether, Noah lived
950 years, and then he died.

Chapter 10 Theme ______________________

10 This is the account[c] of Shem, Ham and Japheth, Noah's sons, who themselves had sons after the flood.

[2]The sons[d] of Japheth:

Gomer,[d] Magog,[e] Madai, Javan, Tubal,[f] Meshech and Tiras.

[3]The sons of Gomer:

Ashkenaz,[g] Riphath and Togarmah.[h]

[4]The sons of Javan:

Elishah, Tarshish,[i] the Kittim and the Rodanim.[e] [5](From these the maritime peoples spread out into their territories by their clans within their nations, each with its own language.)

[6]The sons of Ham:

Cush, Mizraim,[f] Put and Canaan.[j]

[7]The sons of Cush:

Seba, Havilah, Sabtah, Raamah and Sabteca.

The sons of Raamah:

Sheba and Dedan.

[8]Cush was the father[g] of Nimrod, who grew to be a mighty
warrior on the earth. [9]He was a mighty hunter before the LORD;
that is why it is said, "Like Nimrod, a mighty hunter before the
LORD." [10]The first centers of his kingdom were Babylon,[k] Erech,

INSIGHT

In order to see where the sons of Shem, Ham, and Japheth settled, refer to the map **The Settlement of the Descendants of Shem, Ham, and Japheth** on page 2306.

9:25 [a]ver 18 [b]Ge 25:23; Jos 9:23
10:1 [c]Ge 2:4
10:2 [d]Eze 38:6 [e]Eze 38:2; Rev 20:8 [f]Isa 66:19
10:3 [g]Jer 51:27 [h]Eze 27:14; 38:6
10:4 [i]Eze 27:12,25; Jnh 1:3
10:6 [j]ver 15; Ge 9:18
10:10 [k]Ge 11:9

[a]26 Or *be his slave* [b]27 *Japheth* sounds like the Hebrew for *extend.* [c]27 Or *their* [d]2 *Sons* may mean *descendants* or *successors* or *nations*; also in verses 3, 4, 6, 7, 20-23, 29 and 31. [e]4 Some manuscripts of the Masoretic Text and Samaritan Pentateuch (see also Septuagint and 1 Chron. 1:7); most manuscripts of the Masoretic Text *Dodanim* [f]6 That is, Egypt; also in verse 13 [g]8 *Father* may mean *ancestor* or *predecessor* or *founder*; also in verses 13, 15, 24 and 26.

Akkad and Calneh, in[a] Shinar.[b][a] 11 From that land he went to
Assyria,[b] where he built Nineveh,[c] Rehoboth Ir,[c] Calah 12 and
Resen, which is between Nineveh and Calah; that is the great city.

13 Mizraim was the father of
the Ludites, Anamites, Lehabites, Naphtuhites, 14 Pathru-
sites, Casluhites (from whom the Philistines[d] came) and
Caphtorites.

15 Canaan[e] was the father of
Sidon[f] his firstborn,[d] and of the Hittites,[g] 16 Jebusites,[h]
Amorites, Girgashites, 17 Hivites, Arkites, Sinites, 18 Arvad-
ites, Zemarites and Hamathites.

Later the Canaanite[i] clans scattered 19 and the borders of Canaan[j] reached from Sidon[k] toward Gerar as far as Gaza, and then
toward Sodom, Gomorrah, Admah and Zeboiim, as far as Lasha.
20 These are the sons of Ham by their clans and languages, in
their territories and nations.

21 Sons were also born to Shem, whose older brother was[e]
Japheth; Shem was the ancestor of all the sons of Eber.[l]

22 The sons of Shem:
Elam,[m] Asshur, Arphaxad,[n] Lud and Aram.

23 The sons of Aram:
Uz,[o] Hul, Gether and Meshech.[f]

24 Arphaxad was the father of[g] Shelah,
and Shelah the father of Eber.[p]

25 Two sons were born to Eber:
One was named Peleg,[h] because in his time the earth was
divided; his brother was named Joktan.

26 Joktan was the father of
Almodad, Sheleph, Hazarmaveth, Jerah, 27 Hadoram, Uzal,
Diklah, 28 Obal, Abimael, Sheba, 29 Ophir, Havilah and
Jobab. All these were sons of Joktan.

30 The region where they lived stretched from Mesha toward
Sephar, in the eastern hill country.
31 These are the sons of Shem by their clans and languages, in
their territories and nations.

32 These are the clans of Noah's sons,[q] according to their lines
of descent, within their nations. From these the nations spread
out over the earth[r] after the flood.

[a] *10* Or *Erech and Akkad—all of them in* [b] *10* That is, Babylonia [c] *11* Or *Nineveh with its city squares* [d] *15* Or *of the Sidonians, the foremost* [e] *21* Or *Shem, the older brother of* [f] *23* See Septuagint and 1 Chron. 1:17; Hebrew *Mash* [g] *24* Hebrew; Septuagint *father of Cainan, and Cainan was the father of* [h] *25* *Peleg* means *division.*

10:10 [a] Ge 11:2

10:11 [b] Ps 83:8; Mic 5:6 [c] Jnh 1:2; 4:11; Na 1:1

10:14 [d] Ge 21:32,34; 26:1,8

10:15 [e] ver 6; Ge 9:18 [f] Eze 28:21 [g] Ge 23:3,20

10:16 [h] 1Ch 11:4

10:18 [i] Ge 12:6; Ex 13:11

10:19 [j] Ge 11:31; 13:12; 17:8 [k] ver 15

10:21 [l] ver 24; Nu 24:24

10:22 [m] Jer 49:34 [n] Lk 3:36

10:23 [o] Job 1:1

10:24 [p] ver 21

10:32 [q] ver 1 [r] Ge 9:19

11:2 [a]Ge 10:10 *Chapter 11 Theme* ____________________

11 Now the whole world had one language and a common
speech. 2As men moved eastward,[a] they found a plain in
Shinar[b][a] and settled there.
3They said to each other, "Come, let's make bricks[b] and bake
11:3 [b]Ex 1:14 them thoroughly." They used brick instead of stone, and tar[c] for
[c]Ge 14:10 mortar. 4Then they said, "Come, let us build ourselves a city, with
a tower that reaches to the heavens,[d] so that we may make a name[e]
for ourselves and not be scattered over the face of the whole
earth."[f]
5But the LORD came down[g] to see the city and the tower that the
11:4 [d]Dt 1:28; 9:1 men were building. 6The LORD said, "If as one people speaking the
[e]Ge 6:4 [f]Dt 4:27 same language they have begun to do this, then nothing they plan
to do will be impossible for them. 7Come, let us[h] go down and
confuse their language so they will not understand each other."[i]
8So the LORD scattered them from there over all the earth,[j] and
they stopped building the city. 9That is why it was called
11:5 Babel[c][k]—because there the LORD confused the language of the
[g]ver 7; Ge 18:21; whole world. From there the LORD scattered them over the face
Ex 3:8; 19:11,18,20 of the whole earth.

10This is the account of Shem.

Two years after the flood, when Shem was 100 years old, he
became the father[d] of Arphaxad. 11And after he became the father
11:7 of Arphaxad, Shem lived 500 years and had other sons and
[h]Ge 1:26 [i]Ge 42:23 daughters.
12When Arphaxad had lived 35 years, he became the father of
Shelah.[l] 13And after he became the father of Shelah, Arphaxad
lived 403 years and had other sons and daughters.[e]
14When Shelah had lived 30 years, he became the father of Eber.
11:8 15And after he became the father of Eber, Shelah lived 403 years
[j]Ge 9:19; Lk 1:51 and had other sons and daughters.
16When Eber had lived 34 years, he became the father of Peleg.
17And after he became the father of Peleg, Eber lived 430 years
and had other sons and daughters.
18When Peleg had lived 30 years, he became the father of Reu.
11:9 19And after he became the father of Reu, Peleg lived 209 years
[k]Ge 10:10 and had other sons and daughters.

[a]2 Or *from the east*; or *in the east* [b]2 That is, Babylonia [c]9 That is, Babylon; *Babel* sounds like the Hebrew for *confused*. [d]*10 Father* may mean *ancestor*; also in verses 11-25. [e]*12,13* Hebrew; Septuagint (see also Luke 3:35, 36 and note at Gen. 10:24) *35 years, he became the father of Cainan. 13And after he became the father of Cainan, Arphaxad lived 430 years and had other sons and daughters, and then he died. When Cainan had lived 130 years, he became the father of Shelah. And after he became the father of Shelah, Cainan lived 330 years and had other sons and daughters*

11:12 [l]Lk 3:35

20 When Reu had lived 32 years, he became the father of Serug.[a]
21 And after he became the father of Serug, Reu lived 207 years
and had other sons and daughters.
22 When Serug had lived 30 years, he became the father of
Nahor. 23 And after he became the father of Nahor, Serug lived
200 years and had other sons and daughters.
24 When Nahor had lived 29 years, he became the father of Terah.[b] 25 And after he became the father of Terah, Nahor lived 119
years and had other sons and daughters.
26 After Terah had lived 70 years, he became the father of
Abram,[c] Nahor[d] and Haran.
27 This is the account of Terah.

Terah became the father of Abram, Nahor and Haran. And
Haran became the father of Lot.[e] 28 While his father Terah was
still alive, Haran died in Ur of the Chaldeans,[f] in the land of his
birth. 29 Abram and Nahor both married. The name of Abram's
wife was Sarai,[g] and the name of Nahor's wife was Milcah;[h] she
was the daughter of Haran, the father of both Milcah and Iscah.
30 Now Sarai was barren; she had no children.[i]
31 Terah took his son Abram, his grandson Lot son of Haran,
and his daughter-in-law Sarai, the wife of his son Abram, and
together they set out from Ur of the Chaldeans[j] to go to Canaan.[k]
But when they came to Haran, they settled there.
32 Terah lived 205 years, and he died in Haran.

Journeys of Abraham

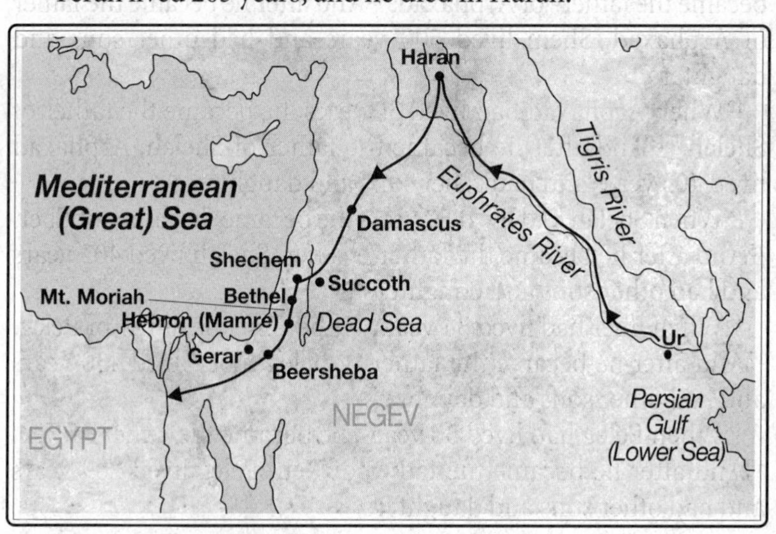

Chapter 12 Theme ______________________________

12 The LORD had said to Abram, "Leave your country, your
people and your father's household and go to the land I
will show you.[l]

11:20 [a] Lk 3:35
11:24 [b] Lk 3:34
11:26 [c] Lk 3:34; [d] Jos 24:2
11:27 [e] ver 31; Ge 12:4; 14:12; 19:1; 2Pe 2:7
11:28 [f] ver 31; Ge 15:7
11:29 [g] Ge 17:15 [h] Ge 22:20
11:30 [i] Ge 16:1; 18:11
11:31 [j] Ge 15:7; Ne 9:7; Ac 7:4 [k] Ge 10:19
12:1 [l] Ac 7:3*; Heb 11:8

2 "I will make you into a great nation[a]
and I will bless you;[b]
I will make your name great,
and you will be a blessing.
3 I will bless those who bless you,
and whoever curses you I will curse;[c]
and all peoples on earth
will be blessed through you.[d]"

4 So Abram left, as the LORD had told him; and Lot went with him. Abram was seventy-five years old when he set out from Haran.[e] 5 He took his wife Sarai, his nephew Lot, all the possessions they had accumulated and the people[f] they had acquired in Haran, and they set out for the land of Canaan, and they arrived there.

6 Abram traveled through the land[g] as far as the site of the great tree of Moreh[h] at Shechem. At that time the Canaanites[i] were in the land. 7 The LORD appeared to Abram[j] and said, "To your offspring[a] I will give this land."[k] So he built an altar there to the LORD,[l] who had appeared to him.

8 From there he went on toward the hills east of Bethel[m] and pitched his tent, with Bethel on the west and Ai on the east. There he built an altar to the LORD and called on the name of the LORD. 9 Then Abram set out and continued toward the Negev.[n]

10 Now there was a famine in the land, and Abram went down to Egypt to live there for a while because the famine was severe. 11 As he was about to enter Egypt, he said to his wife Sarai, "I know what a beautiful woman you are. 12 When the Egyptians see you, they will say, 'This is his wife.' Then they will kill me but will let you live. 13 Say you are my sister,[o] so that I will be treated well for your sake and my life will be spared because of you."

14 When Abram came to Egypt, the Egyptians saw that she was a very beautiful woman. 15 And when Pharaoh's officials saw her, they praised her to Pharaoh, and she was taken into his palace. 16 He treated Abram well for her sake, and Abram acquired sheep and cattle, male and female donkeys, menservants and maidservants, and camels.

17 But the LORD inflicted serious diseases on Pharaoh and his household[p] because of Abram's wife Sarai. 18 So Pharaoh summoned Abram. "What have you done to me?"[q] he said. "Why didn't you tell me she was your wife? 19 Why did you say, 'She is my sister,' so that I took her to be my wife? Now then, here is your wife. Take her and go!" 20 Then Pharaoh gave orders about Abram to his men, and they sent him on his way, with his wife and everything he had.

a 7 Or *seed*

12:2 [a] Ge 15:5; 17:2,4; 18:18; 22:17; Dt 26:5 [b] Ge 24:1,35
12:3 [c] Ge 27:29; Ex 23:22; Nu 24:9 [d] Ge 18:18; 22:18; 26:4; Ac 3:25; Gal 3:8*
12:4 [e] Ge 11:31
12:5 [f] Ge 14:14; 17:23
12:6 [g] Heb 11:9 [h] Ge 35:4; Dt 11:30 [i] Ge 10:18
12:7 [j] Ge 17:1; 18:1; Ex 6:3 [k] Ge 13:15,17; 15:18; 17:8; Ps 105:9-11 [l] Ge 13:4
12:8 [m] Ge 13:3
12:9 [n] Ge 13:1,3
12:13 [o] Ge 20:2; 26:7
12:17 [p] 1Ch 16:21
12:18 [q] Ge 20:9; 26:10

Chapter 13 Theme ______________________________

13 So Abram went up from Egypt to the Negev,[a] with his wife
and everything he had, and Lot went with him. 2 Abram
had become very wealthy in livestock and in silver and gold.
3 From the Negev he went from place to place until he came to
Bethel,[b] to the place between Bethel and Ai where his tent had
been earlier 4 and where he had first built an altar.[c] There Abram
called on the name of the LORD.
5 Now Lot, who was moving about with Abram, also had flocks
and herds and tents. 6 But the land could not support them while
they stayed together, for their possessions were so great that they
were not able to stay together.[d] 7 And quarreling[e] arose between
Abram's herdsmen and the herdsmen of Lot. The Canaanites
and Perizzites were also living in the land[f] at that time.
8 So Abram said to Lot, "Let's not have any quarreling between
you and me,[g] or between your herdsmen and mine, for we are
brothers.[h] 9 Is not the whole land before you? Let's part company.
If you go to the left, I'll go to the right; if you go to the right, I'll
go to the left."
10 Lot looked up and saw that the whole plain of the Jordan was well
watered, like the garden of the LORD,[i] like the land of Egypt, toward
Zoar.[j] (This was before the LORD destroyed Sodom and Gomorrah.)[k] 11 So Lot chose for himself the whole plain of the Jordan and
set out toward the east. The two men parted company: 12 Abram
lived in the land of Canaan, while Lot lived among the cities of
the plain[l] and pitched his tents near Sodom.[m] 13 Now the men of
Sodom were wicked and were sinning greatly against the LORD.[n]
14 The LORD said to Abram after Lot had parted from him,
"Lift up your eyes from where you are and look north and
south, east and west.[o] 15 All the land that you see I will give to
you and your offspring[a] forever.[p] 16 I will make your offspring
like the dust of the earth, so that if anyone could count the dust,
then your offspring could be counted. 17 Go, walk through the
length and breadth of the land,[q] for I am giving it to you."
18 So Abram moved his tents and went to live near the great
trees of Mamre[r] at Hebron,[s] where he built an altar to the LORD.[t]

Chapter 14 Theme ______________________________

14 At this time Amraphel king of Shinar,[b][u] Arioch king of
Ellasar, Kedorlaomer king of Elam and Tidal king of Goiim 2 went to war against Bera king of Sodom, Birsha king of
Gomorrah, Shinab king of Admah, Shemeber king of Zeboiim,[v]
and the king of Bela (that is, Zoar).[w] 3 All these latter kings joined

[a] *15* Or *seed*; also in verse 16 [b] *1* That is, Babylonia; also in verse 9

13:1 [a]Ge 12:9
13:3 [b]Ge 12:8
13:4 [c]Ge 12:7
13:6 [d]Ge 36:7
13:7 [e]Ge 26:20,21 [f]Ge 12:6
13:8 [g]Pr 15:18; 20:3 [h]Ps 133:1
13:10 [i]Ge 2:8-10; Isa 51:3 [j]Ge 19:22,30 [k]Ge 14:8; 19:17-29
13:12 [l]Ge 19:17,25,29 [m]Ge 14:12
13:13 [n]Ge 18:20; Eze 16:49-50; 2Pe 2:8
13:14 [o]Ge 28:14; Dt 3:27
13:15 [p]Ge 12:7; Gal 3:16*
13:17 [q]ver 15; Nu 13:17-25
13:18 [r]Ge 14:13,24; 18:1 [s]Ge 35:27 [t]Ge 8:20
14:1 [u]Ge 10:10
14:2 [v]Ge 10:19 [w]Ge 13:10

forces in the Valley of Siddim (the Salt Sea[a][a]). [4]For twelve years
they had been subject to Kedorlaomer, but in the thirteenth
year they rebelled.
[5]In the fourteenth year, Kedorlaomer and the kings allied with
him went out and defeated the Rephaites[b] in Ashteroth Karnaim,
the Zuzites in Ham, the Emites[c] in Shaveh Kiriathaim [6]and the
Horites[d] in the hill country of Seir,[e] as far as El Paran[f] near the
desert. [7]Then they turned back and went to En Mishpat (that is,
Kadesh), and they conquered the whole territory of the Amalekites, as well as the Amorites who were living in Hazazon Tamar.[g]
[8]Then the king of Sodom, the king of Gomorrah,[h] the king of
Admah, the king of Zeboiim[i] and the king of Bela (that is, Zoar)
marched out and drew up their battle lines in the Valley of Siddim [9]against Kedorlaomer king of Elam, Tidal king of Goiim,
Amraphel king of Shinar and Arioch king of Ellasar—four
kings against five. [10]Now the Valley of Siddim was full of tar
pits, and when the kings of Sodom and Gomorrah fled, some of
the men fell into them and the rest fled to the hills.[j] [11]The four
kings seized all the goods of Sodom and Gomorrah and all their
food; then they went away. [12]They also carried off Abram's
nephew Lot and his possessions, since he was living in Sodom.
[13]One who had escaped came and reported this to Abram the
Hebrew. Now Abram was living near the great trees of Mamre[k]
the Amorite, a brother[b] of Eshcol and Aner, all of whom were
allied with Abram. [14]When Abram heard that his relative had
been taken captive, he called out the 318 trained men born in
his household[l] and went in pursuit as far as Dan.[m] [15]During the
night Abram divided his men to attack them and he routed
them, pursuing them as far as Hobah, north of Damascus. [16]He
recovered all the goods and brought back his relative Lot and
his possessions, together with the women and the other people.
[17]After Abram returned from defeating Kedorlaomer and the
kings allied with him, the king of Sodom came out to meet him
in the Valley of Shaveh (that is, the King's Valley).[n]
[18]Then Melchizedek[o] king of Salem[c][p] brought out bread and
wine. He was priest of God Most High, [19]and he blessed Abram,[q]
saying,

> "Blessed be Abram by God Most High,
> Creator[d] of heaven and earth.[r]
> [20]And blessed be[e] God Most High,[s]
> who delivered your enemies into your hand."

Then Abram gave him a tenth of everything.[t]

[a] 3 That is, the Dead Sea [b] 13 Or *a relative*; or *an ally* [c] 18 That is, Jerusalem [d] 19 Or *Possessor*; also in verse 22 [e] 20 Or *And praise be to*

14:3 *a* Nu 34:3,12; Dt 3:17; Jos 3:16; 15:2,5
14:5 *b* Ge 15:20; Dt 2:11,20 *c* Dt 2:10
14:6 *d* Dt 2:12,22 *e* Dt 2:1,5,22 *f* Ge 21:21; Nu 10:12
14:7 *g* 2Ch 20:2
14:8 *h* Ge 13:10; 19:17-29 *i* Dt 29:23
14:10 *j* Ge 19:17,30
14:13 *k* ver 24; Ge 13:18
14:14 *l* Ge 15:3 *m* Dt 34:1; Jdg 18:29
14:17 *n* 2Sa 18:18
14:18 *o* Ps 110:4; Heb 5:6 *p* Ps 76:2; Heb 7:2
14:19 *q* Heb 7:6 *r* ver 22
14:20 *s* Ge 24:27 *t* Ge 28:22; Dt 26:12; Heb 7:4

21The king of Sodom said to Abram, "Give me the people and
keep the goods for yourself."
22But Abram said to the king of Sodom, "I have raised my
hand[a] to the LORD, God Most High, Creator of heaven and earth,[b]
and have taken an oath 23that I will accept nothing belonging to
you,[c] not even a thread or the thong of a sandal, so that you will
never be able to say, 'I made Abram rich.' 24I will accept nothing
but what my men have eaten and the share that belongs to the
men who went with me—to Aner, Eshcol and Mamre. Let them
have their share."

Chapter 15 Theme __________________________________

15 After this, the word of the LORD came to Abram[d] in a
vision:

"Do not be afraid,[e] Abram.
I am your shield,[a][f]
your very great reward.[b]"

2But Abram said, "O Sovereign LORD, what can you give me
since I remain childless[g] and the one who will inherit[c] my estate
is Eliezer of Damascus?" 3And Abram said, "You have given me
no children; so a servant[h] in my household will be my heir."
4Then the word of the LORD came to him: "This man will not
be your heir, but a son coming from your own body will be your
heir.[i]" 5He took him outside and said, "Look up at the heavens
and count the stars[j]—if indeed you can count them." Then he
said to him, "So shall your offspring be."[k]
6Abram believed the LORD, and he credited it to him as righteousness.[l]
7He also said to him, "I am the LORD, who brought you out of
Ur of the Chaldeans to give you this land to take possession of it."
8But Abram said, "O Sovereign LORD, how can I know[m] that I
will gain possession of it?"
9So the LORD said to him, "Bring me a heifer, a goat and a ram,
each three years old, along with a dove and a young pigeon."
10Abram brought all these to him, cut them in two and arranged
the halves opposite each other;[n] the birds, however, he did not
cut in half.[o] 11Then birds of prey came down on the carcasses,
but Abram drove them away.
12As the sun was setting, Abram fell into a deep sleep,[p] and a
thick and dreadful darkness came over him. 13Then the LORD
said to him, "Know for certain that your descendants will be
strangers in a country not their own, and they will be enslaved[q]

INSIGHT

Beriyt, the Hebrew word for covenant, is a solemn binding agreement made by passing through pieces of flesh. The Greek word for covenant, ***diatheke***, means a testament or an agreement. The Bible is divided into the Old and New Testaments—or covenants. Everything God does is based on covenant.

14:22 [a]Ex 6:8; Da 12:7; Rev 10:5-6 [b]ver 19
14:23 [c]2Ki 5:16
15:1 [d]Da 10:1 [e]Ge 21:17; 26:24; 46:3; 2Ki 6:16; Ps 27:1; Isa 41:10,13-14 [f]Dt 33:29; 2Sa 22:3,31; Ps 3:3
15:2 [g]Ac 7:5
15:3 [h]Ge 24:2,34
15:4 [i]Gal 4:28
15:5 [j]Ps 147:4; Jer 33:22 [k]Ge 12:2; 22:17; Ex 32:13; Ro 4:18*; Heb 11:12
15:6 [l]Ps 106:31; Ro 4:3*, 20-24*; Gal 3:6*; Jas 2:23*
15:8 [m]Lk 1:18
15:10 [n]ver 17; Jer 34:18 [o]Lev 1:17
15:12 [p]Ge 2:21
15:13 [q]Ex 1:11

a *1* Or *sovereign* b *1* Or *shield; / your reward will be very great* c *2* The meaning of the Hebrew for this phrase is uncertain.

and mistreated four hundred years.[a] [14]But I will punish the nation they serve as slaves, and afterward they will come out[b] with great possessions.[c] [15]You, however, will go to your fathers in peace and be buried at a good old age.[d] [16]In the fourth generation your descendants will come back here, for the sin of the Amorites[e] has not yet reached its full measure."

[17]When the sun had set and darkness had fallen, a smoking firepot with a blazing torch appeared and passed between the pieces.[f] [18]On that day the LORD made a covenant with Abram and said, "To your descendants I give this land,[g] from the river[a] of Egypt[h] to the great river, the Euphrates— [19]the land of the Kenites, Kenizzites, Kadmonites, [20]Hittites, Perizzites, Rephaites, [21]Amorites, Canaanites, Girgashites and Jebusites."

Chapter 16 Theme ______________________________

16 Now Sarai, Abram's wife, had borne him no children.[i] But she had an Egyptian maidservant[j] named Hagar; [2]so she said to Abram, "The LORD has kept me from having children. Go, sleep with my maidservant; perhaps I can build a family through her."[k]

Abram agreed to what Sarai said. [3]So after Abram had been living in Canaan[l] ten years, Sarai his wife took her Egyptian maidservant Hagar and gave her to her husband to be his wife. [4]He slept with Hagar, and she conceived.

When she knew she was pregnant, she began to despise her mistress. [5]Then Sarai said to Abram, "You are responsible for the wrong I am suffering. I put my servant in your arms, and now that she knows she is pregnant, she despises me. May the LORD judge between you and me."[m]

[6]"Your servant is in your hands," Abram said. "Do with her whatever you think best." Then Sarai mistreated Hagar; so she fled from her.

[7]The angel of the LORD[n] found Hagar near a spring in the desert; it was the spring that is beside the road to Shur.[o] [8]And he said, "Hagar, servant of Sarai, where have you come from, and where are you going?"

"I'm running away from my mistress Sarai," she answered.

[9]Then the angel of the LORD told her, "Go back to your mistress and submit to her." [10]The angel added, "I will so increase your descendants that they will be too numerous to count."[p]

[11]The angel of the LORD also said to her:

"You are now with child
and you will have a son.

15:13 [a]ver 16; Ex 12:40; Ac 7:6,17
15:14 [b]Ac 7:7*; [c]Ex 12:32-38
15:15 [d]Ge 25:8
15:16 [e]1Ki 21:26
15:17 [f]ver 10
15:18 [g]Ge 12:7; [h]Nu 34:5
16:1 [i]Ge 11:30; Gal 4:24-25; [j]Ge 21:9
16:2 [k]Ge 30:3-4, 9-10
16:3 [l]Ge 12:5
16:5 [m]Ge 31:53
16:7 [n]Ge 21:17; 22:11,15; 31:11; [o]Ge 20:1
16:10 [p]Ge 13:16; 17:20

[a]18 Or *Wadi*

You shall name him Ishmael,[a]
for the LORD has heard of your misery.[a]
12 He will be a wild donkey of a man;
his hand will be against everyone
and everyone's hand against him,
and he will live in hostility
toward[b] all his brothers.[b]"

13 She gave this name to the LORD who spoke to her: "You are the God who sees me," for she said, "I have now seen[c] the One who sees me."[c] 14 That is why the well was called Beer Lahai Roi[d]; it is still there, between Kadesh and Bered.

15 So Hagar bore Abram a son,[d] and Abram gave the name Ishmael to the son she had borne. 16 Abram was eighty-six years old when Hagar bore him Ishmael.

Chapter 17 Theme

17 When Abram was ninety-nine years old, the LORD appeared to him and said, "I am God Almighty[e];[e] walk before me and be blameless.[f] 2 I will confirm my covenant between me and you[g] and will greatly increase your numbers."

3 Abram fell facedown, and God said to him, 4 "As for me, this is my covenant with you:[h] You will be the father of many nations.[i] 5 No longer will you be called Abram[f]; your name will be Abraham,[g][j] for I have made you a father of many nations.[k] 6 I will make you very fruitful;[l] I will make nations of you, and kings will come from you.[m] 7 I will establish my covenant as an everlasting covenant between me and you and your descendants after you for the generations to come, to be your God[n] and the God of your descendants after you.[o] 8 The whole land of Canaan,[p] where you are now an alien,[q] I will give as an everlasting possession to you and your descendants after you;[r] and I will be their God."

9 Then God said to Abraham, "As for you, you must keep my covenant, you and your descendants after you for the generations to come. 10 This is my covenant with you and your descendants after you, the covenant you are to keep: Every male among you shall be circumcised.[s] 11 You are to undergo circumcision,[t] and it will be the sign of the covenant[u] between me and you. 12 For the generations to come every male among you who is eight days old must be circumcised,[v] including those born in your household or bought with money from a foreigner—those who are not your offspring. 13 Whether born

[a] *11 Ishmael* means *God hears.* [b] *12* Or *live to the east / of* [c] *13* Or *seen the back of*
[d] *14 Beer Lahai Roi* means *well of the Living One who sees me.* [e] *1* Hebrew *El-Shaddai*
[f] *5 Abram* means *exalted father.* [g] *5 Abraham* means *father of many.*

16:11 *a* Ex 2:24; 3:7,9
16:12 *b* Ge 25:18
16:13 *c* Ge 32:30
16:15 *d* Gal 4:22
17:1 *e* Ge 28:3; Ex 6:3 *f* Dt 18:13
17:2 *g* Ge 15:18
17:4 *h* Ge 15:18 *i* ver 16; Ge 12:2; 35:11; 48:19
17:5 *j* ver 15; Ne 9:7 *k* Ro 4:17*
17:6 *l* Ge 35:11 *m* Mt 1:6
17:7 *n* Ex 29:45,46 *o* Ro 9:8; Gal 3:16
17:8 *p* Ps 105:9,11 *q* Ge 23:4; 28:4; Ex 6:4 *r* Ge 12:7
17:10 *s* ver 23; Ge 21:4; Jn 7:22; Ac 7:8; Ro 4:11
17:11 *t* Ex 12:48; Dt 10:16 *u* Ro 4:11
17:12 *v* Lev 12:3; Lk 2:21

in your household or bought with your money, they must be circumcised. My covenant in your flesh is to be an everlasting covenant. 14 Any uncircumcised male, who has not been circumcised in the flesh, will be cut off from his people;[a] he has broken my covenant."

15 God also said to Abraham, "As for Sarai your wife, you are no longer to call her Sarai; her name will be Sarah. 16 I will bless her and will surely give you a son by her.[b] I will bless her so that she will be the mother of nations;[c] kings of peoples will come from her."

17 Abraham fell facedown; he laughed[d] and said to himself, "Will a son be born to a man a hundred years old? Will Sarah bear a child at the age of ninety?" 18 And Abraham said to God, "If only Ishmael might live under your blessing!"

19 Then God said, "Yes, but your wife Sarah will bear you a son,[e] and you will call him Isaac.[a] I will establish my covenant with him[f] as an everlasting covenant for his descendants after him. 20 And as for Ishmael, I have heard you: I will surely bless him; I will make him fruitful and will greatly increase his numbers.[g] He will be the father of twelve rulers,[h] and I will make him into a great nation.[i] 21 But my covenant I will establish with Isaac, whom Sarah will bear to you by this time next year."[j] 22 When he had finished speaking with Abraham, God went up from him.

23 On that very day Abraham took his son Ishmael and all those born in his household or bought with his money, every male in his household, and circumcised them, as God told him. 24 Abraham was ninety-nine years old when he was circumcised,[k] 25 and his son Ishmael was thirteen; 26 Abraham and his son Ishmael were both circumcised on that same day. 27 And every male in Abraham's household, including those born in his household or bought from a foreigner, was circumcised with him.

Chapter 18 Theme ________________________________

18

The LORD appeared to Abraham near the great trees of Mamre[l] while he was sitting at the entrance to his tent in the heat of the day. 2 Abraham looked up and saw three men[m] standing nearby. When he saw them, he hurried from the entrance of his tent to meet them and bowed low to the ground.

3 He said, "If I have found favor in your eyes, my lord,[b] do not pass your servant by. 4 Let a little water be brought, and then you may all wash your feet[n] and rest under this tree. 5 Let me get you something to eat,[o] so you can be refreshed and then go on your way—now that you have come to your servant."

[a] 19 *Isaac* means *he laughs.* [b] 3 Or *O Lord*

17:14 [a] Ex 4:24-26
17:16 [b] Ge 18:10 [c] Ge 35:11; Gal 4:31
17:17 [d] Ge 18:12; 21:6
17:19 [e] Ge 18:14; 21:2 [f] Ge 26:3
17:20 [g] Ge 16:10 [h] Ge 25:12-16 [i] Ge 21:18
17:21 [j] Ge 21:2
17:24 [k] Ro 4:11
18:1 [l] Ge 13:18; 14:13
18:2 [m] ver 16,22; Ge 32:24; Jos 5:13; Jdg 13:6-11; Heb 13:2
18:4 [n] Ge 19:2; 43:24
18:5 [o] Jdg 13:15

"Very well," they answered, "do as you say."
6So Abraham hurried into the tent to Sarah. "Quick," he said,
"get three seahs[a] of fine flour and knead it and bake some bread."
7Then he ran to the herd and selected a choice, tender calf and
gave it to a servant, who hurried to prepare it. 8He then brought
some curds and milk and the calf that had been prepared, and
set these before them.[a] While they ate, he stood near them
under a tree.
9"Where is your wife Sarah?" they asked him.
"There, in the tent," he said.
10Then the LORD[b] said, "I will surely return to you about this
time next year, and Sarah your wife will have a son."[b]
Now Sarah was listening at the entrance to the tent, which was
behind him. 11Abraham and Sarah were already old and well
advanced in years,[c] and Sarah was past the age of childbearing.[d]
12So Sarah laughed[e] to herself as she thought, "After I am worn
out and my master[c][f] is old, will I now have this pleasure?"
13Then the LORD said to Abraham, "Why did Sarah laugh and
say, 'Will I really have a child, now that I am old?' 14Is anything
too hard for the LORD?[g] I will return to you at the appointed
time next year and Sarah will have a son."
15Sarah was afraid, so she lied and said, "I did not laugh."
But he said, "Yes, you did laugh."
16When the men got up to leave, they looked down toward
Sodom, and Abraham walked along with them to see them on
their way. 17Then the LORD said, "Shall I hide from Abraham[h]
what I am about to do?[i] 18Abraham will surely become a great
and powerful nation,[j] and all nations on earth will be blessed
through him. 19For I have chosen him, so that he will direct his
children[k] and his household after him to keep the way of the
LORD[l] by doing what is right and just, so that the LORD will bring
about for Abraham what he has promised him."
20Then the LORD said, "The outcry against Sodom and
Gomorrah is so great and their sin so grievous 21that I will go
down[m] and see if what they have done is as bad as the outcry
that has reached me. If not, I will know."
22The men turned away and went toward Sodom,[n] but Abraham remained standing before the LORD.[d] 23Then Abraham
approached him and said: "Will you sweep away the righteous
with the wicked?[o] 24What if there are fifty righteous people in
the city? Will you really sweep it away and not spare[e] the place
for the sake of the fifty righteous people in it?[p] 25Far be it from
you to do such a thing—to kill the righteous with the wicked,

[a]6 That is, probably about 20 quarts (about 22 liters) [b]10 Hebrew *Then he* [c]12 Or *husband*
[d]22 Masoretic Text; an ancient Hebrew scribal tradition *but the LORD remained standing before Abraham* [e]24 Or *forgive*; also in verse 26

18:8 [a]Ge 19:3
18:10 [b]Ro 9:9*
18:11 [c]Ge 17:17 [d]Ro 4:19
18:12 [e]Ge 17:17; 21:6 [f]1Pe 3:6
18:14 [g]Jer 32:17,27; Zec 8:6; Mt 19:26; Lk 1:37; Ro 4:21
18:17 [h]Am 3:7 [i]Ge 19:24
18:18 [j]Gal 3:8*
18:19 [k]Dt 4:9-10; 6:7 [l]Jos 24:15; Eph 6:4
18:21 [m]Ge 11:5
18:22 [n]Ge 19:1
18:23 [o]Nu 16:22
18:24 [p]Jer 5:1

treating the righteous and the wicked alike. Far be it from you! Will not the Judge[a] of all the earth do right?"[a]

26The LORD said, "If I find fifty righteous people in the city of Sodom, I will spare the whole place for their sake.[b]"

27Then Abraham spoke up again: "Now that I have been so bold as to speak to the Lord, though I am nothing but dust and ashes,[c] 28what if the number of the righteous is five less than fifty? Will you destroy the whole city because of five people?"

"If I find forty-five there," he said, "I will not destroy it."

29Once again he spoke to him, "What if only forty are found there?"

He said, "For the sake of forty, I will not do it."

30Then he said, "May the Lord not be angry, but let me speak. What if only thirty can be found there?"

He answered, "I will not do it if I find thirty there."

31Abraham said, "Now that I have been so bold as to speak to the Lord, what if only twenty can be found there?"

He said, "For the sake of twenty, I will not destroy it."

32Then he said, "May the Lord not be angry, but let me speak just once more.[d] What if only ten can be found there?"

He answered, "For the sake of ten,[e] I will not destroy it."

33When the LORD had finished speaking with Abraham, he left, and Abraham returned home.

Chapter 19 Theme ________________________

19 The two angels arrived at Sodom[f] in the evening, and Lot was sitting in the gateway of the city.[g] When he saw them, he got up to meet them and bowed down with his face to the ground. 2"My lords," he said, "please turn aside to your servant's house. You can wash your feet[h] and spend the night and then go on your way early in the morning."

"No," they answered, "we will spend the night in the square."

3But he insisted so strongly that they did go with him and entered his house. He prepared a meal for them, baking bread without yeast, and they ate.[i] 4Before they had gone to bed, all the men from every part of the city of Sodom—both young and old—surrounded the house. 5They called to Lot, "Where are the men who came to you tonight? Bring them out to us so that we can have sex with them."[j]

6Lot went outside to meet them[k] and shut the door behind him 7and said, "No, my friends. Don't do this wicked thing. 8Look, I have two daughters who have never slept with a man. Let me bring them out to you, and you can do what you like

18:25 [a]Job 8:3,20; Ps 58:11; 94:2; Isa 3:10-11; Ro 3:6
18:26 [b]Jer 5:1
18:27 [c]Ge 2:7; 3:19; Job 30:19; 42:6
18:32 [d]Jdg 6:39 [e]Jer 5:1
19:1 [f]Ge 18:22 [g]Ge 18:1
19:2 [h]Ge 18:4; Lk 7:44
19:3 [i]Ge 18:6
19:5 [j]Jdg 19:22; Isa 3:9; Ro 1:24-27
19:6 [k]Jdg 19:23

[a]25 Or *Ruler*

with them. But don't do anything to these men, for they have
come under the protection of my roof."[a]
9"Get out of our way," they replied. And they said, "This fellow came here as an alien, and now he wants to play the judge![b]
We'll treat you worse than them." They kept bringing pressure
on Lot and moved forward to break down the door.
10But the men inside reached out and pulled Lot back into the
house and shut the door. 11Then they struck the men who were
at the door of the house, young and old, with blindness[c] so that
they could not find the door.
12The two men said to Lot, "Do you have anyone else here—
sons-in-law, sons or daughters, or anyone else in the city who
belongs to you?[d] Get them out of here, 13because we are going to
destroy this place. The outcry to the LORD against its people is
so great that he has sent us to destroy it."[e]
14So Lot went out and spoke to his sons-in-law, who were
pledged to marry[a] his daughters. He said, "Hurry and get out of
this place, because the LORD is about to destroy the city![f]" But
his sons-in-law thought he was joking.[g]
15With the coming of dawn, the angels urged Lot, saying,
"Hurry! Take your wife and your two daughters who are here,
or you will be swept away[h] when the city is punished.[i]"
16When he hesitated, the men grasped his hand and the hands
of his wife and of his two daughters and led them safely out of
the city, for the LORD was merciful to them. 17As soon as they
had brought them out, one of them said, "Flee for your lives![j]
Don't look back,[k] and don't stop anywhere in the plain! Flee to
the mountains or you will be swept away!"
18But Lot said to them, "No, my lords,[b] please! 19Your[c] servant has found favor in your[c] eyes, and you[c] have shown great
kindness to me in sparing my life. But I can't flee to the mountains; this disaster will overtake me, and I'll die. 20Look, here is a
town near enough to run to, and it is small. Let me flee to it—it
is very small, isn't it? Then my life will be spared."
21He said to him, "Very well, I will grant this request too; I will
not overthrow the town you speak of. 22But flee there quickly,
because I cannot do anything until you reach it." (That is why
the town was called Zoar.[d])
23By the time Lot reached Zoar, the sun had risen over the
land. 24Then the LORD rained down burning sulfur on Sodom
and Gomorrah[l]—from the LORD out of the heavens.[m] 25Thus he
overthrew those cities and the entire plain, including all those
living in the cities—and also the vegetation in the land.[n] 26But
Lot's wife looked back,[o] and she became a pillar of salt.[p]

[a] *14* Or *were married to* [b] *18* Or *No, Lord;* or *No, my lord* [c] *19* The Hebrew is singular.
[d] *22* *Zoar* means *small.*

19:8 *a* Jdg 19:24
19:9 *b* Ex 2:14; Ac 7:27
19:11 *c* Dt 28:28-29; 2Ki 6:18; Ac 13:11
19:12 *d* Ge 7:1
19:13 *e* 1Ch 21:15
19:14 *f* Nu 16:21 *g* Ex 9:21; Lk 17:28
19:15 *h* Nu 16:26 *i* Rev 18:4
19:17 *j* Jer 48:6 *k* ver 26
19:24 *l* Dt 29:23; Isa 1:9; 13:19 *m* Lk 17:29; 2Pe 2:6; Jude 7
19:25 *n* Ps 107:34; Eze 16:48
19:26 *o* ver 17 *p* Lk 17:32

27Early the next morning Abraham got up and returned to the place where he had stood before the LORD.[a] 28He looked down toward Sodom and Gomorrah, toward all the land of the plain, and he saw dense smoke rising from the land, like smoke from a furnace.[b]

29So when God destroyed the cities of the plain, he remembered Abraham, and he brought Lot out of the catastrophe[c] that overthrew the cities where Lot had lived.

30Lot and his two daughters left Zoar and settled in the mountains,[d] for he was afraid to stay in Zoar. He and his two daughters lived in a cave. 31One day the older daughter said to the younger, "Our father is old, and there is no man around here to lie with us, as is the custom all over the earth. 32Let's get our father to drink wine and then lie with him and preserve our family line through our father."

33That night they got their father to drink wine, and the older daughter went in and lay with him. He was not aware of it when she lay down or when she got up.

34The next day the older daughter said to the younger, "Last night I lay with my father. Let's get him to drink wine again tonight, and you go in and lie with him so we can preserve our family line through our father." 35So they got their father to drink wine that night also, and the younger daughter went and lay with him. Again he was not aware of it when she lay down or when she got up.

36So both of Lot's daughters became pregnant by their father. 37The older daughter had a son, and she named him Moab[a]; he is the father of the Moabites[e] of today. 38The younger daughter also had a son, and she named him Ben-Ammi[b]; he is the father of the Ammonites[f] of today.

Chapter 20 Theme ______________________

20 Now Abraham moved on from there[g] into the region of the Negev and lived between Kadesh and Shur. For a while he stayed in Gerar,[h] 2and there Abraham said of his wife Sarah, "She is my sister.[i]" Then Abimelech king of Gerar sent for Sarah and took her.[j]

3But God came to Abimelech in a dream[k] one night and said to him, "You are as good as dead because of the woman you have taken; she is a married woman."[l]

4Now Abimelech had not gone near her, so he said, "Lord, will you destroy an innocent nation?[m] 5Did he not say to me, 'She is my sister,' and didn't she also say, 'He is my brother'? I have done this with a clear conscience and clean hands."

19:27 [a]Ge 18:22
19:28 [b]Rev 9:2; 18:9
19:29 [c]2Pe 2:7
19:30 [d]ver 19
19:37 [e]Dt 2:9
19:38 [f]Dt 2:19
20:1 [g]Ge 18:1 [h]Ge 26:1,6,17
20:2 [i]ver 12; Ge 12:13; 26:7 [j]Ge 12:15
20:3 [k]Job 33:15; Mt 27:19 [l]Ps 105:14
20:4 [m]Ge 18:25

a 37 *Moab* sounds like the Hebrew for *from father.* b 38 *Ben-Ammi* means *son of my people.*

6Then God said to him in the dream, “Yes, I know you did this
with a clear conscience, and so I have kept[a] you from sinning
against me. That is why I did not let you touch her. 7Now return
the man’s wife, for he is a prophet, and he will pray for you[b] and
you will live. But if you do not return her, you may be sure that
you and all yours will die.”
8Early the next morning Abimelech summoned all his officials,
and when he told them all that had happened, they were very
much afraid. 9Then Abimelech called Abraham in and said,
“What have you done to us? How have I wronged you that you
have brought such great guilt upon me and my kingdom? You
have done things to me that should not be done.[c]” 10And Abimelech asked Abraham, “What was your reason for doing this?”
11Abraham replied, “I said to myself, ‘There is surely no fear
of God[d] in this place, and they will kill me because of my wife.’[e]
12Besides, she really is my sister, the daughter of my father
though not of my mother; and she became my wife. 13And when
God had me wander from my father’s household, I said to her,
‘This is how you can show your love to me: Everywhere we go,
say of me, “He is my brother.” ’ ”
14Then Abimelech brought sheep and cattle and male and
female slaves and gave them to Abraham,[f] and he returned
Sarah his wife to him. 15And Abimelech said, “My land is before
you; live wherever you like.”[g]
16To Sarah he said, “I am giving your brother a thousand
shekels[a] of silver. This is to cover the offense against you before
all who are with you; you are completely vindicated.”
17Then Abraham prayed to God,[h] and God healed Abimelech,
his wife and his slave girls so they could have children again,
18for the LORD had closed up every womb in Abimelech’s household because of Abraham’s wife Sarah.[i]

Chapter 21 Theme __________________________

21

Now the LORD was gracious to Sarah[j] as he had said, and
the LORD did for Sarah what he had promised.[k] 2Sarah
became pregnant and bore a son[l] to Abraham in his old age,[m] at
the very time God had promised him. 3Abraham gave the name
Isaac[b][n] to the son Sarah bore him. 4When his son Isaac was
eight days old, Abraham circumcised him,[o] as God commanded
him. 5Abraham was a hundred years old when his son Isaac was
born to him.
6Sarah said, “God has brought me laughter,[p] and everyone
who hears about this will laugh with me.” 7And she added, “Who

a *16* That is, about 25 pounds (about 11.5 kilograms) b *3* *Isaac* means *he laughs.*

20:6 [a]1Sa 25:26,34
20:7 [b]ver 17; 1Sa 7:5; Job 42:8
20:9 [c]Ge 12:18; 26:10; 34:7
20:11 [d]Ge 42:18; Ps 36:1 [e]Ge 12:12; 26:7
20:14 [f]Ge 12:16
20:15 [g]Ge 13:9
20:17 [h]Job 42:9
20:18 [i]Ge 12:17
21:1 [j]1Sa 2:21 [k]Ge 8:1; 17:16,21; Gal 4:23
21:2 [l]Ge 17:19 [m]Gal 4:22; Heb 11:11
21:3 [n]Ge 17:19
21:4 [o]Ge 17:10,12; Ac 7:8
21:6 [p]Ge 17:17; Isa 54:1

would have said to Abraham that Sarah would nurse children?
Yet I have borne him a son in his old age."
8The child grew and was weaned, and on the day Isaac was
weaned Abraham held a great feast. 9But Sarah saw that the son
whom Hagar the Egyptian had borne to Abraham[a] was mocking,[b] 10and she said to Abraham, "Get rid of that slave woman
and her son, for that slave woman's son will never share in the
inheritance with my son Isaac."[c]
11The matter distressed Abraham greatly because it concerned his son.[d] 12But God said to him, "Do not be so distressed
about the boy and your maidservant. Listen to whatever Sarah
tells you, because it is through Isaac that your offspring[a] will be
reckoned.[e] 13I will make the son of the maidservant into a
nation[f] also, because he is your offspring."
14Early the next morning Abraham took some food and a skin
of water and gave them to Hagar. He set them on her shoulders
and then sent her off with the boy. She went on her way and
wandered in the desert of Beersheba.[g]
15When the water in the skin was gone, she put the boy under
one of the bushes. 16Then she went off and sat down nearby,
about a bowshot away, for she thought, "I cannot watch the boy
die." And as she sat there nearby, she[b] began to sob.
17God heard the boy crying,[h] and the angel of God called to
Hagar from heaven and said to her, "What is the matter, Hagar?
Do not be afraid; God has heard the boy crying as he lies there.
18Lift the boy up and take him by the hand, for I will make him
into a great nation.[i]"
19Then God opened her eyes[j] and she saw a well of water. So
she went and filled the skin with water and gave the boy a drink.
20God was with the boy[k] as he grew up. He lived in the desert
and became an archer. 21While he was living in the Desert of
Paran, his mother got a wife for him[l] from Egypt.
22At that time Abimelech and Phicol the commander of his
forces said to Abraham, "God is with you in everything you do.
23Now swear[m] to me here before God that you will not deal
falsely with me or my children or my descendants. Show to me
and the country where you are living as an alien the same kindness I have shown to you."
24Abraham said, "I swear it."
25Then Abraham complained to Abimelech about a well of
water that Abimelech's servants had seized.[n] 26But Abimelech
said, "I don't know who has done this. You did not tell me, and
I heard about it only today."

21:9 [a]Ge 16:15 [b]Gal 4:29
21:10 [c]Gal 4:30*
21:11 [d]Ge 17:18
21:12 [e]Ro 9:7*; Heb 11:18*
21:13 [f]ver 18
21:14 [g]ver 31,32
21:17 [h]Ex 3:7
21:18 [i]ver 13
21:19 [j]Nu 22:31
21:20 [k]Ge 26:3,24; 28:15; 39:2,21,23
21:21 [l]Ge 24:4,38
21:23 [m]ver 31; Jos 2:12
21:25 [n]Ge 26:15,18, 20-22

a *12* Or *seed* b *16* Hebrew; Septuagint *the child*

27 So Abraham brought sheep and cattle and gave them to Abimelech, and the two men made a treaty.[a] 28 Abraham set apart seven ewe lambs from the flock, 29 and Abimelech asked Abraham, "What is the meaning of these seven ewe lambs you have set apart by themselves?"

30 He replied, "Accept these seven lambs from my hand as a witness[b] that I dug this well."

31 So that place was called Beersheba,[a][c] because the two men swore an oath there.

32 After the treaty had been made at Beersheba, Abimelech and Phicol the commander of his forces returned to the land of the Philistines. 33 Abraham planted a tamarisk tree in Beersheba, and there he called upon the name of the LORD,[d] the Eternal God.[e] 34 And Abraham stayed in the land of the Philistines for a long time.

Chapter 22 Theme

22 Some time later God tested[f] Abraham. He said to him, "Abraham!"

"Here I am," he replied.

2 Then God said, "Take your son[g], your only son, Isaac, whom you love, and go to the region of Moriah.[h] Sacrifice him there as a burnt offering on one of the mountains I will tell you about."

3 Early the next morning Abraham got up and saddled his donkey. He took with him two of his servants and his son Isaac. When he had cut enough wood for the burnt offering, he set out for the place God had told him about. 4 On the third day Abraham looked up and saw the place in the distance. 5 He said to his servants, "Stay here with the donkey while I and the boy go over there. We will worship and then we will come back to you."

6 Abraham took the wood for the burnt offering and placed it on his son Isaac,[i] and he himself carried the fire and the knife. As the two of them went on together, 7 Isaac spoke up and said to his father Abraham, "Father?"

"Yes, my son?" Abraham replied.

"The fire and wood are here," Isaac said, "but where is the lamb[j] for the burnt offering?"

8 Abraham answered, "God himself will provide the lamb for the burnt offering, my son." And the two of them went on together.

9 When they reached the place God had told him about, Abraham built an altar there and arranged the wood on it. He bound his son Isaac and laid him on the altar,[k] on top of the wood. 10 Then he reached out his hand and took the knife to slay his

INSIGHT

The first references to ***love***, ***obedience***, and ***worship*** are found in Genesis 22. Note the context.

21:27 [a]Ge 26:28,31
21:30 [b]Ge 31:44,47, 48,50,52
21:31 [c]Ge 26:33
21:33 [d]Ge 4:26 [e]Dt 33:27
22:1 [f]Dt 8:2,16; Heb 11:17; Jas 1:12-13
22:2 [g]ver 12,16; Jn 3:16; Heb 11:17; 1Jn 4:9 [h]2Ch 3:1
22:6 [i]Jn 19:17
22:7 [j]Lev 1:10
22:9 [k]Heb 11:17-19; Jas 2:21

a 31 *Beersheba* can mean *well of seven* or *well of the oath.*

22:12 [a]1Sa 15:22; son. 11But the angel of the LORD called out to him from heaven,
Jas 2:21-22 “Abraham! Abraham!”
[b]ver 2; Jn 3:16 “Here I am,” he replied.
12“Do not lay a hand on the boy,” he said. “Do not do anything to him. Now I know that you fear God,[a] because you have
22:13 [c]Ro 8:32 not withheld from me your son, your only son.[b]”
13Abraham looked up and there in a thicket he saw a ram[a]
caught by its horns. He went over and took the ram and sacri-
22:14 ficed it as a burnt offering instead of his son.[c] 14So Abraham
[d]ver 8 called that place The LORD Will Provide. And to this day it is
said, “On the mountain of the LORD it will be provided.[d]”
15The angel of the LORD called to Abraham from heaven a sec-
22:16 [e]Lk 1:73; ond time 16and said, “I swear by myself,[e] declares the LORD, that
Heb 6:13 because you have done this and have not withheld your son,
your only son, 17I will surely bless you and make your descen-
22:17 dants[f] as numerous as the stars in the sky[g] and as the sand on
[f]Heb 6:14* [g]Ge 15:5 the seashore.[h] Your descendants will take possession of the cities
[h]Ge 26:24; of their enemies,[i] 18and through your offspring[b] all nations on
32:12 [i]Ge 24:60 earth will be blessed,[j] because you have obeyed me.”[k]
19Then Abraham returned to his servants, and they set off
together for Beersheba. And Abraham stayed in Beersheba.
22:18 20Some time later Abraham was told, “Milcah is also a moth-
[j]Ge 12:2,3; Ac 3:25*; er; she has borne sons to your brother Nahor:[l] 21Uz the first-
Gal 3:8* [k]ver 10 born, Buz his brother, Kemuel (the father of Aram), 22Kesed,
Hazo, Pildash, Jidlaph and Bethuel.” 23Bethuel became the
father of Rebekah.[m] Milcah bore these eight sons to Abraham’s
22:20 brother Nahor. 24His concubine, whose name was Reumah, also
[l]Ge 11:29 had sons: Tebah, Gaham, Tahash and Maacah.

Chapter 23 Theme ______________________

22:23 [m]Ge 24:15 **23** Sarah lived to be a hundred and twenty-seven years old.
2She died at Kiriath Arba[n] (that is, Hebron)[o] in the land
of Canaan, and Abraham went to mourn for Sarah and to weep
23:2 [n]Jos 14:15 over her.
[o]ver 19; Ge 13:18 3Then Abraham rose from beside his dead wife and spoke to
the Hittites.[c] He said, 4“I am an alien and a stranger[p] among
you. Sell me some property for a burial site here so I can bury
23:4 [p]Ge 17:8; my dead.”
1Ch 29:15; 5The Hittites replied to Abraham, 6“Sir, listen to us. You are a
Ps 105:12; Heb 11:9,13 mighty prince[q] among us. Bury your dead in the choicest of our
tombs. None of us will refuse you his tomb for burying your
dead.”

23:6 [q]Ge 14:14-16; 24:35

[a] *13* Many manuscripts of the Masoretic Text, Samaritan Pentateuch, Septuagint and Syriac; most manuscripts of the Masoretic Text *a ram behind* ⌊*him*⌋ [b] *18* Or *seed*
[c] *3* Or *the sons of Heth*; also in verses 5, 7, 10, 16, 18 and 20

7Then Abraham rose and bowed down before the people of
the land, the Hittites. 8He said to them, "If you are willing to let
me bury my dead, then listen to me and intercede with Ephron
son of Zohar[a] on my behalf 9so he will sell me the cave of Machpelah, which belongs to him and is at the end of his field. Ask
him to sell it to me for the full price as a burial site among you."
10Ephron the Hittite was sitting among his people and he
replied to Abraham in the hearing of all the Hittites who had
come to the gate[b] of his city. 11"No, my lord," he said. "Listen to
me; I give[a][c] you the field, and I give[a] you the cave that is in it. I
give[a] it to you in the presence of my people. Bury your dead."

12Again Abraham bowed down before the people of the land
13and he said to Ephron in their hearing, "Listen to me, if you
will. I will pay the price of the field. Accept it from me so I can
bury my dead there."

14Ephron answered Abraham, 15"Listen to me, my lord; the
land is worth four hundred shekels[b] of silver,[d] but what is that
between me and you? Bury your dead."

16Abraham agreed to Ephron's terms and weighed out for
him the price he had named in the hearing of the Hittites: four
hundred shekels of silver,[e] according to the weight current
among the merchants.

17So Ephron's field in Machpelah near Mamre[f]—both the
field and the cave in it, and all the trees within the borders of the
field—was deeded 18to Abraham as his property in the presence
of all the Hittites who had come to the gate of the city. 19After-
ward Abraham buried his wife Sarah in the cave in the field of
Machpelah near Mamre (which is at Hebron) in the land of
Canaan. 20So the field and the cave in it were deeded[g] to Abraham by the Hittites as a burial site.

Chapter 24 Theme ____________________

24 Abraham was now old and well advanced in years, and
the LORD had blessed him in every way.[h] 2He said to the
chief[c] servant in his household, the one in charge of all that he
had,[i] "Put your hand under my thigh.[j] 3I want you to swear by
the LORD, the God of heaven and the God of earth,[k] that you will
not get a wife for my son[l] from the daughters of the Canaanites,[m] among whom I am living, 4but will go to my country and
my own relatives[n] and get a wife for my son Isaac."

5The servant asked him, "What if the woman is unwilling to
come back with me to this land? Shall I then take your son back
to the country you came from?"

a *11* Or *sell* b *15* That is, about 10 pounds (about 4.5 kilograms) c *2* Or *oldest*

23:8 [a]Ge 25:9
23:10 [b]Ge 34:20-24; Ru 4:4
23:11 [c]2Sa 24:23
23:15 [d]Eze 45:12
23:16 [e]Jer 32:9; Zec 11:12
23:17 [f]Ge 25:9; 49:30-32; 50:13; Ac 7:16
23:20 [g]Jer 32:10
24:1 [h]ver 35
24:2 [i]Ge 39:4-6 [j]ver 9; Ge 47:29
24:3 [k]Ge 14:19 [l]Ge 28:1; Dt 7:3 [m]Ge 10:15-19
24:4 [n]Ge 12:1; 28:2

6“Make sure that you do not take my son back there,” Abraham said. 7“The LORD, the God of heaven, who brought me out
of my father’s household and my native land and who spoke to
me and promised me on oath, saying, ‘To your offspring[a][a] I will
give this land’[b]—he will send his angel before you[c] so that you
can get a wife for my son from there. 8If the woman is unwilling
to come back with you, then you will be released from this oath
of mine. Only do not take my son back there.” 9So the servant
put his hand under the thigh[d] of his master Abraham and swore
an oath to him concerning this matter.
10Then the servant took ten of his master’s camels and left, taking with him all kinds of good things from his master. He set out
for Aram Naharaim[b] and made his way to the town of Nahor.
11He had the camels kneel down near the well[e] outside the town;
it was toward evening, the time the women go out to draw water.[f]
12Then he prayed, “O LORD, God of my master Abraham,[g] give
me success today, and show kindness to my master Abraham.
13See, I am standing beside this spring, and the daughters of the
townspeople are coming out to draw water. 14May it be that
when I say to a girl, ‘Please let down your jar that I may have a
drink,’ and she says, ‘Drink, and I’ll water your camels too’—let
her be the one you have chosen for your servant Isaac. By this I
will know[h] that you have shown kindness to my master.”
15Before he had finished praying,[i] Rebekah[j] came out with her
jar on her shoulder. She was the daughter of Bethuel son of
Milcah,[k] who was the wife of Abraham’s brother Nahor.[l] 16The
girl was very beautiful,[m] a virgin; no man had ever lain with her.
She went down to the spring, filled her jar and came up again.
17The servant hurried to meet her and said, “Please give me a
little water from your jar.”
18“Drink,[n] my lord,” she said, and quickly lowered the jar to
her hands and gave him a drink.
19After she had given him a drink, she said, “I’ll draw water
for your camels too,[o] until they have finished drinking.” 20So
she quickly emptied her jar into the trough, ran back to the well
to draw more water, and drew enough for all his camels.
21Without saying a word, the man watched her closely to learn
whether or not the LORD had made his journey successful.[p]
22When the camels had finished drinking, the man took out a
gold nose ring[q] weighing a beka[c] and two gold bracelets weighing ten shekels.[d] 23Then he asked, “Whose daughter are you?
Please tell me, is there room in your father’s house for us to
spend the night?”

24:7 [a]Gal 3:16* [b]Ge 12:7; 13:15 [c]Ex 23:20,23
24:9 [d]ver 2
24:11 [e]Ex 2:15 [f]ver 13; 1Sa 9:11
24:12 [g]ver 27,42,48; Ge 26:24; Ex 3:6,15,16
24:14 [h]Jdg 6:17,37
24:15 [i]ver 45 [j]Ge 22:23 [k]Ge 22:20 [l]Ge 11:29
24:16 [m]Ge 26:7
24:18 [n]ver 14
24:19 [o]ver 14
24:21 [p]ver 12
24:22 [q]ver 47

[a]*7* Or *seed* [b]*10* That is, Northwest Mesopotamia [c]*22* That is, about 1/5 ounce (about 5.5 grams) [d]*22* That is, about 4 ounces (about 110 grams)

24She answered him, "I am the daughter of Bethuel, the son
that Milcah bore to Nahor.[a]" 25And she added, "We have plenty
of straw and fodder, as well as room for you to spend the night."
26Then the man bowed down and worshiped the LORD,[b] 27say-
ing, "Praise be to the LORD,[c] the God of my master Abraham,
who has not abandoned his kindness and faithfulness[d] to my
master. As for me, the LORD has led me on the journey[e] to the
house of my master's relatives."[f]
28The girl ran and told her mother's household about these
things. 29Now Rebekah had a brother named Laban,[g] and he
hurried out to the man at the spring. 30As soon as he had seen
the nose ring, and the bracelets on his sister's arms, and had
heard Rebekah tell what the man said to her, he went out to the
man and found him standing by the camels near the spring.
31"Come, you who are blessed by the LORD,"[h] he said. "Why are
you standing out here? I have prepared the house and a place
for the camels."
32So the man went to the house, and the camels were
unloaded. Straw and fodder were brought for the camels, and
water for him and his men to wash their feet.[i] 33Then food was
set before him, but he said, "I will not eat until I have told you
what I have to say."
"Then tell us," ⌊Laban⌋ said.
34So he said, "I am Abraham's servant. 35The LORD has blessed
my master abundantly,[j] and he has become wealthy. He has giv-
en him sheep and cattle, silver and gold, menservants and maidservants, and camels and donkeys.[k] 36My master's wife Sarah
has borne him a son in her[a] old age,[l] and he has given him
everything he owns.[m] 37And my master made me swear an oath,
and said, 'You must not get a wife for my son from the daughters of the Canaanites, in whose land I live,[n] 38but go to my
father's family and to my own clan, and get a wife for my son.'[o]
39"Then I asked my master, 'What if the woman will not come
back with me?'[p]
40"He replied, 'The LORD, before whom I have walked, will
send his angel with you[q] and make your journey a success, so
that you can get a wife for my son from my own clan and from
my father's family. 41Then, when you go to my clan, you will be
released from my oath even if they refuse to give her to you—
you will be released from my oath.'[r]
42"When I came to the spring today, I said, 'O LORD, God of
my master Abraham, if you will, please grant success[s] to the
journey on which I have come. 43See, I am standing beside this

a36 Or *his*

24:24 [a]ver 15
24:26 [b]ver 48,52; Ex 4:31
24:27 [c]Ex 18:10; Ru 4:14; 1Sa 25:32 [d]ver 49; Ge 32:10; Ps 98:3 [e]ver 21 [f]ver 12,48
24:29 [g]ver 4; Ge 29:5,12,13
24:31 [h]Ge 26:29; Ru 3:10; Ps 115:15
24:32 [i]Ge 43:24; Jdg 19:21
24:35 [j]ver 1 [k]Ge 13:2
24:36 [l]Ge 21:2,10 [m]Ge 25:5
24:37 [n]ver 3
24:38 [o]ver 4
24:39 [p]ver 5
24:40 [q]ver 7
24:41 [r]ver 8
24:42 [s]ver 12

spring;[a] if a maiden comes out to draw water and I say to her,
"Please let me drink a little water from your jar,"[b] 44and if she
says to me, "Drink, and I'll draw water for your camels too," let
her be the one the LORD has chosen for my master's son.'

45"Before I finished praying in my heart,[c] Rebekah came out,
with her jar on her shoulder.[d] She went down to the spring and
drew water, and I said to her, 'Please give me a drink.'[e]

46"She quickly lowered her jar from her shoulder and said,
'Drink, and I'll water your camels too.'[f] So I drank, and she
watered the camels also.

47"I asked her, 'Whose daughter are you?'[g]

"She said, 'The daughter of Bethuel son of Nahor, whom
Milcah bore to him.'[h]

"Then I put the ring in her nose and the bracelets on her arms,[i]
48and I bowed down and worshiped the LORD.[j] I praised the
LORD, the God of my master Abraham, who had led me on the
right road to get the granddaughter of my master's brother for
his son.[k] 49Now if you will show kindness and faithfulness[l] to
my master, tell me; and if not, tell me, so I may know which way
to turn."

50Laban and Bethuel answered, "This is from the LORD;[m] we
can say nothing to you one way or the other.[n] 51Here is Rebekah;
take her and go, and let her become the wife of your master's son,
as the LORD has directed."

52When Abraham's servant heard what they said, he bowed
down to the ground before the LORD.[o] 53Then the servant brought
out gold and silver jewelry and articles of clothing and gave
them to Rebekah; he also gave costly gifts[p] to her brother and to
her mother. 54Then he and the men who were with him ate and
drank and spent the night there.

When they got up the next morning, he said, "Send me on my
way[q] to my master."

55But her brother and her mother replied, "Let the girl remain
with us ten days or so; then you[a] may go."

56But he said to them, "Do not detain me, now that the LORD
has granted success to my journey. Send me on my way so I
may go to my master."

57Then they said, "Let's call the girl and ask her about it." 58So
they called Rebekah and asked her, "Will you go with this man?"

"I will go," she said.

59So they sent their sister Rebekah on her way, along with her
nurse[r] and Abraham's servant and his men. 60And they blessed
Rebekah and said to her,

[a]55 Or *she*

24:43 [a]ver 13 [b]ver 14
24:45 [c]1Sa 1:13 [d]ver 15 [e]ver 17
24:46 [f]ver 18-19
24:47 [g]ver 23 [h]ver 24 [i]Eze 16:11-12
24:48 [j]ver 26 [k]ver 27
24:49 [l]Ge 47:29; Jos 2:14
24:50 [m]Ps 118:23 [n]Ge 31:7,24, 29,42
24:52 [o]ver 26
24:53 [p]ver 10,22
24:54 [q]ver 56,59
24:59 [r]Ge 35:8

"Our sister, may you increase
to thousands upon thousands;[a]
may your offspring possess
the gates of their enemies."[b]

61 Then Rebekah and her maids got ready and mounted their
camels and went back with the man. So the servant took Rebekah
and left.
62 Now Isaac had come from Beer Lahai Roi,[c] for he was living
in the Negev.[d] 63 He went out to the field one evening to meditate,[a][e] and as he looked up, he saw camels approaching. 64 Rebekah also looked up and saw Isaac. She got down from her
camel 65 and asked the servant, "Who is that man in the field
coming to meet us?"
"He is my master," the servant answered. So she took her veil
and covered herself.
66 Then the servant told Isaac all he had done. 67 Isaac brought
her into the tent of his mother Sarah, and he married Rebekah.[f]
So she became his wife, and he loved her;[g] and Isaac was comforted after his mother's death.[h]

Chapter 25 Theme ______________________

25 Abraham took[b] another wife, whose name was Keturah.
2 She bore him Zimran, Jokshan, Medan, Midian, Ishbak
and Shuah.[i] 3 Jokshan was the father of Sheba and Dedan; the
descendants of Dedan were the Asshurites, the Letushites and
the Leummites. 4 The sons of Midian were Ephah, Epher, Hanoch,
Abida and Eldaah. All these were descendants of Keturah.
5 Abraham left everything he owned to Isaac.[j] 6 But while he
was still living, he gave gifts to the sons of his concubines[k] and
sent them away from his son Isaac[l] to the land of the east.
7 Altogether, Abraham lived a hundred and seventy-five years.
8 Then Abraham breathed his last and died at a good old age,[m]
an old man and full of years; and he was gathered to his people.[n] 9 His sons Isaac and Ishmael buried him[o] in the cave of
Machpelah near Mamre, in the field of Ephron son of Zohar the
Hittite,[p] 10 the field Abraham had bought from the Hittites.[c][q]
There Abraham was buried with his wife Sarah. 11 After Abraham's death, God blessed his son Isaac, who then lived near Beer
Lahai Roi.[r]

12 This is the account of Abraham's son Ishmael, whom Sarah's
maidservant, Hagar[s] the Egyptian, bore to Abraham.[t]

a 63 The meaning of the Hebrew for this word is uncertain. b 1 Or *had taken* c 10 Or *the sons of Heth*

24:60
a Ge 17:16
b Ge 22:17

24:62
c Ge 16:14; 25:11
d Ge 20:1

24:63
e Ps 1:2; 77:12; 119:15,27,48, 97,148; 143:5; 145:5

24:67
f Ge 25:20
g Ge 29:18,20
h Ge 23:1-2

25:2
i 1Ch 1:32,33

25:5
j Ge 24:36

25:6
k Ge 22:24
l Ge 21:10,14

25:8
m Ge 15:15
n ver 17; Ge 35:29; 49:29,33

25:9
o Ge 35:29
p Ge 50:13

25:10
q Ge 23:16

25:11
r Ge 16:14

25:12
s Ge 16:1
t Ge 16:15

13 These are the names of the sons of Ishmael, listed in the
order of their birth: Nebaioth the firstborn of Ishmael, Kedar,
Adbeel, Mibsam, 14 Mishma, Dumah, Massa, 15 Hadad, Tema,
Jetur, Naphish and Kedemah. 16 These were the sons of Ishmael,
and these are the names of the twelve tribal rulers[a] according to
their settlements and camps. 17 Altogether, Ishmael lived a hundred and thirty-seven years. He breathed his last and died, and
he was gathered to his people.[b] 18 His descendants settled in the
area from Havilah to Shur, near the border of Egypt, as you go
toward Asshur. And they lived in hostility toward[a] all their
brothers.[c]

19 This is the account of Abraham's son Isaac.

Abraham became the father of Isaac, 20 and Isaac was forty
years old[d] when he married Rebekah[e] daughter of Bethuel the
Aramean from Paddan Aram[b] and sister of Laban[f] the Aramean.
21 Isaac prayed to the LORD on behalf of his wife, because she
was barren. The LORD answered his prayer,[g] and his wife Rebekah
became pregnant. 22 The babies jostled each other within her,
and she said, "Why is this happening to me?" So she went to
inquire of the LORD.[h]
23 The LORD said to her,

"Two nations[i] are in your womb,
and two peoples from within you will be separated;
one people will be stronger than the other,
and the older will serve the younger.[j]"

24 When the time came for her to give birth, there were twin
boys in her womb. 25 The first to come out was red, and his
whole body was like a hairy garment;[k] so they named him Esau.[c]
26 After this, his brother came out, with his hand grasping Esau's
heel;[l] so he was named Jacob.[d][m] Isaac was sixty years old when
Rebekah gave birth to them.
27 The boys grew up, and Esau became a skillful hunter, a man
of the open country,[n] while Jacob was a quiet man, staying
among the tents. 28 Isaac, who had a taste for wild game,[o] loved
Esau, but Rebekah loved Jacob.[p]
29 Once when Jacob was cooking some stew, Esau came in
from the open country, famished. 30 He said to Jacob, "Quick, let
me have some of that red stew! I'm famished!" (That is why he
was also called Edom.[e])
31 Jacob replied, "First sell me your birthright."

[a] 18 Or *lived to the east of* [b] 20 That is, Northwest Mesopotamia [c] 25 *Esau* may mean *hairy*; he was also called Edom, which means *red*. [d] 26 *Jacob* means *he grasps the heel* (figuratively, *he deceives*). [e] 30 *Edom* means *red*.

25:16 [a] Ge 17:20
25:17 [b] ver 8
25:18 [c] Ge 16:12
25:20 [d] ver 26; Ge 26:34 [e] Ge 24:67 [f] Ge 24:29
25:21 [g] 1Ch 5:20; 2Ch 33:13; Ezr 8:23; Ps 127:3; Ro 9:10
25:22 [h] 1Sa 9:9; 10:22
25:23 [i] Ge 17:4 [j] Ge 27:29,40; Mal 1:3; Ro 9:11-12*
25:25 [k] Ge 27:11
25:26 [l] Hos 12:3 [m] Ge 27:36
25:27 [n] Ge 27:3,5
25:28 [o] Ge 27:19 [p] Ge 27:6

32“Look, I am about to die,” Esau said. “What good is the birthright to me?”
33But Jacob said, “Swear to me first.” So he swore an oath to
him, selling his birthright[a] to Jacob.
34Then Jacob gave Esau some bread and some lentil stew. He
ate and drank, and then got up and left.
So Esau despised his birthright.

Chapter 26 Theme ______________________

26 Now there was a famine in the land[b]—besides the earlier
famine of Abraham’s time—and Isaac went to Abimelech
king of the Philistines in Gerar.[c] 2The LORD appeared[d] to Isaac
and said, “Do not go down to Egypt; live in the land where I tell
you to live.[e] 3Stay in this land for a while,[f] and I will be with you
and will bless you.[g] For to you and your descendants I will give
all these lands[h] and will confirm the oath I swore to your father
Abraham. 4I will make your descendants as numerous as the
stars in the sky[i] and will give them all these lands, and through
your offspring[a] all nations on earth will be blessed,[j] 5because
Abraham obeyed me[k] and kept my requirements, my commands,
my decrees and my laws.” 6So Isaac stayed in Gerar.
7When the men of that place asked him about his wife, he
said, “She is my sister,[l]” because he was afraid to say, “She is my
wife.” He thought, “The men of this place might kill me on
account of Rebekah, because she is beautiful.”
8When Isaac had been there a long time, Abimelech king of the
Philistines looked down from a window and saw Isaac caressing
his wife Rebekah. 9So Abimelech summoned Isaac and said, “She
is really your wife! Why did you say, ‘She is my sister’?”
Isaac answered him, “Because I thought I might lose my life
on account of her.”
10Then Abimelech said, “What is this you have done to us?[m]
One of the men might well have slept with your wife, and you
would have brought guilt upon us.”
11So Abimelech gave orders to all the people: “Anyone who
molests[n] this man or his wife shall surely be put to death.”
12Isaac planted crops in that land and the same year reaped a
hundredfold, because the LORD blessed him.[o] 13The man became
rich, and his wealth continued to grow until he became very
wealthy.[p] 14He had so many flocks and herds and servants[q] that
the Philistines envied him.[r] 15So all the wells[s] that his father’s servants had dug in the time of his father Abraham, the Philistines
stopped up,[t] filling them with earth.

a4 Or *seed*

25:33 [a]Ge 27:36; Heb 12:16

26:1 [b]Ge 12:10 [c]Ge 20:1

26:2 [d]Ge 12:7; 17:1; 18:1 [e]Ge 12:1

26:3 [f]Ge 20:1; 28:15 [g]Ge 12:2; 22:16-18 [h]Ge 12:7; 13:15; 15:18

26:4 [i]Ge 15:5; 22:17; Ex 32:13 [j]Ge 12:3; 22:18; Gal 3:8

26:5 [k]Ge 22:16

26:7 [l]Ge 12:13; 20:2,12; Pr 29:25

26:10 [m]Ge 20:9

26:11 [n]Ps 105:15

26:12 [o]ver 3; Job 42:12

26:13 [p]Pr 10:22

26:14 [q]Ge 24:36 [r]Ge 37:11

26:15 [s]Ge 21:30 [t]Ge 21:25

16 Then Abimelech said to Isaac, "Move away from us; you have
become too powerful for us.[a]"
17 So Isaac moved away from there and encamped in the Valley of Gerar and settled there. 18 Isaac reopened the wells[b] that
had been dug in the time of his father Abraham, which the Philistines had stopped up after Abraham died, and he gave them
the same names his father had given them.
19 Isaac's servants dug in the valley and discovered a well of
fresh water there. 20 But the herdsmen of Gerar quarreled with
Isaac's herdsmen and said, "The water is ours!"[c] So he named
the well Esek,[a] because they disputed with him. 21 Then they dug
another well, but they quarreled over that one also; so he named
it Sitnah.[b] 22 He moved on from there and dug another well, and
no one quarreled over it. He named it Rehoboth,[c] saying, "Now
the LORD has given us room and we will flourish[d] in the land."
23 From there he went up to Beersheba. 24 That night the LORD
appeared to him and said, "I am the God of your father Abraham.[e] Do not be afraid,[f] for I am with you; I will bless you and
will increase the number of your descendants[g] for the sake of
my servant Abraham."[h]
25 Isaac built an altar[i] there and called on the name of the LORD.
There he pitched his tent, and there his servants dug a well.
26 Meanwhile, Abimelech had come to him from Gerar, with
Ahuzzath his personal adviser and Phicol the commander of his
forces.[j] 27 Isaac asked them, "Why have you come to me, since
you were hostile to me and sent me away?[k]"
28 They answered, "We saw clearly that the LORD was with you;[l]
so we said, 'There ought to be a sworn agreement between us'—
between us and you. Let us make a treaty with you 29 that you will
do us no harm, just as we did not molest you but always treated
you well and sent you away in peace. And now you are blessed
by the LORD."[m]
30 Isaac then made a feast[n] for them, and they ate and drank.
31 Early the next morning the men swore an oath[o] to each other.
Then Isaac sent them on their way, and they left him in peace.
32 That day Isaac's servants came and told him about the well
they had dug. They said, "We've found water!" 33 He called it Shibah,[d] and to this day the name of the town has been Beersheba.[e][p]
34 When Esau was forty years old,[q] he married Judith daughter
of Beeri the Hittite, and also Basemath daughter of Elon the
Hittite.[r] 35 They were a source of grief to Isaac and Rebekah.[s]

26:16 [a] Ex 1:9
26:18 [b] Ge 21:30
26:20 [c] Ge 21:25
26:22 [d] Ge 17:6; Ex 1:7
26:24 [e] Ge 24:12; Ex 3:6 [f] Ge 15:1 [g] ver 4 [h] Ge 17:7
26:25 [i] Ge 12:7,8; 13:4,18; Ps 116:17
26:26 [j] Ge 21:22
26:27 [k] ver 16
26:28 [l] Ge 21:22
26:29 [m] Ge 24:31; Ps 115:15
26:30 [n] Ge 19:3
26:31 [o] Ge 21:31
26:33 [p] Ge 21:14
26:34 [q] Ge 25:20 [r] Ge 28:9; 36:2
26:35 [s] Ge 27:46

[a] 20 *Esek* means *dispute.* [b] 21 *Sitnah* means *opposition.* [c] 22 *Rehoboth* means *room.* [d] 33 *Shibah* can mean *oath* or *seven.* [e] 33 *Beersheba* can mean *well of the oath* or *well of seven.*

Chapter 27 Theme ______________________

27 When Isaac was old and his eyes were so weak that he could no longer see,[a] he called for Esau his older son[b] and said to him, "My son."

"Here I am," he answered.

2Isaac said, "I am now an old man and don't know the day of my death.[c] 3Now then, get your weapons—your quiver and bow—and go out to the open country[d] to hunt some wild game for me. 4Prepare me the kind of tasty food I like and bring it to me to eat, so that I may give you my blessing[e] before I die."

5Now Rebekah was listening as Isaac spoke to his son Esau. When Esau left for the open country to hunt game and bring it back, 6Rebekah said to her son Jacob,[f] "Look, I overheard your father say to your brother Esau, 7'Bring me some game and prepare me some tasty food to eat, so that I may give you my blessing in the presence of the LORD before I die.' 8Now, my son, listen carefully and do what I tell you:[g] 9Go out to the flock and bring me two choice young goats, so I can prepare some tasty food for your father, just the way he likes it. 10Then take it to your father to eat, so that he may give you his blessing before he dies."

11Jacob said to Rebekah his mother, "But my brother Esau is a hairy man,[h] and I'm a man with smooth skin. 12What if my father touches me?[i] I would appear to be tricking him and would bring down a curse on myself rather than a blessing."

13His mother said to him, "My son, let the curse fall on me.[j] Just do what I say;[k] go and get them for me."

14So he went and got them and brought them to his mother, and she prepared some tasty food, just the way his father liked it. 15Then Rebekah took the best clothes[l] of Esau her older son, which she had in the house, and put them on her younger son Jacob. 16She also covered his hands and the smooth part of his neck with the goatskins. 17Then she handed to her son Jacob the tasty food and the bread she had made.

18He went to his father and said, "My father."

"Yes, my son," he answered. "Who is it?"

19Jacob said to his father, "I am Esau your firstborn. I have done as you told me. Please sit up and eat some of my game so that you may give me your blessing."[m]

20Isaac asked his son, "How did you find it so quickly, my son?"

"The LORD your God gave me success,[n]" he replied.

21Then Isaac said to Jacob, "Come near so I can touch you,[o] my son, to know whether you really are my son Esau or not."

22Jacob went close to his father Isaac, who touched him and said, "The voice is the voice of Jacob, but the hands are the hands

27:1 [a]Ge 48:10; 1Sa 3:2 [b]Ge 25:25
27:2 [c]Ge 47:29
27:3 [d]Ge 25:27
27:4 [e]ver 10,25,31; Ge 49:28; Dt 33:1; Heb 11:20
27:6 [f]Ge 25:28
27:8 [g]ver 13,43
27:11 [h]Ge 25:25
27:12 [i]ver 22
27:13 [j]Mt 27:25 [k]ver 8
27:15 [l]ver 27
27:19 [m]ver 4
27:20 [n]Ge 24:12
27:21 [o]ver 12

of Esau." 23He did not recognize him, for his hands were hairy
like those of his brother Esau;[a] so he blessed him. 24"Are you
really my son Esau?" he asked.

"I am," he replied.

25Then he said, "My son, bring me some of your game to eat,
so that I may give you my blessing."[b]

Jacob brought it to him and he ate; and he brought some wine
and he drank. 26Then his father Isaac said to him, "Come here,
my son, and kiss me."

27So he went to him and kissed him[c]. When Isaac caught the
smell of his clothes,[d] he blessed him and said,

> "Ah, the smell of my son
> is like the smell of a field
> that the LORD has blessed.[e]
> 28May God give you of heaven's dew[f]
> and of earth's richness[g]—
> an abundance of grain and new wine.[h]
> 29May nations serve you
> and peoples bow down to you.[i]
> Be lord over your brothers,
> and may the sons of your mother bow down to you.[j]
> May those who curse you be cursed
> and those who bless you be blessed.[k]"

30After Isaac finished blessing him and Jacob had scarcely left
his father's presence, his brother Esau came in from hunting.
31He too prepared some tasty food and brought it to his father.
Then he said to him, "My father, sit up and eat some of my
game, so that you may give me your blessing."[l]

32His father Isaac asked him, "Who are you?"[m]

"I am your son," he answered, "your firstborn, Esau."

33Isaac trembled violently and said, "Who was it, then, that
hunted game and brought it to me? I ate it just before you came
and I blessed him—and indeed he will be blessed![n]"

34When Esau heard his father's words, he burst out with a
loud and bitter cry[o] and said to his father, "Bless me—me too,
my father!"

35But he said, "Your brother came deceitfully[p] and took your
blessing."

36Esau said, "Isn't he rightly named Jacob[a]?[q] He has deceived
me these two times: He took my birthright,[r] and now he's taken
my blessing!" Then he asked, "Haven't you reserved any blessing
for me?"

a36 *Jacob* means *he grasps the heel* (figuratively, *he deceives*).

27:23 [a]ver 16
27:25 [b]ver 4
27:27 [c]Heb 11:20 [d]SS 4:11 [e]Ps 65:9-13
27:28 [f]Dt 33:13 [g]ver 39 [h]Ge 45:18; Nu 18:12; Dt 33:28
27:29 [i]Isa 45:14,23; 49:7,23 [j]Ge 9:25; 25:23; 37:7 [k]Ge 12:3; Nu 24:9; Zep 2:8
27:31 [l]ver 4
27:32 [m]ver 18
27:33 [n]ver 29; Ge 28:3,4; Ro 11:29
27:34 [o]Heb 12:17
27:35 [p]Jer 9:4; 12:6
27:36 [q]Ge 25:26 [r]Ge 25:33

37Isaac answered Esau, "I have made him lord over you and
have made all his relatives his servants, and I have sustained him
with grain and new wine.[a] So what can I possibly do for you, my
son?"

38Esau said to his father, "Do you have only one blessing, my
father? Bless me too, my father!" Then Esau wept aloud.[b]

39His father Isaac answered him,

"Your dwelling will be
away from the earth's richness,
away from the dew[c] of heaven above.
40You will live by the sword
and you will serve[d] your brother.[e]
But when you grow restless,
you will throw his yoke
from off your neck.[f]"

41Esau held a grudge[g] against Jacob[h] because of the blessing
his father had given him. He said to himself, "The days of mourning[i] for my father are near; then I will kill my brother Jacob."[j]

42When Rebekah was told what her older son Esau had said,
she sent for her younger son Jacob and said to him, "Your
brother Esau is consoling himself with the thought of killing
you. 43Now then, my son, do what I say:[k] Flee at once to my
brother Laban[l] in Haran.[m] 44Stay with him for a while[n] until
your brother's fury subsides. 45When your brother is no longer
angry with you and forgets what you did to him,[o] I'll send word
for you to come back from there. Why should I lose both of you
in one day?"

46Then Rebekah said to Isaac, "I'm disgusted with living
because of these Hittite women. If Jacob takes a wife from among
the women of this land, from Hittite women like these, my life
will not be worth living."[p]

Chapter 28 Theme ________________________

28 So Isaac called for Jacob and blessed[a] him and commanded him: "Do not marry a Canaanite woman.[q] 2Go
at once to Paddan Aram,[b] to the house of your mother's father
Bethuel.[r] Take a wife for yourself there, from among the daughters of Laban, your mother's brother. 3May God Almighty[c][s]
bless you and make you fruitful[t] and increase your numbers
until you become a community of peoples. 4May he give you
and your descendants the blessing given to Abraham,[u] so that
you may take possession of the land where you now live as an

[a] *1* Or *greeted* [b] *2* That is, Northwest Mesopotamia; also in verses 5, 6 and 7
[c] *3* Hebrew *El-Shaddai*

27:37 [a] ver 28
27:38 [b] Heb 12:17
27:39 [c] ver 28
27:40 [d] 2Sa 8:14 [e] Ge 25:23 [f] 2Ki 8:20-22
27:41 [g] Ge 37:4 [h] Ge 32:11 [i] Ge 50:4,10 [j] Ob 1:10
27:43 [k] ver 8 [l] Ge 24:29 [m] Ge 11:31
27:44 [n] Ge 31:38,41
27:45 [o] ver 35
27:46 [p] Ge 26:35
28:1 [q] Ge 24:3
28:2 [r] Ge 25:20
28:3 [s] Ge 17:1 [t] Ge 17:6
28:4 [u] Ge 12:2,3

alien,[a] the land God gave to Abraham." 5 Then Isaac sent Jacob
on his way, and he went to Paddan Aram,[b] to Laban son of
Bethuel the Aramean, the brother of Rebekah,[c] who was the
mother of Jacob and Esau.

6 Now Esau learned that Isaac had blessed Jacob and had sent
him to Paddan Aram to take a wife from there, and that when
he blessed him he commanded him, "Do not marry a Canaanite
woman,"[d] 7 and that Jacob had obeyed his father and mother
and had gone to Paddan Aram. 8 Esau then realized how displeasing the Canaanite women[e] were to his father Isaac;[f] 9 so he
went to Ishmael and married Mahalath, the sister of Nebaioth[g]
and daughter of Ishmael son of Abraham, in addition to the
wives he already had.[h]

10 Jacob left Beersheba and set out for Haran.[i] 11 When he
reached a certain place, he stopped for the night because the
sun had set. Taking one of the stones there, he put it under his
head and lay down to sleep. 12 He had a dream[j] in which he saw
a stairway[a] resting on the earth, with its top reaching to heaven,
and the angels of God were ascending and descending on it.[k]
13 There above it[b] stood the LORD,[l] and he said: "I am the LORD,
the God of your father Abraham and the God of Isaac.[m] I will
give you and your descendants the land[n] on which you are
lying. 14 Your descendants will be like the dust of the earth, and
you[o] will spread out to the west and to the east, to the north and
to the south.[p] All peoples on earth will be blessed through you
and your offspring.[q] 15 I am with you[r] and will watch over you[s]
wherever you go, and I will bring you back to this land. I will
not leave you[t] until I have done what I have promised you."[u]

16 When Jacob awoke from his sleep, he thought, "Surely the
LORD is in this place, and I was not aware of it." 17 He was afraid
and said, "How awesome is this place![v] This is none other than
the house of God; this is the gate of heaven."

18 Early the next morning Jacob took the stone he had placed
under his head and set it up as a pillar[w] and poured oil on top of
it.[x] 19 He called that place Bethel,[c] though the city used to be
called Luz.[y]

20 Then Jacob made a vow,[z] saying, "If God will be with me
and will watch over me[a] on this journey I am taking and will
give me food to eat and clothes to wear 21 so that I return safely[b]
to my father's house, then the LORD[d] will be my God[c] 22 and[e]
this stone that I have set up as a pillar will be God's house,[d] and
of all that you give me I will give you a tenth.[e]"

28:4 [a]Ge 17:8
28:5 [b]Hos 12:12 [c]Ge 24:29
28:6 [d]ver 1
28:8 [e]Ge 24:3 [f]Ge 26:35
28:9 [g]Ge 25:13 [h]Ge 26:34
28:10 [i]Ge 11:31
28:12 [j]Ge 20:3 [k]Jn 1:51
28:13 [l]Ge 12:7; 35:7,9; 48:3 [m]Ge 26:24 [n]Ge 13:15; 35:12
28:14 [o]Ge 26:4 [p]Ge 13:14 [q]Ge 12:3; 18:18; 22:18; Gal 3:8
28:15 [r]Ge 26:3; 48:21 [s]Nu 6:24; Ps 121:5,7-8 [t]Dt 31:6,8 [u]Nu 23:19
28:17 [v]Ex 3:5; Jos 5:15
28:18 [w]Ge 35:14 [x]Lev 8:11
28:19 [y]Jdg 1:23,26
28:20 [z]Ge 31:13; Jdg 11:30; 2Sa 15:8 [a]ver 15
28:21 [b]Jdg 11:31 [c]Dt 26:17
28:22 [d]Ge 35:7,14 [e]Ge 14:20; Lev 27:30

[a]12 Or *ladder* [b]13 Or *There beside him* [c]19 *Bethel* means *house of God.* [d]20,21 Or *Since God . . . father's house, the LORD* [e]21,22 Or *house, and the LORD will be my God,* 22 *then*

Chapter 29 Theme ______________________________

29 Then Jacob continued on his journey and came to the
land of the eastern peoples.[a] 2There he saw a well in the
field, with three flocks of sheep lying near it because the flocks
were watered from that well. The stone over the mouth of the
well was large. 3When all the flocks were gathered there, the
shepherds would roll the stone away from the well's mouth and
water the sheep. Then they would return the stone to its place
over the mouth of the well.

4Jacob asked the shepherds, "My brothers, where are you
from?"

"We're from Haran,[b]" they replied.

5He said to them, "Do you know Laban, Nahor's grandson?"

"Yes, we know him," they answered.

6Then Jacob asked them, "Is he well?"

"Yes, he is," they said, "and here comes his daughter Rachel
with the sheep."

7"Look," he said, "the sun is still high; it is not time for the
flocks to be gathered. Water the sheep and take them back to
pasture."

8"We can't," they replied, "until all the flocks are gathered
and the stone has been rolled away from the mouth of the well.
Then we will water the sheep."

9While he was still talking with them, Rachel came with her
father's sheep,[c] for she was a shepherdess. 10When Jacob saw
Rachel daughter of Laban, his mother's brother, and Laban's
sheep, he went over and rolled the stone away from the mouth
of the well and watered his uncle's sheep.[d] 11Then Jacob kissed
Rachel and began to weep aloud.[e] 12He had told Rachel that he
was a relative[f] of her father and a son of Rebekah. So she ran
and told her father.[g]

13As soon as Laban[h] heard the news about Jacob, his sister's son,
he hurried to meet him. He embraced him and kissed him and
brought him to his home, and there Jacob told him all these things.
14Then Laban said to him, "You are my own flesh and blood."[i]

After Jacob had stayed with him for a whole month, 15Laban
said to him, "Just because you are a relative of mine, should you
work for me for nothing? Tell me what your wages should be."

16Now Laban had two daughters; the name of the older was
Leah, and the name of the younger was Rachel. 17Leah had
weak[a] eyes, but Rachel was lovely in form, and beautiful.
18Jacob was in love with Rachel and said, "I'll work for you sev-
en years in return for your younger daughter Rachel."[j]

[a] 17 Or *delicate*

29:1
[a] Jdg 6:3,33

29:4
[b] Ge 28:10

29:9
[c] Ex 2:16

29:10
[d] Ex 2:17

29:11
[e] Ge 33:4

29:12
[f] Ge 13:8; 14:14,16
[g] Ge 24:28

29:13
[h] Ge 24:29

29:14
[i] Ge 2:23; Jdg 9:2; 2Sa 19:12-13

29:18
[j] Hos 12:12

29:20 [a]SS 8:7; Hos 12:12 [19]Laban said, "It's better that I give her to you than to some
other man. Stay here with me." [20]So Jacob served seven years to
get Rachel, but they seemed like only a few days to him because
29:21 [b]Jdg 15:1 of his love for her.[a]
[21]Then Jacob said to Laban, "Give me my wife. My time is
completed, and I want to lie with her.[b]"
29:22 [c]Jdg 14:10; Jn 2:1-2 [22]So Laban brought together all the people of the place and
gave a feast.[c] [23]But when evening came, he took his daughter
Leah and gave her to Jacob, and Jacob lay with her. [24]And Laban
29:25 [d]Ge 12:18 [e]Ge 27:36 gave his servant girl Zilpah to his daughter as her maidservant.
[25]When morning came, there was Leah! So Jacob said to
Laban, "What is this you have done to me?[d] I served you for
Rachel, didn't I? Why have you deceived me?[e]"
29:27 [f]Jdg 14:12 [26]Laban replied, "It is not our custom here to give the younger
daughter in marriage before the older one. [27]Finish this daugh-
29:29 [g]Ge 30:3 [h]Ge 16:1 ter's bridal week;[f] then we will give you the younger one also, in
return for another seven years of work."
[28]And Jacob did so. He finished the week with Leah, and then
Laban gave him his daughter Rachel to be his wife. [29]Laban gave
29:30 [i]ver 16 [j]Ge 31:41 his servant girl Bilhah[g] to his daughter Rachel as her maidservant.[h] [30]Jacob lay with Rachel also, and he loved Rachel more
than Leah.[i] And he worked for Laban another seven years.[j]
29:31 [k]Dt 21:15-17 [l]Ge 11:30; 30:1; Ps 127:3 [31]When the LORD saw that Leah was not loved,[k] he opened her
womb,[l] but Rachel was barren. [32]Leah became pregnant and
gave birth to a son. She named him Reuben,[a] for she said, "It is
because the LORD has seen my misery.[m] Surely my husband will
29:32 [m]Ge 16:11; 31:42; Ex 4:31; Dt 26:7; Ps 25:18 love me now."
[33]She conceived again, and when she gave birth to a son she
said, "Because the LORD heard that I am not loved, he gave me
this one too." So she named him Simeon.[b][n]
[34]Again she conceived, and when she gave birth to a son she
29:33 [n]Ge 34:25; 49:5 said, "Now at last my husband will become attached to me,[o]
because I have borne him three sons." So he was named Levi.[c][p]
[35]She conceived again, and when she gave birth to a son she
29:34 [o]Ge 30:20; 1Sa 1:2-4 [p]Ge 49:5-7 said, "This time I will praise the LORD." So she named him
Judah.[d][q] Then she stopped having children.

Chapter 30 Theme ______________________

29:35 [q]Ge 49:8; Mt 1:2-3 **30** When Rachel saw that she was not bearing Jacob any
children,[r] she became jealous of her sister.[s] So she said
to Jacob, "Give me children, or I'll die!"

30:1 [r]Ge 29:31; 1Sa 1:5-6 [s]Lev 18:18 [a] 32 *Reuben* sounds like the Hebrew for *he has seen my misery*; the name means *see, a son.* [b] 33 *Simeon* probably means *one who hears.* [c] 34 *Levi* sounds like and may be derived from the Hebrew for *attached.* [d] 35 *Judah* sounds like and may be derived from the Hebrew for *praise.*

2 Jacob became angry with her and said, "Am I in the place of
God, who has kept you from having children?"[a]
3 Then she said, "Here is Bilhah, my maidservant. Sleep with
her so that she can bear children for me and that through her I
too can build a family."[b]
4 So she gave him her servant Bilhah as a wife.[c] Jacob slept with
her,[d] 5 and she became pregnant and bore him a son. 6 Then
Rachel said, "God has vindicated me;[e] he has listened to my plea
and given me a son." Because of this she named him Dan.[a][f]
7 Rachel's servant Bilhah conceived again and bore Jacob a
second son. 8 Then Rachel said, "I have had a great struggle with
my sister, and I have won."[g] So she named him Naphtali.[b][h]
9 When Leah saw that she had stopped having children, she
took her maidservant Zilpah and gave her to Jacob as a wife.[i]
10 Leah's servant Zilpah bore Jacob a son. 11 Then Leah said,
"What good fortune!"[c] So she named him Gad.[d][j]
12 Leah's servant Zilpah bore Jacob a second son. 13 Then Leah
said, "How happy I am! The women will call me[k] happy."[l] So
she named him Asher.[e][m]
14 During wheat harvest, Reuben went out into the fields and
found some mandrake plants,[n] which he brought to his mother
Leah. Rachel said to Leah, "Please give me some of your son's
mandrakes."
15 But she said to her, "Wasn't it enough[o] that you took away
my husband? Will you take my son's mandrakes too?"
"Very well," Rachel said, "he can sleep with you tonight in
return for your son's mandrakes."
16 So when Jacob came in from the fields that evening, Leah
went out to meet him. "You must sleep with me," she said. "I
have hired you with my son's mandrakes." So he slept with her
that night.
17 God listened to Leah,[p] and she became pregnant and bore
Jacob a fifth son. 18 Then Leah said, "God has rewarded me for
giving my maidservant to my husband." So she named him
Issachar.[f][q]
19 Leah conceived again and bore Jacob a sixth son. 20 Then
Leah said, "God has presented me with a precious gift. This time
my husband will treat me with honor, because I have borne him
six sons." So she named him Zebulun.[g][r]
21 Some time later she gave birth to a daughter and named her
Dinah.
22 Then God remembered Rachel;[s] he listened to her and
opened her womb.[t] 23 She became pregnant and gave birth to a

30:2 [a]Ge 16:2; 20:18; 29:31
30:3 [b]Ge 16:2
30:4 [c]ver 9,18 [d]Ge 16:3-4
30:6 [e]Ps 35:24; 43:1; La 3:59 [f]Ge 49:16-17
30:8 [g]Hos 12:3-4 [h]Ge 49:21
30:9 [i]ver 4
30:11 [j]Ge 49:19
30:13 [k]Ps 127:3 [l]Pr 31:28; Lk 1:48 [m]Ge 49:20
30:14 [n]SS 7:13
30:15 [o]Nu 16:9,13
30:17 [p]Ge 25:21
30:18 [q]Ge 49:14
30:20 [r]Ge 35:23; 49:13; Mt 4:13
30:22 [s]Ge 8:1; 1Sa 1:19-20 [t]Ge 29:31

[a] 6 *Dan* here means *he has vindicated.* [b] 8 *Naphtali* means *my struggle.* [c] 11 Or "*A troop is coming!*" [d] 11 *Gad* can mean *good fortune* or *a troop.* [e] 13 *Asher* means *happy.* [f] 18 *Issachar* sounds like the Hebrew for *reward.* [g] 20 *Zebulun* probably means *honor.*

son[a] and said, "God has taken away my disgrace."[b] 24She named
him Joseph,[a][c] and said, "May the LORD add to me another son."[d]
25After Rachel gave birth to Joseph, Jacob said to Laban, "Send
me on my way[e] so I can go back to my own homeland. 26Give me
my wives and children, for whom I have served you,[f] and I will
be on my way. You know how much work I've done for you."
27But Laban said to him, "If I have found favor in your eyes,
please stay. I have learned by divination that[b] the LORD has
blessed me because of you."[g] 28He added, "Name your wages,[h]
and I will pay them."
29Jacob said to him, "You know how I have worked for you[i]
and how your livestock has fared under my care.[j] 30The little
you had before I came has increased greatly, and the LORD has
blessed you wherever I have been. But now, when may I do
something for my own household?[k]"
31"What shall I give you?" he asked.
"Don't give me anything," Jacob replied. "But if you will do
this one thing for me, I will go on tending your flocks and
watching over them: 32Let me go through all your flocks today
and remove from them every speckled or spotted sheep, every
dark-colored lamb and every spotted or speckled goat.[l] They
will be my wages. 33And my honesty will testify for me in the
future, whenever you check on the wages you have paid me.
Any goat in my possession that is not speckled or spotted, or
any lamb that is not dark-colored, will be considered stolen."
34"Agreed," said Laban. "Let it be as you have said." 35That
same day he removed all the male goats that were streaked or
spotted, and all the speckled or spotted female goats (all that
had white on them) and all the dark-colored lambs, and he
placed them in the care of his sons.[m] 36Then he put a three-day
journey between himself and Jacob, while Jacob continued to
tend the rest of Laban's flocks.
37Jacob, however, took fresh-cut branches from poplar,
almond and plane trees and made white stripes on them by
peeling the bark and exposing the white inner wood of the
branches. 38Then he placed the peeled branches in all the watering troughs, so that they would be directly in front of the flocks
when they came to drink. When the flocks were in heat and
came to drink, 39they mated in front of the branches. And they
bore young that were streaked or speckled or spotted. 40Jacob
set apart the young of the flock by themselves, but made the rest
face the streaked and dark-colored animals that belonged to
Laban. Thus he made separate flocks for himself and did not

30:23 [a]ver 6 [b]Isa 4:1; Lk 1:25
30:24 [c]Ge 35:24; 37:2; 39:1; 49:22-26 [d]Ge 35:17
30:25 [e]Ge 24:54
30:26 [f]Ge 29:20,30; Hos 12:12
30:27 [g]Ge 26:24; 39:3,5
30:28 [h]Ge 29:15
30:29 [i]Ge 31:6 [j]Ge 31:38-40
30:30 [k]1Ti 5:8
30:32 [l]Ge 31:8,12
30:35 [m]Ge 31:1

a *24 Joseph* means *may he add.* b *27* Or possibly *have become rich and*

put them with Laban's animals. 41Whenever the stronger females
were in heat, Jacob would place the branches in the troughs in
front of the animals so they would mate near the branches, 42but
if the animals were weak, he would not place them there. So the
weak animals went to Laban and the strong ones to Jacob. 43In
this way the man grew exceedingly prosperous and came to own
large flocks, and maidservants and menservants, and camels and
donkeys.[a]

Chapter 31 Theme ____________________

31 Jacob heard that Laban's sons were saying, "Jacob has
taken everything our father owned and has gained all this
wealth from what belonged to our father." 2And Jacob noticed
that Laban's attitude toward him was not what it had been.
3Then the LORD said to Jacob, "Go back[b] to the land of your
fathers and to your relatives, and I will be with you."[c]
4So Jacob sent word to Rachel and Leah to come out to the
fields where his flocks were. 5He said to them, "I see that your
father's attitude toward me is not what it was before, but the God
of my father has been with me.[d] 6You know that I've worked for
your father with all my strength,[e] 7yet your father has cheated
me by changing my wages ten times.[f] However, God has not
allowed him to harm me.[g] 8If he said, 'The speckled ones will be
your wages,' then all the flocks gave birth to speckled young;
and if he said, 'The streaked ones will be your wages,'[h] then all
the flocks bore streaked young. 9So God has taken away your
father's livestock and has given them to me.[i]
10"In breeding season I once had a dream in which I looked
up and saw that the male goats mating with the flock were
streaked, speckled or spotted. 11The angel of God[j] said to me in
the dream, 'Jacob.' I answered, 'Here I am.' 12And he said, 'Look
up and see that all the male goats mating with the flock are
streaked, speckled or spotted, for I have seen all that Laban has
been doing to you.[k] 13I am the God of Bethel,[l] where you anointed a pillar and where you made a vow to me. Now leave this
land at once and go back to your native land.[m]'"
14Then Rachel and Leah replied, "Do we still have any share in
the inheritance of our father's estate? 15Does he not regard us as
foreigners? Not only has he sold us, but he has used up what
was paid for us.[n] 16Surely all the wealth that God took away
from our father belongs to us and our children. So do whatever
God has told you."
17Then Jacob put his children and his wives on camels, 18and
he drove all his livestock ahead of him, along with all the goods

30:43 [a]ver 30; Ge 12:16; 13:2; 24:35; 26:13-14
31:3 [b]ver 13; Ge 32:9 [c]Ge 21:22; 26:3; 28:15
31:5 [d]Ge 21:22; 26:3
31:6 [e]Ge 30:29
31:7 [f]ver 41; Job 19:3 [g]ver 52; Ps 37:28; 105:14
31:8 [h]Ge 30:32
31:9 [i]ver 1,16; Ge 30:42
31:11 [j]Ge 16:7; 48:16
31:12 [k]Ex 3:7
31:13 [l]Ge 28:10-22 [m]ver 3; Ge 32:9
31:15 [n]Ge 29:20

he had accumulated in Paddan Aram,[a] to go to his father Isaac[a] in the land of Canaan.[b]

19 When Laban had gone to shear his sheep, Rachel stole her father's household gods.[c] 20 Moreover, Jacob deceived[d] Laban the Aramean by not telling him he was running away.[e] 21 So he fled with all he had, and crossing the River,[b] he headed for the hill country of Gilead.[f]

22 On the third day Laban was told that Jacob had fled. 23 Taking his relatives with him, he pursued Jacob for seven days and caught up with him in the hill country of Gilead. 24 Then God came to Laban the Aramean in a dream at night and said to him,[g] "Be careful not to say anything to Jacob, either good or bad."[h]

25 Jacob had pitched his tent in the hill country of Gilead when Laban overtook him, and Laban and his relatives camped there too. 26 Then Laban said to Jacob, "What have you done? You've deceived me,[i] and you've carried off my daughters like captives in war.[j] 27 Why did you run off secretly and deceive me? Why didn't you tell me, so I could send you away with joy and singing to the music of tambourines[k] and harps?[l] 28 You didn't even let me kiss my grandchildren and my daughters good-by.[m] You have done a foolish thing. 29 I have the power to harm you;[n] but last night the God of your father[o] said to me, 'Be careful not to say anything to Jacob, either good or bad.' 30 Now you have gone off because you longed to return to your father's house. But why did you steal my gods?[p]"

31 Jacob answered Laban, "I was afraid, because I thought you would take your daughters away from me by force. 32 But if you find anyone who has your gods, he shall not live.[q] In the presence of our relatives, see for yourself whether there is anything of yours here with me; and if so, take it." Now Jacob did not know that Rachel had stolen the gods.

33 So Laban went into Jacob's tent and into Leah's tent and into the tent of the two maidservants, but he found nothing. After he came out of Leah's tent, he entered Rachel's tent. 34 Now Rachel had taken the household gods and put them inside her camel's saddle and was sitting on them. Laban searched[r] through everything in the tent but found nothing.

35 Rachel said to her father, "Don't be angry, my lord, that I cannot stand up in your presence;[s] I'm having my period." So he searched but could not find the household gods.

36 Jacob was angry and took Laban to task. "What is my crime?" he asked Laban. "What sin have I committed that you hunt me down? 37 Now that you have searched through all my goods,

31:18 [a] Ge 35:27 [b] Ge 10:19
31:19 [c] ver 30,32, 34-35; Ge 35:2; Jdg 17:5; 1Sa 19:13; Hos 3:4
31:20 [d] Ge 27:36 [e] ver 27
31:21 [f] Ge 37:25
31:24 [g] Ge 20:3; Job 33:15 [h] Ge 24:50
31:26 [i] Ge 27:36 [j] 1Sa 30:2-3
31:27 [k] Ex 15:20 [l] Ge 4:21
31:28 [m] ver 55
31:29 [n] ver 7 [o] ver 53
31:30 [p] ver 19; Jdg 18:24
31:32 [q] Ge 44:9
31:34 [r] ver 37; Ge 44:12
31:35 [s] Ex 20:12; Lev 19:3,32

a *18* That is, Northwest Mesopotamia b *21* That is, the Euphrates

what have you found that belongs to your household? Put it
here in front of your relatives[a] and mine, and let them judge
between the two of us.
38“I have been with you for twenty years now. Your sheep and
goats have not miscarried, nor have I eaten rams from your
flocks. 39I did not bring you animals torn by wild beasts; I bore
the loss myself. And you demanded payment from me for whatever was stolen by day or night.[b] 40This was my situation: The
heat consumed me in the daytime and the cold at night, and
sleep fled from my eyes. 41It was like this for the twenty years I
was in your household. I worked for you fourteen years for
your two daughters[c] and six years for your flocks, and you
changed my wages ten times.[d] 42If the God of my father,[e] the
God of Abraham and the Fear of Isaac,[f] had not been with me,[g]
you would surely have sent me away empty-handed. But God
has seen my hardship and the toil of my hands,[h] and last night
he rebuked you.”
43Laban answered Jacob, “The women are my daughters, the
children are my children, and the flocks are my flocks. All you
see is mine. Yet what can I do today about these daughters of
mine, or about the children they have borne? 44Come now, let’s
make a covenant,[i] you and I, and let it serve as a witness
between us.”[j]
45So Jacob took a stone and set it up as a pillar.[k] 46He said to
his relatives, “Gather some stones.” So they took stones and
piled them in a heap, and they ate there by the heap. 47Laban
called it Jegar Sahadutha,[a] and Jacob called it Galeed.[b]
48Laban said, “This heap is a witness between you and me
today.” That is why it was called Galeed. 49It was also called
Mizpah,[c][l] because he said, “May the LORD keep watch between
you and me when we are away from each other. 50If you mistreat my daughters or if you take any wives besides my daughters, even though no one is with us, remember that God is a
witness[m] between you and me.”
51Laban also said to Jacob, “Here is this heap, and here is this
pillar[n] I have set up between you and me. 52This heap is a witness, and this pillar is a witness,[o] that I will not go past this heap
to your side to harm you and that you will not go past this heap
and pillar to my side to harm me.[p] 53May the God of Abraham[q]
and the God of Nahor, the God of their father, judge between us.”[r]
So Jacob took an oath[s] in the name of the Fear of his father
Isaac.[t] 54He offered a sacrifice there in the hill country and

[a]47 The Aramaic *Jegar Sahadutha* means *witness heap.* [b]47 The Hebrew *Galeed* means *witness heap.* [c]49 *Mizpah* means *watchtower.*

31:37 [a]ver 23
31:39 [b]Ex 22:13
31:41 [c]Ge 29:30 [d]ver 7
31:42 [e]ver 5; Ex 3:15; 1Ch 12:17 [f]ver 53; Isa 8:13 [g]Ps 124:1-2 [h]Ge 29:32
31:44 [i]Ge 21:27; 26:28 [j]Jos 24:27
31:45 [k]Ge 28:18
31:49 [l]Jdg 11:29; 1Sa 7:5-6
31:50 [m]Jer 29:23; 42:5
31:51 [n]Ge 28:18
31:52 [o]Ge 21:30 [p]ver 7; Ge 26:29
31:53 [q]Ge 28:13 [r]Ge 16:5 [s]Ge 21:23,27 [t]ver 42

31:55 [a]ver 28 [b]Ge 18:33; 30:25
32:1 [c]Ge 16:11; 2Ki 6:16-17; Ps 34:7; 91:11; Heb 1:14
32:2 [d]Ge 28:17 [e]2Sa 2:8,29
32:3 [f]Ge 27:41-42 [g]Ge 25:30; 36:8,9
32:5 [h]Ge 12:16; 30:43 [i]Ge 33:8,10,15
32:6 [j]Ge 33:1
32:7 [k]ver 11
32:9 [l]Ge 28:13; 31:42 [m]Ge 31:13
32:10 [n]Ge 24:27
32:11 [o]Ps 59:2 [p]Ge 27:41
32:12 [q]Ge 22:17 [r]Ge 28:13-15; Hos 1:10; Ro 9:27
32:13 [s]Ge 43:11, 15,25,26; Pr 18:16

invited his relatives to a meal. After they had eaten, they spent the night there.

55 Early the next morning Laban kissed his grandchildren and his daughters[a] and blessed them. Then he left and returned home.[b]

Chapter 32 Theme ______________________

32 Jacob also went on his way, and the angels of God[c] met him. 2 When Jacob saw them, he said, "This is the camp of God!"[d] So he named that place Mahanaim.[a][e]

3 Jacob sent messengers ahead of him to his brother Esau[f] in the land of Seir, the country of Edom.[g] 4 He instructed them: "This is what you are to say to my master Esau: 'Your servant Jacob says, I have been staying with Laban and have remained there till now. 5 I have cattle and donkeys, sheep and goats, menservants and maidservants.[h] Now I am sending this message to my lord, that I may find favor in your eyes.[i]'"

6 When the messengers returned to Jacob, they said, "We went to your brother Esau, and now he is coming to meet you, and four hundred men are with him."[j]

7 In great fear[k] and distress Jacob divided the people who were with him into two groups,[b] and the flocks and herds and camels as well. 8 He thought, "If Esau comes and attacks one group,[c] the group[c] that is left may escape."

9 Then Jacob prayed, "O God of my father Abraham, God of my father Isaac,[l] O LORD, who said to me, 'Go back to your country and your relatives, and I will make you prosper,'[m] 10 I am unworthy of all the kindness and faithfulness[n] you have shown your servant. I had only my staff when I crossed this Jordan, but now I have become two groups. 11 Save me, I pray, from the hand of my brother Esau, for I am afraid he will come and attack me,[o] and also the mothers with their children.[p] 12 But you have said, 'I will surely make you prosper and will make your descendants like the sand[q] of the sea, which cannot be counted.[r]'"

13 He spent the night there, and from what he had with him he selected a gift[s] for his brother Esau: 14 two hundred female goats and twenty male goats, two hundred ewes and twenty rams, 15 thirty female camels with their young, forty cows and ten bulls, and twenty female donkeys and ten male donkeys. 16 He put them in the care of his servants, each herd by itself, and said to his servants, "Go ahead of me, and keep some space between the herds."

17 He instructed the one in the lead: "When my brother Esau meets you and asks, 'To whom do you belong, and where are

a2 *Mahanaim* means *two camps.* b7 Or *camps*; also in verse 10 c8 Or *camp*

you going, and who owns all these animals in front of you?'
18then you are to say, 'They belong to your servant[a] Jacob. They
are a gift sent to my lord Esau, and he is coming behind us.'"
19He also instructed the second, the third and all the others
who followed the herds: "You are to say the same thing to Esau
when you meet him. 20And be sure to say, 'Your servant Jacob is
coming behind us.'" For he thought, "I will pacify him with
these gifts I am sending on ahead; later, when I see him, perhaps
he will receive me."[b] 21So Jacob's gifts went on ahead of him, but
he himself spent the night in the camp.
22That night Jacob got up and took his two wives, his two
maidservants and his eleven sons and crossed the ford of the
Jabbok.[c] 23After he had sent them across the stream, he sent
over all his possessions. 24So Jacob was left alone, and a man[d]
wrestled with him till daybreak. 25When the man saw that he
could not overpower him, he touched the socket of Jacob's hip[e]
so that his hip was wrenched as he wrestled with the man. 26Then
the man said, "Let me go, for it is daybreak."
But Jacob replied, "I will not let you go unless you bless me."[f]
27The man asked him, "What is your name?"
"Jacob," he answered.
28Then the man said, "Your name will no longer be Jacob, but
Israel,[a][g] because you have struggled with God and with men
and have overcome."
29Jacob said, "Please tell me your name."[h]
But he replied, "Why do you ask my name?"[i] Then he blessed[j]
him there.
30So Jacob called the place Peniel,[b] saying, "It is because I saw
God face to face,[k] and yet my life was spared."
31The sun rose above him as he passed Peniel,[c] and he was
limping because of his hip. 32Therefore to this day the Israelites
do not eat the tendon attached to the socket of the hip, because
the socket of Jacob's hip was touched near the tendon.

Chapter 33 Theme __________________________

33 Jacob looked up and there was Esau, coming with his
four hundred men;[l] so he divided the children among
Leah, Rachel and the two maidservants. 2He put the maidservants and their children in front, Leah and her children next,
and Rachel and Joseph in the rear. 3He himself went on ahead
and bowed down to the ground[m] seven times as he approached
his brother.
4But Esau ran to meet Jacob and embraced him; he threw his
arms around his neck and kissed him. And they wept.[n] 5Then

[a]28 *Israel* means *he struggles with God.* [b]30 *Peniel* means *face of God.* [c]31 Hebrew *Penuel,* a variant of *Peniel*

32:18 [a]Ge 18:3
32:20 [b]Ge 33:10; Pr 21:14
32:22 [c]Dt 2:37; 3:16; Jos 12:2
32:24 [d]Ge 18:2
32:25 [e]ver 32
32:26 [f]Hos 12:4
32:28 [g]Ge 17:5; 35:10; 1Ki 18:31
32:29 [h]Jdg 13:17 [i]Jdg 13:18 [j]Ge 35:9
32:30 [k]Ge 16:13; Ex 24:11; Nu 12:8; Jdg 6:22; 13:22
33:1 [l]Ge 32:6
33:3 [m]Ge 18:2; 42:6
33:4 [n]Ge 45:14-15

33:5 [a]Ge 48:9; Ps 127:3; Isa 8:18 — Esau looked up and saw the women and children. "Who are
these with you?" he asked.
Jacob answered, "They are the children God has graciously
given your servant.[a]"
6Then the maidservants and their children approached and
33:8 [b]Ge 32:14-16 [c]Ge 24:9; 32:5 — bowed down. 7Next, Leah and her children came and bowed
down. Last of all came Joseph and Rachel, and they too bowed
down.
8Esau asked, "What do you mean by all these droves I met?"[b]
"To find favor in your eyes, my lord,"[c] he said.
33:10 [d]Ge 16:13 [e]Ge 32:20 — 9But Esau said, "I already have plenty, my brother. Keep what
you have for yourself."
10"No, please!" said Jacob. "If I have found favor in your eyes,
accept this gift from me. For to see your face is like seeing the
33:11 [f]1Sa 25:27 [g]Ge 30:43 — face of God,[d] now that you have received me favorably.[e] 11Please
accept the present[f] that was brought to you, for God has been
gracious to me[g] and I have all I need." And because Jacob insisted,
Esau accepted it.
12Then Esau said, "Let us be on our way; I'll accompany you."
33:14 [h]Ge 32:3 — 13But Jacob said to him, "My lord knows that the children are
tender and that I must care for the ewes and cows that are nurs-
ing their young. If they are driven hard just one day, all the animals will die. 14So let my lord go on ahead of his servant, while I
33:15 [i]Ge 34:11; 47:25; Ru 2:13 — move along slowly at the pace of the droves before me and that
of the children, until I come to my lord in Seir.[h]"
15Esau said, "Then let me leave some of my men with you."
"But why do that?" Jacob asked. "Just let me find favor in the
eyes of my lord."[i]
33:17 [j]Jos 13:27; Jdg 8:5,6,8, 14-16; Ps 60:6 — 16So that day Esau started on his way back to Seir. 17Jacob,
however, went to Succoth,[j] where he built a place for himself
and made shelters for his livestock. That is why the place is
called Succoth.[a]
18After Jacob came from Paddan Aram,[b][k] he arrived safely at
the[c] city of Shechem[l] in Canaan and camped within sight of the
33:18 [k]Ge 25:20; 28:2 [l]Jos 24:1; Jdg 9:1 — city. 19For a hundred pieces of silver,[d] he bought from the sons
of Hamor, the father of Shechem,[m] the plot of ground[n] where he
pitched his tent. 20There he set up an altar and called it El Elohe
Israel.[e]

Chapter 34 Theme ________________________________

33:19 [m]Jos 24:32 [n]Jn 4:5 — **34** Now Dinah,[o] the daughter Leah had borne to Jacob, went
out to visit the women of the land. 2When Shechem son
of Hamor the Hivite, the ruler of that area, saw her, he took her

34:1 [o]Ge 30:21

[a]17 *Succoth* means *shelters.* [b]18 That is, Northwest Mesopotamia [c]18 Or *arrived at Shalem, a* [d]19 Hebrew *hundred kesitahs;* a kesitah was a unit of money of unknown weight and value. [e]20 *El Elohe Israel* can mean *God, the God of Israel* or *mighty is the God of Israel.*

and violated her. 3His heart was drawn to Dinah daughter of
Jacob, and he loved the girl and spoke tenderly to her. 4And
Shechem said to his father Hamor, "Get me this girl as my wife."
5When Jacob heard that his daughter Dinah had been defiled,
his sons were in the fields with his livestock; so he kept quiet
about it until they came home.
6Then Shechem's father Hamor went out to talk with Jacob.[a]
7Now Jacob's sons had come in from the fields as soon as they
heard what had happened. They were filled with grief and fury,
because Shechem had done a disgraceful thing in[a] Israel[b] by
lying with Jacob's daughter—a thing that should not be done.[c]
8But Hamor said to them, "My son Shechem has his heart set
on your daughter. Please give her to him as his wife. 9Intermar-
ry with us; give us your daughters and take our daughters for
yourselves. 10You can settle among us;[d] the land is open to you.[e]
Live in it, trade[b] in it,[f] and acquire property in it."
11Then Shechem said to Dinah's father and brothers, "Let me
find favor in your eyes, and I will give you whatever you ask.
12Make the price for the bride[g] and the gift I am to bring as great
as you like, and I'll pay whatever you ask me. Only give me the
girl as my wife."
13Because their sister Dinah had been defiled, Jacob's sons
replied deceitfully as they spoke to Shechem and his father
Hamor. 14They said to them, "We can't do such a thing; we can't
give our sister to a man who is not circumcised.[h] That would be
a disgrace to us. 15We will give our consent to you on one condition only: that you become like us by circumcising all your
males.[i] 16Then we will give you our daughters and take your
daughters for ourselves. We'll settle among you and become one
people with you. 17But if you will not agree to be circumcised,
we'll take our sister[c] and go."
18Their proposal seemed good to Hamor and his son Shechem.
19The young man, who was the most honored of all his father's
household, lost no time in doing what they said, because he was
delighted with Jacob's daughter.[j] 20So Hamor and his son
Shechem went to the gate of their city[k] to speak to their fellow
townsmen. 21"These men are friendly toward us," they said. "Let
them live in our land and trade in it; the land has plenty of room
for them. We can marry their daughters and they can marry
ours. 22But the men will consent to live with us as one people
only on the condition that our males be circumcised, as they
themselves are. 23Won't their livestock, their property and all
their other animals become ours? So let us give our consent to
them, and they will settle among us."

[a]7 Or *against* [b]10 Or *move about freely;* also in verse 21 [c]17 Hebrew *daughter*

34:6
[a]Jdg 14:2-5

34:7
[b]Dt 22:21; Jdg 20:6; 2Sa 13:12
[c]Jos 7:15

34:10
[d]Ge 47:6,27
[e]Ge 13:9; 20:15
[f]Ge 42:34

34:12
[g]Ex 22:16; Dt 22:29; 1Sa 18:25

34:14
[h]Ge 17:14; Jdg 14:3

34:15
[i]Ex 12:48

34:19
[j]ver 3

34:20
[k]Ru 4:1; 2Sa 15:2

[24]All the men who went out of the city gate[a] agreed with Hamor
and his son Shechem, and every male in the city was circumcised.
[25]Three days later, while all of them were still in pain, two of
Jacob's sons, Simeon and Levi, Dinah's brothers, took their
swords[b] and attacked the unsuspecting city, killing every male.[c]
[26]They put Hamor and his son Shechem to the sword and took
Dinah from Shechem's house and left. [27]The sons of Jacob came
upon the dead bodies and looted the city where[a] their sister had
been defiled. [28]They seized their flocks and herds and donkeys
and everything else of theirs in the city and out in the fields.
[29]They carried off all their wealth and all their women and children, taking as plunder everything in the houses.
[30]Then Jacob said to Simeon and Levi, "You have brought
trouble on me by making me a stench[d] to the Canaanites and
Perizzites, the people living in this land.[e] We are few in
number,[f] and if they join forces against me and attack me, I and
my household will be destroyed."
[31]But they replied, "Should he have treated our sister like a
prostitute?"

Chapter 35 Theme ________________________

35 Then God said to Jacob, "Go up to Bethel[g] and settle
there, and build an altar there to God, who appeared to
you when you were fleeing from your brother Esau."[h]
[2]So Jacob said to his household[i] and to all who were with him,
"Get rid of the foreign gods[j] you have with you, and purify
yourselves and change your clothes.[k] [3]Then come, let us go up
to Bethel, where I will build an altar to God, who answered me
in the day of my distress[l] and who has been with me wherever I
have gone.[m]" [4]So they gave Jacob all the foreign gods they had
and the rings in their ears, and Jacob buried them under the oak
at Shechem.[n] [5]Then they set out, and the terror of God[o] fell
upon the towns all around them so that no one pursued them.
[6]Jacob and all the people with him came to Luz[p] (that is,
Bethel) in the land of Canaan. [7]There he built an altar, and he
called the place El Bethel,[b] because it was there that God
revealed himself to him[q] when he was fleeing from his brother.
[8]Now Deborah, Rebekah's nurse,[r] died and was buried under
the oak below Bethel. So it was named Allon Bacuth.[c]
[9]After Jacob returned from Paddan Aram,[d] God appeared to
him again and blessed him.[s] [10]God said to him, "Your name is
Jacob,[e] but you will no longer be called Jacob; your name will be
Israel.[f]"[t] So he named him Israel.

34:24 [a]Ge 23:10
34:25 [b]Ge 49:5 [c]Ge 49:7
34:30 [d]Ex 5:21; 1Sa 13:4 [e]Ge 13:7 [f]Ge 46:27; 1Ch 16:19; Ps 105:12
35:1 [g]Ge 28:19 [h]Ge 27:43
35:2 [i]Ge 18:19; Jos 24:15 [j]Ge 31:19 [k]Ex 19:10,14
35:3 [l]Ge 32:7 [m]Ge 28:15, 20-22; 31:3,42
35:4 [n]Jos 24:25-26
35:5 [o]Ex 15:16; 23:27; Jos 2:9
35:6 [p]Ge 28:19; 48:3
35:7 [q]Ge 28:13
35:8 [r]Ge 24:59
35:9 [s]Ge 32:29
35:10 [t]Ge 17:5

[a]27 Or *because* [b]7 *El Bethel* means *God of Bethel.* [c]8 *Allon Bacuth* means *oak of weeping.* [d]9 That is, Northwest Mesopotamia; also in verse 26 [e]10 *Jacob* means *he grasps the heel* (figuratively, *he deceives*). [f]10 *Israel* means *he struggles with God.*

11And God said to him, "I am God Almighty[a];[a] be fruitful and
increase in number. A nation[b] and a community of nations will
come from you, and kings will come from your body.[c] 12The
land I gave to Abraham and Isaac I also give to you, and I will
give this land to your descendants after you.[d]"[e] 13Then God
went up from him[f] at the place where he had talked with him.

14Jacob set up a stone pillar at the place where God had talked
with him, and he poured out a drink offering on it; he also
poured oil on it.[g] 15Jacob called the place where God had talked
with him Bethel.[b][h]

16Then they moved on from Bethel. While they were still some
distance from Ephrath, Rachel began to give birth and had great
difficulty. 17And as she was having great difficulty in childbirth,
the midwife said to her, "Don't be afraid, for you have another
son."[i] 18As she breathed her last—for she was dying—she
named her son Ben-Oni.[c] But his father named him Benjamin.[d]

19So Rachel died and was buried on the way to Ephrath (that
is, Bethlehem[j]). 20Over her tomb Jacob set up a pillar, and to
this day that pillar marks Rachel's tomb.[k]

21Israel moved on again and pitched his tent beyond Migdal
Eder. 22While Israel was living in that region, Reuben went in and
slept with his father's concubine[l] Bilhah,[m] and Israel heard of it.

Jacob had twelve sons:

23The sons of Leah:

Reuben the firstborn[n] of Jacob,

Simeon, Levi, Judah,[o] Issachar and Zebulun.[p]

24The sons of Rachel:

Joseph[q] and Benjamin.[r]

25The sons of Rachel's maidservant Bilhah:

Dan and Naphtali.[s]

26The sons of Leah's maidservant Zilpah:

Gad[t] and Asher.[u]

These were the sons of Jacob, who were born to him in Paddan
Aram.

27Jacob came home to his father Isaac in Mamre,[v] near Kiriath
Arba[w] (that is, Hebron), where Abraham and Isaac had stayed.
28Isaac lived a hundred and eighty years.[x] 29Then he breathed
his last and died and was gathered to his people,[y] old and full of
years.[z] And his sons Esau and Jacob buried him.[a]

a *11* Hebrew *El-Shaddai* b *15* *Bethel* means *house of God.* c *18* *Ben-Oni* means *son of my trouble.* d *18* *Benjamin* means *son of my right hand.*

35:11 [a]Ge 17:1; Ex 6:3 [b]Ge 28:3; 48:4 [c]Ge 17:6
35:12 [d]Ge 13:15; 28:13 [e]Ge 12:7; 26:3
35:13 [f]Ge 17:22
35:14 [g]Ge 28:18
35:15 [h]Ge 28:19
35:17 [i]Ge 30:24
35:19 [j]Ge 48:7; Ru 1:1,19; Mic 5:2; Mt 2:16
35:20 [k]1Sa 10:2
35:22 [l]Ge 49:4; 1Ch 5:1 [m]Ge 29:29; Lev 18:8
35:23 [n]Ge 46:8 [o]Ge 29:35 [p]Ge 30:20
35:24 [q]Ge 30:24 [r]ver 18
35:25 [s]Ge 30:8
35:26 [t]Ge 30:11 [u]Ge 30:13
35:27 [v]Ge 13:18; 18:1 [w]Jos 14:15
35:28 [x]Ge 25:7,20
35:29 [y]Ge 25:8; 49:33 [z]Ge 15:15 [a]Ge 25:9

INSIGHT

The Birth Order of Jacob's (Israel's) Sons

Mother	Son
Leah	Reuben (born 1921 B.C.) Simeon Levi Judah
Bilhah *(Rachel's maidservant)*	Dan Naphtali
Zilpah *(Leah's maidservant)*	Gad Asher
Leah	Issachar Zebulun
Rachel	Joseph (born 1914 B.C.) Benjamin

36:1 [a]Ge 25:30 *Chapter 36 Theme* ______________________________

36

This is the account of Esau (that is, Edom).[a]

36:2 [b]Ge 28:8-9 2Esau took his wives from the women of Canaan:[b] Adah
[c]Ge 26:34 daughter of Elon the Hittite,[c] and Oholibamah daughter of
[d]ver 25 Anah[d] and granddaughter of Zibeon the Hivite— 3also
Basemath daughter of Ishmael and sister of Nebaioth.
4Adah bore Eliphaz to Esau, Basemath bore Reuel,[e] 5and
36:4 [e]1Ch 1:35 Oholibamah bore Jeush, Jalam and Korah. These were the
sons of Esau, who were born to him in Canaan.
6Esau took his wives and sons and daughters and all the
members of his household, as well as his livestock and all his
36:6 [f]Ge 12:5 other animals and all the goods he had acquired in Canaan,[f]
and moved to a land some distance from his brother Jacob.
7Their possessions were too great for them to remain together;
the land where they were staying could not support
36:7 [g]Ge 13:6; 17:8; 28:4 them both because of their livestock.[g] 8So Esau[h] (that is,
Edom) settled in the hill country of Seir.[i]

9This is the account of Esau the father of the Edomites in the
hill country of Seir.

36:8 [h]Dt 2:4 10These are the names of Esau's sons:
[i]Ge 32:3 Eliphaz, the son of Esau's wife Adah, and Reuel, the son
of Esau's wife Basemath.
11The sons of Eliphaz:[j]
36:11 [j]ver 15-16; Job 2:11 Teman,[k] Omar, Zepho, Gatam and Kenaz.
[k]Am 1:12; Hab 3:3 12Esau's son Eliphaz also had a concubine named Timna,
who bore him Amalek.[l] These were grandsons of Esau's
wife Adah.[m]
13The sons of Reuel:
Nahath, Zerah, Shammah and Mizzah. These were
36:12 [l]Ex 17:8,16; grandsons of Esau's wife Basemath.
Nu 24:20; 1Sa 15:2 14The sons of Esau's wife Oholibamah daughter of Anah and
[m]ver 16 granddaughter of Zibeon, whom she bore to Esau:
Jeush, Jalam and Korah.

15These were the chiefs[n] among Esau's descendants:
36:15 [n]Ex 15:15 The sons of Eliphaz the firstborn of Esau:
[o]Job 2:11 Chiefs Teman,[o] Omar, Zepho, Kenaz, 16Korah,[a] Gatam
and Amalek. These were the chiefs descended from Eliphaz
in Edom; they were grandsons of Adah.[p]

36:16 [p]ver 12 [a]*16* Masoretic Text; Samaritan Pentateuch (see also Gen. 36:11 and 1 Chron. 1:36) does not have *Korah*.

[17]The sons of Esau's son Reuel:[a]
Chiefs Nahath, Zerah, Shammah and Mizzah. These were the chiefs descended from Reuel in Edom; they were grandsons of Esau's wife Basemath.
[18]The sons of Esau's wife Oholibamah:
Chiefs Jeush, Jalam and Korah. These were the chiefs descended from Esau's wife Oholibamah daughter of Anah.
[19]These were the sons of Esau (that is, Edom),[b] and these were their chiefs.

[20]These were the sons of Seir the Horite,[c] who were living in the region:
Lotan, Shobal, Zibeon, Anah, [21]Dishon, Ezer and Dishan.
These sons of Seir in Edom were Horite chiefs.
[22]The sons of Lotan:
Hori and Homam.[a] Timna was Lotan's sister.
[23]The sons of Shobal:
Alvan, Manahath, Ebal, Shepho and Onam.
[24]The sons of Zibeon:
Aiah and Anah. This is the Anah who discovered the hot springs[b] in the desert while he was grazing the donkeys of his father Zibeon.
[25]The children of Anah:
Dishon and Oholibamah daughter of Anah.
[26]The sons of Dishon[c]:
Hemdan, Eshban, Ithran and Keran.
[27]The sons of Ezer:
Bilhan, Zaavan and Akan.
[28]The sons of Dishan:
Uz and Aran.
[29]These were the Horite chiefs:
Lotan, Shobal, Zibeon, Anah, [30]Dishon, Ezer and Dishan.
These were the Horite chiefs, according to their divisions, in the land of Seir.

[31]These were the kings who reigned in Edom before any Israelite king[d] reigned[d]:
[32]Bela son of Beor became king of Edom. His city was named Dinhabah.
[33]When Bela died, Jobab son of Zerah from Bozrah[e] succeeded him as king.
[34]When Jobab died, Husham from the land of the Temanites[f] succeeded him as king.

[a]22 Hebrew *Hemam,* a variant of *Homam* (see 1 Chron. 1:39) [b]24 Vulgate; Syriac *discovered water;* the meaning of the Hebrew for this word is uncertain. [c]26 Hebrew *Dishan,* a variant of *Dishon* [d]31 Or *before an Israelite king reigned over them*

36:17 [a]1Ch 1:37
36:19 [b]Ge 25:30
36:20 [c]Ge 14:6; Dt 2:12,22; 1Ch 1:38
36:31 [d]Ge 17:6; 1Ch 1:43
36:33 [e]Jer 49:13,22
36:34 [f]Eze 25:13

36:35 [a]Ge 19:37; Nu 22:1; Dt 1:5; Ru 1:1,6

35When Husham died, Hadad son of Bedad, who defeated
Midian in the country of Moab,[a] succeeded him as king.
His city was named Avith.
36When Hadad died, Samlah from Masrekah succeeded him
as king.
37When Samlah died, Shaul from Rehoboth on the river[a]
succeeded him as king.
38When Shaul died, Baal-Hanan son of Acbor succeeded
him as king.

37:1 [b]Ge 17:8 [c]Ge 10:19

39When Baal-Hanan son of Acbor died, Hadad[b] succeeded
him as king. His city was named Pau, and his wife's name
was Mehetabel daughter of Matred, the daughter of Me-
Zahab.

37:2 [d]Ps 78:71 [e]Ge 35:25 [f]Ge 35:26 [g]1Sa 2:24

40These were the chiefs descended from Esau, by name,
according to their clans and regions:
Timna, Alvah, Jetheth, 41Oholibamah, Elah, Pinon, 42Ke-
naz, Teman, Mibzar, 43Magdiel and Iram. These were the
chiefs of Edom, according to their settlements in the
land they occupied.

This was Esau the father of the Edomites.

37:3 [h]Ge 25:28 [i]Ge 44:20 [j]2Sa 13:18-19

Chapter 37 Theme ______________________

37 Jacob lived in the land where his father had stayed,[b] the
land of Canaan.[c]

2This is the account of Jacob.

Joseph, a young man of seventeen, was tending the flocks[d] with
his brothers, the sons of Bilhah[e] and the sons of Zilpah,[f] his
father's wives, and he brought their father a bad report[g] about
them.

37:4 [k]Ge 27:41; 49:22-23; Ac 7:9

3Now Israel loved Joseph more than any of his other sons,[h]
because he had been born to him in his old age;[i] and he made a
richly ornamented[c] robe[j] for him. 4When his brothers saw that
their father loved him more than any of them, they hated him[k]
and could not speak a kind word to him.

37:5 [l]Ge 20:3; 28:12

5Joseph had a dream,[l] and when he told it to his brothers, they
hated him all the more. 6He said to them, "Listen to this dream I
had: 7We were binding sheaves of grain out in the field when
suddenly my sheaf rose and stood upright, while your sheaves
gathered around mine and bowed down to it."[m]

37:7 [m]Ge 42:6,9; 43:26,28; 44:14; 50:18

a *37* Possibly the Euphrates b *39* Many manuscripts of the Masoretic Text, Samaritan Pentateuch and Syriac (see also 1 Chron. 1:50); most manuscripts of the Masoretic Text *Hadar* c 3 The meaning of the Hebrew for *richly ornamented* is uncertain; also in verses 23 and 32.

8 His brothers said to him, "Do you intend to reign over us?
Will you actually rule us?"[a] And they hated him all the more
because of his dream and what he had said.
9 Then he had another dream, and he told it to his brothers.
"Listen," he said, "I had another dream, and this time the sun
and moon and eleven stars were bowing down to me."
10 When he told his father as well as his brothers,[b] his father
rebuked him and said, "What is this dream you had? Will your
mother and I and your brothers actually come and bow down
to the ground before you?"[c] 11 His brothers were jealous of him,[d]
but his father kept the matter in mind.[e]
12 Now his brothers had gone to graze their father's flocks near
Shechem, 13 and Israel said to Joseph, "As you know, your brothers are grazing the flocks near Shechem. Come, I am going to
send you to them."
"Very well," he replied.
14 So he said to him, "Go and see if all is well with your brothers and with the flocks, and bring word back to me." Then he
sent him off from the Valley of Hebron.[f]
When Joseph arrived at Shechem, 15 a man found him wandering around in the fields and asked him, "What are you looking
for?"
16 He replied, "I'm looking for my brothers. Can you tell me
where they are grazing their flocks?"
17 "They have moved on from here," the man answered. "I
heard them say, 'Let's go to Dothan.[g]'"
So Joseph went after his brothers and found them near
Dothan. 18 But they saw him in the distance, and before he
reached them, they plotted to kill him.[h]
19 "Here comes that dreamer!" they said to each other. 20 "Come
now, let's kill him and throw him into one of these cisterns[i] and
say that a ferocious animal devoured him. Then we'll see what
comes of his dreams."[j]
21 When Reuben heard this, he tried to rescue him from their
hands. "Let's not take his life," he said.[k] 22 "Don't shed any
blood. Throw him into this cistern here in the desert, but don't
lay a hand on him." Reuben said this to rescue him from them
and take him back to his father.
23 So when Joseph came to his brothers, they stripped him of
his robe—the richly ornamented robe he was wearing— 24 and
they took him and threw him into the cistern.[l] Now the cistern
was empty; there was no water in it.
25 As they sat down to eat their meal, they looked up and saw a
caravan of Ishmaelites coming from Gilead. Their camels were
loaded with spices, balm and myrrh,[m] and they were on their
way to take them down to Egypt.[n]

37:8 [a] Ge 49:26
37:10 [b] ver 5 [c] ver 7; Ge 27:29
37:11 [d] Ac 7:9 [e] Lk 2:19,51
37:14 [f] Ge 13:18; 35:27
37:17 [g] 2Ki 6:13
37:18 [h] 1Sa 19:1; Mk 14:1; Ac 23:12
37:20 [i] Jer 38:6,9 [j] Ge 50:20
37:21 [k] Ge 42:22
37:24 [l] Jer 41:7
37:25 [m] Ge 43:11 [n] ver 28

26 Judah said to his brothers, "What will we gain if we kill our brother and cover up his blood?[a] 27 Come, let's sell him to the Ishmaelites and not lay our hands on him; after all, he is our brother,[b] our own flesh and blood." His brothers agreed.

28 So when the Midianite[c] merchants came by, his brothers pulled Joseph up out of the cistern and sold him for twenty shekels[a] of silver to the Ishmaelites, who took him to Egypt.[d]

29 When Reuben returned to the cistern and saw that Joseph was not there, he tore his clothes.[e] 30 He went back to his brothers and said, "The boy isn't there! Where can I turn now?"[f]

31 Then they got Joseph's robe,[g] slaughtered a goat and dipped the robe in the blood. 32 They took the ornamented robe back to their father and said, "We found this. Examine it to see whether it is your son's robe."

33 He recognized it and said, "It is my son's robe! Some ferocious animal[h] has devoured him. Joseph has surely been torn to pieces."[i]

34 Then Jacob tore his clothes,[j] put on sackcloth[k] and mourned for his son many days.[l] 35 All his sons and daughters came to comfort him, but he refused to be comforted. "No," he said, "in mourning will I go down to the grave[b][m] to my son." So his father wept for him.

36 Meanwhile, the Midianites[c] sold Joseph in Egypt to Potiphar, one of Pharaoh's officials, the captain of the guard.[n]

Chapter 38 Theme ______________________________

38 At that time, Judah left his brothers and went down to stay with a man of Adullam named Hirah. 2 There Judah met the daughter of a Canaanite man named Shua.[o] He married her and lay with her; 3 she became pregnant and gave birth to a son, who was named Er.[p] 4 She conceived again and gave birth to a son and named him Onan. 5 She gave birth to still another son and named him Shelah. It was at Kezib that she gave birth to him.

6 Judah got a wife for Er, his firstborn, and her name was Tamar. 7 But Er, Judah's firstborn, was wicked in the LORD's sight; so the LORD put him to death.[q]

8 Then Judah said to Onan, "Lie with your brother's wife and fulfill your duty to her as a brother-in-law to produce offspring for your brother."[r] 9 But Onan knew that the offspring would not be his; so whenever he lay with his brother's wife, he spilled his semen on the ground to keep from producing offspring for his brother. 10 What he did was wicked in the LORD's sight; so he put him to death also.[s]

37:26 [a] ver 20; Ge 4:10
37:27 [b] Ge 42:21
37:28 [c] Ge 25:2; Jdg 6:1-3 [d] Ge 45:4-5; Ps 105:17; Ac 7:9
37:29 [e] ver 34; Ge 44:13; Job 1:20
37:30 [f] ver 22; Ge 42:13,36
37:31 [g] ver 3,23
37:33 [h] ver 20 [i] Ge 44:20,28
37:34 [j] ver 29 [k] 2Sa 3:31 [l] Ge 50:3,10,11
37:35 [m] Ge 42:38; 44:22,29,31
37:36 [n] Ge 39:1
38:2 [o] 1Ch 2:3
38:3 [p] ver 6; Ge 46:12; Nu 26:19
38:7 [q] ver 10; Ge 46:12; 1Ch 2:3
38:8 [r] Dt 25:5-6; Mt 22:24-28
38:10 [s] Ge 46:12; Dt 25:7-10

[a] *28* That is, about 8 ounces (about 0.2 kilogram) [b] *35* Hebrew *Sheol* [c] *36* Samaritan Pentateuch, Septuagint, Vulgate and Syriac (see also verse 28); Masoretic Text *Medanites*

11 Judah then said to his daughter-in-law Tamar, "Live as a widow in your father's house until my son Shelah grows up."[a] For he thought, "He may die too, just like his brothers." So Tamar went to live in her father's house.

12 After a long time Judah's wife, the daughter of Shua, died. When Judah had recovered from his grief, he went up to Timnah,[b] to the men who were shearing his sheep, and his friend Hirah the Adullamite went with him.

13 When Tamar was told, "Your father-in-law is on his way to Timnah to shear his sheep," 14 she took off her widow's clothes, covered herself with a veil to disguise herself, and then sat down at the entrance to Enaim, which is on the road to Timnah. For she saw that, though Shelah[c] had now grown up, she had not been given to him as his wife.

15 When Judah saw her, he thought she was a prostitute, for she had covered her face. 16 Not realizing that she was his daughter-in-law,[d] he went over to her by the roadside and said, "Come now, let me sleep with you."

"And what will you give me to sleep with you?" she asked.

17 "I'll send you a young goat[e] from my flock," he said.

"Will you give me something as a pledge[f] until you send it?" she asked.

18 He said, "What pledge should I give you?"

"Your seal[g] and its cord, and the staff in your hand," she answered. So he gave them to her and slept with her, and she became pregnant by him. 19 After she left, she took off her veil and put on her widow's clothes[h] again.

20 Meanwhile Judah sent the young goat by his friend the Adullamite in order to get his pledge back from the woman, but he did not find her. 21 He asked the men who lived there, "Where is the shrine prostitute[i] who was beside the road at Enaim?"

"There hasn't been any shrine prostitute here," they said.

22 So he went back to Judah and said, "I didn't find her. Besides, the men who lived there said, 'There hasn't been any shrine prostitute here.'"

23 Then Judah said, "Let her keep what she has, or we will become a laughingstock. After all, I did send her this young goat, but you didn't find her."

24 About three months later Judah was told, "Your daughter-in-law Tamar is guilty of prostitution, and as a result she is now pregnant."

Judah said, "Bring her out and have her burned to death!"[j]

25 As she was being brought out, she sent a message to her father-in-law. "I am pregnant by the man who owns these," she said. And she added, "See if you recognize whose seal and cord and staff these are."[k]

38:11 [a]Ru 1:13
38:12 [b]ver 14; Jos 15:10,57
38:14 [c]ver 11
38:16 [d]Lev 18:15; 20:12
38:17 [e]Eze 16:33 [f]ver 20
38:18 [g]ver 25
38:19 [h]ver 14
38:21 [i]Lev 19:29; Hos 4:14
38:24 [j]Lev 21:9; Dt 22:21,22
38:25 [k]ver 18

26 Judah recognized them and said, "She is more righteous than
I,[a] since I wouldn't give her to my son Shelah.[b]" And he did not
sleep with her again.

27 When the time came for her to give birth, there were twin
boys in her womb.[c] 28 As she was giving birth, one of them put
out his hand; so the midwife took a scarlet thread and tied it on
his wrist and said, "This one came out first." 29 But when he drew
back his hand, his brother came out, and she said, "So this is
how you have broken out!" And he was named Perez.[a][d] 30 Then
his brother, who had the scarlet thread on his wrist, came out
and he was given the name Zerah.[b][e]

Chapter 39 Theme ______________________________

39 Now Joseph had been taken down to Egypt. Potiphar, an
Egyptian who was one of Pharaoh's officials, the captain
of the guard,[f] bought him from the Ishmaelites who had taken
him there.[g]

2 The LORD was with Joseph[h] and he prospered, and he lived in
the house of his Egyptian master. 3 When his master saw that the
LORD was with him[i] and that the LORD gave him success in
everything he did,[j] 4 Joseph found favor in his eyes and became
his attendant. Potiphar put him in charge of his household, and
he entrusted to his care everything he owned.[k] 5 From the time he
put him in charge of his household and of all that he owned, the
LORD blessed the household of the Egyptian because of Joseph.[l]
The blessing of the LORD was on everything Potiphar had, both
in the house and in the field. 6 So he left in Joseph's care everything he had; with Joseph in charge, he did not concern himself
with anything except the food he ate.

Now Joseph was well-built and handsome,[m] 7 and after a while
his master's wife took notice of Joseph and said, "Come to bed
with me!"[n]

8 But he refused.[o] "With me in charge," he told her, "my master
does not concern himself with anything in the house; everything he owns he has entrusted to my care. 9 No one is greater in
this house than I am.[p] My master has withheld nothing from
me except you, because you are his wife. How then could I do
such a wicked thing and sin against God?"[q] 10 And though she
spoke to Joseph day after day, he refused to go to bed with her
or even be with her.

11 One day he went into the house to attend to his duties, and
none of the household servants was inside. 12 She caught him by
his cloak[r] and said, "Come to bed with me!" But he left his cloak
in her hand and ran out of the house.

a 29 *Perez* means *breaking out.* b 30 *Zerah* can mean *scarlet* or *brightness.*

38:26 a 1Sa 24:17 b ver 11
38:27 c Ge 25:24
38:29 d Ge 46:12; Nu 26:20,21; Ru 4:12,18; 1Ch 2:4; Mt 1:3
38:30 e 1Ch 2:4
39:1 f Ge 37:36 g Ge 37:25; Ps 105:17
39:2 h Ge 21:20,22; Ac 7:9
39:3 i Ge 21:22; 26:28 j Ps 1:3
39:4 k ver 8,22; Ge 24:2
39:5 l Ge 26:24; 30:27
39:6 m 1Sa 16:12
39:7 n 2Sa 13:11; Pr 7:15-18
39:8 o Pr 6:23-24
39:9 p Ge 41:33,40 q Ge 20:6; 42:18; 2Sa 12:13
39:12 r Pr 7:13

[13]When she saw that he had left his cloak in her hand and had
run out of the house, [14]she called her household servants. "Look,"
she said to them, "this Hebrew has been brought to us to make
sport of us! He came in here to sleep with me, but I screamed.[a]
[15]When he heard me scream for help, he left his cloak beside me
and ran out of the house."

[16]She kept his cloak beside her until his master came home.
[17]Then she told him this story:[b] "That Hebrew slave you brought
us came to me to make sport of me. [18]But as soon as I screamed
for help, he left his cloak beside me and ran out of the house."

[19]When his master heard the story his wife told him, saying,
"This is how your slave treated me," he burned with anger.[c]
[20]Joseph's master took him and put him in prison,[d] the place
where the king's prisoners were confined.

But while Joseph was there in the prison, [21]the LORD was with
him; he showed him kindness and granted him favor in the eyes
of the prison warden.[e] [22]So the warden put Joseph in charge of
all those held in the prison, and he was made responsible for all
that was done there.[f] [23]The warden paid no attention to anything under Joseph's care, because the LORD was with Joseph
and gave him success in whatever he did.[g]

Chapter 40 Theme ____________________________________

40 Some time later, the cupbearer[h] and the baker of the
king of Egypt offended their master, the king of Egypt.
[2]Pharaoh was angry[i] with his two officials, the chief cupbearer
and the chief baker, [3]and put them in custody in the house of the
captain of the guard,[j] in the same prison where Joseph was confined. [4]The captain of the guard assigned them to Joseph,[k] and
he attended them.

After they had been in custody for some time, [5]each of the two
men—the cupbearer and the baker of the king of Egypt, who
were being held in prison—had a dream the same night, and
each dream had a meaning of its own.[l]

[6]When Joseph came to them the next morning, he saw that
they were dejected. [7]So he asked Pharaoh's officials who were in
custody with him in his master's house, "Why are your faces so
sad today?"[m]

[8]"We both had dreams," they answered, "but there is no one
to interpret them."[n]

Then Joseph said to them, "Do not interpretations belong to
God?[o] Tell me your dreams."

[9]So the chief cupbearer told Joseph his dream. He said to him,
"In my dream I saw a vine in front of me, [10]and on the vine were

39:14 [a]Dt 22:24,27
39:17 [b]Ex 23:1,7; Ps 101:5
39:19 [c]Pr 6:34
39:20 [d]Ge 40:3; Ps 105:18
39:21 [e]Ex 3:21
39:22 [f]ver 4
39:23 [g]ver 3
40:1 [h]Ne 1:11
40:2 [i]Pr 16:14,15
40:3 [j]Ge 39:20
40:4 [k]Ge 39:4
40:5 [l]Ge 41:11
40:7 [m]Ne 2:2
40:8 [n]Ge 41:8,15 [o]Ge 41:16; Da 2:22,28,47

three branches. As soon as it budded, it blossomed, and its clusters ripened into grapes. 11 Pharaoh's cup was in my hand, and I
took the grapes, squeezed them into Pharaoh's cup and put the
cup in his hand."
12 "This is what it means,[a]" Joseph said to him. "The three
branches are three days. 13 Within three days Pharaoh will lift up
your head and restore you to your position, and you will put
Pharaoh's cup in his hand, just as you used to do when you were
his cupbearer. 14 But when all goes well with you, remember me[b]
and show me kindness;[c] mention me to Pharaoh and get me out
of this prison. 15 For I was forcibly carried off from the land of the
Hebrews,[d] and even here I have done nothing to deserve being
put in a dungeon."
16 When the chief baker saw that Joseph had given a favorable
interpretation, he said to Joseph, "I too had a dream: On my head
were three baskets of bread.[a] 17 In the top basket were all kinds of
baked goods for Pharaoh, but the birds were eating them out of
the basket on my head."
18 "This is what it means," Joseph said. "The three baskets are
three days.[e] 19 Within three days Pharaoh will lift off your head[f]
and hang you on a tree.[b] And the birds will eat away your flesh."
20 Now the third day was Pharaoh's birthday,[g] and he gave a
feast for all his officials.[h] He lifted up the heads of the chief cupbearer and the chief baker in the presence of his officials: 21 He restored the chief cupbearer to his position, so that he once again
put the cup into Pharaoh's hand,[i] 22 but he hanged[c] the chief
baker,[j] just as Joseph had said to them in his interpretation.[k]
23 The chief cupbearer, however, did not remember Joseph; he
forgot him.[l]

Chapter 41 Theme ________________

41 When two full years had passed, Pharaoh had a dream:[m]
He was standing by the Nile, 2 when out of the river there
came up seven cows, sleek and fat,[n] and they grazed among the
reeds.[o] 3 After them, seven other cows, ugly and gaunt, came up
out of the Nile and stood beside those on the riverbank. 4 And the
cows that were ugly and gaunt ate up the seven sleek, fat cows.
Then Pharaoh woke up.
5 He fell asleep again and had a second dream: Seven heads of
grain, healthy and good, were growing on a single stalk. 6 After
them, seven other heads of grain sprouted—thin and scorched
by the east wind. 7 The thin heads of grain swallowed up the seven
healthy, full heads. Then Pharaoh woke up; it had been a dream.

40:12 [a]Ge 41:12, 15,25; Da 2:36; 4:19
40:14 [b]Lk 23:42 [c]Jos 2:12; 1Sa 20:14,42; 1Ki 2:7
40:15 [d]Ge 37:26-28
40:18 [e]ver 12
40:19 [f]ver 13
40:20 [g]Mt 14:6-10 [h]Mk 6:21
40:21 [i]ver 13
40:22 [j]ver 19 [k]Ps 105:19
40:23 [l]Job 19:14; Ecc 9:15
41:1 [m]Ge 20:3
41:2 [n]ver 26 [o]Isa 19:6

[a]16 Or *three wicker baskets* [b]19 Or *and impale you on a pole* [c]22 Or *impaled*

8In the morning his mind was troubled,[a] so he sent for all the
magicians[b] and wise men of Egypt. Pharaoh told them his dreams,
but no one could interpret them for him.
9Then the chief cupbearer said to Pharaoh, "Today I am
reminded of my shortcomings. 10Pharaoh was once angry with
his servants,[c] and he imprisoned me and the chief baker in the
house of the captain of the guard.[d] 11Each of us had a dream the
same night, and each dream had a meaning of its own.[e] 12Now a
young Hebrew was there with us, a servant of the captain of the
guard. We told him our dreams, and he interpreted them for us,
giving each man the interpretation of his dream.[f] 13And things
turned out exactly as he interpreted them to us: I was restored
to my position, and the other man was hanged.[a][g]"
14So Pharaoh sent for Joseph, and he was quickly brought from
the dungeon.[h] When he had shaved and changed his clothes, he
came before Pharaoh.
15Pharaoh said to Joseph, "I had a dream, and no one can
interpret it. But I have heard it said of you that when you hear a
dream you can interpret it."[i]
16"I cannot do it," Joseph replied to Pharaoh, "but God will
give Pharaoh the answer he desires."[j]
17Then Pharaoh said to Joseph, "In my dream I was standing
on the bank of the Nile, 18when out of the river there came up
seven cows, fat and sleek, and they grazed among the reeds.
19After them, seven other cows came up—scrawny and very ugly
and lean. I had never seen such ugly cows in all the land of Egypt.
20The lean, ugly cows ate up the seven fat cows that came up first.
21But even after they ate them, no one could tell that they had
done so; they looked just as ugly as before. Then I woke up.
22"In my dreams I also saw seven heads of grain, full and good,
growing on a single stalk. 23After them, seven other heads sprouted—withered and thin and scorched by the east wind. 24The
thin heads of grain swallowed up the seven good heads. I told this
to the magicians, but none could explain it to me.[k]"
25Then Joseph said to Pharaoh, "The dreams of Pharaoh are
one and the same. God has revealed to Pharaoh what he is about
to do.[l] 26The seven good cows[m] are seven years, and the seven
good heads of grain are seven years; it is one and the same dream.
27The seven lean, ugly cows that came up afterward are seven
years, and so are the seven worthless heads of grain scorched by
the east wind: They are seven years of famine.[n]
28"It is just as I said to Pharaoh: God has shown Pharaoh what
he is about to do. 29Seven years of great abundance[o] are coming

41:8 [a] Da 2:1,3; 4:5,19 [b] Ex 7:11,22; Da 1:20; 2:2,27; 4:7
41:10 [c] Ge 40:2 [d] Ge 39:20
41:11 [e] Ge 40:5
41:12 [f] Ge 40:12
41:13 [g] Ge 40:22
41:14 [h] Ps 105:20; Da 2:25
41:15 [i] Da 5:16
41:16 [j] Ge 40:8; Da 2:30; Ac 3:12; 2Co 3:5
41:24 [k] ver 8
41:25 [l] Da 2:45
41:26 [m] ver 2
41:27 [n] Ge 12:10; 2Ki 8:1
41:29 [o] ver 47

[a] 13 Or *impaled*

throughout the land of Egypt, 30but seven years of famine[a] will follow them. Then all the abundance in Egypt will be forgotten, and the famine will ravage the land.[b] 31The abundance in the land will not be remembered, because the famine that follows it will be so severe. 32The reason the dream was given to Pharaoh in two forms is that the matter has been firmly decided[c] by God, and God will do it soon.

33"And now let Pharaoh look for a discerning and wise man[d] and put him in charge of the land of Egypt. 34Let Pharaoh appoint commissioners over the land to take a fifth[e] of the harvest of Egypt during the seven years of abundance.[f] 35They should collect all the food of these good years that are coming and store up the grain under the authority of Pharaoh, to be kept in the cities for food.[g] 36This food should be held in reserve for the country, to be used during the seven years of famine that will come upon Egypt,[h] so that the country may not be ruined by the famine."

37The plan seemed good to Pharaoh and to all his officials.[i] 38So Pharaoh asked them, "Can we find anyone like this man, one in whom is the spirit of God[a]?"[j]

39Then Pharaoh said to Joseph, "Since God has made all this known to you, there is no one so discerning and wise as you. 40You shall be in charge of my palace, and all my people are to submit to your orders.[k] Only with respect to the throne will I be greater than you."

41So Pharaoh said to Joseph, "I hereby put you in charge of the whole land of Egypt."[l] 42Then Pharaoh took his signet ring[m] from his finger and put it on Joseph's finger. He dressed him in robes of fine linen and put a gold chain around his neck.[n] 43He had him ride in a chariot as his second-in-command,[b] and men shouted before him, "Make way[c]!"[o] Thus he put him in charge of the whole land of Egypt.

44Then Pharaoh said to Joseph, "I am Pharaoh, but without your word no one will lift hand or foot in all Egypt."[p] 45Pharaoh gave Joseph the name Zaphenath-Paneah and gave him Asenath daughter of Potiphera, priest of On,[d] to be his wife.[q] And Joseph went throughout the land of Egypt.

46Joseph was thirty years old[r] when he entered the service[s] of Pharaoh king of Egypt. And Joseph went out from Pharaoh's presence and traveled throughout Egypt. 47During the seven years of abundance the land produced plentifully. 48Joseph collected all the food produced in those seven years of abundance in Egypt and stored it in the cities. In each city he put the food grown in the fields surrounding it. 49Joseph stored up huge

41:30 [a] ver 54; Ge 47:13 [b] ver 56
41:32 [c] Nu 23:19; Isa 46:10-11
41:33 [d] ver 39
41:34 [e] 1Sa 8:15 [f] ver 48
41:35 [g] ver 48
41:36 [h] ver 56
41:37 [i] Ge 45:16
41:38 [j] Nu 27:18; Job 32:8; Da 4:8,8-9,18; 5:11,14
41:40 [k] Ps 105:21-22; Ac 7:10
41:41 [l] Ge 42:6; Da 6:3
41:42 [m] Est 3:10 [n] Da 5:7,16,29
41:43 [o] Est 6:9
41:44 [p] Ps 105:22
41:45 [q] ver 50; Ge 46:20,27
41:46 [r] Ge 37:2 [s] 1Sa 16:21; Da 1:19

[a] 38 Or *of the gods* [b] 43 Or *in the chariot of his second-in-command*; or *in his second chariot* [c] 43 Or *Bow down* [d] 45 That is, Heliopolis; also in verse 50

quantities of grain, like the sand of the sea; it was so much that
he stopped keeping records because it was beyond measure.
50Before the years of famine came, two sons were born to
Joseph by Asenath daughter of Potiphera, priest of On.[a] 51Joseph
named his firstborn[b] Manasseh[a] and said, "It is because God
has made me forget all my trouble and all my father's household." 52The second son he named Ephraim[b][c] and said, "It is
because God has made me fruitful[d] in the land of my suffering."
53The seven years of abundance in Egypt came to an end,
54and the seven years of famine began,[e] just as Joseph had said.
There was famine in all the other lands, but in the whole land of
Egypt there was food. 55When all Egypt began to feel the
famine,[f] the people cried to Pharaoh for food. Then Pharaoh
told all the Egyptians, "Go to Joseph and do what he tells you."[g]
56When the famine had spread over the whole country, Joseph
opened the storehouses and sold grain to the Egyptians, for the
famine[h] was severe throughout Egypt. 57And all the countries
came to Egypt to buy grain from Joseph,[i] because the famine
was severe in all the world.

Chapter 42 Theme ______

42 When Jacob learned that there was grain in Egypt,[j] he
said to his sons, "Why do you just keep looking at each
other?" 2He continued, "I have heard that there is grain in Egypt.
Go down there and buy some for us, so that we may live and not
die."[k]
3Then ten of Joseph's brothers went down to buy grain from
Egypt. 4But Jacob did not send Benjamin, Joseph's brother, with
the others, because he was afraid that harm might come to him.[l]
5So Israel's sons were among those who went to buy grain,[m] for
the famine was in the land of Canaan also.[n]
6Now Joseph was the governor of the land,[o] the one who sold
grain to all its people. So when Joseph's brothers arrived, they
bowed down to him with their faces to the ground.[p] 7As soon as
Joseph saw his brothers, he recognized them, but he pretended to
be a stranger and spoke harshly to them.[q] "Where do you come
from?" he asked.
"From the land of Canaan," they replied, "to buy food."
8Although Joseph recognized his brothers, they did not recognize him.[r] 9Then he remembered his dreams[s] about them and
said to them, "You are spies! You have come to see where our
land is unprotected."

a 51 *Manasseh* sounds like and may be derived from the Hebrew for *forget.* b 52 *Ephraim* sounds like the Hebrew for *twice fruitful.*

41:50 [a]Ge 46:20; 48:5
41:51 [b]Ge 48:14, 18,20
41:52 [c]Ge 48:1,5; 50:23 [d]Ge 17:6; 28:3; 49:22
41:54 [e]ver 30; Ps 105:11; Ac 7:11
41:55 [f]Dt 32:24 [g]ver 41
41:56 [h]Ge 12:10
41:57 [i]Ge 42:5; 47:15
42:1 [j]Ac 7:12
42:2 [k]Ge 43:8
42:4 [l]ver 38
42:5 [m]Ge 41:57 [n]Ge 12:10; Ac 7:11
42:6 [o]Ge 41:41 [p]Ge 37:7-10
42:7 [q]ver 30
42:8 [r]Ge 37:2
42:9 [s]Ge 37:7

10“No, my lord,” they answered. “Your servants have come to buy food. 11We are all the sons of one man. Your servants are honest men, not spies.”

12“No!” he said to them. “You have come to see where our land is unprotected.”

13But they replied, “Your servants were twelve brothers, the sons of one man, who lives in the land of Canaan. The youngest is now with our father, and one is no more.”[a]

14Joseph said to them, “It is just as I told you: You are spies! 15And this is how you will be tested: As surely as Pharaoh lives,[b] you will not leave this place unless your youngest brother comes here. 16Send one of your number to get your brother; the rest of you will be kept in prison, so that your words may be tested to see if you are telling the truth.[c] If you are not, then as surely as Pharaoh lives, you are spies!” 17And he put them all in custody[d] for three days.

18On the third day, Joseph said to them, “Do this and you will live, for I fear God:[e] 19If you are honest men, let one of your brothers stay here in prison, while the rest of you go and take grain back for your starving households. 20But you must bring your youngest brother to me,[f] so that your words may be verified and that you may not die.” This they proceeded to do.

21They said to one another, “Surely we are being punished because of our brother.[g] We saw how distressed he was when he pleaded with us for his life, but we would not listen; that’s why this distress[h] has come upon us.”

22Reuben replied, “Didn’t I tell you not to sin against the boy?[i] But you wouldn’t listen! Now we must give an accounting[j] for his blood.”[k] 23They did not realize that Joseph could understand them, since he was using an interpreter.

24He turned away from them and began to weep, but then turned back and spoke to them again. He had Simeon taken from them and bound before their eyes.[l]

25Joseph gave orders to fill their bags with grain,[m] to put each man’s silver back in his sack,[n] and to give them provisions for their journey.[o] After this was done for them, 26they loaded their grain on their donkeys and left.

27At the place where they stopped for the night one of them opened his sack to get feed for his donkey, and he saw his silver in the mouth of his sack.[p] 28“My silver has been returned,” he said to his brothers. “Here it is in my sack.”

Their hearts sank and they turned to each other trembling and said, “What is this that God has done to us?”[q]

29When they came to their father Jacob in the land of Canaan, they told him all that had happened to them. They said, 30“The

42:13 [a] Ge 37:30,33; 44:20
42:15 [b] 1Sa 17:55
42:16 [c] ver 11
42:17 [d] Ge 40:4
42:18 [e] Ge 20:11; Lev 25:43
42:20 [f] ver 15,34; Ge 43:5; 44:23
42:21 [g] Ge 37:26-28 [h] Hos 5:15
42:22 [i] Ge 37:21-22 [j] Ge 9:5 [k] 1Ki 2:32; 2Ch 24:22; Ps 9:12
42:24 [l] ver 13; Ge 43:14,23; 45:14-15
42:25 [m] Ge 43:2 [n] Ge 44:1,8 [o] Ro 12:17, 20-21
42:27 [p] Ge 43:21-22
42:28 [q] Ge 43:23

man who is lord over the land spoke harshly to us[a] and treated us as though we were spying on the land. 31But we said to him, 'We are honest men; we are not spies.[b] 32We were twelve brothers, sons of one father. One is no more, and the youngest is now with our father in Canaan.'

33"Then the man who is lord over the land said to us, 'This is how I will know whether you are honest men: Leave one of your brothers here with me, and take food for your starving households and go.[c] 34But bring your youngest brother to me so I will know that you are not spies but honest men. Then I will give your brother back to you, and you can trade[a] in the land.[d]' "

35As they were emptying their sacks, there in each man's sack was his pouch of silver! When they and their father saw the money pouches, they were frightened.[e] 36Their father Jacob said to them, "You have deprived me of my children. Joseph is no more and Simeon is no more, and now you want to take Benjamin.[f] Everything is against me!"

37Then Reuben said to his father, "You may put both of my sons to death if I do not bring him back to you. Entrust him to my care, and I will bring him back."

38But Jacob said, "My son will not go down there with you; his brother is dead[g] and he is the only one left. If harm comes to him[h] on the journey you are taking, you will bring my gray head down to the grave[b][i] in sorrow.[j]"

Chapter 43 Theme ________________________

43 Now the famine was still severe in the land.[k] 2So when they had eaten all the grain they had brought from Egypt, their father said to them, "Go back and buy us a little more food."

3But Judah said to him, "The man warned us solemnly, 'You will not see my face again unless your brother is with you.'[l] 4If you will send our brother along with us, we will go down and buy food for you. 5But if you will not send him, we will not go down, because the man said to us, 'You will not see my face again unless your brother is with you.[m]' "

6Israel asked, "Why did you bring this trouble on me by telling the man you had another brother?"

7They replied, "The man questioned us closely about ourselves and our family. 'Is your father still living?'[n] he asked us. 'Do you have another brother?'[o] We simply answered his questions. How were we to know he would say, 'Bring your brother down here'?"

8Then Judah said to Israel his father, "Send the boy along with me and we will go at once, so that we and you and our children

[a]34 Or *move about freely* [b]38 Hebrew *Sheol*

42:30 [a]ver 7
42:31 [b]ver 11
42:33 [c]ver 19,20
42:34 [d]Ge 34:10
42:35 [e]Ge 43:12,15,18
42:36 [f]Ge 43:14
42:38 [g]Ge 37:33 [h]ver 4 [i]Ge 37:35 [j]Ge 44:29,34
43:1 [k]Ge 12:10; 41:56-57
43:3 [l]Ge 42:15; 44:23
43:5 [m]Ge 42:15; 2Sa 3:13
43:7 [n]ver 27 [o]Ge 42:13

may live and not die.[a] 9I myself will guarantee his safety; you
can hold me personally responsible for him. If I do not bring
him back to you and set him here before you, I will bear the
blame before you all my life.[b] 10As it is, if we had not delayed,
we could have gone and returned twice."

11Then their father Israel said to them, "If it must be, then do
this: Put some of the best products of the land in your bags and
take them down to the man as a gift[c]—a little balm[d] and a little
honey, some spices[e] and myrrh, some pistachio nuts and
almonds. 12Take double the amount of silver with you, for you
must return the silver that was put back into the mouths of your
sacks.[f] Perhaps it was a mistake. 13Take your brother also and
go back to the man at once. 14And may God Almighty[a][g] grant
you mercy before the man so that he will let your other brother
and Benjamin come back with you.[h] As for me, if I am bereaved,
I am bereaved."[i]

15So the men took the gifts and double the amount of silver,
and Benjamin also. They hurried[j] down to Egypt and presented
themselves[k] to Joseph. 16When Joseph saw Benjamin with them,
he said to the steward of his house,[l] "Take these men to my
house, slaughter an animal and prepare dinner;[m] they are to eat
with me at noon."

17The man did as Joseph told him and took the men to
Joseph's house. 18Now the men were frightened[n] when they
were taken to his house. They thought, "We were brought here
because of the silver that was put back into our sacks the first
time. He wants to attack us and overpower us and seize us as
slaves and take our donkeys."

19So they went up to Joseph's steward and spoke to him at the
entrance to the house. 20"Please, sir," they said, "we came down
here the first time to buy food.[o] 21But at the place where we
stopped for the night we opened our sacks and each of us found
his silver—the exact weight—in the mouth of his sack. So we
have brought it back with us.[p] 22We have also brought additional
silver with us to buy food. We don't know who put our silver in
our sacks."

23"It's all right," he said. "Don't be afraid. Your God, the God
of your father, has given you treasure in your sacks;[q] I received
your silver." Then he brought Simeon out to them.[r]

24The steward took the men into Joseph's house,[s] gave them
water to wash their feet[t] and provided fodder for their donkeys.
25They prepared their gifts for Joseph's arrival at noon, because
they had heard that they were to eat there.

43:8 [a]Ge 42:2; Ps 33:18-19

43:9 [b]Ge 42:37; 44:32; Phm 1:18-19

43:11 [c]Ge 32:20; Pr 18:16 [d]Ge 37:25; Jer 8:22 [e]1Ki 10:2

43:12 [f]Ge 42:25

43:14 [g]Ge 17:1; 28:3; 35:11 [h]Ge 42:24 [i]Est 4:16

43:15 [j]Ge 45:9,13 [k]Ge 47:2,7

43:16 [l]Ge 44:1,4,12 [m]ver 31; Lk 15:23

43:18 [n]Ge 42:35

43:20 [o]Ge 42:3

43:21 [p]ver 15; Ge 42:27,35

43:23 [q]Ge 42:28 [r]Ge 42:24

43:24 [s]ver 16 [t]Ge 18:4; 24:32

a *14* Hebrew *El-Shaddai*

26When Joseph came home, they presented to him the gifts[a]
they had brought into the house, and they bowed down before
him to the ground.[b] 27He asked them how they were, and then
he said, "How is your aged father you told me about? Is he still
living?"[c]

28They replied, "Your servant our father is still alive and well."
And they bowed low to pay him honor.[d]

29As he looked about and saw his brother Benjamin, his own
mother's son, he asked, "Is this your youngest brother, the one
you told me about?"[e] And he said, "God be gracious to you,[f] my
son." 30Deeply moved[g] at the sight of his brother, Joseph hurried
out and looked for a place to weep. He went into his private room
and wept[h] there.

31After he had washed his face, he came out and, controlling
himself,[i] said, "Serve the food."

32They served him by himself, the brothers by themselves, and
the Egyptians who ate with him by themselves, because Egyptians
could not eat with Hebrews,[j] for that is detestable to Egyptians.[k]
33The men had been seated before him in the order of their ages,
from the firstborn to the youngest; and they looked at each other in astonishment. 34When portions were served to them from
Joseph's table, Benjamin's portion was five times as much as
anyone else's.[l] So they feasted and drank freely with him.

Chapter 44 Theme

44 Now Joseph gave these instructions to the steward of his
house: "Fill the men's sacks with as much food as they
can carry, and put each man's silver in the mouth of his sack.[m]
2Then put my cup, the silver one, in the mouth of the youngest
one's sack, along with the silver for his grain." And he did as
Joseph said.

3As morning dawned, the men were sent on their way with
their donkeys. 4They had not gone far from the city when Joseph
said to his steward, "Go after those men at once, and when you
catch up with them, say to them, 'Why have you repaid good
with evil?[n] 5Isn't this the cup my master drinks from and also
uses for divination?[o] This is a wicked thing you have done.'"

6When he caught up with them, he repeated these words to
them. 7But they said to him, "Why does my lord say such
things? Far be it from your servants to do anything like that!
8We even brought back to you from the land of Canaan the silver we found inside the mouths of our sacks.[p] So why would we
steal silver or gold from your master's house? 9If any of your
servants is found to have it, he will die;[q] and the rest of us will
become my lord's slaves."

43:26 [a]Mt 2:11 [b]Ge 37:7,10

43:27 [c]ver 7

43:28 [d]Ge 37:7

43:29 [e]Ge 42:13 [f]Nu 6:25; Ps 67:1

43:30 [g]Jn 11:33,38 [h]Ge 42:24; 45:2,14,15; 46:29

43:31 [i]Ge 45:1

43:32 [j]Gal 2:12 [k]Ge 46:34; Ex 8:26

43:34 [l]Ge 37:3; 45:22

44:1 [m]Ge 42:25

44:4 [n]Ps 35:12

44:5 [o]Ge 30:27; Dt 18:10-14

44:8 [p]Ge 42:25; 43:21

44:9 [q]Ge 31:32

10“Very well, then,” he said, “let it be as you say. Whoever is
found to have it will become my slave; the rest of you will be free
from blame.”
11Each of them quickly lowered his sack to the ground and
opened it. 12Then the steward proceeded to search, beginning
with the oldest and ending with the youngest. And the cup was
found in Benjamin’s sack.[a] 13At this, they tore their clothes.[b]
Then they all loaded their donkeys and returned to the city.
14Joseph was still in the house when Judah and his brothers
came in, and they threw themselves to the ground before him.[c]
15Joseph said to them, “What is this you have done? Don’t you
know that a man like me can find things out by divination?[d]”
16“What can we say to my lord?” Judah replied. “What can we
say? How can we prove our innocence? God has uncovered your
servants’ guilt. We are now my lord’s slaves[e]—we ourselves and
the one who was found to have the cup.[f]”
17But Joseph said, “Far be it from me to do such a thing! Only
the man who was found to have the cup will become my slave.
The rest of you, go back to your father in peace.”
18Then Judah went up to him and said: “Please, my lord, let
your servant speak a word to my lord. Do not be angry[g] with
your servant, though you are equal to Pharaoh himself. 19My lord
asked his servants, ‘Do you have a father or a brother?’[h] 20And
we answered, ‘We have an aged father, and there is a young son
born to him in his old age.[i] His brother is dead,[j] and he is the
only one of his mother’s sons left, and his father loves him.’[k]
21“Then you said to your servants, ‘Bring him down to me so I
can see him for myself.’[l] 22And we said to my lord, ‘The boy cannot leave his father; if he leaves him, his father will die.’[m] 23But you
told your servants, ‘Unless your youngest brother comes down
with you, you will not see my face again.’[n] 24When we went back
to your servant my father, we told him what my lord had said.
25“Then our father said, ‘Go back and buy a little more food.’[o]
26But we said, ‘We cannot go down. Only if our youngest brother is with us will we go. We cannot see the man’s face unless our
youngest brother is with us.’
27“Your servant my father said to us, ‘You know that my wife
bore me two sons.[p] 28One of them went away from me, and I
said, “He has surely been torn to pieces.”[q] And I have not seen
him since. 29If you take this one from me too and harm comes to
him, you will bring my gray head down to the grave[a] in misery.’[r]
30“So now, if the boy is not with us when I go back to your servant my father and if my father, whose life is closely bound up
with the boy’s life,[s] 31sees that the boy isn’t there, he will die. Your

44:12 [a]ver 2
44:13 [b]Ge 37:29; Nu 14:6; 2Sa 1:11
44:14 [c]Ge 37:7,10
44:15 [d]ver 5; Ge 30:27
44:16 [e]ver 9; Ge 43:18 [f]ver 2
44:18 [g]Ge 18:30; Ex 32:22
44:19 [h]Ge 43:7
44:20 [i]Ge 37:3 [j]Ge 37:33 [k]Ge 42:13
44:21 [l]Ge 42:15
44:22 [m]Ge 37:35
44:23 [n]Ge 43:5
44:25 [o]Ge 43:2
44:27 [p]Ge 46:19
44:28 [q]Ge 37:33
44:29 [r]Ge 42:38
44:30 [s]1Sa 18:1

a *29* Hebrew *Sheol*; also in verse 31

servants will bring the gray head of our father down to the grave
in sorrow. 32Your servant guaranteed the boy's safety to my
father. I said, 'If I do not bring him back to you, I will bear the
blame before you, my father, all my life!'[a]
33"Now then, please let your servant remain here as my lord's
slave[b] in place of the boy,[c] and let the boy return with his brothers.
34How can I go back to my father if the boy is not with me? No!
Do not let me see the misery that would come upon my father."[d]

Chapter 45 Theme ________________________

45 Then Joseph could no longer control himself[e] before all
his attendants, and he cried out, "Have everyone leave
my presence!" So there was no one with Joseph when he made
himself known to his brothers. 2And he wept[f] so loudly that the
Egyptians heard him, and Pharaoh's household heard about it.[g]
3Joseph said to his brothers, "I am Joseph! Is my father still
living?"[h] But his brothers were not able to answer him,[i] because
they were terrified at his presence.
4Then Joseph said to his brothers, "Come close to me." When
they had done so, he said, "I am your brother Joseph, the one
you sold into Egypt![j] 5And now, do not be distressed[k] and do
not be angry with yourselves for selling me here,[l] because it was
to save lives that God sent me ahead of you.[m] 6For two years
now there has been famine in the land, and for the next five
years there will not be plowing and reaping. 7But God sent me
ahead of you to preserve for you a remnant[n] on earth and to
save your lives by a great deliverance.[a][o]
8"So then, it was not you who sent me here, but God. He made
me father[p] to Pharaoh, lord of his entire household and ruler of
all Egypt.[q] 9Now hurry back to my father and say to him, 'This is
what your son Joseph says: God has made me lord of all Egypt.
Come down to me; don't delay.[r] 10You shall live in the region of
Goshen[s] and be near me—you, your children and grandchildren, your flocks and herds, and all you have. 11I will provide
for you there,[t] because five years of famine are still to come.
Otherwise you and your household and all who belong to you
will become destitute.'
12"You can see for yourselves, and so can my brother Benjamin, that it is really I who am speaking to you. 13Tell my father
about all the honor accorded me in Egypt and about everything
you have seen. And bring my father down here quickly.[u]"
14Then he threw his arms around his brother Benjamin and
wept, and Benjamin embraced him, weeping. 15And he kissed[v]

[a]7 Or *save you as a great band of survivors*

44:32 [a]Ge 43:9
44:33 [b]Ge 43:18 [c]Jn 15:13
44:34 [d]Est 8:6
45:1 [e]Ge 43:31
45:2 [f]Ge 29:11 [g]ver 16; Ge 46:29
45:3 [h]Ac 7:13 [i]ver 15
45:4 [j]Ge 37:28
45:5 [k]Ge 42:21 [l]Ge 42:22 [m]ver 7-8; Ge 50:20; Ps 105:17
45:7 [n]2Ki 19:4, 30,31; Isa 10:20,21; Mic 4:7; Zep 2:7 [o]Ex 15:2; Est 4:14; Isa 25:9
45:8 [p]Jdg 17:10 [q]Ge 41:41
45:9 [r]Ge 43:10
45:10 [s]Ge 46:28,34; 47:1
45:11 [t]Ge 47:12
45:13 [u]Ac 7:14
45:15 [v]Lk 15:20

all his brothers and wept over them. Afterward his brothers talked with him.[a]

16When the news reached Pharaoh's palace that Joseph's brothers had come,[b] Pharaoh and all his officials were pleased. 17Pharaoh said to Joseph, "Tell your brothers, 'Do this: Load your animals and return to the land of Canaan, 18and bring your father and your families back to me. I will give you the best of the land of Egypt[c] and you can enjoy the fat of the land.'[d]

19"You are also directed to tell them, 'Do this: Take some carts[e] from Egypt for your children and your wives, and get your father and come. 20Never mind about your belongings, because the best of all Egypt will be yours.'"

21So the sons of Israel did this. Joseph gave them carts, as Pharaoh had commanded, and he also gave them provisions for their journey.[f] 22To each of them he gave new clothing, but to Benjamin he gave three hundred shekels[a] of silver and five sets of clothes.[g] 23And this is what he sent to his father: ten donkeys loaded with the best things of Egypt, and ten female donkeys loaded with grain and bread and other provisions for his journey. 24Then he sent his brothers away, and as they were leaving he said to them, "Don't quarrel on the way!"[h]

25So they went up out of Egypt and came to their father Jacob in the land of Canaan. 26They told him, "Joseph is still alive! In fact, he is ruler of all Egypt." Jacob was stunned; he did not believe them.[i] 27But when they told him everything Joseph had said to them, and when he saw the carts[j] Joseph had sent to carry him back, the spirit of their father Jacob revived. 28And Israel said, "I'm convinced! My son Joseph is still alive. I will go and see him before I die."

Chapter 46 Theme ______________________

46 So Israel set out with all that was his, and when he reached Beersheba,[k] he offered sacrifices to the God of his father Isaac.[l]

2And God spoke to Israel in a vision at night[m] and said, "Jacob! Jacob!"

"Here I am,"[n] he replied.

3"I am God, the God of your father,"[o] he said. "Do not be afraid to go down to Egypt, for I will make you into a great nation[p] there.[q] 4I will go down to Egypt with you, and I will surely bring you back again.[r] And Joseph's own hand will close your eyes.[s]"

5Then Jacob left Beersheba, and Israel's sons took their father Jacob and their children and their wives in the carts[t] that Pharaoh

45:15 [a]ver 3
45:16 [b]Ac 7:13
45:18 [c]Ge 27:28; 46:34; 47:6,11,27; Nu 18:12,29 [d]Ps 37:19
45:19 [e]Ge 46:5
45:21 [f]Ge 42:25
45:22 [g]Ge 37:3; 43:34
45:24 [h]Ge 42:21-22
45:26 [i]Ge 44:28
45:27 [j]ver 19
46:1 [k]Ge 21:14; 28:10 [l]Ge 26:24; 28:13; 31:42
46:2 [m]Ge 15:1; Job 33:14-15 [n]Ge 22:1; 31:11
46:3 [o]Ge 28:13 [p]Ge 12:2; Dt 26:5 [q]Ex 1:7
46:4 [r]Ge 28:15; 48:21; Ex 3:8 [s]Ge 50:1,24
46:5 [t]Ge 45:19

a *22* That is, about 7 1/2 pounds (about 3.5 kilograms)

had sent to transport him. 6They also took with them their livestock and the possessions they had acquired in Canaan, and Jacob
and all his offspring went to Egypt.[a] 7He took with him to Egypt
his sons and grandsons and his daughters and granddaughters—
all his offspring.[b]

8These are the names of the sons of Israel[c] (Jacob and his
descendants) who went to Egypt:

Reuben the firstborn of Jacob.
9The sons of Reuben:[d]
Hanoch, Pallu, Hezron and Carmi.
10The sons of Simeon:[e]
Jemuel,[f] Jamin, Ohad, Jakin, Zohar and Shaul the son of
a Canaanite woman.
11The sons of Levi:[g]
Gershon, Kohath and Merari.
12The sons of Judah:[h]
Er, Onan, Shelah, Perez and Zerah (but Er and Onan had
died in the land of Canaan).
The sons of Perez:[i]
Hezron and Hamul.
13The sons of Issachar:[j]
Tola, Puah,[a][k] Jashub[b] and Shimron.
14The sons of Zebulun:[l]
Sered, Elon and Jahleel.

15These were the sons Leah bore to Jacob in Paddan Aram,[c]
besides his daughter Dinah. These sons and daughters of his
were thirty-three in all.

16The sons of Gad:[m]
Zephon,[d][n] Haggi, Shuni, Ezbon, Eri, Arodi and Areli.
17The sons of Asher:[o]
Imnah, Ishvah, Ishvi and Beriah.
Their sister was Serah.
The sons of Beriah:
Heber and Malkiel.

18These were the children born to Jacob by Zilpah,[p] whom
Laban had given to his daughter Leah[q]—sixteen in all.

19The sons of Jacob's wife Rachel:
Joseph and Benjamin.[r] 20In Egypt, Manasseh[s] and Ephraim[t] were born to Joseph by Asenath daughter of Potiphera, priest of On.[e]

a *13* Samaritan Pentateuch and Syriac (see also 1 Chron. 7:1); Masoretic Text *Puvah*
b *13* Samaritan Pentateuch and some Septuagint manuscripts (see also Num. 26:24 and 1 Chron. 7:1); Masoretic Text *Iob* c *15* That is, Northwest Mesopotamia d *16* Samaritan Pentateuch and Septuagint (see also Num. 26:15); Masoretic Text *Ziphion* e *20* That is, Heliopolis

46:6 [a] Dt 26:5; Jos 24:4; Ps 105:23; Isa 52:4; Ac 7:15
46:7 [b] Ge 45:10
46:8 [c] Ex 1:1; Nu 26:4
46:9 [d] 1Ch 5:3
46:10 [e] Ge 29:33; Nu 26:14 [f] Ex 6:15
46:11 [g] Ge 29:34; Nu 3:17
46:12 [h] Ge 29:35 [i] 1Ch 2:5 Mt 1:3
46:13 [j] Ge 30:18 [k] 1Ch 7:1
46:14 [l] Ge 30:20
46:16 [m] Ge 30:11 [n] Nu 26:15
46:17 [o] Ge 30:13; 1Ch 7:30-31
46:18 [p] Ge 30:10 [q] Ge 29:24
46:19 [r] Ge 44:27
46:20 [s] Ge 41:51 [t] Ge 41:52

21 The sons of Benjamin:[a]
Bela, Beker, Ashbel, Gera, Naaman, Ehi, Rosh, Muppim,
Huppim and Ard.
22 These were the sons of Rachel who were born to Jacob—
fourteen in all.

23 The son of Dan:
Hushim.
24 The sons of Naphtali:
Jahziel, Guni, Jezer and Shillem.
25 These were the sons born to Jacob by Bilhah,[b] whom Laban
had given to his daughter Rachel[c]—seven in all.

26 All those who went to Egypt with Jacob—those who were
his direct descendants, not counting his sons' wives—numbered sixty-six persons.[d] 27 With the two sons[a] who had been
born to Joseph in Egypt, the members of Jacob's family, which
went to Egypt, were seventy[b] in all.[e]

28 Now Jacob sent Judah ahead of him to Joseph to get directions to Goshen.[f] When they arrived in the region of Goshen,
29 Joseph had his chariot made ready and went to Goshen to
meet his father Israel. As soon as Joseph appeared before him,
he threw his arms around his father[c] and wept for a long time.[g]
30 Israel said to Joseph, "Now I am ready to die, since I have
seen for myself that you are still alive."
31 Then Joseph said to his brothers and to his father's household, "I will go up and speak to Pharaoh and will say to him, 'My
brothers and my father's household, who were living in the land
of Canaan, have come to me.[h] 32 The men are shepherds; they
tend livestock, and they have brought along their flocks and
herds and everything they own.' 33 When Pharaoh calls you in
and asks, 'What is your occupation?'[i] 34 you should answer, 'Your
servants have tended livestock from our boyhood on, just as
our fathers did.' Then you will be allowed to settle in the region
of Goshen,[j] for all shepherds are detestable to the Egyptians.[k]"

Chapter 47 Theme

47 Joseph went and told Pharaoh, "My father and brothers,
with their flocks and herds and everything they own, have
come from the land of Canaan and are now in Goshen."[l] 2 He
chose five of his brothers and presented them before Pharaoh.
3 Pharaoh asked the brothers, "What is your occupation?"[m]
"Your servants are shepherds," they replied to Pharaoh, "just
as our fathers were." 4 They also said to him, "We have come to

46:21 [a] Nu 26:38-41; 1Ch 7:6-12; 8:1
46:25 [b] Ge 30:8 [c] Ge 29:29
46:26 [d] ver 5-7; Ex 1:5; Dt 10:22
46:27 [e] Ac 7:14
46:28 [f] Ge 45:10
46:29 [g] Ge 45:14-15; Lk 15:20
46:31 [h] Ge 47:1
46:33 [i] Ge 47:3
46:34 [j] Ge 45:10 [k] Ge 43:32; Ex 8:26
47:1 [l] Ge 46:31
47:3 [m] Ge 46:33

[a] *27* Hebrew; Septuagint *the nine children* [b] *27* Hebrew (see also Exodus 1:5 and footnote); Septuagint (see also Acts 7:14) *seventy-five* [c] *29* Hebrew *around him*

live here awhile,[a] because the famine is severe in Canaan[b] and
your servants' flocks have no pasture. So now, please let your
servants settle in Goshen."[c]
5 Pharaoh said to Joseph, "Your father and your brothers have
come to you, 6 and the land of Egypt is before you; settle your
father and your brothers in the best part of the land.[d] Let them
live in Goshen. And if you know of any among them with special ability,[e] put them in charge of my own livestock."
7 Then Joseph brought his father Jacob in and presented him
before Pharaoh. After Jacob blessed[a] Pharaoh,[f] 8 Pharaoh asked
him, "How old are you?"
9 And Jacob said to Pharaoh, "The years of my pilgrimage are a
hundred and thirty.[g] My years have been few and difficult,[h] and
they do not equal the years of the pilgrimage of my fathers.[i]"
10 Then Jacob blessed[b] Pharaoh[j] and went out from his presence.
11 So Joseph settled his father and his brothers in Egypt and
gave them property in the best part of the land, the district of
Rameses,[k] as Pharaoh directed. 12 Joseph also provided his
father and his brothers and all his father's household with food,
according to the number of their children.[l]
13 There was no food, however, in the whole region because the
famine was severe; both Egypt and Canaan wasted away because
of the famine.[m] 14 Joseph collected all the money that was to be
found in Egypt and Canaan in payment for the grain they were
buying, and he brought it to Pharaoh's palace.[n] 15 When the money of the people of Egypt and Canaan was gone, all Egypt came to
Joseph and said, "Give us food. Why should we die before your
eyes?[o] Our money is used up."
16 "Then bring your livestock," said Joseph. "I will sell you
food in exchange for your livestock, since your money is gone."
17 So they brought their livestock to Joseph, and he gave them
food in exchange for their horses,[p] their sheep and goats, their
cattle and donkeys. And he brought them through that year with
food in exchange for all their livestock.
18 When that year was over, they came to him the following
year and said, "We cannot hide from our lord the fact that since
our money is gone and our livestock belongs to you, there is
nothing left for our lord except our bodies and our land. 19 Why
should we perish before your eyes—we and our land as well?
Buy us and our land in exchange for food, and we with our land
will be in bondage to Pharaoh. Give us seed so that we may live
and not die, and that the land may not become desolate."
20 So Joseph bought all the land in Egypt for Pharaoh. The
Egyptians, one and all, sold their fields, because the famine was

a 7 Or *greeted* b 10 Or *said farewell to*

47:4 [a] Ge 15:13; Dt 26:5 [b] Ge 43:1 [c] Ge 46:34
47:6 [d] Ge 45:18 [e] Ex 18:21,25
47:7 [f] ver 10; 2Sa 14:22
47:9 [g] Ge 25:7 [h] Heb 11:9,13 [i] Ge 35:28
47:10 [j] ver 7
47:11 [k] Ex 1:11; 12:37
47:12 [l] Ge 45:11
47:13 [m] Ge 41:30; Ac 7:11
47:14 [n] Ge 41:56
47:15 [o] ver 19; Ex 16:3
47:17 [p] Ex 14:9

too severe for them. The land became Pharaoh's, 21 and Joseph
reduced the people to servitude,[a] from one end of Egypt to the
other. 22 However, he did not buy the land of the priests, because
they received a regular allotment from Pharaoh and had food
enough from the allotment[a] Pharaoh gave them. That is why they
did not sell their land.

23 Joseph said to the people, "Now that I have bought you and
your land today for Pharaoh, here is seed for you so you can
plant the ground. 24 But when the crop comes in, give a fifth[b] of
it to Pharaoh. The other four-fifths you may keep as seed for the
fields and as food for yourselves and your households and your
children."

25 "You have saved our lives," they said. "May we find favor in
the eyes of our lord;[c] we will be in bondage to Pharaoh."

26 So Joseph established it as a law concerning land in Egypt—
still in force today—that a fifth of the produce belongs to Pharaoh. It was only the land of the priests that did not become
Pharaoh's.[d]

27 Now the Israelites settled in Egypt in the region of Goshen.
They acquired property there and were fruitful and increased
greatly in number.[e]

28 Jacob lived in Egypt[f] seventeen years, and the years of his life
were a hundred and forty-seven. 29 When the time drew near for
Israel to die,[g] he called for his son Joseph and said to him, "If I
have found favor in your eyes, put your hand under my thigh[h]
and promise that you will show me kindness and faithfulness.[i]
Do not bury me in Egypt, 30 but when I rest with my fathers, carry me out of Egypt and bury me where they are buried."[j]

"I will do as you say," he said.

31 "Swear to me,"[k] he said. Then Joseph swore to him,[l] and
Israel worshiped as he leaned on the top of his staff.[b][m]

Chapter 48 Theme ____________________

48 Some time later Joseph was told, "Your father is ill." So
he took his two sons Manasseh and Ephraim[n] along with
him. 2 When Jacob was told, "Your son Joseph has come to you,"
Israel rallied his strength and sat up on the bed.

3 Jacob said to Joseph, "God Almighty[c] appeared to me at Luz[o]
in the land of Canaan, and there he blessed me[p] 4 and said to me,
'I am going to make you fruitful and will increase your numbers.[q]
I will make you a community of peoples, and I will give this
land as an everlasting possession to your descendants after you.'

[a] *21* Samaritan Pentateuch and Septuagint (see also Vulgate); Masoretic Text *and he moved the people into the cities* [b] *31* Or *Israel bowed down at the head of his bed* [c] *3* Hebrew *El-Shaddai*

47:22 [a] Dt 14:28-29; Ezr 7:24
47:24 [b] Ge 41:34
47:25 [c] Ge 32:5
47:26 [d] ver 22
47:27 [e] Ge 17:6; 46:3; Ex 1:7
47:28 [f] Ps 105:23
47:29 [g] Dt 31:14 [h] Ge 24:2 [i] Ge 24:49
47:30 [j] Ge 49:29-32; 50:5,13; Ac 7:15-16
47:31 [k] Ge 21:23 [l] Ge 24:3 [m] Heb 11:21 *fn;* 1Ki 1:47
48:1 [n] Ge 41:52
48:3 [o] Ge 28:19 [p] Ge 28:13; 35:9-12
48:4 [q] Ge 17:6

5"Now then, your two sons born to you in Egypt[a] before I came
to you here will be reckoned as mine; Ephraim and Manasseh will
be mine,[b] just as Reuben and Simeon are mine. 6Any children
born to you after them will be yours; in the territory they inherit
they will be reckoned under the names of their brothers. 7As I
was returning from Paddan,[a] to my sorrow Rachel died in the
land of Canaan while we were still on the way, a little distance
from Ephrath. So I buried her there beside the road to Ephrath"
(that is, Bethlehem).[c]

8When Israel saw the sons of Joseph, he asked, "Who are these?"

9"They are the sons God has given me here,"[d] Joseph said to
his father.

Then Israel said, "Bring them to me so I may bless[e] them."

10Now Israel's eyes were failing because of old age, and he
could hardly see.[f] So Joseph brought his sons close to him, and
his father kissed them[g] and embraced them.

11Israel said to Joseph, "I never expected to see your face
again, and now God has allowed me to see your children too."[h]

12Then Joseph removed them from Israel's knees and bowed
down with his face to the ground. 13And Joseph took both of
them, Ephraim on his right toward Israel's left hand and Manasseh on his left toward Israel's right hand,[i] and brought them
close to him. 14But Israel reached out his right hand and put it
on Ephraim's head, though he was the younger, and crossing
his arms, he put his left hand on Manasseh's head, even though
Manasseh was the firstborn.[j]

15Then he blessed[k] Joseph and said,

"May the God before whom my fathers
Abraham and Isaac walked,
the God who has been my shepherd[l]
all my life to this day,
16the Angel who has delivered me from all harm
—may he bless these boys.[m]
May they be called by my name
and the names of my fathers Abraham and Isaac,[n]
and may they increase greatly
upon the earth."

17When Joseph saw his father placing his right hand on Ephraim's head[o] he was displeased; so he took hold of his father's hand
to move it from Ephraim's head to Manasseh's head. 18Joseph
said to him, "No, my father, this one is the firstborn; put your
right hand on his head."

[a] 7 That is, Northwest Mesopotamia

48:5 [a] Ge 41:50-52; 46:20 [b] 1Ch 5:1; Jos 14:4
48:7 [c] Ge 35:19
48:9 [d] Ge 33:5 [e] Ge 27:4
48:10 [f] Ge 27:1 [g] Ge 27:27
48:11 [h] Ge 50:23; Ps 128:6
48:13 [i] Ps 110:1
48:14 [j] Ge 41:51
48:15 [k] Ge 17:1 [l] Ge 49:24
48:16 [m] Heb 11:21 [n] Ge 28:13
48:17 [o] ver 14

19 But his father refused and said, "I know, my son, I know. He
too will become a people, and he too will become great.[a] Nevertheless, his younger brother will be greater than he,[b] and his
descendants will become a group of nations." 20 He blessed
them that day and said,

"In your[a] name will Israel pronounce this blessing:
'May God make you like Ephraim[c] and Manasseh.[d]'"

So he put Ephraim ahead of Manasseh.
21 Then Israel said to Joseph, "I am about to die, but God will
be with you[b][e] and take you[b] back to the land of your[b] fathers.[f]
22 And to you, as one who is over your brothers,[g] I give the ridge
of land[c][h] I took from the Amorites with my sword and my bow."

Chapter 49 Theme

49 Then Jacob called for his sons and said: "Gather around
so I can tell you what will happen to you in days to come.[i]

2 "Assemble and listen, sons of Jacob;
listen to your father Israel.[j]

3 "Reuben, you are my firstborn,[k]
my might, the first sign of my strength,[l]
excelling in honor, excelling in power.
4 Turbulent as the waters,[m] you will no longer excel,
for you went up onto your father's bed,
onto my couch and defiled it.[n]

5 "Simeon and Levi are brothers—
their swords[d] are weapons of violence.[o]
6 Let me not enter their council,
let me not join their assembly,[p]
for they have killed men in their anger[q]
and hamstrung oxen as they pleased.
7 Cursed be their anger, so fierce,
and their fury, so cruel!
I will scatter them in Jacob
and disperse them in Israel.[r]

8 "Judah,[e] your brothers will praise you;
your hand will be on the neck of your enemies;
your father's sons will bow down to you.[s]
9 You are a lion[t]'s cub, O Judah;[u]
you return from the prey, my son.

48:19 [a] Ge 17:20 [b] Ge 25:23
48:20 [c] Nu 2:18 [d] Nu 2:20; Ru 4:11
48:21 [e] Ge 26:3; 46:4 [f] Ge 28:13; 50:24
48:22 [g] Ge 37:8 [h] Jos 24:32; Jn 4:5
49:1 [i] Nu 24:14; Jer 23:20
49:2 [j] Ps 34:11
49:3 [k] Ge 29:32 [l] Dt 21:17; Ps 78:51
49:4 [m] Isa 57:20 [n] Ge 35:22; Dt 27:20
49:5 [o] Ge 34:25; Pr 4:17
49:6 [p] Pr 1:15; Eph 5:11 [q] Ge 34:26
49:7 [r] Jos 19:1,9; 21:1-42
49:8 [s] Dt 33:7; 1Ch 5:2
49:9 [t] Nu 24:9; Eze 19:5; Mic 5:8 [u] Rev 5:5

[a] *20* The Hebrew is singular. [b] *21* The Hebrew is plural. [c] *22* Or *And to you I give one portion more than to your brothers—the portion* [d] *5* The meaning of the Hebrew for this word is uncertain. [e] *8* *Judah* sounds like and may be derived from the Hebrew for *praise.*

Like a lion he crouches and lies down,
like a lioness—who dares to rouse him?
10 The scepter will not depart from Judah,[a]
nor the ruler's staff from between his feet,
until he comes to whom it belongs[a]
and the obedience of the nations is his.[b]
11 He will tether his donkey to a vine,
his colt to the choicest branch;
he will wash his garments in wine,
his robes in the blood of grapes.
12 His eyes will be darker than wine,
his teeth whiter than milk.[b]

13 "Zebulun[c] will live by the seashore
and become a haven for ships;
his border will extend toward Sidon.

14 "Issachar[d] is a rawboned[c] donkey
lying down between two saddlebags.[d]
15 When he sees how good is his resting place
and how pleasant is his land,
he will bend his shoulder to the burden
and submit to forced labor.

16 "Dan[e][e] will provide justice for his people
as one of the tribes of Israel.
17 Dan[f] will be a serpent by the roadside,
a viper along the path,
that bites the horse's heels
so that its rider tumbles backward.

18 "I look for your deliverance, O LORD.[g]

19 "Gad[f][h] will be attacked by a band of raiders,
but he will attack them at their heels.

20 "Asher's[i] food will be rich;
he will provide delicacies fit for a king.

21 "Naphtali[j] is a doe set free
that bears beautiful fawns.[g]

22 "Joseph[k] is a fruitful vine,
a fruitful vine near a spring,
whose branches climb over a wall.[h]

[a] *10* Or *until Shiloh comes;* or *until he comes to whom tribute belongs* [b] *12* Or *will be dull from wine, / his teeth white from milk* [c] *14* Or *strong* [d] *14* Or *campfires* [e] *16* *Dan* here means *he provides justice.* [f] *19* *Gad* can mean *attack* and *band of raiders.* [g] *21* Or *free; / he utters beautiful words* [h] *22* Or *Joseph is a wild colt, / a wild colt near a spring, / a wild donkey on a terraced hill*

49:10 [a] Nu 24:17,19; Ps 60:7 [b] Ps 2:9; Isa 42:1,4
49:13 [c] Ge 30:20; Dt 33:18-19; Jos 19:10-11
49:14 [d] Ge 30:18
49:16 [e] Ge 30:6; Dt 33:22; Jdg 18:26-27
49:17 [f] Jdg 18:27
49:18 [g] Ps 119:166,174
49:19 [h] Ge 30:11; Dt 33:20; 1Ch 5:18
49:20 [i] Ge 30:13; Dt 33:24
49:21 [j] Ge 30:8; Dt 33:23
49:22 [k] Ge 30:24; Dt 33:13-17

49:23 [a]Ge 37:24
49:24 [b]Ps 18:34 [c]Ps 132:2,5; Isa 1:24; 41:10 [d]Isa 28:16
49:25 [e]Ge 28:13 [f]Ge 27:28
49:26 [g]Dt 33:15-16
49:27 [h]Ge 35:18; Jdg 20:12-13
49:29 [i]Ge 50:16 [j]Ge 25:8 [k]Ge 15:15; 47:30; 50:13
49:30 [l]Ge 23:9 [m]Ge 23:20
49:31 [n]Ge 25:9 [o]Ge 23:19 [p]Ge 35:29
49:33 [q]ver 29; Ge 25:8; Ac 7:15
50:1 [r]Ge 46:4
50:2 [s]ver 26; 2Ch 16:14
50:3 [t]Ge 37:34; Nu 20:29; Dt 34:8

23 With bitterness archers attacked him;
they shot at him with hostility.[a]
24 But his bow remained steady,
his strong arms[b] stayed[a] limber,
because of the hand of the Mighty One of Jacob,[c]
because of the Shepherd, the Rock of Israel,[d]
25 because of your father's God,[e] who helps you,
because of the Almighty,[b] who blesses you
with blessings of the heavens above,
blessings of the deep that lies below,[f]
blessings of the breast and womb.
26 Your father's blessings are greater
than the blessings of the ancient mountains,
than[c] the bounty of the age-old hills.
Let all these rest on the head of Joseph,
on the brow of the prince among[d] his brothers.[g]
27 "Benjamin[h] is a ravenous wolf;
in the morning he devours the prey,
in the evening he divides the plunder."

28 All these are the twelve tribes of Israel, and this is what their
father said to them when he blessed them, giving each the blessing appropriate to him.
29 Then he gave them these instructions:[i] "I am about to be
gathered to my people.[j] Bury me with my fathers[k] in the cave in
the field of Ephron the Hittite, 30 the cave in the field of Machpelah,[l] near Mamre in Canaan, which Abraham bought as a
burial place from Ephron the Hittite, along with the field.[m]
31 There Abraham[n] and his wife Sarah[o] were buried, there Isaac
and his wife Rebekah[p] were buried, and there I buried Leah.
32 The field and the cave in it were bought from the Hittites.[e]"
33 When Jacob had finished giving instructions to his sons, he
drew his feet up into the bed, breathed his last and was gathered
to his people.[q]

Chapter 50 Theme ______________________________

50 Joseph threw himself upon his father and wept over him
and kissed him.[r] 2 Then Joseph directed the physicians
in his service to embalm his father Israel. So the physicians
embalmed him,[s] 3 taking a full forty days, for that was the time
required for embalming. And the Egyptians mourned for him
seventy days.[t]

[a] *23,24 Or archers will attack . . . will shoot . . . will remain . . . will stay* [b] 25 Hebrew *Shaddai* [c] 26 Or *of my progenitors, / as great as* [d] 26 Or *the one separated from* [e] 32 Or *the sons of Heth*

4When the days of mourning had passed, Joseph said to
Pharaoh's court, "If I have found favor in your eyes, speak to
Pharaoh for me. Tell him, 5'My father made me swear an oath[a]
and said, "I am about to die; bury me in the tomb I dug for myself[b]
in the land of Canaan."[c] Now let me go up and bury my father;
then I will return.'"

6Pharaoh said, "Go up and bury your father, as he made you
swear to do."

7So Joseph went up to bury his father. All Pharaoh's officials
accompanied him—the dignitaries of his court and all the dignitaries of Egypt— 8besides all the members of Joseph's household
and his brothers and those belonging to his father's household.
Only their children and their flocks and herds were left in Goshen.
9Chariots and horsemen[a] also went up with him. It was a very
large company.

10When they reached the threshing floor of Atad, near the Jordan, they lamented loudly and bitterly;[d] and there Joseph
observed a seven-day period[e] of mourning for his father. 11When
the Canaanites who lived there saw the mourning at the threshing floor of Atad, they said, "The Egyptians are holding a solemn
ceremony of mourning." That is why that place near the Jordan
is called Abel Mizraim.[b]

12So Jacob's sons did as he had commanded them: 13They carried him to the land of Canaan and buried him in the cave in the
field of Machpelah, near Mamre, which Abraham had bought
as a burial place from Ephron the Hittite, along with the field.[f]
14After burying his father, Joseph returned to Egypt, together
with his brothers and all the others who had gone with him to
bury his father.

15When Joseph's brothers saw that their father was dead, they
said, "What if Joseph holds a grudge against us and pays us back
for all the wrongs we did to him?"[g] 16So they sent word to Joseph,
saying, "Your father left these instructions before he died: 17'This
is what you are to say to Joseph: I ask you to forgive your brothers the sins and the wrongs they committed in treating you so
badly.' Now please forgive the sins of the servants of the God of
your father." When their message came to him, Joseph wept.

18His brothers then came and threw themselves down before
him.[h] "We are your slaves,"[i] they said.

19But Joseph said to them, "Don't be afraid. Am I in the place
of God?[j] 20You intended to harm me,[k] but God intended[l] it for
good[m] to accomplish what is now being done, the saving of many
lives.[n] 21So then, don't be afraid. I will provide for you and your
children.[o]" And he reassured them and spoke kindly to them.

[a]9 Or *charioteers* [b]11 *Abel Mizraim* means *mourning of the Egyptians.*

50:5 [a]Ge 47:31 [b]2Ch 16:14; Isa 22:16 [c]Ge 47:31

50:10 [d]2Sa 1:17; Ac 8:2 [e]1Sa 31:13; Job 2:13

50:13 [f]Ge 23:20; Ac 7:16

50:15 [g]Ge 37:28; 42:21-22

50:18 [h]Ge 37:7 [i]Ge 43:18

50:19 [j]Ro 12:19; Heb 10:30

50:20 [k]Ge 37:20 [l]Mic 4:11-12 [m]Ro 8:28 [n]Ge 45:5

50:21 [o]Ge 45:11; 47:12

22 Joseph stayed in Egypt, along with all his father's family. He
lived a hundred and ten years[a] 23 and saw the third generation[b]
of Ephraim's children. Also the children of Makir[c] son of Manasseh were placed at birth on Joseph's knees.[a]

24 Then Joseph said to his brothers, "I am about to die.[d] But
God will surely come to your aid[e] and take you up out of this
land to the land[f] he promised on oath to Abraham, Isaac and
Jacob."[g] 25 And Joseph made the sons of Israel swear an oath and
said, "God will surely come to your aid, and then you must carry my bones up from this place."[h]

26 So Joseph died at the age of a hundred and ten. And after
they embalmed him,[i] he was placed in a coffin in Egypt.

50:22 [a]Ge 25:7; Jos 24:29
50:23 [b]Job 42:16 [c]Nu 32:39,40
50:24 [d]Ge 48:21 [e]Ex 3:16-17 [f]Ge 15:14 [g]Ge 12:7; 26:3; 28:13; 35:12
50:25 [h]Ge 47:29-30; Ex 13:19; Jos 24:32; Heb 11:22
50:26 [i]ver 2

[a]23 That is, were counted as his

Genesis at a Glance

Theme of Genesis:

Segment Divisions

	The Firsts		4 Main Events/4 Characters	Time Spans	Chapter Themes
	Man	Beginnings of Man		Approximately 2080 Years	1
	Marriage				2
					3
					4
					5
					6
					7
					8
					9
					10
					11
		Beginnings of Israel *(continued next page)*		Approximately 300 Years *(continued next page)*	12
					13
					14
					15
					16
					17
					18
					19
					20
					21
					22
					23
					24
					25

Author:

Moses
(Luke 24:27)

Date:

Purpose:

Key Words:

God said
(or command

the account of

covenant, trea

altar

circumcised,
circumcision,
circumcising

Abram
(or Abraham)

SEGMENT DIVISIONS

THE FIRSTS		4 MAIN EVENTS/4 CHARACTERS	TIME SPANS		CHAPTER THEMES
	BEGINNINGS OF ISRAEL		APPROXIMATELY 300 YEARS	26	
				27	
				28	
				29	
				30	
				31	
				32	
				33	
				34	
				35	
				36	
				37	
				38	
				39	
				40	
				41	
				42	
				43	
				44	
				45	
				46	
				47	
				48	
				49	
				50	

EXODUS

When Jacob and his family, a relatively small group, went into Egypt, they were welcomed and honored because they were relatives of Joseph. Four hundred and thirty years later the children of Israel were Egypt's slaves, a people so numerous it frightened the Egyptians.

The Israelites were God's covenant people, different from all the nations, a people of his own choosing. And because God is a covenant-keeping God he could not leave Jacob's people in Egypt—they had to be redeemed by the blood of a lamb, a Passover lamb.

THINGS TO DO

General Instructions

1. As Genesis comes to a close, the children of Israel are living in Egypt rather than in Canaan, the land of promise. The book that began with the creation of man in Eden ends with the children of Israel looking into a coffin in Egypt—but not without a promise that someday they would leave Egypt. Read Genesis 50:22-26 and Exodus 1:1-7 and notice how the book of Exodus relates chronologically to the book of Genesis.

2. Exodus can be divided into three segments according to the location of the children of Israel. In Exodus 1 through 12 they are in Egypt. In Exodus 13 through 18 they journey to Sinai and then in Exodus 19 through 40 they camp at Sinai. Record this information on the EXODUS AT A GLANCE chart on pages 159, 160 on the first line for segment divisions. This division will be the basis of some of your instructions.

3. Read through Exodus one chapter at a time. As you read do the following:

   a. Remember that you are reading a historical account. As you read, ask the five W's and an H: Who? What? When? Where? Why? and How? Ask questions such as: Who are the main characters in this chapter? What is happening? When and where is it happening? What were the consequences of their actions? How and why did this occur?

   b. Mark key repeated words. Although a list of the key words for Exodus is recorded on EXODUS AT A GLANCE, remember that there will be other words which are predominant in specific chapters. Don't miss these. You will find it helpful to write the key words on an index card and use it as a bookmark while you study Exodus.

   c. If you glean insights from the repeated use of a key word, list them in the margin of the chapter.

   d. Mark all references to time in a distinctive way so you can immediately notice them.

   e. List in the margin the main points or events covered in a particular chapter or group of chapters. This will give you a concise analysis of the content of the chapter.

   For example, Exodus 2 gives an account of Moses from his birth to the birth of his first son. In the margin you could list the major events in this chapter: Moses' birth, Moses' adoption by Pharaoh's daughter, Moses kills Egyptian, Moses flees to Midian, etc.

4. When you finish reading a chapter, record the main theme or subject of the chapter on EXODUS AT A GLANCE under "Chapter Themes." Also record it in the text next to the chapter number.

Chapters 1-12

1. As you study these chapters, add *Pharaoh* and *staff* to your list of key words. Mark these words and their synonyms in a distinctive way. Then in the margin list everything you observe from marking them.

2. You can gain insights into God's character, power, and dealings with mankind from these chapters. As

you read each chapter, in the margin note what you learn about God. You may want to put a distinguishing mark such as this △ in the margin and then color it yellow so you can easily recognize it. Then list your insights under the symbol for God.

3. There are lessons to be learned from Moses' life in these chapters. Although you will probably want to note these lessons in the margins, you will also find it profitable to record what you learn on LESSONS FROM THE LIFE OF MOSES, a chart on pages 346, 347. When you record an insight, make sure you note the book, chapter, and verse from which it came.

4. As you read chapters 7 through 12, in the margin of the chapter list the plagues as they appear in the text, numbering each one in the order in which they appear.

5. When you come to Exodus 12, in the margin list everything you learn about the Passover. Ask the five W's and an H: Who? What? When? Where? Why? and How?

Chapters 13-18

1. As you read:
   a. Watch for the key words, including those you marked in the first segment. Add *test* and *grumble (grumbled, grumbling)*, along with their synonyms. In the margin note what the tests were and why the people grumbled. Also continue your list of insights on Pharaoh and on Moses' staff.
   b. Mark references to time with a symbol and note where events occur. Locate these places on the map in the text on page 97.

2. Add to your list of insights on Moses and also note in the margin new insights on God. Note what he is called in 15:26 and 17:15 and the circumstances in which these names are revealed.

3. In chapter 16 note in the margin all you learn from the text about manna and why it was given. When you finish you might compare this with Deuteronomy 8:1-3.

4. In chapter 17 note the conditions under which Moses strikes the rock. Compare this with 1 Corinthians 10:1-4 and John 7:37-39. Also note what happens after the rock is smitten and the battle is fought in the valley.

Chapters 19-40

1. In chapters 19 through 24 God gives Moses the law. As you read these important chapters, ask the five W's and an H.
   a. Chapter 20 presents the ten commandments. Number these within the text or list them in the margin.
   b. Chapter 24 is very important because it deals with the inauguration of the law, the old covenant. In the margin note the circumstances and procedure connected with its inauguration and how the people respond.

2. In chapters 25 through 31 God gives the pattern for the tabernacle and all that is necessary for the priests.
   a. Note in the margin the main points of these chapters.
   b. Watch for other key words which are predominant in specific chapters. Mark them.
   c. In chapter 31 notice what is said about the Sabbath. List in the margin everything you learn about it from the text.

3. Chapters 32 through 34 are significant in light of what happens.
   a. Note how Moses deals with this situation. Record your insights in the margin and on the chart LESSONS FROM THE LIFE OF MOSES on pages 346, 347.
   b. Read 2 Corinthians 3:12-18 for additional insights regarding the veil over Moses' face.

4. Chapters 35 through 40 are an account of the construction of the tabernacle and the making of the priests' garments. As you read, highlight or mark in a distinguishable way the specific instructions which are given in regard to each piece of furniture.

5. After you have recorded all the chapter themes on EXODUS AT A GLANCE, see if any of the chapters can be grouped according to main events. Record these segment divisions on the appropriate line next to the chapter themes. Then record the theme of Exodus on the chart.

Things to Think About

1. What have you learned about God, his character, and his ways? What have you seen of his power and sovereignty? When we speak of God as being sovereign, we mean he rules over all. How do you see God's sovereignty and power manifested in Exodus? Meditate on what you have learned and then make it a matter of prayer and application.

2. Since the Bible is a progressive revelation of truth, keep in mind what you have observed about redemption and the Passover. These are Old Testament pictures of the salvation to be offered through the Lord Jesus Christ; therefore, they are pictures of truths to be applied to your life (1 Corinthians 5:6-8). Are you a slave to sin? Jesus Christ has provided for your redemption from sin through his blood. Have you been redeemed?

3. What have you learned from Moses' life? How did he deal with difficult situations and people? What was his overriding passion? What did you learn about Moses' relationship with God that you can apply to your own life today?

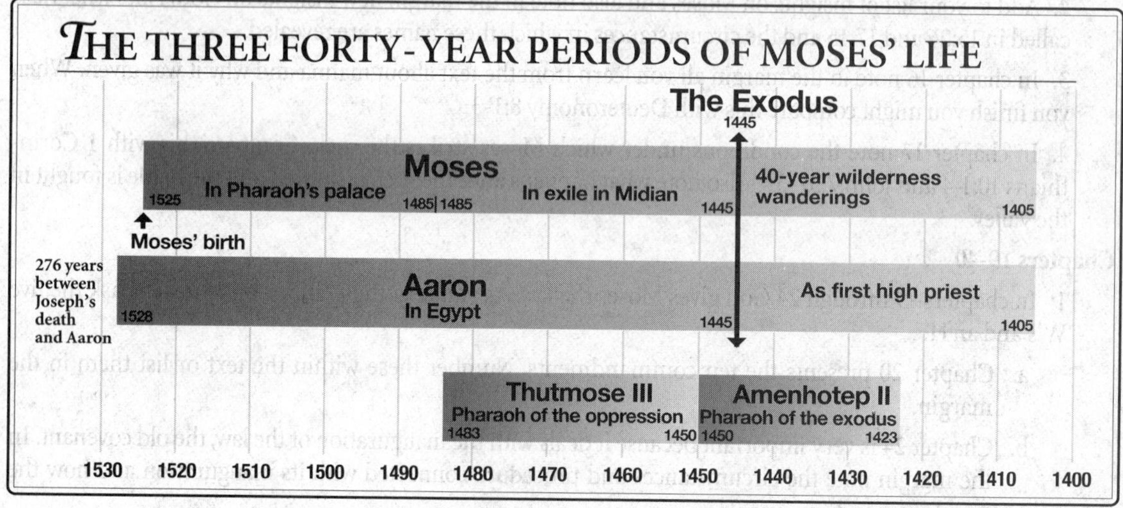

Chapter 1 Theme ______________________

1 These are the names of the sons of Israel[a] who went to Egypt
with Jacob, each with his family: 2Reuben, Simeon, Levi and
Judah; 3Issachar, Zebulun and Benjamin; 4Dan and Naphtali;
Gad and Asher. 5The descendants of Jacob numbered seventy[a]
in all;[b] Joseph was already in Egypt.

1:1 *a* Ge 46:8

1:5 *b* Ge 46:26

a5 Masoretic Text (see also Gen. 46:27); Dead Sea Scrolls and Septuagint (see also Acts 7:14 and note at Gen. 46:27) *seventy-five*

6 Now Joseph and all his brothers and all that generation died,[a]
7 but the Israelites were fruitful and multiplied greatly and became
exceedingly numerous,[b] so that the land was filled with them.
8 Then a new king, who did not know about Joseph, came to
power in Egypt. 9 "Look," he said to his people, "the Israelites
have become much too numerous[c] for us. 10 Come, we must deal
shrewdly[d] with them or they will become even more numerous
and, if war breaks out, will join our enemies, fight against us and
leave the country."[e]
11 So they put slave masters[f] over them to oppress them with
forced labor,[g] and they built Pithom and Rameses[h] as store cities[i]
for Pharaoh. 12 But the more they were oppressed, the more they
multiplied and spread; so the Egyptians came to dread the
Israelites 13 and worked them ruthlessly.[j] 14 They made their lives
bitter with hard labor in brick and mortar and with all kinds of
work in the fields; in all their hard labor the Egyptians used
them ruthlessly.[k]
15 The king of Egypt said to the Hebrew midwives, whose names
were Shiphrah and Puah, 16 "When you help the Hebrew women
in childbirth and observe them on the delivery stool, if it is a boy,
kill him; but if it is a girl, let her live." 17 The midwives, however,
feared[l] God and did not do what the king of Egypt had told them
to do;[m] they let the boys live. 18 Then the king of Egypt summoned
the midwives and asked them, "Why have you done this? Why
have you let the boys live?"
19 The midwives answered Pharaoh, "Hebrew women are not
like Egyptian women; they are vigorous and give birth before
the midwives arrive."[n]
20 So God was kind to the midwives[o] and the people increased
and became even more numerous. 21 And because the midwives
feared God, he gave them families[p] of their own.
22 Then Pharaoh gave this order to all his people: "Every boy that
is born[a] you must throw into the Nile, but let every girl live."[q]

Chapter 2 Theme ______________________

2 Now a man of the house of Levi married a Levite woman,[r]
2 and she became pregnant and gave birth to a son. When
she saw that he was a fine child, she hid him for three months.[s]
3 But when she could hide him no longer, she got a papyrus basket for him and coated it with tar and pitch. Then she placed the
child in it and put it among the reeds along the bank of the Nile.
4 His sister[t] stood at a distance to see what would happen to him.

a22 Masoretic Text; Samaritan Pentateuch, Septuagint and Targums *born to the Hebrews*

1:6 a Ge 50:26
1:7 b Ge 46:3; Dt 26:5; Ac 7:17
1:9 c Ps 105:24-25
1:10 d Ps 83:3 e Ac 7:17-19
1:11 f Ex 3:7 g Ge 15:13; Ex 2:11; 5:4; 6:6-7 h Ge 47:11 i 1Ki 9:19; 2Ch 8:4
1:13 j Dt 4:20
1:14 k Ex 2:23; 6:9; Nu 20:15; Ps 81:6; Ac 7:19
1:17 l ver 21; Pr 16:6 m Da 3:16-18; Ac 4:18-20; 5:29
1:19 n Jos 2:4-6; 2Sa 17:20
1:20 o ver 12; Pr 11:18; Isa 3:10
1:21 p 1Sa 2:35; 2Sa 7:11,27-29; 1Ki 11:38
1:22 q Ac 7:19
2:1 r Ex 6:20; Nu 26:59
2:2 s Ac 7:20; Heb 11:23
2:4 t Ex 15:20; Nu 26:59

5 Then Pharaoh's daughter went down to the Nile to bathe, and
her attendants were walking along the river bank.[a] She saw the
basket among the reeds and sent her slave girl to get it. 6 She
opened it and saw the baby. He was crying, and she felt sorry for
him. "This is one of the Hebrew babies," she said.
7 Then his sister asked Pharaoh's daughter, "Shall I go and get
one of the Hebrew women to nurse the baby for you?"
8 "Yes, go," she answered. And the girl went and got the baby's
mother. 9 Pharaoh's daughter said to her, "Take this baby and
nurse him for me, and I will pay you." So the woman took the
baby and nursed him. 10 When the child grew older, she took
him to Pharaoh's daughter and he became her son. She named
him Moses,[a] saying, "I drew him out of the water."
11 One day, after Moses had grown up, he went out to where his
own people[b] were and watched them at their hard labor. He saw
an Egyptian beating a Hebrew, one of his own people. 12 Glancing
this way and that and seeing no one, he killed the Egyptian and
hid him in the sand. 13 The next day he went out and saw two
Hebrews fighting. He asked the one in the wrong, "Why are you
hitting your fellow Hebrew?"[c]
14 The man said, "Who made you ruler and judge over us?[d] Are
you thinking of killing me as you killed the Egyptian?" Then
Moses was afraid and thought, "What I did must have become
known."
15 When Pharaoh heard of this, he tried to kill Moses, but
Moses fled from Pharaoh and went to live in Midian,[e] where he
sat down by a well. 16 Now a priest of Midian[f] had seven daughters, and they came to draw water[g] and fill the troughs to water
their father's flock. 17 Some shepherds came along and drove
them away, but Moses got up and came to their rescue and
watered their flock.[h]
18 When the girls returned to Reuel[i] their father, he asked them,
"Why have you returned so early today?"
19 They answered, "An Egyptian rescued us from the shepherds.
He even drew water for us and watered the flock."
20 "And where is he?" he asked his daughters. "Why did you
leave him? Invite him to have something to eat."[j]
21 Moses agreed to stay with the man, who gave his daughter
Zipporah[k] to Moses in marriage. 22 Zipporah gave birth to a son,
and Moses named him Gershom,[b] saying, "I have become an
alien[l] in a foreign land."
23 During that long period,[m] the king of Egypt died. The Israelites groaned in their slavery and cried out, and their cry[n] for

[a]10 *Moses* sounds like the Hebrew for *draw out.* [b]22 *Gershom* sounds like the Hebrew for *an alien there.*

2:5 [a] Ex 7:15; 8:20
2:11 [b] Ac 7:23; Heb 11:24-26
2:13 [c] Ac 7:26
2:14 [d] Ac 7:27*
2:15 [e] Ac 7:29; Heb 11:27
2:16 [f] Ex 3:1 [g] Ge 24:11
2:17 [h] Ge 29:10
2:18 [i] Nu 10:29
2:20 [j] Ge 31:54
2:21 [k] Ex 18:2
2:22 [l] Ex 18:3-4; Heb 11:13
2:23 [m] Ac 7:30 [n] Ex 3:7,9; Dt 26:7; Jas 5:4

2:24 [a] Ex 6:5; Ps 105:10,42

help because of their slavery went up to God. 24God heard their
groaning and he remembered his covenant[a] with Abraham, with
Isaac and with Jacob. 25So God looked on the Israelites and was
concerned[b] about them.

2:25 [b] Ex 3:7; 4:31

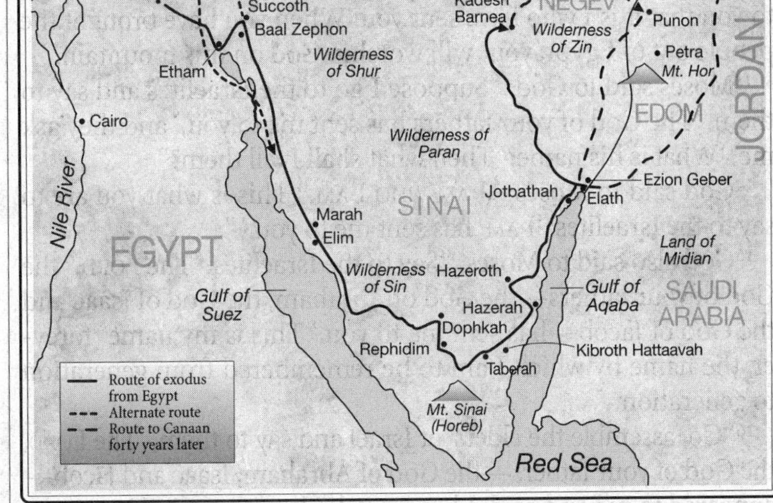

The Exodus from Egypt to Canaan

3:1 [c] Ex 2:18 [d] 1Ki 19:8 [e] Ex 18:5

3:2 [f] Ge 16:7 [g] Dt 33:16; Mk 12:26; Ac 7:30

Chapter 3 Theme ______________________

3 Now Moses was tending the flock of Jethro[c] his father-in-law,
the priest of Midian, and he led the flock to the far side of
the desert and came to Horeb,[d] the mountain[e] of God. 2There
the angel of the LORD[f] appeared to him in flames of fire from
within a bush.[g] Moses saw that though the bush was on fire it did
not burn up. 3So Moses thought, "I will go over and see this
strange sight—why the bush does not burn up."
4When the LORD saw that he had gone over to look, God called
to him from within the bush, "Moses! Moses!"
And Moses said, "Here I am."
5"Do not come any closer," God said. "Take off your sandals, for
the place where you are standing is holy ground."[h] 6Then he said,

3:5 [h] Ge 28:17; Jos 5:15; Ac 7:33*

"I am the God of your father, the God of Abraham, the God of Isaac and the God of Jacob."[a] At this, Moses hid his face, because he was afraid to look at God.

7 The LORD said, "I have indeed seen the misery of my people in Egypt. I have heard them crying out because of their slave drivers, and I am concerned[b] about their suffering. 8 So I have come down[c] to rescue them from the hand of the Egyptians and to bring them up out of that land into a good and spacious land, a land flowing with milk and honey[d]—the home of the Canaanites, Hittites, Amorites, Perizzites, Hivites and Jebusites.[e] 9 And now the cry of the Israelites has reached me, and I have seen the way the Egyptians are oppressing[f] them. 10 So now, go. I am sending you to Pharaoh to bring my people the Israelites out of Egypt."[g]

11 But Moses said to God, "Who am I,[h] that I should go to Pharaoh and bring the Israelites out of Egypt?"

12 And God said, "I will be with you.[i] And this will be the sign to you that it is I who have sent you: When you have brought the people out of Egypt, you[a] will worship God on this mountain."

13 Moses said to God, "Suppose I go to the Israelites and say to them, 'The God of your fathers has sent me to you,' and they ask me, 'What is his name?' Then what shall I tell them?"

14 God said to Moses, "I AM WHO I AM.[b] This is what you are to say to the Israelites: 'I AM[j] has sent me to you.'"

15 God also said to Moses, "Say to the Israelites, 'The LORD,[c] the God of your fathers—the God of Abraham, the God of Isaac and the God of Jacob—has sent me to you.' This is my name[k] forever, the name by which I am to be remembered from generation to generation.

16 "Go, assemble the elders[l] of Israel and say to them, 'The LORD, the God of your fathers—the God of Abraham, Isaac and Jacob—appeared to me and said: I have watched over you and have seen what has been done to you in Egypt. 17 And I have promised to bring you up out of your misery in Egypt[m] into the land of the Canaanites, Hittites, Amorites, Perizzites, Hivites and Jebusites—a land flowing with milk and honey.'

18 "The elders of Israel will listen[n] to you. Then you and the elders are to go to the king of Egypt and say to him, 'The LORD, the God of the Hebrews, has met with us. Let us take a three-day journey into the desert to offer sacrifices[o] to the LORD our God.' 19 But I know that the king of Egypt will not let you go unless a mighty hand[p] compels him. 20 So I will stretch out my hand[q] and strike the Egyptians with all the wonders[r] that I will perform among them. After that, he will let you go.[s]

a *12* The Hebrew is plural. b *14* Or *I WILL BE WHAT I WILL BE* c *15* The Hebrew for *LORD* sounds like and may be derived from the Hebrew for *I AM* in verse 14.

3:6 *a* Ex 4:5; Mt 22:32*; Mk 12:26*; Lk 20:37*; Ac 7:32*

3:7 *b* Ex 2:25

3:8 *c* Ge 50:24 *d* ver 17; Ex 13:5; Dt 1:25 *e* Ge 15:18-21

3:9 *f* Ex 1:14; 2:23

3:10 *g* Mic 6:4

3:11 *h* Ex 6:12,30; 1Sa 18:18

3:12 *i* Ge 31:3; Jos 1:5; Ro 8:31

3:14 *j* Ex 6:2-3; Jn 8:58; Heb 13:8

3:15 *k* Ps 135:13; Hos 12:5

3:16 *l* Ex 4:29

3:17 *m* Ge 15:16; Jos 24:11

3:18 *n* Ex 4:1,8,31 *o* Ex 5:1,3

3:19 *p* Ex 4:21; 5:2

3:20 *q* Ex 6:1,6; 9:15 *r* Dt 6:22; Ne 9:10; Ac 7:36 *s* Ex 12:31-33

21"And I will make the Egyptians favorably disposed[a] toward
this people, so that when you leave you will not go empty-handed.[b]
22Every woman is to ask her neighbor and any woman living in
her house for articles of silver and gold[c] and for clothing, which
you will put on your sons and daughters. And so you will
plunder[d] the Egyptians."

Chapter 4 Theme ______________________

4 Moses answered, "What if they do not believe me or listen[e]
to me and say, 'The LORD did not appear to you'?"
2Then the LORD said to him, "What is that in your hand?"
"A staff,"[f] he replied.
3The LORD said, "Throw it on the ground."
Moses threw it on the ground and it became a snake, and he ran
from it. 4Then the LORD said to him, "Reach out your hand and
take it by the tail." So Moses reached out and took hold of the
snake and it turned back into a staff in his hand. 5"This," said the
LORD, "is so that they may believe[g] that the LORD, the God of their
fathers—the God of Abraham, the God of Isaac and the God of
Jacob—has appeared to you."
6Then the LORD said, "Put your hand inside your cloak." So
Moses put his hand into his cloak, and when he took it out, it
was leprous,[a] like snow.[h]
7"Now put it back into your cloak," he said. So Moses put his
hand back into his cloak, and when he took it out, it was
restored,[i] like the rest of his flesh.
8Then the LORD said, "If they do not believe you or pay attention
to the first miraculous sign, they may believe the second. 9But if
they do not believe these two signs or listen to you, take some
water from the Nile and pour it on the dry ground. The water you
take from the river will become blood[j] on the ground."
10Moses said to the LORD, "O Lord, I have never been eloquent,
neither in the past nor since you have spoken to your servant. I
am slow of speech and tongue."[k]
11The LORD said to him, "Who gave man his mouth? Who
makes him deaf or mute? Who gives him sight or makes him
blind?[l] Is it not I, the LORD? 12Now go; I will help you speak and
will teach you what to say."[m]
13But Moses said, "O Lord, please send someone else to do it."
14Then the LORD's anger burned against Moses and he said,
"What about your brother, Aaron the Levite? I know he can
speak well. He is already on his way to meet[n] you, and his heart

3:21 [a] Ex 12:36 [b] Ps 105:37
3:22 [c] Ex 11:2 [d] Eze 39:10
4:1 [e] Ex 3:18; 6:30
4:2 [f] ver 17,20
4:5 [g] Ex 19:9
4:6 [h] Nu 12:10; 2Ki 5:1,27
4:7 [i] Nu 12:13-15; Dt 32:39; 2Ki 5:14; Mt 8:3
4:9 [j] Ex 7:17-21
4:10 [k] Ex 6:12; Jer 1:6
4:11 [l] Ps 94:9; Mt 11:5
4:12 [m] Isa 50:4; Jer 1:9; Mt 10:19-20; Mk 13:11; Lk 12:12; 21:14-15
4:14 [n] ver 27

[a] *6* The Hebrew word was used for various diseases affecting the skin—not necessarily leprosy.

will be glad when he sees you. 15You shall speak to him and put
words in his mouth;[a] I will help both of you speak and will teach
you what to do. 16He will speak to the people for you, and it will
be as if he were your mouth[b] and as if you were God to him.
17But take this staff[c] in your hand so you can perform miraculous
signs[d] with it."

18Then Moses went back to Jethro his father-in-law and said to
him, "Let me go back to my own people in Egypt to see if any of
them are still alive."

Jethro said, "Go, and I wish you well."

19Now the LORD had said to Moses in Midian, "Go back to
Egypt, for all the men who wanted to kill[e] you are dead.[f]" 20So
Moses took his wife and sons, put them on a donkey and started
back to Egypt. And he took the staff[g] of God in his hand.

21The LORD said to Moses, "When you return to Egypt, see that
you perform before Pharaoh all the wonders[h] I have given you
the power to do. But I will harden his heart[i] so that he will not let
the people go. 22Then say to Pharaoh, 'This is what the LORD
says: Israel is my firstborn son,[j] 23and I told you, "Let my son
go,[k] so he may worship me." But you refused to let him go; so I
will kill your firstborn son.'"[l]

24At a lodging place on the way, the LORD met ⌊Moses⌋[a] and was
about to kill[m] him. 25But Zipporah took a flint knife, cut off her
son's foreskin[n] and touched ⌊Moses'⌋ feet with it.[b] "Surely you are
a bridegroom of blood to me," she said. 26So the LORD let him
alone. (At that time she said "bridegroom of blood," referring to
circumcision.)

27The LORD said to Aaron, "Go into the desert to meet Moses."
So he met Moses at the mountain[o] of God and kissed[p] him.
28Then Moses told Aaron everything the LORD had sent him to
say,[q] and also about all the miraculous signs he had commanded
him to perform.

29Moses and Aaron brought together all the elders[r] of the
Israelites, 30and Aaron told them everything the LORD had said to
Moses. He also performed the signs before the people, 31and they
believed.[s] And when they heard that the LORD was concerned[t]
about them and had seen their misery, they bowed down and
worshiped.

Chapter 5 Theme ______________________

5 Afterward Moses and Aaron went to Pharaoh and said,
"This is what the LORD, the God of Israel, says: 'Let my people go, so that they may hold a festival[u] to me in the desert.'"

a24 Or ⌊*Moses' son*⌋; Hebrew *him* b25 Or *and drew near* ⌊*Moses'*⌋ *feet*

4:15 *a* Nu 23:5,12,16
4:16 *b* Ex 7:1-2
4:17 *c* ver 2 *d* Ex 7:9-21
4:19 *e* Ex 2:15 *f* Ex 2:23
4:20 *g* Ex 17:9; Nu 20:8-9,11
4:21 *h* Ex 3:19,20 *i* Ex 7:3,13; 9:12,35; 14:4, 8; Dt 2:30; Isa 63:17; Jn 12:40; Ro 9:18
4:22 *j* Isa 63:16; 64:8; Jer 31:9; Hos 11:1; Ro 9:4
4:23 *k* Ex 5:1; 7:16 *l* Ex 11:5; 12:12,29
4:24 *m* Nu 22:22
4:25 *n* Ge 17:14; Jos 5:2,3
4:27 *o* Ex 3:1 *p* ver 14
4:28 *q* ver 8-9,16
4:29 *r* Ex 3:16
4:31 *s* ver 8; Ex 3:18 *t* Ex 2:25
5:1 *u* Ex 3:18

5:2 a 2Ki 18:35; 2Pharaoh said, "Who is the LORD,[a] that I should obey him and
Job 21:15 let Israel go? I do not know the LORD and I will not let Israel go."[b]
b Ex 3:19 3Then they said, "The God of the Hebrews has met with us.
Now let us take a three-day journey into the desert to offer sacrifices to the LORD our God, or he may strike us with plagues[c] or
with the sword."
4But the king of Egypt said, "Moses and Aaron, why are you
5:3 taking the people away from their labor?[d] Get back to your
c Ex 3:18 work!" 5Then Pharaoh said, "Look, the people of the land are
now numerous,[e] and you are stopping them from working."
6That same day Pharaoh gave this order to the slave drivers and
foremen in charge of the people: 7"You are no longer to supply
the people with straw for making bricks; let them go and gather
5:4 their own straw. 8But require them to make the same number of
d Ex 1:11 bricks as before; don't reduce the quota. They are lazy; that is
why they are crying out, 'Let us go and sacrifice to our God.'
9Make the work harder for the men so that they keep working
and pay no attention to lies."
10Then the slave drivers and the foremen went out and said to
5:5 the people, "This is what Pharaoh says: 'I will not give you any
e Ex 1:7,9 more straw. 11Go and get your own straw wherever you can find
it, but your work will not be reduced at all.'" 12So the people scattered all over Egypt to gather stubble to use for straw. 13The slave
drivers kept pressing them, saying, "Complete the work required
of you for each day, just as when you had straw." 14The Israelite
5:14 foremen appointed by Pharaoh's slave drivers were beaten[f] and
f Isa 10:24 were asked, "Why didn't you meet your quota of bricks yesterday
or today, as before?"
15Then the Israelite foremen went and appealed to Pharaoh:
"Why have you treated your servants this way? 16Your servants
are given no straw, yet we are told, 'Make bricks!' Your servants
5:17 are being beaten, but the fault is with your own people."
g ver 8 17Pharaoh said, "Lazy, that's what you are—lazy![g] That is why
you keep saying, 'Let us go and sacrifice to the LORD.' 18Now get
to work. You will not be given any straw, yet you must produce
your full quota of bricks."
19The Israelite foremen realized they were in trouble when they
5:21 were told, "You are not to reduce the number of bricks required
h Ge 34:30 of you for each day." 20When they left Pharaoh, they found Moses
i Ex 14:11 and Aaron waiting to meet them, 21and they said, "May the LORD
look upon you and judge you! You have made us a stench[h] to
Pharaoh and his officials and have put a sword in their hand to
kill us."[i]
5:22 22Moses returned to the LORD and said, "O Lord, why have you
j Nu 11:11 brought trouble upon this people?[j] Is this why you sent me?

INSIGHT

Pharaoh is a title that was given to the kings of Egypt. An ancient Pharaoh had absolute power; and during his reign, he was considered a god who owned the lands and the people. He was also the high priest of all religions in Egypt. The Pharaoh mentioned in Exodus chapters 5-12 is believed to have been Amenhotep II.

23Ever since I went to Pharaoh to speak in your name, he has brought trouble upon this people, and you have not rescued[a] your people at all."

Chapter 6 Theme ______________________

6 Then the LORD said to Moses, "Now you will see what I will do to Pharaoh: Because of my mighty hand[b] he will let them go;[c] because of my mighty hand he will drive them out of his country."[d]

2God also said to Moses, "I am the LORD. 3I appeared to Abraham, to Isaac and to Jacob as God Almighty,[a][e] but by my name[f] the LORD[b][g] I did not make myself known to them.[c] 4I also established my covenant[h] with them to give them the land of Canaan, where they lived as aliens.[i] 5Moreover, I have heard the groaning[j] of the Israelites, whom the Egyptians are enslaving, and I have remembered my covenant.

6"Therefore, say to the Israelites: 'I am the LORD, and I will bring you out from under the yoke of the Egyptians. I will free you from being slaves to them, and I will redeem[k] you with an outstretched arm[l] and with mighty acts of judgment. 7I will take you as my own people, and I will be your God.[m] Then you will know[n] that I am the LORD your God, who brought you out from under the yoke of the Egyptians. 8And I will bring you to the land[o] I swore with uplifted hand[p] to give to Abraham, to Isaac and to Jacob.[q] I will give it to you as a possession. I am the LORD.'"

9Moses reported this to the Israelites, but they did not listen to him because of their discouragement and cruel bondage.

10Then the LORD said to Moses, 11"Go, tell Pharaoh king of Egypt to let the Israelites go out of his country."

12But Moses said to the LORD, "If the Israelites will not listen to me, why would Pharaoh listen to me, since I speak with faltering lips[d]?"[r]

13Now the LORD spoke to Moses and Aaron about the Israelites and Pharaoh king of Egypt, and he commanded them to bring the Israelites out of Egypt.

14These were the heads of their families[e]:[s]

The sons of Reuben the firstborn son of Israel were Hanoch and Pallu, Hezron and Carmi. These were the clans of Reuben.

a3 Hebrew *El-Shaddai* b3 See note at Exodus 3:15. c3 Or *Almighty, and by my name the LORD did I not let myself be known to them?* d12 Hebrew *I am uncircumcised of lips*; also in verse 30 e14 The Hebrew for *families* here and in verse 25 refers to units larger than clans.

5:23 [a] Jer 4:10

6:1 [b] Ex 3:19 [c] Ex 3:20 [d] Ex 12:31, 33,39

6:3 [e] Ge 17:1 [f] Ps 68:4; 83:18; Isa 52:6 [g] Ex 3:14

6:4 [h] Ge 15:18 [i] Ge 28:4,13

6:5 [j] Ex 2:23

6:6 [k] Dt 7:8; 1Ch 17:21 [l] Dt 26:8

6:7 [m] Dt 4:20; 2Sa 7:24 [n] Ex 16:12; Isa 41:20

6:8 [o] Ge 15:18; 26:3 [p] Ge 14:22 [q] Ps 136:21-22

6:12 [r] ver 30; Ex 4:10; Jer 1:6

6:14 [s] Ge 46:9

15 The sons of Simeon[a] were Jemuel, Jamin, Ohad, Jakin, Zohar and Shaul the son of a Canaanite woman. These were the clans of Simeon.

16 These were the names of the sons of Levi according to their records: Gershon,[b] Kohath and Merari.[c] Levi lived 137 years.

17 The sons of Gershon, by clans, were Libni and Shimei.[d]

18 The sons of Kohath were Amram, Izhar, Hebron and Uzziel.[e] Kohath lived 133 years.

19 The sons of Merari were Mahli and Mushi.[f]

These were the clans of Levi according to their records.

20 Amram married his father's sister Jochebed, who bore him Aaron and Moses.[g] Amram lived 137 years.

21 The sons of Izhar[h] were Korah, Nepheg and Zicri.

22 The sons of Uzziel were Mishael, Elzaphan[i] and Sithri.

23 Aaron married Elisheba, daughter of Amminadab[j] and sister of Nahshon, and she bore him Nadab and Abihu,[k] Eleazar[l] and Ithamar.[m]

24 The sons of Korah[n] were Assir, Elkanah and Abiasaph. These were the Korahite clans.

25 Eleazar son of Aaron married one of the daughters of Putiel, and she bore him Phinehas.[o]

These were the heads of the Levite families, clan by clan.

26 It was this same Aaron and Moses to whom the LORD said, "Bring the Israelites out of Egypt by their divisions."[p] 27 They were the ones who spoke to Pharaoh king of Egypt about bringing the Israelites out of Egypt. It was the same Moses and Aaron.

28 Now when the LORD spoke to Moses in Egypt, 29 he said to him, "I am the LORD.[q] Tell Pharaoh king of Egypt everything I tell you."

30 But Moses said to the LORD, "Since I speak with faltering lips,[r] why would Pharaoh listen to me?"

Chapter 7 Theme ____________________

7 Then the LORD said to Moses, "See, I have made you like God[s] to Pharaoh, and your brother Aaron will be your prophet. 2 You are to say everything I command you, and your brother Aaron is to tell Pharaoh to let the Israelites go out of his country. 3 But I will harden Pharaoh's heart,[t] and though I multiply my miraculous signs and wonders in Egypt, 4 he will not listen[u] to you. Then I will lay my hand on Egypt and with mighty acts of judgment[v] I will bring out my divisions, my people the Israelites. 5 And the Egyptians will know that I am the LORD[w] when I stretch out my hand[x] against Egypt and bring the Israelites out of it."

6:15 a Ge 46:10; 1Ch 4:24
6:16 b Ge 46:11; c Nu 3:17
6:17 d 1Ch 6:17
6:18 e 1Ch 6:2,18
6:19 f 1Ch 6:19; 23:21
6:20 g Ex 2:1-2; Nu 26:59
6:21 h 1Ch 6:38
6:22 i Lev 10:4; Nu 3:30
6:23 j Ru 4:19,20; k Lev 10:1; l Nu 3:2,32; m Nu 26:60
6:24 n Nu 26:11
6:25 o Nu 25:7,11; Jos 24:33; Ps 106:30
6:26 p Ex 7:4; 12:17,41,51
6:29 q ver 11; Ex 7:2
6:30 r ver 12; Ex 4:10
7:1 s Ex 4:16
7:3 t Ex 4:21; 11:9
7:4 u Ex 11:9; v Ex 3:20; 6:6
7:5 w ver 17; Ex 8:19,22; x Ex 3:20

6Moses and Aaron did just as the LORD commanded[a] them. 7Moses was eighty years old[b] and Aaron eighty-three when they spoke to Pharaoh.

Some of the Gods of Egypt

The god:	Ruled over:	How symbolized:
Aker	Earth-god • Helper of the dead	*Two lion heads*
Aton	Sun-god	
Bes	Protection at birth • Dispenser of virility	*Group of demons*
Heket	Primordial goddess	*Frog*
Isis	Goddess of life and healing	*Human*
Khepri	Primordial god • Rising sun	*Scarabaeus (beetle)*
Khnum	Giver of the Nile • Creator of mankind	*Human with ram's head*
Mut	"Eye of the sun"	*Vulture or human*
Nut	Sky goddess • Mother of heavenly bodies	
Osiris	Dead Pharaohs • Ruler of dead, life, vegetation	
Ra	God of sun, earth, and sky • National god	*Human with falcon head*
Selket	Guardian of life • Protector of dead	*Scorpion*
Seth	God of chaos, desert and storm, crops	
Sothis	God of Nile floodwaters	
Thermuthis	Goddess of fertility and harvest; fate	*Serpent*

8The LORD said to Moses and Aaron, 9"When Pharaoh says to you, 'Perform a miracle,[c]' then say to Aaron, 'Take your staff and throw it down before Pharaoh,' and it will become a snake."[d]

10So Moses and Aaron went to Pharaoh and did just as the LORD commanded. Aaron threw his staff down in front of Pharaoh and his officials, and it became a snake. 11Pharaoh then summoned wise men and sorcerers, and the Egyptian magicians[e] also did the same things by their secret arts:[f] 12Each one threw down his staff and it became a snake. But Aaron's staff swallowed up their staffs. 13Yet Pharaoh's heart[g] became hard and he would not listen to them, just as the LORD had said.

14Then the LORD said to Moses, "Pharaoh's heart is unyielding;[h] he refuses to let the people go. 15Go to Pharaoh in the morning as he goes out to the water. Wait on the bank of the Nile to meet him, and take in your hand the staff that was changed into a snake. 16Then say to him, 'The LORD, the God of the Hebrews, has sent me to say to you: Let my people go, so that they may worship[i] me in the desert. But until now you have not listened. 17This is what the LORD says: By this you will know that I am the LORD:[j] With the staff that is in my hand I will strike the water of the Nile, and it will be changed into blood.[k] 18The fish in the Nile will die, and the river will stink; the Egyptians will not be able to drink its water.'"[l]

7:6 [a] ver 2
7:7 [b] Dt 31:2; 34:7; Ac 7:23,30
7:9 [c] Isa 7:11; Jn 2:18 [d] Ex 4:2-5
7:11 [e] Ge 41:8; 2Ti 3:8 [f] ver 22; Ex 8:7,18
7:13 [g] Ex 4:21
7:14 [h] Ex 8:15,32; 10:1,20,27
7:16 [i] Ex 3:18; 5:1,3
7:17 [j] Ex 5:2 [k] Ex 4:9; Rev 11:6; 16:4
7:18 [l] ver 21,24

19 The LORD said to Moses, "Tell Aaron, 'Take your staff and stretch out your hand[a] over the waters of Egypt—over the streams and canals, over the ponds and all the reservoirs'—and they will turn to blood. Blood will be everywhere in Egypt, even in the wooden buckets and stone jars."

20 Moses and Aaron did just as the LORD had commanded. He raised his staff in the presence of Pharaoh and his officials and struck the water of the Nile,[b] and all the water was changed into blood.[c] 21 The fish in the Nile died, and the river smelled so bad that the Egyptians could not drink its water. Blood was everywhere in Egypt.

22 But the Egyptian magicians did the same things by their secret arts,[d] and Pharaoh's heart became hard; he would not listen to Moses and Aaron, just as the LORD had said. 23 Instead, he turned and went into his palace, and did not take even this to heart. 24 And all the Egyptians dug along the Nile to get drinking water, because they could not drink the water of the river.

Chapter 8 Theme ______________________

8

25 Seven days passed after the LORD struck the Nile. 1 Then the LORD said to Moses, "Go to Pharaoh and say to him, 'This is what the LORD says: Let my people go, so that they may worship[e] me. 2 If you refuse to let them go, I will plague your whole country with frogs. 3 The Nile will teem with frogs. They will come up into your palace and your bedroom and onto your bed, into the houses of your officials and on your people,[f] and into your ovens and kneading troughs. 4 The frogs will go up on you and your people and all your officials.'"

5 Then the LORD said to Moses, "Tell Aaron, 'Stretch out your hand with your staff[g] over the streams and canals and ponds, and make frogs come up on the land of Egypt.'"

6 So Aaron stretched out his hand over the waters of Egypt, and the frogs[h] came up and covered the land. 7 But the magicians did the same things by their secret arts;[i] they also made frogs come up on the land of Egypt.

8 Pharaoh summoned Moses and Aaron and said, "Pray[j] to the LORD to take the frogs away from me and my people, and I will let your people go to offer sacrifices[k] to the LORD."

9 Moses said to Pharaoh, "I leave to you the honor of setting the time for me to pray for you and your officials and your people that you and your houses may be rid of the frogs, except for those that remain in the Nile."

10 "Tomorrow," Pharaoh said.

Moses replied, "It will be as you say, so that you may know there is no one like the LORD our God.[l] 11 The frogs will leave you

7:19 [a] Ex 8:5-6,16; 9:22; 10:12,21; 14:21
7:20 [b] Ex 17:5 [c] Ps 78:44; 105:29
7:22 [d] ver 11
8:1 [e] Ex 3:12,18; 4:23
8:3 [f] Ex 10:6
8:5 [g] Ex 7:19
8:6 [h] Ps 78:45; 105:30
8:7 [i] Ex 7:11
8:8 [j] ver 28; Ex 9:28; 10:17 [k] ver 25
8:10 [l] Ex 9:14; Dt 4:35; 33:26; 2Sa 7:22; 1Ch 17:20; Ps 86:8; Isa 46:9; Jer 10:6

and your houses, your officials and your people; they will remain only in the Nile."

12 After Moses and Aaron left Pharaoh, Moses cried out to the LORD about the frogs he had brought on Pharaoh. 13 And the LORD did what Moses asked. The frogs died in the houses, in the courtyards and in the fields. 14 They were piled into heaps, and the land reeked of them. 15 But when Pharaoh saw that there was relief, he hardened his heart[a] and would not listen to Moses and Aaron, just as the LORD had said.

16 Then the LORD said to Moses, "Tell Aaron, 'Stretch out your staff and strike the dust of the ground,' and throughout the land of Egypt the dust will become gnats." 17 They did this, and when Aaron stretched out his hand with the staff and struck the dust of the ground, gnats[b] came upon men and animals. All the dust throughout the land of Egypt became gnats. 18 But when the magicians[c] tried to produce gnats by their secret arts,[d] they could not. And the gnats were on men and animals.

19 The magicians said to Pharaoh, "This is the finger[e] of God." But Pharaoh's heart was hard and he would not listen, just as the LORD had said.

20 Then the LORD said to Moses, "Get up early in the morning[f] and confront Pharaoh as he goes to the water and say to him, 'This is what the LORD says: Let my people go, so that they may worship[g] me. 21 If you do not let my people go, I will send swarms of flies on you and your officials, on your people and into your houses. The houses of the Egyptians will be full of flies, and even the ground where they are.

22 "'But on that day I will deal differently with the land of Goshen, where my people live;[h] no swarms of flies will be there, so that you will know[i] that I, the LORD, am in this land. 23 I will make a distinction[a] between my people and your people. This miraculous sign will occur tomorrow.'"

24 And the LORD did this. Dense swarms of flies poured into Pharaoh's palace and into the houses of his officials, and throughout Egypt the land was ruined by the flies.[j]

25 Then Pharaoh summoned[k] Moses and Aaron and said, "Go, sacrifice to your God here in the land."

26 But Moses said, "That would not be right. The sacrifices we offer the LORD our God would be detestable to the Egyptians.[l] And if we offer sacrifices that are detestable in their eyes, will they not stone us? 27 We must take a three-day journey into the desert to offer sacrifices[m] to the LORD our God, as he commands us."

28 Pharaoh said, "I will let you go to offer sacrifices to the LORD your God in the desert, but you must not go very far. Now pray[n] for me."

a 23 Septuagint and Vulgate; Hebrew *will put a deliverance*

8:15 a Ex 7:14

8:17 b Ps 105:31

8:18 c Ex 9:11; Da 5:8 d Ex 7:11

8:19 e Ex 7:5; 10:7; Ps 8:3; Lk 11:20

8:20 f Ex 7:15; 9:13 g ver 1; Ex 3:18

8:22 h Ex 9:4,6,26; 10:23; 11:7 i Ex 7:5; 9:29

8:24 j Ps 78:45; 105:31

8:25 k ver 8; Ex 9:27

8:26 l Ge 43:32; 46:34

8:27 m Ex 3:18

8:28 n ver 8; Ex 9:28; 1Ki 13:6

29 Moses answered, "As soon as I leave you, I will pray to the
LORD, and tomorrow the flies will leave Pharaoh and his officials
and his people. Only be sure that Pharaoh does not act deceitfully[a]
again by not letting the people go to offer sacrifices to the LORD."
30 Then Moses left Pharaoh and prayed to the LORD,[b] 31 and the
LORD did what Moses asked: The flies left Pharaoh and his officials and his people; not a fly remained. 32 But this time also
Pharaoh hardened his heart[c] and would not let the people go.

Chapter 9 Theme ____________________

9 Then the LORD said to Moses, "Go to Pharaoh and say to
him, 'This is what the LORD, the God of the Hebrews, says:
"Let my people go, so that they may worship[d] me." 2 If you refuse
to let them go and continue to hold them back, 3 the hand[e] of the
LORD will bring a terrible plague on your livestock in the field—
on your horses and donkeys and camels and on your cattle and
sheep and goats. 4 But the LORD will make a distinction between
the livestock of Israel and that of Egypt,[f] so that no animal
belonging to the Israelites will die.'"
5 The LORD set a time and said, "Tomorrow the LORD will do this
in the land." 6 And the next day the LORD did it: All the livestock[g]
of the Egyptians died,[h] but not one animal belonging to the
Israelites died. 7 Pharaoh sent men to investigate and found that
not even one of the animals of the Israelites had died. Yet his heart
was unyielding and he would not let the people go.[i]
8 Then the LORD said to Moses and Aaron, "Take handfuls of
soot from a furnace and have Moses toss it into the air in the presence of Pharaoh. 9 It will become fine dust over the whole land of
Egypt, and festering boils[j] will break out on men and animals
throughout the land."
10 So they took soot from a furnace and stood before Pharaoh.
Moses tossed it into the air, and festering boils broke out on men
and animals. 11 The magicians[k] could not stand before Moses
because of the boils that were on them and on all the Egyptians.
12 But the LORD hardened Pharaoh's heart[l] and he would not listen to Moses and Aaron, just as the LORD had said to Moses.
13 Then the LORD said to Moses, "Get up early in the morning,
confront Pharaoh and say to him, 'This is what the LORD, the
God of the Hebrews, says: Let my people go, so that they may
worship[m] me, 14 or this time I will send the full force of my
plagues against you and against your officials and your people,
so you may know[n] that there is no one like[o] me in all the earth.
15 For by now I could have stretched out my hand and struck you
and your people[p] with a plague that would have wiped you off
the earth. 16 But I have raised you up[a] for this very purpose,[q] that

8:29 *a* ver 15
8:30 *b* ver 12
8:32 *c* ver 8,15; Ex 4:21
9:1 *d* Ex 8:1
9:3 *e* Ex 7:4
9:4 *f* ver 26; Ex 8:22
9:6 *g* ver 19-21; Ex 11:5 *h* Ps 78:48-50
9:7 *i* Ex 7:14; 8:32
9:9 *j* Dt 28:27,35; Rev 16:2
9:11 *k* Ex 8:18
9:12 *l* Ex 4:21
9:13 *m* Ex 8:20
9:14 *n* Ex 8:10 *o* 2Sa 7:22; 1Ch 17:20; Ps 86:8; Isa 46:9; Jer 10:6
9:15 *p* Ex 3:20
9:16 *q* Pr 16:4

a16 Or *have spared you*

I might show you my power[a] and that my name might be proclaimed in all the earth. 17You still set yourself against my people
and will not let them go. 18Therefore, at this time tomorrow I will
send the worst hailstorm[b] that has ever fallen on Egypt, from the
day it was founded till now.[c] 19Give an order now to bring your
livestock and everything you have in the field to a place of shelter,
because the hail will fall on every man and animal that has not
been brought in and is still out in the field, and they will die.'"

20Those officials of Pharaoh who feared[d] the word of the LORD
hurried to bring their slaves and their livestock inside. 21But
those who ignored the word of the LORD left their slaves and livestock in the field.

22Then the LORD said to Moses, "Stretch out your hand toward
the sky so that hail will fall all over Egypt—on men and animals
and on everything growing in the fields of Egypt." 23When Moses
stretched out his staff toward the sky, the LORD sent thunder[e] and
hail,[f] and lightning flashed down to the ground. So the LORD
rained hail on the land of Egypt; 24hail fell and lightning flashed
back and forth. It was the worst storm in all the land of Egypt
since it had become a nation. 25Throughout Egypt hail struck
everything in the fields—both men and animals; it beat down
everything growing in the fields and stripped every tree.[g] 26The
only place it did not hail was the land of Goshen,[h] where the
Israelites were.[i]

27Then Pharaoh summoned Moses and Aaron. "This time I have
sinned,"[j] he said to them. "The LORD is in the right,[k] and I and
my people are in the wrong. 28Pray[l] to the LORD, for we have had
enough thunder and hail. I will let you go;[m] you don't have to
stay any longer."

29Moses replied, "When I have gone out of the city, I will spread
out my hands[n] in prayer to the LORD. The thunder will stop and
there will be no more hail, so you may know that the earth[o] is the
LORD's. 30But I know that you and your officials still do not fear
the LORD God."

31(The flax and barley[p] were destroyed, since the barley had
headed and the flax was in bloom. 32The wheat and spelt, however, were not destroyed, because they ripen later.)

33Then Moses left Pharaoh and went out of the city. He spread
out his hands toward the LORD; the thunder and hail stopped, and
the rain no longer poured down on the land. 34When Pharaoh saw
that the rain and hail and thunder had stopped, he sinned again:
He and his officials hardened their hearts. 35So Pharaoh's heart[q]
was hard and he would not let the Israelites go, just as the LORD
had said through Moses.

9:16 a Ro 9:17*
9:18 b ver 23 c ver 24
9:20 d Pr 13:13
9:23 e Ps 18:13 f Jos 10:11; Ps 78:47; 105:32; Isa 30:30; Eze 38:22; Rev 8:7; 16:21
9:25 g Ps 105:32-33
9:26 h ver 4 i Ex 8:22; 10:23; 11:7; 12:13
9:27 j Ex 10:16 k 2Ch 12:6; Ps 129:4; La 1:18
9:28 l Ex 10:17 m Ex 8:8
9:29 n 1Ki 8:22,38; Ps 143:6; Isa 1:15 o Ex 19:5; Ps 24:1; 1Co 10:26
9:31 p Ru 1:22; 2:23
9:35 q Ex 4:21

Chapter 10 Theme ______________________________

10

Then the LORD said to Moses, "Go to Pharaoh, for I have
hardened his heart[a] and the hearts of his officials so that I
may perform these miraculous signs[b] of mine among them 2that
you may tell your children[c] and grandchildren how I dealt harshly
with the Egyptians and how I performed my signs among them,
and that you may know that I am the LORD."
3So Moses and Aaron went to Pharaoh and said to him, "This
is what the LORD, the God of the Hebrews, says: 'How long will
you refuse to humble[d] yourself before me? Let my people go, so
that they may worship me. 4If you refuse to let them go, I will
bring locusts[e] into your country tomorrow. 5They will cover the
face of the ground so that it cannot be seen. They will devour
what little you have left[f] after the hail, including every tree that
is growing in your fields. 6They will fill your houses and those
of all your officials and all the Egyptians—something neither
your fathers nor your forefathers have ever seen from the day
they settled in this land till now.'" Then Moses turned and left
Pharaoh.
7Pharaoh's officials said to him, "How long will this man be a
snare[g] to us? Let the people go, so that they may worship the
LORD their God. Do you not yet realize that Egypt is ruined?"[h]
8Then Moses and Aaron were brought back to Pharaoh. "Go,
worship[i] the LORD your God," he said. "But just who will be
going?"
9Moses answered, "We will go with our young and old, with
our sons and daughters, and with our flocks and herds, because
we are to celebrate a festival to the LORD."
10Pharaoh said, "The LORD be with you—if I let you go, along
with your women and children! Clearly you are bent on evil.[a]
11No! Have only the men go; and worship the LORD, since that's
what you have been asking for." Then Moses and Aaron were
driven out of Pharaoh's presence.
12And the LORD said to Moses, "Stretch out your hand[j] over
Egypt so that locusts will swarm over the land and devour
everything growing in the fields, everything left by the hail."
13So Moses stretched out his staff over Egypt, and the LORD
made an east wind blow across the land all that day and all that
night. By morning the wind had brought the locusts;[k] 14they
invaded all Egypt and settled down in every area of the country
in great numbers. Never before had there been such a plague of
locusts,[l] nor will there ever be again. 15They covered all the ground
until it was black. They devoured[m] all that was left after the hail—

[a]10 Or *Be careful, trouble is in store for you!*

10:1 *a* Ex 4:21 *b* Ex 7:3
10:2 *c* Ex 12:26-27; 13:8,14; Dt 4:9; Ps 44:1; 78:4,5; Joel 1:3
10:3 *d* 1Ki 21:29; Jas 4:10; 1Pe 5:6
10:4 *e* Rev 9:3
10:5 *f* Ex 9:32; Joel 1:4
10:7 *g* Ex 23:33; Jos 23:7-13; 1Sa 18:21; Ecc 7:26 *h* Ex 8:19
10:8 *i* Ex 8:8
10:12 *j* Ex 7:19
10:13 *k* Ps 105:34
10:14 *l* Ps 78:46; Joel 2:1-11,25
10:15 *m* ver 5; Ps 105:34-35

everything growing in the fields and the fruit on the trees. Nothing
green remained on tree or plant in all the land of Egypt.
16Pharaoh quickly summoned Moses and Aaron and said, "I
have sinned[a] against the LORD your God and against you. 17Now
forgive my sin once more and pray[b] to the LORD your God to
take this deadly plague away from me."
18Moses then left Pharaoh and prayed to the LORD.[c] 19And the
LORD changed the wind to a very strong west wind, which caught
up the locusts and carried them into the Red Sea.[a] Not a locust
was left anywhere in Egypt. 20But the LORD hardened Pharaoh's
heart,[d] and he would not let the Israelites go.
21Then the LORD said to Moses, "Stretch out your hand toward
the sky so that darkness[e] will spread over Egypt—darkness that
can be felt." 22So Moses stretched out his hand toward the sky,
and total darkness[f] covered all Egypt for three days. 23No one
could see anyone else or leave his place for three days. Yet all the
Israelites had light in the places where they lived.[g]
24Then Pharaoh summoned Moses and said, "Go, worship the
LORD. Even your women and children[h] may go with you; only
leave your flocks and herds behind."
25But Moses said, "You must allow us to have sacrifices and
burnt offerings to present to the LORD our God. 26Our livestock
too must go with us; not a hoof is to be left behind. We have to use
some of them in worshiping the LORD our God, and until we get
there we will not know what we are to use to worship the LORD."
27But the LORD hardened Pharaoh's heart,[i] and he was not
willing to let them go. 28Pharaoh said to Moses, "Get out of my
sight! Make sure you do not appear before me again! The day
you see my face you will die."
29"Just as you say," Moses replied, "I will never appear[j] before
you again."

Chapter 11 Theme ____________________

11 Now the LORD had said to Moses, "I will bring one more
plague on Pharaoh and on Egypt. After that, he will let
you go from here, and when he does, he will drive you out completely. 2Tell the people that men and women alike are to ask their
neighbors for articles of silver and gold."[k] 3(The LORD made the
Egyptians favorably disposed toward the people, and Moses
himself was highly regarded[l] in Egypt by Pharaoh's officials and
by the people.)
4So Moses said, "This is what the LORD says: 'About midnight[m]
I will go throughout Egypt. 5Every firstborn[n] son in Egypt will

a19 Hebrew *Yam Suph*; that is, Sea of Reeds

10:16 [a] Ex 9:27
10:17 [b] Ex 8:8
10:18 [c] Ex 8:30
10:20 [d] Ex 4:21; 11:10
10:21 [e] Dt 28:29
10:22 [f] Ps 105:28; Rev 16:10
10:23 [g] Ex 8:22
10:24 [h] ver 8-10
10:27 [i] ver 20; Ex 4:21
10:29 [j] Heb 11:27
11:2 [k] Ex 3:21,22
11:3 [l] Dt 34:11
11:4 [m] Ex 12:29
11:5 [n] Ex 4:23; Ps 78:51

die, from the firstborn son of Pharaoh, who sits on the throne, to the firstborn son of the slave girl, who is at her hand mill, and all the firstborn of the cattle as well. 6There will be loud wailing[a] throughout Egypt—worse than there has ever been or ever will be again. 7But among the Israelites not a dog will bark at any man or animal.' Then you will know that the LORD makes a distinction[b] between Egypt and Israel. 8All these officials of yours will come to me, bowing down before me and saying, 'Go,[c] you and all the people who follow you!' After that I will leave." Then Moses, hot with anger, left Pharaoh.

9The LORD had said to Moses, "Pharaoh will refuse to listen[d] to you—so that my wonders may be multiplied in Egypt." 10Moses and Aaron performed all these wonders before Pharaoh, but the LORD hardened Pharaoh's heart,[e] and he would not let the Israelites go out of his country.

Chapter 12 Theme ________________________________

12 The LORD said to Moses and Aaron in Egypt, 2"This month is to be for you the first month,[f] the first month of your year. 3Tell the whole community of Israel that on the tenth day of this month each man is to take a lamb[a] for his family, one for each household. 4If any household is too small for a whole lamb, they must share one with their nearest neighbor, having taken into account the number of people there are. You are to determine the amount of lamb needed in accordance with what each person will eat. 5The animals you choose must be year-old males without defect,[g] and you may take them from the sheep or the goats. 6Take care of them until the fourteenth day of the month,[h] when all the people of the community of Israel must slaughter them at twilight.[i] 7Then they are to take some of the blood and put it on the sides and tops of the doorframes of the houses where they eat the lambs. 8That same night[j] they are to eat the meat roasted[k] over the fire, along with bitter herbs,[l] and bread made without yeast.[m] 9Do not eat the meat raw or cooked in water, but roast it over the fire—head, legs and inner parts. 10Do not leave any of it till morning;[n] if some is left till morning, you must burn it. 11This is how you are to eat it: with your cloak tucked into your belt, your sandals on your feet and your staff in your hand. Eat it in haste;[o] it is the LORD's Passover.[p]

12"On that same night I will pass through[q] Egypt and strike down every firstborn—both men and animals—and I will bring judgment on all the gods[r] of Egypt. I am the LORD.[s] 13The blood

11:6 [a] Ex 12:30
11:7 [b] Ex 8:22
11:8 [c] Ex 12:31-33
11:9 [d] Ex 7:4
11:10 [e] Ex 4:21; 10:20,27
12:2 [f] Ex 13:4; Dt 16:1
12:5 [g] Lev 22:18-21; Heb 9:14
12:6 [h] Lev 23:5; Nu 9:1-3,5,11 [i] Ex 16:12; Dt 16:4,6
12:8 [j] Ex 34:25; Nu 9:12 [k] Dt 16:7 [l] Nu 9:11 [m] Dt 16:3-4; 1Co 5:8
12:10 [n] Ex 23:18; 34:25
12:11 [o] Dt 16:3 [p] ver 13,21,27, 43; Dt 16:1
12:12 [q] Ex 11:4; Am 5:17 [r] Nu 33:4 [s] Ex 6:2

a3 The Hebrew word can mean *lamb* or *kid*; also in verse 4.

will be a sign for you on the houses where you are; and when I
see the blood, I will pass over you. No destructive plague will
touch you when I strike Egypt.
14“This is a day you are to commemorate;[a] for the generations
to come you shall celebrate it as a festival to the LORD—a lasting
ordinance.[b] 15For seven days you are to eat bread made without
yeast.[c] On the first day remove the yeast from your houses, for
whoever eats anything with yeast in it from the first day through
the seventh must be cut off[d] from Israel. 16On the first day hold a
sacred assembly, and another one on the seventh day. Do no
work at all on these days, except to prepare food for everyone to
eat—that is all you may do.
17“Celebrate the Feast of Unleavened Bread, because it was on
this very day that I brought your divisions out of Egypt.[e] Celebrate this day as a lasting ordinance for the generations to come.
18In the first month[f] you are to eat bread made without yeast,
from the evening of the fourteenth day until the evening of the
twenty-first day. 19For seven days no yeast is to be found in your
houses. And whoever eats anything with yeast in it must be cut
off from the community of Israel, whether he is an alien or
native-born. 20Eat nothing made with yeast. Wherever you live,
you must eat unleavened bread.”
21Then Moses summoned all the elders of Israel and said to
them, “Go at once and select the animals for your families and
slaughter the Passover[g] lamb. 22Take a bunch of hyssop, dip it into
the blood in the basin and put some of the blood[h] on the top and
on both sides of the doorframe. Not one of you shall go out the
door of his house until morning. 23When the LORD goes through
the land to strike down the Egyptians, he will see the blood[i] on
the top and sides of the doorframe and will pass over[j] that doorway, and he will not permit the destroyer[k] to enter your houses
and strike you down.
24“Obey these instructions as a lasting ordinance for you and
your descendants. 25When you enter the land that the LORD will
give you as he promised, observe this ceremony. 26And when
your children[l] ask you, ‘What does this ceremony mean to you?’
27then tell them, ‘It is the Passover[m] sacrifice to the LORD, who
passed over the houses of the Israelites in Egypt and spared our
homes when he struck down the Egyptians.’ ” Then the people
bowed down and worshiped.[n] 28The Israelites did just what the
LORD commanded Moses and Aaron.
29At midnight[o] the LORD struck down all the firstborn[p] in Egypt,
from the firstborn of Pharaoh, who sat on the throne, to the firstborn of the prisoner, who was in the dungeon, and the firstborn
of all the livestock[q] as well. 30Pharaoh and all his officials and all

12:14
[a] Ex 13:9
[b] ver 17,24; Ex 13:5,10; 2Ki 23:21

12:15
[c] Ex 13:6-7; 23:15; 34:18; Lev 23:6; Dt 16:3
[d] Ge 17:14; Nu 9:13

12:17
[e] ver 41; Ex 13:3

12:18
[f] ver 2; Lev 23:5-8; Nu 28:16-25

12:21
[g] ver 11; Mk 14:12-16

12:22
[h] ver 7; Heb 11:28

12:23
[i] Rev 7:3
[j] ver 13
[k] 1Co 10:10; Heb 11:28

12:26
[l] Ex 10:2; 13:8,14-15; Jos 4:6

12:27
[m] ver 11
[n] Ex 4:31

12:29
[o] Ex 11:4
[p] Ex 4:23; Ps 78:51
[q] Ex 9:6

the Egyptians got up during the night, and there was loud wailing[a] in Egypt, for there was not a house without someone dead.

31During the night Pharaoh summoned Moses and Aaron and said, "Up! Leave my people, you and the Israelites! Go, worship[b] the LORD as you have requested. 32Take your flocks and herds,[c] as you have said, and go. And also bless me."

33The Egyptians urged the people to hurry and leave[d] the country. "For otherwise," they said, "we will all die!" 34So the people took their dough before the yeast was added, and carried it on their shoulders in kneading troughs wrapped in clothing. 35The Israelites did as Moses instructed and asked the Egyptians for articles of silver and gold[e] and for clothing. 36The LORD had made the Egyptians favorably disposed toward the people, and they gave them what they asked for; so they plundered[f] the Egyptians.

37The Israelites journeyed from Rameses to Succoth.[g] There were about six hundred thousand men[h] on foot, besides women and children. 38Many other people[i] went up with them, as well as large droves of livestock, both flocks and herds. 39With the dough they had brought from Egypt, they baked cakes of unleavened bread. The dough was without yeast because they had been driven out[j] of Egypt and did not have time to prepare food for themselves.

40Now the length of time the Israelite people lived in Egypt[a] was 430 years.[k] 41At the end of the 430 years, to the very day, all the LORD's divisions[l] left Egypt.[m] 42Because the LORD kept vigil that night to bring them out of Egypt, on this night all the Israelites are to keep vigil to honor the LORD for the generations to come.[n]

43The LORD said to Moses and Aaron, "These are the regulations for the Passover:[o]

"No foreigner[p] is to eat of it. 44Any slave you have bought may eat of it after you have circumcised[q] him, 45but a temporary resident and a hired worker[r] may not eat of it.

46"It must be eaten inside one house; take none of the meat outside the house. Do not break any of the bones.[s] 47The whole community of Israel must celebrate it.

48"An alien living among you who wants to celebrate the LORD's Passover must have all the males in his household circumcised; then he may take part like one born in the land.[t] No uncircumcised male may eat of it. 49The same law applies to the native-born and to the alien[u] living among you."

50All the Israelites did just what the LORD had commanded Moses and Aaron. 51And on that very day the LORD brought the Israelites out of Egypt by their divisions.[v]

a *40* Masoretic Text; Samaritan Pentateuch and Septuagint *Egypt and Canaan*

12:30 [a] Ex 11:6
12:31 [b] Ex 8:8
12:32 [c] Ex 10:9,26
12:33 [d] Ps 105:38
12:35 [e] Ex 3:22
12:36 [f] Ex 3:22
12:37 [g] Nu 33:3-5 [h] Ex 38:26; Nu 1:46; 11:13,21
12:38 [i] Nu 11:4
12:39 [j] ver 31-33; Ex 6:1; 11:1
12:40 [k] Ge 15:13; Ac 7:6; Gal 3:17
12:41 [l] ver 17; Ex 6:26 [m] Ex 3:10
12:42 [n] Ex 13:10; Dt 16:1,6
12:43 [o] ver 11 [p] ver 48; Nu 9:14
12:44 [q] Ge 17:12-13
12:45 [r] Lev 22:10
12:46 [s] Nu 9:12; Jn 19:36*
12:48 [t] Nu 9:14
12:49 [u] Nu 15:15-16, 29; Gal 3:28
12:51 [v] ver 41; Ex 6:26

Chapter 13 Theme ______________________

13 The LORD said to Moses, 2"Consecrate to me every firstborn male.[a] The first offspring of every womb among the
Israelites belongs to me, whether man or animal."
3Then Moses said to the people, "Commemorate this day, the
day you came out of Egypt, out of the land of slavery, because
the LORD brought you out of it with a mighty hand.[b] Eat nothing
containing yeast.[c] 4Today, in the month of Abib,[d] you are leaving.
5When the LORD brings you into the land of the Canaanites, Hittites, Amorites, Hivites and Jebusites[e]—the land he swore to
your forefathers to give you, a land flowing with milk and honey—you are to observe this ceremony[f] in this month: 6For seven
days eat bread made without yeast and on the seventh day hold a
festival[g] to the LORD. 7Eat unleavened bread during those seven
days; nothing with yeast in it is to be seen among you, nor shall
any yeast be seen anywhere within your borders. 8On that day
tell your son,[h] 'I do this because of what the LORD did for me
when I came out of Egypt.' 9This observance will be for you like
a sign on your hand and a reminder on your forehead[i] that the
law of the LORD is to be on your lips. For the LORD brought you
out of Egypt with his mighty hand. 10You must keep this ordinance[j] at the appointed time year after year.
11"After the LORD brings you into the land of the Canaanites
and gives it to you, as he promised on oath to you and your forefathers, 12you are to give over to the LORD the first offspring of
every womb. All the firstborn males of your livestock belong to the
LORD.[k] 13Redeem with a lamb every firstborn donkey, but if you
do not redeem it, break its neck.[l] Redeem every firstborn among
your sons.[m]
14"In days to come, when your son[n] asks you, 'What does this
mean?' say to him, 'With a mighty hand the LORD brought us out
of Egypt, out of the land of slavery.[o] 15When Pharaoh stubbornly
refused to let us go, the LORD killed every firstborn in Egypt,
both man and animal. This is why I sacrifice to the LORD the first
male offspring of every womb and redeem each of my firstborn
sons.'[p] 16And it will be like a sign on your hand and a symbol on
your forehead[q] that the LORD brought us out of Egypt with his
mighty hand."
17When Pharaoh let the people go, God did not lead them on
the road through the Philistine country, though that was shorter.
For God said, "If they face war, they might change their minds
and return to Egypt."[r] 18So God led[s] the people around by the
desert road toward the Red Sea.[a] The Israelites went up out of
Egypt armed for battle.[t]

a18 Hebrew *Yam Suph*; that is, Sea of Reeds

13:2 [a] ver 12,13,15; Ex 22:29; Nu 3:13; Dt 15:19; Lk 2:23*
13:3 [b] Ex 3:20; 6:1 [c] Ex 12:19
13:4 [d] Ex 12:2
13:5 [e] Ex 3:8 [f] Ex 12:25-26
13:6 [g] Ex 12:15-20
13:8 [h] ver 14; Ex 10:2; Ps 78:5-6
13:9 [i] ver 16; Dt 6:8; 11:18
13:10 [j] Ex 12:24-25
13:12 [k] Lev 27:26; Lk 2:23*
13:13 [l] Ex 34:20 [m] Nu 18:15
13:14 [n] Ex 10:2; 12:26-27; Dt 6:20 [o] ver 3,9
13:15 [p] Ex 12:29
13:16 [q] ver 9
13:17 [r] Ex 14:11; Nu 14:1-4; Dt 17:16
13:18 [s] Ps 136:16 [t] Jos 1:14

19Moses took the bones of Joseph[a] with him because Joseph had made the sons of Israel swear an oath. He had said, "God will surely come to your aid, and then you must carry my bones up with you from this place."[a][b]

20After leaving Succoth they camped at Etham on the edge of the desert.[c] 21By day the LORD went ahead of them in a pillar of cloud[d] to guide them on their way and by night in a pillar of fire to give them light, so that they could travel by day or night. 22Neither the pillar of cloud by day nor the pillar of fire by night left its place in front of the people.

Chapter 14 Theme ____________________

14 Then the LORD said to Moses, 2"Tell the Israelites to turn back and encamp near Pi Hahiroth, between Migdol[e] and the sea. They are to encamp by the sea, directly opposite Baal Zephon. 3Pharaoh will think, 'The Israelites are wandering around the land in confusion, hemmed in by the desert.' 4And I will harden Pharaoh's heart,[f] and he will pursue them. But I will gain glory[g] for myself through Pharaoh and all his army, and the Egyptians will know that I am the LORD."[h] So the Israelites did this.

5When the king of Egypt was told that the people had fled, Pharaoh and his officials changed their minds about them and said, "What have we done? We have let the Israelites go and have lost their services!" 6So he had his chariot made ready and took his army with him. 7He took six hundred of the best chariots, along with all the other chariots of Egypt, with officers over all of them. 8The LORD hardened the heart[i] of Pharaoh king of Egypt, so that he pursued the Israelites, who were marching out boldly.[j] 9The Egyptians—all Pharaoh's horses and chariots, horsemen[b] and troops—pursued the Isrelites and overtook[k] them as they camped by the sea near Pi Hahiroth, opposite Baal Zephon.

10As Pharaoh approached, the Israelites looked up, and there were the Egyptians, marching after them. They were terrified and cried[l] out to the LORD. 11They said to Moses, "Was it because there were no graves in Egypt that you brought us to the desert to die?[m] What have you done to us by bringing us out of Egypt? 12Didn't we say to you in Egypt, 'Leave us alone; let us serve the Egyptians'? It would have been better for us to serve the Egyptians than to die in the desert!"

13Moses answered the people, "Do not be afraid.[n] Stand firm and you will see[o] the deliverance the LORD will bring you today. The Egyptians you see today you will never see[p] again. 14The LORD will fight[q] for you; you need only to be still."[r]

13:19 a Jos 24:32; Ac 7:16 b Ge 50:24-25
13:20 c Nu 33:6
13:21 d Ex 14:19,24; 33:9-10; Nu 9:16; Dt 1:33; Ne 9:12,19; Ps 78:14; 99:7; 105:39; Isa 4:5; 1Co 10:1
14:2 e Nu 33:7; Jer 44:1
14:4 f Ex 4:21 g Ro 9:17, 22-23 h Ex 7:5
14:8 i ver 4; Ex 11:10 j Nu 33:3; Ac 13:17
14:9 k Ex 15:9
14:10 l Jos 24:7; Ne 9:9; Ps 34:17
14:11 m Ps 106:7-8
14:13 n Ge 15:1 o 2Ch 20:17; Isa 41:10, 13-14 p ver 30
14:14 q ver 25; Ex 15:3; Dt 1:30; 3:22; 2Ch 20:29 r Ps 37:7; 46:10; Isa 30:15

a19 See Gen. 50:25. b9 Or *charioteers*; also in verses 17, 18, 23, 26 and 28

15Then the LORD said to Moses, "Why are you crying out to
me? Tell the Israelites to move on. 16Raise your staff[a] and stretch
out your hand over the sea to divide the water[b] so that the Israelites can go through the sea on dry ground. 17I will harden the
hearts of the Egyptians so that they will go in after them.[c] And I
will gain glory through Pharaoh and all his army, through his
chariots and his horsemen. 18The Egyptians will know that I am
the LORD when I gain glory through Pharaoh, his chariots and
his horsemen."

19Then the angel of God, who had been traveling in front of
Israel's army, withdrew and went behind them. The pillar of
cloud[d] also moved from in front and stood behind them, 20com-
ing between the armies of Egypt and Israel. Throughout the
night the cloud brought darkness to the one side and light to the
other side; so neither went near the other all night long.

21Then Moses stretched out his hand over the sea, and all that
night the LORD drove the sea back with a strong east wind[e] and
turned it into dry land. The waters were divided,[f] 22and the Israelites went through the sea on dry ground,[g] with a wall of water
on their right and on their left.

23The Egyptians pursued them, and all Pharaoh's horses and
chariots and horsemen followed them into the sea. 24During the
last watch of the night the LORD looked down from the pillar of
fire and cloud[h] at the Egyptian army and threw it into confusion.
25He made the wheels of their chariots come off[a] so that they had
difficulty driving. And the Egyptians said, "Let's get away from
the Israelites! The LORD is fighting[i] for them against Egypt."

26Then the LORD said to Moses, "Stretch out your hand over the
sea so that the waters may flow back over the Egyptians and their
chariots and horsemen." 27Moses stretched out his hand over the
sea, and at daybreak the sea went back to its place.[j] The Egyptians were fleeing toward[b] it, and the LORD swept them into the
sea.[k] 28The water flowed back and covered the chariots and horsemen—the entire army of Pharaoh that had followed the Israelites
into the sea. Not one of them survived.

29But the Israelites went through the sea on dry ground,[l] with a
wall of water on their right and on their left. 30That day the LORD
saved[m] Israel from the hands of the Egyptians, and Israel saw the
Egyptians lying dead on the shore. 31And when the Israelites saw
the great power the LORD displayed against the Egyptians, the
people feared the LORD and put their trust[n] in him and in Moses
his servant.

14:16 *a* Ex 4:17; Nu 20:8-9,11 *b* Isa 10:26
14:17 *c* ver 4
14:19 *d* Ex 13:21
14:21 *e* Ex 15:8 *f* Ps 74:13; 114:5; Isa 63:12
14:22 *g* Ex 15:19; Ne 9:11; Ps 66:6; Heb 11:29
14:24 *h* Ex 13:21
14:25 *i* ver 14
14:27 *j* Jos 4:18 *k* Ex 15:1,21; Ps 78:53; 106:11
14:29 *l* ver 22
14:30 *m* Ps 106:8, 10,21
14:31 *n* Ps 106:12; Jn 2:11

a25 Or *He jammed the wheels of their chariots* (see Samaritan Pentateuch, Septuagint and Syriac) b27 Or *from*

Chapter 15 Theme ____________________

15

Then Moses and the Israelites sang this song[a] to the LORD:

"I will sing[b] to the LORD,
for he is highly exalted.
The horse and its rider
he has hurled into the sea.
2 The LORD is my strength[c] and my song;
he has become my salvation.[d]
He is my God,[e] and I will praise him,
my father's God, and I will exalt[f] him.
3 The LORD is a warrior;[g]
the LORD is his name.[h]
4 Pharaoh's chariots and his army[i]
he has hurled into the sea.
The best of Pharaoh's officers
are drowned in the Red Sea.[a]
5 The deep waters have covered them;
they sank to the depths like a stone.[j]

6 "Your right hand,[k] O LORD,
was majestic in power.
Your right hand, O LORD,
shattered the enemy.
7 In the greatness of your majesty
you threw down those who opposed you.
You unleashed your burning anger;[l]
it consumed them like stubble.
8 By the blast of your nostrils[m]
the waters piled up.[n]
The surging waters stood firm like a wall;[o]
the deep waters congealed in the heart
of the sea.

9 "The enemy boasted,
'I will pursue,[p] I will overtake them.
I will divide the spoils;[q]
I will gorge myself on them.
I will draw my sword
and my hand will destroy them.'
10 But you blew with your breath,
and the sea covered them.
They sank like lead
in the mighty waters.[r]

15:1 [a] Rev 15:3 [b] Ps 106:12
15:2 [c] Ps 59:17 [d] Ps 18:2,46; Isa 12:2; Hab 3:18 [e] Ge 28:21 [f] Ex 3:6,15-16; Isa 25:1
15:3 [g] Ex 14:14; Ps 24:8; Rev 19:11 [h] Ex 6:2-3,7-8; Ps 83:18
15:4 [i] Ex 14:6-7
15:5 [j] ver 10; Ne 9:11
15:6 [k] Ps 118:15
15:7 [l] Ps 78:49-50
15:8 [m] Ex 14:21 [n] Ps 78:13 [o] Ex 14:22
15:9 [p] Ex 14:5-9 [q] Jdg 5:30; Isa 53:12
15:10 [r] ver 5; Ex 14:27-28

a 4 Hebrew *Yam Suph*; that is, Sea of Reeds; also in verse 22

[11]"Who among the gods is like you,[a] O LORD?
Who is like you—
majestic in holiness,[b]
awesome in glory,[c]
working wonders?
[12]You stretched out your right hand
and the earth swallowed them.

[13]"In your unfailing love you will lead[d]
the people you have redeemed.
In your strength you will guide them
to your holy dwelling.[e]
[14]The nations will hear and tremble;[f]
anguish will grip the people of Philistia.
[15]The chiefs[g] of Edom will be terrified,
the leaders of Moab will be seized with trembling,[h]
the people[a] of Canaan will melt[i] away;
[16] terror[j] and dread will fall upon them.
By the power of your arm
they will be as still as a stone[k]—
until your people pass by, O LORD,
until the people you bought[b][l] pass by.
[17]You will bring them in and plant[m] them
on the mountain[n] of your inheritance—
the place, O LORD, you made for your dwelling,
the sanctuary, O Lord, your hands established.
[18]The LORD will reign
for ever and ever."

[19]When Pharaoh's horses, chariots and horsemen[c] went into
the sea,[o] the LORD brought the waters of the sea back over them,
but the Israelites walked through the sea on dry ground.[p] [20]Then
Miriam[q] the prophetess,[r] Aaron's sister, took a tambourine in
her hand, and all the women followed her, with tambourines and
dancing.[s] [21]Miriam sang to them:

"Sing to the LORD,
for he is highly exalted.
The horse and its rider
he has hurled into the sea."[t]

[22]Then Moses led Israel from the Red Sea and they went into
the Desert of Shur. For three days they traveled in the desert
without finding water. [23]When they came to Marah, they could
not drink its water because it was bitter. (That is why the place is

a15 Or *rulers* b16 Or *created* c19 Or *charioteers*

15:11 [a] Ex 8:10; Dt 3:24; Ps 77:13 [b] Isa 6:3; Rev 4:8 [c] Ps 8:1
15:13 [d] Ne 9:12; Ps 77:20 [e] Ps 78:54
15:14 [f] Dt 2:25
15:15 [g] Ge 36:15 [h] Nu 22:3 [i] Jos 5:1
15:16 [j] Ex 23:27 Jos 2:9 [k] 1Sa 25:37 [l] Ps 74:2
15:17 [m] Ps 44:2 [n] Ps 78:54,68
15:19 [o] Ex 14:28 [p] Ex 14:22
15:20 [q] Nu 26:59 [r] Jdg 4:4 [s] Jdg 11:34; 1Sa 18:6; Ps 30:11; 150:4
15:21 [t] ver 1; Ex 14:27

called Marah.[a][a]) 24So the people grumbled[b] against Moses, saying,
"What are we to drink?"

25Then Moses cried out[c] to the LORD, and the LORD showed him
a piece of wood. He threw it into the water, and the water became
sweet.

There the LORD made a decree and a law for them, and there he
tested[d] them. 26He said, "If you listen carefully to the voice of the
LORD your God and do what is right in his eyes, if you pay attention to his commands and keep all his decrees,[e] I will not bring
on you any of the diseases[f] I brought on the Egyptians, for I am
the LORD, who heals[g] you."

27Then they came to Elim, where there were twelve springs and
seventy palm trees, and they camped[h] there near the water.

Chapter 16 Theme ______________________________

16 The whole Israelite community set out from Elim and came
to the Desert of Sin,[i] which is between Elim and Sinai, on
the fifteenth day of the second month after they had come out of
Egypt. 2In the desert the whole community grumbled[j] against
Moses and Aaron. 3The Israelites said to them, "If only we had
died by the LORD's hand in Egypt![k] There we sat around pots of
meat and ate all the food[l] we wanted, but you have brought us out
into this desert to starve this entire assembly to death."

4Then the LORD said to Moses, "I will rain down bread from
heaven[m] for you. The people are to go out each day and gather
enough for that day. In this way I will test them and see whether
they will follow my instructions. 5On the sixth day they are to
prepare what they bring in, and that is to be twice[n] as much as
they gather on the other days."

6So Moses and Aaron said to all the Israelites, "In the evening
you will know that it was the LORD who brought you out of
Egypt,[o] 7and in the morning you will see the glory[p] of the LORD,
because he has heard your grumbling[q] against him. Who are we,
that you should grumble against us?"[r] 8Moses also said, "You
will know that it was the LORD when he gives you meat to eat in
the evening and all the bread you want in the morning, because
he has heard your grumbling against him. Who are we? You are
not grumbling against us, but against the LORD."[s]

9Then Moses told Aaron, "Say to the entire Israelite community, 'Come before the LORD, for he has heard your grumbling.'"

10While Aaron was speaking to the whole Israelite community,
they looked toward the desert, and there was the glory[t] of the
LORD appearing in the cloud.[u]

15:23 [a] Nu 33:8
15:24 [b] Ex 14:12; 16:2
15:25 [c] Ex 14:10 [d] Jdg 3:4
15:26 [e] Dt 7:12 [f] Dt 28:27, 58-60 [g] Ex 23:25-26
15:27 [h] Nu 33:9
16:1 [i] Nu 33:11,12
16:2 [j] Ex 14:11; 15:24; 1Co 10:10
16:3 [k] Ex 17:3 [l] Nu 11:4,34
16:4 [m] Dt 8:3; Jn 6:31*
16:5 [n] ver 22
16:6 [o] Ex 6:6
16:7 [p] ver 10; Isa 35:2; 40:5 [q] ver 12; Nu 14:2,27,28 [r] Nu 16:11
16:8 [s] 1Sa 8:7; Ro 13:2
16:10 [t] ver 7; Nu 16:19 [u] Ex 13:21; 1Ki 8:10

[a]23 *Marah* means *bitter.*

11The LORD said to Moses, 12"I have heard the grumbling[a] of the
Israelites. Tell them, 'At twilight you will eat meat, and in the
morning you will be filled with bread. Then you will know that I
am the LORD your God.'"
13That evening quail[b] came and covered the camp, and in the
morning there was a layer of dew[c] around the camp. 14When the
dew was gone, thin flakes like frost[d] on the ground appeared on
the desert floor. 15When the Israelites saw it, they said to each
other, "What is it?" For they did not know what it was.
Moses said to them, "It is the bread[e] the LORD has given you to
eat. 16This is what the LORD has commanded: 'Each one is to
gather as much as he needs. Take an omer[a][f] for each person you
have in your tent.'"
17The Israelites did as they were told; some gathered much,
some little. 18And when they measured it by the omer, he who
gathered much did not have too much, and he who gathered little
did not have too little.[g] Each one gathered as much as he needed.
19Then Moses said to them, "No one is to keep any of it until
morning."[h]
20However, some of them paid no attention to Moses; they
kept part of it until morning, but it was full of maggots and
began to smell. So Moses was angry with them.
21Each morning everyone gathered as much as he needed, and
when the sun grew hot, it melted away. 22On the sixth day, they
gathered twice[i] as much—two omers[b] for each person—and the
leaders of the community[j] came and reported this to Moses.
23He said to them, "This is what the LORD commanded: 'Tomorrow is to be a day of rest, a holy Sabbath[k] to the LORD. So bake
what you want to bake and boil what you want to boil. Save
whatever is left and keep it until morning.'"
24So they saved it until morning, as Moses commanded, and it
did not stink or get maggots in it. 25"Eat it today," Moses said,
"because today is a Sabbath to the LORD. You will not find any of
it on the ground today. 26Six days you are to gather it, but on the
seventh day, the Sabbath,[l] there will not be any."
27Nevertheless, some of the people went out on the seventh
day to gather it, but they found none. 28Then the LORD said to
Moses, "How long will you[c] refuse to keep my commands[m] and
my instructions? 29Bear in mind that the LORD has given you the
Sabbath; that is why on the sixth day he gives you bread for two
days. Everyone is to stay where he is on the seventh day; no one
is to go out." 30So the people rested on the seventh day.

a*16* That is, probably about 2 quarts (about 2 liters); also in verses 18, 32, 33 and 36
b*22* That is, probably about 4 quarts (about 4.5 liters) c*28* The Hebrew is plural.

16:12 *a* ver 7
16:13 *b* Nu 11:31; Ps 78:27-28; 105:40 *c* Nu 11:9
16:14 *d* ver 31; Nu 11:7-9; Ps 105:40
16:15 *e* ver 4; Jn 6:31
16:16 *f* ver 32,36
16:18 *g* 2Co 8:15*
16:19 *h* ver 23; Ex 12:10; 23:18
16:22 *i* ver 5 *j* Ex 34:31
16:23 *k* Ge 2:3; Ex 20:8; 23:12; Lev 23:3
16:26 *l* Ex 20:9-10
16:28 *m* 2Ki 17:14; Ps 78:10; 106:13

31 The people of Israel called the bread manna.[a][a] It was white
like coriander seed and tasted like wafers made with honey.
32 Moses said, "This is what the LORD has commanded: 'Take an
omer of manna and keep it for the generations to come, so they
can see the bread I gave you to eat in the desert when I brought
you out of Egypt.'"
33 So Moses said to Aaron, "Take a jar and put an omer of
manna[b] in it. Then place it before the LORD to be kept for the
generations to come."
34 As the LORD commanded Moses, Aaron put the manna in
front of the Testimony,[c] that it might be kept. 35 The Israelites ate
manna[d] forty years,[e] until they came to a land that was settled;
they ate manna until they reached the border of Canaan.[f]
36 (An omer is one tenth of an ephah.)

Chapter 17 Theme ______________________

17

The whole Israelite community set out from the Desert of
Sin,[g] traveling from place to place as the LORD commanded.
They camped at Rephidim, but there was no water[h] for the people
to drink. 2 So they quarreled with Moses and said, "Give us
water[i] to drink."
Moses replied, "Why do you quarrel with me? Why do you put
the LORD to the test?"[j]
3 But the people were thirsty for water there, and they grumbled[k] against Moses. They said, "Why did you bring us up out of
Egypt to make us and our children and livestock die of thirst?"
4 Then Moses cried out to the LORD, "What am I to do with
these people? They are almost ready to stone[l] me."
5 The LORD answered Moses, "Walk on ahead of the people.
Take with you some of the elders of Israel and take in your hand
the staff with which you struck the Nile,[m] and go. 6 I will stand
there before you by the rock at Horeb. Strike the rock, and water[n]
will come out of it for the people to drink." So Moses did this in
the sight of the elders of Israel. 7 And he called the place Massah[b]
and Meribah[c][o] because the Israelites quarreled and because they
tested the LORD saying, "Is the LORD among us or not?"
8 The Amalekites[p] came and attacked the Israelites at Rephidim.
9 Moses said to Joshua, "Choose some of our men and go out to
fight the Amalekites. Tomorrow I will stand on top of the hill
with the staff[q] of God in my hands."
10 So Joshua fought the Amalekites as Moses had ordered, and
Moses, Aaron and Hur[r] went to the top of the hill. 11 As long as

16:31 [a] Nu 11:7-9
16:33 [b] Heb 9:4
16:34 [c] Ex 25:16, 21,22; 40:20; Nu 17:4,10
16:35 [d] Jn 6:31,49 [e] Ne 9:21 [f] Jos 5:12
17:1 [g] Ex 16:1 [h] Nu 33:14
17:2 [i] Nu 20:2 [j] Dt 6:16; Ps 78:18,41; 1Co 10:9
17:3 [k] Ex 15:24; 16:2-3
17:4 [l] Nu 14:10; 1Sa 30:6
17:5 [m] Ex 7:20
17:6 [n] Nu 20:11; Ps 114:8; 1Co 10:4
17:7 [o] Nu 20:13,24; Ps 81:7
17:8 [p] Ge 36:12; Dt 25:17-19
17:9 [q] Ex 4:17
17:10 [r] Ex 24:14

[a] 31 *Manna* means *What is it?* (see verse 15). [b] 7 *Massah* means *testing.* [c] 7 *Meribah* means *quarreling.*

Moses held up his hands, the Israelites were winning,[a] but whenever he lowered his hands, the Amalekites were winning. 12When Moses' hands grew tired, they took a stone and put it under him and he sat on it. Aaron and Hur held his hands up—one on one side, one on the other—so that his hands remained steady till sunset. 13So Joshua overcame the Amalekite army with the sword.

14Then the LORD said to Moses, "Write[b] this on a scroll as something to be remembered and make sure that Joshua hears it, because I will completely blot out the memory of Amalek[c] from under heaven."

15Moses built an altar and called it The LORD is my Banner. 16He said, "For hands were lifted up to the throne of the LORD. The[a] LORD will be at war against the Amalekites from generation to generation."

Chapter 18 Theme ______________________________

18 Now Jethro, the priest of Midian[d] and father-in-law of Moses, heard of everything God had done for Moses and for his people Israel, and how the LORD had brought Israel out of Egypt.

2After Moses had sent away his wife Zipporah,[e] his father-in-law Jethro received her 3and her two sons.[f] One son was named Gershom,[b] for Moses said, "I have become an alien in a foreign land";[g] 4and the other was named Eliezer,[c][h] for he said, "My father's God was my helper; he saved me from the sword of Pharaoh."

5Jethro, Moses' father-in-law, together with Moses' sons and wife, came to him in the desert, where he was camped near the mountain[i] of God. 6Jethro had sent word to him, "I, your father-in-law Jethro, am coming to you with your wife and her two sons."

7So Moses went out to meet his father-in-law and bowed down[j] and kissed[k] him. They greeted each other and then went into the tent. 8Moses told his father-in-law about everything the LORD had done to Pharaoh and the Egyptians for Israel's sake and about all the hardships they had met along the way and how the LORD had saved[l] them.

9Jethro was delighted to hear about all the good things the LORD had done for Israel in rescuing them from the hand of the Egyptians. 10He said, "Praise be to the LORD,[m] who rescued you from the hand of the Egyptians and of Pharaoh, and who rescued the people from the hand of the Egyptians. 11Now I know that the LORD is greater than all other gods,[n] for he did this to

a16 Or "*Because a hand was against the throne of the LORD, the* b3 *Gershom* sounds like the Hebrew for *an alien there.* c4 *Eliezer* means *my God is helper.*

17:11
a Jas 5:16

17:14
b Ex 24:4; 34:27; Nu 33:2
c 1Sa 15:3; 30:17-18

18:1
d Ex 2:16; 3:1

18:2
e Ex 2:21; 4:25

18:3
f Ex 4:20; Ac 7:29
g Ex 2:22

18:4
h 1Ch 23:15

18:5
i Ex 3:1

18:7
j Ge 43:28
k Ge 29:13

18:8
l Ex 15:6,16; Ps 81:7

18:10
m Ge 14:20; Ps 68:19-20

18:11
n Ex 12:12; 15:11; 2Ch 2:5

those who had treated Israel arrogantly."[a] [12]Then Jethro, Moses'
father-in-law, brought a burnt offering and other sacrifices to
God, and Aaron came with all the elders of Israel to eat bread
with Moses' father-in-law in the presence[b] of God.

[13]The next day Moses took his seat to serve as judge for the
people, and they stood around him from morning till evening.
[14]When his father-in-law saw all that Moses was doing for the
people, he said, "What is this you are doing for the people? Why
do you alone sit as judge, while all these people stand around you
from morning till evening?"

[15]Moses answered him, "Because the people come to me to
seek God's will.[c] [16]Whenever they have a dispute, it is brought to
me, and I decide between the parties and inform them of God's
decrees and laws."[d]

[17]Moses' father-in-law replied, "What you are doing is not
good. [18]You and these people who come to you will only wear
yourselves out. The work is too heavy for you; you cannot handle
it alone.[e] [19]Listen now to me and I will give you some advice, and
may God be with you.[f] You must be the people's representative
before God and bring their disputes[g] to him. [20]Teach them the
decrees and laws,[h] and show them the way to live[i] and the duties
they are to perform.[j] [21]But select capable men[k] from all the people—men who fear God, trustworthy men who hate dishonest
gain[l]—and appoint them as officials[m] over thousands, hundreds,
fifties and tens. [22]Have them serve as judges for the people at all
times, but have them bring every difficult case[n] to you; the simple cases they can decide themselves. That will make your load
lighter, because they will share[o] it with you. [23]If you do this and
God so commands, you will be able to stand the strain, and all
these people will go home satisfied."

[24]Moses listened to his father-in-law and did everything he
said. [25]He chose capable men from all Israel and made them
leaders of the people, officials over thousands, hundreds, fifties
and tens.[p] [26]They served as judges for the people at all times. The
difficult cases they brought to Moses, but the simple ones they
decided themselves.[q]

[27]Then Moses sent his father-in-law on his way, and Jethro
returned to his own country.[r]

Chapter 19 Theme ______________________

19 In the third month after the Israelites left Egypt—on the
very day—they came to the Desert of Sinai. [2]After they
set out from Rephidim,[s] they entered the Desert of Sinai, and
Israel camped there in the desert in front of the mountain.[t]

18:11 [a] Lk 1:51
18:12 [b] Dt 12:7
18:15 [c] Nu 9:6,8; Dt 17:8-13
18:16 [d] Lev 24:12
18:18 [e] Nu 11:11, 14,17
18:19 [f] Ex 3:12 [g] Nu 27:5
18:20 [h] Dt 5:1 [i] Ps 143:8 [j] Dt 1:18
18:21 [k] Ac 6:3 [l] Dt 16:19; Ps 15:5; Eze 18:8 [m] Dt 1:13,15; 2Ch 19:5-10
18:22 [n] Dt 1:17-18 [o] Nu 11:17
18:25 [p] Dt 1:13-15
18:26 [q] ver 22
18:27 [r] Nu 10:29-30
19:2 [s] Ex 17:1 [t] Ex 3:1

3Then Moses went up to God, and the LORD called[a] to him
from the mountain and said, "This is what you are to say to the
house of Jacob and what you are to tell the people of Israel: 4'You
yourselves have seen what I did to Egypt,[b] and how I carried you
on eagles' wings[c] and brought you to myself. 5Now if you obey
me fully[d] and keep my covenant,[e] then out of all nations you will
be my treasured possession.[f] Although the whole earth[g] is mine,
6you[a] will be for me a kingdom of priests[h] and a holy nation.'[i]
These are the words you are to speak to the Israelites."

7So Moses went back and summoned the elders of the people
and set before them all the words the LORD had commanded
him to speak. 8The people all responded together, "We will do
everything the LORD has said."[j] So Moses brought their answer
back to the LORD.

9The LORD said to Moses, "I am going to come to you in a
dense cloud,[k] so that the people will hear me speaking[l] with you
and will always put their trust in you." Then Moses told the
LORD what the people had said.

10And the LORD said to Moses, "Go to the people and consecrate[m] them today and tomorrow. Have them wash their clothes[n]
11and be ready by the third day,[o] because on that day the LORD
will come down on Mount Sinai in the sight of all the people.
12Put limits for the people around the mountain and tell them,
'Be careful that you do not go up the mountain or touch the foot
of it. Whoever touches the mountain shall surely be put to death.
13He shall surely be stoned[p] or shot with arrows; not a hand is to
be laid on him. Whether man or animal, he shall not be permitted to live.' Only when the ram's horn sounds a long blast may
they go up to the mountain."

14After Moses had gone down the mountain to the people, he
consecrated them, and they washed their clothes. 15Then he said
to the people, "Prepare yourselves for the third day. Abstain
from sexual relations."

16On the morning of the third day there was thunder and
lightning, with a thick cloud over the mountain, and a very loud
trumpet blast.[q] Everyone in the camp trembled.[r] 17Then Moses
led the people out of the camp to meet with God, and they stood
at the foot of the mountain. 18Mount Sinai was covered with
smoke,[s] because the LORD descended on it in fire.[t] The smoke
billowed up from it like smoke from a furnace,[u] the whole
mountain[b] trembled[v] violently, 19and the sound of the trumpet
grew louder and louder. Then Moses spoke and the voice[w] of
God answered[x] him.[c]

a5,6 Or *possession, for the whole earth is mine.* 6*You* b18 Most Hebrew manuscripts; a few Hebrew manuscripts and Septuagint *all the people* c19 Or *and God answered him with thunder*

19:3 a Ex 3:4; Ac 7:38
19:4 b Dt 29:2 c Isa 63:9
19:5 d Ex 15:26 e Dt 5:2 f Dt 14:2; Ps 135:4 g Ex 9:29; Dt 10:14
19:6 h 1Pe 2:5 i Dt 7:6; 26:19; Isa 62:12
19:8 j Ex 24:3,7; Dt 5:27
19:9 k ver 16; Ex 24:15-16 l Dt 4:12,36
19:10 m Lev 11:44; Heb 10:22 n Ge 35:2
19:11 o ver 16
19:13 p Heb 12:20*
19:16 q Heb 12:18-19; Rev 4:1 r Heb 12:21
19:18 s Ps 104:32 t Ex 3:2; 24:17; Dt 4:11; 2Ch 7:1; Ps 18:8; Heb 12:18 u Ge 19:28 v Jdg 5:5; Ps 68:8; Jer 4:24
19:19 w Ne 9:13 x Ps 81:7

20 The LORD descended to the top of Mount Sinai and called
Moses to the top of the mountain. So Moses went up 21 and the
LORD said to him, "Go down and warn the people so they do not
force their way through to see[a] the LORD and many of them perish. 22 Even the priests, who approach[b] the LORD, must consecrate
themselves, or the LORD will break out against them."[c]
23 Moses said to the LORD, "The people cannot come up Mount
Sinai, because you yourself warned us, 'Put limits[d] around the
mountain and set it apart as holy.'"
24 The LORD replied, "Go down and bring Aaron[e] up with you.
But the priests and the people must not force their way through
to come up to the LORD, or he will break out against them."
25 So Moses went down to the people and told them.

Chapter 20 Theme ______________________________

20 And God spoke all these words:

2 "I am the LORD your God, who brought you out of Egypt,
out of the land of slavery.[f]
3 "You shall have no other gods before[a] me.[g]
4 "You shall not make for yourself an idol[h] in the form of anything in heaven above or on the earth beneath or in the
waters below. 5 You shall not bow down to them or worship[i] them; for I, the LORD your God, am a jealous God,[j]
punishing the children for the sin of the fathers to the
third and fourth generation[k] of those who hate me, 6 but
showing love to a thousand[l] ⌞generations⌟ of those who
love me and keep my commandments.
7 "You shall not misuse the name of the LORD your God, for
the LORD will not hold anyone guiltless who misuses his
name.[m]
8 "Remember the Sabbath[n] day by keeping it holy. 9 Six days
you shall labor and do all your work,[o] 10 but the seventh
day is a Sabbath to the LORD your God. On it you shall
not do any work, neither you, nor your son or daughter,
nor your manservant or maidservant, nor your animals, nor the alien within your gates. 11 For in six days
the LORD made the heavens and the earth, the sea, and
all that is in them, but he rested[p] on the seventh day.
Therefore the LORD blessed the Sabbath day and made
it holy.
12 "Honor your father and your mother,[q] so that you may live
long in the land the LORD your God is giving you.

a3 Or *besides*

19:21 [a] Ex 3:5; 1Sa 6:19
19:22 [b] Lev 10:3 [c] 2Sa 6:7
19:23 [d] ver 12
19:24 [e] Ex 24:1,9
20:2 [f] Ex 13:3
20:3 [g] Dt 6:14; Jer 35:15
20:4 [h] Lev 26:1; Dt 4:15-19,23; 27:15
20:5 [i] Isa 44:15, 17,19 [j] Ex 34:14; Dt 4:24 [k] Nu 14:18; Jer 32:18
20:6 [l] Dt 7:9
20:7 [m] Lev 19:12; Mt 5:33
20:8 [n] Ex 31:13-16; Lev 26:2
20:9 [o] Ex 34:21; Lk 13:14
20:11 [p] Ge 2:2
20:12 [q] Mt 15:4*; Mk 7:10*; Eph 6:2

13“You shall not murder.[a]
14“You shall not commit adultery.[b]
15“You shall not steal.[c]
16“You shall not give false testimony against your neighbor.[d]
17“You shall not covet[e] your neighbor’s house. You shall not
covet your neighbor’s wife, or his manservant or maidservant, his ox or donkey, or anything that belongs to
your neighbor.”

18When the people saw the thunder and lightning and heard the
trumpet[f] and saw the mountain in smoke, they trembled with
fear. They stayed at a distance 19and said to Moses, “Speak to us
yourself and we will listen. But do not have God speak to us or we
will die.”[g]
20Moses said to the people, “Do not be afraid. God has come to
test you, so that the fear[h] of God will be with you to keep you from
sinning.”[i]
21The people remained at a distance, while Moses approached
the thick darkness[j] where God was.
22Then the LORD said to Moses, “Tell the Israelites this: ‘You
have seen for yourselves that I have spoken to you from heaven:[k]
23Do not make any gods to be alongside me;[l] do not make for
yourselves gods of silver or gods of gold.[m]
24“‘Make an altar of earth for me and sacrifice on it your burnt
offerings and fellowship offerings,[a] your sheep and goats and
your cattle. Wherever I cause my name[n] to be honored, I will
come to you and bless[o] you. 25If you make an altar of stones for
me, do not build it with dressed stones, for you will defile it if
you use a tool[p] on it. 26And do not go up to my altar on steps, lest
your nakedness be exposed on it.’

Chapter 21 Theme ________________________

21 “These are the laws[q] you are to set before them:

2“If you buy a Hebrew servant, he is to serve you for six years.
But in the seventh year, he shall go free,[r] without paying anything.
3If he comes alone, he is to go free alone; but if he has a wife when
he comes, she is to go with him. 4If his master gives him a wife
and she bears him sons or daughters, the woman and her children shall belong to her master, and only the man shall go free.
5“But if the servant declares, ‘I love my master and my wife
and children and do not want to go free,’[s] 6then his master must
take him before the judges.[b][t] He shall take him to the door or

a24 Traditionally *peace offerings* b6 Or *before God*

20:13 *a* Mt 5:21*; Ro 13:9*
20:14 *b* Mt 19:18*
20:15 *c* Lev 19:11,13; Mt 19:18*
20:16 *d* Ex 23:1,7; Mt 19:18*
20:17 *e* Ro 7:7*; 13:9*; Eph 5:3
20:18 *f* Ex 19:16-19; Heb 12:18-19
20:19 *g* Dt 5:5,23-27; Gal 3:19
20:20 *h* Dt 4:10; Isa 8:13 *i* Pr 16:6
20:21 *j* Dt 5:22
20:22 *k* Ne 9:13
20:23 *l* ver 3 *m* Ex 32:4, 8,31
20:24 *n* Dt 12:5; 16:6,11; 2Ch 6:6 *o* Ge 12:2
20:25 *p* Dt 27:5-6
21:1 *q* Dt 4:14
21:2 *r* Jer 34:8,14
21:5 *s* Dt 15:16
21:6 *t* Ex 22:8-9

the doorpost and pierce his ear with an awl. Then he will be his
servant for life.[a]
7“If a man sells his daughter as a servant, she is not to go free
as menservants do. 8If she does not please the master who has
selected her for himself,[a] he must let her be redeemed. He has
no right to sell her to foreigners, because he has broken faith
with her. 9If he selects her for his son, he must grant her the
rights of a daughter. 10If he marries another woman, he must not
deprive the first one of her food, clothing and marital rights.[b]
11If he does not provide her with these three things, she is to go
free, without any payment of money.
12“Anyone who strikes a man and kills him shall surely be put
to death.[c] 13However, if he does not do it intentionally, but God
lets it happen, he is to flee to a place[d] I will designate. 14But if a
man schemes and kills another man deliberately,[e] take him away
from my altar and put him to death.[f]
15“Anyone who attacks[b] his father or his mother must be put
to death.
16“Anyone who kidnaps another and either sells[g] him or still
has him when he is caught must be put to death.[h]
17“Anyone who curses his father or mother must be put to
death.[i]
18“If men quarrel and one hits the other with a stone or with his
fist[c] and he does not die but is confined to bed, 19the one who
struck the blow will not be held responsible if the other gets up
and walks around outside with his staff; however, he must pay the
injured man for the loss of his time and see that he is completely
healed.
20“If a man beats his male or female slave with a rod and the
slave dies as a direct result, he must be punished, 21but he is not
to be punished if the slave gets up after a day or two, since the
slave is his property.[j]
22“If men who are fighting hit a pregnant woman and she gives
birth prematurely[d] but there is no serious injury, the offender
must be fined whatever the woman’s husband demands[k] and the
court allows. 23But if there is serious injury, you are to take life
for life,[l] 24eye for eye, tooth for tooth,[m] hand for hand, foot for
foot, 25burn for burn, wound for wound, bruise for bruise.
26“If a man hits a manservant or maidservant in the eye and
destroys it, he must let the servant go free to compensate for the
eye. 27And if he knocks out the tooth of a manservant or maidservant, he must let the servant go free to compensate for the tooth.
28“If a bull gores a man or a woman to death, the bull must be
stoned to death,[n] and its meat must not be eaten. But the owner

a8 Or *master so that he does not choose her* b15 Or *kills* c18 Or *with a tool* d22 Or *she has a miscarriage*

21:6 *a* Ne 5:5
21:10 *b* 1Co 7:3-5
21:12 *c* Ge 9:6; Mt 26:52
21:13 *d* Nu 35:10-34; Dt 19:2-13; Jos 20:9; 1Sa 24:4, 10,18
21:14 *e* Heb 10:26 *f* Dt 19:11-12; 1Ki 2:28-34
21:16 *g* Ge 37:28 *h* Ex 22:4; Dt 24:7
21:17 *i* Lev 20:9-10; Mt 15:4*; Mk 7:10*
21:21 *j* Lev 25:44-46
21:22 *k* ver 30; Dt 22:18-19
21:23 *l* Lev 24:19; Dt 19:21
21:24 *m* Mt 5:38*
21:28 *n* ver 32; Ge 9:5

of the bull will not be held responsible. [29]If, however, the bull has had the habit of goring and the owner has been warned but has not kept it penned up and it kills a man or woman, the bull must be stoned and the owner also must be put to death. [30]However, if payment is demanded of him, he may redeem his life by paying whatever is demanded.[a] [31]This law also applies if the bull gores a son or daughter. [32]If the bull gores a male or female slave, the owner must pay thirty shekels[a][b] of silver to the master of the slave, and the bull must be stoned.

[33]"If a man uncovers a pit or digs one and fails to cover it and an ox or a donkey falls into it, [34]the owner of the pit must pay for the loss; he must pay its owner, and the dead animal will be his.

[35]"If a man's bull injures the bull of another and it dies, they are to sell the live one and divide both the money and the dead animal equally. [36]However, if it was known that the bull had the habit of goring, yet the owner did not keep it penned up, the owner must pay, animal for animal, and the dead animal will be his.

Chapter 22 Theme ______________________________

22

"If a man steals an ox or a sheep and slaughters it or sells it, he must pay back[c] five head of cattle for the ox and four sheep for the sheep.

[2]"If a thief is caught breaking in[d] and is struck so that he dies, the defender is not guilty of bloodshed;[e] [3]but if it happens[b] after sunrise, he is guilty of bloodshed.

"A thief must certainly make restitution, but if he has nothing, he must be sold[f] to pay for his theft.

[4]"If the stolen animal is found alive in his possession—whether ox or donkey or sheep—he must pay back double.[g]

[5]"If a man grazes his livestock in a field or vineyard and lets them stray and they graze in another man's field, he must make restitution from the best of his own field or vineyard.

[6]"If a fire breaks out and spreads into thornbushes so that it burns shocks of grain or standing grain or the whole field, the one who started the fire must make restitution.

[7]"If a man gives his neighbor silver or goods for safekeeping and they are stolen from the neighbor's house, the thief, if he is caught, must pay back double.[h] [8]But if the thief is not found, the owner of the house must appear before the judges[c][i] to determine whether he has laid his hands on the other man's property. [9]In all cases of illegal possession of an ox, a donkey, a sheep, a garment, or any other lost property about which somebody says, 'This is mine,' both parties are to bring their cases before the

21:30 [a] ver 22; Nu 35:31

21:32 [b] Zec 11:12-13; Mt 26:15; 27:3,9

22:1 [c] 2Sa 12:6; Pr 6:31; Lk 19:8

22:2 [d] Mt 6:19-20; 24:43 [e] Nu 35:27

22:3 [f] Ex 21:2; Mt 18:25

22:4 [g] Ge 43:12

22:7 [h] ver 4

22:8 [i] Ex 21:6; Dt 17:8-9; 19:17

a32 That is, about 12 ounces (about 0.3 kilogram) b3 Or *if he strikes him* c8 Or *before God*; also in verse 9

judges.[a] The one whom the judges declare[a] guilty must pay back
double to his neighbor.
10 “If a man gives a donkey, an ox, a sheep or any other animal
to his neighbor for safekeeping and it dies or is injured or is taken
away while no one is looking, 11 the issue between them will be
settled by the taking of an oath[b] before the LORD that the neighbor did not lay hands on the other person’s property. The owner
is to accept this, and no restitution is required. 12 But if the animal
was stolen from the neighbor, he must make restitution to the
owner. 13 If it was torn to pieces by a wild animal, he shall bring in
the remains as evidence and he will not be required to pay for the
torn animal.[c]
14 “If a man borrows an animal from his neighbor and it is
injured or dies while the owner is not present, he must make
restitution. 15 But if the owner is with the animal, the borrower
will not have to pay. If the animal was hired, the money paid for
the hire covers the loss.
16 “If a man seduces a virgin[d] who is not pledged to be married
and sleeps with her, he must pay the bride-price, and she shall
be his wife. 17 If her father absolutely refuses to give her to him,
he must still pay the bride-price for virgins.
18 “Do not allow a sorceress[e] to live.
19 “Anyone who has sexual relations with an animal[f] must be
put to death.
20 “Whoever sacrifices to any god other than the LORD must be
destroyed.[b][g]
21 “Do not mistreat an alien[h] or oppress him, for you were aliens[i]
in Egypt.
22 “Do not take advantage of a widow or an orphan.[j] 23 If you do
and they cry out[k] to me, I will certainly hear their cry.[l] 24 My
anger will be aroused, and I will kill you with the sword; your
wives will become widows and your children fatherless.[m]
25 “If you lend money to one of my people among you who is
needy, do not be like a moneylender; charge him no interest.[c][n]
26 If you take your neighbor’s cloak as a pledge,[o] return it to him
by sunset, 27 because his cloak is the only covering he has for his
body. What else will he sleep in? When he cries out to me, I will
hear, for I am compassionate.[p]
28 “Do not blaspheme God[d][q] or curse the ruler of your people.[r]
29 “Do not hold back offerings[s] from your granaries or your vats.[e]
“You must give me the firstborn of your sons.[t] 30 Do the same
with your cattle and your sheep.[u] Let them stay with their mothers
for seven days, but give them to me on the eighth day.[v]

22:9 [a] ver 28; Dt 25:1
22:11 [b] Heb 6:16
22:13 [c] Ge 31:39
22:16 [d] Dt 22:28
22:18 [e] Lev 20:27; Dt 18:11; 1Sa 28:3
22:19 [f] Lev 18:23; Dt 27:21
22:20 [g] Dt 17:2-5
22:21 [h] Lev 19:33 [i] Dt 10:19
22:22 [j] Dt 24:6, 10,12,17
22:23 [k] Lk 18:7 [l] Dt 15:9; Ps 18:6
22:24 [m] Ps 69:24; 109:9
22:25 [n] Lev 25:35-37; Dt 23:20; Ps 15:5
22:26 [o] Dt 24:6
22:27 [p] Ex 34:6
22:28 [q] Lev 24:11,16 [r] Ecc 10:20; Ac 23:5*
22:29 [s] Ex 23:15,16,19 [t] Ex 13:2
22:30 [u] Ex 13:12; Dt 15:19 [v] Lev 22:27

[a] 9 Or *whom God declares* [b] 20 The Hebrew term refers to the irrevocable giving over of things or persons to the LORD, often by totally destroying them. [c] 25 Or *excessive interest* [d] 28 Or *Do not revile the judges* [e] 29 The meaning of the Hebrew for this phrase is uncertain.

31"You are to be my holy people.[a] So do not eat the meat of an animal torn by wild beasts;[b] throw it to the dogs.

Chapter 23 Theme ______________________

23

"Do not spread false reports.[c] Do not help a wicked man by being a malicious witness.[d]

2"Do not follow the crowd in doing wrong. When you give testimony in a lawsuit, do not pervert justice[e] by siding with the crowd, 3and do not show favoritism to a poor man in his lawsuit.

4"If you come across your enemy's ox or donkey wandering off, be sure to take it back to him.[f] 5If you see the donkey[g] of someone who hates you fallen down under its load, do not leave it there; be sure you help him with it.

6"Do not deny justice[h] to your poor people in their lawsuits. 7Have nothing to do with a false charge[i] and do not put an innocent or honest person to death, for I will not acquit the guilty.

8"Do not accept a bribe,[j] for a bribe blinds those who see and twists the words of the righteous.

9"Do not oppress an alien;[k] you yourselves know how it feels to be aliens, because you were aliens in Egypt.

10"For six years you are to sow your fields and harvest the crops, 11but during the seventh year let the land lie unplowed and unused. Then the poor among your people may get food from it, and the wild animals may eat what they leave. Do the same with your vineyard and your olive grove.

12"Six days do your work,[l] but on the seventh day do not work, so that your ox and your donkey may rest and the slave born in your household, and the alien as well, may be refreshed.

13"Be careful[m] to do everything I have said to you. Do not invoke the names of other gods; do not let them be heard on your lips.

14"Three times[n] a year you are to celebrate a festival to me.

15"Celebrate the Feast of Unleavened Bread;[o] for seven days eat bread made without yeast, as I commanded you. Do this at the appointed time in the month of Abib, for in that month you came out of Egypt.

"No one is to appear before me empty-handed.[p]

16"Celebrate the Feast of Harvest with the firstfruits[q] of the crops you sow in your field.

"Celebrate the Feast of Ingathering at the end of the year, when you gather in your crops from the field.[r]

17"Three times[s] a year all the men are to appear before the Sovereign LORD.

18"Do not offer the blood of a sacrifice to me along with anything containing yeast.[t]

22:31
a Lev 19:2
b Eze 4:14

23:1
c Ex 20:16; Ps 101:5
d Ps 35:11; Ac 6:11

23:2
e Dt 16:19

23:4
f Dt 22:1-3

23:5
g Dt 22:4

23:6
h ver 2

23:7
i Eph 4:25

23:8
j Dt 10:17; 16:19; Pr 15:27

23:9
k Ex 22:21

23:12
l Ex 20:9

23:13
m 1Ti 4:16

23:14
n Ex 34:23,24

23:15
o Ex 12:17

23:15
p Ex 34:20

23:16
q Ex 34:22
r Dt 16:13

23:17
s Dt 16:16

23:18
t Ex 34:25

“The fat of my festival offerings must not be kept until morning.[a]
19“Bring the best of the firstfruits[b] of your soil to the house of
the LORD your God.
“Do not cook a young goat in its mother’s milk.[c]
20“See, I am sending an angel[d] ahead of you to guard you along
the way and to bring you to the place I have prepared.[e] 21Pay
attention to him and listen[f] to what he says. Do not rebel against
him; he will not forgive your rebellion,[g] since my Name is in
him. 22If you listen carefully to what he says and do all that I say,
I will be an enemy[h] to your enemies and will oppose those who
oppose you. 23My angel will go ahead of you and bring you into
the land of the Amorites, Hittites, Perizzites, Canaanites, Hivites
and Jebusites,[i] and I will wipe them out. 24Do not bow down
before their gods or worship[j] them or follow their practices.[k]
You must demolish[l] them and break their sacred stones to
pieces. 25Worship the LORD your God,[m] and his blessing[n] will be
on your food and water. I will take away sickness[o] from among
you, 26and none will miscarry or be barren[p] in your land. I will
give you a full life span.[q]
27“I will send my terror[r] ahead of you and throw into confusion[s] every nation you encounter. I will make all your enemies
turn their backs and run. 28I will send the hornet[t] ahead of you
to drive the Hivites, Canaanites and Hittites out of your way.
29But I will not drive them out in a single year, because the land
would become desolate and the wild animals[u] too numerous for
you. 30Little by little I will drive them out before you, until you
have increased enough to take possession of the land.
31“I will establish your borders from the Red Sea[a] to the Sea of
the Philistines,[b] and from the desert to the River.[c][v] I will hand
over to you the people who live in the land and you will drive
them out[w] before you. 32Do not make a covenant[x] with them or
with their gods. 33Do not let them live in your land, or they will
cause you to sin against me, because the worship of their gods
will certainly be a snare[y] to you.”

Chapter 24 Theme ______________________________

24 Then he said to Moses, “Come up to the LORD, you and
Aaron, Nadab and Abihu,[z] and seventy of the elders[a] of
Israel. You are to worship at a distance, 2but Moses alone is to
approach the LORD; the others must not come near. And the
people may not come up with him.”
3When Moses went and told the people all the LORD’s words
and laws, they responded with one voice, “Everything the LORD

23:18 [a] Dt 16:4
23:19 [b] Ex 22:29; Dt 26:2,10 [c] Dt 14:21
23:20 [d] Ex 14:19; 32:34 [e] Ex 15:17
23:21 [f] Nu 14:11; Dt 18:19 [g] Ps 78:8,40,56
23:22 [h] Ge 12:3; Dt 30:7
23:23 [i] ver 20; Jos 24:8,11
23:24 [j] Ex 20:5 [k] Dt 12:30-31 [l] Ex 34:13; Nu 33:52
23:25 [m] Dt 6:13; Mt 4:10 [n] Dt 7:12-15; 28:1-14 [o] Ex 15:26
23:26 [p] Dt 7:14; Mal 3:11 [q] Job 5:26
23:27 [r] Ex 15:14; Dt 2:25 [s] Dt 7:23
23:28 [t] Dt 7:20; Jos 24:12
23:29 [u] Dt 7:22
23:31 [v] Ge 15:18 [w] Jos 21:44; 24:12,18
23:32 [x] Ex 34:12; Dt 7:2
23:33 [y] Dt 7:16; Ps 106:36
24:1 [z] Ex 6:23; Lev 10:1-2 [a] Nu 11:16

a*31* Hebrew *Yam Suph*; that is, Sea of Reeds b*31* That is, the Mediterranean c*31* That is, the Euphrates

has said we will do."[a] 4Moses then wrote[b] down everything the
LORD had said.
He got up early the next morning and built an altar at the foot
of the mountain and set up twelve stone pillars[c] representing the
twelve tribes of Israel. 5Then he sent young Israelite men, and
they offered burnt offerings and sacrificed young bulls as fellowship offerings[a] to the LORD. 6Moses took half of the blood[d] and
put it in bowls, and the other half he sprinkled on the altar.
7Then he took the Book of the Covenant[e] and read it to the people. They responded, "We will do everything the LORD has said;
we will obey."
8Moses then took the blood, sprinkled it on the people and said,
"This is the blood of the covenant[f] that the LORD has made with
you in accordance with all these words."
9Moses and Aaron, Nadab and Abihu, and the seventy elders[g]
of Israel went up 10and saw[h] the God of Israel. Under his feet was
something like a pavement made of sapphire,[b][i] clear as the sky[j]
itself. 11But God did not raise his hand against these leaders of
the Israelites; they saw[k] God, and they ate and drank.
12The LORD said to Moses, "Come up to me on the mountain
and stay here, and I will give you the tablets of stone,[l] with the
law and commands I have written for their instruction."
13Then Moses set out with Joshua[m] his aide, and Moses went
up on the mountain[n] of God. 14He said to the elders, "Wait here
for us until we come back to you. Aaron and Hur are with you,
and anyone involved in a dispute can go to them."
15When Moses went up on the mountain, the cloud[o] covered it,
16and the glory[p] of the LORD settled on Mount Sinai. For six days
the cloud covered the mountain, and on the seventh day the
LORD called to Moses from within the cloud.[q] 17To the Israelites
the glory of the LORD looked like a consuming fire[r] on top of the
mountain. 18Then Moses entered the cloud as he went on up the
mountain. And he stayed on the mountain forty[s] days and forty
nights.[t]

Chapter 25 Theme ____________________

25 The Lord said to Moses, 2"Tell the Israelites to bring me
an offering. You are to receive the offering for me from
each man whose heart prompts[u] him to give. 3These are the
offerings you are to receive from them: gold, silver and bronze;
4blue, purple and scarlet yarn and fine linen; goat hair; 5ram
skins dyed red and hides of sea cows[c]; acacia wood; 6olive oil[v]
for the light; spices for the anointing oil and for the fragrant

a5 Traditionally *peace offerings* b10 Or *lapis lazuli* c5 That is, dugongs

INSIGHT

Each piece of furniture in the tabernacle was a picture of the work of the Lord Jesus Christ. Think about how each portrays this.

24:3 a Ex 19:8; Dt 5:27
24:4 b Dt 31:9; c Ge 28:18
24:6 d Heb 9:18
24:7 e Heb 9:19
24:8 f Heb 9:20*; 1Pe 1:2
24:9 g ver 1
24:10 h Mt 17:2; Jn 1:18; 6:46; i Eze 1:26; j Rev 4:3
24:11 k Ge 32:30; Ex 19:21
24:12 l Ex 32:15-16
24:13 m Ex 17:9; n Ex 3:1
24:15 o Ex 19:9
24:16 p Ex 16:10; q Ps 99:7
24:17 r Ex 3:2; Dt 4:36; Heb 12:18,29
24:18 s Dt 9:9; t Ex 34:28
25:2 u Ex 35:21; 1Ch 29:5,7,9; Ezr 2:68; 2Co 8:11-12; 9:7
25:6 v Ex 27:20; 30:22-32

incense; [7]and onyx stones and other gems to be mounted on
the ephod[a] and breastpiece.[b]
[8]"Then have them make a sanctuary[c] for me, and I will dwell[d]
among them. [9]Make this tabernacle and all its furnishings
exactly like the pattern[e] I will show you.
[10]"Have them make a chest[f] of acacia wood—two and a half
cubits long, a cubit and a half wide, and a cubit and a half high.[a]
[11]Overlay it with pure gold, both inside and out, and make a
gold molding around it. [12]Cast four gold rings for it and fasten
them to its four feet, with two rings on one side and two rings on
the other. [13]Then make poles of acacia wood and overlay them
with gold. [14]Insert the poles into the rings on the sides of the
chest to carry it. [15]The poles are to remain in the rings of this
ark; they are not to be removed.[g] [16]Then put in the ark the Testimony,[h] which I will give you.
[17]"Make an atonement cover[b][i] of pure gold—two and a half
cubits long and a cubit and a half wide.[c] [18]And make two cherubim out of hammered gold at the ends of the cover. [19]Make one
cherub on one end and the second cherub on the other; make
the cherubim of one piece with the cover, at the two ends. [20]The
cherubim are to have their wings spread upward, overshadowing[j]
the cover with them. The cherubim are to face each other, looking toward the cover. [21]Place the cover on top of the ark[k] and put
in the ark the Testimony,[l] which I will give you. [22]There, above
the cover between the two cherubim[m] that are over the ark of the
Testimony, I will meet[n] with you and give you all my commands
for the Israelites.
[23]"Make a table[o] of acacia wood—two cubits long, a cubit
wide and a cubit and a half high.[d] [24]Overlay it with pure gold
and make a gold molding around it. [25]Also make around it a rim
a handbreadth[e] wide and put a gold molding on the rim. [26]Make
four gold rings for the table and fasten them to the four corners,
where the four legs are. [27]The rings are to be close to the rim to
hold the poles used in carrying the table. [28]Make the poles of
acacia wood, overlay them with gold and carry the table with
them. [29]And make its plates and dishes of pure gold, as well as
its pitchers and bowls for the pouring out of offerings.[p] [30]Put the
bread of the Presence[q] on this table to be before me at all times.
[31]"Make a lampstand[r] of pure gold and hammer it out, base
and shaft; its flowerlike cups, buds and blossoms shall be of one
piece with it. [32]Six branches are to extend from the sides of the

Ark of the Covenant (or Testimony)

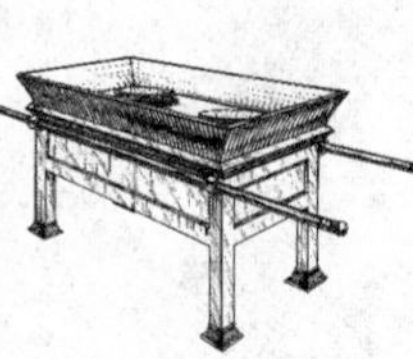

Table for Consecrated Bread

25:7 [a] Ex 28:4,6-14 [b] Ex 28:15-30
25:8 [c] Ex 36:1-5; Heb 9:1-2 [d] Ex 29:45; 1Ki 6:13; 2Co 6:16; Rev 21:3
25:9 [e] ver 40; Ac 7:44; Heb 8:5
25:10 [f] Dt 10:1-5; Heb 9:4
25:15 [g] 1Ki 8:8
25:16 [h] Dt 31:26; Heb 9:4
25:17 [i] Ro 3:25
25:20 [j] 1Ki 8:7; 1Ch 28:18; Heb 9:5
25:21 [k] Ex 26:34 [l] ver 16
25:22 [m] Nu 7:89; 1Sa 4:4; 2Sa 6:2; 2Ki 19:15; Ps 80:1; Isa 37:16 [n] Ex 29:42-43
25:23 [o] Heb 9:2
25:29 [p] Nu 4:7
25:30 [q] Lev 24:5-9
25:31 [r] 1Ki 7:49; Zec 4:2; Heb 9:2; Rev 1:12

[a] *10* That is, about 3 3/4 feet (about 1.1 meters) long and 2 1/4 feet (about 0.7 meter) wide and high [b] *17* Traditionally *a mercy seat* [c] *17* That is, about 3 3/4 feet (about 1.1 meters) long and 2 1/4 feet (about 0.7 meter) wide [d] *23* That is, about 3 feet (about 0.9 meter) long and 1 1/2 feet (about 0.5 meter) wide and 2 1/4 feet (about 0.7 meter) high [e] *25* That is, about 3 inches (about 8 centimeters)

Lampstand

lampstand—three on one side and three on the other. [33]Three
cups shaped like almond flowers with buds and blossoms are to
be on one branch, three on the next branch, and the same for all
six branches extending from the lampstand. [34]And on the lampstand there are to be four cups shaped like almond flowers with
buds and blossoms. [35]One bud shall be under the first pair of
branches extending from the lampstand, a second bud under the
second pair, and a third bud under the third pair—six branches
in all. [36]The buds and branches shall all be of one piece with the
lampstand, hammered out of pure gold.

[37]"Then make its seven lamps[a] and set them up on it so that
they light the space in front of it. [38]Its wick trimmers and trays are
to be of pure gold. [39]A talent[a] of pure gold is to be used for the
lampstand and all these accessories. [40]See that you make them
according to the pattern[b] shown you on the mountain.

Chapter 26 Theme ____________________

26 "Make the tabernacle with ten curtains of finely twisted
linen and blue, purple and scarlet yarn, with cherubim
worked into them by a skilled craftsman. [2]All the curtains are to
be the same size—twenty-eight cubits long and four cubits
wide.[b] [3]Join five of the curtains together, and do the same with
the other five. [4]Make loops of blue material along the edge of the
end curtain in one set, and do the same with the end curtain in
the other set. [5]Make fifty loops on one curtain and fifty loops on
the end curtain of the other set, with the loops opposite each
other. [6]Then make fifty gold clasps and use them to fasten the
curtains together so that the tabernacle is a unit.

[7]"Make curtains of goat hair for the tent over the tabernacle—
eleven altogether. [8]All eleven curtains are to be the same size—
thirty cubits long and four cubits wide.[c] [9]Join five of the curtains
together into one set and the other six into another set. Fold the
sixth curtain double at the front of the tent. [10]Make fifty loops
along the edge of the end curtain in one set and also along the
edge of the end curtain in the other set. [11]Then make fifty bronze
clasps and put them in the loops to fasten the tent together as a
unit. [12]As for the additional length of the tent curtains, the half
curtain that is left over is to hang down at the rear of the tabernacle. [13]The tent curtains will be a cubit[d] longer on both sides; what
is left will hang over the sides of the tabernacle so as to cover it.
[14]Make for the tent a covering of ram skins dyed red, and over
that a covering of hides of sea cows.[e] [c]

[a]39 That is, about 75 pounds (about 34 kilograms) [b]2 That is, about 42 feet (about 12.5 meters) long and 6 feet (about 1.8 meters) wide [c]8 That is, about 45 feet (about 13.5 meters) long and 6 feet (about 1.8 meters) wide [d]13 That is, about 1 1/2 feet (about 0.5 meter) [e]14 That is, dugongs

25:37 [a] Ex 27:21; Lev 24:3-4; Nu 8:2

25:40 [b] Ex 26:30; Nu 8:4; Ac 7:44; Heb 8:5*

26:14 [c] Ex 36:19; Nu 4:25

26:30 [a] Ex 25:9,40; Ac 7:44; Heb 8:5
26:31 [b] 2Ch 3:14; Mt 27:51; Heb 9:3 [c] Ex 36:35
26:33 [d] Ex 40:3,21; Lev 16:2 [e] Heb 9:2-3
26:34 [f] Ex 25:21; 40:20; Heb 9:5
26:35 [g] Heb 9:2 [h] Ex 40:22,24
27:1 [i] Eze 43:13
27:2 [j] Ps 118:27

15 "Make upright frames of acacia wood for the tabernacle. 16 Each frame is to be ten cubits long and a cubit and a half wide,[a] 17 with two projections set parallel to each other. Make all the frames of the tabernacle in this way. 18 Make twenty frames for the south side of the tabernacle 19 and make forty silver bases to go under them—two bases for each frame, one under each projection. 20 For the other side, the north side of the tabernacle, make twenty frames 21 and forty silver bases—two under each frame. 22 Make six frames for the far end, that is, the west end of the tabernacle, 23 and make two frames for the corners at the far end. 24 At these two corners they must be double from the bottom all the way to the top, and fitted into a single ring; both shall be like that. 25 So there will be eight frames and sixteen silver bases—two under each frame.

26 "Also make crossbars of acacia wood: five for the frames on one side of the tabernacle, 27 five for those on the other side, and five for the frames on the west, at the far end of the tabernacle. 28 The center crossbar is to extend from end to end at the middle of the frames. 29 Overlay the frames with gold and make gold rings to hold the crossbars. Also overlay the crossbars with gold.

30 "Set up the tabernacle according to the plan[a] shown you on the mountain.

31 "Make a curtain[b] of blue, purple and scarlet yarn and finely twisted linen, with cherubim[c] worked into it by a skilled craftsman. 32 Hang it with gold hooks on four posts of acacia wood overlaid with gold and standing on four silver bases. 33 Hang the curtain from the clasps and place the ark of the Testimony behind the curtain.[d] The curtain will separate the Holy Place from the Most Holy Place.[e] 34 Put the atonement cover[f] on the ark of the Testimony in the Most Holy Place. 35 Place the table[g] outside the curtain on the north side of the tabernacle and put the lampstand[h] opposite it on the south side.

36 "For the entrance to the tent make a curtain of blue, purple and scarlet yarn and finely twisted linen—the work of an embroiderer. 37 Make gold hooks for this curtain and five posts of acacia wood overlaid with gold. And cast five bronze bases for them.

Chapter 27 Theme ______________________

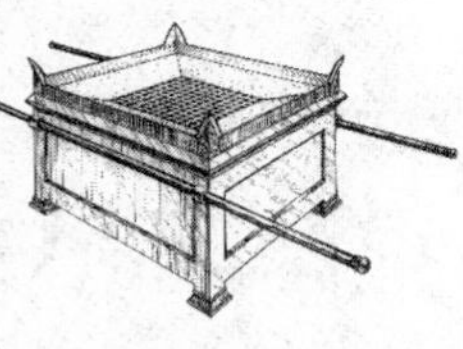
Bronze Altar

27

"Build an altar[i] of acacia wood, three cubits[b] high; it is to be square, five cubits long and five cubits wide.[c] 2 Make a horn[j] at each of the four corners, so that the horns and the altar are of one piece, and overlay the altar with bronze. 3 Make all its utensils of bronze—its pots to remove the ashes, and its shovels,

[a] *16* That is, about 15 feet (about 4.5 meters) long and 2 1/4 feet (about 0.7 meter) wide
[b] *1* That is, about 4 1/2 feet (about 1.3 meters) [c] *1* That is, about 7 1/2 feet (about 2.3 meters) long and wide

sprinkling bowls, meat forks and firepans. 4 Make a grating for it, a bronze network, and make a bronze ring at each of the four corners of the network. 5 Put it under the ledge of the altar so that it is halfway up the altar. 6 Make poles of acacia wood for the altar and overlay them with bronze. 7 The poles are to be inserted into the rings so they will be on two sides of the altar when it is carried. 8 Make the altar hollow, out of boards. It is to be made just as you were shown[a] on the mountain.

9 "Make a courtyard for the tabernacle. The south side shall be a hundred cubits[a] long and is to have curtains of finely twisted linen, 10 with twenty posts and twenty bronze bases and with silver hooks and bands on the posts. 11 The north side shall also be a hundred cubits long and is to have curtains, with twenty posts and twenty bronze bases and with silver hooks and bands on the posts.

12 "The west end of the courtyard shall be fifty cubits[b] wide and have curtains, with ten posts and ten bases. 13 On the east end, toward the sunrise, the courtyard shall also be fifty cubits wide. 14 Curtains fifteen cubits[c] long are to be on one side of the entrance, with three posts and three bases, 15 and curtains fifteen cubits long are to be on the other side, with three posts and three bases.

16 "For the entrance to the courtyard, provide a curtain twenty cubits[d] long, of blue, purple and scarlet yarn and finely twisted linen—the work of an embroiderer—with four posts and four bases. 17 All the posts around the courtyard are to have silver bands and hooks, and bronze bases. 18 The courtyard shall be a hundred cubits long and fifty cubits wide,[e] with curtains of finely twisted linen five cubits[f] high, and with bronze bases. 19 All the other articles used in the service of the tabernacle, whatever their function, including all the tent pegs for it and those for the courtyard, are to be of bronze.

20 "Command the Israelites to bring you clear oil of pressed olives for the light so that the lamps may be kept burning. 21 In the Tent of Meeting,[b] outside the curtain that is in front of the Testimony,[c] Aaron and his sons are to keep the lamps[d] burning before the LORD from evening till morning. This is to be a lasting ordinance[e] among the Israelites for the generations to come.

Chapter 28 Theme ________________________

28 "Have Aaron[f] your brother brought to you from among the Israelites, along with his sons Nadab and Abihu, Eleazar and Ithamar, so they may serve me as priests.[g] 2 Make sacred garments[h] for your brother Aaron, to give him dignity and honor.

a *9* That is, about 150 feet (about 46 meters); also in verse 11 b *12* That is, about 75 feet (about 23 meters); also in verse 13 c *14* That is, about 22 1/2 feet (about 6.9 meters); also in verse 15 d *16* That is, about 30 feet (about 9 meters) e *18* That is, about 150 feet (about 46 meters) long and 75 feet (about 23 meters) wide f *18* That is, about 7 1/2 feet (about 2.3 meters)

27:8
a Ex 25:9,40

27:21
b Ex 28:43
c Ex 26:31,33
d Ex 25:37; 30:8; 1Sa 3:3; 2Ch 13:11
e Ex 29:9; Lev 3:17; 16:34; Nu 18:23; 19:21

28:1
f Heb 5:4
g Nu 18:1-7; Heb 5:1

28:2
h Ex 29:5,29; 31:10; 39:1; Lev 8:7-9,30

28:3
[a] Ex 31:6; 36:1
[b] Ex 31:3

3 Tell all the skilled men[a] to whom I have given wisdom[b] in such
matters that they are to make garments for Aaron, for his consecration, so he may serve me as priest. 4 These are the garments
they are to make: a breastpiece,[c] an ephod, a robe,[d] a woven
tunic,[e] a turban and a sash. They are to make these sacred garments for your brother Aaron and his sons, so they may serve
me as priests. 5 Have them use gold, and blue, purple and scarlet
yarn, and fine linen.

6 "Make the ephod of gold, and of blue, purple and scarlet yarn,
and of finely twisted linen—the work of a skilled craftsman. 7 It
is to have two shoulder pieces attached to two of its corners, so it
can be fastened. 8 Its skillfully woven waistband is to be like it—of
one piece with the ephod and made with gold, and with blue, purple and scarlet yarn, and with finely twisted linen.

9 "Take two onyx stones and engrave on them the names of the
sons of Israel 10 in the order of their birth—six names on one
stone and the remaining six on the other. 11 Engrave the names of
the sons of Israel on the two stones the way a gem cutter engraves
a seal. Then mount the stones in gold filigree settings 12 and fasten them on the shoulder pieces of the ephod as memorial stones
for the sons of Israel. Aaron is to bear the names on his shoulders
as a memorial before the LORD. 13 Make gold filigree settings 14 and
two braided chains of pure gold, like a rope, and attach the chains
to the settings.

15 "Fashion a breastpiece for making decisions—the work of a
skilled craftsman. Make it like the ephod: of gold, and of blue,
purple and scarlet yarn, and of finely twisted linen. 16 It is to be
square—a span[a] long and a span wide—and folded double.
17 Then mount four rows of precious stones on it. In the first row
there shall be a ruby, a topaz and a beryl; 18 in the second row a
turquoise, a sapphire[b] and an emerald; 19 in the third row a jacinth,
an agate and an amethyst; 20 in the fourth row a chrysolite, an onyx
and a jasper.[c] Mount them in gold filigree settings. 21 There are to
be twelve stones, one for each of the names of the sons of Israel,
each engraved like a seal with the name of one of the twelve tribes.

22 "For the breastpiece make braided chains of pure gold, like a
rope. 23 Make two gold rings for it and fasten them to two corners
of the breastpiece. 24 Fasten the two gold chains to the rings at
the corners of the breastpiece, 25 and the other ends of the chains
to the two settings, attaching them to the shoulder pieces of the
ephod at the front. 26 Make two gold rings and attach them to the
other two corners of the breastpiece on the inside edge next to
the ephod. 27 Make two more gold rings and attach them to the

28:4
[c] ver 15-30
[d] ver 31-35
[e] ver 39

[a] 16 That is, about 9 inches (about 22 centimeters) [b] 18 Or *lapis lazuli* [c] 20 The precise identification of some of these precious stones is uncertain.

INSIGHT

The ***ephod*** was used to seek guidance from God. Described in Exodus 28, it was a linen garment worn by the priest and also by David when he was king (2 Samuel 6:14). The ephod was fastened on each shoulder by onyx clasps which had the names of six tribes engraved on one clasp and six tribes engraved on the other. The ***breastpiece***, which was fastened to the ephod, had a linen pouch which held the ***Urim*** and ***Thummim***, which may have been used as sacred lots to reveal God's will (1 Samuel 28:6).

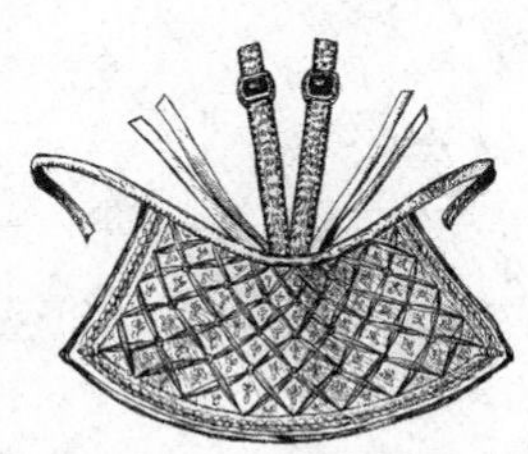

Ephod

High Priest's Garments

Robe of the Ephod

Turban with Plate of Gold

bottom of the shoulder pieces on the front of the ephod, close to
the seam just above the waistband of the ephod. 28The rings of
the breastpiece are to be tied to the rings of the ephod with blue
cord, connecting it to the waistband, so that the breastpiece will
not swing out from the ephod.

29"Whenever Aaron enters the Holy Place,[a] he will bear the
names of the sons of Israel over his heart on the breastpiece of
decision as a continuing memorial before the LORD. 30Also put
the Urim and the Thummim[b] in the breastpiece, so they may be
over Aaron's heart whenever he enters the presence of the LORD.
Thus Aaron will always bear the means of making decisions for
the Israelites over his heart before the LORD.

31"Make the robe of the ephod entirely of blue cloth, 32with an
opening for the head in its center. There shall be a woven edge
like a collar[a] around this opening, so that it will not tear. 33Make
pomegranates of blue, purple and scarlet yarn around the hem
of the robe, with gold bells between them. 34The gold bells and
the pomegranates are to alternate around the hem of the robe.
35Aaron must wear it when he ministers. The sound of the bells
will be heard when he enters the Holy Place before the LORD and
when he comes out, so that he will not die.

36"Make a plate of pure gold and engrave on it as on a seal:
HOLY TO THE LORD.[c] 37Fasten a blue cord to it to attach it to the
turban; it is to be on the front of the turban. 38It will be on
Aaron's forehead, and he will bear the guilt[d] involved in the
sacred gifts the Israelites consecrate, whatever their gifts may be.
It will be on Aaron's forehead continually so that they will be
acceptable to the LORD.

39"Weave the tunic of fine linen and make the turban of fine
linen. The sash is to be the work of an embroiderer. 40Make tunics,
sashes and headbands for Aaron's sons,[e] to give them dignity
and honor. 41After you put these clothes on your brother Aaron
and his sons, anoint[f] and ordain them. Consecrate them so they
may serve me as priests.[g]

42"Make linen undergarments[h] as a covering for the body,
reaching from the waist to the thigh. 43Aaron and his sons must
wear them whenever they enter the Tent of Meeting[i] or approach
the altar to minister in the Holy Place, so that they will not incur
guilt and die.[j]

"This is to be a lasting ordinance[k] for Aaron and his descendants.

Chapter 29 Theme ____________________

29 "This is what you are to do to consecrate them, so they
may serve me as priests: Take a young bull and two rams
without defect. 2And from fine wheat flour, without yeast, make

a32 The meaning of the Hebrew for this word is uncertain.

28:29 *a* ver 12

28:30 *b* Lev 8:8; Nu 27:21; Dt 33:8; Ezr 2:63; Ne 7:65

28:36 *c* Zec 14:20

28:38 *d* Lev 10:17; 22:9,16; Nu 18:1; Heb 9:28; 1Pe 2:24

28:40 *e* ver 4; Ex 39:41

28:41 *f* Ex 29:7; Lev 10:7 *g* Ex 29:7-9; 30:30; 40:15; Lev 8:1-36; Heb 7:28

28:42 *h* Lev 6:10; 16:4,23; Eze 44:18

28:43 *i* Ex 27:21 *j* Ex 20:26 *k* Lev 17:7

bread, and cakes mixed with oil, and wafers spread with oil.[a] 3Put
them in a basket and present them in it—along with the bull and
the two rams. 4Then bring Aaron and his sons to the entrance to
the Tent of Meeting and wash them with water.[b] 5Take the garments[c] and dress Aaron with the tunic, the robe of the ephod,
the ephod itself and the breastpiece. Fasten the ephod on him by
its skillfully woven waistband.[d] 6Put the turban on his head and
attach the sacred diadem[e] to the turban. 7Take the anointing oil[f]
and anoint him by pouring it on his head. 8Bring his sons and
dress them in tunics 9and put headbands on them. Then tie sashes on Aaron and his sons.[a][g] The priesthood is theirs by a lasting
ordinance.[h] In this way you shall ordain Aaron and his sons.

10"Bring the bull to the front of the Tent of Meeting, and Aaron
and his sons shall lay their hands on its head.[i] 11Slaughter it in the
LORD's presence at the entrance to the Tent of Meeting. 12Take
some of the bull's blood and put it on the horns[j] of the altar with
your finger, and pour out the rest of it at the base of the altar.
13Then take all the fat[k] around the inner parts, the covering of
the liver, and both kidneys with the fat on them, and burn them
on the altar. 14But burn the bull's flesh and its hide and its offal
outside the camp.[l] It is a sin offering.

15"Take one of the rams, and Aaron and his sons shall lay their
hands on its head. 16Slaughter it and take the blood and sprinkle
it against the altar on all sides. 17Cut the ram into pieces and wash
the inner parts and the legs, putting them with the head and the
other pieces. 18Then burn the entire ram on the altar. It is a burnt
offering to the LORD, a pleasing aroma,[m] an offering made to the
LORD by fire.

19"Take the other ram,[n] and Aaron and his sons shall lay their
hands on its head. 20Slaughter it, take some of its blood and put
it on the lobes of the right ears of Aaron and his sons, on the
thumbs of their right hands, and on the big toes of their right
feet. Then sprinkle blood against the altar on all sides. 21And take
some of the blood[o] on the altar and some of the anointing oil[p]
and sprinkle it on Aaron and his garments and on his sons and
their garments. Then he and his sons and their garments will be
consecrated.[q]

22"Take from this ram the fat, the fat tail, the fat around the
inner parts, the covering of the liver, both kidneys with the fat on
them, and the right thigh. (This is the ram for the ordination.)
23From the basket of bread made without yeast, which is before
the LORD, take a loaf, and a cake made with oil, and a wafer. 24Put
all these in the hands of Aaron and his sons and wave them before
the LORD as a wave offering.[r] 25Then take them from their hands

29:2 a Lev 2:1,4; 6:19-23
29:4 b Ex 40:12; Heb 10:22
29:5 c Ex 28:2; Lev 8:7 d Ex 28:8
29:6 e Lev 8:9
29:7 f Ex 30:25, 30,31; Lev 8:12; 21:10; Nu 35:25; Ps 133:2
29:9 g Ex 28:40 h Ex 40:15; Nu 3:10; 18:7; 25:13; Dt 18:5
29:10 i Lev 1:4
29:12 j Ex 27:2
29:13 k Lev 3:3,5,9
29:14 l Lev 4:11-12, 21; Heb 13:11
29:18 m Ge 8:21
29:19 n ver 3
29:21 o Heb 9:22 p Ex 30:25,31 q ver 1
29:24 r Lev 7:30

a9 Hebrew; Septuagint *on them*

and burn them on the altar along with the burnt offering for a
pleasing aroma to the LORD, an offering made to the LORD by fire.
26After you take the breast of the ram for Aaron's ordination, wave
it before the LORD as a wave offering, and it will be your share.[a]

27"Consecrate those parts of the ordination ram that belong to
Aaron and his sons:[b] the breast that was waved and the thigh that
was presented. 28This is always to be the regular share from the
Israelites for Aaron and his sons. It is the contribution the Israelites are to make to the LORD from their fellowship offerings.[a][c]

29"Aaron's sacred garments will belong to his descendants so
that they can be anointed and ordained in them.[d] 30The son[e]
who succeeds him as priest and comes to the Tent of Meeting to
minister in the Holy Place is to wear them seven days.

31"Take the ram for the ordination and cook the meat in a
sacred place. 32At the entrance to the Tent of Meeting, Aaron and
his sons are to eat the meat of the ram and the bread[f] that is in
the basket. 33They are to eat these offerings by which atonement
was made for their ordination and consecration. But no one else
may eat[g] them, because they are sacred. 34And if any of the meat
of the ordination ram or any bread is left over till morning,[h]
burn it up. It must not be eaten, because it is sacred.

35"Do for Aaron and his sons everything I have commanded
you, taking seven days to ordain them. 36Sacrifice a bull each
day[i] as a sin offering to make atonement. Purify the altar by
making atonement for it, and anoint it to consecrate[j] it. 37For
seven days make atonement for the altar and consecrate it. Then
the altar will be most holy, and whatever touches it will be holy.[k]

38"This is what you are to offer on the altar regularly each day:[l]
two lambs a year old. 39Offer one in the morning and the other
at twilight.[m] 40With the first lamb offer a tenth of an ephah[b] of
fine flour mixed with a quarter of a hin[c] of oil from pressed
olives, and a quarter of a hin of wine as a drink offering. 41Sacri-
fice the other lamb at twilight with the same grain offering and
its drink offering as in the morning—a pleasing aroma, an
offering made to the LORD by fire.

42"For the generations to come[n] this burnt offering is to be
made regularly at the entrance to the Tent of Meeting before the
LORD. There I will meet you and speak to you;[o] 43there also I will
meet with the Israelites, and the place will be consecrated by my
glory.[p]

44"So I will consecrate the Tent of Meeting and the altar and
will consecrate Aaron and his sons to serve me as priests.[q] 45Then
I will dwell[r] among the Israelites and be their God.[s] 46They will

a*28* Traditionally *peace offerings* b*40* That is, probably about 2 quarts (about 2 liters)
c*40* That is, probably about 1 quart (about 1 liter)

29:26 *a* Lev 7:31-34
29:27 *b* Lev 7:31,34; Dt 18:3
29:28 *c* Lev 10:15
29:29 *d* Nu 20:26,28
29:30 *e* Nu 20:28
29:32 *f* Mt 12:4
29:33 *g* Lev 10:14; 22:10,13
29:34 *h* Ex 12:10
29:36 *i* Heb 10:11 *j* Ex 40:10
29:37 *k* Ex 30:28-29; 40:10; Mt 23:19
29:38 *l* Nu 28:3-8; 1Ch 16:40; Da 12:11
29:39 *m* Eze 46:13-15
29:42 *n* Ex 30:8 *o* Ex 25:22
29:43 *p* 1Ki 8:11
29:44 *q* Lev 21:15
29:45 *r* Ex 25:8; Lev 26:12; Zec 2:10; Jn 14:17 *s* 2Co 6:16; Rev 21:3

29:46 a Ex 20:2 know that I am the LORD their God, who brought them out of
Egypt so that I might dwell among them. I am the LORD their
God.[a]

30:1 b Ex 37:25 c Rev 8:3

Chapter 30 Theme ______________________

30 “Make an altar[b] of acacia wood for burning incense.[c] [2]It is
30:2 d Ex 27:2 to be square, a cubit long and a cubit wide, and two
cubits high[a]—its horns[d] of one piece with it. [3]Overlay the top
and all the sides and the horns with pure gold, and make a gold
30:6 e Ex 25:22; molding around it. [4]Make two gold rings for the altar below the
26:34 molding—two on opposite sides—to hold the poles used to carry
it. [5]Make the poles of acacia wood and overlay them with gold.
30:7 [6]Put the altar in front of the curtain that is before the ark of the
f ver 34-35; Testimony—before the atonement cover[e] that is over the Testi-
Ex 27:21; 1Sa 2:28 mony—where I will meet with you.

Altar of Incense (Gold or Golden Altar)

[7]“Aaron must burn fragrant incense[f] on the altar every morn-
30:9 ing when he tends the lamps. [8]He must burn incense again when
g Lev 10:1 he lights the lamps at twilight so incense will burn regularly before the LORD for the generations to come. [9]Do not offer on this
30:10 altar any other incense[g] or any burnt offering or grain offering,
h Lev 16:18-19, and do not pour a drink offering on it. [10]Once a year Aaron shall
30 make atonement[h] on its horns. This annual atonement must be
made with the blood of the atoning sin offering for the genera-
30:12 tions to come. It is most holy to the LORD.”
i Ex 38:25; Nu 1:2,49; [11]Then the LORD said to Moses, [12]“When you take a census[i] of
2Sa 24:1 j Nu 31:50; the Israelites to count them, each one must pay the LORD a ran-
Mt 20:28 k 2Sa 24:13 som[j] for his life at the time he is counted. Then no plague[k] will
come on them when you number them. [13]Each one who crosses
over to those already counted is to give a half shekel,[b] according
30:13 l Nu 3:47; to the sanctuary shekel,[l] which weighs twenty gerahs. This half
Mt 17:24 shekel is an offering to the LORD. [14]All who cross over, those
twenty years old or more, are to give an offering to the LORD.
30:15 [15]The rich are not to give more than a half shekel and the poor
m Pr 22:2; are not to give less[m] when you make the offering to the LORD to
Eph 6:9 atone for your lives. [16]Receive the atonement money from the
Israelites and use it for the service of the Tent of Meeting.[n] It will
30:16 n Ex 38:25-28 be a memorial for the Israelites before the LORD, making atonement for your lives.”

Bronze Basin

[17]Then the LORD said to Moses, [18]“Make a bronze basin,[o] with
30:18 o Ex 38:8; its bronze stand, for washing. Place it between the Tent of Meeting
40:7,30 and the altar, and put water in it. [19]Aaron and his sons are to wash
their hands and feet[p] with water[q] from it. [20]Whenever they enter
30:19 p Ex 40:31-32; the Tent of Meeting, they shall wash with water so that they will

Isa 52:11 q Ps 26:6

a*2* That is, about 1 1/2 feet (about 0.5 meter) long and wide and about 3 feet (about 0.9 meter) high b*13* That is, about 1/5 ounce (about 6 grams); also in verse 15

not die. Also, when they approach the altar to minister by presenting an offering made to the LORD by fire, 21they shall wash
their hands and feet so that they will not die. This is to be a lasting ordinance[a] for Aaron and his descendants for the generations to come."

22Then the LORD said to Moses, 23"Take the following fine spices:
500 shekels[a] of liquid myrrh,[b] half as much (that is, 250 shekels)
of fragrant cinnamon, 250 shekels of fragrant cane, 24500 shekels
of cassia[c]—all according to the sanctuary shekel—and a hin[b] of
olive oil. 25Make these into a sacred anointing oil, a fragrant
blend, the work of a perfumer.[d] It will be the sacred anointing
oil.[e] 26Then use it to anoint[f] the Tent of Meeting, the ark of the
Testimony, 27the table and all its articles, the lampstand and its
accessories, the altar of incense, 28the altar of burnt offering and
all its utensils, and the basin with its stand. 29You shall consecrate
them so they will be most holy, and whatever touches them will
be holy.[g]

30"Anoint Aaron and his sons and consecrate[h] them so they
may serve me as priests. 31Say to the Israelites, 'This is to be my
sacred anointing oil for the generations to come. 32Do not pour
it on men's bodies and do not make any oil with the same formula. It is sacred, and you are to consider it sacred.[i] 33Whoever
makes perfume like it and whoever puts it on anyone other than
a priest must be cut off[j] from his people.'"

34Then the LORD said to Moses, "Take fragrant spices—gum
resin, onycha and galbanum—and pure frankincense, all in equal
amounts, 35and make a fragrant blend of incense, the work of a
perfumer.[k] It is to be salted and pure and sacred. 36Grind some
of it to powder and place it in front of the Testimony in the Tent
of Meeting, where I will meet with you. It shall be most holy[l] to
you. 37Do not make any incense with this formula for yourselves;
consider it holy[m] to the LORD. 38Whoever makes any like it to
enjoy its fragrance must be cut off[n] from his people."

Chapter 31 Theme ______________________

31 Then the LORD said to Moses, 2"See, I have chosen Bezalel[o]
son of Uri, the son of Hur, of the tribe of Judah, 3and I have
filled him with the Spirit of God, with skill, ability and knowledge in all kinds of crafts[p]— 4to make artistic designs for work
in gold, silver and bronze, 5to cut and set stones, to work in
wood, and to engage in all kinds of craftsmanship. 6Moreover, I
have appointed Oholiab son of Ahisamach, of the tribe of Dan,
to help him. Also I have given skill to all the craftsmen to make

a23 That is, about 12 1/2 pounds (about 6 kilograms) b24 That is, probably about 4 quarts (about 4 liters)

30:21 a Ex 27:21; 28:43
30:23 b Ge 37:25
30:24 c Ps 45:8
30:25 d Ex 37:29 e Ex 40:9
30:26 f Ex 40:9; Lev 8:10; Nu 7:1
30:29 g Ex 29:37
30:30 h Ex 29:7; Lev 8:2,12,30
30:32 i ver 25,37
30:33 j ver 38; Ge 17:14
30:35 k ver 25
30:36 l ver 32; Ex 29:37; Lev 2:3
30:37 m ver 32
30:38 n ver 33
31:2 o Ex 36:1,2; 1Ch 2:20
31:3 p 1Ki 7:14

everything I have commanded you: 7the Tent of Meeting,[a] the ark of the Testimony[b] with the atonement cover[c] on it, and all the other furnishings of the tent— 8the table[d] and its articles, the pure gold lampstand[e] and all its accessories, the altar of incense, 9the altar of burnt offering and all its utensils, the basin with its stand— 10and also the woven garments[f], both the sacred garments for Aaron the priest and the garments for his sons when they serve as priests, 11and the anointing oil[g] and fragrant incense for the Holy Place. They are to make them just as I commanded you."

12Then the LORD said to Moses, 13"Say to the Israelites, 'You must observe my Sabbaths.[h] This will be a sign[i] between me and you for the generations to come, so you may know that I am the LORD, who makes you holy.[a][j]

14"'Observe the Sabbath, because it is holy to you. Anyone who desecrates it must be put to death;[k] whoever does any work on that day must be cut off from his people. 15For six days, work[l] is to be done, but the seventh day is a Sabbath of rest,[m] holy to the LORD. Whoever does any work on the Sabbath day must be put to death. 16The Israelites are to observe the Sabbath, celebrating it for the generations to come as a lasting covenant. 17It will be a sign[n] between me and the Israelites forever, for in six days the LORD made the heavens and the earth, and on the seventh day he abstained from work and rested.[o]'"

18When the LORD finished speaking to Moses on Mount Sinai, he gave him the two tablets of the Testimony, the tablets of stone[p] inscribed by the finger of God.[q]

Chapter 32 Theme ____________________

32 When the people saw that Moses was so long in coming down from the mountain,[r] they gathered around Aaron and said, "Come, make us gods[b] who will go before us. As for this fellow Moses who brought us up out of Egypt, we don't know what has happened to him."[s]

2Aaron answered them, "Take off the gold earrings[t] that your wives, your sons and your daughters are wearing, and bring them to me." 3So all the people took off their earrings and brought them to Aaron. 4He took what they handed him and made it into an idol cast in the shape of a calf,[u] fashioning it with a tool. Then they said, "These are your gods,[c] O Israel, who brought you up out of Egypt."

5When Aaron saw this, he built an altar in front of the calf and announced, "Tomorrow there will be a festival[v] to the LORD." 6So

31:7 [a] Ex 36:8-38 [b] Ex 37:1-5 [c] Ex 37:6
31:8 [d] Ex 37:10-16 [e] Ex 37:17-24
31:10 [f] Ex 28:2; 39:1,41
31:11 [g] Ex 30:22-32
31:13 [h] Ex 20:8; Lev 19:3,30 [i] Eze 20:12,20 [j] Lev 11:44
31:14 [k] Nu 15:32-36
31:15 [l] Ex 20:8-11 [m] Ge 2:3; Ex 16:23
31:17 [n] ver 13 [o] Ge 2:2-3
31:18 [p] Ex 24:12 [q] Ex 32:15-16; 34:1,28; Dt 4:13; 5:22
32:1 [r] Ex 24:18; Dt 9:9-12 [s] Ac 7:40*
32:2 [t] Ex 35:22
32:4 [u] Dt 9:16; Ne 9:18; Ps 106:19; Ac 7:41
32:5 [v] Lev 23:2,37; 2Ki 10:20

[a]13 Or *who sanctifies you*; or *who sets you apart as holy* [b]1 Or *a god*; also in verses 23 and 31
[c]4 Or *This is your god*; also in verse 8

the next day the people rose early and sacrificed burnt offerings
and presented fellowship offerings.[a][a] Afterward they sat down
to eat and drink and got up to indulge in revelry.[b]
7Then the LORD said to Moses, "Go down, because your people, whom you brought up out of Egypt,[c] have become corrupt.[d]
8They have been quick to turn away from what I commanded
them and have made themselves an idol[e] cast in the shape of a
calf. They have bowed down to it and sacrificed[f] to it and have
said, 'These are your gods, O Israel, who brought you up out of
Egypt.'[g]
9"I have seen these people," the LORD said to Moses, "and they
are a stiff-necked[h] people. 10Now leave me alone so that my
anger may burn against them and that I may destroy them.
Then I will make you into a great nation."[i]
11But Moses sought the favor[j] of the LORD his God. "O LORD,"
he said, "why should your anger burn against your people, whom
you brought out of Egypt with great power and a mighty hand?[k]
12Why should the Egyptians say, 'It was with evil intent that he
brought them out, to kill them in the mountains and to wipe
them off the face of the earth'?[l] Turn from your fierce anger;
relent and do not bring disaster on your people. 13Remember[m]
your servants Abraham, Isaac and Israel, to whom you swore by
your own self:[n] 'I will make your descendants as numerous as the
stars[o] in the sky and I will give your descendants all this land[p] I
promised them, and it will be their inheritance forever.'" 14Then
the LORD relented[q] and did not bring on his people the disaster
he had threatened.
15Moses turned and went down the mountain with the two
tablets of the Testimony[r] in his hands.[s] They were inscribed on
both sides, front and back. 16The tablets were the work of God;
the writing was the writing of God, engraved on the tablets.[t]
17When Joshua heard the noise of the people shouting, he said
to Moses, "There is the sound of war in the camp."
18Moses replied:

"It is not the sound of victory,
it is not the sound of defeat;
it is the sound of singing that I hear."

19When Moses approached the camp and saw the calf[u] and the
dancing, his anger burned and he threw the tablets out of his
hands, breaking them to pieces[v] at the foot of the mountain.
20And he took the calf they had made and burned it in the fire;
then he ground it to powder, scattered it on the water[w] and made
the Israelites drink it.

a6 Traditionally *peace offerings*

32:6 *a* Nu 25:2; Ac 7:41 *b* ver 17-19; 1Co 10:7*
32:7 *c* ver 4,11 *d* Ge 6:11-12; Dt 9:12
32:8 *e* Ex 20:4 *f* Ex 22:20 *g* 1Ki 12:28
32:9 *h* Ex 33:3,5; 34:9; Isa 48:4; Ac 7:51
32:10 *i* Nu 14:12; Dt 9:14
32:11 *j* Dt 9:18 *k* Dt 9:26
32:12 *l* Nu 14:13-16; Dt 9:28
32:13 *m* Ex 2:24 *n* Ge 22:16; Heb 6:13 *o* Ge 15:5; 26:4 *p* Ge 12:7
32:14 *q* 2Sa 24:16; Ps 106:45
32:15 *r* Ex 31:18 *s* Dt 9:15
32:16 *t* Ex 31:18
32:19 *u* Dt 9:16 *v* Dt 9:17
32:20 *w* Dt 9:21

21 He said to Aaron, "What did these people do to you, that you led them into such great sin?"

22 "Do not be angry, my lord," Aaron answered. "You know how prone these people are to evil.[a] 23 They said to me, 'Make us gods who will go before us. As for this fellow Moses who brought us up out of Egypt, we don't know what has happened to him.'[b] 24 So I told them, 'Whoever has any gold jewelry, take it off.' Then they gave me the gold, and I threw it into the fire, and out came this calf!"[c]

25 Moses saw that the people were running wild and that Aaron had let them get out of control and so become a laughingstock to their enemies. 26 So he stood at the entrance to the camp and said, "Whoever is for the LORD, come to me." And all the Levites rallied to him.

27 Then he said to them, "This is what the LORD, the God of Israel, says: 'Each man strap a sword to his side. Go back and forth through the camp from one end to the other, each killing his brother and friend and neighbor.'"[d] 28 The Levites did as Moses commanded, and that day about three thousand of the people died. 29 Then Moses said, "You have been set apart to the LORD today, for you were against your own sons and brothers, and he has blessed you this day."

30 The next day Moses said to the people, "You have committed a great sin.[e] But now I will go up to the LORD; perhaps I can make atonement[f] for your sin."

31 So Moses went back to the LORD and said, "Oh, what a great sin these people have committed![g] They have made themselves gods of gold.[h] 32 But now, please forgive their sin—but if not, then blot me[i] out of the book[j] you have written."

33 The LORD replied to Moses, "Whoever has sinned against me I will blot out[k] of my book. 34 Now go, lead the people to the place[l] I spoke of, and my angel[m] will go before you. However, when the time comes for me to punish,[n] I will punish them for their sin."

35 And the LORD struck the people with a plague because of what they did with the calf[o] Aaron had made.

Chapter 33 Theme ______________________________

33 Then the LORD said to Moses, "Leave this place, you and the people you brought up out of Egypt, and go up to the land I promised on oath to Abraham, Isaac and Jacob, saying, 'I will give it to your descendants.'[p] 2 I will send an angel[q] before you and drive out the Canaanites, Amorites, Hittites, Perizzites, Hivites and Jebusites.[r] 3 Go up to the land flowing with milk and honey.[s] But I will not go with you, because you are a stiff-necked[t] people and I might destroy[u] you on the way."

32:22 [a] Dt 9:24
32:23 [b] ver 1
32:24 [c] ver 4
32:27 [d] Nu 25:3,5; Dt 33:9
32:30 [e] 1Sa 12:20 [f] Lev 1:4; Nu 25:13
32:31 [g] Dt 9:18 [h] Ex 20:23
32:32 [i] Ro 9:3 [j] Ps 69:28; Da 12:1; Php 4:3; Rev 3:5; 21:27
32:33 [k] Dt 29:20; Ps 9:5
32:34 [l] Ex 3:17 [m] Ex 23:20 [n] Dt 32:35; Ps 99:8; Ro 2:5-6
32:35 [o] ver 4
33:1 [p] Ge 12:7
33:2 [q] Ex 32:34 [r] Ex 23:27-31; Jos 24:11
33:3 [s] Ex 3:8 [t] Ex 32:9 [u] Ex 32:10

4When the people heard these distressing words, they began to
mourn[a] and no one put on any ornaments. 5For the LORD had said
to Moses, "Tell the Israelites, 'You are a stiff-necked people. If I
were to go with you even for a moment, I might destroy you. Now
take off your ornaments and I will decide what to do with you.'"
6So the Israelites stripped off their ornaments at Mount Horeb.

7Now Moses used to take a tent and pitch it outside the camp
some distance away, calling it the "tent of meeting."[b] Anyone
inquiring of the LORD would go to the tent of meeting outside the
camp. 8And whenever Moses went out to the tent, all the people
rose and stood at the entrances to their tents,[c] watching Moses
until he entered the tent. 9As Moses went into the tent, the pillar
of cloud[d] would come down and stay at the entrance, while the
LORD spoke[e] with Moses. 10Whenever the people saw the pillar of
cloud standing at the entrance to the tent, they all stood and worshiped, each at the entrance to his tent. 11The LORD would speak
to Moses face to face,[f] as a man speaks with his friend. Then
Moses would return to the camp, but his young aide Joshua son
of Nun did not leave the tent.

12Moses said to the LORD, "You have been telling me, 'Lead
these people,'[g] but you have not let me know whom you will send
with me. You have said, 'I know you by name[h] and you have
found favor with me.' 13If you are pleased with me, teach me your
ways[i] so I may know you and continue to find favor with you.
Remember that this nation is your people."[j]

14The LORD replied, "My Presence[k] will go with you, and I will
give you rest."[l]

15Then Moses said to him, "If your Presence does not go with
us, do not send us up from here. 16How will anyone know that
you are pleased with me and with your people unless you go with
us?[m] What else will distinguish me and your people from all the
other people on the face of the earth?"[n]

17And the LORD said to Moses, "I will do the very thing you have
asked, because I am pleased with you and I know you by name."

18Then Moses said, "Now show me your glory."

19And the LORD said, "I will cause all my goodness to pass in
front of you, and I will proclaim my name, the LORD, in your
presence. I will have mercy on whom I will have mercy, and I will
have compassion on whom I will have compassion.[o] 20But," he
said, "you cannot see my face, for no one may see[p] me and live."

21Then the LORD said, "There is a place near me where you
may stand on a rock. 22When my glory passes by, I will put you
in a cleft in the rock and cover you with my hand[q] until I have
passed by. 23Then I will remove my hand and you will see my
back; but my face must not be seen."

33:4 a Nu 14:39
33:7 b Ex 29:42-43
33:8 c Nu 16:27
33:9 d Ex 13:21 e Ex 31:18; Ps 99:7
33:11 f Nu 12:8; Dt 34:10
33:12 g Ex 3:10 h ver 17; Jn 10:14-15; 2Ti 2:19
33:13 i Ps 25:4; 86:11; 119:33 j Ex 34:9; Dt 9:26,29
33:14 k Isa 63:9 l Jos 21:44; 22:4
33:16 m Nu 14:14 n Ex 34:10
33:19 o Ro 9:15*
33:20 p Ge 32:30; Isa 6:5
33:22 q Ps 91:4

Chapter 34 Theme ________________________________

34 The LORD said to Moses, "Chisel out two stone tablets like
the first ones, and I will write on them the words that were
on the first tablets,[a] which you broke.[b] 2 Be ready in the morning,
and then come up on Mount Sinai.[c] Present yourself to me there
on top of the mountain. 3 No one is to come with you or be seen
anywhere on the mountain;[d] not even the flocks and herds may
graze in front of the mountain."
4 So Moses chiseled out two stone tablets like the first ones and
went up Mount Sinai early in the morning, as the LORD had commanded him; and he carried the two stone tablets in his hands.
5 Then the LORD came down in the cloud and stood there with
him and proclaimed his name, the LORD.[e] 6 And he passed in
front of Moses, proclaiming, "The LORD, the LORD, the compassionate[f] and gracious God, slow to anger,[g] abounding in love[h]
and faithfulness,[i] 7 maintaining love to thousands,[j] and forgiving
wickedness, rebellion and sin.[k] Yet he does not leave the guilty
unpunished;[l] he punishes the children and their children for the
sin of the fathers to the third and fourth generation."
8 Moses bowed to the ground at once and worshiped. 9 "O Lord,
if I have found favor in your eyes," he said, "then let the Lord go
with us.[m] Although this is a stiff-necked people, forgive our
wickedness and our sin, and take us as your inheritance."[n]
10 Then the LORD said: "I am making a covenant[o] with you.
Before all your people I will do wonders never before done in any
nation in all the world.[p] The people you live among will see how
awesome is the work that I, the LORD, will do for you. 11 Obey
what I command you today. I will drive out before you the Amorites, Canaanites, Hittites, Perizzites, Hivites and Jebusites.[q] 12 Be
careful not to make a treaty with those who live in the land where
you are going, or they will be a snare[r] among you. 13 Break down
their altars, smash their sacred stones and cut down their Asherah
poles.[a][s] 14 Do not worship any other god,[t] for the LORD, whose
name is Jealous, is a jealous God.[u]
15 "Be careful not to make a treaty with those who live in the
land; for when they prostitute[v] themselves to their gods and sacrifice to them, they will invite you and you will eat their sacrifices.[w]
16 And when you choose some of their daughters as wives[x] for
your sons and those daughters prostitute themselves to their
gods,[y] they will lead your sons to do the same.
17 "Do not make cast idols.[z]
18 "Celebrate the Feast of Unleavened Bread.[a] For seven days
eat bread made without yeast,[b] as I commanded you. Do this at

34:1 [a] Dt 10:2,4 [b] Ex 32:19
34:2 [c] Ex 19:11
34:3 [d] Ex 19:12-13,21
34:5 [e] Ex 33:19
34:6 [f] Ps 86:15 [g] Nu 14:18; Ro 2:4 [h] Ne 9:17; Ps 103:8; Joel 2:13 [i] Ps 108:4
34:7 [j] Ex 20:6 [k] Ps 103:3; 130:4,8; Da 9:9; 1Jn 1:9 [l] Job 10:14; Na 1:3
34:9 [m] Ex 33:15 [n] Ps 33:12
34:10 [o] Dt 5:2-3 [p] Ex 33:16; Dt 4:32
34:11 [q] Ex 33:2
34:12 [r] Ex 23:32-33
34:13 [s] Ex 23:24; Dt 12:3; 2Ki 18:4
34:14 [t] Ex 20:3 [u] Ex 20:5; Dt 4:24
34:15 [v] Jdg 2:17 [w] Nu 25:2; 1Co 8:4
34:16 [x] Dt 7:3 [y] 1Ki 11:4
34:17 [z] Ex 32:8
34:18 [a] Ex 12:17 [b] Ex 12:15

[a]13 That is, symbols of the goddess Asherah

the appointed time in the month of Abib,[a] for in that month you
came out of Egypt.
19“The first offspring[b] of every womb belongs to me, including
all the firstborn males of your livestock, whether from herd or
flock. 20Redeem the firstborn donkey with a lamb, but if you do
not redeem it, break its neck.[c] Redeem all your firstborn sons.
“No one is to appear before me empty-handed.[d]
21“Six days you shall labor, but on the seventh day you shall
rest;[e] even during the plowing season and harvest you must rest.
22“Celebrate the Feast of Weeks with the firstfruits of the wheat
harvest, and the Feast of Ingathering[f] at the turn of the year.[a]
23Three times[g] a year all your men are to appear before the Sovereign LORD, the God of Israel. 24I will drive out nations[h] before you
and enlarge your territory, and no one will covet your land when
you go up three times each year to appear before the LORD your
God.
25“Do not offer the blood of a sacrifice to me along with anything containing yeast,[i] and do not let any of the sacrifice from
the Passover Feast remain until morning.[j]
26“Bring the best of the firstfruits of your soil to the house of
the LORD your God.
“Do not cook a young goat in its mother’s milk.”[k]
27Then the LORD said to Moses, “Write[l] down these words, for
in accordance with these words I have made a covenant with
you and with Israel.” 28Moses was there with the LORD forty
days and forty nights[m] without eating bread or drinking water.
And he wrote on the tablets[n] the words of the covenant—the
Ten Commandments.[o]
29When Moses came down from Mount Sinai with the two
tablets of the Testimony in his hands,[p] he was not aware that his
face was radiant[q] because he had spoken with the LORD. 30When
Aaron and all the Israelites saw Moses, his face was radiant, and
they were afraid to come near him. 31But Moses called to them;
so Aaron and all the leaders of the community came back to him,
and he spoke to them. 32Afterward all the Israelites came near
him, and he gave them all the commands[r] the LORD had given
him on Mount Sinai.
33When Moses finished speaking to them, he put a veil[s] over
his face. 34But whenever he entered the LORD’s presence to speak
with him, he removed the veil until he came out. And when he
came out and told the Israelites what he had been commanded,
35they saw that his face was radiant. Then Moses would put the
veil back over his face until he went in to speak with the LORD.

a22 That is, in the fall

34:18 a Ex 12:2
34:19 b Ex 13:2
34:20 c Ex 13:13,15 d Ex 23:15; Dt 16:16
34:21 e Ex 20:9; Lk 13:14
34:22 f Ex 23:16
34:23 g Ex 23:14
34:24 h Ex 23:28; 33:2; Ps 78:55
34:25 i Ex 23:18 j Ex 12:8,10
34:26 k Ex 23:19
34:27 l Ex 17:14; 24:4
34:28 m Ge 7:4; Ex 24:18; Mt 4:2 n ver 1; Ex 31:18 o Dt 4:13; 10:4
34:29 p Ex 32:15 q Ps 34:5; Mt 17:2; 2Co 3:7,13
34:32 r Ex 24:3
34:33 s 2Co 3:13

35:1 [a] Ex 34:32 *Chapter 35 Theme* ______________________

35 Moses assembled the whole Israelite community and said
to them, "These are the things the LORD has commanded[a]
35:2 [b] Ex 20:9-10; you to do: [2]For six days, work is to be done, but the seventh day
34:21; Lev 23:3 shall be your holy day, a Sabbath[b] of rest to the LORD. Whoever
does any work on it must be put to death. [3]Do not light a fire in
any of your dwellings on the Sabbath day.[c]"
35:3 [4]Moses said to the whole Israelite community, "This is what the
[c] Ex 16:23 LORD has commanded: [5]From what you have, take an offering
for the LORD. Everyone who is willing is to bring to the LORD an
offering of gold, silver and bronze; [6]blue, purple and scarlet yarn
35:10 [d] Ex 31:6 and fine linen; goat hair; [7]ram skins dyed red and hides of sea
cows[a]; acacia wood; [8]olive oil for the light; spices for the anointing
oil and for the fragrant incense; [9]and onyx stones and other gems
35:11 [e] Ex 26:1-37 to be mounted on the ephod and breastpiece.
[10]"All who are skilled among you are to come and make everything the LORD has commanded:[d] [11]the tabernacle[e] with its tent
35:12 and its covering, clasps, frames, crossbars, posts and bases; [12]the
[f] Ex 25:10-22 ark[f] with its poles and the atonement cover and the curtain that
shields it; [13]the table[g] with its poles and all its articles and the
35:13 bread of the Presence; [14]the lampstand[h] that is for light with its
[g] Ex 25:23-30; accessories, lamps and oil for the light; [15]the altar[i] of incense with
Lev 24:5-6 its poles, the anointing oil[j] and the fragrant incense;[k] the curtain
for the doorway at the entrance to the tabernacle; [16]the altar[l] of
35:14 burnt offering with its bronze grating, its poles and all its utensils;
[h] Ex 25:31 the bronze basin with its stand; [17]the curtains of the courtyard
with its posts and bases, and the curtain for the entrance to the
courtyard;[m] [18]the tent pegs for the tabernacle and for the court-
35:15 [i] Ex 30:1-6 yard, and their ropes; [19]the woven garments worn for minister-
[j] Ex 30:25 ing in the sanctuary—both the sacred garments[n] for Aaron the
[k] Ex 30:34-38 priest and the garments for his sons when they serve as priests."
[20]Then the whole Israelite community withdrew from Moses'
presence, [21]and everyone who was willing and whose heart
35:16 [l] Ex 27:1-8 moved him came and brought an offering to the LORD for the
work on the Tent of Meeting, for all its service, and for the sacred
garments. [22]All who were willing, men and women alike, came
35:17 [m] Ex 27:9 and brought gold jewelry of all kinds: brooches, earrings, rings
and ornaments. They all presented their gold as a wave offering
to the LORD. [23]Everyone who had blue, purple or scarlet yarn[o] or
35:19 fine linen, or goat hair, ram skins dyed red or hides of sea cows
[n] Ex 28:2; 31:10; 39:1 brought them. [24]Those presenting an offering of silver or bronze
brought it as an offering to the LORD, and everyone who had aca-
cia wood for any part of the work brought it. [25]Every skilled

35:23 [o] 1Ch 29:8

a7 That is, dugongs; also in verse 23

woman[a] spun with her hands and brought what she had spun—
blue, purple or scarlet yarn or fine linen. 26And all the women
who were willing and had the skill spun the goat hair. 27The leaders[b] brought onyx stones and other gems to be mounted on the
ephod and breastpiece. 28They also brought spices and olive oil for
the light and for the anointing oil and for the fragrant incense.[c]
29All the Israelite men and women who were willing[d] brought to
the LORD freewill offerings[e] for all the work the LORD through
Moses had commanded them to do.

30Then Moses said to the Israelites, "See, the LORD has chosen
Bezalel son of Uri, the son of Hur, of the tribe of Judah, 31and he
has filled him with the Spirit of God, with skill, ability and knowledge in all kinds of crafts[f]— 32to make artistic designs for work
in gold, silver and bronze, 33to cut and set stones, to work in wood
and to engage in all kinds of artistic craftsmanship. 34And he has
given both him and Oholiab[g] son of Ahisamach, of the tribe of
Dan, the ability to teach[h] others. 35He has filled them with skill to
do all kinds of work[i] as craftsmen, designers, embroiderers in
blue, purple and scarlet yarn and fine linen, and weavers—all of
them master craftsmen and designers.

Chapter 36 Theme ________________________

36 So Bezalel, Oholiab and every skilled person[j] to whom
the LORD has given skill and ability to know how to carry
out all the work of constructing the sanctuary[k] are to do the work
just as the Lord has commanded."

2Then Moses summoned Bezalel[l] and Oholiab[m] and every
skilled person to whom the LORD had given ability and who was
willing[n] to come and do the work. 3They received from Moses all
the offerings[o] the Israelites had brought to carry out the work of
constructing the sanctuary. And the people continued to bring
freewill offerings morning after morning. 4So all the skilled
craftsmen who were doing all the work on the sanctuary left their
work 5and said to Moses, "The people are bringing more than
enough[p] for doing the work the LORD commanded to be done."

6Then Moses gave an order and they sent this word throughout the camp: "No man or woman is to make anything else as an
offering for the sanctuary." And so the people were restrained
from bringing more, 7because what they already had was more[q]
than enough to do all the work.

8All the skilled men among the workmen made the tabernacle
with ten curtains of finely twisted linen and blue, purple and scarlet yarn, with cherubim worked into them by a skilled craftsman.
9All the curtains were the same size—twenty-eight cubits long and

35:25
a Ex 28:3

35:27
b 1Ch 29:6; Ezr 2:68

35:28
c Ex 25:6

35:29
d ver 21; 1Ch 29:9
e ver 4-9; Ex 25:1-7; 36:3; 2Ki 12:4

35:31
f ver 35; 2Ch 2:7,14

35:34
g Ex 31:6
h 2Ch 2:14

35:35
i ver 31; Ex 31:3,6; 1Ki 7:14

36:1
j Ex 28:3
k Ex 25:8

36:2
l Ex 31:2
m Ex 31:6
n Ex 25:2; 35:21,26; 1Ch 29:5

36:3
o Ex 35:29

36:5
p 2Ch 24:14; 31:10; 2 Co 8:2-3

36:7
q 1Ki 7:47

36:13 four cubits wide.[a] [10]They joined five of the curtains together and
[a] ver 18 did the same with the other five. [11]Then they made loops of blue
material along the edge of the end curtain in one set, and the
same was done with the end curtain in the other set. [12]They also
made fifty loops on one curtain and fifty loops on the end curtain
of the other set, with the loops opposite each other. [13]Then they
made fifty gold clasps and used them to fasten the two sets of curtains together so that the tabernacle was a unit.[a]

[14]They made curtains of goat hair for the tent over the tabernacle—eleven altogether. [15]All eleven curtains were the same size—
thirty cubits long and four cubits wide.[b] [16]They joined five of the
curtains into one set and the other six into another set. [17]Then
they made fifty loops along the edge of the end curtain in one set
and also along the edge of the end curtain in the other set. [18]They
made fifty bronze clasps to fasten the tent together as a unit.[b]
[19]Then they made for the tent a covering of ram skins dyed red,
and over that a covering of hides of sea cows.[c]

[20]They made upright frames of acacia wood for the tabernacle.
[21]Each frame was ten cubits long and a cubit and a half wide,[d]
[22]with two projections set parallel to each other. They made all the
frames of the tabernacle in this way. [23]They made twenty frames
36:18 for the south side of the tabernacle [24]and made forty silver bases
[b] ver 13 to go under them—two bases for each frame, one under each
projection. [25]For the other side, the north side of the tabernacle,
they made twenty frames [26]and forty silver bases—two under
each frame. [27]They made six frames for the far end, that is, the
west end of the tabernacle, [28]and two frames were made for the
corners of the tabernacle at the far end. [29]At these two corners
the frames were double from the bottom all the way to the top and
fitted into a single ring; both were made alike. [30]So there were
eight frames and sixteen silver bases—two under each frame.

[31]They also made crossbars of acacia wood: five for the frames
on one side of the tabernacle, [32]five for those on the other side,
and five for the frames on the west, at the far end of the tabernacle. [33]They made the center crossbar so that it extended from end
to end at the middle of the frames. [34]They overlaid the frames
with gold and made gold rings to hold the crossbars. They also
overlaid the crossbars with gold.

[35]They made the curtain[c] of blue, purple and scarlet yarn and
finely twisted linen, with cherubim worked into it by a skilled
craftsman. [36]They made four posts of acacia wood for it and overlaid them with gold. They made gold hooks for them and cast

36:35
[c] Ex 39:38; [a]9 That is, about 42 feet (about 12.5 meters) long and 6 feet (about 1.8 meters) wide
Mt 27:51; [b]15 That is, about 45 feet (about 13.5 meters) long and 6 feet (about 1.8 meters) wide
Lk 23:45; [c]19 That is, dugongs [d]21 That is, about 15 feet (about 4.5 meters) long and 2 1/4 feet
Heb 9:3 (about 0.7 meter) wide

their four silver bases. 37 For the entrance to the tent they made a
curtain of blue, purple and scarlet yarn and finely twisted linen—
the work of an embroiderer;[a] 38 and they made five posts with
hooks for them. They overlaid the tops of the posts and their
bands with gold and made their five bases of bronze.

Chapter 37 Theme ____________________

37 Bezalel[b] made the ark[c] of acacia wood—two and a half
cubits long, a cubit and a half wide, and a cubit and a half
high.[a] 2 He overlaid it with pure gold,[d] both inside and out, and
made a gold molding around it. 3 He cast four gold rings for it and
fastened them to its four feet, with two rings on one side and two
rings on the other. 4 Then he made poles of acacia wood and overlaid them with gold. 5 And he inserted the poles into the rings on
the sides of the ark to carry it.

Ark of the Covenant (or Testimony)

6 He made the atonement cover[e] of pure gold—two and a half
cubits long and a cubit and a half wide.[b] 7 Then he made two
cherubim[f] out of hammered gold at the ends of the cover. 8 He
made one cherub on one end and the second cherub on the other;
at the two ends he made them of one piece with the cover. 9 The
cherubim had their wings spread upward, overshadowing[g] the
cover with them. The cherubim faced each other, looking toward
the cover.[h]

Table for Consecrated Bread

10 They[c] made the table[i] of acacia wood—two cubits long, a
cubit wide, and a cubit and a half high.[d] 11 Then they overlaid it
with pure gold[j] and made a gold molding around it. 12 They also
made around it a rim a handbreadth[e] wide and put a gold molding on the rim. 13 They cast four gold rings for the table and fastened them to the four corners, where the four legs were. 14 The
rings[k] were put close to the rim to hold the poles used in carrying
the table. 15 The poles for carrying the table were made of acacia
wood and were overlaid with gold. 16 And they made from pure
gold the articles for the table—its plates and dishes and bowls
and its pitchers for the pouring out of drink offerings.

Lampstand

17 They made the lampstand[l] of pure gold and hammered it
out, base and shaft; its flowerlike cups, buds and blossoms were
of one piece with it. 18 Six branches extended from the sides of the
lampstand—three on one side and three on the other. 19 Three
cups shaped like almond flowers with buds and blossoms were
on one branch, three on the next branch and the same for all six
branches extending from the lampstand. 20 And on the lampstand

36:37 [a] Ex 27:16
37:1 [b] Ex 31:2 [c] Ex 30:6; 39:35; Dt 10:3
37:2 [d] ver 11,26
37:6 [e] Ex 26:34; 31:7; Heb 9:5
37:7 [f] Eze 41:18
37:9 [g] Heb 9:5 [h] Dt 10:3
37:10 [i] Heb 9:2
37:11 [j] ver 2
37:14 [k] ver 27
37:17 [l] Heb 9:2; Rev 1:12

[a] *1* That is, about 3 3/4 feet (about 1.1 meters) long and 2 1/4 feet (about 0.7 meter) wide and high [b] *6* That is, about 3 3/4 feet (about 1.1 meters) long and 2 1/4 feet (about 0.7 meter) wide [c] *10* Or *He;* also in verses 11-29 [d] *10* That is, about 3 feet (about 0.9 meter) long, 1 1/2 feet (about 0.5 meter) wide, and 2 1/4 feet (about 0.7 meter) high [e] *12* That is, about 3 inches (about 8 centimeters)

were four cups shaped like almond flowers with buds and blossoms. 21One bud was under the first pair of branches extending
from the lampstand, a second bud under the second pair, and a
third bud under the third pair—six branches in all. 22The buds
and the branches were all of one piece with the lampstand, hammered out of pure gold.[a]

23They made its seven lamps,[b] as well as its wick trimmers and
trays, of pure gold. 24They made the lampstand and all its accessories from one talent[a] of pure gold.

25They made the altar of incense[c] out of acacia wood. It was
square, a cubit long and a cubit wide, and two cubits high[b]—its
horns[d] of one piece with it. 26They overlaid the top and all the
sides and the horns with pure gold, and made a gold molding
around it. 27They made two gold rings[e] below the molding—two
on opposite sides—to hold the poles used to carry it. 28They
made the poles of acacia wood and overlaid them with gold.[f]

29They also made the sacred anointing oil[g] and the pure, fragrant incense[h]—the work of a perfumer.

Altar of Incense (Gold or Golden Altar)

Chapter 38 Theme ____________________

38 They[c] built the altar of burnt offering of acacia wood,
three cubits[d] high; it was square, five cubits long and five
cubits wide.[e] 2They made a horn at each of the four corners, so
that the horns and the altar were of one piece, and they overlaid
the altar with bronze.[i] 3They made all its utensils[j] of bronze—its
pots, shovels, sprinkling bowls, meat forks and firepans. 4They
made a grating for the altar, a bronze network, to be under its
ledge, halfway up the altar. 5They cast bronze rings to hold the
poles for the four corners of the bronze grating. 6They made the
poles of acacia wood and overlaid them with bronze. 7They
inserted the poles into the rings so they would be on the sides of
the altar for carrying it. They made it hollow, out of boards.

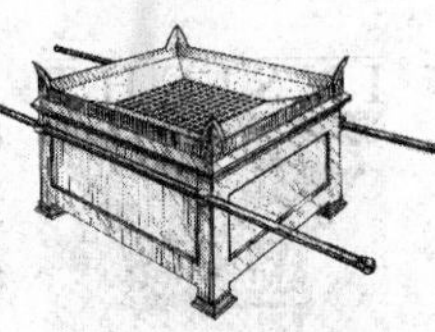
Bronze Altar

8They made the bronze basin[k] and its bronze stand from the
mirrors of the women[l] who served at the entrance to the Tent of
Meeting.

9Next they made the courtyard. The south side was a hundred
cubits[f] long and had curtains of finely twisted linen, 10with
twenty posts and twenty bronze bases, and with silver hooks
and bands on the posts. 11The north side was also a hundred
cubits long and had twenty posts and twenty bronze bases, with
silver hooks and bands on the posts.

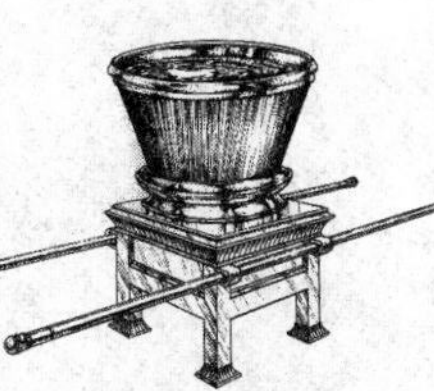
Bronze Basin

37:22 [a] ver 17; Nu 8:4
37:23 [b] Ex 40:4,25
37:25 [c] Ex 30:34-36; Lk 1:11; Heb 9:4; Rev 8:3 [d] Ex 27:2; Rev 9:13
37:27 [e] ver 14
37:28 [f] Ex 25:13
37:29 [g] Ex 31:11 [h] Ex 30:1,25; 39:38
38:2 [i] 2Ch 1:5
38:3 [j] Ex 31:9
38:8 [k] Ex 30:18; 40:7 [l] Dt 23:17; 1Sa 2:22; 1Ki 14:24

[a] *24* That is, about 75 pounds (about 34 kilograms) [b] *25* That is, about 1 1/2 feet (about 0.5 meter) long and wide, and about 3 feet (about 0.9 meter) high [c] *1* Or *He*; also in verses 2-9 [d] *1* That is, about 4 1/2 feet (about 1.3 meters) [e] *1* That is, about 7 1/2 feet (about 2.3 meters) long and wide [f] *9* That is, about 150 feet (about 46 meters)

[12]The west end was fifty cubits[a] wide and had curtains, with ten
posts and ten bases, with silver hooks and bands on the posts.
[13]The east end, toward the sunrise, was also fifty cubits wide.
[14]Curtains fifteen cubits[b] long were on one side of the entrance,
with three posts and three bases, [15]and curtains fifteen cubits
long were on the other side of the entrance to the courtyard, with
three posts and three bases. [16]All the curtains around the courtyard were of finely twisted linen. [17]The bases for the posts were
bronze. The hooks and bands on the posts were silver, and their
tops were overlaid with silver; so all the posts of the courtyard
had silver bands.

[18]The curtain for the entrance to the courtyard was of blue,
purple and scarlet yarn and finely twisted linen—the work of an
embroiderer. It was twenty cubits[c] long and, like the curtains of
the courtyard, five cubits[d] high, [19]with four posts and four bronze
bases. Their hooks and bands were silver, and their tops were
overlaid with silver. [20]All the tent pegs[a] of the tabernacle and of
the surrounding courtyard were bronze.

INSIGHT

See the illustration of the tabernacle on page IISB-34.

[21]These are the amounts of the materials used for the tabernacle, the tabernacle of the Testimony,[b] which were recorded at
Moses' command by the Levites under the direction of Ithamar[c]
son of Aaron, the priest. [22](Bezalel[d] son of Uri, the son of Hur, of
the tribe of Judah, made everything the LORD commanded Moses;
[23]with him was Oholiab[e] son of Ahisamach, of the tribe of Dan—
a craftsman and designer, and an embroiderer in blue, purple and
scarlet yarn and fine linen.) [24]The total amount of the gold from
the wave offering used for all the work on the sanctuary[f] was 29
talents and 730 shekels,[e] according to the sanctuary shekel.[g]

[25]The silver obtained from those of the community who were
counted in the census[h] was 100 talents and 1,775 shekels,[f] according to the sanctuary shekel— [26]one beka per person,[i] that is, half
a shekel,[g] according to the sanctuary shekel,[j] from everyone
who had crossed over to those counted, twenty years old or
more,[k] a total of 603,550 men.[l] [27]The 100 talents[h] of silver were
used to cast the bases[m] for the sanctuary and for the curtain—
100 bases from the 100 talents, one talent for each base. [28]They
used the 1,775 shekels[i] to make the hooks for the posts, to overlay the tops of the posts, and to make their bands.

[29]The bronze from the wave offering was 70 talents and 2,400
shekels.[j] [30]They used it to make the bases for the entrance to the

38:20
[a] Ex 35:18

38:21
[b] Nu 1:50,53; 8:24; 9:15; 10:11; 17:7; 1Ch 23:32; 2Ch 24:6; Ac 7:44; Rev 15:5
[c] Nu 4:28,33

38:22
[d] Ex 31:2

38:23
[e] Ex 31:6

38:24
[f] Ex 30:16
[g] Ex 30:13; Lev 27:25; Nu 3:47; 18:16

38:25
[h] Ex 30:12

38:26
[i] Ex 30:12
[j] Ex 30:13
[k] Ex 30:14
[l] Ex 12:37; Nu 1:46

38:27
[m] Ex 26:19

[a]*12* That is, about 75 feet (about 23 meters) [b]*14* That is, about 22 1/2 feet (about 6.9 meters) [c]*18* That is, about 30 feet (about 9 meters) [d]*18* That is, about 7 1/2 feet (about 2.3 meters) [e]*24* The weight of the gold was a little over one ton (about 1 metric ton). [f]*25* The weight of the silver was a little over 3 3/4 tons (about 3.4 metric tons). [g]*26* That is, about 1/5ounce (about 5.5 grams) [h]*27* That is, about 3 3/4 tons (about 3.4 metric tons) [i]*28* That is, about 45pounds (about 20 kilograms) [j]*29* The weight of the bronze was about 2 1/2 tons (about 2.4 metric tons).

39:1 Tent of Meeting, the bronze altar with its bronze grating and all
[a] Ex 35:23 its utensils, 31the bases for the surrounding courtyard and those
[b] Ex 35:19 for its entrance and all the tent pegs for the tabernacle and those
[c] ver 41; Ex 28:2 for the surrounding courtyard.

Chapter 39 Theme ______________________________

39 From the blue, purple and scarlet yarn[a] they made woven
garments for ministering in the sanctuary.[b] They also made
sacred garments[c] for Aaron, as the LORD commanded Moses.
2They[a] made the ephod of gold, and of blue, purple and scarlet
yarn, and of finely twisted linen. 3They hammered out thin
sheets of gold and cut strands to be worked into the blue, purple
and scarlet yarn and fine linen—the work of a skilled craftsman.
4They made shoulder pieces for the ephod, which were attached
to two of its corners, so it could be fastened. 5Its skillfully woven
39:7 waistband was like it—of one piece with the ephod and made
[d] Lev 24:7; Jos 4:7 with gold, and with blue, purple and scarlet yarn, and with finely
twisted linen, as the LORD commanded Moses.

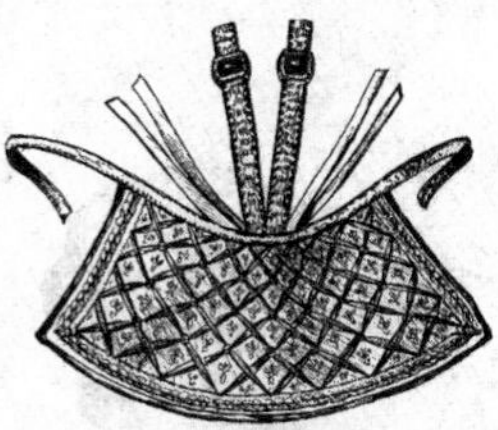

Ephod

6They mounted the onyx stones in gold filigree settings and
engraved them like a seal with the names of the sons of Israel.
7Then they fastened them on the shoulder pieces of the ephod as
memorial[d] stones for the sons of Israel, as the LORD commanded
Moses.
8They fashioned the breastpiece[e]—the work of a skilled craftsman. They made it like the ephod: of gold, and of blue, purple
and scarlet yarn, and of finely twisted linen. 9It was square—a
span[b] long and a span wide—and folded double. 10Then they
mounted four rows of precious stones on it. In the first row there
was a ruby, a topaz and a beryl; 11in the second row a turquoise,
a sapphire[c] and an emerald; 12in the third row a jacinth, an agate
39:8 and an amethyst; 13in the fourth row a chrysolite, an onyx and a
[e] Lev 8:8 jasper.[d] They were mounted in gold filigree settings. 14There were
twelve stones, one for each of the names of the sons of Israel, each
engraved like a seal with the name of one of the twelve tribes.[f]

High Priest's Garments

15For the breastpiece they made braided chains of pure gold,
like a rope. 16They made two gold filigree settings and two gold
rings, and fastened the rings to two of the corners of the breastpiece. 17They fastened the two gold chains to the rings at the corners of the breastpiece, 18and the other ends of the chains to the
two settings, attaching them to the shoulder pieces of the ephod
at the front. 19They made two gold rings and attached them to
the other two corners of the breastpiece on the inside edge next

a2 Or *He*; also in verses 7, 8 and 22 b9 That is, about 9 inches (about 22 centimeters)
39:14 c11 Or *lapis lazuli* d13 The precise identification of some of these precious stones is
[f] Rev 21:12 uncertain.

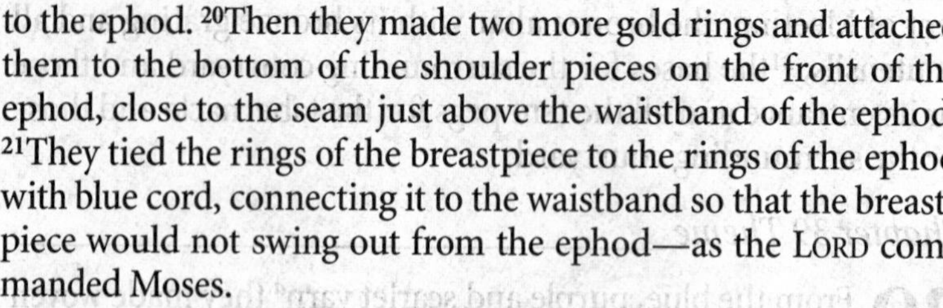

to the ephod. 20Then they made two more gold rings and attached them to the bottom of the shoulder pieces on the front of the ephod, close to the seam just above the waistband of the ephod. 21They tied the rings of the breastpiece to the rings of the ephod with blue cord, connecting it to the waistband so that the breastpiece would not swing out from the ephod—as the LORD commanded Moses.

Robe of the Ephod

22They made the robe of the ephod entirely of blue cloth—the work of a weaver— 23with an opening in the center of the robe like the opening of a collar,[a] and a band around this opening, so that it would not tear. 24They made pomegranates of blue, purple and scarlet yarn and finely twisted linen around the hem of the robe. 25And they made bells of pure gold and attached them around the hem between the pomegranates. 26The bells and pomegranates alternated around the hem of the robe to be worn for ministering, as the LORD commanded Moses.

27For Aaron and his sons, they made tunics of fine linen[*a*]—the work of a weaver— 28and the turban[*b*] of fine linen, the linen headbands and the undergarments of finely twisted linen. 29The sash was of finely twisted linen and blue, purple and scarlet yarn—the work of an embroiderer—as the LORD commanded Moses.

Turban with Plate of Gold

30They made the plate, the sacred diadem, out of pure gold and engraved on it, like an inscription on a seal: HOLY TO THE LORD. 31Then they fastened a blue cord to it to attach it to the turban, as the LORD commanded Moses.

32So all the work on the tabernacle, the Tent of Meeting, was completed. The Israelites did everything just as the LORD commanded Moses.[*c*] 33Then they brought the tabernacle to Moses: the tent and all its furnishings, its clasps, frames, crossbars, posts and bases; 34the covering of ram skins dyed red, the covering of hides of sea cows[b] and the shielding curtain; 35the ark of the Testimony[*d*] with its poles and the atonement cover; 36the table with all its articles and the bread of the Presence; 37the pure gold lampstand[*e*] with its row of lamps and all its accessories, and the oil for the light; 38the gold altar,[*f*] the anointing oil, the fragrant incense, and the curtain[*g*] for the entrance to the tent; 39the bronze altar with its bronze grating, its poles and all its utensils; the basin with its stand; 40the curtains of the courtyard with its posts and bases, and the curtain for the entrance to the courtyard;[*h*] the ropes and tent pegs for the courtyard; all the furnishings for the tabernacle, the Tent of Meeting; 41and the woven garments worn for ministering in the sanctuary, both the sacred garments for Aaron the priest and the garments for his sons when serving as priests.

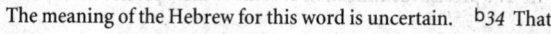

a23 The meaning of the Hebrew for this word is uncertain. b34 That is, dugongs

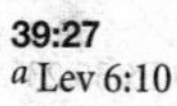

39:27 *a* Lev 6:10

39:28 *b* Ex 28:4

39:32 *c* ver 42-43; Ex 25:9

39:35 *d* Ex 30:6

39:37 *e* Ex 25:31

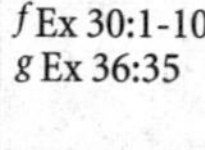

39:38 *f* Ex 30:1-10 *g* Ex 36:35

39:40 *h* Ex 27:9-19

39:42 [a] Ex 25:9
39:43 [b] Lev 9:22,23; Nu 6:23-27; 2Sa 6:18; 1Ki 8:14,55; 2Ch 30:27

42The Israelites had done all the work just as the LORD had commanded Moses.[a] 43Moses inspected the work and saw that they had done it just as the LORD had commanded. So Moses blessed[b] them.

Chapter 40 Theme ______________________

40:2 [c] Nu 1:1 [d] ver 17; Ex 12:2
40:3 [e] ver 21; Nu 4:5; Ex 26:33
40:4 [f] Ex 25:30 [g] ver 22-25; Ex 26:35
40:5 [h] ver 26; Ex 30:1

40 Then the LORD said to Moses: 2"Set up the tabernacle, the Tent of Meeting,[c] on the first day of the first month.[d] 3Place the ark[e] of the Testimony in it and shield the ark with the curtain. 4Bring in the table and set out what belongs on it.[f] Then bring in the lampstand[g] and set up its lamps. 5Place the gold altar[h] of incense in front of the ark of the Testimony and put the curtain at the entrance to the tabernacle.

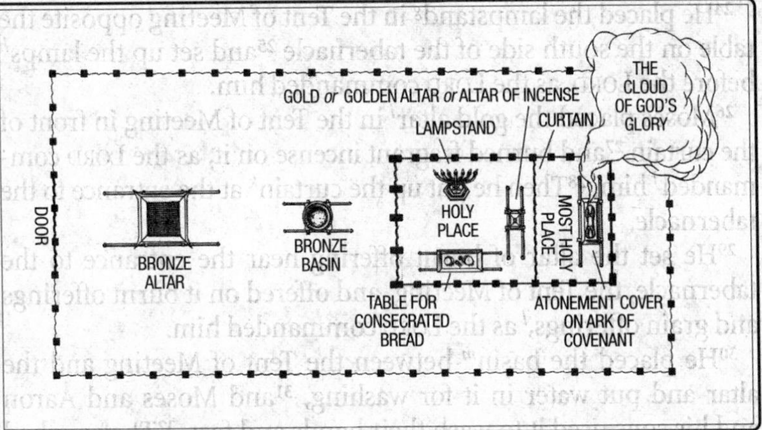

Inside the Tabernacle

40:7 [i] ver 30; Ex 30:18
40:9 [j] Ex 30:26; Lev 8:10
40:10 [k] Ex 29:36
40:12 [l] Lev 8:1-13
40:13 [m] Ex 28:41 [n] Lev 8:12
40:15 [o] Ex 29:9; Nu 25:13

6"Place the altar of burnt offering in front of the entrance to the tabernacle, the Tent of Meeting; 7place the basin[i] between the Tent of Meeting and the altar and put water in it. 8Set up the courtyard around it and put the curtain at the entrance to the courtyard.

9"Take the anointing oil and anoint[j] the tabernacle and everything in it; consecrate it and all its furnishings, and it will be holy. 10Then anoint the altar of burnt offering and all its utensils; consecrate[k] the altar, and it will be most holy. 11Anoint the basin and its stand and consecrate them.

12"Bring Aaron and his sons to the entrance to the Tent of Meeting and wash them with water.[l] 13Then dress Aaron in the sacred garments,[m] anoint him and consecrate[n] him so he may serve me as priest. 14Bring his sons and dress them in tunics. 15Anoint them just as you anointed their father, so they may serve me as priests. Their anointing will be to a priesthood that will continue for all generations to come.[o]" 16Moses did everything just as the LORD commanded him.

17So the tabernacle[a] was set up on the first day of the first
month[b] in the second year. 18When Moses set up the tabernacle,
he put the bases in place, erected the frames, inserted the crossbars and set up the posts. 19Then he spread the tent over the
tabernacle and put the covering over the tent, as the LORD commanded him.

20He took the Testimony[c] and placed it in the ark, attached the
poles to the ark and put the atonement cover over it. 21Then he
brought the ark into the tabernacle and hung the shielding curtain[d] and shielded the ark of the Testimony, as the LORD commanded him.

22Moses placed the table[e] in the Tent of Meeting on the north
side of the tabernacle outside the curtain 23and set out the bread[f]
on it before the LORD, as the LORD commanded him.

24He placed the lampstand[g] in the Tent of Meeting opposite the
table on the south side of the tabernacle 25and set up the lamps[h]
before the LORD, as the LORD commanded him.

26Moses placed the gold altar[i] in the Tent of Meeting in front of
the curtain 27and burned fragrant incense on it, as the LORD commanded[j] him. 28Then he put up the curtain[k] at the entrance to the
tabernacle.

29He set the altar of burnt offering near the entrance to the
tabernacle, the Tent of Meeting, and offered on it burnt offerings
and grain offerings,[l] as the LORD commanded him.

30He placed the basin[m] between the Tent of Meeting and the
altar and put water in it for washing, 31and Moses and Aaron
and his sons used it to wash their hands and feet. 32They washed
whenever they entered the Tent of Meeting or approached the
altar,[n] as the LORD commanded Moses.

33Then Moses set up the courtyard[o] around the tabernacle and
altar and put up the curtain[p] at the entrance to the courtyard.
And so Moses finished the work.

34Then the cloud[q] covered the Tent of Meeting, and the glory of
the LORD filled the tabernacle. 35Moses could not enter the Tent
of Meeting because the cloud had settled upon it, and the glory
of the LORD filled the tabernacle.[r]

36In all the travels of the Israelites, whenever the cloud lifted
from above the tabernacle, they would set out;[s] 37but if the cloud
did not lift, they did not set out—until the day it lifted. 38So the
cloud[t] of the LORD was over the tabernacle by day, and fire was in
the cloud by night, in the sight of all the house of Israel during
all their travels.

40:17 a Nu 7:1; b ver 2
40:20 c Ex 16:34; 25:16; Dt 10:5; 1Ki 8:9; Heb 9:4
40:21 d Ex 26:33
40:22 e Ex 26:35
40:23 f ver 4
40:24 g Ex 26:35
40:25 h ver 4; Ex 25:37
40:26 i ver 5; Ex 30:6
40:27 j Ex 30:7
40:28 k Ex 26:36
40:29 l ver 6; Ex 29:38-42
40:30 m ver 7
40:32 n Ex 30:20
40:33 o Ex 27:9; p ver 8
40:34 q Nu 9:15-23; 1Ki 8:12
40:35 r 1Ki 8:11; 2Ch 5:13-14
40:36 s Nu 9:17-23; 10:13; Ne 9:19
40:38 t Ex 13:21; Nu 9:15; 1Co 10:1

Theme of Exodus:

Author:

Date:

Purpose:

Key Words:

slaves (servant[s]) slavery

rescue, free, hand over (rescued, saved)

holy (sacred)

the Lord commanded (I commanded)

covenant (treaty)

cloud (darkness)

test(ed)

law

tabernacle (tent, Tent of Meeting)

SEGMENT DIVISIONS			CHAPTER THEMES
			1
			2
			3
			4
			5
			6
			7
			8
			9
			10
			11
			12
			13
			14
			15
			16
			17
			18
			19
			20

SEGMENT DIVISIONS

			CHAPTER THEMES
			21
			22
			23
			24
			25
			26
			27
			28
			29
			30
			31
			32
			33
			34
			35
			36
			37
			38
			39
			40

LEVITICUS

In Genesis we see the ruin of man as he listens to the serpent rather than to God. The human race is condemned to sin's awful wage—death. Yet in the mercy and grace of God comes the promise of redemption through the seed of the woman, through the seed of Abraham, as God calls out a people for himself. God makes a covenant with Abraham which he confirms to Isaac and then to Jacob, later to be named Israel.

However, as the book of Genesis comes to a close, the children of Israel are living in Egypt rather than in Canaan, the land of promise. The book that began with the creation of man in Eden ends with the children of Israel looking into a coffin in Egypt, yet not without a promise that someday they would leave Egypt.

Exodus plays out the drama of redemption as the nation of Israel is redeemed from slavery through the blood of the Passover lamb. After the descendants of Abraham were enslaved and oppressed for 400 years, just as God promised, they left Egypt with great possessions as God went before them in his cloud of glory.

And what follows the redemption of ruined man? That is what the book of Leviticus is all about. Study it well, for in picture form Leviticus shows us what God expects from those who have been redeemed.

THINGS TO DO

General Instructions

1. As you read Leviticus watch for the verses which attribute the authorship of this book to Moses. When you come across those references, record them under "Author" on the LEVITICUS AT A GLANCE chart on page 212.

2. Read Exodus 40:17, 32-38 and Leviticus 1:1, 2 and note the uninterrupted transition from one book to the other. Then compare Numbers 1:1 with these verses. As you do this you will see that the book of Leviticus covers a period of one month.

3. As you read through Leviticus one chapter at a time, do the following:
   a. Ask the five W's and an H: Who? What? When? Where? Why? and How? For example: Who is to do what? When are they to do it? How are they to do it? Why? What if they didn't know why? Questions which interrogate the text help you see what is being said.
   b. Mark the key repeated words listed on LEVITICUS AT A GLANCE. You will find it helpful to list these key words on an index card that you can use as a bookmark while you study Leviticus. Also watch for any other key words which might be used in that particular chapter. If you gain insights from marking these words, list what you learn in the margin.
   c. Record the main theme or subject of the chapter on the line next to the chapter number in the text. Then record it on LEVITICUS AT A GLANCE.
   d. You may want to summarize the main points or the order of events covered in the chapter. Record them in the margin.
   e. Record any new insights about the character and ways of God. You could identify your insights on God with this symbol △ and then color it yellow, which would make it easy to recognize.

Chapters 1-7

1. As you read chapters 1 through 7, which give instructions regarding the various sacrifices or offerings, mark the text as instructed under "General Instructions" and then record what you learn about each of the offerings on the chart THE OFFERINGS AND THEIR PURPOSES. This chart is on page 209.

2. Watch what God says about unintentional sin, guilt, and restitution. Note what is to be done when a leader sins and when the congregation sins. Write it in the margin or mark it in the text.

Chapters 8-10

This segment covers the consecration of Aaron and his sons. There is an event in chapter 10 which occurs in conjunction with this. As you read these chapters, list in the margin of each chapter what was to be done and why. In chapter 10 note what happened, why it happened, and who was involved.

Chapters 11-15

This segment deals with laws of cleanliness.

1. In addition to the other key words, also mark *clean* and *unclean*.

2. In the margin record what the law covers. For example: food, women, infections, etc.

Chapters 16, 17

These chapters cover the Day of Atonement and regulations regarding the blood.

1. In the margin of chapter 16 carefully outline what is to be done on the Day of Atonement. As you do, you might want to consult the chart INSIDE THE TABERNACLE on page 187.

2. Note the regulations in chapter 17 regarding sacrifices and blood.

Chapters 18-27

This segment lays out statutes on issues regarding moral laws, the priests, the celebration of annual feasts, the land, etc.

1. As you read each chapter, in the margin list the main topics or situations.

2. If moral laws are given, note the consequences of breaking the laws and the reason for the consequences.

3. In chapter 23 note the feasts, when they are to be celebrated, and how. When you finish studying the chapter, consult the chart THE FEASTS OF ISRAEL on pages 210, 211.

4. Give special attention to any mention of the land—its Sabbath rest, principles of redemption, etc. Mark the words *redeem, redeems, redemption*, and any other synonyms. Record your insights in the margin.

5. When you finish reading through Leviticus, complete LEVITICUS AT A GLANCE.

   a. See if any of the chapters can be grouped categorically. If so, record this under "Segment Divisions" on the chart. Record any other possible segment divisions. For instance, you could do a segment division titled "Laws Regarding."

   b. Record the theme of Leviticus.

❧ Things to Think About

1. What have you learned about God and his attitude toward sin? What happens when sin goes unpunished?

2. What have you learned about the occult and about the types of sexual sin? How severely were these sins to be dealt with? What does this tell you about how God feels regarding these sins and their consequences? What do you think would happen in your country if these sins were dealt with according to God's law? Read 1 Timothy 1:8-11.

3. Jesus told the Jews that the Scriptures—the Old Testament—testified of him. Think about how Jesus Christ and his work are foreshadowed in Leviticus.

4. What have you learned about holiness from Leviticus? If you want to be holy, how will you live your life? Are there any changes you need to make? Are you willing? If not, why not?

Chapter 1 Theme ______________________

1 The LORD called to Moses[a] and spoke to him from the Tent
of Meeting.[b] He said, 2"Speak to the Israelites and say to
them: 'When any of you brings an offering to the LORD, bring
as your offering an animal from either the herd or the flock.[c]
3" 'If the offering is a burnt offering from the herd, he is to offer
a male without defect.[d] He must present it at the entrance to the
Tent[e] of Meeting so that it[a] will be acceptable to the LORD. 4He is
to lay his hand on the head[f] of the burnt offering, and it will be
accepted on his behalf to make atonement[g] for him. 5He is to
slaughter[h] the young bull before the LORD, and then Aaron's sons
the priests shall bring the blood and sprinkle it against the altar
on all sides[i] at the entrance to the Tent of Meeting. 6He is to skin[j]
the burnt offering and cut it into pieces. 7The sons of Aaron the
priest are to put fire on the altar and arrange wood[k] on the fire.
8Then Aaron's sons the priests shall arrange the pieces, including the head and the fat,[l] on the burning wood that is on the
altar. 9He is to wash the inner parts and the legs with water, and
the priest is to burn all of it on the altar.[m] It is a burnt offering,
an offering made by fire, an aroma pleasing to the LORD.[n]
10" 'If the offering is a burnt offering from the flock, from either
the sheep or the goats,[o] he is to offer a male without defect. 11He
is to slaughter it at the north side of the altar before the LORD,
and Aaron's sons the priests shall sprinkle its blood against the
altar on all sides.[p] 12He is to cut it into pieces, and the priest shall
arrange them, including the head and the fat, on the burning
wood that is on the altar. 13He is to wash the inner parts and the
legs with water, and the priest is to bring all of it and burn it on
the altar. It is a burnt offering, an offering made by fire, an aroma pleasing to the LORD.
14" 'If the offering to the LORD is a burnt offering of birds, he is
to offer a dove or a young pigeon.[q] 15The priest shall bring it to
the altar, wring off the head and burn it on the altar; its blood
shall be drained out on the side of the altar.[r] 16He is to remove
the crop with its contents[b] and throw it to the east side of the
altar, where the ashes[s] are. 17He shall tear it open by the wings,
not severing it completely,[t] and then the priest shall burn it on
the wood[u] that is on the fire on the altar. It is a burnt offering, an
offering made by fire, an aroma pleasing to the LORD.

Chapter 2 Theme ______________________

2 " 'When someone brings a grain offering[v] to the LORD, his
offering is to be of fine flour. He is to pour oil[w] on it, put
incense on it 2and take it to Aaron's sons the priests. The priest

1:1 [a]Ex 19:3; 25:22 [b]Nu 7:89
1:2 [c]Lev 22:18-19
1:3 [d]Ex 12:5; Dt 15:21; Heb 9:14; 1Pe 1:19 [e]Lev 17:9
1:4 [f]Ex 29:10,15; Lev 3:2 [g]2Ch 29:23-24
1:5 [h]Lev 3:2,8 [i]Heb 12:24; 1Pe 1:2
1:6 [j]Lev 7:8
1:7 [k]Lev 6:12
1:8 [l]ver 12
1:9 [m]Ex 29:18 [n]ver 13; Ge 8:21; Nu 15:8-10; Eph 5:2
1:10 [o]ver 3; Ex 12:5
1:11 [p]ver 5
1:14 [q]Ge 15:9; Lev 5:7; Lk 2:24
1:15 [r]Lev 5:9
1:16 [s]Lev 6:10
1:17 [t]Ge 15:10 [u]Lev 5:8
2:1 [v]Lev 6:14-18 [w]Nu 15:4

[a]3 Or *he* [b]16 Or *crop and the feathers*; the meaning of the Hebrew for this word is uncertain.

shall take a handful of the fine flour[a] and oil, together with all
the incense,[b] and burn this as a memorial portion[c] on the altar,
an offering made by fire, an aroma pleasing to the Lord. 3The
rest of the grain offering belongs to Aaron and his sons;[d] it is a
most holy part of the offerings made to the LORD by fire.

4" 'If you bring a grain offering baked in an oven, it is to consist
of fine flour: cakes made without yeast and mixed with oil, or[a]
wafers made without yeast and spread with oil.[e] 5If your grain
offering is prepared on a griddle, it is to be made of fine flour
mixed with oil, and without yeast. 6Crumble it and pour oil on
it; it is a grain offering. 7If your grain offering is cooked in a pan,[f]
it is to be made of fine flour and oil. 8Bring the grain offering
made of these things to the LORD; present it to the priest, who
shall take it to the altar. 9He shall take out the memorial portion[g]
from the grain offering and burn it on the altar as an offering
made by fire, an aroma pleasing to the LORD.[h] 10The rest of the
grain offering belongs to Aaron and his sons;[i] it is a most holy
part of the offerings made to the LORD by fire.

11" 'Every grain offering you bring to the LORD must be made
without yeast,[j] for you are not to burn any yeast or honey in an
offering made to the LORD by fire. 12You may bring them to the
LORD as an offering of the firstfruits,[k] but they are not to be
offered on the altar as a pleasing aroma. 13Season all your grain
offerings with salt. Do not leave the salt of the covenant[l] of your
God out of your grain offerings; add salt to all your offerings.

14" 'If you bring a grain offering of firstfruits[m] to the LORD, offer
crushed heads of new grain roasted in the fire. 15Put oil and
incense on it; it is a grain offering. 16The priest shall burn the
memorial portion[n] of the crushed grain and the oil, together
with all the incense, as an offering made to the LORD by fire.

Chapter 3 Theme ________________________

3 " 'If someone's offering is a fellowship offering,[b][o] and he
offers an animal from the herd, whether male or female, he
is to present before the LORD an animal without defect.[p] 2He is to
lay his hand on the head[q] of his offering and slaughter it[r] at the
entrance to the Tent of Meeting. Then Aaron's sons the priests
shall sprinkle the blood against the altar on all sides. 3From the
fellowship offering he is to bring a sacrifice made to the LORD by
fire: all the fat[s] that covers the inner parts or is connected to
them, 4both kidneys with the fat on them near the loins, and the
covering of the liver, which he will remove with the kidneys.
5Then Aaron's sons[t] are to burn it on the altar on top of the burnt

a4 Or *and* b1 Traditionally *peace offering*; also in verses 3, 6 and 9

2:2 [a]Lev 5:11 [b]Lev 6:15; Isa 66:3 [c]ver 9,16; Lev 5:12; 6:15; 24:7; Ac 10:4
2:3 [d]ver 10; Lev 6:16; 10:12,13
2:4 [e]Ex 29:2
2:7 [f]Lev 7:9
2:9 [g]ver 2 [h]Ex 29:18; Lev 6:15
2:10 [i]ver 3
2:11 [j]Ex 23:18; 34:25; Lev 6:16
2:12 [k]Lev 7:13; 23:10
2:13 [l]Nu 18:19; Eze 43:24
2:14 [m]Lev 23:10
2:16 [n]ver 2
3:1 [o]Lev 7:11-34 [p]Lev 1:3; 22:21
3:2 [q]Ex 29:10,15 [r]Lev 1:5
3:3 [s]Ex 29:13
3:5 [t]Lev 7:29-34

offering[a] that is on the burning wood, as an offering made by
fire, an aroma pleasing to the LORD.
6" 'If he offers an animal from the flock as a fellowship offering[b]
to the LORD, he is to offer a male or female without defect. 7If he
offers a lamb, he is to present it before the LORD.[c] 8He is to lay his
hand on the head of his offering and slaughter it[d] in front of the
Tent of Meeting. Then Aaron's sons shall sprinkle its blood
against the altar on all sides. 9From the fellowship offering he is
to bring a sacrifice made to the LORD by fire: its fat, the entire fat
tail cut off close to the backbone, all the fat that covers the inner
parts or is connected to them, 10both kidneys with the fat on them
near the loins, and the covering of the liver, which he will remove
with the kidneys. 11The priest shall burn them on the altar[e] as
food,[f] an offering made to the LORD by fire.
12" 'If his offering is a goat, he is to present it before the LORD.
13He is to lay his hand on its head and slaughter it in front of the
Tent of Meeting. Then Aaron's sons shall sprinkle[g] its blood
against the altar on all sides. 14From what he offers he is to make
this offering to the LORD by fire: all the fat that covers the inner
parts or is connected to them, 15both kidneys with the fat on
them near the loins, and the covering of the liver, which he will
remove with the kidneys. 16The priest shall burn them on the
altar as food, an offering made by fire, a pleasing aroma. All the
fat is the LORD's.[h]
17" 'This is a lasting ordinance for the generations to come,[i]
wherever you live: You must not eat any fat or any blood.[j]' "

Chapter 4 Theme ____________________

4 The LORD said to Moses, 2"Say to the Israelites: 'When anyone sins unintentionally[k] and does what is forbidden in any
of the LORD's commands—
3" 'If the anointed priest sins, bringing guilt on the people, he
must bring to the LORD a young bull[l] without defect as a sin
offering[m] for the sin he has committed. 4He is to present the bull
at the entrance to the Tent of Meeting before the LORD.[n] He is to
lay his hand on its head and slaughter it before the LORD. 5Then
the anointed priest shall take some of the bull's blood[o] and carry
it into the Tent of Meeting. 6He is to dip his finger into the blood
and sprinkle some of it seven times before the LORD, in front of
the curtain of the sanctuary. 7The priest shall then put some of
the blood on the horns of the altar of fragrant incense that is
before the LORD in the Tent of Meeting. The rest of the bull's
blood he shall pour out at the base of the altar[p] of burnt offering[q]
at the entrance to the Tent of Meeting. 8He shall remove all the

3:5 [a]Ex 29:13, 38-42
3:6 [b]ver 1
3:7 [c]Lev 17:8-9
3:8 [d]ver 2; Lev 1:5
3:11 [e]ver 5 [f]ver 16; Lev 21:6,17
3:13 [g]Ex 24:6
3:16 [h]1Sa 2:16
3:17 [i]Lev 6:18; 17:7 [j]Ge 9:4; Lev 7:25-26; 17:10-16; Dt 12:16; Ac 15:20
4:2 [k]Lev 5:15-18; Ps 19:12; Heb 9:7
4:3 [l]ver 14; Ps 66:15 [m]Lev 9:2-22; Heb 9:13-14
4:4 [n]Lev 1:3
4:5 [o]Lev 16:14
4:7 [p]ver 34; Lev 8:15 [q]ver 18,30; Lev 5:9; 9:9; 16:18

fat[a] from the bull of the sin offering—the fat that covers the inner
parts or is connected to them, 9both kidneys with the fat on
them near the loins, and the covering of the liver, which he will
remove with the kidneys[b]— 10just as the fat is removed from the
ox[a] sacrificed as a fellowship offering.[b] Then the priest shall
burn them on the altar of burnt offering. 11But the hide of the
bull and all its flesh, as well as the head and legs, the inner parts
and offal[c]— 12that is, all the rest of the bull—he must take outside the camp[d] to a place ceremonially clean,[e] where the ashes
are thrown, and burn it in a wood fire on the ash heap.

13" 'If the whole Israelite community sins unintentionally[f] and
does what is forbidden in any of the LORD's commands, even
though the community is unaware of the matter, they are guilty.
14When they become aware of the sin they committed, the assembly must bring a young bull[g] as a sin offering[h] and present it
before the Tent of Meeting. 15The elders of the community are to
lay their hands on the bull's head[i] before the LORD, and the bull
shall be slaughtered before the LORD. 16Then the anointed priest
is to take some of the bull's blood[j] into the Tent of Meeting. 17He
shall dip his finger into the blood and sprinkle it before the LORD[k]
seven times in front of the curtain. 18He is to put some of the blood
on the horns of the altar that is before the LORD[l] in the Tent of
Meeting. The rest of the blood he shall pour out at the base of
the altar of burnt offering at the entrance to the Tent of Meeting.
19He shall remove all the fat[m] from it and burn it on the altar,
20and do with this bull just as he did with the bull for the sin
offering. In this way the priest will make atonement[n] for them,
and they will be forgiven.[o] 21Then he shall take the bull outside
the camp and burn it as he burned the first bull. This is the sin
offering for the community.[p]

22" 'When a leader[q] sins unintentionally[r] and does what is forbidden in any of the commands of the LORD his God, he is guilty.
23When he is made aware of the sin he committed, he must bring
as his offering a male goat without defect. 24He is to lay his hand
on the goat's head and slaughter it at the place where the burnt
offering is slaughtered before the LORD. It is a sin offering. 25Then
the priest shall take some of the blood of the sin offering with
his finger and put it on the horns of the altar of burnt offering
and pour out the rest of the blood at the base of the altar.[s] 26He
shall burn all the fat on the altar as he burned the fat of the fellowship offering. In this way the priest will make atonement for
the man's sin, and he will be forgiven.[t]

[a]*10* The Hebrew word can include both male and female. [b]*10* Traditionally *peace offering*; also in verses 26, 31 and 35

4:8 [a]Lev 3:3-5
4:9 [b]Lev 3:4
4:11 [c]Ex 29:14; Lev 9:11; Nu 19:5
4:12 [d]Heb 13:11 [e]Lev 6:11
4:13 [f]ver 2; Lev 5:2-4,17; Nu 15:24-26
4:14 [g]ver 3 [h]ver 23,28
4:15 [i]Lev 1:4; 8:14,22; Nu 8:10
4:16 [j]ver 5
4:17 [k]ver 6
4:18 [l]ver 7
4:19 [m]ver 8
4:20 [n]Heb 10:10-12 [o]Nu 15:25
4:21 [p]Lev 16:5,15
4:22 [q]Nu 31:13 [r]ver 2
4:25 [s]ver 7,18,30,34; Lev 9:9
4:26 [t]Lev 5:10

27“‘If a member of the community sins unintentionally[a] and
does what is forbidden in any of the LORD’s commands, he is
guilty. 28When he is made aware of the sin he committed, he
must bring as his offering[b] for the sin he committed a female
goat[c] without defect. 29He is to lay his hand on the head[d] of the
sin offering[e] and slaughter it at the place of the burnt offering.
30Then the priest is to take some of the blood with his finger and
put it on the horns of the altar of burnt offering[f] and pour out
the rest of the blood at the base of the altar. 31He shall remove all
the fat, just as the fat is removed from the fellowship offering,
and the priest shall burn it on the altar as an aroma pleasing to
the LORD.[g] In this way the priest will make atonement for him,
and he will be forgiven.

32“‘If he brings a lamb as his sin offering, he is to bring a female
without defect.[h] 33He is to lay his hand on its head and slaughter
it for a sin offering at the place where the burnt offering is slaughtered.[i] 34Then the priest shall take some of the blood of the sin
offering with his finger and put it on the horns of the altar of
burnt offering and pour out the rest of the blood at the base of
the altar.[j] 35He shall remove all the fat, just as the fat is removed
from the lamb of the fellowship offering, and the priest shall
burn it on the altar[k] on top of the offerings made to the LORD by
fire. In this way the priest will make atonement for him for the
sin he has committed, and he will be forgiven.

Chapter 5 Theme ____________________________

5 “‘If a person sins because he does not speak up when he
hears a public charge to testify[l] regarding something he has
seen or learned about, he will be held responsible.[m]

2“‘Or if a person touches anything ceremonially unclean—
whether the carcasses of unclean wild animals or of unclean livestock or of unclean creatures that move along the ground[n]—even
though he is unaware of it, he has become unclean and is guilty.

3“‘Or if he touches human uncleanness[o]—anything that would
make him unclean—even though he is unaware of it, when he
learns of it he will be guilty.

4“‘Or if a person thoughtlessly takes an oath[p] to do anything,
whether good or evil—in any matter one might carelessly swear
about—even though he is unaware of it, in any case when he
learns of it he will be guilty.

5“‘When anyone is guilty in any of these ways, he must
confess[q] in what way he has sinned 6and, as a penalty for the sin
he has committed, he must bring to the LORD a female lamb or
goat from the flock as a sin offering;[r] and the priest shall make
atonement for him for his sin.

4:27 [a]ver 2; Nu 15:27
4:28 [b]ver 23 [c]ver 3
4:29 [d]ver 4,24 [e]Lev 1:4
4:30 [f]ver 7
4:31 [g]Ge 8:21
4:32 [h]ver 28
4:33 [i]ver 29
4:34 [j]ver 7
4:35 [k]ver 26,31
5:1 [l]Pr 29:24 [m]ver 17
5:2 [n]Lev 11:11, 24-40; Dt 14:8
5:3 [o]Nu 19:11-16
5:4 [p]Nu 30:6,8
5:5 [q]Lev 16:21; 26:40; Nu 5:7; Pr 28:13
5:6 [r]Lev 4:28

7“‘If he cannot afford[a] a lamb, he is to bring two doves or two
young pigeons to the LORD as a penalty for his sin—one for a sin
offering and the other for a burnt offering. 8He is to bring them
to the priest, who shall first offer the one for the sin offering. He
is to wring its head from its neck,[b] not severing it completely,[c]
9and is to sprinkle some of the blood of the sin offering against
the side of the altar; the rest of the blood must be drained out at
the base of the altar.[d] It is a sin offering. 10The priest shall then
offer the other as a burnt offering in the prescribed way[e] and
make atonement for him for the sin he has committed, and he
will be forgiven.[f]

11“‘If, however, he cannot afford two doves or two young pigeons, he is to bring as an offering for his sin a tenth of an ephah[a]
of fine flour[g] for a sin offering. He must not put oil or incense on
it, because it is a sin offering. 12He is to bring it to the priest, who
shall take a handful of it as a memorial portion and burn it on
the altar on top of the offerings made to the LORD by fire. It is a
sin offering. 13In this way the priest will make atonement[h] for
him for any of these sins he has committed, and he will be forgiven. The rest of the offering will belong to the priest,[i] as in the
case of the grain offering.’”

14The LORD said to Moses: 15“When a person commits a violation and sins unintentionally in regard to any of the LORD’s holy
things, he is to bring to the LORD as a penalty[j] a ram[k] from the
flock, one without defect and of the proper value in silver,
according to the sanctuary shekel.[b][l] It is a guilt offering. 16He
must make restitution[m] for what he has failed to do in regard to
the holy things, add a fifth of the value[n] to that and give it all to
the priest, who will make atonement for him with the ram as a
guilt offering, and he will be forgiven.

17“If a person sins and does what is forbidden in any of the
LORD’s commands, even though he does not know it,[o] he is
guilty and will be held responsible. 18He is to bring to the priest
as a guilt offering a ram from the flock, one without defect and
of the proper value. In this way the priest will make atonement
for him for the wrong he has committed unintentionally, and he
will be forgiven.[p] 19It is a guilt offering; he has been guilty of[c]
wrongdoing against the LORD.”

Chapter 6 Theme ______________________________

6 The LORD said to Moses: 2“If anyone sins and is unfaithful
to the LORD[q] by deceiving his neighbor[r] about something

[a]*11* That is, probably about 2 quarts (about 2 liters) [b]*15* That is, about 2/5 ounce (about 11.5 grams) [c]*19* Or *has made full expiation for his*

5:7 [a]Lev 12:8; 14:21
5:8 [b]Lev 1:15 [c]Lev 1:17
5:9 [d]Lev 4:7,18
5:10 [e]Lev 1:14-17 [f]Lev 4:26
5:11 [g]Lev 2:1
5:13 [h]Lev 4:26 [i]Lev 2:3
5:15 [j]Lev 22:14 [k]Nu 5:8 [l]Ex 30:13
5:16 [m]Lev 6:4 [n]Lev 22:14; Nu 5:7
5:17 [o]ver 15; Lev 4:2
5:18 [p]ver 15
6:2 [q]Nu 5:6; Ac 5:4; Col 3:9 [r]Pr 24:28

entrusted to him or left in his care[a] or stolen, or if he cheats him,
3or if he finds lost property and lies about it,[b] or if he swears
falsely, or if he commits any such sin that people may do—
4when he thus sins and becomes guilty, he must return[c] what he
has stolen or taken by extortion, or what was entrusted to him,
or the lost property he found, 5or whatever it was he swore falsely about. He must make restitution[d] in full, add a fifth of the value to it and give it all to the owner on the day he presents his
guilt offering.[e] 6And as a penalty he must bring to the priest, that
is, to the LORD, his guilt offering,[f] a ram from the flock, one
without defect and of the proper value. 7In this way the priest
will make atonement[g] for him before the LORD, and he will be
forgiven for any of these things he did that made him guilty."

8The LORD said to Moses: 9"Give Aaron and his sons this command: 'These are the regulations for the burnt offering: The
burnt offering is to remain on the altar hearth throughout the
night, till morning, and the fire must be kept burning on the
altar. 10The priest shall then put on his linen clothes, with linen
undergarments next to his body,[h] and shall remove the ashes of
the burnt offering that the fire has consumed on the altar and
place them beside the altar. 11Then he is to take off these clothes
and put on others, and carry the ashes outside the camp to a
place that is ceremonially clean.[i] 12The fire on the altar must be
kept burning; it must not go out. Every morning the priest is to
add firewood and arrange the burnt offering on the fire and
burn the fat of the fellowship offerings[a] on it. 13The fire must be
kept burning on the altar continuously; it must not go out.

14"'These are the regulations for the grain offering:[j] Aaron's
sons are to bring it before the LORD, in front of the altar. 15The
priest is to take a handful of fine flour and oil, together with all
the incense on the grain offering,[k] and burn the memorial portion[l] on the altar as an aroma pleasing to the LORD. 16Aaron and
his sons[m] shall eat the rest[n] of it, but it is to be eaten without
yeast[o] in a holy place;[p] they are to eat it in the courtyard of the
Tent of Meeting. 17It must not be baked with yeast; I have given it
as their share of the offerings made to me by fire. Like the sin
offering and the guilt offering, it is most holy.[q] 18Any male
descendant of Aaron may eat it.[r] It is his regular share of the
offerings made to the LORD by fire for the generations to come.
Whatever touches them will become holy.[b][s]'"

19The LORD also said to Moses, 20"This is the offering Aaron
and his sons are to bring to the LORD on the day he[c] is anointed:
a tenth of an ephah[d][t] of fine flour as a regular grain offering,[u]

6:2 [a]Ex 22:7
6:3 [b]Dt 22:1-3
6:4 [c]Lk 19:8
6:5 [d]Nu 5:7 [e]Lev 5:15
6:6 [f]Lev 5:15
6:7 [g]Lev 4:26
6:10 [h]Ex 28:39-42, 43; 39:28
6:11 [i]Lev 4:12
6:14 [j]Lev 2:1; 15:4
6:15 [k]Lev 2:9 [l]Lev 2:2
6:16 [m]Lev 2:3 [n]Eze 44:29 [o]Lev 2:11 [p]Lev 10:13
6:17 [q]ver 29; Ex 40:10; Nu 18:9,10
6:18 [r]ver 29; Nu 18:9-10 [s]ver 27
6:20 [t]Ex 16:36 [u]Ex 29:2

[a]*12* Traditionally *peace offerings* [b]*18* Or *Whoever touches them must be holy*; similarly in verse 27 [c]*20* Or *each* [d]*20* That is, probably about 2 quarts (about 2 liters)

half of it in the morning and half in the evening. 21 Prepare it
with oil on a griddle;[a] bring it well-mixed and present the grain
offering broken[a] in pieces as an aroma pleasing to the LORD.
22 The son who is to succeed him as anointed priest shall prepare
it. It is the LORD's regular share and is to be burned completely.
23 Every grain offering of a priest shall be burned completely; it
must not be eaten."

24 The LORD said to Moses, 25 "Say to Aaron and his sons: 'These
are the regulations for the sin offering: The sin offering is to be
slaughtered before the LORD[b] in the place[c] the burnt offering is
slaughtered; it is most holy. 26 The priest who offers it shall eat it;
it is to be eaten in a holy place,[d] in the courtyard[e] of the Tent of
Meeting. 27 Whatever touches any of the flesh will become holy,[f]
and if any of the blood is spattered on a garment, you must wash
it in a holy place. 28 The clay pot[g] the meat is cooked in must be
broken; but if it is cooked in a bronze pot, the pot is to be
scoured and rinsed with water. 29 Any male in a priest's family
may eat it;[h] it is most holy.[i] 30 But any sin offering whose blood is
brought into the Tent of Meeting to make atonement in the Holy
Place[j] must not be eaten; it must be burned.[k]

Chapter 7 Theme

7 " 'These are the regulations for the guilt offering,[l] which is
most holy: 2 The guilt offering is to be slaughtered in the
place where the burnt offering is slaughtered, and its blood is to
be sprinkled against the altar on all sides. 3 All its fat[m] shall be
offered: the fat tail and the fat that covers the inner parts, 4 both
kidneys with the fat on them near the loins, and the covering of
the liver, which is to be removed with the kidneys. 5 The priest
shall burn them on the altar as an offering made to the LORD by
fire. It is a guilt offering. 6 Any male in a priest's family may eat
it,[n] but it must be eaten in a holy place; it is most holy.[o]

7 " 'The same law applies to both the sin offering and the guilt
offering: They belong to the priest[p] who makes atonement with
them. 8 The priest who offers a burnt offering for anyone may
keep its hide for himself. 9 Every grain offering baked in an oven
or cooked in a pan or on a griddle[q] belongs to the priest who
offers it, 10 and every grain offering, whether mixed with oil or
dry, belongs equally to all the sons of Aaron.

11 " 'These are the regulations for the fellowship offering[b] a person may present to the LORD:

12 " 'If he offers it as an expression of thankfulness, then along
with this thank offering[r] he is to offer cakes of bread made without

[a]21 The meaning of the Hebrew for this word is uncertain. [b]11 Traditionally *peace offering*; also in verses 13-37

6:21 [a]Lev 2:5
6:25 [b]Lev 1:3 [c]Lev 1:5,11
6:26 [d]ver 16 [e]Lev 10:17-18
6:27 [f]Ex 29:37
6:28 [g]Lev 11:33; 15:12
6:29 [h]ver 18 [i]ver 17
6:30 [j]Lev 4:18 [k]Lev 4:12
7:1 [l]Lev 5:14-6:7
7:3 [m]Ex 29:13; Lev 3:4,9
7:6 [n]Lev 6:18; Nu 18:9-10 [o]Lev 2:3
7:7 [p]Lev 6:17,26; 1Co 9:13
7:9 [q]Lev 2:5
7:12 [r]ver 13,15

yeast and mixed with oil, wafers[a] made without yeast and spread
with oil, and cakes of fine flour well-kneaded and mixed with oil.
13 Along with his fellowship offering of thanksgiving he is to present an offering with cakes of bread made with yeast.[b] 14 He is to
bring one of each kind as an offering, a contribution to the LORD;
it belongs to the priest who sprinkles the blood of the fellowship
offerings. 15 The meat of his fellowship offering of thanksgiving
must be eaten on the day it is offered; he must leave none of it till
morning.[c]

16 " 'If, however, his offering is the result of a vow or is a freewill
offering, the sacrifice shall be eaten on the day he offers it, but
anything left over may be eaten on the next day.[d] 17 Any meat of
the sacrifice left over till the third day must be burned up. 18 If any
meat of the fellowship offering is eaten on the third day, it will not
be accepted.[e] It will not be credited[f] to the one who offered it, for
it is impure; the person who eats any of it will be held responsible.

19 " 'Meat that touches anything ceremonially unclean must not
be eaten; it must be burned up. As for other meat, anyone ceremonially clean may eat it. 20 But if anyone who is unclean eats
any meat of the fellowship offering belonging to the LORD, that
person must be cut off from his people.[g] 21 If anyone touches
something unclean[h]—whether human uncleanness or an unclean
animal or any unclean, detestable thing—and then eats any of
the meat of the fellowship offering belonging to the LORD, that
person must be cut off from his people.' "

22 The LORD said to Moses, 23 "Say to the Israelites: 'Do not eat
any of the fat of cattle, sheep or goats.[i] 24 The fat of an animal
found dead or torn by wild animals[j] may be used for any other
purpose, but you must not eat it. 25 Anyone who eats the fat of an
animal from which an offering by fire may be[a] made to the LORD
must be cut off from his people. 26 And wherever you live, you
must not eat the blood[k] of any bird or animal. 27 If anyone eats
blood,[l] that person must be cut off from his people.' "

28 The LORD said to Moses, 29 "Say to the Israelites: 'Anyone
who brings a fellowship offering to the LORD is to bring part of it
as his sacrifice to the LORD. 30 With his own hands he is to bring
the offering made to the LORD by fire; he is to bring the fat,
together with the breast, and wave the breast before the LORD as
a wave offering.[m] 31 The priest shall burn the fat on the altar, but
the breast belongs to Aaron and his sons.[n] 32 You are to give the
right thigh of your fellowship offerings to the priest as a contribution.[o] 33 The son of Aaron who offers the blood and the fat of
the fellowship offering shall have the right thigh as his share.

7:12 [a]Lev 2:4; Nu 6:15
7:13 [b]Lev 23:17; Am 4:5
7:15 [c]Lev 22:30
7:16 [d]Lev 19:5-8
7:18 [e]Lev 19:7 [f]Nu 18:27
7:20 [g]Lev 22:3-7
7:21 [h]Lev 5:2; 11:24,28
7:23 [i]Lev 3:17; 17:13-14
7:24 [j]Ex 22:31
7:26 [k]Ge 9:4
7:27 [l]Lev 17:10-24; Ac 15:20,29
7:30 [m]Ex 29:24; Nu 6:20
7:31 [n]ver 34
7:32 [o]ver 34; Lev 9:21; Nu 6:20

[a]25 Or *fire is*

34From the fellowship offerings of the Israelites, I have taken the
breast that is waved and the thigh[a] that is presented and have
given them to Aaron the priest and his sons[b] as their regular
share from the Israelites.'"
35This is the portion of the offerings made to the LORD by fire
that were allotted to Aaron and his sons on the day they were
presented to serve the LORD as priests. 36On the day they were
anointed,[c] the LORD commanded that the Israelites give this to
them as their regular share for the generations to come.

37These, then, are the regulations for the burnt offering,[d] the
grain offering,[e] the sin offering, the guilt offering, the ordination
offering[f] and the fellowship offering, 38which the LORD gave
Moses on Mount Sinai on the day he commanded the Israelites
to bring their offerings to the LORD,[g] in the Desert of Sinai.

Chapter 8 Theme ______________________________

8 The LORD said to Moses, 2"Bring Aaron and his sons, their
garments, the anointing oil,[h] the bull for the sin offering, the
two rams and the basket containing bread made without yeast,[i]
3and gather the entire assembly[j] at the entrance to the Tent of
Meeting." 4Moses did as the LORD commanded him, and the
assembly gathered at the entrance to the Tent of Meeting.
5Moses said to the assembly, "This is what the LORD has commanded to be done." 6Then Moses brought Aaron and his sons
forward and washed them with water.[k] 7He put the tunic on
Aaron, tied the sash around him, clothed him with the robe and
put the ephod on him. He also tied the ephod to him by its skillfully woven waistband; so it was fastened on him.[l] 8He placed
the breastpiece on him and put the Urim and Thummim[m] in the
breastpiece. 9Then he placed the turban on Aaron's head and set
the gold plate, the sacred diadem,[n] on the front of it, as the LORD
commanded Moses.
10Then Moses took the anointing oil[o] and anointed[p] the tabernacle and everything in it, and so consecrated them. 11He sprinkled some of the oil on the altar seven times, anointing the altar
and all its utensils and the basin with its stand, to consecrate
them.[q] 12He poured some of the anointing oil on Aaron's head
and anointed[r] him to consecrate him.[s] 13Then he brought Aaron's
sons forward, put tunics on them, tied sashes around them and
put headbands on them, as the LORD commanded Moses.
14He then presented the bull[t] for the sin offering,[u] and Aaron
and his sons laid their hands on its head. 15Moses slaughtered
the bull and took some of the blood, and with his finger he put it
on all the horns of the altar[v] to purify the altar.[w] He poured out the

7:34 [a]Lev 10:15 [b]Ex 29:27; Nu 18:18-19
7:36 [c]Ex 40:13,15; Lev 8:12,30
7:37 [d]Lev 6:9 [e]Lev 6:14 [f]ver 1,11
7:38 [g]Lev 1:2
8:2 [h]Ex 30:23-25, 30 [i]Ex 29:2-3
8:3 [j]Nu 8:9
8:6 [k]Ex 29:4; 30:19; Ps 26:6; Ac 22:16; 1Co 6:11; Eph 5:26
8:7 [l]Ex 28:4
8:8 [m]Ex 28:30
8:9 [n]Ex 28:36
8:10 [o]ver 2 [p]Ex 30:26
8:11 [q]Ex 30:29
8:12 [r]Lev 21:10,12 [s]Ex 30:30
8:14 [t]Lev 4:3 [u]Ps 66:15; Eze 43:19
8:15 [v]Lev 4:7 [w]Heb 9:22

rest of the blood at the base of the altar. So he consecrated it to make atonement for it.[a] 16Moses also took all the fat around the inner parts, the covering of the liver, and both kidneys and their fat, and burned it on the altar. 17But the bull with its hide and its flesh and its offal[b] he burned up outside the camp,[c] as the LORD commanded Moses.

18He then presented the ram[d] for the burnt offering, and Aaron and his sons laid their hands on its head. 19Then Moses slaughtered the ram and sprinkled the blood against the altar on all sides. 20He cut the ram into pieces and burned the head, the pieces and the fat. 21He washed the inner parts and the legs with water and burned the whole ram on the altar as a burnt offering, a pleasing aroma, an offering made to the LORD by fire, as the LORD commanded Moses.

22He then presented the other ram, the ram for the ordination,[e] and Aaron and his sons laid their hands on its head. 23Moses slaughtered the ram and took some of its blood and put it on the lobe of Aaron's right ear, on the thumb of his right hand and on the big toe of his right foot. 24Moses also brought Aaron's sons forward and put some of the blood on the lobes of their right ears, on the thumbs of their right hands and on the big toes of their right feet. Then he sprinkled blood against the altar on all sides.[f] 25He took the fat, the fat tail, all the fat around the inner parts, the covering of the liver, both kidneys and their fat and the right thigh. 26Then from the basket of bread made without yeast, which was before the LORD, he took a cake of bread, and one made with oil, and a wafer; he put these on the fat portions and on the right thigh. 27He put all these in the hands of Aaron and his sons and waved them before the LORD as a wave offering. 28Then Moses took them from their hands and burned them on the altar on top of the burnt offering as an ordination offering, a pleasing aroma, an offering made to the LORD by fire. 29He also took the breast—Moses' share of the ordination ram[g]—and waved it before the LORD as a wave offering, as the LORD commanded Moses.

30Then Moses took some of the anointing oil and some of the blood from the altar and sprinkled them on Aaron and his garments[h] and on his sons and their garments. So he consecrated[i] Aaron and his garments and his sons and their garments.

31Moses then said to Aaron and his sons, "Cook the meat at the entrance to the Tent of Meeting and eat it there with the bread from the basket of ordination offerings, as I commanded, saying,[a] 'Aaron and his sons are to eat it.' 32Then burn up the rest of the

8:15 [a]Eze 43:20
8:17 [b]Lev 4:11 [c]Lev 4:12
8:18 [d]ver 2
8:22 [e]ver 2
8:24 [f]Heb 9:18-22
8:29 [g]Lev 7:31-34
8:30 [h]Ex 28:2 [i]Nu 3:3

a31 Or *I was commanded:*

meat and the bread. 33Do not leave the entrance to the Tent of
Meeting for seven days, until the days of your ordination are completed, for your ordination will last seven days. 34What has been
done today was commanded by the LORD[a] to make atonement for
you. 35You must stay at the entrance to the Tent of Meeting day and
night for seven days and do what the LORD requires,[b] so you will
not die; for that is what I have been commanded." 36So Aaron and
his sons did everything the LORD commanded through Moses.

Chapter 9 Theme ____________________________

9 On the eighth day[c] Moses summoned Aaron and his sons
and the elders of Israel. 2He said to Aaron, "Take a bull calf for
your sin offering and a ram for your burnt offering, both without defect, and present them before the LORD. 3Then say to the
Israelites: 'Take a male goat for a sin offering, a calf and a
lamb—both a year old and without defect—for a burnt offering, 4and an ox[a] and a ram for a fellowship offering[b] to sacrifice
before the LORD, together with a grain offering mixed with oil.
For today the LORD will appear to you.[d]' "
5They took the things Moses commanded to the front of the Tent
of Meeting, and the entire assembly came near and stood before
the LORD. 6Then Moses said, "This is what the LORD has commanded
you to do, so that the glory of the LORD[e] may appear to you."
7Moses said to Aaron, "Come to the altar and sacrifice your sin
offering and your burnt offering and make atonement for yourself and the people; sacrifice the offering that is for the people
and make atonement for them, as the LORD has commanded.[f]"
8So Aaron came to the altar and slaughtered the calf as a sin
offering[g] for himself. 9His sons brought the blood to him,[h] and
he dipped his finger into the blood and put it on the horns of the
altar; the rest of the blood he poured out at the base of the altar.[i]
10On the altar he burned the fat, the kidneys and the covering of
the liver from the sin offering, as the LORD commanded Moses;
11the flesh and the hide[j] he burned up outside the camp.[k]
12Then he slaughtered the burnt offering. His sons handed
him the blood, and he sprinkled it against the altar on all sides.
13They handed him the burnt offering piece by piece, including
the head, and he burned them on the altar.[l] 14He washed the
inner parts and the legs and burned them on top of the burnt
offering on the altar.
15Aaron then brought the offering that was for the people.[m] He
took the goat for the people's sin offering and slaughtered it and
offered it for a sin offering as he did with the first one.

a4 The Hebrew word can include both male and female; also in verses 18 and 19.
b4 Traditionally *peace offering*; also in verses 18 and 22

8:34 [a]Heb 7:16
8:35 [b]Nu 3:7; 9:19; Dt 11:1; 1Ki 2:3; Eze 48:11
9:1 [c]Eze 43:27
9:4 [d]Ex 29:43
9:6 [e]ver 23; Ex 24:16
9:7 [f]Heb 5:1,3; 7:27
9:8 [g]Lev 4:1-12
9:9 [h]ver 12,18 [i]Lev 4:7
9:11 [j]Lev 4:11 [k]Lev 4:12; 8:17
9:13 [l]Lev 1:8
9:15 [m]Lev 4:27-31

16 He brought the burnt offering and offered it in the prescribed
way.[a] 17 He also brought the grain offering, took a handful of it
and burned it on the altar in addition to the morning's burnt
offering.[b]

18 He slaughtered the ox and the ram as the fellowship offering
for the people.[c] His sons handed him the blood, and he sprinkled it against the altar on all sides. 19 But the fat portions of the
ox and the ram—the fat tail, the layer of fat, the kidneys and the
covering of the liver— 20 these they laid on the breasts, and then
Aaron burned the fat on the altar. 21 Aaron waved the breasts and
the right thigh before the LORD as a wave offering,[d] as Moses
commanded.

22 Then Aaron lifted his hands toward the people and blessed
them.[e] And having sacrificed the sin offering, the burnt offering
and the fellowship offering, he stepped down.

23 Moses and Aaron then went into the Tent of Meeting. When
they came out, they blessed the people; and the glory of the
LORD[f] appeared to all the people. 24 Fire[g] came out from the presence of the LORD and consumed the burnt offering and the fat
portions on the altar. And when all the people saw it, they shouted for joy and fell facedown.[h]

Chapter 10 Theme ______________________

10 Aaron's sons Nadab and Abihu[i] took their censers, put
fire in them[j] and added incense; and they offered unauthorized fire before the LORD, contrary to his command.[k] 2 So fire
came out from the presence of the LORD and consumed them,[l]
and they died before the LORD. 3 Moses then said to Aaron, "This
is what the LORD spoke of when he said:

"'Among those who approach me[m]
    I will show myself holy;[n]
in the sight of all the people
    I will be honored.[o]'"

Aaron remained silent.

4 Moses summoned Mishael and Elzaphan,[p] sons of Aaron's
uncle Uzziel,[q] and said to them, "Come here; carry your cousins
outside the camp,[r] away from the front of the sanctuary." 5 So
they came and carried them, still in their tunics,[s] outside the
camp, as Moses ordered.

6 Then Moses said to Aaron and his sons Eleazar and Ithamar,
"Do not let your hair become unkempt,[a][t] and do not tear your
clothes, or you will die and the LORD will be angry with the whole

a6 Or *Do not uncover your heads*

9:16 [a] Lev 1:1-13
9:17 [b] Lev 2:1-2; 3:5
9:18 [c] Lev 3:1-11
9:21 [d] Ex 29:24,26; Lev 7:30-34
9:22 [e] Nu 6:23; Dt 21:5; Lk 24:50
9:23 [f] ver 6
9:24 [g] Jdg 6:21; 2Ch 7:1 [h] 1Ki 18:39
10:1 [i] Ex 24:1; Nu 3:2-4; 26:61 [j] Lev 16:12 [k] Ex 30:9
10:2 [l] Nu 3:4; 16:35; 26:61
10:3 [m] Ex 19:22 [n] Ex 30:29; Lev 21:6; Eze 28:22 [o] Isa 49:3
10:4 [p] Ex 6:22 [q] Ex 6:18 [r] Ac 5:6,9,10
10:5 [s] Lev 8:13
10:6 [t] Lev 21:10

community.[a] But your relatives, all the house of Israel, may mourn
for those the LORD has destroyed by fire. 7Do not leave the entrance
to the Tent of Meeting or you will die, because the LORD's anointing oil[b] is on you." So they did as Moses said.
8Then the LORD said to Aaron, 9"You and your sons are not to
drink wine[c] or other fermented drink[d] whenever you go into the
Tent of Meeting, or you will die. This is a lasting ordinance for
the generations to come. 10You must distinguish between the
holy and the common, between the unclean and the clean,[e] 11and
you must teach[f] the Israelites all the decrees the LORD has given
them through Moses.[g]"
12Moses said to Aaron and his remaining sons, Eleazar and
Ithamar, "Take the grain offering left over from the offerings
made to the LORD by fire and eat it prepared without yeast beside
the altar,[h] for it is most holy. 13Eat it in a holy place, because it is
your share and your sons' share of the offerings made to the
LORD by fire; for so I have been commanded. 14But you and your
sons and your daughters may eat the breast that was waved and
the thigh that was presented. Eat them in a ceremonially clean
place;[i] they have been given to you and your children as your
share of the Israelites' fellowship offerings.[a] 15The thigh[j] that was
presented and the breast that was waved must be brought with
the fat portions of the offerings made by fire, to be waved before
the LORD as a wave offering. This will be the regular share for
you and your children, as the LORD has commanded."
16When Moses inquired about the goat of the sin offering[k] and
found that it had been burned up, he was angry with Eleazar
and Ithamar, Aaron's remaining sons, and asked, 17"Why didn't
you eat the sin offering[l] in the sanctuary area? It is most holy; it
was given to you to take away the guilt of the community by
making atonement for them before the LORD. 18Since its blood
was not taken into the Holy Place,[m] you should have eaten the
goat in the sanctuary area, as I commanded."
19Aaron replied to Moses, "Today they sacrificed their sin
offering and their burnt offering[n] before the LORD, but such
things as this have happened to me. Would the LORD have been
pleased if I had eaten the sin offering today?" 20When Moses
heard this, he was satisfied.

Chapter 11 Theme ______________________

11 The LORD said to Moses and Aaron, 2"Say to the Israelites:
'Of all the animals that live on land, these are the ones you

a *14* Traditionally *peace offerings*

10:6 [a] Nu 1:53; 16:22; Jos 7:1; 22:18; 2Sa 24:1

10:7 [b] Ex 28:41; Lev 21:12

10:9 [c] Hos 4:11 [d] Pr 20:1; Isa 28:7; Eze 44:21; Lk 1:15; Eph 5:18; 1Ti 3:3; Tit 1:7

10:10 [e] Lev 11:47; 20:25; Eze 22:26

10:11 [f] Mal 2:7 [g] Dt 24:8

10:12 [h] Lev 6:14-18; 21:22

10:14 [i] Ex 29:24, 26-27; Lev 7:31,34; Nu 18:11

10:15 [j] Lev 7:34

10:16 [k] Lev 9:3

10:17 [l] Lev 6:24-30

10:18 [m] Lev 6:26,30

10:19 [n] Lev 9:12

may eat:[a] 3You may eat any animal that has a split hoof completely divided and that chews the cud.

4" 'There are some that only chew the cud or only have a split
hoof, but you must not eat them. The camel, though it chews the
cud, does not have a split hoof; it is ceremonially unclean for
you. 5The coney,[a] though it chews the cud, does not have a split
hoof; it is unclean for you. 6The rabbit, though it chews the cud,
does not have a split hoof; it is unclean for you. 7And the pig,[b]
though it has a split hoof completely divided, does not chew the
cud; it is unclean for you. 8You must not eat their meat or touch
their carcasses; they are unclean for you.[c]

9" 'Of all the creatures living in the water of the seas and the
streams, you may eat any that have fins and scales. 10But all creatures in the seas or streams that do not have fins and scales—
whether among all the swarming things or among all the other
living creatures in the water—you are to detest.[d] 11And since you
are to detest them, you must not eat their meat and you must
detest their carcasses. 12Anything living in the water that does
not have fins and scales is to be detestable to you.

13" 'These are the birds you are to detest and not eat because
they are detestable: the eagle, the vulture, the black vulture, 14the
red kite, any kind of black kite, 15any kind of raven, 16the horned
owl, the screech owl, the gull, any kind of hawk, 17the little owl,
the cormorant, the great owl, 18the white owl, the desert owl, the
osprey, 19the stork, any kind of heron, the hoopoe and the bat.[b]

20" 'All flying insects that walk on all fours are to be detestable
to you.[e] 21There are, however, some winged creatures that walk
on all fours that you may eat: those that have jointed legs for
hopping on the ground. 22Of these you may eat any kind of
locust,[f] katydid, cricket or grasshopper. 23But all other winged
creatures that have four legs you are to detest.

24" 'You will make yourselves unclean by these; whoever touches their carcasses will be unclean till evening. 25Whoever picks
up one of their carcasses must wash his clothes,[g] and he will be
unclean till evening.[h]

26" 'Every animal that has a split hoof not completely divided or
that does not chew the cud is unclean for you; whoever touches
⌊the carcass of⌋ any of them will be unclean. 27Of all the animals
that walk on all fours, those that walk on their paws are unclean for
you; whoever touches their carcasses will be unclean till evening.
28Anyone who picks up their carcasses must wash his clothes,
and he will be unclean till evening. They are unclean for you.

11:2 [a]Ac 10:12-14
11:7 [b]Isa 65:4; 66:3,17
11:8 [c]Isa 52:11; Heb 9:10
11:10 [d]Lev 7:18
11:20 [e]Ac 10:14
11:22 [f]Mt 3:4; Mk 1:6
11:25 [g]Lev 14:8,47; 15:5 [h]ver 40; Nu 31:24

a5 That is, the hyrax or rock badger b19 The precise identification of some of the birds, insects and animals in this chapter is uncertain.

29“‘Of the animals that move about on the ground, these are unclean for you: the weasel, the rat,[a] any kind of great lizard, 30the gecko, the monitor lizard, the wall lizard, the skink and the chameleon. 31Of all those that move along the ground, these are unclean for you. Whoever touches them when they are dead will be unclean till evening. 32When one of them dies and falls on something, that article, whatever its use, will be unclean, whether it is made of wood, cloth, hide or sackcloth.[b] Put it in water; it will be unclean till evening, and then it will be clean. 33If one of them falls into a clay pot, everything in it will be unclean, and you must break the pot.[c] 34Any food that could be eaten but has water on it from such a pot is unclean, and any liquid that could be drunk from it is unclean. 35Anything that one of their carcasses falls on becomes unclean; an oven or cooking pot must be broken up. They are unclean, and you are to regard them as unclean. 36A spring, however, or a cistern for collecting water remains clean, but anyone who touches one of these carcasses is unclean. 37If a carcass falls on any seeds that are to be planted, they remain clean. 38But if water has been put on the seed and a carcass falls on it, it is unclean for you.

39“‘If an animal that you are allowed to eat dies, anyone who touches the carcass will be unclean till evening. 40Anyone who eats some of the carcass must wash his clothes, and he will be unclean till evening.[d] Anyone who picks up the carcass must wash his clothes, and he will be unclean till evening.

41“‘Every creature that moves about on the ground is detestable; it is not to be eaten. 42You are not to eat any creature that moves about on the ground, whether it moves on its belly or walks on all fours or on many feet; it is detestable. 43Do not defile yourselves by any of these creatures.[e] Do not make yourselves unclean by means of them or be made unclean by them. 44I am the LORD your God;[f] consecrate yourselves[g] and be holy,[h] because I am holy.[i] Do not make yourselves unclean by any creature that moves about on the ground. 45I am the LORD who brought you up out of Egypt[j] to be your God;[k] therefore be holy, because I am holy.[l]

46“‘These are the regulations concerning animals, birds, every living thing that moves in the water and every creature that moves about on the ground. 47You must distinguish between the unclean and the clean, between living creatures that may be eaten and those that may not be eaten.[m]’ ”

Chapter 12 Theme ____________________

12 The LORD said to Moses, 2“Say to the Israelites: ‘A woman who becomes pregnant and gives birth to a son will be

11:29 [a]Isa 66:17
11:32 [b]Lev 15:12
11:33 [c]Lev 6:28; 15:12
11:40 [d]Lev 17:15; 22:8; Eze 44:31
11:43 [e]Lev 20:25
11:44 [f]Ex 6:2,7; Isa 43:3; 51:15 [g]Lev 20:7 [h]Ex 19:6 [i]Lev 19:2; Ps 99:3; Eph 1:4; 1Th 4:7; 1Pe 1:15,16*
11:45 [j]Lev 25:38,55; Ex 6:7; 20:2 [k]Ge 17:7 [l]Ex 19:6; 1Pe 1:16*
11:47 [m]Lev 10:10

ceremonially unclean for seven days, just as she is unclean during her monthly period.[a] 3On the eighth day the boy is to be circumcised.[b] 4Then the woman must wait thirty-three days to be purified from her bleeding. She must not touch anything sacred or go to the sanctuary until the days of her purification are over. 5If she gives birth to a daughter, for two weeks the woman will be unclean, as during her period. Then she must wait sixty-six days to be purified from her bleeding.

6" 'When the days of her purification for a son or daughter are over,[c] she is to bring to the priest at the entrance to the Tent of Meeting a year-old lamb[d] for a burnt offering and a young pigeon or a dove for a sin offering.[e] 7He shall offer them before the LORD to make atonement for her, and then she will be ceremonially clean from her flow of blood.

" 'These are the regulations for the woman who gives birth to a boy or a girl. 8If she cannot afford a lamb, she is to bring two doves or two young pigeons,[f] one for a burnt offering and the other for a sin offering.[g] In this way the priest will make atonement for her, and she will be clean.[h]' "

Chapter 13 Theme ______________________

13 The LORD said to Moses and Aaron, 2"When anyone has a swelling[i] or a rash or a bright spot[j] on his skin that may become an infectious skin disease,[a][k] he must be brought to Aaron the priest[l] or to one of his sons[b] who is a priest. 3The priest is to examine the sore on his skin, and if the hair in the sore has turned white and the sore appears to be more than skin deep,[c] it is an infectious skin disease. When the priest examines him, he shall pronounce him ceremonially unclean.[m] 4If the spot[n] on his skin is white but does not appear to be more than skin deep and the hair in it has not turned white, the priest is to put the infected person in isolation for seven days.[o] 5On the seventh day[p] the priest is to examine him,[q] and if he sees that the sore is unchanged and has not spread in the skin, he is to keep him in isolation another seven days. 6On the seventh day the priest is to examine him again, and if the sore has faded and has not spread in the skin, the priest shall pronounce him clean;[r] it is only a rash. The man must wash his clothes,[s] and he will be clean.[t] 7But if the rash does spread in his skin after he has shown himself to the priest to be pronounced clean, he must appear before the priest again.[u] 8The priest is to examine him, and if the rash has spread in the skin, he shall pronounce him unclean; it is an infectious disease.

[a]2 Traditionally *leprosy*; the Hebrew word was used for various diseases affecting the skin—not necessarily leprosy; also elsewhere in this chapter. [b]2 Or *descendants*
[c]3 Or *be lower than the rest of the skin*; also elsewhere in this chapter

12:2 [a]Lev 15:19; 18:19
12:3 [b]Ge 17:12; Lk 1:59; 2:21
12:6 [c]Lk 2:22 [d]Ex 29:38; Lev 23:12; Nu 6:12,14; 7:15 [e]Lev 5:7
12:8 [f]Ge 15:9; Lev 14:22 [g]Lev 5:7; Lk 2:22-24* [h]Lev 4:26
13:2 [i]ver 10,19, 28,43 [j]ver 4,38,39; Lev 14:56 [k]ver 3,9,15; Ex 4:6; Lev 14:3,32; Nu 5:2; Dt 24:8 [l]Dt 24:8
13:3 [m]ver 8,11,20,30; Lev 21:1; Nu 9:6
13:4 [n]ver 2 [o]ver 5,21, 26,33,46; Lev 14:38; Nu 12:14,15; Dt 24:9
13:5 [p]Lev 14:9 [q]ver 27,32, 34,51
13:6 [r]ver 13,17, 23,28,34; Mt 8:3; Lk 5:12-14 [s]Lev 11:25 [t]Lev 11:25; 14:8,9, 20,48; 15:8; Nu 8:7
13:7 [u]Lk 5:14

9“When anyone has an infectious skin disease, he must be
brought to the priest. 10The priest is to examine him, and if there
is a white swelling in the skin that has turned the hair white and
if there is raw flesh in the swelling, 11it is a chronic skin disease[a]
and the priest shall pronounce him unclean. He is not to put
him in isolation, because he is already unclean.

12“If the disease breaks out all over his skin and, so far as the
priest can see, it covers all the skin of the infected person from
head to foot, 13the priest is to examine him, and if the disease has
covered his whole body, he shall pronounce that person clean.
Since it has all turned white, he is clean. 14But whenever raw flesh
appears on him, he will be unclean. 15When the priest sees the raw
flesh, he shall pronounce him unclean. The raw flesh is unclean;
he has an infectious disease.[b] 16Should the raw flesh change and
turn white, he must go to the priest. 17The priest is to examine
him, and if the sores have turned white, the priest shall pronounce
the infected person clean;[c] then he will be clean.

18“When someone has a boil[d] on his skin and it heals, 19and in
the place where the boil was, a white swelling or reddish-white[e]
spot[f] appears, he must present himself to the priest. 20The priest
is to examine it, and if it appears to be more than skin deep and
the hair in it has turned white, the priest shall pronounce him
unclean. It is an infectious skin disease[g] that has broken out
where the boil was. 21But if, when the priest examines it, there is
no white hair in it and it is not more than skin deep and has faded, then the priest is to put him in isolation for seven days. 22If it
is spreading in the skin, the priest shall pronounce him unclean;
it is infectious. 23But if the spot is unchanged and has not
spread, it is only a scar from the boil, and the priest shall pronounce him clean.[h]

24“When someone has a burn on his skin and a reddish-white
or white spot appears in the raw flesh of the burn, 25the priest is
to examine the spot, and if the hair in it has turned white, and it
appears to be more than skin deep, it is an infectious disease
that has broken out in the burn. The priest shall pronounce him
unclean; it is an infectious skin disease.[i] 26But if the priest examines it and there is no white hair in the spot and if it is not more
than skin deep and has faded, then the priest is to put him in
isolation for seven days.[j] 27On the seventh day the priest is to
examine him,[k] and if it is spreading in the skin, the priest shall
pronounce him unclean; it is an infectious skin disease. 28If,
however, the spot is unchanged and has not spread in the skin
but has faded, it is a swelling from the burn, and the priest shall
pronounce him clean; it is only a scar from the burn.[l]

13:11 [a]Ex 4:6; Lev 14:8; Nu 12:10; Mt 8:2
13:15 [b]ver 2
13:17 [c]ver 6
13:18 [d]Ex 9:9
13:19 [e]ver 24,42; Lev 14:37 [f]ver 2
13:20 [g]ver 2
13:23 [h]ver 6
13:25 [i]ver 11
13:26 [j]ver 4
13:27 [k]ver 5
13:28 [l]ver 2

13:29 [a]ver 43,44 [29]"If a man or woman has a sore on the head[a] or on the chin,
[30]the priest is to examine the sore, and if it appears to be more
than skin deep and the hair in it is yellow and thin, the priest
shall pronounce that person unclean; it is an itch, an infectious
disease of the head or chin. [31]But if, when the priest examines
13:31 [b]ver 4 this kind of sore, it does not seem to be more than skin deep and
there is no black hair in it, then the priest is to put the infected
person in isolation for seven days.[b] [32]On the seventh day the
priest is to examine the sore,[c] and if the itch has not spread and
13:32 there is no yellow hair in it and it does not appear to be more
[c]ver 5 than skin deep, [33]he must be shaved except for the diseased area,
and the priest is to keep him in isolation another seven days.
[34]On the seventh day the priest is to examine the itch,[d] and if it
has not spread in the skin and appears to be no more than skin
13:34 deep, the priest shall pronounce him clean. He must wash his
[d]ver 5 [e]Lev 11:25 clothes, and he will be clean.[e] [35]But if the itch does spread in the
skin after he is pronounced clean, [36]the priest is to examine him,
and if the itch has spread in the skin, the priest does not need to
look for yellow hair; the person is unclean.[f] [37]If, however, in his
13:36 judgment it is unchanged and black hair has grown in it, the itch
[f]ver 30 is healed. He is clean, and the priest shall pronounce him clean.
[38]"When a man or woman has white spots on the skin, [39]the
priest is to examine them, and if the spots are dull white, it is a
harmless rash that has broken out on the skin; that person is clean.

13:40 [40]"When a man has lost his hair and is bald,[g] he is clean. [41]If
[g]Lev 21:5; 2Ki 2:23; Isa 3:24; 15:2; 22:12; Eze 27:31; 29:18; Am 8:10; Mic 1:16 he has lost his hair from the front of his scalp and has a bald
forehead, he is clean. [42]But if he has a reddish-white sore on his
bald head or forehead, it is an infectious disease breaking out
on his head or forehead. [43]The priest is to examine him, and if
the swollen sore on his head or forehead is reddish-white like
an infectious skin disease, [44]the man is diseased and is unclean.
The priest shall pronounce him unclean because of the sore on
his head.

13:45 [45]"The person with such an infectious disease must wear torn
[h]Lev 10:6 [i]Eze 24:17,22; Mic 3:7 clothes,[h] let his hair be unkempt,[a] cover the lower part of his
[j]Lev 5:2; La 4:15; Lk 17:12 face[i] and cry out, 'Unclean! Unclean!'[j] [46]As long as he has the
infection he remains unclean. He must live alone; he must live
outside the camp.[k]

[47]"If any clothing is contaminated with mildew—any woolen or
linen clothing, [48]any woven or knitted material of linen or wool,
any leather or anything made of leather— [49]and if the contami-
13:46 nation in the clothing, or leather, or woven or knitted material, or
[k]Nu 5:1-4; 12:14; 2Ki 7:3; 15:5; Lk 17:12 any leather article, is greenish or reddish, it is a spreading mildew

[a]45 Or *clothes, uncover his head*

and must be shown to the priest.[a] 50 The priest is to examine the
mildew[b] and isolate the affected article for seven days. 51 On the
seventh day he is to examine it,[c] and if the mildew has spread in
the clothing, or the woven or knitted material, or the leather,
whatever its use, it is a destructive mildew; the article is unclean.[d]
52 He must burn up the clothing, or the woven or knitted material
of wool or linen, or any leather article that has the contamination in it, because the mildew is destructive; the article must be
burned up.[e]

53 "But if, when the priest examines it, the mildew has not
spread in the clothing, or the woven or knitted material, or the
leather article, 54 he shall order that the contaminated article be
washed. Then he is to isolate it for another seven days. 55 After
the affected article has been washed, the priest is to examine it,
and if the mildew has not changed its appearance, even though
it has not spread, it is unclean. Burn it with fire, whether the
mildew has affected one side or the other. 56 If, when the priest
examines it, the mildew has faded after the article has been
washed, he is to tear the contaminated part out of the clothing,
or the leather, or the woven or knitted material. 57 But if it reappears in the clothing, or in the woven or knitted material, or in
the leather article, it is spreading, and whatever has the mildew
must be burned with fire. 58 The clothing, or the woven or knitted material, or any leather article that has been washed and is
rid of the mildew, must be washed again, and it will be clean."

59 These are the regulations concerning contamination by mildew
in woolen or linen clothing, woven or knitted material, or any
leather article, for pronouncing them clean or unclean.

Chapter 14 Theme

14 The LORD said to Moses, 2 "These are the regulations for
the diseased person at the time of his ceremonial cleansing, when he is brought to the priest:[f] 3 The priest is to go outside
the camp and examine him.[g] If the person has been healed of his
infectious skin disease,[a] 4 the priest shall order that two live clean
birds and some cedar wood, scarlet yarn and hyssop be brought
for the one to be cleansed.[h] 5 Then the priest shall order that one
of the birds be killed over fresh water in a clay pot. 6 He is then to
take the live bird and dip it, together with the cedar wood, the
scarlet yarn and the hyssop, into the blood of the bird that was
killed over the fresh water.[i] 7 Seven times he shall sprinkle[j] the
one to be cleansed of the infectious disease and pronounce him
clean. Then he is to release the live bird in the open fields.

a 3 Traditionally *leprosy*; the Hebrew word was used for various diseases affecting the skin—not necessarily leprosy; also elsewhere in this chapter.

13:49 a Mk 1:44
13:50 b Eze 44:23
13:51 c ver 5; d Lev 14:44
13:52 e ver 55,57
14:2 f Mt 8:2-4; Mk 1:40-44; Lk 5:12-14; 17:14
14:3 g Lev 13:46
14:4 h ver 6,49,51,52; Nu 19:6; Ps 51:7
14:6 i ver 4
14:7 j 2Ki 5:10,14; Isa 52:15; Eze 36:25

8"The person to be cleansed must wash his clothes,[a] shave off
all his hair and bathe with water;[b] then he will be ceremonially
clean.[c] After this he may come into the camp,[d] but he must stay
outside his tent for seven days. 9On the seventh day he must
shave off all his hair; he must shave his head, his beard, his eye-
brows and the rest of his hair. He must wash his clothes and
bathe himself with water, and he will be clean.

10"On the eighth day[e] he must bring two male lambs and one
ewe lamb a year old, each without defect, along with three-
tenths of an ephah[a] of fine flour mixed with oil for a grain offering,[f] and one log[b] of oil.[g] 11The priest who pronounces him clean
shall present both the one to be cleansed and his offerings before
the LORD at the entrance to the Tent of Meeting.

12"Then the priest is to take one of the male lambs and offer it
as a guilt offering,[h] along with the log of oil; he shall wave them
before the LORD as a wave offering.[i] 13He is to slaughter the lamb
in the holy place[j] where the sin offering and the burnt offering
are slaughtered. Like the sin offering, the guilt offering belongs
to the priest;[k] it is most holy. 14The priest is to take some of the
blood of the guilt offering and put it on the lobe of the right ear
of the one to be cleansed, on the thumb of his right hand and on
the big toe of his right foot.[l] 15The priest shall then take some of
the log of oil, pour it in the palm of his own left hand, 16dip his
right forefinger into the oil in his palm, and with his finger
sprinkle some of it before the LORD seven times. 17The priest is
to put some of the oil remaining in his palm on the lobe of the
right ear of the one to be cleansed, on the thumb of his right
hand and on the big toe of his right foot, on top of the blood of
the guilt offering. 18The rest of the oil in his palm the priest shall
put on the head of the one to be cleansed and make atonement
for him before the LORD.

19"Then the priest is to sacrifice the sin offering and make
atonement for the one to be cleansed from his uncleanness. After
that, the priest shall slaughter the burnt offering 20and offer it on
the altar, together with the grain offering, and make atonement
for him, and he will be clean.[m]

21"If, however, he is poor[n] and cannot afford these,[o] he must
take one male lamb as a guilt offering to be waved to make
atonement for him, together with a tenth of an ephah[c] of fine
flour mixed with oil for a grain offering, a log of oil, 22and two
doves or two young pigeons,[p] which he can afford, one for a sin
offering and the other for a burnt offering.

14:8 [a]Lev 11:25; 13:6 [b]ver 9 [c]ver 20 [d]Nu 5:2,3; 12:14,15; 2Ch 26:21
14:10 [e]Mt 8:4; Mk 1:44; Lk 5:14 [f]Lev 2:1 [g]ver 12,15, 21,24
14:12 [h]Lev 5:18; 6:6-7 [i]Ex 29:24
14:13 [j]Ex 29:11 [k]Lev 6:24-30; 7:7
14:14 [l]Ex 29:20; Lev 8:23
14:20 [m]ver 8
14:21 [n]Lev 5:7; 12:8 [o]ver 22,32
14:22 [p]Lev 5:7

[a]*10* That is, probably about 6 quarts (about 6.5 liters) [b]*10* That is, probably about 2/3 pint (about 0.3 liter); also in verses 12, 15, 21 and 24 [c]*21* That is, probably about 2 quarts (about 2 liters)

23"On the eighth day he must bring them for his cleansing to the priest at the entrance to the Tent of Meeting, before the LORD.[a] 24The priest is to take the lamb for the guilt offering,[b] together with the log of oil,[c] and wave them before the LORD as a wave offering.[d] 25He shall slaughter the lamb for the guilt offering and take some of its blood and put it on the lobe of the right ear of the one to be cleansed, on the thumb of his right hand and on the big toe of his right foot.[e] 26The priest is to pour some of the oil into the palm of his own left hand,[f] 27and with his right forefinger sprinkle some of the oil from his palm seven times before the LORD. 28Some of the oil in his palm he is to put on the same places he put the blood of the guilt offering—on the lobe of the right ear of the one to be cleansed, on the thumb of his right hand and on the big toe of his right foot. 29The rest of the oil in his palm the priest shall put on the head of the one to be cleansed, to make atonement for him before the LORD.[g] 30Then he shall sacrifice the doves or the young pigeons, which the person can afford,[h] 31one[a] as a sin offering and the other as a burnt offering,[i] together with the grain offering. In this way the priest will make atonement before the LORD on behalf of the one to be cleansed.[j]"

32These are the regulations for anyone who has an infectious skin disease[k] and who cannot afford the regular offerings[l] for his cleansing.

33The LORD said to Moses and Aaron, 34"When you enter the land of Canaan,[m] which I am giving you as your possession,[n] and I put a spreading mildew in a house in that land, 35the owner of the house must go and tell the priest, 'I have seen something that looks like mildew in my house.' 36The priest is to order the house to be emptied before he goes in to examine the mildew, so that nothing in the house will be pronounced unclean. After this the priest is to go in and inspect the house. 37He is to examine the mildew on the walls, and if it has greenish or reddish[o] depressions that appear to be deeper than the surface of the wall, 38the priest shall go out the doorway of the house and close it up for seven days.[p] 39On the seventh day[q] the priest shall return to inspect the house. If the mildew has spread on the walls, 40he is to order that the contaminated stones be torn out and thrown into an unclean place outside the town.[r] 41He must have all the inside walls of the house scraped and the material that is scraped off dumped into an unclean place outside the town. 42Then they are to take other stones to replace these and take new clay and plaster the house.

43"If the mildew reappears in the house after the stones have been torn out and the house scraped and plastered, 44the priest

a31 Septuagint and Syriac; Hebrew *31such as the person can afford, one*

14:23 [a]ver 10,11
14:24 [b]Nu 6:14 [c]ver 10 [d]ver 12
14:25 [e]ver 14; Ex 29:20
14:26 [f]ver 15
14:29 [g]ver 18
14:30 [h]Lev 5:7
14:31 [i]ver 22; Lev 5:7; 15:15,30 [j]ver 18,19
14:32 [k]Lev 13:2 [l]ver 21
14:34 [m]Ge 12:5; Ex 6:4; Nu 13:2 [n]Ge 17:8; 48:4; Nu 27:12; 32:22; Dt 3:27; 7:1; 32:49
14:37 [o]Lev 13:19
14:38 [p]Lev 13:4
14:39 [q]Lev 13:5
14:40 [r]ver 45

is to go and examine it and, if the mildew has spread in the
house, it is a destructive mildew; the house is unclean.[a] 45 It must
be torn down—its stones, timbers and all the plaster—and taken
out of the town to an unclean place.

46 "Anyone who goes into the house while it is closed up will be
unclean till evening.[b] 47 Anyone who sleeps or eats in the house
must wash his clothes.[c]

48 "But if the priest comes to examine it and the mildew has not
spread after the house has been plastered, he shall pronounce
the house clean,[d] because the mildew is gone. 49 To purify the
house he is to take two birds and some cedar wood, scarlet yarn
and hyssop.[e] 50 He shall kill one of the birds over fresh water in a
clay pot.[f] 51 Then he is to take the cedar wood, the hyssop,[g] the
scarlet yarn and the live bird, dip them into the blood of the
dead bird and the fresh water, and sprinkle the house seven
times.[h] 52 He shall purify the house with the bird's blood, the
fresh water, the live bird, the cedar wood, the hyssop and the
scarlet yarn. 53 Then he is to release the live bird in the open
fields[i] outside the town. In this way he will make atonement for
the house, and it will be clean.[j]"

54 These are the regulations for any infectious skin disease,[k] for
an itch, 55 for mildew[l] in clothing or in a house, 56 and for a
swelling, a rash or a bright spot,[m] 57 to determine when something is clean or unclean.

These are the regulations for infectious skin diseases and
mildew.[n]

Chapter 15 Theme ________________________

15 The LORD said to Moses and Aaron, 2 "Speak to the
Israelites and say to them: 'When any man has a bodily
discharge,[o] the discharge is unclean. 3 Whether it continues flowing from his body or is blocked, it will make him unclean. This
is how his discharge will bring about uncleanness:

4 " 'Any bed the man with a discharge lies on will be unclean,
and anything he sits on will be unclean. 5 Anyone who touches
his bed must wash his clothes[p] and bathe with water,[q] and he
will be unclean till evening.[r] 6 Whoever sits on anything that the
man with a discharge sat on must wash his clothes and bathe
with water, and he will be unclean till evening.

7 " 'Whoever touches the man[s] who has a discharge[t] must wash
his clothes and bathe with water, and he will be unclean till
evening.

8 " 'If the man with the discharge spits[u] on someone who is
clean, that person must wash his clothes and bathe with water,
and he will be unclean till evening.

14:44 [a] Lev 13:51
14:46 [b] Lev 11:24
14:47 [c] Lev 11:25
14:48 [d] Lev 13:6
14:49 [e] ver 4; 1Ki 4:33
14:50 [f] ver 5
14:51 [g] ver 6; Ps 51:7 [h] ver 4,7
14:53 [i] ver 7 [j] ver 20
14:54 [k] Lev 13:2,30
14:55 [l] Lev 13:47-52
14:56 [m] Lev 13:2
14:57 [n] Lev 10:10
15:2 [o] ver 16,32; Lev 22:4; Nu 5:2; 2Sa 3:29; Mt 9:20
15:5 [p] Lev 11:25 [q] Lev 14:8 [r] Lev 11:24
15:7 [s] ver 19; Lev 22:5 [t] ver 16; Lev 22:4
15:8 [u] Nu 12:14

[9]" 'Everything the man sits on when riding will be unclean,
[10]and whoever touches any of the things that were under him will
be unclean till evening; whoever picks up those things[a] must wash
his clothes and bathe with water, and he will be unclean till evening.
[11]" 'Anyone the man with a discharge touches without rinsing
his hands with water must wash his clothes and bathe with water,
and he will be unclean till evening.
[12]" 'A clay pot[b] that the man touches must be broken, and any
wooden article[c] is to be rinsed with water.
[13]" 'When a man is cleansed from his discharge, he is to count
off seven days[d] for his ceremonial cleansing; he must wash his
clothes and bathe himself with fresh water, and he will be clean.[e]
[14]On the eighth day he must take two doves or two young pigeons[f]
and come before the LORD to the entrance to the Tent of Meeting
and give them to the priest. [15]The priest is to sacrifice them, the
one for a sin offering[g] and the other for a burnt offering.[h] In this
way he will make atonement before the LORD for the man
because of his discharge.[i]
[16]" 'When a man has an emission of semen,[j] he must bathe his
whole body with water, and he will be unclean till evening.[k]
[17]Any clothing or leather that has semen on it must be washed
with water, and it will be unclean till evening. [18]When a man lies
with a woman and there is an emission of semen,[l] both must
bathe with water, and they will be unclean till evening.
[19]" 'When a woman has her regular flow of blood, the impurity
of her monthly period[m] will last seven days, and anyone who
touches her will be unclean till evening.
[20]" 'Anything she lies on during her period will be unclean,
and anything she sits on will be unclean. [21]Whoever touches her
bed must wash his clothes and bathe with water, and he will be
unclean till evening.[n] [22]Whoever touches anything she sits on
must wash his clothes and bathe with water, and he will be
unclean till evening. [23]Whether it is the bed or anything she was
sitting on, when anyone touches it, he will be unclean till evening.
[24]" 'If a man lies with her and her monthly flow[o] touches him, he
will be unclean for seven days; any bed he lies on will be unclean.
[25]" 'When a woman has a discharge of blood for many days at
a time other than her monthly period[p] or has a discharge that
continues beyond her period, she will be unclean as long as she
has the discharge, just as in the days of her period. [26]Any bed she
lies on while her discharge continues will be unclean, as is her
bed during her monthly period, and anything she sits on will be
unclean, as during her period. [27]Whoever touches them will be
unclean; he must wash his clothes and bathe with water, and he
will be unclean till evening.

15:10 [a]Nu 19:10
15:12 [b]Lev 6:28 [c]Lev 11:32
15:13 [d]Lev 8:33 [e]ver 5
15:14 [f]Lev 14:22
15:15 [g]Lev 5:7 [h]Lev 14:31 [i]Lev 14:18,19
15:16 [j]ver 2; Lev 22:4; Dt 23:10 [k]ver 5; Dt 23:11
15:18 [l]1Sa 21:4
15:19 [m]ver 24; Lev 12:2
15:21 [n]ver 27
15:24 [o]ver 19; Lev 12:2; 18:19; 20:18; Eze 18:6
15:25 [p]Mt 9:20; Mk 5:25; Lk 8:43

28"'When she is cleansed from her discharge, she must count off seven days, and after that she will be ceremonially clean. 29On the eighth day she must take two doves or two young pigeons[a] and bring them to the priest at the entrance to the Tent of Meeting. 30The priest is to sacrifice one for a sin offering and the other for a burnt offering. In this way he will make atonement for her before the LORD for the uncleanness of her discharge.[b]

31"'You must keep the Israelites separate from things that make them unclean, so they will not die in their uncleanness for defiling my dwelling place,[ac] which is among them.'"

32These are the regulations for a man with a discharge, for anyone made unclean by an emission of semen,[d] 33for a woman in her monthly period, for a man or a woman with a discharge, and for a man who lies with a woman who is ceremonially unclean.[e]

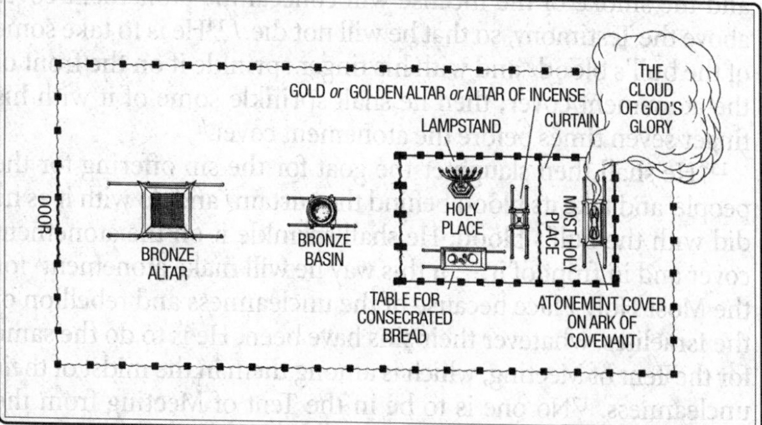

Inside the Tabernacle

Chapter 16 Theme

16 The LORD spoke to Moses after the death of the two sons of Aaron who died when they approached the LORD.[f] 2The LORD said to Moses: "Tell your brother Aaron not to come whenever he chooses[g] into the Most Holy Place[h] behind the curtain in front of the atonement cover on the ark, or else he will die, because I appear[i] in the cloud[j] over the atonement cover.

3"This is how Aaron is to enter the sanctuary area:[k] with a young bull for a sin offering and a ram for a burnt offering. 4He is to put on the sacred linen tunic, with linen undergarments next to his body; he is to tie the linen sash around him and put on the linen turban.[l] These are sacred garments;[m] so he must bathe himself with water[n] before he puts them on. 5From the Israelite community[o] he is to take two male goats[p] for a sin offering and a ram for a burnt offering.

15:29 [a]Lev 14:22
15:30 [b]Lev 5:10; 14:20,31; 18:19; 2Sa 11:4; Mk 5:25; Lk 8:43
15:31 [c]Lev 20:3; Nu 5:3; 19:13,20; 2Sa 15:25; 2Ki 21:7; Ps 33:14; 74:7; 76:2; Eze 5:11; 23:38
15:32 [d]ver 2
15:33 [e]ver 19,24,25
16:1 [f]Lev 10:1
16:2 [g]Ex 30:10; Heb 9:7 [h]Heb 9:25; 10:19 [i]Ex 25:22 [j]Ex 40:34
16:3 [k]Heb 9:24,25
16:4 [l]Ex 28:39 [m]Ex 28:42 [n]ver 24; Heb 10:22
16:5 [o]Lev 4:13-21 [p]2Ch 29:23

INSIGHT

As you study the Day of Atonement in Leviticus, consult the chart **The Feasts of Israel** on pages 210, 211.

a31 Or *my tabernacle*

6“Aaron is to offer the bull for his own sin offering to make
atonement for himself and his household.[a] 7Then he is to take the
two goats and present them before the LORD at the entrance to the
Tent of Meeting. 8He is to cast lots for the two goats—one lot for
the LORD and the other for the scapegoat.[a] 9Aaron shall bring the
goat whose lot falls to the LORD and sacrifice it for a sin offering.
10But the goat chosen by lot as the scapegoat shall be presented
alive before the LORD to be used for making atonement[b] by sending it into the desert as a scapegoat.

11“Aaron shall bring the bull for his own sin offering to make
atonement for himself and his household,[c] and he is to slaughter
the bull for his own sin offering. 12He is to take a censer full of
burning coals[d] from the altar before the LORD and two handfuls
of finely ground fragrant incense[e] and take them behind the
curtain. 13He is to put the incense on the fire before the LORD,
and the smoke of the incense will conceal the atonement cover
above the Testimony, so that he will not die.[f] 14He is to take some
of the bull's blood[g] and with his finger sprinkle it on the front of
the atonement cover; then he shall sprinkle some of it with his
finger seven times before the atonement cover.[h]

15“He shall then slaughter the goat for the sin offering for the
people[i] and take its blood behind the curtain[j] and do with it as he
did with the bull's blood: He shall sprinkle it on the atonement
cover and in front of it. 16In this way he will make atonement[k] for
the Most Holy Place because of the uncleanness and rebellion of
the Israelites, whatever their sins have been. He is to do the same
for the Tent of Meeting, which is among them in the midst of their
uncleanness. 17No one is to be in the Tent of Meeting from the
time Aaron goes in to make atonement in the Most Holy Place
until he comes out, having made atonement for himself, his
household and the whole community of Israel.

18“Then he shall come out to the altar[l] that is before the LORD
and make atonement for it. He shall take some of the bull's blood
and some of the goat's blood and put it on all the horns of the
altar.[m] 19He shall sprinkle some of the blood on it with his finger
seven times to cleanse it and to consecrate it from the uncleanness
of the Israelites.[n]

20“When Aaron has finished making atonement for the Most
Holy Place, the Tent of Meeting and the altar, he shall bring forward the live goat. 21He is to lay both hands on the head of the
live goat and confess[o] over it all the wickedness and rebellion of
the Israelites—all their sins—and put them on the goat's head.
He shall send the goat away into the desert in the care of a man
appointed for the task. 22The goat will carry on itself all their
sins[p] to a solitary place; and the man shall release it in the desert.

a8 That is, the goat of removal; Hebrew *azazel*; also in verses 10 and 26

16:6 [a]Lev 9:7; Heb 5:3; 7:27; 9:7,12
16:10 [b]Isa 53:4-10; Ro 3:25; 1Jn 2:2
16:11 [c]Heb 7:27; 9:7
16:12 [d]Lev 10:1 [e]Ex 30:34-38
16:13 [f]Ex 28:43; Lev 22:9
16:14 [g] Lev 4:5; Heb 9:7,13,25 [h] Lev 4:6
16:15 [i]Heb 9:7,12 [j]Heb 9:3
16:16 [k]Ex 29:36
16:18 [l]Lev 4:7 [m]Lev 4:25
16:19 [n]Eze 43:20
16:21 [o]Lev 5:5
16:22 [p]Isa 53:12

23"Then Aaron is to go into the Tent of Meeting and take off the
linen garments he put on before he entered the Most Holy Place,
and he is to leave them there.[a] 24He shall bathe himself with water
in a holy place and put on his regular garments.[b] Then he shall
come out and sacrifice the burnt offering for himself and the
burnt offering for the people, to make atonement for himself and
for the people. 25He shall also burn the fat of the sin offering on
the altar.
26"The man who releases the goat as a scapegoat must wash his
clothes[c] and bathe himself with water; afterward he may come
into the camp. 27The bull and the goat for the sin offerings, whose
blood was brought into the Most Holy Place to make atonement,
must be taken outside the camp;[d] their hides, flesh and offal are
to be burned up. 28The man who burns them must wash his
clothes and bathe himself with water; afterward he may come
into the camp.
29"This is to be a lasting ordinance for you: On the tenth day of
the seventh month you must deny yourselves[a][e] and not do any
work—whether native-born or an alien living among you—
30because on this day atonement will be made for you, to cleanse
you. Then, before the LORD, you will be clean from all your sins.[f]
31It is a sabbath of rest, and you must deny yourselves;[g] it is a
lasting ordinance. 32The priest who is anointed and ordained to
succeed his father as high priest is to make atonement. He is to
put on the sacred linen garments[h] 33and make atonement for the
Most Holy Place, for the Tent of Meeting and the altar, and for
the priests and all the people of the community.[i]
34"This is to be a lasting ordinance for you: Atonement is to be
made once a year[j] for all the sins of the Israelites."
And it was done, as the LORD commanded Moses.

Chapter 17 Theme

17 The LORD said to Moses, 2"Speak to Aaron and his sons and
to all the Israelites and say to them: 'This is what the LORD
has commanded: 3Any Israelite who sacrifices an ox,[b] a lamb or a
goat in the camp or outside of it 4instead of bringing it to the entrance to the Tent of Meeting to present it as an offering to the
LORD in front of the tabernacle of the LORD[k]—that man shall be
considered guilty of bloodshed; he has shed blood and must be cut
off from his people.[l] 5This is so the Israelites will bring to the
LORD the sacrifices they are now making in the open fields. They
must bring them to the priest, that is, to the LORD, at the entrance
to the Tent of Meeting and sacrifice them as fellowship offerings.[c]

16:23 [a]Eze 42:14; 44:19
16:24 [b]ver 3-5
16:26 [c]Lev 11:25
16:27 [d]Lev 4:12,21; Heb 13:11
16:29 [e]Lev 23:27,32; Nu 29:7; Isa 58:3
16:30 [f]Jer 33:8; Eph 5:26
16:31 [g]Isa 58:3,5
16:32 [h]ver 4; Nu 20:26,28
16:33 [i]ver 11,16-18
16:34 [j]Heb 9:7,25
17:4 [k]Dt 12:5-21 [l]Ge 17:14

[a]29 Or *must fast;* also in verse 31 [b]3 The Hebrew word can include both male and female. [c]5 Traditionally *peace offerings*

6 The priest is to sprinkle the blood against the altar of the LORD[a] at
the entrance to the Tent of Meeting and burn the fat as an aroma
pleasing to the LORD.[b] 7 They must no longer offer any of their
sacrifices to the goat idols[a][c] to whom they prostitute themselves.[d]
This is to be a lasting ordinance for them and for the generations
to come.'

8 "Say to them: 'Any Israelite or any alien living among them
who offers a burnt offering or sacrifice 9 and does not bring it to
the entrance to the Tent of Meeting[e] to sacrifice it to the LORD—
that man must be cut off from his people.

10 " 'Any Israelite or any alien living among them who eats any
blood—I will set my face against that person who eats blood[f] and
will cut him off from his people. 11 For the life of a creature is in the
blood,[g] and I have given it to you to make atonement for yourselves on the altar; it is the blood that makes atonement for one's
life.[h] 12 Therefore I say to the Israelites, "None of you may eat
blood, nor may an alien living among you eat blood."

13 " 'Any Israelite or any alien living among you who hunts any
animal or bird that may be eaten must drain out the blood and
cover it with earth,[i] 14 because the life of every creature is its
blood. That is why I have said to the Israelites, "You must not eat
the blood of any creature, because the life of every creature is its
blood; anyone who eats it must be cut off."[j]

15 " 'Anyone, whether native-born or alien, who eats anything
found dead or torn by wild animals[k] must wash his clothes and
bathe with water, and he will be ceremonially unclean till evening;
then he will be clean. 16 But if he does not wash his clothes and
bathe himself, he will be held responsible.' "

Chapter 18 Theme ________________________

18 The LORD said to Moses, 2 "Speak to the Israelites and say to
them: 'I am the LORD your God.[l] 3 You must not do as they
do in Egypt, where you used to live, and you must not do as they
do in the land of Canaan, where I am bringing you. Do not follow
their practices.[m] 4 You must obey my laws and be careful to follow
my decrees. I am the LORD your God.[n] 5 Keep my decrees and laws,
for the man who obeys them will live by them.[o] I am the LORD.

6 " 'No one is to approach any close relative to have sexual relations. I am the LORD.

7 " 'Do not dishonor your father[p] by having sexual relations with
your mother.[q] She is your mother; do not have relations with her.

8 " 'Do not have sexual relations with your father's wife;[r] that
would dishonor your father.[s]

a7 Or *demons*

17:6 [a] Lev 3:2 [b] Nu 18:17
17:7 [c] Ex 22:20; 2Ch 11:15 [d] Ex 32:8; 34:15; Dt 32:17; 1Co 10:20
17:9 [e] ver 4
17:10 [f] Ge 9:4; Lev 3:17; Dt 12:16,23; 1Sa 14:33
17:11 [g] ver 14; Ge 9:4 [h] Heb 9:22
17:13 [i] Lev 7:26; Dt 12:16
17:14 [j] ver 11; Ge 9:4
17:15 [k] Ex 22:31; Dt 14:21
18:2 [l] Ex 6:7; Lev 11:44; Eze 20:5
18:3 [m] ver 24-30; Ex 23:24; Lev 20:23
18:4 [n] ver 2
18:5 [o] Eze 20:11; Ro 10:5*; Gal 3:12*
18:7 [p] Lev 20:11 [q] Eze 22:10
18:8 [r] 1Co 5:1 [s] Lev 20:11

9 “ ‘Do not have sexual relations with your sister,[a] either your
father’s daughter or your mother’s daughter, whether she was
born in the same home or elsewhere.
10 “ ‘Do not have sexual relations with your son’s daughter or
your daughter’s daughter; that would dishonor you.
11 “ ‘Do not have sexual relations with the daughter of your
father’s wife, born to your father; she is your sister.
12 “ ‘Do not have sexual relations with your father’s sister;[b] she
is your father’s close relative.
13 “ ‘Do not have sexual relations with your mother’s sister,
because she is your mother’s close relative.
14 “ ‘Do not dishonor your father’s brother by approaching his
wife to have sexual relations; she is your aunt.[c]
15 “ ‘Do not have sexual relations with your daughter-in-law.[d]
She is your son’s wife; do not have relations with her.
16 “ ‘Do not have sexual relations with your brother’s wife;[e] that
would dishonor your brother.
17 “ ‘Do not have sexual relations with both a woman and her
daughter.[f] Do not have sexual relations with either her son’s
daughter or her daughter’s daughter; they are her close relatives.
That is wickedness.
18 “ ‘Do not take your wife’s sister as a rival wife and have sexual
relations with her while your wife is living.
19 “ ‘Do not approach a woman to have sexual relations during
the uncleanness of her monthly period.[g]
20 “ ‘Do not have sexual relations with your neighbor’s wife[h] and
defile yourself with her.
21 “ ‘Do not give any of your children[i] to be sacrificed[a] to Molech,[j] for you must not profane the name of your God.[k] I am the
LORD.
22 “ ‘Do not lie with a man as one lies with a woman;[l] that is
detestable.
23 “ ‘Do not have sexual relations with an animal and defile
yourself with it. A woman must not present herself to an animal
to have sexual relations with it; that is a perversion.[m]
24 “ ‘Do not defile yourselves in any of these ways, because this
is how the nations that I am going to drive out before you[n]
became defiled.[o] 25 Even the land was defiled; so I punished it for
its sin,[p] and the land vomited out its inhabitants.[q] 26 But you
must keep my decrees and my laws. The native-born and the
aliens living among you must not do any of these detestable
things, 27 for all these things were done by the people who lived
in the land before you, and the land became defiled. 28 And if you

18:9 [a] Lev 20:17
18:12 [b] Lev 20:19
18:14 [c] Lev 20:20
18:15 [d] Lev 20:12
18:16 [e] Lev 20:21
18:17 [f] Lev 20:14
18:19 [g] Lev 15:24; 20:18
18:20 [h] Ex 20:14; Lev 20:10; Mt 5:27,28; 1Co 6:9; Heb 13:4
18:21 [i] Dt 12:31 [j] Lev 20:2-5 [k] Lev 19:12; 21:6; Eze 36:20
18:22 [l] Lev 20:13; Dt 23:18; Ro 1:27
18:23 [m] Ex 22:19; Lev 20:15; Dt 27:21
18:24 [n] ver 3,27,30 [o] Dt 18:12
18:25 [p] Lev 20:23; Dt 9:5; 18:12 [q] ver 28; Lev 20:22

[a] *21* Or *to be passed through* ⌊*the fire*⌋

defile the land, it will vomit you out as it vomited out the nations
that were before you.
29"'Everyone who does any of these detestable things—such
persons must be cut off from their people. 30Keep my requirements[a] and do not follow any of the detestable customs that were
practiced before you came and do not defile yourselves with
them. I am the LORD your God.[b]'"

Chapter 19 Theme ______________________________

19 The LORD said to Moses, 2"Speak to the entire assembly of
Israel and say to them: 'Be holy because I, the LORD your
God, am holy.[c]
3"'Each of you must respect his mother and father,[d] and you
must observe my Sabbaths. I am the LORD your God.[e]
4"'Do not turn to idols or make gods of cast metal for yourselves.[f] I am the LORD your God.
5"'When you sacrifice a fellowship offering[a] to the LORD, sacrifice it in such a way that it will be accepted on your behalf. 6It
shall be eaten on the day you sacrifice it or on the next day; anything left over until the third day must be burned up. 7If any of it
is eaten on the third day, it is impure and will not be accepted.
8Whoever eats it will be held responsible because he has desecrated what is holy to the LORD; that person must be cut off from
his people.
9"'When you reap the harvest of your land, do not reap to the
very edges of your field or gather the gleanings of your harvest.[g]
10Do not go over your vineyard a second time or pick up the
grapes that have fallen. Leave them for the poor and the alien. I
am the LORD your God.
11"'Do not steal.[h]
"'Do not lie.[i]
"'Do not deceive one another.
12"'Do not swear falsely by my name[j] and so profane the name
of your God. I am the LORD.
13"'Do not defraud your neighbor or rob him.[k]
"'Do not hold back the wages of a hired man overnight.[l]
14"'Do not curse the deaf or put a stumbling block in front of
the blind,[m] but fear your God. I am the LORD.
15"'Do not pervert justice;[n] do not show partiality[o] to the poor
or favoritism to the great, but judge your neighbor fairly.
16"'Do not go about spreading slander[p] among your people.
"'Do not do anything that endangers your neighbor's life.[q] I
am the LORD.

a5 Traditionally *peace offering*

18:30 [a]Dt 11:1 [b]ver 2
19:2 [c]1Pe 1:16*; Lev 11:44
19:3 [d]Ex 20:12 [e]Lev 11:44
19:4 [f]Ex 20:4,23; 34:17; Lev 26:1; Ps 96:5; 115:4-7
19:9 [g]Lev 23:10,22; Dt 24:19-22
19:11 [h]Ex 20:15 [i]Eph 4:25
19:12 [j]Ex 20:7; Mt 5:33
19:13 [k]Ex 22:15, 25-27 [l]Dt 24:15; Jas 5:4
19:14 [m]Dt 27:18
19:15 [n]Ex 23:2,6 [o]Dt 1:17
19:16 [p]Ps 15:3; Eze 22:9 [q]Ex 23:7

17" 'Do not hate your brother in your heart.[a] Rebuke your neighbor frankly[b] so you will not share in his guilt.

18" 'Do not seek revenge[c] or bear a grudge[d] against one of your people, but love your neighbor as yourself.[e] I am the LORD.

19" 'Keep my decrees.

" 'Do not mate different kinds of animals.

" 'Do not plant your field with two kinds of seed.[f]

" 'Do not wear clothing woven of two kinds of material.[g]

20" 'If a man sleeps with a woman who is a slave girl promised to another man but who has not been ransomed or given her freedom, there must be due punishment. Yet they are not to be put to death, because she had not been freed. 21The man, however, must bring a ram to the entrance to the Tent of Meeting for a guilt offering to the LORD.[h] 22With the ram of the guilt offering the priest is to make atonement for him before the LORD for the sin he has committed, and his sin will be forgiven.

23" 'When you enter the land and plant any kind of fruit tree, regard its fruit as forbidden.[a] For three years you are to consider it forbidden[a]; it must not be eaten. 24In the fourth year all its fruit will be holy,[i] an offering of praise to the LORD. 25But in the fifth year you may eat its fruit. In this way your harvest will be increased. I am the LORD your God.

26" 'Do not eat any meat with the blood still in it.[j]

" 'Do not practice divination or sorcery.[k]

27" 'Do not cut the hair at the sides of your head or clip off the edges of your beard.[l]

28" 'Do not cut your bodies for the dead or put tattoo marks on yourselves. I am the LORD.

29" 'Do not degrade your daughter by making her a prostitute,[m] or the land will turn to prostitution and be filled with wickedness.

30" 'Observe my Sabbaths and have reverence for my sanctuary. I am the LORD.[n]

31" 'Do not turn to mediums or seek out spiritists,[o] for you will be defiled by them. I am the LORD your God.

32" 'Rise in the presence of the aged, show respect for the elderly[p] and revere your God. I am the LORD.

33" 'When an alien lives with you in your land, do not mistreat him. 34The alien living with you must be treated as one of your native-born.[q] Love him as yourself, for you were aliens in Egypt.[r] I am the LORD your God.

35" 'Do not use dishonest standards when measuring length, weight or quantity. 36Use honest scales and honest weights, an honest ephah[b] and an honest hin.[c][s] I am the LORD your God, who brought you out of Egypt.

19:17 [a]1Jn 2:9; 3:15 [b]Mt 18:15; Lk 17:3
19:18 [c]Ro 12:19 [d]Ps 103:9 [e]Mt 5:43*; 19:16*; 22:39*; Mk 12:31*; Lk 10:27*; Jn 13:34; Ro 13:9*; Gal 5:14*; Jas 2:8*
19:19 [f]Dt 22:9 [g]Dt 22:11
19:21 [h]Lev 5:15
19:24 [i]Pr 3:9
19:26 [j]Lev 17:10 [k]Dt 18:10
19:27 [l]Lev 21:5
19:29 [m]Dt 23:18
19:30 [n]Lev 26:2
19:31 [o]Lev 20:6; Isa 8:19
19:32 [p]1Ti 5:1
19:34 [q]Ex 12:48 [r]Dt 10:19
19:36 [s]Dt 25:13-15

[a]23 Hebrew *uncircumcised* [b]36 An ephah was a dry measure. [c]36 A hin was a liquid measure.

37“ ‘Keep all my decrees and all my laws and follow them. I am
the LORD.’ ”

Chapter 20 Theme ____________________

20

The LORD said to Moses, 2“Say to the Israelites: ‘Any Israelite or any alien living in Israel who gives[a] any of his
children to Molech must be put to death. The people of the community are to stone him. 3I will set my face against that man and
I will cut him off from his people; for by giving his children to
Molech, he has defiled my sanctuary[a] and profaned my holy
name.[b] 4If the people of the community close their eyes when
that man gives one of his children to Molech and they fail to put
him to death,[c] 5I will set my face against that man and his family
and will cut off from their people both him and all who follow
him in prostituting themselves to Molech.
6“ ‘I will set my face against the person who turns to mediums
and spiritists to prostitute himself by following them, and I will
cut him off from his people.[d]
7“ ‘Consecrate yourselves and be holy,[e] because I am the LORD
your God. 8Keep my decrees and follow them. I am the LORD,
who makes you holy.[b][f]
9“ ‘If anyone curses his father or mother,[g] he must be put to
death.[h] He has cursed his father or his mother, and his blood will
be on his own head.[i]
10“ ‘If a man commits adultery with another man’s wife[j]—with
the wife of his neighbor—both the adulterer and the adulteress
must be put to death.
11“ ‘If a man sleeps with his father’s wife, he has dishonored his
father.[k] Both the man and the woman must be put to death; their
blood will be on their own heads.
12“ ‘If a man sleeps with his daughter-in-law,[l] both of them
must be put to death. What they have done is a perversion; their
blood will be on their own heads.
13“ ‘If a man lies with a man as one lies with a woman, both of
them have done what is detestable.[m] They must be put to death;
their blood will be on their own heads.
14“ ‘If a man marries both a woman and her mother,[n] it is
wicked. Both he and they must be burned in the fire, so that no
wickedness will be among you.[o]
15“ ‘If a man has sexual relations with an animal,[p] he must be
put to death, and you must kill the animal.
16“ ‘If a woman approaches an animal to have sexual relations
with it, kill both the woman and the animal. They must be put to
death; their blood will be on their own heads.

a2 Or *sacrifices*; also in verses 3 and 4 b8 Or *who sanctifies you*; or *who sets you apart as holy*

20:3 [a]Lev 15:31 [b]Lev 18:21
20:4 [c]Dt 17:2-5
20:6 [d]Lev 19:31
20:7 [e]Eph 1:4; 1Pe 1:16*
20:8 [f]Ex 31:13
20:9 [g]Dt 27:16 [h]Ex 21:17; Mt 15:4*; Mk 7:10* [i]ver 11; 2Sa 1:16
20:10 [j]Ex 20:14; Dt 5:18; 22:22
20:11 [k]Lev 18:7; Dt 27:23
20:12 [l]Lev 18:15
20:13 [m]Lev 18:22
20:14 [n]Lev 18:17 [o]Dt 27:23
20:15 [p]Lev 18:23

17" 'If a man marries his sister[a], the daughter of either his father or his mother, and they have sexual relations, it is a disgrace. They must be cut off before the eyes of their people. He has dishonored his sister and will be held responsible.

18" 'If a man lies with a woman during her monthly period[b] and has sexual relations with her, he has exposed the source of her flow, and she has also uncovered it. Both of them must be cut off from their people.

19" 'Do not have sexual relations with the sister of either your mother or your father,[c] for that would dishonor a close relative; both of you would be held responsible.

20" 'If a man sleeps with his aunt,[d] he has dishonored his uncle. They will be held responsible; they will die childless.

21" 'If a man marries his brother's wife,[e] it is an act of impurity; he has dishonored his brother. They will be childless.

22" 'Keep all my decrees and laws and follow them, so that the land[f] where I am bringing you to live may not vomit you out. 23You must not live according to the customs of the nations[g] I am going to drive out before you.[h] Because they did all these things, I abhorred them. 24But I said to you, "You will possess their land; I will give it to you as an inheritance, a land flowing with milk and honey."[i] I am the LORD your God, who has set you apart from the nations.[j]

25" 'You must therefore make a distinction between clean and unclean animals and between unclean and clean birds.[k] Do not defile yourselves by any animal or bird or anything that moves along the ground—those which I have set apart as unclean for you. 26You are to be holy to me[a] because I, the LORD, am holy,[l] and I have set you apart from the nations to be my own.

27" 'A man or woman who is a medium or spiritist among you must be put to death.[m] You are to stone them; their blood will be on their own heads.' "

Chapter 21 Theme ______________________

21 The LORD said to Moses, "Speak to the priests, the sons of Aaron, and say to them: 'A priest must not make himself ceremonially unclean for any of his people who die,[n] 2except for a close relative, such as his mother or father, his son or daughter, his brother, 3or an unmarried sister who is dependent on him since she has no husband—for her he may make himself unclean. 4He must not make himself unclean for people related to him by marriage,[b] and so defile himself.

a26 Or *be my holy ones* b4 Or *unclean as a leader among his people*

20:17 [a]Lev 18:9
20:18 [b]Lev 15:24; 18:19
20:19 [c]Lev 18:12-13
20:20 [d]Lev 18:14
20:21 [e]Lev 18:16
20:22 [f]Lev 18:25-28
20:23 [g]Lev 18:3 [h]Lev 18:24, 27,30
20:24 [i]Ex 3:8; 13:5; 33:3 [j]Ex 33:16
20:25 [k]Lev 11:1-47; Dt 14:3-21
20:26 [l]Lev 19:2
20:27 [m]Lev 19:31
21:1 [n]Eze 44:25

5" 'Priests must not shave their heads or shave off the edges of
their beards[a] or cut their bodies.[b] 6They must be holy to their God
and must not profane the name of their God.[c] Because they present the offerings made to the LORD by fire,[d] the food of their
God, they are to be holy.

7" 'They must not marry women defiled by prostitution or
divorced from their husbands,[e] because priests are holy to their
God.[f] 8Regard them as holy,[g] because they offer up the food of
your God. Consider them holy, because I the LORD am holy—I
who make you holy.[a]

9" 'If a priest's daughter defiles herself by becoming a prostitute,
she disgraces her father; she must be burned in the fire.[h]

10" 'The high priest, the one among his brothers who has had
the anointing oil poured on his head and who has been ordained
to wear the priestly garments,[i] must not let his hair become
unkempt[b] or tear his clothes.[j] 11He must not enter a place where
there is a dead body.[k] He must not make himself unclean,[l] even
for his father or mother, 12nor leave the sanctuary of his God or
desecrate it, because he has been dedicated by the anointing oil[m]
of his God. I am the LORD.

13" 'The woman he marries must be a virgin.[n] 14He must not
marry a widow, a divorced woman, or a woman defiled by prostitution, but only a virgin from his own people, 15so he will not
defile his offspring among his people. I am the LORD, who makes
him holy.[c]' "

16The LORD said to Moses, 17"Say to Aaron: 'For the generations to come none of your descendants who has a defect may
come near to offer the food of his God.[o] 18No man who has any
defect[p] may come near: no man who is blind or lame, disfigured
or deformed; 19no man with a crippled foot or hand, 20or who is
hunchbacked or dwarfed, or who has any eye defect, or who has
festering or running sores or damaged testicles.[q] 21No descendant of Aaron the priest who has any defect is to come near to
present the offerings made to the LORD by fire. He has a defect; he
must not come near to offer the food of his God. 22He may eat the
most holy food of his God,[r] as well as the holy food; 23yet because
of his defect, he must not go near the curtain or approach the
altar, and so desecrate my sanctuary. I am the LORD, who makes
them holy.[d]' "

24So Moses told this to Aaron and his sons and to all the
Israelites.

[a]8 Or *who sanctify you*; or *who set you apart as holy* [b]10 Or *not uncover his head*
[c]15 Or *who sanctifies him*; or *who sets him apart as holy* [d]23 Or *who sanctifies them*; or *who sets them apart as holy*

21:5 [a]Eze 44:20 [b]Lev 19:28; Dt 14:1
21:6 [c]Lev 18:21 [d]Lev 3:11
21:7 [e]ver 13,14 [f]Eze 44:22
21:8 [g]ver 6
21:9 [h]Ge 38:24; Lev 19:29
21:10 [i]Lev 16:32 [j]Lev 10:6
21:11 [k]Nu 19:11,13,14 [l]Lev 19:28
21:12 [m]Ex 29:6-7; Lev 10:7
21:13 [n]Eze 44:22
21:17 [o]ver 6
21:18 [p]Lev 22:19-25
21:20 [q]Dt 23:1; Isa 56:3
21:22 [r]1Co 9:13

Chapter 22 Theme ____________________

22
The LORD said to Moses, 2“Tell Aaron and his sons to treat
with respect the sacred offerings the Israelites consecrate
to me, so they will not profane my holy name. I am the LORD.
3“Say to them: ‘For the generations to come, if any of your
descendants is ceremonially unclean and yet comes near the
sacred offerings that the Israelites consecrate to the LORD, that
person must be cut off from my presence.[a] I am the LORD.
4“ ‘If a descendant of Aaron has an infectious skin disease[a] or a
bodily discharge,[b] he may not eat the sacred offerings until he is
cleansed. He will also be unclean if he touches something defiled
by a corpse[c] or by anyone who has an emission of semen, 5or if
he touches any crawling thing[d] that makes him unclean, or any
person[e] who makes him unclean, whatever the uncleanness may
be. 6The one who touches any such thing will be unclean till
evening. He must not eat any of the sacred offerings unless he has
bathed himself with water. 7When the sun goes down, he will be
clean, and after that he may eat the sacred offerings, for they are
his food.[f] 8He must not eat anything found dead[g] or torn by wild
animals,[h] and so become unclean[i] through it. I am the LORD.
9“ ‘The priests are to keep my requirements so that they do not
become guilty and die[j] for treating them with contempt. I am
the LORD, who makes them holy.[b]
10“ ‘No one outside a priest’s family may eat the sacred offering, nor may the guest of a priest or his hired worker eat it. 11But
if a priest buys a slave with money, or if a slave is born in his
household, that slave may eat his food.[k] 12If a priest’s daughter
marries anyone other than a priest, she may not eat any of the
sacred contributions. 13But if a priest’s daughter becomes a widow
or is divorced, yet has no children, and she returns to live in her
father’s house as in her youth, she may eat of her father’s food.
No unauthorized person, however, may eat any of it.
14“ ‘If anyone eats a sacred offering by mistake, he must make
restitution to the priest for the offering and add a fifth of the value[l] to it. 15The priests must not desecrate the sacred offerings the
Israelites present to the LORD[m] 16by allowing them to eat the
sacred offerings and so bring upon them guilt requiring payment.[n] I am the LORD, who makes them holy.’ ”
17The LORD said to Moses, 18“Speak to Aaron and his sons and
to all the Israelites and say to them: ‘If any of you—either an
Israelite or an alien living in Israel—presents a gift[o] for a burnt
offering to the LORD, either to fulfill a vow or as a freewill offering,

22:3 [a]Lev 7:20,21; Nu 19:13
22:4 [b]Lev 14:1-32; 15:2-15 [c]Lev 11:24-28,39
22:5 [d]Lev 11:24-28,43 [e]Lev 15:7
22:7 [f]Nu 18:11
22:8 [g]Lev 11:39 [h]Ex 22:31; Lev 17:15 [i]Lev 11:40
22:9 [j]ver 16; Ex 28:43
22:11 [k]Ge 17:13; Ex 12:44
22:14 [l]Lev 5:15
22:15 [m]Nu 18:32
22:16 [n]ver 9
22:18 [o]Lev 1:2

a4 Traditionally *leprosy*; the Hebrew word was used for various diseases affecting the skin—not necessarily leprosy. b9 Or *who sanctifies them*; or *who sets them apart as holy*; also in verse 16

19you must present a male without defect[a] from the cattle, sheep
or goats in order that it may be accepted on your behalf. 20Do
not bring anything with a defect,[b] because it will not be accepted
on your behalf. 21When anyone brings from the herd or flock a
fellowship offering[a][c] to the LORD to fulfill a special vow or as a
freewill offering, it must be without defect or blemish to be
acceptable. 22Do not offer to the LORD the blind, the injured or
the maimed, or anything with warts or festering or running
sores. Do not place any of these on the altar as an offering made
to the LORD by fire. 23You may, however, present as a freewill
offering an ox[b] or a sheep that is deformed or stunted, but it will
not be accepted in fulfillment of a vow. 24You must not offer to
the LORD an animal whose testicles are bruised, crushed, torn or
cut.[d] You must not do this in your own land, 25and you must not
accept such animals from the hand of a foreigner and offer them
as the food of your God.[e] They will not be accepted on your
behalf, because they are deformed and have defects.' "
26The LORD said to Moses, 27"When a calf, a lamb or a goat is
born, it is to remain with its mother for seven days.[f] From the
eighth day on, it will be acceptable as an offering made to the
LORD by fire. 28Do not slaughter a cow or a sheep and its young
on the same day.[g]
29"When you sacrifice a thank offering[h] to the LORD, sacrifice it
in such a way that it will be accepted on your behalf. 30It must be
eaten that same day; leave none of it till morning.[i] I am the LORD.
31"Keep[j] my commands and follow them. I am the LORD. 32Do
not profane my holy name.[k] I must be acknowledged as holy by
the Israelites.[l] I am the LORD, who makes[c] you holy[d] 33and who
brought you out of Egypt to be your God.[m] I am the LORD."

Chapter 23 Theme ______________________

23 The LORD said to Moses, 2"Speak to the Israelites and say to
them: 'These are my appointed feasts,[n] the appointed
feasts of the LORD, which you are to proclaim as sacred assemblies.[o]
3" 'There are six days when you may work,[p] but the seventh
day is a Sabbath of rest,[q] a day of sacred assembly. You are not
to do any work; wherever you live, it is a Sabbath to the LORD.
4" 'These are the LORD's appointed feasts, the sacred assemblies you are to proclaim at their appointed times: 5The LORD's
Passover begins at twilight on the fourteenth day of the first
month.[r] 6On the fifteenth day of that month the LORD's Feast of
Unleavened Bread begins; for seven days you must eat bread

INSIGHT

See the chart **The Feasts of Israel** on pages 210, 211.

22:19 [a]Lev 1:3
22:20 [b]Dt 15:21; 17:1; Mal 1:8,14; Heb 9:14; 1Pe 1:19
22:21 [c]Lev 3:6; Nu 15:3,8
22:24 [d]Lev 21:20
22:25 [e]Lev 21:6
22:27 [f]Ex 22:30
22:28 [g]Dt 22:6,7
22:29 [h]Lev 7:12; Ps 107:22
22:30 [i]Lev 7:15
22:31 [j]Dt 4:2,40; Ps 105:45
22:32 [k]Lev 18:21 [l]Lev 10:3
22:33 [m]Lev 11:45
23:2 [n]ver 4,37,44; Nu 29:39 [o]ver 21,27
23:3 [p]Ex 20:9 [q]Ex 20:10; 31:13-17; Lev 19:3; Dt 5:13; Heb 4:9,10
23:5 [r]Ex 12:18-19; Nu 28:16-17; Dt 16:1-8

a21 Traditionally *peace offering* b23 The Hebrew word can include both male and female. c32 Or *made* d32 Or *who sanctifies you*; or *who sets you apart as holy*

The Jewish Calendar

Babylonian names (B) for the months are still used today for the Jewish calendar. Canaanite names (C) were used prior to the Babylonian captivity in 586 B.C. Four are mentioned in the Old Testament.
Adar-Sheni is an intercalary month used every two to three years or seven times in 19 years.

1st month	**2nd month**	**3rd month**	**4th month**
Nisan (B) Abib (C) March-April	Iyyar (B) Ziv (C) April-May	Sivan (B) May-June	Tammuz (B) June-July
7th month	*8th month*	*9th month*	*10th month*
5th month	**6th month**	**7th month**	**8th month**
Ab (B) July-August	Elul (B) August-September	Tishri (B) Ethanim (C) September-October	Marcheshvan (B) Bul (C) October-November
11th month	*12th month*	*1st month*	*2nd month*
9th month	**10th month**	**11th month**	**12th month**
Chislev (B) November-December	Tebeth (B) December-January	Shebat (B) January-February	Adar (B) February-March
3rd month	*4th month*	*5th month*	*6th month*

Sacred calendar appears in black • Civil calendar appears in gray

23:7 made without yeast. [7]On the first day hold a sacred assembly[a]
a ver 3,8 and do no regular work. [8]For seven days present an offering
made to the LORD by fire. And on the seventh day hold a sacred
assembly and do no regular work.' "
23:10 [9]The LORD said to Moses, [10]"Speak to the Israelites and say to
b Ex 23:16,19; 34:26 them: 'When you enter the land I am going to give you and you
reap its harvest, bring to the priest a sheaf[b] of the first grain you
harvest. [11]He is to wave the sheaf before the LORD[c] so it will be
23:11 accepted on your behalf; the priest is to wave it on the day after
c Ex 29:24 the Sabbath. [12]On the day you wave the sheaf, you must sacrifice
as a burnt offering to the LORD a lamb a year old without defect,
[13]together with its grain offering[d] of two-tenths of an ephah[a] of
23:13 fine flour mixed with oil—an offering made to the LORD by fire, a
d Lev 2:14-16; 6:20 pleasing aroma—and its drink offering of a quarter of a hin[b] of
wine. [14]You must not eat any bread, or roasted or new grain, until
the very day you bring this offering to your God.[e] This is to be a
lasting ordinance for the generations to come,[f] wherever you live.
23:14 e Ex 34:26 [15]" 'From the day after the Sabbath, the day you brought the
f Nu 15:21 sheaf of the wave offering, count off seven full weeks. [16]Count off
fifty days up to the day after the seventh Sabbath,[g] and then present an offering of new grain to the LORD. [17]From wherever you
23:16 live, bring two loaves made of two-tenths of an ephah of fine
g Nu 28:26; Ac 2:1 flour, baked with yeast, as a wave offering of firstfruits[h] to the
LORD. [18]Present with this bread seven male lambs, each a year old
and without defect, one young bull and two rams. They will be a
burnt offering to the LORD, together with their grain offerings

23:17 h Ex 34:22; Lev 2:12

a*13* That is, probably about 4 quarts (about 4.5 liters); also in verse 17 b*13* That is, probably about 1quart (about 1liter) and drink offerings—an offering made by fire, an aroma pleasing to the LORD. 19Then sacrifice one male goat for a sin offering and two lambs, each a year old, for a fellowship offering.[a] 20The priest is to wave the two lambs before the LORD as a wave offering, together with the bread of the firstfruits. They are a sacred offering to the LORD for the priest. 21On that same day you are to proclaim a sacred assembly[a] and do no regular work.[b] This is to be a lasting ordinance for the generations to come, wherever you live.

22" 'When you reap the harvest[c] of your land, do not reap to the very edges of your field or gather the gleanings of your harvest.[d] Leave them for the poor and the alien. I am the LORD your God.' "

23The LORD said to Moses, 24"Say to the Israelites: 'On the first day of the seventh month you are to have a day of rest, a sacred assembly commemorated with trumpet blasts.[e] 25Do no regular work,[f] but present an offering made to the LORD by fire.' "

26The LORD said to Moses, 27"The tenth day of this seventh month[g] is the Day of Atonement.[h] Hold a sacred assembly[i] and deny yourselves,[b] and present an offering made to the LORD by fire. 28Do no work on that day, because it is the Day of Atonement, when atonement is made for you before the LORD your God. 29Anyone who does not deny himself on that day must be cut off from his people.[j] 30I will destroy from among his people[k] anyone who does any work on that day. 31You shall do no work at all. This is to be a lasting ordinance for the generations to come, wherever you live. 32It is a sabbath of rest for you, and you must deny yourselves. From the evening of the ninth day of the month until the following evening you are to observe your sabbath."

33The LORD said to Moses, 34"Say to the Israelites: 'On the fifteenth day of the seventh month the LORD's Feast of Tabernacles[l] begins, and it lasts for seven days. 35The first day is a sacred assembly; do no regular work. 36For seven days present offerings made to the LORD by fire, and on the eighth day hold a sacred assembly[m] and present an offering made to the LORD by fire. It is the closing assembly; do no regular work.

37(" 'These are the LORD's appointed feasts, which you are to proclaim as sacred assemblies for bringing offerings made to the LORD by fire—the burnt offerings and grain offerings, sacrifices and drink offerings[n] required for each day. 38These offerings are in addition to those for the LORD's Sabbaths[o] and[c] in addition to your gifts and whatever you have vowed and all the freewill offerings you give to the LORD.)

39" 'So beginning with the fifteenth day of the seventh month, after you have gathered the crops of the land, celebrate the festival to the LORD for seven days;[p] the first day is a day of rest, and the

[a] 19 Traditionally *peace offering* [b] 27 Or *and fast*; also in verses 29 and 32
[c] 38 Or *These feasts are in addition to the Lord's Sabbaths, and these offerings are*

23:21 [a] ver 2 [b] ver 3
23:22 [c] Lev 19:9 [d] Lev 19:10; Dt 24:19-21; Ru 2:15
23:24 [e] Lev 25:9; Nu 10:9,10; 29:1
23:25 [f] ver 21
23:27 [g] Lev 16:29 [h] Ex 30:10 [i] Nu 29:7
23:29 [j] Ge 17:14; Nu 5:2
23:30 [k] Lev 20:3
23:34 [l] Ex 23:16; Dt 16:13; Ezr 3:4; Ne 8:14; Zec 14:16; Jn 7:2
23:36 [m] 2Ch 7:9; Ne 8:18; Jn 7:37
23:37 [n] ver 2,4
23:38 [o] Eze 45:17
23:39 [p] Ex 23:16; Dt 16:13

eighth day also is a day of rest. 40 On the first day you are to take choice fruit from the trees, and palm fronds, leafy branches and poplars,[a] and rejoice before the LORD your God for seven days. 41 Celebrate this as a festival to the LORD for seven days each year. This is to be a lasting ordinance for the generations to come; celebrate it in the seventh month. 42 Live in booths[b] for seven days: All native-born Israelites are to live in booths 43 so your descendants will know[c] that I had the Israelites live in booths when I brought them out of Egypt. I am the LORD your God.' "

44 So Moses announced to the Israelites the appointed feasts of the LORD.

Chapter 24 Theme

24 The LORD said to Moses, 2 "Command the Israelites to bring you clear oil of pressed olives for the light so that the lamps may be kept burning continually. 3 Outside the curtain of the Testimony in the Tent of Meeting, Aaron is to tend the lamps before the LORD from evening till morning, continually. This is to be a lasting ordinance for the generations to come. 4 The lamps on the pure gold lampstand[d] before the LORD must be tended continually.

Lampstand

5 "Take fine flour and bake twelve loaves of bread,[e] using two-tenths of an ephah[a] for each loaf. 6 Set them in two rows, six in each row, on the table of pure gold[f] before the LORD. 7 Along each row put some pure incense as a memorial portion[g] to represent the bread and to be an offering made to the LORD by fire. 8 This bread is to be set out before the LORD regularly,[h] Sabbath after Sabbath,[i] on behalf of the Israelites, as a lasting covenant. 9 It belongs to Aaron and his sons,[j] who are to eat it in a holy place, because it is a most holy part of their regular share of the offerings made to the LORD by fire."

10 Now the son of an Israelite mother and an Egyptian father went out among the Israelites, and a fight broke out in the camp between him and an Israelite. 11 The son of the Israelite woman blasphemed the Name[k] with a curse; so they brought him to Moses. (His mother's name was Shelomith, the daughter of Dibri the Danite.) 12 They put him in custody until the will of the LORD should be made clear to them.[l]

13 Then the LORD said to Moses: 14 "Take the blasphemer outside the camp. All those who heard him are to lay their hands on his head, and the entire assembly is to stone him.[m] 15 Say to the Israelites: 'If anyone curses his God,[n] he will be held responsible; 16 anyone who blasphemes the name of the LORD must be put to death.[o] The entire assembly must stone him. Whether an alien or

[a]5 That is, probably about 4 quarts (about 4.5 liters)

23:40 [a] Ne 8:14-17
23:42 [b] Ne 8:14-16
23:43 [c] Dt 31:13; Ps 78:5
24:4 [d] Ex 25:31; 31:8
24:5 [e] Ex 25:30
24:6 [f] Ex 25:23-30; 1Ki 7:48
24:7 [g] Lev 2:2
24:8 [h] Nu 4:7; 1Ch 9:32; 2Ch 2:4 [i] Mt 12:5
24:9 [j] Lev 8:31; Mt 12:4; Mk 2:26; Lk 6:4
24:11 [k] Ex 3:15
24:12 [l] Ex 18:16; Nu 15:34
24:14 [m] Lev 20:27; Dt 13:9; 17:5,7; 21:21
24:15 [n] Ex 22:28
24:16 [o] 1Ki 21:10,13; Mt 26:66

native-born, when he blasphemes the Name, he must be put to
death.
17“ ‘If anyone takes the life of a human being, he must be put to
death.[a] 18Anyone who takes the life of someone’s animal must
make restitution[b]—life for life. 19If anyone injures his neighbor,
whatever he has done must be done to him: 20fracture for frac-
ture, eye for eye, tooth for tooth.[c] As he has injured the other, so
he is to be injured. 21Whoever kills an animal must make restitution, but whoever kills a man must be put to death.[d] 22You are
to have the same law for the alien[e] and the native-born.[f] I am the
LORD your God.’ ”
23Then Moses spoke to the Israelites, and they took the blasphemer outside the camp and stoned him. The Israelites did as
the LORD commanded Moses.

Chapter 25 Theme ____________________

25 The LORD said to Moses on Mount Sinai, 2“Speak to the
Israelites and say to them: ‘When you enter the land I am
going to give you, the land itself must observe a sabbath to the
LORD. 3For six years sow your fields, and for six years prune your
vineyards and gather their crops.[g] 4But in the seventh year the
land is to have a sabbath of rest, a sabbath to the LORD. Do not sow
your fields or prune your vineyards. 5Do not reap what grows of
itself or harvest the grapes of your untended vines. The land is
to have a year of rest. 6Whatever the land yields during the sabbath year[h] will be food for you—for yourself, your manservant
and maidservant, and the hired worker and temporary resident
who live among you, 7as well as for your livestock and the wild
animals in your land. Whatever the land produces may be eaten.
8“ ‘Count off seven sabbaths of years—seven times seven years—
so that the seven sabbaths of years amount to a period of forty-
nine years. 9Then have the trumpet[i] sounded everywhere on the
tenth day of the seventh month; on the Day of Atonement sound
the trumpet throughout your land. 10Consecrate the fiftieth year
and proclaim liberty[j] throughout the land to all its inhabitants.
It shall be a jubilee[k] for you; each one of you is to return to his
family property and each to his own clan. 11The fiftieth year
shall be a jubilee for you; do not sow and do not reap what grows
of itself or harvest the untended vines. 12For it is a jubilee and is
to be holy for you; eat only what is taken directly from the fields.
13“ ‘In this Year of Jubilee[l] everyone is to return to his own
property.
14“ ‘If you sell land to one of your countrymen or buy any from
him, do not take advantage of each other.[m] 15You are to buy from
your countryman on the basis of the number of years[n] since the

24:17 [a]Ge 9:6; Ex 21:12; Nu 35:30-31; Dt 27:24
24:18 [b]ver 21
24:20 [c]Ex 21:24; Mt 5:38*
24:21 [d]ver 17
24:22 [e]Ex 12:49 [f]Nu 9:14; 15:16
25:3 [g]Ex 23:10
25:6 [h]ver 20
25:9 [i]Lev 23:24
25:10 [j]Isa 61:1; Jer 34:8,15,17; Lk 4:19 [k]Nu 36:4
25:13 [l]ver 10
25:14 [m]Lev 19:13; 1Sa 12:3,4
25:15 [n]Lev 27:18,23

Jubilee. And he is to sell to you on the basis of the number of
years left for harvesting crops. 16When the years are many, you
are to increase the price, and when the years are few, you are to
decrease the price,[a] because what he is really selling you is the
number of crops. 17Do not take advantage of each other,[b] but
fear your God.[c] I am the LORD your God.[d]
18" 'Follow my decrees and be careful to obey my laws, and you
will live safely in the land.[e] 19Then the land will yield its fruit,[f] and
you will eat your fill and live there in safety. 20You may ask, "What
will we eat in the seventh year[g] if we do not plant or harvest our
crops?" 21I will send you such a blessing[h] in the sixth year that
the land will yield enough for three years. 22While you plant during the eighth year, you will eat from the old crop and will continue to eat from it until the harvest of the ninth year comes in.[i]
23" 'The land must not be sold permanently, because the land
is mine[j] and you are but aliens[k] and my tenants. 24Throughout
the country that you hold as a possession, you must provide for
the redemption[l] of the land.
25" 'If one of your countrymen becomes poor and sells some of
his property, his nearest relative[m] is to come and redeem[n] what
his countryman has sold. 26If, however, a man has no one to
redeem it for him but he himself prospers and acquires sufficient
means to redeem it, 27he is to determine the value for the years
since he sold it and refund the balance to the man to whom he
sold it; he can then go back to his own property. 28But if he does
not acquire the means to repay him, what he sold will remain in
the possession of the buyer until the Year of Jubilee. It will be
returned in the Jubilee, and he can then go back to his property.[o]
29" 'If a man sells a house in a walled city, he retains the right of
redemption a full year after its sale. During that time he may
redeem it. 30If it is not redeemed before a full year has passed,
the house in the walled city shall belong permanently to the
buyer and his descendants. It is not to be returned in the Jubilee.
31But houses in villages without walls around them are to be
considered as open country. They can be redeemed, and they
are to be returned in the Jubilee.
32" 'The Levites always have the right to redeem their houses in
the Levitical towns,[p] which they possess. 33So the property of the
Levites is redeemable—that is, a house sold in any town they
hold—and is to be returned in the Jubilee, because the houses in
the towns of the Levites are their property among the Israelites.
34But the pastureland belonging to their towns must not be sold;
it is their permanent possession.[q]
35" 'If one of your countrymen becomes poor[r] and is unable to
support himself among you, help him[s] as you would an alien or
a temporary resident, so he can continue to live among you.

25:16 [a] ver 27,51,52
25:17 [b] Pr 22:22; Jer 7:5,6; 1Th 4:6 [c] Lev 19:14 [d] Lev 19:32
25:18 [e] Lev 26:4,5; Dt 12:10; Ps 4:8; Jer 23:6
25:19 [f] Lev 26:4
25:20 [g] ver 4
25:21 [h] Dt 28:8,12; Hag 2:19; Mal 3:10
25:22 [i] Lev 26:10
25:23 [j] Ex 19:5 [k] Ge 23:4; 1Ch 29:15; Ps 39:12; Heb 11:13; 1Pe 2:11
25:24 [l] ver 29,48; Ru 4:7
25:25 [m] Ru 2:20; Jer 32:7 [n] Lev 27:13, 19,31; Ru 4:4
25:28 [o] ver 10
25:32 [p] Nu 35:1-8; Jos 21:2
25:34 [q] Nu 35:2-5
25:35 [r] Dt 24:14,15 [s] Dt 15:8; Ps 37:21,26; Lk 6:35

36 Do not take interest[a] of any kind[a] from him, but fear your
God, so that your countryman may continue to live among you.
37 You must not lend him money at interest or sell him food at a
profit. 38 I am the LORD your God, who brought you out of Egypt
to give you the land of Canaan and to be your God.[b]
39 " 'If one of your countrymen becomes poor among you and
sells himself to you, do not make him work as a slave.[c] 40 He is to
be treated as a hired worker or a temporary resident among you;
he is to work for you until the Year of Jubilee. 41 Then he and his
children are to be released, and he will go back to his own clan
and to the property[d] of his forefathers. 42 Because the Israelites are
my servants, whom I brought out of Egypt, they must not be sold
as slaves. 43 Do not rule over them ruthlessly,[e] but fear your God.
44 " 'Your male and female slaves are to come from the nations
around you; from them you may buy slaves. 45 You may also buy
some of the temporary residents living among you and members of their clans born in your country, and they will become
your property. 46 You can will them to your children as inherited
property and can make them slaves for life, but you must not
rule over your fellow Israelites ruthlessly.
47 " 'If an alien or a temporary resident among you becomes
rich and one of your countrymen becomes poor and sells himself to the alien living among you or to a member of the alien's
clan, 48 he retains the right of redemption after he has sold himself. One of his relatives[f] may redeem him: 49 An uncle or a
cousin or any blood relative in his clan may redeem him. Or if
he prospers,[g] he may redeem himself. 50 He and his buyer are to
count the time from the year he sold himself up to the Year of
Jubilee. The price for his release is to be based on the rate paid to
a hired man[h] for that number of years. 51 If many years remain,
he must pay for his redemption a larger share of the price paid
for him. 52 If only a few years remain until the Year of Jubilee, he
is to compute that and pay for his redemption accordingly. 53 He
is to be treated as a man hired from year to year; you must see to
it that his owner does not rule over him ruthlessly.
54 " 'Even if he is not redeemed in any of these ways, he and his
children are to be released in the Year of Jubilee, 55 for the
Israelites belong to me as servants. They are my servants, whom
I brought out of Egypt. I am the LORD your God.

Chapter 26 Theme ______________________________

26 " 'Do not make idols[i] or set up an image or a sacred stone[j]
for yourselves, and do not place a carved stone[k] in your
land to bow down before it. I am the LORD your God.

a36 Or *take excessive interest*; similarly in verse 37

25:36 [a]Ex 22:25; Dt 23:19-20
25:38 [b]Ge 17:7; Lev 11:45
25:39 [c]Ex 21:2; Dt 15:12; 1Ki 9:22
25:41 [d]ver 28
25:43 [e]Ex 1:13; Eze 34:4; Col 4:1
25:48 [f]Ne 5:5
25:49 [g]ver 26
25:50 [h]Job 7:1; Isa 16:14; 21:16
26:1 [i]Ex 20:4; Lev 19:4; Dt 5:8 [j]Ex 23:24 [k]Nu 33:52

2" 'Observe my Sabbaths and have reverence for my sanctuary.[a]
I am the LORD.
3" 'If you follow my decrees and are careful to obey[b] my commands, 4I will send you rain[c] in its season, and the ground will
yield its crops and the trees of the field their fruit.[d] 5Your threshing will continue until grape harvest and the grape harvest will
continue until planting, and you will eat all the food you want[e]
and live in safety in your land.[f]
6" 'I will grant peace in the land,[g] and you will lie down[h] and no
one will make you afraid.[i] I will remove savage beasts[j] from the
land, and the sword will not pass through your country. 7You will
pursue your enemies, and they will fall by the sword before you.
8Five of you will chase a hundred, and a hundred of you will chase
ten thousand, and your enemies will fall by the sword before you.[k]
9" 'I will look on you with favor and make you fruitful and
increase your numbers,[l] and I will keep my covenant[m] with you.
10You will still be eating last year's harvest when you will have to
move it out to make room for the new.[n] 11I will put my dwelling
place[a][o] among you, and I will not abhor you. 12I will walk[p]
among you and be your God, and you will be my people.[q] 13I am
the LORD your God, who brought you out of Egypt so that you
would no longer be slaves to the Egyptians; I broke the bars of
your yoke[r] and enabled you to walk with heads held high.
14" 'But if you will not listen to me and carry out all these commands,[s] 15and if you reject my decrees and abhor my laws and
fail to carry out all my commands and so violate my covenant,
16then I will do this to you: I will bring upon you sudden terror,
wasting diseases and fever[t] that will destroy your sight and drain
away your life.[u] You will plant seed in vain, because your enemies will eat it.[v] 17I will set my face[w] against you so that you will
be defeated by your enemies; those who hate you will rule over
you,[x] and you will flee even when no one is pursuing you.[y]
18" 'If after all this you will not listen to me, I will punish you
for your sins seven times over.[z] 19I will break down your stubborn pride[a] and make the sky above you like iron and the
ground beneath you like bronze.[b] 20Your strength will be spent
in vain,[c] because your soil will not yield its crops, nor will the
trees of the land yield their fruit.[d]
21" 'If you remain hostile toward me and refuse to listen to me,
I will multiply your afflictions seven times over,[e] as your sins
deserve. 22I will send wild animals[f] against you, and they will rob
you of your children, destroy your cattle and make you so few in
number that your roads will be deserted.

26:2 [a]Lev 19:30
26:3 [b]Dt 7:12; 11:13,22; 28:1,9
26:4 [c]Dt 11:14 [d]Ps 67:6
26:5 [e]Dt 11:15; Joel 2:19,26; Am 9:13 [f]Lev 25:18
26:6 [g]Ps 29:11; 85:8; 147:14 [h]Ps 4:8 [i]Zep 3:13 [j]ver 22
26:8 [k]Dt 32:30; Jos 23:10
26:9 [l]Ge 17:6; Ne 9:23 [m]Ge 17:7
26:10 [n]Lev 25:22
26:11 [o]Ex 25:8; Ps 76:2; Eze 37:27
26:12 [p]Ge 3:8 [q]2Co 6:16*
26:13 [r]Eze 34:27
26:14 [s]Dt 28:15-68; Mal 2:2
26:16 [t]Dt 28:22,35 [u]1Sa 2:33 [v]Job 31:8
26:17 [w]Lev 17:10 [x]Ps 106:41 [y]ver 36,37; Dt 28:7,25; Ps 53:5
26:18 [z]ver 21
26:19 [a]Isa 25:11 [b]Dt 28:23
26:20 [c]Ps 127:1; Isa 17:11 [d]Dt 11:17
26:21 [e]ver 18
26:22 [f]Dt 32:24

[a]11 Or *my tabernacle*

23“‘If in spite of these things you do not accept my correction[a]
but continue to be hostile toward me, 24I myself will be hostile
toward you and will afflict you for your sins seven times over.
25And I will bring the sword upon you to avenge the breaking of
the covenant. When you withdraw into your cities, I will send a
plague[b] among you, and you will be given into enemy hands.
26When I cut off your supply of bread,[c] ten women will be able to
bake your bread in one oven, and they will dole out the bread by
weight. You will eat, but you will not be satisfied.

27“‘If in spite of this you still do not listen to me but continue
to be hostile toward me, 28then in my anger I will be hostile
toward you, and I myself will punish you for your sins seven
times over. 29You will eat the flesh of your sons and the flesh of
your daughters.[d] 30I will destroy your high places,[e] cut down
your incense altars[f] and pile your dead bodies on the lifeless
forms of your idols,[g] and I will abhor you. 31I will turn your
cities into ruins and lay waste your sanctuaries,[h] and I will take
no delight in the pleasing aroma of your offerings. 32I will lay
waste the land,[i] so that your enemies who live there will be
appalled. 33I will scatter you among the nations[j] and will draw
out my sword and pursue you. Your land will be laid waste, and
your cities will lie in ruins. 34Then the land will enjoy its sabbath
years all the time that it lies desolate and you are in the country
of your enemies;[k] then the land will rest and enjoy its sabbaths.
35All the time that it lies desolate, the land will have the rest it
did not have during the sabbaths you lived in it.

36“‘As for those of you who are left, I will make their hearts so
fearful in the lands of their enemies that the sound of a windblown leaf will put them to flight.[l] They will run as though fleeing from the sword, and they will fall, even though no one is
pursuing them. 37They will stumble over one another as though
fleeing from the sword, even though no one is pursuing them.
So you will not be able to stand before your enemies.[m] 38You will
perish among the nations; the land of your enemies will devour
you.[n] 39Those of you who are left will waste away in the lands of
their enemies because of their sins; also because of their fathers’
sins they will waste away.[o]

40“‘But if they will confess their sins and the sins of their
fathers[p]—their treachery against me and their hostility toward
me, 41which made me hostile toward them so that I sent them
into the land of their enemies—then when their uncircumcised
hearts[q] are humbled and they pay for their sin, 42I will remember my covenant with Jacob[r] and my covenant with Isaac[s] and
my covenant with Abraham, and I will remember the land. 43For
the land will be deserted by them and will enjoy its sabbaths

26:23 [a] Jer 2:30; 5:3
26:25 [b] Nu 14:12; Eze 5:17
26:26 [c] Ps 105:16; Isa 3:1; Mic 6:14
26:29 [d] Dt 28:53
26:30 [e] 2Ch 34:3; Eze 6:3 [f] Eze 6:6 [g] Eze 6:13
26:31 [h] Ps 74:3-7
26:32 [i] Jer 9:11
26:33 [j] Dt 4:27; Eze 12:15; 20:23; Zec 7:14
26:34 [k] ver 43; 2Ch 36:21
26:36 [l] Eze 21:7
26:37 [m] Jos 7:12
26:38 [n] Dt 4:26
26:39 [o] Eze 4:17
26:40 [p] Jer 3:12-15; Lk 15:18; 1Jn 1:9
26:41 [q] Eze 44:7,9; Ac 7:51
26:42 [r] Ge 22:15-18; 28:15; [s] Ge 26:5

while it lies desolate without them. They will pay for their sins
because they rejected my laws and abhorred my decrees. 44Yet in
spite of this, when they are in the land of their enemies, I will not
reject them or abhor[a] them so as to destroy them completely,[b]
breaking my covenant[c] with them. I am the LORD their God.
45But for their sake I will remember[d] the covenant with their
ancestors whom I brought out of Egypt[e] in the sight of the
nations to be their God. I am the LORD.' "

46These are the decrees, the laws and the regulations that the
LORD established on Mount Sinai between himself and the
Israelites through Moses.[f]

Chapter 27 Theme ____________________

27 The LORD said to Moses, 2"Speak to the Israelites and say
to them: 'If anyone makes a special vow[g] to dedicate
persons to the LORD by giving equivalent values, 3set the value of
a male between the ages of twenty and sixty at fifty shekels[a] of
silver, according to the sanctuary shekel[b];[h] 4and if it is a female,
set her value at thirty shekels.[c] 5If it is a person between the ages
of five and twenty, set the value of a male at twenty shekels[d] and
of a female at ten shekels.[e] 6If it is a person between one month
and five years, set the value of a male at five shekels[f][i] of silver
and that of a female at three shekels[g] of silver. 7If it is a person
sixty years old or more, set the value of a male at fifteen shekels[h]
and of a female at ten shekels. 8If anyone making the vow is too
poor to pay[j] the specified amount, he is to present the person to
the priest, who will set the value[k] for him according to what the
man making the vow can afford.

9" 'If what he vowed is an animal that is acceptable as an offering to the LORD, such an animal given to the LORD becomes holy.
10He must not exchange it or substitute a good one for a bad one,
or a bad one for a good one;[l] if he should substitute one animal
for another, both it and the substitute become holy. 11If what he
vowed is a ceremonially unclean animal—one that is not acceptable as an offering to the LORD—the animal must be presented
to the priest, 12who will judge its quality as good or bad. Whatever value the priest then sets, that is what it will be. 13If the owner
wishes to redeem[m] the animal, he must add a fifth to its value.

14" 'If a man dedicates his house as something holy to the LORD,
the priest will judge its quality as good or bad. Whatever value
the priest then sets, so it will remain. 15If the man who dedicates

26:44 [a]Ro 11:2 [b]Dt 4:31; Jer 30:11 [c]Jer 33:26
26:45 [d]Ge 17:7 [e]Ex 6:8; Lev 25:38
26:46 [f]Lev 7:38; 27:34
27:2 [g]Nu 6:2
27:3 [h]Ex 30:13; Nu 3:47; 18:16
27:6 [i]Nu 18:16
27:8 [j]Lev 5:11 [k]ver 12,14
27:10 [l]ver 33
27:13 [m]ver 15,19; Lev 25:25

a3 That is, about 1 1/4 pounds (about 0.6 kilogram); also in verse 16 b3 That is, about 2/5 ounce (about 11.5 grams); also in verse 25 c4 That is, about 12 ounces (about 0.3 kilogram) d5 That is, about 8 ounces (about 0.2 kilogram) e5 That is, about 4 ounces (about 110 grams); also in verse 7 f6 That is, about 2 ounces (about 55 grams) g6 That is, about 1 1/4 ounces (about 35 grams) h7 That is, about 6 ounces (about 170 grams)

his house redeems it,[a] he must add a fifth to its value, and the
house will again become his.
16 "'If a man dedicates to the LORD part of his family land, its
value is to be set according to the amount of seed required for
it—fifty shekels of silver to a homer[a] of barley seed. 17 If he dedicates his field during the Year of Jubilee, the value that has been
set remains. 18 But if he dedicates his field after the Jubilee, the
priest will determine the value according to the number of years
that remain[b] until the next Year of Jubilee, and its set value will be
reduced. 19 If the man who dedicates the field wishes to redeem it,
he must add a fifth to its value, and the field will again become
his. 20 If, however, he does not redeem the field, or if he has sold
it to someone else, it can never be redeemed. 21 When the field is
released in the Jubilee,[c] it will become holy, like a field devoted
to the LORD;[d] it will become the property of the priests.[b]
22 "'If a man dedicates to the LORD a field he has bought, which
is not part of his family land, 23 the priest will determine its value
up to the Year of Jubilee, and the man must pay its value on that
day as something holy to the LORD. 24 In the Year of Jubilee the
field will revert to the person from whom he bought it,[e] the one
whose land it was. 25 Every value is to be set according to the
sanctuary shekel,[f] twenty gerahs[g] to the shekel.
26 "'No one, however, may dedicate the firstborn of an animal,
since the firstborn already belongs to the LORD;[h] whether an ox[c]
or a sheep, it is the LORD's. 27 If it is one of the unclean animals,[i]
he may buy it back at its set value, adding a fifth of the value to
it. If he does not redeem it, it is to be sold at its set value.
28 "'But nothing that a man owns and devotes[d][j] to the LORD—
whether man or animal or family land—may be sold or redeemed;
everything so devoted is most holy to the LORD.
29 "'No person devoted to destruction[e] may be ransomed; he
must be put to death.
30 "'A tithe[k] of everything from the land, whether grain from
the soil or fruit from the trees, belongs to the LORD; it is holy to
the LORD. 31 If a man redeems any of his tithe, he must add a fifth
of the value to it. 32 The entire tithe of the herd and flock—every
tenth animal that passes under the shepherd's rod[l]—will be holy
to the LORD. 33 He must not pick out the good from the bad or
make any substitution.[m] If he does make a substitution, both the
animal and its substitute become holy and cannot be redeemed.'"

34 These are the commands the LORD gave Moses on Mount
Sinai for the Israelites.[n]

[a] *16* That is, probably about 6 bushels (about 220 liters) [b] *21* Or *priest* [c] *26* The Hebrew word can include both male and female. [d] *28* The Hebrew term refers to the irrevocable giving over of things or persons to the LORD. [e] *29* The Hebrew term refers to the irrevocable giving over of things or persons to the LORD, often by totally destroying them.

27:15 [a] ver 13,20
27:18 [b] Lev 25:15
27:21 [c] Lev 25:10 [d] ver 28; Nu 18:14; Eze 44:29
27:24 [e] Lev 25:28
27:25 [f] Ex 30:13; Nu 18:16 [g] Nu 3:47; Eze 45:12
27:26 [h] Ex 13:2,12
27:27 [i] ver 11
27:28 [j] Nu 18:14; Jos 6:17-19
27:30 [k] Ge 28:22; 2Ch 31:6; Mal 3:8
27:32 [l] Jer 33:13; Eze 20:37
27:33 [m] ver 10
27:34 [n] Lev 26:46; Dt 4:5

THE OFFERINGS AND THEIR PURPOSES

THE OFFERING	CHAPTER/ VERSE	VOLUNTARY/ INVOLUNTARY	REASON/PURPOSE

The Feasts of Israel

	1st Month (Nisan) Festival of Passover				3rd Month (Sivan) Festival of Pentecost
Slaves in Egypt	**Passover**	**Yeast Bread**	**Firstfruits**		**Pentecost or Feast of Weeks**
	Slaughter lamb & put blood on doorframe Exodus 12:6, 7	***Purging of all yeast*** (symbol of sin)	***Wave offering of sheaf*** (promise of harvest to come)		***Wave offering of two loaves yeast bread***
	1st month, 14th day Leviticus 23:5	1st month, 15th day for 7 days Leviticus 23:6-8	Day after Sabbath Leviticus 23:9-14		50 days after firstfruits Leviticus 23:15-21
Everyone who sins is a slave to sin	**Christ our Passover Lamb, has been sacrificed**	**Get rid of old yeast that you may be a new batch without yeast**	**Christ has been raised...the first-fruits**	**Going away so Coun-selor can come** **Mount of Olives**	**Promise of the Spirit, mystery of church: Jews-Gentiles in one body**
John 8:34	1 Corinthians 5:7	1 Corinthians 5:7, 8	1 Corinthians 15:20-23	John 16:7 Acts 1:9-12	Acts 2:1-47 1 Corinthians 12:13 Ephesians 2:11-22

Months: Nisan—*March, April* • **Sivan**—*May, June* • **Tishri**—*September, October*

rlude
ween
tivals

7th Month (Tishri)
Festival of Tabernacles

Feast of Trumpets	Day of Atonement	Feast of Booths or Tabernacles	

Trumpet blown — a sacred assembly	*Atonement will be made to cleanse you* Leviticus 16:30	*Harvest celebration memorial of tabernacles in wilderness*	
7th month, 1st day Leviticus 23:23-25	7th month, 10th day Leviticus 23:26-32	7th month, 15th day, for 7 days; 8th day, sacred assembly Leviticus 23:33-44	
Regathering of Israel in preparation for final day of atonement Jeremiah 32:37-41 	**Coming of Christ** **Israel will repent and look to Messiah in one day** Zechariah 3:9,10; 12:10; 13:1; 14:9 	**Peoples of the earth will come to Jerusalem to celebrate the Feast of Tabernacles** Zechariah 14:16-19 	**New heaven and new earth** **God dwells with men** Revelation 21:1-3
Ezekiel 36:24	Ezekiel 36:25-27 Hebrews 9, 10 Romans 11:25-29	Ezekiel 36:28	

Israel had two harvests each year—spring and autumn

Leviticus at a Glance

Theme of Leviticus:

Segment Divisions

	Laws Regarding	Main Division	Chapter Themes
		Worshiping a Holy God	1
			2
			3
			4
			5
			6
			7
			8
			9
			10
			11
			12
			13
			14
			15
			16
			17
		Living a Holy Life	18
			19
			20
			21
			22
			23
			24
			25
			26
			27

Author:

Date:

Purpose:

Key Words:

the Lord said to Moses

tabernacle (dwelling place Tent of Meeting)

law (regulations)

sacrifice(s), do this (offering[s])

sin(s), held responsibl (guilt, guilty)

blood (bleeding)

atonement

holy (sacred)

covenant

NUMBERS

The Israelites cried out to God. And God heard and raised up Moses to deliver the children of Israel out of the land of Egypt, the house of bondage. The children of Israel had lived in Egypt for 430 years, most of those years as slaves. After camping at Sinai, they were to go to Canaan, the land promised to Abraham, Isaac, and Jacob. At last they would see the land with their own eyes. And God would go with them in a pillar of cloud by day and a pillar of fire by night.

Soon the journey would begin, but first there must be a numbering of all the sons of Israel from 20 years of age on up.

THINGS TO DO

General Information

The book of Numbers can be divided into three segments according to the journeys and encampments of the children of Israel. In Numbers 1 through 10:10 they are encamped at Sinai. In Numbers 10:11 the cloud lifts and their journeying begins and does not end for about 39 years. In Numbers 22 Israel camps on the plains of Moab, opposite Jericho, as they prepare to enter the land of promise.

Chapters 1–10:10

1. The first five books of the Bible, Genesis through Deuteronomy, are closely related. They follow each other chronologically. To put Numbers into context:
   a. Read Exodus 40:1, 2, 17, 33-38, which gives an account of the building of the tabernacle at Mount Sinai.
   b. Read Leviticus 1:1 and then 27:34. All of the book of Leviticus takes place at Mount Sinai.
   c. Compare where Leviticus ends and Numbers begins. Read Numbers 1:1, 2.
   d. Look at Exodus 40:17 again and Numbers 1:1, and you will see one month elapsed between the close of Exodus and the beginning of Numbers. Leviticus covers a period of only one month.

2. Read through this first segment chapter by chapter. As you do, do not become discouraged and quit; Numbers becomes more interesting and practical after this segment. As you read:
   a. Mark the following key words in a distinctive way: *number, listing, listed, count(ed)* or *census (have counted)* (and their synonyms), *the Lord spoke to (the Lord said to, the Lord talked with, the Lord also said to, the Lord spoke with), of the sons of (of the people of, from the sons of, from the descendants of)* (then underline whose sons, descendants, or people they were), *service (serve, serving, work, ministering), cloud, desert (tent, Tent of Meeting, Tent of the Testimony, tabernacle),* and *war* (or any reference to being in the army or going to battle or fighting). Write them on an index card and use it as a bookmark as you study Numbers.
   b. Note every reference to time with a symbol.
   c. In the margin of each chapter make lists of key truths you want to be able to find with ease. For instance next to 9:15 you might write: "Instructions re: Cloud" or simply "The Cloud."
   d. Note the theme of each chapter and record it on the NUMBERS AT A GLANCE chart on page 285 and on the line next to the chapter number in the text.

Chapters 10:11–21:35

1. This segment covers about 39 years. As you study you will discover why it takes so long to cover such a relatively short distance. Do the following as you study chapter by chapter:
   a. Since much of what you will read in this segment is historical, you can learn a lot simply by

asking the five W's and an H. Ask: Who are the main characters in this chapter? What is happening? Why is it happening? When and where is it happening? Why are they told to do something? What were the consequences of their actions? How and why did this occur?

1) You might want to note in the margin when and where events occur.
2) Follow the movements of the Israelites on the map at Numbers 11 on page 236.

b. Mark key repeated words. Use the list you used in the first segment. Watch for key words which are not on the list but will be significant in a particular chapter.

c. Write on a piece of paper what you learn about the land the Israelites are to possess and what you learn about Korah and Balaam. (Balaam appears in Numbers 22.) These two men will be mentioned again, even in the New Testament, so it will be helpful to summarize all you learn about them. Record your insights on the chart INSIGHTS FROM NUMBERS on page 284.

d. There are lessons to be learned from Moses' life about leadership and about our relationship to God. Although you will probably want to note these lessons in the chapter margins, you will also find it profitable to summarize what you learn on LESSONS FROM THE LIFE OF MOSES, a chart on pages 346, 347. When you record your insights, make sure you note the book, chapter, and verse from which you took your insight.

2. As you did before, record each chapter theme on NUMBERS AT A GLANCE and in the text.

Chapters 22-36

1. This final segment of Numbers is a mixture of historical events, instructions, and numberings. As you read each chapter, remember to ask the five W's and an H and to record any pertinent insights in the margin.

2. To your list of key words add the following: *Balaam, Moab (Moabite)* (Moab is first mentioned in Numbers 21, so go back and mark Moab in that chapter also), *Midian (Midianite), covenant, burnt offering(s), (offering),* and *sin offering.*

3. Balaam plays a major role in this last segment. Note all you learn about him on INSIGHTS FROM NUMBERS on page 284.

4. Record the main points or events of these chapters in the margin. As you near the end of Numbers you will read more about Balaam, so note in the margin where these final verses on Balaam can be found.

5. Record what you learn about Moses. Give special attention to Numbers 27:12-23 in the light of Numbers 20. Next to Numbers 20:1-13 you might want to write Numbers 27:12-23 as a cross-reference.

6. Record your chapter themes as you did before.

7. Record the predominant theme or event in each of the three segments of Numbers on NUMBERS AT A GLANCE. See if any of the chapters can be grouped according to the types of commands, ordinances, and/or events. In other words, do several chapters cover similar topics or events? For example, chapters 1 and 2 cover the census. Note these in the first column under "Segment Divisions" and complete the NUMBERS AT A GLANCE chart.

❧ Things to Think About

1. Review all you learned from Moses' life and then pray about how it applies to your own life.

2. Remember, God is the same yesterday, today, and forever. His character did not change between the Old Testament and the New Testament. Think about what you have learned about God from the book of Numbers. Are you living accordingly?

3. Are you jealous because the children of Israel had a cloud to guide them? Have you realized that God's presence in the form of the indwelling Spirit is there to guide you? Do you seek and ask for his Spirit to lead and guide you just as surely as he led the children of Israel? What can you learn from the children of Israel so you won't make the same mistakes?

Chapter 1 Theme ______________________________

1 The LORD spoke to Moses in the Tent of Meeting[a] in the
Desert of Sinai[b] on the first day of the second month[c] of the
second year after the Israelites came out of Egypt. He said: 2“Take
a census[d] of the whole Israelite community by their clans and
families, listing every man by name, one by one. 3You and Aaron
are to number by their divisions all the men in Israel twenty
years old or more[e] who are able to serve in the army. 4One man
from each tribe, each the head of his family,[f] is to help you.[g]
5These are the names of the men who are to assist you:

from Reuben,[h] Elizur son of Shedeur;
6from Simeon, Shelumiel son of Zurishaddai;
7from Judah,[i] Nahshon son of Amminadab;[j]
8from Issachar,[k] Nethanel son of Zuar;
9from Zebulun,[l] Eliab son of Helon;
10from the sons of Joseph:
from Ephraim,[m] Elishama son of Ammihud;
from Manasseh, Gamaliel son of Pedahzur;
11from Benjamin, Abidan son of Gideoni;
12from Dan,[n] Ahiezer son of Ammishaddai;
13from Asher,[o] Pagiel son of Ocran;
14from Gad, Eliasaph son of Deuel;[p]
15from Naphtali,[q] Ahira son of Enan.”

16These were the men appointed from the community, the
leaders[r] of their ancestral tribes. They were the heads of the
clans of Israel.[s]
17Moses and Aaron took these men whose names had been
given, 18and they called the whole community together on the
first day of the second month.[t] The people indicated their ancestry[u] by their clans and families, and the men twenty years old
or more were listed by name, one by one, 19as the LORD commanded Moses. And so he counted them in the Desert of Sinai:

20From the descendants of Reuben[v] the firstborn son of Israel:
All the men twenty years old or more who were able to
serve in the army were listed by name, one by one, according to the records of their clans and families. 21The number from the tribe of Reuben was 46,500.

22From the descendants of Simeon:[w]
All the men twenty years old or more who were able to
serve in the army were counted and listed by name, one
by one, according to the records of their clans and families. 23The number from the tribe of Simeon was 59,300.

1:1 [a] Ex 40:2 [b] Ex 19:1 [c] Ex 40:17
1:2 [d] Ex 30:11-16; Nu 26:2
1:3 [e] Ex 30:14
1:4 [f] ver 16 [g] Ex 18:21; Dt 1:15
1:5 [h] Ge 29:32; Dt 33:6; Rev 7:5
1:7 [i] Ge 29:35; Ps 78:68 [j] Ru 4:20; 1Ch 2:10; Lk 3:32
1:8 [k] Ge 30:18
1:9 [l] ver 30
1:10 [m] ver 32
1:12 [n] ver 38
1:13 [o] ver 40
1:14 [p] Nu 2:14
1:15 [q] ver 42
1:16 [r] Ex 18:25 [s] ver 4; Ex 18:21; Nu 7:2
1:18 [t] ver 1 [u] Ezr 2:59; Heb 7:3
1:20 [v] Nu 26:5-11; Rev 7:5
1:22 [w] Nu 26:12-14; Rev 7:7

24From the descendants of Gad:[a]

All the men twenty years old or more who were able to serve in the army were listed by name, according to the records of their clans and families. 25The number from the tribe of Gad was 45,650.

26From the descendants of Judah:[b]

All the men twenty years old or more who were able to serve in the army were listed by name, according to the records of their clans and families. 27The number from the tribe of Judah was 74,600.

28From the descendants of Issachar:[c]

All the men twenty years old or more who were able to serve in the army were listed by name, according to the records of their clans and families. 29The number from the tribe of Issachar was 54,400.

30From the descendants of Zebulun:[d]

All the men twenty years old or more who were able to serve in the army were listed by name, according to the records of their clans and families. 31The number from the tribe of Zebulun was 57,400.

32From the sons of Joseph:

From the descendants of Ephraim:[e]

All the men twenty years old or more who were able to serve in the army were listed by name, according to the records of their clans and families. 33The number from the tribe of Ephraim was 40,500.

34From the descendants of Manasseh:[f]

All the men twenty years old or more who were able to serve in the army were listed by name, according to the records of their clans and families. 35The number from the tribe of Manasseh was 32,200.

36From the descendants of Benjamin:[g]

All the men twenty years old or more who were able to serve in the army were listed by name, according to the records of their clans and families. 37The number from the tribe of Benjamin was 35,400.

38From the descendants of Dan:[h]

All the men twenty years old or more who were able to serve in the army were listed by name, according to the records of their clans and families. 39The number from the tribe of Dan was 62,700.

1:24 [a]Ge 30:11; Nu 26:15-18; Rev 7:5

1:26 [b]Ge 29:35; Nu 26:19-22; Mt 1:2; Rev 7:5

1:28 [c]Nu 26:23-25; Rev 7:7

1:30 [d]Nu 26:26-27; Rev 7:8

1:32 [e]Nu 26:35-37

1:34 [f]Nu 26:28-34; Rev 7:6

1:36 [g]Nu 26:38-41; 2Ch 17:17; Rev 7:8

1:38 [h]Ge 30:6; Nu 26:42-43

1:40 [a]Nu 26:44-47; Rev 7:6 40From the descendants of Asher:[a]
All the men twenty years old or more who were able to
serve in the army were listed by name, according to the
records of their clans and families. 41The number from
1:42 [b]Nu 26:48-50; Rev 7:6 the tribe of Asher was 41,500.

42From the descendants of Naphtali:[b]
All the men twenty years old or more who were able to
1:44 [c]Nu 26:64 serve in the army were listed by name, according to the
records of their clans and families. 43The number from
the tribe of Naphtali was 53,400.

1:46 [d]Ex 12:37; 38:26; Nu 2:32; 26:51 44These were the men counted by Moses and Aaron[c] and the
twelve leaders of Israel, each one representing his family. 45All
the Israelites twenty years old or more who were able to serve in
Israel's army were counted according to their families. 46The total
number was 603,550.[d]
1:47 [e]Nu 2:33; 26:57 [f]Nu 4:3,49 47The families of the tribe of Levi,[e] however, were not counted[f]
along with the others. 48The LORD had said to Moses: 49"You must
not count the tribe of Levi or include them in the census of the
1:50 [g]Ex 38:21; Ac 7:44 other Israelites. 50Instead, appoint the Levites to be in charge of the
tabernacle of the Testimony[g]—over all its furnishings and every-
thing belonging to it. They are to carry the tabernacle and all its
furnishings; they are to take care of it and encamp around it.
1:51 [h]Nu 3:38; 4:1-33 51Whenever the tabernacle is to move, the Levites are to take it
down, and whenever the tabernacle is to be set up, the Levites shall
do it.[h] Anyone else who goes near it shall be put to death. 52The
Israelites are to set up their tents by divisions, each man in his own
1:52 [i]Nu 2:2; Ps 20:5 camp under his own standard.[i] 53The Levites, however, are to set
up their tents around the tabernacle of the Testimony so that
wrath will not fall[j] on the Israelite community. The Levites are to
be responsible for the care of the tabernacle of the Testimony.[k]"
1:53 [j]Lev 10:6; Nu 16:46; 18:5 [k]Nu 18:2-4 54The Israelites did all this just as the LORD commanded Moses.

Chapter 2 Theme ________________________

2:2 [l]Nu 1:52; Ps 74:4; Isa 31:9 **2** The LORD said to Moses and Aaron: 2"The Israelites are to
camp around the Tent of Meeting some distance from it,
each man under his standard[l] with the banners of his family."

3On the east, toward the sunrise, the divisions of the camp
2:3 [m]Nu 10:14; Ru 4:20; 1Ch 2:10 of Judah are to encamp under their standard. The leader of
the people of Judah is Nahshon son of Amminadab.[m] 4His
division numbers 74,600.
5The tribe of Issachar will camp next to them. The leader of
the people of Issachar is Nethanel son of Zuar.[n] 6His division
2:5 [n]Nu 1:8 numbers 54,400.

[7]The tribe of Zebulun will be next. The leader of the people of Zebulun is Eliab son of Helon.[a] [8]His division numbers 57,400.

[9]All the men assigned to the camp of Judah, according to their divisions, number 186,400. They will set out first.[b]

Camp Arrangement of Israel's Tribes

[10]On the south will be the divisions of the camp of Reuben under their standard. The leader of the people of Reuben is Elizur son of Shedeur.[c] [11]His division numbers 46,500.

[12]The tribe of Simeon will camp next to them. The leader of the people of Simeon is Shelumiel son of Zurishaddai.[d] [13]His division numbers 59,300.

[14]The tribe of Gad will be next. The leader of the people of Gad is Eliasaph son of Deuel.[e][a] [15]His division numbers 45,650.

[16]All the men assigned to the camp of Reuben,[f] according to their divisions, number 151,450. They will set out second.

[17]Then the Tent of Meeting and the camp of the Levites[g] will set out in the middle of the camps. They will set out in the same order as they encamp, each in his own place under his standard.

[18]On the west will be the divisions of the camp of Ephraim[h] under their standard. The leader of the people of Ephraim is Elishama son of Ammihud.[i] [19]His division numbers 40,500.

[20]The tribe of Manasseh will be next to them. The leader of the people of Manasseh is Gamaliel son of Pedahzur.[j] [21]His division numbers 32,200.

[22]The tribe of Benjamin will be next. The leader of the people of Benjamin is Abidan son of Gideoni.[k] [23]His division numbers 35,400.

[24]All the men assigned to the camp of Ephraim,[l] according to their divisions, number 108,100. They will set out third.[m]

a *14* Many manuscripts of the Masoretic Text, Samaritan Pentateuch and Vulgate (see also Num. 1:14); most manuscripts of the Masoretic Text *Reuel*

2:7 [a]Nu 1:9
2:9 [b]Nu 10:14
2:10 [c]Nu 1:5
2:12 [d]Nu 1:6
2:14 [e]Nu 1:14
2:16 [f]Nu 10:18
2:17 [g]Nu 1:53; 10:21
2:18 [h]Ge 48:20; Jer 31:18-20 [i]Nu 1:10
2:20 [j]Nu 1:10
2:22 [k]Nu 1:11; Ps 68:27
2:24 [l]Nu 10:22 [m]Ps 80:2

25 On the north will be the divisions of the camp of Dan,
under their standard. The leader of the people of Dan is Ahiezer son of Ammishaddai.[a] 26 His division numbers 62,700.
27 The tribe of Asher will camp next to them. The leader of
the people of Asher is Pagiel son of Ocran.[b] 28 His division
numbers 41,500.
29 The tribe of Naphtali will be next. The leader of the people of Naphtali is Ahira son of Enan.[c] 30 His division numbers
53,400.
31 All the men assigned to the camp of Dan number
157,600. They will set out last,[d] under their standards.

32 These are the Israelites, counted according to their families.
All those in the camps, by their divisions, number 603,550.[e]
33 The Levites, however, were not counted[f] along with the
other Israelites, as the LORD commanded Moses.

34 So the Israelites did everything the LORD commanded Moses;
that is the way they encamped under their standards, and that is
the way they set out, each with his clan and family.

Chapter 3 Theme ____________________

3 This is the account of the family of Aaron and Moses[g] at the
time the LORD talked with Moses on Mount Sinai.
2 The names of the sons of Aaron were Nadab the firstborn and
Abihu, Eleazar and Ithamar.[h] 3 Those were the names of Aaron's
sons, the anointed priests,[i] who were ordained to serve as priests.
4 Nadab and Abihu, however, fell dead before the LORD[j] when
they made an offering with unauthorized fire before him in the
Desert of Sinai.[k] They had no sons; so only Eleazar and Ithamar
served as priests during the lifetime of their father Aaron.[l]
5 The LORD said to Moses, 6 "Bring the tribe of Levi[m] and present them to Aaron the priest to assist him.[n] 7 They are to perform
duties for him and for the whole community at the Tent of Meeting by doing the work[o] of the tabernacle. 8 They are to take care
of all the furnishings of the Tent of Meeting, fulfilling the obligations of the Israelites by doing the work of the tabernacle. 9 Give
the Levites to Aaron and his sons;[p] they are the Israelites who are
to be given wholly to him.[a] 10 Appoint Aaron and his sons to serve
as priests;[q] anyone else who approaches the sanctuary must be
put to death."[r]
11 The LORD also said to Moses, 12 "I have taken the Levites[s] from
among the Israelites in place of the first male offspring[t] of every
Israelite woman. The Levites are mine,[u] 13 for all the firstborn are

2:25 [a] Nu 1:12
2:27 [b] Nu 1:13
2:29 [c] Nu 1:15
2:31 [d] Nu 10:25
2:32 [e] Ex 38:26; Nu 1:46
2:33 [f] Nu 1:47; 26:57-62
3:1 [g] Ex 6:27
3:2 [h] Ex 6:23; Nu 26:60
3:3 [i] Ex 28:41
3:4 [j] Lev 10:2 [k] Lev 10:1 [l] 1Ch 24:1
3:6 [m] Dt 10:8; 31:9; 1Ch 15:2 [n] Nu 8:6-22; 18:1-7; 2Ch 29:11
3:7 [o] Lev 8:35; Nu 1:50
3:9 [p] Nu 8:19; 18:6
3:10 [q] Ex 29:9 [r] Nu 1:51
3:12 [s] Mal 2:4 [t] ver 41; Nu 8:16,18 [u] Ex 13:2

a 9 Most manuscripts of the Masoretic Text; some manuscripts of the Masoretic Text, Samaritan Pentateuch and Septuagint (see also Num. 8:16) *to me*

mine.[a] When I struck down all the firstborn in Egypt, I set apart
for myself every firstborn in Israel, whether man or animal.
They are to be mine. I am the LORD."

14 The LORD said to Moses in the Desert of Sinai, 15 "Count[b] the
Levites by their families and clans. Count every male a month
old or more."[c] 16 So Moses counted them, as he was commanded
by the word of the LORD.

17 These were the names of the sons of Levi:[d]
Gershon, Kohath and Merari.[e]
18 These were the names of the Gershonite clans:
Libni and Shimei.[f]
19 The Kohathite clans:
Amram, Izhar, Hebron and Uzziel.[g]
20 The Merarite clans:[h]
Mahli and Mushi.[i]
These were the Levite clans, according to their families.

21 To Gershon belonged the clans of the Libnites and Shimeites;[j]
these were the Gershonite clans. 22 The number of all the males a
month old or more who were counted was 7,500. 23 The Gershonite clans were to camp on the west, behind the tabernacle.
24 The leader of the families of the Gershonites was Eliasaph son
of Lael. 25 At the Tent of Meeting the Gershonites were responsible for the care of the tabernacle[k] and tent, its coverings,[l] the
curtain at the entrance[m] to the Tent of Meeting, 26 the curtains of
the courtyard[n], the curtain at the entrance to the courtyard surrounding the tabernacle and altar, and the ropes[o]—and everything related to their use.

27 To Kohath belonged the clans of the Amramites, Izharites,
Hebronites and Uzzielites;[p] these were the Kohathite clans.
28 The number of all the males a month old or more was 8,600.[a]
The Kohathites were responsible for the care of the sanctuary.
29 The Kohathite clans were to camp on the south side[q] of the
tabernacle. 30 The leader of the families of the Kohathite clans
was Elizaphan son of Uzziel. 31 They were responsible for the care
of the ark,[r] the table,[s] the lampstand,[t] the altars,[u] the articles of
the sanctuary used in ministering, the curtain,[v] and everything
related to their use.[w] 32 The chief leader of the Levites was Eleazar
son of Aaron, the priest. He was appointed over those who were
responsible for the care of the sanctuary.

33 To Merari belonged the clans of the Mahlites and the Mu-
shites;[x] these were the Merarite clans. 34 The number of all the
males a month old or more who were counted was 6,200. 35 The

a 28 Hebrew; some Septuagint manuscripts *8,300*

3:13 [a] Ex 13:12
3:15 [b] ver 39 [c] Nu 26:62
3:17 [d] Ge 46:11 [e] Ex 6:16
3:18 [f] Ex 6:17
3:19 [g] Ex 6:18
3:20 [h] Ge 46:11 [i] Ex 6:19
3:21 [j] Ex 6:17
3:25 [k] Ex 25:9 [l] Ex 26:14 [m] Ex 26:36; Nu 4:25
3:26 [n] Ex 27:9 [o] Ex 35:18
3:27 [p] 1Ch 26:23
3:29 [q] Nu 1:53
3:31 [r] Ex 25:10-22 [s] Ex 25:23 [t] Ex 25:31 [u] Ex 27:1; 30:1 [v] Ex 26:33 [w] Nu 4:15
3:33 [x] Ex 6:19

leader of the families of the Merarite clans was Zuriel son of Abihail; they were to camp on the north side of the tabernacle.[a] 36The
Merarites were appointed[b] to take care of the frames of the
tabernacle, its crossbars, posts, bases, all its equipment, and
everything related to their use, 37as well as the posts of the surrounding courtyard with their bases, tent pegs and ropes.

38Moses and Aaron and his sons were to camp to the east[c] of
the tabernacle, toward the sunrise, in front of the Tent of Meeting.[d] They were responsible for the care of the sanctuary[e] on
behalf of the Israelites. Anyone else who approached the sanctuary was to be put to death.[f]

39The total number of Levites counted at the LORD's command
by Moses and Aaron according to their clans, including every
male a month old or more, was 22,000.[g]

40The LORD said to Moses, "Count all the firstborn Israelite
males who are a month old or more[h] and make a list of their
names. 41Take the Levites for me in place of all the firstborn of
the Israelites,[i] and the livestock of the Levites in place of all the
firstborn of the livestock of the Israelites. I am the LORD."
42So Moses counted all the firstborn of the Israelites, as the
LORD commanded him. 43The total number of firstborn males a
month old or more, listed by name, was 22,273.[j]
44The LORD also said to Moses, 45"Take the Levites in place of all
the firstborn of Israel, and the livestock of the Levites in place of
their livestock. The Levites are to be mine. I am the LORD. 46To
redeem[k] the 273 firstborn Israelites who exceed the number of the
Levites, 47collect five shekels[a][l] for each one, according to the sanctuary shekel,[m] which weighs twenty gerahs.[n] 48Give the money for
the redemption of the additional Israelites to Aaron and his sons."
49So Moses collected the redemption money from those who
exceeded the number redeemed by the Levites. 50From the firstborn of the Israelites he collected silver weighing 1,365 shekels,[b][o]
according to the sanctuary shekel. 51Moses gave the redemption
money to Aaron and his sons, as he was commanded by the word
of the LORD.

Chapter 4 Theme ________________________

4 The LORD said to Moses and Aaron: 2"Take a census[p] of the
Kohathite branch of the Levites by their clans and families.
3Count all the men from thirty to fifty years of age[q] who come to
serve in the work in the Tent of Meeting.

3:35 [a]Nu 1:53; 2:25
3:36 [b]Nu 4:32
3:38 [c]Nu 2:3 [d]Nu 1:53 [e]ver 7; Nu 18:5 [f]ver 10; Nu 1:51
3:39 [g]Nu 26:62
3:40 [h]ver 15
3:41 [i]ver 12
3:43 [j]ver 39
3:46 [k]Ex 13:13; Nu 18:15
3:47 [l]Lev 27:6 [m]Ex 30:13 [n]Lev 27:25
3:50 [o]ver 46-48
4:2 [p]Ex 30:12
4:3 [q]ver 23; Nu 8:25; 1Ch 23:3,24,27; Ezr 3:8

[a]47 That is, about 2 ounces (about 55 grams) [b]50 That is, about 35 pounds (about 15.5 kilograms)

4“This is the work of the Kohathites in the Tent of Meeting: the
care of the most holy things.[a] 5When the camp is to move, Aaron
and his sons are to go in and take down the shielding curtain[b]
and cover the ark of the Testimony with it.[c] 6Then they are to
cover this with hides of sea cows,[a] spread a cloth of solid blue
over that and put the poles[d] in place.
7“Over the table of the Presence[e] they are to spread a blue cloth
and put on it the plates, dishes and bowls, and the jars for drink
offerings; the bread that is continually there[f] is to remain on it.
8Over these they are to spread a scarlet cloth, cover that with
hides of sea cows and put its poles in place.
9“They are to take a blue cloth and cover the lampstand that is
for light, together with its lamps, its wick trimmers and trays,[g]
and all its jars for the oil used to supply it. 10Then they are to
wrap it and all its accessories in a covering of hides of sea cows
and put it on a carrying frame.
11“Over the gold altar[h] they are to spread a blue cloth and cover
that with hides of sea cows and put its poles in place.
12“They are to take all the articles used for ministering in the
sanctuary, wrap them in a blue cloth, cover that with hides of sea
cows and put them on a carrying frame.
13“They are to remove the ashes from the bronze altar[i] and
spread a purple cloth over it. 14Then they are to place on it all the
utensils used for ministering at the altar, including the firepans,
meat forks,[j] shovels and sprinkling bowls.[k] Over it they are to
spread a covering of hides of sea cows and put its poles[l] in place.
15“After Aaron and his sons have finished covering the holy
furnishings and all the holy articles, and when the camp is ready
to move, the Kohathites are to come to do the carrying.[m] But they
must not touch the holy things or they will die.[n] The Kohathites
are to carry those things that are in the Tent of Meeting.
16“Eleazar[o] son of Aaron, the priest, is to have charge of the oil
for the light,[p] the fragrant incense, the regular grain offering[q] and
the anointing oil. He is to be in charge of the entire tabernacle
and everything in it, including its holy furnishings and articles.”
17The LORD said to Moses and Aaron, 18“See that the Kohathite
tribal clans are not cut off from the Levites. 19So that they may
live and not die when they come near the most holy things,[r] do
this for them: Aaron and his sons are to go into the sanctuary
and assign to each man his work and what he is to carry. 20But
the Kohathites must not go in to look[s] at the holy things, even
for a moment, or they will die.”
21The LORD said to Moses, 22“Take a census also of the Gershonites by their families and clans. 23Count all the men from

[a]6 That is, dugongs; also in verses 8, 10, 11, 12, 14 and 25

4:4 [a]ver 19
4:5 [b]Ex 26:31,33 [c]Ex 25:10,16
4:6 [d]Ex 25:13-15; 1Ki 8:7; 2Ch 5:8
4:7 [e]Ex 25:23,29; Lev 24:6 [f]Ex 25:30
4:9 [g]Ex 25:31,37,38
4:11 [h]Ex 30:1
4:13 [i]Ex 27:1-8
4:14 [j]2Ch 4:16 [k]Jer 52:18 [l]Ex 27:6
4:15 [m]Nu 7:9 [n]Nu 1:51; 2Sa 6:6,7
4:16 [o]Lev 10:6 [p]Ex 25:6 [q]Ex 29:41; Lev 6:14-23
4:19 [r]ver 15
4:20 [s]Ex 19:21; 1Sa 6:19

4:23 [a]ver 3; 1Ch 23:3,24,27

thirty to fifty years of age[a] who come to serve in the work at the
Tent of Meeting.
24“This is the service of the Gershonite clans as they work and
carry burdens: 25They are to carry the curtains of the tabernacle,[b]
the Tent of Meeting,[c] its covering[d] and the outer covering of hides
of sea cows, the curtains for the entrance to the Tent of Meeting,

4:25 [b]Ex 27:10-18; Nu 3:26 [c]Nu 3:25 [d]Ex 26:14

26the curtains of the courtyard surrounding the tabernacle and
altar, the curtain for the entrance, the ropes and all the equipment used in its service. The Gershonites are to do all that needs
to be done with these things. 27All their service, whether carrying
or doing other work, is to be done under the direction of Aaron
and his sons. You shall assign to them as their responsibility all
they are to carry. 28This is the service of the Gershonite clans[e] at

4:28 [e]Nu 7:7

the Tent of Meeting. Their duties are to be under the direction of
Ithamar son of Aaron, the priest.
29“Count the Merarites by their clans and families.[f] 30Count all
the men from thirty to fifty years of age who come to serve in the
work at the Tent of Meeting. 31This is their duty as they perform

4:29 [f]Ge 46:11

service at the Tent of Meeting: to carry the frames of the tabernacle, its crossbars, posts and bases,[g] 32as well as the posts of the
surrounding courtyard with their bases, tent pegs, ropes, all their
equipment and everything related to their use. Assign to each
man the specific things he is to carry. 33This is the service of the

4:31 [g]Nu 3:36

Merarite clans as they work at the Tent of Meeting under the
direction of Ithamar son of Aaron, the priest.”
34Moses, Aaron and the leaders of the community counted the
Kohathites[h] by their clans and families. 35All the men from thirty
to fifty years of age who came to serve in the work in the Tent of

4:34 [h]ver 2

Meeting, 36counted by clans, were 2,750. 37This was the total of all
those in the Kohathite clans[i] who served in the Tent of Meeting.
Moses and Aaron counted them according to the LORD’s command through Moses.
38The Gershonites[j] were counted by their clans and families.

4:37 [i]Nu 3:27

39All the men from thirty to fifty years of age who came to serve in
the work at the Tent of Meeting, 40counted by their clans and families, were 2,630. 41This was the total of those in the Gershonite
clans who served at the Tent of Meeting. Moses and Aaron counted
them according to the LORD’s command.

4:38 [j]Ge 46:11

42The Merarites were counted by their clans and families. 43All the
men from thirty to fifty years of age who came to serve in the work
at the Tent of Meeting, 44counted by their clans, were 3,200. 45This
was the total of those in the Merarite clans.[k] Moses and Aaron
counted them according to the LORD’s command through Moses.

4:45 [k]ver 29

46So Moses, Aaron and the leaders of Israel counted all the
Levites by their clans and families. 47All the men from thirty to

fifty years of age[a] who came to do the work of serving and carrying the Tent of Meeting 48numbered 8,580.[b] 49At the LORD's command through Moses, each was assigned his work and told what to carry.

Thus they were counted,[c] as the LORD commanded Moses.

Chapter 5 Theme ____

5 The LORD said to Moses, 2"Command the Israelites to send
away from the camp anyone who has an infectious skin disease[a][d] or a discharge[e] of any kind, or who is ceremonially unclean[f] because of a dead body. 3Send away male and female alike;
send them outside the camp so they will not defile their camp,
where I dwell among them.[g]" 4The Israelites did this; they sent
them outside the camp. They did just as the LORD had instructed
Moses.

5The LORD said to Moses, 6"Say to the Israelites: 'When a man or
woman wrongs another in any way[b] and so is unfaithful[h] to the
LORD, that person is guilty[i] 7and must confess[j] the sin he has
committed. He must make full restitution[k] for his wrong, add one
fifth to it and give it all to the person he has wronged. 8But if that
person has no close relative to whom restitution can be made for
the wrong, the restitution belongs to the LORD and must be given
to the priest, along with the ram with which atonement is made
for him.[l] 9All the sacred contributions the Israelites bring to a
priest will belong to him.[m] 10Each man's sacred gifts are his own,
but what he gives to the priest will belong to the priest.[n]' "

11Then the LORD said to Moses, 12"Speak to the Israelites and say
to them: 'If a man's wife goes astray[o] and is unfaithful to him 13by
sleeping with another man,[p] and this is hidden from her husband
and her impurity is undetected (since there is no witness against
her and she has not been caught in the act), 14and if feelings of
jealousy[q] come over her husband and he suspects his wife and
she is impure—or if he is jealous and suspects her even though
she is not impure— 15then he is to take his wife to the priest. He
must also take an offering of a tenth of an ephah[c][r] of barley
flour[s] on her behalf. He must not pour oil on it or put incense on
it, because it is a grain offering for jealousy, a reminder[t] offering
to draw attention to guilt.

16" 'The priest shall bring her and have her stand before the
LORD. 17Then he shall take some holy water in a clay jar and put
some dust from the tabernacle floor into the water. 18After the
priest has had the woman stand before the LORD, he shall loosen

[a]2 Traditionally *leprosy*; the Hebrew word was used for various diseases affecting the skin—not necessarily leprosy. [b]6 Or *woman commits any wrong common to mankind* [c]15 That is, probably about 2 quarts (about 2 liters)

4:47 [a]ver 3
4:48 [b]Nu 3:39
4:49 [c]Nu 1:47
5:2 [d]Lev 13:46 [e]Lev 15:2; Mt 9:20 [f]Lev 13:3; Nu 9:6-10
5:3 [g]Lev 26:12; Nu 35:34; 2Co 6:16
5:6 [h]Lev 6:2 [i]Lev 5:14–6:7
5:7 [j]Lev 5:5; 26:40; Jos 7:19; Lk 19:8 [k]Lev 6:5
5:8 [l]Lev 6:6,7; 7:7
5:9 [m]Lev 6:17; 7:6-14
5:10 [n]Lev 10:13
5:12 [o]Ex 20:14
5:13 [p]Lev 18:20; 20:10
5:14 [q]Pr 6:34; SS 8:6
5:15 [r]Ex 16:36 [s]Lev 6:20 [t]Eze 29:16

her hair[a] and place in her hands the reminder offering, the grain
offering for jealousy, while he himself holds the bitter water that
brings a curse. 19Then the priest shall put the woman under oath
and say to her, "If no other man has slept with you and you have
not gone astray[b] and become impure while married to your husband, may this bitter water that brings a curse not harm you.
20But if you have gone astray[c] while married to your husband and
you have defiled yourself by sleeping with a man other than your
husband"— 21here the priest is to put the woman under this
curse of the oath[d]—"may the LORD cause your people to curse
and denounce you when he causes your thigh to waste away and
your abdomen to swell.[a] 22May this water[e] that brings a curse[f]
enter your body so that your abdomen swells and your thigh
wastes away.[b]"

" 'Then the woman is to say, "Amen. So be it.[g]"
23" 'The priest is to write these curses on a scroll[h] and then wash
them off into the bitter water. 24He shall have the woman drink the
bitter water that brings a curse, and this water will enter her and
cause bitter suffering. 25The priest is to take from her hands the
grain offering for jealousy, wave it before the LORD[i] and bring it to
the altar. 26The priest is then to take a handful of the grain offering
as a memorial offering and burn it on the altar; after that, he is to
have the woman drink the water. 27If she has defiled herself and
been unfaithful to her husband, then when she is made to drink
the water that brings a curse, it will go into her and cause bitter
suffering; her abdomen will swell and her thigh waste away,[c] and
she will become accursed[j] among her people. 28If, however, the
woman has not defiled herself and is free from impurity, she will
be cleared of guilt and will be able to have children.

29" 'This, then, is the law of jealousy when a woman goes astray[k]
and defiles herself while married to her husband, 30or when feelings of jealousy come over a man because he suspects his wife.
The priest is to have her stand before the LORD and is to apply this
entire law to her. 31The husband will be innocent of any wrongdoing, but the woman will bear the consequences[l] of her sin.' "

Chapter 6 Theme ______________________________

6 The LORD said to Moses, 2"Speak to the Israelites and say to
them: 'If a man or woman wants to make a special vow[m], a
vow of separation to the LORD as a Nazirite,[n] 3he must abstain
from wine[o] and other fermented drink and must not drink vinegar[p] made from wine or from other fermented drink. He must not

5:18 [a]Lev 10:6; 1Co 11:6
5:19 [b]ver 12,29
5:20 [c]ver 12
5:21 [d]Jos 6:26; 1Sa 14:24; Ne 10:29
5:22 [e]Ps 109:18 [f]ver 18 [g]Dt 27:15
5:23 [h]Jer 45:1
5:25 [i]Lev 8:27
5:27 [j]Isa 43:28; 65:15; Jer 26:6; 29:18; 42:18; 44:12,22; Zec 8:13
5:29 [k]ver 19
5:31 [l]Lev 5:1; 20:17
6:2 [m]Ge 28:20; Ac 21:23 [n]Jdg 13:5; 16:17; Am 2:11,12
6:3 [o]Lk 1:15 [p]Ru 2:14; Ps 69:21; Pr 10:26

[a]21 Or *causes you to have a miscarrying womb and barrenness* [b]22 Or *body and cause you to be barren and have a miscarrying womb* [c]27 Or *suffering; she will have barrenness and a miscarrying womb*

drink grape juice or eat grapes or raisins. 4As long as he is a
Nazirite, he must not eat anything that comes from the grapevine,
not even the seeds or skins.
5"'During the entire period of his vow of separation no razor[a]
may be used on his head.[b] He must be holy until the period of his
separation to the LORD is over; he must let the hair of his head
grow long. 6Throughout the period of his separation to the LORD
he must not go near a dead body.[c] 7Even if his own father or
mother or brother or sister dies, he must not make himself ceremonially unclean[d] on account of them, because the symbol of his
separation to God is on his head. 8Throughout the period of his
separation he is consecrated to the LORD.
9"'If someone dies suddenly in his presence, thus defiling the
hair he has dedicated,[e] he must shave his head on the day of his
cleansing[f]—the seventh day. 10Then on the eighth day he must
bring two doves or two young pigeons[g] to the priest at the
entrance to the Tent of Meeting. 11The priest is to offer one as a sin
offering and the other as a burnt offering[h] to make atonement[i]
for him because he sinned by being in the presence of the dead
body. That same day he is to consecrate his head. 12He must dedicate himself to the LORD for the period of his separation and must
bring a year-old male lamb as a guilt offering. The previous days
do not count, because he became defiled during his separation.
13"'Now this is the law for the Nazirite when the period of his
separation is over.[j] He is to be brought to the entrance to the Tent
of Meeting. 14There he is to present his offerings to the LORD: a
year-old male lamb without defect for a burnt offering, a year-
old ewe lamb without defect for a sin offering,[k] a ram without
defect for a fellowship offering,[a] 15together with their grain
offerings and drink offerings,[l] and a basket of bread made without yeast—cakes made of fine flour mixed with oil, and wafers
spread with oil.[m]
16"'The priest is to present them before the LORD and make the
sin offering and the burnt offering. 17He is to present the basket
of unleavened bread and is to sacrifice the ram as a fellowship
offering to the LORD, together with its grain offering and drink
offering.
18"'Then at the entrance to the Tent of Meeting, the Nazirite
must shave off the hair that he dedicated.[n] He is to take the hair
and put it in the fire that is under the sacrifice of the fellowship
offering.
19"'After the Nazirite has shaved off the hair of his dedication,
the priest is to place in his hands a boiled shoulder of the ram,
and a cake and a wafer from the basket, both made without

a *14* Traditionally *peace offering*; also in verses 17 and 18

6:5 [a]Ps 52:2; 57:4; 59:7; Isa 7:20; Eze 5:1 [b]1Sa 1:11
6:6 [c]Lev 21:1-3; Nu 19:11-22
6:7 [d]Nu 9:6
6:9 [e]ver 18 [f]Lev 14:9
6:10 [g]Lev 5:7; 14:22
6:11 [h]Ge 8:20 [i]Ex 29:36
6:13 [j]Ac 21:26
6:14 [k]Lev 14:10; Nu 15:27
6:15 [l]Nu 15:1-7 [m]Ex 29:2; Lev 2:4
6:18 [n]ver 9; Ac 21:24

yeast. 20The priest shall then wave them before the LORD as a wave
offering; they are holy and belong to the priest, together with the
breast that was waved and the thigh that was presented. After that,
the Nazirite may drink wine.[a]
21"'This is the law of the Nazirite who vows his offering to the
LORD in accordance with his separation, in addition to whatever
else he can afford. He must fulfill the vow he has made, according
to the law of the Nazirite.'"
22The LORD said to Moses, 23"Tell Aaron and his sons, 'This is
how you are to bless[b] the Israelites. Say to them:

24" ' "The LORD bless you[c]
and keep you;[d]
25the LORD make his face shine upon you[e]
and be gracious to you;[f]
26the LORD turn his face[g] toward you
and give you peace.[h]" '

27"So they will put my name[i] on the Israelites, and I will bless
them."

Chapter 7 Theme ____________________

7 When Moses finished setting up the tabernacle,[j] he anointed
it and consecrated it and all its furnishings.[k] He also anointed
and consecrated the altar and all its utensils.[l] 2Then the leaders
of Israel,[m] the heads of families who were the tribal leaders in
charge of those who were counted, made offerings. 3They brought
as their gifts before the LORD six covered carts and twelve oxen—
an ox from each leader and a cart from every two. These they
presented before the tabernacle.
4The LORD said to Moses, 5"Accept these from them, that they
may be used in the work at the Tent of Meeting. Give them to the
Levites as each man's work requires."
6So Moses took the carts and oxen and gave them to the Levites.
7He gave two carts and four oxen to the Gershonites,[n] as their
work required, 8and he gave four carts and eight oxen to the Merarites,[o] as their work required. They were all under the direction
of Ithamar son of Aaron, the priest. 9But Moses did not give any
to the Kohathites, because they were to carry on their shoulders[p]
the holy things, for which they were responsible.
10When the altar was anointed,[q] the leaders brought their offerings for its dedication[r] and presented them before the altar. 11For
the LORD had said to Moses, "Each day one leader is to bring his
offering for the dedication of the altar."

12The one who brought his offering on the first day was Nahshon
son of Amminadab of the tribe of Judah.

6:20 [a] Ecc 9:7
6:23 [b] Dt 21:5; 1Ch 23:13
6:24 [c] Dt 28:3-6; Ps 28:9 [d] 1Sa 2:9; Ps 17:8
6:25 [e] Job 29:24; Ps 31:16; 80:3; 119:135 [f] Ge 43:29; Ps 25:16; 86:16
6:26 [g] Ps 4:6; 44:3 [h] Ps 29:11; 37:11,37; Jn 14:27
6:27 [i] Dt 28:10; 2Sa 7:23; 2Ch 7:14; Ne 9:10; Jer 25:29
7:1 [j] Ex 40:17 [k] Ex 40:9 [l] ver 84,88; Ex 40:10
7:2 [m] Nu 1:5-16
7:7 [n] Nu 4:24-26,28
7:8 [o] Nu 4:31-33
7:9 [p] Nu 4:15
7:10 [q] ver 1 [r] 2Ch 7:9

13 His offering was one silver plate weighing a hundred and
thirty shekels,[a] and one silver sprinkling bowl weighing seventy shekels,[b] both according to the sanctuary shekel,[a] each
filled with fine flour mixed with oil as a grain offering;[b] 14 one
gold dish weighing ten shekels,[c] filled with incense;[c] 15 one
young bull,[d] one ram and one male lamb a year old, for a
burnt offering;[e] 16 one male goat for a sin offering;[f] 17 and two
oxen, five rams, five male goats and five male lambs a year old,
to be sacrificed as a fellowship offering.[d][g] This was the offering
of Nahshon son of Amminadab.[h]

18 On the second day Nethanel son of Zuar,[i] the leader of Issachar,
brought his offering.

19 The offering he brought was one silver plate weighing a
hundred and thirty shekels, and one silver sprinkling bowl
weighing seventy shekels, both according to the sanctuary
shekel, each filled with fine flour mixed with oil as a grain
offering; 20 one gold dish[j] weighing ten shekels, filled with
incense; 21 one young bull, one ram and one male lamb a year
old, for a burnt offering; 22 one male goat for a sin offering;
23 and two oxen, five rams, five male goats and five male
lambs a year old, to be sacrificed as a fellowship offering. This
was the offering of Nethanel son of Zuar.

24 On the third day, Eliab son of Helon,[k] the leader of the people of
Zebulun, brought his offering.

25 His offering was one silver plate weighing a hundred and
thirty shekels, and one silver sprinkling bowl weighing seventy shekels, both according to the sanctuary shekel, each
filled with fine flour mixed with oil as a grain offering; 26 one
gold dish weighing ten shekels, filled with incense; 27 one
young bull, one ram and one male lamb a year old, for a burnt
offering; 28 one male goat for a sin offering; 29 and two oxen,
five rams, five male goats and five male lambs a year old, to
be sacrificed as a fellowship offering. This was the offering of
Eliab son of Helon.

30 On the fourth day Elizur son of Shedeur,[l] the leader of the people of Reuben, brought his offering.

31 His offering was one silver plate weighing a hundred and
thirty shekels, and one silver sprinkling bowl weighing seventy shekels, both according to the sanctuary shekel, each
filled with fine flour mixed with oil as a grain offering; 32 one
gold dish weighing ten shekels, filled with incense; 33 one

7:13 [a] Ex 30:13; Nu 3:47 [b] Lev 2:1
7:14 [c] Ex 30:34
7:15 [d] Ex 24:5; 29:3; Nu 28:11 [e] Lev 1:3
7:16 [f] Lev 4:3,23
7:17 [g] Lev 3:1 [h] Nu 1:7
7:18 [i] Nu 1:8
7:20 [j] ver 14
7:24 [k] Nu 1:9
7:30 [l] Nu 1:5

a *13* That is, about 3 1/4 pounds (about 1.5 kilograms); also elsewhere in this chapter
b *13* That is, about 1 3/4 pounds (about 0.8 kilogram); also elsewhere in this chapter
c *14* That is, about 4 ounces (about 110 grams); also elsewhere in this chapter
d *17* Traditionally *peace offering*; also elsewhere in this chapter

7:36 young bull, one ram and one male lamb a year old, for a burnt
[a]Nu 1:6 offering; 34one male goat for a sin offering; 35and two oxen,
five rams, five male goats and five male lambs a year old, to
be sacrificed as a fellowship offering. This was the offering of
Elizur son of Shedeur.

36On the fifth day Shelumiel son of Zurishaddai,[a] the leader of the
people of Simeon, brought his offering.

37His offering was one silver plate weighing a hundred and
thirty shekels, and one silver sprinkling bowl weighing seventy shekels, both according to the sanctuary shekel, each
7:42 filled with fine flour mixed with oil as a grain offering; 38one
[b]Nu 1:14 gold dish weighing ten shekels, filled with incense; 39one
young bull, one ram and one male lamb a year old, for a burnt
offering; 40one male goat for a sin offering; 41and two oxen,
five rams, five male goats and five male lambs a year old, to
be sacrificed as a fellowship offering. This was the offering of
Shelumiel son of Zurishaddai.

42On the sixth day Eliasaph son of Deuel,[b] the leader of the people
of Gad, brought his offering.

43His offering was one silver plate weighing a hundred and
thirty shekels, and one silver sprinkling bowl weighing sev-
7:48 enty shekels, both according to the sanctuary shekel, each
[c]Nu 1:10 filled with fine flour mixed with oil as a grain offering; 44one
gold dish weighing ten shekels, filled with incense; 45one
young bull, one ram and one male lamb a year old, for a burnt
offering; 46one male goat for a sin offering; 47and two oxen,
five rams, five male goats and five male lambs a year old, to
be sacrificed as a fellowship offering. This was the offering of
Eliasaph son of Deuel.

48On the seventh day Elishama son of Ammihud,[c] the leader of
the people of Ephraim, brought his offering.

7:53 49His offering was one silver plate weighing a hundred and
[d]Nu 1:10 thirty shekels, and one silver sprinkling bowl weighing seventy shekels, both according to the sanctuary shekel, each
filled with fine flour mixed with oil as a grain offering; 50one
gold dish weighing ten shekels, filled with incense; 51one
young bull, one ram and one male lamb a year old, for a burnt
offering; 52one male goat for a sin offering; 53and two oxen,
five rams, five male goats and five male lambs a year old, to
be sacrificed as a fellowship offering. This was the offering of
Elishama son of Ammihud.[d]

54On the eighth day Gamaliel son of Pedahzur,[e] the leader of the
7:54
[e]Nu 1:10; 2:20 people of Manasseh, brought his offering.

55His offering was one silver plate weighing a hundred and
thirty shekels, and one silver sprinkling bowl weighing seventy shekels, both according to the sanctuary shekel, each
filled with fine flour mixed with oil as a grain offering; 56one
gold dish weighing ten shekels, filled with incense; 57one
young bull, one ram and one male lamb a year old, for a burnt
offering; 58one male goat for a sin offering; 59and two oxen,
five rams, five male goats and five male lambs a year old, to
be sacrificed as a fellowship offering. This was the offering of
Gamaliel son of Pedahzur.

60On the ninth day Abidan son of Gideoni,[a] the leader of the people of Benjamin, brought his offering.
61His offering was one silver plate weighing a hundred and
thirty shekels, and one silver sprinkling bowl weighing seventy shekels, both according to the sanctuary shekel, each
filled with fine flour mixed with oil as a grain offering; 62one
gold dish weighing ten shekels, filled with incense; 63one
young bull, one ram and one male lamb a year old, for a burnt
offering; 64one male goat for a sin offering; 65and two oxen,
five rams, five male goats and five male lambs a year old, to
be sacrificed as a fellowship offering. This was the offering of
Abidan son of Gideoni.

66On the tenth day Ahiezer son of Ammishaddai,[b] the leader of
the people of Dan, brought his offering.
67His offering was one silver plate weighing a hundred and
thirty shekels, and one silver sprinkling bowl weighing seventy shekels, both according to the sanctuary shekel, each
filled with fine flour mixed with oil as a grain offering; 68one
gold dish weighing ten shekels, filled with incense; 69one young
bull, one ram and one male lamb a year old, for a burnt offering; 70one male goat for a sin offering; 71and two oxen, five
rams, five male goats and five male lambs a year old, to be
sacrificed as a fellowship offering. This was the offering of
Ahiezer son of Ammishaddai.

72On the eleventh day Pagiel son of Ocran,[c] the leader of the people of Asher, brought his offering.
73His offering was one silver plate weighing a hundred and
thirty shekels, and one silver sprinkling bowl weighing seventy shekels, both according to the sanctuary shekel, each
filled with fine flour mixed with oil as a grain offering; 74one
gold dish weighing ten shekels, filled with incense; 75one
young bull, one ram and one male lamb a year old, for a burnt
offering; 76one male goat for a sin offering; 77and two oxen,

7:60 [a] Nu 1:11

7:66 [b] Nu 1:12; 2:25

7:72 [c] Nu 1:13

7:78 [a]Nu 1:15; 2:29

five rams, five male goats and five male lambs a year old, to be sacrificed as a fellowship offering. This was the offering of Pagiel son of Ocran.

78On the twelfth day Ahira son of Enan,[a] the leader of the people of Naphtali, brought his offering.

79His offering was one silver plate weighing a hundred and thirty shekels, and one silver sprinkling bowl weighing seventy shekels, both according to the sanctuary shekel, each filled with fine flour mixed with oil as a grain offering; 80one gold dish weighing ten shekels, filled with incense; 81one young bull, one ram and one male lamb a year old, for a burnt offering; 82one male goat for a sin offering; 83and two oxen, five rams, five male goats and five male lambs a year old, to be sacrificed as a fellowship offering. This was the offering of Ahira son of Enan.

7:84 [b]ver 1,10 [c]Nu 4:14 [d]ver 14

84These were the offerings of the Israelite leaders for the dedication of the altar when it was anointed:[b] twelve silver plates, twelve silver sprinkling bowls[c] and twelve gold dishes.[d] 85Each silver plate weighed a hundred and thirty shekels, and each sprinkling bowl seventy shekels. Altogether, the silver dishes weighed two thousand four hundred shekels,[a] according to the sanctuary shekel. 86The twelve gold dishes filled with incense weighed ten shekels each, according to the sanctuary shekel. Altogether, the gold dishes weighed a hundred and twenty shekels.[b] 87The total number of animals for the burnt offering came to twelve young bulls, twelve rams and twelve male lambs a year old, together with their grain offering. Twelve male goats were used for the sin offering. 88The total number of animals for the sacrifice of the fellowship offering came to twenty-four oxen, sixty rams, sixty male goats and sixty male lambs a year old. These were the offerings for the dedication of the altar after it was anointed.[e]

7:88 [e]ver 1,10

7:89 [f]Ex 25:21,22; 33:9,11 [g]Ps 80:1; 99:1

89When Moses entered the Tent of Meeting to speak with the LORD,[f] he heard the voice speaking to him from between the two cherubim above the atonement cover[g] on the ark of the Testimony. And he spoke with him.

Chapter 8 Theme ______________________

Lampstand

8 The LORD said to Moses, 2"Speak to Aaron and say to him, 'When you set up the seven lamps, they are to light the area in front of the lampstand.[h]'"

3Aaron did so; he set up the lamps so that they faced forward on the lampstand, just as the LORD commanded Moses. 4This is

8:2 [h]Ex 25:37; Lev 24:2,4

[a]85 That is, about 60 pounds (about 28 kilograms) [b]86 That is, about 3 pounds (about 1.4 kilograms)

how the lampstand was made: It was made of hammered gold[a]—
from its base to its blossoms. The lampstand was made exactly
like the pattern[b] the LORD had shown Moses.
5The LORD said to Moses: 6"Take the Levites from among the
other Israelites and make them ceremonially clean.[c] 7To purify
them, do this: Sprinkle the water of cleansing[d] on them; then
have them shave their whole bodies[e] and wash their clothes,[f] and
so purify themselves. 8Have them take a young bull with its grain
offering of fine flour mixed with oil;[g] then you are to take a second young bull for a sin offering. 9Bring the Levites to the front
of the Tent of Meeting[h] and assemble the whole Israelite community.[i] 10You are to bring the Levites before the LORD, and the
Israelites are to lay their hands on them.[j] 11Aaron is to present
the Levites before the LORD as a wave offering[k] from the Israelites,
so that they may be ready to do the work of the LORD.
12"After the Levites lay their hands on the heads of the bulls,[l]
use the one for a sin offering to the LORD and the other for a burnt
offering, to make atonement[m] for the Levites. 13Have the Levites
stand in front of Aaron and his sons and then present them as a
wave offering to the LORD. 14In this way you are to set the Levites
apart from the other Israelites, and the Levites will be mine.[n]
15"After you have purified the Levites and presented them as a
wave offering,[o] they are to come to do their work at the Tent of
Meeting. 16They are the Israelites who are to be given wholly to
me. I have taken them as my own in place of the firstborn, the first
male offspring[p] from every Israelite woman. 17Every firstborn
male in Israel, whether man or animal,[q] is mine. When I struck
down all the firstborn in Egypt, I set them apart for myself.[r] 18And I
have taken the Levites in place of all the firstborn sons in Israel.[s]
19Of all the Israelites, I have given the Levites as gifts to Aaron and
his sons[t] to do the work at the Tent of Meeting on behalf of the
Israelites[u] and to make atonement for them[v] so that no plague will
strike the Israelites when they go near the sanctuary."
20Moses, Aaron and the whole Israelite community did with the
Levites just as the LORD commanded Moses. 21The Levites purified themselves and washed their clothes.[w] Then Aaron presented them as a wave offering before the LORD and made
atonement for them to purify them.[x] 22After that, the Levites
came to do their work at the Tent of Meeting under the supervision of Aaron and his sons. They did with the Levites just as the
LORD commanded Moses.
23The LORD said to Moses, 24"This applies to the Levites: Men
twenty-five years old or more[y] shall come to take part in the work
at the Tent of Meeting,[z] 25but at the age of fifty, they must retire
from their regular service and work no longer. 26They may assist
their brothers in performing their duties at the Tent of Meeting,

8:4 [a] Ex 25:18,36 [b] Ex 25:9
8:6 [c] Lev 22:2; Isa 1:16; 52:11
8:7 [d] Nu 19:9,17 [e] Lev 14:9; Dt 21:12 [f] Lev 14:8
8:8 [g] Lev 2:1; Nu 15:8-10
8:9 [h] Ex 40:12 [i] Lev 8:3
8:10 [j] Ac 6:6
8:11 [k] Lev 7:30
8:12 [l] Ex 29:10 [m] Ex 29:36
8:14 [n] Nu 3:12
8:15 [o] Ex 29:24
8:16 [p] Nu 3:12
8:17 [q] Ex 4:23 [r] Ex 13:2; Lk 2:23
8:18 [s] Nu 3:12
8:19 [t] Nu 3:9 [u] Nu 1:53 [v] Nu 16:46
8:21 [w] ver 7 [x] ver 12
8:24 [y] 1Ch 23:3 [z] Ex 38:21; Nu 4:3

but they themselves must not do the work. This, then, is how you
are to assign the responsibilities of the Levites.”

Chapter 9 Theme ____

9 The LORD spoke to Moses in the Desert of Sinai in the first
month[a] of the second year after they came out of Egypt.[b] He
said, 2“Have the Israelites celebrate the Passover at the appointed
time. 3Celebrate it at the appointed time, at twilight on the fourteenth day of this month, in accordance with all its rules and
regulations.[c]”
4So Moses told the Israelites to celebrate the Passover, 5and they
did so in the Desert of Sinai at twilight on the fourteenth day of
the first month.[d] The Israelites did everything just as the LORD
commanded Moses.
6But some of them could not celebrate the Passover on that day
because they were ceremonially unclean[e] on account of a dead
body. So they came to Moses and Aaron[f] that same day 7and said
to Moses, “We have become unclean because of a dead body, but
why should we be kept from presenting the LORD’s offering with
the other Israelites at the appointed time?”
8Moses answered them, “Wait until I find out what the LORD
commands concerning you.”[g]
9Then the LORD said to Moses, 10“Tell the Israelites: ‘When any
of you or your descendants are unclean because of a dead body
or are away on a journey, they may still celebrate[h] the LORD’s
Passover. 11They are to celebrate it on the fourteenth day of the
second month at twilight. They are to eat the lamb, together with
unleavened bread and bitter herbs.[i] 12They must not leave any of
it till morning[j] or break any of its bones.[k] When they celebrate
the Passover, they must follow all the regulations. 13But if a man
who is ceremonially clean and not on a journey fails to celebrate
the Passover, that person must be cut off from his people[l]
because he did not present the LORD’s offering at the appointed
time. That man will bear the consequences of his sin.
14“ ‘An alien[m] living among you who wants to celebrate the
LORD’s Passover must do so in accordance with its rules and regulations. You must have the same regulations for the alien and
the native-born.’ ”
15On the day the tabernacle, the Tent of the Testimony, was set
up, the cloud[n] covered it. From evening till morning the cloud
above the tabernacle looked like fire.[o] 16That is how it continued
to be; the cloud covered it, and at night it looked like fire. 17When-
ever the cloud lifted from above the Tent, the Israelites set out;
wherever the cloud settled, the Israelites encamped.[p] 18At the
LORD’s command the Israelites set out, and at his command they

9:1 [a] Ex 40:2 [b] Nu 1:1
9:3 [c] Ex 12:2-11, 43-49; Lev 23:5-8; Dt 16:1-8
9:5 [d] Ex 12:1-13; Jos 5:10
9:6 [e] Lev 5:3 [f] Ex 18:15; Nu 27:2
9:8 [g] Ex 18:15; Nu 27:5,21; Ps 85:8
9:10 [h] 2Ch 30:2
9:11 [i] Ex 12:8
9:12 [j] Ex 12:10,43 [k] Ex 12:46; Jn 19:36*
9:13 [l] Ge 17:14; Ex 12:15
9:14 [m] Ex 12:48,49
9:15 [n] Ex 40:34 [o] Ex 13:21
9:17 [p] Ex 40:36-38; Nu 10:11,12; 1Co 10:1

encamped. As long as the cloud stayed over the tabernacle, they
remained in camp. 19When the cloud remained over the tabernacle a long time, the Israelites obeyed the LORD's order and did not
set out. 20Sometimes the cloud was over the tabernacle only a few
days; at the LORD's command they would encamp, and then at his
command they would set out. 21Sometimes the cloud stayed only
from evening till morning, and when it lifted in the morning, they
set out. Whether by day or by night, whenever the cloud lifted,
they set out. 22Whether the cloud stayed over the tabernacle for
two days or a month or a year, the Israelites would remain in
camp and not set out; but when it lifted, they would set out. 23At
the LORD's command they encamped, and at the LORD's command they set out. They obeyed the LORD's order, in accordance
with his command through Moses.

Chapter 10 Theme ______________________

10 The LORD said to Moses: 2"Make two trumpets[a] of hammered silver, and use them for calling the community[b]
together and for having the camps set out. 3When both are
sounded, the whole community is to assemble before you at the
entrance to the Tent of Meeting. 4If only one is sounded, the leaders[c]—the heads of the clans of Israel—are to assemble before
you. 5When a trumpet blast is sounded, the tribes camping on
the east are to set out.[d] 6At the sounding of a second blast, the
camps on the south are to set out.[e] The blast will be the signal for
setting out. 7To gather the assembly, blow the trumpets,[f] but not
with the same signal.[g]

8"The sons of Aaron, the priests, are to blow the trumpets. This
is to be a lasting ordinance for you and the generations to come.[h]
9When you go into battle in your own land against an enemy who
is oppressing you,[i] sound a blast on the trumpets. Then you will
be remembered[j] by the LORD your God and rescued from your
enemies.[k] 10Also at your times of rejoicing—your appointed
feasts and New Moon festivals[l]—you are to sound the trumpets[m]
over your burnt offerings and fellowship offerings,[a] and they will
be a memorial for you before your God. I am the LORD your God."

11On the twentieth day of the second month of the second year,[n]
the cloud lifted[o] from above the tabernacle of the Testimony.
12Then the Israelites set out from the Desert of Sinai and traveled
from place to place until the cloud came to rest in the Desert of
Paran. 13They set out, this first time, at the LORD's command
through Moses.[p]

14The divisions of the camp of Judah went first, under their
standard.[q] Nahshon son of Amminadab[r] was in command.

a *10* Traditionally *peace offerings*

10:2 [a] Ne 12:35; Ps 47:5 [b] Jer 4:5,19; 6:1; Hos 5:8; Joel 2:1,15; Am 3:6
10:4 [c] Ex 18:21; Nu 1:16; 7:2
10:5 [d] ver 14
10:6 [e] ver 18
10:7 [f] Eze 33:3; Joel 2:1 [g] 1Co 14:8
10:8 [h] Nu 31:6
10:9 [i] Jdg 2:18; 6:9; 1Sa 10:18; Ps 106:42 [j] Ge 8:1 [k] Ps 106:4
10:10 [l] Ps 81:3 [m] Lev 23:24
10:11 [n] Ex 40:17 [o] Nu 9:17
10:13 [p] Dt 1:6
10:14 [q] Nu 2:3-9 [r] Nu 1:7

15 Nethanel son of Zuar was over the division of the tribe of
Issachar, 16 and Eliab son of Helon was over the division of the
tribe of Zebulun. 17 Then the tabernacle was taken down, and the
Gershonites and Merarites, who carried it, set out.[a]

18 The divisions of the camp of Reuben went next, under their
standard.[b] Elizur son of Shedeur was in command. 19 Shelumiel
son of Zurishaddai was over the division of the tribe of Simeon,
20 and Eliasaph son of Deuel was over the division of the tribe of
Gad. 21 Then the Kohathites set out, carrying the holy things.[c]
The tabernacle was to be set up before they arrived.[d]

22 The divisions of the camp of Ephraim[e] went next, under their
standard. Elishama son of Ammihud was in command. 23 Gamaliel
son of Pedahzur was over the division of the tribe of Manasseh,
24 and Abidan son of Gideoni was over the division of the tribe of
Benjamin.

25 Finally, as the rear guard[f] for all the units, the divisions of
the camp of Dan set out, under their standard. Ahiezer son of
Ammishaddai was in command. 26 Pagiel son of Ocran was over
the division of the tribe of Asher, 27 and Ahira son of Enan was
over the division of the tribe of Naphtali. 28 This was the order of
march for the Israelite divisions as they set out.

29 Now Moses said to Hobab[g] son of Reuel[h] the Midianite, Moses'
father-in-law,[i] "We are setting out for the place about which the
LORD said, 'I will give it to you.'[j] Come with us and we will treat
you well, for the LORD has promised good things to Israel."

30 He answered, "No, I will not go;[k] I am going back to my own
land and my own people."

31 But Moses said, "Please do not leave us. You know where we
should camp in the desert, and you can be our eyes.[l] 32 If you
come with us, we will share with you[m] whatever good things the
LORD gives us.[n]"

33 So they set out[o] from the mountain of the LORD and traveled
for three days. The ark of the covenant of the LORD[p] went before
them during those three days to find them a place to rest. 34 The
cloud of the LORD was over them by day when they set out from
the camp.[q]

35 Whenever the ark set out, Moses said,

"Rise up, O LORD!
May your enemies be scattered;[r]
may your foes flee before you.[s]"

36 Whenever it came to rest, he said,

"Return,[t] O LORD,
to the countless thousands of Israel.[u]"

10:17 [a] Nu 4:21-32
10:18 [b] Nu 2:10-16
10:21 [c] Nu 4:20 [d] ver 17
10:22 [e] Nu 2:24
10:25 [f] Nu 2:31; Jos 6:9
10:29 [g] Jdg 4:11 [h] Ex 2:18 [i] Ex 3:1 [j] Ge 12:7
10:30 [k] Mt 21:29
10:31 [l] Job 29:15
10:32 [m] Dt 10:18 [n] Ps 22:27-31; 67:5-7
10:33 [o] ver 12; Dt 1:33 [p] Jos 3:3
10:34 [q] Nu 9:15-23
10:35 [r] Ps 68:1 [s] Dt 7:10; 32:41; Ps 68:2; Isa 17:12-14
10:36 [t] Isa 63:17 [u] Dt 1:10

The Exodus from Egypt to Canaan

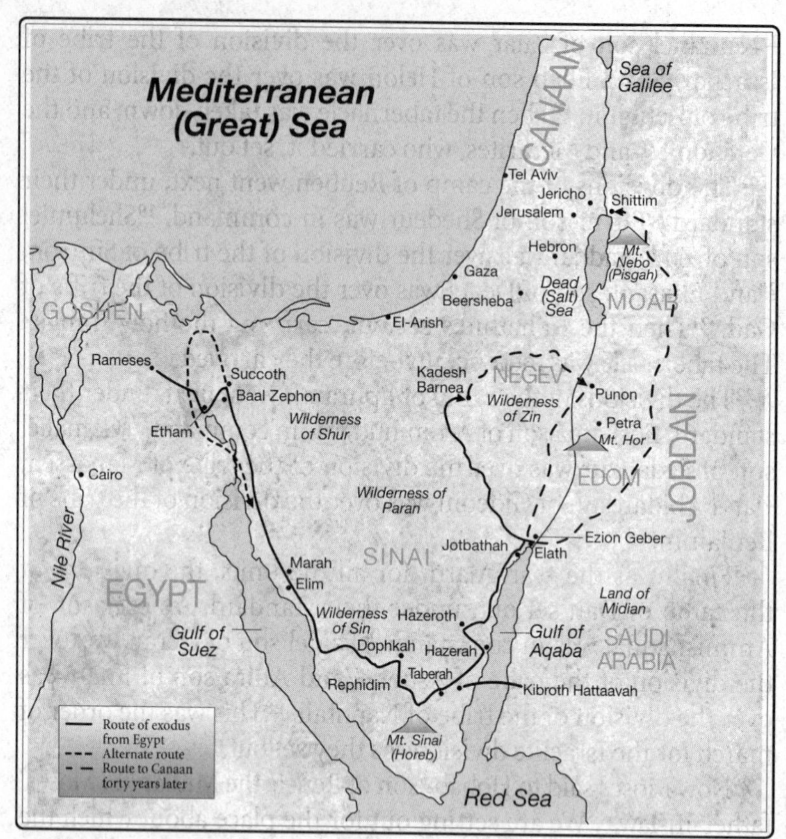

Chapter 11 Theme ____

11 Now the people complained about their hardships in the
hearing of the LORD, and when he heard them his anger was
aroused. Then fire from the LORD burned among them[a] and consumed some of the outskirts of the camp. 2 When the people cried
out to Moses, he prayed to the LORD[b] and the fire died down. 3 So
that place was called Taberah,[a][c] because fire from the LORD had
burned among them.

4 The rabble with them began to crave other food,[d] and again
the Israelites started wailing[e] and said, "If only we had meat to
eat! 5 We remember the fish we ate in Egypt at no cost—also the
cucumbers, melons, leeks, onions and garlic.[f] 6 But now we have
lost our appetite; we never see anything but this manna!"

7 The manna was like coriander seed[g] and looked like resin.[h]
8 The people went around gathering it, and then ground it in a
handmill or crushed it in a mortar. They cooked it in a pot or
made it into cakes. And it tasted like something made with olive
oil. 9 When the dew[i] settled on the camp at night, the manna also
came down.

[a]3 *Taberah* means *burning.*

11:1 [a]Lev 10:2
11:2 [b]Nu 21:7
11:3 [c]Dt 9:22
11:4 [d]Ex 12:38 [e]Ps 78:18; 1Co 10:6
11:5 [f]Ex 16:3
11:7 [g]Ex 16:31 [h]Ge 2:12
11:9 [i]Ex 16:13

10Moses heard the people of every family wailing, each at the
entrance to his tent. The LORD became exceedingly angry, and
Moses was troubled. 11He asked the LORD, "Why have you brought
this trouble on your servant? What have I done to displease you
that you put the burden of all these people on me?[a] 12Did I conceive all these people? Did I give them birth? Why do you tell me
to carry them in my arms, as a nurse carries an infant,[b] to the
land you promised on oath to their forefathers?[c] 13Where can I
get meat for all these people?[d] They keep wailing to me, 'Give us
meat to eat!' 14I cannot carry all these people by myself; the burden is too heavy for me.[e] 15If this is how you are going to treat me,
put me to death[f] right now[g]—if I have found favor in your eyes—
and do not let me face my own ruin."
16The LORD said to Moses: "Bring me seventy of Israel's elders
who are known to you as leaders and officials among the people.
Have them come to the Tent of Meeting, that they may stand
there with you. 17I will come down and speak with you there, and
I will take of the Spirit that is on you and put the Spirit on them.[h]
They will help you carry the burden of the people so that you will
not have to carry it alone.[i]
18"Tell the people: 'Consecrate yourselves[j] in preparation for
tomorrow, when you will eat meat. The LORD heard you when
you wailed,[k] "If only we had meat to eat! We were better off in
Egypt!"[l] Now the LORD will give you meat, and you will eat it.
19You will not eat it for just one day, or two days, or five, ten or
twenty days, 20but for a whole month—until it comes out of your
nostrils and you loathe it[m]—because you have rejected the LORD,[n]
who is among you, and have wailed before him, saying, "Why did
we ever leave Egypt?"'"
21But Moses said, "Here I am among six hundred thousand
men[o] on foot, and you say, 'I will give them meat to eat for a whole
month!' 22Would they have enough if flocks and herds were
slaughtered for them? Would they have enough if all the fish in
the sea were caught for them?"[p]
23The LORD answered Moses, "Is the LORD's arm too short?[q] You
will now see whether or not what I say will come true for you.[r]"
24So Moses went out and told the people what the LORD had
said. He brought together seventy of their elders and had them
stand around the Tent. 25Then the LORD came down in the
cloud[s] and spoke with him,[t] and he took of the Spirit[u] that was
on him and put the Spirit on the seventy elders.[v] When the Spirit
rested on them, they prophesied,[w] but they did not do so again.[a]
26However, two men, whose names were Eldad and Medad,
had remained in the camp. They were listed among the elders,

11:11 [a] Ex 5:22
11:12 [b] Isa 40:11; 49:23 [c] Ex 13:5
11:13 [d] Jn 6:5-9
11:14 [e] Ex 18:18
11:15 [f] Ex 32:32 [g] 1Ki 19:4; Jnh 4:3
11:17 [h] ver 25,29; 1Sa 10:6; 2Ki 2:9,15; Joel 2:28 [i] Ex 18:18
11:18 [j] Ex 19:10 [k] Ex 16:7 [l] ver 5; Ac 7:39
11:20 [m] Ps 78:29; 106:14,15 [n] Jos 24:27; 1Sa 10:19
11:21 [o] Ex 12:37
11:22 [p] Mt 15:33
11:23 [q] Isa 50:2; 59:1 [r] Nu 23:19; Eze 12:25; 24:14
11:25 [s] Nu 12:5 [t] ver 17 [u] 1Sa 10:6 [v] Ac 2:17 [w] 1Sa 10:10

[a] 25 Or *prophesied and continued to do so*

but did not go out to the Tent. Yet the Spirit also rested on them,
and they prophesied in the camp. 27A young man ran and told
Moses, "Eldad and Medad are prophesying in the camp."
28Joshua son of Nun, who had been Moses' aide[a] since youth,
spoke up and said, "Moses, my lord, stop them!"[b]
29But Moses replied, "Are you jealous for my sake? I wish that
all the LORD's people were prophets[c] and that the LORD would
put his Spirit on them!" 30Then Moses and the elders of Israel
returned to the camp.
31Now a wind went out from the LORD and drove quail[d] in from
the sea. It brought them[a] down all around the camp to about
three feet[b] above the ground, as far as a day's walk in any direction. 32All that day and night and all the next day the people went
out and gathered quail. No one gathered less than ten homers.[c]
Then they spread them out all around the camp. 33But while the
meat was still between their teeth[e] and before it could be consumed, the anger of the LORD burned against the people, and he
struck them with a severe plague.[f] 34Therefore the place was
named Kibroth Hattaavah,[d][g] because there they buried the people
who had craved other food.
35From Kibroth Hattaavah the people traveled to Hazeroth[h]
and stayed there.

Chapter 12 Theme ______________________________

12 Miriam and Aaron began to talk against Moses because
of his Cushite wife,[i] for he had married a Cushite. 2"Has
the LORD spoken only through Moses?" they asked. "Hasn't he
also spoken through us?"[j] And the LORD heard this.[k]
3(Now Moses was a very humble man,[l] more humble than anyone else on the face of the earth.)
4At once the LORD said to Moses, Aaron and Miriam, "Come
out to the Tent of Meeting, all three of you." So the three of them
came out. 5Then the LORD came down in a pillar of cloud;[m] he
stood at the entrance to the Tent and summoned Aaron and
Miriam. When both of them stepped forward, 6he said, "Listen
to my words:

"When a prophet of the LORD is among you,
  I reveal myself to him in visions,[n]
  I speak to him in dreams.[o]
7But this is not true of my servant Moses;[p]
  he is faithful in all my house.[q]

[a]31 Or *They flew* [b]31 Hebrew *two cubits* (about 1 meter) [c]32 That is, probably about 60 bushels (about 2.2 kiloliters) [d]34 *Kibroth Hattaavah* means *graves of craving.*

11:28 [a]Ex 33:11; Jos 1:1 [b]Mk 9:38-40
11:29 [c]1Co 14:5
11:31 [d]Ex 16:13; Ps 78:26-28
11:33 [e]Ps 78:30 [f]Ps 106:15
11:34 [g]Dt 9:22
11:35 [h]Nu 33:17
12:1 [i]Ex 2:21
12:2 [j]Nu 16:3 [k]Nu 11:1
12:3 [l]Mt 11:29
12:5 [m]Nu 11:25
12:6 [n]Ge 15:1; 46:2 [o]Ge 31:10; 1Ki 3:5; Heb 1:1
12:7 [p]Jos 1:1-2; Ps 105:26 [q]Heb 3:2,5

8 With him I speak face to face,
clearly and not in riddles;[a]
he sees the form of the LORD.[b]
Why then were you not afraid
to speak against my servant Moses?"

9 The anger of the LORD burned against them, and he left them.[c]
10 When the cloud lifted from above the Tent, there stood Miriam—leprous,[a] like snow.[d] Aaron turned toward her and saw that
she had leprosy;[e] 11 and he said to Moses, "Please, my lord, do not
hold against us the sin we have so foolishly committed.[f] 12 Do not
let her be like a stillborn infant coming from its mother's womb
with its flesh half eaten away."
13 So Moses cried out to the LORD, "O God, please heal her![g]"
14 The LORD replied to Moses, "If her father had spit in her face,[h]
would she not have been in disgrace for seven days? Confine her
outside the camp[i] for seven days; after that she can be brought
back." 15 So Miriam was confined outside the camp for seven days,
and the people did not move on till she was brought back.
16 After that, the people left Hazeroth[j] and encamped in the
Desert of Paran.

Chapter 13 Theme ____________________

13 The LORD said to Moses, 2 "Send some men to explore[k]
the land of Canaan, which I am giving to the Israelites.
From each ancestral tribe send one of its leaders."
3 So at the LORD's command Moses sent them out from the
Desert of Paran. All of them were leaders of the Israelites. 4 These
are their names:

from the tribe of Reuben, Shammua son of Zaccur;
5 from the tribe of Simeon, Shaphat son of Hori;
6 from the tribe of Judah, Caleb son of Jephunneh;[l]
7 from the tribe of Issachar, Igal son of Joseph;
8 from the tribe of Ephraim, Hoshea son of Nun;
9 from the tribe of Benjamin, Palti son of Raphu;
10 from the tribe of Zebulun, Gaddiel son of Sodi;
11 from the tribe of Manasseh (a tribe of Joseph), Gaddi son
of Susi;
12 from the tribe of Dan, Ammiel son of Gemalli;
13 from the tribe of Asher, Sethur son of Michael;
14 from the tribe of Naphtali, Nahbi son of Vophsi;
15 from the tribe of Gad, Geuel son of Maki.

a *10* The Hebrew word was used for various diseases affecting the skin—not necessarily leprosy.

12:8 [a] Dt 34:10 [b] Ex 20:4; Ps 17:15
12:9 [c] Ge 17:22
12:10 [d] Ex 4:6; Dt 24:9 [e] 2Ki 5:1,27
12:11 [f] 2Sa 19:19; 24:10
12:13 [g] Isa 30:26; Jer 17:14
12:14 [h] Dt 25:9; Job 17:6; 30:9-10; Isa 50:6 [i] Lev 13:46; Nu 5:2-3
12:16 [j] Nu 11:35
13:2 [k] Dt 1:22
13:6 [l] ver 30; Nu 14:6,24; 34:19; Jdg 1:12-15

16 These are the names of the men Moses sent to explore the land.
(Moses gave Hoshea son of Nun[a] the name Joshua.)[b]
17 When Moses sent them to explore Canaan, he said, "Go up
through the Negev[c] and on into the hill country.[d] 18 See what the
land is like and whether the people who live there are strong or
weak, few or many. 19 What kind of land do they live in? Is it good
or bad? What kind of towns do they live in? Are they unwalled
or fortified? 20 How is the soil? Is it fertile or poor? Are there trees
on it or not? Do your best to bring back some of the fruit of the
land.[e]" (It was the season for the first ripe grapes.)
21 So they went up and explored the land from the Desert of Zin[f]
as far as Rehob,[g] toward Lebo[a] Hamath.[h] 22 They went up through
the Negev and came to Hebron, where Ahiman, Sheshai and Talmai,[i] the descendants of Anak,[j] lived. (Hebron had been built
seven years before Zoan in Egypt.)[k] 23 When they reached the
Valley of Eshcol,[b] they cut off a branch bearing a single cluster of
grapes. Two of them carried it on a pole between them, along
with some pomegranates and figs. 24 That place was called the
Valley of Eshcol because of the cluster of grapes the Israelites cut
off there. 25 At the end of forty days they returned from exploring
the land.

26 They came back to Moses and Aaron and the whole Israelite
community at Kadesh in the Desert of Paran. There they reported
to them[l] and to the whole assembly and showed them the fruit of
the land. 27 They gave Moses this account: "We went into the land
to which you sent us, and it does flow with milk and honey![m]
Here is its fruit.[n] 28 But the people who live there are powerful,
and the cities are fortified and very large.[o] We even saw descendants of Anak there. 29 The Amalekites live in the Negev; the Hittites, Jebusites and Amorites live in the hill country; and the
Canaanites live near the sea and along the Jordan."
30 Then Caleb silenced the people before Moses and said, "We
should go up and take possession of the land, for we can certainly
do it."
31 But the men who had gone up with him said, "We can't attack
those people; they are stronger than we are."[p] 32 And they spread
among the Israelites a bad report[q] about the land they had explored. They said, "The land we explored devours[r] those living
in it. All the people we saw there are of great size.[s] 33 We saw the
Nephilim[t] there (the descendants of Anak[u] come from the Nephilim). We seemed like grasshoppers in our own eyes, and we
looked the same to them."

a *21* Or *toward the entrance to* b *23* *Eshcol* means *cluster*; also in verse 24.

13:16 [a] ver 8 [b] Dt 32:44
13:17 [c] Ge 12:9 [d] Jdg 1:9
13:20 [e] Dt 1:25
13:21 [f] Nu 20:1; 27:14; 33:36; Jos 15:1 [g] Jos 19:28 [h] Jos 13:5
13:22 [i] Jos 15:14 [j] Jos 15:13 [k] Ps 78:12,43; Isa 19:11,13
13:26 [l] Nu 32:8
13:27 [m] Ex 3:8 [n] Dt 1:25
13:28 [o] Dt 1:28; 9:1,2
13:31 [p] Dt 1:28; 9:1; Jos 14:8
13:32 [q] Nu 14:36,37 [r] Eze 36:13,14 [s] Am 2:9
13:33 [t] Ge 6:4 [u] Dt 1:28

14:2 [a]Nu 11:1
14:4 [b]Ne 9:17
14:5 [c]Nu 16:4,22,45
14:7 [d]Nu 13:27; Dt 1:25
14:8 [e]Dt 10:15 [f]Nu 13:27
14:9 [g]Dt 1:26; 9:7,23,24 [h]Dt 1:21; 7:18; 20:1
14:10 [i]Ex 17:4 [j]Lev 9:23
14:11 [k]Ps 78:22; 106:24
14:12 [l]Ex 32:10
14:13 [m]Ex 32:11-14; Ps 106:23
14:14 [n]Ex 15:14 [o]Ex 13:21
14:16 [p]Jos 7:7
14:18 [q]Ex 34:6; Ps 145:8; Jnh 4:2 [r]Ex 20:5
14:19 [s]Ex34:9 [t]Ps 106:45 [u]Ps 78:38
14:20 [v]Ps 106:23; Mic 7:18-20
14:21 [w]Dt 32:40; Isa 49:18

Chapter 14 Theme ________________________

14 That night all the people of the community raised their voices and wept aloud. 2All the Israelites grumbled against Moses and Aaron, and the whole assembly said to them, "If only we had died in Egypt! Or in this desert![a] 3Why is the LORD bringing us to this land only to let us fall by the sword? Our wives and children will be taken as plunder. Wouldn't it be better for us to go back to Egypt?" 4And they said to each other, "We should choose a leader and go back to Egypt.[b]"

5Then Moses and Aaron fell facedown[c] in front of the whole Israelite assembly gathered there. 6Joshua son of Nun and Caleb son of Jephunneh, who were among those who had explored the land, tore their clothes 7and said to the entire Israelite assembly, "The land we passed through and explored is exceedingly good.[d] 8If the LORD is pleased with us,[e] he will lead us into that land, a land flowing with milk and honey,[f] and will give it to us. 9Only do not rebel[g] against the LORD. And do not be afraid of the people of the land,[h] because we will swallow them up. Their protection is gone, but the LORD is with us. Do not be afraid of them."

10But the whole assembly talked about stoning[i] them. Then the glory of the LORD[j] appeared at the Tent of Meeting to all the Israelites. 11The LORD said to Moses, "How long will these people treat me with contempt? How long will they refuse to believe in me,[k] in spite of all the miraculous signs I have performed among them? 12I will strike them down with a plague and destroy them, but I will make you into a nation[l] greater and stronger than they."

13Moses said to the LORD, "Then the Egyptians will hear about it! By your power you brought these people up from among them.[m] 14And they will tell the inhabitants of this land about it. They have already heard[n] that you, O LORD, are with these people and that you, O LORD, have been seen face to face, that your cloud stays over them, and that you go before them in a pillar of cloud by day and a pillar of fire by night.[o] 15If you put these people to death all at one time, the nations who have heard this report about you will say, 16'The LORD was not able to bring these people into the land he promised them on oath; so he slaughtered them in the desert.'[p]

17"Now may the Lord's strength be displayed, just as you have declared: 18'The LORD is slow to anger, abounding in love and forgiving sin and rebellion.[q] Yet he does not leave the guilty unpunished; he punishes the children for the sin of the fathers to the third and fourth generation.'[r] 19In accordance with your great love, forgive[s] the sin of these people,[t] just as you have pardoned them from the time they left Egypt until now."[u]

20The LORD replied, "I have forgiven them,[v] as you asked. 21Nevertheless, as surely as I live[w] and as surely as the glory of the LORD

fills the whole earth,[a] 22not one of the men who saw my glory and
the miraculous signs I performed in Egypt and in the desert but
who disobeyed me and tested me ten times[b]— 23not one of them
will ever see the land I promised on oath[c] to their forefathers. No
one who has treated me with contempt will ever see it.[d] 24But
because my servant Caleb has a different spirit and follows me
wholeheartedly,[e] I will bring him into the land he went to, and his
descendants will inherit it.[f] 25Since the Amalekites and Canaanites
are living in the valleys, turn[g] back tomorrow and set out toward
the desert along the route to the Red Sea.[a]"

26The LORD said to Moses and Aaron: 27"How long will this
wicked community grumble against me? I have heard the complaints of these grumbling Israelites.[h] 28So tell them, 'As surely as
I live,[i] declares the LORD, I will do to you the very things I heard
you say: 29In this desert your bodies will fall[j]—every one of you
twenty years old or more[k] who was counted in the census and
who has grumbled against me. 30Not one of you will enter the
land I swore with uplifted hand to make your home, except Caleb
son of Jephunneh and Joshua son of Nun. 31As for your children
that you said would be taken as plunder, I will bring them in to
enjoy the land you have rejected.[l] 32But you—your bodies will
fall[m] in this desert. 33Your children will be shepherds here for
forty years, suffering for your unfaithfulness, until the last of your
bodies lies in the desert. 34For forty years—one year for each of
the forty days you explored the land[n]—you will suffer for your
sins and know what it is like to have me against you.' 35I, the LORD,
have spoken, and I will surely do these things[o] to this whole
wicked community, which has banded together against me. They
will meet their end in this desert; here they will die."

36So the men Moses had sent[p] to explore the land, who returned
and made the whole community grumble against him by
spreading a bad report[q] about it— 37these men responsible for
spreading the bad report[r] about the land were struck down and
died of a plague[s] before the LORD. 38Of the men who went to
explore the land, only Joshua son of Nun and Caleb son of Jephunneh survived.[t]

39When Moses reported this to all the Israelites, they mourned[u]
bitterly. 40Early the next morning they went up toward the high
hill country. "We have sinned[v]," they said. "We will go up to the
place the LORD promised."

41But Moses said, "Why are you disobeying the LORD's command? This will not succeed![w] 42Do not go up, because the LORD
is not with you. You will be defeated by your enemies,[x] 43for the

14:21 [a]Ps 72:19; Isa 6:3; Hab 2:14
14:22 [b]Ex 14:11; 32:1; 1Co 10:5
14:23 [c]Nu 32:11 [d]Heb 3:18
14:24 [e]ver 6-9; Jos 14:8,14 [f]Nu 32:12
14:25 [g]Dt 1:40
14:27 [h]Ex 16:12
14:28 [i]ver 21
14:29 [j]Nu 26:65 [k]Nu 1:45
14:31 [l]Ps 106:24
14:32 [m]1Co 10:5
14:34 [n]Nu 13:25
14:35 [o]Nu 23:19
14:36 [p]Nu 13:4-16 [q]Nu 13:32
14:37 [r]1Co 10:10 [s]Nu 16:49
14:38 [t]Jos 14:6
14:39 [u]Ex 33:4
14:40 [v]Dt 1:41
14:41 [w]2Ch 24:20
14:42 [x]Dt 1:42

[a]25 Hebrew *Yam Suph*; that is, Sea of Reeds

Amalekites and Canaanites will face you there. Because you have turned away from the LORD, he will not be with you and you will fall by the sword."

44 Nevertheless, in their presumption they went up[a] toward the high hill country, though neither Moses nor the ark of the LORD's covenant moved from the camp.[b] 45 Then the Amalekites and Canaanites who lived in that hill country came down and attacked them and beat them down all the way to Hormah.[c]

Chapter 15 Theme ______________________

15 The LORD said to Moses, 2 "Speak to the Israelites and say to them: 'After you enter the land I am giving you[d] as a home 3 and you present to the LORD offerings made by fire, from the herd or the flock,[e] as an aroma pleasing to the LORD[f]—whether burnt offerings[g] or sacrifices, for special vows or freewill offerings[h] or festival offerings[i]— 4 then the one who brings his offering shall present to the LORD a grain offering[j] of a tenth of an ephah[a] of fine flour mixed with a quarter of a hin[b] of oil. 5 With each lamb for the burnt offering or the sacrifice, prepare a quarter of a hin of wine[k] as a drink offering.

6 " 'With a ram[l] prepare a grain offering[m] of two-tenths of an ephah[c] of fine flour mixed with a third of a hin[d] of oil,[n] 7 and a third of a hin of wine as a drink offering. Offer it as an aroma pleasing to the LORD.

8 " 'When you prepare a young bull as a burnt offering or sacrifice, for a special vow or a fellowship offering[e][o] to the LORD, 9 bring with the bull a grain offering of three-tenths of an ephah[f][p] of fine flour mixed with half a hin[g] of oil. 10 Also bring half a hin of wine as a drink offering. It will be an offering made by fire, an aroma pleasing to the LORD. 11 Each bull or ram, each lamb or young goat, is to be prepared in this manner. 12 Do this for each one, for as many as you prepare.

13 " 'Everyone who is native-born[q] must do these things in this way when he brings an offering made by fire as an aroma pleasing to the LORD. 14 For the generations to come, whenever an alien or anyone else living among you presents an offering made by fire as an aroma pleasing to the LORD, he must do exactly as you do. 15 The community is to have the same rules for you and for the alien living among you; this is a lasting ordinance for the generations to come.[r] You and the alien shall be the same before the LORD: 16 The same laws and regulations will apply both to you and to the alien living among you.[s] ' "

14:44 [a] Dt 1:43 [b] Nu 31:6
14:45 [c] Nu 21:3; Dt 1:44; Jdg 1:17
15:2 [d] Lev 23:10
15:3 [e] Lev 1:2 [f] ver 24; Ge 8:21; Ex 29:18 [g] Nu 28:19,27 [h] Lev 22:18,21; Ezr 1:4 [i] Lev 23:1-44
15:4 [j] Lev 2:1; 6:14
15:5 [k] Nu 28:7,14
15:6 [l] Lev 5:15 [m] Nu 28:12 [n] Eze 46:14
15:8 [o] Lev 1:3; 3:1
15:9 [p] Lev 14:10
15:13 [q] Lev 16:29
15:15 [r] ver 29; Nu 9:14
15:16 [s] Nu 9:14

[a] *4* That is, probably about 2 quarts (about 2 liters) [b] *4* That is, probably about 1 quart (about 1 liter); also in verse 5 [c] *6* That is, probably about 4 quarts (about 4.5 liters) [d] *6* That is, probably about 1 1/4 quarts (about 1.2 liters); also in verse 7 [e] *8* Traditionally *peace offering* [f] *9* That is, probably about 6 quarts (about 6.5 liters) [g] *9* That is, probably about 2 quarts (about 2 liters); also in verse 10

17The LORD said to Moses, 18"Speak to the Israelites and say to
them: 'When you enter the land to which I am taking you 19and
you eat the food of the land,[a] present a portion as an offering to
the LORD. 20Present a cake from the first of your ground meal[b] and
present it as an offering from the threshing floor.[c] 21Throughout
the generations to come you are to give this offering to the LORD
from the first of your ground meal.[d]

22" 'Now if you unintentionally fail to keep any of these commands the LORD gave Moses[e]— 23any of the LORD's commands
to you through him, from the day the LORD gave them and continuing through the generations to come— 24and if this is done
unintentionally without the community being aware of it,[f] then
the whole community is to offer a young bull for a burnt offering[g]
as an aroma pleasing to the LORD, along with its prescribed grain
offering and drink offering, and a male goat for a sin offering.[h]
25The priest is to make atonement for the whole Israelite community, and they will be forgiven,[i] for it was not intentional and
they have brought to the LORD for their wrong an offering made
by fire and a sin offering. 26The whole Israelite community and
the aliens living among them will be forgiven, because all the
people were involved in the unintentional wrong.[j]

27" 'But if just one person sins unintentionally,[k] he must bring
a year-old female goat for a sin offering. 28The priest is to make
atonement before the LORD for the one who erred by sinning
unintentionally, and when atonement has been made for him,
he will be forgiven.[l] 29One and the same law applies to everyone
who sins unintentionally, whether he is a native-born Israelite or
an alien.

30" 'But anyone who sins defiantly,[m] whether native-born or
alien,[n] blasphemes the LORD, and that person must be cut off
from his people. 31Because he has despised the LORD's word and
broken his commands,[o] that person must surely be cut off; his
guilt remains on him.[p]' "

32While the Israelites were in the desert, a man was found gathering wood on the Sabbath day.[q] 33Those who found him gathering
wood brought him to Moses and Aaron and the whole assembly,
34and they kept him in custody, because it was not clear what
should be done to him.[r] 35Then the LORD said to Moses, "The
man must die.[s] The whole assembly must stone him outside the
camp.[t]" 36So the assembly took him outside the camp and stoned
him to death, as the LORD commanded Moses.

37The LORD said to Moses, 38"Speak to the Israelites and say to
them: 'Throughout the generations to come you are to make tassels on the corners of your garments,[u] with a blue cord on each
tassel. 39You will have these tassels to look at and so you will

15:19 [a] Jos 5:11,12
15:20 [b] Ex 34:26; Lev 23:14; Dt 26:2,10 [c] Lev 2:14
15:21 [d] Ro 11:16
15:22 [e] Lev 4:2
15:24 [f] Lev 5:15 [g] Lev 4:14 [h] Lev 4:3
15:25 [i] Lev 4:20; Ro 3:25; Heb 2:17
15:26 [j] ver 24
15:27 [k] Lev 4:27
15:28 [l] Lev 4:35
15:30 [m] Nu 14:40-44; Dt 1:43; 17:13; Ps 19:13 [n] ver 14
15:31 [o] 2Sa 12:9; Ps 119:126; Pr 13:13 [p] Lev 5:1; Eze 18:20
15:32 [q] Ex 31:14,15; 35:2,3
15:34 [r] Nu 9:8
15:35 [s] Ex 31:14,15; Dt 21:21 [t] Lev 20:2; 24:14; Ac 7:58
15:38 [u] Dt 22:12; Mt 23:5

remember[a] all the commands of the LORD, that you may obey
them and not prostitute yourselves by going after the lusts of your
own hearts and eyes. 40 Then you will remember to obey all my
commands and will be consecrated to your God.[b] 41 I am the LORD
your God, who brought you out of Egypt to be your God. I am the
LORD your God.'"

Chapter 16 Theme ____________________________

16 Korah[c] son of Izhar, the son of Kohath, the son of Levi, and
certain Reubenites—Dathan and Abiram, sons of Eliab,[d]
and On son of Peleth—became insolent[a] 2 and rose up against
Moses. With them were 250 Israelite men, well-known community leaders who had been appointed members of the council.[e]
3 They came as a group to oppose Moses and Aaron[f] and said to
them, "You have gone too far! The whole community is holy,[g]
every one of them, and the LORD is with them.[h] Why then do you
set yourselves above the LORD's assembly?"[i]
4 When Moses heard this, he fell facedown.[j] 5 Then he said to
Korah and all his followers: "In the morning the LORD will show
who belongs to him and who is holy,[k] and he will have that person come near him. The man he chooses[l] he will cause to come
near him. 6 You, Korah, and all your followers are to do this: Take
censers 7 and tomorrow put fire and incense in them before the
LORD. The man the LORD chooses will be the one who is holy.
You Levites have gone too far!"
8 Moses also said to Korah, "Now listen, you Levites! 9 Isn't it
enough for you that the God of Israel has separated you from the
rest of the Israelite community and brought you near himself to
do the work at the LORD's tabernacle and to stand before the
community and minister to them?[m] 10 He has brought you and
all your fellow Levites near himself, but now you are trying to
get the priesthood too.[n] 11 It is against the LORD that you and all
your followers have banded together. Who is Aaron that you
should grumble[o] against him?[p]"
12 Then Moses summoned Dathan and Abiram, the sons of Eliab.
But they said, "We will not come! 13 Isn't it enough that you have
brought us up out of a land flowing with milk and honey to kill us
in the desert?[q] And now you also want to lord it over us?[r] 14 Moreover, you haven't brought us into a land flowing with milk and
honey[s] or given us an inheritance of fields and vineyards.[t] Will
you gouge out the eyes of[b] these men?[u] No, we will not come!"
15 Then Moses became very angry and said to the LORD, "Do
not accept their offering. I have not taken so much as a donkey[v]
from them, nor have I wronged any of them."

[a] 1 Or *Peleth—took ⌊men⌋* [b] 14 Or *you make slaves of*; or *you deceive*

15:39 [a] Dt 4:23; 6:12; Ps 73:27
15:40 [b] Lev 11:44; Ro 12:1; Col 1:22; 1Pe 1:15
16:1 [c] Jude 1:11 [d] Nu 26:8; Dt 11:6
16:2 [e] Nu 1:16; 26:9
16:3 [f] ver 7; Ps 106:16 [g] Ex 19:6 [h] Nu 14:14 [i] Nu 12:2
16:4 [j] Nu 14:5
16:5 [k] Lev 10:3; 2Ti 2:19* [l] Nu 17:5; Ps 65:4
16:9 [m] Nu 3:6; Dt 10:8
16:10 [n] Nu 3:10; 18:7
16:11 [o] 1Co 10:10 [p] Ex 16:7
16:13 [q] Nu 14:2 [r] Ac 7:27,35
16:14 [s] Lev 20:24 [t] Ex 22:5; 23:11; Nu 20:5 [u] Jdg 16:21; 1Sa 11:2
16:15 [v] 1Sa 12:3

[16]Moses said to Korah, "You and all your followers are to appear before the LORD tomorrow—you and they and Aaron.[a] [17]Each man is to take his censer and put incense in it—250 censers in all—and present it before the LORD. You and Aaron are to present your censers also." [18]So each man took his censer, put fire and incense in it, and stood with Moses and Aaron at the entrance to the Tent of Meeting. [19]When Korah had gathered all his followers in opposition to them[b] at the entrance to the Tent of Meeting, the glory of the LORD[c] appeared to the entire assembly. [20]The LORD said to Moses and Aaron, [21]"Separate yourselves from this assembly so I can put an end to them at once."[d]

[22]But Moses and Aaron fell facedown[e] and cried out, "O God, God of the spirits of all mankind,[f] will you be angry with the entire assembly when only one man sins?"[g]

[23]Then the LORD said to Moses, [24]"Say to the assembly, 'Move away from the tents of Korah, Dathan and Abiram.'"

[25]Moses got up and went to Dathan and Abiram, and the elders of Israel followed him. [26]He warned the assembly, "Move back from the tents of these wicked men![h] Do not touch anything belonging to them, or you will be swept away[i] because of all their sins." [27]So they moved away from the tents of Korah, Dathan and Abiram. Dathan and Abiram had come out and were standing with their wives, children and little ones at the entrances to their tents.

[28]Then Moses said, "This is how you will know that the LORD has sent me[j] to do all these things and that it was not my idea: [29]If these men die a natural death and experience only what usually happens to men, then the LORD has not sent me.[k] [30]But if the LORD brings about something totally new, and the earth opens its mouth and swallows them, with everything that belongs to them, and they go down alive into the grave,[a][l] then you will know that these men have treated the LORD with contempt."

[31]As soon as he finished saying all this, the ground under them split apart[m] [32]and the earth opened its mouth and swallowed them,[n] with their households and all Korah's men and all their possessions. [33]They went down alive into the grave, with everything they owned; the earth closed over them, and they perished and were gone from the community. [34]At their cries, all the Israelites around them fled, shouting, "The earth is going to swallow us too!"

[35]And fire came out from the LORD[o] and consumed[p] the 250 men who were offering the incense.

[36]The LORD said to Moses, [37]"Tell Eleazar son of Aaron, the priest, to take the censers out of the smoldering remains and

a *30* Hebrew *Sheol*; also in verse 33

16:16 [a]ver 6
16:19 [b]ver 42 [c]Ex 16:7; Nu 14:10; 20:6
16:21 [d]Ex 32:10
16:22 [e]Nu 14:5 [f]Nu 27:16; Job 12:10; Heb 12:9 [g]Ge 18:23
16:26 [h]Isa 52:11 [i]Ge 19:15
16:28 [j]Ex 3:12; Jn 5:36; 6:38
16:29 [k]Ecc 3:19
16:30 [l]ver 33; Ps 55:15
16:31 [m]Mic 1:3-4
16:32 [n]Nu 26:11; Dt 11:6; Ps 106:17
16:35 [o]Nu 11:1-3; 26:10 [p]Lev 10:2

scatter the coals some distance away, for the censers are holy—
38 the censers of the men who sinned at the cost of their lives.[a]
Hammer the censers into sheets to overlay the altar, for they were
presented before the LORD and have become holy. Let them be a
sign[b] to the Israelites."

39 So Eleazar the priest collected the bronze censers brought by
those who had been burned up, and he had them hammered out
to overlay the altar, 40 as the LORD directed him through Moses.
This was to remind the Israelites that no one except a descendant
of Aaron should come to burn incense[c] before the LORD,[d] or he
would become like Korah and his followers.[e]

41 The next day the whole Israelite community grumbled against
Moses and Aaron. "You have killed the LORD's people," they said.

42 But when the assembly gathered in opposition[f] to Moses and
Aaron and turned toward the Tent of Meeting, suddenly the cloud
covered it and the glory of the LORD appeared. 43 Then Moses and
Aaron went to the front of the Tent of Meeting, 44 and the LORD
said to Moses, 45 "Get away from this assembly so I can put an end
to them at once." And they fell facedown.

46 Then Moses said to Aaron, "Take your censer and put incense
in it, along with fire from the altar, and hurry to the assembly[g] to
make atonement[h] for them. Wrath has come out from the LORD;
the plague[i] has started." 47 So Aaron did as Moses said, and ran
into the midst of the assembly. The plague had already started
among the people,[j] but Aaron offered the incense and made
atonement for them. 48 He stood between the living and the dead,
and the plague stopped.[k] 49 But 14,700 people died from the
plague, in addition to those who had died because of Korah.[l]
50 Then Aaron returned to Moses at the entrance to the Tent of
Meeting, for the plague had stopped.

Chapter 17 Theme ______________________

17 The LORD said to Moses, 2 "Speak to the Israelites and get
twelve staffs from them, one from the leader of each of
their ancestral tribes. Write the name of each man on his staff.
3 On the staff of Levi write Aaron's name,[m] for there must be one
staff for the head of each ancestral tribe. 4 Place them in the Tent of
Meeting in front of the Testimony,[n] where I meet with you.[o] 5 The
staff belonging to the man I choose[p] will sprout, and I will rid
myself of this constant grumbling against you by the Israelites."

6 So Moses spoke to the Israelites, and their leaders gave him
twelve staffs, one for the leader of each of their ancestral tribes,
and Aaron's staff was among them. 7 Moses placed the staffs
before the LORD in the Tent of the Testimony.[q]

8 The next day Moses entered the Tent of the Testimony and
saw that Aaron's staff, which represented the house of Levi, had

16:38 [a] Pr 20:2 [b] Nu 26:10; Eze 14:8; 2Pe 2:6
16:40 [c] Ex 30:7-10; Nu 1:51 [d] 2Ch 26:18 [e] Nu 3:10
16:42 [f] ver 19; Nu 20:6
16:46 [g] Lev 10:6 [h] Nu 18:5; 25:13; Dt 9:22 [i] Nu 8:19; Ps 106:29
16:47 [j] Nu 25:6-8
16:48 [k] Nu 25:8; Ps 106:30
16:49 [l] ver 32
17:3 [m] Nu 1:3
17:4 [n] ver 7 [o] Ex 25:22
17:5 [p] Nu 16:5
17:7 [q] Ex 38:21; Ac 7:44

not only sprouted but had budded, blossomed and produced
almonds.[a] 9Then Moses brought out all the staffs from the LORD's
presence to all the Israelites. They looked at them, and each man
took his own staff.

10The LORD said to Moses, "Put back Aaron's staff in front of
the Testimony, to be kept as a sign to the rebellious.[b] This will put
an end to their grumbling against me, so that they will not die."
11Moses did just as the LORD commanded him.

12The Israelites said to Moses, "We will die! We are lost, we are
all lost![c] 13Anyone who even comes near the tabernacle of the
LORD will die.[d] Are we all going to die?"

Chapter 18 Theme ______________________________

18 The LORD said to Aaron, "You, your sons and your father's
family are to bear the responsibility for offenses against the
sanctuary,[e] and you and your sons alone are to bear the responsibility for offenses against the priesthood. 2Bring your fellow
Levites from your ancestral tribe to join you and assist you when
you and your sons minister[f] before the Tent of the Testimony.
3They are to be responsible to you and are to perform all the
duties of the Tent,[g] but they must not go near the furnishings of
the sanctuary or the altar, or both they and you will die.[h] 4They
are to join you and be responsible for the care of the Tent of
Meeting—all the work at the Tent—and no one else may come
near where you are.

5"You are to be responsible for the care of the sanctuary and the
altar,[i] so that wrath will not fall on the Israelites again. 6I myself
have selected your fellow Levites from among the Israelites as a
gift to you,[j] dedicated to the LORD to do the work at the Tent of
Meeting. 7But only you and your sons may serve as priests in
connection with everything at the altar and inside the curtain.[k] I
am giving you the service of the priesthood as a gift.[l] Anyone
else who comes near the sanctuary must be put to death.[m]"

8Then the LORD said to Aaron, "I myself have put you in charge
of the offerings presented to me; all the holy offerings the
Israelites give me I give to you and your sons as your portion and
regular share.[n] 9You are to have the part of the most holy offerings that is kept from the fire. From all the gifts they bring me as
most holy offerings, whether grain[o] or sin[p] or guilt offerings,[q]
that part belongs to you and your sons. 10Eat it as something
most holy; every male shall eat it.[r] You must regard it as holy.

11"This also is yours: whatever is set aside from the gifts of all
the wave offerings[s] of the Israelites. I give this to you and your
sons and daughters as your regular share. Everyone in your
household who is ceremonially clean[t] may eat it.

17:8 [a] Eze 17:24; Heb 9:4
17:10 [b] Dt 9:24
17:12 [c] Isa 6:5
17:13 [d] Nu 1:51
18:1 [e] Ex 28:38
18:2 [f] Nu 3:10
18:3 [g] Nu 1:51 [h] ver 7; Nu 4:15
18:5 [i] Nu 16:46
18:6 [j] Nu 3:9
18:7 [k] Heb 9:3,6 [l] ver 20; Ex 29:9 [m] Nu 3:10
18:8 [n] Lev 6:16; 7:6,31-34,36
18:9 [o] Lev 2:1 [p] Lev 6:25 [q] Lev 5:15; 7:7
18:10 [r] Lev 6:16
18:11 [s] Ex 29:26 [t] Lev 22:1-16

12“I give you all the finest olive oil and all the finest new wine
and grain they give the LORD as the firstfruits of their harvest.[a]
13All the land’s firstfruits that they bring to the LORD will be
yours.[b] Everyone in your household who is ceremonially clean
may eat it.
14“Everything in Israel that is devoted[a] to the LORD[c] is yours.
15The first offspring of every womb, both man and animal, that is
offered to the LORD is yours.[d] But you must redeem[e] every firstborn son and every firstborn male of unclean animals.[f] 16When
they are a month old, you must redeem them at the redemption
price set at five shekels[b][g] of silver, according to the sanctuary
shekel,[h] which weighs twenty gerahs.
17“But you must not redeem the firstborn of an ox, a sheep or a
goat; they are holy.[i] Sprinkle their blood[j] on the altar and burn
their fat as an offering made by fire, an aroma pleasing to the
LORD. 18Their meat is to be yours, just as the breast of the wave
offering[k] and the right thigh are yours. 19Whatever is set aside
from the holy offerings the Israelites present to the LORD I give to
you and your sons and daughters as your regular share. It is an
everlasting covenant of salt[l] before the LORD for both you and
your offspring.”
20The LORD said to Aaron, “You will have no inheritance in their
land, nor will you have any share among them;[m] I am your share
and your inheritance[n] among the Israelites.
21“I give to the Levites all the tithes[o] in Israel as their inheritance[p] in return for the work they do while serving at the Tent of
Meeting. 22From now on the Israelites must not go near the Tent
of Meeting, or they will bear the consequences of their sin and
will die.[q] 23It is the Levites who are to do the work at the Tent of
Meeting and bear the responsibility for offenses against it. This is
a lasting ordinance for the generations to come. They will receive
no inheritance[r] among the Israelites. 24Instead, I give to the Levites
as their inheritance the tithes that the Israelites present as an
offering to the LORD. That is why I said concerning them: ‘They
will have no inheritance among the Israelites.’ ”
25The LORD said to Moses, 26“Speak to the Levites and say to
them: ‘When you receive from the Israelites the tithe I give you[s]
as your inheritance, you must present a tenth of that tithe as the
LORD’s offering.[t] 27Your offering will be reckoned to you as grain
from the threshing floor or juice from the winepress. 28In this
way you also will present an offering to the LORD from all the
tithes[u] you receive from the Israelites. From these tithes you must
give the LORD’s portion to Aaron the priest. 29You must present as

18:12 [a]Ex 23:19; Ne 10:35
18:13 [b]Ex 22:29; 23:19
18:14 [c]Lev 27:28
18:15 [d]Ex 13:2 [e]Nu 3:46 [f]Ex 13:13
18:16 [g]Lev 27:6 [h]Ex 30:13
18:17 [i]Dt 15:19 [j]Lev 3:2
18:18 [k]Lev 7:30
18:19 [l]Lev 2:13; 2Ch 13:5
18:20 [m]Dt 12:12 [n]Dt 10:9; 14:27; 18:1-2; Jos 13:33; Eze 44:28
18:21 [o]Dt 14:22; Mal 3:8 [p]Lev 27:30-33; Heb 7:5
18:22 [q]Lev 22:9; Nu 1:51
18:23 [r]ver 20
18:26 [s]ver 21 [t]Ne 10:38
18:28 [u]Mal 3:8

[a] *14* The Hebrew term refers to the irrevocable giving over of things or persons to the LORD.
[b] *16* That is, about 2 ounces (about 55 grams)

the LORD's portion the best and holiest part of everything given
to you.'
30"Say to the Levites: 'When you present the best part, it will be
reckoned to you as the product of the threshing floor or the winepress.[a] 31You and your households may eat the rest of it anywhere,
for it is your wages for your work at the Tent of Meeting. 32By presenting the best part[b] of it you will not be guilty in this matter;
then you will not defile the holy offerings[c] of the Israelites, and
you will not die.' "

Chapter 19 Theme

19 The LORD said to Moses and Aaron: 2"This is a requirement
of the law that the LORD has commanded: Tell the Israelites
to bring you a red heifer[d] without defect or blemish[e] and that has
never been under a yoke.[f] 3Give it to Eleazar[g] the priest; it is to be
taken outside the camp[h] and slaughtered in his presence. 4Then
Eleazar the priest is to take some of its blood on his finger and
sprinkle[i] it seven times toward the front of the Tent of Meeting.
5While he watches, the heifer is to be burned—its hide, flesh,
blood and offal.[j] 6The priest is to take some cedar wood, hyssop[k]
and scarlet wool[l] and throw them onto the burning heifer. 7After
that, the priest must wash his clothes and bathe himself with
water.[m] He may then come into the camp, but he will be ceremonially unclean till evening. 8The man who burns it must also
wash his clothes and bathe with water, and he too will be unclean
till evening.
9"A man who is clean shall gather up the ashes of the heifer[n]
and put them in a ceremonially clean place outside the camp.
They shall be kept by the Israelite community for use in the water
of cleansing;[o] it is for purification from sin. 10The man who gathers
up the ashes of the heifer must also wash his clothes, and he too
will be unclean till evening. This will be a lasting ordinance both
for the Israelites and for the aliens living among them.
11"Whoever touches the dead body[p] of anyone will be unclean
for seven days.[q] 12He must purify himself with the water on the
third day and on the seventh day;[r] then he will be clean. But if he
does not purify himself on the third and seventh days, he will not
be clean. 13Whoever touches the dead body[s] of anyone and fails to
purify himself defiles the LORD's tabernacle.[t] That person must be
cut off from Israel.[u] Because the water of cleansing has not been
sprinkled on him, he is unclean;[v] his uncleanness remains on him.
14"This is the law that applies when a person dies in a tent: Anyone who enters the tent and anyone who is in it will be unclean
for seven days, 15and every open container without a lid fastened
on it will be unclean.

18:30 [a]ver 27
18:32 [b]Lev 22:15 [c]Lev 19:8
19:2 [d]Ge 15:9; Heb 9:13 [e]Lev 22:19-25 [f]Dt 21:3; 1Sa 6:7
19:3 [g]Nu 3:4 [h]Lev 4:12,21; Heb 13:11
19:4 [i]Lev 4:17
19:5 [j]Ex 29:14
19:6 [k]ver 18; Ps 51:7 [l]Lev 14:4
19:7 [m]Lev 11:25; 16:26,28; 22:6
19:9 [n]Heb 9:13 [o]ver 13; Nu 8:7
19:11 [p]Lev 21:1; Nu 5:2 [q]Nu 31:19
19:12 [r]ver 19; Nu 31:19
19:13 [s]Lev 20:3 [t]Lev 15:31; 2Ch 36:14 [u]Lev 7:20; 22:3 [v]Hag 2:13

16"Anyone out in the open who touches someone who has been killed with a sword or someone who has died a natural death,[a] or anyone who touches a human bone or a grave,[b] will be unclean for seven days.

17"For the unclean person, put some ashes[c] from the burned purification offering into a jar and pour fresh water over them. 18Then a man who is ceremonially clean is to take some hyssop,[d] dip it in the water and sprinkle the tent and all the furnishings and the people who were there. He must also sprinkle anyone who has touched a human bone or a grave or someone who has been killed or someone who has died a natural death. 19The man who is clean is to sprinkle the unclean person on the third and seventh days, and on the seventh day he is to purify him.[e] The person being cleansed must wash his clothes and bathe with water, and that evening he will be clean. 20But if a person who is unclean does not purify himself, he must be cut off from the community, because he has defiled the sanctuary of the LORD. The water of cleansing has not been sprinkled on him, and he is unclean. 21This is a lasting ordinance for them.

"The man who sprinkles the water of cleansing must also wash his clothes, and anyone who touches the water of cleansing will be unclean till evening. 22Anything that an unclean[f] person touches becomes unclean, and anyone who touches it becomes unclean till evening."

Chapter 20 Theme ______________________

20 In the first month the whole Israelite community arrived at the Desert of Zin,[g] and they stayed at Kadesh.[h] There Miriam[i] died and was buried.

2Now there was no water for the community,[j] and the people gathered in opposition[k] to Moses and Aaron. 3They quarreled[l] with Moses and said, "If only we had died when our brothers fell dead before the LORD![m] 4Why did you bring the LORD's community into this desert, that we and our livestock should die here?[n] 5Why did you bring us up out of Egypt to this terrible place? It has no grain or figs, grapevines or pomegranates.[o] And there is no water to drink!"

6Moses and Aaron went from the assembly to the entrance to the Tent of Meeting and fell facedown,[p] and the glory of the LORD[q] appeared to them. 7The LORD said to Moses, 8"Take the staff,[r] and you and your brother Aaron gather the assembly together. Speak to that rock before their eyes and it will pour out its water.[s] You will bring water out of the rock for the community so they and their livestock can drink."

9So Moses took the staff from the LORD's presence,[t] just as he commanded him. 10He and Aaron gathered the assembly together

19:16 [a] Nu 31:19 [b] Mt 23:27
19:17 [c] ver 9
19:18 [d] ver 6
19:19 [e] Eze 36:25; Heb 10:22
19:22 [f] Lev 5:2; Hag 2:13,14
20:1 [g] Nu 13:21 [h] Nu 33:36 [i] Ex 15:20
20:2 [j] Ex 17:1 [k] Nu 16:19
20:3 [l] Ex 17:2 [m] Nu 14:2; 16:31-35
20:4 [n] Ex 14:11; 17:3; Nu 14:3; 16:13
20:5 [o] Nu 16:14
20:6 [p] Nu 14:5 [q] Nu 16:19
20:8 [r] Ex 4:17,20 [s] Ex 17:6; Isa 43:20
20:9 [t] Nu 17:10

in front of the rock and Moses said to them, “Listen, you rebels,
must we bring you water out of this rock?”[a] 11Then Moses raised
his arm and struck the rock twice with his staff. Water[b] gushed
out, and the community and their livestock drank.
12But the LORD said to Moses and Aaron, “Because you did not
trust in me enough to honor me as holy[c] in the sight of the
Israelites, you will not bring this community into the land I give
them.”[d]
13These were the waters of Meribah,[a][e] where the Israelites quarreled[f] with the LORD and where he showed himself holy among
them.

14Moses sent messengers from Kadesh[g] to the king of Edom,[h]
saying:

“This is what your brother Israel says: You know[i] about all
the hardships that have come upon us. 15Our forefathers went
down into Egypt,[j] and we lived there many years.[k] The Egyptians mistreated[l] us and our fathers, 16but when we cried out
to the LORD, he heard our cry[m] and sent an angel[n] and brought
us out of Egypt.
“Now we are here at Kadesh, a town on the edge of your
territory. 17Please let us pass through your country. We will
not go through any field or vineyard, or drink water from
any well. We will travel along the king’s highway and not
turn to the right or to the left until we have passed through
your territory.[o]”

18But Edom answered:

“You may not pass through here; if you try, we will march
out and attack you with the sword.”

19The Israelites replied:

“We will go along the main road, and if we or our livestock[p]
drink any of your water, we will pay for it.[q] We only want to
pass through on foot—nothing else.”

20Again they answered:

“You may not pass through.”

Then Edom came out against them with a large and powerful
army. 21Since Edom refused to let them go through their territory,
Israel turned away from them.[r]
22The whole Israelite community set out from Kadesh and came
to Mount Hor.[s] 23At Mount Hor, near the border of Edom,[t] the
LORD said to Moses and Aaron, 24“Aaron will be gathered to his

a 13 *Meribah* means *quarreling.*

20:10 [a] Ps 106:32,33

20:11 [b] Ex 17:6; Dt 8:15; Ps 78:16; Isa 48:2; 1Co 10:4

20:12 [c] Nu 27:14 [d] ver 24; Dt 1:37; 3:27

20:13 [e] Ex 17:7 [f] Dt 33:8; Ps 95:8; 106:32

20:14 [g] Jdg 11:16-17 [h] Dt 2:4 [i] Jos 2:11; 9:9

20:15 [j] Ge 46:6 [k] Ge 15:13; Ex 12:40 [l] Ex 1:11; Dt 26:6

20:16 [m] Ex 2:23; 3:7 [n] Ex 14:19

20:17 [o] Nu 21:22

20:19 [p] Ex 12:38 [q] Dt 2:6,28

20:21 [r] Dt 2:8; Jdg 11:18

20:22 [s] Nu 33:37

20:23 [t] Nu 33:37

people.[a] He will not enter the land I give the Israelites, because
both of you rebelled against my command[b] at the waters of
Meribah. [25]Get Aaron and his son Eleazar and take them up
Mount Hor.[c] [26]Remove Aaron's garments and put them on his
son Eleazar, for Aaron will be gathered to his people;[d] he will die
there."

[27]Moses did as the LORD commanded: They went up Mount Hor
in the sight of the whole community. [28]Moses removed Aaron's
garments and put them on his son Eleazar.[e] And Aaron died
there[f] on top of the mountain. Then Moses and Eleazar came
down from the mountain, [29]and when the whole community
learned that Aaron had died, the entire house of Israel mourned
for him[g] thirty days.

Chapter 21 Theme ______________________

21 When the Canaanite king of Arad,[h] who lived in the
Negev,[i] heard that Israel was coming along the road to
Atharim, he attacked the Israelites and captured some of them.
[2]Then Israel made this vow to the LORD: "If you will deliver these
people into our hands, we will totally destroy[a] their cities." [3]The
LORD listened to Israel's plea and gave the Canaanites over to
them. They completely destroyed them and their towns; so the
place was named Hormah.[b]

[4]They traveled from Mount Hor[j] along the route to the Red Sea,[c]
to go around Edom. But the people grew impatient on the way;[k]
[5]they spoke against God[l] and against Moses, and said, "Why have
you brought us up out of Egypt to die in the desert?[m] There is no
bread! There is no water! And we detest this miserable food!"[n]

[6]Then the LORD sent venomous snakes[o] among them; they bit
the people and many Israelites died.[p] [7]The people came to Moses[q]
and said, "We sinned when we spoke against the LORD and against
you. Pray that the LORD[r] will take the snakes away from us." So
Moses prayed[s] for the people.

[8]The LORD said to Moses, "Make a snake and put it up on a
pole;[t] anyone who is bitten can look at it and live." [9]So Moses
made a bronze snake[u] and put it up on a pole. Then when anyone
was bitten by a snake and looked at the bronze snake, he lived.[v]

[10]The Israelites moved on and camped at Oboth.[w] [11]Then they
set out from Oboth and camped in Iye Abarim, in the desert that
faces Moab[x] toward the sunrise. [12]From there they moved on
and camped in the Zered Valley.[y] [13]They set out from there and
camped alongside the Arnon[z], which is in the desert extending

20:24 [a]Ge 25:8 [b]ver 10
20:25 [c]Nu 33:38
20:26 [d]ver 24
20:28 [e]Ex 29:29 [f]Nu 33:38; Dt 10:6; 32:50
20:29 [g]Dt 34:8
21:1 [h]Nu 33:40; Jos 12:14 [i]Jdg 1:9,16
21:4 [j]Nu 20:22 [k]Dt 2:8; Jdg 11:18
21:5 [l]Ps 78:19 [m]Nu 14:2,3 [n]Nu 11:6
21:6 [o]Dt 8:15; Jer 8:17 [p]1Co 10:9
21:7 [q]Ps 78:34; Hos 5:15 [r]Ex 8:8; Ac 8:24 [s]Nu 11:2
21:8 [t]Jn 3:14
21:9 [u]2Ki 18:4 [v]Jn 3:14-15
21:10 [w]Nu 33:43
21:11 [x]Nu 33:44
21:12 [y]Dt 2:13,14
21:13 [z]Nu 22:36; Jdg 11:13,18

[a]*2* The Hebrew term refers to the irrevocable giving over of things or persons to the LORD, often by totally destroying them; also in verse 3. [b]*3* *Hormah* means *destruction.*
[c]*4* Hebrew *Yam Suph*; that is, Sea of Reeds

into Amorite territory. The Arnon is the border of Moab, between
Moab and the Amorites. 14That is why the Book of the Wars of the
LORD says:

> "...Waheb in Suphah[a] and the ravines,
> the Arnon 15and[b] the slopes of the ravines
> that lead to the site of Ar[a]
> and lie along the border of Moab."

16From there they continued on to Beer,[b] the well where the LORD
said to Moses, "Gather the people together and I will give them
water."
17Then Israel sang this song:[c]

> "Spring up, O well!
> Sing about it,
> 18about the well that the princes dug,
> that the nobles of the people sank—
> the nobles with scepters and staffs."

Then they went from the desert to Mattanah, 19from Mattanah to
Nahaliel, from Nahaliel to Bamoth, 20and from Bamoth to the valley in Moab where the top of Pisgah overlooks the wasteland.

21Israel sent messengers to say to Sihon[d] king of the Amorites:

> 22"Let us pass through your country. We will not turn aside into any field or vineyard, or drink water from any well. We will travel along the king's highway until we have passed through your territory.[e]"

23But Sihon would not let Israel pass through his territory.[f] He
mustered his entire army and marched out into the desert against
Israel. When he reached Jahaz,[g] he fought with Israel. 24Israel,
however, put him to the sword[h] and took over his land from the
Arnon to the Jabbok, but only as far as the Ammonites,[i] because
their border was fortified. 25Israel captured all the cities of the
Amorites[j] and occupied them, including Heshbon and all its
surrounding settlements. 26Heshbon was the city of Sihon[k] king
of the Amorites, who had fought against the former king of
Moab and had taken from him all his land as far as the Arnon.
27That is why the poets say:

> "Come to Heshbon and let it be rebuilt;
> let Sihon's city be restored.
>
> 28"Fire went out from Heshbon,
> a blaze from the city of Sihon.[l]

a *14* The meaning of the Hebrew for this phrase is uncertain. b *14,15* Or *"I have been given from Suphah and the ravines / of the Arnon* *15to*

21:15 [a] ver 28; Dt 2:9,18
21:16 [b] Jdg 9:21
21:17 [c] Ex 15:1
21:21 [d] Dt 1:4; 2:26-27; Jdg 11:19-21
21:22 [e] Nu 20:17
21:23 [f] Nu 20:21 [g] Dt 2:32; Jdg 11:20
21:24 [h] Dt 2:33; Ps 135:10-11; Am 2:9 [i] Dt 2:37
21:25 [j] Nu 13:29; Jdg 10:11; Am 2:10
21:26 [k] Dt 29:7; Ps 135:11
21:28 [l] Jer 48:45

It consumed Ar[a] of Moab,
the citizens of Arnon's heights.[b]
29 Woe to you, O Moab![c]
You are destroyed, O people of Chemosh![d]
He has given up his sons as fugitives[e]
and his daughters as captives[f]
to Sihon king of the Amorites.
30 "But we have overthrown them;
Heshbon is destroyed all the way to Dibon.[g]
We have demolished them as far as Nophah,
which extends to Medeba."

31 So Israel settled in the land of the Amorites.
32 After Moses had sent spies to Jazer,[h] the Israelites captured
its surrounding settlements and drove out the Amorites who
were there. 33 Then they turned and went up along the road
toward Bashan[i],[j] and Og king of Bashan and his whole army
marched out to meet them in battle at Edrei.[k]
34 The LORD said to Moses, "Do not be afraid of him, for I have
handed him over to you, with his whole army and his land. Do
to him what you did to Sihon king of the Amorites, who reigned
in Heshbon.[l]"
35 So they struck him down, together with his sons and his
whole army, leaving them no survivors. And they took possession of his land.

Chapter 22 Theme ______________________________

22 Then the Israelites traveled to the plains of Moab and
camped along the Jordan across from Jericho.[a][m]
2 Now Balak son of Zippor[n] saw all that Israel had done to the
Amorites, 3 and Moab was terrified because there were so many
people. Indeed, Moab was filled with dread[o] because of the
Israelites.
4 The Moabites said to the elders of Midian, "This horde is going
to lick up everything around us, as an ox licks up the grass of the
field."
So Balak son of Zippor, who was king of Moab at that time, 5 sent
messengers to summon Balaam son of Beor,[p] who was at Pethor,
near the River,[b] in his native land. Balak said:

"A people has come out of Egypt; they cover the face of the
land and have settled next to me. 6 Now come and put a curse[q]
on these people, because they are too powerful for me. Perhaps

21:28 [a]ver 15 [b]Nu 22:41; Isa 15:2
21:29 [c]Isa 25:10; Jer 48:46 [d]Jdg 11:24; 1Ki 11:7,33; 2Ki 23:13; Jer 48:7,46 [e]Isa 15:5 [f]Isa 16:2
21:30 [g]Nu 32:3; Isa 15:2; Jer 48:18,22
21:32 [h]Nu 32:1,3,35; Jer 48:32
21:33 [i]Dt 3:3 [j]Dt 3:4 [k]Dt 1:4; 3:1,10; Jos 13:12,31
21:34 [l]Dt 3:2
22:1 [m]Nu 33:48
22:2 [n]Jdg 11:25
22:3 [o]Ex 15:15
22:5 [p]Dt 23:4; Jos 13:22; 24:9; Ne 13:2; Mic 6:5; 2Pe 2:15
22:6 [q]ver 12,17; Nu 23:7,11,13

a *1* Hebrew *Jordan of Jericho*; possibly an ancient name for the Jordan River b *5* That is, the Euphrates

then I will be able to defeat them and drive them out of the
country. For I know that those you bless are blessed, and those
you curse are cursed."

7The elders of Moab and Midian left, taking with them the fee
for divination.[a] When they came to Balaam, they told him what
Balak had said.
8"Spend the night here," Balaam said to them, "and I will
bring you back the answer the LORD gives me.[b]" So the Moabite
princes stayed with him.
9God came to Balaam[c] and asked,[d] "Who are these men with
you?"
10Balaam said to God, "Balak son of Zippor, king of Moab, sent
me this message: 11'A people that has come out of Egypt covers
the face of the land. Now come and put a curse on them for me.
Perhaps then I will be able to fight them and drive them away.' "
12But God said to Balaam, "Do not go with them. You must not
put a curse on those people, because they are blessed.[e]"
13The next morning Balaam got up and said to Balak's princes,
"Go back to your own country, for the LORD has refused to let me
go with you."

INSIGHT

Midian was the son of Abraham by his wife Keturah (Genesis 25:2). Midian's descendants, the Midianites, took Joseph to Egypt (Genesis 37:28,36). After killing the Egyptian, Moses fled to Midian and there married the daughter of a priest.

The Lands of Israel's Journey from Mt. Hor to Moab

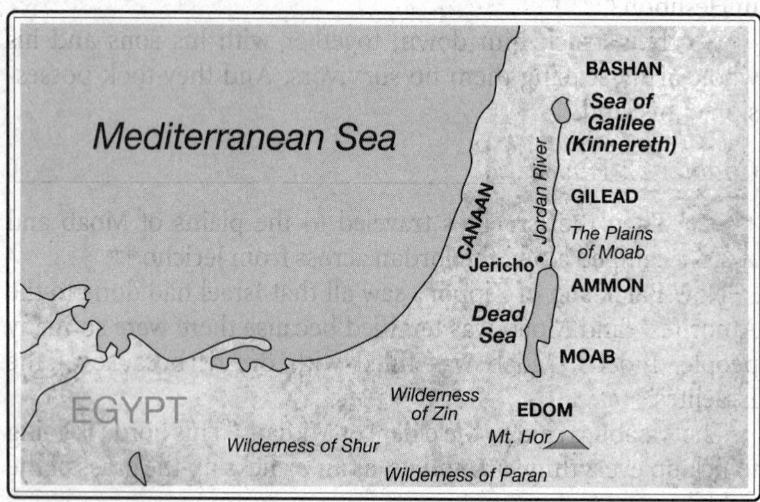

14So the Moabite princes returned to Balak and said, "Balaam
refused to come with us."
15Then Balak sent other princes, more numerous and more
distinguished than the first. 16They came to Balaam and said:

"This is what Balak son of Zippor says: Do not let anything
keep you from coming to me, 17because I will reward you
handsomely[f] and do whatever you say. Come and put a curse[g]
on these people for me."

22:7 [a] Nu 23:23; 24:1
22:8 [b] ver 19
22:9 [c] Ge 20:3 [d] ver 20
22:12 [e] Ge 12:2; 22:17; Nu 23:20
22:17 [f] ver 37; Nu 24:11 [g] ver 6

18 But Balaam answered them, "Even if Balak gave me his palace
filled with silver and gold, I could not do anything great or small
to go beyond the command of the LORD my God.[a] 19 Now stay
here tonight as the others did, and I will find out what else the
LORD will tell me.[b]"

20 That night God came to Balaam[c] and said, "Since these men
have come to summon you, go with them, but do only what I tell
you."[d]

21 Balaam got up in the morning, saddled his donkey and went
with the princes of Moab. 22 But God was very angry[e] when he
went, and the angel of the LORD[f] stood in the road to oppose
him. Balaam was riding on his donkey, and his two servants were
with him. 23 When the donkey saw the angel of the LORD standing
in the road with a drawn sword[g] in his hand, she turned off the
road into a field. Balaam beat her[h] to get her back on the road.

24 Then the angel of the LORD stood in a narrow path between
two vineyards, with walls on both sides. 25 When the donkey saw
the angel of the LORD, she pressed close to the wall, crushing Balaam's foot against it. So he beat her again.

26 Then the angel of the LORD moved on ahead and stood in a
narrow place where there was no room to turn, either to the
right or to the left. 27 When the donkey saw the angel of the LORD,
she lay down under Balaam, and he was angry[i] and beat her
with his staff. 28 Then the LORD opened the donkey's mouth,[j] and
she said to Balaam, "What have I done to you to make you beat
me these three times?[k]"

29 Balaam answered the donkey, "You have made a fool of me!
If I had a sword in my hand, I would kill you right now.[l]"

30 The donkey said to Balaam, "Am I not your own donkey,
which you have always ridden, to this day? Have I been in the
habit of doing this to you?"

"No," he said.

31 Then the LORD opened Balaam's eyes,[m] and he saw the angel
of the LORD standing in the road with his sword drawn. So he
bowed low and fell facedown.

32 The angel of the LORD asked him, "Why have you beaten
your donkey these three times? I have come here to oppose you
because your path is a reckless one before me.[a] 33 The donkey saw
me and turned away from me these three times. If she had not
turned away, I would certainly have killed you by now,[n] but I
would have spared her."

34 Balaam said to the angel of the LORD, "I have sinned.[o] I did not
realize you were standing in the road to oppose me. Now if you
are displeased, I will go back."

22:18 [a] ver 38; Nu 23:12,26; 24:13; 1Ki 22:14; 2Ch 18:13; Jer 42:4
22:19 [b] ver 8
22:20 [c] Ge 20:3 [d] ver 35,38; Nu 23:5,12,16,26; 24:13; 2Ch 18:13
22:22 [e] Ex 4:14 [f] Ge 16:7; Ex 23:20; Jdg 13:3,6,13
22:23 [g] Jos 5:13 [h] ver 25,27
22:27 [i] Nu 11:1; Jas 1:19
22:28 [j] 2Pe 2:16 [k] ver 32
22:29 [l] Dt 25:4; Pr 12:10; 27:23-27; Mt 15:19
22:31 [m] Ge 21:19
22:33 [n] ver 29
22:34 [o] Ge 39:9; Nu 14:40; 1Sa 15:24,30; 2Sa 12:13; 24:10; Job 33:27; Ps 51:4

a *32* The meaning of the Hebrew for this clause is uncertain.

35 The angel of the LORD said to Balaam, “Go with the men, but
speak only what I tell you.” So Balaam went with the princes of
Balak.

36 When Balak heard that Balaam was coming, he went out to
meet him at the Moabite town on the Arnon[a] border, at the edge
of his territory. 37 Balak said to Balaam, “Did I not send you an
urgent summons? Why didn’t you come to me? Am I really not
able to reward you?”

38 “Well, I have come to you now,” Balaam replied. “But can I say
just anything? I must speak only what God puts in my mouth.”[b]

39 Then Balaam went with Balak to Kiriath Huzoth. 40 Balak sacrificed cattle and sheep,[c] and gave some to Balaam and the princes
who were with him. 41 The next morning Balak took Balaam up
to Bamoth Baal,[d] and from there he saw part of the people.[e]

Chapter 23 Theme ________________________________

23 Balaam said, “Build me seven altars here, and prepare sev-
en bulls and seven rams[f] for me.” 2 Balak did as Balaam
said, and the two of them offered a bull and a ram on each altar.[g]

3 Then Balaam said to Balak, “Stay here beside your offering
while I go aside. Perhaps the LORD will come to meet with me.[h]
Whatever he reveals to me I will tell you.” Then he went off to a
barren height.

4 God met with him,[i] and Balaam said, “I have prepared seven
altars, and on each altar I have offered a bull and a ram.”

5 The LORD put a message in Balaam’s mouth[j] and said, “Go
back to Balak and give him this message.”[k]

6 So he went back to him and found him standing beside his
offering, with all the princes of Moab.[l] 7 Then Balaam[m] uttered
his oracle:[n]

“Balak brought me from Aram,
    the king of Moab from the eastern mountains.
‘Come,’ he said, ‘curse Jacob for me;
    come, denounce Israel.’[o]
8 How can I curse
    those whom God has not cursed?[p]
How can I denounce
    those whom the LORD has not denounced?
9 From the rocky peaks I see them,
    from the heights I view them.
I see a people who live apart
    and do not consider themselves one of the nations.[q]
10 Who can count the dust of Jacob[r]
    or number the fourth part of Israel?

22:36 [a] Nu 21:13
22:38 [b] Nu 23:5,16, 26
22:40 [c] Nu 23:1,14, 29; Eze 45:23
22:41 [d] Nu 21:28 [e] Nu 23:13
23:1 [f] Nu 22:40
23:2 [g] ver 14,30
23:3 [h] ver 15
23:4 [i] ver 16
23:5 [j] Dt 18:18; Jer 1:9 [k] Nu 22:20
23:6 [l] ver 17
23:7 [m] Nu 22:5 [n] ver 18; Nu 24:3,21 [o] Nu 22:6; Dt 23:4
23:8 [p] Nu 22:12
23:9 [q] Ex 33:16; Dt 32:8; 33:28
23:10 [r] Ge 13:16

Let me die the death of the righteous,[a]
and may my end be like theirs![b]"

11 Balak said to Balaam, "What have you done to me? I brought
you to curse my enemies, but you have done nothing but bless
them!"[c]
12 He answered, "Must I not speak what the LORD puts in my
mouth?"[d]
13 Then Balak said to him, "Come with me to another place
where you can see them; you will see only a part but not all of
them. And from there, curse them for me." 14 So he took him to
the field of Zophim on the top of Pisgah, and there he built sev-
en altars and offered a bull and a ram on each altar.[e]
15 Balaam said to Balak, "Stay here beside your offering while I
meet with him over there."
16 The LORD met with Balaam and put a message in his mouth[f]
and said, "Go back to Balak and give him this message."
17 So he went to him and found him standing beside his offering, with the princes of Moab. Balak asked him, "What did the
LORD say?"
18 Then he uttered his oracle:

"Arise, Balak, and listen;
hear me, son of Zippor.
19 God is not a man,[g] that he should lie,
nor a son of man, that he should change his mind.[h]
Does he speak and then not act?
Does he promise and not fulfill?
20 I have received a command to bless;
he has blessed,[i] and I cannot change it.[j]

21 "No misfortune is seen in Jacob,[k]
no misery observed in Israel.[a][l]
The LORD their God is with them;[m]
the shout of the King[n] is among them.
22 God brought them out of Egypt;[o]
they have the strength of a wild ox.[p]
23 There is no sorcery against Jacob,
no divination[q] against Israel.
It will now be said of Jacob
and of Israel, 'See what God has done!'
24 The people rise like a lioness;[r]
they rouse themselves like a lion[s]
that does not rest till he devours his prey
and drinks the blood of his victims."

23:10 [a] Ps 116:15; Isa 57:1 [b] Ps 37:37
23:11 [c] Nu 24:10; Ne 13:2
23:12 [d] Nu 22:20,38
23:14 [e] ver 2
23:16 [f] Nu 22:38
23:19 [g] Isa 55:9; Hos 11:9 [h] 1Sa 15:29; Mal 3:6; Tit 1:2; Jas 1:17
23:20 [i] Ge 22:17; Nu 22:12 [j] Isa 43:13
23:21 [k] Ps 32:2,5; Ro 4:7-8 [l] Isa 40:2; Jer 50:20 [m] Ex 29:45,46; Ps 145:18 [n] Dt 33:5; Ps 89:15-18
23:22 [o] Nu 24:8 [p] Dt 33:17; Job 39:9
23:23 [q] Nu 24:1; Jos 13:22
23:24 [r] Na 2:11 [s] Ge 49:9

a *21* Or *He has not looked on Jacob's offenses / or on the wrongs found in Israel.*

25 Then Balak said to Balaam, "Neither curse them at all nor
bless them at all!"
26 Balaam answered, "Did I not tell you I must do whatever the
LORD says?"
27 Then Balak said to Balaam, "Come, let me take you to another
place.[a] Perhaps it will please God to let you curse them for me
from there." 28 And Balak took Balaam to the top of Peor,[b] overlooking the wasteland.
29 Balaam said, "Build me seven altars here, and prepare seven
bulls and seven rams for me." 30 Balak did as Balaam had said, and
offered a bull and a ram on each altar.

Chapter 24 Theme ______________________________

24 Now when Balaam saw that it pleased the LORD to bless
Israel, he did not resort to sorcery[c] as at other times, but
turned his face toward the desert.[d] 2 When Balaam looked out and
saw Israel encamped tribe by tribe, the Spirit of God came upon
him[e] 3 and he uttered his oracle:

"The oracle of Balaam son of Beor,
 the oracle of one whose eye sees clearly,
4 the oracle of one who hears the words of God,[f]
 who sees a vision from the Almighty,[a][g]
 who falls prostrate, and whose eyes are opened:

5 "How beautiful are your tents, O Jacob,
 your dwelling places, O Israel!

6 "Like valleys they spread out,
 like gardens beside a river,
like aloes[h] planted by the LORD,
 like cedars beside the waters.[i]
7 Water will flow from their buckets;
 their seed will have abundant water.

"Their king will be greater than Agag;[j]
 their kingdom will be exalted.[k]

8 "God brought them out of Egypt;
 they have the strength of a wild ox.
They devour hostile nations
 and break their bones in pieces;[l]
 with their arrows they pierce them.[m]
9 Like a lion they crouch and lie down,
 like a lioness[n]—who dares to rouse them?

"May those who bless you be blessed
 and those who curse you be cursed!"[o]

a 4 Hebrew *Shaddai*; also in verse 16

23:27 [a] ver 13
23:28 [b] Ps 106:28
24:1 [c] Nu 23:23 [d] Nu 23:28
24:2 [e] Nu 11:25,26; 1Sa 10:10; 19:20; 2Ch 15:1
24:4 [f] Nu 22:20 [g] Ge 15:1
24:6 [h] Ps 45:8 [i] Ps 1:3; 104:16
24:7 [j] 1Sa 15:8 [k] 2Sa 5:12; 1Ch 14:2; Ps 145:11-13
24:8 [l] Ps 2:9; Jer 50:17 [m] Ps 45:5
24:9 [n] Ge 49:9; Nu 23:24 [o] Ge 12:3

10Then Balak's anger burned against Balaam. He struck his
hands together[a] and said to him, "I summoned you to curse my
enemies, but you have blessed them[b] these three times.[c] 11Now
leave at once and go home! I said I would reward you handsomely,[d] but the LORD has kept you from being rewarded."
12Balaam answered Balak, "Did I not tell the messengers you
sent me,[e] 13'Even if Balak gave me his palace filled with silver and
gold, I could not do anything of my own accord, good or bad, to
go beyond the command of the LORD[f]—and I must say only
what the LORD says'?[g] 14Now I am going back to my people, but
come, let me warn you of what this people will do to your people
in days to come."[h]
15Then he uttered his oracle:

"The oracle of Balaam son of Beor,
  the oracle of one whose eye sees clearly,
16the oracle of one who hears the words of God,
  who has knowledge from the Most High,
who sees a vision from the Almighty,
  who falls prostrate, and whose eyes
    are opened:

17"I see him, but not now;
  I behold him, but not near.[i]
A star will come out of Jacob;[j]
  a scepter will rise out of Israel.[k]
He will crush the foreheads of Moab,[l]
  the skulls[a] of[b] all the sons of Sheth.[c]
18Edom[m] will be conquered;
  Seir, his enemy, will be conquered,
  but Israel will grow strong.
19A ruler will come out of Jacob[n]
  and destroy the survivors of the city."

20Then Balaam saw Amalek[o] and uttered his oracle:

"Amalek was first among the nations,
  but he will come to ruin at last."

21Then he saw the Kenites[p] and uttered his oracle:

"Your dwelling place is secure,
  your nest is set in a rock;
22yet you Kenites will be destroyed
  when Asshur[q] takes you captive."

24:10 [a]Eze 21:14 [b]Nu 23:11 [c]Ne 13:2
24:11 [d]Nu 22:17
24:12 [e]Nu 22:18
24:13 [f]Nu 22:18 [g]Nu 22:20
24:14 [h]Ge 49:1; Nu 31:8,16; Da 2:28; Mic 6:5
24:17 [i]Rev 1:7 [j]Mt 2:2 [k]Ge 49:10 [l]Nu 21:29; Isa 15:1–16:14
24:18 [m]Am 9:12
24:19 [n]Ge 49:10; Mic 5:2
24:20 [o]Ex 17:14
24:21 [p]Ge 15:19
24:22 [q]Ge 10:22

[a] *17* Samaritan Pentateuch (see also Jer. 48:45); the meaning of the word in the Masoretic Text is uncertain. [b] *17* Or possibly *Moab, / batter* [c] *17* Or *all the noisy boasters*

23 Then he uttered his oracle:

> "Ah, who can live when God does this?[a]
> 24 Ships will come from the shores of Kittim;[a]
> they will subdue Asshur and Eber,[b]
> but they too will come to ruin.[c]"

25 Then Balaam[d] got up and returned home and Balak went his
own way.

Chapter 25 Theme

25 While Israel was staying in Shittim,[e] the men began to
indulge in sexual immorality[f] with Moabite women,[g] 2 who
invited them to the sacrifices[h] to their gods.[i] The people ate and
bowed down before these gods. 3 So Israel joined in worshiping
the Baal of Peor.[j] And the LORD's anger burned against them.
4 The LORD said to Moses, "Take all the leaders of these people,
kill them and expose them in broad daylight before the LORD,[k] so
that the LORD's fierce anger[l] may turn away from Israel."
5 So Moses said to Israel's judges, "Each of you must put to
death[m] those of your men who have joined in worshiping the Baal
of Peor."
6 Then an Israelite man brought to his family a Midianite
woman right before the eyes of Moses and the whole assembly of
Israel while they were weeping at the entrance to the Tent of Meeting. 7 When Phinehas son of Eleazar, the son of Aaron, the priest,
saw this, he left the assembly, took a spear in his hand 8 and followed the Israelite into the tent. He drove the spear through both
of them—through the Israelite and into the woman's body. Then
the plague against the Israelites was stopped;[n] 9 but those who died
in the plague[o] numbered 24,000.[p]
10 The LORD said to Moses, 11 "Phinehas son of Eleazar, the son of
Aaron, the priest, has turned my anger away from the Israelites;[q]
for he was as zealous as I am for my honor[r] among them, so that
in my zeal I did not put an end to them. 12 Therefore tell him I am
making my covenant of peace[s] with him. 13 He and his descendants will have a covenant of a lasting priesthood,[t] because he
was zealous for the honor of his God and made atonement[u] for
the Israelites."
14 The name of the Israelite who was killed with the Midianite
woman was Zimri son of Salu, the leader of a Simeonite family.
15 And the name of the Midianite woman who was put to death
was Cozbi[v] daughter of Zur, a tribal chief of a Midianite family.[w]

a 23 Masoretic Text; with a different word division of the Hebrew *A people will gather from the north.*

24:24 [a] Ge 10:4 [b] Ge 10:21 [c] ver 20

24:25 [d] Nu 31:8

25:1 [e] Jos 2:1; Mic 6:5 [f] 1Co 10:8; Rev 2:14 [g] Nu 31:16

25:2 [h] Ex 34:15 [i] Ex 20:5; Dt 32:38; 1Co 10:20

25:3 [j] Ps 106:28; Hos 9:10

25:4 [k] Dt 4:3 [l] Dt 13:17

25:5 [m] Ex 32:27

25:8 [n] Nu 16:46-48; Ps 106:30

25:9 [o] Nu 14:37; 1Co 10:8 [p] Nu 31:16

25:11 [q] Ps 106:30 [r] Ex 20:5; Dt 32:16,21; Ps 78:58

25:12 [s] Isa 54:10; Eze 34:25; Mal 2:4,5

25:13 [t] Ex 29:9 [u] Nu 16:46

25:15 [v] ver 18 [w] Nu 31:8; Jos 13:21

16The LORD said to Moses, 17"Treat the Midianites[a] as enemies and kill them, 18because they treated you as enemies when they deceived you in the affair of Peor[b] and their sister Cozbi, the daughter of a Midianite leader, the woman who was killed when the plague came as a result of Peor."

Chapter 26 Theme ______________________

26 After the plague the LORD said to Moses and Eleazar son of Aaron, the priest, 2"Take a census[c] of the whole Israelite community by families—all those twenty years old or more who are able to serve in the army[d] of Israel." 3So on the plains of Moab[e] by the Jordan across from Jericho,[a][f] Moses and Eleazar the priest spoke with them and said, 4"Take a census of the men twenty years old or more, as the LORD commanded Moses."

These were the Israelites who came out of Egypt:

5The descendants of Reuben, the firstborn son of Israel, were:
through Hanoch,[g] the Hanochite clan;
through Pallu,[h] the Palluite clan;
6through Hezron, the Hezronite clan;
through Carmi, the Carmite clan.
7These were the clans of Reuben; those numbered were 43,730.

8The son of Pallu was Eliab, 9and the sons of Eliab[i] were Nemuel, Dathan and Abiram. The same Dathan and Abiram were the community[j] officials who rebelled against Moses and Aaron and were among Korah's followers when they rebelled against the LORD.[k] 10The earth opened its mouth and swallowed them along with Korah, whose followers died when the fire devoured the 250 men. And they served as a warning sign.[l] 11The line of Korah,[m] however, did not die out.[n]

12The descendants of Simeon by their clans were:
through Nemuel, the Nemuelite clan;
through Jamin,[o] the Jaminite clan;
through Jakin, the Jakinite clan;
13through Zerah,[p] the Zerahite clan;
through Shaul, the Shaulite clan.
14These were the clans of Simeon; there were 22,200 men.[q]

15The descendants of Gad by their clans were:
through Zephon,[r] the Zephonite clan;
through Haggi, the Haggite clan;
through Shuni, the Shunite clan;
16through Ozni, the Oznite clan;
through Eri, the Erite clan;

25:17 [a]Nu 31:1-3
25:18 [b]Nu 31:16
26:2 [c]Ex 30:11-16; 38:25-26; Nu 1:2 [d]Nu 1:3
26:3 [e]Nu 33:48 [f]Nu 22:1
26:5 [g]Ge 46:9 [h]1Ch 5:3
26:9 [i]Nu 16:1 [j]Nu 1:16 [k]Nu 16:2
26:10 [l]Nu 16:35,38
26:11 [m]Ex 6:24 [n]Nu 16:33; Dt 24:16
26:12 [o]1Ch 4:24
26:13 [p]Ge 46:10
26:14 [q]Nu 1:23
26:15 [r]Ge 46:16

a3 Hebrew *Jordan of Jericho*; possibly an ancient name for the Jordan River; also in verse 63

[17]through Arodi,[a] the Arodite clan;
through Areli, the Arelite clan.
[18]These were the clans of Gad;[a] those numbered were 40,500.
[19]Er and Onan were sons of Judah, but they died[b] in Canaan.
[20]The descendants of Judah by their clans were:
through Shelah,[c] the Shelanite clan;
through Perez, the Perezite clan;
through Zerah, the Zerahite clan.[d]
[21]The descendants of Perez were:
through Hezron,[e] the Hezronite clan;
through Hamul, the Hamulite clan.
[22]These were the clans of Judah;[f] those numbered were 76,500.

[23]The descendants of Issachar by their clans were:
through Tola,[g] the Tolaite clan;
through Puah, the Puite[b] clan;
[24]through Jashub,[h] the Jashubite clan;
through Shimron, the Shimronite clan.
[25]These were the clans of Issachar;[i] those numbered were 64,300.

[26]The descendants of Zebulun by their clans were:
through Sered, the Seredite clan;
through Elon, the Elonite clan;
through Jahleel, the Jahleelite clan.
[27]These were the clans of Zebulun;[j] those numbered were 60,500.

[28]The descendants of Joseph by their clans through Manasseh and Ephraim were:
[29]The descendants of Manasseh:
through Makir,[k] the Makirite clan (Makir was the father of Gilead[l]);
through Gilead, the Gileadite clan.
[30]These were the descendants of Gilead:
through Iezer,[m] the Iezerite clan;
through Helek, the Helekite clan;
[31]through Asriel, the Asrielite clan;
through Shechem, the Shechemite clan;
[32]through Shemida, the Shemidaite clan;
through Hepher, the Hepherite clan.
[33](Zelophehad[n] son of Hepher had no sons; he had only daughters, whose names were Mahlah, Noah, Hoglah, Milcah and Tirzah.)[o]

a *17* Samaritan Pentateuch and Syriac (see also Gen. 46:16); Masoretic Text *Arod*
b *23* Samaritan Pentateuch, Septuagint, Vulgate and Syriac (see also 1 Chron. 7:1); Masoretic Text *through Puvah, the Punite*

26:18 [a] Nu 1:25; Jos 13:24-28
26:19 [b] Ge 38:2-10; 46:12
26:20 [c] 1Ch 2:3 [d] Jos 7:17
26:21 [e] Ru 4:19; 1Ch 2:9
26:22 [f] Nu 1:27
26:23 [g] Ge 46:13; 1Ch 7:1
26:24 [h] Ge 46:13
26:25 [i] Nu 1:29
26:27 [j] Nu 1:31
26:29 [k] Jos 17:1 [l] Jdg 11:1
26:30 [m] Jos 17:2; Jdg 6:11
26:33 [n] Nu 27:1 [o] Nu 36:11

26:34 [a] Nu 1:35

34 These were the clans of Manasseh; those numbered were 52,700.[a]

35 These were the descendants of Ephraim by their clans:
through Shuthelah, the Shuthelahite clan;
through Beker, the Bekerite clan;
through Tahan, the Tahanite clan.

26:37 [b] Nu 1:33

36 These were the descendants of Shuthelah:
through Eran, the Eranite clan.
37 These were the clans of Ephraim;[b] those numbered were 32,500.

These were the descendants of Joseph by their clans.

26:38 [c] Ge 46:21; 1Ch 7:6

38 The descendants of Benjamin[c] by their clans were:
through Bela, the Belaite clan;
through Ashbel, the Ashbelite clan;
through Ahiram, the Ahiramite clan;
39 through Shupham,[a] the Shuphamite clan;
through Hupham, the Huphamite clan.

26:40 [d] Ge 46:21; 1Ch 8:3

40 The descendants of Bela through Ard[d] and Naaman were:
through Ard,[b] the Ardite clan;
through Naaman, the Naamite clan.
41 These were the clans of Benjamin;[e] those numbered were 45,600.

26:41 [e] Nu 1:37

42 These were the descendants of Dan by their clans:
through Shuham,[f] the Shuhamite clan.
These were the clans of Dan: 43 All of them were Shuhamite clans;
and those numbered were 64,400.

26:42 [f] Ge 46:23

44 The descendants of Asher by their clans were:
through Imnah, the Imnite clan;
through Ishvi, the Ishvite clan;
through Beriah, the Beriite clan;
45 and through the descendants of Beriah:
through Heber, the Heberite clan;
through Malkiel, the Malkielite clan.

26:47 [g] Nu 1:41

46 (Asher had a daughter named Serah.)
47 These were the clans of Asher;[g] those numbered were 53,400.

26:48 [h] Ge 46:24; 1Ch 7:13

48 The descendants of Naphtali[h] by their clans were:
through Jahzeel, the Jahzeelite clan;
through Guni, the Gunite clan;
49 through Jezer, the Jezerite clan;
through Shillem, the Shillemite clan.
50 These were the clans of Naphtali;[i] those numbered were 45,400.

26:50 [i] Nu 1:43

a *39* A few manuscripts of the Masoretic Text, Samaritan Pentateuch, Vulgate and Syriac (see also Septuagint); most manuscripts of the Masoretic Text *Shephupham*
b *40* Samaritan Pentateuch and Vulgate (see also Septuagint); Masoretic Text does not have *through Ard*.

51The total number of the men of Israel was 601,730.[a]

52The LORD said to Moses, 53"The land is to be allotted to them
as an inheritance based on the number of names.[b] 54To a larger
group give a larger inheritance, and to a smaller group a smaller
one; each is to receive its inheritance according to the number[c] of
those listed. 55Be sure that the land is distributed by lot.[d] What
each group inherits will be according to the names for its ancestral tribe. 56Each inheritance is to be distributed by lot among the
larger and smaller groups."

57These were the Levites[e] who were counted by their clans:
through Gershon, the Gershonite clan;
through Kohath, the Kohathite clan;
through Merari, the Merarite clan.
58These also were Levite clans:
the Libnite clan,
the Hebronite clan,
the Mahlite clan,
the Mushite clan,
the Korahite clan.
(Kohath was the forefather of Amram;[f] 59the name of
Amram's wife was Jochebed,[g] a descendant of Levi, who was
born to the Levites[a] in Egypt. To Amram she bore Aaron,
Moses[h] and their sister Miriam. 60Aaron was the father of
Nadab and Abihu, Eleazar and Ithamar.[i] 61But Nadab and
Abihu[j] died when they made an offering before the LORD with
unauthorized fire.)[k]

62All the male Levites a month old or more numbered 23,000.[l]
They were not counted[m] along with the other Israelites because
they received no inheritance[n] among them.[o]

63These are the ones counted by Moses and Eleazar the priest
when they counted the Israelites on the plains of Moab[p] by the
Jordan across from Jericho. 64Not one of them was among those
counted[q] by Moses and Aaron the priest when they counted the
Israelites in the Desert of Sinai. 65For the LORD had told those
Israelites they would surely die in the desert,[r] and not one of them
was left except Caleb son of Jephunneh and Joshua son of Nun.[s]

Chapter 27 Theme ______________________

27 The daughters of Zelophehad[t] son of Hepher,[u] the son of
Gilead, the son of Makir,[v] the son of Manasseh, belonged
to the clans of Manasseh son of Joseph. The names of the daughters were Mahlah, Noah, Hoglah, Milcah and Tirzah. They approached 2the entrance to the Tent of Meeting and stood before

a59 Or *Jochebed, a daughter of Levi, who was born to Levi*

26:51 [a] Ex 12:37; 38:26; Nu 1:46; 11:21
26:53 [b] Jos 11:23; 14:1; Eze 45:8
26:54 [c] Nu 33:54
26:55 [d] Nu 34:14
26:57 [e] Ge 46:11; Ex 6:16-19
26:58 [f] Ex 6:20
26:59 [g] Ex 2:1 [h] Ex 6:20
26:60 [i] Nu 3:2
26:61 [j] Lev 10:1-2 [k] Nu 3:4
26:62 [l] Nu 3:39 [m] Nu 1:47 [n] Nu 18:23 [o] Nu 2:33; Dt 10:9
26:63 [p] ver 3
26:64 [q] Nu 14:29; Dt 2:14-15; Heb 3:17
26:65 [r] Nu 14:28; 1Co 10:5 [s] Jos 14:6-10
27:1 [t] Nu 26:33 [u] Jos 17:2,3 [v] Nu 36:1

Moses, Eleazar the priest, the leaders and the whole assembly, and
said, 3"Our father died in the desert.[a] He was not among Korah's
followers, who banded together against the LORD,[b] but he died for
his own sin and left no sons.[c] 4Why should our father's name disappear from his clan because he had no son? Give us property
among our father's relatives."

5So Moses brought their case[d] before the LORD[e] 6and the LORD
said to him, 7"What Zelophehad's daughters are saying is right.
You must certainly give them property as an inheritance[f] among
their father's relatives and turn their father's inheritance over to
them.[g]

8"Say to the Israelites, 'If a man dies and leaves no son, turn his
inheritance over to his daughter. 9If he has no daughter, give his
inheritance to his brothers. 10If he has no brothers, give his inheritance to his father's brothers. 11If his father had no brothers, give his
inheritance to the nearest relative in his clan, that he may possess it.
This is to be a legal requirement[h] for the Israelites, as the LORD commanded Moses.' "

12Then the LORD said to Moses, "Go up this mountain in the
Abarim range[i] and see the land[j] I have given the Israelites. 13After
you have seen it, you too will be gathered to your people,[k] as your
brother Aaron[l] was, 14for when the community rebelled at the
waters in the Desert of Zin, both of you disobeyed my command
to honor me as holy[m] before their eyes." (These were the waters
of Meribah[n] Kadesh, in the Desert of Zin.)

15Moses said to the LORD, 16"May the LORD, the God of the spirits
of all mankind,[o] appoint a man over this community 17to go out
and come in before them, one who will lead them out and bring
them in, so the LORD's people will not be like sheep without a
shepherd."[p]

18So the LORD said to Moses, "Take Joshua son of Nun, a man
in whom is the spirit,[a][q] and lay your hand on him.[r] 19Have him
stand before Eleazar the priest and the entire assembly and
commission him[s] in their presence.[t] 20Give him some of your
authority so the whole Israelite community will obey him.[u] 21He
is to stand before Eleazar the priest, who will obtain decisions
for him by inquiring[v] of the Urim[w] before the LORD. At his command he and the entire community of the Israelites will go out,
and at his command they will come in."

22Moses did as the LORD commanded him. He took Joshua and
had him stand before Eleazar the priest and the whole assembly.
23Then he laid his hands on him and commissioned him, as the
LORD instructed through Moses.

27:3 [a]Nu 26:65 [b]Nu 16:2 [c]Nu 26:33
27:5 [d]Ex 18:19 [e]Nu 9:8
27:7 [f]Job 42:15 [g]Jos 17:4
27:11 [h]Nu 35:29
27:12 [i]Nu 33:47; Jer 22:20 [j]Dt 3:23-27; 32:48-52
27:13 [k]Nu 31:2 [l]Nu 20:28
27:14 [m]Nu 20:12 [n]Ex 17:7; Dt 32:51; Ps 106:32
27:16 [o]Nu 16:22
27:17 [p]Dt 31:2; 1Ki 22:17; Eze 34:5; Zec 10:2; Mt 9:36; Mk 6:34
27:18 [q]Ge 41:38; Nu 11:25-29 [r]ver 23; Dt 34:9
27:19 [s]Dt 3:28; 31:14,23 [t]Dt 31:7
27:20 [u]Jos 1:16,17
27:21 [v]Jos 9:14 [w]Ex 28:30

a *18* Or *Spirit*

Chapter 28 Theme ______________________________

28 The LORD said to Moses, 2“Give this command to the
Israelites and say to them: ‘See that you present to me at
the appointed time the food[a] for my offerings made by fire, as an
aroma pleasing to me.’ 3Say to them: ‘This is the offering made
by fire that you are to present to the LORD: two lambs a year old
without defect, as a regular burnt offering each day.[b] 4Prepare
one lamb in the morning and the other at twilight, 5together
with a grain offering of a tenth of an ephah[a] of fine flour mixed
with a quarter of a hin[b] of oil[c] from pressed olives. 6This is the
regular burnt offering instituted at Mount Sinai[d] as a pleasing
aroma, an offering made to the LORD by fire. 7The accompany-
ing drink offering[e] is to be a quarter of a hin of fermented drink
with each lamb. Pour out the drink offering to the LORD at the
sanctuary.[f] 8Prepare the second lamb at twilight, along with the
same kind of grain offering and drink offering that you prepare in
the morning. This is an offering made by fire, an aroma pleasing
to the LORD.[g]

9“ ‘On the Sabbath[h] day, make an offering of two lambs a year
old without defect, together with its drink offering and a grain
offering of two-tenths of an ephah[c][i] of fine flour mixed with oil.
10This is the burnt offering for every Sabbath, in addition to the
regular burnt offering[j] and its drink offering.

11“ ‘On the first of every month,[k] present to the LORD a burnt
offering of two young bulls, one ram and seven male lambs a year
old, all without defect.[l] 12With each bull there is to be a grain
offering[m] of three-tenths of an ephah[d][n] of fine flour mixed with
oil; with the ram, a grain offering of two-tenths of an ephah of
fine flour mixed with oil; 13and with each lamb, a grain offering[o]
of a tenth of an ephah of fine flour mixed with oil. This is for a
burnt offering, a pleasing aroma, an offering made to the LORD
by fire. 14With each bull there is to be a drink offering[p] of half a
hin[e] of wine; with the ram, a third of a hin[f]; and with each lamb,
a quarter of a hin. This is the monthly burnt offering to be made
at each new moon[q] during the year. 15Besides the regular burnt
offering[r] with its drink offering, one male goat is to be presented
to the LORD as a sin offering.[s]

16“ ‘On the fourteenth day of the first month the LORD’s Passover[t] is to be held. 17On the fifteenth day of this month there is to
be a festival; for seven days[u] eat bread made without yeast.[v] 18On

[a] *5* That is, probably about 2 quarts (about 2 liters); also in verses 13, 21 and 29 [b] *5* That is, probably about 1 quart (about 1 liter); also in verses 7 and 14 [c] *9* That is, probably about 4 quarts (about 4.5 liters); also in verses 12, 20 and 28 [d] *12* That is, probably about 6 quarts (about 6.5 liters); also in verses 20 and 28 [e] *14* That is, probably about 2 quarts (about 2 liters) [f] *14* That is, probably about 1 1/4 quarts (about 1.2 liters)

28:2 [a] Lev 3:11
28:3 [b] Ex 29:38
28:5 [c] Lev 2:1; Nu 15:4
28:6 [d] Ex 19:3
28:7 [e] Ex 29:41 [f] Lev 3:7
28:8 [g] Lev 1:9
28:9 [h] Ex 20:10 [i] Lev 23:13
28:10 [j] ver 3
28:11 [k] Nu 10:10 [l] Lev 1:3
28:12 [m] Nu 15:6 [n] Nu 15:9
28:13 [o] Lev 6:14
28:14 [p] Nu 15:7 [q] Ezr 3:5
28:15 [r] ver 3,23,24 [s] Lev 4:3
28:16 [t] Ex 12:6,18; Lev 23:5; Dt 16:1
28:17 [u] Ex 12:19 [v] Ex 23:15; 34:18; Lev 23:6; Dt 16:3-8

28:18 the first day hold a sacred assembly and do no regular work.[a]
a Ex 12:16; 19 Present to the LORD an offering made by fire, a burnt offering
Lev 23:7 of two young bulls, one ram and seven male lambs a year old, all
without defect. 20 With each bull prepare a grain offering of three-
28:20 tenths of an ephah[b] of fine flour mixed with oil; with the ram,
b Lev 14:10 two-tenths; 21 and with each of the seven lambs, one-tenth.
22 Include one male goat as a sin offering[c] to make atonement for
you.[d] 23 Prepare these in addition to the regular morning burnt
28:22 offering. 24 In this way prepare the food for the offering made by
c Ro 8:3; d Nu 15:28 fire every day for seven days as an aroma pleasing to the LORD; it
is to be prepared in addition to the regular burnt offering and its
drink offering. 25 On the seventh day hold a sacred assembly and
28:26 do no regular work.
e Ex 34:22; f Ex 23:16 26 " 'On the day of firstfruits,[e] when you present to the LORD an
g ver 18; offering of new grain during the Feast of Weeks,[f] hold a sacred
Dt 16:10 assembly and do no regular work.[g] 27 Present a burnt offering of
two young bulls, one ram and seven male lambs a year old as an
aroma pleasing to the LORD. 28 With each bull there is to be a grain
28:29 offering of three-tenths of an ephah of fine flour mixed with oil;
h ver 13 with the ram, two-tenths; 29 and with each of the seven lambs,
one-tenth.[h] 30 Include one male goat to make atonement for you.
31 Prepare these together with their drink offerings, in addition
28:31 i ver 3,19 to the regular burnt offering[i] and its grain offering. Be sure the
animals are without defect.

Chapter 29 Theme

29:1 j Lev 23:24 **29** " 'On the first day of the seventh month hold a sacred assembly and do no regular work.[j] It is a day for you to
sound the trumpets. 2 As an aroma pleasing to the LORD,[k] prepare
29:2 k Nu 28:2 a burnt offering of one young bull, one ram and seven male
l Nu 28:3 lambs a year old, all without defect.[l] 3 With the bull prepare a
grain offering of three-tenths of an ephah[a] of fine flour mixed
with oil; with the ram, two-tenths[b]; 4 and with each of the seven
29:5 lambs, one-tenth.[c] 5 Include one male goat[m] as a sin offering to
m Nu 28:15 make atonement for you. 6 These are in addition to the monthly[n]
and daily burnt offerings[o] with their grain offerings and drink
offerings as specified. They are offerings made to the LORD by
29:6 n Nu 28:11 fire—a pleasing aroma.
o Nu 28:3 7 " 'On the tenth day of this seventh month hold a sacred assembly. You must deny yourselves[d][p] and do no work.[q] 8 Present as an
aroma pleasing to the LORD a burnt offering of one young bull,
29:7 one ram and seven male lambs a year old, all without defect.

p Ac 27:9; q Ex 31:15; Lev 16:29; 23:26-32

[a] 3 That is, probably about 6 quarts (about 6.5 liters); also in verses 9 and 14 [b] 3 That is, probably about 4 quarts (about 4.5 liters); also in verses 9 and 14 [c] 4 That is, probably about 2 quarts (about 2 liters); also in verses 10 and 15 [d] 7 Or *must fast*

9 With the bull prepare a grain offering[a] of three-tenths of an ephah of fine flour mixed with oil; with the ram, two-tenths; 10 and with each of the seven lambs, one-tenth.[b] 11 Include one male goat as a sin offering, in addition to the sin offering for atonement and the regular burnt offering[c] with its grain offering, and their drink offerings.

12 " 'On the fifteenth day of the seventh[d] month,[e] hold a sacred assembly and do no regular work. Celebrate a festival to the LORD for seven days. 13 Present an offering made by fire as an aroma pleasing to the LORD, a burnt offering of thirteen young bulls, two rams and fourteen male lambs a year old, all without defect. 14 With each of the thirteen bulls prepare a grain offering[f] of three-tenths of an ephah of fine flour mixed with oil; with each of the two rams, two-tenths; 15 and with each of the fourteen lambs, one-tenth. 16 Include one male goat as a sin offering, in addition to the regular burnt offering with its grain offering and drink offering.[g]

17 " 'On the second day[h] prepare twelve young bulls, two rams and fourteen male lambs a year old, all without defect.[i] 18 With the bulls, rams and lambs, prepare their grain offerings[j] and drink offerings[k] according to the number specified.[l] 19 Include one male goat as a sin offering,[m] in addition to the regular burnt offering with its grain offering, and their drink offerings.

20 " 'On the third day prepare eleven bulls, two rams and fourteen male lambs a year old, all without defect.[n] 21 With the bulls, rams and lambs, prepare their grain offerings and drink offerings according to the number specified.[o] 22 Include one male goat as a sin offering, in addition to the regular burnt offering with its grain offering and drink offering.

23 " 'On the fourth day prepare ten bulls, two rams and fourteen male lambs a year old, all without defect. 24 With the bulls, rams and lambs, prepare their grain offerings and drink offerings according to the number specified. 25 Include one male goat as a sin offering, in addition to the regular burnt offering with its grain offering and drink offering.

26 " 'On the fifth day prepare nine bulls, two rams and fourteen male lambs a year old, all without defect. 27 With the bulls, rams and lambs, prepare their grain offerings and drink offerings according to the number specified. 28 Include one male goat as a sin offering, in addition to the regular burnt offering with its grain offering and drink offering.

29 " 'On the sixth day prepare eight bulls, two rams and fourteen male lambs a year old, all without defect. 30 With the bulls, rams and lambs, prepare their grain offerings and drink offerings according to the number specified. 31 Include one male goat as a sin

29:9 [a] ver 3,18
29:10 [b] Nu 28:13
29:11 [c] Lev 16:3; Nu 28:3
29:12 [d] 1Ki 8:2 [e] Lev 23:24
29:14 [f] ver 3
29:16 [g] ver 6
29:17 [h] Lev 23:36 [i] Nu 28:3
29:18 [j] ver 9 [k] Nu 28:7 [l] Nu 15:4-12
29:19 [m] Nu 28:15
29:20 [n] ver 17
29:21 [o] ver 18

offering, in addition to the regular burnt offering with its grain offering and drink offering.

32 " 'On the seventh day prepare seven bulls, two rams and fourteen male lambs a year old, all without defect. 33 With the bulls, rams and lambs, prepare their grain offerings and drink offerings according to the number specified. 34 Include one male goat as a sin offering, in addition to the regular burnt offering with its grain offering and drink offering.

35 " 'On the eighth day hold an assembly[a] and do no regular work. 36 Present an offering made by fire as an aroma pleasing to the LORD,[b] a burnt offering of one bull, one ram and seven male lambs a year old,[c] all without defect. 37 With the bull, the ram and the lambs, prepare their grain offerings and drink offerings according to the number specified. 38 Include one male goat as a sin offering, in addition to the regular burnt offering with its grain offering and drink offering.

39 " 'In addition to what you vow[d] and your freewill offerings, prepare these for the LORD at your appointed feasts:[e] your burnt offerings,[f] grain offerings, drink offerings and fellowship offerings.[a]' "

40 Moses told the Israelites all that the LORD commanded him.

Chapter 30 Theme ______________________

30 Moses said to the heads of the tribes of Israel:[g] "This is what the LORD commands: 2 When a man makes a vow to the LORD or takes an oath to obligate himself by a pledge, he must not break his word but must do everything he said.[h]

3 "When a young woman still living in her father's house makes a vow to the LORD or obligates herself by a pledge 4 and her father hears about her vow or pledge but says nothing to her, then all her vows and every pledge by which she obligated herself will stand.[i] 5 But if her father forbids her when he hears about it, none of her vows or the pledges by which she obligated herself will stand; the LORD will release her because her father has forbidden her.

6 "If she marries after she makes a vow[j] or after her lips utter a rash promise by which she obligates herself 7 and her husband hears about it but says nothing to her, then her vows or the pledges by which she obligated herself will stand. 8 But if her husband[k] forbids her when he hears about it, he nullifies the vow that obligates her or the rash promise by which she obligates herself, and the LORD will release her.

9 "Any vow or obligation taken by a widow or divorced woman will be binding on her.

29:35 [a] Lev 23:36
29:36 [b] Lev 1:9 [c] ver 2
29:39 [d] Nu 6:2 [e] Lev 23:2 [f] Lev 1:3; 1Ch 23:31; 2Ch 31:3
30:1 [g] Nu 1:4
30:2 [h] Dt 23:21-23; Jdg 11:35; Job 22:27; Ps 22:25; 50:14; 116:14; Pr 20:25; Ecc 5:4,5; Jnh 1:16
30:4 [i] ver 7
30:6 [j] Lev 5:4
30:8 [k] Ge 3:16

[a] 39 Traditionally *peace offerings*

10“If a woman living with her husband makes a vow or obligates herself by a pledge under oath 11and her husband hears about it but says nothing to her and does not forbid her, then all her vows or the pledges by which she obligated herself will stand. 12But if her husband nullifies them when he hears about them, then none of the vows or pledges that came from her lips will stand.[a] Her husband has nullified them, and the LORD will release her. 13Her husband may confirm or nullify any vow she makes or any sworn pledge to deny herself. 14But if her husband says nothing to her about it from day to day, then he confirms all her vows or the pledges binding on her. He confirms them by saying nothing to her when he hears about them. 15If, however, he nullifies them some time after he hears about them, then he is responsible for her guilt.”

16These are the regulations the LORD gave Moses concerning relationships between a man and his wife, and between a father and his young daughter still living in his house.

Chapter 31 Theme ________________

31 The LORD said to Moses, 2“Take vengeance on the Midianites[b] for the Israelites. After that, you will be gathered to your people.[c]”

3So Moses said to the people, “Arm some of your men to go to war against the Midianites and to carry out the LORD’s vengeance[d] on them. 4Send into battle a thousand men from each of the tribes of Israel.” 5So twelve thousand men armed for battle, a thousand from each tribe, were supplied from the clans of Israel. 6Moses sent them into battle, a thousand from each tribe, along with Phinehas son of Eleazar, the priest, who took with him articles from the sanctuary[e] and the trumpets[f] for signaling.

7They fought against Midian, as the LORD commanded Moses, and killed every man.[g] 8Among their victims were Evi, Rekem, Zur, Hur and Reba[h]—the five kings of Midian.[i] They also killed Balaam son of Beor with the sword.[j] 9The Israelites captured the Midianite women and children and took all the Midianite herds, flocks and goods as plunder. 10They burned all the towns where the Midianites had settled, as well as all their camps.[k] 11They took all the plunder and spoils, including the people and animals,[l] 12and brought the captives, spoils and plunder to Moses and Eleazar the priest and the Israelite assembly[m] at their camp on the plains of Moab, by the Jordan across from Jericho.[a]

13Moses, Eleazar the priest and all the leaders of the community went to meet them outside the camp. 14Moses was angry with the

a *12* Hebrew *Jordan of Jericho*; possibly an ancient name for the Jordan River

30:12 [a]Eph 5:22; Col 3:18
31:2 [b]Ge 25:2 [c]Nu 20:26; 27:13
31:3 [d]Jdg 11:36; 1Sa 24:12; 2Sa 4:8; 22:48; Ps 94:1; 149:7
31:6 [e]Nu 14:44 [f]Nu 10:9
31:7 [g]Dt 20:13; Jdg 21:11; 1Ki 11:15,16
31:8 [h]Jos 13:21 [i]Nu 25:15 [j]Jos 13:22
31:10 [k]Ge 25:16; 1Ch 6:54; Ps 69:25; Eze 25:4
31:11 [l]Dt 20:14
31:12 [m]Nu 27:2

officers of the army[a]—the commanders of thousands and commanders of hundreds—who returned from the battle.
15“Have you allowed all the women to live?” he asked them.
16“They were the ones who followed Balaam’s advice[b] and were
the means of turning the Israelites away from the LORD in what
happened at Peor,[c] so that a plague struck the LORD’s people.
17Now kill all the boys. And kill every woman who has slept with
a man,[d] 18but save for yourselves every girl who has never slept
with a man.
19“All of you who have killed anyone or touched anyone who
was killed[e] must stay outside the camp seven days. On the third
and seventh days you must purify yourselves[f] and your captives.
20Purify every garment[g] as well as everything made of leather,
goat hair or wood.”
21Then Eleazar the priest said to the soldiers who had gone into
battle, “This is the requirement of the law that the LORD gave
Moses: 22Gold, silver, bronze, iron,[h] tin, lead 23and anything else
that can withstand fire must be put through the fire,[i] and then it
will be clean. But it must also be purified with the water of
cleansing.[j] And whatever cannot withstand fire must be put
through that water. 24On the seventh day wash your clothes and
you will be clean.[k] Then you may come into the camp.”
25The LORD said to Moses, 26“You and Eleazar the priest and the
family heads of the community are to count all the people[l] and
animals that were captured. 27Divide[m] the spoils between the soldiers who took part in the battle and the rest of the community.
28From the soldiers who fought in the battle, set apart as tribute
for the LORD[n] one out of every five hundred, whether persons, cattle, donkeys, sheep or goats. 29Take this tribute from their half
share and give it to Eleazar the priest as the LORD’s part. 30From
the Israelites’ half, select one out of every fifty, whether persons,
cattle, donkeys, sheep, goats or other animals. Give them to the
Levites, who are responsible for the care of the LORD’s tabernacle.[o]” 31So Moses and Eleazar the priest did as the LORD commanded Moses.
32The plunder remaining from the spoils that the soldiers took
was 675,000 sheep, 3372,000 cattle, 3461,000 donkeys 35and 32,000
women who had never slept with a man.
36The half share of those who fought in the battle was:

337,500 sheep, 37of which the tribute for the LORD[p] was 675;
3836,000 cattle, of which the tribute for the LORD was 72;
3930,500 donkeys, of which the tribute for the LORD was 61;
4016,000 people, of which the tribute for the LORD was 32.

31:14 [a]ver 48; Ex 18:21; Dt 1:15
31:16 [b]2Pe 2:15; Rev 2:14 [c]Nu 25:1-9
31:17 [d]Dt 7:2; 20:16-18; Jdg 21:11
31:19 [e]Nu 19:16 [f]Nu 19:12
31:20 [g]Nu 19:19
31:22 [h]Jos 6:19; 22:8
31:23 [i]1Co 3:13 [j]Nu 19:9,17
31:24 [k]Lev 11:25
31:26 [l]Nu 1:19
31:27 [m]Jos 22:8; 1Sa 30:24
31:28 [n]Nu 18:21
31:30 [o]Nu 3:7; 18:3
31:37 [p]ver 38-41

41Moses gave the tribute to Eleazar the priest as the LORD's
part,[a] as the LORD commanded Moses.
42The half belonging to the Israelites, which Moses set apart
from that of the fighting men— 43the community's half—was
337,500 sheep, 4436,000 cattle, 4530,500 donkeys 46and 16,000
people. 47From the Israelites' half, Moses selected one out of
every fifty persons and animals, as the LORD commanded him,
and gave them to the Levites, who were responsible for the care
of the LORD's tabernacle.
48Then the officers who were over the units of the army—the
commanders of thousands and commanders of hundreds—
went to Moses 49and said to him, "Your servants have counted
the soldiers under our command, and not one is missing.[b] 50So
we have brought as an offering to the LORD the gold articles each
of us acquired—armlets, bracelets, signet rings, earrings and
necklaces—to make atonement for ourselves[c] before the LORD."
51Moses and Eleazar the priest accepted from them the gold—
all the crafted articles. 52All the gold from the commanders of
thousands and commanders of hundreds that Moses and Eleazar
presented as a gift to the LORD weighed 16,750 shekels.[a] 53Each
soldier had taken plunder[d] for himself. 54Moses and Eleazar the
priest accepted the gold from the commanders of thousands and
commanders of hundreds and brought it into the Tent of Meeting
as a memorial[e] for the Israelites before the LORD.

Chapter 32 Theme ______________________

32 The Reubenites and Gadites, who had very large herds
and flocks, saw that the lands of Jazer[f] and Gilead were
suitable for livestock.[g] 2So they came to Moses and Eleazar the
priest and to the leaders of the community, and said, 3"Ataroth,[h]
Dibon, Jazer, Nimrah,[i] Heshbon, Elealeh,[j] Sebam, Nebo and
Beon[k]— 4the land the LORD subdued[l] before the people of
Israel—are suitable for livestock,[m] and your servants have livestock. 5If we have found favor in your eyes," they said, "let this
land be given to your servants as our possession. Do not make us
cross the Jordan."
6Moses said to the Gadites and Reubenites, "Shall your countrymen go to war while you sit here? 7Why do you discourage the
Israelites from going over into the land the LORD has given them?[n]
8This is what your fathers did when I sent them from Kadesh
Barnea to look over the land.[o] 9After they went up to the Valley of
Eshcol[p] and viewed the land, they discouraged the Israelites from
entering the land the LORD had given them. 10The LORD's anger
was aroused[q] that day and he swore this oath: 11'Because they

[a]52 That is, about 420 pounds (about 190 kilograms)

31:41 [a]Nu 5:9; 18:8
31:49 [b]Jer 23:4
31:50 [c]Ex 30:16
31:53 [d]Dt 20:14
31:54 [e]Ex 28:12
32:1 [f]Nu 21:32 [g]Ex 12:38
32:3 [h]ver 34 [i]ver 36 [j]ver 37; Isa 15:4; 16:9; Jer 48:34 [k]ver 38; Jos 13:17; Eze 25:9
32:4 [l]Nu 21:34 [m]Ex 12:38
32:7 [n]Nu 13:27–14:4
32:8 [o]Nu 13:3,26; Dt 1:19-25
32:9 [p]Nu 13:23; Dt 1:24
32:10 [q]Nu 11:1

have not followed me wholeheartedly, not one of the men twenty
years old or more[a] who came up out of Egypt will see the land I
promised on oath[b] to Abraham, Isaac and Jacob[c]— 12not one
except Caleb son of Jephunneh the Kenizzite and Joshua son of
Nun, for they followed the LORD wholeheartedly.'[d] 13The LORD's
anger burned against Israel[e] and he made them wander in the
desert forty years, until the whole generation of those who had
done evil in his sight was gone.[f]

14"And here you are, a brood of sinners, standing in the place
of your fathers and making the LORD even more angry with
Israel.[g] 15If you turn away from following him, he will again leave
all this people in the desert, and you will be the cause of their
destruction.[h]"

16Then they came up to him and said, "We would like to build
pens here for our livestock[i] and cities for our women and children. 17But we are ready to arm ourselves and go ahead of the
Israelites[j] until we have brought them to their place.[k] Meanwhile
our women and children will live in fortified cities, for protection
from the inhabitants of the land. 18We will not return to our
homes until every Israelite has received his inheritance.[l] 19We
will not receive any inheritance with them on the other side of
the Jordan, because our inheritance has come to us on the east
side of the Jordan."[m]

20Then Moses said to them, "If you will do this—if you will arm
yourselves before the LORD for battle,[n] 21and if all of you will go
armed over the Jordan before the LORD until he has driven his
enemies out before him— 22then when the land is subdued before
the LORD, you may return[o] and be free from your obligation to the
LORD and to Israel. And this land will be your possession before
the LORD.[p]

23"But if you fail to do this, you will be sinning against the LORD;
and you may be sure that your sin will find you out.[q] 24Build cities
for your women and children, and pens for your flocks,[r] but do
what you have promised.[s]"

25The Gadites and Reubenites said to Moses, "We your servants
will do as our lord commands. 26Our children and wives, our
flocks and herds will remain here in the cities of Gilead.[t] 27But
your servants, every man armed for battle, will cross over to fight
before the LORD, just as our lord says."

28Then Moses gave orders about them[u] to Eleazar the priest and
Joshua son of Nun and to the family heads of the Israelite tribes.
29He said to them, "If the Gadites and Reubenites, every man
armed for battle, cross over the Jordan with you before the LORD,
then when the land is subdued before you, give them the land of
Gilead as their possession. 30But if they do not cross over with you
armed, they must accept their possession with you in Canaan."

32:11 [a]Ex 30:14 [b]Nu 14:23 [c]Nu 14:28-30
32:12 [d]Nu 14:24,30; Dt 1:36; Ps 63:8
32:13 [e]Ex 4:14 [f]Nu 14:28-35; 26:64,65
32:14 [g]ver 10; Dt 1:34; Ps 78:59
32:15 [h]Dt 30:17-18; 2Ch 7:20
32:16 [i]Ex 12:38; Dt 3:19
32:17 [j]Jos 4:12,13 [k]Nu 22:4; Dt 3:20
32:18 [l]Jos 22:1-4
32:19 [m]Jos 12:1
32:20 [n]Dt 3:18
32:22 [o]Jos 22:4 [p]Dt 3:18-20
32:23 [q]Ge 4:7; 44:16; Isa 59:12
32:24 [r]ver 1,16 [s]Nu 30:2
32:26 [t]Jos 1:14
32:28 [u]Dt 3:18-20; Jos 1:13

31 The Gadites and Reubenites answered, "Your servants will do
what the LORD has said.[a] 32 We will cross over before the LORD into
Canaan armed, but the property we inherit will be on this side of
the Jordan."

33 Then Moses gave to the Gadites,[b] the Reubenites and the half-
tribe of Manasseh son of Joseph the kingdom of Sihon king of the
Amorites[c] and the kingdom of Og king of Bashan—the whole
land with its cities and the territory around them.[d]

34 The Gadites built up Dibon, Ataroth, Aroer,[e] 35 Atroth Sho-
phan, Jazer,[f] Jogbehah, 36 Beth Nimrah[g] and Beth Haran as fortified cities, and built pens for their flocks. 37 And the Reubenites
rebuilt Heshbon, Elealeh and Kiriathaim, 38 as well as Nebo[h] and
Baal Meon (these names were changed) and Sibmah. They gave
names to the cities they rebuilt.

39 The descendants of Makir[i] son of Manasseh went to Gilead,
captured it and drove out the Amorites who were there. 40 So
Moses gave Gilead to the Makirites,[j] the descendants of Manasseh, and they settled there. 41 Jair, a descendant of Manasseh,
captured their settlements and called them Havvoth Jair.[a][k] 42 And
Nobah captured Kenath and its surrounding settlements and
called it Nobah after himself.[l]

Chapter 33 Theme ____________________________

33 Here are the stages in the journey of the Israelites when
they came out of Egypt[m] by divisions under the leadership
of Moses and Aaron.[n] 2 At the LORD's command Moses recorded
the stages in their journey. This is their journey by stages:

3 The Israelites set out from Rameses on the fifteenth day of
the first month, the day after the Passover.[o] They marched out
boldly[p] in full view of all the Egyptians, 4 who were burying
all their firstborn, whom the LORD had struck down among
them; for the LORD had brought judgment on their gods.[q]

5 The Israelites left Rameses and camped at Succoth.[r]

6 They left Succoth and camped at Etham, on the edge of
the desert.[s]

7 They left Etham, turned back to Pi Hahiroth, to the east of
Baal Zephon,[t] and camped near Migdol.[u]

8 They left Pi Hahiroth[b] and passed through the sea[v] into
the desert, and when they had traveled for three days in the
Desert of Etham, they camped at Marah.[w]

9 They left Marah and went to Elim, where there were twelve
springs and seventy palm trees, and they camped[x] there.

32:31 [a] ver 29
32:33 [b] Jos 13:24-28; 1Sa 13:7 [c] Dt 2:26 [d] Nu 21:24; Jos 12:6
32:34 [e] Dt 2:36; Jdg 11:26
32:35 [f] ver 3
32:36 [g] ver 3
32:38 [h] ver 3; Isa 15:2; Jer 48:1,22
32:39 [i] Ge 50:23
32:40 [j] Dt 3:15; Jos 17:1
32:41 [k] Dt 3:14; Jos 13:30; Jdg 10:4; 1Ch 2:23
32:42 [l] 2Sa 18:18; Ps 49:11
33:1 [m] Mic 6:4 [n] Ps 77:20
33:3 [o] Ex 13:4 [p] Ex 14:8
33:4 [q] Ex 12:12
33:5 [r] Ex 12:37
33:6 [s] Ex 13:20
33:7 [t] Ex 14:9 [u] Ex 14:2
33:8 [v] Ex 14:22 [w] Ex 15:23
33:9 [x] Ex 15:27

[a] 41 Or *them the settlements of Jair* [b] 8 Many manuscripts of the Masoretic Text, Samaritan Pentateuch and Vulgate; most manuscripts of the Masoretic Text *left from before Hahiroth*

10 They left Elim and camped by the Red Sea.[a]

11 They left the Red Sea and camped in the Desert of Sin.[a]

12 They left the Desert of Sin and camped at Dophkah.

13 They left Dophkah and camped at Alush.

14 They left Alush and camped at Rephidim, where there was no water for the people to drink.

15 They left Rephidim[b] and camped in the Desert of Sinai.[c]

16 They left the Desert of Sinai and camped at Kibroth Hattaavah.[d]

17 They left Kibroth Hattaavah and camped at Hazeroth.[e]

18 They left Hazeroth and camped at Rithmah.

19 They left Rithmah and camped at Rimmon Perez.

20 They left Rimmon Perez and camped at Libnah.[f]

21 They left Libnah and camped at Rissah.

22 They left Rissah and camped at Kehelathah.

23 They left Kehelathah and camped at Mount Shepher.

24 They left Mount Shepher and camped at Haradah.

25 They left Haradah and camped at Makheloth.

26 They left Makheloth and camped at Tahath.

27 They left Tahath and camped at Terah.

28 They left Terah and camped at Mithcah.

29 They left Mithcah and camped at Hashmonah.

30 They left Hashmonah and camped at Moseroth.[g]

31 They left Moseroth and camped at Bene Jaakan.

32 They left Bene Jaakan and camped at Hor Haggidgad.

33 They left Hor Haggidgad and camped at Jotbathah.[h]

34 They left Jotbathah and camped at Abronah.

35 They left Abronah and camped at Ezion Geber.[i]

36 They left Ezion Geber and camped at Kadesh, in the Desert of Zin.[j]

37 They left Kadesh and camped at Mount Hor,[k] on the border of Edom.[l] 38 At the LORD's command Aaron the priest
went up Mount Hor, where he died[m] on the first day of the
fifth month of the fortieth year after the Israelites came out
of Egypt.[n] 39 Aaron was a hundred and twenty-three years
old when he died on Mount Hor.

40 The Canaanite king of Arad,[o] who lived in the Negev of Canaan, heard that the Israelites were coming.

41 They left Mount Hor and camped at Zalmonah.

42 They left Zalmonah and camped at Punon.

43 They left Punon and camped at Oboth.[p]

44 They left Oboth and camped at Iye Abarim, on the border of Moab.[q]

45 They left Iyim[b] and camped at Dibon Gad.

33:11 *a*Ex 16:1
33:15 *b*Ex 17:1 *c*Ex 19:1
33:16 *d*Nu 11:34
33:17 *e*Nu 11:35
33:20 *f*Jos 10:29
33:30 *g*Dt 10:6
33:33 *h*Dt 10:7
33:35 *i*Dt 2:8; 1Ki 9:26; 22:48
33:36 *j*Nu 20:1
33:37 *k*Nu 20:22 *l*Nu 20:16; 21:4
33:38 *m*Dt 10:6 *n*Nu 20:25-28
33:40 *o*Nu 21:1
33:43 *p*Nu 21:10
33:44 *q*Nu 21:11

a *10* Hebrew *Yam Suph*; that is, Sea of Reeds; also in verse 11 b *45* That is, Iye Abarim

46They left Dibon Gad and camped at Almon Diblathaim.

47They left Almon Diblathaim and camped in the mountains of Abarim,[a] near Nebo.

48They left the mountains of Abarim and camped on the plains of Moab by the Jordan across from Jericho.[a][b] 49There on the plains of Moab they camped along the Jordan from Beth Jeshimoth to Abel Shittim.[c]

50On the plains of Moab by the Jordan across from Jericho the LORD said to Moses, 51"Speak to the Israelites and say to them: 'When you cross the Jordan into Canaan,[d] 52drive out all the inhabitants of the land before you. Destroy all their carved images and their cast idols, and demolish all their high places.[e] 53Take possession of the land and settle in it, for I have given you the land to possess.[f] 54Distribute the land by lot, according to your clans.[g] To a larger group give a larger inheritance, and to a smaller group a smaller one. Whatever falls to them by lot will be theirs. Distribute it according to your ancestral tribes.

55" 'But if you do not drive out the inhabitants of the land, those you allow to remain will become barbs in your eyes and thorns[h] in your sides. They will give you trouble in the land where you will live. 56And then I will do to you what I plan to do to them.' "

Chapter 34 Theme _____________________________

34 The LORD said to Moses, 2"Command the Israelites and say to them: 'When you enter Canaan, the land that will be allotted to you as an inheritance[i] will have these boundaries:[j]

3" 'Your southern side will include some of the Desert of Zin[k] along the border of Edom. On the east, your southern boundary will start from the end of the Salt Sea,[b][l] 4cross south of Scorpion[c] Pass,[m] continue on to Zin and go south of Kadesh Barnea.[n] Then it will go to Hazar Addar and over to Azmon, 5where it will turn, join the Wadi of Egypt[o] and end at the Sea.[d]

6" 'Your western boundary will be the coast of the Great Sea. This will be your boundary on the west.

7" 'For your northern boundary,[p] run a line from the Great Sea to Mount Hor 8and from Mount Hor to Lebo[e] Hamath.[q] Then the boundary will go to Zedad, 9continue to Ziphron and end at Hazar Enan. This will be your boundary on the north.

10" 'For your eastern boundary, run a line from Hazar Enan to Shepham. 11The boundary will go down from Shepham to Riblah[r]

[a]48 Hebrew *Jordan of Jericho*; possibly an ancient name for the Jordan River; also in verse 50 [b]3 That is, the Dead Sea; also in verse 12 [c]4 Hebrew *Akrabbim* [d]5 That is, the Mediterranean; also in verses 6 and 7 [e]8 Or *to the entrance to*

33:47 [a]Nu 27:12

33:48 [b]Nu 22:1

33:49 [c]Nu 25:1

33:51 [d]Jos 3:17

33:52 [e]Ex 23:24; 34:13; Lev 26:1; Dt 7:2,5; 12:3; Jos 11:12; Ps 106:34-36

33:53 [f]Dt 11:31; Jos 21:43

33:54 [g]Nu 26:54

33:55 [h]Jos 23:13; Jdg 2:3; Ps 106:36

34:2 [i]Ge 17:8; Dt 1:7-8; Ps 78:54-55 [j]Eze 47:15

34:3 [k]Jos 15:1-3 [l]Ge 14:3

34:4 [m]Jos 15:3 [n]Nu 32:8

34:5 [o]Ge 15:18; Jos 15:4

34:7 [p]Eze 47:15-17

34:8 [q]Nu 13:21; Jos 13:5

34:11 [r]2Ki 23:33; Jer 39:5

Border of Canaan

34:11 [a]Dt 3:17; Jos 11:2; 13:27
34:13 [b]Jos 14:1-5
34:14 [c]Nu 32:33; Jos 14:3
34:17 [d]Jos 14:1
34:18 [e]Nu 1:4,16
34:19 [f]Nu 26:65 [g]Ge 29:35; Dt 33:7

on the east side of Ain and continue along the slopes east of the
Sea of Kinnereth.[a][a] 12Then the boundary will go down along the
Jordan and end at the Salt Sea.

"'This will be your land, with its boundaries on every side.'"

13Moses commanded the Israelites: "Assign this land by lot as
an inheritance.[b] The LORD has ordered that it be given to the nine
and a half tribes, 14because the families of the tribe of Reuben,
the tribe of Gad and the half-tribe of Manasseh have received
their inheritance.[c] 15These two and a half tribes have received
their inheritance on the east side of the Jordan of Jericho,[b] toward
the sunrise."

16The LORD said to Moses, 17"These are the names of the men
who are to assign the land for you as an inheritance: Eleazar the
priest and Joshua[d] son of Nun. 18And appoint one leader from
each tribe to help[e] assign the land. 19These are their names:

Caleb[f] son of Jephunneh,
    from the tribe of Judah;[g]

[a] *11* That is, Galilee [b] *15* *Jordan of Jericho* was possibly an ancient name for the Jordan River.

20 Shemuel son of Ammihud,
  from the tribe of Simeon;[a]
21 Elidad son of Kislon,
  from the tribe of Benjamin;[b]
22 Bukki son of Jogli,
  the leader from the tribe of Dan;
23 Hanniel son of Ephod,
  the leader from the tribe of Manasseh son of Joseph;
24 Kemuel son of Shiphtan,
  the leader from the tribe of Ephraim son of Joseph;
25 Elizaphan son of Parnach,
  the leader from the tribe of Zebulun;
26 Paltiel son of Azzan,
  the leader from the tribe of Issachar;
27 Ahihud son of Shelomi,
  the leader from the tribe of Asher;[c]
28 Pedahel son of Ammihud,
  the leader from the tribe of Naphtali."

29 These are the men the LORD commanded to assign the inheritance to the Israelites in the land of Canaan.

Chapter 35 Theme ______________________

35 On the plains of Moab by the Jordan across from Jericho,[a]
the LORD said to Moses, 2 "Command the Israelites to give
the Levites towns to live in[d] from the inheritance the Israelites
will possess. And give them pasturelands around the towns.
3 Then they will have towns to live in and pasturelands for their
cattle, flocks and all their other livestock.
4 "The pasturelands around the towns that you give the Levites
will extend out fifteen hundred feet[b] from the town wall. 5 Outside the town, measure three thousand feet[c] on the east side,
three thousand on the south side, three thousand on the west
and three thousand on the north, with the town in the center.
They will have this area as pastureland for the towns.
6 "Six of the towns you give the Levites will be cities of refuge, to
which a person who has killed someone may flee.[e] In addition,
give them forty-two other towns. 7 In all you must give the Levites
forty-eight towns, together with their pasturelands. 8 The towns
you give the Levites from the land the Israelites possess are to be
given in proportion to the inheritance of each tribe: Take many
towns from a tribe that has many, but few from one that has few."[f]
9 Then the LORD said to Moses: 10 "Speak to the Israelites and say
to them: 'When you cross the Jordan into Canaan,[g] 11 select some

[a] *1* Hebrew *Jordan of Jericho*; possibly an ancient name for the Jordan River [b] *4* Hebrew *a thousand cubits* (about 450 meters) [c] *5* Hebrew *two thousand cubits* (about 900 meters)

34:20 [a] Ge 49:5
34:21 [b] Ge 49:27; Ps 68:27
34:27 [c] Nu 1:40
35:2 [d] Lev 25:32-34; Jos 14:3,4
35:6 [e] Jos 20:7-9; 21:3,13
35:8 [f] Nu 26:54; 33:54; Jos 21:1-42
35:10 [g] Jos 20:2

Cities of Refuge

35:11 [a]ver 22-25 [b]Ex 21:13; Dt 19:1-13
35:12 [c]Dt 19:6; Jos 20:3
35:16 [d]Ex 21:12; Lev 24:17
35:19 [e]ver 21
35:20 [f]Ge 4:8; Ex 21:14; Dt 19:11; 2Sa 3:27; 20:10
35:22 [g]ver 11; Ex 21:13
35:24 [h]ver 12; Jos 20:6

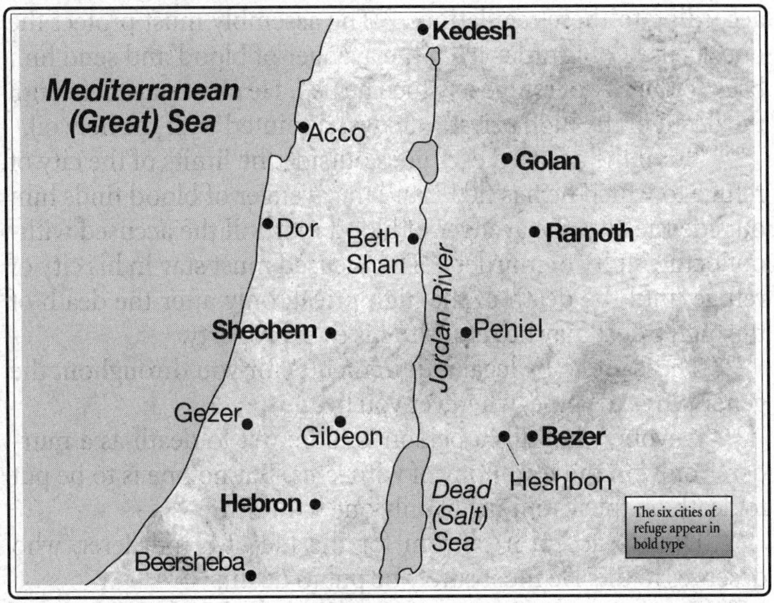

The six cities of refuge appear in bold type

towns to be your cities of refuge, to which a person who has killed
someone[a] accidentally[b] may flee. 12They will be places of refuge
from the avenger,[c] so that a person accused of murder may not
die before he stands trial before the assembly. 13These six towns
you give will be your cities of refuge. 14Give three on this side of
the Jordan and three in Canaan as cities of refuge. 15These six
towns will be a place of refuge for Israelites, aliens and any other
people living among them, so that anyone who has killed another
accidentally can flee there.

16" 'If a man strikes someone with an iron object so that he dies,
he is a murderer; the murderer shall be put to death.[d] 17Or if anyone has a stone in his hand that could kill, and he strikes someone
so that he dies, he is a murderer; the murderer shall be put to
death. 18Or if anyone has a wooden object in his hand that could
kill, and he hits someone so that he dies, he is a murderer; the
murderer shall be put to death. 19The avenger of blood shall put
the murderer to death; when he meets him, he shall put him to
death.[e] 20If anyone with malice aforethought shoves another or
throws something at him intentionally[f] so that he dies 21or if in
hostility he hits him with his fist so that he dies, that person shall
be put to death; he is a murderer. The avenger of blood shall put
the murderer to death when he meets him.

22" 'But if without hostility someone suddenly shoves another
or throws something at him unintentionally[g] 23or, without seeing
him, drops a stone on him that could kill him, and he dies, then
since he was not his enemy and he did not intend to harm him,
24the assembly[h] must judge between him and the avenger of blood

according to these regulations. 25The assembly must protect the one accused of murder from the avenger of blood and send him back to the city of refuge to which he fled. He must stay there until the death of the high priest, who was anointed with the holy oil.[a]

26" 'But if the accused ever goes outside the limits of the city of refuge to which he has fled 27and the avenger of blood finds him outside the city, the avenger of blood may kill the accused without being guilty of murder. 28The accused must stay in his city of refuge until the death of the high priest; only after the death of the high priest may he return to his own property.

29" 'These are to be legal requirements[b] for you throughout the generations to come, wherever you live.

30" 'Anyone who kills a person is to be put to death as a murderer only on the testimony of witnesses. But no one is to be put to death on the testimony of only one witness.[c]

31" 'Do not accept a ransom for the life of a murderer, who deserves to die. He must surely be put to death.

32" 'Do not accept a ransom for anyone who has fled to a city of refuge and so allow him to go back and live on his own land before the death of the high priest.

33" 'Do not pollute the land where you are. Bloodshed pollutes the land,[d] and atonement cannot be made for the land on which blood has been shed, except by the blood of the one who shed it. 34Do not defile the land[e] where you live and where I dwell,[f] for I, the LORD, dwell among the Israelites.' "

Chapter 36 Theme ______________________

36 The family heads of the clan of Gilead[g] son of Makir, the son of Manasseh, who were from the clans of the descendants of Joseph, came and spoke before Moses and the leaders,[h] the heads of the Israelite families. 2They said, "When the LORD commanded my lord to give the land as an inheritance to the Israelites by lot, he ordered you to give the inheritance of our brother Zelophehad[i] to his daughters. 3Now suppose they marry men from other Israelite tribes; then their inheritance will be taken from our ancestral inheritance and added to that of the tribe they marry into. And so part of the inheritance allotted to us will be taken away. 4When the Year of Jubilee[j] for the Israelites comes, their inheritance will be added to that of the tribe into which they marry, and their property will be taken from the tribal inheritance of our forefathers."

5Then at the LORD's command Moses gave this order to the Israelites: "What the tribe of the descendants of Joseph is saying is right. 6This is what the LORD commands for Zelophehad's daughters: They may marry anyone they please as long as they

35:25 [a]Ex 29:7
35:29 [b]Nu 27:11
35:30 [c]ver 16; Dt 17:6; 19:15; Mt 18:16; Jn 7:51; 2Co 13:1; Heb 10:28
35:33 [d]Ge 9:6; Ps 106:38; Mic 4:11
35:34 [e]Lev 18:24,25 [f]Ex 29:45
36:1 [g]Nu 26:29 [h]Nu 27:2
36:2 [i]Nu 26:33; 27:1,7
36:4 [j]Lev 25:10

36:7 [a]1Ki 21:3 marry within the tribal clan of their father. 7No inheritance[a] in
Israel is to pass from tribe to tribe, for every Israelite shall keep
the tribal land inherited from his forefathers. 8Every daughter
who inherits land in any Israelite tribe must marry someone in
her father's tribal clan,[b] so that every Israelite will possess the
36:8 [b]1Ch 23:22 inheritance of his fathers. 9No inheritance may pass from tribe
to tribe, for each Israelite tribe is to keep the land it inherits."

10So Zelophehad's daughters did as the LORD commanded
Moses. 11Zelophehad's daughters—Mahlah, Tirzah, Hoglah, Milcah and Noah[c]—married their cousins on their father's side.
36:11 [c]Nu 26:33; 27:1 12They married within the clans of the descendants of Manasseh
son of Joseph, and their inheritance remained in their father's clan
and tribe.

13These are the commands and regulations the LORD gave
through Moses[d] to the Israelites on the plains of Moab by the
36:13 [d]Lev 26:46; 27:34 [e]Nu 22:1 Jordan across from Jericho.[a][e]

[a] 13 Hebrew *Jordan of Jericho*; possibly an ancient name for the Jordan River

Insights from Numbers

Land of Canaan	Balaam	Korah

NUMBERS AT A GLANCE

Theme of Numbers:

Author:

Date:

Purpose:

Key Words:

SEGMENT DIVISIONS		
	JOURNEYS/ ENCAMP-MENTS	CHAPTER THEMES
		1
		2
		3
		4
		5
		6
		7
		8
		9
		10
		11
		12
		13
		14
		15
		16
		17
		18
		19
		20
		21
		22
		23
		24
		25
		26
		27
		28
		29
		30
		31
		32
		33
		34
		35
		36

DEUTERONOMY

Deuteronomy is the crown jewel of the Pentateuch. It lays before us clearly what God expects from those who have been redeemed: a life of uncompromising obedience.

God raised up Moses to deliver his people from the land of Egypt, the land of bondage. That Moses had done. Now he stood at Pisgah near the land of promise. He was 120 years old.

When Moses struck the rock a second time, he failed to treat God as holy. Because of this he could not enter the land of promise. But the people he had led so faithfully for the last 40 years would go in and possess it.

Moses had to do one more thing before God took him home: tell God's children how to live in the land which the God of their fathers was giving them.

Things to Do

General Instructions

1. For the book's historical context, read Numbers 21:21–22:1; 36:13; Deuteronomy 1:1-5.
   a. Record the author, date, and geographical setting of the book on the DEUTERONOMY AT A GLANCE chart on page 345.
   b. When you study Deuteronomy watch for any verses which confirm Moses' authorship. Although the last chapter tells of Moses' death, this doesn't negate the fact that Moses wrote the rest of the book. The last chapter would be an appropriate postscript after his death.
2. Read Romans 15:4 and 1 Corinthians 10:1-14 and keep these verses in mind as you study.
   a. As you study each chapter, note in the margin insights you glean in respect to the character of God and the ways he deals with his children and with unbelievers.
   b. Also note in the margin any specific instructions or admonitions that are to be followed in respect to God—for example, "Fear him."
   c. Record in the margin any "Lessons for Life" you learn from the text under the heading "LFL." Mark or color them in a distinctive way so you can recognize them immediately.
3. There are insightful lessons to be learned from Moses' life about leadership and about our relationship to God. As you study Deuteronomy note these lessons in the chapter margins. Also record all you learn about Moses on the chart LESSONS FROM THE LIFE OF MOSES on pages 346, 347. When you record your insights, make sure you note the book, chapter, and verse from which they came.

Chapters 1-3

Moses rehearses what happened from the time they left Horeb (Mount Sinai) until they camped in the valley opposite Beth Peor at the foot of Mount Nebo (Pisgah).

1. As you read these three chapters:
   a. Ask the five W's and an H: Who? What? When? Where? Why? and How? Watch what happens in each chapter, where it happens and to whom, why it happens, and what the consequences or results are. Also note how things are accomplished.
   b. Mark every use of *then (and, when, next, after that,* or *until)* so you can see the sequence of events.
   c. Look at the map in chapter 1 on page 289 to see where the events took place.
2. In a distinctive way mark these key words and their synonyms: *fear (be afraid, revere, revering), heart(s) (yourselves, yourself, integrity, hardhearted, disheartened, mind,* or *way), command(s) (orders,*

commanding, commanded), give(n), gave, giving, send, told, directed, or *forbidden),* and *listen (pay attention, hear, obey,* or *obeying).* Write these on an index card to use as a bookmark while studying Deuteronomy.

3. Choose the theme of each chapter and record it in the text on the line next to the chapter number and on DEUTERONOMY AT A GLANCE.

Chapters 4-11

Moses instructs the children of Israel regarding what they are to do when they enter the land.

1. Read this segment chapter by chapter, keeping in mind the five W's and an H. Words such as *when, after, since, how, in the future, then, but now, watch, be careful, hear, listen, proclaim, pay attention, obey, therefore* will come to your attention. When you see the word "when," look and see if "then" eventually follows it. If so, circle each word and connect them with a line.

2. Add the following key words to your list and mark them when you come to them in the text: *observe (follow, obey, be careful, keep, pay attention to, keeping, do, doing, go well, done), love (affection, loved, loves), remember,* and *commandment (commands, law(s), statutes, decrees).*

3. Record the main points of each chapter in the margin, or underline and note them in the text with a number 1, 2, 3, etc.

4. Record the chapter themes as you did previously.

Chapters 12-26

Moses gives the people the statutes and the judgments they are to observe.

1. Add the following phrase to your list of key words and make sure you mark every occurrence of it in these chapters: *you must purge* [remove] *the evil.* Also add the words *life (live, livelihood, kill him), death (die), curse,* and *blessing(s) (blessed).*

2. As you read these chapters note in the margin of the text what the people are to do and why.

3. Go back and read number 2 under "General Instructions." Don't forget this important process.

4. Record the theme of the chapters on DEUTERONOMY AT A GLANCE and in the text.

Chapters 27-30

Moses tells the people about the necessity of obedience and that if they obey they will be blessed, but if they disobey they will be cursed.

1. Add to your list of key words the following words along with their synonyms and pronouns: *curse(s) (oath), blessing(s), the Lord will (it will please him), nation (nations, enemies, people, countries), captivity,* and *covenant.* List in the margin what you observe from marking these words.

2. As you read these chapters keep asking the five W's and an H. Note who and/or what will be affected by their obedience or disobedience. Also note everything that will happen if they obey or disobey.

3. Don't forget to note what you learn about God from these chapters and to record the theme of each chapter.

Chapters 31-34

This segment contains Moses' parting words, song, and blessing, as well as the account of his death.

1. Mark the key repeated words listed on your index card.

2. As Moses sings his song in chapter 32 he recounts Israel's relationship to God and God's dealings with them. *Jeshurun* in 32:15 is a reference to Israel.

   a. Pay attention to what you learn about Israel. Observe what leads to Israel's downfall and what the consequences are.

   b. Remember that although Moses begged God to change his mind and allow him to enter the promised land, God said no. Keep this in mind as you read these chapters and see Moses' heart and hear his words in respect to God. Take note of all you learn about God from these significant chapters. Make a list in the margin of what you learn about "the Rock."

3. Observe what Moses says will happen after his death and note this in the margin.

4. When you study chapter 33, mark the name of each of the tribes of Israel and carefully observe how they are described and what is said about each one of them. Underline every occurrence of *they will.*

5. Record what you learn about Moses from chapter 34 on the chart LESSONS FROM THE LIFE OF MOSES on pages 346, 347. Then complete DEUTERONOMY AT A GLANCE.

THINGS TO THINK ABOUT

1. Since we are under the new covenant of grace, what is our relationship to the commands of God? Do you think grace allows us to continue in sin and disobedience without any consequences or chastening from the Father?

2. What kind of allegiance does God call for from Israel? Do you think he expects anything less from the church, the body of the Lord Jesus Christ?

3. What have you learned regarding the slowness of God's anger and his gracious ways with his covenant people?

4. How does a child of God demonstrate his love for the Lord?

Chapter 1 Theme ____________________

1 These are the words Moses spoke to all Israel in the desert east
of the Jordan—that is, in the Arabah—opposite Suph, between
Paran and Tophel, Laban, Hazeroth and Dizahab. 2(It takes
eleven days to go from Horeb[a] to Kadesh Barnea[b] by the Mount
Seir road.)
3In the fortieth year,[c] on the first day of the eleventh month,
Moses proclaimed[d] to the Israelites all that the LORD had commanded him concerning them. 4This was after he had defeated
Sihon[e] king of the Amorites, who reigned in Heshbon,[f] and at
Edrei had defeated Og[g] king of Bashan, who reigned in Ashtaroth.
5East of the Jordan in the territory of Moab, Moses began to
expound this law, saying:

6The LORD our God said to us[h] at Horeb,[i] "You have stayed
long enough at this mountain. 7Break camp and advance into
the hill country of the Amorites; go to all the neighboring peoples in the Arabah, in the mountains, in the western foothills, in
the Negev[j] and along the coast, to the land of the Canaanites and
to Lebanon,[k] as far as the great river, the Euphrates. 8See, I have
given you this land. Go in and take possession of the land that
the LORD swore[l] he would give to your fathers—to Abraham,
Isaac and Jacob—and to their descendants after them."
9At that time I said to you, "You are too heavy a burden for me to
carry alone.[m] 10The LORD your God has increased your numbers

1:2 [a] Ex 3:1 [b] Nu 13:26; Dt 9:23
1:3 [c] Nu 33:38 [d] Dt 4:1-2
1:4 [e] Nu 21:21-26 [f] Nu 21:25 [g] Nu 21:33-35; Jos 13:12
1:6 [h] Nu 10:13 [i] Ex 3:1
1:7 [j] Jos 10:40 [k] Dt 11:24
1:8 [l] Ge 12:7; 15:18; 17:7-8; 26:4; 28:13
1:9 [m] Ex 18:18

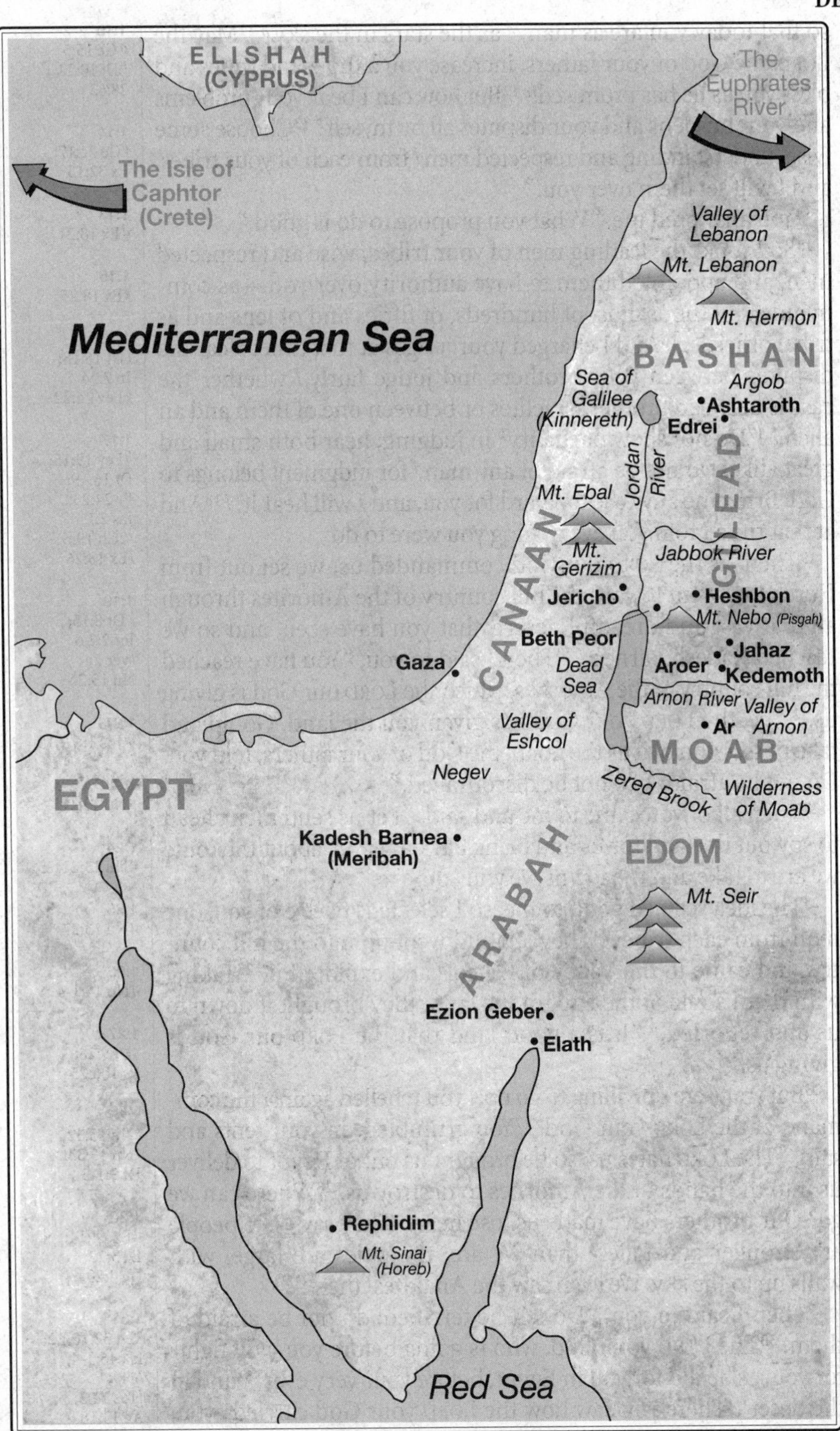
ELISHAH
(CYPRUS)
The Euphrates River
The Isle of Caphtor (Crete)
Valley of Lebanon
Mt. Lebanon
Mt. Hermon
Mediterranean Sea
BASHAN
Sea of Galilee (Kinnereth)
Argob
Ashtaroth
Edrei
Jordan River
GILEAD
Mt. Ebal
Mt. Gerizim
Jabbok River
CANAAN
Jericho
Heshbon
Mt. Nebo (Pisgah)
Beth Peor
Gaza
Dead Sea
Jahaz
Aroer
Kedemoth
Arnon River
Valley of Arnon
Valley of Eshcol
Ar
MOAB
Negev
Zered Brook
Wilderness of Moab
EGYPT
Kadesh Barnea (Meribah)
EDOM
Mt. Seir
ARABAH
Ezion Geber
Elath
Rephidim
Mt. Sinai (Horeb)
Red Sea

The Lands of Israel's Journeys after the Exodus

so that today you are as many[a] as the stars in the sky.[b] 11 May the
LORD, the God of your fathers, increase you a thousand times and
bless you as he has promised![c] 12 But how can I bear your problems
and your burdens and your disputes all by myself? 13 Choose some
wise, understanding and respected men[d] from each of your tribes,
and I will set them over you."

14 You answered me, "What you propose to do is good."

15 So I took[e] the leading men of your tribes, wise and respected
men, and appointed them to have authority over you—as commanders of thousands, of hundreds, of fifties and of tens and as
tribal officials. 16 And I charged your judges at that time: Hear the
disputes between your brothers and judge fairly,[f] whether the
case is between brother Israelites or between one of them and an
alien.[g] 17 Do not show partiality[h] in judging; hear both small and
great alike. Do not be afraid of any man,[i] for judgment belongs to
God. Bring me any case too hard for you, and I will hear it.[j] 18 And
at that time I told you everything you were to do.

19 Then, as the LORD our God commanded us, we set out from
Horeb and went toward the hill country of the Amorites through
all that vast and dreadful desert[k] that you have seen, and so we
reached Kadesh Barnea.[l] 20 Then I said to you, "You have reached
the hill country of the Amorites, which the LORD our God is giving
us. 21 See, the LORD your God has given you the land. Go up and
take possession of it as the LORD, the God of your fathers, told you.
Do not be afraid;[m] do not be discouraged."

22 Then all of you came to me and said, "Let us send men ahead
to spy out the land for us and bring back a report about the route
we are to take and the towns we will come to."

23 The idea seemed good to me; so I selected[n] twelve of you, one
man from each tribe. 24 They left and went up into the hill country, and came to the Valley of Eshcol[o] and explored it. 25 Taking
with them some of the fruit of the land, they brought it down to
us and reported,[p] "It is a good land that the LORD our God is
giving us."

26 But you were unwilling to go up;[q] you rebelled against the command of the LORD your God. 27 You grumbled[r] in your tents and
said, "The LORD hates us; so he brought us out of Egypt to deliver
us into the hands of the Amorites to destroy us. 28 Where can we
go? Our brothers have made us lose heart. They say, 'The people
are stronger and taller[s] than we are; the cities are large, with
walls up to the sky. We even saw the Anakites[t] there.'"

29 Then I said to you, "Do not be terrified; do not be afraid of
them. 30 The LORD your God, who is going before you, will fight[u]
for you, as he did for you in Egypt, before your very eyes, 31 and in
the desert. There you saw how the LORD your God carried[v] you,

1:10 [a] Ge 15:5 [b] Dt 10:22; 28:62
1:11 [c] Ge 22:17; Ex 32:13
1:13 [d] Ex 18:21
1:15 [e] Ex 18:25
1:16 [f] Dt 16:18; Jn 7:24 [g] Lev 24:22
1:17 [h] Lev 19:15; Dt 16:19; Pr 24:23; Jas 2:1 [i] 2Ch 19:6 [j] Ex 18:26
1:19 [k] Dt 8:15; Jer 2:2,6 [l] ver 2; Nu 13:26
1:21 [m] Jos 1:6,9,18
1:23 [n] Nu 13:1-3
1:24 [o] Nu 13:21-25
1:25 [p] Nu 13:27
1:26 [q] Nu 14:1-4
1:27 [r] Dt 9:28; Ps 106:25
1:28 [s] Nu 13:32 [t] Nu 13:33; Dt 9:1-3
1:30 [u] Ex 14:14; Dt 3:22; Ne 4:20
1:31 [v] Dt 32:10-12; Isa 46:3-4; 63:9; Hos 11:3; Ac 13:18

as a father carries his son, all the way you went until you reached
this place."
32 In spite of this, you did not trust[a] in the LORD your God,
33 who went ahead of you on your journey, in fire by night and in
a cloud by day,[b] to search[c] out places for you to camp and to
show you the way you should go.
34 When the LORD heard what you said, he was angry and
solemnly swore:[d] 35 "Not a man of this evil generation shall see
the good land[e] I swore to give your forefathers, 36 except Caleb
son of Jephunneh. He will see it, and I will give him and his
descendants the land he set his feet on, because he followed the
LORD wholeheartedly.[f]"
37 Because of you the LORD became angry[g] with me also and
said, "You shall not enter[h] it, either. 38 But your assistant, Joshua[i]
son of Nun, will enter it. Encourage[j] him, because he will lead[k]
Israel to inherit it. 39 And the little ones that you said would be
taken captive,[l] your children who do not yet know[m] good from
bad—they will enter the land. I will give it to them and they will
take possession of it. 40 But as for you, turn around and set out
toward the desert along the route to the Red Sea.[a][n]"
41 Then you replied, "We have sinned against the LORD. We will
go up and fight, as the LORD our God commanded us." So every
one of you put on his weapons, thinking it easy to go up into the
hill country.
42 But the LORD said to me, "Tell them, 'Do not go up and fight,
because I will not be with you. You will be defeated by your enemies.'"[o]
43 So I told you, but you would not listen. You rebelled against
the LORD's command and in your arrogance you marched up
into the hill country. 44 The Amorites who lived in those hills
came out against you; they chased you like a swarm of bees[p] and
beat you down from Seir all the way to Hormah. 45 You came
back and wept before the LORD, but he paid no attention to your
weeping and turned a deaf ear to you. 46 And so you stayed in
Kadesh[q] many days—all the time you spent there.

Chapter 2 Theme ________________________

2 Then we turned back and set out toward the desert along
the route to the Red Sea,[a][r] as the LORD had directed me. For
a long time we made our way around the hill country of Seir.
2 Then the LORD said to me, 3 "You have made your way around
this hill country long enough; now turn north. 4 Give the people
these orders:[s] 'You are about to pass through the territory of your
brothers the descendants of Esau, who live in Seir. They will be

1:32 [a]Ps 106:24; Jude 1:5
1:33 [b]Ex 13:21; Ps 78:14 [c]Nu 10:33
1:34 [d]Nu 14:23, 28-30
1:35 [e]Ps 95:11
1:36 [f]Nu 14:24; Jos 14:9
1:37 [g]Dt 3:26; 4:21 [h]Nu 20:12
1:38 [i]Nu 14:30 [j]Dt 31:7 [k]Dt 3:28
1:39 [l]Nu 14:3 [m]Isa 7:15-16
1:40 [n]Nu 14:25
1:42 [o]Nu 14:41-43
1:44 [p]Ps 118:12
1:46 [q]Nu 20:1; Jdg 11:17
2:1 [r]Nu 21:4
2:4 [s]Nu 20:14-21

a *40, 1* Hebrew *Yam Suph*; that is, Sea of Reeds

afraid of you, but be very careful. 5Do not provoke them to war,
for I will not give you any of their land, not even enough to put
your foot on. I have given Esau the hill country of Seir as his
own.[a] 6You are to pay them in silver for the food you eat and the
water you drink.'"

7The LORD your God has blessed you in all the work of your
hands. He has watched[b] over your journey through this vast
desert. These forty years the LORD your God has been with you,
and you have not lacked anything.

8So we went on past our brothers the descendants of Esau,
who live in Seir. We turned from the Arabah road, which comes
up from Elath and Ezion Geber,[c] and traveled along the desert
road of Moab.[d]

9Then the LORD said to me, "Do not harass the Moabites or
provoke them to war, for I will not give you any part of their land.
I have given Ar[e] to the descendants of Lot[f] as a possession."

10(The Emites[g] used to live there—a people strong and numerous, and as tall as the Anakites.[h] 11Like the Anakites, they too
were considered Rephaites, but the Moabites called them Emites.
12Horites used to live in Seir, but the descendants of Esau drove
them out. They destroyed the Horites from before them and settled in their place, just as Israel did[i] in the land the LORD gave
them as their possession.)

13And the LORD said, "Now get up and cross the Zered Valley."
So we crossed the valley.

14Thirty-eight years passed from the time we left Kadesh
Barnea[j] until we crossed the Zered Valley. By then, that entire
generation[k] of fighting men had perished from the camp, as the
LORD had sworn to them.[l] 15The LORD's hand was against them
until he had completely eliminated[m] them from the camp.

16Now when the last of these fighting men among the people
had died, 17the LORD said to me, 18"Today you are to pass by the
region of Moab at Ar. 19When you come to the Ammonites,[n] do
not harass them or provoke them to war, for I will not give you
possession of any land belonging to the Ammonites. I have giv-
en it as a possession to the descendants of Lot.[o]"

20(That too was considered a land of the Rephaites, who used
to live there; but the Ammonites called them Zamzummites.
21They were a people strong and numerous, and as tall as the Anakites.[p] The LORD destroyed them from before the Ammonites,
who drove them out and settled in their place. 22The LORD had
done the same for the descendants of Esau, who lived in Seir,[q]
when he destroyed the Horites from before them. They drove
them out and have lived in their place to this day. 23And as for
the Avvites[r] who lived in villages as far as Gaza, the Caphtorites[s]

2:5 [a] Ge 36:8; Jos 24:4
2:7 [b] Dt 8:2-4
2:8 [c] 1Ki 9:26 [d] Jdg 11:18
2:9 [e] Nu 21:15 [f] Ge 19:36-38
2:10 [g] Ge 14:5 [h] Nu 13:22,33
2:12 [i] ver 22
2:14 [j] Nu 13:26 [k] Nu 14:29-35 [l] Dt 1:34-35
2:15 [m] Ps 106:26
2:19 [n] Ge 19:38 [o] ver 9
2:21 [p] ver 10
2:22 [q] Ge 36:8
2:23 [r] Jos 13:3 [s] Ge 10:14

2:23 coming out from Caphtor[a][a] destroyed them and settled in their
[a]Am 9:7 place.)
24"Set out now and cross the Arnon Gorge.[b] See, I have given
2:24 [b]Nu 21:13-14; into your hand Sihon the Amorite, king of Heshbon, and his
Jdg 11:13,18 country. Begin to take possession of it and engage him in battle.
25This very day I will begin to put the terror[c] and fear[d] of you on
2:25 all the nations under heaven. They will hear reports of you and
[c]Dt 11:25 [d]Jos 2:9,11 will tremble[e] and be in anguish because of you."
[e]Ex 15:14-16 26From the desert of Kedemoth I sent messengers to Sihon
king of Heshbon offering peace and saying, 27"Let us pass
2:27 through your country. We will stay on the main road; we will not
[f]Nu 21:21-22 turn aside to the right or to the left.[f] 28Sell us food to eat and
water to drink for their price in silver. Only let us pass through
2:28 on foot[g]— 29as the descendants of Esau, who live in Seir, and the
[g]Nu 20:19 Moabites, who live in Ar, did for us—until we cross the Jordan
into the land the LORD our God is giving us." 30But Sihon king of
2:30 [h]Jos 11:20 Heshbon refused to let us pass through. For the LORD[h] your God
[i]Ex 4:21; Nu 21:23; had made his spirit stubborn[i] and his heart obstinate in order to
Ro 9:18 give him into your hands, as he has now done.
31The LORD said to me, "See, I have begun to deliver Sihon and
2:31 his country over to you. Now begin to conquer and possess his
[j]Dt 1:8 land."[j]
32When Sihon and all his army came out to meet us in battle[k]
2:32 at Jahaz, 33the LORD our God delivered him over to us and we
[k]Nu 21:23 struck him down,[l] together with his sons and his whole army. 34At
that time we took all his towns and completely destroyed[b][m]
2:33 them—men, women and children. We left no survivors. 35But
[l]Dt 29:7 the livestock and the plunder from the towns we had captured
we carried off for ourselves. 36From Aroer[n] on the rim of the
2:34 [m]Dt 3:6; 7:2 Arnon Gorge, and from the town in the gorge, even as far as
Gilead, not one town was too strong for us. The LORD our God
2:36 gave[o] us all of them. 37But in accordance with the command of the
[n]Dt 3:12; LORD our God,[p] you did not encroach on any of the land of the
4:48; Ammonites,[q] neither the land along the course of the Jabbok[r]
Jos 13:9 [o]Ps 44:3 nor that around the towns in the hills.

2:37 *Chapter 3 Theme* ______________________

[p]ver 18-19 [q]Nu 21:24 **3** Next we turned and went up along the road toward Bashan,
[r]Ge 32:22; Dt 3:16 and Og king of Bashan with his whole army marched out to
meet us in battle at Edrei.[s] 2The LORD said to me, "Do not be
afraid[t] of him, for I have handed him over to you with his whole
3:1 [s]Nu 21:33 army and his land. Do to him what you did to Sihon king of the
Amorites, who reigned in Heshbon."

3:2 [t]Nu 21:34 [a]*23* That is, Crete [b]*34* The Hebrew term refers to the irrevocable giving over of things or persons to the LORD, often by totally destroying them.

3 So the LORD our God also gave into our hands Og king of Bashan and all his army. We struck them down, leaving no survivors.[a] 4 At that time we took all his cities. There was not one of the sixty cities that we did not take from them—the whole region of Argob, Og's kingdom in Bashan.[b] 5 All these cities were fortified with high walls and with gates and bars, and there were also a great many unwalled villages. 6 We completely destroyed[a] them, as we had done with Sihon king of Heshbon, destroying[a][c] every city—men, women and children. 7 But all the livestock and the plunder from their cities we carried off for ourselves.

8 So at that time we took from these two kings of the Amorites the territory east of the Jordan, from the Arnon Gorge as far as Mount Hermon. 9 (Hermon is called Sirion[d] by the Sidonians; the Amorites call it Senir.)[e] 10 We took all the towns on the plateau, and all Gilead, and all Bashan as far as Salecah[f] and Edrei, towns of Og's kingdom in Bashan. 11 (Only Og king of Bashan was left of the remnant of the Rephaites.[g] His bed[b] was made of iron and was more than thirteen feet long and six feet wide.[c] It is still in Rabbah[h] of the Ammonites.)

12 Of the land that we took over at that time, I gave the Reubenites and the Gadites the territory north of Aroer[i] by the Arnon Gorge, including half the hill country of Gilead, together with its towns. 13 The rest of Gilead and also all of Bashan, the kingdom of Og, I gave to the half tribe of Manasseh. (The whole region of Argob in Bashan used to be known as a land of the Rephaites. 14 Jair,[j] a descendant of Manasseh, took the whole region of Argob as far as the border of the Geshurites and the Maacathites; it was named after him, so that to this day Bashan is called Havvoth Jair.[d]) 15 And I gave Gilead to Makir.[k] 16 But to the Reubenites and the Gadites I gave the territory extending from Gilead down to the Arnon Gorge (the middle of the gorge being the border) and out to the Jabbok River,[l] which is the border of the Ammonites. 17 Its western border was the Jordan in the Arabah, from Kinnereth[m] to the Sea of the Arabah (the Salt Sea[e][n]), below the slopes of Pisgah.

18 I commanded you at that time: "The LORD your God has given you this land to take possession of it. But all your able-bodied men, armed for battle, must cross over ahead of your brother Israelites.[o] 19 However, your wives, your children and your livestock (I know you have much livestock) may stay in the towns I have given you, 20 until the LORD gives rest to your brothers as he has to you, and they too have taken over the land that the LORD your

[a]6 The Hebrew term refers to the irrevocable giving over of things or persons to the LORD, often by totally destroying them. [b]11 Or *sarcophagus* [c]11 Hebrew *nine cubits long and four cubits wide* (about 4 meters long and 1.8 meters wide) [d]14 Or *called the settlements of Jair* [e]17 That is, the Dead Sea

3:3 [a]Nu 21:35
3:4 [b]1Ki 4:13
3:6 [c]Dt 2:24,34
3:9 [d]Dt 4:48; Ps 29:6 [e]1Ch 5:23
3:10 [f]Jos 13:11
3:11 [g]Ge 14:5 [h]2Sa 12:26; Jer 49:2
3:12 [i]Nu 32:32-38; Dt 2:36; Jos 13:8-13
3:14 [j]Nu 32:41; 1Ch 2:22
3:15 [k]Nu 32:39-40
3:16 [l]Nu 21:24
3:17 [m]Nu 34:11; Jos 13:27 [n]Ge 14:3; Jos 12:3
3:18 [o]Nu 32:17

God is giving them, across the Jordan. After that, each of you may
go back to the possession I have given you."
21 At that time I commanded Joshua: "You have seen with your
own eyes all that the LORD your God has done to these two kings.
The LORD will do the same to all the kingdoms over there where
you are going. 22 Do not be afraid[a] of them; the LORD your God
himself will fight[b] for you."
23 At that time I pleaded with the LORD: 24 "O Sovereign LORD, you
have begun to show to your servant your greatness[c] and your
strong hand. For what god[d] is there in heaven or on earth who
can do the deeds and mighty works[e] you do?[f] 25 Let me go over
and see the good land[g] beyond the Jordan—that fine hill country and Lebanon."
26 But because of you the LORD was angry[h] with me and would
not listen to me. "That is enough," the LORD said. "Do not speak
to me anymore about this matter. 27 Go up to the top of Pisgah
and look west and north and south and east. Look at the land
with your own eyes, since you are not going to cross this Jordan.[i]
28 But commission[j] Joshua, and encourage and strengthen him,
for he will lead this people across[k] and will cause them to inherit
the land that you will see." 29 So we stayed in the valley near Beth
Peor.[l]

Chapter 4 Theme ______________________

4 Hear now, O Israel, the decrees and laws I am about to teach
you. Follow them so that you may live[m] and may go in and
take possession of the land that the LORD, the God of your fathers,
is giving you. 2 Do not add[n] to what I command you and do not
subtract from it, but keep the commands of the LORD your God
that I give you.
3 You saw with your own eyes what the LORD did at Baal Peor.[o]
The LORD your God destroyed from among you everyone who
followed the Baal of Peor, 4 but all of you who held fast to the
LORD your God are still alive today.
5 See, I have taught you decrees and laws as the LORD my God
commanded me, so that you may follow them in the land you
are entering to take possession of it. 6 Observe them carefully, for
this will show your wisdom[p] and understanding to the nations,
who will hear about all these decrees and say, "Surely this great
nation is a wise and understanding people."[q] 7 What other nation
is so great[r] as to have their gods near[s] them the way the LORD our
God is near us whenever we pray to him? 8 And what other nation
is so great as to have such righteous decrees and laws as this body
of laws I am setting before you today?
9 Only be careful,[t] and watch yourselves closely so that you do
not forget the things your eyes have seen or let them slip from

3:22 [a]Dt 1:29 [b]Ex 14:14; Dt 20:4
3:24 [c]Dt 11:2 [d]Ex 15:11; Ps 86:8 [e]Ps 71:16,19 [f]2Sa 7:22
3:25 [g]Dt 4:22
3:26 [h]Dt 1:37; 31:2
3:27 [i]Nu 27:12
3:28 [j]Nu 27:18-23 [k]Dt 31:3,23
3:29 [l]Dt 4:46; 34:6
4:1 [m]Dt 5:33; 8:1; 16:20; 30:15-20; Eze 20:11; Ro 10:5
4:2 [n]Dt 12:32; Jos 1:7; Rev 22:18-19
4:3 [o]Nu 25:1-9; Ps 106:28
4:6 [p]Dt 30:19-20; Ps 19:7; Pr 1:7 [q]Job 28:28
4:7 [r]2Sa 7:23 [s]Ps 46:1; Isa 55:6
4:9 [t]Pr 4:23

your heart as long as you live. Teach[a] them to your children[b] and
to their children after them. 10Remember the day you stood before
the LORD your God at Horeb,[c] when he said to me, "Assemble the
people before me to hear my words so that they may learn to revere
me as long as they live in the land and may teach them to their
children." 11You came near and stood at the foot of the mountain
while it blazed with fire[d] to the very heavens, with black clouds
and deep darkness. 12Then the LORD spoke[e] to you out of the fire.
You heard the sound of words but saw no form; there was only a
voice. 13He declared to you his covenant,[f] the Ten Commandments,[g] which he commanded you to follow and then wrote them
on two stone tablets. 14And the LORD directed me at that time to
teach you the decrees and laws you are to follow in the land that
you are crossing the Jordan to possess.

15You saw no form[h] of any kind the day the LORD spoke to you
at Horeb out of the fire. Therefore watch yourselves very carefully,[i]
16so that you do not become corrupt and make for yourselves an
idol,[j] an image of any shape, whether formed like a man or a
woman, 17or like any animal on earth or any bird that flies in the
air, 18or like any creature that moves along the ground or any
fish in the waters below. 19And when you look up to the sky and
see the sun,[k] the moon and the stars—all the heavenly array[l]—
do not be enticed into bowing down to them and worshiping
things the LORD your God has apportioned to all the nations
under heaven. 20But as for you, the LORD took you and brought
you out of the iron-smelting furnace,[m] out of Egypt, to be the people of his inheritance,[n] as you now are.

21The LORD was angry with me[o] because of you, and he solemnly swore that I would not cross the Jordan and enter the good
land the LORD your God is giving you as your inheritance. 22I
will die in this land; I will not cross the Jordan; but you are
about to cross over and take possession of that good land.[p] 23Be
careful not to forget the covenant[q] of the LORD your God that he
made with you; do not make for yourselves an idol[r] in the form
of anything the LORD your God has forbidden. 24For the LORD
your God is a consuming fire,[s] a jealous God.

25After you have had children and grandchildren and have
lived in the land a long time—if you then become corrupt and
make any kind of idol, doing evil[t] in the eyes of the LORD your God
and provoking him to anger, 26I call heaven and earth as witnesses against you[u] this day that you will quickly perish from the land
that you are crossing the Jordan to possess. You will not live there
long but will certainly be destroyed. 27The LORD will scatter[v] you
among the peoples, and only a few of you will survive among the
nations to which the LORD will drive you. 28There you will worship

4:9 [a]Ge 18:19; Eph 6:4 [b]Ps 78:5-6
4:10 [c]Ex 19:9,16
4:11 [d]Ex 19:18; Heb 12:18-19
4:12 [e]Ex 20:22; Dt 5:4,22
4:13 [f]Dt 9:9,11 [g]Ex 24:12; 31:18; 34:28
4:15 [h]Isa 40:18 [i]Jos 23:11
4:16 [j]Ex 20:4-5; 32:7; Dt 5:8; Ro 1:23
4:19 [k]Dt 17:3; Job 31:26 [l]2Ki 17:16; 21:3; Ro 1:25
4:20 [m]1Ki 8:51; Jer 11:4 [n]Ex 19:5; Dt 9:29
4:21 [o]Nu 20:12; Dt 1:37
4:22 [p]Dt 3:25
4:23 [q]ver 9,16 [r]Ex 20:4
4:24 [s]Ex 24:17; Dt 9:3; Heb 12:29
4:25 [t]2Ki 17:2,17
4:26 [u]Dt 30:18-19; Isa 1:2; Mic 6:2
4:27 [v]Lev 26:33; Dt 28:36,64; Ne 1:8

man-made gods[a] of wood and stone, which cannot see or hear or
eat or smell.[b] 29But if from there you seek[c] the LORD your God,
you will find him if you look for him with all your heart[d] and with
all your soul.[e] 30When you are in distress and all these things have
happened to you, then in later days[f] you will return to the LORD
your God and obey him. 31For the LORD your God is a merciful[g]
God; he will not abandon or destroy you or forget the covenant
with your forefathers, which he confirmed to them by oath.

32Ask[h] now about the former days, long before your time,
from the day God created man on the earth;[i] ask from one end
of the heavens to the other.[j] Has anything so great as this ever
happened, or has anything like it ever been heard of? 33Has any
other people heard the voice of God[a] speaking out of fire, as you
have, and lived?[k] 34Has any god ever tried to take for himself one
nation out of another nation,[l] by testings, by miraculous signs[m]
and wonders,[n] by war, by a mighty hand and an outstretched
arm,[o] or by great and awesome deeds,[p] like all the things the
LORD your God did for you in Egypt before your very eyes?

35You were shown these things so that you might know that the
LORD is God; besides him there is no other.[q] 36From heaven he
made you hear his voice[r] to discipline you. On earth he showed
you his great fire, and you heard his words from out of the fire.
37Because he loved[s] your forefathers and chose their descendants after them, he brought you out of Egypt by his Presence
and his great strength,[t] 38to drive out before you nations greater
and stronger than you and to bring you into their land to give it
to you for your inheritance,[u] as it is today.

39Acknowledge and take to heart this day that the LORD is God
in heaven above and on the earth below. There is no other.[v]
40Keep[w] his decrees and commands, which I am giving you today,
so that it may go well[x] with you and your children after you and
that you may live long[y] in the land the LORD your God gives you
for all time.

41Then Moses set aside three cities east of the Jordan, 42to which
anyone who had killed a person could flee if he had unintentionally killed his neighbor without malice aforethought. He could flee
into one of these cities and save his life. 43The cities were these:
Bezer in the desert plateau, for the Reubenites; Ramoth in Gilead,
for the Gadites; and Golan in Bashan, for the Manassites.

44This is the law Moses set before the Israelites. 45These are the
stipulations, decrees and laws Moses gave them when they came
out of Egypt 46and were in the valley near Beth Peor east of the
Jordan, in the land of Sihon[z] king of the Amorites, who reigned

4:28 [a] Dt 28:36,64; 1Sa 26:19; Jer 16:13 [b] Ps 115:4-8; 135:15-18
4:29 [c] 2Ch 15:4; Isa 55:6 [d] Jer 29:13 [e] Dt 30:1-3,10
4:30 [f] Dt 31:29; Jer 23:20; Hos 3:5
4:31 [g] 2Ch 30:9; Ne 9:31; Ps 116:5; Jnh 4:2
4:32 [h] Dt 32:7; Job 8:8 [i] Ge 1:27 [j] Mt 24:31
4:33 [k] Ex 20:22; Dt 5:24-26
4:34 [l] Ex 6:6 [m] Ex 7:3 [n] Dt 7:19; 26:8 [o] Ex 13:3 [p] Dt 34:12
4:35 [q] Dt 32:39; 1Sa 2:2; Isa 45:5,18
4:36 [r] Ex 19:9,19
4:37 [s] Dt 10:15 [t] Ex 13:3,9,14
4:38 [u] Dt 7:1; 9:5
4:39 [v] ver 35; Jos 2:11
4:40 [w] Lev 22:31; Dt 5:33 [x] Dt 5:16 [y] Dt 6:3,18; Eph 6:2-3
4:46 [z] Nu 21:26; Dt 3:29

[a] 33 Or *of a god*

in Heshbon and was defeated by Moses and the Israelites as they
came out of Egypt. 47They took possession of his land and the land
of Og king of Bashan, the two Amorite kings east of the Jordan.
48This land extended from Aroer[a] on the rim of the Arnon Gorge
to Mount Siyon[a][b] (that is, Hermon), 49and included all the Arabah
east of the Jordan, as far as the Sea of the Arabah,[b] below the slopes
of Pisgah.

Chapter 5 Theme ______________________

5 Moses summoned all Israel and said:
Hear, O Israel, the decrees and laws I declare in your hearing
today. Learn them and be sure to follow them. 2The LORD our God
made a covenant[c] with us at Horeb. 3It was not with our fathers
that the LORD made this covenant, but with us, with all of us who
are alive here today.[d] 4The LORD spoke[e] to you face to face out of
the fire on the mountain. 5(At that time I stood between[f] the
LORD and you to declare to you the word of the LORD, because you
were afraid[g] of the fire and did not go up the mountain.) And he
said:

6"I am the LORD your God, who brought you out of
Egypt, out of the land of slavery.
7"You shall have no other gods before[c] me.
8"You shall not make for yourself an idol in the form of anything in heaven above or on the earth beneath or in the
waters below. 9You shall not bow down to them or worship them; for I, the LORD your God, am a jealous God,
punishing the children for the sin of the fathers to the
third and fourth generation of those who hate me,[h] 10but
showing love to a thousand ⌊generations⌋ of those who
love me and keep my commandments.[i]
11"You shall not misuse the name of the LORD your God, for the
LORD will not hold anyone guiltless who misuses his
name.[j]
12"Observe the Sabbath day by keeping it holy,[k] as the LORD
your God has commanded you. 13Six days you shall labor
and do all your work, 14but the seventh day[l] is a Sabbath to the LORD your God. On it you shall not do any
work, neither you, nor your son or daughter, nor your
manservant or maidservant, nor your ox, your donkey
or any of your animals, nor the alien within your gates,
so that your manservant and maidservant may rest, as
you do. 15Remember that you were slaves in Egypt and
that the LORD your God brought you out of there with a

4:48 [a] Dt 2:36 [b] Dt 3:9
5:2 [c] Ex 19:5
5:3 [d] Heb 8:9
5:4 [e] Dt 4:12,33,36
5:5 [f] Gal 3:19 [g] Ex 20:18,21
5:9 [h] Ex 34:7
5:10 [i] Jer 32:18
5:11 [j] Lev 19:12; Mt 5:33-37
5:12 [k] Ex 20:8
5:14 [l] Ge 2:2; Heb 4:4

a 48 Hebrew; Syriac (see also Deut. 3:9) *Sirion* b 49 That is, the Dead Sea c 7 Or *besides*

mighty hand and an outstretched arm.[a] Therefore the
LORD your God has commanded you to observe the
Sabbath day.
16"Honor your father and your mother,[b] as the LORD your God
has commanded you, so that you may live long[c] and
that it may go well with you in the land the LORD your
God is giving you.
17"You shall not murder.[d]
18"You shall not commit adultery.[e]
19"You shall not steal.
20"You shall not give false testimony against your neighbor.
21"You shall not covet your neighbor's wife. You shall not set
your desire on your neighbor's house or land, his manservant or maidservant, his ox or donkey, or anything
that belongs to your neighbor."[f]

22These are the commandments the LORD proclaimed in a loud
voice to your whole assembly there on the mountain from out of
the fire, the cloud and the deep darkness; and he added nothing
more. Then he wrote them on two stone tablets[g] and gave them
to me.
23When you heard the voice out of the darkness, while the
mountain was ablaze with fire, all the leading men of your tribes
and your elders came to me. 24And you said, "The LORD our God
has shown us his glory and his majesty, and we have heard his
voice from the fire. Today we have seen that a man can live even
if God speaks with him.[h] 25But now, why should we die? This
great fire will consume us, and we will die if we hear the voice of
the LORD our God any longer.[i] 26For what mortal man has ever
heard the voice of the living God speaking out of fire, as we have,
and survived?[j] 27Go near and listen to all that the LORD our God
says. Then tell us whatever the LORD our God tells you. We will
listen and obey."
28The LORD heard you when you spoke to me and the LORD
said to me, "I have heard what this people said to you. Everything
they said was good.[k] 29Oh, that their hearts would be inclined to
fear me[l] and keep all my commands[m] always, so that it might go
well with them and their children forever![n]
30"Go, tell them to return to their tents. 31But you stay here[o] with
me so that I may give you all the commands, decrees and laws you
are to teach them to follow in the land I am giving them to possess."
32So be careful to do what the LORD your God has commanded
you; do not turn aside to the right or to the left.[p] 33Walk in all the
way that the LORD your God has commanded you,[q] so that you

5:15 [a] Dt 4:34
5:16 [b] Ex 20:12; Lev 19:3; Dt 27:16; Eph 6:2-3*; Col 3:20 [c] Dt 4:40
5:17 [d] Mt 5:21-22*
5:18 [e] Mt 5:27-30; Lk 18:20*; Jas 2:11*
5:21 [f] Ro 7:7*; 13:9*
5:22 [g] Ex 24:12; 31:18; Dt 4:13
5:24 [h] Ex 19:19
5:25 [i] Dt 18:16
5:26 [j] Dt 4:33
5:28 [k] Dt 18:17
5:29 [l] Ps 81:8,13 [m] Dt 11:1; Isa 48:18 [n] Dt 4:1,40
5:31 [o] Ex 24:12
5:32 [p] Dt 17:11,20; 28:14; Jos 1:7; 23:6; Pr 4:27
5:33 [q] Jer 7:23

may live and prosper and prolong your days[a] in the land that you
will possess.

Chapter 6 Theme ______________________

6 These are the commands, decrees and laws the LORD your God
directed me to teach you to observe in the land that you are
crossing the Jordan to possess, 2so that you, your children and
their children after them may fear[b] the LORD your God as long as
you live by keeping all his decrees and commands that I give
you, and so that you may enjoy long life. 3Hear, O Israel, and be
careful to obey so that it may go well with you and that you may
increase greatly[c] in a land flowing with milk and honey,[d] just as
the LORD, the God of your fathers, promised you.
4Hear, O Israel: The LORD our God, the LORD is one.[a][e] 5Love[f] the
LORD your God with all your heart and with all your soul and with
all your strength.[g] 6These commandments that I give you today
are to be upon your hearts.[h] 7Impress them on your children.
Talk about them when you sit at home and when you walk along
the road, when you lie down and when you get up.[i] 8Tie them as
symbols on your hands and bind them on your foreheads.[j] 9Write
them on the doorframes of your houses and on your gates.[k]
10When the LORD your God brings you into the land he swore
to your fathers, to Abraham, Isaac and Jacob, to give you—a land
with large, flourishing cities you did not build,[l] 11houses filled
with all kinds of good things you did not provide, wells you did not
dig, and vineyards and olive groves you did not plant—then when
you eat and are satisfied,[m] 12be careful that you do not forget the
LORD, who brought you out of Egypt, out of the land of slavery.
13Fear the LORD[n] your God, serve him only[o] and take your oaths
in his name. 14Do not follow other gods, the gods of the peoples
around you; 15for the LORD your God[p], who is among you, is a jealous God and his anger will burn against you, and he will destroy
you from the face of the land. 16Do not test the LORD your God[q]
as you did at Massah. 17Be sure to keep the commands of the
LORD your God and the stipulations and decrees he has given
you.[r] 18Do what is right and good in the LORD's sight, so that it
may go well[s] with you and you may go in and take over the good
land that the LORD promised on oath to your forefathers, 19thrust-
ing out all your enemies before you, as the LORD said.
20In the future, when your son asks you,[t] "What is the meaning
of the stipulations, decrees and laws the LORD our God has commanded you?" 21tell him: "We were slaves of Pharaoh in Egypt, but
the LORD brought us out of Egypt with a mighty hand. 22Before

a4 Or *The LORD our God is one LORD*; or *The LORD is our God, the LORD is one*; or *The LORD is our God, the LORD alone*

5:33 [a]Dt 4:40
6:2 [b]Ex 20:20; Dt 10:12-13
6:3 [c]Dt 5:33 [d]Ex 3:8
6:4 [e]Mk 12:29*; 1Co 8:4
6:5 [f]Mt 22:37*; Mk 12:30*; Lk 10:27* [g]Dt 10:12
6:6 [h]Dt 11:18
6:7 [i]Dt 4:9; 11:19; Eph 6:4
6:8 [j]Ex 13:9,16; Dt 11:18
6:9 [k]Dt 11:20
6:10 [l]Jos 24:13
6:11 [m]Dt 8:10
6:13 [n]Dt 10:20 [o]Mt 4:10*; Lk 4:8*
6:15 [p]Dt 4:24
6:16 [q]Ex 17:7; Mt 4:7*; Lk 4:12*
6:17 [r]Dt 11:22; Ps 119:4
6:18 [s]Dt 4:40
6:20 [t]Ex 13:14

our eyes the LORD sent miraculous signs and wonders—great
and terrible—upon Egypt and Pharaoh and his whole household. 23But he brought us out from there to bring us in and give
us the land that he promised on oath to our forefathers. 24The
LORD commanded us to obey all these decrees and to fear the
LORD our God,[a] so that we might always prosper and be kept
alive, as is the case today.[b] 25And if we are careful to obey all this
law before the LORD our God, as he has commanded us, that will
be our righteousness.[c]"

Chapter 7 Theme

7 When the LORD your God brings you into the land you are
entering to possess and drives out before you many nations[d]—
the Hittites, Girgashites, Amorites, Canaanites, Perizzites, Hivites
and Jebusites, seven nations larger and stronger than you—
2and when the LORD your God has delivered them over to you
and you have defeated them, then you must destroy them totally.[a]
Make no treaty[e] with them, and show them no mercy.[f] 3Do not
intermarry with them.[g] Do not give your daughters to their sons
or take their daughters for your sons, 4for they will turn your sons
away from following me to serve other gods, and the LORD's anger
will burn against you and will quickly destroy[h] you. 5This is
what you are to do to them: Break down their altars, smash their
sacred stones, cut down their Asherah poles[b] and burn their idols
in the fire.[i] 6For you are a people holy[j] to the LORD your God.[k] The
LORD your God has chosen[l] you out of all the peoples on the face
of the earth to be his people, his treasured possession.

7The LORD did not set his affection on you and choose you
because you were more numerous than other peoples, for you were
the fewest of all peoples.[m] 8But it was because the LORD loved[n]
you and kept the oath he swore[o] to your forefathers that he
brought you out with a mighty hand and redeemed you from
the land of slavery,[p] from the power of Pharaoh king of Egypt.
9Know therefore that the LORD your God is God;[q] he is the faithful God,[r] keeping his covenant of love[s] to a thousand generations
of those who love him and keep his commands. 10But

> those who hate him he will repay to their face by
> destruction;
> he will not be slow to repay to their face those
> who hate him.

11Therefore, take care to follow the commands, decrees and laws
I give you today.

[a]2 The Hebrew term refers to the irrevocable giving over of things or persons to the LORD, often by totally destroying them; also in verse 26. [b]5 That is, symbols of the goddess Asherah; here and elsewhere in Deuteronomy

6:24 [a]Dt 10:12; Jer 32:39 [b]Ps 41:2
6:25 [c]Dt 24:13; Ro 10:3,5
7:1 [d]Dt 31:3; Ac 13:19
7:2 [e]Ex 23:32 [f]Dt 13:8
7:3 [g]Ex 34:15-16; Ezr 9:2
7:4 [h]Dt 6:15
7:5 [i]Ex 23:24; Dt 12:2-3
7:6 [j]Ex 19:5-6; 1Pe 2:9 [k]Ps 50:5; Jer 2:3 [l]Dt 14:2
7:7 [m]Dt 10:22
7:8 [n]Dt 10:15 [o]Ex 32:13 [p]Ex 13:14
7:9 [q]Dt 4:35 [r]1Co 1:9; 2Ti 2:13 [s]Ne 1:5; Da 9:4

12If you pay attention to these laws and are careful to follow
them, then the LORD your God will keep his covenant of love with
you, as he swore to your forefathers.[a] 13He will love you and bless
you[b] and increase your numbers. He will bless the fruit of your
womb, the crops of your land—your grain, new wine and oil—
the calves of your herds and the lambs of your flocks in the land
that he swore to your forefathers to give you.[c] 14You will be blessed
more than any other people; none of your men or women will be
childless, nor any of your livestock without young.[d] 15The LORD
will keep you free from every disease.[e] He will not inflict on you
the horrible diseases you knew in Egypt, but he will inflict them
on all who hate you. 16You must destroy all the peoples the LORD
your God gives over to you. Do not look on them with pity[f] and do
not serve their gods, for that will be a snare[g] to you.

17You may say to yourselves, "These nations are stronger than
we are. How can we drive them out?[h]" 18But do not be afraid[i] of
them; remember well what the LORD your God did to Pharaoh
and to all Egypt.[j] 19You saw with your own eyes the great trials,
the miraculous signs and wonders, the mighty hand and outstretched arm, with which the LORD your God brought you out.
The LORD your God will do the same to all the peoples you now
fear.[k] 20Moreover, the LORD your God will send the hornet[l] among
them until even the survivors who hide from you have perished.
21Do not be terrified by them, for the LORD your God, who is
among you,[m] is a great and awesome God.[n] 22The LORD your
God will drive out those nations before you, little by little.[o] You
will not be allowed to eliminate them all at once, or the wild animals will multiply around you. 23But the LORD your God will
deliver them over to you, throwing them into great confusion
until they are destroyed. 24He will give their kings into your
hand, and you will wipe out their names from under heaven. No
one will be able to stand up against you;[p] you will destroy them.
25The images of their gods you are to burn[q] in the fire. Do not
covet[r] the silver and gold on them, and do not take it for yourselves, or you will be ensnared[s] by it, for it is detestable[t] to the
LORD your God. 26Do not bring a detestable thing into your
house or you, like it, will be set apart for destruction.[u] Utterly
abhor and detest it, for it is set apart for destruction.

Chapter 8 Theme ______________________

8 Be careful to follow every command I am giving you today,
so that you may live[v] and increase and may enter and possess
the land that the LORD promised on oath to your forefathers.
2Remember how the LORD your God led[w] you all the way in the
desert these forty years, to humble you and to test you in order to

7:12 [a]Lev 26:3-13; Dt 28:1-14; Ps 105:8-9
7:13 [b]Jn 14:21 [c]Dt 28:4
7:14 [d]Ex 23:26
7:15 [e]Ex 15:26
7:16 [f]ver 2; Ex 23:33 [g]Jdg 8:27
7:17 [h]Nu 33:53
7:18 [i]Dt 31:6 [j]Ps 105:5
7:19 [k]Dt 4:34
7:20 [l]Ex 23:28; Jos 24:12
7:21 [m]Jos 3:10 [n]Dt 10:17; Ne 9:32
7:22 [o]Ex 23:28-30
7:24 [p]Jos 23:9
7:25 [q]Ex 32:20; 1Ch 14:12 [r]Jos 7:21 [s]Jdg 8:27 [t]Dt 17:1
7:26 [u]Lev 27:28-29
8:1 [v]Dt 4:1
8:2 [w]Am 2:10

know what was in your heart, whether or not you would keep his
commands. 3He humbled you, causing you to hunger and then
feeding you with manna,[a] which neither you nor your fathers had
known, to teach you that man does not live on bread alone but
on every word that comes from the mouth of the LORD.[b] 4Your
clothes did not wear out and your feet did not swell during these
forty years.[c] 5Know then in your heart that as a man disciplines
his son, so the LORD your God disciplines you.[d]
6Observe the commands of the LORD your God, walking in his
ways and revering him.[e] 7For the LORD your God is bringing you
into a good land—a land with streams and pools of water, with
springs flowing in the valleys and hills;[f] 8a land with wheat and barley, vines and fig trees, pomegranates, olive oil and honey; 9a land
where bread will not be scarce and you will lack nothing; a land
where the rocks are iron and you can dig copper out of the hills.
10When you have eaten and are satisfied,[g] praise the LORD your
God for the good land he has given you. 11Be careful that you do
not forget the LORD your God, failing to observe his commands,
his laws and his decrees that I am giving you this day. 12Otherwise,
when you eat and are satisfied, when you build fine houses and
settle down,[h] 13and when your herds and flocks grow large and
your silver and gold increase and all you have is multiplied, 14then
your heart will become proud and you will forget[i] the LORD your
God, who brought you out of Egypt, out of the land of slavery.
15He led you through the vast and dreadful desert,[j] that thirsty and
waterless land, with its venomous snakes[k] and scorpions. He
brought you water out of hard rock.[l] 16He gave you manna to eat
in the desert, something your fathers had never known,[m] to humble and to test you so that in the end it might go well with you.
17You may say to yourself,[n] "My power and the strength of my
hands have produced this wealth for me." 18But remember the
LORD your God, for it is he who gives you the ability to produce
wealth,[o] and so confirms his covenant, which he swore to your
forefathers, as it is today.
19If you ever forget the LORD your God and follow other gods and
worship and bow down to them, I testify against you today that
you will surely be destroyed.[p] 20Like the nations the LORD destroyed
before you, so you will be destroyed for not obeying the LORD
your God.

Chapter 9 Theme ____________________________

9 Hear, O Israel. You are now about to cross the Jordan to go in
and dispossess nations greater and stronger than you,[q] with
large cities that have walls up to the sky.[r] 2The people are strong
and tall—Anakites! You know about them and have heard it said:

8:3 [a]Ex 16:12,14,35 [b]Ex 16:2-3; Mt 4:4*; Lk 4:4*
8:4 [c]Dt 29:5; Ne 9:21
8:5 [d]2Sa 7:14; Pr 3:11-12; Heb 12:5-11; Rev 3:19
8:6 [e]Dt 5:33
8:7 [f]Dt 11:9-12
8:10 [g]Dt 6:10-12
8:12 [h]Hos 13:6
8:14 [i]Ps 106:21
8:15 [j]Jer 2:6 [k]Nu 21:6 [l]Nu 20:11; Ps 78:15; 114:8
8:16 [m]Ex 16:15
8:17 [n]Dt 9:4,7,24
8:18 [o]Pr 10:22; Hos 2:8
8:19 [p]Dt 4:26; 30:18
9:1 [q]Dt 4:38; 11:23,31 [r]Dt 1:28

"Who can stand up against the Anakites?"[a] 3But be assured today
that the LORD your God is the one who goes across ahead of you[b]
like a devouring fire.[c] He will destroy them; he will subdue them
before you. And you will drive them out and annihilate them
quickly,[d] as the LORD has promised you.
4After the LORD your God has driven them out before you, do not
say to yourself,[e] "The LORD has brought me here to take possession of this land because of my righteousness." No, it is on account
of the wickedness of these nations[f] that the LORD is going to
drive them out before you. 5It is not because of your righteousness or your integrity[g] that you are going in to take possession of
their land; but on account of the wickedness of these nations, the
LORD your God will drive them out before you, to accomplish what
he swore[h] to your fathers, to Abraham, Isaac and Jacob. 6Under-
stand, then, that it is not because of your righteousness that the
LORD your God is giving you this good land to possess, for you
are a stiff-necked people.[i]
7Remember this and never forget how you provoked the LORD
your God to anger in the desert. From the day you left Egypt until
you arrived here, you have been rebellious against the LORD. 8At
Horeb you aroused the LORD's wrath so that he was angry enough
to destroy you.[j] 9When I went up on the mountain to receive the
tablets of stone, the tablets of the covenant that the LORD had made
with you, I stayed on the mountain forty days and forty nights; I
ate no bread and drank no water.[k] 10The LORD gave me two stone
tablets inscribed by the finger of God.[l] On them were all the
commandments the LORD proclaimed to you on the mountain
out of the fire, on the day of the assembly.
11At the end of the forty days and forty nights, the LORD gave me
the two stone tablets, the tablets of the covenant. 12Then the LORD
told me, "Go down from here at once, because your people whom
you brought out of Egypt have become corrupt.[m] They have
turned away quickly[n] from what I commanded them and have
made a cast idol for themselves."
13And the LORD said to me, "I have seen this people[o], and they are
a stiff-necked people indeed! 14Let me alone,[p] so that I may destroy
them and blot out[q] their name from under heaven. And I will
make you into a nation stronger and more numerous than they."
15So I turned and went down from the mountain while it was
ablaze with fire. And the two tablets of the covenant were in my
hands.[a][r] 16When I looked, I saw that you had sinned against the
LORD your God; you had made for yourselves an idol cast in the
shape of a calf.[s] You had turned aside quickly from the way that
the LORD had commanded you. 17So I took the two tablets and

[a] 15 Or *And I had the two tablets of the covenant with me, one in each hand*

9:2 [a]Nu 13:22,28, 32-33
9:3 [b]Dt 31:3; Jos 3:11 [c]Dt 4:24; Heb 12:29 [d]Ex 23:31; Dt 7:23-24
9:4 [e]Dt 8:17 [f]Lev 18:21, 24-30; Dt 18:9-14
9:5 [g]Tit 3:5 [h]Ge 12:7; 13:15; 15:7; 17:8; 26:4
9:6 [i]ver 13; Ex 32:9; Dt 31:27
9:8 [j]Ex 32:7-10; Ps 106:19
9:9 [k]Ex 24:12, 15,18; 34:28
9:10 [l]Ex 31:18; Dt 4:13
9:12 [m]Ex 32:7-8; Dt 31:29 [n]Jdg 2:17
9:13 [o]ver 6; Ex 32:9; Dt 10:16
9:14 [p]Ex 32:10 [q]Nu 14:12; Dt 29:20
9:15 [r]Ex 19:18; 32:15
9:16 [s]Ex 32:19

threw them out of my hands, breaking them to pieces before
your eyes.
18Then once again I fell[a] prostrate before the LORD for forty days
and forty nights; I ate no bread and drank no water, because of
all the sin you had committed, doing what was evil in the LORD's
sight and so provoking him to anger. 19I feared the anger and
wrath of the LORD, for he was angry enough with you to destroy
you.[b] But again the LORD listened to me.[c] 20And the LORD was
angry enough with Aaron to destroy him, but at that time I prayed
for Aaron too. 21Also I took that sinful thing of yours, the calf
you had made, and burned it in the fire. Then I crushed it and
ground it to powder as fine as dust and threw the dust into a
stream that flowed down the mountain.[d]
22You also made the LORD angry at Taberah,[e] at Massah[f] and at
Kibroth Hattaavah.[g]
23And when the LORD sent you out from Kadesh Barnea, he
said, "Go up and take possession of the land I have given you."
But you rebelled against the command of the LORD your God.
You did not trust[h] him or obey him. 24You have been rebellious
against the LORD ever since I have known you.[i]
25I lay prostrate before the LORD those forty days and forty nights
because the LORD had said he would destroy you.[j] 26I prayed to
the LORD and said, "O Sovereign LORD, do not destroy your people,
your own inheritance that you redeemed by your great power
and brought out of Egypt with a mighty hand.[k] 27Remember
your servants Abraham, Isaac and Jacob. Overlook the stubbornness of this people, their wickedness and their sin. 28Other-
wise, the country from which you brought us will say, 'Because
the LORD was not able to take them into the land he had promised
them, and because he hated them, he brought them out to put
them to death in the desert.'[l] 29But they are your people, your
inheritance[m] that you brought out by your great power and your
outstretched arm.[n]"

Chapter 10 Theme ____________________________________

10 At that time the LORD said to me, "Chisel out two stone
tablets[o] like the first ones and come up to me on the mountain. Also make a wooden chest.[a] 2I will write on the tablets the
words that were on the first tablets, which you broke. Then you
are to put them in the chest."[p]
3So I made the ark out of acacia wood[q] and chiseled[r] out two
stone tablets like the first ones, and I went up on the mountain
with the two tablets in my hands. 4The LORD wrote on these
tablets what he had written before, the Ten Commandments he

a *1* That is, an ark

9:18 [a]Ex 34:28
9:19 [b]Ex 32:10-11,14 [c]Dt 10:10
9:21 [d]Ex 32:20
9:22 [e]Nu 11:3 [f]Ex 17:7 [g]Nu 11:34
9:23 [h]Ps 106:24
9:24 [i]ver 7; Dt 31:27
9:25 [j]ver 18
9:26 [k]Ex 32:11
9:28 [l]Ex 32:12; Nu 14:16
9:29 [m]Dt 4:20; 1Ki 8:51 [n]Dt 4:34; Ne 1:10
10:1 [o]Ex 25:10; 34:1-2
10:2 [p]Ex 25:16,21; Dt 4:13
10:3 [q]Ex 25:5,10; 37:1-9 [r]Ex 34:4

had proclaimed[a] to you on the mountain, out of the fire, on the
day of the assembly. And the LORD gave them to me. 5Then I
came back down the mountain[b] and put the tablets in the ark[c] I
had made, as the LORD commanded me, and they are there now.[d]
6(The Israelites traveled from the wells of the Jaakanites to
Moserah.[e] There Aaron died and was buried, and Eleazar his son
succeeded him as priest.[f] 7From there they traveled to Gudgodah
and on to Jotbathah, a land with streams of water.[g] 8At that time
the LORD set apart the tribe of Levi[h] to carry the ark of the
covenant of the LORD, to stand before the LORD to minister[i] and to
pronounce blessings[j] in his name, as they still do today. 9That is
why the Levites have no share or inheritance among their brothers;
the LORD is their inheritance,[k] as the LORD your God told them.)
10Now I had stayed on the mountain forty days and nights, as I
did the first time, and the LORD listened to me at this time also. It
was not his will to destroy you.[l] 11"Go," the LORD said to me,
"and lead the people on their way, so that they may enter and
possess the land that I swore to their fathers to give them."
12And now, O Israel, what does the LORD your God ask of you[m]
but to fear the LORD your God, to walk in all his ways, to love
him,[n] to serve the LORD your God with all your heart[o] and with
all your soul, 13and to observe the LORD's commands and decrees
that I am giving you today for your own good?
14To the LORD your God belong the heavens, even the highest
heavens,[p] the earth and everything in it.[q] 15Yet the LORD set his
affection on your forefathers and loved[r] them, and he chose you,
their descendants, above all the nations, as it is today. 16Circum-
cise[s] your hearts, therefore, and do not be stiff-necked[t] any
longer. 17For the LORD your God is God of gods[u] and Lord of
lords, the great God, mighty and awesome, who shows no partiality[v] and accepts no bribes. 18He defends the cause of the fatherless
and the widow,[w] and loves the alien, giving him food and clothing.
19And you are to love those who are aliens, for you yourselves were
aliens in Egypt.[x] 20Fear the LORD your God and serve him.[y] Hold
fast[z] to him and take your oaths in his name.[a] 21He is your praise;[b]
he is your God, who performed for you those great and awesome
wonders[c] you saw with your own eyes. 22Your forefathers who
went down into Egypt were seventy in all,[d] and now the LORD
your God has made you as numerous as the stars in the sky.[e]

Chapter 11 Theme ____________________

11 Love[f] the LORD your God and keep his requirements, his
decrees, his laws and his commands always.[g] 2Remember
today that your children were not the ones who saw and experienced the discipline of the LORD your God:[h] his majesty, his mighty

10:4 [a]Ex 20:1
10:5 [b]Ex 34:29 [c]Ex 40:20 [d]1Ki 8:9
10:6 [e]Nu 33:30-31,38 [f]Nu 20:25-28
10:7 [g]Nu 33:32-34
10:8 [h]Nu 3:6 [i]Dt 18:5 [j]Dt 21:5
10:9 [k]Nu 18:20; Dt 18:1-2; Eze 44:28
10:10 [l]Ex 33:17; 34:28; Dt 9:18-19,25
10:12 [m]Mic 6:8 [n]Dt 5:33; 6:13; Mt 22:37 [o]Dt 6:5
10:14 [p]1Ki 8:27 [q]Ex 19:5
10:15 [r]Dt 4:37
10:16 [s]Jer 4:4 [t]Dt 9:6
10:17 [u]Jos 22:22; Da 2:47 [v]Ac 10:34; Ro 2:11; Eph 6:9
10:18 [w]Ps 68:5
10:19 [x]Lev 19:34
10:20 [y]Mt 4:10 [z]Dt 11:22 [a]Ps 63:11
10:21 [b]Ex 15:2; Jer 17:14 [c]Ps 106:21-22
10:22 [d]Ge 46:26-27 [e]Ge 15:5; Dt 1:10
11:1 [f]Dt 10:12 [g]Zec 3:7
11:2 [h]Dt 5:24; 8:5

hand, his outstretched arm; 3the signs he performed and the things he did in the heart of Egypt, both to Pharaoh king of Egypt and to his whole country; 4what he did to the Egyptian army, to its horses and chariots, how he overwhelmed them with the waters of the Red Sea[a][a] as they were pursuing you, and how the LORD brought lasting ruin on them. 5It was not your children who saw what he did for you in the desert until you arrived at this place, 6and what he did[b] to Dathan and Abiram, sons of Eliab the Reubenite, when the earth opened its mouth right in the middle of all Israel and swallowed them up with their households, their tents and every living thing that belonged to them. 7But it was your own eyes that saw all these great things the LORD has done.

8Observe therefore all the commands I am giving you today, so that you may have the strength to go in and take over the land that you are crossing the Jordan to possess,[c] 9and so that you may live long[d] in the land that the LORD swore[e] to your forefathers to give to them and their descendants, a land flowing with milk and honey.[f] 10The land you are entering to take over is not like the land of Egypt, from which you have come, where you planted your seed and irrigated it by foot as in a vegetable garden. 11But the land you are crossing the Jordan to take possession of is a land of mountains and valleys that drinks rain from heaven.[g] 12It is a land the LORD your God cares for; the eyes[h] of the LORD your God are continually on it from the beginning of the year to its end.

13So if you faithfully obey[i] the commands I am giving you today—to love[j] the LORD your God and to serve him with all your heart and with all your soul— 14then I will send rain[k] on your land in its season, both autumn and spring rains,[l] so that you may gather in your grain, new wine and oil. 15I will provide grass[m] in the fields for your cattle, and you will eat and be satisfied.[n]

16Be careful, or you will be enticed to turn away and worship other gods and bow down to them.[o] 17Then the LORD's anger[p] will burn against you, and he will shut[q] the heavens so that it will not rain and the ground will yield no produce, and you will soon perish[r] from the good land the LORD is giving you. 18Fix these words of mine in your hearts and minds; tie them as symbols on your hands and bind them on your foreheads.[s] 19Teach them to your children,[t] talking about them when you sit at home and when you walk along the road, when you lie down and when you get up.[u] 20Write them on the doorframes of your houses and on your gates,[v] 21so that your days and the days of your children may be many[w] in the land that the LORD swore to give your forefathers, as many as the days that the heavens are above the earth.[x]

11:4 [a]Ex 14:27
11:6 [b]Nu 16:1-35
11:8 [c]Jos 1:7
11:9 [d]Dt 4:40; Pr 10:27 [e]Dt 9:5 [f]Ex 3:8
11:11 [g]Dt 8:7
11:12 [h]1Ki 9:3
11:13 [i]Dt 6:17 [j]Dt 10:12
11:14 [k]Lev 26:4; Dt 28:12 [l]Joel 2:23; Jas 5:7
11:15 [m]Ps 104:14 [n]Dt 6:11
11:16 [o]Dt 8:19; 29:18; Job 31:9,27
11:17 [p]Dt 6:15 [q]1Ki 8:35; 2Ch 6:26 [r]Dt 4:26
11:18 [s]Dt 6:6-8
11:19 [t]Dt 6:7 [u]Dt 4:9-10
11:20 [v]Dt 6:9
11:21 [w]Pr 3:2; 4:10 [x]Ps 72:5

[a]4 Hebrew *Yam Suph*; that is, Sea of Reeds

22If you carefully observe[a] all these commands I am giving you to follow—to love the LORD your God, to walk in all his ways and to hold fast[b] to him— 23then the LORD will drive out all these nations before you, and you will dispossess nations larger and stronger than you.[c] 24Every place where you set your foot will be yours:[d] Your territory will extend from the desert to Lebanon, and from the Euphrates River to the western sea.[a] 25No man will be able to stand against you. The LORD your God, as he promised you, will put the terror and fear of you on the whole land, wherever you go.[e]

26See, I am setting before you today a blessing and a curse[f]— 27the blessing[g] if you obey the commands of the LORD your God that I am giving you today; 28the curse if you disobey[h] the commands of the LORD your God and turn from the way that I command you today by following other gods, which you have not known. 29When the LORD your God has brought you into the land you are entering to possess, you are to proclaim on Mount Gerizim the blessings, and on Mount Ebal the curses.[i] 30As you know, these mountains are across the Jordan, west of the road,[b] toward the setting sun, near the great trees of Moreh,[j] in the territory of those Canaanites living in the Arabah in the vicinity of Gilgal.[k] 31You are about to cross the Jordan to enter and take possession[l] of the land the LORD your God is giving you. When you have taken it over and are living there, 32be sure that you obey all the decrees and laws I am setting before you today.

Chapter 12 Theme ______________________________

12 These are the decrees and laws you must be careful to follow in the land that the LORD, the God of your fathers, has given you to possess—as long as you live in the land.[m] 2Destroy completely all the places on the high mountains and on the hills and under every spreading tree[n] where the nations you are dispossessing worship their gods. 3Break down their altars, smash[o] their sacred stones and burn their Asherah poles in the fire; cut down the idols of their gods and wipe out their names from those places.

4You must not worship the LORD your God in their way. 5But you are to seek the place the LORD your God will choose from among all your tribes to put his Name there for his dwelling.[p] To that place you must go; 6there bring your burnt offerings and sacrifices, your tithes[q] and special gifts, what you have vowed to give and your freewill offerings, and the firstborn of your herds and

11:22 [a]Dt 6:17 [b]Dt 10:20
11:23 [c]Dt 4:38; 9:1
11:24 [d]Ge 15:18; Ex 23:31; Jos 1:3; 14:9
11:25 [e]Ex 23:27; Dt 7:24
11:26 [f]Dt 30:1,15,19
11:27 [g]Dt 28:1-14
11:28 [h]Dt 28:15
11:29 [i]Dt 27:12-13; Jos 8:33
11:30 [j]Ge 12:6 [k]Jos 4:19
11:31 [l]Dt 9:1; Jos 1:11
12:1 [m]Dt 4:9-10; 1Ki 8:40
12:2 [n]2Ki 16:4; 17:10
12:3 [o]Nu 33:52; Dt 7:5; Jdg 2:2
12:5 [p]ver 11,13; 2Ch 7:12,16
12:6 [q]Dt 14:22-23

[a]24 That is, the Mediterranean [b]30 Or *Jordan, westward*

flocks. 7There, in the presence of the LORD your God, you and
your families shall eat and shall rejoice[a] in everything you have
put your hand to, because the LORD your God has blessed you.
8You are not to do as we do here today, everyone as he sees fit,
9since you have not yet reached the resting place and the inheritance the LORD your God is giving you. 10But you will cross the
Jordan and settle in the land the LORD your God is giving[b] you as
an inheritance, and he will give you rest from all your enemies
around you so that you will live in safety. 11Then to the place the
LORD your God will choose as a dwelling for his Name[c]—there
you are to bring everything I command you: your burnt offerings
and sacrifices, your tithes and special gifts, and all the choice
possessions you have vowed to the LORD. 12And there rejoice[d]
before the LORD your God, you, your sons and daughters, your
menservants and maidservants, and the Levites from your
towns, who have no allotment or inheritance[e] of their own. 13Be
careful not to sacrifice your burnt offerings anywhere you please.
14Offer them only at the place the LORD will choose[f] in one of your
tribes, and there observe everything I command you.
15Nevertheless, you may slaughter your animals in any of your
towns and eat as much of the meat as you want, as if it were
gazelle or deer,[g] according to the blessing the LORD your God
gives you. Both the ceremonially unclean and the clean may eat
it. 16But you must not eat the blood;[h] pour it out on the ground
like water.[i] 17You must not eat in your own towns the tithe of
your grain and new wine and oil, or the firstborn of your herds
and flocks, or whatever you have vowed to give, or your freewill
offerings or special gifts. 18Instead, you are to eat[j] them in the
presence of the LORD your God at the place the LORD your God
will choose[k]—you, your sons and daughters, your menservants
and maidservants, and the Levites from your towns—and you
are to rejoice[l] before the LORD your God in everything you put
your hand to. 19Be careful not to neglect the Levites[m] as long as
you live in your land.
20When the LORD your God has enlarged your territory[n] as he
promised[o] you, and you crave meat and say, "I would like some
meat," then you may eat as much of it as you want. 21If the place
where the LORD your God chooses to put his Name is too far away
from you, you may slaughter animals from the herds and flocks
the LORD has given you, as I have commanded you, and in your
own towns you may eat as much of them as you want. 22Eat them
as you would gazelle or deer.[p] Both the ceremonially unclean
and the clean may eat. 23But be sure you do not eat the blood,[q]
because the blood is the life, and you must not eat the life with
the meat. 24You must not eat the blood; pour it out on the ground

12:7 [a] ver 12,18; Lev 23:40; Dt 14:26
12:10 [b] Dt 11:31
12:11 [c] ver 5; Dt 15:20; 16:2
12:12 [d] ver 7 [e] Dt 10:9; 14:29
12:14 [f] ver 11
12:15 [g] ver 20-23; Dt 14:5; 15:22
12:16 [h] Ge 9:4; Lev 7:26; 17:10-12 [i] Dt 15:23
12:18 [j] Dt 14:23 [k] ver 5 [l] ver 7,12
12:19 [m] Dt 14:27
12:20 [n] Dt 19:8 [o] Ge 15:18; Dt 11:24
12:22 [p] ver 15
12:23 [q] ver 16; Ge 9:4; Lev 17:11,14

like water. 25 Do not eat it, so that it may go well[a] with you and your children after you, because you will be doing what is right[b] in the eyes of the LORD.

26 But take your consecrated things and whatever you have vowed to give,[c] and go to the place the LORD will choose. 27 Present your burnt offerings[d] on the altar of the LORD your God, both the meat and the blood. The blood of your sacrifices must be poured beside the altar of the LORD your God, but you may eat the meat. 28 Be careful to obey all these regulations I am giving you, so that it may always go well[e] with you and your children after you, because you will be doing what is good and right in the eyes of the LORD your God.

29 The LORD your God will cut off[f] before you the nations you are about to invade and dispossess. But when you have driven them out and settled in their land, 30 and after they have been destroyed before you, be careful not to be ensnared by inquiring about their gods, saying, "How do these nations serve their gods? We will do the same." 31 You must not worship the LORD your God in their way, because in worshiping their gods, they do all kinds of detestable things the LORD hates.[g] They even burn their sons[h] and daughters in the fire as sacrifices to their gods.

32 See that you do all I command you; do not add[i] to it or take away from it.

Chapter 13 Theme ______________________

13 If a prophet,[j] or one who foretells by dreams, appears among you and announces to you a miraculous sign or wonder, 2 and if the sign or wonder of which he has spoken takes place, and he says, "Let us follow other gods"[k] (gods you have not known) "and let us worship them," 3 you must not listen to the words of that prophet or dreamer. The LORD your God is testing[l] you to find out whether you love him with all your heart and with all your soul. 4 It is the LORD your God you must follow,[m] and him you must revere. Keep his commands and obey him; serve him and hold fast[n] to him. 5 That prophet or dreamer must be put to death, because he preached rebellion against the LORD your God, who brought you out of Egypt and redeemed you from the land of slavery; he has tried to turn you from the way the LORD your God commanded you to follow. You must purge the evil[o] from among you.

6 If your very own brother, or your son or daughter, or the wife you love, or your closest friend secretly entices[p] you, saying, "Let us go and worship other gods" (gods that neither you nor your fathers have known, 7 gods of the peoples around you, whether near or far, from one end of the land to the other), 8 do not yield[q]

12:25 [a] Dt 4:40; Isa 3:10 [b] Ex 15:26; Dt 13:18; 1Ki 11:38

12:26 [c] ver 17; Nu 5:9-10

12:27 [d] Lev 1:5,9,13

12:28 [e] ver 25; Dt 4:40

12:29 [f] Jos 23:4

12:31 [g] Dt 9:5 [h] Dt 18:10; Jer 32:35

12:32 [i] Dt 4:2; Jos 1:7; Rev 22:18-19

13:1 [j] Mt 24:24; Mk 13:22; 2Th 2:9

13:2 [k] ver 6,13

13:3 [l] Dt 8:2,16

13:4 [m] 2Ki 23:3; 2Ch 34:31 [n] Dt 10:20

13:5 [o] Dt 17:7,12; 1Co 5:13

13:6 [p] Dt 17:2-7; 29:18

13:8 [q] Pr 1:10

13:9 [a]Dt 17:5,7 to him or listen to him. Show him no pity. Do not spare him or
shield him. 9 You must certainly put him to death.[a] Your hand
must be the first in putting him to death, and then the hands of
13:11 all the people. 10 Stone him to death, because he tried to turn you
[b]Dt 19:20 away from the LORD your God, who brought you out of Egypt,
out of the land of slavery. 11 Then all Israel will hear and be
13:13 afraid,[b] and no one among you will do such an evil thing again.
[c]ver 2,6; 12 If you hear it said about one of the towns the LORD your God
1Jn 2:19 is giving you to live in 13 that wicked men[c] have arisen among you
and have led the people of their town astray, saying, "Let us go
13:16 and worship other gods" (gods you have not known), 14 then you
[d]Jos 6:24 must inquire, probe and investigate it thoroughly. And if it is true
[e]Jos 8:28; Jer 49:2 and it has been proved that this detestable thing has been done
among you, 15 you must certainly put to the sword all who live in
that town. Destroy it completely,[a] both its people and its livestock.
13:17 [f]Nu 25:4 16 Gather all the plunder of the town into the middle of the public
[g]Dt 30:3 square and completely burn the town and all its plunder as a
[h]Dt 7:13 [i]Ge 22:17; whole burnt offering to the LORD your God.[d] It is to remain a
26:4,24; 28:14 ruin[e] forever, never to be rebuilt. 17 None of those condemned
things[a] shall be found in your hands, so that the LORD will turn
from his fierce anger;[f] he will show you mercy, have compassion[g]
13:18 on you, and increase your numbers,[h] as he promised[i] on oath to
[j]Dt 12:25,28 your forefathers, 18 because you obey the LORD your God, keeping
all his commands that I am giving you today and doing what is
14:1 right[j] in his eyes.

Chapter 14 Theme ______________________

[k]Lev 19:28; 21:5; Jer 16:6; 41:5; Ro 8:14; 9:8; Gal 3:26

14 You are the children[k] of the LORD your God. Do not cut
yourselves or shave the front of your heads for the dead,
2 for you are a people holy to the LORD your God.[l] Out of all the
peoples on the face of the earth, the LORD has chosen you to be
his treasured possession.[m]
14:2 [l]Lev 20:26 [m]Dt 7:6; 26:18-19 3 Do not eat any detestable thing.[n] 4 These are the animals you
may eat:[o] the ox, the sheep, the goat, 5 the deer, the gazelle, the roe
deer, the wild goat, the ibex, the antelope and the mountain sheep.[b]
6 You may eat any animal that has a split hoof divided in two and
14:3 [n]Eze 4:14 that chews the cud. 7 However, of those that chew the cud or that
have a split hoof completely divided you may not eat the camel,
the rabbit or the coney.[c] Although they chew the cud, they do not
14:4 [o]Lev 11:2-45; Ac 10:14 have a split hoof; they are ceremonially unclean for you. 8 The pig
is also unclean; although it has a split hoof, it does not chew the
cud. You are not to eat their meat or touch their carcasses.[p]

[a] *15, 17* The Hebrew term refers to the irrevocable giving over of things or persons to the LORD, often by totally destroying them. [b] *5* The precise identification of some of the birds and animals in this chapter is uncertain. [c] *7* That is, the hyrax or rock badger

14:8 [p]Lev 11:26-27

9Of all the creatures living in the water, you may eat any that has
fins and scales. 10But anything that does not have fins and scales
you may not eat; for you it is unclean.
11You may eat any clean bird. 12But these you may not eat: the
eagle, the vulture, the black vulture, 13the red kite, the black kite,
any kind of falcon, 14any kind of raven, 15the horned owl, the
screech owl, the gull, any kind of hawk, 16the little owl, the great
owl, the white owl, 17the desert owl, the osprey, the cormorant,
18the stork, any kind of heron, the hoopoe and the bat.
19All flying insects that swarm are unclean to you; do not eat
them. 20But any winged creature that is clean you may eat.
21Do not eat anything you find already dead.[a] You may give it to
an alien living in any of your towns, and he may eat it, or you may
sell it to a foreigner. But you are a people holy to the LORD your
God.[b]

Do not cook a young goat in its mother's milk.[c]
22Be sure to set aside a tenth[d] of all that your fields produce
each year. 23Eat the tithe of your grain, new wine and oil, and the
firstborn of your herds and flocks in the presence of the LORD
your God at the place he will choose as a dwelling for his Name,[e]
so that you may learn[f] to revere the LORD your God always. 24But
if that place is too distant and you have been blessed by the LORD
your God and cannot carry your tithe (because the place where
the LORD will choose to put his Name is so far away), 25then
exchange your tithe for silver, and take the silver with you and go
to the place the LORD your God will choose. 26Use the silver to buy
whatever you like: cattle, sheep, wine or other fermented drink,
or anything you wish. Then you and your household shall eat
there in the presence of the LORD your God and rejoice.[g] 27And
do not neglect the Levites[h] living in your towns, for they have no
allotment or inheritance of their own.[i]
28At the end of every three years, bring all the tithes of that
year's produce and store it in your towns,[j] 29so that the Levites
(who have no allotment[k] or inheritance of their own) and the
aliens,[l] the fatherless and the widows who live in your towns may
come and eat and be satisfied, and so that the LORD your God may
bless[m] you in all the work of your hands.

Chapter 15 Theme ______________________________

15 At the end of every seven years you must cancel debts.[n]
2This is how it is to be done: Every creditor shall cancel
the loan he has made to his fellow Israelite. He shall not require
payment from his fellow Israelite or brother, because the LORD's
time for canceling debts has been proclaimed. 3You may require
payment from a foreigner,[o] but you must cancel any debt your

14:21 [a] Lev 17:15; 22:8 [b] ver 2 [c] Ex 23:19; 34:26
14:22 [d] Lev 27:30; Dt 12:6,17; Ne 10:37
14:23 [e] Dt 12:5 [f] Dt 4:10
14:26 [g] Dt 12:7-8
14:27 [h] Dt 12:19 [i] Nu 18:20
14:28 [j] Dt 26:12
14:29 [k] ver 27 [l] Dt 26:12 [m] Dt 15:10; Mal 3:10
15:1 [n] Dt 31:10
15:3 [o] Dt 23:20

brother owes you. 4However, there should be no poor among you,
for in the land the LORD your God is giving you to possess as your
inheritance, he will richly bless[a] you, 5if only you fully obey the
LORD your God and are careful to follow[b] all these commands I
am giving you today. 6For the LORD your God will bless you as he
has promised, and you will lend to many nations but will borrow
from none. You will rule over many nations but none will rule
over you.[c]

7If there is a poor man among your brothers in any of the
towns of the land that the LORD your God is giving you, do not be
hardhearted or tightfisted[d] toward your poor brother. 8Rather be
openhanded[e] and freely lend him whatever he needs. 9Be careful
not to harbor this wicked thought: "The seventh year, the year for
canceling debts,[f] is near," so that you do not show ill will[g] toward
your needy brother and give him nothing. He may then appeal to
the LORD against you, and you will be found guilty of sin.[h] 10Give
generously to him and do so without a grudging heart;[i] then
because of this the LORD your God will bless[j] you in all your work
and in everything you put your hand to. 11There will always be
poor people in the land. Therefore I command you to be openhanded toward your brothers and toward the poor and needy in
your land.[k]

12If a fellow Hebrew, a man or a woman, sells himself to you
and serves you six years, in the seventh year you must let him go
free.[l] 13And when you release him, do not send him away empty-
handed. 14Supply him liberally from your flock, your threshing
floor and your winepress. Give to him as the LORD your God has
blessed you. 15Remember that you were slaves[m] in Egypt and the
LORD your God redeemed you.[n] That is why I give you this command today.

16But if your servant says to you, "I do not want to leave you,"
because he loves you and your family and is well off with you,
17then take an awl and push it through his ear lobe into the door,
and he will become your servant for life. Do the same for your
maidservant.

18Do not consider it a hardship to set your servant free, because
his service to you these six years has been worth twice as much
as that of a hired hand. And the LORD your God will bless you in
everything you do.

19Set apart for the LORD your God every firstborn male[o] of your
herds and flocks. Do not put the firstborn of your oxen to work,
and do not shear the firstborn of your sheep. 20Each year you and
your family are to eat them in the presence of the LORD your God
at the place he will choose.[p] 21If an animal has a defect, is lame
or blind, or has any serious flaw, you must not sacrifice it to the

15:4 [a]Dt 28:8
15:5 [b]Dt 28:1
15:6 [c]Dt 28:12-13,44
15:7 [d]1Jn 3:17
15:8 [e]Mt 5:42; Lk 6:34
15:9 [f]ver 1 [g]Mt 20:15 [h]Dt 24:15
15:10 [i]2Co 9:5 [j]Dt 14:29; 24:19
15:11 [k]Mt 26:11; Mk 14:7; Jn 12:8
15:12 [l]Ex 21:2; Lev 25:39; Jer 34:14
15:15 [m]Dt 5:15 [n]Dt 16:12
15:19 [o]Ex 13:2
15:20 [p]Dt 12:5-7, 17,18; 14:23

LORD your God.[a] 22You are to eat it in your own towns. Both the
ceremonially unclean and the clean may eat it, as if it were gazelle
or deer.[b] 23But you must not eat the blood; pour it out on the
ground like water.[c]

Chapter 16 Theme ________________________________

16 Observe the month of Abib[d] and celebrate the Passover of
the LORD your God, because in the month of Abib he
brought you out of Egypt by night. 2Sacrifice as the Passover to the
LORD your God an animal from your flock or herd at the place the
LORD will choose as a dwelling for his Name.[e] 3Do not eat it with
bread made with yeast, but for seven days eat unleavened bread,
the bread of affliction,[f] because you left Egypt in haste[g]—so that
all the days of your life you may remember the time of your departure from Egypt.[h] 4Let no yeast be found in your possession
in all your land for seven days. Do not let any of the meat you
sacrifice on the evening of the first day remain until morning.[i]

5You must not sacrifice the Passover in any town the LORD your
God gives you 6except in the place he will choose as a dwelling for
his Name. There you must sacrifice the Passover in the evening,
when the sun goes down, on the anniversary[a][j] of your departure
from Egypt. 7Roast[k] it and eat it at the place the LORD your God
will choose. Then in the morning return to your tents. 8For six
days eat unleavened bread and on the seventh day hold an
assembly[l] to the LORD your God and do no work.

9Count off seven weeks[m] from the time you begin to put the
sickle to the standing grain.[n] 10Then celebrate the Feast of Weeks
to the LORD your God by giving a freewill offering in proportion
to the blessings the LORD your God has given you. 11And rejoice[o]
before the LORD your God at the place he will choose as a dwelling
for his Name—you, your sons and daughters, your menservants
and maidservants, the Levites[p] in your towns, and the aliens, the
fatherless and the widows living among you. 12Remember that
you were slaves in Egypt,[q] and follow carefully these decrees.

13Celebrate the Feast of Tabernacles for seven days after you
have gathered the produce of your threshing floor[r] and your
winepress.[s] 14Be joyful[t] at your Feast—you, your sons and
daughters, your menservants and maidservants, and the Levites,
the aliens, the fatherless and the widows who live in your towns.
15For seven days celebrate the Feast to the LORD your God at the
place the LORD will choose. For the LORD your God will bless you
in all your harvest and in all the work of your hands, and your
joy[u] will be complete.

[a]6 Or *down, at the time of day*

15:21 [a]Lev 22:19-25
15:22 [b]Dt 12:15,22
15:23 [c]Dt 12:16
16:1 [d]Ex 12:2; 13:4
16:2 [e]Dt 12:5,26
16:3 [f]Ex 12:8,39; 34:18 [g]Ex 12:11, 15,19 [h]Ex 13:3,6-7
16:4 [i]Ex 12:10; 34:25
16:6 [j]Ex 12:6; Dt 12:5
16:7 [k]Ex 12:8; 2Ch 35:13
16:8 [l]Ex 12:16; 13:6; Lev 23:8
16:9 [m]Ex 34:22; Lev 23:15 [n]Ex 23:16; Nu 28:26
16:11 [o]Dt 12:7 [p]Dt 12:12
16:12 [q]Dt 15:15
16:13 [r]Lev 23:34 [s]Ex 23:16
16:14 [t]ver 11
16:15 [u]Lev 23:39

16Three times a year all your men must appear before the LORD your God at the place he will choose: at the Feast of Unleavened Bread, the Feast of Weeks and the Feast of Tabernacles.[a] No man should appear before the LORD empty-handed:[b] 17Each of you must bring a gift in proportion to the way the LORD your God has blessed you.

18Appoint judges[c] and officials for each of your tribes in every town the LORD your God is giving you, and they shall judge the people fairly. 19Do not pervert justice[d] or show partiality.[e] Do not accept a bribe,[f] for a bribe blinds the eyes of the wise and twists the words of the righteous. 20Follow justice and justice alone, so that you may live and possess the land the LORD your God is giving you.

21Do not set up any wooden Asherah pole[ag] beside the altar you build to the LORD your God,[h] 22and do not erect a sacred stone,[i] for these the LORD your God hates.

Chapter 17 Theme ____________________

17 Do not sacrifice to the LORD your God an ox or a sheep that has any defect[j] or flaw in it, for that would be detestable to him.[k]

2If a man or woman living among you in one of the towns the LORD gives you is found doing evil in the eyes of the LORD your God in violation of his covenant,[l] 3and contrary to my command[m] has worshiped other gods, bowing down to them or to the sun[n] or the moon or the stars of the sky, 4and this has been brought to your attention, then you must investigate it thoroughly. If it is true and it has been proved that this detestable thing has been done in Israel,[o] 5take the man or woman who has done this evil deed to your city gate and stone that person to death.[p] 6On the testimony of two or three witnesses a man shall be put to death, but no one shall be put to death on the testimony of only one witness.[q] 7The hands of the witnesses must be the first in putting him to death, and then the hands of all the people. You must purge the evil[r] from among you.

8If cases come before your courts that are too difficult for you to judge—whether bloodshed, lawsuits or assaults[s]—take them to the place the LORD your God will choose.[t] 9Go to the priests, who are Levites, and to the judge who is in office at that time. Inquire of them and they will give you the verdict.[u] 10You must act according to the decisions they give you at the place the LORD will choose. Be careful to do everything they direct you to do. 11Act according to the law they teach you and the decisions they give

[a]21 Or *Do not plant any tree dedicated to Asherah*

16:16 [a]Ex 23:14,16 [b]Ex 34:20
16:18 [c]Dt 1:16
16:19 [d]Ex 23:2,8 [e]Lev 19:15; Dt 1:17 [f]Ecc 7:7
16:21 [g]Dt 7:5 [h]Ex 34:13; 2Ki 17:16; 21:3; 2Ch 33:3
16:22 [i]Lev 26:1
17:1 [j]Mal 1:8,13 [k]Dt 15:21
17:2 [l]Dt 13:6-11
17:3 [m]Jer 7:22-23 [n]Job 31:26
17:4 [o]Dt 13:12-14
17:5 [p]Lev 24:14
17:6 [q]Nu 35:30; Dt 19:15; Jos 7:25; Mt 18:16; Jn 8:17; 2Co 13:1; 1Ti 5:19; Heb 10:28
17:7 [r]Dt 13:5,9
17:8 [s]2Ch 19:10 [t]Dt 12:5; Hag 2:11
17:9 [u]Dt 19:17; Eze 44:24

you. Do not turn aside from what they tell you, to the right or to
the left.[a] 12The man who shows contempt[b] for the judge or for the
priest who stands ministering there to the LORD your God must
be put to death. You must purge the evil from Israel. 13All the people will hear and be afraid, and will not be contemptuous again.[c]
14When you enter the land the LORD your God is giving you and
have taken possession of it and settled in it, and you say, "Let us
set a king over us like all the nations around us,"[d] 15be sure to
appoint over you the king the LORD your God chooses. He must
be from among your own brothers.[e] Do not place a foreigner over
you, one who is not a brother Israelite. 16The king, moreover,
must not acquire great numbers of horses for himself[f] or make
the people return to Egypt[g] to get more of them,[h] for the LORD
has told you, "You are not to go back that way again."[i] 17He must
not take many wives,[j] or his heart will be led astray. He must not
accumulate large amounts of silver and gold.
18When he takes the throne of his kingdom, he is to write[k] for
himself on a scroll a copy of this law, taken from that of the
priests, who are Levites. 19It is to be with him, and he is to read it
all the days of his life[l] so that he may learn to revere the LORD his
God and follow carefully all the words of this law and these
decrees 20and not consider himself better than his brothers and
turn from the law[m] to the right or to the left.[n] Then he and his
descendants will reign a long time over his kingdom in Israel.

Chapter 18 Theme ______________________

18 The priests, who are Levites—indeed the whole tribe of
Levi—are to have no allotment or inheritance with Israel.
They shall live on the offerings made to the LORD by fire, for that
is their inheritance.[o] 2They shall have no inheritance among their
brothers; the LORD is their inheritance, as he promised them.
3This is the share due the priests from the people who sacrifice
a bull or a sheep: the shoulder, the jowls and the inner parts.[p]
4You are to give them the firstfruits of your grain, new wine and
oil, and the first wool from the shearing of your sheep,[q] 5for the
LORD your God has chosen them[r] and their descendants out of
all your tribes to stand and minister[s] in the LORD's name always.
6If a Levite moves from one of your towns anywhere in Israel
where he is living, and comes in all earnestness to the place the
LORD will choose,[t] 7he may minister in the name of the LORD his
God like all his fellow Levites who serve there in the presence of
the LORD. 8He is to share equally in their benefits, even though he
has received money from the sale of family possessions.[u]
9When you enter the land the LORD your God is giving you, do
not learn to imitate[v] the detestable ways of the nations there. 10Let

17:11 [a] Dt 25:1

17:12 [b] Nu 15:30

17:13 [c] Dt 13:11; 19:20

17:14 [d] Dt 11:31; 1Sa 8:5,19-20

17:15 [e] Jer 30:21

17:16 [f] 1Ki 4:26; 10:26 [g] Isa 31:1; Hos 11:5 [h] 1Ki 10:28; Eze 17:15 [i] Ex 13:17

17:17 [j] 1Ki 11:3

17:18 [k] Dt 31:22,24

17:19 [l] Jos 1:8

17:20 [m] 1Ki 15:5 [n] Dt 5:32

18:1 [o] Dt 10:9; 1Co 9:13

18:3 [p] Lev 7:28-34

18:4 [q] Ex 22:29; Nu 18:12

18:5 [r] Ex 28:1 [s] Dt 10:8

18:6 [t] Nu 35:2-3

18:8 [u] 2Ch 31:4; Ne 12:44,47

18:9 [v] Dt 12:29-31

no one be found among you who sacrifices his son or daughter in[a]
the fire, who practices divination[a] or sorcery, interprets omens,
engages in witchcraft,[b] 11 or casts spells, or who is a medium or
spiritist or who consults the dead. 12 Anyone who does these
things is detestable to the LORD, and because of these detestable
practices the LORD your God will drive out those nations before
you.[c] 13 You must be blameless before the LORD your God.

14 The nations you will dispossess listen to those who practice
sorcery or divination. But as for you, the LORD your God has not
permitted you to do so. 15 The LORD your God will raise up for you
a prophet like me from among your own brothers.[d] You must listen to him. 16 For this is what you asked of the LORD your God at
Horeb on the day of the assembly when you said, "Let us not hear
the voice of the LORD our God nor see this great fire anymore, or
we will die."[e]

17 The LORD said to me: "What they say is good. 18 I will raise up
for them a prophet like you from among their brothers; I will
put my words[f] in his mouth, and he will tell them everything I
command him.[g] 19 If anyone does not listen to my words that the
prophet speaks in my name, I myself will call him to account.[h]
20 But a prophet who presumes to speak in my name anything I
have not commanded him to say, or a prophet who speaks in the
name of other gods,[i] must be put to death."[j]

21 You may say to yourselves, "How can we know when a message has not been spoken by the LORD?" 22 If what a prophet proclaims in the name of the LORD does not take place or come true,
that is a message the LORD has not spoken.[k] That prophet has
spoken presumptuously.[l] Do not be afraid of him.

Chapter 19 Theme ________________________

19 When the LORD your God has destroyed the nations whose
land he is giving you, and when you have driven them out
and settled in their towns and houses,[m] 2 then set aside for yourselves three cities centrally located in the land the LORD your God
is giving you to possess. 3 Build roads to them and divide into
three parts the land the LORD your God is giving you as an inheritance, so that anyone who kills a man may flee there.

4 This is the rule concerning the man who kills another and flees
there to save his life—one who kills his neighbor unintentionally,
without malice aforethought. 5 For instance, a man may go into
the forest with his neighbor to cut wood, and as he swings his ax
to fell a tree, the head may fly off and hit his neighbor and kill
him. That man may flee to one of these cities and save his life.

[a] *10 Or who makes his son or daughter pass through*

18:10 [a] Dt 12:31 [b] Lev 19:31
18:12 [c] Lev 18:24; Dt 9:4
18:15 [d] Jn 1:21; Ac 3:22*; 7:37*
18:16 [e] Ex 20:19; Dt 5:23-27
18:18 [f] Isa 51:16; Jn 17:8 [g] Jn 4:25-26; 8:28; 12:49-50
18:19 [h] Ac 3:23*
18:20 [i] Jer 14:14 [j] Dt 13:1-5
18:22 [k] Jer 28:9 [l] ver 20
19:1 [m] Dt 12:29

6Otherwise, the avenger of blood[a] might pursue him in a rage,
overtake him if the distance is too great, and kill him even though
he is not deserving of death, since he did it to his neighbor without malice aforethought. 7This is why I command you to set aside
for yourselves three cities.

8If the LORD your God enlarges your territory, as he promised
on oath to your forefathers, and gives you the whole land he
promised them, 9because you carefully follow all these laws I
command you today—to love the LORD your God and to walk
always in his ways[b]—then you are to set aside three more cities.
10Do this so that innocent blood will not be shed in your land,
which the LORD your God is giving you as your inheritance, and
so that you will not be guilty of bloodshed.[c]

11But if a man hates his neighbor and lies in wait for him,
assaults and kills him,[d] and then flees to one of these cities, 12the
elders of his town shall send for him, bring him back from the
city, and hand him over to the avenger of blood to die. 13Show him
no pity.[e] You must purge from Israel the guilt of shedding innocent blood,[f] so that it may go well with you.

14Do not move your neighbor's boundary stone set up by your
predecessors in the inheritance you receive in the land the LORD
your God is giving you to possess.[g]

15One witness is not enough to convict a man accused of any
crime or offense he may have committed. A matter must be
established by the testimony of two or three witnesses.[h]

16If a malicious witness[i] takes the stand to accuse a man of a
crime, 17the two men involved in the dispute must stand in the
presence of the LORD before the priests and the judges[j] who are
in office at the time. 18The judges must make a thorough investigation, and if the witness proves to be a liar, giving false testimony against his brother, 19then do to him as he intended to do to
his brother.[k] You must purge the evil from among you. 20The rest
of the people will hear of this and be afraid,[l] and never again
will such an evil thing be done among you. 21Show no pity:[m] life
for life, eye for eye, tooth for tooth, hand for hand, foot for foot.[n]

Chapter 20 Theme ________________________________

20 When you go to war against your enemies and see horses
and chariots and an army greater than yours,[o] do not be
afraid[p] of them,[q] because the LORD your God, who brought you
up out of Egypt, will be with you. 2When you are about to go into
battle, the priest shall come forward and address the army. 3He
shall say: "Hear, O Israel, today you are going into battle against
your enemies. Do not be fainthearted[r] or afraid; do not be terrified or give way to panic before them. 4For the LORD your God is

19:6 [a]Nu 35:12
19:9 [b]Jos 20:7-8
19:10 [c]Nu 35:33; Dt 21:1-9
19:11 [d]Nu 35:16
19:13 [e]Dt 7:2 [f]1Ki 2:31
19:14 [g]Dt 27:17; Pr 22:28; Hos 5:10
19:15 [h]Nu 35:30; Dt 17:6; Mt 18:16*; Jn 8:17; 2Co 13:1*; 1Ti 5:19; Heb 10:28
19:16 [i]Ex 23:1; Ps 27:12
19:17 [j]Dt 17:9
19:19 [k]Pr 19:5,9
19:20 [l]Dt 17:13; 21:21
19:21 [m]ver 13 [n]Ex 21:24; Lev 24:20; Mt 5:38*
20:1 [o]Ps 20:7; Isa 31:1 [p]Dt 31:6,8 [q]2Ch 32:7-8
20:3 [r]Jos 23:10

the one who goes with you to fight[a] for you against your enemies to give you victory."

5 The officers shall say to the army: "Has anyone built a new house and not dedicated[b] it? Let him go home, or he may die in battle and someone else may dedicate it. 6 Has anyone planted a vineyard and not begun to enjoy it? Let him go home, or he may die in battle and someone else enjoy it. 7 Has anyone become pledged to a woman and not married her? Let him go home, or he may die in battle and someone else marry her.[c]" 8 Then the officers shall add, "Is any man afraid or fainthearted? Let him go home so that his brothers will not become disheartened too."[d] 9 When the officers have finished speaking to the army, they shall appoint commanders over it.

10 When you march up to attack a city, make its people an offer of peace.[e] 11 If they accept and open their gates, all the people in it shall be subject to forced labor[f] and shall work for you. 12 If they refuse to make peace and they engage you in battle, lay siege to that city. 13 When the LORD your God delivers it into your hand, put to the sword all the men in it.[g] 14 As for the women, the children, the livestock[h] and everything else in the city, you may take these as plunder for yourselves. And you may use the plunder the LORD your God gives you from your enemies. 15 This is how you are to treat all the cities that are at a distance from you and do not belong to the nations nearby.

16 However, in the cities of the nations the LORD your God is giving you as an inheritance, do not leave alive anything that breathes.[i] 17 Completely destroy[a] them—the Hittites, Amorites, Canaanites, Perizzites, Hivites and Jebusites—as the LORD your God has commanded you. 18 Otherwise, they will teach you to follow all the detestable things they do in worshiping their gods,[j] and you will sin[k] against the LORD your God.

19 When you lay siege to a city for a long time, fighting against it to capture it, do not destroy its trees by putting an ax to them, because you can eat their fruit. Do not cut them down. Are the trees of the field people, that you should besiege them?[b] 20 However, you may cut down trees that you know are not fruit trees and use them to build siege works until the city at war with you falls.

Chapter 21 Theme ____________________

21

If a man is found slain, lying in a field in the land the LORD your God is giving you to possess, and it is not known who killed him, 2 your elders and judges shall go out and measure the

20:4 [a]Dt 1:30; 3:22; Jos 23:10
20:5 [b]Ne 12:27
20:7 [c]Dt 24:5
20:8 [d]Jdg 7:3
20:10 [e]Lk 14:31-32
20:11 [f]1Ki 9:21
20:13 [g]Nu 31:7
20:14 [h]Jos 8:2; 22:8
20:16 [i]Ex 23:31-33; Nu 21:2-3; Dt 7:2; Jos 11:14
20:18 [j]Ex 34:16; Dt 7:4; 12:30-31 [k]Ex 23:33

[a] *17* The Hebrew term refers to the irrevocable giving over of things or persons to the LORD, often by totally destroying them. [b] *19* Or *down to use in the siege, for the fruit trees are for the benefit of man.*

distance from the body to the neighboring towns. 3Then the
elders of the town nearest the body shall take a heifer that has
never been worked and has never worn a yoke 4and lead her
down to a valley that has not been plowed or planted and where
there is a flowing stream. There in the valley they are to break the
heifer's neck. 5The priests, the sons of Levi, shall step forward,
for the LORD your God has chosen them to minister and to pronounce blessings[a] in the name of the LORD and to decide all cases
of dispute and assault.[b] 6Then all the elders of the town nearest
the body shall wash their hands[c] over the heifer whose neck was
broken in the valley, 7and they shall declare: "Our hands did not
shed this blood, nor did our eyes see it done. 8Accept this atonement for your people Israel, whom you have redeemed, O LORD,
and do not hold your people guilty of the blood of an innocent
man." And the bloodshed will be atoned for.[d] 9So you will purge[e]
from yourselves the guilt of shedding innocent blood, since you
have done what is right in the eyes of the LORD.

10When you go to war against your enemies and the LORD your
God delivers them into your hands[f] and you take captives, 11if you
notice among the captives a beautiful woman and are attracted
to her, you may take her as your wife. 12Bring her into your home
and have her shave her head,[g] trim her nails 13and put aside the
clothes she was wearing when captured. After she has lived in
your house and mourned her father and mother for a full
month,[h] then you may go to her and be her husband and she
shall be your wife. 14If you are not pleased with her, let her go
wherever she wishes. You must not sell her or treat her as a slave,
since you have dishonored her.[i]

15If a man has two wives, and he loves one but not the other,
and both bear him sons but the firstborn is the son of the wife he
does not love,[j] 16when he wills his property to his sons, he must
not give the rights of the firstborn to the son of the wife he loves
in preference to his actual firstborn, the son of the wife he does
not love.[k] 17He must acknowledge the son of his unloved wife as
the firstborn by giving him a double share of all he has. That son
is the first sign of his father's strength.[l] The right of the firstborn
belongs to him.[m]

18If a man has a stubborn and rebellious son who does not obey
his father and mother[n] and will not listen to them when they
discipline him, 19his father and mother shall take hold of him
and bring him to the elders at the gate of his town. 20They shall
say to the elders, "This son of ours is stubborn and rebellious.
He will not obey us. He is a profligate and a drunkard." 21Then
all the men of his town shall stone him to death. You must purge
the evil[o] from among you. All Israel will hear of it and be afraid.[p]

21:5 [a] 1Ch 23:13 [b] Dt 17:8-11
21:6 [c] Mt 27:24
21:8 [d] Nu 35:33-34
21:9 [e] Dt 19:13
21:10 [f] Jos 21:44
21:12 [g] Lev 14:9; Nu 6:9
21:13 [h] Ps 45:10
21:14 [i] Ge 34:2
21:15 [j] Ge 29:33
21:16 [k] 1Ch 26:10
21:17 [l] Ge 49:3 [m] Ge 25:31
21:18 [n] Pr 1:8; Isa 30:1; Eph 6:1-3
21:21 [o] Dt 19:19 [p] Dt 13:11

22If a man guilty of a capital offense[a] is put to death and his
body is hung on a tree, 23you must not leave his body on the tree
overnight.[b] Be sure to bury him that same day, because anyone
who is hung on a tree is under God's curse.[c] You must not desecrate[d] the land the LORD your God is giving you as an inheritance.

Chapter 22 Theme ____________________

22 If you see your brother's ox or sheep straying, do not
ignore it but be sure to take it back to him.[e] 2If the brother does not live near you or if you do not know who he is, take it
home with you and keep it until he comes looking for it. Then
give it back to him. 3Do the same if you find your brother's donkey or his cloak or anything he loses. Do not ignore it.

4If you see your brother's donkey[f] or his ox fallen on the road,
do not ignore it. Help him get it to its feet.

5A woman must not wear men's clothing, nor a man wear
women's clothing, for the LORD your God detests anyone who
does this.

6If you come across a bird's nest beside the road, either in a tree
or on the ground, and the mother is sitting on the young or on
the eggs, do not take the mother with the young.[g] 7You may take
the young, but be sure to let the mother go, so that it may go well
with you and you may have a long life.[h]

8When you build a new house, make a parapet around your
roof so that you may not bring the guilt of bloodshed on your
house if someone falls from the roof.

9Do not plant two kinds of seed in your vineyard;[i] if you do,
not only the crops you plant but also the fruit of the vineyard will
be defiled.[a]

10Do not plow with an ox and a donkey yoked together.[j]

11Do not wear clothes of wool and linen woven together.[k]

12Make tassels on the four corners of the cloak you wear.[l]

13If a man takes a wife and, after lying with her[m], dislikes her
14and slanders her and gives her a bad name, saying, "I married
this woman, but when I approached her, I did not find proof of
her virginity," 15then the girl's father and mother shall bring proof
that she was a virgin to the town elders at the gate. 16The girl's
father will say to the elders, "I gave my daughter in marriage to
this man, but he dislikes her. 17Now he has slandered her and said,
'I did not find your daughter to be a virgin.' But here is the proof
of my daughter's virginity." Then her parents shall display the
cloth before the elders of the town, 18and the elders[n] shall take the
man and punish him. 19They shall fine him a hundred shekels of

21:22 [a]Dt 22:26; Mk 14:64; Ac 23:29
21:23 [b]Jos 8:29; 10:27; Jn 19:31 [c]Gal 3:13* [d]Lev 18:25; Nu 35:34
22:1 [e]Ex 23:4-5
22:4 [f]Ex 23:5
22:6 [g]Lev 22:28
22:7 [h]Dt 4:40
22:9 [i]Lev 19:19
22:10 [j]2Co 6:14
22:11 [k]Lev 19:19
22:12 [l]Nu 15:37-41; Mt 23:5
22:13 [m]Dt 24:1
22:18 [n]Ex 18:21

a9 Or *be forfeited to the sanctuary*

silver[a] and give them to the girl's father, because this man has
given an Israelite virgin a bad name. She shall continue to be his
wife; he must not divorce her as long as he lives.
20If, however, the charge is true and no proof of the girl's virginity can be found, 21she shall be brought to the door of her
father's house and there the men of her town shall stone her to
death. She has done a disgraceful thing[a] in Israel by being promiscuous while still in her father's house. You must purge the evil
from among you.
22If a man is found sleeping with another man's wife, both the
man who slept with her and the woman must die.[b] You must
purge the evil from Israel.
23If a man happens to meet in a town a virgin pledged to be
married and he sleeps with her, 24you shall take both of them to
the gate of that town and stone them to death—the girl because
she was in a town and did not scream for help, and the man
because he violated another man's wife. You must purge the evil
from among you.[c]
25But if out in the country a man happens to meet a girl pledged
to be married and rapes her, only the man who has done this shall
die. 26Do nothing to the girl; she has committed no sin deserving
death. This case is like that of someone who attacks and murders
his neighbor, 27for the man found the girl out in the country, and
though the betrothed girl screamed, there was no one to rescue
her.
28If a man happens to meet a virgin who is not pledged to be
married and rapes her and they are discovered,[d] 29he shall pay
the girl's father fifty shekels of silver.[b] He must marry the girl, for
he has violated her. He can never divorce her as long as he lives.
30A man is not to marry his father's wife; he must not dishon-
or his father's bed.[e]

Chapter 23 Theme ______________________________

23 No one who has been emasculated by crushing or cutting
may enter the assembly of the LORD.
2No one born of a forbidden marriage[c] nor any of his descendants may enter the assembly of the LORD, even down to the
tenth generation.
3No Ammonite or Moabite or any of his descendants may
enter the assembly of the LORD, even down to the tenth generation.[f] 4For they did not come to meet you with bread and water
on your way when you came out of Egypt, and they hired Balaam[g]
son of Beor from Pethor in Aram Naharai[d] to pronounce a curse

a *19* That is, about 2 1/2 pounds (about 1 kilogram) b *29* That is, about 1 1/4 pounds (about 0.6 kilogram) c *2* Or *one of illegitimate birth* d *4* That is, Northwest Mesopotamia

22:21 *a* Ge 34:7; Dt 13:5; 23:17-18; Jdg 20:6; 2Sa 13:12
22:22 *b* Lev 20:10; Jn 8:5
22:24 *c* ver 21-22; 1Co 5:13*
22:28 *d* Ex 22:16
22:30 *e* Lev 18:8; 20:11; Dt 27:20; 1Co 5:1
23:3 *f* Ne 13:2
23:4 *g* Nu 22:5-6; 23:7; 2Pe 2:15

on you. 5However, the LORD your God would not listen to Balaam
but turned the curse[a] into a blessing for you, because the LORD
your God loves you. 6Do not seek a treaty of friendship with them
as long as you live.[b]

7Do not abhor an Edomite, for he is your brother.[c] Do not abhor
an Egyptian, because you lived as an alien in his country.[d] 8The
third generation of children born to them may enter the assembly
of the LORD.

9When you are encamped against your enemies, keep away
from everything impure. 10If one of your men is unclean because
of a nocturnal emission, he is to go outside the camp and stay
there.[e] 11But as evening approaches he is to wash himself, and at
sunset he may return to the camp.

12Designate a place outside the camp where you can go to
relieve yourself. 13As part of your equipment have something to
dig with, and when you relieve yourself, dig a hole and cover up
your excrement. 14For the LORD your God moves[f] about in your
camp to protect you and to deliver your enemies to you. Your
camp must be holy,[g] so that he will not see among you anything
indecent and turn away from you.

15If a slave has taken refuge with you, do not hand him over to
his master.[h] 16Let him live among you wherever he likes and in
whatever town he chooses. Do not oppress[i] him.

17No Israelite man[j] or woman is to become a shrine prostitute.[k]
18You must not bring the earnings of a female prostitute or of a
male prostitute[a] into the house of the LORD your God to pay any
vow, because the LORD your God detests them both.

19Do not charge your brother interest, whether on money or
food or anything else that may earn interest.[l] 20You may charge a
foreigner interest, but not a brother Israelite, so that the LORD
your God may bless[m] you in everything you put your hand to in
the land you are entering to possess.

21If you make a vow to the LORD your God, do not be slow to
pay it, for the LORD your God will certainly demand it of you and
you will be guilty of sin.[n] 22But if you refrain from making a vow,
you will not be guilty. 23Whatever your lips utter you must be
sure to do, because you made your vow freely to the LORD your
God with your own mouth.

24If you enter your neighbor's vineyard, you may eat all the
grapes you want, but do not put any in your basket. 25If you enter
your neighbor's grainfield, you may pick kernels with your hands,
but you must not put a sickle to his standing grain.[o]

23:5 [a] Pr 26:2
23:6 [b] Ezr 9:12
23:7 [c] Ge 25:26; Ob 1:10,12 [d] Ex 22:21; 23:9; Lev 19:34; Dt 10:19
23:10 [e] Lev 15:16
23:14 [f] Lev 26:12 [g] Ex 3:5
23:15 [h] 1Sa 30:15
23:16 [i] Ex 22:21
23:17 [j] Ge 19:25; 2Ki 23:7 [k] Lev 19:29; Dt 22:21
23:19 [l] Ex 22:25; Lev 25:35-37
23:20 [m] Dt 15:10; 28:12
23:21 [n] Nu 30:1-2; Ecc 5:4-5; Mt 5:33
23:25 [o] Mt 12:1; Mk 2:23; Lk 6:1

a *18* Hebrew *of a dog*

Chapter 24 Theme ______________________________

24 If a man marries a woman who becomes displeasing to
him[a] because he finds something indecent about her,
and he writes her a certificate of divorce,[b] gives it to her and
sends her from his house, 2and if after she leaves his house she
becomes the wife of another man, 3and her second husband dislikes her and writes her a certificate of divorce, gives it to her and
sends her from his house, or if he dies, 4then her first husband,
who divorced her, is not allowed to marry her again after she has
been defiled. That would be detestable in the eyes of the LORD.
Do not bring sin upon the land the LORD[c] your God is giving you
as an inheritance.
5If a man has recently married, he must not be sent to war or
have any other duty laid on him. For one year he is to be free to
stay at home and bring happiness to the wife he has married.[d]
6Do not take a pair of millstones—not even the upper one—as
security for a debt, because that would be taking a man's livelihood as security.
7If a man is caught kidnapping one of his brother Israelites
and treats him as a slave or sells him, the kidnapper must die.[e]
You must purge the evil from among you.
8In cases of leprous[a] diseases be very careful to do exactly as the
priests, who are Levites, instruct you. You must follow carefully
what I have commanded them.[f] 9Remember what the LORD your
God did to Miriam along the way after you came out of Egypt.[g]
10When you make a loan of any kind to your neighbor, do not
go into his house to get what he is offering as a pledge. 11Stay outside and let the man to whom you are making the loan bring the
pledge out to you. 12If the man is poor, do not go to sleep with his
pledge in your possession. 13Return his cloak to him by sunset[h]
so that he may sleep in it. Then he will thank you, and it will be
regarded as a righteous act in the sight of the LORD your God.[i]
14Do not take advantage of a hired man who is poor and
needy, whether he is a brother Israelite or an alien living in one
of your towns.[j] 15Pay him his wages each day before sunset,
because he is poor[k] and is counting on it.[l] Otherwise he may cry
to the LORD against you, and you will be guilty of sin.[m]
16Fathers shall not be put to death for their children, nor children put to death for their fathers; each is to die for his own sin.[n]
17Do not deprive the alien or the fatherless of justice,[o] or take
the cloak of the widow as a pledge. 18Remember that you were
slaves in Egypt and the LORD your God redeemed you from there.
That is why I command you to do this.

[a]8 The Hebrew word was used for various diseases affecting the skin—not necessarily leprosy.

24:1 [a]Dt 22:13 [b]Mt 5:31*; 19:7-9; Mk 10:4-5
24:4 [c]Jer 3:1
24:5 [d]Dt 20:7
24:7 [e]Ex 21:16
24:8 [f]Lev 13:1-46; 14:2
24:9 [g]Nu 12:10
24:13 [h]Ex 22:26 [i]Dt 6:25; Da 4:27
24:14 [j]Lev 25:35-43; Dt 15:12-18
24:15 [k]Jer 22:13 [l]Lev 19:13 [m]Dt 15:9; Jas 5:4
24:16 [n]2Ki 14:6; 2Ch 25:4; Jer 31:29-30; Eze 18:20
24:17 [o]Dt 1:17; 10:17-18; 16:19

24:19 [a]Lev 19:9; 23:22 [19]When you are harvesting in your field and you overlook a
[b]Pr 19:17 sheaf, do not go back to get it.[a] Leave it for the alien, the fatherless and the widow, so that the LORD your God may bless[b] you in
24:20 all the work of your hands. [20]When you beat the olives from your
[c]Lev 19:10 trees, do not go over the branches a second time.[c] Leave what
remains for the alien, the fatherless and the widow. [21]When you
24:22 [d]ver 18 harvest the grapes in your vineyard, do not go over the vines
again. Leave what remains for the alien, the fatherless and the
25:1 widow. [22]Remember that you were slaves in Egypt. That is why I
[e]Dt 19:17 [f]Dt 1:16-17 command you to do this.[d]

Chapter 25 Theme ____________________

25:2 [g]Lk 12:47-48 **25** When men have a dispute, they are to take it to court and
the judges will decide the case,[e] acquitting the innocent
25:3 and condemning the guilty.[f] [2]If the guilty man deserves to be
[h]2Co 11:24 beaten,[g] the judge shall make him lie down and have him flogged
[i]Job 18:3 in his presence with the number of lashes his crime deserves,
25:4 [3]but he must not give him more than forty lashes.[h] If he is flogged
[j]Pr 12:10; more than that, your brother will be degraded in your eyes.[i]
1Co 9:9*; 1Ti 5:18* [4]Do not muzzle an ox while it is treading out the grain.[j]
[5]If brothers are living together and one of them dies without a
son, his widow must not marry outside the family. Her hus-
25:5 [k]Mt 22:24; band's brother shall take her and marry her and fulfill the duty
Mk 12:19; of a brother-in-law to her.[k] [6]The first son she bears shall carry on
Lk 20:28 the name of the dead brother so that his name will not be blotted
out from Israel.[l]
25:6 [l]Ge 38:9; [7]However, if a man does not want to marry his brother's wife,
Ru 4:5,10 she shall go to the elders at the town gate and say, "My husband's
brother refuses to carry on his brother's name in Israel. He will not
25:7 fulfill the duty of a brother-in-law to me."[m] [8]Then the elders of his
[m]Ru 4:1-2,5-6 town shall summon him and talk to him. If he persists in saying,
"I do not want to marry her," [9]his brother's widow shall go up to
25:9 [n]Ru 4:7-8,11 him in the presence of the elders, take off one of his sandals,[n]
spit in his face and say, "This is what is done to the man who will
25:12 not build up his brother's family line." [10]That man's line shall be
[o]Dt 19:13 known in Israel as The Family of the Unsandaled.
[11]If two men are fighting and the wife of one of them comes to
25:13 rescue her husband from his assailant, and she reaches out and
[p]Lev 19:35-37; Pr 11:1; seizes him by his private parts, [12]you shall cut off her hand. Show
Eze 45:10; her no pity.[o]
Mic 6:11 [13]Do not have two differing weights in your bag—one heavy,
one light.[p] [14]Do not have two differing measures in your house—
25:15 one large, one small. [15]You must have accurate and honest weights
[q]Ex 20:12 and measures, so that you may live long[q] in the land the LORD
25:16 your God is giving you. [16]For the LORD your God detests anyone
[r]Pr 11:1 who does these things, anyone who deals dishonestly.[r]

17 Remember what the Amalekites[a] did to you along the way
when you came out of Egypt. 18 When you were weary and worn
out, they met you on your journey and cut off all who were lag-
ging behind; they had no fear of God.[b] 19 When the LORD your God
gives you rest from all the enemies around you in the land he is
giving you to possess as an inheritance, you shall blot out the
memory of Amalek[c] from under heaven. Do not forget!

Chapter 26 Theme ______________________

26 When you have entered the land the LORD your God is
giving you as an inheritance and have taken possession
of it and settled in it, 2 take some of the firstfruits[d] of all that you
produce from the soil of the land the LORD your God is giving
you and put them in a basket. Then go to the place the LORD your
God will choose as a dwelling for his Name[e] 3 and say to the priest
in office at the time, "I declare today to the LORD your God that I
have come to the land the LORD swore to our forefathers to give
us." 4 The priest shall take the basket from your hands and set it
down in front of the altar of the LORD your God. 5 Then you shall
declare before the LORD your God: "My father was a wandering
Aramean,[f] and he went down into Egypt with a few people[g] and
lived there and became a great nation, powerful and numerous.
6 But the Egyptians mistreated us and made us suffer,[h] putting us
to hard labor. 7 Then we cried out to the LORD, the God of our
fathers, and the LORD heard our voice[i] and saw[j] our misery, toil
and oppression. 8 So the LORD brought us out of Egypt with a
mighty hand and an outstretched arm, with great terror and with
miraculous signs and wonders.[k] 9 He brought us to this place and
gave us this land, a land flowing with milk and honey;[l] 10 and
now I bring the firstfruits of the soil that you, O LORD, have given
me." Place the basket before the LORD your God and bow down
before him. 11 And you and the Levites[m] and the aliens among you
shall rejoice[n] in all the good things the LORD your God has given
to you and your household.

12 When you have finished setting aside a tenth[o] of all your produce in the third year, the year of the tithe,[p] you shall give it to the
Levite, the alien, the fatherless and the widow, so that they may
eat in your towns and be satisfied. 13 Then say to the LORD your
God: "I have removed from my house the sacred portion and
have given it to the Levite, the alien, the fatherless and the widow,
according to all you commanded. I have not turned aside from
your commands nor have I forgotten any of them.[q] 14 I have not
eaten any of the sacred portion while I was in mourning, nor
have I removed any of it while I was unclean,[r] nor have I offered
any of it to the dead. I have obeyed the LORD my God; I have done

25:17 [a] Ex 17:8
25:18 [b] Ps 36:1; Ro 3:18
25:19 [c] 1Sa 15:2-3
26:2 [d] Ex 22:29; 23:16,19; Nu 18:13; Pr 3:9 [e] Dt 12:5
26:5 [f] Hos 12:12 [g] Ge 43:1-2; 45:7,11; 46:27; Dt 10:22
26:6 [h] Ex 1:11,14
26:7 [i] Ex 2:23-25 [j] Ex 3:9
26:8 [k] Dt 4:34
26:9 [l] Ex 3:8
26:11 [m] Dt 12:7 [n] Dt 16:11
26:12 [o] Lev 27:30 [p] Nu 18:24; Dt 14:28-29; Heb 7:5,9
26:13 [q] Ps 119:141, 153,176
26:14 [r] Lev 7:20; Hos 9:4

everything you commanded me. 15 Look down from heaven,[a] your holy dwelling place, and bless your people Israel and the land you have given us as you promised on oath to our forefathers, a land flowing with milk and honey."

16 The LORD your God commands you this day to follow these decrees and laws; carefully observe them with all your heart and with all your soul.[b] 17 You have declared this day that the LORD is your God and that you will walk in his ways, that you will keep his decrees, commands and laws, and that you will obey him. 18 And the LORD has declared this day that you are his people, his treasured possession[c] as he promised, and that you are to keep all his commands. 19 He has declared that he will set you in praise, fame and honor high above all the nations[d] he has made and that you will be a people holy[e] to the LORD your God, as he promised.

Chapter 27 Theme ________________________

27 Moses and the elders of Israel commanded the people: "Keep all these commands that I give you today. 2 When you have crossed the Jordan into the land the LORD your God is giving you, set up some large stones and coat them with plaster.[f] 3 Write on them all the words of this law when you have crossed over to enter the land the LORD your God is giving you, a land flowing with milk and honey,[g] just as the LORD, the God of your fathers, promised you. 4 And when you have crossed the Jordan, set up these stones on Mount Ebal,[h] as I command you today, and coat them with plaster. 5 Build there an altar[i] to the LORD your God, an altar of stones. Do not use any iron tool[j] upon them. 6 Build the altar of the LORD your God with fieldstones and offer burnt offerings on it to the LORD your God. 7 Sacrifice fellowship offerings[a] there, eating them and rejoicing in the presence of the LORD your God. 8 And you shall write very clearly all the words of this law on these stones you have set up."

9 Then Moses and the priests, who are Levites, said to all Israel, "Be silent, O Israel, and listen! You have now become the people of the LORD your God.[k] 10 Obey the LORD your God and follow his commands and decrees that I give you today."

11 On the same day Moses commanded the people:

12 When you have crossed the Jordan, these tribes shall stand on Mount Gerizim[l] to bless the people: Simeon, Levi, Judah, Issachar, Joseph and Benjamin.[m] 13 And these tribes shall stand on Mount Ebal to pronounce curses: Reuben, Gad, Asher, Zebulun, Dan and Naphtali.

14 The Levites shall recite to all the people of Israel in a loud voice:

26:15 [a] Isa 63:15; Zec 2:13
26:16 [b] Dt 4:29
26:18 [c] Ex 6:7; 19:5; Dt 7:6; 14:2; 28:9
26:19 [d] Dt 4:7-8; 28:1,13,44 [e] Ex 19:6; Dt 7:6; 1Pe 2:9
27:2 [f] Jos 8:31
27:3 [g] Dt 26:9
27:4 [h] Dt 11:29
27:5 [i] Jos 8:31 [j] Ex 20:25
27:9 [k] Dt 26:18
27:12 [l] Dt 11:29 [m] Jos 8:35

[a] 7 Traditionally *peace offerings*

[15]"Cursed is the man who carves an image or casts an idol[a]—a thing detestable to the LORD, the work of the craftsman's hands—and sets it up in secret."
Then all the people shall say, "Amen!"
[16]"Cursed is the man who dishonors his father or his mother."[b]
Then all the people shall say, "Amen!"
[17]"Cursed is the man who moves his neighbor's boundary stone."[c]
Then all the people shall say, "Amen!"
[18]"Cursed is the man who leads the blind astray on the road."[d]
Then all the people shall say, "Amen!"
[19]"Cursed is the man who withholds justice from the alien,[e] the fatherless or the widow."[f]
Then all the people shall say, "Amen!"
[20]"Cursed is the man who sleeps with his father's wife, for he dishonors his father's bed."[g]
Then all the people shall say, "Amen!"
[21]"Cursed is the man who has sexual relations with any animal."[h]
Then all the people shall say, "Amen!"
[22]"Cursed is the man who sleeps with his sister, the daughter of his father or the daughter of his mother."[i]
Then all the people shall say, "Amen!"
[23]"Cursed is the man who sleeps with his mother-in-law."[j]
Then all the people shall say, "Amen!"
[24]"Cursed is the man who kills[k] his neighbor secretly."
Then all the people shall say, "Amen!"
[25]"Cursed is the man who accepts a bribe to kill an innocent person."[l]
Then all the people shall say, "Amen!"
[26]"Cursed is the man who does not uphold the words of this law by carrying them out."[m]
Then all the people shall say, "Amen!"

Chapter 28 Theme __________________________

28 If you fully obey the LORD your God and carefully follow all his commands[n] I give you today, the LORD your God will set you high above all the nations on earth.[o] [2]All these blessings will come upon you[p] and accompany you if you obey the LORD your God:

[3]You will be blessed[q] in the city and blessed in the country.[r]

27:15 [a]Ex 20:4; 34:17; Lev 19:4; 26:1; Dt 4:16,23; 5:8; Isa 44:9
27:16 [b]Ex 20:12; 21:17; Lev 19:3; 20:9
27:17 [c]Dt 19:14; Pr 22:28
27:18 [d]Lev 19:14
27:19 [e]Ex 22:21; Dt 24:19 [f]Dt 10:18
27:20 [g]Lev 18:7; Dt 22:30
27:21 [h]Lev 18:23
27:22 [i]Lev 18:9; 20:17
27:23 [j]Lev 20:14
27:24 [k]Lev 24:17; Nu 35:31
27:25 [l]Ex 23:7-8; Dt 10:17; Eze 22:12
27:26 [m]Jer 11:3; Gal 3:10*
28:1 [n]Ex 15:26; Lev 26:3; Dt 7:12-26 [o]Dt 26:19
28:2 [p]Zec 1:6
28:3 [q]Ps 128:1,4 [r]Ge 39:5

28:4 [4]The fruit of your womb will be blessed, and the crops of
[a]Ge 49:25; your land and the young of your livestock—the calves of your
Pr 10:22 herds and the lambs of your flocks.[a]

[5]Your basket and your kneading trough will be blessed.

28:6 [6]You will be blessed when you come in and blessed when
[b]Ps 121:8 you go out.[b]

[7]The LORD will grant that the enemies who rise up against you
will be defeated before you. They will come at you from one
28:7 direction but flee from you in seven.[c]
[c]Lev 26:8,17 [8]The LORD will send a blessing on your barns and on everything
you put your hand to. The LORD your God will bless you in the
land he is giving you.
28:9 [9]The LORD will establish you as his holy people,[d] as he promised
[d]Ex 19:6; you on oath, if you keep the commands of the LORD your God
Dt 7:6 and walk in his ways. [10]Then all the peoples on earth will see that
you are called by the name[e] of the LORD, and they will fear you.
[11]The LORD will grant you abundant prosperity—in the fruit of
28:10 your womb, the young of your livestock and the crops of your
[e]2Ch 7:14 ground—in the land he swore to your forefathers to give you.[f]
[12]The LORD will open the heavens, the storehouse of his bounty,
to send rain[g] on your land in season and to bless all the work of
28:11 your hands. You will lend to many nations but will borrow from
[f]Dt 30:9; none.[h] [13]The LORD will make you the head, not the tail. If you pay
Pr 10:22 attention to the commands of the LORD your God that I give you
this day and carefully follow them, you will always be at the top,
never at the bottom. [14]Do not turn aside from any of the com-
28:12 mands I give you today, to the right or to the left,[i] following other
[g]Lev 26:4 [h]Dt 15:3,6 gods and serving them.
[15]However, if you do not obey[j] the LORD your God and do not
carefully follow all his commands and decrees I am giving you
today, all these curses will come upon you and overtake you:[k]

28:14 [i]Dt 5:32 [16]You will be cursed in the city and cursed in the country.

[17]Your basket and your kneading trough will be cursed.

[18]The fruit of your womb will be cursed, and the crops of
28:15 your land, and the calves of your herds and the lambs of
[j]Lev 26:14 your flocks.

[k]Jos 23:15; [19]You will be cursed when you come in and cursed when
Da 9:11; Mal 2:2 you go out.

[20]The LORD will send on you curses,[l] confusion and rebuke[m] in
everything you put your hand to, until you are destroyed and
28:20 come to sudden ruin[n] because of the evil you have done in for-
[l]Mal 2:2 [m]Isa 51:20; saking him.[a] [21]The LORD will plague you with diseases until he
66:15 [n]Dt 4:26 [a]*20* Hebrew *me*

has destroyed you from the land you are entering to possess.[a] 22The LORD will strike you with wasting disease, with fever and inflammation, with scorching heat and drought,[b] with blight and mildew, which will plague you until you perish.[c] 23The sky over your head will be bronze, the ground beneath you iron.[d] 24The LORD will turn the rain of your country into dust and powder; it will come down from the skies until you are destroyed.

25The LORD will cause you to be defeated before your enemies. You will come at them from one direction but flee from them in seven,[e] and you will become a thing of horror to all the kingdoms on earth.[f] 26Your carcasses will be food for all the birds of the air and the beasts of the earth, and there will be no one to frighten them away.[g] 27The LORD will afflict you with the boils of Egypt[h] and with tumors, festering sores and the itch, from which you cannot be cured. 28The LORD will afflict you with madness, blindness and confusion of mind. 29At midday you will grope[i] about like a blind man in the dark. You will be unsuccessful in everything you do; day after day you will be oppressed and robbed, with no one to rescue you.

30You will be pledged to be married to a woman, but another will take her and ravish her.[j] You will build a house, but you will not live in it.[k] You will plant a vineyard, but you will not even begin to enjoy its fruit.[l] 31Your ox will be slaughtered before your eyes, but you will eat none of it. Your donkey will be forcibly taken from you and will not be returned. Your sheep will be given to your enemies, and no one will rescue them. 32Your sons and daughters will be given to another nation,[m] and you will wear out your eyes watching for them day after day, powerless to lift a hand. 33A people that you do not know will eat what your land and labor produce, and you will have nothing but cruel oppression all your days.[n] 34The sights you see will drive you mad. 35The LORD will afflict your knees and legs with painful boils[o] that cannot be cured, spreading from the soles of your feet to the top of your head.

36The LORD will drive you and the king[p] you set over you to a nation unknown to you or your fathers.[q] There you will worship other gods, gods of wood and stone.[r] 37You will become a thing of horror and an object of scorn and ridicule to all the nations where the LORD will drive you.[s]

38You will sow much seed in the field but you will harvest little,[t] because locusts will devour[u] it. 39You will plant vineyards and cultivate them but you will not drink the wine or gather the grapes, because worms will eat them.[v] 40You will have olive trees throughout your country but you will not use the oil, because the olives will drop off.[w] 41You will have sons and daughters but you

28:21 [a] Lev 26:25; Jer 24:10

28:22 [b] Lev 26:16 [c] Am 4:9

28:23 [d] Lev 26:19

28:25 [e] Isa 30:17 [f] Jer 15:4; 24:9; Eze 23:46

28:26 [g] Jer 7:33; 16:4; 34:20

28:27 [h] ver 60-61; 1Sa 5:6

28:29 [i] Job 5:14; Isa 59:10

28:30 [j] Job 31:10; Jer 8:10 [k] Am 5:11 [l] Jer 12:13

28:32 [m] ver 41

28:33 [n] Jer 5:15-17

28:35 [o] ver 27

28:36 [p] 2Ki 17:4,6; 24:12,14; 25:7,11 [q] Jer 16:13 [r] Dt 4:28

28:37 [s] Jer 24:9

28:38 [t] Mic 6:15; Hag 1:6,9 [u] Joel 1:4

28:39 [v] Isa 5:10; 17:10-11

28:40 [w] Mic 6:15

will not keep them, because they will go into captivity.[a] 42Swarms
of locusts will take over all your trees and the crops of your land.
43The alien who lives among you will rise above you higher and
higher, but you will sink lower and lower.[b] 44He will lend to you,
but you will not lend to him.[c] He will be the head, but you will be
the tail.[d]
45All these curses will come upon you. They will pursue you
and overtake you until you are destroyed,[e] because you did not
obey the LORD your God and observe the commands and decrees
he gave you. 46They will be a sign and a wonder to you and your
descendants forever.[f] 47Because you did not serve[g] the LORD your
God joyfully and gladly[h] in the time of prosperity, 48therefore in
hunger and thirst, in nakedness and dire poverty, you will serve
the enemies the LORD sends against you. He will put an iron
yoke[i] on your neck until he has destroyed you.
49The LORD will bring a nation against you from far away, from
the ends of the earth,[j] like an eagle[k] swooping down, a nation
whose language you will not understand, 50a fierce-looking nation
without respect for the old[l] or pity for the young. 51They will
devour the young of your livestock and the crops of your land
until you are destroyed. They will leave you no grain, new wine
or oil, nor any calves of your herds or lambs of your flocks until
you are ruined.[m] 52They will lay siege to all the cities throughout
your land until the high fortified walls in which you trust fall
down. They will besiege all the cities throughout the land the
LORD your God is giving you.[n]
53Because of the suffering that your enemy will inflict on you
during the siege, you will eat the fruit of the womb, the flesh of
the sons and daughters the LORD your God has given you.[o] 54Even
the most gentle and sensitive man among you will have no compassion on his own brother or the wife he loves or his surviving
children, 55and he will not give to one of them any of the flesh of
his children that he is eating. It will be all he has left because of
the suffering your enemy will inflict on you during the siege of all
your cities. 56The most gentle and sensitive[p] woman among you—
so sensitive and gentle that she would not venture to touch the
ground with the sole of her foot—will begrudge the husband
she loves and her own son or daughter 57the afterbirth from her
womb and the children she bears. For she intends to eat them
secretly during the siege and in the distress that your enemy will
inflict on you in your cities.
58If you do not carefully follow all the words of this law, which are
written in this book, and do not revere[q] this glorious and awesome name[r]—the LORD your God— 59the LORD will send fearful
plagues on you and your descendants, harsh and prolonged

28:41 [a] ver 32
28:43 [b] ver 13
28:44 [c] ver 12 [d] ver 13
28:45 [e] ver 15
28:46 [f] Isa 8:18; Eze 14:8
28:47 [g] Dt 32:15 [h] Ne 9:35
28:48 [i] Jer 28:13-14
28:49 [j] Jer 5:15; 6:22 [k] La 4:19; Hos 8:1
28:50 [l] Isa 47:6
28:51 [m] ver 33
28:52 [n] Jer 10:18; Zep 1:14-16,17
28:53 [o] Lev 26:29; 2Ki 6:28-29; Jer 19:9; La 2:20; 4:10
28:56 [p] ver 54
28:58 [q] Mal 1:14 [r] Ex 6:3

disasters, and severe and lingering illnesses. 60He will bring upon you all the diseases of Egypt[a] that you dreaded, and they will cling to you. 61The LORD will also bring on you every kind of sickness and disaster not recorded in this Book of the Law, until you are destroyed.[b] 62You who were as numerous as the stars in the sky[c] will be left but few in number, because you did not obey the LORD your God. 63Just as it pleased[d] the LORD to make you prosper and increase in number, so it will please[e] him to ruin and destroy you. You will be uprooted[f] from the land you are entering to possess.

64Then the LORD will scatter[g] you among all nations,[h] from one end of the earth to the other. There you will worship other gods—gods of wood and stone, which neither you nor your fathers have known. 65Among those nations you will find no repose, no resting place for the sole of your foot. There the LORD will give you an anxious mind, eyes weary with longing, and a despairing heart.[i] 66You will live in constant suspense, filled with dread both night and day, never sure of your life. 67In the morning you will say, "If only it were evening!" and in the evening, "If only it were morning!"—because of the terror that will fill your hearts and the sights that your eyes will see.[j] 68The LORD will send you back in ships to Egypt on a journey I said you should never make again. There you will offer yourselves for sale to your enemies as male and female slaves, but no one will buy you.

Chapter 29 Theme ______________________________

29

These are the terms of the covenant the LORD commanded Moses to make with the Israelites in Moab, in addition to the covenant he had made with them at Horeb.[k]

2Moses summoned all the Israelites and said to them:

Your eyes have seen all that the LORD did in Egypt to Pharaoh, to all his officials and to all his land.[l] 3With your own eyes you saw those great trials, those miraculous signs and great wonders.[m] 4But to this day the LORD has not given you a mind that understands or eyes that see or ears that hear.[n] 5During the forty years that I led you through the desert, your clothes did not wear out, nor did the sandals on your feet.[o] 6You ate no bread and drank no wine or other fermented drink. I did this so that you might know that I am the LORD your God.[p]

7When you reached this place, Sihon[q] king of Heshbon and Og king of Bashan came out to fight against us, but we defeated them.[r] 8We took their land and gave it as an inheritance to the Reubenites, the Gadites and the half-tribe of Manasseh.[s]

9Carefully follow[t] the terms of this covenant, so that you may prosper in everything you do.[u] 10All of you are standing today in

28:60 [a] ver 27

28:61 [b] Dt 4:25-26

28:62 [c] Dt 4:27; 10:22; Ne 9:23

28:63 [d] Jer 32:41 [e] Pr 1:26 [f] Jer 12:14; 45:4

28:64 [g] Lev 26:33; Dt 4:27 [h] Ne 1:8

28:65 [i] Lev 26:16,36

28:67 [j] ver 34; Job 7:4

29:1 [k] Dt 5:2-3

29:2 [l] Ex 19:4

29:3 [m] Dt 4:34; 7:19

29:4 [n] Isa 6:10; Ac 28:26-27; Ro 11:8*; Eph 4:18

29:5 [o] Dt 8:4

29:6 [p] Dt 8:3

29:7 [q] Dt 2:32; 3:1 [r] Nu 21:21-24, 33-35

29:8 [s] Nu 32:33; Dt 3:12-13

29:9 [t] Dt 4:6; Jos 1:7 [u] 1Ki 2:3

the presence of the LORD your God—your leaders and chief men,
your elders and officials, and all the other men of Israel, 11 together
with your children and your wives, and the aliens living in your
camps who chop your wood and carry your water.[a] 12 You are
standing here in order to enter into a covenant with the LORD
your God, a covenant the LORD is making with you this day and
sealing with an oath, 13 to confirm you this day as his people,[b] that
he may be your God[c] as he promised you and as he swore to your
fathers, Abraham, Isaac and Jacob. 14 I am making this covenant,[d]
with its oath, not only with you 15 who are standing here with us
today in the presence of the LORD our God but also with those
who are not here today.[e]

16 You yourselves know how we lived in Egypt and how we
passed through the countries on the way here. 17 You saw among
them their detestable images and idols of wood and stone, of silver and gold.[f] 18 Make sure there is no man or woman, clan or
tribe among you today whose heart turns away from the LORD
our God to go and worship the gods of those nations; make sure
there is no root among you that produces such bitter poison.[g]

19 When such a person hears the words of this oath, he invokes
a blessing on himself and therefore thinks, "I will be safe, even
though I persist in going my own way." This will bring disaster
on the watered land as well as the dry.[a] 20 The LORD will never be
willing to forgive him; his wrath and zeal[h] will burn[i] against that
man. All the curses written in this book will fall upon him, and
the LORD will blot[j] out his name from under heaven. 21 The LORD
will single him out from all the tribes of Israel for disaster, according to all the curses of the covenant written in this Book of the Law.

22 Your children who follow you in later generations and foreigners who come from distant lands will see the calamities that
have fallen on the land and the diseases with which the LORD has
afflicted it.[k] 23 The whole land will be a burning waste[l] of salt[m]
and sulfur—nothing planted, nothing sprouting, no vegetation
growing on it. It will be like the destruction of Sodom and
Gomorrah,[n] Admah and Zeboiim, which the LORD overthrew in
fierce anger. 24 All the nations will ask: "Why has the LORD done
this to this land?[o] Why this fierce, burning anger?"

25 And the answer will be: "It is because this people abandoned
the covenant of the LORD, the God of their fathers, the covenant
he made with them when he brought them out of Egypt. 26 They
went off and worshiped other gods and bowed down to them,
gods they did not know, gods he had not given them. 27 Therefore
the LORD's anger burned against this land, so that he brought on

29:11 [a] Jos 9:21,23,27
29:13 [b] Dt 28:9 [c] Ge 17:7; Ex 6:7
29:14 [d] Jer 31:31
29:15 [e] Ac 2:39
29:17 [f] Dt 28:36
29:18 [g] Dt 11:16; Heb 12:15
29:20 [h] Eze 23:25 [i] Ps 74:1; 79:5 [j] Ex 32:33; Dt 9:14
29:22 [k] Jer 19:8
29:23 [l] Isa 34:9 [m] Jer 17:6 [n] Ge 19:24,25; Zep 2:9
29:24 [o] 1Ki 9:8; Jer 22:8-9

a *19* Or *way, in order to add drunkenness to thirst."*

it all the curses written in this book.[a] 28In furious anger and in
great wrath the LORD uprooted[b] them from their land and thrust
them into another land, as it is now."

29The secret things belong to the LORD our God, but the things
revealed belong to us and to our children forever, that we may
follow all the words of this law.

Chapter 30 Theme ______________________

30 When all these blessings and curses[c] I have set before
you come upon you and you take them to heart wherever
the LORD your God disperses you among the nations,[d] 2and
when you and your children return[e] to the LORD your God and
obey him with all your heart and with all your soul according to
everything I command you today, 3then the LORD your God will
restore your fortunes[a][f] and have compassion on you and gather[g]
you again from all the nations where he scattered you.[h] 4Even if
you have been banished to the most distant land under the heavens, from there the LORD your God will gather you and bring
you back.[i] 5He will bring[j] you to the land that belonged to your
fathers, and you will take possession of it. He will make you more
prosperous and numerous than your fathers. 6The LORD your
God will circumcise your hearts and the hearts of your descendants,[k] so that you may love him with all your heart and with all
your soul, and live. 7The LORD your God will put all these curses
on your enemies who hate and persecute you.[l] 8You will again
obey the LORD and follow all his commands I am giving you
today. 9Then the LORD your God will make you most prosperous
in all the work of your hands and in the fruit of your womb, the
young of your livestock and the crops of your land.[m] The LORD
will again delight in you and make you prosperous, just as he
delighted in your fathers, 10if you obey the LORD your God and
keep his commands and decrees that are written in this Book of
the Law and turn to the LORD your God with all your heart and
with all your soul.[n]

11Now what I am commanding you today is not too difficult for
you or beyond your reach.[o] 12It is not up in heaven, so that you
have to ask, "Who will ascend into heaven to get it and proclaim
it to us so we may obey it?"[p] 13Nor is it beyond the sea, so that you
have to ask, "Who will cross the sea to get it and proclaim it to us
so we may obey it?" 14No, the word is very near you; it is in your
mouth and in your heart so you may obey it.

15See, I set before you today life and prosperity, death and
destruction.[q] 16For I command you today to love the LORD your

[a]3 Or *will bring you back from captivity*

29:27 [a]Da 9:11,13,14

29:28 [b]1Ki 14:15; 2Ch 7:20; Ps 52:5; Pr 2:22

30:1 [c]ver 15,19; Dt 11:26 [d]Lev 26:40-45; Dt 28:64; 29:28; 1Ki 8:47

30:2 [e]Dt 4:30; Ne 1:9

30:3 [f]Ps 126:4 [g]Ps 147:2; Jer 32:37; Eze 34:13 [h]Jer 29:14

30:4 [i]Ne 1:8-9; Isa 43:6

30:5 [j]Jer 29:14

30:6 [k]Dt 10:16; Jer 32:39

30:7 [l]Dt 7:15

30:9 [m]Dt 28:11; Jer 31:28; 32:41

30:10 [n]Dt 4:29

30:11 [o]Isa 45:19,23

30:12 [p]Ro 10:6*

30:15 [q]Dt 11:26

God, to walk in his ways, and to keep his commands, decrees and
laws; then you will live and increase, and the LORD your God will
bless you in the land you are entering to possess.
17 But if your heart turns away and you are not obedient, and if
you are drawn away to bow down to other gods and worship them,
18 I declare to you this day that you will certainly be destroyed.[a]
You will not live long in the land you are crossing the Jordan to
enter and possess.
19 This day I call heaven and earth as witnesses against you[b] that
I have set before you life and death, blessings and curses.[c] Now
choose life, so that you and your children may live 20 and that
you may love[d] the LORD your God, listen to his voice, and hold
fast to him. For the LORD is your life,[e] and he will give you many
years in the land he swore to give to your fathers, Abraham,
Isaac and Jacob.

Chapter 31 Theme ____________________

31 Then Moses went out and spoke these words to all Israel:
2 "I am now a hundred and twenty years old[f] and I am no
longer able to lead you.[g] The LORD has said to me, 'You shall not
cross the Jordan.'[h] 3 The LORD your God himself will cross[i] over
ahead of you.[j] He will destroy these nations before you, and you
will take possession of their land. Joshua also will cross[k] over
ahead of you, as the LORD said. 4 And the LORD will do to them
what he did to Sihon and Og, the kings of the Amorites, whom
he destroyed along with their land. 5 The LORD will deliver[l] them
to you, and you must do to them all that I have commanded you.
6 Be strong and courageous.[m] Do not be afraid or terrified[n]
because of them, for the LORD your God goes with you;[o] he will
never leave you[p] nor forsake[q] you."
7 Then Moses summoned Joshua and said[r] to him in the presence of all Israel, "Be strong and courageous, for you must go
with this people into the land that the LORD swore to their forefathers to give them, and you must divide it among them as their
inheritance. 8 The LORD himself goes before you and will be with
you;[s] he will never leave you nor forsake you. Do not be afraid;
do not be discouraged."
9 So Moses wrote down this law and gave it to the priests, the
sons of Levi, who carried[t] the ark of the covenant of the LORD,
and to all the elders of Israel. 10 Then Moses commanded them:
"At the end of every seven years, in the year for canceling debts,[u]
during the Feast of Tabernacles,[v] 11 when all Israel comes to
appear[w] before the LORD your God at the place he will choose,
you shall read this law[x] before them in their hearing. 12 Assemble
the people—men, women and children, and the aliens living in

30:18 [a]Dt 8:19
30:19 [b]Dt 4:26 [c]ver 1
30:20 [d]Dt 6:5; 10:20 [e]Ps 27:1; Jn 11:25
31:2 [f]Dt 34:7 [g]Nu 27:17; 1Ki 3:7 [h]Dt 3:23,26
31:3 [i]Nu 27:18 [j]Dt 9:3 [k]Dt 3:28
31:5 [l]Dt 7:2
31:6 [m]Jos 10:25; 1Ch 22:13 [n]Dt 7:18 [o]Dt 1:29; 20:4 [p]Jos 1:5 [q]Heb 13:5*
31:7 [r]Dt 1:38; 3:28
31:8 [s]Ex 13:21; 33:14
31:9 [t]ver 25; Nu 4:15; Jos 3:3
31:10 [u]Dt 15:1 [v]Lev 23:34
31:11 [w]Dt 16:16 [x]Jos 8:34-35; 2Ki 23:2

your towns—so they can listen and learn[a] to fear the LORD your God and follow carefully all the words of this law. 13Their children,[b] who do not know this law, must hear it and learn to fear the LORD your God as long as you live in the land you are crossing the Jordan to possess."

14The LORD said to Moses, "Now the day of your death[c] is near. Call Joshua and present yourselves at the Tent of Meeting, where I will commission him." So Moses and Joshua came and presented themselves at the Tent of Meeting.

15Then the LORD appeared at the Tent in a pillar of cloud, and the cloud stood over the entrance to the Tent.[d] 16And the LORD said to Moses: "You are going to rest with your fathers, and these people will soon prostitute[e] themselves to the foreign gods of the land they are entering. They will forsake[f] me and break the covenant I made with them. 17On that day I will become angry[g] with them and forsake[h] them; I will hide[i] my face from them, and they will be destroyed. Many disasters and difficulties will come upon them, and on that day they will ask, 'Have not these disasters come upon us because our God is not with us?'[j] 18And I will certainly hide my face on that day because of all their wickedness in turning to other gods.

19"Now write down for yourselves this song and teach it to the Israelites and have them sing it, so that it may be a witness for me against them. 20When I have brought them into the land flowing with milk and honey, the land I promised on oath to their forefathers,[k] and when they eat their fill and thrive, they will turn to other gods[l] and worship them, rejecting me and breaking my covenant.[m] 21And when many disasters and difficulties come upon them,[n] this song will testify against them, because it will not be forgotten by their descendants. I know what they are disposed to do,[o] even before I bring them into the land I promised them on oath." 22So Moses wrote[p] down this song that day and taught it to the Israelites.

23The LORD gave this command[q] to Joshua son of Nun: "Be strong and courageous,[r] for you will bring the Israelites into the land I promised them on oath, and I myself will be with you."

24After Moses finished writing in a book the words of this law from beginning to end, 25he gave this command to the Levites who carried the ark of the covenant of the LORD: 26"Take this Book of the Law and place it beside the ark of the covenant of the LORD your God. There it will remain as a witness against you.[s] 27For I know how rebellious and stiff-necked[t] you are. If you have been rebellious against the LORD while I am still alive and with you, how much more will you rebel after I die! 28Assemble before me all the elders of your tribes and all your officials, so that I can

31:12 [a] Dt 4:10
31:13 [b] Dt 11:2; Ps 78:6-7
31:14 [c] Nu 27:13; Dt 32:49-50
31:15 [d] Ex 33:9
31:16 [e] Jdg 2:12 [f] Jdg 10:6,13
31:17 [g] Jdg 2:14,20 [h] Jdg 6:13; 2Ch 15:2 [i] Dt 32:20; Isa 1:15; 8:17 [j] Nu 14:42
31:20 [k] Dt 6:10-12 [l] Dt 32:15-17 [m] ver 16
31:21 [n] ver 17 [o] Hos 5:3
31:22 [p] ver 19
31:23 [q] ver 7 [r] Jos 1:6
31:26 [s] ver 19
31:27 [t] Ex 32:9; Dt 9:6,24

speak these words in their hearing and call heaven and earth to
testify against them.[a] 29 For I know that after my death you are
sure to become utterly corrupt[b] and to turn from the way I have
commanded you. In days to come, disaster[c] will fall upon you
because you will do evil in the sight of the LORD and provoke
him to anger by what your hands have made."

Chapter 32 Theme ______________________________

30 And Moses recited the words of this song from beginning to
end in the hearing of the whole assembly of Israel:

32

Listen, O heavens,[d] and I will speak;
 hear, O earth, the words of my mouth.
2 Let my teaching fall like rain
 and my words descend like dew,[e]
like showers[f] on new grass,
 like abundant rain on tender plants.

3 I will proclaim the name of the LORD.[g]
 Oh, praise the greatness[h] of our God!
4 He is the Rock,[i] his works are perfect,[j]
 and all his ways are just.
A faithful God[k] who does no wrong,
 upright and just is he.

5 They have acted corruptly toward him;
 to their shame they are no longer his children,
 but a warped and crooked generation.[a][l]
6 Is this the way you repay[m] the LORD,
 O foolish and unwise people?[n]
Is he not your Father,[o] your Creator,[b]
 who made you and formed you?[p]

7 Remember the days of old;
 consider the generations long past.
Ask your father and he will tell you,
 your elders, and they will explain to you.[q]
8 When the Most High gave the nations their inheritance,
 when he divided all mankind,[r]
he set up boundaries for the peoples
 according to the number of the sons of Israel.[c]
9 For the LORD's portion[s] is his people,
 Jacob his allotted inheritance.[t]

[a]5 Or *Corrupt are they and not his children, / a generation warped and twisted to their shame* [b]6 Or *Father, who bought you* [c]8 Masoretic Text; Dead Sea Scrolls (see also Septuagint) *sons of God*

31:28 [a]Dt 4:26; 30:19; 32:1
31:29 [b]Dt 32:5; Jdg 2:19 [c]Dt 28:15
32:1 [d]Isa 1:2
32:2 [e]Isa 55:11 [f]Ps 72:6
32:3 [g]Ex 33:19 [h]Dt 3:24
32:4 [i]ver 15,18,30 [j]2Sa 22:31 [k]Dt 7:9
32:5 [l]Dt 31:29
32:6 [m]Ps 116:12 [n]Ps 74:2 [o]Dt 1:31; Isa 63:16 [p]ver 15
32:7 [q]Ex 13:14
32:8 [r]Ge 11:8; Ac 17:26
32:9 [s]Jer 10:16 [t]1Ki 8:51,53

[10]In a desert[a] land he found him,
in a barren and howling waste.
He shielded him and cared for him;
he guarded him as the apple of his eye,[b]
[11]like an eagle that stirs up its nest
and hovers over its young,[c]
that spreads its wings to catch them
and carries them on its pinions.
[12]The LORD alone led him;
no foreign god was with him.[d]

[13]He made him ride on the heights[e] of the land
and fed him with the fruit of the fields.
He nourished him with honey from the rock,
and with oil[f] from the flinty crag,
[14]with curds and milk from herd and flock
and with fattened lambs and goats,
with choice rams of Bashan
and the finest kernels of wheat.[g]
You drank the foaming blood of the grape.[h]

[15]Jeshurun[a] grew fat[i] and kicked;
filled with food, he became heavy and sleek.
He abandoned[j] the God who made him
and rejected the Rock[k] his Savior.
[16]They made him jealous[l] with their foreign gods
and angered[m] him with their detestable idols.
[17]They sacrificed to demons, which are not God—
gods they had not known,[n]
gods that recently appeared,[o]
gods your fathers did not fear.
[18]You deserted the Rock, who fathered you;
you forgot[p] the God who gave you birth.

[19]The LORD saw this and rejected them[q]
because he was angered by his sons and daughters.[r]
[20]"I will hide my face[s] from them," he said,
"and see what their end will be;
for they are a perverse generation,[t]
children who are unfaithful.
[21]They made me jealous[u] by what is no god
and angered me with their worthless idols.[v]
I will make them envious by those who are not a people;
I will make them angry by a nation that has no
understanding.[w]

a *15 Jeshurun* means *the upright one*, that is, Israel.

32:10 [a]Jer 2:6 [b]Ps 17:8; Zec 2:8
32:11 [c]Ex 19:4
32:12 [d]ver 39
32:13 [e]Isa 58:14 [f]Job 29:6
32:14 [g]Ps 81:16; 147:14 [h]Ge 49:11
32:15 [i]Dt 31:20 [j]ver 6; Isa 1:4,28 [k]ver 4
32:16 [l]1Co 10:22 [m]Ps 78:58
32:17 [n]Dt 28:64 [o]Jdg 5:8
32:18 [p]Isa 17:10
32:19 [q]Jer 44:21-23 [r]Ps 106:40
32:20 [s]Dt 31:17,29 [t]ver 5
32:21 [u]1Co 10:22 [v]1Ki 16:13,26 [w]Ro 10:19*

22 For a fire has been kindled by my wrath,
one that burns to the realm of death[a] below.[a]
It will devour the earth and its harvests
and set afire the foundations of the mountains.

23 "I will heap calamities[b] upon them
and spend my arrows[c] against them.
24 I will send wasting famine against them,
consuming pestilence[d] and deadly plague;[e]
I will send against them the fangs of wild beasts,[f]
the venom of vipers[g] that glide in the dust.
25 In the street the sword will make them childless;
in their homes terror will reign.[h]
Young men and young women will perish,
infants and gray-haired men.[i]
26 I said I would scatter[j] them
and blot out their memory from mankind,[k]
27 but I dreaded the taunt of the enemy,
lest the adversary misunderstand
and say, 'Our hand has triumphed;
the LORD has not done all this.'"[l]

28 They are a nation without sense,
there is no discernment in them.
29 If only they were wise and would understand this[m]
and discern what their end will be!
30 How could one man chase a thousand,
or two put ten thousand to flight,[n]
unless their Rock had sold them,
unless the LORD had given them up?[o]
31 For their rock is not like our Rock,
as even our enemies concede.
32 Their vine comes from the vine of Sodom
and from the fields of Gomorrah.
Their grapes are filled with poison,
and their clusters with bitterness.
33 Their wine is the venom of serpents,
the deadly poison of cobras.[p]

34 "Have I not kept this in reserve
and sealed it in my vaults?[q]
35 It is mine to avenge; I will repay.[r]
In due time their foot will slip;[s]
their day of disaster is near
and their doom rushes upon them.[t]"

32:22 [a] Ps 18:7-8; Jer 15:14; La 4:11
32:23 [b] Dt 29:21 [c] Ps 7:13; Eze 5:16
32:24 [d] Dt 28:22 [e] Ps 91:6 [f] Lev 26:22 [g] Am 5:18-19
32:25 [h] Eze 7:15 [i] 2Ch 36:17; La 2:21
32:26 [j] Dt 4:27 [k] Ps 34:16
32:27 [l] Isa 10:13
32:29 [m] Dt 5:29; Ps 81:13
32:30 [n] Lev 26:8 [o] Ps 44:12
32:33 [p] Ps 58:4
32:34 [q] Jer 2:22; Hos 13:12
32:35 [r] Ro 12:19*; Heb 10:30* [s] Jer 23:12 [t] Eze 7:8-9

a 22 Hebrew *to Sheol*

[36]The LORD will judge his people
and have compassion on his servants[a]
when he sees their strength is gone
and no one is left, slave or free.
[37]He will say: "Now where are their gods,
the rock they took refuge in,[b]
[38]the gods who ate the fat of their sacrifices
and drank the wine of their drink offerings?
Let them rise up to help you!
Let them give you shelter!

[39]"See now that I myself am He![c]
There is no god besides me.[d]
I put to death and I bring to life,[e]
I have wounded and I will heal,[f]
and no one can deliver out of my hand.[g]
[40]I lift my hand to heaven and declare:
As surely as I live forever,
[41]when I sharpen my flashing sword[h]
and my hand grasps it in judgment,
I will take vengeance on my adversaries
and repay those who hate me.[i]
[42]I will make my arrows drunk with blood,[j]
while my sword devours flesh:[k]
the blood of the slain and the captives,
the heads of the enemy leaders."

[43]Rejoice,[l] O nations, with his people,[a, b]
for he will avenge the blood of his servants;[m]
he will take vengeance on his enemies
and make atonement for his land and people.[n]

[44]Moses came with Joshua[c][o] son of Nun and spoke all the
words of this song in the hearing of the people. [45]When Moses
finished reciting all these words to all Israel, [46]he said to them,
"Take to heart all the words I have solemnly declared to you this
day,[p] so that you may command your children to obey carefully
all the words of this law. [47]They are not just idle words for you—
they are your life.[q] By them you will live long in the land you are
crossing the Jordan to possess."

[48]On that same day the LORD told Moses, [49]"Go up into the
Abarim[r] Range to Mount Nebo in Moab, across from Jericho,
and view Canaan, the land I am giving the Israelites as their own
possession. [50]There on the mountain that you have climbed you

32:36 [a]Dt 30:1-3; Ps 135:14; Joel 2:14
32:37 [b]Jdg 10:14; Jer 2:28
32:39 [c]Isa 41:4 [d]Isa 45:5 [e]1Sa 2:6; Ps 68:20 [f]Hos 6:1 [g]Ps 50:22
32:41 [h]Isa 34:6; 66:16; Eze 21:9-10 [i]Jer 50:29
32:42 [j]ver 23 [k]Jer 46:10,14
32:43 [l]Ro 15:10* [m]2Ki 9:7 [n]Ps 65:3; 85:1; Rev 19:2
32:44 [o]Nu 13:8,16
32:46 [p]Eze 40:4
32:47 [q]Dt 30:20
32:49 [r]Nu 27:12

a 43 Or *Make his people rejoice, O nations* b 43 Masoretic Text; Dead Sea Scrolls (see also Septuagint) *people, / and let all the angels worship him /* c 44 Hebrew *Hoshea,* a variant of *Joshua*

will die[a] and be gathered to your people, just as your brother
Aaron died on Mount Hor and was gathered to his people. 51 This
is because both of you broke faith with me in the presence of the
Israelites at the waters of Meribah Kadesh in the Desert of Zin[b]
and because you did not uphold my holiness among the
Israelites.[c] 52 Therefore, you will see the land only from a distance;[d]
you will not enter[e] the land I am giving to the people of Israel."

Chapter 33 Theme ______________________

33 This is the blessing that Moses the man of God[f] pronounced on the Israelites before his death. 2 He said:

"The LORD came from Sinai[g]
  and dawned over them from Seir;[h]
  he shone forth from Mount Paran.[i]
He came with[a] myriads of holy ones[j]
  from the south, from his mountain slopes.[b]
3 Surely it is you who love[k] the people;
  all the holy ones are in your hand.[l]
At your feet they all bow down,[m]
  and from you receive instruction,
4 the law that Moses gave us,[n]
  the possession of the assembly of Jacob.[o]
5 He was king over Jeshurun[c]
  when the leaders of the people assembled,
  along with the tribes of Israel.

6 "Let Reuben live and not die,
  nor[d] his men be few."

7 And this he said about Judah:[p]

"Hear, O LORD, the cry of Judah;
  bring him to his people.
With his own hands he defends his cause.
  Oh, be his help against his foes!"

8 About Levi he said:

"Your Thummim and Urim[q] belong
  to the man you favored.
You tested him at Massah;
  you contended with him at the waters of Meribah.[r]
9 He said of his father and mother,[s]
  'I have no regard for them.'

[a] 2 Or *from* [b] 2 The meaning of the Hebrew for this phrase is uncertain. [c] 5 *Jeshurun* means *the upright one,* that is, Israel; also in verse 26. [d] 6 Or *but let*

32:50 [a] Ge 25:8
32:51 [b] Nu 20:11-13 [c] Nu 27:14
32:52 [d] Dt 34:1-3 [e] Dt 1:37
33:1 [f] Jos 14:6
33:2 [g] Ex 19:18; Ps 68:8 [h] Jdg 5:4 [i] Hab 3:3 [j] Da 7:10; Ac 7:53; Rev 5:11
33:3 [k] Hos 11:1 [l] Dt 14:2 [m] Lk 10:39
33:4 [n] Jn 1:17 [o] Ps 119:111
33:7 [p] Ge 49:10
33:8 [q] Ex 28:30 [r] Ex 17:7
33:9 [s] Ex 32:26-29

He did not recognize his brothers
or acknowledge his own children,
but he watched over your word
and guarded your covenant.[a]
10He teaches your precepts to Jacob
and your law to Israel.[b]
He offers incense before you
and whole burnt offerings on your altar.[c]
11Bless all his skills, O LORD,
and be pleased with the work of his hands.[d]
Smite the loins of those who rise up against him;
strike his foes till they rise no more."

12About Benjamin he said:

"Let the beloved of the LORD rest secure in him,[e]
for he shields him all day long,
and the one the LORD loves rests between his shoulders.[f]"

13About Joseph[g] he said:

"May the LORD bless his land
with the precious dew from heaven above
and with the deep waters that lie below;[h]
14with the best the sun brings forth
and the finest the moon can yield;
15with the choicest gifts of the ancient mountains[i]
and the fruitfulness of the everlasting hills;
16with the best gifts of the earth and its fullness
and the favor of him who dwelt in the burning bush.[j]
Let all these rest on the head of Joseph,
on the brow of the prince among[a] his brothers.
17In majesty he is like a firstborn bull;
his horns are the horns of a wild ox.[k]
With them he will gore[l] the nations,
even those at the ends of the earth.
Such are the ten thousands of Ephraim;
such are the thousands of Manasseh."

18About Zebulun[m] he said:

"Rejoice, Zebulun, in your going out,
and you, Issachar, in your tents.
19They will summon peoples to the mountain[n]
and there offer sacrifices of righteousness;[o]

[a] 16 Or *of the one separated from*

33:9 [a] Mal 2:5
33:10 [b] Lev 10:11; Dt 31:9-13 [c] Ps 51:19
33:11 [d] 2Sa 24:23
33:12 [e] Dt 12:10 [f] Ex 28:12
33:13 [g] Ge 49:25 [h] Ge 27:28
33:15 [i] Hab 3:6
33:16 [j] Ex 3:2
33:17 [k] Nu 23:22 [l] 1Ki 22:11; Ps 44:5
33:18 [m] Ge 49:13-15
33:19 [n] Ex 15:17; Isa 2:3 [o] Ps 4:5

they will feast on the abundance of the seas,[a]
on the treasures hidden in the sand."

20About Gad[b] he said:

"Blessed is he who enlarges Gad's domain!
Gad lives there like a lion,
tearing at arm or head.
21He chose the best land for himself;[c]
the leader's portion was kept for him.
When the heads of the people assembled,
he carried out the LORD's righteous will,[d]
and his judgments concerning Israel."

22About Dan[e] he said:

"Dan is a lion's cub,
springing out of Bashan."

23About Naphtali he said:

"Naphtali is abounding with the favor of the LORD
and is full of his blessing;
he will inherit southward to the lake."

24About Asher[f] he said:

"Most blessed of sons is Asher;
let him be favored by his brothers,
and let him bathe his feet in oil.[g]
25The bolts of your gates will be iron and bronze,
and your strength will equal your days.[h]

26"There is no one like the God of Jeshurun,[i]
who rides on the heavens to help you[j]
and on the clouds in his majesty.
27The eternal God is your refuge,[k]
and underneath are the everlasting arms.
He will drive out your enemy before you,[l]
saying, 'Destroy him!'[m]
28So Israel will live in safety alone;[n]
Jacob's spring is secure
in a land of grain and new wine,
where the heavens drop dew.[o]
29Blessed are you, O Israel![p]
Who is like you,[q]
a people saved by the LORD?[r]
He is your shield and helper[s]
and your glorious sword.

33:19 [a]Isa 60:5,11
33:20 [b]Ge 49:19
33:21 [c]Nu 32:1-5, 31-32 [d]Jos 4:12; 22:1-3
33:22 [e]Ge 49:16
33:24 [f]Ge 49:21 [g]Ge 49:20; Job 29:6
33:25 [h]Dt 4:40; 32:47
33:26 [i]Ex 15:11 [j]Ps 104:3
33:27 [k]Ps 90:1 [l]Jos 24:18 [m]Dt 7:2
33:28 [n]Nu 23:9; Jer 23:6 [o]Ge 27:28
33:29 [p]Ps 144:15 [q]Ps 18:44 [r]2Sa 7:23 [s]Ps 115:9-11

Your enemies will cower before you,
and you will trample down their high places.[a] [a]"

Chapter 34 Theme ______________________________

34 Then Moses climbed Mount Nebo from the plains of
Moab to the top of Pisgah, across from Jericho.[b] There
the LORD showed[c] him the whole land—from Gilead to Dan, 2all
of Naphtali, the territory of Ephraim and Manasseh, all the land
of Judah as far as the western sea,[b] [d] 3the Negev and the whole
region from the Valley of Jericho, the City of Palms,[e] as far as
Zoar. 4Then the LORD said to him, "This is the land I promised
on oath[f] to Abraham, Isaac and Jacob when I said, 'I will give it[g]
to your descendants.' I have let you see it with your eyes, but you
will not cross[h] over into it."
5And Moses the servant of the LORD[i] died[j] there in Moab, as
the LORD had said. 6He buried him[c] in Moab, in the valley opposite Beth Peor,[k] but to this day no one knows where his grave is.[l]
7Moses was a hundred and twenty years old[m] when he died, yet
his eyes were not weak[n] nor his strength gone. 8The Israelites
grieved for Moses in the plains of Moab thirty days, until the
time of weeping and mourning[o] was over.
9Now Joshua son of Nun was filled with the spirit[d] of wisdom[p]
because Moses had laid his hands on him.[q] So the Israelites listened to him and did what the LORD had commanded Moses.
10Since then, no prophet has risen in Israel like Moses,[r] whom
the LORD knew face to face,[s] 11who did all those miraculous signs
and wonders[t] the LORD sent him to do in Egypt—to Pharaoh
and to all his officials[u] and to his whole land. 12For no one has
ever shown the mighty power or performed the awesome deeds
that Moses did in the sight of all Israel.

a 29 Or *will tread upon their bodies* b 2 That is, the Mediterranean c 6 Or *He was buried*
d 9 Or *Spirit*

33:29 a Dt 32:13
34:1 b Dt 32:49 c Dt 32:52
34:2 d Dt 11:24
34:3 e Jdg 1:16; 3:13; 2Ch 28:15
34:4 f Ge 28:13 g Ge 12:7 h Dt 3:27
34:5 i Nu 12:7 j Dt 32:50; Jos 1:1-2
34:6 k Dt 3:29 l Jude 1:9
34:7 m Dt 31:2 n Ge 27:1
34:8 o Ge 50:3,10; 2Sa 11:27
34:9 p Ge 41:38; Isa 11:2; Da 6:3 q Nu 27:18,23
34:10 r Dt 18:15,18 s Ex 33:11; Nu 12:6,8; Dt 5:4
34:11 t Dt 4:34 u Dt 7:19

Deuteronomy at a Glance

Theme of Deuteronomy:

Author:

Date:

Geographical Location:

Purpose:

Key Words:

Segment Divisions		Chapter Themes
		1
		2
		3
		4
		5
		6
		7
		8
		9
		10
		11
		12
		13
		14
		15
		16
		17
		18
		19
		20
		21
		22
		23
		24
		25
		26
		27
		28
		29
		30
		31
		32
		33
		34

Lessons from the Life of Moses

Book/ Chapter/ Verse	Lessons for My Life

(continued)

BOOK/ CHAPTER/ VERSE	LESSONS FOR MY LIFE

JOSHUA

For years Joshua had faithfully served Moses—and God. How well Joshua understood the meaning of his name, "The Lord is salvation." All his contemporaries, except Caleb, had died in the wilderness because they had not believed God. But God had spared Joshua and Caleb because they had followed him fully.

Now Moses was dead and God had appointed Joshua to lead the children of Israel into the land of promise. Their salvation from their enemies would not come from the east nor from the west but from the one who made the heaven and the earth!

God's words rang in Joshua's heart: "Be strong and courageous."

Things to Do

General Instructions

1. If you are not familiar with who Joshua is, before you begin studying the book, read Numbers 13; 14; 27:18-23; Deuteronomy 34:9.

2. As you study Joshua one chapter at a time, it will help you keep everything in context if you will remember that Joshua falls into four segments. In chapters 1 through 5 the children of Israel prepare to enter the land. Chapters 6 through 12 describe the conquest of the land. Chapters 13 through 21 tell of the allocation of the land. In chapters 22 through 24 Joshua calls Israel to serve the Lord, who gave them the land.

3. As you read each chapter, ask the five W's and an H: Who? What? When? Where? Why? and How? For example, in a historical book such as Joshua ask: What is this chapter about? Who are the main characters? What is taking place? Where is it happening and when? Who is involved? Why is this occurring, being said, or to be done? What are the consequences? How is it going to happen? How should it be done? Record the main points or events of the chapter in the margin.

4. On the map on page 351 you will find many of the various cities and places mentioned throughout this book. Look them up so you can keep the book in its geographical context.

5. Mark every reference to time with a symbol. This will help you see when events occurred and the chronological relationship of one event to another.

6. After you finish studying each chapter, write the theme or event covered in that chapter on the line next to the chapter number. Then record it on the JOSHUA AT A GLANCE chart on page 391.

Chapters 1-5

1. As you read these chapters, mark the following key words and their synonyms: *Joshua, land (country), strong, courageous, firm, command (tell, word, commanded, directed, ordered, giving orders), occupy (for your own, take possession), covenant, ark of the Lord (ark of the covenant),* and *Israel (Israelites).* Write these on an index card that you can use as a bookmark while studying this segment.

2. Watch how the events or the instructions prepare the Israelites to enter the land. Also note the procedure for entering the land and the requirements placed on them as they arrive in the land. You might list these in the margin under the heading "Occupying the Land."

3. If while reading chapter 5 you need a review of circumcision, read Genesis 17 and Exodus 4:24-26.

4. Don't forget to record the theme of each chapter in the text and on JOSHUA AT A GLANCE.

Chapters 6-12

1. As you study this section keep in mind the general instructions above.

2. Although you will mark many of the same key words, make a new bookmark of the following key words: *God, Lord, Joshua, covenant (treaty), strong, courageous, land (region, country, territory), be afraid, commanded (ordered, instructed, gave the order), fight (make war, fought, attacked, was fighting), captured (taken, took), ark of the covenant,* and *Israel (Israelites).*

3. Carefully observe what God tells the people to do when they conquer a city. Read Genesis 15:7-21 and note that God told Abraham he would bring his descendants into Canaan when "the sin of the Amorites has not yet reached its full measure." Also recall the covenant God made with Abraham on that day. You might write "Genesis 15:7-21" in the margin of this section as a cross-reference.

4. As you read, watch what happens when the people fail to consult God or to obey his commands in respect to the inhabitants of the land. Note this in the margin.

5. When you come to chapter 8, note where Mount Ebal and Mount Gerizim are located and what takes place there. Refer back to Deuteronomy 11:29 and Deuteronomy 27:11-14. Use the map on page 351 to locate these places. Also mark all clues to time with a symbol in the margin or above the verses where they occur.

6. Record the theme of each chapter.

Chapters 13-21

1. Once again make a new bookmark of the following key words, although some words will remain the same: *Israel (Israelites), land (area, country, region, plain), Joshua, Caleb, strong (stronger), fear, command (commanded, instructed), attacked, captured (took), inheritance(s), possession (occupy, territory), taken over* (also mark *possession (inheritance)* in chapter 12), and *promised.*

2. Continue to consult the map on page 351 so you are aware of the geographical location of the places mentioned in this segment. Also mark in the text the name of each tribe as it is allotted its portion of the land.

3. As you read, watch for any mention of Caleb. Remember what you read about Joshua and Caleb in Numbers 13 and 14. There are important lessons to be learned from their example.

4. Pay careful attention to chapter 20 and what you learn about the cities of refuge.

5. Also note the inheritance given to the Levites in Joshua 21.

6. Don't forget to record the chapter themes.

Chapters 22-24

1. Make this final bookmark of key words and mark them in the text: *land (border, country), possess, possession (acquired), covenant, powerful, strong, fear, command (commandment, commanded, gave), serve (serving, served, worshiped), Israel (Israelite(s)), Joshua, promised, fought (fight),* and *inheritance.*

2. In the margin also list God's instructions and what the people are to do in order to keep them. Also note in the margin the consequences of disobedience.

3. As you read Joshua 23, mark the words *hold fast* and *ally* and think of the illustration God uses in Jeremiah 13:1-11 of a belt and how Israel and Judah used to hold fast to him—to be bound to him. Then read Jeremiah 13:1-11.

4. Complete JOSHUA AT A GLANCE. Fill in the four main segment divisions and any others you see.

5. Compare what Joshua tells the children of Israel in chapter 23 with God's word to Joshua in chapter 1. You might write "Joshua 1:7-9" in the margin of Joshua 23.

Things to Think About

1. Do you consult the Lord and his Word and then walk in obedience to what he says?
2. Joshua was admonished to be strong and courageous. What do you think this means? Read Revelation 21:8 and note what is said about the cowardly.
3. Have you decided whom you are going to follow? Have you counted the cost? What would cause you to compromise? Could you get away with compromise? What would it cost you? Would it be worth it?

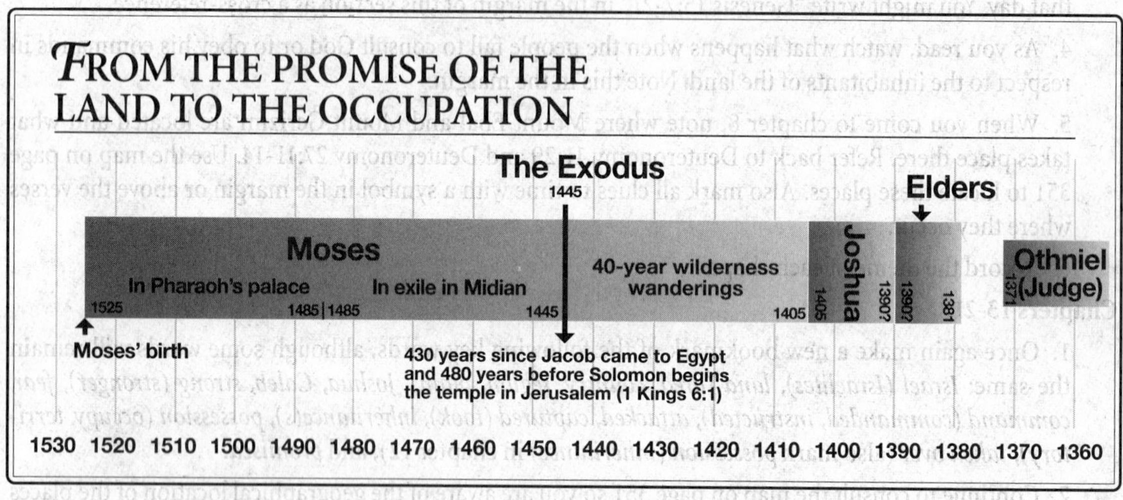

Chapter 1 Theme ________________________

1 After the death of Moses the servant of the LORD,[a] the LORD
said to Joshua[b] son of Nun, Moses' aide: 2"Moses my servant
is dead. Now then, you and all these people, get ready to cross
the Jordan River[c] into the land I am about to give to them—to
the Israelites. 3I will give you every place where you set your
foot,[d] as I promised Moses. 4Your territory will extend from the
desert to Lebanon, and from the great river, the Euphrates[e]—all
the Hittite country—to the Great Sea[a] on the west.[f] 5No one will
be able to stand up against you[g] all the days of your life. As I was
with[h] Moses, so I will be with you; I will never leave you nor forsake[i] you.

6"Be strong and courageous, because you will lead these people to inherit the land I swore to their forefathers[j] to give them.
7Be strong and very courageous. Be careful to obey all the law
my servant Moses gave you; do not turn from it to the right or to

1:1 [a]Nu 12:7; Dt 34:5 [b]Ex 24:13; Dt 1:38
1:2 [c]ver 11
1:3 [d]Dt 11:24
1:4 [e]Ge 15:18 [f]Nu 34:2-12
1:5 [g]Dt 7:24 [h]Jos 3:7; 6:27 [i]Dt 31:6-8
1:6 [j]Dt 31:23

[a]4 That is, the Mediterranean

Joshua: Occupying the Promised Land

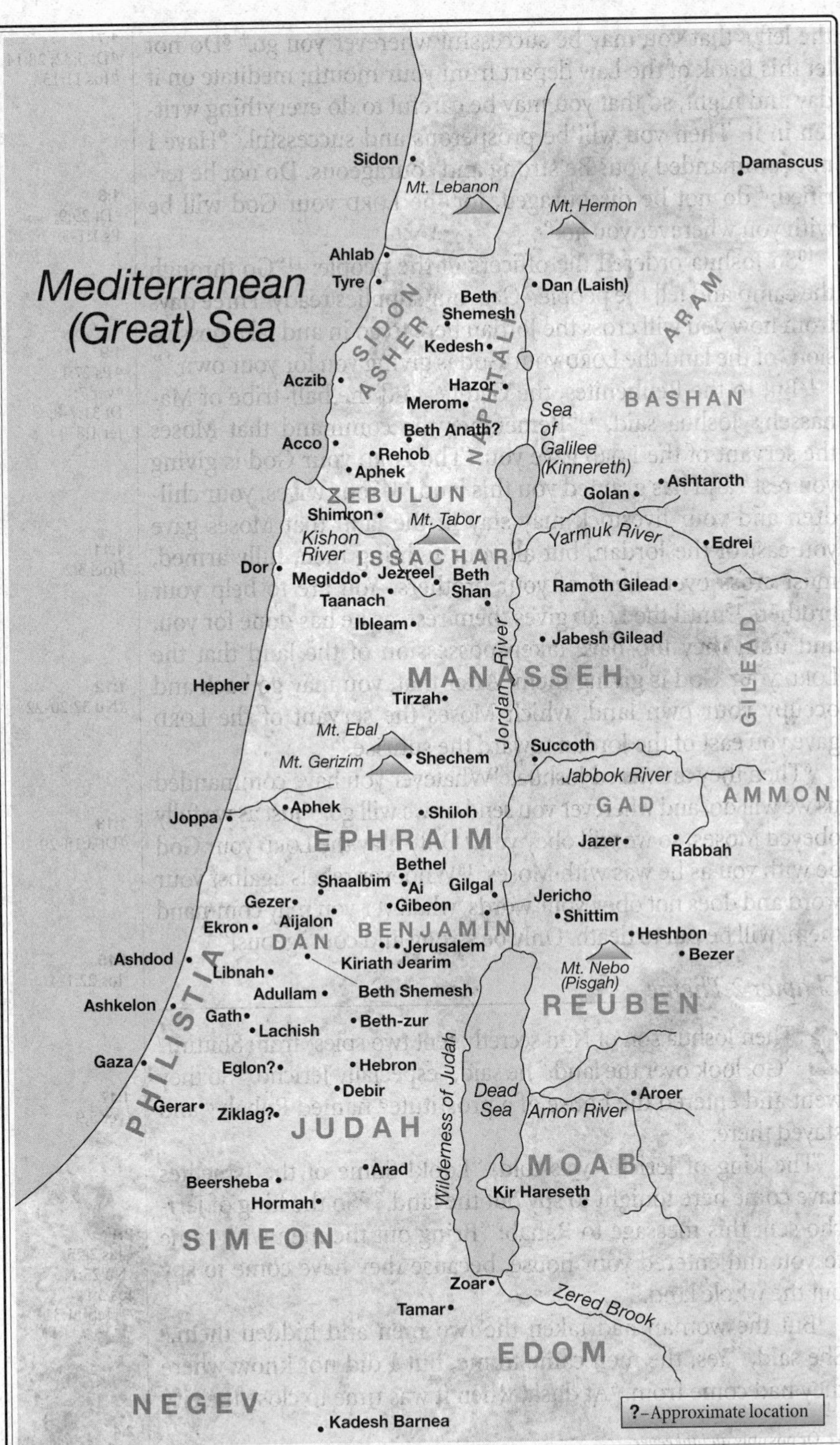

Sidon
Damascus
Mt. Lebanon
Mt. Hermon
Ahlab
Mediterranean (Great) Sea
Tyre
Dan (Laish)
Beth Shemesh
SIDON
ASHER
ARAM
Kedesh
NAPHTALI
Aczib
Hazor
BASHAN
Merom
Sea of Galilee (Kinnereth)
Beth Anath?
Acco
Rehob
Aphek
Ashtaroth
ZEBULUN
Golan
Shimron
Mt. Tabor
Kishon River
Yarmuk River
Edrei
ISSACHAR
Dor
Megiddo
Jezreel
Beth Shan
Ramoth Gilead
Taanach
Ibleam
Jabesh Gilead
Jordan River
MANASSEH
GILEAD
Hepher
Tirzah
Mt. Ebal
Succoth
Mt. Gerizim
Shechem
Jabbok River
AMMON
GAD
Aphek
Joppa
Shiloh
EPHRAIM
Jazer
Rabbah
Bethel
Shaalbim
Ai
Gilgal
Jericho
Gezer
Gibeon
Shittim
Aijalon
Ekron
BENJAMIN
Heshbon
DAN
Jerusalem
Bezer
Ashdod
Kiriath Jearim
Mt. Nebo (Pisgah)
Libnah
Adullam
Beth Shemesh
Ashkelon
REUBEN
Gath
Beth-zur
Lachish
Gaza
Hebron
Eglon?
Debir
Dead Sea
Aroer
PHILISTIA
Arnon River
Gerar
Ziklag?
JUDAH
Wilderness of Judah
MOAB
Arad
Kir Hareseth
Beersheba
Hormah
SIMEON
Zoar
Zered Brook
Tamar
EDOM
NEGEV
?–Approximate location
Kadesh Barnea

the left,[a] that you may be successful wherever you go.[b] 8Do not let this Book of the Law depart from your mouth; meditate on it day and night, so that you may be careful to do everything written in it. Then you will be prosperous and successful.[c] 9Have I not commanded you? Be strong and courageous. Do not be terrified;[d] do not be discouraged, for the LORD your God will be with you wherever you go."[e]

10So Joshua ordered the officers of the people: 11"Go through the camp and tell the people, 'Get your supplies ready. Three days from now you will cross the Jordan here to go in and take possession[f] of the land the LORD your God is giving you for your own.'"

12But to the Reubenites, the Gadites and the half-tribe of Manasseh,[g] Joshua said, 13"Remember the command that Moses the servant of the LORD gave you: 'The LORD your God is giving you rest[h] and has granted you this land.' 14Your wives, your children and your livestock may stay in the land that Moses gave you east of the Jordan, but all your fighting men, fully armed, must cross over ahead of your brothers. You are to help your brothers 15until the LORD gives them rest, as he has done for you, and until they too have taken possession of the land that the LORD your God is giving them. After that, you may go back and occupy your own land, which Moses the servant of the LORD gave you east of the Jordan toward the sunrise."[i]

16Then they answered Joshua, "Whatever you have commanded us we will do, and wherever you send us we will go. 17Just as we fully obeyed Moses, so we will obey you.[j] Only may the LORD your God be with you as he was with Moses. 18Whoever rebels against your word and does not obey your words, whatever you may command them, will be put to death. Only be strong and courageous!"

Chapter 2 Theme ____________________________________

2 Then Joshua son of Nun secretly sent two spies[k] from Shittim.[l] "Go, look over the land," he said, "especially Jericho." So they went and entered the house of a prostitute[a] named Rahab[m] and stayed there.

2The king of Jericho was told, "Look! Some of the Israelites have come here tonight to spy out the land." 3So the king of Jericho sent this message to Rahab: "Bring out the men who came to you and entered your house, because they have come to spy out the whole land."

4But the woman had taken the two men and hidden them.[n] She said, "Yes, the men came to me, but I did not know where they had come from. 5At dusk, when it was time to close the city

a *1* Or possibly *an innkeeper*

1:7 [a]Dt 5:32; 28:14 [b]Jos 11:15
1:8 [c]Dt 29:9; Ps 1:1-3
1:9 [d]Ps 27:1 [e]ver 7; Dt 31:7-8; Jer 1:8
1:11 [f]Joel 3:2
1:12 [g]Nu 32:20-22
1:13 [h]Dt 3:18-20
1:15 [i]Jos 22:1-4
1:17 [j]ver 5,9
2:1 [k]Jas 2:25 [l]Nu 25:1; Jos 3:1 [m]Heb 11:31
2:4 [n]2Sa 17:19-20

gate, the men left. I don't know which way they went. Go after
them quickly. You may catch up with them." 6(But she had taken
them up to the roof and hidden them under the stalks of flax[a]
she had laid out on the roof.)[b] 7So the men set out in pursuit of
the spies on the road that leads to the fords of the Jordan, and as
soon as the pursuers had gone out, the gate was shut.

8Before the spies lay down for the night, she went up on the
roof 9and said to them, "I know that the LORD has given this land
to you and that a great fear[c] of you has fallen on us, so that all
who live in this country are melting in fear because of you. 10We
have heard how the LORD dried up[d] the water of the Red Sea[a] for
you when you came out of Egypt,[e] and what you did to Sihon
and Og,[f] the two kings of the Amorites east of the Jordan, whom
you completely destroyed.[b] 11When we heard of it, our hearts
melted and everyone's courage failed because of you,[g] for the
LORD your God is God in heaven above and on the earth[h] below.
12Now then, please swear to me by the LORD that you will show
kindness to my family, because I have shown kindness to you.
Give me a sure sign[i] 13that you will spare the lives of my father
and mother, my brothers and sisters, and all who belong to them,
and that you will save us from death."

14"Our lives for your lives!" the men assured her. "If you don't
tell what we are doing, we will treat you kindly and faithfully[j]
when the LORD gives us the land."

15So she let them down by a rope through the window,[k] for the
house she lived in was part of the city wall. 16Now she had said to
them, "Go to the hills so the pursuers will not find you. Hide
yourselves there three days[l] until they return, and then go on
your way."[m]

17The men said to her, "This oath[n] you made us swear will not
be binding on us 18unless, when we enter the land, you have tied
this scarlet cord in the window through which you let us down,
and unless you have brought your father and mother, your
brothers and all your family[o] into your house. 19If anyone goes
outside your house into the street, his blood will be on his own
head;[p] we will not be responsible. As for anyone who is in the
house with you, his blood will be on our head[q] if a hand is laid
on him. 20But if you tell what we are doing, we will be released
from the oath you made us swear."

21"Agreed," she replied. "Let it be as you say." So she sent
them away and they departed. And she tied the scarlet cord in
the window.

a *10* Hebrew *Yam Suph*; that is, Sea of Reeds b *10* The Hebrew term refers to the irrevocable giving over of things or persons to the LORD, often by totally destroying them.

2:6 [a]Jas 2:25 [b]Ex 1:17,19; 2Sa 17:19
2:9 [c]Ge 35:5; Ex 23:27; Dt 2:25
2:10 [d]Ex 14:21 [e]Nu 23:22 [f]Nu 21:21,24, 34-35
2:11 [g]Ex 15:14; Jos 5:1; 7:5; Ps 22:14; Isa 13:7 [h]Dt 4:39
2:12 [i]ver 18
2:14 [j]Jdg 1:24; Mt 5:7
2:15 [k]Ac 9:25
2:16 [l]Jas 2:25 [m]Heb 11:31
2:17 [n]Ge 24:8
2:18 [o]ver 12; Jos 6:23
2:19 [p]Eze 33:4 [q]Mt 27:25

22When they left, they went into the hills and stayed there
three days, until the pursuers had searched all along the road
and returned without finding them. 23Then the two men started
back. They went down out of the hills, forded the river and came
to Joshua son of Nun and told him everything that had happened to them. 24They said to Joshua, "The LORD has surely giv-
en the whole land into our hands;[a] all the people are melting in
fear because of us."

Chapter 3 Theme ______________________________________

3 Early in the morning Joshua and all the Israelites set out
from Shittim[b] and went to the Jordan, where they camped
before crossing over. 2After three days the officers went throughout the camp,[c] 3giving orders to the people: "When you see the
ark of the covenant[d] of the LORD your God, and the priests,[e] who
are Levites, carrying it, you are to move out from your positions
and follow it. 4Then you will know which way to go, since you
have never been this way before. But keep a distance of about a
thousand yards[a] between you and the ark; do not go near it."

5Joshua told the people, "Consecrate yourselves,[f] for tomorrow the LORD will do amazing things among you."

6Joshua said to the priests, "Take up the ark of the covenant
and pass on ahead of the people." So they took it up and went
ahead of them.

7And the LORD said to Joshua, "Today I will begin to exalt you[g]
in the eyes of all Israel, so they may know that I am with you as I
was with Moses.[h] 8Tell the priests[i] who carry the ark of the covenant: 'When you reach the edge of the Jordan's waters, go and
stand in the river.'"

9Joshua said to the Israelites, "Come here and listen to the words
of the LORD your God. 10This is how you will know that the living
God[j] is among you and that he will certainly drive out before you
the Canaanites, Hittites, Hivites, Perizzites, Girgashites, Amorites
and Jebusites.[k] 11See, the ark of the covenant of the Lord of all the
earth[l] will go into the Jordan ahead of you. 12Now then, choose
twelve men[m] from the tribes of Israel, one from each tribe.
13And as soon as the priests who carry the ark of the LORD—the
Lord of all the earth[n]—set foot in the Jordan, its waters flowing
downstream[o] will be cut off and stand up in a heap.[p]"

14So when the people broke camp to cross the Jordan, the
priests carrying the ark of the covenant[q] went ahead[r] of them.
15Now the Jordan is at flood stage[s] all during harvest. Yet as soon
as the priests who carried the ark reached the Jordan and their
feet touched the water's edge, 16the water from upstream stopped
flowing.[t] It piled up in a heap a great distance away, at a town

a 4 Hebrew *about two thousand cubits* (about 900 meters)

2:24 [a]ver 9; Jos 6:2
3:1 [b]Jos 2:1
3:2 [c]Jos 1:11
3:3 [d]Nu 10:33 [e]Dt 31:9
3:5 [f]Ex 19:10,14; Lev 20:7; Jos 7:13; 1Sa 16:5; Joel 2:16
3:7 [g]Jos 4:14; 1Ch 29:25 [h]Jos 1:5
3:8 [i]ver 3
3:10 [j]Dt 5:26; 1Sa 17:26,36; 2Ki 19:4,16; Hos 1:10; Mt 16:16; 1Th 1:9 [k]Ex 33:2; Dt 7:1
3:11 [l]ver 13; Job 41:11; Zec 6:5
3:12 [m]Jos 4:2,4
3:13 [n]ver 11 [o]ver 16 [p]Ex 15:8; Ps 78:13
3:14 [q]Ps 132:8 [r]Ac 7:44-45
3:15 [s]Jos 4:18; 1Ch 12:15
3:16 [t]Ps 66:6; 74:15

called Adam in the vicinity of Zarethan,[a] while the water flowing down[b] to the Sea of the Arabah[c] (the Salt Sea[a][d]) was completely cut off. So the people crossed over opposite Jericho. 17The priests who carried the ark of the covenant of the LORD stood firm on dry ground in the middle of the Jordan, while all Israel passed by until the whole nation had completed the crossing on dry ground.[e]

Chapter 4 Theme ______________________________

4 When the whole nation had finished crossing the Jordan,[f] the LORD said to Joshua, 2"Choose twelve men[g] from among the people, one from each tribe, 3and tell them to take up twelve stones[h] from the middle of the Jordan from right where the priests stood and to carry them over with you and put them down at the place where you stay tonight.[i]"

4So Joshua called together the twelve men he had appointed from the Israelites, one from each tribe, 5and said to them, "Go over before the ark of the LORD your God into the middle of the Jordan. Each of you is to take up a stone on his shoulder, according to the number of the tribes of the Israelites, 6to serve as a sign among you. In the future, when your children ask you, 'What do these stones mean?'[j] 7tell them that the flow of the Jordan was cut off[k] before the ark of the covenant of the LORD. When it crossed the Jordan, the waters of the Jordan were cut off. These stones are to be a memorial[l] to the people of Israel forever."

8So the Israelites did as Joshua commanded them. They took twelve stones from the middle of the Jordan, according to the number of the tribes of the Israelites, as the LORD had told Joshua;[m] and they carried them over with them to their camp, where they put them down. 9Joshua set up the twelve stones[n] that had been[b] in the middle of the Jordan at the spot where the priests who carried the ark of the covenant had stood. And they are there to this day.

10Now the priests who carried the ark remained standing in the middle of the Jordan until everything the LORD had commanded Joshua was done by the people, just as Moses had directed Joshua. The people hurried over, 11and as soon as all of them had crossed, the ark of the LORD and the priests came to the other side while the people watched. 12The men of Reuben, Gad and the half-tribe of Manasseh crossed over, armed, in front of the Israelites,[o] as Moses had directed them. 13About forty thousand armed for battle crossed over before the LORD to the plains of Jericho for war.

3:16 [a] 1Ki 4:12; 7:46 [b] ver 13 [c] Dt 1:1 [d] Ge 14:3
3:17 [e] Ex 14:22,29
4:1 [f] Dt 27:2
4:2 [g] Jos 3:12
4:3 [h] ver 20 [i] ver 19
4:6 [j] ver 21; Ex 12:26; 13:14
4:7 [k] Jos 3:13 [l] Ex 12:14
4:8 [m] ver 20
4:9 [n] Ge 28:18; Jos 24:26; 1Sa 7:12
4:12 [o] Nu 32:27

a *16* That is, the Dead Sea   b *9* Or *Joshua also set up twelve stones*

14That day the LORD exalted[a] Joshua in the sight of all Israel; and
they revered him all the days of his life, just as they had revered
Moses.
15Then the LORD said to Joshua, 16"Command the priests carrying the ark of the Testimony[b] to come up out of the Jordan."
17So Joshua commanded the priests, "Come up out of the Jordan."
18And the priests came up out of the river carrying the ark of
the covenant of the LORD. No sooner had they set their feet on
the dry ground than the waters of the Jordan returned to their
place and ran at flood stage[c] as before.
19On the tenth day of the first month the people went up from
the Jordan and camped at Gilgal[d] on the eastern border of Jericho. 20And Joshua set up at Gilgal the twelve stones[e] they had
taken out of the Jordan. 21He said to the Israelites, "In the future
when your descendants ask their fathers, 'What do these stones
mean?'[f] 22tell them, 'Israel crossed the Jordan on dry ground.'[g]
23For the LORD your God dried up the Jordan before you until
you had crossed over. The LORD your God did to the Jordan just
what he had done to the Red Sea[a] when he dried it up before us
until we had crossed over.[h] 24He did this so that all the peoples of
the earth might know[i] that the hand of the LORD is powerful[j]
and so that you might always fear the LORD your God.[k]"

Chapter 5 Theme

5 Now when all the Amorite kings west of the Jordan and all
the Canaanite kings along the coast[l] heard how the LORD
had dried up the Jordan before the Israelites until we had
crossed over, their hearts melted[m] and they no longer had the
courage to face the Israelites.
2At that time the LORD said to Joshua, "Make flint knives[n] and
circumcise the Israelites again." 3So Joshua made flint knives
and circumcised the Israelites at Gibeath Haaraloth.[b]
4Now this is why he did so: All those who came out of Egypt—
all the men of military age—died in the desert on the way after
leaving Egypt.[o] 5All the people that came out had been circumcised, but all the people born in the desert during the journey
from Egypt had not. 6The Israelites had moved about in the
desert forty years[p] until all the men who were of military age
when they left Egypt had died, since they had not obeyed the
LORD. For the LORD had sworn to them that they would not see
the land that he had solemnly promised their fathers to give us,[q]
a land flowing with milk and honey.[r] 7So he raised up their sons

[a]23 Hebrew *Yam Suph*; that is, Sea of Reeds [b]3 *Gibeath Haaraloth* means *hill of foreskins.*

4:14 [a]Jos 3:7
4:16 [b]Ex 25:22
4:18 [c]Jos 3:15
4:19 [d]Jos 5:9
4:20 [e]ver 3,8
4:21 [f]ver 6
4:22 [g]Jos 3:17
4:23 [h]Ex 14:21
4:24 [i]1Ki 8:42-43; 2Ki 19:19; Ps 106:8; Jer 10:7 [j]Ex 15:16; 1Ch 29:12; Ps 89:13 [k]Ex 14:31
5:1 [l]Nu 13:29 [m]Jos 2:9-11
5:2 [n]Ex 4:25
5:4 [o]Dt 2:14
5:6 [p]Dt 2:7 [q]Nu 14:23, 29-35; Dt 2:14 [r]Ex 3:8

5:8 in their place, and these were the ones Joshua circumcised. They
[a]Ge 34:25 were still uncircumcised because they had not been circumcised
on the way. 8And after the whole nation had been circumcised,
5:10 they remained where they were in camp until they were healed.[a]
[b]Ex 12:6 9Then the LORD said to Joshua, "Today I have rolled away the
reproach of Egypt from you." So the place has been called Gilgal[a]
to this day.

5:11 10On the evening of the fourteenth day of the month,[b] while
[c]Nu 15:19 [d]Lev 23:14 camped at Gilgal on the plains of Jericho, the Israelites celebrated the Passover. 11The day after the Passover, that very day, they
ate some of the produce of the land:[c] unleavened bread and
5:12 roasted grain.[d] 12The manna stopped the day after[b] they ate this
[e]Ex 16:35 food from the land; there was no longer any manna for the
Israelites, but that year they ate of the produce of Canaan.[e]

13Now when Joshua was near Jericho, he looked up and saw a
5:13 [f]Ge 18:2; 32:24 man[f] standing in front of him with a drawn sword[g] in his hand.
[g]Nu 22:23 Joshua went up to him and asked, "Are you for us or for our enemies?"

14"Neither," he replied, "but as commander of the army of the
5:14 [h]Ge 17:3 LORD I have now come." Then Joshua fell facedown[h] to the
ground in reverence, and asked him, "What message does my
Lord[c] have for his servant?"

5:15 15The commander of the LORD's army replied, "Take off your
[i]Ex 3:5; Ac 7:33 sandals, for the place where you are standing is holy."[i] And Joshua
did so.

6:1 [j]Jos 24:11

Chapter 6 Theme __________________________

6 Now Jericho[j] was tightly shut up because of the Israelites.
No one went out and no one came in.

6:2 [k]Dt 7:24; 2Then the LORD said to Joshua, "See, I have delivered[k] Jericho
Jos 2:9,24; 8:1 into your hands, along with its king and its fighting men.
3March around the city once with all the armed men. Do this for
six days. 4Have seven priests carry trumpets of rams' horns in
6:4 front of the ark. On the seventh day, march around the city sev-
[l]Lev 25:9; Nu 10:8 en times, with the priests blowing the trumpets.[l] 5When you
hear them sound a long blast[m] on the trumpets, have all the people give a loud shout;[n] then the wall of the city will collapse and
6:5 the people will go up, every man straight in."
[m]Ex 19:13 [n]ver 20; 6So Joshua son of Nun called the priests and said to them,
1Sa 4:5; Ps 42:4; "Take up the ark of the covenant of the LORD and have seven
Isa 42:13 priests carry trumpets in front of it." 7And he ordered the people, "Advance[o]! March around the city, with the armed guard
going ahead of the ark of the LORD."

6:7 [o]Ex 14:15

a9 *Gilgal* sounds like the Hebrew for *roll.* b12 Or *the day* c14 Or *lord*

8When Joshua had spoken to the people, the seven priests carrying the seven trumpets before the LORD went forward, blowing
their trumpets, and the ark of the LORD's covenant followed
them. 9The armed guard marched ahead of the priests who blew
the trumpets, and the rear guard[a] followed the ark. All this time
the trumpets were sounding. 10But Joshua had commanded the
people, "Do not give a war cry, do not raise your voices, do not
say a word until the day I tell you to shout. Then shout![b]" 11So he
had the ark of the LORD carried around the city, circling it once.
Then the people returned to camp and spent the night there.
12Joshua got up early the next morning and the priests took up
the ark of the LORD. 13The seven priests carrying the seven trumpets went forward, marching before the ark of the LORD and
blowing the trumpets. The armed men went ahead of them and
the rear guard followed the ark of the LORD, while the trumpets
kept sounding. 14So on the second day they marched around the
city once and returned to the camp. They did this for six days.
15On the seventh day, they got up at daybreak and marched
around the city seven times in the same manner, except that on
that day they circled the city seven times.[c] 16The seventh time
around, when the priests sounded the trumpet blast, Joshua
commanded the people, "Shout! For the LORD has given you the
city! 17The city and all that is in it are to be devoted[a][d] to the
LORD. Only Rahab the prostitute[b] and all who are with her in her
house shall be spared, because she hid[e] the spies we sent. 18But
keep away from the devoted things,[f] so that you will not bring
about your own destruction by taking any of them. Otherwise
you will make the camp of Israel liable to destruction[g] and bring
trouble[h] on it. 19All the silver and gold and the articles of bronze
and iron[i] are sacred to the LORD and must go into his treasury."
20When the trumpets sounded,[j] the people shouted, and at the
sound of the trumpet, when the people gave a loud shout,[k] the
wall collapsed; so every man charged straight in, and they took
the city.[l] 21They devoted the city to the LORD and destroyed[m]
with the sword every living thing in it—men and women, young
and old, cattle, sheep and donkeys.
22Joshua said to the two men who had spied out the land, "Go
into the prostitute's house and bring her out and all who belong
to her, in accordance with your oath to her.[n]" 23So the young
men who had done the spying went in and brought out Rahab,
her father and mother and brothers and all who belonged to
her.[o] They brought out her entire family and put them in a place
outside the camp of Israel.

a *17* The Hebrew term refers to the irrevocable giving over of things or persons to the LORD, often by totally destroying them; also in verses 18 and 21. b *17* Or possibly *innkeeper*; also in verses 22 and 25

6:9 [a] ver 13; Isa 52:12
6:10 [b] ver 20
6:15 [c] 1Ki 18:44
6:17 [d] Lev 27:28; Dt 20:17 [e] Jos 2:4
6:18 [f] Jos 7:1 [g] Jos 7:12 [h] Jos 7:25,26
6:19 [i] ver 24; Nu 31:22
6:20 [j] Jdg 6:34; Jer 4:21; Am 2:2 [k] ver 5 [l] Heb 11:30
6:21 [m] Dt 20:16
6:22 [n] Jos 2:14; Heb 11:31
6:23 [o] Jos 2:13

6:24 24Then they burned the whole city and everything in it, but
[a]ver 19 they put the silver and gold and the articles of bronze and iron[a]
into the treasury of the LORD's house. 25But Joshua spared Rahab
the prostitute,[b] with her family and all who belonged to her,
6:25 [b]Heb 11:31 because she hid the men Joshua had sent as spies to Jericho[c]—
[c]Jos 2:6 and she lives among the Israelites to this day.
26At that time Joshua pronounced this solemn oath: "Cursed
before the LORD is the man who undertakes to rebuild this city,
6:26 Jericho:
[d]1Ki 16:34

"At the cost of his firstborn son
will he lay its foundations;
6:27 at the cost of his youngest
[e]Ge 39:2; will he set up its gates."[d]

Jos 1:5; [f]Jos 9:1 27So the LORD was with Joshua,[e] and his fame spread[f] throughout
the land.

7:1 *Chapter 7 Theme* ____________________

[g]Jos 6:18; [h]Jos 22:20 **7** But the Israelites acted unfaithfully in regard to the devoted
things[a];[g] Achan son of Carmi, the son of Zimri,[b] the son of
Zerah,[h] of the tribe of Judah, took some of them. So the LORD's
7:2 anger burned against Israel.
[i]Jos 18:12; 2Now Joshua sent men from Jericho to Ai, which is near Beth
1Sa 13:5; 14:23 Aven[i] to the east of Bethel, and told them, "Go up and spy out
the region." So the men went up and spied out Ai.
3When they returned to Joshua, they said, "Not all the people
7:4 [j]Lev 26:17; will have to go up against Ai. Send two or three thousand men to
Dt 28:25 take it and do not weary all the people, for only a few men are
there." 4So about three thousand men went up; but they were
routed by the men of Ai,[j] 5who killed about thirty-six of them.
7:5 They chased the Israelites from the city gate as far as the stone
[k]Lev 26:36; Jos 2:9,11; quarries[c] and struck them down on the slopes. At this the hearts
Eze 21:7; Na 2:10 of the people melted[k] and became like water.
6Then Joshua tore his clothes[l] and fell facedown to the ground
before the ark of the LORD, remaining there till evening. The
elders of Israel did the same, and sprinkled dust[m] on their
7:6 [l]Ge 37:29 heads. 7And Joshua said, "Ah, Sovereign LORD, why did you ever
[m]1Sa 4:12; 2Sa 13:19; bring this people across the Jordan to deliver us into the hands
Ne 9:1; of the Amorites to destroy us?[n] If only we had been content to
Job 2:12; La 2:10; stay on the other side of the Jordan! 8O Lord, what can I say, now
Rev 18:19 that Israel has been routed by its enemies? 9The Canaanites and
the other people of the country will hear about this and they will

a *1* The Hebrew term refers to the irrevocable giving over of things or persons to the LORD, often by totally destroying them; also in verses 11, 12, 13 and 15. b *1* See Septuagint and 1 Chron. 2:6; Hebrew *Zabdi*; also in verses 17 and 18. c *5* Or *as far as Shebarim*

7:7 [n]Ex 5:22

surround us and wipe out our name from the earth.[a] What then
will you do for your own great name?"
10The LORD said to Joshua, "Stand up! What are you doing
down on your face? 11Israel has sinned; they have violated my
covenant,[b] which I commanded them to keep. They have taken
some of the devoted things; they have stolen, they have lied,[c]
they have put them with their own possessions. 12That is why
the Israelites cannot stand against their enemies;[d] they turn
their backs and run because they have been made liable to
destruction.[e] I will not be with you anymore unless you destroy
whatever among you is devoted to destruction.
13"Go, consecrate the people. Tell them, 'Consecrate yourselves[f]
in preparation for tomorrow; for this is what the LORD, the God
of Israel, says: That which is devoted is among you, O Israel. You
cannot stand against your enemies until you remove it.
14" 'In the morning, present yourselves tribe by tribe. The tribe
that the LORD takes[g] shall come forward clan by clan; the clan
that the LORD takes shall come forward family by family; and the
family that the LORD takes shall come forward man by man. 15He
who is caught with the devoted things shall be destroyed by fire,
along with all that belongs to him.[h] He has violated the covenant[i]
of the LORD and has done a disgraceful thing in Israel!' "[j]
16Early the next morning Joshua had Israel come forward by
tribes, and Judah was taken. 17The clans of Judah came forward,
and he took the Zerahites.[k] He had the clan of the Zerahites
come forward by families, and Zimri was taken. 18Joshua had his
family come forward man by man, and Achan son of Carmi, the
son of Zimri, the son of Zerah, of the tribe of Judah, was taken.
19Then Joshua said to Achan, "My son, give glory[l] to the
LORD,[a] the God of Israel, and give him the praise.[b] Tell[m] me what
you have done; do not hide it from me."
20Achan replied, "It is true! I have sinned against the LORD, the
God of Israel. This is what I have done: 21When I saw in the
plunder a beautiful robe from Babylonia,[c] two hundred shekels[d]
of silver and a wedge of gold weighing fifty shekels,[e] I coveted[n]
them and took them. They are hidden in the ground inside my
tent, with the silver underneath."
22So Joshua sent messengers, and they ran to the tent, and
there it was, hidden in his tent, with the silver underneath.
23They took the things from the tent, brought them to Joshua
and all the Israelites and spread them out before the LORD.

a*19* A solemn charge to tell the truth b*19* Or *and confess to him* c*21* Hebrew *Shinar*
d*21* That is, about 5 pounds (about 2.3 kilograms) e*21* That is, about 1 1/4 pounds (about 0.6 kilogram)

7:9 *a*Ex 32:12; Dt 9:28
7:11 *b*Jos 6:17-19 *c*Ac 5:1-2
7:12 *d*Nu 14:45; Jdg 2:14 *e*Jos 6:18
7:13 *f*Jos 3:5; 6:18
7:14 *g*Pr 16:33
7:15 *h*1Sa 14:39 *i*ver 11 *j*Ge 34:7
7:17 *k*Nu 26:20
7:19 *l*1Sa 6:5; Jer 13:16; Jn 9:24* *m*1Sa 14:43
7:21 *n*Dt 7:25; Eph 5:5; 1Ti 6:10

7:24 [a]ver 26; Jos 15:7

24 Then Joshua, together with all Israel, took Achan son of Zerah, the silver, the robe, the gold wedge, his sons and daughters,
his cattle, donkeys and sheep, his tent and all that he had, to the
Valley of Achor.[a] 25 Joshua said, "Why have you brought this trouble[b] on us? The LORD will bring trouble on you today."
Then all Israel stoned him,[c] and after they had stoned the rest,
they burned them. 26 Over Achan they heaped up a large pile of
rocks, which remains to this day. Then the LORD turned from his
fierce anger.[d] Therefore that place has been called the Valley of
Achor[a][e] ever since.

7:25 [b]Jos 6:18 [c]Dt 17:5

Chapter 8 Theme ______________________

8 Then the LORD said to Joshua, "Do not be afraid;[f] do not be
discouraged.[g] Take the whole army[h] with you, and go up
and attack Ai. For I have delivered[i] into your hands the king of
Ai, his people, his city and his land. 2 You shall do to Ai and its
king as you did to Jericho and its king, except that you may carry off their plunder and livestock for yourselves.[j] Set an ambush
behind the city."

7:26 [d]Nu 25:4; Dt 13:17 [e]ver 24; Isa 65:10; Hos 2:15

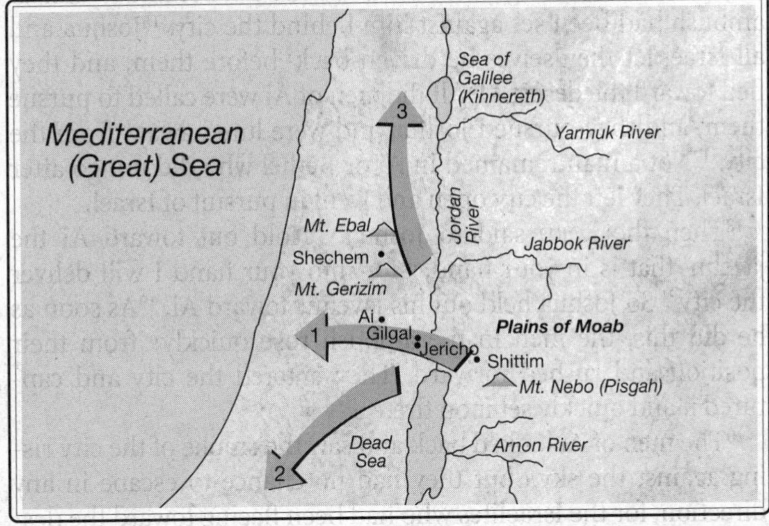

Joshua's 3-Pronged Invasion

8:1 [f]Dt 31:6 [g]Dt 1:21; 7:18; Jos 1:9 [h]Jos 10:7 [i]Jos 6:2

3 So Joshua and the whole army moved out to attack Ai. He
chose thirty thousand of his best fighting men and sent them
out at night 4 with these orders: "Listen carefully. You are to set
an ambush behind the city. Don't go very far from it. All of you
be on the alert. 5 I and all those with me will advance on the city,
and when the men come out against us, as they did before, we
will flee from them. 6 They will pursue us until we have lured
them away from the city, for they will say, 'They are running away

8:2 [j]ver 27; Dt 20:14

[a]26 *Achor* means *trouble.*

from us as they did before.' So when we flee from them, 7you are to rise up from ambush and take the city. The LORD your God will give it into your hand.[a] 8When you have taken the city, set it on fire.[b] Do what the LORD has commanded.[c] See to it; you have my orders."

9Then Joshua sent them off, and they went to the place of ambush[d] and lay in wait between Bethel and Ai, to the west of Ai—but Joshua spent that night with the people.

10Early the next morning[e] Joshua mustered his men, and he and the leaders of Israel[f] marched before them to Ai. 11The entire force that was with him marched up and approached the city and arrived in front of it. They set up camp north of Ai, with the valley between them and the city. 12Joshua had taken about five thousand men and set them in ambush between Bethel and Ai, to the west of the city. 13They had the soldiers take up their positions—all those in the camp to the north of the city and the ambush to the west of it. That night Joshua went into the valley.

14When the king of Ai saw this, he and all the men of the city hurried out early in the morning to meet Israel in battle at a certain place overlooking the Arabah.[g] But he did not know[h] that an ambush had been set against him behind the city. 15Joshua and all Israel let themselves be driven back[i] before them, and they fled toward the desert.[j] 16All the men of Ai were called to pursue them, and they pursued Joshua and were lured away[k] from the city. 17Not a man remained in Ai or Bethel who did not go after Israel. They left the city open and went in pursuit of Israel.

18Then the LORD said to Joshua, "Hold out toward Ai the javelin[l] that is in your hand,[m] for into your hand I will deliver the city." So Joshua held out his javelin[n] toward Ai. 19As soon as he did this, the men in the ambush rose quickly[o] from their position and rushed forward. They entered the city and captured it and quickly set it on fire.[p]

20The men of Ai looked back and saw the smoke of the city rising against the sky,[q] but they had no chance to escape in any direction, for the Israelites who had been fleeing toward the desert had turned back against their pursuers. 21For when Joshua and all Israel saw that the ambush had taken the city and that smoke was going up from the city, they turned around and attacked the men of Ai. 22The men of the ambush also came out of the city against them, so that they were caught in the middle, with Israelites on both sides. Israel cut them down, leaving them neither survivors nor fugitives.[r] 23But they took the king of Ai alive[s] and brought him to Joshua.

24When Israel had finished killing all the men of Ai in the fields and in the desert where they had chased them, and when

8:7 [a] Jdg 7:7; 1Sa 23:4
8:8 [b] Jdg 20:29-38 [c] ver 19
8:9 [d] 2Ch 13:13
8:10 [e] Ge 22:3 [f] Jos 7:6
8:14 [g] Dt 1:1 [h] Jdg 20:34
8:15 [i] Jdg 20:36 [j] Jos 15:61; 16:1; 18:12
8:16 [k] Jdg 20:31
8:18 [l] Job 41:26; Ps 35:3 [m] Ex 4:2; 14:16; 17:9-12 [n] ver 26
8:19 [o] Jdg 20:33 [p] ver 8
8:20 [q] Jdg 20:40
8:22 [r] Dt 7:2; Jos 10:1
8:23 [s] 1Sa 15:8

every one of them had been put to the sword, all the Israelites
returned to Ai and killed those who were in it. 25 Twelve thousand men and women fell that day—all the people of Ai.[a] 26 For
Joshua did not draw back the hand that held out his javelin
until he had destroyed[a][b] all who lived in Ai.[c] 27 But Israel did
carry off for themselves the livestock and plunder of this city, as
the LORD had instructed Joshua.[d]

28 So Joshua burned[e] Ai[f] and made it a permanent heap of
ruins,[g] a desolate place to this day.[h] 29 He hung the king of Ai on
a tree and left him there until evening. At sunset,[i] Joshua
ordered them to take his body from the tree and throw it down
at the entrance of the city gate. And they raised a large pile of
rocks[j] over it, which remains to this day.

30 Then Joshua built on Mount Ebal[k] an altar[l] to the LORD, the
God of Israel, 31 as Moses the servant of the LORD had commanded the Israelites. He built it according to what is written in
the Book of the Law of Moses—an altar of uncut stones, on
which no iron tool[m] had been used. On it they offered to the
LORD burnt offerings and sacrificed fellowship offerings.[b][n]
32 There, in the presence of the Israelites, Joshua copied on
stones the law of Moses, which he had written.[o] 33 All Israel,
aliens and citizens[p] alike, with their elders, officials and judges,
were standing on both sides of the ark of the covenant of the
LORD, facing those who carried it—the priests, who were Levites.[q] Half of the people stood in front of Mount Gerizim and
half of them in front of Mount Ebal,[r] as Moses the servant of the
LORD had formerly commanded when he gave instructions to
bless the people of Israel.

34 Afterward, Joshua read all the words of the law—the blessings and the curses—just as it is written in the Book of the
Law.[s] 35 There was not a word of all that Moses had commanded
that Joshua did not read to the whole assembly of Israel, including the women and children, and the aliens who lived among
them.[t]

Chapter 9 Theme ________________________

9 Now when all the kings west of the Jordan heard about
these things—those in the hill country, in the western
foothills, and along the entire coast of the Great Sea[c][u] as far as
Lebanon (the kings of the Hittites, Amorites, Canaanites, Perizzites, Hivites and Jebusites)[v]— 2 they came together to make
war against Joshua and Israel.

8:25 [a] Dt 20:16-18
8:26 [b] Nu 21:2 [c] Ex 17:12
8:27 [d] ver 2
8:28 [e] Nu 31:10 [f] Jos 7:2; Jer 49:3 [g] Dt 13:16; Jos 10:1 [h] Ge 35:20
8:29 [i] Dt 21:23; Jn 19:31 [j] 2Sa 18:17
8:30 [k] Dt 11:29 [l] Ex 20:24
8:31 [m] Ex 20:25 [n] Dt 27:6-7
8:32 [o] Dt 27:8
8:33 [p] Lev 16:29 [q] Dt 31:12 [r] Dt 11:29; 27:11-14
8:34 [s] Dt 28:61; 31:11; Jos 1:8
8:35 [t] Ex 12:38; Dt 31:12
9:1 [u] Nu 34:6 [v] Ex 3:17; Jos 3:10

[a] *26* The Hebrew term refers to the irrevocable giving over of things or persons to the LORD, often by totally destroying them. [b] *31* Traditionally *peace offerings* [c] *1* That is, the Mediterranean

3However, when the people of Gibeon[a] heard what Joshua had
done to Jericho and Ai, 4they resorted to a ruse: They went as a
delegation whose donkeys were loaded[a] with worn-out sacks and
old wineskins, cracked and mended. 5The men put worn and
patched sandals on their feet and wore old clothes. All the bread
of their food supply was dry and moldy. 6Then they went to Joshua in the camp at Gilgal[b] and said to him and the men of Israel,
"We have come from a distant country; make a treaty with us."
7The men of Israel said to the Hivites,[c] "But perhaps you live
near us. How then can we make a treaty[d] with you?"
8"We are your servants,[e]" they said to Joshua.
But Joshua asked, "Who are you and where do you come from?"
9They answered: "Your servants have come from a very distant
country[f] because of the fame of the LORD your God. For we have
heard reports[g] of him: all that he did in Egypt, 10and all that he
did to the two kings of the Amorites east of the Jordan—Sihon
king of Heshbon, and Og king of Bashan,[h] who reigned in
Ashtaroth.[i] 11And our elders and all those living in our country
said to us, 'Take provisions for your journey; go and meet them
and say to them, "We are your servants; make a treaty with
us."' 12This bread of ours was warm when we packed it at home
on the day we left to come to you. But now see how dry and
moldy it is. 13And these wineskins that we filled were new, but
see how cracked they are. And our clothes and sandals are worn
out by the very long journey."
14The men of Israel sampled their provisions but did not
inquire[j] of the LORD. 15Then Joshua made a treaty of peace[k] with
them to let them live, and the leaders of the assembly ratified it
by oath.
16Three days after they made the treaty with the Gibeonites,
the Israelites heard that they were neighbors, living near them.
17So the Israelites set out and on the third day came to their cities: Gibeon, Kephirah, Beeroth[l] and Kiriath Jearim.[m] 18But the
Israelites did not attack them, because the leaders of the assembly had sworn an oath[n] to them by the LORD, the God of Israel.
The whole assembly grumbled[o] against the leaders, 19but all
the leaders answered, "We have given them our oath by the
LORD, the God of Israel, and we cannot touch them now. 20This is
what we will do to them: We will let them live, so that wrath will
not fall on us for breaking the oath we swore to them." 21They
continued, "Let them live,[p] but let them be woodcutters and
water carriers[q] for the entire community." So the leaders'
promise to them was kept.

[a] 4 Most Hebrew manuscripts; some Hebrew manuscripts, Vulgate and Syriac (see also Septuagint) *They prepared provisions and loaded their donkeys*

9:3 [a] ver 17; Jos 10:2; 2Sa 2:12; 2Ch 1:3; Isa 28:21
9:6 [b] Jos 5:10
9:7 [c] ver 1; Jos 11:19 [d] Ex 23:32; Dt 7:2
9:8 [e] Dt 20:11; 2Ki 10:5
9:9 [f] Dt 20:15 [g] ver 24; Jos 2:9
9:10 [h] Nu 21:33 [i] Nu 21:24,35
9:14 [j] Nu 27:21
9:15 [k] Ex 23:32; Jos 11:19; 2Sa 21:2
9:17 [l] Jos 18:25 [m] 1Sa 7:1-2
9:18 [n] Ps 15:4 [o] Ex 15:24
9:21 [p] ver 15 [q] Dt 29:11

9:22 a ver 6 22 Then Joshua summoned the Gibeonites and said, "Why did
b ver 16 you deceive us by saying, 'We live a long way[a] from you,' while
actually you live near[b] us? 23 You are now under a curse:[c] You will
never cease to serve as woodcutters and water carriers for the
9:23 c Ge 9:25 house of my God."

24 They answered Joshua, "Your servants were clearly told[d] how
the LORD your God had commanded his servant Moses to give
9:24 you the whole land and to wipe out all its inhabitants from
d ver 9 before you. So we feared for our lives because of you, and that is
why we did this. 25 We are now in your hands.[e] Do to us whatever
9:25 seems good and right to you."

e Ge 16:6 26 So Joshua saved them from the Israelites, and they did not kill
them. 27 That day he made the Gibeonites woodcutters and water
9:27 carriers for the community and for the altar of the LORD at the
f Dt 12:5 place the LORD would choose.[f] And that is what they are to this day.

Chapter 10 Theme

10:1 **10** Now Adoni-Zedek king of Jerusalem[g] heard that Joshua
g Jdg 1:7
h Jos 8:1 had taken Ai[h] and totally destroyed[a][i] it, doing to Ai and
i Dt 20:16; its king as he had done to Jericho and its king, and that the peo-
Jos 8:22
j Jos 9:15 ple of Gibeon had made a treaty of peace[j] with Israel and were
living near them. 2 He and his people were very much alarmed at
this, because Gibeon was an important city, like one of the royal
10:3 cities; it was larger than Ai, and all its men were good fighters.
k Ge 13:18
l 2Ch 11:9; 3 So Adoni-Zedek king of Jerusalem appealed to Hoham king of
25:27;
Ne 11:30; Hebron,[k] Piram king of Jarmuth, Japhia king of Lachish[l] and
Isa 36:2; 37:8; Debir king of Eglon. 4 "Come up and help me attack Gibeon," he
Jer 34:7;
Mic 1:13 said, "because it has made peace[m] with Joshua and the Israelites."

5 Then the five kings of the Amorites[n]—the kings of Jerusalem, Hebron, Jarmuth, Lachish and Eglon—joined forces. They
10:4 moved up with all their troops and took up positions against
m Jos 9:15 Gibeon and attacked it.

6 The Gibeonites then sent word to Joshua in the camp at Gil-
10:5 gal: "Do not abandon your servants. Come up to us quickly and
n Nu 13:29 save us! Help us, because all the Amorite kings from the hill
country have joined forces against us."

10:7 7 So Joshua marched up from Gilgal with his entire army,[o]
o Jos 8:1 including all the best fighting men. 8 The LORD said to Joshua,
"Do not be afraid[p] of them; I have given them into your hand.
Not one of them will be able to withstand you."

10:8 9 After an all-night march from Gilgal, Joshua took them by
p Dt 3:2;
Jos 1:9 surprise. 10 The LORD threw them into confusion before Israel,[q]
who defeated them in a great victory at Gibeon. Israel pursued

10:10 a *1* The Hebrew term refers to the irrevocable giving over of things or persons to the LORD, often
q Dt 7:23 by totally destroying them; also in verses 28, 35, 37, 39 and 40.

them along the road going up to Beth Horon[a] and cut them
down all the way to Azekah[b] and Makkedah. 11As they fled before
Israel on the road down from Beth Horon to Azekah, the LORD
hurled large hailstones[c] down on them from the sky, and more
of them died from the hailstones than were killed by the swords
of the Israelites.
12On the day the LORD gave the Amorites[d] over to Israel,
Joshua said to the LORD in the presence of Israel:

> "O sun, stand still over Gibeon,
> O moon, over the Valley of Aijalon.[e]"
> 13So the sun stood still,[f]
> and the moon stopped,
> till the nation avenged itself on[a] its enemies,

as it is written in the Book of Jashar.[g]
The sun stopped[h] in the middle of the sky and delayed going
down about a full day. 14There has never been a day like it before
or since, a day when the LORD listened to a man. Surely the LORD
was fighting[i] for Israel!
15Then Joshua returned with all Israel to the camp at Gilgal.[j]
16Now the five kings had fled and hidden in the cave at
Makkedah. 17When Joshua was told that the five kings had been
found hiding in the cave at Makkedah, 18he said, "Roll large
rocks up to the mouth of the cave, and post some men there to
guard it. 19But don't stop! Pursue your enemies, attack them
from the rear and don't let them reach their cities, for the LORD
your God has given them into your hand."
20So Joshua and the Israelites destroyed them completely[k]—
almost to a man—but the few who were left reached their fortified cities. 21The whole army then returned safely to Joshua in
the camp at Makkedah, and no one uttered a word against the
Israelites.
22Joshua said, "Open the mouth of the cave and bring those
five kings out to me." 23So they brought the five kings out of the
cave—the kings of Jerusalem, Hebron, Jarmuth, Lachish and
Eglon. 24When they had brought these kings to Joshua, he summoned all the men of Israel and said to the army commanders
who had come with him, "Come here and put your feet[l] on the
necks of these kings." So they came forward and placed their
feet[m] on their necks.
25Joshua said to them, "Do not be afraid; do not be discouraged. Be strong and courageous.[n] This is what the LORD will do
to all the enemies you are going to fight." 26Then Joshua struck

INSIGHT

The ***Book of Jashar*** was a collection of poetical writings of important events in Israel's history which was gathered in the time of David or Solomon. It is often compared to "The Book of Wars of the Lord." Bible authors are believed to have quoted from this book.

10:10 [a]Jos 16:3,5 [b]Jos 15:35
10:11 [c]Ps 18:12; Isa 28:2,17
10:12 [d]Am 2:9 [e]Jdg 1:35; 12:12
10:13 [f]Hab 3:11 [g]2Sa 1:18 [h]Isa 38:8
10:14 [i]ver 42; Ex 14:14; Dt 1:30; Ps 106:43; 136:24
10:15 [j]ver 43
10:20 [k]Dt 20:16
10:24 [l]Mal 4:3 [m]Ps 110:1
10:25 [n]Dt 31:6

[a] 13 Or *nation triumphed over*

and killed the kings and hung them on five trees, and they were
left hanging on the trees until evening.
27 At sunset[a] Joshua gave the order and they took them down
from the trees and threw them into the cave where they had
been hiding. At the mouth of the cave they placed large rocks,
which are there to this day.
28 That day Joshua took Makkedah. He put the city and its king
to the sword and totally destroyed everyone in it. He left no survivors.[b] And he did to the king of Makkedah as he had done to
the king of Jericho.[c]
29 Then Joshua and all Israel with him moved on from
Makkedah to Libnah and attacked it. 30 The LORD also gave that
city and its king into Israel's hand. The city and everyone in it
Joshua put to the sword. He left no survivors there. And he did
to its king as he had done to the king of Jericho.
31 Then Joshua and all Israel with him moved on from Libnah
to Lachish; he took up positions against it and attacked it. 32 The
LORD handed Lachish over to Israel, and Joshua took it on the
second day. The city and everyone in it he put to the sword, just
as he had done to Libnah. 33 Meanwhile, Horam king of Gezer[d]
had come up to help Lachish, but Joshua defeated him and his
army—until no survivors were left.
34 Then Joshua and all Israel with him moved on from Lachish
to Eglon; they took up positions against it and attacked it.
35 They captured it that same day and put it to the sword and
totally destroyed everyone in it, just as they had done to Lachish.
36 Then Joshua and all Israel with him went up from Eglon to
Hebron[e] and attacked it. 37 They took the city and put it to the
sword, together with its king, its villages and everyone in it.
They left no survivors. Just as at Eglon, they totally destroyed it
and everyone in it.
38 Then Joshua and all Israel with him turned around and
attacked Debir.[f] 39 They took the city, its king and its villages,
and put them to the sword. Everyone in it they totally destroyed.
They left no survivors. They did to Debir and its king as they
had done to Libnah and its king and to Hebron.
40 So Joshua subdued the whole region, including the hill country, the Negev,[g] the western foothills and the mountain slopes,[h]
together with all their kings.[i] He left no survivors. He totally destroyed all who breathed, just as the LORD, the God of Israel, had
commanded.[j] 41 Joshua subdued them from Kadesh Barnea[k] to
Gaza[l] and from the whole region of Goshen[m] to Gibeon. 42 All
these kings and their lands Joshua conquered in one campaign,
because the LORD, the God of Israel, fought[n] for Israel.
43 Then Joshua returned with all Israel to the camp at Gilgal.[o]

10:27 [a]Dt 21:23; Jos 8:9,29
10:28 [b]Dt 20:16 [c]Jos 6:21
10:33 [d]Jos 16:3,10; Jdg 1:29; 1Ki 9:15
10:36 [e]Jos 14:13; 15:13; Jdg 1:10
10:38 [f]Jos 15:15; Jdg 1:11
10:40 [g]Ge 12:9; Jos 12:8 [h]Dt 1:7 [i]Dt 7:24 [j]Dt 20:16-17
10:41 [k]Ge 14:7 [l]Ge 10:19 [m]Jos 11:16; 15:51
10:42 [n]ver 14
10:43 [o]ver 15; Jos 5:9

Chapter 11 Theme ____________________

11 When Jabin[a] king of Hazor[b] heard of this, he sent word to Jobab king of Madon, to the kings of Shimron[c] and Acshaph, 2and to the northern kings who were in the mountains, in the Arabah[d] south of Kinnereth,[e] in the western foothills and in Naphoth Dor[a][f] on the west; 3to the Canaanites in the east and west; to the Amorites, Hittites, Perizzites and Jebusites in the hill country; and to the Hivites[g] below Hermon in the region of Mizpah.[h] 4They came out with all their troops and a large number of horses and chariots—a huge army, as numerous as the sand on the seashore.[i] 5All these kings joined forces[j] and made camp together at the Waters of Merom, to fight against Israel.

6The LORD said to Joshua, "Do not be afraid of them, because by this time tomorrow I will hand all of them over[k] to Israel, slain. You are to hamstring[l] their horses and burn their chariots."

7So Joshua and his whole army came against them suddenly at the Waters of Merom and attacked them, 8and the LORD gave them into the hand of Israel. They defeated them and pursued them all the way to Greater Sidon, to Misrephoth Maim,[m] and to the Valley of Mizpah on the east, until no survivors were left. 9Joshua did to them as the LORD had directed: He hamstrung their horses and burned their chariots.

10At that time Joshua turned back and captured Hazor and put its king to the sword. (Hazor had been the head of all these kingdoms.) 11Everyone in it they put to the sword. They totally destroyed[b] them, not sparing anything that breathed,[n] and he burned up Hazor itself.

12Joshua took all these royal cities and their kings and put them to the sword. He totally destroyed them, as Moses the servant of the LORD had commanded.[o] 13Yet Israel did not burn any of the cities built on their mounds—except Hazor, which Joshua burned. 14The Israelites carried off for themselves all the plunder and livestock of these cities, but all the people they put to the sword until they completely destroyed them, not sparing anyone that breathed.[p] 15As the LORD commanded his servant Moses, so Moses commanded Joshua, and Joshua did it; he left nothing undone of all that the LORD commanded Moses.[q]

16So Joshua took this entire land: the hill country, all the Negev, the whole region of Goshen, the western foothills,[r] the Arabah and the mountains of Israel with their foothills, 17from Mount Halak, which rises toward Seir, to Baal Gad in the Valley

a *2* Or *in the heights of Dor* b *11* The Hebrew term refers to the irrevocable giving over of things or persons to the LORD, often by totally destroying them; also in verses 12, 20 and 21.

11:1 [a]Jdg 4:2,7,23 [b]ver 10; 1Sa 12:9 [c]Jos 19:15
11:2 [d]Jos 12:3 [e]Nu 34:11 [f]Jos 17:11; Jdg 1:27; 1Ki 4:11
11:3 [g]Dt 7:1; Jdg 3:3,5; 1Ki 9:20 [h]Ge 31:49; Jos 15:38; 18:26
11:4 [i]Jdg 7:12; 1Sa 13:5
11:5 [j]Jdg 5:19
11:6 [k]Jos 10:8 [l]2Sa 8:4
11:8 [m]Jos 13:6
11:11 [n]Dt 20:16-17
11:12 [o]Nu 33:50-52; Dt 7:2
11:14 [p]Nu 31:11-12
11:15 [q]Ex 34:11; Jos 1:7
11:16 [r]Jos 10:41

of Lebanon[a] below Mount Hermon. He captured all their kings
and struck them down, putting them to death.[b] 18 Joshua waged
war against all these kings for a long time. 19 Except for the
Hivites living in Gibeon,[c] not one city made a treaty of peace
with the Israelites, who took them all in battle. 20 For it was the
LORD himself who hardened their hearts[d] to wage war against
Israel, so that he might destroy them totally, exterminating them
without mercy, as the LORD had commanded Moses.[e]
21 At that time Joshua went and destroyed the Anakites[f] from
the hill country: from Hebron, Debir and Anab, from all the hill
country of Judah, and from all the hill country of Israel. Joshua
totally destroyed them and their towns. 22 No Anakites were left
in Israelite territory; only in Gaza, Gath[g] and Ashdod[h] did any
survive. 23 So Joshua took the entire land,[i] just as the LORD had
directed Moses, and he gave it as an inheritance[j] to Israel
according to their tribal divisions.[k]
Then the land had rest from war.[l]

Chapter 12 Theme ______________________

12 These are the kings of the land whom the Israelites had
defeated and whose territory they took over east of the
Jordan, from the Arnon Gorge to Mount Hermon,[m] including all
the eastern side of the Arabah:

2 Sihon king of the Amorites,
who reigned in Heshbon. He ruled from Aroer on the rim of
the Arnon Gorge—from the middle of the gorge—to the
Jabbok River, which is the border of the Ammonites. This
included half of Gilead.[n] 3 He also ruled over the eastern
Arabah from the Sea of Kinnereth[a][o] to the Sea of the Arabah
(the Salt Sea[b]), to Beth Jeshimoth,[p] and then southward
below the slopes of Pisgah.

4 And the territory of Og king of Bashan,[q]
one of the last of the Rephaites, who reigned in Ashtaroth[r]
and Edrei. 5 He ruled over Mount Hermon, Salecah,[s] all of
Bashan to the border of the people of Geshur[t] and Maacah,[u]
and half of Gilead to the border of Sihon king of Heshbon.

6 Moses, the servant of the LORD, and the Israelites conquered
them. And Moses the servant of the LORD gave their land to the
Reubenites, the Gadites and the half-tribe of Manasseh to be
their possession.[v]
7 These are the kings of the land that Joshua and the Israelites
conquered on the west side of the Jordan, from Baal Gad in the

11:17 [a] Jos 12:7 [b] Dt 7:24
11:19 [c] Jos 9:3
11:20 [d] Ex 14:17; Ro 9:18 [e] Dt 7:16; Jdg 14:4
11:21 [f] Nu 13:22,33; Dt 9:2
11:22 [g] 1Sa 17:4; 1Ki 2:39; 1Ch 8:13 [h] 1Sa 5:1; Isa 20:1
11:23 [i] Jos 21:43-45 [j] Dt 1:38; 12:9-10; 25:19 [k] Nu 26:53 [l] Jos 14:15
12:1 [m] Dt 3:8
12:2 [n] Dt 2:36
12:3 [o] Jos 11:2 [p] Jos 13:20
12:4 [q] Nu 21:21,33; Dt 3:11 [r] Dt 1:4
12:5 [s] Dt 3:10 [t] 1Sa 27:8 [u] Dt 3:14
12:6 [v] Nu 32:29,33; Jos 13:8

a3 That is, Galilee b3 That is, the Dead Sea

Valley of Lebanon[a] to Mount Halak, which rises toward Seir
(their lands Joshua gave as an inheritance to the tribes of Israel
according to their tribal divisions— 8the hill country, the western foothills, the Arabah, the mountain slopes, the desert and
the Negev[b]—the lands of the Hittites, Amorites, Canaanites,
Perizzites, Hivites and Jebusites):

9the king of Jericho[c]	one
the king of Ai[d] (near Bethel)	one
10the king of Jerusalem[e]	one
the king of Hebron	one
11the king of Jarmuth	one
the king of Lachish	one
12the king of Eglon	one
the king of Gezer[f]	one
13the king of Debir	one
the king of Geder	one
14the king of Hormah	one
the king of Arad[g]	one
15the king of Libnah	one
the king of Adullam	one
16the king of Makkedah	one
the king of Bethel[h]	one
17the king of Tappuah	one
the king of Hepher[i]	one
18the king of Aphek[j]	one
the king of Lasharon	one
19the king of Madon	one
the king of Hazor	one
20the king of Shimron Meron	one
the king of Acshaph[k]	one
21the king of Taanach	one
the king of Megiddo	one
22the king of Kedesh[l]	one
the king of Jokneam in Carmel[m]	one
23the king of Dor (in Naphoth Dor[a][n])	one
the king of Goyim in Gilgal	one
24the king of Tirzah	one

thirty-one kings in all.[o]

Chapter 13 Theme

13 When Joshua was old and well advanced in years,[p] the
LORD said to him, "You are very old, and there are still
very large areas of land to be taken over.

a23 Or *in the heights of Dor*

12:7 [a]Jos 11:17
12:8 [b]Jos 11:16
12:9 [c]Jos 6:2 [d]Jos 8:29
12:10 [e]Jos 10:23
12:12 [f]Jos 10:33
12:14 [g]Nu 21:1
12:16 [h]Jos 7:2
12:17 [i]1Ki 4:10
12:18 [j]Jos 13:4
12:20 [k]Jos 11:1
12:22 [l]Jos 19:37; 20:7; 21:32 [m]1Sa 15:12
12:23 [n]Jos 11:2
12:24 [o]Ps 135:11; Dt 7:24
13:1 [p]Ge 24:1; Jos 14:10

2 “This is the land that remains: all the regions of the
Philistines and Geshurites: 3 from the Shihor River[a] on the
east of Egypt to the territory of Ekron[b] on the north, all of it
counted as Canaanite (the territory of the five Philistine
rulers[c] in Gaza, Ashdod, Ashkelon, Gath and Ekron—that
of the Avvites);[d] 4 from the south, all the land of the Canaanites, from Arah of the Sidonians as far as Aphek,[e] the region
of the Amorites,[f] 5 the area of the Gebalites[a];[g] and all
Lebanon[h] to the east, from Baal Gad below Mount Hermon
to Lebo[b] Hamath.

6 “As for all the inhabitants of the mountain regions from
Lebanon to Misrephoth Maim,[i] that is, all the Sidonians, I
myself will drive them out before the Israelites. Be sure to allo-
cate this land to Israel for an inheritance, as I have instructed
you,[j] 7 and divide it as an inheritance[k] among the nine tribes and
half of the tribe of Manasseh.”

8 The other half of Manasseh,[c] the Reubenites and the Gadites had
received the inheritance that Moses had given them east of the
Jordan, as he, the servant of the LORD, had assigned[l] it to them.

9 It extended from Aroer[m] on the rim of the Arnon Gorge,
and from the town in the middle of the gorge, and included
the whole plateau[n] of Medeba as far as Dibon,[o] 10 and all the
towns of Sihon king of the Amorites, who ruled in Heshbon,
out to the border of the Ammonites.[p] 11 It also included
Gilead, the territory of the people of Geshur and Maacah, all
of Mount Hermon and all Bashan as far as Salecah[q]— 12 that
is, the whole kingdom of Og in Bashan,[r] who had reigned in
Ashtaroth[s] and Edrei and had survived as one of the last of
the Rephaites.[t] Moses had defeated them and taken over
their land. 13 But the Israelites did not drive out the people of
Geshur[u] and Maacah,[v] so they continue to live among the
Israelites to this day.

14 But to the tribe of Levi he gave no inheritance, since the offerings made by fire to the LORD, the God of Israel, are their inheritance, as he promised them.[w]

15 This is what Moses had given to the tribe of Reuben, clan by
clan:

16 The territory from Aroer[x] on the rim of the Arnon Gorge,
and from the town in the middle of the gorge, and the whole

13:3 [a] Jer 2:18 [b] Jdg 1:18 [c] Jdg 3:3 [d] Dt 2:23
13:4 [e] Jos 12:18; 19:30 [f] Am 2:10
13:5 [g] 1Ki 5:18; Ps 83:7; Eze 27:9 [h] Jos 12:7
13:6 [i] Jos 11:8 [j] Nu 33:54
13:7 [k] Jos 11:23; Ps 78:55
13:8 [l] Jos 12:6
13:9 [m] ver 16; Jdg 11:26 [n] Jer 48:8,21 [o] Nu 21:30
13:10 [p] Nu 21:24
13:11 [q] Jos 12:5
13:12 [r] Dt 3:11 [s] Jos 12:4 [t] Ge 14:5
13:13 [u] Jos 12:5 [v] Dt 3:14
13:14 [w] ver 33; Dt 18:1-2
13:16 [x] ver 9; Jos 12:2

[a] 5 That is, the area of Byblos [b] 5 Or *to the entrance to* [c] 8 Hebrew *With it* (that is, with the other half of Manasseh)

plateau past Medeba[a] 17to Heshbon and all its towns on the plateau, including Dibon,[b] Bamoth Baal, Beth Baal Meon,[c] 18Jahaz,[d] Kedemoth, Mephaath,[e] 19Kiriathaim,[f] Sibmah, Zereth Shahar on the hill in the valley, 20Beth Peor,[g] the slopes of Pisgah, and Beth Jeshimoth 21—all the towns on the plateau and the entire realm of Sihon king of the Amorites, who ruled at Heshbon. Moses had defeated him and the Midianite chiefs,[h] Evi, Rekem, Zur, Hur and Reba[i]—princes allied with Sihon—who lived in that country. 22In addition to those slain in battle, the Israelites had put to the sword Balaam son of Beor,[j] who practiced divination. 23The boundary of the Reubenites was the bank of the Jordan. These towns and their villages were the inheritance of the Reubenites, clan by clan.

24This is what Moses had given to the tribe of Gad, clan by clan:

25The territory of Jazer,[k] all the towns of Gilead and half the Ammonite country as far as Aroer, near Rabbah; 26and from Heshbon[l] to Ramath Mizpah and Betonim, and from Mahanaim to the territory of Debir;[m] 27and in the valley, Beth Haram, Beth Nimrah, Succoth[n] and Zaphon with the rest of the realm of Sihon king of Heshbon (the east side of the Jordan, the territory up to the end of the Sea of Kinnereth[a][o]). 28These towns and their villages were the inheritance of the Gadites,[p] clan by clan.

29This is what Moses had given to the half-tribe of Manasseh, that is, to half the family of the descendants of Manasseh, clan by clan:

30The territory extending from Mahanaim[q] and including all of Bashan, the entire realm of Og king of Bashan—all the settlements of Jair[r] in Bashan, sixty towns, 31half of Gilead, and Ashtaroth and Edrei (the royal cities of Og in Bashan). This was for the descendants of Makir[s] son of Manasseh—for half of the sons of Makir, clan by clan.

32This is the inheritance Moses had given when he was in the plains of Moab across the Jordan east of Jericho. 33But to the tribe of Levi, Moses had given no inheritance; the LORD, the God of Israel, is their inheritance,[t] as he promised them.[u]

Chapter 14 Theme ________________________

14 Now these are the areas the Israelites received as an inheritance in the land of Canaan, which Eleazar the priest, Joshua son of Nun and the heads of the tribal clans of Israel allotted

a 27 That is, Galilee

13:16 [a]Nu 21:30
13:17 [b]Nu 32:3 [c]1Ch 5:8
13:18 [d]Nu 21:23 [e]Jer 48:21
13:19 [f]Nu 32:37
13:20 [g]Dt 3:29
13:21 [h]Nu 25:15 [i]Nu 31:8
13:22 [j]Nu 22:5; 31:8
13:25 [k]Nu 21:32; Jos 21:39
13:26 [l]Nu 21:25; Jer 49:3 [m]Jos 10:3
13:27 [n]Ge 33:17 [o]Nu 34:11
13:28 [p]Nu 32:33
13:30 [q]Ge 32:2 [r]Nu 32:41
13:31 [s]Ge 50:23
13:33 [t]Nu 18:20 [u]ver 14; Jos 18:7

to them.[a] 2Their inheritances were assigned by lot[b] to the nine-
and-a-half tribes, as the LORD had commanded through Moses.
3Moses had granted the two-and-a-half tribes their inheritance
east of the Jordan[c] but had not granted the Levites an inheritance among the rest,[d] 4for the sons of Joseph had become two
tribes—Manasseh and Ephraim.[e] The Levites received no share
of the land but only towns to live in, with pasturelands for their
flocks and herds. 5So the Israelites divided the land, just as the
LORD had commanded Moses.[f]

6Now the men of Judah approached Joshua at Gilgal, and
Caleb son of Jephunneh[g] the Kenizzite said to him, "You know
what the LORD said to Moses the man of God at Kadesh Barnea[h]
about you and me. 7I was forty years old when Moses the servant of the LORD sent me from Kadesh Barnea to explore the
land.[i] And I brought him back a report according to my convictions,[j] 8but my brothers who went up with me made the hearts
of the people melt with fear.[k] I, however, followed the LORD my
God wholeheartedly.[l] 9So on that day Moses swore to me, 'The
land on which your feet have walked will be your inheritance
and that of your children[m] forever, because you have followed
the LORD my God wholeheartedly.'[a]

10"Now then, just as the LORD promised,[n] he has kept me alive
for forty-five years since the time he said this to Moses, while
Israel moved about in the desert. So here I am today, eighty-five
years old! 11I am still as strong[o] today as the day Moses sent me
out; I'm just as vigorous to go out to battle now as I was then.
12Now give me this hill country that the LORD promised me that
day. You yourself heard then that the Anakites[p] were there and
their cities were large and fortified,[q] but, the LORD helping me, I
will drive them out just as he said."

13Then Joshua blessed[r] Caleb son of Jephunneh and gave him
Hebron[s] as his inheritance.[t] 14So Hebron has belonged to Caleb
son of Jephunneh the Kenizzite ever since, because he followed
the LORD, the God of Israel, wholeheartedly. 15(Hebron used to
be called Kiriath Arba[u] after Arba,[v] who was the greatest man
among the Anakites.)

Then the land had rest[w] from war.

Chapter 15 Theme ____________________

15 The allotment for the tribe of Judah, clan by clan, extended down to the territory of Edom,[x] to the Desert of Zin[y]
in the extreme south.

a9 Deut. 1:36

14:1 [a]Nu 34:17-18
14:2 [b]Nu 26:55
14:3 [c]Nu 32:33 [d]Jos 13:14
14:4 [e]Ge 41:52; 48:5
14:5 [f]Nu 34:13; 35:2; Jos 21:2
14:6 [g]Nu 13:6; 14:30 [h]Nu 13:26
14:7 [i]Nu 13:17 [j]Nu 13:30; 14:6-9
14:8 [k]Nu 13:31 [l]Nu 14:24
14:9 [m]Nu 14:24; Dt 1:36
14:10 [n]Nu 14:30
14:11 [o]Dt 34:7
14:12 [p]Nu 13:33 [q]Nu 13:28
14:13 [r]Jos 22:6,7 [s]Jos 10:36 [t]Jdg 1:20; 1Ch 6:56
14:15 [u]Ge 23:2 [v]Jos 15:13 [w]Jos 11:23
15:1 [x]Nu 34:3 [y]Nu 33:36

[2]Their southern boundary started from the bay at the southern end of the Salt Sea,[a] [3]crossed south of Scorpion[b] Pass,[a] continued on to Zin and went over to the south of Kadesh Barnea. Then it ran past Hezron up to Addar and curved around to Karka. [4]It then passed along to Azmon[b] and joined the Wadi of Egypt,[c] ending at the sea. This is their[c] southern boundary.

[5]The eastern boundary[d] is the Salt Sea as far as the mouth of the Jordan.

The northern boundary[e] started from the bay of the sea at the mouth of the Jordan, [6]went up to Beth Hoglah[f] and continued north of Beth Arabah to the Stone of Bohan[g] son of Reuben. [7]The boundary then went up to Debir from the Valley of Achor[h] and turned north to Gilgal, which faces the Pass of Adummim south of the gorge. It continued along to the waters of En Shemesh and came out at En Rogel.[i] [8]Then it ran up the Valley of Ben Hinnom along the southern slope of the Jebusite[j] city (that is, Jerusalem). From there it climbed to the top of the hill west of the Hinnom Valley at the northern end of the Valley of Rephaim. [9]From the hilltop the boundary headed toward the spring of the waters of Nephtoah,[k] came out at the towns of Mount Ephron and went down toward Baalah[l] (that is, Kiriath Jearim). [10]Then it curved westward from Baalah to Mount Seir, ran along the northern slope of Mount Jearim (that is, Kesalon), continued down to Beth Shemesh and crossed to Timnah.[m] [11]It went to the northern slope of Ekron, turned toward Shikkeron, passed along to Mount Baalah and reached Jabneel.[n] The boundary ended at the sea.

[12]The western boundary is the coastline of the Great Sea.[d][o] These are the boundaries around the people of Judah by their clans.

[13]In accordance with the LORD's command to him, Joshua gave to Caleb son of Jephunneh a portion in Judah—Kiriath Arba, that is, Hebron. (Arba was the forefather of Anak.)[p] [14]From Hebron Caleb drove out the three Anakites[q]—Sheshai, Ahiman and Talmai[r]—descendants of Anak.[s] [15]From there he marched against the people living in Debir (formerly called Kiriath Sepher). [16]And Caleb said, "I will give my daughter Acsah[t] in marriage to the man who attacks and captures Kiriath Sepher." [17]Othniel[u] son of Kenaz, Caleb's brother, took it; so Caleb gave his daughter Acsah to him in marriage.

[a]*2* That is, the Dead Sea; also in verse 5 [b]*3* Hebrew *Akrabbim* [c]*4* Hebrew *your* [d]*12* That is, the Mediterranean; also in verse 47

15:3 [a]Nu 34:4

15:4 [b]Nu 34:5 [c]Ge 15:18

15:5 [d]Nu 34:10 [e]Jos 18:15-19

15:6 [f]Jos 18:19,21 [g]Jos 18:17

15:7 [h]Jos 7:24 [i]2Sa 17:17; 1Ki 1:9

15:8 [j]ver 63; Jos 18:16,28; Jdg 1:21; 19:10

15:9 [k]Jos 18:15 [l]1Ch 13:6

15:10 [m]Ge 38:12; Jdg 14:1

15:11 [n]Jos 19:33

15:12 [o]Nu 34:6

15:13 [p]Jos 14:13-15

15:14 [q]Nu 13:33 [r]Nu 13:22 [s]Jdg 1:10,20

15:16 [t]Jdg 1:12

15:17 [u]Jdg 3:9,11

18 One day when she came to Othniel, she urged him[a] to ask
her father for a field. When she got off her donkey, Caleb asked
her, "What can I do for you?"

19 She replied, "Do me a special favor. Since you have given me
land in the Negev, give me also springs of water." So Caleb gave
her the upper and lower springs.

20 This is the inheritance of the tribe of Judah, clan by clan:

21 The southernmost towns of the tribe of Judah in the Negev
toward the boundary of Edom were:

Kabzeel, Eder,[a] Jagur, 22 Kinah, Dimonah, Adadah, 23 Kedesh,
Hazor, Ithnan, 24 Ziph,[b] Telem, Bealoth, 25 Hazor Hadattah,
Kerioth Hezron (that is, Hazor), 26 Amam, Shema, Moladah,[c]
27 Hazar Gaddah, Heshmon, Beth Pelet, 28 Hazar Shual, Beer-
sheba,[d] Biziothiah, 29 Baalah,[e] Iim, Ezem, 30 Eltolad,[f] Kesil,
Hormah, 31 Ziklag,[g] Madmannah, Sansannah, 32 Lebaoth,
Shilhim, Ain and Rimmon[h]—a total of twenty-nine towns
and their villages.

33 In the western foothills:

Eshtaol,[i] Zorah, Ashnah, 34 Zanoah,[j] En Gannim, Tappuah,
Enam, 35 Jarmuth,[k] Adullam,[l] Socoh, Azekah, 36 Shaaraim,
Adithaim and Gederah[m] (or Gederothaim)[b]—fourteen towns
and their villages.

37 Zenan, Hadashah, Migdal Gad, 38 Dilean, Mizpah, Joktheel,[n] 39 Lachish,[o] Bozkath,[p] Eglon, 40 Cabbon, Lahmas, Kitlish,
41 Gederoth, Beth Dagon, Naamah and Makkedah[q]—sixteen
towns and their villages.

42 Libnah, Ether, Ashan,[r] 43 Iphtah, Ashnah, Nezib, 44 Keilah,
Aczib[s] and Mareshah[t]—nine towns and their villages.

45 Ekron, with its surrounding settlements and villages;
46 west of Ekron, all that were in the vicinity of Ashdod, together
with their villages; 47 Ashdod,[u] its surrounding settlements
and villages; and Gaza, its settlements and villages, as far as
the Wadi of Egypt[v] and the coastline of the Great Sea.[w]

48 In the hill country:

Shamir, Jattir,[x] Socoh, 49 Dannah, Kiriath Sannah (that is,
Debir[y]), 50 Anab, Eshtemoh,[z] Anim, 51 Goshen,[a] Holon and
Giloh—eleven towns and their villages.

52 Arab, Dumah,[b] Eshan, 53 Janim, Beth Tappuah, Aphekah,
54 Humtah, Kiriath Arba (that is, Hebron) and Zior—nine
towns and their villages.

15:21 [a] Ge 35:21
15:24 [b] 1Sa 23:14
15:26 [c] 1Ch 4:28
15:28 [d] Ge 21:31
15:29 [e] ver 9
15:30 [f] Jos 19:4
15:31 [g] 1Sa 27:6
15:32 [h] Jdg 20:45
15:33 [i] Jdg 13:25; 16:31
15:34 [j] 1Ch 4:18; Ne 3:13
15:35 [k] Jos 10:3 [l] 1Sa 22:1
15:36 [m] 1Ch 12:4
15:38 [n] 2Ki 14:7
15:39 [o] Jos 10:3; 2Ki 14:19 [p] 2Ki 22:1
15:41 [q] Jos 10:10
15:42 [r] 1Sa 30:30
15:44 [s] Jdg 1:31 [t] Mic 1:15
15:47 [u] Jos 11:22 [v] ver 4 [w] Nu 34:6
15:48 [x] 1Sa 30:27
15:49 [y] Jos 10:3
15:50 [z] Jos 21:14
15:51 [a] Jos 10:41; 11:16
15:52 [b] Ge 25:14

[a] *18* Hebrew and some Septuagint manuscripts; other Septuagint manuscripts (see also note at Judges 1:14) *Othniel, he urged her* [b] *36* Or *Gederah and Gederothaim*

[55]Maon, Carmel,[a] Ziph, Juttah, [56]Jezreel,[b] Jokdeam, Zanoah,
[57]Kain, Gibeah[c] and Timnah—ten towns and their villages.
[58]Halhul, Beth Zur,[d] Gedor, [59]Maarath, Beth Anoth and
Eltekon—six towns and their villages.
[60]Kiriath Baal (that is, Kiriath Jearim[e]) and Rabbah[f]—two
towns and their villages.

[61]In the desert:

Beth Arabah, Middin, Secacah, [62]Nibshan, the City of Salt
and En Gedi[g]—six towns and their villages.
[63]Judah could not[h] dislodge the Jebusites[i], who were living in
Jerusalem; to this day the Jebusites live there with the people of
Judah.

Chapter 16 Theme ____________________________

16 The allotment for Joseph began at the Jordan of
Jericho,[a] east of the waters of Jericho, and went up from
there through the desert[j] into the hill country of Bethel. [2]It
went on from Bethel (that is, Luz[k]),[b] crossed over to the territory of the Arkites in Ataroth, [3]descended westward to the
territory of the Japhletites as far as the region of Lower Beth
Horon[l] and on to Gezer,[m] ending at the sea.
[4]So Manasseh and Ephraim, the descendants of Joseph, received
their inheritance.[n]

[5]This was the territory of Ephraim, clan by clan:

The boundary of their inheritance went from Ataroth
Addar[o] in the east to Upper Beth Horon [6]and continued to the
sea. From Micmethath[p] on the north it curved eastward to
Taanath Shiloh, passing by it to Janoah on the east. [7]Then it
went down from Janoah to Ataroth[q] and Naarah, touched Jericho and came out at the Jordan. [8]From Tappuah the border
went west to the Kanah Ravine[r] and ended at the sea. This was
the inheritance of the tribe of the Ephraimites, clan by clan. [9]It
also included all the towns and their villages that were set aside
for the Ephraimites within the inheritance of the Manassites.
[10]They did not dislodge the Canaanites living in Gezer; to this
day the Canaanites live among the people of Ephraim but are
required to do forced labor.[s]

Chapter 17 Theme ____________________________

17 This was the allotment for the tribe of Manasseh as Joseph's
firstborn,[t] that is, for Makir,[u] Manasseh's firstborn.

[a] *1 Jordan of Jericho* was possibly an ancient name for the Jordan River. [b] *2* Septuagint; Hebrew *Bethel to Luz*

15:55 [a]Jos 12:22
15:56 [b]Jos 17:16
15:57 [c]Jos 18:28; Jdg 19:12
15:58 [d]1Ch 2:45
15:60 [e]Jos 18:14 [f]Dt 3:11
15:62 [g]1Sa 23:29
15:63 [h]Jdg 1:21 [i]2Sa 5:6
16:1 [j]Jos 8:15; 18:12
16:2 [k]Jos 18:13
16:3 [l]2Ch 8:5 [m]Jos 10:33; 1Ki 9:15
16:4 [n]Jos 17:14
16:5 [o]Jos 18:13
16:6 [p]Jos 17:7
16:7 [q]1Ch 7:28
16:8 [r]Jos 17:9
16:10 [s]Jos 17:13; Jdg 1:28-29; 1Ki 9:16
17:1 [t]Ge 41:51 [u]Ge 50:23

Makir was the ancestor of the Gileadites, who had received
Gilead and Bashan because the Makirites were great soldiers.
2 So this allotment was for the rest of the people of Manasseh—
the clans of Abiezer,[a] Helek, Asriel, Shechem, Hepher and Shemida. These are the other male descendants of Manasseh son of
Joseph by their clans.

3 Now Zelophehad son of Hepher,[b] the son of Gilead, the son of
Makir, the son of Manasseh, had no sons but only daughters,[c]
whose names were Mahlah, Noah, Hoglah, Milcah and Tirzah.
4 They went to Eleazar the priest, Joshua son of Nun, and the
leaders and said, "The LORD commanded Moses to give us an
inheritance among our brothers." So Joshua gave them an
inheritance along with the brothers of their father, according to
the LORD's command.[d] 5 Manasseh's share consisted of ten tracts
of land besides Gilead and Bashan east of the Jordan, 6 because
the daughters of the tribe of Manasseh received an inheritance
among the sons. The land of Gilead belonged to the rest of the
descendants of Manasseh.

7 The territory of Manasseh extended from Asher to
Micmethath[e] east of Shechem.[f] The boundary ran southward from there to include the people living at En Tappuah.
8 (Manasseh had the land of Tappuah, but Tappuah[g] itself, on
the boundary of Manasseh, belonged to the Ephraimites.)
9 Then the boundary continued south to the Kanah Ravine.[h]
There were towns belonging to Ephraim lying among the towns
of Manasseh, but the boundary of Manasseh was the northern
side of the ravine and ended at the sea. 10 On the south the
land belonged to Ephraim, on the north to Manasseh. The
territory of Manasseh reached the sea and bordered Asher
on the north and Issachar[i] on the east.

11 Within Issachar and Asher, Manasseh also had Beth
Shan,[j] Ibleam and the people of Dor,[k] Endor,[l] Taanach and
Megiddo,[m] together with their surrounding settlements (the
third in the list is Naphoth[a]).
12 Yet the Manassites were not able[n] to occupy these towns, for
the Canaanites were determined to live in that region. 13 However,
when the Israelites grew stronger, they subjected the Canaanites
to forced labor but did not drive them out completely.[o]

14 The people of Joseph said to Joshua, "Why have you given us
only one allotment and one portion for an inheritance? We are a
numerous people and the LORD has blessed us abundantly."[p]

15 "If you are so numerous," Joshua answered, "and if the hill
country of Ephraim is too small for you, go up into the forest

[a] *11* That is, Naphoth Dor

17:2 [a] Nu 26:30; 1Ch 7:18
17:3 [b] Nu 27:1 [c] Nu 26:33
17:4 [d] Nu 27:5-7
17:7 [e] Jos 16:6 [f] Ge 12:6; Jos 21:21
17:8 [g] Jos 16:8
17:9 [h] Jos 16:8
17:10 [i] Ge 30:18
17:11 [j] 1Sa 31:10; 1Ki 4:12; 1Ch 7:29 [k] Jos 11:2 [l] 1Sa 28:7; Ps 83:10 [m] 1Ki 9:15
17:12 [n] Jdg 1:27
17:13 [o] Jos 16:10
17:14 [p] Nu 26:28-37

and clear land for yourselves there in the land of the Perizzites and Rephaites.[a]"

16The people of Joseph replied, "The hill country is not enough for us, and all the Canaanites who live in the plain have iron chariots,[b] both those in Beth Shan and its settlements and those in the Valley of Jezreel."

17But Joshua said to the house of Joseph—to Ephraim and Manasseh—"You are numerous and very powerful. You will have not only one allotment 18but the forested hill country as well. Clear it, and its farthest limits will be yours; though the Canaanites have iron chariots[c] and though they are strong, you can drive them out."

Chapter 18 Theme

18 The whole assembly of the Israelites gathered at Shiloh[d] and set up the Tent of Meeting[e] there. The country was brought under their control, 2but there were still seven Israelite tribes who had not yet received their inheritance.

3So Joshua said to the Israelites: "How long will you wait before you begin to take possession of the land that the LORD, the God of your fathers, has given you? 4Appoint three men from each tribe. I will send them out to make a survey of the land and to write a description of it, according to the inheritance of each.[f] Then they will return to me. 5You are to divide the land into seven parts. Judah is to remain in its territory on the south[g] and the house of Joseph in its territory on the north.[h] 6After you have written descriptions of the seven parts of the land, bring them here to me and I will cast lots[i] for you in the presence of the LORD our God. 7The Levites, however, do not get a portion among you, because the priestly service of the LORD is their inheritance.[j] And Gad, Reuben and the half-tribe of Manasseh have already received their inheritance on the east side of the Jordan. Moses the servant of the LORD gave it to them.[k]"

8As the men started on their way to map out the land, Joshua instructed them, "Go and make a survey of the land and write a description of it. Then return to me, and I will cast lots for you here at Shiloh[l] in the presence of the LORD." 9So the men left and went through the land. They wrote its description on a scroll, town by town, in seven parts, and returned to Joshua in the camp at Shiloh. 10Joshua then cast lots[m] for them in Shiloh in the presence[n] of the LORD, and there he distributed the land to the Israelites according to their tribal divisions.[o]

11The lot came up for the tribe of Benjamin, clan by clan. Their allotted territory lay between the tribes of Judah and Joseph:

17:15 [a] Ge 14:5
17:16 [b] Jdg 1:19; 4:3,13
17:18 [c] ver 16
18:1 [d] Jos 19:51; 21:2; Jdg 18:31; 21:12,19; 1Sa 1:3; 4:3; Jer 7:12; 26:6 [e] Ex 27:21
18:4 [f] Mic 2:5
18:5 [g] Jos 15:1 [h] Jos 16:1-4
18:6 [i] Jos 14:2
18:7 [j] Jos 13:33 [k] Jos 13:8
18:8 [l] ver 1
18:10 [m] Nu 34:13 [n] ver 1; Jer 7:12 [o] Nu 33:54; Jos 19:51

12On the north side their boundary began at the Jordan,
passed the northern slope of Jericho and headed west into
the hill country, coming out at the desert[a] of Beth Aven.[b]
13From there it crossed to the south slope of Luz[c] (that is,
Bethel[d]) and went down to Ataroth Addar[e] on the hill south
of Lower Beth Horon.

14From the hill facing Beth Horon[f] on the south the bound-
ary turned south along the western side and came out at
Kiriath Baal (that is, Kiriath Jearim), a town of the people of
Judah. This was the western side.

15The southern side began at the outskirts of Kiriath
Jearim on the west, and the boundary came out at the spring
of the waters of Nephtoah.[g] 16The boundary went down to
the foot of the hill facing the Valley of Ben Hinnom, north of
the Valley of Rephaim. It continued down the Hinnom Valley[h] along the southern slope of the Jebusite city and so to En
Rogel.[i] 17It then curved north, went to En Shemesh, continued to Geliloth, which faces the Pass of Adummim, and ran
down to the Stone of Bohan[j] son of Reuben. 18It continued
to the northern slope of Beth Arabah[a][k] and on down into
the Arabah. 19It then went to the northern slope of Beth
Hoglah and came out at the northern bay of the Salt Sea,[b][l] at
the mouth of the Jordan in the south. This was the southern
boundary.

20The Jordan formed the boundary on the eastern side.
These were the boundaries that marked out the inheritance of
the clans of Benjamin on all sides.[m]

21The tribe of Benjamin, clan by clan, had the following cities:
Jericho, Beth Hoglah, Emek Keziz, 22Beth Arabah, Zema-
raim, Bethel,[n] 23Avvim, Parah, Ophrah, 24Kephar Ammoni,
Ophni and Geba[o]—twelve towns and their villages.

25Gibeon,[p] Ramah,[q] Beeroth,[r] 26Mizpah,[s] Kephirah, Mozah,
27Rekem, Irpeel, Taralah, 28Zelah,[t] Haeleph, the Jebusite city[u]
(that is, Jerusalem[v]), Gibeah[w] and Kiriath—fourteen towns
and their villages.

This was the inheritance of Benjamin for its clans.

Chapter 19 Theme ________________________

19 The second lot came out for the tribe of Simeon, clan by
clan. Their inheritance lay within the territory of Judah.[x]
2It included:

Beersheba[y] (or Sheba),[c] Moladah, 3Hazar Shual, Balah,
Ezem, 4Eltolad, Bethul, Hormah, 5Ziklag, Beth Marcaboth,

18:12 [a]Jos 16:1 [b]Jos 7:2
18:13 [c]Ge 28:19 [d]Jdg 1:23 [e]Jos 16:5
18:14 [f]Jos 10:10
18:15 [g]Jos 15:9
18:16 [h]Jos 15:8; 2Ki 23:10 [i]Jos 15:7
18:17 [j]Jos 15:6
18:18 [k]Jos 15:6
18:19 [l]Ge 14:3
18:20 [m]Jos 21:4,17; 1Sa 9:1
18:22 [n]Jos 16:1
18:24 [o]Isa 10:29
18:25 [p]Jos 9:3 [q]Jdg 4:5 [r]Jos 9:17
18:26 [s]Jos 11:3
18:28 [t]2Sa 21:14 [u]Jos 15:8 [v]Jos 10:1 [w]Jos 15:57
19:1 [x]ver 9; Ge 49:7
19:2 [y]Ge 21:14; 1Ki 19:3

a *18* Septuagint; Hebrew *slope facing the Arabah* b *19* That is, the Dead Sea c *2* Or *Beersheba, Sheba*; 1 Chron. 4:28 does not have *Sheba.*

Hazar Susah, 6 Beth Lebaoth and Sharuhen—thirteen towns
and their villages;

7 Ain, Rimmon, Ether and Ashan[a]—four towns and their
villages— 8 and all the villages around these towns as far as
Baalath Beer (Ramah in the Negev).[b]
This was the inheritance of the tribe of the Simeonites, clan by
clan. 9 The inheritance of the Simeonites was taken from the share
of Judah,[c] because Judah's portion was more than they needed.
So the Simeonites received their inheritance within the territory
of Judah.[d]

10 The third lot came up for Zebulun,[e] clan by clan:

The boundary of their inheritance went as far as Sarid.
11 Going west it ran to Maralah, touched Dabbesheth, and
extended to the ravine near Jokneam.[f] 12 It turned east from
Sarid toward the sunrise to the territory of Kisloth Tabor and
went on to Daberath and up to Japhia. 13 Then it continued
eastward to Gath Hepher and Eth Kazin; it came out at Rimmon[g] and turned toward Neah. 14 There the boundary went
around on the north to Hannathon and ended at the Valley
of Iphtah El. 15 Included were Kattath, Nahalal, Shimron, Idalah
and Bethlehem.[h] There were twelve towns and their villages.
16 These towns and their villages were the inheritance of
Zebulun,[i] clan by clan.[j]

17 The fourth lot came out for Issachar,[k] clan by clan. 18 Their territory included:

Jezreel,[l] Kesulloth, Shunem,[m] 19 Hapharaim, Shion, Ana-
harath, 20 Rabbith, Kishion, Ebez, 21 Remeth, En Gannim, En
Haddah and Beth Pazzez. 22 The boundary touched Tabor,[n]
Shahazumah and Beth Shemesh,[o] and ended at the Jordan.
There were sixteen towns and their villages.
23 These towns and their villages were the inheritance of the tribe
of Issachar,[p] clan by clan.[q]

24 The fifth lot came out for the tribe of Asher,[r] clan by clan.
25 Their territory included:

Helkath, Hali, Beten, Acshaph, 26 Allammelech, Amad and
Mishal. On the west the boundary touched Carmel[s] and Shihor Libnath. 27 It then turned east toward Beth Dagon,
touched Zebulun[t] and the Valley of Iphtah El, and went north
to Beth Emek and Neiel, passing Cabul[u] on the left. 28 It went
to Abdon,[a] Rehob,[v] Hammon[w] and Kanah, as far as Greater
Sidon.[x] 29 The boundary then turned back toward Ramah[y]
and went to the fortified city of Tyre,[z] turned toward Hosah

[a] 28 Some Hebrew manuscripts (see also Joshua 21:30); most Hebrew manuscripts *Ebron*

19:7 [a] Jos 15:42
19:8 [b] Jos 10:40
19:9 [c] Ge 49:7 [d] Eze 48:24
19:10 [e] Jos 21:7,34
19:11 [f] Jos 12:22
19:13 [g] Jos 15:32
19:15 [h] Ge 35:19
19:16 [i] ver 10; Jos 21:7 [j] Eze 48:26
19:17 [k] Ge 30:18
19:18 [l] Jos 15:56 [m] 1Sa 28:4; 2Ki 4:8
19:22 [n] Jdg 4:6,12; Ps 89:12 [o] Jos 15:10
19:23 [p] Jos 17:10 [q] Ge 49:15; Eze 48:25
19:24 [r] Jos 17:7
19:26 [s] Jos 12:22
19:27 [t] ver 10 [u] 1Ki 9:13
19:28 [v] Jdg 1:31 [w] 1Ch 6:76 [x] Ge 10:19; Jos 11:8
19:29 [y] Jos 18:25 [z] 2Sa 5:11; 24:7; Isa 23:1; Jer 25:22; Eze 26:2

and came out at the sea in the region of Aczib,[a] 30 Ummah,
Aphek and Rehob. There were twenty-two towns and their
villages.
31 These towns and their villages were the inheritance of the tribe
of Asher,[b] clan by clan.

32 The sixth lot came out for Naphtali, clan by clan:
33 Their boundary went from Heleph and the large tree in
Zaanannim, passing Adami Nekeb and Jabneel to Lakkum
and ending at the Jordan. 34 The boundary ran west through
Aznoth Tabor and came out at Hukkok. It touched Zebulun
on the south, Asher on the west and the Jordan[a] on the east.
35 The fortified cities were Ziddim, Zer, Hammath, Rakkath,
Kinnereth,[c] 36 Adamah, Ramah,[d] Hazor,[e] 37 Kedesh, Edrei,[f] En
Hazor, 38 Iron, Migdal El, Horem, Beth Anath and Beth Shemesh. There were nineteen towns and their villages.
39 These towns and their villages were the inheritance of the tribe
of Naphtali, clan by clan.[g]

40 The seventh lot came out for the tribe of Dan, clan by clan.
41 The territory of their inheritance included:
Zorah, Eshtaol, Ir Shemesh, 42 Shaalabbin, Aijalon,[h] Ithlah,
43 Elon, Timnah,[i] Ekron, 44 Eltekeh, Gibbethon, Baalath, 45 Je-
hud, Bene Berak, Gath Rimmon,[j] 46 Me Jarkon and Rakkon,
with the area facing Joppa.[k]
47 (But the Danites had difficulty taking possession of their territory,[l] so they went up and attacked Leshem[m], took it, put it to
the sword and occupied it. They settled in Leshem and named it
Dan after their forefather.)[n]
48 These towns and their villages were the inheritance of the tribe
of Dan,[o] clan by clan.

49 When they had finished dividing the land into its allotted
portions, the Israelites gave Joshua son of Nun an inheritance
among them, 50 as the LORD had commanded. They gave him the
town he asked for—Timnath Serah[b][p] in the hill country of Ephraim. And he built up the town and settled there.
51 These are the territories that Eleazar the priest, Joshua son of
Nun and the heads of the tribal clans of Israel assigned by lot at
Shiloh in the presence of the LORD at the entrance to the Tent of
Meeting. And so they finished dividing the land.[q]

Chapter 20 Theme ______________________________

20 Then the LORD said to Joshua: 2 "Tell the Israelites to designate the cities of refuge, as I instructed you through

[a] *34* Septuagint; Hebrew *west, and Judah, the Jordan,* [b] *50* Also known as *Timnath Heres* (see Judges 2:9)

19:29 [a] Jdg 1:31
19:31 [b] Ge 30:13; Eze 48:2
19:35 [c] Jos 11:2
19:36 [d] Jos 18:25 [e] Jos 11:1
19:37 [f] Nu 21:33
19:39 [g] Dt 33:23; Eze 48:3
19:42 [h] Jdg 1:35
19:43 [i] Ge 38:12
19:45 [j] Jos 21:24; 1Ch 6:69
19:46 [k] 2Ch 2:16; Jnh 1:3
19:47 [l] Jdg 18:1 [m] Jdg 18:7,14 [n] Jdg 18:27,29
19:48 [o] Ge 30:6
19:50 [p] Jos 24:30
19:51 [q] Jos 14:1; 18:10; Ac 13:19

Moses, [3]so that anyone who kills a person accidentally and unintentionally[a] may flee there and find protection from the avenger of blood.[b]

[4]"When he flees to one of these cities, he is to stand in the entrance of the city gate[c] and state his case before the elders[d] of that city. Then they are to admit him into their city and give him a place to live with them. [5]If the avenger of blood pursues him, they must not surrender the one accused, because he killed his neighbor unintentionally and without malice aforethought. [6]He is to stay in that city until he has stood trial before the assembly[e] and until the death of the high priest who is serving at that time. Then he may go back to his own home in the town from which he fled."

[7]So they set apart Kedesh[f] in Galilee in the hill country of Naphtali, Shechem[g] in the hill country of Ephraim, and Kiriath Arba (that is, Hebron[h]) in the hill country of Judah.[i] [8]On the east side of the Jordan of Jericho[a] they designated Bezer[j] in the desert on the plateau in the tribe of Reuben, Ramoth in Gilead[k] in the tribe of Gad, and Golan in Bashan in the tribe of Manasseh. [9]Any of the Israelites or any alien living among them who killed someone accidentally could flee to these designated cities and not be killed by the avenger of blood prior to standing trial before the assembly.[l]

Chapter 21 Theme

21 Now the family heads of the Levites approached Eleazar the priest, Joshua son of Nun, and the heads of the other tribal families of Israel[m] [2]at Shiloh[n] in Canaan and said to them, "The LORD commanded through Moses that you give us towns to live in, with pasturelands for our livestock."[o] [3]So, as the LORD had commanded, the Israelites gave the Levites the following towns and pasturelands out of their own inheritance:

[4]The first lot came out for the Kohathites, clan by clan. The Levites who were descendants of Aaron the priest were allotted thirteen towns from the tribes of Judah, Simeon and Benjamin.[p] [5]The rest of Kohath's descendants were allotted ten towns from the clans of the tribes of Ephraim, Dan and half of Manasseh.[q]

[6]The descendants of Gershon were allotted thirteen towns from the clans of the tribes of Issachar,[r] Asher, Naphtali and the half-tribe of Manasseh in Bashan.

[7]The descendants of Merari,[s] clan by clan, received twelve towns from the tribes of Reuben, Gad and Zebulun.[t]

[8]So the Israelites allotted to the Levites these towns and their pasturelands, as the LORD had commanded through Moses.

[a]8 *Jordan of Jericho* was possibly an ancient name for the Jordan River.

20:3 [a]Lev 4:2 [b]Nu 35:12
20:4 [c]Ru 4:1; Jer 38:7 [d]Jos 7:6
20:6 [e]Nu 35:12
20:7 [f]Jos 21:32; 1Ch 6:76 [g]Ge 12:6 [h]Jos 10:36; 21:11 [i]Lk 1:39
20:8 [j]Jos 21:36; 1Ch 6:78 [k]Jos 12:2
20:9 [l]Ex 21:13; Nu 35:15
21:1 [m]Jos 14:1
21:2 [n]Jos 18:1 [o]Nu 35:2-3
21:4 [p]ver 19
21:5 [q]ver 26
21:6 [r]Ge 30:18
21:7 [s]Ex 6:16 [t]Jos 19:10

9 From the tribes of Judah and Simeon they allotted the following
towns by name 10 (these towns were assigned to the descendants
of Aaron who were from the Kohathite clans of the Levites,
because the first lot fell to them):

11 They gave them Kiriath Arba (that is, Hebron[a]), with its
surrounding pastureland, in the hill country of Judah. (Arba
was the forefather of Anak.) 12 But the fields and villages
around the city they had given to Caleb son of Jephunneh as
his possession.

13 So to the descendants of Aaron the priest they gave Hebron (a city of refuge for one accused of murder), Libnah,[b]
14 Jattir,[c] Eshtemoa,[d] 15 Holon,[e] Debir, 16 Ain, Juttah[f] and Beth
Shemesh,[g] together with their pasturelands—nine towns from
these two tribes.

17 And from the tribe of Benjamin they gave them Gibeon,
Geba,[h] 18 Anathoth and Almon, together with their pasturelands—four towns.

19 All the towns for the priests, the descendants of Aaron, were
thirteen, together with their pasturelands.

20 The rest of the Kohathite clans of the Levites were allotted
towns from the tribe of Ephraim:

21 In the hill country of Ephraim they were given Shechem[i]
(a city of refuge for one accused of murder) and Gezer,
22 Kibzaim and Beth Horon,[j] together with their pasturelands—four towns.[k]

23 Also from the tribe of Dan they received Eltekeh, Gibbethon, 24 Aijalon and Gath Rimmon,[l] together with their
pasturelands—four towns.

25 From half the tribe of Manasseh they received Taanach and
Gath Rimmon, together with their pasturelands—two towns.

26 All these ten towns and their pasturelands were given to the
rest of the Kohathite clans.

27 The Levite clans of the Gershonites were given:
from the half-tribe of Manasseh,
Golan in Bashan[m] (a city of refuge for one accused of murder[n]) and Be Eshtarah, together with their pasturelands—
two towns;
28 from the tribe of Issachar,[o]
Kishion, Daberath, 29 Jarmuth and En Gannim, together
with their pasturelands—four towns;
30 from the tribe of Asher,[p]
Mishal, Abdon, 31 Helkath and Rehob, together with their
pasturelands—four towns;
32 from the tribe of Naphtali,

21:11 [a] Jos 15:13; 1Ch 6:55
21:13 [b] Jos 15:42; 1Ch 6:57
21:14 [c] Jos 15:48 [d] Jos 15:50
21:15 [e] Jos 15:51
21:16 [f] Jos 15:55 [g] Jos 15:10
21:17 [h] Jos 18:24
21:21 [i] Jos 17:7; 20:7
21:22 [j] Jos 10:10 [k] 1Sa 1:1
21:24 [l] Jos 19:45
21:27 [m] Jos 12:5 [n] Nu 35:6
21:28 [o] Ge 30:18
21:30 [p] Jos 17:7

Kedesh[a] in Galilee (a city of refuge for one accused of
murder[b]), Hammoth Dor and Kartan, together with their
pasturelands—three towns.
33 All the towns of the Gershonite[c] clans were thirteen, together
with their pasturelands.

34 The Merarite clans (the rest of the Levites) were given:
from the tribe of Zebulun,[d]
Jokneam, Kartah, 35 Dimnah and Nahalal, together with their
pasturelands—four towns;
36 from the tribe of Reuben,
Bezer,[e] Jahaz, 37 Kedemoth and Mephaath, together with their
pasturelands—four towns;
38 from the tribe of Gad,
Ramoth[f] in Gilead (a city of refuge for one accused of murder), Mahanaim,[g] 39 Heshbon and Jazer, together with their
pasturelands—four towns in all.
40 All the towns allotted to the Merarite clans, who were the rest of
the Levites, were twelve.
41 The towns of the Levites in the territory held by the Israelites
were forty-eight in all, together with their pasturelands.[h] 42 Each of
these towns had pasturelands surrounding it; this was true for all
these towns.

43 So the LORD gave Israel all the land he had sworn to give their
forefathers,[i] and they took possession[j] of it and settled there.[k]
44 The LORD gave them rest[l] on every side, just as he had sworn to
their forefathers. Not one of their enemies[m] withstood them; the
LORD handed all their enemies[n] over to them.[o] 45 Not one of all the
LORD's good promises[p] to the house of Israel failed; every one was
fulfilled.

Chapter 22 Theme ______________________

22 Then Joshua summoned the Reubenites, the Gadites and
the half-tribe of Manasseh 2 and said to them, "You have
done all that Moses the servant of the LORD commanded,[q] and
you have obeyed me in everything I commanded. 3 For a long
time now—to this very day—you have not deserted your brothers but have carried out the mission the LORD your God gave
you. 4 Now that the LORD your God has given your brothers rest
as he promised, return to your homes[r] in the land that Moses
the servant of the LORD gave you on the other side of the Jordan.[s]
5 But be very careful to keep the commandment[t] and the law that
Moses the servant of the LORD gave you: to love the LORD your
God, to walk in all his ways, to obey his commands,[u] to hold fast
to him and to serve him with all your heart and all your soul.[v]"

21:32 [a] Jos 12:22 [b] Nu 35:6; Jos 20:7
21:33 [c] ver 6
21:34 [d] Jos 19:10; 1Ch 6:77
21:36 [e] Jos 20:8
21:38 [f] Dt 4:43 [g] Ge 32:2
21:41 [h] Nu 35:7
21:43 [i] Dt 34:4 [j] Dt 11:31 [k] Dt 17:14
21:44 [l] Ex 33:14; Jos 1:13 [m] Dt 6:19 [n] Ex 23:31 [o] Dt 7:24; 21:10
21:45 [p] Jos 23:14; Ne 9:8
22:2 [q] Nu 32:25
22:4 [r] Nu 32:22; Dt 3:20 [s] Nu 32:18; Jos 1:13-15
22:5 [t] Isa 43:22 [u] Dt 5:29 [v] Dt 6:6,17

6 Then Joshua blessed[a] them and sent them away, and they went to their homes. 7 (To the half-tribe of Manasseh Moses had given land in Bashan,[b] and to the other half of the tribe Joshua gave land on the west side[c] of the Jordan with their brothers.) When Joshua sent them home, he blessed them, 8 saying, "Return to your homes with your great wealth—with large herds of livestock,[d] with silver, gold, bronze and iron, and a great quantity of clothing—and divide[e] with your brothers the plunder[f] from your enemies."

9 So the Reubenites, the Gadites and the half-tribe of Manasseh left the Israelites at Shiloh in Canaan to return to Gilead,[g] their own land, which they had acquired in accordance with the command of the LORD through Moses.

10 When they came to Geliloth near the Jordan in the land of Canaan, the Reubenites, the Gadites and the half-tribe of Manasseh built an imposing altar there by the Jordan. 11 And when the Israelites heard that they had built the altar on the border of Canaan at Geliloth near the Jordan on the Israelite side, 12 the whole assembly of Israel gathered at Shiloh[h] to go to war against them.

13 So the Israelites sent Phinehas[i] son of Eleazar,[j] the priest, to the land of Gilead—to Reuben, Gad and the half-tribe of Manasseh. 14 With him they sent ten of the chief men, one for each of the tribes of Israel, each the head of a family division among the Israelite clans.[k]

15 When they went to Gilead—to Reuben, Gad and the half-tribe of Manasseh—they said to them: 16 "The whole assembly of the LORD says: 'How could you break faith[l] with the God of Israel like this? How could you turn away from the LORD and build yourselves an altar in rebellion[m] against him now? 17 Was not the sin of Peor[n] enough for us? Up to this very day we have not cleansed ourselves from that sin, even though a plague fell on the community of the LORD! 18 And are you now turning away from the LORD?

"'If you rebel against the LORD today, tomorrow he will be angry with the whole community[o] of Israel. 19 If the land you possess is defiled, come over to the LORD's land, where the LORD's tabernacle stands, and share the land with us. But do not rebel against the LORD or against us by building an altar for yourselves, other than the altar of the LORD our God. 20 When Achan son of Zerah acted unfaithfully regarding the devoted things,[a][p] did not wrath[q] come upon the whole community of Israel? He was not the only one who died for his sin.'"[r]

22:6 [a] Ex 39:43
22:7 [b] Nu 32:33; Jos 12:5 [c] Jos 17:2,5
22:8 [d] Dt 20:14 [e] Nu 31:27 [f] Ge 49:27; 1Sa 30:16; Isa 9:3
22:9 [g] Nu 32:26,29
22:12 [h] Jos 18:1
22:13 [i] Nu 25:7 [j] Nu 3:32; Jos 24:33
22:14 [k] Nu 1:4
22:16 [l] Dt 13:14 [m] Dt 12:13-14
22:17 [n] Nu 25:1-9
22:18 [o] Lev 10:6; Nu 16:22
22:20 [p] Jos 7:1 [q] Ps 7:11 [r] Jos 7:5

a *20* The Hebrew term refers to the irrevocable giving over of things or persons to the LORD, often by totally destroying them.

21 Then Reuben, Gad and the half-tribe of Manasseh replied to the heads of the clans of Israel: 22 "The Mighty One, God, the LORD! The Mighty One, God,[a] the LORD![b] He knows![c] And let Israel know! If this has been in rebellion or disobedience to the LORD, do not spare us this day. 23 If we have built our own altar to turn away from the LORD and to offer burnt offerings and grain offerings,[d] or to sacrifice fellowship offerings[a] on it, may the LORD himself call us to account.[e]

24 "No! We did it for fear that some day your descendants might say to ours, 'What do you have to do with the LORD, the God of Israel? 25 The LORD has made the Jordan a boundary between us and you—you Reubenites and Gadites! You have no share in the LORD.' So your descendants might cause ours to stop fearing the LORD.

26 "That is why we said, 'Let us get ready and build an altar—but not for burnt offerings or sacrifices.' 27 On the contrary, it is to be a witness[f] between us and you and the generations that follow, that we will worship the LORD at his sanctuary with our burnt offerings, sacrifices and fellowship offerings.[g] Then in the future your descendants will not be able to say to ours, 'You have no share in the LORD.'

28 "And we said, 'If they ever say this to us, or to our descendants, we will answer: Look at the replica of the LORD's altar, which our fathers built, not for burnt offerings and sacrifices, but as a witness between us and you.'

29 "Far be it from us to rebel[h] against the LORD and turn away from him today by building an altar for burnt offerings, grain offerings and sacrifices, other than the altar of the LORD our God that stands before his tabernacle.[i]"

30 When Phinehas the priest and the leaders of the community—the heads of the clans of the Israelites—heard what Reuben, Gad and Manasseh had to say, they were pleased. 31 And Phinehas son of Eleazar, the priest, said to Reuben, Gad and Manasseh, "Today we know that the LORD is with us,[j] because you have not acted unfaithfully toward the LORD in this matter. Now you have rescued the Israelites from the LORD's hand."

32 Then Phinehas son of Eleazar, the priest, and the leaders returned to Canaan from their meeting with the Reubenites and Gadites in Gilead and reported to the Israelites. 33 They were glad to hear the report and praised God.[k] And they talked no more about going to war against them to devastate the country where the Reubenites and the Gadites lived.

34 And the Reubenites and the Gadites gave the altar this name: A Witness[l] Between Us that the LORD is God.

a *23* Traditionally *peace offerings*; also in verse 27

22:22 [a] Dt 10:17 [b] Ps 50:1 [c] 1Ki 8:39; Job 10:7; Ps 44:21; Jer 17:10

22:23 [d] Jer 41:5 [e] Dt 12:11; 18:19; 1Sa 20:16

22:27 [f] Ge 21:30; Jos 24:27 [g] Dt 12:6

22:29 [h] Jos 24:16 [i] Dt 12:13-14

22:31 [j] Lev 26:11-12; 2Ch 15:2

22:33 [k] 1Ch 29:20; Da 2:19; Lk 2:28

22:34 [l] Ge 21:30

Chapter 23 Theme ______________________________

23 After a long time had passed and the LORD had given Israel rest[a] from all their enemies around them, Joshua, by then old and well advanced in years,[b] 2summoned all Israel—their elders,[c] leaders, judges and officials[d]—and said to them: "I am old and well advanced in years. 3You yourselves have seen everything the LORD your God has done to all these nations for your sake; it was the LORD your God who fought for you.[e] 4Remember how I have allotted[f] as an inheritance for your tribes all the land of the nations that remain—the nations I conquered—between the Jordan and the Great Sea[a][g] in the west. 5The LORD your God himself will drive them out of your way. He will push them out before you, and you will take possession of their land, as the LORD your God promised you.[h]

6"Be very strong; be careful to obey all that is written in the Book of the Law of Moses, without turning aside to the right or to the left.[i] 7Do not associate with these nations that remain among you; do not invoke the names of their gods or swear[j] by them. You must not serve them or bow down[k] to them. 8But you are to hold fast to the LORD[l] your God, as you have until now.

9"The LORD has driven out before you great and powerful nations;[m] to this day no one has been able to withstand you.[n] 10One of you routs a thousand,[o] because the LORD your God fights for you,[p] just as he promised. 11So be very careful to love the LORD[q] your God.

12"But if you turn away and ally yourselves with the survivors of these nations that remain among you and if you intermarry with them[r] and associate with them,[s] 13then you may be sure that the LORD your God will no longer drive out these nations before you. Instead, they will become snares[t] and traps for you, whips on your backs and thorns in your eyes,[u] until you perish from this good land, which the LORD your God has given you.

14"Now I am about to go the way of all the earth.[v] You know with all your heart and soul that not one of all the good promises the LORD your God gave you has failed. Every promise has been fulfilled; not one has failed.[w] 15But just as every good promise of the LORD your God has come true, so the LORD will bring on you all the evil he has threatened, until he has destroyed you from this good land he has given you.[x] 16If you violate the covenant of the LORD your God, which he commanded you, and go and serve other gods and bow down to them, the LORD's anger will burn against you, and you will quickly perish from the good land he has given you.[y]"

23:1 [a]Dt 12:9; Jos 21:44 [b]Jos 13:1
23:2 [c]Jos 7:6 [d]Jos 24:1
23:3 [e]Ex 14:14
23:4 [f]Jos 19:51 [g]Nu 34:6
23:5 [h]Ex 23:30; Nu 33:53
23:6 [i]Dt 5:32; Jos 1:7
23:7 [j]Ex 23:13; Ps 16:4; Jer 5:7 [k]Ex 20:5
23:8 [l]Dt 10:20
23:9 [m]Dt 11:23 [n]Dt 7:24
23:10 [o]Lev 26:8 [p]Ex 14:14; Dt 3:22
23:11 [q]Jos 22:5
23:12 [r]Dt 7:3 [s]Ex 34:16; Ps 106:34-35
23:13 [t]Ex 23:33 [u]Nu 33:55
23:14 [v]1Ki 2:2 [w]Jos 21:45
23:15 [x]Lev 26:17; Dt 28:15
23:16 [y]Dt 4:25-26

[a]4 That is, the Mediterranean

Chapter 24 Theme ______________________

24 Then Joshua assembled all the tribes of Israel at Shechem.
He summoned the elders, leaders, judges and officials of
Israel,[a] and they presented themselves before God.
[2]Joshua said to all the people, "This is what the LORD, the God
of Israel, says: 'Long ago your forefathers, including Terah the
father of Abraham and Nahor, lived beyond the River[a] and worshiped other gods.[b] [3]But I took your father Abraham from the
land beyond the River and led him throughout Canaan[c] and
gave him many descendants.[d] I gave him Isaac,[e] [4]and to Isaac I
gave Jacob and Esau.[f] I assigned the hill country of Seir[g] to Esau,
but Jacob and his sons went down to Egypt.[h]
[5]"'Then I sent Moses and Aaron,[i] and I afflicted the Egyptians
by what I did there, and I brought you out. [6]When I brought
your fathers out of Egypt, you came to the sea, and the Egyptians pursued them with chariots and horsemen[b][j] as far as the
Red Sea.[c] [7]But they cried to the LORD for help, and he put darkness[k] between you and the Egyptians; he brought the sea over
them and covered them.[l] You saw with your own eyes what I did
to the Egyptians. Then you lived in the desert for a long time.[m]
[8]"'I brought you to the land of the Amorites who lived east of
the Jordan. They fought against you, but I gave them into your
hands. I destroyed them from before you, and you took possession of their land.[n] [9]When Balak son of Zippor,[o] the king of
Moab, prepared to fight against Israel, he sent for Balaam son of
Beor to put a curse on you.[p] [10]But I would not listen to Balaam,
so he blessed you[q] again and again, and I delivered you out of
his hand.
[11]"'Then you crossed the Jordan[r] and came to Jericho.[s] The
citizens of Jericho fought against you, as did also the Amorites,
Perizzites, Canaanites, Hittites, Girgashites, Hivites and Jebusites, but I gave them into your hands.[t] [12]I sent the hornet[u]
ahead of you, which drove them out before you—also the two
Amorite kings. You did not do it with your own sword and bow.
[13]So I gave you a land on which you did not toil and cities you
did not build; and you live in them and eat from vineyards and
olive groves that you did not plant.'[v]
[14]"Now fear the LORD and serve him with all faithfulness.[w]
Throw away the gods[x] your forefathers worshiped beyond the
River and in Egypt,[y] and serve the LORD. [15]But if serving the
LORD seems undesirable to you, then choose for yourselves this
day whom you will serve, whether the gods your forefathers served

[a]2 That is, the Euphrates; also in verses 3, 14 and 15 [b]6 Or *charioteers* [c]6 Hebrew *Yam Suph*; that is, Sea of Reeds

24:1 [a]Jos 23:2
24:2 [b]Ge 11:32
24:3 [c]Ge 12:1 [d]Ge 15:5 [e]Ge 21:3
24:4 [f]Ge 25:26 [g]Dt 2:5 [h]Ge 46:5-6
24:5 [i]Ex 3:10
24:6 [j]Ex 14:9
24:7 [k]Ex 14:20 [l]Ex 14:28 [m]Dt 1:46
24:8 [n]Nu 21:31
24:9 [o]Nu 22:2 [p]Nu 22:6
24:10 [q]Nu 23:11; Dt 23:5
24:11 [r]Jos 3:16-17 [s]Jos 6:1 [t]Ex 23:23; Dt 7:1
24:12 [u]Ex 23:28; Dt 7:20; Ps 44:3,6-7
24:13 [v]Dt 6:10-11
24:14 [w]Dt 10:12; 18:13; 1Sa 12:24; 2Co 1:12 [x]ver 23 [y]Eze 23:3

beyond the River, or the gods of the Amorites,[a] in whose land
you are living. But as for me and my household, we will serve
the LORD."[b]

16 Then the people answered, "Far be it from us to forsake the
LORD to serve other gods! 17 It was the LORD our God himself who
brought us and our fathers up out of Egypt, from that land of
slavery, and performed those great signs before our eyes. He
protected us on our entire journey and among all the nations
through which we traveled. 18 And the LORD drove out before us
all the nations, including the Amorites, who lived in the land.
We too will serve the LORD, because he is our God."

19 Joshua said to the people, "You are not able to serve the
LORD. He is a holy God;[c] he is a jealous God.[d] He will not forgive
your rebellion[e] and your sins. 20 If you forsake the LORD[f] and
serve foreign gods, he will turn[g] and bring disaster on you and
make an end of you,[h] after he has been good to you."

21 But the people said to Joshua, "No! We will serve the LORD."

22 Then Joshua said, "You are witnesses against yourselves that
you have chosen[i] to serve the LORD."

"Yes, we are witnesses," they replied.

23 "Now then," said Joshua, "throw away the foreign gods[j] that are
among you and yield your hearts[k] to the LORD, the God of Israel."

24 And the people said to Joshua, "We will serve the LORD our
God and obey him."[l]

25 On that day Joshua made a covenant[m] for the people, and
there at Shechem he drew up for them decrees and laws.[n] 26 And
Joshua recorded these things in the Book of the Law of God.[o]
Then he took a large stone[p] and set it up there under the oak
near the holy place of the LORD.

27 "See!" he said to all the people. "This stone will be a witness[q]
against us. It has heard all the words the LORD has said to us. It
will be a witness against you if you are untrue to your God."

28 Then Joshua sent the people away, each to his own inheritance.

29 After these things, Joshua son of Nun, the servant of the
LORD, died at the age of a hundred and ten.[r] 30 And they buried
him in the land of his inheritance, at Timnath Serah[a][s] in the hill
country of Ephraim, north of Mount Gaash.

31 Israel served the LORD throughout the lifetime of Joshua and
of the elders[t] who outlived him and who had experienced everything the LORD had done for Israel.

32 And Joseph's bones, which the Israelites had brought up from
Egypt,[u] were buried at Shechem in the tract of land[v] that Jacob
bought for a hundred pieces of silver[b] from the sons of Hamor,

24:15 [a] Jdg 6:10; Ru 1:15 [b] Ru 1:16; 1Ki 18:21
24:19 [c] Lev 19:2; 20:26 [d] Ex 20:5 [e] Ex 23:21
24:20 [f] 1Ch 28:9,20 [g] Ac 7:42 [h] Jos 23:15
24:22 [i] Ps119:30,173
24:23 [j] ver 14 [k] 1Ki 8:58; Ps 119:36; 141:4
24:24 [l] Ex 19:8; 24:3,7; Dt 5:27
24:25 [m] Ex 24:8 [n] Ex 15:25
24:26 [o] Dt 31:24 [p] Ge 28:18
24:27 [q] Jos 22:27
24:29 [r] Jdg 2:8
24:30 [s] Jos 19:50
24:31 [t] Jdg 2:7
24:32 [u] Ge 50:25; Ex 13:19 [v] Ge 33:19; Jn 4:5; Ac 7:16

[a] *30* Also known as *Timnath Heres* (see Judges 2:9) [b] *32* Hebrew *hundred kesitahs*; a kesitah was a unit of money of unknown weight and value.

the father of Shechem. This became the inheritance of Joseph's
descendants.
33And Eleazar son of Aaron[a] died and was buried at Gibeah,
which had been allotted to his son Phinehas[b] in the hill country
of Ephraim.

24:33
[a] Jos 22:13
[b] Ex 6:25

Theme of Joshua:

thor:

te:

rpose:

y Words:

SEGMENT DIVISIONS		CHAPTER THEMES
		1
		2
		3
		4
		5
		6
		7
		8
		9
		10
		11
		12
		13
		14
		15
		16
		17
		18
		19
		20
		21
		22
		23
		24

JUDGES

During Joshua's leadership Israel finally entered the land promised to Abraham. There were giants in the land, but none who were greater than God. The commander of the Lord's army was able to subdue all Israel's enemies. In one battle the sun even stood still and the moon stopped until the people of Israel avenged themselves on their enemies.

Then there arose a generation which did not know war, nor did they know the Lord or the work he had done for Israel. Israel went from victory to defeat and plunged into more than 300 years of darkness. These were the days of the judges, days from which we can learn valuable lessons.

Things to Do

Chapters 1, 2

1. Because the book of Judges is not strictly chronological, it is helpful to understand the setting of the book. Read chapters 1 and 2. Then go to the end of Judges and read Judges 17:6; 18:1; 19:1; 21:25 and look for the key repeated phrase. Mark this phrase in a distinctive way and record it on the JUDGES AT A GLANCE chart on page 433 under "Key Words."

2. Now read chapters 1 and 2 again and do the following:

   a. Mark in the text the key words and phrases listed on JUDGES AT A GLANCE. Put these on an index card that you can use as a bookmark while you study Judges.

   b. Chapter 1 also contains an important key phrase which is not on this list because it is not used after this chapter. Look for that phrase and mark its repeated use in a distinctive way. Then look up Exodus 23:20-33, Deuteronomy 7:1-11, 16, and Joshua 23:5-13. Record these references in the margin of chapter 1 for cross-references.

   c. As you read each chapter, question the text with the five W's and an H: Who? What? When? Where? Why? and How? You will not always find the answer to every question. As you read make sure you note who does what and why. Watch for where events take place and when. Always ask how something was accomplished, happened, or is to be done.

   d. Write in the chapter margin the names of key persons or groups of people (such as "the sons of Israel" and "judges"). Then list everything you learn about them from that chapter. Do this with the references to the Lord also.

3. When you finish your observations of chapter 2, review all you have learned, especially from verses 11 through 23. Notice the cycle of events. Make sure you record this in the margin; it sets the pattern for chapters 3 through 16.

4. Discern the themes of these chapters and record them on JUDGES AT A GLANCE and in the text on the line next to the chapter number.

Chapters 3-16

1. Study chapters 3 through 16 the same way you did chapters 1 and 2: Mark key words, ask the five W's and an H, list your insights in the margin, and record the theme of each chapter in the appropriate places.

2. As you read Judges 3 through 16, note the names of the judges and record them in the chapter margin where they appear. List everything you learn about them from the text. Then record this information on the chart THE JUDGES OF ISRAEL on page 432. To understand when these judges ruled and what their relationship was to one another, carefully study the historical chart before Judges chapter 1.

3. On page 394 is a map showing many locations mentioned in Judges. As you study each judge, note where the judge is from and write his or her name on the map next to the proper location.

Chapters 17-21

1. There is no indication that chapters 17 through 21 chronologically follow chapters 3 through 16. Rather, they give an overview of the moral setting of the time. Examine each chapter carefully as you have done the other chapters of Judges and note your insights. Watch the progression of events.

2. As you read these chapters, keep in mind the key phrase you marked when you began your study. Note how the result of this phrase is manifested in the way the people live.

3. Record the chapter themes as you have done previously on JUDGES AT A GLANCE. Also record the main theme of each segment division and any other segment division you may see. Finally, record the main theme of Judges.

Things to Think About

1. What have you learned from Judges about carefully listening to and obeying the commands of the Lord? What have you seen about the consequences of doing as you see fit with your life? What parallels do you see between the sins committed in Judges 17 through 21 and today? What does it tell you?

2. Why wasn't the cycle of sin broken in the days of the judges? Are you caught in a cycle of sin in your own life? What will it take to break it?

3. What have you learned by studying the lives of the judges? Carefully review your chart on the judges on page 432 and meditate on the lessons you can apply to your own life.

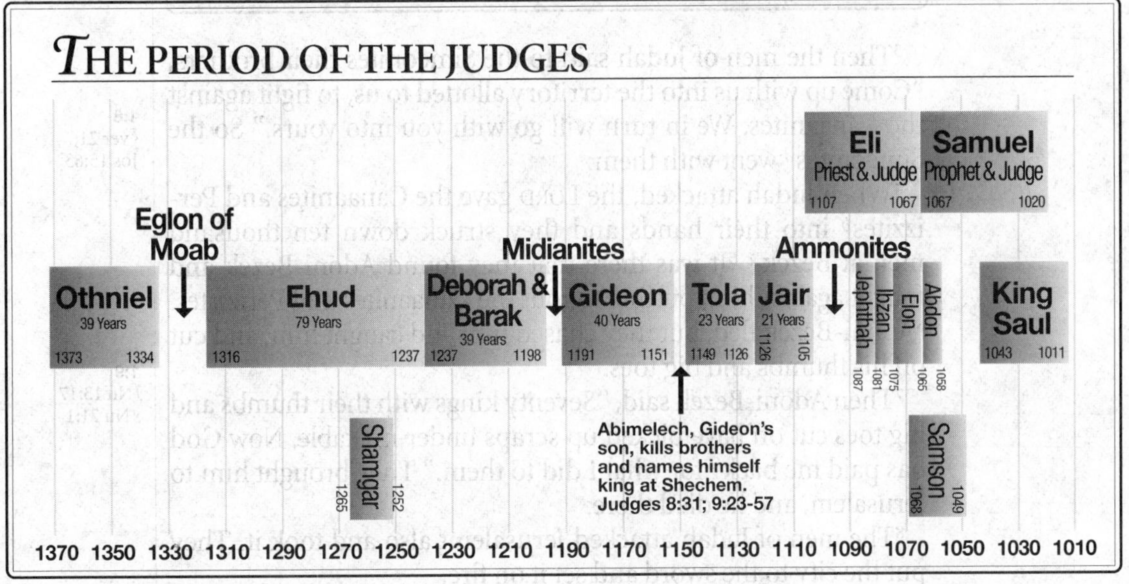

Chapter 1 Theme ________________

1:1 [a]Jos 24:29 [b]Nu 27:21 [c]ver 27; Jdg 3:1-6
1:2 [d]Ge 49:8 [e]ver 4; Jdg 3:28

1 After the death[a] of Joshua, the Israelites asked the LORD, "Who
will be the first[b] to go up and fight for us against the Canaanites?[c]"
2The LORD answered, "Judah[d] is to go; I have given the land into
their hands.[e]"

Israelite Cities and Settlements in the Time of the Judges

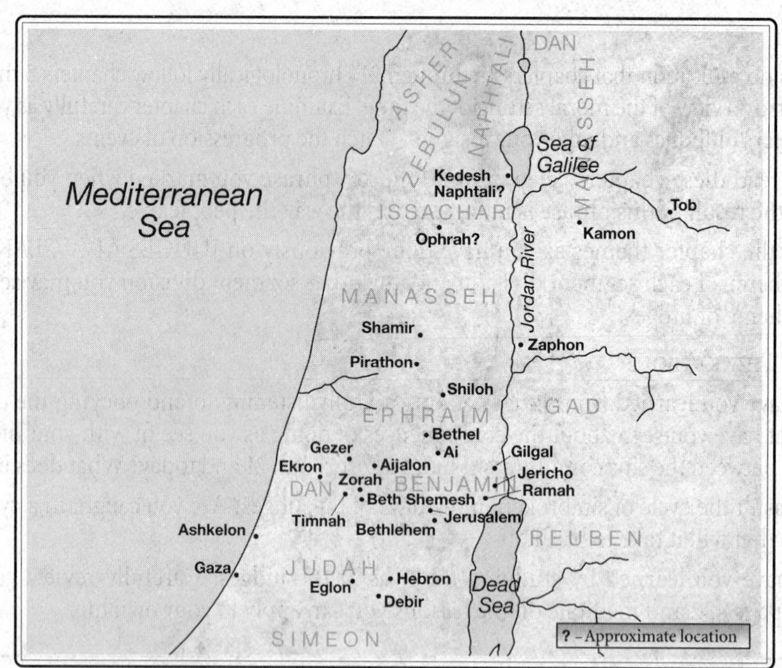

3 Then the men of Judah said to the Simeonites their brothers,
"Come up with us into the territory allotted to us, to fight against
the Canaanites. We in turn will go with you into yours." So the
Simeonites[a] went with them.
4 When Judah attacked, the LORD gave the Canaanites and Perizzites[b] into their hands and they struck down ten thousand
men at Bezek.[c] 5 It was there that they found Adoni-Bezek and
fought against him, putting to rout the Canaanites and Perizzites.
6 Adoni-Bezek fled, but they chased him and caught him, and cut
off his thumbs and big toes.
7 Then Adoni-Bezek said, "Seventy kings with their thumbs and
big toes cut off have picked up scraps under my table. Now God
has paid me back[d] for what I did to them." They brought him to
Jerusalem, and he died there.
8 The men of Judah attacked Jerusalem[e] also and took it. They
put the city to the sword and set it on fire.
9 After that, the men of Judah went down to fight against the
Canaanites living in the hill country,[f] the Negev[g] and the western
foothills. 10 They advanced against the Canaanites living in Hebron[h]
(formerly called Kiriath Arba[i]) and defeated Sheshai, Ahiman
and Talmai.[j]
11 From there they advanced against the people living in Debir[k]
(formerly called Kiriath Sepher). 12 And Caleb said, "I will give my
daughter Acsah in marriage to the man who attacks and captures
Kiriath Sepher." 13 Othniel son of Kenaz, Caleb's younger brother,
took it; so Caleb gave his daughter Acsah to him in marriage.

1:3 [a] ver 17
1:4 [b] Ge 13:7; Jos 3:10 [c] 1Sa 11:8
1:7 [d] Lev 24:19
1:8 [e] ver 21; Jos 15:63
1:9 [f] Nu 13:17 [g] Nu 21:1
1:10 [h] Ge 13:18 [i] Ge 35:27 [j] Jos 15:14
1:11 [k] Jos 15:15

14 One day when she came to Othniel, she urged him[a] to ask her
father for a field. When she got off her donkey, Caleb asked her,
"What can I do for you?"
15 She replied, "Do me a special favor. Since you have given me
land in the Negev, give me also springs of water." Then Caleb
gave her the upper and lower springs.
16 The descendants of Moses' father-in-law,[a] the Kenite,[b] went
up from the City of Palms[b][c] with the men of Judah to live among
the people of the Desert of Judah in the Negev near Arad.[d]
17 Then the men of Judah went with the Simeonites[e] their
brothers and attacked the Canaanites living in Zephath, and they
totally destroyed[c] the city. Therefore it was called Hormah.[d][f]
18 The men of Judah also took[e] Gaza,[g] Ashkelon and Ekron—each
city with its territory.
19 The LORD was with[h] the men of Judah. They took possession
of the hill country, but they were unable to drive the people from
the plains, because they had iron chariots.[i] 20 As Moses had
promised, Hebron[j] was given to Caleb, who drove from it the
three sons of Anak.[k] 21 The Benjamites, however, failed[l] to dislodge the Jebusites, who were living in Jerusalem;[m] to this day
the Jebusites live there with the Benjamites.
22 Now the house of Joseph attacked Bethel, and the LORD was
with them. 23 When they sent men to spy out Bethel (formerly
called Luz),[n] 24 the spies saw a man coming out of the city and
they said to him, "Show us how to get into the city and we will
see that you are treated well.[o]" 25 So he showed them, and they
put the city to the sword but spared[p] the man and his whole
family. 26 He then went to the land of the Hittites, where he built
a city and called it Luz, which is its name to this day.
27 But Manasseh did not drive out the people of Beth Shan or
Taanach or Dor or Ibleam[q] or Megiddo and their surrounding
settlements, for the Canaanites[r] were determined to live in that
land. 28 When Israel became strong, they pressed the Canaanites
into forced labor but never drove them out completely. 29 Nor did
Ephraim drive out the Canaanites living in Gezer,[s] but the Canaanites continued to live there among them.[t] 30 Neither did Zebulun
drive out the Canaanites living in Kitron or Nahalol, who remained
among them; but they did subject them to forced labor. 31 Nor
did Asher drive out those living in Acco or Sidon or Ahlab or Aczib[u] or Helbah or Aphek or Rehob, 32 and because of this the people of Asher lived among the Canaanite inhabitants of the land.

1:16 [a] Nu 10:29 [b] Ge 15:19; Jdg 4:11 [c] Dt 34:3; Jdg 3:13 [d] Nu 21:1
1:17 [e] ver 3 [f] Nu 21:3
1:18 [g] Jos 11:22
1:19 [h] ver 2 [i] Jos 17:16
1:20 [j] Jos 14:9; 15:13-14 [k] ver 10; Jos 14:13
1:21 [l] Jos 15:63 [m] ver 8
1:23 [n] Ge 28:19
1:24 [o] Jos 2:12,14
1:25 [p] Jos 6:25
1:27 [q] Jos 17:11 [r] ver 1
1:29 [s] 1Ki 9:16 [t] Jos 16:10
1:31 [u] Jdg 10:6

[a] *14* Hebrew; Septuagint and Vulgate *Othniel, he urged her* [b] *16* That is, Jericho
[c] *17* The Hebrew term refers to the irrevocable giving over of things or persons to the LORD, often by totally destroying them. [d] *17* *Hormah* means *destruction.* [e] *18* Hebrew; Septuagint *Judah did not take*

33Neither did Naphtali drive out those living in Beth Shemesh or
Beth Anath[a]; but the Naphtalites too lived among the Canaanite
inhabitants of the land, and those living in Beth Shemesh and
Beth Anath became forced laborers for them. 34The Amorites[b]
confined the Danites to the hill country, not allowing them to
come down into the plain. 35And the Amorites were determined
also to hold out in Mount Heres, Aijalon[c] and Shaalbim, but
when the power of the house of Joseph increased, they too were
pressed into forced labor. 36The boundary of the Amorites was
from Scorpion[a] Pass[d] to Sela and beyond.

Chapter 2 Theme

2 The angel of the LORD[e] went up from Gilgal to Bokim[f] and
said, "I brought you up out of Egypt[g] and led you into the
land that I swore to give to your forefathers.[h] I said, 'I will never
break my covenant with you,[i] 2and you shall not make a covenant
with the people of this land,[j] but you shall break down their
altars.[k]' Yet you have disobeyed me. Why have you done this?
3Now therefore I tell you that I will not drive them out before
you;[l] they will be ⌊thorns⌋[m] in your sides and their gods will be a
snare[n] to you."

4When the angel of the LORD had spoken these things to all the
Israelites, the people wept aloud, 5and they called that place
Bokim.[b] There they offered sacrifices to the LORD.

6After Joshua had dismissed the Israelites, they went to take
possession of the land, each to his own inheritance. 7The people
served the LORD throughout the lifetime of Joshua and of the
elders who outlived him and who had seen all the great things
the LORD had done for Israel.

8Joshua son of Nun, the servant of the LORD, died at the age of a
hundred and ten. 9And they buried him in the land of his inheritance, at Timnath Heres[c][o] in the hill country of Ephraim, north
of Mount Gaash.

10After that whole generation had been gathered to their fathers,
another generation grew up, who knew neither the LORD nor
what he had done for Israel.[p] 11Then the Israelites did evil in the
eyes of the LORD[q] and served the Baals.[r] 12They forsook the LORD,
the God of their fathers, who had brought them out of Egypt.
They followed and worshiped various gods[s] of the peoples
around them.[t] They provoked the LORD to anger 13because they
forsook him and served Baal and the Ashtoreths.[u] 14In his anger[v]
against Israel the LORD handed them over[w] to raiders who plundered them. He sold them[x] to their enemies all around, whom

INSIGHT

Baal, which meant "lord, owner, possessor, or husband," was the Canaanite god of fertility. ***Baal*** was part of several compound names for locations where Canaanite deities were worshiped, such as Baal Peor.

Ashtoreth is the Canaanite goddess of fertility, love, and war. According to Greek mythology she was the wife of Baal.

[a]36 Hebrew *Akrabbim* [b]5 *Bokim* means *weepers.* [c]9 Also known as *Timnath Serah* (see Joshua 19:50 and 24:30)

1:33 [a]Jos 19:38
1:34 [b]Ex 3:17
1:35 [c]Jos 19:42
1:36 [d]Jos 15:3
2:1 [e]Jdg 6:11 [f]ver 5 [g]Ex 20:2 [h]Ge 17:8 [i]Lev 26:42-44; Dt 7:9
2:2 [j]Ex 23:32; 34:12; Dt 7:2 [k]Ex 34:13
2:3 [l]Jos 23:13 [m]Nu 33:55 [n]Dt 7:16; Jdg 3:6; Ps 106:36
2:9 [o]Jos 19:50
2:10 [p]Ex 5:2; 1Sa 2:12; 1Ch 28:9; Gal 4:8
2:11 [q]Jdg 3:12; 4:1; 6:1; 10:6 [r]Jdg 3:7; 8:33
2:12 [s]Ps 106:36 [t]Dt 31:16; Jdg 10:6
2:13 [u]Jdg 10:6
2:14 [v]Dt 31:17 [w]Ps 106:41 [x]Dt 32:30; Jdg 3:8

2:14 [a]Dt 28:25 they were no longer able to resist.[a] 15Whenever Israel went out to
fight, the hand of the LORD was against them to defeat them, just
2:16 as he had sworn to them. They were in great distress.
[b]Ac 13:20 16Then the LORD raised up judges,[a][b] who saved[c] them out of the
[c]Ps 106:43 hands of these raiders. 17Yet they would not listen to their judges
but prostituted[d] themselves to other gods and worshiped them.
2:17 [d]Ex 34:15 Unlike their fathers, they quickly turned from the way in which
[e]ver 7 their fathers had walked, the way of obedience to the LORD's
commands.[e] 18Whenever the LORD raised up a judge for them, he
2:18 [f]Dt 32:36; was with the judge and saved them out of the hands of their ene-
Jos 1:5 mies as long as the judge lived; for the LORD had compassion[f] on
[g]Ps 106:44 them as they groaned[g] under those who oppressed and afflicted
them. 19But when the judge died, the people returned to ways
2:19 [h]Jdg 3:12 even more corrupt[h] than those of their fathers, following other
[i]Jdg 4:1; 8:33 gods and serving and worshiping them.[i] They refused to give up
their evil practices and stubborn ways.
2:20 20Therefore the LORD was very angry[j] with Israel and said,
[j]ver 14; "Because this nation has violated the covenant that I laid down
Jos 23:16 for their forefathers and has not listened to me, 21I will no longer
drive out[k] before them any of the nations Joshua left when he
2:21 [k]Jos 23:13 died. 22I will use them to test[l] Israel and see whether they will
keep the way of the LORD and walk in it as their forefathers did."
2:22 23The LORD had allowed those nations to remain; he did not drive
[l]Dt 8:2,16; Jdg 3:1,14 them out at once by giving them into the hands of Joshua.

Chapter 3 Theme ____________________

3:1 [m]Jdg 2:21-22 **3** These are the nations the LORD left to test[m] all those Israelites
who had not experienced any of the wars in Canaan 2(he
3:3 [n]Jos 13:3 did this only to teach warfare to the descendants of the Israelites
who had not had previous battle experience): 3the five[n] rulers of
3:4 the Philistines, all the Canaanites, the Sidonians, and the Hivites
[o]Dt 8:2; living in the Lebanon mountains from Mount Baal Hermon to
Jdg 2:22 Lebo[b] Hamath. 4They were left to test[o] the Israelites to see
whether they would obey the LORD's commands, which he had
3:5 [p]Ps 106:35 given their forefathers through Moses.
5The Israelites lived[p] among the Canaanites, Hittites, Amorites,
Perizzites, Hivites and Jebusites. 6They took their daughters in
3:6 [q]Ex 34:16; marriage and gave their own daughters to their sons, and served
Dt 7:3-4 their gods.[q]
7The Israelites did evil in the eyes of the LORD; they forgot the
3:7 [r]Dt 4:9 LORD[r] their God and served the Baals and the Asherahs.[s] 8The
[s]Ex 34:13; Jdg 2:11,13 anger of the LORD burned against Israel so that he sold[t] them
into the hands of Cushan-Rishathaim king of Aram Naharaim,[c]

3:8 [t]Jdg 2:14 [a]16 Or *leaders*; similarly in verses 17-19 [b]3 Or *to the entrance to* [c]8 That is, Northwest Mesopotamia

to whom the Israelites were subject for eight years. 9But when
they cried out[a] to the LORD, he raised up for them a deliverer,
Othniel[b] son of Kenaz, Caleb's younger brother, who saved
them. 10The Spirit of the LORD came upon him,[c] so that he
became Israel's judge[a] and went to war. The LORD gave Cushan-
Rishathaim king of Aram into the hands of Othniel, who overpowered him. 11So the land had peace for forty years, until Othniel
son of Kenaz died.

12Once again the Israelites did evil in the eyes of the LORD,[d] and
because they did this evil the LORD gave Eglon king of Moab[e]
power over Israel. 13Getting the Ammonites and Amalekites to
join him, Eglon came and attacked Israel, and they took possession of the City of Palms.[b][f] 14The Israelites were subject to Eglon
king of Moab for eighteen years.

15Again the Israelites cried out to the LORD, and he gave them a
deliverer[g]—Ehud, a left-handed man, the son of Gera the Benjamite. The Israelites sent him with tribute to Eglon king of
Moab. 16Now Ehud had made a double-edged sword about a foot
and a half[c] long, which he strapped to his right thigh under his
clothing. 17He presented the tribute to Eglon king of Moab, who
was a very fat man.[h] 18After Ehud had presented the tribute, he
sent on their way the men who had carried it. 19At the idols[d] near
Gilgal he himself turned back and said, "I have a secret message
for you, O king."

The king said, "Quiet!" And all his attendants left him.

20Ehud then approached him while he was sitting alone in the
upper room of his summer palace[e] and said, "I have a message
from God for you." As the king rose from his seat, 21Ehud
reached with his left hand, drew the sword from his right thigh
and plunged it into the king's belly. 22Even the handle sank in
after the blade, which came out his back. Ehud did not pull the
sword out, and the fat closed in over it. 23Then Ehud went out to
the porch[f]; he shut the doors of the upper room behind him and
locked them.

24After he had gone, the servants came and found the doors of
the upper room locked. They said, "He must be relieving himself[i]
in the inner room of the house." 25They waited to the point of
embarrassment,[j] but when he did not open the doors of the
room, they took a key and unlocked them. There they saw their
lord fallen to the floor, dead.

26While they waited, Ehud got away. He passed by the idols and
escaped to Seirah. 27When he arrived there, he blew a trumpet[k]

[a]*10* Or *leader* [b]*13* That is, Jericho [c]*16* Hebrew *a cubit* (about 0.5 meter) [d]*19* Or *the stone quarries*; also in verse 26 [e]*20* The meaning of the Hebrew for this phrase is uncertain. [f]*23* The meaning of the Hebrew for this word is uncertain.

3:9 [a] ver 15; Jdg 6:6,7; 10:10; Ps 106:44 [b] Jdg 1:13

3:10 [c] Nu 11:25,29; 24:2; Jdg 6:34; 11:29; 13:25; 14:6,19; 1Sa 11:6

3:12 [d] Jdg 2:11,14 [e] 1Sa 12:9

3:13 [f] Jdg 1:16

3:15 [g] ver 9; Ps 78:34; 107:13

3:17 [h] ver 12

3:24 [i] 1Sa 24:3

3:25 [j] 2Ki 2:17; 8:11

3:27 [k] Jdg 6:34; 1Sa 13:3

in the hill country of Ephraim, and the Israelites went down with
him from the hills, with him leading them.
28"Follow me," he ordered, "for the LORD has given Moab, your
enemy, into your hands.[a]" So they followed him down and, taking
possession of the fords of the Jordan[b] that led to Moab, they
allowed no one to cross over. 29At that time they struck down
about ten thousand Moabites, all vigorous and strong; not a man
escaped. 30That day Moab was made subject to Israel, and the
land had peace[c] for eighty years.
31After Ehud came Shamgar son of Anath,[d] who struck down
six hundred[e] Philistines with an oxgoad. He too saved Israel.

Chapter 4 Theme ______________________________

4 After Ehud died, the Israelites once again did evil[f] in the
eyes of the LORD. 2So the LORD sold them into the hands of
Jabin, a king of Canaan, who reigned in Hazor.[g] The commander
of his army was Sisera,[h] who lived in Harosheth Haggoyim.
3Because he had nine hundred iron chariots[i] and had cruelly oppressed[j] the Israelites for twenty years, they cried to the LORD
for help.
4Deborah, a prophetess, the wife of Lappidoth, was leading[a]
Israel at that time. 5She held court under the Palm of Deborah
between Ramah and Bethel[k] in the hill country of Ephraim, and
the Israelites came to her to have their disputes decided. 6She sent
for Barak son of Abinoam[l] from Kedesh in Naphtali and said to
him, "The LORD, the God of Israel, commands you: 'Go, take with
you ten thousand men of Naphtali and Zebulun and lead the way
to Mount Tabor. 7I will lure Sisera, the commander of Jabin's
army, with his chariots and his troops to the Kishon River[m] and
give him into your hands.'"
8Barak said to her, "If you go with me, I will go; but if you don't
go with me, I won't go."
9"Very well," Deborah said, "I will go with you. But because of
the way you are going about this,[b] the honor will not be yours, for
the LORD will hand Sisera over to a woman." So Deborah went
with Barak to Kedesh,[n] 10where he summoned[o] Zebulun and
Naphtali. Ten thousand men followed him, and Deborah also
went with him.
11Now Heber the Kenite had left the other Kenites,[p] the descendants of Hobab,[q] Moses' brother-in-law,[c] and pitched his tent by
the great tree in Zaanannim[r] near Kedesh.
12When they told Sisera that Barak son of Abinoam had gone
up to Mount Tabor, 13Sisera gathered together his nine hundred

3:28 [a]Jdg 7:9,15 [b]Jos 2:7; Jdg 7:24; 12:5
3:30 [c]ver 11
3:31 [d]Jdg 5:6 [e]Jos 23:10
4:1 [f]Jdg 2:19
4:2 [g]Jos 11:1 [h]ver 13,16; 1Sa 12:9; Ps 83:9
4:3 [i]Jdg 1:19 [j]Ps 106:42
4:5 [k]Ge 35:8
4:6 [l]Heb 11:32
4:7 [m]Ps 83:9
4:9 [n]ver 21; Jdg 2:14
4:10 [o]ver 14; Jdg 5:15,18
4:11 [p]Jdg 1:16 [q]Nu 10:29 [r]Jos 19:33

[a]4 Traditionally *judging* [b]9 Or *But on the expedition you are undertaking* [c]11 Or *father-in-law*

iron chariots[a] and all the men with him, from Harosheth Haggoyim to the Kishon River.

14Then Deborah said to Barak, "Go! This is the day the LORD has given Sisera into your hands. Has not the LORD gone ahead[b] of you?" So Barak went down Mount Tabor, followed by ten thousand men. 15At Barak's advance, the LORD routed[c] Sisera and all his chariots and army by the sword, and Sisera abandoned his chariot and fled on foot. 16But Barak pursued the chariots and army as far as Harosheth Haggoyim. All the troops of Sisera fell by the sword; not a man was left.[d]

17Sisera, however, fled on foot to the tent of Jael, the wife of Heber the Kenite, because there were friendly relations between Jabin king of Hazor and the clan of Heber the Kenite.

18Jael went out to meet Sisera and said to him, "Come, my lord, come right in. Don't be afraid." So he entered her tent, and she put a covering over him.

19"I'm thirsty," he said. "Please give me some water." She opened a skin of milk,[e] gave him a drink, and covered him up.

20"Stand in the doorway of the tent," he told her. "If someone comes by and asks you, 'Is anyone here?' say 'No.'"

21But Jael, Heber's wife, picked up a tent peg and a hammer and went quietly to him while he lay fast asleep, exhausted. She drove the peg through his temple into the ground, and he died.[f]

22Barak came by in pursuit of Sisera, and Jael went out to meet him. "Come," she said, "I will show you the man you're looking for." So he went in with her, and there lay Sisera with the tent peg through his temple—dead.

23On that day God subdued[g] Jabin, the Canaanite king, before the Israelites. 24And the hand of the Israelites grew stronger and stronger against Jabin, the Canaanite king, until they destroyed him.

Chapter 5 Theme ______________________

5 On that day Deborah and Barak son of Abinoam sang this song:[h]

2"When the princes in Israel take the lead,
when the people willingly offer[i] themselves—
praise the LORD![j]

3"Hear this, you kings! Listen, you rulers!
I will sing to[a] the LORD, I will sing;
I will make music to[b] the LORD, the God of Israel.[k]

4"O LORD, when you went out from Seir,[l]
when you marched from the land of Edom,

[a]3 Or *of* [b]3 Or */ with song I will praise*

4:13 [a]ver 3
4:14 [b]Dt 9:3; 2Sa 5:24; Ps 68:7
4:15 [c]Jos 10:10; Ps 83:9-10
4:16 [d]Ex 14:28; Ps 83:9
4:19 [e]Jdg 5:25
4:21 [f]Jdg 5:26
4:23 [g]Ne 9:24; Ps 18:47
5:1 [h]Ex 15:1
5:2 [i]2Ch 17:16; Ps 110:3 [j]ver 9
5:3 [k]Ps 27:6
5:4 [l]Dt 33:2

the earth shook, the heavens poured,
the clouds poured down water.[a]
5The mountains quaked[b] before the LORD, the One of Sinai,
before the LORD, the God of Israel.

6"In the days of Shamgar son of Anath,[c]
in the days of Jael,[d] the roads[e] were abandoned;
travelers took to winding paths.
7Village life[a] in Israel ceased,
ceased until I,[b] Deborah, arose,
arose a mother in Israel.
8When they chose new gods,[f]
war came to the city gates,
and not a shield or spear was seen
among forty thousand in Israel.
9My heart is with Israel's princes,
with the willing volunteers[g] among the people.
Praise the LORD!

10"You who ride on white donkeys,[h]
sitting on your saddle blankets,
and you who walk along the road,
consider 11the voice of the singers[c] at the watering places.
They recite the righteous acts[i] of the LORD,
the righteous acts of his warriors[d] in Israel.

"Then the people of the LORD
went down to the city gates.[j]
12'Wake up,[k] wake up, Deborah!
Wake up, wake up, break out in song!
Arise, O Barak!
Take captive your captives,[l] O son of Abinoam.'

13"Then the men who were left
came down to the nobles;
the people of the LORD
came to me with the mighty.
14Some came from Ephraim, whose roots were in Amalek;[m]
Benjamin was with the people who followed you.
From Makir captains came down,
from Zebulun those who bear a commander's staff.
15The princes of Issachar were with Deborah;[n]
yes, Issachar was with Barak,
rushing after him into the valley.

5:4 [a]Ps 68:8
5:5 [b]Ex 19:18; Ps 68:8; 97:5; Isa 64:3
5:6 [c]Jdg 3:31 [d]Jdg 4:17 [e]Isa 33:8
5:8 [f]Dt 32:17
5:9 [g]ver 2
5:10 [h]Jdg 10:4; 12:14
5:11 [i]1Sa 12:7; Mic 6:5 [j]ver 8
5:12 [k]Ps 57:8 [l]Ps 68:18; Eph 4:8
5:14 [m]Jdg 3:13
5:15 [n]Jdg 4:10

[a]7 Or *Warriors* [b]7 Or *you* [c]11 Or *archers*; the meaning of the Hebrew for this word is uncertain. [d]11 Or *villagers*

In the districts of Reuben
there was much searching of heart.
16Why did you stay among the campfires[a]
to hear the whistling for the flocks?[a]
In the districts of Reuben
there was much searching of heart.
17Gilead stayed beyond the Jordan.
And Dan, why did he linger by the ships?
Asher remained on the coast[b]
and stayed in his coves.
18The people of Zebulun risked their very lives;
so did Naphtali on the heights of the field.[c]

19"Kings came[d], they fought;
the kings of Canaan fought
at Taanach by the waters of Megiddo,[e]
but they carried off no silver, no plunder.[f]
20From the heavens[g] the stars fought,
from their courses they fought against Sisera.
21The river Kishon[h] swept them away,
the age-old river, the river Kishon.
March on, my soul; be strong!
22Then thundered the horses' hoofs—
galloping, galloping go his mighty steeds.
23'Curse Meroz,' said the angel of the LORD.
'Curse its people bitterly,
because they did not come to help the LORD,
to help the LORD against the mighty.'

24"Most blessed of women be Jael,[i]
the wife of Heber the Kenite,
most blessed of tent-dwelling women.
25He asked for water, and she gave him milk;[j]
in a bowl fit for nobles she brought him curdled milk.
26Her hand reached for the tent peg,
her right hand for the workman's hammer.
She struck Sisera, she crushed his head,
she shattered and pierced his temple.[k]
27At her feet he sank,
he fell; there he lay.
At her feet he sank, he fell;
where he sank, there he fell—dead.

28"Through the window peered Sisera's mother;
behind the lattice she cried out,[l]

5:16 [a]Nu 32:1
5:17 [b]Jos 19:29
5:18 [c]Jdg 4:6,10
5:19 [d]Jos 11:5; Jdg 4:13 [e]Jdg 1:27 [f]ver 30
5:20 [g]Jos 10:11
5:21 [h]Jdg 4:7
5:24 [i]Jdg 4:17
5:25 [j]Jdg 4:19
5:26 [k]Jdg 4:21
5:28 [l]Pr 7:6

[a]16 Or *saddlebags*

'Why is his chariot so long in coming?
Why is the clatter of his chariots delayed?'
29The wisest of her ladies answer her;
indeed, she keeps saying to herself,
30'Are they not finding and dividing the spoils:[a]
a girl or two for each man,
colorful garments as plunder for Sisera,
colorful garments embroidered,
highly embroidered garments for my neck—
all this as plunder?'
31"So may all your enemies perish, O LORD!
But may they who love you be like the sun[b]
when it rises in its strength."

Then the land had peace[c] forty years.

Chapter 6 Theme ________________________

6 Again the Israelites did evil in the eyes of the LORD,[d] and for
seven years he gave them into the hands of the Midianites.[e]
2Because the power of Midian was so oppressive,[f] the Israelites
prepared shelters for themselves in mountain clefts, caves and
strongholds.[g] 3Whenever the Israelites planted their crops, the Midianites, Amalekites[h] and other eastern peoples invaded the country. 4They camped on the land and ruined the crops[i] all the way
to Gaza and did not spare a living thing for Israel, neither sheep
nor cattle nor donkeys. 5They came up with their livestock and
their tents like swarms of locusts.[j] It was impossible to count the
men and their camels;[k] they invaded the land to ravage it. 6Midi-
an so impoverished the Israelites that they cried out[l] to the LORD
for help.

7When the Israelites cried to the LORD because of Midian, 8he
sent them a prophet, who said, "This is what the LORD, the God
of Israel, says: I brought you up out of Egypt,[m] out of the land of
slavery. 9I snatched you from the power of Egypt and from the
hand of all your oppressors. I drove them from before you and
gave you their land.[n] 10I said to you, 'I am the LORD your God; do
not worship[o] the gods of the Amorites,[p] in whose land you live.'
But you have not listened to me."

11The angel of the LORD[q] came and sat down under the oak in
Ophrah that belonged to Joash the Abiezrite,[r] where his son
Gideon[s] was threshing wheat in a winepress to keep it from the
Midianites. 12When the angel of the LORD appeared to Gideon, he
said, "The LORD is with you,[t] mighty warrior."

13"But sir," Gideon replied, "if the LORD is with us, why has all
this happened to us? Where are all his wonders that our fathers

5:30 [a]Ex 15:9; 1Sa 30:24
5:31 [b]2Sa 23:4; Ps 19:4; 89:36 [c]Jdg 3:11
6:1 [d]Jdg 2:11 [e]Nu 25:15-18; 31:1-3
6:2 [f]1Sa 13:6; Isa 8:21 [g]Heb 11:38
6:3 [h]Jdg 3:13
6:4 [i]Lev 26:16; Dt 28:30,51
6:5 [j]Jdg 7:12 [k]Jdg 8:10
6:6 [l]Jdg 3:9
6:8 [m]Jdg 2:1
6:9 [n]Ps 44:2
6:10 [o]2Ki 17:35 [p]Jer 10:2
6:11 [q]Ge 16:7 [r]Jos 17:2 [s]Heb 11:32
6:12 [t]Jos 1:5; Jdg 13:3; Lk 1:11,28

told[a] us about when they said, 'Did not the LORD bring us up out
of Egypt?' But now the LORD has abandoned[b] us and put us into
the hand of Midian."
14 The LORD turned to him and said, "Go in the strength you
have[c] and save Israel out of Midian's hand. Am I not sending you?"
15 "But Lord,[a]" Gideon asked, "how can I save Israel? My clan is
the weakest in Manasseh, and I am the least in my family.[d]"
16 The LORD answered, "I will be with you[e], and you will strike
down all the Midianites together."
17 Gideon replied, "If now I have found favor in your eyes, give
me a sign[f] that it is really you talking to me. 18 Please do not go
away until I come back and bring my offering and set it before
you."
And the LORD said, "I will wait until you return."
19 Gideon went in, prepared a young goat, and from an ephah[b]
of flour he made bread without yeast. Putting the meat in a basket and its broth in a pot, he brought them out and offered them
to him under the oak.[g]
20 The angel of God said to him, "Take the meat and the unleavened bread, place them on this rock,[h] and pour out the broth."
And Gideon did so. 21 With the tip of the staff that was in his
hand, the angel of the LORD touched the meat and the unleavened
bread.[i] Fire flared from the rock, consuming the meat and the
bread. And the angel of the LORD disappeared. 22 When Gideon
realized[j] that it was the angel of the LORD, he exclaimed, "Ah,
Sovereign LORD! I have seen the angel of the LORD face to face!"[k]
23 But the LORD said to him, "Peace! Do not be afraid.[l] You are
not going to die."
24 So Gideon built an altar to the LORD there and called[m] it The
LORD is Peace. To this day it stands in Ophrah[n] of the Abiezrites.
25 That same night the LORD said to him, "Take the second bull
from your father's herd, the one seven years old.[c] Tear down your
father's altar to Baal and cut down the Asherah pole[d][o] beside it.
26 Then build a proper kind of[e] altar to the LORD your God on the
top of this height. Using the wood of the Asherah pole that you
cut down, offer the second[f] bull as a burnt offering."
27 So Gideon took ten of his servants and did as the LORD told
him. But because he was afraid of his family and the men of the
town, he did it at night rather than in the daytime.
28 In the morning when the men of the town got up, there was
Baal's altar,[p] demolished, with the Asherah pole beside it cut
down and the second bull sacrificed on the newly built altar!

[a] 15 Or *sir* [b] 19 That is, probably about 3/5 bushel (about 22 liters) [c] 25 Or *Take a full-grown, mature bull from your father's herd* [d] 25 That is, a symbol of the goddess Asherah; here and elsewhere in Judges [e] 26 Or *build with layers of stone an* [f] 26 Or *full-grown;* also in verse 28

6:13 [a] Ps 44:1 [b] 2Ch 15:2
6:14 [c] Heb 11:34
6:15 [d] Ex 3:11; 1Sa 9:21
6:16 [e] Ex 3:12; Jos 1:5
6:17 [f] ver 36-37; Ge 24:14; Isa 38:7-8
6:19 [g] Ge 18:7-8
6:20 [h] Jdg 13:19
6:21 [i] Lev 9:24
6:22 [j] Jdg 13:16,21 [k] Ge 32:30; Ex 33:20; Jdg 13:22
6:23 [l] Da 10:19
6:24 [m] Ge 22:14 [n] Jdg 8:32
6:25 [o] Ex 34:13; Dt 7:5
6:28 [p] 1Ki 16:32

29 They asked each other, "Who did this?"
When they carefully investigated, they were told, "Gideon son
of Joash did it."
30 The men of the town demanded of Joash, "Bring out your
son. He must die, because he has broken down Baal's altar and
cut down the Asherah pole beside it."
31 But Joash replied to the hostile crowd around him, "Are you
going to plead Baal's cause? Are you trying to save him? Whoever fights for him shall be put to death by morning! If Baal really
is a god, he can defend himself when someone breaks down his
altar." 32 So that day they called Gideon "Jerub-Baal,[a] [a]" saying,
"Let Baal contend with him," because he broke down Baal's altar.
33 Now all the Midianites, Amalekites and other eastern peoples[b] joined forces and crossed over the Jordan and camped in
the Valley of Jezreel.[c] 34 Then the Spirit of the LORD came upon[d]
Gideon, and he blew a trumpet,[e] summoning the Abiezrites to
follow him. 35 He sent messengers throughout Manasseh, calling
them to arms, and also into Asher, Zebulun and Naphtali,[f] so
that they too went up to meet them.
36 Gideon said to God, "If you will save[g] Israel by my hand as you
have promised— 37 look, I will place a wool fleece on the threshing
floor.[h] If there is dew only on the fleece and all the ground is dry,
then I will know[i] that you will save Israel by my hand, as you said."
38 And that is what happened. Gideon rose early the next day; he
squeezed the fleece and wrung out the dew—a bowlful of water.
39 Then Gideon said to God, "Do not be angry with me. Let me
make just one more request.[j] Allow me one more test with the
fleece. This time make the fleece dry and the ground covered with
dew." 40 That night God did so. Only the fleece was dry; all the
ground was covered with dew.

Chapter 7 Theme

7

Early in the morning, Jerub-Baal[k] (that is, Gideon) and all
his men camped at the spring of Harod. The camp of Midian
was north of them in the valley near the hill of Moreh.[l] 2 The LORD
said to Gideon, "You have too many men for me to deliver Midian
into their hands. In order that Israel may not boast against me
that her own strength[m] has saved her, 3 announce now to the people, 'Anyone who trembles with fear may turn back and leave
Mount Gilead.[n]'" So twenty-two thousand men left, while ten
thousand remained.
4 But the LORD said to Gideon, "There are still too many[o] men.
Take them down to the water, and I will sift them for you there. If

a 32 *Jerub-Baal* means *let Baal contend.*

6:32 [a] Jdg 7:1; 8:29,35; 1Sa 12:11
6:33 [b] ver 3 [c] Jos 17:16
6:34 [d] Jdg 3:10; 1Ch 12:18; 2Ch 24:20 [e] Jdg 3:27
6:35 [f] Jdg 4:6
6:36 [g] ver 14
6:37 [h] Ex 4:3-7 [i] Ge 24:14
6:39 [j] Ge 18:32
7:1 [k] Jdg 6:32 [l] Ge 12:6
7:2 [m] Dt 8:17; 2Co 4:7
7:3 [n] Dt 20:8
7:4 [o] 1Sa 14:6

I say, 'This one shall go with you,' he shall go; but if I say, 'This
one shall not go with you,' he shall not go."
5So Gideon took the men down to the water. There the LORD
told him, "Separate those who lap the water with their tongues
like a dog from those who kneel down to drink." 6Three hundred
men lapped with their hands to their mouths. All the rest got
down on their knees to drink.
7The LORD said to Gideon, "With the three hundred men that
lapped I will save you and give the Midianites into your hands.
Let all the other men go, each to his own place."[a] 8So Gideon sent
the rest of the Israelites to their tents but kept the three hundred,
who took over the provisions and trumpets of the others.
Now the camp of Midian lay below him in the valley. 9During
that night the LORD said to Gideon, "Get up, go down against the
camp, because I am going to give it into your hands.[b] 10If you are
afraid to attack, go down to the camp with your servant Purah
11and listen to what they are saying. Afterward, you will be
encouraged to attack the camp." So he and Purah his servant
went down to the outposts of the camp. 12The Midianites, the
Amalekites[c] and all the other eastern peoples had settled in the
valley, thick as locusts.[d] Their camels[e] could no more be counted
than the sand on the seashore.[f]
13Gideon arrived just as a man was telling a friend his dream. "I
had a dream," he was saying. "A round loaf of barley bread came
tumbling into the Midianite camp. It struck the tent with such
force that the tent overturned and collapsed."
14His friend responded, "This can be nothing other than the
sword of Gideon son of Joash, the Israelite. God has given the
Midianites and the whole camp into his hands."
15When Gideon heard the dream and its interpretation, he
worshiped God.[g] He returned to the camp of Israel and called
out, "Get up! The LORD has given the Midianite camp into your
hands." 16Dividing the three hundred men[h] into three companies,[i] he placed trumpets and empty jars in the hands of all of
them, with torches inside.
17"Watch me," he told them. "Follow my lead. When I get to the
edge of the camp, do exactly as I do. 18When I and all who are
with me blow our trumpets,[j] then from all around the camp blow
yours and shout, 'For the LORD and for Gideon.'"
19Gideon and the hundred men with him reached the edge of
the camp at the beginning of the middle watch, just after they
had changed the guard. They blew their trumpets and broke the
jars that were in their hands. 20The three companies blew the
trumpets and smashed the jars. Grasping the torches in their left
hands and holding in their right hands the trumpets they were to

7:7
[a] 1Sa 14:6

7:9
[b] Jos 2:24; 10:8; 11:6

7:12
[c] Jdg 8:10
[d] Jdg 6:5
[e] Jer 49:29
[f] Jos 11:4

7:15
[g] 1Sa 15:31

7:16
[h] Ge 14:15
[i] 2Sa 18:2

7:18
[j] Jdg 3:27

blow, they shouted, "A sword[a] for the LORD and for Gideon!"
21While each man held his position around the camp, all the
Midianites ran, crying out as they fled.[b]
22When the three hundred trumpets sounded,[c] the LORD caused
the men throughout the camp to turn on each other[d] with their
swords. The army fled to Beth Shittah toward Zererah as far as the
border of Abel Meholah[e] near Tabbath. 23Israelites from Naphtali,
Asher and all Manasseh were called out,[f] and they pursued the
Midianites. 24Gideon sent messengers throughout the hill country
of Ephraim, saying, "Come down against the Midianites and seize
the waters of the Jordan[g] ahead of them as far as Beth Barah."
So all the men of Ephraim were called out and they took the
waters of the Jordan as far as Beth Barah. 25They also captured
two of the Midianite leaders, Oreb and Zeeb[h]. They killed Oreb
at the rock of Oreb,[i] and Zeeb at the winepress of Zeeb. They
pursued the Midianites and brought the heads of Oreb and Zeeb
to Gideon, who was by the Jordan.[j]

Chapter 8 Theme ______________________

8 Now the Ephraimites asked Gideon, "Why have you treated
us like this? Why didn't you call us when you went to fight
Midian?"[k] And they criticized him sharply.[l]
2But he answered them, "What have I accomplished compared
to you? Aren't the gleanings of Ephraim's grapes better than the
full grape harvest of Abiezer? 3God gave Oreb and Zeeb,[m] the
Midianite leaders, into your hands. What was I able to do compared to you?" At this, their resentment against him subsided.
4Gideon and his three hundred men, exhausted yet keeping up
the pursuit, came to the Jordan[n] and crossed it. 5He said to the men
of Succoth,[o] "Give my troops some bread; they are worn out, and I
am still pursuing Zebah and Zalmunna,[p] the kings of Midian."
6But the officials of Succoth said, "Do you already have the
hands of Zebah and Zalmunna in your possession? Why should
we give bread[q] to your troops?"[r]
7Then Gideon replied, "Just for that, when the LORD has given
Zebah and Zalmunna[s] into my hand, I will tear your flesh with
desert thorns and briers."
8From there he went up to Peniel[a][t] and made the same request
of them, but they answered as the men of Succoth had. 9So he said
to the men of Peniel, "When I return in triumph, I will tear down
this tower."[u]
10Now Zebah and Zalmunna were in Karkor with a force of
about fifteen thousand men, all that were left of the armies of the
eastern peoples; a hundred and twenty thousand swordsmen had

7:20 a ver 14
7:21 b 2Ki 7:7
7:22 c Jos 6:20 d 1Sa 14:20; 2Ch 20:23 e 1Ki 4:12; 19:16
7:23 f Jdg 6:35
7:24 g Jdg 3:28
7:25 h Jdg 8:3; Ps 83:11 i Isa 10:26 j Jdg 8:4
8:1 k Jdg 12:1 l 2Sa 19:41
8:3 m Jdg 7:25; Pr 15:1
8:4 n Jdg 7:25
8:5 o Ge 33:17 p Ps 83:11
8:6 q 1Sa 25:11 r ver 15
8:7 s Jdg 7:15
8:8 t Ge 32:30; 1Ki 12:25
8:9 u ver 17

a8 Hebrew *Penuel,* a variant of *Peniel*; also in verses 9 and 17

fallen.[a] 11Gideon went up by the route of the nomads east of
Nobah[b] and Jogbehah[c] and fell upon the unsuspecting army.
12Zebah and Zalmunna, the two kings of Midian, fled, but he
pursued them and captured them, routing their entire army.
13Gideon son of Joash then returned from the battle by the Pass
of Heres. 14He caught a young man of Succoth and questioned
him, and the young man wrote down for him the names of the
seventy-seven officials of Succoth, the elders of the town. 15Then
Gideon came and said to the men of Succoth, "Here are Zebah
and Zalmunna, about whom you taunted me by saying, 'Do you
already have the hands of Zebah and Zalmunna in your possession? Why should we give bread to your exhausted men?[d]'" 16He
took the elders of the town and taught the men of Succoth a
lesson[e] by punishing them with desert thorns and briers. 17He
also pulled down the tower of Peniel and killed the men of the
town.[f]
18Then he asked Zebah and Zalmunna, "What kind of men did
you kill at Tabor?[g]"

"Men like you," they answered, "each one with the bearing of
a prince."

19Gideon replied, "Those were my brothers, the sons of my own
mother. As surely as the LORD lives, if you had spared their lives,
I would not kill you." 20Turning to Jether, his oldest son, he said,
"Kill them!" But Jether did not draw his sword, because he was
only a boy and was afraid.

21Zebah and Zalmunna said, "Come, do it yourself. 'As is the
man, so is his strength.'" So Gideon stepped forward and killed
them, and took the ornaments[h] off their camels' necks.

22The Israelites said to Gideon, "Rule over us—you, your son
and your grandson—because you have saved us out of the hand
of Midian."

23But Gideon told them, "I will not rule over you, nor will my
son rule over you. The LORD will rule[i] over you." 24And he said,
"I do have one request, that each of you give me an earring from
your share of the plunder." (It was the custom of the Ishmaelites[j]
to wear gold earrings.)

25They answered, "We'll be glad to give them." So they spread
out a garment, and each man threw a ring from his plunder onto
it. 26The weight of the gold rings he asked for came to seventeen
hundred shekels,[a] not counting the ornaments, the pendants and
the purple garments worn by the kings of Midian or the chains
that were on their camels' necks. 27Gideon made the gold into an
ephod,[k] which he placed in Ophrah, his town. All Israel prostituted

a26 That is, about 43 pounds (about 19.5 kilograms)

8:10 [a] Jdg 6:5; 7:12; Isa 9:4
8:11 [b] Nu 32:42 [c] Nu 32:35
8:15 [d] ver 6
8:16 [e] ver 7
8:17 [f] ver 9
8:18 [g] Jos 19:22; Jdg 4:6
8:21 [h] ver 26; Ps 83:11
8:23 [i] Ex 16:8; 1Sa 8:7; 10:19; 12:12
8:24 [j] Ge 25:13
8:27 [k] Jdg 17:5; 18:14

themselves by worshiping it there, and it became a snare[a] to
Gideon and his family.
28 Thus Midian was subdued before the Israelites and did not
raise its head again. During Gideon's lifetime, the land enjoyed
peace[b] forty years.
29 Jerub-Baal[c] son of Joash went back home to live. 30 He had seventy sons[d] of his own, for he had many wives. 31 His concubine,
who lived in Shechem, also bore him a son, whom he named
Abimelech.[e] 32 Gideon son of Joash died at a good old age[f] and was
buried in the tomb of his father Joash in Ophrah of the Abiezrites.
33 No sooner had Gideon died than the Israelites again prostituted themselves to the Baals.[g] They set up Baal-Berith[h] as their
god[i] and 34 did not remember[j] the LORD their God, who had rescued them from the hands of all their enemies on every side.
35 They also failed to show kindness to the family of Jerub-Baal
(that is, Gideon) for all the good things he had done for them.[k]

Chapter 9 Theme ______________________________

9 Abimelech[l] son of Jerub-Baal went to his mother's brothers
in Shechem and said to them and to all his mother's clan,
2 "Ask all the citizens of Shechem, 'Which is better for you: to have
all seventy of Jerub-Baal's sons rule over you, or just one man?'
Remember, I am your flesh and blood.[m]"
3 When the brothers repeated all this to the citizens of Shechem,
they were inclined to follow Abimelech, for they said, "He is our
brother." 4 They gave him seventy shekels[a] of silver from the
temple of Baal-Berith,[n] and Abimelech used it to hire reckless
adventurers,[o] who became his followers. 5 He went to his father's
home in Ophrah and on one stone murdered his seventy brothers,[p] the sons of Jerub-Baal. But Jotham, the youngest son of
Jerub-Baal, escaped by hiding.[q] 6 Then all the citizens of Shechem
and Beth Millo gathered beside the great tree at the pillar in
Shechem to crown Abimelech king.
7 When Jotham was told about this, he climbed up on the top of
Mount Gerizim[r] and shouted to them, "Listen to me, citizens of
Shechem, so that God may listen to you. 8 One day the trees went
out to anoint a king for themselves. They said to the olive tree,
'Be our king.'
9 "But the olive tree answered, 'Should I give up my oil, by which
both gods and men are honored, to hold sway over the trees?'
10 "Next, the trees said to the fig tree, 'Come and be our king.'
11 "But the fig tree replied, 'Should I give up my fruit, so good
and sweet, to hold sway over the trees?'
12 "Then the trees said to the vine, 'Come and be our king.'

8:27 [a] Dt 7:16; Ps 106:39
8:28 [b] Jdg 5:31
8:29 [c] Jdg 7:1
8:30 [d] Jdg 9:2,5, 18,24
8:31 [e] Jdg 9:1
8:32 [f] Ge 25:8
8:33 [g] Jdg 2:11,13,19 [h] Jdg 9:4 [i] Jdg 9:27,46
8:34 [j] Jdg 3:7; Dt 4:9; Ps 78:11,42
8:35 [k] Jdg 9:16
9:1 [l] Jdg 8:31
9:2 [m] Ge 29:14; Jdg 8:30
9:4 [n] Jdg 8:33 [o] Jdg 11:3; 2Ch 13:7
9:5 [p] ver 2; Jdg 8:30 [q] 2Ki 11:2
9:7 [r] Dt 11:29; 27:12; Jn 4:20

[a] *4* That is, about 1 3/4 pounds (about 0.8 kilogram)

13"But the vine answered, 'Should I give up my wine,[a] which
cheers both gods and men, to hold sway over the trees?'
14"Finally all the trees said to the thornbush, 'Come and be our
king.'
15"The thornbush said to the trees, 'If you really want to anoint
me king over you, come and take refuge in my shade;[b] but if not,
then let fire come out[c] of the thornbush and consume the cedars
of Lebanon!'[d]
16"Now if you have acted honorably and in good faith when
you made Abimelech king, and if you have been fair to Jerub-
Baal and his family, and if you have treated him as he deserves—
17and to think that my father fought for you, risked his life to rescue you from the hand of Midian 18(but today you have revolted
against my father's family, murdered his seventy sons[e] on a single stone, and made Abimelech, the son of his slave girl, king
over the citizens of Shechem because he is your brother)— 19if
then you have acted honorably and in good faith toward Jerub-
Baal and his family today, may Abimelech be your joy, and may
you be his, too! 20But if you have not, let fire come out[f] from
Abimelech and consume you, citizens of Shechem and Beth Millo, and let fire come out from you, citizens of Shechem and Beth
Millo, and consume Abimelech!"
21Then Jotham fled, escaping to Beer, and he lived there because
he was afraid of his brother Abimelech.
22After Abimelech had governed Israel three years, 23God sent an
evil spirit[g] between Abimelech and the citizens of Shechem, who
acted treacherously against Abimelech. 24God did this in order
that the crime against Jerub-Baal's seventy sons, the shedding[h] of
their blood, might be avenged[i] on their brother Abimelech and
on the citizens of Shechem, who had helped him[j] murder his
brothers. 25In opposition to him these citizens of Shechem set
men on the hilltops to ambush and rob everyone who passed by,
and this was reported to Abimelech.
26Now Gaal son of Ebed moved with his brothers into Shechem,
and its citizens put their confidence in him. 27After they had gone
out into the fields and gathered the grapes and trodden[k] them,
they held a festival in the temple of their god.[l] While they were
eating and drinking, they cursed Abimelech. 28Then Gaal son of
Ebed said, "Who[m] is Abimelech, and who is Shechem, that we
should be subject to him? Isn't he Jerub-Baal's son, and isn't
Zebul his deputy? Serve the men of Hamor,[n] Shechem's father!
Why should we serve Abimelech? 29If only this people were under
my command![o] Then I would get rid of him. I would say to Abimelech, 'Call out your whole army!' "[a]

a 29 Septuagint; Hebrew *him." Then he said to Abimelech, "Call out your whole army!"*

9:13 [a] Ecc 2:3
9:15 [b] Isa 30:2 [c] ver 20 [d] Isa 2:13
9:18 [e] ver 5-6; Jdg 8:30
9:20 [f] ver 15
9:23 [g] 1Sa 16:14,23; 18:10; 1Ki 22:22; Isa 19:14; 33:1
9:24 [h] Nu 35:33; 1Ki 2:32 [i] ver 56-57 [j] Dt 27:25
9:27 [k] Am 9:13 [l] Jdg 8:33
9:28 [m] 1Sa 25:10; 1Ki 12:16 [n] Ge 34:2,6
9:29 [o] 2Sa 15:4

9:32 [a]Jos 8:2 [30]When Zebul the governor of the city heard what Gaal son of
Ebed said, he was very angry. [31]Under cover he sent messengers to
Abimelech, saying, "Gaal son of Ebed and his brothers have come
to Shechem and are stirring up the city against you. [32]Now then,
during the night you and your men should come and lie in wait[a]
in the fields. [33]In the morning at sunrise, advance against the city.
9:33 [b]1Sa 10:7 When Gaal and his men come out against you, do whatever your
hand finds to do.[b]"

[34]So Abimelech and all his troops set out by night and took up
concealed positions near Shechem in four companies. [35]Now Gaal
son of Ebed had gone out and was standing at the entrance to the
city gate just as Abimelech and his soldiers came out from their
9:35 [c]Ps 32:7; Jer 49:10 hiding place.[c]

[36]When Gaal saw them, he said to Zebul, "Look, people are
coming down from the tops of the mountains!"

Zebul replied, "You mistake the shadows of the mountains for
men."

[37]But Gaal spoke up again: "Look, people are coming down
from the center of the land, and a company is coming from the
9:38 [d]ver 28-29 direction of the soothsayers' tree."

[38]Then Zebul said to him, "Where is your big talk now, you who
said, 'Who is Abimelech that we should be subject to him?' Aren't
these the men you ridiculed?[d] Go out and fight them!"

[39]So Gaal led out[a] the citizens of Shechem and fought Abimelech. [40]Abimelech chased him, and many fell wounded in the
9:43 [e]Jdg 7:16 flight—all the way to the entrance to the gate. [41]Abimelech stayed
in Arumah, and Zebul drove Gaal and his brothers out of Shechem.

[42]The next day the people of Shechem went out to the fields,
and this was reported to Abimelech. [43]So he took his men, divided them into three companies[e] and set an ambush in the fields.
When he saw the people coming out of the city, he rose to attack
9:45 [f]ver 20; 2Ki 3:25 [g]Dt 29:23 them. [44]Abimelech and the companies with him rushed forward
to a position at the entrance to the city gate. Then two companies
rushed upon those in the fields and struck them down. [45]All that
day Abimelech pressed his attack against the city until he had
captured it and killed its people. Then he destroyed the city[f] and
scattered salt[g] over it.

[46]On hearing this, the citizens in the tower of Shechem went into
9:46 [h]Jdg 8:33 the stronghold of the temple[h] of El-Berith. [47]When Abimelech
heard that they had assembled there, [48]he and all his men went up
Mount Zalmon.[i] He took an ax and cut off some branches, which
he lifted to his shoulders. He ordered the men with him, "Quick!
Do what you have seen me do!" [49]So all the men cut branches
and followed Abimelech. They piled them against the stronghold

9:48 [i]Ps 68:14 a39 Or *Gaal went out in the sight of*

and set it on fire over the people inside. So all the people in the
tower of Shechem, about a thousand men and women, also died.
50Next Abimelech went to Thebez[a] and besieged it and captured
it. 51Inside the city, however, was a strong tower, to which all the
men and women—all the people of the city—fled. They locked
themselves in and climbed up on the tower roof. 52Abimelech
went to the tower and stormed it. But as he approached the
entrance to the tower to set it on fire, 53a woman dropped an
upper millstone on his head and cracked his skull.[b]
54Hurriedly he called to his armor-bearer, "Draw your sword
and kill me,[c] so that they can't say, 'A woman killed him.'" So his
servant ran him through, and he died. 55When the Israelites saw
that Abimelech was dead, they went home.
56Thus God repaid the wickedness that Abimelech had done to
his father by murdering his seventy brothers. 57God also made
the men of Shechem pay for all their wickedness.[d] The curse of
Jotham son of Jerub-Baal came on them.

Chapter 10 Theme

10 After the time of Abimelech a man of Issachar,[e] Tola son
of Puah,[f] the son of Dodo, rose to save[g] Israel. He lived in
Shamir, in the hill country of Ephraim. 2He led[a] Israel twenty-
three years; then he died, and was buried in Shamir.
3He was followed by Jair of Gilead, who led Israel twenty-two
years. 4He had thirty sons, who rode thirty donkeys. They controlled thirty towns in Gilead, which to this day are called Havvoth
Jair.[b][h] 5When Jair died, he was buried in Kamon.
6Again the Israelites did evil in the eyes of the LORD.[i] They
served the Baals and the Ashtoreths,[j] and the gods of Aram, the
gods of Sidon, the gods of Moab, the gods of the Ammonites and
the gods of the Philistines.[k] And because the Israelites forsook
the LORD[l] and no longer served him, 7he became angry[m] with
them. He sold them[n] into the hands of the Philistines and the
Ammonites, 8who that year shattered and crushed them. For
eighteen years they oppressed all the Israelites on the east side of
the Jordan in Gilead, the land of the Amorites. 9The Ammonites
also crossed the Jordan to fight against Judah, Benjamin and the
house of Ephraim; and Israel was in great distress. 10Then the
Israelites cried out to the LORD, "We have sinned against you,
forsaking our God and serving the Baals."[o]
11The LORD replied, "When the Egyptians,[p] the Amorites, the
Ammonites,[q] the Philistines,[r] 12the Sidonians, the Amalekites and
the Maonites[c] oppressed you[s] and you cried to me for help, did I

[a] 2 Traditionally *judged*; also in verse 3 [b] 4 Or *called the settlements of Jair*
[c] 12 Hebrew; some Septuagint manuscripts *Midianites*

9:50 [a] 2Sa 11:21
9:53 [b] 2Sa 11:21
9:54 [c] 1Sa 31:4; 2Sa 1:9
9:57 [d] ver 20
10:1 [e] Ge 30:18 [f] Ge 46:13 [g] Jdg 2:16; 6:14
10:4 [h] Nu 32:41
10:6 [i] Jdg 2:11 [j] Jdg 2:13 [k] Jdg 2:12 [l] Dt 32:15
10:7 [m] Dt 31:17 [n] Dt 32:30; Jdg 2:14; 1Sa 12:9
10:10 [o] 1Sa 12:10
10:11 [p] Ex 14:30 [q] Nu 21:21; Jdg 3:13 [r] Jdg 3:31
10:12 [s] Ps 106:42

not save you from their hands? 13But you have forsaken me and served other gods, so I will no longer save you. 14Go and cry out to the gods you have chosen. Let them save you when you are in trouble![a]"

15But the Israelites said to the LORD, "We have sinned. Do with us whatever you think best,[b] but please rescue us now." 16Then they got rid of the foreign gods among them and served the LORD.[c] And he could bear Israel's misery[d] no longer.[e]

17When the Ammonites were called to arms and camped in Gilead, the Israelites assembled and camped at Mizpah.[f] 18The leaders of the people of Gilead said to each other, "Whoever will launch the attack against the Ammonites will be the head[g] of all those living in Gilead."

Chapter 11 Theme

11 Jephthah[h] the Gileadite was a mighty warrior.[i] His father was Gilead; his mother was a prostitute. 2Gilead's wife also bore him sons, and when they were grown up, they drove Jephthah away. "You are not going to get any inheritance in our family," they said, "because you are the son of another woman." 3So Jephthah fled from his brothers and settled in the land of Tob,[j] where a group of adventurers[k] gathered around him and followed him.

4Some time later, when the Ammonites[l] made war on Israel, 5the elders of Gilead went to get Jephthah from the land of Tob. 6"Come," they said, "be our commander, so we can fight the Ammonites."

7Jephthah said to them, "Didn't you hate me and drive me from my father's house?[m] Why do you come to me now, when you're in trouble?"

8The elders of Gilead said to him, "Nevertheless, we are turning to you now; come with us to fight the Ammonites, and you will be our head[n] over all who live in Gilead."

9Jephthah answered, "Suppose you take me back to fight the Ammonites and the LORD gives them to me—will I really be your head?"

10The elders of Gilead replied, "The LORD is our witness;[o] we will certainly do as you say." 11So Jephthah went with the elders of Gilead, and the people made him head and commander over them. And he repeated all his words before the LORD in Mizpah.[p]

12Then Jephthah sent messengers to the Ammonite king with the question: "What do you have against us that you have attacked our country?"

13The king of the Ammonites answered Jephthah's messengers, "When Israel came up out of Egypt, they took away my land from

10:14 [a]Dt 32:37
10:15 [b]1Sa 3:18; 2Sa 15:26
10:16 [c]Jos 24:23; Jer 18:8 [d]Isa 63:9 [e]Dt 32:36; Ps 106:44-45
10:17 [f]Ge 31:49; Jdg 11:29
10:18 [g]Jdg 11:8,9
11:1 [h]Heb 11:32 [i]Jdg 6:12
11:3 [j]2Sa 10:6,8 [k]Jdg 9:4
11:4 [l]Jdg 10:9
11:7 [m]Ge 26:27
11:8 [n]Jdg 10:18
11:10 [o]Ge 31:50; Jer 42:5
11:11 [p]Jos 11:3; Jdg 10:17; 20:1; 1Sa 10:17

the Arnon to the Jabbok,[a] all the way to the Jordan. Now give it
back peaceably."
[14]Jephthah sent back messengers to the Ammonite king, [15]say-
ing:

"This is what Jephthah says: Israel did not take the land of
Moab[b] or the land of the Ammonites.[c] [16]But when they came
up out of Egypt, Israel went through the desert to the Red
Sea[a][d] and on to Kadesh.[e] [17]Then Israel sent messengers[f] to the
king of Edom, saying, 'Give us permission to go through your
country,'[g] but the king of Edom would not listen. They sent
also to the king of Moab, and he refused.[h] So Israel stayed at
Kadesh.
[18]"Next they traveled through the desert, skirted the lands
of Edom[i] and Moab, passed along the eastern side[j] of the
country of Moab, and camped on the other side of the Arnon.[k] They did not enter the territory of Moab, for the Arnon
was its border.
[19]"Then Israel sent messengers to Sihon king of the Amorites, who ruled in Heshbon, and said to him, 'Let us pass
through your country to our own place.'[l] [20]Sihon, however,
did not trust Israel[b] to pass through his territory. He mustered
all his men and encamped at Jahaz and fought with Israel.[m]
[21]"Then the LORD, the God of Israel, gave Sihon and all his
men into Israel's hands, and they defeated them. Israel took
over all the land of the Amorites who lived in that country,
[22]capturing all of it from the Arnon to the Jabbok and from
the desert to the Jordan.[n]
[23]"Now since the LORD, the God of Israel, has driven the
Amorites out before his people Israel, what right have you to
take it over? [24]Will you not take what your god Chemosh[o]
gives you? Likewise, whatever the LORD our God has given us,
we will possess. [25]Are you better than Balak son of Zippor,[p]
king of Moab? Did he ever quarrel with Israel or fight with
them?[q] [26]For three hundred years Israel occupied[r] Heshbon,
Aroer, the surrounding settlements and all the towns along
the Arnon. Why didn't you retake them during that time? [27]I
have not wronged you, but you are doing me wrong by waging war against me. Let the LORD, the Judge,[c][s] decide[t] the dispute this day between the Israelites and the Ammonites."

[28]The king of Ammon, however, paid no attention to the message
Jephthah sent him.

[a] *16* Hebrew *Yam Suph*; that is, Sea of Reeds [b] *20* Or *however, would not make an agreement for Israel* [c] *27* Or *Ruler*

11:13 [a]Ge 32:22; Nu 21:24
11:15 [b]Dt 2:9 [c]Dt 2:19
11:16 [d]Nu 14:25; Dt 1:40 [e]Nu 20:1
11:17 [f]Nu 20:14 [g]Nu 20:18,21 [h]Jos 24:9
11:18 [i]Nu 21:4 [j]Dt 2:8 [k]Nu 21:13
11:19 [l]Nu 21:21-22; Dt 2:26-27
11:20 [m]Nu 21:23; Dt 2:32
11:22 [n]Dt 2:36
11:24 [o]Nu 21:29; Jos 3:10; 1Ki 11:7
11:25 [p]Nu 22:2 [q]Jos 24:9
11:26 [r]Nu 21:25
11:27 [s]Ge 18:25 [t]Ge 16:5; 31:53; 1Sa 24:12,15

29Then the Spirit[a] of the LORD came upon Jephthah. He crossed
Gilead and Manasseh, passed through Mizpah of Gilead, and
from there he advanced against the Ammonites. 30And Jephthah
made a vow[b] to the LORD: "If you give the Ammonites into my
hands, 31whatever comes out of the door of my house to meet me
when I return in triumph from the Ammonites will be the LORD's,
and I will sacrifice it as a burnt offering."

32Then Jephthah went over to fight the Ammonites, and the
LORD gave them into his hands. 33He devastated twenty towns
from Aroer to the vicinity of Minnith,[c] as far as Abel Keramim.
Thus Israel subdued Ammon.

34When Jephthah returned to his home in Mizpah, who should
come out to meet him but his daughter, dancing to the sound of
tambourines![d] She was an only child. Except for her he had neither son nor daughter. 35When he saw her, he tore his clothes
and cried, "Oh! My daughter! You have made me miserable and
wretched, because I have made a vow to the LORD that I cannot
break.[e]"

36"My father," she replied, "you have given your word to the
LORD. Do to me just as you promised,[f] now that the LORD has
avenged you of your enemies,[g] the Ammonites. 37But grant me
this one request," she said. "Give me two months to roam the hills
and weep with my friends, because I will never marry."

38"You may go," he said. And he let her go for two months. She
and the girls went into the hills and wept because she would never
marry. 39After the two months, she returned to her father and he
did to her as he had vowed. And she was a virgin.

From this comes the Israelite custom 40that each year the young
women of Israel go out for four days to commemorate the daughter of Jephthah the Gileadite.

Chapter 12 Theme ______________________________

12 The men of Ephraim called out their forces, crossed over
to Zaphon and said to Jephthah, "Why did you go to fight
the Ammonites without calling us to go with you?[h] We're going
to burn down your house over your head."

2Jephthah answered, "I and my people were engaged in a great
struggle with the Ammonites, and although I called, you didn't
save me out of their hands. 3When I saw that you wouldn't help, I
took my life in my hands[i] and crossed over to fight the Ammonites, and the LORD gave me the victory over them. Now why have
you come up today to fight me?"

4Jephthah then called together the men of Gilead and fought
against Ephraim. The Gileadites struck them down because the
Ephraimites had said, "You Gileadites are renegades from Ephraim

11:29 [a]Nu 11:25; Jdg 3:10; 6:34; 14:6,19; 15:14; 1Sa 11:6; 16:13; Isa 11:2
11:30 [b]Ge 28:20
11:33 [c]Eze 27:17
11:34 [d]Ex 15:20; Jer 31:4
11:35 [e]Nu 30:2; Ecc 5:2,4,5
11:36 [f]Lk 1:38 [g]2Sa 18:19
12:1 [h]Jdg 8:1
12:3 [i]1Sa 19:5; 28:21; Job 13:14

and Manasseh." 5The Gileadites captured the fords of the Jordan[a] leading to Ephraim, and whenever a survivor of Ephraim said, "Let me cross over," the men of Gilead asked him, "Are you an Ephraimite?" If he replied, "No," 6they said, "All right, say 'Shibboleth.' " If he said, "Sibboleth," because he could not pronounce the word correctly, they seized him and killed him at the fords of the Jordan. Forty-two thousand Ephraimites were killed at that time.

7Jephthah led[a] Israel six years. Then Jephthah the Gileadite died, and was buried in a town in Gilead.

8After him, Ibzan of Bethlehem led Israel. 9He had thirty sons and thirty daughters. He gave his daughters away in marriage to those outside his clan, and for his sons he brought in thirty young women as wives from outside his clan. Ibzan led Israel seven years. 10Then Ibzan died, and was buried in Bethlehem.

11After him, Elon the Zebulunite led Israel ten years. 12Then Elon died, and was buried in Aijalon in the land of Zebulun.

13After him, Abdon son of Hillel, from Pirathon, led Israel. 14He had forty sons and thirty grandsons,[b] who rode on seventy donkeys.[c] He led Israel eight years. 15Then Abdon son of Hillel died, and was buried at Pirathon in Ephraim, in the hill country of the Amalekites.[d]

Chapter 13 Theme ______________________

13 Again the Israelites did evil in the eyes of the LORD, so the LORD delivered them into the hands of the Philistines[e] for forty years.

2A certain man of Zorah,[f] named Manoah, from the clan of the Danites, had a wife who was sterile and remained childless. 3The angel of the LORD[g] appeared to her[h] and said, "You are sterile and childless, but you are going to conceive and have a son.[i] 4Now see to it that you drink no wine or other fermented drink and that you do not eat anything unclean,[j] 5because you will conceive and give birth to a son. No razor[k] may be used on his head, because the boy is to be a Nazirite,[l] set apart to God from birth, and he will begin[m] the deliverance of Israel from the hands of the Philistines."

6Then the woman went to her husband and told him, "A man of God[n] came to me. He looked like an angel of God,[o] very awesome. I didn't ask him where he came from, and he didn't tell me his name. 7But he said to me, 'You will conceive and give birth to a son. Now then, drink no wine or other fermented drink and do not eat anything unclean, because the boy will be a Nazirite of God from birth until the day of his death.' "

a 7 Traditionally *judged*; also in verses 8-14

12:5
[a] Jos 22:11; Jdg 3:28

12:14
[b] Jdg 10:4
[c] Jdg 5:10

12:15
[d] Jdg 5:14

13:1
[e] Jdg 2:11; 1Sa 12:9

13:2
[f] Jos 15:33; 19:41

13:3
[g] ver 6,8; Jdg 6:12
[h] ver 10
[i] Lk 1:13

13:4
[j] ver 14; Nu 6:2-4; Lk 1:15

13:5
[k] Nu 6:5; 1Sa 1:11
[l] Nu 6:2,13
[m] 1Sa 7:13

13:6
[n] ver 8; 1Sa 2:27; 9:6
[o] ver 17-18; Mt 28:3

8Then Manoah prayed to the LORD: "O Lord, I beg you, let the
man of God you sent to us come again to teach us how to bring
up the boy who is to be born."
9God heard Manoah, and the angel of God came again to the
woman while she was out in the field; but her husband Manoah
was not with her. 10The woman hurried to tell her husband, "He's
here! The man who appeared to me the other day!"
11Manoah got up and followed his wife. When he came to the
man, he said, "Are you the one who talked to my wife?"
"I am," he said.
12So Manoah asked him, "When your words are fulfilled, what
is to be the rule for the boy's life and work?"
13The angel of the LORD answered, "Your wife must do all that I
have told her. 14She must not eat anything that comes from the
grapevine, nor drink any wine or other fermented drink[a] nor eat
anything unclean.[b] She must do everything I have commanded
her."
15Manoah said to the angel of the LORD, "We would like you to
stay until we prepare a young goat[c] for you."
16The angel of the LORD replied, "Even though you detain me, I
will not eat any of your food. But if you prepare a burnt
offering,[d] offer it to the LORD." (Manoah did not realize that it
was the angel of the LORD.)
17Then Manoah inquired of the angel of the LORD, "What is your
name,[e] so that we may honor you when your word comes true?"
18He replied, "Why do you ask my name?[f] It is beyond understanding.[a]" 19Then Manoah took a young goat, together with the
grain offering, and sacrificed it on a rock[g] to the LORD. And the
LORD did an amazing thing while Manoah and his wife watched:
20As the flame[h] blazed up from the altar toward heaven, the angel
of the LORD ascended in the flame. Seeing this, Manoah and his
wife fell with their faces to the ground.[i] 21When the angel of the
LORD did not show himself again to Manoah and his wife,
Manoah realized[j] that it was the angel of the LORD.
22"We are doomed[k] to die!" he said to his wife. "We have seen[l]
God!"
23But his wife answered, "If the LORD had meant to kill us, he
would not have accepted a burnt offering and grain offering from
our hands, nor shown us all these things or now told us this."[m]
24The woman gave birth to a boy and named him Samson.[n] He
grew[o] and the LORD blessed him,[p] 25and the Spirit of the LORD
began to stir[q] him while he was in Mahaneh Dan,[r] between Zorah
and Eshtaol.

13:14 [a]Nu 6:4 [b]ver 4
13:15 [c]ver 3; Jdg 6:19
13:16 [d]Jdg 6:20
13:17 [e]Ge 32:29
13:18 [f]Isa 9:6
13:19 [g]Jdg 6:20
13:20 [h]Lev 9:24 [i]1Ch 21:16; Eze 1:28; Mt 17:6
13:21 [j]ver 16; Jdg 6:22
13:22 [k]Dt 5:26 [l]Ge 32:30; Jdg 6:22
13:23 [m]Ps 25:14
13:24 [n]Heb 11:32 [o]1Sa 3:19 [p]Lk 1:80
13:25 [q]Jdg 3:10 [r]Jdg 18:12

[a] *18* Or *is wonderful*

Chapter 14 Theme ______________________________

14

14 Samson went down to Timnah[a] and saw there a young
Philistine woman. 2When he returned, he said to his
father and mother, "I have seen a Philistine woman in Timnah;
now get her for me as my wife."[b]
3His father and mother replied, "Isn't there an acceptable
woman among your relatives or among all our people?[c] Must you
go to the uncircumcised[d] Philistines to get a wife?[e]"
But Samson said to his father, "Get her for me. She's the right
one for me." 4(His parents did not know that this was from the
LORD, who was seeking an occasion to confront the Philistines;[f]
for at that time they were ruling over Israel.)[g] 5Samson went
down to Timnah together with his father and mother. As they
approached the vineyards of Timnah, suddenly a young lion came
roaring toward him. 6The Spirit of the LORD came upon him in
power[h] so that he tore the lion apart with his bare hands as he
might have torn a young goat. But he told neither his father nor
his mother what he had done. 7Then he went down and talked
with the woman, and he liked her.
8Some time later, when he went back to marry her, he turned
aside to look at the lion's carcass. In it was a swarm of bees and
some honey, 9which he scooped out with his hands and ate as he
went along. When he rejoined his parents, he gave them some,
and they too ate it. But he did not tell them that he had taken the
honey from the lion's carcass.
10Now his father went down to see the woman. And Samson
made a feast there, as was customary for bridegrooms. 11When
he appeared, he was given thirty companions.
12"Let me tell you a riddle,[i]" Samson said to them. "If you can
give me the answer within the seven days of the feast,[j] I will give
you thirty linen garments and thirty sets of clothes.[k] 13If you can't
tell me the answer, you must give me thirty linen garments and
thirty sets of clothes."
"Tell us your riddle," they said. "Let's hear it."
14He replied,

> "Out of the eater, something to eat;
> out of the strong, something sweet."

For three days they could not give the answer.
15On the fourth[a] day, they said to Samson's wife, "Coax[l] your
husband into explaining the riddle for us, or we will burn you
and your father's household to death.[m] Did you invite us here to
rob us?"

14:1 [a]Ge 38:12
14:2 [b]Ge 21:21; 34:4
14:3 [c]Ge 24:4 [d]Dt 7:3 [e]Ex 34:16
14:4 [f]Jos 11:20 [g]Jdg 13:1
14:6 [h]Jdg 3:10; 13:25
14:12 [i]1Ki 10:1; Eze 17:2 [j]Ge 29:27 [k]Ge 45:22; 2Ki 5:5
14:15 [l]Jdg 16:5; Ecc 7:26 [m]Jdg 15:6

[a] *15* Some Septuagint manuscripts and Syriac; Hebrew *seventh*

14:16
[a]Jdg 16:15

16 Then Samson's wife threw herself on him, sobbing, "You hate
me! You don't really love me.[a] You've given my people a riddle,
but you haven't told me the answer."
"I haven't even explained it to my father or mother," he replied,
"so why should I explain it to you?" 17 She cried the whole seven
days[b] of the feast. So on the seventh day he finally told her, because she continued to press him. She in turn explained the riddle
to her people.

14:17
[b]Est 1:5

18 Before sunset on the seventh day the men of the town said to
him,

14:18
[c]ver 14

> "What is sweeter than honey?
> What is stronger than a lion?"[c]

Samson said to them,

> "If you had not plowed with my heifer,
> you would not have solved my riddle."

14:19
[d]Nu 11:25; Jdg 3:10; 6:34; 11:29; 13:25; 15:14; 1Sa 11:6; 16:13; 1Ki 18:46; 2Ch 24:20; Isa 11:2
[e]1Sa 11:6

19 Then the Spirit of the LORD came upon him in power.[d] He
went down to Ashkelon, struck down thirty of their men, stripped
them of their belongings and gave their clothes to those who had
explained the riddle. Burning with anger,[e] he went up to his
father's house. 20 And Samson's wife was given to the friend[f] who
had attended him at his wedding.

Chapter 15 Theme ______________________

14:20
[f]Jdg 15:2,6; Jn 3:29

15 Later on, at the time of wheat harvest, Samson took a
young goat[g] and went to visit his wife. He said, "I'm going
to my wife's room." But her father would not let him go in.
2 "I was so sure you thoroughly hated her," he said, "that I gave
her to your friend.[h] Isn't her younger sister more attractive? Take
her instead."
3 Samson said to them, "This time I have a right to get even with
the Philistines; I will really harm them." 4 So he went out and
caught three hundred foxes and tied them tail to tail in pairs. He
then fastened a torch to every pair of tails, 5 lit the torches and let
the foxes loose in the standing grain of the Philistines. He burned
up the shocks and standing grain, together with the vineyards
and olive groves.
6 When the Philistines asked, "Who did this?" they were told,
"Samson, the Timnite's son-in-law, because his wife was given to
his friend."
So the Philistines went up and burned her and her father to
death.[i] 7 Samson said to them, "Since you've acted like this, I
won't stop until I get my revenge on you." 8 He attacked them
viciously and slaughtered many of them. Then he went down
and stayed in a cave in the rock of Etam.

15:1
[g]Ge 38:17

15:2
[h]Jdg 14:20

15:6
[i]Jdg 14:15

9The Philistines went up and camped in Judah, spreading out
near Lehi.[a] 10The men of Judah asked, "Why have you come to
fight us?"

"We have come to take Samson prisoner," they answered, "to
do to him as he did to us."

11Then three thousand men from Judah went down to the cave
in the rock of Etam and said to Samson, "Don't you realize that
the Philistines are rulers over us?[b] What have you done to us?"

He answered, "I merely did to them what they did to me."

12They said to him, "We've come to tie you up and hand you
over to the Philistines."

Samson said, "Swear to me that you won't kill me yourselves."

13"Agreed," they answered. "We will only tie you up and hand
you over to them. We will not kill you." So they bound him with
two new ropes and led him up from the rock. 14As he approached
Lehi, the Philistines came toward him shouting. The Spirit of the
LORD came upon him in power.[c] The ropes on his arms became
like charred flax, and the bindings dropped from his hands.
15Finding a fresh jawbone of a donkey, he grabbed it and struck
down a thousand men.[d]

16Then Samson said,

"With a donkey's jawbone
I have made donkeys of them.[a]
With a donkey's jawbone
I have killed a thousand men."

17When he finished speaking, he threw away the jawbone; and
the place was called Ramath Lehi.[b]

18Because he was very thirsty, he cried out to the LORD,[e] "You
have given your servant this great victory. Must I now die of
thirst and fall into the hands of the uncircumcised?" 19Then God
opened up the hollow place in Lehi, and water came out of it.
When Samson drank, his strength returned and he revived.[f] So
the spring was called En Hakkore,[c] and it is still there in Lehi.

20Samson led[d] Israel for twenty years[g] in the days of the
Philistines.

Chapter 16 Theme ______________________________

16 One day Samson went to Gaza, where he saw a prostitute.
He went in to spend the night with her. 2The people of
Gaza were told, "Samson is here!" So they surrounded the place
and lay in wait for him all night at the city gate.[h] They made no
move during the night, saying, "At dawn we'll kill him."

[a] *16* Or *made a heap or two*; the Hebrew for *donkey* sounds like the Hebrew for *heap*.
[b] *17* *Ramath Lehi* means *jawbone hill.* [c] *19* *En Hakkore* means *caller's spring.*
[d] *20* Traditionally *judged*

15:9
[a] ver 14,17,19

15:11
[b] Jdg 13:1; 14:4; Ps 106:40-42

15:14
[c] Jdg 3:10; 14:19; 1Sa 11:6

15:15
[d] Lev 26:8; Jos 23:10; Jdg 3:31

15:18
[e] Jdg 16:28

15:19
[f] Ge 45:27; Isa 40:29

15:20
[g] Jdg 13:1; 16:31; Heb 11:32

16:2
[h] 1Sa 23:26; Ps 118:10-12; Ac 9:24

16:3 [a]Jos 10:36 3But Samson lay there only until the middle of the night. Then
he got up and took hold of the doors of the city gate, together
with the two posts, and tore them loose, bar and all. He lifted
them to his shoulders and carried them to the top of the hill that
faces Hebron.[a]

4Some time later, he fell in love[b] with a woman in the Valley of
16:4 [b]Ge 24:67 Sorek whose name was Delilah. 5The rulers of the Philistines[c]
went to her and said, "See if you can lure[d] him into showing you
the secret of his great strength and how we can overpower him so
we may tie him up and subdue him. Each one of us will give you
eleven hundred shekels[a] of silver."[e]

6So Delilah said to Samson, "Tell me the secret of your great
16:5 [c]Jos 13:3 strength and how you can be tied up and subdued."
[d]Ex 10:7; 7Samson answered her, "If anyone ties me with seven fresh
Jdg 14:15 [e]ver 18 thongs[b] that have not been dried, I'll become as weak as any other
man."

8Then the rulers of the Philistines brought her seven fresh
thongs that had not been dried, and she tied him with them.
9With men hidden in the room,[f] she called to him, "Samson, the
16:9 Philistines are upon you!" But he snapped the thongs as easily as
[f]ver 12 a piece of string snaps when it comes close to a flame. So the
secret of his strength was not discovered.

10Then Delilah said to Samson, "You have made a fool of me;[g]
you lied to me. Come now, tell me how you can be tied."

11He said, "If anyone ties me securely with new ropes[h] that have
16:10 never been used, I'll become as weak as any other man."

[g]ver 13 12So Delilah took new ropes and tied him with them. Then,
with men hidden in the room, she called to him, "Samson, the
Philistines are upon you!" But he snapped the ropes off his arms
as if they were threads.

13Delilah then said to Samson, "Until now, you have been mak-
16:11 ing a fool of me and lying to me. Tell me how you can be tied."

[h]Jdg 15:13 He replied, "If you weave the seven braids of my head into the
fabric ⌞on the loom⌟ and tighten it with the pin, I'll become as
weak as any other man." So while he was sleeping, Delilah took
the seven braids of his head, wove them into the fabric 14and[c]
tightened it with the pin.

16:14 Again she called to him, "Samson, the Philistines are upon
[i]ver 9,20 you!"[i] He awoke from his sleep and pulled up the pin and the
loom, with the fabric.

15Then she said to him, "How can you say, 'I love you,'[j] when
you won't confide in me? This is the third time[k] you have made a
fool of me and haven't told me the secret of your great strength.[l]"

16:15 [j]Jdg 14:16 [k]Nu 24:10 [l]ver 5

a5 That is, about 28 pounds (about 13 kilograms) b7 Or *bowstrings*; also in verses 8 and 9 c13,14 Some Septuagint manuscripts; Hebrew "⌞*I can*⌟ *if you weave the seven braids of my head into the fabric* ⌞*on the loom*⌟." *14So she*

16 With such nagging she prodded him day after day until he was
tired to death.
17 So he told her everything.[a] "No razor has ever been used on
my head," he said, "because I have been a Nazirite[b] set apart to
God since birth. If my head were shaved, my strength would leave
me, and I would become as weak as any other man."
18 When Delilah saw that he had told her everything, she sent
word to the rulers of the Philistines[c], "Come back once more; he
has told me everything." So the rulers of the Philistines returned
with the silver in their hands. 19 Having put him to sleep on her
lap, she called a man to shave off the seven braids of his hair, and
so began to subdue him.[a] And his strength left him.[d]
20 Then she called, "Samson, the Philistines are upon you!"
He awoke from his sleep and thought, "I'll go out as before and
shake myself free." But he did not know that the LORD had left
him.[e]
21 Then the Philistines[f] seized him, gouged out his eyes[g] and
took him down to Gaza. Binding him with bronze shackles, they
set him to grinding[h] in the prison. 22 But the hair on his head
began to grow again after it had been shaved.
23 Now the rulers of the Philistines assembled to offer a great
sacrifice to Dagon[i] their god and to celebrate, saying, "Our god
has delivered Samson, our enemy, into our hands."
24 When the people saw him, they praised their god,[j] saying,

"Our god has delivered our enemy
 into our hands,[k]
the one who laid waste our land
 and multiplied our slain."

25 While they were in high spirits,[l] they shouted, "Bring out
Samson to entertain us." So they called Samson out of the prison,
and he performed for them.
When they stood him among the pillars, 26 Samson said to the
servant who held his hand, "Put me where I can feel the pillars
that support the temple, so that I may lean against them." 27 Now
the temple was crowded with men and women; all the rulers of
the Philistines were there, and on the roof[m] were about three
thousand men and women watching Samson perform. 28 Then
Samson prayed to the LORD,[n] "O Sovereign LORD, remember me.
O God, please strengthen me just once more, and let me with
one blow get revenge[o] on the Philistines for my two eyes." 29 Then
Samson reached toward the two central pillars on which the temple stood. Bracing himself against them, his right hand on the one
and his left hand on the other, 30 Samson said, "Let me die with the
Philistines!" Then he pushed with all his might, and down came

a *19* Hebrew; some Septuagint manuscripts *and he began to weaken*

16:17 [a] Mic 7:5 [b] Nu 6:2,5; Jdg 13:5
16:18 [c] Jos 13:3; 1Sa 5:8
16:19 [d] Pr 7:26-27
16:20 [e] Nu 14:42; Jos 7:12; 1Sa 16:14; 18:12; 28:15
16:21 [f] Jer 47:1 [g] Nu 16:14 [h] Job 31:10; Isa 47:2
16:23 [i] 1Sa 5:2; 1Ch 10:10
16:24 [j] Da 5:4 [k] 1Sa 31:9; 1Ch 10:9
16:25 [l] Jdg 9:27; Ru 3:7; Est 1:10
16:27 [m] Dt 22:8; Jos 2:8
16:28 [n] Jdg 15:18 [o] Jer 15:15

the temple on the rulers and all the people in it. Thus he killed
many more when he died than while he lived.
31 Then his brothers and his father's whole family went down to
get him. They brought him back and buried him between Zorah
and Eshtaol in the tomb of Manoah[a] his father. He had led[a][b] Israel
twenty years.[c]

Chapter 17 Theme ________________________________

17 Now a man named Micah[d] from the hill country of Ephraim 2 said to his mother, "The eleven hundred shekels[b] of
silver that were taken from you and about which I heard you utter
a curse—I have that silver with me; I took it."
Then his mother said, "The LORD bless you,[e] my son!"
3 When he returned the eleven hundred shekels of silver to his
mother, she said, "I solemnly consecrate my silver to the LORD for
my son to make a carved image and a cast idol.[f] I will give it back
to you."
4 So he returned the silver to his mother, and she took two hundred shekels[c] of silver and gave them to a silversmith, who made
them into the image and the idol.[g] And they were put in Micah's
house.
5 Now this man Micah had a shrine,[h] and he made an ephod[i]
and some idols[j] and installed[k] one of his sons as his priest.[l] 6 In
those days Israel had no king;[m] everyone did as he saw fit.[n]
7 A young Levite from Bethlehem in Judah,[o] who had been living within the clan of Judah, 8 left that town in search of some
other place to stay. On his way[d] he came to Micah's house in the
hill country of Ephraim.
9 Micah asked him, "Where are you from?"
"I'm a Levite from Bethlehem in Judah," he said, "and I'm
looking for a place to stay."
10 Then Micah said to him, "Live with me and be my father and
priest,[p] and I'll give you ten shekels[e] of silver a year, your clothes
and your food." 11 So the Levite agreed to live with him, and the
young man was to him like one of his sons. 12 Then Micah
installed[q] the Levite, and the young man became his priest and
lived in his house. 13 And Micah said, "Now I know that the LORD
will be good to me, since this Levite has become my priest."

Chapter 18 Theme ________________________________

18 In those days Israel had no king.[r]
And in those days the tribe of the Danites was seeking a
place of their own where they might settle, because they had not

16:31 [a] Jdg 13:2 [b] Ru 1:1; 1Sa 4:18 [c] Jdg 15:20
17:1 [d] Jdg 18:2,13
17:2 [e] Ru 2:20; 1Sa 15:13; 2Sa 2:5
17:3 [f] Ex 20:4,23; 34:17; Lev 19:4
17:4 [g] Ex 32:4; Isa 17:8
17:5 [h] Isa 44:13; Eze 8:10 [i] Jdg 8:27 [j] Ge 31:19; Jdg 18:14 [k] Nu 16:10 [l] Ex 29:9; Jdg 18:24
17:6 [m] Jdg 18:1; 19:1; 21:25 [n] Dt 12:8
17:7 [o] Jdg 19:1; Ru 1:1-2; Mic 5:2; Mt 2:1
17:10 [p] Jdg 18:19
17:12 [q] Nu 16:10
18:1 [r] Jdg 17:6; 19:1

[a] *31* Traditionally *judged* [b] *2* That is, about 28 pounds (about 13 kilograms) [c] *4* That is, about 5 pounds (about 2.3 kilograms) [d] *8* Or *To carry on his profession* [e] *10* That is, about 4 ounces (about 110 grams)

yet come into an inheritance among the tribes of Israel.[a] 2So the
Danites[b] sent five warriors from Zorah and Eshtaol to spy out the
land and explore it. These men represented all their clans. They
told them, "Go, explore the land."[c]
The men entered the hill country of Ephraim and came to the
house of Micah,[d] where they spent the night. 3When they were
near Micah's house, they recognized the voice of the young
Levite; so they turned in there and asked him, "Who brought you
here? What are you doing in this place? Why are you here?"
4He told them what Micah had done for him, and said, "He has
hired me and I am his priest.[e]"
5Then they said to him, "Please inquire of God[f] to learn whether
our journey will be successful."
6The priest answered them, "Go in peace[g]. Your journey has the
LORD's approval."
7So the five men left and came to Laish,[h] where they saw that
the people were living in safety, like the Sidonians, unsuspecting
and secure. And since their land lacked nothing, they were prosperous.[a] Also, they lived a long way from the Sidonians[i] and had
no relationship with anyone else.[b]
8When they returned to Zorah and Eshtaol, their brothers asked
them, "How did you find things?"
9They answered, "Come on, let's attack them! We have seen that
the land is very good. Aren't you going to do something? Don't
hesitate to go there and take it over.[j] 10When you get there, you
will find an unsuspecting people and a spacious land that God
has put into your hands, a land that lacks nothing[k] whatever.[l]"
11Then six hundred men[m] from the clan of the Danites,[n] armed
for battle, set out from Zorah and Eshtaol. 12On their way they set
up camp near Kiriath Jearim in Judah. This is why the place west
of Kiriath Jearim is called Mahaneh Dan[c][o] to this day. 13From
there they went on to the hill country of Ephraim and came to
Micah's house.
14Then the five men who had spied out the land of Laish said
to their brothers, "Do you know that one of these houses has an
ephod, other household gods, a carved image and a cast idol?[p]
Now you know what to do." 15So they turned in there and went
to the house of the young Levite at Micah's place and greeted
him. 16The six hundred Danites,[q] armed for battle, stood at the
entrance to the gate. 17The five men who had spied out the land
went inside and took the carved image, the ephod, the other
household gods[r] and the cast idol while the priest and the six
hundred armed men stood at the entrance to the gate.

[a] *7* The meaning of the Hebrew for this clause is uncertain. [b] *7* Hebrew; some Septuagint manuscripts *with the Arameans* [c] *12* *Mahaneh Dan* means *Dan's camp.*

18:1 [a] Jos 19:47
18:2 [b] Jdg 13:25 [c] Jos 2:1 [d] Jdg 17:1
18:4 [e] Jdg 17:12
18:5 [f] 1Ki 22:5
18:6 [g] 1Ki 22:6
18:7 [h] Jos 19:47 [i] ver 28
18:9 [j] Nu 13:30; 1Ki 22:3
18:10 [k] ver 7,27; Dt 8:9 [l] 1Ch 4:40
18:11 [m] ver 16,17 [n] Jdg 13:2
18:12 [o] Jdg 13:25
18:14 [p] Ge 31:19; Jdg 17:5
18:16 [q] ver 11
18:17 [r] Ge 31:19; Mic 5:13

18When these men went into Micah's house and took[a] the
carved image, the ephod, the other household gods and the cast
idol, the priest said to them, "What are you doing?"
19They answered him, "Be quiet![b] Don't say a word. Come with
us, and be our father and priest.[c] Isn't it better that you serve a
tribe and clan in Israel as priest rather than just one man's
household?" 20Then the priest was glad. He took the ephod, the
other household gods and the carved image and went along with
the people. 21Putting their little children, their livestock and their
possessions in front of them, they turned away and left.
22When they had gone some distance from Micah's house, the
men who lived near Micah were called together and overtook the
Danites. 23As they shouted after them, the Danites turned and
said to Micah, "What's the matter with you that you called out
your men to fight?"
24He replied, "You took the gods I made, and my priest, and
went away. What else do I have? How can you ask, 'What's the
matter with you?'"
25The Danites answered, "Don't argue with us, or some hot-
tempered men will attack you, and you and your family will lose
your lives." 26So the Danites went their way, and Micah, seeing
that they were too strong for him,[d] turned around and went back
home.
27Then they took what Micah had made, and his priest, and
went on to Laish, against a peaceful and unsuspecting people.[e]
They attacked them with the sword and burned down their city.[f]
28There was no one to rescue them because they lived a long way
from Sidon[g] and had no relationship with anyone else. The city
was in a valley near Beth Rehob.[h]
The Danites rebuilt the city and settled there. 29They named it
Dan[i] after their forefather Dan, who was born to Israel—though
the city used to be called Laish.[j] 30There the Danites set up for
themselves the idols, and Jonathan son of Gershom,[k] the son of
Moses,[a] and his sons were priests for the tribe of Dan until the
time of the captivity of the land. 31They continued to use the idols
Micah had made, all the time the house of God[l] was in Shiloh.[m]

Chapter 19 Theme ____________________

19 In those days Israel had no king.
Now a Levite who lived in a remote area in the hill country of Ephraim[n] took a concubine from Bethlehem in Judah.[o]
2But she was unfaithful to him. She left him and went back to
her father's house in Bethlehem, Judah. After she had been there

a 30 An ancient Hebrew scribal tradition, some Septuagint manuscripts and Vulgate; Masoretic Text *Manasseh*

18:18 [a] Isa 46:2; Jer 43:11; Hos 10:5
18:19 [b] Job 21:5; 29:9; 40:4; Mic 7:16 [c] Jdg 17:10
18:26 [d] Ps 18:17; 35:10
18:27 [e] ver 7,10 [f] Ge 49:17; Jos 19:47
18:28 [g] ver 7 [h] Nu 13:21; 2Sa 10:6
18:29 [i] Ge 14:14 [j] Jos 19:47; 1Ki 15:20
18:30 [k] Ex 2:22; Jdg 17:3,5
18:31 [l] Jdg 19:18 [m] Jos 18:1; Jer 7:14
19:1 [n] Jdg 18:1 [o] Ru 1:1

four months, 3her husband went to her to persuade her to return.
He had with him his servant and two donkeys. She took him into
her father's house, and when her father saw him, he gladly welcomed him. 4His father-in-law, the girl's father, prevailed upon
him to stay; so he remained with him three days, eating and
drinking,[a] and sleeping there.
5On the fourth day they got up early and he prepared to leave,
but the girl's father said to his son-in-law, "Refresh yourself[b]
with something to eat; then you can go." 6So the two of them sat
down to eat and drink together. Afterward the girl's father said,
"Please stay tonight and enjoy yourself.[c]" 7And when the man
got up to go, his father-in-law persuaded him, so he stayed there
that night. 8On the morning of the fifth day, when he rose to go,
the girl's father said, "Refresh yourself. Wait till afternoon!" So
the two of them ate together.
9Then when the man, with his concubine and his servant, got
up to leave, his father-in-law, the girl's father, said, "Now look,
it's almost evening. Spend the night here; the day is nearly over.
Stay and enjoy yourself. Early tomorrow morning you can get
up and be on your way home." 10But, unwilling to stay another
night, the man left and went toward Jebus[d] (that is, Jerusalem),
with his two saddled donkeys and his concubine.
11When they were near Jebus and the day was almost gone, the
servant said to his master, "Come, let's stop at this city of the
Jebusites[e] and spend the night."
12His master replied, "No. We won't go into an alien city, whose
people are not Israelites. We will go on to Gibeah." 13He added,
"Come, let's try to reach Gibeah or Ramah[f] and spend the night
in one of those places." 14So they went on, and the sun set as they
neared Gibeah in Benjamin.[g] 15There they stopped to spend the
night. They went and sat in the city square,[h] but no one took them
into his home for the night.
16That evening[i] an old man from the hill country of Ephraim,[j]
who was living in Gibeah (the men of the place were Benjamites),
came in from his work in the fields. 17When he looked and saw
the traveler in the city square, the old man asked, "Where are you
going? Where did you come from?"[k]
18He answered, "We are on our way from Bethlehem in Judah to
a remote area in the hill country of Ephraim where I live. I have
been to Bethlehem in Judah and now I am going to the house of
the LORD.[l] No one has taken me into his house. 19We have both
straw and fodder[m] for our donkeys and bread and wine[n] for ourselves your servants—me, your maidservant, and the young man
with us. We don't need anything."
20"You are welcome at my house," the old man said. "Let me
supply whatever you need. Only don't spend the night in the

19:4 [a] Ex 32:6
19:5 [b] ver 8; Ge 18:5
19:6 [c] ver 9,22; Jdg 16:25
19:10 [d] Ge 10:16; Jos 15:8; 1Ch 11:4-5
19:11 [e] Jos 3:10
19:13 [f] Jos 18:25
19:14 [g] 1Sa 10:26; Isa 10:29
19:15 [h] Ge 19:2
19:16 [i] Ps 104:23 [j] ver 1
19:17 [k] Ge 29:4
19:18 [l] Jdg 18:31
19:19 [m] Ge 24:25 [n] Ge 14:18

square." [21]So he took him into his house and fed his donkeys. After they had washed their feet, they had something to eat and drink.[a]

[22]While they were enjoying themselves,[b] some of the wicked men[c] of the city surrounded the house. Pounding on the door, they shouted to the old man who owned the house, "Bring out the man who came to your house so we can have sex with him.[d]"

[23]The owner of the house went outside[e] and said to them, "No, my friends, don't be so vile. Since this man is my guest, don't do this disgraceful thing.[f] [24]Look, here is my virgin daughter,[g] and his concubine. I will bring them out to you now, and you can use them and do to them whatever you wish. But to this man, don't do such a disgraceful thing."

[25]But the men would not listen to him. So the man took his concubine and sent her outside to them, and they raped her and abused her[h] throughout the night, and at dawn they let her go. [26]At daybreak the woman went back to the house where her master was staying, fell down at the door and lay there until daylight.

[27]When her master got up in the morning and opened the door of the house and stepped out to continue on his way, there lay his concubine, fallen in the doorway of the house, with her hands on the threshold. [28]He said to her, "Get up; let's go." But there was no answer. Then the man put her on his donkey and set out for home.

[29]When he reached home, he took a knife[i] and cut up his concubine, limb by limb, into twelve parts and sent them into all the areas of Israel.[j] [30]Everyone who saw it said, "Such a thing has never been seen or done, not since the day the Israelites came up out of Egypt.[k] Think about it! Consider it! Tell us what to do![l]"

Chapter 20 Theme ______________________________

20 Then all the Israelites[m] from Dan to Beersheba[n] and from the land of Gilead came out as one man[o] and assembled[p] before the LORD in Mizpah. [2]The leaders of all the people of the tribes of Israel took their places in the assembly of the people of God, four hundred thousand soldiers[q] armed with swords. [3](The Benjamites heard that the Israelites had gone up to Mizpah.) Then the Israelites said, "Tell us how this awful thing happened."

[4]So the Levite, the husband of the murdered woman, said, "I and my concubine came to Gibeah[r] in Benjamin to spend the night.[s] [5]During the night the men of Gibeah came after me and surrounded the house, intending to kill me.[t] They raped my concubine, and she died.[u] [6]I took my concubine, cut her into pieces and sent one piece to each region of Israel's inheritance,[v] because they committed this lewd and disgraceful act[w] in Israel. [7]Now, all you Israelites, speak up and give your verdict.[x]"

19:21 [a]Ge 24:32-33; Lk 7:44
19:22 [b]Jdg 16:25 [c]Dt 13:13 [d]Ge 19:4-5; Jdg 20:5; Ro 1:26-27
19:23 [e]Ge 19:6 [f]Ge 34:7; Lev 19:29; Dt 22:21; Jdg 20:6; 2Sa 13:12; Ro 1:27
19:24 [g]Ge 19:8; Dt 21:14
19:25 [h]1Sa 31:4
19:29 [i]Ge 22:6 [j]Jdg 20:6; 1Sa 11:7
19:30 [k]Hos 9:9 [l]Jdg 20:7; Pr 13:10
20:1 [m]Jdg 21:5 [n]1Sa 3:20; 2Sa 3:10; 1Ki 4:25 [o]1Sa 11:7 [p]1Sa 7:5
20:2 [q]Jdg 8:10
20:4 [r]Jos 15:57 [s]Jdg 19:15
20:5 [t]Jdg 19:22 [u]Jdg 19:25-26
20:6 [v]Jdg 19:29 [w]Jos 7:15; Jdg 19:23
20:7 [x]Jdg 19:30

8All the people rose as one man, saying, "None of us will go
home. No, not one of us will return to his house. 9But now this is
what we'll do to Gibeah: We'll go up against it as the lot directs.[a]
10We'll take ten men out of every hundred from all the tribes of
Israel, and a hundred from a thousand, and a thousand from ten
thousand, to get provisions for the army. Then, when the army
arrives at Gibeah[a] in Benjamin, it can give them what they deserve
for all this vileness done in Israel." 11So all the men of Israel got
together and united as one man[b] against the city.

12The tribes of Israel sent men throughout the tribe of Benjamin, saying, "What about this awful crime that was committed
among you? 13Now surrender those wicked men[c] of Gibeah so
that we may put them to death and purge the evil from Israel.[d]"

But the Benjamites would not listen to their fellow Israelites.
14From their towns they came together at Gibeah to fight against
the Israelites. 15At once the Benjamites mobilized twenty-six
thousand swordsmen from their towns, in addition to seven hundred chosen men from those living in Gibeah. 16Among all these
soldiers there were seven hundred chosen men who were left-
handed,[e] each of whom could sling a stone at a hair and not miss.

17Israel, apart from Benjamin, mustered four hundred thousand swordsmen, all of them fighting men.

18The Israelites went up to Bethel[b] and inquired of God.[f] They
said, "Who of us shall go first to fight[g] against the Benjamites?"

The LORD replied, "Judah shall go first."

19The next morning the Israelites got up and pitched camp
near Gibeah. 20The men of Israel went out to fight the Benjamites
and took up battle positions against them at Gibeah. 21The Benjamites came out of Gibeah and cut down twenty-two thousand
Israelites[h] on the battlefield that day. 22But the men of Israel
encouraged one another and again took up their positions where
they had stationed themselves the first day. 23The Israelites went
up and wept before the LORD until evening,[i] and they inquired of
the LORD. They said, "Shall we go up again to battle[j] against the
Benjamites, our brothers?"

The LORD answered, "Go up against them."

24Then the Israelites drew near to Benjamin the second day.
25This time, when the Benjamites came out from Gibeah to oppose
them, they cut down another eighteen thousand Israelites,[k] all of
them armed with swords.

26Then the Israelites, all the people, went up to Bethel, and there
they sat weeping before the LORD.[l] They fasted that day until
evening and presented burnt offerings and fellowship offerings[c]

[a] *10* One Hebrew manuscript; most Hebrew manuscripts *Geba,* a variant of *Gibeah*
[b] *18* Or *to the house of God*; also in verse26 [c] *26* Traditionally *peace offerings*

20:9 [a]Lev 16:8
20:11 [b]ver 1
20:13 [c]Dt 13:13; Jdg 19:22 [d]Dt 17:12
20:16 [e]Jdg 3:15; 1Ch 12:2
20:18 [f]ver 26-27; Nu 27:21 [g]ver 23,28
20:21 [h]ver 25
20:23 [i]Jos 7:6 [j]ver 18
20:25 [k]ver 21
20:26 [l]ver 23

20:26 to the LORD.[a] 27 And the Israelites inquired of the LORD. (In those
a Jdg 21:4 days the ark of the covenant of God[b] was there, 28 with Phinehas
son of Eleazar,[c] the son of Aaron, ministering before it.)[d] They
20:27 asked, "Shall we go up again to battle with Benjamin our brother,
b Jos 18:1 or not?"

The LORD responded, "Go, for tomorrow I will give them into
20:28 your hands.[e]"

c Jos 24:33 29 Then Israel set an ambush[f] around Gibeah. 30 They went up
d Dt 18:5 against the Benjamites on the third day and took up positions
e Jdg 7:9 against Gibeah as they had done before. 31 The Benjamites came
out to meet them and were drawn away[g] from the city. They
20:29 began to inflict casualties on the Israelites as before, so that
f Jos 8:2,4 about thirty men fell in the open field and on the roads—the
one leading to Bethel and the other to Gibeah.

20:31 32 While the Benjamites were saying, "We are defeating them as
g Jos 8:16 before,"[h] the Israelites were saying, "Let's retreat and draw them
away from the city to the roads."

20:32 33 All the men of Israel moved from their places and took up
h ver 39 positions at Baal Tamar, and the Israelite ambush charged out of
its place[i] on the west[a] of Gibeah.[b] 34 Then ten thousand of Israel's
finest men made a frontal attack on Gibeah. The fighting was so
20:33 heavy that the Benjamites did not realize[j] how near disaster was.[k]
i Jos 8:19 35 The LORD defeated Benjamin[l] before Israel, and on that day the
Israelites struck down 25,100 Benjamites, all armed with swords.
20:34 36 Then the Benjamites saw that they were beaten.

j Jos 8:14 Now the men of Israel had given way[m] before Benjamin, because
k Isa 47:11 they relied on the ambush they had set near Gibeah. 37 The men
who had been in ambush made a sudden dash into Gibeah,
20:35 spread out and put the whole city to the sword.[n] 38 The men of
l 1Sa 9:21 Israel had arranged with the ambush that they should send up a
great cloud of smoke[o] from the city, 39 and then the men of Israel
20:36 would turn in the battle.

m Jos 8:15 The Benjamites had begun to inflict casualties on the men of
Israel (about thirty), and they said, "We are defeating them as in
20:37 the first battle."[p] 40 But when the column of smoke began to rise
n Jos 8:19 from the city, the Benjamites turned and saw the smoke of the
whole city going up into the sky.[q] 41 Then the men of Israel turned
on them, and the men of Benjamin were terrified, because they
20:38 realized that disaster had come upon them. 42 So they fled before
o Jos 8:20 the Israelites in the direction of the desert, but they could not
escape the battle. And the men of Israel who came out of the
20:39 towns cut them down there. 43 They surrounded the Benjamites,
p ver 32 chased them and easily[c] overran them in the vicinity of Gibeah

[a] *33* Some Septuagint manuscripts and Vulgate; the meaning of the Hebrew for this word
20:40 is uncertain. [b] *33* Hebrew *Geba,* a variant of *Gibeah* [c] *43* The meaning of the Hebrew
q Jos 8:20 for this word is uncertain.

on the east. 44Eighteen thousand Benjamites fell, all of them
valiant fighters.[a] 45As they turned and fled toward the desert to
the rock of Rimmon,[b] the Israelites cut down five thousand men
along the roads. They kept pressing after the Benjamites as far as
Gidom and struck down two thousand more.
46On that day twenty-five thousand Benjamite swordsmen fell,
all of them valiant fighters. 47But six hundred men turned and
fled into the desert to the rock of Rimmon, where they stayed
four months. 48The men of Israel went back to Benjamin and put
all the towns to the sword, including the animals and everything
else they found. All the towns they came across they set on fire.[c]

Chapter 21 Theme

21 The men of Israel had taken an oath[d] at Mizpah:[e] "Not one
of us will give[f] his daughter in marriage to a Benjamite."
2The people went to Bethel,[a] where they sat before God until
evening, raising their voices and weeping bitterly. 3"O LORD, the
God of Israel," they cried, "why has this happened to Israel? Why
should one tribe be missing from Israel today?"
4Early the next day the people built an altar and presented burnt
offerings and fellowship offerings.[b][g]
5Then the Israelites asked, "Who from all the tribes of Israel[h]
has failed to assemble before the LORD?" For they had taken a
solemn oath that anyone who failed to assemble before the LORD
at Mizpah should certainly be put to death.
6Now the Israelites grieved for their brothers, the Benjamites.
"Today one tribe is cut off from Israel," they said. 7"How can we
provide wives for those who are left, since we have taken an oath[i]
by the LORD not to give them any of our daughters in marriage?"
8Then they asked, "Which one of the tribes of Israel failed to
assemble before the LORD at Mizpah?" They discovered that no
one from Jabesh Gilead[j] had come to the camp for the assembly.
9For when they counted the people, they found that none of the
people of Jabesh Gilead were there.
10So the assembly sent twelve thousand fighting men with
instructions to go to Jabesh Gilead and put to the sword those
living there, including the women and children. 11"This is what
you are to do," they said. "Kill every male and every woman who
is not a virgin.[k]" 12They found among the people living in Jabesh
Gilead four hundred young women who had never slept with a
man, and they took them to the camp at Shiloh[l] in Canaan.
13Then the whole assembly sent an offer of peace[m] to the Benjamites at the rock of Rimmon.[n] 14So the Benjamites returned at

a2 Or *to the house of God* b4 Traditionally *peace offerings*

20:44 [a]Ps 76:5
20:45 [b]Jos 15:32; Jdg 21:13
20:48 [c]Jdg 21:23
21:1 [d]Jos 9:18 [e]Jdg 20:1 [f]ver 7,18
21:4 [g]Jdg 20:26; 2Sa 24:25
21:5 [h]Jdg 5:23; 20:1
21:7 [i]ver 1
21:8 [j]1Sa 11:1; 31:11
21:11 [k]Nu 31:17-18
21:12 [l]Jos 18:1
21:13 [m]Dt 20:10 [n]Jdg 20:47

that time and were given the women of Jabesh Gilead who had
been spared. But there were not enough for all of them.
[15]The people grieved for Benjamin,[a] because the LORD had
made a gap in the tribes of Israel. [16]And the elders of the assembly
said, "With the women of Benjamin destroyed, how shall we provide wives for the men who are left? [17]The Benjamite survivors
must have heirs," they said, "so that a tribe of Israel will not be
wiped out. [18]We can't give them our daughters as wives, since we
Israelites have taken this oath: 'Cursed be anyone who gives[b] a
wife to a Benjamite.' [19]But look, there is the annual festival of the
LORD in Shiloh,[c] to the north of Bethel, and east of the road that
goes from Bethel to Shechem, and to the south of Lebonah."
[20]So they instructed the Benjamites, saying, "Go and hide in
the vineyards [21]and watch. When the girls of Shiloh come out to
join in the dancing,[d] then rush from the vineyards and each of
you seize a wife from the girls of Shiloh and go to the land of
Benjamin. [22]When their fathers or brothers complain to us, we
will say to them, 'Do us a kindness by helping them, because we
did not get wives for them during the war, and you are innocent,
since you did not give[e] your daughters to them.' "
[23]So that is what the Benjamites did. While the girls were dancing, each man caught one and carried her off to be his wife. Then
they returned to their inheritance and rebuilt the towns and settled in them.[f]
[24]At that time the Israelites left that place and went home to
their tribes and clans, each to his own inheritance.
[25]In those days Israel had no king; everyone did as he saw fit.[g]

21:15 [a]ver 6
21:18 [b]ver 1
21:19 [c]Jos 18:1; Jdg 18:31; 1Sa 1:3
21:21 [d]Ex 15:20; Jdg 11:34
21:22 [e]ver 1,18
21:23 [f]Jdg 20:48
21:25 [g]Dt 12:8; Jdg 17:6; 18:1; 19:1

The Judges of Israel

Judge	Chapter/ Verse	Years Judged	Major Facts/Accomplishments	Lessons for My Life

Judges at a Glance

Theme of Judges:

Author:

Date:

Purpose:

Key Words:

Israelites did evil (Israelites once again did evil)

sold (served, serving, were subject)

Israelites cried out (they cried out, Israelites cried, they cried to the Lord)

he raised up for them a deliverer, he gave them a deliverer (the Lord raised up a judge)

judge(s)

Segment Divisions		Chapter Themes
		1
		2
		3
		4
		5
		6
		7
		8
		9
		10
		11
		12
		13
		14
		15
		16
		17
		18
		19
		20
		21

RUTH

The book of Ruth is set chronologically in the midst of the dark years of the judges. It offers encouragement and hope to those who decide to follow God. This story of love and dedication revolves around three people who determine in their hearts to walk in integrity, clinging to their God and his precepts—three people who know who their king is and who do what is right in his eyes.

Things to Do

1. As you read Ruth one chapter at a time:

   a. First read each chapter simply to catch the flavor of the lives of these people.

   b. Then read each chapter again, observing the events of that chapter. Examine what you read in light of the five W's and an H, asking questions such as: Who are these people? What can I learn about them? What is happening to them? When is it happening, and where? Why do they do what they do? How will they accomplish their tasks? What will be the end result? Record pertinent insights in the margin.

   c. Watch for and mark the key repeated words listed on the RUTH AT A GLANCE chart on page 441. After you finish marking key words in a chapter, observe what you learn about each. If there is something significant you want to remember, write it in the margin.

2. Determine the theme of each chapter and record it on RUTH AT A GLANCE and on the line next to the chapter number in the text.

3. When you finish reading Ruth and marking every reference to *redeem (redemption), kinsman-redeemer, kinsman,* and *close relative (near of kin, relative):*

   a. List everything you learn about the process of redeeming a close relative. Pay attention to the process in chapter 4.

   b. Look up the laws regarding redemption in Leviticus 25:23-28 and Deuteronomy 25:5-10. You may want to record these cross-references in the margin next to your insights on redemption.

4. Complete RUTH AT A GLANCE.

Things to Think About

1. What have you learned about loyalty from the story of Ruth? What does it mean to be loyal to God, to his people, to his precepts, and to trust God to do what he says he will do?

2. As you think of Boaz redeeming Ruth, remember that you have a kinsman-redeemer, the Lord Jesus Christ. Think of how the Lord has acted on your behalf as your kinsman-redeemer by becoming a man so he could break death's hold by paying for your sin (Hebrews 2:14, 15). Remember that you were not redeemed from your empty way of life with silver or gold, but with the precious blood of the Lamb of God, a Lamb without spot or blemish (1 Peter 1:18, 19).

3. The final verses of Ruth show us that Ruth was included in the genealogy of David and therefore in the human lineage of our Lord Jesus Christ. Not only did a sovereign God include the harlot, Rahab, in the genealogy of his Son, but he also chose a Gentile, Ruth. Both of these women chose to believe God when those around them didn't! Consider how their example might apply to your life.

4. In the book of Judges Israel forsook the true God and turned to idols, while in Ruth the opposite is seen. One Gentile woman turns from idols to serve the only true God. In which category do you find yourself?

Chapter 1 Theme ________________

1 In the days when the judges ruled,[a][a] there was a famine in the
land,[b] and a man from Bethlehem in Judah, together with his
wife and two sons, went to live for a while in the country of
Moab.[c] 2 The man's name was Elimelech, his wife's name Naomi,
and the names of his two sons were Mahlon and Kilion. They
were Ephrathites from Bethlehem,[d] Judah. And they went to
Moab and lived there.
3 Now Elimelech, Naomi's husband, died, and she was left with
her two sons. 4 They married Moabite women, one named Orpah
and the other Ruth.[e] After they had lived there about ten years,
5 both Mahlon and Kilion also died, and Naomi was left without
her two sons and her husband.
6 When she heard in Moab that the LORD had come to the aid of his
people[f] by providing food[g] for them, Naomi and her daughters-
in-law prepared to return home from there. 7 With her two
daughters-in-law she left the place where she had been living and
set out on the road that would take them back to the land of Judah.
8 Then Naomi said to her two daughters-in-law, "Go back, each of
you, to your mother's home. May the LORD show kindness[h] to you,
as you have shown to your dead[i] and to me. 9 May the LORD grant
that each of you will find rest[j] in the home of another husband."
Then she kissed them and they wept aloud 10 and said to her,
"We will go back with you to your people."
11 But Naomi said, "Return home,
my daughters. Why would you come
with me? Am I going to have any
more sons, who could become your
husbands?[k] 12 Return home, my
daughters; I am too old to have
another husband. Even if I thought
there was still hope for me—even if
I had a husband tonight and then
gave birth to sons— 13 would you
wait until they grew up? Would you
remain unmarried for them? No,
my daughters. It is more bitter for
me than for you, because the LORD's
hand has gone out against me![l]"
14 At this they wept again. Then
Orpah kissed her mother-in-law[m] good-by, but Ruth clung to her.[n]
15 "Look," said Naomi, "your sister-in-law is going back to her
people and her gods.[o] Go back with her."

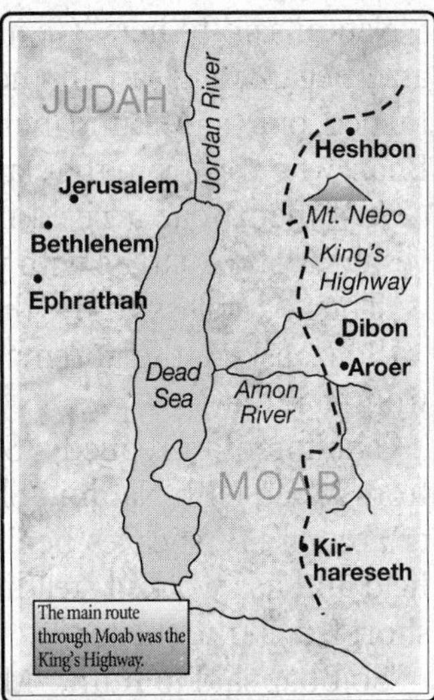

The main route through Moab was the King's Highway.

Ruth's Journey from Moab to Bethlehem

1:1 [a]Jdg 2:16-18 [b]Ge 12:10; Ps 105:16 [c]Jdg 3:30
1:2 [d]Ge 35:19
1:4 [e]Mt 1:5
1:6 [f]Ex 4:31; Jer 29:10; Zep 2:7 [g]Ps 132:15; Mt 6:11
1:8 [h]Ru 2:20; 2Ti 1:16 [i]ver 5
1:9 [j]Ru 3:1
1:11 [k]Ge 38:11; Dt 25:5
1:13 [l]Jdg 2:15; Job 4:5; 19:21; Ps 32:4
1:14 [m]Ru 2:11 [n]Pr 17:17; 18:24
1:15 [o]Jos 24:14; Jdg 11:24

[a] *1* Traditionally *judged*

16But Ruth replied, "Don't urge me to leave you[a] or to turn
back from you. Where you go I will go, and where you stay I will
stay. Your people will be my people and your God my God.[b]
17Where you die I will die, and there I will be buried. May the
LORD deal with me, be it ever so severely,[c] if anything but death
separates you and me." 18When Naomi realized that Ruth was
determined to go with her, she stopped urging her.[d]
19So the two women went on until they came to Bethlehem.
When they arrived in Bethlehem, the whole town was stirred[e]
because of them, and the women exclaimed, "Can this be Naomi?"
20"Don't call me Naomi,[a]" she told them. "Call me Mara,[b]
because the Almighty[c][f] has made my life very bitter.[g] 21I went
away full, but the LORD has brought me back empty.[h] Why call
me Naomi? The LORD has afflicted[d] me; the Almighty has
brought misfortune upon me."
22So Naomi returned from Moab accompanied by Ruth the
Moabitess, her daughter-in-law, arriving in Bethlehem as the
barley harvest[i] was beginning.[j]

Chapter 2 Theme ______________________________

2 Now Naomi had a relative[k] on her husband's side, from the
clan of Elimelech,[l] a man of standing, whose name was Boaz.[m]
2And Ruth the Moabitess said to Naomi, "Let me go to the
fields and pick up the leftover grain[n] behind anyone in whose
eyes I find favor."
Naomi said to her, "Go ahead, my daughter." 3So she went out
and began to glean in the fields behind the harvesters. As it
turned out, she found herself working in a field belonging to
Boaz, who was from the clan of Elimelech.
4Just then Boaz arrived from Bethlehem and greeted the harvesters, "The LORD be with you![o]"
"The LORD bless you![p]" they called back.
5Boaz asked the foreman of his harvesters, "Whose young
woman is that?"
6The foreman replied, "She is the Moabitess[q] who came back
from Moab with Naomi. 7She said, 'Please let me glean and gather among the sheaves behind the harvesters.' She went into the
field and has worked steadily from morning till now, except for a
short rest in the shelter."
8So Boaz said to Ruth, "My daughter, listen to me. Don't go and
glean in another field and don't go away from here. Stay here
with my servant girls. 9Watch the field where the men are harvesting, and follow along after the girls. I have told the men not

1:16 [a]2Ki 2:2 [b]Ru 2:11,12
1:17 [c]1Sa 3:17; 25:22; 2Sa 19:13; 2Ki 6:31
1:18 [d]Ac 21:14
1:19 [e]Mt 21:10
1:20 [f]Ex 6:3 [g]ver 13; Job 6:4
1:21 [h]Job 1:21
1:22 [i]Ex 9:31; Ru 2:23 [j]2Sa 21:9
2:1 [k]Ru 3:2,12 [l]Ru 1:2 [m]Ru 4:21
2:2 [n]ver 7; Lev 19:9; 23:22; Dt 24:19
2:4 [o]Jdg 6:12; Lk 1:28; 2Th 3:16 [p]Ps 129:7-8
2:6 [q]Ru 1:22

[a]20 *Naomi* means *pleasant*; also in verse 21. [b]20 *Mara* means *bitter*. [c]20 Hebrew *Shaddai*; also in verse 21 [d]21 Or *has testified against*

to touch you. And whenever you are thirsty, go and get a drink from the water jars the men have filled."

10 At this, she bowed down with her face to the ground.[a] She exclaimed, "Why have I found such favor in your eyes that you notice me[b]—a foreigner?[c]"

11 Boaz replied, "I've been told all about what you have done for your mother-in-law[d] since the death of your husband—how you left your father and mother and your homeland and came to live with a people you did not know before.[e] 12 May the LORD repay you for what you have done. May you be richly rewarded by the LORD,[f] the God of Israel, under whose wings[g] you have come to take refuge.[h]"

13 "May I continue to find favor in your eyes, my lord," she said. "You have given me comfort and have spoken kindly to your servant—though I do not have the standing of one of your servant girls."

14 At mealtime Boaz said to her, "Come over here. Have some bread and dip it in the wine vinegar."

When she sat down with the harvesters, he offered her some roasted grain. She ate all she wanted and had some left over.[i] 15 As she got up to glean, Boaz gave orders to his men, "Even if she gathers among the sheaves, don't embarrass her. 16 Rather, pull out some stalks for her from the bundles and leave them for her to pick up, and don't rebuke her."

17 So Ruth gleaned in the field until evening. Then she threshed the barley she had gathered, and it amounted to about an ephah.[a] 18 She carried it back to town, and her mother-in-law saw how much she had gathered. Ruth also brought out and gave her what she had left over[j] after she had eaten enough.

19 Her mother-in-law asked her, "Where did you glean today? Where did you work? Blessed be the man who took notice of you![k]"

Then Ruth told her mother-in-law about the one at whose place she had been working. "The name of the man I worked with today is Boaz," she said.

20 "The LORD bless him!" Naomi said to her daughter-in-law. "He has not stopped showing his kindness[l] to the living and the dead." She added, "That man is our close relative; he is one of our kinsman-redeemers.[m]"

21 Then Ruth the Moabitess said, "He even said to me, 'Stay with my workers until they finish harvesting all my grain.'"

22 Naomi said to Ruth her daughter-in-law, "It will be good for you, my daughter, to go with his girls, because in someone else's field you might be harmed."

2:10 [a] 1Sa 25:23 [b] Ps 41:1 [c] Dt 15:3
2:11 [d] Ru 1:14 [e] Ru 1:16-17
2:12 [f] 1Sa 24:19 [g] Ps 17:8; 36:7; 57:1; 61:4; 63:7; 91:4 [h] Ru 1:16
2:14 [i] ver 18
2:18 [j] ver 14
2:19 [k] ver 10; Ps 41:1
2:20 [l] Ru 3:10; 2Sa 2:5; Pr 17:17 [m] Ru 3:9,12; 4:1,14

a *17* That is, probably about 3/5 bushel (about 22 liters)

23So Ruth stayed close to the servant girls of Boaz to glean until
the barley and wheat harvests[a] were finished. And she lived with
her mother-in-law.

Chapter 3 Theme ______________________

3 One day Naomi her mother-in-law said to her, "My daughter,
should I not try to find a home[a][b] for you, where you will be
well provided for? 2Is not Boaz, with whose servant girls you have
been, a kinsman[c] of ours? Tonight he will be winnowing barley on
the threshing floor. 3Wash and perfume yourself,[d] and put on your
best clothes. Then go down to the threshing floor, but don't let him
know you are there until he has finished eating and drinking.
4When he lies down, note the place where he is lying. Then go and
uncover his feet and lie down. He will tell you what to do."
5"I will do whatever you say,"[e] Ruth answered. 6So she went
down to the threshing floor and did everything her mother-in-law
told her to do.
7When Boaz had finished eating and drinking and was in good
spirits,[f] he went over to lie down at the far end of the grain pile.
Ruth approached quietly, uncovered his feet and lay down. 8In the
middle of the night something startled the man, and he turned
and discovered a woman lying at his feet.
9"Who are you?" he asked.

"I am your servant Ruth," she said. "Spread the corner of your
garment[g] over me, since you are a kinsman-redeemer.[h]"
10"The LORD bless you, my daughter," he replied. "This kindness
is greater than that which you showed earlier: You have not run
after the younger men, whether rich or poor. 11And now, my
daughter, don't be afraid. I will do for you all you ask. All my
fellow townsmen know that you are a woman of noble character.[i]
12Although it is true that I am near of kin, there is a kinsman-
redeemer[j] nearer than[k] I. 13Stay here for the night, and in the
morning if he wants to redeem,[l] good; let him redeem. But if he is
not willing, as surely as the LORD lives[m] I will do it. Lie here until
morning."
14So she lay at his feet until morning, but got up before anyone
could be recognized; and he said, "Don't let it be known that a
woman came to the threshing floor."[n]
15He also said, "Bring me the shawl you are wearing and hold it
out." When she did so, he poured into it six measures of barley
and put it on her. Then he[b] went back to town.
16When Ruth came to her mother-in-law, Naomi asked, "How
did it go, my daughter?"

[a] *1* Hebrew *find rest* (see Ruth 1:9) [b] *15* Most Hebrew manuscripts; many Hebrew manuscripts, Vulgate and Syriac *she*

2:23 [a]Dt 16:9
3:1 [b]Ru 1:9
3:2 [c]Dt 25:5-10; Ru 2:1
3:3 [d]2Sa 14:2
3:5 [e]Eph 6:1; Col 3:20
3:7 [f]Jdg 19:6,9,22; 2Sa 13:28; 1Ki 21:7; Est 1:10
3:9 [g]Eze 16:8 [h]ver 12; Ru 2:20
3:11 [i]Pr 12:4; 31:10
3:12 [j]ver 9 [k]Ru 4:1
3:13 [l]Dt 25:5; Ru 4:5; Mt 22:24 [m]Jdg 8:19; Jer 4:2
3:14 [n]Ro 14:16; 2Co 8:21

3:18 [a]Ps 37:3-5 Then she told her everything Boaz had done for her 17and
added, "He gave me these six measures of barley, saying, 'Don't
go back to your mother-in-law empty-handed.'"
18Then Naomi said, "Wait, my daughter, until you find out
what happens. For the man will not rest until the matter is settled
4:1 [b]Ru 3:12 today."[a]

Chapter 4 Theme ____

4 Meanwhile Boaz went up to the town gate and sat there.
When the kinsman-redeemer he had mentioned[b] came
4:2 [c]1Ki 21:8; Pr 31:23 along, Boaz said, "Come over here, my friend, and sit down." So
he went over and sat down.
2Boaz took ten of the elders[c] of the town and said, "Sit here,"
and they did so. 3Then he said to the kinsman-redeemer, "Naomi, who has come back from Moab, is selling the piece of land
4:4 that belonged to our brother Elimelech. 4I thought I should bring
[d]Lev 25:25; Jer 32:7-8 the matter to your attention and suggest that you buy it in the
presence of these seated here and in the presence of the elders of
my people. If you will redeem it, do so. But if you[a] will not, tell
me, so I will know. For no one has the right to do it except you,[d]
and I am next in line."
4:5 "I will redeem it," he said.
[e]Ge 38:8; Dt 25:5-6; 5Then Boaz said, "On the day you buy the land from Naomi and
Ru 3:13; Mt 22:24 from Ruth the Moabitess, you acquire[b] the dead man's widow, in
order to maintain the name of the dead with his property."[e]
6At this, the kinsman-redeemer said, "Then I cannot redeem[f] it
because I might endanger my own estate. You redeem it yourself.
I cannot do it."
4:6 7(Now in earlier times in Israel, for the redemption and transfer
[f]Lev 25:25; Ru 3:13 of property to become final, one party took off his sandal and
gave it to the other. This was the method of legalizing transactions in Israel.)[g]
8So the kinsman-redeemer said to Boaz, "Buy it yourself." And
he removed his sandal.
4:7 [g]Dt 25:7-9 9Then Boaz announced to the elders and all the people, "Today
you are witnesses that I have bought from Naomi all the property
of Elimelech, Kilion and Mahlon. 10I have also acquired Ruth the
Moabitess, Mahlon's widow, as my wife, in order to maintain the
name of the dead with his property, so that his name will not dis-
4:10 [h]Dt 25:6 appear from among his family or from the town records.[h] Today
you are witnesses!"
11Then the elders and all those at the gate said, "We are witnesses.[i] May the LORD make the woman who is coming into your

4:11 [i]Dt 25:9

[a]4 Many Hebrew manuscripts, Septuagint, Vulgate and Syriac; most Hebrew manuscripts *he* [b]5 Hebrew; Vulgate and Syriac *Naomi, you acquire Ruth the Moabitess,*

INSIGHT

The Genealogy of Boaz

Abram + Sarai (Abraham + Sarah)
↓
Isaac + Rebekah
↓
Jacob + Leah
↓
Judah + Tamar
↓
Perez
↓
Hezron
↓
Ram
↓
Admin (included in some manuscripts)
↓
Amminadab
↓
Nahshon
↓
Salmon + ***Rahab*** (the harlot)
↓
Boaz + ***Ruth*** (the Gentile)
↓
Obed
↓
Jesse
↓
David from whom came "Mary, of whom was born Jesus"

See **The Genealogy of Jesus the Christ** on page 1665.

home like Rachel and Leah,[a] who together built up the house of
Israel. May you have standing in Ephrathah[b] and be famous in
Bethlehem. 12 Through the offspring the LORD gives you by this
young woman, may your family be like that of Perez,[c] whom Tamar bore to Judah."

13 So Boaz took Ruth and she became his wife. Then he went to
her, and the LORD enabled her to conceive,[d] and she gave birth to a
son. 14 The women[e] said to Naomi: "Praise be to the LORD, who this
day has not left you without a kinsman-redeemer. May he become
famous throughout Israel! 15 He will renew your life and sustain
you in your old age. For your daughter-in-law, who loves you and
who is better to you than seven sons,[f] has given him birth."

16 Then Naomi took the child, laid him in her lap and cared for
him. 17 The women living there said, "Naomi has a son." And they
named him Obed. He was the father of Jesse,[g] the father of David.

18 This, then, is the family line of Perez[h]:

Perez was the father of Hezron,
19 Hezron the father of Ram,
Ram the father of Amminadab,[i]
20 Amminadab the father of Nahshon,
Nahshon the father of Salmon,[a]
21 Salmon the father of Boaz,[j]
Boaz the father of Obed,
22 Obed the father of Jesse,
and Jesse the father of David.

a *20* A few Hebrew manuscripts, some Septuagint manuscripts and Vulgate (see also verse 21 and Septuagint of 1 Chron. 2:11); most Hebrew manuscripts *Salma*

4:11
a Ps 127:3; 128:3
b Ge 35:16

4:12
c ver 18; Ge 38:29

4:13
d Ge 29:31; 33:5; Ru 3:11

4:14
e Lk 1:58

4:15
f Ru 1:16-17; 2:11-12; 1Sa 1:8

4:17
g ver 22; 1Sa 16:1,18; 1Ch 2:12,13

4:18
h Mt 1:3-6

4:19
i Ex 6:23

4:21
j Ru 2:1

Ruth at a Glance

Theme of Ruth:

Author:

Date:

Purpose:

Key Words:

redeem (redemption)

close relative (near of kin, kinsman, kinsman-redeemer, relative)

Naomi

Ruth

Boaz

Segment Divisions	Chapter Themes
	1
	2
	3
	4

1 SAMUEL

The days of the judges were dark until God raised up Samuel as a prophet, priest, and judge. Samuel would do what was right in God's eyes. But the people weren't satisfied. They cried, "Now appoint a king to lead us, such as all the other nations have!" With that plea they rejected the Lord as their King. What would it be like to live under a monarchy rather than a theocracy? The children of Israel were soon to find out as the times of the kings began. The kingdom, at first united, was divided because of the disobedience of the kings.

The books of 1 and 2 Samuel, 1 and 2 Kings, and 1 and 2 Chronicles record the days of the kings of Israel. Children of God who have been made "to be a kingdom and priests" and who "will reign on the earth" (Revelation 1:6; 5:10) can learn many valuable lessons from these books. The lessons begin in 1 Samuel as God rejects Saul and chooses as king a man after his own heart. And what will such a man be like? Will he live a perfect life? Is this what will make him a man after God's own heart, or are there other reasons?

~ THINGS TO DO

General Instructions

As you study this book never forget that these are actual people, frail but not without access to God, nor to his precepts and statutes of life. Observe the text prayerfully and carefully, and as you study, note in the margin God's lessons for life. You might want to give these the heading "LFL" (Lessons for Life) and color them in a distinctive way so you can recognize them immediately.

Chapters 1-7: Samuel, the Last Judge

1. As you observe these first seven chapters, mark the following words in a distinctive way and then note in the margin what you learn from observing each word in its context:
   a. *Ark (of the Lord, of God, of the Lord's covenant), ephod, judge (judged, led, was leader, judging), king, Ichabod,* and *Ebenezer.* The last three words are used only one time in these chapters but are significant. *Ephod* is used only twice in this segment but will have greater significance in the last segment of 1 Samuel. List these key words on an index card you can use as a bookmark for this segment.
   b. Mark selected geographical references on the map on page 497. This will help you gain perspective of events and familiarity with biblical locations.
2. Since 1 Samuel is a historical account, note the focus of each chapter. Who and/or what event does the chapter center on?
   a. In the margin list your insights about the main characters in each chapter. You might note who they are. For example, Elkanah's two wives:
      1) Hannah (childless)
      2) Peninnah (had sons/daughters)
   b. Especially observe the lives of Hannah, Samuel, and Eli, and list what you learn.
   c. In the margin list any progression of events which occurs. For example, in chapter 1 Hannah:
      1) Weeps because barren
      2) Asks for son/makes vow to God
      3) Is confronted by Eli
      4) Conceives
      5) Keeps vow to God

d. Note in the margin your insights about God and his ways. For instance, in chapter 1 God closes the womb and opens the womb.

3. Record the theme of each chapter on the 1 SAMUEL AT A GLANCE chart on page 496 and in the text next to the chapter number.

Chapters 8-15: From Samuel to Saul, from Judge to King

1. As you observe this segment of 1 Samuel:

a. Mark the following key words: *judge (judges), king* (don't include foreign kings), *sin (sins, sinned), evil, Spirit of God (of the Lord), ark of God,* and *ephod.* Put them on an index card to use as a bookmark.

b. In the margin list what you learn about Samuel, Saul, King Agag, and the Amalekites.

c. Note all you learn about God and his ways.

d. Mark any reference to time (when Saul begins his reign, etc.). Mark these with a symbol.

e. There are no references to the ark in 1 Samuel after this segment. Review what you learned about the ark in this book and note in the margin where it is last mentioned and its location. (Read "The Ark of the Covenant" on page 2203.)

2. Carefully observe all you learn from marking the word *king.* Watch for the following and record your insights in the margin:

a. Why the people wanted a king, how they perceived the kingship, and what kind of king they wanted.

b. How God responded to the people's request, what God desired in a kingship, and how the success or failure of a king was determined.

3. Examine each chapter as you did in the previous segment, watching for and recording the main event of each chapter and any pertinent subpoints. Don't forget to record the chapter theme on 1 SAMUEL AT A GLANCE and in the text.

Chapters 16-31: The Preparation of Another King

1. In this segment:

a. Make a new bookmark and mark the following key words: *kings (king's)* (not foreign kings), *evil (harm, wrongdoing, mean, disaster, doing wrong, no fault, wrong), evil spirit, sin (sinned, wronged), judge, covenant, inquire (inquired, inquiring, find out),* and *ephod.* Don't forget to record what you are learning from marking *king* and *ephod.*

b. Mark all references to time and to geographical locations as before.

2. Observe and record in the margin of each chapter what you learn about Samuel, Saul, and David. Give special attention to all that happens to David and how he responds to God and to man. Watch for and note in the margin the "LFL" (Lessons for Life).

3. In the margin write "Covenant" and list what you have observed from the text. Ask the five W's and an H: Who makes the covenant? How is it made? What is done? What is promised? What are the conditions? When is it made? Where is it made? Why? Remember that you are in covenant with God if you are a child of God (Matthew 26:26-29); watch for any principles which might apply to you. (See the "Insight" on covenant at Genesis 15:10.)

4. As you read each chapter watch for insights about God, note the events of each chapter and the subpoints of the chapter, and record the chapter themes.

5. Complete 1 SAMUEL AT A GLANCE. Watch for any additional segment divisions in 1 Samuel. Look at the chapter themes and see if there is any other way 1 Samuel might be segmented: Can any chapters be grouped in respect to David's relationship to Saul, to Jonathan, to the Philistines, or to others? Or is there any geographical segmentation, such as where Samuel, Saul, and David spend their time?

6. Record the theme of 1 Samuel on 1 SAMUEL AT A GLANCE.

Things to Think About

1. What lessons did you learn from Eli's dealings with his sons? Do you see your accountability before God to discipline your children?
2. What do you learn from Samuel, Saul, and David's lives regarding seeking God, listening to him, and obeying him? Are there consequences when you don't?
3. Did you notice how much time has elapsed since David was anointed to be king? Still, as 1 Samuel comes to a close, David is not king over Israel. Think about all that transpired since Samuel anointed David. What can you learn from this about God's promises, his purpose, and his timing? Are you waiting patiently on God for the fulfillment of his promise to you?
4. Review the "Lessons for Life" you observed and the insights you recorded about God in the margins of 1 Samuel. Make these a matter of prayer.

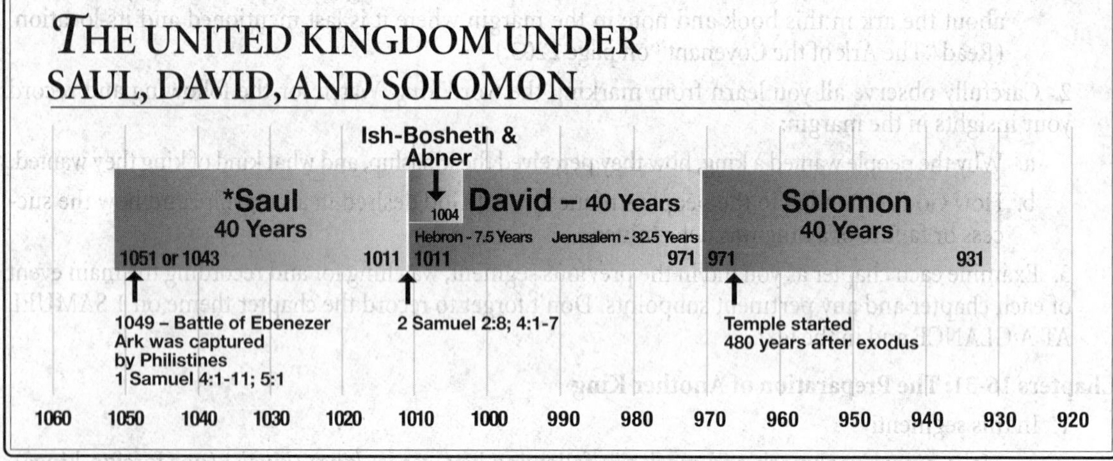

First Samuel 13:1 says that Saul was king for thirty-two years.
Acts 13:21 says that Saul was king for forty years.
In Hebrew, numbers from 1-19 are singular and numbers 20 and above are plural.
In this case, the number is plural, so we know it is 20+ years.

In Hebrew, the numbers are missing in 1 Samuel 13:1. Any number given is supplied or guessed.
The first word of 1 Samuel 13:2 is a connector word. It can be used in ten different ways. "And" would be a good translation.
In any case, that connector word tells us Saul was in his thirty-second year when what follows happened.

Chapter 1 Theme ____________

1 There was a certain man from Ramathaim, a Zuphite[a] from
the hill country[a] of Ephraim, whose name was Elkanah[b] son
of Jeroham, the son of Elihu, the son of Tohu, the son of Zuph, an
Ephraimite. 2 He had two wives;[c] one was called Hannah and the
other Peninnah. Peninnah had children, but Hannah had none.
3 Year after year[d] this man went up from his town to worship[e]
and sacrifice to the LORD Almighty at Shiloh,[f] where Hophni and
Phinehas, the two sons of Eli, were priests of the LORD. 4 Whenever
the day came for Elkanah to sacrifice,[g] he would give portions of
the meat to his wife Peninnah and to all her sons and daughters.
5 But to Hannah he gave a double portion because he loved her,

a1 Or *from Ramathaim Zuphim*

1:1
a Jos 17:17-18
b 1Ch 6:27,34

1:2
c Dt 21:15-17; Lk 2:36

1:3
d ver 21; Ex 23:14; 34:23; Lk 2:41
e Dt 12:5-7
f Jos 18:1

1:4
g Dt 12:17-18

and the LORD had closed her womb.[a] 6And because the LORD had
closed her womb, her rival kept provoking her in order to irritate
her.[b] 7This went on year after year. Whenever Hannah went up to
the house of the LORD, her rival provoked her till she wept and
would not eat. 8Elkanah her husband would say to her, "Hannah,
why are you weeping? Why don't you eat? Why are you down-
hearted? Don't I mean more to you than ten sons?[c] "

9Once when they had finished eating and drinking in Shiloh,
Hannah stood up. Now Eli the priest was sitting on a chair by the
doorpost of the LORD's temple.a[d] 10In bitterness of soul[e] Hannah
wept much and prayed to the LORD. 11And she made a vow, saying,
"O LORD Almighty, if you will only look upon your servant's misery and remember[f] me, and not forget your servant but give her a
son, then I will give him to the LORD for all the days of his life, and
no razor[g] will ever be used on his head."

12As she kept on praying to the LORD, Eli observed her mouth.
13Hannah was praying in her heart, and her lips were moving but
her voice was not heard. Eli thought she was drunk 14and said to
her, "How long will you keep on getting drunk? Get rid of your
wine."

15"Not so, my lord," Hannah replied, "I am a woman who is
deeply troubled. I have not been drinking wine or beer; I was
pouring[h] out my soul to the LORD. 16Do not take your servant for a
wicked woman; I have been praying here out of my great anguish
and grief."

17Eli answered, "Go in peace,[i] and may the God of Israel grant
you what you have asked of him.[j]"

18She said, "May your servant find favor in your eyes.[k]" Then
she went her way and ate something, and her face was no longer
downcast.[l]

19Early the next morning they arose and worshiped before the
LORD and then went back to their home at Ramah. Elkanah lay
with Hannah his wife, and the LORD remembered[m] her. 20So in
the course of time Hannah conceived and gave birth to a son. She
named[n] him Samuel,b saying, "Because I asked the LORD for him."

21When the man Elkanah went up with all his family to offer the
annual[o] sacrifice to the LORD and to fulfill his vow,[p] 22Hannah did
not go. She said to her husband, "After the boy is weaned, I will
take him and present[q] him before the LORD, and he will live there
always."

23"Do what seems best to you," Elkanah her husband told her.
"Stay here until you have weaned him; only may the LORD make
good[r] hisc word." So the woman stayed at home and nursed her
son until she had weaned him.

INSIGHT

A *Nazirite* (which means "consecration, devotion, and separation") was someone who was bound by a vow of consecration to God's service for either a specific period of time or for life. A Nazirite's devotion to God was evidenced outwardly by not cutting the hair, abstaining from wine and alcoholic drinks, and avoiding contact with the dead. Violation of these brought defilement and need of purification.

a 9 That is, tabernacle b 20 *Samuel* sounds like the Hebrew for *heard of God.* c 23 Masoretic Text; Dead Sea Scrolls, Septuagint and Syriac *your*

1:5 [a] Ge 16:1; 30:2
1:6 [b] Job 24:21
1:8 [c] Ru 4:15
1:9 [d] 1Sa 3:3
1:10 [e] Job 7:11
1:11 [f] Ge 8:1; 28:20; 29:32 [g] Nu 6:1-21; Jdg 13:5
1:15 [h] Ps 42:4; 62:8; La 2:19
1:17 [i] Jdg 18:6; 1Sa 25:35; 2Ki 5:19; Mk 5:34 [j] Ps 20:3-5
1:18 [k] Ru 2:13 [l] Ecc 9:7; Ro 15:13
1:19 [m] Ge 4:1; 30:22
1:20 [n] Ge 41:51-52; Ex 2:10,22; Mt 1:21
1:21 [o] ver 3 [p] Dt 12:11
1:22 [q] ver 11,28; Lk 2:22
1:23 [r] ver 17; Nu 30:7

24 After he was weaned, she took the boy with her, young as he
was, along with a three-year-old bull,[a][a] an ephah[b] of flour and a
skin of wine, and brought him to the house of the LORD at Shiloh.
25 When they had slaughtered the bull, they brought the boy to
Eli, 26 and she said to him, "As surely as you live, my lord, I am the
woman who stood here beside you praying to the LORD. 27 I prayed[b]
for this child, and the LORD has granted me what I asked of him.
28 So now I give him to the LORD. For his whole life[c] he will be given
over to the LORD." And he worshiped the LORD there.

Chapter 2 Theme ______________________

2

Then Hannah prayed and said:[d]

"My heart rejoices[e] in the LORD;
in the LORD my horn[c][f] is lifted high.
My mouth boasts over my enemies,
for I delight in your deliverance.

2 "There is no one holy[d][g] like the LORD;
there is no one besides you;
there is no Rock[h] like our God.

3 "Do not keep talking so proudly
or let your mouth speak such arrogance,[i]
for the LORD is a God who knows,
and by him deeds[j] are weighed.[k]

4 "The bows of the warriors are broken,[l]
but those who stumbled are armed with strength.
5 Those who were full hire themselves out for food,
but those who were hungry hunger no more.
She who was barren[m] has borne seven children,
but she who has had many sons pines away.

6 "The LORD brings death and makes alive;[n]
he brings down to the grave[e] and raises up.[o]
7 The LORD sends poverty and wealth;[p]
he humbles and he exalts.[q]
8 He raises[r] the poor from the dust
and lifts the needy from the ash heap;
he seats them with princes
and has them inherit a throne of honor.[s]

"For the foundations[t] of the earth are the LORD's;
upon them he has set the world.

[a] *24* Dead Sea Scrolls, Septuagint and Syriac; Masoretic Text *with three bulls* [b] *24* That is, probably about 3/5 bushel (about 22 liters) [c] *1* *Horn* here symbolizes strength; also in verse 10. [d] *2* Or *no Holy One* [e] *6* Hebrew *Sheol*

1:24
[a] Nu 15:8-10; Dt 12:5; Jos 18:1

1:27
[b] ver 11-13; Ps 66:19-20

1:28
[c] ver 11,22; Ge 24:26,52

2:1
[d] Lk 1:46-55
[e] Ps 9:14; 13:5
[f] Ps 89:17,24; 92:10; Isa 12:2-3

2:2
[g] Ex 15:11; Lev 19:2
[h] Dt 32:30-31; 2Sa 22:2,32

2:3
[i] Pr 8:13
[j] 1Sa 16:7; 1Ki 8:39
[k] Pr 16:2; 24:11-12

2:4
[l] Ps 37:15

2:5
[m] Ps 113:9; Jer 15:9

2:6
[n] Dt 32:39
[o] Isa 26:19

2:7
[p] Dt 8:18
[q] Job 5:11; Ps 75:7

2:8
[r] Ps 113:7-8
[s] Job 36:7
[t] Job 38:4

9He will guard the feet[a] of his saints,
but the wicked will be silenced in darkness.[b]

"It is not by strength[c] that one prevails;
10 those who oppose the LORD will be shattered.[d]
He will thunder[e] against them from heaven;
the LORD will judge[f] the ends of the earth.

"He will give strength[g] to his king
and exalt the horn[h] of his anointed."

11Then Elkanah went home to Ramah, but the boy ministered[i]
before the LORD under Eli the priest.
12Eli's sons were wicked men; they had no regard[j] for the LORD.
13Now it was the practice of the priests with the people that whenever anyone offered a sacrifice and while the meat[k] was being
boiled, the servant of the priest would come with a three-pronged
fork in his hand. 14He would plunge it into the pan or kettle or caldron or pot, and the priest would take for himself whatever the
fork brought up. This is how they treated all the Israelites who
came to Shiloh. 15But even before the fat was burned, the servant
of the priest would come and say to the man who was sacrificing,
"Give the priest some meat to roast; he won't accept boiled meat
from you, but only raw."
16If the man said to him, "Let the fat be burned up first, and then
take whatever you want," the servant would then answer, "No, hand
it over now; if you don't, I'll take it by force."
17This sin of the young men was very great in the LORD's sight,
for they[a] were treating the LORD's offering with contempt.[l]
18But Samuel was ministering[m] before the LORD—a boy wearing
a linen ephod.[n] 19Each year his mother made him a little robe and
took it to him when she went up with her husband to offer the
annual[o] sacrifice. 20Eli would bless Elkanah and his wife, saying,
"May the LORD give you children by this woman to take the place
of the one she prayed[p] for and gave to the LORD." Then they would
go home. 21And the LORD was gracious to Hannah;[q] she conceived
and gave birth to three sons and two daughters. Meanwhile, the
boy Samuel grew[r] up in the presence of the LORD.
22Now Eli, who was very old, heard about everything his sons
were doing to all Israel and how they slept with the women[s] who
served at the entrance to the Tent of Meeting. 23So he said to them,
"Why do you do such things? I hear from all the people about
these wicked deeds of yours. 24No, my sons; it is not a good report
that I hear spreading among the LORD's people. 25If a man sins
against another man, God[b] may mediate for him; but if a man sins
against the LORD, who will[t] intercede[u] for him?" His sons, however,

2:9 [a]Ps 91:12 [b]Mt 8:12 [c]Ps 33:16-17
2:10 [d]Ps 2:9 [e]Ps 18:13 [f]Ps 96:13 [g]Ps 21:1 [h]Ps 89:24
2:11 [i]ver 18; 1Sa 3:1
2:12 [j]Jer 2:8; 9:6
2:13 [k]Lev 7:29-34
2:17 [l]Mal 2:7-9
2:18 [m]ver 11; 1Sa 3:1 [n]ver 28
2:19 [o]1Sa 1:3
2:20 [p]1Sa 1:11, 27-28; Lk 2:34
2:21 [q]Ge 21:1 [r]ver 26; Jdg 13:24; 1Sa 3:19; Lk 2:40
2:22 [s]Ex 38:8
2:25 [t]Nu 15:30; Jos 11:20 [u]Dt 1:17; 1Sa 3:14; Heb 10:26

[a]17 Or *men* [b]25 Or *the judges*

INSIGHT

The *ephod* was used to seek guidance from God. Described in Exodus 28, it was a linen garment worn by the priest and also by David when he was king (2 Samuel 6:14). The ephod was fastened on each shoulder by onyx clasps which had the names of six tribes engraved on one clasp and six tribes engraved on the other. The *breastpiece*, which was fastened to the ephod, had a linen pouch which held the *Urim* and *Thummim*, which may have been used as sacred lots to reveal God's will (1 Samuel 28:6).

did not listen to their father's rebuke, for it was the LORD's will to put them to death.

26 And the boy Samuel continued to grow[a] in stature and in favor with the LORD and with men.

27 Now a man of God[b] came to Eli and said to him, "This is what the LORD says: 'Did I not clearly reveal myself to your father's house when they were in Egypt under Pharaoh? 28 I chose[c] your father out of all the tribes of Israel to be my priest, to go up to my altar, to burn incense, and to wear an ephod[d] in my presence. I also gave your father's house all the offerings made with fire by the Israelites. 29 Why do you[a] scorn my sacrifice and offering[e] that I prescribed for my dwelling?[f] Why do you honor your sons more than me by fattening yourselves on the choice parts of every offering made by my people Israel?'

30 "Therefore the LORD, the God of Israel, declares: 'I promised that your house and your father's house would minister before me forever.[g]' But now the LORD declares: 'Far be it from me! Those who honor me I will honor,[h] but those who despise[i] me will be disdained. 31 The time is coming when I will cut short your strength and the strength of your father's house, so that there will not be an old man in your family line[j] 32 and you will see distress in my dwelling. Although good will be done to Israel, in your family line there will never be an old man.[k] 33 Every one of you that I do not cut off from my altar will be spared only to blind your eyes with tears and to grieve your heart, and all your descendants will die in the prime of life.

34 " 'And what happens to your two sons, Hophni and Phinehas, will be a sign to you—they will both die[l] on the same day.[m] 35 I will raise up for myself a faithful priest,[n] who will do according to what is in my heart and mind. I will firmly establish his house, and he will minister before my anointed[o] one always. 36 Then everyone left in your family line will come and bow down before him for a piece of silver and a crust of bread and plead, "Appoint me to some priestly office so I can have food to eat.[p]" ' "

Chapter 3 Theme

3 The boy Samuel ministered[q] before the LORD under Eli. In those days the word of the LORD was rare;[r] there were not many visions.[s]

2 One night Eli, whose eyes[t] were becoming so weak that he could barely see, was lying down in his usual place. 3 The lamp[u] of God had not yet gone out, and Samuel was lying down in the temple[b] of the LORD, where the ark of God was. 4 Then the LORD called Samuel.

Samuel answered, "Here I am.[v]" 5 And he ran to Eli and said, "Here I am; you called me."

[a] 29 The Hebrew is plural. [b] 3 That is, tabernacle

2:26 [a] ver 21; Lk 2:52
2:27 [b] Ex 4:14-16; 1Ki 13:1
2:28 [c] Ex 28:1 [d] Lev 8:7-8
2:29 [e] ver 12-17 [f] Dt 12:5; Mt 10:37
2:30 [g] Ex 29:9 [h] Ps 50:23; 91:15 [i] Mal 2:9
2:31 [j] 1Sa 4:11-18; 22:16-20
2:32 [k] 1Ki 2:26-27; Zec 8:4
2:34 [l] 1Sa 4:11 [m] 1Ki 13:3
2:35 [n] 1Sa 12:3; 1Ki 2:35 [o] 1Sa 16:13; 2Sa 7:11,27; 1Ki 11:38
2:36 [p] 1Ki 2:27
3:1 [q] 1Sa 2:11 [r] Ps 74:9 [s] Am 8:11
3:2 [t] 1Sa 4:15
3:3 [u] Lev 24:1-4
3:4 [v] Isa 6:8

3:7 [a]Ac 19:12 But Eli said, "I did not call; go back and lie down." So he went
and lay down.
6Again the LORD called, "Samuel!" And Samuel got up and went
to Eli and said, "Here I am; you called me."
3:11 [b]2Ki 21:12; Jer 19:3 "My son," Eli said, "I did not call; go back and lie down."
7Now Samuel did not yet know the LORD: The word of the LORD
had not yet been revealed[a] to him.
8The LORD called Samuel a third time, and Samuel got up and
3:12 [c]1Sa 2:27-36 went to Eli and said, "Here I am; you called me."
Then Eli realized that the LORD was calling the boy. 9So Eli told
Samuel, "Go and lie down, and if he calls you, say, 'Speak, LORD,
for your servant is listening.'" So Samuel went and lay down in
3:13 [d]1Sa 2:12,17, 22;29-31 his place.
10The LORD came and stood there, calling as at the other times,
"Samuel! Samuel!"
Then Samuel said, "Speak, for your servant is listening."
3:14 [e]Lev 15:30-31; 1Sa 2:25; Isa 22:14 11And the LORD said to Samuel: "See, I am about to do something in Israel that will make the ears of everyone who hears of it
tingle.[b] 12At that time I will carry out against Eli everything[c] I
spoke against his family—from beginning to end. 13For I told him
that I would judge his family forever because of the sin he knew
3:17 [f]Ru 1:17; 2Sa 3:35 about; his sons made themselves contemptible,[a] and he failed to
restrain[d] them. 14Therefore, I swore to the house of Eli, 'The guilt
of Eli's house will never be atoned[e] for by sacrifice or offering.'"
15Samuel lay down until morning and then opened the doors of
the house of the LORD. He was afraid to tell Eli the vision, 16but Eli
3:18 [g]Job 2:10; Isa 39:8 called him and said, "Samuel, my son."
Samuel answered, "Here I am."
17"What was it he said to you?" Eli asked. "Do not hide it from
me. May God deal with you, be it ever so severely,[f] if you hide
3:19 [h]Ge 21:22; 39:2 [i]1Sa 2:21 [j]1Sa 9:6 from me anything he told you." 18So Samuel told him everything,
hiding nothing from him. Then Eli said, "He is the LORD; let him
do what is good in his eyes."[g]
19The LORD was with[h] Samuel as he grew[i] up, and he let none[j] of
his words fall to the ground. 20And all Israel from Dan to Beershe-
3:20 [k]Jdg 20:1 ba[k] recognized that Samuel was attested as a prophet of the LORD.
21The LORD continued to appear at Shiloh, and there he revealed[l]
himself to Samuel through his word.

3:21 [l]ver 10

Chapter 4 Theme ______________________

4 And Samuel's word came to all Israel.
Now the Israelites went out to fight against the Philistines.
4:1 [m]1Sa 7:12 [n]Jos 12:18; 1Sa 29:1 The Israelites camped at Ebenezer,[m] and the Philistines at Aphek.[n]
2The Philistines deployed their forces to meet Israel, and as the

[a] *13* Masoretic Text; an ancient Hebrew scribal tradition and Septuagint *sons blasphemed God*

battle spread, Israel was defeated by the Philistines, who killed
about four thousand of them on the battlefield. 3When the soldiers returned to camp, the elders of Israel asked, "Why[a] did the
LORD bring defeat upon us today before the Philistines? Let us
bring the ark[b] of the LORD's covenant from Shiloh, so that it[a] may
go with us and save us from the hand of our enemies."

4So the people sent men to Shiloh, and they brought back the ark
of the covenant of the LORD Almighty, who is enthroned between
the cherubim.[c] And Eli's two sons, Hophni and Phinehas, were
there with the ark of the covenant of God.

5When the ark of the LORD's covenant came into the camp, all
Israel raised such a great shout[d] that the ground shook. 6Hearing
the uproar, the Philistines asked, "What's all this shouting in the
Hebrew camp?"

When they learned that the ark of the LORD had come into the
camp, 7the Philistines were afraid.[e] "A god has come into the
camp," they said. "We're in trouble! Nothing like this has happened before. 8Woe to us! Who will deliver us from the hand of
these mighty gods? They are the gods who struck the Egyptians
with all kinds of plagues in the desert. 9Be strong, Philistines! Be
men, or you will be subject to the Hebrews, as they[f] have been to
you. Be men, and fight!"

10So the Philistines fought, and the Israelites were defeated[g] and
every man fled to his tent. The slaughter was very great; Israel lost
thirty thousand foot soldiers. 11The ark of God was captured, and
Eli's two sons, Hophni and Phinehas, died.[h]

12That same day a Benjamite ran from the battle line and went
to Shiloh, his clothes torn and dust[i] on his head. 13When he
arrived, there was Eli[j] sitting on his chair by the side of the road,
watching, because his heart feared for the ark of God. When the
man entered the town and told what had happened, the whole
town sent up a cry.

14Eli heard the outcry and asked, "What is the meaning of this
uproar?"

The man hurried over to Eli, 15who was ninety-eight years old
and whose eyes[k] were set so that he could not see. 16He told Eli, "I
have just come from the battle line; I fled from it this very day."

Eli asked, "What happened, my son?"

17The man who brought the news replied, "Israel fled before the
Philistines, and the army has suffered heavy losses. Also your two
sons, Hophni and Phinehas, are dead, and the ark of God has been
captured."

18When he mentioned the ark of God, Eli fell backward off his
chair by the side of the gate. His neck was broken and he died, for
he was an old man and heavy. He had led[b][l] Israel forty years.

[a] 3 Or *he* [b] 18 Traditionally *judged*

4:3 [a] Jos 7:7 [b] Nu 10:35; Jos 6:7
4:4 [c] Ex 25:22; 2Sa 6:2
4:5 [d] Jos 6:5,10
4:7 [e] Ex 15:14
4:9 [f] Jdg 13:1; 1Co 16:13
4:10 [g] ver 2; Dt 28:25; 2Sa 18:17; 2Ki 14:12
4:11 [h] 1Sa 2:34; Ps 78:61,64
4:12 [i] Jos 7:6; 2Sa 1:2; 15:32; Ne 9:1; Job 2:12
4:13 [j] ver 18; 1Sa 1:9
4:15 [k] 1Sa 3:2
4:18 [l] ver 13

4:21
[a]Ge 35:18
[b]Ps 26:8;
Jer 2:11

19His daughter-in-law, the wife of Phinehas, was pregnant and
near the time of delivery. When she heard the news that the ark of
God had been captured and that her father-in-law and her husband
were dead, she went into labor and gave birth, but was overcome
by her labor pains. 20As she was dying, the women attending her
said, "Don't despair; you have given birth to a son." But she did
not respond or pay any attention.
21She named the boy Ichabod,[a][a] saying, "The glory[b] has departed
from Israel"—because of the capture of the ark of God and the
deaths of her father-in-law and her husband. 22She said, "The glory
has departed from Israel, for the ark of God has been captured."

INSIGHT

Dagon, the chief deity of the Philistines, dates back to Mesopotamia and the third millennium B.C. According to ancient literature Dagon was the father of Baal. (See Judges 16:23; 1 Chronicles 10:10.)

5:1
[c]1Sa 4:1; 7:12
[d]Jos 13:3

5:2
[e]Jdg 16:23

Chapter 5 Theme ______________________

5 After the Philistines had captured the ark of God, they took it
from Ebenezer[c] to Ashdod.[d] 2Then they carried the ark into
Dagon's temple and set it beside Dagon.[e] 3When the people of
Ashdod rose early the next day, there was Dagon, fallen[f] on his
face on the ground before
the ark of the LORD! They
took Dagon and put him
back in his place. 4But the
following morning when
they rose, there was Dagon,
fallen on his face on the
ground before the ark of the
LORD! His head and hands
had been broken[g] off and
were lying on the threshold;
only his body remained.
5That is why to this day neither the priests of Dagon
nor any others who enter
Dagon's temple at Ashdod
step on the threshold.[h]
6The LORD's hand[i] was
heavy upon the people of
Ashdod and its vicinity; he brought devastation[j] upon them and
afflicted them with tumors.[b][k] 7When the men of Ashdod saw
what was happening, they said, "The ark of the god of Israel must
not stay here with us, because his hand is heavy upon us and
upon Dagon our god." 8So they called together all the rulers of the
Philistines and asked them, "What shall we do with the ark of the
god of Israel?"

5:3
[f]Isa 19:1;
46:7

5:4
[g]Eze 6:6;
Mic 1:7

5:5
[h]Zep 1:9

5:6
[i]ver 7;
Ex 9:3;
Ps 32:4;
Ac 13:11
[j]ver 11;
Ps 78:66
[k]Dt 28:27;
1Sa 6:5

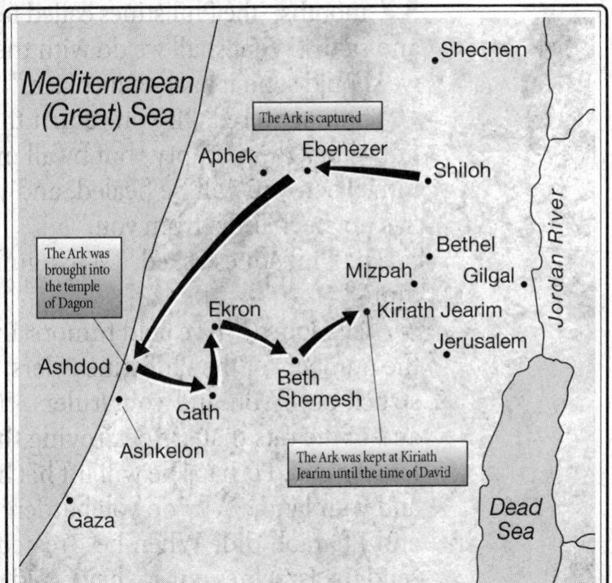

The Wanderings of the Ark

(see page 2703)

[a]*21 Ichabod* means *no glory.* [b]*6* Hebrew; Septuagint and Vulgate *tumors. And rats appeared in their land, and death and destruction were throughout the city*

They answered, "Have the ark of the god of Israel moved to
Gath.[a]" So they moved the ark of the God of Israel.
9But after they had moved it, the LORD's hand was against that
city, throwing it into a great panic.[b] He afflicted the people of the
city, both young and old, with an outbreak of tumors.[a] 10So they
sent the ark of God to Ekron.
As the ark of God was entering Ekron, the people of Ekron cried
out, "They have brought the ark of the god of Israel around to us to
kill us and our people." 11So they called together all the rulers[c] of
the Philistines and said, "Send the ark of the god of Israel away; let
it go back to its own place, or it[b] will kill us and our people." For
death had filled the city with panic; God's hand was very heavy
upon it. 12Those who did not die were afflicted with tumors, and
the outcry of the city went up to heaven.

Chapter 6 Theme ____________________________

6 When the ark of the LORD had been in Philistine territory seven
months, 2the Philistines called for the priests and the diviners[d]
and said, "What shall we do with the ark of the LORD? Tell us how
we should send it back to its place."
3They answered, "If you return the ark of the god of Israel, do
not send it away empty,[e] but by all means send a guilt offering[f] to
him. Then you will be healed, and you will know why his hand[g]
has not been lifted from you."
4The Philistines asked, "What guilt offering should we send to
him?"
They replied, "Five gold tumors and five gold rats, according to
the number[h] of the Philistine rulers, because the same plague has
struck both you and your rulers. 5Make models of the tumors[i]
and of the rats that are destroying the country, and pay honor[j] to
Israel's god. Perhaps he will lift his hand from you and your gods
and your land. 6Why do you harden[k] your hearts as the Egyptians
and Pharaoh did? When he[c] treated them harshly, did they[l] not
send the Israelites out so they could go on their way?
7"Now then, get a new cart[m] ready, with two cows that have
calved and have never been yoked.[n] Hitch the cows to the cart, but
take their calves away and pen them up. 8Take the ark of the LORD
and put it on the cart, and in a chest beside it put the gold objects
you are sending back to him as a guilt offering. Send it on its way,
9but keep watching it. If it goes up to its own territory, toward
Beth Shemesh,[o] then the LORD has brought this great disaster on
us. But if it does not, then we will know that it was not his hand
that struck us and that it happened to us by chance."

a9 Or *with tumors in the groin* (see Septuagint) b11 Or *he* c6 That is, God

5:8 [a]ver 11
5:9 [b]ver 6,11; Dt 2:15; 1Sa 7:13; Ps 78:66
5:11 [c]ver 6,8-9
6:2 [d]Ge 41:8; Ex 7:11; Isa 2:6
6:3 [e]Ex 23:15; Dt 16:16 [f]Lev 5:15 [g]ver 9
6:4 [h]ver 17-18; Jos 13:3; Jdg 3:3
6:5 [i]1Sa 5:6-11 [j]Jos 7:19; Isa 42:12; Jn 9:24; Rev 14:7
6:6 [k]Ex 7:13; 8:15; 9:34; 14:17 [l]Ex 12:31,33
6:7 [m]2Sa 6:3 [n]Nu 19:2
6:9 [o]ver 3; Jos 15:10; 21:16

6:14 [a]2Sa 24:22; 10So they did this. They took two such cows and hitched them to
1Ki 19:21 the cart and penned up their calves. 11They placed the ark of the
LORD on the cart and along with it the chest containing the gold
rats and the models of the tumors. 12Then the cows went straight
up toward Beth Shemesh, keeping on the road and lowing all the
way; they did not turn to the right or to the left. The rulers of the
Philistines followed them as far as the border of Beth Shemesh.

6:15 [b]Jos 3:3 13Now the people of Beth Shemesh were harvesting their wheat
in the valley, and when they looked up and saw the ark, they
rejoiced at the sight. 14The cart came to the field of Joshua of Beth
Shemesh, and there it stopped beside a large rock. The people
chopped up the wood of the cart and sacrificed the cows as a
burnt offering[a] to the LORD. 15The Levites[b] took down the ark of
6:17 the LORD, together with the chest containing the gold objects, and
[c]ver 4 placed them on the large rock. On that day the people of Beth
Shemesh offered burnt offerings and made sacrifices to the LORD.
16The five rulers of the Philistines saw all this and then returned
that same day to Ekron.

17These are the gold tumors the Philistines sent as a guilt offering to the LORD—one each[c] for Ashdod, Gaza, Ashkelon, Gath
6:19 [d]2Sa 6:7 and Ekron. 18And the number of the gold rats was according to
[e]Ex 19:21; the number of Philistine towns belonging to the five rulers—the
Nu 4:5,15,20 fortified towns with their country villages. The large rock, on
which[a] they set the ark of the LORD, is a witness to this day in the
field of Joshua of Beth Shemesh.

19But God struck down[d] some of the men of Beth Shemesh,
putting seventy[b] of them to death because they had looked[e] into
6:20 the ark of the LORD. The people mourned because of the heavy
[f]2Sa 6:9; blow the LORD had dealt them, 20and the men of Beth Shemesh
Mal 3:2; asked, "Who can stand[f] in the presence of the LORD, this holy[g]
Rev 6:17 [g]Lev 11:45 God? To whom will the ark go up from here?"

21Then they sent messengers to the people of Kiriath Jearim,[h]
saying, "The Philistines have returned the ark of the LORD. Come
down and take it up to your place."

Chapter 7 Theme

6:21 [h]Jos 9:17; 7 So the men of Kiriath Jearim came and took up the ark of the
15:9,60; LORD. They took it to Abinadab's[i] house on the hill and con-
1Ch 13:5-6 secrated Eleazar his son to guard the ark of the LORD.

2It was a long time, twenty years in all, that the ark remained at
Kiriath Jearim, and all the people of Israel mourned and sought
after the LORD. 3And Samuel said to the whole house of Israel, "If

[a] *18* A few Hebrew manuscripts (see also Septuagint); most Hebrew manuscripts *villages as far as Greater Abel, where* [b] *19* A few Hebrew manuscripts; most Hebrew manuscripts and Septuagint *50,070*

7:1 [i]2Sa 6:3

you are returning[a] to the LORD with all your hearts, then rid[b] yourselves of the foreign gods and the Ashtoreths[c] and commit[d] yourselves to the LORD and serve him only,[e] and he will deliver you out
of the hand of the Philistines." 4So the Israelites put away their
Baals and Ashtoreths, and served the LORD only.
5Then Samuel said, "Assemble all Israel at Mizpah[f] and I will
intercede with the LORD for you." 6When they had assembled at
Mizpah, they drew water and poured[g] it out before the LORD. On
that day they fasted and there they confessed, "We have sinned
against the LORD." And Samuel was leader[a][h] of Israel at Mizpah.
7When the Philistines heard that Israel had assembled at Mizpah, the rulers of the Philistines came up to attack them. And
when the Israelites heard of it, they were afraid[i] because of the
Philistines. 8They said to Samuel, "Do not stop crying[j] out to
the LORD our God for us, that he may rescue us from the hand of
the Philistines." 9Then Samuel[k] took a suckling lamb and offered
it up as a whole burnt offering to the LORD. He cried out to the
LORD on Israel's behalf, and the LORD answered him.[l]
10While Samuel was sacrificing the burnt offering, the Philistines
drew near to engage Israel in battle. But that day the LORD thundered[m] with loud thunder against the Philistines and threw them
into such a panic[n] that they were routed before the Israelites. 11The
men of Israel rushed out of Mizpah and pursued the Philistines,
slaughtering them along the way to a point below Beth Car.
12Then Samuel took a stone[o] and set it up between Mizpah and
Shen. He named it Ebenezer,[b] saying, "Thus far has the LORD
helped us." 13So the Philistines were subdued[p] and did not invade
Israelite territory again.
Throughout Samuel's lifetime, the hand of the LORD was
against the Philistines. 14The towns from Ekron to Gath that the
Philistines had captured from Israel were restored to her, and
Israel delivered the neighboring territory from the power of the
Philistines. And there was peace between Israel and the Amorites.
15Samuel[q] continued as judge over Israel all the days of his life.
16From year to year he went on a circuit from Bethel to Gilgal to
Mizpah, judging Israel in all those places. 17But he always went
back to Ramah,[r] where his home was, and there he also judged
Israel. And he built an altar[s] there to the LORD.

Chapter 8 Theme ________________________

8 When Samuel grew old, he appointed[t] his sons as judges for
Israel. 2The name of his firstborn was Joel and the name of
his second was Abijah, and they served at Beersheba.[u] 3But his

a6 Traditionally *judge* b12 *Ebenezer* means *stone of help.*

7:3 [a]Dt 30:10; Isa 55:7; Hos 6:1 [b]Ge 35:2; Jos 24:14 [c]Jdg 2:12-13; 1Sa 31:10 [d]Joel 2:12 [e]Dt 6:13; Mt 4:10; Lk 4:8
7:5 [f]Jdg 20:1
7:6 [g]Ps 62:8; La 2:19 [h]Jdg 10:10; Ne 9:1; Ps 106:6
7:7 [i]1Sa 17:11
7:8 [j]1Sa 12:19,23; Isa 37:4; Jer 15:1
7:9 [k]Ps 99:6 [l]Jer 15:1
7:10 [m]1Sa 2:10; 2Sa 22:14-15 [n]Jos 10:10
7:12 [o]Ge 35:14; Jos 4:9
7:13 [p]Jdg 13:1,5; 1Sa 13:5
7:15 [q]ver 6; 1Sa 12:11
7:17 [r]1Sa 1:19; 8:4 [s]Jdg 21:4
8:1 [t]Dt 16:18-19
8:2 [u]Ge 22:19; 1Ki 19:3; Am 5:4-5

sons did not walk in his ways. They turned aside after dishonest
gain and accepted bribes[a] and perverted justice.
4 So all the elders of Israel gathered together and came to Samuel
at Ramah.[b] 5 They said to him, "You are old, and your sons do not
walk in your ways; now appoint a king[c] to lead[a] us, such as all the
other nations have."
6 But when they said, "Give us a king to lead us," this displeased[d]
Samuel; so he prayed to the LORD. 7 And the LORD told him: "Listen
to all that the people are saying to you; it is not you they have
rejected, but they have rejected me as their king.[e] 8 As they have
done from the day I brought them up out of Egypt until this day,
forsaking me and serving other gods, so they are doing to you.
9 Now listen to them; but warn them solemnly and let them know[f]
what the king who will reign over them will do."
10 Samuel told all the words of the LORD to the people who were
asking him for a king. 11 He said, "This is what the king who will
reign over you will do: He will take[g] your sons and make them
serve with his chariots and horses, and they will run in front of his
chariots.[h] 12 Some he will assign to be commanders[i] of thousands
and commanders of fifties, and others to plow his ground and
reap his harvest, and still others to make weapons of war and
equipment for his chariots. 13 He will take your daughters to be
perfumers and cooks and bakers. 14 He will take the best of your[j]
fields and vineyards[k] and olive groves and give them to his attendants. 15 He will take a tenth of your grain and of your vintage and
give it to his officials and attendants. 16 Your menservants and
maidservants and the best of your cattle[b] and donkeys he will take
for his own use. 17 He will take a tenth of your flocks, and you
yourselves will become his slaves. 18 When that day comes, you
will cry out for relief from the king you have chosen, and the LORD
will not answer[l] you in that day."
19 But the people refused[m] to listen to Samuel. "No!" they said. "We
want a king over us. 20 Then we will be like all the other nations,[n]
with a king to lead us and to go out before us and fight our battles."
21 When Samuel heard all that the people said, he repeated[o] it
before the LORD. 22 The LORD answered, "Listen[p] to them and give
them a king."
Then Samuel said to the men of Israel, "Everyone go back to his
town."

Chapter 9 Theme ____________________________

9 There was a Benjamite, a man of standing, whose name was
Kish[q] son of Abiel, the son of Zeror, the son of Becorath, the son
of Aphiah of Benjamin. 2 He had a son named Saul, an impressive

8:3 [a] Ex 23:8; Dt 16:19; Ps 15:5
8:4 [b] 1Sa 7:17
8:5 [c] Dt 17:14-20
8:6 [d] 1Sa 15:11
8:7 [e] Ex 16:8; 1Sa 10:19
8:9 [f] ver 11-18; 1Sa 10:25
8:11 [g] 1Sa 10:25; 14:52 [h] Dt 17:16; 2Sa 15:1
8:12 [i] 1Sa 22:7
8:14 [j] Eze 46:18 [k] 1Ki 21:7,15
8:18 [l] Pr 1:28; Isa 1:15; Mic 3:4
8:19 [m] Isa 66:4; Jer 44:16
8:20 [n] ver 5
8:21 [o] Jdg 11:11
8:22 [p] ver 7
9:1 [q] 1Sa 14:51; 1Ch 8:33; 9:39

[a] 5 Traditionally *judge*; also in verses 6 and 20 [b] 16 Septuagint; Hebrew *young men*

young man without equal[a] among the Israelites—a head taller[b] than any of the others.

3 Now the donkeys belonging to Saul's father Kish were lost, and Kish said to his son Saul, "Take one of the servants with you and go and look for the donkeys." 4 So he passed through the hill[c] country of Ephraim and through the area around Shalisha,[d] but they did not find them. They went on into the district of Shaalim, but the donkeys were not there. Then he passed through the territory of Benjamin, but they did not find them.

5 When they reached the district of Zuph,[e] Saul said to the servant who was with him, "Come, let's go back, or my father will stop thinking about the donkeys and start worrying[f] about us."

6 But the servant replied, "Look, in this town there is a man of God;[g] he is highly respected, and everything[h] he says comes true. Let's go there now. Perhaps he will tell us what way to take."

7 Saul said to his servant, "If we go, what can we give the man? The food in our sacks is gone. We have no gift[i] to take to the man of God. What do we have?"

8 The servant answered him again. "Look," he said, "I have a quarter of a shekel[a] of silver. I will give it to the man of God so that he will tell us what way to take." 9 (Formerly in Israel, if a man went to inquire of God, he would say, "Come, let us go to the seer," because the prophet of today used to be called a seer.)[j]

10 "Good," Saul said to his servant. "Come, let's go." So they set out for the town where the man of God was.

11 As they were going up the hill to the town, they met some girls coming out to draw[k] water, and they asked them, "Is the seer here?"

12 "He is," they answered. "He's ahead of you. Hurry now; he has just come to our town today, for the people have a sacrifice[l] at the high place.[m] 13 As soon as you enter the town, you will find him before he goes up to the high place to eat. The people will not begin eating until he comes, because he must bless the sacrifice; afterward, those who are invited will eat. Go up now; you should find him about this time."

14 They went up to the town, and as they were entering it, there was Samuel, coming toward them on his way up to the high place.

15 Now the day before Saul came, the LORD had revealed this to Samuel: 16 "About this time tomorrow I will send you a man from the land of Benjamin. Anoint[n] him leader over my people Israel; he will deliver[o] my people from the hand of the Philistines. I have looked upon my people, for their cry has reached me."

17 When Samuel caught sight of Saul, the LORD said to him, "This[p] is the man I spoke to you about; he will govern my people."

a 8 That is, about 1/10 ounce (about 3 grams)

9:2 a 1Sa 10:24 b 1Sa 10:23
9:4 c Jos 24:33 d 2Ki 4:42
9:5 e 1Sa 1:1 f 1Sa 10:2
9:6 g Dt 33:1; 1Ki 13:1 h 1Sa 3:19
9:7 i 1Ki 14:3; 2Ki 5:5,15; 8:8
9:9 j 2Sa 24:11; 2Ki 17:13; 1Ch 9:22; 26:28; 29:29; Isa 30:10; Am 7:12
9:11 k Ge 24:11,13
9:12 l Nu 28:11-15; 1Sa 7:17 m Ge 31:54; 1Sa 10:5; 1Ki 3:2
9:16 n 1Sa 10:1 o Ex 3:7-9
9:17 p 1Sa 16:12

9:20 [a] ver 3 18Saul approached Samuel in the gateway and asked, "Would you
[b] 1Sa 8:5; 12:13 please tell me where the seer's house is?"
19"I am the seer," Samuel replied. "Go up ahead of me to the high
place, for today you are to eat with me, and in the morning I will
let you go and will tell you all that is in your heart. 20As for the
donkeys[a] you lost three days ago, do not worry about them; they
have been found. And to whom is all the desire[b] of Israel turned, if
9:21 [c] 1Sa 15:17 not to you and all your father's family?"
[d] Jdg 20:35,46 21Saul answered, "But am I not a Benjamite, from the smallest
tribe[c] of Israel, and is not my clan the least of all the clans of the
tribe of Benjamin?[d] Why do you say such a thing to me?"
22Then Samuel brought Saul and his servant into the hall and
seated them at the head of those who were invited—about thirty
9:24 in number. 23Samuel said to the cook, "Bring the piece of meat I
[e] Lev 7:32-34; Nu 18:18 gave you, the one I told you to lay aside."
24So the cook took up the leg[e] with what was on it and set it in
front of Saul. Samuel said, "Here is what has been kept for you. Eat,
because it was set aside for you for this occasion, from the time I
said, 'I have invited guests.'" And Saul dined with Samuel that day.
25After they came down from the high place to the town, Samuel
9:25 talked with Saul on the roof[f] of his house. 26They rose about day-
[f] Dt 22:8; Ac 10:9 break and Samuel called to Saul on the roof, "Get ready, and I will
send you on your way." When Saul got ready, he and Samuel went
outside together. 27As they were going down to the edge of the
town, Samuel said to Saul, "Tell the servant to go on ahead of
us"—and the servant did so—"but you stay here awhile, so that I
may give you a message from God."

10:1 [g] 1Sa 16:13; 2Ki 9:1,3,6 [h] Ps 2:12 [i] Dt 32:9; Ps 78:62,71

Chapter 10 Theme ______________________

10 Then Samuel took a flask[g] of oil and poured it on Saul's
head and kissed him, saying, "Has not the LORD anointed[h]
you leader over his inheritance?[a][i] 2When you leave me today, you
will meet two men near Rachel's tomb,[j] at Zelzah on the border
of Benjamin. They will say to you, 'The donkeys[k] you set out to
look for have been found. And now your father has stopped
10:2 thinking about them and is worried[l] about you. He is asking,
[j] Ge 35:20 [k] 1Sa 9:4 "What shall I do about my son?"'
[l] 1Sa 9:5 3"Then you will go on from there until you reach the great tree of
Tabor. Three men going up to God at Bethel[m] will meet you there.
One will be carrying three young goats, another three loaves of
bread, and another a skin of wine. 4They will greet you and offer
you two loaves of bread, which you will accept from them.

10:3 [m] Ge 28:22; 35:7-8

[a] *1* Hebrew; Septuagint and Vulgate *over his people Israel? You will reign over the LORD's people and save them from the power of their enemies round about. And this will be a sign to you that the LORD has anointed you leader over his inheritance:*

5“After that you will go to Gibeah of God, where there is a
Philistine outpost.[a] As you approach the town, you will meet a
procession of prophets coming down from the high place[b] with
lyres, tambourines, flutes and harps[c] being played before them,
and they will be prophesying.[d] 6The Spirit[e] of the LORD will come
upon you in power, and you will prophesy with them; and you
will be changed into a different person. 7Once these signs are fulfilled, do whatever[f] your hand finds to do, for God is with[g] you.
8“Go down ahead of me to Gilgal.[h] I will surely come down to
you to sacrifice burnt offerings and fellowship offerings,[a] but you
must wait seven days until I come to you and tell you what you are
to do.”
9As Saul turned to leave Samuel, God changed[i] Saul’s heart,
and all these signs were fulfilled that day. 10When they arrived at
Gibeah, a procession of prophets met him; the Spirit of God came
upon him in power, and he joined in their prophesying.[j] 11When
all those who had formerly known him saw him prophesying
with the prophets, they asked each other, “What is this[k] that has
happened to the son of Kish? Is Saul also among the prophets?”[l]
12A man who lived there answered, “And who is their father?”
So it became a saying: “Is Saul also among the prophets?” 13After
Saul stopped prophesying, he went to the high place.
14Now Saul’s uncle[m] asked him and his servant, “Where have
you been?”

“Looking for the donkeys,” he said. “But when we saw they were not to be found, we went to Samuel.”

15Saul’s uncle said, “Tell me what Samuel said to you.”

16Saul replied, “He assured us that the donkeys[n] had been
found.” But he did not tell his uncle what Samuel had said about
the kingship.
17Samuel summoned the people of Israel to the LORD at Mizpah[o]
18and said to them, “This is what the LORD, the God of Israel,
says: ‘I brought Israel up out of Egypt, and I delivered you from
the power of Egypt and all the kingdoms that oppressed[p] you.’
19But you have now rejected your God, who saves you out of all
your calamities and distresses. And you have said, ‘No, set a king[q]
over us.’ So now present[r] yourselves before the LORD by your tribes
and clans.”
20When Samuel brought all the tribes of Israel near, the tribe of
Benjamin was chosen. 21Then he brought forward the tribe of
Benjamin, clan by clan, and Matri’s clan was chosen. Finally Saul
son of Kish was chosen. But when they looked for him, he was
not to be found. 22So they inquired[s] further of the LORD, “Has the
man come here yet?”

a 8 Traditionally *peace offerings*

10:5 a 1Sa 13:3 b 1Sa 9:12 c 2Ki 3:15 d 1Sa 19:20; 1Co 14:1
10:6 e ver 10; Nu 11:25; 1Sa 19:23-24
10:7 f Ecc 9:10 g Jos 1:5; Jdg 6:12; Heb 13:5
10:8 h 1Sa 11:14-15
10:9 i ver 6
10:10 j ver 5-6; 1Sa 19:20
10:11 k Mt 13:54; Jn 7:15 l 1Sa 19:24
10:14 m 1Sa 14:50
10:16 n 1Sa 9:20
10:17 o Jdg 20:1; 1Sa 7:5
10:18 p Jdg 6:8-9
10:19 q 1Sa 8:5-7; 12:12 r Jos 7:14; 24:1
10:22 s 1Sa 23:2,4, 9-11

And the LORD said, "Yes, he has hidden himself among the bag-
gage."
23 They ran and brought him out, and as he stood among the
people he was a head taller[a] than any of the others. 24 Samuel said
to all the people, "Do you see the man the LORD has chosen?[b] There
is no one like him among all the people."
Then the people shouted, "Long live[c] the king!"
25 Samuel explained to the people the regulations[d] of the kingship. He wrote them down on a scroll and deposited it before the
LORD. Then Samuel dismissed the people, each to his own home.
26 Saul also went to his home in Gibeah,[e] accompanied by valiant
men whose hearts God had touched. 27 But some troublemakers[f]
said, "How can this fellow save us?" They despised him and
brought him no gifts.[g] But Saul kept silent.

Chapter 11 Theme ______________________

Saul's Ascent to Kingship

11 Nahash[h] the Ammonite went up and besieged Jabesh Gilead.[i]
And all the men of Jabesh said to him, "Make a treaty[j] with
us, and we will be subject to you."
2 But Nahash the Ammonite replied, "I will make a treaty with
you only on the condition
that I gouge[k] out the right eye
of every one of you and so
bring disgrace[l] on all Israel."
3 The elders of Jabesh said
to him, "Give us seven days
so we can send messengers
throughout Israel; if no one
comes to rescue us, we will
surrender to you."
4 When the messengers
came to Gibeah[m] of Saul and
reported these terms to the
people, they all wept[n] aloud.
5 Just then Saul was returning
from the fields, behind his
oxen, and he asked, "What is
wrong with the people? Why
are they weeping?" Then they
repeated to him what the men of Jabesh had said.
6 When Saul heard their words, the Spirit[o] of God came upon
him in power, and he burned with anger. 7 He took a pair of oxen,
cut them into pieces, and sent the pieces by messengers throughout Israel,[p] proclaiming, "This is what will be done to the oxen of
anyone[q] who does not follow Saul and Samuel." Then the terror

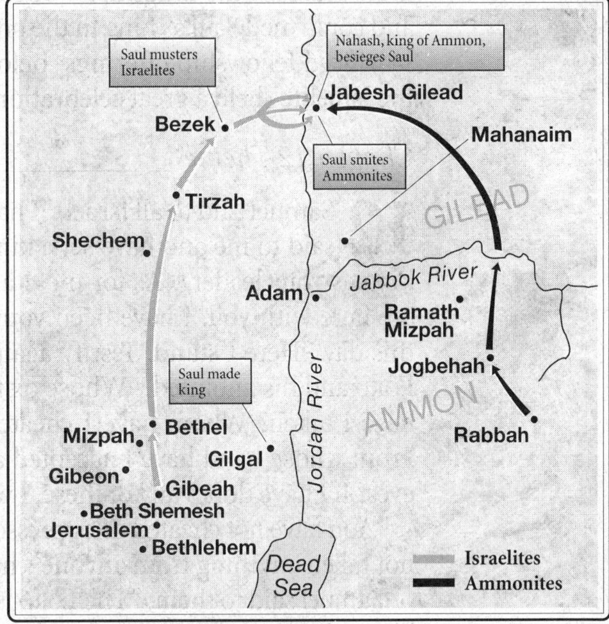

10:23 [a] 1Sa 9:2
10:24 [b] Dt 17:15; 2Sa 21:6 [c] 1Ki 1:25,34,39
10:25 [d] Dt 17:14-20; 1Sa 8:11-18
10:26 [e] 1Sa 11:4
10:27 [f] Dt 13:13 [g] 1Ki 10:25; 2Ch 17:5
11:1 [h] 1Sa 12:12 [i] Jdg 21:8 [j] 1Ki 20:34; Eze 17:13
11:2 [k] Nu 16:14 [l] 1Sa 17:26
11:4 [m] 1Sa 10:5,26; 15:34 [n] Jdg 2:4; 1Sa 30:4
11:6 [o] Jdg 3:10; 6:34; 13:25; 14:6; 1Sa 10:10; 16:13
11:7 [p] Jdg 19:29 [q] Jdg 21:5

of the LORD fell on the people, and they turned out as one man. 8When Saul mustered[a] them at Bezek,[b] the men of Israel numbered three hundred thousand and the men of Judah thirty thousand.

9They told the messengers who had come, "Say to the men of Jabesh Gilead, 'By the time the sun is hot tomorrow, you will be delivered.'" When the messengers went and reported this to the men of Jabesh, they were elated. 10They said to the Ammonites, "Tomorrow we will surrender[c] to you, and you can do to us whatever seems good to you."

11The next day Saul separated his men into three divisions;[d] during the last watch of the night they broke into the camp of the Ammonites and slaughtered them until the heat of the day. Those who survived were scattered, so that no two of them were left together.

12The people then said to Samuel, "Who[e] was it that asked, 'Shall Saul reign over us?' Bring these men to us and we will put them to death."

13But Saul said, "No one shall be put to death today,[f] for this day the LORD has rescued[g] Israel."

14Then Samuel said to the people, "Come, let us go to Gilgal[h] and there reaffirm the kingship.[i]" 15So all the people went to Gilgal[j] and confirmed Saul as king in the presence of the LORD. There they sacrificed fellowship offerings[a] before the LORD, and Saul and all the Israelites held a great celebration.

Chapter 12 Theme ____________________

12 Samuel said to all Israel, "I have listened[k] to everything you said to me and have set a king[l] over you. 2Now you have a king as your leader.[m] As for me, I am old and gray, and my sons are here with you. I have been your leader from my youth until this day. 3Here I stand. Testify against me in the presence of the LORD and his anointed.[n] Whose ox have I taken? Whose donkey[o] have I taken? Whom have I cheated? Whom have I oppressed? From whose hand have I accepted a bribe[p] to make me shut my eyes? If I have done[q] any of these, I will make it right."

4"You have not cheated or oppressed us," they replied. "You have not taken anything from anyone's hand."

5Samuel said to them, "The LORD is witness against you, and also his anointed is witness this day, that you have not found anything[r] in my hand.[s]"

"He is witness," they said.

6Then Samuel said to the people, "It is the LORD who appointed Moses and Aaron and brought[t] your forefathers up out of Egypt.

a 15 Traditionally *peace offerings*

11:8 [a] Jdg 20:2 [b] Jdg 1:4
11:10 [c] ver 3
11:11 [d] Jdg 7:16
11:12 [e] 1Sa 10:27; Lk 19:27
11:13 [f] 2Sa 19:22 [g] Ex 14:13; 1Sa 19:5
11:14 [h] 1Sa 10:8 [i] 1Sa 10:25
11:15 [j] 1Sa 10:8,17
12:1 [k] 1Sa 8:7 [l] 1Sa 10:24; 11:15
12:2 [m] 1Sa 8:5
12:3 [n] 1Sa 10:1; 24:6; 2Sa 1:14 [o] Nu 16:15 [p] Dt 16:19 [q] Ac 20:33
12:5 [r] Ac 23:9; 24:20 [s] Ex 22:4
12:6 [t] Ex 6:26; Mic 6:4

7 Now then, stand here, because I am going to confront[a] you with
evidence before the LORD as to all the righteous acts performed
by the LORD for you and your fathers.
8 "After Jacob entered Egypt, they cried[b] to the LORD for help, and
the LORD sent[c] Moses and Aaron, who brought your forefathers out
of Egypt and settled them in this place.
9 "But they forgot[d] the LORD their God; so he sold them into the
hand of Sisera,[e] the commander of the army of Hazor, and into
the hands of the Philistines[f] and the king of Moab,[g] who fought
against them. 10 They cried out to the LORD and said, 'We have
sinned; we have forsaken[h] the LORD and served the Baals and the
Ashtoreths.[i] But now deliver us from the hands of our enemies,
and we will serve you.' 11 Then the LORD sent Jerub-Baal,[a][j] Barak,[b][k]
Jephthah[l] and Samuel,[c] and he delivered you from the hands of
your enemies on every side, so that you lived securely.
12 "But when you saw that Nahash[m] king[n] of the Ammonites
was moving against you, you said to me, 'No, we want a king to
rule[o] over us'—even though the LORD your God was your king.
13 Now here is the king[p] you have chosen, the one you asked[q] for;
see, the LORD has set a king over you. 14 If you fear[r] the LORD and
serve and obey him and do not rebel against his commands, and
if both you and the king who reigns over you follow the LORD
your God—good! 15 But if you do not obey the LORD, and if you
rebel against[s] his commands, his hand will be against you, as it
was against your fathers.
16 "Now then, stand still and see[t] this great thing the LORD is
about to do before your eyes! 17 Is it not wheat harvest[u] now? I will
call[v] upon the LORD to send thunder and rain.[w] And you will realize
what an evil[x] thing you did in the eyes of the LORD when you asked
for a king."
18 Then Samuel called upon the LORD, and that same day the
LORD sent thunder and rain. So all the people stood in awe[y] of the
LORD and of Samuel.
19 The people all said to Samuel, "Pray[z] to the LORD your God for
your servants so that we will not die, for we have added to all our
other sins the evil of asking for a king."
20 "Do not be afraid," Samuel replied. "You have done all this
evil; yet do not turn away from the LORD, but serve the LORD with
all your heart. 21 Do not turn away after useless[a] idols.[b] They can
do you no good, nor can they rescue you, because they are useless.
22 For the sake[c] of his great name[d] the LORD will not reject[e] his people, because the LORD was pleased to make[f] you his own. 23 As for
me, far be it from me that I should sin against the LORD by failing

12:7 [a] Isa 1:18; Mic 6:1-5
12:8 [b] Ex 2:23 [c] Ex 3:10; 4:16
12:9 [d] Jdg 3:7 [e] Jdg 4:2 [f] Jdg 10:7; 13:1 [g] Jdg 3:12
12:10 [h] Jdg 10:10,15 [i] Jdg 2:13
12:11 [j] Jdg 6:14,32 [k] Jdg 4:6 [l] Jdg 11:1
12:12 [m] 1Sa 11:1 [n] 1Sa 8:5 [o] Jdg 8:23; 1Sa 8:6,19
12:13 [p] 1Sa 8:5; Hos 13:11 [q] 1Sa 10:24
12:14 [r] Jos 24:14
12:15 [s] ver 9; Jos 24:20; Isa 1:20
12:16 [t] Ex 14:13
12:17 [u] 1Sa 7:9-10 [v] Jas 5:18 [w] Pr 26:1 [x] 1Sa 8:6-7
12:18 [y] Ex 14:31
12:19 [z] ver 23; Ex 9:28; Jas 5:18; 1Jn 5:16
12:21 [a] Isa 41:24,29; Jer 16:19; Hab 2:18 [b] Dt 11:16
12:22 [c] Ps 106:8 [d] Jos 7:9 [e] 1Ki 6:13 [f] Dt 7:7; 1Pe 2:9

[a] *11* Also called *Gideon* [b] *11* Some Septuagint manuscripts and Syriac; Hebrew *Bedan*
[c] *11* Hebrew; some Septuagint manuscripts and Syriac *Samson*

to pray[a] for you. And I will teach[b] you the way that is good and
right. 24But be sure to fear[c] the LORD and serve him faithfully with
all your heart; consider[d] what great[e] things he has done for you.
25Yet if you persist[f] in doing evil, both you and your king will be
swept[g] away."

Chapter 13 Theme

The Philistines' Attack on the Israelites

(See master map on page 497)

13 Saul was ⌊thirty⌋[a] years old when he became king, and he
reigned over Israel ⌊forty-⌋[b] two years.
2Saul[c] chose three thousand men from Israel; two thousand were
with him at Micmash and in the hill country of Bethel, and a thousand were with Jonathan at Gibeah[h] in Benjamin. The rest of the
men he sent back to their homes.
3Jonathan attacked the Philistine outpost[i] at Geba, and the 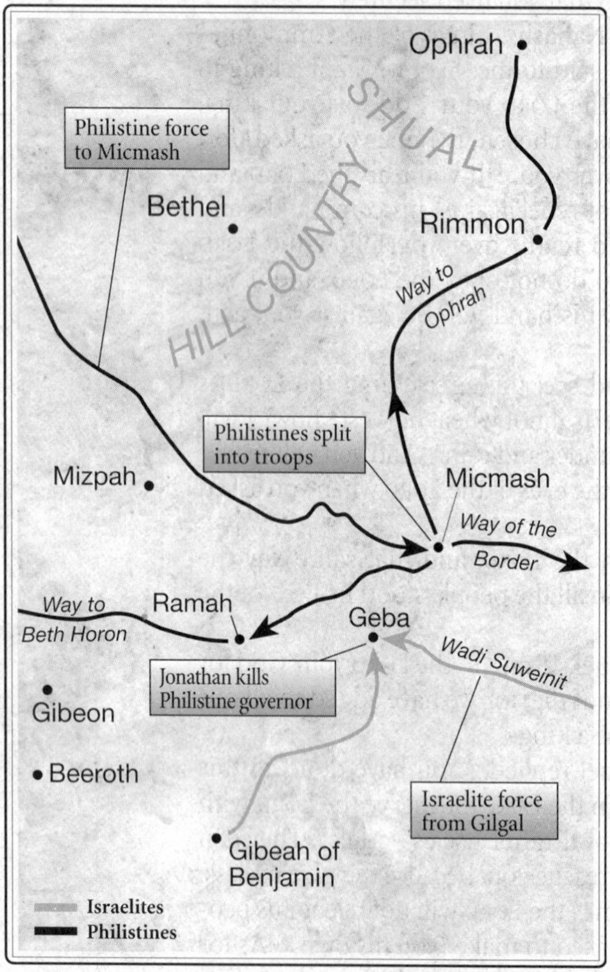
Philistines heard about it.
Then Saul had the trumpet
blown throughout the land
and said, "Let the Hebrews
hear!" 4So all Israel heard
the news: "Saul has attacked
the Philistine outpost, and
now Israel has become a
stench[j] to the Philistines."
And the people were sum-
moned to join Saul at Gilgal.
5The Philistines assembled
to fight Israel, with three
thousand[d] chariots, six thousand charioteers, and soldiers as numerous as the
sand[k] on the seashore. They
went up and camped at Micmash, east of Beth Aven.
6When the men of Israel saw
that their situation was critical and that their army was
hard pressed, they hid in
caves and thickets, among
the rocks, and in pits and
cisterns.[l] 7Some Hebrews
even crossed the Jordan to
the land of Gad[m] and Gilead.

a *1* A few late manuscripts of the Septuagint; Hebrew does not have *thirty.* b *1* See the round number in Acts 13:21; Hebrew does not have *forty-.* c *1,2* Or *and when he had reigned over Israel two years, 2he* d *5* Some Septuagint manuscripts and Syriac; Hebrew *thirty thousand*

12:23 [a]Ro 1:9-10; Col 1:9; 2Ti 1:3 [b]1Ki 8:36; Ps 34:11; Pr 4:11
12:24 [c]Ecc 12:13 [d]Isa 5:12 [e]Dt 10:21
12:25 [f]1Sa 31:1-5 [g]Jos 24:20
13:2 [h]1Sa 10:26
13:3 [i]1Sa 10:5
13:4 [j]Ge 34:30
13:5 [k]Jos 11:4
13:6 [l]Jdg 6:2
13:7 [m]Nu 32:33

Saul remained at Gilgal, and all the troops with him were quaking with fear. 8He waited seven[a] days, the time set by Samuel; but
Samuel did not come to Gilgal, and Saul's men began to scatter.
9So he said, "Bring me the burnt offering and the fellowship offerings.[a]" And Saul offered[b] up the burnt offering. 10Just as he finished making the offering, Samuel[c] arrived, and Saul went out to
greet him.

11"What have you done?" asked Samuel.

Saul replied, "When I saw that the men were scattering, and that
you did not come at the set time, and that the Philistines were
assembling at Micmash,[d] 12I thought, 'Now the Philistines will
come down against me at Gilgal, and I have not sought the LORD's
favor.[e]' So I felt compelled to offer the burnt offering."

13"You acted foolishly,[f]" Samuel said. "You have not kept[g] the
command the LORD your God gave you; if you had, he would have
established your kingdom over Israel for all time. 14But now your
kingdom[h] will not endure; the LORD has sought out a man after
his own heart[i] and appointed[j] him leader of his people, because
you have not kept the LORD's command."

15Then Samuel left Gilgal[b] and went up to Gibeah[k] in Benjamin,
and Saul counted the men who were with him. They numbered
about six hundred.

16Saul and his son Jonathan and the men with them were staying
in Gibeah[c] in Benjamin, while the Philistines camped at Micmash.
17Raiding[l] parties went out from the Philistine camp in three
detachments. One turned toward Ophrah[m] in the vicinity of Shual,
18another toward Beth Horon,[n] and the third toward the border-
land overlooking the Valley of Zeboim[o] facing the desert.

19Not a blacksmith[p] could be found in the whole land of Israel,
because the Philistines had said, "Otherwise the Hebrews will
make swords or spears!" 20So all Israel went down to the Philistines
to have their plowshares, mattocks, axes and sickles[d] sharpened.
21The price was two thirds of a shekel[e] for sharpening plowshares
and mattocks, and a third of a shekel[f] for sharpening forks and
axes and for repointing goads.

22So on the day of the battle not a soldier with Saul and Jonathan[q]
had a sword or spear[r] in his hand; only Saul and his son Jonathan
had them.

23Now a detachment of Philistines had gone out to the pass[s] at
Micmash.

[a] *9* Traditionally *peace offerings* [b] *15* Hebrew; Septuagint *Gilgal and went his way; the rest of the people went after Saul to meet the army, and they went out of Gilgal* [c] *16* Two Hebrew manuscripts; most Hebrew manuscripts *Geba,* a variant of *Gibeah* [d] *20* Septuagint; Hebrew *plowshares* [e] *21* Hebrew *pim;* that is, about 1/4 ounce (about 8 grams) [f] *21* That is, about 1/8 ounce (about 4 grams)

13:8 [a] 1Sa 10:8
13:9 [b] 2Sa 24:25; 1Ki 3:4
13:10 [c] 1Sa 15:13
13:11 [d] ver 2,5,16, 23
13:12 [e] Jer 26:19
13:13 [f] 2Ch 16:9 [g] 1Sa 15:23,24
13:14 [h] 1Sa 15:28 [i] Ac 7:46; 13:22 [j] 2Sa 6:21
13:15 [k] 1Sa 14:2
13:17 [l] 1Sa 14:15 [m] Jos 18:23
13:18 [n] Jos 18:13-14 [o] Ne 11:34
13:19 [p] 2Ki 24:14; Jer 24:1
13:22 [q] 1Ch 9:39 [r] Jdg 5:8
13:23 [s] 1Sa 14:4

Chapter 14 Theme ____

14 One day Jonathan son of Saul said to the young man bearing his armor, "Come, let's go over to the Philistine outpost
on the other side." But he did not tell his father.

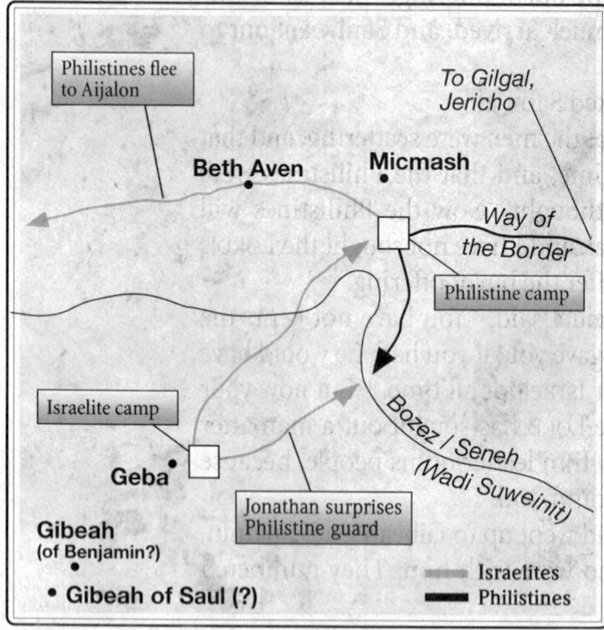

2Saul was staying on the
outskirts of Gibeah[a] under
a pomegranate tree in Migron.[b] With him were about
six hundred men, 3among
whom was Ahijah, who was
wearing an ephod. He was a
son of Ichabod's[c] brother
Ahitub[d] son of Phinehas, the
son of Eli,[e] the LORD's priest
in Shiloh. No one was aware
that Jonathan had left.
4On each side of the pass[f]
that Jonathan intended to
cross to reach the Philistine
outpost was a cliff; one was
called Bozez, and the other
Seneh. 5One cliff stood to the
north toward Micmash, the
other to the south toward Geba.

The Battle at Micmash

6Jonathan said to his young armor-bearer, "Come, let's go over
to the outpost of those uncircumcised[g] fellows. Perhaps the LORD
will act in our behalf. Nothing[h] can hinder the LORD from saving,
whether by many[i] or by few.[j]"
7"Do all that you have in mind," his armor-bearer said. "Go
ahead; I am with you heart and soul."
8Jonathan said, "Come, then; we will cross over toward the men
and let them see us. 9If they say to us, 'Wait there until we come to
you,' we will stay where we are and not go up to them. 10But if they
say, 'Come up to us,' we will climb up, because that will be our
sign[k] that the LORD has given them into our hands."
11So both of them showed themselves to the Philistine outpost.
"Look!" said the Philistines. "The Hebrews are crawling out of the
holes they were hiding[l] in." 12The men of the outpost shouted to
Jonathan and his armor-bearer, "Come up to us and we'll teach
you a lesson.[m]"
So Jonathan said to his armor-bearer, "Climb up after me; the
LORD has given them into the hand[n] of Israel."
13Jonathan climbed up, using his hands and feet, with his armor-
bearer right behind him. The Philistines fell before Jonathan, and
his armor-bearer followed and killed behind him. 14In that first

14:2
[a] 1Sa 13:15
[b] Isa 10:28

14:3
[c] 1Sa 4:21
[d] 1Sa 22:11,20
[e] 1Sa 2:28

14:4
[f] 1Sa 13:23

14:6
[g] 1Sa 17:26,36; Jer 9:26
[h] Heb 11:34
[i] Jdg 7:4
[j] 1Sa 17:46-47

14:10
[k] Ge 24:14; Jdg 6:36-37

14:11
[l] 1Sa 13:6

14:12
[m] 1Sa 17:43-44
[n] 2Sa 5:24

attack Jonathan and his armor-bearer killed some twenty men in
an area of about half an acre.[a]
15Then panic[a] struck the whole army—those in the camp and
field, and those in the outposts and raiding[b] parties—and the
ground shook. It was a panic sent by God.[b]
16Saul's lookouts[c] at Gibeah in Benjamin saw the army melting
away in all directions. 17Then Saul said to the men who were with
him, "Muster the forces and see who has left us." When they did,
it was Jonathan and his armor-bearer who were not there.
18Saul said to Ahijah, "Bring[d] the ark of God." (At that time it
was with the Israelites.)[c] 19While Saul was talking to the priest, the
tumult in the Philistine camp increased more and more. So Saul
said to the priest,[e] "Withdraw your hand."
20Then Saul and all his men assembled and went to the battle.
They found the Philistines in total confusion, striking[f] each other
with their swords. 21Those Hebrews who had previously been with
the Philistines and had gone up with them to their camp went[g]
over to the Israelites who were with Saul and Jonathan. 22When
all the Israelites who had hidden[h] in the hill country of Ephraim
heard that the Philistines were on the run, they joined the battle in
hot pursuit. 23So the LORD rescued[i] Israel that day, and the battle
moved on beyond Beth Aven.[j]
24Now the men of Israel were in distress that day, because Saul
had bound the people under an oath,[k] saying, "Cursed be any man
who eats food before evening comes, before I have avenged myself
on my enemies!" So none of the troops tasted food.
25The entire army[d] entered the woods, and there was honey on
the ground. 26When they went into the woods, they saw the honey
oozing out, yet no one put his hand to his mouth, because they
feared the oath. 27But Jonathan had not heard that his father had
bound the people with the oath, so he reached out the end of the
staff that was in his hand and dipped it into the honeycomb.[l] He
raised his hand to his mouth, and his eyes brightened.[e] 28Then
one of the soldiers told him, "Your father bound the army under a
strict oath, saying, 'Cursed be any man who eats food today!' That
is why the men are faint."
29Jonathan said, "My father has made trouble[m] for the country.
See how my eyes brightened[f] when I tasted a little of this honey.
30How much better it would have been if the men had eaten today
some of the plunder they took from their enemies. Would not the
slaughter of the Philistines have been even greater?"

14:15 [a] Ge 35:5; 2Ki 7:5-7 [b] 1Sa 13:17
14:16 [c] 2Sa 18:24
14:18 [d] 1Sa 30:7
14:19 [e] Nu 27:21
14:20 [f] Jdg 7:22; 2Ch 20:23
14:21 [g] 1Sa 29:4
14:22 [h] 1Sa 13:6
14:23 [i] Ex 14:30; Ps 44:6-7 [j] 1Sa 13:5
14:24 [k] Jos 6:26
14:27 [l] ver 43; 1Sa 30:12
14:29 [m] Jos 7:25; 1Ki 18:18

[a] *14* Hebrew *half a yoke*; a "yoke" was the land plowed by a yoke of oxen in one day. [b] *15* Or *a terrible panic* [c] *18* Hebrew; Septuagint *"Bring the ephod." (At that time he wore the ephod before the Israelites.)* [d] *25* Or *Now all the people of the land* [e] *27* Or *his strength was renewed* [f] *29* Or *my strength was renewed*

31 That day, after the Israelites had struck down the Philistines
from Micmash to Aijalon,[a] they were exhausted. 32 They pounced
on the plunder[b] and, taking sheep, cattle and calves, they
butchered them on the ground and ate them, together with the
blood.[c] 33 Then someone said to Saul, "Look, the men are sinning
against the LORD by eating meat that has blood in it."
"You have broken faith," he said. "Roll a large stone over here at
once." 34 Then he said, "Go out among the men and tell them,
'Each of you bring me your cattle and sheep, and slaughter them
here and eat them. Do not sin against the LORD by eating meat
with blood still in it.'"
So everyone brought his ox that night and slaughtered it there.
35 Then Saul built an altar[d] to the LORD; it was the first time he had
done this.
36 Saul said, "Let us go down after the Philistines by night and
plunder them till dawn, and let us not leave one of them alive."
"Do whatever seems best to you," they replied.
But the priest said, "Let us inquire of God here."
37 So Saul asked God, "Shall I go down after the Philistines? Will
you give them into Israel's hand?" But God did not answer[e] him
that day.
38 Saul therefore said, "Come here, all you who are leaders of the
army, and let us find out what sin has been committed[f] today. 39 As
surely as the LORD who rescues Israel lives,[g] even if it lies with my
son Jonathan, he must die." But not one of the men said a word.
40 Saul then said to all the Israelites, "You stand over there; I and
Jonathan my son will stand over here."
"Do what seems best to you," the men replied.
41 Then Saul prayed to the LORD, the God of Israel, "Give[h] me the
right[i] answer."[a] And Jonathan and Saul were taken by lot, and the
men were cleared. 42 Saul said, "Cast the lot between me and Jonathan my son." And Jonathan was taken.
43 Then Saul said to Jonathan, "Tell me what you have done."[j]
So Jonathan told him, "I merely tasted a little honey[k] with the
end of my staff. And now must I die?"
44 Saul said, "May God deal with me, be it ever so severely,[l] if
you do not die, Jonathan.[m]"
45 But the men said to Saul, "Should Jonathan die—he who has
brought about this great deliverance in Israel? Never! As surely as
the LORD lives, not a hair[n] of his head will fall to the ground, for he
did this today with God's help." So the men rescued[o] Jonathan,
and he was not put to death.

[a] *41* Hebrew; Septuagint *"Why have you not answered your servant today? If the fault is in me or my son Jonathan, respond with Urim, but if the men of Israel are at fault, respond with Thummim."*

14:31 [a] Jos 10:12

14:32 [b] 1Sa 15:19 [c] Ge 9:4; Lev 3:17; 7:26; 17:10-14; 19:26; Dt 12:16, 23-24

14:35 [d] 1Sa 7:17

14:37 [e] 1Sa 10:22; 28:6,15

14:38 [f] Jos 7:11; 1Sa 10:19

14:39 [g] 2Sa 12:5

14:41 [h] Ac 1:24 [i] Pr 16:33

14:43 [j] Jos 7:19 [k] ver 27

14:44 [l] Ru 1:17 [m] ver 39

14:45 [n] 1Ki 1:52; Lk 21:18; Ac 27:34 [o] 2Sa 14:11

46 Then Saul stopped pursuing the Philistines, and they withdrew to their own land.
47 After Saul had assumed rule over Israel, he fought against their
enemies on every side: Moab, the Ammonites,[a] Edom, the kings[a]
of Zobah,[b] and the Philistines. Wherever he turned, he inflicted
punishment on them.[b] 48 He fought valiantly and defeated the
Amalekites,[c] delivering Israel from the hands of those who had
plundered them.
49 Saul's sons were Jonathan, Ishvi and Malki-Shua.[d] The name
of his older daughter was Merab, and that of the younger was
Michal.[e] 50 His wife's name was Ahinoam daughter of Ahimaaz.
The name of the commander of Saul's army was Abner son of
Ner, and Ner was Saul's uncle. 51 Saul's father Kish[f] and Abner's
father Ner were sons of Abiel.
52 All the days of Saul there was bitter war with the Philistines,
and whenever Saul saw a mighty or brave man, he took[g] him into
his service.

Chapter 15 Theme ______________________________

15 Samuel said to Saul, "I am the one the LORD sent to anoint[h]
you king over his people Israel; so listen now to the message
from the LORD. 2 This is what the LORD Almighty says: 'I will punish the Amalekites[i] for what they did to Israel when they waylaid
them as they came up from Egypt. 3 Now go, attack the Amalekites
and totally[j] destroy[c] everything that belongs to them. Do not spare
them; put to death men and women, children and infants, cattle
and sheep, camels and donkeys.'"
4 So Saul summoned the men and mustered them at Telaim—
two hundred thousand foot soldiers and ten thousand men from
Judah. 5 Saul went to the city of Amalek and set an ambush in the
ravine. 6 Then he said to the Kenites,[k] "Go away, leave the Amalekites so that I do not destroy you along with them; for you showed

14:47 [a] 1Sa 11:1-13 [b] ver 52; 2Sa 10:6
14:48 [c] 1Sa 15:2,7
14:49 [d] 1Sa 31:2; 1Ch 8:33 [e] 1Sa 18:17-20
14:51 [f] 1Sa 9:1
14:52 [g] 1Sa 8:11
15:1 [h] 1Sa 9:16
15:2 [i] Ex 17:8-14; Nu 24:20; Dt 25:17-19
15:3 [j] Nu 24:20; Dt 20:16-18; Jos 6:17; 1Sa 22:19
15:6 [k] Ex 18:10,19; Nu 10:29-32; 24:22; Jdg 1:16; 4:1

[a] *47* Masoretic Text; Dead Sea Scrolls and Septuagint *king* [b] *47* Hebrew; Septuagint *he was victorious* [c] *3* The Hebrew term refers to the irrevocable giving over of things or persons to the LORD, often by totally destroying them; also in verses 8, 9, 15, 18, 20 and 21.

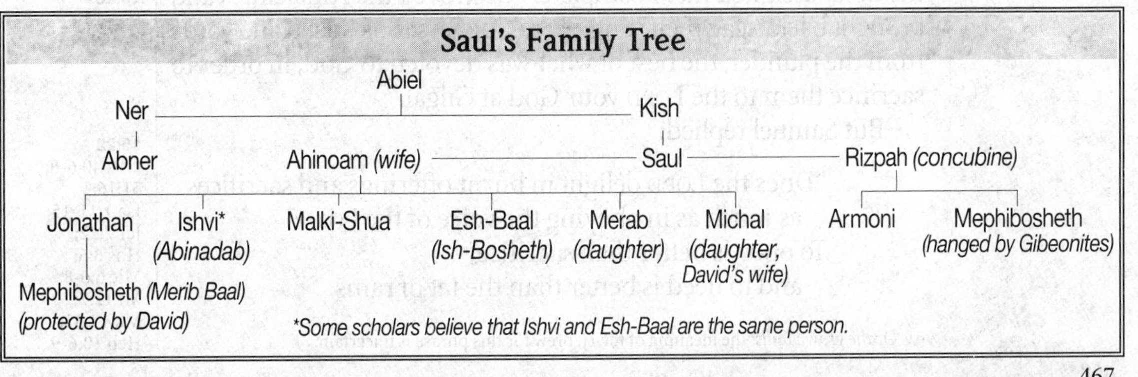

kindness to all the Israelites when they came up out of Egypt." So the Kenites moved away from the Amalekites.

7Then Saul attacked the Amalekites[a] all the way from Havilah to Shur,[b] to the east of Egypt. 8He took Agag king of the Amalekites alive,[c] and all his people he totally destroyed with the sword. 9But Saul and the army spared[d] Agag and the best of the sheep and cattle, the fat calves[a] and lambs—everything that was good. These they were unwilling to destroy completely, but everything that was despised and weak they totally destroyed.

10Then the word of the LORD came to Samuel: 11"I am grieved[e] that I have made Saul king, because he has turned[f] away from me and has not carried out my instructions."[g] Samuel was troubled,[h] and he cried out to the LORD all that night.

12Early in the morning Samuel got up and went to meet Saul, but he was told, "Saul has gone to Carmel.[i] There he has set up a monument in his own honor and has turned and gone on down to Gilgal."

13When Samuel reached him, Saul said, "The LORD bless you! I have carried out the LORD's instructions."

14But Samuel said, "What then is this bleating of sheep in my ears? What is this lowing of cattle that I hear?"

15Saul answered, "The soldiers brought them from the Amalekites; they spared the best of the sheep and cattle to sacrifice to the LORD your God, but we totally destroyed the rest."

16"Stop!" Samuel said to Saul. "Let me tell you what the LORD said to me last night."

"Tell me," Saul replied.

17Samuel said, "Although you were once small[j] in your own eyes, did you not become the head of the tribes of Israel? The LORD anointed you king over Israel. 18And he sent you on a mission, saying, 'Go and completely destroy those wicked people, the Amalekites; make war on them until you have wiped them out.' 19Why did you not obey the LORD? Why did you pounce on the plunder[k] and do evil in the eyes of the LORD?"

20"But I did obey[l] the LORD," Saul said. "I went on the mission the LORD assigned me. I completely destroyed the Amalekites and brought back Agag their king. 21The soldiers took sheep and cattle from the plunder, the best of what was devoted to God, in order to sacrifice them to the LORD your God at Gilgal."

22But Samuel replied:

> "Does the LORD delight in burnt offerings and sacrifices
> as much as in obeying the voice of the LORD?
> To obey is better than sacrifice,[m]
> and to heed is better than the fat of rams.

15:7 [a] 1Sa 14:48 [b] Ge 16:7; 25:17-18; Ex 15:22
15:8 [c] 1Sa 30:1
15:9 [d] ver 3,15
15:11 [e] Ge 6:6; 2Sa 24:16 [f] Jos 22:16 [g] 1Sa 13:13; 1Ki 9:6-7 [h] ver 35
15:12 [i] Jos 15:55
15:17 [j] 1Sa 9:21
15:19 [k] 1Sa 14:32
15:20 [l] ver 13
15:22 [m] Ps 40:6-8; 51:16; Isa 1:11-15; Jer 7:22; Hos 6:6; Mic 6:6-8; Mt 12:7; Mk 12:33; Heb 10:6-9

a9 Or *the grown bulls;* the meaning of the Hebrew for this phrase is uncertain.

23 For rebellion is like the sin of divination,[a]
and arrogance like the evil of idolatry.
Because you have rejected[b] the word of the LORD,
he has rejected you as king."

24 Then Saul said to Samuel, "I have sinned.[c] I violated the LORD's command and your instructions. I was afraid[d] of the people and so I gave in to them. 25 Now I beg you, forgive[e] my sin and come back with me, so that I may worship the LORD."

26 But Samuel said to him, "I will not go back with you. You have rejected[f] the word of the LORD, and the LORD has rejected you as king over Israel!"

27 As Samuel turned to leave, Saul caught hold of the hem of his robe, and it tore.[g] 28 Samuel said to him, "The LORD has torn[h] the kingdom of Israel from you today and has given it to one of your neighbors—to one better than you. 29 He who is the Glory of Israel does not lie[i] or change[j] his mind; for he is not a man, that he should change his mind."

30 Saul replied, "I have sinned. But please honor[k] me before the elders of my people and before Israel; come back with me, so that I may worship the LORD your God." 31 So Samuel went back with Saul, and Saul worshiped the LORD.

32 Then Samuel said, "Bring me Agag king of the Amalekites."

Agag came to him confidently,[a] thinking, "Surely the bitterness of death is past."

33 But Samuel said,

"As your sword has made women childless,
so will your mother be childless among women."[l]

And Samuel put Agag to death before the LORD at Gilgal.

34 Then Samuel left for Ramah,[m] but Saul went up to his home in Gibeah[n] of Saul. 35 Until the day Samuel[o] died, he did not go to see Saul again, though Samuel mourned[p] for him. And the LORD was grieved that he had made Saul king over Israel.

Chapter 16 Theme ______________________________

16 The LORD said to Samuel, "How long will you mourn[q] for Saul, since I have rejected[r] him as king over Israel? Fill your horn with oil[s] and be on your way; I am sending you to Jesse[t] of Bethlehem. I have chosen[u] one of his sons to be king."

2 But Samuel said, "How can I go? Saul will hear about it and kill me."

The LORD said, "Take a heifer with you and say, 'I have come to sacrifice to the LORD.' 3 Invite Jesse to the sacrifice, and I will show[v] you what to do. You are to anoint[w] for me the one I indicate."

15:23 [a] Dt 18:10 [b] 1Sa 13:13
15:24 [c] 2Sa 12:13 [d] Pr 29:25; Isa 51:12-13
15:25 [e] Ex 10:17
15:26 [f] 1Sa 13:14
15:27 [g] 1Ki 11:11,31
15:28 [h] 1Sa 28:17; 1Ki 11:31
15:29 [i] 1Ch 29:11; Tit 1:2 [j] Nu 23:19; Eze 24:14
15:30 [k] Isa 29:13; Jn 5:44; 12:43
15:33 [l] Ge 9:6; Jdg 1:7
15:34 [m] 1Sa 7:17 [n] 1Sa 11:4
15:35 [o] 1Sa 19:24 [p] 1Sa 16:1
16:1 [q] 1Sa 15:35 [r] 1Sa 15:23 [s] 2Ki 9:1 [t] Ru 4:17; 1Sa 9:16 [u] Ps 78:70; Ac 13:22
16:3 [v] Ex 4:15 [w] Dt 17:15; 1Sa 9:16

a 32 Or *him trembling, yet*

4Samuel did what the LORD said. When he arrived at Bethlehem,[a] the elders of the town trembled when they met him. They
asked, "Do you come in peace?[b]"

5Samuel replied, "Yes, in peace; I have come to sacrifice to the
LORD. Consecrate[c] yourselves and come to the sacrifice with me."
Then he consecrated Jesse and his sons and invited them to the
sacrifice.

6When they arrived, Samuel saw Eliab[d] and thought, "Surely the
LORD's anointed stands here before the LORD."

7But the LORD said to Samuel, "Do not consider his appearance
or his height, for I have rejected him. The LORD does not look at
the things man looks at. Man looks at the outward appearance,[e]
but the LORD looks at the heart."[f]

8Then Jesse called Abinadab[g] and had him pass in front of
Samuel. But Samuel said, "The LORD has not chosen this one
either." 9Jesse then had Shammah pass by, but Samuel said, "Nor
has the LORD chosen this one." 10Jesse had seven of his sons pass
before Samuel, but Samuel said to him, "The LORD has not chosen
these." 11So he asked Jesse, "Are these all[h] the sons you have?"

"There is still the youngest," Jesse answered, "but he is tending
the sheep."

Samuel said, "Send for him; we will not sit down[a] until he
arrives."

12So he[i] sent and had him brought in. He was ruddy, with a fine
appearance and handsome[j] features.

Then the LORD said, "Rise and anoint him; he is the one."

13So Samuel took the horn of oil and anointed him in the presence of his brothers, and from that day on the Spirit of the LORD[k]
came upon David in power.[l] Samuel then went to Ramah.

14Now the Spirit of the LORD had departed[m] from Saul, and an
evil[b] spirit[n] from the LORD tormented him.

15Saul's attendants said to him, "See, an evil spirit from God is
tormenting you. 16Let our lord command his servants here to
search for someone who can play the harp.[o] He will play when the
evil spirit from God comes upon you, and you will feel better."

17So Saul said to his attendants, "Find someone who plays well
and bring him to me."

18One of the servants answered, "I have seen a son of Jesse of
Bethlehem who knows how to play the harp. He is a brave man
and a warrior. He speaks well and is a fine-looking man. And the
LORD is with[p] him."

19Then Saul sent messengers to Jesse and said, "Send me your
son David, who is with the sheep." 20So Jesse took a donkey loaded

[a] *11* Some Septuagint manuscripts; Hebrew *not gather around* [b] *14* Or *injurious*; also in verses 15, 16 and 23

16:4 [a] Ge 48:7; Lk 2:4 [b] 1Ki 2:13; 2Ki 9:17
16:5 [c] Ex 19:10,22
16:6 [d] 1Sa 17:13
16:7 [e] Ps 147:10 [f] 1Ki 8:39; 1Ch 28:9; Isa 55:8
16:8 [g] 1Sa 17:13
16:11 [h] 1Sa 17:12
16:12 [i] 1Sa 9:17 [j] Ge 39:6; 1Sa 17:42
16:13 [k] Nu 27:18; Jdg 11:29 [l] 1Sa 10:1,6, 9-10; 11:6
16:14 [m] Jdg 16:20 [n] Jdg 9:23; 1Sa 18:10
16:16 [o] ver 23; 1Sa 18:10; 19:9; 2Ki 3:15
16:18 [p] 1Sa 3:19; 17:32-37

16:20 [a]1Sa 10:27; Pr 18:16
with bread,[a] a skin of wine and a young goat and sent them with
his son David to Saul.
21David came to Saul and entered his service.[b] Saul liked him
16:21 [b]Ge 41:46; Pr 22:29
very much, and David became one of his armor-bearers. 22Then
Saul sent word to Jesse, saying, "Allow David to remain in my
service, for I am pleased with him."
23Whenever the spirit from God came upon Saul, David would
16:23 [c]ver 14-16
take his harp and play. Then relief would come to Saul; he would
feel better, and the evil spirit[c] would leave him.

Chapter 17 Theme ____________________________

17:1 [d]1Sa 13:5 [e]Jos 15:35; 2Ch 28:18
17 Now the Philistines gathered their forces for war and
assembled[d] at Socoh in Judah. They pitched camp at Ephes
Dammim, between Socoh[e] and Azekah. 2Saul and the Israelites
17:2 [f]1Sa 21:9
assembled and camped in the Valley of Elah[f] and drew up their
battle line to meet the Philistines. 3The Philistines occupied one
hill and the Israelites another, with the valley between them.
17:4 [g]Jos 11:21-22; 2Sa 21:19
4A champion named Goliath,[g] who was from Gath, came out of
the Philistine camp. He was over nine feet[a] tall. 5He had a bronze
helmet on his head and wore a coat of scale armor of bronze weighing five thousand shekels[b]; 6on his legs he wore bronze greaves,
17:6 [h]ver 45
and a bronze javelin[h] was slung on his back. 7His spear shaft was
like a weaver's rod,[i] and its iron point weighed six hundred
shekels.[c] His shield bearer[j] went ahead of him.
17:7 [i]2Sa 21:19 [j]ver 41
8Goliath stood and shouted to the ranks of Israel, "Why do you
come out and line up for battle? Am I not a Philistine, and are
you not the servants of Saul? Choose[k] a man and have him come
17:8 [k]1Sa 8:17
down to me. 9If he is able to fight and kill me, we will become
your subjects; but if I overcome him and kill him, you will become
our subjects and serve us." 10Then the Philistine said, "This day I
defy[l] the ranks of Israel! Give me a man and let us fight each other."
17:10 [l]ver 26,45; 2Sa 21:21
11On hearing the Philistine's words, Saul and all the Israelites were
dismayed and terrified.
12Now David was the son of an Ephrathite named Jesse,[m] who
17:12 [m]Ru 4:17; 1Ch 2:13-15 [n]Ge 35:19 [o]1Sa 16:11
was from Bethlehem[n] in Judah. Jesse had eight[o] sons, and in Saul's
time he was old and well advanced in years. 13Jesse's three oldest
sons had followed Saul to the war: The firstborn was Eliab;[p] the
second, Abinadab; and the third, Shammah.[q] 14David was the
youngest. The three oldest followed Saul, 15but David went back
17:13 [p]1Sa 16:6 [q]1Sa 16:9
and forth from Saul to tend his father's sheep[r] at Bethlehem.
16For forty days the Philistine came forward every morning
and evening and took his stand.

17:15 [r]1Sa 16:19

[a]4 Hebrew *was six cubits and a span* (about 3 meters) [b]5 That is, about 125 pounds (about 57 kilograms) [c]7 That is, about 15 pounds (about 7 kilograms)

[17]Now Jesse said to his son David, "Take this ephah[a] of roasted
grain[a] and these ten loaves of bread for your brothers and hurry
to their camp. [18]Take along these ten cheeses to the commander
of their unit.[b] See how your brothers[b] are and bring back some
assurance[c] from them. [19]They are with Saul and all the men of
Israel in the Valley of Elah, fighting against the Philistines."
[20]Early in the morning David left the flock with a shepherd,
loaded up and set out, as Jesse had directed. He reached the camp
as the army was going out to its battle positions, shouting the war
cry. [21]Israel and the Philistines were drawing up their lines facing
each other. [22]David left his things with the keeper of supplies, ran
to the battle lines and greeted his brothers. [23]As he was talking
with them, Goliath, the Philistine champion from Gath, stepped
out from his lines and shouted his usual[c] defiance, and David
heard it. [24]When the Israelites saw the man, they all ran from him
in great fear.
[25]Now the Israelites had been saying, "Do you see how this man
keeps coming out? He comes out to defy Israel. The king will give
great wealth to the man who kills him. He will also give him his
daughter[d] in marriage and will exempt his father's family from
taxes in Israel."
[26]David asked the men standing near him, "What will be done
for the man who kills this Philistine and removes this disgrace[e]
from Israel? Who is this uncircumcised[f] Philistine that he should
defy[g] the armies of the living[h] God?"
[27]They repeated to him what they had been saying and told him,
"This is what will be done for the man who kills him."
[28]When Eliab, David's oldest brother, heard him speaking with
the men, he burned with anger[i] at him and asked, "Why have you
come down here? And with whom did you leave those few sheep
in the desert? I know how conceited you are and how wicked your
heart is; you came down only to watch the battle."
[29]"Now what have I done?" said David. "Can't I even speak?"
[30]He then turned away to someone else and brought up the same
matter, and the men answered him as before. [31]What David said
was overheard and reported to Saul, and Saul sent for him.
[32]David said to Saul, "Let no one lose heart[j] on account of this
Philistine; your servant will go and fight him."
[33]Saul replied,[k] "You are not able to go out against this Philistine
and fight him; you are only a boy, and he has been a fighting man
from his youth."
[34]But David said to Saul, "Your servant has been keeping his
father's sheep. When a lion[l] or a bear came and carried off a sheep

17:17 *a* 1Sa 25:18
17:18 *b* Ge 37:14
17:23 *c* ver 8-10
17:25 *d* Jos 15:16; 1Sa 18:17
17:26 *e* 1Sa 11:2 *f* 1Sa 14:6 *g* ver 10 *h* Dt 5:26
17:28 *i* Ge 37:4,8,11; Pr 18:19; Mt 10:36
17:32 *j* Dt 20:3; 1Sa 16:18
17:33 *k* Nu 13:31
17:34 *l* Jer 49:19; Am 3:12

a *17* That is, probably about 3/5 bushel (about 22 liters) b *18* Hebrew *thousand* c *18* Or *some token*; or *some pledge of spoils*

from the flock, 35I went after it, struck it and rescued the sheep
from its mouth. When it turned on me, I seized it by its hair, struck
it and killed it. 36Your servant has killed both the lion and the
bear; this uncircumcised Philistine will be like one of them,
because he has defied the armies of the living God. 37The LORD
who delivered[a] me from the paw of the lion[b] and the paw of the
bear will deliver me from the hand of this Philistine."

Saul said to David, "Go, and the LORD be with[c] you."

38Then Saul dressed David in his own tunic. He put a coat of
armor on him and a bronze helmet on his head. 39David fastened
on his sword over the tunic and tried walking around, because he
was not used to them.

"I cannot go in these," he said to Saul, "because I am not used to
them." So he took them off. 40Then he took his staff in his hand,
chose five smooth stones from the stream, put them in the pouch
of his shepherd's bag and, with his sling in his hand, approached
the Philistine.

41Meanwhile, the Philistine, with his shield bearer in front of
him, kept coming closer to David. 42He looked David over and saw
that he was only a boy, ruddy and handsome,[d] and he despised[e]
him. 43He said to David, "Am I a dog,[f] that you come at me with
sticks?" And the Philistine cursed David by his gods. 44"Come
here," he said, "and I'll give your flesh to the birds of the air and
the beasts of the field![g]"

45David said to the Philistine, "You come against me with sword
and spear and javelin, but I come against you in the name[h] of the
LORD Almighty, the God of the armies of Israel, whom you have
defied.[i] 46This day the LORD will hand you over to me, and I'll
strike you down and cut off your head. Today I will give the carcasses[j] of the Philistine army to the birds of the air and the beasts
of the earth, and the whole world[k] will know that there is a God in
Israel.[l] 47All those gathered here will know that it is not by sword[m]
or spear that the LORD saves;[n] for the battle[o] is the LORD's, and he
will give all of you into our hands."

48As the Philistine moved closer to attack him, David ran quickly toward the battle line to meet him. 49Reaching into his bag and
taking out a stone, he slung it and struck the Philistine on the
forehead. The stone sank into his forehead, and he fell facedown
on the ground.

50So David triumphed over the Philistine with a sling[p] and a
stone; without a sword in his hand he struck down the Philistine
and killed him.

51David ran and stood over him. He took hold of the Philistine's
sword and drew it from the scabbard. After he killed him, he cut[q]
off his head with the sword.[r]

17:37 [a]2Co 1:10 [b]2Ti 4:17 [c]1Sa 20:13; 1Ch 22:11,16
17:42 [d]1Sa 16:12 [e]Ps 123:3-4; Pr 16:18
17:43 [f]1Sa 24:14; 2Sa 3:8; 9:8; 2Ki 8:13
17:44 [g]1Ki 20:10-11
17:45 [h]2Sa 22:33,35; 2Ch 32:8; Ps 124:8; Heb 11:32-34 [i]ver 10
17:46 [j]Dt 28:26 [k]Jos 4:24; 1Ki 8:43; Isa 52:10 [l]1Ki 18:36; 2Ki 19:19; Isa 37:20
17:47 [m]Hos 1:7; Zec 4:6 [n]1Sa 14:6; 2Ch 14:11 [o]2Ch 20:15; Ps 44:6-7
17:50 [p]2Sa 23:21
17:51 [q]Heb 11:34 [r]1Sa 21:9

When the Philistines saw that their hero was dead, they turned
and ran. 52Then the men of Israel and Judah surged forward with
a shout and pursued the Philistines to the entrance of Gath[a] and
to the gates of Ekron.[a] Their dead were strewn along the Shaaraim[b]
road to Gath and Ekron. 53When the Israelites returned from
chasing the Philistines, they plundered their camp. 54David took
the Philistine's head and brought it to Jerusalem, and he put the
Philistine's weapons in his own tent.

55As Saul watched David[c] going out to meet the Philistine, he
said to Abner, commander of the army, "Abner, whose son is that
young man?"

Abner replied, "As surely as you live, O king, I don't know."

56The king said, "Find out whose son this young man is."

57As soon as David returned from killing the Philistine, Abner
took him and brought him before Saul, with David still holding
the Philistine's head.

58"Whose son are you, young man?" Saul asked him.

David said, "I am the son of your servant Jesse[d] of Bethlehem."

Chapter 18 Theme ____________________

18 After David had finished talking with Saul, Jonathan became
one in spirit with David, and he loved[e] him as himself.[f]
2From that day Saul kept David with him and did not let him
return to his father's house. 3And Jonathan made a covenant[g] with
David because he loved him as himself. 4Jonathan took off the
robe[h] he was wearing and gave it to David, along with his tunic,
and even his sword, his bow and his belt.

5Whatever Saul sent him to do, David did it so successfully[b] that
Saul gave him a high rank in the army. This pleased all the people,
and Saul's officers as well.

6When the men were returning home after David had killed the
Philistine, the women came out from all the towns of Israel to meet
King Saul with singing and dancing,[i] with joyful songs and with
tambourines[j] and lutes. 7As they danced, they sang:[k]

> "Saul has slain his thousands,
> and David his tens[l] of thousands."

8Saul was very angry; this refrain galled him. "They have credited
David with tens of thousands," he thought, "but me with only
thousands. What more can he get but the kingdom?[m]" 9And from
that time on Saul kept a jealous eye on David.

10The next day an evil[c] spirit[n] from God came forcefully upon
Saul. He was prophesying in his house, while David was playing

17:52 [a]Jos 15:11 [b]Jos 15:36
17:55 [c]1Sa 16:21
17:58 [d]ver 12
18:1 [e]2Sa 1:26 [f]Ge 44:30
18:3 [g]1Sa 20:8,16, 17,42
18:4 [h]Ge 41:42
18:6 [i]Ex 15:20 [j]Jdg 11:34; Ps 68:25
18:7 [k]Ex 15:21 [l]1Sa 21:11; 29:5
18:8 [m]1Sa 15:8
18:10 [n]1Sa 16:14

[a]52 Some Septuagint manuscripts; Hebrew *a valley* [b]5 Or *wisely* [c]10 Or *injurious*

the harp, as he usually[a] did. Saul had a spear in his hand 11 and he hurled it, saying to himself,[b] "I'll pin David to the wall." But David eluded[c] him twice.

12 Saul was afraid[d] of David, because the LORD[e] was with[f] David but had left Saul. 13 So he sent David away from him and gave him command over a thousand men, and David led[g] the troops in their campaigns.[h] 14 In everything he did he had great success,[a][i] because the LORD was with[j] him. 15 When Saul saw how successful[b] he was, he was afraid of him. 16 But all Israel and Judah loved David, because he led them in their campaigns.[k]

17 Saul said to David, "Here is my older daughter[l] Merab. I will give her to you in marriage; only serve me bravely and fight the battles[m] of the LORD." For Saul said to himself,[n] "I will not raise a hand against him. Let the Philistines do that!"

18 But David said to Saul, "Who am I,[o] and what is my family or my father's clan in Israel, that I should become the king's son-in-law?[p]" 19 So[c] when the time came for Merab,[q] Saul's daughter, to be given to David, she was given in marriage to Adriel of Meholah.[r]

20 Now Saul's daughter Michal[s] was in love with David, and when they told Saul about it, he was pleased. 21 "I will give her to him," he thought, "so that she may be a snare[t] to him and so that the hand of the Philistines may be against him." So Saul said to David, "Now you have a second opportunity to become my son-in-law."

22 Then Saul ordered his attendants: "Speak to David privately and say, 'Look, the king is pleased with you, and his attendants all like you; now become his son-in-law.' "

23 They repeated these words to David. But David said, "Do you think it is a small matter to become the king's son-in-law? I'm only a poor man and little known."

24 When Saul's servants told him what David had said, 25 Saul replied, "Say to David, 'The king wants no other price[u] for the bride than a hundred Philistine foreskins, to take revenge on his enemies.' " Saul's plan[v] was to have David fall by the hands of the Philistines.

26 When the attendants told David these things, he was pleased to become the king's son-in-law. So before the allotted time elapsed, 27 David and his men went out and killed two hundred Philistines. He brought their foreskins and presented the full number to the king so that he might become the king's son-in-law. Then Saul gave him his daughter Michal[w] in marriage.

28 When Saul realized that the LORD was with David and that his daughter Michal loved David, 29 Saul became still more afraid of him, and he remained his enemy the rest of his days.

18:10 [a] 1Sa 19:7
18:11 [b] 1Sa 20:7,33 [c] 1Sa 19:10
18:12 [d] ver 15,29 [e] 1Sa 16:13 [f] 1Sa 28:15
18:13 [g] ver 16; Nu 27:17 [h] 2Sa 5:2
18:14 [i] Ge 39:3 [j] Ge 39:2,23; Jos 6:27; 1Sa 16:18
18:16 [k] ver 5
18:17 [l] 1Sa 17:25 [m] Nu 21:14; 1Sa 25:28 [n] ver 25
18:18 [o] 1Sa 9:21; 2Sa 7:18 [p] ver 23
18:19 [q] 2Sa 21:8 [r] Jdg 7:22
18:20 [s] ver 28
18:21 [t] ver 17,26
18:25 [u] Ge 34:12; Ex 22:17; 1Sa 14:24 [v] ver 17
18:27 [w] ver 13; 2Sa 3:14

[a] 14 Or *he was very wise* [b] 15 Or *wise* [c] 19 Or *However,*

30 The Philistine commanders continued to go out to battle, and
as often as they did, David met with more success[a][a] than the rest
of Saul's officers, and his name became well known.

Chapter 19 Theme ______________________________

19 Saul told his son Jonathan[b] and all the attendants to kill[c]
David. But Jonathan was very fond of David 2 and warned
him, "My father Saul is looking for a chance to kill you. Be on your
guard tomorrow morning; go into hiding and stay there. 3 I will go
out and stand with my father in the field where you are. I'll speak[d]
to him about you and will tell you what I find out."

4 Jonathan spoke[e] well of David to Saul his father and said to
him, "Let not the king do wrong[f] to his servant David; he has not
wronged you, and what he has done has benefited you greatly. 5 He
took his life in his hands when he killed the Philistine. The LORD
won a great victory[g] for all Israel, and you saw it and were glad.
Why then would you do wrong to an innocent[h] man like David
by killing him for no reason?"

6 Saul listened to Jonathan and took this oath: "As surely as the
LORD lives, David will not be put to death."

7 So Jonathan called David and told him the whole conversation.
He brought him to Saul, and David was with Saul as before.[i]

8 Once more war broke out, and David went out and fought the
Philistines. He struck them with such force that they fled before
him.

9 But an evil[b] spirit[j] from the LORD came upon Saul as he was sitting in his house with his spear in his hand. While David was
playing the harp, 10 Saul tried to pin him to the wall with his spear,
but David eluded[k] him as Saul drove the spear into the wall. That
night David made good his escape.

11 Saul sent men to David's house to watch[l] it and to kill him in
the morning. But Michal, David's wife, warned him, "If you don't
run for your life tonight, tomorrow you'll be killed." 12 So Michal
let David down through a window,[m] and he fled and escaped.
13 Then Michal took an idol[c] and laid it on the bed, covering it with
a garment and putting some goats' hair at the head.

14 When Saul sent the men to capture David, Michal said,[n] "He
is ill."

15 Then Saul sent the men back to see David and told them,
"Bring him up to me in his bed so that I may kill him." 16 But when
the men entered, there was the idol in the bed, and at the head was
some goats' hair.

17 Saul said to Michal, "Why did you deceive me like this and
send my enemy away so that he escaped?"

18:30 [a] ver 5; 2Sa 11:1

19:1 [b] 1Sa 18:1 [c] 1Sa 18:9

19:3 [d] 1Sa 20:12

19:4 [e] 1Sa 20:32; Pr 31:8,9; Jer 18:20 [f] Ge 42:22; Pr 17:13

19:5 [g] 1Sa 11:13; 17:49-50; 1Ch 11:14 [h] Dt 19:10-13; 1Sa 20:32; Mt 27:4

19:7 [i] 1Sa 16:21; 18:2,13

19:9 [j] 1Sa 16:14; 18:10-11

19:10 [k] 1Sa 18:11

19:11 [l] Ps 59 Title

19:12 [m] Jos 2:15; Ac 9:25

19:14 [n] Jos 2:4

[a] 30 Or *David acted more wisely* [b] 9 Or *injurious* [c] 13 Hebrew *teraphim;* also in verse 16

19:18 [a]1Sa 7:17

Michal told him, "He said to me, 'Let me get away. Why should
I kill you?' "
18 When David had fled and made his escape, he went to Samuel
at Ramah[a] and told him all that Saul had done to him. Then he and

19:20 [b]ver 11,14; Jn 7:32,45 [c]Nu 11:25 [d]1Sa 10:5; Joel 2:28

Samuel went to Naioth and stayed there. 19 Word came to Saul:
"David is in Naioth at Ramah"; 20 so he sent men to capture him.
But when they saw a group of prophets[b] prophesying, with Samuel
standing there as their leader, the Spirit of God came upon[c] Saul's
men and they also prophesied.[d] 21 Saul was told about it, and he
sent more men, and they prophesied too. Saul sent men a third
time, and they also prophesied. 22 Finally, he himself left for Ramah

19:23 [e]1Sa 10:13

and went to the great cistern at Secu. And he asked, "Where are
Samuel and David?"
"Over in Naioth at Ramah," they said.
23 So Saul went to Naioth at Ramah. But the Spirit of God came

19:24 [f]2Sa 6:20; Isa 20:2; Mic 1:8 [g]1Sa 10:11

even upon him, and he walked along prophesying[e] until he came
to Naioth. 24 He stripped[f] off his robes and also prophesied in
Samuel's presence. He lay that way all that day and night. This is
why people say, "Is Saul also among the prophets?"[g]

Chapter 20 Theme ____________________

20:1 [h]1Sa 24:9

20 Then David fled from Naioth at Ramah and went to Jonathan and asked, "What have I done? What is my crime? How
have I wronged[h] your father, that he is trying to take my life?"
2 "Never!" Jonathan replied. "You are not going to die! Look, my

20:3 [i]Dt 6:13

father doesn't do anything, great or small, without confiding in
me. Why would he hide this from me? It's not so!"
3 But David took an oath[i] and said, "Your father knows very well
that I have found favor in your eyes, and he has said to himself,

20:5 [j]Nu 10:10; 28:11 [k]1Sa 19:2

'Jonathan must not know this or he will be grieved.' Yet as surely
as the LORD lives and as you live, there is only a step between me
and death."
4 Jonathan said to David, "Whatever you want me to do, I'll do
for you."

20:6 [l]1Sa 17:58 [m]Dt 12:5

5 So David said, "Look, tomorrow is the New Moon festival,[j] and
I am supposed to dine with the king; but let me go and hide[k] in the
field until the evening of the day after tomorrow. 6 If your father
misses me at all, tell him, 'David earnestly asked my permission
to hurry to Bethlehem,[l] his hometown, because an annual[m] sacri-

20:7 [n]1Sa 25:17

fice is being made there for his whole clan.' 7 If he says, 'Very well,'
then your servant is safe. But if he loses his temper,[n] you can be
sure that he is determined to harm me. 8 As for you, show kindness to your servant, for you have brought him into a covenant[o]

20:8 [o]1Sa 18:3; 23:18 [p]2Sa 14:32

with you before the LORD. If I am guilty, then kill[p] me yourself!
Why hand me over to your father?"

9"Never!" Jonathan said. "If I had the least inkling that my father
was determined to harm you, wouldn't I tell you?"
10David asked, "Who will tell me if your father answers you
harshly?"
11"Come," Jonathan said, "let's go out into the field." So they
went there together.
12Then Jonathan said to David: "By the LORD, the God of Israel, I
will surely sound out my father by this time the day after tomorrow!
If he is favorably disposed toward you, will I not send you
word and let you know? 13But if my father is inclined to harm you,
may the LORD deal with me, be it ever so severely,[a] if I do not let
you know and send you away safely. May the LORD be with[b] you as
he has been with my father. 14But show me unfailing kindness like
that of the LORD as long as I live, so that I may not be killed, 15and
do not ever cut off your kindness from my family[c]—not even
when the LORD has cut off every one of David's enemies from the
face of the earth."
16So Jonathan made a covenant[d] with the house of David, saying,
"May the LORD call David's enemies to account." 17And Jonathan
had David reaffirm his oath[e] out of love for him, because he loved
him as he loved himself.
18Then Jonathan said to David: "Tomorrow is the New Moon
festival. You will be missed, because your seat will be empty.[f]
19The day after tomorrow, toward evening, go to the place where
you hid[g] when this trouble began, and wait by the stone Ezel. 20I
will shoot three arrows to the side of it, as though I were shooting
at a target. 21Then I will send a boy and say, 'Go, find the arrows.'
If I say to him, 'Look, the arrows are on this side of you; bring
them here,' then come, because, as surely as the LORD lives, you
are safe; there is no danger. 22But if I say to the boy, 'Look, the
arrows are beyond[h] you,' then you must go, because the LORD has
sent you away. 23And about the matter you and I discussed—
remember, the LORD is witness[i] between you and me forever."
24So David hid in the field, and when the New Moon festival
came, the king sat down to eat. 25He sat in his customary place by
the wall, opposite Jonathan,[a] and Abner sat next to Saul, but
David's place was empty.[j] 26Saul said nothing that day, for he
thought, "Something must have happened to David to make him
ceremonially unclean—surely he is unclean.[k]" 27But the next day,
the second day of the month, David's place was empty again. Then
Saul said to his son Jonathan, "Why hasn't the son of Jesse come to
the meal, either yesterday or today?"
28Jonathan answered, "David earnestly asked me for permission[l]
to go to Bethlehem. 29He said, 'Let me go, because our family is

[a] 25 Septuagint; Hebrew *wall. Jonathan arose*

20:13 [a] Ru 1:17; 1Sa 3:17 [b] Jos 1:5; 1Sa 17:37; 18:12; 1Ch 22:11,16
20:15 [c] 2Sa 9:7
20:16 [d] 1Sa 25:22
20:17 [e] 1Sa 18:3
20:18 [f] ver 5,25
20:19 [g] 1Sa 19:2
20:22 [h] ver 37
20:23 [i] ver 14-15; Ge 31:50
20:25 [j] ver 18
20:26 [k] Lev 7:20-21; 15:5; 1Sa 16:5
20:28 [l] ver 6

20:32
[a]1Sa 19:4;
Mt 27:23
[b]Ge 31:36;
Lk 23:22

observing a sacrifice in the town and my brother has ordered me
to be there. If I have found favor in your eyes, let me get away to see
my brothers.’ That is why he has not come to the king’s table.”
30Saul’s anger flared up at Jonathan and he said to him, “You son
of a perverse and rebellious woman! Don’t I know that you have
sided with the son of Jesse to your own shame and to the shame
of the mother who bore you? 31As long as the son of Jesse lives on
this earth, neither you nor your kingdom will be established. Now
send and bring him to me, for he must die!”
32“Why[a] should he be put to death? What[b] has he done?” Jonathan asked his father. 33But Saul hurled his spear at him to kill
him. Then Jonathan knew that his father intended[c] to kill David.
34Jonathan got up from the table in fierce anger; on that second
day of the month he did not eat, because he was grieved at his
father’s shameful treatment of David.

20:33
[c]ver 7;
1Sa 18:11,17

35In the morning Jonathan went out to the field for his meeting
with David. He had a small boy with him, 36and he said to the
boy, “Run and find the arrows I shoot.” As the boy ran, he shot
an arrow beyond him. 37When the boy came to the place where
Jonathan’s arrow had fallen, Jonathan called out after him, “Isn’t
the arrow beyond[d] you?” 38Then he shouted, “Hurry! Go quickly!
Don’t stop!” The boy picked up the arrow and returned to his
master. 39(The boy knew nothing of all this; only Jonathan and
David knew.) 40Then Jonathan gave his weapons to the boy and
said, “Go, carry them back to town.”

20:37
[d]ver 22

41After the boy had gone, David got up from the south side ⌊of the
stone⌋ and bowed down before Jonathan three times, with his face
to the ground. Then they kissed each other and wept together—
but David wept the most.
42Jonathan said to David, “Go in peace,[e] for we have sworn
friendship[f] with each other in the name of the LORD, saying, ‘The
LORD is witness between you and me, and between your descendants and my descendants forever.’” Then David left, and Jonathan went back to the town.

20:42
[e]ver 22;
1Sa 1:17
[f]2Sa 1:26;
Pr 18:24

Chapter 21 Theme ______________________________

21 David went to Nob,[g] to Ahimelech the priest. Ahimelech
trembled[h] when he met him, and asked, “Why are you
alone? Why is no one with you?”
2David answered Ahimelech the priest, “The king charged me
with a certain matter and said to me, ‘No one is to know anything
about your mission and your instructions.’ As for my men, I have
told them to meet me at a certain place. 3Now then, what do you
have on hand? Give me five loaves of bread, or whatever you can
find.”

21:1
[g]1Sa 14:3;
22:9,19;
Ne 11:32;
Isa 10:32
[h]1Sa 16:4

4But the priest answered David, "I don't have any ordinary bread[a]
on hand; however, there is some consecrated[b] bread here—provided the men have kept[c] themselves from women."
5David replied, "Indeed women have been kept from us, as usual
whenever[a] I set out. The men's things[b] are holy[d] even on missions
that are not holy. How much more so today!" 6So the priest gave
him the consecrated bread,[e] since there was no bread there except
the bread of the Presence that had been removed from before the
LORD and replaced by hot bread on the day it was taken away.
7Now one of Saul's servants was there that day, detained before
the LORD; he was Doeg[f] the Edomite,[g] Saul's head shepherd.
8David asked Ahimelech, "Don't you have a spear or a sword
here? I haven't brought my sword or any other weapon, because
the king's business was urgent."
9The priest replied, "The sword[h] of Goliath the Philistine, whom
you killed in the Valley of Elah,[i] is here; it is wrapped in a cloth
behind the ephod. If you want it, take it; there is no sword here but
that one."
David said, "There is none like it; give it to me."
10That day David fled from Saul and went[j] to Achish king of
Gath. 11But the servants of Achish said to him, "Isn't this David, the
king of the land? Isn't he the one they sing about in their dances:

> "'Saul has slain his thousands,
> and David his tens of thousands'?"[k]

12David took these words to heart and was very much afraid of
Achish king of Gath. 13So he pretended to be insane[l] in their presence; and while he was in their hands he acted like a madman,
making marks on the doors of the gate and letting saliva run
down his beard.
14Achish said to his servants, "Look at the man! He is insane!
Why bring him to me? 15Am I so short of madmen that you have
to bring this fellow here to carry on like this in front of me? Must
this man come into my house?"

Chapter 22 Theme ______________________

22 David left Gath and escaped to the cave[m] of Adullam.
When his brothers and his father's household heard about
it, they went down to him there. 2All those who were in distress or
in debt or discontented gathered[n] around him, and he became
their leader. About four hundred men were with him.
3From there David went to Mizpah in Moab and said to the king
of Moab, "Would you let my father and mother come and stay with

a5 Or *from us in the past few days since* b5 Or *bodies*

21:4 *a* Lev 24:8-9 *b* Ex 25:30; Mt 12:4 *c* Ex 19:15
21:5 *d* 1Th 4:4
21:6 *e* Lev 24:8-9; Mt 12:3-4; Mk 2:25-28; Lk 6:1-5
21:7 *f* 1Sa 22:9,22 *g* 1Sa 14:47; Ps 52 Title
21:9 *h* 1Sa 17:51 *i* 1Sa 17:2
21:10 *j* 1Sa 27:2
21:11 *k* 1Sa 18:7; 29:5; Ps 56 Title
21:13 *l* Ps 34 Title
22:1 *m* 2Sa 23:13; Ps 57 Title; 142 Title
22:2 *n* 1Sa 23:13; 25:13; 2Sa 15:20

you until I learn what God will do for me?" 4So he left them with
the king of Moab, and they stayed with him as long as David was
in the stronghold.
5But the prophet Gad[a] said to David, "Do not stay in the stronghold. Go into the land of Judah." So David left and went to the
forest of Hereth.
6Now Saul heard that David and his men had been discovered.
And Saul, spear in hand, was seated[b] under the tamarisk[c] tree on
the hill at Gibeah, with all his officials standing around him. 7Saul
said to them, "Listen, men of Benjamin! Will the son of Jesse give
all of you fields and vineyards? Will he make all of you commanders[d] of thousands and commanders of hundreds? 8Is that why
you have all conspired against me? No one tells me when my son
makes a covenant[e] with the
son of Jesse. None of you is
concerned[f] about me or tells
me that my son has incited
my servant to lie in wait for
me, as he does today."
9But Doeg[g] the Edomite,
who was standing with Saul's
officials, said, "I saw the son
of Jesse come to Ahimelech
son of Ahitub at Nob.[h]
10Ahimelech inquired[i] of the
LORD for him; he also gave
him provisions[j] and the
sword of Goliath the Philistine."
11Then the king sent for
the priest Ahimelech son of
Ahitub and his father's whole
family, who were the priests at Nob, and they all came to the king.
12Saul said, "Listen now, son of Ahitub."
"Yes, my lord," he answered.
13Saul said to him, "Why have you conspired[k] against me, you
and the son of Jesse, giving him bread and a sword and inquiring
of God for him, so that he has rebelled against me and lies in wait
for me, as he does today?"
14Ahimelech answered the king, "Who[l] of all your servants is as
loyal as David, the king's son-in-law, captain of your bodyguard
and highly respected in your household? 15Was that day the first
time I inquired of God for him? Of course not! Let not the king
accuse your servant or any of his father's family, for your servant
knows nothing at all about this whole affair."

INSIGHT

A ***stronghold*** was a fortified or secure location.

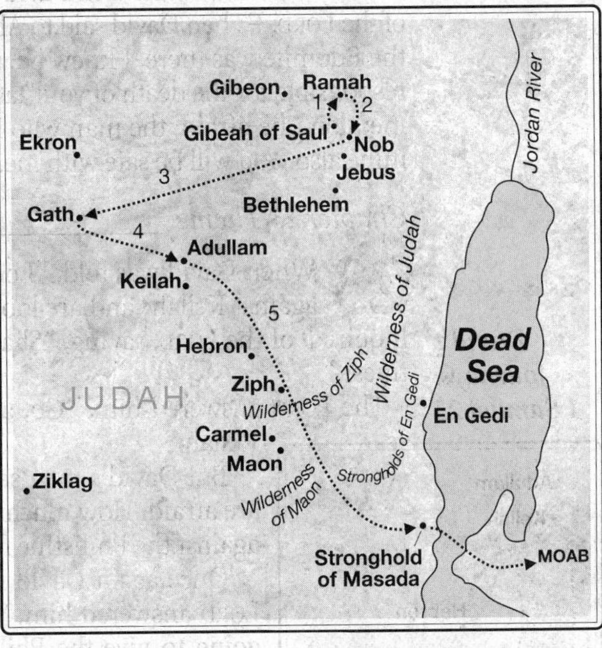

David's Journeys: 1 Samuel 21–22
(Numbers on the following maps indicate the progression of David's journey.)

22:5 [a] 2Sa 24:11; 1Ch 21:9; 29:29; 2Ch 29:25
22:6 [b] Jdg 4:5 [c] Ge 21:33
22:7 [d] 1Sa 8:14
22:8 [e] 1Sa 18:3; 20:16 [f] 1Sa 23:21
22:9 [g] 1Sa 21:7; Ps 52 Title [h] 1Sa 21:1
22:10 [i] Nu 27:21; 1Sa 10:22 [j] 1Sa 21:6
22:13 [k] ver 8
22:14 [l] 1Sa 19:4

16But the king said, "You will surely die, Ahimelech, you and your father's whole family."

17Then the king ordered the guards at his side: "Turn and kill the priests of the LORD, because they too have sided with David. They knew he was fleeing, yet they did not tell me."

But the king's officials were not willing[a] to raise a hand to strike the priests of the LORD.

18The king then ordered Doeg, "You turn and strike down the priests." So Doeg the Edomite turned and struck them down. That day he killed eighty-five men who wore the linen ephod.[b] 19He also put to the sword[c] Nob, the town of the priests, with its men and women, its children and infants, and its cattle, donkeys and sheep.

20But Abiathar,[d] a son of Ahimelech son of Ahitub, escaped and fled to join David.[e] 21He told David that Saul had killed the priests of the LORD. 22Then David said to Abiathar: "That day, when Doeg[f] the Edomite was there, I knew he would be sure to tell Saul. I am responsible for the death of your father's whole family. 23Stay with me; don't be afraid; the man who is seeking your life[g] is seeking mine also. You will be safe with me."

Chapter 23 Theme ______________________

David's Journeys: 1 Samuel 23

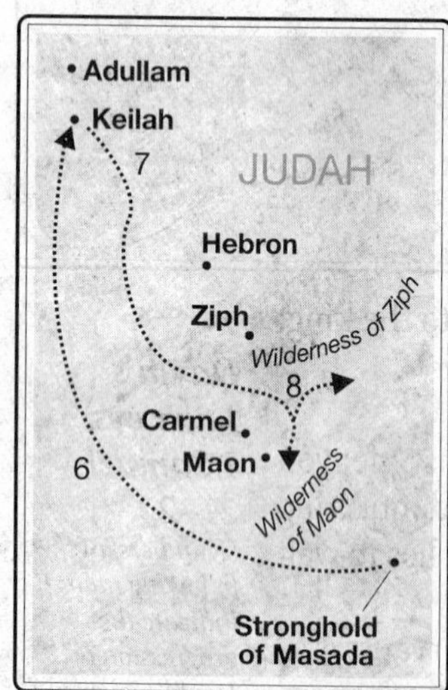

23

When David was told, "Look, the Philistines are fighting against Keilah[h] and are looting the threshing floors," 2he inquired[i] of the LORD, saying, "Shall I go and attack these Philistines?"

The LORD answered him, "Go, attack the Philistines and save Keilah."

3But David's men said to him, "Here in Judah we are afraid. How much more, then, if we go to Keilah against the Philistine forces!"

4Once again David inquired of the LORD, and the LORD answered him, "Go down to Keilah, for I am going to give the Philistines into your hand.[j]" 5So David and his men went to Keilah, fought the Philistines and carried off their livestock. He inflicted heavy losses on the Philistines and saved the people of Keilah. 6(Now Abiathar[k] son of Ahimelech had brought the ephod down with him when he fled to David at Keilah.)

7Saul was told that David had gone to Keilah, and he said, "God has handed him over to me, for David has imprisoned himself by entering a town with gates and bars." 8And Saul called up all his forces for battle, to go down to Keilah to besiege David and his men.

9When David learned that Saul was plotting against him, he said to Abiathar[l] the priest, "Bring the ephod." 10David said, "O LORD,

22:17 [a] Ex 1:17
22:18 [b] 1Sa 2:18,31
22:19 [c] 1Sa 15:3
22:20 [d] 1Sa 23:6,9; 30:7; 1Ki 2:22, 26,27 [e] 1Sa 2:32
22:22 [f] 1Sa 21:7
22:23 [g] 1Ki 2:26
23:1 [h] Jos 15:44
23:2 [i] ver 4,12; 1Sa 30:8; 2Sa 5:19,23
23:4 [j] Jos 8:7; Jdg 7:7
23:6 [k] 1Sa 22:20
23:9 [l] ver 6; 1Sa 22:20; 30:7

God of Israel, your servant has heard definitely that Saul plans to
come to Keilah and destroy the town on account of me. 11 Will the
citizens of Keilah surrender me to him? Will Saul come down, as
your servant has heard? O LORD, God of Israel, tell your servant."
And the LORD said, "He will."
12 Again David asked, "Will the citizens of Keilah surrender[a] me
and my men to Saul?"
And the LORD said, "They will."
13 So David and his men,[b] about six hundred in number, left
Keilah and kept moving from place to place. When Saul was told
that David had escaped from Keilah, he did not go there.
14 David stayed in the desert strongholds and in the hills of the
Desert of Ziph.[c] Day after day Saul searched[d] for him, but God did
not[e] give David into his hands.
15 While David was at Horesh in the Desert of Ziph, he learned
that Saul had come out to take his life. 16 And Saul's son Jonathan
went to David at Horesh and helped him find strength[f] in God.
17 "Don't be afraid," he said. "My father Saul will not lay a hand on
you. You will be king[g] over Israel, and I will be second to you.
Even my father Saul knows this." 18 The two of them made a covenant[h] before the LORD. Then Jonathan went home, but David
remained at Horesh.
19 The Ziphites[i] went up to Saul at Gibeah and said, "Is not David
hiding among us[j] in the strongholds at Horesh, on the hill of Hakilah,[k] south of Jeshimon? 20 Now, O king, come down whenever it
pleases you to do so, and we will be responsible for handing[l] him
over to the king."
21 Saul replied, "The LORD bless you for your concern[m] for me.
22 Go and make further preparation. Find out where David usually
goes and who has seen him there. They tell me he is very crafty.
23 Find out about all the hiding places he uses and come back to
me with definite information.[a] Then I will go with you; if he is in
the area, I will track him down among all the clans of Judah."
24 So they set out and went to Ziph ahead of Saul. Now David and
his men were in the Desert of Maon,[n] in the Arabah south of Jeshimon. 25 Saul and his men began the search, and when David was
told about it, he went down to the rock and stayed in the Desert of
Maon. When Saul heard this, he went into the Desert of Maon in
pursuit of David.
26 Saul[o] was going along one side of the mountain, and David and
his men were on the other side, hurrying to get away from Saul. As
Saul and his forces were closing in on David and his men to capture them, 27 a messenger came to Saul, saying, "Come quickly! The
Philistines are raiding the land." 28 Then Saul broke off his pursuit

23:12 [a] ver 20
23:13 [b] 1Sa 22:2; 25:13
23:14 [c] Jos 15:24,55 [d] Ps 54:3-4 [e] Ps 32:7
23:16 [f] 1Sa 30:6
23:17 [g] 1Sa 20:31; 24:20
23:18 [h] 1Sa 18:3; 20:16,42; 2Sa 9:1; 21:7
23:19 [i] 1Sa 26:1 [j] Ps 54 Title [k] 1Sa 26:3
23:20 [l] ver 12
23:21 [m] 1Sa 22:8
23:24 [n] Jos 15:55; 1Sa 25:2
23:26 [o] Ps 17:9

a 23 Or *me at Nacon*

of David and went to meet the Philistines. That is why they call this
place Sela Hammahlekoth.[a] 29And David went up from there and
lived in the strongholds of En Gedi.[a]

Chapter 24 Theme ______________________________

24 After Saul returned from pursuing the Philistines, he was
told, "David is in the Desert of En Gedi.[b]" 2So Saul took
three thousand chosen men from all Israel and set out to look[c] for
David and his men near the Crags of the Wild Goats.
3He came to the sheep pens along the way; a cave[d] was there, and
Saul went in to relieve[e] himself. David and his men were far back
in the cave. 4The men said, "This is the day the LORD spoke[f] of
when he said[b] to you, 'I will give your enemy into your hands for
you to deal with as you wish.' "[g] Then David crept up unnoticed
and cut off a corner of Saul's robe.
5Afterward, David was conscience-stricken[h] for
having cut off a corner of his robe. 6He said to his
men, "The LORD forbid that I should do such a thing
to my master, the LORD's anointed,[i] or lift my hand
against him; for he is the anointed of the LORD."
7With these words David rebuked his men and did
not allow them to attack Saul. And Saul left the cave
and went his way.
8Then David went out of the cave and called out to
Saul, "My lord the king!" When Saul looked behind
him, David bowed down and prostrated himself with
his face to the ground.[j] 9He said to Saul, "Why do
you listen when men say, 'David is bent on harming
you'? 10This day you have seen with your own eyes
how the LORD delivered you into my hands in the
cave. Some urged me to kill you, but I spared you; I said, 'I will not
lift my hand against my master, because he is the LORD's anointed.'
11See, my father, look at this piece of your robe in my hand! I cut
off the corner of your robe but did not kill you. Now understand
and recognize that I am not guilty[k] of wrongdoing or rebellion. I
have not wronged you, but you are hunting[l] me down to take my
life. 12May the LORD judge[m] between you and me. And may the
LORD avenge[n] the wrongs you have done to me, but my hand will
not touch you. 13As the old saying goes, 'From evildoers come evil
deeds,[o]' so my hand will not touch you.
14"Against whom has the king of Israel come out? Whom are
you pursuing? A dead dog?[p] A flea?[q] 15May the LORD be our judge[r]
and decide between us. May he consider my cause and uphold[s] it;
may he vindicate[t] me by delivering[u] me from your hand."

En Gedi
Dead Sea
9
Strongholds of En Gedi
Stronghold of Masada

David's Journeys: 1 Samuel 24

[a]28 *Sela Hammahlekoth* means *rock of parting.* [b]4 Or *"Today the LORD is saying*

23:29 [a]2Ch 20:2
24:1 [b]1Sa 23:28-29
24:2 [c]1Sa 26:2
24:3 [d]Ps 57 Title; 142 Title [e]Jdg 3:24
24:4 [f]1Sa 25:28-30 [g]1Sa 23:17; 26:8
24:5 [h]2Sa 24:10
24:6 [i]1Sa 26:11
24:8 [j]1Sa 25:23-24
24:11 [k]Ps 7:3 [l]1Sa 23:14,23; 1Sa 26:20
24:12 [m]Ge 16:5; 31:53; Job 5:8 [n]Jdg 11:27; 1Sa 26:10
24:13 [o]Mt 7:20
24:14 [p]1Sa 17:43; 2Sa 9:8 [q]1Sa 26:20
24:15 [r]ver 12 [s]Ps 35:1,23; Mic 7:9 [t]Ps 43:1 [u]Ps 119:134,154

24:16
[a] 1Sa 26:17
24:17
[b] Ge 38:26; 1Sa 26:21
[c] Mt 5:44
24:18
[d] 1Sa 26:23
24:20
[e] 1Sa 23:17
[f] 1Sa 13:14
24:21
[g] Ge 21:23; 2Sa 21:1-9
[h] 1Sa 20:14-15
24:22
[i] 1Sa 23:29
25:1
[j] 1Sa 28:3
[k] Nu 20:29; Dt 34:8
[l] Ge 21:21; 2Ch 33:20
25:2
[m] Jos 15:55; 1Sa 23:24
25:3
[n] Pr 31:10
[o] Jos 15:13
25:6
[p] Ps 122:7; Lk 10:5
[q] 1Ch 12:18
25:7
[r] ver 15
25:8
[s] Ne 8:10
25:10
[t] Jdg 9:28
25:11
[u] Jdg 8:6

16 When David finished saying this, Saul asked, "Is that your
voice,[a] David my son?" And he wept aloud. 17 "You are more righteous than I,"[b] he said. "You have treated me well,[c] but I have treated you badly. 18 You have just now told me of the good you did to
me; the LORD delivered[d] me into your hands, but you did not kill
me. 19 When a man finds his enemy, does he let him get away
unharmed? May the LORD reward you well for the way you treated
me today. 20 I know that you will surely be king[e] and that the kingdom[f] of Israel will be established in your hands. 21 Now swear[g] to
me by the LORD that you will not cut off my descendants or wipe
out my name from my father's family.[h]"
22 So David gave his oath to Saul. Then Saul returned home, but
David and his men went up to the stronghold.[i]

Chapter 25 Theme ____________________

25 Now Samuel died,[j] and all Israel assembled and mourned[k]
for him; and they buried him at his home in Ramah.[l]
Then David moved down into the Desert of Maon.[a]
2 A certain man in Maon,[m] who had property there at
Carmel, was very wealthy. He had a thousand goats
and three thousand sheep, which he was shearing in
Carmel. 3 His name was Nabal and his wife's name
was Abigail.[n] She was an intelligent and beautiful
woman, but her husband, a Calebite,[o] was surly and
mean in his dealings.
4 While David was in the desert, he heard that Nabal
was shearing sheep. 5 So he sent ten young men and
said to them, "Go up to Nabal at Carmel and greet
him in my name. 6 Say to him: 'Long life to you!
Good health[p] to you and your household! And good
health to all that is yours![q]
7 " 'Now I hear that it is sheep-shearing time. When
your shepherds were with us, we did not mistreat[r]
them, and the whole time they were at Carmel nothing of theirs
was missing. 8 Ask your own servants and they will tell you. Therefore be favorable toward my young men, since we come at a festive
time. Please give your servants and your son David whatever[s] you
can find for them.' "
9 When David's men arrived, they gave Nabal this message in
David's name. Then they waited.
10 Nabal answered David's servants, "Who[t] is this David? Who
is this son of Jesse? Many servants are breaking away from their
masters these days. 11 Why should I take my bread[u] and water, and

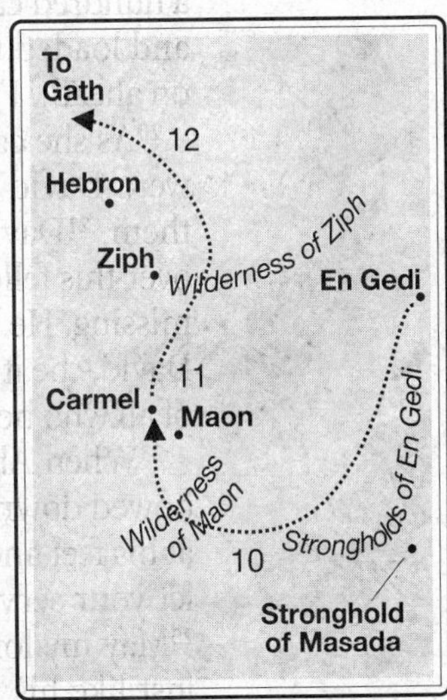

David's Journeys: 1 Samuel 25–27:2

a 1 Some Septuagint manuscripts; Hebrew *Paran*

the meat I have slaughtered for my shearers, and give it to men
coming from who knows where?"
12David's men turned around and went back. When they arrived,
they reported every word. 13David said to his men, "Put on your
swords!" So they put on their swords, and David put on his. About
four hundred men went[a] up with David, while two hundred stayed
with the supplies.[b]
14One of the servants told Nabal's wife Abigail: "David sent
messengers from the desert to give our master his greetings,[c] but
he hurled insults at them. 15Yet these men were very good to us.
They did not mistreat[d] us, and the whole time we were out in the
fields near them nothing was missing.[e] 16Night and day they were
a wall[f] around us all the time we were herding our sheep near
them. 17Now think it over and see what you can do, because disaster is hanging over our master and his whole household. He is
such a wicked[g] man that no one can talk to him."
18Abigail lost no time. She took two hundred loaves of bread,
two skins of wine, five dressed sheep, five seahs[a] of roasted grain,
a hundred cakes of raisins[h] and two hundred cakes of pressed figs,
and loaded them on donkeys.[i] 19Then she told her servants, "Go
on ahead;[j] I'll follow you." But she did not tell her husband Nabal.
20As she came riding her donkey into a mountain ravine, there
were David and his men descending toward her, and she met
them. 21David had just said, "It's been useless—all my watching
over this fellow's property in the desert so that nothing of his was
missing. He has paid[k] me back evil for good. 22May God deal with
David,[b] be it ever so severely,[l] if by morning I leave alive one male[m]
of all who belong to him!"
23When Abigail saw David, she quickly got off her donkey and
bowed down before David with her face to the ground.[n] 24She fell
at his feet and said: "My lord, let the blame be on me alone. Please
let your servant speak to you; hear what your servant has to say.
25May my lord pay no attention to that wicked man Nabal. He is
just like his name—his name is Fool,[o] and folly goes with him.
But as for me, your servant, I did not see the men my master sent.
26"Now since the LORD has kept you, my master, from bloodshed[p]
and from avenging[q] yourself with your own hands, as surely as
the LORD lives and as you live, may your enemies and all who
intend to harm my master be like Nabal.[r] 27And let this gift,[s]
which your servant has brought to my master, be given to the men
who follow you. 28Please forgive[t] your servant's offense, for the
LORD will certainly make a lasting[u] dynasty for my master, because
he fights the LORD's battles.[v] Let no wrongdoing[w] be found in you
as long as you live. 29Even though someone is pursuing you to take

[a] *18* That is, probably about a bushel (about 37 liters) [b] *22* Some Septuagint manuscripts; Hebrew *with David's enemies*

25:13
[a] 1Sa 23:13
[b] 1Sa 30:24

25:14
[c] 1Sa 13:10

25:15
[d] ver 7
[e] ver 21

25:16
[f] Ex 14:22; Job 1:10

25:17
[g] 1Sa 20:7

25:18
[h] 1Ch 12:40
[i] 2Sa 16:1

25:19
[j] Ge 32:20

25:21
[k] Ps 109:5

25:22
[l] 1Sa 3:17; 20:13
[m] 1Ki 14:10; 21:21; 2Ki 9:8

25:23
[n] 1Sa 20:41

25:25
[o] Pr 14:16

25:26
[p] ver 33
[q] Heb 10:30
[r] 2Sa 18:32

25:27
[s] Ge 33:11; 1Sa 30:26

25:28
[t] ver 24
[u] 2Sa 7:11,26
[v] 1Sa 18:17
[w] 1Sa 24:11

25:29 [a]Jer 10:18 your life, the life of my master will be bound securely in the bundle
of the living by the LORD your God. But the lives of your enemies
he will hurl[a] away as from the pocket of a sling. 30When the LORD
25:30 [b]1Sa 13:14 has done for my master every good thing he promised concerning him and has appointed him leader[b] over Israel, 31my master
will not have on his conscience the staggering burden of needless
25:31 [c]Ge 40:14 bloodshed or of having avenged himself. And when the LORD has
brought my master success, remember[c] your servant."

32David said to Abigail, "Praise[d] be to the LORD, the God of Israel,
25:32 [d]Ge 24:27; who has sent you today to meet me. 33May you be blessed for your
Ex 18:10; good judgment and for keeping me from bloodshed[e] this day
Lk 1:68 and from avenging myself with my own hands. 34Otherwise, as
surely as the LORD, the God of Israel, lives, who has kept me from
25:33 harming you, if you had not come quickly to meet me, not one
[e]ver 26 male belonging to Nabal would have been left alive by daybreak."

35Then David accepted from her hand what she had brought
25:35 him and said, "Go home in peace. I have heard your words and
[f]Ge 19:21; 1Sa 20:42; granted[f] your request."

2Ki 5:19 36When Abigail went to Nabal, he was in the house holding a
banquet like that of a king. He was in high[g] spirits and very
drunk.[h] So she told[i] him nothing until daybreak. 37Then in the
25:36 [g]2Sa 13:23 morning, when Nabal was sober, his wife told him all these things,
[h]Pr 20:1; Isa 5:11,22; and his heart failed him and he became like a stone. 38About ten
Hos 4:11 days later, the LORD struck[j] Nabal and he died.

[i]ver 19 39When David heard that Nabal was dead, he said, "Praise be to
the LORD, who has upheld my cause against Nabal for treating me
25:38 with contempt. He has kept his servant from doing wrong and has
[j]1Sa 26:10; 2Sa 6:7 brought Nabal's wrongdoing down on his own head."

Then David sent word to Abigail, asking her to become his wife.
40His servants went to Carmel and said to Abigail, "David has sent
25:42 [k]Ge 24:61-67 us to you to take you to become his wife."

41She bowed down with her face to the ground and said, "Here is
your maidservant, ready to serve you and wash the feet of my mas-
25:43 ter's servants." 42Abigail[k] quickly got on a donkey and, attended by
[l]Jos 15:56 [m]1Sa 27:3; 30:5 her five maids, went with David's messengers and became his wife.
43David had also married Ahinoam[l] of Jezreel, and they both were
his wives.[m] 44But Saul had given his daughter Michal, David's
25:44 [n]2Sa 3:15 wife, to Paltiel[a][n] son of Laish, who was from Gallim.[o]
[o]Isa 10:30

Chapter 26 Theme ____________________________

26:1 [p]1Sa 23:19 **26** The Ziphites[p] went to Saul at Gibeah and said, "Is not David
[q]Ps 54 Title hiding[q] on the hill of Hakilah, which faces Jeshimon?"

2So Saul went down to the Desert of Ziph, with his three thousand chosen men of Israel, to search[r] there for David. 3Saul made

26:2 [r]1Sa 13:2; 24:2

a 44 Hebrew *Palti*, a variant of *Paltiel*

his camp beside the road on the hill of Hakilah facing Jeshimon,
but David stayed in the desert. When he saw that Saul had followed
him there, 4he sent out scouts and learned that Saul had definitely
arrived.[a]
5Then David set out and went to the place where Saul had
camped. He saw where Saul and Abner[a] son of Ner, the commander of the army, had lain down. Saul was lying inside the
camp, with the army encamped around him.
6David then asked Ahimelech the Hittite and Abishai son of
Zeruiah,[b] Joab's brother, "Who will go down into the camp with
me to Saul?"
"I'll go with you," said Abishai.
7So David and Abishai went to the army by night, and there was
Saul, lying asleep inside the camp with his spear stuck in the ground
near his head. Abner and the soldiers were lying around him.
8Abishai said to David, "Today God has delivered your enemy
into your hands. Now let me pin him to the ground with one thrust
of my spear; I won't strike him twice."
9But David said to Abishai, "Don't destroy him! Who can lay a
hand on the LORD's anointed[c] and be guiltless?[d] 10As surely as the
LORD lives," he said, "the LORD himself will strike[e] him; either his
time[f] will come and he will die,[g] or he will go into battle and perish. 11But the LORD forbid that I should lay a hand on the LORD's
anointed. Now get the spear and water jug that are near his head,
and let's go."
12So David took the spear and water jug near Saul's head, and
they left. No one saw or knew about it, nor did anyone wake up.
They were all sleeping, because the LORD had put them into a
deep sleep.[h]
13Then David crossed over to the other side and stood on top of
the hill some distance away; there was a wide space between them.
14He called out to the army and to Abner son of Ner, "Aren't you
going to answer me, Abner?"
Abner replied, "Who are you who calls to the king?"
15David said, "You're a man, aren't you? And who is like you in
Israel? Why didn't you guard your lord the king? Someone came
to destroy your lord the king. 16What you have done is not good.
As surely as the LORD lives, you and your men deserve to die, because you did not guard your master, the LORD's anointed. Look
around you. Where are the king's spear and water jug that were
near his head?"
17Saul recognized David's voice and said, "Is that your voice,[i]
David my son?"
David replied, "Yes it is, my lord the king." 18And he added,
"Why is my lord pursuing his servant? What have I done, and what

[a]4 Or *had come to Nacon*

26:5 [a]1Sa 14:50; 17:55
26:6 [b]Jdg 7:10-11; 1Ch 2:16
26:9 [c]2Sa 1:14 [d]1Sa 24:5
26:10 [e]1Sa 25:38; Ro 12:19 [f]Ge 47:29; Dt 31:14; Ps 37:13 [g]1Sa 31:6; 2Sa 1:1
26:12 [h]Ge 2:21; 15:12
26:17 [i]1Sa 24:16

wrong[a] am I guilty of? 19 Now let my lord the king listen to his servant's words. If the LORD has incited you against me, then may he
accept an offering.[b] If, however, men have done it, may they be
cursed before the LORD! They have now driven me from my share
in the LORD's inheritance[c] and have said, 'Go, serve other gods.'
20 Now do not let my blood fall to the ground far from the presence of the LORD. The king of Israel has come out to look for a
flea[d]—as one hunts a partridge in the mountains."
21 Then Saul said, "I have sinned.[e] Come back, David my son.
Because you considered my life precious[f] today, I will not try to
harm you again. Surely I have acted like a fool and have erred
greatly."
22 "Here is the king's spear," David answered. "Let one of your
young men come over and get it. 23 The LORD rewards[g] every man
for his righteousness[h] and faithfulness. The LORD delivered you
into my hands today, but I would not lay a hand on the LORD's
anointed. 24 As surely as I valued your life today, so may the LORD
value my life and deliver[i] me from all trouble."
25 Then Saul said to David, "May you be blessed, my son David;
you will do great things and surely triumph."
So David went on his way, and Saul returned home.

Chapter 27 Theme ______________________

David's Journeys: 1 Samuel 27

27

But David thought to himself, "One of these days I will be
destroyed by the hand of Saul. The best thing I can do is to
escape to the land of the Philistines. Then Saul will give up searching for me anywhere in Israel, and I will slip out of his hand."
2 So David and the six hundred men[j] with him left
and went[k] over to Achish[l] son of Maoch king of Gath.
3 David and his men settled in Gath with Achish.
Each man had his family with him, and David had
his two wives:[m] Ahinoam of Jezreel and Abigail of
Carmel, the widow of Nabal. 4 When Saul was told
that David had fled to Gath, he no longer searched
for him.
5 Then David said to Achish, "If I have found favor
in your eyes, let a place be assigned to me in one of
the country towns, that I may live there. Why should
your servant live in the royal city with you?"
6 So on that day Achish gave him Ziklag,[n] and it has
belonged to the kings of Judah ever since. 7 David
lived[o] in Philistine territory a year and four months.
8 Now David and his men went up and raided the
Geshurites,[p] the Girzites and the Amalekites.[q] (From ancient times
these peoples had lived in the land extending to Shur[r] and Egypt.)
9 Whenever David attacked an area, he did not leave a man or

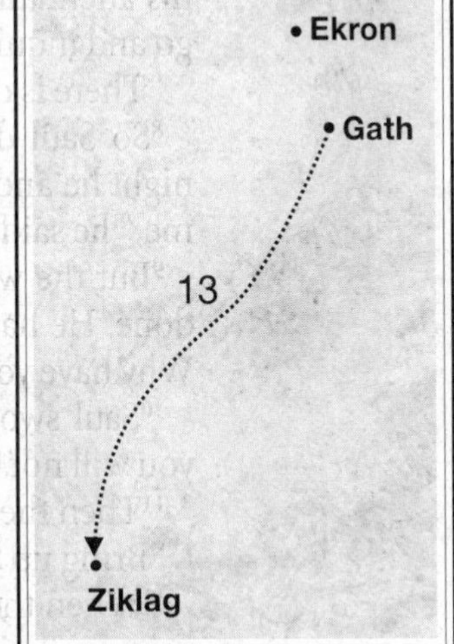

26:18 [a] 1Sa 24:9,11-14
26:19 [b] 2Sa 16:11 [c] 2Sa 14:16
26:20 [d] 1Sa 24:14
26:21 [e] Ex 9:27; 1Sa 15:24 [f] 1Sa 24:17
26:23 [g] Ps 62:12 [h] Ps 7:8; 18:20,24
26:24 [i] Ps 54:7
27:2 [j] 1Sa 25:13 [k] 1Sa 21:10 [l] 1Ki 2:39
27:3 [m] 1Sa 25:43; 30:3
27:6 [n] Jos 15:31; 19:5; Ne 11:28
27:7 [o] 1Sa 29:3
27:8 [p] Jos 13:2,13 [q] Ex 17:8; 1Sa 15:7-8 [r] Ex 15:22

woman alive,[a] but took sheep and cattle, donkeys and camels, and
clothes. Then he returned to Achish.
10 When Achish asked, "Where did you go raiding today?" David
would say, "Against the Negev of Judah" or "Against the Negev of
Jerahmeel[b]" or "Against the Negev of the Kenites.[c]" 11 He did not
leave a man or woman alive to be brought to Gath, for he thought,
"They might inform on us and say, 'This is what David did.' "
And such was his practice as long as he lived in Philistine territory.
12 Achish trusted David and said to himself, "He has become so odi-
ous to his people, the Israelites, that he will be my servant forever."

Chapter 28 Theme ______________________________

28 In those days the Philistines gathered[d] their forces to fight
against Israel. Achish said to David, "You must understand
that you and your men will accompany me in the army."
2 David said, "Then you will see for yourself what your servant
can do."
Achish replied, "Very well, I will make you my bodyguard for
life."
3 Now Samuel was dead,[e] and all Israel had mourned for him and
buried him in his own town of Ramah.[f] Saul had expelled the
mediums and spiritists[g] from the land.
4 The Philistines assembled and came and set up camp at
Shunem,[h] while Saul gathered all the Israelites and set up camp
at Gilboa.[i] 5 When Saul saw the Philistine army, he was afraid; terror filled his heart. 6 He inquired[j] of the LORD, but the LORD did not
answer him by dreams[k] or Urim[l] or prophets. 7 Saul then said to
his attendants, "Find me a woman who is a medium,[m] so I may
go and inquire of her."
"There is one in Endor,[n] " they said.
8 So Saul disguised[o] himself, putting on other clothes, and at
night he and two men went to the woman. "Consult[p] a spirit for
me," he said, "and bring up for me the one I name."
9 But the woman said to him, "Surely you know what Saul has
done. He has cut off[q] the mediums and spiritists from the land.
Why have you set a trap for my life to bring about my death?"
10 Saul swore to her by the LORD, "As surely as the LORD lives,
you will not be punished for this."
11 Then the woman asked, "Whom shall I bring up for you?"
"Bring up Samuel," he said.
12 When the woman saw Samuel, she cried out at the top of her
voice and said to Saul, "Why have you deceived me? You are Saul!"
13 The king said to her, "Don't be afraid. What do you see?"
The woman said, "I see a spirit[a] coming up out of the ground."

[a] 13 Or *see spirits*; or *see gods*

27:9 [a] 1Sa 15:3
27:10 [b] 1Sa 30:29; 1Ch 2:9,25 [c] Jdg 1:16
28:1 [d] 1Sa 29:1
28:3 [e] 1Sa 25:1 [f] 1Sa 7:17 [g] Ex 22:18; Lev 19:31; 20:27; Dt 18:10-11; 1Sa 15:23
28:4 [h] Jos 19:18; 2Ki 4:8 [i] 1Sa 31:1,3
28:6 [j] 1Sa 14:37; 1Ch 10:13-14; Pr 1:28 [k] Nu 12:6 [l] Ex 28:30; Nu 27:21
28:7 [m] Ac 16:16 [n] Jos 17:11
28:8 [o] 2Ch 18:29; 35:22 [p] Dt 18:10-11; 1Ch 10:13; Isa 8:19
28:9 [q] ver 3

14“What does he look like?” he asked.
“An old man wearing a robe[a] is coming up,” she said.
Then Saul knew it was Samuel, and he bowed down and prostrated himself with his face to the ground.
15Samuel said to Saul, “Why have you disturbed me by bringing
me up?”
“I am in great distress,” Saul said. “The Philistines are fighting
against me, and God has turned[b] away from me. He no longer
answers me, either by prophets or by dreams. So I have called on
you to tell me what to do.”
16Samuel said, “Why do you consult me, now that the LORD has
turned away from you and become your enemy? 17The LORD has
done what he predicted through me. The LORD has torn[c] the kingdom out of your hands and given it to one of your neighbors—to
David. 18Because you did not obey[d] the LORD or carry out his fierce
wrath[e] against the Amalekites, the LORD has done this to you today.
19The LORD will hand over both Israel and you to the Philistines,
and tomorrow you and your sons[f] will be with me. The LORD will
also hand over the army of Israel to the Philistines.”
20Immediately Saul fell full length on the ground, filled with fear
because of Samuel’s words. His strength was gone, for he had eaten
nothing all that day and night.
21When the woman came to Saul and saw that he was greatly
shaken, she said, “Look, your maidservant has obeyed you. I took
my life[g] in my hands and did what you told me to do. 22Now
please listen to your servant and let me give you some food so you
may eat and have the strength to go on your way.”
23He refused[h] and said, “I will not eat.”
But his men joined the woman in urging him, and he listened
to them. He got up from the ground and sat on the couch.
24The woman had a fattened calf at the house, which she butchered at once. She took some flour, kneaded it and baked bread
without yeast. 25Then she set it before Saul and his men, and they
ate. That same night they got up and left.

Chapter 29 Theme ______________________

29 The Philistines gathered[i] all their forces at Aphek,[j] and
Israel camped by the spring in Jezreel.[k] 2As the Philistine
rulers marched with their units of hundreds and thousands, David
and his men were marching at the rear[l] with Achish. 3The commanders of the Philistines asked, “What about these Hebrews?”
Achish replied, “Is this not David, who was an officer of Saul
king of Israel? He has already been with me for over a year,[m] and
from the day he left Saul until now, I have found no fault in him.”
4But the Philistine commanders were angry with him and said,
“Send[n] the man back, that he may return to the place you assigned

28:14 [a] 1Sa 15:27; 24:8
28:15 [b] ver 6; 1Sa 18:12
28:17 [c] 1Sa 15:28
28:18 [d] 1Sa 15:20 [e] 1Ki 20:42
28:19 [f] 1Sa 31:2
28:21 [g] Jdg 12:3; 1Sa 19:5; Job 13:14
28:23 [h] 2Ki 5:13
29:1 [i] 1Sa 28:1 [j] Jos 12:18; 1Sa 4:1 [k] 2Ki 9:30
29:2 [l] 1Sa 28:2
29:3 [m] 1Sa 27:7; Da 6:5
29:4 [n] 1Ch 12:19

him. He must not go with us into battle, or he will turn[a] against us
during the fighting. How better could he regain his master's favor
than by taking the heads of our own men? 5Isn't this the David
they sang about in their dances:

"'Saul has slain his thousands,
and David his tens of thousands'?"[b]

6So Achish called David and said to him, "As surely as the LORD
lives, you have been reliable, and I would be pleased to have you
serve with me in the army. From the day[c] you came to me until
now, I have found no fault in you, but the rulers[d] don't approve of
you. 7Turn back and go in peace; do nothing to displease the
Philistine rulers."

8"But what have I done?" asked David. "What have you found
against your servant from the day I came to you until now? Why
can't I go and fight against the enemies of my lord the king?"
9Achish answered, "I know that you have been as pleasing in my
eyes as an angel[e] of God; nevertheless, the Philistine commanders[f]
have said, 'He must not go up with us into battle.' 10Now get up
early, along with your master's servants who have come with you,
and leave[g] in the morning as soon as it is light."
11So David and his men got up early in the morning to go back
to the land of the Philistines, and the Philistines went up to Jezreel.

Chapter 30 Theme

30 David and his men reached Ziklag[h] on the third day. Now
the Amalekites[i] had raided the Negev and Ziklag. They had
attacked Ziklag and burned it, 2and had taken captive the women
and all who were in it, both young and old. They killed none of
them, but carried them off as they went on their way.
3When David and his men came to Ziklag, they found it
destroyed by fire and their wives and sons and daughters taken
captive. 4So David and his men wept aloud until they had no
strength left to weep. 5David's two wives[j] had been captured—
Ahinoam of Jezreel and Abigail, the widow of Nabal of Carmel.
6David was greatly distressed because the men were talking of
stoning[k] him; each one was bitter in spirit because of his sons and
daughters. But David found strength[l] in the LORD his God.
7Then David said to Abiathar[m] the priest, the son of Ahimelech,
"Bring me the ephod.[n]" Abiathar brought it to him, 8and David
inquired[o] of the LORD, "Shall I pursue this raiding party? Will I
overtake them?"

"Pursue them," he answered. "You will certainly overtake them
and succeed[p] in the rescue."

29:4 [a] 1Sa 14:21
29:5 [b] 1Sa 18:7; 21:11
29:6 [c] 1Sa 27:8-12 [d] ver 3
29:9 [e] 2Sa 14:17,20; 19:27 [f] ver 4
29:10 [g] 1Ch 12:19
30:1 [h] 1Sa 29:4,11 [i] 1Sa 15:7; 27:8
30:5 [j] 1Sa 25:43; 2Sa 2:2
30:6 [k] Ex 17:4; Jn 8:59 [l] Ps 27:14; 56:3-4,11; Ro 4:20
30:7 [m] 1Sa 22:20 [n] 1Sa 23:9
30:8 [o] 1Sa 23:2 [p] ver 18

INSIGHT

The ***ephod*** was used to seek guidance from God. Described in Exodus 28, it was a linen garment worn by the priest and also by David when he was king (2 Samuel 6:14). The ephod was fastened on each shoulder by onyx clasps which had the names of six tribes engraved on one clasp and six tribes engraved on the other. The ***breastpiece***, which was fastened to the ephod, had a linen pouch which held the ***Urim*** and ***Thummim***, which may have been used as sacred lots to reveal God's will (1 Samuel 28:6).

30:9 [a]1Sa 27:2 [9]David and the six hundred men[a] with him came to the Besor
Ravine, where some stayed behind, [10]for two hundred men were
too exhausted[b] to cross the ravine. But David and four hundred
men continued the pursuit.
[11]They found an Egyptian in a field and brought him to David.
30:10 They gave him water to drink and food to eat— [12]part of a cake of
[b]ver 9,21 pressed figs and two cakes of raisins. He ate and was revived,[c] for
he had not eaten any food
or drunk any water for three
days and three nights.
[13]David asked him, "To
30:12 whom do you belong, and
[c]Jdg 15:19 where do you come from?"
He said, "I am an Egyptian,
the slave of an Amalekite.
My master abandoned
me when I became ill three
30:14 days ago. [14]We raided the
[d]2Sa 8:18; 1Ki 1:38,44; Negev of the Kerethites[d] and
Eze 25:16; the territory belonging to Ju-
Zep 2:5 [e]ver 16; dah and the Negev of Caleb.[e]
Jos 14:13; 15:13 [f]ver 1 And we burned[f] Ziklag."
[15]David asked him, "Can
you lead me down to this
raiding party?"

Amalekites raid Ziklag
Eglon
Hebron
Ziph
Negev of the Kerethites
Debir
Carmel
Ziklag
Eshtemoa
Gerar
Rimmon
Madmannah
Jattir
Negev of Caleb
Besor Brook
Negev of Judah
Arad
Beersheba
Negev of the Kenites
Hormah
Aroer
David pursues Amalekites
Negev of the Jerahmeelites
Baalath Beer
Locations unknown: Siphmoth, Bor Ashan, and Athach

He answered, "Swear to me
30:16 before God that you will not kill me or hand me over to my master,
[g]Lk 12:19 [h]ver 14 and I will take you down to them."
[16]He led David down, and there they were, scattered over the
countryside, eating, drinking and reveling[g] because of the great
amount of plunder[h] they had taken from the land of the Philistines
and from Judah. [17]David fought[i] them from dusk until the
30:17 evening of the next day, and none of them got away, except four
[i]1Sa 11:11 [j]1Sa 15:3 hundred young men who rode off on camels and fled.[j] [18]David
recovered[k] everything the Amalekites had taken, including his
two wives. [19]Nothing was missing: young or old, boy or girl, plunder or anything else they had taken. David brought everything
back. [20]He took all the flocks and herds, and his men drove them
30:18 ahead of the other livestock, saying, "This is David's plunder."
[k]Ge 14:16 [21]Then David came to the two hundred men who had been too
exhausted[l] to follow him and who were left behind at the Besor
Ravine. They came out to meet David and the people with him. As
David and his men approached, he greeted them. [22]But all the evil
men and troublemakers among David's followers said, "Because
30:21 [l]ver 10 they did not go out with us, we will not share with them the plunder

Ziklag and the Plunder

we recovered. However, each man may take his wife and children
and go."
23David replied, "No, my brothers, you must not do that with
what the LORD has given us. He has protected us and handed over
to us the forces that came against us. 24Who will listen to what you
say? The share of the man who stayed with the supplies is to be the
same as that of him who went down to the battle. All will share
alike.[a]" 25David made this a statute and ordinance for Israel from
that day to this.
26When David arrived in Ziklag, he sent some of the plunder to
the elders of Judah, who were his friends, saying, "Here is a present
for you from the plunder of the LORD's enemies."
27He sent it to those who were in Bethel,[b] Ramoth[c] Negev and
Jattir;[d] 28to those in Aroer,[e] Siphmoth, Eshtemoa[f] 29and Racal; to
those in the towns of the Jerahmeelites[g] and the Kenites;[h] 30to those
in Hormah,[i] Bor Ashan,[j] Athach 31and Hebron;[k] and to those in
all the other places where David and his men had roamed.

Chapter 31 Theme ______________________

31 Now the Philistines fought against Israel; the Israelites fled
before them, and many fell slain on Mount Gilboa.[l] 2The
Philistines pressed hard after Saul and his sons, and
they killed his sons Jonathan, Abinadab and Malki-
Shua. 3The fighting grew fierce around Saul, and
when the archers overtook him, they wounded[m] him
critically.
4Saul said to his armor-bearer, "Draw your sword
and run me through,[n] or these uncircumcised[o] fellows will come and run me through and abuse me."
But his armor-bearer was terrified and would not
do it; so Saul took his own sword and fell on it. 5When
the armor-bearer saw that Saul was dead, he too fell
on his sword and died with him. 6So Saul and his
three sons and his armor-bearer and all his men died
together that same day.
7When the Israelites along the valley and those
across the Jordan saw that the Israelite army had fled
and that Saul and his sons had died, they abandoned their towns
and fled. And the Philistines came and occupied them.
8The next day, when the Philistines came to strip the dead, they
found Saul and his three sons fallen on Mount Gilboa. 9They cut
off his head and stripped off his armor, and they sent messengers
throughout the land of the Philistines to proclaim the news[p] in
the temple of their idols and among their people.[q] 10They put his
armor in the temple of the Ashtoreths[r] and fastened his body to
the wall of Beth Shan.[s]

The Death of Saul and His Sons

30:24 [a]Nu 31:27; Jos 22:8
30:27 [b]Jos 7:2 [c]Jos 19:8 [d]Jos 15:48
30:28 [e]Jos 13:16 [f]Jos 15:50
30:29 [g]1Sa 27:10 [h]Jdg 1:16; 1Sa 15:6
30:30 [i]Nu 14:45; Jdg 1:17 [j]Jos 15:42
30:31 [k]Jos 14:13; 2Sa 2:1,4
31:1 [l]1Sa 28:4; 1Ch 10:1-12
31:3 [m]2Sa 1:6
31:4 [n]Jdg 9:54; 2Sa 1:6,10 [o]1Sa 14:6
31:9 [p]2Sa 1:20 [q]Jdg 16:24
31:10 [r]Jdg 2:12-13; 1Sa 7:3 [s]Jos 17:11; 2Sa 21:12

31:11 [a]1Sa 11:1

31:12 [b]2Sa 2:4-7; 2Ch 16:14; Am 6:10

11When the people of Jabesh Gilead[a] heard of what the Philistines had done to Saul, 12all their valiant men journeyed through
the night to Beth Shan. They took down the bodies of Saul and his
sons from the wall of Beth Shan and went to Jabesh, where they
burned[b] them. 13Then they took their bones[c] and buried them
under a tamarisk[d] tree at Jabesh, and they fasted[e] seven days.[f]

31:13 [c]2Sa 21:12-14 [d]1Sa 22:6 [e]2Sa 1:12 [f]Ge 50:10

1 Samuel at a Glance

Theme of 1 Samuel:

Segment Divisions

		Main Divisions	Chapter Themes
		Samuel, the Last Judge	1
			2
			3
			4
			5
			6
			7
		From Samuel to Saul From Judges to Kings	8
			9
			10
			11
			12
			13
			14
			15
		The Preparation of Another King	16
			17
			18
			19
			20
			21
			22
			23
			24
			25
			26
			27
			28
			29
			30
			31

Author:

Date:

Purpose:

Key Words:

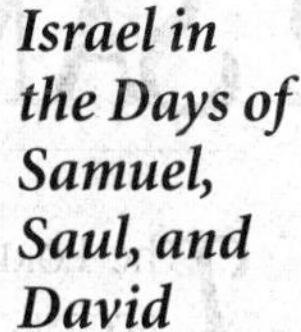

Israel in the Days of Samuel, Saul, and David

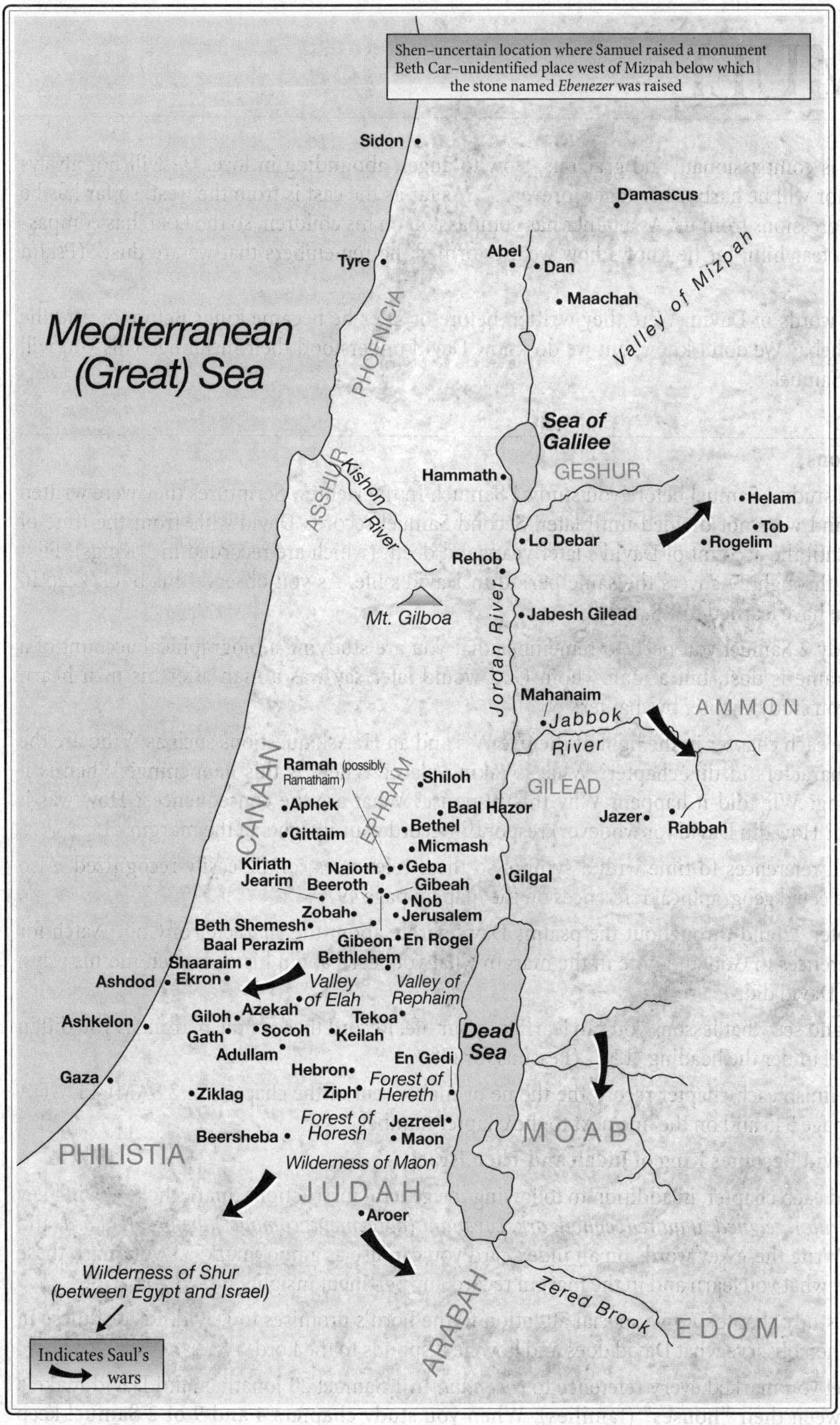

Shen–uncertain location where Samuel raised a monument
Beth Car–unidentified place west of Mizpah below which the stone named *Ebenezer* was raised

Mediterranean (Great) Sea

Sidon

Damascus

Abel

Dan

Tyre

Valley of Mizpah

Maachah

PHOENICIA

Sea of Galilee

ASSHUR

Kishon River

Hammath

GESHUR

Helam

Tob

Rogelim

Lo Debar

Rehob

Mt. Gilboa

Jabesh Gilead

Jordan River

Mahanaim

Jabbok River

AMMON

GILEAD

CANAAN

EPHRAIM

Ramah (possibly Ramathaim)

Shiloh

Aphek

Baal Hazor

Jazer

Rabbah

Gittaim

Bethel

Micmash

Kiriath Jearim

Naioth

Geba

Gilgal

Beeroth

Gibeah

Nob

Zobah

Jerusalem

Beth Shemesh

Gibeon

En Rogel

Baal Perazim

Bethlehem

Shaaraim

Ashdod

Ekron

Valley of Elah

Valley of Rephaim

Giloh

Azekah

Tekoa

Ashkelon

Gath

Socoh

Keilah

Dead Sea

Adullam

En Gedi

Hebron

Gaza

Forest of Hereth

Ziklag

Ziph

Forest of Horesh

Jezreel

Beersheba

Maon

MOAB

PHILISTIA

Wilderness of Maon

JUDAH

Aroer

Wilderness of Shur (between Egypt and Israel)

ARABAH

Zered Brook

EDOM

Indicates Saul's wars

2 SAMUEL

"The LORD is compassionate and gracious, slow to anger, abounding in love. He will not always accuse, nor will he harbor his anger forever. . . . As far as the east is from the west, so far has he removed our transgressions from us. As a father has compassion on his children, so the LORD has compassion on those who fear him; for he knows how we are formed, he remembers that we are dust" (Psalm 103:8, 9, 12-14).

These are the words of David. Were they written before or after he became king? Before or after he sinned with Bathsheba? We don't know, but we do know David understood their meaning. This you will see as you study 2 Samuel.

THINGS TO DO

General Instructions

1. You should study 1 Samuel before you study 2 Samuel. In the Hebrew Scriptures they were written as one book and were not divided until later. Second Samuel records David's life from the time of Saul's death until the account of David's later years and death (which are recorded in 1 Kings). First Chronicles 10 through 29 covers the same period in David's life. As you observe this book keep in mind what you have learned in 1 Samuel.

2. As you study 2 Samuel you need to remember that you are studying a biographical account of a man whose frame is dust, but a man whom God would later say was a man after his own heart. Therefore as you study chapter by chapter:

   a. Observe each chapter in the light of the five W's and an H. Ask questions such as: Who are the main characters in this chapter? What is taking place? Where is this happening? When is it occurring? Why did it happen? Why this response? What are the consequences? How was it handled? How did David (or whoever) respond? Record your insights in the margin.

   b. Mark all references to time with a symbol so these references can be easily recognized. Also mark selected geographical references on the map on page 497.

   c. In chapter 22 and throughout the psalms David wrote about the character of God. Watch for the references to God and note in the margin what you learn about his character and his ways, even as David did.

   d. Watch and see what lessons you can learn for your life. Record these in the margin as you did in 1 Samuel under the heading "LFL" (Lessons for Life).

3. When you finish each chapter record the theme or main event of the chapter on 2 SAMUEL AT A GLANCE on page 545 and on the line next to the chapter number.

Chapters 1-10: David Becomes King of Judah and Then Israel

1. As you read each chapter, in addition to following the general instructions, mark the following key words: *king, (rule), reigned, inquired, ephod, ark, covenant (agreement, compact), before the Lord,* and *evil (wrong)*. Write these key words on an index card you can use as a bookmark. As you mark these words observe what you learn and in the margin record any pertinent insights.

2. When you study chapter 7 give special attention to the Lord's promises to David. Record these in the margin. Then observe what David does and how he responds to the Lord.

3. In 1 Samuel you marked every reference to *covenant*. In 1 Samuel 20 Jonathan and David make a covenant between their "houses" (families). When you study chapters 4 and 9 of 2 Samuel keep

in mind the covenant David and Jonathan made in regard to their houses and notice how David fulfills this covenant. Also when you study Mephibosheth, remember 2 Samuel 5:6-8.

Chapters 11, 12: David's Sins

1. Mark the following key words: *find out (pleaded with), ark,* and *evil (displeased, calamity, sinned, sin).* Make a new bookmark for this segment.
2. Carefully watch the progression of events in these two chapters. Note in the margin the progression of sin and the things which could have served as admonitions against sin had David heeded them. Also list the consequences of David's sin and how the consequences parallel his sin.
3. Remember to follow the "General Instructions." Don't forget the "Lessons for Life" (LFL).
4. Study Psalm 51. Note when the psalm was written.

Chapters 13-24: Consequences of David's Sins

1. Mark the following key words: *inquires, ark, covenant (sworn), before the Lord, evil (come to ruin, harm, calamities, blame, guilt, guilty, sin, sinned),* and *Spirit.* Make a new bookmark for this segment.
2. Follow the "General Instructions." Pay attention to who's who in these chapters—there are many key characters. Record their names in the margin along with a brief description of who they are. Observe the consequences of their actions.
3. Note who David's children are and how he deals with them. Watch Absalom carefully and keep a running record in the margin of what you learn about him. Record your "LFL" in the margin.
4. As you study these final chapters give special attention to David's relationship to the Lord and to what David has to say about God even after God told him he would chasten him. Spend time meditating on chapter 22 and 23:1-7. When you come to *covenant (sworn),* review what you learned in chapter 7 and add any new insights.
5. Then complete 2 SAMUEL AT A GLANCE.

Things to Think About

1. What have you learned about sin and its consequences? Did you think that if God forgave you, you would never reap sin's harvest? What do you think now?
2. In light of all you have learned, why do you think God referred to David as a man after his own heart (1 Samuel 13:14; Acts 13:22)? Give this some serious thought. Then think about what such a statement about David, made after his death, would mean to you. If you wanted to be a man, a woman, a teen, a child after God's own heart, what do you think it would require on your part?
3. Review the "Lessons for Life" you marked in the margin. What did you see that you can make a matter of prayer? Did you learn anything about inquiring or sitting before the Lord? Did you learn anything from marking "before the Lord"?

1:1
[a]1Sa 31:6
[b]1Sa 30:17

Chapter 1 Theme ______________________

1 After the death[a] of Saul, David returned from defeating[b] the
Amalekites and stayed in Ziklag two days. 2On the third day a
man[c] arrived from Saul's camp, with his clothes torn and with
dust on his head.[d] When he came to David, he fell to the ground
to pay him honor.
3"Where have you come from?" David asked him.
He answered, "I have escaped from the Israelite camp."
4"What happened?" David asked. "Tell me."

1:2
[c]2Sa 4:10
[d]1Sa 4:12

He said, "The men fled from the battle. Many of them fell and
died. And Saul and his son Jonathan are dead."
5Then David said to the young man who brought him the report,
"How do you know that Saul and his son Jonathan are dead?"
6"I happened to be on Mount Gilboa,[a]" the young man said,
"and there was Saul, leaning on his spear, with the chariots and
riders almost upon him. 7When he turned around and saw me,
he called out to me, and I said, 'What can I do?'
8"He asked me, 'Who are you?'
"'An Amalekite,[b]' I answered.
9"Then he said to me, 'Stand over me and kill me! I am in the
throes of death, but I'm still alive.'
10"So I stood over him and killed him, because I knew that
after he had fallen he could not survive. And I took the crown[c]
that was on his head and the band on his arm and have brought
them here to my lord."
11Then David and all the men with him took hold of their clothes
and tore[d] them. 12They mourned and wept and fasted till evening
for Saul and his son Jonathan, and for the army of the LORD and
the house of Israel, because they had fallen by the sword.
13David said to the young man who brought him the report,
"Where are you from?"
"I am the son of an alien, an Amalekite,[e]" he answered.
14David asked him, "Why were you not afraid to lift your hand
to destroy the LORD's anointed?[f]"
15Then David called one of his men and said, "Go, strike him
down!"[g] So he struck him down, and he died.[h] 16For David had
said to him, "Your blood be on your own head.[i] Your own mouth
testified against you when you said, 'I killed the LORD's anointed.'"
17David took up this lament[j] concerning Saul and his son
Jonathan, 18and ordered that the men of Judah be taught this
lament of the bow (it is written in the Book of Jashar):[k]

19"Your glory, O Israel, lies slain on your heights.
How the mighty have fallen![l]

20"Tell it not in Gath,[m]
proclaim it not in the streets of Ashkelon,
lest the daughters of the Philistines[n] be glad,
lest the daughters of the uncircumcised rejoice.[o]

21"O mountains of Gilboa,[p]
may you have neither dew nor rain,
nor fields that yield offerings[q] ⌊of grain⌋.
For there the shield of the mighty was defiled,
the shield of Saul—no longer rubbed with oil.[r]

INSIGHT

The *Book of Jashar* was a collection of poetical writings of important events in Israel's history which was gathered in the time of David or Solomon. It is often compared to "The Book of the Wars of the Lord." Bible authors are believed to have quoted occasionally from this book.

1:6 [a] 1Sa 28:4; 31:2-4
1:8 [b] 1Sa 15:2; 30:13,17
1:10 [c] Jdg 9:54; 2Ki 11:12
1:11 [d] Ge 37:29; 2Sa 3:31; 13:31
1:13 [e] ver 8
1:14 [f] 1Sa 24:6; 26:9
1:15 [g] 2Sa 4:12 [h] 2Sa 4:10
1:16 [i] Lev 20:9; 2Sa 3:28-29; 1Ki 2:32; Mt 27:24-25; Ac 18:6
1:17 [j] 2Ch 35:25
1:18 [k] Jos 10:13; 1Sa 31:3
1:19 [l] ver 27
1:20 [m] Mic 1:10 [n] 1Sa 31:8 [o] Ex 15:20; 1Sa 18:6
1:21 [p] ver 6; 1Sa 31:1 [q] Eze 31:15 [r] Isa 21:5

22From the blood[a] of the slain,
from the flesh of the mighty,
the bow[b] of Jonathan did not turn back,
the sword of Saul did not return unsatisfied.

23“Saul and Jonathan—
in life they were loved and gracious,
and in death they were not parted.
They were swifter than eagles,[c]
they were stronger than lions.[d]

24“O daughters of Israel,
weep for Saul,
who clothed you in scarlet and finery,
who adorned your garments with ornaments of gold.

25“How the mighty have fallen in battle!
Jonathan lies slain on your heights.
26I grieve for you, Jonathan my brother;[e]
you were very dear to me.
Your love for me was wonderful,[f]
more wonderful than that of women.

27“How the mighty have fallen!
The weapons of war have perished!”[g]

Chapter 2 Theme ____________________________________

2 In the course of time, David inquired[h] of the LORD. “Shall I
go up to one of the towns of Judah?” he asked.
The LORD said, “Go up.”
David asked, “Where shall I go?”
“To Hebron,”[i] the LORD answered.
2So David went up there with his two wives,[j] Ahinoam of Jezreel
and Abigail,[k] the widow of Nabal of Carmel. 3David also took the
men who were with him,[l] each with his family, and they settled in
Hebron and its towns. 4Then the men of Judah came to Hebron[m]
and there they anointed[n] David king over the house of Judah.
When David was told that it was the men of Jabesh Gilead[o] who
had buried Saul, 5he sent messengers to the men of Jabesh Gilead
to say to them, “The LORD bless[p] you for showing this kindness
to Saul your master by burying him. 6May the LORD now show
you kindness and faithfulness,[q] and I too will show you the same
favor because you have done this. 7Now then, be strong and
brave, for Saul your master is dead, and the house of Judah has
anointed me king over them.”
8Meanwhile, Abner[r] son of Ner, the commander of Saul’s army,
had taken Ish-Bosheth son of Saul and brought him over to

1:22 [a]Isa 34:3,7 [b]Dt 32:42; 1Sa 18:4
1:23 [c]Dt 28:49; Jer 4:13 [d]Jdg 14:18
1:26 [e]1Sa 20:42 [f]1Sa 18:1
1:27 [g]ver 19,25; 1Sa 2:4
2:1 [h]1Sa 23:2,11-12 [i]Ge 13:18; 1Sa 30:31
2:2 [j]1Sa 25:43; 30:5 [k]1Sa 25:42
2:3 [l]1Sa 27:2; 30:9
2:4 [m]1Sa 30:31 [n]1Sa 2:35; 2Sa 5:3-5 [o]1Sa 31:11-13
2:5 [p]1Sa 23:21
2:6 [q]Ex 34:6; 1Ti 1:16
2:8 [r]1Sa 14:50

Mahanaim.[a] 9He made him king over Gilead,[b] Ashuri[a] [c] and Jezreel,
and also over Ephraim, Benjamin and all Israel.[d]
10Ish-Bosheth son of Saul was forty years old when he became
king over Israel, and he reigned two years. The house of Judah,
however, followed David. 11The length of time David was king in
Hebron over the house of Judah was seven years and six months.[e]
12Abner son of Ner, together with the men of Ish-Bosheth son
of Saul, left Mahanaim and went to Gibeon.[f] 13Joab[g] son of
Zeruiah and David's men went out and met them at the pool of
Gibeon. One group sat down on one side of the pool and one
group on the other side.
14Then Abner said to Joab, "Let's have some of the young men
get up and fight hand to hand in front of us."
"All right, let them do it," Joab said.
15So they stood up and were counted off—twelve men for Benjamin and Ish-Bosheth son of Saul, and twelve for David. 16Then
each man grabbed his opponent by the head and thrust his dagger into his opponent's side, and they fell down together. So that
place in Gibeon was called Helkath Hazzurim.[b]
17The battle that day was very fierce, and Abner and the men of
Israel were defeated[h] by David's men.
18The three sons of Zeruiah[i] were there: Joab,[j] Abishai[k] and Asahel.[l] Now Asahel was as fleet-footed as a wild gazelle.[m] 19He chased
Abner, turning neither to the right nor to the left as he pursued
him. 20Abner looked behind him and asked, "Is that you, Asahel?"
"It is," he answered.
21Then Abner said to him, "Turn aside to the right or to the left;
take on one of the young men and strip him of his weapons." But
Asahel would not stop chasing him.
22Again Abner warned Asahel, "Stop chasing me! Why should I
strike you down? How could I look your brother Joab in the face?"[n]
23But Asahel refused to give up the pursuit; so Abner thrust the
butt of his spear into Asahel's stomach,[o] and the spear came out
through his back. He fell there and died on the spot. And every
man stopped when he came to the place where Asahel had fallen
and died.[p]
24But Joab and Abishai pursued Abner, and as the sun was setting, they came to the hill of Ammah, near Giah on the way to the
wasteland of Gibeon. 25Then the men of Benjamin rallied behind
Abner. They formed themselves into a group and took their
stand on top of a hill.
26Abner called out to Joab, "Must the sword devour[q] forever?
Don't you realize that this will end in bitterness? How long before
you order your men to stop pursuing their brothers?"

[a] 9 Or *Asher* [b] 16 *Helkath Hazzurim* means *field of daggers* or *field of hostilities.*

2:8
[a] Ge 32:2

2:9
[b] Nu 32:26
[c] Jdg 1:32
[d] 1Ch 12:29

2:11
[e] 2Sa 5:5

2:12
[f] Jos 18:25

2:13
[g] 2Sa 8:16; 1Ch 2:16; 11:6

2:17
[h] 2Sa 3:1

2:18
[i] 2Sa 3:39
[j] 2Sa 3:30
[k] 1Sa 26:6
[l] 1Ch 2:16
[m] 1Ch 12:8

2:22
[n] 2Sa 3:27

2:23
[o] 2Sa 3:27; 4:6
[p] 2Sa 20:12

2:26
[q] Dt 32:42; Jer 46:10,14

27 Joab answered, "As surely as God lives, if you had not spoken, the men would have continued the pursuit of their brothers until morning.[a]"

28 So Joab[a] blew the trumpet,[b] and all the men came to a halt; they no longer pursued Israel, nor did they fight anymore.

29 All that night Abner and his men marched through the Arabah. They crossed the Jordan, continued through the whole Bithron[b] and came to Mahanaim.[c]

30 Then Joab returned from pursuing Abner and assembled all his men. Besides Asahel, nineteen of David's men were found missing. 31 But David's men had killed three hundred and sixty Benjamites who were with Abner. 32 They took Asahel and buried him in his father's tomb[d] at Bethlehem. Then Joab and his men marched all night and arrived at Hebron by daybreak.

Chapter 3 Theme ______________________________________

3 The war between the house of Saul and the house of David lasted a long time.[e] David grew stronger and stronger,[f] while the house of Saul grew weaker and weaker.[g]

2 Sons were born to David in Hebron:

His firstborn was Amnon the son of Ahinoam[h] of Jezreel;
3 his second, Kileab the son of Abigail[i] the widow of Nabal of Carmel;
the third, Absalom[j] the son of Maacah daughter of Talmai king of Geshur;[k]
4 the fourth, Adonijah[l] the son of Haggith;
the fifth, Shephatiah the son of Abital;
5 and the sixth, Ithream the son of David's wife Eglah.
These were born to David in Hebron.

6 During the war between the house of Saul and the house of David, Abner had been strengthening his own position in the house of Saul. 7 Now Saul had had a concubine[m] named Rizpah[n] daughter of Aiah. And Ish-Bosheth said to Abner, "Why did you sleep with my father's concubine?"

8 Abner was very angry because of what Ish-Bosheth said and he answered, "Am I a dog's head[o]—on Judah's side? This very day I am loyal to the house of your father Saul and to his family and friends. I haven't handed you over to David. Yet now you accuse me of an offense involving this woman! 9 May God deal with Abner, be it ever so severely, if I do not do for David what the LORD promised[p] him on oath 10 and transfer the kingdom from the house of Saul and establish David's throne over Israel

2:28 [a]2Sa 18:16 [b]Jdg 3:27
2:29 [c]ver 8
2:32 [d]Ge 49:29
3:1 [e]1Ki 14:30 [f]2Sa 5:10 [g]2Sa 2:17
3:2 [h]1Sa 25:43; 1Ch 3:1-3
3:3 [i]1Sa 25:42 [j]2Sa 13:1,28 [k]1Sa 27:8; 2Sa 13:37; 14:32; 15:8
3:4 [l]1Ki 1:5,11
3:7 [m]2Sa 16:21-22 [n]2Sa 21:8-11
3:8 [o]1Sa 24:14; 2Sa 9:8; 16:9
3:9 [p]1Sa 15:28; 1Ki 19:2

[a] *27* Or *spoken this morning, the men would not have taken up the pursuit of their brothers*; or *spoken, the men would have given up the pursuit of their brothers by morning* [b] *29* Or *morning*; or *ravine*; the meaning of the Hebrew for this word is uncertain.

and Judah from Dan to Beersheba."[a] 11Ish-Bosheth did not dare
to say another word to Abner, because he was afraid of him.

12Then Abner sent messengers on his behalf to say to David,
"Whose land is it? Make an agreement with me, and I will help
you bring all Israel over to you."

13"Good," said David. "I will make an agreement with you. But
I demand one thing of you: Do not come into my presence unless
you bring Michal daughter of Saul when you come to see me."[b]
14Then David sent messengers to Ish-Bosheth son of Saul,
demanding, "Give me my wife Michal,[c] whom I betrothed to
myself for the price of a hundred Philistine foreskins."

15So Ish-Bosheth gave orders and had her taken away from her
husband[d] Paltiel[e] son of Laish. 16Her husband, however, went
with her, weeping behind her all the way to Bahurim.[f] Then Abner said to him, "Go back home!" So he went back.

17Abner conferred with the elders[g] of Israel and said, "For some
time you have wanted to make David your king. 18Now do it! For
the LORD promised David, 'By my servant David I will rescue my
people Israel from the hand of the Philistines[h] and from the hand
of all their enemies.[i]' "

19Abner also spoke to the Benjamites in person. Then he went
to Hebron to tell David everything that Israel and the whole
house of Benjamin[j] wanted to do. 20When Abner, who had twenty men with him, came to David at Hebron, David prepared a
feast for him and his men. 21Then Abner said to David, "Let me
go at once and assemble all Israel for my lord the king, so that
they may make a compact[k] with you, and that you may rule over
all that your heart desires."[l] So David sent Abner away, and he
went in peace.

22Just then David's men and Joab returned from a raid and
brought with them a great deal of plunder. But Abner was no longer
with David in Hebron, because David had sent him away, and he
had gone in peace. 23When Joab and all the soldiers with him
arrived, he was told that Abner son of Ner had come to the king and
that the king had sent him away and that he had gone in peace.

24So Joab went to the king and said, "What have you done?
Look, Abner came to you. Why did you let him go? Now he is
gone! 25You know Abner son of Ner; he came to deceive you and
observe your movements and find out everything you are doing."

26Joab then left David and sent messengers after Abner, and
they brought him back from the well of Sirah. But David did not
know it. 27Now when Abner[m] returned to Hebron, Joab took him
aside into the gateway, as though to speak with him privately.
And there, to avenge the blood of his brother Asahel, Joab stabbed
him in the stomach, and he died.[n]

3:10 [a] Jdg 20:1; 1Sa 3:20

3:13 [b] Ge 43:5; 1Sa 18:20

3:14 [c] 1Sa 18:27

3:15 [d] Dt 24:1-4 [e] 1Sa 25:44

3:16 [f] 2Sa 16:5; 19:16

3:17 [g] Jdg 11:11

3:18 [h] 1Sa 9:16 [i] 1Sa 15:28; 2Sa 8:6

3:19 [j] 1Sa 10:20-21; 1Ch 12:2,16,29

3:21 [k] ver 10,12 [l] 1Ki 11:37

3:27 [m] 2Sa 2:8 [n] 2Sa 2:22; 20:9-10; 1Ki 2:5

28Later, when David heard about this, he said, “I and my kingdom are forever innocent[a] before the LORD concerning the blood
of Abner son of Ner. 29May his blood[b] fall upon the head of Joab
and upon all his father’s house![c] May Joab’s house never be without someone who has a running sore[d] or leprosy[a] or who leans
on a crutch or who falls by the sword or who lacks food.”

30(Joab and his brother Abishai murdered Abner because he
had killed their brother Asahel in the battle at Gibeon.)

31Then David said to Joab and all the people with him, “Tear
your clothes and put on sackcloth[e] and walk in mourning[f] in
front of Abner.” King David himself walked behind the bier.
32They buried Abner in Hebron, and the king wept[g] aloud at
Abner’s tomb. All the people wept also.

33The king sang this lament[h] for Abner:

“Should Abner have died as the lawless die?
34 Your hands were not bound,
your feet were not fettered.
You fell as one falls before wicked men.”

And all the people wept over him again.

35Then they all came and urged David to eat something while it
was still day; but David took an oath, saying, “May God deal with
me, be it ever so severely,[i] if I taste bread[j] or anything else before
the sun sets!”

36All the people took note and were pleased; indeed, everything
the king did pleased them. 37So on that day all the people and all
Israel knew that the king had no part[k] in the murder of Abner
son of Ner.

38Then the king said to his men, “Do you not realize that a
prince and a great man has fallen[l] in Israel this day? 39And today,
though I am the anointed king, I am weak, and these sons of Zeruiah[m] are too strong for me.[n] May the LORD repay[o] the evildoer
according to his evil deeds!”

Chapter 4 Theme ____________________

4 When Ish-Bosheth son of Saul heard that Abner[p] had died
in Hebron, he lost courage, and all Israel became alarmed.
2Now Saul’s son had two men who were leaders of raiding bands.
One was named Baanah and the other Recab; they were sons of
Rimmon the Beerothite from the tribe of Benjamin—Beeroth[q] is
considered part of Benjamin, 3because the people of Beeroth fled
to Gittaim[r] and have lived there as aliens to this day.

4(Jonathan[s] son of Saul had a son who was lame in both feet.
He was five years old when the news[t] about Saul and Jonathan

3:28 [a]ver 37; Dt 21:9
3:29 [b]Lev 20:9 [c]1Ki 2:31-33 [d]Lev 15:2
3:31 [e]2Sa 1:2,11; Ps 30:11; Isa 20:2 [f]Ge 37:34
3:32 [g]Nu 14:1; Pr 24:17
3:33 [h]2Sa 1:17
3:35 [i]Ru 1:17; 1Sa 3:17 [j]1Sa 31:13; 2Sa 1:12; 12:17; Jer 16:7
3:37 [k]ver 28
3:38 [l]2Sa 1:19
3:39 [m]2Sa 2:18 [n]2Sa 19:5-7 [o]1Ki 2:5-6, 33-34; Ps 41:10; 101:8
4:1 [p]2Sa 3:27; Ezr 4:4
4:2 [q]Jos 9:17; 18:25
4:3 [r]Ne 11:33
4:4 [s]1Sa 18:1 [t]1Sa 31:1-4

a 29 The Hebrew word was used for various diseases affecting the skin—not necessarily leprosy.

came from Jezreel. His nurse picked him up and fled, but as she
hurried to leave, he fell and became crippled.[a] His name was
Mephibosheth.)[b]
5Now Recab and Baanah, the sons of Rimmon the Beerothite,
set out for the house of Ish-Bosheth,[c] and they arrived there in
the heat of the day while he was taking his noonday rest. 6They
went into the inner part of the house as if to get some wheat, and
they stabbed[d] him in the stomach. Then Recab and his brother
Baanah slipped away.
7They had gone into the house while he was lying on the bed in
his bedroom. After they stabbed and killed him, they cut off his
head. Taking it with them, they traveled all night by way of the
Arabah. 8They brought the head of Ish-Bosheth to David at
Hebron and said to the king, "Here is the head of Ish-Bosheth son
of Saul,[e] your enemy, who tried to take your life. This day the LORD
has avenged my lord the king against Saul and his offspring."
9David answered Recab and his brother Baanah, the sons of
Rimmon the Beerothite, "As surely as the LORD lives, who has
delivered[f] me out of all trouble, 10when a man told me, 'Saul is
dead,' and thought he was bringing good news, I seized him and
put him to death in Ziklag.[g] That was the reward I gave him for his
news! 11How much more—when wicked men have killed an innocent man in his own house and on his own bed—should I not now
demand his blood[h] from your hand and rid the earth of you!"
12So David gave an order to his men, and they killed them.[i]
They cut off their hands and feet and hung the bodies by the pool
in Hebron. But they took the head of Ish-Bosheth and buried it
in Abner's tomb at Hebron.

Chapter 5 Theme ________________________________

5 All the tribes of Israel[j] came to David at Hebron and said,
"We are your own flesh and blood.[k] 2In the past, while Saul
was king over us, you were the one who led Israel on their military campaigns.[l] And the LORD said to you, 'You will shepherd[m]
my people Israel, and you will become their ruler.[n]'"
3When all the elders of Israel had come to King David at
Hebron, the king made a compact[o] with them at Hebron before
the LORD, and they anointed[p] David king over Israel.
4David was thirty years old[q] when he became king, and he
reigned[r] forty[s] years. 5In Hebron he reigned over Judah seven
years and six months,[t] and in Jerusalem he reigned over all Israel
and Judah thirty-three years.
6The king and his men marched to Jerusalem[u] to attack the
Jebusites,[v] who lived there. The Jebusites said to David, "You will
not get in here; even the blind and the lame can ward you off."

4:4
[a] Lev 21:18
[b] 2Sa 9:3,6; 1Ch 8:34; 9:40

4:5
[c] 2Sa 2:8

4:6
[d] 2Sa 2:23

4:8
[e] 1Sa 24:4; 25:29

4:9
[f] Ge 48:16; 1Ki 1:29

4:10
[g] 2Sa 1:2-16

4:11
[h] Ge 9:5; Ps 9:12

4:12
[i] 2Sa 1:15

5:1
[j] 2Sa 19:43
[k] 1Ch 11:1

5:2
[l] 1Sa 18:5,13,16
[m] 1Sa 16:1; 2Sa 7:7
[n] 1Sa 25:30

5:3
[o] 2Sa 3:21
[p] 2Sa 2:4

5:4
[q] Lk 3:23
[r] 1Ki 2:11; 1Ch 3:4
[s] 1Ch 26:31; 29:27

5:5
[t] 2Sa 2:11; 1Ch 3:4

5:6
[u] Jdg 1:8
[v] Jos 15:8

They thought, "David cannot get in here." 7Nevertheless, David
captured the fortress of Zion, the City of David.[a]
8On that day, David said, "Anyone who conquers the Jebusites
will have to use the water shaft[a] to reach those 'lame and blind'
who are David's enemies.[b]" That is why they say, "The 'blind and
lame' will not enter the palace."
9David then took up residence in the fortress and called it the
City of David. He built up the area around it, from the supporting terraces[c][b] inward. 10And he became more and more powerful,[c] because the LORD God Almighty was with him.
11Now Hiram[d] king of Tyre sent messengers to David, along
with cedar logs and carpenters and stonemasons, and they built
a palace for David. 12And David knew that the LORD had established him as king over Israel and had exalted his kingdom for
the sake of his people Israel.
13After he left Hebron, David took more concubines and wives[e]
in Jerusalem, and more sons and daughters were born to him.
14These are the names of the children born to him there:[f] Shammua, Shobab, Nathan, Solomon, 15Ibhar, Elishua, Nepheg, Japhia,
16Elishama, Eliada and Eliphelet.
17When the Philistines heard that David had been anointed
king over Israel, they went up in full force to search for him, but
David heard about it and went down to the stronghold.[g] 18Now
the Philistines had come and spread out in the Valley of Rephaim;[h]
19so David inquired[i] of the LORD, "Shall I go and attack the Philistines? Will you hand them over to me?"
The LORD answered him, "Go, for I will surely hand the Philistines over to you."
20So David went to Baal Perazim, and there he defeated them.
He said, "As waters break out, the LORD has broken out against
my enemies before me." So that place was called Baal Perazim.[d][j]
21The Philistines abandoned their idols there, and David and his
men carried them off.[k]
22Once more the Philistines came up and spread out in the Valley of Rephaim; 23so David inquired of the LORD, and he answered,
"Do not go straight up, but circle around behind them and attack
them in front of the balsam trees. 24As soon as you hear the sound[l]
of marching in the tops of the balsam trees, move quickly,
because that will mean the LORD has gone out in front[m] of you to
strike the Philistine army." 25So David did as the LORD commanded him, and he struck down the Philistines all the way from
Gibeon[e][n] to Gezer.[o]

5:7 [a] 2Sa 6:12,16; 1Ki 2:10
5:9 [b] ver 7; 1Ki 9:15,24
5:10 [c] 2Sa 3:1
5:11 [d] 1Ki 5:1,18; 1Ch 14:1
5:13 [e] Dt 17:17; 1Ch 3:9
5:14 [f] 1Ch 3:5
5:17 [g] 2Sa 23:14; 1Ch 11:16
5:18 [h] Jos 15:8; 17:15; 18:16
5:19 [i] 1Sa 23:2; 2Sa 2:1
5:20 [j] Isa 28:21
5:21 [k] Dt 7:5; 1Ch 14:12; Isa 46:2
5:24 [l] 2Ki 7:6 [m] Jdg 4:14
5:25 [n] Isa 28:21 [o] 1Ch 14:16

[a]8 Or *use scaling hooks* [b]8 Or *are hated by David* [c]9 Or *the Millo* [d]20 *Baal Perazim* means *the lord who breaks out.* [e]25 Septuagint (see also 1 Chron. 14:16); Hebrew *Geba*

Chapter 6 Theme ______________________________

6 David again brought together out of Israel chosen men, thirty thousand in all. 2He and all his men set out from Baalah[a]
of Judah[a] to bring up from there the ark[b] of God, which is called by
the Name,[b][c] the name of the LORD Almighty, who is enthroned[d]
between the cherubim[e] that are on the ark. 3They set the ark of
God on a new cart[f] and brought it from the house of Abinadab,
which was on the hill. Uzzah and Ahio, sons of Abinadab, were
guiding the new cart 4with the ark of God on it,[c] and Ahio was
walking in front of it. 5David and the whole house of Israel were
celebrating with all their might before the LORD, with songs[d] and
with harps, lyres, tambourines, sistrums and cymbals.[g]
6When they came to the threshing floor of Nacon, Uzzah
reached out and took hold of[h] the ark of God, because the oxen
stumbled. 7The LORD's anger burned against Uzzah because of
his irreverent act;[i] therefore God struck him down[j] and he died
there beside the ark of God.
8Then David was angry because the LORD's wrath[k] had broken
out against Uzzah, and to this day that place is called Perez Uzzah.[e][l]
9David was afraid of the LORD that day and said, "How[m] can the
ark of the LORD ever come to me?" 10He was not willing to take
the ark of the LORD to be with him in the City of David. Instead, he
took it aside to the house of Obed-Edom[n] the Gittite. 11The ark of
the LORD remained in the house of Obed-Edom the Gittite for
three months, and the LORD blessed him and his entire household.[o]
12Now King David[p] was told, "The LORD has blessed the household of Obed-Edom and everything he has, because of the ark of
God." So David went down and brought up the ark of God from
the house of Obed-Edom to the City of David with rejoicing.
13When those who were carrying the ark of the LORD had taken
six steps, he sacrificed[q] a bull and a fattened calf. 14David, wearing a linen ephod,[r] danced[s] before the LORD with all his might,
15while he and the entire house of Israel brought up the ark of the
LORD with shouts and the sound of trumpets.[t]
16As the ark of the LORD was entering the City of David,[u] Michal
daughter of Saul watched from a window. And when she saw
King David leaping and dancing before the LORD, she despised
him in her heart.
17They brought the ark of the LORD and set it in its place inside
the tent that David had pitched for it,[v] and David sacrificed burnt

[a] *2* That is, Kiriath Jearim; Hebrew *Baale Judah,* a variant of *Baalah of Judah* [b] *2* Hebrew; Septuagint and Vulgate do not have *the Name.* [c] *3,4* Dead Sea Scrolls and some Septuagint manuscripts; Masoretic Text *cart* [4]*and they brought it with the ark of God from the house of Abinadab, which was on the hill* [d] *5* See Dead Sea Scrolls, Septuagint and 1 Chronicles 13:8; Masoretic Text *celebrating before the LORD with all kinds of instruments made of pine.* [e] *8 Perez Uzzah* means *outbreak against Uzzah.*

6:2
[a] Jos 15:9
[b] 1Sa 4:4; 7:1
[c] Lev 24:16; Isa 63:14
[d] Ps 99:1
[e] Ex 25:22; 1Ch 13:5-6

6:3
[f] Nu 7:4-9; 1Sa 6:7

6:5
[g] 1Sa 18:6-7; Ezr 3:10; Ps 150:5

6:6
[h] Nu 4:15, 19-20; 1Ch 13:9

6:7
[i] 1Ch 15:13-15
[j] Ex 19:22; 1Sa 6:19

6:8
[k] Ps 7:11
[l] Ge 38:29

6:9
[m] Ps 119:120

6:10
[n] 1Ch 13:13; 26:4-5

6:11
[o] Ge 30:27; 39:5

6:12
[p] 1Ki 8:1; 1Ch 15:25

6:13
[q] 1Ki 8:5,62

6:14
[r] Ex 19:6; 1Sa 2:18
[s] Ex 15:20

6:15
[t] Ps 47:5; 98:6

6:16
[u] 2Sa 5:7

6:17
[v] 1Ch 15:1; 2Ch 1:4

offerings[a] and fellowship offerings[a] before the LORD. 18After he
had finished sacrificing[b] the burnt offerings and fellowship offerings, he blessed the people in the name of the LORD Almighty.
19Then he gave a loaf of bread, a cake of dates and a cake of
raisins[c] to each person in the whole crowd of Israelites, both men
and women.[d] And all the people went to their homes.
20When David returned home to bless his household, Michal
daughter of Saul came out to meet him and said, "How the king
of Israel has distinguished himself today, disrobing[e] in the sight
of the slave girls of his servants as any vulgar fellow would!"
21David said to Michal, "It was before the LORD, who chose me
rather than your father or anyone from his house when he
appointed[f] me ruler over the LORD's people Israel—I will celebrate before the LORD. 22I will become even more undignified
than this, and I will be humiliated in my own eyes. But by these
slave girls you spoke of, I will be held in honor."
23And Michal daughter of Saul had no children to the day of
her death.

Chapter 7 Theme ______________________

7 After the king was settled in his palace[g] and the LORD had
given him rest from all his enemies around him, 2he said to
Nathan the prophet, "Here I am, living in a palace[h] of cedar, while
the ark of God remains in a tent."[i]
3Nathan replied to the king, "Whatever you have in mind, go
ahead and do it, for the LORD is with you."
4That night the word of the LORD came to Nathan, saying:

5"Go and tell my servant David, 'This is what the LORD says:
Are you[j] the one to build me a house to dwell in?[k] 6I have not
dwelt in a house from the day I brought the Israelites up out
of Egypt to this day. I have been moving from place to place
with a tent[l] as my dwelling.[m] 7Wherever I have moved with all
the Israelites,[n] did I ever say to any of their rulers whom I
commanded to shepherd[o] my people Israel, "Why have you
not built me a house of cedar?[p]"'
8"Now then, tell my servant David, 'This is what the LORD
Almighty says: I took you from the pasture and from following
the flock[q] to be ruler[r] over my people Israel.[s] 9I have been with
you wherever you have gone,[t] and I have cut off all your enemies from before you.[u] Now I will make your name great, like
the names of the greatest men of the earth. 10And I will provide
a place for my people Israel and will plant[v] them so that they
can have a home of their own and no longer be disturbed.

6:17 [a]Lev 1:1-17; 1Ki 8:62-64
6:18 [b]1Ki 8:22
6:19 [c]Hos 3:1 [d]Ne 8:10
6:20 [e]ver 14,16
6:21 [f]1Sa 13:14; 15:28
7:1 [g]1Ch 17:1
7:2 [h]2Sa 5:11 [i]Ex 26:1; Ac 7:45-46
7:5 [j]1Ki 8:19; 1Ch 22:8 [k]1Ki 5:3-5
7:6 [l]Ex 40:18,34 [m]1Ki 8:16
7:7 [n]Dt 23:14 [o]2Sa 5:2 [p]Lev 26:11-12
7:8 [q]1Sa 16:11 [r]2Sa 6:21 [s]Ps 78:70-72; 2Co 6:18*
7:9 [t]2Sa 5:10 [u]Ps 18:37-42
7:10 [v]Ex 15:17; Isa 5:1-7

[a]17 Traditionally *peace offerings*; also in verse 18

Wicked[a] people will not oppress them anymore,[b] as they did
at the beginning 11 and have done ever since the time I
appointed leaders[a][c] over my people Israel. I will also give you
rest from all your enemies.[d]
"'The LORD declares to you that the LORD himself will establish[e] a house[f] for you: 12 When your days are over and you
rest[g] with your fathers, I will raise up your offspring to succeed you, who will come from your own body,[h] and I will establish his kingdom. 13 He is the one who will build a house
for my Name,[i] and I will establish the throne of his kingdom
forever.[j] 14 I will be his father, and he will be my son.[k] When
he does wrong, I will punish him with the rod[l] of men, with
floggings inflicted by men. 15 But my love will never be taken
away from him, as I took it away from Saul,[m] whom I removed
from before you. 16 Your house and your kingdom will endure
forever before me[b]; your throne[n] will be established forever.[o]'"

17 Nathan reported to David all the words of this entire revelation.

18 Then King David went in and sat before the LORD, and he said:

"Who am I,[p] O Sovereign LORD, and what is my family, that
you have brought me this far? 19 And as if this were not
enough in your sight, O Sovereign LORD, you have also spoken about the future of the house of your servant. Is this your
usual way of dealing with man,[q] O Sovereign LORD?
20 "What more can David say to you? For you know[r] your
servant,[s] O Sovereign LORD. 21 For the sake of your word and
according to your will, you have done this great thing and
made it known to your servant.
22 "How great[t] you are,[u] O Sovereign LORD! There is no one
like you, and there is no God[v] but you, as we have heard with
our own ears.[w] 23 And who is like your people Israel[x]—the
one nation on earth that God went out to redeem as a people
for himself, and to make a name for himself, and to perform
great and awesome wonders[y] by driving out nations and their
gods from before your people, whom you redeemed[z] from
Egypt?[c] 24 You have established your people Israel as your
very own[a] forever, and you, O LORD, have become their God.[b]
25 "And now, LORD God, keep forever the promise you have
made concerning your servant and his house. Do as you
promised, 26 so that your name will be great forever. Then
men will say, 'The LORD Almighty is God over Israel!' And the
house of your servant David will be established before you.

7:10 [a]Ps 89:22-23 [b]Isa 60:18
7:11 [c]Jdg 2:16; 1Sa 12:9-11 [d]ver 1 [e]1Sa 25:28 [f]ver 27
7:12 [g]1Ki 2:1 [h]Ps 132:11-12
7:13 [i]1Ki 5:5; 8:19,29 [j]Isa 9:7
7:14 [k]Ps 89:26; Heb 1:5* [l]Ps 89:30-33
7:15 [m]1Sa 15:23,28
7:16 [n]Ps 89:36-37 [o]ver 13
7:18 [p]Ex 3:11; 1Sa 18:18
7:19 [q]Isa 55:8-9
7:20 [r]Jn 21:17 [s]1Sa 16:7
7:22 [t]Ps 48:1; 86:10; Jer 10:6 [u]Dt 3:24 [v]Ex 15:11 [w]Ex 10:2; Ps 44:1
7:23 [x]Dt 4:32-38 [y]Dt 10:21 [z]Dt 9:26; 15:15
7:24 [a]Dt 26:18 [b]Ex 6:6-7; Ps 48:14

[a] *11* Traditionally *judges* [b] *16* Some Hebrew manuscripts and Septuagint; most Hebrew manuscripts *you* [c] *23* See Septuagint and 1 Chron. 17:21; Hebrew *wonders for your land and before your people, whom you redeemed from Egypt, from the nations and their gods.*

27“O LORD Almighty, God of Israel, you have revealed this
to your servant, saying, ‘I will build a house for you.’ So your
servant has found courage to offer you this prayer. 28O Sovereign LORD, you are God! Your words are trustworthy,[a] and
you have promised these good things to your servant. 29Now
be pleased to bless the house of your servant, that it may continue forever in your sight; for you, O Sovereign LORD, have
spoken, and with your blessing[b] the house of your servant
will be blessed forever.”

Chapter 8 Theme ______________

8 In the course of time, David defeated the Philistines and
subdued them, and he took Metheg Ammah from the control of the Philistines.

2David also defeated the Moabites.[c] He made them lie down on
the ground and measured them off with a length of cord. Every
two lengths of them were put to death, and the third length was
allowed to live. So the Moabites became subject to David and
brought tribute.

3Moreover, David fought Hadadezer[d] son of Rehob, king of
Zobah,[e] when he went to restore his control along the Euphrates
River. 4David captured a thousand of his chariots, seven thousand charioteers[a] and twenty thousand foot soldiers. He hamstrung[f] all but a hundred of the chariot horses.

5When the Arameans of Damascus[g] came to help Hadadezer
king of Zobah, David struck down twenty-two thousand of them.
6He put garrisons in the Aramean kingdom of Damascus, and
the Arameans became subject to him and brought tribute. The
LORD gave David victory wherever he went.[h]

7David took the gold shields[i] that belonged to the officers of
Hadadezer and brought them to Jerusalem. 8From Tebah[b] and
Berothai,[j] towns that belonged to Hadadezer, King David took a
great quantity of bronze.

9When Tou[c] king of Hamath[k] heard that David had defeated the
entire army of Hadadezer, 10he sent his son Joram[d] to King David
to greet him and congratulate him on his victory in battle over
Hadadezer, who had been at war with Tou. Joram brought with
him articles of silver and gold and bronze.

11King David dedicated[l] these articles to the LORD, as he had
done with the silver and gold from all the nations he had subdued: 12Edom[e] and Moab,[m] the Ammonites[n] and the Philistines,[o]

7:28 [a]Ex 34:6; Jn 17:17
7:29 [b]Nu 6:23-27
8:2 [c]Ge 19:37; Nu 24:17
8:3 [d]2Sa 10:16,19 [e]1Sa 14:47
8:4 [f]Jos 11:9
8:5 [g]1Ki 11:24
8:6 [h]ver 14; 2Sa 3:18; 7:9
8:7 [i]1Ki 10:16
8:8 [j]Eze 47:16
8:9 [k]1Ki 8:65; 2Ch 8:4
8:11 [l]1Ki 7:51; 1Ch 26:26
8:12 [m]ver 2 [n]2Sa 10:14 [o]2Sa 5:25

[a] *4* Septuagint (see also Dead Sea Scrolls and 1 Chron. 18:4); Masoretic Text *captured seventeen hundred of his charioteers* [b] *8* See some Septuagint manuscripts (see also 1 Chron. 18:8); Hebrew *Betah.* [c] *9* Hebrew *Toi,* a variant of *Tou;* also in verse 10 [d] *10* A variant of *Hadoram* [e] *12* Some Hebrew manuscripts, Septuagint and Syriac (see also 1 Chron. 18:11); most Hebrew manuscripts *Aram*

and Amalek.[a] He also dedicated the plunder taken from Hadadezer
son of Rehob, king of Zobah.
13And David became famous[b] after he returned from striking
down eighteen thousand Edomites[a] in the Valley of Salt.[c]
14He put garrisons throughout Edom, and all the Edomites[d]
became subject to David.[e] The LORD gave David victory wherever
he went.[f]
15David reigned over all Israel, doing what was just and right
for all his people. 16Joab[g] son of Zeruiah was over the army;
Jehoshaphat[h] son of Ahilud was recorder; 17Zadok[i] son of Ahitub
and Ahimelech son of Abiathar were priests; Seraiah was secretary;[j] 18Benaiah[k] son of Jehoiada was over the Kerethites[l] and
Pelethites; and David's sons were royal advisers.[b]

Chapter 9 Theme ______

9 David asked, "Is there anyone still left of the house of Saul to
whom I can show kindness for Jonathan's sake?"[m]
2Now there was a servant of Saul's household named Ziba.[n]
They called him to appear before David, and the king said to
him, "Are you Ziba?"
"Your servant," he replied.
3The king asked, "Is there no one still left of the house of Saul to
whom I can show God's kindness?"
Ziba answered the king, "There is still a son of Jonathan;[o] he is
crippled[p] in both feet."

a *13* A few Hebrew manuscripts, Septuagint and Syriac (see also 1 Chron. 18:12); most Hebrew manuscripts *Aram* (that is, Arameans) b *18* Or *were priests*

8:12 [a] 1Sa 27:8
8:13 [b] 2Sa 7:9 [c] 2Ki 14:7; 1Ch 18:12
8:14 [d] Nu 24:17-18 [e] Ge 27:29,37-40 [f] ver 6
8:16 [g] 2Sa 19:13; 1Ch 11:6 [h] 2Sa 20:24; 1Ki 4:3
8:17 [i] 2Sa 15:24,29; 1Ch 16:39; 24:3 [j] 1Ki 4:3; 2Ki 12:10
8:18 [k] 2Sa 20:23; 1Ki 1:8,38; 1Ch 18:17 [l] 1Sa 30:14
9:1 [m] 1Sa 20:14-17, 42
9:2 [n] 2Sa 16:1-4; 19:17,26,29
9:3 [o] 1Sa 20:14 [p] 2Sa 4:4

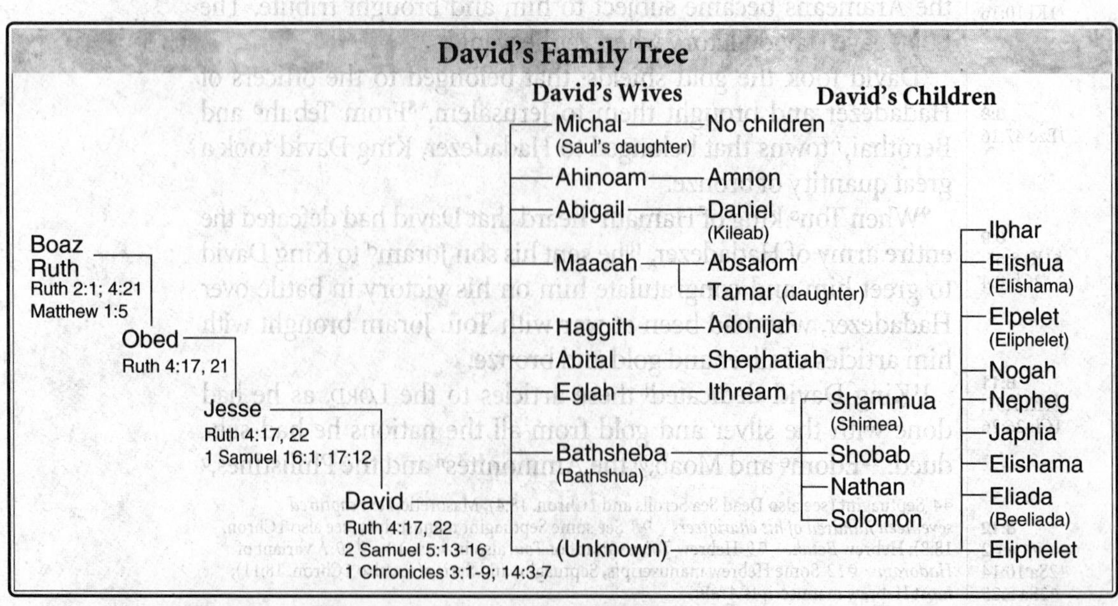

4 “Where is he?” the king asked.
Ziba answered, “He is at the house of Makir[a] son of Ammiel in
Lo Debar.”
5 So King David had him brought from Lo Debar, from the
house of Makir son of Ammiel.
6 When Mephibosheth son of Jonathan, the son of Saul, came to
David, he bowed down to pay him honor.[b]
David said, “Mephibosheth!”
“Your servant,” he replied.
7 “Don't be afraid,” David said to him, “for I will surely show
you kindness for the sake of your father Jonathan. I will restore to
you all the land that belonged to your grandfather Saul, and you
will always eat at my table.[c]”
8 Mephibosheth bowed down and said, “What is your servant,
that you should notice a dead dog[d] like me?”
9 Then the king summoned Ziba, Saul's servant, and said to
him, “I have given your master's grandson everything that
belonged to Saul and his family. 10 You and your sons and your servants are to farm the land for him and bring in the crops, so that
your master's grandson[e] may be provided for. And Mephibosheth, grandson of your master, will always eat at my table.”
(Now Ziba had fifteen sons and twenty servants.)
11 Then Ziba said to the king, “Your servant will do whatever
my lord the king commands his servant to do.” So Mephibosheth
ate at David's[a] table like one of the king's sons.[f]
12 Mephibosheth had a young son named Mica, and all the
members of Ziba's household were servants of Mephibosheth.[g]
13 And Mephibosheth lived in Jerusalem, because he always ate at
the king's table, and he was crippled in both feet.

Chapter 10 Theme __________________________________

10 In the course of time, the king of the Ammonites died, and
his son Hanun succeeded him as king. 2 David thought, “I
will show kindness to Hanun son of Nahash,[h] just as his father
showed kindness to me.” So David sent a delegation to express
his sympathy to Hanun concerning his father.
When David's men came to the land of the Ammonites, 3 the
Ammonite nobles said to Hanun their lord, “Do you think David
is honoring your father by sending men to you to express sympathy? Hasn't David sent them to you to explore the city and spy it
out and overthrow it?” 4 So Hanun seized David's men, shaved off
half of each man's beard,[i] cut off their garments in the middle at
the buttocks,[j] and sent them away.

9:4 [a] 2Sa 17:27-29
9:6 [b] 2Sa 16:4; 19:24-30
9:7 [c] ver 1,3; 2Sa 12:8; 19:28; 1Ki 2:7; 2Ki 25:29
9:8 [d] 2Sa 16:9
9:10 [e] ver 7,11,13; 2Sa 19:28
9:11 [f] Job 36:7; Ps 113:8
9:12 [g] 1Ch 8:34
10:2 [h] 1Sa 11:1
10:4 [i] Lev 19:27; Isa 15:2; Jer 48:37 [j] Isa 20:4

[a] *11* Septuagint; Hebrew *my*

5When David was told about this, he sent messengers to meet
the men, for they were greatly humiliated. The king said, "Stay at
Jericho till your beards have grown, and then come back."

6When the Ammonites realized that they had become a stench[a]
in David's nostrils, they hired twenty thousand Aramean[b] foot soldiers from Beth Rehob[c] and Zobah, as well as the king of Maacah[d]
with a thousand men, and also twelve thousand men from Tob.

7On hearing this, David sent Joab out with the entire army of
fighting men. 8The Ammonites came out and drew up in battle
formation at the entrance to their city gate, while the Arameans
of Zobah and Rehob and the men of Tob and Maacah were by
themselves in the open country.

9Joab saw that there were battle lines in front of him and
behind him; so he selected some of the best troops in Israel and
deployed them against the Arameans. 10He put the rest of the
men under the command of Abishai his brother and deployed
them against the Ammonites. 11Joab said, "If the Arameans are
too strong for me, then you are to come to my rescue; but if the
Ammonites are too strong for you, then I will come to rescue
you. 12Be strong[e] and let us fight bravely for our people and the
cities of our God. The LORD will do what is good in his sight."[f]

13Then Joab and the troops with him advanced to fight the
Arameans, and they fled before him. 14When the Ammonites saw
that the Arameans were fleeing, they fled before Abishai and
went inside the city. So Joab returned from fighting the Ammonites
and came to Jerusalem.

15After the Arameans saw that they had been routed by Israel,
they regrouped. 16Hadadezer had Arameans brought from beyond
the River[a]; they went to Helam, with Shobach the commander of
Hadadezer's army leading them.

17When David was told of this, he gathered all Israel, crossed
the Jordan and went to Helam. The Arameans formed their battle lines to meet David and fought against him. 18But they fled
before Israel, and David killed seven hundred of their charioteers
and forty thousand of their foot soldiers.[b] He also struck down
Shobach the commander of their army, and he died there.
19When all the kings who were vassals of Hadadezer saw that
they had been defeated by Israel, they made peace with the
Israelites and became subject[g] to them.

So the Arameans[h] were afraid to help the Ammonites anymore.

Chapter 11 Theme

11 In the spring,[i] at the time when kings go off to war, David
sent Joab[j] out with the king's men and the whole Israelite

10:6
[a] Ge 34:30
[b] 2Sa 8:5
[c] Jdg 18:28
[d] Dt 3:14

10:12
[e] Dt 31:6; 1Co 16:13; Eph 6:10
[f] Jdg 10:15; 1Sa 3:18; Ne 4:14

10:19
[g] 2Sa 8:6
[h] 1Ki 11:25; 2Ki 5:1

11:1
[i] 1Ki 20:22,26
[j] 2Sa 2:18

[a] *16* That is, the Euphrates
[b] *18* Some Septuagint manuscripts (see also 1 Chron. 19:18); Hebrew *horsemen*

army.[a] They destroyed the Ammonites and besieged Rabbah.[b]
But David remained in Jerusalem.
2One evening David got up from his bed and walked around on
the roof[c] of the palace. From the roof he saw[d] a woman bathing.
The woman was very beautiful, 3and David sent someone to find
out about her. The man said, "Isn't this Bathsheba,[e] the daughter
of Eliam[f] and the wife of Uriah[g] the Hittite?" 4Then David sent
messengers to get her.[h] She came to him, and he slept[i] with her.
(She had purified herself from her uncleanness.)[j] Then[a] she went
back home. 5The woman conceived and sent word to David, saying, "I am pregnant."
6So David sent this word to Joab: "Send me Uriah[k] the Hittite."
And Joab sent him to David. 7When Uriah came to him, David
asked him how Joab was, how the soldiers were and how the war
was going. 8Then David said to Uriah, "Go down to your house and
wash your feet."[l] So Uriah left the palace, and a gift from the king
was sent after him. 9But Uriah slept at the entrance to the palace
with all his master's servants and did not go down to his house.
10When David was told, "Uriah did not go home," he asked him,
"Haven't you just come from a distance? Why didn't you go home?"
11Uriah said to David, "The ark[m] and Israel and Judah are staying in tents, and my master Joab and my lord's men are camped in
the open fields. How could I go to my house to eat and drink and
lie with my wife? As surely as you live, I will not do such a thing!"
12Then David said to him, "Stay here one more day, and tomorrow I will send you back." So Uriah remained in Jerusalem that day
and the next. 13At David's invitation, he ate and drank with him,
and David made him drunk. But in the evening Uriah went out to
sleep on his mat among his master's servants; he did not go home.
14In the morning David wrote a letter[n] to Joab and sent it with
Uriah. 15In it he wrote, "Put Uriah in the front line where the
fighting is fiercest. Then withdraw from him so he will be struck
down[o] and die.[p]"
16So while Joab had the city under siege, he put Uriah at a place
where he knew the strongest defenders were. 17When the men of
the city came out and fought against Joab, some of the men in
David's army fell; moreover, Uriah the Hittite died.
18Joab sent David a full account of the battle. 19He instructed
the messenger: "When you have finished giving the king this
account of the battle, 20the king's anger may flare up, and he may
ask you, 'Why did you get so close to the city to fight? Didn't you
know they would shoot arrows from the wall? 21Who killed Abimelech[q] son of Jerub-Besheth[b]? Didn't a woman throw an upper
millstone on him from the wall,[r] so that he died in Thebez? Why

11:1 [a] 1Ch 20:1 [b] 2Sa 12:26-28
11:2 [c] Dt 22:8; Jos 2:8 [d] Mt 5:28
11:3 [e] 1Ch 3:5 [f] 2Sa 23:34 [g] 2Sa 23:39
11:4 [h] Lev 20:10; Ps 51 Title; Jas 1:14-15 [i] Dt 22:22 [j] Lev 15:25-30; 18:19
11:6 [k] 1Ch 11:41
11:8 [l] Ge 18:4; 43:24; Lk 7:44
11:11 [m] 2Sa 7:2
11:14 [n] 1Ki 21:8
11:15 [o] 2Sa 12:9 [p] 2Sa 12:12
11:21 [q] Jdg 8:31 [r] Jdg 9:50-54

[a] 4 Or *with her. When she purified herself from her uncleanness,* [b] 21 Also known as *Jerub-Baal* (that is, Gideon)

did you get so close to the wall?' If he asks you this, then say to
him, 'Also, your servant Uriah the Hittite is dead.'"
22 The messenger set out, and when he arrived he told David
everything Joab had sent him to say. 23 The messenger said to
David, "The men overpowered us and came out against us in the
open, but we drove them back to the entrance to the city gate.
24 Then the archers shot arrows at your servants from the wall,
and some of the king's men died. Moreover, your servant Uriah
the Hittite is dead."
25 David told the messenger, "Say this to Joab: 'Don't let this
upset you; the sword devours one as well as another. Press the
attack against the city and destroy it.' Say this to encourage Joab."
26 When Uriah's wife heard that her husband was dead, she
mourned for him. 27 After the time of mourning was over, David
had her brought to his house, and she became his wife and bore
him a son. But the thing David had done displeased[a] the LORD.

Chapter 12 Theme ____________________

12 The LORD sent Nathan[b] to David.[c] When he came to him,[d]
he said, "There were two men in a certain town, one rich
and the other poor. 2 The rich man had a very large number of
sheep and cattle, 3 but the poor man had nothing except one little
ewe lamb he had bought. He raised it, and it grew up with him
and his children. It shared his food, drank from his cup and even
slept in his arms. It was like a daughter to him.
4 "Now a traveler came to the rich man, but the rich man
refrained from taking one of his own sheep or cattle to prepare a
meal for the traveler who had come to him. Instead, he took the
ewe lamb that belonged to the poor man and prepared it for the
one who had come to him."
5 David[e] burned with anger against the man and said to Nathan,
"As surely as the LORD lives, the man who did this deserves to
die! 6 He must pay for that lamb four times over,[f] because he did
such a thing and had no pity."
7 Then Nathan said to David, "You are the man! This is what the
LORD, the God of Israel, says: 'I anointed[g] you[h] king over Israel,
and I delivered you from the hand of Saul. 8 I gave your master's
house to you,[i] and your master's wives into your arms. I gave you
the house of Israel and Judah. And if all this had been too little, I
would have given you even more. 9 Why did you despise[j] the
word of the LORD by doing what is evil in his eyes? You struck
down[k] Uriah the Hittite with the sword and took his wife to be
your own. You killed him with the sword of the Ammonites.
10 Now, therefore, the sword[l] will never depart from your house,
because you despised me and took the wife of Uriah the Hittite to
be your own.'

11:27 [a] 2Sa 12:9; Ps 51:4-5

12:1 [b] 2Sa 7:2; 1Ki 20:35-41 [c] Ps 51 Title [d] 2Sa 14:4

12:5 [e] 1Ki 20:40

12:6 [f] Ex 22:1; Lk 19:8

12:7 [g] 1Sa 16:13 [h] 1Ki 20:42

12:8 [i] 2Sa 9:7

12:9 [j] Nu 15:31; 1Sa 15:19 [k] 2Sa 11:15

12:10 [l] 2Sa 13:28; 18:14-15; 1Ki 2:25

11“This is what the LORD says: ‘Out of your own household I am
going to bring calamity upon you.[a] Before your very eyes I will
take your wives and give them to one who is close to you, and he
will lie with your wives in broad daylight. 12You did it in secret,[b]
but I will do this thing in broad daylight[c] before all Israel.’ ”
13Then David said to Nathan, “I have sinned[d] against the LORD.”
Nathan replied, “The LORD has taken away[e] your sin.[f] You are
not going to die.[g] 14But because by doing this you have made the
enemies of the LORD show utter contempt,[a][h] the son born to you
will die.”
15After Nathan had gone home, the LORD struck[i] the child that
Uriah’s wife had borne to David, and he became ill. 16David
pleaded with God for the child. He fasted and went into his house
and spent the nights lying[j] on the ground. 17The elders of his
household stood beside him to get him up from the ground, but
he refused, and he would not eat any food with them.[k]
18On the seventh day the child died. David’s servants were
afraid to tell him that the child was dead, for they thought, “While
the child was still living, we spoke to David but he would not listen to us. How can we tell him the child is dead? He may do something desperate.”
19David noticed that his servants were whispering among
themselves and he realized the child was dead. “Is the child
dead?” he asked.
“Yes,” they replied, “he is dead.”
20Then David got up from the ground. After he had washed,[l]
put on lotions and changed his clothes,[m] he went into the house
of the LORD and worshiped. Then he went to his own house, and
at his request they served him food, and he ate.
21His servants asked him, “Why are you acting this way? While
the child was alive, you fasted and wept,[n] but now that the child is
dead, you get up and eat!”
22He answered, “While the child was still alive, I fasted and
wept. I thought, ‘Who knows?[o] The LORD may be gracious to me
and let the child live.’[p] 23But now that he is dead, why should I
fast? Can I bring him back again? I will go to him,[q] but he will not
return to me.”[r]
24Then David comforted his wife Bathsheba,[s] and he went to her
and lay with her. She gave birth to a son, and they named him
Solomon.[t] The LORD loved him; 25and because the LORD loved him,
he sent word through Nathan the prophet to name him Jedidiah.[b][u]
26Meanwhile Joab fought against Rabbah[v] of the Ammonites
and captured the royal citadel. 27Joab then sent messengers to

12:11 [a]Dt 28:30; 2Sa 16:21-22
12:12 [b]2Sa 11:4-15 [c]2Sa 16:22
12:13 [d]Ge 13:13; Nu 22:34; 1Sa 15:24; 2Sa 24:10 [e]Ps 32:1-5; 51:1,9; 103:12; Zec 3:4,9 [f]Pr 28:13; Mic 7:18-19 [g]Lev 20:10; 24:17
12:14 [h]Isa 52:5; Ro 2:24
12:15 [i]1Sa 25:38
12:16 [j]2Sa 13:31; Ps 5:7
12:17 [k]2Sa 3:35
12:20 [l]Mt 6:17 [m]Job 1:20
12:21 [n]Jdg 20:26
12:22 [o]Jnh 3:9 [p]Isa 38:1-5
12:23 [q]Ge 37:35 [r]1Sa 31:13; 2Sa 13:39; Job 7:10; 10:21
12:24 [s]1Ki 1:11 [t]1Ki 1:10; 1Ch 22:9; 28:5; Mt 1:6
12:25 [u]Ne 13:26
12:26 [v]Dt 3:11; 1Ch 20:1-3

[a]14 Masoretic Text; an ancient Hebrew scribal tradition *this you have shown utter contempt for the LORD* [b]25 *Jedidiah* means *loved by the LORD.*

David, saying, "I have fought against Rabbah and taken its water
supply. 28Now muster the rest of the troops and besiege the city
and capture it. Otherwise I will take the city, and it will be named
after me."

29So David mustered the entire army and went to Rabbah, and
attacked and captured it. 30He took the crown[a] from the head of
their king[a]—its weight was a talent[b] of gold, and it was set with
precious stones—and it was placed on David's head. He took a
great quantity of plunder from the city 31and brought out the
people who were there, consigning them to labor with saws and
with iron picks and axes, and he made them work at brickmak-
ing.[c] He did this to all the Ammonite[b] towns. Then David and his
entire army returned to Jerusalem.

Chapter 13 Theme ____________________

13 In the course of time, Amnon[c] son of David fell in love
with Tamar,[d] the beautiful sister of Absalom[e] son of David.
2Amnon became frustrated to the point of illness on account of
his sister Tamar, for she was a virgin, and it seemed impossible
for him to do anything to her.

3Now Amnon had a friend named Jonadab son of Shimeah,[f]
David's brother. Jonadab was a very shrewd man. 4He asked
Amnon, "Why do you, the king's son, look so haggard morning
after morning? Won't you tell me?"

Amnon said to him, "I'm in love with Tamar, my brother Absalom's sister."

5"Go to bed and pretend to be ill," Jonadab said. "When your
father comes to see you, say to him, 'I would like my sister Tamar
to come and give me something to eat. Let her prepare the food
in my sight so I may watch her and then eat it from her hand.'"

6So Amnon lay down and pretended to be ill. When the king
came to see him, Amnon said to him, "I would like my sister
Tamar to come and make some special bread in my sight, so I
may eat from her hand."

7David sent word to Tamar at the palace: "Go to the house of
your brother Amnon and prepare some food for him." 8So
Tamar went to the house of her brother Amnon, who was lying
down. She took some dough, kneaded it, made the bread in his
sight and baked it. 9Then she took the pan and served him the
bread, but he refused to eat.

"Send everyone out of here,"[g] Amnon said. So everyone left
him. 10Then Amnon said to Tamar, "Bring the food here into my
bedroom so I may eat from your hand." And Tamar took the

12:30 [a] 1Ch 20:2; Est 8:15; Ps 21:3; 132:18

12:31 [b] 1Sa 14:47

13:1 [c] 2Sa 3:2 [d] 2Sa 14:27; 1Ch 3:9 [e] 2Sa 3:3

13:3 [f] 1Sa 16:9

13:9 [g] Ge 45:1

[a] *30* Or *of Milcom* (that is, Molech) [b] *30* That is, about 75 pounds (about 34 kilograms)
[c] *31* The meaning of the Hebrew for this clause is uncertain.

bread she had prepared and brought it to her brother Amnon in his bedroom. 11But when she took it to him to eat, he grabbed[a] her and said, "Come to bed with me, my sister."[b]

12"Don't, my brother!" she said to him. "Don't force me. Such a thing should not be done in Israel![c] Don't do this wicked thing.[d] 13What about me?[e] Where could I get rid of my disgrace? And what about you? You would be like one of the wicked fools in Israel. Please speak to the king; he will not keep me from being married to you." 14But he refused to listen to her, and since he was stronger than she, he raped her.[f]

15Then Amnon hated her with intense hatred. In fact, he hated her more than he had loved her. Amnon said to her, "Get up and get out!"

16"No!" she said to him. "Sending me away would be a greater wrong than what you have already done to me."

But he refused to listen to her. 17He called his personal servant and said, "Get this woman out of here and bolt the door after her." 18So his servant put her out and bolted the door after her. She was wearing a richly ornamented[a] robe,[g] for this was the kind of garment the virgin daughters of the king wore. 19Tamar put ashes[h] on her head and tore the ornamented[b] robe she was wearing. She put her hand on her head and went away, weeping aloud as she went.

20Her brother Absalom said to her, "Has that Amnon, your brother, been with you? Be quiet now, my sister; he is your brother. Don't take this thing to heart." And Tamar lived in her brother Absalom's house, a desolate woman.

21When King David heard all this, he was furious.[i] 22Absalom never said a word to Amnon, either good or bad;[j] he hated[k] Amnon because he had disgraced his sister Tamar.

23Two years later, when Absalom's sheepshearers[l] were at Baal Hazor near the border of Ephraim, he invited all the king's sons to come there. 24Absalom went to the king and said, "Your servant has had shearers come. Will the king and his officials please join me?"

25"No, my son," the king replied. "All of us should not go; we would only be a burden to you." Although Absalom urged him, he still refused to go, but gave him his blessing.

26Then Absalom said, "If not, please let my brother Amnon come with us."

The king asked him, "Why should he go with you?" 27But Absalom urged him, so he sent with him Amnon and the rest of the king's sons.

13:11 [a]Ge 39:12 [b]Ge 38:16
13:12 [c]Lev 20:17; Jdg 20:6 [d]Ge 34:7; Jdg 19:23
13:13 [e]Ge 20:12; Lev 18:9; Dt 22:21,23-24
13:14 [f]Ge 34:2; Dt 22:25; Eze 22:11
13:18 [g]Ge 37:23; Jdg 5:30
13:19 [h]Jos 7:6; 1Sa 4:12; 2Sa 1:2; Est 4:1; Da 9:3
13:21 [i]Ge 34:7
13:22 [j]Ge 31:24 [k]Lev 19:17-18; 1Jn 2:9-11
13:23 [l]1Sa 25:7

[a] *18* The meaning of the Hebrew for this phrase is uncertain. [b] *19* The meaning of the Hebrew for this word is uncertain.

28 Absalom[a] ordered his men, "Listen! When Amnon is in high[b] spirits from drinking wine and I say to you, 'Strike Amnon down,' then kill him. Don't be afraid. Have not I given you this order? Be strong and brave.[c]" 29 So Absalom's men did to Amnon what Absalom had ordered. Then all the king's sons got up, mounted their mules and fled.

30 While they were on their way, the report came to David: "Absalom has struck down all the king's sons; not one of them is left." 31 The king stood up, tore[d] his clothes and lay down on the ground; and all his servants stood by with their clothes torn.

32 But Jonadab son of Shimeah, David's brother, said, "My lord should not think that they killed all the princes; only Amnon is dead. This has been Absalom's expressed intention ever since the day Amnon raped his sister Tamar. 33 My lord the king should not be concerned about the report that all the king's sons are dead. Only Amnon is dead."

34 Meanwhile, Absalom had fled.

Now the man standing watch looked up and saw many people on the road west of him, coming down the side of the hill. The watchman went and told the king, "I see men in the direction of Horonaim, on the side of the hill."[a]

35 Jonadab said to the king, "See, the king's sons are here; it has happened just as your servant said."

36 As he finished speaking, the king's sons came in, wailing loudly. The king, too, and all his servants wept very bitterly.

37 Absalom fled and went to Talmai[e] son of Ammihud, the king of Geshur. But King David mourned for his son every day.

38 After Absalom fled and went to Geshur, he stayed there three years. 39 And the spirit of the king[b] longed to go to Absalom,[f] for he was consoled[g] concerning Amnon's death.

Chapter 14 Theme ____________________________

14 Joab[h] son of Zeruiah knew that the king's heart longed for Absalom. 2 So Joab sent someone to Tekoa[i] and had a wise woman[j] brought from there. He said to her, "Pretend you are in mourning. Dress in mourning clothes, and don't use any cosmetic lotions.[k] Act like a woman who has spent many days grieving for the dead. 3 Then go to the king and speak these words to him." And Joab[l] put the words in her mouth.

4 When the woman from Tekoa went[c] to the king, she fell with her face to the ground to pay him honor, and she said, "Help me, O king!"

[a] 34 Septuagint; Hebrew does not have this sentence. [b] 39 Dead Sea Scrolls and some Septuagint manuscripts; Masoretic Text *But* ⌊*the spirit of*⌋ *David the king* [c] 4 Many Hebrew manuscripts, Septuagint, Vulgate and Syriac; most Hebrew manuscripts *spoke*

13:28 [a] 2Sa 3:3 [b] Jdg 19:6,9,22; Ru 3:7; 1Sa 25:36 [c] 2Sa 12:10

13:31 [d] Nu 14:6; 2Sa 1:11; 12:16

13:37 [e] ver 34; 2Sa 3:3; 14:23,32

13:39 [f] 2Sa 14:13 [g] 2Sa 12:19-23

14:1 [h] 2Sa 2:18

14:2 [i] 2Ch 11:6; Ne 3:5; Jer 6:1; Am 1:1 [j] 2Sa 20:16 [k] Ru 3:3; 2Sa 12:20; Isa 1:6

14:3 [l] ver 19

5 The king asked her, "What is troubling you?"
She said, "I am indeed a widow; my husband is dead. 6 I your
servant had two sons. They got into a fight with each other in the
field, and no one was there to separate them. One struck the other and killed him. 7 Now the whole clan has risen up against your
servant; they say, 'Hand over the one who struck his brother down,
so that we may put him to death[a] for the life of his brother whom
he killed; then we will get rid of the heir[b] as well.' They would put
out the only burning coal I have left,[c] leaving my husband neither
name nor descendant on the face of the earth."
8 The king said to the woman, "Go home,[d] and I will issue an
order in your behalf."
9 But the woman from Tekoa said to him, "My lord the king, let
the blame[e] rest on me and on my father's family,[f] and let the king
and his throne be without guilt.[g]"
10 The king replied, "If anyone says anything to you, bring him
to me, and he will not bother you again."
11 She said, "Then let the king invoke the LORD his God to prevent the avenger[h] of blood from adding to the destruction, so
that my son will not be destroyed."
"As surely as the LORD lives," he said, "not one hair[i] of your
son's head will fall to the ground.[j]"
12 Then the woman said, "Let your servant speak a word to my
lord the king."
"Speak," he replied.
13 The woman said, "Why then have you devised a thing like
this against the people of God? When the king says this, does he
not convict himself,[k] for the king has not brought back his banished son?[l] 14 Like water[m] spilled on the ground, which cannot be
recovered, so we must die.[n] But God does not take away life;
instead, he devises ways so that a banished person[o] may not
remain estranged from him.
15 "And now I have come to say this to my lord the king because
the people have made me afraid. Your servant thought, 'I will
speak to the king; perhaps he will do what his servant asks. 16 Perhaps the king will agree to deliver his servant from the hand of
the man who is trying to cut off both me and my son from the
inheritance[p] God gave us.'
17 "And now your servant says, 'May the word of my lord the
king bring me rest, for my lord the king is like an angel[q] of God in
discerning[r] good and evil. May the LORD your God be with you.'"
18 Then the king said to the woman, "Do not keep from me the
answer to what I am going to ask you."
"Let my lord the king speak," the woman said.
19 The king asked, "Isn't the hand of Joab[s] with you in all this?"
The woman answered, "As surely as you live, my lord the king,

14:7 [a] Nu 35:19 [b] Mt 21:38 [c] Dt 19:10-13
14:8 [d] 1Sa 25:35
14:9 [e] 1Sa 25:24 [f] Mt 27:25 [g] 1Sa 25:28; 1Ki 2:33
14:11 [h] Nu 35:12,21 [i] Mt 10:30 [j] 1Sa 14:45
14:13 [k] 2Sa 12:7; 1Ki 20:40 [l] 2Sa 13:38-39
14:14 [m] Job 14:11; Ps 58:7; Isa 19:5 [n] Job 10:8; 17:13; 30:23; Ps 22:15; Heb 9:27 [o] Nu 35:15, 25-28; Job 34:15
14:16 [p] Ex 34:9; 1Sa 26:19
14:17 [q] ver 20; 1Sa 29:9; 2Sa 19:27 [r] 1Ki 3:9; Da 2:21
14:19 [s] ver 3

no one can turn to the right or to the left from anything my lord
the king says. Yes, it was your servant Joab who instructed me to
do this and who put all these words into the mouth of your servant. 20Your servant Joab did this to change the present situation.
My lord has wisdom[a] like that of an angel of God—he knows
everything that happens in the land.[b]"
21The king said to Joab, "Very well, I will do it. Go, bring back
the young man Absalom."
22Joab fell with his face to the ground to pay him honor, and he
blessed the king.[c] Joab said, "Today your servant knows that he
has found favor in your eyes, my lord the king, because the king
has granted his servant's request."
23Then Joab went to Geshur and brought Absalom back to
Jerusalem. 24But the king said, "He must go to his own house; he
must not see my face." So Absalom went to his own house and did
not see the face of the king.
25In all Israel there was not a man so highly praised for his
handsome appearance as Absalom. From the top of his head to
the sole of his foot there was no blemish in him. 26Whenever he
cut the hair of his head[d]—he used to cut his hair from time to
time when it became too heavy for him—he would weigh it, and
its weight was two hundred shekels[a] by the royal standard.
27Three sons[e] and a daughter were born to Absalom. The daughter's name was Tamar,[f] and she became a beautiful woman.
28Absalom lived two years in Jerusalem without seeing the
king's face. 29Then Absalom sent for Joab in order to send him to
the king, but Joab refused to come to him. So he sent a second
time, but he refused to come. 30Then he said to his servants,
"Look, Joab's field is next to mine, and he has barley[g] there. Go
and set it on fire." So Absalom's servants set the field on fire.
31Then Joab did go to Absalom's house and he said to him,
"Why have your servants set my field on fire?[h]"
32Absalom said to Joab, "Look, I sent word to you and said,
'Come here so I can send you to the king to ask, "Why have I
come from Geshur?[i] It would be better for me if I were still there!"'
Now then, I want to see the king's face, and if I am guilty of anything, let him put me to death."[j]
33So Joab went to the king and told him this. Then the king
summoned Absalom, and he came in and bowed down with his
face to the ground before the king. And the king kissed[k] Absalom.

Chapter 15 Theme ______________________

15 In the course of time,[l] Absalom provided himself with a
chariot[m] and horses and with fifty men to run ahead of

14:20 [a] 1Ki 3:12,28; Isa 28:6 [b] ver 17; 2Sa 18:13; 19:27
14:22 [c] Ge 47:7
14:26 [d] 2Sa 18:9; Eze 44:20
14:27 [e] 2Sa 18:18 [f] 2Sa 13:1
14:30 [g] Ex 9:31
14:31 [h] Jdg 15:5
14:32 [i] 2Sa 3:3 [j] 1Sa 20:8
14:33 [k] Ge 33:4; Lk 15:20
15:1 [l] 2Sa 12:11 [m] 1Sa 8:11; 1Ki 1:5

[a] *26* That is, about 5 pounds (about 2.3 kilograms)

him. 2He would get up early and stand by the side of the road
leading to the city gate.[a] Whenever anyone came with a complaint to be placed before the king for a decision, Absalom would
call out to him, "What town are you from?" He would answer,
"Your servant is from one of the tribes of Israel." 3Then Absalom
would say to him, "Look, your claims are valid and proper, but
there is no representative of the king to hear you."[b] 4And Absalom would add, "If only I were appointed judge in the land![c]
Then everyone who has a complaint or case could come to me
and I would see that he gets justice."

5Also, whenever anyone approached him to bow down before
him, Absalom would reach out his hand, take hold of him and
kiss him. 6Absalom behaved in this way toward all the Israelites
who came to the king asking for justice, and so he stole the
hearts[d] of the men of Israel.

7At the end of four[a] years, Absalom said to the king, "Let me go
to Hebron and fulfill a vow I made to the LORD. 8While your servant was living at Geshur[e] in Aram, I made this vow:[f] 'If the LORD
takes me back to Jerusalem, I will worship the LORD in Hebron.[b]'"

9The king said to him, "Go in peace." So he went to Hebron.

10Then Absalom sent secret messengers throughout the tribes
of Israel to say, "As soon as you hear the sound of the trumpets,[g]
then say, 'Absalom is king in Hebron.'" 11Two hundred men from
Jerusalem had accompanied Absalom. They had been invited as
guests and went quite innocently, knowing nothing about the
matter. 12While Absalom was offering sacrifices, he also sent for
Ahithophel[h] the Gilonite, David's counselor,[i] to come from Giloh,[j]
his hometown. And so the conspiracy gained strength, and Absalom's following kept on increasing.[k]

13A messenger came and told David, "The hearts of the men of
Israel are with Absalom."

14Then David said to all his officials who were with him in
Jerusalem, "Come! We must flee,[l] or none of us will escape from
Absalom.[m] We must leave immediately, or he will move quickly to
overtake us and bring ruin upon us and put the city to the sword."

15The king's officials answered him, "Your servants are ready to
do whatever our lord the king chooses."

16The king set out, with his entire household following him; but
he left ten concubines[n] to take care of the palace. 17So the king set
out, with all the people following him, and they halted at a place
some distance away. 18All his men marched past him, along with
all the Kerethites[o] and Pelethites; and all the six hundred Gittites
who had accompanied him from Gath marched before the king.

15:2 [a]Ge 23:10; 2Sa 19:8
15:3 [b]Pr 12:2
15:4 [c]Jdg 9:29
15:6 [d]Ro 16:18
15:8 [e]2Sa 3:3; 13:37-38 [f]Ge 28:20
15:10 [g]1Ki 1:34,39; 2Ki 9:13
15:12 [h]ver 31,34; 2Sa 16:15,23; 1Ch 27:33 [i]Job 19:14; Ps 41:9; 55:13; Jer 9:4 [j]Jos 15:51 [k]Ps 3:1
15:14 [l]2Sa 12:11; 1Ki 2:26; Ps 132:1; Ps 3 Title [m]2Sa 19:9
15:16 [n]2Sa 16:21-22; 20:3
15:18 [o]1Sa 30:14; 2Sa 8:18; 20:7,23; 1Ki 1:38,44; 1Ch 18:17

[a]7 Some Septuagint manuscripts, Syriac and Josephus; Hebrew *forty* [b]8 Some Septuagint manuscripts; Hebrew does not have *in Hebron.*

19The king said to Ittai[a] the Gittite, "Why should you come
along with us? Go back and stay with King Absalom. You are a
foreigner,[b] an exile from your homeland. 20You came only yesterday. And today shall I make you wander[c] about with us, when I
do not know where I am going? Go back, and take your countrymen. May kindness and faithfulness[d] be with you."
21But Ittai replied to the king, "As surely as the LORD lives, and
as my lord the king lives, wherever my lord the king may be,
whether it means life or death, there will your servant be."[e]
22David said to Ittai, "Go ahead, march on." So Ittai the Gittite
marched on with all his men and the families that were with him.
23The whole countryside wept aloud as all the people passed by.
The king also crossed the Kidron Valley,[f] and all the people moved
on toward the desert.
24Zadok[g] was there, too, and all the Levites who were with him
were carrying the ark[h] of the covenant of God. They set down the
ark of God, and Abiathar[i] offered sacrifices[a] until all the people
had finished leaving the city.
25Then the king said to Zadok, "Take the ark of God back into
the city. If I find favor in the LORD's eyes, he will bring me back
and let me see it and his dwelling place[j] again. 26But if he says, 'I
am not pleased with you,' then I am ready; let him do to me
whatever seems good to him.[k]"
27The king also said to Zadok the priest, "Aren't you a seer?[l] Go
back to the city in peace, with your son Ahimaaz and Jonathan[m] son
of Abiathar. You and Abiathar take your two sons with you. 28I
will wait at the fords[n] in the desert until word comes from you to
inform me." 29So Zadok and Abiathar took the ark of God back
to Jerusalem and stayed there.
30But David continued up the Mount of Olives, weeping[o] as he
went; his head[p] was covered and he was barefoot. All the people
with him covered their heads too and were weeping as they went
up. 31Now David had been told, "Ahithophel[q] is among the con-
spirators with Absalom." So David prayed, "O LORD, turn Ahithophel's counsel into foolishness."
32When David arrived at the summit, where people used to
worship God, Hushai the Arkite[r] was there to meet him, his robe
torn and dust[s] on his head. 33David said to him, "If you go with
me, you will be a burden[t] to me. 34But if you return to the city
and say to Absalom, 'I will be your servant, O king; I was your
father's servant in the past, but now I will be your servant,'[u] then
you can help me by frustrating Ahithophel's advice. 35Won't the
priests Zadok and Abiathar be there with you? Tell them anything you hear in the king's palace.[v] 36Their two sons, Ahimaaz

[a]24 Or *Abiathar went up*

15:19 [a]2Sa 18:2 [b]Ge 31:15
15:20 [c]1Sa 23:13 [d]2Sa 2:6
15:21 [e]Ru 1:16-17; Pr 17:17
15:23 [f]2Ch 29:16
15:24 [g]2Sa 8:17 [h]Nu 4:15 [i]1Sa 22:20
15:25 [j]Ex 15:13; Ps 43:3; Jer 25:30
15:26 [k]1Sa 3:18; 2Sa 22:20; 1Ki 10:9
15:27 [l]1Sa 9:9 [m]2Sa 17:17
15:28 [n]2Sa 17:16
15:30 [o]2Sa 19:4; Ps 126:6 [p]Est 6:12; Isa 20:2-4
15:31 [q]ver 12; 2Sa 16:23; 17:14,23
15:32 [r]Jos 16:2 [s]2Sa 1:2
15:33 [t]2Sa 19:35
15:34 [u]2Sa 16:19
15:35 [v]2Sa 17:15-16

son of Zadok and Jonathan[a] son of Abiathar, are there with them. Send them to me with anything you hear."

37 So David's friend Hushai[b] arrived at Jerusalem as Absalom[c] was entering the city.

Chapter 16 Theme ____

16 When David had gone a short distance beyond the summit, there was Ziba,[d] the steward of Mephibosheth, waiting to meet him. He had a string of donkeys saddled and loaded with two hundred loaves of bread, a hundred cakes of raisins, a hundred cakes of figs and a skin of wine.[e]

2 The king asked Ziba, "Why have you brought these?"

Ziba answered, "The donkeys are for the king's household to ride on, the bread and fruit are for the men to eat, and the wine is to refresh[f] those who become exhausted in the desert."

3 The king then asked, "Where is your master's grandson?"[g]

Ziba said to him, "He is staying in Jerusalem, because he thinks, 'Today the house of Israel will give me back my grandfather's kingdom.'"

4 Then the king said to Ziba, "All that belonged to Mephibosheth is now yours."

"I humbly bow," Ziba said. "May I find favor in your eyes, my lord the king."

5 As King David approached Bahurim,[h] a man from the same clan as Saul's family came out from there. His name was Shimei[i] son of Gera, and he cursed[j] as he came out. 6 He pelted David and all the king's officials with stones, though all the troops and the special guard were on David's right and left. 7 As he cursed, Shimei said, "Get out, get out, you man of blood, you scoundrel! 8 The LORD has repaid you for all the blood you shed in the household of Saul, in whose place you have reigned.[k] The LORD has handed the kingdom over to your son Absalom. You have come to ruin because you are a man of blood!"

9 Then Abishai[l] son of Zeruiah said to the king, "Why should this dead dog curse my lord the king? Let me go over and cut off his head."[m]

10 But the king said, "What do you and I have in common, you sons of Zeruiah?[n] If he is cursing because the LORD said to him, 'Curse David,' who can ask, 'Why do you do this?'"[o]

11 David then said to Abishai and all his officials, "My son,[p] who is of my own flesh, is trying to take my life. How much more, then, this Benjamite! Leave him alone; let him curse, for the LORD has told him to.[q] 12 It may be that the LORD will see my distress[r] and repay me with good[s] for the cursing I am receiving today.[t]"

13 So David and his men continued along the road while Shimei was going along the hillside opposite him, cursing as he went and

15:36 [a] ver 27; 2Sa 17:17
15:37 [b] 2Sa 16:16-17; 1Ch 27:33 [c] 2Sa 16:15
16:1 [d] 2Sa 9:1-13 [e] 1Sa 25:18
16:2 [f] 2Sa 17:27-29
16:3 [g] 2Sa 9:9-10; 19:26-27
16:5 [h] 2Sa 3:16 [i] 2Sa 19:16-23; 1Ki 2:8-9,36,44 [j] Ex 22:28
16:8 [k] 2Sa 21:9
16:9 [l] 2Sa 9:8 [m] Ex 22:28; Lk 9:54
16:10 [n] 2Sa 19:22 [o] Ro 9:20
16:11 [p] 2Sa 12:11 [q] Ge 45:5
16:12 [r] Ps 4:1; 25:18 [s] Dt 23:5; Ro 8:28 [t] Ps 109:28

throwing stones at him and showering him with dirt. 14The king and all the people with him arrived at their destination exhausted.[a] And there he refreshed himself.

15Meanwhile, Absalom[b] and all the men of Israel came to Jerusalem, and Ahithophel[c] was with him. 16Then Hushai[d] the Arkite, David's friend, went to Absalom and said to him, "Long live the king! Long live the king!"

17Absalom asked Hushai, "Is this the love you show your friend? Why didn't you go with your friend?"[e]

18Hushai said to Absalom, "No, the one chosen by the LORD, by these people, and by all the men of Israel—his I will be, and I will remain with him. 19Furthermore, whom should I serve? Should I not serve the son? Just as I served your father, so I will serve you."[f]

20Absalom said to Ahithophel, "Give us your advice. What should we do?"

21Ahithophel answered, "Lie with your father's concubines whom he left to take care of the palace. Then all Israel will hear that you have made yourself a stench in your father's nostrils, and the hands of everyone with you will be strengthened." 22So they pitched a tent for Absalom on the roof, and he lay with his father's concubines in the sight of all Israel.[g]

23Now in those days the advice[h] Ahithophel gave was like that of one who inquires of God. That was how both David[i] and Absalom regarded all of Ahithophel's advice.

Chapter 17 Theme ______________________________

17 Ahithophel said to Absalom, "I would[a] choose twelve thousand men and set out tonight in pursuit of David. 2I would[b] attack him while he is weary and weak.[j] I would[b] strike him with terror, and then all the people with him will flee. I would[b] strike down only the king[k] 3and bring all the people back to you. The death of the man you seek will mean the return of all; all the people will be unharmed." 4This plan seemed good to Absalom and to all the elders of Israel.

5But Absalom said, "Summon also Hushai[l] the Arkite, so we can hear what he has to say." 6When Hushai came to him, Absalom said, "Ahithophel has given this advice. Should we do what he says? If not, give us your opinion."

7Hushai replied to Absalom, "The advice Ahithophel has given is not good this time. 8You know your father and his men; they are fighters, and as fierce as a wild bear robbed of her cubs.[m] Besides, your father is an experienced fighter;[n] he will not spend the night with the troops. 9Even now, he is hidden in a cave or

a1 Or *Let me* b2 Or *will*

16:14
a 2Sa 17:2

16:15
b 2Sa 15:37
c 2Sa 15:12

16:16
d 2Sa 15:37

16:17
e 2Sa 19:25

16:19
f 2Sa 15:34

16:22
g 2Sa 12:11-12; 15:16

16:23
h 2Sa 17:14,23
i 2Sa 15:12

17:2
j 2Sa 16:14
k 1Ki 22:31; Zec 13:7

17:5
l 2Sa 15:32

17:8
m Hos 13:8
n 1Sa 16:18

some other place.[a] If he should attack your troops first,[a] whoever
hears about it will say, 'There has been a slaughter among the
troops who follow Absalom.' 10 Then even the bravest soldier,
whose heart is like the heart of a lion,[b] will melt[c] with fear, for all
Israel knows that your father is a fighter and that those with him
are brave.[d]

11 "So I advise you: Let all Israel, from Dan to Beersheba[e]—as
numerous as the sand[f] on the seashore—be gathered to you,
with you yourself leading them into battle. 12 Then we will attack
him wherever he may be found, and we will fall on him as dew
settles on the ground. Neither he nor any of his men will be left
alive. 13 If he withdraws into a city, then all Israel will bring ropes
to that city, and we will drag it down to the valley[g] until not even
a piece of it can be found."

14 Absalom and all the men of Israel said, "The advice[h] of Hushai
the Arkite is better than that of Ahithophel."[i] For the LORD had
determined to frustrate[j] the good advice of Ahithophel in order
to bring disaster[k] on Absalom.[l]

15 Hushai told Zadok and Abiathar, the priests, "Ahithophel has
advised Absalom and the elders of Israel to do such and such, but
I have advised them to do so and so. 16 Now send a message immediately and tell David, 'Do not spend the night at the fords in the
desert;[m] cross over without fail, or the king and all the people
with him will be swallowed up.[n]' "

17 Jonathan[o] and Ahimaaz were staying at En Rogel.[p] A servant
girl was to go and inform them, and they were to go and tell King
David, for they could not risk being seen entering the city. 18 But a
young man saw them and told Absalom. So the two of them left
quickly and went to the house of a man in Bahurim.[q] He had a
well in his courtyard, and they climbed down into it. 19 His wife
took a covering and spread it out over the opening of the well and
scattered grain over it. No one knew anything about it.[r]

20 When Absalom's men came to the woman[s] at the house, they
asked, "Where are Ahimaaz and Jonathan?"

The woman answered them, "They crossed over the brook."[b] The
men searched but found no one, so they returned to Jerusalem.

21 After the men had gone, the two climbed out of the well and
went to inform King David. They said to him, "Set out and cross the
river at once; Ahithophel has advised such and such against you."
22 So David and all the people with him set out and crossed the Jordan. By daybreak, no one was left who had not crossed the Jordan.

23 When Ahithophel saw that his advice[t] had not been followed,
he saddled his donkey and set out for his house in his hometown.

17:9 [a]Jer 41:9
17:10 [b]1Ch 12:8 [c]Jos 2:9,11; Eze 21:15 [d]2Sa 23:8; 1Ch 11:11
17:11 [e]Jdg 20:1 [f]Ge 12:2; 22:17; Jos 11:4
17:13 [g]Mic 1:6
17:14 [h]2Sa 16:23 [i]2Sa 15:12 [j]2Sa 15:34; Ne 4:15 [k]Ps 9:16 [l]2Ch 10:8
17:16 [m]2Sa 15:28 [n]2Sa 15:35
17:17 [o]2Sa 15:27,36 [p]Jos 15:7; 18:16
17:18 [q]2Sa 3:16; 16:5
17:19 [r]Jos 2:6
17:20 [s]Ex 1:19; Jos 2:3-5; 1Sa 19:12-17
17:23 [t]2Sa 15:12; 16:23

[a]9 Or *When some of the men fall at the first attack* [b]20 Or *"They passed by the sheep pen toward the water."*

He put his house in order[a] and then hanged himself. So he died and was buried in his father's tomb.

24 David went to Mahanaim,[b] and Absalom crossed the Jordan with all the men of Israel. 25 Absalom had appointed Amasa[c] over the army in place of Joab. Amasa was the son of a man named Jether,[a][d] an Israelite[b] who had married Abigail,[c] the daughter of Nahash and sister of Zeruiah the mother of Joab. 26 The Israelites and Absalom camped in the land of Gilead.

27 When David came to Mahanaim, Shobi son of Nahash[e] from Rabbah[f] of the Ammonites, and Makir[g] son of Ammiel from Lo Debar, and Barzillai[h] the Gileadite[i] from Rogelim 28 brought bedding and bowls and articles of pottery. They also brought wheat and barley, flour and roasted grain, beans and lentils,[d] 29 honey and curds, sheep, and cheese from cows' milk for David and his people to eat.[j] For they said, "The people have become hungry and tired and thirsty in the desert.[k]"

Chapter 18 Theme ________________________________

18 David mustered the men who were with him and appointed over them commanders of thousands and commanders of hundreds. 2 David sent the troops out[l]—a third under the command of Joab, a third under Joab's brother Abishai[m] son of Zeruiah, and a third under Ittai[n] the Gittite. The king told the troops, "I myself will surely march out with you."

3 But the men said, "You must not go out; if we are forced to flee, they won't care about us. Even if half of us die, they won't care; but you are worth ten[o] thousand of us.[e] It would be better now for you to give us support from the city."[p]

4 The king answered, "I will do whatever seems best to you."

So the king stood beside the gate while all the men marched out in units of hundreds and of thousands. 5 The king commanded Joab, Abishai and Ittai, "Be gentle with the young man Absalom for my sake." And all the troops heard the king giving orders concerning Absalom to each of the commanders.

6 The army marched into the field to fight Israel, and the battle took place in the forest[q] of Ephraim. 7 There the army of Israel was defeated by David's men, and the casualties that day were great—twenty thousand men. 8 The battle spread out over the whole countryside, and the forest claimed more lives that day than the sword.

[a]25 Hebrew *Ithra,* a variant of *Jether* [b]25 Hebrew and some Septuagint manuscripts; other Septuagint manuscripts (see also 1 Chron. 2:17) *Ishmaelite* or *Jezreelite* [c]25 Hebrew *Abigal,* a variant of *Abigail* [d]28 Most Septuagint manuscripts and Syriac; Hebrew *lentils, and roasted grain* [e]3 Two Hebrew manuscripts, some Septuagint manuscripts and Vulgate; most Hebrew manuscripts *care; for now there are ten thousand like us*

17:23 *a* 2Ki 20:1; Mt 27:5
17:24 *b* Ge 32:2; 2Sa 2:8
17:25 *c* 2Sa 19:13; 20:4,9-12; 1Ki 2:5,32; 1Ch 12:18 *d* 1Ch 2:13-17
17:27 *e* 1Sa 11:1 *f* Dt 3:11; 2Sa 10:1-2; 12:26,29 *g* 2Sa 9:4 *h* 2Sa 19:31-39; 1Ki 2:7 *i* 2Sa 19:31; Ezr 2:61
17:29 *j* 1Ch 12:40 *k* 2Sa 16:2; Ro 12:13
18:2 *l* Jdg 7:16; 1Sa 11:11 *m* 1Sa 26:6 *n* 2Sa 15:19
18:3 *o* 1Sa 18:7 *p* 2Sa 21:17
18:6 *q* Jos 17:18

9Now Absalom happened to meet David's men. He was riding
his mule, and as the mule went under the thick branches of a large
oak, Absalom's head[a] got caught in the tree. He was left hanging
in midair, while the mule he was riding kept on going.
10When one of the men saw this, he told Joab, "I just saw Absalom hanging in an oak tree."
11Joab said to the man who had told him this, "What! You saw
him? Why didn't you strike[b] him to the ground right there? Then
I would have had to give you ten shekels[a] of silver and a warrior's
belt.[c]"
12But the man replied, "Even if a thousand shekels[b] were
weighed out into my hands, I would not lift my hand against the
king's son. In our hearing the king commanded you and Abishai
and Ittai, 'Protect the young man Absalom for my sake.[c]' 13And if
I had put my life in jeopardy[d]—and nothing is hidden from the
king[d]—you would have kept your distance from me."
14Joab[e] said, "I'm not going to wait like this for you." So he took
three javelins in his hand and plunged them into Absalom's heart
while Absalom was still alive in the oak tree. 15And ten of Joab's
armor-bearers surrounded Absalom, struck him and killed him.[f]
16Then Joab[g] sounded the trumpet, and the troops stopped pursuing Israel, for Joab halted them. 17They took Absalom, threw
him into a big pit in the forest and piled up[h] a large heap of rocks[i]
over him. Meanwhile, all the Israelites fled to their homes.
18During his lifetime Absalom had taken a pillar and erected it
in the King's Valley[j] as a monument[k] to himself, for he thought,
"I have no son[l] to carry on the memory of my name." He named
the pillar after himself, and it is called Absalom's Monument to
this day.
19Now Ahimaaz[m] son of Zadok said, "Let me run and take the
news to the king that the LORD has delivered him from the hand
of his enemies.[n]"
20"You are not the one to take the news today," Joab told him.
"You may take the news another time, but you must not do so
today, because the king's son is dead."
21Then Joab said to a Cushite, "Go, tell the king what you have
seen." The Cushite bowed down before Joab and ran off.
22Ahimaaz son of Zadok again said to Joab, "Come what may,
please let me run behind the Cushite."
But Joab replied, "My son, why do you want to go? You don't
have any news that will bring you a reward."
23He said, "Come what may, I want to run."

18:9 *a* 2Sa 14:26
18:11 *b* 2Sa 3:39 *c* 1Sa 18:4
18:13 *d* 2Sa 14:19-20
18:14 *e* 2Sa 2:18; 14:30
18:15 *f* 2Sa 12:10
18:16 *g* 2Sa 2:28; 20:22
18:17 *h* Jos 7:26 *i* Jos 8:29
18:18 *j* Ge 14:17 *k* Ge 50:5; Nu 32:42; 1Sa 15:12 *l* 2Sa 14:27
18:19 *m* 2Sa 15:36 *n* ver 31; Jdg 11:36

a *11* That is, about 4 ounces (about 115 grams) b *12* That is, about 25 pounds (about 11 kilograms) c *12* A few Hebrew manuscripts, Septuagint, Vulgate and Syriac; most Hebrew manuscripts may be translated *Absalom, whoever you may be.* d *13* Or *Otherwise, if I had acted treacherously toward him*

So Joab said, "Run!" Then Ahimaaz ran by way of the plain[a] and outran the Cushite.

24While David was sitting between the inner and outer gates, the watchman[a] went up to the roof of the gateway by the wall. As he looked out, he saw a man running alone. 25The watchman called out to the king and reported it.

The king said, "If he is alone, he must have good news." And the man came closer and closer.

26Then the watchman saw another man running, and he called down to the gatekeeper, "Look, another man running alone!"

The king said, "He must be bringing good news,[b] too."

27The watchman said, "It seems to me that the first one runs like[c] Ahimaaz son of Zadok."

"He's a good man," the king said. "He comes with good news."

28Then Ahimaaz called out to the king, "All is well!" He bowed down before the king with his face to the ground and said, "Praise be to the LORD your God! He has delivered up the men who lifted their hands against my lord the king."

29The king asked, "Is the young man Absalom safe?"

Ahimaaz answered, "I saw great confusion just as Joab was about to send the king's servant and me, your servant, but I don't know what it was."

30The king said, "Stand aside and wait here." So he stepped aside and stood there.

31Then the Cushite arrived and said, "My lord the king, hear the good news! The LORD has delivered you today from all who rose up against you."

32The king asked the Cushite, "Is the young man Absalom safe?"

The Cushite replied, "May the enemies of my lord the king and all who rise up to harm you be like that young man."[d]

33The king was shaken. He went up to the room over the gateway and wept. As he went, he said: "O my son Absalom! My son, my son Absalom! If only I had died[e] instead of you—O Absalom, my son, my son!"[f]

Chapter 19 Theme ______________________

19 Joab was told, "The king is weeping and mourning for Absalom." 2And for the whole army the victory that day was turned into mourning, because on that day the troops heard it said, "The king is grieving for his son." 3The men stole into the city that day as men steal in who are ashamed when they flee from battle. 4The king covered his face and cried aloud, "O my son Absalom! O Absalom, my son, my son!"

[a]*23* That is, the plain of the Jordan

18:24
[a] 1Sa 14:16; 2Sa 19:8; 2Ki 9:17; Jer 51:12

18:26
[b] 1Ki 1:42; Isa 52:7; 61:1

18:27
[c] 2Ki 9:20

18:32
[d] Jdg 5:31; 1Sa 25:26

18:33
[e] Ex 32:32
[f] Ge 43:14; 2Sa 19:4; Ro 9:3

5Then Joab went into the house to the king and said, “Today
you have humiliated all your men, who have just saved your life
and the lives of your sons and daughters and the lives of your
wives and concubines. 6You love those who hate you and hate
those who love you. You have made it clear today that the commanders and their men mean nothing to you. I see that you
would be pleased if Absalom were alive today and all of us were
dead. 7Now go out and encourage your men. I swear by the LORD
that if you don’t go out, not a man will be left with you by nightfall. This will be worse for you than all the calamities that have
come upon you from your youth till now.”[a]
8So the king got up and took his seat in the gateway. When the
men were told, “The king is sitting in the gateway,[b]” they all came
before him.
Meanwhile, the Israelites had fled to their homes. 9Throughout
the tribes of Israel, the people were all arguing with each other,
saying, “The king delivered us from the hand of our enemies; he
is the one who rescued us from the hand of the Philistines.[c] But
now he has fled the country because of Absalom;[d] 10and Absalom,
whom we anointed to rule over us, has died in battle. So why do
you say nothing about bringing the king back?”
11King David sent this message to Zadok[e] and Abiathar, the
priests: “Ask the elders of Judah, ‘Why should you be the last to
bring the king back to his palace, since what is being said throughout Israel has reached the king at his quarters? 12You are my
brothers, my own flesh and blood. So why should you be the last
to bring back the king?’ 13And say to Amasa,[f] ‘Are you not my
own flesh and blood?[g] May God deal with me, be it ever so
severely,[h] if from now on you are not the commander of my army
in place of Joab.[i]’”
14He won over the hearts of all the men of Judah as though they
were one man. They sent word to the king, “Return, you and all
your men.” 15Then the king returned and went as far as the Jordan.
Now the men of Judah had come to Gilgal[j] to go out and meet
the king and bring him across the Jordan. 16Shimei[k] son of Gera,
the Benjamite from Bahurim, hurried down with the men of
Judah to meet King David. 17With him were a thousand Benjamites, along with Ziba,[l] the steward of Saul’s household,[m] and
his fifteen sons and twenty servants. They rushed to the Jordan,
where the king was. 18They crossed at the ford to take the king’s
household over and to do whatever he wished.
When Shimei son of Gera crossed the Jordan, he fell prostrate
before the king 19and said to him, “May my lord not hold me
guilty. Do not remember how your servant did wrong on the day
my lord the king left Jerusalem.[n] May the king put it out of his

19:7 [a]Pr 14:28
19:8 [b]2Sa 15:2
19:9 [c]2Sa 8:1-14 [d]2Sa 15:14
19:11 [e]2Sa 15:24
19:13 [f]2Sa 17:25 [g]Ge 29:14 [h]Ru 1:17; 1Ki 19:2; 8:16 [i]2Sa 2:13
19:15 [j]Jos 5:9; 1Sa 11:15
19:16 [k]2Sa 16:5-13; 1Ki 2:8
19:17 [l]2Sa 9:2; 16:1-2 [m]Ge 43:16
19:19 [n]1Sa 22:15; 2Sa 16:6-8

mind. 20 For I your servant know that I have sinned, but today I have come here as the first of the whole house of Joseph to come down and meet my lord the king."

21 Then Abishai[a] son of Zeruiah said, "Shouldn't Shimei be put to death for this? He cursed[b] the LORD's anointed."[c]

22 David replied, "What do you and I have in common, you sons of Zeruiah?[d] This day you have become my adversaries! Should anyone be put to death in Israel today?[e] Do I not know that today I am king over Israel?" 23 So the king said to Shimei, "You shall not die." And the king promised him on oath.[f]

24 Mephibosheth,[g] Saul's grandson, also went down to meet the king. He had not taken care of his feet or trimmed his mustache or washed his clothes from the day the king left until the day he returned safely. 25 When he came from Jerusalem to meet the king, the king asked him, "Why didn't you go with me,[h] Mephibosheth?"

26 He said, "My lord the king, since I your servant am lame,[i] I said, 'I will have my donkey saddled and will ride on it, so I can go with the king.' But Ziba[j] my servant betrayed me. 27 And he has slandered your servant to my lord the king. My lord the king is like an angel[k] of God; so do whatever pleases you. 28 All my grandfather's descendants deserved nothing but death[l] from my lord the king, but you gave your servant a place among those who eat at your table.[m] So what right do I have to make any more appeals to the king?"

29 The king said to him, "Why say more? I order you and Ziba to divide the fields."

30 Mephibosheth said to the king, "Let him take everything, now that my lord the king has arrived home safely."

31 Barzillai[n] the Gileadite also came down from Rogelim to cross the Jordan with the king and to send him on his way from there. 32 Now Barzillai was a very old man, eighty years of age. He had provided for the king during his stay in Mahanaim, for he was a very wealthy[o] man. 33 The king said to Barzillai, "Cross over with me and stay with me in Jerusalem, and I will provide for you."

34 But Barzillai answered the king, "How many more years will I live, that I should go up to Jerusalem with the king? 35 I am now eighty[p] years old. Can I tell the difference between what is good and what is not? Can your servant taste what he eats and drinks? Can I still hear the voices of men and women singers?[q] Why should your servant be an added[r] burden to my lord the king? 36 Your servant will cross over the Jordan with the king for a short distance, but why should the king reward me in this way? 37 Let your servant return, that I may die in my own town near the tomb of my father[s] and mother. But here is your servant Kimham.[t] Let him cross over with my lord the king. Do for him whatever pleases you."

19:21 [a] 1Sa 26:6 [b] Ex 22:28 [c] 1Sa 12:3; 26:9; 2Sa 16:7-8

19:22 [d] 2Sa 2:18; 16:10 [e] 1Sa 11:13

19:23 [f] 1Ki 2:8,42

19:24 [g] 2Sa 4:4; 9:6-10

19:25 [h] 2Sa 16:17

19:26 [i] Lev 21:18 [j] 2Sa 9:2

19:27 [k] 1Sa 29:9; 2Sa 14:17,20

19:28 [l] 2Sa 16:8; 21:6-9 [m] 2Sa 9:7,13

19:31 [n] 2Sa 17:27-29, 27; 1Ki 2:7

19:32 [o] 1Sa 25:2; 2Sa 17:27

19:35 [p] Ps 90:10 [q] 2Ch 35:25; Ezr 2:65; Ecc 2:8; 12:1; Isa 5:11-12 [r] 2Sa 15:33

19:37 [s] Ge 49:29; 1Ki 2:7 [t] ver 40; Jer 41:17

19:39 [a]Ge 31:55; Ge 47:7

38The king said, "Kimham shall cross over with me, and I will do for him whatever pleases you. And anything you desire from me I will do for you."

39So all the people crossed the Jordan, and then the king crossed over. The king kissed Barzillai and gave him his blessing,[a] and Barzillai returned to his home.

40When the king crossed over to Gilgal, Kimham crossed with him. All the troops of Judah and half the troops of Israel had taken the king over.

19:41 [b]Jdg 8:1; 12:1

41Soon all the men of Israel were coming to the king and saying to him, "Why did our brothers, the men of Judah, steal the king away and bring him and his household across the Jordan, together with all his men?"[b]

42All the men of Judah answered the men of Israel, "We did this because the king is closely related to us. Why are you angry about it? Have we eaten any of the king's provisions? Have we taken anything for ourselves?"

19:43 [c]2Sa 5:1

43Then the men of Israel[c] answered the men of Judah, "We have ten shares in the king; and besides, we have a greater claim on David than you have. So why do you treat us with contempt? Were we not the first to speak of bringing back our king?"

But the men of Judah responded even more harshly than the men of Israel.

20:1 [d]Ge 31:14 [e]Ge 29:14; 1Ki 12:16 [f]1Sa 22:7-8; 2Ch 10:16

Chapter 20 Theme ____________________________

20

Now a troublemaker named Sheba son of Bicri, a Benjamite, happened to be there. He sounded the trumpet and shouted,

"We have no share[d] in David,[e]
no part in Jesse's son![f]
Every man to his tent, O Israel!"

20:3 [g]2Sa 15:16; 16:21-22

2So all the men of Israel deserted David to follow Sheba son of Bicri. But the men of Judah stayed by their king all the way from the Jordan to Jerusalem.

3When David returned to his palace in Jerusalem, he took the ten concubines[g] he had left to take care of the palace and put them in a house under guard. He provided for them, but did not lie with them. They were kept in confinement till the day of their death, living as widows.

20:4 [h]2Sa 17:25; 19:13

4Then the king said to Amasa,[h] "Summon the men of Judah to come to me within three days, and be here yourself." 5But when Amasa went to summon Judah, he took longer than the time the king had set for him.

20:6 [i]2Sa 21:17

6David said to Abishai,[i] "Now Sheba son of Bicri will do us more harm than Absalom did. Take your master's men and pursue

him, or he will find fortified cities and escape from us." 7So Joab's
men and the Kerethites[a] and Pelethites and all the mighty warriors went out under the command of Abishai. They marched out
from Jerusalem to pursue Sheba son of Bicri.
8While they were at the great rock in Gibeon,[b] Amasa came to
meet them. Joab[c] was wearing his military tunic, and strapped
over it at his waist was a belt with a dagger in its sheath. As he
stepped forward, it dropped out of its sheath.
9Joab said to Amasa, "How are you, my brother?" Then Joab
took Amasa by the beard with his right hand to kiss him. 10Amasa
was not on his guard against the dagger[d] in Joab's[e] hand, and
Joab plunged it into his belly, and his intestines spilled out on the
ground. Without being stabbed again, Amasa died. Then Joab
and his brother Abishai pursued Sheba son of Bicri.
11One of Joab's men stood beside Amasa and said, "Whoever
favors Joab, and whoever is for David, let him follow Joab!"
12Amasa lay wallowing in his blood in the middle of the road,
and the man saw that all the troops came to a halt[f] there. When
he realized that everyone who came up to Amasa stopped, he
dragged him from the road into a field and threw a garment over
him. 13After Amasa had been removed from the road, all the men
went on with Joab to pursue Sheba son of Bicri.
14Sheba passed through all the tribes of Israel to Abel Beth
Maacah[a] and through the entire region of the Berites,[g] who gathered together and followed him. 15All the troops with Joab came
and besieged Sheba in Abel Beth Maacah.[h] They built a siege
ramp[i] up to the city, and it stood against the outer fortifications.
While they were battering the wall to bring it down, 16a wise
woman[j] called from the city, "Listen! Listen! Tell Joab to come
here so I can speak to him." 17He went toward her, and she asked,
"Are you Joab?"

"I am," he answered.

She said, "Listen to what your servant has to say."

"I'm listening," he said.

18She continued, "Long ago they used to say, 'Get your answer
at Abel,' and that settled it. 19We are the peaceful[k] and faithful in
Israel. You are trying to destroy a city that is a mother in Israel.
Why do you want to swallow up the LORD's inheritance?"[l]
20"Far be it from me!" Joab replied, "Far be it from me to swallow up or destroy! 21That is not the case. A man named Sheba
son of Bicri, from the hill country of Ephraim, has lifted up his
hand against the king, against David. Hand over this one man,
and I'll withdraw from the city."

a *14* Or *Abel, even Beth Maacah*; also in verse 15

20:7 [a] 1Sa 30:14; 2Sa 8:18; 15:18; 1Ki 1:38

20:8 [b] Jos 9:3 [c] 2Sa 2:18

20:10 [d] Jdg 3:21; 2Sa 2:23; 3:27 [e] 1Ki 2:5

20:12 [f] 2Sa 2:23

20:14 [g] Nu 21:16

20:15 [h] 1Ki 15:20; 2Ki 15:29 [i] 2Ki 19:32; Isa 37:33; Jer 6:6; 32:24

20:16 [j] 2Sa 14:2

20:19 [k] Dt 2:26 [l] 1Sa 26:19; 2Sa 21:3

The woman said to Joab, "His head[a] will be thrown to you from
the wall."
22Then the woman went to all the people with her wise advice,[b]
and they cut off the head of Sheba son of Bicri and threw it to
Joab. So he sounded the trumpet, and his men dispersed from
the city, each returning to his home. And Joab went back to the
king in Jerusalem.
23Joab[c] was over Israel's entire army; Benaiah son of Jehoiada
was over the Kerethites and Pelethites; 24Adoniram[a][d] was in charge
of forced labor; Jehoshaphat[e] son of Ahilud was recorder; 25Sheva
was secretary; Zadok[f] and Abiathar were priests; 26and Ira the
Jairite was David's priest.

Chapter 21 Theme ________________________

21 During the reign of David, there was a famine[g] for three
successive years; so David sought[h] the face of the LORD.
The LORD said, "It is on account of Saul and his blood-stained
house; it is because he put the Gibeonites to death."
2The king summoned the Gibeonites[i] and spoke to them. (Now
the Gibeonites were not a part of Israel but were survivors of the
Amorites; the Israelites had sworn to ⌊spare⌋ them, but Saul in his
zeal for Israel and Judah had tried to annihilate them.) 3David
asked the Gibeonites, "What shall I do for you? How shall I make
amends so that you will bless the LORD's inheritance?"[j]
4The Gibeonites answered him, "We have no right to demand
silver or gold from Saul or his family, nor do we have the right to
put anyone in Israel to death."[k]
"What do you want me to do for you?" David asked.
5They answered the king, "As for the man who destroyed us
and plotted against us so that we have been decimated and have
no place anywhere in Israel, 6let seven of his male descendants be
given to us to be killed and exposed[l] before the LORD at Gibeah of
Saul—the LORD's chosen[m] one."
So the king said, "I will give them to you."
7The king spared Mephibosheth[n] son of Jonathan, the son of
Saul, because of the oath[o] before the LORD between David and
Jonathan son of Saul. 8But the king took Armoni and Mephibosheth, the two sons of Aiah's daughter Rizpah,[p] whom she had
borne to Saul, together with the five sons of Saul's daughter
Merab,[b] whom she had borne to Adriel son of Barzillai the Meho-
lathite.[q] 9He handed them over to the Gibeonites, who killed and

20:21 [a] 2Sa 4:8
20:22 [b] Ecc 9:13
20:23 [c] 2Sa 2:28; 8:16-18; 24:2
20:24 [d] 1Ki 4:6; 5:14; 12:18; 2Ch 10:18 [e] 2Sa 8:16; 1Ki 4:3
20:25 [f] 1Sa 2:35; 2Sa 8:17
21:1 [g] Ge 12:10; Dt 32:24 [h] Ex 32:11
21:2 [i] Jos 9:15
21:3 [j] 1Sa 26:19; 2Sa 20:19
21:4 [k] Nu 35:33-34
21:6 [l] Nu 25:4 [m] 1Sa 10:24
21:7 [n] 2Sa 4:4 [o] 1Sa 18:3; 20:8,15; 2Sa 9:7
21:8 [p] 2Sa 3:7 [q] 1Sa 18:19

[a] *24* Some Septuagint manuscripts (see also 1 Kings 4:6 and 5:14); Hebrew *Adoram* [b] *8* Two Hebrew manuscripts, some Septuagint manuscripts and Syriac (see also 1 Samuel 18:19); most Hebrew and Septuagint manuscripts *Michal*

exposed them on a hill before the LORD. All seven of them fell
together; they were put to death[a] during the first days of the harvest, just as the barley harvest was beginning.[b]
10 Rizpah daughter of Aiah took sackcloth and spread it out for
herself on a rock. From the beginning of the harvest till the rain
poured down from the heavens on the bodies, she did not let the
birds of the air touch them by day or the wild animals by night.[c]
11 When David was told what Aiah's daughter Rizpah, Saul's
concubine, had done, 12 he went and took the bones of Saul[d] and
his son Jonathan from the citizens of Jabesh Gilead. (They had
taken them secretly from the public square at Beth Shan,[e] where
the Philistines had hung[f] them after they struck Saul down on
Gilboa.) 13 David brought the bones of Saul and his son Jonathan
from there, and the bones of those who had been killed and
exposed were gathered up.
14 They buried the bones of Saul and his son Jonathan in the
tomb of Saul's father Kish, at Zela[g] in Benjamin, and did everything the king commanded. After that,[h] God answered prayer[i] in
behalf of the land.
15 Once again there was a battle between the Philistines[j] and Israel.
David went down with his men to fight against the Philistines,
and he became exhausted. 16 And Ishbi-Benob, one of the descendants of Rapha, whose bronze spearhead weighed three hundred
shekels[a] and who was armed with a new ⌊sword⌋, said he would
kill David. 17 But Abishai[k] son of Zeruiah came to David's rescue;
he struck the Philistine down and killed him. Then David's men
swore to him, saying, "Never again will you go out with us to battle, so that the lamp[l] of Israel will not be extinguished.[m]"
18 In the course of time, there was another battle with the
Philistines, at Gob. At that time Sibbecai[n] the Hushathite killed
Saph, one of the descendants of Rapha.
19 In another battle with the Philistines at Gob, Elhanan son of
Jaare-Oregim[b] the Bethlehemite killed Goliath[c] the Gittite, who
had a spear with a shaft like a weaver's rod.[o]
20 In still another battle, which took place at Gath, there was a
huge man with six fingers on each hand and six toes on each
foot—twenty-four in all. He also was descended from Rapha.
21 When he taunted Israel, Jonathan son of Shimeah,[p] David's
brother, killed him.
22 These four were descendants of Rapha in Gath, and they fell
at the hands of David and his men.

[a] *16* That is, about 7 1/2 pounds (about 3.5 kilograms) [b] *19* Or *son of Jair the weaver*
[c] *19* Hebrew and Septuagint; 1 Chron. 20:5 *son of Jair killed Lahmi the brother of Goliath*

21:9
[a] 2Sa 16:8
[b] Ru 1:22

21:10
[c] ver 8; Dt 21:23; 1Sa 17:44

21:12
[d] 1Sa 31:11-13
[e] Jos 17:11
[f] 1Sa 31:10

21:14
[g] Jos 18:28
[h] Jos 7:26
[i] 2Sa 24:25

21:15
[j] 2Sa 5:25

21:17
[k] 2Sa 20:6
[l] 1Ki 11:36
[m] 2Sa 18:3

21:18
[n] 1Ch 11:29; 20:4; 27:11

21:19
[o] 1Sa 17:7

21:21
[p] 1Sa 16:9

Chapter 22 Theme ____________________

22

David sang[a] to the LORD the words of this song when the
LORD delivered him from the hand of all his enemies and
from the hand of Saul. 2He said:

"The LORD is my rock,[b] my fortress[c] and my deliverer;[d]
3 my God is my rock, in whom I take refuge,[e]
my shield[f] and the horn[a][g] of my salvation.
He is my stronghold,[h] my refuge and my savior—
from violent men you save me.
4I call to the LORD, who is worthy[i] of praise,
and I am saved from my enemies.

5"The waves[j] of death swirled about me;
the torrents of destruction overwhelmed me.
6The cords of the grave[b][k] coiled around me;
the snares of death confronted me.
7In my distress[l] I called[m] to the LORD;
I called out to my God.
From his temple he heard my voice;
my cry came to his ears.

8"The earth[n] trembled and quaked,[o]
the foundations[p] of the heavens[c] shook;
they trembled because he was angry.
9Smoke rose from his nostrils;
consuming fire[q] came from his mouth,
burning coals blazed out of it.
10He parted the heavens and came down;
dark clouds[r] were under his feet.
11He mounted the cherubim and flew;
he soared[d] on the wings of the wind.[s]
12He made darkness his canopy around him—
the dark[e] rain clouds of the sky.
13Out of the brightness of his presence
bolts of lightning[t] blazed forth.
14The LORD thundered[u] from heaven;
the voice of the Most High resounded.
15He shot arrows[v] and scattered ⌊the enemies⌋,
bolts of lightning and routed them.
16The valleys of the sea were exposed
and the foundations of the earth laid bare
at the rebuke[w] of the LORD,
at the blast of breath from his nostrils.

22:1 [a]Ex 15:1; Jdg 5:1; Ps 18:2-50
22:2 [b]Dt 32:4; Ps 71:3 [c]Ps 31:3; 91:2 [d]Ps 144:2
22:3 [e]Dt 32:37; Jer 16:19 [f]Ge 15:1 [g]Lk 1:69 [h]Ps 9:9
22:4 [i]Ps 48:1; 96:4
22:5 [j]Ps 69:14-15; 93:4; Jnh 2:3
22:6 [k]Ps 116:3
22:7 [l]Ps 120:1 [m]Ps 34:6,15; 116:4
22:8 [n]Jdg 5:4; Ps 97:4 [o]Ps 77:18 [p]Job 26:11
22:9 [q]Ps 97:3; Heb 12:29
22:10 [r]1Ki 8:12; Na 1:3
22:11 [s]Ps 104:3
22:13 [t]ver 9
22:14 [u]1Sa 2:10
22:15 [v]Dt 32:23
22:16 [w]Na 1:4

a3 *Horn* here symbolizes strength. b6 Hebrew *Sheol* c8 Hebrew; Vulgate and Syriac (see also Psalm 18:7) *mountains* d11 Many Hebrew manuscripts (see also Psalm 18:10); most Hebrew manuscripts *appeared* e12 Septuagint and Vulgate (see also Psalm 18:11); Hebrew *massed*

17"He reached down from on high[a] and took hold of me;
he drew[b] me out of deep waters.
18He rescued me from my powerful enemy,
from my foes, who were too strong for me.
19They confronted me in the day of my disaster,
but the LORD was my support.[c]
20He brought me out into a spacious[d] place;
he rescued[e] me because he delighted[f] in me.[g]

21"The LORD has dealt with me according to my
righteousness;[h]
according to the cleanness of my hands[i] he has
rewarded me.
22For I have kept[j] the ways of the LORD;
I have not done evil by turning from my God.
23All his laws are before me;[k]
I have not turned[l] away from his decrees.
24I have been blameless[m] before him
and have kept myself from sin.
25The LORD has rewarded me according to my
righteousness,[n]
according to my cleanness[a] in his sight.

26"To the faithful you show yourself faithful,
to the blameless you show yourself blameless,
27to the pure[o] you show yourself pure,
but to the crooked you show yourself shrewd.[p]
28You save the humble,[q]
but your eyes are on the haughty to bring
them low.[r]
29You are my lamp,[s] O LORD;
the LORD turns my darkness into light.
30With your help I can advance against a troop[b];
with my God I can scale a wall.

31"As for God, his way is perfect;[t]
the word of the LORD is flawless.[u]
He is a shield
for all who take refuge in him.
32For who is God besides the LORD?
And who is the Rock[v] except our God?
33It is God who arms me with strength[c]
and makes my way perfect.

22:17 [a]Ps 144:7 [b]Ex 2:10
22:19 [c]Ps 23:4
22:20 [d]Ps 31:8 [e]Ps 118:5 [f]Ps 22:8 [g]2Sa 15:26
22:21 [h]1Sa 26:23 [i]Ps 24:4
22:22 [j]Ge 18:19; Ps 128:1; Pr 8:32
22:23 [k]Dt 6:4-9; Ps 119:30-32 [l]Ps 119:102
22:24 [m]Ge 6:9; Eph 1:4
22:25 [n]ver 21
22:27 [o]Mt 5:8 [p]Lev 26:23-24
22:28 [q]Ex 3:8; Ps 72:12-13 [r]Isa 2:12,17; 5:15
22:29 [s]Ps 27:1
22:31 [t]Dt 32:4; Mt 5:48 [u]Ps 12:6; 119:140; Pr 30:5-6
22:32 [v]1Sa 2:2

[a] *25* Hebrew; Septuagint and Vulgate (see also Psalm 18:24) *to the cleanness of my hands*
[b] *30* Or *can run through a barricade* [c] *33* Dead Sea Scrolls, some Septuagint manuscripts, Vulgate and Syriac (see also Psalm 18:32); Masoretic Text *who is my strong refuge*

34 He makes my feet like the feet of a deer;[a]
he enables me to stand on the heights.[b]
35 He trains my hands[c] for battle;
my arms can bend a bow of bronze.
36 You give me your shield[d] of victory;
you stoop down to make me great.
37 You broaden the path[e] beneath me,
so that my ankles do not turn.

38 "I pursued my enemies and crushed them;
I did not turn back till they were destroyed.
39 I crushed[f] them completely, and they could not rise;
they fell beneath my feet.
40 You armed me with strength for battle;
you made my adversaries bow at my feet.[g]
41 You made my enemies turn their backs[h] in flight,
and I destroyed my foes.
42 They cried for help,[i] but there was no one to save them—[j]
to the LORD, but he did not answer.
43 I beat them as fine as the dust of the earth;
I pounded and trampled[k] them like mud[l] in the streets.

44 "You have delivered[m] me from the attacks of my people;
you have preserved[n] me as the head of nations.
People[o] I did not know are subject to me,
45 and foreigners come cringing[p] to me;
as soon as they hear me, they obey me.
46 They all lose heart;
they come trembling[a][q] from their strongholds.

47 "The LORD lives! Praise be to my Rock!
Exalted be God, the Rock, my Savior![r]
48 He is the God who avenges me,[s]
who puts the nations under me,
49 who sets me free from my enemies.[t]
You exalted me above my foes;
from violent men you rescued me.
50 Therefore I will praise you, O LORD, among the nations;
I will sing praises to your name.[u]
51 He gives his king great victories;[v]
he shows unfailing kindness to his anointed,[w]
to David[x] and his descendants forever."[y]

a 46 Some Septuagint manuscripts and Vulgate (see also Psalm 18:45); Masoretic Text *they arm themselves.*

22:34 [a]Hab 3:19 [b]Dt 32:13
22:35 [c]Ps 144:1
22:36 [d]Eph 6:16
22:37 [e]Pr 4:11
22:39 [f]Mal 4:3
22:40 [g]Ps 44:5
22:41 [h]Ex 23:27
22:42 [i]Isa 1:15 [j]Ps 50:22
22:43 [k]Mic 7:10 [l]Isa 10:6; Mic 7:10
22:44 [m]2Sa 3:1 [n]Dt 28:13 [o]2Sa 8:1-14; Isa 55:3-5
22:45 [p]Ps 66:3; 81:15
22:46 [q]Mic 7:17
22:47 [r]Ps 89:26
22:48 [s]Ps 94:1; 144:2; 1Sa 25:39
22:49 [t]Ps 140:1,4
22:50 [u]Ro 15:9*
22:51 [v]Ps 144:9-10 [w]Ps 89:20 [x]2Sa 7:13 [y]Ps 89:24,29

Chapter 23 Theme ______________________________

23

These are the last words of David:

"The oracle of David son of Jesse,
the oracle of the man exalted[a] by the Most High,
the man anointed[b] by the God of Jacob,
Israel's singer of songs[a]:

2 "The Spirit[c] of the LORD spoke through me;
his word was on my tongue.
3 The God of Israel spoke,
the Rock[d] of Israel said to me:
'When one rules over men in righteousness,[e]
when he rules in the fear of God,[f]
4 he is like the light of morning at sunrise[g]
on a cloudless morning,
like the brightness after rain
that brings the grass from the earth.'

5 "Is not my house right with God?
Has he not made with me an everlasting covenant,[h]
arranged and secured in every part?
Will he not bring to fruition my salvation
and grant me my every desire?
6 But evil men are all to be cast aside like thorns,[i]
which are not gathered with the hand.
7 Whoever touches thorns
uses a tool of iron or the shaft of a spear;
they are burned up where they lie."

8 These are the names of David's mighty men:
Josheb-Basshebeth,[b] a Tahkemonite,[c] was chief of the Three; he
raised his spear against eight hundred men, whom he killed[d] in
one encounter.
9 Next to him was Eleazar son of Dodai[j] the Ahohite.[k] As one of
the three mighty men, he was with David when they taunted the
Philistines gathered ⌊at Pas Dammim⌋[e] for battle. Then the men
of Israel retreated, 10 but he stood his ground and struck down
the Philistines till his hand grew tired and froze to the sword. The
LORD brought about a great victory that day. The troops returned
to Eleazar, but only to strip the dead.
11 Next to him was Shammah son of Agee the Hararite. When
the Philistines banded together at a place where there was a field

23:1 [a] 2Sa 7:8-9; Ps 78:70-71; 89:27 [b] 1Sa 16:12-13; Ps 89:20
23:2 [c] Mt 22:43; 2Pe 1:21
23:3 [d] Dt 32:4; 2Sa 22:2,32 [e] Ps 72:3 [f] 2Ch 19:7,9; Isa 11:1-5
23:4 [g] Jdg 5:31; Ps 89:36
23:5 [h] Ps 89:29; Isa 55:3
23:6 [i] Mt 13:40-41
23:9 [j] 1Ch 27:4 [k] 1Ch 8:4

[a] *1* Or *Israel's beloved singer* [b] *8* Hebrew; some Septuagint manuscripts suggest *Ish-Bosheth*, that is, *Esh-Baal* (see also 1 Chron. 11:11 *Jashobeam*). [c] *8* Probably a variant of *Hacmonite* (see 1 Chron. 11:11) [d] *8* Some Septuagint manuscripts (see also 1 Chron. 11:11); Hebrew and other Septuagint manuscripts *Three; it was Adino the Eznite who killed eight hundred men* [e] *9* See 1 Chron. 11:13; Hebrew *gathered there.*

full of lentils, Israel's troops fled from them. 12But Shammah took
his stand in the middle of the field. He defended it and struck the
Philistines down, and the LORD brought about a great victory.
13During harvest time, three of the thirty chief men came down
to David at the cave of Adullam,[a] while a band of Philistines was
encamped in the Valley of Rephaim.[b] 14At that time David was in
the stronghold,[c] and the Philistine garrison was at Bethlehem.[d]
15David longed for water and said, "Oh, that someone would get
me a drink of water from the well near the gate of Bethlehem!"
16So the three mighty men broke through the Philistine lines,
drew water from the well near the gate of Bethlehem and carried
it back to David. But he refused to drink it; instead, he poured[e] it
out before the LORD. 17"Far be it from me, O LORD, to do this!" he
said. "Is it not the blood[f] of men who went at the risk of their
lives?" And David would not drink it.

Such were the exploits of the three mighty men.

18Abishai[g] the brother of Joab son of Zeruiah was chief of the
Three.[a] He raised his spear against three hundred men, whom he
killed, and so he became as famous as the Three. 19Was he not held
in greater honor than the Three? He became their commander,
even though he was not included among them.

20Benaiah[h] son of Jehoiada was a valiant fighter from Kabzeel,[i]
who performed great exploits. He struck down two of Moab's best
men. He also went down into a pit on a snowy day and killed a lion.
21And he struck down a huge Egyptian. Although the Egyptian had
a spear in his hand, Benaiah went against him with a club. He
snatched the spear from the Egyptian's hand and killed him with
his own spear. 22Such were the exploits of Benaiah son of Jehoiada; he too was as famous as the three mighty men. 23He was held
in greater honor than any of the Thirty, but he was not included
among the Three. And David put him in charge of his bodyguard.

24Among the Thirty were:
Asahel[j] the brother of Joab,
Elhanan son of Dodo from Bethlehem,
25Shammah the Harodite,[k]
Elika the Harodite,
26Helez[l] the Paltite,
Ira son of Ikkesh from Tekoa,
27Abiezer from Anathoth,[m]
Mebunnai[b] the Hushathite,
28Zalmon the Ahohite,
Maharai[n] the Netophathite,[o]

23:13 [a] 1Sa 22:1 [b] 2Sa 5:18
23:14 [c] 1Sa 22:4-5 [d] Ru 1:19
23:16 [e] Ge 35:14
23:17 [f] Lev 17:10-12
23:18 [g] 2Sa 10:10,14; 1Ch 11:20
23:20 [h] 2Sa 8:18; 20:23 [i] Jos 15:21
23:24 [j] 2Sa 2:18
23:25 [k] Jdg 7:1; 1Ch 11:27
23:26 [l] 1Ch 27:10
23:27 [m] Jos 21:18
23:28 [n] 1Ch 27:13 [o] 2Ki 25:23; Ne 7:26

a *18* Most Hebrew manuscripts (see also 1 Chron. 11:20); two Hebrew manuscripts and Syriac *Thirty* b *27* Hebrew; some Septuagint manuscripts (see also 1 Chron. 11:29) *Sibbecai*

29Heled[a] son of Baanah the Netophathite,
Ithai son of Ribai from Gibeah[a] in Benjamin,
30Benaiah the Pirathonite,[b]
Hiddai[b] from the ravines of Gaash,[c]
31Abi-Albon the Arbathite,
Azmaveth the Barhumite,[d]
32Eliahba the Shaalbonite,
the sons of Jashen,
Jonathan 33son of[c] Shammah the Hararite,
Ahiam son of Sharar[d] the Hararite,
34Eliphelet son of Ahasbai the Maacathite,
Eliam[e] son of Ahithophel[f] the Gilonite,
35Hezro the Carmelite,[g]
Paarai the Arbite,
36Igal son of Nathan from Zobah,[h]
the son of Hagri,[e]
37Zelek the Ammonite,
Naharai the Beerothite, the armor-bearer of Joab son of Zeruiah,
38Ira the Ithrite,[i]
Gareb the Ithrite
39and Uriah[j] the Hittite.
There were thirty-seven in all.

Chapter 24 Theme

24 Again[k] the anger of the LORD burned against Israel, and he
incited David against them, saying, "Go and take a census of[l] Israel and Judah."
2So the king said to Joab[m] and the army commanders[f] with him,
"Go throughout the tribes of Israel from Dan to Beersheba[n] and
enroll the fighting men, so that I may know how many there are."
3But Joab replied to the king, "May the LORD your God multiply
the troops a hundred times over,[o] and may the eyes of my lord the
king see it. But why does my lord the king want to do such a thing?"
4The king's word, however, overruled Joab and the army commanders; so they left the presence of the king to enroll the fighting men of Israel.
5After crossing the Jordan, they camped near Aroer,[p] south of
the town in the gorge, and then went through Gad and on to Jazer.[q] 6They went to Gilead and the region of Tahtim Hodshi, and

a29 Some Hebrew manuscripts and Vulgate (see also 1 Chron. 11:30); most Hebrew manuscripts *Heleb* b30 Hebrew; some Septuagint manuscripts (see also 1 Chron. 11:32) *Hurai* c33 Some Septuagint manuscripts (see also 1 Chron. 11:34); Hebrew does not have *son of.* d33 Hebrew; some Septuagint manuscripts (see also 1 Chron. 11:35) *Sacar* e36 Some Septuagint manuscripts (see also 1 Chron. 11:38); Hebrew *Haggadi* f2 Septuagint (see also verse 4 and 1 Chron. 21:2); Hebrew *Joab the army commander*

23:29 *a* Jos 15:57
23:30 *b* Jdg 12:13 *c* Jos 24:30
23:31 *d* 2Sa 3:16
23:34 *e* 2Sa 11:3 *f* 2Sa 15:12
23:35 *g* Jos 12:22
23:36 *h* 1Sa 14:47
23:38 *i* 2Sa 20:26; 1Ch 2:53
23:39 *j* 2Sa 11:3
24:1 *k* Jos 9:15 *l* 1Ch 27:23
24:2 *m* 2Sa 20:23 *n* Jdg 20:1; 2Sa 3:10
24:3 *o* Dt 1:11
24:5 *p* Dt 2:36; Jos 13:9 *q* Nu 21:32

on to Dan Jaan and around toward Sidon.[a] 7Then they went toward
the fortress of Tyre[b] and all the towns of the Hivites and Canaanites. Finally, they went on to Beersheba[c] in the Negev[d] of Judah.
8After they had gone through the entire land, they came back
to Jerusalem at the end of nine months and twenty days.
9Joab reported the number of the fighting men to the king: In
Israel there were eight hundred thousand able-bodied men who
could handle a sword, and in Judah five hundred thousand.[e]
10David was conscience-stricken[f] after he had counted the
fighting men, and he said to the LORD, "I have sinned[g] greatly in
what I have done. Now, O LORD, I beg you, take away the guilt of
your servant. I have done a very foolish thing.[h]"
11Before David got up the next morning, the word of the LORD
had come to Gad[i] the prophet, David's seer:[j] 12"Go and tell
David, 'This is what the LORD says: I am giving you three options.
Choose one of them for me to carry out against you.'"
13So Gad went to David and said to him, "Shall there come
upon you three[a] years of famine[k] in your land? Or three months
of fleeing from your enemies while they pursue you? Or three
days of plague[l] in your land? Now then, think it over and decide
how I should answer the one who sent me."
14David said to Gad, "I am in deep distress. Let us fall into the
hands of the LORD, for his mercy[m] is great; but do not let me fall
into the hands of men."
15So the LORD sent a plague on Israel from that morning until
the end of the time designated, and seventy thousand of the people from Dan to Beersheba died.[n] 16When the angel stretched out
his hand to destroy Jerusalem, the LORD was grieved[o] because of
the calamity and said to the angel who was afflicting the people,
"Enough! Withdraw your hand." The angel of the LORD[p] was
then at the threshing floor of Araunah the Jebusite.
17When David saw the angel who was striking down the people, he said to the LORD, "I am the one who has sinned and done
wrong. These are but sheep.[q] What have they done? Let your hand
fall upon me and my family."[r]
18On that day Gad went to David and said to him, "Go up and
build an altar to the LORD on the threshing floor of Araunah the
Jebusite." 19So David went up, as the LORD had commanded
through Gad. 20When Araunah looked and saw the king and his
men coming toward him, he went out and bowed down before
the king with his face to the ground.
21Araunah said, "Why has my lord the king come to his servant?"
"To buy your threshing floor," David answered, "so I can build an
altar to the LORD, that the plague on the people may be stopped."[s]

24:6 [a] Ge 10:19; Jos 19:28; Jdg 1:31
24:7 [b] Jos 19:29 [c] Ge 21:22-33 [d] Dt 1:7; Jos 11:3
24:9 [e] Nu 1:44-46; 1Ch 21:5
24:10 [f] 1Sa 24:5 [g] 2Sa 12:13 [h] Nu 12:11; 1Sa 13:13
24:11 [i] 1Sa 22:5 [j] 1Sa 9:9; 1Ch 29:29
24:13 [k] Dt 28:38-42, 48; Eze 14:21 [l] Lev 26:25
24:14 [m] Ne 9:28; Ps 51:1; 103:8,13; 130:4
24:15 [n] 1Ch 27:24
24:16 [o] Ge 6:6; 1Sa 15:11 [p] Ex 12:23; Ac 12:23
24:17 [q] Ps 74:1 [r] Jnh 1:12
24:21 [s] Nu 16:44-50

[a] *13* Septuagint (see also 1 Chron. 21:12); Hebrew *seven*

[22]Araunah said to David, "Let my lord the king take whatever
pleases him and offer it up. Here are oxen[a] for the burnt offering, and here are threshing sledges and ox yokes for the wood.
[23]O king, Araunah gives[b] all this to the king." Araunah also said
to him, "May the LORD your God accept you."

[24]But the king replied to Araunah, "No, I insist on paying you
for it. I will not sacrifice to the LORD my God burnt offerings that
cost me nothing."[c]

So David bought the threshing floor and the oxen and paid fifty
shekels[a] of silver for them. [25]David built an altar[d] to the LORD there
and sacrificed burnt offerings and fellowship offerings.[b] Then the
LORD answered prayer[e] in behalf of the land, and the plague on
Israel was stopped.

[a] *24* That is, about 1 1/4 pounds (about 0.6 kilogram) [b] *25* Traditionally *peace offerings*

24:22
a 1Sa 6:14; 1Ki 19:21

24:23
b Eze 20:40-41

24:24
c Mal 1:13-14

24:25
d 1Sa 7:17
e 2Sa 21:14

2 Samuel at a Glance

heme of 2 Samuel:

uthor:

ate:

urpose:

ey Words:

Segment Divisions		Chapter Themes
		1
		2
		3
		4
		5
		6
		7
		8
		9
		10
		11
		12
		13
		14
		15
		16
		17
		18
		19
		20
		21
		22
		23
		24

1 KINGS

David—the warrior, the great king, the man loved but chastened by God—was getting old. At the end of his life many people were vying for his throne. First Kings, which records the final events of David's life, begins a new era for Israel, one that begins with untold glory and ends with apostasy.

The account of the kings who followed David is full of wonderful but sobering lessons. It is the history of Israel and their God, who made them a people of his own possession.

We don't know who wrote 1 Kings. We only know that this is God's Word preserved "to teach us, so that through endurance and the encouragement of the Scriptures we might have hope" (Romans 15:4).

Things to Do

General Information

Chapter 12 of 1 Kings records a dramatic, pivotal point in the history of Israel. Therefore as we study 1 Kings, we will divide it into two segments with two sets of instructions.

Chapters 1-11

Read through this first segment of 1 Kings one chapter at a time.

1. Remember, you are studying the lives of real people. Observe the opportunities God gives them, his instructions to them, and how they respond. Watch when they succeed and when they fail; note why—and learn! Ask God to speak to your heart. In the margin of each chapter, if applicable, make a list of these two things: "Lessons for Life" (LFL) and "Insights about God" (△).

2. Mark in a distinctive way the following words and phrases: *word (promise, command)*, or any reference to the *word of the Lord, heart (wholeheartedly, hearts, mind, thought), pray (prays, praying, cry, cried, called, declared, shouted), covenant (treaty), wisdom (wise), command (give orders, told, word, commands), promise (word, promises, promised), high places, house* (when it refers to God's house, their place of worship), and *sin (commit, wrong, sinned, committed)*. The first occurrence of the word *sin* is in chapter 8.

   a. List the key words on an index card and use it as a bookmark while you study this segment of 1 Kings.

   b. When you read "*and the Lord said,*" "*the Lord said,*" or "*the Lord asked,*" highlight or underline what the Lord said. Then underline anything you want to remember.

3. The main characters of these first chapters are David and Solomon. List in the margins what you learn about them.

   a. When you come to Solomon's reign, read Deuteronomy 7:2-6 and 17:14-20 to understand Solomon's actions as he took over the kingdom. Remember that sin was to be judged and murderers were to be put to death; otherwise the land would be polluted.

   b. Second Chronicles 1 through 9 is an excellent cross-reference on 1 Kings 1 through 11.

4. Mark every reference to time.

5. After you finish reading a chapter, record the theme or subject of that chapter next to the chapter number in the text and on the appropriate place on 1 KINGS AT A GLANCE on page 598.

6. When you finish chapter 11 see if any of the first eleven chapters can be grouped under a common theme or as part of an event: e.g. the building of the temple. These are called segment divisions and can be recorded in the designated place on 1 KINGS AT A GLANCE.

Chapters 12-22

1. As you read chapter 12 study the chart ISRAEL'S DIVISION AND CAPTIVITY on page 575. Note the division of the kingdom which occurred in 931 B.C. Write this date at the beginning of chapter 12. From this point on whenever "Israel" is used you will need to distinguish whether it is a reference to the ten tribes of the northern kingdom (which it will usually be) or to the nation of Israel as a whole.

2. Add *according to, like, as, in accordance with,* and *keeping with* to your key word list. When you come to these phrases, note what was "according to," "in accordance with," or "in keeping with" what. You will gain some important insights. Mark your key words in this section.

3. Watch for insights the Lord gives you about himself, his ways, and about life in general through the example of the kings and God's people. Record these in the margin under "Insights about God" or "Lessons for Life" just as you did in the first segment of 1 Kings.

4. When you read of a king or another key figure consult THE HISTORICAL CHART OF THE KINGS AND PROPHETS OF ISRAEL AND JUDAH, which is located on pages 651 through 653 between 2 Kings and 1 Chronicles.

5. Each time you finish reading about a king, record your insights on the chart THE KINGS OF ISRAEL AND JUDAH on pages 654 and 655 between 2 Kings and 1 Chronicles. Also fill in the information on Solomon.

   a. Make sure you note on the chart whether each king ruled over the northern (Israel) or southern (Judah) kingdom.

   b. Mark every reference to time. You might find it helpful to record in the margin the dates the king reigned. These are on the chart THE KINGS OF ISRAEL AND JUDAH.

6. In chapter 17, when you come to Elijah, in the margin compile a list of everything you learn about this prophet. Also compare 17:1 with Deuteronomy 28:1, 2, 12, 15, 23, 24 and James 5:17, 18. What could be the scriptural basis for Elijah's prayer and word to Ahab? Think about it.

7. Record the chapter themes and any segment divisions you see on 1 KINGS AT A GLANCE. Also fill in any other pertinent information. Choose a theme for 1 Kings which best describes what happens during this period in Israel's history.

8. Second Kings is a continuation of 1 Kings. You will want to study it next.

Things to Think About

1. Have you seen God's graciousness and slowness to anger? God doesn't retaliate, but rather brings us to repentance and obedience. What does this provoke in your heart? And how should you live if he is in control of your life?

2. Have you seen how a person can start well in his walk with the Lord and then turn away? What do you think causes this? What can you do to prevent this in your own life? Go back and review what you have listed in the margin regarding the kings and their relationship with the Lord. What lessons have you learned that you can apply to your life?

3. Did you notice the sovereignty of God—how he turns hearts, directs spirits, raises up and puts down kings and others in order to accomplish his purpose and will? Are you living in the light of this truth about God?

4. Have you been thinking that you had to be absolutely perfect before God could use you? Did you see how Elijah was a man "of like passions" just like you and yet God used him? What have you learned in 1 Kings? When David's life was over, didn't God call David a man after his own heart? Frailties and all, David was a man of God because he believed and obeyed God.

David's Family Tree Related to 1 Kings

David

Amnon (killed by Absalom) — **Daniel** (Kileab) (died in youth) — **Absalom** (killed by Joab) — **Adonijah** (deposed by Solomon and killed by Benaiah, son of Jehoiada, by order of Solomon) — **Solomon**

According to 2 Samuel 5:13-16; 1 Chronicles 3:1-9; 14:3-7, there were fourteen other sons: **Shephatiah, Ithream, Eliphelet, Shammua, Shobab, Nathan, Ibhar, Elishama, Eliphelet, Nogah, Nepheg, Japhia, Eliada, Elishua.**

Chapter 1 Theme ______________________

1 When King David was old and well advanced in years, he could
not keep warm even when they put covers over him. 2 So his
servants said to him, "Let us look for a young virgin to attend the
king and take care of him. She can lie beside him so that our lord
the king may keep warm."
3 Then they searched throughout Israel for a beautiful girl and
found Abishag, a Shunammite,[a] and brought her to the king. 4 The
girl was very beautiful; she took care of the king and waited on
him, but the king had no intimate relations with her.
5 Now Adonijah,[b] whose mother was Haggith, put himself forward and said, "I will be king." So he got chariots[c] and horses[a]
ready, with fifty men to run ahead of him. 6 (His father had never
interfered[d] with him by asking, "Why do you behave as you do?"
He was also very handsome and was born next after Absalom.)
7 Adonijah conferred with Joab[e] son of Zeruiah and with Abiathar[f] the priest, and they gave him their support. 8 But Zadok[g]
the priest, Benaiah[h] son of Jehoiada, Nathan[i] the prophet, Shimei[j]
and Rei[b] and David's special guard[k] did not join Adonijah.
9 Adonijah then sacrificed sheep, cattle and fattened calves at
the Stone of Zoheleth near En Rogel.[l] He invited all his brothers,
the king's sons, and all the men of Judah who were royal officials,
10 but he did not invite Nathan the prophet or Benaiah or the special guard or his brother Solomon.[m]
11 Then Nathan asked Bathsheba,[n] Solomon's mother, "Have
you not heard that Adonijah,[o] the son of Haggith, has become
king without our lord David's knowing it? 12 Now then, let me
advise[p] you how you can save your own life and the life of your
son Solomon. 13 Go in to King David and say to him, 'My lord the
king, did you not swear[q] to me your servant: "Surely Solomon
your son shall be king after me, and he will sit on my throne"?
Why then has Adonijah become king?' 14 While you are still there
talking to the king, I will come in and confirm what you have said."

[a] 5 Or *charioteers* [b] 8 Or *and his friends*

1:3 [a] Jos 19:18
1:5 [b] 2Sa 3:4 [c] 2Sa 15:1
1:6 [d] 2Sa 3:3-4
1:7 [e] 1Ki 2:22,28; 1Ch 11:6 [f] 1Sa 22:20; 2Sa 20:25
1:8 [g] 2Sa 20:25 [h] 2Sa 8:18 [i] 2Sa 12:1 [j] 1Ki 4:18 [k] 2Sa 23:8
1:9 [l] 2Sa 17:17
1:10 [m] 2Sa 12:24
1:11 [n] 2Sa 12:24 [o] 2Sa 3:4
1:12 [p] Pr 15:22
1:13 [q] ver 30; 1Ch 22:9-13

1:15 15So Bathsheba went to see the aged king in his room, where
[a]ver 1 Abishag[a] the Shunammite was attending him. 16Bathsheba bowed
low and knelt before the king.
"What is it you want?" the king asked.
17She said to him, "My lord, you yourself swore[b] to me your ser-
1:17 [b]ver 13,30 vant by the LORD your God: 'Solomon your son shall be king after
me, and he will sit on my throne.' 18But now Adonijah has become
king, and you, my lord the king, do not know about it. 19He has
sacrificed[c] great numbers of cattle, fattened calves, and sheep, and
has invited all the king's sons, Abiathar the priest and Joab the
1:19 [c]ver 9 commander of the army, but he has not invited Solomon your
servant. 20My lord the king, the eyes of all Israel are on you, to
learn from you who will sit on the throne of my lord the king after
him. 21Otherwise, as soon as my lord the king is laid to rest[d] with
his fathers, I and my son Solomon will be treated as criminals."
1:21 [d]Dt 31:16; 1Ki 2:10 22While she was still speaking with the king, Nathan the prophet
arrived. 23And they told the king, "Nathan the prophet is here." So
he went before the king and bowed with his face to the ground.
24Nathan said, "Have you, my lord the king, declared that Adonijah shall be king after you, and that he will sit on your throne?
1:26 [e]ver 8,10 25Today he has gone down and sacrificed great numbers of cattle,
fattened calves, and sheep. He has invited all the king's sons, the
commanders of the army and Abiathar the priest. Right now they
are eating and drinking with him and saying, 'Long live King
Adonijah!' 26But me your servant, and Zadok the priest, and
1:29 [f]2Sa 4:9 Benaiah son of Jehoiada, and your servant Solomon he did not
invite.[e] 27Is this something my lord the king has done without letting his servants know who should sit on the throne of my lord
the king after him?"
28Then King David said, "Call in Bathsheba." So she came into
1:30 [g]ver 13,17 the king's presence and stood before him.
29The king then took an oath: "As surely as the LORD lives, who
has delivered me out of every trouble,[f] 30I will surely carry out
today what I swore[g] to you by the LORD, the God of Israel: Solomon
1:33 your son shall be king after me, and he will sit on my throne in
[h]2Sa 20:6-7 my place."
[i]2Ch 32:30; 33:14 31Then Bathsheba bowed low with her face to the ground and,
kneeling before the king, said, "May my lord King David live forever!"
32King David said, "Call in Zadok the priest, Nathan the prophet
1:34 and Benaiah son of Jehoiada." When they came before the king,
[j]1Sa 10:1; 33he said to them: "Take your lord's servants with you and set
16:3,12; Solomon my son on my own mule[h] and take him down to Gihon.[i]
1Ki 19:16; 2Ki 9:3,13 34There have Zadok the priest and Nathan the prophet anoint[j]
[k]ver 25; 2Sa 5:3; 15:10 him king over Israel. Blow the trumpet[k] and shout, 'Long live King

Solomon!' 35Then you are to go up with him, and he is to come and sit on my throne and reign in my place. I have appointed him ruler over Israel and Judah."

36Benaiah son of Jehoiada answered the king, "Amen! May the LORD, the God of my lord the king, so declare it. 37As the LORD was with my lord the king, so may he be with[a] Solomon to make his throne even greater[b] than the throne of my lord King David!"

38So Zadok[c] the priest, Nathan the prophet, Benaiah son of Jehoiada, the Kerethites[d] and the Pelethites went down and put Solomon on King David's mule and escorted him to Gihon.[e] 39Zadok the priest took the horn of oil[f] from the sacred tent and anointed Solomon. Then they sounded the trumpet and all the people shouted,[g] "Long live King Solomon!" 40And all the people went up after him, playing flutes and rejoicing greatly, so that the ground shook with the sound.

41Adonijah and all the guests who were with him heard it as they were finishing their feast. On hearing the sound of the trumpet, Joab asked, "What's the meaning of all the noise in the city?"

42Even as he was speaking, Jonathan[h] son of Abiathar the priest arrived. Adonijah said, "Come in. A worthy man like you must be bringing good news."[i]

43"Not at all!" Jonathan answered. "Our lord King David has made Solomon king. 44The king has sent with him Zadok the priest, Nathan the prophet, Benaiah son of Jehoiada, the Kerethites and the Pelethites, and they have put him on the king's mule, 45and Zadok the priest and Nathan the prophet have anointed him king at Gihon. From there they have gone up cheering, and the city resounds[j] with it. That's the noise you hear. 46Moreover, Solomon has taken his seat on the royal throne. 47Also, the royal officials have come to congratulate our lord King David, saying, 'May your God make Solomon's name more famous than yours and his throne greater[k] than yours!' And the king bowed in worship on his bed 48and said, 'Praise be to the LORD, the God of Israel, who has allowed my eyes to see a successor[l] on my throne today.'"

49At this, all Adonijah's guests rose in alarm and dispersed. 50But Adonijah, in fear of Solomon, went and took hold of the horns[m] of the altar. 51Then Solomon was told, "Adonijah is afraid of King Solomon and is clinging to the horns of the altar. He says, 'Let King Solomon swear to me today that he will not put his servant to death with the sword.'"

52Solomon replied, "If he shows himself to be a worthy man, not a hair[n] of his head will fall to the ground; but if evil is found in him, he will die." 53Then King Solomon sent men, and they brought him down from the altar. And Adonijah came and bowed down to King Solomon, and Solomon said, "Go to your home."

1:37 [a] Jos 1:5,17; 1Sa 20:13 [b] ver 47
1:38 [c] ver 8 [d] 2Sa 8:18 [e] ver 33
1:39 [f] Ex 30:23-32; Ps 89:20 [g] ver 34; 1Sa 10:24
1:42 [h] 2Sa 15:27,36 [i] 2Sa 18:26
1:45 [j] ver 40
1:47 [k] ver 37; Ge 47:31
1:48 [l] 2Sa 7:12; 1Ki 3:6
1:50 [m] 1Ki 2:28
1:52 [n] 1Sa 14:45; 2Sa 14:11

Chapter 2 Theme ______________________________

2

When the time drew near for David to die,[a] he gave a charge
to Solomon his son.
2“I am about to go the way of all the earth,”[b] he said. “So be
strong,[c] show yourself a man, 3and observe[d] what the LORD your
God requires: Walk in his ways, and keep his decrees and commands, his laws and requirements, as written in the Law of
Moses, so that you may prosper[e] in all you do and wherever you
go, 4and that the LORD may keep his promise[f] to me: ‘If your
descendants watch how they live, and if they walk faithfully[g]
before me with all their heart and soul, you will never fail to have
a man on the throne of Israel.’
5“Now you yourself know what Joab[h] son of Zeruiah did to
me—what he did to the two commanders of Israel’s armies,
Abner[i] son of Ner and Amasa[j] son of Jether. He killed them,
shedding their blood in peacetime as if in battle, and with that
blood stained the belt around his waist and the sandals on his
feet. 6Deal with him according to your wisdom,[k] but do not let
his gray head go down to the grave[a] in peace.
7“But show kindness to the sons of Barzillai[l] of Gilead and let
them be among those who eat at your table.[m] They stood by me
when I fled from your brother Absalom.
8“And remember, you have with you Shimei[n] son of Gera, the
Benjamite from Bahurim, who called down bitter curses on me
the day I went to Mahanaim. When he came down to meet me at
the Jordan, I swore[o] to him by the LORD: ‘I will not put you to
death by the sword.’ 9But now, do not consider him innocent.
You are a man of wisdom;[p] you will know what to do to him.
Bring his gray head down to the grave in blood.”
10Then David rested with his fathers and was buried[q] in the City
of David.[r] 11He had reigned[s] forty years over Israel—seven years
in Hebron and thirty-three in Jerusalem. 12So Solomon sat on the
throne[t] of his father David, and his rule was firmly established.[u]
13Now Adonijah, the son of Haggith, went to Bathsheba, Solomon’s mother. Bathsheba asked him, “Do you come peacefully?”[v]
He answered, “Yes, peacefully.” 14Then he added, “I have something to say to you.”
“You may say it,” she replied.
15“As you know,” he said, “the kingdom was mine. All Israel
looked to me as their king. But things changed, and the kingdom
has gone to my brother; for it has come to him from the LORD.
16Now I have one request to make of you. Do not refuse me.”
“You may make it,” she said.

2:1 [a] Ge 47:29; Dt 31:14
2:2 [b] Jos 23:14 [c] Dt 31:7,23; Jos 1:6
2:3 [d] Dt 17:14-20; Jos 1:7 [e] 1Ch 22:13
2:4 [f] 2Sa 7:13,25; 1Ki 8:25 [g] 2Ki 20:3; Ps 132:12
2:5 [h] 2Sa 2:18; 18:5,12,14 [i] 2Sa 3:27 [j] 2Sa 20:10
2:6 [k] ver 9
2:7 [l] 2Sa 17:27; 19:31-39 [m] 2Sa 9:7
2:8 [n] 2Sa 16:5-13 [o] 2Sa 19:18-23
2:9 [p] ver 6
2:10 [q] Ac 2:29; 13:36 [r] 2Sa 5:7
2:11 [s] 2Sa 5:4,5
2:12 [t] 1Ch 29:23 [u] 2Ch 1:1
2:13 [v] 1Sa 16:4

[a] 6 Hebrew *Sheol*; also in verse 9

17 So he continued, "Please ask King Solomon—he will not
refuse you—to give me Abishag[a] the Shunammite as my wife."
18 "Very well," Bathsheba replied, "I will speak to the king for
you."
19 When Bathsheba went to King Solomon to speak to him for
Adonijah, the king stood up to meet her, bowed down to her and
sat down on his throne. He had a throne brought for the king's
mother,[b] and she sat down at his right hand.[c]
20 "I have one small request to make of you," she said. "Do not
refuse me."
The king replied, "Make it, my mother; I will not refuse you."
21 So she said, "Let Abishag[d] the Shunammite be given in marriage to your brother Adonijah."
22 King Solomon answered his mother, "Why do you request
Abishag[e] the Shunammite for Adonijah? You might as well request
the kingdom for him—after all, he is my older brother[f]—yes, for
him and for Abiathar the priest and Joab son of Zeruiah!"
23 Then King Solomon swore by the LORD: "May God deal with
me, be it ever so severely,[g] if Adonijah does not pay with his life
for this request! 24 And now, as surely as the LORD lives—he who
has established me securely on the throne of my father David and
has founded a dynasty for me as he promised[h]—Adonijah shall
be put to death today!" 25 So King Solomon gave orders to Benaiah[i] son of Jehoiada, and he struck down Adonijah and he died.
26 To Abiathar[j] the priest the king said, "Go back to your fields in
Anathoth.[k] You deserve to die, but I will not put you to death now,
because you carried the ark[l] of the Sovereign LORD before my
father David and shared all my father's hardships."[m] 27 So Solomon
removed Abiathar from the priesthood of the LORD, fulfilling[n] the
word the LORD had spoken at Shiloh about the house of Eli.
28 When the news reached Joab, who had conspired with Adonijah though not with Absalom, he fled to the tent of the LORD and
took hold of the horns[o] of the altar. 29 King Solomon was told that
Joab had fled to the tent of the LORD and was beside the altar.
Then Solomon ordered Benaiah[p] son of Jehoiada, "Go, strike
him down!"
30 So Benaiah entered the tent of the LORD and said to Joab,
"The king says, 'Come out![q]'"
But he answered, "No, I will die here."
Benaiah reported to the king, "This is how Joab answered me."
31 Then the king commanded Benaiah, "Do as he says. Strike
him down and bury him, and so clear me and my father's house
of the guilt of the innocent blood[r] that Joab shed. 32 The LORD will
repay[s] him for the blood he shed,[t] because without the knowledge of my father David he attacked two men and killed them

2:17 [a] 1Ki 1:3
2:19 [b] 1Ki 15:13 [c] Ps 45:9
2:21 [d] 1Ki 1:3
2:22 [e] 2Sa 12:8; 1Ki 1:3 [f] 1Ch 3:2
2:23 [g] Ru 1:17
2:24 [h] 2Sa 7:11; 1Ch 22:10
2:25 [i] 2Sa 8:18
2:26 [j] 1Sa 22:20 [k] Jos 21:18 [l] 2Sa 15:24 [m] 1Sa 23:6
2:27 [n] 1Sa 2:27-36
2:28 [o] 1Ki 1:7,50
2:29 [p] ver 25
2:30 [q] Ex 21:14
2:31 [r] Nu 35:33; Dt 19:13; 21:8-9
2:32 [s] Jdg 9:57; Ps 7:16 [t] Jdg 9:24

with the sword. Both of them—Abner son of Ner, commander
of Israel's army, and Amasa[a] son of Jether, commander of Judah's
army—were better[b] men and more upright than he. 33 May the
guilt of their blood rest on the head of Joab and his descendants
forever. But on David and his descendants, his house and his
throne, may there be the LORD's peace forever."
34 So Benaiah son of Jehoiada went up and struck down Joab
and killed him, and he was buried on his own land[a] in the desert.
35 The king put Benaiah[c] son of Jehoiada over the army in Joab's
position and replaced Abiathar with Zadok[d] the priest.
36 Then the king sent for Shimei[e] and said to him, "Build yourself a house in Jerusalem and live there, but do not go anywhere
else. 37 The day you leave and cross the Kidron Valley,[f] you can be
sure you will die; your blood will be on your own head."[g]
38 Shimei answered the king, "What you say is good. Your servant will do as my lord the king has said." And Shimei stayed in
Jerusalem for a long time.
39 But three years later, two of Shimei's slaves ran off to Achish[h]
son of Maacah, king of Gath, and Shimei was told, "Your slaves
are in Gath." 40 At this, he saddled his donkey and went to Achish
at Gath in search of his slaves. So Shimei went away and brought
the slaves back from Gath.
41 When Solomon was told that Shimei had gone from Jerusalem
to Gath and had returned, 42 the king summoned Shimei and said
to him, "Did I not make you swear by the LORD and warn you,
'On the day you leave to go anywhere else, you can be sure you
will die'? At that time you said to me, 'What you say is good. I will
obey.' 43 Why then did you not keep your oath to the LORD and obey
the command I gave you?"
44 The king also said to Shimei, "You know in your heart all the
wrong[i] you did to my father David. Now the LORD will repay you
for your wrongdoing. 45 But King Solomon will be blessed, and
David's throne will remain secure[j] before the LORD forever."
46 Then the king gave the order to Benaiah son of Jehoiada, and
he went out and struck Shimei down and killed him.
The kingdom was now firmly established[k] in Solomon's hands.

Chapter 3 Theme ______________________________

3 Solomon made an alliance with Pharaoh king of Egypt and
married[l] his daughter.[m] He brought her to the City of David[n]
until he finished building his palace[o] and the temple of the LORD,
and the wall around Jerusalem. 2 The people, however, were still sacrificing at the high places,[p] because a temple had not yet been built

2:32
[a] 2Sa 3:27; 20:10
[b] 2Ch 21:13
2:35
[c] 1Ki 4:4
[d] ver 27; 1Ch 29:22
2:36
[e] ver 8; 2Sa 16:5
2:37
[f] 2Sa 15:23
[g] Lev 20:9; Jos 2:19; 2Sa 1:16
2:39
[h] 1Sa 27:2
2:44
[i] 1Sa 25:39; 2Sa 16:5-13; Eze 17:19
2:45
[j] 2Sa 7:13; Pr 25:5
2:46
[k] ver 12; 2Ch 1:1
3:1
[l] 1Ki 7:8
[m] 1Ki 9:24
[n] 2Sa 5:7
[o] 1Ki 7:1; 9:15,19
3:2
[p] Lev 17:3-5; Dt 12:2,4-5; 1Ki 22:43

[a] *34* Or *buried in his tomb*

for the Name of the LORD. 3Solomon showed his love[a] for the LORD by walking according to the statutes[b] of his father David, except that he offered sacrifices and burned incense on the high places.

4The king went to Gibeon[c] to offer sacrifices, for that was the most important high place, and Solomon offered a thousand burnt offerings on that altar. 5At Gibeon the LORD appeared[d] to Solomon during the night in a dream,[e] and God said, "Ask for whatever you want me to give you."

6Solomon answered, "You have shown great kindness to your servant, my father David, because he was faithful[f] to you and righteous and upright in heart. You have continued this great kindness to him and have given him a son[g] to sit on his throne this very day.

7"Now, O LORD my God, you have made your servant king in place of my father David. But I am only a little child[h] and do not know how to carry out my duties. 8Your servant is here among the people you have chosen,[i] a great people, too numerous to count or number.[j] 9So give your servant a discerning[k] heart to govern your people and to distinguish[l] between right and wrong. For who is able[m] to govern this great people of yours?"

10The Lord was pleased that Solomon had asked for this. 11So God said to him, "Since you have asked[n] for this and not for long life or wealth for yourself, nor have asked for the death of your enemies but for discernment in administering justice, 12I will do what you have asked.[o] I will give you a wise[p] and discerning heart, so that there will never have been anyone like you, nor will there ever be. 13Moreover, I will give you what you have not[q] asked for—both riches and honor[r]—so that in your lifetime you will have no equal[s] among kings. 14And if you walk[t] in my ways and obey my statutes and commands as David your father did, I will give you a long life."[u] 15Then Solomon awoke[v]—and he realized it had been a dream.

He returned to Jerusalem, stood before the ark of the Lord's covenant and sacrificed burnt offerings[w] and fellowship offerings.[a][x] Then he gave a feast[y] for all his court.

16Now two prostitutes came to the king and stood before him. 17One of them said, "My lord, this woman and I live in the same house. I had a baby while she was there with me. 18The third day after my child was born, this woman also had a baby. We were alone; there was no one in the house but the two of us.

19"During the night this woman's son died because she lay on him. 20So she got up in the middle of the night and took my son from my side while I your servant was asleep. She put him by her breast and put her dead son by my breast. 21The next morning, I

3:3 [a]Dt 6:5; Ps 31:23; 1Co 8:3 [b]1Ki 2:3; 9:4; 11:4,6,38

3:4 [c]1Ch 16:39

3:5 [d]1Ki 9:2 [e]Nu 12:6; Mt 1:20

3:6 [f]1Ki 2:4; 9:4 [g]1Ki 1:48

3:7 [h]Nu 27:17; 1Ch 29:1

3:8 [i]Dt 7:6 [j]Ge 15:5

3:9 [k]2Sa 14:17; Jas 1:5 [l]Pr 2:3-9; Heb 5:14 [m]Ps 72:1-2

3:11 [n]Jas 4:3

3:12 [o]1Jn 5:14-15 [p]1Ki 4:29,30,31; 5:12; 10:23; Ecc 1:16

3:13 [q]Mt 6:33; Eph 3:20 [r]1Ki 4:21-24; Pr 3:1-2,16 [s]1Ki 10:23

3:14 [t]ver 6; Pr 3:1-2,16 [u]Ps 61:6; 91:16

3:15 [v]Ge 41:7 [w]1Ki 8:65 [x]Mk 6:21 [y]Est 1:3,9; Da 5:1

a *15* Traditionally *peace offerings*

3:26 [a]Ge 43:30; Isa 49:15; Jer 31:20; Hos 11:8
3:28 [b]ver 9,11-12; Col 2:3
4:2 [c]1Ch 6:10
4:3 [d]2Sa 8:16
4:4 [e]1Ki 2:35 [f]1Ki 2:27
4:8 [g]Jos 24:33
4:9 [h]Jdg 1:35 [i]Jos 21:16

got up to nurse my son—and he was dead! But when I looked at
him closely in the morning light, I saw that it wasn't the son I had
borne."

22 The other woman said, "No! The living one is my son; the
dead one is yours."

But the first one insisted, "No! The dead one is yours; the living
one is mine." And so they argued before the king.

23 The king said, "This one says, 'My son is alive and your son is
dead,' while that one says, 'No! Your son is dead and mine is alive.'"

24 Then the king said, "Bring me a sword." So they brought a
sword for the king.
25 He then gave an order: "Cut the living child
in two and give half to one and half to the other."

26 The woman whose son was alive was filled with compassion[a]
for her son and said to the king, "Please, my lord, give her the living baby! Don't kill him!"

But the other said, "Neither I nor you shall have him. Cut him
in two!"

27 Then the king gave his ruling: "Give the living baby to the
first woman. Do not kill him; she is his mother."

28 When all Israel heard the verdict the king had given, they
held the king in awe, because they saw that he had wisdom[b] from
God to administer justice.

Chapter 4 Theme ____________________

4 So King Solomon ruled over all Israel.
2 And these were his
chief officials:

Azariah[c] son of Zadok—the priest;
3 Elihoreph and Ahijah, sons of Shisha—secretaries;
Jehoshaphat[d] son of Ahilud—recorder;
4 Benaiah[e] son of Jehoiada—commander in chief;
Zadok[f] and Abiathar—priests;
5 Azariah son of Nathan—in charge of the district officers;
Zabud son of Nathan—a priest and personal adviser to the king;
6 Ahishar—in charge of the palace;
Adoniram son of Abda—in charge of forced labor.

7 Solomon also had twelve district governors over all Israel,
who supplied provisions for the king and the royal household.
Each one had to provide supplies for one month in the year.
8 These are their names:

Ben-Hur—in the hill country[g] of Ephraim;
9 Ben-Deker—in Makaz, Shaalbim,[h] Beth Shemesh[i] and Elon Bethhanan;

[10]Ben-Hesed—in Arubboth (Socoh[a] and all the land of Hepher[b] were his);
[11]Ben-Abinadab—in Naphoth Dor[a c] (he was married to Taphath daughter of Solomon);
[12]Baana son of Ahilud—in Taanach and Megiddo, and in all of Beth Shan[d] next to Zarethan[e] below Jezreel, from Beth Shan to Abel Meholah[f] across to Jokmeam;[g]
[13]Ben-Geber—in Ramoth Gilead (the settlements of Jair[h] son of Manasseh in Gilead were his, as well as the district of Argob in Bashan and its sixty large walled cities[i] with bronze gate bars);

Solomon's Kingdom

[14]Ahinadab son of Iddo—in Mahanaim;[j]
[15]Ahimaaz[k]—in Naphtali (he had married Basemath daughter of Solomon);
[16]Baana son of Hushai[l]—in Asher and in Aloth;
[17]Jehoshaphat son of Paruah—in Issachar;
[18]Shimei[m] son of Ela—in Benjamin;
[19]Geber son of Uri—in Gilead (the country of Sihon king of the Amorites and the country of Og[n] king of Bashan). He was the only governor over the district.

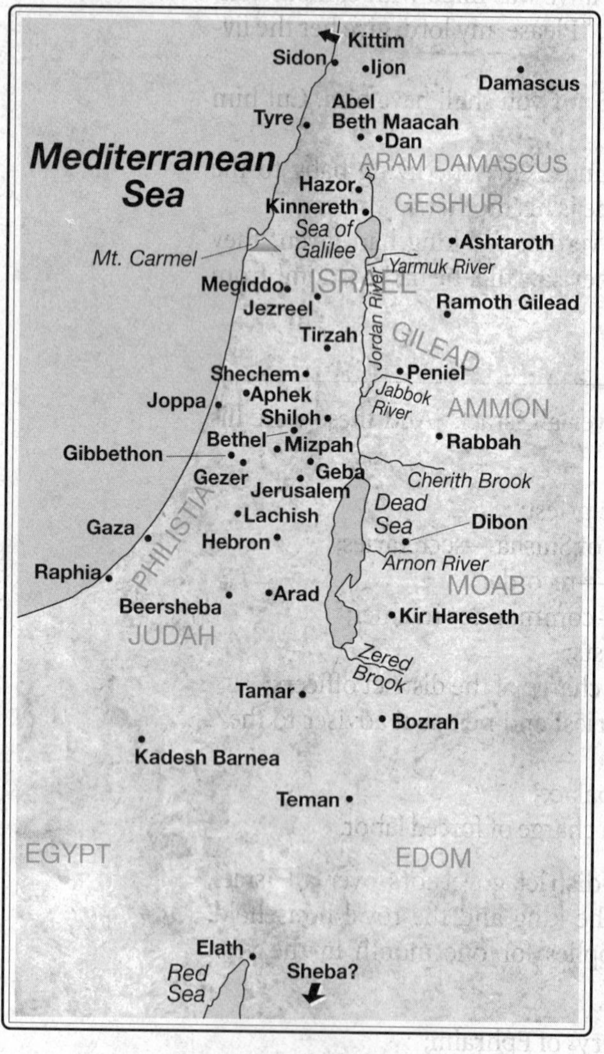

[20]The people of Judah and Israel were as numerous as the sand[o] on the seashore; they ate, they drank and they were happy.
[21]And Solomon ruled[p] over all the kingdoms from the River[b q] to the land of the Philistines, as far as the border of Egypt.[r] These countries brought tribute[s] and were Solomon's subjects all his life.

[22]Solomon's daily provisions were thirty cors[c] of fine flour and sixty cors[d] of meal,

[a]*11* Or *in the heights of Dor* [b]*21* That is, the Euphrates; also in verse 24 [c]*22* That is, probably about 185 bushels (about 6.6 kiloliters) [d]*22* That is, probably about 375 bushels (about 13.2 kiloliters)

4:10 [a]Jos 15:35 [b]Jos 12:17
4:11 [c]Jos 11:2
4:12 [d]Jos 17:11; Jdg 5:19 [e]Jos 3:16 [f]1Ki 19:16 [g]1Ch 6:68
4:13 [h]Nu 32:41 [i]Dt 3:4
4:14 [j]Jos 13:26
4:15 [k]2Sa 15:27
4:16 [l]2Sa 15:32
4:18 [m]1Ki 1:8
4:19 [n]Dt 3:8-10
4:20 [o]Ge 22:17; 32:12; 1Ki 3:8
4:21 [p]2Ch 9:26; Ps 72:11 [q]Jos 1:4; Ps 72:8 [r]Ge 15:18 [s]Ps 68:29

23ten head of stall-fed cattle, twenty of pasture-fed cattle and a
hundred sheep and goats, as well as deer, gazelles, roebucks and
choice fowl. 24For he ruled over all the kingdoms west of the River, from Tiphsah[a] to Gaza, and had peace[b] on all sides. 25During
Solomon's lifetime Judah and Israel, from Dan to Beersheba,[c]
lived in safety,[d] each man under his own vine and fig tree.[e]

26Solomon had four[a] thousand stalls for chariot horses,[f] and
twelve thousand horses.[b]

27The district officers,[g] each in his month, supplied provisions
for King Solomon and all who came to the king's table. They saw
to it that nothing was lacking. 28They also brought to the proper
place their quotas of barley and straw for the chariot horses and
the other horses.

29God gave Solomon wisdom[h] and very great insight, and a
breadth of understanding as measureless as the sand on the
seashore. 30Solomon's wisdom was greater than the wisdom of all
the men of the East,[i] and greater than all the wisdom of Egypt.[j]
31He was wiser[k] than any other man, including Ethan the Ezrahite—wiser than Heman, Calcol and Darda, the sons of Mahol.
And his fame spread to all the surrounding nations. 32He spoke
three thousand proverbs[l] and his songs[m] numbered a thousand
and five. 33He described plant life, from the cedar of Lebanon to
the hyssop that grows out of walls. He also taught about animals
and birds, reptiles and fish. 34Men of all nations came to listen to
Solomon's wisdom, sent by all the kings[n] of the world, who had
heard of his wisdom.

Chapter 5 Theme ________________

5 When Hiram[o] king of Tyre heard that Solomon had been
anointed king to succeed his father David, he sent his envoys to Solomon, because he had always been on friendly terms
with David. 2Solomon sent back this message to Hiram:

3"You know that because of the wars[p] waged against my
father David from all sides, he could not build a temple for
the Name of the LORD his God until the LORD put his enemies
under his feet. 4But now the LORD my God has given me rest[q]
on every side, and there is no adversary or disaster. 5I intend,
therefore, to build a temple[r] for the Name of the LORD my
God, as the LORD told my father David, when he said, 'Your
son whom I will put on the throne in your place will build the
temple for my Name.'[s]

6"So give orders that cedars of Lebanon be cut for me. My
men will work with yours, and I will pay you for your men

4:24 [a]Ps 72:11 [b]1Ch 22:9
4:25 [c]Jdg 20:1 [d]Jer 23:6 [e]Mic 4:4; Zec 3:10
4:26 [f]1Ki 10:26; 2Ch 1:14
4:27 [g]ver 7
4:29 [h]1Ki 3:12
4:30 [i]Ge 25:6 [j]Ac 7:22
4:31 [k]1Ki 3:12; 1Ch 2:6; 6:33; 15:19; Ps 89 Title
4:32 [l]Pr 1:1; Ecc 12:9 [m]SS 1:1
4:34 [n]1Ki 10:1; 2Ch 9:23
5:1 [o]ver 10,18; 2Sa 5:11; 1Ch 14:1
5:3 [p]1Ch 22:8; 28:3
5:4 [q]1Ki 4:24; 1Ch 22:9
5:5 [r]1Ch 17:12 [s]2Sa 7:13; 1Ch 22:10

[a]26 Some Septuagint manuscripts (see also 2 Chron. 9:25); Hebrew *forty* [b]26 Or *charioteers*

whatever wages you set. You know that we have no one so
skilled in felling timber as the Sidonians."

7When Hiram heard Solomon's message, he was greatly pleased
and said, "Praise be to the LORD today, for he has given David a
wise son to rule over this great nation."
8So Hiram sent word to Solomon:

> "I have received the message you sent me and will do all
> you want in providing the cedar and pine logs. 9My men will
> haul them down from Lebanon to the sea[a], and I will float
> them in rafts by sea to the place you specify. There I will sepa-
> rate them and you can take them away. And you are to grant
> my wish by providing food[b] for my royal household."

10In this way Hiram kept Solomon supplied with all the cedar
and pine logs he wanted, 11and Solomon gave Hiram twenty thousand cors[a] of wheat as food for his household, in addition to twenty thousand baths[b,c] of pressed olive oil. Solomon continued to do
this for Hiram year after year. 12The LORD gave Solomon wisdom,[c]
just as he had promised him. There were peaceful relations between Hiram and Solomon, and the two of them made a treaty.[d]
13King Solomon conscripted laborers[e] from all Israel—thirty
thousand men. 14He sent them off to Lebanon in shifts of ten
thousand a month, so that they spent one month in Lebanon and
two months at home. Adoniram[f] was in charge of the forced
labor. 15Solomon had seventy thousand carriers and eighty thousand stonecutters in the hills, 16as well as thirty-three hundred[d]
foremen[g] who supervised the project and directed the workmen.
17At the king's command they removed from the quarry[h] large
blocks of quality stone[i] to provide a foundation of dressed stone
for the temple. 18The craftsmen of Solomon and Hiram and the
men of Gebal[e][j] cut and prepared the timber and stone for the
building of the temple.

Chapter 6 Theme ________________________________

6 In the four hundred and eightieth[f] year after the Israelites
had come out of Egypt, in the fourth year of Solomon's reign
over Israel, in the month of Ziv, the second month, he began to
build the temple of the LORD.[k]
2The temple[l] that King Solomon built for the LORD was sixty
cubits long, twenty wide and thirty high.[g] 3The portico at the front
of the main hall of the temple extended the width of the temple,

[a] *11* That is, probably about 125,000 bushels (about 4,400 kiloliters) [b] *11* Septuagint (see also 2 Chron. 2:10); Hebrew *twenty cors* [c] *11* That is, about 115,000 gallons (about 440 kiloliters) [d] *16* Hebrew; some Septuagint manuscripts (see also 2 Chron. 2:2, 18) *thirty-six hundred* [e] *18* That is, Byblos [f] *1* Hebrew; Septuagint *four hundred and fortieth* [g] *2* That is, about 90 feet (about 27 meters) long and 30 feet (about 9 meters) wide and 45 feet (about 13.5 meters) high

5:9 [a] Ezr 3:7 [b] Eze 27:17; Ac 12:20
5:12 [c] 1Ki 3:12 [d] Am 1:9
5:13 [e] 1Ki 9:15
5:14 [f] 1Ki 4:6; 2Ch 10:18
5:16 [g] 1Ki 9:23
5:17 [h] 1Ki 6:7 [i] 1Ch 22:2
5:18 [j] Jos 13:5
6:1 [k] Ac 7:47
6:2 [l] Eze 41:1

The Jewish Calendar

Babylonian names (B) for the months are still used today for the Jewish calendar. Canaanite names (C) were used prior to the Babylonian captivity in 586 B.C. Four are mentioned in the Old Testament. **Adar-Sheni** is an intercalary month used every two to three years or seven times in 19 years.

1st month	2nd month	3rd month	4th month
Nisan (B) Abib (C) March-April	Iyyar (B) Ziv (C) April-May	Sivan (B) May-June	Tammuz (B) June-July
7th month	*8th month*	*9th month*	*10th month*
5th month	**6th month**	**7th month**	**8th month**
Ab (B) July-August	Elul (B) August-September	Tishri (B) Ethanim (C) September-October	Marcheshvan (B) Bul (C) October-November
11th month	*12th month*	*1st month*	*2nd month*
9th month	**10th month**	**11th month**	**12th month**
Chislev (B) November-December	Tebeth (B) December-January	Shebat (B) January-February	Adar (B) February-March
3rd month	*4th month*	*5th month*	*6th month*

Sacred calendar appears in black • Civil calendar appears in gray

that is twenty cubits,[a] and projected ten cubits[b] from the front of
the temple. 4He made narrow clerestory windows[a] in the temple.
5Against the walls of the main hall and inner sanctuary he built a
structure around the building, in which there were side rooms.[b]
6The lowest floor was five cubits[c] wide, the middle floor six cubits[d]
and the third floor seven.[e] He made offset ledges around the outside of the temple so that nothing would be inserted into the temple
walls.

7In building the temple, only blocks dressed[c] at the quarry were
used, and no hammer, chisel or any other iron tool[d] was heard at
the temple site while it was being built.

8The entrance to the lowest[f] floor was on the south side of the
temple; a stairway led up to the middle level and from there to
the third. 9So he built the temple and completed it, roofing it with
beams and cedar[e] planks. 10And he built the side rooms all along
the temple. The height of each was five cubits, and they were attached to the temple by beams of cedar.

11The word of the LORD came to Solomon: 12"As for this temple
you are building, if you follow my decrees, carry out my regulations and keep all my commands and obey them, I will fulfill
through you the promise[f] I gave to David your father. 13And I will
live among the Israelites and will not abandon[g] my people Israel."

14So Solomon built the temple and completed[h] it. 15He lined its
interior walls with cedar boards, paneling them from the floor of
the temple to the ceiling,[i] and covered the floor of the temple

6:4 *a* Eze 40:16; 41:16
6:5 *b* ver 16,19-21; Eze 41:5-6
6:7 *c* Ex 20:25 *d* Dt 27:5
6:9 *e* ver 14,38
6:12 *f* 2Sa 7:12-16; 1Ki 2:4; 9:5
6:13 *g* Ex 25:8; Lev 26:11; Dt 31:6; Heb 13:5
6:14 *h* ver 9,38
6:15 *i* 1Ki 7:7

a3 That is, about 30 feet (about 9 meters) b3 That is, about 15 feet (about 4.5 meters) c6 That is, about 7 1/2 feet (about 2.3 meters); also in verses 10 and 24 d6 That is, about 9 feet (about 2.7 meters) e6 That is, about 10 1/2 feet (about 3.1 meters) f8 Septuagint; Hebrew *middle*

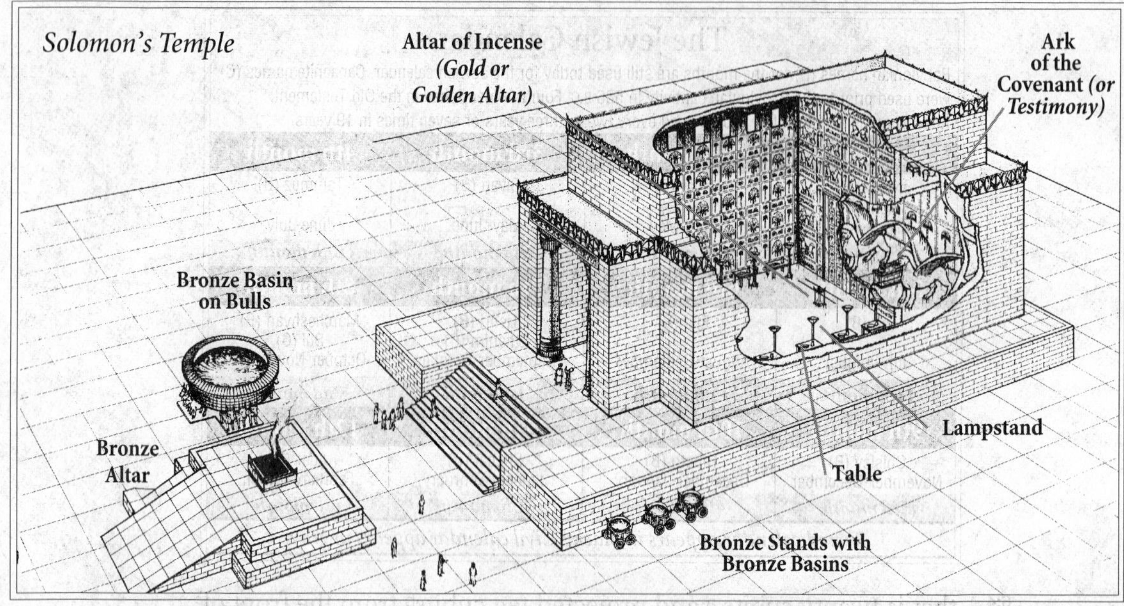

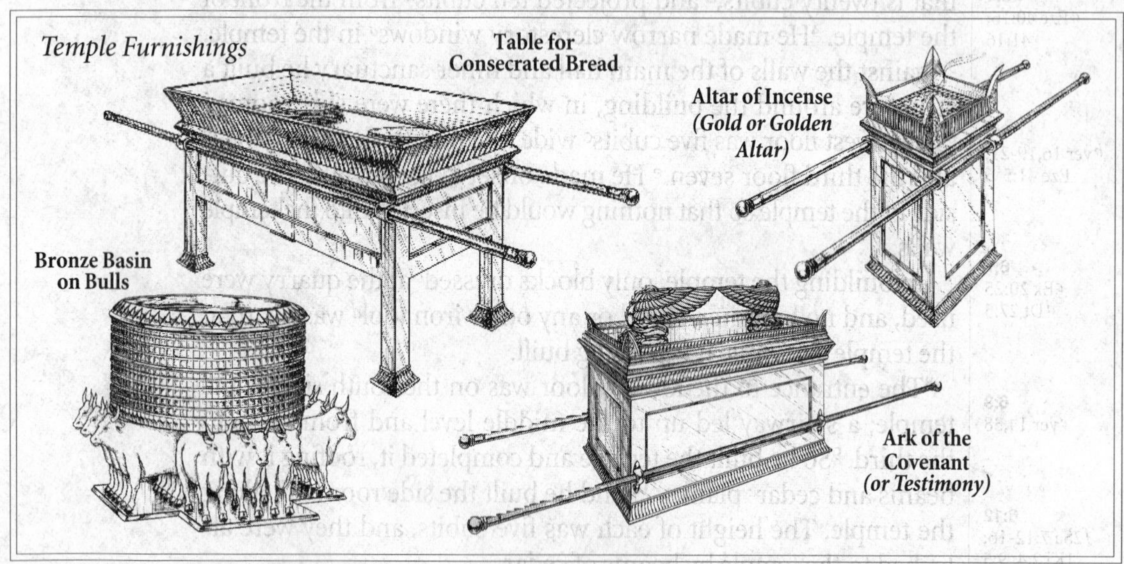

with planks of pine. 16He partitioned off twenty cubits[a] at the rear
of the temple with cedar boards from floor to ceiling to form
within the temple an inner sanctuary, the Most Holy Place.[a] 17The
main hall in front of this room was forty cubits[b] long. 18The inside
of the temple was cedar,[b] carved with gourds and open flowers.
Everything was cedar; no stone was to be seen.
19He prepared the inner sanctuary[c] within the temple to set the
ark of the covenant[d] of the LORD there. 20The inner sanctuary[e] was
twenty cubits long, twenty wide and twenty high.[c] He overlaid

a *16* That is, about 30 feet (about 9 meters) b *17* That is, about 60 feet (about 18 meters)
c *20* That is, about 30 feet (about 9 meters) long, wide and high

6:16 *a* Ex 26:33; Lev 16:2; 1Ki 8:6
6:18 *b* 1Ki 7:24; Ps 74:6
6:19 *c* 1Ki 8:6 *d* 1Sa 3:3
6:20 *e* Eze 41:3-4

6:23 the inside with pure gold, and he also overlaid the altar of cedar.
[a]Ex 37:1-9 21 Solomon covered the inside of the temple with pure gold, and
he extended gold chains across the front of the inner sanctuary,
which was overlaid with gold. 22 So he overlaid the whole interior
with gold. He also overlaid with gold the altar that belonged to
the inner sanctuary.

23 In the inner sanctuary he made a pair of cherubim[a] of olive
6:27 wood, each ten cubits[a] high. 24 One wing of the first cherub was
[b]Ex 25:20; 37:9; 1Ki 8:7; 2Ch 5:8 five cubits long, and the other wing five cubits—ten cubits from
wing tip to wing tip. 25 The second cherub also measured ten
cubits, for the two cherubim were identical in size and shape.
26 The height of each cherub was ten cubits. 27 He placed the
cherubim[b] inside the innermost room of the temple, with their
wings spread out. The wing of one cherub touched one wall,
6:29 while the wing of the other touched the other wall, and their
[c]ver 32,35 wings touched each other in the middle of the room. 28 He overlaid the cherubim with gold.

29 On the walls all around the temple, in both the inner and outer rooms, he carved cherubim,[c] palm trees and open flowers.
30 He also covered the floors of both the inner and outer rooms of
the temple with gold.

6:36 [d]1Ki 7:12; 31 For the entrance of the inner sanctuary he made doors of
Ezr 6:4 olive wood with five-sided jambs. 32 And on the two olive wood
doors he carved cherubim, palm trees and open flowers, and
overlaid the cherubim and palm trees with beaten gold. 33 In the
same way he made four-sided jambs of olive wood for the entrance to the main hall. 34 He also made two pine doors, each having two leaves that turned in sockets. 35 He carved cherubim, palm
6:38 trees and open flowers on them and overlaid them with gold ham-
[e]Heb 8:5 mered evenly over the carvings.

36 And he built the inner courtyard of three courses[d] of dressed
stone and one course of trimmed cedar beams.

37 The foundation of the temple of the LORD was laid in the
fourth year, in the month of Ziv. 38 In the eleventh year in the
month of Bul, the eighth month, the temple was finished in all its
7:1 details according to its specifications.[e] He had spent seven years
[f]1Ki 9:10; 2Ch 8:1 building it.

Chapter 7 Theme ______________________________

7 It took Solomon thirteen years, however, to complete the
construction of his palace.[f] 2 He built the Palace[g] of the Forest of Lebanon[h] a hundred cubits long, fifty wide and thirty
7:2 high,[b] with four rows of cedar columns supporting trimmed

[g]2Sa 7:2
[h]1Ki 10:17; 2Ch 9:16

Close-up of Most Holy Place

[a] *23* That is, about 15 feet (about 4.5 meters) [b] *2* That is, about 150 feet (about 46 meters)
long, 75 feet (about 23 meters) wide and 45 feet (about 13.5 meters) high

cedar beams. 3It was roofed with cedar above the beams that rested on the columns—forty-five beams, fifteen to a row. 4Its windows were placed high in sets of three, facing each other. 5All the
doorways had rectangular frames; they were in the front part in
sets of three, facing each other.[a]

6He made a colonnade fifty cubits long and thirty wide.[b] In front
of it was a portico, and in front of that were pillars and an overhanging roof.

7He built the throne hall, the Hall of Justice, where he was to
judge,[a] and he covered it with cedar from floor to ceiling.[c][b] 8And
the palace in which he was to live, set farther back, was similar in
design. Solomon also made a palace like this hall for Pharaoh's
daughter, whom he had married.[c]

9All these structures, from the outside to the great courtyard and
from foundation to eaves, were made of blocks of high-grade stone
cut to size and trimmed with a saw on their inner and outer faces.
10The foundations were laid with large stones of good quality,
some measuring ten cubits[d] and some eight.[e] 11Above were high-
grade stones, cut to size, and cedar beams. 12The great courtyard
was surrounded by a wall of three courses[d] of dressed stone and
one course of trimmed cedar beams, as was the inner courtyard
of the temple of the LORD with its portico.

13King Solomon sent to Tyre and brought Huram,[f][e] 14whose
mother was a widow from the tribe of Naphtali and whose father
was a man of Tyre and a craftsman in bronze. Huram was highly
skilled[f] and experienced in all kinds of bronze work. He came to
King Solomon and did all[g] the work assigned to him.

15He cast two bronze pillars,[h] each eighteen cubits high and
twelve cubits around,[g] by line. 16He also made two capitals[i] of cast
bronze to set on the tops of the pillars; each capital was five cubits[h]
high. 17A network of interwoven chains festooned the capitals on
top of the pillars, seven for each capital. 18He made pomegranates
in two rows[i] encircling each network to decorate the capitals on
top of the pillars.[j] He did the same for each capital. 19The capitals
on top of the pillars in the portico were in the shape of lilies, four
cubits[k] high. 20On the capitals of both pillars, above the bowl-
shaped part next to the network, were the two hundred pomegranates[j] in rows all around. 21He erected the pillars at the
portico of the temple. The pillar to the south he named Jakin[l] and

7:7 [a]Ps 122:5; Pr 20:8 [b]1Ki 6:15
7:8 [c]1Ki 3:1; 2Ch 8:11
7:12 [d]1Ki 6:36
7:13 [e]2Ch 2:13
7:14 [f]Ex 31:2-5; 35:31; 36:1; 2Ch 2:14 [g]2Ch 4:11,16
7:15 [h]2Ki 25:17; 2Ch 3:15; 4:12; 52:17,21
7:16 [i]2Ki 25:17
7:20 [j]2Ch 3:16; 4:13; Jer 52:23

[a] *5* The meaning of the Hebrew for this verse is uncertain. [b] *6* That is, about 75 feet (about 23 meters) long and 45 feet (about 13.5 meters) wide [c] *7* Vulgate and Syriac; Hebrew *floor* [d] *10* That is, about 15 feet (about 4.5 meters) [e] *10* That is, about 12 feet (about 3.6 meters) [f] *13* Hebrew *Hiram,* a variant of *Huram;* also in verses 40 and 45 [g] *15* That is, about 27 feet (about 8.1 meters) high and 18 feet (about 5.4 meters) around [h] *16* That is, about 7 1/2 feet (about 2.3 meters); also in verse 23 [i] *18* Two Hebrew manuscripts and Septuagint; most Hebrew manuscripts *made the pillars, and there were two rows* [j] *18* Many Hebrew manuscripts and Syriac; most Hebrew manuscripts *pomegranates* [k] *19* That is, about 6 feet (about 1.8 meters); also in verse 38 [l] *21* *Jakin* probably means *he establishes.*

7:21 [a] 1Ki 6:3; the one to the north Boaz.[a] [a] 22The capitals on top were in the shape
2Ch 3:17 of lilies. And so the work on the pillars was completed.
23He made the Sea[b] of cast metal, circular in shape, measuring
ten cubits[b] from rim to rim and five cubits high. It took a line of
thirty cubits[c] to measure around it. 24Below the rim, gourds encircled it—ten to a cubit. The gourds were cast in two rows in
one piece with the Sea.
25The Sea stood on twelve bulls,[c] three facing north, three facing
7:23 west, three facing south and three facing east. The Sea rested on
[b] 2Ki 25:13; top of them, and their hindquarters were toward the center. 26It
1Ch 18:8; was a handbreadth[d] in thickness, and its rim was like the rim of a
Jer 52:17 cup, like a lily blossom. It held two thousand baths.[e]
27He also made ten movable stands[d] of bronze; each was four
cubits long, four wide and three high.[f] 28This is how the stands
were made: They had side panels attached to uprights. 29On the
panels between the uprights were lions, bulls and cherubim—and
on the uprights as well. Above and below the lions and bulls were
wreaths of hammered work. 30Each stand[e] had four bronze wheels
7:25 with bronze axles, and each had a basin resting on four supports,
[c] 2Ch 4:4-5; cast with wreaths on each side. 31On the inside of the stand there
Jer 52:20 was an opening that had a circular frame one cubit[g] deep. This
opening was round, and with its basework it measured a cubit
and a half.[h] Around its opening there was engraving. The panels
of the stands were square, not round. 32The four wheels were
under the panels, and the axles of the wheels were attached to the
stand. The diameter of each wheel was a cubit and a half. 33The
7:27 wheels were made like chariot wheels; the axles, rims, spokes and
[d] ver 38; hubs were all of cast metal.
2Ch 4:14 34Each stand had four handles, one on each corner, projecting
from the stand. 35At the top of the stand there was a circular band
half a cubit[i] deep. The supports and panels were attached to the
top of the stand. 36He engraved cherubim, lions and palm trees on
the surfaces of the supports and on the panels, in every available
space, with wreaths all around. 37This is the way he made the ten
stands. They were all cast in the same molds and were identical in
7:30 size and shape.
[e] 2Ki 16:17 38He then made ten bronze basins,[f] each holding forty baths[j]
and measuring four cubits across, one basin to go on each of the
ten stands. 39He placed five of the stands on the south side of the
temple and five on the north. He placed the Sea on the south side,

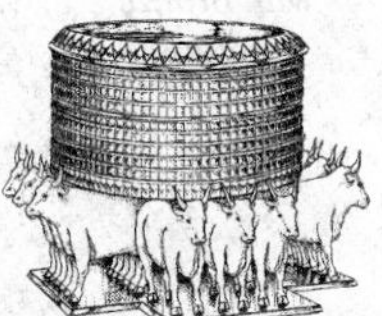

Bronze Basin on Bulls

[a] *21* *Boaz* probably means *in him is strength.* [b] *23* That is, about 15 feet (about 4.5 meters)
[c] *23* That is, about 45 feet (about 13.5 meters) [d] *26* That is, about 3 inches (about 8
centimeters) [e] *26* That is, probably about 11,500 gallons (about 44 kiloliters); the Septuagint
does not have this sentence. [f] *27* That is, about 6 feet (about 1.8 meters) long and wide and
7:38 about 4 1/2 feet (about 1.3 meters) high [g] *31* That is, about 1 1/2 feet (about 0.5 meter)
[f] Ex 30:18; [h] *31* That is, about 2 1/4 feet (about 0.7 meter); also in verse 32 [i] *35* That is, about 3/4 foot
2Ch 4:6 (about 0.2 meter) [j] *38* That is, about 230 gallons (about 880 liters)

Bronze Stand
with Bronze
Basin

at the southeast corner of the temple. 40He also made the basins
and shovels and sprinkling bowls.

So Huram finished all the work he had undertaken for King
Solomon in the temple of the LORD:

41the two pillars;
the two bowl-shaped capitals on top of the pillars;
the two sets of network decorating the two bowl-shaped
capitals on top of the pillars;
42the four hundred pomegranates for the two sets of network
(two rows of pomegranates for each network, decorating
the bowl-shaped capitals[a] on top of the pillars);
43the ten stands with their ten basins;
44the Sea and the twelve bulls under it;
45the pots, shovels and sprinkling bowls.[b]

All these objects that Huram made for King Solomon for the
temple of the LORD were of burnished bronze. 46The king had them
cast in clay molds in the plain[c] of the Jordan between Succoth[d] and
Zarethan.[e] 47Solomon left all these things unweighed,[f] because
there were so many; the weight of the bronze was not determined.

48Solomon also made all the furnishings that were in the LORD's
temple:

the golden altar;
the golden table[g] on which was the bread of the Presence;[h]
49the lampstands[i] of pure gold (five on the right and five on
the left, in front of the inner sanctuary);
the gold floral work and lamps and tongs;
50the pure gold basins, wick trimmers, sprinkling bowls,
dishes and censers;[j]
and the gold sockets for the doors of the innermost room,
the Most Holy Place, and also for the doors of the main
hall of the temple.

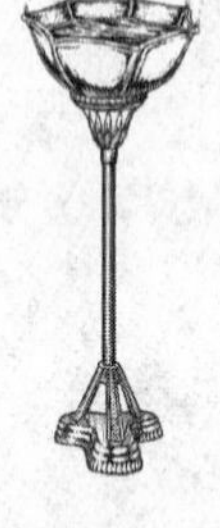

Lampstand

51When all the work King Solomon had done for the temple of
the LORD was finished, he brought in the things his father David
had dedicated[k]—the silver and gold and the furnishings—and
he placed them in the treasuries of the LORD's temple.

Chapter 8 Theme

8 Then King Solomon summoned into his presence at Jerusalem the elders of Israel, all the heads of the tribes and the
chiefs[l] of the Israelite families, to bring up the ark[m] of the LORD's
covenant from Zion, the City of David.[n] 2All the men of Israel
came together to King Solomon at the time of the festival[o] in the
month of Ethanim, the seventh month.[p]

7:42 [a]ver 20
7:45 [b]Ex 27:3
7:46 [c]2Ch 4:17 [d]Ge 33:17; Jos 13:27 [e]Jos 3:16
7:47 [f]1Ch 22:3
7:48 [g]Ex 37:10 [h]Ex 25:30
7:49 [i]Ex 25:31-38
7:50 [j]2Ki 25:13
7:51 [k]2Sa 8:11
8:1 [l]Nu 7:2 [m]2Sa 6:17 [n]2Sa 5:7
8:2 [o]2Ch 7:8 [p]Lev 23:34

3 When all the elders of Israel had arrived, the priests[a] took up
the ark, 4 and they brought up the ark of the LORD and the Tent of
Meeting[b] and all the sacred furnishings in it. The priests and
Levites carried them up, 5 and King Solomon and the entire
assembly of Israel that had gathered about him were before the
ark, sacrificing[c] so many sheep and cattle that they could not be
recorded or counted.

6 The priests then brought the ark of the LORD's covenant[d] to its
place in the inner sanctuary of the temple, the Most Holy Place,
and put it beneath the wings of the cherubim.[e] 7 The cherubim
spread their wings over the place of the ark and overshadowed the
ark and its carrying poles. 8 These poles were so long that their
ends could be seen from the Holy Place in front of the inner sanctuary, but not from outside the Holy Place; and they are still there
today.[f] 9 There was nothing in the ark except the two stone tablets[g]
that Moses had placed in it at Horeb, where the LORD made a
covenant with the Israelites after they came out of Egypt.

10 When the priests withdrew from the Holy Place, the cloud[h]
filled the temple of the LORD. 11 And the priests could not perform
their service because of the cloud, for the glory of the LORD filled
his temple.

12 Then Solomon said, "The LORD has said that he would dwell in
a dark cloud;[i] 13 I have indeed built a magnificent temple for you, a
place for you to dwell[j] forever."

14 While the whole assembly of Israel was standing there, the king
turned around and blessed[k] them. 15 Then he said:

"Praise be to the LORD,[l] the God of Israel, who with his own
hand has fulfilled what he promised with his own mouth to my
father David. For he said, 16 'Since the day I brought my people
Israel out of Egypt, I have not chosen a city in any tribe of Israel to have a temple built for my Name[m] to be there, but I have
chosen[n] David[o] to rule my people Israel.'

17 "My father David had it in his heart to build a temple[p] for
the Name of the LORD, the God of Israel. 18 But the LORD said
to my father David, 'Because it was in your heart to build a
temple for my Name, you did well to have this in your heart.
19 Nevertheless, you[q] are not the one to build the temple, but
your son, who is your own flesh and blood—he is the one
who will build the temple for my Name.'[r]

20 "The LORD has kept the promise he made: I have succeeded
David my father and now I sit on the throne of Israel, just as
the LORD promised, and I have built[s] the temple for the Name
of the LORD, the God of Israel. 21 I have provided a place there
for the ark, in which is the covenant of the LORD that he made
with our fathers when he brought them out of Egypt."

8:3 [a] Nu 7:9; Jos 3:3
8:4 [b] 1Ki 3:4; 2Ch 1:3
8:5 [c] 2Sa 6:13
8:6 [d] 2Sa 6:17 [e] 1Ki 6:19,27
8:8 [f] Ex 25:13-15
8:9 [g] Ex 24:7-8; 25:21; 40:20; Dt 10:2-5; Heb 9:4
8:10 [h] Ex 40:34-35; 2Ch 7:1-2
8:12 [i] Ps 18:11; 97:2
8:13 [j] Ex 15:17; 2Sa 7:13; Ps 132:13
8:14 [k] 2Sa 6:18
8:15 [l] 2Sa 7:12-13; 1Ch 29:10,20; Ne 9:5; Lk 1:68
8:16 [m] Dt 12:5 [n] 1Sa 16:1 [o] 2Sa 7:4-6,8
8:17 [p] 2Sa 7:2; 1Ch 17:1
8:19 [q] 2Sa 7:5 [r] 2Sa 7:13; 1Ki 5:3,5
8:20 [s] 1Ch 28:6

INSIGHT

See the illustration of Solomon's Temple on page IISB-36.

[22]Then Solomon stood before the altar of the LORD in front of
the whole assembly of Israel, spread out his hands[a] toward heaven
[23]and said:

"O LORD, God of Israel, there is no God like[b] you in heaven
above or on earth below—you who keep your covenant of
love[c] with your servants who continue wholeheartedly in your
way. [24]You have kept your promise to your servant David my
father; with your mouth you have promised and with your
hand you have fulfilled it—as it is today.

[25]"Now LORD, God of Israel, keep for your servant David my
father the promises[d] you made to him when you said, 'You
shall never fail to have a man to sit before me on the throne of
Israel, if only your sons are careful in all they do to walk
before me as you have done.' [26]And now, O God of Israel, let
your word that you promised[e] your servant David my father
come true.

[27]"But will God really dwell[f] on earth? The heavens, even the
highest heaven, cannot contain[g] you. How much less this temple I have built! [28]Yet give attention to your servant's prayer
and his plea for mercy, O LORD my God. Hear the cry and the
prayer that your servant is praying in your presence this day.
[29]May your eyes be open[h] toward[i] this temple night and day,
this place of which you said, 'My Name[j] shall be there,' so that
you will hear the prayer your servant prays toward this place.
[30]Hear the supplication of your servant and of your people
Israel when they pray toward this place. Hear from heaven,
your dwelling place, and when you hear, forgive.[k]

[31]"When a man wrongs his neighbor and is required to take
an oath and he comes and swears the oath[l] before your altar
in this temple, [32]then hear from heaven and act. Judge between
your servants, condemning the guilty and bringing down on
his own head what he has done. Declare the innocent not
guilty, and so establish his innocence.[m]

[33]"When your people Israel have been defeated[n] by an enemy
because they have sinned[o] against you, and when they turn
back to you and confess your name, praying and making supplication to you in this temple, [34]then hear from heaven and
forgive the sin of your people Israel and bring them back to the
land you gave to their fathers.

[35]"When the heavens are shut up and there is no rain[p]
because your people have sinned against you, and when they
pray toward this place and confess your name and turn from
their sin because you have afflicted them, [36]then hear from
heaven and forgive the sin of your servants, your people Israel.

8:22 [a]Ex 9:29; Ezr 9:5
8:23 [b]1Sa 2:2; 2Sa 7:22 [c]Dt 7:9,12; Ne 1:5; 9:32; Da 9:4
8:25 [d]1Ki 2:4
8:26 [e]2Sa 7:25
8:27 [f]Ac 7:48 [g]2Ch 2:6; Ps 139:7-16; Isa 66:1; Jer 23:24
8:29 [h]2Ch 7:15; Ne 1:6 [i]Da 6:10 [j]Dt 12:11
8:30 [k]Ps 85:2
8:31 [l]Ex 22:11
8:32 [m]Dt 25:1
8:33 [n]Lev 26:17; Dt 28:25 [o]Lev 26:39
8:35 [p]Lev 26:19; Dt 28:24

Teach[a] them the right way[b] to live, and send rain on the land
you gave your people for an inheritance.
37“When famine[c] or plague comes to the land, or blight[d] or
mildew, locusts or grasshoppers, or when an enemy besieges
them in any of their cities, whatever disaster or disease may
come, 38and when a prayer or plea is made by any of your people Israel—each one aware of the afflictions of his own heart,
and spreading out his hands toward this temple— 39then hear
from heaven, your dwelling place. Forgive and act; deal with
each man according to all he does, since you know[e] his heart
(for you alone know the hearts of all men), 40so that they will
fear[f] you all the time they live in the land you gave our fathers.
41“As for the foreigner who does not belong to your people
Israel but has come from a distant land because of your
name— 42for men will hear of your great name and your
mighty hand[g] and your outstretched arm—when he comes
and prays toward this temple, 43then hear from heaven, your
dwelling place, and do whatever the foreigner asks of you, so
that all the peoples of the earth may know[h] your name and
fear[i] you, as do your own people Israel, and may know that
this house I have built bears your Name.
44“When your people go to war against their enemies, wherever you send them, and when they pray to the LORD toward
the city you have chosen and the temple I have built for your
Name, 45then hear from heaven their prayer and their plea,
and uphold their cause.
46“When they sin against you—for there is no one who does
not sin[j]—and you become angry with them and give them
over to the enemy, who takes them captive[k] to his own land, far
away or near; 47and if they have a change of heart in the land
where they are held captive, and repent and plead[l] with you in
the land of their conquerors and say, ‘We have sinned, we have
done wrong, we have acted wickedly’;[m] 48and if they turn back
to you with all their heart[n] and soul in the land of their enemies
who took them captive, and pray[o] to you toward the land you
gave their fathers, toward the city you have chosen and the
temple[p] I have built for your Name; 49then from heaven, your
dwelling place, hear their prayer and their plea, and uphold
their cause. 50And forgive your people, who have sinned against
you; forgive all the offenses they have committed against you,
and cause their conquerors to show them mercy;[q] 51for they
are your people and your inheritance,[r] whom you brought out
of Egypt, out of that iron-smelting furnace.[s]
52“May your eyes be open to your servant’s plea and to the
plea of your people Israel, and may you listen to them whenever

8:36 [a] 1Sa 12:23; Ps 25:4; 94:12 [b] Ps 5:8; 27:11; Jer 6:16
8:37 [c] Lev 26:26 [d] Dt 28:22
8:39 [e] 1Sa 16:7; 1Ch 28:9; Ps 11:4; Jer 17:10; Jn 2:24; Ac 1:24
8:40 [f] Ps 130:4
8:42 [g] Dt 3:24
8:43 [h] 1Sa 17:46; 2Ki 19:19 [i] Ps 102:15
8:46 [j] Pr 20:9; Ecc 7:20; Ro 3:9; 1Jn 1:8-10 [k] Lev 26:33-39; Dt 28:64
8:47 [l] Lev 26:40; Ne 1:6 [m] Ps 106:6; Da 9:5
8:48 [n] Dt 4:29; Jer 29:12-14 [o] Da 6:10 [p] Jnh 2:4
8:50 [q] 2Ch 30:9; Ps 106:46
8:51 [r] Dt 4:20; 9:29; Ne 1:10 [s] Jer 11:4

they cry out to you. 53 For you singled them out from all the
nations of the world to be your own inheritance,[a] just as you
declared through your servant Moses when you, O Sovereign
LORD, brought our fathers out of Egypt."

54 When Solomon had finished all these prayers and supplications to the LORD, he rose from before the altar of the LORD, where
he had been kneeling with his hands spread out toward heaven.
55 He stood and blessed[b] the whole assembly of Israel in a loud
voice, saying:

56 "Praise be to the LORD, who has given rest[c] to his people
Israel just as he promised. Not one word has failed of all the
good promises[d] he gave through his servant Moses. 57 May the
LORD our God be with us as he was with our fathers; may he
never leave us nor forsake[e] us. 58 May he turn our hearts[f] to
him, to walk in all his ways and to keep the commands,
decrees and regulations he gave our fathers. 59 And may these
words of mine, which I have prayed before the LORD, be near
to the LORD our God day and night, that he may uphold the
cause of his servant and the cause of his people Israel according to each day's need, 60 so that all the peoples[g] of the
earth may know that the LORD is God and that there is no
other.[h] 61 But your hearts must be fully committed[i] to the LORD
our God, to live by his decrees and obey his commands, as at
this time."

62 Then the king and all Israel with him offered sacrifices before
the LORD. 63 Solomon offered a sacrifice of fellowship offerings[a] to
the LORD: twenty-two thousand cattle and a hundred and twenty
thousand sheep and goats. So the king and all the Israelites dedicated the temple of the LORD.

64 On that same day the king consecrated the middle part of the
courtyard in front of the temple of the LORD, and there he offered
burnt offerings, grain offerings and the fat of the fellowship offerings, because the bronze altar[j] before the LORD was too small to
hold the burnt offerings, the grain offerings and the fat of the fellowship offerings.

65 So Solomon observed the festival[k] at that time, and all Israel
with him—a vast assembly, people from Lebo[b] Hamath[l] to the
Wadi of Egypt.[m] They celebrated it before the LORD our God for
seven days and seven days more, fourteen days in all. 66 On the
following day he sent the people away. They blessed the king and
then went home, joyful and glad in heart for all the good things
the LORD had done for his servant David and his people Israel.

[a]63 Traditionally *peace offerings*; also in verse 64 [b]65 Or *from the entrance to*

8:53 [a]Ex 19:5; Dt 9:26-29

8:55 [b]ver 14; 2Sa 6:18

8:56 [c]Dt 12:10 [d]Jos 21:45; 23:15

8:57 [e]Dt 31:6; Jos 1:5; Heb 13:5

8:58 [f]Ps 119:36

8:60 [g]Jos 4:24; 1Sa 17:46 [h]Dt 4:35; 1Ki 18:39; Jer 10:10-12

8:61 [i]1Ki 11:4; 15:3,14; 2Ki 20:3

8:64 [j]2Ch 4:1

8:65 [k]ver 2; Lev 23:34 [l]Nu 34:8; Jos 13:5; Jdg 3:3; 2Ki 14:25 [m]Ge 15:18

Chapter 9 Theme ____

9 When Solomon had finished[a] building the temple of the LORD and the royal palace, and had achieved all he had desired to do, 2the LORD appeared[b] to him a second time, as he had appeared to him at Gibeon. 3The LORD said to him:

"I have heard[c] the prayer and plea you have made before me; I have consecrated this temple, which you have built, by putting my Name there forever. My eyes[d] and my heart will always be there.

4"As for you, if you walk before me in integrity of heart[e] and uprightness, as David[f] your father did, and do all I command and observe my decrees and laws, 5I will establish[g] your royal throne over Israel forever, as I promised David your father when I said, 'You shall never fail[h] to have a man on the throne of Israel.'

6"But if you[a] or your sons turn away[i] from me and do not observe the commands and decrees I have given you[a] and go off to serve other gods and worship them, 7then I will cut off Israel from the land[j] I have given them and will reject this temple I have consecrated for my Name.[k] Israel will then become a byword[l] and an object of ridicule[m] among all peoples. 8And though this temple is now imposing, all who pass by will be appalled and will scoff and say, 'Why has the LORD done such a thing to this land and to this temple?'[n] 9People will answer, 'Because they have forsaken the LORD their God, who brought their fathers out of Egypt, and have embraced other gods, worshiping and serving them—that is why the LORD brought all this disaster on them.'"

10At the end of twenty years, during which Solomon built these two buildings—the temple of the LORD and the royal palace—11King Solomon gave twenty towns in Galilee to Hiram king of Tyre, because Hiram had supplied him with all the cedar and pine and gold[o] he wanted. 12But when Hiram went from Tyre to see the towns that Solomon had given him, he was not pleased with them. 13"What kind of towns are these you have given me, my brother?" he asked. And he called them the Land of Cabul,[b][p] a name they have to this day. 14Now Hiram had sent to the king 120 talents[c] of gold.

15Here is the account of the forced labor King Solomon conscripted[q] to build the LORD's temple, his own palace, the supporting terraces,[d][r] the wall of Jerusalem, and Hazor,[s] Megiddo and

a 6 The Hebrew is plural. b 13 *Cabul* sounds like the Hebrew for *good-for-nothing.*
c 14 That is, about 4 1/2 tons (about 4 metric tons) d 15 Or *the Millo;* also in verse 24

9:1 a 1Ki 7:1; 2Ch 8:6
9:2 b 1Ki 3:5
9:3 c 2Ki 20:5; Ps 10:17 d Dt 11:12; 1Ki 8:29
9:4 e Ge 17:1 f 1Ki 15:5
9:5 g 1Ch 22:10 h 2Sa 7:15; 1Ki 2:4
9:6 i 2Sa 7:14
9:7 j 2Ki 17:23; 25:21 k Jer 7:14 l Ps 44:14 m Dt 28:37
9:8 n Dt 29:24; Jer 22:8-9
9:11 o 2Ch 8:2
9:13 p Jos 19:27
9:15 q Jos 16:10; 1Ki 5:13 r ver 24; 2Sa 5:9 s Jos 19:36

Gezer.[a] 16(Pharaoh king of Egypt had attacked and captured Gezer.
He had set it on fire. He killed its Canaanite inhabitants and then
gave it as a wedding gift to his daughter, Solomon's wife. 17And
Solomon rebuilt Gezer.) He built up Lower Beth Horon,[b] 18Baal-
ath,[c] and Tadmor[a] in the desert, within his land, 19as well as all
his store cities[d] and the towns for his chariots[e] and for his
horses[b]—whatever he desired to build in Jerusalem, in Lebanon
and throughout all the territory he ruled.

20All the people left from the Amorites, Hittites, Perizzites,
Hivites and Jebusites (these peoples were not Israelites), 21that is,
their descendants[f] remaining in the land, whom the Israelites
could not exterminate[c][g]—these Solomon conscripted for his slave
labor force,[h] as it is to this day. 22But Solomon did not make slaves[i]
of any of the Israelites; they were his fighting men, his government
officials, his officers, his captains, and the commanders of his
chariots and charioteers. 23They were also the chief officials[j] in
charge of Solomon's projects—550 officials supervising the men
who did the work.

24After Pharaoh's daughter[k] had come up from the City of David
to the palace Solomon had built for her, he constructed the supporting terraces.[l]

25Three[m] times a year Solomon sacrificed burnt offerings and
fellowship offerings[d] on the altar he had built for the LORD, burning incense before the LORD along with them, and so fulfilled the
temple obligations.

26King Solomon also built ships[n] at Ezion Geber,[o] which is near
Elath in Edom, on the shore of the Red Sea.[e] 27And Hiram sent his
men—sailors[p] who knew the sea—to serve in the fleet with Solomon's men. 28They sailed to Ophir[q] and brought back 420 talents[f]
of gold, which they delivered to King Solomon.

Chapter 10 Theme ______________________

10 When the queen of Sheba[r] heard about the fame of Solomon and his relation to the name of the LORD, she came to
test him with hard questions.[s] 2Arriving at Jerusalem with a very
great caravan—with camels carrying spices, large quantities of
gold, and precious stones—she came to Solomon and talked with
him about all that she had on her mind. 3Solomon answered all
her questions; nothing was too hard for the king to explain to her.
4When the queen of Sheba saw all the wisdom of Solomon and
the palace he had built, 5the food on his table,[t] the seating of his

a *18* The Hebrew may also be read *Tamar.* b *19* Or *charioteers* c *21* The Hebrew term refers to the irrevocable giving over of things or persons to the LORD, often by totally destroying them. d *25* Traditionally *peace offerings* e *26* Hebrew *Yam Suph*; that is, Sea of Reeds f *28* That is, about 16 tons (about 14.5 metric tons)

9:15 [a] Jos 17:11
9:17 [b] Jos 16:3; 2Ch 8:5
9:18 [c] Jos 19:44
9:19 [d] ver 1 [e] 1Ki 4:26
9:21 [f] Ge 9:25-26 [g] Jos 15:63; 17:12; Jdg 1:21,27,29 [h] Ezr 2:55,58
9:22 [i] Lev 25:39
9:23 [j] 1Ki 5:16
9:24 [k] 1Ki 3:1; 7:8 [l] 2Sa 5:9; 1Ki 11:27; 2Ch 32:5
9:25 [m] Ex 23:14; 2Ch 8:12-13,16
9:26 [n] 1Ki 22:48 [o] Nu 33:35; Dt 2:8
9:27 [p] 1Ki 10:11; Eze 27:8
9:28 [q] 1Ch 29:4
10:1 [r] Ge 10:7,28; Mt 12:42; Lk 11:31 [s] Jdg 14:12
10:5 [t] 1Ch 26:16

10:7 [a]1Ch 29:25 officials, the attending servants in their robes, his cupbearers, and
the burnt offerings he made at[a] the temple of the LORD, she was
overwhelmed.
6 She said to the king, "The report I heard in my own country
about your achievements and your wisdom is true. 7 But I did not
believe these things until I came and saw with my own eyes. In-
10:8 [b]Pr 8:34 deed, not even half was told me; in wisdom and wealth[a] you have
far exceeded the report I heard. 8 How happy your men must be!
How happy your officials, who continually stand before you and
hear[b] your wisdom! 9 Praise[c] be to the LORD your God, who has
delighted in you and placed you on the throne of Israel. Because of
the LORD's eternal love for Israel, he has made you king, to main-
10:9 tain justice[d] and righteousness."
[c]1Ki 5:7 [d]2Sa 8:15; 10 And she gave the king 120 talents[b] of gold,[e] large quantities of
Ps 33:5; 72:2 spices, and precious stones. Never again were so many spices
brought in as those the queen of Sheba gave to King Solomon.
11 (Hiram's ships brought gold from Ophir;[f] and from there they
brought great cargoes of almugwood[c] and precious stones. 12 The
king used the almugwood to make supports for the temple of the
10:10 [e]ver 2 LORD and for the royal palace, and to make harps and lyres for the
musicians. So much almugwood has never been imported or seen
since that day.)
13 King Solomon gave the queen of Sheba all she desired and
asked for, besides what he had given her out of his royal bounty.
Then she left and returned with her retinue to her own country.
10:11 14 The weight of the gold[g] that Solomon received yearly was 666
[f]Ge 10:29; 1Ki 9:27-28 talents,[d] 15 not including the revenues from merchants and traders
and from all the Arabian kings and the governors of the land.
16 King Solomon made two hundred large shields[h] of hammered
gold; six hundred bekas[e] of gold went into each shield. 17 He also
made three hundred small shields of hammered gold, with three
minas[f] of gold in each shield. The king put them in the Palace of
10:14 [g]1Ki 9:28 the Forest of Lebanon.[i]
18 Then the king made a great throne inlaid with ivory and overlaid with fine gold. 19 The throne had six steps, and its back had a
rounded top. On both sides of the seat were armrests, with a lion
standing beside each of them. 20 Twelve lions stood on the six
steps, one at either end of each step. Nothing like it had ever been
10:16 [h]1Ki 14:26-28 made for any other kingdom. 21 All King Solomon's goblets were
gold, and all the household articles in the Palace of the Forest of
Lebanon were pure gold. Nothing was made of silver, because silver was considered of little value in Solomon's days. 22 The king

[a]5 Or *the ascent by which he went up to* [b]*10* That is, about 4 1/2 tons (about 4 metric tons)
[c]*11* Probably a variant of *algumwood*; also in verse 12 [d]*14* That is, about 25 tons (about 23
10:17 [i]1Ki 7:2 metric tons) [e]*16* That is, about 7 1/2 pounds (about 3.5 kilograms) [f]*17* That is, about 3 3/4
pounds (about 1.7 kilograms)

had a fleet of trading ships[a][a] at sea along with the ships of Hiram.
Once every three years it returned, carrying gold, silver and ivory,
and apes and baboons.
23King Solomon was greater in riches[b] and wisdom[c] than all the
other kings of the earth. 24The whole world sought audience with
Solomon to hear the wisdom[d] God had put in his heart. 25Year
after year, everyone who came brought a gift—articles of silver
and gold, robes, weapons and spices, and horses and mules.
26Solomon accumulated chariots and horses;[e] he had fourteen
hundred chariots and twelve thousand horses,[b] which he kept in
the chariot cities and also with him in Jerusalem. 27The king made
silver as common[f] in Jerusalem as stones, and cedar as plentiful
as sycamore-fig trees in the foothills. 28Solomon's horses were
imported from Egypt[c] and from Kue[d]—the royal merchants purchased them from Kue. 29They imported a chariot from Egypt for
six hundred shekels[e] of silver, and a horse for a hundred and fifty.[f]
They also exported them to all the kings of the Hittites[g] and of the
Arameans.

Chapter 11 Theme

11 King Solomon, however, loved many foreign women[h] besides
Pharaoh's daughter—Moabites, Ammonites, Edomites, Sidonians and Hittites. 2They were from nations about which the LORD
had told the Israelites, "You must not intermarry[i] with them,
because they will surely turn your hearts after their gods." Nevertheless, Solomon held fast to them in love. 3He had seven hundred
wives of royal birth and three hundred concubines, and his wives
led him astray. 4As Solomon grew old, his wives turned his heart
after other gods, and his heart was not fully devoted[j] to the LORD
his God, as the heart of David his father had been. 5He followed
Ashtoreth[k] the goddess of the Sidonians, and Molech[g][l] the detestable god of the Ammonites. 6So Solomon did evil in the eyes of
the LORD; he did not follow the LORD completely, as David his
father had done.
7On a hill east[m] of Jerusalem, Solomon built a high place for Chemosh[n] the detestable god of Moab, and for Molech[o] the detestable
god of the Ammonites. 8He did the same for all his foreign wives,
who burned incense and offered sacrifices to their gods.
9The LORD became angry with Solomon because his heart had
turned away from the LORD, the God of Israel, who had appeared[p]
to him twice. 10Although he had forbidden Solomon to follow other

10:22 [a] 1Ki 9:26
10:23 [b] 1Ki 3:13 [c] 1Ki 4:30
10:24 [d] 1Ki 3:9,12,28
10:26 [e] Dt 17:16; 1Ki 4:26; 9:19; 2Ch 1:14; 9:25
10:27 [f] Dt 17:17
10:29 [g] 2Ki 7:6-7
11:1 [h] Dt 17:17; Ne 13:26
11:2 [i] Ex 34:16; Dt 7:3-4
11:4 [j] 1Ki 8:61; 9:4
11:5 [k] ver 33; Jdg 2:13; 2Ki 23:13 [l] ver 7
11:7 [m] 2Ki 23:13 [n] Nu 21:29; Jdg 11:24 [o] Lev 20:2-5; Ac 7:43
11:9 [p] ver 2-3; 1Ki 3:5; 9:2

[a] 22 Hebrew *of ships of Tarshish* [b] 26 Or *charioteers* [c] 28 Or possibly *Muzur*, a region in Cilicia; also in verse 29 [d] 28 Probably *Cilicia* [e] 29 That is, about 15 pounds (about 7 kilograms) [f] 29 That is, about 3 3/4 pounds (about 1.7 kilograms) [g] 5 Hebrew *Milcom*; also in verse 33

gods,[a] Solomon did not keep the LORD's command.[b] 11So the LORD
said to Solomon, "Since this is your attitude and you have not
kept my covenant and my decrees, which I commanded you, I will
most certainly tear[c] the kingdom away from you and give it to one
of your subordinates. 12Nevertheless, for the sake of David your
father, I will not do it during your lifetime. I will tear it out of the
hand of your son. 13Yet I will not tear the whole kingdom from
him, but will give him one tribe[d] for the sake[e] of David my servant
and for the sake of Jerusalem, which I have chosen."[f]

14Then the LORD raised up against Solomon an adversary,
Hadad the Edomite, from the royal line of Edom. 15Earlier when
David was fighting with Edom, Joab the commander of the army,
who had gone up to bury the dead, had struck down all the men
in Edom.[g] 16Joab and all the Israelites stayed there for six months,
until they had destroyed all the men in Edom. 17But Hadad, still
only a boy, fled to Egypt with some Edomite officials who had
served his father. 18They set out from Midian and went to Paran.[h]
Then taking men from Paran with them, they went to Egypt, to
Pharaoh king of Egypt, who gave Hadad a house and land and
provided him with food.

19Pharaoh was so pleased with Hadad that he gave him a sister
of his own wife, Queen Tahpenes, in marriage. 20The sister of Tahpenes bore him a son named Genubath, whom Tahpenes brought
up in the royal palace. There Genubath lived with Pharaoh's own
children.

21While he was in Egypt, Hadad heard that David rested with his
fathers and that Joab the commander of the army was also dead.
Then Hadad said to Pharaoh, "Let me go, that I may return to my
own country."

22"What have you lacked here that you want to go back to your
own country?" Pharaoh asked.

"Nothing," Hadad replied, "but do let me go!"

23And God raised up against Solomon another adversary,[i]
Rezon son of Eliada, who had fled from his master, Hadadezer[j]
king of Zobah. 24He gathered men around him and became the
leader of a band of rebels when David destroyed the forces[a] ⌊of
Zobah⌋; the rebels went to Damascus,[k] where they settled and took
control. 25Rezon was Israel's adversary as long as Solomon lived,
adding to the trouble caused by Hadad. So Rezon ruled in Aram[l]
and was hostile toward Israel.

26Also, Jeroboam son of Nebat rebelled[m] against the king. He
was one of Solomon's officials, an Ephraimite from Zeredah, and
his mother was a widow named Zeruah.

11:10 [a] 1Ki 9:6 [b] 1Ki 6:12
11:11 [c] ver 31; 1Ki 12:15-16; 2Ki 17:21
11:13 [d] 1Ki 12:20 [e] 2Sa 7:15 [f] Dt 12:11
11:15 [g] Dt 20:13; 2Sa 8:14; 1Ch 18:12
11:18 [h] Nu 10:12
11:23 [i] ver 14 [j] 2Sa 8:3
11:24 [k] 2Sa 8:5; 10:8,18
11:25 [l] 2Sa 10:19
11:26 [m] 2Sa 20:21; 1Ki 12:2; 2Ch 13:6

[a] 24 Hebrew *destroyed them*

INSIGHT

Religious Influences of Solomon's Wives

1. The Gods of Egypt (see page 104).
2. Ashtoreth*—Sidonian* (Canaanite) goddess of fertility, love, and war. Later she became the spouse of Baal (2 Kings 23:13).
3. Chemosh*—god of Moab*—meaning "to subdue." Solomon erected a sanctuary for Chemosh on a mountain east of Jerusalem (2 Kings 23:13; Jeremiah 48:7, 13, 46).
4. Molech—(also known as *Milcom*)—*Ammonite* god whose name means "king." At the request of his pagan wives, Solomon built sanctuaries to Molech (Milcom) on the Mount of Olives. Human sacrifices, usually children, were made to Molech. This practice was condemned by God (Leviticus 18:21; 20:3-5; 2 Kings 23:10; Jeremiah 32:35). Compare with 2 Kings 17:31 and Jeremiah 7:31; 19:5.

For more information, look up these names in a Bible dictionary.

27 Here is the account of how he rebelled against the king:
Solomon had built the supporting terraces[a][a] and had filled in the
gap in the wall of the city of David his father. 28 Now Jeroboam was
a man of standing,[b] and when Solomon saw how well[c] the young
man did his work, he put him in charge of the whole labor force
of the house of Joseph.
29 About that time Jeroboam was going out of Jerusalem, and
Ahijah[d] the prophet of Shiloh met him on the way, wearing a new
cloak. The two of them were alone out in the country, 30 and Ahijah
took hold of the new cloak he was wearing and tore[e] it into twelve
pieces. 31 Then he said to Jeroboam, "Take ten pieces for yourself,
for this is what the LORD, the God of Israel, says: 'See, I am going to
tear[f] the kingdom out of Solomon's hand and give you ten tribes.
32 But for the sake of my servant David and the city of Jerusalem,
which I have chosen out of all the tribes of Israel, he will have one
tribe. 33 I will do this because they have[b] forsaken me and worshiped[g] Ashtoreth the goddess of the Sidonians, Chemosh the god
of the Moabites, and Molech the god of the Ammonites, and have
not walked in my ways, nor done what is right in my eyes, nor
kept my statutes[h] and laws as David, Solomon's father, did.
34 " 'But I will not take the whole kingdom out of Solomon's
hand; I have made him ruler all the days of his life for the sake of
David my servant, whom I chose and who observed my commands and statutes. 35 I will take the kingdom from his son's
hands and give you ten tribes. 36 I will give one tribe[i] to his son so
that David my servant may always have a lamp[j] before me in
Jerusalem, the city where I chose to put my Name. 37 However, as
for you, I will take you, and you will rule over all that your heart
desires;[k] you will be king over Israel. 38 If you do whatever I command you and walk in my ways and do what is right in my eyes by
keeping my statutes[l] and commands, as David my servant did, I
will be with you. I will build you a dynasty[m] as enduring as the
one I built for David and will give Israel to you. 39 I will humble
David's descendants because of this, but not forever.' "
40 Solomon tried to kill Jeroboam, but Jeroboam fled to Egypt,
to Shishak[n] the king, and stayed there until Solomon's death.
41 As for the other events of Solomon's reign—all he did and the
wisdom he displayed—are they not written in the book of the
annals of Solomon? 42 Solomon reigned in Jerusalem over all Israel
forty years. 43 Then he rested with his fathers and was buried in
the city of David his father. And Rehoboam[o] his son succeeded
him as king.

[a] 27 Or *the Millo* [b] 33 Hebrew; Septuagint, Vulgate and Syriac *because he has*

11:27 [a] 1Ki 9:24
11:28 [b] Ru 2:1 [c] Pr 22:29
11:29 [d] 1Ki 12:15; 14:2; 2Ch 9:29
11:30 [e] 1Sa 15:27
11:31 [f] ver 11
11:33 [g] ver 5-7 [h] 1Ki 3:3
11:36 [i] ver 13; 1Ki 12:17 [j] 1Ki 15:4; 2Ki 8:19
11:37 [k] 2Sa 3:21
11:38 [l] Dt 17:19 [m] Jos 1:5; 2Sa 7:11,27
11:40 [n] 2Ch 12:2
11:43 [o] 1Ki 14:21; Mt 1:7

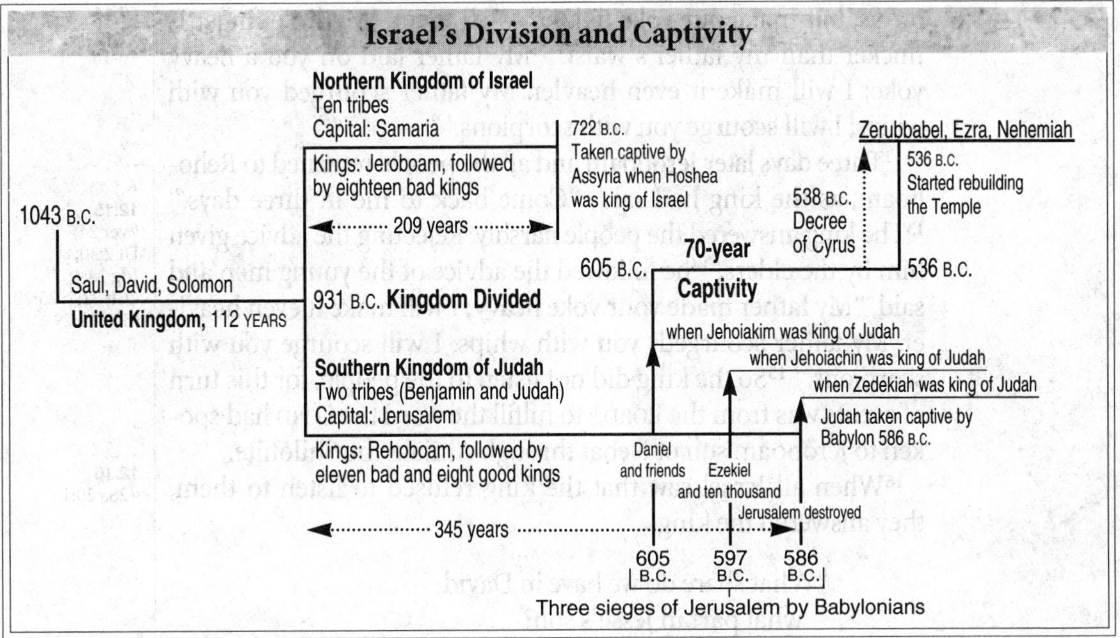

12:2
a 1Ki 11:40

Chapter 12 Theme ________________

12 Rehoboam went to Shechem, for all the Israelites had gone
there to make him king. 2When Jeroboam son of Nebat
heard this (he was still in Egypt, where he had fled[a] from King
Solomon), he returned from[a] Egypt. 3So they sent for Jeroboam,
and he and the whole assembly of Israel went to Rehoboam and
said to him: 4"Your father put a heavy yoke[b] on us, but now lighten
the harsh labor and the heavy yoke he put on us, and we will serve
you."

5Rehoboam answered, "Go away for three days and then come
back to me." So the people went away.

6Then King Rehoboam consulted the elders[c] who had served
his father Solomon during his lifetime. "How would you advise
me to answer these people?" he asked.

7They replied, "If today you will be a servant to these people and
serve them and give them a favorable answer,[d] they will always be
your servants."

8But Rehoboam rejected the advice the elders gave him and
consulted the young men who had grown up with him and were
serving him. 9He asked them, "What is your advice? How should
we answer these people who say to me, 'Lighten the yoke your
father put on us'?"

10The young men who had grown up with him replied, "Tell
these people who have said to you, 'Your father put a heavy yoke

12:4
b 1Sa 8:11-18; 1Ki 4:20-28

12:6
c 1Ki 4:2

12:7
d Pr 15:1

a 2 Or *he remained in*

on us, but make our yoke lighter'—tell them, 'My little finger is
thicker than my father's waist. 11 My father laid on you a heavy
yoke; I will make it even heavier. My father scourged you with
whips; I will scourge you with scorpions.' "

12 Three days later Jeroboam and all the people returned to Rehoboam, as the king had said, "Come back to me in three days."
13 The king answered the people harshly. Rejecting the advice given
him by the elders, 14 he followed the advice of the young men and
said, "My father made your yoke heavy; I will make it even heavier. My father scourged[a] you with whips; I will scourge you with
scorpions." 15 So the king did not listen to the people, for this turn
of events was from the LORD,[b] to fulfill the word the LORD had spoken to Jeroboam son of Nebat through Ahijah[c] the Shilonite.

16 When all Israel saw that the king refused to listen to them,
they answered the king:

> "What share do we have in David,
> what part in Jesse's son?
> To your tents, O Israel![d]
> Look after your own house, O David!"

So the Israelites went home. 17 But as for the Israelites who were
living in the towns of Judah,[e] Rehoboam still ruled over them.

18 King Rehoboam sent out Adoniram,[a][f] who was in charge of
forced labor, but all Israel stoned him to death. King Rehoboam,
however, managed to get into his chariot and escape to Jerusalem.
19 So Israel has been in rebellion against the house of David[g] to
this day.

20 When all the Israelites heard that Jeroboam had returned,
they sent and called him to the assembly and made him king over
all Israel. Only the tribe of Judah remained loyal to the house of
David.[h]

21 When Rehoboam arrived in Jerusalem, he mustered the whole
house of Judah and the tribe of Benjamin—a hundred and eighty
thousand fighting men—to make war[i] against the house of Israel
and to regain the kingdom for Rehoboam son of Solomon.

22 But this word of God came to Shemaiah[j] the man of God:
23 "Say to Rehoboam son of Solomon king of Judah, to the whole
house of Judah and Benjamin, and to the rest of the people, 24 'This
is what the LORD says: Do not go up to fight against your brothers,
the Israelites. Go home, every one of you, for this is my doing.' "
So they obeyed the word of the LORD and went home again, as the
LORD had ordered.

[a] *18* Some Septuagint manuscripts and Syriac (see also 1 Kings 4:6 and 5:14); Hebrew *Adoram*

12:14 [a] Ex 1:14; 5:5-9, 16-18
12:15 [b] ver 24; Dt 2:30; Jdg 14:4; 2Ch 22:7; 25:20 [c] 1Ki 11:29
12:16 [d] 2Sa 20:1
12:17 [e] 1Ki 11:13,36
12:18 [f] 2Sa 20:24; 1Ki 4:6; 5:14
12:19 [g] 2Ki 17:21
12:20 [h] 1Ki 11:13,32
12:21 [i] 2Ch 11:1
12:22 [j] 2Ch 12:5-7

12:25 [a]Jdg 9:45 [b]Jdg 8:8,17 25Then Jeroboam fortified Shechem[a] in the hill country of
Ephraim and lived there. From there he went out and built up
Peniel.[a][b]
26Jeroboam thought to himself, "The kingdom will now likely
12:27 [c]Dt 12:5-6 revert to the house of David. 27If these people go up to offer sacrifices at the temple of the LORD in Jerusalem,[c] they
will again give their allegiance to their lord, Reho-
12:28 [d]Ex 32:4; 2Ki 10:29; 17:16 [e]Ex 32:8 boam king of Judah. They will kill me and return to
King Rehoboam."
28After seeking advice, the king made two golden
calves.[d] He said to the people, "It is too much for you
to go up to Jerusalem. Here are your gods, O Israel,
12:29 [f]Ge 28:19 [g]Jdg 18:27-31 who brought you up out of Egypt."[e] 29One he set up
in Bethel,[f] and the other in Dan.[g] 30And this thing
became a sin;[h] the people went even as far as Dan to
worship the one there.
12:30 [h]1Ki 13:34; 2Ki 17:21 31Jeroboam built shrines[i] on high places and
appointed priests[j] from all sorts of people, even
though they were not Levites. 32He instituted a festival on the fifteenth day of the eighth[k] month, like the
12:31 [i]1Ki 13:32 [j]Nu 3:10; 1Ki 13:33; 2Ki 17:32; 2Ch 11:14-15; 13:9 festival held in Judah, and offered sacrifices on the
altar. This he did in Bethel, sacrificing to the calves he had made.
And at Bethel he also installed priests at the high places he had
made. 33On the fifteenth day of the eighth month, a month of his
own choosing, he offered sacrifices on the altar he had built at
Bethel.[l] So he instituted the festival for the Israelites and went up
12:32 [k]Lev 23:33-34; Nu 29:12 to the altar to make offerings.

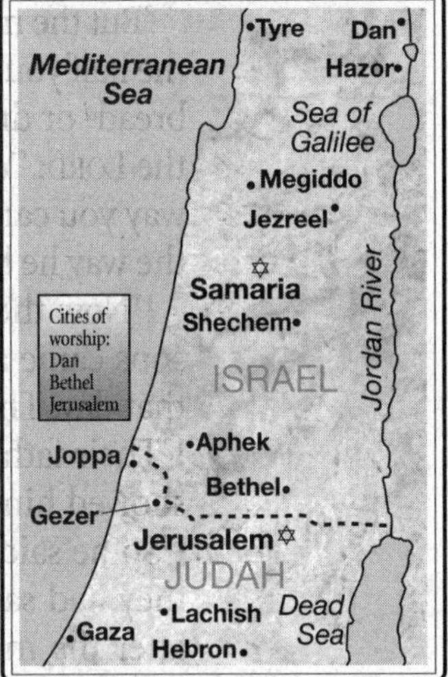

Chapter 13 Theme

12:33 [l]Nu 15:39; 1Ki 13:1; Am 7:13 **13** By the word of the LORD a man of God[m] came from Judah to
Bethel,[n] as Jeroboam was standing by the altar to make an
offering. 2He cried out against the altar by the word of the LORD:
"O altar, altar! This is what the LORD says: 'A son named Josiah[o]
will be born to the house of David. On you he will sacrifice the
13:1 [m]2Ki 23:17 [n]1Ki 12:32-33 priests of the high places who now make offerings here, and
human bones will be burned on you.'" 3That same day the man
of God gave a sign:[p] "This is the sign the LORD has declared: The
altar will be split apart and the ashes on it will be poured out."
13:2 [o]2Ki 23:15-16, 20 4When King Jeroboam heard what the man of God cried out
against the altar at Bethel, he stretched out his hand from the
altar and said, "Seize him!" But the hand he stretched out toward
the man shriveled up, so that he could not pull it back. 5Also, the
13:3 [p]Jdg 6:17; Isa 7:14; Jn 2:11; 1Co 1:22 altar was split apart and its ashes poured out according to the
sign given by the man of God by the word of the LORD.

[a]25 Hebrew *Penuel,* a variant of *Peniel*

6Then the king said to the man of God, "Intercede[a] with the
LORD your God and pray for me that my hand may be restored."
So the man of God interceded with the LORD, and the king's hand
was restored and became as it was before.
7The king said to the man of God, "Come home with me and
have something to eat, and I will give you a gift."[b]
8But the man of God answered the king, "Even if you were to give
me half your possessions,[c] I would not go with you, nor would I eat
bread[d] or drink water here. 9For I was commanded by the word of
the LORD: 'You must not eat bread or drink water or return by the
way you came.'" 10So he took another road and did not return by
the way he had come to Bethel.
11Now there was a certain old prophet living in Bethel, whose
sons came and told him all that the man of God had done there
that day. They also told their father what he had said to the king.
12Their father asked them, "Which way did he go?" And his sons
showed him which road the man of God from Judah had taken.
13So he said to his sons, "Saddle the donkey for me." And when
they had saddled the donkey for him, he mounted it 14and rode
after the man of God. He found him sitting under an oak tree
and asked, "Are you the man of God who came from Judah?"
"I am," he replied.
15So the prophet said to him, "Come home with me and eat."
16The man of God said, "I cannot turn back and go with you,
nor can I eat bread[e] or drink water with you in this place. 17I have
been told by the word of the LORD: 'You must not eat bread or
drink water there or return by the way you came.'"
18The old prophet answered, "I too am a prophet, as you are.
And an angel said to me by the word of the LORD: 'Bring him back
with you to your house so that he may eat bread and drink water.'"
(But he was lying[f] to him.) 19So the man of God returned with him
and ate and drank in his house.
20While they were sitting at the table, the word of the LORD came
to the old prophet who had brought him back. 21He cried out to
the man of God who had come from Judah, "This is what the LORD
says: 'You have defied[g] the word of the LORD and have not kept the
command the LORD your God gave you. 22You came back and ate
bread and drank water in the place where he told you not to eat or
drink. Therefore your body will not be buried in the tomb of your
fathers.'"
23When the man of God had finished eating and drinking, the
prophet who had brought him back saddled his donkey for him.
24As he went on his way, a lion[h] met him on the road and killed
him, and his body was thrown down on the road, with both the
donkey and the lion standing beside it. 25Some people who passed

13:6 [a] Ex 8:8; 9:28; 10:17; Lk 6:27-28; Ac 8:24; Jas 5:16
13:7 [b] 1Sa 9:7; 2Ki 5:15
13:8 [c] Nu 22:18; 24:13 [d] ver 16
13:16 [e] ver 8
13:18 [f] Dt 13:3
13:21 [g] ver 26
13:24 [h] 1Ki 20:36

by saw the body thrown down there, with the lion standing beside
the body, and they went and reported it in the city where the old
prophet lived.

26When the prophet who had brought him back from his journey
heard of it, he said, "It is the man of God who defied the word of the
LORD. The LORD has given him over to the lion, which has mauled
him and killed him, as the word of the LORD had warned him."

27The prophet said to his sons, "Saddle the donkey for me," and
they did so. 28Then he went out and found the body thrown down
on the road, with the donkey and the lion standing beside it. The
lion had neither eaten the body nor mauled the donkey. 29So the
prophet picked up the body of the man of God, laid it on the
donkey, and brought it back to his own city to mourn for him
and bury him. 30Then he laid the body in his own tomb, and they
mourned over him and said, "Oh, my brother!"[a]

31After burying him, he said to his sons, "When I die, bury me
in the grave where the man of God is buried; lay my bones[b] beside
his bones. 32For the message he declared by the word of the LORD
against the altar in Bethel and against all the shrines on the high
places[c] in the towns of Samaria[d] will certainly come true."[e]

33Even after this, Jeroboam did not change his evil ways, but
once more appointed priests for the high places from all sorts[f] of
people. Anyone who wanted to become a priest he consecrated for
the high places. 34This was the sin[g] of the house of Jeroboam that
led to its downfall and to its destruction[h] from the face of the earth.

Chapter 14 Theme ____

14 At that time Abijah son of Jeroboam became ill, 2and Jeroboam said to his wife, "Go, disguise yourself, so you won't
be recognized as the wife of Jeroboam. Then go to Shiloh. Ahijah[i]
the prophet is there—the one who told me I would be king over
this people. 3Take ten loaves of bread[j] with you, some cakes and a
jar of honey, and go to him. He will tell you what will happen to the
boy." 4So Jeroboam's wife did what he said and went to Ahijah's
house in Shiloh.

Now Ahijah could not see; his sight was gone because of his age.
5But the LORD had told Ahijah, "Jeroboam's wife is coming to ask
you about her son, for he is ill, and you are to give her such and such
an answer. When she arrives, she will pretend to be someone else."

6So when Ahijah heard the sound of her footsteps at the door,
he said, "Come in, wife of Jeroboam. Why this pretense? I have
been sent to you with bad news. 7Go, tell Jeroboam that this is what
the LORD, the God of Israel, says: 'I raised you up from among the
people and made you a leader[k] over my people Israel. 8I tore[l] the
kingdom away from the house of David and gave it to you, but

13:30 [a]Jer 22:18
13:31 [b]2Ki 23:18
13:32 [c]ver 2; Lev 26:30 [d]1Ki 16:24,28 [e]2Ki 23:16
13:33 [f]1Ki 12:31; 2Ch 11:15; 13:9
13:34 [g]1Ki 12:30 [h]1Ki 14:10
14:2 [i]1Sa 28:8; 2Sa 14:2; 1Ki 11:29
14:3 [j]1Sa 9:7
14:7 [k]2Sa 12:7-8; 1Ki 16:2
14:8 [l]1Ki 11:31, 33,38

you have not been like my servant David, who kept my commands
and followed me with all his heart, doing only what was right[a] in
my eyes. 9You have done more evil than all who lived before you.
You have made for yourself other gods, idols[b] made of metal; you
have provoked me to anger and thrust me behind your back.[c]
10" 'Because of this, I am going to bring disaster on the house of
Jeroboam. I will cut off from Jeroboam every last male in Israel—
slave or free.[d] I will burn up the house of Jeroboam as one burns
dung, until it is all gone.[e] 11Dogs[f] will eat those belonging to Jeroboam who die in the city, and the birds of the air will feed on
those who die in the country. The LORD has spoken!'
12"As for you, go back home. When you set foot in your city, the
boy will die. 13All Israel will mourn for him and bury him. He is
the only one belonging to Jeroboam who will be buried, because
he is the only one in the house of Jeroboam in whom the LORD, the
God of Israel, has found anything good.[g]
14"The LORD will raise up for himself a king over Israel who will
cut off the family of Jeroboam. This is the day! What? Yes, even
now.[a] 15And the LORD will strike Israel, so that it will be like a reed
swaying in the water. He will uproot[h] Israel from this good land
that he gave to their forefathers and scatter them beyond the River,[b]
because they provoked[i] the LORD to anger by making Asherah[j]
poles.[c] 16And he will give Israel up because of the sins[k] Jeroboam
has committed and has caused Israel to commit."
17Then Jeroboam's wife got up and left and went to Tirzah.[l] As
soon as she stepped over the threshold of the house, the boy died.
18They buried him, and all Israel mourned for him, as the LORD
had said through his servant the prophet Ahijah.
19The other events of Jeroboam's reign, his wars and how he
ruled, are written in the book of the annals of the kings of Israel.
20He reigned for twenty-two years and then rested with his
fathers. And Nadab his son succeeded him as king.
21Rehoboam son of Solomon was king in Judah. He was forty-
one years old when he became king, and he reigned seventeen
years in Jerusalem, the city the LORD had chosen out of all the
tribes of Israel in which to put his Name. His mother's name was
Naamah; she was an Ammonite.[m]
22Judah[n] did evil in the eyes of the LORD. By the sins they committed they stirred up his jealous anger[o] more than their fathers
had done. 23They also set up for themselves high places, sacred
stones[p] and Asherah poles on every high hill and under every
spreading tree.[q] 24There were even male shrine prostitutes[r] in the
land; the people engaged in all the detestable practices of the nations the LORD had driven out before the Israelites.

a *14* The meaning of the Hebrew for this sentence is uncertain. b *15* That is, the Euphrates
c *15* That is, symbols of the goddess Asherah; here and elsewhere in 1 Kings

14:8 [a] 1Ki 15:5
14:9 [b] Ex 34:17; 1Ki 12:28; 2Ch 11:15 [c] Ne 9:26; Ps 50:17; Eze 23:35
14:10 [d] Dt 32:36; 1Ki 21:21; 2Ki 9:8-9; 14:26 [e] 1Ki 15:29
14:11 [f] 1Ki 16:4; 21:24
14:13 [g] 2Ch 12:12; 19:3
14:15 [h] Dt 29:28; 2Ki 15:29; 17:6; Ps 52:5 [i] Jos 23:15-16 [j] Ex 34:13; Dt 12:3
14:16 [k] 1Ki 12:30; 13:34; 15:30,34; 16:2
14:17 [l] ver 12; 1Ki 15:33; 16:6-9
14:21 [m] ver 31; 1Ki 11:1; 2Ch 12:13
14:22 [n] 2Ch 12:1 [o] Dt 32:21; Ps 78:58; 1Co 10:22
14:23 [p] Dt 16:22; 2Ki 17:9-10; Eze 16:24-25 [q] Dt 12:2; Isa 57:5
14:24 [r] Dt 23:17; 1Ki 15:12; 2Ki 23:7

14:25 [a]1Ki 11:40; [25]In the fifth year of King Rehoboam, Shishak king of Egypt
2Ch 12:2 attacked[a] Jerusalem. [26]He carried off the treasures of the temple[b] of
the LORD and the treasures of the royal palace. He took everything,
including all the gold shields[c] Solomon had made. [27]So King Reho-
14:26 boam made bronze shields to replace them and assigned these to
[b]1Ki 15:15,18 [c]1Ki 10:17 the commanders of the guard on duty at the entrance to the royal
palace. [28]Whenever the king went to the LORD's temple, the guards
bore the shields, and afterward they returned them to the guardroom.

14:30 [d]1Ki 12:21; 15:6 [29]As for the other events of Rehoboam's reign, and all he did, are
they not written in the book of the annals of the kings of Judah?
[30]There was continual warfare[d] between Rehoboam and Jerobo-
14:31 am. [31]And Rehoboam rested with his fathers and was buried with
[e]ver 21; them in the City of David. His mother's name was Naamah; she
2Ch 12:16 was an Ammonite.[e] And Abijah[a] his son succeeded him as king.

Chapter 15 Theme

15:2 [f]2Ch 11:20; 13:2 **15** In the eighteenth year of the reign of Jeroboam son of
Nebat, Abijah[b] became king of Judah, [2]and he reigned in
Jerusalem three years. His mother's name was Maacah[f] daughter
of Abishalom.[c]

15:3 [g]1Ki 11:4; [3]He committed all the sins his father had done before him; his
Ps 119:80 heart was not fully devoted[g] to the LORD his God, as the heart of
David his forefather had been. [4]Nevertheless, for David's sake the
LORD his God gave him a lamp[h] in Jerusalem by raising up a son
15:4 to succeed him and by making Jerusalem strong. [5]For David had
[h]2Sa 21:17; 1Ki 11:36; done what was right in the eyes of the LORD and had not failed to
2Ch 21:7 keep[i] any of the LORD's commands all the days of his life—except
in the case of Uriah[j] the Hittite.

[6]There was war[k] between Rehoboam[d] and Jeroboam through-
15:5 out ⌊Abijah's⌋ lifetime. [7]As for the other events of Abijah's reign,
[i]1Ki 9:4; 14:8 [j]2Sa 11:2-27; and all he did, are they not written in the book of the annals of the
12:9 kings of Judah? There was war between Abijah and Jeroboam.
[8]And Abijah rested with his fathers and was buried in the City of
David. And Asa his son succeeded him as king.

15:6 [9]In the twentieth year of Jeroboam king of Israel, Asa became
[k]1Ki 14:30 king of Judah, [10]and he reigned in Jerusalem forty-one years. His
grandmother's name was Maacah[l] daughter of Abishalom.

[11]Asa did what was right in the eyes of the LORD, as his father
15:10 [l]ver 2 David had done. [12]He expelled the male shrine prostitutes[m] from
the land and got rid of all the idols his fathers had made. [13]He even

15:12 [m]1Ki 14:24; 22:46

[a]31 Some Hebrew manuscripts and Septuagint (see also 2 Chron. 12:16); most Hebrew manuscripts *Abijam* [b]1 Some Hebrew manuscripts and Septuagint (see also 2 Chron. 12:16); most Hebrew manuscripts *Abijam*; also in verses 7 and 8 [c]2 A variant of *Absalom*; also in verse 10 [d]6 Most Hebrew manuscripts; some Hebrew manuscripts and Syriac *Abijam* (that is, Abijah)

deposed his grandmother Maacah from her position as queen
mother, because she had made a repulsive Asherah pole. Asa cut
the pole down[a] and burned it in the Kidron Valley. 14Although he
did not remove the high places, Asa's heart was fully committed[b] to
the LORD all his life. 15He brought into the temple of the LORD the silver and gold and the articles that he and his father had dedicated.[c]

16There was war[d] between Asa and Baasha king of Israel
throughout their reigns. 17Baasha king of Israel went up against
Judah and fortified Ramah[e] to prevent anyone from leaving or
entering the territory of Asa king of Judah.

18Asa then took all the silver and gold that was left in the treasuries of the LORD's temple[f] and of his own palace. He entrusted it
to his officials and sent[g] them to Ben-Hadad[h] son of Tabrimmon,
the son of Hezion, the king of Aram, who was ruling in Damascus.
19"Let there be a treaty between me and you," he said, "as there
was between my father and your father. See, I am sending you a
gift of silver and gold. Now break your treaty with Baasha king of
Israel so he will withdraw from me."

20Ben-Hadad agreed with King Asa and sent the commanders
of his forces against the towns of Israel. He conquered[i] Ijon, Dan,
Abel Beth Maacah and all Kinnereth in addition to Naphtali.
21When Baasha heard this, he stopped building Ramah and withdrew to Tirzah. 22Then King Asa issued an order to all Judah—no
one was exempt—and they carried away from Ramah the stones
and timber Baasha had been using there. With them King Asa
built up Geba[j] in Benjamin, and also Mizpah.

23As for all the other events of Asa's reign, all his achievements,
all he did and the cities he built, are they not written in the book
of the annals of the kings of Judah? In his old age, however, his feet
became diseased. 24Then Asa rested with his fathers and was buried
with them in the city of his father David. And Jehoshaphat[k] his son
succeeded him as king.

25Nadab son of Jeroboam became king of Israel in the second
year of Asa king of Judah, and he reigned over Israel two years.
26He did evil in the eyes of the LORD, walking in the ways of his
father[l] and in his sin, which he had caused Israel to commit.

27Baasha son of Ahijah of the house of Issachar plotted against
him, and he struck him down[m] at Gibbethon,[n] a Philistine town,
while Nadab and all Israel were besieging it. 28Baasha killed Nadab
in the third year of Asa king of Judah and succeeded him as king.

29As soon as he began to reign, he killed Jeroboam's whole
family.[o] He did not leave Jeroboam anyone that breathed, but
destroyed them all, according to the word of the LORD given
through his servant Ahijah the Shilonite— 30because of the sins[p]
Jeroboam had committed and had caused Israel to commit, and
because he provoked the LORD, the God of Israel, to anger.

15:13 [a] Ex 32:20
15:14 [b] ver 3; 1Ki 8:61; 22:43
15:15 [c] 1Ki 7:51
15:16 [d] ver 32
15:17 [e] Jos 18:25; 1Ki 12:27
15:18 [f] ver 15; 1Ki 14:26 [g] 2Ki 12:18 [h] 1Ki 11:23-24
15:20 [i] Jdg 18:29; 2Sa 20:14; 2Ki 15:29
15:22 [j] Jos 18:24; 21:17
15:24 [k] Mt 1:8
15:26 [l] 1Ki 12:30; 14:16
15:27 [m] 1Ki 14:14 [n] Jos 19:44; 21:23
15:29 [o] 1Ki 14:10,14
15:30 [p] 1Ki 14:9,16

31 As for the other events of Nadab's reign, and all he did, are
they not written in the book of the annals of the kings of Israel?
32 There was war[a] between Asa and Baasha king of Israel throughout their reigns.
33 In the third year of Asa king of Judah, Baasha son of Ahijah
became king of all Israel in Tirzah, and he reigned twenty-four
years. 34 He did evil[b] in the eyes of the LORD, walking in the ways of
Jeroboam and in his sin, which he had caused Israel to commit.

Chapter 16 Theme ______________________________

16 Then the word of the LORD came to Jehu[c] son of Hanani[d]
against Baasha: 2 "I lifted you up from the dust[e] and made
you leader[f] of my people Israel, but you walked in the ways of Jeroboam and caused[g] my people Israel to sin and to provoke me to
anger by their sins. 3 So I am about to consume Baasha and his
house,[h] and I will make your house like that of Jeroboam son of
Nebat. 4 Dogs[i] will eat those belonging to Baasha who die in the
city, and the birds of the air will feed on those who die in the
country."
5 As for the other events of Baasha's reign, what he did and his
achievements, are they not written in the book of the annals[j] of
the kings of Israel? 6 Baasha rested with his fathers and was buried
in Tirzah.[k] And Elah his son succeeded him as king.
7 Moreover, the word of the LORD came[l] through the prophet
Jehu[m] son of Hanani to Baasha and his house, because of all the evil
he had done in the eyes of the LORD, provoking him to anger by the
things he did, and becoming like the house of Jeroboam—and
also because he destroyed it.
8 In the twenty-sixth year of Asa king of Judah, Elah son of Baasha
became king of Israel, and he reigned in Tirzah two years.
9 Zimri, one of his officials, who had command of half his chariots, plotted against him. Elah was in Tirzah at the time, getting
drunk[n] in the home of Arza, the man in charge[o] of the palace at
Tirzah. 10 Zimri came in, struck him down and killed him in the
twenty-seventh year of Asa king of Judah. Then he succeeded
him as king.
11 As soon as he began to reign and was seated on the throne, he
killed off Baasha's whole family.[p] He did not spare a single male,
whether relative or friend. 12 So Zimri destroyed the whole family
of Baasha, in accordance with the word of the LORD spoken against
Baasha through the prophet Jehu— 13 because of all the sins
Baasha and his son Elah had committed and had caused Israel to
commit, so that they provoked the LORD, the God of Israel, to anger
by their worthless idols.[q]
14 As for the other events of Elah's reign, and all he did, are they
not written in the book of the annals of the kings of Israel?

15:32 [a] ver 16
15:34 [b] ver 26; 1Ki 12:28-29; 13:33; 14:16
16:1 [c] ver 7; 2Ch 19:2; 20:34 [d] 2Ch 16:7
16:2 [e] 1Sa 2:8 [f] 1Ki 14:7-9 [g] 1Ki 15:34
16:3 [h] ver 11; 1Ki 14:10; 15:29; 21:22
16:4 [i] 1Ki 14:11
16:5 [j] 1Ki 14:19; 15:31
16:6 [k] 1Ki 14:17; 15:33
16:7 [l] 1Ki 15:27,29 [m] ver 1
16:9 [n] 2Ki 9:30-33 [o] 1Ki 18:3
16:11 [p] ver 3
16:13 [q] Dt 32:21; 1Sa 12:21; Isa 41:29

15 In the twenty-seventh year of Asa king of Judah, Zimri reigned
in Tirzah seven days. The army was encamped near Gibbethon,[a] a
Philistine town. 16 When the Israelites in the camp heard that Zimri
had plotted against the king and murdered him, they proclaimed
Omri, the commander of the army, king over Israel that very day
there in the camp. 17 Then Omri and all the Israelites with him
withdrew from Gibbethon and laid siege to Tirzah. 18 When Zimri saw that the city was taken, he went into the citadel of the royal
palace and set the palace on fire around him. So he died, 19 because
of the sins he had committed, doing evil in the eyes of the LORD
and walking in the ways of Jeroboam and in the sin he had committed and had caused Israel to commit.

20 As for the other events of Zimri's reign, and the rebellion he
carried out, are they not written in the book of the annals of the
kings of Israel?

21 Then the people of Israel were split into two factions; half supported Tibni son of Ginath for king, and the other half supported
Omri. 22 But Omri's followers proved stronger than those of Tibni
son of Ginath. So Tibni died and Omri became king.

23 In the thirty-first year of Asa king of Judah, Omri became king
of Israel, and he reigned twelve years, six of them in Tirzah.[b] 24 He
bought the hill of Samaria from Shemer for two talents[a] of silver
and built a city on the hill, calling it Samaria,[c] after Shemer, the
name of the former owner of the hill.

25 But Omri did evil[d] in the eyes of the LORD and sinned more
than all those before him. 26 He walked in all the ways of Jeroboam
son of Nebat and in his sin, which he had caused[e] Israel to commit,
so that they provoked the LORD, the God of Israel, to anger by their
worthless idols.[f]

27 As for the other events of Omri's reign, what he did and the
things he achieved, are they not written in the book of the annals
of the kings of Israel? 28 Omri rested with his fathers and was
buried in Samaria. And Ahab his son succeeded him as king.

29 In the thirty-eighth year of Asa king of Judah, Ahab son of
Omri became king of Israel, and he reigned in Samaria over Israel
twenty-two years. 30 Ahab son of Omri did more[g] evil in the eyes
of the LORD than any of those before him. 31 He not only considered it trivial to commit the sins of Jeroboam son of Nebat, but he
also married[h] Jezebel daughter[i] of Ethbaal king of the Sidonians,
and began to serve Baal[j] and worship him. 32 He set up an altar for
Baal in the temple[k] of Baal that he built in Samaria. 33 Ahab also
made an Asherah pole[l] and did more[m] to provoke the LORD, the
God of Israel, to anger than did all the kings of Israel before him.

a *24* That is, about 150 pounds (about 70 kilograms)

16:15 [a] Jos 19:44; 1Ki 15:27
16:23 [b] 1Ki 15:21
16:24 [c] 1Ki 13:32; Jn 4:4
16:25 [d] Dt 4:25; Mic 6:16
16:26 [e] ver 19 [f] Dt 32:21
16:30 [g] ver 25; 1Ki 14:9
16:31 [h] Dt 7:3; 1Ki 11:2 [i] Jdg 18:7; 2Ki 9:34 [j] 2Ki 10:18; 17:16
16:32 [k] 2Ki 10:21,27; 11:18
16:33 [l] 2Ki 13:6 [m] ver 29,30; 1Ki 14:9; 21:25

34 In Ahab's time, Hiel of Bethel rebuilt Jericho. He laid its foundations at the cost of his firstborn son Abiram, and he set up its gates at the cost of his youngest son Segub, in accordance with the word of the LORD spoken by Joshua son of Nun.[a]

Chapter 17 Theme ______________________

17 Now Elijah[b] the Tishbite, from Tishbe[a] in Gilead,[c] said to Ahab, "As the LORD, the God of Israel, lives, whom I serve, there will be neither dew nor rain[d] in the next few years except at my word."

2 Then the word of the LORD came to Elijah: 3 "Leave here, turn eastward and hide in the Kerith Ravine, east of the Jordan. 4 You will drink from the brook, and I have ordered the ravens[e] to feed you there."

5 So he did what the LORD had told him. He went to the Kerith Ravine, east of the Jordan, and stayed there. 6 The ravens brought him bread and meat in the morning[f] and bread and meat in the evening, and he drank from the brook.

7 Some time later the brook dried up because there had been no rain in the land. 8 Then the word of the LORD came to him: 9 "Go at once to Zarephath[g] of Sidon and stay there. I have commanded a widow[h] in that place to supply you with food." 10 So he went to Zarephath. When he came to the town gate, a widow was there gathering sticks. He called to her and asked, "Would you bring me a little water in a jar so I may have a drink?"[i] 11 As she was going to get it, he called, "And bring me, please, a piece of bread."

12 "As surely as the LORD your God lives," she replied, "I don't have any bread—only a handful of flour in a jar and a little oil[j] in a jug. I am gathering a few sticks to take home and make a meal for myself and my son, that we may eat it—and die."

13 Elijah said to her, "Don't be afraid. Go home and do as you have said. But first make a small cake of bread for me from what you have and bring it to me, and then make something for yourself and your son. 14 For this is what the LORD, the God of Israel, says: 'The jar of flour will not be used up and the jug of oil will not run dry until the day the LORD gives rain on the land.'"

15 She went away and did as Elijah had told her. So there was food every day for Elijah and for the woman and her family. 16 For the jar of flour was not used up and the jug of oil did not run dry, in keeping with the word of the LORD spoken by Elijah.

17 Some time later the son of the woman who owned the house became ill. He grew worse and worse, and finally stopped breathing. 18 She said to Elijah, "What do you have against me, man of God? Did you come to remind me of my sin[k] and kill my son?"

16:34 [a] Jos 6:26
17:1 [b] Mal 4:5; Jas 5:17 [c] Jdg 12:4 [d] Dt 10:8; 1Ki 18:1; 2Ki 3:14; Lk 4:25
17:4 [e] Ge 8:7
17:6 [f] Ex 16:8
17:9 [g] Ob 1:20 [h] Lk 4:26
17:10 [i] Ge 24:17; Jn 4:7
17:12 [j] ver 1; 2Ki 4:2
17:18 [k] 2Ki 3:13; Lk 5:8

a *1* Or *Tishbite, of the settlers*

19“Give me your son,” Elijah replied. He took him from her
arms, carried him to the upper room where he was staying, and
laid him on his bed. 20Then he cried out to the LORD, “O LORD my
God, have you brought tragedy also upon this widow I am staying
with, by causing her son to die?” 21Then he stretched[a] himself out
on the boy three times and cried to the LORD, “O LORD my God, let
this boy’s life return to him!”

22The LORD heard Elijah’s cry, and the boy’s life returned to him,
and he lived. 23Elijah picked up the child and carried him down
from the room into the house. He gave him to his mother and said,
“Look, your son is alive!”

24Then the woman said to Elijah, “Now I know[b] that you are a
man of God and that the word of the LORD from your mouth is the
truth.”[c]

Chapter 18 Theme ____

18 After a long time, in the third[d] year, the word of the LORD
came to Elijah: “Go and present yourself to Ahab, and I will
send rain[e] on the land.” 2So Elijah went to present himself to Ahab.

Now the famine was severe in Samaria, 3and Ahab had summoned Obadiah, who was in charge[f] of his palace. (Obadiah was
a devout believer[g] in the LORD. 4While Jezebel[h] was killing off the
LORD’s prophets, Obadiah had taken a hundred prophets and hidden[i] them in two caves, fifty in each, and had supplied them with
food and water.) 5Ahab had said to Obadiah, “Go through the
land to all the springs and valleys. Maybe we can find some grass
to keep the horses and mules alive so we will not have to kill any of
our animals.” 6So they divided the land they were to cover, Ahab
going in one direction and Obadiah in another.

7As Obadiah was walking along, Elijah met him. Obadiah recognized[j] him, bowed down to the ground, and said, “Is it really
you, my lord Elijah?”

8“Yes,” he replied. “Go tell your master, ‘Elijah is here.’ ”

9“What have I done wrong,” asked Obadiah, “that you are handing your servant over to Ahab to be put to death? 10As surely as
the LORD your God lives, there is not a nation or kingdom where
my master has not sent someone to look[k] for you. And whenever
a nation or kingdom claimed you were not there, he made them
swear they could not find you. 11But now you tell me to go to my
master and say, ‘Elijah is here.’ 12I don’t know where the Spirit[l] of
the LORD may carry you when I leave you. If I go and tell Ahab
and he doesn’t find you, he will kill me. Yet I your servant have
worshiped the LORD since my youth. 13Haven’t you heard, my
lord, what I did while Jezebel was killing the prophets of the LORD?
I hid a hundred of the LORD’s prophets in two caves, fifty in each,

17:21 [a] 2Ki 4:34; Ac 20:10

17:24 [b] Jn 3:2; 16:30 [c] Ps 119:43; Jn 17:17

18:1 [d] 1Ki 17:1; Lk 4:25; Jas 5:17 [e] Dt 28:12

18:3 [f] 1Ki 16:9 [g] Ne 7:2

18:4 [h] 2Ki 9:7 [i] ver 13; Isa 16:3

18:7 [j] 2Ki 1:8

18:10 [k] 1Ki 17:3

18:12 [l] 2Ki 2:16; Eze 3:14; Ac 8:39

and supplied them with food and water. 14And now you tell me to
go to my master and say, 'Elijah is here.' He will kill me!"
15Elijah said, "As the LORD Almighty lives, whom I serve, I will
surely present[a] myself to Ahab today."
16So Obadiah went to meet Ahab and told him, and Ahab went
to meet Elijah. 17When he saw Elijah, he said to him, "Is that you,
you troubler[b] of Israel?"
18"I have not made trouble for Israel," Elijah replied. "But you[c]
and your father's family have. You have abandoned[d] the LORD's
commands and have followed the Baals. 19Now summon the people from all over Israel to meet me on Mount Carmel.[e] And bring
the four hundred and fifty prophets of Baal and the four hundred
prophets of Asherah, who eat at Jezebel's table."
20So Ahab sent word throughout all Israel and assembled the
prophets on Mount Carmel. 21Elijah went before the people and
said, "How long will you waver[f] between two opinions? If the LORD
is God, follow him; but if Baal is God, follow him."
But the people said nothing.
22Then Elijah said to them, "I am the only one of the LORD's
prophets left,[g] but Baal has four hundred and fifty prophets.[h]
23Get two bulls for us. Let them choose one for themselves, and let
them cut it into pieces and put it on the wood but not set fire to it.
I will prepare the other bull and put it on the wood but not set fire
to it. 24Then you call on the name of your god, and I will call on
the name of the LORD. The god who answers by fire[i]—he is God."
Then all the people said, "What you say is good."
25Elijah said to the prophets of Baal, "Choose one of the bulls
and prepare it first, since there are so many of you. Call on the
name of your god, but do not light the fire." 26So they took the
bull given them and prepared it.
Then they called on the name of Baal from morning till noon.
"O Baal, answer us!" they shouted. But there was no response;[j] no
one answered. And they danced around the altar they had made.
27At noon Elijah began to taunt them. "Shout louder!" he said.
"Surely he is a god! Perhaps he is deep in thought, or busy, or traveling. Maybe he is sleeping and must be awakened."[k] 28So they
shouted louder and slashed[l] themselves with swords and spears, as
was their custom, until their blood flowed. 29Midday passed, and
they continued their frantic prophesying until the time for the evening sacrifice.[m] But there was no response, no one answered, no
one paid attention.[n]
30Then Elijah said to all the people, "Come here to me." They
came to him, and he repaired the altar[o] of the LORD, which was in
ruins. 31Elijah took twelve stones, one for each of the tribes descended from Jacob, to whom the word of the LORD had come,

18:15 [a] 1Ki 17:1
18:17 [b] Jos 7:25; 1Ki 21:20; Ac 16:20
18:18 [c] 1Ki 16:31,33; 21:25 [d] 2Ch 15:2
18:19 [e] Jos 19:26
18:21 [f] Jos 24:15; 2Ki 17:41; Mt 6:24
18:22 [g] 1Ki 19:10 [h] ver 19
18:24 [i] ver 38; 1Ch 21:26
18:26 [j] Ps 115:4-5; Jer 10:5; 1Co 8:4; 12:2
18:27 [k] Hab 2:19
18:28 [l] Lev 19:28; Dt 14:1
18:29 [m] Ex 29:41 [n] ver 26
18:30 [o] 1Ki 19:10

saying, "Your name shall be Israel."[a] 32With the stones he built an
altar in the name[b] of the LORD, and he dug a trench around it large
enough to hold two seahs[a] of seed. 33He arranged[c] the wood, cut
the bull into pieces and laid it on the wood. Then he said to them,
"Fill four large jars with water and pour it on the offering and on
the wood."
34"Do it again," he said, and they did it again.
"Do it a third time," he ordered, and they did it the third time.
35The water ran down around the altar and even filled the trench.
36At the time of sacrifice, the prophet Elijah stepped forward
and prayed: "O LORD, God of Abraham,[d] Isaac and Israel, let it be
known[e] today that you are God in Israel and that I am your servant
and have done all these things at your command.[f] 37Answer me,
O LORD, answer me, so these people will know that you, O LORD,
are God, and that you are turning their hearts back again."
38Then the fire[g] of the LORD fell and burned up the sacrifice, the
wood, the stones and the soil, and also licked up the water in the
trench.
39When all the people saw this, they fell prostrate and cried, "The
LORD—he is God! The LORD—he is God!"[h]
40Then Elijah commanded them, "Seize the prophets of Baal.
Don't let anyone get away!" They seized them, and Elijah had them
brought down to the Kishon Valley[i] and slaughtered[j] there.
41And Elijah said to Ahab, "Go, eat and drink, for there is the
sound of a heavy rain." 42So Ahab went off to eat and drink, but
Elijah climbed to the top of Carmel, bent down to the ground
and put his face between his knees.[k]
43"Go and look toward the sea," he told his servant. And he went
up and looked.
"There is nothing there," he said.
Seven times Elijah said, "Go back."
44The seventh time the servant reported, "A cloud[l] as small as a
man's hand is rising from the sea."
So Elijah said, "Go and tell Ahab, 'Hitch up your chariot and go
down before the rain stops you.'"
45Meanwhile, the sky grew black with clouds, the wind rose, a
heavy rain came on and Ahab rode off to Jezreel. 46The power[m] of
the LORD came upon Elijah and, tucking his cloak into his belt,[n] he
ran ahead of Ahab all the way to Jezreel.

Chapter 19 Theme ______________________

19 Now Ahab told Jezebel everything Elijah had done and
how he had killed[o] all the prophets with the sword. 2So
Jezebel sent a messenger to Elijah to say, "May the gods deal with

[a]32 That is, probably about 13 quarts (about 15 liters)

18:31 [a]Ge 32:28; 35:10; 2Ki 17:34
18:32 [b]Col 3:17
18:33 [c]Ge 22:9; Lev 1:6-8
18:36 [d]Ex 3:6; Mt 22:32 [e]1Ki 8:43; 2Ki 19:19 [f]Nu 16:28
18:38 [g]Lev 9:24; Jdg 6:21; 1Ch 21:26; 2Ch 7:1; Job 1:16
18:39 [h]ver 24
18:40 [i]Jdg 4:7 [j]Dt 13:5; 18:20; 2Ki 10:24-25
18:42 [k]ver 19-20; Jas 5:18
18:44 [l]Lk 12:54
18:46 [m]2Ki 3:15 [n]2Ki 4:29; 9:1
19:1 [o]1Ki 18:40

me, be it ever so severely,[a] if by this time tomorrow I do not make
your life like that of one of them."
3Elijah was afraid[a] and ran[b] for his life. When he came to Beersheba in Judah, he left his servant there, 4while he himself went a day's journey into the desert. He came to a broom tree, sat down under it and prayed that he might die. "I have had enough, LORD," he said. "Take my life;[c] I am no better than my ancestors." 5Then he lay down under the tree and fell asleep.[d]

All at once an angel touched him and said, "Get up and eat." 6He looked around, and there by his head was a cake of bread baked over hot coals, and a jar of water. He ate and drank and then lay down again.

7The angel of the LORD came back a second time and touched him and said, "Get up and eat, for the journey is too much for you." 8So he got up and ate and drank. Strengthened by that food, he traveled forty[e] days and forty nights until he reached Horeb,[f] the mountain of God. 9There he went into a cave[g] and spent the night.

And the word of the LORD came to him: "What are you doing here, Elijah?"

10He replied, "I have been very zealous[h] for the LORD God Almighty. The Israelites have rejected your covenant, broken down your altars, and put your prophets to death with the sword. I am the only one left,[i] and now they are trying to kill me too."

11The LORD said, "Go out and stand on the mountain[j] in the presence of the LORD, for the LORD is about to pass by."

Then a great and powerful wind[k] tore the mountains apart and shattered the rocks before the LORD, but the LORD was not in the wind. After the wind there was an earthquake, but the LORD was

Elijah's Ministry

19:2 [a]1Ki 20:10; 2Ki 6:31; Ru 1:17
19:3 [b]Ge 31:21
19:4 [c]Nu 11:15; Jer 20:18; Jnh 4:8
19:5 [d]Ge 28:11
19:8 [e]Ex 24:18; 34:28; Dt 9:9-11,18; Mt 4:2 [f]Ex 3:1
19:9 [g]Ex 33:22
19:10 [h]Nu 25:13 [i]1Ki 18:4,22; Ro 11:3*
19:11 [j]Ex 24:12 [k]Eze 1:4; 37:7

[a]3 Or *Elijah saw*

not in the earthquake. 12After the earthquake came a fire, but the
LORD was not in the fire. And after the fire came a gentle whisper.[a]
13When Elijah heard it, he pulled his cloak over his face[b] and went
out and stood at the mouth of the cave.
Then a voice said to him, "What are you doing here, Elijah?"
14He replied, "I have been very zealous for the LORD God Almighty. The Israelites have rejected your covenant, broken down
your altars, and put your prophets to death with the sword. I am
the only one left,[c] and now they are trying to kill me too."
15The LORD said to him, "Go back the way you came, and go to
the Desert of Damascus. When you get there, anoint Hazael[d] king
over Aram. 16Also, anoint[e] Jehu son of Nimshi king over Israel,
and anoint Elisha[f] son of Shaphat from Abel Meholah to succeed
you as prophet. 17Jehu will put to death any who escape the sword
of Hazael,[g] and Elisha will put to death any who escape the sword
of Jehu. 18Yet I reserve[h] seven thousand in Israel—all whose knees
have not bowed down to Baal and all whose mouths have not
kissed[i] him."
19So Elijah went from there and found Elisha son of Shaphat. He
was plowing with twelve yoke of oxen, and he himself was driving
the twelfth pair. Elijah went up to him and threw his cloak[j] around
him. 20Elisha then left his oxen and ran after Elijah. "Let me kiss
my father and mother good-by,"[k] he said, "and then I will come
with you."
"Go back," Elijah replied. "What have I done to you?"
21So Elisha left him and went back. He took his yoke of oxen[l]
and slaughtered them. He burned the plowing equipment to cook
the meat and gave it to the people, and they ate. Then he set out to
follow Elijah and became his attendant.[m]

Chapter 20 Theme ______________________________

20 Now Ben-Hadad[n] king of Aram mustered his entire army.
Accompanied by thirty-two kings with their horses and
chariots, he went up and besieged Samaria and attacked it. 2He
sent messengers into the city to Ahab king of Israel, saying, "This
is what Ben-Hadad says: 3'Your silver and gold are mine, and the
best of your wives and children are mine.' "
4The king of Israel answered, "Just as you say, my lord the king.
I and all I have are yours."
5The messengers came again and said, "This is what Ben-Hadad
says: 'I sent to demand your silver and gold, your wives and your
children. 6But about this time tomorrow I am going to send my
officials to search your palace and the houses of your officials.
They will seize everything you value and carry it away.' "
7The king of Israel summoned all the elders of the land and
said to them, "See how this man is looking for trouble![o] When he

19:12 [a]Job 4:16; Zec 4:6
19:13 [b]ver 9; Ex 3:6
19:14 [c]ver 10
19:15 [d]2Ki 8:7-15
19:16 [e]2Ki 9:1-3,6 [f]ver 21; 2Ki 2:9,15
19:17 [g]2Ki 8:12,29; 9:14; 13:3,7,22
19:18 [h]Ro 11:4* [i]Hos 13:2
19:19 [j]2Ki 2:8,14
19:20 [k]Mt 8:21-22; Lk 9:61
19:21 [l]2Sa 24:22 [m]ver 16
20:1 [n]1Ki 15:18; 22:31; 2Ki 6:24
20:7 [o]2Ki 5:7

sent for my wives and my children, my silver and my gold, I did not refuse him."

8The elders and the people all answered, "Don't listen to him or agree to his demands."

9So he replied to Ben-Hadad's messengers, "Tell my lord the king, 'Your servant will do all you demanded the first time, but this demand I cannot meet.'" They left and took the answer back to Ben-Hadad.

10Then Ben-Hadad sent another message to Ahab: "May the gods deal with me, be it ever so severely, if enough dust[a] remains in Samaria to give each of my men a handful."

11The king of Israel answered, "Tell him: 'One who puts on his armor should not boast[b] like one who takes it off.'"

12Ben-Hadad heard this message while he and the kings were drinking[c] in their tents,[a] and he ordered his men: "Prepare to attack." So they prepared to attack the city.

13Meanwhile a prophet came to Ahab king of Israel and announced, "This is what the LORD says: 'Do you see this vast army? I will give it into your hand today, and then you will know[d] that I am the LORD.'"

14"But who will do this?" asked Ahab.

The prophet replied, "This is what the LORD says: 'The young officers of the provincial commanders will do it.'"

"And who will start[e] the battle?" he asked.

The prophet answered, "You will."

15So Ahab summoned the young officers of the provincial commanders, 232 men. Then he assembled the rest of the Israelites, 7,000 in all. 16They set out at noon while Ben-Hadad and the 32 kings allied with him were in their tents getting drunk.[f] 17The young officers of the provincial commanders went out first.

Now Ben-Hadad had dispatched scouts, who reported, "Men are advancing from Samaria."

18He said, "If they have come out for peace, take them alive; if they have come out for war, take them alive."

19The young officers of the provincial commanders marched out of the city with the army behind them 20and each one struck down his opponent. At that, the Arameans fled, with the Israelites in pursuit. But Ben-Hadad king of Aram escaped on horseback with some of his horsemen. 21The king of Israel advanced and overpowered the horses and chariots and inflicted heavy losses on the Arameans.

22Afterward, the prophet[g] came to the king of Israel and said, "Strengthen your position and see what must be done, because next spring[h] the king of Aram will attack you again."

20:10 [a]2Sa 22:43; 1Ki 19:2
20:11 [b]Pr 27:1; Jer 9:23
20:12 [c]ver 16; 1Ki 16:9
20:13 [d]ver 28; Ex 6:7
20:14 [e]Jdg 1:1
20:16 [f]ver 12; 1Ki 16:9
20:22 [g]ver 13 [h]ver 26; 2Sa 11:1

a *12* Or *in Succoth*; also in verse 16

23 Meanwhile, the officials of the king of Aram advised him, “Their gods are gods[a] of the hills. That is why they were too strong for us. But if we fight them on the plains, surely we will be stronger than they. 24 Do this: Remove all the kings from their commands and replace them with other officers. 25 You must also raise an army like the one you lost—horse for horse and chariot for chariot—so we can fight Israel on the plains. Then surely we will be stronger than they.” He agreed with them and acted accordingly.

26 The next spring[b] Ben-Hadad mustered the Arameans and went up to Aphek[c] to fight against Israel. 27 When the Israelites were also mustered and given provisions, they marched out to meet them. The Israelites camped opposite them like two small flocks of goats, while the Arameans covered the countryside.[d]

28 The man of God came up and told the king of Israel, “This is what the LORD says: ‘Because the Arameans think the LORD is a god of the hills and not a god[e] of the valleys, I will deliver this vast army into your hands, and you will know[f] that I am the LORD.’ ”

29 For seven days they camped opposite each other, and on the seventh day the battle was joined. The Israelites inflicted a hundred thousand casualties on the Aramean foot soldiers in one day. 30 The rest of them escaped to the city of Aphek,[g] where the wall collapsed on twenty-seven thousand of them. And Ben-Hadad fled to the city and hid[h] in an inner room.

31 His officials said to him, “Look, we have heard that the kings of the house of Israel are merciful. Let us go to the king of Israel with sackcloth[i] around our waists and ropes around our heads. Perhaps he will spare your life.”

32 Wearing sackcloth around their waists and ropes around their heads, they went to the king of Israel and said, “Your servant Ben-Hadad says: ‘Please let me live.’ ”

The king answered, “Is he still alive? He is my brother.”

33 The men took this as a good sign and were quick to pick up his word. “Yes, your brother Ben-Hadad!” they said.

“Go and get him,” the king said. When Ben-Hadad came out, Ahab had him come up into his chariot.

34 “I will return the cities[j] my father took from your father,” Ben-Hadad offered. “You may set up your own market areas in Damascus,[k] as my father did in Samaria.”

⌊Ahab said,⌋ “On the basis of a treaty[l] I will set you free.” So he made a treaty with him, and let him go.

35 By the word of the LORD one of the sons of the prophets said to his companion, “Strike me with your weapon,” but the man refused.[m]

36 So the prophet said, “Because you have not obeyed the LORD, as soon as you leave me a lion[n] will kill you.” And after the man went away, a lion found him and killed him.

20:23 [a] 1Ki 14:23; Ro 1:21-23
20:26 [b] ver 22 [c] 2Ki 13:17
20:27 [d] Jdg 6:6; 1Sa 13:6
20:28 [e] ver 23 [f] ver 13
20:30 [g] ver 26 [h] 1Ki 22:25; 2Ch 18:24
20:31 [i] Ge 37:34
20:34 [j] 1Ki 15:20 [k] Jer 49:23-27 [l] Ex 23:32
20:35 [m] 1Ki 13:21; 2Ki 2:3-7
20:36 [n] 1Ki 13:24

37The prophet found another man and said, "Strike me, please."
So the man struck him and wounded him. 38Then the prophet
went and stood by the road waiting for the king. He disguised
himself with his headband down over his eyes. 39As the king
passed by, the prophet called out to him, "Your servant went into
the thick of the battle, and someone came to me with a captive
and said, 'Guard this man. If he is missing, it will be your life for
his life,[a] or you must pay a talent[a] of silver.' 40While your servant
was busy here and there, the man disappeared."

"That is your sentence," the king of Israel said. "You have pronounced it yourself."

41Then the prophet quickly removed the headband from his
eyes, and the king of Israel recognized him as one of the prophets.
42He said to the king, "This is what the LORD says: 'You have set free
a man I had determined should die.[b][b] Therefore it is your life for
his life,[c] your people for his people.'" 43Sullen and angry,[d] the king
of Israel went to his palace in Samaria.

Chapter 21 Theme __________________________

21 Some time later there was an incident involving a vineyard
belonging to Naboth[e] the Jezreelite. The vineyard was in
Jezreel,[f] close to the palace of Ahab king of Samaria. 2Ahab said to
Naboth, "Let me have your vineyard to use for a vegetable garden,
since it is close to my palace. In exchange I will give you a better
vineyard or, if you prefer, I will pay you whatever it is worth."

3But Naboth replied, "The LORD forbid that I should give you the
inheritance[g] of my fathers."

4So Ahab went home, sullen and angry[h] because Naboth the
Jezreelite had said, "I will not give you the inheritance of my fathers."
He lay on his bed sulking and refused to eat.

5His wife Jezebel came in and asked him, "Why are you so sullen?
Why won't you eat?"

6He answered her, "Because I said to Naboth the Jezreelite, 'Sell
me your vineyard; or if you prefer, I will give you another vineyard
in its place.' But he said, 'I will not give you my vineyard.'"

7Jezebel his wife said, "Is this how you act as king over Israel?
Get up and eat! Cheer up. I'll get you the vineyard[i] of Naboth the
Jezreelite."

8So she wrote letters in Ahab's name, placed his seal[j] on them,
and sent them to the elders and nobles who lived in Naboth's city
with him. 9In those letters she wrote:

> "Proclaim a day of fasting and seat Naboth in a prominent
> place among the people. 10But seat two scoundrels[k] opposite

20:39 [a]2Ki 10:24
20:42 [b]Jer 48:10 [c]ver 39; Jos 2:14; 1Ki 22:31-37
20:43 [d]1Ki 21:4
21:1 [e]2Ki 9:21 [f]1Ki 18:45-46
21:3 [g]Lev 25:23; Nu 36:7; Eze 46:18
21:4 [h]1Ki 20:43
21:7 [i]1Sa 8:14
21:8 [j]Ge 38:18; Est 3:12; 8:8,10
21:10 [k]Ac 6:11

[a]*39* That is, about 75 pounds (about 34 kilograms) [b]*42* The Hebrew term refers to the irrevocable giving over of things or persons to the LORD, often by totally destroying them.

him and have them testify that he has cursed[a] both God and
the king. Then take him out and stone him to death."

11So the elders and nobles who lived in Naboth's city did as
Jezebel directed in the letters she had written to them. 12They proclaimed a fast[b] and seated Naboth in a prominent place among the
people. 13Then two scoundrels came and sat opposite him and
brought charges against Naboth before the people, saying, "Naboth
has cursed both God and the king." So they took him outside the
city and stoned him to death.[c] 14Then they sent word to Jezebel:
"Naboth has been stoned and is dead."

15As soon as Jezebel heard that Naboth had been stoned to death,
she said to Ahab, "Get up and take possession of the vineyard[d] of
Naboth the Jezreelite that he refused to sell you. He is no longer
alive, but dead." 16When Ahab heard that Naboth was dead, he got
up and went down to take possession of Naboth's vineyard.

17Then the word of the LORD came to Elijah the Tishbite: 18"Go
down to meet Ahab king of Israel, who rules in Samaria. He is now
in Naboth's vineyard, where he has gone to take possession of it.
19Say to him, 'This is what the LORD says: Have you not murdered
a man and seized his property?' Then say to him, 'This is what
the LORD says: In the place where dogs licked up Naboth's blood,[e]
dogs[f] will lick up your blood—yes, yours!'"

20Ahab said to Elijah, "So you have found me, my enemy!"[g]

"I have found you," he answered, "because you have sold[h] yourself to do evil in the eyes of the LORD. 21'I am going to bring disaster
on you. I will consume your descendants and cut off from Ahab
every last male[i] in Israel—slave or free. 22I will make your house[j]
like that of Jeroboam son of Nebat and that of Baasha son of Ahijah, because you have provoked me to anger and have caused Israel
to sin.'[k]

23"And also concerning Jezebel the LORD says: 'Dogs[l] will devour
Jezebel by the wall of[a] Jezreel.'

24"Dogs[m] will eat those belonging to Ahab who die in the city,
and the birds of the air will feed on those who die in the country."

25(There was never[n] a man like Ahab, who sold himself to do evil
in the eyes of the LORD, urged on by Jezebel his wife. 26He behaved
in the vilest manner by going after idols, like the Amorites[o] the
LORD drove out before Israel.)

27When Ahab heard these words, he tore his clothes, put on sackcloth[p] and fasted. He lay in sackcloth and went around meekly.

28Then the word of the LORD came to Elijah the Tishbite: 29"Have
you noticed how Ahab has humbled himself before me? Because

[a] 23 Most Hebrew manuscripts; a few Hebrew manuscripts, Vulgate and Syriac (see also 2 Kings 9:26) *the plot of ground at*

21:10 [a] Ex 22:28; Lev 24:15-16
21:12 [b] Isa 58:4
21:13 [c] 2Ki 9:26
21:15 [d] 1Sa 8:14
21:19 [e] 2Ki 9:26; Ps 9:12; Isa 14:20 [f] 1Ki 22:38
21:20 [g] 1Ki 18:17 [h] ver 25; 2Ki 17:17; Ro 7:14
21:21 [i] 1Ki 14:10; 2Ki 9:8
21:22 [j] 1Ki 15:29; 16:3 [k] 1Ki 12:30
21:23 [l] 2Ki 9:10, 34-36
21:24 [m] 1Ki 14:11; 16:4
21:25 [n] ver 20; 1Ki 16:33
21:26 [o] Ge 15:16; Lev 18:25-30; 2Ki 21:11
21:27 [p] Ge 37:34; 2Sa 3:31; 2Ki 6:30

21:29 [a]2Ki 9:26 he has humbled himself, I will not bring this disaster in his day, but
I will bring it on his house in the days of his son."[a]

Chapter 22 Theme ______________________________

22:3 [b]Dt 4:43; **22** For three years there was no war between Aram and Israel.
Jos 21:38 2But in the third year Jehoshaphat king of Judah went down
to see the king of Israel. 3The king of Israel had said to his officials,
"Don't you know that Ramoth Gilead[b] belongs to us and yet we are
doing nothing to retake it from the king of Aram?"
4So he asked Jehoshaphat, "Will you go with me to fight[c] against
22:4 [c]2Ki 3:7 Ramoth Gilead?"
Jehoshaphat replied to the king of Israel, "I am as you are, my
people as your people, my horses as your horses." 5But Jehoshaphat
also said to the king of Israel, "First seek the counsel[d] of the LORD."
22:5 [d]Ex 33:7; 6So the king of Israel brought together the prophets—about
2Ki 3:11 four hundred men—and asked them, "Shall I go to war against
Ramoth Gilead, or shall I refrain?"
"Go,"[e] they answered, "for the Lord will give it into the king's
hand."
22:6 7But Jehoshaphat asked, "Is there not a prophet[f] of the LORD here
[e]1Ki 18:19 whom we can inquire of?"
8The king of Israel answered Jehoshaphat, "There is still one
man through whom we can inquire of the LORD, but I hate[g] him
because he never prophesies anything good[h] about me, but always
22:7 [f]2Ki 3:11 bad. He is Micaiah son of Imlah."
"The king should not say that," Jehoshaphat replied.
9So the king of Israel called one of his officials and said, "Bring
Micaiah son of Imlah at once."
22:8 10Dressed in their royal robes, the king of Israel and Jehoshaphat
[g]Am 5:10 king of Judah were sitting on their thrones at the threshing floor[i]
[h]Isa 5:20 by the entrance of the gate of Samaria, with all the prophets
prophesying before them. 11Now Zedekiah son of Kenaanah had
made iron horns[j] and he declared, "This is what the LORD says:
'With these you will gore the Arameans until they are destroyed.'"
22:10 [i]ver 6 12All the other prophets were prophesying the same thing. "Attack Ramoth Gilead and be victorious," they said, "for the LORD
will give it into the king's hand."
13The messenger who had gone to summon Micaiah said to him,
22:11 [j]Dt 33:17; "Look, as one man the other prophets are predicting success for
Zec 1:18-21 the king. Let your word agree with theirs, and speak favorably."
14But Micaiah said, "As surely as the LORD lives, I can tell him
only what the LORD tells me."[k]
15When he arrived, the king asked him, "Micaiah, shall we go to
22:14 war against Ramoth Gilead, or shall I refrain?"
[k]Nu 22:18; 24:13; "Attack and be victorious," he answered, "for the LORD will give it
1Ki 18:10,15 into the king's hand."

16 The king said to him, "How many times must I make you
swear to tell me nothing but the truth in the name of the LORD?"
17 Then Micaiah answered, "I saw all Israel scattered on the hills
like sheep without a shepherd,[a] and the LORD said, 'These people
have no master. Let each one go home in peace.' "
18 The king of Israel said to Jehoshaphat, "Didn't I tell you that he
never prophesies anything good about me, but only bad?"
19 Micaiah continued, "Therefore hear the word of the LORD: I
saw the LORD sitting on his throne[b] with all the host[c] of heaven
standing around him on his right and on his left. 20 And the LORD
said, 'Who will entice Ahab into attacking Ramoth Gilead and
going to his death there?'
"One suggested this, and another that. 21 Finally, a spirit came
forward, stood before the LORD and said, 'I will entice him.'
22 " 'By what means?' the LORD asked.
" 'I will go out and be a lying[d] spirit in the mouths of all his prophets,' he said.
" 'You will succeed in enticing him,' said the LORD. 'Go and do it.'
23 "So now the LORD has put a lying spirit in the mouths of all
these prophets[e] of yours. The LORD has decreed disaster for you."
24 Then Zedekiah[f] son of Kenaanah went up and slapped[g] Micaiah in the face. "Which way did the spirit from[a] the LORD go when
he went from me to speak to you?" he asked.
25 Micaiah replied, "You will find out on the day you go to hide[h]
in an inner room."
26 The king of Israel then ordered, "Take Micaiah and send him
back to Amon the ruler of the city and to Joash the king's son
27 and say, 'This is what the king says: Put this fellow in prison[i] and
give him nothing but bread and water until I return safely.' "
28 Micaiah declared, "If you ever return safely, the LORD has not
spoken[j] through me." Then he added, "Mark my words, all you
people!"
29 So the king of Israel and Jehoshaphat king of Judah went up to
Ramoth Gilead. 30 The king of Israel said to Jehoshaphat, "I will
enter the battle in disguise,[k] but you wear your royal robes." So the
king of Israel disguised himself and went into battle.
31 Now the king of Aram had ordered his thirty-two chariot commanders, "Do not fight with anyone, small or great, except the
king[l] of Israel." 32 When the chariot commanders saw Jehoshaphat,
they thought, "Surely this is the king of Israel." So they turned to
attack him, but when Jehoshaphat cried out, 33 the chariot commanders saw that he was not the king of Israel and stopped pursuing him.
34 But someone drew his bow[m] at random and hit the king of Israel
between the sections of his armor. The king told his chariot driver,

a 24 Or *Spirit of*

22:17 [a] ver 34-36; Nu 27:17; Mt 9:36
22:19 [b] Isa 6:1; Eze 1:26; Da 7:9 [c] Job 1:6; 2:1; Ps 103:20-21; Mt 18:10; Heb 1:7,14
22:22 [d] Jdg 9:23; 1Sa 16:14; 18:10; 19:9; Eze 14:9; 2Th 2:11
22:23 [e] Eze 14:9
22:24 [f] ver 11 [g] Ac 23:2
22:25 [h] 1Ki 20:30
22:27 [i] 2Ch 16:10
22:28 [j] Dt 18:22
22:30 [k] 2Ch 35:32
22:31 [l] 2Sa 17:2
22:34 [m] 2Ch 35:23

“Wheel around and get me out of the fighting. I’ve been wounded.” 35All day long the battle raged, and the king was propped up
in his chariot facing the Arameans. The blood from his wound ran
onto the floor of the chariot, and that evening he died. 36As the sun
was setting, a cry spread through the army: “Every man to his
town; everyone to his land!”[a]

37So the king died and was brought to Samaria, and they buried
him there. 38They washed the chariot at a pool in Samaria (where
the prostitutes bathed),[a] and the dogs[b] licked up his blood, as the
word of the LORD had declared.

39As for the other events of Ahab’s reign, including all he did, the
palace he built and inlaid with ivory,[c] and the cities he fortified, are
they not written in the book of the annals of the kings of Israel?
40Ahab rested with his fathers. And Ahaziah his son succeeded
him as king.

41Jehoshaphat son of Asa became king of Judah in the fourth
year of Ahab king of Israel. 42Jehoshaphat was thirty-five years old
when he became king, and he reigned in Jerusalem twenty-five
years. His mother’s name was Azubah daughter of Shilhi. 43In
everything he walked in the ways of his father Asa[d] and did not
stray from them; he did what was right in the eyes of the LORD. The
high places,[e] however, were not removed, and the people continued
to offer sacrifices and burn incense there. 44Jehoshaphat was also at
peace with the king of Israel.

45As for the other events of Jehoshaphat’s reign, the things he
achieved and his military exploits, are they not written in the
book of the annals of the kings of Judah? 46He rid the land of the
rest of the male shrine prostitutes[f] who remained there even after
the reign of his father Asa. 47There was then no king[g] in Edom; a
deputy ruled.

48Now Jehoshaphat built a fleet of trading ships[b][h] to go to Ophir
for gold, but they never set sail—they were wrecked at Ezion
Geber. 49At that time Ahaziah son of Ahab said to Jehoshaphat,
“Let my men sail with your men,” but Jehoshaphat refused.

50Then Jehoshaphat rested with his fathers and was buried with
them in the city of David his father. And Jehoram his son succeeded him.

51Ahaziah son of Ahab became king of Israel in Samaria in the
seventeenth year of Jehoshaphat king of Judah, and he reigned over
Israel two years. 52He did evil[i] in the eyes of the LORD, because he
walked in the ways of his father and mother and in the ways of
Jeroboam son of Nebat, who caused Israel to sin. 53He served and
worshiped Baal[j] and provoked the LORD, the God of Israel, to
anger, just as his father[k] had done.

22:36 [a]2Ki 14:12
22:38 [b]1Ki 21:19
22:39 [c]2Ch 9:17; Am 3:15
22:43 [d]2Ch 17:3 [e]1Ki 3:2; 15:14; 2Ki 12:3
22:46 [f]Dt 23:17; 1Ki 14:24; 15:12
22:47 [g]2Sa 8:14; 2Ki 3:9; 8:20
22:48 [h]1Ki 9:26; 10:22
22:52 [i]1Ki 15:26; 21:25
22:53 [j]Jdg 2:11 [k]1Ki 16:30-32

[a]38 Or *Samaria and cleaned the weapons* [b]48 Hebrew *of ships of Tarshish*

1 Kings at a Glance

Theme of 1 Kings:

Segment Divisions

		Chapter Themes
		1
		2
		3
		4
		5
		6
		7
		8
		9
		10
		11
		12
		13
		14
		15
		16
		17
		18
		19
		20
		21
		22

Author:

Date:

Purpose:

Key Words:

2 KINGS

"Where now is the LORD, the God of Elijah?"

As you study 2 Kings, the continuation of 1 Kings, you will see God at work setting up and removing kings and kingdoms. You will be introduced to his spokesmen, the prophets, who spoke his Word until Israel and then Judah were led into captivity.

THINGS TO DO

1. As you read through 2 Kings one chapter at a time:
   a. Mark the following key repeated words: *according to the word of the Lord (as the Lord had said, in accordance with the word of the Lord), heart (spirit, in accord, mind, wholehearted), sin (sins, which he caused Israel to commit), high places (high place, shrine),* and *covenant.* Always watch for and mark words which are distinctive to a particular chapter such as *practices* in chapter 17. Write these key words on an index card you can use as a bookmark while studying 2 Kings.

   b. Look for what you learn about God: his requirements, his ways, his judgments, and his character. Record your insights in the margin of the text. Be sure to note "Lessons for Life" (LFL).

   c. Watch for any reforms instituted by a king. In the margin note these reforms and the results. As you finish reading about the reign of a king, record what you learn on the chart THE KINGS OF ISRAEL AND JUDAH on pages 654 and 655.

   d. Record the theme or main event of each chapter on 2 KINGS AT A GLANCE on page 650 and in the text next to the chapter number.

2. Second Kings has some key or pivotal events:
   a. In 1:1 through 8:15 the prophetic ministries of Elijah and then Elisha are prominent. List in the margin the miracles accomplished through these men. Several miraculous things occur after 8:15; watch for them.

   b. Second Kings gives the account of the Assyrian invasion and subsequent captivity of the northern kingdom of Israel. Give special attention to the details of this invasion and why it came about. Note these in the margin of the text under the heading "The Assyrian Captivity."

   c. After the Assyrian captivity all that is left is the southern kingdom of Judah. Watch how Judah conducts herself after seeing God's judgment on the northern kingdom. All this came to pass just as God's prophets said it would.

   d. Watch for the account of the Babylonian captivity of the southern kingdom of Judah and the ensuing events. Record this in the margin as you did the Assyrian captivity.

3. There are two charts which identify the major characters and events of 2 Kings.
   a. The first chart, ISRAEL'S DIVISION AND CAPTIVITY, on page 649, gives a broad overview of the division of the kingdom through the three sieges of Jerusalem by the Babylonians.

   b. The second is a three-part chart: THE HISTORICAL CHART OF THE KINGS AND PROPHETS OF ISRAEL AND JUDAH, on pages 651 through 653. This chart shows the relationship of the kings and prophets to one another and to other foreign kings and their kingdoms. You might color these charts so that the kings of the northern and southern kingdoms and the prophets can be readily distinguished from one another.

   c. When you read of key figures or events in 2 Kings consult these charts.

4. Complete the chart 2 KINGS AT A GLANCE. Considering the key events or personages featured in 2 Kings, see which chapters of 2 Kings can be grouped together under a common theme or topic. Record the theme of each segment under "Segment Divisions." Also, you might want to note on the chart the chapters which tell when the Assyrian and Babylonian invasions occur. Remember to record the theme of 2 Kings.

Things to Think About

1. As you consider the lives of Elijah and Elisha, what do you learn about faith and trusting God?

2. As you think about the captivity of Israel and Judah, and the reasons for their captivity, what do you learn about the necessity of living a righteous life? What practical applications can you make to your own life? Remember, walking your own way may be pleasurable for awhile, but a just God must hold you accountable.

3. As you studied 1 and 2 Kings you saw that what God says will happen eventually comes to pass. Since his Word stands and none can alter it, can you see how critical it is that you believe God and hold to his Word no matter what others say or do?

Chapter 1 Theme ____________________

1 After Ahab's death, Moab[a] rebelled against Israel. 2Now Ahaziah had fallen through the lattice of his upper room in Samaria
and injured himself. So he sent messengers,[b] saying to them, "Go
and consult Baal-Zebub,[c] the god of Ekron,[d] to see if I will recover[e]
from this injury."
3But the angel[f] of the LORD said to Elijah[g] the Tishbite, "Go up
and meet the messengers of the king of Samaria and ask them, 'Is
it because there is no God in Israel[h] that you are going off to consult Baal-Zebub, the god of Ekron?' 4Therefore this is what the
LORD says: 'You will not leave[i] the bed you are lying on. You will
certainly die!'" So Elijah went.
5When the messengers returned to the king, he asked them,
"Why have you come back?"
6"A man came to meet us," they replied. "And he said to us, 'Go
back to the king who sent you and tell him, "This is what the LORD
says: Is it because there is no God in Israel that you are sending
men to consult Baal-Zebub, the god of Ekron? Therefore you will
not leave the bed you are lying on. You will certainly die!"'"
7The king asked them, "What kind of man was it who came to
meet you and told you this?"
8They replied, "He was a man with a garment of hair[j] and with
a leather belt around his waist."
The king said, "That was Elijah the Tishbite."
9Then he sent[k] to Elijah a captain[l] with his company of fifty men.
The captain went up to Elijah, who was sitting on the top of a hill,
and said to him, "Man of God, the king says, 'Come down!'"

1:1 [a]Ge 19:37; 2Sa 8:2; 2Ki 3:5

1:2 [b]ver 16 [c]Mk 3:22 [d]1Sa 6:2; Isa 2:6; 14:29; Mt 10:25 [e]Jdg 18:5; 2Ki 8:7-10

1:3 [f]ver 15; Ge 16:7 [g]1Ki 17:1 [h]1Sa 28:8

1:4 [i]ver 6,16; Ps 41:8

1:8 [j]1Ki 18:7; Zec 13:4; Mt 3:4; Mk 1:6

1:9 [k]2Ki 6:14 [l]Ex 18:25; Isa 3:3

10 Elijah answered the captain, "If I am a man of God, may fire
come down from heaven and consume you and your fifty men!"
Then fire[a] fell from heaven and consumed the captain and his men.
11 At this the king sent to Elijah another captain with his fifty
men. The captain said to him, "Man of God, this is what the king
says, 'Come down at once!' "
12 "If I am a man of God," Elijah replied, "may fire come down
from heaven and consume you and your fifty men!" Then the fire
of God fell from heaven and consumed him and his fifty men.
13 So the king sent a third captain with his fifty men. This third
captain went up and fell on his knees before Elijah. "Man of
God," he begged, "please have respect for my life[b] and the lives of
these fifty men, your servants! 14 See, fire has fallen from heaven
and consumed the first two captains and all their men. But now
have respect for my life!"
15 The angel[c] of the LORD said to Elijah, "Go down with him; do
not be afraid[d] of him." So Elijah got up and went down with him
to the king.
16 He told the king, "This is what the LORD says: Is it because
there is no God in Israel for you to consult that you have sent
messengers[e] to consult Baal-Zebub, the god of Ekron? Because
you have done this, you will never leave[f] the bed you are lying on.
You will certainly die!" 17 So he died,[g] according to the word of the
LORD that Elijah had spoken.
Because Ahaziah had no son, Joram[a][h] succeeded him as king
in the second year of Jehoram son of Jehoshaphat king of Judah.
18 As for all the other events of Ahaziah's reign, and what he did,
are they not written in the book of the annals of the kings of Israel?

Chapter 2 Theme ________________________

2 When the LORD was about to take[i] Elijah up to heaven in a
whirlwind,[j] Elijah and Elisha[k] were on their way from Gilgal.[l]
2 Elijah said to Elisha, "Stay here;[m] the LORD has sent me to Bethel."
But Elisha said, "As surely as the LORD lives and as you live, I
will not leave you."[n] So they went down to Bethel.
3 The company[o] of the prophets at Bethel came out to Elisha
and asked, "Do you know that the LORD is going to take your
master from you today?"
"Yes, I know," Elisha replied, "but do not speak of it."
4 Then Elijah said to him, "Stay here, Elisha; the LORD has sent
me to Jericho.[p]"
And he replied, "As surely as the LORD lives and as you live, I
will not leave you." So they went to Jericho.

a 17 Hebrew *Jehoram,* a variant of *Joram*

1:10 a 1Ki 18:38; Lk 9:54; Rev 11:5; 13:13
1:13 b 1Sa 26:21; Ps 72:14
1:15 c ver 3 d Isa 51:12; 57:11; Jer 1:17; Eze 2:6
1:16 e ver 2 f ver 4
1:17 g 2Ki 8:15; Jer 20:6; 28:17 h 2Ki 3:1; 8:16
2:1 i Ge 5:24; Heb 11:5 j ver 11; 1Ki 19:11; Isa 5:28; 66:15; Jer 4:13; Na 1:3 k 1Ki 19:16,21 l Dt 11:30; 2Ki 4:38
2:2 m ver 6 n Ru 1:16; 1Sa 1:26; 2Ki 4:30
2:3 o 1Sa 10:5; 2Ki 4:1,38
2:4 p Jos 3:16; 6:26

5The company[a] of the prophets at Jericho went up to Elisha and
asked him, "Do you know that the LORD is going to take your
master from you today?"
"Yes, I know," he replied, "but do not speak of it."
6Then Elijah said to him, "Stay here;[b] the LORD has sent me to
the Jordan."[c]
And he replied, "As surely as the LORD lives and as you live, I
will not leave you."[d] So the two of them walked on.
7Fifty men of the company of the prophets went and stood at a
distance, facing the place where Elijah and Elisha had stopped at
the Jordan. 8Elijah took his cloak,[e] rolled it up and struck[f] the
water with it. The water divided[g] to the right and to the left, and
the two of them crossed over on dry[h] ground.

Elisha's Ministry

9When they had crossed, Elijah said to Elisha, "Tell me, what
can I do for you before I am taken from you?"
"Let me inherit a double[i]
portion of your spirit,"[j] Elisha replied.
10"You have asked a difficult thing," Elijah said, "yet
if you see me when I am
taken from you, it will be
yours—otherwise not."
11As they were walking
along and talking together,
suddenly a chariot of fire[k]
and horses of fire appeared
and separated the two of
them, and Elijah went up to
heaven[l] in a whirlwind.[m]
12Elisha saw this and cried
out, "My father! My father!
The chariots[n] and horsemen of Israel!" And Elisha
saw him no more. Then he
took hold of his own clothes
and tore[o] them apart.
13He picked up the cloak
that had fallen from Elijah
and went back and stood on
the bank of the Jordan.
14Then he took the cloak[p]
that had fallen from him
and struck[q] the water with
it. "Where now is the LORD,

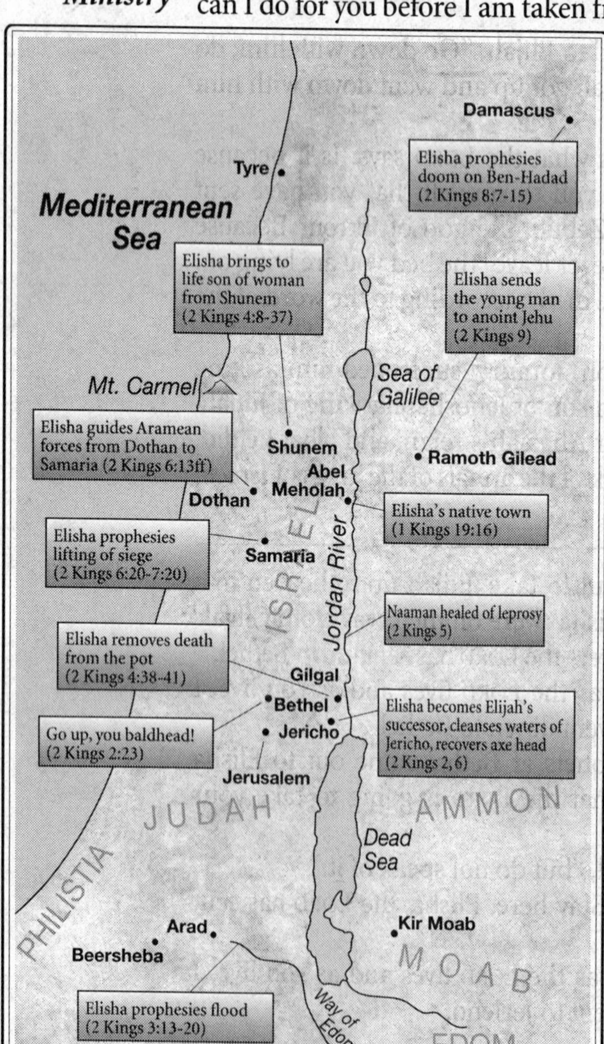

2:5 [a]ver 3
2:6 [b]ver 2 [c]Jos 3:15 [d]Ru 1:16
2:8 [e]1Ki 19:19 [f]ver 14 [g]Ex 14:21 [h]Ex 14:22,29
2:9 [i]Dt 21:17 [j]Nu 11:17
2:11 [k]2Ki 6:17; Ps 68:17; 104:3,4; Isa 66:15; Hab 3:8; Zec 6:1 [l]Ge 5:24 [m]ver 1
2:12 [n]2Ki 6:17; 13:14 [o]Ge 37:29
2:14 [p]1Ki 19:19 [q]ver 8

2:15 [a]ver 7; 1Sa 10:5 [b]Nu 11:17

the God of Elijah?" he asked. When he struck the water, it divided to the right and to the left, and he crossed over.
15The company[a] of the prophets from Jericho, who were watching, said, "The spirit[b] of Elijah is resting on Elisha." And they
went to meet him and bowed to the ground before him. 16"Look,"
they said, "we your servants have fifty able men. Let them go and
look for your master. Perhaps the Spirit[c] of the LORD has picked
him up[d] and set him down on some mountain or in some valley."
"No," Elisha replied, "do not send them."

2:16 [c]1Ki 18:12 [d]Ac 8:39

17But they persisted until he was too ashamed[e] to refuse. So he
said, "Send them." And they sent fifty men, who searched for
three days but did not find him. 18When they returned to Elisha,
who was staying in Jericho, he said to them, "Didn't I tell you not
to go?"
19The men of the city
said to Elisha, "Look, our
lord, this town is well situated, as you can see, but

2:17 [e]2Ki 8:11

the water is bad and the
land is unproductive."
20"Bring me a new
bowl," he said, "and put
salt in it." So they brought
it to him.
21Then he went out to
the spring and threw[f] the

2:21 [f]Ex 15:25; 2Ki 4:41; 6:6

salt into it, saying, "This
is what the LORD says: 'I
have healed this water.
Never again will it cause
death or make the land
unproductive.'" 22And
the water has remained
wholesome[g] to this day,

2:22 [g]Ex 15:25

according to the word
Elisha had spoken.
23From there Elisha
went up to Bethel. As he
was walking along the
road, some youths came
out of the town and
jeered[h] at him. "Go on

2:23 [h]Ex 22:28; 2Ch 36:16; Job 19:18; Ps 31:18

up, you baldhead!" they
said. "Go on up, you
baldhead!" 24He turned

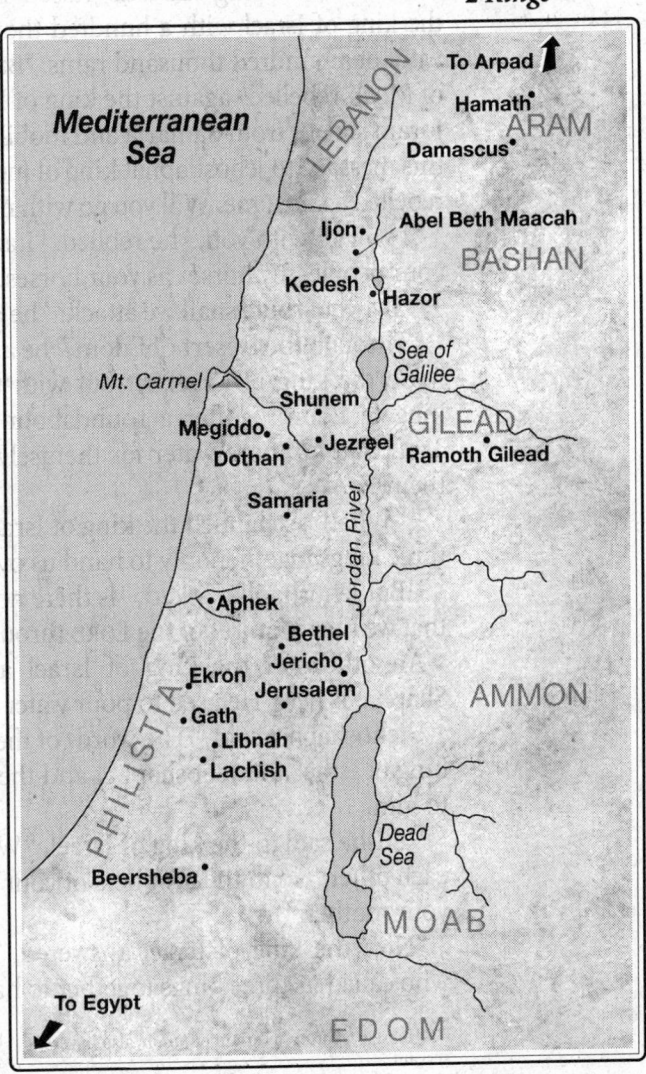

The Cities and Geography of 2 Kings

around, looked at them and called down a curse[a] on them in the
name[b] of the LORD. Then two bears came out of the woods and
mauled forty-two of the youths. 25And he went on to Mount
Carmel[c] and from there returned to Samaria.

Chapter 3 Theme ________________________________

3 Joram[a][d] son of Ahab became king of Israel in Samaria in the
eighteenth year of Jehoshaphat king of Judah, and he reigned
twelve years. 2He did evil[e] in the eyes of the LORD, but not as his
father[f] and mother had done. He got rid of the sacred stone[g] of
Baal that his father had made. 3Nevertheless he clung to the sins[h]
of Jeroboam son of Nebat, which he had caused Israel to commit;
he did not turn away from them.

4Now Mesha king of Moab[i] raised sheep, and he had to supply
the king of Israel with a hundred thousand lambs[j] and with the
wool of a hundred thousand rams. 5But after Ahab died, the king
of Moab rebelled[k] against the king of Israel. 6So at that time King
Joram set out from Samaria and mobilized all Israel. 7He also sent
this message to Jehoshaphat king of Judah: "The king of Moab has
rebelled against me. Will you go with me to fight[l] against Moab?"

"I will go with you," he replied. "I am as you are, my people as
your people, my horses as your horses."

8"By what route shall we attack?" he asked.

"Through the Desert of Edom," he answered.

9So the king of Israel set out with the king of Judah and the
king of Edom.[m] After a roundabout march of seven days, the
army had no more water for themselves or for the animals with
them.

10"What!" exclaimed the king of Israel. "Has the LORD called us
three kings together only to hand us over to Moab?"

11But Jehoshaphat asked, "Is there no prophet of the LORD here,
that we may inquire[n] of the LORD through him?"

An officer of the king of Israel answered, "Elisha[o] son of
Shaphat is here. He used to pour water on the hands of Elijah.[b][p]"

12Jehoshaphat said, "The word[q] of the LORD is with him." So the
king of Israel and Jehoshaphat and the king of Edom went down
to him.

13Elisha said to the king of Israel, "What do we have to do with
each other? Go to the prophets of your father and the prophets of
your mother."

"No," the king of Israel answered, "because it was the LORD
who called us three kings together to hand us over to Moab."

2:24 [a]Ge 4:11; Ne 13:25-27 [b]Dt 18:19
2:25 [c]1Ki 18:20; 2Ki 4:25
3:1 [d]2Ki 1:17
3:2 [e]1Ki 15:26 [f]1Ki 16:30-32 [g]Ex 23:24; 2Ki 10:18, 26-28
3:3 [h]1Ki 12:28-32; 14:9,16
3:4 [i]Ge 19:37; 2Ki 1:1 [j]Ezr 7:17; Isa 16:1
3:5 [k]2Ki 1:1
3:7 [l]1Ki 22:4
3:9 [m]1Ki 22:47
3:11 [n]Ge 25:22; 1Ki 22:7 [o]Ge 20:7 [p]1Ki 19:16
3:12 [q]Nu 11:17

a *1* Hebrew *Jehoram*, a variant of *Joram*; also in verse 6 b *11* That is, he was Elijah's personal servant.

14Elisha said, "As surely as the LORD Almighty lives, whom I serve, if I did not have respect for the presence of Jehoshaphat king of Judah, I would not look at you or even notice you. 15But now bring me a harpist."[a]

While the harpist was playing, the hand[b] of the LORD came upon Elisha 16and he said, "This is what the LORD says: Make this valley full of ditches. 17For this is what the LORD says: You will see neither wind nor rain, yet this valley will be filled with water,[c] and you, your cattle and your other animals will drink. 18This is an easy[d] thing in the eyes of the LORD; he will also hand Moab over to you. 19You will overthrow every fortified city and every major town. You will cut down every good tree, stop up all the springs, and ruin every good field with stones."

20The next morning, about the time[e] for offering the sacrifice, there it was—water flowing from the direction of Edom! And the land was filled with water.[f]

21Now all the Moabites had heard that the kings had come to fight against them; so every man, young and old, who could bear arms was called up and stationed on the border. 22When they got up early in the morning, the sun was shining on the water. To the Moabites across the way, the water looked red—like blood. 23"That's blood!" they said. "Those kings must have fought and slaughtered each other. Now to the plunder, Moab!"

24But when the Moabites came to the camp of Israel, the Israelites rose up and fought them until they fled. And the Israelites invaded the land and slaughtered the Moabites. 25They destroyed the towns, and each man threw a stone on every good field until it was covered. They stopped up all the springs and cut down every good tree. Only Kir Hareseth[g] was left with its stones in place, but men armed with slings surrounded it and attacked it as well.

26When the king of Moab saw that the battle had gone against him, he took with him seven hundred swordsmen to break through to the king of Edom, but they failed. 27Then he took his firstborn[h] son, who was to succeed him as king, and offered him as a sacrifice on the city wall. The fury against Israel was great; they withdrew and returned to their own land.

Chapter 4 Theme ______________________

4 The wife of a man from the company[i] of the prophets cried out to Elisha, "Your servant my husband is dead, and you know that he revered the LORD. But now his creditor[j] is coming to take my two boys as his slaves."

2Elisha replied to her, "How can I help you? Tell me, what do you have in your house?"

3:15 [a] 1Sa 16:23 [b] Jer 15:17; Eze 1:3
3:17 [c] Ps 107:35; Isa 32:2; 35:6; 41:18
3:18 [d] Ge 18:14; 2Ki 20:10; Isa 49:6; Jer 32:17,27; Mk 10:27
3:20 [e] Ex 29:39-40 [f] Ex 17:6
3:25 [g] ver 19; Isa 15:1; 16:7; Jer 48:31,36
3:27 [h] Dt 12:31; 2Ki 16:3; 21:6; 2Ch 28:3; Ps 106:38; Jer 19:4-5; Am 2:1; Mic 6:7
4:1 [i] 1Sa 10:5; 2Ki 2:3 [j] Ex 22:26; Lev 25:39-43; Ne 5:3-5; Job 22:6; 24:9

"Your servant has nothing there at all," she said, "except a little oil."[a]

3Elisha said, "Go around and ask all your neighbors for empty jars. Don't ask for just a few. 4Then go inside and shut the door behind you and your sons. Pour oil into all the jars, and as each is filled, put it to one side."

5She left him and afterward shut the door behind her and her sons. They brought the jars to her and she kept pouring. 6When all the jars were full, she said to her son, "Bring me another one."

But he replied, "There is not a jar left." Then the oil stopped flowing.

7She went and told the man of God,[b] and he said, "Go, sell the oil and pay your debts. You and your sons can live on what is left."

8One day Elisha went to Shunem.[c] And a well-to-do woman was there, who urged him to stay for a meal. So whenever he came by, he stopped there to eat. 9She said to her husband, "I know that this man who often comes our way is a holy man of God. 10Let's make a small room on the roof and put in it a bed and a table, a chair and a lamp for him. Then he can stay[d] there whenever he comes to us."

11One day when Elisha came, he went up to his room and lay down there. 12He said to his servant Gehazi, "Call the Shunammite."[e] So he called her, and she stood before him. 13Elisha said to him, "Tell her, 'You have gone to all this trouble for us. Now what can be done for you? Can we speak on your behalf to the king or the commander of the army?' "

She replied, "I have a home among my own people."

14"What can be done for her?" Elisha asked.

Gehazi said, "Well, she has no son and her husband is old."

15Then Elisha said, "Call her." So he called her, and she stood in the doorway. 16"About this time[f] next year," Elisha said, "you will hold a son in your arms."

"No, my lord," she objected. "Don't mislead your servant, O man of God!"

17But the woman became pregnant, and the next year about that same time she gave birth to a son, just as Elisha had told her.

18The child grew, and one day he went out to his father, who was with the reapers.[g] 19"My head! My head!" he said to his father.

His father told a servant, "Carry him to his mother." 20After the servant had lifted him up and carried him to his mother, the boy sat on her lap until noon, and then he died. 21She went up and laid him on the bed[h] of the man of God, then shut the door and went out.

22She called her husband and said, "Please send me one of the servants and a donkey so I can go to the man of God quickly and return."

4:2 [a] 1Ki 17:12
4:7 [b] 1Ki 12:22
4:8 [c] Jos 19:18
4:10 [d] Mt 10:41; Ro 12:13
4:12 [e] 2Ki 8:1
4:16 [f] Ge 18:10
4:18 [g] Ru 2:3
4:21 [h] ver 32

23“Why go to him today?” he asked. “It’s not the New Moon[a] or the Sabbath.”

“It’s all right,” she said.

24She saddled the donkey and said to her servant, “Lead on; don’t slow down for me unless I tell you.” 25So she set out and came to the man of God at Mount Carmel.[b]

When he saw her in the distance, the man of God said to his servant Gehazi, “Look! There’s the Shunammite! 26Run to meet her and ask her, ‘Are you all right? Is your husband all right? Is your child all right?’ ”

“Everything is all right,” she said.

27When she reached the man of God at the mountain, she took hold of his feet. Gehazi came over to push her away, but the man of God said, “Leave her alone! She is in bitter distress,[c] but the LORD has hidden it from me and has not told me why.”

28“Did I ask you for a son, my lord?” she said. “Didn’t I tell you, ‘Don’t raise my hopes’?”

29Elisha said to Gehazi, “Tuck your cloak into your belt,[d] take my staff[e] in your hand and run. If you meet anyone, do not greet him, and if anyone greets you, do not answer. Lay my staff on the boy’s face.”

30But the child’s mother said, “As surely as the LORD lives and as you live, I will not leave you.” So he got up and followed her.

31Gehazi went on ahead and laid the staff on the boy’s face, but there was no sound or response. So Gehazi went back to meet Elisha and told him, “The boy has not awakened.”

32When Elisha reached the house, there was the boy lying dead on his couch.[f] 33He went in, shut the door on the two of them and prayed[g] to the LORD. 34Then he got on the bed and lay upon the boy, mouth to mouth, eyes to eyes, hands to hands. As he stretched[h] himself out upon him, the boy’s body grew warm. 35Elisha turned away and walked back and forth in the room and then got on the bed and stretched out upon him once more. The boy sneezed seven times[i] and opened his eyes.[j]

36Elisha summoned Gehazi and said, “Call the Shunammite.” And he did. When she came, he said, “Take your son.”[k] 37She came in, fell at his feet and bowed to the ground. Then she took her son and went out.

38Elisha returned to Gilgal[l] and there was a famine[m] in that region. While the company of the prophets was meeting with him, he said to his servant, “Put on the large pot and cook some stew for these men.”

39One of them went out into the fields to gather herbs and found a wild vine. He gathered some of its gourds and filled the fold of his cloak. When he returned, he cut them up into the pot of

4:23 [a]Nu 10:10; 1Ch 23:31; Ps 81:3
4:25 [b]1Ki 18:20; 2Ki 2:25
4:27 [c]1Sa 1:15
4:29 [d]1Ki 18:46; 2Ki 2:8, 14; 9:1 [e]Ex 4:2; 7:19; 14:16
4:32 [f]ver 21
4:33 [g]1Ki 17:20; Mt 6:6
4:34 [h]1Ki 17:21; Ac 20:10
4:35 [i]Jos 6:15 [j]2Ki 8:5
4:36 [k]Heb 11:35
4:38 [l]2Ki 2:1 [m]Lev 26:26; 2Ki 8:1

INSIGHT

The land of ***Baal Shalishah***, meaning "the third," was evidently the tribal territory of Ephraim (1 Samuel 9:4). Modern-day Kefr Thilth may be on the site of the ancient city. However, the exact location of Baal Shalishah has recently been questioned.

stew, though no one knew what they were. 40The stew was poured
out for the men, but as they began to eat it, they cried out, "O
man of God, there is death in the pot!" And they could not eat it.
41Elisha said, "Get some flour." He put it into the pot and said,
"Serve it to the people to eat." And there was nothing harmful in
the pot.[a]
42A man came from Baal Shalishah,[b] bringing the man of God
twenty loaves[c] of barley bread[d] baked from the first ripe grain,
along with some heads of new grain. "Give it to the people to eat,"
Elisha said.
43"How can I set this before a hundred men?" his servant asked.
But Elisha answered, "Give it to the people to eat.[e] For this is
what the LORD says: 'They will eat and have some left over.[f]'"
44Then he set it before them, and they ate and had some left over,
according to the word of the LORD.

Chapter 5 Theme ______________________________

5 Now Naaman was commander of the army of the king of
Aram.[g] He was a great man in the sight of his master and
highly regarded, because through him the LORD had given victory to
Aram. He was a valiant soldier, but he had leprosy.[a][h]
2Now bands[i] from Aram had gone out and had taken captive a
young girl from Israel, and she served Naaman's wife. 3She said
to her mistress, "If only my master would see the prophet[j] who is
in Samaria! He would cure him of his leprosy."
4Naaman went to his master and told him what the girl from
Israel had said. 5"By all means, go," the king of Aram replied. "I
will send a letter to the king of Israel." So Naaman left, taking with
him ten talents[b] of silver, six thousand shekels[c] of gold and ten
sets of clothing.[k] 6The letter that he took to the king of Israel read:
"With this letter I am sending my servant Naaman to you so that
you may cure him of his leprosy."
7As soon as the king of Israel read the letter,[l] he tore his robes
and said, "Am I God?[m] Can I kill and bring back to life?[n] Why
does this fellow send someone to me to be cured of his leprosy? See
how he is trying to pick a quarrel[o] with me!"
8When Elisha the man of God heard that the king of Israel had
torn his robes, he sent him this message: "Why have you torn
your robes? Have the man come to me and he will know that there
is a prophet[p] in Israel." 9So Naaman went with his horses and
chariots and stopped at the door of Elisha's house. 10Elisha sent a

4:41 [a] Ex 15:25; 2Ki 2:21

4:42 [b] 1Sa 9:4 [c] Mt 14:17; 15:36 [d] 1Sa 9:7

4:43 [e] Lk 9:13 [f] Mt 14:20; Jn 6:12

5:1 [g] Ge 10:22; 2Sa 10:19 [h] Ex 4:6; Nu 12:10; Lk 4:27

5:2 [i] 2Ki 6:23; 13:20; 24:2

5:3 [j] Ge 20:7

5:5 [k] ver 22; Ge 24:53; Jdg 14:12; 1Sa 9:7

5:7 [l] 2Ki 19:14 [m] Ge 30:2 [n] Dt 32:39; 1Sa 2:6 [o] 1Ki 20:7

5:8 [p] 1Ki 22:7

[a] *1* The Hebrew word was used for various diseases affecting the skin—not necessarily leprosy; also in verses 3, 6, 7, 11 and 27. [b] *5* That is, about 750 pounds (about 340 kilograms)
[c] *5* That is, about 150 pounds (about 70 kilograms)

messenger to say to him, "Go, wash[a] yourself seven times[b] in the
Jordan, and your flesh will be restored and you will be cleansed."
11But Naaman went away angry and said, "I thought that he
would surely come out to me and stand and call on the name of
the LORD his God, wave his hand[c] over the spot and cure me of my
leprosy. 12Are not Abana and Pharpar, the rivers of Damascus,
better than any of the waters[d] of Israel? Couldn't I wash in them
and be cleansed?" So he turned and went off in a rage.[e]
13Naaman's servants went to him and said, "My father,[f] if the
prophet had told you to do some great thing, would you not have
done it? How much more, then, when he tells you, 'Wash and be
cleansed'!" 14So he went down and dipped himself in the Jordan
seven times,[g] as the man of God had told him, and his flesh was
restored[h] and became clean like that of a young boy.[i]
15Then Naaman and all his attendants went back to the man of
God[j]. He stood before him and said, "Now I know[k] that there is no
God in all the world except in Israel. Please accept now a gift[l]
from your servant."
16The prophet answered, "As surely as the LORD lives, whom I
serve, I will not accept a thing." And even though Naaman urged
him, he refused.[m]
17"If you will not," said Naaman, "please let me, your servant, be
given as much earth[n] as a pair of mules can carry, for your servant
will never again make burnt offerings and sacrifices to any other
god but the LORD. 18But may the LORD forgive your servant for
this one thing: When my master enters the temple of Rimmon to
bow down and he is leaning[o] on my arm and I bow there also—
when I bow down in the temple of Rimmon, may the LORD forgive your servant for this."
19"Go in peace,"[p] Elisha said.
After Naaman had traveled some distance, 20Gehazi, the servant
of Elisha the man of God, said to himself, "My master was too
easy on Naaman, this Aramean, by not accepting from him what
he brought. As surely as the LORD[q] lives, I will run after him and
get something from him."
21So Gehazi hurried after Naaman. When Naaman saw him
running toward him, he got down from the chariot to meet him.
"Is everything all right?" he asked.
22"Everything is all right," Gehazi answered. "My master sent
me to say, 'Two young men from the company of the prophets
have just come to me from the hill country of Ephraim. Please
give them a talent[a] of silver and two sets of clothing.' "[r]
23"By all means, take two talents," said Naaman. He urged
Gehazi to accept them, and then tied up the two talents of silver in

5:10 [a]Jn 9:7 [b]Ge 33:3; Lev 14:7
5:11 [c]Ex 7:19
5:12 [d]Isa 8:6 [e]Pr 14:17,29; 19:11; 29:11
5:13 [f]2Ki 6:21; 13:14
5:14 [g]Ge 33:3; Lev 14:7; Jos 6:15 [h]Ex 4:7 [i]Job 33:25; Lk 4:27
5:15 [j]Jos 2:11 [k]Jos 4:24; 1Sa 17:46; Da 2:47 [l]1Sa 9:7; 25:27
5:16 [m]ver 20,26; Ge 14:23; Da 5:17
5:17 [n]Ex 20:24
5:18 [o]2Ki 7:2
5:19 [p]1Sa 1:17; Ac 15:33
5:20 [q]Ex 20:7
5:22 [r]ver 5; Ge 45:22

INSIGHT

The *Arameans*, the descendants of Noah through Shem, lived in a confederation of towns and settlements in what is now Syria. Some settled as far as Babylon. Jacob's grandfather, Abraham, was Aramean (Deuteronomy 26:5).

a *22* That is, about 75 pounds (about 34 kilograms)

two bags, with two sets of clothing. He gave them to two of his servants, and they carried them ahead of Gehazi. 24When Gehazi came to the hill, he took the things from the servants and put them away in the house. He sent the men away and they left. 25Then he went in and stood before his master Elisha.

"Where have you been, Gehazi?" Elisha asked.

"Your servant didn't go anywhere," Gehazi answered.

26But Elisha said to him, "Was not my spirit with you when the man got down from his chariot to meet you? Is this the time[a] to take money, or to accept clothes, olive groves, vineyards, flocks, herds, or menservants and maidservants?[b] 27Naaman's leprosy[c] will cling to you and to your descendants forever." Then Gehazi[d] went from Elisha's presence and he was leprous, as white as snow.[e]

Chapter 6 Theme ______________________________

6 The company[f] of the prophets said to Elisha, "Look, the place where we meet with you is too small for us. 2Let us go to the Jordan, where each of us can get a pole; and let us build a place there for us to live."

And he said, "Go."

3Then one of them said, "Won't you please come with your servants?"

"I will," Elisha replied. 4And he went with them.

They went to the Jordan and began to cut down trees. 5As one of them was cutting down a tree, the iron axhead fell into the water. "Oh, my lord," he cried out, "it was borrowed!"

6The man of God asked, "Where did it fall?" When he showed him the place, Elisha cut a stick and threw[g] it there, and made the iron float. 7"Lift it out," he said. Then the man reached out his hand and took it.

8Now the king of Aram was at war with Israel. After conferring with his officers, he said, "I will set up my camp in such and such a place."

9The man of God sent word to the king[h] of Israel: "Beware of passing that place, because the Arameans are going down there." 10So the king of Israel checked on the place indicated by the man of God. Time and again Elisha warned[i] the king, so that he was on his guard in such places.

11This enraged the king of Aram. He summoned his officers and demanded of them, "Will you not tell me which of us is on the side of the king of Israel?"

12"None of us, my lord the king,[j]" said one of his officers, "but Elisha, the prophet who is in Israel, tells the king of Israel the very words you speak in your bedroom."

5:26 [a] ver 16 [b] Jer 45:5
5:27 [c] Nu 12:10; 2Ki 15:5 [d] Col 3:5 [e] Ex 4:6
6:1 [f] 1Sa 10:5; 2Ki 4:38
6:6 [g] Ex 15:25; 2Ki 2:21
6:9 [h] ver 12
6:10 [i] Jer 11:18
6:12 [j] ver 9

13“Go, find out where he is,” the king ordered, “so I can send
men and capture him.” The report came back: “He is in
Dothan.”[a] 14Then he sent[b] horses and chariots and a strong force
there. They went by night and surrounded the city.
15When the servant of the man of God got up and went out early the next morning, an army with horses and chariots had surrounded the city. “Oh, my lord, what shall we do?” the servant
asked.
16“Don’t be afraid,”[c] the prophet answered. “Those who are
with us are more[d] than those who are with them.”
17And Elisha prayed, “O LORD, open his eyes so he may see.”
Then the LORD opened the servant’s eyes, and he looked and saw
the hills full of horses and chariots[e] of fire all around Elisha.
18As the enemy came down toward him, Elisha prayed to the
LORD, “Strike these people with blindness.”[f] So he struck them
with blindness, as Elisha had asked.
19Elisha told them, “This is not the road and this is not the city.
Follow me, and I will lead you to the man you are looking for.”
And he led them to Samaria.
20After they entered the city, Elisha said, “LORD, open the eyes
of these men so they can see.” Then the LORD opened their eyes
and they looked, and there they were, inside Samaria.
21When the king of Israel saw them, he asked Elisha, “Shall I
kill them, my father?[g] Shall I kill them?”
22“Do not kill them,” he answered. “Would you kill men you
have captured[h] with your own sword or bow? Set food and water
before them so that they may eat and drink and then go back to
their master.” 23So he prepared a great feast for them, and after
they had finished eating and drinking, he sent them away, and
they returned to their master. So the bands[i] from Aram stopped
raiding Israel’s territory.
24Some time later, Ben-Hadad[j] king of Aram mobilized his
entire army and marched up and laid siege[k] to Samaria. 25There
was a great famine[l] in the city; the siege lasted so long that a donkey’s head sold for eighty shekels[a] of silver, and a quarter of a
cab[b] of seed pods[c][m] for five shekels.[d]
26As the king of Israel was passing by on the wall, a woman
cried to him, “Help me, my lord the king!”
27The king replied, “If the LORD does not help you, where can I
get help for you? From the threshing floor? From the winepress?”
28Then he asked her, “What’s the matter?”
She answered, “This woman said to me, ‘Give up your son so
we may eat him today, and tomorrow we’ll eat my son.’ 29So we

[a] *25* That is, about 2 pounds (about 1 kilogram) [b] *25* That is, probably about 1/2 pint (about 0.3 liter) [c] *25* Or *of dove’s dung* [d] *25* That is, about 2 ounces (about 55 grams)

6:13 [a] Ge 37:17
6:14 [b] 2Ki 1:9
6:16 [c] Ge 15:1 [d] 2Ch 32:7; Ps 55:18; Ro 8:31; 1Jn 4:4
6:17 [e] 2Ki 2:11,12; Ps 68:17; Zec 6:1-7
6:18 [f] Ge 19:11; Ac 13:11
6:21 [g] 2Ki 5:13
6:22 [h] Dt 20:11; 2Ch 28:8-15; Ro 12:20
6:23 [i] 2Ki 5:2
6:24 [j] 1Ki 15:18; 20:1; 2Ki 8:7 [k] Dt 28:52
6:25 [l] Lev 26:26; Ru 1:1 [m] Isa 36:12

cooked my son and ate[a] him. The next day I said to her, 'Give up
your son so we may eat him,' but she had hidden him."
30When the king heard the woman's words, he tore[b] his robes.
As he went along the wall, the people looked, and there, underneath, he had sackcloth[c] on his body. 31He said, "May God deal
with me, be it ever so severely, if the head of Elisha son of
Shaphat remains on his shoulders today!"
32Now Elisha was sitting in his house, and the elders[d] were sitting with him. The king sent a messenger ahead, but before he
arrived, Elisha said to the elders, "Don't you see how this murderer[e] is sending someone to cut off my head?[f] Look, when the
messenger comes, shut the door and hold it shut against him. Is
not the sound of his master's footsteps behind him?"
33While he was still talking to them, the messenger came down
to him. And ⌊the king⌋ said, "This disaster is from the LORD. Why
should I wait[g] for the LORD any longer?"

Chapter 7 Theme

7 Elisha said, "Hear the word of the LORD. This is what the
LORD says: About this time tomorrow, a seah[a] of flour will
sell for a shekel[b] and two seahs[c] of barley for a shekel[h] at the gate
of Samaria."
2The officer on whose arm the king was leaning[i] said to the
man of God, "Look, even if the LORD should open the floodgates[j]
of the heavens, could this happen?"
"You will see it with your own eyes," answered Elisha, "but you
will not eat[k] any of it!"
3Now there were four men with leprosy[d][l] at the entrance of the
city gate. They said to each other, "Why stay here until we die? 4If
we say, 'We'll go into the city'—the famine is there, and we will
die. And if we stay here, we will die. So let's go over to the camp
of the Arameans and surrender. If they spare us, we live; if they
kill us, then we die."
5At dusk they got up and went to the camp of the Arameans.
When they reached the edge of the camp, not a man was there,
6for the Lord had caused the Arameans to hear the sound[m] of
chariots and horses and a great army, so that they said to one
another, "Look, the king of Israel has hired[n] the Hittite[o] and
Egyptian kings to attack us!" 7So they got up and fled[p] in the
dusk and abandoned their tents and their horses and donkeys.
They left the camp as it was and ran for their lives.

a *1* That is, probably about 7 quarts (about 7.3 liters); also in verses 16 and 18 b *1* That is, about 2/5 ounce (about 11 grams); also in verses 16 and 18 c *1* That is, probably about 13 quarts (about 15 liters); also in verses 16 and 18 d *3* The Hebrew word is used for various diseases affecting the skin—not necessarily leprosy; also in verse 8.

6:29 [a] Lev 26:29; Dt 28:53-55
6:30 [b] 2Ki 18:37; Isa 22:15 [c] Ge 37:34; 1Ki 21:27
6:32 [d] Eze 8:1; 14:1; 20:1 [e] 1Ki 18:4 [f] ver 31
6:33 [g] Lev 24:11; Job 2:9; 14:14; Isa 40:31
7:1 [h] ver 16
7:2 [i] 2Ki 5:18 [j] ver 19; Ge 7:11; Ps 78:23; Mal 3:10 [k] ver 17
7:3 [l] Lev 13:45-46; Nu 5:1-4
7:6 [m] Ex 14:24; 2Sa 5:24; Eze 1:24 [n] 2Sa 10:6; Jer 46:21 [o] Nu 13:29
7:7 [p] Jdg 7:21; Ps 48:4-6; Pr 28:1; Isa 30:17

7:8 [a]Isa 33:23; 35:6

8 The men who had leprosy[a] reached the edge of the camp and
entered one of the tents. They ate and drank, and carried away silver, gold and clothes, and went off and hid them. They returned
and entered another tent and took some things from it and hid
them also.
9 Then they said to each other, "We're not doing right. This is a
day of good news and we are keeping it to ourselves. If we wait
until daylight, punishment will overtake us. Let's go at once and
report this to the royal palace."
10 So they went and called out to the city gatekeepers and told
them, "We went into the Aramean camp and not a man was
there—not a sound of anyone—only tethered horses and donkeys,
and the tents left just as they were." 11 The gatekeepers shouted
the news, and it was reported within the palace.

7:12 [b]Jos 8:4; 2Ki 6:25-29

12 The king got up in the night and said to his officers, "I will tell
you what the Arameans have done to us. They know we are
starving; so they have left the camp to hide[b] in the countryside,
thinking, 'They will surely come out, and then we will take them
alive and get into the city.' "
13 One of his officers answered, "Have some men take five of the
horses that are left in the city. Their plight will be like that of all the
Israelites left here—yes, they will only be like all these Israelites
who are doomed. So let us send them to find out what happened."
14 So they selected two chariots with their horses, and the king
sent them after the Aramean army. He commanded the drivers,
"Go and find out what has happened." 15 They followed them as
far as the Jordan, and they found the whole road strewn with the
clothing and equipment the Arameans had thrown away in their
headlong flight. So the messengers returned and reported to the
king. 16 Then the people went out and plundered[c] the camp of the
Arameans. So a seah of flour sold for a shekel, and two seahs of
barley sold for a shekel,[d] as the LORD had said.

7:16 [c]Isa 33:4,23 [d]ver 1

17 Now the king had put the officer on whose arm he leaned in
charge of the gate, and the people trampled him in the gateway,
and he died,[e] just as the man of God had foretold when the king
came down to his house. 18 It happened as the man of God had
said to the king: "About this time tomorrow, a seah of flour will
sell for a shekel and two seahs of barley for a shekel at the gate of
Samaria."
19 The officer had said to the man of God, "Look, even if the LORD
should open the floodgates[f] of the heavens, could this happen?"
The man of God had replied, "You will see it with your own eyes,
but you will not eat any of it!" 20 And that is exactly what happened
to him, for the people trampled him in the gateway, and he died.

7:17 [e]ver 2; 2Ki 6:32

7:19 [f]ver 2

Chapter 8 Theme

8 Now Elisha had said to the woman[a] whose son he had
restored to life, "Go away with your family and stay for a
while wherever you can, because the LORD has decreed a famine[b]
in the land that will last seven years."[c] 2The woman proceeded to
do as the man of God said. She and her family went away and
stayed in the land of the Philistines seven years.
3At the end of the seven years she came back from the land of
the Philistines and went to the king to beg for her house and
land. 4The king was talking to Gehazi, the servant of the man of
God, and had said, "Tell me about all the great things Elisha has
done." 5Just as Gehazi was telling the king how Elisha had
restored[d] the dead to life, the woman whose son Elisha had
brought back to life came to beg the king for her house and land.
Gehazi said, "This is the woman, my lord the king, and this is
her son whom Elisha restored to life." 6The king asked the
woman about it, and she told him.

Then he assigned an official to her case and said to him, "Give
back everything that belonged to her, including all the income
from her land from the day she left the country until now."
7Elisha went to Damascus,[e] and Ben-Hadad[f] king of Aram was
ill. When the king was told, "The man of God has come all the
way up here," 8he said to Hazael,[g] "Take a gift[h] with you and go to
meet the man of God. Consult[i] the LORD through him; ask him,
'Will I recover from this illness?'"
9Hazael went to meet Elisha, taking with him as a gift forty
camel-loads of all the finest wares of Damascus. He went in and
stood before him, and said, "Your son Ben-Hadad king of Aram
has sent me to ask, 'Will I recover from this illness?'"
10Elisha answered, "Go and say to him, 'You will certainly
recover';[j] but[a] the LORD has revealed to me that he will in fact
die." 11He stared at him with a fixed gaze until Hazael felt
ashamed.[k] Then the man of God began to weep.[l]
12"Why is my lord weeping?" asked Hazael.

"Because I know the harm[m] you will do to the Israelites," he
answered. "You will set fire to their fortified places, kill their young
men with the sword, dash[n] their little children[o] to the ground,
and rip open[p] their pregnant women."
13Hazael said, "How could your servant, a mere dog,[q] accomplish such a feat?"

"The LORD has shown me that you will become king[r] of Aram,"
answered Elisha.
14Then Hazael left Elisha and returned to his master. When
Ben-Hadad asked, "What did Elisha say to you?" Hazael replied,

[a] *10* The Hebrew may also be read *Go and say, 'You will certainly not recover,' for.*

8:1
[a] 2Ki 4:8-37
[b] Lev 26:26; Dt 28:22; Ru 1:1
[c] Ge 12:10; Ps 105:16; Hag 1:11

8:5
[d] 2Ki 4:35

8:7
[e] 2Sa 8:5; 1Ki 11:24
[f] 2Ki 6:24

8:8
[g] 1Ki 19:15
[h] Ge 32:20; 1Sa 9:7; 2Ki 1:2
[i] Jdg 18:5

8:10
[j] Isa 38:1

8:11
[k] Jdg 3:25
[l] Lk 19:41

8:12
[m] 1Ki 19:17; 2Ki 10:32; 12:17; 13:3,7
[n] Ps 137:9; Isa 13:16; Hos 13:16; Na 3:10; Lk 19:44
[o] Ge 34:29
[p] 2Ki 15:16; Am 1:13

8:13
[q] 1Sa 17:43; 2Sa 3:8
[r] 1Ki 19:15

"He told me that you would certainly recover." 15 But the next day
he took a thick cloth, soaked it in water and spread it over the
king's face, so that he died.[a] Then Hazael succeeded him as king.
16 In the fifth year of Joram[b] son of Ahab king of Israel, when
Jehoshaphat was king of Judah, Jehoram[c] son of Jehoshaphat
began his reign as king of Judah. 17 He was thirty-two years old
when he became king, and he reigned in Jerusalem eight years.
18 He walked in the ways of the kings of Israel, as the house of Ahab
had done, for he married a daughter[d] of Ahab. He did evil in the
eyes of the LORD. 19 Nevertheless, for the sake of his servant David,
the LORD was not willing to destroy[e] Judah. He had promised to
maintain a lamp[f] for David and his descendants forever.
20 In the time of Jehoram, Edom rebelled against Judah and set
up its own king.[g] 21 So Jehoram[a] went to Zair with all his chariots.
The Edomites surrounded him and his chariot commanders, but
he rose up and broke through by night; his army, however, fled
back home. 22 To this day Edom has been in rebellion[h] against
Judah. Libnah[i] revolted at the same time.
23 As for the other events of Jehoram's reign, and all he did, are
they not written in the book of the annals of the kings of Judah?
24 Jehoram rested with his fathers and was buried with them in
the City of David. And Ahaziah his son succeeded him as king.
25 In the twelfth[j] year of Joram son of Ahab king of Israel,
Ahaziah son of Jehoram king of Judah began to reign. 26 Ahaziah
was twenty-two years old when he became king, and he reigned in
Jerusalem one year. His mother's name was Athaliah,[k] a granddaughter of Omri[l] king of Israel. 27 He walked in the ways of the
house of Ahab[m] and did evil[n] in the eyes of the LORD, as the house
of Ahab had done, for he was related by marriage to Ahab's family.
28 Ahaziah went with Joram son of Ahab to war against Hazael
king of Aram at Ramoth Gilead.[o] The Arameans wounded
Joram; 29 so King Joram returned to Jezreel[p] to recover from the
wounds the Arameans had inflicted on him at Ramoth[b] in his
battle with Hazael[q] king of Aram.
Then Ahaziah son of Jehoram king of Judah went down to
Jezreel to see Joram son of Ahab, because he had been wounded.

Chapter 9 Theme ____________________

9 The prophet Elisha summoned a man from the company[r] of
the prophets and said to him, "Tuck your cloak into your
belt,[s] take this flask of oil[t] with you and go to Ramoth Gilead.[u]
2 When you get there, look for Jehu son of Jehoshaphat, the son of
Nimshi. Go to him, get him away from his companions and take

8:15 [a]2Ki 1:17
8:16 [b]2Ki 1:17; 3:1 [c]2Ch 21:1-4
8:18 [d]ver 26; 2Ki 11:1
8:19 [e]Ge 6:13 [f]2Sa 21:17; 7:13; 1Ki 11:36; Rev 21:23
8:20 [g]1Ki 22:47
8:22 [h]Ge 27:40 [i]Nu 33:20; Jos 21:13; 2Ki 19:8
8:25 [j]2Ki 9:29
8:26 [k]ver 18 [l]1Ki 16:23
8:27 [m]1Ki 16:30 [n]1Ki 15:26
8:28 [o]Dt 4:43; Ki 22:3,29
8:29 [p]2Ki 9:15 [q]1Ki 19:15,17
9:1 [r]1Sa 10:5 [s]2Ki 4:29 [t]1Sa 10:1 [u]2Ki 8:28

INSIGHT

Zair's exact location is in question. The name means "small." Some believe it was south of the Dead (Salt) Sea near Edom, while others equate it with Zoar (Genesis 13:10) or Zior (Joshua 15:54).

a *21* Hebrew *Joram,* a variant of *Jehoram;* also in verses 23 and 24 b *29* Hebrew *Ramah,* a variant of *Ramoth*

him into an inner room. 3Then take the flask and pour the oil[a] on
his head and declare, 'This is what the LORD says: I anoint you king
over Israel.' Then open the door and run; don't delay!"
4So the young man, the prophet, went to Ramoth Gilead. 5When
he arrived, he found the army officers sitting together. "I have a
message for you, commander," he said.
"For which of us?" asked Jehu.
"For you, commander," he replied.
6Jehu got up and went into the house. Then the prophet poured
the oil[b] on Jehu's head and declared, "This is what the LORD, the
God of Israel, says: 'I anoint you king over the LORD's people
Israel. 7You are to destroy the house of Ahab your master, and I will
avenge[c] the blood of my servants[d] the prophets and the blood of
all the LORD's servants shed by Jezebel.[e] 8The whole house[f] of
Ahab will perish. I will cut off from Ahab every last male[g] in
Israel—slave or free. 9I will make the house of Ahab like the
house of Jeroboam[h] son of Nebat and like the house of Baasha[i] son
of Ahijah. 10As for Jezebel, dogs[j] will devour her on the plot of
ground at Jezreel, and no one will bury her.' " Then he opened the
door and ran.
11When Jehu went out to his fellow officers, one of them asked
him, "Is everything all right? Why did this madman[k] come to
you?"
"You know the man and the sort of things he says," Jehu replied.
12"That's not true!" they said. "Tell us."
Jehu said, "Here is what he told me: 'This is what the LORD says:
I anoint you king over Israel.' "
13They hurried and took their cloaks and spread[l] them under
him on the bare steps. Then they blew the trumpet[m] and shouted,
"Jehu is king!"
14So Jehu son of Jehoshaphat, the son of Nimshi, conspired
against Joram. (Now Joram and all Israel had been defending
Ramoth Gilead[n] against Hazael king of Aram, 15but King Joram[a]
had returned to Jezreel to recover[o] from the wounds the Arameans had inflicted on him in the battle with Hazael king of
Aram.) Jehu said, "If this is the way you feel, don't let anyone slip
out of the city to go and tell the news in Jezreel." 16Then he got
into his chariot and rode to Jezreel, because Joram was resting
there and Ahaziah[p] king of Judah had gone down to see him.
17When the lookout[q] standing on the tower in Jezreel saw Jehu's
troops approaching, he called out, "I see some troops coming."
"Get a horseman," Joram ordered. "Send him to meet them and
ask, 'Do you come in peace?[r] ' "

a *15* Hebrew *Jehoram,* a variant of *Joram;* also in verses 17 and 21-24

9:3 [a] 1Ki 19:16
9:6 [b] 1Ki 19:16; 2Ch 22:7
9:7 [c] Ge 4:24; Rev 6:10 [d] Dt 32:43 [e] 1Ki 18:4; 21:15
9:8 [f] 2Ki 10:17 [g] Dt 32:36; 1Sa 25:22; 1Ki 21:21; 2Ki 14:26
9:9 [h] 1Ki 14:10; 15:29; 16:3,11 [i] 1Ki 16:3
9:10 [j] ver 35-36; 1Ki 21:23
9:11 [k] Jer 29:26; Jn 10:20; Ac 26:24
9:13 [l] Mt 21:8; Lk 19:36 [m] 2Sa 15:10; 1Ki 1:34,39
9:14 [n] Dt 4:43; 2Ki 8:28
9:15 [o] 2Ki 8:29
9:16 [p] 2Ch 22:7
9:17 [q] Isa 21:6 [r] 1Sa 16:4

18The horseman rode off to meet Jehu and said, "This is what
the king says: 'Do you come in peace?' "
"What do you have to do with peace?" Jehu replied. "Fall in
behind me."
The lookout reported, "The messenger has reached them, but
he isn't coming back."
19So the king sent out a second horseman. When he came to
them he said, "This is what the king says: 'Do you come in peace?' "
Jehu replied, "What do you have to do with peace? Fall in
behind me."
20The lookout reported, "He has reached them, but he isn't
coming back either. The driving is like[a] that of Jehu son of
Nimshi—he drives like a madman."
21"Hitch up my chariot," Joram ordered. And when it was
hitched up, Joram king of Israel and Ahaziah king of Judah rode
out, each in his own chariot, to meet Jehu. They met him at the
plot of ground that had belonged to Naboth[b] the Jezreelite. 22When
Joram saw Jehu he asked, "Have you come in peace, Jehu?"
"How can there be peace," Jehu replied, "as long as all the idolatry and witchcraft of your mother Jezebel[c] abound?"
23Joram turned about and fled, calling out to Ahaziah, "Treachery,[d] Ahaziah!"
24Then Jehu drew his bow[e] and shot Joram between the shoulders. The arrow pierced his heart and he slumped down in his
chariot. 25Jehu said to Bidkar, his chariot officer, "Pick him up and
throw him on the field that belonged to Naboth the Jezreelite.
Remember how you and I were riding together in chariots behind
Ahab his father when the LORD made this prophecy[f] about him:
26'Yesterday I saw the blood of Naboth[g] and the blood of his sons,
declares the LORD, and I will surely make you pay for it on this plot
of ground, declares the LORD.'[a] Now then, pick him up and throw
him on that plot, in accordance with the word of the LORD."[h]
27When Ahaziah king of Judah saw what had happened, he fled
up the road to Beth Haggan.[b] Jehu chased him, shouting, "Kill
him too!" They wounded him in his chariot on the way up to Gur
near Ibleam,[i] but he escaped to Megiddo[j] and died there. 28His
servants took him by chariot[k] to Jerusalem and buried him with
his fathers in his tomb in the City of David. 29(In the eleventh[l]
year of Joram son of Ahab, Ahaziah had become king of Judah.)
30Then Jehu went to Jezreel. When Jezebel heard about it, she
painted[m] her eyes, arranged her hair and looked out of a window.
31As Jehu entered the gate, she asked, "Have you come in peace,
Zimri,[n] you murderer of your master?"[c]

9:20 [a] 2Sa 18:27
9:21 [b] ver 26; 1Ki 21:1-7, 15-19
9:22 [c] 1Ki 16:30-33; 18:19; 2Ch 21:13; Rev 2:20
9:23 [d] 2Ki 11:14
9:24 [e] 1Ki 22:34
9:25 [f] 1Ki 21:19-22, 24-29
9:26 [g] 1Ki 21:19 [h] 1Ki 21:29
9:27 [i] Jdg 1:27 [j] 2Ki 23:29
9:28 [k] 2Ki 14:20; 23:30
9:29 [l] 2Ki 8:25
9:30 [m] Jer 4:30; Eze 23:40
9:31 [n] 1Ki 16:9-10

[a] *26* See 1 Kings 21:19. [b] *27* Or *fled by way of the garden house* [c] *31* Or *"Did Zimri have peace, who murdered his master?"*

32He looked up at the window and called out, "Who is on my
side? Who?" Two or three eunuchs looked down at him.
33"Throw her down!" Jehu said. So they threw her down, and some
of her blood spattered the wall and the horses as they trampled
her underfoot.[a]

34Jehu went in and ate and drank. "Take care of that cursed
woman," he said, "and bury her, for she was a king's daughter."[b]
35But when they went out to bury her, they found nothing except
her skull, her feet and her hands. 36They went back and told Jehu,
who said, "This is the word of the LORD that he spoke through his
servant Elijah the Tishbite: On the plot of ground at Jezreel dogs[c]
will devour Jezebel's flesh.[a][d] 37Jezebel's body will be like refuse[e] on
the ground in the plot at Jezreel, so that no one will be able to say,
'This is Jezebel.'"

Chapter 10 Theme ______________________________

10 Now there were in Samaria[f] seventy sons[g] of the house of
Ahab. So Jehu wrote letters and sent them to Samaria: to
the officials of Jezreel,[b][h] to the elders and to the guardians[i] of
Ahab's children. He said, 2"As soon as this letter reaches you, since
your master's sons are with you and you have chariots and horses,
a fortified city and weapons, 3choose the best and most worthy of
your master's sons and set him on his father's throne. Then fight
for your master's house."

4But they were terrified and said, "If two kings could not resist
him, how can we?"

5So the palace administrator, the city governor, the elders and
the guardians sent this message to Jehu: "We are your servants[j]
and we will do anything you say. We will not appoint anyone as
king; you do whatever you think best."

6Then Jehu wrote them a second letter, saying, "If you are on
my side and will obey me, take the heads of your master's sons and
come to me in Jezreel by this time tomorrow."

Now the royal princes, seventy of them, were with the leading
men of the city, who were rearing them. 7When the letter arrived,
these men took the princes and slaughtered all seventy[k] of them.
They put their heads[l] in baskets and sent them to Jehu in Jezreel.
8When the messenger arrived, he told Jehu, "They have brought
the heads of the princes."

Then Jehu ordered, "Put them in two piles at the entrance of
the city gate until morning."

9The next morning Jehu went out. He stood before all the people
and said, "You are innocent. It was I who conspired against my

9:33 [a]Ps 7:5

9:34 [b]1Ki 16:31; 21:25

9:36 [c]Ps 68:23; Jer 15:3 [d]1Ki 21:23

9:37 [e]Ps 83:10; Isa 5:25; Jer 8:2; 9:22; 16:4; 25:33; Zep 1:17

10:1 [f]1Ki 13:32 [g]Jdg 8:30 [h]1Ki 21:1 [i]ver 5

10:5 [j]Jos 9:8; 1Ki 20:4,32

10:7 [k]1Ki 21:21 [l]2Sa 4:8

[a] *36* See 1 Kings 21:23. [b] *1* Hebrew; some Septuagint manuscripts and Vulgate *of the city*

master and killed him, but who killed all these? 10Know then,
that not a word the LORD has spoken against the house of Ahab
will fail. The LORD has done what he promised[a] through his servant Elijah."[b] 11So Jehu[c] killed everyone in Jezreel who remained
of the house of Ahab, as well as all his chief men, his close friends
and his priests, leaving him no survivor.[d]
12Jehu then set out and went toward Samaria. At Beth Eked of
the Shepherds, 13he met some relatives of Ahaziah king of Judah
and asked, "Who are you?"

They said, "We are relatives of Ahaziah,[e] and we have come
down to greet the families of the king and of the queen mother.[f]"
14"Take them alive!" he ordered. So they took them alive and
slaughtered them by the well of Beth Eked—forty-two men. He
left no survivor.
15After he left there, he came upon Jehonadab[g] son of Recab,[h]
who was on his way to meet him. Jehu greeted him and said, "Are
you in accord with me, as I am with you?"

"I am," Jehonadab answered.

"If so," said Jehu, "give me your hand."[i] So he did, and Jehu
helped him up into the chariot. 16Jehu said, "Come with me and
see my zeal[j] for the LORD." Then he had him ride along in his
chariot.
17When Jehu came to Samaria, he killed all who were left there
of Ahab's family;[k] he destroyed them, according to the word of
the LORD spoken to Elijah.
18Then Jehu brought all the people together and said to them,
"Ahab served[l] Baal a little; Jehu will serve him much. 19Now summon[m] all the prophets of Baal, all his ministers and all his priests.
See that no one is missing, because I am going to hold a great
sacrifice for Baal. Anyone who fails to come will no longer live."
But Jehu was acting deceptively in order to destroy the ministers
of Baal.
20Jehu said, "Call an assembly[n] in honor of Baal." So they proclaimed it. 21Then he sent word throughout Israel, and all the
ministers of Baal came; not one stayed away. They crowded into
the temple of Baal until it was full from one end to the other.
22And Jehu said to the keeper of the wardrobe, "Bring robes for
all the ministers of Baal." So he brought out robes for them.
23Then Jehu and Jehonadab son of Recab went into the temple of
Baal. Jehu said to the ministers of Baal, "Look around and see
that no servants of the LORD are here with you—only ministers of
Baal." 24So they went in to make sacrifices and burnt offerings.
Now Jehu had posted eighty men outside with this warning: "If
one of you lets any of the men I am placing in your hands escape, it
will be your life for his life."[o]

10:10 [a] 2Ki 9:7-10 [b] 1Ki 21:29
10:11 [c] Hos 1:4 [d] ver 14; Job 18:19
10:13 [e] 2Ki 8:24,29; 2Ch 22:8 [f] 1Ki 2:19
10:15 [g] Jer 35:6, 14-19 [h] 1Ch 2:55; Jer 35:2 [i] Ezr 10:19; Eze 17:18
10:16 [j] Nu 25:13; 1Ki 19:10
10:17 [k] 2Ki 9:8
10:18 [l] Jdg 2:11; 1Ki 16:31-32
10:19 [m] 1Ki 18:19; 22:6
10:20 [n] Ex 32:5; Joel 1:14
10:24 [o] 1Ki 20:39

[25]As soon as Jehu had finished making the burnt offering, he
ordered the guards and officers: "Go in and kill[a] them; let no one
escape."[b] So they cut them down with the sword. The guards and
officers threw the bodies out and then entered the inner shrine of
the temple of Baal. [26]They brought the sacred stone[c] out of the
temple of Baal and burned it. [27]They demolished the sacred stone
of Baal and tore down the temple[d] of Baal, and people have used
it for a latrine to this day.

[28]So Jehu[e] destroyed Baal worship in Israel. [29]However, he did
not turn away from the sins[f] of Jeroboam son of Nebat, which he
had caused Israel to commit—the worship of the golden calves[g] at
Bethel[h] and Dan.

[30]The LORD said to Jehu, "Because you have done well in
accomplishing what is right in my eyes and have done to the
house of Ahab all I had in mind to do, your descendants will sit on
the throne of Israel to the fourth generation."[i] [31]Yet Jehu was not
careful[j] to keep the law of the LORD, the God of Israel, with all his
heart. He did not turn away from the sins[k] of Jeroboam, which he
had caused Israel to commit.

[32]In those days the LORD began to reduce[l] the size of Israel.
Hazael[m] overpowered the Israelites throughout their territory
[33]east of the Jordan in all the land of Gilead (the region of Gad,
Reuben and Manasseh), from Aroer[n] by the Arnon Gorge
through Gilead to Bashan.

[34]As for the other events of Jehu's reign, all he did, and all his
achievements, are they not written in the book of the annals[o] of the
kings of Israel?

[35]Jehu rested with his fathers and was buried in Samaria. And
Jehoahaz his son succeeded him as king. [36]The time that Jehu
reigned over Israel in Samaria was twenty-eight years.

Chapter 11 Theme ________________________

11 When Athaliah[p] the mother of Ahaziah saw that her son was
dead, she proceeded to destroy the whole royal family. [2]But
Jehosheba, the daughter of King Jehoram[a] and sister of Ahaziah,
took Joash[q] son of Ahaziah and stole him away from among the
royal princes, who were about to be murdered. She put him and
his nurse in a bedroom to hide him from Athaliah; so he was not
killed.[r] [3]He remained hidden with his nurse at the temple of the
LORD for six years while Athaliah ruled the land.

[4]In the seventh year Jehoiada sent for the commanders of units
of a hundred, the Carites[s] and the guards and had them brought
to him at the temple of the LORD. He made a covenant with them

[a]2 Hebrew *Joram*, a variant of *Jehoram*

10:25 [a]Ex 22:20; 2Ki 11:18 [b]1Ki 18:40
10:26 [c]1Ki 14:23
10:27 [d]1Ki 16:32
10:28 [e]1Ki 19:17
10:29 [f]1Ki 12:30 [g]1Ki 12:28-29 [h]1Ki 12:32
10:30 [i]ver 35; 2Ki 15:12
10:31 [j]Pr 4:23 [k]1Ki 12:30
10:32 [l]2Ki 13:25 [m]1Ki 19:17; 2Ki 8:12
10:33 [n]Nu 32:34; Dt 2:36; Jdg 11:26; Isa 17:2
10:34 [o]1Ki 15:31
11:1 [p]2Ki 8:18
11:2 [q]ver 21; 2Ki 12:1 [r]Jdg 9:5
11:4 [s]ver 19

and put them under oath at the temple of the LORD. Then he
showed them the king's son. 5He commanded them, saying,
"This is what you are to do: You who are in the three companies
that are going on duty on the Sabbath[a]—a third of you guarding
the royal palace,[b] 6a third at the Sur Gate, and a third at the gate
behind the guard, who take turns guarding the temple— 7and
you who are in the other two companies that normally go off
Sabbath duty are all to guard the temple for the king. 8Station
yourselves around the king, each man with his weapon in his
hand. Anyone who approaches your ranks[a] must be put to death.
Stay close to the king wherever he goes."

9The commanders of units of a hundred did just as Jehoiada
the priest ordered. Each one took his men—those who were
going on duty on the Sabbath and those who were going off
duty—and came to Jehoiada the priest. 10Then he gave the commanders the spears and shields[c] that had belonged to King David
and that were in the temple of the LORD. 11The guards, each with
his weapon in his hand, stationed themselves around the king—
near the altar and the temple, from the south side to the north
side of the temple.

12Jehoiada brought out the king's son and put the crown on
him; he presented him with a copy of the covenant[d] and proclaimed him king. They anointed[e] him, and the people clapped
their hands[f] and shouted, "Long live the king!"[g]

13When Athaliah heard the noise made by the guards and the
people, she went to the people at the temple of the LORD. 14She
looked and there was the king, standing by the pillar,[h] as the custom was. The officers and the trumpeters were beside the king,
and all the people of the land were rejoicing and blowing trumpets.[i] Then Athaliah tore[j] her robes and called out, "Treason!
Treason!"[k]

15Jehoiada the priest ordered the commanders of units of a
hundred, who were in charge of the troops: "Bring her out
between the ranks[b] and put to the sword anyone who follows
her." For the priest had said, "She must not be put to death in the
temple[l] of the LORD." 16So they seized her as she reached the place
where the horses enter[m] the palace grounds, and there she was
put to death.[n]

17Jehoiada then made a covenant[o] between the LORD and the
king and people that they would be the LORD's people. He also
made a covenant between the king and the people.[p] 18All the people of the land went to the temple[q] of Baal and tore it down. They
smashed[r] the altars and idols to pieces and killed Mattan the
priest[s] of Baal in front of the altars.

11:5 [a]1Ch 9:25 [b]1Ki 14:27
11:10 [c]2Sa 8:7; 1Ch 18:7
11:12 [d]Ex 25:16; 2Ki 23:3 [e]1Sa 9:16; 1Ki 1:39 [f]Ps 47:1; 98:8; Isa 55:12 [g]1Sa 10:24
11:14 [h]1Ki 7:15; 2Ki 23:3; 2Ch 34:31 [i]1Ki 1:39 [j]Ge 37:29 [k]2Ki 9:23
11:15 [l]1Ki 2:30
11:16 [m]Ne 3:28; Jer 31:40 [n]Ge 4:14
11:17 [o]Ex 24:8; 2Sa 5:3; 2Ch 15:12; 23:3; 29:10; 34:31; Ezr 10:3 [p]2Ki 23:3; Jer 34:8
11:18 [q]1Ki 16:32 [r]Dt 12:3 [s]1Ki 18:40; 2Ki 10:25; 23:20

[a]8 Or *approaches the precincts* [b]15 Or *out from the precincts*

Then Jehoiada the priest posted guards at the temple of the
LORD. 19He took with him the commanders of hundreds, the
Carites,[a] the guards and all the people of the land, and together
they brought the king down from the temple of the LORD and
went into the palace, entering by way of the gate of the guards.
The king then took his place on the royal throne, 20and all the
people of the land rejoiced.[b] And the city was quiet, because
Athaliah had been slain with the sword at the palace.
21Joash[a] was seven years old when he began to reign.

Chapter 12 Theme ______________________

12 In the seventh year of Jehu, Joash[b][c] became king, and he
reigned in Jerusalem forty years. His mother's name was
Zibiah; she was from Beersheba. 2Joash did what was right in the
eyes of the LORD all the years Jehoiada the priest instructed him.
3The high places,[d] however, were not removed; the people continued to offer sacrifices and burn incense there.
4Joash said to the priests, "Collect[e] all the money that is
brought as sacred offerings[f] to the temple of the LORD—the money collected in the census,[g] the money received from personal
vows and the money brought voluntarily[h] to the temple. 5Let
every priest receive the money from one of the treasurers, and let
it be used to repair whatever damage is found in the temple."
6But by the twenty-third year of King Joash the priests still had
not repaired the temple. 7Therefore King Joash summoned
Jehoiada the priest and the other priests and asked them, "Why
aren't you repairing the damage done to the temple? Take no
more money from your treasurers, but hand it over for repairing
the temple." 8The priests agreed that they would not collect any
more money from the people and that they would not repair the
temple themselves.
9Jehoiada the priest took a chest and bored a hole in its lid. He
placed it beside the altar, on the right side as one enters the temple of the LORD. The priests who guarded the entrance[i] put into
the chest all the money[j] that was brought to the temple of the
LORD. 10Whenever they saw that there was a large amount of
money in the chest, the royal secretary[k] and the high priest came,
counted the money that had been brought into the temple of the
LORD and put it into bags. 11When the amount had been determined, they gave the money to the men appointed to supervise
the work on the temple. With it they paid those who worked on
the temple of the LORD—the carpenters and builders, 12the
masons and stonecutters.[l] They purchased timber and dressed

11:19 [a] ver 4
11:20 [b] Pr 11:10; 28:12; 29:2
12:1 [c] 2Ki 11:2
12:3 [d] 1Ki 3:3; 2Ki 14:4; 15:35; 18:4
12:4 [e] 2Ki 22:4 [f] Ex 35:5 [g] Ex 30:12 [h] Ex 35:29; 1Ch 29:3-9
12:9 [i] Jer 35:4 [j] 2Ch 24:8; Mk 12:41; Lk 21:1
12:10 [k] 2Sa 8:17
12:12 [l] 2Ki 22:5-6

[a] *21* Hebrew *Jehoash,* a variant of *Joash* [b] *1* Hebrew *Jehoash,* a variant of *Joash*; also in verses 2, 4, 6, 7 and 18

stone for the repair of the temple of the LORD, and met all the other expenses of restoring the temple.

13 The money brought into the temple was not spent for making silver basins, wick trimmers, sprinkling bowls, trumpets or any other articles of gold[a] or silver for the temple of the LORD; 14 it was paid to the workmen, who used it to repair the temple. 15 They did not require an accounting from those to whom they gave the money to pay the workers, because they acted with complete honesty.[b] 16 The money from the guilt offerings[c] and sin offerings[d] was not brought into the temple of the LORD; it belonged[e] to the priests.

17 About this time Hazael[f] king of Aram went up and attacked Gath and captured it. Then he turned to attack Jerusalem. 18 But Joash king of Judah took all the sacred objects dedicated by his fathers—Jehoshaphat, Jehoram and Ahaziah, the kings of Judah—and the gifts he himself had dedicated and all the gold found in the treasuries of the temple of the LORD and of the royal palace, and he sent[g] them to Hazael king of Aram, who then withdrew[h] from Jerusalem.

19 As for the other events of the reign of Joash, and all he did, are they not written in the book of the annals of the kings of Judah? 20 His officials[i] conspired against him and assassinated[j] him at Beth Millo,[k] on the road down to Silla. 21 The officials who murdered him were Jozabad son of Shimeath and Jehozabad son of Shomer. He died and was buried with his fathers in the City of David. And Amaziah his son succeeded him as king.

Chapter 13 Theme ____________________

13 In the twenty-third year of Joash son of Ahaziah king of Judah, Jehoahaz son of Jehu became king of Israel in Samaria, and he reigned seventeen years. 2 He did evil[l] in the eyes of the LORD by following the sins of Jeroboam son of Nebat, which he had caused Israel to commit, and he did not turn away from them. 3 So the LORD's anger[m] burned against Israel, and for a long time he kept them under the power[n] of Hazael king of Aram and Ben-Hadad[o] his son.

4 Then Jehoahaz sought[p] the LORD's favor, and the LORD listened to him, for he saw[q] how severely the king of Aram was oppressing[r] Israel. 5 The LORD provided a deliverer[s] for Israel, and they escaped from the power of Aram. So the Israelites lived in their own homes as they had before. 6 But they did not turn away from the sins[t] of the house of Jeroboam, which he had caused Israel to commit; they continued in them. Also, the Asherah pole[a][u] remained standing in Samaria.

a6 That is, a symbol of the goddess Asherah; here and elsewhere in 2 Kings

12:13 [a] 1Ki 7:48-51; 2Ch 24:14
12:15 [b] 2Ki 22:7; 1Co 4:2
12:16 [c] Lev 5:14-19; Nu 18:9 [d] Lev 4:1-35 [e] Lev 7:7
12:17 [f] 2Ki 8:12
12:18 [g] 1Ki 15:18; 2Ch 21:16-17 [h] 1Ki 15:21
12:20 [i] 2Ki 14:5 [j] 2Ch 24:25 [k] Jdg 9:6
13:2 [l] 1Ki 12:26-33
13:3 [m] Dt 31:17; Jdg 2:14 [n] 1Ki 8:12; 12:17; 19:17 [o] ver 24
13:4 [p] Dt 4:29; Ps 78:34 [q] Ex 3:7; Dt 26:7 [r] 2Ki 14:26
13:5 [s] ver 25; 2Ki 14:25,27
13:6 [t] 1Ki 12:30 [u] 1Ki 16:33

INSIGHT

Silla's exact location is indefinite, but is believed to be near Jerusalem.

7 Nothing had been left[a] of the army of Jehoahaz except fifty
horsemen, ten chariots and ten thousand foot soldiers, for the king
of Aram had destroyed the rest and made them like the dust[b] at
threshing time.
8 As for the other events of the reign of Jehoahaz, all he did and
his achievements, are they not written in the book of the annals
of the kings of Israel? 9 Jehoahaz rested with his fathers and was
buried in Samaria. And Jehoash[a] his son succeeded him as king.
10 In the thirty-seventh year of Joash king of Judah, Jehoash son
of Jehoahaz became king of Israel in Samaria, and he reigned sixteen years. 11 He did evil in the eyes of the LORD and did not turn
away from any of the sins of Jeroboam son of Nebat, which he
had caused Israel to commit; he continued in them.
12 As for the other events of the reign of Jehoash, all he did and
his achievements, including his war against Amaziah[c] king of
Judah, are they not written in the book of the annals[d] of the kings
of Israel? 13 Jehoash rested with his fathers, and Jeroboam[e] succeeded him on the throne. Jehoash was buried in Samaria with the
kings of Israel.
14 Now Elisha was suffering from the illness from which he died.
Jehoash king of Israel went down to see him and wept over him.
"My father! My father!" he cried. "The chariots[f] and horsemen of
Israel!"
15 Elisha said, "Get a bow and some arrows,"[g] and he did so.
16 "Take the bow in your hands," he said to the king of Israel.
When he had taken it, Elisha put his hands on the king's hands.
17 "Open the east window," he said, and he opened it. "Shoot!"[h]
Elisha said, and he shot. "The LORD's arrow of victory, the arrow
of victory over Aram!" Elisha declared. "You will completely
destroy the Arameans at Aphek."[i]
18 Then he said, "Take the arrows," and the king took them.
Elisha told him, "Strike the ground." He struck it three times and
stopped. 19 The man of God was angry with him and said, "You
should have struck the ground five or six times; then you would
have defeated Aram and completely destroyed it. But now you will
defeat it only three times."[j]
20 Elisha died and was buried.
Now Moabite raiders[k] used to enter the country every spring.
21 Once while some Israelites were burying a man, suddenly they
saw a band of raiders; so they threw the man's body into Elisha's
tomb. When the body touched Elisha's bones, the man came to
life[l] and stood up on his feet.
22 Hazael king of Aram oppressed[m] Israel throughout the reign
of Jehoahaz. 23 But the LORD was gracious to them and had

13:7 [a] 2Ki 10:32-33 [b] 2Sa 22:43
13:12 [c] 2Ki 14:15 [d] 1Ki 15:31
13:13 [e] 2Ki 14:23; Hos 1:1
13:14 [f] 2Ki 2:12
13:15 [g] 1Sa 20:20
13:17 [h] Jos 8:18 [i] 1Ki 20:26
13:19 [j] ver 25
13:20 [k] 2Ki 3:7; 24:2
13:21 [l] Mt 27:52
13:22 [m] 1Ki 19:17; 2Ki 8:12

[a] 9 Hebrew *Joash,* a variant of *Jehoash;* also in verses 12-14 and 25

compassion and showed concern for them because of his
covenant[a] with Abraham, Isaac and Jacob. To this day he has been
unwilling to destroy[b] them or banish them from his presence.[c]
24Hazael king of Aram died, and Ben-Hadad[d] his son succeeded him as king. 25Then Jehoash son of Jehoahaz recaptured from
Ben-Hadad son of Hazael the towns he had taken in battle from
his father Jehoahaz. Three times[e] Jehoash defeated him, and so
he recovered[f] the Israelite towns.

Chapter 14 Theme ________________________

14 In the second year of Jehoash[a] son of Jehoahaz king of
Israel, Amaziah son of Joash king of Judah began to reign.
2He was twenty-five years old when he became king, and he
reigned in Jerusalem twenty-nine years. His mother's name was
Jehoaddin; she was from Jerusalem. 3He did what was right in the
eyes of the LORD, but not as his father David had done. In everything he followed the example of his father Joash. 4The high
places,[g] however, were not removed; the people continued to
offer sacrifices and burn incense there.
5After the kingdom was firmly in his grasp, he executed[h] the
officials[i] who had murdered his father the king. 6Yet he did not
put the sons of the assassins to death, in accordance with what is
written in the Book of the Law[j] of Moses where the LORD commanded: "Fathers shall not be put to death for their children, nor
children put to death for their fathers; each is to die for his own
sins."[b][k]
7He was the one who defeated ten thousand Edomites in the
Valley of Salt[l] and captured Sela[m] in battle, calling it Joktheel, the
name it has to this day.
8Then Amaziah sent messengers to Jehoash son of Jehoahaz,
the son of Jehu, king of Israel, with the challenge:
"Come, meet me face to face."
9But Jehoash king of Israel replied to Amaziah
king of Judah: "A thistle[n] in Lebanon sent a message
to a cedar in Lebanon, 'Give your daughter to my
son in marriage.' Then a wild beast in Lebanon
came along and trampled the thistle underfoot.
10You have indeed defeated Edom and now you are
arrogant.[o] Glory in your victory, but stay at home!
Why ask for trouble and cause your own downfall
and that of Judah also?"
11Amaziah, however, would not listen, so Jehoash
king of Israel attacked. He and Amaziah king of
Judah faced each other at Beth Shemesh[p] in Judah.

a *1* Hebrew *Joash*, a variant of *Jehoash*; also in verses 13, 23 and 27
b *6* Deut. 24:16

13:23 [a]Ge 13:16-17; Ex 2:24 [b]Dt 29:20 [c]Ex 33:15; 2Ki 14:27; 17:18; 24:3,20
13:24 [d]ver 3
13:25 [e]ver 18,19 [f]2Ki 10:32
14:4 [g]2Ki 12:3; 16:4
14:5 [h]2Ki 21:24 [i]2Ki 12:20
14:6 [j]Dt 28:61 [k]Nu 26:11; Job 21:20; Jer 31:30; 44:3; Eze 18:4,20
14:7 [l]2Sa 8:13; 2Ch 25:11 [m]Jdg 1:36
14:9 [n]Jdg 9:8-15
14:10 [o]Dt 8:14; 2Ch 26:16; 32:25
14:11 [p]Jos 15:10

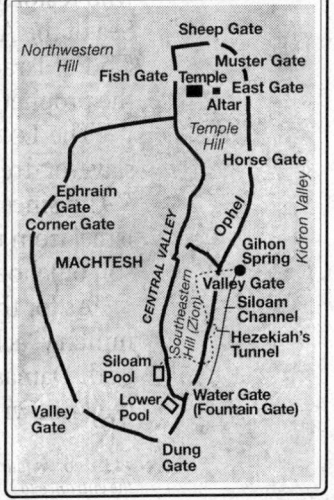

Jerusalem of the Old Testament

Northwestern Hill
Sheep Gate
Muster Gate
Fish Gate
Temple
East Gate
Altar
Temple Hill
Horse Gate
Ephraim Gate
Corner Gate
MACHTESH
CENTRAL VALLEY
Ophel
Kidron Valley
Gihon Spring
Valley Gate
Southeastern Hill (Zion)
Siloam Channel
Hezekiah's Tunnel
Siloam Pool
Lower Pool
Water Gate (Fountain Gate)
Valley Gate
Dung Gate

12 Judah was routed by Israel, and every man fled to his home.[a]
13 Jehoash king of Israel captured Amaziah king of Judah, the son
of Joash, the son of Ahaziah, at Beth Shemesh. Then Jehoash
went to Jerusalem and broke down the wall[b] of Jerusalem from the
Ephraim Gate[c] to the Corner Gate[d]—a section about six hundred
feet long.[a] 14 He took all the gold and silver and all the articles
found in the temple of the LORD and in the treasuries of the royal
palace. He also took hostages and returned to Samaria.

15 As for the other events of the reign of Jehoash, what he did and
his achievements, including his war[e] against Amaziah king of
Judah, are they not written in the book of the annals of the kings of
Israel? 16 Jehoash rested with his fathers and was buried in
Samaria with the kings of Israel. And Jeroboam his son succeeded
him as king.

17 Amaziah son of Joash king of Judah lived for fifteen years after
the death of Jehoash son of Jehoahaz king of Israel. 18 As for the
other events of Amaziah's reign, are they not written in the book
of the annals of the kings of Judah?

19 They conspired[f] against him in Jerusalem, and he fled to
Lachish,[g] but they sent men after him to Lachish and killed him
there. 20 He was brought back by horse[h] and was buried in
Jerusalem with his fathers, in the City of David.

21 Then all the people of Judah took Azariah,[b][i] who was sixteen
years old, and made him king in place of his father Amaziah.
22 He was the one who rebuilt Elath[j] and restored it to Judah after
Amaziah rested with his fathers.

23 In the fifteenth year of Amaziah son of Joash king of Judah,
Jeroboam[k] son of Jehoash king of Israel became king in Samaria,
and he reigned forty-one years. 24 He did evil in the eyes of the
LORD and did not turn away from any of the sins of Jeroboam son
of Nebat, which he had caused Israel to commit.[l] 25 He was the one
who restored the boundaries of Israel from Lebo[c] Hamath[m] to the
Sea of the Arabah,[d][n] in accordance with the word of the LORD, the
God of Israel, spoken through his servant Jonah[o] son of Amittai,
the prophet from Gath Hepher.

26 The LORD had seen how bitterly everyone in Israel, whether
slave or free,[p] was suffering;[q] there was no one to help them.[r]
27 And since the LORD had not said he would blot out[s] the name of
Israel from under heaven, he saved[t] them by the hand of Jeroboam
son of Jehoash.

28 As for the other events of Jeroboam's reign, all he did, and his
military achievements, including how he recovered for Israel
both Damascus[u] and Hamath,[v] which had belonged to Yaudi,[e] are
they not written in the book of the annals[w] of the kings of Israel?

[a] *13* Hebrew *four hundred cubits* (about 180 meters) [b] *21* Also called *Uzziah* [c] *25* Or *from the entrance to* [d] *25* That is, the Dead Sea [e] *28* Or *Judah*

14:12 [a] 2Sa 18:17
14:13 [b] 1Ki 3:1; 2Ch 33:14; 36:19; Jer 39:2 [c] Ne 8:16; 12:39 [d] 2Ch 25:23; Jer 31:38; Zec 14:10
14:15 [e] 2Ki 13:12
14:19 [f] 2Ki 12:20 [g] Jos 10:3; 2Ki 18:14,17
14:20 [h] 2Ki 9:28
14:21 [i] 2Ki 15:1; 2Ch 26:23
14:22 [j] 1Ki 9:26; 2Ki 16:6
14:23 [k] 2Ki 13:13
14:24 [l] 1Ki 15:30
14:25 [m] Nu 13:21; 1Ki 8:65 [n] Dt 3:17 [o] Jnh 1:1; Mt 12:39
14:26 [p] Dt 32:36 [q] 2Ki 13:4 [r] Ps 18:41; 22:11; 72:12; 107:12; Isa 63:5; La 1:7
14:27 [s] 2Ki 13:23 [t] Jdg 6:14
14:28 [u] 2Sa 8:5; 1Ki 11:24 [v] 2Ch 8:3 [w] 1Ki 15:31

15:1 [a]ver 32; 2Ki 14:21

29 Jeroboam rested with his fathers, the kings of Israel. And Zechariah his son succeeded him as king.

Chapter 15 Theme

15 In the twenty-seventh year of Jeroboam king of Israel,
Azariah[a] son of Amaziah king of Judah began to reign. 2 He
was sixteen years old when he became king, and he reigned in Jerusalem fifty-two years. His mother's name was Jecoliah; she was
from Jerusalem. 3 He did what was right in the eyes of the LORD, just
as his father Amaziah had done. 4 The high places, however, were
not removed; the people continued to offer sacrifices and burn
incense there.

15:5 [b]Ge 12:17 [c]Lev 13:46 [d]2Ch 27:1 [e]Ge 41:40

5 The LORD afflicted[b] the king with leprosy[a] until the day he died,
and he lived in a separate house.[b][c] Jotham[d] the king's son had
charge of the palace[e] and governed the people of the land.
6 As for the other events of Azariah's reign, and all he did, are
they not written in the book of the annals of the kings of Judah?
7 Azariah rested[f] with his fathers and was buried near them in the
City of David. And Jotham[g] his son succeeded him as king.
8 In the thirty-eighth year of Azariah king of Judah, Zechariah
son of Jeroboam became king of Israel in Samaria, and he reigned
six months. 9 He did evil[h] in the eyes of the LORD, as his fathers
had done. He did not turn away from the sins of Jeroboam son of
Nebat, which he had caused Israel to commit.

15:7 [f]Isa 6:1; 14:28 [g]ver 5

15:9 [h]1Ki 15:26

[a] 5 The Hebrew word was used for various diseases affecting the skin—not necessarily leprosy.
[b] 5 Or *in a house where he was relieved of responsibility*

Some of the Pagan Gods Worshiped by the Israelites

The god:	Ruled over / description:	Reference:
Adrammelech	War, love	2 Kings 17:31
Anammelech	Demanded child sacrifice	2 Kings 17:31
Asherah	Wife of Baal	2 Kings 13:6
Ashima	God of Hittites	2 Kings 17:30
Ashtoreth (Astarte, Ishtar)	Sex, fertility, queen of heaven	2 Kings 23:13
Baal	Rain, wind, clouds, fertility of land	2 Kings 3:2
Baal-Zebub	God of Ekron	2 Kings 1:2
Chemosh	Provider of land	2 Kings 23:13
Molech (Milcom)	National god of Moabites, worship involved human sacrifice	2 Kings 23:10
Nebo	Wisdom, literature, arts	1 Chronicles 5:8
Nergal	Underworld, death	2 Kings 17:30
Nibhaz	Worshiped by the Avvites *(a people transplanted to Samaria from Assyria)*	2 Kings 17:31
Nisroch	God worshiped in Nineveh	2 Kings 19:37
Rimmon	Thunder, lightning, rain	2 Kings 5:18
Succoth Benoth	Mistress of Marduk, goddess of war	2 Kings 17:30
Tartak	Fertility (worshiped by Avvites)	2 Kings 17:31

10 Shallum son of Jabesh conspired against Zechariah. He
attacked him in front of the people,[a] assassinated[a] him and succeeded him as king. 11 The other events of Zechariah's reign are
written in the book of the annals[b] of the kings of Israel. 12 So the
word of the LORD spoken to Jehu was fulfilled:[c] "Your descendants will sit on the throne of Israel to the fourth generation."[b]
13 Shallum son of Jabesh became king in the thirty-ninth year of
Uzziah king of Judah, and he reigned in Samaria[d] one month.
14 Then Menahem son of Gadi went from Tirzah[e] up to Samaria.
He attacked Shallum son of Jabesh in Samaria, assassinated[f] him
and succeeded him as king.
15 The other events of Shallum's reign, and the conspiracy he
led, are written in the book of the annals[g] of the kings of Israel.
16 At that time Menahem, starting out from Tirzah, attacked
Tiphsah[h] and everyone in the city and its vicinity, because they
refused to open[i] their gates. He sacked Tiphsah and ripped open
all the pregnant women.
17 In the thirty-ninth year of Azariah king of Judah, Menahem
son of Gadi became king of Israel, and he reigned in Samaria ten
years. 18 He did evil in the eyes of the LORD. During his entire
reign he did not turn away from the sins of Jeroboam son of
Nebat, which he had caused Israel to commit.
19 Then Pul[c][j] king of Assyria invaded the land, and Menahem
gave him a thousand talents[d] of silver to gain his support and
strengthen his own hold on the kingdom. 20 Menahem exacted
this money from Israel. Every wealthy man had to contribute
fifty shekels[e] of silver to be given to the king of Assyria. So the
king of Assyria withdrew[k] and stayed in the land no longer.
21 As for the other events of Menahem's reign, and all he did,
are they not written in the book of the annals of the kings of
Israel? 22 Menahem rested with his fathers. And Pekahiah his son
succeeded him as king.
23 In the fiftieth year of Azariah king of Judah, Pekahiah son of
Menahem became king of Israel in Samaria, and he reigned two
years. 24 Pekahiah did evil in the eyes of the LORD. He did not turn
away from the sins of Jeroboam son of Nebat, which he had
caused Israel to commit. 25 One of his chief officers, Pekah[l] son of
Remaliah, conspired against him. Taking fifty men of Gilead
with him, he assassinated[m] Pekahiah, along with Argob and
Arieh, in the citadel of the royal palace at Samaria. So Pekah
killed Pekahiah and succeeded him as king.
26 The other events of Pekahiah's reign, and all he did, are written
in the book of the annals of the kings of Israel.

[a] *10* Hebrew; some Septuagint manuscripts *in Ibleam* [b] *12* 2 Kings 10:30 [c] *19* Also called *Tiglath-Pileser* [d] *19* That is, about 37 tons (about 34 metric tons) [e] *20* That is, about 1 1/4 pounds (about 0.6 kilogram)

15:10 [a] 2Ki 12:20
15:11 [b] 1Ki 15:31
15:12 [c] 2Ki 10:30
15:13 [d] ver 1,8
15:14 [e] 1Ki 14:17 [f] 2Ki 12:20
15:15 [g] 1Ki 15:31
15:16 [h] 1Ki 4:24 [i] 2Ki 8:12; Hos 13:16
15:19 [j] 1Ch 5:6,26
15:20 [k] 2Ki 12:18
15:25 [l] 2Ch 28:6; Isa 7:1 [m] 2Ki 12:20

27 In the fifty-second year of Azariah king of Judah, Pekah[a] son
of Remaliah[b] became king of Israel in Samaria, and he reigned
twenty years. 28 He did evil in the eyes of the LORD. He did not turn
away from the sins of Jeroboam son of Nebat, which he had caused
Israel to commit.
29 In the time of Pekah king of Israel, Tiglath-Pileser[c] king of
Assyria came and took Ijon,[d] Abel Beth Maacah, Janoah, Kedesh
and Hazor. He took Gilead and Galilee, including all the land of
Naphtali,[e] and deported[f] the people to Assyria. 30 Then Hoshea[g]
son of Elah conspired against Pekah son of Remaliah. He
attacked and assassinated[h] him, and then succeeded him as king
in the twentieth year of Jotham son of Uzziah.
31 As for the other events of Pekah's reign, and all he did, are
they not written in the book of the annals of the kings of Israel?
32 In the second year of Pekah son of Remaliah king of Israel,
Jotham[i] son of Uzziah king of Judah began to reign. 33 He was
twenty-five years old when he became king, and he reigned in
Jerusalem sixteen years. His mother's name was Jerusha daughter
of Zadok. 34 He did what was right[j] in the eyes of the LORD, just as
his father Uzziah had done. 35 The high places,[k] however, were not
removed; the people continued to offer sacrifices and burn incense
there. Jotham rebuilt the Upper Gate[l] of the temple of the LORD.
36 As for the other events of Jotham's reign, and what he did, are
they not written in the book of the annals of the kings of Judah?
37 (In those days the LORD began to send Rezin[m] king of Aram
and Pekah son of Remaliah against Judah.) 38 Jotham rested with
his fathers and was buried with them in the City of David, the
city of his father. And Ahaz his son succeeded him as king.

Chapter 16 Theme ______________________

16 In the seventeenth year of Pekah son of Remaliah, Ahaz[n]
son of Jotham king of Judah began to reign. 2 Ahaz was
twenty years old when he became king, and he reigned in Jerusalem sixteen years. Unlike David his father, he did not do what
was right[o] in the eyes of the LORD his God. 3 He walked in the ways
of the kings of Israel and even sacrificed his son[p] in[a] the fire, following the detestable[q] ways of the nations the LORD had driven out
before the Israelites. 4 He offered sacrifices and burned incense at
the high places, on the hilltops and under every spreading tree.[r]
5 Then Rezin[s] king of Aram and Pekah son of Remaliah king of
Israel marched up to fight against Jerusalem and besieged Ahaz,
but they could not overpower him. 6 At that time, Rezin[t] king of
Aram recovered Elath[u] for Aram by driving out the men of Judah.
Edomites then moved into Elath and have lived there to this day.

15:27 [a] 2Ch 28:6; Isa 7:1 [b] Isa 7:4
15:29 [c] 2Ki 16:7; 17:6; 1Ch 5:26; 2Ch 28:20; Jer 50:17 [d] 1Ki 15:20 [e] 2Ki 16:9; 17:24; 2Ch 16:4; Isa 9:1 [f] 2Ki 24:14-16; 1Ch 5:22; Isa 14:6,17; 36:17; 45:13
15:30 [g] 2Ki 17:1 [h] 2Ki 12:20
15:32 [i] 1Ch 5:17
15:34 [j] ver 3; 1Ki 14:8; 2Ch 26:4-5
15:35 [k] 2Ki 12:3 [l] 2Ch 23:20
15:37 [m] 2Ki 16:5; Isa 7:1
16:1 [n] Isa 1:1; 14:28
16:2 [o] 1Ki 14:8
16:3 [p] Lev 18:21; 2Ki 21:6 [q] Lev 18:3; Dt 9:4; 12:31
16:4 [r] Dt 12:2; Eze 6:13
16:5 [s] 2Ki 15:37; Isa 7:1,4
16:6 [t] Isa 9:12 [u] 2Ki 14:22; 2Ch 26:2

a 3 Or *even made his son pass through*

7 Ahaz sent messengers to say to Tiglath-Pileser[a] king of Assyria,
"I am your servant and vassal. Come up and save[b] me out of the
hand of the king of Aram and of the king of Israel, who are
attacking me." 8 And Ahaz took the silver and gold found in the
temple of the LORD and in the treasuries of the royal palace and
sent it as a gift[c] to the king of Assyria. 9 The king of Assyria complied by attacking Damascus[d] and capturing it. He deported its
inhabitants to Kir[e] and put Rezin to death.
10 Then King Ahaz went to Damascus to meet Tiglath-Pileser
king of Assyria. He saw an altar in Damascus and sent to Uriah[f]
the priest a sketch of the altar, with detailed plans for its construction. 11 So Uriah the priest built an altar in accordance with
all the plans that King Ahaz had sent from Damascus and finished it before King Ahaz returned. 12 When the king came back
from Damascus and saw the altar, he approached it and presented offerings[a][g] on it. 13 He offered up his burnt offering[h] and grain
offering, poured out his drink offering, and sprinkled the blood
of his fellowship offerings[b][i] on the altar. 14 The bronze altar[j] that
stood before the LORD he brought from the front of the temple—
from between the new altar and the temple of the LORD—and put
it on the north side of the new altar.

16:7 [a] 2Ki 15:29 [b] Isa 2:6; Jer 2:18; Eze 16:28; Hos 10:6

16:8 [c] 2Ki 12:18

16:9 [d] 2Ki 15:29 [e] Isa 22:6; Am 1:5; 9:7

16:10 [f] Isa 8:2

16:12 [g] 2Ch 26:16

16:13 [h] Lev 6:8-13 [i] Lev 7:11-21

16:14 [j] 2Ch 4:1

[a] 12 Or *and went up* [b] 13 Traditionally *peace offerings*

The Assyrian Captivity of Israel

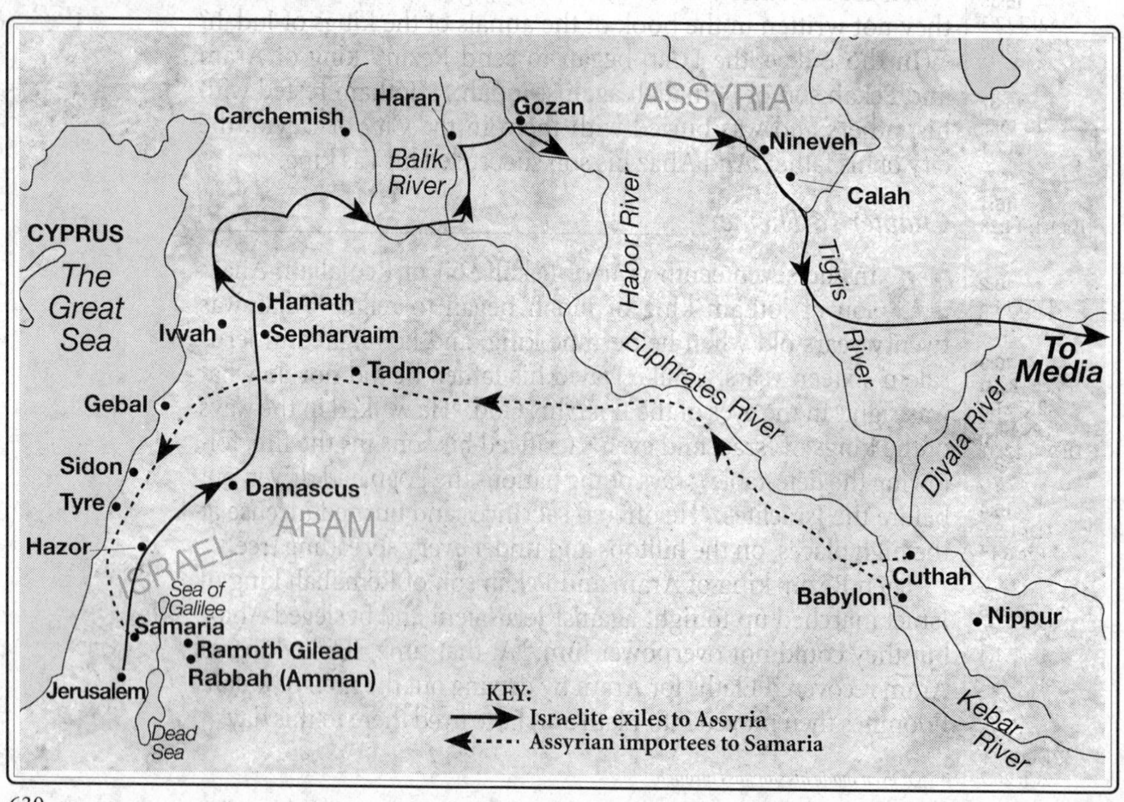

15 King Ahaz then gave these orders to Uriah the priest: "On the
large new altar, offer the morning[a] burnt offering and the evening
grain offering, the king's burnt offering and his grain offering,
and the burnt offering of all the people of the land, and their
grain offering and their drink offering. Sprinkle on the altar all the
blood of the burnt offerings and sacrifices. But I will use the
bronze altar for seeking guidance."[b] 16 And Uriah the priest did just
as King Ahaz had ordered.

17 King Ahaz took away the side panels and removed the basins
from the movable stands. He removed the Sea from the bronze
bulls that supported it and set it on a stone base.[c] 18 He took away
the Sabbath canopy[a] that had been built at the temple and
removed the royal entryway outside the temple of the LORD, in
deference to the king of Assyria.[d]

19 As for the other events of the reign of Ahaz, and what he did, are
they not written in the book of the annals of the kings of Judah?
20 Ahaz rested with his fathers and was buried with them in the
City of David. And Hezekiah his son succeeded him as king.

Chapter 17 Theme

17 In the twelfth year of Ahaz king of Judah, Hoshea[e] son of
Elah became king of Israel in Samaria, and he reigned nine
years. 2 He did evil in the eyes of the LORD, but not like the kings of
Israel who preceded him.

3 Shalmaneser[f] king of Assyria came up to attack Hoshea, who
had been Shalmaneser's vassal and had paid him tribute. 4 But
the king of Assyria discovered that Hoshea was a traitor, for he
had sent envoys to So[b] king of Egypt, and he no longer paid tribute
to the king of Assyria, as he had done year by year. Therefore
Shalmaneser seized him and put him in prison. 5 The king of
Assyria invaded the entire land, marched against Samaria and
laid siege[g] to it for three years. 6 In the ninth year of Hoshea, the
king of Assyria captured Samaria[h] and deported[i] the Israelites to
Assyria. He settled them in Halah, in Gozan[j] on the Habor River
and in the towns of the Medes.

7 All this took place because the Israelites had sinned[k] against the
LORD their God, who had brought them up out of Egypt[l] from
under the power of Pharaoh king of Egypt. They worshiped other gods 8 and followed the practices of the nations[m] the LORD had
driven out before them, as well as the practices that the kings of
Israel had introduced. 9 The Israelites secretly did things against
the LORD their God that were not right. From watchtower to fortified city[n] they built themselves high places in all their towns.

[a] 18 Or *the dais of his throne* (see Septuagint) [b] 4 Or *to Sais, to the*; *So* is possibly an abbreviation for *Osorkon*.

16:15 [a] Ex 29:38-41 [b] 1Sa 9:9
16:17 [c] 1Ki 7:27
16:18 [d] Eze 16:28
17:1 [e] 2Ki 15:30
17:3 [f] 2Ki 18:9-12; Hos 10:14
17:5 [g] Hos 13:16
17:6 [h] Hos 13:16 [i] Dt 28:36,64; 2Ki 18:10-11 [j] 1Ch 5:26
17:7 [k] Jos 23:16; Jdg 6:10 [l] Ex 14:15-31
17:8 [m] Lev 18:3; Dt 18:9; 2Ki 16:3
17:9 [n] 2Ki 18:8

[10]They set up sacred stones and Asherah poles[a] on every high hill
and under every spreading tree.[b] [11]At every high place they
burned incense, as the nations whom the LORD had driven out
before them had done. They did wicked things that provoked the
LORD to anger. [12]They worshiped idols,[c] though the LORD had
said, "You shall not do this."[a] [13]The LORD warned Israel and
Judah through all his prophets and seers:[d] "Turn from your evil
ways.[e] Observe my commands and decrees, in accordance with the
entire Law that I commanded your fathers to obey and that I
delivered to you through my servants the prophets."

[14]But they would not listen and were as stiff-necked[f] as their
fathers, who did not trust in the LORD their God. [15]They rejected
his decrees and the covenant[g] he had made with their fathers and
the warnings he had given them. They followed worthless idols[h]
and themselves became worthless. They imitated the nations[i]
around them although the LORD had ordered them, "Do not do as
they do," and they did the things the LORD had forbidden them
to do.

[16]They forsook all the commands of the LORD their God and
made for themselves two idols cast in the shape of calves,[j] and an
Asherah[k] pole. They bowed down to all the starry hosts,[l] and they
worshiped Baal.[m] [17]They sacrificed[n] their sons and daughters in[b]
the fire. They practiced divination and sorcery[o] and sold[p] themselves to do evil in the eyes of the LORD, provoking him to anger.

[18]So the LORD was very angry with Israel and removed them
from his presence. Only the tribe of Judah was left, [19]and even
Judah did not keep the commands of the LORD their God. They
followed the practices Israel had introduced.[q] [20]Therefore the
LORD rejected all the people of Israel; he afflicted them and gave
them into the hands of plunderers,[r] until he thrust them from his
presence.

[21]When he tore[s] Israel away from the house of David, they
made Jeroboam son of Nebat their king.[t] Jeroboam enticed Israel
away from following the LORD and caused them to commit a great
sin. [22]The Israelites persisted in all the sins of Jeroboam and did
not turn away from them [23]until the LORD removed them from
his presence, as he had warned through all his servants the
prophets. So the people of Israel were taken from their homeland
into exile in Assyria, and they are still there.

[24]The king of Assyria[u] brought people from Babylon, Cuthah,
Avva, Hamath and Sepharvaim[v] and settled them in the towns of
Samaria to replace the Israelites. They took over Samaria and lived
in its towns. [25]When they first lived there, they did not worship
the LORD; so he sent lions[w] among them and they killed some of

[a] 12 Exodus 20:4, 5 [b] 17 Or *They made their sons and daughters pass through*

INSIGHT

Cuthah (or Cuth), located in Mesopotamia about eighteen miles northeast of Babylon, was the center of worship for Nergal, the god of death or the underworld. The Assyrians took the people of Cuthah captive and exiled them to Israel (2 Kings 17:24). There they made an idol to Nergal (2 Kings 17:30), and became yet another influence upon the people's tendency to worship other gods alongside Yahweh of Israel.

17:10 [a]Ex 34:13; Mic 5:14 [b]1Ki 14:23
17:12 [c]Ex 20:4
17:13 [d]1Sa 9:9 [e]Jer 18:11; 25:5; 35:15
17:14 [f]Ex 32:9; Dt 31:27; Ac 7:51
17:15 [g]Dt 29:25 [h]Dt 32:21; Ro 1:21-23 [i]Dt 12:30-31
17:16 [j]1Ki 12:28 [k]1Ki 14:15,23 [l]2Ki 21:3 [m]1Ki 16:31
17:17 [n]Dt 18:10-12; 2Ki 16:3 [o]Lev 19:26 [p]1Ki 21:20
17:19 [q]1Ki 14:22-23; 2Ki 16:3
17:20 [r]2Ki 15:29
17:21 [s]1Ki 11:11 [t]1Ki 12:20
17:24 [u]Ezr 4:2,10 [v]2Ki 18:34
17:25 [w]Ge 37:20

the people. 26It was reported to the king of Assyria: "The people
you deported and resettled in the towns of Samaria do not know
what the god of that country requires. He has sent lions among
them, which are killing them off, because the people do not know
what he requires."

27Then the king of Assyria gave this order: "Have one of the
priests you took captive from Samaria go back to live there and
teach the people what the god of the land requires." 28So one of the
priests who had been exiled from Samaria came to live in Bethel
and taught them how to worship the LORD.

29Nevertheless, each national group made its own gods in the
several towns[a] where they settled, and set them up in the shrines[b]
the people of Samaria had made at the high places.[c] 30The men
from Babylon made Succoth Benoth, the men from Cuthah
made Nergal, and the men from Hamath made Ashima; 31the
Avvites made Nibhaz and Tartak, and the Sepharvites burned their
children in the fire as sacrifices to Adrammelech[d] and Anam-
melech, the gods of Sepharvaim.[e] 32They worshiped the LORD,
but they also appointed all sorts[f] of their own people to officiate
for them as priests in the shrines at the high places. 33They worshiped the LORD, but they also served their own gods in accordance with the customs of the nations from which they had
been brought.

34To this day they persist in their former practices. They neither
worship the LORD nor adhere to the decrees and ordinances, the
laws and commands that the LORD gave the descendants of Jacob,
whom he named Israel.[g] 35When the LORD made a covenant with
the Israelites, he commanded them: "Do not worship[h] any other
gods or bow down to them, serve them or sacrifice to them. 36But
the LORD, who brought you up out of Egypt with mighty power
and outstretched arm,[i] is the one you must worship. To him you
shall bow down and to him offer sacrifices. 37You must always be
careful[j] to keep the decrees and ordinances, the laws and commands he wrote for you. Do not worship other gods. 38Do not
forget[k] the covenant I have made with you, and do not worship
other gods. 39Rather, worship the LORD your God; it is he who
will deliver you from the hand of all your enemies."

40They would not listen, however, but persisted in their former
practices. 41Even while these people were worshiping the LORD,[l]
they were serving their idols. To this day their children and
grandchildren continue to do as their fathers did.

Chapter 18 Theme ________________________

18 In the third year of Hoshea son of Elah king of Israel,
Hezekiah[m] son of Ahaz king of Judah began to reign. 2He

17:29 [a]Jer 2:28 [b]1Ki 12:31 [c]Mic 4:5
17:31 [d]2Ki 19:37 [e]ver 24
17:32 [f]1Ki 12:31
17:34 [g]Ge 32:28; 35:10; 1Ki 18:31
17:35 [h]Ex 20:5; Jdg 6:10
17:36 [i]Ex 3:20; 6:6; Ps 136:12
17:37 [j]Dt 5:32
17:38 [k]Dt 4:23; 6:12
17:41 [l]ver 32-33; 1Ki 18:21; Mt 6:24
18:1 [m]Isa 1:1; 2Ch 28:27

was twenty-five years old when he became king, and he reigned
in Jerusalem twenty-nine years.[a] His mother's name was Abijah[a]
daughter of Zechariah. 3He did what was right in the eyes of the
LORD, just as his father David[b] had done. 4He removed[c] the high
places, smashed the sacred stones[d] and cut down the Asherah
poles. He broke into pieces the bronze snake[e] Moses had made, for
up to that time the Israelites had been burning incense to it. (It was
called[b] Nehushtan.[c])

5Hezekiah trusted[f] in the LORD, the God of Israel. There was no
one like him among all the kings of Judah, either before him or
after him. 6He held fast[g] to the LORD and did not cease to follow
him; he kept the commands the LORD had given Moses. 7And the
LORD was with him; he was successful[h] in whatever he undertook.
He rebelled[i] against the king of Assyria and did not serve him.
8From watchtower to fortified city,[j] he defeated the Philistines, as
far as Gaza and its territory.

9In King Hezekiah's fourth year,[k] which was the seventh year of
Hoshea son of Elah king of Israel, Shalmaneser king of Assyria
marched against Samaria and laid siege to it. 10At the end of three
years the Assyrians took it. So Samaria was captured in Hezekiah's
sixth year, which was the ninth year of Hoshea king of Israel.
11The king[l] of Assyria deported Israel to Assyria and settled them
in Halah, in Gozan on the Habor River and in towns of the
Medes. 12This happened because they had not obeyed the LORD
their God, but had violated his covenant[m]—all that Moses the
servant of the LORD commanded.[n] They neither listened to the
commands[o] nor carried them out.

13In the fourteenth year of King Hezekiah's reign, Sennacherib
king of Assyria attacked all the fortified cities of Judah[p] and captured them. 14So Hezekiah king of Judah sent this message to the
king of Assyria at Lachish: "I have done wrong.[q] Withdraw from
me, and I will pay whatever you demand of me." The king of
Assyria exacted from Hezekiah king of Judah three hundred talents[d] of silver and thirty talents[e] of gold. 15So Hezekiah gave[r] him
all the silver that was found in the temple of the LORD and in the
treasuries of the royal palace.

16At this time Hezekiah king of Judah stripped off the gold with
which he had covered the doors and doorposts of the temple of the
LORD, and gave it to the king of Assyria.

17The king of Assyria sent his supreme commander,[s] his chief
officer and his field commander with a large army, from Lachish
to King Hezekiah at Jerusalem. They came up to Jerusalem and
stopped at the aqueduct of the Upper Pool,[t] on the road to the

[a] 2 Hebrew *Abi*, a variant of *Abijah* [b] 4 Or *He called it* [c] 4 *Nehushtan* sounds like the Hebrew for *bronze* and *snake* and *unclean thing*. [d] 14 That is, about 11 tons (about 10 metric tons) [e] 14 That is, about 1 ton (about 1 metric ton)

18:2 [a]Isa 38:5
18:3 [b]Isa 38:5
18:4 [c]2Ch 31:1 [d]Ex 23:24 [e]Nu 21:9
18:5 [f]2Ki 19:10; 23:25
18:6 [g]Dt 10:20; Jos 23:8
18:7 [h]Ge 39:3; 1Sa 18:14 [i]2Ki 16:7
18:8 [j]2Ki 17:9; Isa 14:29
18:9 [k]Isa 1:1
18:11 [l]Isa 37:12
18:12 [m]2Ki 17:15 [n]Da 9:6,10 [o]1Ki 9:6
18:13 [p]2Ch 32:1; Isa 1:7; Mic 1:9
18:14 [q]Isa 24:5
18:15 [r]1Ki 15:18; 2Ki 16:8
18:17 [s]Isa 20:1 [t]2Ki 20:20; 2Ch 32:4,30; Isa 7:3

Washerman's Field. 18They called for the king; and Eliakim[a] son of
Hilkiah the palace administrator, Shebna[b] the secretary, and Joah
son of Asaph the recorder went out to them.
19The field commander said to them, "Tell Hezekiah:

"'This is what the great king, the king of Assyria, says: On
what are you basing this confidence of yours? 20You say you
have strategy and military strength—but you speak only
empty words. On whom are you depending, that you rebel
against me? 21Look now, you are depending on Egypt,[c] that
splintered reed of a staff,[d] which pierces a man's hand and
wounds him if he leans on it! Such is Pharaoh king of Egypt
to all who depend on him. 22And if you say to me, "We are
depending on the LORD our God"—isn't he the one whose
high places and altars Hezekiah removed, saying to Judah and
Jerusalem, "You must worship before this altar in Jerusalem"?
23"'Come now, make a bargain with my master, the king of
Assyria: I will give you two thousand horses—if you can put
riders on them! 24How can you repulse one officer[e] of the
least of my master's officials, even though you are depending
on Egypt for chariots and horsemen[a]? 25Furthermore, have I
come to attack and destroy this place without word from the
LORD?[f] The LORD himself told me to march against this country and destroy it.'"

26Then Eliakim son of Hilkiah, and Shebna and Joah said to the
field commander, "Please speak to your servants in Aramaic,[g]
since we understand it. Don't speak to us in Hebrew in the hearing of the people on the wall."
27But the commander replied, "Was it only to your master and
you that my master sent me to say these things, and not to the
men sitting on the wall—who, like you, will have to eat their own
filth and drink their own urine?"
28Then the commander stood and called out in Hebrew: "Hear
the word of the great king, the king of Assyria! 29This is what the
king says: Do not let Hezekiah deceive[h] you. He cannot deliver
you from my hand. 30Do not let Hezekiah persuade you to trust
in the LORD when he says, 'The LORD will surely deliver us; this
city will not be given into the hand of the king of Assyria.'
31"Do not listen to Hezekiah. This is what the king of Assyria
says: Make peace with me and come out to me. Then every one of
you will eat from his own vine and fig tree[i] and drink water from
his own cistern,[j] 32until I come and take you to a land like your
own, a land of grain and new wine, a land of bread and vineyards,
a land of olive trees and honey. Choose life[k] and not death!

a 24 Or *charioteers*

18:18 [a]2Ki 19:2; Isa 22:20 [b]Isa 22:15
18:21 [c]Isa 20:5; Eze 29:6 [d]Isa 30:5,7
18:24 [e]Isa 10:8
18:25 [f]2Ki 19:6,22
18:26 [g]Ezr 4:7
18:29 [h]2Ki 19:10
18:31 [i]Nu 13:23; 1Ki 4:25 [j]Jer 14:3; La 4:4
18:32 [k]Dt 8:7-9; 30:19

"Do not listen to Hezekiah, for he is misleading you when he says, 'The LORD will deliver us.' [33]Has the god[a] of any nation ever delivered his land from the hand of the king of Assyria? [34]Where are the gods of Hamath[b] and Arpad?[c] Where are the gods of Sepharvaim, Hena and Ivvah? Have they rescued Samaria from my hand? [35]Who of all the gods of these countries has been able to save his land from me? How then can the LORD deliver Jerusalem from my hand?"[d]

[36]But the people remained silent and said nothing in reply, because the king had commanded, "Do not answer him."

[37]Then Eliakim son of Hilkiah the palace administrator, Shebna the secretary and Joah son of Asaph the recorder went to Hezekiah, with their clothes torn,[e] and told him what the field commander had said.

INSIGHT

Ivvah (also spelled Ava or Avva) refers to the people the Assyrians conquered and took to Israel to replace the people taken into exile (2 Kings 17:24). Since the gods of the Ivvahian people did not come to their rescue against the Assyrians, they were used by Sennacherib as an example to call Jerusalem to surrender in 701 B.C. (2 Kings 18:34). Ivvah is believed to have been in Syria. Sennacherib used the same ploy against the city of Hena, which could possibly have been Ana or Anat on the Euphrates River.

Chapter 19 Theme

19 When King Hezekiah heard this, he tore[f] his clothes and put on sackcloth and went into the temple of the LORD. [2]He sent Eliakim the palace administrator, Shebna the secretary and the leading priests, all wearing sackcloth, to the prophet Isaiah[g] son of Amoz. [3]They told him, "This is what Hezekiah says: This day is a day of distress and rebuke and disgrace, as when children come to the point of birth and there is no strength to deliver them. [4]It may be that the LORD your God will hear all the words of the field commander, whom his master, the king of Assyria, has sent to ridicule[h] the living God, and that he will rebuke[i] him for the words the LORD your God has heard. Therefore pray for the remnant that still survives."

[5]When King Hezekiah's officials came to Isaiah, [6]Isaiah said to them, "Tell your master, 'This is what the LORD says: Do not be afraid of what you have heard—those words with which the underlings of the king of Assyria have blasphemed[j] me. [7]Listen! I am going to put such a spirit in him that when he hears a certain report, he will return to his own country, and there I will have him cut down with the sword.[k]'"

[8]When the field commander heard that the king of Assyria had left Lachish,[l] he withdrew and found the king fighting against Libnah.

[9]Now Sennacherib received a report that Tirhakah, the Cushite[a] king ⌞of Egypt⌟, was marching out to fight against him. So he again sent messengers to Hezekiah with this word: [10]"Say to Hezekiah king of Judah: Do not let the god you depend[m] on deceive[n] you when he says, 'Jerusalem will not be handed over to

[a]9 That is, from the upper Nile region

18:33 [a]2Ki 19:12; Isa 10:10-11
18:34 [b]2Ki 17:24; 19:13 [c]Isa 10:9
18:35 [d]Ps 2:1-2
18:37 [e]2Ki 6:30
19:1 [f]Ge 37:34; 1Ki 21:27; 2Ch 32:20-22
19:2 [g]Isa 1:1
19:4 [h]2Ki 18:35 [i]2Sa 16:12
19:6 [j]2Ki 18:25
19:7 [k]ver 37
19:8 [l]2Ki 18:14
19:10 [m]2Ki 18:5 [n]2Ki 18:29

the king of Assyria.' 11Surely you have heard what the kings of
Assyria have done to all the countries, destroying them completely.
And will you be delivered? 12Did the gods of the nations that were
destroyed by my forefathers deliver[a] them: the gods of Gozan,[b]
Haran,[c] Rezeph and the people of Eden who were in Tel Assar?
13Where is the king of Hamath, the king of Arpad, the king of the
city of Sepharvaim, or of Hena or Ivvah?"[d]

14Hezekiah received the letter from the messengers and read it.
Then he went up to the temple of the LORD and spread it out before
the LORD. 15And Hezekiah prayed to the LORD: "O LORD, God of
Israel, enthroned between the cherubim,[e] you alone are God over
all the kingdoms of the earth. You have made heaven and earth.
16Give ear,[f] O LORD, and hear;[g] open your eyes,[h] O LORD, and see;
listen to the words Sennacherib has sent to insult the living God.

17"It is true, O LORD, that the Assyrian kings have laid waste
these nations and their lands. 18They have thrown their gods into
the fire and destroyed them, for they were not gods[i] but only
wood and stone, fashioned by men's hands.[j] 19Now, O LORD our
God, deliver us from his hand, so that all kingdoms[k] on earth may
know[l] that you alone, O LORD, are God."

20Then Isaiah son of Amoz sent a message to Hezekiah: "This is
what the LORD, the God of Israel, says: I have heard[m] your prayer
concerning Sennacherib king of Assyria. 21This is the word that
the LORD has spoken against him:

"'The Virgin Daughter[n] of Zion
  despises you and mocks[o] you.
The Daughter of Jerusalem
  tosses her head[p] as you flee.
22Who is it you have insulted and blasphemed?
  Against whom have you raised your voice
and lifted your eyes in pride?
  Against the Holy One[q] of Israel!
23By your messengers
  you have heaped insults on the Lord.
And you have said,[r]
  "With my many chariots[s]
I have ascended the heights of the mountains,
  the utmost heights of Lebanon.
I have cut down its tallest cedars,
  the choicest of its pines.
I have reached its remotest parts,
  the finest of its forests.
24I have dug wells in foreign lands
  and drunk the water there.

19:12 [a]2Ki 18:33 [b]2Ki 17:6 [c]Ge 11:31
19:13 [d]2Ki 18:34
19:15 [e]Ex 25:22
19:16 [f]Ps 31:2 [g]1Ki 8:29 [h]ver 4; 2Ch 6:40
19:18 [i]Isa 44:9-11; Jer 10:3-10 [j]Ps 115:4; Ac 17:29
19:19 [k]1Ki 8:43 [l]Ps 83:18
19:20 [m]2Ki 20:5
19:21 [n]Jer 14:17; La 2:13 [o]Ps 22:7-8 [p]Job 16:4; Ps 109:25
19:22 [q]Ps 71:22; Isa 5:24
19:23 [r]Isa 10:18 [s]Ps 20:7

With the soles of my feet
I have dried up all the streams of Egypt."

25"'Have you not heard?[a]
Long ago I ordained it.
In days of old I planned[b] it;
now I have brought it to pass,
that you have turned fortified cities
into piles of stone.[c]
26Their people, drained of power,
are dismayed[d] and put to shame.
They are like plants in the field,
like tender green shoots,[e]
like grass sprouting on the roof,
scorched[f] before it grows up.

27"'But I know[g] where you stay
and when you come and go
and how you rage against me.
28Because you rage against me
and your insolence has reached my ears,
I will put my hook[h] in your nose
and my bit[i] in your mouth,
and I will make you return[j]
by the way you came.'

29"This will be the sign[k] for you, O Hezekiah:

"This year you will eat what grows by itself,[l]
and the second year what springs from that.
But in the third year sow and reap,
plant vineyards[m] and eat their fruit.
30Once more a remnant of the house of Judah
will take root[n] below and bear fruit above.
31For out of Jerusalem will come a remnant,
and out of Mount Zion a band of survivors.

The zeal[o] of the LORD Almighty will accomplish this.

32"Therefore this is what the LORD says concerning the king of Assyria:

"He will not enter this city
or shoot an arrow here.
He will not come before it with shield
or build a siege ramp against it.
33By the way that he came he will return;[p]
he will not enter this city,
declares the LORD.

19:25 [a]Isa 40:21,28 [b]Isa 10:5; 45:7 [c]Mic 1:6
19:26 [d]Ps 6:10 [e]Isa 4:2 [f]Ps 129:6
19:27 [g]Ps 139:1-4
19:28 [h]Eze 19:9; 29:4 [i]Isa 30:28 [j]ver 33
19:29 [k]2Ki 20:8-9; Lk 2:12 [l]Lev 25:5 [m]Ps 107:37
19:30 [n]2Ch 32:22-23
19:31 [o]Isa 9:7
19:33 [p]ver 28

34 I will defend[a] this city and save it,
for my sake and for the sake of David[b] my servant."

35 That night the angel of the LORD[c] went out and put to death a
hundred and eighty-five thousand men in the Assyrian camp.
When the people got up the next morning—there were all the
dead bodies![d] 36 So Sennacherib king of Assyria broke camp and
withdrew. He returned to Nineveh[e] and stayed there.
37 One day, while he was worshiping in the temple of his god
Nisroch, his sons Adrammelech and Sharezer cut him down with
the sword,[f] and they escaped to the land of Ararat.[g] And Esar-
haddon[h] his son succeeded him as king.

Chapter 20 Theme

20 In those days Hezekiah became ill and was at the point of
death. The prophet Isaiah son of Amoz went to him and
said, "This is what the LORD says: Put your house in order, because
you are going to die; you will not recover."
2 Hezekiah turned his face to the wall and prayed to the LORD,
3 "Remember,[i] O LORD, how I have walked before you faithfully[j]
and with wholehearted devotion and have done what is good in
your eyes." And Hezekiah wept bitterly.
4 Before Isaiah had left the middle court, the word of the LORD
came to him: 5 "Go back and tell Hezekiah, the leader of my people,
'This is what the LORD, the God of your father David, says: I have
heard[k] your prayer and seen your tears;[l] I will heal you. On the
third day from now you will go up to the temple of the LORD. 6 I
will add fifteen years to your life. And I will deliver you and this
city from the hand of the king of Assyria. I will defend[m] this city
for my sake and for the sake of my servant David.' "
7 Then Isaiah said, "Prepare a poultice of figs." They did so and
applied it to the boil,[n] and he recovered.
8 Hezekiah had asked Isaiah, "What will be the sign that the
LORD will heal me and that I will go up to the temple of the LORD
on the third day from now?"
9 Isaiah answered, "This is the LORD's sign[o] to you that the LORD
will do what he has promised: Shall the shadow go forward ten
steps, or shall it go back ten steps?"
10 "It is a simple matter for the shadow to go forward ten steps,"
said Hezekiah. "Rather, have it go back ten steps."
11 Then the prophet Isaiah called upon the LORD, and the LORD
made the shadow go back[p] the ten steps it had gone down on the
stairway of Ahaz.
12 At that time Merodach-Baladan son of Baladan king of Babylon sent Hezekiah letters and a gift, because he had heard of
Hezekiah's illness. 13 Hezekiah received the messengers and

19:34 [a] 2Ki 20:6 [b] 1Ki 11:12-13
19:35 [c] Ex 12:23 [d] Job 24:24
19:36 [e] Ge 10:11; Jnh 1:2
19:37 [f] ver 7 [g] Ge 8:4 [h] Ezr 4:2
20:3 [i] Ne 13:22 [j] 2Ki 18:3-6
20:5 [k] 1Sa 9:16; 1Ki 9:3; 2Ki 19:20 [l] Ps 39:12; 56:8
20:6 [m] 2Ki 19:34
20:7 [n] Isa 38:21
20:9 [o] Dt 13:2; Jer 44:29
20:11 [p] Jos 10:13

showed them all that was in his storehouses—the silver, the gold,
the spices and the fine oil—his armory and everything found
among his treasures. There was nothing in his palace or in all his
kingdom that Hezekiah did not show them.
14 Then Isaiah the prophet went to King Hezekiah and asked,
"What did those men say, and where did they come from?"
"From a distant land," Hezekiah replied. "They came from
Babylon."
15 The prophet asked, "What did they see in your palace?"
"They saw everything in my palace," Hezekiah said. "There is
nothing among my treasures that I did not show them."
16 Then Isaiah said to Hezekiah, "Hear the word of the LORD:
17 The time will surely come when everything in your palace, and
all that your fathers have stored up until this day, will be carried
off to Babylon.[a] Nothing will be left, says the LORD. 18 And some of
your descendants,[b] your own flesh and blood, that will be born to
you, will be taken away, and they will become eunuchs in the
palace of the king of Babylon."
19 "The word of the LORD you have spoken is good," Hezekiah
replied. For he thought, "Will there not be peace and security in
my lifetime?"
20 As for the other events of Hezekiah's reign, all his achievements and how he made the pool[c] and the tunnel by which he
brought water into the city, are they not written in the book of
the annals of the kings of Judah? 21 Hezekiah rested with his
fathers. And Manasseh his son succeeded him as king.

Chapter 21 Theme ______________________

21 Manasseh was twelve years old when he became king, and
he reigned in Jerusalem fifty-five years. His mother's name
was Hephzibah.[d] 2 He did evil[e] in the eyes of the LORD, following
the detestable practices[f] of the nations the LORD had driven out
before the Israelites. 3 He rebuilt the high places[g] his father
Hezekiah had destroyed; he also erected altars to Baal[h] and made
an Asherah pole, as Ahab king of Israel had done. He bowed
down to all the starry hosts[i] and worshiped them. 4 He built
altars[j] in the temple of the LORD, of which the LORD had said, "In
Jerusalem I will put my Name."[k] 5 In both courts[l] of the temple of
the LORD, he built altars to all the starry hosts. 6 He sacrificed his
own son[m] in[a] the fire, practiced sorcery and divination, and consulted mediums and spiritists.[n] He did much evil in the eyes of
the LORD, provoking him to anger.

a6 Or *He made his own son pass through*

20:17 [a] 2Ki 24:13; 25:13; 2Ch 36:10; Jer 27:22; 52:17-23
20:18 [b] 2Ki 24:15; 2Ch 33:11; Da 1:3
20:20 [c] Ne 3:16
21:1 [d] Isa 62:4
21:2 [e] Jer 15:4 [f] 2Ki 16:3
21:3 [g] 2Ki 18:4 [h] Jdg 6:28; 1Ki 16:32 [i] Dt 17:3; 2Ki 17:16
21:4 [j] Jer 32:34 [k] 2Sa 7:13; 1Ki 8:29
21:5 [l] 1Ki 7:12; 2Ki 23:12
21:6 [m] Lev 18:21; Dt 18:10; 2Ki 16:3; 17:17 [n] Lev 19:31

7He took the carved Asherah pole[a] he had made and put it in
the temple, of which the LORD had said to David and to his son
Solomon, "In this temple and in Jerusalem, which I have chosen
out of all the tribes of Israel, I will put my Name[b] forever. 8I will
not again[c] make the feet of the Israelites wander from the land I
gave their forefathers, if only they will be careful to do everything
I commanded them and will keep the whole Law that my servant
Moses[d] gave them." 9But the people did not listen. Manasseh led
them astray, so that they did more evil[e] than the nations[f] the
LORD had destroyed before the Israelites.

10The LORD said through his servants the prophets: 11"Manasseh king of Judah has committed these detestable sins. He has
done more evil[g] than the Amorites[h] who preceded him and has
led Judah into sin with his idols. 12Therefore this is what the
LORD, the God of Israel, says: I am going to bring such disaster[i]
on Jerusalem and Judah that the ears of everyone who hears of it
will tingle.[j] 13I will stretch out over Jerusalem the measuring line
used against Samaria and the plumb line[k] used against the house
of Ahab. I will wipe[l] out Jerusalem as one wipes a dish, wiping it
and turning it upside down. 14I will forsake[m] the remnant[n] of my
inheritance and hand them over to their enemies. They will be
looted and plundered by all their foes, 15because they have done
evil[o] in my eyes and have provoked[p] me to anger from the day
their forefathers came out of Egypt until this day."

16Moreover, Manasseh also shed so much innocent blood[q] that
he filled Jerusalem from end to end—besides the sin that he had
caused Judah to commit, so that they did evil in the eyes of the
LORD.

17As for the other events of Manasseh's reign, and all he did,
including the sin he committed, are they not written in the book
of the annals of the kings of Judah? 18Manasseh rested with his
fathers and was buried in his palace garden,[r] the garden of Uzza.
And Amon his son succeeded him as king.

19Amon was twenty-two years old when he became king, and
he reigned in Jerusalem two years. His mother's name was
Meshullemeth daughter of Haruz; she was from Jotbah. 20He did
evil[s] in the eyes of the LORD, as his father Manasseh had done.
21He walked in all the ways of his father; he worshiped the idols
his father had worshiped, and bowed down to them. 22He forsook
the LORD, the God of his fathers, and did not walk[t] in the way of
the LORD.

23Amon's officials conspired against him and assassinated[u] the
king in his palace. 24Then the people of the land killed[v] all who
had plotted against King Amon, and they made Josiah his son
king in his place.

21:7 [a]Dt 16:21; 2Ki 23:4 [b]2Sa 7:13; 1Ki 8:29; 9:3; 2Ki 23:27; Jer 32:34
21:8 [c]2Sa 7:10 [d]2Ki 18:12
21:9 [e]Pr 29:12 [f]Dt 9:4
21:11 [g]2Ki 24:3-4 [h]Ge 15:16; 1Ki 21:26
21:12 [i]2Ki 23:26; 24:3; Jer 15:4 [j]1Sa 3:11; Jer 19:3
21:13 [k]Isa 34:11; La 2:8; Am 7:7-9 [l]2Ki 23:27
21:14 [m]Ps 78:58-60 [n]2Ki 19:4; Mic 2:12
21:15 [o]Ex 32:22 [p]Jer 25:7
21:16 [q]2Ki 24:4
21:18 [r]ver 26
21:20 [s]ver 2-6
21:22 [t]1Ki 11:33
21:23 [u]2Ki 12:20; 2Ch 33:24-25
21:24 [v]2Ki 14:5

25 As for the other events of Amon's reign, and what he did, are
they not written in the book of the annals of the kings of Judah?
26 He was buried in his grave in the garden[a] of Uzza. And Josiah
his son succeeded him as king.

Chapter 22 Theme ________________________

22 Josiah was eight years old when he became king, and he
reigned in Jerusalem thirty-one years. His mother's name
was Jedidah daughter of Adaiah; she was from Bozkath.[b] 2 He did
what was right[c] in the eyes of the LORD and walked in all the ways
of his father David, not turning aside to the right[d] or to the left.
3 In the eighteenth year of his reign, King Josiah sent the secretary, Shaphan[e] son of Azaliah, the son of Meshullam, to the temple
of the LORD. He said: 4 "Go up to Hilkiah the high priest and have
him get ready the money that has been brought into the temple
of the LORD, which the doorkeepers have collected[f] from the people. 5 Have them entrust it to the men appointed to supervise the
work on the temple. And have these men pay the workers who
repair[g] the temple of the LORD— 6 the carpenters, the builders
and the masons. Also have them purchase timber and dressed
stone to repair the temple.[h] 7 But they need not account for the
money entrusted to them, because they are acting faithfully."[i]
8 Hilkiah the high priest said to Shaphan the secretary, "I have
found the Book of the Law[j] in the temple of the LORD." He gave it
to Shaphan, who read it. 9 Then Shaphan the secretary went to the
king and reported to him: "Your officials have paid out the money that was in the temple of the LORD and have entrusted it to the
workers and supervisors at the temple." 10 Then Shaphan the secretary informed the king, "Hilkiah the priest has given me a
book." And Shaphan read from it in the presence of the king.[k]
11 When the king heard the words of the Book of the Law, he
tore his robes. 12 He gave these orders to Hilkiah the priest,
Ahikam[l] son of Shaphan, Acbor son of Micaiah, Shaphan the
secretary and Asaiah the king's attendant: 13 "Go and inquire of
the LORD for me and for the people and for all Judah about what
is written in this book that has been found. Great is the LORD's
anger[m] that burns against us because our fathers have not obeyed
the words of this book; they have not acted in accordance with all
that is written there concerning us."
14 Hilkiah the priest, Ahikam, Acbor, Shaphan and Asaiah went
to speak to the prophetess Huldah, who was the wife of Shallum
son of Tikvah, the son of Harhas, keeper of the wardrobe. She
lived in Jerusalem, in the Second District.
15 She said to them, "This is what the LORD, the God of Israel,
says: Tell the man who sent you to me, 16 'This is what the LORD

21:26 [a] ver 18
22:1 [b] Jos 15:39
22:2 [c] Dt 17:19 [d] Dt 5:32
22:3 [e] 2Ch 34:20; Jer 39:14
22:4 [f] 2Ki 12:4-5
22:5 [g] 2Ki 12:5, 11-14
22:6 [h] 2Ki 12:11-12
22:7 [i] 2Ki 12:15
22:8 [j] Dt 31:24
22:10 [k] Jer 36:21
22:12 [l] 2Ki 25:22; Jer 26:24
22:13 [m] Dt 29:24-28; 31:17

says: I am going to bring disaster[a] on this place and its people, according to everything written in the book[b] the king of Judah has read. 17Because they have forsaken[c] me and burned incense to other gods and provoked me to anger by all the idols their hands have made,[a] my anger will burn against this place and will not be quenched.' 18Tell the king of Judah, who sent you to inquire[d] of the LORD, 'This is what the LORD, the God of Israel, says concerning the words you heard: 19Because your heart was responsive and you humbled[e] yourself before the LORD when you heard what I have spoken against this place and its people, that they would become accursed[f] and laid waste,[g] and because you tore your robes and wept in my presence, I have heard you, declares the LORD. 20Therefore I will gather you to your fathers, and you will be buried in peace.[h] Your eyes will not see all the disaster I am going to bring on this place.' "

So they took her answer back to the king.

Chapter 23 Theme ____

23 Then the king called together all the elders of Judah and Jerusalem. 2He went up to the temple of the LORD with the men of Judah, the people of Jerusalem, the priests and the prophets—all the people from the least to the greatest. He read[i] in their hearing all the words of the Book of the Covenant, which had been found in the temple of the LORD. 3The king stood by the pillar and renewed the covenant[j] in the presence of the LORD—to follow[k] the LORD and keep his commands, regulations and decrees with all his heart and all his soul, thus confirming the words of the covenant written in this book. Then all the people pledged themselves to the covenant.

4The king ordered Hilkiah the high priest, the priests next in rank and the doorkeepers[l] to remove[m] from the temple of the LORD all the articles made for Baal and Asherah and all the starry hosts. He burned them outside Jerusalem in the fields of the Kidron Valley and took the ashes to Bethel. 5He did away with the pagan priests appointed by the kings of Judah to burn incense on the high places of the towns of Judah and on those around Jerusalem—those who burned incense to Baal, to the sun and moon, to the constellations and to all the starry hosts.[n] 6He took the Asherah pole from the temple of the LORD to the Kidron Valley outside Jerusalem and burned it there. He ground it to powder and scattered the dust over the graves of the common people.[o] 7He also tore down the quarters of the male shrine prostitutes,[p] which were in the temple of the LORD and where women did weaving for Asherah.

22:16 [a]Dt 31:29; Jos 23:15 [b]Dt 29:27; Da 9:11
22:17 [c]Dt 29:25-27
22:18 [d]2Ch 34:26; Jer 21:2
22:19 [e]Ex 10:3; 1Ki 21:29; Ps 51:17; Isa 57:15; Mic 6:8 [f]Jer 26:6 [g]Lev 26:31
22:20 [h]Isa 57:1
23:2 [i]Dt 31:11; 2Ki 22:8
23:3 [j]2Ki 11:14,17 [k]Dt 13:4
23:4 [l]2Ki 25:18 [m]2Ki 21:7
23:5 [n]2Ki 21:3; Jer 8:2
23:6 [o]Jer 26:23
23:7 [p]1Ki 14:24; 15:12; Eze 16:16

a 17 Or *by everything they have done*

8Josiah brought all the priests from the towns of Judah and desecrated the high places, from Geba[a] to Beersheba, where the
priests had burned incense. He broke down the shrines[a] at the
gates—at the entrance to the Gate of Joshua, the city governor,
which is on the left of the city gate. 9Although the priests of the
high places did not serve[b] at the altar of the LORD in Jerusalem,
they ate unleavened bread with their fellow priests.
10He desecrated Topheth,[c] which was in the Valley of Ben Hinnom,[d] so no one could use it to sacrifice his son[e] or daughter in[b] the
fire to Molech. 11He removed from the entrance to the temple of the
LORD the horses that the kings of Judah had dedicated to the sun.
They were in the court near the room of an official named Nathan-
Melech. Josiah then burned the chariots dedicated to the sun.[f]
12He pulled down the altars the kings of Judah had erected on
the roof[g] near the upper room of Ahaz, and the altars Manasseh
had built in the two courts[h] of the temple of the LORD. He
removed them from there, smashed them to pieces and threw the
rubble into the Kidron Valley. 13The king also desecrated the high
places that were east of Jerusalem on the south of the Hill of Corruption—the ones Solomon[i] king of Israel had built for Ashtoreth the vile goddess of the Sidonians, for Chemosh the vile
god of Moab, and for Molech[c] the detestable god of the people of
Ammon. 14Josiah smashed[j] the sacred stones and cut down the
Asherah poles and covered the sites with human bones.
15Even the altar[k] at Bethel, the high place made by Jeroboam[l]
son of Nebat, who had caused Israel to sin—even that altar and
high place he demolished. He burned the high place and ground
it to powder, and burned the Asherah pole also. 16Then Josiah[m]
looked around, and when he saw the tombs that were there on
the hillside, he had the bones removed from them and burned on
the altar to defile it, in accordance with the word of the LORD proclaimed by the man of God who foretold these things.
17The king asked, "What is that tombstone I see?"
The men of the city said, "It marks the tomb of the man of God
who came from Judah and pronounced against the altar of Bethel
the very things you have done to it."
18"Leave it alone," he said. "Don't let anyone disturb his bones[n]."
So they spared his bones and those of the prophet who had come
from Samaria.
19Just as he had done at Bethel, Josiah removed and defiled all
the shrines at the high places that the kings of Israel had built in
the towns of Samaria that had provoked the LORD to anger. 20Josiah
slaughtered[o] all the priests of those high places on the altars and
burned human bones[p] on them. Then he went back to Jerusalem.

23:8 [a] 1Ki 15:22
23:9 [b] Eze 44:10-14
23:10 [c] Isa 30:33; Jer 7:31,32; 19:6 [d] Jos 15:8 [e] Lev 18:21; Dt 18:10
23:11 [f] Dt 4:19
23:12 [g] Jer 19:13; Zep 1:5 [h] 2Ki 21:5
23:13 [i] 1Ki 11:7
23:14 [j] Ex 23:24; Dt 7:5,25
23:15 [k] 1Ki 13:1-3 [l] 1Ki 12:33
23:16 [m] 1Ki 13:2
23:18 [n] 1Ki 13:31
23:20 [o] Ex 22:20; 2Ki 10:25; 11:18 [p] 1Ki 13:2

[a] 8 Or *high places* [b] *10* Or *to make his son or daughter pass through* [c] *13* Hebrew *Milcom*

21 The king gave this order to all the people: "Celebrate the Passover[a] to the LORD your God, as it is written in this Book of the Covenant." 22 Not since the days of the judges who led Israel, nor throughout the days of the kings of Israel and the kings of Judah, had any such Passover been observed. 23 But in the eighteenth year of King Josiah, this Passover was celebrated to the LORD in Jerusalem.

24 Furthermore, Josiah got rid of the mediums and spiritists,[b] the household gods,[c] the idols and all the other detestable things seen in Judah and Jerusalem. This he did to fulfill the requirements of the law written in the book that Hilkiah the priest had discovered in the temple of the LORD. 25 Neither before nor after Josiah was there a king like him who turned[d] to the LORD as he did—with all his heart and with all his soul and with all his strength, in accordance with all the Law of Moses.

26 Nevertheless, the LORD did not turn away from the heat of his fierce anger, which burned against Judah because of all that Manasseh[e] had done to provoke him to anger. 27 So the LORD said, "I will remove[f] Judah also from my presence[g] as I removed Israel, and I will reject Jerusalem, the city I chose, and this temple, about which I said, 'There shall my Name be.'[a]"

28 As for the other events of Josiah's reign, and all he did, are they not written in the book of the annals of the kings of Judah?

29 While Josiah was king, Pharaoh Neco[h] king of Egypt went up to the Euphrates River to help the king of Assyria. King Josiah marched out to meet him in battle, but Neco faced him and killed him at Megiddo.[i] 30 Josiah's servants brought his body in a chariot[j] from Megiddo to Jerusalem and buried him in his own tomb. And the people of the land took Jehoahaz son of Josiah and anointed him and made him king in place of his father.

31 Jehoahaz[k] was twenty-three years old when he became king, and he reigned in Jerusalem three months. His mother's name was Hamutal[l] daughter of Jeremiah; she was from Libnah. 32 He did evil in the eyes of the LORD, just as his fathers had done. 33 Pharaoh Neco put him in chains at Riblah[m] in the land of Hamath[b][n] so that he might not reign in Jerusalem, and he imposed on Judah a levy of a hundred talents[c] of silver and a talent[d] of gold. 34 Pharaoh Neco made Eliakim[o] son of Josiah king in place of his father Josiah and changed Eliakim's name to Jehoiakim. But he took Jehoahaz and carried him off to Egypt, and there he died.[p] 35 Jehoiakim paid Pharaoh Neco the silver and gold he demanded. In order to do so, he taxed the land and

23:21 [a] Ex 12:11; Nu 9:2; Dt 16:1-8
23:24 [b] Lev 19:31; Dt 18:11; 2Ki 21:6 [c] Ge 31:19
23:25 [d] 2Ki 18:5
23:26 [e] 2Ki 21:12; Jer 15:4
23:27 [f] 2Ki 21:13 [g] 2Ki 18:11
23:29 [h] Jer 46:2 [i] Zec 12:11
23:30 [j] 2Ki 9:28
23:31 [k] 1Ch 3:15; Jer 22:11 [l] 2Ki 24:18
23:33 [m] 2Ki 25:6 [n] 1Ki 8:65
23:34 [o] 1Ch 3:15; 2Ch 36:5-8 [p] Jer 22:12; Eze 19:3-4

[a] *27* 1 Kings 8:29 [b] *33* Hebrew; Septuagint (see also 2 Chron. 36:3) *Neco at Riblah in Hamath removed him* [c] *33* That is, about 3 3/4 tons (about 3.4 metric tons) [d] *33* That is, about 75 pounds (about 34 kilograms)

exacted the silver and gold from the people of the land according
to their assessments.[a]
36 Jehoiakim[b] was twenty-five years old when he became king,
and he reigned in Jerusalem eleven years. His mother's name was
Zebidah daughter of Pedaiah; she was from Rumah. 37 And he did
evil in the eyes of the LORD, just as his fathers had done.

Chapter 24 Theme

24 During Jehoiakim's reign, Nebuchadnezzar[c] king of Babylon invaded the land, and Jehoiakim became his vassal
for three years. But then he changed his mind and rebelled against
Nebuchadnezzar. 2 The LORD sent Babylonian,[a] Aramean,[d] Moabite and Ammonite raiders against him. He sent them to destroy[e]
Judah, in accordance with the word of the LORD proclaimed by
his servants the prophets. 3 Surely these things happened to Judah
according to the LORD's command,[f] in order to remove them from
his presence because of the sins of Manasseh[g] and all he had
done, 4 including the shedding of innocent blood.[h] For he had
filled Jerusalem with innocent blood, and the LORD was not willing
to forgive.
5 As for the other events of Jehoiakim's reign, and all he did, are
they not written in the book of the annals of the kings of Judah?
6 Jehoiakim rested[i] with his fathers. And Jehoiachin his son succeeded him as king.
7 The king of Egypt[j] did not march out from his own country
again, because the king of Babylon[k] had taken all his territory,
from the Wadi of Egypt to the Euphrates River.
8 Jehoiachin[l] was eighteen years old when he became king, and
he reigned in Jerusalem three months. His mother's name was
Nehushta daughter of Elnathan; she was from Jerusalem. 9 He did
evil in the eyes of the LORD, just as his father had done.
10 At that time the officers of Nebuchadnezzar[m] king of Babylon
advanced on Jerusalem and laid siege to it, 11 and Nebuchadnezzar
himself came up to the city while his officers were besieging it.
12 Jehoiachin king of Judah, his mother, his attendants, his nobles
and his officials all surrendered[n] to him.
In the eighth year of the reign of the king of Babylon, he took
Jehoiachin prisoner. 13 As the LORD had declared,[o] Nebuchadnezzar
removed all the treasures[p] from the temple of the LORD and from
the royal palace, and took away all the gold articles[q] that Solomon[r]
king of Israel had made for the temple of the LORD. 14 He carried
into exile[s] all Jerusalem: all the officers and fighting men, and all
the craftsmen and artisans—a total of ten thousand. Only the
poorest[t] people of the land were left.

[a]2 Or *Chaldean*

23:35 [a]ver 33
23:36 [b]Jer 26:1
24:1 [c]Jer 25:1,9; Da 1:1
24:2 [d]Jer 35:11 [e]Jer 25:9
24:3 [f]2Ki 18:25 [g]2Ki 21:12; 23:26
24:4 [h]2Ki 21:16
24:6 [i]Jer 22:19
24:7 [j]Ge 15:18 [k]Jer 37:5-7; 46:2
24:8 [l]1Ch 3:16
24:10 [m]Da 1:1
24:12 [n]2Ki 25:27; Jer 22:24-30; 24:1; 25:1; 29:2; 52:28
24:13 [o]2Ki 20:17 [p]2Ki 25:15; Isa 39:6 [q]2Ki 25:14; Jer 20:5 [r]1Ki 7:51
24:14 [s]Jer 24:1; 52:28 [t]2Ki 25:12; Jer 40:7; 52:16

[15]Nebuchadnezzar took Jehoiachin captive to Babylon.
He also took from Jerusalem
to Babylon the king's mother,[a] his wives, his officials
and the leading men[b] of the
land. [16]The king of Babylon
also deported to Babylon the
entire force of seven thousand fighting men, strong
and fit for war, and a thousand craftsmen and artisans.[c]
[17]He made Mattaniah, Jehoiachin's uncle, king in his place and
changed his name to Zedekiah.[d]

[18]Zedekiah[e] was twenty-one years old when he became king,
and he reigned in Jerusalem eleven years. His mother's name was
Hamutal[f] daughter of Jeremiah; she was from Libnah. [19]He did
evil in the eyes of the LORD, just as Jehoiakim had done. [20]It was
because of the LORD's anger that all this happened to Jerusalem
and Judah, and in the end he thrust[g] them from his presence.

Now Zedekiah rebelled against the king of Babylon.

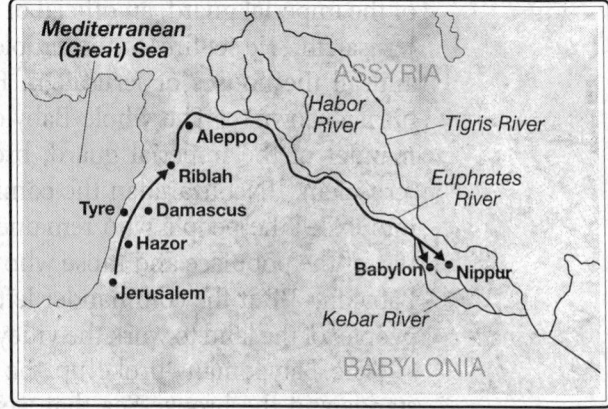

Mediterranean (Great) Sea
ASSYRIA
Habor River
Tigris River
Aleppo
Riblah
Euphrates River
Tyre
Damascus
Hazor
Babylon
Nippur
Jerusalem
Kebar River
BABYLONIA

Exiles of Judah to Babylon

Chapter 25 Theme

25 So in the ninth year of Zedekiah's reign, on the tenth day
of the tenth month, Nebuchadnezzar[h] king of Babylon
marched against Jerusalem with his whole army. He encamped
outside the city and built siege works[i] all around it. [2]The city was
kept under siege until the eleventh year of King Zedekiah. [3]By the
ninth day of the ⌊fourth⌋[a] month the famine[j] in the city had become so severe that there was no food for the people to eat. [4]Then
the city wall was broken through,[k] and the whole army fled at
night through the gate between the two walls near the king's garden, though the Babylonians[b] were surrounding[l] the city. They
fled toward the Arabah,[c] [5]but the Babylonian[d] army pursued the
king and overtook him in the plains of Jericho. All his soldiers
were separated from him and scattered,[m] [6]and he was captured.[n]
He was taken to the king of Babylon at Riblah,[o] where sentence
was pronounced on him. [7]They killed the sons of Zedekiah
before his eyes. Then they put out his eyes, bound him with
bronze shackles and took him to Babylon.[p]

[8]On the seventh day of the fifth month, in the nineteenth year
of Nebuchadnezzar king of Babylon, Nebuzaradan commander

24:15 [a]Jer 22:24-28 [b]Est 2:6; Eze 17:12-14
24:16 [c]Jer 52:28
24:17 [d]1Ch 3:15; 2Ch 36:11; Jer 37:1
24:18 [e]Jer 52:1 [f]2Ki 23:31
24:20 [g]Dt 4:26; 29:27
25:1 [h]Jer 34:1-7 [i]Eze 24:2
25:3 [j]Jer 14:18; La 4:9
25:4 [k]Eze 33:21 [l]Jer 4:17
25:5 [m]Eze 12:14
25:6 [n]Jer 34:21-22 [o]2Ki 23:33
25:7 [p]Jer 21:7; 32:4-5; Eze 12:11

[a] *3* See Jer. 52:6. [b] *4* Or *Chaldeans*; also in verses 13, 25 and 26 [c] *4* Or *the Jordan Valley*
[d] *5* Or *Chaldean*; also in verses 10 and 24

of the imperial guard, an official of the king of Babylon, came to
Jerusalem. 9He set fire[a] to the temple of the LORD, the royal palace
and all the houses of Jerusalem. Every important building he
burned down.[b] 10The whole Babylonian army, under the commander of the imperial guard, broke down the walls[c] around
Jerusalem. 11Nebuzaradan the commander of the guard carried
into exile[d] the people who remained in the city, along with the
rest of the populace and those who had gone over to the king of
Babylon.[e] 12But the commander left behind some of the poorest
people[f] of the land to work the vineyards and fields.

13The Babylonians broke up the bronze pillars, the movable
stands and the bronze Sea that were at the temple of the LORD
and they carried the bronze to Babylon. 14They also took away
the pots, shovels, wick trimmers, dishes and all the bronze articles[g] used in the temple service. 15The commander of the imperial guard took away the censers and sprinkling bowls—all
that were made of pure gold or silver.

16The bronze from the two pillars, the Sea and the movable
stands, which Solomon had made for the temple of the LORD, was
more than could be weighed. 17Each pillar[h] was twenty-seven feet[a]
high. The bronze capital on top of one pillar was four and a half
feet[b] high and was decorated with a network and pomegranates of
bronze all around. The other pillar, with its network, was similar.

18The commander of the guard took as prisoners Seraiah[i] the
chief priest, Zephaniah[j] the priest next in rank and the three
doorkeepers. 19Of those still in the city, he took the officer in
charge of the fighting men and five royal advisers. He also took
the secretary who was chief officer in charge of conscripting the
people of the land and sixty of his men who were found in the
city. 20Nebuzaradan the commander took them all and brought
them to the king of Babylon at Riblah. 21There at Riblah, in the
land of Hamath, the king had them executed.

So Judah went into captivity, away from her land.[k]

22Nebuchadnezzar king of Babylon appointed Gedaliah[l] son of
Ahikam, the son of Shaphan, to be over the people he had left
behind in Judah. 23When all the army officers and their men
heard that the king of Babylon had appointed Gedaliah as governor, they came to Gedaliah at Mizpah—Ishmael son of Nethaniah, Johanan son of Kareah, Seraiah son of Tanhumeth the
Netophathite, Jaazaniah the son of the Maacathite, and their men.
24Gedaliah took an oath to reassure them and their men. "Do not
be afraid of the Babylonian officials," he said. "Settle down in the
land and serve the king of Babylon, and it will go well with you."

a 17 Hebrew *eighteen cubits* (about 8.1 meters) b 17 Hebrew *three cubits* (about 1.3 meters)

25:9 [a]Isa 60:7 [b]Ps 74:3-8; Jer 2:15; Am 2:5; Mic 3:12

25:10 [c]Ne 1:3

25:11 [d]2Ki 24:14 [e]2Ki 24:1

25:12 [f]2Ki 24:14

25:14 [g]Ex 27:3; 1Ki 7:47-50

25:17 [h]1Ki 7:15-22

25:18 [i]1Ch 6:14; Ezr 7:1; Ne 11:11 [j]Jer 21:1; 29:25

25:21 [k]Ge 12:7; Dt 28:64; Jos 23:13; 2Ki 23:27

25:22 [l]Jer 39:14; 40:5,7

25:26 [a]Isa 30:2; Jer 43:7
25:27 [b]2Ki 24:12; Jer 52:31-34
25:28 [c]Ezr 5:5; Ne 2:1; Da 2:48
25:29 [d]2Sa 9:7
25:30 [e]Est 2:9; Jer 28:4

25In the seventh month, however, Ishmael son of Nethaniah,
the son of Elishama, who was of royal blood, came with ten men
and assassinated Gedaliah and also the men of Judah and the
Babylonians who were with him at Mizpah. 26At this, all the people from the least to the greatest, together with the army officers,
fled to Egypt[a] for fear of the Babylonians.
27In the thirty-seventh year of the exile of Jehoiachin king of
Judah, in the year Evil-Merodach[a] became king of Babylon, he
released Jehoiachin[b] from prison on the twenty-seventh day of
the twelfth month. 28He spoke kindly to him and gave him a seat
of honor[c] higher than those of the other kings who were with
him in Babylon. 29So Jehoiachin put aside his prison clothes and
for the rest of his life ate regularly at the king's table.[d] 30Day by day
the king gave Jehoiachin a regular allowance as long as he lived.[e]

[a]27 Also called *Amel-Marduk*

Israel's Division and Captivity

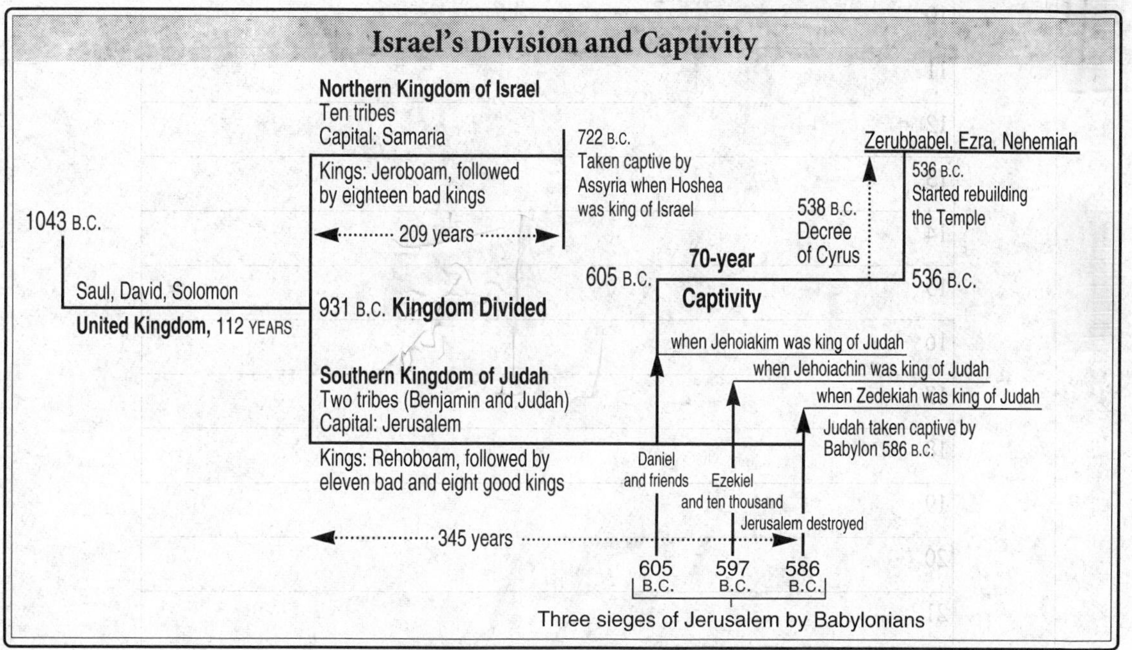

2 Kings at a Glance

Theme of 2 Kings:

Segment Divisions		Chapter Themes
		1
		2
		3
		4
		5
		6
		7
		8
		9
		10
		11
		12
		13
		14
		15
		16
		17
		18
		19
		20
		21
		22
		23
		24
		25

Author:

Date:

Purpose:

Key Words:

THE HISTORICAL CHART OF THE KINGS AND PROPHETS OF ISRAEL AND JUDAH

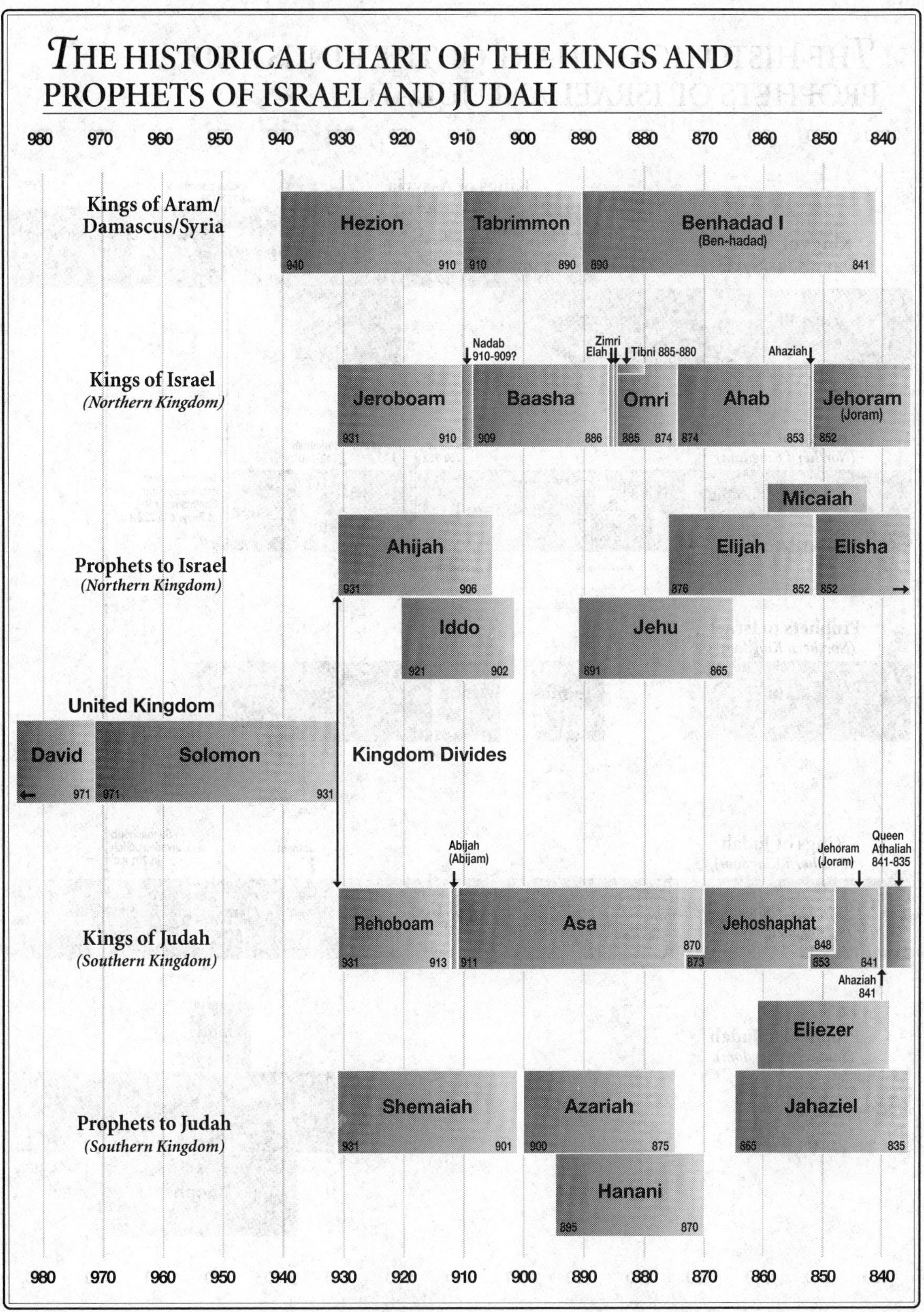

980 970 960 950 940 930 920 910 900 890 880 870 860 850 840
Kings of Aram/ Damascus/Syria
Hezion 940 910
Tabrimmon 910 890
Benhadad I (Ben-hadad) 890 841
Kings of Israel (Northern Kingdom)
Jeroboam 931 910
Nadab 910-909?
Baasha 909 886
Elah
Zimri
Tibni 885-880
Omri 885 874
Ahab 874 853
Ahaziah
Jehoram (Joram) 852
Prophets to Israel (Northern Kingdom)
Micaiah
Ahijah 931 906
Elijah 876 852
Elisha 852
Iddo 921 902
Jehu 891 865
United Kingdom
David 971
Solomon 971 931
Kingdom Divides
Kings of Judah (Southern Kingdom)
Rehoboam 931 913
Abijah (Abijam)
Asa 911 870
Jehoshaphat 873 848
Jehoram (Joram) 853 841
Queen Athaliah 841-835
Ahaziah 841
Prophets to Judah (Southern Kingdom)
Eliezer
Shemaiah 931 901
Azariah 900 875
Jahaziel 865 835
Hanani 895 870
980 970 960 950 940 930 920 910 900 890 880 870 860 850 840

THE HISTORICAL CHART OF THE KINGS AND PROPHETS OF ISRAEL AND JUDAH

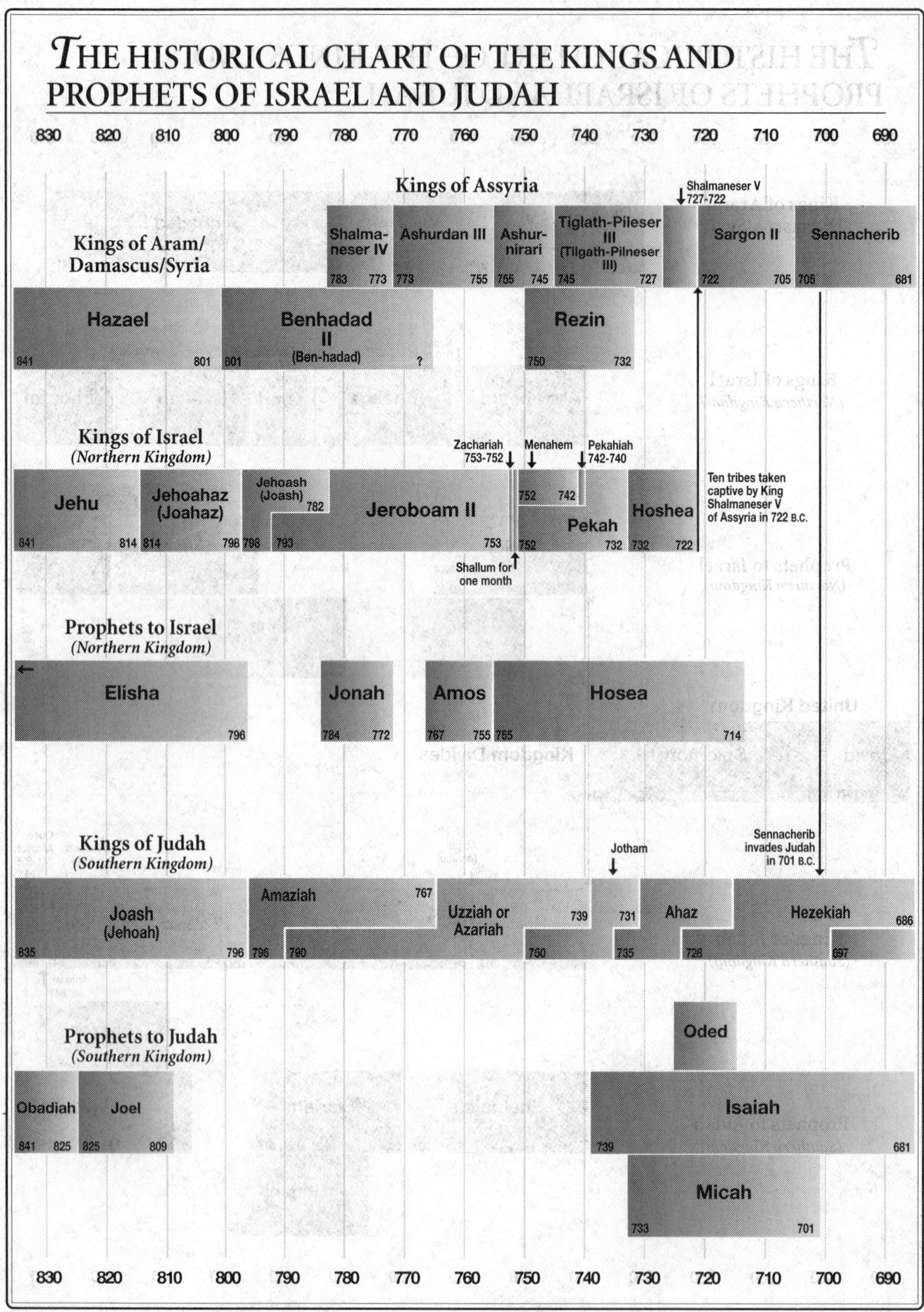

830 820 810 800 790 780 770 760 750 740 730 720 710 700 690
Kings of Assyria
Shalmaneser V 727-722
Shalma-neser IV 783 773
Ashurdan III 773 755
Ashur-nirari 755 745
Tiglath-Pileser III (Tilgath-Pilneser III) 745 727
Sargon II 722 705
Sennacherib 705 681
Kings of Aram/ Damascus/Syria
Hazael 841 801
Benhadad II (Ben-hadad) 801 ?
Rezin 750 732
Kings of Israel (Northern Kingdom)
Zachariah 753-752
Menahem
Pekahiah 742-740
Jehu 841 814
Jehoahaz (Joahaz) 814 798
Jehoash (Joash) 782 798 793
Jeroboam II 753
752 742
Pekah 752 732
Hoshea 732 722
Shallum for one month
Ten tribes taken captive by King Shalmaneser V of Assyria in 722 B.C.
Prophets to Israel (Northern Kingdom)
Elisha 796
Jonah 784 772
Amos 767 755
Hosea 755 714
Kings of Judah (Southern Kingdom)
Jotham
Sennacherib invades Judah in 701 B.C.
Joash (Jehoah) 835 796
Amaziah 767 796 790
Uzziah or Azariah 739 750
731 735
Ahaz 728
Hezekiah 686 697
Prophets to Judah (Southern Kingdom)
Oded
Obadiah 841 825
Joel 825 809
Isaiah 739 681
Micah 733 701
830 820 810 800 790 780 770 760 750 740 730 720 710 700 690

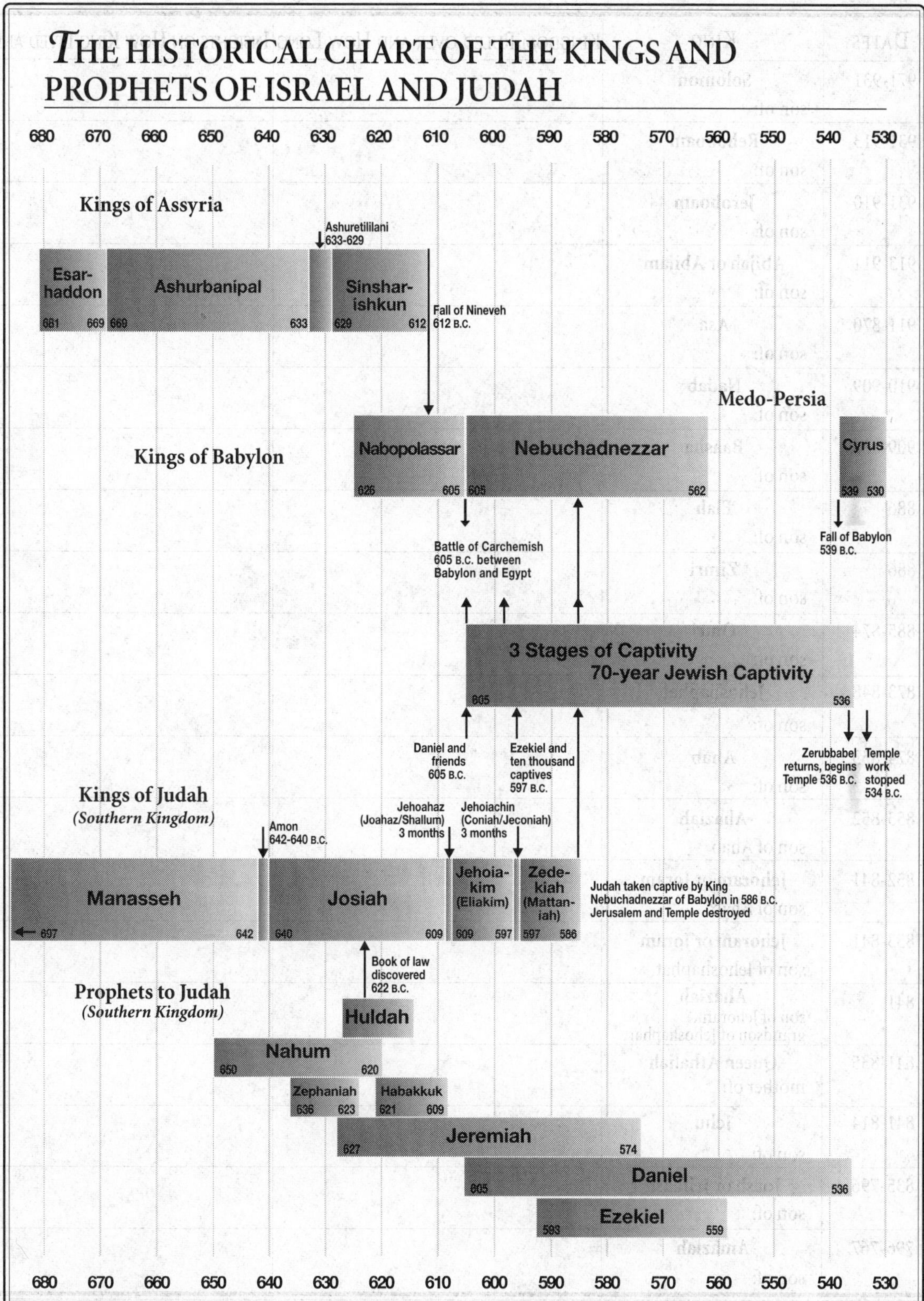
THE HISTORICAL CHART OF THE KINGS AND PROPHETS OF ISRAEL AND JUDAH
680 670 660 650 640 630 620 610 600 590 580 570 560 550 540 530
Kings of Assyria
Ashuretililani 633-629
Esar-haddon 681 669
Ashurbanipal 669 633
Sinshar-ishkun 629 612
Fall of Nineveh 612 B.C.
Medo-Persia
Kings of Babylon
Nabopolassar 626 605
Nebuchadnezzar 605 562
Cyrus 539 530
Fall of Babylon 539 B.C.
Battle of Carchemish 605 B.C. between Babylon and Egypt
3 Stages of Captivity
70-year Jewish Captivity
605 536
Daniel and friends 605 B.C.
Ezekiel and ten thousand captives 597 B.C.
Zerubbabel returns, begins Temple 536 B.C.
Temple work stopped 534 B.C.
Kings of Judah
(Southern Kingdom)
Jehoahaz (Joahaz/Shallum) 3 months
Jehoiachin (Coniah/Jeconiah) 3 months
Amon 642-640 B.C.
Manasseh 697 642
Josiah 640 609
Jehoia-kim (Eliakim) 609 597
Zede-kiah (Mattan-iah) 597 586
Judah taken captive by King Nebuchadnezzar of Babylon in 586 B.C. Jerusalem and Temple destroyed
Book of law discovered 622 B.C.
Prophets to Judah
(Southern Kingdom)
Huldah
Nahum 650 620
Zephaniah 636 623
Habakkuk 621 609
Jeremiah 627 574
Daniel 605 536
Ezekiel 593 559
680 670 660 650 640 630 620 610 600 590 580 570 560 550 540 530

THE KINGS OF ISRAEL AND JUDAH

DATES	KING	KINGDOM RULED OVER AND HOW LONG	INSIGHTS ON HOW KING LIVED AND DIED
971-931	**Solomon** son of:		
931-913	**Rehoboam** son of:		
931-910	**Jeroboam** son of:		
913-911	**Abijah** or **Abijam** son of:		
911-870	**Asa** son of:		
910-909	**Nadab** son of:		
909-886	**Baasha** son of:		
886	**Elah** son of:		
886	**Zimri** son of:		
885-874	**Omri** son of:		
873-848	**Jehoshaphat** son of:		
874-853	**Ahab** son of:		
853-852	**Ahaziah** son of Ahab		
852-841	**Jehoram** or **Joram** son of Ahab		
853-841	**Jehoram** or **Joram** son of Jehoshaphat		
841	**Ahaziah** son of Jehoram, grandson of Jehoshaphat		
841-835	**Queen Athaliah** mother of:		
841-814	**Jehu** son of:		
835-796	**Joash** or **Jehoash** son of:		
796-767	**Amaziah** son of:		

If a king ruled for any portion of a year, customarily that year was included as part of his reign.
An overlap in reigns indicates a co-regency, such as a son ruling alongside his father.

The Kings of Israel and Judah

Dates	King	Kingdom Ruled over and How Long	Insights on How King Lived and Died
814-798	**Jehoahaz or Joahaz** son of:		
798-782	**Jehoash or Joash** son of:		
790-739	**Azariah or Uzziah** son of:		
793-753	**Jeroboam II** son of:		
753-752	**Zechariah** son of:		
752	**Shallum** son of:		
752-742	**Menahem** son of:		
742-740	**Pekahiah** son of:		
752-732	**Pekah** son of:		
750-731	**Jotham** son of:		
735-715	**Ahaz** son of:		
732-722	**Hoshea** son of:		
728-686	**Hezekiah** son of:		
697-642	**Manasseh** son of:		
642-640	**Amon** son of:		
640-609	**Josiah** son of:		
609	**Jehoahaz or Joahaz or Shallum** son of:		
609-597	**Jehoiakim or Eliakim** son of:		
597	**Jehoiachin or Coniah or Jeconiah** son of:		
597-586	**Zedekiah or Mattaniah** son of:		

If a king ruled for any portion of a year, customarily that year was included as part of his reign.
An overlap in reigns indicates a co-regency, such as a son ruling alongside his father.

1 CHRONICLES

Judah had watched Assyria capture Israel in 722 B.C. In 586 B.C., when the Babylonians besieged Jerusalem for the third and final time, Judah lost her temple, the city of David, and the reign of the sons of David came to a halt. All seemed lost. Judah was held captive for 70 years. Then a Persian king, Cyrus, sent out a decree telling the exiles they could return and rebuild Jerusalem and their temple.

But if they did, could they be assured that the God of Abraham, Isaac, and Jacob would be with them? Had he abandoned his people and his promise to Abraham because of their sin? Would the northern and southern kingdoms ever be united again? Would God still send Messiah? Would David have a descendant who would sit on the throne of David forever?

And the temple? Between the time of Solomon and the Babylonian captivity, king after king had neglected it or desecrated it with idols. If they were to restore it, would it do any good?

And what of the prophets? What was God's Word, the prophets' message, regarding Israel, Judah, and their future? Would the Word of God change? Would the messages of the prophets be valid after Israel and Judah had so grievously sinned?

Having returned from captivity, God's people had to be reminded of "the events or annals of the days, the years," and so Chronicles was written. We don't know for certain who wrote it; perhaps it was Ezra. However, we do know that it was part of God's plan, for God included it in the canon of Scripture.

THINGS TO DO

General Instructions

1. If possible, study 1 and 2 Samuel and then 1 and 2 Kings before you study 1 and 2 Chronicles. Chronicles is to these other historical books what John is to the synoptic Gospels (Matthew, Mark, and Luke). Both John and Chronicles are supplemental and yet bring unique insight and understanding. Study the HISTORICAL PARALLEL OF SAMUEL, KINGS, AND CHRONICLES on page 659.

2. First and 2 Chronicles have time gaps in them. Keep this in mind as you study. When you wonder about the timing of something, look at the HISTORICAL PARALLEL again.

3. As you read 1 Chronicles watch for references to time, to any mention of dates or periods of time as well as who is reigning at the time. Mark these with an appropriate symbol.

4. When you finish observing each chapter, record its theme on 1 CHRONICLES AT A GLANCE on page 715 and on the line next to the chapter number in the text.

Chapters 1-9: The Genealogies of the Nation of Israel

1. This section may seem boring because it is primarily genealogies with a few historical sidelights. However, remember that this information has a purpose, and that is why God included it in his Word. Some genealogies, such as 4:1-23, are not included anywhere else.

   a. Don't skip this section; you will gain valuable insights which will help you in the study of the rest of the book.

   b. To discover the scope of the genealogies, read verses 1:1 and 9:1, 2. Then write in the margin of 1:1 when the genealogies begin and end according to the historical events they represent. Keeping in mind what was said in the introduction to 1 Chronicles, notice in 9:2 the words "the first to resettle on their own property in their own towns."

2. In this segment the key words to mark or underline are the names of people who play vital roles in Israel's history.

a. Mark the following key words in a distinctive way: *Adam, Noah,* and Noah's three sons: *Shem, Ham,* and *Japheth*. Then mark the phrases *the sons of Japheth, the sons of Ham,* and *the sons of Shem.*

b. Mark *the sons of Abraham: Isaac and Ishmael,* and *Abraham was the father of Isaac,* and *the sons of Isaac: Esau and Israel* (remember that Israel was called Jacob until God changed his name to Israel).

c. In chapter 2 mark *these were the sons of Israel.* Then count the sons. How many were there? They became the heads of the tribes of Israel. Record their names on an index card and look for any place where they are repeated in this segment. Use this card as a bookmark.

1) Read Genesis 49:1-28 where Jacob (Israel) gives a prophetic blessing to each of these men.

2) Look at the "Insight" on page 662 which shows the birth order and mother of each of Israel's sons.

d. In 2:3-15 mark *the sons of Judah (the people of Judah),* and then look for *David*. In the margin list David's genealogy from Judah through David's immediate father, Jesse. Remember that the author of Chronicles gives the genealogy of Judah before the other sons of Israel. Why? What would be important to the exiles who now repossessed their cities? Wouldn't it be God's promises to David? Keep this in mind as you study the second-to-the-last segment of 1 Chronicles.

e. In 3:1 mark the names of the sons of David, then list their names in the margin.

f. First Chronicles 3:10-16 gives the line of kings which come from David through Solomon.

1) List these names in the margin.

2) Then turn to the "Insight" next to Jeremiah 1:2-9 and look at this partial list of kings and note their alternate names. Write these names next to the names you listed in the margin of 1 Chronicles 3:10-16.

g. First Chronicles 3:17-24 lists the genealogy through Jeconiah (Jehoiachin). He was the king who reigned three months and ten days before he was taken into exile in Babylon, put in prison, and then released. See 2 Kings 24:8-16 and 2 Chronicles 36:9, 10.

3. When you read chapters 4 through 9 watch for any mention of the twelve sons of Israel and their genealogy. As you do:

a. Notice that not all twelve are mentioned in chapters 4 through 9.

b. Joseph's sons Manasseh and Ephraim are mentioned in Scripture as part of the twelve tribes of Israel. The reason for this is given in 1 Chronicles 5:1, 2. Take special note of this.

1) Write "Joseph's son" next to any mention of Manasseh and/or Ephraim.

2) Manasseh is named twice. The tribe split when Canaan was divided. Half the tribe of Manasseh took land east of the Jordan and the other half went west of the Jordan; thus the reference to the "half-tribe of Manasseh."

4. Read the section on the sons of Levi carefully and either underline what they were to do or note it in the margin. Also observe and note what Aaron and his sons were to do. This will help when you come to the final chapters of 1 Chronicles.

5. Don't forget to record the chapter themes in the text and on 1 CHRONICLES AT A GLANCE.

Chapters 10-19: God Turns the Kingdom to David

1. As you read this segment see how it fits with 1 and 2 Samuel. To do this consult the chart THE HISTORICAL PARALLEL OF SAMUEL, KINGS, AND CHRONICLES on page 659.

a. Read 1 Chronicles 10, mark any reference to *kingdom,* and list the events of that chapter.

b. Also note where it says whose son David was. Keep in mind what you just studied in the first segment.

c. Note in the margin why Saul died, who died with him, and what happened to Saul's body.

2. Read this segment chapter by chapter and do the following:

   a. Mark the following key words: *City of David, ark,* and *covenant (compact)*. Observe what you learn from these words and record your insights in the margin.

   b. Ask the five W's and an H as you read each chapter. Who are the key characters? What happens? When? (Draw a symbol next to any mention of time.) Where do events occur? Why do they occur? How do things happen? Record your insights in the margin.

   c. Don't forget to record chapter themes on 1 CHRONICLES AT A GLANCE and in the text next to the chapter number.

3. Watch for any prophecies (promises), speeches, songs, or psalms of praise. Who gives them? Why? What is said in each? Record your insights in the margin. Also ask: How can I apply these truths in my life?

Chapters 20-29: David Builds an Altar and Prepares for God's House

1. Note where this portion of 1 Chronicles comes in respect to 2 Samuel.

   a. When you read chapter 20, compare the wording of verse 1 with 2 Samuel 11:1. Then as you look at the content of 2 Samuel 11, 12, note what the author of Chronicles leaves out.

   b. Now compare 1 Chronicles 21 with 2 Samuel 24. Why was this event included in 1 Chronicles when David's other sin was omitted? See the "Insight" on page 700 next to 1 Chronicles 22. Remember, the temple is very important to the returning exiles.

2. As you read each chapter, mark the following key words and note in the margin what you learn from each: *house (temple, family, palatial structure, sanctuary), ark, heart (hearts, wholehearted, wholeheartedly), Levi (Levite, Levites),* and *Aaron.*

   a. The word *house* has been used numerous times in 1 Chronicles; however, with one or two exceptions "house" referred to someone's family, such as the house of David. In this segment it is used primarily for the house of the Lord. As you mark it note what you learn. Keep in mind that this is the book for the exiles who had returned to rebuild the temple and thus the emphasis is on the house of God and its importance. When difficulties arose this historical account would affirm God's enduring purpose and promises.

   b. As you mark the references to the Levites and to Aaron and his sons, observe carefully the types of duties they were to perform and which Levite family was to perform each type of duty. Also go back and review what you marked in the first segment regarding Levi, Aaron, and Aaron's other sons.

3. Read each chapter as you did in the last segment, asking the five W's and an H. Note in the margin what you observe. Also as you did in the last segment, watch for any speeches, prophecies, etc., and note the same things you looked for previously.

4. Complete 1 CHRONICLES AT A GLANCE. There are two lines for any additional segment divisions you might see and want to mark.

Things to Think About

1. Second Timothy 2:13 says, "If we are faithless, he will remain faithful, for he cannot disown himself." What have you seen of the faithfulness of God in the book of 1 Chronicles? What assurance does this give you for your life?

2. You marked the word *heart* in this last segment. Go back over these references in chapter 29 and review what you observed about the heart. Also review what you observed as David blessed the Lord.

Think about your own heart. What is your heart like in respect to the Lord? How can you turn what David did into a prayer to the Lord?

3. As you think about all you learned about the priests and their duties and you think of yourself and other Christians as a kingdom of priests unto God (Revelation 1 and 5), do you see any application you can make to your responsibilities as a priest unto God?

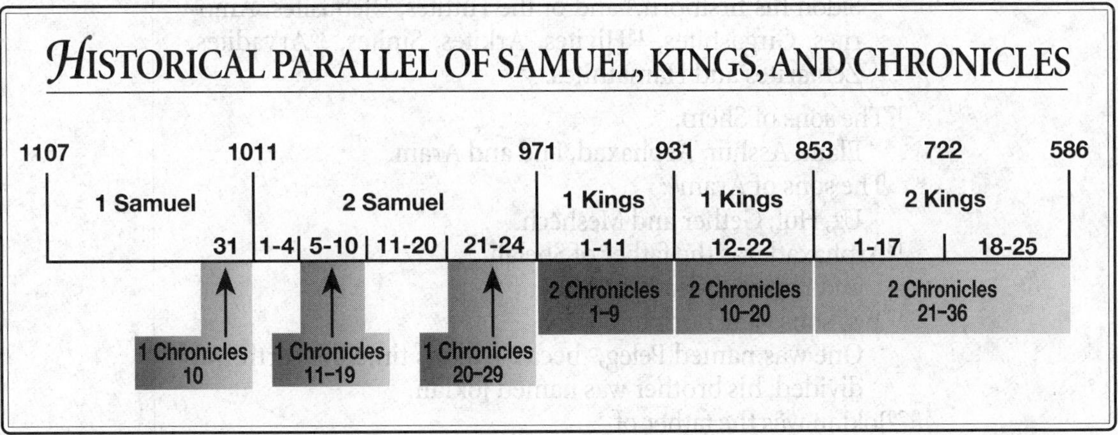

Chapter 1 Theme ____________________

1:1 [a]Ge 5:1-32; Lk 3:36-38

1 Adam,[a] Seth, Enosh, [2]Kenan,[b] Mahalalel,[c] Jared,[d] [3]Enoch,[e]
Methuselah,[f] Lamech,[g] Noah.[h]

[4]The sons of Noah:[a][i]
Shem, Ham and Japheth.[j]

1:2 [b]Ge 5:9 [c]Ge 5:12 [d]Ge 5:15

[5]The sons[b] of Japheth:
Gomer, Magog, Madai, Javan, Tubal, Meshech and Tiras.
[6]The sons of Gomer:
Ashkenaz, Riphath[c] and Togarmah.
[7]The sons of Javan:
Elishah, Tarshish, the Kittim and the Rodanim.

1:3 [e]Ge 5:18; Jude 14 [f]Ge 5:21 [g]Ge 5:25 [h]Ge 5:29

[8]The sons of Ham:
Cush, Mizraim,[d] Put and Canaan.
[9]The sons of Cush:
Seba, Havilah, Sabta, Raamah and Sabteca.
The sons of Raamah:
Sheba and Dedan.
[10]Cush was the father[e] of
Nimrod, who grew to be a mighty warrior on earth.

1:4 [i]Ge 6:10; 10:1 [j]Ge 5:32

[a]*4* Septuagint; Hebrew does not have *The sons of Noah:* [b]*5* *Sons* may mean *descendants* or *successors* or *nations*; also in verses 6-10, 17 and 20. [c]*6* Many Hebrew manuscripts and Vulgate (see also Septuagint and Gen. 10:3); most Hebrew manuscripts *Diphath* [d]*8* That is, Egypt; also in verse 11 [e]*10* *Father* may mean *ancestor* or *predecessor* or *founder*; also in verses 11, 13, 18 and 20.

[11]Mizraim was the father of
the Ludites, Anamites, Lehabites, Naphtuhites, [12]Pathru-
sites, Casluhites (from whom the Philistines came) and
Caphtorites.
[13]Canaan was the father of
Sidon his firstborn,[a] and of the Hittites, [14]Jebusites, Amorites, Girgashites, [15]Hivites, Arkites, Sinites, [16]Arvadites,
Zemarites and Hamathites.

[17]The sons of Shem:
Elam, Asshur, Arphaxad, Lud and Aram.
The sons of Aram[b]:
Uz, Hul, Gether and Meshech.
[18]Arphaxad was the father of Shelah,
and Shelah the father of Eber.
[19]Two sons were born to Eber:
One was named Peleg,[c] because in his time the earth was
divided; his brother was named Joktan.
[20]Joktan was the father of
Almodad, Sheleph, Hazarmaveth, Jerah, [21]Hadoram, Uzal,
Diklah, [22]Obal,[d] Abimael, Sheba, [23]Ophir, Havilah and
Jobab. All these were sons of Joktan.

[24]Shem,[a] Arphaxad,[e] Shelah,
[25]Eber, Peleg, Reu,
[26]Serug, Nahor, Terah
[27]and Abram (that is, Abraham).

[28]The sons of Abraham:
Isaac and Ishmael.
[29]These were their descendants:
Nebaioth the firstborn of Ishmael, Kedar, Adbeel, Mibsam,
[30]Mishma, Dumah, Massa, Hadad, Tema, [31]Jetur, Naphish
and Kedemah. These were the sons of Ishmael.

[32]The sons born to Keturah, Abraham's concubine:[b]
Zimran, Jokshan, Medan, Midian, Ishbak and Shuah.
The sons of Jokshan:
Sheba and Dedan.[c]
[33]The sons of Midian:
Ephah, Epher, Hanoch, Abida and Eldaah.
All these were descendants of Keturah.

[34]Abraham[d] was the father of Isaac.[e]
The sons of Isaac:
Esau and Israel.[f]

1:24
[a]Ge 10:21-25; Lk 3:34-36

1:32
[b]Ge 22:24
[c]Ge 10:7

1:34
[d]Lk 3:34
[e]Ge 21:2-3; Mt 1:2; Ac 7:8
[f]Ge 17:5; 25:25-26

[a]13 Or *of the Sidonians, the foremost* [b]17 One Hebrew manuscript and some Septuagint manuscripts (see also Gen. 10:23); most Hebrew manuscripts do not have this line. [c]19 *Peleg* means *division.* [d]22 Some Hebrew manuscripts and Syriac (see also Gen. 10:28); most Hebrew manuscripts *Ebal* [e]24 Hebrew; some Septuagint manuscripts *Arphaxad, Cainan* (see also note at Gen. 11:10)

1:35 [a]Ge 36:19 35The sons of Esau:[a]
[b]Ge 36:4 Eliphaz, Reuel,[b] Jeush, Jalam and Korah.
36The sons of Eliphaz:
Teman, Omar, Zepho,[a] Gatam and Kenaz;
by Timna: Amalek.[b][c]
37The sons of Reuel:[d]
Nahath, Zerah, Shammah and Mizzah.
38The sons of Seir:
Lotan, Shobal, Zibeon, Anah, Dishon, Ezer and Dishan.
39The sons of Lotan:
Hori and Homam. Timna was Lotan's sister.
1:36 40The sons of Shobal:
[c]Ex 17:14 Alvan,[c] Manahath, Ebal, Shepho and Onam.
The sons of Zibeon:
Aiah and Anah.[e]
41The son of Anah:
Dishon.
The sons of Dishon:
Hemdan,[d] Eshban, Ithran and Keran.
42The sons of Ezer:
Bilhan, Zaavan and Akan.[e]
The sons of Dishan[f]:
1:37 [d]Ge 36:17 Uz and Aran.

43These were the kings who reigned in Edom before any Israelite king reigned[g]:
Bela son of Beor, whose city was named Dinhabah.
44When Bela died, Jobab son of Zerah from Bozrah succeeded him as king.
45When Jobab died, Husham from the land of the Temanites[f]
succeeded him as king.
46When Husham died, Hadad son of Bedad, who defeated Midian in the country of Moab, succeeded him as king.
His city was named Avith.
1:40 [e]Ge 36:2 47When Hadad died, Samlah from Masrekah succeeded him as king.
48When Samlah died, Shaul from Rehoboth on the river[h] succeeded him as king.
49When Shaul died, Baal-Hanan son of Acbor succeeded him as king.

[a] *36* Many Hebrew manuscripts, some Septuagint manuscripts and Syriac (see also Gen. 36:11); most Hebrew manuscripts *Zephi* [b] *36* Some Septuagint manuscripts (see also Gen. 36:12); Hebrew *Gatam, Kenaz, Timna and Amalek* [c] *40* Many Hebrew manuscripts and some Septuagint manuscripts (see also Gen. 36:23); most Hebrew manuscripts *Alian* [d] *41* Many Hebrew manuscripts and some Septuagint manuscripts (see also Gen. 36:26); most Hebrew manuscripts *Hamran* [e] *42* Many Hebrew and Septuagint manuscripts (see also Gen. 36:27);
1:45 most Hebrew manuscripts *Zaavan, Jaakan* [f] *42* Hebrew *Dishon,* a variant of *Dishan* [g] *43* Or
[f]Ge 36:11 *before an Israelite king reigned over them* [h] *48* Possibly the Euphrates

[50]When Baal-Hanan died, Hadad succeeded him as king. His city was named Pau,[a] and his wife's name was Mehetabel daughter of Matred, the daughter of Me-Zahab. [51]Hadad also died.

The chiefs of Edom were:
Timna, Alvah, Jetheth, [52]Oholibamah, Elah, Pinon, [53]Kenaz, Teman, Mibzar, [54]Magdiel and Iram. These were the chiefs of Edom.

Chapter 2 Theme ______________________

INSIGHT

The Birth Order of Jacob's (Israel's) Sons

Mother	Son
Leah	Reuben (born 1921 B.C.) Simeon Levi Judah
Bilhah *(Rachel's maid-servant)*	Dan Naphtali
Zilpah *(Leah's maid-servant)*	Gad Asher
Leah	Issachar Zebulun
Rachel	Joseph (born 1914 B.C.) Benjamin

2 These were the sons of Israel:
Reuben, Simeon, Levi, Judah, Issachar, Zebulun, [2]Dan,
Joseph, Benjamin, Naphtali, Gad and Asher.

[3]The sons of Judah:[a]
Er, Onan and Shelah.[b] These three were born to him by a Canaanite woman, the daughter of Shua.[c] Er, Judah's firstborn, was wicked in the LORD's sight; so the LORD put him to death.[d]
[4]Tamar,[e] Judah's daughter-in-law,[f] bore him Perez[g] and Zerah. Judah had five sons in all.

[5]The sons of Perez:[h]
Hezron[i] and Hamul.
[6]The sons of Zerah:
Zimri, Ethan, Heman, Calcol and Darda[b]—five in all.
[7]The son of Carmi:
Achar,[c][j] who brought trouble on Israel by violating the ban on taking devoted things.[d][k]
[8]The son of Ethan:
Azariah.
[9]The sons born to Hezron[l] were:
Jerahmeel, Ram and Caleb.[e]

[10]Ram[m] was the father of
Amminadab[n], and Amminadab the father of Nahshon,[o] the leader of the people of Judah.
[11]Nahshon was the father of Salmon,[f] Salmon the father of Boaz,
[12]Boaz[p] the father of Obed and Obed the father of Jesse.[q]
[13]Jesse[r] was the father of
Eliab[s] his firstborn; the second son was Abinadab, the third Shimea,
[14]the fourth Nethanel, the fifth Raddai,
[15]the sixth Ozem and the seventh David.
[16]Their sisters were Zeruiah[t]

[a]50 Many Hebrew manuscripts, some Septuagint manuscripts, Vulgate and Syriac (see also Gen. 36:39); most Hebrew manuscripts *Pai* [b]6 Many Hebrew manuscripts, some Septuagint manuscripts and Syriac (see also 1 Kings 4:31); most Hebrew manuscripts *Dara* [c]7 *Achar* means *trouble; Achar* is called *Achan* in Joshua. [d]7 The Hebrew term refers to the irrevocable giving over of things or persons to the LORD, often by totally destroying them. [e]9 Hebrew *Kelubai,* a variant of *Caleb* [f]11 Septuagint (see also Ruth 4:21); Hebrew *Salma*

2:3 [a]Ge 29:35; 38:2-10 [b]Ge 38:5 [c]Ge 38:2 [d]Nu 26:19
2:4 [e]Ge 38:11-30 [f]Ge 11:31 [g]Ge 38:29
2:5 [h]Ge 46:12 [i]Nu 26:21
2:7 [j]Jos 7:1 [k]Jos 6:18
2:9 [l]Nu 26:21
2:10 [m]Lk 3:32-33 [n]Ex 6:23 [o]Nu 1:7
2:12 [p]Ru 2:1 [q]Ru 4:17
2:13 [r]Ru 4:17 [s]1Sa 16:6
2:16 [t]1Sa 26:6

2:16 [a]2Sa 2:18 [b]2Sa 2:13 and Abigail. Zeruiah's[a] three sons were Abishai, Joab[b] and
Asahel. 17 Abigail was the mother of Amasa,[c] whose father
was Jether the Ishmaelite.

18 Caleb son of Hezron had children by his wife Azubah (and by
Jerioth). These were her sons: Jesher, Shobab and Ardon.
19 When Azubah died, Caleb[d] married Ephrath, who bore
him Hur. 20 Hur was the father of Uri, and Uri the father of
2:17 [c]2Sa 17:25 Bezalel.[e]
21 Later, Hezron lay with the daughter of Makir the father of
Gilead[f] (he had married her when he was sixty years old),
and she bore him Segub. 22 Segub was the father of Jair, who
controlled twenty-three towns in Gilead. 23 (But Geshur
and Aram captured Havvoth Jair,[a][g] as well as Kenath[h] with
2:19 its surrounding settlements—sixty towns.) All these were
[d]ver 42,50 descendants of Makir the father of Gilead.

24 After Hezron died in Caleb Ephrathah, Abijah the wife of
Hezron bore him Ashhur[i] the father[b] of Tekoa.

25 The sons of Jerahmeel the firstborn of Hezron:
Ram his firstborn, Bunah, Oren, Ozem and[c] Ahijah. 26 Je-
2:20 rahmeel had another wife, whose name was Atarah; she
[e]Ex 31:2 was the mother of Onam.
27 The sons of Ram the firstborn of Jerahmeel:
Maaz, Jamin and Eker.
28 The sons of Onam:
Shammai and Jada.
The sons of Shammai:
2:21 Nadab and Abishur.
[f]Nu 27:1 29 Abishur's wife was named Abihail, who bore him Ahban and
Molid.
30 The sons of Nadab:
Seled and Appaim. Seled died without children.
31 The son of Appaim:
Ishi, who was the father of Sheshan.
2:23 Sheshan was the father of Ahlai.
[g]Nu 32:41; Dt 3:14; 32 The sons of Jada, Shammai's brother:
Jos 13:30 [h]Nu 32:42 Jether and Jonathan. Jether died without children.
33 The sons of Jonathan:
Peleth and Zaza.
These were the descendants of Jerahmeel.
34 Sheshan had no sons—only daughters.
He had an Egyptian servant named Jarha. 35 Sheshan gave

2:24 [i]1Ch 4:5

[a] 23 Or *captured the settlements of Jair* [b] 24 *Father* may mean *civic leader* or *military leader*; also in verses 42, 45, 49-52 and possibly elsewhere. [c] 25 Or *Oren and Ozem, by*

his daughter in marriage to his servant Jarha, and she bore him Attai.

36 Attai was the father of Nathan,
Nathan the father of Zabad,[a]
37 Zabad the father of Ephlal,
Ephlal the father of Obed,
38 Obed the father of Jehu,
Jehu the father of Azariah,
39 Azariah the father of Helez,
Helez the father of Eleasah,
40 Eleasah the father of Sismai,
Sismai the father of Shallum,
41 Shallum the father of Jekamiah,
and Jekamiah the father of Elishama.

42 The sons of Caleb[b] the brother of Jerahmeel:
Mesha his firstborn, who was the father of Ziph, and his son Mareshah,[a] who was the father of Hebron.
43 The sons of Hebron:
Korah, Tappuah, Rekem and Shema.
44 Shema was the father of Raham, and Raham the father of Jorkeam. Rekem was the father of Shammai.
45 The son of Shammai was Maon[c], and Maon was the father of Beth Zur.[d]
46 Caleb's concubine Ephah was the mother of Haran, Moza and Gazez. Haran was the father of Gazez.
47 The sons of Jahdai:
Regem, Jotham, Geshan, Pelet, Ephah and Shaaph.
48 Caleb's concubine Maacah was the mother of Sheber and Tirhanah.
49 She also gave birth to Shaaph the father of Madmannah[e] and to Sheva the father of Macbenah and Gibea. Caleb's daughter was Acsah.[f]
50 These were the descendants of Caleb.

The sons of Hur[g] the firstborn of Ephrathah:
Shobal the father of Kiriath Jearim,[h]
51 Salma the father of Bethlehem, and Hareph the father of Beth Gader.
52 The descendants of Shobal the father of Kiriath Jearim were:
Haroeh, half the Manahathites,
53 and the clans of Kiriath Jearim: the Ithrites,[i] Puthites, Shumathites and Mishraites. From these descended the Zorathites and Eshtaolites.
54 The descendants of Salma:
Bethlehem, the Netophathites,[j] Atroth Beth Joab, half the Manahathites, the Zorites,
55 and the clans of scribes[b] who lived at Jabez: the Tirathites, Shimeathites and Sucathites.

[a] *42* The meaning of the Hebrew for this phrase is uncertain. [b] *55* Or *of the Sopherites*

2:36 [a] 1Ch 11:41
2:42 [b] ver 19
2:45 [c] Jos 15:55 [d] Jos 15:58
2:49 [e] Jos 15:31 [f] Jos 15:16
2:50 [g] 1Ch 4:4 [h] ver 19
2:53 [i] 2Sa 23:38
2:54 [j] Ezr 2:22; Ne 7:26; 12:28

These are the Kenites[a] who came from Hammath,[b] the
father of the house of Recab.[a][c]

Chapter 3 Theme ______________________________

3

These were the sons of David[d] born to him in Hebron:
1 The firstborn was Amnon the son of Ahinoam of Jezreel;[e]
the second, Daniel the son of Abigail[f] of Carmel;
2the third, Absalom the son of Maacah daughter of Talmai
king of Geshur;
the fourth, Adonijah[g] the son of Haggith;
3the fifth, Shephatiah the son of Abital;
and the sixth, Ithream, by his wife Eglah.
4These six were born to David in Hebron,[h] where he
reigned seven years and six months.[i]
David reigned in Jerusalem thirty-three years, 5and these were
the children born to him there:
Shammua,[b] Shobab, Nathan and Solomon. These four were
by Bathsheba[c][j] daughter of Ammiel. 6There were also Ibhar,
Elishua,[d] Eliphelet, 7Nogah, Nepheg, Japhia, 8Elishama, Eliada and Eliphelet—nine in all. 9All these were the sons of
David, besides his sons by his concubines. And Tamar[k] was
their sister.[l]

10Solomon's son was Rehoboam,[m]
Abijah his son,
Asa his son,
Jehoshaphat[n] his son,
11Jehoram[e][o] his son,
Ahaziah[p] his son,
Joash[q] his son,
12Amaziah[r] his son,
Azariah his son,
Jotham[s] his son,
13Ahaz[t] his son,
Hezekiah[u] his son,
Manasseh[v] his son,
14Amon[w] his son,
Josiah[x] his son.
15The sons of Josiah:
Johanan the firstborn,
Jehoiakim[y] the second son,
Zedekiah[z] the third,
Shallum[a] the fourth.

[a]55 Or *father of Beth Recab* [b]5 Hebrew *Shimea,* a variant of *Shammua* [c]5 One Hebrew manuscript and Vulgate (see also Septuagint and 2 Samuel 11:3); most Hebrew manuscripts *Bathshua* [d]6 Two Hebrew manuscripts (see also 2 Samuel 5:15 and 1 Chron. 14:5); most Hebrew manuscripts *Elishama* [e]11 Hebrew *Joram,* a variant of *Jehoram*

2:55 [a]Ge 15:19; Jdg 1:16; Jdg 4:11 [b]Jos 19:35 [c]2Ki 10:15, 23; Jer 35:2-19

3:1 [d]1Ch 14:3; 28:5 [e]Jos 15:56 [f]1Sa 25:42

3:2 [g]1Ki 2:22

3:4 [h]2Sa 5:4; 1Ch 29:27 [i]2Sa 2:11; 5:5

3:5 [j]2Sa 11:3; 12:24

3:9 [k]2Sa 13:1 [l]1Ch 14:4

3:10 [m]1Ki 11:43; 14:21-31; 2Ch 12:16 [n]2Ch 17:1–21:3

3:11 [o]2Ki 8:16-24; 2Ch 21:1 [p]2Ch 22:1-10 [q]2Ki 11:1–12:21

3:12 [r]2Ki 14:1-22; 2Ch 25:1-28 [s]Isa 1:1; Hos 1:1; Mic 1:1

3:13 [t]2Ki 16:1-20; 2Ch 28:1; Isa 7:1 [u]2Ki 18:1–20:21; 2Ch 29:1; Jer 26:19 [v]2Ch 33:1

3:14 [w]2Ki 21:19-26; 2Ch 33:21; Zep 1:1 [x]2Ch 34:1; Jer 1:2; 3:6; 25:3

3:15 [y]2Ki 23:34 [z]Jer 37:1 [a]2Ki 23:31

The Land Allotted to the Twelve Tribes

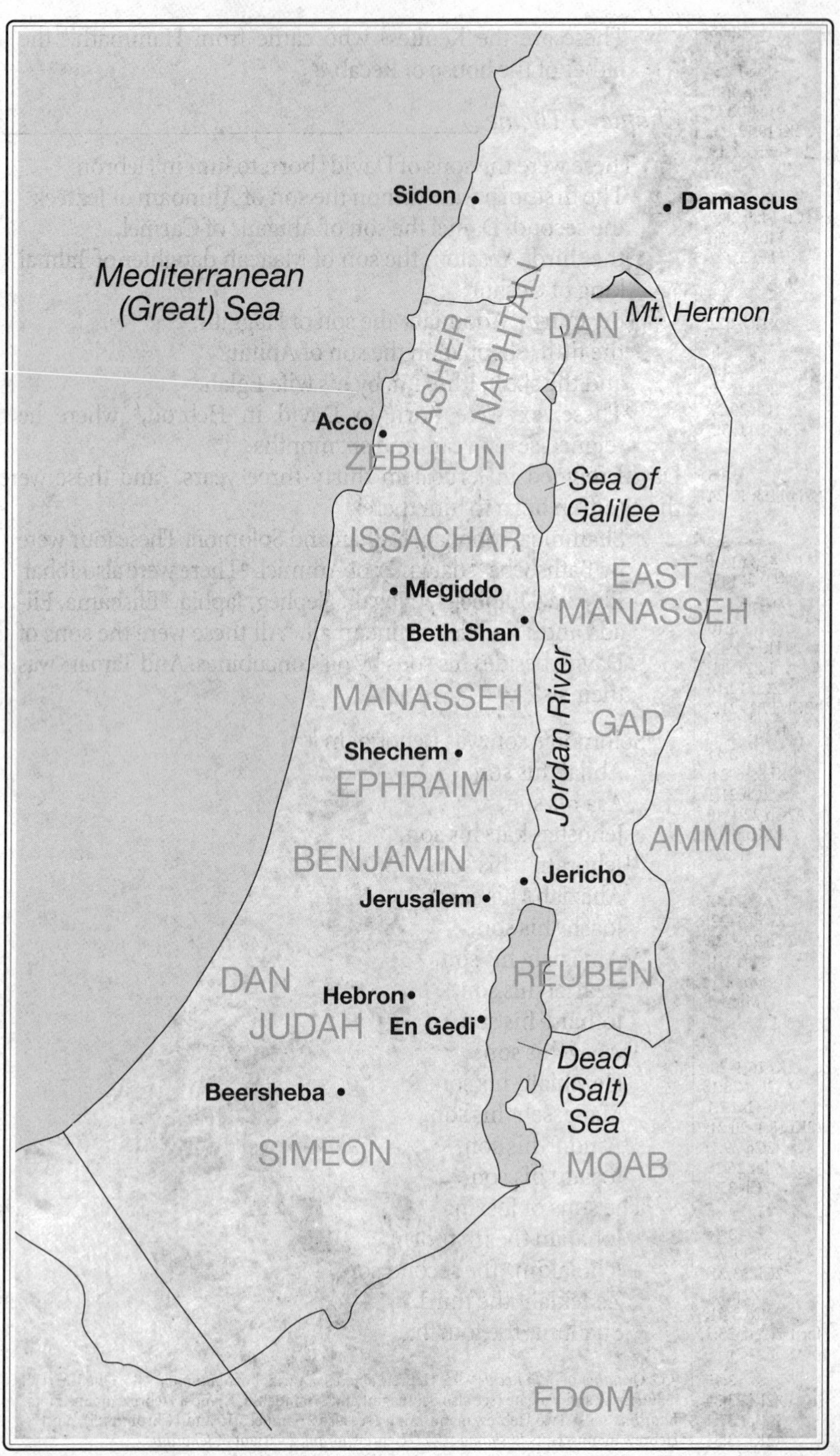

3:16 [a]2Ki 24:6,8; Mt 1:11 [b]2Ki 24:18

16 The successors of Jehoiakim:
Jehoiachin[a][a] his son,
and Zedekiah.[b]

17 The descendants of Jehoiachin the captive:
Shealtiel[c] his son, 18 Malkiram, Pedaiah, Shenazzar,[d] Jekamiah, Hoshama and Nedabiah.[e]

3:17 [c]Ezr 3:2

19 The sons of Pedaiah:
Zerubbabel[f] and Shimei.

The sons of Zerubbabel:
Meshullam and Hananiah.
Shelomith was their sister.

20 There were also five others:
Hashubah, Ohel, Berekiah, Hasadiah and Jushab-Hesed.

3:18 [d]Ezr 1:8; 5:14 [e]Jer 22:30

21 The descendants of Hananiah:
Pelatiah and Jeshaiah, and the sons of Rephaiah, of Arnan,
of Obadiah and of Shecaniah.

22 The descendants of Shecaniah:
Shemaiah and his sons:
Hattush,[g] Igal, Bariah, Neariah and Shaphat—six in all.

3:19 [f]Ezr 2:2; 3:2; 5:2; Ne 7:7; 12:1; Hag 1:1; 2:2; Zec 4:6

23 The sons of Neariah:
Elioenai, Hizkiah and Azrikam—three in all.

24 The sons of Elioenai:
Hodaviah, Eliashib, Pelaiah, Akkub, Johanan, Delaiah and
Anani—seven in all.

3:22 [g]Ezr 8:2-3

Chapter 4 Theme ____________________________

4

The descendants of Judah:[h]
Perez, Hezron,[i] Carmi, Hur and Shobal.

2 Reaiah son of Shobal was the father of Jahath, and Jahath
the father of Ahumai and Lahad. These were the clans of
the Zorathites.

4:1 [h]Ge 29:35; 46:12; 1Ch 2:3 [i]Nu 26:21

3 These were the sons[b] of Etam:
Jezreel, Ishma and Idbash. Their sister was named Hazze-
lelponi. 4 Penuel was the father of Gedor, and Ezer the father
of Hushah.

These were the descendants of Hur,[j] the firstborn of Ephrathah and father[c] of Bethlehem.[k]

4:4 [j]1Ch 2:50 [k]Ru 1:19

5 Ashhur[l] the father of Tekoa had two wives, Helah and Naarah.

6 Naarah bore him Ahuzzam, Hepher, Temeni and Haa-
hashtari. These were the descendants of Naarah.

7 The sons of Helah:
Zereth, Zohar, Ethnan, 8 and Koz, who was the father of

4:5 [l]1Ch 2:24

[a]16 Hebrew *Jeconiah,* a variant of *Jehoiachin;* also in verse 17 [b]3 Some Septuagint manuscripts (see also Vulgate); Hebrew *father* [c]4 *Father* may mean *civic leader* or *military leader;* also in verses 12, 14, 17, 18 and possibly elsewhere.

Anub and Hazzobebah and of the clans of Aharhel son of
Harum.

9Jabez was more honorable than his brothers. His mother had
named him Jabez,[a] saying, "I gave birth to him in pain." 10Jabez
cried out to the God of Israel, "Oh, that you would bless me and
enlarge my territory! Let your hand be with me, and keep me
from harm so that I will be free from pain." And God granted his
request.

11Kelub, Shuhah's brother, was the father of Mehir, who was the
father of Eshton. 12Eshton was the father of Beth Rapha,
Paseah and Tehinnah the father of Ir Nahash.[b] These were
the men of Recah.

13The sons of Kenaz:
Othniel[a] and Seraiah.
The sons of Othniel:
Hathath and Meonothai.[c] 14Meonothai was the father of
Ophrah.
Seraiah was the father of Joab,
the father of Ge Harashim.[d] It was called this because its
people were craftsmen.
15The sons of Caleb son of Jephunneh:
Iru, Elah and Naam.
The son of Elah:
Kenaz.
16The sons of Jehallelel:
Ziph, Ziphah, Tiria and Asarel.
17The sons of Ezrah:
Jether, Mered, Epher and Jalon. One of Mered's wives gave
birth to Miriam,[b] Shammai and Ishbah the father of Eshtemoa. 18(His Judean wife gave birth to Jered the father of
Gedor, Heber the father of Soco, and Jekuthiel the father
of Zanoah.[c]) These were the children of Pharaoh's daughter Bithiah, whom Mered had married.
19The sons of Hodiah's wife, the sister of Naham:
the father of Keilah[d] the Garmite, and Eshtemoa the Maacathite.[e]
20The sons of Shimon:
Amnon, Rinnah, Ben-Hanan and Tilon.
The descendants of Ishi:
Zoheth and Ben-Zoheth.

4:13
[a]Jos 15:17

4:17
[b]Ex 15:20

4:18
[c]Jos 15:34

4:19
[d]Jos 15:44
[e]Dt 3:14

[a]9 *Jabez* sounds like the Hebrew for *pain.* [b]12 Or *of the city of Nahash* [c]13 Some Septuagint manuscripts and Vulgate; Hebrew does not have *and Meonothai.* [d]14 *Ge Harashim* means *valley of craftsmen.*

21The sons of Shelah[a] son of Judah:
Er the father of Lecah, Laadah the father of Mareshah and
the clans of the linen workers at Beth Ashbea, 22Jokim, the
men of Cozeba, and Joash and Saraph, who ruled in Moab
and Jashubi Lehem. (These records are from ancient
times.) 23They were the potters who lived at Netaim and
Gederah; they stayed there and worked for the king.

24The descendants of Simeon:[b]
Nemuel, Jamin, Jarib,[c] Zerah and Shaul;
25Shallum was Shaul's son, Mibsam his son and Mishma his
son.

26The descendants of Mishma:
Hammuel his son, Zaccur his son and Shimei his son.

27Shimei had sixteen sons and six daughters, but his brothers
did not have many children; so their entire clan did not become
as numerous as the people of Judah. 28They lived in Beersheba,[d]
Moladah,[e] Hazar Shual, 29Bilhah, Ezem,[f] Tolad, 30Bethuel, Hormah,[g] Ziklag, 31Beth Marcaboth, Hazar Susim, Beth Biri and
Shaaraim.[h] These were their towns until the reign of David.
32Their surrounding villages were Etam, Ain,[i] Rimmon, Token and
Ashan[j]—five towns— 33and all the villages around these towns
as far as Baalath.[a] These were their settlements. And they kept a
genealogical record.

34Meshobab, Jamlech, Joshah son of Amaziah, 35Joel, Jehu
son of Joshibiah, the son of Seraiah, the son of Asiel, 36also
Elioenai, Jaakobah, Jeshohaiah, Asaiah, Adiel, Jesimiel, Benaiah, 37and Ziza son of Shiphi, the son of Allon, the son of
Jedaiah, the son of Shimri, the son of Shemaiah.

38The men listed above by name were leaders of their clans. Their
families increased greatly, 39and they went to the outskirts of Gedor[k]
to the east of the valley in search of pasture for their flocks. 40They
found rich, good pasture, and the land was spacious, peaceful and
quiet.[l] Some Hamites had lived there formerly.

41The men whose names were listed came in the days of Hezekiah king of Judah. They attacked the Hamites in their dwellings
and also the Meunites[m] who were there and completely destroyed[b]
them, as is evident to this day. Then they settled in their place,
because there was pasture for their flocks. 42And five hundred of
these Simeonites, led by Pelatiah, Neariah, Rephaiah and Uzziel,
the sons of Ishi, invaded the hill country of Seir.[n] 43They killed the
remaining Amalekites[o] who had escaped, and they have lived there
to this day.

4:21 [a] Ge 38:5
4:24 [b] Ge 29:33 [c] Nu 26:12
4:28 [d] Ge 21:14 [e] Jos 15:26
4:29 [f] Jos 15:29
4:30 [g] Nu 14:45
4:31 [h] Jos 15:36
4:32 [i] Nu 34:11 [j] Jos 15:42
4:39 [k] Jos 15:58
4:40 [l] Jdg 18:7-10
4:41 [m] 2Ch 20:1; 26:7
4:42 [n] Ge 14:6
4:43 [o] 1Sa 15:8; 30:17; 2Sa 8:12; Est 3:1; 9:16

[a] *33* Some Septuagint manuscripts (see also Joshua 19:8); Hebrew *Baal* [b] *41* The Hebrew term refers to the irrevocable giving over of things or persons to the LORD, often by totally destroying them.

Chapter 5 Theme ___________________

5

The sons of Reuben[a] the firstborn of Israel (he was the firstborn, but when he defiled his father's marriage bed,[b] his
rights as firstborn were given to the sons of Joseph[c] son of Israel;[d]
so he could not be listed in the genealogical record in accordance
with his birthright,[e] 2and though Judah[f] was the strongest of his
brothers and a ruler[g] came from him, the rights of the firstborn[h]
belonged to Joseph)— 3the sons of Reuben[i] the firstborn of Israel:

Hanoch, Pallu,[j] Hezron and Carmi.

4The descendants of Joel:

Shemaiah his son, Gog his son,
Shimei his son, 5Micah his son,
Reaiah his son, Baal his son,
6and Beerah his son, whom Tiglath-Pileser[a][k] king of Assyria took into exile. Beerah was a leader of the Reubenites.

7Their relatives by clans,[l] listed according to their genealogical
records:

Jeiel the chief, Zechariah, 8and Bela son of Azaz, the son of
Shema, the son of Joel. They settled in the area from Aroer[m]
to Nebo and Baal Meon.[n] 9To the east they occupied the
land up to the edge of the desert that extends to the
Euphrates River, because their livestock had increased in
Gilead.[o]

10During Saul's reign they waged war against the Hagrites[p], who were defeated at their hands; they occupied the
dwellings of the Hagrites throughout the entire region east
of Gilead.

11The Gadites[q] lived next to them in Bashan, as far as Salecah:[r]

12Joel was the chief, Shapham the second, then Janai and
Shaphat, in Bashan.

13Their relatives, by families, were:

Michael, Meshullam, Sheba, Jorai, Jacan, Zia and Eber—
seven in all.

14These were the sons of Abihail son of Huri, the son of
Jaroah, the son of Gilead, the son of Michael, the son of
Jeshishai, the son of Jahdo, the son of Buz.

15Ahi son of Abdiel, the son of Guni, was head of their family.

16The Gadites lived in Gilead, in Bashan and its outlying villages,
and on all the pasturelands of Sharon as far as they extended.

17All these were entered in the genealogical records during the
reigns of Jotham[s] king of Judah and Jeroboam[t] king of Israel.

18The Reubenites, the Gadites and the half-tribe of Manasseh
had 44,760 men ready for military service[u]—able-bodied men

[a]6 Hebrew *Tilgath-Pilneser,* a variant of *Tiglath-Pileser*; also in verse 26

5:1
[a]Ge 29:32
[b]Ge 35:22; 49:4
[c]Ge 48:16,22; 49:26
[d]Ge 48:5
[e]1Ch 26:10

5:2
[f]Ge 49:10,12
[g]1Sa 9:16; 12:12; 2Sa 6:21; 1Ch 11:2; 2Ch 7:18; Ps 60:7; Mic 5:2; Mt 2:6
[h]Ge 25:31

5:3
[i]Ge 29:32; 46:9; Ex 6:14; Nu 26:5-11
[j]Nu 26:5

5:6
[k]ver 26; 2Ki 15:19; 16:10; 2Ch 28:20

5:7
[l]ver 17

5:8
[m]Nu 32:34
[n]Jos 13:17

5:9
[o]Nu 32:26; Jos 22:9

5:10
[p]ver 18-21

5:11
[q]Jos 13:24-28
[r]Dt 3:10; Jos 13:11

5:17
[s]2Ki 15:32
[t]2Ki 14:16,28

5:18
[u]Nu 1:3

who could handle shield and sword, who could use a bow, and
who were trained for battle. 19 They waged war against the Hagrites, Jetur,[a] Naphish and Nodab. 20 They were helped[b] in fighting
them, and God handed the Hagrites and all their allies over to
them, because they cried[c] out to him during the battle. He answered their prayers, because they trusted[d] in him. 21 They seized
the livestock of the Hagrites—fifty thousand camels, two hundred
fifty thousand sheep and two thousand donkeys. They also took
one hundred thousand people captive, 22 and many others fell slain,
because the battle[e] was God's. And they occupied the land until
the exile.[f]

23 The people of the half-tribe of Manasseh were numerous; they
settled in the land from Bashan to Baal Hermon, that is, to Senir
(Mount Hermon).[g]

24 These were the heads of their families: Epher, Ishi, Eliel, Azriel,
Jeremiah, Hodaviah and Jahdiel. They were brave warriors, famous
men, and heads of their families. 25 But they were unfaithful[h] to the
God of their fathers and prostituted[i] themselves to the gods of the
peoples of the land, whom God had destroyed before them. 26 So
the God of Israel stirred up the spirit of Pul[j] king of Assyria (that
is, Tiglath-Pileser[k] king of Assyria), who took the Reubenites, the
Gadites and the half-tribe of Manasseh into exile. He took them
to Halah,[l] Habor, Hara and the river of Gozan, where they are to
this day.

Chapter 6 Theme ______________________

6 The sons of Levi:[m]
Gershon, Kohath and Merari.
2 The sons of Kohath:
Amram, Izhar, Hebron and Uzziel.
3 The children of Amram:
Aaron, Moses and Miriam.
The sons of Aaron:
Nadab, Abihu,[n] Eleazar and Ithamar.
4 Eleazar was the father of Phinehas,
Phinehas the father of Abishua,
5 Abishua the father of Bukki,
Bukki the father of Uzzi,
6 Uzzi the father of Zerahiah,
Zerahiah the father of Meraioth,
7 Meraioth the father of Amariah,
Amariah the father of Ahitub,
8 Ahitub the father of Zadok,[o]
Zadok the father of Ahimaaz,
9 Ahimaaz the father of Azariah,
Azariah the father of Johanan,

5:19 [a] ver 10; Ge 25:15; 1Ch 1:31
5:20 [b] Ps 37:40 [c] 1Ki 8:44; 2Ch 13:14; 14:11; Ps 20:7-9; 22:5 [d] Ps 26:1; Da 6:23
5:22 [e] 2Ch 32:8 [f] 2Ki 15:29; 17:6
5:23 [g] Dt 3:8,9; SS 4:8
5:25 [h] Dt 32:15-18; 2Ki 17:7; 1Ch 9:1; 2Ch 26:16 [i] Ex 34:15
5:26 [j] 2Ki 15:19 [k] 2Ki 15:29 [l] 2Ki 17:6; 18:11
6:1 [m] Ge 46:11; Ex 6:16; Nu 26:57; 1Ch 23:6
6:3 [n] Lev 10:1
6:8 [o] 2Sa 8:17; 15:27; Ezr 7:2

[10]Johanan the father of Azariah[a] (it was he who served as
priest in the temple Solomon built in Jerusalem),
[11]Azariah the father of Amariah,
Amariah the father of Ahitub,
[12]Ahitub the father of Zadok,
Zadok the father of Shallum,
[13]Shallum the father of Hilkiah,[b]
Hilkiah the father of Azariah,
[14]Azariah the father of Seraiah,[c]
and Seraiah the father of Jehozadak.

[15]Jehozadak[d] was deported when the LORD sent Judah and
Jerusalem into exile by the hand of Nebuchadnezzar.

[16]The sons of Levi:[e]
Gershon,[a] Kohath and Merari.[f]
[17]These are the names of the sons of Gershon:
Libni and Shimei.
[18]The sons of Kohath:
Amram, Izhar, Hebron and Uzziel.
[19]The sons of Merari:[g]
Mahli and Mushi.

These are the clans of the Levites listed according to their
fathers:
[20]Of Gershon:
Libni his son, Jehath his son,
Zimmah his son, [21]Joah his son,
Iddo his son, Zerah his son
and Jeatherai his son.
[22]The descendants of Kohath:
Amminadab his son, Korah[h] his son,
Assir his son, [23]Elkanah his son,
Ebiasaph his son, Assir his son,
[24]Tahath his son, Uriel[i] his son,
Uzziah his son and Shaul his son.
[25]The descendants of Elkanah:
Amasai, Ahimoth,
[26]Elkanah his son,[b] Zophai his son,
Nahath his son, [27]Eliab his son,
Jeroham his son, Elkanah[j] his son
and Samuel[k] his son.[c]
[28]The sons of Samuel:
Joel[d][l] the firstborn
and Abijah the second son.

[a] *16* Hebrew *Gershom,* a variant of *Gershon*; also in verses 17, 20, 43, 62 and 71 [b] *26* Some Hebrew manuscripts, Septuagint and Syriac; most Hebrew manuscripts *Ahimoth* [26]*and Elkanah. The sons of Elkanah:* [c] *27* Some Septuagint manuscripts (see also 1 Samuel 1:19,20 and 1 Chron. 6:33,34); Hebrew does not have *and Samuel his son.* [d] *28* Some Septuagint manuscripts and Syriac (see also 1 Samuel 8:2 and 1 Chron. 6:33); Hebrew does not have *Joel.*

6:10 [a] 1Ki 4:2; 6:1; 2Ch 3:1; 26:17-18
6:13 [b] 2Ki 22:1-20; 2Ch 34:9; 35:8
6:14 [c] 2Ki 25:18; Ezr 2:2; Ne 11:11
6:15 [d] 2Ki 25:18; Ne 12:1; Hag 1:1,14; 2:2,4; Zec 6:11
6:16 [e] Ge 29:34; Ex 6:16; Nu 3:17-20 [f] Nu 26:57
6:19 [g] Ge 46:11; 1Ch 23:21; 24:26
6:22 [h] Ex 6:24
6:24 [i] 1Ch 15:5
6:27 [j] 1Sa 1:1 [k] 1Sa 1:20
6:28 [l] ver 33; 1Sa 8:2

29 The descendants of Merari:
Mahli, Libni his son,
Shimei his son, Uzzah his son,
30 Shimea his son, Haggiah his son
and Asaiah his son.

31 These are the men[a] David put in charge of the music[b] in the
house of the LORD after the ark came to rest there. 32 They ministered with music before the tabernacle, the Tent of Meeting, until
Solomon built the temple of the LORD in Jerusalem. They performed their duties according to the regulations laid down for them.
33 Here are the men who served, together with their sons:
From the Kohathites:
Heman,[c] the musician,
the son of Joel,[d] the son of Samuel,
34 the son of Elkanah,[e] the son of Jeroham,
the son of Eliel, the son of Toah,
35 the son of Zuph, the son of Elkanah,
the son of Mahath, the son of Amasai,
36 the son of Elkanah, the son of Joel,
the son of Azariah, the son of Zephaniah,
37 the son of Tahath, the son of Assir,
the son of Ebiasaph, the son of Korah,[f]
38 the son of Izhar,[g] the son of Kohath,
the son of Levi, the son of Israel;
39 and Heman's associate Asaph,[h] who served at his right hand:
Asaph son of Berekiah, the son of Shimea,[i]
40 the son of Michael, the son of Baaseiah,[a]
the son of Malkijah, 41 the son of Ethni,
the son of Zerah, the son of Adaiah,
42 the son of Ethan, the son of Zimmah,
the son of Shimei, 43 the son of Jahath,
the son of Gershon, the son of Levi;
44 and from their associates, the Merarites, at his left hand:
Ethan son of Kishi, the son of Abdi,
the son of Malluch, 45 the son of Hashabiah,
the son of Amaziah, the son of Hilkiah,
46 the son of Amzi, the son of Bani,
the son of Shemer, 47 the son of Mahli,
the son of Mushi, the son of Merari,
the son of Levi.

48 Their fellow Levites[j] were assigned to all the other duties of the
tabernacle, the house of God. 49 But Aaron and his descendants

6:31 [a] 1Ch 25:1; 2Ch 29:25-26; Ne 12:45 [b] 1Ch 9:33; 15:19; Ezr 3:10; Ps 68:25
6:33 [c] 1Ki 4:31; 1Ch 15:17; 25:1 [d] ver 28
6:34 [e] 1Sa 1:1
6:37 [f] Ex 6:24
6:38 [g] Ex 6:21
6:39 [h] 1Ch 25:1,9; 2Ch 29:13; Ne 11:17 [i] 1Ch 15:17
6:48 [j] 1Ch 23:32

a *40* Most Hebrew manuscripts; some Hebrew manuscripts, one Septuagint manuscript and Syriac *Maaseiah*

were the ones who presented offerings on the altar[a] of burnt offering and on the altar of incense[b] in connection with all that was done in the Most Holy Place, making atonement for Israel, in accordance with all that Moses the servant of God had commanded.

50These were the descendants of Aaron:
Eleazar his son, Phinehas his son,
Abishua his son, 51Bukki his son,
Uzzi his son, Zerahiah his son,
52Meraioth his son, Amariah his son,
Ahitub his son, 53Zadok[c] his son
and Ahimaaz his son.

54These were the locations of their settlements[d] allotted as their territory (they were assigned to the descendants of Aaron who were from the Kohathite clan, because the first lot was for them):

55They were given Hebron in Judah with its surrounding
pasturelands. 56But the fields and villages around the city
were given to Caleb son of Jephunneh.[e]
57So the descendants of Aaron were given Hebron (a city
of refuge), and Libnah,[a] [f] Jattir,[g] Eshtemoa, 58Hilen, Debir,[h]
59Ashan,[i] Juttah[b] and Beth Shemesh, together with their pasturelands. 60And from the tribe of Benjamin they were given
Gibeon,[c] Geba, Alemeth and Anathoth,[j] together with their
pasturelands.

These towns, which were distributed among the Kohathite clans, were thirteen in all.

61The rest of Kohath's descendants were allotted ten towns from
the clans of half the tribe of Manasseh.
62The descendants of Gershon, clan by clan, were allotted thirteen towns from the tribes of Issachar, Asher and Naphtali, and
from the part of the tribe of Manasseh that is in Bashan.
63The descendants of Merari, clan by clan, were allotted twelve
towns from the tribes of Reuben, Gad and Zebulun.
64So the Israelites gave the Levites these towns[k] and their pasturelands. 65From the tribes of Judah, Simeon and Benjamin they
allotted the previously named towns.
66Some of the Kohathite clans were given as their territory
towns from the tribe of Ephraim.
67In the hill country of Ephraim they were given Shechem
(a city of refuge), and Gezer,[d] [l] 68Jokmeam,[m] Beth Horon,[n]
69Aijalon[o] and Gath Rimmon,[p] together with their pasturelands.

[a]57 See Joshua 21:13; Hebrew *given the cities of refuge: Hebron, Libnah.* [b]59 Syriac (see also Septuagint and Joshua 21:16); Hebrew does not have *Juttah.* [c]60 See Joshua 21:17; Hebrew does not have *Gibeon.* [d]67 See Joshua 21:21; Hebrew *given the cities of refuge: Shechem, Gezer.*

6:49 [a]Ex 27:1-8 [b]Ex 30:1-7,10; 2Ch 26:18
6:53 [c]2Sa 8:17
6:54 [d]Nu 31:10
6:56 [e]Jos 14:13; 15:13
6:57 [f]Nu 33:20 [g]Jos 15:48
6:58 [h]Jos 10:3
6:59 [i]Jos 15:42
6:60 [j]Jer 1:1
6:64 [k]Nu 35:1-8; Jos 21:3, 41-42
6:67 [l]Jos 10:33
6:68 [m]1Ki 4:12 [n]Jos 10:10
6:69 [o]Jos 10:12 [p]Jos 19:45

70 And from half the tribe of Manasseh the Israelites gave
Aner and Bileam, together with their pasturelands, to the rest
of the Kohathite clans.

71 The Gershonites[a] received the following:
From the clan of the half-tribe of Manasseh
they received Golan in Bashan[b] and also Ashtaroth, together
with their pasturelands;
72 from the tribe of Issachar
they received Kedesh, Daberath,[c] 73 Ramoth and Anem,
together with their pasturelands;
74 from the tribe of Asher
they received Mashal, Abdon,[d] 75 Hukok[e] and Rehob,[f]
together with their pasturelands;
76 and from the tribe of Naphtali
they received Kedesh in Galilee, Hammon[g] and Kiriathaim,[h] together with their pasturelands.

77 The Merarites (the rest of the Levites) received the following:
From the tribe of Zebulun
they received Jokneam, Kartah,[a] Rimmono and Tabor,
together with their pasturelands;
78 from the tribe of Reuben across the Jordan east of Jericho
they received Bezer[i] in the desert, Jahzah, 79 Kedemoth[j]
and Mephaath, together with their pasturelands;
80 and from the tribe of Gad
they received Ramoth in Gilead,[k] Mahanaim,[l] 81 Heshbon
and Jazer,[m] together with their pasturelands.[n]

Chapter 7 Theme ______________________

7 The sons of Issachar:[o]
Tola, Puah,[p] Jashub and Shimron—four in all.
2 The sons of Tola:
Uzzi, Rephaiah, Jeriel, Jahmai, Ibsam and Samuel—heads
of their families. During the reign of David, the descendants
of Tola listed as fighting men in their genealogy numbered
22,600.
3 The son of Uzzi:
Izrahiah.
The sons of Izrahiah:
Michael, Obadiah, Joel and Isshiah. All five of them were
chiefs. 4 According to their family genealogy, they had
36,000 men ready for battle, for they had many wives and
children.

6:71 [a] 1Ch 23:7 [b] Jos 20:8
6:72 [c] Jos 19:12
6:74 [d] Jos 19:28
6:75 [e] Jos 19:34 [f] Nu 13:21
6:76 [g] Jos 19:28 [h] Nu 32:37
6:78 [i] Jos 20:8
6:79 [j] Dt 2:26
6:80 [k] Jos 20:8 [l] Ge 32:2
6:81 [m] Nu 21:32 [n] 2Ch 11:14
7:1 [o] Ge 30:18; Nu 26:23 [p] Ge 46:13

[a] 77 See Septuagint and Joshua 21:34; Hebrew does not have *Jokneam, Kartah*.

5 The relatives who were fighting men belonging to all the clans
of Issachar, as listed in their genealogy, were 87,000 in all.

6 Three sons of Benjamin:[a]
Bela, Beker and Jediael.
7 The sons of Bela:
Ezbon, Uzzi, Uzziel, Jerimoth and Iri, heads of families—
five in all. Their genealogical record listed 22,034 fighting
men.
8 The sons of Beker:
Zemirah, Joash, Eliezer, Elioenai, Omri, Jeremoth, Abijah,
Anathoth and Alemeth. All these were the sons of Beker.
9 Their genealogical record listed the heads of families and
20,200 fighting men.
10 The son of Jediael:
Bilhan.
The sons of Bilhan:
Jeush, Benjamin, Ehud, Kenaanah, Zethan, Tarshish and
Ahishahar. 11 All these sons of Jediael were heads of families. There were 17,200 fighting men ready to go out to war.
12 The Shuppites and Huppites were the descendants of Ir, and
the Hushites the descendants of Aher.

13 The sons of Naphtali:[b]
Jahziel, Guni, Jezer and Shillem[a]—the descendants of
Bilhah.

14 The descendants of Manasseh:[c]
Asriel was his descendant through his Aramean concubine. She gave birth to Makir the father of Gilead.[d]
15 Makir took a wife from among the Huppites and Shuppites. His sister's name was Maacah.
Another descendant was named Zelophehad,[e] who had
only daughters.
16 Makir's wife Maacah gave birth to a son and named
him Peresh. His brother was named Sheresh, and his sons
were Ulam and Rakem.
17 The son of Ulam:
Bedan.
These were the sons of Gilead[f] son of Makir, the son of Manasseh. 18 His sister Hammoleketh gave birth to Ishhod,
Abiezer[g] and Mahlah.
19 The sons of Shemida were:
Ahian, Shechem, Likhi and Aniam.
20 The descendants of Ephraim:[h]
Shuthelah, Bered his son,
Tahath his son, Eleadah his son,

7:6 [a] Ge 46:21; Nu 26:38; 1Ch 8:1-40
7:13 [b] Ge 30:8; 46:24
7:14 [c] Ge 41:51; Jos 17:1; 1Ch 5:23 [d] Nu 26:30
7:15 [e] Nu 26:33; 36:1-12
7:17 [f] Nu 26:30; 1Sa 12:11
7:18 [g] Jos 17:2
7:20 [h] Ge 41:52; Nu 1:33; 26:35

a *13* Some Hebrew and Septuagint manuscripts (see also Gen. 46:24 and Num. 26:49); most Hebrew manuscripts *Shallum*

7:24
[a]Jos 10:10; 16:3,5

Tahath his son, [21]Zabad his son
and Shuthelah his son.

Ezer and Elead were killed by the native-born men of Gath,
when they went down to seize their livestock. [22]Their father
Ephraim mourned for them many days, and his relatives
came to comfort him. [23]Then he lay with his wife again, and
she became pregnant and gave birth to a son. He named him
Beriah,[a] because there had been misfortune in his family.
[24]His daughter was Sheerah, who built Lower and Upper
Beth Horon[a] as well as Uzzen Sheerah.

[25]Rephah was his son, Resheph his son,[b]
Telah his son, Tahan his son,
[26]Ladan his son, Ammihud his son,
Elishama his son, [27]Nun his son
and Joshua his son.

7:28
[b]Jos 10:33; 16:7

[28]Their lands and settlements included Bethel and its surrounding villages, Naaran to the east, Gezer[b] and its villages to the west,
and Shechem and its villages all the way to Ayyah and its villages.
[29]Along the borders of Manasseh were Beth Shan,[c] Taanach,
Megiddo and Dor,[d] together with their villages. The descendants
of Joseph son of Israel lived in these towns.

[30]The sons of Asher:[e]
Imnah, Ishvah, Ishvi and Beriah. Their sister was Serah.
[31]The sons of Beriah:
Heber and Malkiel, who was the father of Birzaith.
[32]Heber was the father of Japhlet, Shomer and Hotham and of
their sister Shua.
[33]The sons of Japhlet:
Pasach, Bimhal and Ashvath.

7:29
[c]Jos 17:11
[d]Jos 11:2

These were Japhlet's sons.
[34]The sons of Shomer:
Ahi, Rohgah,[c] Hubbah and Aram.
[35]The sons of his brother Helem:
Zophah, Imna, Shelesh and Amal.
[36]The sons of Zophah:
Suah, Harnepher, Shual, Beri, Imrah, [37]Bezer, Hod, Sham-
ma, Shilshah, Ithran[d] and Beera.
[38]The sons of Jether:
Jephunneh, Pispah and Ara.
[39]The sons of Ulla:
Arah, Hanniel and Rizia.

[40]All these were descendants of Asher—heads of families, choice
men, brave warriors and outstanding leaders. The number of men
ready for battle, as listed in their genealogy, was 26,000.

7:30
[e]Ge 46:17; Nu 1:40; 26:44

[a] 23 *Beriah* sounds like the Hebrew for *misfortune.* [b] 25 Some Septuagint manuscripts; Hebrew does not have *his son.* [c] 34 Or *of his brother Shomer: Rohgah* [d] 37 Possibly a variant of *Jether*

Chapter 8 Theme ______________________

8 Benjamin[a] was the father of Bela his firstborn,
Ashbel the second son, Aharah the third,
2Nohah the fourth and Rapha the fifth.
3The sons of Bela were:
Addar,[b] Gera, Abihud,[a] 4Abishua, Naaman, Ahoah,[c] 5Gera,
Shephuphan and Huram.
6These were the descendants of Ehud,[d] who were heads of
families of those living in Geba and were deported to
Manahath:
7Naaman, Ahijah, and Gera, who deported them and who
was the father of Uzza and Ahihud.
8Sons were born to Shaharaim in Moab after he had divorced
his wives Hushim and Baara. 9By his wife Hodesh he had
Jobab, Zibia, Mesha, Malcam, 10Jeuz, Sakia and Mirmah.
These were his sons, heads of families. 11By Hushim he
had Abitub and Elpaal.
12The sons of Elpaal:
Eber, Misham, Shemed (who built Ono[e] and Lod with its
surrounding villages), 13and Beriah and Shema, who were
heads of families of those living in Aijalon[f] and who drove
out the inhabitants of Gath.[g]
14Ahio, Shashak, Jeremoth, 15Zebadiah, Arad, Eder, 16Michael,
Ishpah and Joha were the sons of Beriah.
17Zebadiah, Meshullam, Hizki, Heber, 18Ishmerai, Izliah and
Jobab were the sons of Elpaal.
19Jakim, Zicri, Zabdi, 20Elienai, Zillethai, Eliel, 21Adaiah, Beraiah
and Shimrath were the sons of Shimei.
22Ishpan, Eber, Eliel, 23Abdon, Zicri, Hanan, 24Hananiah, Elam,
Anthothijah, 25Iphdeiah and Penuel were the sons of
Shashak.
26Shamsherai, Shehariah, Athaliah, 27Jaareshiah, Elijah and
Zicri were the sons of Jeroham.
28All these were heads of families, chiefs as listed in their genealogy,
and they lived in Jerusalem.

29Jeiel[b] the father[c] of Gibeon lived in Gibeon.[h]
His wife's name was Maacah, 30and his firstborn son was
Abdon, followed by Zur, Kish, Baal, Ner,[d] Nadab, 31Gedor,
Ahio, Zeker 32and Mikloth, who was the father of Shimeah.
They too lived near their relatives in Jerusalem.

a3 Or *Gera the father of Ehud* b29 Some Septuagint manuscripts (see also 1 Chron. 9:35); Hebrew does not have *Jeiel.* c29 *Father* may mean *civic leader* or *military leader.* d30 Some Septuagint manuscripts (see also 1 Chron. 9:36); Hebrew does not have *Ner.*

8:1 [a] Ge 46:21; 1Ch 7:6
8:3 [b] Ge 46:21
8:4 [c] 2Sa 23:9
8:6 [d] Jdg 3:12-30; 1Ch 2:52
8:12 [e] Ezr 2:33; Ne 6:2; 7:37; 11:35
8:13 [f] Jos 10:12 [g] Jos 11:22
8:29 [h] Jos 9:3

33 Ner[a] was the father of Kish,[b] Kish the father of Saul[c], and
Saul the father of Jonathan, Malki-Shua, Abinadab and
Esh-Baal.[a][d]

34 The son of Jonathan:[e]
Merib-Baal,[b][f] who was the father of Micah.

35 The sons of Micah:
Pithon, Melech, Tarea and Ahaz.

36 Ahaz was the father of Jehoaddah, Jehoaddah was the
father of Alemeth, Azmaveth and Zimri, and Zimri was
the father of Moza. 37 Moza was the father of Binea; Raphah
was his son, Eleasah his son and Azel his son.

38 Azel had six sons, and these were their names:
Azrikam, Bokeru, Ishmael, Sheariah, Obadiah and Hanan.
All these were the sons of Azel.

39 The sons of his brother Eshek:
Ulam his firstborn, Jeush the second son and Eliphelet the
third. 40 The sons of Ulam were brave warriors who could
handle the bow. They had many sons and grandsons—
150 in all.

All these were the descendants of Benjamin.[g]

Chapter 9 Theme ____________________

9 All Israel was listed in the genealogies recorded in the book
of the kings of Israel.

The people of Judah were taken captive to Babylon because of
their unfaithfulness.[h] 2 Now the first to resettle on their own property in their own towns[i] were some Israelites, priests, Levites and
temple servants.[j]

3 Those from Judah, from Benjamin, and from Ephraim and
Manasseh who lived in Jerusalem were:

4 Uthai son of Ammihud, the son of Omri, the son of Imri,
the son of Bani, a descendant of Perez son of Judah.[k]

5 Of the Shilonites:
Asaiah the firstborn and his sons.

6 Of the Zerahites:
Jeuel.
The people from Judah numbered 690.

7 Of the Benjamites:
Sallu son of Meshullam, the son of Hodaviah, the son of
Hassenuah;

8 Ibneiah son of Jeroham; Elah son of Uzzi, the son of Micri;
and Meshullam son of Shephatiah, the son of Reuel, the
son of Ibnijah.

8:33 a 1Sa 28:19; b 1Sa 9:1; c 1Sa 14:49; d 2Sa 2:8
8:34 e 2Sa 9:12; f 2Sa 4:4
8:40 g Nu 26:38
9:1 h 1Ch 5:25
9:2 i Jos 9:27; Ezr 2:70; j Ezr 2:43,58; 8:20; Ne 7:60
9:4 k Ge 38:29; 46:12

a 33 Also known as *Ish-Bosheth* b 34 Also known as *Mephibosheth*

9The people from Benjamin, as listed in their genealogy,
numbered 956. All these men were heads of their families.
10Of the priests:
Jedaiah; Jehoiarib; Jakin;
11Azariah son of Hilkiah, the son of Meshullam, the son of
Zadok, the son of Meraioth, the son of Ahitub, the official
in charge of the house of God;
12Adaiah son of Jeroham, the son of Pashhur,[a] the son of
Malkijah; and Maasai son of Adiel, the son of Jahzerah,
the son of Meshullam, the son of Meshillemith, the son of
Immer.
13The priests, who were heads of families, numbered 1,760.
They were able men, responsible for ministering in the
house of God.
14Of the Levites:
Shemaiah son of Hasshub, the son of Azrikam, the son of
Hashabiah, a Merarite; 15Bakbakkar, Heresh, Galal and
Mattaniah[b] son of Mica, the son of Zicri, the son of Asaph;
16Obadiah son of Shemaiah, the son of Galal, the son of
Jeduthun; and Berekiah son of Asa, the son of Elkanah,
who lived in the villages of the Netophathites.[c]
17The gatekeepers:[d]
Shallum, Akkub, Talmon, Ahiman and their brothers,
Shallum their chief 18being stationed at the King's Gate[e] on
the east, up to the present time. These were the gatekeepers belonging to the camp of the Levites. 19Shallum[f] son of
Kore, the son of Ebiasaph, the son of Korah, and his fellow
gatekeepers from his family (the Korahites) were responsible for guarding the thresholds of the Tent[a] just as their
fathers had been responsible for guarding the entrance to
the dwelling of the LORD. 20In earlier times Phinehas[g] son
of Eleazar was in charge of the gatekeepers, and the LORD
was with him. 21Zechariah[h] son of Meshelemiah was the
gatekeeper at the entrance to the Tent of Meeting.
22Altogether, those chosen to be gatekeepers[i] at the thresholds
numbered 212. They were registered by genealogy in their villages.
The gatekeepers had been assigned to their positions of trust by
David and Samuel the seer.[j] 23They and their descendants were in
charge of guarding the gates of the house of the LORD—the house
called the Tent. 24The gatekeepers were on the four sides: east,
west, north and south. 25Their brothers in their villages had to
come from time to time and share their duties for seven-day[k]
periods. 26But the four principal gatekeepers, who were Levites,
were entrusted with the responsibility for the rooms and treasuries[l]

a 19 That is, the temple; also in verses 21 and 23

9:12 a Ezr 2:38; 10:22; Ne 10:3; Jer 21:1; 38:1
9:15 b 2Ch 20:14; Ne 11:22
9:16 c Ne 12:28
9:17 d ver 22; 1Ch 26:1; 2Ch 8:14; 31:14; Ezr 2:42; Ne 7:45
9:18 e 1Ch 26:14; Eze 43:1; 46:1
9:19 f Jer 35:4
9:20 g Nu 25:7-13
9:21 h 1Ch 26:2,14
9:22 i ver 17; 1Ch 26:1-2; 2Ch 31:15,18 j 1Sa 9:9
9:25 k 2Ki 11:5; 2Ch 23:8
9:26 l 1Ch 26:22

in the house of God. 27They would spend the night stationed
around the house of God,[a] because they had to guard it; and they
had charge of the key[b] for opening it each morning.

28Some of them were in charge of the articles used in the temple
service; they counted them when they were brought in and when
they were taken out. 29Others were assigned to take care of the
furnishings and all the other articles of the sanctuary,[c] as well as
the flour and wine, and the oil, incense and spices. 30But some[d] of
the priests took care of mixing the spices. 31A Levite named Mattithiah, the firstborn son of Shallum the Korahite, was entrusted
with the responsibility for baking the offering bread. 32Some of
their Kohathite brothers were in charge of preparing for every
Sabbath the bread set out on the table.[e]

33Those who were musicians,[f] heads of Levite families, stayed
in the rooms of the temple and were exempt from other duties
because they were responsible for the work day and night.[g]

34All these were heads of Levite families, chiefs as listed in their
genealogy, and they lived in Jerusalem.

35Jeiel[h] the father[a] of Gibeon lived in Gibeon.

His wife's name was Maacah, 36and his firstborn son was
Abdon, followed by Zur, Kish, Baal, Ner, Nadab, 37Gedor,
Ahio, Zechariah and Mikloth. 38Mikloth was the father of
Shimeam. They too lived near their relatives in Jerusalem.

39Ner[i] was the father of Kish,[j] Kish the father of Saul, and Saul
the father of Jonathan,[k] Malki-Shua, Abinadab and Esh-
Baal.[b][l]

40The son of Jonathan:

Merib-Baal,[c][m] who was the father of Micah.

41The sons of Micah:

Pithon, Melech, Tahrea and Ahaz.[d]

42Ahaz was the father of Jadah, Jadah[e] was the father of
Alemeth, Azmaveth and Zimri, and Zimri was the father
of Moza. 43Moza was the father of Binea; Rephaiah was his
son, Eleasah his son and Azel his son.

44Azel had six sons, and these were their names:

Azrikam, Bokeru, Ishmael, Sheariah, Obadiah and Hanan.
These were the sons of Azel.

Chapter 10 Theme ____________________

10 Now the Philistines fought against Israel; the Israelites fled
before them, and many fell slain on Mount Gilboa. 2The
Philistines pressed hard after Saul and his sons, and they killed

9:27 [a]Nu 3:38; 1Ch 23:30-32 [b]Isa 22:22
9:29 [c]Nu 3:28; 1Ch 23:29
9:30 [d]Ex 30:23-25
9:32 [e]Lev 24:5-8; 1Ch 23:29; 2Ch 13:11
9:33 [f]1Ch 6:31; 25:1-31 [g]Ps 134:1
9:35 [h]1Ch 8:29
9:39 [i]1Ch 8:33 [j]1Sa 9:1 [k]1Sa 13:22 [l]2Sa 2:8
9:40 [m]2Sa 4:4

[a]35 *Father* may mean *civic leader* or *military leader.* [b]39 Also known as *Ish-Bosheth*
[c]40 Also known as *Mephibosheth* [d]41 Vulgate and Syriac (see also Septuagint and 1 Chron. 8:35); Hebrew does not have *and Ahaz.* [e]42 Some Hebrew manuscripts and Septuagint (see also 1 Chron. 8:36); most Hebrew manuscripts *Jarah, Jarah*

his sons Jonathan, Abinadab and Malki-Shua. 3The fighting grew
fierce around Saul, and when the archers overtook him, they
wounded him.
4Saul said to his armor-bearer, "Draw your sword and run me
through, or these uncircumcised fellows will come and abuse me."
But his armor-bearer was terrified and would not do it; so Saul
took his own sword and fell on it. 5When the armor-bearer saw
that Saul was dead, he too fell on his sword and died. 6So Saul and
his three sons died, and all his house died together.
7When all the Israelites in the valley saw that the army had fled
and that Saul and his sons had died, they abandoned their towns
and fled. And the Philistines came and occupied them.
8The next day, when the Philistines came to strip the dead, they
found Saul and his sons fallen on Mount Gilboa. 9They stripped
him and took his head and his armor, and sent messengers
throughout the land of the Philistines to proclaim the news among
their idols and their people. 10They put his armor in the temple of
their gods and hung up his head in the temple of Dagon.[a]
11When all the inhabitants of Jabesh Gilead[b] heard of everything
the Philistines had done to Saul, 12all their valiant men went and
took the bodies of Saul and his sons and brought them to Jabesh.
Then they buried their bones under the great tree in Jabesh, and
they fasted seven days.
13Saul died[c] because he was unfaithful[d] to the LORD; he did not
keep[e] the word of the LORD and even consulted a medium[f] for
guidance, 14and did not inquire of the LORD. So the LORD put him
to death and turned[g] the kingdom[h] over to David son of Jesse.

Chapter 11 Theme ____________________

11 All Israel[i] came together to David at Hebron[j] and said, "We
are your own flesh and blood. 2In the past, even while Saul
was king, you were the one who led Israel on their military campaigns.[k] And the LORD your God said to you, 'You will shepherd[l]
my people Israel, and you will become their ruler.[m]'"
3When all the elders of Israel had come to King David at Hebron,
he made a compact with them at Hebron before the LORD, and
they anointed[n] David king over Israel, as the LORD had promised
through Samuel.
4David and all the Israelites marched to Jerusalem (that is,
Jebus). The Jebusites[o] who lived there 5said to David, "You will not
get in here." Nevertheless, David captured the fortress of Zion, the
City of David.
6David had said, "Whoever leads the attack on the Jebusites will
become commander-in-chief." Joab[p] son of Zeruiah went up first,
and so he received the command.

10:10 [a] Jdg 16:23
10:11 [b] Jdg 21:8
10:13 [c] 2Sa 1:1 [d] 1Sa 15:23; 1Ch 5:25 [e] 1Sa 13:13 [f] Lev 19:31; 20:6; Dt 18:9-14; 1Sa 28:7
10:14 [g] 1Ch 12:23 [h] 1Sa 13:14; 15:28
11:1 [i] 1Ch 9:1 [j] Ge 13:18; 23:19
11:2 [k] 1Sa 18:5,16 [l] Ps 78:71; Mt 2:6 [m] 1Ch 5:2
11:3 [n] 1Sa 16:1-13
11:4 [o] Ge 10:16; 15:18-21; Jos 3:10; 15:8; Jdg 1:21; 19:10
11:6 [p] 2Sa 2:13; 8:16

11:8 [7]David then took up residence in the fortress, and so it was called
[a]2Sa 5:9; the City of David. [8]He built up the city around it, from the sup-
2Ch 32:5 porting terraces[a][a] to the surrounding wall, while Joab restored the
rest of the city. [9]And David became more and more powerful,[b]
11:9 because the LORD Almighty was with him.
[b]2Sa 3:1; [10]These were the chiefs of David's mighty men—they, together
Est 9:4 with all Israel,[c] gave his kingship strong support to extend it over
the whole land, as the LORD had promised[d]— [11]this is the list of
David's mighty men:[e]
11:10 Jashobeam,[b] a Hacmonite, was chief of the officers[c]; he raised his
[c]ver 1 [d]ver 3; spear against three hundred men, whom he killed in one encounter.
1Ch 12:23 [12]Next to him was Eleazar son of Dodai the Ahohite, one of the
three mighty men. [13]He was with David at Pas Dammim when the
Philistines gathered there for battle. At a place where there was a
11:11 field full of barley, the troops fled from the Philistines. [14]But they
[e]2Sa 17:10 took their stand in the middle of the field. They defended it and
struck the Philistines down, and the LORD brought about a great
victory.[f]
11:14 [15]Three of the thirty chiefs came down to David to the rock at the
[f]Ex 14:30; cave of Adullam, while a band of Philistines was encamped in the
1Sa 11:13 Valley[g] of Rephaim. [16]At that time David was in the stronghold,[h]
and the Philistine garrison was at Bethlehem. [17]David longed for
water and said, "Oh, that someone would get me a drink of water
11:15 [g]1Ch 14:9; from the well near the gate of Bethlehem!" [18]So the Three broke
Isa 17:5 through the Philistine lines, drew water from the well near the gate
of Bethlehem and carried it back to David. But he refused to drink
it; instead, he poured[i] it out before the LORD. [19]"God forbid that I
11:16 should do this!" he said. "Should I drink the blood of these men
[h]2Sa 5:17 who went at the risk of their lives?" Because they risked their lives
to bring it back, David would not drink it.
Such were the exploits of the three mighty men.
11:18 [20]Abishai[j] the brother of Joab was chief of the Three. He raised
[i]Dt 12:16 his spear against three hundred men, whom he killed, and so he
became as famous as the Three. [21]He was doubly honored above
the Three and became their commander, even though he was not
11:20 included among them.
[j]1Sa 26:6 [22]Benaiah son of Jehoiada was a valiant fighter from Kabzeel,[k]
who performed great exploits. He struck down two of Moab's
best men. He also went down into a pit on a snowy day and killed a
11:22 lion.[l] [23]And he struck down an Egyptian who was seven and a half
[k]Jos 15:21 [l]1Sa 17:36 feet[d] tall. Although the Egyptian had a spear like a weaver's rod[m]
in his hand, Benaiah went against him with a club. He snatched
the spear from the Egyptian's hand and killed him with his own

11:23 [m]1Sa 17:7 [a]8 Or *the Millo* [b]11 Possibly a variant of *Jashob-Baal* [c]11 Or *Thirty*; some Septuagint manuscripts *Three* (see also 2 Samuel 23:8) [d]23 Hebrew *five cubits* (about 2.3 meters)

spear. 24Such were the exploits of Benaiah son of Jehoiada; he too
was as famous as the three mighty men. 25He was held in greater
honor than any of the Thirty, but he was not included among the
Three. And David put him in charge of his bodyguard.

26The mighty men were:
Asahel[a] the brother of Joab,
Elhanan son of Dodo from Bethlehem,
27Shammoth[b] the Harorite,
Helez the Pelonite,
28Ira son of Ikkesh from Tekoa,
Abiezer[c] from Anathoth,
29Sibbecai[d] the Hushathite,
Ilai the Ahohite,
30Maharai the Netophathite,
Heled son of Baanah the Netophathite,
31Ithai son of Ribai from Gibeah in Benjamin,
Benaiah[e] the Pirathonite,[f]
32Hurai from the ravines of Gaash,
Abiel the Arbathite,
33Azmaveth the Baharumite,
Eliahba the Shaalbonite,
34the sons of Hashem the Gizonite,
Jonathan son of Shagee the Hararite,
35Ahiam son of Sacar the Hararite,
Eliphal son of Ur,
36Hepher the Mekerathite,
Ahijah the Pelonite,
37Hezro the Carmelite,
Naarai son of Ezbai,
38Joel the brother of Nathan,
Mibhar son of Hagri,
39Zelek the Ammonite,
Naharai the Berothite, the armor-bearer of Joab son of Zeruiah,
40Ira the Ithrite,
Gareb the Ithrite,
41Uriah[g] the Hittite,
Zabad[h] son of Ahlai,
42Adina son of Shiza the Reubenite, who was chief of the Reubenites, and the thirty with him,
43Hanan son of Maacah,
Joshaphat the Mithnite,
44Uzzia the Ashterathite,[i]
Shama and Jeiel the sons of Hotham the Aroerite,

11:26 [a] 2Sa 2:18
11:27 [b] 1Ch 27:8
11:28 [c] 1Ch 27:12
11:29 [d] 2Sa 21:18
11:31 [e] 1Ch 27:14 [f] Jdg 12:13
11:41 [g] 2Sa 11:6 [h] 1Ch 2:36
11:44 [i] Dt 1:4

45 Jediael son of Shimri,
his brother Joha the Tizite,
46 Eliel the Mahavite,
Jeribai and Joshaviah the sons of Elnaam,
Ithmah the Moabite,
47 Eliel, Obed and Jaasiel the Mezobaite.

Chapter 12 Theme ______________________________

12

These were the men who came to David at Ziklag,[a] while
he was banished from the presence of Saul son of Kish
(they were among the warriors who helped him in battle; 2 they
were armed with bows and were able to shoot arrows or to sling
stones right-handed or left-handed;[b] they were kinsmen of Saul[c]
from the tribe of Benjamin):

3 Ahiezer their chief and Joash the sons of Shemaah the
Gibeathite; Jeziel and Pelet the sons of Azmaveth; Beracah,
Jehu the Anathothite, 4 and Ishmaiah the Gibeonite, a mighty
man among the Thirty, who was a leader of the Thirty;
Jeremiah, Jahaziel, Johanan, Jozabad the Gederathite,[d] 5 Eluzai,
Jerimoth, Bealiah, Shemariah and Shephatiah the Haruphite;
6 Elkanah, Isshiah, Azarel, Joezer and Jashobeam the Korahites;
7 and Joelah and Zebadiah the sons of Jeroham from Gedor.[e]

8 Some Gadites[f] defected to David at his stronghold in the desert.
They were brave warriors, ready for battle and able to handle the
shield and spear. Their faces were the faces of lions,[g] and they were
as swift as gazelles[h] in the mountains.

9 Ezer was the chief,
Obadiah the second in command, Eliab the third,
10 Mishmannah the fourth, Jeremiah the fifth,
11 Attai the sixth, Eliel the seventh,
12 Johanan the eighth, Elzabad the ninth,
13 Jeremiah the tenth and Macbannai the eleventh.

14 These Gadites were army commanders; the least was a match
for a hundred,[i] and the greatest for a thousand.[j] 15 It was they who
crossed the Jordan in the first month when it was overflowing all
its banks,[k] and they put to flight everyone living in the valleys, to
the east and to the west.

16 Other Benjamites[l] and some men from Judah also came to
David in his stronghold. 17 David went out to meet them and said
to them, "If you have come to me in peace, to help me, I am ready
to have you unite with me. But if you have come to betray me to
my enemies when my hands are free from violence, may the God
of our fathers see it and judge you."

12:1 [a] Jos 15:31; 1Sa 27:2-6
12:2 [b] Jdg 3:15; 20:16 [c] 2Sa 3:19
12:4 [d] Jos 15:36
12:7 [e] Jos 15:58
12:8 [f] Ge 30:11 [g] 2Sa 17:10 [h] 2Sa 2:18
12:14 [i] Lev 26:8 [j] Dt 32:30
12:15 [k] Jos 3:15
12:16 [l] 2Sa 3:19

18Then the Spirit[a] came upon Amasai,[b] chief of the Thirty, and
he said:

"We are yours, O David!
We are with you, O son of Jesse!
Success,[c] success to you,
and success to those who help you,
for your God will help you."

So David received them and made them leaders of his raiding
bands.
19Some of the men of Manasseh defected to David when he went
with the Philistines to fight against Saul. (He and his men did not
help the Philistines because, after consultation, their rulers sent
him away. They said, "It will cost us our heads if he deserts to his
master Saul.")[d] 20When David went to Ziklag,[e] these were the
men of Manasseh who defected to him: Adnah, Jozabad, Jediael,
Michael, Jozabad, Elihu and Zillethai, leaders of units of a thousand in Manasseh. 21They helped David against raiding bands,
for all of them were brave warriors, and they were commanders
in his army. 22Day after day men came to help David, until he had
a great army, like the army of God.[a]

23These are the numbers of the men armed for battle who came
to David at Hebron[f] to turn[g] Saul's kingdom over to him, as the
LORD had said:[h]

24men of Judah, carrying shield and spear—6,800 armed for battle;
25men of Simeon, warriors ready for battle—7,100;
26men of Levi—4,600, 27including Jehoiada, leader of the family of Aaron, with 3,700 men, 28and Zadok,[i] a brave young warrior, with 22 officers from his family;
29men of Benjamin,[j] Saul's kinsmen—3,000, most[k] of whom had remained loyal to Saul's house until then;
30men of Ephraim, brave warriors, famous in their own clans—20,800;
31men of half the tribe of Manasseh, designated by name to come and make David king—18,000;
32men of Issachar, who understood the times and knew what Israel should do[l]—200 chiefs, with all their relatives under their command;
33men of Zebulun, experienced soldiers prepared for battle with every type of weapon, to help David with undivided loyalty—50,000;
34men of Naphtali—1,000 officers, together with 37,000 men carrying shields and spears;
35men of Dan, ready for battle—28,600;

a 22 Or *a great and mighty army*

12:18 [a] Jdg 3:10; 6:34; 1Ch 28:12; 2Ch 15:1; 20:14; 24:20 [b] 2Sa 17:25 [c] 1Sa 25:5-6
12:19 [d] 1Sa 29:2-11
12:20 [e] 1Sa 27:6
12:23 [f] 2Sa 2:3-4 [g] 1Ch 10:14 [h] 1Sa 16:1; 1Ch 11:10
12:28 [i] 2Sa 8:17; 1Ch 6:8; 15:11; 16:39; 27:17
12:29 [j] 2Sa 3:19 [k] 2Sa 2:8-9
12:32 [l] Est 1:13

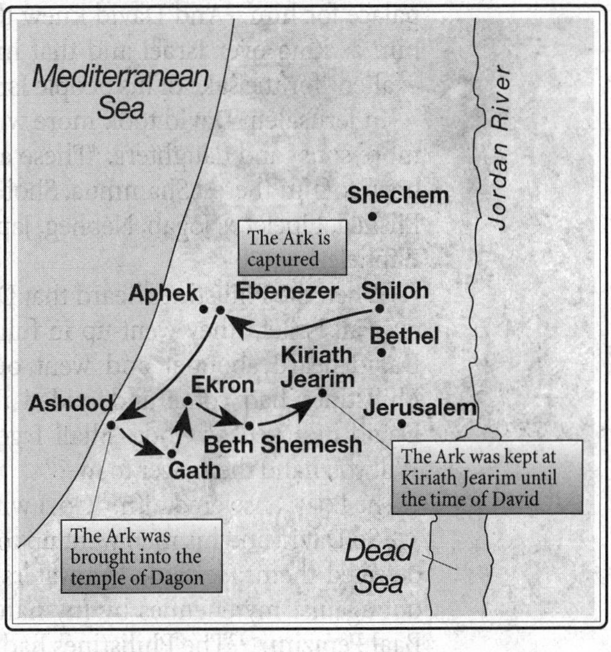

12:38 [a]2Sa 5:1-3; 1Ch 9:1
12:39 [b]2Sa 3:20; Isa 25:6-8
12:40 [c]2Sa 16:1; 17:29 [d]1Sa 25:18 [e]1Ch 29:22

36 men of Asher, experienced soldiers prepared for battle—
40,000;
37 and from east of the Jordan, men of Reuben, Gad and the half-
tribe of Manasseh, armed with every type of weapon—
120,000.
38 All these were fighting men who volunteered to serve in the
ranks. They came to Hebron fully determined to make David king
over all Israel.[a] All the rest of the Israelites were also of one mind
to make David king. 39 The men spent three days there with David,
eating and drinking,[b] for their families had supplied provisions for
them. 40 Also, their neighbors from as far away as Issachar, Zebulun
and Naphtali came bringing food on donkeys, camels, mules and
oxen. There were plentiful supplies[c] of flour, fig cakes, raisin[d] cakes,
wine, oil, cattle and sheep, for there was joy[e] in Israel.

Chapter 13 Theme ______________________________

The Wanderings of the Ark
(see page 2203)

13:3 [f]1Sa 7:1-2 [g]2Ch 1:5
13:5 [h]1Ch 11:1; 15:3 [i]Jos 13:3 [j]Nu 13:21 [k]1Sa 6:21; 7:2
13:6 [l]Jos 15:9; 2Sa 6:2 [m]Ex 25:22; 2Ki 19:15
13:7 [n]Nu 4:15; 1Sa 7:1

13

David conferred with each of his officers, the commanders of thousands and commanders of hundreds. 2 He then
said to the whole assembly of Israel, "If it seems good to you and
if it is the will of the LORD
our God, let us send word
far and wide to the rest of
our brothers throughout the
territories of Israel, and also
to the priests and Levites
who are with them in their
towns and pasturelands, to
come and join us. 3 Let us
bring the ark of our God
back to us,[f] for we did not
inquire[g] of[a] it[b] during the
reign of Saul." 4 The whole
assembly agreed to do this,
because it seemed right to
all the people.
5 So David assembled all
the Israelites,[h] from the Shihor River[i] in Egypt to Lebo[c]
Hamath,[j] to bring the ark
of God from Kiriath Jearim.[k] 6 David and all the Israelites with
him went to Baalah[l] of Judah (Kiriath Jearim) to bring up from
there the ark of God the LORD, who is enthroned between the
cherubim[m]—the ark that is called by the Name.
7 They moved the ark of God from Abinadab's[n] house on a new
cart, with Uzzah and Ahio guiding it. 8 David and all the Israelites

[a]3 Or *we neglected* [b]3 Or *him* [c]5 Or *to the entrance to*

were celebrating with all their might before God, with songs and with harps, lyres, tambourines, cymbals and trumpets.[a]

9When they came to the threshing floor of Kidon, Uzzah reached out his hand to steady the ark, because the oxen stumbled. 10The LORD's anger[b] burned against Uzzah, and he struck him down[c] because he had put his hand on the ark. So he died there before God.

11Then David was angry because the LORD's wrath had broken out against Uzzah, and to this day that place is called Perez Uzzah.[a][d]

12David was afraid of God that day and asked, "How can I ever bring the ark of God to me?" 13He did not take the ark to be with him in the City of David. Instead, he took it aside to the house of Obed-Edom[e] the Gittite. 14The ark of God remained with the family of Obed-Edom in his house for three months, and the LORD blessed his household[f] and everything he had.

Chapter 14 Theme ______________________________________

14 Now Hiram king of Tyre sent messengers to David, along with cedar logs,[g] stonemasons and carpenters to build a palace for him. 2And David knew that the LORD had established him as king over Israel and that his kingdom had been highly exalted[h] for the sake of his people Israel.

3In Jerusalem David took more wives and became the father of more sons[i] and daughters. 4These are the names of the children born to him there:[j] Shammua, Shobab, Nathan, Solomon, 5Ibhar, Elishua, Elpelet, 6Nogah, Nepheg, Japhia, 7Elishama, Beeliada[b] and Eliphelet.

8When the Philistines heard that David had been anointed king over all Israel,[k] they went up in full force to search for him, but David heard about it and went out to meet them. 9Now the Philistines had come and raided the Valley[l] of Rephaim; 10so David inquired of God: "Shall I go and attack the Philistines? Will you hand them over to me?"

The LORD answered him, "Go, I will hand them over to you."

11So David and his men went up to Baal Perazim,[m] and there he defeated them. He said, "As waters break out, God has broken out against my enemies by my hand." So that place was called Baal Perazim.[c] 12The Philistines had abandoned their gods there, and David gave orders to burn[n] them in the fire.[o]

13Once more the Philistines raided the valley;[p] 14so David inquired of God again, and God answered him, "Do not go straight up, but circle around them and attack them in front of the balsam trees. 15As soon as you hear the sound of marching in the tops of

[a]11 *Perez Uzzah* means *outbreak against Uzzah.* [b]7 A variant of *Eliada* [c]11 *Baal Perazim* means *the lord who breaks out.*

13:8 [a]2Sa 6:5; 1Ch 15:16, 19,24; 2Ch 5:12; Ps 92:3
13:10 [b]1Ch 15:13,15 [c]Lev 10:2
13:11 [d]1Ch 15:13; Ps 7:11
13:13 [e]1Ch 15:18, 24; 16:38; 26:4-5,15
13:14 [f]2Sa 6:11; 1Ch 26:4-5
14:1 [g]2Ch 2:3; Ezr 3:7
14:2 [h]Nu 24:7; Dt 26:19
14:3 [i]1Ch 3:1
14:4 [j]1Ch 3:9
14:8 [k]1Ch 11:1
14:9 [l]ver 13; Jos 15:8; 1Ch 11:15
14:11 [m]Isa 28:21
14:12 [n]Ex 32:20 [o]Jos 7:15
14:13 [p]ver 9

the balsam trees, move out to battle, because that will mean God
has gone out in front of you to strike the Philistine army." 16So
David did as God commanded him, and they struck down the
Philistine army, all the way from Gibeon[a] to Gezer.[b]
17So David's fame[c] spread throughout every land, and the LORD
made all the nations fear[d] him.

Chapter 15 Theme ____________________

15 After David had constructed buildings for himself in the
City of David, he prepared[e] a place for the ark of God and
pitched[f] a tent for it. 2Then David said, "No one but the Levites[g]
may carry[h] the ark of God, because the LORD chose them to carry
the ark of the LORD and to minister[i] before him forever."
3David assembled all Israel[j] in Jerusalem to bring up the ark of
the LORD to the place he had prepared for it. 4He called together
the descendants of Aaron and the Levites:

5From the descendants of Kohath,
Uriel the leader and 120 relatives;
6from the descendants of Merari,
Asaiah the leader and 220 relatives;
7from the descendants of Gershon,[a]
Joel the leader and 130 relatives;
8from the descendants of Elizaphan,[k]
Shemaiah the leader and 200 relatives;
9from the descendants of Hebron,[l]
Eliel the leader and 80 relatives;
10from the descendants of Uzziel,
Amminadab the leader and 112 relatives.

11Then David summoned Zadok[m] and Abiathar[n] the priests, and
Uriel, Asaiah, Joel, Shemaiah, Eliel and Amminadab the Levites.
12He said to them, "You are the heads of the Levitical families; you
and your fellow Levites are to consecrate[o] yourselves and bring up
the ark of the LORD, the God of Israel, to the place I have prepared
for it. 13It was because you, the Levites,[p] did not bring it up the first
time that the LORD our God broke out in anger against us.[q] We did
not inquire of him about how to do it in the prescribed way." 14So
the priests and Levites consecrated themselves in order to bring
up the ark of the LORD, the God of Israel. 15And the Levites carried
the ark of God with the poles on their shoulders, as Moses had
commanded[r] in accordance with the word of the LORD.

16David told the leaders of the Levites to appoint their brothers
as singers[s] to sing joyful songs, accompanied by musical instruments: lyres, harps and cymbals.[t]

[a]7 Hebrew *Gershom,* a variant of *Gershon*

14:16 [a]Jos 9:3 [b]Jos 10:33
14:17 [c]Jos 6:27; 2Ch 26:8 [d]Ex 15:14-16; Dt 2:25
15:1 [e]Ps 132:1-18 [f]1Ch 16:1; 17:1
15:2 [g]Nu 4:15; Dt 10:8; 2Ch 5:5 [h]Dt 31:9 [i]1Ch 23:13
15:3 [j]1Ki 8:1; 1Ch 13:5
15:8 [k]Ex 6:22
15:9 [l]Ex 6:18
15:11 [m]1Ch 12:28 [n]1Sa 22:20
15:12 [o]Ex 19:14-15; Lev 11:44; 2Ch 35:6
15:13 [p]1Ki 8:4 [q]2Sa 6:3; 1Ch 13:7-10
15:15 [r]Ex 25:14; Nu 4:5,15
15:16 [s]Ps 68:25 [t]1Ch 13:8; 25:1; Ne 12:27,36

[17]So the Levites appointed Heman[a] son of Joel; from his brothers,
Asaph[b] son of Berekiah; and from their brothers the Merarites,[c]
Ethan son of Kushaiah; [18]and with them their brothers next in
rank: Zechariah,[a] Jaaziel, Shemiramoth, Jehiel, Unni, Eliab, Benaiah, Maaseiah, Mattithiah, Eliphelehu, Mikneiah, Obed-Edom[d]
and Jeiel,[b] the gatekeepers.
[19]The musicians Heman,[e] Asaph and Ethan were to sound the
bronze cymbals; [20]Zechariah, Aziel, Shemiramoth, Jehiel, Unni,
Eliab, Maaseiah and Benaiah were to play the lyres according to
alamoth,[c] [21]and Mattithiah, Eliphelehu, Mikneiah, Obed-Edom,
Jeiel and Azaziah were to play the harps, directing according to
sheminith.[c] [22]Kenaniah the head Levite was in charge of the
singing; that was his responsibility because he was skillful at it.
[23]Berekiah and Elkanah were to be doorkeepers for the ark.
[24]Shebaniah, Joshaphat, Nethanel, Amasai, Zechariah, Benaiah and
Eliezer the priests were to blow trumpets[f] before the ark of God.
Obed-Edom and Jehiah were also to be doorkeepers for the ark.
[25]So David and the elders of Israel and the commanders of units
of a thousand went to bring up the ark[g] of the covenant of the LORD
from the house of Obed-Edom, with rejoicing. [26]Because God
had helped the Levites who were carrying the ark of the covenant
of the LORD, seven bulls and seven rams[h] were sacrificed. [27]Now
David was clothed in a robe of fine linen, as were all the Levites
who were carrying the ark, and as were the singers, and Kenaniah,
who was in charge of the singing of the choirs. David also wore a
linen ephod. [28]So all Israel brought up the ark of the covenant of
the LORD with shouts, with the sounding of rams' horns[i] and
trumpets, and of cymbals, and the playing of lyres and harps.

Robe of the Ephod

[29]As the ark of the covenant of the LORD was entering the City
of David, Michal daughter of Saul watched from a window. And
when she saw King David dancing and celebrating, she despised
him in her heart.

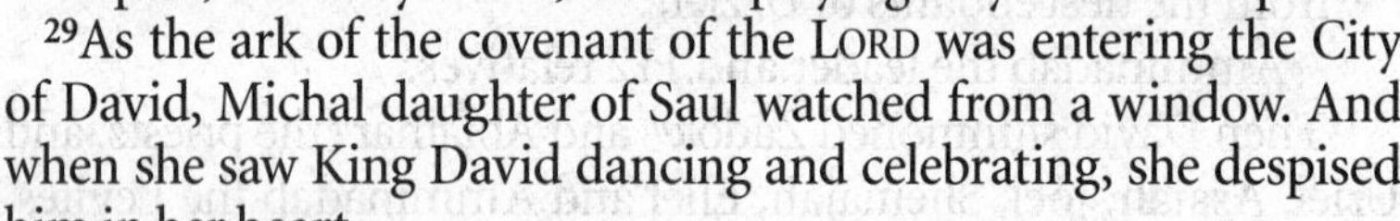

Chapter 16 Theme

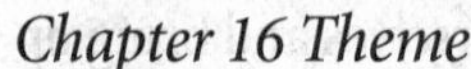

16 They brought the ark of God and set it inside the tent that
David had pitched[j] for it, and they presented burnt offerings
and fellowship offerings[d] before God. [2]After David had finished
sacrificing the burnt offerings and fellowship offerings, he blessed[k]
the people in the name of the LORD. [3]Then he gave a loaf of bread, a
cake of dates and a cake of raisins to each Israelite man and woman.
[4]He appointed some of the Levites to minister[l] before the ark of
the LORD, to make petition, to give thanks, and to praise the LORD,
the God of Israel: [5]Asaph was the chief, Zechariah second, then

15:17 *a* 1Ch 6:33 *b* 1Ch 6:39 *c* 1Ch 6:44
15:18 *d* 1Ch 26:4-5
15:19 *e* 1Ch 25:6
15:24 *f* ver 28; 1Ch 16:6; 2Ch 7:6
15:25 *g* 1Ch 13:13; 2Ch 1:4
15:26 *h* Nu 23:1-4,29
15:28 *i* 1Ch 13:8
16:1 *j* 1Ch 15:1
16:2 *k* Ex 39:43
16:4 *l* 1Ch 15:2

a *18* Three Hebrew manuscripts and most Septuagint manuscripts (see also verse 20 and 1Chron. 16:5); most Hebrew manuscripts *Zechariah son and* or *Zechariah, Ben and*
b *18* Hebrew; Septuagint (see also verse 21) *Jeiel and Azaziah* c *20,21* Probably a musical term
d *1* Traditionally *peace offerings*; also in verse 2

Jeiel, Shemiramoth, Jehiel, Mattithiah, Eliab, Benaiah, Obed-
Edom and Jeiel. They were to play the lyres and harps, Asaph was
to sound the cymbals, 6and Benaiah and Jahaziel the priests were
to blow the trumpets regularly before the ark of the covenant of
God.

7That day David first committed to Asaph and his associates
this psalm[a] of thanks to the LORD:

> 8Give thanks[b] to the LORD, call on his name;
>   make known among the nations[c] what he has done.
> 9Sing to him, sing praise[d] to him;
>   tell of all his wonderful acts.
> 10Glory in his holy name;
>   let the hearts of those who seek the LORD rejoice.
> 11Look to the LORD and his strength;
>   seek[e] his face always.
> 12Remember[f] the wonders he has done,
>   his miracles,[g] and the judgments he pronounced,
> 13O descendants of Israel his servant,
>   O sons of Jacob, his chosen ones.
>
> 14He is the LORD our God;
>   his judgments[h] are in all the earth.
> 15He remembers[a] his covenant forever,
>   the word he commanded, for a thousand generations,
> 16the covenant[i] he made with Abraham,
>   the oath he swore to Isaac.
> 17He confirmed it to Jacob[j] as a decree,
>   to Israel as an everlasting covenant:
> 18"To you I will give the land of Canaan[k]
>   as the portion you will inherit."
>
> 19When they were but few in number,[l]
>   few indeed, and strangers in it,
> 20they[b] wandered from nation to nation,
>   from one kingdom to another.
> 21He allowed no man to oppress them;
>   for their sake he rebuked kings:[m]
> 22"Do not touch my anointed ones;
>   do my prophets[n] no harm."
>
> 23Sing to the LORD, all the earth;
>   proclaim his salvation day after day.
> 24Declare his glory among the nations,

16:7 [a]2Sa 23:1
16:8 [b]ver 34; Ps 136:1 [c]2Ki 19:19
16:9 [d]Ex 15:1
16:11 [e]1Ch 28:9; 2Ch 7:14; Ps 24:6; 119:2,58
16:12 [f]Ps 77:11 [g]Ps 78:43
16:14 [h]Isa 26:9
16:16 [i]Ge 12:7; 15:18; 17:2; 22:16-18; 26:3; 28:13; 35:11
16:17 [j]Ge 35:9-12
16:18 [k]Ge 13:14-17
16:19 [l]Ge 34:30; Dt 7:7
16:21 [m]Ge 12:17; 20:3; Ex 7:15-18
16:22 [n]Ge 20:7

[a] *15* Some Septuagint manuscripts (see also Psalm 105:8); Hebrew *Remember* [b] *18-20* One Hebrew manuscript, Septuagint and Vulgate (see also Psalm 105:12); most Hebrew manuscripts *inherit, / 19though you are but few in number, / few indeed, and strangers in it." / 20They*

his marvelous deeds among all peoples.
[25]For great is the LORD and most worthy of praise;[a]
he is to be feared[b] above all gods.[c]
[26]For all the gods of the nations are idols,
but the LORD made the heavens.[d]
[27]Splendor and majesty are before him;
strength and joy in his dwelling place.
[28]Ascribe to the LORD, O families of nations,
ascribe to the LORD glory and strength,[e]
[29] ascribe to the LORD the glory due his name.
Bring an offering and come before him;
worship the LORD in the splendor of his[a] holiness.[f]
[30]Tremble[g] before him, all the earth!
The world is firmly established; it cannot be moved.
[31]Let the heavens rejoice, let the earth be glad;[h]
let them say among the nations, "The LORD reigns![i]"
[32]Let the sea resound, and all that is in it;[j]
let the fields be jubilant, and everything in them!
[33]Then the trees[k] of the forest will sing,
they will sing for joy before the LORD,
for he comes to judge[l] the earth.

[34]Give thanks[m] to the LORD, for he is good;[n]
his love endures forever.[o]
[35]Cry out, "Save us, O God our Savior;[p]
gather us and deliver us from the nations,
that we may give thanks to your holy name,
that we may glory in your praise."
[36]Praise be to the LORD, the God of Israel,[q]
from everlasting to everlasting.

Then all the people said "Amen" and "Praise the LORD."

[37]David left Asaph and his associates before the ark of the covenant of the LORD to minister there regularly, according to each
day's requirements.[r] [38]He also left Obed-Edom[s] and his sixty-eight
associates to minister with them. Obed-Edom son of Jeduthun,
and also Hosah,[t] were gatekeepers.
[39]David left Zadok[u] the priest and his fellow priests before the
tabernacle of the LORD at the high place in Gibeon[v] [40]to present
burnt offerings to the LORD on the altar of burnt offering regularly,
morning and evening, in accordance with everything written in
the Law[w] of the LORD, which he had given Israel. [41]With them were
Heman[x] and Jeduthun and the rest of those chosen and designated
by name to give thanks to the LORD, "for his love endures forever."
[42]Heman and Jeduthun were responsible for the sounding of the

a 29 Or *LORD with the splendor of*

16:25 [a]Ps 48:1 [b]Ps 76:7; 89:7 [c]Dt 32:39
16:26 [d]Lev 19:4; Ps 102:25
16:28 [e]Ps 29:1-2
16:29 [f]Ps 29:1-2
16:30 [g]Ps 114:7
16:31 [h]Isa 44:23; 49:13 [i]Ps 93:1
16:32 [j]Ps 98:7
16:33 [k]Isa 55:12 [l]Ps 96:10; 98:9
16:34 [m]ver 8 [n]Na 1:7 [o]2Ch 5:13; 7:3; Ezr 3:11; Ps 136:1-26; Jer 33:11
16:35 [p]Mic 7:7
16:36 [q]Dt 27:15; 1Ki 8:15; Ps 72:18-19
16:37 [r]2Ch 8:14
16:38 [s]1Ch 13:13 [t]1Ch 26:10
16:39 [u]2Sa 8:17; 1Ch 15:11 [v]1Ki 3:4; 2Ch 1:3
16:40 [w]Ex 29:38; Nu 28:1-8
16:41 [x]1Ch 6:33; 25:1-6; 2Ch 5:13

16:42 [a]2Ch 7:6 trumpets and cymbals and for the playing of the other instruments
for sacred song.[a] The sons of Jeduthun were stationed at the gate.
43Then all the people left, each for his own home, and David
returned home to bless his family.

17:1 [b]1Ch 15:1

Chapter 17 Theme ____

17 After David was settled in his palace, he said to Nathan the
prophet, "Here I am, living in a palace of cedar, while the
ark of the covenant of the LORD is under a tent.[b]"
2Nathan replied to David, "Whatever you have in mind,[c] do it,
17:2 [c]2Ch 6:7 for God is with you."
3That night the word of God came to Nathan, saying:
4"Go and tell my servant David, 'This is what the LORD says:
You[d] are not the one to build me a house to dwell in. 5I have not
17:4 dwelt in a house from the day I brought Israel up out of Egypt
[d]1Ch 28:3 to this day. I have moved from one tent site to another, from
one dwelling place to another. 6Wherever I have moved with
all the Israelites, did I ever say to any of their leaders[a] whom I
commanded to shepherd my people, "Why have you not built
17:7 me a house of cedar?"'
[e]2Sa 6:21 7"Now then, tell my servant David, 'This is what the LORD
Almighty says: I took you from the pasture and from following
the flock, to be ruler[e] over my people Israel. 8I have been with
you wherever you have gone, and I have cut off all your ene-
17:10 mies from before you. Now I will make your name like the
[f]Jdg 2:16 names of the greatest men of the earth. 9And I will provide a
place for my people Israel and will plant them so that they can
have a home of their own and no longer be disturbed. Wicked
people will not oppress them anymore, as they did at the begin-
17:12 ning 10and have done ever since the time I appointed leaders[f]
[g]1Ki 5:5 [h]2Ch 7:18 over my people Israel. I will also subdue all your enemies.
"'I declare to you that the LORD will build a house for you:
11When your days are over and you go to be with your fathers,
I will raise up your offspring to succeed you, one of your own
sons, and I will establish his kingdom. 12He is the one who will
17:13 [i]2Co 6:18 build[g] a house for me, and I will establish his throne forever.[h]
[j]Lk 1:32; Heb 1:5* 13I will be his father,[i] and he will be my son.[j] I will never take
my love away from him, as I took it away from your predeces-
sor. 14I will set him over my house and my kingdom forever;
his throne[k] will be established forever.[l]'"

17:14 15Nathan reported to David all the words of this entire revelation.
[k]1Ki 2:12; 1Ch 28:5 16Then King David went in and sat before the LORD, and he said:

[l]Ps 132:11; Jer 33:17

[a]6 Traditionally *judges*; also in verse 10

"Who am I, O LORD God, and what is my family, that you
have brought me this far? 17And as if this were not enough in
your sight, O God, you have spoken about the future of the
house of your servant. You have looked on me as though I were
the most exalted of men, O LORD God.
18"What more can David say to you for honoring your servant? For you know your servant, 19O LORD. For the sake[a] of
your servant and according to your will, you have done this
great thing and made known all these great promises.[b]
20"There is no one like you, O LORD, and there is no God but
you,[c] as we have heard with our own ears. 21And who is like
your people Israel—the one nation on earth whose God went
out to redeem[d] a people for himself, and to make a name for
yourself, and to perform great and awesome wonders by driving
out nations from before your people, whom you redeemed
from Egypt? 22You made your people Israel your very own forever,[e] and you, O LORD, have become their God.
23"And now, LORD, let the promise[f] you have made concerning your servant and his house be established forever. Do as
you promised, 24so that it will be established and that your
name will be great forever. Then men will say, 'The LORD
Almighty, the God over Israel, is Israel's God!' And the house
of your servant David will be established before you.
25"You, my God, have revealed to your servant that you will
build a house for him. So your servant has found courage to
pray to you. 26O LORD, you are God! You have promised these
good things to your servant. 27Now you have been pleased to
bless the house of your servant, that it may continue forever
in your sight;[g] for you, O LORD, have blessed it, and it will be
blessed forever."

Chapter 18 Theme ______________________________

18 In the course of time, David defeated the Philistines and
subdued them, and he took Gath and its surrounding villages from the control of the Philistines.
2David also defeated the Moabites,[h] and they became subject to
him and brought tribute.
3Moreover, David fought Hadadezer king of Zobah,[i] as far as
Hamath, when he went to establish his control along the Euphrates
River.[j] 4David captured a thousand of his chariots, seven thousand
charioteers and twenty thousand foot soldiers. He hamstrung[k] all
but a hundred of the chariot horses.
5When the Arameans of Damascus[l] came to help Hadadezer
king of Zobah, David struck down twenty-two thousand of them.
6He put garrisons in the Aramean kingdom of Damascus, and

17:19 [a] 2Sa 7:16-17; 2Ki 20:6; Isa 9:7; 37:35; 55:3 [b] 2Sa 7:25
17:20 [c] Ex 8:10; 9:14; 15:11; Isa 44:6; 46:9
17:21 [d] Ex 6:6
17:22 [e] Ex 19:5-6
17:23 [f] 1Ki 8:25
17:27 [g] Ps 16:11; 21:6
18:2 [h] Nu 21:29
18:3 [i] 1Ch 19:6 [j] Ge 2:14
18:4 [k] Ge 49:6
18:5 [l] 2Ki 16:9; 1Ch 19:6

the Arameans became subject to him and brought tribute. The LORD gave David victory everywhere he went.

7 David took the gold shields carried by the officers of Hadadezer and brought them to Jerusalem. 8 From Tebah[a] and Cun, towns that belonged to Hadadezer, David took a great quantity of bronze, which Solomon used to make the bronze Sea,[a] the pillars and various bronze articles.

9 When Tou king of Hamath heard that David had defeated the entire army of Hadadezer king of Zobah, 10 he sent his son Hadoram to King David to greet him and congratulate him on his victory in battle over Hadadezer, who had been at war with Tou. Hadoram brought all kinds of articles of gold and silver and bronze.

11 King David dedicated these articles to the LORD, as he had done with the silver and gold he had taken from all these nations: Edom[b] and Moab, the Ammonites and the Philistines, and Amalek.[c]

12 Abishai son of Zeruiah struck down eighteen thousand Edomites[d] in the Valley of Salt. 13 He put garrisons in Edom, and all the Edomites became subject to David. The LORD gave David victory everywhere he went.

14 David reigned[e] over all Israel,[f] doing what was just and right for all his people. 15 Joab[g] son of Zeruiah was over the army; Jehoshaphat son of Ahilud was recorder; 16 Zadok[h] son of Ahitub and Ahimelech[b][i] son of Abiathar were priests; Shavsha was secretary; 17 Benaiah son of Jehoiada was over the Kerethites and Pelethites;[j] and David's sons were chief officials at the king's side.

- - - - - Border of David's empire

The Borders of David's Empire

18:8 [a] 1Ki 7:23; 2Ch 4:12, 15-16
18:11 [b] Nu 24:18 [c] Nu 24:20
18:12 [d] 1Ki 11:15
18:14 [e] 1Ch 29:26 [f] 1Ch 11:1
18:15 [g] 2Sa 5:6-8; 1Ch 11:6
18:16 [h] 2Sa 8:17; 1Ch 6:8 [i] 1Ch 24:6
18:17 [j] 1Sa 30:14; 2Sa 8:18; 15:18

[a] 8 Hebrew *Tibhath,* a variant of *Tebah* [b] *16* Some Hebrew manuscripts, Vulgate and Syriac (see also 2 Samuel 8:17); most Hebrew manuscripts *Abimelech*

Chapter 19 Theme ____

19 In the course of time, Nahash king of the Ammonites[a] died,
and his son succeeded him as king. 2David thought, "I will
show kindness to Hanun son of Nahash, because his father showed
kindness to me." So David sent a delegation to express his sympathy to Hanun concerning his father.

When David's men came to Hanun in the land of the Ammonites to express sympathy to him, 3the Ammonite nobles said to
Hanun, "Do you think David is honoring your father by sending
men to you to express sympathy? Haven't his men come to you to
explore and spy out[b] the country and overthrow it?" 4So Hanun
seized David's men, shaved them, cut off their garments in the
middle at the buttocks, and sent them away.

5When someone came and told David about the men, he sent
messengers to meet them, for they were greatly humiliated. The
king said, "Stay at Jericho till your beards have grown, and then
come back."

6When the Ammonites realized that they had become a stench[c] in
David's nostrils, Hanun and the Ammonites sent a thousand talents[a] of silver to hire chariots and charioteers from Aram Naharaim,[b] Aram Maacah and Zobah.[d] 7They hired thirty-two thousand
chariots and charioteers, as well as the king of Maacah with his
troops, who came and camped near Medeba,[e] while the Ammonites
were mustered from their towns and moved out for battle.

8On hearing this, David sent Joab out with the entire army of
fighting men. 9The Ammonites came out and drew up in battle
formation at the entrance to their city, while the kings who had
come were by themselves in the open country.

10Joab saw that there were battle lines in front of him and behind
him; so he selected some of the best troops in Israel and deployed
them against the Arameans. 11He put the rest of the men under the
command of Abishai[f] his brother, and they were deployed against
the Ammonites. 12Joab said, "If the Arameans are too strong for
me, then you are to rescue me; but if the Ammonites are too strong
for you, then I will rescue you. 13Be strong and let us fight bravely
for our people and the cities of our God. The LORD will do what is
good in his sight."

14Then Joab and the troops with him advanced to fight the
Arameans, and they fled before him. 15When the Ammonites saw
that the Arameans were fleeing, they too fled before his brother
Abishai and went inside the city. So Joab went back to Jerusalem.

16After the Arameans saw that they had been routed by Israel,
they sent messengers and had Arameans brought from beyond the

19:1 [a]Ge 19:38; Jdg 10:17–11:33; 2Ch 20:1-2; Zep 2:8-11

19:3 [b]Nu 21:32

19:6 [c]Ge 34:30 [d]1Ch 18:3,5,9

19:7 [e]Nu 21:30; Jos 13:9,16

19:11 [f]1Sa 26:6

a6 That is, about 37 tons (about 34 metric tons) b6 That is, Northwest Mesopotamia

River,[a] with Shophach the commander of Hadadezer's army leading them.

17When David was told of this, he gathered all Israel[a] and crossed the Jordan; he advanced against them and formed his battle lines opposite them. David formed his lines to meet the Arameans in battle, and they fought against him. 18But they fled before Israel, and David killed seven thousand of their charioteers and forty thousand of their foot soldiers. He also killed Shophach the commander of their army.

19When the vassals of Hadadezer saw that they had been defeated by Israel, they made peace with David and became subject to him.

So the Arameans were not willing to help the Ammonites anymore.

Chapter 20 Theme ____________________

20

In the spring, at the time when kings go off to war, Joab led out the armed forces. He laid waste the land of the Ammonites and went to Rabbah[b] and besieged it, but David remained in Jerusalem. Joab attacked Rabbah and left it in ruins.[c] 2David took the crown from the head of their king[b]—its weight was found to be a talent[c] of gold, and it was set with precious stones—and it was placed on David's head. He took a great quantity of plunder from the city 3and brought out the people who were there, consigning them to labor with saws and with iron picks and axes.[d] David did this to all the Ammonite towns. Then David and his entire army returned to Jerusalem.

4In the course of time, war broke out with the Philistines, at Gezer.[e] At that time Sibbecai the Hushathite killed Sippai, one of the descendants of the Rephaites,[f] and the Philistines were subjugated.

5In another battle with the Philistines, Elhanan son of Jair killed Lahmi the brother of Goliath the Gittite, who had a spear with a shaft like a weaver's rod.[g]

6In still another battle, which took place at Gath, there was a huge man with six fingers on each hand and six toes on each foot—twenty-four in all. He also was descended from Rapha. 7When he taunted Israel, Jonathan son of Shimea, David's brother, killed him.

8These were descendants of Rapha in Gath, and they fell at the hands of David and his men.

Chapter 21 Theme ____________________

21

Satan[h] rose up against Israel and incited David to take a census[i] of Israel. 2So David said to Joab and the commanders of the troops, "Go and count[j] the Israelites from Beersheba to

19:17 [a] 1Ch 9:1
20:1 [b] Dt 3:11; 2Sa 12:26 [c] Am 1:13-15
20:3 [d] Dt 29:11
20:4 [e] Jos 10:33 [f] Ge 14:5
20:5 [g] 1Sa 17:7
21:1 [h] 2Ch 18:21; Ps 109:6 [i] 2Ch 14:8; 25:5
21:2 [j] 1Ch 27:23-24

[a] 16 That is, the Euphrates [b] 2 Or *of Milcom,* that is, Molech [c] 2 That is, about 75 pounds (about 34 kilograms)

Dan. Then report back to me so that I may know how many there are."

3 But Joab replied, "May the LORD multiply his troops a hundred times over.[a] My lord the king, are they not all my lord's subjects? Why does my lord want to do this? Why should he bring guilt on Israel?"

4 The king's word, however, overruled Joab; so Joab left and went throughout Israel and then came back to Jerusalem. 5 Joab reported the number of the fighting men to David: In all Israel[b] there were one million one hundred thousand men who could handle a sword, including four hundred and seventy thousand in Judah.

6 But Joab did not include Levi and Benjamin in the numbering, because the king's command was repulsive to him. 7 This command was also evil in the sight of God; so he punished Israel.

8 Then David said to God, "I have sinned greatly by doing this. Now, I beg you, take away the guilt of your servant. I have done a very foolish thing."

9 The LORD said to Gad,[c] David's seer,[d] 10 "Go and tell David, 'This is what the LORD says: I am giving you three options. Choose one of them for me to carry out against you.'"

11 So Gad went to David and said to him, "This is what the LORD says: 'Take your choice: 12 three years of famine,[e] three months of being swept away[a] before your enemies, with their swords overtaking you, or three days of the sword[f] of the LORD[g]—days of plague in the land, with the angel of the LORD ravaging every part of Israel.' Now then, decide how I should answer the one who sent me."

13 David said to Gad, "I am in deep distress. Let me fall into the hands of the LORD, for his mercy[h] is very great; but do not let me fall into the hands of men."

14 So the LORD sent a plague on Israel, and seventy thousand men of Israel fell dead.[i] 15 And God sent an angel[j] to destroy Jerusalem.[k] But as the angel was doing so, the LORD saw it and was grieved[l] because of the calamity and said to the angel who was destroying[m] the people, "Enough! Withdraw your hand." The angel of the LORD was then standing at the threshing floor of Araunah[b] the Jebusite.

16 David looked up and saw the angel of the LORD standing between heaven and earth, with a drawn sword in his hand extended over Jerusalem. Then David and the elders, clothed in sackcloth, fell facedown.[n]

17 David said to God, "Was it not I who ordered the fighting men to be counted? I am the one who has sinned and done wrong. These are but sheep.[o] What have they done? O LORD my God, let

[a] 12 Hebrew; Septuagint and Vulgate (see also 2 Samuel 24:13) *of fleeing* [b] 15 Hebrew *Ornan*, a variant of *Araunah*; also in verses 18-28

21:3 [a] Dt 1:11
21:5 [b] 1Ch 9:1
21:9 [c] 1Sa 22:5 [d] 1Sa 9:9
21:12 [e] Dt 32:24 [f] Eze 30:25 [g] Ge 19:13
21:13 [h] Ps 6:4; 86:15; 130:4,7
21:14 [i] 1Ch 27:24
21:15 [j] Ge 32:1 [k] Ps 125:2 [l] Ge 6:6; Ex 32:14 [m] Ge 19:13
21:16 [n] Nu 14:5; Jos 7:6
21:17 [o] 2Sa 7:8; Ps 74:1

21:17 your hand fall upon me and my family,[a] but do not let this plague
[a]Jnh 1:12 remain on your people."
[18]Then the angel of the LORD ordered Gad to tell David to go up
and build an altar to the LORD on the threshing floor[b] of Araunah
the Jebusite. [19]So David went up in obedience to the word that
21:18 Gad had spoken in the name of the LORD.
[b]2Ch 3:1 [20]While Araunah was threshing wheat,[c] he turned and saw the
angel; his four sons who were with him hid themselves. [21]Then
David approached, and when Araunah looked and saw him, he left
the threshing floor and bowed down before David with his face to
the ground.
21:20 [22]David said to him, "Let me have the site of your threshing floor
[c]Jdg 6:11 so I can build an altar to the LORD, that the plague on the people
may be stopped. Sell it to me at the full price."
[23]Araunah said to David, "Take it! Let my lord the king do whatever pleases him. Look, I will give the oxen for the burnt offerings,
21:26 the threshing sledges for the wood, and the wheat for the grain
[d]Lev 9:24; offering. I will give all this."
Jdg 6:21 [24]But King David replied to Araunah, "No, I insist on paying the
full price. I will not take for the LORD what is yours, or sacrifice a
burnt offering that costs me nothing."
[25]So David paid Araunah six hundred shekels[a] of gold for the
21:29 site. [26]David built an altar to the LORD there and sacrificed burnt
[e]1Ki 3:4; offerings and fellowship offerings.[b] He called on the LORD, and the
1Ch 16:39 LORD answered him with fire[d] from heaven on the altar of burnt
offering.
[27]Then the LORD spoke to the angel, and he put his sword back
into its sheath. [28]At that time, when David saw that the LORD had
22:1 answered him on the threshing floor of Araunah the Jebusite, he
[f]Ge 28:17; offered sacrifices there. [29]The tabernacle of the LORD, which Moses
1Ch 21:18-29; had made in the desert, and the altar of burnt offering were at that
2Ch 3:1 time on the high place at Gibeon.[e] [30]But David could not go before
it to inquire of God, because he was afraid of the sword of the angel
of the LORD.

INSIGHT

See 2 Chronicles 3:1 for what happened at this threshing floor.

22:2 *Chapter 22 Theme* ______________________

[g]1Ki 9:21; Isa 56:6 **22** Then David said, "The house of the LORD God[f] is to be here,
[h]1Ki 5:17-18 and also the altar of burnt offering for Israel."
[2]So David gave orders to assemble the aliens[g] living in Israel, and
from among them he appointed stonecutters[h] to prepare dressed
stone for building the house of God. [3]He provided a large amount
22:3 of iron to make nails for the doors of the gateways and for the fit-
[i]ver 14; 1Ki 7:47; 1Ch 29:2-5 tings, and more bronze than could be weighed.[i] [4]He also provided

a *25* That is, about 15 pounds (about 7 kilograms) b *26* Traditionally *peace offerings*

more cedar logs[a] than could be counted, for the Sidonians and Tyri-
ans had brought large numbers of them to David.
5David said, "My son Solomon is young[b] and inexperienced, and
the house to be built for the LORD should be of great magnificence
and fame and splendor in the sight of all the nations. Therefore I
will make preparations for it." So David made extensive preparations before his death.
6Then he called for his son Solomon and charged him to build[c]
a house for the LORD, the God of Israel. 7David said to Solomon:
"My son, I had it in my heart[d] to build[e] a house for the Name[f] of
the LORD my God. 8But this word of the LORD came to me: 'You
have shed much blood and have fought many wars.[g] You are not
to build a house for my Name,[h] because you have shed much
blood on the earth in my sight. 9But you will have a son who will
be a man of peace[i] and rest, and I will give him rest from all his
enemies on every side. His name will be Solomon,[a] [j] and I will
grant Israel peace and quiet[k] during his reign. 10He is the one who
will build a house for my Name.[l] He will be my son,[m] and I will
be his father. And I will establish the throne of his kingdom over
Israel forever.'[n]
11"Now, my son, the LORD be with[o] you, and may you have success and build the house of the LORD your God, as he said you
would. 12May the LORD give you discretion and understanding[p]
when he puts you in command over Israel, so that you may keep
the law of the LORD your God. 13Then you will have success if you
are careful to observe the decrees and laws[q] that the LORD gave
Moses for Israel. Be strong and courageous.[r] Do not be afraid or
discouraged.
14"I have taken great pains to provide for the temple of the LORD
a hundred thousand talents[b] of gold, a million talents[c] of silver,
quantities of bronze and iron too great to be weighed, and wood
and stone. And you may add to them.[s] 15You have many workmen: stonecutters, masons and carpenters, as well as men skilled
in every kind of work 16in gold and silver, bronze and iron—
craftsmen[t] beyond number. Now begin the work, and the LORD
be with you."
17Then David ordered[u] all the leaders of Israel to help his son
Solomon. 18He said to them, "Is not the LORD your God with you?
And has he not granted you rest[v] on every side?[w] For he has handed
the inhabitants of the land over to me, and the land is subject to
the LORD and to his people. 19Now devote your heart and soul to
seeking the LORD your God.[x] Begin to build the sanctuary of the
LORD God, so that you may bring the ark of the covenant of the

INSIGHT

There were basically three historical temples: ***Solomon's*** (pre-exilic), ***Zerubbabel's***, called the second temple (post-exilic), and ***Herod's*** (New Testament). Since Herod's Temple was an expansion/rebuilding of the second temple, it is often referred to as the second temple rather than "the third." All were located on a hill north of David's capital city, which he took from the Jebusites (2 Samuel 5:6, 7). David acquired the temple hill to build an altar and offer sacrifices (2 Samuel 24:18-25). Second Chronicles identifies this hill with Mount Moriah, where Abraham was willing to offer Isaac (2 Chronicles 3:1; Genesis 22:1-14).

22:4 [a] 1Ki 5:6
22:5 [b] 1Ki 3:7; 1Ch 29:1
22:6 [c] Ac 7:47
22:7 [d] 1Ch 17:2 [e] 2Sa 7:2; 1Ki 8:17 [f] Dt 12:5,11
22:8 [g] 1Ki 5:3 [h] 1Ch 28:3
22:9 [i] 1Ki 5:4 [j] 2Sa 12:24 [k] 1Ki 4:20
22:10 [l] 1Ch 17:12 [m] 2Sa 7:13 [n] 2Sa 7:14; 2Ch 6:15
22:11 [o] ver 16
22:12 [p] 1Ki 3:9-12; 2Ch 1:10
22:13 [q] 1Ch 28:7 [r] Dt 31:6; Jos 1:6-9; 1Ch 28:20
22:14 [s] ver 3; 1Ch 29:2-5,19
22:16 [t] ver 11; 2Ch 2:7
22:17 [u] 1Ch 28:1-6
22:18 [v] ver 9; 1Ch 23:25 [w] 2Sa 7:1
22:19 [x] ver 7; 1Ki 8:6; 1Ch 28:9; 2Ch 5:7; 7:14

a 9 *Solomon* sounds like and may be derived from the Hebrew for *peace.* b 14 That is, about 3,750 tons (about 3,450 metric tons) c 14 That is, about 37,500 tons (about 34,500 metric tons)

LORD and the sacred articles belonging to God into the temple that
will be built for the Name of the LORD."

Chapter 23 Theme ______________________________

23

When David was old and full of years, he made his son
Solomon[a] king over Israel.[b]
2He also gathered together all the leaders of Israel, as well as the
priests and Levites. 3The Levites thirty years old or more[c] were
counted, and the total number of men was thirty-eight thousand.[d]
4David said, "Of these, twenty-four thousand are to supervise[e] the
work of the temple of the LORD and six thousand are to be officials
and judges.[f] 5Four thousand are to be gatekeepers and four thousand are to praise the LORD with the musical instruments[g] I have
provided for that purpose."[h]

6David divided[i] the Levites into groups corresponding to the
sons of Levi: Gershon, Kohath and Merari.

7Belonging to the Gershonites:
Ladan and Shimei.
8The sons of Ladan:
Jehiel the first, Zetham and Joel—three in all.
9The sons of Shimei:
Shelomoth, Haziel and Haran—three in all.
These were the heads of the families of Ladan.
10And the sons of Shimei:
Jahath, Ziza,[a] Jeush and Beriah.
These were the sons of Shimei—four in all.
11Jahath was the first and Ziza the second, but Jeush and
Beriah did not have many sons; so they were counted as
one family with one assignment.

12The sons of Kohath:[j]
Amram, Izhar, Hebron and Uzziel—four in all.
13The sons of Amram:[k]
Aaron and Moses.
Aaron was set apart,[l] he and his descendants forever, to
consecrate the most holy things, to offer sacrifices before
the LORD, to minister before him and to pronounce blessings[m] in his name forever. 14The sons of Moses the man[n] of
God were counted as part of the tribe of Levi.
15The sons of Moses:
Gershom and Eliezer.[o]
16The descendants of Gershom:[p]
Shubael was the first.

23:1 [a] 1Ki 1:33-39; 1Ch 28:5 [b] 1Ki 1:30; 1Ch 29:28
23:3 [c] ver 24; Nu 8:24 [d] Nu 4:3-49
23:4 [e] Ezr 3:8 [f] 1Ch 26:29; 2Ch 19:8
23:5 [g] 1Ch 15:16 [h] Ne 12:45
23:6 [i] 2Ch 8:14; 29:25
23:12 [j] Ex 6:18
23:13 [k] Ex 6:20; 28:1 [l] Ex 30:7-10; Dt 21:5 [m] Nu 6:23
23:14 [n] Dt 33:1
23:15 [o] Ex 18:4
23:16 [p] 1Ch 26:24-28

a *10* One Hebrew manuscript, Septuagint and Vulgate (see also verse 11); most Hebrew manuscripts *Zina*

17The descendants of Eliezer:
Rehabiah was the first.
Eliezer had no other sons, but the sons of Rehabiah were very numerous.
18The sons of Izhar:
Shelomith was the first.
19The sons of Hebron:[a]
Jeriah the first, Amariah the second, Jahaziel the third and Jekameam the fourth.
20The sons of Uzziel:
Micah the first and Isshiah the second.

21The sons of Merari:[b]
Mahli and Mushi.
The sons of Mahli:
Eleazar and Kish.
22Eleazar died without having sons: he had only daughters. Their cousins, the sons of Kish, married them.
23The sons of Mushi:
Mahli, Eder and Jerimoth—three in all.

24These were the descendants of Levi by their families—the
heads of families as they were registered under their names and
counted individually, that is, the workers twenty years old or more[c]
who served in the temple of the LORD. 25For David had said, "Since
the LORD, the God of Israel, has granted rest[d] to his people and has
come to dwell in Jerusalem forever, 26the Levites no longer need
to carry the tabernacle or any of the articles used in its service."[e]
27According to the last instructions of David, the Levites were
counted from those twenty years old or more.

28The duty of the Levites was to help Aaron's descendants in
the service of the temple of the LORD: to be in charge of the courtyards, the side rooms, the purification[f] of all sacred things and
the performance of other duties at the house of God. 29They were
in charge of the bread set out on the table,[g] the flour for the grain
offerings,[h] the unleavened wafers, the baking and the mixing, and
all measurements of quantity and size.[i] 30They were also to stand
every morning to thank and praise the LORD. They were to do the
same in the evening[j] 31and whenever burnt offerings were presented to the LORD on Sabbaths and at New Moon[k] festivals and
at appointed feasts.[l] They were to serve before the LORD regularly
in the proper number and in the way prescribed for them.

32And so the Levites[m] carried out their responsibilities for the
Tent of Meeting,[n] for the Holy Place and, under their brothers the
descendants of Aaron, for the service of the temple of the LORD.[o]

23:19 [a]1Ch 24:23
23:21 [b]1Ch 24:26
23:24 [c]Nu 4:3; 10:17,21
23:25 [d]1Ch 22:9
23:26 [e]Nu 4:5,15; 7:9; Dt 10:8
23:28 [f]2Ch 29:15; Ne 13:9; Mal 3:3
23:29 [g]Ex 25:30 [h]Lev 2:4-7; 6:20-23 [i]Lev 19:35-36; 1Ch 9:29,32
23:30 [j]1Ch 9:33; Ps 134:1
23:31 [k]2Ki 4:23 [l]Lev 23:4; Nu 28:9–29:39; Isa 1:13-14; Col 2:16
23:32 [m]Nu 1:53; 1Ch 6:48 [n]Nu 3:6-8,38 [o]2Ch 23:18; 31:2; Eze 44:14

Chapter 24 Theme ______________________

24 These were the divisions[a] of the sons of Aaron:[b]
The sons of Aaron were Nadab, Abihu, Eleazar and Ithamar.[c] 2 But Nadab and Abihu died before their father did,[d] and
they had no sons; so Eleazar and Ithamar served as the priests.
3 With the help of Zadok[e] a descendant of Eleazar and Ahimelech a
descendant of Ithamar, David separated them into divisions for
their appointed order of ministering. 4 A larger number of leaders
were found among Eleazar's descendants than among Ithamar's,
and they were divided accordingly: sixteen heads of families from
Eleazar's descendants and eight heads of families from Ithamar's
descendants. 5 They divided them impartially by drawing lots,[f] for
there were officials of the sanctuary and officials of God among the
descendants of both Eleazar and Ithamar.

6 The scribe Shemaiah son of Nethanel, a Levite, recorded their
names in the presence of the king and of the officials: Zadok the
priest, Ahimelech[g] son of Abiathar and the heads of families of the
priests and of the Levites—one family being taken from Eleazar
and then one from Ithamar.

7 The first lot fell to Jehoiarib,
the second to Jedaiah,[h]
8 the third to Harim,[i]
the fourth to Seorim,
9 the fifth to Malkijah,
the sixth to Mijamin,
10 the seventh to Hakkoz,
the eighth to Abijah,[j]
11 the ninth to Jeshua,
the tenth to Shecaniah,
12 the eleventh to Eliashib,
the twelfth to Jakim,
13 the thirteenth to Huppah,
the fourteenth to Jeshebeab,
14 the fifteenth to Bilgah,
the sixteenth to Immer,[k]
15 the seventeenth to Hezir,[l]
the eighteenth to Happizzez,
16 the nineteenth to Pethahiah,
the twentieth to Jehezkel,
17 the twenty-first to Jakin,
the twenty-second to Gamul,
18 the twenty-third to Delaiah
and the twenty-fourth to Maaziah.

24:1
[a] 1Ch 23:6; 28:13; 2Ch 5:11; 8:14; 23:8; 31:2; 35:4,5; Ezr 6:18
[b] Nu 3:2-4
[c] Ex 6:23

24:2
[d] Lev 10:1-2; Nu 3:4

24:3
[e] 2Sa 8:17

24:5
[f] ver 31; 1Ch 25:8

24:6
[g] 1Ch 18:16

24:7
[h] Ezr 2:36; Ne 12:6

24:8
[i] Ezr 2:39; Ne 10:5

24:10
[j] Ne 12:4,17; Lk 1:5

24:14
[k] Jer 20:1

24:15
[l] Ne 10:20

19This was their appointed order of ministering when they
entered the temple of the LORD, according to the regulations prescribed for them by their forefather Aaron, as the LORD, the God
of Israel, had commanded him.

20As for the rest of the descendants of Levi:[a]
from the sons of Amram: Shubael;
from the sons of Shubael: Jehdeiah.
21As for Rehabiah,[b] from his sons:
Isshiah was the first.
22From the Izharites: Shelomoth;
from the sons of Shelomoth: Jahath.
23The sons of Hebron:[c] Jeriah the first,[a] Amariah the second,
Jahaziel the third and Jekameam the fourth.
24The son of Uzziel: Micah;
from the sons of Micah: Shamir.
25The brother of Micah: Isshiah;
from the sons of Isshiah: Zechariah.
26The sons of Merari:[d] Mahli and Mushi.
The son of Jaaziah: Beno.
27The sons of Merari:
from Jaaziah: Beno, Shoham, Zaccur and Ibri.
28From Mahli: Eleazar, who had no sons.
29From Kish: the son of Kish:
Jerahmeel.
30And the sons of Mushi: Mahli, Eder and Jerimoth.

These were the Levites, according to their families. 31They also
cast lots,[e] just as their brothers the descendants of Aaron did, in
the presence of King David and of Zadok, Ahimelech, and the
heads of families of the priests and of the Levites. The families of
the oldest brother were treated the same as those of the youngest.

Chapter 25 Theme ______________________

25 David, together with the commanders of the army, set apart
some of the sons of Asaph,[f] Heman[g] and Jeduthun[h] for the
ministry of prophesying,[i] accompanied by harps, lyres and cymbals.[j] Here is the list of the men[k] who performed this service:[l]

2From the sons of Asaph:
Zaccur, Joseph, Nethaniah and Asarelah. The sons of Asaph
were under the supervision of Asaph, who prophesied under
the king's supervision.
3As for Jeduthun, from his sons:[m]
Gedaliah, Zeri, Jeshaiah, Shimei,[b]Hashabiah and Mattithiah,

[a]23 Two Hebrew manuscripts and some Septuagint manuscripts (see also 1 Chron. 23:19); most Hebrew manuscripts *The sons of Jeriah:* [b]3 One Hebrew manuscript and some Septuagint manuscripts (see also verse 17); most Hebrew manuscripts do not have *Shimei.*

24:20 [a]1Ch 23:6
24:21 [b]1Ch 23:17
24:23 [c]1Ch 23:19
24:26 [d]1Ch 6:19; 23:21
24:31 [e]ver 5
25:1 [f]1Ch 6:39 [g]1Ch 6:33 [h]1Ch 16:41,42; Ne 11:17 [i]1Sa 10:5; 2Ki 3:15 [j]1Ch 15:16 [k]1Ch 6:31 [l]2Ch 5:12; 8:14; 34:12; 35:15; Ezr 3:10
25:3 [m]1Ch 16:41-42

25:3 [a]Ge 4:21; Ps 33:2

six in all, under the supervision of their father Jeduthun, who
prophesied, using the harp[a] in thanking and praising the LORD.
4As for Heman, from his sons:
Bukkiah, Mattaniah, Uzziel, Shubael and Jerimoth; Hananiah,
Hanani, Eliathah, Giddalti and Romamti-Ezer; Joshbekashah,
Mallothi, Hothir and Mahazioth. 5All these were sons of
Heman the king's seer. They were given him through the
promises of God to exalt him.[a] God gave Heman fourteen sons
and three daughters.

6All these men were under the supervision of their fathers[b] for
the music of the temple of the LORD, with cymbals, lyres and harps,
for the ministry at the house of God. Asaph, Jeduthun and Heman[c]
were under the supervision of the king.[d] 7Along with their relatives—all of them trained and skilled in music for the LORD—they
numbered 288. 8Young and old alike, teacher as well as student,
cast lots[e] for their duties.

25:6 [b]1Ch 15:16 [c]1Ch 15:19 [d]2Ch 23:18; 29:25

9The first lot, which was for Asaph,[f] fell to Joseph,
his sons and relatives,[b] 12[c]
the second to Gedaliah,
he and his relatives and sons, 12
10the third to Zaccur,
his sons and relatives, 12
11the fourth to Izri,[d]
his sons and relatives, 12
12the fifth to Nethaniah,
his sons and relatives, 12
13the sixth to Bukkiah,
his sons and relatives, 12
14the seventh to Jesarelah,[e]
his sons and relatives, 12
15the eighth to Jeshaiah,
his sons and relatives, 12
16the ninth to Mattaniah,
his sons and relatives, 12
17the tenth to Shimei,
his sons and relatives, 12
18the eleventh to Azarel,[f]
his sons and relatives, 12
19the twelfth to Hashabiah,
his sons and relatives, 12
20the thirteenth to Shubael,
his sons and relatives, 12

25:8 [e]1Ch 26:13

25:9 [f]1Ch 6:39

[a]5 Hebrew *exalt the horn* [b]9 See Septuagint; Hebrew does not have *his sons and relatives.* [c]9 See the total in verse 7; Hebrew does not have *twelve.* [d]11 A variant of *Zeri* [e]14 A variant of *Asarelah* [f]18 A variant of *Uzziel*

21the fourteenth to Mattithiah,
his sons and relatives, 12
22the fifteenth to Jerimoth,
his sons and relatives, 12
23the sixteenth to Hananiah,
his sons and relatives, 12
24the seventeenth to Joshbekashah,
his sons and relatives, 12
25the eighteenth to Hanani,
his sons and relatives, 12
26the nineteenth to Mallothi,
his sons and relatives, 12
27the twentieth to Eliathah,
his sons and relatives, 12
28the twenty-first to Hothir,
his sons and relatives, 12
29the twenty-second to Giddalti,
his sons and relatives, 12
30the twenty-third to Mahazioth,
his sons and relatives, 12
31the twenty-fourth to Romamti-Ezer,
his sons and relatives, 12[a]

Chapter 26 Theme ______________________

26 The divisions of the gatekeepers:[b]

From the Korahites: Meshelemiah son of Kore, one of the sons of Asaph.
2Meshelemiah had sons:
Zechariah[c] the firstborn,
Jediael the second,
Zebadiah the third,
Jathniel the fourth,
3Elam the fifth,
Jehohanan the sixth
and Eliehoenai the seventh.
4Obed-Edom also had sons:
Shemaiah the firstborn,
Jehozabad the second,
Joah the third,
Sacar the fourth,
Nethanel the fifth,
5Ammiel the sixth,
Issachar the seventh
and Peullethai the eighth.
(For God had blessed Obed-Edom.[d])

25:31 [a] 1Ch 9:33
26:1 [b] 1Ch 9:17
26:2 [c] 1Ch 9:21
26:5 [d] 2Sa 6:10; 1Ch 13:13; 16:38

6 His son Shemaiah also had sons, who were leaders in their father's family because they were very capable men. 7 The sons of Shemaiah: Othni, Rephael, Obed and Elzabad; his relatives Elihu and Semakiah were also able men. 8 All these were descendants of Obed-Edom; they and their sons and their relatives were capable men with the strength to do the work—descendants of Obed-Edom, 62 in all.

9 Meshelemiah had sons and relatives, who were able men—18 in all.

10 Hosah the Merarite had sons: Shimri the first (although he was not the firstborn, his father had appointed him the first),[a] 11 Hilkiah the second, Tabaliah the third and Zechariah the fourth. The sons and relatives of Hosah were 13 in all.

12 These divisions of the gatekeepers, through their chief men, had duties for ministering[b] in the temple of the LORD, just as their relatives had. 13 Lots[c] were cast for each gate, according to their families, young and old alike.

14 The lot for the East Gate[d] fell to Shelemiah.[a] Then lots were cast for his son Zechariah,[e] a wise counselor, and the lot for the North Gate fell to him. 15 The lot for the South Gate fell to Obed-Edom,[f] and the lot for the storehouse fell to his sons. 16 The lots for the West Gate and the Shalleketh Gate on the upper road fell to Shuppim and Hosah.

Guard was alongside of guard: 17 There were six Levites a day on the east, four a day on the north, four a day on the south and two at a time at the storehouse. 18 As for the court to the west, there were four at the road and two at the court itself.

19 These were the divisions of the gatekeepers who were descendants of Korah and Merari.[g]

20 Their fellow Levites[h] were[b] in charge of the treasuries of the house of God and the treasuries for the dedicated things.[i]

21 The descendants of Ladan, who were Gershonites through Ladan and who were heads of families belonging to Ladan the Gershonite,[j] were Jehieli, 22 the sons of Jehieli, Zetham and his brother Joel. They were in charge of the treasuries[k] of the temple of the LORD.

23 From the Amramites, the Izharites, the Hebronites and the Uzzielites:[l]

24 Shubael,[m] a descendant of Gershom son of Moses, was the officer in charge of the treasuries. 25 His relatives through Eliezer: Rehabiah his son, Jeshaiah his son, Joram his son, Zicri his son and Shelomith[n] his son. 26 Shelomith and his

26:10 [a] Dt 21:16; 1Ch 5:1
26:12 [b] 1Ch 9:22
26:13 [c] 1Ch 24:5,31; 25:8
26:14 [d] 1Ch 9:18 [e] 1Ch 9:21
26:15 [f] 1Ch 13:13; 2Ch 25:24
26:19 [g] 2Ch 35:15; Ne 7:1; Eze 44:11
26:20 [h] 2Ch 24:5 [i] 1Ch 28:12
26:21 [j] 1Ch 23:7; 29:8
26:22 [k] 1Ch 9:26
26:23 [l] Nu 3:27
26:24 [m] 1Ch 23:16
26:25 [n] 1Ch 23:18

a *14* A variant of *Meshelemiah* b *20* Septuagint; Hebrew *As for the Levites, Ahijah was*

relatives were in charge of all the treasuries for the things
dedicated[a] by King David, by the heads of families who
were the commanders of thousands and commanders of
hundreds, and by the other army commanders. 27Some of
the plunder taken in battle they dedicated for the repair
of the temple of the LORD. 28And everything dedicated by
Samuel the seer[b] and by Saul son of Kish, Abner son of Ner
and Joab son of Zeruiah, and all the other dedicated things
were in the care of Shelomith and his relatives.

29From the Izharites: Kenaniah and his sons were assigned
duties away from the temple, as officials and judges[c] over
Israel.

30From the Hebronites: Hashabiah[d] and his relatives—seventeen hundred able men—were responsible in Israel west of
the Jordan for all the work of the LORD and for the king's
service. 31As for the Hebronites,[e] Jeriah was their chief
according to the genealogical records of their families. In
the fortieth[f] year of David's reign a search was made in
the records, and capable men among the Hebronites were
found at Jazer in Gilead. 32Jeriah had twenty-seven hundred relatives, who were able men and heads of families,
and King David put them in charge of the Reubenites, the
Gadites and the half-tribe of Manasseh for every matter
pertaining to God and for the affairs of the king.

Chapter 27 Theme ______________________

27 This is the list of the Israelites—heads of families, commanders of thousands and commanders of hundreds,
and their officers, who served the king in all that concerned the
army divisions that were on duty month by month throughout
the year. Each division consisted of 24,000 men.

2In charge of the first division, for the first month, was Jashobeam[g]
son of Zabdiel. There were 24,000 men in his division. 3He was
a descendant of Perez and chief of all the army officers for the
first month.

4In charge of the division for the second month was Dodai[h] the
Ahohite; Mikloth was the leader of his division. There were
24,000 men in his division.

5The third army commander, for the third month, was Benaiah[i]
son of Jehoiada the priest. He was chief and there were 24,000
men in his division. 6This was the Benaiah who was a mighty
man among the Thirty and was over the Thirty. His son
Ammizabad was in charge of his division.

26:26 [a] 2Sa 8:11
26:28 [b] 1Sa 9:9
26:29 [c] Dt 17:8-13; 1Ch 23:4; Ne 11:16
26:30 [d] 1Ch 27:17
26:31 [e] 1Ch 23:19 [f] 2Sa 5:4
27:2 [g] 2Sa 23:8; 1Ch 11:11
27:4 [h] 2Sa 23:9
27:5 [i] 2Sa 23:20

27:7 [a]2Sa 2:18; 1Ch 11:26
7 The fourth, for the fourth month, was Asahel[a] the brother of
Joab; his son Zebadiah was his successor. There were 24,000
men in his division.
8 The fifth, for the fifth month, was the commander Shamhuth[b]
27:8 [b]1Ch 11:27
the Izrahite. There were 24,000 men in his division.
9 The sixth, for the sixth month, was Ira[c] the son of Ikkesh the Teko-
ite. There were 24,000 men in his division.
27:9 [c]2Sa 23:26; 1Ch 11:28
10 The seventh, for the seventh month, was Helez[d] the Pelonite, an
Ephraimite. There were 24,000 men in his division.
11 The eighth, for the eighth month, was Sibbecai[e] the Hushathite,
a Zerahite. There were 24,000 men in his division.
27:10 [d]2Sa 23:26; 1Ch 11:27
12 The ninth, for the ninth month, was Abiezer[f] the Anathothite, a
Benjamite. There were 24,000 men in his division.
13 The tenth, for the tenth month, was Maharai[g] the Netophathite,
a Zerahite. There were 24,000 men in his division.
27:11 [e]2Sa 21:18
14 The eleventh, for the eleventh month, was Benaiah[h] the Pirathonite, an Ephraimite. There were 24,000 men in his division.
15 The twelfth, for the twelfth month, was Heldai[i] the Netophathite,
from the family of Othniel.[j] There were 24,000 men in his divi-
27:12 [f]2Sa 23:27; 1Ch 11:28
sion.

16 The officers over the tribes of Israel:

over the Reubenites: Eliezer son of Zicri;
27:13 [g]2Sa 23:28; 1Ch 11:30
over the Simeonites: Shephatiah son of Maacah;
17 over Levi: Hashabiah[k] son of Kemuel;
over Aaron: Zadok;[l]
18 over Judah: Elihu, a brother of David;
27:14 [h]1Ch 11:31
over Issachar: Omri son of Michael;
19 over Zebulun: Ishmaiah son of Obadiah;
over Naphtali: Jerimoth son of Azriel;
27:15 [i]2Sa 23:29 [j]Jos 15:17
20 over the Ephraimites: Hoshea son of Azaziah;
over half the tribe of Manasseh: Joel son of Pedaiah;
21 over the half-tribe of Manasseh in Gilead: Iddo son of Zechariah;
27:17 [k]1Ch 26:30 [l]2Sa 8:17; 1Ch 12:28
over Benjamin: Jaasiel son of Abner;
22 over Dan: Azarel son of Jeroham.
These were the officers over the tribes of Israel.

23 David did not take the number of the men twenty years old or
27:23 [m]1Ch 21:2-5 [n]Ge 15:5
less,[m] because the LORD had promised to make Israel as numerous
as the stars[n] in the sky. 24 Joab son of Zeruiah began to count the
men but did not finish. Wrath came on Israel on account of this
numbering,[o] and the number was not entered in the book[a] of the
annals of King David.
27:24 [o]2Sa 24:15; 1Ch 21:7

a 24 Septuagint; Hebrew *number*

25Azmaveth son of Adiel was in charge of the royal storehouses.
Jonathan son of Uzziah was in charge of the storehouses in the
outlying districts, in the towns, the villages and the watchtowers.
26Ezri son of Kelub was in charge of the field workers who
farmed the land.
27Shimei the Ramathite was in charge of the vineyards.
Zabdi the Shiphmite was in charge of the produce of the vineyards for the wine vats.
28Baal-Hanan the Gederite was in charge of the olive and
sycamore-fig[a] trees in the western foothills.
Joash was in charge of the supplies of olive oil.
29Shitrai the Sharonite was in charge of the herds grazing in
Sharon.
Shaphat son of Adlai was in charge of the herds in the valleys.
30Obil the Ishmaelite was in charge of the camels.
Jehdeiah the Meronothite was in charge of the donkeys.
31Jaziz the Hagrite[b] was in charge of the flocks.
All these were the officials in charge of King David's property.

32Jonathan, David's uncle, was a counselor, a man of insight and
a scribe. Jehiel son of Hacmoni took care of the king's sons.
33Ahithophel[c] was the king's counselor.
Hushai[d] the Arkite was the king's friend. 34Ahithophel was succeeded by Jehoiada son of Benaiah and by Abiathar.[e]
Joab[f] was the commander of the royal army.

Chapter 28 Theme ______________________

28 David summoned all the officials[g] of Israel to assemble at
Jerusalem: the officers over the tribes, the commanders of
the divisions in the service of the king, the commanders of thousands and commanders of hundreds, and the officials in charge of
all the property and livestock belonging to the king and his sons,
together with the palace officials, the mighty men and all the
brave warriors.
2King David rose to his feet and said: "Listen to me, my brothers
and my people. I had it in my heart[h] to build a house as a place of
rest for the ark of the covenant of the LORD, for the footstool[i] of
our God, and I made plans to build it. 3But God said to me,[j] 'You
are not to build a house for my Name,[k] because you are a warrior
and have shed blood.'[l]
4"Yet the LORD, the God of Israel, chose me[m] from my whole
family[n] to be king over Israel forever. He chose Judah[o] as leader,
and from the house of Judah he chose my family, and from my
father's sons he was pleased to make me king over all Israel. 5Of
all my sons—and the LORD has given me many[p]—he has chosen

27:28 [a] 1Ki 10:27; 2Ch 1:15
27:31 [b] 1Ch 5:10
27:33 [c] 2Sa 15:12 [d] 2Sa 15:37
27:34 [e] 1Ki 1:7 [f] 1Ch 11:6
28:1 [g] 1Ch 11:10; 27:1-31
28:2 [h] 1Ch 17:2 [i] Ps 99:5; 132:7
28:3 [j] 2Sa 7:5 [k] 1Ch 22:8 [l] 1Ki 5:3; 1Ch 17:4
28:4 [m] 1Ch 17:23,27; 2Ch 6:6 [n] 1Sa 16:1-13 [o] Ge 49:10; 1Ch 5:2
28:5 [p] 1Ch 3:1

28:5 [a]1Ch 22:9; 23:1 my son Solomon[a] to sit on the throne of the kingdom of the LORD
over Israel. 6He said to me: 'Solomon your son is the one who will
28:6 build my house and my courts, for I have chosen him to be my
[b]2Sa 7:13; son,[b] and I will be his father. 7I will establish his kingdom forever
1Ch 22:9-10 if he is unswerving in carrying out my commands and laws,[c] as is
being done at this time.'
28:7 [c]1Ch 22:13 8"So now I charge you in the sight of all Israel and of the assembly of the LORD, and in the hearing of our God: Be careful to follow
28:8 all the commands[d] of the LORD your God, that you may possess
[d]Dt 6:1 this good land and pass it on as an inheritance to your descendants
[e]Dt 4:1 forever.[e]
9"And you, my son Solomon, acknowledge the God of your
28:9 [f]1Ch 29:19 father, and serve him with wholehearted devotion[f] and with a
[g]1Sa 16:7; willing mind, for the LORD searches every heart[g] and understands
Ps 7:9 [h]Ps 40:16; every motive behind the thoughts. If you seek him,[h] he will be
Jer 29:13 [i]Jos 24:20; found by you; but if you forsake[i] him, he will reject[j] you forever.
2Ch 15:2 10Consider now, for the LORD has chosen you to build a temple as
[j]Ps 44:23 a sanctuary. Be strong and do the work."
11Then David gave his son Solomon the plans[k] for the portico of
28:11 [k]Ex 25:9 the temple, its buildings, its storerooms, its upper parts, its inner
rooms and the place of atonement. 12He gave him the plans of all
28:12 that the Spirit[l] had put in his mind for the courts of the temple of
[l]1Ch 12:18 the LORD and all the surrounding rooms, for the treasuries of the
[m]1Ch 26:20 temple of God and for the treasuries for the dedicated things.[m]
13He gave him instructions for the divisions[n] of the priests and
28:13 [n]1Ch 24:1 Levites, and for all the work of serving in the temple of the LORD,
as well as for all the articles to be used in its service. 14He designated
28:15 the weight of gold for all the gold articles to be used in various kinds
[o]Ex 25:31 of service, and the weight of silver for all the silver articles to be
used in various kinds of service: 15the weight of gold for the gold
28:16 [p]Ex 25:23 lampstands[o] and their lamps, with the weight for each lampstand
and its lamps; and the weight of silver for each silver lampstand and
28:17 its lamps, according to the use of each lampstand; 16the weight of
[q]Ex 27:3 gold for each table[p] for consecrated bread; the weight of silver for
the silver tables; 17the weight of pure gold for the forks, sprinkling
28:18 bowls[q] and pitchers; the weight of gold for each gold dish; the
[r]Ex 30:1-10 [s]Ex 25:18-22 weight of silver for each silver dish; 18and the weight of the refined
[t]Ex 25:20 gold for the altar of incense.[r] He also gave him the plan for the
chariot,[s] that is, the cherubim of gold that spread their wings and
28:19 [u]1Ki 6:38 shelter[t] the ark of the covenant of the LORD.
[v]Ex 25:9 19"All this," David said, "I have in writing from the hand of the
LORD upon me, and he gave me understanding in all the details[u]
28:20 [w]Dt 31:6; of the plan.[v] "
1Ch 22:13; 2Ch 19:11; 20David also said to Solomon his son, "Be strong and coura-
Hag 2:4 geous,[w] and do the work. Do not be afraid or discouraged, for the

LORD God, my God, is with you. He will not fail you or forsake[a] you until all the work for the service of the temple of the LORD is finished.[b] 21The divisions of the priests and Levites are ready for all the work on the temple of God, and every willing man skilled[c] in any craft will help you in all the work. The officials and all the people will obey your every command."

Chapter 29 Theme ______________________

29 Then King David said to the whole assembly: "My son Solomon, the one whom God has chosen, is young and inexperienced.[d] The task is great, because this palatial structure is not for man but for the LORD God. 2With all my resources I have provided for the temple of my God—gold[e] for the gold work, silver for the silver, bronze for the bronze, iron for the iron and wood for the wood, as well as onyx for the settings, turquoise,[a][f] stones of various colors, and all kinds of fine stone and marble—all of these in large quantities.[g] 3Besides, in my devotion to the temple of my God I now give my personal treasures of gold and silver for the temple of my God, over and above everything I have provided[h] for this holy temple: 4three thousand talents[b] of gold (gold of Ophir)[i] and seven thousand talents[c] of refined silver,[j] for the overlaying of the walls of the buildings, 5for the gold work and the silver work, and for all the work to be done by the craftsmen. Now, who is willing to consecrate himself today to the LORD?"

6Then the leaders of families, the officers of the tribes of Israel, the commanders of thousands and commanders of hundreds, and the officials[k] in charge of the king's work gave willingly.[l] 7They[m] gave toward the work on the temple of God five thousand talents[d] and ten thousand darics[e] of gold, ten thousand talents[f] of silver, eighteen thousand talents[g] of bronze and a hundred thousand talents[h] of iron. 8Any who had precious stones[n] gave them to the treasury of the temple of the LORD in the custody of Jehiel the Gershonite.[o] 9The people rejoiced at the willing response of their leaders, for they had given freely and wholeheartedly[p] to the LORD. David the king also rejoiced greatly.

10David praised the LORD in the presence of the whole assembly, saying,

"Praise be to you, O LORD,
God of our father Israel,
from everlasting to everlasting.

[a]2 The meaning of the Hebrew for this word is uncertain. [b]4 That is, about 110 tons (about 100 metric tons) [c]4 That is, about 260 tons (about 240 metric tons) [d]7 That is, about 190 tons (about 170 metric tons) [e]7 That is, about 185 pounds (about 84 kilograms) [f]7 That is, about 375 tons (about 345 metric tons) [g]7 That is, about 675 tons (about 610 metric tons) [h]7 That is, about 3,750 tons (about 3,450 metric tons)

28:20 [a]Dt 4:31; Jos 24:20 [b]1Ki 6:14; 2Ch 7:11
28:21 [c]Ex 35:25–36:5
29:1 [d]1Ki 3:7; 1Ch 22:5; 2Ch 13:7
29:2 [e]ver 7,14,16; Ezr 1:4; 6:5; Hag 2:8 [f]Isa 54:11 [g]1Ch 22:2-5
29:3 [h]2Ch 24:10; 31:3; 35:8
29:4 [i]Ge 10:29 [j]1Ch 22:14
29:6 [k]1Ch 27:1; 28:1 [l]ver 9; Ex 25:1-8; 35:20-29; 36:2; 2Ch 24:10; Ezr 7:15
29:7 [m]Ex 25:2; Ne 7:70-71
29:8 [n]Ex 35:27 [o]1Ch 26:21
29:9 [p]1Ki 8:61; 2Co 9:7

29:11 [a]Ps 24:8; 59:17; 62:11 [b]Ps 89:11 [c]Rev 5:12-13

11 Yours, O LORD, is the greatness and the power[a]
and the glory and the majesty and the splendor,
for everything in heaven and earth is yours.[b]
Yours, O LORD, is the kingdom;
you are exalted as head over all.[c]

29:12 [d]2Ch 1:12 [e]2Ch 20:6; Ro 11:36

12 Wealth and honor[d] come from you;
you are the ruler[e] of all things.
In your hands are strength and power
to exalt and give strength to all.
13 Now, our God, we give you thanks,
and praise your glorious name.

29:15 [f]Ps 39:12; Heb 11:13 [g]Job 14:2

14 "But who am I, and who are my people, that we should be able
to give as generously as this? Everything comes from you, and we
have given you only what comes from your hand. 15 We are aliens
and strangers[f] in your sight, as were all our forefathers. Our days
on earth are like a shadow,[g] without hope. 16 O LORD our God, as

29:17 [h]Ps 139:23; Pr 15:11; 17:3; Jer 11:20; 17:10 [i]1Ch 28:9; Ps 15:1-5

for all this abundance that we have provided for building you a
temple for your Holy Name, it comes from your hand, and all of it
belongs to you. 17 I know, my God, that you test the heart[h] and are
pleased with integrity. All these things have I given willingly and
with honest intent. And now I have seen with joy how willingly
your people who are here have given to you.[i] 18 O LORD, God of our
fathers Abraham, Isaac and Israel, keep this desire in the hearts of

29:19 [j]1Ch 28:9 [k]Ps 72:1 [l]1Ch 22:14

your people forever, and keep their hearts loyal to you. 19 And give
my son Solomon the wholehearted devotion[j] to keep your commands, requirements and decrees[k] and to do everything to build
the palatial structure for which I have provided."[l]

20 Then David said to the whole assembly, "Praise the LORD your

29:21 [m]1Ki 8:62

God." So they all praised the LORD, the God of their fathers; they
bowed low and fell prostrate before the LORD and the king.

21 The next day they made sacrifices to the LORD and presented
burnt offerings to him:[m] a thousand bulls, a thousand rams and a

29:22 [n]1Ch 23:1 [o]1Ki 1:33-39

thousand male lambs, together with their drink offerings, and
other sacrifices in abundance for all Israel. 22 They ate and drank
with great joy[n] in the presence of the LORD that day.

Then they acknowledged Solomon son of David as king a second time, anointing him before the LORD to be ruler and Zadok[o]

29:23 [p]1Ki 2:12

to be priest. 23 So Solomon sat on the throne[p] of the LORD as king
in place of his father David. He prospered and all Israel obeyed
him. 24 All the officers and mighty men, as well as all of King
David's sons, pledged their submission to King Solomon.

29:25 [q]2Ch 1:1,12 [r]1Ki 3:13; Ecc 2:9

25 The LORD highly exalted Solomon in the sight of all Israel and
bestowed on him royal splendor[q] such as no king over Israel ever
had before.[r]

[26]David son of Jesse was king[a] over all Israel. [27]He ruled over
Israel forty years—seven in Hebron and thirty-three in Jerusalem.[b]
[28]He died[c] at a good old age, having enjoyed long life, wealth and
honor. His son Solomon succeeded him as king.[d]
[29]As for the events of King David's reign, from beginning to end,
they are written in the records of Samuel the seer,[e] the records of
Nathan[f] the prophet and the records of Gad[g] the seer, [30]together
with the details of his reign and power, and the circumstances
that surrounded him and Israel and the kingdoms of all the other
lands.

29:26 [a]1Ch 18:14
29:27 [b]2Sa 5:4-5; 1Ki 2:11; 1Ch 3:4
29:28 [c]Ge 15:15; Ac 13:36 [d]1Ch 23:1
29:29 [e]1Sa 9:9 [f]2Sa 7:2 [g]1Sa 22:5

1 Chronicles at a Glance

heme of 1 Chronicles:

uthor:

ate:

urpose:

ey Words:

Segment Divisions

		Main Divisions		Chapter Themes
		The Genealogies of Israel	1	
			2	
			3	
			4	
			5	
			6	
			7	
			8	
			9	
		God Turns Kingdom to David	10	
			11	
			12	
			13	
			14	
			15	
			16	
			17	
			18	
			19	
			20	
		David Builds Altar, Prepares for God's Temple	21	
			22	
			23	
			24	
			25	
			26	
			27	
			28	
			29	

2 CHRONICLES

King David wanted to build a house for the Lord, but instead the Lord promised David he would establish David's house forever and that David's son would build God's house. At this point in the record of David's life the writers of the Septuagint divided Chronicles. Second Chronicles tells of the house of David and of the house that David's son built for the Lord.

Things to Do

If you haven't already done so, study 1 Chronicles (at the very least read the introduction to 1 Chronicles) before you begin your study of 2 Chronicles.

Second Chronicles is filled with truths and lessons for life which, if heeded, will help you in your pursuit of holiness. Second Chronicles focuses on the reigns of the kings of Judah and their relationship to God and his house from the time of Solomon until the Babylonian exile. Read all the instructions before you begin.

1. Examine every chapter in the light of the five W's and an H. Record your insights in the margin.
   a. Look for three *who's:* the king, the prophet, and the Lord. Of the three, the Lord and the king are most prominent. Ask: Who are the associates of the king? Who influences, opposes, or assists him?
   b. Look for *what* each king does, *what* God does in respect to that king, and *what* role the prophet plays, if any. In 2 Chronicles the "house" of God takes center stage; therefore, in each reign observe what the king's relationship is to the Lord and to his house.
   c. Also keep track of *when* events occur. Don't forget to note references to time with a symbol.
   d. Because this is a historical book, also watch *where* things occur.
   e. Observing *why* events occur will bring insight into the character and sovereignty of God in the affairs of men and nations. Keep asking why. If the king does evil, ask why.
   f. Ask *how*. How did the king seek the Lord? How did the king do evil? How did God respond?

2. Record your insights on the kings mentioned in 2 Chronicles. Transfer these insights to the chart THE KINGS OF ISRAEL AND JUDAH located on pages 654 and 655 between 2 Kings and 1 Chronicles.

3. On an index card make a list of the key repeated words printed on the 2 CHRONICLES AT A GLANCE chart on page 771. Use this list as a bookmark while you study 2 Chronicles.
   a. In the margin record all you learn from marking each of these key words. Note that after chapter 8, *ark,* one of the key words, is used once more in chapter 35.
   b. You will also observe key words and phrases which will play a major role in only one or two chapters. Don't miss these. They will come to the surface as you prayerfully read and meditate on a chapter.

4. As you study each chapter take notes in the margin of all you learn about God. You will gain rich and perhaps surprising insights. Also mark and record any lessons for life ("LFL").

5. Remember that 1 and 2 Chronicles were written as one book. Second Chronicles is a continuation of 1 Chronicles. Chronicles has a number of speeches, prophecies, and prayers, some of which are not mentioned in Samuel or Kings. Watch for these and pay attention to what is said, by whom, and why. Highlight or note your insights in the margin.

6. When you finish reading each chapter, record its theme on 2 CHRONICLES AT A GLANCE and on the line next to the chapter number. Also watch for the major historical events which occur in 2 Chronicles. Highlight these on the chart.

7. Complete 2 CHRONICLES AT A GLANCE. As you review the chapter themes you have recorded, see how this book could be segmented and record this under "Segment Divisions." Also, record the book's theme.

Things to Think About

1. Many lessons about prayer and seeking God can be learned from this book. Review what you have seen from marking the key words. Think about what you learned regarding sin, prayer, confession, and repentance in 2 Chronicles 6.

2. Second Chronicles is filled with illustrations of how people dealt with difficulties and testings. How did you relate to these people? What did you learn from their lives—men such as Asa, Jehoshaphat, Hezekiah, Uzziah? As you studied them, did God prick your heart? With what warnings or cautions?

3. What did you learn about the heart from this book? Do you serve the Lord wholeheartedly or half-heartedly? What did you learn about crying to the Lord? What happened to those who cried out to him? Did they always deserve to be heard?

4. What did you learn about the sovereignty of God? How active or involved is God in the affairs of men? What were the different ways God afflicted those who disobeyed? Do you have a healthy fear of God?

Chapter 1 Theme ____________________

1 Solomon son of David established[a] himself firmly over his
kingdom, for the LORD his God was with[b] him and made him
exceedingly great.[c]
2Then Solomon spoke to all Israel[d]—to the commanders of
thousands and commanders of hundreds, to the judges and to all
the leaders in Israel, the heads of families— 3and Solomon and
the whole assembly went to the high place at Gibeon, for God's
Tent of Meeting[e] was there, which Moses[f] the LORD's servant had
made in the desert. 4Now David had brought up the ark[g] of God
from Kiriath Jearim to the place he had prepared for it, because
he had pitched a tent[h] for it in Jerusalem. 5But the bronze altar[i] that
Bezalel[j] son of Uri, the son of Hur, had made was in Gibeon in
front of the tabernacle of the LORD; so Solomon and the assembly
inquired[k] of him there. 6Solomon went up to the bronze altar
before the LORD in the Tent of Meeting and offered a thousand
burnt offerings on it.
7That night God appeared[l] to Solomon and said to him, "Ask
for whatever you want me to give you."
8Solomon answered God, "You have shown great kindness to
David my father and have made me[m] king in his place. 9Now, LORD
God, let your promise[n] to my father David be confirmed, for you
have made me king over a people who are as numerous as the dust

1:1 [a]1Ki 2:12,26; 2Ch 12:1 [b]Ge 21:22; 39:2; Nu 14:43 [c]1Ch 29:25
1:2 [d]1Ch 9:1; 28:1
1:3 [e]Ex 36:8 [f]Ex 40:18
1:4 [g]2Sa 6:2; 1Ch 15:25 [h]2Sa 6:17; 1Ch 15:1
1:5 [i]Ex 38:2 [j]Ex 31:2 [k]1Ch 13:3
1:7 [l]2Ch 7:12
1:8 [m]1Ch 23:1; 28:5
1:9 [n]2Sa 7:25; 1Ki 8:25

INSIGHT

Read **The Ark of the Covenant** on page 2203.

of the earth.[a] 10Give me wisdom and knowledge, that I may lead[b] this people, for who is able to govern this great people of yours?"

11God said to Solomon, "Since this is your heart's desire and you have not asked for wealth,[c] riches or honor, nor for the death of your enemies, and since you have not asked for a long life but for wisdom and knowledge to govern my people over whom I have made you king, 12therefore wisdom and knowledge will be given you. And I will also give you wealth, riches and honor,[d] such as no king who was before you ever had and none after you will have.[e]"

13Then Solomon went to Jerusalem from the high place at Gibeon, from before the Tent of Meeting. And he reigned over Israel.

14Solomon accumulated chariots[f] and horses; he had fourteen hundred chariots and twelve thousand horses,[a] which he kept in the chariot cities and also with him in Jerusalem. 15The king made silver and gold[g] as common in Jerusalem as stones, and cedar as plentiful as sycamore-fig trees in the foothills. 16Solomon's horses were imported from Egypt[b] and from Kue[c]—the royal merchants purchased them from Kue. 17They imported a chariot[h] from Egypt for six hundred shekels[d] of silver, and a horse for a hundred and fifty.[e] They also exported them to all the kings of the Hittites and of the Arameans.

Chapter 2 Theme ________________________

2 Solomon gave orders to build a temple[i] for the Name of the LORD and a royal palace for himself.[j] 2He conscripted seventy thousand men as carriers and eighty thousand as stonecutters in the hills and thirty-six hundred as foremen over them.[k]

3Solomon sent this message to Hiram[f][l] king of Tyre:

"Send me cedar logs[m] as you did for my father David when you sent him cedar to build a palace to live in. 4Now I am about to build a temple[n] for the Name of the LORD my God and to dedicate it to him for burning fragrant incense[o] before him, for setting out the consecrated bread[p] regularly, and for making burnt offerings[q] every morning and evening and on Sabbaths[r] and New Moons and at the appointed feasts of the LORD our God. This is a lasting ordinance for Israel.

5"The temple I am going to build will be great,[s] because our God is greater than all other gods.[t] 6But who is able to build a temple for him, since the heavens, even the highest heavens, cannot contain him?[u] Who then am I[v] to build a temple for him, except as a place to burn sacrifices before him?

[a] *14* Or *charioteers* [b] *16* Or possibly *Muzur,* a region in Cilicia; also in verse 17 [c] *16* Probably Cilicia [d] *17* That is, about 15 pounds (about 7 kilograms) [e] *17* That is, about 3 3/4 pounds (about 1.7 kilograms) [f] *3* Hebrew *Huram,* a variant of *Hiram;* also in verses 11 and 12

1:9 [a] Ge 12:2

1:10 [b] Nu 27:17; 2Sa 5:2; Pr 8:15-16

1:11 [c] Dt 17:17

1:12 [d] 1Ch 29:12 [e] 1Ch 29:25; 2Ch 9:22; Ne 13:26

1:14 [f] 1Sa 8:11; 1Ki 4:26; 9:19

1:15 [g] 1Ki 9:28; Isa 60:5

1:17 [h] SS 1:9

2:1 [i] Dt 12:5 [j] Ecc 2:4

2:2 [k] ver 18; 2Ch 10:4

2:3 [l] 2Sa 5:11 [m] 1Ch 14:1

2:4 [n] ver 1; Dt 12:5 [o] Ex 30:7 [p] Ex 25:30 [q] Ex 29:42; 2Ch 13:11 [r] Nu 28:9-10

2:5 [s] 1Ch 22:5; Ps 135:5 [t] 1Ch 16:25

2:6 [u] 1Ki 8:27; 2Ch 6:18; Jer 23:24 [v] Ex 3:11

2:7 [a]ver 13-14; Ex 35:31; 1Ch 22:16
2:10 [b]Ezr 3:7
2:11 [c]1Ki 10:9; 2Ch 9:8
2:12 [d]Ne 9:6; Ps 8:3; 33:6; 102:25
2:13 [e]1Ki 7:13
2:14 [f]Ex 31:6 [g]Ex 35:31 [h]Ex 35:35
2:15 [i]ver 10; Ezr 3:7
2:16 [j]Jos 19:46; Jnh 1:3
2:17 [k]1Ch 22:2 [l]2Sa 24:2
2:18 [m]ver 2; 1Ch 22:2; 2Ch 8:8

7"Send me, therefore, a man skilled to work in gold and silver, bronze and iron, and in purple, crimson and blue yarn, and experienced in the art of engraving, to work in Judah and Jerusalem with my skilled craftsmen,[a] whom my father David provided.

8"Send me also cedar, pine and algum[a] logs from Lebanon, for I know that your men are skilled in cutting timber there. My men will work
with yours 9to provide me with plenty of lumber,
because the temple I build must be large and
magnificent. 10I will give your servants, the woodsmen who cut the timber, twenty thousand cors[b] of ground wheat, twenty thousand cors of barley, twenty thousand baths[c] of wine and twenty thousand baths of olive oil.[b]"

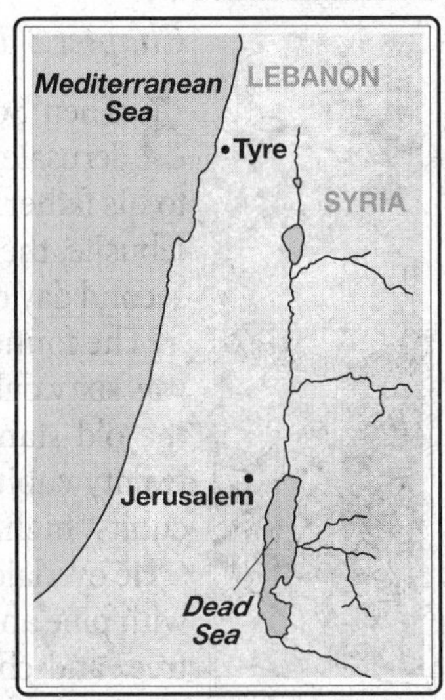

Cedar from Lebanon

11Hiram king of Tyre replied by letter to Solomon:

"Because the LORD loves[c] his people, he has made you their king."

12And Hiram added:

"Praise be to the LORD, the God of Israel, who made heaven and earth![d] He has given King David a wise son, endowed with intelligence and discernment, who will build a temple for the LORD and a palace for himself.

13"I am sending you Huram-Abi,[e] a man of great skill,
14whose mother was from Dan[f] and whose father was from Tyre. He is trained[g] to work in gold and silver, bronze and iron, stone and wood, and with purple and blue[h] and crimson yarn and fine linen. He is experienced in all kinds of engraving and can execute any design given to him. He will work with your craftsmen and with those of my lord, David your father.

15"Now let my lord send his servants the wheat and barley
and the olive oil[i] and wine he promised, 16and we will cut all
the logs from Lebanon that you need and will float them in rafts by sea down to Joppa.[j] You can then take them up to Jerusalem."

17Solomon took a census of all the aliens[k] who were in Israel, after the census[l] his father David had taken; and they were found
to be 153,600. 18He assigned[m] 70,000 of them to be carriers and 80,000 to be stonecutters in the hills, with 3,600 foremen over them to keep the people working.

[a]8 Probably a variant of *almug*; possibly juniper [b]10 That is, probably about 125,000 bushels (about 4,400 kiloliters) [c]10 That is, probably about 115,000 gallons (about 440 kiloliters)

Chapter 3 Theme ____________________

3

Then Solomon began to build[a] the temple of the LORD[b] in
Jerusalem on Mount Moriah, where the LORD had appeared
to his father David. It was on the threshing floor of Araunah[a,c] the
Jebusite, the place provided by David. 2He began building on the
second day of the second month in the fourth year of his reign.[d]

Close-up of Most Holy Place

3The foundation Solomon laid for building the temple of God
was sixty cubits long and twenty cubits wide[b,e] (using the cubit of
the old standard). 4The portico at the front of the temple was
twenty cubits[c] long across the width of the building and twenty
cubits[d] high.
He overlaid the inside with pure gold. 5He paneled the main hall
with pine and covered it with fine gold and decorated it with palm
tree[f] and chain designs. 6He adorned the temple with precious
stones. And the gold he used was gold of Parvaim. 7He overlaid
the ceiling beams, doorframes, walls and doors of the temple with
gold, and he carved cherubim[g] on the walls.
8He built the Most Holy Place,[h] its length corresponding to the
width of the temple—twenty cubits long and twenty cubits wide.
He overlaid the inside with six hundred talents[e] of fine gold. 9The
gold nails[i] weighed fifty shekels.[f] He also overlaid the upper parts
with gold.
10In the Most Holy Place he made a pair[j] of sculptured cherubim and overlaid them with gold. 11The total wingspan of the
cherubim was twenty cubits. One wing of the first cherub was five
cubits[g] long and touched the temple wall, while its other wing,
also five cubits long, touched the wing of the other cherub. 12Sim-
ilarly one wing of the second cherub was five cubits long and
touched the other temple wall, and its other wing, also five cubits
long, touched the wing of the first cherub. 13The wings of these
cherubim[k] extended twenty cubits. They stood on their feet, facing
the main hall.[h]
14He made the curtain[l] of blue, purple and crimson yarn and
fine linen, with cherubim[m] worked into it.
15In the front of the temple he made two pillars,[n] which ⌊togeth-
er⌋ were thirty-five cubits[i] long, each with a capital[o] on top measuring five cubits. 16He made interwoven chains[j][p] and put them
on top of the pillars. He also made a hundred pomegranates[q] and
attached them to the chains. 17He erected the pillars in the front of

[a] *1* Hebrew *Ornan*, a variant of *Araunah* [b] *3* That is, about 90 feet (about 27 meters) long and 30 feet (about 9 meters) wide [c] *4* That is, about 30 feet (about 9 meters); also in verses 8, 11 and 13 [d] *4* Some Septuagint and Syriac manuscripts; Hebrew *and a hundred and twenty* [e] *8* That is, about 23 tons (about 21 metric tons) [f] *9* That is, about 1 1/4 pounds (about 0.6 kilogram) [g] *11* That is, about 7 1/2 feet (about 2.3 meters); also in verse 15 [h] *13* Or *facing inward* [i] *15* That is, about 52 feet (about 16 meters) [j] *16* Or possibly *made chains in the inner sanctuary*; the meaning of the Hebrew for this phrase is uncertain.

3:1 [a] Ac 7:47 [b] Ge 28:17 [c] 2Sa 24:18; 1Ch 21:18
3:2 [d] Ezr 5:11
3:3 [e] Eze 41:2
3:5 [f] Eze 40:16
3:7 [g] Ge 3:24; 1Ki 6:29-35; Eze 41:18
3:8 [h] Ex 26:33
3:9 [i] Ex 26:32
3:10 [j] Ex 25:18
3:13 [k] Ex 25:18
3:14 [l] Ex 26:31,33; Heb 9:3 [m] Ge 3:24
3:15 [n] 1Ki 7:15; Rev 3:12 [o] 1Ki 7:22
3:16 [p] 1Ki 7:17 [q] 1Ki 7:20

the temple, one to the south and one to the north. The one to the
south he named Jakin[a] and the one to the north Boaz.[b]

Chapter 4 Theme

4

He made a bronze altar[a] twenty cubits long, twenty cubits
wide and ten cubits high.[c] 2He made the Sea[b] of cast metal,
circular in shape, measuring ten cubits from rim to rim and five
cubits[d] high. It took a line of thirty cubits[e] to measure around it.
3Below the rim, figures of bulls encircled it—ten to a cubit.[f] The
bulls were cast in two rows in one piece with the Sea.
4The Sea stood on twelve bulls, three facing north, three facing
west, three facing south and three facing east.[c] The Sea rested on
top of them, and their hindquarters were toward the center. 5It
was a handbreadth[g] in thickness, and its rim was like the rim of a
cup, like a lily blossom. It held three thousand baths.[h]
6He then made ten basins[d] for washing and placed five on the
south side and five on the north. In them the things to be used for
the burnt offerings[e] were rinsed, but the Sea was to be used by the
priests for washing.
7He made ten gold lampstands[f] according to the specifications[g]
for them and placed them in the temple, five on the south side and
five on the north.
8He made ten tables[h] and placed them in the temple, five on the
south side and five on the north. He also made a hundred gold
sprinkling bowls.[i]
9He made the courtyard[j] of the priests, and the large court and
the doors for the court, and overlaid the doors with bronze. 10He
placed the Sea on the south side, at the southeast corner.
11He also made the pots and shovels and sprinkling bowls.
So Huram finished[k] the work he had undertaken for King Solomon in the temple of God:

12the two pillars;
the two bowl-shaped capitals on top of the pillars;
the two sets of network decorating the two bowl-shaped capitals on top of the pillars;
13the four hundred pomegranates for the two sets of network
(two rows of pomegranates for each network, decorating
the bowl-shaped capitals on top of the pillars);
14the stands[l] with their basins;
15the Sea and the twelve bulls under it;
16the pots, shovels, meat forks and all related articles.

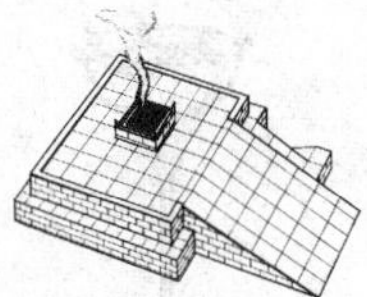
Bronze Altar

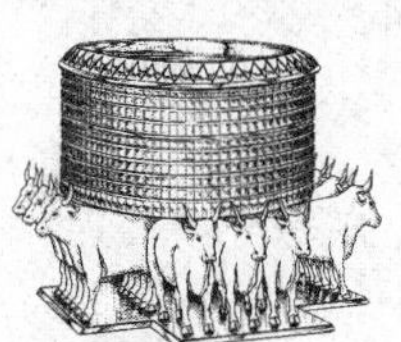
Bronze Basin on Bulls

Bronze Stand with Bronze Basin

Table

4:1 [a]Ex 20:24; 27:1-2; 40:6; 1Ki 8:64; 2Ki 16:14
4:2 [b]Rev 4:6; 15:2
4:4 [c]Nu 2:3-25; Eze 48:30-34; Rev 21:13
4:6 [d]Ex 30:18 [e]Ne 13:5,9; Eze 40:38
4:7 [f]Ex 25:31 [g]Ex 25:40
4:8 [h]Ex 25:23 [i]Nu 4:14
4:9 [j]1Ki 6:36; 2Ki 21:5; 2Ch 33:5
4:11 [k]1Ki 7:14
4:14 [l]1Ki 7:27-30

[a] *17 Jakin* probably means *he establishes.* [b] *17 Boaz* probably means *in him is strength.*
[c] *1* That is, about 30 feet (about 9 meters) long and wide, and about 15 feet (about 4.5 meters) high [d] *2* That is, about 7 1/2 feet (about 2.3 meters) [e] *2* That is, about 45 feet (about 13.5 meters) [f] *3* That is, about 1 1/2 feet (about 0.5 meter) [g] *5* That is, about 3 inches (about 8 centimeters) [h] *5* That is, about 17,500 gallons (about 66 kiloliters)

All the objects that Huram-Abi[a] made for King Solomon for the
temple of the LORD were of polished bronze. 17The king had them
cast in clay molds in the plain of the Jordan between Succoth[b] and
Zarethan.[a] 18All these things that Solomon made amounted to so
much that the weight of the bronze[c] was not determined.

19Solomon also made all the furnishings that were in God's
temple:

Lampstand

the golden altar;
the tables[d] on which was the bread of the Presence;
20the lampstands[e] of pure gold with their lamps, to burn in front of the inner sanctuary as prescribed;
21the gold floral work and lamps and tongs (they were solid gold);
22the pure gold wick trimmers, sprinkling bowls, dishes[f] and censers;[g] and the gold doors of the temple: the inner doors to the Most Holy Place and the doors of the main hall.

Chapter 5 Theme ______________________

5 When all the work Solomon had done for the temple of the
LORD was finished,[h] he brought in the things his father David
had dedicated[i]—the silver and gold and all the furnishings—and
he placed them in the treasuries of God's temple.

2Then Solomon summoned to Jerusalem the elders of Israel, all
the heads of the tribes and the chiefs of the Israelite families, to
bring up the ark[j] of the LORD's covenant from Zion, the City of
David. 3And all the men of Israel[k] came together to the king at
the time of the festival in the seventh month.

4When all the elders of Israel had arrived, the Levites took up the
ark, 5and they brought up the ark and the Tent of Meeting and all
the sacred furnishings in it. The priests, who were Levites,[l] carried
them up; 6and King Solomon and the entire assembly of Israel
that had gathered about him were before the ark, sacrificing so
many sheep and cattle that they could not be recorded or counted.

Ark of the Covenant (or Testimony)

7The priests then brought the ark[m] of the LORD's covenant to its
place in the inner sanctuary of the temple, the Most Holy Place,
and put it beneath the wings of the cherubim. 8The cherubim[n]
spread their wings over the place of the ark and covered the ark
and its carrying poles. 9These poles were so long that their ends,
extending from the ark, could be seen from in front of the inner
sanctuary, but not from outside the Holy Place; and they are still
there today. 10There was nothing in the ark except[o] the two tablets[p]
that Moses had placed in it at Horeb, where the LORD made a covenant with the Israelites after they came out of Egypt.

[a] 17 Hebrew *Zeredatha,* a variant of *Zarethan*

4:16 [a] 1Ki 7:13
4:17 [b] Ge 33:17
4:18 [c] 1Ki 7:23
4:19 [d] Ex 25:23,30
4:20 [e] Ex 25:31
4:22 [f] Nu 7:14 [g] Lev 10:1
5:1 [h] 1Ki 6:14 [i] 2Sa 8:11
5:2 [j] Nu 3:31; 2Sa 6:12; 1Ch 15:25
5:3 [k] 1Ch 9:1; 2Ch 7:8-10
5:5 [l] Nu 3:31; 1Ch 15:2
5:7 [m] Rev 11:19
5:8 [n] Ge 3:24
5:10 [o] Heb 9:4 [p] Ex 16:34; Dt 10:2

[11]The priests then withdrew from the Holy Place. All the priests
who were there had consecrated themselves, regardless of their
divisions.[a] [12]All the Levites who were musicians[b]—Asaph, Heman,
Jeduthun and their sons and relatives—stood on the east side of
the altar, dressed in fine linen and playing cymbals, harps and
lyres. They were accompanied by 120 priests sounding trumpets.[c]
[13]The trumpeters and singers joined in unison, as with one voice,
to give praise and thanks to the LORD. Accompanied by trumpets,
cymbals and other instruments, they raised their voices in praise
to the LORD and sang:

> "He is good;
> his love endures forever."[d]

Then the temple of the LORD was filled with a cloud, [14]and the
priests could not perform[e] their service because of the cloud,[f] for
the glory[g] of the LORD filled the temple of God.

Chapter 6 Theme ____________________

6 Then Solomon said, "The LORD has said that he would dwell
in a dark cloud;[h] [2]I have built a magnificent temple for you, a
place for you to dwell forever.[i]"

[3]While the whole assembly of Israel was standing there, the king
turned around and blessed them. [4]Then he said:

"Praise be to the LORD, the God of Israel, who with his
hands has fulfilled what he promised with his mouth to my
father David. For he said, [5]'Since the day I brought my people
out of Egypt, I have not chosen a city in any tribe of Israel to
have a temple built for my Name to be there, nor have I chosen
anyone to be the leader over my people Israel. [6]But now I have
chosen Jerusalem[j] for my Name[k] to be there, and I have chosen David[l] to rule my people Israel.'

[7]"My father David had it in his heart[m] to build a temple for
the Name of the LORD, the God of Israel. [8]But the LORD said to
my father David, 'Because it was in your heart to build a temple for my Name, you did well to have this in your heart.
[9]Nevertheless, you are not the one to build the temple, but
your son, who is your own flesh and blood—he is the one
who will build the temple for my Name.'

[10]"The LORD has kept the promise he made. I have succeeded
David my father and now I sit on the throne of Israel, just as
the LORD promised, and I have built the temple for the Name
of the LORD, the God of Israel. [11]There I have placed the ark,
in which is the covenant[n] of the LORD that he made with the
people of Israel."

5:11 [a]1Ch 24:1
5:12 [b]1Ki 10:12; 1Ch 25:1; Ps 68:25 [c]1Ch 13:8; 15:24
5:13 [d]1Ch 16:34, 41; 2Ch 7:3; 20:21; Ezr 3:11; Ps 100:5; 136:1; Jer 33:11
5:14 [e]Ex 40:35; Rev 15:8 [f]Ex 19:16 [g]Ex 29:43; 2Ch 7:2
6:1 [h]Ex 19:9; 1Ki 8:12-50
6:2 [i]Ezr 6:12; 7:15; Ps 135:21
6:6 [j]Dt 12:5; Isa 14:1 [k]Ex 20:24; 2Ch 12:13 [l]1Ch 28:4
6:7 [m]1Sa 10:7; 1Ch 17:2; 28:2; Ac 7:46
6:11 [n]Dt 10:2; 2Ch 5:10; Ps 25:10; 50:5

INSIGHT

See the illustration of Solomon's Temple on page IISB-36.

12 Then Solomon stood before the altar of the LORD in front of
the whole assembly of Israel and spread out his hands. 13 Now he
had made a bronze platform,[a] five cubits[a] long, five cubits wide
and three cubits[b] high, and had placed it in the center of the outer
court. He stood on the platform and then knelt down[b] before the
whole assembly of Israel and spread out his hands toward heaven.
14 He said:

"O LORD, God of Israel, there is no God like you[c] in heaven
or on earth—you who keep your covenant of love[d] with your
servants who continue wholeheartedly in your way. 15 You have
kept your promise to your servant David my father; with your
mouth you have promised[e] and with your hand you have fulfilled it—as it is today.
16 "Now LORD, God of Israel, keep for your servant David my
father the promises you made to him when you said, 'You shall
never fail[f] to have a man to sit before me on the throne of Israel,
if only your sons are careful in all they do to walk before me
according to my law,[g] as you have done.' 17 And now, O LORD,
God of Israel, let your word that you promised your servant
David come true.
18 "But will God really dwell[h] on earth with men? The heavens,[i] even the highest heavens, cannot contain you. How much
less this temple I have built! 19 Yet give attention to your servant's prayer and his plea for mercy, O LORD my God. Hear the
cry and the prayer that your servant is praying in your presence. 20 May your eyes[j] be open toward this temple day and
night, this place of which you said you would put your Name[k]
there. May you hear[l] the prayer your servant prays toward this
place. 21 Hear the supplications of your servant and of your
people Israel when they pray toward this place. Hear from
heaven, your dwelling place; and when you hear, forgive.[m]
22 "When a man wrongs his neighbor and is required to take
an oath[n] and he comes and swears the oath before your altar in
this temple, 23 then hear from heaven and act. Judge between
your servants, repaying[o] the guilty by bringing down on his
own head what he has done. Declare the innocent not guilty
and so establish his innocence.
24 "When your people Israel have been defeated[p] by an enemy
because they have sinned against you and when they turn back
and confess your name, praying and making supplication
before you in this temple, 25 then hear from heaven and forgive
the sin of your people Israel and bring them back to the land
you gave to them and their fathers.

[a] *13* That is, about 7 1/2 feet (about 2.3 meters) [b] *13* That is, about 4 1/2 feet (about 1.3 meters)

6:13 [a]Ne 8:4 [b]Ps 95:6
6:14 [c]Ex 8:10; 15:11 [d]Dt 7:9
6:15 [e]1Ch 22:10
6:16 [f]2Sa 7:13,15; 1Ki 2:4; 2Ch 7:18; 23:3 [g]Ps 132:12
6:18 [h]Rev 21:3 [i]2Ch 2:6; Ps 11:4; Isa 40:22; 66:1; Ac 7:49
6:20 [j]Ex 3:16; Ps 34:15 [k]Dt 12:11 [l]2Ch 7:14; 30:20
6:21 [m]Ps 51:1; Isa 33:24; 40:2; 43:25; 44:22; 55:7; Mic 7:18
6:22 [n]Ex 22:11
6:23 [o]Isa 3:11; 65:6; Mt 16:27
6:24 [p]Lev 26:17

26 "When the heavens are shut up and there is no rain[a]
because your people have sinned against you, and when they
pray toward this place and confess your name and turn from
their sin because you have afflicted them, 27 then hear from
heaven and forgive[b] the sin of your servants, your people Israel.
Teach them the right way to live, and send rain on the land
you gave your people for an inheritance.

28 "When famine[c] or plague comes to the land, or blight or
mildew, locusts or grasshoppers, or when enemies besiege
them in any of their cities, whatever disaster or disease may
come, 29 and when a prayer or plea is made by any of your people Israel—each one aware of his afflictions and pains, and
spreading out his hands toward this temple— 30 then hear from
heaven, your dwelling place. Forgive,[d] and deal with each man
according to all he does, since you know his heart (for you
alone know the hearts of men),[e] 31 so that they will fear you[f]
and walk in your ways all the time they live in the land you
gave our fathers.

32 "As for the foreigner who does not belong to your people
Israel but has come[g] from a distant land because of your great
name and your mighty hand[h] and your outstretched arm—
when he comes and prays toward this temple, 33 then hear from
heaven, your dwelling place, and do whatever the foreigner[i]
asks of you, so that all the peoples of the earth may know your
name and fear you, as do your own people Israel, and may
know that this house I have built bears your Name.

34 "When your people go to war against their enemies,[j]
wherever you send them, and when they pray[k] to you toward
this city you have chosen and the temple I have built for your
Name, 35 then hear from heaven their prayer and their plea,
and uphold their cause.

36 "When they sin against you—for there is no one who does
not sin[l]—and you become angry with them and give them
over to the enemy, who takes them captive[m] to a land far away
or near; 37 and if they have a change of heart[n] in the land where
they are held captive, and repent and plead with you in the
land of their captivity and say, 'We have sinned, we have done
wrong and acted wickedly'; 38 and if they turn back to you with
all their heart and soul in the land of their captivity where they
were taken, and pray toward the land you gave their fathers,
toward the city you have chosen and toward the temple I have
built for your Name; 39 then from heaven, your dwelling place,
hear their prayer and their pleas, and uphold their cause. And
forgive your people, who have sinned against you.

6:26 [a] Lev 26:19; Dt 11:17; 28:24; 2Sa 1:21; 1Ki 17:1
6:27 [b] ver 30,39; 2Ch 7:14
6:28 [c] 2Ch 20:9
6:30 [d] ver 27 [e] 1Sa 16:7; 1Ch 28:9; Ps 7:9; 44:21; Pr 16:2; 17:3
6:31 [f] Ps 103:11, 13; Pr 8:13
6:32 [g] 2Ch 9:6; Jn 12:20; Ac 8:27 [h] Ex 3:19,20
6:33 [i] 2Ch 7:14
6:34 [j] Dt 28:7 [k] 1Ch 5:20
6:36 [l] Job 15:14; Ps 143:2; Ecc 7:20; Jer 17:9; Jas 3:1; 1Jn 1:8-10 [m] Lev 26:44
6:37 [n] 2Ch 7:14; 33:12,19,23; Jer 29:13

40“Now, my God, may your eyes be open and your ears attentive[a] to the prayers offered in this place.

41“Now arise,[b] O Lord God, and come to your resting place,[c]
you and the ark of your might.
May your priests,[d] O Lord God, be clothed with salvation,
may your saints rejoice in your goodness.[e]
42O Lord God, do not reject your anointed one.
Remember the great love[f] promised to
David your servant.”

Chapter 7 Theme ___________________________________

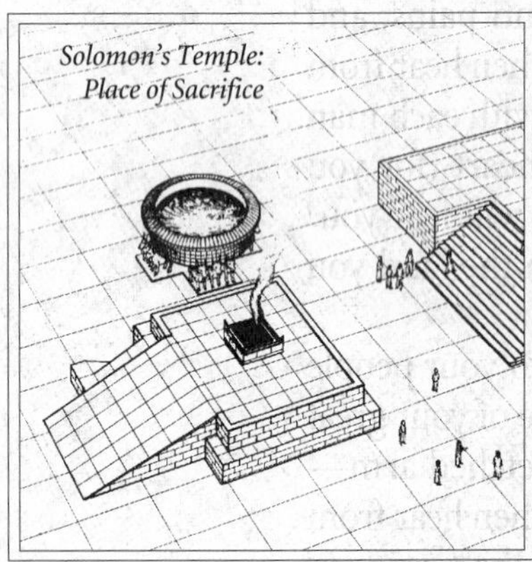
Solomon’s Temple: Place of Sacrifice

7 When Solomon finished praying, fire[g] came
down from heaven and consumed the burnt
offering and the sacrifices, and the glory of the
LORD filled[h] the temple.[i] 2The priests could not
enter[j] the temple of the LORD because the glory[k]
of the LORD filled it. 3When all the Israelites saw
the fire coming down and the glory of the LORD
above the temple, they knelt on the pavement
with their faces to the ground, and they worshiped and gave thanks to the LORD, saying,

“He is good;
his love endures forever.”[l]

4Then the king and all the people offered sacrifices before the
LORD. 5And King Solomon offered a sacrifice of twenty-two thousand head of cattle and a hundred and twenty thousand sheep
and goats. So the king and all the people dedicated the temple of
God. 6The priests took their positions, as did the Levites[m] with
the LORD’s musical instruments,[n] which King David had made
for praising the LORD and which were used when he gave thanks,
saying, “His love endures forever.” Opposite the Levites, the
priests blew their trumpets, and all the Israelites were standing.
7Solomon consecrated the middle part of the courtyard in front
of the temple of the LORD, and there he offered burnt offerings
and the fat of the fellowship offerings,[a] because the bronze altar
he had made could not hold the burnt offerings, the grain offerings and the fat portions.
8So Solomon observed the festival[o] at that time for seven days,
and all Israel with him—a vast assembly, people from Lebo[b]
Hamath to the Wadi of Egypt.[p] 9On the eighth day they held an
assembly, for they had celebrated the dedication of the altar for
seven days and the festival[q] for seven days more. 10On the twenty-
third day of the seventh month he sent the people to their homes,

[a]7 Traditionally *peace offerings* [b]8 Or *from the entrance to*

6:40 [a]2Ch 7:15; Ne 1:6,11; Ps 17:1,6
6:41 [b]Isa 33:10 [c]1Ch 28:2 [d]Ps 132:16 [e]Ps 116:12
6:42 [f]Ps 89:24,28; Isa 55:3
7:1 [g]Lev 9:24; 1Ki 18:38 [h]Ex 16:10 [i]Ps 26:8
7:2 [j]1Ki 8:11 [k]Ex 29:43; 40:35; 2Ch 5:14
7:3 [l]1Ch 16:34; 2Ch 5:13; 20:21
7:6 [m]1Ch 15:16 [n]2Ch 5:12
7:8 [o]2Ch 30:26 [p]Ge 15:18
7:9 [q]Lev 23:36

7:12 [a]Dt 12:5 joyful and glad in heart for the good things the LORD had done
for David and Solomon and for his people Israel.
11When Solomon had finished the temple of the LORD and the
7:13 royal palace, and had succeeded in carrying out all he had in mind
[b]2Ch 6:26-28; Am 4:7 to do in the temple of the LORD and in his own palace, 12the LORD
appeared to him at night and said:

"I have heard your prayer and have chosen this place for
7:14 [c]Lev 26:41; myself[a] as a temple for sacrifices.
2Ch 6:37; Jas 4:10 13"When I shut up the heavens so that there is no rain,[b] or
[d]1Ch 16:11 [e]Isa 55:7; command locusts to devour the land or send a plague among
Zec 1:4 my people, 14if my people, who are called by my name, will
[f]2Ch 6:27 [g]2Ch 30:20; humble[c] themselves and pray and seek my face[d] and turn[e]
Isa 30:26; 57:18 from their wicked ways, then will I hear from heaven and will
forgive[f] their sin and will heal[g] their land. 15Now my eyes will
be open and my ears attentive to the prayers offered in this
7:15 place.[h] 16I have chosen[i] and consecrated this temple so that
[h]2Ch 6:40 my Name may be there forever. My eyes and my heart will
always be there.
17"As for you, if you walk before me[j] as David your father
7:16 [i]ver 12; 2Ch 6:6 did, and do all I command, and observe my decrees and laws,
18I will establish your royal throne, as I covenanted with David
your father when I said, 'You shall never fail to have a man[k] to
7:17 rule over Israel.'[l]
[j]1Ki 9:4 19"But if you[a] turn away[m] and forsake[n] the decrees and commands I have given you[a] and go off to serve other gods and
worship them, 20then I will uproot[o] Israel from my land,[p]
7:18 [k]2Ch 6:16 which I have given them, and will reject this temple I have con-
[l]2Sa 7:13; 2Ch 13:5 secrated for my Name. I will make it a byword and an object of
ridicule[q] among all peoples. 21And though this temple is now
so imposing, all who pass by will be appalled and say,[r] 'Why
7:19 has the LORD done such a thing to this land and to this temple?'
[m]Dt 28:15 [n]Lev 26:14,33 22People will answer, 'Because they have forsaken the LORD, the
God of their fathers, who brought them out of Egypt, and have
embraced other gods, worshiping and serving them—that is
7:20 why he brought all this disaster on them.' "

[o]Dt 29:28 [p]1Ki 14:15 [q]Dt 28:37

Chapter 8 Theme ______________________________

8 At the end of twenty years, during which Solomon built the
temple of the LORD and his own palace, 2Solomon rebuilt the
7:21 [r]Dt 29:24 villages that Hiram[b] had given him, and settled Israelites in them.
3Solomon then went to Hamath Zobah and captured it. 4He also
built up Tadmor in the desert and all the store cities he had built
8:5 in Hamath. 5He rebuilt Upper Beth Horon[s] and Lower Beth Horon

[s]1Ch 7:24; 2Ch 14:7

[a]*19* The Hebrew is plural. [b]*2* Hebrew *Huram,* a variant of *Hiram*; also in verse 18

as fortified cities, with walls and with gates and bars, 6as well as
Baalath and all his store cities, and all the cities for his chariots
and for his horses[a]—whatever he desired to build in Jerusalem,
in Lebanon and throughout all the territory he ruled.
7All the people left from the Hittites, Amorites, Perizzites,
Hivites and Jebusites[a] (these peoples were not Israelites), 8that is,
their descendants remaining in the land, whom the Israelites had
not destroyed—these Solomon conscripted[b] for his slave labor
force, as it is to this day. 9But Solomon did not make slaves of the
Israelites for his work; they were his fighting men, commanders
of his captains, and commanders of his chariots and charioteers.
10They were also King Solomon's chief officials—two hundred
and fifty officials supervising the men.
11Solomon brought Pharaoh's daughter[c] up from the City of
David to the palace he had built for her, for he said, "My wife must
not live in the palace of David king of Israel, because the places the
ark of the LORD has entered are holy."
12On the altar[d] of the LORD that he had built in front of the portico, Solomon sacrificed burnt offerings to the LORD, 13according
to the daily requirement[e] for offerings commanded by Moses for
Sabbaths,[f] New Moons and the three[g] annual feasts—the Feast
of Unleavened Bread, the Feast of Weeks[h] and the Feast of Tabernacles. 14In keeping with the ordinance of his father David, he
appointed the divisions[i] of the priests for their duties, and the
Levites[j] to lead the praise and to assist the priests according to
each day's requirement. He also appointed the gatekeepers[k] by
divisions for the various gates, because this was what David the
man of God[l] had ordered.[m] 15They did not deviate from the king's
commands to the priests or to the Levites in any matter, including
that of the treasuries.
16All Solomon's work was carried out, from the day the foundation of the temple of the LORD was laid until its completion. So the
temple of the LORD was finished.
17Then Solomon went to Ezion Geber and Elath on the coast of
Edom. 18And Hiram sent him ships commanded by his own officers, men who knew the sea. These, with Solomon's men, sailed
to Ophir and brought back four hundred and fifty talents[b] of
gold,[n] which they delivered to King Solomon.

Chapter 9 Theme

9 When the queen of Sheba[o] heard of Solomon's fame, she came
to Jerusalem to test him with hard questions. Arriving with a
very great caravan—with camels carrying spices, large quantities
of gold, and precious stones—she came to Solomon and talked
with him about all she had on her mind. 2Solomon answered all

[a]6 Or *charioteers* [b]18 That is, about 17 tons (about 16 metric tons)

8:7 [a]Ge 10:16
8:8 [b]1Ki 4:6; 9:21
8:11 [c]1Ki 3:1; 7:8
8:12 [d]1Ki 8:64; 2Ch 4:1; 15:8
8:13 [e]Ex 29:38; Nu 28:3 [f]Nu 28:9 [g]Ex 23:14; Dt 16:16 [h]Ex 23:16
8:14 [i]1Ch 24:1 [j]1Ch 25:1 [k]1Ch 9:17; 26:1 [l]Ne 12:24,36 [m]1Ch 23:6; Ne 12:45
8:18 [n]2Ch 9:9
9:1 [o]Ge 10:7; Eze 23:42; Mt 12:42; Lk 11:31

her questions; nothing was too hard for him to explain to her. 3When the queen of Sheba saw the wisdom of Solomon,[a] as well as the palace he had built, 4the food on his table, the seating of his officials, the attending servants in their robes, the cupbearers in their robes and the burnt offerings he made at[a] the temple of the LORD, she was overwhelmed.

5She said to the king, "The report I heard in my own country about your achievements and your wisdom is true. 6But I did not believe what they said until I came[b] and saw with my own eyes. Indeed, not even half the greatness of your wisdom was told me; you have far exceeded the report I heard. 7How happy your men must be! How happy your officials, who continually stand before you and hear your wisdom! 8Praise be to the LORD your God, who has delighted in you and placed you on his throne[c] as king to rule for the LORD your God. Because of the love of your God for Israel and his desire to uphold them forever, he has made you king[d] over them, to maintain justice and righteousness."

9Then she gave the king 120 talents[b] of gold,[e] large quantities of spices, and precious stones. There had never been such spices as those the queen of Sheba gave to King Solomon.

10(The men of Hiram and the men of Solomon brought gold from Ophir;[f] they also brought algumwood[c] and precious stones. 11The king used the algumwood to make steps for the temple of the LORD and for the royal palace, and to make harps and lyres for the musicians. Nothing like them had ever been seen in Judah.)

12King Solomon gave the queen of Sheba all she desired and asked for; he gave her more than she had brought to him. Then she left and returned with her retinue to her own country.

13The weight of the gold that Solomon received yearly was 666 talents,[d] 14not including the revenues brought in by merchants and traders. Also all the kings of Arabia[g] and the governors of the land brought gold and silver to Solomon.

15King Solomon made two hundred large shields of hammered gold; six hundred bekas[e] of hammered gold went into each shield. 16He also made three hundred small shields[h] of hammered gold, with three hundred bekas[f] of gold in each shield. The king put them in the Palace of the Forest of Lebanon.[i]

17Then the king made a great throne inlaid with ivory[j] and overlaid with pure gold. 18The throne had six steps, and a footstool of gold was attached to it. On both sides of the seat were armrests, with a lion standing beside each of them. 19Twelve lions stood on the six steps, one at either end of each step. Nothing like it had ever

9:3 *a* 1Ki 5:12
9:6 *b* 2Ch 6:32
9:8 *c* 1Ki 2:12; 1Ch 17:14; 28:5; 29:23; 2Ch 13:8 *d* 2Ch 2:11
9:9 *e* 2Ch 8:18
9:10 *f* 2Ch 8:18
9:14 *g* 2Ch 17:11; Isa 21:13; Jer 25:24; Eze 27:21; 30:5
9:16 *h* 2Ch 12:9 *i* 1Ki 7:2
9:17 *j* 1Ki 22:39

a *4* Or *the ascent by which he went up to* b *9* That is, about 4 1/2 tons (about 4 metric tons) c *10* Probably a variant of *almugwood* d *13* That is, about 25 tons (about 23 metric tons) e *15* That is, about 7 1/2 pounds (about 3.5 kilograms) f *16* That is, about 3 3/4 pounds (about 1.7 kilograms)

been made for any other kingdom. 20 All King Solomon's goblets were gold, and all the household articles in the Palace of the Forest of Lebanon were pure gold. Nothing was made of silver, because silver was considered of little value in Solomon's day. 21 The king had a fleet of trading ships[a] manned by Hiram's[b] men. Once every three years it returned, carrying gold, silver and ivory, and apes and baboons.

22 King Solomon was greater in riches and wisdom than all the other kings of the earth.[a] 23 All the kings[b] of the earth sought audience with Solomon to hear the wisdom God had put in his heart. 24 Year after year, everyone who came brought a gift[c]—articles of silver and gold, and robes, weapons and spices, and horses and mules.

25 Solomon had four thousand stalls for horses and chariots,[d] and twelve thousand horses,[c] which he kept in the chariot cities and also with him in Jerusalem. 26 He ruled[e] over all the kings from the River[d][f] to the land of the Philistines, as far as the border of Egypt.[g] 27 The king made silver as common in Jerusalem as stones, and cedar as plentiful as sycamore-fig trees in the foothills. 28 Solomon's horses were imported from Egypt[e] and from all other countries.

29 As for the other events of Solomon's reign, from beginning to end, are they not written in the records of Nathan[h] the prophet, in the prophecy of Ahijah[i] the Shilonite and in the visions of Iddo the seer concerning Jeroboam[j] son of Nebat? 30 Solomon reigned in Jerusalem over all Israel forty years. 31 Then he rested with his fathers and was buried in the city of David[k] his father. And Rehoboam his son succeeded him as king.

Chapter 10 Theme ____

10 Rehoboam went to Shechem, for all the Israelites had gone there to make him king. 2 When Jeroboam[l] son of Nebat heard this (he was in Egypt, where he had fled[m] from King Solomon), he returned from Egypt. 3 So they sent for Jeroboam, and he and all Israel[n] went to Rehoboam and said to him: 4 "Your father put a heavy yoke on us,[o] but now lighten the harsh labor and the heavy yoke he put on us, and we will serve you."

5 Rehoboam answered, "Come back to me in three days." So the people went away.

6 Then King Rehoboam consulted the elders[p] who had served his father Solomon during his lifetime. "How would you advise me to answer these people?" he asked.

7 They replied, "If you will be kind to these people and please them and give them a favorable answer,[q] they will always be your servants."

[a]21 Hebrew *of ships that could go to Tarshish* [b]21 Hebrew *Huram,* a variant of *Hiram*
[c]25 Or *charioteers* [d]26 That is, the Euphrates [e]28 Or possibly *Muzur,* a region in Cilicia

9:22 [a]1Ki 3:13; 2Ch 1:12
9:23 [b]1Ki 4:34
9:24 [c]2Ch 32:23; Ps 45:12; 68:29; 72:10; Isa 18:7
9:25 [d]1Sa 8:11; 1Ki 4:26
9:26 [e]1Ki 4:21 [f]Ps 72:8-9 [g]Ge 15:18-21
9:29 [h]2Sa 7:2; 1Ch 29:29 [i]1Ki 11:29 [j]2Ch 10:2
9:31 [k]1Ki 2:10
10:2 [l]2Ch 9:29 [m]1Ki 11:40
10:3 [n]1Ch 9:1
10:4 [o]2Ch 2:2
10:6 [p]Job 8:8-9; 12:12; 15:10; 32:7
10:7 [q]Pr 15:1

10:8 [a]2Sa 17:14 [b]Pr 13:20

8 But Rehoboam rejected[a] the advice the elders[b] gave him and consulted the young men who had grown up with him and were serving him. 9 He asked them, "What is your advice? How should we answer these people who say to me, 'Lighten the yoke your father put on us'?"

10 The young men who had grown up with him replied, "Tell the people who have said to you, 'Your father put a heavy yoke on us, but make our yoke lighter'—tell them, 'My little finger is thicker than my father's waist. 11 My father laid on you a heavy yoke; I will make it even heavier. My father scourged you with whips; I will scourge you with scorpions.'"

10:15 [c]2Ch 11:4; 25:16-20 [d]1Ki 11:29

12 Three days later Jeroboam and all the people returned to Rehoboam, as the king had said, "Come back to me in three days." 13 The king answered them harshly. Rejecting the advice of the elders, 14 he followed the advice of the young men and said, "My father made your yoke heavy; I will make it even heavier. My father scourged you with whips; I will scourge you with scorpions." 15 So the king did not listen to the people, for this turn of events was from God,[c] to fulfill the word the LORD had spoken to Jeroboam son of Nebat through Ahijah the Shilonite.[d]

10:16 [e]1Ch 9:1 [f]ver 19; 2Sa 20:1

16 When all Israel[e] saw that the king refused to listen to them, they answered the king:

> "What share do we have in David,[f]
>   what part in Jesse's son?
> To your tents, O Israel!
>   Look after your own house, O David!"

10:18 [g]1Ki 5:14

So all the Israelites went home. 17 But as for the Israelites who were living in the towns of Judah, Rehoboam still ruled over them.

18 King Rehoboam sent out Adoniram,[a][g] who was in charge of forced labor, but the Israelites stoned him to death. King Rehoboam, however, managed to get into his chariot and escape to Jerusalem. 19 So Israel has been in rebellion against the house of David to this day.

Chapter 11 Theme

11:1 [h]1Ki 12:21

11 When Rehoboam arrived in Jerusalem,[h] he mustered the house of Judah and Benjamin—a hundred and eighty thousand fighting men—to make war against Israel and to regain the kingdom for Rehoboam.

11:2 [i]2Ch 12:5-7, 15

2 But this word of the LORD came to Shemaiah[i] the man of God: 3 "Say to Rehoboam son of Solomon king of Judah and to all the Israelites in Judah and Benjamin, 4 'This is what the LORD says:

[a] *18* Hebrew *Hadoram,* a variant of *Adoniram*

Do not go up to fight against your brothers.[a] Go home, every one
of you, for this is my doing.'" So they obeyed the words of the
LORD and turned back from marching against Jeroboam.
5Rehoboam lived in Jerusalem and built up towns for defense in
Judah: 6Bethlehem, Etam, Tekoa, 7Beth Zur, Soco, Adullam, 8Gath,
Mareshah, Ziph, 9Adoraim, Lachish, Azekah, 10Zorah, Aijalon and
Hebron. These were fortified cities in Judah and Benjamin. 11He
strengthened their defenses and put commanders in
them, with supplies of food, olive oil and wine. 12He
put shields and spears in all the cities, and made
them very strong. So Judah and Benjamin were his.
13The priests and Levites from all their districts
throughout Israel sided with him. 14The Levites[b] even
abandoned their pasturelands and property,[c] and
came to Judah and Jerusalem because Jeroboam and
his sons had rejected them as priests of the LORD.
15And he appointed[d] his own priests[e] for the high
places and for the goat[f] and calf[g] idols he had made.
16Those from every tribe of Israel[h] who set their
hearts on seeking the LORD, the God of Israel, followed the Levites to Jerusalem to offer sacrifices to
the LORD, the God of their fathers. 17They strengthened[i] the kingdom of Judah and supported Rehoboam son of Solomon three years, walking in the ways of David
and Solomon during this time.
18Rehoboam married Mahalath, who was the daughter of
David's son Jerimoth and of Abihail, the daughter of Jesse's son
Eliab. 19She bore him sons: Jeush, Shemariah and Zaham. 20Then
he married Maacah[j] daughter of Absalom, who bore him Abijah,[k]
Attai, Ziza and Shelomith. 21Rehoboam loved Maacah daughter of
Absalom more than any of his other wives and concubines. In all,
he had eighteen wives[l] and sixty concubines, twenty-eight sons
and sixty daughters.
22Rehoboam appointed Abijah[m] son of Maacah to be the chief
prince among his brothers, in order to make him king. 23He acted
wisely, dispersing some of his sons throughout the districts of
Judah and Benjamin, and to all the fortified cities. He gave them
abundant provisions and took many wives for them.

The Divided Kingdom 931–586 B.C.

Chapter 12 Theme ____________________

12 After Rehoboam's position as king was established[n] and
he had become strong,[o] he and all Israel[a] with him abandoned the law of the LORD. 2Because they had been unfaithful[p] to
the LORD, Shishak[q] king of Egypt attacked Jerusalem in the fifth

a *1* That is, Judah, as frequently in 2 Chronicles

11:4 [a] 2Ch 28:8-11
11:14 [b] Nu 35:2-5 [c] 2Ch 13:9
11:15 [d] 1Ki 13:33 [e] 1Ki 12:31 [f] Lev 17:7 [g] 1Ki 12:28; 2Ch 13:8
11:16 [h] 2Ch 15:9
11:17 [i] 2Ch 12:1
11:20 [j] 1Ki 15:2 [k] 2Ch 13:2
11:21 [l] Dt 17:17
11:22 [m] Dt 21:15-17
12:1 [n] ver 13 [o] 2Ch 11:17
12:2 [p] 1Ki 14:22-24 [q] 1Ki 11:40

year of King Rehoboam. 3With twelve hundred chariots and sixty
thousand horsemen and the innumerable troops of Libyans, Suk-
kites and Cushites[a][a] that came with him from Egypt, 4he captured
the fortified cities[b] of Judah and came as far as Jerusalem.
5Then the prophet Shemaiah[c] came to Rehoboam and to the
leaders of Judah who had assembled in Jerusalem for fear of Shishak, and he said to them, "This is what the LORD says, 'You have
abandoned me; therefore, I now abandon[d] you to Shishak.' "
6The leaders of Israel and the king humbled themselves and said,
"The LORD is just."[e]
7When the LORD saw that they humbled themselves, this word
of the LORD came to Shemaiah: "Since they have humbled themselves, I will not destroy them but will soon give them deliverance.[f]
My wrath will not be poured out on Jerusalem through Shishak.
8They will, however, become subjects[g] to him, so that they may
learn the difference between serving me and serving the kings of
other lands."
9When Shishak king of Egypt attacked Jerusalem, he carried
off the treasures of the temple of the LORD and the treasures of
the royal palace. He took everything, including the gold shields[h]
Solomon had made. 10So King Rehoboam made bronze shields to
replace them and assigned these to the commanders of the guard
on duty at the entrance to the royal palace. 11Whenever the king
went to the LORD's temple, the guards went with him, bearing the
shields, and afterward they returned them to the guardroom.
12Because Rehoboam humbled himself, the LORD's anger turned
from him, and he was not totally destroyed. Indeed, there was some
good[i] in Judah.
13King Rehoboam established himself firmly in Jerusalem and
continued as king. He was forty-one years old when he became
king, and he reigned seventeen years in Jerusalem, the city the
LORD had chosen out of all the tribes of Israel in which to put his
Name.[j] His mother's name was Naamah; she was an Ammonite.
14He did evil because he had not set his heart on seeking the LORD.
15As for the events of Rehoboam's reign, from beginning to
end, are they not written in the records of Shemaiah[k] the prophet
and of Iddo the seer that deal with genealogies? There was continual warfare between Rehoboam and Jeroboam. 16Rehoboam
rested with his fathers and was buried in the City of David. And
Abijah[l] his son succeeded him as king.

Chapter 13 Theme ____________________

13 In the eighteenth year of the reign of Jeroboam, Abijah became king of Judah, 2and he reigned in Jerusalem three

[a] 3 That is, people from the upper Nile region

12:3 *a* 2Ch 16:8; Na 3:9
12:4 *b* 2Ch 11:10
12:5 *c* 2Ch 11:2 *d* Dt 28:15; 2Ch 15:2
12:6 *e* Ex 9:27; Da 9:14
12:7 *f* 1Ki 21:29; Ps 78:38
12:8 *g* Dt 28:48
12:9 *h* 2Ch 9:16
12:12 *i* 1Ki 14:13; 2Ch 19:3
12:13 *j* Dt 12:5; 2Ch 6:6
12:15 *k* 2Ch 9:29; 11:2
12:16 *l* 2Ch 11:20

years. His mother's name was Maacah,[a] a daughter[b] of Uriel of
Gibeah.
There was war between Abijah[a] and Jeroboam.[b] 3 Abijah went
into battle with a force of four hundred thousand able fighting
men, and Jeroboam drew up a battle line against him with eight
hundred thousand able troops.
4 Abijah stood on Mount Zemaraim,[c] in the hill country of
Ephraim, and said, "Jeroboam and all Israel,[d] listen to me! 5 Don't
you know that the LORD, the God of Israel, has given the kingship of
Israel to David and his descendants forever[e] by a covenant of salt?[f]
6 Yet Jeroboam son of Nebat, an official of Solomon son of David,
rebelled[g] against his master. 7 Some worthless scoundrels[h] gathered
around him and opposed Rehoboam son of Solomon when he was
young and indecisive and not strong enough to resist them.
8 "And now you plan to resist the kingdom of the LORD, which is
in the hands of David's descendants. You are indeed a vast army
and have with you the golden calves[i] that Jeroboam made to be
your gods. 9 But didn't you drive out the priests of the LORD,[j] the
sons of Aaron, and the Levites, and make priests of your own as
the peoples of other lands do? Whoever comes to consecrate himself with a young bull[k] and seven rams may become a priest of what
are not gods.[l]
10 "As for us, the LORD is our God, and we have not forsaken him.
The priests who serve the LORD are sons of Aaron, and the Levites
assist them. 11 Every morning and evening[m] they present burnt
offerings and fragrant incense to the LORD. They set out the bread
on the ceremonially clean table[n] and light the lamps on the gold
lampstand every evening. We are observing the requirements of
the LORD our God. But you have forsaken him. 12 God is with us; he
is our leader. His priests with their trumpets will sound the battle
cry against you.[o] Men of Israel, do not fight against the LORD,[p] the
God of your fathers, for you will not succeed."
13 Now Jeroboam had sent troops around to the rear, so that
while he was in front of Judah the ambush[q] was behind them.
14 Judah turned and saw that they were being attacked at both
front and rear. Then they cried out[r] to the LORD. The priests blew
their trumpets 15 and the men of Judah raised the battle cry. At
the sound of their battle cry, God routed Jeroboam and all Israel[s]
before Abijah and Judah. 16 The Israelites fled before Judah, and
God delivered[t] them into their hands. 17 Abijah and his men
inflicted heavy losses on them, so that there were five hundred
thousand casualties among Israel's able men. 18 The men of Israel
were subdued on that occasion, and the men of Judah were victorious because they relied[u] on the LORD, the God of their fathers.

[a]2 Most Septuagint manuscripts and Syriac (see also 2 Chron. 11:20 and 1 Kings 15:2); Hebrew *Micaiah* [b]2 Or *granddaughter*

13:2 [a] 2Ch 11:20 [b] 1Ki 15:6
13:4 [c] Jos 18:22 [d] 1Ch 11:1
13:5 [e] 2Sa 7:13 [f] Lev 2:13 Nu 18:19
13:6 [g] 1Ki 11:26
13:7 [h] Jdg 9:4
13:8 [i] 1Ki 12:28 2Ch 11:15
13:9 [j] 2Ch 11:14-15 [k] Ex 29:35-36 [l] Jer 2:11
13:11 [m] Ex 29:39 2Ch 2:4 [n] 2Lev 24:5-9
13:12 [o] Nu 10:8-9 [p] Ac 5:39
13:13 [q] Jos 8:9
13:14 [r] 2Ch 14:11
13:15 [s] 2Ch 14:12
13:16 [t] 2Ch 16:8
13:18 [u] 1Ch 5:20; 2Ch 14:11; Ps 22:5

19 Abijah pursued Jeroboam and took from him the towns of
Bethel, Jeshanah and Ephron, with their surrounding villages.
20 Jeroboam did not regain power during the time of Abijah. And
the LORD struck him down and he died.
21 But Abijah grew in strength. He married fourteen wives and
had twenty-two sons and sixteen daughters.
22 The other events of Abijah's reign, what he did and what he
said, are written in the annotations of the prophet Iddo.

Chapter 14 Theme ____________________

14 And Abijah rested with his fathers and was buried in the
City of David. Asa his son succeeded him as king, and in his
days the country was at peace for ten years.
2 Asa did what was good and right in the eyes of the LORD his
God. 3 He removed the foreign altars and the high places, smashed
the sacred stones and cut down the Asherah poles.[a][a] 4 He commanded Judah to seek the LORD, the God of their fathers, and to
obey his laws and commands. 5 He removed the high places and
incense altars[b] in every town in Judah, and the kingdom was at
peace under him. 6 He built up the fortified cities of Judah, since
the land was at peace. No one was at war with him during those
years, for the LORD gave him rest.[c]
7 "Let us build up these towns," he said to Judah, "and put walls
around them, with towers, gates and bars. The land is still ours,
because we have sought the LORD our God; we sought him and he
has given us rest on every side." So they built and prospered.
8 Asa had an army of three hundred thousand men from Judah,
equipped with large shields and with spears, and two hundred and
eighty thousand from Benjamin, armed with small shields and
with bows. All these were brave fighting men.
9 Zerah the Cushite[d] marched out against them with a vast army[b]
and three hundred chariots, and came as far as Mareshah.[e] 10 Asa
went out to meet him, and they took up battle positions in the
Valley of Zephathah near Mareshah.
11 Then Asa called[f] to the LORD his God and said, "LORD, there is
no one like you to help the powerless against the mighty. Help us,
O LORD our God, for we rely[g] on you, and in your name[h] we have
come against this vast army. O LORD, you are our God; do not let
man prevail[i] against you."
12 The LORD struck down[j] the Cushites before Asa and Judah.
The Cushites fled, 13 and Asa and his army pursued them as far as
Gerar.[k] Such a great number of Cushites fell that they could not

[a]3 That is, symbols of the goddess Asherah; here and elsewhere in 2 Chronicles [b]9 Hebrew *with an army of a thousand thousands* or *with an army of thousands upon thousands*

14:3 [a] Ex 34:13; Dt 7:5; 1Ki 15:12-14
14:5 [b] 2Ch 34:4,7
14:6 [c] 1Ch 22:9; 2Ch 15:15
14:9 [d] 2Ch 12:3; 16:8 [e] 2Ch 11:8
14:11 [f] 2Ch 13:14 [g] 2Ch 13:18 [h] 1Sa 17:45 [i] 1Sa 14:6; Ps 9:19
14:12 [j] 2Ch 13:15
14:13 [k] Ge 10:19

recover; they were crushed before the LORD and his forces. The
men of Judah carried off a large amount of plunder. 14They destroyed all the villages around Gerar, for the terror[a] of the LORD
had fallen upon them. They plundered all these villages, since
there was much booty there. 15They also attacked the camps of the
herdsmen and carried off droves of sheep and goats and camels.
Then they returned to Jerusalem.

Chapter 15 Theme ______________________

15 The Spirit of God came upon[b] Azariah son of Oded. 2He
went out to meet Asa and said to him, "Listen to me, Asa
and all Judah and Benjamin. The LORD is with you[c] when you are
with him.[d] If you seek[e] him, he will be found by you, but if you forsake him, he will forsake you.[f] 3For a long time Israel was without
the true God, without a priest to teach[g] and without the law.[h] 4But
in their distress they turned to the LORD, the God of Israel, and
sought him,[i] and he was found by them. 5In those days it was not
safe to travel about,[j] for all the inhabitants of the lands were in
great turmoil. 6One nation was being crushed by another and one
city by another,[k] because God was troubling them with every kind
of distress. 7But as for you, be strong[l] and do not give up, for your
work will be rewarded."[m]

8When Asa heard these words and the prophecy of Azariah son
of[a] Oded the prophet, he took courage. He removed the detestable
idols from the whole land of Judah and Benjamin and from the
towns he had captured[n] in the hills of Ephraim. He repaired the
altar[o] of the LORD that was in front of the portico of the LORD's
temple.

9Then he assembled all Judah and Benjamin and the people
from Ephraim, Manasseh and Simeon who had settled among
them, for large numbers[p] had come over to him from Israel when
they saw that the LORD his God was with him.

10They assembled at Jerusalem in the third month of the fifteenth year of Asa's reign. 11At that time they sacrificed to the LORD
seven hundred head of cattle and seven thousand sheep and goats
from the plunder[q] they had brought back. 12They entered into a
covenant[r] to seek the LORD,[s] the God of their fathers, with all their
heart and soul. 13All who would not seek the LORD, the God of
Israel, were to be put to death,[t] whether small or great, man or
woman. 14They took an oath to the LORD with loud acclamation,
with shouting and with trumpets and horns. 15All Judah rejoiced
about the oath because they had sworn it wholeheartedly. They
sought God[u] eagerly, and he was found by them. So the LORD gave
them rest[v] on every side.

[a]8 Vulgate and Syriac (see also Septuagint and verse 1); Hebrew does not have *Azariah son of.*

14:14 [a]Ge 35:5; 2Ch 17:10
15:1 [b]Nu 11:25,26; 24:2; 2Ch 20:14; 24:20
15:2 [c]ver 4,15; 2Ch 20:17 [d]Jas 4:8 [e]Jer 29:13 [f]1Ch 28:9; 2Ch 24:20
15:3 [g]Lev 10:11 [h]2Ch 17:9; La 2:9
15:4 [i]Dt 4:29
15:5 [j]Jdg 5:6
15:6 [k]Mt 24:7
15:7 [l]Jos 1:7,9 [m]Ps 58:11
15:8 [n]2Ch 13:19 [o]2Ch 8:12
15:9 [p]2Ch 11:16-17
15:11 [q]2Ch 14:13
15:12 [r]2Ki 11:17; 2Ch 23:16; 34:31 [s]1Ch 16:11
15:13 [t]Ex 22:20; Dt 13:9-16
15:15 [u]Dt 4:29 [v]1Ch 22:9; 2Ch 14:7

15:16 [a]Ex 34:13; 2Ch 14:2-5 [16]King Asa also deposed his grandmother Maacah from her position as queen mother, because she had made a repulsive Asherah
pole.[a] Asa cut the pole down, broke it up and burned it in the
Kidron Valley. [17]Although he did not remove the high places from
Israel, Asa's heart was fully committed ⌊to the LORD⌋ all his life.
[18]He brought into the temple of God the silver and gold and the
articles that he and his father had dedicated.

[19]There was no more war until the thirty-fifth year of Asa's reign.

16:1 [b]Jer 41:9

Chapter 16 Theme ____________________

16 In the thirty-sixth year of Asa's reign Baasha[b] king of Israel
went up against Judah and fortified Ramah to prevent anyone from leaving or entering the territory of Asa king of Judah.

[2]Asa then took the silver and gold out of the treasuries of the
LORD's temple and of his own palace and sent it to Ben-Hadad king
of Aram, who was ruling in Damascus. [3]"Let there be a treaty[c]
between me and you," he said, "as there was between my father
16:3 [c]2Ch 20:35 and your father. See, I am sending you silver and gold. Now break
your treaty with Baasha king of Israel so he will withdraw
from me."

[4]Ben-Hadad agreed with King Asa and sent the commanders of
his forces against the towns of Israel. They conquered Ijon, Dan,
Abel Maim[a] and all the store cities of Naphtali. [5]When Baasha
heard this, he stopped building Ramah and abandoned his work.
[6]Then King Asa brought all the men of Judah, and they carried
16:7 [d]1Ki 16:1 away from Ramah the stones and timber Baasha had been using.
With them he built up Geba and Mizpah.

[7]At that time Hanani[d] the seer came to Asa king of Judah and
said to him: "Because you relied on the king of Aram and not on
the LORD your God, the army of the king of Aram has escaped
from your hand. [8]Were not the Cushites[b][e] and Libyans a mighty
army with great numbers of chariots and horsemen[c]? Yet when
you relied on the LORD, he delivered[f] them into your hand. [9]For the
16:8 [e]2Ch 12:3; 14:9 [f]2Ch 13:16 eyes[g] of the LORD range throughout the earth to strengthen those
whose hearts are fully committed to him. You have done a foolish[h]
thing, and from now on you will be at war."

[10]Asa was angry with the seer because of this; he was so enraged
that he put him in prison. At the same time Asa brutally oppressed
some of the people.

[11]The events of Asa's reign, from beginning to end, are written in
the book of the kings of Judah and Israel. [12]In the thirty-ninth year
of his reign Asa was afflicted with a disease in his feet. Though his
16:9 [g]Pr 15:3; Jer 16:17; Zec 4:10 [h]1Sa 13:13 disease was severe, even in his illness he did not seek help from the

[a]4 Also known as *Abel Beth Maacah* [b]8 That is, people from the upper Nile region
[c]8 Or *charioteers*

LORD,[a] but only from the physicians. 13Then in the forty-first year
of his reign Asa died and rested with his fathers. 14They buried him
in the tomb that he had cut out for himself in the City of David.
They laid him on a bier covered with spices and various blended
perfumes,[b] and they made a huge fire[c] in his honor.

Chapter 17 Theme ______________________

17 Jehoshaphat his son succeeded him as king and strengthened himself against Israel. 2He stationed troops in all the
fortified cities of Judah and put garrisons in Judah and in the
towns of Ephraim that his father Asa had captured.[d]
3The LORD was with Jehoshaphat because in his early years he
walked in the ways his father David[e] had followed. He did not
consult the Baals 4but sought[f] the God of his father and followed
his commands rather than the practices of Israel. 5The LORD
established the kingdom under his control; and all Judah brought
gifts[g] to Jehoshaphat, so that he had great wealth and honor.[h]
6His heart was devoted[i] to the ways of the LORD; furthermore, he
removed the high places[j] and the Asherah poles[k] from Judah.[l]
7In the third year of his reign he sent his officials Ben-Hail, Obadiah, Zechariah, Nethanel and Micaiah to teach[m] in the towns of
Judah. 8With them were certain Levites[n]—Shemaiah, Nethaniah,
Zebadiah, Asahel, Shemiramoth, Jehonathan, Adonijah, Tobijah
and Tob-Adonijah—and the priests Elishama and Jehoram. 9They
taught throughout Judah, taking with them the Book of the Law[o]
of the LORD; they went around to all the towns of Judah and taught
the people.
10The fear[p] of the LORD fell on all the kingdoms of the lands surrounding Judah, so that they did not make war with Jehoshaphat.
11Some Philistines brought Jehoshaphat gifts and silver as tribute,
and the Arabs[q] brought him flocks:[r] seven thousand seven hundred rams and seven thousand seven hundred goats.
12Jehoshaphat became more and more powerful; he built forts
and store cities in Judah 13and had large supplies in the towns of
Judah. He also kept experienced fighting men in Jerusalem. 14Their
enrollment[s] by families was as follows:

From Judah, commanders of units of 1,000:
Adnah the commander, with 300,000 fighting men;
15next, Jehohanan the commander, with 280,000;
16next, Amasiah son of Zicri, who volunteered[t] himself for the
service of the LORD, with 200,000.
17From Benjamin:[u]
Eliada, a valiant soldier, with 200,000 men armed with bows
and shields;
18next, Jehozabad, with 180,000 men armed for battle.

16:12 [a]Jer 17:5-6
16:14 [b]Ge 50:2; Jn 19:39-40 [c]2Ch 21:19; Jer 34:5
17:2 [d]2Ch 15:8
17:3 [e]1Ki 22:43
17:4 [f]1Ki 12:28; 2Ch 22:9
17:5 [g]1Sa 10:27 [h]2Ch 18:1
17:6 [i]1Ki 8:61; 2Ch 15:17 [j]1Ki 15:14; 2Ch 19:3; 20:33 [k]Ex 34:13 [l]2Ch 21:12
17:7 [m]Lev 10:11; Dt 6:4-9; 2Ch 15:3; 35:3
17:8 [n]2Ch 19:8; Ne 8:7-8
17:9 [o]Dt 6:4-9; 28:61
17:10 [p]Ge 35:5; Dt 2:25; 2Ch 14:14
17:11 [q]2Ch 9:14; 26:8 [r]2Ch 21:16
17:14 [s]2Sa 24:2
17:16 [t]Jdg 5:9; 1Ch 29:9
17:17 [u]Nu 1:36

17:19 [a]2Ch 11:10 19These were the men who served the king, besides those he sta-
[b]2Ch 25:5 tioned in the fortified cities[a] throughout Judah.[b]

Chapter 18 Theme ________________________

18 Now Jehoshaphat had great wealth and honor,[c] and he
allied[d] himself with Ahab[e] by marriage. 2Some years later
he went down to visit Ahab in Samaria. Ahab slaughtered many
sheep and cattle for him and the people with him and urged him
to attack Ramoth Gilead. 3Ahab king of Israel asked Jehoshaphat
king of Judah, "Will you go with me against Ramoth Gilead?"
Jehoshaphat replied, "I am as you are, and my people as your
people; we will join you in the war." 4But Jehoshaphat also said to
the king of Israel, "First seek the counsel of the LORD."
5So the king of Israel brought together the prophets—four hun-
18:1 dred men—and asked them, "Shall we go to war against Ramoth
[c]2Ch 17:5 Gilead, or shall I refrain?"
[d]2Ch 19:1-3; "Go," they answered, "for God will give it into the king's hand."
22:3 [e]2Ch 21:6 6But Jehoshaphat asked, "Is there not a prophet of the LORD here
whom we can inquire of?"
7The king of Israel answered Jehoshaphat, "There is still one man
through whom we can inquire of the LORD, but I hate him because
he never prophesies anything good about me, but always bad. He
is Micaiah son of Imlah."
"The king should not say that," Jehoshaphat replied.
8So the king of Israel called one of his officials and said, "Bring
Micaiah son of Imlah at once."
9Dressed in their royal robes, the king of Israel and Jehoshaphat
king of Judah were sitting on their thrones at the threshing floor by
the entrance to the gate of Samaria, with all the prophets prophesying before them. 10Now Zedekiah son of Kenaanah had made
18:11 iron horns, and he declared, "This is what the LORD says: 'With
[f]2Ch 22:5 these you will gore the Arameans until they are destroyed.'"
11All the other prophets were prophesying the same thing. "Attack Ramoth Gilead[f] and be victorious," they said, "for the LORD
will give it into the king's hand."
12The messenger who had gone to summon Micaiah said to him,
"Look, as one man the other prophets are predicting success for
the king. Let your word agree with theirs, and speak favorably."
13But Micaiah said, "As surely as the LORD lives, I can tell him only
what my God says."[g]
14When he arrived, the king asked him, "Micaiah, shall we go to
war against Ramoth Gilead, or shall I refrain?"
"Attack and be victorious," he answered, "for they will be given
into your hand."
18:13 15The king said to him, "How many times must I make you swear
[g]Nu 22:18, 20,35 to tell me nothing but the truth in the name of the LORD?"

16Then Micaiah answered, "I saw all Israel[a] scattered on the hills
like sheep without a shepherd,[b] and the LORD said, 'These people
have no master. Let each one go home in peace.' "
17The king of Israel said to Jehoshaphat, "Didn't I tell you that he
never prophesies anything good about me, but only bad?"
18Micaiah continued, "Therefore hear the word of the LORD: I
saw the LORD sitting on his throne[c] with all the host of heaven
standing on his right and on his left. 19And the LORD said, 'Who
will entice Ahab king of Israel into attacking Ramoth Gilead and
going to his death there?'
"One suggested this, and another that. 20Finally, a spirit came
forward, stood before the LORD and said, 'I will entice him.'
" 'By what means?' the LORD asked.
21" 'I will go and be a lying spirit[d] in the mouths of all his prophets,' he said.
" 'You will succeed in enticing him,' said the LORD. 'Go and do it.'
22"So now the LORD has put a lying spirit in the mouths of these
prophets of yours.[e] The LORD has decreed disaster for you."
23Then Zedekiah son of Kenaanah went up and slapped[f] Micaiah in the face. "Which way did the spirit from[a] the LORD go when
he went from me to speak to you?" he asked.
24Micaiah replied, "You will find out on the day you go to hide
in an inner room."
25The king of Israel then ordered, "Take Micaiah and send him
back to Amon the ruler of the city and to Joash the king's son,
26and say, 'This is what the king says: Put this fellow in prison[g] and
give him nothing but bread and water until I return safely.' "
27Micaiah declared, "If you ever return safely, the LORD has not
spoken through me." Then he added, "Mark my words, all you
people!"
28So the king of Israel and Jehoshaphat king of Judah went up to
Ramoth Gilead. 29The king of Israel said to Jehoshaphat, "I will
enter the battle in disguise, but you wear your royal robes." So the
king of Israel disguised[h] himself and went into battle.
30Now the king of Aram had ordered his chariot commanders,
"Do not fight with anyone, small or great, except the king of Israel."
31When the chariot commanders saw Jehoshaphat, they thought,
"This is the king of Israel." So they turned to attack him, but
Jehoshaphat cried out,[i] and the LORD helped him. God drew them
away from him, 32for when the chariot commanders saw that he
was not the king of Israel, they stopped pursuing him.
33But someone drew his bow at random and hit the king of
Israel between the sections of his armor. The king told the chariot
driver, "Wheel around and get me out of the fighting. I've been

[a]23 Or *Spirit of*

18:16 [a]1Ch 9:1 [b]Nu 27:17; Eze 34:5-8
18:18 [c]Da 7:9
18:21 [d]1Ch 21:1; Job 1:6; Zec 3:1; Jn 8:44
18:22 [e]Job 12:16; Isa 19:14; Eze 14:9
18:23 [f]Jer 20:2; Mk 14:65; Ac 23:2
18:26 [g]2Ch 16:10; Heb 11:36
18:29 [h]1Sa 28:8
18:31 [i]2Ch 13:14

wounded." 34All day long the battle raged, and the king of Israel propped himself up in his chariot facing the Arameans until evening. Then at sunset he died.[a]

Chapter 19 Theme ____________________

19 When Jehoshaphat king of Judah returned safely to his palace in Jerusalem, 2Jehu[b] the seer, the son of Hanani, went out to meet him and said to the king, "Should you help the wicked[c] and love[a] those who hate the LORD?[d] Because of this, the wrath[e] of the LORD is upon you. 3There is, however, some good[f] in you, for you have rid the land of the Asherah poles[g] and have set your heart on seeking God.[h]"

4Jehoshaphat lived in Jerusalem, and he went out again among the people from Beersheba to the hill country of Ephraim and turned them back to the LORD, the God of their fathers. 5He appointed judges[i] in the land, in each of the fortified cities of Judah. 6He told them, "Consider carefully what you do,[j] because you are not judging for man[k] but for the LORD, who is with you whenever you give a verdict. 7Now let the fear of the LORD be upon you. Judge carefully, for with the LORD our God there is no injustice[l] or partiality[m] or bribery."

8In Jerusalem also, Jehoshaphat appointed some of the Levites, priests and heads of Israelite families to administer[n] the law of the LORD and to settle disputes. And they lived in Jerusalem. 9He gave them these orders: "You must serve faithfully and wholeheartedly in the fear of the LORD. 10In every case that comes before you from your fellow countrymen who live in the cities—whether bloodshed or other concerns of the law, commands, decrees or ordinances—you are to warn them not to sin against the LORD;[o] otherwise his wrath will come on you and your brothers. Do this, and you will not sin.

11"Amariah the chief priest will be over you in any matter concerning the LORD, and Zebadiah son of Ishmael, the leader of the tribe of Judah, will be over you in any matter concerning the king, and the Levites will serve as officials before you. Act with courage,[p] and may the LORD be with those who do well."

Chapter 20 Theme ____________________

20 After this, the Moabites and Ammonites with some of the Meunites[b][q] came to make war on Jehoshaphat.

2Some men came and told Jehoshaphat, "A vast army is coming against you from Edom,[c] from the other side of the Sea.[d] It is

18:34
[a]2Ch 22:5

19:2
[b]1Ki 16:1
[c]2Ch 16:2-9
[d]Ps 139:21-22
[e]2Ch 24:18; 32:25; Ps 7:11

19:3
[f]1Ki 14:13; 2Ch 12:12
[g]2Ch 17:6
[h]2Ch 18:1; 20:35; 25:7; Ezr 7:10

19:5
[i]Ge 47:6; Ex 18:26

19:6
[j]Lev 19:15
[k]Dt 1:17; 16:18-20; 17:8-13

19:7
[l]Ge 18:25; Dt 32:4
[m]Dt 10:17; Job 34:19; Ro 2:11; Col 3:25

19:8
[n]2Ch 17:8-9

19:10
[o]Dt 17:8-13

19:11
[p]1Ch 28:20

20:1
[q]1Ch 4:41

[a]2 Or *and make alliances with* [b]1 Some Septuagint manuscripts; Hebrew *Ammonites*
[c]2 One Hebrew manuscript; most Hebrew manuscripts, Septuagint and Vulgate *Aram*
[d]2 That is, the Dead Sea

already in Hazazon Tamar[a]" (that is, En Gedi). 3Alarmed, Jehoshaphat resolved to inquire of the LORD, and he proclaimed a fast[b] for
all Judah. 4The people of Judah came together to seek help from the
LORD; indeed, they came from every town in Judah to seek him.
5Then Jehoshaphat stood up in the assembly of Judah and Jerusalem at the temple of the LORD in the front of the new courtyard
6and said:

"O LORD, God of our fathers,[c] are you not the God who is in
heaven?[d] You rule over all the kingdoms[e] of the nations. Power
and might are in your hand, and no one can withstand you.
7O our God, did you not drive out the inhabitants of this land
before your people Israel and give it forever to the descendants
of Abraham your friend?[f] 8They have lived in it and have built
in it a sanctuary[g] for your Name, saying, 9'If calamity comes
upon us, whether the sword of judgment, or plague or famine,[h]
we will stand in your presence before this temple that bears
your Name and will cry out to you in our distress, and you will
hear us and save us.'

10"But now here are men from Ammon, Moab and Mount
Seir, whose territory you would not allow Israel to invade when
they came from Egypt;[i] so they turned away from them and
did not destroy them. 11See how they are repaying us by coming
to drive us out of the possession[j] you gave us as an inheritance.
12O our God, will you not judge them?[k] For we have no power
to face this vast army that is attacking us. We do not know
what to do, but our eyes are upon you.[l]"

13All the men of Judah, with their wives and children and little
ones, stood there before the LORD.

14Then the Spirit[m] of the LORD came upon Jahaziel son of Zechariah, the son of Benaiah, the son of Jeiel, the son of Mattaniah, a
Levite and descendant of Asaph, as he stood in the assembly.

15He said: "Listen, King Jehoshaphat and all who live in Judah
and Jerusalem! This is what the LORD says to you: 'Do not be afraid
or discouraged[n] because of this vast army. For the battle[o] is not
yours, but God's. 16Tomorrow march down against them. They
will be climbing up by the Pass of Ziz, and you will find them at the
end of the gorge in the Desert of Jeruel. 17You will not have to fight
this battle. Take up your positions; stand firm and see[p] the deliverance the LORD will give you, O Judah and Jerusalem. Do not be
afraid; do not be discouraged. Go out to face them tomorrow, and
the LORD will be with you.'"

18Jehoshaphat bowed[q] with his face to the ground, and all the
people of Judah and Jerusalem fell down in worship before the
LORD. 19Then some Levites from the Kohathites and Korahites

20:2 [a]Ge 14:7
20:3 [b]1Sa 7:6; 2Ch 19:3; Ezr 8:21; Jer 36:9; Jnh 3:5,7
20:6 [c]Mt 6:9 [d]Dt 4:39 [e]1Ch 29:11-12
20:7 [f]Isa 41:8; Jas 2:23
20:8 [g]2Ch 6:20
20:9 [h]2Ch 6:28
20:10 [i]Nu 20:14-21; Dt 2:4-6,9, 18-19
20:11 [j]Ps 83:1-12
20:12 [k]Jdg 11:27 [l]Ps 25:15; 121:1-2
20:14 [m]2Ch 15:1
20:15 [n]2Ch 32:7 [o]Ex 14:13-14; 1Sa 17:47
20:17 [p]Ex 14:13; 2Ch 15:2
20:18 [q]Ex 4:31

stood up and praised the LORD, the God of Israel, with very loud
voice.
20 Early in the morning they left for the Desert of Tekoa. As they
set out, Jehoshaphat stood and said, "Listen to me, Judah and
people of Jerusalem! Have faith[a] in the LORD your God and you
will be upheld; have faith in his prophets and you will be successful.[b]" 21 After consulting the people, Jehoshaphat appointed men
to sing to the LORD and to praise him for the splendor of his[a] holiness[c] as they went out at the head of the army, saying:

> "Give thanks to the LORD,
> for his love endures forever."[d]

22 As they began to sing and praise, the LORD set ambushes[e]
against the men of Ammon and Moab and Mount Seir who were
invading Judah, and they were defeated. 23 The men of Ammon[f]
and Moab rose up against the men from Mount Seir[g] to destroy
and annihilate them. After they finished slaughtering the men
from Seir, they helped to destroy one another.[h]
24 When the men of Judah came to the place that overlooks the
desert and looked toward the vast army, they saw only dead bodies
lying on the ground; no one had escaped. 25 So Jehoshaphat and
his men went to carry off their plunder, and they found among
them a great amount of equipment and clothing[b] and also articles
of value—more than they could take away. There was so much
plunder that it took three days to collect it. 26 On the fourth day
they assembled in the Valley of Beracah, where they praised the
LORD. This is why it is called the Valley of Beracah[c] to this day.
27 Then, led by Jehoshaphat, all the men of Judah and Jerusalem
returned joyfully to Jerusalem, for the LORD had given them cause
to rejoice over their enemies. 28 They entered Jerusalem and went to
the temple of the LORD with harps and lutes and trumpets.
29 The fear[i] of God came upon all the kingdoms of the countries
when they heard how the LORD had fought[j] against the enemies of
Israel. 30 And the kingdom of Jehoshaphat was at peace, for his God
had given him rest[k] on every side.
31 So Jehoshaphat reigned over Judah. He was thirty-five years
old when he became king of Judah, and he reigned in Jerusalem
twenty-five years. His mother's name was Azubah daughter of
Shilhi. 32 He walked in the ways of his father Asa and did not stray
from them; he did what was right in the eyes of the LORD. 33 The
high places,[l] however, were not removed, and the people still had
not set their hearts on the God of their fathers.

20:20 [a]Isa 7:9 [b]Ge 39:3; Pr 16:3
20:21 [c]1Ch 16:29; Ps 29:2 [d]2Ch 5:13; Ps 136:1
20:22 [e]Jdg 7:22; 2Ch 13:13
20:23 [f]Ge 19:38 [g]2Ch 21:8 [h]Jdg 7:22; 1Sa 14:20; Eze 38:21
20:29 [i]Ge 35:5; Dt 2:25; 2Ch 14:14; 17:10 [j]Ex 14:14
20:30 [k]1Ch 22:9; 2Ch 14:6-7; 15:15
20:33 [l]2Ch 17:6; 19:3

[a] 21 Or *him with the splendor of* [b] 25 Some Hebrew manuscripts and Vulgate; most Hebrew manuscripts *corpses* [c] 26 *Beracah* means *praise.*

34 The other events of Jehoshaphat's reign, from beginning to
end, are written in the annals of Jehu[a] son of Hanani, which are
recorded in the book of the kings of Israel.
35 Later, Jehoshaphat king of Judah made an alliance[b] with Ahaziah king of Israel, who was guilty of wickedness.[c] 36 He agreed with
him to construct a fleet of trading ships.[a] After these were built at
Ezion Geber, 37 Eliezer son of Dodavahu of Mareshah prophesied
against Jehoshaphat, saying, "Because you have made an alliance
with Ahaziah, the LORD will destroy what you have made." The
ships[d] were wrecked and were not able to set sail to trade.[b]

Chapter 21 Theme ____________________________

21 Then Jehoshaphat rested with his fathers and was buried
with them in the City of David. And Jehoram[e] his son succeeded him as king. 2 Jehoram's brothers, the sons of Jehoshaphat,
were Azariah, Jehiel, Zechariah, Azariahu, Michael and Shephatiah.
All these were sons of Jehoshaphat king of Israel.[c] 3 Their father
had given them many gifts[f] of silver and gold and articles of value,
as well as fortified cities[g] in Judah, but he had given the kingdom
to Jehoram because he was his firstborn son.
4 When Jehoram established[h] himself firmly over his father's
kingdom, he put all his brothers[i] to the sword along with some of
the princes of Israel. 5 Jehoram was thirty-two years old when he
became king, and he reigned in Jerusalem eight years. 6 He walked
in the ways of the kings of Israel,[j] as the house of Ahab had done,
for he married a daughter of Ahab.[k] He did evil in the eyes of the
LORD. 7 Nevertheless, because of the covenant the LORD had made
with David,[l] the LORD was not willing to destroy the house of
David.[m] He had promised to maintain a lamp[n] for him and his
descendants forever.
8 In the time of Jehoram, Edom[o] rebelled against Judah and set
up its own king. 9 So Jehoram went there with his officers and all
his chariots. The Edomites surrounded him and his chariot commanders, but he rose up and broke through by night. 10 To this day
Edom has been in rebellion against Judah.

Libnah[p] revolted at the same time, because Jehoram had forsaken
the LORD, the God of his fathers. 11 He had also built high places on
the hills of Judah and had caused the people of Jerusalem to prostitute themselves and had led Judah astray.
12 Jehoram received a letter from Elijah[q] the prophet, which said:

"This is what the LORD, the God of your father[r] David, says:
'You have not walked in the ways of your father Jehoshaphat or

20:34 [a] 1Ki 16:1
20:35 [b] 2Ch 16:3 [c] 2Ch 19:1-3
20:37 [d] 1Ki 9:26; 2Ch 9:21
21:1 [e] 1Ch 3:11
21:3 [f] 2Ch 11:23 [g] 2Ch 11:10
21:4 [h] 1Ki 2:12 [i] Jdg 9:5
21:6 [j] 1Ki 12:28-30 [k] 2Ch 18:1; 22:3
21:7 [l] 2Sa 7:13 [m] 2Sa 7:15; 2Ch 23:3 [n] 2Sa 21:17; 1Ki 11:36
21:8 [o] 2Ch 20:22-23
21:10 [p] Nu 33:20
21:12 [q] 2Ki 1:16-17 [r] 2Ch 17:3-6

[a] 36 Hebrew *of ships that could go to Tarshish* [b] 37 Hebrew *sail for Tarshish* [c] 2 That is, Judah, as frequently in 2 Chronicles

of Asa[a] king of Judah. 13 But you have walked in the ways of the kings of Israel, and you have led Judah and the people of Jerusalem to prostitute themselves, just as the house of Ahab did.[b] You have also murdered your own brothers, members of your father's house, men who were better[c] than you. 14 So now the LORD is about to strike your people, your sons, your wives and everything that is yours, with a heavy blow. 15 You yourself will be very ill with a lingering disease[d] of the bowels, until the disease causes your bowels to come out.' "

16 The LORD aroused against Jehoram the hostility of the Philistines and of the Arabs[e] who lived near the Cushites. 17 They attacked Judah, invaded it and carried off all the goods found in the king's palace, together with his sons and wives. Not a son was left to him except Ahaziah,[a] the youngest.[f]

18 After all this, the LORD afflicted Jehoram with an incurable disease of the bowels. 19 In the course of time, at the end of the second year, his bowels came out because of the disease, and he died in great pain. His people made no fire in his honor,[g] as they had for his fathers.

20 Jehoram was thirty-two years old when he became king, and he reigned in Jerusalem eight years. He passed away, to no one's regret, and was buried[h] in the City of David, but not in the tombs of the kings.

Chapter 22 Theme __________________________

22 The people[i] of Jerusalem[j] made Ahaziah, Jehoram's youngest son, king in his place, since the raiders,[k] who came with the Arabs into the camp, had killed all the older sons. So Ahaziah son of Jehoram king of Judah began to reign.

2 Ahaziah was twenty-two[b] years old when he became king, and he reigned in Jerusalem one year. His mother's name was Athaliah, a granddaughter of Omri.

3 He too walked[l] in the ways of the house of Ahab,[m] for his mother encouraged him in doing wrong. 4 He did evil in the eyes of the LORD, as the house of Ahab had done, for after his father's death they became his advisers, to his undoing. 5 He also followed their counsel when he went with Joram[c] son of Ahab king of Israel to war against Hazael king of Aram at Ramoth Gilead.[n] The Arameans wounded Joram; 6 so he returned to Jezreel to recover from the wounds they had inflicted on him at Ramoth[d] in his battle with Hazael[o] king of Aram.

21:12 a 2Ch 14:2
21:13 b ver 6,11; 1Ki 16:29-33 c ver 4; 1Ki 2:32
21:15 d ver 18-19; Nu 12:10
21:16 e 2Ch 17:10-11; 22:1; 26:7
21:17 f 2Ki 12:18; 2Ch 22:1; 25:23; Joel 3:5
21:19 g 2Ch 16:14
21:20 h 2Ch 24:25; 28:27; 33:20; Jer 22:18,28
22:1 i 2Ch 33:25; 36:1 j 2Ch 23:20-21; 26:1 k 2Ch 21:16-17
22:3 l 2Ch 18:1 m 2Ch 21:6
22:5 n 2Ch 18:11,34
22:6 o 1Ki 19:15; 2Ki 8:13-15; 9:15

a 17 Hebrew *Jehoahaz,* a variant of *Ahaziah* b 2 Some Septuagint manuscripts and Syriac (see also 2 Kings 8:26); Hebrew *forty-two* c 5 Hebrew *Jehoram,* a variant of *Joram;* also in verses 6 and 7 d 6 Hebrew *Ramah,* a variant of *Ramoth*

Then Ahaziah[a] son of Jehoram king of Judah went down to
Jezreel to see Joram son of Ahab because he had been wounded.
7Through Ahaziah's[a] visit to Joram, God brought about Ahaziah's downfall. When Ahaziah arrived, he went out with Joram to
meet Jehu son of Nimshi, whom the LORD had anointed to destroy
the house of Ahab. 8While Jehu was executing judgment on the
house of Ahab,[b] he found the princes of Judah and the sons of
Ahaziah's relatives, who had been attending Ahaziah, and he
killed them. 9He then went in search of Ahaziah, and his men captured him while he was hiding[c] in Samaria. He was brought to Jehu
and put to death. They buried him, for they said, "He was a son of
Jehoshaphat, who sought[d] the LORD with all his heart." So there
was no one in the house of Ahaziah powerful enough to retain the
kingdom.
10When Athaliah the mother of Ahaziah saw that her son was
dead, she proceeded to destroy the whole royal family of the house
of Judah. 11But Jehosheba,[b] the daughter of King Jehoram, took
Joash son of Ahaziah and stole him away from among the royal
princes who were about to be murdered and put him and his nurse
in a bedroom. Because Jehosheba,[b] the daughter of King Jehoram and wife of the priest Jehoiada, was Ahaziah's sister, she hid
the child from Athaliah so she could not kill him. 12He remained
hidden with them at the temple of God for six years while Athaliah ruled the land.

Chapter 23 Theme ____________________

23 In the seventh year Jehoiada showed his strength. He made
a covenant with the commanders of units of a hundred:
Azariah son of Jeroham, Ishmael son of Jehohanan, Azariah son of
Obed, Maaseiah son of Adaiah, and Elishaphat son of Zicri. 2They
went throughout Judah and gathered the Levites[e] and the heads of
Israelite families from all the towns. When they came to Jerusalem,
3the whole assembly made a covenant[f] with the king at the temple
of God.
Jehoiada said to them, "The king's son shall reign, as the LORD
promised concerning the descendants of David.[g] 4Now this is what
you are to do: A third of you priests and Levites who are going on
duty on the Sabbath are to keep watch at the doors, 5a third of you
at the royal palace and a third at the Foundation Gate, and all the
other men are to be in the courtyards of the temple of the LORD.
6No one is to enter the temple of the LORD except the priests and
Levites on duty; they may enter because they are consecrated, but
all the other men are to guard[h] what the LORD has assigned to

[a]6 Some Hebrew manuscripts, Septuagint, Vulgate and Syriac (see also 2 Kings 8:29); most Hebrew manuscripts *Azariah* [b]*11* Hebrew *Jehoshabeath,* a variant of *Jehosheba*

22:7 *a* 2Ki 9:16; 2Ch 10:15
22:8 *b* 2Ki 10:13
22:9 *c* Jdg 9:5 *d* 2Ch 17:4
23:2 *e* Nu 35:2-5
23:3 *f* 2Ki 11:17 *g* 2Sa 7:12; 1Ki 2:4; 2Ch 6:16; 7:18; 21:7
23:6 *h* 1Ch 23:28-29; Zec 3:7

them.[a] [7]The Levites are to station themselves around the king, each
man with his weapons in his hand. Anyone who enters the temple
must be put to death. Stay close to the king wherever he goes."

[8]The Levites and all the men of Judah did just as Jehoiada the
priest ordered.[a] Each one took his men—those who were going
on duty on the Sabbath and those who were going off duty—for
Jehoiada the priest had not released any of the divisions.[b] [9]Then
he gave the commanders of units of a hundred the spears and the
large and small shields that had belonged to King David and that
were in the temple of God. [10]He stationed all the men, each with
his weapon in his hand, around the king—near the altar and the
temple, from the south side to the north side of the temple.

[11]Jehoiada and his sons brought out the king's son and put the
crown on him; they presented him with a copy[c] of the covenant
and proclaimed him king. They anointed him and shouted, "Long
live the king!"

[12]When Athaliah heard the noise of the people running and
cheering the king, she went to them at the temple of the LORD.
[13]She looked, and there was the king,[d] standing by his pillar[e] at the
entrance. The officers and the trumpeters were beside the king,
and all the people of the land were rejoicing and blowing trumpets,
and singers with musical instruments were leading the praises.
Then Athaliah tore her robes and shouted, "Treason! Treason!"

[14]Jehoiada the priest sent out the commanders of units of a hundred, who were in charge of the troops, and said to them: "Bring
her out between the ranks[b] and put to the sword anyone who follows her." For the priest had said, "Do not put her to death at the
temple of the LORD." [15]So they seized her as she reached the
entrance of the Horse Gate[f] on the palace grounds, and there they
put her to death.

[16]Jehoiada then made a covenant[g] that he and the people and
the king[c] would be the LORD's people. [17]All the people went to
the temple of Baal and tore it down. They smashed the altars and
idols and killed[h] Mattan the priest of Baal in front of the altars.

[18]Then Jehoiada placed the oversight of the temple of the LORD
in the hands of the priests, who were Levites,[i] to whom David had
made assignments in the temple,[j] to present the burnt offerings
of the LORD as written in the Law of Moses, with rejoicing and
singing, as David had ordered. [19]He also stationed doorkeepers[k]
at the gates of the LORD's temple so that no one who was in any
way unclean might enter.

[20]He took with him the commanders of hundreds, the nobles,
the rulers of the people and all the people of the land and brought

23:8 [a]2Ki 11:9 [b]1Ch 24:1
23:11 [c]Ex 25:16; Dt 17:18; 1Sa 10:24
23:13 [d]1Ki 1:41 [e]1Ki 7:15
23:15 [f]Ne 3:28; Jer 31:40
23:16 [g]2Ch 29:10; 34:31; Ne 9:38
23:17 [h]Dt 13:6-9
23:18 [i]1Ch 23:28-32; 2Ch 5:5 [j]1Ch 23:6; 25:6
23:19 [k]1Ch 9:22

[a]6 Or *to observe the LORD's command ⌊not to enter⌋* [b]14 Or *out from the precincts* [c]16 Or *covenant between ⌊the LORD⌋ and the people and the king that they* (see 2 Kings 11:17)

the king down from the temple of the LORD. They went into the
palace through the Upper Gate[a] and seated the king on the royal
throne, 21and all the people of the land rejoiced. And the city was
quiet, because Athaliah had been slain with the sword.[b]

Chapter 24 Theme ______________________

24 Joash was seven years old when he became king, and he
reigned in Jerusalem forty years. His mother's name was
Zibiah; she was from Beersheba. 2Joash did what was right in the
eyes of the LORD[c] all the years of Jehoiada the priest. 3Jehoiada
chose two wives for him, and he had sons and daughters.
4Some time later Joash decided to restore the temple of the LORD.
5He called together the priests and Levites and said to them, "Go
to the towns of Judah and collect the money[d] due annually from
all Israel,[e] to repair the temple of your God. Do it now." But the
Levites[f] did not act at once.
6Therefore the king summoned Jehoiada the chief priest and said
to him, "Why haven't you required the Levites to bring in from
Judah and Jerusalem the tax imposed by Moses the servant of the
LORD and by the assembly of Israel for the Tent of the Testimony?"[g]
7Now the sons of that wicked woman Athaliah had broken into
the temple of God and had used even its sacred objects for the
Baals.
8At the king's command, a chest was made and placed outside,
at the gate of the temple of the LORD. 9A proclamation was then
issued in Judah and Jerusalem that they should bring to the LORD
the tax that Moses the servant of God had required of Israel in
the desert. 10All the officials and all the people brought their contributions gladly,[h] dropping them into the chest until it was full.
11Whenever the chest was brought in by the Levites to the king's
officials and they saw that there was a large amount of money, the
royal secretary and the officer of the chief priest would come and
empty the chest and carry it back to its place. They did this regularly and collected a great amount of money. 12The king and
Jehoiada gave it to the men who carried out the work required for
the temple of the LORD. They hired[i] masons and carpenters to
restore the LORD's temple, and also workers in iron and bronze to
repair the temple.
13The men in charge of the work were diligent, and the repairs
progressed under them. They rebuilt the temple of God according
to its original design and reinforced it. 14When they had finished,
they brought the rest of the money to the king and Jehoiada, and
with it were made articles for the LORD's temple: articles for the
service and for the burnt offerings, and also dishes and other
objects of gold and silver. As long as Jehoiada lived, burnt offerings
were presented continually in the temple of the LORD.

23:20 [a] 2Ki 15:35
23:21 [b] 2Ch 22:1
24:2 [c] 2Ch 25:2; 26:5
24:5 [d] Ex 30:16; Ne 10:32-33; Mt 17:24 [e] 1Ch 11:1 [f] 1Ch 26:20
24:6 [g] Ex 30:12-16; Nu 1:50
24:10 [h] Ex 25:2; 1Ch 29:3,6,9
24:12 [i] 2Ch 34:11

15Now Jehoiada was old and full of years, and he died at the age
of a hundred and thirty. 16He was buried with the kings in the City
of David, because of the good he had done in Israel for God and
his temple.
17After the death of Jehoiada, the officials of Judah came and paid
homage to the king, and he listened to them. 18They abandoned[a]
the temple of the LORD, the God of their fathers, and worshiped
Asherah poles and idols.[b] Because of their guilt, God's anger[c] came
upon Judah and Jerusalem. 19Although the LORD sent prophets to
the people to bring them back to him, and though they testified
against them, they would not listen.[d]
20Then the Spirit[e] of God came upon Zechariah[f] son of Jehoiada
the priest. He stood before the people and said, "This is what God
says: 'Why do you disobey the LORD's commands? You will not
prosper.[g] Because you have forsaken the LORD, he has forsaken[h]
you.'"
21But they plotted against him, and by order of the king they
stoned[i] him to death[j] in the courtyard of the LORD's temple.[k]
22King Joash did not remember the kindness Zechariah's father
Jehoiada had shown him but killed his son, who said as he lay
dying, "May the LORD see this and call you to account."[l]
23At the turn of the year,[a] the army of Aram marched against
Joash; it invaded Judah and Jerusalem and killed all the leaders of
the people.[m] They sent all the plunder to their king in Damascus.
24Although the Aramean army had come with only a few men,[n]
the LORD delivered into their hands a much larger army.[o] Because
Judah had forsaken the LORD, the God of their fathers, judgment
was executed on Joash. 25When the Arameans withdrew, they left
Joash severely wounded. His officials conspired against him for
murdering the son of Jehoiada the priest, and they killed him in
his bed. So he died and was buried[p] in the City of David, but not
in the tombs of the kings.
26Those who conspired against him were Zabad,[b] son of Shimeath an Ammonite woman, and Jehozabad, son of Shimrith[c][q] a
Moabite woman.[r] 27The account of his sons, the many prophecies
about him, and the record of the restoration of the temple of God
are written in the annotations on the book of the kings. And
Amaziah his son succeeded him as king.

Chapter 25 Theme ______________________

25 Amaziah was twenty-five years old when he became king,
and he reigned in Jerusalem twenty-nine years. His mother's
name was Jehoaddin[d]; she was from Jerusalem. 2He did what was
right in the eyes of the LORD, but not wholeheartedly.[s] 3After the

24:18 [a]ver 4; Jos 24:20; 2Ch 7:19 [b]Ex 34:13; 1Ki 14:23; 2Ch 33:3; Jer 17:2 [c]Jos 22:20; 2Ch 19:2
24:19 [d]Nu 11:29; Jer 7:25; Zec 1:4
24:20 [e]Jdg 3:10; 1Ch 12:18; 2Ch 20:14 [f]Mt 23:35; Lk 11:51 [g]Nu 14:41 [h]Dt 31:17; 2Ch 15:2
24:21 [i]Jos 7:25; Ac 7:58-59 [j]Ne 9:26; Jer 26:21 [k]Jer 20:2; Mt 23:35
24:22 [l]Ge 9:5
24:23 [m]2Ki 12:17-18
24:24 [n]2Ch 14:9; 16:8; 20:2,12 [o]Lev 26:23-25; Dt 28:25
24:25 [p]2Ch 21:20
24:26 [q]2Ki 12:21 [r]Ru 1:4
25:2 [s]ver 14; 1Ki 8:61; 2Ch 24:2

[a] *23* Probably in the spring [b] *26* A variant of *Jozabad* [c] *26* A variant of *Shomer*
[d] *1* Hebrew *Jehoaddan,* a variant of *Jehoaddin*

kingdom was firmly in his control, he executed the officials who
had murdered his father the king. 4Yet he did not put their sons to
death, but acted in accordance with what is written in the Law, in
the Book of Moses,[a] where the LORD commanded: "Fathers shall
not be put to death for their children, nor children put to death for
their fathers; each is to die for his own sins."[a][b]

5Amaziah called the people of Judah together and assigned them
according to their families to commanders of thousands and
commanders of hundreds for all Judah and Benjamin. He then
mustered[c] those twenty years old[d] or more and found that there
were three hundred thousand men ready for military service,[e]
able to handle the spear and shield. 6He also hired a hundred
thousand fighting men from Israel for a hundred talents[b] of silver.

7But a man of God came to him and said, "O king, these troops
from Israel[f] must not march with you, for the LORD is not with
Israel—not with any of the people of Ephraim. 8Even if you go
and fight courageously in battle, God will overthrow you before
the enemy, for God has the power to help or to overthrow."[g]

9Amaziah asked the man of God, "But what about the hundred
talents I paid for these Israelite troops?"

The man of God replied, "The LORD can give you much more
than that."[h]

10So Amaziah dismissed the troops who had come to him from
Ephraim and sent them home. They were furious with Judah and
left for home in a great rage.[i]

11Amaziah then marshaled his strength and led his army to the
Valley of Salt, where he killed ten thousand men of Seir. 12The
army of Judah also captured ten thousand men alive, took them
to the top of a cliff and threw them down so that all were dashed
to pieces.[j]

13Meanwhile the troops that Amaziah had sent back and had not
allowed to take part in the war raided Judean towns from Samaria
to Beth Horon. They killed three thousand people and carried off
great quantities of plunder.

14When Amaziah returned from slaughtering the Edomites, he
brought back the gods of the people of Seir. He set them up as his
own gods,[k] bowed down to them and burned sacrifices to them.
15The anger of the LORD burned against Amaziah, and he sent a
prophet to him, who said, "Why do you consult this people's gods,
which could not save[l] their own people from your hand?"

16While he was still speaking, the king said to him, "Have we
appointed you an adviser to the king? Stop! Why be struck down?"

So the prophet stopped but said, "I know that God has determined to destroy you, because you have done this and have not
listened to my counsel."

a *4* Deut. 24:16 b *6* That is, about 3 3/4 tons (about 3.4 metric tons); also in verse 9

25:4 [a]Dt 28:61 [b]Nu 26:11; Dt 24:16

25:5 [c]2Sa 24:2 [d]Ex 30:14 [e]Nu 1:3; 1Ch 21:1; 2Ch 17:14-19

25:7 [f]2Ch 16:2-9; 19:1-3

25:8 [g]2Ch 14:11; 20:6

25:9 [h]Dt 8:18; Pr 10:22

25:10 [i]ver 13

25:12 [j]Ps 141:6; Ob 3

25:14 [k]Ex 20:3; 2Ch 28:23; Isa 44:15

25:15 [l]Ps 96:5; Isa 36:20

25:18 [a]Jdg 9:8-15

17After Amaziah king of Judah consulted his advisers, he sent
this challenge to Jehoash[a] son of Jehoahaz, the son of Jehu, king of
Israel: "Come, meet me face to face."
18But Jehoash king of Israel replied to Amaziah king of Judah:
"A thistle[a] in Lebanon sent a message to a cedar in Lebanon, 'Give
your daughter to my son in marriage.' Then a wild beast in Lebanon came along and trampled the thistle underfoot. 19You say to
yourself that you have defeated Edom, and now you are arrogant

25:20 [b]1Ki 12:15; 2Ch 10:15; 22:7

and proud. But stay at home! Why ask for trouble and cause your
own downfall and that of Judah also?"
20Amaziah, however, would not listen, for God so worked that he
might hand them over to ⌞Jehoash⌟, because they sought the gods
of Edom.[b] 21So Jehoash king of Israel attacked. He and Amaziah
king of Judah faced each other at Beth Shemesh in Judah. 22Judah
was routed by Israel, and every man fled to his home. 23Jehoash
king of Israel captured Amaziah king of Judah, the son of Joash,
the son of Ahaziah,[b] at Beth Shemesh. Then Jehoash brought

25:23 [c]2Ki 14:13; Ne 8:16; 12:39 [d]2Ch 26:9; Jer 31:38

him to Jerusalem and broke down the wall of Jerusalem from the
Ephraim Gate[c] to the Corner Gate[d]—a section about six hundred
feet[c] long. 24He took all the gold and silver and all the articles
found in the temple of God that had been in the care of Obed-
Edom,[e] together with the palace treasures and the hostages, and
returned to Samaria.
25Amaziah son of Joash king of Judah lived for fifteen years after
the death of Jehoash son of Jehoahaz king of Israel. 26As for the
other events of Amaziah's reign, from beginning to end, are they
not written in the book of the kings of Judah and Israel? 27From

25:24 [e]1Ch 26:15

the time that Amaziah turned away from following the LORD, they
conspired against him in Jerusalem and he fled to Lachish[f], but
they sent men after him to Lachish and killed him there. 28He was
brought back by horse and was buried with his fathers in the City
of Judah.

Chapter 26 Theme ____________________

25:27 [f]Jos 10:3

26 Then all the people of Judah[g] took Uzziah,[d] who was sixteen years old, and made him king in place of his father
Amaziah. 2He was the one who rebuilt Elath and restored it to
Judah after Amaziah rested with his fathers.
3Uzziah was sixteen years old when he became king, and he
reigned in Jerusalem fifty-two years. His mother's name was Jecoliah; she was from Jerusalem. 4He did what was right in the eyes
of the LORD, just as his father Amaziah had done. 5He sought God

[a]*17* Hebrew *Joash,* a variant of *Jehoash*; also in verses 18, 21, 23 and 25 [b]*23* Hebrew *Jehoahaz,* a variant of *Ahaziah* [c]*23* Hebrew *four hundred cubits* (about 180 meters)
[d]*1* Also called *Azariah*

26:1 [g]2Ch 22:1

during the days of Zechariah, who instructed him in the fear[a] of
God.[a] As long as he sought the LORD, God gave him success.[b]
6He went to war against the Philistines[c] and broke down the
walls of Gath, Jabneh and Ashdod.[d] He then rebuilt towns near
Ashdod and elsewhere among the Philistines. 7God helped him
against the Philistines and against the Arabs[e] who lived in Gur
Baal and against the Meunites.[f] 8The Ammonites[g] brought tribute to Uzziah, and his fame spread as far as the border of Egypt,
because he had become very powerful.
9Uzziah built towers in Jerusalem at the Corner Gate,[h] at the Valley Gate[i] and at the angle of the wall, and he fortified them. 10He
also built towers in the desert and dug many cisterns, because he
had much livestock in the foothills and in the plain. He had people
working his fields and vineyards in the hills and in the fertile lands,
for he loved the soil.
11Uzziah had a well-trained army, ready to go out by divisions
according to their numbers as mustered by Jeiel the secretary and
Maaseiah the officer under the direction of Hananiah, one of the
royal officials. 12The total number of family leaders over the fighting men was 2,600. 13Under their command was an army of
307,500 men trained for war, a powerful force to support the king
against his enemies. 14Uzziah provided shields, spears, helmets,
coats of armor, bows and slingstones for the entire army.[j] 15In
Jerusalem he made machines designed by skillful men for use on
the towers and on the corner defenses to shoot arrows and hurl
large stones. His fame spread far and wide, for he was greatly
helped until he became powerful.
16But after Uzziah became powerful, his pride[k] led to his downfall.[l] He was unfaithful[m] to the LORD his God, and entered the temple of the LORD to burn incense[n] on the altar of incense. 17Azariah[o]
the priest with eighty other courageous priests of the LORD followed him in. 18They confronted him and said, "It is not right for
you, Uzziah, to burn incense to the LORD. That is for the priests,[p]
the descendants[q] of Aaron,[r] who have been consecrated to burn
incense.[s] Leave the sanctuary, for you have been unfaithful; and
you will not be honored by the LORD God."
19Uzziah, who had a censer in his hand ready to burn incense,
became angry. While he was raging at the priests in their presence
before the incense altar in the LORD's temple, leprosy[b][t] broke out
on his forehead. 20When Azariah the chief priest and all the other
priests looked at him, they saw that he had leprosy on his forehead,
so they hurried him out. Indeed, he himself was eager to leave,
because the LORD had afflicted him.

26:5 [a] 2Ch 15:2; 24:2; Da 1:17 [b] 2Ch 27:6
26:6 [c] Isa 2:6; 11:14; 14:29; Jer 25:20 [d] Am 1:8; 3:9
26:7 [e] 2Ch 21:16 [f] 2Ch 20:1
26:8 [g] Ge 19:38; 2Ch 17:11
26:9 [h] 2Ki 14:13; 2Ch 25:23 [i] Ne 2:13; 3:13
26:14 [j] Jer 46:4
26:16 [k] 2Ki 14:10 [l] Dt 32:15; 2Ch 25:19 [m] 1Ch 5:25 [n] 2Ki 16:12
26:17 [o] 1Ki 4:2; 1Ch 6:10
26:18 [p] Nu 16:39 [q] Nu 18:1-7 [r] Ex 30:7 [s] 1Ch 6:49
26:19 [t] Nu 12:10; 2Ki 5:25-27

[a] *5* Many Hebrew manuscripts, Septuagint and Syriac; other Hebrew manuscripts *vision*
[b] *19* The Hebrew word was used for various diseases affecting the skin—not necessarily leprosy; also in verses 20, 21 and 23.

21 King Uzziah had leprosy until the day he died. He lived in a
separate house[a][a]—leprous, and excluded from the temple of the
LORD. Jotham his son had charge of the palace and governed the
people of the land.
22 The other events of Uzziah's reign, from beginning to end, are
recorded by the prophet Isaiah[b] son of Amoz. 23 Uzziah[c] rested with
his fathers and was buried near them in a field for burial that belonged to the kings, for people said, "He had leprosy." And Jotham
his son succeeded him as king.[d]

Chapter 27 Theme ____________________

27 Jotham[e] was twenty-five years old when he became king,
and he reigned in Jerusalem sixteen years. His mother's
name was Jerusha daughter of Zadok. 2 He did what was right in
the eyes of the LORD, just as his father Uzziah had done, but unlike
him he did not enter the temple of the LORD. The people, however,
continued their corrupt practices. 3 Jotham rebuilt the Upper Gate
of the temple of the LORD and did extensive work on the wall at the
hill of Ophel.[f] 4 He built towns in the Judean hills and forts and
towers in the wooded areas.
5 Jotham made war on the king of the Ammonites[g] and conquered them. That year the Ammonites paid him a hundred talents[b] of silver, ten thousand cors[c] of wheat and ten thousand cors
of barley. The Ammonites brought him the same amount also in
the second and third years.
6 Jotham grew powerful[h] because he walked steadfastly before the
LORD his God.
7 The other events in Jotham's reign, including all his wars and the
other things he did, are written in the book of the kings of Israel
and Judah. 8 He was twenty-five years old when he became king,
and he reigned in Jerusalem sixteen years. 9 Jotham rested with his
fathers and was buried in the City of David. And Ahaz his son succeeded him as king.

Chapter 28 Theme ____________________

28 Ahaz[i] was twenty years old when he became king, and he
reigned in Jerusalem sixteen years. Unlike David his father,
he did not do what was right in the eyes of the LORD. 2 He walked in
the ways of the kings of Israel and also made cast idols[j] for worshiping the Baals. 3 He burned sacrifices in the Valley of Ben Hinnom[k] and sacrificed his sons[l] in the fire, following the detestable[m]
ways of the nations the LORD had driven out before the Israelites.
4 He offered sacrifices and burned incense at the high places, on
the hilltops and under every spreading tree.

26:21 [a]Ex 4:6; Lev 13:46; 14:8; Nu 5:2; 19:12
26:22 [b]2Ki 15:1; Isa 1:1; 6:1
26:23 [c]Isa 1:1; 6:1 [d]2Ki 14:21; 15:7; Am 1:1
27:1 [e]2Ki 15:5,32; 1Ch 3:12
27:3 [f]2Ch 33:14; Ne 3:26
27:5 [g]Ge 19:38
27:6 [h]2Ch 26:5
28:1 [i]1Ch 3:13; Isa 1:1
28:2 [j]Ex 34:17; 2Ch 22:3
28:3 [k]Jos 15:8; 2Ki 23:10 [l]Lev 18:21; 2Ki 3:27; 2Ch 33:6; Eze 20:26 [m]Dt 18:9; 2Ch 33:2

[a] 21 Or *in a house where he was relieved of responsibilities* [b] 5 That is, about 3 3/4 tons (about 3.4 metric tons) [c] 5 That is, probably about 62,000 bushels (about 2,200 kiloliters)

5 Therefore the LORD his God handed him over to the king of
Aram.[a] The Arameans defeated him and took many of his people
as prisoners and brought them to Damascus.
He was also given into the hands of the king of Israel, who inflicted heavy casualties on him. 6 In one day Pekah[b] son of Remaliah
killed a hundred and twenty thousand soldiers in Judah[c]—
because Judah had forsaken the LORD, the God of their fathers.
7 Zicri, an Ephraimite warrior, killed Maaseiah the king's son,
Azrikam the officer in charge of the palace, and Elkanah, second
to the king. 8 The Israelites took captive from their kinsmen[d] two
hundred thousand wives, sons and daughters. They also took a
great deal of plunder, which they carried back to Samaria.[e]
9 But a prophet of the LORD named Oded was there, and he went
out to meet the army when it returned to Samaria. He said to
them, "Because the LORD, the God of your fathers, was angry[f] with
Judah, he gave them into your hand. But you have slaughtered them
in a rage that reaches to heaven.[g] 10 And now you intend to make
the men and women of Judah and Jerusalem your slaves.[h] But
aren't you also guilty of sins against the LORD your God? 11 Now
listen to me! Send back your fellow countrymen you have taken as
prisoners, for the LORD's fierce anger rests on you.[i]"
12 Then some of the leaders in Ephraim—Azariah son of Jehohanan, Berekiah son of Meshillemoth, Jehizkiah son of Shallum,
and Amasa son of Hadlai—confronted those who were arriving
from the war. 13 "You must not bring those prisoners here," they
said, "or we will be guilty before the LORD. Do you intend to add
to our sin and guilt? For our guilt is already great, and his fierce
anger rests on Israel."
14 So the soldiers gave up the prisoners and plunder in the presence of the officials and all the assembly. 15 The men designated by
name took the prisoners, and from the plunder they clothed all
who were naked. They provided them with clothes and sandals,
food and drink,[j] and healing balm. All those who were weak they
put on donkeys. So they took them back to their fellow countrymen at Jericho, the City of Palms,[k] and returned to Samaria.
16 At that time King Ahaz sent to the king[a] of Assyria[l] for help.
17 The Edomites[m] had again come and attacked Judah and carried
away prisoners,[n] 18 while the Philistines[o] had raided towns in the
foothills and in the Negev of Judah. They captured and occupied
Beth Shemesh, Aijalon[p] and Gederoth, as well as Soco, Timnah
and Gimzo, with their surrounding villages. 19 The LORD had humbled Judah because of Ahaz king of Israel,[b] for he had promoted
wickedness in Judah and had been most unfaithful[q] to the LORD.

[a] *16* One Hebrew manuscript, Septuagint and Vulgate (see also 2 Kings 16:7); most Hebrew manuscripts *kings* [b] *19* That is, Judah, as frequently in 2 Chronicles

28:5 [a] Isa 7:1
28:6 [b] 2Ki 15:25,27 [c] ver 8; Isa 9:21; 11:13
28:8 [d] Dt 28:25-41; 2Ch 11:4 [e] 2Ch 29:9
28:9 [f] 2Ch 25:15; Isa 10:6; 47:6; Zec 1:15 [g] Ezr 9:6; Rev 18:5
28:10 [h] Lev 25:39-46
28:11 [i] 2Ch 11:4; Jas 2:13
28:15 [j] 2Ki 6:22; Pr 25:21-22 [k] Dt 34:3; Jdg 1:16
28:16 [l] 2Ki 16:7
28:17 [m] Ps 137:7; Isa 34:5 [n] 2Ch 29:9
28:18 [o] Eze 16:27,57 [p] Jos 10:12
28:19 [q] 2Ch 21:2

20 Tiglath-Pileser[a] [a] king of Assyria came to him, but he gave him
trouble instead of help.[b] 21 Ahaz took some of the things from the
temple of the LORD and from the royal palace and from the princes
and presented them to the king of Assyria, but that did not help
him.

22 In his time of trouble King Ahaz became even more unfaithful[c]
to the LORD. 23 He offered sacrifices to the gods[d] of Damascus, who
had defeated him; for he thought, "Since the gods of the kings of
Aram have helped them, I will sacrifice to them so they will help
me."[e] But they were his downfall and the downfall of all Israel.

24 Ahaz gathered together the furnishings from the temple of
God[f] and took them away.[b] He shut the doors[g] of the LORD's temple and set up altars[h] at every street corner in Jerusalem. 25 In every
town in Judah he built high places to burn sacrifices to other gods
and provoked the LORD, the God of his fathers, to anger.

26 The other events of his reign and all his ways, from beginning
to end, are written in the book of the kings of Judah and Israel.
27 Ahaz rested[i] with his fathers and was buried[j] in the city of Jerusalem, but he was not placed in the tombs of the kings of Israel.
And Hezekiah his son succeeded him as king.

Chapter 29 Theme ____________________

29 Hezekiah[k] was twenty-five years old when he became king,
and he reigned in Jerusalem twenty-nine years. His mother's name was Abijah daughter of Zechariah. 2 He did what was
right in the eyes of the LORD, just as his father David[l] had done.

3 In the first month of the first year of his reign, he opened the
doors of the temple of the LORD and repaired[m] them. 4 He brought
in the priests and the Levites, assembled them in the square on
the east side 5 and said: "Listen to me, Levites! Consecrate[n] yourselves now and consecrate the temple of the LORD, the God of your
fathers. Remove all defilement from the sanctuary. 6 Our fathers[o]
were unfaithful;[p] they did evil in the eyes of the LORD our God
and forsook him. They turned their faces away from the LORD's
dwelling place and turned their backs on him. 7 They also shut the
doors of the portico and put out the lamps. They did not burn
incense or present any burnt offerings at the sanctuary to the God
of Israel. 8 Therefore, the anger of the LORD has fallen on Judah and
Jerusalem; he has made them an object of dread and horror[q] and
scorn,[r] as you can see with your own eyes. 9 This is why our fathers
have fallen by the sword and why our sons and daughters and our
wives are in captivity.[s] 10 Now I intend to make a covenant[t] with the
LORD, the God of Israel, so that his fierce anger will turn away from

28:20 [a] 2Ki 15:29; 1Ch 5:6 [b] 2Ki 16:7
28:22 [c] Jer 5:3
28:23 [d] 2Ch 25:14 [e] Jer 44:17-18
28:24 [f] 2Ki 16:18 [g] 2Ch 29:7 [h] 2Ch 30:14
28:27 [i] Isa 14:28-32 [j] 2Ch 21:20; 24:25
29:1 [k] 1Ch 3:13
29:2 [l] 2Ch 28:1; 34:2
29:3 [m] 2Ch 28:24
29:5 [n] 2Ch 35:6
29:6 [o] Ps 106:6-47; Jer 2:27 [p] 1Ch 5:25; Eze 8:16
29:8 [q] Dt 28:25; 2Ch 24:18 [r] Jer 18:16; 19:8; 25:9,18
29:9 [s] 2Ch 28:5-8, 17
29:10 [t] 2Ch 15:12; 23:16

[a] *20* Hebrew *Tilgath-Pilneser,* a variant of *Tiglath-Pileser* [b] *24* Or *and cut them up*

us. 11My sons, do not be negligent now, for the LORD has chosen
you to stand before him and serve him,[a] to minister[b] before him
and to burn incense."

12Then these Levites[c] set to work:
from the Kohathites,
Mahath son of Amasai and Joel son of Azariah;
from the Merarites,
Kish son of Abdi and Azariah son of Jehallelel;
from the Gershonites,
Joah son of Zimmah and Eden[d] son of Joah;
13from the descendants of Elizaphan,
Shimri and Jeiel;
from the descendants of Asaph,[e]
Zechariah and Mattaniah;
14from the descendants of Heman,
Jehiel and Shimei;
from the descendants of Jeduthun,
Shemaiah and Uzziel.

15When they had assembled their brothers and consecrated
themselves, they went in to purify[f] the temple of the LORD, as the
king had ordered, following the word of the LORD. 16The priests
went into the sanctuary of the LORD to purify it. They brought out
to the courtyard of the LORD's temple everything unclean that they
found in the temple of the LORD. The Levites took it and carried it
out to the Kidron Valley.[g] 17They began the consecration on the
first day of the first month, and by the eighth day of the month
they reached the portico of the LORD. For eight more days they
consecrated the temple of the LORD itself, finishing on the sixteenth
day of the first month.

18Then they went in to King Hezekiah and reported: "We have
purified the entire temple of the LORD, the altar of burnt offering
with all its utensils, and the table for setting out the consecrated
bread, with all its articles. 19We have prepared and consecrated all
the articles[h] that King Ahaz removed in his unfaithfulness while
he was king. They are now in front of the LORD's altar."

20Early the next morning King Hezekiah gathered the city officials together and went up to the temple of the LORD. 21They
brought seven bulls, seven rams, seven male lambs and seven male
goats as a sin offering[i] for the kingdom, for the sanctuary and for
Judah. The king commanded the priests, the descendants of Aaron,
to offer these on the altar of the LORD. 22So they slaughtered the
bulls, and the priests took the blood and sprinkled it on the altar;
next they slaughtered the rams and sprinkled their blood on the
altar; then they slaughtered the lambs and sprinkled their blood[j]
on the altar. 23The goats for the sin offering were brought before

29:11 [a]Nu 3:6; 8:6,14 [b]1Ch 15:2

29:12 [c]Nu 3:17-20 [d]2Ch 31:15

29:13 [e]1Ch 6:39

29:15 [f]ver 5; 1Ch 23:28; 2Ch 30:12

29:16 [g]2Sa 15:23

29:19 [h]2Ch 28:24

29:21 [i]Lev 4:13-14

29:22 [j]Lev 4:18

the king and the assembly, and they laid their hands[a] on them.
24 The priests then slaughtered the goats and presented their blood
on the altar for a sin offering to atone[b] for all Israel, because the king
had ordered the burnt offering and the sin offering for all Israel.

25 He stationed the Levites in the temple of the LORD with cymbals, harps and lyres in the way prescribed by David[c] and Gad[d]
the king's seer and Nathan the prophet; this was commanded by
the LORD through his prophets. 26 So the Levites stood ready with
David's instruments,[e] and the priests with their trumpets.[f]

27 Hezekiah gave the order to sacrifice the burnt offering on the
altar. As the offering began, singing to the LORD began also,
accompanied by trumpets and the instruments[g] of David king of
Israel. 28 The whole assembly bowed in worship, while the singers
sang and the trumpeters played. All this continued until the sacrifice of the burnt offering was completed.

29 When the offerings were finished, the king and everyone
present with him knelt down and worshiped.[h] 30 King Hezekiah
and his officials ordered the Levites to praise the LORD with the
words of David and of Asaph the seer. So they sang praises with
gladness and bowed their heads and worshiped.

31 Then Hezekiah said, "You have now dedicated yourselves to the
LORD. Come and bring sacrifices[i] and thank offerings to the temple
of the LORD." So the assembly brought sacrifices and thank offerings, and all whose hearts were willing[j] brought burnt offerings.

32 The number of burnt offerings the assembly brought was seventy bulls, a hundred rams and two hundred male lambs—all of
them for burnt offerings to the LORD. 33 The animals consecrated as
sacrifices amounted to six hundred bulls and three thousand sheep
and goats. 34 The priests, however, were too few to skin all the burnt
offerings;[k] so their kinsmen the Levites helped them until the task
was finished and until other priests had been consecrated,[l] for the
Levites had been more conscientious in consecrating themselves
than the priests had been. 35 There were burnt offerings in abundance, together with the fat[m] of the fellowship offerings[a][n] and the
drink offerings[o] that accompanied the burnt offerings.

So the service of the temple of the LORD was reestablished.
36 Hezekiah and all the people rejoiced at what God had brought
about for his people, because it was done so quickly.

Chapter 30 Theme ________________________________

30 Hezekiah sent word to all Israel and Judah and also wrote
letters to Ephraim and Manasseh,[p] inviting them to come
to the temple of the LORD in Jerusalem and celebrate the Passover[q]

29:23 [a] Lev 4:15
29:24 [b] Ex 29:36; Lev 4:26
29:25 [c] 1Ch 25:6; 2Ch 8:14 [d] 1Sa 22:5; 2Sa 24:11
29:26 [e] 1Ch 15:16 [f] 1Ch 15:24; 23:5; 2Ch 5:12
29:27 [g] 2Ch 23:18
29:29 [h] 2Ch 20:18
29:31 [i] Heb 13:15-16 [j] Ex 25:2; 35:22
29:34 [k] 2Ch 35:11 [l] 2Ch 30:3,15
29:35 [m] Ex 29:13; Lev 3:16 [n] Lev 7:11-21 [o] Nu 15:5-10
30:1 [p] Ge 41:52 [q] Ex 12:11; Nu 28:16

[a] 35 Traditionally *peace offerings*

to the LORD, the God of Israel. 2The king and his officials and the
whole assembly in Jerusalem decided to celebrate[a] the Passover in
the second month. 3They had not been able to celebrate it at the
regular time because not enough priests had consecrated[b] themselves and the people had not assembled in Jerusalem. 4The plan
seemed right both to the king and to the whole assembly. 5They
decided to send a proclamation throughout Israel, from Beersheba
to Dan,[c] calling the people to come to Jerusalem and celebrate the
Passover to the LORD, the God of Israel. It had not been celebrated
in large numbers according to what was written.

6At the king's command, couriers went throughout Israel and
Judah with letters from the king and from his officials, which read:

"People of Israel, return to the LORD, the God of Abraham,
Isaac and Israel, that he may return to you who are left, who
have escaped from the hand of the kings of Assyria. 7Do not
be like your fathers[d] and brothers, who were unfaithful to the
LORD, the God of their fathers, so that he made them an object
of horror,[e] as you see. 8Do not be stiff-necked,[f] as your fathers
were; submit to the LORD. Come to the sanctuary, which he
has consecrated forever. Serve the LORD your God, so that his
fierce anger[g] will turn away from you. 9If you return[h] to the
LORD, then your brothers and your children will be shown
compassion[i] by their captors and will come back to this land,
for the LORD your God is gracious and compassionate.[j] He
will not turn his face from you if you return to him."

10The couriers went from town to town in Ephraim and Manasseh, as far as Zebulun, but the people scorned and ridiculed[k]
them. 11Nevertheless, some men of Asher, Manasseh and Zebulun
humbled themselves and went to Jerusalem.[l] 12Also in Judah the
hand of God was on the people to give them unity[m] of mind to
carry out what the king and his officials had ordered, following
the word of the LORD.

13A very large crowd of people assembled in Jerusalem to celebrate the Feast of Unleavened Bread[n] in the second month. 14They
removed the altars[o] in Jerusalem and cleared away the incense
altars and threw them into the Kidron Valley.[p]

15They slaughtered the Passover lamb on the fourteenth day of
the second month. The priests and the Levites were ashamed and
consecrated[q] themselves and brought burnt offerings to the temple
of the LORD. 16Then they took up their regular positions[r] as prescribed in the Law of Moses the man of God. The priests sprinkled
the blood handed to them by the Levites. 17Since many in the
crowd had not consecrated themselves, the Levites had to kill[s] the
Passover lambs for all those who were not ceremonially clean and

30:2 [a]Nu 9:10
30:3 [b]2Ch 29:34
30:5 [c]Jdg 20:1
30:7 [d]Ps 78:8,57; 106:6; Eze 20:18 [e]2Ch 29:8
30:8 [f]Ex 32:9 [g]Nu 25:4; 2Ch 29:10
30:9 [h]Dt 30:2-5; Isa 1:16; 55:7 [i]1Ki 8:50; Ps 106:46 [j]Ex 34:6-7; Dt 4:31; Mic 7:18
30:10 [k]2Ch 36:16
30:11 [l]ver 25
30:12 [m]Jer 32:39; Eze 11:19; Php 2:13
30:13 [n]Nu 28:16
30:14 [o]2Ch 28:24 [p]2Sa 15:23
30:15 [q]2Ch 29:34
30:16 [r]2Ch 35:10
30:17 [s]2Ch 29:34

could not consecrate ⌊their lambs⌋ to the LORD. 18Although most of
the many people who came from Ephraim, Manasseh, Issachar
and Zebulun had not purified themselves,[a] yet they ate the Passover, contrary to what was written. But Hezekiah prayed for them,
saying, "May the LORD, who is good, pardon everyone 19who sets
his heart on seeking God—the LORD, the God of his fathers—even
if he is not clean according to the rules of the sanctuary." 20And
the LORD heard[b] Hezekiah and healed[c] the people.[d]
21The Israelites who were present in Jerusalem celebrated the
Feast of Unleavened Bread[e] for seven days with great rejoicing,
while the Levites and priests sang to the LORD every day, accompanied by the LORD's instruments of praise.[a]
22Hezekiah spoke encouragingly to all the Levites, who showed
good understanding of the service of the LORD. For the seven days
they ate their assigned portion and offered fellowship offerings[b]
and praised the LORD, the God of their fathers.
23The whole assembly then agreed to celebrate[f] the festival sev-
en more days; so for another seven days they celebrated joyfully.
24Hezekiah king of Judah provided[g] a thousand bulls and seven
thousand sheep and goats for the assembly, and the officials provided them with a thousand bulls and ten thousand sheep and
goats. A great number of priests consecrated themselves. 25The
entire assembly of Judah rejoiced, along with the priests and
Levites and all who had assembled from Israel[h], including the
aliens who had come from Israel and those who lived in Judah.
26There was great joy in Jerusalem, for since the days of Solomon[i]
son of David king of Israel there had been nothing like this in
Jerusalem. 27The priests and the Levites stood to bless[j] the people,
and God heard them, for their prayer reached heaven, his holy
dwelling place.

Chapter 31 Theme

31 When all this had ended, the Israelites who were there went
out to the towns of Judah, smashed the sacred stones and
cut down[k] the Asherah poles. They destroyed the high places and
the altars throughout Judah and Benjamin and in Ephraim and
Manasseh. After they had destroyed all of them, the Israelites
returned to their own towns and to their own property.
2Hezekiah[l] assigned the priests and Levites to divisions[m]—each
of them according to their duties as priests or Levites—to offer
burnt offerings and fellowship offerings,[b] to minister,[n] to give
thanks and to sing praises[o] at the gates of the LORD's dwelling.[p]
3The king contributed[q] from his own possessions for the morning

30:18 [a]Ex 12:43-49; Nu 9:6-10
30:20 [b]2Ch 6:20 [c]2Ch 7:14; Mal 4:2 [d]Jas 5:16
30:21 [e]Ex 12:15,17; 13:6
30:23 [f]1Ki 8:65; 2Ch 7:9
30:24 [g]1Ki 8:5; 2Ch 29:34; 35:7; Ezr 6:17; 8:35
30:25 [h]ver 11
30:26 [i]2Ch 7:8
30:27 [j]Ex 39:43; Nu 6:23; Dt 26:15; 2Ch 23:18; Ps 68:5
31:1 [k]2Ki 18:4; 2Ch 32:12; Isa 36:7
31:2 [l]2Ch 29:9 [m]1Ch 24:1 [n]1Ch 15:2 [o]Ps 7:17; 9:2; 47:6; 71:22 [p]1Ch 23:28-32
31:3 [q]1Ch 29:3; 2Ch 35:7; Eze 45:17

[a] *21* Or *priests praised the LORD every day with resounding instruments belonging to the LORD*
[b] *22, 2* Traditionally *peace offerings*

and evening burnt offerings and for the burnt offerings on the
Sabbaths, New Moons and appointed feasts as written in the Law
of the LORD.[a] 4He ordered the people living in Jerusalem to give
the portion[b] due the priests and Levites so they could devote
themselves to the Law of the LORD. 5As soon as the order went out,
the Israelites generously gave the firstfruits[c] of their grain, new
wine,[d] oil and honey and all that the fields produced. They brought
a great amount, a tithe of everything. 6The men of Israel and Judah
who lived in the towns of Judah also brought a tithe[e] of their herds
and flocks and a tithe of the holy things dedicated to the LORD their
God, and they piled them in heaps.[f] 7They began doing this in the
third month and finished in the seventh month.[g] 8When Hezekiah
and his officials came and saw the heaps, they praised the LORD
and blessed[h] his people Israel.

9Hezekiah asked the priests and Levites about the heaps; 10and
Azariah the chief priest, from the family of Zadok,[i] answered,
"Since the people began to bring their contributions to the temple of the LORD, we have had enough to eat and plenty to spare,
because the LORD has blessed his people, and this great amount is
left over."[j]

11Hezekiah gave orders to prepare storerooms in the temple of
the LORD, and this was done. 12Then they faithfully brought in the
contributions, tithes and dedicated gifts. Conaniah,[k] a Levite, was
in charge of these things, and his brother Shimei was next in rank.
13Jehiel, Azaziah, Nahath, Asahel, Jerimoth, Jozabad,[l] Eliel, Isma-
kiah, Mahath and Benaiah were supervisors under Conaniah and
Shimei his brother, by appointment of King Hezekiah and Azariah
the official in charge of the temple of God.

14Kore son of Imnah the Levite, keeper of the East Gate, was in
charge of the freewill offerings given to God, distributing the contributions made to the LORD and also the consecrated gifts. 15Eden,[m]
Miniamin, Jeshua, Shemaiah, Amariah and Shecaniah assisted
him faithfully in the towns[n] of the priests, distributing to their fellow priests according to their divisions, old and young alike.

16In addition, they distributed to the males three years old or
more whose names were in the genealogical records[o]—all who
would enter the temple of the LORD to perform the daily duties of
their various tasks, according to their responsibilities and their
divisions. 17And they distributed to the priests enrolled by their
families in the genealogical records and likewise to the Levites
twenty years old or more, according to their responsibilities and
their divisions. 18They included all the little ones, the wives, and
the sons and daughters of the whole community listed in these
genealogical records. For they were faithful in consecrating
themselves.

31:3 [a] Nu 28:1–29:40
31:4 [b] Nu 18:8; Dt 18:8; Ne 13:10; Mal 2:7
31:5 [c] Nu 18:12,24; Ne 13:12; Eze 44:30 [d] Dt 12:17
31:6 [e] Lev 27:30; Ne 13:10-12 [f] Dt 14:28; Ru 3:7
31:7 [g] Ex 23:16
31:8 [h] Ps 144:13-15
31:10 [i] 2Sa 8:17 [j] Ex 36:5; Eze 44:30; Mal 3:10-12
31:12 [k] 2Ch 35:9
31:13 [l] 2Ch 35:9
31:15 [m] 2Ch 29:12 [n] Jos 21:9-19
31:16 [o] 1Ch 23:3; Ezr 3:4

19 As for the priests, the descendants of Aaron, who lived on the
farm lands around their towns or in any other towns,[a] men were
designated by name to distribute portions to every male among
them and to all who were recorded in the genealogies of the
Levites.
20 This is what Hezekiah did throughout Judah, doing what was
good and right and faithful[b] before the LORD his God. 21 In everything that he undertook in the service of God's temple and in
obedience to the law and the commands, he sought his God and
worked wholeheartedly. And so he prospered.[c]

Chapter 32 Theme ______________________

32 After all that Hezekiah had so faithfully done, Sennacherib[d] king of Assyria came and invaded Judah. He laid
siege to the fortified cities, thinking to conquer them for himself.
2 When Hezekiah saw that Sennacherib had come and that he
intended to make war on Jerusalem,[e] 3 he consulted with his officials and military staff about blocking off the water from the
springs outside the city, and they helped him. 4 A large force of
men assembled, and they blocked all the springs[f] and the stream
that flowed through the land. "Why should the kings[a] of Assyria
come and find plenty of water?" they said. 5 Then he worked hard
repairing all the broken sections of the wall[g] and building towers
on it. He built another wall outside that one and reinforced the
supporting terraces[b][h] of the City of David. He also made large
numbers of weapons[i] and shields.
6 He appointed military officers over the people and assembled
them before him in the square at the city gate and encouraged
them with these words: 7 "Be strong and courageous.[j] Do not be
afraid or discouraged[k] because of the king of Assyria and the vast
army with him, for there is a greater power with us than with him.[l]
8 With him is only the arm of flesh,[m] but with us[n] is the LORD our
God to help us and to fight our battles."[o] And the people gained
confidence from what Hezekiah the king of Judah said.
9 Later, when Sennacherib king of Assyria and all his forces were
laying siege to Lachish,[p] he sent his officers to Jerusalem with this
message for Hezekiah king of Judah and for all the people of Judah
who were there:

10 "This is what Sennacherib king of Assyria says: On what
are you basing your confidence,[q] that you remain in Jerusalem
under siege? 11 When Hezekiah says, 'The LORD our God will
save us from the hand of the king of Assyria,' he is misleading[r]
you, to let you die of hunger and thirst. 12 Did not Hezekiah

31:19 [a] ver 12-15; Lev 25:34; Nu 35:2-5
31:20 [b] 2Ki 20:3; 22:2
31:21 [c] Dt 29:9
32:1 [d] 2Ki 18:13-19; Isa 36:1; 37:9,17,37
32:2 [e] Isa 22:7; Jer 1:15
32:4 [f] 2Ki 18:17; 20:20; Isa 22:9,11; Na 3:14
32:5 [g] 2Ch 25:23; Isa 22:10 [h] 1Ki 9:24; 1Ch 11:8 [i] Isa 22:8
32:7 [j] Dt 31:6; 1Ch 22:13 [k] 2Ch 20:15 [l] Nu 14:9; 2Ki 6:16
32:8 [m] Job 40:9; Isa 52:10; Jer 17:5; 32:21 [n] Dt 3:22; 1Sa 17:45; 2Ch 13:12 [o] 1Ch 5:22; 2Ch 20:17; Ps 20:7; Isa 28:6
32:9 [p] Jos 10:3,31
32:10 [q] Eze 29:16
32:11 [r] Isa 37:10

[a] 4 Hebrew; Septuagint and Syriac *king* [b] 5 Or *the Millo*

himself remove this god’s high places and altars, saying to
Judah and Jerusalem, ‘You must worship before one altar[a] and
burn sacrifices on it’?

13 “Do you not know what I and my fathers have done to all
the peoples of the other lands? Were the gods of those nations
ever able to deliver their land from my hand?[b] 14 Who of all the
gods of these nations that my fathers destroyed has been able
to save his people from me? How then can your god deliver
you from my hand? 15 Now do not let Hezekiah deceive[c] you
and mislead you like this. Do not believe him, for no god of
any nation or kingdom has been able to deliver[d] his people
from my hand or the hand of my fathers.[e] How much less will
your god deliver you from my hand!”

16 Sennacherib’s officers spoke further against the LORD God
and against his servant Hezekiah. 17 The king also wrote letters[f]
insulting[g] the LORD, the God of Israel, and saying this against him:
“Just as the gods[h] of the peoples of the other lands did not rescue
their people from my hand, so the god of Hezekiah will not rescue
his people from my hand.” 18 Then they called out in Hebrew to
the people of Jerusalem who were on the wall, to terrify them and
make them afraid in order to capture the city. 19 They spoke about
the God of Jerusalem as they did about the gods of the other peoples of the world—the work of men’s hands.[i]

20 King Hezekiah and the prophet Isaiah son of Amoz cried out in
prayer to heaven about this. 21 And the LORD sent an angel,[j] who
annihilated all the fighting men and the leaders and officers in the
camp of the Assyrian king. So he withdrew to his own land in disgrace. And when he went into the temple of his god, some of his
sons cut him down with the sword.[k]

22 So the LORD saved Hezekiah and the people of Jerusalem from
the hand of Sennacherib king of Assyria and from the hand of all
others. He took care of them[a] on every side. 23 Many brought
offerings to Jerusalem for the LORD and valuable gifts[l] for Hezekiah king of Judah. From then on he was highly regarded by all the
nations.

24 In those days Hezekiah became ill and was at the point of
death. He prayed to the LORD, who answered him and gave him a
miraculous sign. 25 But Hezekiah’s heart was proud[m] and he did not
respond to the kindness shown him; therefore the LORD’s wrath[n]
was on him and on Judah and Jerusalem. 26 Then Hezekiah
repented[o] of the pride of his heart, as did the people of Jerusalem;
therefore the LORD’s wrath did not come upon them during the
days of Hezekiah.[p]

[a] 22 Hebrew; Septuagint and Vulgate *He gave them rest*

32:12 [a] 2Ch 31:1
32:13 [b] ver 15
32:15 [c] Isa 37:10 [d] Da 3:15 [e] Ex 5:2
32:17 [f] Isa 37:14 [g] Ps 74:22; Isa 37:4,17 [h] 2Ki 19:12
32:19 [i] 2Ki 19:18; Ps 115:4,4-8; Isa 2:8; 17:8
32:21 [j] Ge 19:13 [k] 2Ki 19:7
32:23 [l] 2Ch 9:24; 17:5; Isa 45:14; Zec 14:16-17
32:25 [m] 2Ki 14:10; 2Ch 26:16 [n] 2Ch 19:2; 24:18
32:26 [o] Jer 26:18-19 [p] 2Ch 34:27,28; Isa 39:8

27 Hezekiah had very great riches and honor,[a] and he made treasuries for his silver and gold and for his precious stones, spices,
shields and all kinds of valuables. 28 He also made buildings to store
the harvest of grain, new wine and oil; and he made stalls for various kinds of cattle, and pens for the flocks. 29 He built villages and
acquired great numbers of flocks and herds, for God had given
him very great riches.[b]

30 It was Hezekiah who blocked[c] the upper outlet of the Gihon[d]
spring and channeled the water down to the west side of the City
of David. He succeeded in everything he undertook. 31 But when
envoys were sent by the rulers of Babylon[e] to ask him about the
miraculous sign[f] that had occurred in the land, God left him to
test[g] him and to know everything that was in his heart.

32 The other events of Hezekiah's reign and his acts of devotion
are written in the vision of the prophet Isaiah son of Amoz in the
book of the kings of Judah and Israel. 33 Hezekiah rested with his
fathers and was buried on the hill where the tombs of David's
descendants are. All Judah and the people of Jerusalem honored
him when he died. And Manasseh his son succeeded him as king.

Chapter 33 Theme

33 Manasseh[h] was twelve years old when he became king, and
he reigned in Jerusalem fifty-five years. 2 He did evil in the
eyes of the LORD,[i] following the detestable[j] practices of the nations
the LORD had driven out before the Israelites. 3 He rebuilt the high
places his father Hezekiah had demolished; he also erected altars
to the Baals and made Asherah poles.[k] He bowed down[l] to all the
starry hosts and worshiped them. 4 He built altars in the temple of
the LORD, of which the LORD had said, "My Name[m] will remain in
Jerusalem forever." 5 In both courts of the temple of the LORD,[n] he
built altars to all the starry hosts. 6 He sacrificed his sons[o] in[a] the
fire in the Valley of Ben Hinnom, practiced sorcery, divination and
witchcraft, and consulted mediums[p] and spiritists.[q] He did much
evil in the eyes of the LORD, provoking him to anger.

7 He took the carved image he had made and put it in God's
temple,[r] of which God had said to David and to his son Solomon,
"In this temple and in Jerusalem, which I have chosen out of all
the tribes of Israel, I will put my Name forever. 8 I will not again
make the feet of the Israelites leave the land[s] I assigned to your
forefathers, if only they will be careful to do everything I commanded them concerning all the laws, decrees and ordinances
given through Moses." 9 But Manasseh led Judah and the people
of Jerusalem astray, so that they did more evil than the nations
the LORD had destroyed before the Israelites.[t]

a6 Or *He made his sons pass through*

32:27 a 1Ch 29:12
32:29 b 1Ch 29:12
32:30 c 2Ki 18:17; d 1Ki 1:33
32:31 e Isa 39:1; f ver 24; Isa 38:7; g Ge 22:1; Dt 8:16
33:1 h 1Ch 3:13
33:2 i Jer 15:4; j Dt 18:9; 2Ch 28:3
33:3 k Dt 16:21-22; l Dt 17:3; 2Ch 31:1
33:4 m 2Ch 7:16
33:5 n 2Ch 4:9
33:6 o Lev 18:21; Dt 18:10; 2Ch 28:3; p Lev 19:31; q 1Sa 28:13
33:7 r 2Ch 7:16
33:8 s 2Sa 7:10
33:9 t Jer 15:4

10The LORD spoke to Manasseh and his people, but they paid no
attention. 11So the LORD brought against them the army commanders of the king of Assyria, who took Manasseh prisoner,[a] put a
hook in his nose, bound him with bronze shackles[b] and took him
to Babylon. 12In his distress he sought the favor of the LORD his
God and humbled[c] himself greatly before the God of his fathers.
13And when he prayed to him, the LORD was moved by his entreaty
and listened to his plea; so he brought him back to Jerusalem and
to his kingdom. Then Manasseh knew that the LORD is God.
14Afterward he rebuilt the outer wall of the City of David, west
of the Gihon[d] spring in the valley, as far as the entrance of the Fish
Gate[e] and encircling the hill of Ophel;[f] he also made it much higher. He stationed military commanders in all the fortified cities in
Judah.
15He got rid of the foreign gods and removed[g] the image from
the temple of the LORD, as well as all the altars he had built on the
temple hill and in Jerusalem; and he threw them out of the city.
16Then he restored the altar of the LORD and sacrificed fellowship
offerings[a] and thank offerings[h] on it, and told Judah to serve the
LORD, the God of Israel. 17The people, however, continued to sacrifice at the high places, but only to the LORD their God.
18The other events of Manasseh's reign, including his prayer to
his God and the words the seers spoke to him in the name of the
LORD, the God of Israel, are written in the annals of the kings of
Israel.[b] 19His prayer and how God was moved by his entreaty, as
well as all his sins and unfaithfulness, and the sites where he built
high places and set up Asherah poles and idols before he humbled[i]
himself—all are written in the records of the seers.[c][j] 20Manasseh
rested with his fathers and was buried[k] in his palace. And Amon
his son succeeded him as king.
21Amon[l] was twenty-two years old when he became king, and
he reigned in Jerusalem two years. 22He did evil in the eyes of the
LORD, as his father Manasseh had done. Amon worshiped and
offered sacrifices to all the idols Manasseh had made. 23But unlike
his father Manasseh, he did not humble[m] himself before the LORD;
Amon increased his guilt.
24Amon's officials conspired against him and assassinated him in
his palace. 25Then the people[n] of the land killed all who had plotted
against King Amon, and they made Josiah his son king in his place.

Chapter 34 Theme ____________________

34 Josiah[o] was eight years old when he became king,[p] and he
reigned in Jerusalem thirty-one years. 2He did what was

33:11 [a]Dt 28:36 [b]Ps 149:8
33:12 [c]2Ch 6:37; 32:26; 1Pe 5:6
33:14 [d]1Ki 1:33 [e]Ne 3:3; 12:39; Zep 1:10 [f]2Ch 27:3; Ne 3:26
33:15 [g]ver 3-7; 2Ki 23:12
33:16 [h]Lev 7:11-18
33:19 [i]2Ch 6:37 [j]2Ki 21:17
33:20 [k]2Ki 21:18; 2Ch 21:20
33:21 [l]1Ch 3:14
33:23 [m]ver 12; Ex 10:3; 2Ch 7:14; Ps 18:27; 147:6; Pr 3:34
33:25 [n]2Ch 22:1
34:1 [o]1Ch 3:14 [p]Zep 1:1

a *16* Traditionally *peace offerings* b *18* That is, Judah, as frequently in 2 Chronicles c *19* One Hebrew manuscript and Septuagint; most Hebrew manuscripts *of Hozai*

right in the eyes of the LORD and walked in the ways of his father
David,[a] not turning aside to the right or to the left.
3In the eighth year of his reign, while he was still young, he began
to seek the God[b] of his father David. In his twelfth year he began to
purge Judah and Jerusalem of high places, Asherah poles, carved
idols and cast images. 4Under his direction the altars of the Baals
were torn down; he cut to pieces the incense altars that were above
them, and smashed the Asherah poles,[c] the idols and the images.
These he broke to pieces and scattered over the graves of those who
had sacrificed to them.[d] 5He burned[e] the bones of the priests on
their altars, and so he purged Judah and Jerusalem. 6In the towns
of Manasseh, Ephraim and Simeon, as far as Naphtali, and in the
ruins around them, 7he tore down the altars and the Asherah poles
and crushed the idols to powder[f] and cut to pieces all the incense
altars throughout Israel. Then he went back to Jerusalem.
8In the eighteenth year of Josiah's reign, to purify the land and
the temple, he sent Shaphan son of Azaliah and Maaseiah the
ruler of the city, with Joah son of Joahaz, the recorder, to repair
the temple of the LORD his God.
9They went to Hilkiah[g] the high priest and gave him the money
that had been brought into the temple of God, which the Levites
who were the doorkeepers had collected from the people of
Manasseh, Ephraim and the entire remnant of Israel and from all
the people of Judah and Benjamin and the inhabitants of Jerusalem. 10Then they entrusted it to the men appointed to supervise
the work on the LORD's temple. These men paid the workers who
repaired and restored the temple. 11They also gave money[h] to the
carpenters and builders to purchase dressed stone, and timber
for joists and beams for the buildings that the kings of Judah had
allowed to fall into ruin.[i]
12The men did the work faithfully.[j] Over them to direct them
were Jahath and Obadiah, Levites descended from Merari, and
Zechariah and Meshullam, descended from Kohath. The Levites—
all who were skilled in playing musical instruments—[k] 13had
charge of the laborers[l] and supervised all the workers from job to
job. Some of the Levites were secretaries, scribes and doorkeepers.
14While they were bringing out the money that had been taken
into the temple of the LORD, Hilkiah the priest found the Book of
the Law of the LORD that had been given through Moses. 15Hilkiah
said to Shaphan the secretary, "I have found the Book of the
Law[m] in the temple of the LORD." He gave it to Shaphan.
16Then Shaphan took the book to the king and reported to him:
"Your officials are doing everything that has been committed to
them. 17They have paid out the money that was in the temple of
the LORD and have entrusted it to the supervisors and workers."

34:2 [a]2Ch 29:2
34:3 [b]1Ki 13:2; 1Ch 16:11; 2Ch 15:2; 33:17,22
34:4 [c]Ex 34:13 [d]Ex 32:20; Lev 26:30; 2Ki 23:11; Mic 1:5
34:5 [e]1Ki 13:2
34:7 [f]Ex 32:20; 2Ch 31:1
34:9 [g]1Ch 6:13; 2Ch 35:8
34:11 [h]2Ch 24:12 [i]2Ch 33:4-7
34:12 [j]2Ki 12:15 [k]1Ch 25:1
34:13 [l]1Ch 23:4
34:15 [m]2Ki 22:8; Ezr 7:6; Ne 8:1

18 Then Shaphan the secretary informed the king, "Hilkiah the
priest has given me a book." And Shaphan read from it in the
presence of the king.
19 When the king heard the words of the Law,[a] he tore[b] his robes.
20 He gave these orders to Hilkiah, Ahikam son of Shaphan[c], Abdon son of Micah,[a] Shaphan the secretary and Asaiah the king's
attendant: 21 "Go and inquire of the LORD for me and for the remnant in Israel and Judah about what is written in this book that has
been found. Great is the LORD's anger that is poured out[d] on us
because our fathers have not kept the word of the LORD; they have
not acted in accordance with all that is written in this book."
22 Hilkiah and those the king had sent with him[b] went to speak
to the prophetess[e] Huldah, who was the wife of Shallum son of
Tokhath,[c] the son of Hasrah,[d] keeper of the wardrobe. She lived in
Jerusalem, in the Second District.
23 She said to them, "This is what the LORD, the God of Israel,
says: Tell the man who sent you to me, 24 'This is what the LORD
says: I am going to bring disaster[f] on this place and its people[g]—
all the curses[h] written in the book that has been read in the presence of the king of Judah. 25 Because they have forsaken me[i] and
burned incense to other gods and provoked me to anger by all that
their hands have made,[e] my anger will be poured out on this place
and will not be quenched.' 26 Tell the king of Judah, who sent you to
inquire of the LORD, 'This is what the LORD, the God of Israel, says
concerning the words you heard: 27 Because your heart was responsive[j] and you humbled[k] yourself before God when you heard
what he spoke against this place and its people, and because you
humbled yourself before me and tore your robes and wept in my
presence, I have heard you, declares the LORD. 28 Now I will gather
you to your fathers,[l] and you will be buried in peace. Your eyes
will not see all the disaster I am going to bring on this place and
on those who live here.' "[m]
So they took her answer back to the king.
29 Then the king called together all the elders of Judah and Jerusalem. 30 He went up to the temple of the LORD[n] with the men of
Judah, the people of Jerusalem, the priests and the Levites—all the
people from the least to the greatest. He read in their hearing all
the words of the Book of the Covenant, which had been found in
the temple of the LORD. 31 The king stood by his pillar[o] and renewed
the covenant[p] in the presence of the LORD—to follow[q] the LORD
and keep his commands, regulations and decrees with all his heart
and all his soul, and to obey the words of the covenant written in
this book.

a 20 Also called *Acbor son of Micaiah* b 22 One Hebrew manuscript, Vulgate and Syriac; most Hebrew manuscripts do not have *had sent with him.* c 22 Also called *Tikvah* d 22 Also called *Harhas* e 25 Or *by everything they have done*

34:19 a Dt 28:3-68 b Jos 7:6; Isa 36:22; 37:1
34:20 c 2Ki 22:3
34:21 d 2Ch 29:8; La 2:4; 4:11; Eze 36:18
34:22 e Ex 15:20; Ne 6:14
34:24 f Pr 16:4; Isa 3:9; Jer 40:2; 42:10; 44:2,11 g 2Ch 36:14-20 h Dt 28:15-68
34:25 i 2Ch 33:3-6; Jer 22:9
34:27 j 2Ch 12:7; 32:26 k Ex 10:3; 2Ch 6:37
34:28 l 2Ch 35:20-25 m 2Ch 32:26
34:30 n 2Ki 23:2; Ne 8:1-3
34:31 o 1Ki 7:15; 2Ki 11:14 p 2Ki 11:17; 2Ch 23:16; 29:10 q Dt 13:4

32 Then he had everyone in Jerusalem and Benjamin pledge themselves to it; the people of Jerusalem did this in accordance with the
covenant of God, the God of their fathers.

33 Josiah removed all the detestable[a] idols from all the territory
belonging to the Israelites, and he had all who were present in
Israel serve the LORD their God. As long as he lived, they did not
fail to follow the LORD, the God of their fathers.

Chapter 35 Theme ____________________

35 Josiah celebrated the Passover[b] to the LORD in Jerusalem,
and the Passover lamb was slaughtered on the fourteenth
day of the first month. 2 He appointed the priests to their duties
and encouraged them in the service of the LORD's temple. 3 He said
to the Levites, who instructed[c] all Israel and who had been consecrated to the LORD: "Put the sacred ark in the temple that Solomon son of David king of Israel built. It is not to be carried about
on your shoulders. Now serve the LORD your God and his people
Israel. 4 Prepare yourselves by families in your divisions,[d] according to the directions written by David king of Israel and by his
son Solomon.

5 "Stand in the holy place with a group of Levites for each sub-
division of the families of your fellow countrymen, the lay people.
6 Slaughter the Passover lambs, consecrate yourselves[e] and prepare
⌊the lambs⌋ for your fellow countrymen, doing what the LORD
commanded through Moses."

7 Josiah provided for all the lay people who were there a total of
thirty thousand sheep and goats for the Passover offerings,[f] and
also three thousand cattle—all from the king's own possessions.[g]

8 His officials also contributed[h] voluntarily to the people and the
priests and Levites. Hilkiah,[i] Zechariah and Jehiel, the administrators of God's temple, gave the priests twenty-six hundred Passover
offerings and three hundred cattle. 9 Also Conaniah[j] along with
Shemaiah and Nethanel, his brothers, and Hashabiah, Jeiel and
Jozabad,[k] the leaders of the Levites, provided five thousand Passover offerings and five hundred head of cattle for the Levites.

10 The service was arranged and the priests stood in their places
with the Levites in their divisions[l] as the king had ordered.[m] 11 The
Passover lambs were slaughtered,[n] and the priests sprinkled the
blood handed to them, while the Levites skinned the animals.
12 They set aside the burnt offerings to give them to the subdivisions
of the families of the people to offer to the LORD, as is written in the
Book of Moses. They did the same with the cattle. 13 They roasted
the Passover animals over the fire as prescribed,[o] and boiled the
holy offerings in pots, caldrons and pans and served them quickly
to all the people. 14 After this, they made preparations for themselves

34:33 [a] ver 3-7; Dt 18:9
35:1 [b] Ex 12:1-30; Nu 9:3; 28:16
35:3 [c] Dt 33:10; 1Ch 23:26; 2Ch 5:7; 17:7
35:4 [d] ver 10; 1Ch 9:10-13; 24:1; 2Ch 8:14; Ezr 6:18
35:6 [e] Lev 11:44; 2Ch 29:5,15
35:7 [f] 2Ch 30:24 [g] 2Ch 31:3
35:8 [h] 1Ch 29:3; 2Ch 29:31-36 [i] 1Ch 6:13
35:9 [j] 2Ch 31:12 [k] 2Ch 31:13
35:10 [l] ver 4; Ezr 6:18 [m] 2Ch 30:16
35:11 [n] 2Ch 29:22,34; 30:17
35:13 [o] Ex 12:2-11; Lev 6:25; 1Sa 2:13-15

and for the priests, because the priests, the descendants of Aaron,
were sacrificing the burnt offerings and the fat portions[a] until
nightfall. So the Levites made preparations for themselves and for
the Aaronic priests.
15 The musicians,[b] the descendants of Asaph, were in the places
prescribed by David, Asaph, Heman and Jeduthun the king's seer.
The gatekeepers at each gate did not need to leave their posts,
because their fellow Levites made the preparations for them.
16 So at that time the entire service of the LORD was carried out for
the celebration of the Passover and the offering of burnt offerings
on the altar of the LORD, as King Josiah had ordered. 17 The Israelites
who were present celebrated the Passover at that time and observed
the Feast of Unleavened Bread for seven days. 18 The Passover had
not been observed like this in Israel since the days of the prophet
Samuel; and none of the kings of Israel had ever celebrated such a
Passover as did Josiah, with the priests, the Levites and all Judah
and Israel who were there with the people of Jerusalem. 19 This
Passover was celebrated in the eighteenth year of Josiah's reign.
20 After all this, when Josiah had set the temple in order, Neco
king of Egypt went up to fight at Carchemish[c] on the Euphrates,[d]
and Josiah marched out to meet him in battle. 21 But Neco sent
messengers to him, saying, "What quarrel is there between you
and me, O king of Judah? It is not you I am attacking at this time,
but the house with which I am at war. God has told[e] me to hurry;
so stop opposing God, who is with me, or he will destroy you."
22 Josiah, however, would not turn away from him, but disguised[f]
himself to engage him in battle. He would not listen to what Neco
had said at God's command but went to fight him on the plain of
Megiddo.
23 Archers[g] shot King Josiah, and he told his officers, "Take me
away; I am badly wounded." 24 So they took him out of his chariot,
put him in the other chariot he had and brought him to Jerusalem,
where he died. He was buried in the tombs of his fathers, and all
Judah and Jerusalem mourned for him.
25 Jeremiah composed laments for Josiah, and to this day all the
men and women singers commemorate Josiah in the laments.[h]
These became a tradition in Israel and are written in the Laments.
26 The other events of Josiah's reign and his acts of devotion,
according to what is written in the Law of the LORD— 27 all the
events, from beginning to end, are written in the book of the kings
of Israel and Judah.

Chapter 36 Theme ____________________________

36 And the people of the land took Jehoahaz son of Josiah
and made him king in Jerusalem in place of his father.

35:14 [a] Ex 29:13
35:15 [b] 1Ch 25:1; 26:12-19; 2Ch 29:30; Ne 12:46; Ps 68:25
35:20 [c] Isa 10:9; Jer 46:2 [d] Ge 2:14
35:21 [e] 1Ki 13:18; 2Ki 18:25
35:22 [f] Jdg 5:19; 1Sa 28:8; 2Ch 18:29
35:23 [g] 1Ki 22:34
35:25 [h] Jer 22:10, 15-16

2 Jehoahaz[a] was twenty-three years old when he became king,
and he reigned in Jerusalem three months. 3 The king of Egypt
dethroned him in Jerusalem and imposed on Judah a levy of a
hundred talents[b] of silver and a talent[c] of gold. 4 The king of
Egypt made Eliakim, a brother of Jehoahaz, king over Judah and
Jerusalem and changed Eliakim's name to Jehoiakim. But Neco[a]
took Eliakim's brother Jehoahaz and carried him off to Egypt.

5 Jehoiakim[b] was twenty-five years old when he became king, and
he reigned in Jerusalem eleven years. He did evil in the eyes of the
LORD his God. 6 Nebuchadnezzar[c] king of Babylon attacked him
and bound him with bronze shackles to take him to Babylon.[d]
7 Nebuchadnezzar also took to Babylon articles from the temple of
the LORD and put them in his temple[d] there.[e]

8 The other events of Jehoiakim's reign, the detestable things he
did and all that was found against him, are written in the book of
the kings of Israel and Judah. And Jehoiachin his son succeeded
him as king.

9 Jehoiachin[f] was eighteen[e] years old when he became king, and
he reigned in Jerusalem three months and ten days. He did evil in
the eyes of the LORD. 10 In the spring, King Nebuchadnezzar sent for
him and brought him to Babylon,[g] together with articles of value
from the temple of the LORD, and he made Jehoiachin's uncle,[f]
Zedekiah, king over Judah and Jerusalem.

11 Zedekiah[h] was twenty-one years old when he became king,
and he reigned in Jerusalem eleven years. 12 He did evil in the eyes
of the LORD[i] his God and did not humble[j] himself before Jeremiah
the prophet, who spoke the word of the LORD. 13 He also rebelled
against King Nebuchadnezzar, who had made him take an oath[k] in
God's name. He became stiff-necked[l] and hardened his heart and
would not turn to the LORD, the God of Israel. 14 Furthermore, all
the leaders of the priests and the people became more and more
unfaithful,[m] following all the detestable practices of the nations
and defiling the temple of the LORD, which he had consecrated in
Jerusalem.

15 The LORD, the God of their fathers, sent word to them through
his messengers[n] again and again,[o] because he had pity on his people
and on his dwelling place. 16 But they mocked God's messengers,
despised his words and scoffed[p] at his prophets until the wrath[q] of
the LORD was aroused against his people and there was no remedy.[r]
17 He brought up against them the king of the Babylonians,[g] who
killed their young men with the sword in the sanctuary, and spared

36:4 *a* Jer 22:10-12
36:5 *b* Jer 22:18; 26:1; 35:1
36:6 *c* Jer 25:9; 27:6; Eze 29:18 *d* 2Ch 33:11; Eze 19:9; Da 1:1
36:7 *e* 2Ki 24:13; Ezr 1:7; Da 1:2
36:9 *f* Jer 22:24-28; 52:31
36:10 *g* ver 18; 2Ki 20:17; Ezr 1:7; Jer 22:25; 24:1; 29:1; 37:1; Eze 17:12
36:11 *h* 2Ki 24:17; Jer 27:1; 28:1
36:12 *i* Jer 37:1-39:18 *j* Dt 8:3; 2Ch 7:14; 2Ch 33:23; Jer 21:3-7
36:13 *k* Eze 17:13 *l* 2Ki 17:14; 2Ch 30:8
36:14 *m* 1Ch 5:25
36:15 *n* Isa 5:4; 44:26; Jer 7:25; Hag 1:13; Zec 1:4; Mal 2:7; 3:1 *o* Jer 7:13,25; 25:3-4; 35:14,15; 44:4-6
36:16 *p* 2Ki 2:23; Pr 1:25; Jer 5:13 *q* Ezr 5:12; Pr 1:30-31 *r* 2Ch 30:10; Pr 29:1; Zec 1:2

a *2* Hebrew *Joahaz,* a variant of *Jehoahaz;* also in verse 4 b *3* That is, about 3 3/4 tons (about 3.4 metric tons) c *3* That is, about 75 pounds (about 34 kilograms) d *7* Or *palace* e *9* One Hebrew manuscript, some Septuagint manuscripts and Syriac (see also 2 Kings 24:8); most Hebrew manuscripts *eight* f *10* Hebrew *brother,* that is, relative (see 2 Kings 24:17) g *17* Or *Chaldeans*

neither young man[a] nor young woman, old man or aged. God
handed all of them over to Nebuchadnezzar.[b] 18He carried to Babylon all the articles[c] from the temple of God, both large and
small, and the treasures of the LORD's temple and the treasures of
the king and his officials. 19They set fire[d] to God's temple[e] and
broke down the wall[f] of Jerusalem; they burned all the palaces
and destroyed[g] everything of value there.[h]
20He carried into exile[i] to Babylon the remnant, who escaped
from the sword, and they became servants[j] to him and his sons
until the kingdom of Persia came to power. 21The land enjoyed its
sabbath rests;[k] all the time of its desolation it rested,[l] until the seventy years[m] were completed in fulfillment of the word of the LORD
spoken by Jeremiah.
22In the first year of Cyrus[n] king of Persia, in order to fulfill the
word of the LORD spoken by Jeremiah, the LORD moved the heart
of Cyrus king of Persia to make a proclamation throughout his
realm and to put it in writing:

23"This is what Cyrus king of Persia says:

"'The LORD, the God of heaven, has given me all the kingdoms of the earth and he has appointed[o] me to build a temple for him at Jerusalem in Judah. Anyone of his people among you—may the LORD his God be with him, and let him go up.'"

36:22 [n] Isa 44:28; 45:1,13; Jer 25:12; 29:10; Da 1:21; 6:28; 10:1 **36:23** [o] Jdg 4:10

36:17 [a] Jer 6:11 [b] Ezr 5:12; Jer 32:28
36:18 [c] ver 7,10
36:19 [d] Jer 11:16; 17:27; 21:10,14; 22:7; 32:29; 39:8; La 4:11; Eze 20:47; Am 2:5; Zec 11:1; [e] 1Ki 9:8-9 [f] 2Ki 14:13 [g] La 2:6 [h] Ps 79:1-3
36:20 [i] Lev 26:44; 2Ki 24:14; Ezr 2:1; Ne 7:6 [j] Jer 27:7
36:21 [k] Lev 25:4; 26:34 [l] 1Ch 22:9 [m] Jer 1:1; 25:11; 27:22; 29:10; 40:1; Da 9:2; Zec 1:12; 7:5

heme of 2 Chronicles:

uthor:

ate:

urpose:

ey Words:

temple

palace

ark

covenant

cry (cried)

seek, seeking, consult, inquire of, sought (inquired of, took, in search of)

heart

pray (prayer[s], prayed, prays)

prophet(s)

SEGMENT DIVISIONS			CHAPTER THEMES
			1
			2
			3
			4
			5
			6
			7
			8
			9
			10
			11
			12
			13
			14
			15
			16
			17
			18
			19
			20
			21
			22
			23
			24
			25
			26
			27
			28
			29
			30
			31
			32
			33
			34
			35
			36

EZRA

Every seventh year the land was to lie fallow. This was God's ordinance to his people, part of his law by which they were to govern their lives.

However, for 490 years God's people had not paid attention to this statute, nor to others. The land had missed 70 Sabbaths. As prophesied by Jeremiah, God would exact 70 years for the land. Then the Spirit of God would move on behalf of his people. He would stir up the spirit of Cyrus, king of Persia, so that Cyrus would send out a written decree proclaiming, "The LORD, the God of heaven, has given me all the kingdoms of the earth and he has appointed me to build a temple for him at Jerusalem in Judah. Anyone of his people among you—may the LORD his God be with him, and let him go up" (2 Chronicles 36:23).

And so a remnant returned from the land of exile to the land promised to Abraham, Isaac, and Jacob as an everlasting possession. Ezra tells us what happened.

Things to Do

To better understand Ezra, look at Isaiah's prophecy in 44:28–45:7. This was written about 175 years before Cyrus was born.

Ezra falls into two main segments: chapters 1 through 6 and chapters 7 through 10. There is a lapse of approximately 58 to 60 years between these two segments.

Chapters 1-6

1. Read this segment chapter by chapter and do the following:
   a. In a distinctive way mark in the text the key words listed on the EZRA AT A GLANCE chart on page 791.
   b. Pay attention to any references to time. Mark these in a way that will enable you to spot them immediately. You may want to put a symbol in the margin next to the references to time.
   c. When you come to a reference of a particular king, consult the historical chart THE TIMES OF EZRA, NEHEMIAH, AND ESTHER, on page 774. This will help you appreciate the historical setting of the book of Ezra and see the relationship of Ezra to Esther and Nehemiah, who were contemporaries of Ezra.
   d. If specific people play a significant role, record their names in the margin and briefly describe what they did.

2. There are seven official documents or letters in the book of Ezra, all of which (except the first) were written in Aramaic, the international language of the times. The first document, written by Cyrus, the Persian king, is in Hebrew. These documents or letters are found in Ezra 1:2-4; 4:11-16; 4:17-22; 5:7-17; 6:2-5; and 6:6-12. The last one is in the second segment of the book, 7:12-26.

   As you come to each document or letter in the text, underline who presented it. Then in the margin list the major points of the document or letter. This information will help you keep track of the opposition the Jews faced and how God moved on their behalf.

3. After you finish reading each chapter, identify the main subject, theme, or event and record it on the line next to the chapter number and on EZRA AT A GLANCE.

4. The book of Ezra records when the temple construction began and when it was completed. Write this information in the margin in bold print so you can easily find it.

5. For a better understanding of the Jewish feasts, consult the chart THE FEASTS OF ISRAEL on pages 210 and 211.

Chapters 7-10

1. This is the first time Ezra's name appears in this book. Note how he is described. Observe this man and the lessons you can learn from his life. List your insights in the margin under LFL, "Lessons for Life."

2. Don't forget to mark the key words listed on EZRA AT A GLANCE. Also, note your insights on the last official document in 7:12-26.

3. Watch for and mark references to time and to kings. Note these as you did before.

4. Record the theme of each chapter as you did in the first segment of Ezra.

5. How does the second segment of Ezra, chapters 7 through 10, differ from the first?

   a. Record the theme or subject of the first six chapters on EZRA AT A GLANCE under "Segment Divisions." Do the same for the last segment, chapters 7 through 10.

   b. On the second line for segment divisions write in the name(s) of the central character(s) of each segment.

   c. Consult the historical chart THE TIMES OF EZRA, NEHEMIAH, AND ESTHER on page 774 and then record on the chart the number of years covered in each segment.

6. What is the theme or teaching of Ezra? Record this and any other requested information in the appropriate place on EZRA AT A GLANCE.

Things to Think About

1. How did the people in Ezra's time deal with their sin? What showed you whether their sorrow led to repentance or simply regret? How do you deal with sin in your own life? How is it dealt with within your church congregation?

2. What did you learn about prayer and fasting? Are either of these integral parts of your walk with the Lord? Why?

3. As you review what you have learned in Ezra, what have you learned about your God, his promises, and his ways? What difference can this knowledge make in your life?

1:1 [a] Jer 25:11-12; 29:10-14 [b] 2Ch 36:22,23

Chapter 1 Theme ________________

1 In the first year of Cyrus king of Persia, in order to fulfill the
word of the LORD spoken by Jeremiah,[a] the LORD moved the
heart[b] of Cyrus king of Persia to make a proclamation throughout his realm and to put it in writing:

1:2 [c] Isa 44:28; 45:13 [d] Ezr 5:13

2"This is what Cyrus king of Persia says:
" 'The LORD, the God of heaven, has given me all the kingdoms of the earth and he has appointed[c] me to build[d] a temple
for him at Jerusalem in Judah. 3Anyone of his people among
you—may his God be with him, and let him go up to Jerusalem in Judah and build the temple of the LORD, the God of
Israel, the God who is in Jerusalem. 4And the people of any

1:4 [e] Isa 10:20-22

place where survivors[e] may now be living are to provide him

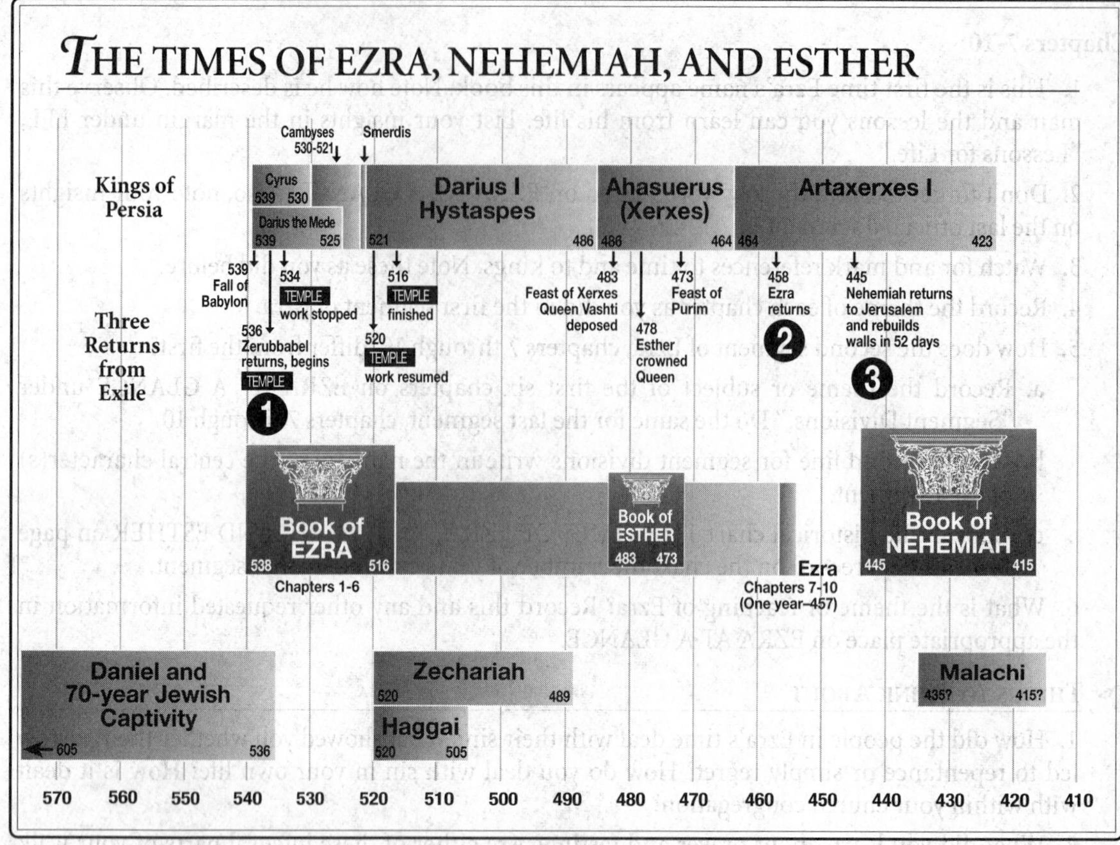

with silver and gold, with goods and livestock, and with freewill offerings[a] for the temple of God in Jerusalem.' "[b]

5 Then the family heads of Judah and Benjamin,[c] and the priests
and Levites—everyone whose heart God had moved[d]—prepared
to go up and build the house[e] of the LORD in Jerusalem. 6 All their
neighbors assisted them with articles of silver and gold, with
goods and livestock, and with valuable gifts, in addition to all the
freewill offerings. 7 Moreover, King Cyrus brought out the articles
belonging to the temple of the LORD, which Nebuchadnezzar had
carried away from Jerusalem and had placed in the temple of his
god.[a][f] 8 Cyrus king of Persia had them brought by Mithredath the
treasurer, who counted them out to Sheshbazzar[g] the prince of
Judah.

9 This was the inventory:

gold dishes	30
silver dishes	1,000
silver pans[b]	29

[a] 7 Or *gods* [b] 9 The meaning of the Hebrew for this word is uncertain.

1:4 [a] Nu 15:3; Ps 50:14; 54:6; 116:17 [b] Ezr 4:3; 5:13; 6:3,14

1:5 [c] Ezr 4:1; Ne 11:4 [d] ver 1; Ex 35:20-22; 2Ch 36:22; Hag 1:14; Php 2:13 [e] Ps 127:1

1:7 [f] 2Ki 24:13; 2Ch 36:7,10; Ezr 5:14; 6:5

1:8 [g] Ezr 5:14

2:1 [a]2Ch 36:20; Ne 7:6 [b]2Ki 24:16; 25:12 [c]Ne 7:73

[10]gold bowls	30
matching silver bowls	410
other articles	1,000

[11]In all, there were 5,400 articles of gold and of silver. Sheshbazzar brought all these along when the exiles came up from Babylon to Jerusalem.

Chapter 2 Theme ______________________________

2:2 [d]1Ch 3:19 [e]Ezr 3:2 [f]Ne 10:2

2 Now these are the people of the province who came up from
the captivity of the exiles,[a] whom Nebuchadnezzar king of
Babylon[b] had taken captive to Babylon (they returned to Jerusalem
and Judah, each to his own town,[c] [2]in company with Zerubbabel,[d]
Jeshua,[e] Nehemiah, Seraiah,[f] Reelaiah, Mordecai, Bilshan, Mispar,
Bigvai, Rehum and Baanah):

The list of the men of the people of Israel:

2:3 [g]Ezr 8:3

2:13 [h]Ezr 8:13

2:21 [i]Mic 5:2

2:26 [j]Jos 18:25

[3]the descendants of Parosh[g]	2,172
[4]of Shephatiah	372
[5]of Arah	775
[6]of Pahath-Moab (through the line of Jeshua and Joab)	2,812
[7]of Elam	1,254
[8]of Zattu	945
[9]of Zaccai	760
[10]of Bani	642
[11]of Bebai	623
[12]of Azgad	1,222
[13]of Adonikam[h]	666
[14]of Bigvai	2,056
[15]of Adin	454
[16]of Ater (through Hezekiah)	98
[17]of Bezai	323
[18]of Jorah	112
[19]of Hashum	223
[20]of Gibbar	95
[21]the men of Bethlehem[i]	123
[22]of Netophah	56
[23]of Anathoth	128
[24]of Azmaveth	42
[25]of Kiriath Jearim,[a] Kephirah and Beeroth	743
[26]of Ramah[j] and Geba	621
[27]of Micmash	122

[a]*25* See Septuagint (see also Neh. 7:29); Hebrew *Kiriath Arim.*

28 of Bethel and Ai[a] 223
29 of Nebo 52
30 of Magbish 156
31 of the other Elam 1,254
32 of Harim 320
33 of Lod, Hadid and Ono 725
34 of Jericho[b] 345
35 of Senaah 3,630

36 The priests:

the descendants of Jedaiah[c]
(through the family of Jeshua) 973
37 of Immer[d] 1,052
38 of Pashhur[e] 1,247
39 of Harim[f] 1,017

40 The Levites:[g]

the descendants of Jeshua[h] and Kadmiel
(through the line of Hodaviah) 74

41 The singers:[i]

the descendants of Asaph 128

42 The gatekeepers[j] of the temple:

the descendants of
Shallum, Ater, Talmon,
Akkub, Hatita and Shobai 139

43 The temple servants:[k]

the descendants of
Ziha, Hasupha, Tabbaoth,
44 Keros, Siaha, Padon,
45 Lebanah, Hagabah, Akkub,
46 Hagab, Shalmai, Hanan,
47 Giddel, Gahar, Reaiah,
48 Rezin, Nekoda, Gazzam,
49 Uzza, Paseah, Besai,
50 Asnah, Meunim, Nephussim,
51 Bakbuk, Hakupha, Harhur,
52 Bazluth, Mehida, Harsha,
53 Barkos, Sisera, Temah,
54 Neziah and Hatipha

55 The descendants of the servants of Solomon:

the descendants of
Sotai, Hassophereth, Peruda,

2:28 [a] Ge 12:8
2:34 [b] 1Ki 16:34; 2Ch 28:15
2:36 [c] 1Ch 24:7
2:37 [d] 1Ch 24:14
2:38 [e] 1Ch 9:12
2:39 [f] 1Ch 24:8
2:40 [g] Ge 29:34; Nu 3:9; Dt 18:6-7; 1Ch 16:4; Ezr 7:7; 8:15; Ne 12:24 [h] Ezr 3:9
2:41 [i] 1Ch 15:16
2:42 [j] 1Sa 3:15; 1Ch 9:17
2:43 [k] 1Ch 9:2; Ne 11:21

56 Jaala, Darkon, Giddel,
57 Shephatiah, Hattil,
Pokereth-Hazzebaim and Ami

58 The temple servants[a] and the descendants
of the servants of Solomon 392

59 The following came up from the towns of Tel Melah, Tel Harsha, Kerub, Addon and Immer, but they could not show that their families were descended[b] from Israel:

60 The descendants of
Delaiah, Tobiah and Nekoda 652

61 And from among the priests:

The descendants of
Hobaiah, Hakkoz and Barzillai (a man who had married a daughter of Barzillai the Gileadite[c] and was called by that name).

62 These searched for their family records, but they could not find them and so were excluded from the priesthood[d] as unclean. 63 The governor ordered them not to eat any of the most sacred food[e] until there was a priest ministering with the Urim and Thummim.[f]

64 The whole company numbered 42,360, 65 besides their 7,337 menservants and maidservants; and they also had 200 men and women singers.[g] 66 They had 736 horses,[h] 245 mules, 67 435 camels and 6,720 donkeys.

68 When they arrived at the house of the LORD in Jerusalem, some of the heads of the families[i] gave freewill offerings toward the rebuilding of the house of God on its site. 69 According to their ability they gave to the treasury for this work 61,000 drachmas[a] of gold, 5,000 minas[b] of silver and 100 priestly garments.
70 The priests, the Levites, the singers, the gatekeepers and the temple servants settled in their own towns, along with some of the other people, and the rest of the Israelites settled in their towns.[j]

Chapter 3 Theme ______________________________

3

When the seventh month came and the Israelites had settled in their towns,[k] the people assembled[l] as one man in Jerusalem. 2 Then Jeshua[m] son of Jozadak[n] and his fellow priests and Zerubbabel son of Shealtiel[o] and his associates began to build the altar of the God of Israel to sacrifice burnt offerings on it, in accordance

2:58 a 1Ki 9:21; 1Ch 9:2
2:59 b Nu 1:18
2:61 c 2Sa 17:27
2:62 d Nu 3:10; 16:39-40
2:63 e Lev 2:3,10 f Ex 28:30; Nu 27:21
2:65 g 2Sa 19:35
2:66 h Isa 66:20
2:68 i Ex 25:2
2:70 j ver 1; 1Ch 9:2; Ne 11:3-4
3:1 k Ne 7:73; 8:1 l Lev 23:24
3:2 m Ezr 2:2; Ne 12:1,8; Hag 2:2 n Hag 1:1; Zec 6:11 o 1Ch 3:17

a 69 That is, about 1,100 pounds (about 500 kilograms) b 69 That is, about 3 tons (about 2.9 metric tons)

with what is written in the Law of Moses[a] the man of God. 3 Despite
their fear[b] of the peoples around them, they built the altar on its
foundation and sacrificed burnt offerings on it to the LORD, both
the morning and evening sacrifices.[c] 4 Then in accordance with
what is written, they celebrated the Feast of Tabernacles[d] with the
required number of burnt offerings prescribed for each day. 5 After
that, they presented the regular burnt offerings, the New Moon[e]
sacrifices and the sacrifices for all the appointed sacred feasts of
the LORD,[f] as well as those brought as freewill offerings to the
LORD. 6 On the first day of the seventh month they began to offer
burnt offerings to the LORD, though the foundation of the LORD's
temple had not yet been laid.

7 Then they gave money to the masons and carpenters, and gave
food and drink and oil to the people of Sidon and Tyre, so that
they would bring cedar logs[g] by sea from Lebanon[h] to Joppa, as
authorized by Cyrus[i] king of Persia.

8 In the second month of the second year after their arrival at
the house of God in Jerusalem, Zerubbabel[j] son of Shealtiel,
Jeshua son of Jozadak and the rest of their brothers (the priests
and the Levites and all who had returned from the captivity to
Jerusalem) began the work, appointing Levites twenty[k] years of
age and older to supervise the building of the house of the LORD.
9 Jeshua[l] and his sons and brothers and Kadmiel and his sons
(descendants of Hodaviah[a]) and the sons of Henadad and their
sons and brothers—all Levites—joined together in supervising
those working on the house of God.

10 When the builders laid[m] the foundation of the temple of the
LORD, the priests in their vestments and with trumpets,[n] and the
Levites (the sons of Asaph) with cymbals, took their places to
praise[o] the LORD, as prescribed by David[p] king of Israel.[q] 11 With
praise and thanksgiving they sang to the LORD:

> "He is good;
> his love to Israel endures forever."[r]

And all the people gave a great shout[s] of praise to the LORD,
because the foundation of the house of the LORD was laid. 12 But
many of the older priests and Levites and family heads, who had
seen the former temple,[t] wept aloud when they saw the foundation
of this temple being laid, while many others shouted for joy. 13 No
one could distinguish the sound of the shouts of joy[u] from the
sound of weeping, because the people made so much noise. And
the sound was heard far away.

[a] 9 Hebrew *Yehudah,* probably a variant of *Hodaviah*

3:2 [a] Ex 20:24; Dt 12:5-6
3:3 [b] Ezr 4:4; Da 9:25 [c] Ex 29:39; Nu 28:1-8
3:4 [d] Ex 23:16; Nu 29:12-38; Ne 8:14-18; Zec 14:16-19
3:5 [e] Nu 28:3,11,14; Col 2:16 [f] Lev 23:1-44; Nu 29:39
3:7 [g] 1Ch 14:1 [h] Isa 35:2 [i] Ezr 1:2-4; 6:3
3:8 [j] Zec 4:9 [k] 1Ch 23:24
3:9 [l] Ezr 2:40
3:10 [m] Ezr 5:16 [n] Nu 10:2; 1Ch 16:6 [o] 1Ch 25:1 [p] 1Ch 6:31 [q] Zec 6:12
3:11 [r] 1Ch 16:34,41; 2Ch 7:3; Ps 107:1; 118:1 [s] Ne 12:24
3:12 [t] Hag 2:3,9
3:13 [u] Job 8:21; Ps 27:6; Isa 16:9

Chapter 4 Theme ________________________

4

When the enemies of Judah and Benjamin heard that the exiles were building a temple for the LORD, the God of Israel, 2they came to Zerubbabel and to the heads of the families and said, "Let us help you build because, like you, we seek your God and have been sacrificing to him since the time of Esarhaddon[a] king of Assyria, who brought us here."[b]

3But Zerubbabel, Jeshua and the rest of the heads of the families of Israel answered, "You have no part with us in building a temple to our God. We alone will build it for the LORD, the God of Israel, as King Cyrus, the king of Persia, commanded us."[c]

4Then the peoples around them set out to discourage the people of Judah and make them afraid to go on building.[a][d] 5They hired counselors to work against them and frustrate their plans during the entire reign of Cyrus king of Persia and down to the reign of Darius king of Persia.

6At the beginning of the reign of Xerxes,[b][e] they lodged an accusation against the people of Judah and Jerusalem.[f]

7And in the days of Artaxerxes[g] king of Persia, Bishlam, Mithredath, Tabeel and the rest of his associates wrote a letter to Artaxerxes. The letter was written in Aramaic script and in the Aramaic[h] language.[c,d]

8Rehum the commanding officer and Shimshai the secretary wrote a letter against Jerusalem to Artaxerxes the king as follows:

9Rehum the commanding officer and Shimshai the secretary, together with the rest of their associates[i]—the judges and officials over the men from Tripolis, Persia,[e] Erech and Babylon, the Elamites of Susa, 10and the other people whom the great and honorable Ashurbanipal[f] deported and settled in the city of Samaria and elsewhere in Trans-Euphrates.[j]

11(This is a copy of the letter they sent him.)

To King Artaxerxes,

From your servants, the men of Trans-Euphrates:

12The king should know that the Jews who came up to us from you have gone to Jerusalem and are rebuilding that rebellious and wicked city. They are restoring the walls and repairing the foundations.[k]

13Furthermore, the king should know that if this city is built and its walls are restored, no more taxes, tribute or duty[l] will

4:2 [a]2Ki 17:24; 19:37 [b]2Ki 17:41
4:3 [c]Ezr 1:1-4; Ne 2:20
4:4 [d]Ezr 3:3
4:6 [e]Est 1:1; Da 9:1 [f]Est 3:13; 9:5
4:7 [g]Ezr 7:1; Ne 2:1 [h]2Ki 18:26; Isa 36:11; Da 2:4
4:9 [i]Ezr 5:6; 6:6,13
4:10 [j]ver 17; Ne 4:2
4:12 [k]Ezr 5:3,9
4:13 [l]Ezr 7:24; Ne 5:4

[a]*4* Or *and troubled them as they built* [b]*6* Hebrew *Ahasuerus,* a variant of Xerxes' Persian name [c]*7* Or *written in Aramaic and translated* [d]*7* The text of Ezra 4:8—6:18 is in Aramaic. [e]*9* Or *officials, magistrates and governors over the men from* [f]*10* Aramaic *Osnappar,* a variant of *Ashurbanipal*

be paid, and the royal revenues will suffer. 14Now since we are
under obligation to the palace and it is not proper for us to
see the king dishonored, we are sending this message to inform the king, 15so that a search may be made in the archives[a]
of your predecessors. In these records you will find that this
city is a rebellious city, troublesome to kings and provinces, a
place of rebellion from ancient times. That is why this city was
destroyed.[b] 16We inform the king that if this city is built and
its walls are restored, you will be left with nothing in Trans-
Euphrates.

17The king sent this reply:

To Rehum the commanding officer, Shimshai the secretary and the rest of their associates living in Samaria and elsewhere in Trans-Euphrates:[c]

Greetings.

18The letter you sent us has been read and translated in my
presence. 19I issued an order and a search was made, and it was
found that this city has a long history of revolt[d] against kings
and has been a place of rebellion and sedition. 20Jerusalem has
had powerful kings ruling over the whole of Trans-Euphrates,[e]
and taxes, tribute and duty were paid to them. 21Now issue an
order to these men to stop work, so that this city will not be
rebuilt until I so order. 22Be careful not to neglect this matter.
Why let this threat grow, to the detriment of the royal interests?[f]

23As soon as the copy of the letter of King Artaxerxes was read to Rehum and Shimshai the secretary and their associates,[g] they went immediately to the Jews in Jerusalem and compelled them by force to stop.

24Thus the work on the house of God in Jerusalem came to a standstill until the second year of the reign of Darius[h] king of Persia.

Chapter 5 Theme ______________________________

5 Now Haggai[i] the prophet and Zechariah[j] the prophet, a descendant of Iddo, prophesied[k] to the Jews in Judah and
Jerusalem in the name of the God of Israel, who was over them.
2Then Zerubbabel[l] son of Shealtiel and Jeshua[m] son of Jozadak
set to work[n] to rebuild the house of God in Jerusalem. And the
prophets of God were with them, helping them.
3At that time Tattenai,[o] governor of Trans-Euphrates, and
Shethar-Bozenai[p] and their associates went to them and asked,
"Who authorized you to rebuild this temple and restore this

4:15
[a] Ezr 5:17; 6:1
[b] Est 3:8

4:17
[c] ver 10

4:19
[d] 2Ki 18:7

4:20
[e] Ge 15:18-21; Ex 23:31; Jos 1:4; 1Ki 4:21; 1Ch 18:3; Ps 72:8-11

4:22
[f] Da 6:2

4:23
[g] ver 9

4:24
[h] Ne 2:1-8; Da 9:25; Hag 1:1,15; Zec 1:1

5:1
[i] Ezr 6:14; Hag 1:1,3,12; 2:1,10,20
[j] Zec 1:1; 7:1
[k] Hag 1:14–2:9; Zec 4:9-10; 8:9

5:2
[l] 1Ch 3:19; Hag 1:14; 2:21; Zec 4:6-10
[m] Ezr 2:2; 3:2
[n] ver 8; Hag 2:2-5

5:3
[o] Ezr 6:6
[p] Ezr 6:6

structure?"[a] 4They also asked, "What are the names of the men
constructing this building?"[a] 5But the eye of their God[b] was watching over the elders of the Jews, and they were not stopped until a
report could go to Darius and his written reply be received.
6This is a copy of the letter that Tattenai, governor of Trans-
Euphrates, and Shethar-Bozenai and their associates, the officials
of Trans-Euphrates, sent to King Darius. 7The report they sent
him read as follows:

To King Darius:

Cordial greetings.

8The king should know that we went to the district of Judah,
to the temple of the great God. The people are building it with
large stones and placing the timbers in the walls. The work[c] is
being carried on with diligence and is making rapid progress
under their direction.
9We questioned the elders and asked them, "Who authorized
you to rebuild this temple and restore this structure?"[d] 10We
also asked them their names, so that we could write down the
names of their leaders for your information.
11This is the answer they gave us:

"We are the servants of the God of heaven and earth, and we
are rebuilding the temple[e] that was built many years ago, one
that a great king of Israel built and finished. 12But because our
fathers angered[f] the God of heaven, he handed them over to
Nebuchadnezzar the Chaldean, king of Babylon, who destroyed
this temple and deported the people to Babylon.[g]
13"However, in the first year of Cyrus king of Babylon, King
Cyrus issued a decree[h] to rebuild this house of God. 14He even
removed from the temple[b] of Babylon the gold and silver articles of the house of God, which Nebuchadnezzar had taken
from the temple in Jerusalem and brought to the temple[b] in
Babylon.[i]
"Then King Cyrus gave them to a man named Sheshbazzar,[j]
whom he had appointed governor, 15and he told him, 'Take
these articles and go and deposit them in the temple in
Jerusalem. And rebuild the house of God on its site.' 16So this
Sheshbazzar came and laid the foundations of the house of
God[k] in Jerusalem. From that day to the present it has been
under construction but is not yet finished."

17Now if it pleases the king, let a search be made in the royal
archives[l] of Babylon to see if King Cyrus did in fact issue a

5:3 [a] ver 9; Ezr 1:3; 4:12
5:5 [b] 2Ki 25:28; Ezr 7:6,9,28; 8:18,22,31; Ne 2:8,18; Ps 33:18; Isa 66:14
5:8 [c] ver 2
5:9 [d] Ezr 4:12
5:11 [e] 1Ki 6:1; 2Ch 3:1-2
5:12 [f] 2Ch 36:16 [g] Dt 21:10; 28:36; 2Ki 24:1; 25:8,9,11; Jer 1:3
5:13 [h] Ezr 1:1
5:14 [i] Ezr 1:7; 6:5; Da 5:2 [j] 1Ch 3:18
5:16 [k] Ezr 3:10; 6:15
5:17 [l] Ezr 4:15; 6:1,2

a *4* See Septuagint; Aramaic *4We told them the names of the men constructing this building.*
b *14* Or *palace*

decree to rebuild this house of God in Jerusalem. Then let the
king send us his decision in this matter.

Chapter 6 Theme ____

6 King Darius then issued an order, and they searched in the
archives[a] stored in the treasury at Babylon. 2A scroll was found
in the citadel of Ecbatana in the province of Media, and this was
written on it:

Memorandum:

3In the first year of King Cyrus, the king issued a decree
concerning the temple of God in Jerusalem:

Let the temple be rebuilt as a place to present sacrifices, and
let its foundations be laid.[b] It is to be ninety feet[a] high and
ninety feet wide, 4with three courses[c] of large stones and one of
timbers. The costs are to be paid by the royal treasury.[d] 5Also,
the gold[e] and silver articles of the house of God, which Nebuchadnezzar took from the temple in Jerusalem and brought
to Babylon, are to be returned to their places in the temple in
Jerusalem; they are to be deposited in the house of God.[f]

6Now then, Tattenai,[g] governor of Trans-Euphrates, and
Shethar-Bozenai[h] and you, their fellow officials of that province,
stay away from there. 7Do not interfere with the work on this
temple of God. Let the governor of the Jews and the Jewish
elders rebuild this house of God on its site.
8Moreover, I hereby decree what you are to do for these
elders of the Jews in the construction of this house of God:
The expenses of these men are to be fully paid out of the
royal treasury,[i] from the revenues[j] of Trans-Euphrates, so that
the work will not stop. 9Whatever is needed—young bulls,
rams, male lambs for burnt offerings[k] to the God of heaven,
and wheat, salt, wine and oil, as requested by the priests in
Jerusalem—must be given them daily without fail, 10so that
they may offer sacrifices pleasing to the God of heaven and
pray for the well-being of the king and his sons.[l]
11Furthermore, I decree that if anyone changes this edict, a
beam is to be pulled from his house and he is to be lifted up
and impaled[m] on it. And for this crime his house is to be made
a pile of rubble.[n] 12May God, who has caused his Name to
dwell there,[o] overthrow any king or people who lifts a hand to
change this decree or to destroy this temple in Jerusalem.
I Darius[p] have decreed it. Let it be carried out with diligence.

a3 Aramaic *sixty cubits* (about 27 meters)

6:1
[a] Ezr 4:15; 5:17

6:3
[b] Ezr 3:10; Hag 2:3

6:4
[c] 1Ki 6:36
[d] ver 8; Ezr 7:20

6:5
[e] 1Ch 29:2
[f] Ezr 1:7; 5:14

6:6
[g] Ezr 5:3
[h] Ezr 5:3

6:8
[i] ver 4
[j] 1Sa 9:20

6:9
[k] Lev 1:3,10

6:10
[l] Ezr 7:23; 1Ti 2:1-2

6:11
[m] Dt 21:22-23; Est 2:23; 5:14; 9:14
[n] Ezr 7:26; Da 2:5; 3:29

6:12
[o] Ex 20:24; Dt 12:5; 1Ki 9:3; 2Ch 6:2
[p] ver 14

13 Then, because of the decree King Darius had sent, Tattenai, governor of Trans-Euphrates, and Shethar-Bozenai and their associates[a] carried it out with diligence. 14 So the elders of the Jews continued to build and prosper under the preaching[b] of Haggai the prophet and Zechariah, a descendant of Iddo. They finished building the temple according to the command of the God of Israel and the decrees of Cyrus,[c] Darius[d] and Artaxerxes,[e] kings of Persia. 15 The temple was completed on the third day of the month Adar, in the sixth year of the reign of King Darius.[f]

16 Then the people of Israel—the priests, the Levites and the rest of the exiles—celebrated the dedication[g] of the house of God with joy. 17 For the dedication of this house of God they offered[h] a hundred bulls, two hundred rams, four hundred male lambs and, as a sin offering for all Israel, twelve male goats, one for each of the tribes of Israel. 18 And they installed the priests in their divisions[i] and the Levites in their groups[j] for the service of God at Jerusalem, according to what is written in the Book of Moses.[k]

19 On the fourteenth day of the first month, the exiles celebrated the Passover.[l] 20 The priests and Levites had purified themselves and were all ceremonially clean. The Levites slaughtered[m] the Passover lamb for all the exiles, for their brothers the priests and for themselves. 21 So the Israelites who had returned from the exile ate it, together with all who had separated themselves[n] from the unclean practices[o] of their Gentile neighbors in order to seek the LORD,[p] the God of Israel. 22 For seven days they celebrated with joy the Feast of Unleavened Bread,[q] because the LORD had filled them with joy by changing the attitude[r] of the king of Assyria, so that he assisted them in the work on the house of God, the God of Israel.

Chapter 7 Theme

7 After these things, during the reign of Artaxerxes[s] king of Persia, Ezra son of Seraiah, the son of Azariah, the son of Hilkiah,[t] 2 the son of Shallum, the son of Zadok,[u] the son of Ahitub,[v] 3 the son of Amariah, the son of Azariah, the son of Meraioth, 4 the son of Zerahiah, the son of Uzzi, the son of Bukki, 5 the son of Abishua, the son of Phinehas, the son of Eleazar, the son of Aaron the chief priest— 6 this Ezra[w] came up from Babylon. He was a teacher well versed in the Law of Moses, which the LORD, the God of Israel, had given. The king had granted him everything he asked, for the hand of the LORD his God was on him.[x] 7 Some of the Israelites, including priests, Levites, singers, gatekeepers and temple servants, also came up to Jerusalem in the seventh year of King Artaxerxes.[y]

8 Ezra arrived in Jerusalem in the fifth month of the seventh year of the king. 9 He had begun his journey from Babylon on the

6:13 [a] Ezr 4:9
6:14 [b] Ezr 5:1 [c] Ezr 1:1-4 [d] ver 12 [e] Ezr 7:1; Ne 2:1
6:15 [f] Zec 1:1; 4:9
6:16 [g] 1Ki 8:63; 2Ch 7:5
6:17 [h] 2Sa 6:13; 2Ch 29:21; 30:24; Ezr 8:35
6:18 [i] 1Ch 23:6; 2Ch 35:4; Lk 1:5 [j] 1Ch 24:1 [k] Nu 3:6-9; 8:9-11; 18:1-32
6:19 [l] Ex 12:11; Nu 28:16
6:20 [m] 2Ch 30:15, 17; 35:11
6:21 [n] Ezr 9:1; Ne 9:2 [o] Dt 18:9; Ezr 9:11; Eze 36:25 [p] 1Ch 22:19; Ps 14:2
6:22 [q] Ex 12:17 [r] Ezr 1:1
7:1 [s] Ezr 4:7; 6:14; Ne 2:1 [t] 2Ki 22:4
7:2 [u] 1Ki 1:8; 1Ch 6:8 [v] Ne 11:11
7:6 [w] Ne 12:36 [x] Ezr 5:5; Isa 41:20
7:7 [y] Ezr 8:1

first day of the first month, and he arrived in Jerusalem on the first
day of the fifth month, for the gracious hand of his God was on
him.[a] 10For Ezra had devoted himself to the study and observance
of the Law of the LORD, and to teaching[b] its decrees and laws in
Israel.

11This is a copy of the letter King Artaxerxes had given to Ezra
the priest and teacher, a man learned in matters concerning the
commands and decrees of the LORD for Israel:

12[a]Artaxerxes, king of kings,[c]

To Ezra the priest, a teacher of the Law of the God of heaven:
Greetings.

13Now I decree that any of the Israelites in my kingdom,
including priests and Levites, who wish to go to Jerusalem
with you, may go. 14You are sent by the king and his seven
advisers[d] to inquire about Judah and Jerusalem with regard
to the Law of your God, which is in your hand. 15Moreover,
you are to take with you the silver and gold that the king and
his advisers have freely given[e] to the God of Israel, whose
dwelling[f] is in Jerusalem, 16together with all the silver and
gold[g] you may obtain from the province of Babylon, as well as
the freewill offerings of the people and priests for the temple
of their God in Jerusalem.[h] 17With this money be sure to buy
bulls, rams and male lambs,[i] together with their grain offerings and drink offerings,[j] and sacrifice[k] them on the altar of
the temple of your God in Jerusalem.

18You and your brother Jews may then do whatever seems
best with the rest of the silver and gold, in accordance with the
will of your God. 19Deliver[l] to the God of Jerusalem all the articles entrusted to you for worship in the temple of your God.
20And anything else needed for the temple of your God that
you may have occasion to supply, you may provide from the
royal treasury.[m]

21Now I, King Artaxerxes, order all the treasurers of Trans-
Euphrates to provide with diligence whatever Ezra the priest,
a teacher of the Law of the God of heaven, may ask of you—
22up to a hundred talents[b] of silver, a hundred cors[c] of wheat, a
hundred baths[d] of wine, a hundred baths[d] of olive oil, and salt
without limit. 23Whatever the God of heaven has prescribed,
let it be done with diligence for the temple of the God of heav-
en. Why should there be wrath against the realm of the king

[a] *12* The text of Ezra 7:12-26 is in Aramaic. [b] *22* That is, about 3 3/4 tons (about 3.4 metric tons) [c] *22* That is, probably about 600 bushels (about 22 kiloliters) [d] *22* That is, probably about 600 gallons (about 2.2 kiloliters)

7:9 [a]ver 6
7:10 [b]ver 25; Dt 33:10; Ne 8:1-8
7:12 [c]Eze 26:7; Da 2:37
7:14 [d]Est 1:14
7:15 [e]1Ch 29:6 [f]1Ch 29:6,9; 2Ch 6:2
7:16 [g]Ezr 8:25 [h]Zec 6:10
7:17 [i]2Ki 3:4 [j]Nu 15:5-12 [k]Dt 12:5-11
7:19 [l]Ezr 5:14; Jer 27:22
7:20 [m]Ezr 6:4

and of his sons?[a] 24You are also to know that you have no authority to impose taxes, tribute or duty[b] on any of the priests, Levites, singers, gatekeepers, temple servants or other workers at this house of God.[c]

25And you, Ezra, in accordance with the wisdom of your God, which you possess, appoint[d] magistrates and judges to administer justice to all the people of Trans-Euphrates—all who know the laws of your God. And you are to teach[e] any who do not know them. 26Whoever does not obey the law of your God and the law of the king must surely be punished by death, banishment, confiscation of property, or imprisonment.[f]

27Praise be to the LORD, the God of our fathers, who has put it into the king's heart[g] to bring honor[h] to the house of the LORD in Jerusalem in this way 28and who has extended his good favor[i] to me before the king and his advisers and all the king's powerful officials. Because the hand of the LORD my God was on me,[j] I took courage and gathered leading men from Israel to go up with me.

Chapter 8 Theme

8 These are the family heads and those registered with them who came up with me from Babylon during the reign of King Artaxerxes:[k]

2of the descendants of Phinehas, Gershom;
of the descendants of Ithamar, Daniel;
of the descendants of David, Hattush 3of the descendants of Shecaniah;[l]

of the descendants of Parosh,[m] Zechariah, and with him were registered 150 men;
4of the descendants of Pahath-Moab,[n] Eliehoenai son of Zerahiah, and with him 200 men;
5of the descendants of Zattu,[a] Shecaniah son of Jahaziel, and with him 300 men;
6of the descendants of Adin,[o] Ebed son of Jonathan, and with him 50 men;
7of the descendants of Elam, Jeshaiah son of Athaliah, and with him 70 men;
8of the descendants of Shephatiah, Zebadiah son of Michael, and with him 80 men;
9of the descendants of Joab, Obadiah son of Jehiel, and with him 218 men;
10of the descendants of Bani,[b] Shelomith son of Josiphiah, and with him 160 men;

7:23 [a]Ezr 6:10
7:24 [b]Ezr 4:13 [c]Ezr 8:36
7:25 [d]Ex 18:21,26; Dt 16:18 [e]ver 10; Lev 10:11
7:26 [f]Ezr 6:11
7:27 [g]Ezr 1:1; 6:22 [h]1Ch 29:12
7:28 [i]2Ki 25:28 [j]Ezr 5:5; 9:9
8:1 [k]Ezr 7:7
8:3 [l]1Ch 3:22 [m]Ezr 2:3
8:4 [n]Ezr 2:6
8:6 [o]Ezr 2:15; Ne 7:20; 10:16

a*5* Some Septuagint manuscripts (also 1 Esdras 8:32); Hebrew does not have *Zattu.* b*10* Some Septuagint manuscripts (also 1 Esdras 8:36); Hebrew does not have *Bani.*

[11]of the descendants of Bebai, Zechariah son of Bebai, and with
him 28 men;
[12]of the descendants of Azgad, Johanan son of Hakkatan, and
with him 110 men;
[13]of the descendants of Adonikam,[a] the last ones, whose names
were Eliphelet, Jeuel and Shemaiah, and with them 60 men;
[14]of the descendants of Bigvai, Uthai and Zaccur, and with them
70 men.

[15]I assembled them at the canal that flows toward Ahava,[b] and we
camped there three days. When I checked among the people and
the priests, I found no Levites[c] there. [16]So I summoned Eliezer,
Ariel, Shemaiah, Elnathan, Jarib, Elnathan, Nathan, Zechariah
and Meshullam, who were leaders, and Joiarib and Elnathan,
who were men of learning, [17]and I sent them to Iddo, the leader
in Casiphia. I told them what to say to Iddo and his kinsmen, the
temple servants[d] in Casiphia, so that they might bring attendants
to us for the house of our God. [18]Because the gracious hand of
our God was on us,[e] they brought us Sherebiah, a capable man,
from the descendants of Mahli son of Levi, the son of Israel, and
Sherebiah's sons and brothers, 18 men; [19]and Hashabiah, together
with Jeshaiah from the descendants of Merari, and his brothers
and nephews, 20 men. [20]They also brought 220 of the temple servants[f]—a body that David and the officials had established to assist
the Levites. All were registered by name.

[21]There, by the Ahava Canal,[g] I proclaimed a fast, so that we
might humble ourselves before our God and ask him for a safe
journey[h] for us and our children, with all our possessions. [22]I was
ashamed to ask the king for soldiers[i] and horsemen to protect us
from enemies on the road, because we had told the king, "The
gracious hand of our God is on everyone[j] who looks to him, but
his great anger is against all who forsake him.[k]" [23]So we fasted[l]
and petitioned our God about this, and he answered our prayer.

[24]Then I set apart twelve of the leading priests, together with
Sherebiah,[m] Hashabiah and ten of their brothers, [25]and I weighed
out[n] to them the offering of silver and gold and the articles that the
king, his advisers, his officials and all Israel present there had
donated for the house of our God. [26]I weighed out to them 650 talents[a] of silver, silver articles weighing 100 talents,[b] 100 talents[b] of
gold, [27]20 bowls of gold valued at 1,000 darics,[c] and two fine articles
of polished bronze, as precious as gold.

[28]I said to them, "You as well as these articles are consecrated to
the LORD.[o] The silver and gold are a freewill offering to the LORD,

[a]*26* That is, about 25 tons (about 22 metric tons) [b]*26* That is, about 3 3/4 tons (about 3.4 metric tons) [c]*27* That is, about 19 pounds (about 8.5 kilograms)

8:13 [a]Ezr 2:13
8:15 [b]ver 21,31 [c]Ezr 2:40; 7:7
8:17 [d]Ezr 2:43
8:18 [e]Ezr 5:5
8:20 [f]1Ch 9:2; Ezr 2:43
8:21 [g]ver 15; 2Ch 20:3 [h]Ps 5:8; 107:7
8:22 [i]Ne 2:9; Ezr 7:6,9,28 [j]Ezr 5:5 [k]Dt 31:17; 2Ch 15:2
8:23 [l]2Ch 20:3; 33:13
8:24 [m]ver 18
8:25 [n]ver 33; Ezr 7:15,16
8:28 [o]Lev 21:6; 22:2-3

the God of your fathers. 29Guard them carefully until you weigh
them out in the chambers of the house of the LORD in Jerusalem
before the leading priests and the Levites and the family heads of
Israel." 30Then the priests and Levites received the silver and gold
and sacred articles that had been weighed out to be taken to the
house of our God in Jerusalem.

31On the twelfth day of the first month we set out from the Ahava
Canal[a] to go to Jerusalem. The hand of our God was on us, and
he protected us from enemies and bandits along the way. 32So we
arrived in Jerusalem, where we rested three days.[b]

33On the fourth day, in the house of our God, we weighed out
the silver and gold and the sacred articles into the hands of Meremoth[c] son of Uriah, the priest. Eleazar son of Phinehas was with
him, and so were the Levites Jozabad son of Jeshua and Noadiah
son of Binnui.[d] 34Everything was accounted for by number and
weight, and the entire weight was recorded at that time.

35Then the exiles who had returned from captivity sacrificed
burnt offerings to the God of Israel: twelve bulls for all Israel,
ninety-six rams, seventy-seven male lambs and, as a sin offering,
twelve male goats.[e] All this was a burnt offering to the LORD.
36They also delivered the king's orders[f] to the royal satraps and to
the governors of Trans-Euphrates, who then gave assistance to the
people and to the house of God.[g]

Chapter 9 Theme ______________________________

9 After these things had been done, the leaders came to me and
said, "The people of Israel, including the priests and the
Levites, have not kept themselves separate[h] from the neighboring
peoples with their detestable practices, like those of the Canaanites,
Hittites, Perizzites, Jebusites, Ammonites,[i] Moabites, Egyptians
and Amorites.[j] 2They have taken some of their daughters[k] as wives
for themselves and their sons, and have mingled the holy race[l]
with the peoples around them. And the leaders and officials have
led the way in this unfaithfulness."[m]

3When I heard this, I tore my tunic and cloak, pulled hair from
my head and beard and sat down appalled. 4Then everyone who
trembled[n] at the words of the God of Israel gathered around me
because of this unfaithfulness of the exiles. And I sat there appalled
until the evening sacrifice.

5Then, at the evening sacrifice,[o] I rose from my self-abasement,
with my tunic and cloak torn, and fell on my knees with my hands
spread out to the LORD my God 6and prayed:

"O my God, I am too ashamed and disgraced to lift up my
face to you, my God, because our sins are higher than our

8:31 [a]ver 15
8:32 [b]Ge 40:13; Ne 2:11
8:33 [c]Ne 3:4,21 [d]Ne 3:24
8:35 [e]2Ch 29:21; Ezr 6:17
8:36 [f]Ezr 7:21-24 [g]Est 9:3
9:1 [h]Ezr 6:21; Ne 9:2 [i]Ge 19:38 [j]Ex 13:5
9:2 [k]Ex 34:16 [l]Ex 22:31 [m]Ezr 10:2
9:4 [n]Ezr 10:3
9:5 [o]Ex 29:41

heads and our guilt has reached to the heavens.[a] 7From the days of our forefathers[b] until now, our guilt has been great. Because of our sins, we and our kings and our priests have been subjected to the sword[c] and captivity,[d] to pillage and humiliation[e] at the hand of foreign kings, as it is today.

8"But now, for a brief moment, the LORD our God has been gracious[f] in leaving us a remnant[g] and giving us a firm place[h] in his sanctuary, and so our God gives light to our eyes[i] and a little relief in our bondage. 9Though we are slaves,[j] our God has not deserted us in our bondage. He has shown us kindness[k] in the sight of the kings of Persia: He has granted us new life to rebuild the house of our God and repair its ruins,[l] and he has given us a wall of protection in Judah and Jerusalem.

10"But now, O our God, what can we say after this? For we have disregarded the commands[m] 11you gave through your servants the prophets when you said: 'The land you are entering to possess is a land polluted[n] by the corruption of its peoples. By their detestable practices[o] they have filled it with their impurity from one end to the other. 12Therefore, do not give your daughters in marriage to their sons or take their daughters for your sons. Do not seek a treaty of friendship with them[p] at any time, that you may be strong and eat the good things of the land and leave it to your children as an everlasting inheritance.'

13"What has happened to us is a result of our evil deeds and our great guilt, and yet, our God, you have punished us less than our sins have deserved[q] and have given us a remnant like this. 14Shall we again break your commands and intermarry[r] with the peoples who commit such detestable practices? Would you not be angry enough with us to destroy us,[s] leaving us no remnant[t] or survivor? 15O LORD, God of Israel, you are righteous![u] We are left this day as a remnant. Here we are before you in our guilt, though because of it not one of us can stand[v] in your presence.[w]"

Chapter 10 Theme ______________________

10 While Ezra was praying and confessing,[x] weeping and throwing himself down before the house of God, a large crowd of Israelites—men, women and children—gathered around him. They too wept bitterly. 2Then Shecaniah son of Jehiel, one of the descendants of Elam, said to Ezra, "We have been unfaithful[y] to our God by marrying foreign women from the peoples around us. But in spite of this, there is still hope for Israel.[z] 3Now let us make a covenant[a] before our God to send away[b] all these women and their children, in accordance with the counsel of my lord and of those who fear the commands of our God. Let it be done

9:6
[a] 2Ch 28:9; Job 42:6; Ps 38:4; Rev 18:5

9:7
[b] 2Ch 29:6
[c] Eze 21:1-32
[d] Dt 28:64
[e] Dt 28:37

9:8
[f] Ps 25:16; Isa 33:2
[g] Ge 45:7
[h] Ecc 12:11; Isa 22:23
[i] Ps 13:3

9:9
[j] Ex 1:14; Ne 9:36
[k] Ezr 7:28
[l] Ps 69:35; Isa 43:1; Jer 32:44

9:10
[m] Dt 11:8; Isa 1:19-20

9:11
[n] Lev 18:25-28
[o] Dt 9:4

9:12
[p] Ex 34:15; Dt 7:3; 23:6

9:13
[q] Job 11:6; Ps 103:10

9:14
[r] Ne 13:27
[s] Dt 9:8
[t] Dt 9:14

9:15
[u] Ge 18:25; Ps 51:4; Jer 12:1; Da 9:7
[v] Ne 9:33; Ps 130:3; Mal 3:2
[w] 1Ki 8:47

10:1
[x] 2Ch 20:9; Da 9:20

10:2
[y] Ezr 9:2; Ne 13:27
[z] Dt 30:8-10

10:3
[a] 2Ch 34:31
[b] Ex 34:16; Dt 7:2-3; Ezr 9:4

10:5 [a]Ne 5:12; 13:25 according to the Law. 4 Rise up; this matter is in your hands. We
will support you, so take courage and do it."

5 So Ezra rose up and put the leading priests and Levites and all
Israel under oath[a] to do what had been suggested. And they took
the oath. 6 Then Ezra withdrew from before the house of God and
10:6 [b]Ex 34:28; Dt 9:18 went to the room of Jehohanan son of Eliashib. While he was
there, he ate no food and drank no water,[b] because he continued
to mourn over the unfaithfulness of the exiles.

7 A proclamation was then issued throughout Judah and Jerusalem for all the exiles to assemble in Jerusalem. 8 Anyone who
failed to appear within three days would forfeit all his property, in
10:9 [c]Ezr 1:5 accordance with the decision of the officials and elders, and would
himself be expelled from the assembly of the exiles.

9 Within the three days, all the men of Judah and Benjamin[c] had
gathered in Jerusalem. And on the twentieth day of the ninth
month, all the people were sitting in the square before the house
10:11 [d]ver 3; Dt 24:1; Ne 9:2; Mal 2:10-16 of God, greatly distressed by the occasion and because of the rain.
10 Then Ezra the priest stood up and said to them, "You have been
unfaithful; you have married foreign women, adding to Israel's
guilt. 11 Now make confession to the LORD, the God of your fathers,
and do his will. Separate yourselves from the peoples around you
and from your foreign wives."[d]

12 The whole assembly responded with a loud voice:[e] "You are
right! We must do as you say. 13 But there are many people here
10:12 [e]Jos 6:5 and it is the rainy season; so we cannot stand outside. Besides, this
matter cannot be taken care of in a day or two, because we have
sinned greatly in this thing. 14 Let our officials act for the whole
assembly. Then let everyone in our towns who has married a foreign woman come at a set time, along with the elders and judges[f]
10:14 [f]Dt 16:18 [g]Nu 25:4; 2Ch 29:10; 30:8 of each town, until the fierce anger[g] of our God in this matter is
turned away from us." 15 Only Jonathan son of Asahel and Jahzeiah
son of Tikvah, supported by Meshullam and Shabbethai[h] the
Levite, opposed this.

16 So the exiles did as was proposed. Ezra the priest selected men
who were family heads, one from each family division, and all of
them designated by name. On the first day of the tenth month they
sat down to investigate the cases, 17 and by the first day of the first
10:15 [h]Ne 11:16 month they finished dealing with all the men who had married
foreign women.

18 Among the descendants of the priests, the following had
married foreign women:[i]

10:18 [i]Jdg 3:6 [j]Ezr 2:2 From the descendants of Jeshua[j] son of Jozadak, and his
brothers: Maaseiah, Eliezer, Jarib and Gedaliah. 19 (They

all gave their hands[a] in pledge to put away their wives, and for their guilt they each presented a ram from the flock as a guilt offering.)[b]

[20]From the descendants of Immer:[c]
Hanani and Zebadiah.
[21]From the descendants of Harim:[d]
Maaseiah, Elijah, Shemaiah, Jehiel and Uzziah.
[22]From the descendants of Pashhur:[e]
Elioenai, Maaseiah, Ishmael, Nethanel, Jozabad and Elasah.

[23]Among the Levites:[f]
Jozabad, Shimei, Kelaiah (that is, Kelita), Pethahiah, Judah and Eliezer.
[24]From the singers:
Eliashib.[g]
From the gatekeepers:
Shallum, Telem and Uri.

[25]And among the other Israelites:

From the descendants of Parosh:[h]
Ramiah, Izziah, Malkijah, Mijamin, Eleazar, Malkijah and Benaiah.
[26]From the descendants of Elam:[i]
Mattaniah, Zechariah, Jehiel, Abdi, Jeremoth and Elijah.
[27]From the descendants of Zattu:
Elioenai, Eliashib, Mattaniah, Jeremoth, Zabad and Aziza.
[28]From the descendants of Bebai:
Jehohanan, Hananiah, Zabbai and Athlai.
[29]From the descendants of Bani:
Meshullam, Malluch, Adaiah, Jashub, Sheal and Jeremoth.
[30]From the descendants of Pahath-Moab:
Adna, Kelal, Benaiah, Maaseiah, Mattaniah, Bezalel, Binnui and Manasseh.
[31]From the descendants of Harim:
Eliezer, Ishijah, Malkijah, Shemaiah, Shimeon, [32]Benjamin, Malluch and Shemariah.
[33]From the descendants of Hashum:
Mattenai, Mattattah, Zabad, Eliphelet, Jeremai, Manasseh and Shimei.
[34]From the descendants of Bani:
Maadai, Amram, Uel, [35]Benaiah, Bedeiah, Keluhi, [36]Vaniah, Meremoth, Eliashib, [37]Mattaniah, Mattenai and Jaasu.
[38]From the descendants of Binnui:[a]
Shimei, [39]Shelemiah, Nathan, Adaiah, [40]Macnadebai, Shashai,

a *37,38* See Septuagint (also 1 Esdras 9:34); Hebrew *Jaasu* [38]*and Bani and Binnui,*

10:19 [a]2Ki 10:15 [b]Lev 5:15; 6:6
10:20 [c]1Ch 24:14
10:21 [d]1Ch 24:8
10:22 [e]1Ch 9:12
10:23 [f]Ne 8:7; 9:4
10:24 [g]Ne 3:1; 12:10; 13:7,28
10:25 [h]Ezr 2:3
10:26 [i]ver 2

Sharai, 41Azarel, Shelemiah, Shemariah, 42Shallum, Amariah
and Joseph.
43From the descendants of Nebo:
Jeiel, Mattithiah, Zabad, Zebina, Jaddai, Joel and Benaiah.

44All these had married foreign women, and some of them had
children by these wives.[a]

[a] 44 Or *and they sent them away with their children*

Ezra at a Glance

eme of Ezra:

thor:

te:

rpose:

y Words:

nouse, temple (or any reference to God's house)

decree (decrees, order, authorized, letter)

the law, the Law (of Moses, of the Lord, of your God)

commands

Segment Divisions			
	Years Covered	Central Characters	Chapter Themes
			1
			2
			3
			4
			5
			6
			7
			8
			9
			10

NEHEMIAH

Since the third millennium B.C. the cities of the Middle East were surrounded by walls of stones while guarded gates acted as sentinels opening to or shutting out all who wanted to enter. From the tops of these walls, watchmen could survey the landscape for great distances, seeing everyone who approached the city either as visitors or invaders.

The city fathers would gather at the city gates to carry out their business transactions and pass their judgments on civic affairs. The condition of the walls of the city was a matter of either pride or reproach.

Jerusalem's walls had been destroyed during the Babylonian invasion. The walls and its many gates stood in ruins, a rebuke to the newly returned exiles and a cause of mourning to Nehemiah, although he was over 600 miles away serving as cupbearer to Artaxerxes. Nehemiah had not forgotten his beloved city or people.

While Ezra gives the account of the rebuilding of the temple under Zerubbabel, Nehemiah (Ezra's contemporary) gives the account of the rebuilding of Jerusalem's walls. His account begins in 445 B.C. in Susa, the Persian capital.

Things to Do

1. Nehemiah is a continuation of Ezra. As a matter of fact, Ezra and Nehemiah were treated as one book in the earliest Hebrew manuscripts. Therefore to put this book into context, study the historical chart THE TIMES OF EZRA, NEHEMIAH, AND ESTHER on page 793.
2. As you read Nehemiah chapter by chapter:
   a. Look for the theme of each chapter. Record this next to the chapter number on the NEHEMIAH AT A GLANCE chart on page 818 and record it in the text next to the chapter number.
   b. Read each chapter again. This time make a list of the points you want to remember about the main topic or event within each chapter.

      1) For example, in chapter 1 the theme is Nehemiah's concern for Jerusalem. In the margin opposite the first three verses you could write "Remnant's Distress." Then underneath it write "walls broken down, gates burned."

      2) Then next to verses 4 through 11 you could write "Nehemiah's Prayer" and list the main parts or points of his prayer; for example, a) weeps, mourns, fasts, b) reminds God of who he is and his covenant, and c) confesses his and Israel's sins.

      3) As you summarize each chapter, list what you learn about God.

   c. While there are many key repeated words you could mark—such as *wall, gate, rebuilding, repairs,* etc.—you may want to observe them without marking them because of the nature of Nehemiah's writing. Some key words are used so many times within specific chapters that you may become overwhelmed by all the markings.

      1) However, you will find it beneficial to mark every occurrence of *remember* and *remember me* and then in the margin note what or who is to be remembered and why.

      2) Also mark *commands (ordinances, gave, over, regulations, law, laws)* and note in the margin what you learn from marking these words.

d. Note any references to time by drawing a symbol next to the verse.

e. As you read through Nehemiah, note in the margin when the wall is started, when it is completed, and when it is dedicated.

3. There are valuable lessons to be learned from observing how Nehemiah handled situations. As you see how Nehemiah related to God in each situation, how he dealt with the people (including those who opposed him), and the example he set, you will see principles you can apply to your life. As you study, record your insights on the chart LESSONS FROM THE LIFE OF NEHEMIAH on page 819.

4. When you finish recording the theme of every chapter on NEHEMIAH AT A GLANCE, look for the main division of the book, where one emphasis ends and another begins. On the line under the chapter themes, record this division and the theme or subject of the two segments of the book. Also fill in the rest of the chart and record the theme of Nehemiah.

Things to Think About

1. Read Nehemiah chapter 9 again and think about the character of God and how he dealt with Israel. What can you learn about God and also about Israel's behavior that you can apply to your own life?

2. Have you thought about what could happen if the congregation of a church gathered together and publicly confessed their sins and then the sins of their nation?

3. What have you learned from Nehemiah's life? How are you going to apply it to your life in a practical way?

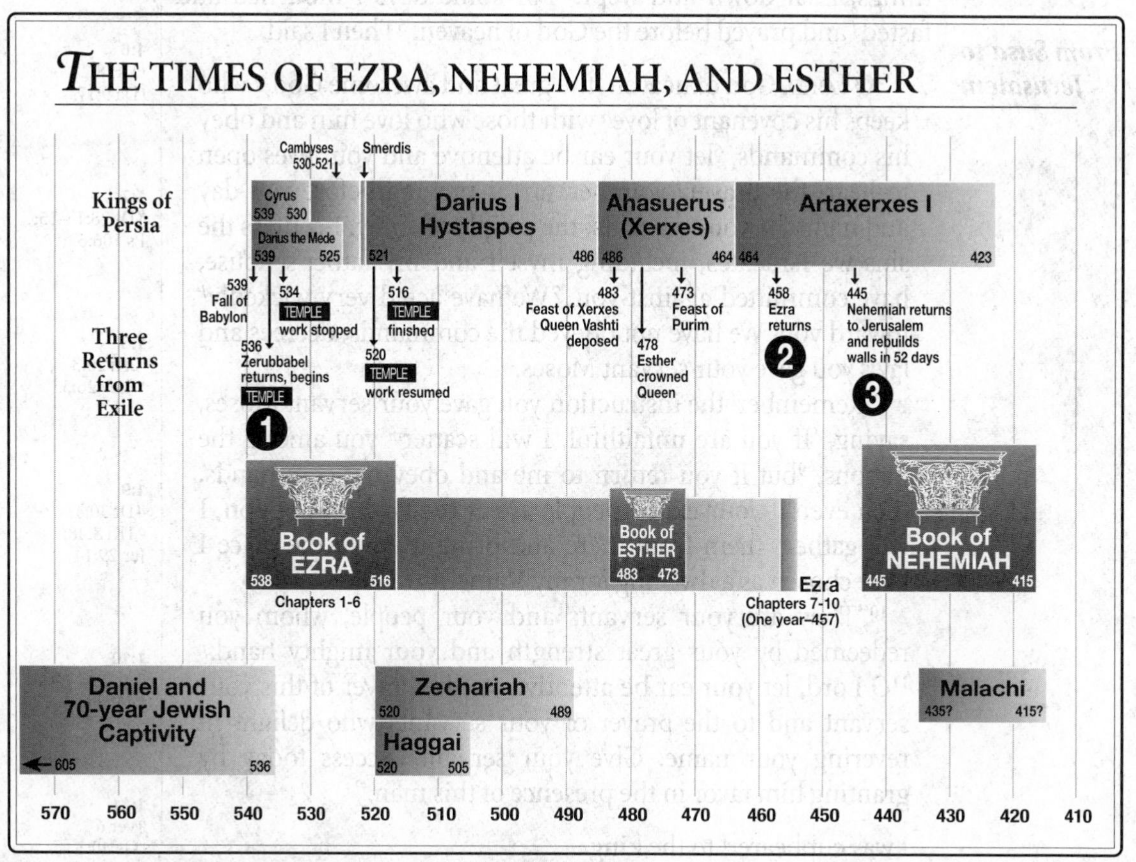

Chapter 1 Theme ________________________________

1

The words of Nehemiah son of Hacaliah:

In the month of Kislev[a] in the twentieth year, while I was in the
citadel of Susa, 2Hanani,[b] one of my brothers, came from Judah
with some other men, and I questioned them about the Jewish
remnant[c] that survived
the exile, and also about
Jerusalem.
3They said to me,
"Those who survived
the exile and are back
in the province are in
great trouble and disgrace.
The wall of Jerusalem
is broken down,
and its gates have been
burned with fire.[d]"
4When I heard these
things, I sat down and wept.[e] For some days I mourned and
fasted[f] and prayed before the God of heaven. 5Then I said:

From Susa to Jerusalem

"O LORD, God of heaven, the great and awesome God,[g] who
keeps his covenant of love[h] with those who love him and obey
his commands, 6let your ear be attentive and your eyes open
to hear[i] the prayer[j] your servant is praying before you day
and night for your servants, the people of Israel. I confess the
sins we Israelites, including myself and my father's house,
have committed against you. 7We have acted very wickedly[k]
toward you. We have not obeyed the commands, decrees and
laws you gave your servant Moses.

8"Remember[l] the instruction you gave your servant Moses,
saying, 'If you are unfaithful, I will scatter[m] you among the
nations, 9but if you return to me and obey my commands,
then even if your exiled people are at the farthest horizon, I
will gather[n] them from there and bring them to the place I
have chosen as a dwelling for my Name.'[o]

10"They are your servants and your people, whom you
redeemed by your great strength and your mighty hand.[p]
11O Lord, let your ear be attentive[q] to the prayer of this your
servant and to the prayer of your servants who delight in
revering your name. Give your servant success today by
granting him favor in the presence of this man."

I was cupbearer[r] to the king.

1:1 [a] Ne 10:1; Zec 7:1
1:2 [b] Ne 7:2 [c] Jer 52:28
1:3 [d] 2Ki 25:10; Ne 2:3,13,17
1:4 [e] Ps 137:1 [f] Ezr 9:4
1:5 [g] Dt 7:21; Ne 4:14 [h] Ex 20:6; Da 9:4
1:6 [i] 1Ki 8:29 [j] Da 9:17
1:7 [k] Dt 28:14-15; Ps 106:6
1:8 [l] 2Ki 20:3 [m] Lev 26:33
1:9 [n] Dt 30:4 [o] 1Ki 8:48; Jer 29:14
1:10 [p] Ex 32:11; Dt 9:29
1:11 [q] ver 6 [r] Ge 40:1

Chapter 2 Theme ______________________

2 In the month of Nisan in the twentieth year of King Artaxerxes,[a] when wine was brought for him, I took the wine and
gave it to the king. I had not been sad in his presence before; 2so
the king asked me, "Why does your face look so sad when you
are not ill? This can be nothing but sadness of heart."
I was very much afraid, 3but I said to the king, "May the king
live forever![b] Why should my face not look sad when the city[c]
where my fathers are buried lies in ruins, and its gates have been
destroyed by fire?[d]"
4The king said to me, "What is it you want?"
Then I prayed to the God of heaven, 5and I answered the king,
"If it pleases the king and if your servant has found favor in his
sight, let him send me to the city in Judah where my fathers are
buried so that I can rebuild it."
6Then the king[e], with the queen sitting beside him, asked me,
"How long will your journey take, and when will you get back?"
It pleased the king to send me; so I set a time.
7I also said to him, "If it pleases the king, may I have letters to
the governors of Trans-Euphrates,[f] so that they will provide me
safe-conduct until I arrive in Judah? 8And may I have a letter to
Asaph, keeper of the king's forest, so he will give me timber to
make beams for the gates of the citadel[g] by the temple and for the
city wall and for the residence I will occupy?" And because the
gracious hand of my God was upon me,[h] the king granted my
requests. 9So I went to the governors of Trans-Euphrates and gave
them the king's letters. The king had also sent army officers and
cavalry[i] with me.
10When Sanballat[j] the Horonite and Tobiah[k] the Ammonite
official heard about this, they were very much disturbed that
someone had come to promote the welfare of the Israelites.[l]

11I went to Jerusalem, and after staying there three days[m] 12I set
out during the night with a few men. I had not told anyone what
my God had put in my heart to do for Jerusalem. There were no
mounts with me except the one I was riding on.
13By night I went out through the Valley Gate[n] toward the Jackal[a]
Well and the Dung Gate,[o] examining the walls[p] of Jerusalem,
which had been broken down, and its gates, which had been
destroyed by fire. 14Then I moved on toward the Fountain Gate[q]
and the King's Pool,[r] but there was not enough room for my
mount to get through; 15so I went up the valley by night, examining the wall. Finally, I turned back and reentered through the Valley Gate. 16The officials did not know where I had gone or what I

2:1 [a]Ezr 7:1
2:3 [b]1Ki 1:31; Da 2:4; 5:10; 6:6,21 [c]Ps 137:6 [d]Ne 1:3
2:6 [e]Ne 5:14; 13:6
2:7 [f]Ezr 8:36
2:8 [g]Ne 7:2 [h]ver 18; Ezr 5:5; 7:6
2:9 [i]Ezr 8:22
2:10 [j]ver 19; Ne 4:1,7 [k]Ne 4:3; 13:4-7 [l]Est 10:3
2:11 [m]Ge 40:13
2:13 [n]2Ch 26:9 [o]Ne 3:13 [p]Ne 1:3
2:14 [q]Ne 3:15 [r]2Ki 18:17

[a]13 Or *Serpent* or *Fig*

was doing, because as yet I had said nothing to the Jews or the
priests or nobles or officials or any others who would be doing
the work.
[17]Then I said to them, "You see the trouble we are in: Jerusalem
lies in ruins, and its gates have been burned with fire.[a] Come, let
us rebuild the wall[b] of Jerusalem, and we will no longer be in disgrace.[c]" [18]I also told them about the gracious hand of my God
upon me[d] and what the king had said to me.
They replied, "Let us start rebuilding." So they began this good
work.
[19]But when Sanballat the Horonite, Tobiah the Ammonite official
and Geshem[e] the Arab heard about it, they mocked and ridiculed
us.[f] "What is this you are doing?" they asked. "Are you rebelling
against the king?"
[20]I answered them by saying, "The God of heaven will give us
success. We his servants will start rebuilding, but as for you, you
have no share[g] in Jerusalem or any claim or historic right to it."

Chapter 3 Theme ____________________

3 Eliashib[h] the high priest and his fellow priests went to work
and rebuilt[i] the Sheep Gate.[j] They dedicated it and set its
doors in place, building as far as the Tower of the
Hundred, which they dedicated, and as far as the
Tower of Hananel.[k] [2]The men of Jericho[l] built the adjoining section, and Zaccur son of Imri built next to
them.
[3]The Fish Gate[m] was rebuilt by the sons of Hasse-
naah. They laid its beams and put its doors and bolts
and bars in place. [4]Meremoth son of Uriah, the son
of Hakkoz, repaired the next section. Next to him
Meshullam son of Berekiah, the son of Meshezabel,
made repairs, and next to him Zadok son of Baana
also made repairs. [5]The next section was repaired by
the men of Tekoa,[n] but their nobles would not put
their shoulders to the work under their supervisors.[a]
[6]The Jeshanah[b] Gate[o] was repaired by Joiada son
of Paseah and Meshullam son of Besodeiah. They laid its beams
and put its doors and bolts and bars in place. [7]Next to them,
repairs were made by men from Gibeon[p] and Mizpah—Melatiah
of Gibeon and Jadon of Meronoth—places under the authority of
the governor of Trans-Euphrates. [8]Uzziel son of Harhaiah, one
of the goldsmiths, repaired the next section; and Hananiah, one of
the perfume-makers, made repairs next to that. They restored[c]

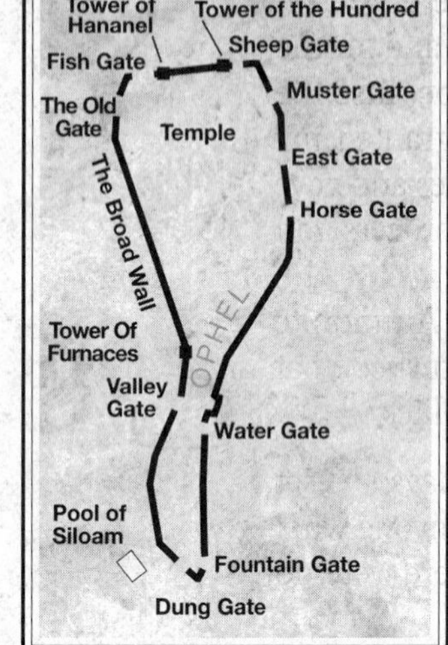

The Gates in Nehemiah's Time

2:17 [a]Ne 1:3 [b]Ps 102:16; Isa 30:13; 58:12 [c]Eze 5:14
2:18 [d]2Sa 2:7
2:19 [e]Ne 6:1,2,6 [f]Ps 44:13-16
2:20 [g]Ezr 4:3
3:1 [h]Ezr 10:24 [i]Isa 58:12 [j]ver 32; Ne 12:39 [k]Ne 12:39; Jer 31:38; Zec 14:10
3:2 [l]Ne 7:36
3:3 [m]2Ch 33:14; Ne 12:39
3:5 [n]2Sa 14:2
3:6 [o]Ne 12:39
3:7 [p]Jos 9:3; Ne 2:7

[a]5 Or *their Lord* or *the governor* [b]6 Or *Old* [c]8 Or *They left out part of*

Jerusalem as far as the Broad Wall.[a] 9Rephaiah son of Hur, ruler
of a half-district of Jerusalem, repaired the next section. 10Adjoin-
ing this, Jedaiah son of Harumaph made repairs opposite his
house, and Hattush son of Hashabneiah made repairs next to
him. 11Malkijah son of Harim and Hasshub son of Pahath-Moab
repaired another section and the Tower of the Ovens.[b] 12Shallum
son of Hallohesh, ruler of a half-district of Jerusalem, repaired
the next section with the help of his daughters.

13The Valley Gate[c] was repaired by Hanun and the residents of
Zanoah.[d] They rebuilt it and put its doors and bolts and bars in
place. They also repaired five hundred yards[a] of the wall as far as
the Dung Gate.[e]

14The Dung Gate was repaired by Malkijah son of Recab, ruler
of the district of Beth Hakkerem.[f] He rebuilt it and put its doors
and bolts and bars in place.

15The Fountain Gate was repaired by Shallun son of Col-Hozeh,
ruler of the district of Mizpah. He rebuilt it, roofing it over and
putting its doors and bolts and bars in place. He also repaired the
wall of the Pool of Siloam,[b][g] by the King's Garden, as far as the
steps going down from the City of David. 16Beyond him, Nehemiah son of Azbuk, ruler of a half-district of Beth Zur,[h] made repairs
up to a point opposite the tombs[c][i] of David, as far as the artificial
pool and the House of the Heroes.

17Next to him, the repairs were made by the Levites under
Rehum son of Bani. Beside him, Hashabiah, ruler of half the district of Keilah,[j] carried out repairs for his district. 18Next to him,
the repairs were made by their countrymen under Binnui[d] son of
Henadad, ruler of the other half-district of Keilah. 19Next to him,
Ezer son of Jeshua, ruler of Mizpah, repaired another section,
from a point facing the ascent to the armory as far as the angle.
20Next to him, Baruch son of Zabbai zealously repaired another
section, from the angle to the entrance of the house of Eliashib
the high priest. 21Next to him, Meremoth[k] son of Uriah, the son
of Hakkoz, repaired another section, from the entrance of
Eliashib's house to the end of it.

22The repairs next to him were made by the priests from the
surrounding region. 23Beyond them, Benjamin and Hasshub
made repairs in front of their house; and next to them, Azariah
son of Maaseiah, the son of Ananiah, made repairs beside his
house. 24Next to him, Binnui[l] son of Henadad repaired another

3:8 [a] Ne 12:38
3:11 [b] Ne 12:38
3:13 [c] 2Ch 26:9 [d] Jos 15:34 [e] Ne 2:13
3:14 [f] Jer 6:1
3:15 [g] Isa 8:6; Jn 9:7
3:16 [h] Jos 15:58 [i] Ac 2:29
3:17 [j] Jos 15:44
3:21 [k] Ezr 8:33
3:24 [l] Ezr 8:33

a *13* Hebrew *a thousand cubits* (about 450 meters) b *15* Hebrew *Shelah,* a variant of *Shiloah,* that is, Siloam c *16* Hebrew; Septuagint, some Vulgate manuscripts and Syriac *tomb*
d *18* Two Hebrew manuscripts and Syriac (see also Septuagint and verse 24); most Hebrew manuscripts *Bavvai*

section, from Azariah's house to the angle and the corner, 25and
Palal son of Uzai worked opposite the angle and the tower projecting from the upper palace near the court of the guard.[a] Next
to him, Pedaiah son of Parosh[b] 26and the temple servants[c] living
on the hill of Ophel[d] made repairs up to a point opposite the
Water Gate[e] toward the east and the projecting tower. 27Next to
them, the men of Tekoa[f] repaired another section, from the great
projecting tower[g] to the wall of Ophel.

28Above the Horse Gate,[h] the priests made repairs, each in front
of his own house. 29Next to them, Zadok son of Immer made
repairs opposite his house. Next to him, Shemaiah son of Shecaniah, the guard at the East Gate, made repairs. 30Next to him,
Hananiah son of Shelemiah, and Hanun, the sixth son of Zalaph,
repaired another section. Next to them, Meshullam son of Berekiah made repairs opposite his living quarters. 31Next to him,
Malkijah, one of the goldsmiths, made repairs as far as the house
of the temple servants and the merchants, opposite the Inspec-
tion Gate, and as far as the room above the corner; 32and between
the room above the corner and the Sheep Gate[i] the goldsmiths
and merchants made repairs.

Chapter 4 Theme __________________________

4 When Sanballat[j] heard that we were rebuilding the wall, he
became angry and was greatly incensed. He ridiculed the
Jews, 2and in the presence of his associates[k] and the army of
Samaria, he said, "What are those feeble Jews doing? Will they
restore their wall? Will they offer sacrifices? Will they finish in a
day? Can they bring the stones back to life from those heaps of
rubble[l]—burned as they are?"

3Tobiah[m] the Ammonite, who was at his side, said, "What they
are building—if even a fox climbed up on it, he would break
down their wall of stones!"[n]

4Hear us, O our God, for we are despised.[o] Turn their insults back
on their own heads. Give them over as plunder in a land of captivity. 5Do not cover up their guilt[p] or blot out their sins from your
sight,[q] for they have thrown insults in the face of[a] the builders.

6So we rebuilt the wall till all of it reached half its height, for the
people worked with all their heart.

7But when Sanballat, Tobiah,[r] the Arabs, the Ammonites and
the men of Ashdod heard that the repairs to Jerusalem's walls
had gone ahead and that the gaps were being closed, they were
very angry. 8They all plotted together[s] to come and fight against

a5 Or *have provoked you to anger before*

3:25 [a]Jer 32:2; 37:21; 39:14 [b]Ezr 2:3
3:26 [c]Ne 7:46; 11:21 [d]2Ch 33:14 [e]Ne 8:1,3,16; 12:37
3:27 [f]ver 5 [g]Ps 48:12
3:28 [h]2Ki 11:16; 2Ch 23:15; Jer 31:40
3:32 [i]ver 1; Jn 5:2
4:1 [j]Ne 2:10
4:2 [k]Ezr 4:9-10 [l]Ps 79:1; Jer 26:18
4:3 [m]Ne 2:10 [n]Job 13:12; 15:3
4:4 [o]Ps 44:13; 79:12; 123:3-4; Jer 33:24
4:5 [p]Isa 2:9; La 1:22 [q]2Ki 14:27; Ps 51:1; 69:27-28; 109:14; Jer 18:23
4:7 [r]Ne 2:10
4:8 [s]Ps 2:2; 83:1-18

Jerusalem and stir up trouble against it. 9 But we prayed to our
God and posted a guard day and night to meet this threat.
10 Meanwhile, the people in Judah said, "The strength of the
laborers[a] is giving out, and there is so much rubble that we cannot
rebuild the wall."
11 Also our enemies said, "Before they know it or see us, we will
be right there among them and will kill them and put an end to
the work."
12 Then the Jews who lived near them came and told us ten times
over, "Wherever you turn, they will attack us."
13 Therefore I stationed some of the people behind the lowest
points of the wall at the exposed places, posting them by families,
with their swords, spears and bows. 14 After I looked things over, I
stood up and said to the nobles, the officials and the rest of the
people, "Don't be afraid[b] of them. Remember[c] the Lord, who is
great and awesome,[d] and fight[e] for your brothers, your sons and
your daughters, your wives and your homes."
15 When our enemies heard that we were aware of their plot and
that God had frustrated it,[f] we all returned to the wall, each to his
own work.
16 From that day on, half of my men did the work, while the other half were equipped with spears, shields, bows and armor. The
officers posted themselves behind all the people of Judah 17 who
were building the wall. Those who carried materials did their
work with one hand and held a weapon[g] in the other, 18 and each
of the builders wore his sword at his side as he worked. But the
man who sounded the trumpet[h] stayed with me.
19 Then I said to the nobles, the officials and the rest of the people, "The work is extensive and spread out, and we are widely separated from each other along the wall. 20 Wherever you hear the
sound of the trumpet,[i] join us there. Our God will fight[j] for us!"
21 So we continued the work with half the men holding spears,
from the first light of dawn till the stars came out. 22 At that time I
also said to the people, "Have every man and his helper stay inside Jerusalem at night, so they can serve us as guards by night
and workmen by day." 23 Neither I nor my brothers nor my men
nor the guards with me took off our clothes; each had his weapon,
even when he went for water.[a]

Chapter 5 Theme ______________________________________

5 Now the men and their wives raised a great outcry against
their Jewish brothers. 2 Some were saying, "We and our sons
and daughters are numerous; in order for us to eat and stay alive,
we must get grain."

4:10 [a] 1Ch 23:4
4:14 [b] Ge 28:15; Nu 14:9; Dt 1:29 [c] Ne 1:8 [d] Ne 1:5 [e] 2Sa 10:12
4:15 [f] 2Sa 17:14; Job 5:12
4:17 [g] Ps 149:6
4:18 [h] Nu 10:2
4:20 [i] Eze 33:3 [j] Ex 14:14; Dt 1:30; 20:4; Jos 10:14

a *23* The meaning of the Hebrew for this clause is uncertain.

3 Others were saying, "We are mortgaging our fields,[a] our vineyards and our homes to get grain during the famine."[b]
4 Still others were saying, "We have had to borrow money to pay
the king's tax[c] on our fields and vineyards. 5 Although we are of
the same flesh and blood[d] as our countrymen and though our
sons are as good as theirs, yet we have to subject our sons and
daughters to slavery.[e] Some of our daughters have already been
enslaved, but we are powerless, because our fields and our vineyards belong to others."[f]
6 When I heard their outcry and these charges, I was very angry.
7 I pondered them in my mind and then accused the nobles and
officials. I told them, "You are exacting usury[g] from your own
countrymen!" So I called together a large meeting to deal with
them 8 and said: "As far as possible, we have bought[h] back our Jewish brothers who were sold to the Gentiles. Now you are selling
your brothers, only for them to be sold back to us!" They kept
quiet, because they could find nothing to say.[i]
9 So I continued, "What you are doing is not right. Shouldn't you
walk in the fear of our God to avoid the reproach[j] of our Gentile
enemies? 10 I and my brothers and my men are also lending the
people money and grain. But let the exacting of usury stop![k]
11 Give back to them immediately their fields, vineyards, olive
groves and houses, and also the usury[l] you are charging them—
the hundredth part of the money, grain, new wine and oil."
12 "We will give it back," they said. "And we will not demand
anything more from them. We will do as you say."
Then I summoned the priests and made the nobles and officials
take an oath[m] to do what they had promised. 13 I also shook[n] out
the folds of my robe and said, "In this way may God shake out of
his house and possessions every man who does not keep this
promise. So may such a man be shaken out and emptied!"
At this the whole assembly said, "Amen,"[o] and praised the
LORD. And the people did as they had promised.
14 Moreover, from the twentieth year of King Artaxerxes,[p] when
I was appointed to be their governor[q] in the land of Judah, until
his thirty-second year—twelve years—neither I nor my brothers
ate the food allotted to the governor. 15 But the earlier governors—those preceding me—placed a heavy burden on the people and took forty shekels[a] of silver from them in addition to
food and wine. Their assistants also lorded it over the people. But
out of reverence for God[r] I did not act like that. 16 Instead,[s] I
devoted myself to the work on this wall. All my men were assembled there for the work; we[b] did not acquire any land.

[a] *15* That is, about 1 pound (about 0.5 kilogram) [b] *16* Most Hebrew manuscripts; some Hebrew manuscripts, Septuagint, Vulgate and Syriac *I*

5:3 [a] Ps 109:11 [b] Ge 47:23
5:4 [c] Ezr 4:13
5:5 [d] Ge 29:14 [e] Lev 25:39-43, 47; 2Ki 4:1; Isa 50:1 [f] Dt 15:7-11; 2Ki 4:1
5:7 [g] Ex 22:25-27; Lev 25:35-37; Dt 23:19-20; 24:10-13
5:8 [h] Lev 25:47 [i] Jer 34:8
5:9 [j] Isa 52:5
5:10 [k] Ex 22:25
5:11 [l] Isa 58:6
5:12 [m] Ezr 10:5
5:13 [n] Mt 10:14; Ac 18:6 [o] Dt 27:15-26
5:14 [p] Ne 2:6; 13:6 [q] Ge 42:6; Ezr 6:7; Jer 40:7; Hag 1:1
5:15 [r] Ge 20:11
5:16 [s] 2Th 3:7-10

5:18 [a]1Ki 4:23 17 Furthermore, a hundred and fifty Jews and officials ate at my
table, as well as those who came to us from the surrounding
nations. 18 Each day one ox, six choice sheep and some poultry[a]
were prepared for me, and every ten days an abundant supply of
wine of all kinds. In spite of all this, I never demanded the food
allotted to the governor, because the demands were heavy on
these people.
5:19 [b]Ge 8:1; 19 Remember[b] me with favor, O my God, for all I have done for
2Ki 20:3; these people.
Ne 1:8;
13:14,22,31

Chapter 6 Theme ______________________________

6 When word came to Sanballat, Tobiah,[c] Geshem[d] the Arab
and the rest of our enemies that I had rebuilt the wall and not
a gap was left in it—though up to that time I had not set the
doors in the gates— 2 Sanballat and Geshem sent me this mes-
6:1 sage: "Come, let us meet together in one of the villages[a] on the
[c]Ne 2:10
[d]Ne 2:19 plain of Ono.[e]"
But they were scheming to harm me; 3 so I sent messengers to
them with this reply: "I am carrying on a great project and cannot go down. Why should the work stop while I leave it and go
down to you?" 4 Four times they sent me the same message, and
each time I gave them the same answer.
6:2 5 Then, the fifth time, Sanballat[f] sent his aide to me with the
[e]1Ch 8:12 same message, and in his hand was an unsealed letter 6 in which
was written:

"It is reported among the nations—and Geshem[b][g] says it is
true—that you and the Jews are plotting to revolt, and therefore you are building the wall. Moreover, according to these
reports you are about to become their king 7 and have even
6:5 appointed prophets to make this proclamation about you in
[f]Ne 2:10 Jerusalem: 'There is a king in Judah!' Now this report will get
back to the king; so come, let us confer together."

8 I sent him this reply: "Nothing like what you are saying is happening; you are just making it up out of your head."
9 They were all trying to frighten us, thinking, "Their hands will
6:6 get too weak for the work, and it will not be completed."
[g]Ne 2:19 ⌊But I prayed,⌋ "Now strengthen my hands."
10 One day I went to the house of Shemaiah son of Delaiah, the
son of Mehetabel, who was shut in at his home. He said, "Let us
meet in the house of God, inside the temple[h], and let us close the
temple doors, because men are coming to kill you—by night
they are coming to kill you."

6:10
[h]Nu 18:7 a2 Or *in Kephirim* b6 Hebrew *Gashmu,* a variant of *Geshem*

11But I said, "Should a man like me run away? Or should one
like me go into the temple to save his life? I will not go!" 12I realized that God had not sent him, but that he had prophesied
against me[a] because Tobiah and Sanballat[b] had hired him. 13He
had been hired to intimidate me so that I would commit a sin by
doing this, and then they would give me a bad name to
discredit me.[c]

14Remember[d] Tobiah and Sanballat,[e] O my God, because of what
they have done; remember also the prophetess[f] Noadiah and the
rest of the prophets[g] who have been trying to intimidate me.

15So the wall was completed on the twenty-fifth of Elul, in fifty-
two days. 16When all our enemies heard about this, all the surrounding nations were afraid and lost their self-confidence,
because they realized that this work had been done with the help
of our God.

17Also, in those days the nobles of Judah were sending many
letters to Tobiah, and replies from Tobiah kept coming to them.
18For many in Judah were under oath to him, since he was son-
in-law to Shecaniah son of Arah, and his son Jehohanan had
married the daughter of Meshullam son of Berekiah. 19Moreover,
they kept reporting to me his good deeds and then telling him
what I said. And Tobiah sent letters to intimidate me.

Chapter 7 Theme ________________________

7 After the wall had been rebuilt and I had set the doors in
place, the gatekeepers[h] and the singers[i] and the Levites[j] were
appointed. 2I put in charge of Jerusalem my brother Hanani,[k]
along with[a] Hananiah[l] the commander of the citadel,[m] because
he was a man of integrity and feared[n] God more than most men
do. 3I said to them, "The gates of Jerusalem are not to be opened
until the sun is hot. While the gatekeepers are still on duty, have
them shut the doors and bar them. Also appoint residents of
Jerusalem as guards, some at their posts and some near their
own houses."

4Now the city was large and spacious, but there were few people
in it,[o] and the houses had not yet been rebuilt. 5So my God put it
into my heart to assemble the nobles, the officials and the common people for registration by families. I found the genealogical
record of those who had been the first to return. This is what I
found written there:

6These are the people of the province who came up from
the captivity of the exiles[p] whom Nebuchadnezzar king of

[a] 2 Or *Hanani, that is,*

6:12
[a] Eze 13:22-23
[b] Ne 2:10

6:13
[c] Jer 20:10

6:14
[d] Ne 1:8
[e] Ne 2:10
[f] Ex 15:20; Eze 13:17-23; Ac 21:9; Rev 2:20
[g] Ne 13:29; Jer 23:9-40; Zec 13:2-3

7:1
[h] 1Ch 9:27; 26:12-19; Ne 6:1,15
[i] Ps 68:25
[j] Ne 8:9

7:2
[k] Ne 1:2
[l] Ne 10:23
[m] Ne 2:8
[n] 1Ki 18:3

7:4
[o] Ne 11:1

7:6
[p] 2Ch 36:20; Ezr 2:1-70; Ne 1:2

7:7 [a] 1Ch 3:19; Ezr 2:2

Babylon had taken captive (they returned to Jerusalem and
Judah, each to his own town, 7 in company with Zerubbabel,[a]
Jeshua, Nehemiah, Azariah, Raamiah, Nahamani, Mordecai,
Bilshan, Mispereth, Bigvai, Nehum and Baanah):

The list of the men of Israel:

8 the descendants of Parosh	2,172
9 of Shephatiah	372
10 of Arah	652
11 of Pahath-Moab (through the line of Jeshua and Joab)	2,818
12 of Elam	1,254
13 of Zattu	845
14 of Zaccai	760
15 of Binnui	648
16 of Bebai	628
17 of Azgad	2,322
18 of Adonikam	667
19 of Bigvai	2,067
20 of Adin[b]	655
21 of Ater (through Hezekiah)	98
22 of Hashum	328
23 of Bezai	324
24 of Hariph	112
25 of Gibeon	95
26 the men of Bethlehem and Netophah[c]	188
27 of Anathoth[d]	128
28 of Beth Azmaveth	42
29 of Kiriath Jearim, Kephirah[e] and Beeroth[f]	743
30 of Ramah and Geba	621
31 of Micmash	122
32 of Bethel and Ai[g]	123
33 of the other Nebo	52
34 of the other Elam	1,254
35 of Harim	320
36 of Jericho[h]	345
37 of Lod, Hadid and Ono[i]	721
38 of Senaah	3,930

39 The priests:

the descendants of Jedaiah (through the family of Jeshua)	973
40 of Immer	1,052
41 of Pashhur	1,247
42 of Harim	1,017

7:20 [b] Ezr 8:6
7:26 [c] 2Sa 23:28; 1Ch 2:54
7:27 [d] Jos 21:18
7:29 [e] Jos 18:26 [f] Jos 18:25
7:32 [g] Ge 12:8
7:36 [h] Ne 3:2
7:37 [i] 1Ch 8:12

43The Levites:

the descendants of Jeshua
(through Kadmiel through the line of Hodaviah) 74

44The singers:[a]

the descendants of Asaph 148

45The gatekeepers:[b]

the descendants of
Shallum, Ater, Talmon, Akkub, Hatita and Shobai 138

46The temple servants:[c]

the descendants of
Ziha, Hasupha, Tabbaoth,
47Keros, Sia, Padon,
48Lebana, Hagaba, Shalmai,
49Hanan, Giddel, Gahar,
50Reaiah, Rezin, Nekoda,
51Gazzam, Uzza, Paseah,
52Besai, Meunim, Nephussim,
53Bakbuk, Hakupha, Harhur,
54Bazluth, Mehida, Harsha,
55Barkos, Sisera, Temah,
56Neziah and Hatipha

57The descendants of the servants of Solomon:

the descendants of
Sotai, Sophereth, Perida,
58Jaala, Darkon, Giddel,
59Shephatiah, Hattil,
Pokereth-Hazzebaim and Amon

60The temple servants and the descendants of the servants of
Solomon[d] 392

61The following came up from the towns of Tel Melah, Tel
Harsha, Kerub, Addon and Immer, but they could not show
that their families were descended from Israel:

62the descendants of
Delaiah, Tobiah and Nekoda 642

63And from among the priests:

the descendants of
Hobaiah, Hakkoz and Barzillai (a man who had
married a daughter of Barzillai the Gileadite and was
called by that name).

7:44 [a]Ne 11:23

7:45 [b]1Ch 9:17

7:46 [c]Ne 3:26

7:60 [d]1Ch 9:2

7:65
[a]Ex 28:30;
Ne 8:9

64 These searched for their family records, but they could not find them and so were excluded from the priesthood as unclean. 65 The governor, therefore, ordered them not to eat any of the most sacred food until there should be a priest ministering with the Urim and Thummim.[a]

7:71
[b]1Ch 29:7

66 The whole company numbered 42,360, 67 besides their 7,337 menservants and maidservants; and they also had 245 men and women singers. 68 There were 736 horses, 245 mules,[a] 69 435 camels and 6,720 donkeys.

7:72
[c]Ex 25:2

70 Some of the heads of the families contributed to the work. The governor gave to the treasury 1,000 drachmas[b] of gold, 50 bowls and 530 garments for priests. 71 Some of the heads of the families[b] gave to the treasury for the work 20,000 drach-

7:73
[d]Ne 1:10;
Ps 34:22;
103:21; 113:1;
135:1
[e]Ezr 3:1;
Ne 11:1
[f]Ezr 3:1

mas[c] of gold and 2,200 minas[d] of silver. 72 The total given by the rest of the people was 20,000 drachmas of gold, 2,000 minas[e] of silver and 67 garments for priests.[c]

73 The priests, the Levites, the gatekeepers, the singers and the temple servants,[d] along with certain of the people and the rest of the Israelites, settled in their own towns.[e]

Chapter 8 Theme ____________________

8:1
[g]Ne 3:26
[h]Dt 28:61;
2Ch 34:15;
Ezr 7:6

8 When the seventh month came and the Israelites had settled in their towns,[f] 1 all the people assembled as one man in the square before the Water Gate.[g] They told Ezra the scribe to bring out the Book of the Law of Moses,[h] which the LORD had commanded for Israel.

2 So on the first day of the seventh month[i] Ezra the priest brought

8:2
[i]Lev 23:23-25;
Nu 29:1-6
[j]Dt 31:11

the Law[j] before the assembly, which was made up of men and women and all who were able to understand. 3 He read it aloud from daybreak till noon as he faced the square before the Water Gate[k] in the presence of the men, women and others who could understand. And all the people listened attentively to the Book of the Law.

8:3
[k]Ne 3:26

4 Ezra the scribe stood on a high wooden platform[l] built for the occasion. Beside him on his right stood Mattithiah, Shema, Anaiah, Uriah, Hilkiah and Maaseiah; and on his left were Pedaiah, Mishael, Malkijah, Hashum, Hashbaddanah, Zechariah and

8:4
[l]2Ch 6:13

Meshullam.

5 Ezra opened the book. All the people could see him because he was standing[m] above them; and as he opened it, the people all

8:5
[m]Jdg 3:20

[a]*68* Some Hebrew manuscripts (see also Ezra 2:66); most Hebrew manuscripts do not have this verse. [b]*70* That is, about 19 pounds (about 8.5 kilograms) [c]*71* That is, about 375 pounds (about 170 kilograms); also in verse 72 [d]*71* That is, about 1 1/3 tons (about 1.2 metric tons) [e]*72* That is, about 1 1/4 tons (about 1.1 metric tons)

stood up. 6Ezra praised the LORD, the great God; and all the people lifted their hands[a] and responded, "Amen! Amen!" Then they
bowed down and worshiped the LORD with their faces to the
ground.
7The Levites[b]—Jeshua, Bani, Sherebiah, Jamin, Akkub, Shabbethai, Hodiah, Maaseiah, Kelita, Azariah, Jozabad, Hanan and
Pelaiah—instructed[c] the people in the Law while the people were
standing there. 8They read from the Book of the Law of God,
making it clear[a] and giving the meaning so that the people could
understand what was being read.
9Then Nehemiah the governor, Ezra the priest and scribe, and
the Levites[d] who were instructing the people said to them all,
"This day is sacred to the LORD your God. Do not mourn or weep."[e]
For all the people had been weeping as they listened to the words
of the Law.
10Nehemiah said, "Go and enjoy choice food and sweet drinks,
and send some to those who have nothing[f] prepared. This day is
sacred to our Lord. Do not grieve, for the joy[g] of the LORD is your
strength."
11The Levites calmed all the people, saying, "Be still, for this is
a sacred day. Do not grieve."
12Then all the people went away to eat and drink, to send portions of food and to celebrate with great joy,[h] because they now
understood the words that had been made known to them.
13On the second day of the month, the heads of all the families,
along with the priests and the Levites, gathered around Ezra the
scribe to give attention to the words of the Law. 14They found
written in the Law, which the LORD had commanded through
Moses, that the Israelites were to live in booths during the feast of
the seventh month 15and that they should proclaim this word and
spread it throughout their towns and in Jerusalem: "Go out into
the hill country and bring back branches from olive and wild
olive trees, and from myrtles, palms and shade trees, to make
booths"—as it is written.[b]
16So the people went out and brought back branches and built
themselves booths on their own roofs, in their courtyards, in the
courts of the house of God and in the square by the Water Gate
and the one by the Gate of Ephraim.[i] 17The whole company that
had returned from exile built booths and lived in them. From the
days of Joshua son of Nun until that day, the Israelites had not
celebrated[j] it like this. And their joy was very great.
18Day after day, from the first day to the last, Ezra read[k] from
the Book of the Law of God. They celebrated the feast for seven

[a]8 Or *God, translating it* [b]15 See Lev. 23:37-40.

8:6 [a]Ex 4:31; Ezr 9:5; 1Ti 2:8

8:7 [b]Ezr 10:23 [c]Lev 10:11; 2Ch 17:7

8:9 [d]Ne 7:1,65,70 [e]Dt 12:7,12; 16:14-15

8:10 [f]1Sa 25:8; Lk 14:12-14 [g]Lev 23:40; Dt 12:18; 16:11,14-15

8:12 [h]Est 9:22

8:16 [i]2Ki 14:13; Ne 12:39

8:17 [j]2Ch 7:8; 8:13; 30:21

8:18 [k]Dt 31:11

days, and on the eighth day, in accordance with the regulation,[a]
there was an assembly.

Chapter 9 Theme ______________________________________

9 On the twenty-fourth day of the same month, the Israelites
gathered together, fasting and wearing sackcloth and having
dust on their heads.[b] 2Those of Israelite descent had separated
themselves from all foreigners.[c] They stood in their places and
confessed their sins and the wickedness of their fathers.[d] 3They
stood where they were and read from the Book of the Law of the
LORD their God for a quarter of the day, and spent another quarter in confession and in worshiping the LORD their God. 4Standing
on the stairs were the Levites[e]—Jeshua, Bani, Kadmiel, Shebaniah, Bunni, Sherebiah, Bani and Kenani—who called with loud
voices to the LORD their God. 5And the Levites—Jeshua, Kadmiel,
Bani, Hashabneiah, Sherebiah, Hodiah, Shebaniah and Pethahiah—said: "Stand up and praise the LORD your God,[f] who is from
everlasting to everlasting.[a]"

"Blessed be your glorious name, and may it be exalted
above all blessing and praise. 6You alone are the LORD.[g] You
made the heavens,[h] even the highest heavens, and all their
starry host, the earth[i] and all that is on it, the seas[j] and all that
is in them.[k] You give life to everything, and the multitudes of
heaven worship you.

7"You are the LORD God, who chose Abram and brought
him out of Ur of the Chaldeans[l] and named him Abraham.[m]
8You found his heart faithful to you, and you made a covenant
with him to give to his descendants the land of the Canaanites, Hittites, Amorites, Perizzites, Jebusites and Girgashites.[n]
You have kept your promise[o] because you are righteous.[p]

9"You saw the suffering of our forefathers in Egypt;[q] you
heard their cry at the Red Sea.[b][r] 10You sent miraculous signs[s]
and wonders against Pharaoh, against all his officials and all
the people of his land, for you knew how arrogantly the Egyptians treated them. You made a name[t] for yourself, which
remains to this day. 11You divided the sea before them,[u] so that
they passed through it on dry ground, but you hurled their
pursuers into the depths, like a stone into mighty waters.[v] 12By
day you led[w] them with a pillar of cloud,[x] and by night with a
pillar of fire to give them light on the way they were to take.

13"You came down on Mount Sinai;[y] you spoke[z] to them
from heaven. You gave them regulations and laws that are
just[a] and right, and decrees and commands that are good.[b]

a5 Or *God for ever and ever* b9 Hebrew *Yam Suph*; that is, Sea of Reeds

8:18 [a]Lev 23:36,40; Nu 29:35
9:1 [b]Jos 7:6; 1Sa 4:12
9:2 [c]Ne 13:3,30 [d]Ezr 10:11; Ps 106:6
9:4 [e]Ezr 10:23
9:5 [f]Ps 78:4
9:6 [g]Dt 6:4 [h]2Ki 19:15 [i]Ge 1:1; Isa 37:16 [j]Ps 95:5 [k]Dt 10:14
9:7 [l]Ge 11:31 [m]Ge 17:5
9:8 [n]Ge 15:18-21 [o]Jos 21:45 [p]Ge 15:6; Ezr 9:15
9:9 [q]Ex 3:7 [r]Ex 14:10-30
9:10 [s]Ex 10:1 [t]Jer 32:20; Da 9:15
9:11 [u]Ex 14:21; Ps 78:13 [v]Ex 15:4-5,10; Heb 11:29
9:12 [w]Ex 15:13 [x]Ex 13:21
9:13 [y]Ex 19:11 [z]Ex 19:19 [a]Ps 119:137 [b]Ex 20:1

14You made known to them your holy Sabbath[a] and gave them
commands, decrees and laws through your servant Moses. 15In
their hunger you gave them bread from heaven[b] and in their
thirst you brought them water from the rock;[c] you told them
to go in and take possession of the land you had sworn with
uplifted hand to give them.[d]
16"But they, our forefathers, became arrogant and stiff-
necked, and did not obey your commands.[e] 17They refused to
listen and failed to remember[f] the miracles you performed
among them. They became stiff-necked and in their rebellion
appointed a leader in order to return to their slavery.[g] But you
are a forgiving God, gracious and compassionate, slow to
anger[h] and abounding in love.[i] Therefore you did not desert
them,[j] 18even when they cast for themselves an image of a
calf[k] and said, 'This is your god, who brought you up out of
Egypt,' or when they committed awful blasphemies.
19"Because of your great compassion you did not abandon
them in the desert. By day the pillar of cloud did not cease to
guide them on their path, nor the pillar of fire by night to
shine on the way they were to take. 20You gave your good
Spirit[l] to instruct them. You did not withhold your manna[m]
from their mouths, and you gave them water[n] for their thirst.
21For forty years you sustained them in the desert; they
lacked nothing,[o] their clothes did not wear out nor did their
feet become swollen.[p]
22"You gave them kingdoms and nations, allotting to them
even the remotest frontiers. They took over the country of Sihon[a][q] king of Heshbon and the country of Og king of Bashan.[r]
23You made their sons as numerous as the stars in the sky, and
you brought them into the land that you told their fathers to
enter and possess. 24Their sons went in and took possession
of the land.[s] You subdued before them the Canaanites, who
lived in the land; you handed the Canaanites over to them,
along with their kings and the peoples of the land, to deal
with them as they pleased. 25They captured fortified cities
and fertile land; they took possession of houses filled with all
kinds of good things, wells already dug, vineyards, olive groves
and fruit trees in abundance. They ate to the full and were
well-nourished;[t] they reveled in your great goodness.[u]
26"But they were disobedient and rebelled against you; they
put your law behind their backs.[v] They killed your prophets,[w]
who had admonished them in order to turn them back to you;
they committed awful blasphemies.[x] 27So you handed them
over to their enemies,[y] who oppressed them. But when they

a 22 One Hebrew manuscript and Septuagint; most Hebrew manuscripts *Sihon, that is, the country of the*

9:14 [a] Ge 2:3; Ex 20:8-11

9:15 [b] Ex 16:4; Jn 6:31 [c] Ex 17:6; Nu 20:7-13 [d] Dt 1:8,21

9:16 [e] Dt 1:26-33; 31:29

9:17 [f] Ps 78:42 [g] Nu 14:1-4 [h] Ex 34:6 [i] Nu 14:17-19 [j] Ps 78:11

9:18 [k] Ex 32:4

9:20 [l] Nu 11:17; Isa 63:11,14 [m] Ex 16:15 [n] Ex 17:6

9:21 [o] Dt 2:7 [p] Dt 8:4

9:22 [q] Nu 21:21 [r] Nu 21:33

9:24 [s] Jos 11:23

9:25 [t] Dt 6:10-12 [u] Nu 13:27; Dt 32:12-15

9:26 [v] 1Ki 14:9 [w] Mt 21:35-36 [x] Jdg 2:12-13

9:27 [y] Jdg 2:14

9:27 [a]Ps 106:45
were oppressed they cried out to you. From heaven you heard
them, and in your great compassion[a] you gave them deliverers, who rescued them from the hand of their enemies.

9:28
28"But as soon as they were at rest, they again did what was
[b]Ps 106:43
evil in your sight. Then you abandoned them to the hand of
their enemies so that they ruled over them. And when they
9:29
cried out to you again, you heard from heaven, and in your
[c]Ps 5:5; Isa 2:11; Jer 43:2
compassion you delivered them[b] time after time.
[d]Dt 30:16
29"You warned them to return to your law, but they became
[e]Zec 7:11-12
arrogant[c] and disobeyed your commands. They sinned against
your ordinances, by which a man will live if he obeys them.[d]
9:30
Stubbornly they turned their backs on you, became stiff-
[f]2Ki 17:13-18; 2Ch 36:16
necked and refused to listen.[e] 30For many years you were
patient with them. By your Spirit you admonished them
through your prophets.[f] Yet they paid no attention, so you
9:31
handed them over to the neighboring peoples. 31But in your
[g]Isa 48:9; Jer 4:27
great mercy you did not put an end[g] to them or abandon
them, for you are a gracious and merciful God.

32"Now therefore, O our God, the great, mighty[h] and awe-
9:32
some God, who keeps his covenant of love,[i] do not let all this
[h]Ps 24:8
[i]Dt 7:9
hardship seem trifling in your eyes—the hardship that has
come upon us, upon our kings and leaders, upon our priests
and prophets, upon our fathers and all your people, from the
9:33
days of the kings of Assyria until today. 33In all that has hap-
[j]Ge 18:25
[k]Jer 44:3; Da 9:7-8,14
pened to us, you have been just;[j] you have acted faithfully,
while we did wrong.[k] 34Our kings,[l] our leaders, our priests
and our fathers[m] did not follow your law; they did not pay
9:34
attention to your commands or the warnings you gave them.
[l]2Ki 23:11
[m]Jer 44:17
35Even while they were in their kingdom, enjoying your great
goodness[n] to them in the spacious and fertile land you gave
them, they did not serve you[o] or turn from their evil ways.

36"But see, we are slaves[p] today, slaves in the land you gave
9:35
[n]Isa 63:7
[o]Dt 28:45-48
our forefathers so they could eat its fruit and the other good
things it produces. 37Because of our sins, its abundant harvest
goes to the kings you have placed over us. They rule over our
9:36
bodies and our cattle as they please. We are in great distress.[q]
[p]Dt 28:48; Ezr 9:9

38"In view of all this, we are making a binding agreement,[r]
putting it in writing,[s] and our leaders, our Levites and our priests
9:37
are affixing their seals to it."
[q]Dt 28:33; La 5:5

Chapter 10 Theme ______________________

10

Those who sealed it were:

9:38
[r]2Ch 23:16
[s]Isa 44:5
Nehemiah the governor, the son of Hacaliah.

Zedekiah, 2Seraiah,[a] Azariah, Jeremiah,
3Pashhur,[b] Amariah, Malkijah,
4Hattush, Shebaniah, Malluch,
5Harim,[c] Meremoth, Obadiah,
6Daniel, Ginnethon, Baruch,
7Meshullam, Abijah, Mijamin,
8Maaziah, Bilgai and Shemaiah.
These were the priests.

9The Levites:[d]

Jeshua son of Azaniah, Binnui of the sons of Henadad, Kadmiel,
10and their associates: Shebaniah,
Hodiah, Kelita, Pelaiah, Hanan,
11Mica, Rehob, Hashabiah,
12Zaccur, Sherebiah, Shebaniah,
13Hodiah, Bani and Beninu.

14The leaders of the people:

Parosh, Pahath-Moab, Elam, Zattu, Bani,
15Bunni, Azgad, Bebai,
16Adonijah, Bigvai, Adin,[e]
17Ater, Hezekiah, Azzur,
18Hodiah, Hashum, Bezai,
19Hariph, Anathoth, Nebai,
20Magpiash, Meshullam, Hezir,[f]
21Meshezabel, Zadok, Jaddua,
22Pelatiah, Hanan, Anaiah,
23Hoshea, Hananiah,[g] Hasshub,
24Hallohesh, Pilha, Shobek,
25Rehum, Hashabnah, Maaseiah,
26Ahiah, Hanan, Anan,
27Malluch, Harim and Baanah.

28"The rest of the people—priests, Levites, gatekeepers, singers, temple servants[h] and all who separated themselves from the neighboring peoples[i] for the sake of the Law of God, together with their wives and all their sons and daughters who are able to understand— 29all these now join their brothers the nobles, and bind themselves with a curse and an oath[j] to follow the Law of God given through Moses the servant of God and to obey carefully all the commands, regulations and decrees of the LORD our Lord.

30"We promise not to give our daughters in marriage to the peoples around us or take their daughters for our sons.[k]

10:2 [a] Ezr 2:2
10:3 [b] 1Ch 9:12
10:5 [c] 1Ch 24:8
10:9 [d] Ne 12:1
10:16 [e] Ezr 8:6
10:20 [f] 1Ch 24:15
10:23 [g] Ne 7:2
10:28 [h] Ps 135:1 [i] 2Ch 6:26; Ne 9:2
10:29 [j] Nu 5:21; Ps 119:106
10:30 [k] Ex 34:16; Dt 7:3; Ne 13:23

31"When the neighboring peoples bring merchandise or
grain to sell on the Sabbath,[a] we will not buy from them on the
Sabbath or on any holy day. Every seventh year we will forgo
working the land[b] and will cancel all debts.[c]
32"We assume the responsibility for carrying out the commands to give a third of a shekel[a] each year for the service of
the house of our God: 33for the bread set out on the table;[d] for
the regular grain offerings and burnt offerings; for the offerings on the Sabbaths, New Moon[e] festivals and appointed
feasts; for the holy offerings; for sin offerings to make atonement for Israel; and for all the duties of the house of our God.[f]
34"We—the priests, the Levites and the people—have cast
lots[g] to determine when each of our families is to bring to the
house of our God at set times each year a contribution of
wood[h] to burn on the altar of the LORD our God, as it is written in the Law.
35"We also assume responsibility for bringing to the house
of the LORD each year the firstfruits[i] of our crops and of every
fruit tree.[j]
36"As it is also written in the Law, we will bring the firstborn[k]
of our sons and of our cattle, of our herds and of our flocks to
the house of our God, to the priests ministering there.[l]
37"Moreover, we will bring to the storerooms of the house
of our God, to the priests, the first of our ground meal, of our
⌊grain⌋ offerings, of the fruit of all our trees and of our new
wine and oil.[m] And we will bring a tithe[n] of our crops to the
Levites,[o] for it is the Levites who collect the tithes in all the
towns where we work.[p] 38A priest descended from Aaron is to
accompany the Levites when they receive the tithes, and the
Levites are to bring a tenth of the tithes[q] up to the house of
our God, to the storerooms of the treasury. 39The people of
Israel, including the Levites, are to bring their contributions
of grain, new wine and oil to the storerooms where the articles for the sanctuary are kept and where the ministering
priests, the gatekeepers and the singers stay.
"We will not neglect the house of our God."[r]

Chapter 11 Theme ______________________________

11 Now the leaders of the people settled in Jerusalem, and the
rest of the people cast lots to bring one out of every ten to
live in Jerusalem,[s] the holy city,[t] while the remaining nine were to
stay in their own towns.[u] 2The people commended all the men
who volunteered to live in Jerusalem.

10:31 [a]Ne 13:16,18; Jer 17:27; Eze 23:38; Am 8:5 [b]Ex 23:11; Lev 25:1-7 [c]Dt 15:1
10:33 [d]Lev 24:6 [e]Nu 10:10; Ps 81:3; Isa 1:14 [f]2Ch 24:5
10:34 [g]Lev 16:8 [h]Ne 13:31
10:35 [i]Ex 22:29; 23:19; Nu 18:12 [j]Dt 26:1-11
10:36 [k]Ex 13:2; Nu 18:14-16 [l]Ne 13:31
10:37 [m]Lev 23:17; Nu 18:12 [n]Lev 27:30; Nu 18:21 [o]Dt 14:22-29 [p]Eze 44:30
10:38 [q]Nu 18:26
10:39 [r]Dt 12:6; Ne 13:11,12
11:1 [s]Ne 7:4 [t]ver 18; Isa 48:2; 52:1; 64:10; Zec 14:20-21 [u]Ne 7:73

[a] *32* That is, about 1/8 ounce (about 4 grams)

3These are the provincial leaders who settled in Jerusalem (now
some Israelites, priests, Levites, temple servants and descendants
of Solomon's servants lived in the towns of Judah, each on his
own property in the various towns,[a] 4while other people from
both Judah and Benjamin[b] lived in Jerusalem):[c]

From the descendants of Judah:

Athaiah son of Uzziah, the son of Zechariah, the son of Amariah, the son of Shephatiah, the son of Mahalalel, a descendant
of Perez; 5and Maaseiah son of Baruch, the son of Col-Hozeh,
the son of Hazaiah, the son of Adaiah, the son of Joiarib, the
son of Zechariah, a descendant of Shelah. 6The descendants
of Perez who lived in Jerusalem totaled 468 able men.

7From the descendants of Benjamin:

Sallu son of Meshullam, the son of Joed, the son of Pedaiah,
the son of Kolaiah, the son of Maaseiah, the son of Ithiel, the
son of Jeshaiah, 8and his followers, Gabbai and Sallai—928
men. 9Joel son of Zicri was their chief officer, and Judah son
of Hassenuah was over the Second District of the city.

10From the priests:

Jedaiah; the son of Joiarib; Jakin; 11Seraiah[d] son of Hilkiah,
the son of Meshullam, the son of Zadok, the son of Meraioth,
the son of Ahitub,[e] supervisor in the house of God, 12and their
associates, who carried on work for the temple—822 men;
Adaiah son of Jeroham, the son of Pelaliah, the son of Amzi,
the son of Zechariah, the son of Pashhur, the son of Malkijah,
13and his associates, who were heads of families—242 men;
Amashsai son of Azarel, the son of Ahzai, the son of Meshillemoth, the son of Immer, 14and his[a] associates, who were able
men—128. Their chief officer was Zabdiel son of Haggedolim.

15From the Levites:

Shemaiah son of Hasshub, the son of Azrikam, the son of
Hashabiah, the son of Bunni; 16Shabbethai[f] and Jozabad,[g]
two of the heads of the Levites, who had charge of the outside
work of the house of God; 17Mattaniah[h] son of Mica, the son
of Zabdi, the son of Asaph,[i] the director who led in thanksgiving and prayer; Bakbukiah, second among his associates;
and Abda son of Shammua, the son of Galal, the son of
Jeduthun.[j] 18The Levites in the holy city[k] totaled 284.

11:3 [a] 1Ch 9:2-3; Ezr 2:1
11:4 [b] Ezr 1:5 [c] Ezr 2:70
11:11 [d] 2Ki 25:18; Ezr 2:2 [e] Ezr 7:2
11:16 [f] Ezr 10:15 [g] Ezr 8:33
11:17 [h] 1Ch 9:15; Ne 12:8 [i] 2Ch 5:12 [j] 1Ch 25:1
11:18 [k] Rev 21:2

a *14* Most Septuagint manuscripts; Hebrew *their*

19 The gatekeepers:

Akkub, Talmon and their associates, who kept watch at the gates—172 men.

20 The rest of the Israelites, with the priests and Levites, were in all the towns of Judah, each on his ancestral property.

21 The temple servants[a] lived on the hill of Ophel, and Ziha and Gishpa were in charge of them.

22 The chief officer of the Levites in Jerusalem was Uzzi son of Bani, the son of Hashabiah, the son of Mattaniah,[b] the son of Mica. Uzzi was one of Asaph's descendants, who were the singers responsible for the service of the house of God. 23 The singers[c] were under the king's orders, which regulated their daily activity.

24 Pethahiah son of Meshezabel, one of the descendants of Zerah[d] son of Judah, was the king's agent in all affairs relating to the people.

25 As for the villages with their fields, some of the people of Judah lived in Kiriath Arba[e] and its surrounding settlements, in Dibon[f] and its settlements, in Jekabzeel and its villages, 26 in Jeshua, in Moladah, in Beth Pelet,[g] 27 in Hazar Shual, in Beersheba[h] and its settlements, 28 in Ziklag,[i] in Meconah and its settlements, 29 in En Rimmon, in Zorah,[j] in Jarmuth,[k] 30 Zanoah, Adullam[l] and their villages, in Lachish[m] and its fields, and in Azekah[n] and its settlements. So they were living all the way from Beersheba[o] to the Valley of Hinnom.

31 The descendants of the Benjamites from Geba[p] lived in Micmash,[q] Aija, Bethel and its settlements, 32 in Anathoth,[r] Nob[s] and Ananiah, 33 in Hazor,[t] Ramah and Gittaim,[u] 34 in Hadid, Zeboim[v] and Neballat, 35 in Lod and Ono,[w] and in the Valley of the Craftsmen.

36 Some of the divisions of the Levites of Judah settled in Benjamin.

Chapter 12 Theme

12 These were the priests[x] and Levites who returned with Zerubbabel[y] son of Shealtiel and with Jeshua:[z]

Seraiah,[a] Jeremiah, Ezra,
2 Amariah, Malluch, Hattush,
3 Shecaniah, Rehum, Meremoth,
4 Iddo,[b] Ginnethon,[a] Abijah,[c]
5 Mijamin,[b] Moadiah, Bilgah,
6 Shemaiah, Joiarib, Jedaiah,[d]
7 Sallu, Amok, Hilkiah and Jedaiah.

These were the leaders of the priests and their associates in the days of Jeshua.

11:21 [a] Ezr 2:43; Ne 3:26
11:22 [b] 1Ch 9:15
11:23 [c] Ne 7:44
11:24 [d] Ge 38:30
11:25 [e] Ge 35:27; Jos 14:15 [f] Nu 21:30
11:26 [g] Jos 15:27
11:27 [h] Ge 21:14
11:28 [i] 1Sa 27:6
11:29 [j] Jos 15:33 [k] Jos 10:3
11:30 [l] Jos 15:35 [m] Jos 10:3 [n] Jos 10:10 [o] Jos 15:28
11:31 [p] Jos 21:17; Isa 10:29 [q] 1Sa 13:2
11:32 [r] Jos 21:18; Isa 10:30 [s] 1Sa 21:1
11:33 [t] Jos 11:1 [u] 2Sa 4:3
11:34 [v] 1Sa 13:18
11:35 [w] 1Ch 8:12
12:1 [x] Ne 10:1-8 [y] 1Ch 3:19 [z] Ezr 2:2 [a] Ezr 2:2
12:4 [b] Zec 1:1 [c] Lk 1:5
12:6 [d] 1Ch 24:7

[a] *4* Many Hebrew manuscripts and Vulgate (see also Neh. 12:16); most Hebrew manuscripts *Ginnethoi* [b] *5* A variant of *Miniamin*

8 The Levites were Jeshua, Binnui, Kadmiel, Sherebiah, Judah,
and also Mattaniah,[a] who, together with his associates, was in
charge of the songs of thanksgiving. 9 Bakbukiah and Unni, their
associates, stood opposite them in the services.
10 Jeshua was the father of Joiakim, Joiakim the father of Eliashib,[b] Eliashib the father of Joiada, 11 Joiada the father of Jonathan,
and Jonathan the father of Jaddua.
12 In the days of Joiakim, these were the heads of the priestly
families:
of Seraiah's family, Meraiah;
of Jeremiah's, Hananiah;
13 of Ezra's, Meshullam;
of Amariah's, Jehohanan;
14 of Malluch's, Jonathan;
of Shecaniah's,[a] Joseph;
15 of Harim's, Adna;
of Meremoth's,[b] Helkai;
16 of Iddo's,[c] Zechariah;
of Ginnethon's, Meshullam;
17 of Abijah's, Zicri;
of Miniamin's and of Moadiah's, Piltai;
18 of Bilgah's, Shammua;
of Shemaiah's, Jehonathan;
19 of Joiarib's, Mattenai;
of Jedaiah's, Uzzi;
20 of Sallu's, Kallai;
of Amok's, Eber;
21 of Hilkiah's, Hashabiah;
of Jedaiah's, Nethanel.
22 The family heads of the Levites in the days of Eliashib, Joiada,
Johanan and Jaddua, as well as those of the priests, were recorded
in the reign of Darius the Persian. 23 The family heads among the
descendants of Levi up to the time of Johanan son of Eliashib
were recorded in the book of the annals. 24 And the leaders of the
Levites[d] were Hashabiah, Sherebiah, Jeshua son of Kadmiel, and
their associates, who stood opposite them to give praise and
thanksgiving, one section responding to the other, as prescribed
by David the man of God.
25 Mattaniah, Bakbukiah, Obadiah, Meshullam, Talmon and
Akkub were gatekeepers who guarded the storerooms at the
gates. 26 They served in the days of Joiakim son of Jeshua, the son
of Jozadak, and in the days of Nehemiah the governor and of
Ezra the priest and scribe.

12:8 [a] Ne 11:17

12:10 [b] Ezr 10:24

12:16 [c] ver 4

12:24 [d] Ezr 2:40

[a] *14* Very many Hebrew manuscripts, some Septuagint manuscripts and Syriac (see also Neh. 12:3); most Hebrew manuscripts *Shebaniah's* [b] *15* Some Septuagint manuscripts (see also Neh. 12:3); Hebrew *Meraioth's*

27 At the dedication[a] of the wall of Jerusalem, the Levites were
sought out from where they lived and were brought to Jerusalem to
celebrate joyfully the dedication with songs of thanksgiving and
with the music of cymbals,[b] harps and lyres.[c] 28 The singers also
were brought together from the region around Jerusalem—from
the villages of the Netophathites,[d] 29 from Beth Gilgal, and from the
area of Geba and Azmaveth, for the singers had built villages for
themselves around Jerusalem. 30 When the priests and Levites had
purified themselves ceremonially, they purified the people,[e] the
gates and the wall.

31 I had the leaders of Judah go up on top[a] of the wall. I also
assigned two large choirs to give thanks. One was to proceed on
top[b] of the wall to the right, toward the Dung Gate.[f] 32 Hoshaiah
and half the leaders of Judah followed them, 33 along with Azariah, Ezra, Meshullam, 34 Judah, Benjamin,[g] Shemaiah, Jeremiah,
35 as well as some priests with trumpets,[h] and also Zechariah son
of Jonathan, the son of Shemaiah, the son of Mattaniah, the son
of Micaiah, the son of Zaccur, the son of Asaph, 36 and his associates—Shemaiah, Azarel, Milalai, Gilalai, Maai, Nethanel, Judah
and Hanani—with musical instruments[i] ⌊prescribed by⌋ David
the man of God.[j] Ezra[k] the scribe led the procession. 37 At the
Fountain Gate[l] they continued directly up the steps of the City of
David on the ascent to the wall and passed above the house of
David to the Water Gate[m] on the east.

38 The second choir proceeded in the opposite direction. I followed them on top[c] of the wall, together with half the people—
past the Tower of the Ovens[n] to the Broad Wall,[o] 39 over the Gate
of Ephraim,[p] the Jeshanah[d] Gate,[q] the Fish Gate,[r] the Tower of
Hananel[s] and the Tower of the Hundred,[t] as far as the Sheep
Gate.[u] At the Gate of the Guard they stopped.

40 The two choirs that gave thanks then took their places in the
house of God; so did I, together with half the officials, 41 as well as
the priests—Eliakim, Maaseiah, Miniamin, Micaiah, Elioenai,
Zechariah and Hananiah with their trumpets— 42 and also Maaseiah, Shemaiah, Eleazar, Uzzi, Jehohanan, Malkijah, Elam and
Ezer. The choirs sang under the direction of Jezrahiah. 43 And on
that day they offered great sacrifices, rejoicing because God had
given them great joy. The women and children also rejoiced. The
sound of rejoicing in Jerusalem could be heard far away.

44 At that time men were appointed to be in charge of the storerooms[v] for the contributions, firstfruits and tithes.[w] From the
fields around the towns they were to bring into the storerooms
the portions required by the Law for the priests and the Levites,
for Judah was pleased with the ministering priests and Levites.[x]

12:27 [a] Dt 20:5 [b] 2Sa 6:5 [c] 1Ch 15:16,28; 25:6; Ps 92:3
12:28 [d] 1Ch 2:54; 9:16
12:30 [e] Ex 19:10; Job 1:5
12:31 [f] Ne 2:13
12:34 [g] Ezr 1:5
12:35 [h] Ezr 3:10
12:36 [i] 1Ch 15:16 [j] 2Ch 8:14 [k] Ezr 7:6
12:37 [l] Ne 2:14; 3:15 [m] Ne 3:26
12:38 [n] Ne 3:11 [o] Ne 3:8
12:39 [p] 2Ki 14:13; Ne 8:16 [q] Ne 3:6 [r] 2Ch 33:14; Ne 3:3 [s] Ne 3:1 [t] Ne 3:1 [u] Ne 3:1
12:44 [v] Ne 13:4,13 [w] Lev 27:30 [x] Dt 18:8

[a] 31 Or *go alongside* [b] 31 Or *proceed alongside* [c] 38 Or *them alongside* [d] 39 Or *Old*

45They performed the service of their God and the service of
purification, as did also the singers and gatekeepers, according to
the commands of David[a] and his son Solomon.[b] 46For long ago,
in the days of David and Asaph,[c] there had been directors for the
singers and for the songs of praise[d] and thanksgiving to God.
47So in the days of Zerubbabel and of Nehemiah, all Israel contributed the daily portions for the singers and gatekeepers. They
also set aside the portion for the other Levites, and the Levites set
aside the portion for the descendants of Aaron.[e]

Chapter 13 Theme ______________________

13 On that day the Book of Moses was read aloud in the hearing of the people and there it was found written that no
Ammonite or Moabite should ever be admitted into the assembly
of God,[f] 2because they had not met the Israelites with food and
water but had hired Balaam[g] to call a curse down on them.[h] (Our
God, however, turned the curse into a blessing.)[i] 3When the people heard this law, they excluded from Israel all who were of foreign descent.[j]
4Before this, Eliashib the priest had been put in charge of the
storerooms[k] of the house of our God. He was closely associated
with Tobiah,[l] 5and he had provided him with a large room formerly used to store the grain offerings and incense and temple articles,
and also the tithes[m] of grain, new wine and oil prescribed for the
Levites, singers and gatekeepers, as well as the contributions for
the priests.
6But while all this was going on, I was not in Jerusalem, for in
the thirty-second year of Artaxerxes[n] king of Babylon I had
returned to the king. Some time later I asked his permission 7and
came back to Jerusalem. Here I learned about the evil thing
Eliashib[o] had done in providing Tobiah a room in the courts of
the house of God. 8I was greatly displeased and threw all Tobiah's
household goods out of the room.[p] 9I gave orders to purify the
rooms,[q] and then I put back into them the equipment of the
house of God, with the grain offerings and the incense.
10I also learned that the portions assigned to the Levites had
not been given to them,[r] and that all the Levites and singers
responsible for the service had gone back to their own fields. 11So
I rebuked the officials and asked them, "Why is the house of God
neglected?"[s] Then I called them together and stationed them at
their posts.
12All Judah brought the tithes[t] of grain, new wine and oil into
the storerooms.[u] 13I put Shelemiah the priest, Zadok the scribe,
and a Levite named Pedaiah in charge of the storerooms and
made Hanan son of Zaccur, the son of Mattaniah, their assistant,
because these men were considered trustworthy. They were made
responsible for distributing the supplies to their brothers.[v]

12:45 [a] 1Ch 25:1; 2Ch 8:14 [b] 1Ch 6:31; 23:5
12:46 [c] 2Ch 35:15 [d] 2Ch 29:27; Ps 137:4
12:47 [e] Nu 18:21; Dt 18:8
13:1 [f] ver 23; Dt 23:3
13:2 [g] Nu 22:3-11 [h] Nu 23:7; Dt 23:3 [i] Nu 23:11; Dt 23:4-5
13:3 [j] ver 23; Ne 9:2
13:4 [k] Ne 12:44 [l] Ne 2:10
13:5 [m] Lev 27:30; Nu 18:21
13:6 [n] Ne 2:6; 5:14
13:7 [o] Ezr 10:24
13:8 [p] Mt 21:12-13; Jn 2:13-16
13:9 [q] 1Ch 23:28; 2Ch 29:5
13:10 [r] Dt 12:19
13:11 [s] Ne 10:37-39; Hag 1:1-9
13:12 [t] 2Ch 31:6 [u] 1Ki 7:51; Ne 10:37-39; Mal 3:10
13:13 [v] Ne 12:44; Ac 6:1-5

14Remember[a] me for this, O my God, and do not blot out what I have so faithfully done for the house of my God and its services.

15In those days I saw men in Judah treading winepresses on the Sabbath and bringing in grain and loading it on donkeys, together with wine, grapes, figs and all other kinds of loads. And they were bringing all this into Jerusalem on the Sabbath.[b] Therefore I warned them against selling food on that day. 16Men from Tyre who lived in Jerusalem were bringing in fish and all kinds of merchandise and selling them in Jerusalem on the Sabbath[c] to the people of Judah. 17I rebuked the nobles of Judah and said to them, "What is this wicked thing you are doing—desecrating the Sabbath day? 18Didn't your forefathers do the same things, so that our God brought all this calamity upon us and upon this city? Now you are stirring up more wrath against Israel by desecrating the Sabbath."[d]

19When evening shadows fell on the gates of Jerusalem before the Sabbath,[e] I ordered the doors to be shut and not opened until the Sabbath was over. I stationed some of my own men at the gates so that no load could be brought in on the Sabbath day. 20Once or twice the merchants and sellers of all kinds of goods spent the night outside Jerusalem. 21But I warned them and said, "Why do you spend the night by the wall? If you do this again, I will lay hands on you." From that time on they no longer came on the Sabbath. 22Then I commanded the Levites to purify themselves and go and guard the gates in order to keep the Sabbath day holy.

Remember[f] me for this also, O my God, and show mercy to me according to your great love.

23Moreover, in those days I saw men of Judah who had married[g] women from Ashdod, Ammon and Moab.[h] 24Half of their children spoke the language of Ashdod or the language of one of the other peoples, and did not know how to speak the language of Judah. 25I rebuked them and called curses down on them. I beat some of the men and pulled out their hair. I made them take an oath[i] in God's name and said: "You are not to give your daughters in marriage to their sons, nor are you to take their daughters in marriage for your sons or for yourselves. 26Was it not because of marriages like these that Solomon king of Israel sinned? Among the many nations there was no king like him.[j] He was loved by his God,[k] and God made him king over all Israel, but even he was led into sin by foreign women.[l] 27Must we hear now that you too are doing all this terrible wickedness and are being unfaithful to our God by marrying[m] foreign women?"

13:14 [a]Ge 8:1
13:15 [b]Ex 20:8-11; 34:21; Dt 5:12-15; Ne 10:31
13:16 [c]Ne 10:31
13:18 [d]Ne 10:31; Jer 17:21-23
13:19 [e]Lev 23:32
13:22 [f]Ge 8:1; Ne 12:30
13:23 [g]Ezr 9:1-2; Mal 2:11 [h]ver 1; Ne 10:30
13:25 [i]Ezr 10:5
13:26 [j]1Ki 3:13; 2Ch 1:12 [k]2Sa 12:25 [l]1Ki 11:3
13:27 [m]Ezr 9:14; 10:2

28 One of the sons of Joiada son of Eliashib[a] the high priest was
son-in-law to Sanballat[b] the Horonite. And I drove him away
from me.

29 Remember[c] them, O my God, because they defiled the priestly office and the covenant of the priesthood and of the Levites.

30 So I purified the priests and the Levites of everything foreign,[d]
and assigned them duties, each to his own task. 31 I also made provision for contributions of wood[e] at designated times, and for the
firstfruits.

Remember[f] me with favor, O my God.

13:28 [a] Ezr 10:24 [b] Ne 2:10
13:29 [c] Ne 6:14
13:30 [d] Ne 10:30
13:31 [e] Ne 10:34 [f] ver 14,22; Ge 8:1

Nehemiah at a Glance

Theme of Nehemiah:

Segment Divisions

		Chapter Themes
		1
		2
		3
		4
		5
		6
		7
		8
		9
		10
		11
		12
		13

Author:

Date:

Purpose:

Key Words:

Lessons from the Life of Nehemiah

The Situation	How Nehemiah Related to God	How Nehemiah Related to People	Nehemiah's Example

ESTHER

Throughout time people have attempted to destroy the nation of Israel, the "apple of his eye." Why? Because from the Jews came the covenants, the promises, the law, and the Messiah—salvation for the world. The people of God are the enemy of Satan, the prince of this world.

While a remnant from Judah returned to the land promised to Abraham, Isaac, and Jacob, other Jews remained in the cities of their captivity. Some were welcomed as valuable members of their communities, but others were despised and hated. Some were even targeted for extermination.

Esther tells the story. The book of Esther records a ten-year span during the 58- to 60-year interlude in the book of Ezra. Esther tells us of the inauguration of a feast which has endured over 2000 years because of one woman who, for the sake of her people, was willing to say, "If I perish, I perish."

Things to Do

Esther is a story of intrigue—a divinely inspired one. It reveals the sovereignty of God, although God is never mentioned in this book. As you read:

1. Consult the historical chart THE TIMES OF EZRA, NEHEMIAH, AND ESTHER on page 821 in order to see the setting of Esther.

2. Observe the main events which occur in each chapter. Examine each chapter under the scrutiny of the five W's and an H: Who? What? When? Where? Why? and How? Ask: Who was involved? What happened? When did it occur? Where did it take place and why? How did it come about? etc.

   a. List in the margin the major points you want to remember about each event under the heading you give that event. For example, Esther 1:3, 4 could be titled "King Ahasuerus' Banquet." Then under the heading you could list these major points: 1) attended by his princes, attendants, etc., 2) given to display riches, 3) lasted 180 days.

   b. While the main event of each chapter will not always be a banquet, banquets play an important role in Esther. So mark in a distinctive way each use of the words *banquet, dinner, feast,* or *feasting*. Ask the five W's and an H about each banquet and list your insights in the margin.

   c. Make sure you underline or mark in a distinctive way the main characters in each chapter.

3. Mark every reference to time with a symbol so it can be seen immediately. This will help you see the timing of the events. Also consult the calendar on page 822 so you can keep track of the references to the various months.

4. Mark every occurrence of the words *Jew* or *Jews* (with their pronouns and synonyms, such as *her people, her kindred, people, nationality, my family, her family background*). *Jews* was a term used to describe the people who came from Judah.

5. Carefully observe the timing of events, such as when the king can't sleep and needs something to read. Remember the truth in Daniel 4:34, 35.

6. When you finish studying each chapter, record the theme of that chapter in the appropriate place on the ESTHER AT A GLANCE chart on page 834. Also record this in the text next to the chapter number.

7. In a chapter margin, list all you learn about Esther and then list all you learn about Mordecai.

8. When you finish reading Esther, complete ESTHER AT A GLANCE. See if any of the chapters can be grouped according to events. If so, record these segment divisions on the AT A GLANCE chart.

Things to Think About

1. What can you learn from the lives of each of the main characters of this historical event? Review what you have listed about Esther and Mordecai. Have you ever realized that you too have come to the

kingdom for such a time as this? What are the good works that God would have you do? Read John 15:16 and Ephesians 2:8-10.

2. Have you thought about why Mordecai was unwilling to bow before Haman? Have you "bowed" to someone or something and in so doing compromised your calling and position as a child of God? Read Galatians 1:10.

3. Esther and Mordecai relied heavily on fasting and prayer to turn the tide of events. What about you?

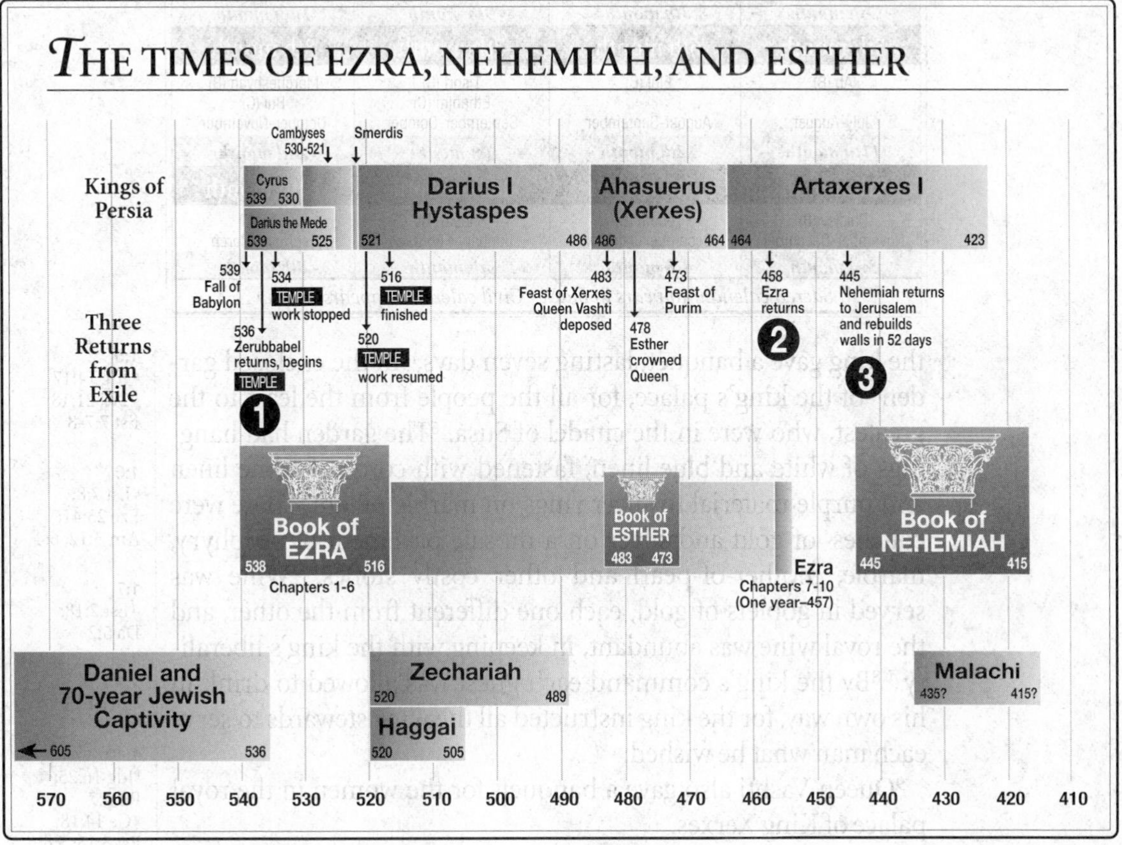

Chapter 1 Theme

1:1 [a]Ezr 4:6; Da 9:1 [b]Est 9:30; Da 3:2; 6:1 [c]Est 8:9
1:2 [d]Ezr 4:9; Ne 1:1; Est 2:8
1:3 [e]1Ki 3:15; Est 2:18

1 This is what happened during the time of Xerxes,[a][a] the Xerxes
who ruled over 127 provinces[b] stretching from India to Cush[b]:[c]
2At that time King Xerxes reigned from his royal throne in the
citadel of Susa,[d] 3and in the third year of his reign he gave a banquet[e]
for all his nobles and officials. The military leaders of Persia and
Media, the princes, and the nobles of the provinces were present.
4For a full 180 days he displayed the vast wealth of his kingdom and
the splendor and glory of his majesty. 5When these days were over,

[a] *1* Hebrew *Ahasuerus*, a variant of Xerxes' Persian name; here and throughout Esther
[b] *1* That is, the upper Nile region

The Jewish Calendar

Babylonian names (B) for the months are still used today for the Jewish calendar. Canaanite names (C) were used prior to the Babylonian captivity in 586 B.C. Four are mentioned in the Old Testament.
Adar-Sheni is an intercalary month used every two to three years or seven times in 19 years.

1st month	2nd month	3rd month	4th month
Nisan (B) Abib (C) March-April	Iyyar (B) Ziv (C) April-May	Sivan (B) May-June	Tammuz (B) June-July
7th month	*8th month*	*9th month*	*10th month*
5th month	**6th month**	**7th month**	**8th month**
Ab (B) July-August	Elul (B) August-September	Tishri (B) Ethanim (C) September-October	Marcheshvan (B) Bul (C) October-November
11th month	*12th month*	*1st month*	*2nd month*
9th month	**10th month**	**11th month**	**12th month**
Chislev (B) November-December	Tebeth (B) December-January	Shebat (B) January-February	Adar (B) February-March
3rd month	*4th month*	*5th month*	*6th month*

Sacred calendar appears in black • Civil calendar appears in gray

the king gave a banquet, lasting seven days,[a] in the enclosed garden[b] of the king's palace, for all the people from the least to the
greatest, who were in the citadel of Susa. 6The garden had hang-
ings of white and blue linen, fastened with cords of white linen
and purple material to silver rings on marble pillars. There were
couches[c] of gold and silver on a mosaic pavement of porphyry,
marble, mother-of-pearl and other costly stones. 7Wine was
served in goblets of gold, each one different from the other, and
the royal wine was abundant, in keeping with the king's liberality.[d] 8By the king's command each guest was allowed to drink in
his own way, for the king instructed all the wine stewards to serve
each man what he wished.

9Queen Vashti also gave a banquet[e] for the women in the royal
palace of King Xerxes.

10On the seventh day, when King Xerxes was in high spirits[f] from
wine,[g] he commanded the seven eunuchs who served him—
Mehuman, Biztha, Harbona,[h] Bigtha, Abagtha, Zethar and Car-
cas— 11to bring[i] before him Queen Vashti, wearing her royal
crown, in order to display her beauty[j] to the people and nobles,
for she was lovely to look at. 12But when the attendants delivered
the king's command, Queen Vashti refused to come. Then the
king became furious and burned with anger.[k]

13Since it was customary for the king to consult experts in matters of law and justice, he spoke with the wise men who understood the times[l] 14and were closest to the king—Carshena, Shethar,
Admatha, Tarshish, Meres, Marsena and Memucan, the seven
nobles[m] of Persia and Media who had special access to the king
and were highest in the kingdom.

1:5 [a] Jdg 14:17 [b] 2Ki 21:18; Est 7:7-8
1:6 [c] Est 7:8; Eze 23:41; Am 3:12; 6:4
1:7 [d] Est 2:18; Da 5:2
1:9 [e] 1Ki 3:15
1:10 [f] Jdg 16:25; Ru 3:7 [g] Ge 14:18; Est 3:15; 5:6; 7:2; Pr 31:4-7; Da 5:1-4 [h] Est 7:9
1:11 [i] SS 2:4 [j] Ps 45:11; Eze 16:14
1:12 [k] Ge 39:19; Est 2:21; 7:7; Pr 19:12
1:13 [l] 1Ch 12:32; Jer 10:7; Da 2:12
1:14 [m] 2Ki 25:19; Ezr 7:14

15"According to law, what must be done to Queen Vashti?" he
asked. "She has not obeyed the command of King Xerxes that the
eunuchs have taken to her."
16Then Memucan replied in the presence of the king and the
nobles, "Queen Vashti has done wrong, not only against the king
but also against all the nobles and the peoples of all the provinces
of King Xerxes. 17For the queen's conduct will become known to
all the women, and so they will despise their husbands and say,
'King Xerxes commanded Queen Vashti to be brought before
him, but she would not come.' 18This very day the Persian and
Median women of the nobility who have heard about the queen's
conduct will respond to all the king's nobles in the same way.
There will be no end of disrespect and discord.[a]
19"Therefore, if it pleases the king,[b] let him issue a royal decree
and let it be written in the laws of Persia and Media, which cannot be repealed,[c] that Vashti is never again to enter the presence
of King Xerxes. Also let the king give her royal position to someone else who is better than she. 20Then when the king's edict is
proclaimed throughout all his vast realm, all the women will
respect their husbands, from the least to the greatest."
21The king and his nobles were pleased with this advice, so the
king did as Memucan proposed. 22He sent dispatches to all parts
of the kingdom, to each province in its own script and to each
people in its own language,[d] proclaiming in each people's tongue
that every man should be ruler over his own household.

Chapter 2 Theme

2 Later when the anger of King Xerxes had subsided,[e] he
remembered Vashti and what she had done and what he had
decreed about her. 2Then the king's personal attendants proposed, "Let a search be made for beautiful young virgins for the
king. 3Let the king appoint commissioners in every province of
his realm to bring all these beautiful girls into the harem at the
citadel of Susa. Let them be placed under the care of Hegai, the
king's eunuch, who is in charge of the women; and let beauty
treatments be given to them. 4Then let the girl who pleases the
king be queen instead of Vashti." This advice appealed to the
king, and he followed it.
5Now there was in the citadel of Susa a Jew of the tribe of Benjamin, named Mordecai son of Jair, the son of Shimei, the son of
Kish,[f] 6who had been carried into exile from Jerusalem by Nebuchadnezzar king of Babylon, among those taken captive with
Jehoiachin[a][g] king of Judah.[h] 7Mordecai had a cousin named

1:18
[a]Pr 19:13; 27:15

1:19
[b]Ecc 8:4
[c]Est 8:8; Da 6:8,12

1:22
[d]Ne 13:24; Est 8:9; Eph 5:22-24; 1Ti 2:12

2:1
[e]Est 1:19-20; 7:10

2:5
[f]1Sa 9:1; Est 3:2

2:6
[g]2Ki 24:6,15; 2Ch 36:10,20
[h]Da 1:1-5; 5:13

[a]6 Hebrew *Jeconiah*, a variant of *Jehoiachin*

Hadassah, whom he had brought up because she had neither father
nor mother. This girl, who was also known as Esther,[a] was lovely[b] in
form and features, and Mordecai had taken her as his own daughter
when her father and mother died.
8 When the king's order and edict had been proclaimed, many
girls were brought to the citadel of Susa[c] and put under the care
of Hegai. Esther also was taken to the king's palace and entrusted
to Hegai, who had charge of the harem. 9 The girl pleased him
and won his favor.[d] Immediately he provided her with her beauty
treatments and special food.[e] He assigned to her seven maids selected from the king's palace and moved her and her maids into
the best place in the harem.
10 Esther had not revealed her nationality and family background, because Mordecai had forbidden her to do so.[f] 11 Every
day he walked back and forth near the courtyard of the harem to
find out how Esther was and what was happening to her.
12 Before a girl's turn came to go in to King Xerxes, she had to
complete twelve months of beauty treatments prescribed for the
women, six months with oil of myrrh and six with perfumes[g] and
cosmetics. 13 And this is how she would go to the king: Anything
she wanted was given her to take with her from the harem to the
king's palace. 14 In the evening she would go there and in the
morning return to another part of the harem to the care of
Shaashgaz, the king's eunuch who was in charge of the concubines.[h] She would not return to the king unless he was pleased
with her and summoned her by name.[i]
15 When the turn came for Esther (the girl Mordecai had adopted,
the daughter of his uncle Abihail[j]) to go to the king,[k] she asked
for nothing other than what Hegai, the king's eunuch who was in
charge of the harem, suggested. And Esther won the favor[l] of
everyone who saw her. 16 She was taken to King Xerxes in the royal residence in the tenth month, the month of Tebeth, in the seventh year of his reign.
17 Now the king was attracted to Esther more than to any of the
other women, and she won his favor and approval more than any
of the other virgins. So he set a royal crown on her head and
made her queen[m] instead of Vashti. 18 And the king gave a great
banquet,[n] Esther's banquet, for all his nobles and officials.[o] He
proclaimed a holiday throughout the provinces and distributed
gifts with royal liberality.[p]
19 When the virgins were assembled a second time, Mordecai
was sitting at the king's gate.[q] 20 But Esther had kept secret her
family background and nationality just as Mordecai had told her
to do, for she continued to follow Mordecai's instructions as she
had done when he was bringing her up.[r]

2:7 [a] Ge 41:45 [b] Ge 39:6

2:8 [c] ver 3,15; Ne 1:1; Est 1:2; Da 8:2

2:9 [d] Ge 39:21 [e] ver 3,12; Ge 37:3; 1Sa 9:22-24; 2Ki 25:30; Eze 16:9-13; Da 1:5

2:10 [f] ver 20

2:12 [g] Pr 27:9; SS 1:3; Isa 3:24

2:14 [h] 1Ki 11:3; SS 6:8; Da 5:2 [i] Est 4:11

2:15 [j] Est 9:29 [k] Ps 45:14 [l] Ge 18:3; 30:27; Est 5:8

2:17 [m] Est 1:11; Eze 16:9-13

2:18 [n] 1Ki 3:15; Est 1:3 [o] Ge 40:20 [p] Est 1:7

2:19 [q] ver 21; Est 3:2; 4:2; 5:13

2:20 [r] ver 10

21 During the time Mordecai was sitting at the king's gate, Bigthana[a] and Teresh, two of the king's officers[a] who guarded the doorway, became angry[b] and conspired to assassinate King Xerxes.
22 But Mordecai found out about the plot and told Queen Esther,
who in turn reported it to the king, giving credit to Mordecai.
23 And when the report was investigated and found to be true, the
two officials were hanged[c] on a gallows.[b] All this was recorded in
the book of the annals[d] in the presence of the king.

Chapter 3 Theme ______________________

3 After these events, King Xerxes honored Haman son of
Hammedatha, the Agagite,[e] elevating him and giving him a
seat of honor higher than that of all the other nobles. 2 All the royal officials at the king's gate knelt down and paid honor to
Haman, for the king had commanded this concerning him. But
Mordecai would not kneel down or pay him honor.
3 Then the royal officials at the king's gate asked Mordecai,
"Why do you disobey the king's command?"[f] 4 Day after day they
spoke to him but he refused to comply.[g] Therefore they told
Haman about it to see whether Mordecai's behavior would be tol-
erated, for he had told them he was a Jew.
5 When Haman saw that Mordecai would not kneel down or pay
him honor, he was enraged.[h] 6 Yet having learned who Mordecai's
people were, he scorned the idea of killing only Mordecai.
Instead Haman looked for a way[i] to destroy[j] all Mordecai's people, the Jews,[k] throughout the whole kingdom of Xerxes.
7 In the twelfth year of King Xerxes, in the first month, the
month of Nisan, they cast the *pur*[l] (that is, the lot[m]) in the presence of Haman to select a day and month. And the lot fell on[c] the
twelfth month, the month of Adar.[n]
8 Then Haman said to King Xerxes, "There is a certain people
dispersed and scattered among the peoples in all the provinces of
your kingdom whose customs[o] are different from those of all
other people and who do not obey[p] the king's laws; it is not in the
king's best interest to tolerate them.[q] 9 If it pleases the king, let a
decree be issued to destroy them, and I will put ten thousand talents[d] of silver into the royal treasury for the men who carry out
this business."[r]
10 So the king took his signet ring[s] from his finger and gave it to
Haman son of Hammedatha, the Agagite, the enemy of the Jews.
11 "Keep the money," the king said to Haman, "and do with the
people as you please."

2:21 [a] Ge 40:2; Est 6:2 [b] Est 1:12; 3:5; 5:9; 7:7
2:23 [c] Ge 40:19; Ps 7:14-16; Pr 26:27 [d] Est 6:1; 10:2
3:1 [e] ver 10; Ex 17:8-16; Nu 24:7; Dt 25:17-19; 1Sa 14:48; Est 5:11
3:3 [f] Est 5:9; Da 3:12
3:4 [g] Ge 39:10
3:5 [h] Est 2:21; 5:9
3:6 [i] Pr 16:25 [j] Ps 74:8; 83:4 [k] Est 9:24
3:7 [l] Est 9:24,26 [m] Lev 16:8; 1Sa 10:21 [n] ver 13; Ezr 6:15; Est 9:19
3:8 [o] Ac 16:20-21 [p] Jer 29:7; Da 6:13 [q] Ezr 4:15
3:9 [r] Est 7:4
3:10 [s] Ge 41:42; Est 7:6; 8:2

INSIGHT

Agagite, possibly a synonym for Amalekite, is a reference to a descendant of Agag. Agag was king of the Amalekites, a tribal people whom the Lord ordered King Saul to destroy completely. However, Saul spared King Agag. Haman, the arch villain in Esther, was an Agagite.

[a] *21* Hebrew *Bigthan,* a variant of *Bigthana* [b] *23* Or *were hung* (or *impaled*) *on poles*; similarly elsewhere in Esther [c] *7* Septuagint; Hebrew does not have *And the lot fell on.* [d] *9* That is, about 375 tons (about 345 metric tons)

12Then on the thirteenth day of the first month the royal secretaries were summoned. They wrote out in the script of each
province and in the language[a] of each people all Haman's orders
to the king's satraps, the governors of the various provinces and
the nobles of the various peoples. These were written in the name
of King Xerxes himself and sealed[b] with his own ring. 13Dis-
patches were sent by couriers to all the king's provinces with the
order to destroy, kill and annihilate all the Jews[c]—young and old,
women and little children—on a single day, the thirteenth day of
the twelfth month, the month of Adar,[d] and to plunder[e] their
goods. 14A copy of the text of the edict was to be issued as law in
every province and made known to the people of every nationality so they would be ready for that day.[f]
15Spurred on by the king's command, the couriers went out,
and the edict was issued in the citadel of Susa.[g] The king and
Haman sat down to drink,[h] but the city of Susa was bewildered.[i]

Chapter 4 Theme ______________________

4 When Mordecai learned of all that had been done, he tore his
clothes,[j] put on sackcloth and ashes,[k] and went out into the
city, wailing[l] loudly and bitterly. 2But he went only as far as the
king's gate,[m] because no one clothed in sackcloth was allowed to
enter it. 3In every province to which the edict and order of the
king came, there was great mourning among the Jews, with fasting, weeping and wailing. Many lay in sackcloth and ashes.
4When Esther's maids and eunuchs came and told her about
Mordecai, she was in great distress. She sent clothes for him to
put on instead of his sackcloth, but he would not accept them.
5Then Esther summoned Hathach, one of the king's eunuchs
assigned to attend her, and ordered him to find out what was
troubling Mordecai and why.
6So Hathach went out to Mordecai in the open square of the
city in front of the king's gate. 7Mordecai told him everything
that had happened to him, including the exact amount of money
Haman had promised to pay into the royal treasury for the
destruction of the Jews.[n] 8He also gave him a copy of the text of
the edict for their annihilation, which had been published in
Susa, to show to Esther and explain it to her, and he told him to
urge her to go into the king's presence to beg for mercy and plead
with him for her people.
9Hathach went back and reported to Esther what Mordecai had
said. 10Then she instructed him to say to Mordecai, 11"All the
king's officials and the people of the royal provinces know that
for any man or woman who approaches the king in the inner
court without being summoned[o] the king has but one law:[p] that

3:12
[a] Ne 13:24
[b] Ge 38:18; 1Ki 21:8; Est 8:8-10

3:13
[c] 1Sa 15:3; Ezr 4:6; Est 8:10-14
[d] ver 7
[e] Est 8:11; 9:10

3:14
[f] Est 8:8; 9:1

3:15
[g] Est 8:14
[h] Est 1:10
[i] Est 8:15

4:1
[j] Nu 14:6
[k] 2Sa 13:19; Eze 27:30-31; Jnh 3:5-6
[l] Ex 11:6; Ps 30:11

4:2
[m] Est 2:19

4:7
[n] Est 3:9; 7:4

4:11
[o] Est 2:14
[p] Da 2:9

he be put to death. The only exception to this is for the king to
extend the gold scepter[a] to him and spare his life. But thirty days
have passed since I was called to go to the king."
12When Esther's words were reported to Mordecai, 13he sent
back this answer: "Do not think that because you are in the
king's house you alone of all the Jews will escape. 14For if you
remain silent[b] at this time, relief[c] and deliverance[d] for the Jews
will arise from another place, but you and your father's family
will perish. And who knows but that you have come to royal
position for such a time as this?"[e]
15Then Esther sent this reply to Mordecai: 16"Go, gather together all the Jews who are in Susa, and fast[f] for me. Do not eat or
drink for three days, night or day. I and my maids will fast as you
do. When this is done, I will go to the king, even though it is
against the law. And if I perish, I perish."[g]
17So Mordecai went away and carried out all of Esther's
instructions.

Chapter 5 Theme ______________________

5 On the third day Esther put on her royal robes[h] and stood in
the inner court of the palace, in front of the king's[i] hall. The
king was sitting on his royal throne in the hall, facing the entrance.
2When he saw Queen Esther standing in the court, he was pleased
with her and held out to her the gold scepter that was in his hand.
So Esther approached and touched the tip of the scepter.[j]
3Then the king asked, "What is it, Queen Esther? What is your
request? Even up to half the kingdom,[k] it will be given you."
4"If it pleases the king," replied Esther, "let the king, together
with Haman, come today to a banquet I have prepared for him."
5"Bring Haman at once," the king said, "so that we may do
what Esther asks."
So the king and Haman went to the banquet Esther had prepared. 6As they were drinking wine,[l] the king again asked Esther,
"Now what is your petition? It will be given you. And what is
your request? Even up to half the kingdom,[m] it will be granted."[n]
7Esther replied, "My petition and my request is this: 8If the king
regards me with favor[o] and if it pleases the king to grant my petition and fulfill my request, let the king and Haman come tomorrow to the banquet[p] I will prepare for them. Then I will answer
the king's question."
9Haman went out that day happy and in high spirits. But when
he saw Mordecai at the king's gate and observed that he neither
rose nor showed fear in his presence, he was filled with rage[q]
against Mordecai.[r] 10Nevertheless, Haman restrained himself and
went home.

4:11 [a] Est 5:1,2; 8:4
4:14 [b] Ecc 3:7; Isa 62:1; Am 5:13 [c] Est 9:16,22 [d] Ge 45:7; Dt 28:29 [e] Ge 50:20
4:16 [f] 2Ch 20:3; Est 9:31 [g] Ge 43:14
5:1 [h] Est 4:16; Eze 16:13 [i] Est 6:4; Pr 21:1
5:2 [j] Est 4:11; 8:4; Pr 21:1
5:3 [k] Est 7:2; Da 5:16; Mk 6:23
5:6 [l] Est 1:10 [m] Mk 6:23 [n] Est 7:2; 9:12
5:8 [o] Est 2:15; 7:3; 8:5 [p] 1Ki 3:15; Est 6:14
5:9 [q] Est 2:21; Pr 14:17 [r] Est 3:3,5

Calling together his friends and Zeresh,[a] his wife, 11Haman boasted[b] to them about his vast wealth, his many sons,[c] and all the ways the king had honored him and how he had elevated him above the other nobles and officials. 12"And that's not all," Haman added. "I'm the only person[d] Queen Esther invited to accompany the king to the banquet she gave. And she has invited me along with the king tomorrow. 13But all this gives me no satisfaction as long as I see that Jew Mordecai sitting at the king's gate.[e]"

14His wife Zeresh and all his friends said to him, "Have a gallows built, seventy-five feet[a] high,[f] and ask the king in the morning to have Mordecai hanged[g] on it. Then go with the king to the dinner and be happy." This suggestion delighted Haman, and he had the gallows built.

Chapter 6 Theme ____________________

6 That night the king could not sleep;[h] so he ordered the book of the chronicles,[i] the record of his reign, to be brought in and read to him. 2It was found recorded there that Mordecai had exposed Bigthana and Teresh, two of the king's officers who guarded the doorway, who had conspired to assassinate King Xerxes.

3"What honor and recognition has Mordecai received for this?" the king asked.

"Nothing has been done for him,"[j] his attendants answered.

4The king said, "Who is in the court?" Now Haman had just entered the outer court of the palace to speak to the king about hanging Mordecai on the gallows he had erected for him.

5His attendants answered, "Haman is standing in the court."

"Bring him in," the king ordered.

6When Haman entered, the king asked him, "What should be done for the man the king delights to honor?"

Now Haman thought to himself, "Who is there that the king would rather honor than me?" 7So he answered the king, "For the man the king delights to honor, 8have them bring a royal robe[k] the king has worn and a horse[l] the king has ridden, one with a royal crest placed on its head. 9Then let the robe and horse be entrusted to one of the king's most noble princes. Let them robe the man the king delights to honor, and lead him on the horse through the city streets, proclaiming before him, 'This is what is done for the man the king delights to honor![m]' "

10"Go at once," the king commanded Haman. "Get the robe and the horse and do just as you have suggested for Mordecai the Jew, who sits at the king's gate. Do not neglect anything you have recommended."

a *14* Hebrew *fifty cubits* (about 23 meters)

5:10 [a] Est 6:13
5:11 [b] Pr 13:16 [c] Est 9:7-10,13
5:12 [d] Job 22:29; Pr 16:18; 29:23
5:13 [e] Est 2:19
5:14 [f] Est 7:9 [g] Ezr 6:11; Est 6:4
6:1 [h] Da 2:1; 6:18 [i] Est 2:23; 10:2
6:3 [j] Ecc 9:13-16
6:8 [k] Ge 41:42; Isa 52:1 [l] 1Ki 1:33
6:9 [m] Ge 41:43

11 So Haman got[a] the robe and the horse. He robed Mordecai,
and led him on horseback through the city streets, proclaiming
before him, "This is what is done for the man the king delights to
honor!"
12 Afterward Mordecai returned to the king's gate. But Haman
rushed home, with his head covered[b] in grief, 13 and told Zeresh[c]
his wife and all his friends everything that had happened to him.
His advisers and his wife Zeresh said to him, "Since Mordecai,
before whom your downfall[d] has started, is of Jewish origin, you
cannot stand against him—you will surely come to ruin!" 14 While
they were still talking with him, the king's eunuchs arrived and
hurried Haman away to the banquet[e] Esther had prepared.

Chapter 7 Theme ________________________________

7 So the king and Haman went to dine[f] with Queen Esther,
2 and as they were drinking wine[g] on that second day, the
king again asked, "Queen Esther, what is your petition? It will be
given you. What is your request? Even up to half the kingdom,[h] it
will be granted.[i]"
3 Then Queen Esther answered, "If I have found favor[j] with you,
O king, and if it pleases your majesty, grant me my life—this is
my petition. And spare my people—this is my request. 4 For I and
my people have been sold for destruction and slaughter and
annihilation.[k] If we had merely been sold as male and female
slaves, I would have kept quiet, because no such distress would
justify disturbing the king.[a]"
5 King Xerxes asked Queen Esther, "Who is he? Where is the
man who has dared to do such a thing?"
6 Esther said, "The adversary and enemy is this vile Haman."
Then Haman was terrified before the king and queen. 7 The
king got up in a rage,[l] left his wine and went out into the palace
garden.[m] But Haman, realizing that the king had already decided
his fate,[n] stayed behind to beg Queen Esther for his life.
8 Just as the king returned from the palace garden to the banquet hall, Haman was falling on the couch[o] where Esther was
reclining.[p]
The king exclaimed, "Will he even molest the queen while she
is with me in the house?"[q]
As soon as the word left the king's mouth, they covered
Haman's face.[r] 9 Then Harbona,[s] one of the eunuchs attending the
king, said, "A gallows seventy-five feet[b] high[t] stands by Haman's
house. He had it made for Mordecai, who spoke up to help the
king."

6:11 [a] Ge 41:42
6:12 [b] 2Sa 15:30; Jer 14:3,4; Mic 3:7
6:13 [c] Est 5:10 [d] Ps 57:6; Pr 26:27; 28:18
6:14 [e] 1Ki 3:15; Est 5:8
7:1 [f] Ge 40:20-22; Mt 22:1-14
7:2 [g] Est 1:10 [h] Est 5:3 [i] Est 9:12
7:3 [j] Est 2:15
7:4 [k] Est 3:9
7:7 [l] Ge 34:7; Est 1:12; Pr 19:12; 20:1-2 [m] 2Ki 21:18 [n] Est 6:13
7:8 [o] Est 1:6 [p] Ge 39:14 [q] Ge 34:7 [r] Est 6:12
7:9 [s] Est 1:10 [t] Est 5:14

[a] 4 Or *quiet, but the compensation our adversary offers cannot be compared with the loss the king would suffer* [b] 9 Hebrew *fifty cubits* (about 23 meters)

The king said, "Hang him on it!"[a] 10So they hanged Haman[b] on
the gallows[c] he had prepared for Mordecai.[d] Then the king's fury
subsided.[e]

Chapter 8 Theme ________________________

8 That same day King Xerxes gave Queen Esther the estate of
Haman,[f] the enemy of the Jews. And Mordecai came into the
presence of the king, for Esther had told how he was related to
her. 2The king took off his signet ring,[g] which he had reclaimed
from Haman, and presented it to Mordecai. And Esther appointed him over Haman's estate.[h]

3Esther again pleaded with the king, falling at his feet and
weeping. She begged him to put an end to the evil plan of Haman
the Agagite, which he had devised against the Jews. 4Then the
king extended the gold scepter[i] to Esther and she arose and stood
before him.

5"If it pleases the king," she said, "and if he regards me with
favor and thinks it the right thing to do, and if he is pleased with
me, let an order be written overruling the dispatches that Haman
son of Hammedatha, the Agagite, devised and wrote to destroy
the Jews in all the king's provinces. 6For how can I bear to see
disaster fall on my people? How can I bear to see the destruction
of my family?"[j]

7King Xerxes replied to Queen Esther and to Mordecai the Jew,
"Because Haman attacked the Jews, I have given his estate to
Esther, and they have hanged him on the gallows. 8Now write
another decree[k] in the king's name in behalf of the Jews as seems
best to you, and seal it with the king's signet ring[l]—for no document written in the king's name and sealed with his ring can be
revoked."[m]

9At once the royal secretaries were summoned—on the twenty-
third day of the third month, the month of Sivan. They wrote out
all Mordecai's orders to the Jews, and to the satraps, governors and
nobles of the 127 provinces stretching from India to Cush.[a][n] These
orders were written in the script of each province and the language
of each people and also to the Jews in their own script and language.[o] 10Mordecai wrote in the name of King Xerxes, sealed the
dispatches with the king's signet ring, and sent them by mounted
couriers, who rode fast horses especially bred for the king.

11The king's edict granted the Jews in every city the right to
assemble and protect themselves; to destroy, kill and annihilate
any armed force of any nationality or province that might attack
them and their women and children; and to plunder[p] the property

a9 That is, the upper Nile region

7:9 [a]Ps 7:14-16; 9:16; Pr 11:5-6; 26:27; Mt 7:2
7:10 [b]Pr 10:28 [c]Est 9:25 [d]Da 6:24 [e]Est 2:1
8:1 [f]Est 2:7; 7:6; Pr 22:22-23
8:2 [g]Ge 41:42; Est 3:10 [h]Pr 13:22; Da 2:48
8:4 [i]Est 4:11; 5:2
8:6 [j]Est 7:4; 9:1
8:8 [k]Est 3:12-14 [l]Ge 41:42 [m]Est 1:19; Da 6:15
8:9 [n]Est 1:1 [o]Est 1:22
8:11 [p]Est 9:10, 15,16

of their enemies. 12 The day appointed for the Jews to do this in all
the provinces of King Xerxes was the thirteenth day of the twelfth
month, the month of Adar.[a] 13 A copy of the text of the edict was
to be issued as law in every province and made known to the
people of every nationality so that the Jews would be ready on
that day[b] to avenge themselves on their enemies.

14 The couriers, riding the royal horses, raced out, spurred on
by the king's command. And the edict was also issued in the
citadel of Susa.

15 Mordecai[c] left the king's presence wearing royal garments of
blue and white, a large crown of gold and a purple robe of fine
linen.[d] And the city of Susa held a joyous celebration.[e] 16 For the
Jews it was a time of happiness and joy,[f] gladness and honor.[g]
17 In every province and in every city, wherever the edict of the
king went, there was joy[h] and gladness among the Jews, with
feasting and celebrating. And many people of other nationalities
became Jews because fear[i] of the Jews had seized them.[j]

Chapter 9 Theme ________________________

9 On the thirteenth day of the twelfth month, the month of
Adar,[k] the edict commanded by the king was to be carried
out. On this day the enemies of the Jews had hoped to overpower
them, but now the tables were turned and the Jews got the upper
hand[l] over those who hated them.[m] 2 The Jews assembled in their
cities[n] in all the provinces of King Xerxes to attack those seeking
their destruction. No one could stand against them,[o] because the
people of all the other nationalities were afraid of them. 3 And all
the nobles of the provinces, the satraps, the governors and the
king's administrators helped the Jews,[p] because fear of Mordecai
had seized them. 4 Mordecai was prominent[q] in the palace; his
reputation spread throughout the provinces, and he became
more and more powerful.[r]

5 The Jews struck down all their enemies with the sword, killing
and destroying them,[s] and they did what they pleased to those who
hated them. 6 In the citadel of Susa, the Jews killed and destroyed
five hundred men. 7 They also killed Parshandatha, Dalphon,
Aspatha, 8 Poratha, Adalia, Aridatha, 9 Parmashta, Arisai, Aridai
and Vaizatha, 10 the ten sons[t] of Haman son of Hammedatha, the
enemy of the Jews. But they did not lay their hands on the
plunder.[u]

11 The number of those slain in the citadel of Susa was reported
to the king that same day. 12 The king said to Queen Esther, "The
Jews have killed and destroyed five hundred men and the ten
sons of Haman in the citadel of Susa. What have they done in the
rest of the king's provinces? Now what is your petition? It will be
given you. What is your request? It will also be granted."[v]

8:12 [a] Est 3:13; 9:1
8:13 [b] Est 3:14
8:15 [c] Est 9:4 [d] Ge 41:42 [e] Est 3:15
8:16 [f] Ps 97:10-12 [g] Ps 112:4
8:17 [h] Est 9:19,27; Ps 35:27; Pr 11:10 [i] Ex 15:14,16; Dt 11:25 [j] Est 9:3
9:1 [k] Est 8:12 [l] Jer 29:4-7 [m] Est 3:12-14; Pr 22:22-23
9:2 [n] ver 15-18 [o] Est 8:11,17; Ps 71:13,24
9:3 [p] Ezr 8:36
9:4 [q] Ex 11:3 [r] 2Sa 3:1; 1Ch 11:9
9:5 [s] Ezr 4:6
9:10 [t] Est 5:11 [u] Ge 14:23; 1Sa 14:32; Est 3:13; 8:11
9:12 [v] Est 5:6; 7:2

13"If it pleases the king," Esther answered, "give the Jews in Susa
permission to carry out this day's edict tomorrow also, and let
Haman's ten sons[a] be hanged[b] on gallows."
14So the king commanded that this be done. An edict was
issued in Susa, and they hanged[c] the ten sons of Haman. 15The
Jews in Susa came together on the fourteenth day of the month of
Adar, and they put to death in Susa three hundred men, but they
did not lay their hands on the plunder.[d]
16Meanwhile, the remainder of the Jews who were in the king's
provinces also assembled to protect themselves and get relief[e]
from their enemies.[f] They killed seventy-five thousand of them[g]
but did not lay their hands on the plunder. 17This happened on
the thirteenth day of the month of Adar, and on the fourteenth
they rested and made it a day of feasting[h] and joy.
18The Jews in Susa, however, had assembled on the thirteenth
and fourteenth, and then on the fifteenth they rested and made it
a day of feasting and joy.
19That is why rural Jews—those living in villages—observe the
fourteenth of the month of Adar[i] as a day of joy and feasting, a
day for giving presents to each other.[j]
20Mordecai recorded these events, and he sent letters to all the
Jews throughout the provinces of King Xerxes, near and far, 21to
have them celebrate annually the fourteenth and fifteenth days of
the month of Adar 22as the time when the Jews got relief[k] from
their enemies, and as the month when their sorrow was turned
into joy and their mourning into a day of celebration.[l] He wrote
them to observe the days as days of feasting and joy and giving
presents of food[m] to one another and gifts to the poor.
23So the Jews agreed to continue the celebration they had
begun, doing what Mordecai had written to them. 24For Haman
son of Hammedatha, the Agagite,[n] the enemy of all the Jews, had
plotted against the Jews to destroy them and had cast the *pur*[o]
(that is, the lot[p]) for their ruin and destruction. 25But when the
plot came to the king's attention,[a] he issued written orders that
the evil scheme Haman had devised against the Jews should come
back onto his own head,[q] and that he and his sons should be
hanged[r] on the gallows.[s] 26(Therefore these days were called
Purim, from the word *pur*.[t]) Because of everything written in this
letter and because of what they had seen and what had happened
to them, 27the Jews took it upon themselves to establish the custom that they and their descendants and all who join them
should without fail observe these two days every year, in the way
prescribed and at the time appointed. 28These days should be

a 25 Or *when Esther came before the king*

9:13 [a] Est 5:11 [b] Dt 21:22-23
9:14 [c] Ezr 6:11
9:15 [d] Ge 14:23; Est 8:11
9:16 [e] Est 4:14 [f] Dt 25:19 [g] 1Ch 4:43
9:17 [h] 1Ki 3:15
9:19 [i] Est 3:7 [j] ver 22; Dt 16:11,14; Ne 8:10,12; Est 2:9; Rev 11:10
9:22 [k] Est 4:14 [l] Ne 8:12; Ps 30:11-12 [m] 2Ki 25:30
9:24 [n] Ex 17:8-16 [o] Est 3:7 [p] Lev 16:8
9:25 [q] Ps 7:16 [r] Dt 21:22-23 [s] Est 7:10
9:26 [t] ver 20; Est 3:7

remembered and observed in every generation by every family,
and in every province and in every city. And these days of Purim
should never cease to be celebrated by the Jews, nor should the
memory of them die out among their descendants.
29 So Queen Esther, daughter of Abihail,[a] along with Mordecai
the Jew, wrote with full authority to confirm this second letter
concerning Purim. 30 And Mordecai sent letters to all the Jews in
the 127 provinces[b] of the kingdom of Xerxes—words of goodwill
and assurance— 31 to establish these days of Purim at their designated times, as Mordecai the Jew and Queen Esther had decreed
for them, and as they had established for themselves and their
descendants in regard to their times of fasting[c] and lamentation.[d]
32 Esther's decree confirmed these regulations about Purim, and
it was written down in the records.

Chapter 10 Theme ______________________________

10 King Xerxes imposed tribute throughout the empire, to its
distant shores.[e] 2 And all his acts of power and might,
together with a full account of the greatness of Mordecai[f] to
which the king had raised him,[g] are they not written in the book
of the annals[h] of the kings of Media and Persia? 3 Mordecai the
Jew was second[i] in rank[j] to King Xerxes,[k] preeminent among the
Jews, and held in high esteem by his many fellow Jews, because
he worked for the good of his people and spoke up for the welfare
of all the Jews.[l]

9:29 [a] Est 2:15
9:30 [b] Est 1:1
9:31 [c] Est 4:16 [d] Est 4:1-3
10:1 [e] Ps 72:10; 97:1; Isa 24:15
10:2 [f] Est 8:15; 9:4 [g] Ge 41:44 [h] Est 2:23
10:3 [i] Da 5:7 [j] Ge 41:43 [k] Ge 41:40 [l] Ne 2:10; Jer 29:4-7; Da 6:3

Esther at a Glance

Theme of Esther:

Author:

Date:

Purpose:

Key Words:

Segment Divisions

		Chapter Themes
		1
		2
		3
		4
		5
		6
		7
		8
		9
		10

JOB

Job is a book born out of pain. Job's pain was so crushing he wanted to die; he wished he had never been born. His pain was compounded because his friends wrestled with the reason for his suffering. Job's affliction brought God's character and ways into question. Yet ultimately it brought deeper intimacy with God.

Job, the first and probably oldest of the poetical books of the Bible, is for those who need answers from God, for those who want to say with Job, "Then I would still have this consolation—my joy in unrelenting pain—that I had not denied the words of the Holy One" (6:10).

Things to Do

1. Chapters 1 and 2 provide the setting of Job's pain. Read through these two chapters. Mark every reference to Satan and to God. Then on the OBSERVATIONS CHART on page 893:
   a. List what you learn about Satan—his person and his relationship to God and to Job.
   b. List what you learn about God.
   c. List what you learn about Job: what God says about him; what Satan says; how he responds to God, to his pain, and to the counsel of his wife.
2. In order to understand Job and the ensuing discourses of his friends, read Job 1:8 and 2:3, 11-13 again and then Job 42:7-9. Stop and do this before you proceed any further. Pay attention to what God says about Job and to what God says about what Job's three friends said.
3. In chapter 3 Job pours out his anguish, and then in chapters 4 through 42:6 there is a series of discourses given either by Job, his friends, or God himself. Read through this section chapter by chapter and do the following:
   a. At the top of every chapter, on the line next to the chapter number, note who is speaking and to whom. Then record this under chapter themes on the JOB AT A GLANCE chart on page 894.
   b. Job 42:7 says that Job's friends did not speak what was right concerning God. Therefore if one of these three men speaks, in the margin note how his reasoning is wrong in respect to God and to Job's suffering. Watch carefully to see where or how (if it tells) Job's friend came up with his conclusion. Then watch how Job answers each of his friends. Record pertinent notes in the margin.
4. As you read Job 4 through 42 observe what the text says about:
   a. Man and God
   b. What God expects from man and what he does not expect
   c. Nature
   d. Sin and righteousness
   e. Physical life and death
   f. How to deal with those in pain

   Record your insights on the OBSERVATIONS CHART on page 893 as you read each chapter.
5. Mark key words or phrases which play a significant role in a particular chapter or which recur throughout the book (for instance, the words *wisdom, victory,* and *insight*). Note in the margin the insights you glean from marking *wisdom* and other key words. Also highlight or underline verses which speak to your heart.
6. Don't fail to compare Job's end with his beginning and to notice what came from Satan's challenge.
7. When you finish reading Job and you have filled in JOB AT A GLANCE, note how the book divides itself into a pattern of discourses. Record this under "Segment Divisions."

Things to Think About

1. Think about Job's end compared to his beginning and then ask yourself if Job's suffering was worth it. What about your suffering? What can it produce if you will respond in the proper way? What is the proper way? What did you learn from Job?
2. What have you learned about Satan and Satan's relationship to God from this book? How can those insights comfort you?
3. Read Job 31 again, and if you did not mark it the first time, mark in a distinctive way every *if* and every *if I have.* Think about how Job appealed to his own integrity in various matters of life. Examine those areas carefully. How does your own integrity measure up in those areas? What do you need to remember, do, hold onto, let go of, begin, or stop?

Chapter 1 Theme

1 In the land of Uz[a] there lived a man whose name was Job.[b] This
man was blameless[c] and upright; he feared God[d] and shunned
evil. 2 He had seven sons and three daughters,[e] 3 and he owned sev-
en thousand sheep, three thousand camels, five hundred yoke of
oxen and five hundred donkeys, and had a large number of servants. He was the greatest man[f] among all the people of the East.
4 His sons used to take turns holding feasts in their homes, and
they would invite their three sisters to eat and drink with them.
5 When a period of feasting had run its course, Job would send
and have them purified. Early in the morning he would sacrifice a
burnt offering[g] for each of them, thinking, "Perhaps my children
have sinned[h] and cursed God[i] in their hearts." This was Job's regular custom.
6 One day the angels[a] [j] came to present themselves before the
LORD, and Satan[b] also came with them.[k] 7 The LORD said to Satan,
"Where have you come from?"
Satan answered the LORD, "From roaming through the earth
and going back and forth in it."[l]
8 Then the LORD said to Satan, "Have you considered my servant Job?[m] There is no one on earth like him; he is blameless and
upright, a man who fears God and shuns evil."[n]
9 "Does Job fear God for nothing?"[o] Satan replied. 10 "Have you
not put a hedge around him and his household and everything
he has?[p] You have blessed the work of his hands, so that his flocks
and herds are spread throughout the land.[q] 11 But stretch out your
hand and strike everything he has,[r] and he will surely curse you
to your face."[s]
12 The LORD said to Satan, "Very well, then, everything he has is
in your hands, but on the man himself do not lay a finger."
Then Satan went out from the presence of the LORD.

a6 Hebrew *the sons of God* b6 *Satan* means *accuser.*

1:1 [a] Jer 25:20 [b] Eze 14:14, 20; Jas 5:11 [c] Ge 6:9; 17:1 [d] Ge 22:12; Ex 18:21
1:2 [e] Job 42:13
1:3 [f] Job 29:25
1:5 [g] Ge 8:20; Job 42:8 [h] Job 8:4 [i] 1Ki 21:10,13
1:6 [j] Job 38:7 [k] Job 2:1
1:7 [l] 1Pe 5:8
1:8 [m] Jos 1:7; Job 42:7-8 [n] ver 1
1:9 [o] 1Ti 6:5
1:10 [p] Ps 34:7 [q] ver 3; Job 29:6; 31:25; Ps 128:1-2
1:11 [r] Job 19:21 [s] Job 2:5

13 One day when Job's sons and daughters were feasting and drinking wine at the oldest brother's house, 14 a messenger came to Job and said, "The oxen were plowing and the donkeys were grazing nearby, 15 and the Sabeans[a] attacked and carried them off. They put the servants to the sword, and I am the only one who has escaped to tell you!"

16 While he was still speaking, another messenger came and said, "The fire of God fell from the sky[b] and burned up the sheep and the servants,[c] and I am the only one who has escaped to tell you!"

17 While he was still speaking, another messenger came and said, "The Chaldeans[d] formed three raiding parties and swept down on your camels and carried them off. They put the servants to the sword, and I am the only one who has escaped to tell you!"

18 While he was still speaking, yet another messenger came and said, "Your sons and daughters were feasting and drinking wine at the oldest brother's house, 19 when suddenly a mighty wind[e] swept in from the desert and struck the four corners of the house. It collapsed on them and they are dead, and I am the only one who has escaped to tell you!"

20 At this, Job got up and tore his robe[f] and shaved his head. Then he fell to the ground in worship[g] 21 and said:

> "Naked I came from my mother's womb,
> and naked I will depart.[a][h]
> The LORD gave and the LORD has taken away;[i]
> may the name of the LORD be praised."[j]

22 In all this, Job did not sin by charging God with wrongdoing.[k]

Chapter 2 Theme ________________________________

2 On another day the angels[b] came to present themselves before the LORD, and Satan also came with them[l] to present himself before him. 2 And the LORD said to Satan, "Where have you come from?"

Satan answered the LORD, "From roaming through the earth and going back and forth in it."

3 Then the LORD said to Satan, "Have you considered my servant Job? There is no one on earth like him; he is blameless and upright, a man who fears God and shuns evil.[m] And he still maintains his integrity,[n] though you incited me against him to ruin him without any reason."[o]

4 "Skin for skin!" Satan replied. "A man will give all he has for his own life. 5 But stretch out your hand and strike his flesh and bones,[p] and he will surely curse you to your face."[q]

1:15 [a] Ge 10:7; Job 6:19
1:16 [b] Ge 19:24 [c] Lev 10:2; Nu 11:1-3
1:17 [d] Ge 11:28,31
1:19 [e] Jer 4:11; 13:24
1:20 [f] Ge 37:29 [g] 1Pe 5:6
1:21 [h] Ecc 5:15; 1Ti 6:7 [i] 1Sa 2:7 [j] Job 2:10; Eph 5:20; 1Th 5:18
1:22 [k] Job 2:10
2:1 [l] Job 1:6
2:3 [m] Job 1:1,8 [n] Job 27:6 [o] Job 9:17
2:5 [p] Job 19:20 [q] Job 1:11

[a] 21 Or *will return there* [b] 1 Hebrew *the sons of God*

[6]The LORD said to Satan, "Very well, then, he is in your hands;
but you must spare his life."[a]
[7]So Satan went out from the presence of the LORD and afflicted
Job with painful sores from the soles of his feet to the top of his
head.[b] [8]Then Job took a piece of broken pottery and scraped himself with it as he sat among the ashes.[c]
[9]His wife said to him, "Are you still holding on to your integrity? Curse God and die!"
[10]He replied, "You are talking like a foolish[a] woman. Shall we
accept good from God, and not trouble?"[d]
In all this, Job did not sin in what he said.[e]
[11]When Job's three friends, Eliphaz the Temanite,[f] Bildad the
Shuhite[g] and Zophar the Naamathite, heard about all the troubles
that had come upon him, they set out from their homes and met
together by agreement to go and sympathize with him and comfort him.[h] [12]When they saw him from a distance, they could hardly recognize him; they began to weep aloud, and they tore their
robes and sprinkled dust on their heads.[i] [13]Then they sat on the
ground with him for seven days and seven nights.[j] No one said a
word to him, because they saw how great his suffering was.

Chapter 3 Theme ______________________

3

After this, Job opened his mouth and cursed the day of his
birth. [2]He said:

[3]"May the day of my birth perish,
and the night it was said, 'A boy is born!'[k]
[4]That day—may it turn to darkness;
may God above not care about it;
may no light shine upon it.
[5]May darkness and deep shadow[b][l] claim it once more;
may a cloud settle over it;
may blackness overwhelm its light.
[6]That night—may thick darkness[m] seize it;
may it not be included among the days of the year
nor be entered in any of the months.
[7]May that night be barren;
may no shout of joy be heard in it.
[8]May those who curse days[c] curse that day,
those who are ready to rouse Leviathan.[n]
[9]May its morning stars become dark;
may it wait for daylight in vain
and not see the first rays of dawn,[o]

2:6 [a]Job 1:12
2:7 [b]Dt 28:35; Job 7:5
2:8 [c]Job 42:6; Jer 6:26; Eze 27:30; Mt 11:21
2:10 [d]Job 1:21 [e]Job 1:22; Ps 39:1; Jas 1:12; 5:11
2:11 [f]Ge 36:11; Jer 49:7 [g]Ge 25:2 [h]Job 42:11; Ro 12:15
2:12 [i]Jos 7:6; Ne 9:1; La 2:10; Eze 27:30
2:13 [j]Ge 50:10; Eze 3:15
3:3 [k]Job 10:18-19; Jer 20:14-18
3:5 [l]Job 10:21,22; Ps 23:4; Jer 2:6; 13:16
3:6 [m]Job 23:17
3:8 [n]Job 41:1,8, 10,25
3:9 [o]Job 41:18

[a]*10* The Hebrew word rendered *foolish* denotes moral deficiency. [b]*5* Or *and the shadow of death* [c]*8* Or *the sea*

[10]for it did not shut the doors of the womb on me
to hide trouble from my eyes.

[11]"Why did I not perish at birth,
and die as I came from the womb?[a]
[12]Why were there knees to receive me[b]
and breasts that I might be nursed?
[13]For now I would be lying down[c] in peace;
I would be asleep and at rest[d]
[14]with kings and counselors of the earth,[e]
who built for themselves places now lying in ruins,[f]
[15]with rulers[g] who had gold,
who filled their houses with silver.[h]
[16]Or why was I not hidden in the ground like a
stillborn child,[i]
like an infant who never saw the light of day?
[17]There the wicked cease from turmoil,
and there the weary are at rest.[j]
[18]Captives also enjoy their ease;
they no longer hear the slave driver's shout.[k]
[19]The small and the great are there,
and the slave is freed from his master.

[20]"Why is light given to those in misery,
and life to the bitter of soul,[l]
[21]to those who long for death that does not come,[m]
who search for it more than for hidden treasure,[n]
[22]who are filled with gladness
and rejoice when they reach the grave?
[23]Why is life given to a man
whose way is hidden,
whom God has hedged in?[o]
[24]For sighing comes to me instead of food;[p]
my groans pour out like water.[q]
[25]What I feared has come upon me;
what I dreaded[r] has happened to me.
[26]I have no peace, no quietness;
I have no rest,[s] but only turmoil."

Chapter 4 Theme ______________________

4

Then Eliphaz the Temanite replied:

[2]"If someone ventures a word with you, will you
be impatient?
But who can keep from speaking?[t]

3:11 [a]Job 10:18
3:12 [b]Ge 30:3; Isa 66:12
3:13 [c]Job 17:13 [d]Job 7:8-10,21; 10:22; 14:10-12; 19:27; 21:13,23
3:14 [e]Job 12:17 [f]Job 15:28
3:15 [g]Job 12:21 [h]Job 27:17
3:16 [i]Ps 58:8; Ecc 6:3
3:17 [j]Job 17:16
3:18 [k]Job 39:7
3:20 [l]1Sa 1:10; Jer 20:18; Eze 27:30-31
3:21 [m]Rev 9:6 [n]Pr 2:4
3:23 [o]Job 19:6,8, 12; Ps 88:8; La 3:7
3:24 [p]Job 6:7; 33:20 [q]Ps 42:3,4
3:25 [r]Job 30:15
3:26 [s]Job 7:4,14
4:2 [t]Job 32:20

3Think how you have instructed many,
how you have strengthened feeble hands.[a]
4Your words have supported those who stumbled;
you have strengthened faltering knees.[b]
5But now trouble comes to you, and you are discouraged;
it strikes[c] you, and you are dismayed.[d]
6Should not your piety be your confidence[e]
and your blameless[f] ways your hope?

7"Consider now: Who, being innocent, has
ever perished?[g]
Where were the upright ever destroyed?[h]
8As I have observed, those who plow evil[i]
and those who sow trouble reap it.[j]
9At the breath of God[k] they are destroyed;
at the blast of his anger they perish.[l]
10The lions may roar and growl,
yet the teeth of the great lions are broken.[m]
11The lion perishes for lack of prey,[n]
and the cubs of the lioness are scattered.

12"A word was secretly brought to me,
my ears caught a whisper[o] of it.[p]
13Amid disquieting dreams in the night,
when deep sleep falls on men,[q]
14fear and trembling seized me
and made all my bones shake.[r]
15A spirit glided past my face,
and the hair on my body stood on end.
16It stopped,
but I could not tell what it was.
A form stood before my eyes,
and I heard a hushed voice:
17'Can a mortal be more righteous than God?[s]
Can a man be more pure than his Maker?[t]
18If God places no trust in his servants,
if he charges his angels with error,[u]
19how much more those who live in houses of clay,[v]
whose foundations[w] are in the dust,[x]
who are crushed more readily than a moth!
20Between dawn and dusk they are broken to pieces;
unnoticed, they perish forever.[y]
21Are not the cords of their tent pulled up,[z]
so that they die without wisdom?'[a][a]

a 21 Some interpreters end the quotation after verse 17.

4:3 [a]Isa 35:3; Heb 12:12
4:4 [b]Isa 35:3; Heb 12:12
4:5 [c]Job 19:21 [d]Job 6:14
4:6 [e]Pr 3:26 [f]Job 1:1
4:7 [g]Job 36:7 [h]Job 8:20; Ps 37:25
4:8 [i]Job 15:35 [j]Pr 22:8; Hos 10:13; Gal 6:7-8
4:9 [k]Job 15:30; Isa 30:33; 2Th 2:8 [l]Job 40:13
4:10 [m]Job 5:15; Ps 58:6
4:11 [n]Job 27:14; Ps 34:10
4:12 [o]Job 26:14 [p]Job 33:14
4:13 [q]Job 33:15
4:14 [r]Jer 23:9; Hab 3:16
4:17 [s]Job 9:2 [t]Job 35:10
4:18 [u]Job 15:15
4:19 [v]Job 10:9 [w]Job 22:16 [x]Ge 2:7
4:20 [y]Job 14:2,20; 20:7; Ps 90:5-6
4:21 [z]Job 8:22 [a]Job 18:21; 36:12

Chapter 5 Theme ____________________

5

"Call if you will, but who will answer you?
To which of the holy ones[a] will you turn?
2 Resentment kills a fool,
and envy slays the simple.[b]
3 I myself have seen a fool taking root,[c]
but suddenly his house was cursed.[d]
4 His children are far from safety,[e]
crushed in court[f] without a defender.
5 The hungry consume his harvest,[g]
taking it even from among thorns,
and the thirsty pant after his wealth.
6 For hardship does not spring from the soil,
nor does trouble sprout from the ground.
7 Yet man is born to trouble[h]
as surely as sparks fly upward.

8 "But if it were I, I would appeal to God;
I would lay my cause before him.[i]
9 He performs wonders that cannot be fathomed,[j]
miracles that cannot be counted.
10 He bestows rain on the earth;
he sends water upon the countryside.[k]
11 The lowly he sets on high,[l]
and those who mourn are lifted to safety.
12 He thwarts the plans[m] of the crafty,
so that their hands achieve no success.
13 He catches the wise in their craftiness,[n]
and the schemes of the wily are swept away.
14 Darkness[o] comes upon them in the daytime;
at noon they grope as in the night.[p]
15 He saves the needy[q] from the sword in their mouth;
he saves them from the clutches of the powerful.[r]
16 So the poor have hope,
and injustice shuts its mouth.[s]

17 "Blessed is the man whom God corrects;[t]
so do not despise the discipline[u] of the Almighty.[a][v]
18 For he wounds, but he also binds up;[w]
he injures, but his hands also heal.[x]
19 From six calamities he will rescue you;
in seven no harm will befall you.[y]
20 In famine[z] he will ransom you from death,
and in battle from the stroke of the sword.[a]

5:1 [a] Job 15:15
5:2 [b] Pr 12:16
5:3 [c] Ps 37:35; Jer 12:2 [d] Job 24:18
5:4 [e] Job 4:11 [f] Am 5:12
5:5 [g] Job 18:8-10
5:7 [h] Job 14:1
5:8 [i] Ps 35:23; 50:15
5:9 [j] Job 42:3; Ps 40:5
5:10 [k] Job 36:28
5:11 [l] Ps 113:7-8
5:12 [m] Ne 4:15; Ps 33:10
5:13 [n] 1Co 3:19*
5:14 [o] Job 12:25 [p] Dt 28:29
5:15 [q] Ps 35:10 [r] Job 4:10
5:16 [s] Ps 107:42
5:17 [t] Jas 1:12 [u] Ps 94:12; Pr 3:11 [v] Heb 12:5-11
5:18 [w] Isa 30:26 [x] 1Sa 2:6
5:19 [y] Ps 34:19; 91:10
5:20 [z] Ps 33:19 [a] Ps 144:10

a *17* Hebrew *Shaddai*; here and throughout Job

21You will be protected from the lash of the tongue,[a]
and need not fear[b] when destruction comes.
22You will laugh at destruction and famine,
and need not fear the beasts of the earth.[c]
23For you will have a covenant with the stones[d] of the field,
and the wild animals will be at peace with you.[e]
24You will know that your tent is secure;
you will take stock of your property and find
nothing missing.[f]
25You will know that your children will be many,[g]
and your descendants like the grass of the earth.[h]
26You will come to the grave in full vigor,[i]
like sheaves gathered in season.

27"We have examined this, and it is true.
So hear it and apply it to yourself."

Chapter 6 Theme ____________________

6 Then Job replied:

2"If only my anguish could be weighed
and all my misery be placed on the scales![j]
3It would surely outweigh the sand[k] of the seas—
no wonder my words have been impetuous.[l]
4The arrows[m] of the Almighty are in me,[n]
my spirit drinks[o] in their poison;
God's terrors[p] are marshaled against me.[q]
5Does a wild donkey bray when it has grass,
or an ox bellow when it has fodder?
6Is tasteless food eaten without salt,
or is there flavor in the white of an egg[a]?
7I refuse to touch it;
such food makes me ill.[r]

8"Oh, that I might have my request,
that God would grant what I hope for,[s]
9that God would be willing to crush me,
to let loose his hand and cut me off![t]
10Then I would still have this consolation—
my joy in unrelenting pain—
that I had not denied the words[u] of the Holy One.[v]

11"What strength do I have, that I should still hope?
What prospects, that I should be patient?[w]

a6 The meaning of the Hebrew for this phrase is uncertain.

5:21 [a]Ps 31:20 [b]Ps 91:5
5:22 [c]Ps 91:13; Eze 34:25
5:23 [d]Ps 91:12 [e]Isa 11:6-9
5:24 [f]Job 8:6
5:25 [g]Ps 112:2 [h]Ps 72:16; Isa 44:3-4
5:26 [i]Ge 15:15
6:2 [j]Job 31:6
6:3 [k]Pr 27:3 [l]Job 23:2
6:4 [m]Ps 38:2 [n]Job 16:12,13 [o]Job 21:20 [p]Job 30:15 [q]Ps 88:15-18
6:7 [r]Job 3:24
6:8 [s]Job 14:13
6:9 [t]Nu 11:15; 1Ki 19:4
6:10 [u]Job 22:22; 23:12 [v]Lev 19:2; Isa 57:15
6:11 [w]Job 21:4

12 Do I have the strength of stone?
Is my flesh bronze?
13 Do I have any power to help myself,[a]
now that success has been driven from me?

14 "A despairing man[b] should have the devotion[c] of
his friends,
even though he forsakes the fear of the Almighty.
15 But my brothers are as undependable as
intermittent streams,[d]
as the streams that overflow
16 when darkened by thawing ice
and swollen with melting snow,
17 but that cease to flow in the dry season,
and in the heat[e] vanish from their channels.
18 Caravans turn aside from their routes;
they go up into the wasteland and perish.
19 The caravans of Tema[f] look for water,
the traveling merchants of Sheba look in hope.
20 They are distressed, because they had been confident;
they arrive there, only to be disappointed.[g]
21 Now you too have proved to be of no help;
you see something dreadful and are afraid.[h]
22 Have I ever said, 'Give something on my behalf,
pay a ransom for me from your wealth,
23 deliver me from the hand of the enemy,
ransom me from the clutches of the ruthless'?

24 "Teach me, and I will be quiet;[i]
show me where I have been wrong.
25 How painful are honest words![j]
But what do your arguments prove?
26 Do you mean to correct what I say,
and treat the words of a despairing man as wind?[k]
27 You would even cast lots[l] for the fatherless
and barter away your friend.

28 "But now be so kind as to look at me.
Would I lie to your face?[m]
29 Relent, do not be unjust;
reconsider, for my integrity is at stake.[a][n]
30 Is there any wickedness on my lips?[o]
Can my mouth not discern[p] malice?

6:13 [a]Job 26:2
6:14 [b]Job 4:5 [c]Job 15:4
6:15 [d]Ps 38:11; Jer 15:18
6:17 [e]Job 24:19
6:19 [f]Ge 25:15; Isa 21:14
6:20 [g]Jer 14:3
6:21 [h]Ps 38:11
6:24 [i]Ps 39:1
6:25 [j]Ecc 12:11
6:26 [k]Job 8:2; 15:3
6:27 [l]Joel 3:3; Na 3:10; 2Pe 2:3
6:28 [m]Job 27:4; 33:1,3; 36:3,4
6:29 [n]Job 23:7,10; 34:5,36; 42:6
6:30 [o]Job 27:4 [p]Job 12:11

a 29 Or *my righteousness still stands*

Chapter 7 Theme ______________________

7

"Does not man have hard service[a] on earth?[b]
Are not his days like those of a hired man?[c]
2 Like a slave longing for the evening shadows,
or a hired man waiting eagerly for his wages,[d]
3 so I have been allotted months of futility,
and nights of misery have been assigned to me.[e]
4 When I lie down I think, 'How long before I get up?'[f]
The night drags on, and I toss till dawn.
5 My body is clothed with worms[g] and scabs,
my skin is broken and festering.

6 "My days are swifter than a weaver's shuttle,[h]
and they come to an end without hope.[i]
7 Remember, O God, that my life is but a breath;[j]
my eyes will never see happiness again.[k]
8 The eye that now sees me will see me no longer;
you will look for me, but I will be no more.[l]
9 As a cloud vanishes and is gone,
so he who goes down to the grave[a][m] does not return.[n]
10 He will never come to his house again;
his place[o] will know him no more.[p]

11 "Therefore I will not keep silent;[q]
I will speak out in the anguish of my spirit,
I will complain in the bitterness of my soul.[r]
12 Am I the sea, or the monster of the deep,[s]
that you put me under guard?
13 When I think my bed will comfort me
and my couch will ease my complaint,[t]
14 even then you frighten me with dreams
and terrify[u] me with visions,
15 so that I prefer strangling and death,[v]
rather than this body of mine.
16 I despise my life;[w] I would not live forever.
Let me alone; my days have no meaning.

17 "What is man that you make so much of him,
that you give him so much attention,[x]
18 that you examine him every morning
and test him every moment?[y]
19 Will you never look away from me,
or let me alone even for an instant?[z]
20 If I have sinned, what have I done to you,[a]
O watcher of men?

a 9 Hebrew *Sheol*

7:1 [a] Job 14:14; Isa 40:2 [b] Job 5:7 [c] Job 14:6
7:2 [d] Lev 19:13
7:3 [e] Job 16:7; Ps 6:6
7:4 [f] Dt 28:67
7:5 [g] Job 17:14; Isa 14:11
7:6 [h] Job 9:25 [i] Job 13:15; 17:11,15
7:7 [j] Ps 78:39; Jas 4:14 [k] Job 9:25
7:8 [l] Job 20:7,9,21
7:9 [m] Job 11:8 [n] 2Sa 12:23; Job 30:15
7:10 [o] Job 27:21,23 [p] Job 8:18
7:11 [q] Ps 40:9 [r] 1Sa 1:10
7:12 [s] Eze 32:2-3
7:13 [t] Job 9:27
7:14 [u] Job 9:34
7:15 [v] 1Ki 19:4
7:16 [w] Job 9:21; 10:1
7:17 [x] Ps 8:4; 144:3; Heb 2:6
7:18 [y] Job 14:3
7:19 [z] Job 9:18
7:20 [a] Job 35:6

Why have you made me your target?[a]
Have I become a burden to you?[a]
[21]Why do you not pardon my offenses
and forgive my sins?[b]
For I will soon lie down in the dust;[c]
you will search for me, but I will be no more."

Chapter 8 Theme

8

Then Bildad the Shuhite replied:

[2]"How long will you say such things?
Your words are a blustering wind.[d]
[3]Does God pervert justice?[e]
Does the Almighty pervert what is right?[f]
[4]When your children sinned against him,
he gave them over to the penalty of their sin.[g]
[5]But if you will look to God
and plead[h] with the Almighty,
[6]if you are pure and upright,
even now he will rouse himself on your behalf[i]
and restore you to your rightful place.[j]
[7]Your beginnings will seem humble,
so prosperous[k] will your future be.

[8]"Ask the former generations[l]
and find out what their fathers learned,
[9]for we were born only yesterday and know nothing,[m]
and our days on earth are but a shadow.[n]
[10]Will they not instruct you and tell you?
Will they not bring forth words from
their understanding?
[11]Can papyrus grow tall where there is no marsh?
Can reeds thrive without water?
[12]While still growing and uncut,
they wither more quickly than grass.[o]
[13]Such is the destiny of all who forget God;[p]
so perishes the hope of the godless.[q]
[14]What he trusts in is fragile[b];
what he relies on is a spider's web.[r]
[15]He leans on his web,[s] but it gives way;
he clings to it, but it does not hold.[t]
[16]He is like a well-watered plant in the sunshine,
spreading its shoots[u] over the garden;[v]

7:20 [a]Job 16:12
7:21 [b]Job 10:14 [c]Job 10:9; Ps 104:29
8:2 [d]Job 6:26
8:3 [e]Dt 32:4; 2Ch 19:7; Ro 3:5 [f]Ge 18:25
8:4 [g]Job 1:19
8:5 [h]Job 11:13
8:6 [i]Ps 7:6 [j]Job 5:24
8:7 [k]Job 42:12
8:8 [l]Dt 4:32; 32:7; Job 15:18
8:9 [m]Ge 47:9 [n]1Ch 29:15; Job 7:6
8:12 [o]Ps 129:6; Jer 17:6
8:13 [p]Ps 9:17 [q]Job 11:20; 13:16; 15:34; Pr 10:28
8:14 [r]Isa 59:5
8:15 [s]Job 27:18 [t]Ps 49:11
8:16 [u]Ps 80:11 [v]Ps 37:35; Jer 11:16

a *20* A few manuscripts of the Masoretic Text, an ancient Hebrew scribal tradition and Septuagint; most manuscripts of the Masoretic Text *I have become a burden to myself.*
b *14* The meaning of the Hebrew for this word is uncertain.

[17]it entwines its roots around a pile of rocks
and looks for a place among the stones.
[18]But when it is torn from its spot,
that place disowns it and says, 'I never saw you.'[a]
[19]Surely its life withers[b] away,
and[a] from the soil other plants grow.[c]

[20]"Surely God does not reject a blameless[d] man
or strengthen the hands of evildoers.[e]
[21]He will yet fill your mouth with laughter[f]
and your lips with shouts of joy.[g]
[22]Your enemies will be clothed in shame,[h]
and the tents of the wicked will be no more."[i]

Chapter 9 Theme

9

Then Job replied:

[2]"Indeed, I know that this is true.
But how can a mortal be righteous before God?[j]
[3]Though one wished to dispute with him,
he could not answer him one time out of a thousand.[k]
[4]His wisdom[l] is profound, his power is vast.[m]
Who has resisted him and come out unscathed?[n]
[5]He moves mountains without their knowing it
and overturns them in his anger.[o]
[6]He shakes the earth[p] from its place
and makes its pillars tremble.[q]
[7]He speaks to the sun and it does not shine;
he seals off the light of the stars.[r]
[8]He alone stretches out the heavens[s]
and treads on the waves of the sea.[t]
[9]He is the Maker of the Bear and Orion,
the Pleiades and the constellations of the south.[u]
[10]He performs wonders[v] that cannot be fathomed,
miracles that cannot be counted.[w]
[11]When he passes me, I cannot see him;
when he goes by, I cannot perceive him.[x]
[12]If he snatches away, who can stop him?[y]
Who can say to him, 'What are you doing?'[z]
[13]God does not restrain his anger;
even the cohorts of Rahab[a] cowered at his feet.

[14]"How then can I dispute with him?
How can I find words to argue with him?

a *19* Or *Surely all the joy it has / is that*

8:18 [a]Job 7:8; Ps 37:36
8:19 [b]Job 20:5 [c]Ecc 1:4
8:20 [d]Job 1:1 [e]Job 21:30
8:21 [f]Job 5:22 [g]Ps 126:2; 132:16
8:22 [h]Ps 35:26; 109:29; 132:18 [i]Job 18:6, 14,21
9:2 [j]Job 4:17; Ps 143:2; Ro 3:20
9:3 [k]Job 10:2; 40:2
9:4 [l]Job 11:6 [m]Job 36:5 [n]2Ch 13:12
9:5 [o]Mic 1:4
9:6 [p]Isa 2:21; Hag 2:6; Heb 12:26 [q]Job 26:11
9:7 [r]Isa 13:10; Eze 32:8
9:8 [s]Ge 1:6; Ps 104:2-3 [t]Job 38:16; Ps 77:19
9:9 [u]Ge 1:16; Job 38:31; Am 5:8
9:10 [v]Ps 71:15 [w]Job 5:9
9:11 [x]Job 23:8-9; 35:14
9:12 [y]Job 11:10 [z]Isa 45:9; Ro 9:20
9:13 [a]Job 26:12; Ps 89:10; Isa 30:7; 51:9

15 Though I were innocent, I could not answer him;[a]
I could only plead[b] with my Judge for mercy.
16 Even if I summoned him and he responded,
I do not believe he would give me a hearing.
17 He would crush me[c] with a storm[d]
and multiply[e] my wounds for no reason.[f]
18 He would not let me regain my breath
but would overwhelm me with misery.[g]
19 If it is a matter of strength, he is mighty!
And if it is a matter of justice, who will summon him[a]?
20 Even if I were innocent, my mouth would condemn me;
if I were blameless, it would pronounce me guilty.

21 "Although I am blameless,[h]
I have no concern for myself;
I despise my own life.[i]
22 It is all the same; that is why I say,
'He destroys both the blameless and the wicked.'[j]
23 When a scourge[k] brings sudden death,
he mocks the despair of the innocent.[l]
24 When a land falls into the hands of the wicked,[m]
he blindfolds its judges.[n]
If it is not he, then who is it?

25 "My days are swifter than a runner;[o]
they fly away without a glimpse of joy.
26 They skim past like boats of papyrus,[p]
like eagles swooping down on their prey.[q]
27 If I say, 'I will forget my complaint,[r]
I will change my expression, and smile,'
28 I still dread[s] all my sufferings,
for I know you will not hold me innocent.[t]
29 Since I am already found guilty,
why should I struggle in vain?[u]
30 Even if I washed myself with soap[b]
and my hands[v] with washing soda,[w]
31 you would plunge me into a slime pit
so that even my clothes would detest me.

32 "He is not a man like me that I might answer him,[x]
that we might confront each other in court.[y]
33 If only there were someone to arbitrate between us,[z]
to lay his hand upon us both,
34 someone to remove God's rod from me,[a]
so that his terror would frighten me no more.

9:15 [a] Job 10:15 [b] Job 8:5
9:17 [c] Job 16:12 [d] Job 30:22 [e] Job 16:14 [f] Job 2:3
9:18 [g] Job 7:19; 27:2
9:21 [h] Job 1:1 [i] Job 7:16
9:22 [j] Job 10:8; Ecc 9:2,3; Eze 21:3
9:23 [k] Heb 11:36 [l] Job 24:1,12
9:24 [m] Job 10:3; 16:11 [n] Job 12:6
9:25 [o] Job 7:6
9:26 [p] Isa 18:2 [q] Hab 1:8
9:27 [r] Job 7:11
9:28 [s] Job 3:25; Ps 119:120 [t] Job 7:21
9:29 [u] Ps 37:33
9:30 [v] Job 31:7 [w] Jer 2:22
9:32 [x] Ro 9:20 [y] Ps 143:2; Ecc 6:10
9:33 [z] 1Sa 2:25
9:34 [a] Job 13:21; Ps 39:10

[a] *19* See Septuagint; Hebrew *me.* [b] *30* Or *snow*

35Then I would speak up without fear of him,
but as it now stands with me, I cannot.[a]

Chapter 10 Theme

10 "I loathe my very life;[b]
therefore I will give free rein to my complaint
and speak out in the bitterness of my soul.[c]
2I will say to God: Do not condemn me,
but tell me what charges[d] you have against me.
3Does it please you to oppress me,[e]
to spurn the work of your hands,[f]
while you smile on the schemes of the wicked?[g]
4Do you have eyes of flesh?
Do you see as a mortal sees?[h]
5Are your days like those of a mortal
or your years like those of a man,[i]
6that you must search out my faults
and probe after my sin[j]—
7though you know that I am not guilty
and that no one can rescue me from your hand?

8"Your hands shaped[k] me and made me.
Will you now turn and destroy me?
9Remember that you molded me like clay.[l]
Will you now turn me to dust again?[m]
10Did you not pour me out like milk
and curdle me like cheese,
11clothe me with skin and flesh
and knit me together[n] with bones and sinews?
12You gave me life[o] and showed me kindness,
and in your providence watched over my spirit.

13"But this is what you concealed in your heart,
and I know that this was in your mind:[p]
14If I sinned, you would be watching me
and would not let my offense go unpunished.[q]
15If I am guilty—woe to me![r]
Even if I am innocent, I cannot lift my head,[s]
for I am full of shame
and drowned in[a] my affliction.
16If I hold my head high, you stalk me like a lion[t]
and again display your awesome power against me.[u]
17You bring new witnesses against me[v]
and increase your anger toward me;[w]
your forces come against me wave upon wave.

9:35 [a] Job 13:21
10:1 [b] 1Ki 19:4 [c] Job 7:11
10:2 [d] Job 9:29
10:3 [e] Job 9:22 [f] Job 14:15; Ps 138:8; Isa 64:8 [g] Job 21:16; 22:18
10:4 [h] 1Sa 16:7
10:5 [i] Ps 90:2,4; 2Pe 3:8
10:6 [j] Job 14:16
10:8 [k] Ps 119:73
10:9 [l] Isa 64:8 [m] Ge 2:7
10:11 [n] Ps 139:13,15
10:12 [o] Job 33:4
10:13 [p] Job 23:13
10:14 [q] Job 7:21
10:15 [r] Job 9:13; Isa 3:11 [s] Job 9:15
10:16 [t] Isa 38:13; La 3:10 [u] Job 5:9
10:17 [v] Job 16:8 [w] Ru 1:21

[a] 15 Or *and aware of*

18 “Why then did you bring me out of the womb?[a]
I wish I had died before any eye saw me.
19 If only I had never come into being,
or had been carried straight from the womb to
the grave!
20 Are not my few days[b] almost over?[c]
Turn away from me[d] so I can have a moment's joy
21 before I go to the place of no return,[e]
to the land of gloom and deep shadow,[a][f]
22 to the land of deepest night,
of deep shadow and disorder,
where even the light is like darkness.”

Chapter 11 Theme ____________________________

11

Then Zophar the Naamathite replied:

2 “Are all these words to go unanswered?[g]
Is this talker to be vindicated?
3 Will your idle talk reduce men to silence?
Will no one rebuke you when you mock?[h]
4 You say to God, ‘My beliefs are flawless[i]
and I am pure[j] in your sight.’
5 Oh, how I wish that God would speak,
that he would open his lips against you
6 and disclose to you the secrets of wisdom,[k]
for true wisdom has two sides.
Know this: God has even forgotten some of your sin.[l]

7 “Can you fathom[m] the mysteries of God?
Can you probe the limits of the Almighty?
8 They are higher than the heavens[n]—what can you do?
They are deeper than the depths of the grave[b]—what
can you know?
9 Their measure is longer than the earth
and wider than the sea.

10 “If he comes along and confines you in prison
and convenes a court, who can oppose him?[o]
11 Surely he recognizes deceitful men;
and when he sees evil, does he not take note?[p]
12 But a witless man can no more become wise
than a wild donkey's colt can be born a man.[c]

13 “Yet if you devote your heart[q] to him
and stretch out your hands to him,[r]

10:18 [a]Job 3:11
10:20 [b]Job 14:1 [c]Job 7:19 [d]Job 7:16
10:21 [e]2Sa 12:23; Job 3:13; 16:22 [f]Ps 23:4; 88:12
11:2 [g]Job 8:2
11:3 [h]Job 17:2; 21:3
11:4 [i]Job 6:10 [j]Job 10:7
11:6 [k]Job 9:4 [l]Ezr 9:13; Job 15:5
11:7 [m]Ecc 3:11; Ro 11:33
11:8 [n]Job 22:12
11:10 [o]Job 9:12; Rev 3:7
11:11 [p]Job 34:21-25; Ps 10:14
11:13 [q]1Sa 7:3; Ps 78:8 [r]Ps 88:9

[a] *21* Or *and the shadow of death*; also in verse 22 [b] *8* Hebrew *than Sheol* [c] *12* Or *wild donkey can be born tame*

[14]if you put away the sin that is in your hand
and allow no evil[a] to dwell in your tent,[b]
[15]then you will lift up your face[c] without shame;
you will stand firm and without fear.
[16]You will surely forget your trouble,[d]
recalling it only as waters gone by.[e]
[17]Life will be brighter than noonday,[f]
and darkness will become like morning.
[18]You will be secure, because there is hope;
you will look about you and take your rest[g] in safety.[h]
[19]You will lie down, with no one to make you afraid,[i]
and many will court your favor.[j]
[20]But the eyes of the wicked will fail,[k]
and escape will elude them;[l]
their hope will become a dying gasp."[m]

Chapter 12 Theme

12 Then Job replied:

[2]"Doubtless you are the people,
and wisdom will die with you![n]
[3]But I have a mind as well as you;
I am not inferior to you.
Who does not know all these things?[o]

[4]"I have become a laughingstock[p] to my friends,
though I called upon God and he answered[q]—
a mere laughingstock, though righteous
and blameless![r]
[5]Men at ease have contempt for misfortune
as the fate of those whose feet are slipping.
[6]The tents of marauders are undisturbed,[s]
and those who provoke God are secure[t]—
those who carry their god in their hands.[a]

[7]"But ask the animals, and they will teach you,
or the birds of the air, and they will tell you;
[8]or speak to the earth, and it will teach you,
or let the fish of the sea inform you.
[9]Which of all these does not know
that the hand of the LORD has done this?[u]
[10]In his hand is the life of every creature
and the breath of all mankind.[v]
[11]Does not the ear test words
as the tongue tastes food?[w]

[a]6 Or *secure / in what God's hand brings them*

11:14 [a]Ps 101:4 [b]Job 22:23
11:15 [c]Job 22:26; 1Jn 3:21
11:16 [d]Isa 65:16 [e]Job 22:11
11:17 [f]Job 22:28; Ps 37:6; Isa 58:8,10
11:18 [g]Ps 3:5 [h]Lev 26:6; Pr 3:24
11:19 [i]Lev 26:6 [j]Isa 45:14
11:20 [k]Dt 28:65; Job 17:5 [l]Job 27:22; 34:22 [m]Job 8:13
12:2 [n]Job 17:10
12:3 [o]Job 13:2
12:4 [p]Job 21:3 [q]Ps 91:15 [r]Job 6:29
12:6 [s]Job 22:18 [t]Job 9:24; 21:9
12:9 [u]Isa 41:20
12:10 [v]Job 27:3; 33:4; Ac 17:28
12:11 [w]Job 34:3

12 Is not wisdom found among the aged?[a]
Does not long life bring understanding?[b]

13 "To God belong wisdom[c] and power;[d]
counsel and understanding are his.[e]
14 What he tears down[f] cannot be rebuilt;[g]
the man he imprisons cannot be released.
15 If he holds back the waters,[h] there is drought;[i]
if he lets them loose, they devastate the land.[j]
16 To him belong strength and victory;
both deceived and deceiver are his.[k]
17 He leads counselors away stripped[l]
and makes fools of judges.[m]
18 He takes off the shackles[n] put on by kings
and ties a loincloth[a] around their waist.
19 He leads priests away stripped
and overthrows men long established.[o]
20 He silences the lips of trusted advisers
and takes away the discernment of elders.[p]
21 He pours contempt on nobles
and disarms the mighty.
22 He reveals the deep things of darkness[q]
and brings deep shadows[r] into the light.[s]
23 He makes nations great, and destroys them;[t]
he enlarges nations,[u] and disperses them.
24 He deprives the leaders of the earth of their reason;
he sends them wandering through a trackless waste.[v]
25 They grope in darkness with no light;[w]
he makes them stagger like drunkards.[x]

Chapter 13 Theme ________________________

13

"My eyes have seen all this,
my ears have heard and understood it.
2 What you know, I also know;
I am not inferior to you.[y]
3 But I desire to speak to the Almighty
and to argue my case with God.[z]
4 You, however, smear me with lies;[a]
you are worthless physicians, all of you!
5 If only you would be altogether silent!
For you, that would be wisdom.[b]
6 Hear now my argument;
listen to the plea of my lips.

12:12 [a] Job 15:10 [b] Job 32:7,9
12:13 [c] Job 11:6 [d] Job 9:4 [e] Job 32:8; 38:36
12:14 [f] Job 19:10 [g] Job 37:7; Isa 25:2
12:15 [h] 1Ki 8:35 [i] 1Ki 17:1 [j] Ge 7:11
12:16 [k] Job 13:7,9
12:17 [l] Job 19:9 [m] Job 3:14
12:18 [n] Ps 116:16
12:19 [o] Job 24:12,22; 34:20,28; 35:9
12:20 [p] Job 32:9
12:22 [q] 1Co 4:5 [r] Job 3:5 [s] Da 2:22
12:23 [t] Jer 25:9 [u] Ps 107:38; Isa 9:3; 26:15
12:24 [v] Ps 107:40
12:25 [w] Job 5:14 [x] Ps 107:27; Isa 24:20
13:2 [y] Job 12:3
13:3 [z] Job 23:3-4
13:4 [a] Ps 119:69; Jer 23:32
13:5 [b] Pr 17:28

a *18* Or *shackles of kings / and ties a belt*

[7]Will you speak wickedly on God's behalf?
Will you speak deceitfully for him?[a]
[8]Will you show him partiality?[b]
Will you argue the case for God?
[9]Would it turn out well if he examined you?
Could you deceive him as you might deceive men?[c]
[10]He would surely rebuke you
if you secretly showed partiality.
[11]Would not his splendor[d] terrify you?
Would not the dread of him fall on you?
[12]Your maxims are proverbs of ashes;
your defenses are defenses of clay.

[13]"Keep silent and let me speak;
then let come to me what may.
[14]Why do I put myself in jeopardy
and take my life in my hands?
[15]Though he slay me, yet will I hope[e] in him;[f]
I will surely[a] defend my ways to his face.[g]
[16]Indeed, this will turn out for my deliverance,[h]
for no godless man would dare come before him!
[17]Listen carefully to my words;[i]
let your ears take in what I say.
[18]Now that I have prepared my case,[j]
I know I will be vindicated.
[19]Can anyone bring charges against me?[k]
If so, I will be silent and die.[l]

[20]"Only grant me these two things, O God,
and then I will not hide from you:
[21]Withdraw your hand[m] far from me,
and stop frightening me with your terrors.
[22]Then summon me and I will answer,[n]
or let me speak, and you reply.[o]
[23]How many wrongs and sins have I committed?[p]
Show me my offense and my sin.
[24]Why do you hide your face[q]
and consider me your enemy?[r]
[25]Will you torment a windblown leaf?[s]
Will you chase after dry chaff?[t]
[26]For you write down bitter things against me
and make me inherit the sins of my youth.[u]
[27]You fasten my feet in shackles;[v]
you keep close watch on all my paths
by putting marks on the soles of my feet.

[a]15 Or *He will surely slay me; I have no hope— / yet I will*

13:7 [a]Job 36:4
13:8 [b]Lev 19:15
13:9 [c]Job 12:16; Gal 6:7
13:11 [d]Job 31:23
13:15 [e]Job 7:6 [f]Ps 23:4; Pr 14:32 [g]Job 27:5
13:16 [h]Isa 12:1
13:17 [i]Job 21:2
13:18 [j]Job 23:4
13:19 [k]Job 40:4; Isa 50:8 [l]Job 10:8
13:21 [m]Ps 39:10
13:22 [n]Job 14:15 [o]Job 9:16
13:23 [p]1Sa 26:18
13:24 [q]Dt 32:20; Ps 13:1; Isa 8:17 [r]Job 19:11; La 2:5
13:25 [s]Lev 26:36 [t]Job 21:18; Isa 42:3
13:26 [u]Ps 25:7
13:27 [v]Job 33:11

28 "So man wastes away like something rotten,
like a garment eaten by moths.[a]

Chapter 14 Theme ______________________

14

"Man born of woman
is of few days and full of trouble.[b]
2 He springs up like a flower[c] and withers away;[d]
like a fleeting shadow,[e] he does not endure.
3 Do you fix your eye on such a one?[f]
Will you bring him[a] before you for judgment?[g]
4 Who can bring what is pure[h] from the impure?[i]
No one![j]
5 Man's days are determined;
you have decreed the number of his months[k]
and have set limits he cannot exceed.
6 So look away from him and let him alone,[l]
till he has put in his time like a hired man.[m]

7 "At least there is hope for a tree:
If it is cut down, it will sprout again,
and its new shoots will not fail.
8 Its roots may grow old in the ground
and its stump die in the soil,
9 yet at the scent of water it will bud
and put forth shoots like a plant.
10 But man dies and is laid low;
he breathes his last and is no more.[n]
11 As water disappears from the sea
or a riverbed becomes parched and dry,[o]
12 so man lies down and does not rise;
till the heavens are no more,[p] men will not awake
or be roused from their sleep.[q]

13 "If only you would hide me in the grave[b]
and conceal me till your anger has passed![r]
If only you would set me a time
and then remember me!
14 If a man dies, will he live again?
All the days of my hard service
I will wait for my renewal[c] to come.
15 You will call and I will answer you;[s]
you will long for the creature your hands have made.
16 Surely then you will count my steps[t]
but not keep track of my sin.[u]

13:28 [a]Isa 50:9; Jas 5:2
14:1 [b]Job 5:7; Ecc 2:23
14:2 [c]Jas 1:10 [d]Ps 90:5-6 [e]Job 8:9
14:3 [f]Ps 8:4; 144:3 [g]Ps 143:2
14:4 [h]Ps 51:10 [i]Eph 2:1-3 [j]Jn 3:6; Ro 5:12
14:5 [k]Job 21:21
14:6 [l]Job 7:19 [m]Job 7:1,2; Ps 39:13
14:10 [n]Job 13:19
14:11 [o]Isa 19:5
14:12 [p]Rev 20:11; 21:1 [q]Ac 3:21
14:13 [r]Isa 26:20
14:15 [s]Job 13:22
14:16 [t]Ps 139:1-3; Pr 5:21; Jer 32:19 [u]Job 10:6

[a] *3* Septuagint, Vulgate and Syriac; Hebrew *me* [b] *13* Hebrew *Sheol* [c] *14* Or *release*

17My offenses will be sealed up in a bag;[a]
you will cover over my sin.[b]

18"But as a mountain erodes and crumbles
and as a rock is moved from its place,
19as water wears away stones
and torrents wash away the soil,
so you destroy man's hope.[c]
20You overpower him once for all, and he is gone;
you change his countenance and send him away.
21If his sons are honored, he does not know it;
if they are brought low, he does not see it.[d]
22He feels but the pain of his own body
and mourns only for himself."

Chapter 15 Theme ______________________

15 Then Eliphaz the Temanite replied:

2"Would a wise man answer with empty notions
or fill his belly with the hot east wind?[e]
3Would he argue with useless words,
with speeches that have no value?
4But you even undermine piety
and hinder devotion to God.
5Your sin prompts your mouth;
you adopt the tongue of the crafty.[f]
6Your own mouth condemns you, not mine;
your own lips testify against you.[g]

7"Are you the first man ever born?[h]
Were you brought forth before the hills?[i]
8Do you listen in on God's council?[j]
Do you limit wisdom to yourself?
9What do you know that we do not know?
What insights do you have that we do not have?[k]
10The gray-haired and the aged[l] are on our side,
men even older than your father.
11Are God's consolations[m] not enough for you,
words[n] spoken gently to you?[o]
12Why has your heart[p] carried you away,
and why do your eyes flash,
13so that you vent your rage against God
and pour out such words from your mouth?

14"What is man, that he could be pure,
or one born of woman,[q] that he could be righteous?[r]

14:17 [a]Dt 32:34 [b]Hos 13:12
14:19 [c]Job 7:6
14:21 [d]Ecc 9:5; Isa 63:16
15:2 [e]Job 6:26
15:5 [f]Job 5:13
15:6 [g]Lk 19:22
15:7 [h]Job 38:21 [i]Ps 90:2; Pr 8:25
15:8 [j]Ro 11:34; 1Co 2:11
15:9 [k]Job 13:2
15:10 [l]Job 32:6-7
15:11 [m]2Co 1:3-4 [n]Zec 1:13 [o]Job 36:16
15:12 [p]Job 11:13
15:14 [q]Job 14:4; 25:4 [r]Pr 20:9; Ecc 7:20

15 If God places no trust in his holy ones,
if even the heavens are not pure in his eyes,[a]
16 how much less man, who is vile and corrupt,[b]
who drinks up evil like water![c]

17 "Listen to me and I will explain to you;
let me tell you what I have seen,
18 what wise men have declared,
hiding nothing received from their fathers[d]
19 (to whom alone the land was given
when no alien passed among them):
20 All his days the wicked man suffers torment,
the ruthless through all the years stored up for him.[e]
21 Terrifying sounds fill his ears;[f]
when all seems well, marauders attack him.[g]
22 He despairs of escaping the darkness;
he is marked for the sword.[h]
23 He wanders about[i]—food for vultures[a];
he knows the day of darkness is at hand.[j]
24 Distress and anguish fill him with terror;
they overwhelm him, like a king poised to attack,
25 because he shakes his fist at God
and vaunts himself against the Almighty,[k]
26 defiantly charging against him
with a thick, strong shield.

27 "Though his face is covered with fat
and his waist bulges with flesh,[l]
28 he will inhabit ruined towns
and houses where no one lives,[m]
houses crumbling to rubble.[n]
29 He will no longer be rich and his wealth will
not endure,[o]
nor will his possessions spread over the land.
30 He will not escape the darkness;[p]
a flame[q] will wither his shoots,
and the breath of God's mouth[r] will carry him away.
31 Let him not deceive himself by trusting what
is worthless,[s]
for he will get nothing in return.
32 Before his time[t] he will be paid in full,[u]
and his branches will not flourish.[v]
33 He will be like a vine stripped of its unripe grapes,[w]
like an olive tree shedding its blossoms.

15:15 [a] Job 4:18; 25:5
15:16 [b] Ps 14:1 [c] Job 34:7; Pr 19:28
15:18 [d] Job 8:8
15:20 [e] Job 24:1; 27:13-23
15:21 [f] Job 18:11; 20:25 [g] Job 27:20; 1Th 5:3
15:22 [h] Job 19:29; 27:14
15:23 [i] Ps 59:15; 109:10 [j] Job 18:12
15:25 [k] Job 36:9
15:27 [l] Ps 17:10
15:28 [m] Isa 5:9 [n] Job 3:14
15:29 [o] Job 27:16-17
15:30 [p] Job 5:14 [q] Job 22:20 [r] Job 4:9
15:31 [s] Isa 59:4
15:32 [t] Ecc 7:17 [u] Job 22:16; Ps 55:23 [v] Job 18:16
15:33 [w] Hab 3:17

a 23 Or *about, looking for food*

34For the company of the godless will be barren,
and fire will consume the tents of those who
love bribes.[a]
35They conceive trouble and give birth to evil;[b]
their womb fashions deceit."

Chapter 16 Theme ______________________

16 Then Job replied:
2"I have heard many things like these;
miserable comforters are you all![c]
3Will your long-winded speeches never end?
What ails you that you keep on arguing?[d]
4I also could speak like you,
if you were in my place;
I could make fine speeches against you
and shake my head[e] at you.
5But my mouth would encourage you;
comfort from my lips would bring you relief.

6"Yet if I speak, my pain is not relieved;
and if I refrain, it does not go away.
7Surely, O God, you have worn me out;[f]
you have devastated my entire household.
8You have bound me—and it has become a witness;
my gauntness[g] rises up and testifies against me.[h]
9God assails me and tears[i] me in his anger
and gnashes his teeth at me;[j]
my opponent fastens on me his piercing eyes.[k]
10Men open their mouths[l] to jeer at me;
they strike my cheek[m] in scorn
and unite together against me.[n]
11God has turned me over to evil men
and thrown me into the clutches of the wicked.[o]
12All was well with me, but he shattered me;
he seized me by the neck and crushed me.[p]
He has made me his target;[q]
13 his archers surround me.
Without pity, he pierces[r] my kidneys
and spills my gall on the ground.
14Again and again[s] he bursts upon me;
he rushes at me like a warrior.[t]

15"I have sewed sackcloth[u] over my skin
and buried my brow in the dust.
16My face is red with weeping,
deep shadows ring my eyes;

15:34 [a]Job 8:22
15:35 [b]Ps 7:14; Isa 59:4; Hos 10:13
16:2 [c]Job 13:4
16:3 [d]Job 6:26
16:4 [e]Ps 22:7; 109:25; La 2:15; Zep 2:15; Mt 27:39
16:7 [f]Job 7:3
16:8 [g]Job 19:20 [h]Job 10:17
16:9 [i]Hos 6:1 [j]Ps 35:16; La 2:16; Ac 7:54 [k]Job 13:24
16:10 [l]Ps 22:13 [m]Isa 50:6; La 3:30; Mic 5:1; Ac 23:2 [n]Ps 35:15
16:11 [o]Job 1:15,17
16:12 [p]Job 9:17 [q]La 3:12
16:13 [r]Job 20:24
16:14 [s]Job 9:17 [t]Joel 2:7
16:15 [u]Ge 37:34

17 yet my hands have been free of violence[a]
and my prayer is pure.

18 "O earth, do not cover my blood;[b]
may my cry never be laid to rest![c]
19 Even now my witness[d] is in heaven;
my advocate is on high.
20 My intercessor is my friend[a]
as my eyes pour out[e] tears to God;
21 on behalf of a man he pleads[f] with God
as a man pleads for his friend.

22 "Only a few years will pass
before I go on the journey of no return.[g]

Chapter 17 Theme

17 My spirit is broken,
my days are cut short,
the grave awaits me.[h]
2 Surely mockers[i] surround me;
my eyes must dwell on their hostility.

3 "Give me, O God, the pledge you demand.[j]
Who else will put up security[k] for me?[l]
4 You have closed their minds to understanding;
therefore you will not let them triumph.
5 If a man denounces his friends for reward,
the eyes of his children will fail.[m]

6 "God has made me a byword[n] to everyone,
a man in whose face people spit.
7 My eyes have grown dim with grief;[o]
my whole frame is but a shadow.
8 Upright men are appalled at this;
the innocent are aroused[p] against the ungodly.
9 Nevertheless, the righteous[q] will hold to their ways,
and those with clean hands[r] will grow stronger.

10 "But come on, all of you, try again!
I will not find a wise man among you.[s]
11 My days have passed, my plans are shattered,
and so are the desires of my heart.[t]
12 These men turn night into day;
in the face of darkness they say, 'Light is near.'
13 If the only home I hope for is the grave,[b][u]
if I spread out my bed in darkness,

16:17 [a]Isa 59:6; Jnh 3:8
16:18 [b]Isa 26:21 [c]Ps 66:18-19
16:19 [d]Ge 31:50; Ro 1:9; 1Th 2:5
16:20 [e]La 2:19
16:21 [f]Ps 9:4
16:22 [g]Ecc 12:5
17:1 [h]Ps 88:3-4
17:2 [i]1Sa 1:6-7
17:3 [j]Ps 119:122 [k]Pr 6:1 [l]Isa 38:14
17:5 [m]Job 11:20
17:6 [n]Job 30:9
17:7 [o]Job 16:8
17:8 [p]Job 22:19
17:9 [q]Pr 4:18 [r]Job 22:30
17:10 [s]Job 12:2
17:11 [t]Job 7:6
17:13 [u]Job 3:13

a 20 Or *My friends treat me with scorn* b 13 Hebrew *Sheol*

[14]if I say to corruption,[a] 'You are my father,'
and to the worm,[b] 'My mother' or 'My sister,'
[15]where then is my hope?[c]
Who can see any hope for me?
[16]Will it go down to the gates of death[a]?[d]
Will we descend together into the dust?"

Chapter 18 Theme ______________________________

18

Then Bildad the Shuhite replied:

[2]"When will you end these speeches?
Be sensible, and then we can talk.
[3]Why are we regarded as cattle
and considered stupid in your sight?[e]
[4]You who tear yourself[f] to pieces in your anger,
is the earth to be abandoned for your sake?
Or must the rocks be moved from their place?

[5]"The lamp of the wicked is snuffed out;[g]
the flame of his fire stops burning.
[6]The light in his tent becomes dark;
the lamp beside him goes out.
[7]The vigor of his step is weakened;[h]
his own schemes[i] throw him down.[j]
[8]His feet thrust him into a net[k]
and he wanders into its mesh.
[9]A trap seizes him by the heel;
a snare holds him fast.
[10]A noose is hidden for him on the ground;
a trap lies in his path.
[11]Terrors startle him on every side[l]
and dog[m] his every step.
[12]Calamity is hungry[n] for him;
disaster is ready for him when he falls.
[13]It eats away parts of his skin;
death's firstborn devours his limbs.[o]
[14]He is torn from the security of his tent[p]
and marched off to the king of terrors.
[15]Fire resides[b] in his tent;
burning sulfur[q] is scattered over his dwelling.
[16]His roots dry up below[r]
and his branches wither above.[s]
[17]The memory of him perishes from the earth;
he has no name in the land.[t]

[a]16 Hebrew *Sheol* [b]15 Or *Nothing he had remains*

17:14 [a]Job 13:28; 30:28,30; Ps 16:10 [b]Job 21:26
17:15 [c]Job 7:6
17:16 [d]Job 3:17-19; Jnh 2:6
18:3 [e]Ps 73:22
18:4 [f]Job 13:14
18:5 [g]Job 21:17; Pr 13:9; 20:20; 24:20
18:7 [h]Pr 4:12 [i]Job 5:13 [j]Job 15:6
18:8 [k]Job 22:10; Ps 9:15; 35:7
18:11 [l]Job 15:21; Jer 6:25; 20:3 [m]Job 20:8
18:12 [n]Isa 8:21
18:13 [o]Zec 14:12
18:14 [p]Job 8:22
18:15 [q]Ps 11:6
18:16 [r]Isa 5:24; Hos 9:1-16; Am 2:9 [s]Job 15:30; Mal 4:1
18:17 [t]Ps 34:16; Pr 2:22; 10:7

18 He is driven from light into darkness[a]
and is banished from the world.
19 He has no offspring[b] or descendants[c] among his people,
no survivor where once he lived.[d]
20 Men of the west are appalled at his fate;[e]
men of the east are seized with horror.
21 Surely such is the dwelling[f] of an evil man;
such is the place of one who knows not God."[g]

Chapter 19 Theme ______________________________

19

Then Job replied:

2 "How long will you torment me
and crush me with words?
3 Ten times now you have reproached me;
shamelessly you attack me.
4 If it is true that I have gone astray,
my error[h] remains my concern alone.
5 If indeed you would exalt yourselves above me[i]
and use my humiliation against me,
6 then know that God has wronged me[j]
and drawn his net[k] around me.

7 "Though I cry, 'I've been wronged!' I get no response;[l]
though I call for help, there is no justice.[m]
8 He has blocked my way so I cannot pass;[n]
he has shrouded my paths in darkness.[o]
9 He has stripped[p] me of my honor
and removed the crown from my head.[q]
10 He tears me down[r] on every side till I am gone;
he uproots my hope[s] like a tree.[t]
11 His anger[u] burns against me;
he counts me among his enemies.[v]
12 His troops advance in force;[w]
they build a siege ramp[x] against me
and encamp around my tent.

13 "He has alienated my brothers[y] from me;
my acquaintances are completely estranged from me.[z]
14 My kinsmen have gone away;
my friends have forgotten me.
15 My guests and my maidservants count me a stranger;
they look upon me as an alien.
16 I summon my servant, but he does not answer,
though I beg him with my own mouth.
17 My breath is offensive to my wife;
I am loathsome to my own brothers.

18:18 [a] Job 5:14
18:19 [b] Jer 22:30 [c] Isa 14:22 [d] Job 27:14-15
18:20 [e] Ps 37:13; Jer 50:27,31
18:21 [f] Job 21:28 [g] Jer 9:3; 1Th 4:5
19:4 [h] Job 6:24
19:5 [i] Ps 35:26; 38:16; 55:12
19:6 [j] Job 27:2 [k] Job 18:8
19:7 [l] Job 30:20 [m] Job 9:24; Hab 1:2-4
19:8 [n] Job 3:23; La 3:7 [o] Job 30:26
19:9 [p] Job 12:17 [q] Ps 89:39,44; La 5:16
19:10 [r] Job 12:14 [s] Job 7:6 [t] Job 24:20
19:11 [u] Job 16:9 [v] Job 13:24
19:12 [w] Job 16:13 [x] Job 30:12
19:13 [y] Ps 69:8 [z] Job 16:7; Ps 88:8

18Even the little boys[a] scorn me;
when I appear, they ridicule me.
19All my intimate friends[b] detest me;[c]
those I love have turned against me.
20I am nothing but skin and bones;[d]
I have escaped with only the skin of my teeth.[a]

21"Have pity on me, my friends, have pity,
for the hand of God has struck me.
22Why do you pursue[e] me as God does?
Will you never get enough of my flesh?[f]

23"Oh, that my words were recorded,
that they were written on a scroll,[g]
24that they were inscribed with an iron tool on[b] lead,
or engraved in rock forever!
25I know that my Redeemer[c][h] lives,[i]
and that in the end he will stand upon the earth.[d]
26And after my skin has been destroyed,
yet[e] in[f] my flesh I will see God;[j]
27I myself will see him
with my own eyes—I, and not another.
How my heart yearns[k] within me!
28"If you say, 'How we will hound him,
since the root of the trouble lies in him,[g]'
29you should fear the sword yourselves;
for wrath will bring punishment by the sword,[l]
and then you will know that there is judgment.[h]"[m]

Chapter 20 Theme ______________________

20

Then Zophar the Naamathite replied:

2"My troubled thoughts prompt me to answer
because I am greatly disturbed.
3I hear a rebuke[n] that dishonors me,
and my understanding inspires me to reply.

4"Surely you know how it has been from of old,
ever since man[i] was placed on the earth,
5that the mirth of the wicked is brief,
the joy of the godless lasts but a moment.[o]
6Though his pride reaches to the heavens
and his head touches the clouds,[p]

[a] 20 Or *only my gums* [b] 24 Or *and* [c] 25 Or *defender* [d] 25 Or *upon my grave* [e] 26 Or *And after I awake, / though this ⌊body⌋ has been destroyed, / then* [f] 26 Or */ apart from* [g] 28 Many Hebrew manuscripts, Septuagint and Vulgate; most Hebrew manuscripts *me* [h] 29 Or */ that you may come to know the Almighty* [i] 4 Or *Adam*

19:18 [a] 2Ki 2:23
19:19 [b] Ps 55:12-13 [c] Ps 38:11
19:20 [d] Job 33:21; Ps 102:5
19:22 [e] Job 13:25; 16:11 [f] Ps 69:26
19:23 [g] Isa 30:8
19:25 [h] Ps 78:35; Pr 23:11; Isa 43:14; Jer 50:34 [i] Job 16:19
19:26 [j] Ps 17:15; Mt 5:8; 1Co 13:12; 1Jn 3:2
19:27 [k] Ps 73:26
19:29 [l] Job 15:22 [m] Job 22:4; Ps 1:5; 9:7
20:3 [n] Job 19:3
20:5 [o] Job 8:12; Ps 37:35-36; 73:19
20:6 [p] Isa 14:13-14; Ob 3-4

7 he will perish forever,[a] like his own dung;
those who have seen him will say, 'Where is he?'[b]
8 Like a dream[c] he flies away,[d] no more to be found,
banished[e] like a vision of the night.[f]
9 The eye that saw him will not see him again;
his place will look on him no more.[g]
10 His children[h] must make amends to the poor;
his own hands must give back his wealth.[i]
11 The youthful vigor[j] that fills his bones
will lie with him in the dust.[k]

12 "Though evil is sweet in his mouth
and he hides it under his tongue,
13 though he cannot bear to let it go
and keeps it in his mouth,[l]
14 yet his food will turn sour in his stomach;
it will become the venom of serpents within him.
15 He will spit out the riches he swallowed;
God will make his stomach vomit them up.
16 He will suck the poison[m] of serpents;
the fangs of an adder will kill him.[n]
17 He will not enjoy the streams,
the rivers flowing with honey[o] and cream.[p]
18 What he toiled for he must give back uneaten;
he will not enjoy the profit from his trading.
19 For he has oppressed the poor and left them destitute;[q]
he has seized houses he did not build.

20 "Surely he will have no respite from his craving;[r]
he cannot save himself by his treasure.
21 Nothing is left for him to devour;
his prosperity will not endure.[s]
22 In the midst of his plenty, distress will overtake him;
the full force of misery will come upon him.
23 When he has filled his belly,
God will vent his burning anger against him
and rain down his blows upon him.[t]
24 Though he flees[u] from an iron weapon,
a bronze-tipped arrow pierces him.
25 He pulls it out of his back,
the gleaming point out of his liver.
Terrors[v] will come over him;[w]
26 total darkness[x] lies in wait for his treasures.
A fire unfanned will consume him[y]
and devour what is left in his tent.

20:7 [a] Job 4:20 [b] Job 7:10; 8:18
20:8 [c] Ps 73:20 [d] Job 27:21-23 [e] Job 18:18 [f] Ps 90:5
20:9 [g] Job 7:8
20:10 [h] Job 5:4 [i] Job 27:16-17
20:11 [j] Job 13:26 [k] Job 21:26
20:13 [l] Nu 11:18-20
20:16 [m] Dt 32:32 [n] Dt 32:24
20:17 [o] Dt 32:13 [p] Job 29:6
20:19 [q] Job 24:4,14; 35:9
20:20 [r] Ecc 5:12-14
20:21 [s] Job 15:29
20:23 [t] Ps 78:30-31
20:24 [u] Isa 24:18; Am 5:19
20:25 [v] Job 18:11 [w] Job 16:13
20:26 [x] Job 18:18 [y] Ps 21:9

27The heavens will expose his guilt;
the earth will rise up against him.[a]
28A flood will carry off his house,[b]
rushing waters[a] on the day of God's wrath.[c]
29Such is the fate God allots the wicked,
the heritage appointed for them by God."[d]

Chapter 21 Theme ______________________________

21 Then Job replied:

2"Listen carefully to my words;
let this be the consolation you give me.
3Bear with me while I speak,
and after I have spoken, mock on.[e]

4"Is my complaint directed to man?
Why should I not be impatient?[f]
5Look at me and be astonished;
clap your hand over your mouth.[g]
6When I think about this, I am terrified;
trembling seizes my body.
7Why do the wicked live on,
growing old and increasing in power?[h]
8They see their children established around them,
their offspring before their eyes.[i]
9Their homes are safe and free from fear;[j]
the rod of God is not upon them.
10Their bulls never fail to breed;
their cows calve and do not miscarry.[k]
11They send forth their children as a flock;
their little ones dance about.
12They sing to the music of tambourine and harp;
they make merry to the sound of the flute.[l]
13They spend their years in prosperity[m]
and go down to the grave[b] in peace.[c]
14Yet they say to God, 'Leave us alone![n]
We have no desire to know your ways.[o]
15Who is the Almighty, that we should serve him?
What would we gain by praying to him?'[p]
16But their prosperity is not in their own hands,
so I stand aloof from the counsel of the wicked.

17"Yet how often is the lamp of the wicked snuffed out?[q]
How often does calamity come upon them,
the fate God allots in his anger?

a 28 Or *The possessions in his house will be carried off, / washed away* b 13 Hebrew *Sheol*
c 13 Or *in an instant*

20:27 *a* Dt 31:28
20:28 *b* Dt 28:31 *c* Job 21:17, 20,30
20:29 *d* Job 27:13
21:3 *e* Job 16:10
21:4 *f* Job 6:11
21:5 *g* Jdg 18:19; Job 29:9; 40:4
21:7 *h* Job 12:6; Ps 73:3; Jer 12:1; Hab 1:13
21:8 *i* Ps 17:14
21:9 *j* Ps 73:5
21:10 *k* Ex 23:26
21:12 *l* Ps 81:2
21:13 *m* Job 36:11
21:14 *n* Job 22:17 *o* Pr 1:29
21:15 *p* Ex 5:2; Job 34:9; Mal 3:14
21:17 *q* Job 18:5

18How often are they like straw before the wind,
like chaff[a] swept away by a gale?
19⌊It is said,⌋ 'God stores up a man's punishment for his sons.'[b]
Let him repay the man himself, so that he will know it!
20Let his own eyes see his destruction;
let him drink[c] of the wrath of the Almighty.[a][d]
21For what does he care about the family he leaves behind
when his allotted months[e] come to an end?

22"Can anyone teach knowledge to God,[f]
since he judges even the highest?[g]
23One man dies in full vigor,
completely secure and at ease,
24his body[b] well nourished,
his bones rich with marrow.[h]
25Another man dies in bitterness of soul,
never having enjoyed anything good.
26Side by side they lie in the dust,
and worms cover them both.[i]

27"I know full well what you are thinking,
the schemes by which you would wrong me.
28You say, 'Where now is the great man's[j] house,
the tents where wicked men lived?'[k]
29Have you never questioned those who travel?
Have you paid no regard to their accounts—
30that the evil man is spared from the day of calamity,[l]
that he is delivered from[c] the day of wrath?[m]
31Who denounces his conduct to his face?
Who repays him for what he has done?
32He is carried to the grave,
and watch is kept over his tomb.
33The soil in the valley is sweet to him;[n]
all men follow after him,
and a countless throng goes[d] before him.[o]
34"So how can you console me[p] with your nonsense?
Nothing is left of your answers but falsehood!"

Chapter 22 Theme ______________________

22

Then Eliphaz the Temanite replied:

2"Can a man be of benefit to God?[q]
Can even a wise man benefit him?

21:18 [a]Job 13:25; Ps 1:4
21:19 [b]Ex 20:5; Jer 31:29; Eze 18:2
21:20 [c]Ps 75:8; Isa 51:17 [d]Jer 25:15; Rev 14:10
21:21 [e]Job 14:5
21:22 [f]Job 35:11; 36:22; Isa 40:13-14; Ro 11:34 [g]Ps 82:1
21:24 [h]Pr 3:8
21:26 [i]Job 24:20; Ecc 9:2-3; Isa 14:11
21:28 [j]Job 1:3; 12:21; 31:37 [k]Job 8:22
21:30 [l]Pr 16:4 [m]Job 20:22,28; 2Pe 2:9
21:33 [n]Job 3:22; 17:16; 24:24 [o]Job 3:19
21:34 [p]Job 16:2
22:2 [q]Lk 17:10

[a] *17-20* Verses 17 and 18 may be taken as exclamations and 19 and 20 as declarations.
[b] *24* The meaning of the Hebrew for this word is uncertain. [c] *30* Or *man is reserved for the day of calamity, / that he is brought forth to* [d] *33* Or / *as a countless throng went*

3What pleasure would it give the Almighty if you
were righteous?
What would he gain if your ways were blameless?

4"Is it for your piety that he rebukes you
and brings charges against you?[a]
5Is not your wickedness great?
Are not your sins[b] endless?
6You demanded security[c] from your brothers for
no reason;
you stripped men of their clothing, leaving
them naked.
7You gave no water to the weary
and you withheld food from the hungry,[d]
8though you were a powerful man, owning land—
an honored man,[e] living on it.
9And you sent widows away empty-handed[f]
and broke the strength of the fatherless.
10That is why snares are all around you,
why sudden peril terrifies you,
11why it is so dark[g] you cannot see,
and why a flood of water covers you.[h]

12"Is not God in the heights of heaven?[i]
And see how lofty are the highest stars!
13Yet you say, 'What does God know?[j]
Does he judge through such darkness?[k]
14Thick clouds[l] veil him, so he does not see us
as he goes about in the vaulted heavens.'
15Will you keep to the old path
that evil men have trod?
16They were carried off before their time,[m]
their foundations washed away by a flood.[n]
17They said to God, 'Leave us alone!
What can the Almighty do to us?'[o]
18Yet it was he who filled their houses with good things,[p]
so I stand aloof from the counsel of the wicked.[q]

19"The righteous see their ruin and rejoice;[r]
the innocent mock[s] them, saying,
20'Surely our foes are destroyed,
and fire[t] devours their wealth.'

21"Submit to God and be at peace with him;
in this way prosperity will come to you.[u]
22Accept instruction from his mouth
and lay up his words in your heart.

22:4 [a]Job 14:3; 19:29; Ps 143:2
22:5 [b]Job 11:6; 15:5
22:6 [c]Ex 22:26; Dt 24:6,17; Eze 18:12,16
22:7 [d]Job 31:17, 21,31
22:8 [e]Isa 3:3; 9:15
22:9 [f]Job 24:3,21
22:11 [g]Job 5:14 [h]Ps 69:1-2; 124:4-5; La 3:54
22:12 [i]Job 11:8
22:13 [j]Ps 10:11; Isa 29:15 [k]Eze 8:12
22:14 [l]Job 26:9
22:16 [m]Job 15:32 [n]Job 14:19; Mt 7:26-27
22:17 [o]Job 21:15
22:18 [p]Job 12:6 [q]Job 21:16
22:19 [r]Ps 58:10; 107:42 [s]Ps 52:6
22:20 [t]Job 15:30
22:21 [u]Ps 34:8-10

23 If you return[a] to the Almighty, you will be restored:[b]
If you remove wickedness far from your tent[c]
24 and assign your nuggets to the dust,
your gold of Ophir to the rocks in the ravines,[d]
25 then the Almighty will be your gold,
the choicest silver for you.[e]
26 Surely then you will find delight in the Almighty[f]
and will lift up your face to God.
27 You will pray to him,[g] and he will hear you,
and you will fulfill your vows.
28 What you decide on will be done,
and light will shine on your ways.
29 When men are brought low and you say, 'Lift them up!'
then he will save the downcast.[h]
30 He will deliver even one who is not innocent,
who will be delivered through the cleanness of
your hands."[i]

Chapter 23 Theme ______________________

23

Then Job replied:

2 "Even today my complaint[j] is bitter;[k]
his hand[a] is heavy in spite of[b] my groaning.
3 If only I knew where to find him;
if only I could go to his dwelling!
4 I would state my case[l] before him
and fill my mouth with arguments.
5 I would find out what he would answer me,
and consider what he would say.
6 Would he oppose me with great power?[m]
No, he would not press charges against me.
7 There an upright man could present his case before him,[n]
and I would be delivered forever from my judge.

8 "But if I go to the east, he is not there;
if I go to the west, I do not find him.
9 When he is at work in the north, I do not see him;
when he turns to the south, I catch no glimpse of him.[o]
10 But he knows the way that I take;
when he has tested me,[p] I will come forth as gold.[q]
11 My feet have closely followed his steps;[r]
I have kept to his way without turning aside.[s]
12 I have not departed from the commands of his lips;[t]
I have treasured the words of his mouth more than my
daily bread.[u]

22:23 [a] Job 8:5; Isa 31:6; Zec 1:3 [b] Isa 19:22; Ac 20:32 [c] Job 11:14
22:24 [d] Job 31:25
22:25 [e] Isa 33:6
22:26 [f] Job 27:10; Isa 58:14
22:27 [g] Job 33:26; 34:28; Isa 58:9
22:29 [h] Mt 23:12; 1Pe 5:5
22:30 [i] Job 42:7-8
23:2 [j] Job 7:11 [k] Job 6:3
23:4 [l] Job 13:18
23:6 [m] Job 9:4
23:7 [n] Job 13:3
23:9 [o] Job 9:11
23:10 [p] Ps 66:10; 139:1-3 [q] 1Pe 1:7
23:11 [r] Ps 17:5 [s] Ps 44:18
23:12 [t] Job 6:10 [u] Jn 4:32,34

[a] 2 Septuagint and Syriac; Hebrew / *the hand on me* [b] 2 Or *heavy on me in*

13"But he stands alone, and who can oppose him?
He does whatever he pleases.[a]
14He carries out his decree against me,
and many such plans he still has in store.[b]
15That is why I am terrified before him;
when I think of all this, I fear him.
16God has made my heart faint;[c]
the Almighty[d] has terrified me.
17Yet I am not silenced by the darkness,[e]
by the thick darkness that covers my face.

Chapter 24 Theme ____________________

24 "Why does the Almighty not set times for judgment?[f]
Why must those who know him look in vain for such days?[g]
2Men move boundary stones;[h]
they pasture flocks they have stolen.
3They drive away the orphan's donkey
and take the widow's ox in pledge.[i]
4They thrust the needy from the path
and force all the poor[j] of the land into hiding.[k]
5Like wild donkeys in the desert,
the poor go about their labor[l] of foraging food;
the wasteland provides food for their children.
6They gather fodder in the fields
and glean in the vineyards of the wicked.
7Lacking clothes, they spend the night naked;
they have nothing to cover themselves in the cold.[m]
8They are drenched by mountain rains
and hug[n] the rocks for lack of shelter.
9The fatherless[o] child is snatched from the breast;
the infant of the poor is seized for a debt.
10Lacking clothes, they go about naked;
they carry the sheaves, but still go hungry.
11They crush olives among the terraces[a];
they tread the winepresses, yet suffer thirst.
12The groans of the dying rise from the city,
and the souls of the wounded cry out for help.[p]
But God charges no one with wrongdoing.[q]

13"There are those who rebel against the light,[r]
who do not know its ways
or stay in its paths.[s]
14When daylight is gone, the murderer rises up

23:13 [a]Ps 115:3
23:14 [b]1Th 3:3
23:16 [c]Dt 20:3; Ps 22:14; Jer 51:46 [d]Job 27:2
23:17 [e]Job 19:8
24:1 [f]Jer 46:10 [g]Ac 1:7
24:2 [h]Dt 19:14; 27:17; Pr 23:10
24:3 [i]Dt 24:6,10, 12,17; Job 22:6
24:4 [j]Job 29:12; 30:25; Ps 41:1 [k]Pr 28:28
24:5 [l]Ps 104:23
24:7 [m]Ex 22:27; Job 22:6
24:8 [n]La 4:5
24:9 [o]Dt 24:17
24:12 [p]Eze 26:15 [q]Job 9:23
24:13 [r]Jn 3:19-20 [s]Isa 5:20

a *11* Or *olives between the millstones*; the meaning of the Hebrew for this word is uncertain.

and kills the poor and needy;
in the night he steals forth like a thief.[a]
15 The eye of the adulterer watches for dusk;[b]
he thinks, 'No eye will see me,'[c]
and he keeps his face concealed.
16 In the dark, men break into houses,[d]
but by day they shut themselves in;
they want nothing to do with the light.[e]
17 For all of them, deep darkness is their morning[a];
they make friends with the terrors of darkness.[b]

18 "Yet they are foam[f] on the surface of the water;[g]
their portion of the land is cursed,
so that no one goes to the vineyards.
19 As heat and drought snatch away the melted snow,[h]
so the grave[c] [i] snatches away those who have sinned.
20 The womb forgets them,
the worm feasts on them;
evil men are no longer remembered[j]
but are broken like a tree.[k]
21 They prey on the barren and childless woman,
and to the widow show no kindness.[l]
22 But God drags away the mighty by his power;
though they become established, they have no
assurance of life.[m]
23 He may let them rest in a feeling of security,[n]
but his eyes are on their ways.[o]
24 For a little while they are exalted, and then they
are gone;[p]
they are brought low and gathered up like all others;
they are cut off like heads of grain.[q]

25 "If this is not so, who can prove me false
and reduce my words to nothing?"[r]

Chapter 25 Theme

25

Then Bildad the Shuhite replied:

2 "Dominion and awe belong to God;[s]
he establishes order in the heights of heaven.
3 Can his forces be numbered?
Upon whom does his light not rise?[t]
4 How then can a man be righteous before God?
How can one born of woman be pure?[u]

24:14 [a]Ps 10:9
24:15 [b]Pr 7:8-9 [c]Ps 10:11
24:16 [d]Ex 22:2; Mt 6:19 [e]Jn 3:20
24:18 [f]Job 9:26 [g]Job 22:16
24:19 [h]Job 6:17 [i]Job 21:13
24:20 [j]Job 18:17; Pr 10:7 [k]Ps 31:12; Da 4:14
24:21 [l]Job 22:9
24:22 [m]Dt 28:66
24:23 [n]Job 12:6 [o]Job 11:11
24:24 [p]Job 14:21; Ps 37:10 [q]Isa 17:5
24:25 [r]Job 6:28; 27:4
25:2 [s]Job 9:4; Rev 1:6
25:3 [t]Jas 1:17
25:4 [u]Job 4:17; 14:4

a *17* Or *them, their morning is like the shadow of death* b *17* Or *of the shadow of death*
c *19* Hebrew *Sheol*

5If even the moon[a] is not bright
and the stars are not pure in his eyes,[b]
6how much less man, who is but a maggot—
a son of man,[c] who is only a worm!"[d]

Chapter 26 Theme ______________________

26

Then Job replied:

2"How you have helped the powerless![e]
How you have saved the arm that is feeble![f]
3What advice you have offered to one without wisdom!
And what great insight you have displayed!
4Who has helped you utter these words?
And whose spirit spoke from your mouth?

5"The dead are in deep anguish,[g]
those beneath the waters and all that live in them.
6Death[a][h] is naked before God;
Destruction[b] lies uncovered.[i]
7He spreads out the northern ⌊skies⌋[j] over empty space;
he suspends the earth over nothing.
8He wraps up the waters[k] in his clouds,[l]
yet the clouds do not burst under their weight.
9He covers the face of the full moon,
spreading his clouds[m] over it.
10He marks out the horizon on the face of the waters[n]
for a boundary between light and darkness.[o]
11The pillars of the heavens quake,
aghast at his rebuke.
12By his power he churned up the sea;[p]
by his wisdom[q] he cut Rahab to pieces.
13By his breath the skies became fair;
his hand pierced the gliding serpent.[r]
14And these are but the outer fringe of his works;
how faint the whisper we hear of him!
Who then can understand the thunder of his power?"[s]

Chapter 27 Theme ______________________

27

And Job continued his discourse:[t]

2"As surely as God lives, who has denied me justice,[u]
the Almighty, who has made me taste bitterness
of soul,[v]

a6 Hebrew *Sheol* b6 Hebrew *Abaddon*

25:5 [a]Job 31:26 [b]Job 15:15
25:6 [c]Job 7:17 [d]Ps 22:6
26:2 [e]Job 6:12 [f]Ps 71:9
26:5 [g]Ps 88:10
26:6 [h]Ps 139:8 [i]Job 41:11; Pr 15:11; Heb 4:13
26:7 [j]Job 9:8
26:8 [k]Pr 30:4 [l]Job 37:11
26:9 [m]Job 22:14; Ps 97:2
26:10 [n]Pr 8:27,29 [o]Job 38:8-11
26:12 [p]Ex 14:21; Isa 51:15; Jer 31:35 [q]Job 12:13
26:13 [r]Isa 27:1
26:14 [s]Job 36:29
27:1 [t]Job 29:1
27:2 [u]Job 34:5 [v]Job 9:18

3 as long as I have life within me,
  the breath of God[a] in my nostrils,
4 my lips will not speak wickedness,
  and my tongue will utter no deceit.[b]
5 I will never admit you are in the right;
  till I die, I will not deny my integrity.[c]
6 I will maintain my righteousness and never let go of it;
  my conscience will not reproach me as long as I live.[d]

7 "May my enemies be like the wicked,
  my adversaries like the unjust!
8 For what hope has the godless[e] when he is cut off,
  when God takes away his life?[f]
9 Does God listen to his cry
  when distress comes upon him?[g]
10 Will he find delight in the Almighty?[h]
  Will he call upon God at all times?

11 "I will teach you about the power of God;
  the ways of the Almighty I will not conceal.
12 You have all seen this yourselves.
  Why then this meaningless talk?

13 "Here is the fate God allots to the wicked,
  the heritage a ruthless man receives from
    the Almighty:[i]
14 However many his children, their fate is the sword;[j]
  his offspring will never have enough to eat.[k]
15 The plague will bury those who survive him,
  and their widows will not weep for them.[l]
16 Though he heaps up silver like dust
  and clothes like piles of clay,[m]
17 what he lays up the righteous will wear,[n]
  and the innocent will divide his silver.
18 The house he builds is like a moth's cocoon,[o]
  like a hut[p] made by a watchman.
19 He lies down wealthy, but will do so no more;[q]
  when he opens his eyes, all is gone.
20 Terrors overtake him like a flood;[r]
  a tempest snatches him away in the night.[s]
21 The east wind carries him off, and he is gone;
  it sweeps him out of his place.[t]
22 It hurls itself against him without mercy[u]
  as he flees headlong from its power.[v]
23 It claps its hands in derision
  and hisses him out of his place.[w]

27:3 [a]Job 32:8; 33:4
27:4 [b]Job 6:28
27:5 [c]Job 2:9; 13:15
27:6 [d]Job 2:3
27:8 [e]Job 8:13 [f]Job 11:20; Lk 12:20
27:9 [g]Job 35:12; Pr 1:28; Isa 1:15; Jer 14:12; Mic 3:4
27:10 [h]Job 22:26
27:13 [i]Job 15:20; 20:29
27:14 [j]Dt 28:41; Job 15:22; Hos 9:13 [k]Job 20:10
27:15 [l]Ps 78:64
27:16 [m]Zec 9:3
27:17 [n]Pr 28:8; Ecc 2:26
27:18 [o]Job 8:14 [p]Isa 1:8
27:19 [q]Job 7:8
27:20 [r]Job 15:21 [s]Job 20:8
27:21 [t]Job 7:10; 21:18
27:22 [u]Jer 13:14; Eze 5:11; 24:14 [v]Job 11:20
27:23 [w]Job 18:18

Chapter 28 Theme ____________________

28

"There is a mine for silver
and a place where gold is refined.
2 Iron is taken from the earth,
and copper is smelted from ore.[a]
3 Man puts an end to the darkness;[b]
he searches the farthest recesses
for ore in the blackest darkness.
4 Far from where people dwell he cuts a shaft,
in places forgotten by the foot of man;
far from men he dangles and sways.
5 The earth, from which food comes,[c]
is transformed below as by fire;
6 sapphires[a] come from its rocks,
and its dust contains nuggets of gold.
7 No bird of prey knows that hidden path,
no falcon's eye has seen it.
8 Proud beasts do not set foot on it,
and no lion prowls there.
9 Man's hand assaults the flinty rock
and lays bare the roots of the mountains.
10 He tunnels through the rock;
his eyes see all its treasures.
11 He searches[b] the sources of the rivers
and brings hidden things to light.

12 "But where can wisdom be found?[d]
Where does understanding dwell?
13 Man does not comprehend its worth;[e]
it cannot be found in the land of the living.
14 The deep says, 'It is not in me';
the sea says, 'It is not with me.'
15 It cannot be bought with the finest gold,
nor can its price be weighed in silver.[f]
16 It cannot be bought with the gold of Ophir,
with precious onyx or sapphires.
17 Neither gold nor crystal can compare with it,
nor can it be had for jewels of gold.[g]
18 Coral and jasper are not worthy of mention;
the price of wisdom is beyond rubies.[h]
19 The topaz of Cush cannot compare with it;
it cannot be bought with pure gold.[i]

20 "Where then does wisdom come from?
Where does understanding dwell?[j]

[a] 6 Or *lapis lazuli*; also in verse 16 [b] 11 Septuagint, Aquila and Vulgate; Hebrew *He dams up*

28:2 [a] Dt 8:9
28:3 [b] Ecc 1:13
28:5 [c] Ps 104:14
28:12 [d] Ecc 7:24
28:13 [e] Pr 3:15; Mt 13:44-46
28:15 [f] Pr 3:13-14; 8:10-11; 16:16
28:17 [g] Pr 16:16
28:18 [h] Pr 3:15
28:19 [i] Pr 8:19
28:20 [j] ver 23,28

21 It is hidden from the eyes of every living thing,
concealed even from the birds of the air.
22 Destruction[a] [a] and Death say,
'Only a rumor of it has reached our ears.'
23 God understands the way to it
and he alone knows where it dwells,[b]
24 for he views the ends of the earth[c]
and sees everything under the heavens.[d]
25 When he established the force of the wind
and measured out the waters,[e]
26 when he made a decree for the rain
and a path for the thunderstorm,[f]
27 then he looked at wisdom and appraised it;
he confirmed it and tested it.
28 And he said to man,
'The fear of the Lord—that is wisdom,
and to shun evil is understanding.[g]' "

Chapter 29 Theme ________________________

29 Job continued his discourse:[h]
2 "How I long for the months gone by,
for the days when God watched over me,[i]
3 when his lamp shone upon my head
and by his light I walked through darkness![j]
4 Oh, for the days when I was in my prime,
when God's intimate friendship blessed my house,[k]
5 when the Almighty was still with me
and my children were around me,
6 when my path was drenched with cream[l]
and the rock[m] poured out for me streams of olive oil.[n]

7 "When I went to the gate[o] of the city
and took my seat in the public square,
8 the young men saw me and stepped aside
and the old men rose to their feet;
9 the chief men refrained from speaking
and covered their mouths with their hands;[p]
10 the voices of the nobles were hushed,
and their tongues stuck to the roof of their mouths.[q]
11 Whoever heard me spoke well of me,
and those who saw me commended me,
12 because I rescued the poor[r] who cried for help,
and the fatherless[s] who had none to assist him.[t]

28:22 [a]Job 26:6
28:23 [b]Pr 8:22-31
28:24 [c]Ps 33:13-14 [d]Pr 15:3
28:25 [e]Job 12:15; Ps 135:7
28:26 [f]Job 37:3,8,11; 38:25,27
28:28 [g]Dt 4:6; Ps 111:10; Pr 1:7; 9:10
29:1 [h]Job 13:12; 27:1
29:2 [i]Jer 31:28
29:3 [j]Job 11:17
29:4 [k]Ps 25:14; Pr 3:32
29:6 [l]Job 20:17 [m]Ps 81:16 [n]Dt 32:13
29:7 [o]Job 31:21
29:9 [p]Job 21:5
29:10 [q]Ps 137:6
29:12 [r]Job 24:4 [s]Job 31:17,21 [t]Ps 72:12; Pr 21:13

a 22 Hebrew *Abaddon*

13The man who was dying blessed me;[a]
I made the widow's[b] heart sing.
14I put on righteousness[c] as my clothing;
justice was my robe and my turban.
15I was eyes[d] to the blind
and feet to the lame.
16I was a father to the needy;[e]
I took up the case of the stranger.
17I broke the fangs of the wicked
and snatched the victims from their teeth.[f]

18"I thought, 'I will die in my own house,
my days as numerous as the grains of sand.[g]
19My roots will reach to the water,[h]
and the dew will lie all night on my branches.
20My glory will remain fresh in me,
the bow[i] ever new in my hand.'[j]

21"Men listened to me expectantly,
waiting in silence for my counsel.
22After I had spoken, they spoke no more;
my words fell gently on their ears.[k]
23They waited for me as for showers
and drank in my words as the spring rain.
24When I smiled at them, they scarcely believed it;
the light of my face was precious to them.[a]
25I chose the way for them and sat as their chief;
I dwelt as a king[l] among his troops;
I was like one who comforts mourners.[m]

Chapter 30 Theme ______________________

30

"But now they mock me,[n]
men younger than I,
whose fathers I would have disdained
to put with my sheep dogs.
2Of what use was the strength of their hands to me,
since their vigor had gone from them?
3Haggard from want and hunger,
they roamed[b] the parched land
in desolate wastelands at night.
4In the brush they gathered salt herbs,
and their food[c] was the root of the broom tree.
5They were banished from their fellow men,
shouted at as if they were thieves.

a *24* The meaning of the Hebrew for this clause is uncertain. b *3* Or *gnawed* c *4* Or *fuel*

29:13 [a] Job 31:20 [b] Job 22:9

29:14 [c] Job 27:6; Ps 132:9; Isa 59:17; 61:10; Eph 6:14

29:15 [d] Nu 10:31

29:16 [e] Job 24:4; Pr 29:7

29:17 [f] Ps 3:7

29:18 [g] Ps 30:6

29:19 [h] Job 18:16; Jer 17:8

29:20 [i] Ps 18:34 [j] Ge 49:24

29:22 [k] Dt 32:2

29:25 [l] Job 1:3; 31:37 [m] Job 4:4

30:1 [n] Job 12:4

6 They were forced to live in the dry stream beds,
among the rocks and in holes in the ground.
7 They brayed among the bushes
and huddled in the undergrowth.
8 A base and nameless brood,
they were driven out of the land.

9 "And now their sons mock me[a] in song;[b]
I have become a byword[c] among them.
10 They detest me and keep their distance;
they do not hesitate to spit in my face.[d]
11 Now that God has unstrung my bow and afflicted me,[e]
they throw off restraint[f] in my presence.
12 On my right the tribe[a] attacks;
they lay snares for my feet,[g]
they build their siege ramps against me.[h]
13 They break up my road;[i]
they succeed in destroying me—
without anyone's helping them.[b]
14 They advance as through a gaping breach;
amid the ruins they come rolling in.
15 Terrors overwhelm me;[j]
my dignity is driven away as by the wind,
my safety vanishes like a cloud.[k]

16 "And now my life ebbs away;[l]
days of suffering grip me.
17 Night pierces my bones;
my gnawing pains never rest.
18 In his great power ⌊God⌋ becomes like clothing to me[c];
he binds me like the neck of my garment.
19 He throws me into the mud,[m]
and I am reduced to dust and ashes.

20 "I cry out to you, O God, but you do not answer;[n]
I stand up, but you merely look at me.
21 You turn on me ruthlessly;[o]
with the might of your hand[p] you attack me.[q]
22 You snatch me up and drive me before the wind;[r]
you toss me about in the storm.[s]
23 I know you will bring me down to death,[t]
to the place appointed for all the living.[u]

24 "Surely no one lays a hand on a broken man
when he cries for help in his distress.[v]

30:9 [a] Ps 69:11 [b] Job 12:4; La 3:14,63 [c] Job 17:6
30:10 [d] Nu 12:14; Dt 25:9; Isa 50:6; Mt 26:67
30:11 [e] Ru 1:21 [f] Ps 32:9
30:12 [g] Ps 140:4-5 [h] Job 19:12
30:13 [i] Isa 3:12
30:15 [j] Job 31:23; Ps 55:4-5 [k] Job 3:25; Hos 13:3
30:16 [l] Job 3:24; Ps 22:14; 42:4
30:19 [m] Ps 69:2,14
30:20 [n] Job 19:7
30:21 [o] Job 19:6,22 [p] Job 16:9,14 [q] Job 10:3
30:22 [r] Job 27:21 [s] Job 9:17
30:23 [t] Job 9:22; 10:8 [u] Job 3:19
30:24 [v] Job 19:7

a *12* The meaning of the Hebrew for this word is uncertain. b *13* Or *me. / 'No one can help him,' ⌊they say⌋.* c *18* Hebrew; Septuagint *⌊God⌋ grasps my clothing*

25Have I not wept for those in trouble?
Has not my soul grieved for the poor?[a]
26Yet when I hoped for good, evil came;
when I looked for light, then came darkness.[b]
27The churning inside me never stops;[c]
days of suffering confront me.
28I go about blackened,[d] but not by the sun;
I stand up in the assembly and cry for help.[e]
29I have become a brother of jackals,[f]
a companion of owls.[g]
30My skin grows black and peels;[h]
my body burns with fever.[i]
31My harp is tuned to mourning,[j]
and my flute to the sound of wailing.

Chapter 31 Theme ______________________

31

"I made a covenant with my eyes
not to look lustfully at a girl.[k]
2For what is man's lot from God above,
his heritage from the Almighty on high?[l]
3Is it not ruin[m] for the wicked,
disaster for those who do wrong?[n]
4Does he not see my ways[o]
and count my every step?[p]

5"If I have walked in falsehood
or my foot has hurried after deceit[q]—
6let God weigh me in honest scales[r]
and he will know that I am blameless—
7if my steps have turned from the path,[s]
if my heart has been led by my eyes,
or if my hands[t] have been defiled,
8then may others eat what I have sown,[u]
and may my crops be uprooted.[v]

9"If my heart has been enticed[w] by a woman,
or if I have lurked at my neighbor's door,
10then may my wife grind another man's grain,
and may other men sleep with her.[x]
11For that would have been shameful,
a sin to be judged.[y]
12It is a fire[z] that burns to Destruction[a];[a]
it would have uprooted my harvest.[b]

a 12 Hebrew *Abaddon*

30:25 [a]Job 24:4; Ps 35:13-14; Ro 12:15
30:26 [b]Job 3:25-26; 19:8; Jer 8:15
30:27 [c]La 2:11
30:28 [d]Ps 38:6; 42:9; 43:2 [e]Job 19:7
30:29 [f]Ps 44:19 [g]Ps 102:6; Mic 1:8
30:30 [h]La 4:8 [i]Ps 102:3
30:31 [j]Isa 24:8
31:1 [k]Mt 5:28
31:2 [l]Job 20:29
31:3 [m]Job 21:30 [n]Job 34:22
31:4 [o]2Ch 16:9 [p]Pr 5:21
31:5 [q]Mic 2:11
31:6 [r]Job 6:2; 27:5-6
31:7 [s]Job 23:11 [t]Job 9:30
31:8 [u]Lev 26:16; Job 20:18 [v]Mic 6:15
31:9 [w]Job 24:15
31:10 [x]Dt 28:30; Jer 8:10
31:11 [y]Ge 38:24; Lev 20:10; Dt 22:22-24
31:12 [z]Job 15:30 [a]Job 26:6 [b]Job 20:28

13 “If I have denied justice to my menservants
and maidservants
when they had a grievance against me,[a]
14 what will I do when God confronts me?
What will I answer when called to account?
15 Did not he who made me in the womb make them?
Did not the same one form us both within
our mothers?[b]

16 “If I have denied the desires of the poor[c]
or let the eyes of the widow[d] grow weary,
17 if I have kept my bread to myself,
not sharing it with the fatherless[e]—
18 but from my youth I reared him as would a father,
and from my birth I guided the widow—
19 if I have seen anyone perishing for lack of clothing,[f]
or a needy[g] man without a garment,
20 and his heart did not bless me
for warming him with the fleece from my sheep,
21 if I have raised my hand against the fatherless,[h]
knowing that I had influence in court,
22 then let my arm fall from the shoulder,
let it be broken off at the joint.[i]
23 For I dreaded destruction from God,
and for fear of his splendor[j] I could not do
such things.

24 “If I have put my trust in gold[k]
or said to pure gold, ‘You are my security,’[l]
25 if I have rejoiced over my great wealth,[m]
the fortune my hands had gained,
26 if I have regarded the sun[n] in its radiance
or the moon moving in splendor,
27 so that my heart was secretly enticed
and my hand offered them a kiss of homage,
28 then these also would be sins to be judged,[o]
for I would have been unfaithful to God on high.

29 “If I have rejoiced at my enemy’s misfortune[p]
or gloated over the trouble that came to him[q]—
30 I have not allowed my mouth to sin
by invoking a curse against his life—
31 if the men of my household have never said,
‘Who has not had his fill of Job’s meat?’[r]—
32 but no stranger had to spend the night in the street,
for my door was always open to the traveler[s]—

31:13 [a]Dt 24:14-15
31:15 [b]Job 10:3
31:16 [c]Job 5:16; 20:19 [d]Job 22:9
31:17 [e]Job 22:7; 29:12
31:19 [f]Job 22:6 [g]Job 24:4
31:21 [h]Job 22:9
31:22 [i]Job 38:15
31:23 [j]Job 13:11
31:24 [k]Job 22:25 [l]Mt 6:24; Mk 10:24
31:25 [m]Ps 62:10
31:26 [n]Eze 8:16
31:28 [o]Dt 17:2-7
31:29 [p]Ob 12 [q]Pr 17:5; 24:17-18
31:31 [r]Job 22:7
31:32 [s]Ge 19:2-3; Ro 12:13

33 if I have concealed[a] my sin as men do,[a]
by hiding[b] my guilt in my heart
34 because I so feared the crowd[c]
and so dreaded the contempt of the clans
that I kept silent and would not go outside

35 ("Oh, that I had someone to hear me![d]
I sign now my defense—let the Almighty answer me;
let my accuser[e] put his indictment in writing.
36 Surely I would wear it on my shoulder,
I would put it on like a crown.
37 I would give him an account of my every step;
like a prince[f] I would approach him.)—

38 "if my land cries out against me[g]
and all its furrows are wet with tears,
39 if I have devoured its yield without payment[h]
or broken the spirit of its tenants,[i]
40 then let briers[j] come up instead of wheat
and weeds instead of barley."

The words of Job are ended.

Chapter 32 Theme ______________________________

32 So these three men stopped answering Job, because he
was righteous in his own eyes.[k] 2 But Elihu son of Barakel
the Buzite,[l] of the family of Ram, became very angry with Job for
justifying himself rather than God.[m] 3 He was also angry with the
three friends, because they had found no way to refute Job, and
yet had condemned him.[b] 4 Now Elihu had waited before speaking to Job because they were older than he. 5 But when he saw that
the three men had nothing more to say, his anger was aroused.
6 So Elihu son of Barakel the Buzite said:

"I am young in years,
and you are old;[n]
that is why I was fearful,
not daring to tell you what I know.
7 I thought, 'Age should speak;
advanced years should teach wisdom.'
8 But it is the spirit[c] in a man,
the breath of the Almighty,[o] that gives him
understanding.[p]
9 It is not only the old[d] who are wise,[q]
not only the aged who understand what is right.

[a] 33 Or *as Adam did* [b] 3 Masoretic Text; an ancient Hebrew scribal tradition *Job, and so had condemned God* [c] 8 Or *Spirit*; also in verse 18 [d] 9 Or *many*; or *great*

31:33 *a* Pr 28:13 *b* Ge 3:8
31:34 *c* Ex 23:2
31:35 *d* Job 19:7; 30:28 *e* Job 27:7; 35:14
31:37 *f* Job 1:3; 29:25
31:38 *g* Ge 4:10
31:39 *h* 1Ki 21:19 *i* Lev 19:13; Jas 5:4
31:40 *j* Ge 3:18
32:1 *k* Job 10:7; 33:9
32:2 *l* Ge 22:21 *m* Job 27:5; 30:21
32:6 *n* Job 15:10
32:8 *o* Job 27:3; 33:4 *p* Pr 2:6
32:9 *q* 1Co 1:26

32:13
[a]Jer 9:23

32:21
[b]Lev 19:15; Job 13:10
[c]Mt 22:16

33:1
[d]Job 13:6

33:3
[e]Job 6:28; 27:4; 36:4

33:4
[f]Ge 2:7; Job 10:3
[g]Job 27:3

33:5
[h]ver 32
[i]Job 13:18

33:6
[j]Job 4:19

33:7
[k]Job 9:34; 13:21; 2Co 2:4

10“Therefore I say: Listen to me;
I too will tell you what I know.
11I waited while you spoke,
I listened to your reasoning;
while you were searching for words,
12 I gave you my full attention.
But not one of you has proved Job wrong;
none of you has answered his arguments.
13Do not say, ‘We have found wisdom;[a]
let God refute him, not man.’
14But Job has not marshaled his words against me,
and I will not answer him with your arguments.

15“They are dismayed and have no more to say;
words have failed them.
16Must I wait, now that they are silent,
now that they stand there with no reply?
17I too will have my say;
I too will tell what I know.
18For I am full of words,
and the spirit within me compels me;
19inside I am like bottled-up wine,
like new wineskins ready to burst.
20I must speak and find relief;
I must open my lips and reply.
21I will show partiality[b] to no one,[c]
nor will I flatter any man;
22for if I were skilled in flattery,
my Maker would soon take me away.

Chapter 33 Theme ______________________________

33

“But now, Job, listen to my words;
pay attention to everything I say.[d]
2I am about to open my mouth;
my words are on the tip of my tongue.
3My words come from an upright heart;
my lips sincerely speak what I know.[e]
4The Spirit of God has made me;[f]
the breath of the Almighty[g] gives me life.
5Answer me[h] then, if you can;
prepare[i] yourself and confront me.
6I am just like you before God;
I too have been taken from clay.[j]
7No fear of me should alarm you,
nor should my hand be heavy upon you.[k]

8"But you have said in my hearing—
I heard the very words—
9'I am pure[a] and without sin;[b]
I am clean and free from guilt.
10Yet God has found fault with me;
he considers me his enemy.[c]
11He fastens my feet in shackles;[d]
he keeps close watch on all my paths.'[e]

12"But I tell you, in this you are not right,
for God is greater than man.[f]
13Why do you complain to him[g]
that he answers none of man's words[a]?
14For God does speak[h]—now one way, now another—
though man may not perceive it.
15In a dream,[i] in a vision of the night,
when deep sleep falls on men
as they slumber in their beds,
16he may speak[j] in their ears
and terrify them with warnings,
17to turn man from wrongdoing
and keep him from pride,
18to preserve his soul from the pit,[b][k]
his life from perishing by the sword.[c][l]
19Or a man may be chastened on a bed of pain
with constant distress in his bones,[m]
20so that his very being finds food[n] repulsive
and his soul loathes the choicest meal.[o]
21His flesh wastes away to nothing,
and his bones, once hidden, now stick out.[p]
22His soul draws near to the pit,[d]
and his life to the messengers of death.[e][q]

23"Yet if there is an angel on his side
as a mediator, one out of a thousand,
to tell a man what is right for him,[r]
24to be gracious to him and say,
'Spare him from going down to the pit[f];[s]
I have found a ransom for him'—
25then his flesh is renewed like a child's;
it is restored as in the days of his youth.[t]
26He prays to God and finds favor with him,[u]
he sees God's face and shouts for joy;[v]
he is restored by God to his righteous state.[w]

a 13 Or *that he does not answer for any of his actions* b 18 Or *preserve him from the grave*
c 18 Or *from crossing the River* d 22 Or *He draws near to the grave* e 22 Or *to the dead*
f 24 Or *grave*

33:9 [a]Job 10:7 [b]Job 13:23; 16:17
33:10 [c]Job 13:24
33:11 [d]Job 13:27 [e]Job 14:16
33:12 [f]Ecc 7:20
33:13 [g]Job 40:2; Isa 45:9
33:14 [h]Ps 62:11
33:15 [i]Job 4:13
33:16 [j]Job 36:10,15
33:18 [k]ver 22,24, 28,30 [l]Job 15:22
33:19 [m]Job 30:17
33:20 [n]Ps 107:18 [o]Job 3:24; 6:6
33:21 [p]Job 16:8; 19:20
33:22 [q]Ps 88:3
33:23 [r]Mic 6:8
33:24 [s]Isa 38:17
33:25 [t]2Ki 5:14
33:26 [u]Job 34:28 [v]Job 22:26 [w]Ps 50:15; 51:12

27Then he comes to men and says,
'I sinned,[a] and perverted what was right,[b]
but I did not get what I deserved.[c]
28He redeemed my soul from going down to the pit,[a]
and I will live to enjoy the light.'[d]

29"God does all these things to a man[e]—
twice, even three times—
30to turn back his soul from the pit,[b]
that the light of life[f] may shine on him.

31"Pay attention, Job, and listen to me;
be silent, and I will speak.
32If you have anything to say, answer me;
speak up, for I want you to be cleared.
33But if not, then listen to me;
be silent, and I will teach you wisdom.[g]"

Chapter 34 Theme

34 Then Elihu said:

2"Hear my words, you wise men;
listen to me, you men of learning.
3For the ear tests words
as the tongue tastes food.[h]
4Let us discern for ourselves what is right;
let us learn together what is good.[i]

5"Job says, 'I am innocent,[j]
but God denies me justice.[k]
6Although I am right,
I am considered a liar;
although I am guiltless,
his arrow inflicts an incurable wound.'[l]
7What man is like Job,
who drinks scorn like water?[m]
8He keeps company with evildoers;
he associates with wicked men.[n]
9For he says, 'It profits a man nothing
when he tries to please God.'[o]

10"So listen to me, you men of understanding.
Far be it from God to do evil,[p]
from the Almighty to do wrong.[q]
11He repays a man for what he has done;[r]
he brings upon him what his conduct deserves.[s]

33:27 [a]2Sa 12:13 [b]Lk 15:21 [c]Ro 6:21
33:28 [d]Job 22:28
33:29 [e]1Co 12:6; Eph 1:11; Php 2:13
33:30 [f]Ps 56:13
33:33 [g]Ps 34:11
34:3 [h]Job 12:11
34:4 [i]1Th 5:21
34:5 [j]Job 33:9 [k]Job 27:2
34:6 [l]Job 6:4
34:7 [m]Job 15:16
34:8 [n]Job 22:15; Ps 50:18
34:9 [o]Job 21:15; 35:3
34:10 [p]Ge 18:25 [q]Dt 32:4; Job 8:3; Ro 9:14
34:11 [r]Ps 62:12; Mt 16:27; Ro 2:6; 2 Co 5:10 [s]Jer 32:19; Eze 33:20

a 28 Or *redeemed me from going down to the grave* b 30 Or *turn him back from the grave*

[12]It is unthinkable that God would do wrong,
that the Almighty would pervert justice.[a]
[13]Who appointed him over the earth?
Who put him in charge of the whole world?[b]
[14]If it were his intention
and he withdrew his spirit[a] and breath,[c]
[15]all mankind would perish together
and man would return to the dust.[d]

[16]"If you have understanding, hear this;
listen to what I say.
[17]Can he who hates justice govern?[e]
Will you condemn the just and mighty One?[f]
[18]Is he not the One who says to kings, 'You are worthless,'
and to nobles, 'You are wicked,'[g]
[19]who shows no partiality[h] to princes
and does not favor the rich over the poor,[i]
for they are all the work of his hands?[j]
[20]They die in an instant, in the middle of the night;[k]
the people are shaken and they pass away;
the mighty are removed without human hand.[l]

[21]"His eyes are on the ways of men;
he sees their every step.[m]
[22]There is no dark place,[n] no deep shadow,[o]
where evildoers can hide.
[23]God has no need to examine men further,
that they should come before him for judgment.[p]
[24]Without inquiry he shatters the mighty[q]
and sets up others in their place.[r]
[25]Because he takes note of their deeds,
he overthrows them in the night and they are crushed.
[26]He punishes them for their wickedness
where everyone can see them,
[27]because they turned from following him[s]
and had no regard for any of his ways.[t]
[28]They caused the cry of the poor to come before him,
so that he heard the cry of the needy.[u]
[29]But if he remains silent, who can condemn him?
If he hides his face, who can see him?
Yet he is over man and nation alike,
[30] to keep a godless man from ruling,
from laying snares for the people.[v]

[31]"Suppose a man says to God,
'I am guilty but will offend no more.

a 14 Or *Spirit*

34:12 [a]Job 8:3
34:13 [b]Job 38:4,6
34:14 [c]Ps 104:29
34:15 [d]Ge 3:19; Job 9:22
34:17 [e]2Sa 23:3-4 [f]Job 40:8
34:18 [g]Ex 22:28
34:19 [h]Dt 10:17; Ac 10:34 [i]Lev 19:15 [j]Job 10:3
34:20 [k]Ex 12:29 [l]Job 12:19
34:21 [m]Job 31:4; Pr 15:3
34:22 [n]Ps 139:12 [o]Am 9:2-3
34:23 [p]Job 11:11
34:24 [q]Job 12:19 [r]Da 2:21
34:27 [s]Ps 28:5; Isa 5:12 [t]1Sa 15:11
34:28 [u]Ex 22:23; Job 35:9; Jas 5:4
34:30 [v]Pr 29:2-12

32 Teach me what I cannot see;[a]
if I have done wrong, I will not do so again.'[b]
33 Should God then reward you on your terms,
when you refuse to repent?[c]
You must decide, not I;
so tell me what you know.

34 "Men of understanding declare,
wise men who hear me say to me,
35 'Job speaks without knowledge;[d]
his words lack insight.'
36 Oh, that Job might be tested to the utmost
for answering like a wicked man![e]
37 To his sin he adds rebellion;
scornfully he claps his hands[f] among us
and multiplies his words against God."[g]

Chapter 35 Theme ______________________

35

Then Elihu said:

2 "Do you think this is just?
You say, 'I will be cleared by God.[a]'
3 Yet you ask him, 'What profit is it to me,[b]
and what do I gain by not sinning?'[h]

4 "I would like to reply to you
and to your friends with you.
5 Look up at the heavens[i] and see;
gaze at the clouds so high above you.[j]
6 If you sin, how does that affect him?
If your sins are many, what does that do to him?[k]
7 If you are righteous, what do you give to him,[l]
or what does he receive[m] from your hand?[n]
8 Your wickedness affects only a man like yourself,
and your righteousness only the sons of men.

9 "Men cry out[o] under a load of oppression;
they plead for relief from the arm of the powerful.[p]
10 But no one says, 'Where is God my Maker,[q]
who gives songs in the night,[r]
11 who teaches[s] more to us than to[c] the beasts of the earth
and makes us wiser than[d] the birds of the air?'
12 He does not answer[t] when men cry out
because of the arrogance of the wicked.
13 Indeed, God does not listen to their empty plea;
the Almighty pays no attention to it.[u]

34:32 [a] Job 35:11; Ps 25:4 [b] Job 33:27
34:33 [c] Job 41:11
34:35 [d] Job 35:16; 38:2
34:36 [e] Job 22:15
34:37 [f] Job 27:23 [g] Job 23:2
35:3 [h] Job 9:29-31; 34:9
35:5 [i] Ge 15:5 [j] Job 22:12
35:6 [k] Pr 8:36
35:7 [l] Ro 11:35 [m] Pr 9:12 [n] Job 22:2-3; Lk 17:10
35:9 [o] Ex 2:23 [p] Job 12:19
35:10 [q] Job 27:10; Isa 51:13 [r] Ps 42:8; 149:5; Ac 16:25
35:11 [s] Ps 94:12
35:12 [t] Pr 1:28
35:13 [u] Job 27:9; Pr 15:29; Isa 1:15; Jer 11:11

[a] 2 Or *My righteousness is more than God's* [b] 3 Or *you* [c] 11 Or *teaches us by* [d] 11 Or *us wise by*

[14]How much less, then, will he listen
when you say that you do not see him,[a]
that your case[b] is before him
and you must wait for him,
[15]and further, that his anger never punishes
and he does not take the least notice of wickedness.[a]
[16]So Job opens his mouth with empty talk;
without knowledge he multiplies words."[c]

Chapter 36 Theme ______________________

36

Elihu continued:

[2]"Bear with me a little longer and I will show you
that there is more to be said in God's behalf.
[3]I get my knowledge from afar;
I will ascribe justice to my Maker.[d]
[4]Be assured that my words are not false;[e]
one perfect in knowledge[f] is with you.

[5]"God is mighty, but does not despise men;[g]
he is mighty, and firm in his purpose.[h]
[6]He does not keep the wicked alive[i]
but gives the afflicted their rights.[j]
[7]He does not take his eyes off the righteous;[k]
he enthrones them with kings[l]
and exalts them forever.
[8]But if men are bound in chains,[m]
held fast by cords of affliction,
[9]he tells them what they have done—
that they have sinned arrogantly.[n]
[10]He makes them listen[o] to correction
and commands them to repent of their evil.[p]
[11]If they obey and serve him,[q]
they will spend the rest of their days in prosperity
and their years in contentment.
[12]But if they do not listen,
they will perish by the sword[b] [r]
and die without knowledge.[s]

[13]"The godless in heart[t] harbor resentment;
even when he fetters them, they do not cry for help.
[14]They die in their youth,
among male prostitutes of the shrines.[u]

[a] *15* Symmachus, Theodotion and Vulgate; the meaning of the Hebrew for this word is uncertain. [b] *12* Or *will cross the River*

35:14 [a]Job 9:11 [b]Ps 37:6
35:16 [c]Job 34:35,37
36:3 [d]Job 8:3; 37:23
36:4 [e]Job 33:3 [f]Job 37:5, 16,23
36:5 [g]Ps 22:24 [h]Job 12:13
36:6 [i]Job 8:22 [j]Job 5:15
36:7 [k]Ps 33:18 [l]Ps 113:8
36:8 [m]Ps 107:10,14
36:9 [n]Job 15:25
36:10 [o]Job 33:16 [p]2Ki 17:13
36:11 [q]Isa 1:19
36:12 [r]Job 15:22 [s]Job 4:21
36:13 [t]Ro 2:5
36:14 [u]Dt 23:17

15But those who suffer he delivers in their suffering;
he speaks to them in their affliction.

16"He is wooing[a] you from the jaws of distress
to a spacious place free from restriction,
to the comfort of your table[b] laden with choice food.
17But now you are laden with the judgment due
the wicked;
judgment and justice have taken hold of you.[c]
18Be careful that no one entices you by riches;
do not let a large bribe turn you aside.[d]
19Would your wealth
or even all your mighty efforts
sustain you so you would not be in distress?
20Do not long for the night,[e]
to drag people away from their homes.[a]
21Beware of turning to evil,[f]
which you seem to prefer to affliction.[g]

22"God is exalted in his power.
Who is a teacher like him?[h]
23Who has prescribed his ways for him,[i]
or said to him, 'You have done wrong'?[j]
24Remember to extol his work,[k]
which men have praised in song.[l]
25All mankind has seen it;
men gaze on it from afar.
26How great is God—beyond our understanding![m]
The number of his years is past finding out.[n]

27"He draws up the drops of water,
which distill as rain to the streams[b];[o]
28the clouds pour down their moisture
and abundant showers fall on mankind.[p]
29Who can understand how he spreads out the clouds,
how he thunders from his pavilion?[q]
30See how he scatters his lightning about him,
bathing the depths of the sea.
31This is the way he governs[c] the nations[r]
and provides food in abundance.[s]
32He fills his hands with lightning
and commands it to strike its mark.[t]
33His thunder announces the coming storm;
even the cattle make known its approach.[d]

36:16 [a]Hos 2:14 [b]Ps 23:5
36:17 [c]Job 22:11
36:18 [d]Job 34:33
36:20 [e]Job 34:20,25
36:21 [f]Ps 66:18 [g]Heb 11:25
36:22 [h]Isa 40:13; 1Co 2:16
36:23 [i]Job 34:13 [j]Job 8:3
36:24 [k]Ps 92:5; 138:5 [l]Ps 59:16; Rev 15:3
36:26 [m]1Co 13:12 [n]Job 10:5; Ps 90:2; 102:24; Heb 1:12
36:27 [o]Job 38:28; Ps 147:8
36:28 [p]Job 5:10
36:29 [q]Job 26:14; 37:16
36:31 [r]Job 37:13 [s]Ps 136:25; Ac 14:17
36:32 [t]Job 37:12,15

[a] *20* The meaning of the Hebrew for verses 18-20 is uncertain. [b] *27* Or *distill from the mist as rain* [c] *31* Or *nourishes* [d] *33* Or *announces his coming— / the One zealous against evil*

Chapter 37 Theme ____________________

37

"At this my heart pounds
and leaps from its place.
2 Listen! Listen to the roar of his voice,
to the rumbling that comes from his mouth.[a]
3 He unleashes his lightning beneath the whole heaven
and sends it to the ends of the earth.
4 After that comes the sound of his roar;
he thunders with his majestic voice.
When his voice resounds,
he holds nothing back.
5 God's voice thunders in marvelous ways;
he does great things beyond our understanding.[b]
6 He says to the snow,[c] 'Fall on the earth,'
and to the rain shower, 'Be a mighty downpour.'[d]
7 So that all men he has made may know his work,
he stops every man from his labor.[a][e]
8 The animals take cover;
they remain in their dens.[f]
9 The tempest comes out from its chamber,
the cold from the driving winds.
10 The breath of God produces ice,
and the broad waters become frozen.[g]
11 He loads the clouds with moisture;
he scatters his lightning through them.[h]
12 At his direction they swirl around
over the face of the whole earth
to do whatever he commands them.[i]
13 He brings the clouds to punish men,[j]
or to water his earth[b] and show his love.[k]

14 "Listen to this, Job;
stop and consider God's wonders.
15 Do you know how God controls the clouds
and makes his lightning flash?
16 Do you know how the clouds hang poised,
those wonders of him who is perfect in knowledge?[l]
17 You who swelter in your clothes
when the land lies hushed under the south wind,
18 can you join him in spreading out the skies,[m]
hard as a mirror of cast bronze?

19 "Tell us what we should say to him;
we cannot draw up our case because of our darkness.

a 7 Or / *he fills all men with fear by his power* b 13 Or *to favor them*

37:2 [a] Ps 29:3-9
37:5 [b] Job 5:9
37:6 [c] Job 38:22 [d] Job 36:27
37:7 [e] Job 12:14
37:8 [f] Job 38:40; Ps 104:22
37:10 [g] Job 38:29-30; Ps 147:17
37:11 [h] Job 36:27,29
37:12 [i] Ps 148:8
37:13 [j] 1Sa 12:17 [k] Ex 9:18; 1Ki 18:45; Job 38:27
37:16 [l] Job 36:4
37:18 [m] Job 9:8; Ps 104:2; Isa 44:24

37:23 [a]Job 9:4; 36:4; 1Ti 6:16 [b]Job 8:3 [c]Isa 63:9; Eze 18:23,32

[20]Should he be told that I want to speak?
Would any man ask to be swallowed up?
[21]Now no one can look at the sun,
bright as it is in the skies
after the wind has swept them clean.
[22]Out of the north he comes in golden splendor;
God comes in awesome majesty.
[23]The Almighty is beyond our reach and exalted in power;[a]
in his justice[b] and great righteousness, he does not oppress.[c]
[24]Therefore, men revere him,[d]
for does he not have regard for all the wise[e] in heart?[a]"

37:24 [d]Mt 10:28 [e]Mt 11:25

38:1 [f]Job 40:6

38:2 [g]Job 35:16; 42:3; 1Ti 1:7

Chapter 38 Theme ______________________

38 Then the LORD answered Job out of the storm.[f] He said:

[2]"Who is this that darkens my counsel
with words without knowledge?[g]
[3]Brace yourself like a man;
I will question you,
and you shall answer me.[h]

38:3 [h]Job 40:7

38:4 [i]Ps 104:5; Pr 8:29

[4]"Where were you when I laid the earth's foundation?[i]
Tell me, if you understand.
[5]Who marked off its dimensions?[j] Surely you know!
Who stretched a measuring line across it?
[6]On what were its footings set,
or who laid its cornerstone[k]—
[7]while the morning stars sang together
and all the angels[b] shouted for joy?

38:5 [j]Pr 8:29; Isa 40:12

38:6 [k]Job 26:7

[8]"Who shut up the sea behind doors[l]
when it burst forth from the womb,[m]
[9]when I made the clouds its garment
and wrapped it in thick darkness,
[10]when I fixed limits for it[n]
and set its doors and bars in place,[o]
[11]when I said, 'This far you may come and no farther;
here is where your proud waves halt'?[p]

38:8 [l]Jer 5:22 [m]Ge 1:9-10

38:10 [n]Ps 33:7; 104:9 [o]Job 26:10

[12]"Have you ever given orders to the morning,
or shown the dawn its place,
[13]that it might take the earth by the edges
and shake the wicked[q] out of it?

38:11 [p]Ps 89:9

38:13 [q]Ps 104:35

[a]24 Or *for he does not have regard for any who think they are wise.* [b]7 Hebrew *the sons of God*

14The earth takes shape like clay under a seal;
its features stand out like those of a garment.
15The wicked are denied their light,[a]
and their upraised arm is broken.[b]

16"Have you journeyed to the springs of the sea
or walked in the recesses of the deep?[c]
17Have the gates of death[d] been shown to you?
Have you seen the gates of the shadow of death[a]?
18Have you comprehended the vast expanses of the earth?[e]
Tell me, if you know all this.

19"What is the way to the abode of light?
And where does darkness reside?
20Can you take them to their places?
Do you know the paths[f] to their dwellings?
21Surely you know, for you were already born![g]
You have lived so many years!

22"Have you entered the storehouses of the snow[h]
or seen the storehouses of the hail,
23which I reserve for times of trouble,[i]
for days of war and battle?[j]
24What is the way to the place where the lightning
is dispersed,
or the place where the east winds are scattered over
the earth?
25Who cuts a channel for the torrents of rain,
and a path for the thunderstorm,[k]
26to water[l] a land where no man lives,
a desert with no one in it,
27to satisfy a desolate wasteland
and make it sprout with grass?[m]
28Does the rain have a father?[n]
Who fathers the drops of dew?
29From whose womb comes the ice?
Who gives birth to the frost from the heavens[o]
30when the waters become hard as stone,
when the surface of the deep is frozen?[p]

31"Can you bind the beautiful[b] Pleiades?
Can you loose the cords of Orion?[q]
32Can you bring forth the constellations in their seasons[c]
or lead out the Bear[d] with its cubs?

38:15 [a]Job 18:5 [b]Ps 10:15
38:16 [c]Ps 77:19
38:17 [d]Ps 9:13
38:18 [e]Job 28:24
38:20 [f]Job 26:10
38:21 [g]Job 15:7
38:22 [h]Job 37:6
38:23 [i]Isa 30:30; Eze 13:11 [j]Ex 9:18; Jos 10:11; Rev 16:21
38:25 [k]Job 28:26
38:26 [l]Job 36:27
38:27 [m]Ps 104:14; 107:35
38:28 [n]Ps 147:8; Jer 14:22
38:29 [o]Ps 147:16-17
38:30 [p]Job 37:10
38:31 [q]Job 9:9; Am 5:8

a 17 Or *gates of deep shadows* b 31 Or *the twinkling*; or *the chains of the* c 32 Or *the morning star in its season* d 32 Or *out Leo*

38:33 [a]Ps 148:6; Jer 31:36
38:34 [b]Job 22:11; 36:27-28
38:35 [c]Job 36:32; 37:3
38:36 [d]Job 9:4 [e]Job 32:8; Ps 51:6; Ecc 2:26
38:39 [f]Ps 104:21
38:40 [g]Job 37:8
38:41 [h]Lk 12:24 [i]Ps 147:9; Mt 6:26
39:1 [j]Dt 14:5
39:5 [k]Job 6:5; 11:12; 24:5
39:6 [l]Job 24:5; Ps 107:34; Jer 2:24 [m]Hos 8:9
39:7 [n]Job 3:18
39:9 [o]Nu 23:22; Dt 33:17

33Do you know the laws[a] of the heavens?
Can you set up ⌊God's[a]⌋ dominion over the earth?

34"Can you raise your voice to the clouds
and cover yourself with a flood of water?[b]
35Do you send the lightning bolts on their way?[c]
Do they report to you, 'Here we are'?
36Who endowed the heart[b] with wisdom[d]
or gave understanding[e] to the mind[b]?
37Who has the wisdom to count the clouds?
Who can tip over the water jars of the heavens
38when the dust becomes hard
and the clods of earth stick together?
39"Do you hunt the prey for the lioness
and satisfy the hunger of the lions[f]
40when they crouch in their dens[g]
or lie in wait in a thicket?
41Who provides food for the raven[h]
when its young cry out to God
and wander about for lack of food?[i]

Chapter 39 Theme ______________________

39 "Do you know when the mountain goats[j]
give birth?
Do you watch when the doe bears her fawn?
2Do you count the months till they bear?
Do you know the time they give birth?
3They crouch down and bring forth their young;
their labor pains are ended.
4Their young thrive and grow strong in the wilds;
they leave and do not return.

5"Who let the wild donkey[k] go free?
Who untied his ropes?
6I gave him the wasteland[l] as his home,
the salt flats as his habitat.[m]
7He laughs at the commotion in the town;
he does not hear a driver's shout.[n]
8He ranges the hills for his pasture
and searches for any green thing.

9"Will the wild ox[o] consent to serve you?
Will he stay by your manger at night?
10Can you hold him to the furrow with a harness?
Will he till the valleys behind you?

[a]*33* Or *his*; or *their* [b]*36* The meaning of the Hebrew for this word is uncertain.

11Will you rely on him for his great strength?
Will you leave your heavy work to him?
12Can you trust him to bring in your grain
and gather it to your threshing floor?

13"The wings of the ostrich flap joyfully,
but they cannot compare with the pinions and feathers of the stork.
14She lays her eggs on the ground
and lets them warm in the sand,
15unmindful that a foot may crush them,
that some wild animal may trample them.
16She treats her young harshly,[a] as if they were not hers;
she cares not that her labor was in vain,
17for God did not endow her with wisdom
or give her a share of good sense.[b]
18Yet when she spreads her feathers to run,
she laughs at horse and rider.

19"Do you give the horse his strength
or clothe his neck with a flowing mane?
20Do you make him leap like a locust,[c]
striking terror with his proud snorting?[d]
21He paws fiercely, rejoicing in his strength,
and charges into the fray.[e]
22He laughs at fear, afraid of nothing;
he does not shy away from the sword.
23The quiver rattles against his side,
along with the flashing spear and lance.
24In frenzied excitement he eats up the ground;
he cannot stand still when the trumpet sounds.[f]
25At the blast of the trumpet[g] he snorts, 'Aha!'
He catches the scent of battle from afar,
the shout of commanders and the battle cry.[h]

26"Does the hawk take flight by your wisdom
and spread his wings toward the south?
27Does the eagle soar at your command
and build his nest on high?[i]
28He dwells on a cliff and stays there at night;
a rocky crag is his stronghold.
29From there he seeks out his food;[j]
his eyes detect it from afar.
30His young ones feast on blood,
and where the slain are, there is he."[k]

39:16
[a] La 4:3

39:17
[b] Job 35:11

39:20
[c] Joel 2:4-5
[d] Jer 8:16

39:21
[e] Jer 8:6

39:24
[f] Jer 4:5,19; Eze 7:14; Am 3:6

39:25
[g] Jos 6:5
[h] Am 1:14; 2:2

39:27
[i] Jer 49:16; Ob 4

39:29
[j] Job 9:26

39:30
[k] Mt 24:28; Lk 17:37

Chapter 40 Theme ______________________

40

The LORD said to Job:[a]

2"Will the one who contends with the Almighty
correct him?
Let him who accuses God answer him!"

3Then Job answered the LORD:

4"I am unworthy[b]—how can I reply to you?
I put my hand over my mouth.[c]
5I spoke once, but I have no answer[d]—
twice, but I will say no more."[e]

6Then the LORD spoke to Job out of the storm:[f]

7"Brace yourself like a man;
I will question you,
and you shall answer me.[g]

8"Would you discredit my justice?[h]
Would you condemn me to justify yourself?
9Do you have an arm like God's,[i]
and can your voice thunder like his?[j]
10Then adorn yourself with glory and splendor,
and clothe yourself in honor and majesty.[k]
11Unleash the fury of your wrath,[l]
look at every proud man and bring him low,[m]
12look at every proud man and humble him,[n]
crush[o] the wicked where they stand.
13Bury them all in the dust together;
shroud their faces in the grave.
14Then I myself will admit to you
that your own right hand can save you.[p]

15"Look at the behemoth,[a]
which I made along with you
and which feeds on grass like an ox.
16What strength he has in his loins,
what power in the muscles of his belly!
17His tail[b] sways like a cedar;
the sinews of his thighs are close-knit.
18His bones are tubes of bronze,
his limbs like rods of iron.
19He ranks first among the works of God,[q]
yet his Maker can approach him with his sword.

40:1 [a] Job 10:2; 13:3; 23:4; 31:35; 33:13
40:4 [b] Job 42:6 [c] Job 29:9
40:5 [d] Job 9:3 [e] Job 9:15
40:6 [f] Job 38:1
40:7 [g] Job 38:3; 42:4
40:8 [h] Job 27:2; Ro 3:3
40:9 [i] 2Ch 32:8 [j] Job 37:5; Ps 29:3-4
40:10 [k] Ps 93:1; 104:1
40:11 [l] Isa 42:25; Na 1:6 [m] Isa 2:11,12,17; Da 4:37
40:12 [n] 1Sa 2:7 [o] Isa 13:11; 63:2-3,6
40:14 [p] Ps 20:6; 60:5; 108:6
40:19 [q] Job 41:33

a *15* Possibly the hippopotamus or the elephant b *17* Possibly trunk

20The hills bring him their produce,[a]
and all the wild animals play[b] nearby.
21Under the lotus plants he lies,
hidden among the reeds in the marsh.
22The lotuses conceal him in their shadow;
the poplars by the stream[c] surround him.
23When the river rages, he is not alarmed;
he is secure, though the Jordan should surge against
his mouth.
24Can anyone capture him by the eyes,[a]
or trap him and pierce his nose?[d]

Chapter 41 Theme ______________________

41

"Can you pull in the leviathan[b][e] with a fishhook
or tie down his tongue with a rope?
2Can you put a cord through his nose
or pierce his jaw with a hook?[f]
3Will he keep begging you for mercy?
Will he speak to you with gentle words?
4Will he make an agreement with you
for you to take him as your slave for life?[g]
5Can you make a pet of him like a bird
or put him on a leash for your girls?
6Will traders barter for him?
Will they divide him up among the merchants?
7Can you fill his hide with harpoons
or his head with fishing spears?
8If you lay a hand on him,
you will remember the struggle and never do it again!
9Any hope of subduing him is false;
the mere sight of him is overpowering.
10No one is fierce enough to rouse him.[h]
Who then is able to stand against me?[i]
11Who has a claim against me that I must pay?[j]
Everything under heaven belongs to me.[k]

12"I will not fail to speak of his limbs,
his strength and his graceful form.
13Who can strip off his outer coat?
Who would approach him with a bridle?
14Who dares open the doors of his mouth,
ringed about with his fearsome teeth?
15His back has[c] rows of shields
tightly sealed together;

40:20
[a]Ps 104:14
[b]Ps 104:26

40:22
[c]Isa 44:4

40:24
[d]Job 41:2,7,26

41:1
[e]Job 3:8;
Ps 104:26;
Isa 27:1

41:2
[f]Isa 37:29

41:4
[g]Ex 21:6

41:10
[h]Job 3:8
[i]Jer 50:44

41:11
[j]Ro 11:35
[k]Ex 19:5;
Dt 10:14;
Ps 24:1; 50:12;
1Co 10:26

[a]24 Or *by a water hole* [b]1 Possibly the crocodile [c]15 Or *His pride is his*

41:18 [a]Job 3:9

16 each is so close to the next
that no air can pass between.
17 They are joined fast to one another;
they cling together and cannot be parted.
18 His snorting throws out flashes of light;
his eyes are like the rays of dawn.[a]
19 Firebrands stream from his mouth;

41:21 [b]Isa 40:7 [c]Ps 18:8

sparks of fire shoot out.
20 Smoke pours from his nostrils
as from a boiling pot over a fire of reeds.
21 His breath[b] sets coals ablaze,
and flames dart from his mouth.[c]
22 Strength resides in his neck;
dismay goes before him.
23 The folds of his flesh are tightly joined;

41:30 [d]Isa 41:15

they are firm and immovable.
24 His chest is hard as rock,
hard as a lower millstone.
25 When he rises up, the mighty are terrified;
they retreat before his thrashing.
26 The sword that reaches him has no effect,
nor does the spear or the dart or the javelin.

41:33 [e]Job 40:19

27 Iron he treats like straw
and bronze like rotten wood.
28 Arrows do not make him flee;
slingstones are like chaff to him.
29 A club seems to him but a piece of straw;
he laughs at the rattling of the lance.
30 His undersides are jagged potsherds,

41:34 [f]Job 28:8

leaving a trail in the mud like a threshing sledge.[d]
31 He makes the depths churn like a boiling caldron
and stirs up the sea like a pot of ointment.
32 Behind him he leaves a glistening wake;
one would think the deep had white hair.
33 Nothing on earth is his equal[e]—
a creature without fear.

42:2 [g]Ge 18:14; Mt 19:26 [h]2Ch 20:6

34 He looks down on all that are haughty;
he is king over all that are proud.[f]"

Chapter 42 Theme ____________________

42

Then Job replied to the LORD:

2 "I know that you can do all things;[g]
no plan of yours can be thwarted.[h]
3 ⌊You asked,⌋ 'Who is this that obscures my counsel
without knowledge?'[i]

42:3 [i]Job 38:2

Surely I spoke of things I did not understand,
things too wonderful for me to know.[a]

4⌞"You said,⌟ 'Listen now, and I will speak;
I will question you,
and you shall answer me.'[b]
5My ears had heard of you[c]
but now my eyes have seen you.[d]
6Therefore I despise myself[e]
and repent in dust and ashes."[f]

7After the LORD had said these things to Job, he said to Eliphaz
the Temanite, "I am angry with you and your two friends,[g]
because you have not spoken of me what is right, as my servant
Job has. 8So now take seven bulls and seven rams[h] and go to my
servant Job and sacrifice a burnt offering[i] for yourselves. My servant Job will pray for you, and I will accept his prayer[j] and not
deal with you according to your folly.[k] You have not spoken of me
what is right, as my servant Job has." 9So Eliphaz the Temanite,
Bildad the Shuhite and Zophar the Naamathite did what the
LORD told them; and the LORD accepted Job's prayer.

10After Job had prayed for his friends, the LORD made him
prosperous again[l] and gave him twice as much as he had before.[m]
11All his brothers and sisters and everyone who had known him
before[n] came and ate with him in his house. They comforted and
consoled him over all the trouble the LORD had brought upon
him, and each one gave him a piece of silver[a] and a gold ring.

12The LORD blessed the latter part of Job's life more than the
first. He had fourteen thousand sheep, six thousand camels, a
thousand yoke of oxen and a thousand donkeys. 13And he also had
seven sons and three daughters. 14The first daughter he named
Jemimah, the second Keziah and the third Keren-Happuch.
15Nowhere in all the land were there found women as beautiful as
Job's daughters, and their father granted them an inheritance
along with their brothers.

16After this, Job lived a hundred and forty years; he saw his
children and their children to the fourth generation. 17And so he
died, old and full of years.[o]

a *11* Hebrew ; a kesitah was a unit of money of unknown weight and value.

42:3
[a] Ps 40:5; 131:1; 139:6

42:4
[b] Job 38:3; 40:7

42:5
[c] Job 26:14; Ro 10:17
[d] Jdg 13:22; Isa 6:5; Eph 1:17-18

42:6
[e] Job 40:4
[f] Ezr 9:6

42:7
[g] Job 32:3

42:8
[h] Nu 23:1,29
[i] Job 1:5
[j] Ge 20:17; Jas 5:15-16; 1Jn 5:16
[k] Job 22:30

42:10
[l] Dt 30:3; Ps 14:7
[m] Job 1:3; Ps 85:1-3; 126:5-6

42:11
[n] Job 19:13

42:17
[o] Ge 15:15; 25:8

Job Observations Chart

Insights Regarding Satan	Insights Regarding Job
Character	Character
Tactics	Relationship to God
Power	Relationship to His Friends

Insights Regarding God	What God Says Regarding
His Character	Job
	Job's Friends
	Insights Regarding God's Expectations of Man
His Ways	
His Power	
Over Satan	
	Insights into Life and Death
Over Nature	
Over Man	

Lessons I Learned about Dealing with Those in Pain

Theme of Job:

Segment Divisions

		Chapter Themes
		1
		2
		3
		4
		5
		6
		7
		8
		9
		10
		11
		12
		13
		14
		15
		16
		17
		18
		19
		20
		21
		22
		23
		24
		25
		26
		27
		28
		29
		30
		31
		32
		33
		34
		35
		36
		37
		38
		39
		40
		41
		42

Author:

Date:

Purpose:

Key Words:

PSALMS

Man needs to communicate with God in prayer and in song. He needs to come before him and honestly present that which is on his heart—whether it be distress or joy, confusion or confidence. Man needs to lift up his voice in worship, to speak to God and to others in psalms and hymns and spiritual songs, singing and making melody with his heart to the Lord (see Ephesians 5:19).

Thus the psalms—praises, prayers, and songs—are to be accompanied on stringed instruments. So David, writer of many psalms, appointed Levites over the service of song in the house of the Lord. They ministered with song before the tabernacle of the tent of meeting until Solomon built the house of the Lord in Jerusalem (see 1 Chronicles 6:31, 32).

Receiving worship is befitting to God alone. Psalms is a book of prayer and praise, written by men but inspired by God. "For from him and through him and to him are all things. To him be the glory forever! Amen" (Romans 11:36).

Things to Do

1. As you study Psalms, remember that the psalms are poetry whether they are prayers or songs. Hebrew poetry does not contain rhyme and meter. Rather, its distinctive feature is parallelism of some form, where one line relates to another in various ways. Usually the poetic lines are composed of two (or sometimes three) balanced segments in which the second is shorter than the first and repeats, contrasts, or completes the first segment.

   The psalms vary in design. Nine are alphabetical, with each stanza beginning with the next letter from the Hebrew alphabet. The alphabetical psalms are 9, 10, 25, 34, 37, 111, 112, 119, and 145.

2. The majority of the psalms have a superscription at the beginning, which designates one or several things: the composer, the occasion of the psalm, who it is for, how it is to be accompanied, and what kind of psalm it is. If a psalm has a superscription, read it and consult the cross-references (if it is referenced). This will help put the psalm into context.

3. Watch for the theme of the psalm and how it is developed. Sometimes the theme will be stated at the very beginning of the psalm, while at other times the key thematic scheme will be found in the center of the psalm. Each will have a theme and will be developed in accordance with the author's design for the psalm.

   a. Some of the psalms give insights into the history of Israel, such as Psalm 78. Study these carefully. Note the events, God's intervention, and God's watchful care.

   b. If a psalm makes reference to a person or circumstance which is discussed in one of the historical books of the Bible, you might go back to that book and record the psalm that applies to that person or circumstance. For instance, in the margin of 2 Samuel 12, note "Psalm 51" as a cross-reference.

4. Key words bring out the theme of the psalm's song or prayer. Sometimes a key phrase will open and close the psalm. Watch for and mark these phrases. Also watch for the following key words and mark them in a distinctive way: *righteous (right, righteousness), wicked (evil, vile, evildoers), sin (sins, condemns him, malice, iniquity, wrong, iniquities, affliction, sinful, crime), prayer (prayers, pray, plea), praise (praises, glorify, commend, extol), sing (shout, make music, cry out, jubilant song with music), fear (dread, afraid, be afraid), refuge (stronghold, shelter, hide), hope (hopes, wait for, trust in), save (saves, victory, deliver, saved, salvation, deliverance, Savior, deliverer, victories),* and *cry (call, called, cried).* Write these key words on an index card and use it as a bookmark when you study and meditate on the psalms.

5. Don't miss the central focus of these psalms—God. There is so much to be learned about him, and

then he is to be worshiped and adored. Observe his names, his titles, his attributes, and how man is to respond to him.

a. Don't forget to look for Jesus, who is God, one with the Father, for he said, "Everything must be fulfilled that is written about me in the Law of Moses, the Prophets and the Psalms" (Luke 24:44).

b. The psalms are for the heart and soul, but they also address the mind. In the margin record your insights about God (use a △ as a heading). As you do this, meditate on what you learn. Spend time in praise and prayer. Let the book of Psalms help you love the Lord your God with all your heart, mind, body, soul, and strength.

6. When you finish each psalm, record the theme of that psalm on the line in the text next to the number of the psalm and on the PSALMS AT A GLANCE chart on pages 1061 through 1066.

7. Psalms has five segments, which are marked on PSALMS AT A GLANCE.

a. Give each segment a title or record its theme.

b. Read Psalms 41:13; 72:18, 19; 89:52; 106:48; and 150:6. Notice what is said and how each segment concludes.

c. Complete PSALMS AT A GLANCE.

Things to Think About

1. When you are distressed, confused, afraid, or hurt, or when you need to talk with someone who will understand, turn to Psalms. With the psalmist, be still (cease striving) and know that he is God.

2. Think about the practical value of Psalms and let it serve as your primary counselor when you need wisdom and understanding. Remember, blessed is the man who does not walk in the counsel of the wicked, but whose delight is in the law of the Lord, and who meditates in that law day and night (see Psalm 1).

3. Have you thought about ending each day as the book of Psalms ends—with a psalm of praise? "Let the saints rejoice in this honor and sing for joy on their beds. May the praise of God be in their mouths. . . . Let everything that has breath praise the LORD. Praise the LORD" (Psalm 149:5, 6; Psalm 150:6). Try it and see what God does.

BOOK I

Psalms 1–41

Psalm 1

*Psalm 1 Theme*____________________

1Blessed is the man
who does not walk[a] in the counsel of the wicked
or stand in the way of sinners
or sit[b] in the seat of mockers.
2But his delight[c] is in the law of the LORD,[d]
and on his law he meditates[e] day and night.
3He is like a tree[f] planted by streams of water,[g]
which yields its fruit[h] in season

1:1 [a]Pr 4:14 [b]Ps 26:4; Jer 15:17
1:2 [c]Ps 119:16,35 [d]Ps 119:1 [e]Jos 1:8
1:3 [f]Ps 128:3 [g]Jer 17:8 [h]Eze 47:12

1:3 [a]Ge 39:3

and whose leaf does not wither.
Whatever he does prospers.[a]

1:4 [b]Job 21:18; Isa 17:13

4 Not so the wicked!
They are like chaff[b]
that the wind blows away.
5 Therefore the wicked will not stand[c] in the judgment,[d]
nor sinners in the assembly of the righteous.

1:5 [c]Ps 5:5 [d]Ps 9:7-8,16

6 For the LORD watches over[e] the way of the righteous,
but the way of the wicked will perish.[f]

1:6 [e]Ps 37:18; 2Ti 2:19 [f]Ps 9:6

Psalm 2

*Psalm 2 Theme*______________________________

2:1 [g]Ps 21:11

1 Why do the nations conspire[a]
and the peoples plot[g] in vain?
2 The kings[h] of the earth take their stand
and the rulers gather together
against the LORD
and against his Anointed[i] One.[b][j]

2:2 [h]Ps 48:4 [i]Jn 1:41 [j]Ps 74:18,23; Ac 4:25-26*

3 "Let us break their chains," they say,
"and throw off their fetters."[k]

2:3 [k]Jer 5:5

4 The One enthroned in heaven laughs;[l]
the Lord scoffs at them.
5 Then he rebukes them in his anger
and terrifies them in his wrath,[m] saying,
6 "I have installed my King[c]
on Zion, my holy hill."

2:4 [l]Ps 37:13; 59:8; Pr 1:26

2:5 [m]Ps 21:9; 78:49-50

7 I will proclaim the decree of the LORD:

He said to me, "You are my Son[d];
today I have become your Father.[e][n]
8 Ask of me,
and I will make the nations your inheritance,
the ends of the earth[o] your possession.
9 You will rule them with an iron scepter[f];[p]
you will dash them to pieces[q] like pottery.[r]"

2:7 [n]Ac 13:33*; Heb 1:5*

2:8 [o]Ps 22:27

10 Therefore, you kings, be wise;
be warned, you rulers of the earth.
11 Serve the LORD with fear
and rejoice[s] with trembling.[t]

2:9 [p]Rev 12:5 [q]Ps 89:23 [r]Rev 2:27*

2:11 [s]Heb 12:28 [t]Ps 119:119-120

[a]*1* Hebrew; Septuagint *rage* [b]*2* Or *anointed one* [c]*6* Or *king* [d]*7* Or *son*; also in verse 12
[e]*7* Or *have begotten you* [f]*9* Or *will break them with a rod of iron*

[12]Kiss the Son,[a] lest he be angry
and you be destroyed in your way,
for his wrath[b] can flare up in a moment.
Blessed are all who take refuge[c] in him.

2:12
[a]Jn 5:23
[b]Rev 6:16
[c]Ps 34:8; Ro 9:33

Psalm 3

A psalm of David. When he fled from his son Absalom.[d]

3:Title
[d]2Sa 15:14

*Psalm 3 Theme*____

[1]O LORD, how many are my foes!
How many rise up against me!
[2]Many are saying of me,
"God will not deliver him.[e]"
Selah[a]

[3]But you are a shield[f] around me, O LORD;
you bestow glory on me and lift[b] up my head.[g]
[4]To the LORD I cry aloud,
and he answers me from his holy hill.[h] *Selah*

[5]I lie down and sleep;[i]
I wake again, because the LORD sustains me.
[6]I will not fear[j] the tens of thousands
drawn up against me on every side.

[7]Arise,[k] O LORD!
Deliver me,[l] O my God!
Strike[m] all my enemies on the jaw;
break the teeth[n] of the wicked.

[8]From the LORD comes deliverance.[o]
May your blessing be on your people. *Selah*

3:2
[e]Ps 71:11

3:3
[f]Ge 15:1; Ps 28:7
[g]Ps 27:6

3:4
[h]Ps 2:6

3:5
[i]Lev 26:6; Pr 3:24

3:6
[j]Ps 27:3

3:7
[k]Ps 7:6
[l]Ps 6:4
[m]Job 16:10
[n]Ps 58:6

3:8
[o]Isa 43:3,11

Psalm 4

For the director of music. With stringed instruments. A psalm of David.

*Psalm 4 Theme*____

[1]Answer me when I call to you,
O my righteous God.
Give me relief from my distress;
be merciful[p] to me and hear my prayer.[q]

4:1
[p]Ps 25:16
[q]Ps 17:6

a 2 A word of uncertain meaning, occurring frequently in the Psalms; possibly a musical term
b 3 Or *LORD, / my Glorious One, who lifts*

2 How long, O men, will you turn my glory into shame[a]?
How long will you love delusions and seek
false gods[b]?[a] *Selah*
3 Know that the LORD has set apart the godly[b] for himself;
the LORD will hear[c] when I call to him.

4 In your anger do not sin;[d]
when you are on your beds,[e]
search your hearts and be silent. *Selah*
5 Offer right sacrifices
and trust in the LORD.[f]

6 Many are asking, "Who can show us any good?"
Let the light of your face shine upon us,[g] O LORD.
7 You have filled my heart[h] with greater joy[i]
than when their grain and new wine abound.
8 I will lie down and sleep[j] in peace,
for you alone, O LORD,
make me dwell in safety.[k]

Psalm 5

For the director of music. For flutes. A psalm of David.

*Psalm 5 Theme*____

1 Give ear to my words, O LORD,
consider my sighing.
2 Listen to my cry for help,[l]
my King and my God,[m]
for to you I pray.
3 In the morning,[n] O LORD, you hear my voice;
in the morning I lay my requests before you
and wait in expectation.

4 You are not a God who takes pleasure in evil;
with you the wicked[o] cannot dwell.
5 The arrogant[p] cannot stand[q] in your presence;
you hate[r] all who do wrong.
6 You destroy those who tell lies;[s]
bloodthirsty and deceitful men
the LORD abhors.

7 But I, by your great mercy,
will come into your house;

4:2 [a]Ps 31:6
4:3 [b]Ps 31:23 [c]Ps 6:8
4:4 [d]Eph 4:26* [e]Ps 77:6
4:5 [f]Dt 33:19; Ps 37:3
4:6 [g]Nu 6:25
4:7 [h]Ac 14:17 [i]Isa 9:3
4:8 [j]Ps 3:5 [k]Lev 25:18
5:2 [l]Ps 3:4 [m]Ps 84:3
5:3 [n]Ps 88:13
5:4 [o]Ps 11:5; 92:15
5:5 [p]Ps 73:3 [q]Ps 1:5 [r]Ps 11:5
5:6 [s]Ps 55:23; Rev 21:8

[a]2 Or *you dishonor my Glorious One* [b]2 Or *seek lies*

in reverence will I bow down[a]
toward your holy temple.
8Lead me, O LORD, in your righteousness[b]
because of my enemies—
make straight your way[c] before me.

9Not a word from their mouth can be trusted;
their heart is filled with destruction.
Their throat is an open grave;[d]
with their tongue they speak deceit.[e]
10Declare them guilty, O God!
Let their intrigues be their downfall.
Banish them for their many sins,[f]
for they have rebelled[g] against you.

11But let all who take refuge in you be glad;
let them ever sing for joy.[h]
Spread your protection over them,
that those who love your name[i] may rejoice in you.[j]
12For surely, O LORD, you bless the righteous;
you surround them[k] with your favor as with a shield.

Psalm 6

For the director of music. With stringed instruments. According to *sheminith*.[a]
A psalm of David.

*Psalm 6 Theme*______________________________

1O LORD, do not rebuke me in your anger[l]
or discipline me in your wrath.
2Be merciful to me, LORD, for I am faint;
O LORD, heal me,[m] for my bones are in agony.[n]
3My soul is in anguish.[o]
How long,[p] O LORD, how long?

4Turn, O LORD, and deliver me;
save me because of your unfailing love.[q]
5No one remembers you when he is dead.
Who praises you from the grave[b]?[r]

6I am worn out[s] from groaning;
all night long I flood my bed with weeping
and drench my couch with tears.[t]
7My eyes grow weak[u] with sorrow;
they fail because of all my foes.

[a]Title: Probably a musical term [b]5 Hebrew *Sheol*

5:7
[a]Ps 138:2

5:8
[b]Ps 31:1
[c]Ps 27:11

5:9
[d]Lk 11:44
[e]Ro 3:13*

5:10
[f]Ps 9:16
[g]Ps 107:11

5:11
[h]Ps 2:12
[i]Ps 69:36
[j]Isa 65:13

5:12
[k]Ps 32:7

6:1
[l]Ps 38:1

6:2
[m]Hos 6:1
[n]Ps 22:14; 31:10

6:3
[o]Jn 12:27
[p]Ps 90:13

6:4
[q]Ps 17:13

6:5
[r]Ps 30:9; 88:10-12; Ecc 9:10; Isa 38:18

6:6
[s]Ps 69:3
[t]Ps 42:3

6:7
[u]Ps 31:9

8 Away from me,[a] all you who do evil,[b]
for the LORD has heard my weeping.
9 The LORD has heard my cry for mercy;[c]
the LORD accepts my prayer.
10 All my enemies will be ashamed and dismayed;
they will turn back in sudden disgrace.[d]

Psalm 7

A *shiggaion*[a] of David, which he sang to the LORD concerning Cush, a Benjamite.

*Psalm 7 Theme*________________________________

1 O LORD my God, I take refuge in you;
save and deliver me from all who pursue me,[e]
2 or they will tear me like a lion[f]
and rip me to pieces with no one to rescue[g] me.

3 O LORD my God, if I have done this
and there is guilt on my hands[h]—
4 if I have done evil to him who is at peace with me
or without cause have robbed my foe—
5 then let my enemy pursue and overtake me;
let him trample my life to the ground
and make me sleep in the dust.

Selah

6 Arise,[i] O LORD, in your anger;
rise up against the rage of my enemies.[j]
Awake,[k] my God; decree justice.
7 Let the assembled peoples gather around you.
Rule over them from on high;
8 let the LORD judge the peoples.
Judge me, O LORD, according to my righteousness,[l]
according to my integrity, O Most High.
9 O righteous God,[m]
who searches minds and hearts,[n]
bring to an end the violence of the wicked
and make the righteous secure.[o]

10 My shield[b] is God Most High,
who saves the upright in heart.[p]
11 God is a righteous judge,[q]
a God who expresses his wrath every day.
12 If he does not relent,
he[c] will sharpen his sword;[r]

[a] Title: Probably a literary or musical term [b] 10 Or *sovereign* [c] 12 Or *If a man does not repent, / God*

6:8 [a] Ps 119:115 [b] Mt 7:23; Lk 13:27
6:9 [c] Ps 116:1
6:10 [d] Ps 71:24; 73:19
7:1 [e] Ps 31:15
7:2 [f] Isa 38:13 [g] Ps 50:22
7:3 [h] 1Sa 24:11; Isa 59:3
7:6 [i] Ps 94:2 [j] Ps 138:7 [k] Ps 44:23
7:8 [l] Ps 18:20; 96:13
7:9 [m] Jer 11:20 [n] 1Ch 28:9; Ps 26:2; Rev 2:23 [o] Ps 37:23
7:10 [p] Ps 125:4
7:11 [q] Ps 50:6
7:12 [r] Dt 32:41

he will bend and string his bow.
13He has prepared his deadly weapons;
he makes ready his flaming arrows.

14He who is pregnant with evil
and conceives trouble gives birth[a] to disillusionment.
15He who digs a hole and scoops it out
falls into the pit he has made.[b]
16The trouble he causes recoils on himself;
his violence comes down on his own head.

17I will give thanks to the LORD because of his
righteousness[c]
and will sing praise[d] to the name of the LORD
Most High.

Psalm 8

For the director of music. According to *gittith*.[a] A psalm of David.

Psalm 8 Theme ______________________

1O LORD, our Lord,
how majestic is your name in all the earth!

You have set your glory
above the heavens.[e]
2From the lips of children and infants
you have ordained praise[b][f]
because of your enemies,
to silence the foe[g] and the avenger.

3When I consider your heavens,[h]
the work of your fingers,
the moon and the stars,[i]
which you have set in place,
4what is man that you are mindful of him,
the son of man that you care for him?[j]
5You made him a little lower than the heavenly beings[c]
and crowned him with glory and honor.[k]

6You made him ruler[l] over the works of your hands;
you put everything under his feet:[m n]
7all flocks and herds,
and the beasts of the field,

[a]Title: Probably a musical term [b]2 Or *strength* [c]5 Or *than God*

7:14 [a]Job 15:35; Isa 59:4; Jas 1:15
7:15 [b]Job 4:8
7:17 [c]Ps 71:15-16 [d]Ps 9:2
8:1 [e]Ps 57:5; 113:4; 148:13
8:2 [f]Mt 21:16* [g]Ps 44:16; 1Co 1:27
8:3 [h]Ps 89:11 [i]Ps 136:9
8:4 [j]Job 7:17; Ps 144:3; Heb 2:6
8:5 [k]Ps 21:5; 103:4
8:6 [l]Ge 1:28 [m]Heb 2:6-8* [n]1Co 15:25,27*; Eph 1:22

8 the birds of the air,
and the fish of the sea,
all that swim the paths of the seas.

9 O LORD, our Lord,
how majestic is your name in all the earth![a]

Psalm 9[a]

For the director of music. To ⌊the tune of⌋ "The Death of the Son." A psalm of David.

*Psalm 9 Theme*________________________

1 I will praise you, O LORD, with all my heart;[b]
I will tell of all your wonders.[c]
2 I will be glad and rejoice[d] in you;
I will sing praise to your name,[e] O Most High.

3 My enemies turn back;
they stumble and perish before you.
4 For you have upheld my right and my cause;[f]
you have sat on your throne, judging righteously.[g]
5 You have rebuked the nations and destroyed the wicked;
you have blotted out their name[h] for ever and ever.
6 Endless ruin has overtaken the enemy,
you have uprooted their cities;
even the memory of them[i] has perished.

7 The LORD reigns forever;
he has established his throne[j] for judgment.
8 He will judge the world in righteousness;[k]
he will govern the peoples with justice.
9 The LORD is a refuge for the oppressed,
a stronghold in times of trouble.[l]
10 Those who know your name[m] will trust in you,
for you, LORD, have never forsaken[n] those who
seek you.

11 Sing praises to the LORD, enthroned in Zion;[o]
proclaim among the nations[p] what he has done.[q]
12 For he who avenges blood[r] remembers;
he does not ignore the cry of the afflicted.

13 O LORD, see how my enemies[s] persecute me!
Have mercy and lift me up from the gates of death,
14 that I may declare your praises[t]

8:9 [a] ver 1
9:1 [b] Ps 86:12 [c] Ps 26:7
9:2 [d] Ps 5:11 [e] Ps 92:1; 83:18
9:4 [f] Ps 140:12 [g] 1Pe 2:23
9:5 [h] Pr 10:7
9:6 [i] Ps 34:16
9:7 [j] Ps 89:14
9:8 [k] Ps 96:13
9:9 [l] Ps 32:7
9:10 [m] Ps 91:14 [n] Ps 37:28
9:11 [o] Ps 76:2 [p] Ps 107:22 [q] Ps 105:1
9:12 [r] Ge 9:5
9:13 [s] Ps 38:19
9:14 [t] Ps 106:2

[a] Psalms 9 and 10 may have been originally a single acrostic poem, the stanzas of which begin with the successive letters of the Hebrew alphabet. In the Septuagint they constitute one psalm.

in the gates of the Daughter of Zion
and there rejoice in your salvation.[a]
15The nations have fallen into the pit they have dug;[b]
their feet are caught in the net they have hidden.[c]
16The LORD is known by his justice;
the wicked are ensnared by the work of their hands.
Higgaion.[a] *Selah*

17The wicked return to the grave,[b][d]
all the nations that forget God.[e]
18But the needy will not always be forgotten,
nor the hope[f] of the afflicted[g] ever perish.

19Arise, O LORD, let not man triumph;
let the nations be judged in your presence.
20Strike them with terror, O LORD;
let the nations know they are but men.[h] *Selah*

Psalm 10[c]

Psalm 10 Theme ________________________________

1Why, O LORD, do you stand far off?[i]
Why do you hide yourself[j] in times of trouble?

2In his arrogance the wicked man hunts down the weak,
who are caught in the schemes he devises.
3He boasts[k] of the cravings of his heart;
he blesses the greedy and reviles the LORD.
4In his pride the wicked does not seek him;
in all his thoughts there is no room for God.[l]
5His ways are always prosperous;
he is haughty and your laws are far from him;
he sneers at all his enemies.
6He says to himself, "Nothing will shake me;
I'll always be happy[m] and never have trouble."
7His mouth is full of curses[n] and lies and threats;[o]
trouble and evil are under his tongue.[p]
8He lies in wait near the villages;
from ambush he murders the innocent,[q]
watching in secret for his victims.
9He lies in wait like a lion in cover;
he lies in wait to catch the helpless;[r]
he catches the helpless and drags them off in his net.
10His victims are crushed, they collapse;
they fall under his strength.

a *16* Or *Meditation*; possibly a musical notation b *17* Hebrew *Sheol* c Psalms 9 and 10 may have been originally a single acrostic poem, the stanzas of which begin with the successive letters of the Hebrew alphabet. In the Septuagint they constitute one psalm.

9:14 [a]Ps 13:5; 51:12
9:15 [b]Ps 7:15-16 [c]Ps 35:8; 57:6
9:17 [d]Ps 49:14 [e]Job 8:13; Ps 50:22
9:18 [f]Ps 71:5; Pr 23:18 [g]Ps 12:5
9:20 [h]Ps 62:9; Isa 31:3
10:1 [i]Ps 22:1,11 [j]Ps 13:1
10:3 [k]Ps 94:4
10:4 [l]Ps 14:1; 36:1
10:6 [m]Rev 18:7
10:7 [n]Ro 3:14* [o]Ps 73:8 [p]Ps 140:3
10:8 [q]Ps 94:6
10:9 [r]Ps 17:12; 59:3; 140:5

10:11 [a]Job 22:13 [11]He says to himself, "God has forgotten;[a]
he covers his face and never sees."

[12]Arise, LORD! Lift up your hand,[b] O God.
10:12 [b]Ps 17:7; Mic 5:9 [c]Ps 9:12 Do not forget the helpless.[c]
[13]Why does the wicked man revile God?
Why does he say to himself,
"He won't call me to account"?
10:14 [d]Ps 22:11 [e]Ps 37:5 [f]Ps 68:5 [14]But you, O God, do see trouble[d] and grief;
you consider it to take it in hand.
The victim commits himself to you;[e]
you are the helper[f] of the fatherless.
[15]Break the arm of the wicked and evil man;[g]
10:15 [g]Ps 37:17 call him to account for his wickedness
that would not be found out.

10:16 [h]Ps 29:10 [i]Dt 8:20 [16]The LORD is King for ever and ever;[h]
the nations[i] will perish from his land.
[17]You hear, O LORD, the desire of the afflicted;[j]
you encourage them, and you listen to their cry,
10:17 [j]1Ch 29:18; Ps 34:15 [18]defending the fatherless[k] and the oppressed,[l]
in order that man, who is of the earth, may terrify
no more.

10:18 [k]Ps 82:3 [l]Ps 9:9

Psalm 11

For the director of music. Of David.

11:1 [m]Ps 56:11

Psalm 11 Theme

[1]In the LORD I take refuge.[m]
How then can you say to me:
11:2 [n]Ps 7:13 [o]Ps 64:3-4 "Flee like a bird to your mountain.
[2]For look, the wicked bend their bows;
they set their arrows[n] against the strings
11:3 [p]Ps 82:5 to shoot from the shadows
at the upright in heart.[o]
[3]When the foundations[p] are being destroyed,
what can the righteous do[a]?"

11:4 [q]Ps 18:6 [r]Ps 103:19 [s]Ps 33:13 [t]Ps 34:15-16 [4]The LORD is in his holy temple;[q]
the LORD is on his heavenly throne.[r]
He observes the sons of men;[s]
his eyes examine[t] them.
[5]The LORD examines the righteous,[u]

11:5 [u]Ge 22:1; Jas 1:12

[a]3 Or *what is the Righteous One doing*

but the wicked[a] and those who love violence
his soul hates.[a]
6On the wicked he will rain
fiery coals and burning sulfur;[b]
a scorching wind[c] will be their lot.
7For the LORD is righteous,[d]
he loves justice;[e]
upright men will see his face.[f]

Psalm 12

For the director of music. According to *sheminith*.[b] A psalm of David.

Psalm 12 Theme ______________________

1Help, LORD, for the godly are no more;[g]
the faithful have vanished from among men.
2Everyone lies to his neighbor;
their flattering lips speak with deception.[h]
3May the LORD cut off all flattering lips
and every boastful tongue[i]
4that says, "We will triumph with our tongues;
we own our lips[c]—who is our master?"

5"Because of the oppression of the weak
and the groaning of the needy,
I will now arise," says the LORD.
"I will protect them[j] from those who malign them."
6And the words of the LORD are flawless,[k]
like silver refined in a furnace of clay,
purified seven times.

7O LORD, you will keep us safe
and protect us from such people forever.[l]
8The wicked freely strut[m] about
when what is vile is honored among men.

Psalm 13

For the director of music. A psalm of David.

Psalm 13 Theme ______________________

1How long, O LORD? Will you forget me forever?
How long will you hide your face[n] from me?

a5 Or *The LORD, the Righteous One, examines the wicked, /* b Title: Probably a musical term
c4 Or */ our lips are our plowshares*

11:5
[a] Ps 5:5

11:6
[b] Eze 38:22
[c] Jer 4:11-12

11:7
[d] Ps 7:9,11; 45:7
[e] Ps 33:5
[f] Ps 17:15

12:1
[g] Isa 57:1

12:2
[h] Ps 10:7; 41:6; 55:21; Ro 16:18

12:3
[i] Da 7:8; Rev 13:5

12:5
[j] Ps 10:18; 34:6

12:6
[k] 2Sa 22:31; Ps 18:30; Pr 30:5

12:7
[l] Ps 37:28

12:8
[m] Ps 55:10-11

13:1
[n] Job 13:24; Ps 44:24

2 How long must I wrestle with my thoughts[a]
and every day have sorrow in my heart?
How long will my enemy triumph over me?[b]

3 Look on me and answer,[c] O LORD my God.
Give light to my eyes,[d] or I will sleep in death;[e]
4 my enemy will say, "I have overcome him,[f]"
and my foes will rejoice when I fall.

5 But I trust in your unfailing love;[g]
my heart rejoices in your salvation.[h]
6 I will sing[i] to the LORD,
for he has been good to me.

Psalm 14

For the director of music. Of David.

Psalm 14 Theme ______________________________

1 The fool[a] says in his heart,
"There is no God."[j]
They are corrupt, their deeds are vile;
there is no one who does good.

2 The LORD looks down from heaven[k]
on the sons of men
to see if there are any who understand,[l]
any who seek God.
3 All have turned aside,
they have together become corrupt;[m]
there is no one who does good,[n]
not even one.[o]

4 Will evildoers never learn—[p]
those who devour my people[q] as men eat bread
and who do not call on the LORD?[r]
5 There they are, overwhelmed with dread,
for God is present in the company of the righteous.
6 You evildoers frustrate the plans of the poor,
but the LORD is their refuge.[s]

7 Oh, that salvation for Israel would come out of Zion!
When the LORD restores the fortunes[t] of his people,
let Jacob rejoice and Israel be glad!

13:2 [a]Ps 42:4 [b]Ps 42:9
13:3 [c]Ps 5:1 [d]Ezr 9:8 [e]Jer 51:39
13:4 [f]Ps 25:2
13:5 [g]Ps 52:8 [h]Ps 9:14
13:6 [i]Ps 116:7
14:1 [j]Ps 10:4
14:2 [k]Ps 33:13 [l]Ps 92:6
14:3 [m]Ps 58:3 [n]Ps 143:2 [o]Ro 3:10-12*
14:4 [p]Ps 82:5 [q]Ps 27:2 [r]Ps 79:6; Isa 64:7
14:6 [s]Ps 9:9; 40:17
14:7 [t]Ps 53:6

a *1* The Hebrew words rendered *fool* in Psalms denote one who is morally deficient.

Psalm 15

A psalm of David.

*Psalm 15 Theme*______________________________________

1 LORD, who may dwell in your sanctuary?[a]
Who may live on your holy hill?[b]

2 He whose walk is blameless
and who does what is righteous,
who speaks the truth[c] from his heart
3 and has no slander[d] on his tongue,
who does his neighbor no wrong
and casts no slur on his fellowman,
4 who despises a vile man
but honors[e] those who fear the LORD,
who keeps his oath[f]
even when it hurts,
5 who lends his money without usury[g]
and does not accept a bribe[h] against the innocent.

He who does these things
will never be shaken.[i]

Psalm 16

A *miktam*[a] of David.

*Psalm 16 Theme*______________________________________

1 Keep me safe,[j] O God,
for in you I take refuge.[k]

2 I said to the LORD, "You are my Lord;
apart from you I have no good thing."[l]
3 As for the saints who are in the land,[m]
they are the glorious ones in whom is all my delight.[b]
4 The sorrows[n] of those will increase
who run after other gods.[o]
I will not pour out their libations of blood
or take up their names[p] on my lips.

5 LORD, you have assigned me my portion[q] and my cup;[r]
you have made my lot secure.

15:1
[a] Ps 27:5-6
[b] Ps 24:3-5

15:2
[c] Ps 24:4; Zec 8:3,16; Eph 4:25

15:3
[d] Ex 23:1

15:4
[e] Ac 28:10
[f] Jdg 11:35

15:5
[g] Ex 22:25
[h] Ex 23:8; Dt 16:19
[i] 2Pe 1:10

16:1
[j] Ps 17:8
[k] Ps 7:1

16:2
[l] Ps 73:25

16:3
[m] Ps 101:6

16:4
[n] Ps 32:10
[o] Ps 106:37-38
[p] Ex 23:13

16:5
[q] Ps 73:26
[r] Ps 23:5

[a] Title: Probably a literary or musical term [b] 3 Or *As for the pagan priests who are in the land / and the nobles in whom all delight, I said:*

16:6 [a]Ps 78:55; Jer 3:19
16:7 [b]Ps 73:24 [c]Ps 77:6
16:8 [d]Ps 73:23
16:9 [e]Ps 4:7; 30:11 [f]Ps 4:8
16:10 [g]Ac 13:35*
16:11 [h]Mt 7:14 [i]Ac 2:25-28* [j]Ps 36:7-8

6 The boundary lines have fallen for me in pleasant places;
surely I have a delightful inheritance.[a]

7 I will praise the LORD, who counsels me;[b]
even at night[c] my heart instructs me.
8 I have set the LORD always before me.
Because he is at my right hand,[d]
I will not be shaken.

9 Therefore my heart is glad[e] and my tongue rejoices;
my body also will rest secure,[f]
10 because you will not abandon me to the grave,[a]
nor will you let your Holy One[b] see decay.[g]
11 You have made[c] known to me the path of life;[h]
you will fill me with joy in your presence,[i]
with eternal pleasures[j] at your right hand.

Psalm 17

A prayer of David.

*Psalm 17 Theme*____________________________

17:1 [k]Ps 61:1 [l]Isa 29:13
17:3 [m]Ps 26:2; 66:10 [n]Job 23:10; Jer 50:20 [o]Ps 39:1
17:5 [p]Ps 44:18; 119:133 [q]Ps 18:36
17:6 [r]Ps 86:7 [s]Ps 116:2 [t]Ps 88:2
17:7 [u]Ps 31:21 [v]Ps 20:6

1 Hear, O LORD, my righteous plea;
listen to my cry.[k]
Give ear to my prayer—
it does not rise from deceitful lips.[l]
2 May my vindication come from you;
may your eyes see what is right.

3 Though you probe my heart and examine me at night,
though you test me,[m] you will find nothing;[n]
I have resolved that my mouth will not sin.[o]
4 As for the deeds of men—
by the word of your lips
I have kept myself
from the ways of the violent.
5 My steps have held to your paths;[p]
my feet have not slipped.[q]

6 I call on you, O God, for you will answer me;[r]
give ear to me[s] and hear my prayer.[t]
7 Show the wonder of your great love,[u]
you who save by your right hand[v]
those who take refuge in you from their foes.

[a] *10* Hebrew *Sheol* [b] *10* Or *your faithful one* [c] *11* Or *You will make*

8Keep me as the apple of your eye;[a]
hide me in the shadow of your wings
9from the wicked who assail me,
from my mortal enemies who surround me.[b]

10They close up their callous hearts,[c]
and their mouths speak with arrogance.[d]
11They have tracked me down, they now surround me,[e]
with eyes alert, to throw me to the ground.
12They are like a lion[f] hungry for prey,
like a great lion crouching in cover.

13Rise up, O LORD, confront them, bring them down;[g]
rescue me from the wicked by your sword.
14O LORD, by your hand save me from such men,
from men of this world[h] whose reward is in this life.

You still the hunger of those you cherish;
their sons have plenty,
and they store up wealth[i] for their children.
15And I—in righteousness I will see your face;
when I awake, I will be satisfied with seeing your
likeness.[j]

Psalm 18

For the director of music. Of David the servant of the LORD. He sang to the LORD the words of this song when the LORD delivered him from the hand of all his enemies and from the hand of Saul. He said:

Psalm 18 Theme ________________________

1I love you, O LORD, my strength.

2The LORD is my rock,[k] my fortress and my deliverer;
my God is my rock, in whom I take refuge.
He is my shield[l] and the horn[a] of my salvation,[m]
my stronghold.
3I call to the LORD, who is worthy of praise,[n]
and I am saved from my enemies.

4The cords of death[o] entangled me;
the torrents[p] of destruction overwhelmed me.
5The cords of the grave[b] coiled around me;
the snares of death[q] confronted me.
6In my distress I called to the LORD;
I cried to my God for help.

a2 *Horn* here symbolizes strength. b5 Hebrew *Sheol*

17:8 [a] Dt 32:10
17:9 [b] Ps 31:20; 109:3
17:10 [c] Ps 73:7 [d] 1Sa 2:3
17:11 [e] Ps 37:14; 88:17
17:12 [f] Ps 7:2; 10:9
17:13 [g] Ps 7:12; 22:20; 73:18
17:14 [h] Lk 16:8 [i] Ps 73:3-7
17:15 [j] Nu 12:8; Ps 4:6-7; 16:11; 1Jn 3:2
18:2 [k] Ps 19:14 [l] Ps 59:11 [m] Ps 75:10
18:3 [n] Ps 48:1
18:4 [o] Ps 116:3 [p] Ps 124:4
18:5 [q] Ps 116:3

From his temple he heard my voice;[a]
my cry came before him, into his ears.

7 The earth trembled and quaked,[b]
and the foundations of the mountains shook;
they trembled because he was angry.[c]
8 Smoke rose from his nostrils;
consuming fire[d] came from his mouth,
burning coals blazed out of it.
9 He parted the heavens and came down;[e]
dark clouds were under his feet.
10 He mounted the cherubim[f] and flew;
he soared on the wings of the wind.[g]
11 He made darkness his covering,[h] his canopy
around him—
the dark rain clouds of the sky.
12 Out of the brightness of his presence[i] clouds advanced,
with hailstones and bolts of lightning.[j]
13 The LORD thundered[k] from heaven;
the voice of the Most High resounded.[a]
14 He shot his arrows and scattered ⌊the enemies⌋,
great bolts of lightning and routed them.[l]
15 The valleys of the sea were exposed
and the foundations of the earth laid bare
at your rebuke,[m] O LORD,
at the blast of breath from your nostrils.

16 He reached down from on high and took hold of me;
he drew me out of deep waters.[n]
17 He rescued me from my powerful enemy,
from my foes, who were too strong for me.[o]
18 They confronted me in the day of my disaster,
but the LORD was my support.[p]
19 He brought me out into a spacious place;[q]
he rescued me because he delighted in me.[r]

20 The LORD has dealt with me according to
my righteousness;
according to the cleanness of my hands[s] he has
rewarded me.
21 For I have kept the ways of the LORD;[t]
I have not done evil by turning[u] from my God.
22 All his laws are before me;[v]
I have not turned away from his decrees.

18:6 [a]Ps 34:15
18:7 [b]Jdg 5:4 [c]Ps 68:7-8
18:8 [d]Ps 50:3
18:9 [e]Ps 144:5
18:10 [f]Ps 80:1 [g]Ps 104:3
18:11 [h]Dt 4:11; Ps 97:2
18:12 [i]Ps 104:2 [j]Ps 97:3
18:13 [k]Ps 29:3; 104:7
18:14 [l]Ps 144:6
18:15 [m]Ps 76:6; 106:9
18:16 [n]Ps 144:7
18:17 [o]Ps 35:10
18:18 [p]Ps 59:16
18:19 [q]Ps 31:8 [r]Ps 118:5
18:20 [s]Ps 24:4
18:21 [t]2Ch 34:33 [u]Ps 119:102
18:22 [v]Ps 119:30

[a] *13* Some Hebrew manuscripts and Septuagint (see also 2 Samuel 22:14); most Hebrew manuscripts *resounded, / amid hailstones and bolts of lightning*

[23]I have been blameless before him
and have kept myself from sin.
[24]The LORD has rewarded me according to my
righteousness,[a]
according to the cleanness of my hands in his sight.

[25]To the faithful[b] you show yourself faithful,
to the blameless you show yourself blameless,
[26]to the pure you show yourself pure,
but to the crooked you show yourself shrewd.[c]
[27]You save the humble
but bring low those whose eyes are haughty.[d]
[28]You, O LORD, keep my lamp burning;
my God turns my darkness into light.[e]
[29]With your help[f] I can advance against a troop[a];
with my God I can scale a wall.

[30]As for God, his way is perfect;[g]
the word of the LORD is flawless.[h]
He is a shield
for all who take refuge[i] in him.
[31]For who is God besides the LORD?[j]
And who is the Rock[k] except our God?
[32]It is God who arms me with strength[l]
and makes my way perfect.
[33]He makes my feet like the feet of a deer;[m]
he enables me to stand on the heights.[n]
[34]He trains my hands for battle;[o]
my arms can bend a bow of bronze.
[35]You give me your shield of victory,
and your right hand sustains[p] me;
you stoop down to make me great.
[36]You broaden the path beneath me,
so that my ankles do not turn.

[37]I pursued my enemies[q] and overtook them;
I did not turn back till they were destroyed.
[38]I crushed them so that they could not rise;[r]
they fell beneath my feet.[s]
[39]You armed me with strength for battle;
you made my adversaries bow at my feet.
[40]You made my enemies turn their backs[t] in flight,
and I destroyed[u] my foes.
[41]They cried for help, but there was no one to
save them[v]—
to the LORD, but he did not answer.[w]

18:24 [a]1Sa 26:23
18:25 [b]1Ki 8:32; Ps 62:12; Mt 5:7
18:26 [c]Pr 3:34
18:27 [d]Pr 6:17
18:28 [e]Job 18:6; 29:3
18:29 [f]Heb 11:34
18:30 [g]Dt 32:4; Rev 15:3 [h]Ps 12:6 [i]Ps 17:7
18:31 [j]Dt 32:39; 86:8; Isa 45:5,6,14, 18,21 [k]Dt 32:31; 1Sa 2:2
18:32 [l]Isa 45:5
18:33 [m]Hab 3:19 [n]Dt 32:13
18:34 [o]Ps 144:1
18:35 [p]Ps 119:116
18:37 [q]Ps 37:20; 44:5
18:38 [r]Ps 36:12 [s]Ps 47:3
18:40 [t]Ps 21:12 [u]Ps 94:23
18:41 [v]Ps 50:22 [w]Job 27:9; Pr 1:28

[a]29 Or *can run through a barricade*

42 I beat them as fine as dust borne on the wind;
I poured them out like mud in the streets.

43 You have delivered me from the attacks of the people;
you have made me the head of nations;[a]
people I did not know[b] are subject to me.
44 As soon as they hear me, they obey me;
foreigners[c] cringe before me.
45 They all lose heart;
they come trembling from their strongholds.[d]

46 The LORD lives! Praise be to my Rock!
Exalted be God my Savior![e]
47 He is the God who avenges me,
who subdues nations[f] under me,
48 who saves[g] me from my enemies.
You exalted me above my foes;
from violent men you rescued me.
49 Therefore I will praise you among the nations, O LORD;
I will sing[h] praises to your name.[i]
50 He gives his king great victories;
he shows unfailing kindness to his anointed,
to David[j] and his descendants forever.[k]

Psalm 19

For the director of music. A psalm of David.

*Psalm 19 Theme*________________________

1 The heavens[l] declare[m] the glory of God;
the skies proclaim the work of his hands.
2 Day after day they pour forth speech;
night after night they display knowledge.[n]
3 There is no speech or language
where their voice is not heard.[a]
4 Their voice[b] goes out into all the earth,
their words to the ends of the world.[o]

In the heavens he has pitched a tent[p] for the sun,
5 which is like a bridegroom coming forth from
his pavilion,
like a champion rejoicing to run his course.
6 It rises at one end of the heavens

18:43 [a] 2Sa 8:1-14 [b] Isa 52:15; 55:5
18:44 [c] Ps 66:3
18:45 [d] Mic 7:17
18:46 [e] Ps 51:14
18:47 [f] Ps 47:3
18:48 [g] Ps 59:1
18:49 [h] Ps 108:1 [i] Ro 15:9*
18:50 [j] Ps 144:10 [k] Ps 89:4
19:1 [l] Isa 40:22 [m] Ps 50:6; Ro 1:19
19:2 [n] Ps 74:16
19:4 [o] Ro 10:18* [p] Ps 104:2

[a] 3 Or *They have no speech, there are no words; / no sound is heard from them* [b] 4 Septuagint, Jerome and Syriac; Hebrew *line*

and makes its circuit to the other;[a]
nothing is hidden from its heat.

7The law of the LORD is perfect,
reviving the soul.[b]
The statutes of the LORD are trustworthy,[c]
making wise the simple.[d]
8The precepts of the LORD are right,[e]
giving joy to the heart.
The commands of the LORD are radiant,
giving light to the eyes.
9The fear of the LORD is pure,
enduring forever.
The ordinances of the LORD are sure
and altogether righteous.[f]
10They are more precious than gold,[g]
than much pure gold;
they are sweeter than honey,
than honey from the comb.
11By them is your servant warned;
in keeping them there is great reward.

12Who can discern his errors?
Forgive my hidden faults.[h]
13Keep your servant also from willful sins;
may they not rule over me.
Then will I be blameless,
innocent of great transgression.

14May the words of my mouth and the meditation of my heart
be pleasing[i] in your sight,
O LORD, my Rock[j] and my Redeemer.[k]

Psalm 20

For the director of music. A psalm of David.

*Psalm 20 Theme*____________________________________

1May the LORD answer you when you are in distress;
may the name of the God of Jacob[l] protect you.[m]
2May he send you help from the sanctuary[n]
and grant you support from Zion.
3May he remember[o] all your sacrifices
and accept your burnt offerings.[p] *Selah*

19:6 [a]Ps 113:3; Ecc 1:5
19:7 [b]Ps 23:3 [c]Ps 93:5; 111:7 [d]Ps 119:98-100
19:8 [e]Ps 12:6; 119:128
19:9 [f]Ps 119:138,142
19:10 [g]Pr 8:10
19:12 [h]Ps 51:2; 90:8; 139:6
19:14 [i]Ps 104:34 [j]Ps 18:2 [k]Isa 47:4
20:1 [l]Ps 46:7,11 [m]Ps 91:14
20:2 [n]Ps 3:4
20:3 [o]Ac 10:4 [p]Ps 51:19

20:4 [a]Ps 21:2; 145:16,19

20:5 [b]Ps 9:14; 60:4 [c]1Sa 1:17

20:6 [d]Ps 28:8; 41:11; Isa 58:9

20:7 [e]Ps 33:17; Isa 31:1 [f]2Ch 32:8

20:8 [g]Mic 7:8 [h]Ps 37:23

20:9 [i]Ps 3:7; 17:6

21:1 [j]Ps 59:16-17

21:2 [k]Ps 37:4

21:3 [l]2Sa 12:30

21:4 [m]Ps 61:5-6; 91:16; 133:3

21:5 [n]Ps 18:50

21:6 [o]Ps 43:4 [p]1Ch 17:27

21:8 [q]Isa 10:10

21:9 [r]Ps 50:3; La 2:2; Mal 4:1

4 May he give you the desire of your heart[a]
and make all your plans succeed.
5 We will shout for joy when you are victorious
and will lift up our banners[b] in the name of our God.
May the LORD grant all your requests.[c]

6 Now I know that the LORD saves his anointed;[d]
he answers him from his holy heaven
with the saving power of his right hand.
7 Some trust in chariots and some in horses,[e]
but we trust in the name of the LORD our God.[f]
8 They are brought to their knees and fall,
but we rise up[g] and stand firm.[h]

9 O LORD, save the king!
Answer[a] us[i] when we call!

Psalm 21

For the director of music. A psalm of David.

*Psalm 21 Theme*______________________________

1 O LORD, the king rejoices in your strength.
How great is his joy in the victories you give![j]
2 You have granted him the desire of his heart[k]
and have not withheld the request of his lips. *Selah*
3 You welcomed him with rich blessings
and placed a crown of pure gold[l] on his head.
4 He asked you for life, and you gave it to him—
length of days, for ever and ever.[m]
5 Through the victories[n] you gave, his glory is great;
you have bestowed on him splendor and majesty.
6 Surely you have granted him eternal blessings
and made him glad with the joy[o] of your presence.[p]
7 For the king trusts in the LORD;
through the unfailing love of the Most High
he will not be shaken.

8 Your hand will lay hold[q] on all your enemies;
your right hand will seize your foes.
9 At the time of your appearing
you will make them like a fiery furnace.
In his wrath the LORD will swallow them up,
and his fire will consume them.[r]

a9 Or *save! / O King, answer*

[10]You will destroy their descendants from the earth,
their posterity from mankind.[a]
[11]Though they plot evil[b] against you
and devise wicked schemes,[c] they cannot succeed;
[12]for you will make them turn their backs[d]
when you aim at them with drawn bow.

[13]Be exalted, O LORD, in your strength;
we will sing and praise your might.

Psalm 22

For the director of music. To ⌊the tune of⌋ "The Doe of the Morning."
A psalm of David.

*Psalm 22 Theme*____________________

[1]My God, my God, why have you forsaken me?[e]
Why are you so far[f] from saving me,
so far from the words of my groaning?
[2]O my God, I cry out by day, but you do not answer,
by night,[g] and am not silent.

[3]Yet you are enthroned as the Holy One;[h]
you are the praise[i] of Israel.[a]
[4]In you our fathers put their trust;
they trusted and you delivered them.
[5]They cried to you and were saved;
in you they trusted and were not disappointed.[j]

[6]But I am a worm[k] and not a man,
scorned by men[l] and despised[m] by the people.
[7]All who see me mock me;
they hurl insults,[n] shaking their heads:[o]
[8]"He trusts in the LORD;
let the LORD rescue him.[p]
Let him deliver him,
since he delights[q] in him."

[9]Yet you brought me out of the womb;[r]
you made me trust in you
even at my mother's breast.
[10]From birth[s] I was cast upon you;
from my mother's womb you have been my God.
[11]Do not be far from me,
for trouble is near
and there is no one to help.[t]

a 3 Or *Yet you are holy, / enthroned on the praises of Israel*

21:10
[a]Dt 28:18; Ps 37:28

21:11
[b]Ps 2:1
[c]Ps 10:2

21:12
[d]Ps 7:12-13; 18:40

22:1
[e]Mt 27:46*; Mk 15:34*
[f]Ps 10:1

22:2
[g]Ps 42:3

22:3
[h]Ps 99:9
[i]Dt 10:21

22:5
[j]Isa 49:23

22:6
[k]Job 25:6; Isa 41:14
[l]Ps 31:11
[m]Isa 49:7; 53:3

22:7
[n]Mt 27:39,44
[o]Mk 15:29

22:8
[p]Ps 91:14
[q]Mt 27:43

22:9
[r]Ps 71:6

22:10
[s]Isa 46:3

22:11
[t]Ps 72:12

[12]Many bulls[a] surround me;
strong bulls of Bashan[b] encircle me.
[13]Roaring lions[c] tearing their prey
open their mouths wide[d] against me.
[14]I am poured out like water,
and all my bones are out of joint.[e]
My heart has turned to wax;
it has melted away[f] within me.
[15]My strength is dried up like a potsherd,
and my tongue sticks to the roof of my mouth;[g]
you lay me[a] in the dust[h] of death.
[16]Dogs[i] have surrounded me;
a band of evil men has encircled me,
they have pierced[b][j] my hands and my feet.
[17]I can count all my bones;
people stare[k] and gloat over me.[l]
[18]They divide my garments among them
and cast lots[m] for my clothing.

[19]But you, O LORD, be not far off;
O my Strength, come quickly[n] to help me.
[20]Deliver my life from the sword,
my precious life[o] from the power of the dogs.
[21]Rescue me from the mouth of the lions;
save[c] me from the horns of the wild oxen.

[22]I will declare your name to my brothers;
in the congregation I will praise you.[p]
[23]You who fear the LORD, praise him![q]
All you descendants of Jacob, honor him!
Revere him,[r] all you descendants of Israel!
[24]For he has not despised or disdained
the suffering of the afflicted one;
he has not hidden his face[s] from him
but has listened to his cry for help.[t]

[25]From you comes the theme of my praise in the great
assembly;[u]
before those who fear you[d] will I fulfill my vows.[v]
[26]The poor will eat[w] and be satisfied;
they who seek the LORD will praise him—[x]
may your hearts live forever!
[27]All the ends of the earth[y]
will remember and turn to the LORD,
and all the families of the nations
will bow down before him,[z]

22:12 [a]Ps 68:30 [b]Dt 32:14
22:13 [c]Ps 17:12 [d]Ps 35:21
22:14 [e]Ps 31:10 [f]Job 30:16; Da 5:6
22:15 [g]Ps 38:10; Jn 19:28 [h]Ps 104:29
22:16 [i]Ps 59:6 [j]Isa 53:5; Zec 12:10; Jn 19:34
22:17 [k]Lk 23:35 [l]Lk 23:27
22:18 [m]Mt 27:35*; Lk 23:34; Jn 19:24*
22:19 [n]Ps 70:5
22:20 [o]Ps 35:17
22:22 [p]Heb 2:12*
22:23 [q]Ps 86:12; 135:19 [r]Ps 33:8
22:24 [s]Ps 69:17 [t]Heb 5:7
22:25 [u]Ps 35:18 [v]Ecc 5:4
22:26 [w]Ps 107:9 [x]Ps 40:16
22:27 [y]Ps 2:8 [z]Ps 86:9

[a]*15* Or */ I am laid* [b]*16* Some Hebrew manuscripts, Septuagint and Syriac; most Hebrew manuscripts */ like the lion,* [c]*21* Or */ you have heard* [d]*25* Hebrew *him*

[28]for dominion belongs to the LORD[a]
and he rules over the nations.

[29]All the rich[b] of the earth will feast and worship;
all who go down to the dust[c] will kneel before him—
those who cannot keep themselves alive.
[30]Posterity[d] will serve him;
future generations will be told about the Lord.
[31]They will proclaim his righteousness
to a people yet unborn[e]—
for he has done it.

Psalm 23

A psalm of David.

*Psalm 23 Theme*________________________

[1]The LORD is my shepherd,[f] I shall not be in want.[g]
[2] He makes me lie down in green pastures,
he leads me beside quiet waters,[h]
[3] he restores my soul.[i]
He guides me in paths of righteousness[j]
for his name's sake.
[4]Even though I walk
through the valley of the shadow of death,[a][k]
I will fear no evil,[l]
for you are with me;[m]
your rod and your staff,
they comfort me.

[5]You prepare a table before me
in the presence of my enemies.
You anoint my head with oil;[n]
my cup[o] overflows.
[6]Surely goodness and love will follow me
all the days of my life,
and I will dwell in the house of the LORD forever.

Psalm 24

Of David. A psalm.

*Psalm 24 Theme*________________________

[1]The earth is the LORD's,[p] and everything in it,
the world, and all who live in it;[q]

a4 Or *through the darkest valley*

22:28 [a]Ps 47:7-8
22:29 [b]Ps 45:12 [c]Isa 26:19
22:30 [d]Ps 102:28
22:31 [e]Ps 78:6
23:1 [f]Isa 40:11; Jn 10:11; 1Pe 2:25 [g]Php 4:19
23:2 [h]Eze 34:14; Rev 7:17
23:3 [i]Ps 19:7 [j]Ps 5:8; 85:13
23:4 [k]Job 10:21-22 [l]Ps 3:6; 27:1 [m]Isa 43:2
23:5 [n]Ps 92:10 [o]Ps 16:5
24:1 [p]Ex 9:29; Job 41:11; Ps 89:11 [q]1Co 10:26*

24:3 [a]Ps 2:6 [b]Ps 15:1; 65:4

2 for he founded it upon the seas
and established it upon the waters.

3 Who may ascend the hill[a] of the LORD?
Who may stand in his holy place?[b]
4 He who has clean hands[c] and a pure heart,[d]
who does not lift up his soul to an idol
or swear by what is false.[a]

24:4 [c]Job 17:9 [d]Mt 5:8

5 He will receive blessing from the LORD
and vindication from God his Savior.
6 Such is the generation of those who seek him,
who seek your face,[e] O God of Jacob.[b] *Selah*

24:6 [e]Ps 27:8

7 Lift up your heads, O you gates;[f]
be lifted up, you ancient doors,
that the King of glory[g] may come in.
8 Who is this King of glory?
The LORD strong and mighty,
the LORD mighty in battle.[h]

24:7 [f]Isa 26:2 [g]Ps 97:6; 1Co 2:8

9 Lift up your heads, O you gates;
lift them up, you ancient doors,
that the King of glory may come in.
10 Who is he, this King of glory?
The LORD Almighty—
he is the King of glory. *Selah*

24:8 [h]Ps 76:3-6

Psalm 25[c]

Of David.

*Psalm 25 Theme*____________________________

25:1 [i]Ps 86:4

1 To you, O LORD, I lift up my soul;[i]
2 in you I trust,[j] O my God.
Do not let me be put to shame,
nor let my enemies triumph over me.
3 No one whose hope is in you
will ever be put to shame,[k]
but they will be put to shame
who are treacherous without excuse.

25:2 [j]Ps 41:11

4 Show me your ways, O LORD,
teach me your paths;[l]
5 guide me in your truth and teach me,
for you are God my Savior,
and my hope is in you all day long.

25:3 [k]Isa 49:23

25:4 [l]Ex 33:13

[a]4 Or *swear falsely* [b]6 Two Hebrew manuscripts and Syriac (see also Septuagint); most Hebrew manuscripts *face, Jacob* [c]This psalm is an acrostic poem, the verses of which begin with the successive letters of the Hebrew alphabet.

6 Remember, O LORD, your great mercy and love,[a]
for they are from of old.
7 Remember not the sins of my youth[b]
and my rebellious ways;
according to your love[c] remember me,
for you are good, O LORD.

8 Good and upright[d] is the LORD;
therefore he instructs[e] sinners in his ways.
9 He guides[f] the humble in what is right
and teaches them[g] his way.
10 All the ways of the LORD are loving and faithful[h]
for those who keep the demands of his covenant.[i]
11 For the sake of your name,[j] O LORD,
forgive my iniquity, though it is great.
12 Who, then, is the man that fears the LORD?
He will instruct him in the way[k] chosen for him.
13 He will spend his days in prosperity,[l]
and his descendants will inherit the land.[m]
14 The LORD confides[n] in those who fear him;
he makes his covenant known[o] to them.
15 My eyes are ever on the LORD,[p]
for only he will release my feet from the snare.

16 Turn to me[q] and be gracious to me,
for I am lonely and afflicted.
17 The troubles of my heart have multiplied;
free me from my anguish.[r]
18 Look upon my affliction and my distress[s]
and take away all my sins.
19 See how my enemies[t] have increased
and how fiercely they hate me!
20 Guard my life[u] and rescue me;
let me not be put to shame,
for I take refuge in you.
21 May integrity[v] and uprightness protect me,
because my hope is in you.

22 Redeem Israel,[w] O God,
from all their troubles!

Psalm 26

Of David.

Psalm 26 Theme ______________________________

1 Vindicate me, O LORD,
for I have led a blameless life;[x]

25:6 [a]Ps 103:17; Isa 63:7,15
25:7 [b]Job 13:26; Jer 3:25 [c]Ps 51:1
25:8 [d]Ps 92:15 [e]Ps 32:8
25:9 [f]Ps 23:3 [g]Ps 27:11
25:10 [h]Ps 40:11 [i]Ps 103:18
25:11 [j]Ps 31:3; 79:9
25:12 [k]Ps 37:23
25:13 [l]Pr 19:23 [m]Ps 37:11
25:14 [n]Pr 3:32 [o]Jn 7:17
25:15 [p]Ps 141:8
25:16 [q]Ps 69:16
25:17 [r]Ps 107:6
25:18 [s]2Sa 16:12
25:19 [t]Ps 3:1
25:20 [u]Ps 86:2
25:21 [v]Ps 41:12
25:22 [w]Ps 130:8
26:1 [x]Ps 7:8; Pr 20:7

I have trusted[a] in the LORD
without wavering.[b]
2Test me,[c] O LORD, and try me,
examine my heart and my mind;[d]
3for your love is ever before me,
and I walk continually[e] in your truth.
4I do not sit[f] with deceitful men,
nor do I consort with hypocrites;
5I abhor[g] the assembly of evildoers
and refuse to sit with the wicked.
6I wash my hands in innocence,[h]
and go about your altar, O LORD,
7proclaiming aloud your praise
and telling of all your wonderful deeds.[i]
8I love[j] the house where you live, O LORD,
the place where your glory dwells.

9Do not take away my soul along with sinners,
my life with bloodthirsty men,[k]
10in whose hands are wicked schemes,
whose right hands are full of bribes.[l]
11But I lead a blameless life;
redeem me[m] and be merciful to me.

12My feet stand on level ground;[n]
in the great assembly[o] I will praise the LORD.

Psalm 27

Of David.

*Psalm 27 Theme*____________________________

1The LORD is my light[p] and my salvation[q]—
whom shall I fear?
The LORD is the stronghold of my life—
of whom shall I be afraid?[r]
2When evil men advance against me
to devour my flesh,[a]
when my enemies and my foes attack me,
they will stumble and fall.[s]
3Though an army besiege me,
my heart will not fear;[t]
though war break out against me,
even then will I be confident.[u]

26:1 [a]Ps 28:7 [b]2Ki 20:3; Heb 10:23
26:2 [c]Ps 17:3 [d]Ps 7:9
26:3 [e]2Ki 20:3
26:4 [f]Ps 1:1
26:5 [g]Ps 31:6; 139:21
26:6 [h]Ps 73:13
26:7 [i]Ps 9:1
26:8 [j]Ps 27:4
26:9 [k]Ps 28:3
26:10 [l]1Sa 8:3
26:11 [m]Ps 69:18
26:12 [n]Ps 27:11; 40:2 [o]Ps 22:22
27:1 [p]Isa 60:19 [q]Ex 15:2 [r]Ps 118:6
27:2 [s]Ps 9:3; 14:4
27:3 [t]Ps 3:6 [u]Job 4:6

[a]2 Or *to slander me*

[4]One thing[a] I ask of the LORD,
this is what I seek:
that I may dwell in the house of the LORD
all the days of my life,[b]
to gaze upon the beauty of the LORD
and to seek him in his temple.
[5]For in the day of trouble
he will keep me safe in his dwelling;
he will hide me[c] in the shelter of his tabernacle
and set me high upon a rock.[d]
[6]Then my head will be exalted[e]
above the enemies who surround me;
at his tabernacle will I sacrifice[f] with shouts of joy;
I will sing and make music to the LORD.

[7]Hear my voice when I call, O LORD;
be merciful to me and answer me.[g]
[8]My heart says of you, "Seek his[a] face!"
Your face, LORD, I will seek.
[9]Do not hide your face[h] from me,
do not turn your servant away in anger;
you have been my helper.
Do not reject me or forsake me,
O God my Savior.
[10]Though my father and mother forsake me,
the LORD will receive me.
[11]Teach me your way, O LORD;
lead me in a straight path[i]
because of my oppressors.
[12]Do not turn me over to the desire of my foes,
for false witnesses[j] rise up against me,
breathing out violence.

[13]I am still confident of this:
I will see the goodness of the LORD[k]
in the land of the living.[l]
[14]Wait[m] for the LORD;
be strong and take heart
and wait for the LORD.

Psalm 28

Of David.

Psalm 28 Theme ______________________________

[1]To you I call, O LORD my Rock;
do not turn a deaf ear to me.

[a]8 Or *To you, O my heart, he has said, "Seek my*

27:4
[a]Ps 90:17
[b]Ps 23:6; 26:8

27:5
[c]Ps 17:8; 31:20
[d]Ps 40:2

27:6
[e]Ps 3:3
[f]Ps 107:22

27:7
[g]Ps 13:3

27:9
[h]Ps 69:17

27:11
[i]Ps 5:8; 25:4; 86:11

27:12
[j]Mt 26:60; Ac 9:1

27:13
[k]Ps 31:19
[l]Jer 11:19; Eze 26:20

27:14
[m]Ps 40:1

28:1 [a]Ps 83:1 [b]Ps 88:4

For if you remain silent,[a]
I will be like those who have gone down to the pit.[b]

28:2 [c]Ps 138:2; 140:6 [d]Ps 5:7

2 Hear my cry for mercy[c]
as I call to you for help,
as I lift up my hands
toward your Most Holy Place.[d]

28:3 [e]Ps 12:2; Ps 26:9; Jer 9:8

3 Do not drag me away with the wicked,
with those who do evil,
who speak cordially with their neighbors
but harbor malice in their hearts.[e]

28:4 [f]2Ti 4:14; Rev 22:12 [g]Rev 18:6

4 Repay them for their deeds
and for their evil work;
repay them for what their hands have done[f]
and bring back upon them what they deserve.[g]

28:5 [h]Isa 5:12

5 Since they show no regard for the works of the LORD
and what his hands have done,[h]
he will tear them down
and never build them up again.

28:7 [i]Ps 18:1 [j]Ps 13:5 [k]Ps 40:3; 69:30

6 Praise be to the LORD,
for he has heard my cry for mercy.
7 The LORD is my strength[i] and my shield;
my heart trusts[j] in him, and I am helped.
My heart leaps for joy
and I will give thanks to him in song.[k]

28:8 [l]Ps 20:6

28:9 [m]Dt 9:29; Ezr 1:4 [n]Isa 40:11 [o]Dt 1:31; 32:11

8 The LORD is the strength of his people,
a fortress of salvation for his anointed one.[l]
9 Save your people and bless your inheritance;[m]
be their shepherd[n] and carry them[o] forever.

Psalm 29

A psalm of David.

Psalm 29 Theme ______________________

29:1 [p]1Ch 16:28 [q]Ps 96:7-9

1 Ascribe to the LORD,[p] O mighty ones,
ascribe to the LORD glory[q] and strength.

29:2 [r]2Ch 20:21

2 Ascribe to the LORD the glory due his name;
worship the LORD in the splendor of his[a] holiness.[r]

29:3 [s]Job 37:5 [t]Ps 18:13

3 The voice[s] of the LORD is over the waters;
the God of glory thunders,[t]
the LORD thunders over the mighty waters.

[a] 2 Or *LORD with the splendor of*

[4]The voice of the LORD is powerful;[a]
the voice of the LORD is majestic.
[5]The voice of the LORD breaks the cedars;
the LORD breaks in pieces the cedars of Lebanon.[b]
[6]He makes Lebanon skip[c] like a calf,
Sirion[a] [d] like a young wild ox.
[7]The voice of the LORD strikes
with flashes of lightning.
[8]The voice of the LORD shakes the desert;
the LORD shakes the Desert of Kadesh.[e]
[9]The voice of the LORD twists the oaks[b]
and strips the forests bare.
And in his temple all cry, "Glory!"[f]
[10]The LORD sits[c] enthroned over the flood;[g]
the LORD is enthroned as King forever.[h]
[11]The LORD gives strength to his people;[i]
the LORD blesses his people with peace.[j]

Psalm 30

A psalm. A song. For the dedication of the temple.[d] Of David.

*Psalm 30 Theme*____________________________________

[1]I will exalt you, O Lord,
for you lifted me out of the depths
and did not let my enemies gloat over me.[k]
[2]O LORD my God, I called to you for help[l]
and you healed me.[m]
[3]O LORD, you brought me up from the grave[e];
you spared me from going down into the pit.[n]

[4]Sing to the LORD, you saints[o] of his;
praise his holy name.[p]
[5]For his anger[q] lasts only a moment,
but his favor lasts a lifetime;
weeping may remain for a night,
but rejoicing comes in the morning.[r]

[6]When I felt secure, I said,
"I will never be shaken."
[7]O LORD, when you favored me,
you made my mountain[f] stand firm;
but when you hid your face,[s]
I was dismayed.

[a] 6 That is, Mount Hermon [b] 9 Or *LORD makes the deer give birth* [c] *10* Or *sat* [d] Title: Or *palace* [e] 3 Hebrew *Sheol* [f] 7 Or *hill country*

29:4 [a] Ps 68:33
29:5 [b] Jdg 9:15
29:6 [c] Ps 114:4 [d] Dt 3:9
29:8 [e] Nu 13:26
29:9 [f] Ps 26:8
29:10 [g] Ge 6:17 [h] Ps 10:16
29:11 [i] Ps 28:8 [j] Ps 37:11
30:1 [k] Ps 25:2; 28:9
30:2 [l] Ps 88:13 [m] Ps 6:2
30:3 [n] Ps 28:1; 86:13
30:4 [o] Ps 149:1 [p] Ps 97:12
30:5 [q] Ps 103:9 [r] 2Co 4:17
30:7 [s] Dt 31:17; Ps 104:29

8 To you, O LORD, I called;
to the Lord I cried for mercy:
9 "What gain is there in my destruction,[a]
in my going down into the pit?
Will the dust praise you?
Will it proclaim your faithfulness?[a]
10 Hear, O LORD, and be merciful to me;
O LORD, be my help."

11 You turned my wailing into dancing;
you removed my sackcloth and clothed me with joy,[b]
12 that my heart may sing to you and not be silent.
O LORD my God, I will give you thanks[c] forever.[d]

Psalm 31

For the director of music. A psalm of David.

*Psalm 31 Theme*________________________________

1 In you, O LORD, I have taken refuge;
let me never be put to shame;
deliver me in your righteousness.
2 Turn your ear to me,
come quickly to my rescue;
be my rock of refuge,[e]
a strong fortress to save me.
3 Since you are my rock and my fortress,[f]
for the sake of your name[g] lead and guide me.
4 Free me from the trap that is set for me,
for you are my refuge.[h]
5 Into your hands I commit my spirit;[i]
redeem me, O LORD, the God of truth.

6 I hate those who cling to worthless idols;
I trust in the LORD.[j]
7 I will be glad and rejoice in your love,
for you saw my affliction[k]
and knew the anguish[l] of my soul.
8 You have not handed me over[m] to the enemy
but have set my feet in a spacious place.

9 Be merciful to me, O LORD, for I am in distress;
my eyes grow weak with sorrow,[n]
my soul and my body with grief.

30:9 [a]Ps 6:5
30:11 [b]Ps 4:7; Jer 31:4,13
30:12 [c]Ps 16:9 [d]Ps 44:8
31:2 [e]Ps 18:2
31:3 [f]Ps 18:2 [g]Ps 23:3
31:4 [h]Ps 25:15
31:5 [i]Lk 23:46; Ac 7:59
31:6 [j]Jnh 2:8
31:7 [k]Ps 90:14 [l]Ps 10:14; Jn 10:27
31:8 [m]Dt 32:30
31:9 [n]Ps 6:7

a9 Or *there if I am silenced*

[10]My life is consumed by anguish
and my years by groaning;[a]
my strength fails because of my affliction,[a]
and my bones grow weak.[b]
[11]Because of all my enemies,
I am the utter contempt of my neighbors;[c]
I am a dread to my friends—
those who see me on the street flee from me.
[12]I am forgotten by them as though I were dead;[d]
I have become like broken pottery.
[13]For I hear the slander of many;
there is terror on every side;[e]
they conspire against me
and plot to take my life.[f]

[14]But I trust[g] in you, O LORD;
I say, "You are my God."
[15]My times[h] are in your hands;
deliver me from my enemies
and from those who pursue me.
[16]Let your face shine[i] on your servant;
save me in your unfailing love.
[17]Let me not be put to shame,[j] O LORD,
for I have cried out to you;
but let the wicked be put to shame
and lie silent[k] in the grave.[b]
[18]Let their lying lips[l] be silenced,
for with pride and contempt
they speak arrogantly[m] against the righteous.
[19]How great is your goodness,[n]
which you have stored up for those who fear you,
which you bestow in the sight of men[o]
on those who take refuge in you.
[20]In the shelter of your presence you hide[p] them
from the intrigues of men;[q]
in your dwelling you keep them safe
from accusing tongues.

[21]Praise be to the LORD,
for he showed his wonderful love[r] to me
when I was in a besieged city.[s]
[22]In my alarm[t] I said,
"I am cut off from your sight!"
Yet you heard my cry[u] for mercy
when I called to you for help.

a *10* Or *guilt*   b *17* Hebrew *Sheol*

31:10 [a]Ps 13:2 [b]Ps 38:3; 39:11

31:11 [c]Job 19:13; Ps 38:11; 64:8; Isa 53:4

31:12 [d]Ps 88:4

31:13 [e]Jer 20:3,10; La 2:22 [f]Mt 27:1

31:14 [g]Ps 140:6

31:15 [h]Job 24:1; Ps 143:9

31:16 [i]Nu 6:25; Ps 4:6

31:17 [j]Ps 25:2-3 [k]Ps 115:17

31:18 [l]Ps 120:2 [m]Ps 94:4

31:19 [n]Ro 11:22 [o]Isa 64:4

31:20 [p]Ps 27:5 [q]Job 5:21

31:21 [r]Ps 17:7 [s]1Sa 23:7

31:22 [t]Ps 116:11 [u]La 3:54

23 Love the LORD, all his saints![a]
The LORD preserves the faithful,[b]
but the proud he pays back[c] in full.
24 Be strong and take heart,[d]
all you who hope in the LORD.

Psalm 32

Of David. A *maskil*.[a]

Psalm 32 Theme ______________________________

1 Blessed is he
whose transgressions are forgiven,
whose sins are covered.[e]
2 Blessed is the man
whose sin the LORD does not count against him[f]
and in whose spirit is no deceit.[g]

3 When I kept silent,
my bones wasted away[h]
through my groaning all day long.
4 For day and night
your hand was heavy[i] upon me;
my strength was sapped
as in the heat of summer. *Selah*
5 Then I acknowledged my sin to you
and did not cover up my iniquity.
I said, "I will confess[j]
my transgressions[k] to the LORD"—
and you forgave
the guilt of my sin.[l] *Selah*

6 Therefore let everyone who is godly pray to you
while you may be found;[m]
surely when the mighty waters rise,
they will not reach him.[n]
7 You are my hiding place;
you will protect me from trouble[o]
and surround me with songs of deliverance.[p] *Selah*

8 I will instruct[q] you and teach you in the way
you should go;
I will counsel you and watch over[r] you.

31:23 [a]Ps 34:9 [b]Ps 145:20 [c]Ps 94:2
31:24 [d]Ps 27:14
32:1 [e]Ps 85:2
32:2 [f]Ro 4:7-8*; 2Co 5:19 [g]Jn 1:47
32:3 [h]Ps 31:10
32:4 [i]Job 33:7
32:5 [j]Pr 28:13 [k]Ps 103:12 [l]Lev 26:40
32:6 [m]Ps 69:13; Isa 55:6 [n]Isa 43:2
32:7 [o]Ps 9:9 [p]Ex 15:1
32:8 [q]Ps 25:8 [r]Ps 33:18

[a] Title: Probably a literary or musical term

[9]Do not be like the horse or the mule,
which have no understanding
but must be controlled by bit and bridle[a]
or they will not come to you.
[10]Many are the woes of the wicked,[b]
but the LORD's unfailing love
surrounds the man who trusts[c] in him.

[11]Rejoice in the LORD[d] and be glad, you righteous;
sing, all you who are upright in heart!

Psalm 33

*Psalm 33 Theme*___________________________________

[1]Sing joyfully to the LORD, you righteous;
it is fitting[e] for the upright[f] to praise him.
[2]Praise the LORD with the harp;
make music to him on the ten-stringed lyre.[g]
[3]Sing to him a new song;[h]
play skillfully, and shout for joy.

[4]For the word of the LORD is right[i] and true;
he is faithful in all he does.
[5]The LORD loves righteousness and justice;[j]
the earth is full of his unfailing love.[k]

[6]By the word[l] of the LORD were the heavens made,
their starry host by the breath of his mouth.
[7]He gathers the waters of the sea into jars[a];
he puts the deep into storehouses.
[8]Let all the earth fear the LORD;
let all the people of the world revere him.[m]
[9]For he spoke, and it came to be;
he commanded,[n] and it stood firm.
[10]The LORD foils the plans of the nations;[o]
he thwarts the purposes of the peoples.
[11]But the plans of the LORD stand firm forever,
the purposes[p] of his heart through all generations.

[12]Blessed is the nation whose God is the LORD,[q]
the people he chose[r] for his inheritance.
[13]From heaven the LORD looks down
and sees all mankind;[s]
[14]from his dwelling place[t] he watches
all who live on earth—

[a]7 Or *sea as into a heap*

32:9 [a]Pr 26:3
32:10 [b]Ro 2:9 [c]Pr 16:20
32:11 [d]Ps 64:10
33:1 [e]Ps 147:1 [f]Ps 32:11
33:2 [g]Ps 92:3
33:3 [h]Ps 96:1
33:4 [i]Ps 19:8
33:5 [j]Ps 11:7 [k]Ps 119:64
33:6 [l]Heb 11:3
33:8 [m]Ps 67:7; 96:9
33:9 [n]Ge 1:3; Ps 148:5
33:10 [o]Isa 8:10
33:11 [p]Job 23:13
33:12 [q]Ps 144:15 [r]Ex 19:5; Dt 7:6
33:13 [s]Job 28:24; Ps 11:4
33:14 [t]1Ki 8:39

33:15 [a]Job 10:8 [b]Jer 32:19
33:16 [c]Ps 44:6
33:17 [d]Ps 20:7; Pr 21:31
33:18 [e]Job 36:7; Ps 34:15 [f]Ps 147:11
33:19 [g]Job 5:20
33:20 [h]Ps 130:6
33:21 [i]Zec 10:7; Jn 16:22

15he who forms[a] the hearts of all,
who considers everything they do.[b]
16No king is saved by the size of his army;[c]
no warrior escapes by his great strength.
17A horse[d] is a vain hope for deliverance;
despite all its great strength it cannot save.
18But the eyes[e] of the LORD are on those who fear him,
on those whose hope is in his unfailing love,[f]
19to deliver them from death
and keep them alive in famine.[g]

20We wait[h] in hope for the LORD;
he is our help and our shield.
21In him our hearts rejoice,[i]
for we trust in his holy name.
22May your unfailing love rest upon us, O LORD,
even as we put our hope in you.

Psalm 34[a]

Of David. When he pretended to be insane before Abimelech,
who drove him away, and he left.

*Psalm 34 Theme*____________________________

34:1 [j]Ps 71:6; Eph 5:20
34:2 [k]Jer 9:24; 1Co 1:31 [l]Ps 119:74
34:3 [m]Lk 1:46
34:4 [n]Mt 7:7
34:5 [o]Ps 36:9 [p]Ps 25:3
34:7 [q]2Ki 6:17; Da 6:22
34:8 [r]1Pe 2:3 [s]Ps 2:12

1I will extol the LORD at all times;[j]
his praise will always be on my lips.
2My soul will boast[k] in the LORD;
let the afflicted hear and rejoice.[l]
3Glorify the LORD with me;
let us exalt[m] his name together.

4I sought the LORD,[n] and he answered me;
he delivered me from all my fears.
5Those who look to him are radiant;[o]
their faces are never covered with shame.[p]
6This poor man called, and the LORD heard him;
he saved him out of all his troubles.
7The angel of the LORD[q] encamps around those
who fear him,
and he delivers them.

8Taste and see that the LORD is good;[r]
blessed is the man who takes refuge[s] in him.

a This psalm is an acrostic poem, the verses of which begin with the successive letters of the Hebrew alphabet.

[9]Fear the LORD, you his saints,
for those who fear him lack nothing.[a]
[10]The lions may grow weak and hungry,
but those who seek the LORD lack no good thing.[b]

[11]Come, my children, listen to me;
I will teach you[c] the fear of the LORD.
[12]Whoever of you loves life[d]
and desires to see many good days,
[13]keep your tongue from evil
and your lips from speaking lies.[e]
[14]Turn from evil and do good;[f]
seek peace[g] and pursue it.

[15]The eyes of the LORD[h] are on the righteous[i]
and his ears are attentive to their cry;
[16]the face of the LORD is against[j] those who do evil,[k]
to cut off the memory[l] of them from the earth.

[17]The righteous cry out, and the LORD hears[m] them;
he delivers them from all their troubles.
[18]The LORD is close[n] to the brokenhearted[o]
and saves those who are crushed in spirit.

[19]A righteous man may have many troubles,[p]
but the LORD delivers him from them all;[q]
[20]he protects all his bones,
not one of them will be broken.[r]

[21]Evil will slay the wicked;[s]
the foes of the righteous will be condemned.
[22]The LORD redeems[t] his servants;
no one will be condemned who takes refuge in him.

Psalm 35

Of David.

*Psalm 35 Theme*______________________________

[1]Contend, O LORD, with those who contend with me;
fight[u] against those who fight against me.
[2]Take up shield and buckler;
arise[v] and come to my aid.
[3]Brandish spear and javelin[a]
against those who pursue me.
Say to my soul,
"I am your salvation."

[a]3 Or *and block the way*

34:9 [a]Ps 23:1
34:10 [b]Ps 84:11
34:11 [c]Ps 32:8
34:12 [d]1Pe 3:10
34:13 [e]1Pe 2:22
34:14 [f]Ps 37:27 [g]Heb 12:14
34:15 [h]Ps 33:18 [i]Job 36:7
34:16 [j]Lev 17:10; Jer 44:11 [k]1Pe 3:10-12* [l]Pr 10:7
34:17 [m]Ps 145:19
34:18 [n]Ps 145:18 [o]Isa 57:15
34:19 [p]ver 17 [q]ver 4,6; Pr 24:16
34:20 [r]Jn 19:36*
34:21 [s]Ps 94:23
34:22 [t]1Ki 1:29; Ps 71:23
35:1 [u]Ps 43:1
35:2 [v]Ps 62:2

4 May those who seek my life
be disgraced[a] and put to shame;
may those who plot my ruin
be turned back in dismay.
5 May they be like chaff[b] before the wind,
with the angel of the LORD driving them away;
6 may their path be dark and slippery,
with the angel of the LORD pursuing them.
7 Since they hid their net for me without cause
and without cause dug a pit for me,
8 may ruin overtake them by surprise—[c]
may the net they hid entangle them,
may they fall into the pit,[d] to their ruin.
9 Then my soul will rejoice[e] in the LORD
and delight in his salvation.[f]
10 My whole being will exclaim,
"Who is like you,[g] O LORD?
You rescue the poor from those too strong[h] for them,
the poor and needy[i] from those who rob them."

11 Ruthless witnesses[j] come forward;
they question me on things I know nothing about.
12 They repay me evil for good[k]
and leave my soul forlorn.
13 Yet when they were ill, I put on sackcloth
and humbled myself with fasting.[l]
When my prayers returned to me unanswered,
14 I went about mourning
as though for my friend or brother.
I bowed my head in grief
as though weeping for my mother.
15 But when I stumbled, they gathered in glee;
attackers gathered against me when I was unaware.
They slandered[m] me without ceasing.
16 Like the ungodly they maliciously mocked[a];
they gnashed their teeth[n] at me.
17 O Lord, how long[o] will you look on?
Rescue my life from their ravages,
my precious life[p] from these lions.
18 I will give you thanks in the great assembly;[q]
among throngs of people I will praise you.[r]

19 Let not those gloat over me
who are my enemies without cause;

35:4 [a]Ps 70:2
35:5 [b]Job 21:18; Ps 1:4; Isa 29:5
35:8 [c]1Th 5:3 [d]Ps 9:15
35:9 [e]Lk 1:47 [f]Isa 61:10
35:10 [g]Ex 15:11 [h]Ps 18:17 [i]Ps 37:14
35:11 [j]Ps 27:12
35:12 [k]Jn 10:32
35:13 [l]Job 30:25; Ps 69:10
35:15 [m]Job 30:1,8
35:16 [n]Job 16:9; La 2:16
35:17 [o]Hab 1:13 [p]Ps 22:20
35:18 [q]Ps 22:25 [r]Ps 22:22

a *16* Septuagint; Hebrew may mean *ungodly circle of mockers.*

let not those who hate me without reason[a]
maliciously wink the eye.[b]
20They do not speak peaceably,
but devise false accusations
against those who live quietly in the land.
21They gape[c] at me and say, "Aha! Aha![d]
With our own eyes we have seen it."

22O LORD, you have seen[e] this; be not silent.
Do not be far[f] from me, O Lord.
23Awake,[g] and rise to my defense!
Contend for me, my God and Lord.
24Vindicate me in your righteousness, O LORD my God;
do not let them gloat over me.
25Do not let them think, "Aha, just what we wanted!"
or say, "We have swallowed him up."[h]

26May all who gloat over my distress
be put to shame[i] and confusion;
may all who exalt themselves over me[j]
be clothed with shame and disgrace.
27May those who delight in my vindication[k]
shout for joy[l] and gladness;
may they always say, "The LORD be exalted,
who delights[m] in the well-being of his servant."
28My tongue will speak of your righteousness[n]
and of your praises all day long.

Psalm 36

For the director of music. Of David the servant of the LORD.

*Psalm 36 Theme*________________________________

1An oracle is within my heart
concerning the sinfulness of the wicked:[a]
There is no fear of God
before his eyes.[o]
2For in his own eyes he flatters himself
too much to detect or hate his sin.
3The words of his mouth[p] are wicked and deceitful;
he has ceased to be wise[q] and to do good.[r]
4Even on his bed he plots evil;[s]
he commits himself to a sinful course[t]
and does not reject what is wrong.[u]

a *1* Or *heart: / Sin proceeds from the wicked.*

35:19
[a]Ps 38:19; 69:4; Jn 15:25*
[b]Ps 13:4; Pr 6:13

35:21
[c]Ps 22:13
[d]Ps 40:15

35:22
[e]Ex 3:7
[f]Ps 10:1; 28:1

35:23
[g]Ps 44:23

35:25
[h]La 2:16

35:26
[i]Ps 40:14; 109:29
[j]Ps 38:16

35:27
[k]Ps 9:4
[l]Ps 32:11
[m]Ps 40:16; 147:11

35:28
[n]Ps 51:14

36:1
[o]Ro 3:18*

36:3
[p]Ps 10:7
[q]Ps 94:8
[r]Jer 4:22

36:4
[s]Pr 4:16; Mic 2:1
[t]Isa 65:2
[u]Ps 52:3; Ro 12:9

5 Your love, O LORD, reaches to the heavens,
your faithfulness to the skies.
6 Your righteousness is like the mighty mountains,
your justice like the great deep.[a]
O LORD, you preserve both man and beast.
7 How priceless is your unfailing love!
Both high and low among men
find[a] refuge in the shadow of your wings.[b]
8 They feast on the abundance of your house;[c]
you give them drink from your river[d] of delights.
9 For with you is the fountain of life;[e]
in your light[f] we see light.

10 Continue your love to those who know you,
your righteousness to the upright in heart.
11 May the foot of the proud not come against me,
nor the hand of the wicked drive me away.
12 See how the evildoers lie fallen—
thrown down, not able to rise![g]

Psalm 37[b]

Of David.

Psalm 37 Theme ______________________________

1 Do not fret because of evil men
or be envious[h] of those who do wrong;[i]
2 for like the grass they will soon wither,
like green plants they will soon die away.[j]

3 Trust in the LORD and do good;
dwell in the land[k] and enjoy safe pasture.[l]
4 Delight[m] yourself in the LORD
and he will give you the desires of your heart.

5 Commit your way to the LORD;
trust in him[n] and he will do this:
6 He will make your righteousness[o] shine like the dawn,[p]
the justice of your cause like the noonday sun.

7 Be still[q] before the LORD and wait patiently[r] for him;
do not fret when men succeed in their ways,
when they carry out their wicked schemes.

36:6 [a] Job 11:8; Ps 77:19; Ro 11:33
36:7 [b] Ru 2:12; Ps 17:8
36:8 [c] Ps 65:4 [d] Job 20:17; Rev 22:1
36:9 [e] Jer 2:13 [f] 1Pe 2:9
36:12 [g] Ps 140:10
37:1 [h] Pr 23:17-18 [i] Ps 73:3
37:2 [j] Ps 90:6
37:3 [k] Dt 30:20 [l] Isa 40:11; Jn 10:9
37:4 [m] Isa 58:14
37:5 [n] Ps 4:5; Ps 55:22; Pr 16:3; 1Pe 5:7
37:6 [o] Mic 7:9 [p] Job 11:17
37:7 [q] Ps 62:5; La 3:26 [r] Ps 40:1

[a] 7 Or *love, O God! / Men find*; or *love! / Both heavenly beings and men / find* [b] This psalm is an acrostic poem, the stanzas of which begin with the successive letters of the Hebrew alphabet.

[8]Refrain from anger[a] and turn from wrath;
do not fret—it leads only to evil.
[9]For evil men will be cut off,
but those who hope in the LORD will inherit the land.[b]

[10]A little while, and the wicked will be no more;[c]
though you look for them, they will not be found.
[11]But the meek will inherit the land[d]
and enjoy great peace.

[12]The wicked plot against the righteous
and gnash their teeth[e] at them;
[13]but the Lord laughs at the wicked,
for he knows their day is coming.[f]

[14]The wicked draw the sword
and bend the bow[g]
to bring down the poor and needy,[h]
to slay those whose ways are upright.
[15]But their swords will pierce their own hearts,[i]
and their bows will be broken.

[16]Better the little that the righteous have
than the wealth[j] of many wicked;
[17]for the power of the wicked will be broken,[k]
but the LORD upholds the righteous.

[18]The days of the blameless are known to the LORD,[l]
and their inheritance will endure forever.
[19]In times of disaster they will not wither;
in days of famine they will enjoy plenty.

[20]But the wicked will perish:
The LORD's enemies will be like the beauty
of the fields,
they will vanish—vanish like smoke.[m]

[21]The wicked borrow and do not repay,
but the righteous give generously;[n]
[22]those the LORD blesses will inherit the land,
but those he curses[o] will be cut off.

[23]If the LORD delights[p] in a man's way,
he makes his steps firm;[q]
[24]though he stumble, he will not fall,[r]
for the LORD upholds[s] him with his hand.

[25]I was young and now I am old,
yet I have never seen the righteous forsaken[t]
or their children begging bread.
[26]They are always generous and lend freely;
their children will be blessed.[u]

37:8 [a]Eph 4:31; Col 3:8
37:9 [b]Isa 57:13; 60:21
37:10 [c]Job 7:10; 24:24
37:11 [d]Mt 5:5
37:12 [e]Ps 35:16
37:13 [f]1Sa 26:10; Ps 2:4
37:14 [g]Ps 11:2 [h]Ps 35:10
37:15 [i]Ps 9:16
37:16 [j]Pr 15:16
37:17 [k]Job 38:15; Ps 10:15
37:18 [l]Ps 1:6
37:20 [m]Ps 102:3
37:21 [n]Ps 112:5
37:22 [o]Job 5:3; Pr 3:33
37:23 [p]Ps 147:11 [q]1Sa 2:9
37:24 [r]Pr 24:16 [s]Ps 145:14; 147:6
37:25 [t]Heb 13:5
37:26 [u]Ps 147:13

27 Turn from evil and do good;[a]
then you will dwell in the land forever.
28 For the LORD loves the just
and will not forsake his faithful ones.

They will be protected forever,
but the offspring of the wicked will be cut off;[b]
29 the righteous will inherit the land[c]
and dwell in it forever.

30 The mouth of the righteous man utters wisdom,
and his tongue speaks what is just.
31 The law of his God is in his heart;[d]
his feet do not slip.[e]

32 The wicked lie in wait[f] for the righteous,
seeking their very lives;
33 but the LORD will not leave them in their power
or let them be condemned when brought to trial.[g]

34 Wait for the LORD[h]
and keep his way.
He will exalt you to inherit the land;
when the wicked are cut off, you will see[i] it.

35 I have seen a wicked and ruthless man
flourishing[j] like a green tree in its native soil,
36 but he soon passed away and was no more;
though I looked for him, he could not be found.[k]

37 Consider the blameless, observe the upright;
there is a future[a] for the man of peace.[l]
38 But all sinners will be destroyed;
the future[b] of the wicked will be cut off.[m]

39 The salvation[n] of the righteous comes from the LORD;
he is their stronghold in time of trouble.[o]
40 The LORD helps[p] them and delivers[q] them;
he delivers them from the wicked and saves them,
because they take refuge in him.

Psalm 38

A psalm of David. A petition.

Psalm 38 Theme ______________________________

1 O LORD, do not rebuke me in your anger
or discipline me in your wrath.[r]

37:27 [a]Ps 34:14
37:28 [b]Ps 21:10; Isa 14:20
37:29 [c]ver 9; Pr 2:21
37:31 [d]Dt 6:6; Ps 40:8; Isa 51:7 [e]ver 23
37:32 [f]Ps 10:8
37:33 [g]Ps 109:31; 2Pe 2:9
37:34 [h]Ps 27:14 [i]Ps 52:6
37:35 [j]Job 5:3
37:36 [k]Job 20:5
37:37 [l]Isa 57:1-2
37:38 [m]Ps 1:4
37:39 [n]Ps 3:8 [o]Ps 9:9
37:40 [p]1Ch 5:20 [q]Isa 31:5
38:1 [r]Ps 6:1

[a] 37 Or *there will be posterity* [b] 38 Or *posterity*

[2]For your arrows[a] have pierced me,
and your hand has come down upon me.
[3]Because of your wrath there is no health in my body;
my bones[b] have no soundness because of my sin.
[4]My guilt has overwhelmed me
like a burden too heavy to bear.[c]

[5]My wounds fester and are loathsome
because of my sinful folly.[d]
[6]I am bowed down and brought very low;
all day long I go about mourning.[e]
[7]My back is filled with searing pain;[f]
there is no health in my body.
[8]I am feeble and utterly crushed;
I groan[g] in anguish of heart.

[9]All my longings lie open before you, O Lord;
my sighing[h] is not hidden from you.
[10]My heart pounds, my strength fails[i] me;
even the light has gone from my eyes.[j]
[11]My friends and companions avoid me because
of my wounds;[k]
my neighbors stay far away.
[12]Those who seek my life set their traps,[l]
those who would harm me talk of my ruin;[m]
all day long they plot deception.[n]

[13]I am like a deaf man, who cannot hear,
like a mute, who cannot open his mouth;
[14]I have become like a man who does not hear,
whose mouth can offer no reply.
[15]I wait[o] for you, O LORD;
you will answer,[p] O Lord my God.
[16]For I said, "Do not let them gloat[q]
or exalt themselves over me when my foot slips."[r]

[17]For I am about to fall,
and my pain is ever with me.
[18]I confess my iniquity;[s]
I am troubled by my sin.
[19]Many are those who are my vigorous enemies;[t]
those who hate me without reason[u] are numerous.
[20]Those who repay my good with evil[v]
slander me when I pursue what is good.

[21]O LORD, do not forsake me;
be not far[w] from me, O my God.
[22]Come quickly to help me,[x]
O Lord my Savior.[y]

38:2 [a]Job 6:4; Ps 32:4
38:3 [b]Ps 6:2; Isa 1:6
38:4 [c]Ezr 9:6
38:5 [d]Ps 69:5
38:6 [e]Job 30:28; Ps 35:14; 42:9
38:7 [f]Ps 102:3
38:8 [g]Ps 22:1
38:9 [h]Job 3:24; Ps 6:6; 10:17
38:10 [i]Ps 31:10 [j]Ps 6:7
38:11 [k]Ps 31:11
38:12 [l]Ps 140:5 [m]Ps 35:4; 54:3 [n]Ps 35:20
38:15 [o]Ps 39:7 [p]Ps 17:6
38:16 [q]Ps 35:26 [r]Ps 13:4
38:18 [s]Ps 32:5
38:19 [t]Ps 18:17 [u]Ps 35:19
38:20 [v]Ps 35:12; 1Jn 3:12
38:21 [w]Ps 35:22
38:22 [x]Ps 40:13 [y]Ps 27:1

Psalm 39

For the director of music. For Jeduthun. A psalm of David.

Psalm 39 Theme ______________________________

1 I said, "I will watch my ways[a]
and keep my tongue from sin;[b]
I will put a muzzle on my mouth
as long as the wicked are in my presence."
2 But when I was silent[c] and still,
not even saying anything good,
my anguish increased.
3 My heart grew hot within me,
and as I meditated, the fire burned;
then I spoke with my tongue:

4 "Show me, O LORD, my life's end
and the number of my days;[d]
let me know how fleeting is my life.[e]
5 You have made my days[f] a mere handbreadth;
the span of my years is as nothing before you.
Each man's life is but a breath.[g] *Selah*
6 Man is a mere phantom[h] as he goes to and fro:
He bustles about, but only in vain;[i]
he heaps up wealth, not knowing who will get it.[j]

7 "But now, Lord, what do I look for?
My hope is in you.[k]
8 Save me[l] from all my transgressions;[m]
do not make me the scorn of fools.
9 I was silent; I would not open my mouth,[n]
for you are the one who has done this.
10 Remove your scourge from me;
I am overcome by the blow of your hand.[o]
11 You rebuke[p] and discipline men for their sin;
you consume their wealth like a moth[q]—
each man is but a breath. *Selah*

12 "Hear my prayer, O LORD,
listen to my cry for help;
be not deaf to my weeping.
For I dwell with you as an alien,[r]
a stranger,[s] as all my fathers were.
13 Look away from me, that I may rejoice again
before I depart and am no more."[t]

39:1 [a] 1Ki 2:4 [b] Job 2:10; Jas 3:2
39:2 [c] Ps 38:13
39:4 [d] Ps 90:12 [e] Ps 103:14
39:5 [f] Ps 89:45 [g] Ps 62:9
39:6 [h] 1Pe 1:24 [i] Ps 127:2 [j] Lk 12:20
39:7 [k] Ps 38:15
39:8 [l] Ps 51:9 [m] Ps 44:13
39:9 [n] Job 2:10
39:10 [o] Job 9:34; Ps 32:4
39:11 [p] 2Pe 2:16 [q] Job 13:28
39:12 [r] 1Pe 2:11 [s] Heb 11:13
39:13 [t] Job 10:21; 14:10

Psalm 40

For the director of music. Of David. A psalm.

Psalm 40 Theme ____

1 I waited patiently[a] for the LORD;
he turned to me and heard my cry.[b]
2 He lifted me out of the slimy pit,
out of the mud and mire;[c]
he set my feet on a rock[d]
and gave me a firm place to stand.
3 He put a new song[e] in my mouth,
a hymn of praise to our God.
Many will see and fear
and put their trust in the LORD.

4 Blessed is the man[f]
who makes the LORD his trust,[g]
who does not look to the proud,
to those who turn aside to false gods.[a]
5 Many, O LORD my God,
are the wonders[h] you have done.
The things you planned for us
no one can recount[i] to you;
were I to speak and tell of them,
they would be too many to declare.

6 Sacrifice and offering you did not desire,[j]
but my ears you have pierced[b,c];
burnt offerings[k] and sin offerings
you did not require.
7 Then I said, "Here I am, I have come—
it is written about me in the scroll.[d]
8 I desire to do your will,[l] O my God;
your law is within my heart."[m]

9 I proclaim righteousness in the great assembly;[n]
I do not seal my lips,
as you know,[o] O LORD.
10 I do not hide your righteousness in my heart;
I speak of your faithfulness[p] and salvation.
I do not conceal your love and your truth
from the great assembly.[q]

11 Do not withhold your mercy from me, O LORD;
may your love[r] and your truth[s] always protect me.

[a]4 Or *to falsehood* [b]6 Hebrew; Septuagint *but a body you have prepared for me* (see also Symmachus and Theodotion) [c]6 Or *opened* [d]7 Or *come / with the scroll written for me*

40:1
[a]Ps 27:14
[b]Ps 34:15

40:2
[c]Ps 69:14
[d]Ps 27:5

40:3
[e]Ps 33:3

40:4
[f]Ps 34:8
[g]Ps 84:12

40:5
[h]Ps 136:4
[i]Ps 139:18; Isa 55:8

40:6
[j]1Sa 15:22; Am 5:22
[k]Isa 1:11

40:8
[l]Jn 4:34
[m]Ps 37:31

40:9
[n]Ps 22:25
[o]Jos 22:22; Ps 119:13

40:10
[p]Ps 89:1
[q]Ac 20:20

40:11
[r]Pr 20:28
[s]Ps 43:3

12 For troubles[a] without number surround me;
my sins have overtaken me, and I cannot see.[b]
They are more than the hairs of my head,[c]
and my heart fails[d] within me.

13 Be pleased, O LORD, to save me;
O LORD, come quickly to help me.[e]
14 May all who seek to take my life
be put to shame and confusion;
may all who desire my ruin[f]
be turned back in disgrace.
15 May those who say to me, "Aha! Aha!"
be appalled at their own shame.
16 But may all who seek you
rejoice and be glad in you;
may those who love your salvation always say,
"The LORD be exalted!"[g]

17 Yet I am poor and needy;
may the Lord think of me.
You are my help and my deliverer;
O my God, do not delay.[h]

Psalm 41

For the director of music. A psalm of David.

Psalm 41 Theme ______________________________

1 Blessed is he who has regard for the weak;[i]
the LORD delivers him in times of trouble.
2 The LORD will protect him and preserve his life;
he will bless him in the land[j]
and not surrender him to the desire of his foes.[k]
3 The LORD will sustain him on his sickbed
and restore him from his bed of illness.

4 I said, "O LORD, have mercy[l] on me;
heal me, for I have sinned[m] against you."
5 My enemies say of me in malice,
"When will he die and his name perish?[n]"
6 Whenever one comes to see me,
he speaks falsely,[o] while his heart gathers slander;[p]
then he goes out and spreads it abroad.

7 All my enemies whisper together[q] against me;
they imagine the worst for me, saying,

40:12 [a]Ps 116:3 [b]Ps 38:4 [c]Ps 69:4 [d]Ps 73:26
40:13 [e]Ps 70:1
40:14 [f]Ps 35:4
40:16 [g]Ps 35:27
40:17 [h]Ps 70:5
41:1 [i]Ps 82:3-4; Pr 14:21
41:2 [j]Ps 37:22 [k]Ps 27:12
41:4 [l]Ps 6:2 [m]Ps 51:4
41:5 [n]Ps 38:12
41:6 [o]Ps 12:2 [p]Pr 26:24
41:7 [q]Ps 56:5; 71:10-11

[8]"A vile disease has beset him;
he will never get up from the place where he lies."
[9]Even my close friend,[a] whom I trusted,
he who shared my bread,
has lifted up his heel against me.[b]

[10]But you, O LORD, have mercy on me;
raise me up,[c] that I may repay them.
[11]I know that you are pleased with me,[d]
for my enemy does not triumph over me.[e]
[12]In my integrity you uphold me[f]
and set me in your presence forever.[g]

[13]Praise be to the LORD, the God of Israel,[h]
from everlasting to everlasting.
Amen and Amen.[i]

BOOK II

Psalms 42-72

Psalm 42[a]

For the director of music. A *maskil* [b] of the Sons of Korah.

*Psalm 42 Theme*________________________________

[1]As the deer pants for streams of water,
so my soul pants[j] for you, O God.
[2]My soul thirsts[k] for God, for the living God.[l]
When can I go[m] and meet with God?
[3]My tears[n] have been my food
day and night,
while men say to me all day long,
"Where is your God?"[o]
[4]These things I remember
as I pour out my soul:
how I used to go with the multitude,
leading the procession to the house of God,[p]
with shouts of joy and thanksgiving[q]
among the festive throng.

[5]Why are you downcast,[r] O my soul?
Why so disturbed within me?
Put your hope in God,[s]
for I will yet praise him,
my Savior[t] and [6]my God.

[a]In many Hebrew manuscripts Psalms 42 and 43 constitute one psalm. [b]Title: Probably a literary or musical term

41:9 [a]2Sa 15:12; Ps 55:12 [b]Job 19:19; Ps 55:20; Mt 26:23; Jn 13:18*

41:10 [c]Ps 3:3

41:11 [d]Ps 147:11 [e]Ps 25:2

41:12 [f]Ps 37:17 [g]Job 36:7

41:13 [h]Ps 72:18 [i]Ps 89:52; 106:48

42:1 [j]Ps 119:131

42:2 [k]Ps 63:1 [l]Jer 10:10 [m]Ps 43:4

42:3 [n]Ps 80:5 [o]Ps 79:10

42:4 [p]Isa 30:29 [q]Ps 100:4

42:5 [r]Ps 38:6; 77:3 [s]La 3:24 [t]Ps 44:3

42:7
[a]Ps 88:7; Jnh 2:3

My[a] soul is downcast within me;
therefore I will remember you
from the land of the Jordan,
the heights of Hermon—from Mount Mizar.
7Deep calls to deep
in the roar of your waterfalls;
all your waves and breakers
have swept over me.[a]

42:8
[b]Ps 57:3
[c]Job 35:10
[d]Ps 63:6; 149:5

8By day the LORD directs his love,[b]
at night[c] his song[d] is with me—
a prayer to the God of my life.

42:9
[e]Ps 38:6

9I say to God my Rock,
"Why have you forgotten me?
Why must I go about mourning,[e]
oppressed by the enemy?"
10My bones suffer mortal agony
as my foes taunt me,
saying to me all day long,
"Where is your God?"

42:11
[f]Ps 43:5

11Why are you downcast, O my soul?
Why so disturbed within me?
Put your hope in God,
for I will yet praise him,
my Savior and my God.[f]

43:1
[g]1Sa 24:15; Ps 26:1; 35:1
[h]Ps 5:6

Psalm 43[b]

*Psalm 43 Theme*______________________________

1Vindicate me, O God,
and plead my cause[g] against an ungodly nation;
rescue me from deceitful and wicked men.[h]

43:2
[i]Ps 44:9
[j]Ps 42:9

2You are God my stronghold.
Why have you rejected[i] me?
Why must I go about mourning,
oppressed by the enemy?[j]

43:3
[k]Ps 36:9
[l]Ps 42:4
[m]Ps 84:1

3Send forth your light[k] and your truth,
let them guide me;
let them bring me to your holy mountain,[l]
to the place where you dwell.[m]

43:4
[n]Ps 26:6

4Then will I go to the altar[n] of God,
to God, my joy and my delight.

[a]5,6 A few Hebrew manuscripts, Septuagint and Syriac; most Hebrew manuscripts *praise him for his saving help. / 6O my God, my* [b]In many Hebrew manuscripts Psalms 42 and 43 constitute one psalm.

I will praise you with the harp,[a]
O God, my God.

5Why are you downcast, O my soul?
Why so disturbed within me?
Put your hope in God,
for I will yet praise him,
my Savior and my God.[b]

Psalm 44

For the director of music. Of the Sons of Korah. A *maskil*.[a]

*Psalm 44 Theme*________________________

1We have heard with our ears, O God;
our fathers have told us[c]
what you did in their days,
in days long ago.
2With your hand you drove out[d] the nations
and planted[e] our fathers;
you crushed the peoples
and made our fathers flourish.[f]
3It was not by their sword[g] that they won the land,
nor did their arm bring them victory;
it was your right hand, your arm,[h]
and the light of your face, for you loved[i] them.

4You are my King[j] and my God,
who decrees[b] victories for Jacob.
5Through you we push back our enemies;
through your name we trample[k] our foes.
6I do not trust in my bow,[l]
my sword does not bring me victory;
7but you give us victory[m] over our enemies,
you put our adversaries to shame.[n]
8In God we make our boast[o] all day long,
and we will praise your name forever.[p] *Selah*

9But now you have rejected[q] and humbled us;
you no longer go out with our armies.[r]
10You made us retreat[s] before the enemy,
and our adversaries have plundered us.
11You gave us up to be devoured like sheep[t]
and have scattered us among the nations.[u]

[a]Title: Probably a literary or musical term [b]4 Septuagint, Aquila and Syriac; Hebrew *King, O God; / command*

43:4 [a]Ps 33:2
43:5 [b]Ps 42:6
44:1 [c]Ex 12:26; Ps 78:3
44:2 [d]Ps 78:55 [e]Ex 15:17 [f]Ps 80:9
44:3 [g]Dt 8:17; Jos 24:12 [h]Ps 77:15 [i]Dt 4:37; 7:7-8
44:4 [j]Ps 74:12
44:5 [k]Ps 108:13
44:6 [l]Ps 33:16
44:7 [m]Ps 136:24 [n]Ps 53:5
44:8 [o]Ps 34:2 [p]Ps 30:12
44:9 [q]Ps 74:1 [r]Ps 60:1,10
44:10 [s]Lev 26:17; Jos 7:8; Ps 89:41
44:11 [t]Ro 8:36 [u]Dt 4:27; 28:64; Ps 106:27

12 You sold your people for a pittance,[a]
gaining nothing from their sale.

13 You have made us a reproach to our neighbors,[b]
the scorn[c] and derision of those around us.
14 You have made us a byword among the nations;
the peoples shake their heads[d] at us.
15 My disgrace is before me all day long,
and my face is covered with shame
16 at the taunts of those who reproach and revile[e] me,
because of the enemy, who is bent on revenge.

17 All this happened to us,
though we had not forgotten[f] you
or been false to your covenant.
18 Our hearts had not turned[g] back;
our feet had not strayed from your path.
19 But you crushed[h] us and made us a haunt for jackals
and covered us over with deep darkness.[i]

20 If we had forgotten[j] the name of our God
or spread out our hands to a foreign god,[k]
21 would not God have discovered it,
since he knows the secrets of the heart?[l]
22 Yet for your sake we face death all day long;
we are considered as sheep to be slaughtered.[m]

23 Awake,[n] O Lord! Why do you sleep?[o]
Rouse yourself! Do not reject us forever.[p]
24 Why do you hide your face[q]
and forget our misery and oppression?[r]

25 We are brought down to the dust;[s]
our bodies cling to the ground.
26 Rise up[t] and help us;
redeem[u] us because of your unfailing love.

Psalm 45

For the director of music. To ⌊the tune of⌋ "Lilies." Of the Sons of Korah. A *maskil*.[a]
A wedding song.

Psalm 45 Theme ________________________________

1 My heart is stirred by a noble theme
as I recite my verses for the king;
my tongue is the pen of a skillful writer.

44:12 [a] Isa 52:3; Jer 15:13
44:13 [b] Ps 79:4; 80:6 [c] Dt 28:37
44:14 [d] Ps 109:25; Jer 24:9
44:16 [e] Ps 74:10
44:17 [f] Ps 78:7,57; Da 9:13
44:18 [g] Job 23:11
44:19 [h] Ps 51:8 [i] Job 3:5
44:20 [j] Ps 78:11 [k] Dt 6:14; Ps 81:9
44:21 [l] Ps 139:1-2; Jer 17:10
44:22 [m] Isa 53:7; Ro 8:36*
44:23 [n] Ps 7:6 [o] Ps 78:65 [p] Ps 77:7
44:24 [q] Job 13:24 [r] Ps 42:9
44:25 [s] Ps 119:25
44:26 [t] Ps 35:2 [u] Ps 25:22

[a] Title: Probably a literary or musical term

[2]You are the most excellent of men
and your lips have been anointed with grace,[a]
since God has blessed you forever.
[3]Gird your sword[b] upon your side, O mighty one;[c]
clothe yourself with splendor and majesty.
[4]In your majesty ride forth victoriously[d]
in behalf of truth, humility and righteousness;
let your right hand display awesome deeds.
[5]Let your sharp arrows pierce the hearts of the
king's enemies;
let the nations fall beneath your feet.
[6]Your throne, O God, will last for ever and ever;[e]
a scepter of justice will be the scepter of
your kingdom.
[7]You love righteousness[f] and hate wickedness;
therefore God, your God, has set you above
your companions
by anointing[g] you with the oil of joy.[h]
[8]All your robes are fragrant[i] with myrrh and aloes
and cassia;
from palaces adorned with ivory
the music of the strings makes you glad.
[9]Daughters of kings[j] are among your honored women;
at your right hand[k] is the royal bride in gold of Ophir.

[10]Listen, O daughter, consider and give ear:
Forget your people[l] and your father's house.
[11]The king is enthralled by your beauty;
honor[m] him, for he is your lord.[n]
[12]The Daughter of Tyre will come with a gift,[a][o]
men of wealth will seek your favor.

[13]All glorious[p] is the princess within ⌊her chamber⌋;
her gown is interwoven with gold.
[14]In embroidered garments she is led to the king;[q]
her virgin companions follow her
and are brought to you.
[15]They are led in with joy and gladness;
they enter the palace of the king.

[16]Your sons will take the place of your fathers;
you will make them princes throughout the land.
[17]I will perpetuate your memory through all generations;[r]
therefore the nations will praise you[s] for ever and ever.

[a]12 Or *A Tyrian robe is among the gifts*

45:2 [a]Lk 4:22
45:3 [b]Heb 4:12; Rev 1:16 [c]Isa 9:6
45:4 [d]Rev 6:2
45:6 [e]Ps 93:2; 98:9
45:7 [f]Ps 33:5 [g]Isa 61:1 [h]Ps 21:6; Heb 1:8-9*
45:8 [i]SS 1:3
45:9 [j]SS 6:8 [k]1Ki 2:19
45:10 [l]Dt 21:13
45:11 [m]Ps 95:6 [n]Isa 54:5
45:12 [o]Ps 22:29; Isa 49:23
45:13 [p]Isa 61:10
45:14 [q]SS 1:4
45:17 [r]Mal 1:11 [s]Ps 138:4

Psalm 46

For the director of music. Of the Sons of Korah. According to *alamoth*.[a] A song.

Psalm 46 Theme ______________________

1 God is our refuge[a] and strength,
an ever-present[b] help in trouble.
2 Therefore we will not fear,[c] though the earth give way[d]
and the mountains fall[e] into the heart of the sea,
3 though its waters roar[f] and foam
and the mountains quake with their surging. *Selah*

4 There is a river whose streams make glad the
city of God,[g]
the holy place where the Most High dwells.
5 God is within her,[h] she will not fall;
God will help[i] her at break of day.
6 Nations[j] are in uproar, kingdoms[k] fall;
he lifts his voice, the earth melts.[l]

7 The LORD Almighty is with us;[m]
the God of Jacob is our fortress.[n] *Selah*

8 Come and see the works of the LORD,[o]
the desolations[p] he has brought on the earth.
9 He makes wars[q] cease to the ends of the earth;
he breaks the bow[r] and shatters the spear,
he burns the shields[b] with fire.[s]
10 "Be still, and know that I am God;[t]
I will be exalted[u] among the nations,
I will be exalted in the earth."

11 The LORD Almighty is with us;
the God of Jacob is our fortress. *Selah*

Psalm 47

For the director of music. Of the Sons of Korah. A psalm.

Psalm 47 Theme ______________________

1 Clap your hands,[v] all you nations;
shout to God with cries of joy.[w]
2 How awesome[x] is the LORD Most High,
the great King[y] over all the earth!

46:1 [a] Ps 9:9; 14:6 [b] Dt 4:7
46:2 [c] Ps 23:4 [d] Ps 82:5 [e] Ps 18:7
46:3 [f] Ps 93:3
46:4 [g] Ps 48:1,8; Isa 60:14
46:5 [h] Isa 12:6; Eze 43:7 [i] Ps 37:40
46:6 [j] Ps 2:1 [k] Ps 68:32 [l] Mic 1:4
46:7 [m] 2Ch 13:12 [n] Ps 9:9
46:8 [o] Ps 66:5 [p] Isa 61:4
46:9 [q] Isa 2:4 [r] Ps 76:3 [s] Eze 39:9
46:10 [t] Ps 100:3 [u] Isa 2:11
47:1 [v] Ps 98:8; Isa 55:12 [w] Ps 106:47
47:2 [x] Dt 7:21 [y] Mal 1:14

[a] Title: Probably a musical term [b] 9 Or *chariots*

[3]He subdued[a] nations under us,
peoples under our feet.
[4]He chose our inheritance[b] for us,
the pride of Jacob, whom he loved. *Selah*

[5]God has ascended amid shouts of joy,
the LORD amid the sounding of trumpets.[c]
[6]Sing praises[d] to God, sing praises;
sing praises to our King, sing praises.

[7]For God is the King of all the earth;[e]
sing to him a psalm[a][f] of praise.
[8]God reigns[g] over the nations;
God is seated on his holy throne.
[9]The nobles of the nations assemble
as the people of the God of Abraham,
for the kings[b] of the earth belong to God;[h]
he is greatly exalted.[i]

47:3 [a]Ps 18:39,47
47:4 [b]1Pe 1:4
47:5 [c]Ps 68:33; 98:6
47:6 [d]Ps 68:4; 89:18
47:7 [e]Zec 14:9 [f]Col 3:16
47:8 [g]1Ch 16:31
47:9 [h]Ps 72:11; 89:18 [i]Ps 97:9

Psalm 48

A song. A psalm of the Sons of Korah.

*Psalm 48 Theme*________________________

[1]Great is the LORD,[j] and most worthy of praise,
in the city of our God,[k] his holy mountain.[l]
[2]It is beautiful[m] in its loftiness,
the joy of the whole earth.
Like the utmost heights of Zaphon[c] is Mount Zion,
the[d] city of the Great King.[n]
[3]God is in her citadels;
he has shown himself to be her fortress.[o]

[4]When the kings joined forces,
when they advanced together,[p]
[5]they saw ⌊her⌋ and were astounded;
they fled in terror.[q]
[6]Trembling seized them there,
pain like that of a woman in labor.
[7]You destroyed them like ships of Tarshish
shattered by an east wind.[r]

[8]As we have heard,
so have we seen

48:1 [j]Ps 96:4 [k]Ps 46:4 [l]Isa 2:2-3; Mic 4:1; Zec 8:3
48:2 [m]Ps 50:2; La 2:15 [n]Mt 5:35
48:3 [o]Ps 46:7
48:4 [p]2Sa 10:1-19
48:5 [q]Ex 15:16
48:7 [r]Jer 18:17; Eze 27:26

[a]7 Or *a maskil* (probably a literary or musical term) [b]9 Or *shields* [c]2 *Zaphon* can refer to a sacred mountain or the direction north. [d]2 Or *earth, / Mount Zion, on the northern side / of the*

in the city of the LORD Almighty,
in the city of our God:
God makes her secure forever.[a] *Selah*

9 Within your temple, O God,
we meditate on your unfailing love.[b]
10 Like your name,[c] O God,
your praise reaches to the ends of the earth;[d]
your right hand is filled with righteousness.
11 Mount Zion rejoices,
the villages of Judah are glad
because of your judgments.[e]

12 Walk about Zion, go around her,
count her towers,
13 consider well her ramparts,
view her citadels,[f]
that you may tell of them to the next generation.[g]
14 For this God is our God for ever and ever;
he will be our guide[h] even to the end.

Psalm 49

For the director of music. Of the Sons of Korah. A psalm.

Psalm 49 Theme ________________________

1 Hear this, all you peoples;[i]
listen, all who live in this world,[j]
2 both low and high,
rich and poor alike:
3 My mouth will speak words of wisdom;[k]
the utterance from my heart will give understanding.[l]
4 I will turn my ear to a proverb;[m]
with the harp I will expound my riddle:[n]

5 Why should I fear[o] when evil days come,
when wicked deceivers surround me—
6 those who trust in their wealth[p]
and boast of their great riches?
7 No man can redeem the life of another
or give to God a ransom for him—
8 the ransom for a life is costly,
no payment is ever enough—[q]
9 that he should live on[r] forever
and not see decay.

48:8 [a]Ps 87:5
48:9 [b]Ps 26:3
48:10 [c]Dt 28:58; Jos 7:9 [d]Isa 41:10
48:11 [e]Ps 97:8
48:13 [f]ver 3; Ps 122:7 [g]Ps 78:6
48:14 [h]Ps 23:4
49:1 [i]Ps 78:1 [j]Ps 33:8
49:3 [k]Ps 37:30 [l]Ps 119:130
49:4 [m]Ps 78:2 [n]Nu 12:8
49:5 [o]Ps 23:4
49:6 [p]Job 31:24
49:8 [q]Mt 16:26
49:9 [r]Ps 22:29; 89:48

10For all can see that wise men die;[a]
the foolish and the senseless alike perish
and leave their wealth to others.[b]
11Their tombs will remain their houses[a] forever,
their dwellings for endless generations,
though they had[b] named[c] lands after themselves.

12But man, despite his riches, does not endure;
he is[c] like the beasts that perish.

13This is the fate of those who trust in themselves,[d]
and of their followers, who approve their sayings. *Selah*
14Like sheep they are destined for the grave,[d][e]
and death will feed on them.
The upright will rule[f] over them in the morning;
their forms will decay in the grave,[d]
far from their princely mansions.
15But God will redeem my life[e] from the grave;[g]
he will surely take me to himself.[h] *Selah*

16Do not be overawed when a man grows rich,
when the splendor of his house increases;
17for he will take nothing with him when he dies,
his splendor will not descend with him.[i]
18Though while he lived he counted himself blessed—[j]
and men praise you when you prosper—
19he will join the generation of his fathers,[k]
who will never see the light[l] ⌞of life⌟.

20A man who has riches without understanding
is like the beasts that perish.[m]

Psalm 50

A psalm of Asaph.

Psalm 50 Theme ____________________

1The Mighty One, God, the LORD,[n]
speaks and summons the earth
from the rising of the sun to the place where it sets.[o]
2From Zion, perfect in beauty,[p]
God shines forth.[q]

[a] *11* Septuagint and Syriac; Hebrew *In their thoughts their houses will remain* [b] *11* Or */ for they have* [c] *12* Hebrew; Septuagint and Syriac read verse 12 the same as verse 20. [d] *14* Hebrew *Sheol*; also in verse 15 [e] *15* Or *soul*

49:10
[a] Ecc 2:16
[b] Ecc 2:18,21

49:11
[c] Ge 4:17; Dt 3:14

49:13
[d] Lk 12:20

49:14
[e] Job 24:19; Ps 9:17
[f] Da 7:18; Mal 4:3; 1Co 6:2; Rev 2:26

49:15
[g] Ps 56:13; Hos 13:14
[h] Ps 73:24

49:17
[i] Ps 17:14; 1Ti 6:7

49:18
[j] Dt 29:19; Lk 12:19

49:19
[k] Ge 15:15
[l] Job 33:30

49:20
[m] Ecc 3:19

50:1
[n] Jos 22:22
[o] Ps 113:3

50:2
[p] Ps 48:2
[q] Dt 33:2; Ps 80:1

3 Our God comes[a] and will not be silent;
a fire devours before him,[b]
and around him a tempest rages.
4 He summons the heavens above,
and the earth,[c] that he may judge his people:
5 "Gather to me my consecrated ones,[d]
who made a covenant[e] with me by sacrifice."
6 And the heavens proclaim[f] his righteousness,
for God himself is judge.[g] *Selah*

7 "Hear, O my people, and I will speak,
O Israel, and I will testify[h] against you:
I am God, your God.[i]
8 I do not rebuke you for your sacrifices
or your burnt offerings,[j] which are ever before me.
9 I have no need of a bull[k] from your stall
or of goats from your pens,
10 for every animal of the forest is mine,
and the cattle on a thousand hills.[l]
11 I know every bird in the mountains,
and the creatures of the field are mine.
12 If I were hungry I would not tell you,
for the world[m] is mine, and all that is in it.
13 Do I eat the flesh of bulls
or drink the blood of goats?
14 Sacrifice thank offerings[n] to God,
fulfill your vows[o] to the Most High,
15 and call[p] upon me in the day of trouble;
I will deliver you, and you will honor[q] me."

16 But to the wicked, God says:

"What right have you to recite my laws
or take my covenant on your lips?[r]
17 You hate my instruction
and cast my words behind[s] you.
18 When you see a thief, you join[t] with him;
you throw in your lot with adulterers.
19 You use your mouth for evil
and harness your tongue to deceit.[u]
20 You speak continually against your brother[v]
and slander your own mother's son.
21 These things you have done and I kept silent;[w]
you thought I was altogether[a] like you.
But I will rebuke you
and accuse[x] you to your face.

50:3 *a* Ps 96:13 *b* Ps 97:3; Da 7:10
50:4 *c* Dt 4:26; Isa 1:2
50:5 *d* Ps 30:4 *e* Ex 24:7
50:6 *f* Ps 89:5 *g* Ps 75:7
50:7 *h* Ps 81:8 *i* Ex 20:2
50:8 *j* Ps 40:6; Hos 6:6
50:9 *k* Ps 69:31
50:10 *l* Ps 104:24
50:12 *m* Ex 19:5
50:14 *n* Heb 13:15 *o* Dt 23:21
50:15 *p* Ps 81:7 *q* Ps 22:23
50:16 *r* Isa 29:13
50:17 *s* Ne 9:26; Ro 2:21-22
50:18 *t* Ro 1:32; 1Ti 5:22
50:19 *u* Ps 10:7; 52:2
50:20 *v* Mt 10:21
50:21 *w* Ecc 8:11; Isa 42:14 *x* Ps 90:8

a *21 Or thought the 'I AM' was*

[22]"Consider this, you who forget God,[a]
or I will tear you to pieces, with none to rescue:[b]
[23]He who sacrifices thank offerings honors me,
and he prepares the way[c]
so that I may show him[a] the salvation of God.[d]"

Psalm 51

For the director of music. A psalm of David. When the prophet Nathan came to him after David had committed adultery with Bathsheba.

*Psalm 51 Theme*________________________________

[1]Have mercy on me, O God,
according to your unfailing love;
according to your great compassion
blot out[e] my transgressions.[f]
[2]Wash away[g] all my iniquity
and cleanse[h] me from my sin.

[3]For I know my transgressions,
and my sin is always before me.[i]
[4]Against you, you only, have I sinned
and done what is evil in your sight,[j]
so that you are proved right when you speak
and justified when you judge.[k]
[5]Surely I was sinful[l] at birth,
sinful from the time my mother conceived me.
[6]Surely you desire truth in the inner parts[b];
you teach[c] me wisdom[m] in the inmost place.[n]

[7]Cleanse me with hyssop,[o] and I will be clean;
wash me, and I will be whiter than snow.[p]
[8]Let me hear joy and gladness;[q]
let the bones you have crushed rejoice.
[9]Hide your face from my sins[r]
and blot out all my iniquity.

[10]Create in me a pure heart,[s] O God,
and renew a steadfast spirit within me.[t]
[11]Do not cast me from your presence
or take your Holy Spirit[u] from me.
[12]Restore to me the joy of your salvation[v]
and grant me a willing spirit, to sustain me.

[13]Then I will teach transgressors your ways,[w]
and sinners will turn back to you.[x]

50:22 [a]Job 8:13; Ps 9:17 [b]Ps 7:2
50:23 [c]Ps 85:13 [d]Ps 91:16
51:1 [e]Ac 3:19 [f]Isa 43:25; Col 2:14
51:2 [g]1Jn 1:9 [h]Heb 9:14
51:3 [i]Isa 59:12
51:4 [j]Ge 20:6; Lk 15:21 [k]Ro 3:4*
51:5 [l]Job 14:4
51:6 [m]Pr 2:6 [n]Ps 15:2
51:7 [o]Lev 14:4; Heb 9:19 [p]Isa 1:18
51:8 [q]Isa 35:10
51:9 [r]Jer 16:17
51:10 [s]Ps 78:37; Ac 15:9 [t]Eze 18:31
51:11 [u]Eph 4:30
51:12 [v]Ps 13:5
51:13 [w]Ac 9:21-22 [x]Ps 22:27

[a]23 Or *and to him who considers his way / I will show* [b]6 The meaning of the Hebrew for this phrase is uncertain. [c]6 Or *you desired . . . ; / you taught*

[14]Save me from bloodguilt,[a] O God,
the God who saves me,[b]
and my tongue will sing of your righteousness.[c]
[15]O Lord, open my lips,[d]
and my mouth will declare your praise.
[16]You do not delight in sacrifice,[e] or I would bring it;
you do not take pleasure in burnt offerings.
[17]The sacrifices of God are[a] a broken spirit;
a broken and contrite heart,[f]
O God, you will not despise.

[18]In your good pleasure make Zion[g] prosper;
build up the walls of Jerusalem.
[19]Then there will be righteous sacrifices,[h]
whole burnt offerings[i] to delight you;
then bulls[j] will be offered on your altar.

Psalm 52

For the director of music. A *maskil*[b] of David. When Doeg the Edomite[k] had gone to Saul and told him: "David has gone to the house of Ahimelech."

*Psalm 52 Theme*______________________________

[1]Why do you boast of evil, you mighty man?
Why do you boast[l] all day long,
you who are a disgrace in the eyes of God?
[2]Your tongue plots destruction;
it is like a sharpened razor,[m]
you who practice deceit.[n]
[3]You love evil rather than good,
falsehood[o] rather than speaking the truth. *Selah*
[4]You love every harmful word,
O you deceitful tongue![p]

[5]Surely God will bring you down to everlasting ruin:
He will snatch you up and tear[q] you from your tent;
he will uproot[r] you from the land of the living.[s] *Selah*
[6]The righteous will see and fear;
they will laugh[t] at him, saying,
[7]"Here now is the man
who did not make God his stronghold
but trusted in his great wealth[u]
and grew strong by destroying others!"

[8]But I am like an olive tree[v]
flourishing in the house of God;

[a] *17* Or *My sacrifice, O God, is* [b] Title: Probably a literary or musical term

51:14 [a] 2Sa 12:9 [b] Ps 25:5 [c] Ps 35:28
51:15 [d] Ps 9:14
51:16 [e] 1Sa 15:22; Ps 40:6
51:17 [f] Ps 34:18
51:18 [g] Ps 102:16; Isa 51:3
51:19 [h] Ps 4:5 [i] Ps 66:13 [j] Ps 66:15
52:Title [k] 1Sa 22:9
52:1 [l] Ps 94:4
52:2 [m] Ps 57:4 [n] Ps 50:19
52:3 [o] Jer 9:5
52:4 [p] Ps 120:2,3
52:5 [q] Isa 22:19 [r] Pr 2:22 [s] Ps 27:13
52:6 [t] Job 22:19; Ps 37:34; 40:3
52:7 [u] Ps 49:6
52:8 [v] Jer 11:16

I trust[a] in God's unfailing love
for ever and ever.
9I will praise you forever[b] for what you have done;
in your name I will hope, for your name is good.[c]
I will praise you in the presence of your saints.

Psalm 53

For the director of music. According to *mahalath*.[a] A *maskil*[b] of David.

*Psalm 53 Theme*____________________

1The fool[d] says in his heart,
"There is no God."[e]
They are corrupt, and their ways are vile;
there is no one who does good.

2God looks down from heaven[f]
on the sons of men
to see if there are any who understand,
any who seek God.[g]
3Everyone has turned away,
they have together become corrupt;
there is no one who does good,
not even one.[h]
4Will the evildoers never learn—
those who devour my people as men eat bread
and who do not call on God?
5There they were, overwhelmed with dread,
where there was nothing to dread.[i]
God scattered the bones[j] of those who attacked you;
you put them to shame, for God despised them.

6Oh, that salvation for Israel would come out of Zion!
When God restores the fortunes of his people,
let Jacob rejoice and Israel be glad!

Psalm 54

For the director of music. With stringed instruments. A *maskil*[b] of David. When the Ziphites had gone to Saul and said, "Is not David hiding among us?"

*Psalm 54 Theme*____________________

1Save me, O God, by your name;[k]
vindicate me by your might.[l]

[a]Title: Probably a musical term [b]Title: Probably a literary or musical term

52:8
[a]Ps 13:5

52:9
[b]Ps 30:12
[c]Ps 54:6

53:1
[d]Ps 14:1-7; Ro 3:10
[e]Ps 10:4

53:2
[f]Ps 33:13
[g]2Ch 15:2

53:3
[h]Ro 3:10-12*

53:5
[i]Lev 26:17
[j]Eze 6:5

54:1
[k]Ps 20:1
[l]2Ch 20:6

54:2 [a]Ps 5:1; 55:1

2 Hear my prayer, O God;[a]
listen to the words of my mouth.

54:3 [b]Ps 86:14 [c]Ps 40:14 [d]Ps 36:1

3 Strangers are attacking me;[b]
ruthless men seek my life[c]—
men without regard for God.[d] *Selah*

54:4 [e]Ps 118:7 [f]Ps 41:12

4 Surely God is my help;[e]
the Lord is the one who sustains me.[f]

54:5 [g]Ps 94:23 [h]Ps 89:49; 143:12

5 Let evil recoil[g] on those who slander me;
in your faithfulness[h] destroy them.

54:6 [i]Ps 50:14 [j]Ps 52:9

6 I will sacrifice a freewill offering[i] to you;
I will praise your name, O LORD,
for it is good.[j]

54:7 [k]Ps 34:6 [l]Ps 59:10

7 For he has delivered me[k] from all my troubles,
and my eyes have looked in triumph on my foes.[l]

Psalm 55

For the director of music. With stringed instruments. A *maskil* [a] of David.

*Psalm 55 Theme*____________________________

55:1 [m]Ps 27:9; 61:1

1 Listen to my prayer, O God,
do not ignore my plea;[m]
2 hear me and answer me.[n]

55:2 [n]Ps 66:19 [o]Ps 77:3; Isa 38:14

My thoughts trouble me and I am distraught[o]
3 at the voice of the enemy,
at the stares of the wicked;
for they bring down suffering upon me[p]
and revile me in their anger.[q]

55:3 [p]2Sa 16:6-8; Ps 17:9 [q]Ps 71:11

4 My heart is in anguish within me;
the terrors[r] of death assail me.

55:4 [r]Ps 116:3

5 Fear and trembling[s] have beset me;
horror has overwhelmed me.
6 I said, "Oh, that I had the wings of a dove!
I would fly away and be at rest—

55:5 [s]Job 21:6; Ps 119:120

7 I would flee far away
and stay in the desert; *Selah*
8 I would hurry to my place of shelter,
far from the tempest and storm.[t]"

55:8 [t]Isa 4:6

9 Confuse the wicked, O Lord, confound their speech,
for I see violence and strife[u] in the city.

55:9 [u]Jer 6:7

[a]Title: Probably a literary or musical term

[10]Day and night they prowl about on its walls;
malice and abuse are within it.
[11]Destructive forces[a] are at work in the city;
threats and lies[b] never leave its streets.

[12]If an enemy were insulting me,
I could endure it;
if a foe were raising himself against me,
I could hide from him.
[13]But it is you, a man like myself,
my companion, my close friend,[c]
[14]with whom I once enjoyed sweet fellowship
as we walked with the throng at the house of God.[d]

[15]Let death take my enemies by surprise;[e]
let them go down alive to the grave,[a][f]
for evil finds lodging among them.

[16]But I call to God,
and the LORD saves me.
[17]Evening,[g] morning[h] and noon
I cry out in distress,
and he hears my voice.
[18]He ransoms me unharmed
from the battle waged against me,
even though many oppose me.
[19]God, who is enthroned forever,[i]
will hear[j] them and afflict them— *Selah*
men who never change their ways
and have no fear of God.

[20]My companion attacks his friends;[k]
he violates his covenant.[l]
[21]His speech is smooth as butter,
yet war is in his heart;
his words are more soothing than oil,[m]
yet they are drawn swords.[n]

[22]Cast your cares on the LORD
and he will sustain you;[o]
he will never let the righteous fall.[p]
[23]But you, O God, will bring down the wicked
into the pit[q] of corruption;
bloodthirsty and deceitful men[r]
will not live out half their days.[s]

But as for me, I trust in you.[t]

[a]*15* Hebrew *Sheol*

55:11 [a]Ps 5:9 [b]Ps 10:7
55:13 [c]2Sa 15:12; Ps 41:9
55:14 [d]Ps 42:4
55:15 [e]Ps 64:7 [f]Nu 16:30,33
55:17 [g]Ps 141:2; Ac 3:1 [h]Ps 5:3
55:19 [i]Dt 33:27 [j]Ps 78:59
55:20 [k]Ps 7:4 [l]Ps 89:34
55:21 [m]Pr 5:3 [n]Ps 28:3; Ps 57:4; 59:7
55:22 [o]Ps 37:5; Mt 6:25-34; 1Pe 5:7 [p]Ps 37:24
55:23 [q]Ps 73:18 [r]Ps 5:6 [s]Job 15:32; Pr 10:27 [t]Ps 25:2

Psalm 56

For the director of music. To ⌊the tune of⌋ "A Dove on Distant Oaks." Of David.
A *miktam*.[a] When the Philistines had seized him in Gath.

Psalm 56 Theme ______________________________

1 Be merciful to me, O God, for men hotly pursue me;[a]
all day long they press their attack.
2 My slanderers pursue me all day long;[b]
many are attacking me in their pride.[c]

3 When I am afraid,[d]
I will trust in you.
4 In God, whose word I praise,
in God I trust; I will not be afraid.
What can mortal man do to me?[e]

5 All day long they twist my words;[f]
they are always plotting to harm me.
6 They conspire,[g] they lurk,
they watch my steps,
eager to take my life.[h]

7 On no account let them escape;
in your anger, O God, bring down the nations.[i]
8 Record my lament;
list my tears on your scroll[b]—
are they not in your record?[j]

9 Then my enemies will turn back[k]
when I call for help.[l]
By this I will know that God is for me.[m]
10 In God, whose word I praise,
in the LORD, whose word I praise—
11 in God I trust; I will not be afraid.
What can man do to me?

12 I am under vows[n] to you, O God;
I will present my thank offerings to you.
13 For you have delivered me[c] from death[o]
and my feet from stumbling,
that I may walk before God
in the light of life.[d][p]

56:1 [a] Ps 57:1-3
56:2 [b] Ps 57:3 [c] Ps 35:1
56:3 [d] Ps 55:4-5
56:4 [e] Ps 118:6; Heb 13:6
56:5 [f] Ps 41:7
56:6 [g] Ps 59:3 [h] Ps 71:10
56:7 [i] Ps 36:12; 55:23
56:8 [j] Mal 3:16
56:9 [k] Ps 9:3 [l] Ps 102:2 [m] Ro 8:31
56:12 [n] Ps 50:14
56:13 [o] Ps 116:8 [p] Job 33:30

[a] Title: Probably a literary or musical term [b] 8 Or / *put my tears in your wineskin* [c] 13 Or *my soul* [d] 13 Or *the land of the living*

Psalm 57

For the director of music. ⌊To the tune of⌋ "Do Not Destroy." Of David. A *miktam*.[a]
When he had fled from Saul into the cave.

*Psalm 57 Theme*____________________________________

1Have mercy on me, O God, have mercy on me,
for in you my soul takes refuge.[a]
I will take refuge in the shadow of your wings[b]
until the disaster has passed.[c]

2I cry out to God Most High,
to God, who fulfills ⌊his purpose⌋ for me.[d]
3He sends from heaven and saves me,[e]
rebuking those who hotly pursue me;[f] *Selah*
God sends his love and his faithfulness.[g]

4I am in the midst of lions;[h]
I lie among ravenous beasts—
men whose teeth are spears and arrows,
whose tongues are sharp swords.[i]

5Be exalted, O God, above the heavens;
let your glory be over all the earth.[j]

6They spread a net for my feet—
I was bowed down[k] in distress.
They dug a pit[l] in my path—
but they have fallen into it themselves.[m] *Selah*

7My heart is steadfast, O God,
my heart is steadfast;[n]
I will sing and make music.
8Awake, my soul!
Awake, harp and lyre![o]
I will awaken the dawn.

9I will praise you, O Lord, among the nations;
I will sing of you among the peoples.
10For great is your love, reaching to the heavens;
your faithfulness reaches to the skies.[p]

11Be exalted, O God, above the heavens;
let your glory be over all the earth.[q]

[a] Title: Probably a literary or musical term

57:1 [a]Ps 2:12 [b]Ps 17:8 [c]Isa 26:20
57:2 [d]Ps 138:8
57:3 [e]Ps 18:9,16 [f]Ps 56:1 [g]Ps 40:11
57:4 [h]Ps 35:17 [i]Ps 55:21; Pr 30:14
57:5 [j]Ps 108:5
57:6 [k]Ps 145:14 [l]Ps 35:7 [m]Ps 7:15; Pr 28:10
57:7 [n]Ps 108:1
57:8 [o]Ps 16:9; 30:12; 150:3
57:10 [p]Ps 36:5; 103:11
57:11 [q]ver 5

58:1 [a]Ps 82:2
58:2 [b]Ps 94:20; Mal 3:15
58:4 [c]Ps 140:3; Ecc 10:11
58:6 [d]Ps 3:7 [e]Job 4:10
58:7 [f]Jos 7:5; Ps 112:10 [g]Ps 64:3
58:8 [h]Job 3:16
58:9 [i]Ps 118:12 [j]Pr 10:25
58:10 [k]Ps 64:10; 91:8 [l]Ps 68:23
58:11 [m]Ps 9:8; 18:20
59:1 [n]Ps 143:9
59:2 [o]Ps 139:19

Psalm 58

For the director of music. ⌊To the tune of⌋ "Do Not Destroy." Of David. A *miktam.*[a]

*Psalm 58 Theme*____________________________________

1Do you rulers indeed speak justly?[a]
Do you judge uprightly among men?
2No, in your heart you devise injustice,
and your hands mete out violence on the earth.[b]
3Even from birth the wicked go astray;
from the womb they are wayward and speak lies.
4Their venom is like the venom of a snake,[c]
like that of a cobra that has stopped its ears,
5that will not heed the tune of the charmer,
however skillful the enchanter may be.

6Break the teeth in their mouths, O God;[d]
tear out, O LORD, the fangs of the lions![e]
7Let them vanish like water that flows away;[f]
when they draw the bow, let their arrows be blunted.[g]
8Like a slug melting away as it moves along,
like a stillborn child,[h] may they not see the sun.

9Before your pots can feel ⌊the heat of⌋ the thorns[i]—
whether they be green or dry—the wicked will be
swept away.[b][j]
10The righteous will be glad when they are avenged,[k]
when they bathe their feet in the blood of the wicked.[l]
11Then men will say,
"Surely the righteous still are rewarded;
surely there is a God who judges the earth."[m]

Psalm 59

For the director of music. ⌊To the tune of⌋ "Do Not Destroy." Of David. A *miktam.*[a]
When Saul had sent men to watch David's house in order to kill him.

*Psalm 59 Theme*____________________________________

1Deliver me from my enemies, O God;[n]
protect me from those who rise up against me.
2Deliver me from evildoers
and save me from bloodthirsty men.[o]

[a]Title: Probably a literary or musical term [b]9 The meaning of the Hebrew for this verse is uncertain.

[3]See how they lie in wait for me!
Fierce men conspire[a] against me
for no offense or sin of mine, O LORD.
[4]I have done no wrong, yet they are ready to attack me.[b]
Arise to help me; look on my plight!
[5]O LORD God Almighty, the God of Israel,
rouse yourself to punish all the nations;
show no mercy to wicked traitors.[c] *Selah*

[6]They return at evening,
snarling like dogs,[d]
and prowl about the city.
[7]See what they spew from their mouths—
they spew out swords[e] from their lips,
and they say, "Who can hear us?"[f]
[8]But you, O LORD, laugh at them;[g]
you scoff at all those nations.[h]

[9]O my Strength, I watch for you;
you, O God, are my fortress,[i] [10]my loving God.

God will go before me
and will let me gloat over those who slander me.
[11]But do not kill them, O Lord our shield,[a][j]
or my people will forget.[k]
In your might make them wander about,
and bring them down.[l]
[12]For the sins of their mouths,[m]
for the words of their lips,[n]
let them be caught in their pride.[o]
For the curses and lies they utter,
[13] consume them in wrath,
consume them till they are no more.[p]
Then it will be known to the ends of the earth
that God rules over Jacob.[q] *Selah*

[14]They return at evening,
snarling like dogs,
and prowl about the city.
[15]They wander about for food[r]
and howl if not satisfied.
[16]But I will sing of your strength,[s]
in the morning[t] I will sing of your love;[u]
for you are my fortress,
my refuge in times of trouble.[v]

[17]O my Strength, I sing praise to you;
you, O God, are my fortress, my loving God.

[a]11 Or *sovereign*

59:3
[a]Ps 56:6

59:4
[b]Ps 35:19,23

59:5
[c]Jer 18:23

59:6
[d]ver 14

59:7
[e]Ps 57:4
[f]Ps 10:11

59:8
[g]Ps 37:13; Pr 1:26
[h]Ps 2:4

59:9
[i]Ps 9:9; 62:2

59:11
[j]Ps 84:9
[k]Dt 4:9
[l]Ps 106:27

59:12
[m]Ps 10:7
[n]Pr 12:13
[o]Zep 3:11

59:13
[p]Ps 104:35
[q]Ps 83:18

59:15
[r]Job 15:23

59:16
[s]Ps 21:13
[t]Ps 88:13
[u]Ps 101:1
[v]Ps 46:1

60:1
[a]2Sa 5:20; Ps 44:9
[b]Ps 79:5
[c]Ps 80:3

Psalm 60

For the director of music. To [the tune of] "The Lily of the Covenant." A *miktam*[a] of David. For teaching. When he fought Aram Naharaim[b] and Aram Zobah,[c] and when Joab returned and struck down twelve thousand Edomites in the Valley of Salt.

Psalm 60 Theme ______________________

60:2
[d]Ps 18:7
[e]2Ch 7:14

[1]You have rejected us,[a] O God, and burst forth upon us;
you have been angry[b]—now restore us![c]
[2]You have shaken the land[d] and torn it open;
mend its fractures,[e] for it is quaking.

60:3
[f]Ps 71:20
[g]Isa 51:17; Jer 25:16

[3]You have shown your people desperate times;[f]
you have given us wine that makes us stagger.[g]

[4]But for those who fear you, you have raised a banner
to be unfurled against the bow. *Selah*

60:5
[h]Ps 17:7; 108:6
[i]Ps 127:2

[5]Save us and help us with your right hand,[h]
that those you love[i] may be delivered.
[6]God has spoken from his sanctuary:
"In triumph I will parcel out Shechem[j]
and measure off the Valley of Succoth.

60:6
[j]Ge 12:6

[7]Gilead[k] is mine, and Manasseh is mine;
Ephraim is my helmet,
Judah[l] my scepter.[m]
[8]Moab is my washbasin,
upon Edom I toss my sandal;
over Philistia I shout in triumph.[n]"

60:7
[k]Jos 13:31
[l]Dt 33:17
[m]Ge 49:10

[9]Who will bring me to the fortified city?
Who will lead me to Edom?
[10]Is it not you, O God, you who have rejected us
and no longer go out with our armies?[o]
[11]Give us aid against the enemy,
for the help of man is worthless.[p]
[12]With God we will gain the victory,
and he will trample down our enemies.[q]

60:8
[n]2Sa 8:1

60:10
[o]Jos 7:12; Ps 44:9; 108:11

60:11
[p]Ps 146:3

Psalm 61

For the director of music. With stringed instruments. Of David.

60:12
[q]Nu 24:18; Ps 44:5

Psalm 61 Theme ______________________

[1]Hear my cry, O God;[r]
listen to my prayer.[s]

61:1
[r]Ps 64:1
[s]Ps 86:6

[a]Title: Probably a literary or musical term [b]Title: That is, Arameans of Northwest Mesopotamia [c]Title: That is, Arameans of central Syria

[2]From the ends of the earth I call to you,
I call as my heart grows faint;[a]
lead me to the rock[b] that is higher than I.
[3]For you have been my refuge,[c]
a strong tower against the foe.[d]

[4]I long to dwell[e] in your tent forever
and take refuge in the shelter of your wings.[f] *Selah*
[5]For you have heard my vows,[g] O God;
you have given me the heritage of those who fear
your name.[h]

[6]Increase the days of the king's life,
his years for many generations.[i]
[7]May he be enthroned in God's presence forever;[j]
appoint your love and faithfulness to protect him.[k]

[8]Then will I ever sing praise to your name[l]
and fulfill my vows day after day.

Psalm 62

For the director of music. For Jeduthun. A psalm of David.

*Psalm 62 Theme*____

[1]My soul finds rest[m] in God alone;
my salvation comes from him.
[2]He alone is my rock[n] and my salvation;
he is my fortress, I will never be shaken.

[3]How long will you assault a man?
Would all of you throw him down—
this leaning wall,[o] this tottering fence?
[4]They fully intend to topple him
from his lofty place;
they take delight in lies.
With their mouths they bless,
but in their hearts they curse.[p] *Selah*

[5]Find rest, O my soul, in God alone;
my hope comes from him.
[6]He alone is my rock and my salvation;
he is my fortress, I will not be shaken.
[7]My salvation and my honor depend on God[a];
he is my mighty rock, my refuge.[q]

a 7 Or / *God Most High is my salvation and my honor*

61:2
[a]Ps 77:3
[b]Ps 18:2

61:3
[c]Ps 62:7
[d]Pr 18:10

61:4
[e]Ps 23:6
[f]Ps 91:4

61:5
[g]Ps 56:12
[h]Ps 86:11

61:6
[i]Ps 21:4

61:7
[j]Ps 41:12
[k]Ps 40:11

61:8
[l]Ps 65:1; 71:22

62:1
[m]Ps 33:20

62:2
[n]Ps 89:26

62:3
[o]Isa 30:13

62:4
[p]Ps 28:3

62:7
[q]Ps 46:1; 85:9;
Jer 3:23

8Trust in him at all times, O people;
pour out your hearts to him,[a]
for God is our refuge. *Selah*

9Lowborn men are but a breath,[b]
the highborn are but a lie;
if weighed on a balance,[c] they are nothing;
together they are only a breath.
10Do not trust in extortion
or take pride in stolen goods;[d]
though your riches increase,
do not set your heart on them.[e]

11One thing God has spoken,
two things have I heard:
that you, O God, are strong,
12 and that you, O Lord, are loving.
Surely you will reward each person
according to what he has done.[f]

Psalm 63

A psalm of David. When he was in the Desert of Judah.

*Psalm 63 Theme*____________________

1O God, you are my God,
earnestly I seek you;
my soul thirsts for you,[g]
my body longs for you,
in a dry and weary land
where there is no water.
2I have seen you in the sanctuary[h]
and beheld your power and your glory.
3Because your love is better than life,[i]
my lips will glorify you.
4I will praise you as long as I live,[j]
and in your name I will lift up my hands.[k]
5My soul will be satisfied as with the richest of foods;[l]
with singing lips my mouth will praise you.

6On my bed I remember you;
I think of you through the watches of the night.[m]
7Because you are my help,[n]
I sing in the shadow of your wings.
8My soul clings to you;
your right hand upholds me.[o]

62:8 [a]1Sa 1:15; Ps 42:4; La 2:19
62:9 [b]Ps 39:5,11 [c]Isa 40:15
62:10 [d]Isa 61:8 [e]Job 31:25; 1Ti 6:6-10
62:12 [f]Job 34:11; Mt 16:27
63:1 [g]Ps 42:2; 84:2
63:2 [h]Ps 27:4
63:3 [i]Ps 69:16
63:4 [j]Ps 104:33 [k]Ps 28:2
63:5 [l]Ps 36:8
63:6 [m]Ps 42:8
63:7 [n]Ps 27:9
63:8 [o]Ps 18:35

[9]They who seek my life will be destroyed;[a]
they will go down to the depths of the earth.[b]
[10]They will be given over to the sword
and become food for jackals.

[11]But the king will rejoice in God;
all who swear by God's name will praise him,[c]
while the mouths of liars will be silenced.

63:9
[a]Ps 40:14
[b]Ps 55:15

63:11
[c]Dt 6:13; Ps 21:1; Isa 45:23

Psalm 64

For the director of music. A psalm of David.

*Psalm 64 Theme*____________________

[1]Hear me, O God, as I voice my complaint;[d]
protect my life from the threat of the enemy.[e]
[2]Hide me from the conspiracy of the wicked,[f]
from that noisy crowd of evildoers.

[3]They sharpen their tongues like swords
and aim their words like deadly arrows.[g]
[4]They shoot from ambush at the innocent man;[h]
they shoot at him suddenly, without fear.[i]

[5]They encourage each other in evil plans,
they talk about hiding their snares;
they say, "Who will see them[a]?"[j]
[6]They plot injustice and say,
"We have devised a perfect plan!"
Surely the mind and heart of man are cunning.

[7]But God will shoot them with arrows;
suddenly they will be struck down.
[8]He will turn their own tongues against them[k]
and bring them to ruin;
all who see them will shake their heads[l] in scorn.
[9]All mankind will fear;
they will proclaim the works of God
and ponder what he has done.[m]
[10]Let the righteous rejoice in the LORD
and take refuge in him;[n]
let all the upright in heart praise him![o]

64:1
[d]Ps 55:2
[e]Ps 140:1

64:2
[f]Ps 56:6; 59:2

64:3
[g]Ps 58:7

64:4
[h]Ps 11:2
[i]Ps 55:19

64:5
[j]Ps 10:11

64:8
[k]Ps 9:3; Pr 18:7
[l]Ps 22:7

64:9
[m]Jer 51:10

64:10
[n]Ps 25:20
[o]Ps 32:11

[a]5 Or *us*

Psalm 65

For the director of music. A psalm of David. A song.

Psalm 65 Theme ______________________________

1 Praise awaits[a] you, O God, in Zion;
to you our vows will be fulfilled.[a]
2 O you who hear prayer,
to you all men will come.[b]
3 When we were overwhelmed by sins,[c]
you forgave[b] our transgressions.[d]
4 Blessed are those you choose[e]
and bring near to live in your courts!
We are filled with the good things of your house,[f]
of your holy temple.

5 You answer us with awesome deeds of righteousness,
O God our Savior,[g]
the hope of all the ends of the earth
and of the farthest seas,[h]
6 who formed the mountains by your power,
having armed yourself with strength,[i]
7 who stilled the roaring of the seas,[j]
the roaring of their waves,
and the turmoil of the nations.[k]
8 Those living far away fear your wonders;
where morning dawns and evening fades
you call forth songs of joy.

9 You care for the land and water it;[l]
you enrich it abundantly.
The streams of God are filled with water
to provide the people with grain,[m]
for so you have ordained it.[c]
10 You drench its furrows
and level its ridges;
you soften it with showers
and bless its crops.
11 You crown the year with your bounty,
and your carts overflow with abundance.
12 The grasslands of the desert overflow;[n]
the hills are clothed with gladness.

65:1 *a* Ps 116:18
65:2 *b* Isa 66:23
65:3 *c* Ps 38:4 *d* Heb 9:14
65:4 *e* Ps 4:3; 33:12 *f* Ps 36:8
65:5 *g* Ps 85:4 *h* Ps 107:23
65:6 *i* Ps 93:1
65:7 *j* Mt 8:26 *k* Isa 17:12-13
65:9 *l* Ps 68:9-10 *m* Ps 46:4; 104:14
65:12 *n* Job 28:26

[a] *1* Or *befits*; the meaning of the Hebrew for this word is uncertain. [b] *3* Or *made atonement for*
[c] *9* Or *for that is how you prepare the land*

[13]The meadows are covered with flocks[a]
and the valleys are mantled with grain;[b]
they shout for joy and sing.[c]

Psalm 66

For the director of music. A song. A psalm.

*Psalm 66 Theme*______________________________

[1]Shout with joy to God, all the earth![d]
[2] Sing the glory of his name;[e]
make his praise glorious!
[3]Say to God, "How awesome are your deeds![f]
So great is your power
that your enemies cringe[g] before you.
[4]All the earth bows down[h] to you;
they sing praise[i] to you,
they sing praise to your name." *Selah*

[5]Come and see what God has done,
how awesome his works[j] in man's behalf!
[6]He turned the sea into dry land,[k]
they passed through the waters on foot—
come, let us rejoice in him.
[7]He rules forever[l] by his power,
his eyes watch[m] the nations—
let not the rebellious[n] rise up against him. *Selah*

[8]Praise[o] our God, O peoples,
let the sound of his praise be heard;
[9]he has preserved our lives
and kept our feet from slipping.[p]
[10]For you, O God, tested us;
you refined us like silver.[q]
[11]You brought us into prison
and laid burdens[r] on our backs.
[12]You let men ride over our heads;[s]
we went through fire and water,
but you brought us to a place of abundance.[t]

[13]I will come to your temple with burnt offerings
and fulfill my vows[u] to you—
[14]vows my lips promised and my mouth spoke
when I was in trouble.
[15]I will sacrifice fat animals to you
and an offering of rams;
I will offer bulls and goats.[v] *Selah*

65:13 [a]Ps 144:13 [b]Ps 72:16 [c]Ps 98:8; Isa 55:12

66:1 [d]Ps 100:1

66:2 [e]Ps 79:9

66:3 [f]Ps 65:5 [g]Ps 18:44

66:4 [h]Ps 22:27 [i]Ps 67:3

66:5 [j]Ps 106:22

66:6 [k]Ex 14:22

66:7 [l]Ps 145:13 [m]Ps 11:4 [n]Ps 140:8

66:8 [o]Ps 98:4

66:9 [p]Ps 121:3

66:10 [q]Ps 17:3; Isa 48:10; Zec 13:9; 1Pe 1:6-7

66:11 [r]La 1:13

66:12 [s]Isa 51:23 [t]Isa 43:2

66:13 [u]Ecc 5:4

66:15 [v]Nu 6:14; Ps 51:19

66:16 [a]Ps 34:11 [b]Ps 71:15,24

16 Come and listen,[a] all you who fear God;
let me tell[b] you what he has done for me.
17 I cried out to him with my mouth;
his praise was on my tongue.

66:18 [c]Job 36:21; Isa 1:15; Jas 4:3

18 If I had cherished sin in my heart,
the Lord would not have listened;[c]
19 but God has surely listened
and heard my voice[d] in prayer.

66:19 [d]Ps 116:1-2

20 Praise be to God,
who has not rejected[e] my prayer
or withheld his love from me!

66:20 [e]Ps 22:24; 68:35

Psalm 67

For the director of music. With stringed instruments. A psalm. A song.

*Psalm 67 Theme*______________________________

67:1 [f]Nu 6:24-26; Ps 4:6

1 May God be gracious to us and bless us
and make his face shine upon us,[f] *Selah*
2 that your ways may be known on earth,
your salvation[g] among all nations.[h]

67:2 [g]Isa 52:10 [h]Tit 2:11

3 May the peoples praise you, O God;
may all the peoples praise you.
4 May the nations be glad and sing for joy,
for you rule the peoples justly[i]
and guide the nations of the earth. *Selah*

67:4 [i]Ps 96:10-13

5 May the peoples praise you, O God;
may all the peoples praise you.

67:6 [j]Lev 26:4; Ps 85:12; Eze 34:27

6 Then the land will yield its harvest,[j]
and God, our God, will bless us.
7 God will bless us,
and all the ends of the earth will fear him.[k]

67:7 [k]Ps 33:8

Psalm 68

For the director of music. Of David. A psalm. A song.

68:1 [l]Nu 10:35; Isa 33:3

*Psalm 68 Theme*______________________________

1 May God arise, may his enemies be scattered;
may his foes flee[l] before him.
2 As smoke[m] is blown away by the wind,
may you blow them away;

68:2 [m]Hos 13:3

as wax melts[a] before the fire,
may the wicked perish before God.
3But may the righteous be glad
and rejoice[b] before God;
may they be happy and joyful.

4Sing to God, sing praise to his name,[c]
extol him who rides on the clouds[a][d]—
his name is the LORD[e]—
and rejoice before him.
5A father to the fatherless,[f] a defender of widows,[g]
is God in his holy dwelling.[h]
6God sets the lonely in families,[b][i]
he leads forth the prisoners[j] with singing;
but the rebellious live in a sun-scorched land.[k]

7When you went out[l] before your people, O God,
when you marched through the wasteland, *Selah*
8the earth shook,
the heavens poured down rain,[m]
before God, the One of Sinai,[n]
before God, the God of Israel.
9You gave abundant showers,[o] O God;
you refreshed your weary inheritance.
10Your people settled in it,
and from your bounty, O God, you provided[p]
for the poor.

11The Lord announced the word,
and great was the company of those who
proclaimed it:
12"Kings and armies flee[q] in haste;
in the camps men divide the plunder.
13Even while you sleep among the campfires,[c][r]
the wings of ⌊my⌋ dove are sheathed with silver,
its feathers with shining gold."
14When the Almighty[d] scattered[s] the kings in the land,
it was like snow fallen on Zalmon.

15The mountains of Bashan are majestic mountains;
rugged are the mountains of Bashan.
16Why gaze in envy, O rugged mountains,
at the mountain where God chooses[t] to reign,
where the LORD himself will dwell forever?

[a]4 Or / *prepare the way for him who rides through the deserts* [b]6 Or *the desolate in a homeland* [c]13 Or *saddlebags* [d]14 Hebrew *Shaddai*

68:2 [a]Isa 9:18; Mic 1:4
68:3 [b]Ps 32:11
68:4 [c]Ps 66:2 [d]Dt 33:26 [e]Ex 6:3; Ps 83:18
68:5 [f]Ps 10:14 [g]Dt 10:18 [h]Dt 26:15
68:6 [i]Ps 113:9 [j]Ac 12:6 [k]Ps 107:34
68:7 [l]Ex 13:21; Jdg 4:14
68:8 [m]Jdg 5:4 [n]Ex 19:16,18
68:9 [o]Dt 11:11
68:10 [p]Ps 74:19
68:12 [q]Jos 10:16
68:13 [r]Ge 49:14
68:14 [s]Jos 10:10
68:16 [t]Dt 12:5

17 The chariots of God are tens of thousands
and thousands of thousands;[a]
the Lord ⌊has come⌋ from Sinai into his sanctuary.
18 When you ascended on high,
you led captives[b] in your train;
you received gifts from men,[c]
even from[a] the rebellious—
that you,[b] O LORD God, might dwell there.

19 Praise be to the Lord, to God our Savior,[d]
who daily bears our burdens.[e] *Selah*
20 Our God is a God who saves;
from the Sovereign LORD comes escape from death.[f]

21 Surely God will crush the heads[g] of his enemies,
the hairy crowns of those who go on in their sins.
22 The Lord says, "I will bring them from Bashan;
I will bring them from the depths of the sea,[h]
23 that you may plunge your feet in the blood of your foes,[i]
while the tongues of your dogs[j] have their share."

24 Your procession has come into view, O God,
the procession of my God and King into
the sanctuary.[k]
25 In front are the singers, after them the musicians;
with them are the maidens playing tambourines.[l]
26 Praise God in the great congregation;
praise the LORD in the assembly of Israel.[m]
27 There is the little tribe[n] of Benjamin, leading them,
there the great throng of Judah's princes,
and there the princes of Zebulun and of Naphtali.

28 Summon your power, O God[c];
show us your strength, O God, as you have
done before.
29 Because of your temple at Jerusalem
kings will bring you gifts.[o]
30 Rebuke the beast among the reeds,
the herd of bulls[p] among the calves of the nations.
Humbled, may it bring bars of silver.
Scatter the nations[q] who delight in war.
31 Envoys will come from Egypt;[r]
Cush[d] will submit herself to God.

68:17 [a] Dt 33:2; Da 7:10
68:18 [b] Jdg 5:12 [c] Eph 4:8*
68:19 [d] Ps 65:5 [e] Ps 55:22
68:20 [f] Ps 56:13
68:21 [g] Ps 110:5; Hab 3:13
68:22 [h] Nu 21:33
68:23 [i] Ps 58:10 [j] 1Ki 21:19
68:24 [k] Ps 63:2
68:25 [l] Jdg 11:34; 1Ch 13:8
68:26 [m] Ps 26:12; Isa 48:1
68:27 [n] 1Sa 9:21
68:29 [o] Ps 72:10
68:30 [p] Ps 22:12 [q] Ps 89:10
68:31 [r] Isa 19:19; 45:14

[a] *18* Or *gifts for men, / even* [b] *18* Or *they* [c] *28* Many Hebrew manuscripts, Septuagint and Syriac; most Hebrew manuscripts *Your God has summoned power for you* [d] *31* That is, the upper Nile region

[32]Sing to God, O kingdoms of the earth,
sing praise to the Lord, *Selah*
[33]to him who rides[a] the ancient skies above,
who thunders with mighty voice.[b]
[34]Proclaim the power[c] of God,
whose majesty is over Israel,
whose power is in the skies.
[35]You are awesome, O God, in your sanctuary;
the God of Israel gives power and strength to
his people.[d]

Praise be to God![e]

Psalm 69

For the director of music. To ⌊the tune of⌋ "Lilies." Of David.

Psalm 69 Theme ______________________________

[1]Save me, O God,
for the waters have come up to my neck.[f]
[2]I sink in the miry depths,[g]
where there is no foothold.
I have come into the deep waters;
the floods engulf me.
[3]I am worn out calling for help;[h]
my throat is parched.
My eyes fail,[i]
looking for my God.
[4]Those who hate me without reason[j]
outnumber the hairs of my head;
many are my enemies without cause,[k]
those who seek to destroy me.
I am forced to restore
what I did not steal.

[5]You know my folly,[l] O God;
my guilt is not hidden from you.[m]

[6]May those who hope in you
not be disgraced because of me,
O Lord, the LORD Almighty;
may those who seek you
not be put to shame because of me,
O God of Israel.
[7]For I endure scorn for your sake,[n]
and shame covers my face.[o]

68:33
[a]Ps 18:10
[b]Ps 29:4

68:34
[c]Ps 29:1

68:35
[d]Ps 29:11
[e]Ps 66:20

69:1
[f]Jnh 2:5

69:2
[g]Ps 40:2

69:3
[h]Ps 6:6
[i]Ps 119:82; Isa 38:14

69:4
[j]Jn 15:25*
[k]Ps 35:19; 38:19

69:5
[l]Ps 38:5
[m]Ps 44:21

69:7
[n]Jer 15:15
[o]Ps 44:15

69:8 [a]Ps 31:11; Isa 53:3
69:9 [b]Jn 2:17* [c]Ps 89:50-51; Ro 15:3*
69:10 [d]Ps 35:13
69:11 [e]Ps 35:13
69:12 [f]Job 30:9
69:13 [g]Isa 49:8; 2Co 6:2 [h]Ps 51:1
69:14 [i]ver 2; Ps 144:7
69:15 [j]Ps 124:4-5 [k]Nu 16:33
69:16 [l]Ps 63:3
69:17 [m]Ps 27:9 [n]Ps 66:14
69:18 [o]Ps 49:15
69:19 [p]Ps 22:6
69:20 [q]Job 16:2 [r]Isa 63:5
69:21 [s]Mt 27:34; Mk 15:23; Jn 19:28-30
69:23 [t]Isa 6:9-10; Ro 11:9-10*
69:24 [u]Ps 79:6
69:25 [v]Mt 23:38 [w]Ac 1:20*

8 I am a stranger to my brothers,
an alien to my own mother's sons;[a]
9 for zeal for your house consumes me,[b]
and the insults of those who insult you fall on me.[c]
10 When I weep and fast,[d]
I must endure scorn;
11 when I put on sackcloth,[e]
people make sport of me.
12 Those who sit at the gate mock me,
and I am the song of the drunkards.[f]

13 But I pray to you, O LORD,
in the time of your favor;[g]
in your great love,[h] O God,
answer me with your sure salvation.
14 Rescue me from the mire,
do not let me sink;
deliver me from those who hate me,
from the deep waters.[i]
15 Do not let the floodwaters[j] engulf me
or the depths swallow me up[k]
or the pit close its mouth over me.
16 Answer me, O LORD, out of the goodness of your love;[l]
in your great mercy turn to me.
17 Do not hide your face[m] from your servant;
answer me quickly, for I am in trouble.[n]
18 Come near and rescue me;
redeem[o] me because of my foes.

19 You know how I am scorned,[p] disgraced and shamed;
all my enemies are before you.
20 Scorn has broken my heart
and has left me helpless;
I looked for sympathy, but there was none,
for comforters,[q] but I found none.[r]
21 They put gall in my food
and gave me vinegar for my thirst.[s]

22 May the table set before them become a snare;
may it become retribution and[a] a trap.
23 May their eyes be darkened so they cannot see,
and their backs be bent forever.[t]
24 Pour out your wrath[u] on them;
let your fierce anger overtake them.
25 May their place be deserted;[v]
let there be no one to dwell in their tents.[w]

a 22 Or *snare / and their fellowship become*

[26]For they persecute those you wound
and talk about the pain of those you hurt.[a]
[27]Charge them with crime upon crime;[b]
do not let them share in your salvation.[c]
[28]May they be blotted out of the book of life[d]
and not be listed with the righteous.[e]

[29]I am in pain and distress;
may your salvation, O God, protect me.[f]

[30]I will praise God's name in song[g]
and glorify him[h] with thanksgiving.
[31]This will please the LORD more than an ox,
more than a bull with its horns and hoofs.[i]
[32]The poor will see and be glad[j]—
you who seek God, may your hearts live![k]
[33]The LORD hears the needy[l]
and does not despise his captive people.

[34]Let heaven and earth praise him,
the seas and all that move in them,[m]
[35]for God will save Zion[n]
and rebuild the cities of Judah.[o]
Then people will settle there and possess it;
36 the children of his servants will inherit it,
and those who love his name will dwell there.[p]

Psalm 70

For the director of music. Of David. A petition.

*Psalm 70 Theme*________________________________

[1]Hasten, O God, to save me;
O LORD, come quickly to help me.[q]
[2]May those who seek my life[r]
be put to shame and confusion;
may all who desire my ruin
be turned back in disgrace.[s]
[3]May those who say to me, "Aha! Aha!"
turn back because of their shame.
[4]But may all who seek you
rejoice and be glad in you;
may those who love your salvation always say,
"Let God be exalted!"

69:26 [a]Isa 53:4; Zec 1:15
69:27 [b]Ne 4:5 [c]Ps 109:14; Isa 26:10
69:28 [d]Ex 32:32-33; Lk 10:20; Php 4:3 [e]Eze 13:9
69:29 [f]Ps 59:1; 70:5
69:30 [g]Ps 28:7 [h]Ps 34:3
69:31 [i]Ps 50:9-13
69:32 [j]Ps 34:2 [k]Ps 22:26
69:33 [l]Ps 12:5; 68:6
69:34 [m]Ps 96:11; 148:1; Isa 44:23; 49:13; 55:12
69:35 [n]Ob 17 [o]Ps 51:18; Isa 44:26
69:36 [p]Ps 37:29; 102:28
70:1 [q]Ps 40:13
70:2 [r]Ps 35:4 [s]Ps 35:26

5 Yet I am poor and needy;[a]
come quickly to me,[b] O God.
You are my help and my deliverer;
O LORD, do not delay.

Psalm 71

Psalm 71 Theme ____________________

1 In you, O LORD, I have taken refuge;
let me never be put to shame.[c]
2 Rescue me and deliver me in your righteousness;
turn your ear[d] to me and save me.
3 Be my rock of refuge,
to which I can always go;
give the command to save me,
for you are my rock and my fortress.[e]
4 Deliver me, O my God, from the hand of the wicked,[f]
from the grasp of evil and cruel men.

5 For you have been my hope, O Sovereign LORD,
my confidence[g] since my youth.
6 From birth[h] I have relied on you;
you brought me forth from my mother's womb.[i]
I will ever praise[j] you.
7 I have become like a portent[k] to many,
but you are my strong refuge.[l]
8 My mouth[m] is filled with your praise,
declaring your splendor[n] all day long.

9 Do not cast[o] me away when I am old;[p]
do not forsake me when my strength is gone.
10 For my enemies speak against me;
those who wait to kill[q] me conspire[r] together.
11 They say, "God has forsaken him;
pursue him and seize him,
for no one will rescue[s] him."
12 Be not far[t] from me, O God;
come quickly, O my God, to help[u] me.
13 May my accusers perish in shame;
may those who want to harm me
be covered with scorn and disgrace.[v]

14 But as for me, I will always have hope;[w]
I will praise you more and more.
15 My mouth will tell[x] of your righteousness,
of your salvation all day long,
though I know not its measure.

70:5 [a]Ps 40:17 [b]Ps 141:1
71:1 [c]Ps 25:2-3; 31:1
71:2 [d]Ps 17:6
71:3 [e]Ps 18:2; 31:2-3; 44:4
71:4 [f]Ps 140:4
71:5 [g]Job 4:6; Jer 17:7
71:6 [h]Ps 22:10 [i]Ps 22:9; Isa 46:3 [j]Ps 9:1; 34:1; 52:9; 119:164; 145:2
71:7 [k]Isa 8:18; 1Co 4:9 [l]2Sa 22:3; Ps 61:3
71:8 [m]Ps 51:15; 63:5 [n]Ps 35:28; 96:6; 104:1
71:9 [o]Ps 51:11 [p]ver 18; Ps 92:14; Isa 46:4
71:10 [q]Ps 10:8; 59:3; Pr 1:18 [r]Ps 31:13; 56:6; Mt 12:14
71:11 [s]Ps 7:2
71:12 [t]Ps 35:22; 38:21 [u]Ps 38:22; 70:1
71:13 [v]ver 24
71:14 [w]Ps 130:7
71:15 [x]Ps 35:28; 40:5

[16]I will come and proclaim your mighty acts,[a]
O Sovereign LORD;
I will proclaim your righteousness, yours alone.
[17]Since my youth, O God, you have taught[b] me,
and to this day I declare your marvelous deeds.[c]
[18]Even when I am old and gray,[d]
do not forsake me, O God,
till I declare your power to the next generation,
your might to all who are to come.[e]

[19]Your righteousness reaches to the skies,[f] O God,
you who have done great things.[g]
Who, O God, is like you?[h]
[20]Though you have made me see troubles,[i] many
and bitter,
you will restore[j] my life again;
from the depths of the earth
you will again bring me up.
[21]You will increase my honor[k]
and comfort[l] me once again.

[22]I will praise you with the harp[m]
for your faithfulness, O my God;
I will sing praise to you with the lyre,[n]
O Holy One of Israel.[o]
[23]My lips will shout for joy
when I sing praise to you—
I, whom you have redeemed.[p]
[24]My tongue will tell of your righteous acts
all day long,[q]
for those who wanted to harm me[r]
have been put to shame and confusion.

Psalm 72

Of Solomon.

Psalm 72 Theme ____________________

[1]Endow the king with your justice, O God,
the royal son with your righteousness.
[2]He will[a] judge your people in righteousness,[s]
your afflicted ones with justice.
[3]The mountains will bring prosperity to the people,
the hills the fruit of righteousness.

a2 Or *May he*; similarly in verses 3-11 and 17

71:16
[a]Ps 106:2

71:17
[b]Dt 4:5
[c]Ps 26:7

71:18
[d]ver 9
[e]Ps 22:30,31; 78:4

71:19
[f]Ps 36:5; 57:10
[g]Ps 126:2; Lk 1:49
[h]Ps 35:10

71:20
[i]Ps 60:3
[j]Hos 6:2

71:21
[k]Ps 18:35
[l]Ps 23:4; 86:17; Isa 12:1; 49:13

71:22
[m]Ps 33:2
[n]Ps 92:3; 144:9
[o]2Ki 19:22

71:23
[p]Ps 103:4

71:24
[q]Ps 35:28
[r]ver 13

72:2
[s]Isa 9:7; 11:4-5; 32:1

4He will defend the afflicted among the people
 and save the children of the needy;[a]
 he will crush the oppressor.

5He will endure[a] as long as the sun,
 as long as the moon, through all generations.
6He will be like rain[b] falling on a mown field,
 like showers watering the earth.
7In his days the righteous will flourish;[c]
 prosperity will abound till the moon is no more.

8He will rule from sea to sea
 and from the River[d][b] to the ends of the earth.[c][e]
9The desert tribes will bow before him
 and his enemies will lick the dust.
10The kings of Tarshish and of distant shores
 will bring tribute to him;
the kings of Sheba[f] and Seba
 will present him gifts.[g]
11All kings will bow down to him
 and all nations will serve him.

12For he will deliver the needy who cry out,
 the afflicted who have no one to help.
13He will take pity on the weak and the needy
 and save the needy from death.
14He will rescue[h] them from oppression and violence,
 for precious[i] is their blood in his sight.

15Long may he live!
 May gold from Sheba[j] be given him.
May people ever pray for him
 and bless him all day long.
16Let grain abound throughout the land;
 on the tops of the hills may it sway.
Let its fruit flourish like Lebanon;[k]
 let it thrive like the grass of the field.
17May his name endure forever;[l]
 may it continue as long as the sun.[m]

All nations will be blessed through him,
 and they will call him blessed.[n]

18Praise be to the LORD God, the God of Israel,[o]
 who alone does marvelous deeds.[p]
19Praise be to his glorious name forever;

72:4 [a]Isa 11:4
72:6 [b]Dt 32:2; Hos 6:3
72:7 [c]Ps 92:12; Isa 2:4
72:8 [d]Ex 23:31 [e]Zec 9:10
72:10 [f]Ge 10:7 [g]2Ch 9:24
72:14 [h]Ps 69:18 [i]1Sa 26:21; Ps 116:15
72:15 [j]Isa 60:6
72:16 [k]Ps 104:16
72:17 [l]Ex 3:15 [m]Ps 89:36 [n]Ge 12:3; Lk 1:48
72:18 [o]1Ch 29:10; Ps 41:13; 106:48 [p]Job 5:9

a5 Septuagint; Hebrew *You will be feared* b8 That is, the Euphrates c8 Or *the end of the land*

may the whole earth be filled with his glory.[a]
Amen and Amen.[b]

[20]This concludes the prayers of David son of Jesse.

BOOK III

Psalms 73–89

Psalm 73

A psalm of Asaph.

Psalm 73 Theme ____________________

[1]Surely God is good to Israel,
to those who are pure in heart.[c]

[2]But as for me, my feet had almost slipped;
I had nearly lost my foothold.
[3]For I envied[d] the arrogant
when I saw the prosperity of the wicked.[e]

[4]They have no struggles;
their bodies are healthy and strong.[a]
[5]They are free[f] from the burdens common to man;
they are not plagued by human ills.
[6]Therefore pride is their necklace;[g]
they clothe themselves with violence.[h]
[7]From their callous hearts[i] comes iniquity[b];
the evil conceits of their minds know no limits.
[8]They scoff, and speak with malice;
in their arrogance[j] they threaten oppression.
[9]Their mouths lay claim to heaven,
and their tongues take possession of the earth.
[10]Therefore their people turn to them
and drink up waters in abundance.[c]
[11]They say, "How can God know?
Does the Most High have knowledge?"

[12]This is what the wicked are like—
always carefree, they increase in wealth.[k]

[13]Surely in vain[l] have I kept my heart pure;
in vain have I washed my hands in innocence.[m]
[14]All day long I have been plagued;
I have been punished every morning.

[a] *4* With a different word division of the Hebrew; Masoretic Text *struggles at their death; / their bodies are healthy* [b] *7* Syriac (see also Septuagint); Hebrew *Their eyes bulge with fat*
[c] *10* The meaning of the Hebrew for this verse is uncertain.

72:19 [a]Nu 14:21; Ne 9:5 [b]Ps 41:13
73:1 [c]Mt 5:8
73:3 [d]Ps 37:1; Pr 23:17 [e]Job 21:7; Jer 12:1
73:5 [f]Job 21:9
73:6 [g]Ge 41:42 [h]Ps 109:18
73:7 [i]Ps 17:10
73:8 [j]Ps 17:10; Jude 16
73:12 [k]Ps 49:6
73:13 [l]Job 21:15; 34:9 [m]Ps 26:6

15 If I had said, "I will speak thus,"
I would have betrayed your children.
16 When I tried to understand[a] all this,
it was oppressive to me
17 till I entered the sanctuary[b] of God;
then I understood their final destiny.[c]

18 Surely you place them on slippery ground;[d]
you cast them down to ruin.
19 How suddenly[e] are they destroyed,
completely swept away by terrors!
20 As a dream[f] when one awakes,[g]
so when you arise, O Lord,
you will despise them as fantasies.

21 When my heart was grieved
and my spirit embittered,
22 I was senseless[h] and ignorant;
I was a brute beast[i] before you.

23 Yet I am always with you;
you hold me by my right hand.
24 You guide[j] me with your counsel,[k]
and afterward you will take me into glory.
25 Whom have I in heaven but you?
And earth has nothing I desire besides you.[l]
26 My flesh and my heart[m] may fail,[n]
but God is the strength of my heart
and my portion forever.

27 Those who are far from you will perish;[o]
you destroy all who are unfaithful to you.
28 But as for me, it is good to be near God.[p]
I have made the Sovereign LORD my refuge;
I will tell of all your deeds.[q]

Psalm 74

A *maskil*[a] of Asaph.

*Psalm 74 Theme*____________________________

1 Why have you rejected us forever,[r] O God?
Why does your anger smolder against the sheep
of your pasture?[s]

73:16 [a] Ecc 8:17
73:17 [b] Ps 77:13 [c] Ps 37:38
73:18 [d] Ps 35:6
73:19 [e] Isa 47:11
73:20 [f] Job 20:8 [g] Ps 78:65
73:22 [h] Ps 49:10; 92:6 [i] Ecc 3:18
73:24 [j] Ps 48:14 [k] Ps 32:8
73:25 [l] Php 3:8
73:26 [m] Ps 84:2 [n] Ps 40:12
73:27 [o] Ps 119:155
73:28 [p] Heb 10:22; Jas 4:8 [q] Ps 40:5
74:1 [r] Dt 29:20; Ps 44:23 [s] Ps 79:13; 95:7; 100:3

[a] Title: Probably a literary or musical term

[2]Remember the people you purchased[a] of old,[b]
the tribe of your inheritance, whom you redeemed[c]—
Mount Zion, where you dwelt.[d]
[3]Turn your steps toward these everlasting ruins,
all this destruction the enemy has brought on
the sanctuary.

[4]Your foes roared[e] in the place where you met with us;
they set up their standards[f] as signs.
[5]They behaved like men wielding axes
to cut through a thicket of trees.[g]
[6]They smashed all the carved[h] paneling
with their axes and hatchets.
[7]They burned your sanctuary to the ground;
they defiled the dwelling place of your Name.
[8]They said in their hearts, "We will crush[i] them
completely!"
They burned every place where God was
worshiped in the land.
[9]We are given no miraculous signs;
no prophets[j] are left,
and none of us knows how long this will be.

[10]How long will the enemy mock you, O God?
Will the foe revile[k] your name forever?
[11]Why do you hold back your hand, your right hand?[l]
Take it from the folds of your garment and
destroy them!

[12]But you, O God, are my king[m] from of old;
you bring salvation upon the earth.
[13]It was you who split open the sea[n] by your power;
you broke the heads of the monster[o] in the waters.
[14]It was you who crushed the heads of Leviathan
and gave him as food to the creatures of the desert.
[15]It was you who opened up springs[p] and streams;
you dried up[q] the ever flowing rivers.
[16]The day is yours, and yours also the night;
you established the sun and moon.[r]
[17]It was you who set all the boundaries[s] of the earth;
you made both summer and winter.[t]

[18]Remember how the enemy has mocked you, O LORD,
how foolish people[u] have reviled your name.
[19]Do not hand over the life of your dove to wild beasts;
do not forget the lives of your afflicted[v]
people forever.

74:2 [a]Ex 15:16 [b]Dt 32:7 [c]Ex 15:13 [d]Ps 68:16
74:4 [e]La 2:7 [f]Nu 2:2
74:5 [g]Jer 46:22
74:6 [h]1Ki 6:18
74:8 [i]Ps 83:4
74:9 [j]1Sa 3:1
74:10 [k]Ps 44:16
74:11 [l]La 2:3
74:12 [m]Ps 44:4
74:13 [n]Ex 14:21 [o]Isa 51:9; Eze 29:3
74:15 [p]Ex 17:6; Nu 20:11 [q]Jos 2:10; 3:13
74:16 [r]Ge 1:16; Ps 136:7-9
74:17 [s]Dt 32:8; Ac 17:26 [t]Ge 8:22
74:18 [u]Dt 32:6; Ps 39:8
74:19 [v]Ps 9:18

20Have regard for your covenant,[a]
because haunts of violence fill the dark places of the land.
21Do not let the oppressed[b] retreat in disgrace;
may the poor and needy[c] praise your name.

22Rise up, O God, and defend your cause;
remember how fools[d] mock you all day long.
23Do not ignore the clamor of your adversaries,[e]
the uproar of your enemies, which rises continually.

Psalm 75

For the director of music. ⌊To the tune of⌋ "Do Not Destroy." A psalm of Asaph. A song.

*Psalm 75 Theme*______________________________

1We give thanks to you, O God,
we give thanks, for your Name is near;[f]
men tell of your wonderful deeds.[g]

2You say, "I choose the appointed time;
it is I who judge uprightly.
3When the earth and all its people quake,[h]
it is I who hold its pillars[i] firm. *Selah*
4To the arrogant I say, 'Boast no more,'
and to the wicked, 'Do not lift up your horns.[j]
5Do not lift your horns against heaven;
do not speak with outstretched neck.'"

6No one from the east or the west
or from the desert can exalt a man.
7But it is God who judges:[k]
He brings one down, he exalts another.[l]
8In the hand of the LORD is a cup
full of foaming wine mixed[m] with spices;
he pours it out, and all the wicked of the earth
drink it down to its very dregs.[n]

9As for me, I will declare[o] this forever;
I will sing praise to the God of Jacob.
10I will cut off the horns of all the wicked,
but the horns of the righteous will be lifted up.[p]

74:20 [a]Ge 17:7; Ps 106:45
74:21 [b]Ps 103:6 [c]Ps 35:10
74:22 [d]Ps 53:1
74:23 [e]Ps 65:7
75:1 [f]Ps 145:18 [g]Ps 44:1; 71:16
75:3 [h]Isa 24:19 [i]1Sa 2:8
75:4 [j]Zec 1:21
75:7 [k]Ps 50:6 [l]1Sa 2:7; Ps 147:6; Da 2:21
75:8 [m]Pr 23:30 [n]Job 21:20; Jer 25:15
75:9 [o]Ps 40:10
75:10 [p]Ps 89:17; 92:10; 148:14

Psalm 76

For the director of music. With stringed instruments. A psalm of Asaph. A song.

*Psalm 76 Theme*__________________________

1In Judah God is known;
his name is great in Israel.
2His tent is in Salem,[a]
his dwelling place in Zion.
3There he broke the flashing arrows,
the shields and the swords, the weapons of war.[b] *Selah*

4You are resplendent with light,
more majestic than mountains rich with game.
5Valiant men lie plundered,
they sleep their last sleep;[c]
not one of the warriors
can lift his hands.
6At your rebuke, O God of Jacob,
both horse and chariot[d] lie still.
7You alone are to be feared.[e]
Who can stand[f] before you when you are angry?[g]
8From heaven you pronounced judgment,
and the land feared[h] and was quiet—
9when you, O God, rose up to judge,[i]
to save all the afflicted of the land. *Selah*
10Surely your wrath against men brings you praise,[j]
and the survivors of your wrath are restrained.[a]

11Make vows to the LORD your God and fulfill them;[k]
let all the neighboring lands
bring gifts[l] to the One to be feared.
12He breaks the spirit of rulers;
he is feared by the kings of the earth.

Psalm 77

For the director of music. For Jeduthun. Of Asaph. A psalm.

*Psalm 77 Theme*__________________________

1I cried out to God[m] for help;
I cried out to God to hear me.

a *10* Or *Surely the wrath of men brings you praise,/ and with the remainder of wrath you arm yourself*

76:2 [a]Ge 14:18
76:3 [b]Ps 46:9
76:5 [c]Ps 13:3
76:6 [d]Ex 15:1
76:7 [e]1Ch 16:25 [f]Ezr 9:15; Rev 6:17 [g]Ps 2:5; Na 1:6
76:8 [h]1Ch 16:30; 2Ch 20:29-30
76:9 [i]Ps 9:8
76:10 [j]Ex 9:16; Ro 9:17
76:11 [k]Ps 50:14; Ecc 5:4-5 [l]2Ch 32:23; Ps 68:29
77:1 [m]Ps 3:4

2When I was in distress,[a] I sought the Lord;
at night I stretched out untiring hands[b]
and my soul refused to be comforted.[c]

3I remembered you, O God, and I groaned;
I mused, and my spirit grew faint.[d] *Selah*
4You kept my eyes from closing;
I was too troubled to speak.
5I thought about the former days,[e]
the years of long ago;
6I remembered my songs in the night.
My heart mused and my spirit inquired:

7"Will the Lord reject forever?
Will he never show his favor[f] again?
8Has his unfailing love vanished forever?
Has his promise[g] failed for all time?
9Has God forgotten to be merciful?[h]
Has he in anger withheld his compassion?[i]" *Selah*

10Then I thought, "To this I will appeal:
the years of the right hand[j] of the Most High."
11I will remember the deeds of the LORD;
yes, I will remember your miracles[k] of long ago.
12I will meditate on all your works
and consider all your mighty deeds.

13Your ways, O God, are holy.
What god is so great as our God?[l]
14You are the God who performs miracles;
you display your power among the peoples.
15With your mighty arm you redeemed your people,[m]
the descendants of Jacob and Joseph. *Selah*

16The waters[n] saw you, O God,
the waters saw you and writhed;[o]
the very depths were convulsed.
17The clouds poured down water,[p]
the skies resounded with thunder;
your arrows flashed back and forth.
18Your thunder was heard in the whirlwind,
your lightning lit up the world;
the earth trembled and quaked.[q]
19Your path led through the sea,[r]
your way through the mighty waters,
though your footprints were not seen.

20You led your people[s] like a flock[t]
by the hand of Moses and Aaron.

77:2 [a]Ps 50:15; Isa 26:9,16 [b]Job 11:13 [c]Ge 37:35
77:3 [d]Ps 143:4
77:5 [e]Dt 32:7; Ps 44:1; 143:5; Isa 51:9
77:7 [f]Ps 85:1
77:8 [g]2Pe 3:9
77:9 [h]Ps 25:6; 40:11; 51:1 [i]Isa 49:15
77:10 [j]Ps 31:22
77:11 [k]Ps 143:5
77:13 [l]Ex 15:11; Ps 71:19; 86:8
77:15 [m]Ex 6:6; Dt 9:29
77:16 [n]Ex 14:21,28; Hab 3:8 [o]Ps 114:4; Hab 3:10
77:17 [p]Jdg 5:4
77:18 [q]Jdg 5:4
77:19 [r]Hab 3:15
77:20 [s]Ex 13:21 [t]Ps 78:52; Isa 63:11

Psalm 78

A *maskil*[a] of Asaph.

*Psalm 78 Theme*__________________________________

1O my people, hear my teaching;[a]
listen to the words of my mouth.
2I will open my mouth in parables,[b]
I will utter hidden things, things from of old—
3what we have heard and known,
what our fathers have told us.[c]
4We will not hide them from their children;[d]
we will tell the next generation
the praiseworthy deeds[e] of the LORD,
his power, and the wonders he has done.
5He decreed statutes[f] for Jacob[g]
and established the law in Israel,
which he commanded our forefathers
to teach their children,
6so the next generation would know them,
even the children yet to be born,[h]
and they in turn would tell their children.
7Then they would put their trust in God
and would not forget[i] his deeds
but would keep his commands.[j]
8They would not be like their forefathers[k]—
a stubborn[l] and rebellious[m] generation,
whose hearts were not loyal to God,
whose spirits were not faithful to him.

9The men of Ephraim, though armed with bows,[n]
turned back on the day of battle;[o]
10they did not keep God's covenant[p]
and refused to live by his law.
11They forgot what he had done,[q]
the wonders he had shown them.
12He did miracles[r] in the sight of their fathers
in the land of Egypt,[s] in the region of Zoan.[t]
13He divided the sea[u] and led them through;
he made the water stand firm like a wall.[v]
14He guided them with the cloud by day
and with light from the fire all night.[w]
15He split the rocks[x] in the desert
and gave them water as abundant as the seas;

[a]Title: Probably a literary or musical term

78:1 [a]Isa 51:4; 55:3
78:2 [b]Ps 49:4; Mt 13:35*
78:3 [c]Ps 44:1
78:4 [d]Dt 11:19 [e]Ps 26:7; 71:17
78:5 [f]Ps 19:7; 81:5 [g]Ps 147:19
78:6 [h]Ps 22:31; 102:18
78:7 [i]Dt 6:12 [j]Dt 5:29
78:8 [k]2Ch 30:7 [l]Ex 32:9 [m]ver 37; Isa 30:9
78:9 [n]ver 57; 1Ch 12:2 [o]Jdg 20:39
78:10 [p]2Ki 17:15
78:11 [q]Ps 106:13
78:12 [r]Ps 106:22 [s]Ex 7-12 [t]Nu 13:22
78:13 [u]Ex 14:21; Ps 136:13 [v]Ex 15:8
78:14 [w]Ex 13:21; Ps 105:39
78:15 [x]Nu 20:11; 1Co 10:4

16 he brought streams out of a rocky crag
  and made water flow down like rivers.

17 But they continued to sin[a] against him,
  rebelling in the desert against the Most High.
18 They willfully put God to the test[b]
  by demanding the food they craved.[c]
19 They spoke against God,[d] saying,
  "Can God spread a table in the desert?
20 When he struck the rock, water gushed out,[e]
  and streams flowed abundantly.
But can he also give us food?
  Can he supply meat[f] for his people?"
21 When the LORD heard them, he was very angry;
  his fire broke out[g] against Jacob,
  and his wrath rose against Israel,
22 for they did not believe in God
  or trust[h] in his deliverance.
23 Yet he gave a command to the skies above
  and opened the doors of the heavens;[i]
24 he rained down manna[j] for the people to eat,
  he gave them the grain of heaven.
25 Men ate the bread of angels;
  he sent them all the food they could eat.
26 He let loose the east wind[k] from the heavens
  and led forth the south wind by his power.
27 He rained meat down on them like dust,
  flying birds like sand on the seashore.
28 He made them come down inside their camp,
  all around their tents.
29 They ate till they had more than enough,[l]
  for he had given them what they craved.
30 But before they turned from the food they craved,
  even while it was still in their mouths,[m]
31 God's anger rose against them;
  he put to death the sturdiest[n] among them,
  cutting down the young men of Israel.

32 In spite of all this, they kept on sinning;
  in spite of his wonders,[o] they did not believe.[p]
33 So he ended their days in futility[q]
  and their years in terror.
34 Whenever God slew them, they would seek[r] him;
  they eagerly turned to him again.
35 They remembered that God was their Rock,[s]
  that God Most High was their Redeemer.[t]

78:17 [a] Dt 9:22; Isa 63:10; Heb 3:16
78:18 [b] 1Co 10:9 [c] Ex 16:2; Nu 11:4
78:19 [d] Nu 21:5
78:20 [e] Nu 20:11 [f] Nu 11:18
78:21 [g] Nu 11:1
78:22 [h] Dt 1:32; Heb 3:19
78:23 [i] Ge 7:11; Mal 3:10
78:24 [j] Ex 16:4; Jn 6:31*
78:26 [k] Nu 11:31
78:29 [l] Nu 11:20
78:30 [m] Nu 11:33
78:31 [n] Isa 10:16
78:32 [o] ver 11 [p] ver 22
78:33 [q] Nu 14:29,35
78:34 [r] Hos 5:15
78:35 [s] Dt 32:4 [t] Dt 9:26

[36]But then they would flatter him with their mouths,[a]
lying to him with their tongues;
[37]their hearts were not loyal[b] to him,
they were not faithful to his covenant.
[38]Yet he was merciful;[c]
he forgave[d] their iniquities[e]
and did not destroy them.
Time after time he restrained his anger
and did not stir up his full wrath.
[39]He remembered that they were but flesh,[f]
a passing breeze[g] that does not return.

[40]How often they rebelled[h] against him in the desert[i]
and grieved him[j] in the wasteland!
[41]Again and again they put God to the test;[k]
they vexed the Holy One of Israel.[l]
[42]They did not remember his power—
the day he redeemed them from the oppressor,
[43]the day he displayed his miraculous signs in Egypt,
his wonders in the region of Zoan.
[44]He turned their rivers to blood;[m]
they could not drink from their streams.
[45]He sent swarms of flies[n] that devoured them,
and frogs[o] that devastated them.
[46]He gave their crops to the grasshopper,
their produce to the locust.[p]
[47]He destroyed their vines with hail[q]
and their sycamore-figs with sleet.
[48]He gave over their cattle to the hail,
their livestock[r] to bolts of lightning.
[49]He unleashed against them his hot anger,[s]
his wrath, indignation and hostility—
a band of destroying angels.
[50]He prepared a path for his anger;
he did not spare them from death
but gave them over to the plague.
[51]He struck down all the firstborn of Egypt,[t]
the firstfruits of manhood in the tents of Ham.[u]
[52]But he brought his people out like a flock;[v]
he led them like sheep through the desert.
[53]He guided them safely, so they were unafraid;
but the sea engulfed[w] their enemies.[x]
[54]Thus he brought them to the border of his holy land,
to the hill country his right hand[y] had taken.
[55]He drove out nations[z] before them
and allotted their lands to them as an inheritance;[a]
he settled the tribes of Israel in their homes.

78:36 [a]Eze 33:31
78:37 [b]ver 8; Ac 8:21
78:38 [c]Ex 34:6 [d]Isa 48:10 [e]Nu 14:18,20
78:39 [f]Ge 6:3; Ps 103:14 [g]Job 7:7; Jas 4:14
78:40 [h]Heb 3:16 [i]Ps 95:8; 106:14 [j]Eph 4:30
78:41 [k]Nu 14:22 [l]2Ki 19:22; Ps 89:18
78:44 [m]Ex 7:20-21; Ps 105:29
78:45 [n]Ex 8:24; Ps 105:31 [o]Ex 8:2,6
78:46 [p]Ex 10:13
78:47 [q]Ex 9:23; Ps 105:32
78:48 [r]Ex 9:25
78:49 [s]Ex 15:7
78:51 [t]Ex 12:29; Ps 135:8 [u]Ps 105:23; 106:22
78:52 [v]Ps 77:20
78:53 [w]Ex 14:28 [x]Ps 106:10
78:54 [y]Ex 15:17; Ps 44:3
78:55 [z]Ps 44:2 [a]Jos 13:7

56 But they put God to the test
and rebelled against the Most High;
they did not keep his statutes.
57 Like their fathers[a] they were disloyal and faithless,
as unreliable as a faulty bow.[b]
58 They angered him[c] with their high places;[d]
they aroused his jealousy with their idols.[e]
59 When God heard them, he was very angry;
he rejected Israel[f] completely.
60 He abandoned the tabernacle of Shiloh,[g]
the tent he had set up among men.
61 He sent ⌊the ark of⌋ his might[h] into captivity,[i]
his splendor into the hands of the enemy.
62 He gave his people over to the sword;
he was very angry with his inheritance.
63 Fire consumed[j] their young men,
and their maidens had no wedding songs;[k]
64 their priests were put to the sword,[l]
and their widows could not weep.

65 Then the Lord awoke as from sleep,[m]
as a man wakes from the stupor of wine.
66 He beat back his enemies;
he put them to everlasting shame.[n]
67 Then he rejected the tents of Joseph,
he did not choose the tribe of Ephraim;
68 but he chose the tribe of Judah,
Mount Zion,[o] which he loved.
69 He built his sanctuary like the heights,
like the earth that he established forever.
70 He chose David[p] his servant
and took him from the sheep pens;
71 from tending the sheep he brought him
to be the shepherd[q] of his people Jacob,
of Israel his inheritance.
72 And David shepherded them with integrity of heart;[r]
with skillful hands he led them.

Psalm 79

A psalm of Asaph.

Psalm 79 Theme ________________________________

1 O God, the nations have invaded your inheritance;[s]
they have defiled your holy temple,
they have reduced Jerusalem to rubble.[t]

78:57 [a] Eze 20:27 [b] Hos 7:16
78:58 [c] Jdg 2:12 [d] Lev 26:30 [e] Ex 20:4; Dt 32:21
78:59 [f] Dt 32:19
78:60 [g] Jos 18:1
78:61 [h] Ps 132:8 [i] 1Sa 4:17
78:63 [j] Nu 11:1 [k] Jer 7:34; 16:9
78:64 [l] 1Sa 4:17; 22:18
78:65 [m] Ps 44:23
78:66 [n] 1Sa 5:6
78:68 [o] Ps 87:2
78:70 [p] 1Sa 16:1
78:71 [q] 2Sa 5:2; Ps 28:9
78:72 [r] 1Ki 9:4
79:1 [s] Ps 74:2 [t] 2Ki 25:9

[2]They have given the dead bodies of
your servants
as food to the birds of the air,
the flesh of your saints to the beasts of
the earth.[a]
[3]They have poured out blood like water
all around Jerusalem,
and there is no one to bury the dead.[b]
[4]We are objects of reproach to our neighbors,
of scorn and derision to those around us.[c]

[5]How long,[d] O LORD? Will you be angry[e] forever?
How long will your jealousy burn like fire?[f]
[6]Pour out your wrath[g] on the nations
that do not acknowledge[h] you,
on the kingdoms
that do not call on your name;[i]
[7]for they have devoured Jacob
and destroyed his homeland.
[8]Do not hold against us the sins of the fathers;[j]
may your mercy come quickly to meet us,
for we are in desperate need.[k]

[9]Help us,[l] O God our Savior,
for the glory of your name;
deliver us and forgive our sins
for your name's sake.[m]
[10]Why should the nations say,
"Where is their God?"[n]
Before our eyes, make known among
the nations
that you avenge[o] the outpoured blood of
your servants.
[11]May the groans of the prisoners come before you;
by the strength of your arm
preserve those condemned to die.

[12]Pay back into the laps[p] of our neighbors seven times[q]
the reproach they have hurled at you, O Lord.
[13]Then we your people, the sheep of your pasture,[r]
will praise you forever;[s]
from generation to generation
we will recount your praise.

79:2 [a]Dt 28:26; Jer 7:33
79:3 [b]Jer 16:4
79:4 [c]Ps 44:13; 80:6
79:5 [d]Ps 74:10 [e]Ps 74:1; 85:5 [f]Dt 29:20; Ps 89:46; Zep 3:8
79:6 [g]Ps 69:24; Rev 16:1 [h]Jer 10:25; 2Th 1:8 [i]Ps 14:4
79:8 [j]Isa 64:9 [k]Ps 116:6; 142:6
79:9 [l]2Ch 14:11 [m]Ps 25:11; 31:3; Jer 14:7
79:10 [n]Ps 42:10 [o]Ps 94:1
79:12 [p]Isa 65:6; Jer 32:18 [q]Ge 4:15
79:13 [r]Ps 74:1; 95:7 [s]Ps 44:8

80:1
[a]Ps 77:20
[b]Ex 25:22

Psalm 80

For the director of music. To ⌊the tune of⌋ "The Lilies of the Covenant."
Of Asaph. A psalm.

80:2
[c]Nu 2:18-24
[d]Ps 35:23

80:3
[e]Ps 85:4;
La 5:21
[f]Nu 6:25

80:5
[g]Ps 42:3;
Isa 30:20

80:6
[h]Ps 79:4

80:8
[i]Isa 5:1-2;
Jer 2:21
[j]Jos 13:6;
Ac 7:45

80:11
[k]Ps 72:8

80:12
[l]Ps 89:40;
Isa 5:5

80:13
[m]Jer 5:6

*Psalm 80 Theme*____________________________

1 Hear us, O Shepherd of Israel,
you who lead Joseph like a flock;[a]
you who sit enthroned between the cherubim,[b]
shine forth
2 before Ephraim, Benjamin and Manasseh.[c]
Awaken[d] your might;
come and save us.

3 Restore[e] us,[f] O God;
make your face shine upon us,
that we may be saved.

4 O LORD God Almighty,
how long will your anger smolder
against the prayers of your people?
5 You have fed them with the bread of tears;
you have made them drink tears by the bowlful.[g]
6 You have made us a source of contention to
our neighbors,
and our enemies mock us.[h]

7 Restore us, O God Almighty;
make your face shine upon us,
that we may be saved.

8 You brought a vine[i] out of Egypt;
you drove out[j] the nations and planted it.
9 You cleared the ground for it,
and it took root and filled the land.
10 The mountains were covered with its shade,
the mighty cedars with its branches.
11 It sent out its boughs to the Sea,[a]
its shoots as far as the River.[b][k]

12 Why have you broken down its walls[l]
so that all who pass by pick its grapes?
13 Boars from the forest ravage[m] it
and the creatures of the field feed on it.

[a] *11* Probably the Mediterranean [b] *11* That is, the Euphrates

14Return to us, O God Almighty!
Look down from heaven and see![a]
Watch over this vine,
15 the root your right hand has planted,
the son[a] you have raised up for yourself.

16Your vine is cut down, it is burned with fire;
at your rebuke[b] your people perish.
17Let your hand rest on the man at your right hand,
the son of man you have raised up for yourself.
18Then we will not turn away from you;
revive us, and we will call on your name.

19Restore us, O LORD God Almighty;
make your face shine upon us,
that we may be saved.

Psalm 81

For the director of music. According to *gittith*.[b] Of Asaph.

*Psalm 81 Theme*______________________________

1Sing for joy to God our strength;
shout aloud to the God of Jacob![c]
2Begin the music, strike the tambourine,[d]
play the melodious harp[e] and lyre.

3Sound the ram's horn at the New Moon,
and when the moon is full, on the day of our Feast;
4this is a decree for Israel,
an ordinance of the God of Jacob.
5He established it as a statute for Joseph
when he went out against Egypt,[f]
where we heard a language we did not understand.[c][g]

6He says, "I removed the burden from their shoulders;[h]
their hands were set free from the basket.
7In your distress you called[i] and I rescued you,
I answered[j] you out of a thundercloud;
I tested you at the waters of Meribah.[k] *Selah*

8"Hear, O my people,[l] and I will warn you—
if you would but listen to me, O Israel!
9You shall have no foreign god[m] among you;
you shall not bow down to an alien god.

[a]*15* Or *branch* [b]Title: Probably a musical term [c]*5* Or / *and we heard a voice we had not known*

80:14 [a]Isa 63:15
80:16 [b]Ps 39:11; 76:6
81:1 [c]Ps 66:1
81:2 [d]Ex 15:20 [e]Ps 92:3
81:5 [f]Ex 11:4 [g]Ps 114:1
81:6 [h]Isa 9:4
81:7 [i]Ex 2:23; Ps 50:15 [j]Ex 19:19 [k]Ex 17:7
81:8 [l]Ps 50:7
81:9 [m]Ex 20:3; Dt 32:12; Isa 43:12

10 I am the LORD your God,
who brought you up out of Egypt.[a]
Open wide your mouth and I will fill[b] it.

11 "But my people would not listen to me;
Israel would not submit to me.[c]
12 So I gave them over[d] to their stubborn hearts
to follow their own devices.

13 "If my people would but listen to me,[e]
if Israel would follow my ways,
14 how quickly would I subdue[f] their enemies
and turn my hand against[g] their foes!
15 Those who hate the LORD would cringe before him,
and their punishment would last forever.
16 But you would be fed with the finest of wheat;[h]
with honey from the rock I would satisfy you."

Psalm 82

A psalm of Asaph.

*Psalm 82 Theme*______________________________________

1 God presides in the great assembly;
he gives judgment[i] among the "gods":

2 "How long will you[a] defend the unjust
and show partiality[j] to the wicked?[k] *Selah*
3 Defend the cause of the weak and fatherless;[l]
maintain the rights of the poor[m] and oppressed.
4 Rescue the weak and needy;
deliver them from the hand of the wicked.

5 "They know nothing, they understand nothing.[n]
They walk about in darkness;[o]
all the foundations[p] of the earth are shaken.

6 "I said, 'You are "gods";[q]
you are all sons of the Most High.'
7 But you will die[r] like mere men;
you will fall like every other ruler."

8 Rise up,[s] O God, judge the earth,
for all the nations are your inheritance.[t]

81:10 [a]Ex 20:2 [b]Ps 107:9
81:11 [c]Ex 32:1-6
81:12 [d]Ac 7:42; Ro 1:24
81:13 [e]Dt 5:29; Isa 48:18
81:14 [f]Ps 47:3 [g]Am 1:8
81:16 [h]Dt 32:14
82:1 [i]Ps 58:11; Isa 3:13
82:2 [j]Dt 1:17 [k]Ps 58:1-2; Pr 18:5
82:3 [l]Dt 24:17 [m]Jer 22:16
82:5 [n]Ps 14:4; Mic 3:1 [o]Isa 59:9 [p]Ps 11:3
82:6 [q]Jn 10:34*
82:7 [r]Ps 49:12; Eze 31:14
82:8 [s]Ps 12:5 [t]Ps 2:8; Rev 11:15

[a]2 The Hebrew is plural.

Psalm 83

A song. A psalm of Asaph.

*Psalm 83 Theme*____

1O God, do not keep silent;[a]
be not quiet, O God, be not still.
2See how your enemies are astir,[b]
how your foes rear their heads.[c]
3With cunning they conspire[d] against your people;
they plot against those you cherish.
4"Come," they say, "let us destroy[e] them as a nation,
that the name of Israel be remembered[f] no more."

5With one mind they plot together;[g]
they form an alliance against you—
6the tents of Edom[h] and the Ishmaelites,
of Moab[i] and the Hagrites,[j]
7Gebal,[a][k] Ammon and Amalek,
Philistia, with the people of Tyre.[l]
8Even Assyria has joined them
to lend strength to the descendants of Lot.[m] *Selah*

9Do to them as you did to Midian,[n]
as you did to Sisera and Jabin at the river Kishon,[o]
10who perished at Endor
and became like refuse[p] on the ground.
11Make their nobles like Oreb and Zeeb,[q]
all their princes like Zebah and Zalmunna,[r]
12who said, "Let us take possession[s]
of the pasturelands of God."

13Make them like tumbleweed, O my God,
like chaff[t] before the wind.
14As fire consumes the forest
or a flame sets the mountains ablaze,[u]
15so pursue them with your tempest
and terrify them with your storm.[v]
16Cover their faces with shame[w]
so that men will seek your name, O LORD.

17May they ever be ashamed and dismayed;
may they perish in disgrace.[x]
18Let them know that you, whose name is the LORD—
that you alone are the Most High over all the earth.[y]

83:1 [a]Ps 28:1; 35:22
83:2 [b]Ps 2:1; Isa 17:12 [c]Jdg 8:28; Ps 81:15
83:3 [d]Ps 31:13
83:4 [e]Est 3:6 [f]Jer 11:19
83:5 [g]Ps 2:2
83:6 [h]Ps 137:7 [i]2Ch 20:1 [j]Ge 25:16
83:7 [k]Jos 13:5 [l]Eze 27:3
83:8 [m]Dt 2:9
83:9 [n]Jdg 7:1-23 [o]Jdg 4:23-24
83:10 [p]Zep 1:17
83:11 [q]Jdg 7:25 [r]Jdg 8:12,21
83:12 [s]2Ch 20:11
83:13 [t]Ps 35:5; Isa 17:13
83:14 [u]Dt 32:22; Isa 9:18
83:15 [v]Job 9:17
83:16 [w]Ps 109:29; 132:18
83:17 [x]Ps 35:4
83:18 [y]Ps 59:13

[a]7 That is, Byblos

Psalm 84

For the director of music. According to *gittith.*[a] Of the Sons of Korah. A psalm.

Psalm 84 Theme ____________________________________

1 How lovely is your dwelling place,[a]
O LORD Almighty!
2 My soul yearns,[b] even faints,
for the courts of the LORD;
my heart and my flesh cry out
for the living God.

3 Even the sparrow has found a home,
and the swallow a nest for herself,
where she may have her young—
a place near your altar,[c]
O LORD Almighty, my King and my God.[d]
4 Blessed are those who dwell in your house;
they are ever praising you. *Selah*

5 Blessed are those whose strength[e] is in you,
who have set their hearts on pilgrimage.[f]
6 As they pass through the Valley of Baca,
they make it a place of springs;
the autumn[g] rains also cover it with pools.[b]
7 They go from strength to strength,[h]
till each appears[i] before God in Zion.

8 Hear my prayer, O LORD God Almighty;
listen to me, O God of Jacob. *Selah*
9 Look upon our shield,[c][j] O God;
look with favor on your anointed one.[k]

10 Better is one day in your courts
than a thousand elsewhere;
I would rather be a doorkeeper[l] in the house of my God
than dwell in the tents of the wicked.
11 For the LORD God is a sun[m] and shield;[n]
the LORD bestows favor and honor;
no good thing does he withhold[o]
from those whose walk is blameless.

12 O LORD Almighty,
blessed[p] is the man who trusts in you.

84:1 [a]Ps 27:4; 43:3; 132:5
84:2 [b]Ps 42:1-2
84:3 [c]Ps 43:4 [d]Ps 5:2
84:5 [e]Ps 81:1 [f]Jer 31:6
84:6 [g]Joel 2:23
84:7 [h]Pr 4:18 [i]Dt 16:16
84:9 [j]Ps 59:11 [k]1Sa 16:6; Ps 2:2; 132:17
84:10 [l]1Ch 23:5
84:11 [m]Isa 60:19; Rev 21:23 [n]Ge 15:1 [o]Ps 34:10
84:12 [p]Ps 2:12

[a]Title: Probably a musical term [b]6 Or *blessings* [c]9 Or *sovereign*

Psalm 85

For the director of music. Of the Sons of Korah. A psalm.

Psalm 85 Theme ______________________________

[1]You showed favor to your land, O LORD;
you restored the fortunes[a] of Jacob.
[2]You forgave[b] the iniquity[c] of your people
and covered all their sins. *Selah*
[3]You set aside all your wrath[d]
and turned from your fierce anger.[e]

[4]Restore[f] us again, O God our Savior,
and put away your displeasure toward us.
[5]Will you be angry with us forever?[g]
Will you prolong your anger through all generations?
[6]Will you not revive[h] us again,
that your people may rejoice in you?
[7]Show us your unfailing love, O LORD,
and grant us your salvation.

[8]I will listen to what God the LORD will say;
he promises peace[i] to his people, his saints—
but let them not return to folly.
[9]Surely his salvation[j] is near those who fear him,
that his glory[k] may dwell in our land.

[10]Love and faithfulness[l] meet together;
righteousness[m] and peace kiss each other.
[11]Faithfulness springs forth from the earth,
and righteousness[n] looks down from heaven.
[12]The LORD will indeed give what is good,[o]
and our land will yield[p] its harvest.
[13]Righteousness goes before him
and prepares the way for his steps.

Psalm 86

A prayer of David.

Psalm 86 Theme ______________________________

[1]Hear, O LORD, and answer[q] me,
for I am poor and needy.
[2]Guard my life, for I am devoted to you.
You are my God; save your servant
who trusts in you.[r]

85:1 [a]Ps 14:7; Jer 30:18; Eze 39:25
85:2 [b]Nu 14:19 [c]Ps 78:38
85:3 [d]Ps 106:23 [e]Ex 32:12; Dt 13:17; Ps 78:38; Jnh 3:9
85:4 [f]Ps 80:3,7
85:5 [g]Ps 79:5
85:6 [h]Ps 80:18; Hab 3:2
85:8 [i]Zec 9:10
85:9 [j]Isa 46:13 [k]Zec 2:5
85:10 [l]Ps 89:14; Pr 3:3 [m]Ps 72:2-3; Isa 32:17
85:11 [n]Isa 45:8
85:12 [o]Ps 84:11; Jas 1:17 [p]Lev 26:4; Ps 67:6; Zec 8:12
86:1 [q]Ps 17:6
86:2 [r]Ps 25:2; 31:14

3 Have mercy[a] on me, O Lord,
for I call[b] to you all day long.
4 Bring joy to your servant,
for to you, O Lord,
I lift[c] up my soul.

5 You are forgiving and good, O Lord,
abounding in love[d] to all who call to you.
6 Hear my prayer, O LORD;
listen to my cry for mercy.
7 In the day of my trouble[e] I will call to you,
for you will answer me.

8 Among the gods there is none like you,[f] O Lord;
no deeds can compare with yours.
9 All the nations you have made
will come and worship[g] before you, O Lord;
they will bring glory[h] to your name.
10 For you are great and do marvelous deeds;[i]
you alone[j] are God.

11 Teach me your way,[k] O LORD,
and I will walk in your truth;
give me an undivided[l] heart,
that I may fear your name.
12 I will praise you, O Lord my God, with all
my heart;
I will glorify your name forever.
13 For great is your love toward me;
you have delivered me from the depths of
the grave.[a]

14 The arrogant are attacking me, O God;
a band of ruthless men seeks my life—
men without regard for you.[m]
15 But you, O Lord, are a compassionate and
gracious[n] God,
slow to anger, abounding in love and faithfulness.[o]
16 Turn to me and have mercy on me;
grant your strength to your servant
and save the son of your maidservant.[b][p]
17 Give me a sign of your goodness,
that my enemies may see it and be put to shame,
for you, O LORD, have helped me and
comforted me.

86:3 [a]Ps 4:1; 57:1 [b]Ps 88:9
86:4 [c]Ps 25:1; 143:8
86:5 [d]Ex 34:6; Ne 9:17; Ps 103:8; 145:8; Joel 2:13; Jnh 4:2
86:7 [e]Ps 50:15
86:8 [f]Ex 15:11; Dt 3:24; Ps 89:6
86:9 [g]Ps 66:4; Rev 15:4 [h]Isa 43:7
86:10 [i]Ps 72:18 [j]Dt 6:4; Mk 12:29; 1Co 8:4
86:11 [k]Ps 25:5 [l]Jer 32:39
86:14 [m]Ps 54:3
86:15 [n]Ps 103:8 [o]Ex 34:6; Ne 9:17; Joel 2:13
86:16 [p]Ps 116:16

[a]13 Hebrew *Sheol* [b]16 Or *save your faithful son*

Psalm 87

Of the Sons of Korah. A psalm. A song.

*Psalm 87 Theme*____________________________________

1He has set his foundation on the holy mountain;
2 the LORD loves the gates of Zion[a]
more than all the dwellings of Jacob.
3Glorious things are said of you,
O city of God:[b] *Selah*
4"I will record Rahab[a][c] and Babylon
among those who acknowledge me—
Philistia too, and Tyre[d], along with Cush[b]—
and will say, 'This[c] one was born in Zion.[e]' "

5Indeed, of Zion it will be said,
"This one and that one were born in her,
and the Most High himself will establish her."
6The LORD will write in the register[f] of the peoples:
"This one was born in Zion." *Selah*
7As they make music[g] they will sing,
"All my fountains[h] are in you."

87:2 [a]Ps 78:68
87:3 [b]Ps 46:4; Isa 60:1
87:4 [c]Job 9:13 [d]Ps 45:12 [e]Isa 19:25
87:6 [f]Ps 69:28; Isa 4:3; Eze 13:9
87:7 [g]Ps 149:3 [h]Ps 36:9

Psalm 88

A song. A psalm of the Sons of Korah. For the director of music. According to *mahalath leannoth.*[d] A *maskil*[e] of Heman the Ezrahite.

*Psalm 88 Theme*____________________________________

1O LORD, the God who saves me,[i]
day and night I cry out[j] before you.
2May my prayer come before you;
turn your ear to my cry.

3For my soul is full of trouble
and my life draws near the grave.[f][k]
4I am counted among those who go down to the pit;[l]
I am like a man without strength.
5I am set apart with the dead,
like the slain who lie in the grave,
whom you remember no more,
who are cut off[m] from your care.

88:1 [i]Ps 51:14 [j]Ps 22:2; 27:9; Lk 18:7
88:3 [k]Ps 107:18,26
88:4 [l]Ps 28:1
88:5 [m]Ps 31:22; Isa 53:8

[a]4 A poetic name for Egypt [b]4 That is, the upper Nile region [c]4 Or *"O Rahab and Babylon, / Philistia, Tyre and Cush, / I will record concerning those who acknowledge me: / 'This* [d]Title: Possibly a tune, "The Suffering of Affliction" [e]Title: Probably a literary or musical term [f]3 Hebrew *Sheol*

88:6 [a]Ps 69:15; La 3:55
88:7 [b]Ps 42:7
88:8 [c]Job 19:13; Ps 31:11 [d]Jer 32:2
88:9 [e]Ps 38:10 [f]Ps 86:3 [g]Job 11:13; Ps 143:6
88:10 [h]Ps 6:5
88:11 [i]Ps 30:9
88:13 [j]Ps 30:2 [k]Ps 5:3 [l]Ps 119:147
88:14 [m]Ps 43:2 [n]Job 13:24; Ps 13:1
88:15 [o]Job 6:4
88:17 [p]Ps 22:16; 124:4
88:18 [q]ver 8; Job 19:13; Ps 38:11
89:1 [r]Ps 59:16; Ps 101:1 [s]Ps 36:5; 40:10
89:2 [t]Ps 36:5

6 You have put me in the lowest pit,
in the darkest depths.[a]
7 Your wrath lies heavily upon me;
you have overwhelmed me with all your waves.[b]
Selah

8 You have taken from me my closest friends[c]
and have made me repulsive to them.
I am confined[d] and cannot escape;
9 my eyes[e] are dim with grief.

I call[f] to you, O LORD, every day;
I spread out my hands[g] to you.
10 Do you show your wonders to the dead?
Do those who are dead rise up and praise you?[h]
Selah

11 Is your love declared in the grave,
your faithfulness[i] in Destruction[a]?
12 Are your wonders known in the place of darkness,
or your righteous deeds in the land of oblivion?

13 But I cry to you for help,[j] O LORD;
in the morning[k] my prayer comes before you.[l]
14 Why, O LORD, do you reject[m] me
and hide your face[n] from me?
15 From my youth I have been afflicted and close to death;
I have suffered your terrors[o] and am in despair.
16 Your wrath has swept over me;
your terrors have destroyed me.
17 All day long they surround me like a flood;[p]
they have completely engulfed me.
18 You have taken my companions[q] and loved ones from me;
the darkness is my closest friend.

Psalm 89

A *maskil*[b] of Ethan the Ezrahite.

Psalm 89 Theme ________________________________

1 I will sing[r] of the LORD's great love forever;
with my mouth I will make your faithfulness known[s]
through all generations.
2 I will declare that your love stands firm forever,
that you established your faithfulness in heaven itself.[t]

[a] *11* Hebrew *Abaddon* [b] Title: Probably a literary or musical term

[3]You said, "I have made a covenant with my chosen one,
I have sworn to David my servant,
[4]'I will establish your line forever
and make your throne firm through all generations.' "[a]
Selah

[5]The heavens[b] praise your wonders, O LORD,
your faithfulness too, in the assembly of the holy ones.
[6]For who in the skies above can compare with the LORD?
Who is like the LORD among the heavenly beings?[c]
[7]In the council of the holy ones God is greatly feared;
he is more awesome than all who surround him.[d]
[8]O LORD God Almighty, who is like you?[e]
You are mighty, O LORD, and your faithfulness
surrounds you.

[9]You rule over the surging sea;
when its waves mount up, you still them.[f]
[10]You crushed Rahab[g] like one of the slain;
with your strong arm you scattered[h] your enemies.
[11]The heavens are yours, and yours also the earth;[i]
you founded the world and all that is in it.[j]
[12]You created the north and the south;
Tabor[k] and Hermon[l] sing for joy[m] at your name.
[13]Your arm is endued with power;
your hand is strong, your right hand exalted.

[14]Righteousness and justice are the foundation of
your throne;[n]
love and faithfulness go before you.
[15]Blessed are those who have learned to acclaim you,
who walk in the light[o] of your presence, O LORD.
[16]They rejoice in your name[p] all day long;
they exult in your righteousness.
[17]For you are their glory and strength,
and by your favor you exalt our horn.[a][q]
[18]Indeed, our shield[b] belongs to the LORD,
our king[r] to the Holy One of Israel.

[19]Once you spoke in a vision,
to your faithful people you said:
"I have bestowed strength on a warrior;
I have exalted a young man from among the people.
[20]I have found David[s] my servant;[t]
with my sacred oil I have anointed[u] him.

a 17 *Horn* here symbolizes strong one. b 18 Or *sovereign*

89:4 [a]2Sa 7:12-16; 1Ki 8:16; Ps 132:11-12; Isa 9:7; Lk 1:33
89:5 [b]Ps 19:1
89:6 [c]Ps 113:5
89:7 [d]Ps 47:2
89:8 [e]Ps 71:19
89:9 [f]Ps 65:7
89:10 [g]Ps 87:4 [h]Ps 68:1
89:11 [i]1Ch 29:11; Ps 24:1 [j]Ge 1:1
89:12 [k]Jos 19:22 [l]Dt 3:8; Jos 12:1 [m]Ps 98:8
89:14 [n]Ps 97:2
89:15 [o]Ps 44:3
89:16 [p]Ps 105:3
89:17 [q]Ps 75:10; 92:10; 148:14
89:18 [r]Ps 47:9
89:20 [s]Ac 13:22 [t]Ps 78:70 [u]1Sa 16:1,12

89:21 [a]Ps 18:35
89:22 [b]2Sa 7:10
89:23 [c]Ps 18:40 [d]2Sa 7:9
89:24 [e]2Sa 7:15
89:25 [f]Ps 72:8
89:26 [g]2Sa 7:14 [h]2Sa 22:47
89:27 [i]Col 1:18 [j]Nu 24:7 [k]Rev 1:5; 19:16
89:28 [l]ver 33-34; Isa 55:3
89:29 [m]ver 4,36; Dt 11:21; Jer 33:17
89:32 [n]2Sa 7:14
89:33 [o]2Sa 7:15
89:34 [p]Nu 23:19
89:38 [q]Dt 32:19; 1Ch 28:9; Ps 44:9
89:39 [r]La 5:16
89:40 [s]Ps 80:12 [t]La 2:2
89:41 [u]Ps 44:13

21 My hand will sustain him;
surely my arm will strengthen him.[a]
22 No enemy will subject him to tribute;
no wicked man will oppress[b] him.
23 I will crush his foes before him[c]
and strike down his adversaries.[d]
24 My faithful love will be with him,[e]
and through my name his horn[a] will be exalted.
25 I will set his hand over the sea,
his right hand over the rivers.[f]
26 He will call out to me, 'You are my Father,[g]
my God, the Rock my Savior.'[h]
27 I will also appoint him my firstborn,[i]
the most exalted[j] of the kings[k] of the earth.
28 I will maintain my love to him forever,
and my covenant with him will never fail.[l]
29 I will establish his line forever,
his throne as long as the heavens endure.[m]

30 "If his sons forsake my law
and do not follow my statutes,
31 if they violate my decrees
and fail to keep my commands,
32 I will punish their sin with the rod,
their iniquity with flogging;[n]
33 but I will not take my love from him,[o]
nor will I ever betray my faithfulness.
34 I will not violate my covenant
or alter what my lips have uttered.[p]
35 Once for all, I have sworn by my holiness—
and I will not lie to David—
36 that his line will continue forever
and his throne endure before me like the sun;
37 it will be established forever like the moon,
the faithful witness in the sky." *Selah*

38 But you have rejected,[q] you have spurned,
you have been very angry with your anointed one.
39 You have renounced the covenant with your servant
and have defiled his crown in the dust.[r]
40 You have broken through all his walls[s]
and reduced his strongholds[t] to ruins.
41 All who pass by have plundered him;
he has become the scorn of his neighbors.[u]

[a] *24 Horn* here symbolizes strength.

[42]You have exalted the right hand of his foes;
you have made all his enemies rejoice.[a]
[43]You have turned back the edge of his sword
and have not supported him in battle.[b]
[44]You have put an end to his splendor
and cast his throne to the ground.
[45]You have cut short the days of his youth;
you have covered him with a mantle of shame.[c]
Selah

[46]How long, O LORD? Will you hide yourself forever?
How long will your wrath burn like fire?[d]
[47]Remember how fleeting is my life.[e]
For what futility you have created all men!
[48]What man can live and not see death,
or save himself from the power of the grave[a]?[f]
Selah
[49]O Lord, where is your former great love,
which in your faithfulness you swore to David?
[50]Remember, Lord, how your servant has[b] been mocked,[g]
how I bear in my heart the taunts of all the nations,
[51]the taunts with which your enemies have mocked,
O LORD,
with which they have mocked every step of your
anointed one.[h]

[52]Praise be to the LORD forever!
Amen and Amen.[i]

BOOK IV

Psalms 90–106

Psalm 90

A prayer of Moses the man of God.

*Psalm 90 Theme*____________________

[1]Lord, you have been our dwelling place[j]
throughout all generations.
[2]Before the mountains were born[k]
or you brought forth the earth and the world,
from everlasting to everlasting you are God.[l]

[3]You turn men back to dust,
saying, "Return to dust, O sons of men."[m]

89:42 [a]Ps 13:2; 80:6
89:43 [b]Ps 44:10
89:45 [c]Ps 44:15; 109:29
89:46 [d]Ps 79:5
89:47 [e]Job 7:7; Ps 39:5
89:48 [f]Ps 22:29; 49:9
89:50 [g]Ps 69:19
89:51 [h]Ps 74:10
89:52 [i]Ps 41:13; 72:19
90:1 [j]Dt 33:27; Eze 11:16
90:2 [k]Job 15:7; Pr 8:25 [l]Ps 102:24-27
90:3 [m]Ge 3:19; Job 34:15

[a]48 Hebrew *Sheol* [b]50 Or *your servants have*

4 For a thousand years in your sight
are like a day that has just gone by,
or like a watch in the night.[a]
5 You sweep men away[b] in the sleep of death;
they are like the new grass of the morning—
6 though in the morning it springs up new,
by evening it is dry and withered.[c]

7 We are consumed by your anger
and terrified by your indignation.
8 You have set our iniquities before you,
our secret sins[d] in the light of your presence.
9 All our days pass away under your wrath;
we finish our years with a moan.[e]
10 The length of our days is seventy years—
or eighty, if we have the strength;
yet their span[a] is but trouble and sorrow,
for they quickly pass, and we fly away.[f]

11 Who knows the power of your anger?
For your wrath is as great as the fear that is due you.[g]
12 Teach us to number our days[h] aright,
that we may gain a heart of wisdom.[i]

13 Relent, O LORD! How long[j] will it be?
Have compassion on your servants.[k]
14 Satisfy[l] us in the morning with your unfailing love,
that we may sing for joy[m] and be glad all our days.[n]
15 Make us glad for as many days as you have afflicted us,
for as many years as we have seen trouble.
16 May your deeds be shown to your servants,
your splendor to their children.[o]

17 May the favor[b] of the Lord our God rest upon us;
establish the work of our hands for us—
yes, establish the work of our hands.[p]

Psalm 91

*Psalm 91 Theme*________________________________

1 He who dwells in the shelter[q] of the Most High
will rest in the shadow[r] of the Almighty.[c]
2 I will say[d] of the LORD, "He is my refuge[s] and
my fortress,
my God, in whom I trust."

90:4 [a] 2Pe 3:8
90:5 [b] Ps 73:20; Isa 40:6
90:6 [c] Mt 6:30; Jas 1:10
90:8 [d] Ps 19:12
90:9 [e] Ps 78:33
90:10 [f] Job 20:8
90:11 [g] Ps 76:7
90:12 [h] Ps 39:4 [i] Dt 32:29
90:13 [j] Ps 6:3 [k] Dt 32:36; Ps 135:14
90:14 [l] Ps 103:5 [m] Ps 85:6 [n] Ps 31:7
90:16 [o] Ps 44:1; Hab 3:2
90:17 [p] Isa 26:12
91:1 [q] Ps 31:20 [r] Ps 17:8
91:2 [s] Ps 142:5

[a] *10* Or *yet the best of them* [b] *17* Or *beauty* [c] *1* Hebrew *Shaddai* [d] *2* Or *He says*

[3]Surely he will save you from the fowler's snare[a]
and from the deadly pestilence.[b]
[4]He will cover you with his feathers,
and under his wings you will find refuge;[c]
his faithfulness will be your shield[d] and rampart.
[5]You will not fear[e] the terror of night,
nor the arrow that flies by day,
[6]nor the pestilence that stalks in the darkness,
nor the plague that destroys at midday.
[7]A thousand may fall at your side,
ten thousand at your right hand,
but it will not come near you.
[8]You will only observe with your eyes
and see the punishment of the wicked.[f]

[9]If you make the Most High your dwelling—
even the LORD, who is my refuge—
[10]then no harm[g] will befall you,
no disaster will come near your tent.
[11]For he will command his angels[h] concerning you
to guard you in all your ways;[i]
[12]they will lift you up in their hands,
so that you will not strike your foot against a stone.[j]
[13]You will tread upon the lion and the cobra;
you will trample the great lion and the serpent.[k]

[14]"Because he loves me," says the LORD, "I will rescue him;
I will protect him, for he acknowledges my name.
[15]He will call upon me, and I will answer him;
I will be with him in trouble,
I will deliver him and honor him.[l]
[16]With long life[m] will I satisfy him
and show him my salvation.[n]"

Psalm 92

A psalm. A song. For the Sabbath day.

Psalm 92 Theme ______________________________

[1]It is good to praise the LORD
and make music to your name,[o] O Most High,[p]
[2]to proclaim your love in the morning[q]
and your faithfulness at night,
[3]to the music of the ten-stringed lyre
and the melody of the harp.[r]

91:3 [a]Ps 124:7; Pr 6:5 [b]1Ki 8:37
91:4 [c]Ps 17:8 [d]Ps 35:2
91:5 [e]Job 5:21
91:8 [f]Ps 37:34; 58:10; Mal 1:5
91:10 [g]Pr 12:21
91:11 [h]Heb 1:14 [i]Ps 34:7
91:12 [j]Mt 4:6*; Lk 4:10-11*
91:13 [k]Da 6:22; Lk 10:19
91:15 [l]1Sa 2:30; Ps 50:15; Jn 12:26
91:16 [m]Dt 6:2; Ps 21:4 [n]Ps 50:23
92:1 [o]Ps 147:1 [p]Ps 135:3
92:2 [q]Ps 89:1
92:3 [r]1Sa 10:5; Ne 12:27; Ps 33:2

4 For you make me glad by your deeds, O LORD;
I sing for joy at the works of your hands.[a]
5 How great are your works,[b] O LORD,
how profound your thoughts![c]
6 The senseless man[d] does not know,
fools do not understand,
7 that though the wicked spring up like grass
and all evildoers flourish,
they will be forever destroyed.

8 But you, O LORD, are exalted forever.

9 For surely your enemies, O LORD,
surely your enemies will perish;
all evildoers will be scattered.[e]
10 You have exalted my horn[a][f] like that of a wild ox;
fine oils[g] have been poured upon me.
11 My eyes have seen the defeat of my adversaries;
my ears have heard the rout of my wicked foes.[h]

12 The righteous will flourish like a palm tree,
they will grow like a cedar of Lebanon;[i]
13 planted in the house of the LORD,
they will flourish in the courts of our God.[j]
14 They will still bear fruit[k] in old age,
they will stay fresh and green,
15 proclaiming, "The LORD is upright;
he is my Rock, and there is no wickedness in him.[l]"

Psalm 93

Psalm 93 Theme ______________________________

1 The LORD reigns,[m] he is robed in majesty;[n]
the LORD is robed in majesty
and is armed with strength.[o]
The world is firmly established;
it cannot be moved.[p]
2 Your throne was established long ago;
you are from all eternity.[q]

3 The seas[r] have lifted up, O LORD,
the seas have lifted up their voice;
the seas have lifted up their pounding waves.
4 Mightier than the thunder[s] of the great waters,
mightier than the breakers of the sea—
the LORD on high is mighty.

a *10 Horn* here symbolizes strength.

92:4 [a] Ps 8:6; 143:5
92:5 [b] Rev 15:3 [c] Ps 40:5; 139:17; Isa 28:29; Ro 11:33
92:6 [d] Ps 73:22
92:9 [e] Ps 68:1; 89:10
92:10 [f] Ps 89:17 [g] Ps 23:5
92:11 [h] Ps 54:7; 91:8
92:12 [i] Ps 1:3; 52:8; Jer 17:8; Hos 14:6
92:13 [j] Ps 100:4
92:14 [k] Jn 15:2
92:15 [l] Job 34:10
93:1 [m] Ps 97:1 [n] Ps 104:1 [o] Ps 65:6 [p] Ps 96:10
93:2 [q] Ps 45:6
93:3 [r] Ps 96:11
93:4 [s] Ps 65:7

5Your statutes stand firm;
holiness[a] adorns your house
for endless days, O LORD.

Psalm 94

Psalm 94 Theme

1O LORD, the God who avenges,[b]
O God who avenges, shine forth.[c]
2Rise up, O Judge[d] of the earth;
pay back[e] to the proud what they deserve.
3How long will the wicked, O LORD,
how long will the wicked be jubilant?

4They pour out arrogant[f] words;
all the evildoers are full of boasting.[g]
5They crush your people,[h] O LORD;
they oppress your inheritance.
6They slay the widow and the alien;
they murder the fatherless.
7They say, "The LORD does not see;[i]
the God of Jacob pays no heed."

8Take heed, you senseless ones[j] among the people;
you fools, when will you become wise?
9Does he who implanted the ear not hear?
Does he who formed the eye not see?[k]
10Does he who disciplines nations not punish?
Does he who teaches[l] man lack knowledge?
11The LORD knows the thoughts of man;
he knows that they are futile.[m]

12Blessed is the man you discipline,[n] O LORD,
the man you teach[o] from your law;
13you grant him relief from days of trouble,
till a pit[p] is dug for the wicked.
14For the LORD will not reject his people;[q]
he will never forsake his inheritance.
15Judgment will again be founded on righteousness,[r]
and all the upright in heart will follow it.

16Who will rise up[s] for me against the wicked?
Who will take a stand for me against evildoers?[t]
17Unless the LORD had given me help,[u]
I would soon have dwelt in the silence of death.
18When I said, "My foot is slipping,[v]"
your love, O LORD, supported me.

93:5 [a]Ps 29:2
94:1 [b]Na 1:2; Ro 12:19 [c]Ps 80:1
94:2 [d]Ge 18:25 [e]Ps 31:23
94:4 [f]Ps 31:18 [g]Ps 52:1
94:5 [h]Isa 3:15
94:7 [i]Job 22:14; Ps 10:11
94:8 [j]Ps 92:6
94:9 [k]Ex 4:11; Pr 20:12
94:10 [l]Job 35:11; Isa 28:26
94:11 [m]1Co 3:20*
94:12 [n]Job 5:17; Heb 12:5 [o]Dt 8:3
94:13 [p]Ps 55:23
94:14 [q]1Sa 12:22; Ps 37:28; Ro 11:2
94:15 [r]Ps 97:2
94:16 [s]Nu 10:35; Ps 17:13 [t]Ps 59:2
94:17 [u]Ps 124:2
94:18 [v]Ps 38:16

94:20 [a]Ps 58:2
94:21 [b]Ps 56:6 [c]Ps 106:38; Pr 17:15,26
94:22 [d]Ps 18:2; 59:9
94:23 [e]Ps 7:16
95:1 [f]Ps 81:1 [g]2Sa 22:47
95:2 [h]Mic 6:6 [i]Ps 81:2; Eph 5:19
95:3 [j]Ps 48:1; 145:3 [k]Ps 96:4; 97:9
95:5 [l]Ge 1:9; Ps 146:6
95:6 [m]Php 2:10 [n]2Ch 6:13 [o]Ps 100:3; 149:2; Isa 17:7; Da 6:10-11; Hos 8:14
95:7 [p]Ps 74:1; 79:13
95:8 [q]Ex 17:7
95:9 [r]Nu 14:22; Ps 78:18; 1Co 10:9
95:10 [s]Ac 7:36; Heb 3:17
95:11 [t]Nu 14:23 [u]Dt 1:35; Heb 4:3*

19 When anxiety was great within me,
your consolation brought joy to my soul.

20 Can a corrupt throne be allied with you—
one that brings on misery by its decrees?[a]
21 They band together[b] against the righteous
and condemn the innocent[c] to death.
22 But the LORD has become my fortress,
and my God the rock in whom I take refuge.[d]
23 He will repay[e] them for their sins
and destroy them for their wickedness;
the LORD our God will destroy them.

Psalm 95

Psalm 95 Theme ____________________

1 Come, let us sing for joy to the LORD;
let us shout aloud[f] to the Rock[g] of our salvation.
2 Let us come before him[h] with thanksgiving
and extol him with music[i] and song.

3 For the LORD is the great God,[j]
the great King above all gods.[k]
4 In his hand are the depths of the earth,
and the mountain peaks belong to him.
5 The sea is his, for he made it,
and his hands formed the dry land.[l]

6 Come, let us bow down[m] in worship,
let us kneel[n] before the LORD our Maker;[o]
7 for he is our God
and we are the people of his pasture,[p]
the flock under his care.

Today, if you hear his voice,
8 do not harden your hearts as you did at Meribah,[a][q]
as you did that day at Massah[b] in the desert,
9 where your fathers tested[r] and tried me,
though they had seen what I did.
10 For forty years[s] I was angry with that generation;
I said, "They are a people whose hearts go astray,
and they have not known my ways."
11 So I declared on oath[t] in my anger,
"They shall never enter my rest."[u]

[a] 8 *Meribah* means *quarreling.* [b] 8 *Massah* means *testing.*

Psalm 96

*Psalm 96 Theme*______________________________

1Sing to the LORD[a] a new song;
sing to the LORD, all the earth.
2Sing to the LORD, praise his name;
proclaim his salvation[b] day after day.
3Declare his glory among the nations,
his marvelous deeds among all peoples.

4For great is the LORD and most worthy of praise;[c]
he is to be feared[d] above all gods.[e]
5For all the gods of the nations are idols,
but the LORD made the heavens.[f]
6Splendor and majesty are before him;
strength and glory[g] are in his sanctuary.

7Ascribe to the LORD,[h] O families of nations,[i]
ascribe to the LORD glory and strength.
8Ascribe to the LORD the glory due his name;
bring an offering[j] and come into his courts.
9Worship the LORD in the splendor of his[a] holiness;[k]
tremble[l] before him, all the earth.[m]

10Say among the nations, "The LORD reigns.[n]"
The world is firmly established, it cannot be moved;[o]
he will judge the peoples with equity.[p]
11Let the heavens rejoice, let the earth be glad;[q]
let the sea resound, and all that is in it;
12 let the fields be jubilant, and everything in them.
Then all the trees of the forest[r] will sing for joy;[s]
13 they will sing before the LORD, for he comes,
he comes to judge[t] the earth.
He will judge the world in righteousness
and the peoples in his truth.

Psalm 97

*Psalm 97 Theme*______________________________

1The LORD reigns,[u] let the earth be glad;[v]
let the distant shores rejoice.

2Clouds and thick darkness[w] surround him;
righteousness and justice are the foundation of
his throne.[x]

[a]9 Or *LORD with the splendor of*

96:1 [a]1Ch 16:23
96:2 [b]Ps 71:15
96:4 [c]Ps 18:3; 145:3 [d]Ps 89:7 [e]Ps 95:3
96:5 [f]Ps 115:15
96:6 [g]Ps 29:1
96:7 [h]Ps 29:1 [i]Ps 22:27
96:8 [j]Ps 45:12; 72:10
96:9 [k]Ps 29:2 [l]Ps 114:7 [m]Ps 33:8
96:10 [n]Ps 97:1 [o]Ps 93:1 [p]Ps 67:4
96:11 [q]Ps 97:1; 98:7; Isa 49:13
96:12 [r]Isa 44:23 [s]Ps 65:13
96:13 [t]Rev 19:11
97:1 [u]Ps 96:10 [v]Ps 96:11
97:2 [w]Ex 19:9; Ps 18:11 [x]Ps 89:14

3Fire[a] goes before[b] him
and consumes[c] his foes on every side.
4His lightning lights up the world;
the earth sees and trembles.[d]
5The mountains melt[e] like wax before the LORD,
before the Lord of all the earth.[f]
6The heavens proclaim his righteousness,[g]
and all the peoples see his glory.[h]

7All who worship images[i] are put to shame,[j]
those who boast in idols—
worship him,[k] all you gods!

8Zion hears and rejoices
and the villages of Judah are glad
because of your judgments,[l] O LORD.
9For you, O LORD, are the Most High over all the earth;[m]
you are exalted[n] far above all gods.

10Let those who love the LORD hate evil,[o]
for he guards the lives of his faithful ones[p]
and delivers[q] them from the hand of the wicked.[r]
11Light is shed[s] upon the righteous
and joy on the upright in heart.
12Rejoice in the LORD, you who are righteous,
and praise his holy name.[t]

Psalm 98

A psalm.

*Psalm 98 Theme*______________________________

1Sing to the LORD a new song,[u]
for he has done marvelous things;[v]
his right hand[w] and his holy arm[x]
have worked salvation for him.
2The LORD has made his salvation known[y]
and revealed his righteousness to the nations.
3He has remembered[z] his love
and his faithfulness to the house of Israel;
all the ends of the earth have seen
the salvation of our God.

4Shout for joy[a] to the LORD, all the earth,
burst into jubilant song with music;

97:3 [a]Da 7:10 [b]Hab 3:5 [c]Ps 18:8
97:4 [d]Ps 104:32
97:5 [e]Ps 46:2,6; Mic 1:4 [f]Jos 3:11
97:6 [g]Ps 50:6 [h]Ps 19:1
97:7 [i]Lev 26:1 [j]Jer 10:14 [k]Heb 1:6
97:8 [l]Ps 48:11
97:9 [m]Ps 83:18; 95:3 [n]Ex 18:11
97:10 [o]Ps 34:14; Am 5:15; Ro 12:9 [p]Pr 2:8 [q]Da 3:28 [r]Ps 37:40; Jer 15:21
97:11 [s]Job 22:28
97:12 [t]Ps 30:4
98:1 [u]Ps 96:1 [v]Ps 96:3 [w]Ex 15:6 [x]Isa 52:10
98:2 [y]Isa 52:10
98:3 [z]Lk 1:54
98:4 [a]Isa 44:23

[5]make music to the LORD with the harp,[a]
with the harp and the sound of singing,[b]
[6]with trumpets[c] and the blast of the ram's horn—
shout for joy before the LORD, the King.[d]

[7]Let the sea resound, and everything in it,
the world, and all who live in it.[e]
[8]Let the rivers clap their hands,
let the mountains[f] sing together for joy;
[9]let them sing before the LORD,
for he comes to judge the earth.
He will judge the world in righteousness
and the peoples with equity.[g]

Psalm 99

Psalm 99 Theme

[1]The LORD reigns,[h]
let the nations tremble;
he sits enthroned between the cherubim,[i]
let the earth shake.
[2]Great is the LORD[j] in Zion;
he is exalted[k] over all the nations.
[3]Let them praise your great and awesome name[l]—
he is holy.

[4]The King is mighty, he loves justice[m]—
you have established equity;[n]
in Jacob you have done
what is just and right.
[5]Exalt[o] the LORD our God
and worship at his footstool;
he is holy.

[6]Moses[p] and Aaron were among his priests,
Samuel[q] was among those who called on his name;
they called on the LORD
and he answered[r] them.
[7]He spoke to them from the pillar of cloud;[s]
they kept his statutes and the decrees he gave them.

[8]O LORD our God,
you answered them;
you were to Israel[a] a forgiving God,[t]
though you punished their misdeeds.[b]

[a]8 Hebrew *them* [b]8 Or / *an avenger of the wrongs done to them*

98:5
[a]Ps 92:3
[b]Isa 51:3

98:6
[c]Nu 10:10
[d]Ps 47:7

98:7
[e]Ps 24:1

98:8
[f]Isa 55:12

98:9
[g]Ps 96:10

99:1
[h]Ps 97:1
[i]Ex 25:22

99:2
[j]Ps 48:1
[k]Ps 97:9; 113:4

99:3
[l]Ps 76:1

99:4
[m]Ps 11:7
[n]Ps 98:9

99:5
[o]Ps 132:7

99:6
[p]Ex 24:6
[q]Jer 15:1
[r]1Sa 7:9

99:7
[s]Ex 33:9

99:8
[t]Nu 14:20

100:1 [a]Ps 98:4

9 Exalt the LORD our God
and worship at his holy mountain,
for the LORD our God is holy.

Psalm 100

100:2 [b]Ps 95:2

A psalm. For giving thanks.

Psalm 100 Theme ______________________________

100:3 [c]Ps 46:10 [d]Job 10:3 [e]Ps 74:1; Eze 34:31

1 Shout for joy[a] to the LORD, all the earth.
2 Worship the LORD with gladness;
come before him[b] with joyful songs.
3 Know that the LORD is God.[c]
It is he who made us,[d] and we are his[a];
we are his people, the sheep of his pasture.[e]

100:4 [f]Ps 116:17

4 Enter his gates with thanksgiving
and his courts with praise;
give thanks to him and praise his name.[f]
5 For the LORD is good[g] and his love endures forever;[h]
his faithfulness[i] continues through all generations.

100:5 [g]1Ch 16:34; Ps 25:8 [h]Ezr 3:11; Ps 106:1 [i]Ps 119:90

Psalm 101

Of David. A psalm.

Psalm 101 Theme ______________________________

101:1 [j]Ps 51:14; 89:1; 145:7

1 I will sing of your love[j] and justice;
to you, O LORD, I will sing praise.
2 I will be careful to lead a blameless life—
when will you come to me?

I will walk in my house
with blameless heart.

101:3 [k]Dt 15:9 [l]Ps 40:4

3 I will set before my eyes
no vile thing.[k]

The deeds of faithless men I hate;[l]
they will not cling to me.

101:4 [m]Pr 11:20

4 Men of perverse heart[m] shall be far from me;
I will have nothing to do with evil.

5 Whoever slanders his neighbor[n] in secret,
him will I put to silence;

101:5 [n]Ps 50:20

[a]3 Or *and not we ourselves*

whoever has haughty eyes[a] and a proud heart,
him will I not endure.

[6]My eyes will be on the faithful in the land,
that they may dwell with me;
he whose walk is blameless[b]
will minister to me.

[7]No one who practices deceit
will dwell in my house;
no one who speaks falsely
will stand in my presence.

[8]Every morning[c] I will put to silence
all the wicked[d] in the land;
I will cut off every evildoer[e]
from the city of the LORD.[f]

Psalm 102

A prayer of an afflicted man. When he is faint and pours out his lament before the LORD.

Psalm 102 Theme ______________________

[1]Hear my prayer, O LORD;
let my cry for help[g] come to you.
[2]Do not hide your face[h] from me
when I am in distress.
Turn your ear to me;
when I call, answer me quickly.
[3]For my days vanish like smoke;[i]
my bones burn like glowing embers.
[4]My heart is blighted and withered like grass;[j]
I forget to eat my food.
[5]Because of my loud groaning
I am reduced to skin and bones.
[6]I am like a desert owl,[k]
like an owl among the ruins.
[7]I lie awake;[l] I have become
like a bird alone[m] on a roof.
[8]All day long my enemies taunt me;
those who rail against me use my name as a curse.
[9]For I eat ashes as my food
and mingle my drink with tears[n]

101:5 [a]Ps 10:5; Pr 6:17
101:6 [b]Ps 119:1
101:8 [c]Jer 21:12 [d]Ps 75:10 [e]Ps 118:10-12 [f]Ps 46:4
102:1 [g]Ex 2:23
102:2 [h]Ps 69:17
102:3 [i]Jas 4:14
102:4 [j]Ps 37:2
102:6 [k]Job 30:29; Isa 34:11
102:7 [l]Ps 77:4 [m]Ps 38:11
102:9 [n]Ps 42:3

[10]because of your great wrath,[a]
for you have taken me up and thrown me aside.
[11]My days are like the evening shadow;[b]
I wither away like grass.

[12]But you, O LORD, sit enthroned forever;[c]
your renown endures[d] through all generations.
[13]You will arise and have compassion[e] on Zion,
for it is time to show favor to her;
the appointed time has come.
[14]For her stones are dear to your servants;
her very dust moves them to pity.
[15]The nations will fear[f] the name of the LORD,
all the kings[g] of the earth will revere your glory.
[16]For the LORD will rebuild Zion
and appear in his glory.[h]
[17]He will respond to the prayer[i] of the destitute;
he will not despise their plea.

[18]Let this be written[j] for a future generation,
that a people not yet created[k] may praise the LORD:
[19]"The LORD looked down[l] from his sanctuary on high,
from heaven he viewed the earth,
[20]to hear the groans of the prisoners[m]
and release those condemned to death."
[21]So the name of the LORD will be declared[n] in Zion
and his praise in Jerusalem
[22]when the peoples and the kingdoms
assemble to worship the LORD.

[23]In the course of my life[a] he broke my strength;
he cut short my days.
[24]So I said:
"Do not take me away, O my God, in the midst of
my days;
your years go on[o] through all generations.
[25]In the beginning[p] you laid the foundations of the earth,
and the heavens are the work of your hands.
[26]They will perish,[q] but you remain;
they will all wear out like a garment.
Like clothing you will change them
and they will be discarded.
[27]But you remain the same,[r]
and your years will never end.
[28]The children of your servants[s] will live in your presence;
their descendants[t] will be established before you."

102:10 [a]Ps 38:3
102:11 [b]Job 14:2
102:12 [c]Ps 9:7 [d]Ps 135:13
102:13 [e]Isa 60:10
102:15 [f]1Ki 8:43 [g]Ps 138:4
102:16 [h]Isa 60:1-2
102:17 [i]Ne 1:6
102:18 [j]Ro 15:4 [k]Ps 22:31
102:19 [l]Dt 26:15
102:20 [m]Ps 79:11
102:21 [n]Ps 22:22
102:24 [o]Ps 90:2; Isa 38:10
102:25 [p]Ge 1:1; Heb 1:10-12*
102:26 [q]Isa 34:4; Mt 24:35; 2Pe 3:7-10; Rev 20:11
102:27 [r]Mal 3:6; Heb 13:8; Jas 1:17
102:28 [s]Ps 69:36 [t]Ps 89:4

[a]23 Or *By his power*

Psalm 103

Of David.

Psalm 103 Theme ____________________

1Praise the LORD, O my soul;[a]
all my inmost being, praise his holy name.
2Praise the LORD, O my soul,
and forget not all his benefits—
3who forgives all your sins[b]
and heals[c] all your diseases,
4who redeems your life from the pit
and crowns you with love and compassion,
5who satisfies your desires with good things
so that your youth is renewed like the eagle's.[d]

6The LORD works righteousness
and justice for all the oppressed.

7He made known[e] his ways[f] to Moses,
his deeds[g] to the people of Israel:
8The LORD is compassionate and gracious,[h]
slow to anger, abounding in love.
9He will not always accuse,
nor will he harbor his anger forever;[i]
10he does not treat us as our sins deserve[j]
or repay us according to our iniquities.
11For as high as the heavens are above the earth,
so great is his love[k] for those who fear him;
12as far as the east is from the west,
so far has he removed our transgressions[l] from us.
13As a father has compassion[m] on his children,
so the LORD has compassion on those who fear him;
14for he knows how we are formed,[n]
he remembers that we are dust.
15As for man, his days are like grass,[o]
he flourishes like a flower[p] of the field;
16the wind blows[q] over it and it is gone,
and its place[r] remembers it no more.
17But from everlasting to everlasting
the LORD's love is with those who fear him,
and his righteousness with their children's children—
18with those who keep his covenant
and remember to obey his precepts.[s]

19The LORD has established his throne in heaven,
and his kingdom rules[t] over all.

103:1 [a]Ps 104:1
103:3 [b]Ps 130:8 [c]Ex 15:26
103:5 [d]Isa 40:31
103:7 [e]Ps 99:7; 147:19 [f]Ex 33:13 [g]Ps 106:22
103:8 [h]Ex 34:6; Ps 86:15; Jas 5:11
103:9 [i]Ps 30:5; Isa 57:16; Jer 3:5,12; Mic 7:18
103:10 [j]Ezr 9:13
103:11 [k]Ps 57:10
103:12 [l]2Sa 12:13
103:13 [m]Mal 3:17
103:14 [n]Isa 29:16
103:15 [o]Ps 90:5 [p]Job 14:2; Jas 1:10; 1Pe 1:24
103:16 [q]Isa 40:7 [r]Job 7:10
103:18 [s]Dt 7:9
103:19 [t]Ps 47:2

20 Praise the LORD, you his angels,[a]
you mighty ones[b] who do his bidding,
who obey his word.
21 Praise the LORD, all his heavenly hosts,[c]
you his servants who do his will.
22 Praise the LORD, all his works[d]
everywhere in his dominion.

Praise the LORD, O my soul.

Psalm 104

Psalm 104 Theme ______________________________

1 Praise the LORD, O my soul.[e]

O LORD my God, you are very great;
you are clothed with splendor and majesty.
2 He wraps[f] himself in light as with a garment;
he stretches out the heavens[g] like a tent
3 and lays the beams[h] of his upper chambers on
their waters.
He makes the clouds[i] his chariot
and rides on the wings of the wind.[j]
4 He makes winds his messengers,[a][k]
flames of fire[l] his servants.

5 He set the earth[m] on its foundations;
it can never be moved.
6 You covered it[n] with the deep[o] as with a garment;
the waters stood above the mountains.
7 But at your rebuke[p] the waters fled,
at the sound of your thunder they took to flight;
8 they flowed over the mountains,
they went down into the valleys,
to the place you assigned[q] for them.
9 You set a boundary they cannot cross;
never again will they cover the earth.

10 He makes springs[r] pour water into the ravines;
it flows between the mountains.
11 They give water to all the beasts of the field;
the wild donkeys quench their thirst.
12 The birds of the air[s] nest by the waters;
they sing among the branches.
13 He waters the mountains[t] from his upper chambers;
the earth is satisfied by the fruit of his work.

103:20 [a]Ps 148:2; Heb 1:14 [b]Ps 29:1
103:21 [c]1Ki 22:19
103:22 [d]Ps 145:10
104:1 [e]Ps 103:22
104:2 [f]Da 7:9 [g]Isa 40:22
104:3 [h]Am 9:6 [i]Isa 19:1 [j]Ps 18:10
104:4 [k]Ps 148:8; Heb 1:7* [l]2Ki 2:11
104:5 [m]Job 26:7; Ps 24:1-2
104:6 [n]Ge 7:19 [o]Ge 1:2
104:7 [p]Ps 18:15
104:8 [q]Ps 33:7
104:10 [r]Ps 107:33; Isa 41:18
104:12 [s]Mt 8:20
104:13 [t]Ps 147:8; Jer 10:13

[a] 4 Or *angels*

[14]He makes grass grow[a] for the cattle,
and plants for man to cultivate—
bringing forth food[b] from the earth:
[15]wine[c] that gladdens the heart of man,
oil[d] to make his face shine,
and bread that sustains his heart.
[16]The trees of the LORD are well watered,
the cedars of Lebanon that he planted.
[17]There the birds[e] make their nests;
the stork has its home in the pine trees.
[18]The high mountains belong to the wild goats;
the crags are a refuge for the coneys.[a][f]

[19]The moon marks off the seasons,[g]
and the sun[h] knows when to go down.
[20]You bring darkness,[i] it becomes night,[j]
and all the beasts of the forest[k] prowl.
[21]The lions roar for their prey
and seek their food from God.[l]
[22]The sun rises, and they steal away;
they return and lie down in their dens.[m]
[23]Then man goes out to his work,[n]
to his labor until evening.

[24]How many are your works,[o] O LORD!
In wisdom you made[p] them all;
the earth is full of your creatures.
[25]There is the sea,[q] vast and spacious,
teeming with creatures beyond number—
living things both large and small.
[26]There the ships[r] go to and fro,
and the leviathan,[s] which you formed to frolic there.

[27]These all look to you
to give them their food[t] at the proper time.
[28]When you give it to them,
they gather it up;
when you open your hand,
they are satisfied[u] with good things.
[29]When you hide your face,[v]
they are terrified;
when you take away their breath,
they die and return to the dust.[w]
[30]When you send your Spirit,
they are created,
and you renew the face of the earth.

[a]*18* That is, the hyrax or rock badger

104:14 [a]Job 38:27; Ps 147:8 [b]Ge 1:30; Job 28:5
104:15 [c]Jdg 9:13 [d]Ps 23:5; 92:10; Lk 7:46
104:17 [e]ver 12
104:18 [f]Pr 30:26
104:19 [g]Ge 1:14 [h]Ps 19:6
104:20 [i]Isa 45:7 [j]Ps 74:16 [k]Ps 50:10
104:21 [l]Job 38:39; Ps 145:15; Joel 1:20
104:22 [m]Job 37:8
104:23 [n]Ge 3:19
104:24 [o]Ps 40:5 [p]Pr 3:19
104:25 [q]Ps 69:34
104:26 [r]Ps 107:23; Eze 27:9 [s]Job 41:1
104:27 [t]Job 36:31; Ps 136:25; 145:15; 147:9
104:28 [u]Ps 145:16
104:29 [v]Dt 31:17 [w]Job 34:14; Ecc 12:7

31 May the glory of the LORD endure forever;
may the LORD rejoice in his works[a]—
32 he who looks at the earth, and it trembles,[b]
who touches the mountains,[c] and they smoke.[d]

33 I will sing[e] to the LORD all my life;
I will sing praise to my God as long as I live.
34 May my meditation be pleasing to him,
as I rejoice[f] in the LORD.
35 But may sinners vanish[g] from the earth
and the wicked be no more.

Praise the LORD, O my soul.

Praise the LORD.[a][h]

Psalm 105

Psalm 105 Theme ____________________

1 Give thanks to the LORD,[i] call on his name;[j]
make known among the nations what he has done.
2 Sing to him,[k] sing praise to him;
tell of all his wonderful acts.
3 Glory in his holy name;
let the hearts of those who seek the LORD rejoice.
4 Look to the LORD and his strength;
seek his face[l] always.

5 Remember the wonders[m] he has done,
his miracles, and the judgments he pronounced,[n]
6 O descendants of Abraham his servant,[o]
O sons of Jacob, his chosen[p] ones.
7 He is the LORD our God;
his judgments are in all the earth.

8 He remembers his covenant[q] forever,
the word he commanded, for a thousand generations,
9 the covenant he made with Abraham,[r]
the oath he swore to Isaac.
10 He confirmed it[s] to Jacob as a decree,
to Israel as an everlasting covenant:
11 "To you I will give the land of Canaan[t]
as the portion you will inherit."

12 When they were but few in number,[u]
few indeed, and strangers in it,[v]

104:31 [a] Ge 1:31
104:32 [b] Ps 97:4 [c] Ex 19:18 [d] Ps 144:5
104:33 [e] Ps 63:4
104:34 [f] Ps 9:2
104:35 [g] Ps 37:38 [h] Ps 105:45; 106:48
105:1 [i] 1Ch 16:34 [j] Ps 99:6
105:2 [k] Ps 96:1
105:4 [l] Ps 27:8
105:5 [m] Ps 40:5 [n] Ps 77:11
105:6 [o] ver 42 [p] Ps 106:5
105:8 [q] Ps 106:45; Lk 1:72
105:9 [r] Ge 12:7; 17:2; 22:16-18; Gal 3:15-18
105:10 [s] Ge 28:13-15
105:11 [t] Ge 13:15; 15:18
105:12 [u] Ge 34:30; Dt 7:7 [v] Ge 23:4; Heb 11:9

a 35 Hebrew *Hallelu Yah*; in the Septuagint this line stands at the beginning of Psalm 105.

[13]they wandered from nation to nation,
from one kingdom to another.
[14]He allowed no one to oppress[a] them;
for their sake he rebuked kings:[b]
[15]"Do not touch[c] my anointed ones;
do my prophets no harm."

[16]He called down famine[d] on the land
and destroyed all their supplies of food;
[17]and he sent a man before them—
Joseph, sold as a slave.[e]
[18]They bruised his feet with shackles,[f]
his neck was put in irons,
[19]till what he foretold[g] came to pass,
till the word of the LORD proved him true.
[20]The king sent and released him,
the ruler of peoples set him free.[h]
[21]He made him master of his household,
ruler over all he possessed,
[22]to instruct his princes[i] as he pleased
and teach his elders wisdom.

[23]Then Israel entered Egypt;[j]
Jacob lived as an alien in the land of Ham.
[24]The LORD made his people very fruitful;
he made them too numerous[k] for their foes,
[25]whose hearts he turned[l] to hate his people,
to conspire[m] against his servants.
[26]He sent Moses[n] his servant,
and Aaron, whom he had chosen.[o]
[27]They performed[p] his miraculous signs among them,
his wonders in the land of Ham.
[28]He sent darkness[q] and made the land dark—
for had they not rebelled against his words?
[29]He turned their waters into blood,[r]
causing their fish to die.[s]
[30]Their land teemed with frogs,[t]
which went up into the bedrooms of their rulers.
[31]He spoke, and there came swarms of flies,[u]
and gnats[v] throughout their country.
[32]He turned their rain into hail,[w]
with lightning throughout their land;
[33]he struck down their vines[x] and fig trees
and shattered the trees of their country.
[34]He spoke, and the locusts came,[y]
grasshoppers without number;

105:14
[a]Ge 35:5
[b]Ge 12:17-20

105:15
[c]Ge 26:11

105:16
[d]Ge 41:54; Lev 26:26; Isa 3:1; Eze 4:16

105:17
[e]Ge 37:28; 45:5; Ac 7:9

105:18
[f]Ge 40:15

105:19
[g]Ge 40:20-22

105:20
[h]Ge 41:14

105:22
[i]Ge 41:43-44

105:23
[j]Ge 46:6; Ac 13:17

105:24
[k]Ex 1:7,9

105:25
[l]Ex 4:21
[m]Ex 1:6-10; Ac 7:19

105:26
[n]Ex 3:10
[o]Nu 16:5; 17:5-8

105:27
[p]Ex 7:8–12:51

105:28
[q]Ex 10:22

105:29
[r]Ps 78:44
[s]Ex 7:21

105:30
[t]Ex 8:2,6

105:31
[u]Ex 8:21-24
[v]Ex 8:16-18

105:32
[w]Ex 9:22-25

105:33
[x]Ps 78:47

105:34
[y]Ex 10:4,12-15

35they ate up every green thing in their land,
ate up the produce of their soil.
36Then he struck down all the firstborn[a] in their land,
the firstfruits of all their manhood.

37He brought out Israel, laden with silver and gold,[b]
and from among their tribes no one faltered.
38Egypt was glad when they left,
because dread of Israel[c] had fallen on them.
39He spread out a cloud[d] as a covering,
and a fire to give light at night.[e]
40They asked,[f] and he brought them quail[g]
and satisfied them with the bread of heaven.[h]
41He opened the rock,[i] and water gushed out;
like a river it flowed in the desert.

42For he remembered his holy promise[j]
given to his servant Abraham.
43He brought out his people with rejoicing,[k]
his chosen ones with shouts of joy;
44he gave them the lands of the nations,[l]
and they fell heir to what others had toiled for—
45that they might keep his precepts
and observe his laws.[m]

Praise the LORD.[a]

105:36 [a]Ex 12:29
105:37 [b]Ex 12:35
105:38 [c]Ex 12:33; 15:16
105:39 [d]Ex 13:21 [e]Ne 9:12; Ps 78:14
105:40 [f]Ps 78:18,24 [g]Ex 16:13 [h]Jn 6:31
105:41 [i]Ex 17:6; Nu 20:11; Ps 78:15-16; 1Co 10:4
105:42 [j]Ge 15:13-16
105:43 [k]Ex 15:1-18; Ps 106:12
105:44 [l]Jos 13:6-7
105:45 [m]Dt 4:40; 6:21-24

Psalm 106

Psalm 106 Theme ______________________________

1Praise the LORD.[b]

Give thanks to the LORD, for he is good;[n]
his love endures forever.
2Who can proclaim the mighty acts[o] of the LORD
or fully declare his praise?
3Blessed are they who maintain justice,
who constantly do what is right.[p]
4Remember me,[q] O LORD, when you show favor to
your people,
come to my aid when you save them,
5that I may enjoy the prosperity[r] of your chosen ones,
that I may share in the joy[s] of your nation
and join your inheritance in giving praise.

106:1 [n]Ps 100:5; 105:1
106:2 [o]Ps 145:4,12
106:3 [p]Ps 15:2
106:4 [q]Ps 119:132
106:5 [r]Ps 1:3 [s]Ps 118:15

[a]45 Hebrew *Hallelu Yah* [b]1 Hebrew *Hallelu Yah*; also in verse 48

[6]We have sinned,[a] even as our fathers did;
we have done wrong and acted wickedly.
[7]When our fathers were in Egypt,
they gave no thought to your miracles;
they did not remember[b] your many kindnesses,
and they rebelled by the sea,[c] the Red Sea.[a]
[8]Yet he saved them for his name's sake,[d]
to make his mighty power known.
[9]He rebuked[e] the Red Sea, and it dried up;[f]
he led them through[g] the depths as through a desert.
[10]He saved them[h] from the hand of the foe;
from the hand of the enemy he redeemed them.[i]
[11]The waters covered[j] their adversaries;
not one of them survived.
[12]Then they believed his promises
and sang his praise.[k]

[13]But they soon forgot[l] what he had done
and did not wait for his counsel.
[14]In the desert they gave in to their craving;
in the wasteland they put God to the test.[m]
[15]So he gave them[n] what they asked for,
but sent a wasting disease[o] upon them.

[16]In the camp they grew envious[p] of Moses
and of Aaron, who was consecrated to the LORD.
[17]The earth opened[q] up and swallowed Dathan;
it buried the company of Abiram.
[18]Fire blazed[r] among their followers;
a flame consumed the wicked.

[19]At Horeb they made a calf[s]
and worshiped an idol cast from metal.
[20]They exchanged their Glory[t]
for an image of a bull, which eats grass.
[21]They forgot the God[u] who saved them,
who had done great things[v] in Egypt,
[22]miracles in the land of Ham[w]
and awesome deeds by the Red Sea.
[23]So he said he would destroy[x] them—
had not Moses, his chosen one,
stood in the breach[y] before him
to keep his wrath from destroying them.

[24]Then they despised the pleasant land;[z]
they did not believe[a] his promise.

106:6 [a]Da 9:5
106:7 [b]Ps 78:11,42 [c]Ex 14:11-12
106:8 [d]Ex 9:16
106:9 [e]Ps 18:15 [f]Ex 14:21; Na 1:4 [g]Isa 63:11-14
106:10 [h]Ex 14:30 [i]Ps 107:2
106:11 [j]Ex 14:28; 15:5
106:12 [k]Ex 15:1-21
106:13 [l]Ex 15:24
106:14 [m]1Co 10:9
106:15 [n]Nu 11:31 [o]Isa 10:16
106:16 [p]Nu 16:1-3
106:17 [q]Dt 11:6
106:18 [r]Nu 16:35
106:19 [s]Ex 32:4
106:20 [t]Jer 2:11; Ro 1:23
106:21 [u]Ps 78:11 [v]Dt 10:21
106:22 [w]Ps 105:27
106:23 [x]Ex 32:10 [y]Ex 32:11-14
106:24 [z]Dt 8:7; Eze 20:6 [a]Heb 3:18-19

[a]7 Hebrew *Yam Suph*; that is, Sea of Reeds; also in verses 9 and 22

25 They grumbled[a] in their tents
and did not obey the LORD.
26 So he swore[b] to them with uplifted hand
that he would make them fall in the desert,[c]
27 make their descendants fall among the nations
and scatter[d] them throughout the lands.

28 They yoked themselves to the Baal of Peor[e]
and ate sacrifices offered to lifeless gods;
29 they provoked the LORD to anger by their wicked deeds,
and a plague broke out among them.
30 But Phinehas stood up and intervened,
and the plague was checked.[f]
31 This was credited to him[g] as righteousness
for endless generations to come.

32 By the waters of Meribah[h] they angered the LORD,
and trouble came to Moses because of them;
33 for they rebelled against the Spirit of God,
and rash words came from Moses' lips.[a][i]

34 They did not destroy[j] the peoples
as the LORD had commanded[k] them,
35 but they mingled[l] with the nations
and adopted their customs.
36 They worshiped their idols,[m]
which became a snare to them.
37 They sacrificed their sons[n]
and their daughters to demons.
38 They shed innocent blood,
the blood of their sons[o] and daughters,
whom they sacrificed to the idols of Canaan,
and the land was desecrated by their blood.
39 They defiled themselves[p] by what they did;
by their deeds they prostituted[q] themselves.

40 Therefore the LORD was angry[r] with his people
and abhorred his inheritance.[s]
41 He handed them over[t] to the nations,
and their foes ruled over them.
42 Their enemies oppressed them
and subjected them to their power.
43 Many times he delivered them,
but they were bent on rebellion[u]
and they wasted away in their sin.

106:25 [a]Nu 14:2
106:26 [b]Eze 20:15; Heb 3:11 [c]Nu 14:28-35
106:27 [d]Lev 26:33; Ps 44:11
106:28 [e]Nu 25:2-3; Hos 9:10
106:30 [f]Nu 25:8
106:31 [g]Nu 25:11-13
106:32 [h]Nu 20:2-13; Ps 81:7
106:33 [i]Nu 20:8-12
106:34 [j]Jdg 1:21 [k]Dt 7:16
106:35 [l]Jdg 3:5-6
106:36 [m]Jdg 2:12
106:37 [n]2Ki 16:3; 17:17
106:38 [o]Nu 35:33
106:39 [p]Eze 20:18 [q]Lev 17:7; Nu 15:39
106:40 [r]Jdg 2:14; Ps 78:59 [s]Dt 9:29
106:41 [t]Jdg 2:14; Ne 9:27
106:43 [u]Jdg 2:16-19

[a] 33 Or *against his spirit, / and rash words came from his lips*

[44]But he took note of their distress
when he heard their cry;[a]
[45]for their sake he remembered his covenant[b]
and out of his great love[c] he relented.
[46]He caused them to be pitied[d]
by all who held them captive.

[47]Save us, O LORD our God,
and gather us[e] from the nations,
that we may give thanks to your holy name
and glory in your praise.

[48]Praise be to the LORD, the God of Israel,
from everlasting to everlasting.
Let all the people say, "Amen!"[f]

Praise the LORD.

BOOK V

Psalms 107–150

Psalm 107

Psalm 107 Theme ____________________

[1]Give thanks to the LORD,[g] for he is good;
his love endures forever.
[2]Let the redeemed[h] of the LORD say this—
those he redeemed from the hand of the foe,
[3]those he gathered[i] from the lands,
from east and west, from north and south.[a]

[4]Some wandered in desert[j] wastelands,
finding no way to a city where they could settle.
[5]They were hungry and thirsty,
and their lives ebbed away.
[6]Then they cried out[k] to the LORD in their trouble,
and he delivered them from their distress.
[7]He led them by a straight way[l]
to a city where they could settle.
[8]Let them give thanks to the LORD for his unfailing love
and his wonderful deeds for men,
[9]for he satisfies[m] the thirsty
and fills the hungry with good things.[n]

[10]Some sat in darkness[o] and the deepest gloom,
prisoners suffering in iron chains,[p]
[11]for they had rebelled[q] against the words of God
and despised the counsel[r] of the Most High.

106:44 [a]Jdg 3:9; 10:10
106:45 [b]Lev 26:42; Ps 105:8 [c]Jdg 2:18
106:46 [d]Ezr 9:9; Jer 42:12
106:47 [e]Ps 147:2
106:48 [f]Ps 41:13
107:1 [g]Ps 106:1
107:2 [h]Ps 106:10
107:3 [i]Ps 106:47; Isa 43:5-6
107:4 [j]Nu 14:33; 32:13
107:6 [k]Ps 50:15
107:7 [l]Ezr 8:21
107:9 [m]Ps 22:26; Lk 1:53 [n]Ps 34:10
107:10 [o]Lk 1:79 [p]Job 36:8
107:11 [q]Ps 106:7; La 3:42 [r]2Ch 36:16

[a]3 Hebrew *north and the sea*

12So he subjected them to bitter labor;
they stumbled, and there was no one to help.[a]
13Then they cried to the LORD in their trouble,
and he saved them from their distress.
14He brought them out of darkness and the deepest gloom
and broke away their chains.[b]
15Let them give thanks to the LORD for his unfailing love
and his wonderful deeds for men,
16for he breaks down gates of bronze
and cuts through bars of iron.

17Some became fools through their rebellious ways
and suffered affliction[c] because of their iniquities.
18They loathed all food[d]
and drew near the gates of death.[e]
19Then they cried to the LORD in their trouble,
and he saved them from their distress.
20He sent forth his word[f] and healed them;[g]
he rescued[h] them from the grave.[i]
21Let them give thanks to the LORD for his unfailing love
and his wonderful deeds for men.
22Let them sacrifice thank offerings[j]
and tell of his works[k] with songs of joy.

23Others went out on the sea in ships;
they were merchants on the mighty waters.
24They saw the works of the LORD,
his wonderful deeds in the deep.
25For he spoke[l] and stirred up a tempest[m]
that lifted high the waves.[n]
26They mounted up to the heavens and went down to
the depths;
in their peril their courage melted[o] away.
27They reeled and staggered like drunken men;
they were at their wits' end.
28Then they cried out to the LORD in their trouble,
and he brought them out of their distress.
29He stilled the storm[p] to a whisper;
the waves[q] of the sea were hushed.
30They were glad when it grew calm,
and he guided them to their desired haven.
31Let them give thanks to the LORD for his unfailing love
and his wonderful deeds for men.
32Let them exalt him in the assembly[r] of the people
and praise him in the council of the elders.

107:12 [a]Ps 22:11
107:14 [b]Ps 116:16; Lk 13:16; Ac 12:7
107:17 [c]Isa 65:6-7; La 3:39
107:18 [d]Job 33:20 [e]Job 33:22; Ps 9:13; 88:3
107:20 [f]Mt 8:8 [g]Ps 103:3 [h]Job 33:28 [i]Ps 30:3; 49:15
107:22 [j]Lev 7:12; Ps 50:14; 116:17 [k]Ps 9:11; 73:28; 118:17
107:25 [l]Ps 105:31 [m]Jnh 1:4 [n]Ps 93:3
107:26 [o]Ps 22:14
107:29 [p]Mt 8:26 [q]Ps 89:9
107:32 [r]Ps 22:22,25; 35:18

[33]He turned rivers into a desert,[a]
flowing springs into thirsty ground,
[34]and fruitful land into a salt waste,[b]
because of the wickedness of those who lived there.
[35]He turned the desert into pools of water[c]
and the parched ground into flowing springs;
[36]there he brought the hungry to live,
and they founded a city where they could settle.
[37]They sowed fields and planted vineyards[d]
that yielded a fruitful harvest;
[38]he blessed them, and their numbers greatly increased,[e]
and he did not let their herds diminish.

[39]Then their numbers decreased,[f] and they were humbled
by oppression, calamity and sorrow;
[40]he who pours contempt on nobles[g]
made them wander in a trackless waste.[h]
[41]But he lifted the needy[i] out of their affliction
and increased their families like flocks.
[42]The upright see and rejoice,[j]
but all the wicked shut their mouths.[k]

[43]Whoever is wise,[l] let him heed these things
and consider the great love[m] of the LORD.

Psalm 108

A song. A psalm of David.

*Psalm 108 Theme*______________________________

[1]My heart is steadfast, O God;
I will sing and make music with all my soul.
[2]Awake, harp and lyre!
I will awaken the dawn.
[3]I will praise you, O LORD, among the nations;
I will sing of you among the peoples.
[4]For great is your love, higher than the heavens;
your faithfulness reaches to the skies.
[5]Be exalted, O God, above the heavens,
and let your glory be over all the earth.[n]

[6]Save us and help us with your right hand,
that those you love may be delivered.
[7]God has spoken from his sanctuary:
"In triumph I will parcel out Shechem
and measure off the Valley of Succoth.

107:33 [a]1Ki 17:1; Ps 74:15
107:34 [b]Ge 13:10; 14:3; 19:25
107:35 [c]Ps 114:8; Isa 41:18
107:37 [d]Isa 65:21
107:38 [e]Ge 12:2; 17:16,20; Ex 1:7
107:39 [f]2Ki 10:32; Eze 5:12
107:40 [g]Job 12:21 [h]Job 12:24
107:41 [i]1Sa 2:8; Ps 113:7-9
107:42 [j]Job 22:19 [k]Job 5:16; Ps 63:11; Ro 3:19
107:43 [l]Jer 9:12; Hos 14:9 [m]Ps 64:9
108:5 [n]Ps 57:5

108:8 [a]Ge 49:10
108:11 [b]Ps 44:9
109:1 [c]Ps 83:1
109:2 [d]Ps 52:4; 120:2
109:3 [e]Ps 69:4 [f]Ps 35:7; Jn 15:25
109:4 [g]Ps 69:13
109:5 [h]Ps 35:12; 38:20
109:6 [i]Zec 3:1
109:7 [j]Pr 28:9
109:8 [k]Ac 1:20*
109:9 [l]Ex 22:24

8Gilead is mine, Manasseh is mine;
Ephraim is my helmet,
Judah[a] my scepter.
9Moab is my washbasin,
upon Edom I toss my sandal;
over Philistia I shout in triumph."

10Who will bring me to the fortified city?
Who will lead me to Edom?
11Is it not you, O God, you who have rejected us
and no longer go out with our armies?[b]
12Give us aid against the enemy,
for the help of man is worthless.
13With God we will gain the victory,
and he will trample down our enemies.

Psalm 109

For the director of music. Of David. A psalm.

Psalm 109 Theme ______________________

1O God, whom I praise,
do not remain silent,[c]
2for wicked and deceitful men
have opened their mouths against me;
they have spoken against me with lying tongues.[d]
3With words of hatred[e] they surround me;
they attack me without cause.[f]
4In return for my friendship they accuse me,
but I am a man of prayer.[g]
5They repay me evil for good,[h]
and hatred for my friendship.

6Appoint[a] an evil man[b] to oppose him;
let an accuser[c][i] stand at his right hand.
7When he is tried, let him be found guilty,
and may his prayers condemn[j] him.
8May his days be few;
may another take his place[k] of leadership.
9May his children be fatherless
and his wife a widow.[l]
10May his children be wandering beggars;
may they be driven[d] from their ruined homes.

[a]6 Or ⌊They say:⌋ "Appoint (with quotation marks at the end of verse 19) [b]6 Or *the Evil One*
[c]6 Or *let Satan* [d]10 Septuagint; Hebrew *sought*

[11]May a creditor seize all he has;
may strangers plunder the fruits of his labor.[a]
[12]May no one extend kindness to him
or take pity[b] on his fatherless children.
[13]May his descendants be cut off,[c]
their names blotted out[d] from the next generation.
[14]May the iniquity of his fathers[e] be remembered before
the LORD;
may the sin of his mother never be blotted out.
[15]May their sins always remain before the LORD,
that he may cut off the memory[f] of them from
the earth.

[16]For he never thought of doing a kindness,
but hounded to death the poor
and the needy[g] and the brokenhearted.[h]
[17]He loved to pronounce a curse—
may it[a] come on him;[i]
he found no pleasure in blessing—
may it be[b] far from him.
[18]He wore cursing[j] as his garment;
it entered into his body like water,[k]
into his bones like oil.
[19]May it be like a cloak wrapped about him,
like a belt tied forever around him.
[20]May this be the LORD's payment[l] to my accusers,
to those who speak evil[m] of me.

[21]But you, O Sovereign LORD,
deal well with me for your name's sake;[n]
out of the goodness of your love,[o] deliver me.
[22]For I am poor and needy,
and my heart is wounded within me.
[23]I fade away like an evening shadow;[p]
I am shaken off like a locust.
[24]My knees give[q] way from fasting;
my body is thin and gaunt.
[25]I am an object of scorn[r] to my accusers;
when they see me, they shake their heads.[s]

[26]Help me,[t] O LORD my God;
save me in accordance with your love.
[27]Let them know[u] that it is your hand,
that you, O LORD, have done it.
[28]They may curse,[v] but you will bless;

[a]17 Or *curse, / and it has* [b]17 Or *blessing, / and it is*

109:11 [a]Job 5:5
109:12 [b]Isa 9:17
109:13 [c]Job 18:19; Ps 37:28 [d]Pr 10:7
109:14 [e]Ex 20:5; Ne 4:5; Jer 18:23
109:15 [f]Job 18:17; Ps 34:16
109:16 [g]Ps 37:14,32 [h]Ps 34:18
109:17 [i]Pr 14:14; Eze 35:6
109:18 [j]Ps 73:6 [k]Nu 5:22
109:20 [l]Ps 94:23; 2Ti 4:14 [m]Ps 71:10
109:21 [n]Ps 79:9 [o]Ps 69:16
109:23 [p]Ps 102:11
109:24 [q]Heb 12:12
109:25 [r]Ps 22:6 [s]Mt 27:39; Mk 15:29
109:26 [t]Ps 119:86
109:27 [u]Job 37:7
109:28 [v]2Sa 16:12

when they attack they will be put to shame,
but your servant will rejoice.[a]
29 My accusers will be clothed with disgrace
and wrapped in shame[b] as in a cloak.

30 With my mouth I will greatly extol the LORD;
in the great throng[c] I will praise him.
31 For he stands at the right hand[d] of the needy one,
to save his life from those who condemn him.

Psalm 110

Of David. A psalm.

Psalm 110 Theme ____________________

1 The LORD says[e] to my Lord:
"Sit at my right hand
until I make your enemies
a footstool for your feet."[f]
2 The LORD will extend your mighty scepter[g] from Zion;
you will rule in the midst of your enemies.
3 Your troops will be willing
on your day of battle.
Arrayed in holy majesty,[h]
from the womb of the dawn
you will receive the dew of your youth.[a]

4 The LORD has sworn
and will not change his mind:[i]
"You are a priest forever,[j]
in the order of Melchizedek.[k]"

5 The Lord is at your right hand;[l]
he will crush kings[m] on the day of his wrath.[n]
6 He will judge the nations,[o] heaping up the dead[p]
and crushing the rulers[q] of the whole earth.
7 He will drink from a brook beside the way[b];
therefore he will lift up his head.[r]

Psalm 111[c]

Psalm 111 Theme ____________________

1 Praise the LORD.[d]

I will extol the LORD with all my heart
in the council of the upright and in the assembly.

a 3 Or / *your young men will come to you like the dew* b 7 Or / *The One who grants succession will set him in authority* c This psalm is an acrostic poem, the lines of which begin with the successive letters of the Hebrew alphabet. d 1 Hebrew *Hallelu Yah*

109:28 a Isa 65:14
109:29 b Ps 35:26; 132:18
109:30 c Ps 35:18; 111:1
109:31 d Ps 16:8; 73:23; 121:5
110:1 e Mt 22:44*; Mk 12:36*; Lk 20:42*; Ac 2:34* f 1Co 15:25
110:2 g Ps 45:6
110:3 h Jdg 5:2; Ps 96:9
110:4 i Nu 23:19 j Heb 5:6*; 7:21* k Heb 7:15-17*
110:5 l Ps 16:8 m Ps 2:12 n Ps 2:5; Ro 2:5
110:6 o Isa 2:4 p Isa 66:24 q Ps 68:21
110:7 r Ps 27:6

[2]Great are the works[a] of the LORD;
they are pondered by all who delight in them.
[3]Glorious and majestic are his deeds,
and his righteousness endures forever.
[4]He has caused his wonders to be remembered;
the LORD is gracious and compassionate.[b]
[5]He provides food[c] for those who fear him;
he remembers his covenant forever.
[6]He has shown his people the power of his works,
giving them the lands of other nations.
[7]The works of his hands are faithful and just;
all his precepts are trustworthy.[d]
[8]They are steadfast for ever[e] and ever,
done in faithfulness and uprightness.
[9]He provided redemption[f] for his people;
he ordained his covenant forever—
holy and awesome[g] is his name.

[10]The fear of the LORD is the beginning of wisdom;[h]
all who follow his precepts have good understanding.[i]
To him belongs eternal praise.[j]

Psalm 112[a]

Psalm 112 Theme ______________________________

[1]Praise the LORD.[b]

Blessed is the man who fears the LORD,[k]
who finds great delight[l] in his commands.

[2]His children will be mighty in the land;
the generation of the upright will be blessed.
[3]Wealth and riches are in his house,
and his righteousness endures forever.
[4]Even in darkness light dawns[m] for the upright,
for the gracious and compassionate and
righteous[n] man.[c]
[5]Good will come to him who is generous and
lends freely,[o]
who conducts his affairs with justice.
[6]Surely he will never be shaken;
a righteous man will be remembered[p] forever.
[7]He will have no fear of bad news;
his heart is steadfast,[q] trusting in the LORD.

[a]This psalm is an acrostic poem, the lines of which begin with the successive letters of the Hebrew alphabet. [b]*1* Hebrew *Hallelu Yah* [c]*4* Or / *for* ⌊*the* LORD⌋ *is gracious and compassionate and righteous*

111:2 [a]Ps 92:5; 143:5
111:4 [b]Ps 103:8
111:5 [c]Mt 6:26,31-33
111:7 [d]Ps 19:7; Rev 15:3
111:8 [e]Isa 40:8; Mt 5:18
111:9 [f]Lk 1:68 [g]Ps 99:3; Lk 1:49
111:10 [h]Pr 9:10 [i]Ecc 12:13 [j]Ps 145:2
112:1 [k]Ps 128:1 [l]Ps 119:14, 16,47,92
112:4 [m]Job 11:17 [n]Ps 97:11
112:5 [o]Ps 37:21,26
112:6 [p]Pr 10:7
112:7 [q]Ps 57:7; Pr 1:33

8 His heart is secure, he will have no fear;
in the end he will look in triumph on his foes.[a]
9 He has scattered abroad his gifts to the poor,[b]
his righteousness endures forever;
his horn[a] will be lifted[c] high in honor.

10 The wicked man will see[d] and be vexed,
he will gnash his teeth[e] and waste away;[f]
the longings of the wicked will come to nothing.[g]

Psalm 113

*Psalm 113 Theme*____________________________

1 Praise the LORD.[b]

Praise, O servants of the LORD,[h]
praise the name of the LORD.
2 Let the name of the LORD be praised,
both now and forevermore.[i]
3 From the rising of the sun[j] to the place where it sets,
the name of the LORD is to be praised.

4 The LORD is exalted[k] over all the nations,
his glory above the heavens.[l]
5 Who is like the LORD our God,[m]
the One who sits enthroned[n] on high,
6 who stoops down to look[o]
on the heavens and the earth?

7 He raises the poor[p] from the dust
and lifts the needy[q] from the ash heap;
8 he seats them[r] with princes,
with the princes of their people.
9 He settles the barren[s] woman in her home
as a happy mother of children.

Praise the LORD.

Psalm 114

*Psalm 114 Theme*____________________________

1 When Israel came out of Egypt,[t]
the house of Jacob from a people of foreign tongue,
2 Judah became God's sanctuary,
Israel his dominion.

112:8 [a] Ps 59:10
112:9 [b] 2Co 9:9* [c] Ps 75:10
112:10 [d] Ps 86:17 [e] Ps 37:12 [f] Ps 58:7-8 [g] Pr 11:7
113:1 [h] Ps 135:1
113:2 [i] Da 2:20
113:3 [j] Isa 59:19; Mal 1:11
113:4 [k] Ps 99:2 [l] Ps 8:1; 97:9
113:5 [m] Ps 89:6 [n] Ps 103:19
113:6 [o] Ps 11:4; 138:6; Isa 57:15
113:7 [p] 1Sa 2:8 [q] Ps 107:41
113:8 [r] Job 36:7
113:9 [s] 1Sa 2:5; Ps 68:6; Isa 54:1
114:1 [t] Ex 13:3

a 9 *Horn* here symbolizes dignity. b 1 Hebrew *Hallelu Yah*; also in verse 9

[3]The sea looked and fled,[a]
the Jordan turned back;[b]
[4]the mountains skipped like rams,
the hills like lambs.

[5]Why was it, O sea, that you fled,
O Jordan, that you turned back,
[6]you mountains, that you skipped like rams,
you hills, like lambs?

[7]Tremble, O earth,[c] at the presence of the Lord,
at the presence of the God of Jacob,
[8]who turned the rock into a pool,
the hard rock into springs of water.[d]

Psalm 115

Psalm 115 Theme ____________________

[1]Not to us, O LORD, not to us
but to your name be the glory,[e]
because of your love and faithfulness.

[2]Why do the nations say,
"Where is their God?"[f]
[3]Our God is in heaven;[g]
he does whatever pleases him.[h]
[4]But their idols are silver and gold,
made by the hands of men.[i]
[5]They have mouths, but cannot speak,[j]
eyes, but they cannot see;
[6]they have ears, but cannot hear,
noses, but they cannot smell;
[7]they have hands, but cannot feel,
feet, but they cannot walk;
nor can they utter a sound with their throats.
[8]Those who make them will be like them,
and so will all who trust in them.

[9]O house of Israel, trust in the LORD—
he is their help and shield.
[10]O house of Aaron,[k] trust in the LORD—
he is their help and shield.
[11]You who fear him, trust in the LORD—
he is their help and shield.

[12]The LORD remembers us and will bless us:
He will bless the house of Israel,
he will bless the house of Aaron,

114:3 [a]Ex 14:21; Ps 77:16 [b]Jos 3:16
114:7 [c]Ps 96:9
114:8 [d]Ex 17:6; Nu 20:11; Ps 107:35
115:1 [e]Ps 96:8; Isa 48:11; Eze 36:32
115:2 [f]Ps 42:3; 79:10
115:3 [g]Ps 103:19 [h]Ps 135:6; Da 4:35
115:4 [i]Dt 4:28; Jer 10:3-5
115:5 [j]Jer 10:5
115:10 [k]Ps 118:3

13 he will bless those who fear[a] the LORD—
small and great alike.

14 May the LORD make you increase,[b]
both you and your children.
15 May you be blessed by the LORD,
the Maker of heaven[c] and earth.

16 The highest heavens belong to the LORD,[d]
but the earth he has given[e] to man.
17 It is not the dead[f] who praise the LORD,
those who go down to silence;
18 it is we who extol the LORD,
both now and forevermore.[g]

Praise the LORD.[a]

Psalm 116

Psalm 116 Theme ______________________________

1 I love the LORD,[h] for he heard my voice;
he heard my cry[i] for mercy.
2 Because he turned his ear[j] to me,
I will call on him as long as I live.

3 The cords of death[k] entangled me,
the anguish of the grave[b] came upon me;
I was overcome by trouble and sorrow.
4 Then I called on the name[l] of the LORD:
"O LORD, save me![m]"

5 The LORD is gracious and righteous;[n]
our God is full of compassion.
6 The LORD protects the simplehearted;
when I was in great need,[o] he saved me.

7 Be at rest[p] once more, O my soul,
for the LORD has been good[q] to you.
8 For you, O LORD, have delivered my soul[r] from death,
my eyes from tears,
my feet from stumbling,
9 that I may walk before the LORD
in the land of the living.[s]
10 I believed;[t] therefore[c] I said,
"I am greatly afflicted."

115:13 [a]Ps 128:1,4
115:14 [b]Dt 1:11
115:15 [c]Ge 1:1; 14:19; Ps 96:5
115:16 [d]Ps 89:11 [e]Ps 8:6-8
115:17 [f]Ps 6:5; 88:10-12; Isa 38:18
115:18 [g]Ps 113:2; Da 2:20
116:1 [h]Ps 18:1 [i]Ps 66:19
116:2 [j]Ps 40:1
116:3 [k]Ps 18:4-5
116:4 [l]Ps 118:5 [m]Ps 22:20
116:5 [n]Ezr 9:15; Ne 9:8; Ps 103:8; 145:17
116:6 [o]Ps 19:7; 79:8
116:7 [p]Jer 6:16; Mt 11:29 [q]Ps 13:6
116:8 [r]Ps 56:13
116:9 [s]Ps 27:13
116:10 [t]2Co 4:13*

[a] *18* Hebrew *Hallelu Yah* [b] *3* Hebrew *Sheol* [c] *10* Or *believed even when*

[11]And in my dismay I said,
"All men are liars."[a]

[12]How can I repay the LORD
for all his goodness to me?
[13]I will lift up the cup of salvation
and call on the name[b] of the LORD.
[14]I will fulfill my vows[c] to the LORD
in the presence of all his people.

[15]Precious in the sight[d] of the LORD
is the death of his saints.
[16]O LORD, truly I am your servant;[e]
I am your servant, the son of your maidservant[a];[f]
you have freed me from my chains.

[17]I will sacrifice a thank offering[g] to you
and call on the name of the LORD.
[18]I will fulfill my vows to the LORD
in the presence of all his people,
[19]in the courts[h] of the house of the LORD—
in your midst, O Jerusalem.

Praise the LORD.[b]

Psalm 117

Psalm 117 Theme ______________________

[1]Praise the LORD, all you nations;[i]
extol him, all you peoples.
[2]For great is his love toward us,
and the faithfulness of the LORD[j] endures forever.

Praise the LORD.[b]

Psalm 118

Psalm 118 Theme ______________________

[1]Give thanks to the LORD,[k] for he is good;
his love endures forever.[l]

[2]Let Israel say:[m]
"His love endures forever."
[3]Let the house of Aaron say:
"His love endures forever."
[4]Let those who fear the LORD say:
"His love endures forever."

[a] 16 Or *servant, your faithful son* [b] 19,2 Hebrew *Hallelu Yah*

116:11 [a]Ro 3:4
116:13 [b]Ps 16:5; 80:18
116:14 [c]Ps 22:25; Jnh 2:9
116:15 [d]Ps 72:14
116:16 [e]Ps 119:125; 143:12 [f]Ps 86:16
116:17 [g]Lev 7:12; Ps 50:14
116:19 [h]Ps 96:8; 135:2
117:1 [i]Ro 15:11*
117:2 [j]Ps 100:5
118:1 [k]1Ch 16:8 [l]Ps 106:1; 136:1
118:2 [m]Ps 115:9

5 In my anguish[a] I cried to the LORD,
and he answered[b] by setting me free.
6 The LORD is with me;[c] I will not be afraid.
What can man do to me?[d]
7 The LORD is with me; he is my helper.[e]
I will look in triumph on my enemies.[f]

8 It is better to take refuge in the LORD[g]
than to trust in man.[h]
9 It is better to take refuge in the LORD
than to trust in princes.[i]

10 All the nations surrounded me,
but in the name of the LORD I cut them off.[j]
11 They surrounded me[k] on every side,[l]
but in the name of the LORD I cut them off.
12 They swarmed around me like bees,[m]
but they died out as quickly as burning thorns;[n]
in the name of the LORD I cut them off.

13 I was pushed back and about to fall,
but the LORD helped me.[o]
14 The LORD is my strength[p] and my song;
he has become my salvation.[q]

15 Shouts of joy[r] and victory
resound in the tents of the righteous:
"The LORD's right hand[s] has done mighty things!
16 The LORD's right hand is lifted high;
the LORD's right hand has done mighty things!"

17 I will not die[t] but live,
and will proclaim[u] what the LORD has done.
18 The LORD has chastened me severely,
but he has not given me over to death.[v]

19 Open for me the gates[w] of righteousness;
I will enter and give thanks to the LORD.
20 This is the gate of the LORD
through which the righteous may enter.[x]
21 I will give you thanks, for you answered me;[y]
you have become my salvation.

22 The stone the builders rejected
has become the capstone;[z]
23 the LORD has done this,
and it is marvelous in our eyes.
24 This is the day the LORD has made;
let us rejoice and be glad in it.

118:5 [a] Ps 120:1 [b] Ps 18:19
118:6 [c] Heb 13:6* [d] Ps 27:1; 56:4
118:7 [e] Ps 54:4 [f] Ps 59:10
118:8 [g] Ps 40:4 [h] Jer 17:5
118:9 [i] Ps 146:3
118:10 [j] Ps 18:40
118:11 [k] Ps 88:17 [l] Ps 3:6
118:12 [m] Dt 1:44 [n] Ps 58:9
118:13 [o] Ps 86:17; 140:4
118:14 [p] Ex 15:2 [q] Isa 12:2
118:15 [r] Ps 68:3 [s] Ps 89:13
118:17 [t] Ps 6:5; Hab 1:12 [u] Ex 15:6; Ps 73:28
118:18 [v] 2Co 6:9
118:19 [w] Isa 26:2
118:20 [x] Ps 24:7; Isa 35:8; Rev 22:14
118:21 [y] Ps 116:1
118:22 [z] Mt 21:42; Mk 12:10; Lk 20:17*; Ac 4:11*; 1Pe 2:7*

[25]O LORD, save us;
O LORD, grant us success.
[26]Blessed is he who comes[a] in the name of the LORD.
From the house of the LORD we bless you.[a]
[27]The LORD is God,
and he has made his light shine[b] upon us.
With boughs in hand, join in the festal procession
up[b] to the horns of the altar.

[28]You are my God, and I will give you thanks;
you are my God,[c] and I will exalt[d] you.

[29]Give thanks to the LORD, for he is good;
his love endures forever.

Psalm 119[c]

*Psalm 119 Theme*________________________________

א Aleph

[1]Blessed are they whose ways are blameless,
who walk[e] according to the law of the LORD.
[2]Blessed are they who keep his statutes
and seek him with all their heart.[f]
[3]They do nothing wrong;[g]
they walk in his ways.
[4]You have laid down precepts
that are to be fully obeyed.
[5]Oh, that my ways were steadfast
in obeying your decrees!
[6]Then I would not be put to shame
when I consider all your commands.
[7]I will praise you with an upright heart
as I learn your righteous laws.
[8]I will obey your decrees;
do not utterly forsake me.

ב Beth

[9]How can a young man keep his way pure?
By living according to your word.[h]
[10]I seek you with all my heart;[i]
do not let me stray from your commands.[j]

118:26 [a]Mt 21:9*; Mk 11:9*; Lk 13:35*; 19:38*; Jn 12:13*
118:27 [b]1Pe 2:9
118:28 [c]Isa 25:1 [d]Ex 15:2
119:1 [e]Ps 128:1
119:2 [f]Dt 6:5
119:3 [g]1Jn 3:9; 5:18
119:9 [h]2Ch 6:16
119:10 [i]2Ch 15:15 [j]ver 21,118

[a]26 The Hebrew is plural. [b]27 Or *Bind the festal sacrifice with ropes / and take it*
[c]This psalm is an acrostic poem; the verses of each stanza begin with the same letter of the Hebrew alphabet.

11 I have hidden your word in my heart[a]
that I might not sin against you.
12 Praise be to you, O LORD;
teach me your decrees.[b]
13 With my lips I recount
all the laws that come from your mouth.[c]
14 I rejoice in following your statutes
as one rejoices in great riches.
15 I meditate on your precepts[d]
and consider your ways.
16 I delight[e] in your decrees;
I will not neglect your word.

ג Gimel

17 Do good to your servant,[f] and I will live;
I will obey your word.
18 Open my eyes that I may see
wonderful things in your law.
19 I am a stranger on earth;[g]
do not hide your commands from me.
20 My soul is consumed[h] with longing
for your laws[i] at all times.
21 You rebuke the arrogant, who are cursed
and who stray[j] from your commands.
22 Remove from me scorn[k] and contempt,
for I keep your statutes.
23 Though rulers sit together and slander me,
your servant will meditate on your decrees.
24 Your statutes are my delight;
they are my counselors.

ד Daleth

25 I am laid low in the dust;[l]
preserve my life[m] according to your word.
26 I recounted my ways and you answered me;
teach me your decrees.[n]
27 Let me understand the teaching of your precepts;
then I will meditate on your wonders.[o]
28 My soul is weary with sorrow;[p]
strengthen me[q] according to your word.
29 Keep me from deceitful ways;
be gracious to me through your law.
30 I have chosen the way of truth;
I have set my heart on your laws.

119:11 [a]Ps 37:31; Lk 2:19,51
119:12 [b]ver 26
119:13 [c]Ps 40:9
119:15 [d]Ps 1:2
119:16 [e]Ps 1:2
119:17 [f]Ps 13:6; 116:7
119:19 [g]1Ch 29:15; Ps 39:12; 2Co 5:6; Heb 11:13
119:20 [h]Ps 42:2; 84:2 [i]Ps 63:1
119:21 [j]ver 10
119:22 [k]Ps 39:8
119:25 [l]Ps 44:25 [m]Ps 143:11
119:26 [n]Ps 25:4; 27:11; 86:11
119:27 [o]Ps 145:5
119:28 [p]Ps 107:26 [q]Ps 20:2; 1Pe 5:10

[31]I hold fast[a] to your statutes, O LORD;
do not let me be put to shame.
[32]I run in the path of your commands,
for you have set my heart free.

ה He

[33]Teach me,[b] O LORD, to follow your decrees;
then I will keep them to the end.
[34]Give me understanding, and I will keep your law
and obey it with all my heart.
[35]Direct me in the path of your commands,
for there I find delight.
[36]Turn my heart[c] toward your statutes
and not toward selfish gain.[d]
[37]Turn my eyes away from worthless things;
preserve my life[e] according to your word.[a]
[38]Fulfill your promise[f] to your servant,
so that you may be feared.
[39]Take away the disgrace I dread,
for your laws are good.
[40]How I long[g] for your precepts!
Preserve my life in your righteousness.

ו Waw

[41]May your unfailing love come to me, O LORD,
your salvation according to your promise;
[42]then I will answer[h] the one who taunts me,
for I trust in your word.
[43]Do not snatch the word of truth from my mouth,
for I have put my hope in your laws.
[44]I will always obey your law,
for ever and ever.
[45]I will walk about in freedom,
for I have sought out your precepts.
[46]I will speak of your statutes before kings[i]
and will not be put to shame,
[47]for I delight in your commands
because I love them.
[48]I lift up my hands to[b] your commands, which I love,
and I meditate on your decrees.

ז Zayin

[49]Remember your word to your servant,
for you have given me hope.

[a]37 Two manuscripts of the Masoretic Text and Dead Sea Scrolls; most manuscripts of the Masoretic Text *life in your way* [b]48 Or *for*

119:31 [a]Dt 11:22
119:33 [b]ver 12
119:36 [c]1Ki 8:58 [d]Eze 33:31; Mk 7:21-22; Lk 12:15; Heb 13:5
119:37 [e]Ps 71:20; Isa 33:15
119:38 [f]2Sa 7:25
119:40 [g]ver 20
119:42 [h]Pr 27:11
119:46 [i]Mt 10:18; Ac 26:1-2

50 My comfort in my suffering is this:
Your promise preserves my life.[a]
51 The arrogant mock me[b] without restraint,
but I do not turn[c] from your law.
52 I remember[d] your ancient laws, O LORD,
and I find comfort in them.
53 Indignation grips me[e] because of the wicked,
who have forsaken your law.[f]
54 Your decrees are the theme of my song
wherever I lodge.
55 In the night I remember[g] your name, O LORD,
and I will keep your law.
56 This has been my practice:
I obey your precepts.

ח Heth

57 You are my portion,[h] O LORD;
I have promised to obey your words.
58 I have sought your face with all my heart;
be gracious to me[i] according to your promise.[j]
59 I have considered my ways[k]
and have turned my steps to your statutes.
60 I will hasten and not delay
to obey your commands.
61 Though the wicked bind me with ropes,
I will not forget[l] your law.
62 At midnight[m] I rise to give you thanks
for your righteous laws.
63 I am a friend to all who fear you,[n]
to all who follow your precepts.
64 The earth is filled with your love,[o] O LORD;
teach me your decrees.

ט Teth

65 Do good to your servant
according to your word, O LORD.
66 Teach me knowledge and good judgment,
for I believe in your commands.
67 Before I was afflicted I went astray,[p]
but now I obey your word.
68 You are good,[q] and what you do is good;
teach me your decrees.[r]
69 Though the arrogant have smeared me with lies,[s]
I keep your precepts with all my heart.

119:50 [a] Ro 15:4
119:51 [b] Jer 20:7 [c] ver 157; Job 23:11; Ps 44:18
119:52 [d] Ps 103:18
119:53 [e] Ezr 9:3 [f] Ps 89:30
119:55 [g] Ps 63:6
119:57 [h] Ps 16:5; La 3:24
119:58 [i] 1Ki 13:6 [j] ver 41
119:59 [k] Lk 15:17-18
119:61 [l] Ps 140:5
119:62 [m] Ac 16:25
119:63 [n] Ps 101:6-7
119:64 [o] Ps 33:5
119:67 [p] Jer 31:18-19; Heb 12:11
119:68 [q] Ps 106:1; 107:1; Mt 19:17 [r] ver 12
119:69 [s] Job 13:4; Ps 109:2

[70]Their hearts are callous[a] and unfeeling,
but I delight in your law.
[71]It was good for me to be afflicted
so that I might learn your decrees.
[72]The law from your mouth is more precious to me
than thousands of pieces of silver and gold.[b]

י Yodh

[73]Your hands made me[c] and formed me;
give me understanding to learn your commands.
[74]May those who fear you rejoice[d] when they see me,
for I have put my hope in your word.
[75]I know, O LORD, that your laws are righteous,
and in faithfulness[e] you have afflicted me.
[76]May your unfailing love be my comfort,
according to your promise to your servant.
[77]Let your compassion[f] come to me that I may live,
for your law is my delight.
[78]May the arrogant[g] be put to shame for wronging me
without cause;[h]
but I will meditate on your precepts.
[79]May those who fear you turn to me,
those who understand your statutes.
[80]May my heart be blameless toward your decrees,
that I may not be put to shame.

כ Kaph

[81]My soul faints[i] with longing for your salvation,
but I have put my hope in your word.
[82]My eyes fail,[j] looking for your promise;
I say, "When will you comfort me?"
[83]Though I am like a wineskin in the smoke,
I do not forget your decrees.
[84]How long[k] must your servant wait?
When will you punish my persecutors?
[85]The arrogant dig pitfalls[l] for me,
contrary to your law.
[86]All your commands are trustworthy;[m]
help me,[n] for men persecute me without cause.[o]
[87]They almost wiped me from the earth,
but I have not forsaken[p] your precepts.
[88]Preserve my life according to your love,
and I will obey the statutes of your mouth.

119:70 [a]Ps 17:10; Isa 6:10; Ac 28:27
119:72 [b]Ps 19:10; Pr 8:10-11,19
119:73 [c]Job 10:8; Ps 100:3; 138:8; 139:13-16
119:74 [d]Ps 34:2
119:75 [e]Heb 12:5-11
119:77 [f]ver 41
119:78 [g]Jer 50:32 [h]ver 86,161
119:81 [i]Ps 84:2
119:82 [j]Ps 69:3; La 2:11
119:84 [k]Ps 39:4; Rev 6:10
119:85 [l]Ps 35:7; Jer 18:20,22
119:86 [m]Ps 35:19 [n]Ps 109:26 [o]ver 78
119:87 [p]Isa 58:2

ל Lamedh

89Your word, O LORD, is eternal;[a]
it stands firm in the heavens.
90Your faithfulness[b] continues through all generations;
you established the earth, and it endures.[c]
91Your laws endure[d] to this day,
for all things serve you.
92If your law had not been my delight,
I would have perished in my affliction.
93I will never forget your precepts,
for by them you have preserved my life.
94Save me, for I am yours;
I have sought out your precepts.
95The wicked are waiting to destroy me,
but I will ponder your statutes.
96To all perfection I see a limit;
but your commands are boundless.

מ Mem

97Oh, how I love your law!
I meditate[e] on it all day long.
98Your commands make me wiser[f] than my enemies,
for they are ever with me.
99I have more insight than all my teachers,
for I meditate on your statutes.
100I have more understanding than the elders,
for I obey your precepts.[g]
101I have kept my feet[h] from every evil path
so that I might obey your word.
102I have not departed from your laws,
for you yourself have taught me.
103How sweet are your words to my taste,
sweeter than honey[i] to my mouth![j]
104I gain understanding from your precepts;
therefore I hate every wrong path.[k]

נ Nun

105Your word is a lamp to my feet
and a light[l] for my path.
106I have taken an oath[m] and confirmed it,
that I will follow your righteous laws.
107I have suffered much;
preserve my life, O LORD, according to your word.

119:89 [a] Mt 24:34-35; 1Pe 1:25
119:90 [b] Ps 36:5 [c] Ps 148:6; Ecc 1:4
119:91 [d] Jer 33:25
119:97 [e] Ps 1:2
119:98 [f] Dt 4:6
119:100 [g] Job 32:7-9
119:101 [h] Pr 1:15
119:103 [i] Ps 19:10; Pr 8:11 [j] Pr 24:13-14
119:104 [k] ver 128
119:105 [l] Pr 6:23
119:106 [m] Ne 10:29

[108]Accept, O LORD, the willing praise of my mouth,[a]
and teach me your laws.
[109]Though I constantly take my life in my hands,[b]
I will not forget your law.
[110]The wicked have set a snare[c] for me,
but I have not strayed[d] from your precepts.
[111]Your statutes are my heritage forever;
they are the joy of my heart.
[112]My heart is set on keeping your decrees
to the very end.[e]

ס Samekh

[113]I hate double-minded men,[f]
but I love your law.
[114]You are my refuge and my shield;[g]
I have put my hope[h] in your word.
[115]Away from me,[i] you evildoers,
that I may keep the commands of my God!
[116]Sustain me[j] according to your promise, and I will live;
do not let my hopes be dashed.[k]
[117]Uphold me, and I will be delivered;
I will always have regard for your decrees.
[118]You reject all who stray from your decrees,
for their deceitfulness is in vain.
[119]All the wicked of the earth you discard like dross;[l]
therefore I love your statutes.
[120]My flesh trembles[m] in fear of you;
I stand in awe of your laws.

ע Ayin

[121]I have done what is righteous and just;
do not leave me to my oppressors.
[122]Ensure your servant's well-being;[n]
let not the arrogant oppress me.
[123]My eyes fail, looking for your salvation,
looking for your righteous promise.[o]
[124]Deal with your servant according to your love
and teach me your decrees.[p]
[125]I am your servant;[q] give me discernment
that I may understand your statutes.
[126]It is time for you to act, O LORD;
your law is being broken.
[127]Because I love your commands
more than gold,[r] more than pure gold,

119:108 [a]Hos 14:2; Heb 13:15
119:109 [b]Jdg 12:3; Job 13:14
119:110 [c]Ps 140:5; 141:9 [d]ver 10
119:112 [e]ver 33
119:113 [f]Jas 1:8
119:114 [g]Ps 32:7; 91:1 [h]ver 74
119:115 [i]Ps 6:8; 139:19; Mt 7:23
119:116 [j]Ps 54:4 [k]Ps 25:2; Ro 5:5; 9:33
119:119 [l]Eze 22:18,19
119:120 [m]Hab 3:16
119:122 [n]Job 17:3
119:123 [o]ver 82
119:124 [p]ver 12
119:125 [q]Ps 116:16
119:127 [r]Ps 19:10

128 and because I consider all your precepts right,
I hate every wrong path.[a]

פ Pe

129 Your statutes are wonderful;
therefore I obey them.
130 The unfolding of your words gives light;[b]
it gives understanding to the simple.[c]
131 I open my mouth and pant,[d]
longing for your commands.[e]
132 Turn to me and have mercy[f] on me,
as you always do to those who love your name.
133 Direct my footsteps according to your word;[g]
let no sin rule[h] over me.
134 Redeem me from the oppression of men,[i]
that I may obey your precepts.
135 Make your face shine[j] upon your servant
and teach me your decrees.
136 Streams of tears[k] flow from my eyes,
for your law is not obeyed.[l]

צ Tsadhe

137 Righteous are you,[m] O LORD,
and your laws are right.[n]
138 The statutes you have laid down are righteous;[o]
they are fully trustworthy.
139 My zeal wears me out,[p]
for my enemies ignore your words.
140 Your promises have been thoroughly tested,[q]
and your servant loves them.
141 Though I am lowly and despised,[r]
I do not forget your precepts.
142 Your righteousness is everlasting
and your law is true.[s]
143 Trouble and distress have come upon me,
but your commands are my delight.
144 Your statutes are forever right;
give me understanding[t] that I may live.

ק Qoph

145 I call with all my heart; answer me, O LORD,
and I will obey your decrees.
146 I call out to you; save me
and I will keep your statutes.

119:128 [a] ver 104,163
119:130 [b] Pr 6:23 [c] Ps 19:7
119:131 [d] Ps 42:1 [e] ver 20
119:132 [f] Ps 25:16; 106:4
119:133 [g] Ps 17:5 [h] Ps 19:13; Ro 6:12
119:134 [i] Ps 142:6; Lk 1:74
119:135 [j] Nu 6:25; Ps 4:6
119:136 [k] Jer 9:1,18 [l] Eze 9:4
119:137 [m] Ezr 9:15; Jer 12:1 [n] Ne 9:13
119:138 [o] Ps 19:7
119:139 [p] Ps 69:9; Jn 2:17
119:140 [q] Ps 12:6
119:141 [r] Ps 22:6
119:142 [s] Ps 19:7
119:144 [t] Ps 19:9

[147]I rise before dawn[a] and cry for help;
I have put my hope in your word.
[148]My eyes stay open through the watches of the night,[b]
that I may meditate on your promises.
[149]Hear my voice in accordance with your love;
preserve my life, O LORD, according to your laws.
[150]Those who devise wicked schemes are near,
but they are far from your law.
[151]Yet you are near,[c] O LORD,
and all your commands are true.[d]
[152]Long ago I learned from your statutes
that you established them to last forever.[e]

ר Resh

[153]Look upon my suffering[f] and deliver me,
for I have not forgotten[g] your law.
[154]Defend my cause[h] and redeem me;[i]
preserve my life according to your promise.
[155]Salvation is far from the wicked,
for they do not seek out[j] your decrees.
[156]Your compassion is great, O LORD;
preserve my life[k] according to your laws.
[157]Many are the foes who persecute me,[l]
but I have not turned from your statutes.
[158]I look on the faithless with loathing,[m]
for they do not obey your word.
[159]See how I love your precepts;
preserve my life, O LORD, according to your love.
[160]All your words are true;
all your righteous laws are eternal.

שׁ Sin and Shin

[161]Rulers persecute me[n] without cause,
but my heart trembles at your word.
[162]I rejoice in your promise
like one who finds great spoil.[o]
[163]I hate and abhor falsehood
but I love your law.
[164]Seven times a day I praise you
for your righteous laws.
[165]Great peace[p] have they who love your law,
and nothing can make them stumble.
[166]I wait for your salvation,[q] O LORD,
and I follow your commands.

119:147 [a]Ps 5:3; 57:8; 108:2
119:148 [b]Ps 63:6
119:151 [c]Ps 34:18; 145:18 [d]ver 142
119:152 [e]Lk 21:33
119:153 [f]La 5:1 [g]Pr 3:1
119:154 [h]Mic 7:9 [i]1Sa 24:15
119:155 [j]Job 5:4
119:156 [k]2Sa 24:14
119:157 [l]Ps 7:1
119:158 [m]Ps 139:21
119:161 [n]1Sa 24:11
119:162 [o]1Sa 30:16
119:165 [p]Pr 3:2; Isa 26:3,12; 32:17
119:166 [q]Ge 49:18

167 I obey your statutes,
for I love them greatly.
168 I obey your precepts and your statutes,
for all my ways are known[a] to you.

ת Taw

169 May my cry come[b] before you, O LORD;
give me understanding according to your word.
170 May my supplication come[c] before you;
deliver me[d] according to your promise.
171 May my lips overflow with praise,[e]
for you teach me[f] your decrees.
172 May my tongue sing of your word,
for all your commands are righteous.
173 May your hand be ready to help[g] me,
for I have chosen[h] your precepts.
174 I long for your salvation,[i] O LORD,
and your law is my delight.
175 Let me live[j] that I may praise you,
and may your laws sustain me.
176 I have strayed like a lost sheep.[k]
Seek your servant,
for I have not forgotten your commands.

Psalm 120

A song of ascents.

Psalm 120 Theme ____________________________________

1 I call on the LORD in my distress,[l]
and he answers me.
2 Save me, O LORD, from lying lips[m]
and from deceitful tongues.[n]

3 What will he do to you,
and what more besides, O deceitful tongue?
4 He will punish you with a warrior's sharp arrows,[o]
with burning coals of the broom tree.

5 Woe to me that I dwell in Meshech,
that I live among the tents of Kedar![p]
6 Too long have I lived
among those who hate peace.
7 I am a man of peace;
but when I speak, they are for war.

119:168 [a] Pr 5:21
119:169 [b] Ps 18:6
119:170 [c] Ps 28:2 [d] Ps 31:2
119:171 [e] Ps 51:15 [f] Ps 94:12
119:173 [g] Ps 37:24 [h] Jos 24:22
119:174 [i] ver 166
119:175 [j] Isa 55:3
119:176 [k] Isa 53:6
120:1 [l] Ps 102:2; Jnh 2:2
120:2 [m] Pr 12:22 [n] Ps 52:4
120:4 [o] Ps 45:5
120:5 [p] Ge 25:13; Jer 49:28

Psalm 121

A song of ascents.

Psalm 121 Theme ________________________________

[1]I lift up my eyes to the hills—
where does my help come from?
[2]My help comes from the LORD,
the Maker of heaven and earth.[a]

[3]He will not let your foot slip—
he who watches over you will not slumber;
[4]indeed, he who watches over Israel
will neither slumber nor sleep.

[5]The LORD watches over[b] you—
the LORD is your shade at your right hand;
[6]the sun[c] will not harm you by day,
nor the moon by night.

[7]The LORD will keep you from all harm[d]—
he will watch over your life;
[8]the LORD will watch over your coming and going
both now and forevermore.[e]

Psalm 122

A song of ascents. Of David.

Psalm 122 Theme ________________________________

[1]I rejoiced with those who said to me,
"Let us go to the house of the LORD."
[2]Our feet are standing
in your gates, O Jerusalem.

[3]Jerusalem is built like a city
that is closely compacted together.
[4]That is where the tribes go up,
the tribes of the LORD,
to praise the name of the LORD
according to the statute given to Israel.
[5]There the thrones for judgment stand,
the thrones of the house of David.

[6]Pray for the peace of Jerusalem:
"May those who love[f] you be secure.

121:2 [a]Ps 115:15; 124:8

121:5 [b]Isa 25:4

121:6 [c]Ps 91:5; Isa 49:10; Rev 7:16

121:7 [d]Ps 41:2; 91:10-12

121:8 [e]Dt 28:6

122:6 [f]Ps 51:18

122:9 [a]Ne 2:10

7 May there be peace within your walls
and security within your citadels."
8 For the sake of my brothers and friends,
I will say, "Peace be within you."
9 For the sake of the house of the LORD our God,
I will seek your prosperity.[a]

Psalm 123

A song of ascents.

123:1 [b]Ps 11:4; 121:1; 141:8

*Psalm 123 Theme*______________________________________

1 I lift up my eyes to you,
to you whose throne[b] is in heaven.
2 As the eyes of slaves look to the hand of their master,
as the eyes of a maid look to the hand of her mistress,
so our eyes look to the LORD[c] our God,
till he shows us his mercy.

3 Have mercy on us, O LORD, have mercy on us,
for we have endured much contempt.
4 We have endured much ridicule from the proud,
123:2 [c]Ps 25:15
much contempt from the arrogant.

Psalm 124

A song of ascents. Of David.

*Psalm 124 Theme*______________________________________

1 If the LORD had not been on our side—
let Israel say[d]—
2 if the LORD had not been on our side
124:1 [d]Ps 129:1
when men attacked us,
3 when their anger flared against us,
they would have swallowed us alive;
4 the flood would have engulfed us,
the torrent would have swept over us,
5 the raging waters
would have swept us away.

6 Praise be to the LORD,
who has not let us be torn by their teeth.
7 We have escaped like a bird
124:7 [e]Ps 91:3; Pr 6:5
out of the fowler's snare;[e]

the snare has been broken,
and we have escaped.
8Our help is in the name of the LORD,
the Maker of heaven[a] and earth.

Psalm 125

A song of ascents.

Psalm 125 Theme ________________________

1Those who trust in the LORD are like Mount Zion,
which cannot be shaken[b] but endures forever.
2As the mountains surround Jerusalem,
so the LORD surrounds[c] his people
both now and forevermore.

3The scepter of the wicked will not remain[d]
over the land allotted to the righteous,
for then the righteous might use
their hands to do evil.[e]

4Do good, O LORD,[f] to those who are good,
to those who are upright in heart.[g]
5But those who turn[h] to crooked ways[i]
the LORD will banish with the evildoers.

Peace be upon Israel.[j]

Psalm 126

A song of ascents.

Psalm 126 Theme ________________________

1When the LORD brought back[k] the captives to[a] Zion,
we were like men who dreamed.[b]
2Our mouths were filled with laughter,
our tongues with songs of joy.[l]
Then it was said among the nations,
"The LORD has done great things[m] for them."
3The LORD has done great things for us,
and we are filled with joy.[n]

4Restore our fortunes,[c] O LORD,
like streams in the Negev.[o]

a *1* Or *LORD restored the fortunes of* b *1* Or *men restored to health* c *4* Or *Bring back our captives*

124:8 [a] Ge 1:1; Ps 121:2; 134:3
125:1 [b] Ps 46:5
125:2 [c] Ps 121:8; Zec 2:4-5
125:3 [d] Ps 89:22; Pr 22:8; Isa 14:5 [e] 1Sa 24:10; Ps 55:20
125:4 [f] Ps 119:68 [g] Ps 7:10; 36:10; 94:15
125:5 [h] Job 23:11 [i] Pr 2:15; Isa 59:8 [j] Ps 128:6
126:1 [k] Ps 85:1; Hos 6:11
126:2 [l] Job 8:21; Ps 51:14 [m] Ps 71:19
126:3 [n] Isa 25:9
126:4 [o] Isa 35:6; 43:19

126:5 [a]Isa 35:10

[5]Those who sow in tears
will reap with songs of joy.[a]
[6]He who goes out weeping,
carrying seed to sow,
will return with songs of joy,
carrying sheaves with him.

127:1 [b]Ps 78:69 [c]Ps 121:4

Psalm 127

A song of ascents. Of Solomon.

Psalm 127 Theme ______________________

127:2 [d]Ge 3:17 [e]Job 11:18

[1]Unless the LORD builds[b] the house,
its builders labor in vain.
Unless the LORD watches[c] over the city,
the watchmen stand guard in vain.
[2]In vain you rise early
and stay up late,
toiling for food[d] to eat—
for he grants sleep[e] to[a] those he loves.

127:3 [f]Ge 33:5

[3]Sons are a heritage from the LORD,
children a reward[f] from him.
[4]Like arrows in the hands of a warrior
are sons born in one's youth.

127:5 [g]Pr 27:11

[5]Blessed is the man
whose quiver is full of them.
They will not be put to shame
when they contend with their enemies[g] in the gate.

128:1 [h]Ps 112:1 [i]Ps 119:1-3

Psalm 128

A song of ascents.

Psalm 128 Theme ______________________

128:2 [j]Isa 3:10 [k]Ecc 8:12

[1]Blessed are all who fear the LORD,[h]
who walk in his ways.[i]
[2]You will eat the fruit of your labor;[j]
blessings and prosperity[k] will be yours.
[3]Your wife will be like a fruitful vine[l]
within your house;
your sons will be like olive shoots[m]
around your table.

128:3 [l]Eze 19:10 [m]Ps 52:8; 144:12

[a]2 Or *eat— / for while they sleep he provides for*

[4]Thus is the man blessed
who fears the LORD.

[5]May the LORD bless you from Zion[a]
all the days of your life;
may you see the prosperity of Jerusalem,
6 and may you live to see your children's children.[b]

Peace be upon Israel.[c]

Psalm 129

A song of ascents.

Psalm 129 Theme ______________________

[1]They have greatly oppressed me from my youth[d]—
let Israel say[e]—
[2]they have greatly oppressed me from my youth,
but they have not gained the victory[f] over me.
[3]Plowmen have plowed my back
and made their furrows long.
[4]But the LORD is righteous;[g]
he has cut me free from the cords of the wicked.

[5]May all who hate Zion[h]
be turned back in shame.[i]
[6]May they be like grass on the roof,
which withers[j] before it can grow;
[7]with it the reaper cannot fill his hands,
nor the one who gathers fill his arms.
[8]May those who pass by not say,
"The blessing of the LORD be upon you;
we bless you[k] in the name of the LORD."

Psalm 130

A song of ascents.

Psalm 130 Theme ______________________

[1]Out of the depths[l] I cry to you, O LORD;
2 O Lord, hear my voice.[m]
Let your ears be attentive[n]
to my cry for mercy.

[3]If you, O LORD, kept a record of sins,
O Lord, who could stand?[o]

128:5 [a]Ps 20:2; 134:3
128:6 [b]Ge 50:23; Job 42:16 [c]Ps 125:5
129:1 [d]Ps 88:15; Hos 2:15 [e]Ps 124:1
129:2 [f]Mt 16:18
129:4 [g]Ps 119:137
129:5 [h]Mic 4:11 [i]Ps 71:13
129:6 [j]Ps 37:2
129:8 [k]Ru 2:4; Ps 118:26
130:1 [l]Ps 42:7; 69:2; La 3:55
130:2 [m]Ps 28:2 [n]2Ch 6:40; Ps 64:1
130:3 [o]Ps 76:7; 143:2

130:4 [a]Ex 34:7; Isa 55:7; Jer 33:8 [b]1Ki 8:40

4 But with you there is forgiveness;[a]
therefore you are feared.[b]

5 I wait for the LORD,[c] my soul waits,
and in his word[d] I put my hope.
6 My soul waits for the Lord
more than watchmen[e] wait for the morning,
more than watchmen wait for the morning.[f]

130:5 [c]Ps 27:14; 33:20; Isa 8:17 [d]Ps 119:81

7 O Israel, put your hope[g] in the LORD,
for with the LORD is unfailing love
and with him is full redemption.
8 He himself will redeem[h] Israel
from all their sins.

130:6 [e]Ps 63:6 [f]Ps 119:147

Psalm 131

A song of ascents. Of David.

130:7 [g]Ps 131:3

*Psalm 131 Theme*______________________________

1 My heart is not proud,[i] O LORD,
my eyes are not haughty;
I do not concern myself with great matters
or things too wonderful for me.

130:8 [h]Lk 1:68

2 But I have stilled and quieted my soul;
like a weaned child with its mother,
like a weaned child is my soul[j] within me.

3 O Israel, put your hope[k] in the LORD
both now and forevermore.

131:1 [i]Ps 101:5; Ro 12:16

Psalm 132

A song of ascents.

131:2 [j]Mt 18:3; 1Co 14:20

*Psalm 132 Theme*______________________________

1 O LORD, remember David
and all the hardships he endured.

2 He swore an oath to the LORD
and made a vow to the Mighty One of Jacob:[l]
3 "I will not enter my house
or go to my bed—
4 I will allow no sleep to my eyes,
no slumber to my eyelids,

131:3 [k]Ps 130:7

132:2 [l]Ge 49:24

[5]till I find a place[a] for the LORD,
a dwelling for the Mighty One of Jacob."

[6]We heard it in Ephrathah,[b]
we came upon it in the fields of Jaar[a]:[b][c]
[7]"Let us go to his dwelling place;[d]
let us worship at his footstool[e]—
[8]arise, O LORD,[f] and come to your resting place,
you and the ark of your might.
[9]May your priests be clothed with righteousness;[g]
may your saints sing for joy."

[10]For the sake of David your servant,
do not reject your anointed one.

[11]The LORD swore an oath to David,[h]
a sure oath that he will not revoke:
"One of your own descendants[i]
I will place on your throne—
[12]if your sons keep my covenant
and the statutes I teach them,
then their sons will sit
on your throne[j] for ever and ever."

[13]For the LORD has chosen Zion,[k]
he has desired it for his dwelling:
[14]"This is my resting place for ever and ever;[l]
here I will sit enthroned, for I have desired it—
[15]I will bless her with abundant provisions;
her poor will I satisfy with food.[m]
[16]I will clothe her priests[n] with salvation,
and her saints will ever sing for joy.

[17]"Here I will make a horn[c] grow[o] for David
and set up a lamp[p] for my anointed one.
[18]I will clothe his enemies with shame,[q]
but the crown on his head will be resplendent."

Psalm 133

A song of ascents. Of David.

Psalm 133 Theme ____________________

[1]How good and pleasant it is
when brothers live together[r] in unity!

[a]6 That is, Kiriath Jearim [b]6 Or *heard of it in Ephrathah, / we found it in the fields of Jaar.* (And no quotes around verses 7-9) [c]17 *Horn* here symbolizes strong one, that is, king.

132:5 [a]Ac 7:46
132:6 [b]1Sa 17:12 [c]1Sa 7:2
132:7 [d]Ps 5:7 [e]Ps 99:5
132:8 [f]Nu 10:35; Ps 78:61
132:9 [g]Job 29:14; Isa 61:3,10
132:11 [h]Ps 89:3-4,35 [i]2Sa 7:12
132:12 [j]Lk 1:32; Ac 2:30
132:13 [k]Ps 48:1-2
132:14 [l]Ps 68:16
132:15 [m]Ps 107:9; 147:14
132:16 [n]2Ch 6:41
132:17 [o]Eze 29:21; Lk 1:69 [p]1Ki 11:36; 2Ch 21:7
132:18 [q]Ps 35:26; 109:29
133:1 [r]Ge 13:8; Heb 13:1

2 It is like precious oil poured on the head,[a]
running down on the beard,
running down on Aaron's beard,
down upon the collar of his robes.
3 It is as if the dew of Hermon[b]
were falling on Mount Zion.
For there the LORD bestows his blessing,[c]
even life forevermore.[d]

Psalm 134

A song of ascents.

Psalm 134 Theme ____________________

1 Praise the LORD, all you servants[e] of the LORD
who minister by night[f] in the house of the LORD.
2 Lift up your hands[g] in the sanctuary
and praise the LORD.

3 May the LORD, the Maker of heaven[h] and earth,
bless you from Zion.[i]

Psalm 135

Psalm 135 Theme ____________________

1 Praise the LORD.[a]

Praise the name of the LORD;
praise him, you servants[j] of the LORD,
2 you who minister in the house[k] of the LORD,
in the courts[l] of the house of our God.

3 Praise the LORD, for the LORD is good;[m]
sing praise to his name, for that is pleasant.[n]
4 For the LORD has chosen Jacob[o] to be his own,
Israel to be his treasured possession.[p]

5 I know that the LORD is great,[q]
that our Lord is greater than all gods.[r]
6 The LORD does whatever pleases him,[s]
in the heavens and on the earth,
in the seas and all their depths.
7 He makes clouds rise from the ends of the earth;
he sends lightning with the rain[t]
and brings out the wind[u] from his storehouses.[v]

133:2 [a]Ex 30:25
133:3 [b]Dt 4:48 [c]Lev 25:21; Dt 28:8 [d]Ps 42:8
134:1 [e]Ps 135:1-2 [f]1Ch 9:33
134:2 [g]Ps 28:2; 1Ti 2:8
134:3 [h]Ps 124:8 [i]Ps 128:5
135:1 [j]Ps 113:1; 134:1
135:2 [k]Lk 2:37 [l]Ps 116:19
135:3 [m]Ps 119:68 [n]Ps 147:1
135:4 [o]Dt 10:15; 1Pe 2:9 [p]Ex 19:5; Dt 7:6
135:5 [q]Ps 48:1 [r]Ps 97:9
135:6 [s]Ps 115:3
135:7 [t]Jer 10:13; Zec 10:1 [u]Job 28:25 [v]Job 38:22

a *1* Hebrew *Hallelu Yah;* also in verses 3 and 21

[8]He struck down the firstborn[a] of Egypt,
the firstborn of men and animals.
[9]He sent his signs[b] and wonders into your midst, O Egypt,
against Pharaoh and all his servants.[c]
[10]He struck down many[d] nations
and killed mighty kings—
[11]Sihon[e] king of the Amorites,
Og king of Bashan
and all the kings of Canaan[f]—
[12]and he gave their land as an inheritance,[g]
an inheritance to his people Israel.

[13]Your name, O LORD, endures forever,[h]
your renown,[i] O LORD, through all generations.
[14]For the LORD will vindicate his people
and have compassion on his servants.[j]

[15]The idols of the nations are silver and gold,
made by the hands of men.
[16]They have mouths, but cannot speak,
eyes, but they cannot see;
[17]they have ears, but cannot hear,
nor is there breath in their mouths.
[18]Those who make them will be like them,
and so will all who trust in them.

[19]O house of Israel, praise the LORD;
O house of Aaron, praise the LORD;
[20]O house of Levi, praise the LORD;
you who fear him, praise the LORD.
[21]Praise be to the LORD from Zion,[k]
to him who dwells in Jerusalem.

Praise the LORD.

Psalm 136

Psalm 136 Theme ______________________

[1]Give thanks to the LORD, for he is good.[l]
His love endures forever.[m]
[2]Give thanks to the God of gods.[n]
His love endures forever.
[3]Give thanks to the Lord of lords:
His love endures forever.
[4]to him who alone does great wonders,[o]
His love endures forever.

135:8 [a]Ex 12:12; Ps 78:51
135:9 [b]Dt 6:22 [c]Ps 136:10-15
135:10 [d]Nu 21:21-25; Ps 136:17-21
135:11 [e]Nu 21:21 [f]Jos 12:7-24
135:12 [g]Ps 78:55
135:13 [h]Ex 3:15 [i]Ps 102:12
135:14 [j]Dt 32:36
135:21 [k]Ps 134:3
136:1 [l]Ps 106:1 [m]1Ch 16:34; 2Ch 20:21
136:2 [n]Dt 10:17
136:4 [o]Ps 72:18

5 who by his understanding[a] made the heavens,[b]
His love endures forever.
6 who spread out the earth[c] upon the waters,[d]
His love endures forever.
7 who made the great lights[e]—
His love endures forever.
8 the sun to govern[f] the day,
His love endures forever.
9 the moon and stars to govern the night;
His love endures forever.

10 to him who struck down the firstborn[g] of Egypt
His love endures forever.
11 and brought Israel out[h] from among them
His love endures forever.
12 with a mighty hand and outstretched arm;[i]
His love endures forever.

13 to him who divided the Red Sea[a][j] asunder
His love endures forever.
14 and brought Israel through[k] the midst of it,
His love endures forever.
15 but swept Pharaoh and his army into the Red Sea;[l]
His love endures forever.

16 to him who led his people through the desert,[m]
His love endures forever.
17 who struck down great kings,[n]
His love endures forever.
18 and killed mighty kings[o]—
His love endures forever.
19 Sihon king of the Amorites[p]
His love endures forever.
20 and Og king of Bashan—
His love endures forever.
21 and gave their land[q] as an inheritance,
His love endures forever.
22 an inheritance to his servant Israel;
His love endures forever.

23 to the One who remembered us[r] in our low estate
His love endures forever.
24 and freed us from our enemies,[s]
His love endures forever.

136:5 [a] Pr 3:19; Jer 51:15 [b] Ge 1:1
136:6 [c] Ge 1:9; Jer 10:12 [d] Ps 24:2
136:7 [e] Ge 1:14,16
136:8 [f] Ge 1:16
136:10 [g] Ex 12:29; Ps 135:8
136:11 [h] Ex 6:6; 12:51
136:12 [i] Dt 4:34; Ps 44:3
136:13 [j] Ex 14:21; Ps 78:13
136:14 [k] Ex 14:22
136:15 [l] Ex 14:27; Ps 135:9
136:16 [m] Ex 13:18
136:17 [n] Ps 135:9-12
136:18 [o] Dt 29:7
136:19 [p] Nu 21:21-25
136:21 [q] Jos 12:1
136:23 [r] Ps 113:7
136:24 [s] Ps 107:2

a *13* Hebrew *Yam Suph*; that is, Sea of Reeds; also in verse 15

[25]and who gives food[a] to every creature.
His love endures forever.

[26]Give thanks to the God of heaven.
His love endures forever.

Psalm 137

Psalm 137 Theme ______________________

[1]By the rivers of Babylon[b] we sat and wept[c]
when we remembered Zion.
[2]There on the poplars
we hung our harps,
[3]for there our captors asked us for songs,
our tormentors demanded[d] songs of joy;
they said, "Sing us one of the songs of Zion!"

[4]How can we sing the songs of the LORD
while in a foreign land?
[5]If I forget you, O Jerusalem,
may my right hand forget ⌊its skill⌋.
[6]May my tongue cling to the roof[e] of my mouth
if I do not remember you,
if I do not consider Jerusalem
my highest joy.

[7]Remember, O LORD, what the Edomites[f] did
on the day Jerusalem fell.[g]
"Tear it down," they cried,
"tear it down to its foundations!"

[8]O Daughter of Babylon, doomed to destruction,[h]
happy is he who repays you
for what you have done to us—
[9]he who seizes your infants
and dashes them[i] against the rocks.

Psalm 138

Of David.

Psalm 138 Theme ______________________

[1]I will praise you, O LORD, with all my heart;
before the "gods"[j] I will sing your praise.
[2]I will bow down toward your holy temple[k]
and will praise your name

136:25
[a]Ps 104:27; 145:15

137:1
[b]Eze 1:1,3
[c]Ne 1:4

137:3
[d]Ps 80:6

137:6
[e]Eze 3:26

137:7
[f]Jer 49:7; La 4:21-22; Eze 25:12
[g]Ob 11

137:8
[h]Isa 13:1,19; Jer 25:12,26; Jer 50:15; Rev 18:6

137:9
[i]2Ki 8:12; Isa 13:16

138:1
[j]Ps 95:3; 96:4

138:2
[k]1Ki 8:29; Ps 5:7; 28:2

for your love and your faithfulness,
for you have exalted above all things
your name and your word.[a]
3 When I called, you answered me;
you made me bold and stouthearted.[b]

4 May all the kings of the earth[c] praise you, O LORD,
when they hear the words of your mouth.
5 May they sing of the ways of the LORD,
for the glory of the LORD is great.

6 Though the LORD is on high, he looks upon the lowly,[d]
but the proud[e] he knows from afar.
7 Though I walk[f] in the midst of trouble,
you preserve my life;
you stretch out your hand against the anger of my foes,[g]
with your right hand[h] you save me.[i]
8 The LORD will fulfill ⌊his purpose⌋[j] for me;
your love, O LORD, endures forever—
do not abandon the works of your hands.[k]

Psalm 139

For the director of music. Of David. A psalm.

Psalm 139 Theme ________________________

1 O LORD, you have searched me[l]
and you know[m] me.
2 You know when I sit and when I rise;[n]
you perceive my thoughts[o] from afar.
3 You discern my going out and my lying down;
you are familiar with all my ways.[p]
4 Before a word is on my tongue
you know it completely,[q] O LORD.

5 You hem me in[r]—behind and before;
you have laid your hand upon me.
6 Such knowledge is too wonderful for me,
too lofty[s] for me to attain.

7 Where can I go from your Spirit?
Where can I flee[t] from your presence?
8 If I go up to the heavens,[u] you are there;
if I make my bed[v] in the depths,[a] you are there.

138:2 [a] Isa 42:21
138:3 [b] Ps 28:7
138:4 [c] Ps 102:15
138:6 [d] Ps 113:6; Isa 57:15 [e] Pr 3:34; Jas 4:6
138:7 [f] Ps 23:4 [g] Jer 51:25 [h] Ps 20:6 [i] Ps 71:20
138:8 [j] Ps 57:2; Php 1:6 [k] Job 10:3,8; 14:15
139:1 [l] Ps 17:3 [m] Jer 12:3
139:2 [n] 2Ki 19:27 [o] Mt 9:4; Jn 2:24
139:3 [p] Job 31:4
139:4 [q] Heb 4:13
139:5 [r] Ps 34:7
139:6 [s] Job 42:3; Ro 11:33
139:7 [t] Jer 23:24; Jnh 1:3
139:8 [u] Am 9:2-3 [v] Pr 15:11

a8 Hebrew *Sheol*

[9]If I rise on the wings of the dawn,
 if I settle on the far side of the sea,
[10]even there your hand will guide me,[a]
 your right hand will hold me fast.

[11]If I say, "Surely the darkness will hide me
 and the light become night around me,"
[12]even the darkness will not be dark[b] to you;
 the night will shine like the day,
 for darkness is as light to you.

[13]For you created my inmost being;[c]
 you knit me together[d] in my mother's womb.
[14]I praise you because I am fearfully and wonderfully
  made;
 your works are wonderful,[e]
 I know that full well.
[15]My frame was not hidden from you
 when I was made in the secret place.
When I was woven together[f] in the depths of the earth,[g]
[16] your eyes saw my unformed body.
All the days ordained for me
 were written in your book
 before one of them came to be.

[17]How precious to[a] me are your thoughts, O God![h]
 How vast is the sum of them!
[18]Were I to count them,
 they would outnumber the grains of sand.
When I awake,
 I am still with you.

[19]If only you would slay the wicked,[i] O God!
 Away from me,[j] you bloodthirsty men!
[20]They speak of you with evil intent;
 your adversaries misuse your name.[k]
[21]Do I not hate those[l] who hate you, O LORD,
 and abhor those who rise up against you?
[22]I have nothing but hatred for them;
 I count them my enemies.

[23]Search me,[m] O God, and know my heart;[n]
 test me and know my anxious thoughts.
[24]See if there is any offensive way in me,
 and lead me[o] in the way everlasting.

[a] *17* Or *concerning*

139:10
[a]Ps 23:3

139:12
[b]Job 34:22; Da 2:22

139:13
[c]Ps 119:73
[d]Job 10:11

139:14
[e]Ps 40:5

139:15
[f]Job 10:11
[g]Ps 63:9

139:17
[h]Ps 40:5

139:19
[i]Isa 11:4
[j]Ps 119:115

139:20
[k]Jude 15

139:21
[l]2Ch 19:2; Ps 31:6; 119:113; Ps 119:158

139:23
[m]Job 31:6; Ps 26:2
[n]Jer 11:20

139:24
[o]Ps 5:8; 143:10; Pr 15:9

Psalm 140

For the director of music. A psalm of David.

Psalm 140 Theme ______________________________

1 Rescue me,[a] O LORD, from evil men;
protect me from men of violence,[b]
2 who devise evil plans[c] in their hearts
and stir up war every day.
3 They make their tongues as sharp as[d] a serpent's;
the poison of vipers[e] is on their lips. *Selah*

4 Keep me,[f] O LORD, from the hands of the wicked;[g]
protect me from men of violence
who plan to trip my feet.
5 Proud men have hidden a snare for me;
they have spread out the cords of their net
and have set traps[h] for me along my path. *Selah*

6 O LORD, I say to you, "You are my God."[i]
Hear, O LORD, my cry for mercy.[j]
7 O Sovereign LORD,[k] my strong deliverer,
who shields my head in the day of battle—
8 do not grant the wicked[l] their desires, O LORD;
do not let their plans succeed,
or they will become proud. *Selah*

9 Let the heads of those who surround me
be covered with the trouble their lips have caused.[m]
10 Let burning coals fall upon them;
may they be thrown into the fire,[n]
into miry pits, never to rise.
11 Let slanderers not be established in the land;
may disaster hunt down men of violence.[o]

12 I know that the LORD secures justice for the poor
and upholds the cause[p] of the needy.[q]
13 Surely the righteous will praise your name[r]
and the upright will live[s] before you.

Psalm 141

A psalm of David.

Psalm 141 Theme ______________________________

1 O LORD, I call to you; come quickly[t] to me.
Hear my voice[u] when I call to you.

140:1 [a]Ps 17:13 [b]Ps 18:48
140:2 [c]Ps 36:4; 56:6
140:3 [d]Ps 57:4 [e]Ps 58:4; Jas 3:8
140:4 [f]Ps 141:9 [g]Ps 71:4
140:5 [h]Ps 31:4; 35:7
140:6 [i]Ps 16:2 [j]Ps 116:1; 143:1
140:7 [k]Ps 28:8
140:8 [l]Ps 10:2-3
140:9 [m]Ps 7:16
140:10 [n]Ps 11:6; 21:9
140:11 [o]Ps 34:21
140:12 [p]Ps 9:4 [q]Ps 35:10
140:13 [r]Ps 97:12 [s]Ps 11:7
141:1 [t]Ps 22:19; 70:5 [u]Ps 143:1

[2]May my prayer be set before you like incense;[a]
may the lifting up of my hands[b] be like the evening sacrifice.[c]

[3]Set a guard over my mouth, O LORD;
keep watch over the door of my lips.
[4]Let not my heart be drawn to what is evil,
to take part in wicked deeds
with men who are evildoers;
let me not eat of their delicacies.[d]

[5]Let a righteous man[a] strike me—it is a kindness;
let him rebuke me[e]—it is oil on my head.[f]
My head will not refuse it.

Yet my prayer is ever against the deeds of evildoers;
[6] their rulers will be thrown down from the cliffs,
and the wicked will learn that my words were well spoken.
[7]⌊They will say,⌋ "As one plows and breaks up the earth,
so our bones have been scattered at the mouth[g] of the grave.[b]"

[8]But my eyes are fixed[h] on you, O Sovereign LORD;
in you I take refuge[i]—do not give me over to death.
[9]Keep me[j] from the snares they have laid for me,
from the traps set[k] by evildoers.
[10]Let the wicked fall[l] into their own nets,
while I pass by in safety.

Psalm 142

A *maskil*[c] of David. When he was in the cave. A prayer.

Psalm 142 Theme ____________________

[1]I cry aloud to the LORD;
I lift up my voice to the LORD for mercy.[m]
[2]I pour out my complaint[n] before him;
before him I tell my trouble.

[3]When my spirit grows faint[o] within me,
it is you who know my way.
In the path where I walk
men have hidden a snare for me.

141:2 [a]Rev 5:8; 8:3 [b]1Ti 2:8 [c]Ex 29:39,41
141:4 [d]Pr 23:6
141:5 [e]Pr 9:8 [f]Ps 23:5
141:7 [g]Ps 53:5
141:8 [h]Ps 25:15 [i]Ps 2:12
141:9 [j]Ps 140:4 [k]Ps 38:12
141:10 [l]Ps 35:8
142:1 [m]Ps 30:8
142:2 [n]Isa 26:16
142:3 [o]Ps 140:5; 143:4,7

[a]5 Or *Let the Righteous One* [b]7 Hebrew *Sheol* [c]Title: Probably a literary or musical term

142:4 [a]Ps 31:11; Jer 30:17

[4]Look to my right and see;
no one is concerned for me.
I have no refuge;
no one cares[a] for my life.

142:5 [b]Ps 46:1 [c]Ps 16:5 [d]Ps 27:13

[5]I cry to you, O LORD;
I say, "You are my refuge,[b]
my portion[c] in the land of the living."[d]

142:6 [e]Ps 17:1 [f]Ps 79:8; 116:6

[6]Listen to my cry,[e]
for I am in desperate need;[f]
rescue me from those who pursue me,
for they are too strong for me.

142:7 [g]Ps 146:7 [h]Ps 13:6

[7]Set me free from my prison,[g]
that I may praise your name.

Then the righteous will gather about me
because of your goodness to me.[h]

Psalm 143

A psalm of David.

Psalm 143 Theme ____________________

143:1 [i]Ps 140:6 [j]Ps 89:1-2 [k]Ps 71:2

[1]O LORD, hear my prayer,
listen to my cry for mercy;[i]
in your faithfulness[j] and righteousness[k]
come to my relief.

143:2 [l]Ps 14:3; Ecc 7:20; Ro 3:20

[2]Do not bring your servant into judgment,
for no one living is righteous[l] before you.

[3]The enemy pursues me,
he crushes me to the ground;
he makes me dwell in darkness
like those long dead.

143:4 [m]Ps 142:3

[4]So my spirit grows faint within me;
my heart within me is dismayed.[m]

143:5 [n]Ps 77:6

[5]I remember[n] the days of long ago;
I meditate on all your works
and consider what your hands have done.

143:6 [o]Ps 63:1; 88:9

[6]I spread out my hands[o] to you;
my soul thirsts for you like a parched land. *Selah*

143:7 [p]Ps 69:17 [q]Ps 27:9; 28:1

[7]Answer me quickly,[p] O LORD;
my spirit fails.
Do not hide your face[q] from me
or I will be like those who go down to the pit.

[8]Let the morning bring me word of your unfailing love,[a]
for I have put my trust in you.
Show me the way[b] I should go,
for to you I lift up my soul.[c]
[9]Rescue me from my enemies,[d] O LORD,
for I hide myself in you.
[10]Teach me to do your will,
for you are my God;
may your good Spirit
lead[e] me on level ground.

[11]For your name's sake, O LORD, preserve my life;[f]
in your righteousness,[g] bring me out of trouble.
[12]In your unfailing love, silence my enemies;
destroy all my foes,[h]
for I am your servant.[i]

Psalm 144

Of David.

Psalm 144 Theme ______________________

[1]Praise be to the LORD my Rock,[j]
who trains my hands for war,
my fingers for battle.
[2]He is my loving God and my fortress,[k]
my stronghold and my deliverer,
my shield,[l] in whom I take refuge,
who subdues peoples[a] under me.

[3]O LORD, what is man[m] that you care for him,
the son of man that you think of him?
[4]Man is like a breath;
his days are like a fleeting shadow.[n]

[5]Part your heavens,[o] O LORD, and come down;
touch the mountains, so that they smoke.[p]
[6]Send forth lightning and scatter ⌊the enemies⌋;
shoot your arrows[q] and rout them.
[7]Reach down your hand from on high;
deliver me and rescue me
from the mighty waters,[r]
from the hands of foreigners[s]

143:8
[a]Ps 46:5; 90:14
[b]Ps 27:11
[c]Ps 25:1-2

143:9
[d]Ps 31:15

143:10
[e]Ne 9:20; Ps 23:3; 25:4-5

143:11
[f]Ps 119:25
[g]Ps 31:1

143:12
[h]Ps 52:5; 54:5
[i]Ps 116:16

144:1
[j]Ps 18:2,34

144:2
[k]Ps 59:9; 91:2
[l]Ps 84:9

144:3
[m]Ps 8:4; Heb 2:6

144:4
[n]Ps 39:11; 102:11

144:5
[o]Ps 18:9; Isa 64:1
[p]Ps 104:32

144:6
[q]Ps 7:12-13; 18:14

144:7
[r]Ps 69:2
[s]Ps 18:44

[a] *2* Many manuscripts of the Masoretic Text, Dead Sea Scrolls, Aquila, Jerome and Syriac; most manuscripts of the Masoretic Text *subdues my people*

8 whose mouths are full of lies,[a]
whose right hands are deceitful.

9 I will sing a new song to you, O God;
on the ten-stringed lyre[b] I will make music to you,
10 to the One who gives victory to kings,
who delivers his servant David[c] from the
deadly sword.

11 Deliver me and rescue me
from the hands of foreigners
whose mouths are full of lies,
whose right hands are deceitful.[d]

12 Then our sons in their youth
will be like well-nurtured plants,[e]
and our daughters will be like pillars
carved to adorn a palace.
13 Our barns will be filled
with every kind of provision.
Our sheep will increase by thousands,
by tens of thousands in our fields;
14 our oxen will draw heavy loads.[a]
There will be no breaching of walls,
no going into captivity,
no cry of distress in our streets.

15 Blessed are the people[f] of whom this is true;
blessed are the people whose God is the LORD.

Psalm 145[b]

A psalm of praise. Of David.

Psalm 145 Theme ____________________

1 I will exalt you,[g] my God the King;[h]
I will praise your name for ever and ever.
2 Every day I will praise[i] you
and extol your name for ever and ever.

3 Great is the LORD and most worthy of praise;
his greatness no one can fathom.[j]
4 One generation[k] will commend your works to another;
they will tell of your mighty acts.

144:8 *a* Ps 12:2
144:9 *b* Ps 33:2-3
144:10 *c* Ps 18:50
144:11 *d* Ps 12:2; Isa 44:20
144:12 *e* Ps 128:3
144:15 *f* Ps 33:12
145:1 *g* Ps 30:1; 34:1 *h* Ps 5:2
145:2 *i* Ps 71:6
145:3 *j* Job 5:9; Ps 147:5; Ro 11:33
145:4 *k* Isa 38:19

a *14* Or *our chieftains will be firmly established* b This psalm is an acrostic poem, the verses of which (including verse 13b) begin with the successive letters of the Hebrew alphabet.

[5]They will speak of the glorious splendor of your majesty,
and I will meditate on your wonderful works.[a] [a]
[6]They will tell of the power of your awesome works,[b]
and I will proclaim[c] your great deeds.
[7]They will celebrate your abundant goodness[d]
and joyfully sing of your righteousness.[e]

[8]The LORD is gracious and compassionate,[f]
slow to anger and rich in love.[g]
[9]The LORD is good[h] to all;
he has compassion on all he has made.
[10]All you have made will praise you,[i] O LORD;
your saints will extol you.[j]
[11]They will tell of the glory of your kingdom
and speak of your might,
[12]so that all men may know of your mighty acts[k]
and the glorious splendor of your kingdom.
[13]Your kingdom is an everlasting kingdom,[l]
and your dominion endures through all generations.

The LORD is faithful to all his promises
and loving toward all he has made.[b]
[14]The LORD upholds[m] all those who fall
and lifts up all[n] who are bowed down.
[15]The eyes of all look to you,
and you give them their food[o] at the proper time.
[16]You open your hand
and satisfy the desires[p] of every living thing.

[17]The LORD is righteous in all his ways
and loving toward all he has made.
[18]The LORD is near[q] to all who call on him,[r]
to all who call on him in truth.
[19]He fulfills the desires[s] of those who fear him;
he hears their cry[t] and saves them.
[20]The LORD watches over all who love him,[u]
but all the wicked he will destroy.[v]

[21]My mouth will speak[w] in praise of the LORD.
Let every creature[x] praise his holy name
for ever and ever.

[a]5 Dead Sea Scrolls and Syriac (see also Septuagint); Masoretic Text *On the glorious splendor of your majesty / and on your wonderful works I will meditate* [b]13 One manuscript of the Masoretic Text, Dead Sea Scrolls and Syriac (see also Septuagint); most manuscripts of the Masoretic Text do not have the last two lines of verse 13.

145:5 [a]Ps 119:27
145:6 [b]Ps 66:3 [c]Dt 32:3
145:7 [d]Isa 63:7 [e]Ps 51:14
145:8 [f]Ps 86:15 [g]Ex 34:6; Nu 14:18
145:9 [h]Ps 100:5
145:10 [i]Ps 19:1 [j]Ps 68:26
145:12 [k]Ps 105:1
145:13 [l]1Ti 1:17; 2Pe 1:11
145:14 [m]Ps 37:24 [n]Ps 146:8
145:15 [o]Ps 104:27; 136:25
145:16 [p]Ps 104:28
145:18 [q]Dt 4:7 [r]Jn 4:24
145:19 [s]Ps 37:4 [t]Pr 15:29
145:20 [u]Ps 31:23; 97:10 [v]Ps 9:5
145:21 [w]Ps 71:8 [x]Ps 65:2

Psalm 146

Psalm 146 Theme ______________________

1 Praise the LORD.[a]

Praise the LORD,[a] O my soul.
2 I will praise the LORD all my life;[b]
I will sing praise to my God as long as I live.

3 Do not put your trust in princes,[c]
in mortal men,[d] who cannot save.
4 When their spirit departs, they return to the ground;[e]
on that very day their plans come to nothing.[f]
5 Blessed is he[g] whose help[h] is the God of Jacob,
whose hope is in the LORD his God,
6 the Maker of heaven[i] and earth,
the sea, and everything in them—
the LORD, who remains faithful[j] forever.
7 He upholds the cause of the oppressed[k]
and gives food to the hungry.[l]
The LORD sets prisoners free,[m]
8 the LORD gives sight to the blind,[n]
the LORD lifts up those who are bowed down,
the LORD loves the righteous.
9 The LORD watches over the alien
and sustains the fatherless and the widow,[o]
but he frustrates the ways of the wicked.

10 The LORD reigns[p] forever,
your God, O Zion, for all generations.

Praise the LORD.

Psalm 147

Psalm 147 Theme ______________________

1 Praise the LORD.[b]

How good it is to sing praises to our God,
how pleasant[q] and fitting to praise him![r]

2 The LORD builds up Jerusalem;[s]
he gathers the exiles[t] of Israel.
3 He heals the brokenhearted
and binds up their wounds.

146:1 [a] Ps 103:1
146:2 [b] Ps 104:33
146:3 [c] Ps 118:9; [d] Isa 2:22
146:4 [e] Ps 104:29; Ecc 12:7; [f] Ps 33:10; 1Co 2:6
146:5 [g] Ps 144:15; Jer 17:7; [h] Ps 71:5
146:6 [i] Ps 115:15; Ac 14:15; Rev 14:7; [j] Ps 117:2
146:7 [k] Ps 103:6; [l] Ps 107:9; [m] Ps 68:6
146:8 [n] Mt 9:30
146:9 [o] Ex 22:22; Dt 10:18; Ps 68:5
146:10 [p] Ex 15:18; Ps 10:16
147:1 [q] Ps 135:3; [r] Ps 33:1
147:2 [s] Ps 102:16; [t] Dt 30:3

a *1* Hebrew *Hallelu Yah*; also in verse 10 b *1* Hebrew *Hallelu Yah*; also in verse 20

[4]He determines the number of the stars[a]
and calls them each by name.
[5]Great is our Lord[b] and mighty in power;
his understanding has no limit.[c]
[6]The LORD sustains the humble[d]
but casts the wicked to the ground.

[7]Sing to the LORD[e] with thanksgiving;
make music to our God on the harp.
[8]He covers the sky with clouds;
he supplies the earth with rain[f]
and makes grass grow[g] on the hills.
[9]He provides food[h] for the cattle
and for the young ravens[i] when they call.
[10]His pleasure is not in the strength[j] of the horse,[k]
nor his delight in the legs of a man;
[11]the LORD delights in those who fear him,
who put their hope in his unfailing love.
[12]Extol the LORD, O Jerusalem;
praise your God, O Zion,
[13]for he strengthens the bars of your gates
and blesses your people within you.
[14]He grants peace[l] to your borders
and satisfies you[m] with the finest of wheat.

[15]He sends his command[n] to the earth;
his word runs swiftly.
[16]He spreads the snow[o] like wool
and scatters the frost[p] like ashes.
[17]He hurls down his hail like pebbles.
Who can withstand his icy blast?
[18]He sends his word[q] and melts them;
he stirs up his breezes, and the waters flow.

[19]He has revealed his word to Jacob,
his laws and decrees[r] to Israel.
[20]He has done this for no other nation;[s]
they do not know his laws.

Praise the LORD.

Psalm 148

Psalm 148 Theme ______________________________

[1]Praise the LORD.[a]

Praise the LORD from the heavens,

[a] *1* Hebrew *Hallelu Yah*; also in verse 14

147:4
[a] Isa 40:26

147:5
[b] Ps 48:1
[c] Isa 40:28

147:6
[d] Ps 146:8-9

147:7
[e] Ps 33:3

147:8
[f] Job 38:26
[g] Ps 104:14

147:9
[h] Ps 104:27-28; Mt 6:26
[i] Job 38:41

147:10
[j] 1Sa 16:7
[k] Ps 33:16-17

147:14
[l] Isa 60:17-18
[m] Ps 132:15

147:15
[n] Job 37:12

147:16
[o] Job 37:6
[p] Job 38:29

147:18
[q] Ps 33:9

147:19
[r] Dt 33:4; Mal 4:4

147:20
[s] Dt 4:7-8,32-34

praise him in the heights above.
2 Praise him, all his angels,[a]
praise him, all his heavenly hosts.
3 Praise him, sun and moon,
praise him, all you shining stars.
4 Praise him, you highest heavens
and you waters above the skies.[b]
5 Let them praise the name of the LORD,
for he commanded[c] and they were created.
6 He set them in place for ever and ever;
he gave a decree[d] that will never pass away.

7 Praise the LORD from the earth,
you great sea creatures[e] and all ocean depths,
8 lightning and hail, snow and clouds,
stormy winds that do his bidding,[f]
9 you mountains and all hills,[g]
fruit trees and all cedars,
10 wild animals and all cattle,
small creatures and flying birds,
11 kings of the earth and all nations,
you princes and all rulers on earth,
12 young men and maidens,
old men and children.

13 Let them praise the name of the LORD,[h]
for his name alone is exalted;
his splendor is above the earth and the heavens.[i]
14 He has raised up for his people a horn,[a][j]
the praise of all his saints,
of Israel, the people close to his heart.

Praise the LORD.

Psalm 149

Psalm 149 Theme ______________________________

1 Praise the LORD.[b][k]

Sing to the LORD a new song,
his praise in the assembly[l] of the saints.

2 Let Israel rejoice in their Maker;[m]
let the people of Zion be glad in their King.[n]
3 Let them praise his name with dancing
and make music to him with tambourine and harp.[o]

148:2 [a] Ps 103:20
148:4 [b] Ge 1:7; 1Ki 8:27
148:5 [c] Ge 1:1,6; Ps 33:6,9
148:6 [d] Job 38:33; Ps 89:37; Jer 33:25
148:7 [e] Ps 74:13-14
148:8 [f] Ps 147:15-18
148:9 [g] Isa 44:23; 49:13; 55:12
148:13 [h] Isa 12:4 [i] Ps 8:1; 113:4
148:14 [j] Ps 75:10
149:1 [k] Ps 33:2 [l] Ps 35:18
149:2 [m] Ps 95:6 [n] Ps 47:6; Zec 9:9
149:3 [o] Ps 81:2; 150:4

[a] 14 *Horn* here symbolizes strong one, that is, king. [b] 1 Hebrew *Hallelu Yah*; also in verse 9

4For the LORD takes delight[a] in his people;
he crowns the humble with salvation.[b]
5Let the saints rejoice[c] in this honor
and sing for joy on their beds.[d]

6May the praise of God be in their mouths[e]
and a double-edged[f] sword in their hands,
7to inflict vengeance on the nations
and punishment on the peoples,
8to bind their kings with fetters,
their nobles with shackles of iron,
9to carry out the sentence written against them.[g]
This is the glory of all his saints.[h]

Praise the LORD.

Psalm 150

Psalm 150 Theme ______________________________

1Praise the LORD.[a]

Praise God in his sanctuary;[i]
praise him in his mighty heavens.[j]
2Praise him for his acts of power;[k]
praise him for his surpassing greatness.[l]
3Praise him with the sounding of the trumpet,
praise him with the harp and lyre,[m]
4praise him with tambourine and dancing,[n]
praise him with the strings[o] and flute,
5praise him with the clash of cymbals,[p]
praise him with resounding cymbals.

6Let everything[q] that has breath praise the LORD.

Praise the LORD.

[a] *1* Hebrew *Hallelu Yah*; also in verse 6

149:4
[a] Ps 35:27
[b] Ps 132:16

149:5
[c] Ps 132:16
[d] Job 35:10

149:6
[e] Ps 66:17
[f] Heb 4:12; Rev 1:16

149:9
[g] Dt 7:1; Eze 28:26
[h] Ps 148:14

150:1
[i] Ps 102:19
[j] Ps 19:1

150:2
[k] Dt 3:24
[l] Ps 145:5-6

150:3
[m] Ps 149:3

150:4
[n] Ex 15:20
[o] Isa 38:20

150:5
[p] 1Ch 13:8; 15:16

150:6
[q] Ps 145:21

eme of Psalms:

EGMENT DIVISIONS		CHAPTER THEMES
		1
		2
		3
		4
		5
		6
		7
		8
		9
		10
		11
		12
		13
		14
		15
		16
		17
		18
		19
		20
		21
		22
		23
		24
		25

Author:

Date:

Purpose:

Key Words:

Segment Divisions		Chapter Themes
		26
		27
		28
		29
		30
		31
		32
		33
		34
		35
		36
		37
		38
		39
		40
		41
		42
		43
		44
		45
		46
		47
		48
		49
		50

SEGMENT DIVISIONS

		CHAPTER THEMES
		51
		52
		53
		54
		55
		56
		57
		58
		59
		60
		61
		62
		63
		64
		65
		66
		67
		68
		69
		70
		71
		72
		73
		74
		75

Segment Divisions

		Chapter Themes
		76
		77
		78
		79
		80
		81
		82
		83
		84
		85
		86
		87
		88
		89
		90
		91
		92
		93
		94
		95
		96
		97
		98
		99
		100

…GMENT DIVISIONS

		CHAPTER THEMES
		101
		102
		103
		104
		105
		106
		107
		108
		109
		110
		111
		112
		113
		114
		115
		116
		117
		118
		119
		120
		121
		122
		123
		124
		125

Segment Divisions

		Chapter Themes
		126
		127
		128
		129
		130
		131
		132
		133
		134
		135
		136
		137
		138
		139
		140
		141
		142
		143
		144
		145
		146
		147
		148
		149
		150

PROVERBS

When God appeared to King Solomon in a dream, he said, "Ask for whatever you want me to give you." Solomon asked for an understanding heart so that he could lead the nation of Israel (see 1 Kings 3). In response to that prayer "God gave Solomon wisdom and very great insight, and a breadth of understanding as measureless as the sand on the seashore. Solomon's wisdom was greater than the wisdom of all the men of the East, and greater than all the wisdom of Egypt. He was wiser than any other man.... He spoke three thousand proverbs" (1 Kings 4:29-32).

A portion of those proverbs has been preserved for us in the book of Proverbs. A proverb is usually a short saying or maxim which gives insight on life and human behavior.

The book of Proverbs, which is wisdom literature, is a compilation of true sayings which give wisdom and instruction. However, these maxims cannot be interpreted as prophecies, nor can they be held as absolute doctrines. For example, Proverbs says a man's enemies will be at peace with him when his ways please the Lord. We can accept this as a valid proverb which generally proves to be true, though not always. Our Lord's enemies were not at peace with him even though he did only those things which pleased the Father.

The Proverbs are inspired by God. Don't rush through them. Give yourself time for meditation and application. Although Proverbs was written between 971 and 686 B.C., the sayings are timeless. They can equip you for life in the home and the marketplace.

Things to Do

1. Proverbs uses figurative language—similes and metaphors. Read the section called "Figures of Speech" on page 2207 before you study Proverbs.

2. Read Proverbs 1:1-7 and note the author, purpose, and theme of the book in the margin of chapter 1. As you look for the purpose, watch the repeated use of *for.* The theme is also repeated in 9:10. Record these insights on the PROVERBS AT A GLANCE chart on page 1120.

3. A wise person appreciates the wisdom of others. Look at PROVERBS AT A GLANCE and note the major segment divisions of this book. You will see that Solomon respected the wisdom of others. Look up the following verses and note whose words or proverbs follow: Proverbs 10:1; 22:17; 25:1; 30:1; 31:1.

4. Mark the key words listed on PROVERBS AT A GLANCE. Keep a list of what you learn about wisdom, especially in the first nine chapters. Note how wisdom is personified. (An abstraction, such as wisdom, is personified when it takes on the characteristics of a person. Proverbs 1:20 is an example.)

5. Watch for and mark the phrase *my son (O son).* Then listen as if it is God the Father speaking to you, his own dear child whom he wants to show the path of life.

6. Develop a code for marking the subjects covered throughout Proverbs: sexual morality, finances, discipline, the heart, the tongue, the company we keep, etc. As you read through Proverbs repeatedly you will learn more and more about mankind and will find yourself much wiser when it comes to living in the "fear of the Lord." You will have a collection of insights on the critical issues of life.

7. Record the theme or themes of each chapter on PROVERBS AT A GLANCE and in the text next to the chapter number. You may find this difficult between chapters 10 and 29 because the proverbs are short and varied. However, simply listing the major topics of each chapter will help you find the major topics at a glance. Color coding or marking each topic throughout the book will help you easily spot what Proverbs teaches about a particular subject. This will be a great help as you share these truths with others or need wisdom on a specific topic.

Things to Think About

1. Are you walking in the fear of the Lord? To fear God is to have an awesome respect of who he is and a reverential trust in his Word and his character, and to live accordingly.

2. Do you rely on your own understanding or do you seek God's wisdom in the matters of everyday life?

3. What do you need to do or change in light of the insight and wisdom you have learned from these proverbs?

4. Since there are 31 chapters in Proverbs, some people read a chapter a day, month after month. This is good as long as you do not neglect other portions of the Word and as long as you give yourself adequate time to meditate on these proverbs.

   a. After chapter 9 many proverbs are only two to four lines long. You may want to choose one or two proverbs a day, evaluating your life and relationships in the light of them.

   b. Or you may want to select a theme you marked throughout Proverbs, list what you learned from the book as a whole, and then meditate on that theme. For example, you might meditate on what you learned about diligence versus laziness, or about the tongue.

Chapter 1 Theme ______

1 The proverbs of Solomon[a] son of David, king of Israel:[b]

[2]for attaining wisdom and discipline;
for understanding words of insight;
[3]for acquiring a disciplined and prudent life,
doing what is right and just and fair;
[4]for giving prudence to the simple,[c]
knowledge and discretion[d] to the young—
[5]let the wise listen and add to their learning,[e]
and let the discerning get guidance—
[6]for understanding proverbs and parables,[f]
the sayings and riddles[g] of the wise.
[7]The fear of the LORD[h] is the beginning of knowledge,
but fools[a] despise wisdom and discipline.

[8]Listen, my son,[i] to your father's instruction
and do not forsake your mother's teaching.[j]
[9]They will be a garland to grace your head
and a chain to adorn your neck.[k]

[10]My son, if sinners entice[l] you,
do not give in[m] to them.[n]
[11]If they say, "Come along with us;
let's lie in wait[o] for someone's blood,
let's waylay some harmless soul;

INSIGHT

To have ***knowledge*** is to have understanding or information about something. To have ***wisdom*** is to have the ability to apply knowledge to daily life.

1:1 [a]1Ki 4:29-34 [b]Pr 10:1; 25:1; Ecc 1:1
1:4 [c]Pr 8:5 [d]Pr 2:10-11; 8:12
1:5 [e]Pr 9:9
1:6 [f]Ps 49:4; 78:2 [g]Nu 12:8
1:7 [h]Job 28:28; Ps 111:10; Pr 9:10; 15:33; Ecc 12:13
1:8 [i]Pr 4:1 [j]Pr 6:20
1:9 [k]Pr 4:1-9
1:10 [l]Ge 39:7 [m]Dt 13:8 [n]Pr 16:29; Eph 5:11
1:11 [o]Ps 10:8

[a]7 The Hebrew words rendered *fool* in Proverbs, and often elsewhere in the Old Testament, denote one who is morally deficient.

1:12
[a] Ps 28:1

1:15
[b] Ps 119:101
[c] Ps 1:1; Pr 4:14

1:16
[d] Pr 6:18; Isa 59:7

1:19
[e] Pr 15:27

1:20
[f] Pr 8:1; 9:1-3,13-15

1:22
[g] Pr 8:5; 9:4,16

1:24
[h] Isa 65:12; 66:4; Jer 7:13; Zec 7:11

1:26
[i] Ps 2:4
[j] Pr 6:15; 10:24

1:28
[k] 1Sa 8:18; Isa 1:15; Jer 11:11; Mic 3:4
[l] Job 27:9; Pr 8:17; Eze 8:18; Zec 7:13

1:29
[m] Job 21:14

1:30
[n] ver 25; Ps 81:11

1:31
[o] Job 4:8; Pr 14:14; Isa 3:11; Jer 6:19

12 let's swallow them alive, like the grave,[a]
and whole, like those who go down to the pit;[a]
13 we will get all sorts of valuable things
and fill our houses with plunder;
14 throw in your lot with us,
and we will share a common purse"—
15 my son, do not go along with them,
do not set foot[b] on their paths;[c]
16 for their feet rush into sin,
they are swift to shed blood.[d]
17 How useless to spread a net
in full view of all the birds!
18 These men lie in wait for their own blood;
they waylay only themselves!
19 Such is the end of all who go after ill-gotten gain;
it takes away the lives of those who get it.[e]

20 Wisdom calls aloud[f] in the street,
she raises her voice in the public squares;
21 at the head of the noisy streets[b] she cries out,
in the gateways of the city she makes her speech:

22 "How long will you simple ones[c][g] love your simple ways?
How long will mockers delight in mockery
and fools hate knowledge?
23 If you had responded to my rebuke,
I would have poured out my heart to you
and made my thoughts known to you.
24 But since you rejected me when I called[h]
and no one gave heed when I stretched out my hand,
25 since you ignored all my advice
and would not accept my rebuke,
26 I in turn will laugh[i] at your disaster;
I will mock when calamity overtakes you[j]—
27 when calamity overtakes you like a storm,
when disaster sweeps over you like a whirlwind,
when distress and trouble overwhelm you.

28 "Then they will call to me but I will not answer;[k]
they will look for me but will not find me.[l]
29 Since they hated knowledge
and did not choose to fear the LORD,[m]
30 since they would not accept my advice
and spurned my rebuke,[n]
31 they will eat the fruit of their ways
and be filled with the fruit of their schemes.[o]

a *12* Hebrew *Sheol* b *21* Hebrew; Septuagint / *on the tops of the walls* c *22* The Hebrew word rendered *simple* in Proverbs generally denotes one without moral direction and inclined to evil.

[32]For the waywardness of the simple will kill them,
and the complacency of fools will destroy them;[a]
[33]but whoever listens to me will live in safety[b]
and be at ease, without fear of harm."[c]

Chapter 2 Theme ____________________

2 My son, if you accept my words
and store up my commands within you,
[2]turning your ear to wisdom
and applying your heart to understanding,[d]
[3]and if you call out for insight
and cry aloud for understanding,
[4]and if you look for it as for silver
and search for it as for hidden treasure,[e]
[5]then you will understand the fear of the LORD
and find the knowledge of God.[f]
[6]For the LORD gives wisdom,[g]
and from his mouth come knowledge and
understanding.
[7]He holds victory in store for the upright,
he is a shield[h] to those whose walk is blameless,[i]
[8]for he guards the course of the just
and protects the way of his faithful ones.[j]

[9]Then you will understand what is right and just
and fair—every good path.
[10]For wisdom will enter your heart,[k]
and knowledge will be pleasant to your soul.
[11]Discretion will protect you,
and understanding will guard you.[l]

[12]Wisdom will save you from the ways of wicked men,
from men whose words are perverse,
[13]who leave the straight paths
to walk in dark ways,[m]
[14]who delight in doing wrong
and rejoice in the perverseness of evil,[n]
[15]whose paths are crooked[o]
and who are devious in their ways.[p]

[16]It will save you also from the adulteress,[q]
from the wayward wife with her seductive words,
[17]who has left the partner of her youth
and ignored the covenant she made before God.[a r]
[18]For her house leads down to death
and her paths to the spirits of the dead.[s]

a 17 *Or covenant of her God*

1:32 [a]Jer 2:19
1:33 [b]Ps 25:12; Pr 3:23 [c]Ps 112:8
2:2 [d]Pr 22:17
2:4 [e]Job 3:21; Pr 3:14; Mt 13:44
2:5 [f]Pr 1:7
2:6 [g]1Ki 3:9,12; Jas 1:5
2:7 [h]Pr 30:5-6 [i]Ps 84:11
2:8 [j]1Sa 2:9; Ps 66:9
2:10 [k]Pr 14:33
2:11 [l]Pr 4:6; 6:22
2:13 [m]Pr 4:19; Jn 3:19
2:14 [n]Pr 10:23; Jer 11:15
2:15 [o]Ps 125:5 [p]Pr 21:8
2:16 [q]Pr 5:1-6; 6:20-29; 7:5-27
2:17 [r]Mal 2:14
2:18 [s]Pr 7:27

19 None who go to her return
or attain the paths of life.[a]

20 Thus you will walk in the ways of good men
and keep to the paths of the righteous.
21 For the upright will live in the land,[b]
and the blameless will remain in it;
22 but the wicked will be cut off from the land,[c]
and the unfaithful will be torn from it.[d]

Chapter 3 Theme ______________________________

3

My son, do not forget my teaching,[e]
but keep my commands in your heart,
2 for they will prolong your life many years[f]
and bring you prosperity.

3 Let love and faithfulness never leave you;
bind them around your neck,
write them on the tablet of your heart.[g]
4 Then you will win favor and a good name
in the sight of God and man.[h]

5 Trust in the LORD[i] with all your heart
and lean not on your own understanding;
6 in all your ways acknowledge him,
and he will make your paths[j] straight.[a][k]

7 Do not be wise in your own eyes;[l]
fear the LORD and shun evil.[m]
8 This will bring health to your body[n]
and nourishment to your bones.[o]

9 Honor the LORD with your wealth,
with the firstfruits[p] of all your crops;
10 then your barns will be filled[q] to overflowing,
and your vats will brim over with new wine.[r]

11 My son, do not despise the LORD's discipline[s]
and do not resent his rebuke,
12 because the LORD disciplines those he loves,[t]
as a father[b] the son he delights in.[u]

13 Blessed is the man who finds wisdom,
the man who gains understanding,
14 for she is more profitable than silver
and yields better returns than gold.[v]
15 She is more precious than rubies;[w]
nothing you desire can compare with her.[x]

2:19 [a] Ecc 7:26
2:21 [b] Ps 37:29
2:22 [c] Job 18:17; Ps 37:38 [d] Dt 28:63; Pr 10:30
3:1 [e] Pr 4:5
3:2 [f] Pr 4:10
3:3 [g] Ex 13:9; Pr 6:21; 7:3; 2Co 3:3
3:4 [h] 1Sa 2:26; Lk 2:52
3:5 [i] Ps 37:3,5
3:6 [j] 1Ch 28:9 [k] Pr 16:3; Isa 45:13
3:7 [l] Ro 12:16 [m] Job 1:1; Pr 16:6
3:8 [n] Pr 4:22 [o] Job 21:24
3:9 [p] Ex 22:29; 23:19; Dt 26:1-15
3:10 [q] Dt 28:8 [r] Joel 2:24
3:11 [s] Job 5:17
3:12 [t] Pr 13:24; Rev 3:19 [u] Dt 8:5; Heb 12:5-6*
3:14 [v] Job 28:15; Pr 8:19; 16:16
3:15 [w] Job 28:18 [x] Pr 8:11

[a] 6 Or *will direct your paths* [b] 12 Hebrew; Septuagint / *and he punishes*

16Long life is in her right hand;
in her left hand are riches and honor.[a]
17Her ways are pleasant ways,
and all her paths are peace.[b]
18She is a tree of life[c] to those who embrace her;
those who lay hold of her will be blessed.

19By wisdom the LORD laid the earth's foundations,[d]
by understanding he set the heavens[e] in place;
20by his knowledge the deeps were divided,
and the clouds let drop the dew.

21My son, preserve sound judgment and discernment,
do not let them out of your sight;[f]
22they will be life for you,
an ornament to grace your neck.[g]
23Then you will go on your way in safety,
and your foot will not stumble;[h]
24when you lie down,[i] you will not be afraid;
when you lie down, your sleep[j] will be sweet.
25Have no fear of sudden disaster
or of the ruin that overtakes the wicked,
26for the LORD will be your confidence
and will keep your foot[k] from being snared.

27Do not withhold good from those who deserve it,
when it is in your power to act.
28Do not say to your neighbor,
"Come back later; I'll give it tomorrow"—
when you now have it with you.[l]
29Do not plot harm against your neighbor,
who lives trustfully near you.
30Do not accuse a man for no reason—
when he has done you no harm.

31Do not envy[m] a violent man
or choose any of his ways,
32for the LORD detests a perverse man[n]
but takes the upright into his confidence.[o]

33The LORD's curse[p] is on the house of the wicked,[q]
but he blesses the home of the righteous.[r]
34He mocks proud mockers
but gives grace to the humble.[s]
35The wise inherit honor,
but fools he holds up to shame.

3:16 [a]Pr 8:18
3:17 [b]Pr 16:7; Mt 11:28-30
3:18 [c]Ge 2:9; Pr 11:30; Rev 2:7
3:19 [d]Ps 104:24 [e]Pr 8:27-29
3:21 [f]Pr 4:20-22
3:22 [g]Pr 1:8-9
3:23 [h]Ps 37:24; Pr 4:12
3:24 [i]Lev 26:6; Ps 3:5 [j]Job 11:18
3:26 [k]1Sa 2:9
3:28 [l]Lev 19:13; Dt 24:15
3:31 [m]Ps 37:1; Pr 24:1-2
3:32 [n]Pr 11:20 [o]Job 29:4; Ps 25:14
3:33 [p]Dt 11:28; Mal 2:2 [q]Zec 5:4 [r]Ps 1:3
3:34 [s]Jas 4:6*; 1Pe 5:5*

Chapter 4 Theme ______________________________

4

Listen, my sons,[a] to a father's instruction;
pay attention and gain understanding.
2 I give you sound learning,
so do not forsake my teaching.
3 When I was a boy in my father's house,
still tender, and an only child of my mother,
4 he taught me and said,
"Lay hold of my words with all your heart;
keep my commands and you will live.[b]
5 Get wisdom,[c] get understanding;
do not forget my words or swerve from them.
6 Do not forsake wisdom, and she will protect you;[d]
love her, and she will watch over you.
7 Wisdom is supreme; therefore get wisdom.
Though it cost all[e] you have,[a] get understanding.[f]
8 Esteem her, and she will exalt you;
embrace her, and she will honor you.[g]
9 She will set a garland of grace on your head
and present you with a crown of splendor.[h]"

10 Listen, my son, accept what I say,
and the years of your life will be many.[i]
11 I guide[j] you in the way of wisdom
and lead you along straight paths.
12 When you walk, your steps will not be hampered;
when you run, you will not stumble.[k]
13 Hold on to instruction, do not let it go;
guard it well, for it is your life.[l]
14 Do not set foot on the path of the wicked
or walk in the way of evil men.[m]
15 Avoid it, do not travel on it;
turn from it and go on your way.
16 For they cannot sleep till they do evil;[n]
they are robbed of slumber till they make someone fall.
17 They eat the bread of wickedness
and drink the wine of violence.

18 The path of the righteous[o] is like the first gleam of dawn,
shining ever brighter till the full light of day.[p]
19 But the way of the wicked is like deep darkness;[q]
they do not know what makes them stumble.

20 My son, pay attention to what I say;
listen closely to my words.[r]

4:1 [a] Pr 1:8
4:4 [b] Pr 7:2
4:5 [c] Pr 16:16
4:6 [d] 2Th 2:10
4:7 [e] Mt 13:44-46 [f] Pr 23:23
4:8 [g] 1Sa 2:30; Pr 3:18
4:9 [h] Pr 1:8-9
4:10 [i] Pr 3:2
4:11 [j] 1Sa 12:23
4:12 [k] Job 18:7; Pr 3:23
4:13 [l] Pr 3:22
4:14 [m] Ps 1:1; Pr 1:15
4:16 [n] Ps 36:4; Mic 2:1
4:18 [o] Isa 26:7 [p] 2Sa 23:4; Da 12:3; Mt 5:14; Php 2:15
4:19 [q] Job 18:5; Pr 2:13; Isa 59:9-10; Jn 12:35
4:20 [r] Pr 5:1

[a] 7 Or *Whatever else you get*

21 Do not let them out of your sight,[a]
keep them within your heart;
22 for they are life to those who find them
and health to a man's whole body.[b]
23 Above all else, guard your heart,
for it is the wellspring of life.[c]
24 Put away perversity from your mouth;
keep corrupt talk far from your lips.
25 Let your eyes look straight ahead,
fix your gaze directly before you.
26 Make level[a] paths for your feet[d]
and take only ways that are firm.
27 Do not swerve to the right or the left;[e]
keep your foot from evil.

Chapter 5 Theme ____________________

5 My son, pay attention to my wisdom,
listen well to my words[f] of insight,
2 that you may maintain discretion
and your lips may preserve knowledge.
3 For the lips of an adulteress drip honey,
and her speech is smoother than oil;[g]
4 but in the end she is bitter as gall,[h]
sharp as a double-edged sword.
5 Her feet go down to death;
her steps lead straight to the grave.[b][i]
6 She gives no thought to the way of life;
her paths are crooked, but she knows it not.[j]

7 Now then, my sons, listen[k] to me;
do not turn aside from what I say.
8 Keep to a path far from her,[l]
do not go near the door of her house,
9 lest you give your best strength to others
and your years to one who is cruel,
10 lest strangers feast on your wealth
and your toil enrich another man's house.
11 At the end of your life you will groan,
when your flesh and body are spent.
12 You will say, "How I hated discipline!
How my heart spurned correction![m]
13 I would not obey my teachers
or listen to my instructors.
14 I have come to the brink of utter ruin
in the midst of the whole assembly."

[a] 26 Or *Consider the* [b] 5 Hebrew *Sheol*

4:21 [a] Pr 3:21; 7:1-2
4:22 [b] Pr 3:8; 12:18
4:23 [c] Mt 12:34; Lk 6:45
4:26 [d] Heb 12:13*
4:27 [e] Dt 5:32; 28:14
5:1 [f] Pr 4:20; 22:17
5:3 [g] Ps 55:21; Pr 2:16; 7:5
5:4 [h] Ecc 7:26
5:5 [i] Pr 7:26-27
5:6 [j] Pr 30:20
5:7 [k] Pr 7:24
5:8 [l] Pr 7:1-27
5:12 [m] Pr 1:29; 12:1

15 Drink water from your own cistern,
running water from your own well.
16 Should your springs overflow in the streets,
your streams of water in the public squares?
17 Let them be yours alone,
never to be shared with strangers.
18 May your fountain[a] be blessed,
and may you rejoice in the wife of your youth.[b]
19 A loving doe, a graceful deer[c]—
may her breasts satisfy you always,
may you ever be captivated by her love.
20 Why be captivated, my son, by an adulteress?
Why embrace the bosom of another man's wife?

21 For a man's ways are in full view[d] of the LORD,
and he examines all his paths.[e]
22 The evil deeds of a wicked man ensnare him;[f]
the cords of his sin hold him fast.[g]
23 He will die for lack of discipline,[h]
led astray by his own great folly.

Chapter 6 Theme ________________________________

6 My son, if you have put up security for your neighbor,[i]
if you have struck hands in pledge[j] for another,
2 if you have been trapped by what you said,
ensnared by the words of your mouth,
3 then do this, my son, to free yourself,
since you have fallen into your neighbor's hands:
Go and humble yourself;
press your plea with your neighbor!
4 Allow no sleep to your eyes,
no slumber to your eyelids.[k]
5 Free yourself, like a gazelle from the hand of the hunter,
like a bird from the snare of the fowler.[l]

6 Go to the ant, you sluggard;[m]
consider its ways and be wise!
7 It has no commander,
no overseer or ruler,
8 yet it stores its provisions in summer
and gathers its food at harvest.[n]

9 How long will you lie there, you sluggard?[o]
When will you get up from your sleep?
10 A little sleep, a little slumber,
a little folding of the hands to rest[p]—

5:18 [a] SS 4:12-15 [b] Ecc 9:9; Mal 2:14
5:19 [c] SS 2:9; 4:5
5:21 [d] Ps 119:168; Hos 7:2 [e] Job 14:16; Job 31:4; 34:21; Pr 15:3; Jer 16:17; 32:19; Heb 4:13
5:22 [f] Ps 9:16 [g] Nu 32:23; Ps 7:15-16; Pr 1:31-32
5:23 [h] Job 4:21; 36:12
6:1 [i] Pr 17:18 [j] Pr 11:15; 22:26-27
6:4 [k] Ps 132:4
6:5 [l] Ps 91:3
6:6 [m] Pr 20:4
6:8 [n] Pr 10:4
6:9 [o] Pr 24:30-34
6:10 [p] Pr 24:33

11and poverty[a] will come on you like a bandit
and scarcity like an armed man.[a]

12A scoundrel and villain,
who goes about with a corrupt mouth,
13 who winks with his eye,[b]
signals with his feet
and motions with his fingers,
14 who plots evil[c] with deceit in his heart—
he always stirs up dissension.[d]
15Therefore disaster will overtake him in an instant;
he will suddenly be destroyed—without remedy.[e]

16There are six things the LORD hates,
seven that are detestable to him:
17 haughty eyes,
a lying tongue,[f]
hands that shed innocent blood,[g]
18 a heart that devises wicked schemes,
feet that are quick to rush into evil,[h]
19 a false witness[i] who pours out lies
and a man who stirs up dissension among brothers.[j]

20My son, keep your father's commands
and do not forsake your mother's teaching.[k]
21Bind them upon your heart forever;
fasten them around your neck.[l]
22When you walk, they will guide you;
when you sleep, they will watch over you;
when you awake, they will speak to you.
23For these commands are a lamp,
this teaching is a light,[m]
and the corrections of discipline
are the way to life,
24keeping you from the immoral woman,
from the smooth tongue of the wayward wife.[n]
25Do not lust in your heart after her beauty
or let her captivate you with her eyes,
26for the prostitute reduces you to a loaf of bread,
and the adulteress preys upon your very life.[o]
27Can a man scoop fire into his lap
without his clothes being burned?
28Can a man walk on hot coals
without his feet being scorched?

6:11 [a]Pr 24:30-34
6:13 [b]Ps 35:19
6:14 [c]Mic 2:1 [d]ver 16-19
6:15 [e]2Ch 36:16
6:17 [f]Ps 120:2; Pr 12:22 [g]Dt 19:10; Isa 1:15; 59:7
6:18 [h]Ge 6:5
6:19 [i]Ps 27:12 [j]ver 12-15
6:20 [k]Pr 1:8
6:21 [l]Pr 3:3; 7:1-3
6:23 [m]Ps 19:8; 119:105
6:24 [n]Pr 2:16; 7:5
6:26 [o]Pr 7:22-23; 29:3

[a] *11* Or *like a vagrant / and scarcity like a beggar*

29So is he who sleeps[a] with another man's wife;[b]
no one who touches her will go unpunished.

30Men do not despise a thief if he steals
to satisfy his hunger when he is starving.
31Yet if he is caught, he must pay sevenfold,[c]
though it costs him all the wealth of his house.
32But a man who commits adultery[d] lacks judgment;[e]
whoever does so destroys himself.
33Blows and disgrace are his lot,
and his shame will never[f] be wiped away;
34for jealousy[g] arouses a husband's fury,[h]
and he will show no mercy when he takes revenge.
35He will not accept any compensation;
he will refuse the bribe, however great it is.[i]

Chapter 7 Theme ______________________

7

My son,[j] keep my words
and store up my commands within you.
2Keep my commands and you will live;[k]
guard my teachings as the apple of your eye.
3Bind them on your fingers;
write them on the tablet of your heart.[l]
4Say to wisdom, "You are my sister,"
and call understanding your kinsman;
5they will keep you from the adulteress,
from the wayward wife with her seductive words.[m]

6At the window of my house
I looked out through the lattice.
7I saw among the simple,
I noticed among the young men,
a youth who lacked judgment.[n]
8He was going down the street near her corner,
walking along in the direction of her house
9at twilight,[o] as the day was fading,
as the dark of night set in.

10Then out came a woman to meet him,
dressed like a prostitute and with crafty intent.
11(She is loud[p] and defiant,
her feet never stay at home;
12now in the street, now in the squares,
at every corner she lurks.)[q]
13She took hold of him[r] and kissed him
and with a brazen face she said:[s]

6:29 [a]Ex 20:14 [b]Pr 2:16-19; 5:8
6:31 [c]Ex 22:1-14
6:32 [d]Ex 20:14 [e]Pr 7:7; 9:4,16
6:33 [f]Pr 5:9-14
6:34 [g]Nu 5:14 [h]Ge 34:7
6:35 [i]Job 31:9-11; SS 8:7
7:1 [j]Pr 1:8; 2:1
7:2 [k]Pr 4:4
7:3 [l]Dt 6:8; Pr 3:3
7:5 [m]ver 21; Job 31:9; Pr 2:16; 6:24
7:7 [n]Pr 1:22; 6:32
7:9 [o]Job 24:15
7:11 [p]Pr 9:13; 1Ti 5:13
7:12 [q]Pr 8:1-36; 23:26-28
7:13 [r]Ge 39:12 [s]Pr 1:20

14"I have fellowship offerings[a][a] at home;
today I fulfilled my vows.
15So I came out to meet you;
I looked for you and have found you!
16I have covered my bed
with colored linens from Egypt.
17I have perfumed my bed[b]
with myrrh,[c] aloes and cinnamon.
18Come, let's drink deep of love till morning;
let's enjoy ourselves with love![d]
19My husband is not at home;
he has gone on a long journey.
20He took his purse filled with money
and will not be home till full moon."

21With persuasive words she led him astray;
she seduced him with her smooth talk.[e]
22All at once he followed her
like an ox going to the slaughter,
like a deer[b] stepping into a noose[c][f]
23 till an arrow pierces[g] his liver,
like a bird darting into a snare,
little knowing it will cost him his life.[h]

24Now then, my sons, listen[i] to me;
pay attention to what I say.
25Do not let your heart turn to her ways
or stray into her paths.[j]
26Many are the victims she has brought down;
her slain are a mighty throng.
27Her house is a highway to the grave,[d]
leading down to the chambers of death.[k]

Chapter 8 Theme ____________________

8 Does not wisdom call out?[l]
Does not understanding raise her voice?
2On the heights along the way,
where the paths meet, she takes her stand;
3beside the gates leading into the city,
at the entrances, she cries aloud:[m]
4"To you, O men, I call out;
I raise my voice to all mankind.
5You who are simple,[n] gain prudence;[o]
you who are foolish, gain understanding.

a *14* Traditionally *peace offerings* b *22* Syriac (see also Septuagint); Hebrew *fool* c *22* The meaning of the Hebrew for this line is uncertain. d *27* Hebrew *Sheol*

7:14 *a*Lev 7:11-18
7:17 *b*Est 1:6; Isa 57:7; Eze 23:41; Am 6:4 *c*Ge 37:25
7:18 *d*Ge 39:7
7:21 *e*Pr 5:3
7:22 *f*Job 18:10
7:23 *g*Job 15:22; 16:13 *h*Pr 6:26; Ecc 7:26; 9:12
7:24 *i*Pr 1:8-9; 5:7; 8:32
7:25 *j*Pr 5:7-8
7:27 *k*Pr 2:18; 5:5; 9:18; Rev 22:15
8:1 *l*Pr 1:20; 9:3
8:3 *m*Job 29:7
8:5 *n*Pr 1:22 *o*Pr 1:4

6 Listen, for I have worthy things to say;
I open my lips to speak what is right.
7 My mouth speaks what is true,[a]
for my lips detest wickedness.
8 All the words of my mouth are just;
none of them is crooked or perverse.
9 To the discerning all of them are right;
they are faultless to those who have knowledge.
10 Choose my instruction instead of silver,
knowledge rather than choice gold,[b]
11 for wisdom is more precious[c] than rubies,
and nothing you desire can compare with her.[d]

12 "I, wisdom, dwell together with prudence;
I possess knowledge and discretion.[e]
13 To fear the LORD is to hate evil;[f]
I hate[g] pride and arrogance,
evil behavior and perverse speech.
14 Counsel and sound judgment are mine;
I have understanding and power.[h]
15 By me kings reign
and rulers[i] make laws that are just;
16 by me princes govern,
and all nobles who rule on earth.[a]
17 I love those who love me,[j]
and those who seek me find me.[k]
18 With me are riches and honor,[l]
enduring wealth and prosperity.[m]
19 My fruit is better than fine gold;
what I yield surpasses choice silver.[n]
20 I walk in the way of righteousness,
along the paths of justice,
21 bestowing wealth on those who love me
and making their treasuries full.[o]

22 "The LORD brought me forth as the first of his works,[b,c]
before his deeds of old;
23 I was appointed[d] from eternity,
from the beginning, before the world began.
24 When there were no oceans, I was given birth,
when there were no springs abounding with water;[p]
25 before the mountains were settled in place,
before the hills, I was given birth,[q]
26 before he made the earth or its fields
or any of the dust of the world.[r]

8:7 [a] Ps 37:30; Jn 8:14
8:10 [b] Pr 3:14-15
8:11 [c] Job 28:17-19 [d] Pr 3:13-15
8:12 [e] Pr 1:4
8:13 [f] Pr 16:6 [g] Jer 44:4
8:14 [h] Pr 21:22; Ecc 7:19
8:15 [i] Da 2:21; Ro 13:1
8:17 [j] 1Sa 2:30; Ps 91:14; Jn 14:21-24 [k] Pr 1:28; Jas 1:5
8:18 [l] Pr 3:16 [m] Dt 8:18; Mt 6:33
8:19 [n] Pr 3:13-14; 10:20
8:21 [o] Pr 24:4
8:24 [p] Ge 7:11
8:25 [q] Job 15:7
8:26 [r] Ps 90:2

[a] *16* Many Hebrew manuscripts and Septuagint; most Hebrew manuscripts *and nobles—all righteous rulers* [b] *22* Or *way;* or *dominion* [c] *22* Or *The LORD possessed me at the beginning of his work;* or *The LORD brought me forth at the beginning of his work* [d] *23* Or *fashioned*

27 I was there when he set the heavens in place,[a]
when he marked out the horizon on the face of the deep,
28 when he established the clouds above
and fixed securely the fountains of the deep,
29 when he gave the sea its boundary[b]
so the waters would not overstep his command,[c]
and when he marked out the foundations of the earth.[d]
30 Then I was the craftsman at his side.[e]
I was filled with delight day after day,
rejoicing always in his presence,
31 rejoicing in his whole world
and delighting in mankind.[f]

32 "Now then, my sons, listen to me;
blessed are[g] those who keep my ways.[h]
33 Listen to my instruction and be wise;
do not ignore it.
34 Blessed is the man who listens[i] to me,
watching daily at my doors,
waiting at my doorway.
35 For whoever finds me[j] finds life
and receives favor from the LORD.[k]
36 But whoever fails to find me harms himself;[l]
all who hate me love death."

Chapter 9 Theme ____________________________

9

Wisdom has built[m] her house;
she has hewn out its seven pillars.
2 She has prepared her meat and mixed her wine;
she has also set her table.[n]
3 She has sent out her maids, and she calls[o]
from the highest point of the city.[p]
4 "Let all who are simple come in here!"
she says to those who lack judgment.[q]
5 "Come, eat my food
and drink the wine I have mixed.[r]
6 Leave your simple ways and you will live;[s]
walk in the way of understanding.

7 "Whoever corrects a mocker invites insult;
whoever rebukes a wicked man incurs abuse.[t]
8 Do not rebuke a mocker[u] or he will hate you;
rebuke a wise man and he will love you.[v]
9 Instruct a wise man and he will be wiser still;
teach a righteous man and he will add to his learning.[w]

8:27 [a] Pr 3:19
8:29 [b] Ge 1:9; Job 38:10; Ps 16:6 [c] Ps 104:9 [d] Job 38:5
8:30 [e] Jn 1:1-3
8:31 [f] Ps 16:3; 104:1-30
8:32 [g] Lk 11:28 [h] Ps 119:1-2
8:34 [i] Pr 3:13,18
8:35 [j] Pr 3:13-18 [k] Pr 12:2
8:36 [l] Pr 15:32
9:1 [m] Eph 2:20-22; 1Pe 2:5
9:2 [n] Lk 14:16-23
9:3 [o] Pr 8:1-3 [p] ver 14
9:4 [q] Pr 6:32
9:5 [r] Isa 55:1
9:6 [s] Pr 8:35
9:7 [t] Pr 23:9
9:8 [u] Pr 15:12 [v] Ps 141:5
9:9 [w] Pr 1:5,7

10"The fear of the LORD[a] is the beginning of wisdom,
and knowledge of the Holy One is understanding.
11For through me your days will be many,
and years will be added to your life.[b]
12If you are wise, your wisdom will reward you;
if you are a mocker, you alone will suffer."

13The woman Folly is loud;[c]
she is undisciplined and without knowledge.[d]
14She sits at the door of her house,
on a seat at the highest point of the city,[e]
15calling out to those who pass by,
who go straight on their way.
16"Let all who are simple come in here!"
she says to those who lack judgment.
17"Stolen water is sweet;
food eaten in secret is delicious![f]"
18But little do they know that the dead are there,
that her guests are in the depths of the grave.[a][g]

Chapter 10 Theme ______________________________

10

The proverbs of Solomon:[h]

A wise son brings joy to his father,[i]
but a foolish son grief to his mother.

2Ill-gotten treasures are of no value,[j]
but righteousness delivers from death.[k]

3The LORD does not let the righteous go hungry[l]
but he thwarts the craving of the wicked.

4Lazy hands make a man poor,[m]
but diligent hands bring wealth.[n]

5He who gathers crops in summer is a wise son,
but he who sleeps during harvest is a disgraceful son.

6Blessings crown the head of the righteous,
but violence overwhelms the mouth of the wicked.[b][o]

7The memory of the righteous[p] will be a blessing,
but the name of the wicked[q] will rot.[r]

8The wise in heart accept commands,
but a chattering fool comes to ruin.[s]

9The man of integrity[t] walks securely,[u]
but he who takes crooked paths will be found out.[v]

9:10 [a]Job 28:28; Pr 1:7
9:11 [b]Pr 3:16; 10:27
9:13 [c]Pr 7:11 [d]Pr 5:6
9:14 [e]ver 3
9:17 [f]Pr 20:17
9:18 [g]Pr 2:18; 7:26-27
10:1 [h]Pr 1:1 [i]Pr 15:20; 29:3
10:2 [j]Pr 21:6 [k]Pr 11:4,19
10:3 [l]Mt 6:25-34
10:4 [m]Pr 19:15 [n]Pr 12:24; 13:4; 21:5
10:6 [o]ver 8,11,14
10:7 [p]Ps 112:6 [q]Ps 109:13 [r]Ps 9:6
10:8 [s]Mt 7:24-27
10:9 [t]Isa 33:15 [u]Ps 23:4 [v]Pr 28:18

[a] *18* Hebrew *Sheol* [b] *6* Or *but the mouth of the wicked conceals violence*; also in verse 11

10 He who winks maliciously[a] causes grief,
and a chattering fool comes to ruin.

11 The mouth of the righteous is a fountain of life,[b]
but violence overwhelms the mouth of the wicked.[c]

12 Hatred stirs up dissension,
but love covers over all wrongs.[d]

13 Wisdom is found on the lips of the discerning,[e]
but a rod is for the back of him who lacks judgment.[f]

14 Wise men store up knowledge,
but the mouth of a fool invites ruin.[g]

15 The wealth of the rich is their fortified city,[h]
but poverty is the ruin of the poor.[i]

16 The wages of the righteous bring them life,
but the income of the wicked brings them punishment.[j]

17 He who heeds discipline shows the way to life,[k]
but whoever ignores correction leads others astray.

18 He who conceals his hatred has lying lips,
and whoever spreads slander is a fool.

19 When words are many, sin is not absent,
but he who holds his tongue is wise.[l]

20 The tongue of the righteous is choice silver,
but the heart of the wicked is of little value.

21 The lips of the righteous nourish many,
but fools die for lack of judgment.[m]

22 The blessing of the LORD brings wealth,[n]
and he adds no trouble to it.

23 A fool finds pleasure in evil conduct,[o]
but a man of understanding delights in wisdom.

24 What the wicked dreads[p] will overtake him;
what the righteous desire will be granted.[q]

25 When the storm has swept by, the wicked are gone,
but the righteous stand firm[r] forever.[s]

26 As vinegar to the teeth and smoke to the eyes,
so is a sluggard to those who send him.[t]

27 The fear of the LORD adds length to life,[u]
but the years of the wicked are cut short.[v]

10:10 [a] Ps 35:19
10:11 [b] Ps 37:30; Pr 13:12,14,19 [c] ver 6
10:12 [d] Pr 17:9; 1Co 13:4-7; 1Pe 4:8
10:13 [e] ver 31 [f] Pr 26:3
10:14 [g] Pr 18:6,7
10:15 [h] Pr 18:11 [i] Pr 19:7
10:16 [j] Pr 11:18-19
10:17 [k] Pr 6:23
10:19 [l] Pr 17:28; Ecc 5:3; Jas 1:19; 3:2-12
10:21 [m] Pr 5:22-23; Hos 4:1,6,14
10:22 [n] Ge 24:35; Ps 37:22
10:23 [o] Pr 2:14; 15:21
10:24 [p] Isa 66:4 [q] Ps 145:17-19; Mt 5:6; 1Jn 5:14-15
10:25 [r] Ps 15:5 [s] Pr 12:3,7; Mt 7:24-27
10:26 [t] Pr 26:6
10:27 [u] Pr 9:10-11 [v] Job 15:32

28 The prospect of the righteous is joy,
but the hopes of the wicked come to nothing.[a]

29 The way of the LORD is a refuge for the righteous,
but it is the ruin of those who do evil.[b]

30 The righteous will never be uprooted,
but the wicked will not remain in the land.[c]

31 The mouth of the righteous brings forth wisdom,[d]
but a perverse tongue will be cut out.

32 The lips of the righteous know what is fitting,[e]
but the mouth of the wicked only what is perverse.

Chapter 11 Theme ____________________________

11 The LORD abhors dishonest scales,[f]
but accurate weights are his delight.[g]

2 When pride comes, then comes disgrace,[h]
but with humility comes wisdom.[i]

3 The integrity of the upright guides them,
but the unfaithful are destroyed by their duplicity.[j]

4 Wealth is worthless in the day of wrath,[k]
but righteousness delivers from death.[l]

5 The righteousness of the blameless makes a straight way
for them,
but the wicked are brought down by their own
wickedness.[m]

6 The righteousness of the upright delivers them,
but the unfaithful are trapped by evil desires.

7 When a wicked man dies, his hope perishes;
all he expected from his power comes to nothing.[n]

8 The righteous man is rescued from trouble,
and it comes on the wicked instead.[o]

9 With his mouth the godless destroys his neighbor,
but through knowledge the righteous escape.

10 When the righteous prosper, the city rejoices;[p]
when the wicked perish, there are shouts of joy.

11 Through the blessing of the upright a city is exalted,
but by the mouth of the wicked it is destroyed.[q]

12 A man who lacks judgment derides his neighbor,[r]
but a man of understanding holds his tongue.

10:28 [a] Job 8:13; Pr 11:7
10:29 [b] Pr 21:15
10:30 [c] Ps 37:9,28-29; Pr 2:20-22
10:31 [d] Ps 37:30
10:32 [e] Ecc 10:12
11:1 [f] Lev 19:36; Dt 25:13-16; Pr 20:10,23 [g] Pr 16:11
11:2 [h] Pr 16:18 [i] Pr 18:12; 29:23
11:3 [j] Pr 13:6
11:4 [k] Eze 7:19; Zep 1:18 [l] Ge 7:1; Pr 10:2
11:5 [m] Pr 5:21-23
11:7 [n] Pr 10:28
11:8 [o] Pr 21:18
11:10 [p] Pr 28:12
11:11 [q] Pr 29:8
11:12 [r] Pr 14:21

13 A gossip betrays a confidence,[a]
but a trustworthy man keeps a secret.

14 For lack of guidance a nation falls,[b]
but many advisers make victory sure.[c]

15 He who puts up security[d] for another will surely suffer,
but whoever refuses to strike hands in pledge is safe.

16 A kindhearted woman gains respect,[e]
but ruthless men gain only wealth.

17 A kind man benefits himself,
but a cruel man brings trouble on himself.

18 The wicked man earns deceptive wages,
but he who sows righteousness reaps a sure reward.[f]

19 The truly righteous man attains life,
but he who pursues evil goes to his death.

20 The LORD detests men of perverse heart
but he delights in those whose ways are blameless.[g]

21 Be sure of this: The wicked will not go unpunished,
but those who are righteous will go free.[h]

22 Like a gold ring in a pig's snout
is a beautiful woman who shows no discretion.

23 The desire of the righteous ends only in good,
but the hope of the wicked only in wrath.

24 One man gives freely, yet gains even more;
another withholds unduly, but comes to poverty.

25 A generous man will prosper;
he who refreshes others will himself be refreshed.[i]

26 People curse the man who hoards grain,
but blessing crowns him who is willing to sell.

27 He who seeks good finds goodwill,
but evil comes to him who searches for it.[j]

28 Whoever trusts in his riches will fall,[k]
but the righteous will thrive like a green leaf.[l]

29 He who brings trouble on his family will inherit
only wind,
and the fool will be servant to the wise.[m]

30 The fruit of the righteous is a tree of life,[n]
and he who wins souls is wise.

11:13
[a] Lev 19:16; Pr 20:19; 1Ti 5:13

11:14
[b] Pr 20:18
[c] Pr 15:22; 24:6

11:15
[d] Pr 6:1

11:16
[e] Pr 31:31

11:18
[f] Hos 10:12-13

11:20
[g] 1Ch 29:17; Ps 119:1; Pr 12:2,22

11:21
[h] Pr 16:5

11:25
[i] Mt 5:7; 2Co 9:6-9

11:27
[j] Est 7:10; Ps 7:15-16

11:28
[k] Job 31:24-28; Ps 49:6; 52:7; Mk 10:25; 1Ti 6:17
[l] Ps 1:3; 92:12-14; Jer 17:8

11:29
[m] Pr 14:19

11:30
[n] Jas 5:20

31 If the righteous receive their due[a] on earth,
how much more the ungodly and the sinner!

Chapter 12 Theme ______________________

12

Whoever loves discipline loves knowledge,
but he who hates correction is stupid.[b]

2 A good man obtains favor from the LORD,
but the LORD condemns a crafty man.

3 A man cannot be established through wickedness,
but the righteous cannot be uprooted.[c]

4 A wife of noble character is her husband's crown,
but a disgraceful wife is like decay in his bones.[d]

5 The plans of the righteous are just,
but the advice of the wicked is deceitful.

6 The words of the wicked lie in wait for blood,
but the speech of the upright rescues them.[e]

7 Wicked men are overthrown and are no more,[f]
but the house of the righteous stands firm.[g]

8 A man is praised according to his wisdom,
but men with warped minds are despised.

9 Better to be a nobody and yet have a servant
than pretend to be somebody and have no food.

10 A righteous man cares for the needs of his animal,
but the kindest acts of the wicked are cruel.

11 He who works his land will have abundant food,
but he who chases fantasies lacks judgment.[h]

12 The wicked desire the plunder of evil men,
but the root of the righteous flourishes.

13 An evil man is trapped by his sinful talk,[i]
but a righteous man escapes trouble.[j]

14 From the fruit of his lips a man is filled with good things[k]
as surely as the work of his hands rewards him.[l]

15 The way of a fool seems right to him,[m]
but a wise man listens to advice.

16 A fool shows his annoyance at once,
but a prudent man overlooks an insult.[n]

17 A truthful witness gives honest testimony,
but a false witness tells lies.[o]

11:31 [a] Pr 13:21; Jer 25:29; 1Pe 4:18
12:1 [b] Pr 9:7-9; 15:5,10,12,32
12:3 [c] Pr 10:25
12:4 [d] Pr 14:30
12:6 [e] Pr 14:3
12:7 [f] Ps 37:36 [g] Pr 10:25
12:11 [h] Pr 28:19
12:13 [i] Pr 18:7 [j] Pr 21:23; 2Pe 2:9
12:14 [k] Pr 13:2; 15:23; 18:20 [l] Isa 3:10-11
12:15 [m] Pr 14:12; 16:2,25; Lk 18:11
12:16 [n] Pr 29:11
12:17 [o] Pr 14:5,25

[18]Reckless words pierce like a sword,[a]
but the tongue of the wise brings healing.[b]

[19]Truthful lips endure forever,
but a lying tongue lasts only a moment.

[20]There is deceit in the hearts of those who plot evil,
but joy for those who promote peace.

[21]No harm befalls the righteous,[c]
but the wicked have their fill of trouble.

[22]The LORD detests lying lips,[d]
but he delights in men who are truthful.[e]

[23]A prudent man keeps his knowledge to himself,[f]
but the heart of fools blurts out folly.

[24]Diligent hands will rule,
but laziness ends in slave labor.[g]

[25]An anxious heart weighs a man down,[h]
but a kind word cheers him up.

[26]A righteous man is cautious in friendship,[a]
but the way of the wicked leads them astray.

[27]The lazy man does not roast[b] his game,
but the diligent man prizes his possessions.

[28]In the way of righteousness there is life;[i]
along that path is immortality.

Chapter 13 Theme ____________________

13 A wise son heeds his father's instruction,
but a mocker does not listen to rebuke.[j]

[2]From the fruit of his lips a man enjoys good things,[k]
but the unfaithful have a craving for violence.

[3]He who guards his lips[l] guards his life,[m]
but he who speaks rashly will come to ruin.[n]

[4]The sluggard craves and gets nothing,
but the desires of the diligent are fully satisfied.

[5]The righteous hate what is false,
but the wicked bring shame and disgrace.

[6]Righteousness guards the man of integrity,
but wickedness overthrows the sinner.[o]

[a]26 Or *man is a guide to his neighbor* [b]27 The meaning of the Hebrew for this word is uncertain.

12:18 [a]Ps 57:4 [b]Pr 15:4
12:21 [c]Ps 91:10
12:22 [d]Pr 6:17; Rev 22:15 [e]Pr 11:20
12:23 [f]Pr 10:14; 13:16
12:24 [g]Pr 10:4
12:25 [h]Pr 15:13; Isa 50:4
12:28 [i]Dt 30:15
13:1 [j]Pr 10:1
13:2 [k]Pr 12:14
13:3 [l]Jas 3:2 [m]Pr 21:23 [n]Pr 18:7,20-21
13:6 [o]Pr 11:3,5

13:7 [a]2Co 6:10

7 One man pretends to be rich, yet has nothing;
another pretends to be poor, yet has great wealth.[a]

8 A man's riches may ransom his life,
but a poor man hears no threat.

13:9 [b]Job 18:5; Pr 4:18-19; 24:20

9 The light of the righteous shines brightly,
but the lamp of the wicked is snuffed out.[b]

10 Pride only breeds quarrels,
but wisdom is found in those who take advice.

13:11 [c]Pr 10:2

11 Dishonest money dwindles away,[c]
but he who gathers money little by little makes it grow.

12 Hope deferred makes the heart sick,
but a longing fulfilled is a tree of life.

13:13 [d]Nu 15:31; 2Ch 36:16

13 He who scorns instruction will pay for it,[d]
but he who respects a command is rewarded.

13:14 [e]Pr 10:11 [f]Pr 14:27

14 The teaching of the wise is a fountain of life,[e]
turning a man from the snares of death.[f]

15 Good understanding wins favor,
but the way of the unfaithful is hard.[a]

13:16 [g]Pr 12:23

16 Every prudent man acts out of knowledge,
but a fool exposes his folly.[g]

13:17 [h]Pr 25:13

17 A wicked messenger falls into trouble,
but a trustworthy envoy brings healing.[h]

13:18 [i]Pr 15:5,31-32

18 He who ignores discipline comes to poverty and shame,
but whoever heeds correction is honored.[i]

19 A longing fulfilled is sweet to the soul,
but fools detest turning from evil.

13:20 [j]Pr 15:31

20 He who walks with the wise grows wise,
but a companion of fools suffers harm.[j]

13:21 [k]Ps 32:10

21 Misfortune pursues the sinner,
but prosperity is the reward of the righteous.[k]

13:22 [l]Job 27:17; Ecc 2:26

22 A good man leaves an inheritance for his children's
children,
but a sinner's wealth is stored up for the righteous.[l]

23 A poor man's field may produce abundant food,
but injustice sweeps it away.

[a] *15* Or *unfaithful does not endure*

[24]He who spares the rod hates his son,
but he who loves him is careful to discipline him.[a]

[25]The righteous eat to their hearts' content,
but the stomach of the wicked goes hungry.[b]

Chapter 14 Theme ______________________

14 The wise woman builds her house,[c]
but with her own hands the foolish one tears hers down.

[2]He whose walk is upright fears the LORD,
but he whose ways are devious despises him.

[3]A fool's talk brings a rod to his back,
but the lips of the wise protect them.[d]

[4]Where there are no oxen, the manger is empty,
but from the strength of an ox comes an abundant harvest.

[5]A truthful witness does not deceive,
but a false witness pours out lies.[e]

[6]The mocker seeks wisdom and finds none,
but knowledge comes easily to the discerning.

[7]Stay away from a foolish man,
for you will not find knowledge on his lips.

[8]The wisdom of the prudent is to give thought to their ways,
but the folly of fools is deception.[f]

[9]Fools mock at making amends for sin,
but goodwill is found among the upright.

[10]Each heart knows its own bitterness,
and no one else can share its joy.

[11]The house of the wicked will be destroyed,
but the tent of the upright will flourish.[g]

[12]There is a way that seems right to a man,[h]
but in the end it leads to death.[i]

[13]Even in laughter[j] the heart may ache,
and joy may end in grief.

[14]The faithless will be fully repaid for their ways,[k]
and the good man rewarded for his.[l]

[15]A simple man believes anything,
but a prudent man gives thought to his steps.

13:24 [a]Pr 19:18; 22:15; 23:13-14; 29:15,17; Heb 12:7
13:25 [b]Ps 34:10; Pr 10:3
14:1 [c]Pr 24:3
14:3 [d]Pr 12:6
14:5 [e]Pr 6:19; 12:17
14:8 [f]ver 24
14:11 [g]Pr 3:33; 12:7
14:12 [h]Pr 12:15 [i]Pr 16:25
14:13 [j]Ecc 2:2
14:14 [k]Pr 1:31 [l]Pr 12:14

14:16 [a]Pr 22:3 — 16 A wise man fears the LORD and shuns evil,[a]
but a fool is hotheaded and reckless.

17 A quick-tempered man does foolish things,[b]
14:17 [b]ver 29 — and a crafty man is hated.

18 The simple inherit folly,
but the prudent are crowned with knowledge.

14:19 [c]Pr 11:29 — 19 Evil men will bow down in the presence of the good,
and the wicked at the gates of the righteous.[c]

20 The poor are shunned even by their neighbors,
14:20 [d]Pr 19:4,7 — but the rich have many friends.[d]

21 He who despises his neighbor sins,[e]
but blessed is he who is kind to the needy.[f]

14:21 [e]Pr 11:12 [f]Ps 41:1; Pr 19:17 — 22 Do not those who plot evil go astray?
But those who plan what is good find[a] love
and faithfulness.

23 All hard work brings a profit,
14:25 [g]ver 5 — but mere talk leads only to poverty.

24 The wealth of the wise is their crown,
but the folly of fools yields folly.

14:26 [h]Pr 18:10; 19:23; Isa 33:6 — 25 A truthful witness saves lives,
but a false witness is deceitful.[g]

26 He who fears the LORD has a secure fortress,[h]
and for his children it will be a refuge.

14:27 [i]Pr 13:14 — 27 The fear of the LORD is a fountain of life,
turning a man from the snares of death.[i]

14:29 [j]Ecc 7:8-9; Jas 1:19 — 28 A large population is a king's glory,
but without subjects a prince is ruined.

29 A patient man has great understanding,
but a quick-tempered man displays folly.[j]

14:30 [k]Pr 12:4 — 30 A heart at peace gives life to the body,
but envy rots the bones.[k]

14:31 [l]Pr 17:5 — 31 He who oppresses the poor shows contempt for
their Maker,[l]
but whoever is kind to the needy honors God.

14:32 [m]Pr 6:15 [n]Job 13:15; 2Ti 4:18 — 32 When calamity comes, the wicked are brought down,[m]
but even in death the righteous have a refuge.[n]

a 22 Or *show*

[33]Wisdom reposes in the heart of the discerning[a]
and even among fools she lets herself be known.[a]

[34]Righteousness exalts a nation,[b]
but sin is a disgrace to any people.

[35]A king delights in a wise servant,
but a shameful servant incurs his wrath.[c]

Chapter 15 Theme ____________________

15 A gentle answer turns away wrath,[d]
but a harsh word stirs up anger.

[2]The tongue of the wise commends knowledge,
but the mouth of the fool gushes folly.[e]

[3]The eyes[f] of the LORD are everywhere,[g]
keeping watch on the wicked and the good.[h]

[4]The tongue that brings healing is a tree of life,
but a deceitful tongue crushes the spirit.

[5]A fool spurns his father's discipline,
but whoever heeds correction shows prudence.[i]

[6]The house of the righteous contains great treasure,[j]
but the income of the wicked brings them trouble.

[7]The lips of the wise spread knowledge;
not so the hearts of fools.

[8]The LORD detests the sacrifice of the wicked,[k]
but the prayer of the upright pleases him.[l]

[9]The LORD detests the way of the wicked
but he loves those who pursue righteousness.[m]

[10]Stern discipline awaits him who leaves the path;
he who hates correction will die.[n]

[11]Death and Destruction[b] lie open before the LORD[o]—
how much more the hearts of men![p]

[12]A mocker resents correction;[q]
he will not consult the wise.

[13]A happy heart makes the face cheerful,
but heartache crushes the spirit.[r]

[14]The discerning heart seeks knowledge,[s]
but the mouth of a fool feeds on folly.

[a] 33 Hebrew; Septuagint and Syriac / *but in the heart of fools she is not known* [b] *11* Hebrew *Sheol and Abaddon*

14:33 [a]Pr 2:6-10
14:34 [b]Pr 11:11
14:35 [c]Mt 24:45-51; 25:14-30
15:1 [d]Pr 25:15
15:2 [e]Pr 12:23
15:3 [f]2Ch 16:9 [g]Job 31:4; Heb 4:13 [h]Job 34:21; Jer 16:17
15:5 [i]Pr 13:1
15:6 [j]Pr 8:21
15:8 [k]Pr 21:27; Isa 1:11; Jer 6:20 [l]ver 29
15:9 [m]Pr 21:21; 1Ti 6:11
15:10 [n]Pr 1:31-32; 5:12
15:11 [o]Job 26:6; Ps 139:8 [p]2Ch 6:30; Ps 44:21
15:12 [q]Am 5:10
15:13 [r]Pr 12:25; 17:22; 18:14
15:14 [s]Pr 18:15

15 All the days of the oppressed are wretched,
but the cheerful heart has a continual feast.[a]

16 Better a little with the fear of the LORD
than great wealth with turmoil.[b]

17 Better a meal of vegetables where there is love
than a fattened calf with hatred.[c]

18 A hot-tempered man stirs up dissension,[d]
but a patient man calms a quarrel.[e]

19 The way of the sluggard is blocked with thorns,[f]
but the path of the upright is a highway.

20 A wise son brings joy to his father,[g]
but a foolish man despises his mother.

21 Folly delights a man who lacks judgment,[h]
but a man of understanding keeps a straight course.

22 Plans fail for lack of counsel,
but with many advisers they succeed.[i]

23 A man finds joy in giving an apt reply[j]—
and how good is a timely word![k]

24 The path of life leads upward for the wise
to keep him from going down to the grave.[a]

25 The LORD tears down the proud man's house[l]
but he keeps the widow's boundaries intact.[m]

26 The LORD detests the thoughts of the wicked,[n]
but those of the pure are pleasing to him.

27 A greedy man brings trouble to his family,
but he who hates bribes will live.[o]

28 The heart of the righteous weighs its answers,[p]
but the mouth of the wicked gushes evil.

29 The LORD is far from the wicked
but he hears the prayer of the righteous.[q]

30 A cheerful look brings joy to the heart,
and good news gives health to the bones.

31 He who listens to a life-giving rebuke
will be at home among the wise.[r]

32 He who ignores discipline despises himself,[s]
but whoever heeds correction gains understanding.

15:15 [a] ver 13
15:16 [b] Ps 37:16-17; Pr 16:8; 1Ti 6:6
15:17 [c] Pr 17:1
15:18 [d] Pr 26:21 [e] Ge 13:8
15:19 [f] Pr 22:5
15:20 [g] Pr 10:1
15:21 [h] Pr 10:23
15:22 [i] Pr 11:14
15:23 [j] Pr 12:14 [k] Pr 25:11
15:25 [l] Pr 12:7 [m] Dt 19:14; Ps 68:5-6; Pr 23:10-11
15:26 [n] Pr 6:16
15:27 [o] Ex 23:8; Isa 33:15
15:28 [p] 1Pe 3:15
15:29 [q] Ps 145:18-19
15:31 [r] ver 5
15:32 [s] Pr 1:7

[a] *24* Hebrew *Sheol*

33The fear of the LORD[a] teaches a man wisdom,[a]
and humility comes before honor.[b]

15:33
[a]Pr 1:7
[b]Pr 18:12

Chapter 16 Theme ________________

16 To man belong the plans of the heart,
but from the LORD comes the reply of the tongue.[c]

2All a man's ways seem innocent to him,
but motives are weighed by the LORD.[d]

3Commit to the LORD whatever you do,
and your plans will succeed.[e]

4The LORD works out everything for his own ends[f]—
even the wicked for a day of disaster.[g]

5The LORD detests all the proud of heart.[h]
Be sure of this: They will not go unpunished.[i]

6Through love and faithfulness sin is atoned for;
through the fear of the LORD a man avoids evil.[j]

7When a man's ways are pleasing to the LORD,
he makes even his enemies live at peace with him.

8Better a little with righteousness
than much gain[k] with injustice.

9In his heart a man plans his course,
but the LORD determines his steps.[l]

10The lips of a king speak as an oracle,
and his mouth should not betray justice.

11Honest scales and balances are from the LORD;
all the weights in the bag are of his making.[m]

12Kings detest wrongdoing,
for a throne is established through righteousness.[n]

13Kings take pleasure in honest lips;
they value a man who speaks the truth.[o]

14A king's wrath is a messenger of death,[p]
but a wise man will appease it.

15When a king's face brightens, it means life;[q]
his favor is like a rain cloud in spring.

16How much better to get wisdom than gold,
to choose understanding rather than silver![r]

16:1
[c]Pr 19:21

16:2
[d]Pr 21:2

16:3
[e]Ps 37:5-6; Pr 3:5-6

16:4
[f]Isa 43:7
[g]Ro 9:22

16:5
[h]Pr 6:16
[i]Pr 11:20-21

16:6
[j]Pr 14:16

16:8
[k]Ps 37:16

16:9
[l]Jer 10:23

16:11
[m]Pr 11:1

16:12
[n]Pr 25:5

16:13
[o]Pr 14:35

16:14
[p]Pr 19:12

16:15
[q]Job 29:24

16:16
[r]Pr 8:10,19

[a]33 Or *Wisdom teaches the fear of the LORD*

16:18 [a] Pr 11:2; 18:12
16:20 [b] Ps 2:12; 34:8; Pr 19:8; Jer 17:7
16:21 [c] ver 23
16:22 [d] Pr 13:14
16:24 [e] Pr 24:13-14
16:25 [f] Pr 12:15 [g] Pr 14:12
16:27 [h] Jas 3:6
16:28 [i] Pr 15:18 [j] Pr 17:9
16:29 [k] Pr 1:10; 12:26
16:31 [l] Pr 20:29
16:33 [m] Pr 18:18; 29:26

17 The highway of the upright avoids evil;
he who guards his way guards his life.

18 Pride goes before destruction,
a haughty spirit before a fall.[a]

19 Better to be lowly in spirit and among the oppressed
than to share plunder with the proud.

20 Whoever gives heed to instruction prospers,
and blessed is he who trusts in the LORD.[b]

21 The wise in heart are called discerning,
and pleasant words promote instruction.[a][c]

22 Understanding is a fountain of life to those who have it,[d]
but folly brings punishment to fools.

23 A wise man's heart guides his mouth,
and his lips promote instruction.[b]

24 Pleasant words are a honeycomb,
sweet to the soul and healing to the bones.[e]

25 There is a way that seems right to a man,[f]
but in the end it leads to death.[g]

26 The laborer's appetite works for him;
his hunger drives him on.

27 A scoundrel plots evil,
and his speech is like a scorching fire.[h]

28 A perverse man stirs up dissension,[i]
and a gossip separates close friends.[j]

29 A violent man entices his neighbor
and leads him down a path that is not good.[k]

30 He who winks with his eye is plotting perversity;
he who purses his lips is bent on evil.

31 Gray hair is a crown of splendor;[l]
it is attained by a righteous life.

32 Better a patient man than a warrior,
a man who controls his temper than one who
takes a city.

33 The lot is cast into the lap,
but its every decision is from the LORD.[m]

[a] *21* Or *words make a man persuasive* [b] *23* Or *mouth / and makes his lips persuasive*

Chapter 17 Theme ______________________________

17

Better a dry crust with peace and quiet
than a house full of feasting,[a] with strife.[a]

2A wise servant will rule over a disgraceful son,
and will share the inheritance as one of the brothers.

3The crucible for silver and the furnace for gold,[b]
but the LORD tests the heart.[c]

4A wicked man listens to evil lips;
a liar pays attention to a malicious tongue.

5He who mocks the poor shows contempt for their Maker;[d]
whoever gloats over disaster[e] will not go unpunished.[f]

6Children's children[g] are a crown to the aged,
and parents are the pride of their children.

7Arrogant[b] lips are unsuited to a fool—
how much worse lying lips to a ruler!

8A bribe is a charm to the one who gives it;
wherever he turns, he succeeds.

9He who covers over an offense promotes love,[h]
but whoever repeats the matter separates close friends.[i]

10A rebuke impresses a man of discernment
more than a hundred lashes a fool.

11An evil man is bent only on rebellion;
a merciless official will be sent against him.

12Better to meet a bear robbed of her cubs
than a fool in his folly.

13If a man pays back evil[j] for good,
evil will never leave his house.

14Starting a quarrel is like breaching a dam;
so drop the matter before a dispute breaks out.[k]

15Acquitting the guilty and condemning the innocent[l]—
the LORD detests them both.[m]

16Of what use is money in the hand of a fool,
since he has no desire to get wisdom?[n]

17A friend loves at all times,
and a brother is born for adversity.

a *1* Hebrew *sacrifices* b *7* Or *Eloquent*

17:1 [a]Pr 15:16,17
17:3 [b]Pr 27:21 [c]1Ch 29:17; Ps 26:2; Jer 17:10
17:5 [d]Pr 14:31 [e]Job 31:29 [f]Ob 1:12
17:6 [g]Pr 13:22
17:9 [h]Pr 10:12 [i]Pr 16:28
17:13 [j]Ps 109:4-5; Jer 18:20
17:14 [k]Pr 20:3
17:15 [l]Pr 18:5 [m]Ex 23:6-7; Isa 5:23
17:16 [n]Pr 23:23

18 A man lacking in judgment strikes hands in pledge
and puts up security for his neighbor.[a]

19 He who loves a quarrel loves sin;
he who builds a high gate invites destruction.

20 A man of perverse heart does not prosper;
he whose tongue is deceitful falls into trouble.

21 To have a fool for a son brings grief;
there is no joy for the father of a fool.[b]

22 A cheerful heart is good medicine,
but a crushed spirit dries up the bones.[c]

23 A wicked man accepts a bribe[d] in secret
to pervert the course of justice.

24 A discerning man keeps wisdom in view,
but a fool's eyes[e] wander to the ends of the earth.

25 A foolish son brings grief to his father
and bitterness to the one who bore him.[f]

26 It is not good to punish an innocent man,[g]
or to flog officials for their integrity.

27 A man of knowledge uses words with restraint,
and a man of understanding is even-tempered.[h]

28 Even a fool is thought wise if he keeps silent,
and discerning if he holds his tongue.[i]

Chapter 18 Theme ________________________________

18 An unfriendly man pursues selfish ends;
he defies all sound judgment.

2 A fool finds no pleasure in understanding
but delights in airing his own opinions.[j]

3 When wickedness comes, so does contempt,
and with shame comes disgrace.

4 The words of a man's mouth are deep waters,
but the fountain of wisdom is a bubbling brook.

5 It is not good to be partial to the wicked[k]
or to deprive the innocent of justice.[l]

6 A fool's lips bring him strife,
and his mouth invites a beating.

7 A fool's mouth is his undoing,
and his lips are a snare[m] to his soul.[n]

17:18 [a] Pr 6:1-5; 11:15; 22:26-27
17:21 [b] Pr 10:1
17:22 [c] Ps 22:15; Pr 15:13
17:23 [d] Ex 23:8
17:24 [e] Ecc 2:14
17:25 [f] Pr 10:1
17:26 [g] Pr 18:5
17:27 [h] Pr 14:29; Jas 1:19
17:28 [i] Job 13:5
18:2 [j] Pr 12:23
18:5 [k] Lev 19:15; Pr 24:23-25; 28:21 [l] Ps 82:2; Pr 17:15
18:7 [m] Ps 140:9 [n] Ps 64:8; Pr 10:14; 12:13; 13:3; Ecc 10:12

[8]The words of a gossip are like choice morsels;
they go down to a man's inmost parts.[a]

[9]One who is slack in his work
is brother to one who destroys.[b]

[10]The name of the LORD is a strong tower;[c]
the righteous run to it and are safe.

[11]The wealth of the rich is their fortified city;[d]
they imagine it an unscalable wall.

[12]Before his downfall a man's heart is proud,
but humility comes before honor.[e]

[13]He who answers before listening—
that is his folly and his shame.[f]

[14]A man's spirit sustains him in sickness,
but a crushed spirit who can bear?[g]

[15]The heart of the discerning acquires knowledge;[h]
the ears of the wise seek it out.

[16]A gift[i] opens the way for the giver
and ushers him into the presence of the great.

[17]The first to present his case seems right,
till another comes forward and questions him.

[18]Casting the lot settles disputes[j]
and keeps strong opponents apart.

[19]An offended brother is more unyielding than a
fortified city,
and disputes are like the barred gates of a citadel.

[20]From the fruit of his mouth a man's stomach
is filled;
with the harvest from his lips he is satisfied.[k]

[21]The tongue has the power of life and death,
and those who love it will eat its fruit.[l]

[22]He who finds a wife finds what is good[m]
and receives favor from the LORD.[n]

[23]A poor man pleads for mercy,
but a rich man answers harshly.

[24]A man of many companions may come to ruin,
but there is a friend who sticks closer than a brother.[o]

18:8 [a]Pr 26:22
18:9 [b]Pr 28:24
18:10 [c]2Sa 22:3; Ps 61:3
18:11 [d]Pr 10:15
18:12 [e]Pr 11:2; 15:33; 16:18
18:13 [f]Pr 20:25; Jn 7:51
18:14 [g]Pr 15:13; 17:22
18:15 [h]Pr 15:14
18:16 [i]Ge 32:20
18:18 [j]Pr 16:33
18:20 [k]Pr 12:14
18:21 [l]Pr 13:2-3; Mt 12:37
18:22 [m]Pr 12:4 [n]Pr 19:14; 31:10
18:24 [o]Pr 17:17; Jn 15:13-15

Chapter 19 Theme ____________________________

19

Better a poor man whose walk is blameless
than a fool whose lips are perverse.[a]

2 It is not good to have zeal without knowledge,
nor to be hasty and miss the way.[b]

3 A man's own folly ruins his life,
yet his heart rages against the LORD.

4 Wealth brings many friends,
but a poor man's friend deserts him.[c]

5 A false witness[d] will not go unpunished,
and he who pours out lies will not go free.[e]

6 Many curry favor with a ruler,[f]
and everyone is the friend of a man who gives gifts.[g]

7 A poor man is shunned by all his relatives—
how much more do his friends avoid him!
Though he pursues them with pleading,
they are nowhere to be found.[a][h]

8 He who gets wisdom loves his own soul;
he who cherishes understanding prospers.[i]

9 A false witness will not go unpunished,
and he who pours out lies will perish.[j]

10 It is not fitting for a fool[k] to live in luxury—
how much worse for a slave to rule over princes![l]

11 A man's wisdom gives him patience;[m]
it is to his glory to overlook an offense.

12 A king's rage is like the roar of a lion,
but his favor is like dew[n] on the grass.[o]

13 A foolish son is his father's ruin,[p]
and a quarrelsome wife is like a constant dripping.[q]

14 Houses and wealth are inherited from parents,[r]
but a prudent wife is from the LORD.[s]

15 Laziness brings on deep sleep,
and the shiftless man goes hungry.[t]

16 He who obeys instructions guards his life,
but he who is contemptuous of his ways will die.[u]

19:1 [a]Pr 28:6
19:2 [b]Pr 29:20
19:4 [c]Pr 14:20
19:5 [d]Ex 23:1 [e]Dt 19:19; Pr 21:28
19:6 [f]Pr 29:26 [g]Pr 17:8; 18:16
19:7 [h]ver 4; Ps 38:11
19:8 [i]Pr 16:20
19:9 [j]ver 5
19:10 [k]Pr 26:1 [l]Pr 30:21-23; Ecc 10:5-7
19:11 [m]Pr 16:32
19:12 [n]Ps 133:3 [o]Pr 16:14-15
19:13 [p]Pr 10:1 [q]Pr 21:9
19:14 [r]2Co 12:14 [s]Pr 18:22
19:15 [t]Pr 6:9; 10:4
19:16 [u]Pr 16:17; Lk 10:28

[a] 7 The meaning of the Hebrew for this sentence is uncertain.

17He who is kind to the poor lends to the LORD,
and he will reward him for what he has done.[a]

18Discipline your son, for in that there is hope;
do not be a willing party to his death.[b]

19A hot-tempered man must pay the penalty;
if you rescue him, you will have to do it again.

20Listen to advice and accept instruction,[c]
and in the end you will be wise.[d]

21Many are the plans in a man's heart,
but it is the LORD's purpose that prevails.[e]

22What a man desires is unfailing love[a];
better to be poor than a liar.

23The fear of the LORD leads to life:
Then one rests content, untouched by trouble.[f]

24The sluggard buries his hand in the dish;
he will not even bring it back to his mouth![g]

25Flog a mocker, and the simple will learn prudence;
rebuke a discerning man, and he will gain knowledge.[h]

26He who robs his father and drives out his mother[i]
is a son who brings shame and disgrace.

27Stop listening to instruction, my son,
and you will stray from the words of knowledge.

28A corrupt witness mocks at justice,
and the mouth of the wicked gulps down evil.[j]

29Penalties are prepared for mockers,
and beatings for the backs of fools.[k]

Chapter 20 Theme ____________________

20 Wine is a mocker and beer a brawler;
whoever is led astray by them is not wise.[l]

2A king's wrath is like the roar of a lion;[m]
he who angers him forfeits his life.[n]

3It is to a man's honor to avoid strife,
but every fool is quick to quarrel.[o]

4A sluggard does not plow in season;
so at harvest time he looks but finds nothing.

19:17 [a] Mt 10:42; 2Co 9:6-8
19:18 [b] Pr 13:24; 23:13-14
19:20 [c] Pr 4:1 [d] Pr 12:15
19:21 [e] Ps 33:11; Pr 16:9; Isa 14:24,27
19:23 [f] Ps 25:13; Pr 12:21; 1Ti 4:8
19:24 [g] Pr 26:15
19:25 [h] Pr 9:9; 21:11
19:26 [i] Pr 28:24
19:28 [j] Job 15:16
19:29 [k] Pr 26:3
20:1 [l] Pr 31:4
20:2 [m] Pr 19:12 [n] Pr 8:36
20:3 [o] Pr 17:14

a 22 Or *A man's greed is his shame*

5 The purposes of a man's heart are deep waters,
but a man of understanding draws them out.

6 Many a man claims to have unfailing love,
but a faithful man who can find?[a]

7 The righteous man leads a blameless life;
blessed are his children after him.[b]

8 When a king sits on his throne to judge,
he winnows out all evil with his eyes.[c]

9 Who can say, "I have kept my heart pure;
I am clean and without sin"?[d]

10 Differing weights and differing measures—
the LORD detests them both.[e]

11 Even a child is known by his actions,
by whether his conduct is pure[f] and right.

12 Ears that hear and eyes that see—
the LORD has made them both.[g]

13 Do not love sleep or you will grow poor;[h]
stay awake and you will have food to spare.

14 "It's no good, it's no good!" says the buyer;
then off he goes and boasts about his purchase.

15 Gold there is, and rubies in abundance,
but lips that speak knowledge are a rare jewel.

16 Take the garment of one who puts up security for
a stranger;
hold it in pledge[i] if he does it for a wayward woman.[j]

17 Food gained by fraud tastes sweet to a man,[k]
but he ends up with a mouth full of gravel.

18 Make plans by seeking advice;
if you wage war, obtain guidance.[l]

19 A gossip betrays a confidence;[m]
so avoid a man who talks too much.

20 If a man curses his father or mother,[n]
his lamp will be snuffed out in pitch darkness.[o]

21 An inheritance quickly gained at the beginning
will not be blessed at the end.

22 Do not say, "I'll pay you back for this wrong!"[p]
Wait for the LORD, and he will deliver you.[q]

20:6 [a] Ps 12:1
20:7 [b] Ps 37:25-26; 112:2
20:8 [c] ver 26; Pr 25:4-5
20:9 [d] 1Ki 8:46; Ecc 7:20; 1Jn 1:8
20:10 [e] ver 23; Pr 11:1
20:11 [f] Mt 7:16
20:12 [g] Ps 94:9
20:13 [h] Pr 6:11; 19:15
20:16 [i] Ex 22:26 [j] Pr 27:13
20:17 [k] Pr 9:17
20:18 [l] Pr 11:14; 24:6
20:19 [m] Pr 11:13
20:20 [n] Pr 30:11 [o] Ex 21:17; Job 18:5
20:22 [p] Pr 24:29 [q] Ro 12:19

[23]The LORD detests differing weights,
and dishonest scales do not please him.[a]

[24]A man's steps are directed by the LORD.
How then can anyone understand his own way?[b]

[25]It is a trap for a man to dedicate something rashly
and only later to consider his vows.[c]

[26]A wise king winnows out the wicked;
he drives the threshing wheel over them.[d]

[27]The lamp of the LORD searches the spirit of a man[a];
it searches out his inmost being.

[28]Love and faithfulness keep a king safe;
through love his throne is made secure.[e]

[29]The glory of young men is their strength,
gray hair the splendor of the old.[f]

[30]Blows and wounds cleanse[g] away evil,
and beatings purge the inmost being.

Chapter 21 Theme ______________________________

21

The king's heart is in the hand of the LORD;
he directs it like a watercourse wherever he pleases.

[2]All a man's ways seem right to him,
but the LORD weighs the heart.[h]

[3]To do what is right and just
is more acceptable to the LORD than sacrifice.[i]

[4]Haughty eyes[j] and a proud heart,
the lamp of the wicked, are sin!

[5]The plans of the diligent lead to profit[k]
as surely as haste leads to poverty.

[6]A fortune made by a lying tongue
is a fleeting vapor and a deadly snare.[b] [l]

[7]The violence of the wicked will drag them away,
for they refuse to do what is right.

[8]The way of the guilty is devious,[m]
but the conduct of the innocent is upright.

[9]Better to live on a corner of the roof
than share a house with a quarrelsome wife.[n]

[a]27 Or *The spirit of man is the LORD's lamp* [b]6 Some Hebrew manuscripts, Septuagint and Vulgate; most Hebrew manuscripts *vapor for those who seek death*

20:23 [a]ver 10
20:24 [b]Jer 10:23
20:25 [c]Ecc 5:2,4-5
20:26 [d]ver 8
20:28 [e]Pr 29:14
20:29 [f]Pr 16:31
20:30 [g]Pr 22:15
21:2 [h]Pr 16:2; 24:12; Lk 16:15
21:3 [i]1Sa 15:22; Pr 15:8; Isa 1:11; Hos 6:6; Mic 6:6-8
21:4 [j]Pr 6:17
21:5 [k]Pr 10:4; 28:22
21:6 [l]2Pe 2:3
21:8 [m]Pr 2:15
21:9 [n]Pr 25:24

10 The wicked man craves evil;
his neighbor gets no mercy from him.

11 When a mocker is punished, the simple gain wisdom;
when a wise man is instructed, he gets knowledge.[a]

12 The Righteous One[a] takes note of the house of the wicked
and brings the wicked to ruin.[b]

13 If a man shuts his ears to the cry of the poor,
he too will cry out and not be answered.[c]

14 A gift given in secret soothes anger,
and a bribe concealed in the cloak pacifies great wrath.[d]

15 When justice is done, it brings joy to the righteous
but terror to evildoers.[e]

16 A man who strays from the path of understanding
comes to rest in the company of the dead.[f]

17 He who loves pleasure will become poor;
whoever loves wine and oil will never be rich.[g]

18 The wicked become a ransom[h] for the righteous,
and the unfaithful for the upright.

19 Better to live in a desert
than with a quarrelsome and ill-tempered wife.[i]

20 In the house of the wise are stores of choice food and oil,
but a foolish man devours all he has.

21 He who pursues righteousness and love
finds life, prosperity[b] and honor.[j]

22 A wise man attacks the city of the mighty[k]
and pulls down the stronghold in which they trust.

23 He who guards his mouth[l] and his tongue
keeps himself from calamity.[m]

24 The proud and arrogant[n] man—"Mocker" is his name;
he behaves with overweening pride.

25 The sluggard's craving will be the death of him,[o]
because his hands refuse to work.

26 All day long he craves for more,
but the righteous give without sparing.[p]

27 The sacrifice of the wicked is detestable[q]—
how much more so when brought with evil intent![r]

21:11 [a] Pr 19:25
21:12 [b] Pr 14:11
21:13 [c] Mt 18:30-34; Jas 2:13
21:14 [d] Pr 18:16; 19:6
21:15 [e] Pr 10:29
21:16 [f] Ps 49:14
21:17 [g] Pr 23:20-21, 29-35
21:18 [h] Pr 11:8; Isa 43:3
21:19 [i] ver 9
21:21 [j] Mt 5:6
21:22 [k] Ecc 9:15-16
21:23 [l] Jas 3:2 [m] Pr 12:13; 13:3
21:24 [n] Ps 1:1; Pr 1:22; Isa 16:6; Jer 48:29
21:25 [o] Pr 13:4
21:26 [p] Ps 37:26; Mt 5:42; Eph 4:28
21:27 [q] Isa 66:3; Jer 6:20; Am 5:22 [r] Pr 15:8

[a] *12* Or *The righteous man* [b] *21* Or *righteousness*

28 A false witness will perish,[a]
and whoever listens to him will be destroyed forever.[a]

29 A wicked man puts up a bold front,
but an upright man gives thought to his ways.

30 There is no wisdom,[b] no insight, no plan
that can succeed against the LORD.[c]

31 The horse is made ready for the day of battle,
but victory rests with the LORD.[d]

Chapter 22 Theme ______________________

22

A good name is more desirable than great riches;
to be esteemed is better than silver or gold.[e]

2 Rich and poor have this in common:
The LORD is the Maker of them all.[f]

3 A prudent man sees danger and takes refuge,[g]
but the simple keep going and suffer for it.[h]

4 Humility and the fear of the LORD
bring wealth and honor and life.

5 In the paths of the wicked lie thorns and snares,[i]
but he who guards his soul stays far from them.

6 Train[b] a child in the way he should go,[j]
and when he is old he will not turn from it.

7 The rich rule over the poor,
and the borrower is servant to the lender.

8 He who sows wickedness reaps trouble,[k]
and the rod of his fury will be destroyed.[l]

9 A generous man will himself be blessed,[m]
for he shares his food with the poor.[n]

10 Drive out the mocker, and out goes strife;
quarrels and insults are ended.[o]

11 He who loves a pure heart and whose speech is gracious
will have the king for his friend.[p]

12 The eyes of the LORD keep watch over knowledge,
but he frustrates the words of the unfaithful.

13 The sluggard says, "There is a lion outside!"[q]
or, "I will be murdered in the streets!"

[a] 28 Or / *but the words of an obedient man will live on* [b] 6 Or *Start*

21:28 [a] Pr 19:5
21:30 [b] Jer 9:23 [c] Isa 8:10; Ac 5:39
21:31 [d] Ps 3:8; 33:12-19; Isa 31:1
22:1 [e] Ecc 7:1
22:2 [f] Job 31:15
22:3 [g] Pr 14:16 [h] Pr 27:12
22:5 [i] Pr 15:19
22:6 [j] Eph 6:4
22:8 [k] Job 4:8 [l] Ps 125:3
22:9 [m] 2Co 9:6 [n] Pr 19:17
22:10 [o] Pr 18:6; 26:20
22:11 [p] Pr 16:13; Mt 5:8
22:13 [q] Pr 26:13

14 The mouth of an adulteress is a deep pit;[a]
he who is under the LORD's wrath will fall into it.[b]

15 Folly is bound up in the heart of a child,
but the rod of discipline will drive it far from him.[c]

16 He who oppresses the poor to increase his wealth
and he who gives gifts to the rich—both come
to poverty.

17 Pay attention and listen to the sayings of the wise;[d]
apply your heart to what I teach,
18 for it is pleasing when you keep them in your heart
and have all of them ready on your lips.
19 So that your trust may be in the LORD,
I teach you today, even you.
20 Have I not written thirty[a] sayings for you,
sayings of counsel and knowledge,
21 teaching you true and reliable words,[e]
so that you can give sound answers
to him who sent you?

22 Do not exploit the poor[f] because they are poor
and do not crush the needy in court,[g]
23 for the LORD will take up their case[h]
and will plunder those who plunder them.[i]

24 Do not make friends with a hot-tempered man,
do not associate with one easily angered,
25 or you may learn his ways
and get yourself ensnared.[j]

26 Do not be a man who strikes hands in pledge[k]
or puts up security for debts;
27 if you lack the means to pay,
your very bed will be snatched from under you.[l]

28 Do not move an ancient boundary stone[m]
set up by your forefathers.

29 Do you see a man skilled in his work?
He will serve[n] before kings;
he will not serve before obscure men.

Chapter 23 Theme ______________________

23 When you sit to dine with a ruler,
note well what[b] is before you,
2 and put a knife to your throat
if you are given to gluttony.

22:14 [a] Pr 2:16; 5:3-5; 7:5; 23:27 [b] Ecc 7:26
22:15 [c] Pr 13:24; 23:14
22:17 [d] Pr 5:1
22:21 [e] Lk 1:3-4; 1Pe 3:15
22:22 [f] Zec 7:10 [g] Ex 23:6; Mal 3:5
22:23 [h] Ps 12:5 [i] 1Sa 25:39; Pr 23:10-11
22:25 [j] 1Co 15:33
22:26 [k] Pr 11:15
22:27 [l] Pr 17:18
22:28 [m] Dt 19:14; Pr 23:10
22:29 [n] Ge 41:46

[a] *20* Or *not formerly written*; or *not written excellent* [b] *1* Or *who*

[3]Do not crave his delicacies,[a]
for that food is deceptive.

[4]Do not wear yourself out to get rich;
have the wisdom to show restraint.
[5]Cast but a glance at riches, and they are gone,
for they will surely sprout wings
and fly off to the sky like an eagle.[b]

[6]Do not eat the food of a stingy man,
do not crave his delicacies;[c]
[7]for he is the kind of man
who is always thinking about the cost.[a]
"Eat and drink," he says to you,
but his heart is not with you.
[8]You will vomit up the little you have eaten
and will have wasted your compliments.

[9]Do not speak to a fool,
for he will scorn the wisdom of your words.[d]

[10]Do not move an ancient boundary stone[e]
or encroach on the fields of the fatherless,
[11]for their Defender[f] is strong;
he will take up their case against you.[g]

[12]Apply your heart to instruction
and your ears to words of knowledge.

[13]Do not withhold discipline from a child;
if you punish him with the rod, he will not die.
[14]Punish him with the rod
and save his soul from death.[b]

[15]My son, if your heart is wise,
then my heart will be glad;
[16]my inmost being will rejoice
when your lips speak what is right.[h]

[17]Do not let your heart envy[i] sinners,
but always be zealous for the fear of the LORD.
[18]There is surely a future hope for you,
and your hope will not be cut off.[j]

[19]Listen, my son, and be wise,
and keep your heart on the right path.
[20]Do not join those who drink too much wine[k]
or gorge themselves on meat,

23:3 [a]ver 6-8
23:5 [b]Pr 27:24
23:6 [c]Ps 141:4
23:9 [d]Pr 1:7; 9:7; Mt 7:6
23:10 [e]Dt 19:14; Pr 22:28
23:11 [f]Job 19:25 [g]Pr 22:22-23
23:16 [h]ver 24; Pr 27:11
23:17 [i]Ps 37:1; Pr 28:14
23:18 [j]Ps 9:18; Pr 24:14,19-20
23:20 [k]Isa 5:11,22; Ro 13:13; Eph 5:18

a *7* Or *for as he thinks within himself, / so he is*; or *for as he puts on a feast, / so he is* b *14* Hebrew *Sheol*

23:21 [a] Pr 21:17
23:22 [b] Lev 19:32; Pr 1:8; 30:17; Eph 6:1-2
23:23 [c] Pr 4:7
23:24 [d] ver 15-16; Pr 10:1; 15:20
23:26 [e] Pr 3:1; 5:1-6 [f] Ps 18:21; Pr 4:4
23:27 [g] Pr 22:14
23:28 [h] Pr 7:11-12; Ecc 7:26
23:30 [i] Ps 75:8; Isa 5:11; Eph 5:18
24:1 [j] Ps 37:1; 73:3; Pr 3:31-32; 23:17-18
24:2 [k] Ps 10:7
24:3 [l] Pr 14:1
24:4 [m] Pr 8:21

21 for drunkards and gluttons become poor,[a]
and drowsiness clothes them in rags.

22 Listen to your father, who gave you life,
and do not despise your mother when she is old.[b]
23 Buy the truth and do not sell it;
get wisdom, discipline and understanding.[c]
24 The father of a righteous man has great joy;
he who has a wise son delights in him.[d]
25 May your father and mother be glad;
may she who gave you birth rejoice!

26 My son,[e] give me your heart
and let your eyes keep to my ways,[f]
27 for a prostitute is a deep pit[g]
and a wayward wife is a narrow well.
28 Like a bandit she lies in wait,[h]
and multiplies the unfaithful among men.

29 Who has woe? Who has sorrow?
Who has strife? Who has complaints?
Who has needless bruises? Who has bloodshot eyes?
30 Those who linger over wine,[i]
who go to sample bowls of mixed wine.
31 Do not gaze at wine when it is red,
when it sparkles in the cup,
when it goes down smoothly!
32 In the end it bites like a snake
and poisons like a viper.
33 Your eyes will see strange sights
and your mind imagine confusing things.
34 You will be like one sleeping on the high seas,
lying on top of the rigging.
35 "They hit me," you will say, "but I'm not hurt!
They beat me, but I don't feel it!
When will I wake up
so I can find another drink?"

Chapter 24 Theme ______________________

24

Do not envy[j] wicked men,
do not desire their company;
2 for their hearts plot violence,
and their lips talk about making trouble.[k]

3 By wisdom a house is built,[l]
and through understanding it is established;
4 through knowledge its rooms are filled
with rare and beautiful treasures.[m]

5A wise man has great power,
and a man of knowledge increases strength;
6for waging war you need guidance,
and for victory many advisers.[a]

7Wisdom is too high for a fool;
in the assembly at the gate he has nothing to say.

8He who plots evil
will be known as a schemer.
9The schemes of folly are sin,
and men detest a mocker.

10If you falter in times of trouble,
how small is your strength![b]

11Rescue those being led away to death;
hold back those staggering toward slaughter.[c]
12If you say, "But we knew nothing about this,"
does not he who weighs[d] the heart perceive it?
Does not he who guards your life know it?
Will he not repay each person according to what
he has done?[e]

13Eat honey, my son, for it is good;
honey from the comb is sweet to your taste.
14Know also that wisdom is sweet to your soul;
if you find it, there is a future hope for you,
and your hope will not be cut off.[f g]

15Do not lie in wait like an outlaw against a righteous
man's house,
do not raid his dwelling place;
16for though a righteous man falls seven times, he
rises again,
but the wicked are brought down by calamity.[h]

17Do not gloat[i] when your enemy falls;
when he stumbles, do not let your heart rejoice,[j]
18or the LORD will see and disapprove
and turn his wrath away from him.

19Do not fret[k] because of evil men
or be envious of the wicked,
20for the evil man has no future hope,
and the lamp of the wicked will be snuffed out.[l]

21Fear the LORD and the king,[m] my son,
and do not join with the rebellious,

24:6 [a]Pr 11:14; 20:18; Lk 14:31

24:10 [b]Job 4:5; Jer 51:46; Heb 12:3

24:11 [c]Ps 82:4; Isa 58:6-7

24:12 [d]Pr 21:2 [e]Job 34:11; Ps 62:12; Ro 2:6*

24:14 [f]Ps 119:103; Pr 16:24 [g]Pr 23:18

24:16 [h]Job 5:19; Ps 34:19; Mic 7:8

24:17 [i]Ob 1:12 [j]Job 31:29

24:19 [k]Ps 37:1

24:20 [l]Job 18:5; Pr 13:9; 23:17-18

24:21 [m]Ro 13:1-5; 1Pe 2:17

22 for those two will send sudden destruction upon them,
and who knows what calamities they can bring?

24:23 [a]Pr 1:6 [b]Lev 19:15 [c]Pr 28:21

23 These also are sayings of the wise:[a]

To show partiality[b] in judging is not good:[c]

24:24 [d]Pr 17:15

24 Whoever says to the guilty, "You are innocent"[d]—
peoples will curse him and nations denounce him.
25 But it will go well with those who convict the guilty,
and rich blessing will come upon them.

24:28 [e]Ps 7:4; Pr 25:18; Eph 4:25

26 An honest answer
is like a kiss on the lips.

27 Finish your outdoor work
and get your fields ready;
after that, build your house.

24:29 [f]Pr 20:22; Mt 5:38-41; Ro 12:17

28 Do not testify against your neighbor without cause,[e]
or use your lips to deceive.
29 Do not say, "I'll do to him as he has done to me;
I'll pay that man back for what he did."[f]

24:30 [g]Pr 6:6-11; 26:13-16

30 I went past the field of the sluggard,[g]
past the vineyard of the man who lacks judgment;
31 thorns had come up everywhere,
the ground was covered with weeds,
and the stone wall was in ruins.

24:33 [h]Pr 6:10

32 I applied my heart to what I observed
and learned a lesson from what I saw:
33 A little sleep, a little slumber,
a little folding of the hands to rest[h]—

24:34 [i]Pr 10:4; Ecc 10:18

34 and poverty will come on you like a bandit
and scarcity like an armed man.[a][i]

Chapter 25 Theme ________________________

25:1 [j]1Ki 4:32 [k]Pr 1:1

25 These are more proverbs[j] of Solomon, copied by the men of Hezekiah king of Judah:[k]

25:2 [l]Pr 16:10-15

2 It is the glory of God to conceal a matter;
to search out a matter is the glory of kings.[l]

3 As the heavens are high and the earth is deep,
so the hearts of kings are unsearchable.

25:5 [m]Pr 20:8 [n]2Sa 7:13 [o]Pr 16:12; 29:14

4 Remove the dross from the silver,
and out comes material for[b] the silversmith;
5 remove the wicked from the king's presence,[m]
and his throne will be established[n] through
righteousness.[o]

[a]34 Or *like a vagrant / and scarcity like a beggar* [b]4 Or *comes a vessel from*

6Do not exalt yourself in the king's presence,
and do not claim a place among great men;
7it is better for him to say to you, "Come up here,"[a]
than for him to humiliate you before a nobleman.

What you have seen with your eyes
8 do not bring[a] hastily to court,
for what will you do in the end
if your neighbor puts you to shame?[b]

9If you argue your case with a neighbor,
do not betray another man's confidence,
10or he who hears it may shame you
and you will never lose your bad reputation.

11A word aptly spoken
is like apples of gold in settings of silver.[c]
12Like an earring of gold or an ornament of fine gold
is a wise man's rebuke to a listening ear.[d]

13Like the coolness of snow at harvest time
is a trustworthy messenger to those who send him;
he refreshes the spirit of his masters.[e]

14Like clouds and wind without rain
is a man who boasts of gifts he does not give.

15Through patience a ruler can be persuaded,[f]
and a gentle tongue can break a bone.[g]

16If you find honey, eat just enough—
too much of it, and you will vomit.[h]
17Seldom set foot in your neighbor's house—
too much of you, and he will hate you.

18Like a club or a sword or a sharp arrow
is the man who gives false testimony against
his neighbor.[i]

19Like a bad tooth or a lame foot
is reliance on the unfaithful in times of trouble.

20Like one who takes away a garment on a cold day,
or like vinegar poured on soda,
is one who sings songs to a heavy heart.

21If your enemy is hungry, give him food to eat;
if he is thirsty, give him water to drink.
22In doing this, you will heap burning coals[j] on his head,
and the LORD will reward you.[k]

25:7 [a]Lk 14:7-10
25:8 [b]Mt 5:25-26
25:11 [c]ver 12; Pr 15:23
25:12 [d]ver 11; Ps 141:5; Pr 13:18; 15:31
25:13 [e]Pr 10:26; 13:17
25:15 [f]Ecc 10:4 [g]Pr 15:1
25:16 [h]ver 27
25:18 [i]Ps 57:4; Pr 12:18
25:22 [j]Ps 18:8 [k]2Sa 16:12; 2Ch 28:15; Mt 5:44; Ro 12:20*

[a]7,8 Or *nobleman / on whom you had set your eyes. /* [8]*Do not go*

25:24
[a]Pr 21:9

25:25
[b]Pr 15:30

25:27
[c]ver 16
[d]Pr 27:2; Mt 23:12

26:1
[e]1Sa 12:17
[f]ver 8; Pr 19:10

26:2
[g]Nu 23:8; Dt 23:5

26:3
[h]Ps 32:9
[i]Pr 10:13

26:4
[j]ver 5; Isa 36:21

26:5
[k]ver 4; Pr 3:7

26:6
[l]Pr 10:26

26:7
[m]ver 9

26:8
[n]ver 1

26:9
[o]ver 7

26:11
[p]2Pe 2:22*
[q]Ex 8:15; Ps 85:8

26:12
[r]Pr 3:7
[s]Pr 29:20

23 As a north wind brings rain,
so a sly tongue brings angry looks.

24 Better to live on a corner of the roof
than share a house with a quarrelsome wife.[a]

25 Like cold water to a weary soul
is good news from a distant land.[b]

26 Like a muddied spring or a polluted well
is a righteous man who gives way to the wicked.

27 It is not good to eat too much honey,[c]
nor is it honorable to seek one's own honor.[d]

28 Like a city whose walls are broken down
is a man who lacks self-control.

Chapter 26 Theme ____________________

26

Like snow in summer or rain[e] in harvest,
honor is not fitting for a fool.[f]

2 Like a fluttering sparrow or a darting swallow,
an undeserved curse does not come to rest.[g]

3 A whip for the horse, a halter for the donkey,[h]
and a rod for the backs of fools![i]

4 Do not answer a fool according to his folly,
or you will be like him yourself.[j]

5 Answer a fool according to his folly,
or he will be wise in his own eyes.[k]

6 Like cutting off one's feet or drinking violence
is the sending of a message by the hand of a fool.[l]

7 Like a lame man's legs that hang limp
is a proverb in the mouth of a fool.[m]

8 Like tying a stone in a sling
is the giving of honor to a fool.[n]

9 Like a thornbush in a drunkard's hand
is a proverb in the mouth of a fool.[o]

10 Like an archer who wounds at random
is he who hires a fool or any passer-by.

11 As a dog returns to its vomit,[p]
so a fool repeats his folly.[q]

12 Do you see a man wise in his own eyes?[r]
There is more hope for a fool than for him.[s]

13The sluggard says,[a] "There is a lion in the road,
a fierce lion roaming the streets!"[b]

14As a door turns on its hinges,
so a sluggard turns on his bed.[c]

15The sluggard buries his hand in the dish;
he is too lazy to bring it back to his mouth.[d]

16The sluggard is wiser in his own eyes
than seven men who answer discreetly.

17Like one who seizes a dog by the ears
is a passer-by who meddles in a quarrel not his own.

18Like a madman shooting
firebrands or deadly arrows
19is a man who deceives his neighbor
and says, "I was only joking!"

20Without wood a fire goes out;
without gossip a quarrel dies down.[e]

21As charcoal to embers and as wood to fire,
so is a quarrelsome man for kindling strife.[f]

22The words of a gossip are like choice morsels;
they go down to a man's inmost parts.[g]

23Like a coating of glaze[a] over earthenware
are fervent lips with an evil heart.

24A malicious man disguises himself with his lips,[h]
but in his heart he harbors deceit.[i]
25Though his speech is charming,[j] do not believe him,
for seven abominations fill his heart.[k]
26His malice may be concealed by deception,
but his wickedness will be exposed in the assembly.

27If a man digs a pit,[l] he will fall into it;[m]
if a man rolls a stone, it will roll back on him.[n]

28A lying tongue hates those it hurts,
and a flattering mouth[o] works ruin.

Chapter 27 Theme ____________________

27

Do not boast[p] about tomorrow,
for you do not know what a day may bring forth.[q]

2Let another praise you, and not your own mouth;
someone else, and not your own lips.[r]

[a]23 With a different word division of the Hebrew; Masoretic Text *of silver dross*

26:13 [a]Pr 6:6-11; 24:30-34 [b]Pr 22:13

26:14 [c]Pr 6:9

26:15 [d]Pr 19:24

26:20 [e]Pr 22:10

26:21 [f]Pr 14:17; 15:18

26:22 [g]Pr 18:8

26:24 [h]Ps 31:18 [i]Ps 41:6; Pr 10:18; 12:20

26:25 [j]Ps 28:3 [k]Jer 9:4-8

26:27 [l]Ps 7:15 [m]Est 6:13 [n]Est 2:23; 7:9; Ps 35:8; 141:10; Pr 28:10; 29:6; Isa 50:11

26:28 [o]Ps 12:3; Pr 29:5

27:1 [p]1Ki 20:11 [q]Mt 6:34; Lk 12:19-20; Jas 4:13-16

27:2 [r]Pr 25:27

3 Stone is heavy and sand[a] a burden,
but provocation by a fool is heavier than both.

4 Anger is cruel and fury overwhelming,
but who can stand before jealousy?[b]

5 Better is open rebuke
than hidden love.

6 Wounds from a friend can be trusted,
but an enemy multiplies kisses.[c]

7 He who is full loathes honey,
but to the hungry even what is bitter tastes sweet.

8 Like a bird that strays from its nest[d]
is a man who strays from his home.

9 Perfume[e] and incense bring joy to the heart,
and the pleasantness of one's friend springs from his
earnest counsel.

10 Do not forsake your friend and the friend of your father,
and do not go to your brother's house when disaster[f]
strikes you—
better a neighbor nearby than a brother far away.

11 Be wise, my son, and bring joy to my heart;[g]
then I can answer anyone who treats me with contempt.[h]

12 The prudent see danger and take refuge,
but the simple keep going and suffer for it.[i]

13 Take the garment of one who puts up security for a
stranger;
hold it in pledge if he does it for a wayward woman.[j]

14 If a man loudly blesses his neighbor early in the morning,
it will be taken as a curse.

15 A quarrelsome wife is like
a constant dripping[k] on a rainy day;
16 restraining her is like restraining the wind
or grasping oil with the hand.

17 As iron sharpens iron,
so one man sharpens another.

18 He who tends a fig tree will eat its fruit,[l]
and he who looks after his master will be honored.[m]

19 As water reflects a face,
so a man's heart reflects the man.

27:3 [a] Job 6:3
27:4 [b] Nu 5:14
27:6 [c] Ps 141:5; Pr 28:23
27:8 [d] Isa 16:2
27:9 [e] Est 2:12; Ps 45:8
27:10 [f] Pr 17:17; 18:24
27:11 [g] Pr 10:1; 23:15-16 [h] Ge 24:60
27:12 [i] Pr 22:3
27:13 [j] Pr 20:16
27:15 [k] Est 1:18; Pr 19:13
27:18 [l] 1Co 9:7 [m] Lk 19:12-27

20 Death and Destruction[a] are never satisfied,[a]
and neither are the eyes of man.[b]

21 The crucible for silver and the furnace for gold,[c]
but man is tested by the praise he receives.

22 Though you grind a fool in a mortar,
grinding him like grain with a pestle,
you will not remove his folly from him.

23 Be sure you know the condition of your flocks,[d]
give careful attention to your herds;
24 for riches do not endure forever,[e]
and a crown is not secure for all generations.
25 When the hay is removed and new growth appears
and the grass from the hills is gathered in,
26 the lambs will provide you with clothing,
and the goats with the price of a field.
27 You will have plenty of goats' milk
to feed you and your family
and to nourish your servant girls.

Chapter 28 Theme ____________________

28

The wicked man flees[f] though no one pursues,[g]
but the righteous are as bold as a lion.[h]

2 When a country is rebellious, it has many rulers,
but a man of understanding and knowledge
maintains order.

3 A ruler[b] who oppresses the poor
is like a driving rain that leaves no crops.

4 Those who forsake the law praise the wicked,
but those who keep the law resist them.

5 Evil men do not understand justice,
but those who seek the LORD understand it fully.

6 Better a poor man whose walk is blameless
than a rich man whose ways are perverse.[i]

7 He who keeps the law is a discerning son,
but a companion of gluttons disgraces his father.[j]

8 He who increases his wealth by exorbitant interest[k]
amasses it for another,[l] who will be kind to the poor.[m]

9 If anyone turns a deaf ear to the law,
even his prayers are detestable.[n]

[a] 20 Hebrew *Sheol and Abaddon* [b] 3 Or *A poor man*

27:20
[a] Pr 30:15-16; Hab 2:5
[b] Ecc 1:8; 6:7

27:21
[c] Pr 17:3

27:23
[d] Pr 12:10

27:24
[e] Pr 23:5

28:1
[f] 2Ki 7:7
[g] Lev 26:17; Ps 53:5
[h] Ps 138:3

28:6
[i] Pr 19:1

28:7
[j] Pr 23:19-21

28:8
[k] Ex 18:21
[l] Job 27:17; Pr 13:22
[m] Ps 112:9; Pr 14:31; Lk 14:12-14

28:9
[n] Ps 66:18; 109:7; Pr 15:8; Isa 1:13

10 He who leads the upright along an evil path
will fall into his own trap,[a]
but the blameless will receive a good inheritance.

11 A rich man may be wise in his own eyes,
but a poor man who has discernment sees through him.

12 When the righteous triumph, there is great elation;[b]
but when the wicked rise to power, men go into hiding.[c]

13 He who conceals his sins[d] does not prosper,
but whoever confesses and renounces them
finds mercy.[e]

14 Blessed is the man who always fears the LORD,
but he who hardens his heart falls into trouble.

15 Like a roaring lion or a charging bear
is a wicked man ruling over a helpless people.

16 A tyrannical ruler lacks judgment,
but he who hates ill-gotten gain will enjoy a long life.

17 A man tormented by the guilt of murder
will be a fugitive[f] till death;
let no one support him.

18 He whose walk is blameless is kept safe,
but he whose ways are perverse will suddenly fall.[g]

19 He who works his land will have abundant food,
but the one who chases fantasies will have his fill
of poverty.[h]

20 A faithful man will be richly blessed,
but one eager to get rich will not go unpunished.[i]

21 To show partiality is not good[j]—
yet a man will do wrong for a piece of bread.[k]

22 A stingy man is eager to get rich
and is unaware that poverty awaits him.[l]

23 He who rebukes a man will in the end gain more favor
than he who has a flattering tongue.[m]

24 He who robs his father or mother[n]
and says, "It's not wrong"—
he is partner to him who destroys.[o]

25 A greedy man stirs up dissension,
but he who trusts in the LORD[p] will prosper.

28:10 [a] Pr 26:27
28:12 [b] 2Ki 11:20 [c] Pr 11:10; 29:2
28:13 [d] Job 31:33 [e] Ps 32:1-5; 1Jn 1:9
28:17 [f] Ge 9:6
28:18 [g] Pr 10:9
28:19 [h] Pr 12:11
28:20 [i] ver 22; Pr 10:6; 1Ti 6:9
28:21 [j] Pr 18:5 [k] Eze 13:19
28:22 [l] ver 20; Pr 23:6
28:23 [m] Pr 27:5-6
28:24 [n] Pr 19:26 [o] Pr 18:9
28:25 [p] Pr 29:25

26He who trusts in himself is a fool,[a]
but he who walks in wisdom is kept safe.

27He who gives to the poor will lack nothing,[b]
but he who closes his eyes to them receives
many curses.

28When the wicked rise to power, people go into hiding;[c]
but when the wicked perish, the righteous thrive.

Chapter 29 Theme ____________________

29

A man who remains stiff-necked after many rebukes
will suddenly be destroyed—without remedy.[d]

2When the righteous thrive, the people rejoice;[e]
when the wicked rule, the people groan.[f]

3A man who loves wisdom brings joy to his father,[g]
but a companion of prostitutes squanders his wealth.[h]

4By justice a king gives a country stability,[i]
but one who is greedy for bribes tears it down.

5Whoever flatters his neighbor
is spreading a net for his feet.

6An evil man is snared by his own sin,[j]
but a righteous one can sing and be glad.

7The righteous care about justice for the poor,[k]
but the wicked have no such concern.

8Mockers stir up a city,
but wise men turn away anger.[l]

9If a wise man goes to court with a fool,
the fool rages and scoffs, and there is no peace.

10Bloodthirsty men hate a man of integrity
and seek to kill the upright.[m]

11A fool gives full vent to his anger,
but a wise man keeps himself under control.[n]

12If a ruler listens to lies,
all his officials become wicked.

13The poor man and the oppressor have this in common:
The LORD gives sight to the eyes of both.[o]

14If a king judges the poor with fairness,
his throne will always be secure.[p]

28:26 [a]Ps 4:5; Pr 3:5

28:27 [b]Dt 15:7; 24:19; Pr 19:17; 22:9

28:28 [c]ver 12

29:1 [d]2Ch 36:16; Pr 6:15

29:2 [e]Est 8:15 [f]Pr 28:12

29:3 [g]Pr 10:1 [h]Pr 5:8-10; Lk 15:11-32

29:4 [i]Pr 8:15-16

29:6 [j]Ecc 9:12

29:7 [k]Job 29:16; Ps 41:1; Pr 31:8-9

29:8 [l]Pr 11:11; 16:14

29:10 [m]1Jn 3:12

29:11 [n]Pr 12:16; 19:11

29:13 [o]Pr 22:2; Mt 5:45

29:14 [p]Ps 72:1-5; Pr 16:12

15 The rod of correction imparts wisdom,
but a child left to himself disgraces his mother.[a]

16 When the wicked thrive, so does sin,
but the righteous will see their downfall.[b]

17 Discipline your son, and he will give you peace;
he will bring delight to your soul.[c]

18 Where there is no revelation, the people cast off restraint;
but blessed is he who keeps the law.[d]

19 A servant cannot be corrected by mere words;
though he understands, he will not respond.

20 Do you see a man who speaks in haste?
There is more hope for a fool than for him.[e]

21 If a man pampers his servant from youth,
he will bring grief[a] in the end.

22 An angry man stirs up dissension,
and a hot-tempered one commits many sins.[f]

23 A man's pride brings him low,
but a man of lowly spirit gains honor.[g]

24 The accomplice of a thief is his own enemy;
he is put under oath and dare not testify.[h]

25 Fear of man will prove to be a snare,
but whoever trusts in the LORD[i] is kept safe.

26 Many seek an audience with a ruler,[j]
but it is from the LORD that man gets justice.

27 The righteous detest the dishonest;
the wicked detest the upright.[k]

Chapter 30 Theme ______________________

30

The sayings of Agur son of Jakeh—an oracle[b]:

This man declared to Ithiel,
to Ithiel and to Ucal:[c]

2 "I am the most ignorant of men;
I do not have a man's understanding.
3 I have not learned wisdom,
nor have I knowledge of the Holy One.[l]

29:15 [a]Pr 10:1; 13:24; 17:21,25
29:16 [b]Ps 37:35-36; 58:10; 91:8; 92:11
29:17 [c]ver 15; Pr 10:1
29:18 [d]Ps 1:1-2; 119:1-2; Jn 13:17
29:20 [e]Pr 26:12; Jas 1:19
29:22 [f]Pr 14:17; 15:18; 26:21
29:23 [g]Pr 11:2; 15:33; 16:18; Isa 66:2; Mt 23:12
29:24 [h]Lev 5:1
29:25 [i]Pr 28:25
29:26 [j]Pr 19:6
29:27 [k]ver 10
30:3 [l]Pr 9:10

[a] *21* The meaning of the Hebrew for this word is uncertain. [b] *1* Or *Jakeh of Massa*
[c] *1* Masoretic Text; with a different word division of the Hebrew *declared, "I am weary, O God; / I am weary, O God, and faint.*

[4]Who has gone up[a] to heaven and come down?
Who has gathered up the wind in the hollow[b] of his hands?
Who has wrapped up the waters[c] in his cloak?[d]
Who has established all the ends of the earth?
What is his name,[e] and the name of his son?
Tell me if you know!

[5]"Every word of God is flawless;[f]
he is a shield[g] to those who take refuge in him.
[6]Do not add[h] to his words,
or he will rebuke you and prove you a liar.

[7]"Two things I ask of you, O LORD;
do not refuse me before I die:
[8]Keep falsehood and lies far from me;
give me neither poverty nor riches,
but give me only my daily bread.[i]
[9]Otherwise, I may have too much and disown[j] you
and say, 'Who is the LORD?'[k]
Or I may become poor and steal,
and so dishonor the name of my God.[l]

[10]"Do not slander a servant to his master,
or he will curse you, and you will pay for it.

[11]"There are those who curse their fathers
and do not bless their mothers;[m]
[12]those who are pure in their own eyes[n]
and yet are not cleansed of their filth;[o]
[13]those whose eyes are ever so haughty,[p]
whose glances are so disdainful;
[14]those whose teeth[q] are swords
and whose jaws are set with knives[r]
to devour[s] the poor[t] from the earth,
the needy from among mankind.[u]

[15]"The leech has two daughters.
'Give! Give!' they cry.

"There are three things that are never satisfied,[v]
four that never say, 'Enough!':
[16]the grave,[a] [w] the barren womb,
land, which is never satisfied with water,
and fire, which never says, 'Enough!'

[17]"The eye that mocks[x] a father,
that scorns obedience to a mother,

a 16 Hebrew *Sheol*

30:4
[a]Ps 24:1-2; Jn 3:13; Eph 4:7-10
[b]Ps 104:3; Isa 40:12
[c]Job 26:8; 38:8-9
[d]Ge 1:2
[e]Rev 19:12

30:5
[f]Ps 12:6; 18:30
[g]Ge 15:1; Ps 84:11

30:6
[h]Dt 4:2; 12:32; Rev 22:18

30:8
[i]Mt 6:11

30:9
[j]Jos 24:27; Isa 1:4; 59:13
[k]Dt 6:12; 8:10-14; Hos 13:6
[l]Dt 8:12

30:11
[m]Pr 20:20

30:12
[n]Pr 16:2; Lk 18:11
[o]Jer 2:23,35

30:13
[p]2Sa 22:28; Job 41:34; Ps 131:1; Pr 6:17

30:14
[q]Job 4:11; 29:17; Ps 3:7
[r]Ps 57:4
[s]Job 24:9; Ps 14:4
[t]Am 8:4; Mic 2:2
[u]Job 19:22

30:15
[v]Pr 27:20

30:16
[w]Pr 27:20; Isa 5:14; 14:9,11; Hab 2:5

30:17
[x]Dt 21:18-21; Pr 23:22

will be pecked out by the ravens of the valley,
will be eaten by the vultures.[a]

18 “There are three things that are too amazing for me,
four that I do not understand:
19 the way of an eagle in the sky,
the way of a snake on a rock,
the way of a ship on the high seas,
and the way of a man with a maiden.

20 “This is the way of an adulteress:
She eats and wipes her mouth
and says, ‘I’ve done nothing wrong.’[b]

21 “Under three things the earth trembles,
under four it cannot bear up:
22 a servant who becomes king,[c]
a fool who is full of food,
23 an unloved woman who is married,
and a maidservant who displaces her mistress.

24 “Four things on earth are small,
yet they are extremely wise:
25 Ants are creatures of little strength,
yet they store up their food in the summer;[d]
26 coneys[a][e] are creatures of little power,
yet they make their home in the crags;
27 locusts[f] have no king,
yet they advance together in ranks;
28 a lizard can be caught with the hand,
yet it is found in kings’ palaces.

29 “There are three things that are stately in
their stride,
four that move with stately bearing:
30 a lion, mighty among beasts,
who retreats before nothing;
31 a strutting rooster, a he-goat,
and a king with his army around him.[b]

32 “If you have played the fool and exalted yourself,
or if you have planned evil,
clap your hand over your mouth![g]
33 For as churning the milk produces butter,
and as twisting the nose produces blood,
so stirring up anger produces strife.”

30:17 [a] Job 15:23
30:20 [b] Pr 5:6
30:22 [c] Pr 19:10; 29:2
30:25 [d] Pr 6:6-8
30:26 [e] Ps 104:18
30:27 [f] Ex 10:4
30:32 [g] Job 21:5; 29:9

[a] *26* That is, the hyrax or rock badger [b] *31* Or *king secure against revolt*

Chapter 31 Theme ______________________________

31

The sayings[a] of King Lemuel—an oracle[a] his mother
taught him:

[2]"O my son, O son of my womb,
O son of my vows,[b][b]
[3]do not spend your strength on women,
your vigor on those who ruin kings.[c]

[4]"It is not for kings, O Lemuel—
not for kings to drink wine,[d]
not for rulers to crave beer,
[5]lest they drink[e] and forget what the law decrees,[f]
and deprive all the oppressed of their rights.
[6]Give beer to those who are perishing,
wine[g] to those who are in anguish;
[7]let them drink[h] and forget their poverty
and remember their misery no more.

[8]"Speak[i] up for those who cannot speak for themselves,
for the rights of all who are destitute.
[9]Speak up and judge fairly;
defend the rights of the poor and needy."[j]

[10][c]A wife of noble character[k] who can find?[l]
She is worth far more than rubies.
[11]Her husband[m] has full confidence in her
and lacks nothing of value.[n]
[12]She brings him good, not harm,
all the days of her life.
[13]She selects wool and flax
and works with eager hands.[o]
[14]She is like the merchant ships,
bringing her food from afar.
[15]She gets up while it is still dark;
she provides food for her family
and portions for her servant girls.
[16]She considers a field and buys it;
out of her earnings she plants a vineyard.
[17]She sets about her work vigorously;
her arms are strong for her tasks.
[18]She sees that her trading is profitable,
and her lamp does not go out at night.
[19]In her hand she holds the distaff
and grasps the spindle with her fingers.

[a] *1* Or *of Lemuel king of Massa, which* [b] *2* Or / *the answer to my prayers* [c] *10* Verses 10-31 are an acrostic, each verse beginning with a successive letter of the Hebrew alphabet.

31:1
[a] Pr 22:17

31:2
[b] Jdg 11:30; Isa 49:15

31:3
[c] Dt 17:17; 1Ki 11:3; Ne 13:26; Pr 5:1-14

31:4
[d] Pr 20:1; Ecc 10:16-17; Isa 5:22

31:5
[e] 1Ki 16:9
[f] Pr 16:12; Hos 4:11

31:6
[g] Ge 14:18

31:7
[h] Est 1:10

31:8
[i] 1Sa 19:4; Job 29:12-17

31:9
[j] Lev 19:15; Dt 1:16; Pr 24:23; 29:7; Isa 1:17; Jer 22:16

31:10
[k] Ru 3:11; Pr 12:4; 18:22
[l] Pr 8:35; 19:14

31:11
[m] Ge 2:18
[n] Pr 12:4

31:13
[o] 1Ti 2:9-10

31:20 [a] Dt 15:11; Eph 4:28; Heb 13:16

31:23 [b] Ex 3:16; Ru 4:1,11; Pr 12:4

31:26 [c] Pr 10:31

31:31 [d] Pr 11:16

20 She opens her arms to the poor
and extends her hands to the needy.[a]
21 When it snows, she has no fear for her household;
for all of them are clothed in scarlet.
22 She makes coverings for her bed;
she is clothed in fine linen and purple.
23 Her husband is respected at the city gate,
where he takes his seat among the elders[b] of the land.
24 She makes linen garments and sells them,
and supplies the merchants with sashes.
25 She is clothed with strength and dignity;
she can laugh at the days to come.
26 She speaks with wisdom,
and faithful instruction is on her tongue.[c]
27 She watches over the affairs of her household
and does not eat the bread of idleness.
28 Her children arise and call her blessed;
her husband also, and he praises her:
29 "Many women do noble things,
but you surpass them all."
30 Charm is deceptive, and beauty is fleeting;
but a woman who fears the LORD is to be praised.
31 Give her the reward she has earned,
and let her works bring her praise[d] at the city gate.

PROVERBS AT A GLANCE

Theme of Proverbs:

SEGMENT DIVISIONS

	MAIN DIVISIONS		CHAPTER THEMES
	THE CRY OF WISDOM, KNOWLEDGE, AND UNDERSTANDING	1	
		2	
		3	
		4	
		5	
		6	
		7	
		8	
		9	
	THE PROVERBS OF SOLOMON AND WISDOM OF WISE MEN	10	
		11	
		12	
		13	
		14	
		15	
		16	
		17	
		18	
		19	
		20	
		21	
		22	
		23	
		24	
	SOLOMON'S PROVERBS TRANSCRIBED	25	
		26	
		27	
		28	
		29	
	WORDS & COUNSEL OF OTHERS	30	
		31	

Author:

Date:

Purpose:

Key Words:

wisdom, gui
(wise)

judgment, v

knowledge

understandi
(discerning,
discernment

fear(s)

my son
(O son)

command(s)

instruction
(discipline, t
teaching, less

tongue

fool, fool's, f
(folly, simple

ECCLESIASTES

Life seems inconsistent, unpredictable, and unfair at times. No matter the generation, no matter the time in history, the righteous and the wicked have the same experiences, face the same trials, grapple with the same problems. And all end up in the grave!

As people grow older they look back and see what a breath, what a vapor, life is. It passes so quickly. What was its purpose? Was what we strove to attain worth it? Did we live as we should have?

"What does man gain from all his labor at which he toils under the sun?" (Ecclesiastes 1:3). And what is the conclusion of it all? (See Ecclesiastes 12:13.)

Things to Do

General Instructions

1. A careful observation of Ecclesiastes gives insight into why this book is included in the Bible. So as you begin your study of this book, do the following:
   a. Remember that all you read must be considered in the context of the whole counsel of God.
   b. Read 1:1-3 and 12:13, 14 to see how Ecclesiastes begins and ends. Keep these verses in mind as you study.
2. In the margin of chapter 1, list what you learn about the author:
   a. Who and/or what he is; how he describes himself; what he pursued, had, or experienced, and what gain it was to him. This is important. You may want to list your insights on a piece of paper first as you go through Ecclesiastes. Then when you have completed your study, summarize and record them in the margin of chapter 1.
   b. As you read the book, observe what the author has seen, come to know, commends, and concludes. Mark or note these insights in a special way, since these usually include important key repeated phrases.
   c. After chapter 4, watch for and list in the margin the author's commands and warnings. For example, in 5:1 he tells us to guard our steps when we go into the house of God.
3. As you read each chapter mark in a distinctive way the key words listed on the ECCLESIASTES AT A GLANCE chart on page 1138. List these key words on an index card that you can use as a bookmark while observing this book.
4. When you finish observing each chapter:
   a. Look at every reference to God. On a piece of paper list all you learn about him, what he does, and what we are to do in respect to him.
   b. Also mark the contrasting groups of people: the righteous and the wicked, the wise and the foolish. On a separate piece of paper list what you learn about these persons from each chapter.
   c. Also make a list of what you learn about *wealth* and *labor (work, toil, effort).*
   d. When you have completed your study of the book, summarize in one of the margins what you learned from compiling the above lists.
5. Record the theme of each chapter on ECCLESIASTES AT A GLANCE and on the line next to the chapter number in the text.

Chapters 1-8: Exploring Life's Inconsistencies

1. As you read, mark the key words listed on ECCLESIASTES AT A GLANCE. Also watch for and mark these words: *explore, discover (comprehend), discovered (find),* and *turned.*

2. Mark the word *meaningless.* The word *meaningless* is from the word *hebel.*
   a. *Hebel* appears more in Ecclesiastes than in any other book of the Bible; half of all its occurrences are in Ecclesiastes.
   b. Except for 11:8 and 12:8, all the occurrences of *meaningless* appear in this first section of Ecclesiastes. Therefore after you finish marking each occurrence of these words, list in one of the chapter margins everything you learn from the text about *meaningless.*

Chapters 9-12: Explaining Life's Inconsistencies

1. Read 9:1 and mark the word *concluded.* Do you see how this verse might be used as a pivotal point in the book? If so, watch for any explanations the author might give to life's inconsistencies.
2. When you finish observing chapter 10, review each reference to wisdom that you have marked and in the margin list everything you learned about wisdom from Ecclesiastes.
3. As you read 12:1-7, think of the human body and the effects of age on its members. See if you find any "pictorial descriptions" of the body and what happens as you get old (e.g., "when the grinders cease because they are few" might be a picture of losing some teeth).
4. Complete ECCLESIASTES AT A GLANCE.

THINGS TO THINK ABOUT

1. Where have you been searching for the meaning of life? What have you been pursuing in order to find fulfillment or happiness?
2. Where can the meaning of life be found? Where can't it be found?
3. The author of Ecclesiastes is Solomon, David's son, who was the richest and wisest of men. What do you learn from his experience that can help you?
4. Review all you have learned about God from this book. Since God is going to bring every act to judgment, even those of Christians (2 Corinthians 5:10; Romans 14:10), what are you doing that you should continue to do and what do you need to stop doing? Will you?

Chapter 1 Theme ____________

1 The words of the Teacher,[a] [a] son of David, king in Jerusalem:[b]

2"Meaningless! Meaningless!"
says the Teacher.
"Utterly meaningless!
Everything is meaningless."[c]

3What does man gain from all his labor
at which he toils under the sun?[d]
4Generations come and generations go,
but the earth remains forever.[e]
5The sun rises and the sun sets,
and hurries back to where it rises.[f]
6The wind blows to the south
and turns to the north;

[a] *1* Or *leader of the assembly*; also in verses 2 and 12

1:1
[a] ver 12; Ecc 7:27; 12:10
[b] Pr 1:1

1:2
[c] Ps 39:5-6; 62:9; 144:4; Ecc 12:8; Ro 8:20-21

1:3
[d] Ecc 2:11,22; 3:9; 5:15-16

1:4
[e] Ps 104:5; 119:90

1:5
[f] Ps 19:5-6

round and round it goes,
ever returning on its course.
7All streams flow into the sea,
yet the sea is never full.
To the place the streams come from,
there they return again.[a]
8All things are wearisome,
more than one can say.
The eye never has enough of seeing,[b]
nor the ear its fill of hearing.
9What has been will be again,
what has been done will be done again;[c]
there is nothing new under the sun.
10Is there anything of which one can say,
"Look! This is something new"?
It was here already, long ago;
it was here before our time.
11There is no remembrance of men of old,
and even those who are yet to come
will not be remembered
by those who follow.[d]

12I, the Teacher,[e] was king over Israel in Jerusalem. 13I devoted
myself to study and to explore by wisdom all that is done under
heaven. What a heavy burden God has laid on men![f] 14I have seen
all the things that are done under the sun; all of them are meaningless, a chasing after the wind.[g]

15What is twisted cannot be straightened;[h]
what is lacking cannot be counted.

16I thought to myself, "Look, I have grown and increased in
wisdom more than anyone who has ruled over Jerusalem before
me;[i] I have experienced much of wisdom and knowledge."17Then
I applied myself to the understanding of wisdom,[j] and also of
madness and folly,[k] but I learned that this, too, is a chasing after
the wind.

18For with much wisdom comes much sorrow;
the more knowledge, the more grief.[l]

Chapter 2 Theme ______________________

2 I thought in my heart, "Come now, I will test you with pleasure[m] to find out what is good." But that also proved to be
meaningless. 2"Laughter,"[n] I said, "is foolish. And what does pleasure accomplish?" 3I tried cheering myself with wine,[o] and
embracing folly[p]—my mind still guiding me with wisdom. I

1:7 [a] Job 36:28
1:8 [b] Pr 27:20
1:9 [c] Ecc 2:12; 3:15
1:11 [d] Ecc 2:16
1:12 [e] ver 1
1:13 [f] Ge 3:17; Ecc 3:10
1:14 [g] Ecc 2:11,17
1:15 [h] Ecc 7:13
1:16 [i] 1Ki 3:12; 4:30; Ecc 2:9
1:17 [j] Ecc 7:23 [k] Ecc 2:3,12; 7:25
1:18 [l] Ecc 2:23; 12:12
2:1 [m] Ecc 7:4; 8:15; Lk 12:19
2:2 [n] Pr 14:13; Ecc 7:6
2:3 [o] ver 24-25; Ecc 3:12-13 [p] Ecc 1:17

wanted to see what was worthwhile for men to do under heaven
during the few days of their lives.

4I undertook great projects: I built houses for myself[a] and
planted vineyards.[b] 5I made gardens and parks and planted all
kinds of fruit trees in them. 6I made reservoirs to water groves of
flourishing trees. 7I bought male and female slaves and had other
slaves who were born in my house. I also owned more herds and
flocks than anyone in Jerusalem before me. 8I amassed silver and
gold[c] for myself, and the treasure of kings and provinces. I
acquired men and women singers,[d] and a harem[a] as well—the
delights of the heart of man. 9I became greater by far than anyone
in Jerusalem before me.[e] In all this my wisdom stayed with me.

10I denied myself nothing my eyes desired;
I refused my heart no pleasure.
My heart took delight in all my work,
and this was the reward for all my labor.
11Yet when I surveyed all that my hands had done
and what I had toiled to achieve,
everything was meaningless, a chasing after the wind;[f]
nothing was gained under the sun.[g]

12Then I turned my thoughts to consider wisdom,
and also madness and folly.[h]
What more can the king's successor do
than what has already been done?[i]
13I saw that wisdom[j] is better than folly,[k]
just as light is better than darkness.
14The wise man has eyes in his head,
while the fool walks in the darkness;
but I came to realize
that the same fate overtakes them both.[l]

15Then I thought in my heart,

"The fate of the fool will overtake me also.
What then do I gain by being wise?"[m]
I said in my heart,
"This too is meaningless."
16For the wise man, like the fool, will not be long
remembered;
in days to come both will be forgotten.[n]
Like the fool, the wise man too must die!

17So I hated life, because the work that is done under the sun
was grievous to me. All of it is meaningless, a chasing after the
wind.[o] 18I hated all the things I had toiled for under the sun,
because I must leave them to the one who comes after me.[p]

a8 The meaning of the Hebrew for this phrase is uncertain.

2:4
[a] 1Ki 7:1-12
[b] SS 8:11

2:8
[c] 1Ki 9:28; 10:10,14,21
[d] 2Sa 19:35

2:9
[e] 1Ch 29:25; Ecc 1:16

2:11
[f] Ecc 1:14
[g] Ecc 1:3

2:12
[h] Ecc 1:17
[i] Ecc 1:9; 7:25

2:13
[j] Ecc 7:19; 9:18
[k] Ecc 7:11-12

2:14
[l] Ps 49:10; Pr 17:24; Ecc 3:19; 6:6; 7:2; 9:3,11-12

2:15
[m] Ecc 6:8

2:16
[n] Ecc 1:11; 9:5

2:17
[o] Ecc 4:2

2:18
[p] Ps 39:6; 49:10

19 And who knows whether he will be a wise man or a fool? Yet he
will have control over all the work into which I have poured my
effort and skill under the sun. This too is meaningless. 20 So my
heart began to despair over all my toilsome labor under the sun.
21 For a man may do his work with wisdom, knowledge and skill,
and then he must leave all he owns to someone who has not
worked for it. This too is meaningless and a great misfortune.
22 What does a man get for all the toil and anxious striving with
which he labors under the sun?[a] 23 All his days his work is pain and
grief;[b] even at night his mind does not rest. This too is meaningless.
24 A man can do nothing better than to eat and drink[c] and find
satisfaction in his work.[d] This too, I see, is from the hand of God,[e]
25 for without him, who can eat or find enjoyment? 26 To the man
who pleases him, God gives wisdom, knowledge and happiness,
but to the sinner he gives the task of gathering and storing up
wealth[f] to hand it over to the one who pleases God.[g] This too is
meaningless, a chasing after the wind.

Chapter 3 Theme ______________________________

3 There is a time[h] for everything,
and a season for every activity under heaven:

2 a time to be born and a time to die,
a time to plant and a time to uproot,
3 a time to kill and a time to heal,
a time to tear down and a time to build,
4 a time to weep and a time to laugh,
a time to mourn and a time to dance,
5 a time to scatter stones and a time to gather them,
a time to embrace and a time to refrain,
6 a time to search and a time to give up,
a time to keep and a time to throw away,
7 a time to tear and a time to mend,
a time to be silent[i] and a time to speak,
8 a time to love and a time to hate,
a time for war and a time for peace.

9 What does the worker gain from his toil?[j] 10 I have seen the
burden God has laid on men.[k] 11 He has made everything beautiful in its time.[l] He has also set eternity in the hearts of men; yet
they cannot fathom[m] what God has done from beginning to
end.[n] 12 I know that there is nothing better for men than to be
happy and do good while they live. 13 That everyone may eat and
drink,[o] and find satisfaction[p] in all his toil—this is the gift of
God.[q] 14 I know that everything God does will endure forever;

2:22 [a]Ecc 1:3; 3:9
2:23 [b]Job 5:7; 14:1; Ecc 1:18
2:24 [c]Ecc 8:15; 1Co 15:32 [d]Ecc 3:22 [e]Ecc 3:12-13; 5:17-19; 9:7-10
2:26 [f]Job 27:17 [g]Pr 13:22
3:1 [h]ver 11,17; Ecc 8:6
3:7 [i]Am 5:13
3:9 [j]Ecc 1:3
3:10 [k]Ecc 1:13
3:11 [l]ver 1 [m]Job 11:7; Ecc 8:17 [n]Job 28:23; Ro 11:33
3:13 [o]Ecc 2:3 [p]Ps 34:12 [q]Dt 12:7,18; Ecc 2:24; 5:19

nothing can be added to it and nothing taken from it. God does it
so that men will revere him.[a]

[15]Whatever is has already been,[b]
and what will be has been before;[c]
and God will call the past to account.[a]

[16]And I saw something else under the sun:

In the place of judgment—wickedness was there,
in the place of justice—wickedness was there.

[17]I thought in my heart,

"God will bring to judgment[d]
both the righteous and the wicked,
for there will be a time for every activity,
a time for every deed."[e]

[18]I also thought, "As for men, God tests them so that they may
see that they are like the animals.[f] [19]Man's fate[g] is like that of the
animals; the same fate awaits them both: As one dies, so dies the
other. All have the same breath[b]; man has no advantage over
the animal. Everything is meaningless. [20]All go to the same place;
all come from dust, and to dust all return.[h] [21]Who knows if the
spirit of man rises upward[i] and if the spirit of the animal[c] goes
down into the earth?"

[22]So I saw that there is nothing better for a man than to enjoy
his work,[j] because that is his lot.[k] For who can bring him to see
what will happen after him?

Chapter 4 Theme ______________________________

4 Again I looked and saw all the oppression[l] that was taking
place under the sun:

I saw the tears of the oppressed—
and they have no comforter;
power was on the side of their oppressors—
and they have no comforter.[m]
[2]And I declared that the dead,[n]
who had already died,
are happier than the living,
who are still alive.[o]
[3]But better than both
is he who has not yet been,[p]
who has not seen the evil
that is done under the sun.[q]

[a]15 *Or God calls back the past* [b]19 *Or spirit* [c]21 Or *Who knows the spirit of man, which rises upward, or the spirit of the animal, which*

3:14 [a]Job 23:15; Ecc 5:7; 7:18; 8:12-13; Jas 1:17
3:15 [b]Ecc 6:10 [c]Ecc 1:9
3:17 [d]Job 19:29; Ecc 11:9; Mt 16:27; Ro 2:6-8; 2Th 1:6-7 [e]ver 1
3:18 [f]Ps 73:22
3:19 [g]Ecc 2:14
3:20 [h]Ge 2:7; 3:19; Job 34:15
3:21 [i]Ecc 12:7
3:22 [j]Ecc 2:24; 5:18 [k]Job 31:2
4:1 [l]Ps 12:5; Ecc 3:16 [m]La 1:16
4:2 [n]Jer 20:17-18; 22:10 [o]Job 3:17; 10:18
4:3 [p]Job 3:16; Ecc 6:3 [q]Job 3:22

4:4 [a]Ecc 1:14

4 And I saw that all labor and all achievement spring from
man's envy of his neighbor. This too is meaningless, a chasing
after the wind.[a]

5 The fool folds his hands[b]
  and ruins himself.
6 Better one handful with tranquillity
  than two handfuls with toil[c]
  and chasing after the wind.

7 Again I saw something meaningless under the sun:

8 There was a man all alone;

4:5 [b]Pr 6:10

  he had neither son nor brother.
There was no end to his toil,
  yet his eyes were not content[d] with his wealth.
"For whom am I toiling," he asked,
  "and why am I depriving myself of enjoyment?"
This too is meaningless—
  a miserable business!

9 Two are better than one,
  because they have a good return for their work:
10 If one falls down,
  his friend can help him up.

4:6 [c]Pr 15:16-17; 16:8

But pity the man who falls
  and has no one to help him up!
11 Also, if two lie down together, they will keep warm.
  But how can one keep warm alone?
12 Though one may be overpowered,
  two can defend themselves.
A cord of three strands is not quickly broken.

13 Better a poor but wise youth than an old but foolish king who
no longer knows how to take warning. 14 The youth may have
come from prison to the kingship, or he may have been born in
poverty within his kingdom. 15 I saw that all who lived and

4:8 [d]Pr 27:20

walked under the sun followed the youth, the king's successor.
16 There was no end to all the people who were before them. But
those who came later were not pleased with the successor. This
too is meaningless, a chasing after the wind.

Chapter 5 Theme ______________________

5

Guard your steps when you go to the house of God. Go near
to listen rather than to offer the sacrifice of fools, who do not
know that they do wrong.

2 Do not be quick with your mouth,
  do not be hasty in your heart

5:2 [e]Jdg 11:35

  to utter anything before God.[e]

God is in heaven
and you are on earth,
so let your words be few.[a]
3 As a dream[b] comes when there are many cares,
so the speech of a fool when there are many words.[c]

4 When you make a vow to God, do not delay in fulfilling it.[d] He
has no pleasure in fools; fulfill your vow.[e] 5 It is better not to vow
than to make a vow and not fulfill it.[f] 6 Do not let your mouth
lead you into sin. And do not protest to the ⌊temple⌋ messenger,
"My vow was a mistake." Why should God be angry at what you
say and destroy the work of your hands? 7 Much dreaming and
many words are meaningless. Therefore stand in awe of God.[g]
8 If you see the poor oppressed[h] in a district, and justice and
rights denied, do not be surprised at such things; for one official
is eyed by a higher one, and over them both are others higher
still. 9 The increase from the land is taken by all; the king himself
profits from the fields.

10 Whoever loves money never has money enough;
whoever loves wealth is never satisfied with his income.
This too is meaningless.

11 As goods increase,
so do those who consume them.
And what benefit are they to the owner
except to feast his eyes on them?

12 The sleep of a laborer is sweet,
whether he eats little or much,
but the abundance of a rich man
permits him no sleep.[i]

13 I have seen a grievous evil under the sun:[j]

wealth hoarded to the harm of its owner,
14 or wealth lost through some misfortune,
so that when he has a son
there is nothing left for him.
15 Naked a man comes from his mother's womb,
and as he comes, so he departs.[k]
He takes nothing from his labor[l]
that he can carry in his hand.[m]

16 This too is a grievous evil:

As a man comes, so he departs,
and what does he gain,
since he toils for the wind?[n]

5:2 [a] Job 6:24; Pr 10:19; 20:25
5:3 [b] Job 20:8 [c] Ecc 10:14
5:4 [d] Dt 23:21; Jdg 11:35; Ps 119:60 [e] Nu 30:2; Ps 66:13-14; 76:11
5:5 [f] Nu 30:2-4; Pr 20:25; Jnh 2:9; Ac 5:4
5:7 [g] Ecc 3:14; 12:13
5:8 [h] Ps 12:5; Ecc 4:1
5:12 [i] Job 20:20
5:13 [j] Ecc 6:1-2
5:15 [k] Job 1:21 [l] Ps 49:17; 1Ti 6:7 [m] Ecc 1:3
5:16 [n] Pr 11:29; Ecc 1:3

17 All his days he eats in darkness,
with great frustration, affliction and anger.

18 Then I realized that it is good and proper for a man to eat and
drink,[a] and to find satisfaction in his toilsome labor[b] under the
sun during the few days of life God has given him—for this is his
lot. 19 Moreover, when God gives any man wealth and possessions,[c]
and enables him to enjoy them,[d] to accept his lot[e] and be happy in
his work—this is a gift of God.[f] 20 He seldom reflects on the days of
his life, because God keeps him occupied with gladness of heart.[g]

Chapter 6 Theme

6 I have seen another evil under the sun, and it weighs heavily
on men: 2 God gives a man wealth, possessions and honor, so
that he lacks nothing his heart desires, but God does not enable
him to enjoy them,[h] and a stranger enjoys them instead. This is
meaningless, a grievous evil.[i]

3 A man may have a hundred children and live many years; yet
no matter how long he lives, if he cannot enjoy his prosperity and
does not receive proper burial, I say that a stillborn[j] child is better off than he.[k] 4 It comes without meaning, it departs in darkness, and in darkness its name is shrouded. 5 Though it never saw
the sun or knew anything, it has more rest than does that man—
6 even if he lives a thousand years twice over but fails to enjoy his
prosperity. Do not all go to the same place?

7 All man's efforts are for his mouth,
yet his appetite is never satisfied.[l]
8 What advantage has a wise man
over a fool?[m]
What does a poor man gain
by knowing how to conduct himself before others?
9 Better what the eye sees
than the roving of the appetite.
This too is meaningless,
a chasing after the wind.[n]

10 Whatever exists has already been named,
and what man is has been known;
no man can contend
with one who is stronger than he.
11 The more the words,
the less the meaning,
and how does that profit anyone?

12 For who knows what is good for a man in life, during the few
and meaningless days[o] he passes through like a shadow?[p] Who
can tell him what will happen under the sun after he is gone?

5:18 [a] Ecc 2:3 [b] Ecc 2:10,24
5:19 [c] 1Ch 29:12; 2Ch 1:12 [d] Ecc 6:2 [e] Job 31:2 [f] Ecc 2:24; 3:13
5:20 [g] Dt 12:7,18
6:2 [h] Ps 17:14; Ecc 5:19 [i] Ecc 5:13
6:3 [j] Job 3:16; Ecc 4:3 [k] Job 3:3
6:7 [l] Pr 16:26; 27:20
6:8 [m] Ecc 2:15
6:9 [n] Ecc 1:14
6:12 [o] Job 10:20 [p] Job 14:2; Ps 39:6; Jas 4:14

Chapter 7 Theme ______________________

7

A good name is better than fine perfume,[a]
and the day of death better than the day of birth.
2It is better to go to a house of mourning
than to go to a house of feasting,
for death[b] is the destiny[c] of every man;
the living should take this to heart.
3Sorrow is better than laughter,[d]
because a sad face is good for the heart.
4The heart of the wise is in the house of mourning,
but the heart of fools is in the house of pleasure.[e]
5It is better to heed a wise man's rebuke[f]
than to listen to the song of fools.
6Like the crackling of thorns[g] under the pot,
so is the laughter[h] of fools.
This too is meaningless.

7Extortion turns a wise man into a fool,
and a bribe[i] corrupts the heart.
8The end of a matter is better than its beginning,
and patience[j] is better than pride.
9Do not be quickly provoked[k] in your spirit,
for anger resides in the lap of fools.

10Do not say, "Why were the old days better than these?"
For it is not wise to ask such questions.

11Wisdom, like an inheritance, is a good thing[l]
and benefits those who see the sun.[m]
12Wisdom is a shelter
as money is a shelter,
but the advantage of knowledge is this:
that wisdom preserves the life of its possessor.

13Consider what God has done:[n]

Who can straighten
what he has made crooked?[o]
14When times are good, be happy;
but when times are bad, consider:
God has made the one
as well as the other.
Therefore, a man cannot discover
anything about his future.

15In this meaningless life[p] of mine I have seen both of these:
a righteous man perishing in his righteousness,
and a wicked man living long in his wickedness.[q]

7:1 [a]Pr 22:1; SS 1:3
7:2 [b]Pr 11:19 [c]Ps 90:12
7:3 [d]Pr 14:13
7:4 [e]Ecc 2:1; Jer 16:8
7:5 [f]Ps 141:5; Pr 13:18; 15:31-32
7:6 [g]Ps 58:9; 118:12 [h]Ecc 2:2
7:7 [i]Ex 18:21; 23:8; Dt 16:19
7:8 [j]Pr 14:29; Gal 5:22; Eph 4:2
7:9 [k]Mt 5:22; Pr 14:17; Jas 1:19
7:11 [l]Pr 8:10-11; Ecc 2:13 [m]Ecc 11:7
7:13 [n]Ecc 2:24 [o]Ecc 1:15
7:15 [p]Job 7:7 [q]Ecc 8:12-14; Jer 12:1

16 Do not be overrighteous,
neither be overwise—
why destroy yourself?
17 Do not be overwicked,
and do not be a fool—
why die before your time?[a]
18 It is good to grasp the one
and not let go of the other.
The man who fears God[b] will avoid all ⌊extremes⌋.[a]

19 Wisdom[c] makes one wise man more powerful[d]
than ten rulers in a city.

20 There is not a righteous man[e] on earth
who does what is right and never sins.[f]

21 Do not pay attention to every word people say,
or you[g] may hear your servant cursing you—
22 for you know in your heart
that many times you yourself have cursed others.

23 All this I tested by wisdom and I said,

"I am determined to be wise"[h]—
but this was beyond me.
24 Whatever wisdom may be,
it is far off and most profound—
who can discover it?[i]
25 So I turned my mind to understand,
to investigate and to search out wisdom and the scheme of things[j]
and to understand the stupidity of wickedness
and the madness of folly.[k]

26 I find more bitter than death
the woman who is a snare,[l]
whose heart is a trap
and whose hands are chains.
The man who pleases God will escape her,
but the sinner she will ensnare.[m]

27 "Look," says the Teacher,[b][n] "this is what I have discovered:

"Adding one thing to another to discover the scheme of things—
28 while I was still searching
but not finding—
I found one ⌊upright⌋ man among a thousand,
but not one ⌊upright⌋ woman[o] among them all.

[a] 18 Or *will follow them both* [b] 27 Or *leader of the assembly*

7:17
[a] Job 15:32; Ps 55:23
7:18
[b] Ecc 3:14
7:19
[c] Ecc 2:13
[d] Ecc 9:13-18
7:20
[e] Ps 14:3
[f] 1Ki 8:46; 2Ch 6:36; Pr 20:9; Ro 3:23
7:21
[g] Pr 30:10
7:23
[h] Ecc 1:17; Ro 1:22
7:24
[i] Job 28:12
7:25
[j] Job 28:3
[k] Ecc 1:17
7:26
[l] Ex 10:7; Jdg 14:15
[m] Pr 2:16-19; 5:3-5; 7:23; 22:14
7:27
[n] Ecc 1:1
7:28
[o] 1Ki 11:3

[29]This only have I found:
God made mankind upright,
but men have gone in search of many schemes."

Chapter 8 Theme ______________________

8

Who is like the wise man?
Who knows the explanation of things?
Wisdom brightens a man's face
and changes its hard appearance.

[2]Obey the king's command, I say, because you took an oath
before God. [3]Do not be in a hurry to leave the king's presence.[a] Do
not stand up for a bad cause, for he will do whatever he pleases.
[4]Since a king's word is supreme, who can say to him, "What are
you doing?[b]"

[5]Whoever obeys his command will come to no harm,
and the wise heart will know the proper time and
procedure.
[6]For there is a proper time and procedure for every matter,[c]
though a man's misery weighs heavily upon him.

[7]Since no man knows the future,
who can tell him what is to come?
[8]No man has power over the wind to contain it[a];
so no one has power over the day of his death.
As no one is discharged in time of war,
so wickedness will not release those who practice it.

[9]All this I saw, as I applied my mind to everything done under
the sun. There is a time when a man lords it over others to his
own[b] hurt. [10]Then too, I saw the wicked buried[d]—those who used
to come and go from the holy place and receive praise[c] in the city
where they did this. This too is meaningless.
[11]When the sentence for a crime is not quickly carried out, the
hearts of the people are filled with schemes to do wrong. [12]Al-
though a wicked man commits a hundred crimes and still lives a
long time, I know that it will go better[e] with God-fearing men,[f]
who are reverent before God.[g] [13]Yet because the wicked do not
fear God,[h] it will not go well with them, and their days[i] will not
lengthen like a shadow.
[14]There is something else meaningless that occurs on earth:
righteous men who get what the wicked deserve, and wicked men
who get what the righteous deserve.[j] This too, I say, is meaningless.[k] [15]So I commend the enjoyment of life[l], because nothing is
better for a man under the sun than to eat and drink[m] and be

[a]8 Or *over his spirit to retain it* [b]9 Or *to their* [c]10 Some Hebrew manuscripts and Septuagint (Aquila); most Hebrew manuscripts *and are forgotten*

8:3
[a]Ecc 10:4

8:4
[b]Job 9:12; Est 1:19; Da 4:35

8:6
[c]Ecc 3:1

8:10
[d]Ecc 1:11

8:12
[e]Dt 12:28; Ps 37:11,18-19; Pr 1:32-33; Isa 3:10-11
[f]Ex 1:20
[g]Ecc 3:14

8:13
[h]Ecc 3:14; Isa 3:11
[i]Dt 4:40; Job 5:26; Ps 34:12; Isa 65:20

8:14
[j]Job 21:7; Ps 73:14; Mal 3:15
[k]Ecc 7:15

8:15
[l]Ps 42:8
[m]Ex 32:6; Ecc 2:3

glad.[a] Then joy will accompany him in his work all the days of
the life God has given him under the sun.
[16]When I applied my mind to know wisdom[b] and to observe
man's labor on earth[c]—his eyes not seeing sleep day or night—
[17]then I saw all that God has done.[d] No one can comprehend
what goes on under the sun. Despite all his efforts to search it
out, man cannot discover its meaning. Even if a wise man claims
he knows, he cannot really comprehend it.[e]

Chapter 9 Theme ____________________

9 So I reflected on all this and concluded that the righteous
and the wise and what they do are in God's hands, but no
man knows whether love or hate awaits him.[f] [2]All share a common destiny—the righteous and the wicked, the good and the
bad,[a] the clean and the unclean, those who offer sacrifices and
those who do not.

As it is with the good man,
  so with the sinner;
as it is with those who take oaths,
  so with those who are afraid to take them.[g]

[3]This is the evil in everything that happens under the sun: The
same destiny overtakes all.[h] The hearts of men, moreover, are full
of evil and there is madness in their hearts while they live,[i] and
afterward they join the dead.[j] [4]Anyone who is among the living
has hope[b]—even a live dog is better off than a dead lion!

[5]For the living know that they will die,
  but the dead know nothing;[k]
they have no further reward,
  and even the memory of them[l] is forgotten.[m]
[6]Their love, their hate
  and their jealousy have long since vanished;
never again will they have a part
  in anything that happens under the sun.[n]

[7]Go, eat your food with gladness, and drink your wine[o] with a
joyful heart,[p] for it is now that God favors what you do. [8]Always
be clothed in white,[q] and always anoint your head with oil.
[9]Enjoy life with your wife,[r] whom you love, all the days of this
meaningless life that God has given you under the sun—all your
meaningless days. For this is your lot[s] in life and in your toilsome
labor under the sun. [10]Whatever[t] your hand finds to do, do it with
all your might,[u] for in the grave,[c][v] where you are going, there is
neither working nor planning nor knowledge nor wisdom.[w]

8:15 [a]Ecc 2:24; 3:12-13; 5:18; 9:7
8:16 [b]Ecc 1:17 [c]Ecc 1:13
8:17 [d]Job 28:3 [e]Job 5:9; 28:23; Ecc 3:11; Ro 11:33
9:1 [f]Dt 33:3; Job 12:10; Ecc 10:14
9:2 [g]Job 9:22; Ecc 2:14; 6:6; 7:2
9:3 [h]Job 9:22; Ecc 2:14 [i]Jer 11:8; 13:10; 16:12; 17:9 [j]Job 21:26
9:5 [k]Job 14:21 [l]Ps 9:6 [m]Ecc 1:11; 2:16; Isa 26:14
9:6 [n]Job 21:21
9:7 [o]Nu 6:20 [p]Ecc 2:24; 8:15
9:8 [q]Ps 23:5; Rev 3:4
9:9 [r]Pr 5:18 [s]Job 31:2
9:10 [t]1Sa 10:7 [u]Ecc 11:6; Ro 12:11; Col 3:23 [v]Nu 16:33 [w]Ecc 2:24

[a]2 Septuagint (Aquila), Vulgate and Syriac; Hebrew does not have *and the bad.* [b]4 Or *What then is to be chosen? With all who live, there is hope* [c]10 Hebrew *Sheol*

11 I have seen something else under the sun:

The race is not to the swift
  or the battle to the strong,[a]
nor does food come to the wise[b]
  or wealth to the brilliant
  or favor to the learned;
but time and chance[c] happen to them all.[d]

12 Moreover, no man knows when his hour will come:

As fish are caught in a cruel net,
  or birds are taken in a snare,
so men are trapped by evil times[e]
  that fall unexpectedly upon them.[f]

13 I also saw under the sun this example of wisdom[g] that greatly
impressed me: 14 There was once a small city with only a few people in it. And a powerful king came against it, surrounded it and
built huge siegeworks against it. 15 Now there lived in that city a
man poor but wise, and he saved the city by his wisdom. But
nobody remembered that poor man.[h] 16 So I said, "Wisdom is
better than strength." But the poor man's wisdom is despised,
and his words are no longer heeded.[i]

17 The quiet words of the wise are more to be heeded
  than the shouts of a ruler of fools.
18 Wisdom[j] is better than weapons of war,
  but one sinner destroys much good.

Chapter 10 Theme ____________________

10

As dead flies give perfume a bad smell,
  so a little folly[k] outweighs wisdom and honor.
2 The heart of the wise inclines to the right,
  but the heart of the fool to the left.
3 Even as he walks along the road,
  the fool lacks sense
  and shows everyone[l] how stupid he is.
4 If a ruler's anger rises against you,
  do not leave your post;[m]
  calmness can lay great errors to rest.[n]

5 There is an evil I have seen under the sun,
  the sort of error that arises from a ruler:
6 Fools are put in many high positions,[o]
  while the rich occupy the low ones.
7 I have seen slaves on horseback,
  while princes go on foot like slaves.[p]

9:11 [a] Am 2:14-15 [b] Job 32:13; Isa 47:10; Jer 9:23 [c] Ecc 2:14 [d] Dt 8:18
9:12 [e] Pr 29:6 [f] Ps 73:22; Ecc 2:14; 8:7
9:13 [g] 2Sa 20:22
9:15 [h] Ge 40:14; Ecc 1:11; 2:16; 4:13
9:16 [i] Pr 21:22; Ecc 7:19
9:18 [j] ver 16
10:1 [k] Pr 13:16; 18:2
10:3 [l] Pr 13:16; 18:2
10:4 [m] Ecc 8:3 [n] Pr 16:14; 25:15
10:6 [o] Pr 29:2
10:7 [p] Pr 19:10

8 Whoever digs a pit may fall into it;[a]
whoever breaks through a wall may be bitten by
a snake.[b]
9 Whoever quarries stones may be injured by them;
whoever splits logs may be endangered by them.[c]

10 If the ax is dull
and its edge unsharpened,
more strength is needed
but skill will bring success.

11 If a snake bites before it is charmed,
there is no profit for the charmer.[d]

12 Words from a wise man's mouth are gracious,[e]
but a fool is consumed by his own lips.[f]
13 At the beginning his words are folly;
at the end they are wicked madness—
14 and the fool multiplies words.[g]

No one knows what is coming—
who can tell him what will happen after him?[h]

15 A fool's work wearies him;
he does not know the way to town.

16 Woe to you, O land whose king was a servant[a] [i]
and whose princes feast in the morning.
17 Blessed are you, O land whose king is of noble birth
and whose princes eat at a proper time—
for strength and not for drunkenness.[j]

18 If a man is lazy, the rafters sag;
if his hands are idle, the house leaks.[k]

19 A feast is made for laughter,
and wine[l] makes life merry,
but money is the answer for everything.

20 Do not revile the king[m] even in your thoughts,
or curse the rich in your bedroom,
because a bird of the air may carry your words,
and a bird on the wing may report what you say.

Chapter 11 Theme ______________________________

11

Cast[n] your bread upon the waters,
for after many days you will find it again.[o]

10:8 [a]Ps 7:15; 57:6; Pr 26:27 [b]Est 2:23; Ps 9:16; Am 5:19
10:9 [c]Pr 26:27
10:11 [d]Ps 58:5; Isa 3:3
10:12 [e]Pr 10:32 [f]Pr 10:14; 14:3; 15:2; 18:7
10:14 [g]Pr 15:2; Ecc 5:3; 6:12; 8:7 [h]Ecc 9:1
10:16 [i]Isa 3:4-5,12
10:17 [j]Dt 14:26; 1Sa 25:36; Pr 31:4
10:18 [k]Pr 20:4; 24:30-34
10:19 [l]Ge 14:18; Jdg 9:13
10:20 [m]Ex 22:28
11:1 [n]ver 6; Isa 32:20; Hos 10:12 [o]Dt 24:19; Pr 19:17; Mt 10:42

[a] *16* Or *king is a child*

[2]Give portions to seven, yes to eight,
for you do not know what disaster may come
upon the land.

[3]If clouds are full of water,
they pour rain upon the earth.
Whether a tree falls to the south or to the north,
in the place where it falls, there will it lie.
[4]Whoever watches the wind will not plant;
whoever looks at the clouds will not reap.

[5]As you do not know the path of the wind,[a]
or how the body is formed[a] in a mother's womb,[b]
so you cannot understand the work of God,
the Maker of all things.

[6]Sow your seed in the morning,
and at evening let not your hands be idle,[c]
for you do not know which will succeed,
whether this or that,
or whether both will do equally well.

[7]Light is sweet,
and it pleases the eyes to see the sun.[d]
[8]However many years a man may live,
let him enjoy them all.
But let him remember[e] the days of darkness,
for they will be many.
Everything to come is meaningless.
[9]Be happy, young man, while you are young,
and let your heart give you joy in the days of your
youth.
Follow the ways of your heart
and whatever your eyes see,
but know that for all these things
God will bring you to judgment.[f]
[10]So then, banish anxiety[g] from your heart
and cast off the troubles of your body,
for youth and vigor are meaningless.[h]

Chapter 12 Theme ______________________

12

Remember[i] your Creator
in the days of your youth,
before the days of trouble[j] come
and the years approach when you will say,
"I find no pleasure in them"—

[a]5 Or *know how life* (or *the spirit*) / *enters the body being formed*

11:5
[a]Jn 3:8-10
[b]Ps 139:14-16

11:6
[c]Ecc 9:10

11:7
[d]Ecc 7:11

11:8
[e]Ecc 12:1

11:9
[f]Job 19:29; Ecc 2:24; 3:17; 12:14; Ro 14:10

11:10
[g]Ps 94:19
[h]Ecc 2:24

12:1
[i]Ecc 11:8
[j]2Sa 19:35

2before the sun and the light
and the moon and the stars grow dark,
and the clouds return after the rain;
3when the keepers of the house tremble,
and the strong men stoop,
when the grinders cease because they are few,
and those looking through the windows grow dim;
4when the doors to the street are closed
and the sound of grinding fades;
when men rise up at the sound of birds,
but all their songs grow faint;[a]
5when men are afraid of heights
and of dangers in the streets;
when the almond tree blossoms
and the grasshopper drags himself along
and desire no longer is stirred.
Then man goes to his eternal home[b]
and mourners[c] go about the streets.

6Remember him—before the silver cord is severed,
or the golden bowl is broken;
before the pitcher is shattered at the spring,
or the wheel broken at the well,
7and the dust returns[d] to the ground it came from,
and the spirit returns to God[e] who gave it.[f]

8"Meaningless! Meaningless!" says the Teacher.[a]
"Everything is meaningless![g]"

9Not only was the Teacher wise, but also he imparted knowledge to the people. He pondered and searched out and set in
order many proverbs.[h] 10The Teacher searched to find just the
right words, and what he wrote was upright and true.[i]
11The words of the wise are like goads, their collected sayings
like firmly embedded nails[j]—given by one Shepherd. 12Be
warned, my son, of anything in addition to them.
Of making many books there is no end, and much study wearies the body.[k]

13Now all has been heard;
here is the conclusion of the matter:
Fear God and keep his commandments,[l]
for this is the whole ⌊duty⌋ of man.[m]
14For God will bring every deed into judgment,[n]
including every hidden thing,[o]
whether it is good or evil.

12:4 [a] Jer 25:10
12:5 [b] Job 17:13; 10:21 [c] Jer 9:17; Am 5:16
12:7 [d] Ge 3:19; Job 34:15; Ps 146:4 [e] Ecc 3:21 [f] Job 20:8; Zec 12:1
12:8 [g] Ecc 1:2
12:9 [h] 1Ki 4:32
12:10 [i] Pr 22:20-21
12:11 [j] Ezr 9:8
12:12 [k] Ecc 1:18
12:13 [l] Dt 4:2; 10:12 [m] Mic 6:8
12:14 [n] Ecc 3:17 [o] Mt 10:26; 1Co 4:5

[a] 8 Or *the leader of the assembly*; also in verses 9 and 10

Ecclesiastes at a Glance

Theme of Ecclesiastes:

Segment Divisions

		Chapter Themes
		1
		2
		3
		4
		5
		6
		7
		8
		9
		10
		11
		12

Author:

Date:

Purpose:

Key Words:

God

meaningless

under the sun (under heaven)

wisdom (wise, skill)

righteous, overrighteous (righteousness, justice, rights)

wicked, overwicked (wickedness)

wise (overwise)

fool(s), fool's

evil (misfortune, wrong, bad, crime[s], trouble)

labor (work[ed], toil[ed], effort[s], toilsome, do his work)

wealthy, much

SONG OF SONGS

Song of Songs is a love story included in the canon of Scripture. On the eighth day of Passover the Jews would sing portions of the Song of Songs, a book they compared to the Most Holy Place in the temple.

Song of Songs is a book never quoted by our Lord, but one from which many Christians sing, "I am my lover's and my lover is mine" and "his banner over me is love."

Many waters cannot quench love;
    rivers cannot wash it away.
If one were to give all the wealth of his house for love,
    it would be utterly scorned (8:7).

Things to Do

1. The Song of Songs is a unified lyrical poem composed of a variety of songs. There is no other book like it in Scripture. Before you begin to analyze its content sit down and read it through slowly without stopping. Remember, the phrases may seem different or unusual because of the culture of the Eastern people.

2. As you read Song of Songs notice who is speaking when. The reference notes of the NIV identify who speaks. If you prefer to identify the speaker yourself, do the following:

   a. Read the book again and mark every time the "woman" speaks and also when the "man" speaks. Watch for pronouns such as *he, him, his,* and *she* and mark them in a distinctive way.

   b. As you read, you will notice there is a third party referred to in the text as the "daughters of Jerusalem" or "daughters of Zion" and in the reference notes in the margin as "Friends." Note when the "daughters of Jerusalem" or "daughters of Zion" (the friends) intervene. When you see any other parties speaking, mark these as well. Note these under "Segment Divisions" on the SONG OF SONGS AT A GLANCE chart on page 1152.

3. Now read through the Song of Songs again. This time do the following:

   a. When you note from the text whose song this is, record it under "Author" on SONG OF SONGS AT A GLANCE.

   b. As you read, mark the key words listed on SONG OF SONGS AT A GLANCE.

   c. Watch for details about the bride and the bridegroom—their position, family, how they met, where they met, etc. A careful reading of the book as a whole can help you piece together these facts. You might want to write your observations on a piece of paper and then transfer them to the margin of the text.

   d. Watch for other segment divisions in the book. For instance, note when the courtship ends, when the wedding takes place, and what occurs in the marriage and why. (Watch for the word *wedding.*) Record these divisions on SONG OF SONGS AT A GLANCE.

   e. Record the theme of each chapter on SONG OF SONGS AT A GLANCE and then on the line next to the chapter number. Complete the chart.

Things to Think About

1. There are many different interpretations about the meaning of this book. Does Song of Songs speak only about the emotional and physical relationship of love and marriage? Or does it symbolize something such as Israel's relationship to God, or the church's relationship to Jesus, their heavenly bridegroom, or the individual's devotion to Christ? If it goes beyond the natural to the spiritual, what would you see that you might apply to your relationship with the Lord Jesus Christ?

2. If this book speaks merely of the physical and emotional bonds of marriage, what do you learn from it that you might apply to your relationship with your mate? Think about the way the bride and bridegroom communicated with each other, what they shared, what their physical relationship was like, what caused problems, and how they solved them.

3. What can you learn from Song of Songs that would help you prepare for marriage? For instance, what can you learn from this book about understanding yourself, your future mate, and the importance of intimacy, purity, and physical oneness?

4. What do you think an adulterous relationship would do to the intimacy between the bride and the bridegroom? James 4:4 tells us that when we become friends with the world (the world system) we are committing spiritual adultery. What does this do to our intimacy with God? Read 2 Corinthians 11:2, 3 and think about it.

Chapter 1 Theme ______________________________

1 Solomon's Song of Songs.[a]

Beloved[a]

[2]Let him kiss me with the kisses of his mouth—
for your love[b] is more delightful than wine.
[3]Pleasing is the fragrance of your perfumes;[c]
your name[d] is like perfume poured out.
No wonder the maidens[e] love you!
[4]Take me away with you—let us hurry!
Let the king bring me into his chambers.[f]

Friends

We rejoice and delight in you[b];
we will praise your love more than wine.

Beloved

How right they are to adore you!

[5]Dark am I, yet lovely,[g]
O daughters of Jerusalem,[h]
dark like the tents of Kedar,
like the tent curtains of Solomon.[c]
[6]Do not stare at me because I am dark,
because I am darkened by the sun.
My mother's sons were angry with me
and made me take care of the vineyards;[i]
my own vineyard I have neglected.

[a]Primarily on the basis of the gender of the Hebrew pronouns used, male and female speakers are indicated in the margins by the captions *Lover* and *Beloved* respectively. The words of others are marked *Friends.* In some instances the divisions and their captions are debatable. [b]4 The Hebrew is masculine singular. [c]5 Or *Salma*

1:1 *a* 1Ki 4:32
1:2 *b* SS 4:10
1:3 *c* SS 4:10 *d* Ecc 7:1 *e* Ps 45:14
1:4 *f* Ps 45:15
1:5 *g* SS 2:14; 4:3 *h* SS 2:7; 5:8; 5:16
1:6 *i* Ps 69:8; SS 8:12

1:7 [a]SS 3:1-4; Isa 13:20

[7]Tell me, you whom I love, where you graze your flock
and where you rest your sheep[a] at midday.
Why should I be like a veiled woman
beside the flocks of your friends?

Friends

1:8 [b]SS 5:9; 6:1

[8]If you do not know, most beautiful of women,[b]
follow the tracks of the sheep
and graze your young goats
by the tents of the shepherds.

Lover

1:9 [c]2Ch 1:17

[9]I liken you, my darling, to a mare
harnessed to one of the chariots[c] of Pharaoh.
[10]Your cheeks[d] are beautiful with earrings,
your neck with strings of jewels.[e]
[11]We will make you earrings of gold,
studded with silver.

1:10 [d]SS 5:13 [e]Isa 61:10

Beloved

[12]While the king was at his table,
my perfume spread its fragrance.[f]
[13]My lover is to me a sachet of myrrh
resting between my breasts.
[14]My lover is to me a cluster of henna[g] blossoms
from the vineyards of En Gedi.[h]

1:12 [f]SS 4:11-14

Lover

1:14 [g]SS 4:13 [h]1Sa 23:29

[15]How beautiful[i] you are, my darling!
Oh, how beautiful!
Your eyes are doves.[j]

Beloved

1:15 [i]SS 4:7 [j]SS 2:14; 4:1; 5:2,12; 6:9

[16]How handsome you are, my lover!
Oh, how charming!
And our bed is verdant.

Lover

[17]The beams of our house are cedars;[k]
our rafters are firs.

1:17 [k]1Ki 6:9

Chapter 2 Theme ________________________

Beloved[a]

2 I am a rose[b] [a] of Sharon,[b]
a lily[c] of the valleys.

Lover

2Like a lily among thorns
is my darling among the maidens.

Beloved

3Like an apple tree among the trees of the forest
is my lover[d] among the young men.
I delight[e] to sit in his shade,
and his fruit is sweet to my taste.[f]
4He has taken me to the banquet hall,[g]
and his banner[h] over me is love.
5Strengthen me with raisins,
refresh me with apples,[i]
for I am faint with love.[j]
6His left arm is under my head,
and his right arm embraces me.[k]
7Daughters of Jerusalem, I charge you[l]
by the gazelles and by the does of the field:
Do not arouse or awaken love
until it so desires.[m]

8Listen! My lover!
Look! Here he comes,
leaping across the mountains,
bounding over the hills.[n]
9My lover is like a gazelle[o] or a young stag.[p]
Look! There he stands behind our wall,
gazing through the windows,
peering through the lattice.
10My lover spoke and said to me,
"Arise, my darling,
my beautiful one, and come with me.
11See! The winter is past;
the rains are over and gone.
12Flowers appear on the earth;
the season of singing has come,
the cooing of doves
is heard in our land.

[a] *1* Or *Lover* [b] *1* Possibly a member of the crocus family

2:1
[a] Isa 35:1
[b] 1Ch 27:29
[c] SS 5:13; Hos 14:5

2:3
[d] SS 1:14
[e] SS 1:4
[f] SS 4:16

2:4
[g] Est 1:11
[h] Nu 1:52

2:5
[i] SS 7:8
[j] SS 5:8

2:6
[k] SS 8:3

2:7
[l] SS 5:8
[m] SS 3:5; 8:4

2:8
[n] ver 17; SS 8:14

2:9
[o] 2Sa 2:18
[p] ver 17; SS 8:14

13 The fig tree forms its early fruit;[a]
the blossoming[b] vines spread their fragrance.
Arise, come, my darling;
my beautiful one, come with me."

Lover

14 My dove[c] in the clefts of the rock,
in the hiding places on the mountainside,
show me your face,
let me hear your voice;
for your voice is sweet,
and your face is lovely.[d]
15 Catch for us the foxes,[e]
the little foxes
that ruin the vineyards,[f]
our vineyards that are in bloom.[g]

Beloved

16 My lover is mine and I am his;[h]
he browses among the lilies.[i]
17 Until the day breaks
and the shadows flee,[j]
turn, my lover,[k]
and be like a gazelle
or like a young stag[l]
on the rugged hills.[a] [m]

Chapter 3 Theme ______________________________

3 All night long on my bed
I looked[n] for the one my heart loves;
I looked for him but did not find him.
2 I will get up now and go about the city,
through its streets and squares;
I will search for the one my heart loves.
So I looked for him but did not find him.
3 The watchmen found me
as they made their rounds in the city.[o]
"Have you seen the one my heart loves?"
4 Scarcely had I passed them
when I found the one my heart loves.
I held him and would not let him go
till I had brought him to my mother's house,[p]
to the room of the one who conceived me.[q]

2:13 [a] Isa 28:4; Jer 24:2; Hos 9:10; Mic 7:1; Na 3:12 [b] SS 7:12
2:14 [c] Ge 8:8; SS 1:15 [d] SS 1:5; 8:13
2:15 [e] Jdg 15:4 [f] SS 1:6 [g] SS 7:12
2:16 [h] SS 7:10 [i] SS 4:5; 6:3
2:17 [j] SS 4:6 [k] SS 1:14 [l] ver 9 [m] ver 8
3:1 [n] SS 5:6; Isa 26:9
3:3 [o] SS 5:7
3:4 [p] SS 8:2 [q] SS 6:9

a 17 Or *the hills of Bether*

5Daughters of Jerusalem, I charge you[a]
by the gazelles and by the does of the field:
Do not arouse or awaken love
until it so desires.[b]

6Who is this coming up from the desert[c]
like a column of smoke,
perfumed with myrrh[d] and incense
made from all the spices[e] of the merchant?
7Look! It is Solomon's carriage,
escorted by sixty warriors,[f]
the noblest of Israel,
8all of them wearing the sword,
all experienced in battle,
each with his sword at his side,
prepared for the terrors of the night.[g]
9King Solomon made for himself the carriage;
he made it of wood from Lebanon.
10Its posts he made of silver,
its base of gold.
Its seat was upholstered with purple,
its interior lovingly inlaid
by[a] the daughters of Jerusalem.
11Come out, you daughters of Zion,[h]
and look at King Solomon wearing the crown,
the crown with which his mother crowned him
on the day of his wedding,
the day his heart rejoiced.[i]

Chapter 4 Theme ________________________

Lover

4 How beautiful you are, my darling!
Oh, how beautiful!
Your eyes behind your veil are doves.[j]
Your hair is like a flock of goats
descending from Mount Gilead.[k]
2Your teeth are like a flock of sheep just shorn,
coming up from the washing.
Each has its twin;
not one of them is alone.[l]
3Your lips are like a scarlet ribbon;
your mouth[m] is lovely.
Your temples behind your veil
are like the halves of a pomegranate.[n]

a *10* Or *its inlaid interior a gift of love / from*

3:5
[a]SS 2:7
[b]SS 8:4

3:6
[c]SS 8:5
[d]SS 1:13; 4:6,14
[e]Ex 30:34

3:7
[f]1Sa 8:11

3:8
[g]Job 15:22; Ps 91:5

3:11
[h]Isa 4:4
[i]Isa 62:5

4:1
[j]SS 1:15; 5:12
[k]SS 6:5; Mic 7:14

4:2
[l]SS 6:6

4:3
[m]SS 5:16
[n]SS 6:7

4Your neck is like the tower[a] of David,
built with elegance[a];
on it hang a thousand shields,[b]
all of them shields of warriors.
5Your two breasts[c] are like two fawns,
like twin fawns of a gazelle[d]
that browse among the lilies.[e]
6Until the day breaks
and the shadows flee,[f]
I will go to the mountain of myrrh[g]
and to the hill of incense.
7All beautiful[h] you are, my darling;
there is no flaw in you.

8Come with me from Lebanon, my bride,[i]
come with me from Lebanon.
Descend from the crest of Amana,
from the top of Senir,[j] the summit of Hermon,[k]
from the lions' dens
and the mountain haunts of the leopards.
9You have stolen my heart, my sister, my bride;
you have stolen my heart
with one glance of your eyes,
with one jewel of your necklace.[l]
10How delightful[m] is your love[n], my sister, my bride!
How much more pleasing is your love than wine,
and the fragrance of your perfume than any spice!
11Your lips drop sweetness as the honeycomb, my bride;
milk and honey are under your tongue.[o]
The fragrance of your garments is like that of Lebanon.[p]
12You are a garden locked up, my sister, my bride;
you are a spring enclosed, a sealed fountain.[q]
13Your plants are an orchard of pomegranates[r]
with choice fruits,
with henna[s] and nard,
14 nard and saffron,
calamus and cinnamon,[t]
with every kind of incense tree,
with myrrh[u] and aloes
and all the finest spices.[v]
15You are[b] a garden fountain,
a well of flowing water
streaming down from Lebanon.

4:4 [a]SS 7:4 [b]Eze 27:10
4:5 [c]SS 7:3 [d]Pr 5:19 [e]SS 2:16; 6:2-3
4:6 [f]SS 2:17 [g]ver 14
4:7 [h]SS 1:15
4:8 [i]SS 5:1 [j]Dt 3:9 [k]1Ch 5:23
4:9 [l]Ge 41:42
4:10 [m]SS 7:6 [n]SS 1:2
4:11 [o]Ps 19:10; SS 5:1 [p]Hos 14:6
4:12 [q]Pr 5:15-18
4:13 [r]SS 6:11; 7:12 [s]SS 1:14
4:14 [t]Ex 30:23 [u]SS 3:6 [v]SS 1:12

a *4* The meaning of the Hebrew for this word is uncertain. b *15* Or *I am* (spoken by the *Beloved*)

Beloved

[16]Awake, north wind,
and come, south wind!
Blow on my garden,
that its fragrance may spread abroad.
Let my lover come into his garden
and taste its choice fruits.[a]

Chapter 5 Theme ______________________

Lover

5

I have come into my garden, my sister, my bride;[b]
I have gathered my myrrh with my spice.
I have eaten my honeycomb and my honey;
I have drunk my wine and my milk. [c]

Friends

Eat, O friends, and drink;
drink your fill, O lovers.

Beloved

[2]I slept but my heart was awake.
Listen! My lover is knocking:
"Open to me, my sister, my darling,
my dove, my flawless[d] one.[e]
My head is drenched with dew,
my hair with the dampness of the night."
[3]I have taken off my robe—
must I put it on again?
I have washed my feet—
must I soil them again?
[4]My lover thrust his hand through the latch-opening;
my heart began to pound for him.
[5]I arose to open for my lover,
and my hands dripped with myrrh,[f]
my fingers with flowing myrrh,
on the handles of the lock.
[6]I opened for my lover,[g]
but my lover had left; he was gone.[h]
My heart sank at his departure.[a]
I looked[i] for him but did not find him.
I called him but he did not answer.

a6 Or *heart had gone out to him when he spoke*

4:16
[a]SS 2:3; 5:1

5:1
[b]SS 4:8
[c]SS 4:11; Isa 55:1

5:2
[d]SS 4:7
[e]SS 6:9

5:5
[f]ver 13

5:6
[g]SS 6:1
[h]SS 6:2
[i]SS 3:1

[7]The watchmen found me
as they made their rounds in the city.[a]
They beat me, they bruised me;
they took away my cloak,
those watchmen of the walls!
[8]O daughters of Jerusalem, I charge you[b]—
if you find my lover,
what will you tell him?
Tell him I am faint with love.[c]

Friends

[9]How is your beloved better than others,
most beautiful of women?[d]
How is your beloved better than others,
that you charge us so?

Beloved

[10]My lover is radiant and ruddy,
outstanding among ten thousand.[e]
[11]His head is purest gold;
his hair is wavy
and black as a raven.
[12]His eyes are like doves[f]
by the water streams,
washed in milk,[g]
mounted like jewels.
[13]His cheeks[h] are like beds of spice[i]
yielding perfume.
His lips are like lilies[j]
dripping with myrrh.
[14]His arms are rods of gold
set with chrysolite.
His body is like polished ivory
decorated with sapphires.[a][k]
[15]His legs are pillars of marble
set on bases of pure gold.
His appearance is like Lebanon,[l]
choice as its cedars.
[16]His mouth[m] is sweetness itself;
he is altogether lovely.
This is my lover,[n] this my friend,
O daughters of Jerusalem.[o]

5:7 [a]SS 3:3
5:8 [b]SS 2:7; 3:5 [c]SS 2:5
5:9 [d]SS 1:8; 6:1
5:10 [e]Ps 45:2
5:12 [f]SS 1:15; 4:1 [g]Ge 49:12
5:13 [h]SS 1:10 [i]SS 6:2 [j]SS 2:1
5:14 [k]Job 28:6
5:15 [l]1Ki 4:33; SS 7:4
5:16 [m]SS 4:3 [n]SS 7:9 [o]SS 1:5

[a]*14* Or *lapis lazuli*

Chapter 6 Theme ______________________

Friends

6

Where has your lover[a] gone,
most beautiful of women?[b]
Which way did your lover turn,
that we may look for him with you?

Beloved

2My lover has gone[c] down to his garden,[d]
to the beds of spices,[e]
to browse in the gardens
and to gather lilies.
3I am my lover's and my lover is mine;[f]
he browses among the lilies.[g]

Lover

4You are beautiful, my darling, as Tirzah,[h]
lovely as Jerusalem,[i]
majestic as troops with banners.[j]
5Turn your eyes from me;
they overwhelm me.
Your hair is like a flock of goats
descending from Gilead.[k]
6Your teeth are like a flock of sheep
coming up from the washing.
Each has its twin,
not one of them is alone.[l]
7Your temples behind your veil[m]
are like the halves of a pomegranate.[n]
8Sixty queens[o] there may be,
and eighty concubines,[p]
and virgins beyond number;
9but my dove,[q] my perfect one,[r] is unique,
the only daughter of her mother,
the favorite of the one who bore her.[s]
The maidens saw her and called her blessed;
the queens and concubines praised her.

Friends

10Who is this that appears like the dawn,
fair as the moon, bright as the sun,
majestic as the stars in procession?

6:1
[a]SS 5:6
[b]SS 1:8

6:2
[c]SS 5:6
[d]SS 4:12
[e]SS 5:13

6:3
[f]SS 7:10
[g]SS 2:16

6:4
[h]Jos 12:24
[i]Ps 48:2; 50:2
[j]ver 10

6:5
[k]SS 4:1

6:6
[l]SS 4:2

6:7
[m]Ge 24:65
[n]SS 4:3

6:8
[o]Ps 45:9
[p]Ge 22:24

6:9
[q]SS 1:15
[r]SS 5:2
[s]SS 3:4

6:11 [a]SS 7:12

Lover

[11]I went down to the grove of nut trees
to look at the new growth in the valley,
to see if the vines had budded
or the pomegranates were in bloom.[a]
[12]Before I realized it,
my desire set me among the royal chariots of my people.[a]

6:13 [b]Ex 15:20

Friends

[13]Come back, come back, O Shulammite;
come back, come back, that we may gaze on you!

7:1 [c]Ps 45:13

Lover

Why would you gaze on the Shulammite
as on the dance[b] of Mahanaim?

Chapter 7 Theme ______________________

7:3 [d]SS 4:5

7 How beautiful your sandaled feet,
O prince's[c] daughter!
Your graceful legs are like jewels,
the work of a craftsman's hands.
[2]Your navel is a rounded goblet
that never lacks blended wine.
Your waist is a mound of wheat
encircled by lilies.
[3]Your breasts[d] are like two fawns,
twins of a gazelle.
[4]Your neck is like an ivory tower.[e]
Your eyes are the pools of Heshbon[f]
by the gate of Bath Rabbim.
Your nose is like the tower of Lebanon[g]
looking toward Damascus.
[5]Your head crowns you like Mount Carmel.[h]
Your hair is like royal tapestry;
the king is held captive by its tresses.
[6]How beautiful[i] you are and how pleasing,
O love, with your delights![j]
[7]Your stature is like that of the palm,
and your breasts[k] like clusters of fruit.
[8]I said, "I will climb the palm tree;
I will take hold of its fruit."
May your breasts be like the clusters of the vine,

7:4 [e]Ps 144:12; SS 4:4 [f]Nu 21:26 [g]SS 5:15

7:5 [h]Isa 35:2

7:6 [i]SS 1:15 [j]SS 4:10

7:7 [k]SS 4:5

a 12 Or *among the chariots of Amminadab*; or *among the chariots of the people of the prince*

the fragrance of your breath like apples,[a]
9 and your mouth like the best wine.

Beloved

May the wine go straight to my lover,[b]
flowing gently over lips and teeth.[a]
10I belong to my lover,
and his desire[c] is for me.[d]
11Come, my lover, let us go to the countryside,
let us spend the night in the villages.[b]
12Let us go early to the vineyards[e]
to see if the vines have budded,[f]
if their blossoms[g] have opened,
and if the pomegranates[h] are in bloom[i]—
there I will give you my love.
13The mandrakes[j] send out their fragrance,
and at our door is every delicacy,
both new and old,
that I have stored up for you, my lover.[k]

Chapter 8 Theme ______________________________

8

If only you were to me like a brother,
who was nursed at my mother's breasts!
Then, if I found you outside,
I would kiss you,
and no one would despise me.
2I would lead you
and bring you to my mother's house[l]—
she who has taught me.
I would give you spiced wine to drink,
the nectar of my pomegranates.
3His left arm is under my head
and his right arm embraces me.[m]
4Daughters of Jerusalem, I charge you:
Do not arouse or awaken love
until it so desires.[n]

Friends

5Who is this coming up from the desert[o]
leaning on her lover?

a9 Septuagint, Aquila, Vulgate and Syriac; Hebrew *lips of sleepers* b11 Or *henna bushes*

7:8
[a]SS 2:5

7:9
[b]SS 5:16

7:10
[c]Ps 45:11
[d]SS 2:16; 6:3

7:12
[e]SS 1:6
[f]SS 2:15
[g]SS 2:13
[h]SS 4:13
[i]SS 6:11

7:13
[j]Ge 30:14
[k]SS 4:16

8:2
[l]SS 3:4

8:3
[m]SS 2:6

8:4
[n]SS 2:7; 3:5

8:5
[o]SS 3:6

Beloved

Under the apple tree I roused you;
there your mother conceived[a] you,
there she who was in labor gave you birth.
6Place me like a seal over your heart,
like a seal on your arm;
for love[b] is as strong as death,
its jealousy[a][c] unyielding as the grave.[b]
It burns like blazing fire,
like a mighty flame.[c]
7Many waters cannot quench love;
rivers cannot wash it away.
If one were to give
all the wealth of his house for love,
it[d] would be utterly scorned.[d]

Friends

8We have a young sister,
and her breasts are not yet grown.
What shall we do for our sister
for the day she is spoken for?
9If she is a wall,
we will build towers of silver on her.
If she is a door,
we will enclose her with panels of cedar.

Beloved

10I am a wall,
and my breasts are like towers.
Thus I have become in his eyes
like one bringing contentment.
11Solomon had a vineyard[e] in Baal Hamon;
he let out his vineyard to tenants.
Each was to bring for its fruit
a thousand shekels[e][f] of silver.
12But my own vineyard[g] is mine to give;
the thousand shekels are for you, O Solomon,
and two hundred[f] are for those who tend its fruit.

8:5 *a*SS 3:4
8:6 *b*SS 1:2 *c*Nu 5:14
8:7 *d*Pr 6:35
8:11 *e*Ecc 2:4 *f*Isa 7:23
8:12 *g*SS 1:6

a6 Or *ardor* b6 Hebrew *Sheol* c6 Or / *like the very flame of the* Lord d7 Or *he*
e11 That is, about 25 pounds (about 11.5 kilograms); also in verse 12 f12 That is, about 5 pounds (about 2.3 kilograms)

Lover

13You who dwell in the gardens
with friends in attendance,
let me hear your voice!

Beloved

14Come away, my lover,
and be like a gazelle[a]
or like a young stag[b]
on the spice-laden mountains.[c]

8:14
[a]Pr 5:19
[b]SS 2:9
[c]SS 2:8,17

Song of Songs at a Glance

Theme of Song of Songs:

Segment Divisions

		Chapter Themes
		1
		2
		3
		4
		5
		6
		7
		8

Author:

Date:

Purpose:

Key Words:

love (ador

beloved (lo

come
(coming, c

beautiful
(delightful

ISAIAH

The messages of the Old Testament prophets addressed the people of Israel and Judah who lived between the years of 840 and 420 B.C. Isaiah is the first of the major prophets. Isaiah's name, *Yeshayahu*, means "Jehovah Saves" or "Salvation of Jehovah." No other prophet gives more prophecies regarding the coming Messiah. Isaiah reveals the Messiah (Christ) as the Suffering Servant and the Conquering King. Under divine inspiration Isaiah announces and declares things that are coming and events which will occur in the future so that God's people might know there is no God besides him.

From Isaiah 37:37, 38 we know Isaiah lived at least until 681 B.C., the year Esarhaddon, the son of Sennacherib, became king of Assyria after his father's death. Tradition says Isaiah was sawn in two by Manasseh, the king of Judah who reigned after Hezekiah (2 Kings 21:16). If tradition is correct, Isaiah might be one of the heroes of faith referred to in Hebrews 11:37.

Things to Do

The basic structure of Isaiah is easy to remember if it is compared to the Bible's structure. The Bible is comprised of 66 books, 39 in the Old Testament and 27 in the New Testament. Isaiah, which focuses on the Holy One of Israel, has 66 chapters which fall into two main divisions: Isaiah 1 through 39 reveals God's character and judgment, and Isaiah 40 through 66 shows God's comfort and redemption. Because Isaiah is a long book filled with discourses and songs, it needs to be studied segment by segment so that you don't miss the wonder of its promises and prophecies. Ask God to help you understand the important message of this book.

General Instructions

1. As you read through Isaiah one chapter at a time, observe each chapter in the light of the five W's and an H. Ask general questions such as: Who does this chapter focus on? What happens or what is this about? When is this happening? Where will it happen? Why is this going to happen and how?

2. Isaiah is a set of discourses or songs rather than a historical chronology of events in the life of Israel. Periodically there are historical interludes which are very important. In these interludes God will often tell Isaiah to do something which will act as a sign to the people. For instance, in Isaiah 8:3 Isaiah is to name his son *Maher-Shalal-Hash-Baz,* which means "quick to the plunder, swift to the spoil." His name pointed the people to the Assyrian invasion, which would come before Maher-Shalal-Hash-Baz would learn to say Momma or Daddy. Observe these interludes carefully.

3. Isaiah recorded many prophecies regarding future events, including the captivity, the birth of Messiah, the reign of Messiah, and the last days. Watch for these prophecies and note them in the margin. Also check the reference notes to see where they are fulfilled.

   a. As you read some of these prophecies you will see that the first and second coming of Messiah (Christ) can be prophesied without any indication that there is an interval of time between these comings. For instance, Isaiah 61:1 through 2a covers the first coming of Jesus Christ. As a matter of fact Jesus read this passage in the synagogue in Nazareth and stopped at this point (Luke 4:18, 19). Why? Because the next part of the verse, "And the day of vengeance of our God," skips to the day of the Lord, which encompasses Christ's judgment and his second coming.

   b. You will find it beneficial to read the section entitled "Guidelines for Interpreting Predictive Prophecy" on page 2205.

c. On page 1158 is a chart called THE PROPHETIC POINTS OF HISTORY. Keeping these prophetic points in mind as you read Isaiah will help you distinguish the time periods to which Isaiah refers. You may want to draw this chart on a card so you can look at it as you study Isaiah.

4. Mark every reference to *the day of the Lord* or *the last days* in a distinctive way, then list your observations in the margin and on the chart THE DAY OF THE LORD that begins on page 2178. It will become a valuable resource on this critical event. Record the book, chapter, and verse from which you took your information. Do this all the way through Isaiah.

5. Babylon plays a significant prophetic role throughout Scripture, even in the day of the Lord. List what you learn about Babylon in the margin of the text. Then record that information on the chart WHAT THE BIBLE TEACHES ABOUT BABYLON beginning on page 2176. When you record your observations on Babylon note the reference (book, chapter, and verse) from which you took your information. You will want this for future reference.

Isaiah 1-39: God's Character and Judgment

Chapters 1-12: Discourses Regarding Judah and Jerusalem

1. Read Isaiah 1 to get the spiritual and moral condition and the historical setting of this book.

   a. Examine Isaiah 1 carefully under the scrutiny of the five W's and an H: Who? What? When? Where? Why? and How? Ask questions such as: Who wrote this? When was it written? Why was it written? To whom was it written? What do you learn about them? What are they to do and why? What will happen? Interrogating the text with such questions will give you great insight into what is being said in this chapter. Record your insights in the margin of chapter 1.

   b. To put the book into its chronological setting, compare Isaiah 1:1 with the historical chart on page 1159. Record your insights under "Author" and "Date" on the ISAIAH AT A GLANCE chart on page 1277.

2. As you read Isaiah 2 through 12 one chapter at a time:

   a. Mark the following key words in a distinctive way: *remnant, Israel, Judah, Samaria, Assyria (Assyrian), woe, Holy One of Israel,* and *the Lord Almighty*. (Although the last two phrases are titles referring to God, it is helpful to see how each is used, so mark them distinctively.)

   b. Also mark every occurrence of *in the last days* and *in that day*. As you mark *in that day* make sure you know what day it is referring to. For instance, in Isaiah 2 *in that day* refers to the last days. Therefore both can be marked in the same way. However, this may not always be the case, so check the context in which "that day" is used.

   c. Write all these key words on an index card that you can use as a bookmark while you study Isaiah. Color code them so you can mark them quickly.

   d. Watch for key repeated words or phrases which are not on the list but are distinctive to certain chapters.

3. As you read each chapter observe the following and record your insights in the margin:

   a. Notice to whom God is speaking and what he says about their behavior.

   b. Observe the consequences of the behavior.

   c. See if there is an exhortation or plea followed by a promise of how God will cleanse them, bless them, or move on their behalf.

4. Isaiah 6 is a strategic chapter. It records Isaiah's call and commission from the Lord.

   a. To get the historical setting of this chapter read 2 Kings 15. Uzziah is called Azariah in 2 Kings 15:1 (see 2 Chronicles 26:1). On the chart on page 1159, you will notice that the reigns of Uzziah and Jotham overlapped. This is because they served as co-regents for a time.

   b. Observe the progression of events in this chapter and note them in the margin.

5. As you study each chapter, don't forget the "General Instructions." These are an important part of the process of carefully observing the text.

6. When you finish observing each chapter record the theme of that chapter on ISAIAH AT A GLANCE and on the line in the text next to the chapter number.

Chapters 13-23: Oracles Against Various Nations

1. As you read this section chapter by chapter:
   a. Watch for and mark in a distinctive way the key repeated phrase, *an oracle concerning* ________________. Note who the oracle concerns and locate each of these on the map at the beginning of chapter 13.
   b. Mark the following key words: *the Lord Almighty, Babylon, day of the Lord,* and *remnant (those who remain, survivors)*. Write these on a new index card to use as a bookmark.
2. As you observe each chapter, note the following in the margin or mark it in the text:
   a. Observe if there is any judgment connected with those to whom the oracle is given and why.
   b. Watch where the judgment comes and if there is any effect on Israel.
   c. Watch for *when* something happens. Note this with a time symbol in the margin.
   d. Notice how God's purposes are being worked out in history.
3. Record the theme of each chapter in the same way you did previously. However, remember that this will not always be easy. The chapter divisions in the Bible are not part of the original Scriptures. Therefore, if you have a hard time summarizing the theme of each chapter, don't be discouraged. When it is not easy to settle on a chapter theme, pick a key verse that the truths of the chapter seem to pivot around, or simply choose some words from the first verse and record these on ISAIAH AT A GLANCE.

Chapters 24-27: Discourses Regarding "That Day"

1. As you read this segment, mark the following key words: *earth('s), in that day, salvation,* and *the Lord Almighty.*
2. As you read each chapter observe the following:
   a. What happens to the earth and its inhabitants (humans and animals)
   b. What the Lord of hosts will do and where he will be
   c. What the people's response will be
3. Record the theme of each chapter on ISAIAH AT A GLANCE and in the text.

Chapters 28-33: Six Woes

1. As you read each chapter watch for and mark the following key words: *woe, the Holy One of Israel, the Lord Almighty, remnant, (the* or *my) Spirit, in that day (on that day),* and *salvation.*
2. As you read each of these chapters, note in the margin or mark in the text the following:
   a. To whom the woe is given
   b. What was done to cause the woe
   c. What the Lord will do and what the result will be
3. Record the chapter themes on ISAIAH AT A GLANCE and in the text.

Chapters 34, 35: God's Recompense and Ransom for Zion

1. As you read these two chapters, mark the following key words: *nations* (and any pronouns), *sword, retribution, glory,* and *ransomed.*

2. Look for and list in the margin on whom God's recompense will come, what it will be, and what will follow. Make sure you note what happens to the ransomed and the redeemed. Also note what this will mean to Zion.

3. Record the chapter themes on ISAIAH AT A GLANCE and in the text.

Chapters 36-39: Historical Account from the Threat of Assyria to the Threat of Babylon

1. Read these chapters and mark the following words: *Assyria (Assyrian), Sennacherib, his field commander (the field commander, the commander)* (also known as Rabshakeh), *Hezekiah('s), Isaiah, Babylon, remnant, the Lord Almighty (O Lord Almighty),* and *prayer (pray, prayed).*

2. Now read the chapters again, observing the words you marked. In the margin note what you learn about each of the characters and what they do, what happens as a result, and how God intervenes. List what you learn about God from these chapters. Don't miss what happens to Assyria and Babylon. This is a pivotal point in respect to these two powers and the nation of Israel.

3. Record the chapter themes on ISAIAH AT A GLANCE and in the text.

Isaiah 40-66: God's Comfort and Redemption

Chapters 40-48: Behold the Lord, Your Redeemer

1. Mark the following references to God in a distinctive way: *the Lord Almighty, the Holy One of Israel, I am the Lord (God), I the Lord, none besides me (no other god, no god),* and *Redeemer.* Then list in the margin all you see about God that you want to remember for future reference. Note God's character, what he does, and to what or whom he is compared.

2. As you do all this don't simply mark these and move on. Meditate on what you see. Think of what these insights can do for your relationship with God. Remember, he is not only Israel's Redeemer but yours also if you have repented and believed in the Lord Jesus Christ.

3. Also mark *servant.* As you read each chapter, check the context (the surrounding verses) in which *servant* is used. This is vital. Note whether *servant* refers to Israel (Jacob) or to the Lord Jesus Christ. Record your insights in the margin. If it seems to be a prophetic reference to Jesus, check a concordance to find the New Testament verses which correspond to the Old Testament passage and see if they show how this prophecy was fulfilled by Jesus. When you make your list in the margin put it under "Israel the Servant" or "Messiah the Servant."

4. Mark every reference to *redeemed* and list in the margin what you learn about the redeemed. Then mark *who remain* (used only one time in this segment), *glory of the Lord, salvation, nation (nations, Gentiles),* and *Babylon.* In the margin record what you learn about each.

5. Put the key words for this segment on an index card to use as a bookmark in studying the remainder of Isaiah. *Remnant (who remain), none besides me (no other god),* and *Babylon* do not appear after this segment.

6. Record your chapter themes as before. Fill in the second line of the segment division for these chapters: Discourses Regarding ____________________.

Chapters 49-57: Your Redeemer Will Save

1. As you read through this segment, add the following key words to your bookmark: *covenant, Zion,* and *Jerusalem.* Mark *Zion* and *Jerusalem* in the same way. In the margin note what you observe from marking these words. Don't forget to delete from your card key words which no longer appear.

2. Do everything you did under numbers 1 through 5 in the previous segment. Watch carefully all that the Lord can and will do and note it in the margin. Observe the text carefully to see why this segment is titled "Your Redeemer Will Save." Watch for God's instructions and take them to heart.

3. Watch for prophetic verses which come in the midst of what Isaiah is saying. Give special attention to 50:6 and 52:13 through 53:12. After you observe Isaiah 53, read it through on your knees and substitute your name every time you see *we* or *us.*

4. Look for and record the theme of each chapter. If you think it will be helpful, summarize and list in the margin the subpoints covered in the chapter. Fill in the second line of the segment division for these chapters.

Chapters 58-66: Your Redeemer Will Come

1. Once again mark the key words on your bookmark. Delete *the Lord Almighty,* as it is not mentioned in this segment. *Servant* becomes *servants* in this segment; don't miss it.

2. There is much in this segment about the events that surround or accompany the Lord's coming to reign and what will follow, even in regard to the new heaven and new earth. In the margin list what you observe. Also watch for practical lessons and list what you learn in the margin. For instance, in Isaiah 58 you will gain insights on fasting.

3. Once again continue marking everything as you did under 1 through 5 (Isaiah 40-48).

4. Record your chapter themes and then complete ISAIAH AT A GLANCE. Fill in the second line of the segment division for these chapters. Write in any new segment divisions you have seen.

Things to Think About

1. God's character never changes; therefore what distressed him in the days of Isaiah still distresses him today. And what he had to judge then, he cannot overlook now. Is there anything in your life you must confess and forsake? And what if you are not willing to do so? Will God be able to overlook it? Think about what you learned about God and his ways.

2. God is sovereign. He ruled over the nations in the days of Israel. Does he do the same today? What then can you know? How will your nation fit into all this?

3. Amos says God doesn't do anything without first revealing it to his servants the prophets (Amos 3:7). Therefore from studying Isaiah what do you know with an absolute certainty is going to come to pass? If the prophecies regarding the first coming of Jesus Christ literally came to pass (and they did), won't the prophecies regarding his second coming be literally fulfilled? How then are you going to live?

Chapter 1 Theme ______________________

1 The vision[a] concerning Judah and Jerusalem[b] that Isaiah son
of Amoz saw[c] during the reigns of Uzziah,[d] Jotham, Ahaz[e]
and Hezekiah, kings of Judah.

2Hear, O heavens! Listen, O earth!
For the LORD has spoken:[f]
"I reared children and brought them up,
but they have rebelled[g] against me.
3The ox knows his master,
the donkey his owner's manger,
but Israel does not know,[h]
my people do not understand."

4Ah, sinful nation,
a people loaded with guilt,
a brood of evildoers,[i]
children given to corruption!
They have forsaken the LORD;
they have spurned the Holy One[j] of Israel
and turned their backs on him.

1:1 [a]Nu 12:6 [b]Isa 40:9 [c]Isa 2:1 [d]2Ch 26:22 [e]2Ki 16:1
1:2 [f]Mic 1:2 [g]Isa 30:1,9; 65:2
1:3 [h]Jer 8:7; 9:3,6
1:4 [i]Isa 14:20 [j]Isa 5:19,24

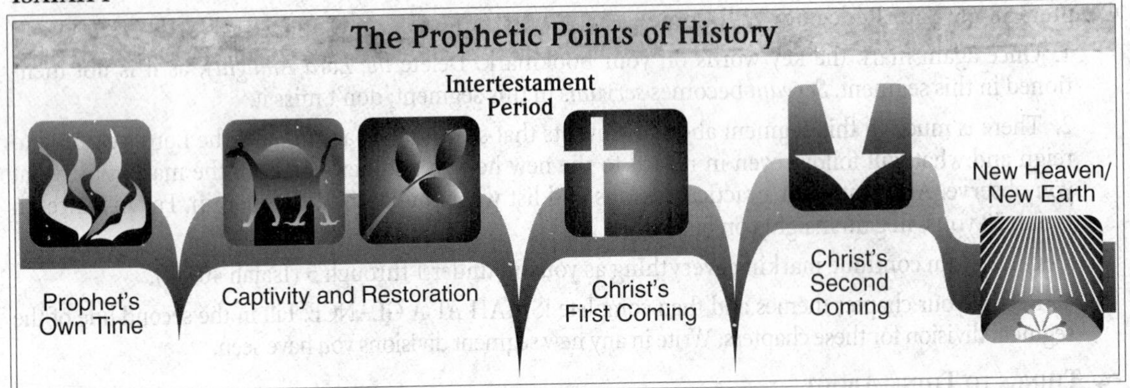

5Why should you be beaten anymore?
Why do you persist in rebellion?[a]
Your whole head is injured,
your whole heart afflicted.[b]
6From the sole of your foot to the top of your head
there is no soundness[c]—
only wounds and welts
and open sores,
not cleansed or bandaged[d]
or soothed with oil.[e]

7Your country is desolate,[f]
your cities burned with fire;
your fields are being stripped by foreigners
right before you,
laid waste as when overthrown by strangers.
8The Daughter of Zion is left
like a shelter in a vineyard,
like a hut[g] in a field of melons,
like a city under siege.
9Unless the LORD Almighty
had left us some survivors,[h]
we would have become like Sodom,
we would have been like Gomorrah.[i]

10Hear the word of the LORD,[j]
you rulers of Sodom;[k]
listen to the law[l] of our God,
you people of Gomorrah!
11"The multitude of your sacrifices—
what are they to me?" says the LORD.
"I have more than enough of burnt offerings,
of rams and the fat of fattened animals;[m]
I have no pleasure
in the blood of bulls[n] and lambs and goats.[o]

1:5 [a]Isa 31:6 [b]Isa 33:6,24
1:6 [c]Ps 38:3 [d]Isa 30:26; Jer 8:22 [e]Lk 10:34
1:7 [f]Lev 26:34
1:8 [g]Job 27:18
1:9 [h]Isa 10:20-22; 37:4,31-32 [i]Ge 19:24; Ro 9:29*
1:10 [j]Isa 28:14 [k]Isa 3:9; Eze 16:49; Ro 9:29; Rev 11:8 [l]Isa 8:20
1:11 [m]Ps 50:8 [n]Jer 6:20 [o]1Sa 15:22; Mal 1:10

12When you come to appear before me,
who has asked this of you,[a]
this trampling of my courts?
13Stop bringing meaningless offerings![b]
Your incense[c] is detestable to me.
New Moons, Sabbaths and convocations[d]—
I cannot bear your evil assemblies.
14Your New Moon festivals and your appointed feasts[e]
my soul hates.
They have become a burden to me;
I am weary[f] of bearing them.
15When you spread out your hands in prayer,
I will hide[g] my eyes from you;
even if you offer many prayers,
I will not listen.
Your hands are full of blood;[h]
16 wash and make yourselves clean.
Take your evil deeds
out of my sight![i]
Stop doing wrong,[j]
17 learn to do right!
Seek justice,[k]
encourage the oppressed.[a]

1:12 [a]Ex 23:17
1:13 [b]Isa 66:3 [c]Jer 7:9 [d]1Ch 23:31
1:14 [e]Lev 23:1-44; Nu 28:11–29:39; Isa 29:1 [f]Isa 7:13; 43:22,24
1:15 [g]Isa 8:17; 59:2; Mic 3:4 [h]Isa 59:3
1:16 [i]Isa 52:11 [j]Isa 55:7; Jer 25:5
1:17 [k]Zep 2:3

a 17 Or / *rebuke the oppressor*

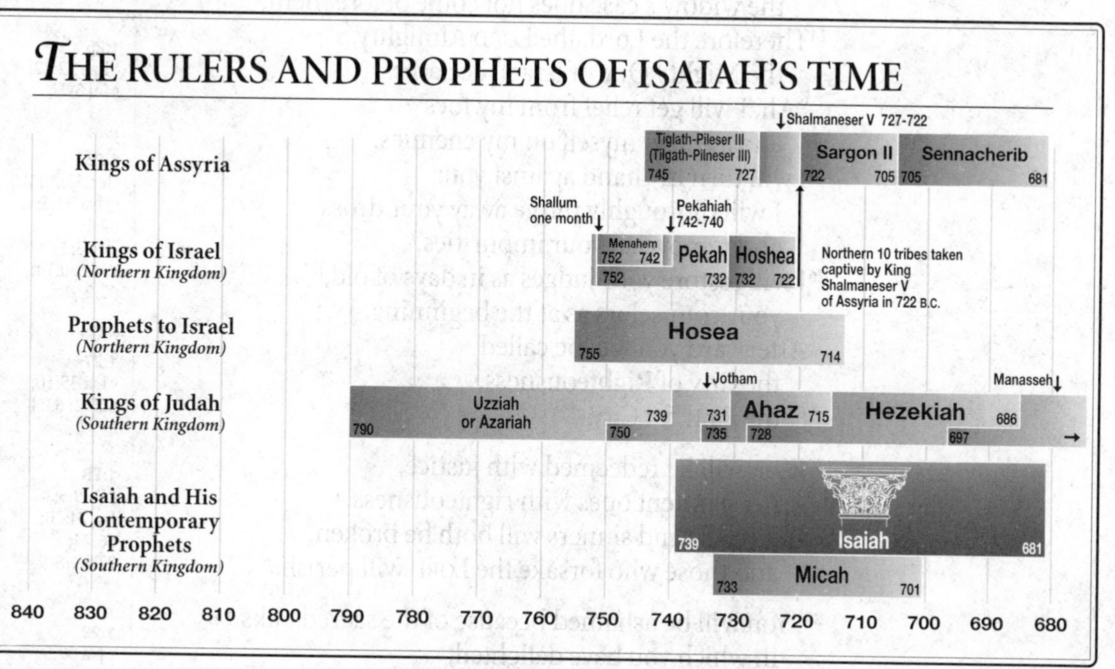

Defend the cause of the fatherless,[a]
plead the case of the widow.

18"Come now, let us reason together,"[b]
says the LORD.
"Though your sins are like scarlet,
they shall be as white as snow;[c]
though they are red as crimson,
they shall be like wool.
19If you are willing and obedient,
you will eat the best from the land;[d]
20but if you resist and rebel,
you will be devoured by the sword."[e]
For the mouth of the LORD has spoken.[f]

21See how the faithful city
has become a harlot![g]
She once was full of justice;
righteousness used to dwell in her—
but now murderers!
22Your silver has become dross,
your choice wine is diluted with water.
23Your rulers are rebels,
companions of thieves;
they all love bribes[h]
and chase after gifts.
They do not defend the cause of the fatherless;
the widow's case does not come before them.[i]
24Therefore the Lord, the LORD Almighty,
the Mighty One of Israel, declares:
"Ah, I will get relief from my foes
and avenge[j] myself on my enemies.
25I will turn my hand against you;
I will thoroughly purge away your dross
and remove all your impurities.[k]
26I will restore your judges as in days of old,[l]
your counselors as at the beginning.
Afterward you will be called
the City of Righteousness,[m]
the Faithful City.[n]"

27Zion will be redeemed with justice,
her penitent ones with righteousness.[o]
28But rebels and sinners will both be broken,
and those who forsake the LORD will perish.[p]

29"You will be ashamed because of the sacred oaks[q]
in which you have delighted;

1:17
[a] Ps 82:3

1:18
[b] Isa 41:1; 43:9,26
[c] Ps 51:7; Rev 7:14

1:19
[d] Dt 30:15-16; Isa 55:2

1:20
[e] Isa 3:25; 65:12
[f] Isa 34:16; 40:5; 58:14; Mic 4:4

1:21
[g] Isa 57:3-9; Jer 2:20

1:23
[h] Ex 23:8
[i] Isa 10:2; Jer 5:28; Eze 22:6-7; Zec 7:10

1:24
[j] Isa 35:4; 59:17; 61:2; 63:4

1:25
[k] Eze 22:22; Mal 3:3

1:26
[l] Jer 33:7,11
[m] Isa 33:5; 62:1; Zec 8:3
[n] Isa 60:14; 62:2

1:27
[o] Isa 35:10; 62:12; 63:4

1:28
[p] Ps 9:5; Isa 24:20; 66:24; 2Th 1:8-9

1:29
[q] Isa 57:5

1:29 [a] Isa 65:3; 66:17

you will be disgraced because of the gardens[a]
that you have chosen.
30 You will be like an oak with fading leaves,
like a garden without water.

1:31 [b] Isa 5:24; 9:18-19; 26:11; 33:14; 66:15-16,24

31 The mighty man will become tinder
and his work a spark;
both will burn together,
with no one to quench the fire.[b]"

Chapter 2 Theme ______________________

2:1 [c] Isa 1:1

2 This is what Isaiah son of Amoz saw concerning Judah and Jerusalem:[c]

2 In the last days

2:2 [d] Isa 27:13; 56:7; 66:20; Mic 4:7

the mountain[d] of the LORD's temple will be established
as chief among the mountains;
it will be raised above the hills,
and all nations will stream to it.

2:3 [e] Isa 51:4,7 [f] Lk 24:47

3 Many peoples will come and say,

"Come, let us go up to the mountain of the LORD,
to the house of the God of Jacob.
He will teach us his ways,
so that we may walk in his paths."
The law[e] will go out from Zion,
the word of the LORD from Jerusalem.[f]

2:4 [g] Joel 3:10 [h] Ps 46:9; Isa 9:5; 11:6-9; 32:18; Hos 2:18; Zec 9:10

4 He will judge between the nations
and will settle disputes for many peoples.
They will beat their swords into plowshares
and their spears into pruning hooks.[g]
Nation will not take up sword against nation,[h]
nor will they train for war anymore.

2:5 [i] Isa 58:1 [j] Isa 60:1,19-20; 1Jn 1:5,7

5 Come, O house of Jacob,[i]
let us walk in the light[j] of the LORD.

2:6 [k] Dt 31:17 [l] 2Ki 1:2 [m] Pr 6:1 [n] 2Ki 16:7

6 You have abandoned[k] your people,
the house of Jacob.
They are full of superstitions from the East;
they practice divination like the Philistines[l]
and clasp hands[m] with pagans.[n]
7 Their land is full of silver and gold;
there is no end to their treasures.

2:7 [o] Dt 17:16 [p] Isa 31:1; Mic 5:10

Their land is full of horses;[o]
there is no end to their chariots.[p]

[8]Their land is full of idols;[a]
they bow down to the work of their hands,
to what their fingers[b] have made.
[9]So man will be brought low[c]
and mankind humbled[d]—
do not forgive them.[a][e]

[10]Go into the rocks,
hide in the ground
from dread of the LORD
and the splendor of his majesty![f]
[11]The eyes of the arrogant man will be humbled
and the pride[g] of men brought low;
the LORD alone will be exalted in that day.

[12]The LORD Almighty has a day in store
for all the proud and lofty,
for all that is exalted[h]
(and they will be humbled),[i]
[13]for all the cedars of Lebanon, tall and lofty,
and all the oaks of Bashan,[j]
[14]for all the towering mountains
and all the high hills,[k]
[15]for every lofty tower
and every fortified wall,[l]
[16]for every trading ship[b][m]
and every stately vessel.
[17]The arrogance of man will be brought low
and the pride of men humbled;
the LORD alone will be exalted in that day,[n]
18 and the idols will totally disappear.[o]

[19]Men will flee to caves in the rocks
and to holes in the ground
from dread of the LORD
and the splendor of his majesty,
when he rises to shake the earth.[p]
[20]In that day men will throw away
to the rodents and bats[q]
their idols of silver and idols of gold,
which they made to worship.
[21]They will flee to caverns in the rocks
and to the overhanging crags
from dread of the LORD
and the splendor of his majesty,
when he rises to shake the earth.[r]

a9 Or *not raise them up* b16 Hebrew *every ship of Tarshish*

2:8 [a]Isa 10:9-11 [b]Isa 17:8
2:9 [c]Ps 62:9 [d]Isa 5:15 [e]Ne 4:5
2:10 [f]2Th 1:9; Rev 6:15-16
2:11 [g]Isa 5:15; 37:23
2:12 [h]Isa 24:4,21; Mal 4:1 [i]Job 40:11
2:13 [j]Zec 11:2
2:14 [k]Isa 30:25; 40:4
2:15 [l]Isa 25:2,12
2:16 [m]1Ki 10:22
2:17 [n]ver 11
2:18 [o]Isa 21:9
2:19 [p]Heb 12:26
2:20 [q]Lev 11:19
2:21 [r]ver 19

22Stop trusting in man,[a]
who has but a breath in his nostrils.
Of what account is he?[b]

Chapter 3 Theme ____________________

3 See now, the Lord,
the LORD Almighty,
is about to take from Jerusalem and Judah
both supply and support:
all supplies of food[c] and all supplies of water,[d]
2 the hero and warrior,[e]
the judge and prophet,
the soothsayer and elder,[f]
3the captain of fifty and man of rank,
the counselor, skilled craftsman and clever enchanter.

4I will make boys their officials;
mere children will govern them.[g]
5People will oppress each other—
man against man, neighbor against neighbor.[h]
The young will rise up against the old,
the base against the honorable.

6A man will seize one of his brothers
at his father's home, and say,
"You have a cloak, you be our leader;
take charge of this heap of ruins!"
7But in that day he will cry out,
"I have no remedy.[i]
I have no food or clothing in my house;
do not make me the leader of the people."

8Jerusalem staggers,
Judah is falling;[j]
their words[k] and deeds are against the LORD,
defying[l] his glorious presence.
9The look on their faces testifies against them;
they parade their sin like Sodom;[m]
they do not hide it.
Woe to them!
They have brought disaster[n] upon themselves.

10Tell the righteous it will be well[o] with them,
for they will enjoy the fruit of their deeds.[p]
11Woe to the wicked! Disaster[q] is upon them!
They will be paid back for what their hands have done.

12Youths[r] oppress my people,
women rule over them.

2:22 [a] Ps 146:3; Jer 17:5 [b] Ps 8:4; 144:3; Isa 40:15; Jas 4:14
3:1 [c] Lev 26:26 [d] Isa 5:13; Eze 4:16
3:2 [e] Eze 17:13 [f] 2Ki 24:14; Isa 9:14-15
3:4 [g] Ecc 10:16*fn*
3:5 [h] Isa 9:19; Jer 9:8; Mic 7:2,6
3:7 [i] Eze 34:4; Hos 5:13
3:8 [j] Isa 1:7 [k] Isa 9:15,17 [l] Ps 73:9,11
3:9 [m] Ge 13:13 [n] Pr 8:36; Ro 6:23
3:10 [o] Dt 28:1-14 [p] Ps 128:2
3:11 [q] Dt 28:15-68
3:12 [r] ver 4

O my people, your guides lead you astray;[a]
they turn you from the path.

13The LORD takes his place in court;
he rises to judge[b] the people.
14The LORD enters into judgment[c]
against the elders and leaders of his people:
"It is you who have ruined my vineyard;
the plunder[d] from the poor is in your houses.
15What do you mean by crushing my people[e]
and grinding the faces of the poor?"
declares the Lord, the LORD Almighty.
16The LORD says,
"The women of Zion[f] are haughty,
walking along with outstretched necks,
flirting with their eyes,
tripping along with mincing steps,
with ornaments jingling on their ankles.
17Therefore the Lord will bring sores on the heads of the
women of Zion;
the LORD will make their scalps bald."

18In that day the Lord will snatch away their finery: the bangles
and headbands and crescent necklaces,[g] 19the earrings and bracelets and veils, 20the headdresses[h] and ankle chains and sashes, the
perfume bottles and charms, 21the signet rings and nose rings,
22the fine robes and the capes and cloaks, the purses 23and mirrors,
and the linen garments and tiaras and shawls.

24Instead of fragrance[i] there will be a stench;
instead of a sash,[j] a rope;
instead of well-dressed hair, baldness;[k]
instead of fine clothing, sackcloth;[l]
instead of beauty,[m] branding.
25Your men will fall by the sword,[n]
your warriors in battle.
26The gates of Zion will lament and mourn;[o]
destitute, she will sit on the ground.[p]

Chapter 4 Theme ____________________

4 In that day seven women
will take hold of one man[q]
and say, "We will eat our own food[r]
and provide our own clothes;
only let us be called by your name.
Take away our disgrace!"[s]

3:12 [a] Isa 9:16
3:13 [b] Mic 6:2
3:14 [c] Job 22:4 [d] Job 24:9; Jas 2:6
3:15 [e] Ps 94:5
3:16 [f] SS 3:11
3:18 [g] Jdg 8:21
3:20 [h] Ex 39:28
3:24 [i] Est 2:12 [j] Pr 31:24 [k] Isa 22:12 [l] La 2:10; Eze 27:30-31 [m] 1Pe 3:3
3:25 [n] Isa 1:20
3:26 [o] Jer 14:2 [p] La 2:10
4:1 [q] Isa 13:12 [r] 2Th 3:12 [s] Ge 30:23

2 In that day the Branch of the LORD[a] will be beautiful and glorious, and the fruit[b] of the land will be the pride and glory of the
survivors in Israel. 3 Those who are left in Zion, who remain[c] in
Jerusalem, will be called holy,[d] all who are recorded[e] among the
living in Jerusalem. 4 The Lord will wash away the filth[f] of the
women of Zion; he will cleanse the bloodstains[g] from Jerusalem
by a spirit[a] of judgment[h] and a spirit[a] of fire.[i] 5 Then the LORD will
create over all of Mount Zion and over those who assemble there
a cloud of smoke by day and a glow of flaming fire by night;[j] over
all the glory[k] will be a canopy. 6 It will be a shelter[l] and shade from
the heat of the day, and a refuge[m] and hiding place from the
storm and rain.

Chapter 5 Theme ______________________

5 I will sing for the one I love
  a song about his vineyard:[n]
My loved one had a vineyard
  on a fertile hillside.
2 He dug it up and cleared it of stones
  and planted it with the choicest vines.[o]
He built a watchtower in it
  and cut out a winepress as well.
Then he looked for a crop of good grapes,
  but it yielded only bad fruit.[p]

3 "Now you dwellers in Jerusalem and men of Judah,
  judge between me and my vineyard.[q]
4 What more could have been done for my vineyard
  than I have done for it?[r]
When I looked for good grapes,
  why did it yield only bad?
5 Now I will tell you
  what I am going to do to my vineyard:
I will take away its hedge,
  and it will be destroyed;
I will break down its wall,[s]
  and it will be trampled.[t]
6 I will make it a wasteland,
  neither pruned nor cultivated,
  and briers and thorns[u] will grow there.
I will command the clouds
  not to rain on it."

7 The vineyard[v] of the LORD Almighty
  is the house of Israel,

4:2 [a] Isa 11:1-5; 53:2; Jer 23:5-6; Zec 3:8; 6:12 [b] Ps 72:16
4:3 [c] Ro 11:5 [d] Isa 52:1; 60:21 [e] Lk 10:20
4:4 [f] Isa 3:24 [g] Isa 1:15 [h] Isa 28:6 [i] Isa 1:31; Mt 3:11
4:5 [j] Ex 13:21 [k] Isa 60:1
4:6 [l] Ps 27:5 [m] Isa 25:4
5:1 [n] Ps 80:8-9
5:2 [o] Jer 2:21 [p] Mt 21:19; Mk 11:13; Lk 13:6
5:3 [q] Mt 21:40
5:4 [r] 2Ch 36:15; Jer 2:5-7; Mic 6:3-4; Mt 23:37
5:5 [s] Ps 80:12 [t] Isa 28:3,18; La 1:15; Lk 21:24
5:6 [u] Isa 7:23,24; Heb 6:8
5:7 [v] Ps 80:8

a 4 Or *the Spirit*

and the men of Judah
are the garden of his delight.
And he looked for justice,[a] but saw bloodshed;
for righteousness, but heard cries of distress.

8 Woe[b] to you who add house to house
and join field to field[c]
till no space is left
and you live alone in the land.

9 The LORD Almighty has declared in my hearing:[d]

"Surely the great houses will become desolate,[e]
the fine mansions left without occupants.
10 A ten-acre[a] vineyard will produce only a bath[b] of wine,
a homer[c] of seed only an ephah[d] of grain."[f]

11 Woe to those who rise early in the morning
to run after their drinks,
who stay up late at night
till they are inflamed with wine.[g]
12 They have harps and lyres at their banquets,
tambourines and flutes and wine,
but they have no regard[h] for the deeds of the LORD,
no respect for the work of his hands.[i]
13 Therefore my people will go into exile[j]
for lack of understanding;[k]
their men of rank will die of hunger
and their masses will be parched with thirst.
14 Therefore the grave[e][l] enlarges its appetite
and opens its mouth[m] without limit;
into it will descend their nobles and masses
with all their brawlers and revelers.
15 So man will be brought low[n]
and mankind humbled,[o]
the eyes of the arrogant[p] humbled.
16 But the LORD Almighty will be exalted by his justice,[q]
and the holy God will show himself holy[r] by his
righteousness.
17 Then sheep will graze as in their own pasture;[s]
lambs will feed[f] among the ruins of the rich.

18 Woe to those who draw sin along with cords of deceit,
and wickedness[t] as with cart ropes,

a 10 Hebrew *ten-yoke,* that is, the land plowed by 10 yoke of oxen in one day b 10 That is, probably about 6 gallons (about 22 liters) c 10 That is, probably about 6 bushels (about 220 liters) d 10 That is, probably about 3/5 bushel (about 22 liters) e 14 Hebrew *Sheol*
f 17 Septuagint; Hebrew / *strangers will eat*

5:7 [a] Isa 59:15
5:8 [b] Jer 22:13 [c] Mic 2:2; Hab 2:9-12
5:9 [d] Isa 22:14 [e] Isa 6:11-12; Mt 23:38
5:10 [f] Lev 26:26
5:11 [g] Pr 23:29-30
5:12 [h] Job 34:27 [i] Ps 28:5; Am 6:5-6
5:13 [j] Hos 4:6 [k] Isa 1:3
5:14 [l] Pr 30:16 [m] Nu 16:30
5:15 [n] Isa 10:33 [o] Isa 2:9 [p] Isa 2:11
5:16 [q] Isa 28:17; 30:18; 33:5; 61:8 [r] Isa 29:23
5:17 [s] Isa 7:25; Zep 2:6,14
5:18 [t] Isa 59:4-8; Jer 23:14

[19]to those who say, "Let God hurry,
let him hasten his work
so we may see it.
Let it approach,
let the plan of the Holy One of Israel come,
so we may know it."[a]

[20]Woe to those who call evil good
and good evil,
who put darkness for light
and light for darkness,[b]
who put bitter for sweet
and sweet for bitter.[c]

[21]Woe to those who are wise in their own eyes[d]
and clever in their own sight.

[22]Woe to those who are heroes at drinking wine[e]
and champions at mixing drinks,
[23]who acquit the guilty for a bribe,[f]
but deny justice[g] to the innocent.[h]
[24]Therefore, as tongues of fire lick up straw
and as dry grass sinks down in the flames,
so their roots will decay[i]
and their flowers blow away like dust;
for they have rejected the law of the LORD Almighty
and spurned the word[j] of the Holy One of Israel.
[25]Therefore the LORD's anger[k] burns against his people;
his hand is raised and he strikes them down.
The mountains shake,
and the dead bodies are like refuse[l] in the streets.

Yet for all this, his anger is not turned away,[m]
his hand is still upraised.[n]

[26]He lifts up a banner for the distant nations,
he whistles[o] for those at the ends of the earth.[p]
Here they come,
swiftly and speedily!
[27]Not one of them grows tired or stumbles,
not one slumbers or sleeps;
not a belt is loosened at the waist,[q]
not a sandal thong is broken.[r]
[28]Their arrows are sharp,[s]
all their bows[t] are strung;
their horses' hoofs seem like flint,
their chariot wheels like a whirlwind.

5:19
[a]Jer 17:15; Eze 12:22; 2Pe 3:4

5:20
[b]Mt 6:22-23; Lk 11:34-35
[c]Am 5:7

5:21
[d]Pr 3:7; Ro 12:16; 1Co 3:18-20

5:22
[e]Pr 23:20

5:23
[f]Ex 23:8
[g]Isa 10:2
[h]Ps 94:21; Jas 5:6

5:24
[i]Job 18:16
[j]Isa 8:6; 30:9,12

5:25
[k]2Ki 22:13
[l]2Ki 9:37
[m]Jer 4:8; Da 9:16
[n]Isa 9:12,17, 21; 10:4

5:26
[o]Isa 7:18; Zec 10:8
[p]Dt 28:49; Isa 13:5; 18:3

5:27
[q]Job 12:18
[r]Joel 2:7-8

5:28
[s]Ps 45:5
[t]Ps 7:12

29 Their roar is like that of the lion,[a]
they roar like young lions;
they growl as they seize[b] their prey
and carry it off with no one to rescue.[c]
30 In that day they will roar over it
like the roaring of the sea.[d]
And if one looks at the land,
he will see darkness and distress;[e]
even the light will be darkened[f] by the clouds.

Chapter 6 Theme ______________________

6 In the year that King Uzziah[g] died,[h] I saw the Lord[i] seated on
a throne,[j] high and exalted, and the train of his robe filled the
temple. 2 Above him were seraphs,[k] each with six wings: With two
wings they covered their faces, with two they covered their feet,[l]
and with two they were flying. 3 And they were calling to one
another:

"Holy, holy, holy is the LORD Almighty;
the whole earth is full of his glory."[m]

4 At the sound of their voices the doorposts and thresholds shook
and the temple was filled with smoke.
5 "Woe to me!" I cried. "I am ruined! For I am a man of unclean
lips, and I live among a people of unclean lips,[n] and my eyes have
seen the King,[o] the LORD Almighty."
6 Then one of the seraphs flew to me with a live coal in his hand,
which he had taken with tongs from the altar. 7 With it he touched
my mouth and said, "See, this has touched your lips;[p] your guilt
is taken away and your sin atoned for.[q]"
8 Then I heard the voice[r] of the Lord saying, "Whom shall I send?
And who will go for us?"
And I said, "Here am I. Send me!"
9 He said, "Go[s] and tell this people:

"'Be ever hearing, but never understanding;
be ever seeing, but never perceiving.'[t]
10 Make the heart of this people calloused;[u]
make their ears dull
and close their eyes.[a]
Otherwise they might see with their eyes,
hear with their ears,[v]
understand with their hearts,
and turn and be healed."[w]

INSIGHT

For the historical background of King Uzziah (also called Azariah), read 2 Kings 15 and 2 Chronicles 26.

5:29 [a] Jer 51:38; Zep 3:3; Zec 11:3 [b] Isa 10:6; 49:24-25 [c] Isa 42:22; Mic 5:8
5:30 [d] Lk 21:25 [e] Isa 8:22; Jer 4:23-28 [f] Joel 2:10
6:1 [g] 2Ch 26:22,23 [h] 2Ki 15:7 [i] Jn 12:41 [j] Rev 4:2
6:2 [k] Rev 4:8 [l] Eze 1:11
6:3 [m] Ps 72:19; Rev 4:8
6:5 [n] Jer 9:3-8 [o] Jer 51:57
6:7 [p] Jer 1:9 [q] 1Jn 1:7
6:8 [r] Ac 9:4
6:9 [s] Eze 3:11 [t] Mt 13:15*; Lk 8:10*
6:10 [u] Dt 32:15; Ps 119:70 [v] Jer 5:21 [w] Mt 13:13-15; Mk 4:12*; Ac 28:26-27*

[a] 9,10 Hebrew; Septuagint *'You will be ever hearing, but never understanding; / you will be ever seeing, but never perceiving.' / 10 This people's heart has become calloused; / they hardly hear with their ears, / and they have closed their eyes*

11 Then I said, "For how long, O Lord?"[a]
And he answered:

> "Until the cities lie ruined[b]
> and without inhabitant,
> until the houses are left deserted
> and the fields ruined and ravaged,
> 12 until the LORD has sent everyone far away[c]
> and the land is utterly forsaken.[d]
> 13 And though a tenth remains[e] in the land,
> it will again be laid waste.
> But as the terebinth and oak
> leave stumps when they are cut down,
> so the holy seed will be the stump in the land."[f]

Chapter 7 Theme

7 When Ahaz son of Jotham, the son of Uzziah, was king of
Judah, King Rezin[g] of Aram[h] and Pekah[i] son of Remaliah king
of Israel marched up to fight against Jerusalem, but they could not
overpower it.
2 Now the house of David[j] was told, "Aram has allied itself with[a]
Ephraim[k]"; so the hearts of Ahaz and his people were shaken, as
the trees of the forest are shaken by the wind.
3 Then the LORD said to Isaiah, "Go out, you and your son Shear-
Jashub,[b] to meet Ahaz at the end of the aqueduct of the Upper
Pool, on the road to the Washerman's Field.[l] 4 Say to him, 'Be careful, keep calm[m] and don't be afraid.[n] Do not lose heart[o] because of
these two smoldering stubs[p] of firewood—because of the fierce
anger[q] of Rezin and Aram and of the son of Remaliah. 5 Aram,
Ephraim and Remaliah's son have plotted your ruin, saying, 6 "Let
us invade Judah; let us tear it apart and divide it among ourselves,
and make the son of Tabeel king over it." 7 Yet this is what the
Sovereign LORD says:

> "'It will not take place,
> it will not happen,[r]
> 8 for the head of Aram is Damascus,[s]
> and the head of Damascus is only Rezin.
> Within sixty-five years
> Ephraim will be too shattered[t] to be a people.
> 9 The head of Ephraim is Samaria,
> and the head of Samaria is only Remaliah's son.
> If you do not stand firm in your faith,[u]
> you will not stand at all.'"[v]

6:11 [a] Ps 79:5 [b] Lev 26:31
6:12 [c] Dt 28:64 [d] Jer 4:29
6:13 [e] Isa 1:9 [f] Job 14:7
7:1 [g] 2Ki 15:37 [h] 2Ch 28:5 [i] 2Ki 15:25
7:2 [j] ver 13; Isa 22:22 [k] Isa 9:9
7:3 [l] 2Ki 18:17; Isa 36:2
7:4 [m] Isa 30:15 [n] Isa 35:4 [o] Dt 20:3 [p] Zec 3:2 [q] Isa 10:24
7:7 [r] Isa 8:10; Ac 4:25
7:8 [s] Ge 14:15 [t] Isa 17:1-3
7:9 [u] 2Ch 20:20 [v] Isa 8:6-8; 30:12-14

[a] 2 Or *has set up camp in* [b] 3 *Shear-Jashub* means *a remnant will return.*

10 Again the LORD spoke to Ahaz, 11 "Ask the LORD your God for a sign, whether in the deepest depths or in the highest heights."

12 But Ahaz said, "I will not ask; I will not put the LORD to the test."

13 Then Isaiah said, "Hear now, you house of David! Is it not enough to try the patience of men? Will you try the patience of my God[a] also? 14 Therefore the Lord himself will give you[a] a sign: The virgin will be with child and will give birth to a son,[b] and[b] will call him Immanuel.[c][c] 15 He will eat curds and honey[d] when he knows enough to reject the wrong and choose the right. 16 But before the boy knows[e] enough to reject the wrong and choose the right, the land of the two kings you dread will be laid waste.[f] 17 The LORD will bring on you and on your people and on the house of your father a time unlike any since Ephraim broke away[g] from Judah—he will bring the king of Assyria.[h]"

18 In that day the LORD will whistle[i] for flies from the distant streams of Egypt and for bees from the land of Assyria.[j] 19 They will all come and settle in the steep ravines and in the crevices[k] in the rocks, on all the thornbushes and at all the water holes. 20 In that day the Lord will use[l] a razor hired from beyond the River[d]—the king of Assyria[m]—to shave your head and the hair of your legs, and to take off your beards also. 21 In that day, a man will keep alive a young cow and two goats. 22 And because of the abundance of the milk they give, he will have curds to eat. All who remain in the land will eat curds and honey. 23 In that day, in every place where there were a thousand vines worth a thousand silver shekels,[e] there will be only briers and thorns.[n] 24 Men will go there with bow and arrow, for the land will be covered with briers and thorns. 25 As for all the hills once cultivated by the hoe, you will no longer go there for fear of the briers and thorns; they will become places where cattle are turned loose and where sheep run.[o]

Chapter 8 Theme

8 The LORD said to me, "Take a large scroll[p] and write on it with an ordinary pen: Maher-Shalal-Hash-Baz.[f][q] 2 And I will call in Uriah[r] the priest and Zechariah son of Jeberekiah as reliable witnesses for me."

3 Then I went to the prophetess, and she conceived and gave birth to a son. And the LORD said to me, "Name him Maher-Shalal-Hash-Baz. 4 Before the boy knows[s] how to say 'My father' or 'My mother,' the wealth of Damascus and the plunder of Samaria will be carried off by the king of Assyria.[t]"

5 The LORD spoke to me again:

7:13 [a] Isa 25:1
7:14 [b] Lk 1:31 [c] Isa 8:8,10; Mt 1:23*
7:15 [d] ver 22
7:16 [e] Isa 8:4 [f] Isa 17:3; Hos 5:9,13; Am 1:3-5
7:17 [g] 1Ki 12:16 [h] 2Ch 28:20
7:18 [i] Isa 5:26 [j] Isa 13:5
7:19 [k] Isa 2:19
7:20 [l] Isa 10:15 [m] Isa 8:7; 10:5
7:23 [n] Isa 5:6
7:25 [o] Isa 5:17
8:1 [p] Isa 30:8; [q] ver 3; Hab 2:2
8:2 [r] 2Ki 16:10
8:4 [s] Isa 7:16 [t] Isa 7:8

a *14* The Hebrew is plural. b *14* Masoretic Text; Dead Sea Scrolls *and he* or *and they* c *14* *Immanuel* means *God with us.* d *20* That is, the Euphrates e *23* That is, about 25 pounds (about 11.5 kilograms) f *1* *Maher-Shalal-Hash-Baz* means *quick to the plunder, swift to the spoil*; also in verse 3.

6"Because this people has rejected[a]
the gently flowing waters of Shiloah[b]
and rejoices over Rezin
and the son of Remaliah,[c]
7therefore the Lord is about to bring against them
the mighty floodwaters[d] of the River[a]—
the king of Assyria[e] with all his pomp.
It will overflow all its channels,
run over all its banks
8and sweep on into Judah, swirling over it,
passing through it and reaching up to the neck.
Its outspread wings will cover the breadth of your land,
O Immanuel[b]!"[f]

9Raise the war cry,[c][g] you nations, and be shattered!
Listen, all you distant lands.
Prepare[h] for battle, and be shattered!
Prepare for battle, and be shattered!
10Devise your strategy, but it will be thwarted;[i]
propose your plan, but it will not stand,[j]
for God is with us.[d][k]

11The LORD spoke to me with his strong hand upon me,[l] warning me not to follow[m] the way of this people. He said:

12"Do not call conspiracy[n]
everything that these people call conspiracy[e];
do not fear what they fear,
and do not dread it.[o]
13The LORD Almighty is the one you are to regard as holy,[p]
he is the one you are to fear,
he is the one you are to dread,[q]
14and he will be a sanctuary;[r]
but for both houses of Israel he will be
a stone that causes men to stumble
and a rock that makes them fall.[s]
And for the people of Jerusalem he will be
a trap and a snare.[t]
15Many of them will stumble;[u]
they will fall and be broken,
they will be snared and captured."

16Bind up the testimony
and seal[v] up the law among my disciples.
17I will wait[w] for the LORD,
who is hiding[x] his face from the house of Jacob.
I will put my trust in him.

8:6 [a] Isa 5:24 [b] Jn 9:7 [c] Isa 7:1
8:7 [d] Isa 17:12-13 [e] Isa 7:20
8:8 [f] Isa 7:14
8:9 [g] Isa 17:12-13 [h] Joel 3:9
8:10 [i] Job 5:12 [j] Isa 7:7 [k] Isa 7:14; Ro 8:31
8:11 [l] Eze 3:14 [m] Eze 2:8
8:12 [n] Isa 7:2; 30:1 [o] 1Pe 3:14*
8:13 [p] Nu 20:12 [q] Isa 29:23
8:14 [r] Isa 4:6; Eze 11:16 [s] Lk 2:34; Ro 9:33*; 1Pe 2:8* [t] Isa 24:17-18
8:15 [u] Isa 28:13; 59:10; Lk 20:18; Ro 9:32
8:16 [v] Isa 29:11-12
8:17 [w] Hab 2:3 [x] Dt 31:17; Isa 54:8

[a] 7 That is, the Euphrates [b] 8 *Immanuel* means *God with us.* [c] 9 Or *Do your worst*
[d] 10 Hebrew *Immanuel* [e] 12 Or *Do not call for a treaty / every time these people call for a treaty*

18Here am I, and the children the LORD has given me.[a] We are
signs[b] and symbols in Israel from the LORD Almighty, who dwells
on Mount Zion.[c]
19When men tell you to consult[d] mediums and spiritists, who
whisper and mutter,[e] should not a people inquire of their God?
Why consult the dead on behalf of the living? 20To the law[f] and to
the testimony! If they do not speak according to this word, they
have no light[g] of dawn. 21Distressed and hungry, they will roam
through the land; when they are famished, they will become
enraged and, looking upward, will curse[h] their king and their God.
22Then they will look toward the earth and see only distress and
darkness and fearful gloom, and they will be thrust into utter
darkness.[i]

Chapter 9 Theme ______________________

9 Nevertheless, there will be no more gloom for those who were
in distress. In the past he humbled the land of Zebulun and the
land of Naphtali,[j] but in the future he will honor Galilee of the
Gentiles, by the way of the sea, along the Jordan—

2The people walking in darkness
have seen a great light;[k]
on those living in the land of the shadow of death[a][l]
a light has dawned.[m]
3You have enlarged the nation
and increased their joy;
they rejoice before you
as people rejoice at the harvest,
as men rejoice
when dividing the plunder.
4For as in the day of Midian's defeat,[n]
you have shattered
the yoke[o] that burdens them,
the bar across their shoulders,[p]
the rod of their oppressor.[q]
5Every warrior's boot used in battle
and every garment rolled in blood
will be destined for burning,[r]
will be fuel for the fire.
6For to us a child is born,[s]
to us a son is given,[t]
and the government[u] will be on his shoulders.
And he will be called
Wonderful Counselor,[b][v] Mighty God,[w]
Everlasting Father, Prince of Peace.[x]

[a]2 Or *land of darkness* [b]6 Or *Wonderful, Counselor*

8:18 [a]Heb 2:13* [b]Lk 2:34 [c]Ps 9:11
8:19 [d]1Sa 28:8 [e]Isa 29:4
8:20 [f]Isa 1:10; Lk 16:29 [g]Mic 3:6
8:21 [h]Rev 16:11
8:22 [i]ver 20; Isa 5:30
9:1 [j]2Ki 15:29
9:2 [k]Eph 5:8 [l]Lk 1:79 [m]Mt 4:15-16*
9:4 [n]Jdg 7:25 [o]Isa 14:25 [p]Isa 10:27 [q]Isa 14:4; 49:26; 51:13; 54:14
9:5 [r]Isa 2:4
9:6 [s]Isa 53:2; Lk 2:11 [t]Jn 3:16 [u]Mt 28:18 [v]Isa 28:29 [w]Isa 10:21; 11:2 [x]Isa 26:3,12; 66:12

7 Of the increase of his government and peace
there will be no end.[a]
He will reign on David's throne
and over his kingdom,
establishing and upholding it
with justice[b] and righteousness
from that time on and forever.
The zeal[c] of the LORD Almighty
will accomplish this.

8 The Lord has sent a message against Jacob;
it will fall on Israel.
9 All the people will know it—
Ephraim and the inhabitants of Samaria[d]—
who say with pride
and arrogance[e] of heart,
10 "The bricks have fallen down,
but we will rebuild with dressed stone;
the fig trees have been felled,
but we will replace them with cedars."
11 But the LORD has strengthened Rezin's[f] foes against them
and has spurred their enemies on.
12 Arameans[g] from the east and Philistines[h] from the west
have devoured[i] Israel with open mouth.

Yet for all this, his anger is not turned away,
his hand is still upraised.[j]

13 But the people have not returned to him who
struck[k] them,
nor have they sought[l] the LORD Almighty.
14 So the LORD will cut off from Israel both head and tail,
both palm branch and reed[m] in a single day;[n]
15 the elders[o] and prominent men are the head,
the prophets who teach lies are the tail.
16 Those who guide[p] this people mislead them,
and those who are guided are led astray.[q]
17 Therefore the Lord will take no pleasure in the
young men,[r]
nor will he pity[s] the fatherless and widows,
for everyone is ungodly[t] and wicked,[u]
every mouth speaks vileness.[v]

Yet for all this, his anger is not turned away,
his hand is still upraised.[w]

18 Surely wickedness burns like a fire;[x]
it consumes briers and thorns,

9:7 [a] Da 2:44; Lk 1:33 [b] Isa 11:4; 16:5; 32:1,16 [c] Isa 37:32; 59:17
9:9 [d] Isa 7:9 [e] Isa 46:12
9:11 [f] Isa 7:8
9:12 [g] 2Ki 16:6 [h] 2Ch 28:18 [i] Ps 79:7 [j] Isa 5:25
9:13 [k] Jer 5:3 [l] Isa 31:1; Hos 7:7,10
9:14 [m] Isa 19:15 [n] Rev 18:8
9:15 [o] Isa 3:2-3
9:16 [p] Mt 15:14; 23:16,24 [q] Isa 3:12
9:17 [r] Jer 18:21 [s] Isa 27:11 [t] Isa 10:6 [u] Isa 1:4 [v] Mt 12:34 [w] Isa 5:25
9:18 [x] Mal 4:1

it sets the forest thickets ablaze,[a]
so that it rolls upward in a column of smoke.
19By the wrath[b] of the LORD Almighty
the land will be scorched
and the people will be fuel for the fire;[c]
no one will spare his brother.[d]
20On the right they will devour,
but still be hungry;[e]
on the left they will eat,[f]
but not be satisfied.
Each will feed on the flesh of his own offspring[a]:
21 Manasseh will feed on Ephraim, and Ephraim on Manasseh;
together they will turn against Judah.[g]

Yet for all this, his anger is not turned away,
his hand is still upraised.[h]

Chapter 10 Theme ____________________

10

Woe to those who make unjust laws,
to those who issue oppressive decrees,[i]
2to deprive[j] the poor of their rights
and withhold justice from the oppressed of my people,[k]
making widows their prey
and robbing the fatherless.
3What will you do on the day of reckoning,[l]
when disaster[m] comes from afar?
To whom will you run for help?[n]
Where will you leave your riches?
4Nothing will remain but to cringe among the captives[o]
or fall among the slain.[p]

Yet for all this, his anger is not turned away,[q]
his hand is still upraised.

5"Woe to the Assyrian,[r] the rod of my anger,
in whose hand is the club[s] of my wrath![t]
6I send him against a godless[u] nation,
I dispatch him against a people who anger me,[v]
to seize loot and snatch plunder,[w]
and to trample them down like mud in the streets.
7But this is not what he intends,[x]
this is not what he has in mind;
his purpose is to destroy,
to put an end to many nations.

a20 Or *arm*

9:18
[a]Ps 83:14

9:19
[b]Isa 13:9,13
[c]Isa 1:31
[d]Mic 7:2,6

9:20
[e]Lev 26:26
[f]Isa 49:26

9:21
[g]2Ch 28:6
[h]Isa 5:25

10:1
[i]Ps 58:2

10:2
[j]Isa 3:14
[k]Isa 5:23

10:3
[l]Job 31:14; Hos 9:7
[m]Lk 19:44
[n]Isa 20:6

10:4
[o]Isa 24:22
[p]Isa 22:2; 34:3; 66:16
[q]Isa 5:25

10:5
[r]Isa 14:25; Zep 2:13
[s]Jer 51:20
[t]Isa 13:3,5,13; 30:30; 66:14

10:6
[u]Isa 9:17
[v]Isa 9:19
[w]Isa 5:29

10:7
[x]Ge 50:20; Ac 4:23-28

8‘Are not my commanders[a] all kings?’ he says.
9 ‘Has not Calno[b] fared like Carchemish?[c]
Is not Hamath like Arpad,
and Samaria[d] like Damascus?[e]
10As my hand seized the kingdoms of the idols,[f]
kingdoms whose images excelled those of Jerusalem
and Samaria—
11shall I not deal with Jerusalem and her images
as I dealt with Samaria and her idols?’ ”

12When the Lord has finished all his work[g] against Mount Zion[h]
and Jerusalem, he will say, “I will punish the king of Assyria[i] for
the willful pride of his heart and the haughty look in his eyes.
13For he says:

“ ‘By the strength of my hand I have done this,[j]
and by my wisdom, because I have understanding.
I removed the boundaries of nations,
I plundered their treasures;[k]
like a mighty one I subdued[a] their kings.
14As one reaches into a nest,[l]
so my hand reached for the wealth[m] of the nations;
as men gather abandoned eggs,
so I gathered all the countries;
not one flapped a wing,
or opened its mouth to chirp.’ ”

15Does the ax raise itself above him who swings it,
or the saw boast against him who uses it?[n]
As if a rod were to wield him who lifts it up,
or a club[o] brandish him who is not wood!
16Therefore, the Lord, the LORD Almighty,
will send a wasting disease[p] upon his sturdy warriors;
under his pomp[q] a fire will be kindled
like a blazing flame.
17The Light of Israel will become a fire,[r]
their Holy One[s] a flame;
in a single day it will burn and consume
his thorns[t] and his briers.[u]
18The splendor of his forests[v] and fertile fields
it will completely destroy,
as when a sick man wastes away.
19And the remaining trees of his forests will be so few[w]
that a child could write them down.

20In that day[x] the remnant of Israel,
the survivors of the house of Jacob,

10:8 [a]2Ki 18:24
10:9 [b]Ge 10:10 [c]2Ch 35:20 [d]2Ki 17:6 [e]2Ki 16:9
10:10 [f]2Ki 19:18
10:12 [g]Isa 28:21-22; 65:7 [h]2Ki 19:31 [i]Jer 50:18
10:13 [j]Isa 37:24; Da 4:30 [k]Eze 28:4
10:14 [l]Jer 49:16; Ob 4 [m]Job 31:25
10:15 [n]Isa 45:9; Ro 9:20-21 [o]ver 5
10:16 [p]ver 18; Isa 17:4 [q]Isa 8:7
10:17 [r]Isa 31:9 [s]Isa 37:23 [t]Nu 11:1-3 [u]Isa 9:18
10:18 [v]2Ki 19:23
10:19 [w]Isa 21:17
10:20 [x]Isa 11:10,11

a *13* Or / *I subdued the mighty,*

will no longer rely[a] on him
who struck them down[b]
but will truly rely[c] on the LORD,
the Holy One of Israel.
21 A remnant[d] will return,[a] a remnant of Jacob
will return to the Mighty God.[e]
22 Though your people, O Israel, be like the sand by the sea,
only a remnant will return.[f]
Destruction has been decreed,[g]
overwhelming and righteous.
23 The Lord, the LORD Almighty, will carry out
the destruction decreed upon the whole land.[h]

24 Therefore, this is what the Lord, the LORD Almighty, says:

"O my people who live in Zion,[i]
do not be afraid of the Assyrians,
who beat[j] you with a rod
and lift up a club against you, as Egypt did.
25 Very soon[k] my anger against you will end
and my wrath[l] will be directed to their destruction."

26 The LORD Almighty will lash[m] them with a whip,
as when he struck down Midian[n] at the rock of Oreb;
and he will raise his staff over the waters,[o]
as he did in Egypt.
27 In that day their burden will be lifted from your shoulders,
their yoke[p] from your neck;[q]
the yoke will be broken
because you have grown so fat.[b]

28 They enter Aiath;
they pass through Migron;[r]
they store supplies at Micmash.[s]
29 They go over the pass, and say,
"We will camp overnight at Geba."
Ramah[t] trembles;
Gibeah of Saul flees.
30 Cry out, O Daughter of Gallim![u]
Listen, O Laishah!
Poor Anathoth![v]
31 Madmenah is in flight;
the people of Gebim take cover.
32 This day they will halt at Nob;[w]
they will shake their fist

a 21 Hebrew *shear-jashub*; also in verse 22 b 27 Hebrew; Septuagint *broken / from your shoulders*

10:20
a 2Ki 16:7
b 2Ch 28:20
c Isa 17:7

10:21
d Isa 6:13
e Isa 9:6

10:22
f Ro 9:27-28
g Isa 28:22; Da 9:27

10:23
h Isa 28:22; Ro 9:27-28*

10:24
i Ps 87:5-6
j Ex 5:14

10:25
k Isa 17:14
l ver 5; Da 11:36

10:26
m Isa 37:36-38
n Isa 9:4
o Ex 14:16

10:27
p Isa 9:4
q Isa 14:25

10:28
r 1Sa 14:2
s 1Sa 13:2

10:29
t Jos 18:25

10:30
u 1Sa 25:44
v Ne 11:32

10:32
w 1Sa 21:1

at the mount of the Daughter of Zion,[a]
at the hill of Jerusalem.

33 See, the Lord, the LORD Almighty,
will lop off the boughs with great power.
The lofty trees will be felled,
the tall[b] ones will be brought low.
34 He will cut down the forest thickets with an ax;
Lebanon will fall before the Mighty One.

Chapter 11 Theme ________________________

11 A shoot will come up from the stump of Jesse;[c]
from his roots a Branch[d] will bear fruit.
2 The Spirit[e] of the LORD will rest on him—
the Spirit of wisdom[f] and of understanding,
the Spirit of counsel and of power,[g]
the Spirit of knowledge and of the fear of the LORD—
3 and he will delight in the fear of the LORD.

He will not judge by what he sees with his eyes,[h]
or decide by what he hears with his ears;[i]
4 but with righteousness[j] he will judge the needy,
with justice[k] he will give decisions for the poor[l] of the earth.
He will strike[m] the earth with the rod of his mouth;
with the breath[n] of his lips he will slay the wicked.
5 Righteousness will be his belt
and faithfulness[o] the sash around his waist.[p]

6 The wolf will live with the lamb,[q]
the leopard will lie down with the goat,
the calf and the lion and the yearling[a] together;
and a little child will lead them.
7 The cow will feed with the bear,
their young will lie down together,
and the lion will eat straw like the ox.
8 The infant will play near the hole of the cobra,
and the young child put his hand into the viper's nest.
9 They will neither harm nor destroy[r]
on all my holy mountain,
for the earth[s] will be full of the knowledge[t] of the LORD
as the waters cover the sea.

10 In that day the Root of Jesse will stand as a banner[u] for the peoples; the nations[v] will rally to him,[w] and his place of rest[x] will be
glorious. 11 In that day[y] the Lord will reach out his hand a second
time to reclaim the remnant that is left of his people from Assyria,[z]

10:32 [a] Jer 6:23
10:33 [b] Am 2:9
11:1 [c] ver 10; Isa 9:7; Rev 5:5 [d] Isa 4:2
11:2 [e] Isa 42:1; 48:16; 61:1; Mt 3:16; Jn 1:32-33 [f] Eph 1:17 [g] 2Ti 1:7
11:3 [h] Jn 7:24 [i] Jn 2:25
11:4 [j] Ps 72:2 [k] Isa 9:7 [l] Isa 3:14 [m] Mal 4:6 [n] Job 4:9; 2Th 2:8
11:5 [o] Isa 25:1 [p] Eph 6:14
11:6 [q] Isa 65:25
11:9 [r] Job 5:23 [s] Ps 98:2-3; Isa 52:10 [t] Isa 45:6,14; Hab 2:14
11:10 [u] Jn 12:32 [v] Isa 49:23; Lk 2:32 [w] Ro 15:12* [x] Isa 14:3; 28:12; 32:17-18
11:11 [y] Isa 10:20 [z] Isa 19:24; Hos 11:11; Mic 7:12; Zec 10:10

[a] 6 Hebrew; Septuagint *lion will feed*

from Lower Egypt, from Upper Egypt,[a] from Cush,[b] from Elam,[a]
from Babylonia,[c] from Hamath and from the islands[b] of the sea.

12He will raise a banner for the nations
and gather the exiles of Israel;
he will assemble the scattered people[c] of Judah
from the four quarters of the earth.
13Ephraim's jealousy will vanish,
and Judah's enemies[d] will be cut off;
Ephraim will not be jealous of Judah,
nor Judah hostile toward Ephraim.[d]
14They will swoop down on the slopes of Philistia to
the west;
together they will plunder the people to the east.
They will lay hands on Edom[e] and Moab,[f]
and the Ammonites will be subject to them.
15The LORD will dry up
the gulf of the Egyptian sea;
with a scorching wind he will sweep his hand[g]
over the Euphrates River.[e][h]
He will break it up into seven streams
so that men can cross over in sandals.
16There will be a highway[i] for the remnant of his people
that is left from Assyria,
as there was for Israel
when they came up from Egypt.[j]

Chapter 12 Theme ______________________

12

In that day you will say:
"I will praise[k] you, O LORD.
Although you were angry with me,
your anger has turned away
and you have comforted me.
2Surely God is my salvation;
I will trust[l] and not be afraid.
The LORD, the LORD, is my strength and my song;
he has become my salvation.[m]"
3With joy you will draw water[n]
from the wells of salvation.

4In that day you will say:

"Give thanks to the LORD, call on his name;[o]
make known among the nations what he has done,
and proclaim that his name is exaltd.

[a] *11* Hebrew *from Pathros* [b] *11* That is, the upper Nile region [c] *11* Hebrew *Shinar*
[d] *13* Or *hostility* [e] *15* Hebrew *the River*

11:11 [a] Ge 10:22 [b] Isa 42:4,10,12; 66:19
11:12 [c] Zep 3:10
11:13 [d] Jer 3:18; Eze 37:16-17,22; Hos 1:11
11:14 [e] Da 11:41; Joel 3:19 [f] Isa 16:14; 25:10
11:15 [g] Isa 19:16 [h] Isa 7:20
11:16 [i] Isa 19:23; 62:10 [j] Ex 14:26-31
12:1 [k] Isa 25:1
12:2 [l] Isa 26:3 [m] Ex 15:2; Ps 118:14
12:3 [n] Jn 4:10,14
12:4 [o] Ps 105:1; Isa 24:15

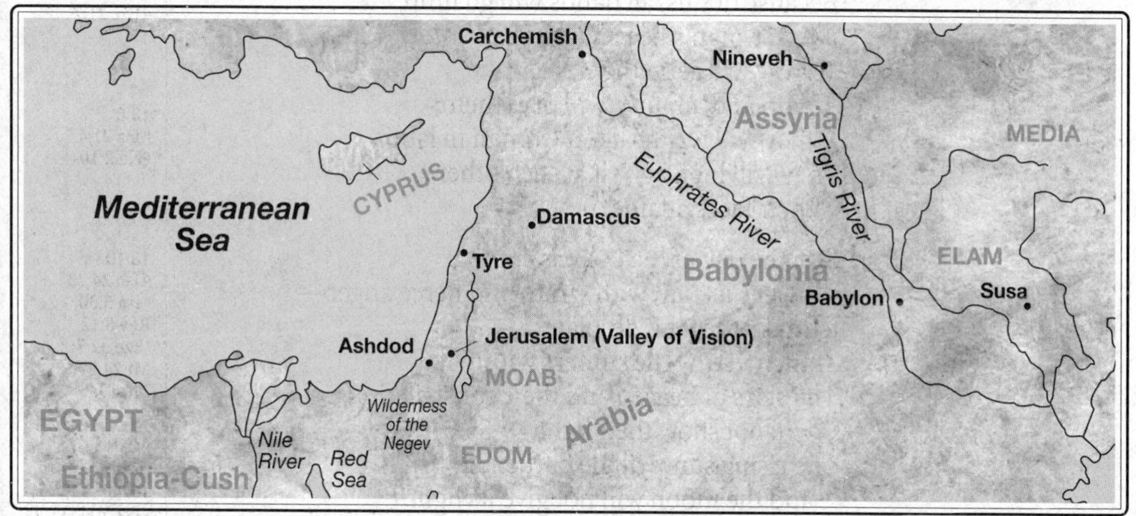

5 Sing[a] to the LORD, for he has done glorious things;[b]
let this be known to all the world.
6 Shout aloud and sing for joy, people of Zion,
for great is the Holy One of Israel[c] among you.[d]"

12:5 [a]Ex 15:1 [b]Ps 98:1
12:6 [c]Isa 49:26 [d]Zep 3:14-17

The Nations That Received the Oracles

Chapter 13 Theme

13

An oracle concerning Babylon that Isaiah son of Amoz saw:

2 Raise a banner[e] on a bare hilltop,
shout to them;
beckon to them
to enter the gates of the nobles.
3 I have commanded my holy ones;
I have summoned my warriors[f] to carry out my wrath—
those who rejoice[g] in my triumph.

4 Listen, a noise on the mountains,
like that of a great multitude![h]
Listen, an uproar among the kingdoms,
like nations massing together!
The LORD Almighty is mustering
an army for war.
5 They come from faraway lands,
from the ends of the heavens[i]—
the LORD and the weapons of his wrath—
to destroy[j] the whole country.

6 Wail,[k] for the day[l] of the LORD is near;
it will come like destruction from the Almighty.[a]

13:2 [e]Jer 50:2; 51:27
13:3 [f]Joel 3:11 [g]Ps 149:2
13:4 [h]Joel 3:14
13:5 [i]Isa 5:26 [j]Isa 24:1
13:6 [k]Eze 30:2 [l]Isa 2:12; Joel 1:15

[a]6 Hebrew *Shaddai*

INSIGHT

From 729 B.C. Babylon was part of the Assyrian Empire. The ruler of Assyria assumed the title "King of Babylon." Babylon then became the capital of the Neo-Babylonian Empire which Nebuchadnezzar ruled after the death of his father, Nabopolassar. Nebuchadnezzar first besieged Jerusalem in 605 B.C. In 586 B.C. he destroyed Jerusalem and the temple.

7Because of this, all hands will go limp,
every man's heart will melt.[a]
8Terror[b] will seize them,
pain and anguish will grip them;
they will writhe like a woman in labor.
They will look aghast at each other,
their faces aflame.[c]

9See, the day of the LORD is coming
—a cruel day, with wrath and fierce anger—
to make the land desolate
and destroy the sinners within it.
10The stars of heaven and their constellations
will not show their light.
The rising sun[d] will be darkened[e]
and the moon will not give its light.[f]
11I will punish[g] the world for its evil,
the wicked for their sins.
I will put an end to the arrogance of the haughty
and will humble the pride of the ruthless.
12I will make man[h] scarcer than pure gold,
more rare than the gold of Ophir.
13Therefore I will make the heavens tremble;[i]
and the earth will shake from its place
at the wrath of the LORD Almighty,
in the day of his burning anger.

14Like a hunted gazelle,
like sheep without a shepherd,[j]
each will return to his own people,
each will flee to his native land.[k]
15Whoever is captured will be thrust through;
all who are caught will fall[l] by the sword.[m]
16Their infants[n] will be dashed to pieces before their eyes;
their houses will be looted and their wives ravished.

17See, I will stir up[o] against them the Medes,
who do not care for silver
and have no delight in gold.[p]
18Their bows will strike down the young men;
they will have no mercy on infants
nor will they look with compassion on children.
19Babylon, the jewel of kingdoms,
the glory[q] of the Babylonians'[a] pride,
will be overthrown[r] by God
like Sodom and Gomorrah.[s]

a19 Or *Chaldeans'*

13:7 [a]Eze 21:7
13:8 [b]Isa 21:4 [c]Na 2:10
13:10 [d]Isa 24:23 [e]Isa 5:30; Rev 8:12 [f]Eze 32:7; Mt 24:29*; Mk 13:24*
13:11 [g]Isa 3:11; 11:4; 26:21
13:12 [h]Isa 4:1
13:13 [i]Isa 34:4; 51:6; Hag 2:6
13:14 [j]1Ki 22:17 [k]Jer 50:16
13:15 [l]Jer 51:4 [m]Isa 14:19; Jer 50:25
13:16 [n]Ps 137:9
13:17 [o]Jer 51:1 [p]Pr 6:34-35
13:19 [q]Da 4:30 [r]Rev 14:8 [s]Ge 19:24

20She will never be inhabited[a]
  or lived in through all generations;
no Arab[b] will pitch his tent there,
  no shepherd will rest his flocks there.
21But desert creatures[c] will lie there,
  jackals will fill her houses;
there the owls will dwell,
  and there the wild goats will leap about.
22Hyenas will howl in her strongholds,[d]
  jackals[e] in her luxurious palaces.
Her time is at hand,[f]
  and her days will not be prolonged.

Chapter 14 Theme ______________________

14 The LORD will have compassion[g] on Jacob;
  once again he will choose[h] Israel
  and will settle them in their own land.
Aliens[i] will join them
  and unite with the house of Jacob.
2Nations will take them
  and bring[j] them to their own place.
And the house of Israel will possess the nations[k]
  as menservants and maidservants in the LORD's land.
They will make captives of their captors
  and rule over their oppressors.[l]

3On the day the LORD gives you relief[m] from suffering and turmoil and cruel bondage, 4you will take up this taunt[n] against the
king of Babylon:

How the oppressor[o] has come to an end!
  How his fury[a] has ended!
5The LORD has broken the rod of the wicked,[p]
  the scepter of the rulers,
6which in anger struck down peoples[q]
  with unceasing blows,
and in fury subdued nations
  with relentless aggression.[r]
7All the lands are at rest and at peace;
  they break into singing.[s]
8Even the pine trees[t] and the cedars of Lebanon
  exult over you and say,
"Now that you have been laid low,
  no woodsman comes to cut us down."

13:20 [a]Isa 14:23; 34:10-15 [b]2Ch 17:11
13:21 [c]Rev 18:2
13:22 [d]Isa 25:2 [e]Isa 34:13 [f]Jer 51:33
14:1 [g]Ps 102:13; Isa 49:10,13; 54:7-8,10 [h]Isa 41:8; 44:1; 49:7; Zec 1:17; 2:12 [i]Eph 2:12-19
14:2 [j]Isa 60:9 [k]Isa 49:7,23 [l]Isa 60:14; 61:5
14:3 [m]Isa 11:10
14:4 [n]Hab 2:6 [o]Isa 9:4
14:5 [p]Ps 125:3
14:6 [q]Isa 10:14 [r]Isa 47:6
14:7 [s]Ps 98:1; 126:1-3
14:8 [t]Eze 31:16

[a]4 Dead Sea Scrolls, Septuagint and Syriac; the meaning of the word in the Masoretic Text is uncertain.

9The grave[a] [a] below is all astir
to meet you at your coming;
it rouses the spirits of the departed to greet you—
all those who were leaders in the world;
it makes them rise from their thrones—
all those who were kings over the nations.
10They will all respond,
they will say to you,
"You also have become weak, as we are;
you have become like us."[b]
11All your pomp has been brought down to the grave,
along with the noise of your harps;
maggots are spread out beneath you
and worms[c] cover you.

12How you have fallen[d] from heaven,
O morning star,[e] son of the dawn!
You have been cast down to the earth,
you who once laid low the nations!
13You said in your heart,
"I will ascend[f] to heaven;
I will raise my throne[g]
above the stars of God;
I will sit enthroned on the mount of assembly,
on the utmost heights of the sacred mountain.[b]
14I will ascend above the tops of the clouds;
I will make myself like the Most High."[h]
15But you are brought down to the grave,
to the depths[i] of the pit.

16Those who see you stare at you,
they ponder your fate:[j]
"Is this the man who shook the earth
and made kingdoms tremble,
17the man who made the world a desert,[k]
who overthrew its cities
and would not let his captives go home?"
18All the kings of the nations lie in state,
each in his own tomb.
19But you are cast out[l] of your tomb
like a rejected branch;
you are covered with the slain,
with those pierced by the sword,
those who descend to the stones of the pit.[m]
Like a corpse trampled underfoot,

a9 Hebrew *Sheol*; also in verses 11 and 15 b13 Or *the north*; Hebrew *Zaphon*

14:9 *a* Eze 32:21
14:10 *b* Eze 32:21
14:11 *c* Isa 51:8
14:12 *d* Isa 34:4; Lk 10:18 *e* 2Pe 1:19; Rev 2:28; 8:10; 9:1
14:13 *f* Da 5:23; 8:10; Mt 11:23 *g* Eze 28:2; 2Th 2:4
14:14 *h* Isa 47:8; 2Th 2:4
14:15 *i* Mt 11:23; Lk 10:15
14:16 *j* Jer 50:23
14:17 *k* Joel 2:3
14:19 *l* Isa 22:16-18 *m* Jer 41:7-9

20 you will not join them in burial,
for you have destroyed your land
and killed your people.
The offspring[a] of the wicked[b]
will never be mentioned[c] again.
21 Prepare a place to slaughter his sons
for the sins of their forefathers;[d]
they are not to rise to inherit the land
and cover the earth with their cities.
22 "I will rise up against them,"
declares the LORD Almighty.
"I will cut off from Babylon her name and survivors,
her offspring and descendants,[e]"
declares the LORD.
23 "I will turn her into a place for owls[f]
and into swampland;
I will sweep her with the broom of destruction,"
declares the LORD Almighty.

24 The LORD Almighty has sworn,[g]

"Surely, as I have planned, so it will be,
and as I have purposed, so it will stand.[h]
25 I will crush the Assyrian[i] in my land;
on my mountains I will trample him down.
His yoke[j] will be taken from my people,
and his burden removed from their shoulders.[k]"
26 This is the plan[l] determined for the whole world;
this is the hand[m] stretched out over all nations.
27 For the LORD Almighty has purposed, and who can thwart him?
His hand is stretched out, and who can turn it back?[n]

28 This oracle[o] came in the year King Ahaz[p] died:

29 Do not rejoice, all you Philistines,[q]
that the rod that struck you is broken;
from the root of that snake will spring up a viper,[r]
its fruit will be a darting, venomous serpent.
30 The poorest of the poor will find pasture,
and the needy[s] will lie down in safety.[t]
But your root I will destroy by famine;[u]
it will slay[v] your survivors.
31 Wail, O gate![w] Howl, O city!
Melt away, all you Philistines!
A cloud of smoke comes from the north,[x]
and there is not a straggler in its ranks.

14:20 [a] Job 18:19 [b] Isa 1:4 [c] Ps 21:10
14:21 [d] Ex 20:5; Lev 26:39
14:22 [e] 1Ki 14:10; Job 18:19
14:23 [f] Isa 34:11-15; Zep 2:14
14:24 [g] Isa 45:23 [h] Ac 4:28
14:25 [i] Isa 10:5,12 [j] Isa 9:4 [k] Isa 10:27
14:26 [l] Isa 23:9 [m] Ex 15:12
14:27 [n] 2Ch 20:6; Isa 43:13; Da 4:35
14:28 [o] Isa 13:1 [p] 2Ki 16:20
14:29 [q] 2Ch 26:6 [r] Isa 11:8
14:30 [s] Isa 3:15 [t] Isa 7:21-22 [u] Isa 8:21; 9:20; 51:19 [v] Jer 25:16
14:31 [w] Isa 3:26 [x] Jer 1:14

32What answer shall be given
to the envoys[a] of that nation?
"The LORD has established Zion,[b]
and in her his afflicted people will find refuge.[c]"

14:32
[a]Isa 37:9
[b]Ps 87:2,5; Isa 44:28; 54:11
[c]Isa 4:6; Jas 2:5

Chapter 15 Theme

15 An oracle concerning Moab:[d]

Ar in Moab is ruined,[e]
destroyed in a night!
Kir in Moab is ruined,
destroyed in a night!
2Dibon goes up to its temple,
to its high places[f] to weep;
Moab wails over Nebo and Medeba.
Every head is shaved[g]
and every beard cut off.
3In the streets they wear sackcloth;
on the roofs and in the public squares[h]
they all wail,
prostrate with weeping.[i]
4Heshbon and Elealeh[j] cry out,
their voices are heard all the way to Jahaz.
Therefore the armed men of Moab cry out,
and their hearts are faint.

5My heart cries out over Moab;[k]
her fugitives flee as far as Zoar,
as far as Eglath Shelishiyah.
They go up the way to Luhith,
weeping as they go;
on the road to Horonaim[l]
they lament their destruction.[m]
6The waters of Nimrim are dried up[n]
and the grass is withered;[o]
the vegetation is gone
and nothing green is left.
7So the wealth they have acquired[p] and stored up
they carry away over the Ravine of the Poplars.
8Their outcry echoes along the border of Moab;
their wailing reaches as far as Eglaim,
their lamentation as far as Beer Elim.
9Dimon's[a] waters are full of blood,
but I will bring still more upon Dimon[a]—

INSIGHT

Moab was a narrow strip of land directly east of the Dead (Salt) Sea. Its inhabitants were called Moabites and were neighbors to the Israelites. Moab, the father of the Moabites, was the son of Lot by his firstborn daughter. Ruth, who is in the genealogy of King David, was a Moabitess.

15:1
[d]Isa 11:14
[e]Jer 48:24,41

15:2
[f]Jer 48:35
[g]Lev 21:5

15:3
[h]Jer 48:38
[i]Isa 22:4

15:4
[j]Nu 32:3

15:5
[k]Jer 48:31
[l]Jer 48:3,34
[m]Jer 4:20; 48:5

15:6
[n]Isa 19:5-7; Jer 48:34
[o]Joel 1:12

15:7
[p]Isa 30:6; Jer 48:36

[a]9 Masoretic Text; Dead Sea Scrolls, some Septuagint manuscripts and Vulgate *Dibon*

a lion[a] upon the fugitives of Moab
and upon those who remain in the land.

Chapter 16 Theme ____________________

16

Send lambs[b] as tribute
to the ruler of the land,
from Sela,[c] across the desert,
to the mount of the Daughter of Zion.[d]
2Like fluttering birds
pushed from the nest,[e]
so are the women of Moab
at the fords of the Arnon.[f]

3"Give us counsel,
render a decision.
Make your shadow like night—
at high noon.
Hide the fugitives,[g]
do not betray the refugees.
4Let the Moabite fugitives stay with you;
be their shelter from the destroyer."

The oppressor[h] will come to an end,
and destruction will cease;
the aggressor will vanish from the land.
5In love a throne[i] will be established;
in faithfulness a man will sit on it—
one from the house[a] of David[j]—
one who in judging seeks justice[k]
and speeds the cause of righteousness.

6We have heard of Moab's[l] pride[m]—
her overweening pride and conceit,
her pride and her insolence—
but her boasts are empty.
7Therefore the Moabites wail,[n]
they wail together for Moab.
Lament and grieve
for the men[b][o] of Kir Hareseth.[p]
8The fields of Heshbon wither,
the vines of Sibmah also.
The rulers of the nations
have trampled down the choicest vines,
which once reached Jazer
and spread toward the desert.

a5 Hebrew *tent* b7 Or "*raisin cakes,*" a wordplay

15:9 [a]2Ki 17:25
16:1 [b]2Ki 3:4 [c]2Ki 14:7 [d]Isa 10:32
16:2 [e]Pr 27:8 [f]Nu 21:13-14; Jer 48:20
16:3 [g]1Ki 18:4
16:4 [h]Isa 9:4
16:5 [i]Da 7:14; Mic 4:7 [j]Lk 1:32 [k]Isa 9:7
16:6 [l]Am 2:1; Zep 2:8 [m]Ob 3; Zep 2:10
16:7 [n]Jer 48:20 [o]1Ch 16:3 [p]2Ki 3:25

Their shoots spread out
and went as far as the sea.
9So I weep,[a] as Jazer weeps,
for the vines of Sibmah.
O Heshbon, O Elealeh,
I drench you with tears!
The shouts of joy over your ripened fruit
and over your harvests[b] have been stilled.
10Joy and gladness are taken away from the orchards;[c]
no one sings or shouts in the vineyards;
no one treads[d] out wine at the presses,[e]
for I have put an end to the shouting.
11My heart laments for Moab[f] like a harp,
my inmost being[g] for Kir Hareseth.
12When Moab appears at her high place,
she only wears herself out;
when she goes to her shrine[h] to pray,
it is to no avail.[i]

13This is the word the LORD has already spoken concerning
Moab. 14But now the LORD says: "Within three years, as a servant
bound by contract would count them, Moab's splendor and all her
many people will be despised,[j] and her survivors will be very few
and feeble."[k]

Chapter 17 Theme ________________

17 An oracle concerning Damascus:[l]

"See, Damascus will no longer be a city
but will become a heap of ruins.[m]
2The cities of Aroer will be deserted
and left to flocks,[n] which will lie down,
with no one to make them afraid.[o]
3The fortified city will disappear from Ephraim,
and royal power from Damascus;
the remnant of Aram will be
like the glory[p] of the Israelites,"[q]
declares the LORD Almighty.

4"In that day the glory of Jacob will fade;
the fat of his body will waste[r] away.
5It will be as when a reaper gathers the standing grain
and harvests[s] the grain with his arm—
as when a man gleans heads of grain
in the Valley of Rephaim.
6Yet some gleanings will remain,[t]
as when an olive tree is beaten,[u]

INSIGHT

Damascus is the capital of Aram (or Syria).

16:9 [a]Isa 15:3 [b]Jer 40:12
16:10 [c]Isa 24:7-8 [d]Jdg 9:27 [e]Job 24:11
16:11 [f]Isa 15:5 [g]Isa 63:15; Hos 11:8; Php 2:1
16:12 [h]Isa 15:2 [i]1Ki 18:29
16:14 [j]Isa 25:10; Jer 48:42 [k]Isa 21:17
17:1 [l]Ge 14:15; Jer 49:23; Ac 9:2 [m]Isa 25:2; Am 1:3; Zec 9:1
17:2 [n]Isa 7:21; Eze 25:5 [o]Jer 7:33; Mic 4:4
17:3 [p]ver 4; Hos 9:11 [q]Isa 7:8,16; 8:4
17:4 [r]Isa 10:16
17:5 [s]ver 11; Jer 51:33; Joel 3:13; Mt 13:30
17:6 [t]Dt 4:27; Isa 24:13 [u]Isa 27:12

17:7 *a* Isa 10:20 *b* Mic 7:7

leaving two or three olives on the topmost branches,
four or five on the fruitful boughs,"
declares the LORD, the God of Israel.

7 In that day men will look[a] to their Maker
and turn their eyes to the Holy One[b] of Israel.

17:8 *c* Isa 2:18,20; 30:22

8 They will not look to the altars,
the work of their hands,[c]
and they will have no regard for the Asherah poles[a]
and the incense altars their fingers have made.

17:10 *d* Isa 51:13 *e* Ps 68:19; Isa 12:2

9 In that day their strong cities, which they left because of the
Israelites, will be like places abandoned to thickets and undergrowth. And all will be desolation.

10 You have forgotten[d] God your Savior;[e]
you have not remembered the Rock, your fortress.

17:11 *f* Ps 90:6 *g* Hos 8:7 *h* Job 4:8

Therefore, though you set out the finest plants
and plant imported vines,
11 though on the day you set them out, you make them grow,
and on the morning[f] when you plant them, you bring
them to bud,
yet the harvest will be as nothing[g]
in the day of disease and incurable pain.[h]

17:12 *i* Ps 18:4; Jer 6:23; Lk 21:25

12 Oh, the raging of many nations—
they rage like the raging sea![i]
Oh, the uproar of the peoples—
they roar like the roaring of great waters!

17:13 *j* Ps 9:5 *k* Isa 13:14 *l* Isa 41:2, 15-16 *m* Job 21:18

13 Although the peoples roar like the roar of surging waters,
when he rebukes[j] them they flee[k] far away,
driven before the wind like chaff[l] on the hills,
like tumbleweed before a gale.[m]
14 In the evening, sudden terror!
Before the morning, they are gone![n]

17:14 *n* 2Ki 19:35

This is the portion of those who loot us,
the lot of those who plunder us.

Chapter 18 Theme ________________________________

18:1 *o* Isa 20:3-5; Eze 30:4-5,9; Zep 2:12; 3:10

18 Woe to the land of whirring wings[b]
along the rivers of Cush,[c] [o]
2 which sends envoys by sea
in papyrus[p] boats over the water.

Go, swift messengers,
to a people tall and smooth-skinned,

18:2 *p* Ex 2:3

[a] *8* That is, symbols of the goddess Asherah [b] *1* Or *of locusts* [c] *1* That is, the upper Nile region

to a people feared far and wide,
an aggressive[a] nation of strange speech,
whose land is divided by rivers.[b]

3 All you people of the world,
you who live on the earth,
when a banner[c] is raised on the mountains,
you will see it,
and when a trumpet sounds,
you will hear it.
4 This is what the LORD says to me:
"I will remain quiet and will look on from my dwelling place,[d]
like shimmering heat in the sunshine,
like a cloud of dew[e] in the heat of harvest."
5 For, before the harvest, when the blossom is gone
and the flower becomes a ripening grape,
he will cut off the shoots with pruning knives,
and cut down and take away the spreading branches.[f]
6 They will all be left to the mountain birds of prey
and to the wild animals;[g]
the birds will feed on them all summer,
the wild animals all winter.

7 At that time gifts will be brought to the LORD Almighty

from a people tall and smooth-skinned,
from a people feared far and wide,
an aggressive nation of strange speech,
whose land is divided by rivers—

the gifts will be brought to Mount Zion, the place of the Name of the LORD Almighty.[h]

Chapter 19 Theme

19 An oracle[i] concerning Egypt:[j k]

See, the LORD rides on a swift cloud[l]
and is coming to Egypt.
The idols of Egypt tremble before him,
and the hearts of the Egyptians melt[m] within them.

2 "I will stir up Egyptian against Egyptian—
brother will fight against brother,[n]
neighbor against neighbor,
city against city,
kingdom against kingdom.[o]

18:2 [a] Ge 10:8-9; 2Ch 12:3 [b] ver 7

18:3 [c] Isa 5:26

18:4 [d] Isa 26:21; Hos 5:15 [e] Isa 26:19; Hos 14:5

18:5 [f] Isa 17:10-11; Eze 17:6

18:6 [g] Isa 56:9; Jer 7:33; Eze 32:4; 39:17

18:7 [h] Ps 68:31

19:1 [i] Isa 13:1; Jer 43:12 [j] Joel 3:19 [k] Ex 12:12 [l] Ps 18:10; 104:3; Rev 1:7 [m] Jos 2:11

19:2 [n] Jdg 7:22; Mt 10:21,36 [o] 2Ch 20:23

3 The Egyptians will lose heart,
and I will bring their plans to nothing;
they will consult the idols and the spirits of the dead,
the mediums and the spiritists.[a]
4 I will hand the Egyptians over
to the power of a cruel master,
and a fierce king[b] will rule over them,"
declares the Lord, the LORD Almighty.

5 The waters of the river will dry up,[c]
and the riverbed will be parched and dry.
6 The canals will stink;[d]
the streams of Egypt will dwindle and dry up.[e]
The reeds and rushes will wither,[f]
7 also the plants along the Nile,
at the mouth of the river.
Every sown field[g] along the Nile
will become parched, will blow away and be no more.
8 The fishermen[h] will groan and lament,
all who cast hooks[i] into the Nile;
those who throw nets on the water
will pine away.
9 Those who work with combed flax will despair,
the weavers of fine linen[j] will lose hope.
10 The workers in cloth will be dejected,
and all the wage earners will be sick at heart.

11 The officials of Zoan[k] are nothing but fools;
the wise counselors of Pharaoh give senseless advice.
How can you say to Pharaoh,
"I am one of the wise men,[l]
a disciple of the ancient kings"?
12 Where are your wise men[m] now?
Let them show you and make known
what the LORD Almighty
has planned[n] against Egypt.
13 The officials of Zoan have become fools,
the leaders of Memphis[a] [o] are deceived;
the cornerstones of her peoples
have led Egypt astray.
14 The LORD has poured into them
a spirit of dizziness;[p]
they make Egypt stagger in all that she does,
as a drunkard staggers around in his vomit.

19:3 [a]Isa 8:19; 47:13; Da 2:2,10
19:4 [b]Isa 20:4; Jer 46:26; Eze 29:19
19:5 [c]Jer 51:36
19:6 [d]Ex 7:18 [e]Isa 37:25; Eze 30:12 [f]Isa 15:6
19:7 [g]Isa 23:3
19:8 [h]Eze 47:10 [i]Hab 1:15
19:9 [j]Pr 7:16; Eze 27:7
19:11 [k]Nu 13:22 [l]1Ki 4:30; Ac 7:22
19:12 [m]1Co 1:20 [n]Isa 14:24; Ro 9:17
19:13 [o]Jer 2:16; Eze 30:13,16
19:14 [p]Mt 17:17

a 13 Hebrew *Noph*

15 There is nothing Egypt can do—
head or tail, palm branch or reed.[a]

16 In that day the Egyptians will be like women.[b] They will shudder with fear[c] at the uplifted hand[d] that the LORD Almighty raises
against them. 17 And the land of Judah will bring terror to the
Egyptians; everyone to whom Judah is mentioned will be terrified,
because of what the LORD Almighty is planning[e] against them.

18 In that day five cities in Egypt will speak the language of Canaan
and swear allegiance[f] to the LORD Almighty. One of them will be
called the City of Destruction.[a]

19 In that day there will be an altar[g] to the LORD in the heart of
Egypt, and a monument[h] to the LORD at its border. 20 It will be a
sign and witness to the LORD Almighty in the land of Egypt. When
they cry out to the LORD because of their oppressors, he will send
them a savior and defender, and he will rescue[i] them. 21 So the
LORD will make himself known to the Egyptians, and in that day
they will acknowledge[j] the LORD. They will worship[k] with sacrifices and grain offerings; they will make vows to the LORD and keep
them. 22 The LORD will strike[l] Egypt with a plague; he will strike
them and heal them. They will turn[m] to the LORD, and he will
respond to their pleas and heal[n] them.

23 In that day there will be a highway[o] from Egypt to Assyria. The
Assyrians will go to Egypt and the Egyptians to Assyria. The
Egyptians and Assyrians will worship[p] together. 24 In that day
Israel will be the third, along with Egypt and Assyria, a blessing on
the earth. 25 The LORD Almighty will bless them, saying, "Blessed
be Egypt my people,[q] Assyria my handiwork,[r] and Israel my
inheritance.[s]"

Chapter 20 Theme ____________________

20 In the year that the supreme commander,[t] sent by Sargon
king of Assyria, came to Ashdod and attacked and captured it— 2 at that time the LORD spoke through Isaiah son of
Amoz.[u] He said to him, "Take off the sackcloth[v] from your body
and the sandals[w] from your feet." And he did so, going around
stripped[x] and barefoot.[y]

3 Then the LORD said, "Just as my servant Isaiah has gone stripped
and barefoot for three years, as a sign[z] and portent against Egypt
and Cush,[b][a] 4 so the king[b] of Assyria will lead away stripped and
barefoot the Egyptian captives and Cushite exiles, young and old,
with buttocks bared—to Egypt's shame.[c] 5 Those who trusted in
Cush and boasted in Egypt[d] will be afraid and put to shame. 6 In

a *18* Most manuscripts of the Masoretic Text; some manuscripts of the Masoretic Text, Dead Sea Scrolls and Vulgate *City of the Sun* (that is, Heliopolis) b *3* That is, the upper Nile region; also in verse 5

19:15 [a]Isa 9:14
19:16 [b]51:30; Na 3:13 [c]Heb 10:31 [d]Isa 11:15
19:17 [e]Isa 14:24
19:18 [f]Zep 3:9
19:19 [g]Jos 22:10 [h]Ge 28:18
19:20 [i]Isa 49:24-26
19:21 [j]Isa 11:9 [k]Isa 56:7; Mal 1:11
19:22 [l]Heb 12:11 [m]Isa 45:14; Hos 14:1 [n]Dt 32:39
19:23 [o]Isa 11:16 [p]Isa 27:13
19:25 [q]Ps 100:3 [r]Isa 29:23; 45:11; 60:21; 64:8; Eph 2:10 [s]Hos 2:23
20:1 [t]2Ki 18:17
20:2 [u]Isa 13:1 [v]Zec 13:4; Mt 3:4 [w]Eze 24:17,23 [x]1Sa 19:24 [y]Mic 1:8
20:3 [z]Isa 8:18 [a]Isa 37:9; 43:3
20:4 [b]Isa 19:4 [c]Isa 47:3; Jer 13:22,26
20:5 [d]2Ki 18:21; Isa 30:5

that day the people who live on this coast will say, 'See what has
happened to those we relied on, those we fled to for help[a] and
deliverance from the king of Assyria! How then can we escape?[b]'"

Chapter 21 Theme ______________________________

21

An oracle concerning the Desert[c] by the Sea:

Like whirlwinds sweeping through the southland,[d]
an invader comes from the desert,
from a land of terror.

2 A dire[e] vision has been shown to me:
The traitor betrays,[f] the looter takes loot.
Elam,[g] attack! Media, lay siege!
I will bring to an end all the groaning she caused.

3 At this my body is racked with pain,
pangs seize me, like those of a woman in labor;[h]
I am staggered by what I hear,
I am bewildered by what I see.
4 My heart falters,
fear makes me tremble;
the twilight I longed for
has become a horror to me.

5 They set the tables,
they spread the rugs,
they eat, they drink![i]
Get up, you officers,
oil the shields!

6 This is what the Lord says to me:

"Go, post a lookout
and have him report what he sees.
7 When he sees chariots[j]
with teams of horses,
riders on donkeys
or riders on camels,
let him be alert,
fully alert."

8 And the lookout[a][k] shouted,

"Day after day, my lord, I stand on the watchtower;
every night I stay at my post.
9 Look, here comes a man in a chariot
with a team of horses.

a8 Dead Sea Scrolls and Syriac; Masoretic Text *A lion*

20:6 [a]Isa 10:3 [b]Jer 30:15-17; Mt 23:33; 1Th 5:3; Heb 2:3
21:1 [c]Isa 13:21; Jer 51:43 [d]Zec 9:14
21:2 [e]Ps 60:3 [f]Isa 33:1 [g]Isa 22:6; Jer 49:34
21:3 [h]Ps 48:6; Isa 26:17
21:5 [i]Jer 51:39,57; Da 5:2
21:7 [j]ver 9
21:8 [k]Hab 2:1

And he gives back the answer:
'Babylon[a] has fallen,[b] has fallen!
All the images of its gods[c]
lie shattered on the ground!'"

10O my people, crushed on the threshing floor,[d]
I tell you what I have heard
from the LORD Almighty,
from the God of Israel.

11An oracle concerning Dumah[a]:[e]

Someone calls to me from Seir,[f]
"Watchman, what is left of the night?
Watchman, what is left of the night?"
12The watchman replies,
"Morning is coming, but also the night.
If you would ask, then ask;
and come back yet again."

13An oracle[g] concerning Arabia:

You caravans of Dedanites,
who camp in the thickets of Arabia,
14 bring water for the thirsty;
you who live in Tema,[h]
bring food for the fugitives.
15They flee[i] from the sword,
from the drawn sword,
from the bent bow
and from the heat of battle.

16This is what the Lord says to me: "Within one year, as a servant
bound by contract[j] would count it, all the pomp[k] of Kedar[l] will
come to an end. 17The survivors of the bowmen, the warriors of
Kedar, will be few.[m]" The LORD, the God of Israel, has spoken.

Chapter 22 Theme ______________________

22

An oracle[n] concerning the Valley[o] of Vision:

What troubles you now,
that you have all gone up on the roofs,
2O town full of commotion,
O city of tumult and revelry?[p]
Your slain were not killed by the sword,
nor did they die in battle.
3All your leaders have fled together;
they have been captured without using the bow.

a *11 Dumah* means *silence* or *stillness,* a wordplay on *Edom.*

21:9 [a]Rev 14:8 [b]Jer 51:8; Rev 18:2 [c]Isa 46:1; Jer 50:2; 51:44
21:10 [d]Jer 51:33
21:11 [e]Ge 25:14 [f]Ge 32:3
21:13 [g]Isa 13:1
21:14 [h]Ge 25:15
21:15 [i]Isa 13:14
21:16 [j]Isa 16:14 [k]Isa 17:3 [l]Ps 120:5; Isa 60:7
21:17 [m]Isa 10:19
22:1 [n]Isa 13:1 [o]Ps 125:2; Jer 21:13; Joel 3:2,12,14
22:2 [p]Isa 32:13

All you who were caught were taken prisoner together,
having fled while the enemy was still far away.
4 Therefore I said, "Turn away from me;
let me weep[a] bitterly.
Do not try to console me
over the destruction of my people."[b]

5 The Lord, the LORD Almighty, has a day
of tumult and trampling and terror[c]
in the Valley of Vision,
a day of battering down walls
and of crying out to the mountains.
6 Elam[d] takes up the quiver,[e]
with her charioteers and horses;
Kir[f] uncovers the shield.
7 Your choicest valleys are full of chariots,
and horsemen are posted at the city gates;[g]
8 the defenses of Judah are stripped away.

And you looked in that day
to the weapons[h] in the Palace of the Forest;[i]
9 you saw that the City of David
had many breaches in its defenses;
you stored up water
in the Lower Pool.[j]
10 You counted the buildings in Jerusalem
and tore down houses to strengthen the wall.
11 You built a reservoir between the two walls[k]
for the water of the Old Pool,[l]
but you did not look to the One who made it,
or have regard for the One who planned it long ago.

12 The Lord, the LORD Almighty,
called you on that day
to weep[m] and to wail,
to tear out your hair[n] and put on sackcloth.[o]
13 But see, there is joy and revelry,
slaughtering of cattle and killing of sheep,
eating of meat and drinking of wine![p]
"Let us eat and drink," you say,
"for tomorrow we die!"[q]

14 The LORD Almighty has revealed this in my hearing:[r] "Till your dying day this sin will not be atoned[s] for," says the Lord, the LORD Almighty.

15 This is what the Lord, the LORD Almighty, says:

22:4 [a] Isa 15:3; Lk 19:41 [b] Jer 9:1
22:5 [c] La 1:5
22:6 [d] Isa 21:2 [e] Jer 49:35 [f] 2Ki 16:9
22:7 [g] 2Ch 32:1-2
22:8 [h] 2Ch 32:5 [i] 1Ki 7:2
22:9 [j] 2Ch 32:4
22:11 [k] 2Ki 25:4; Jer 39:4 [l] 2Ch 32:4
22:12 [m] Joel 2:17 [n] Mic 1:16 [o] Joel 1:13
22:13 [p] Isa 5:22; 28:7-8; 56:12; Lk 17:26-29 [q] 1Co 15:32*
22:14 [r] Isa 5:9 [s] Isa 13:11; 26:21; 30:13-14; Eze 24:13

"Go, say to this steward,
to Shebna,[a] who is in charge of the palace:
16What are you doing here and who gave you permission
to cut out a grave[b] for yourself here,
hewing your grave on the height
and chiseling your resting place in the rock?

17"Beware, the LORD is about to take firm hold of you
and hurl you away, O you mighty man.
18He will roll you up tightly like a ball
and throw[c] you into a large country.
There you will die
and there your splendid chariots will remain—
you disgrace to your master's house!
19I will depose you from your office,
and you will be ousted from your position.

20"In that day I will summon my servant, Eliakim[d] son of Hilkiah. 21I will clothe him with your robe and fasten your sash around
him and hand your authority over to him. He will be a father to
those who live in Jerusalem and to the house of Judah. 22I will place
on his shoulder the key[e] to the house of David;[f] what he opens no
one can shut, and what he shuts no one can open.[g] 23I will drive
him like a peg[h] into a firm place;[i] he will be a seat[a] of honor[j] for
the house of his father. 24All the glory of his family will hang on
him: its offspring and offshoots—all its lesser vessels, from the
bowls to all the jars.

25"In that day," declares the LORD Almighty, "the peg[k] driven into
the firm place will give way; it will be sheared off and will fall, and
the load hanging on it will be cut down." The LORD has spoken.[l]

Chapter 23 Theme ____________________

23 An oracle concerning Tyre:[m]

Wail, O ships[n] of Tarshish![o]
For Tyre is destroyed
and left without house or harbor.
From the land of Cyprus[b]
word has come to them.

2Be silent, you people of the island
and you merchants of Sidon,
whom the seafarers have enriched.
3On the great waters
came the grain of the Shihor;

a23 Or *throne* b1 Hebrew *Kittim*

22:15 [a]2Ki 18:18; Isa 36:3
22:16 [b]Mt 27:60
22:18 [c]Isa 17:13
22:20 [d]2Ki 18:18; Isa 36:3
22:22 [e]Rev 3:7 [f]Isa 7:2 [g]Job 12:14
22:23 [h]Zec 10:4 [i]Ezr 9:8 [j]1Sa 2:7-8; Job 36:7
22:25 [k]ver 23 [l]Isa 46:11; Mic 4:4
23:1 [m]Jos 19:29; 1Ki 5:1; Jer 47:4; Eze 26,27,28; Joel 3:4-8; Am 1:9-10; Zec 9:2-4 [n]1Ki 10:22 [o]Ge 10:4; Isa 2:16*fn*

the harvest of the Nile[a] [a] was the revenue of Tyre,[b]
and she became the marketplace of the nations.

4 Be ashamed, O Sidon,[c] and you, O fortress of the sea,
for the sea has spoken:
"I have neither been in labor nor given birth;
I have neither reared sons nor brought
up daughters."
5 When word comes to Egypt,
they will be in anguish at the report from Tyre.

6 Cross over to Tarshish;
wail, you people of the island.
7 Is this your city of revelry,[d]
the old, old city,
whose feet have taken her
to settle in far-off lands?
8 Who planned this against Tyre,
the bestower of crowns,
whose merchants are princes,
whose traders are renowned in the earth?
9 The LORD Almighty planned it,
to bring low[e] the pride of all glory
and to humble[f] all who are renowned[g] on the earth.

10 Till[b] your land as along the Nile,
O Daughter of Tarshish,
for you no longer have a harbor.
11 The LORD has stretched out his hand[h] over the sea
and made its kingdoms tremble.
He has given an order concerning Phoenicia[c]
that her fortresses be destroyed.[i]
12 He said, "No more of your reveling,[j]
O Virgin Daughter[k] of Sidon, now crushed!

"Up, cross over to Cyprus[d];
even there you will find no rest."
13 Look at the land of the Babylonians,[e]
this people that is now of no account!
The Assyrians[l] have made it
a place for desert creatures;
they raised up their siege towers,
they stripped its fortresses bare
and turned it into a ruin.[m]

23:3 [a] Isa 19:7 [b] Eze 27:3
23:4 [c] Ge 10:15,19
23:7 [d] Isa 22:2; 32:13
23:9 [e] Job 40:11 [f] Isa 13:11 [g] Isa 5:13; 9:15
23:11 [h] Ex 14:21 [i] Isa 25:2; Zec 9:3-4
23:12 [j] Rev 18:22 [k] Isa 47:1
23:13 [l] Isa 10:5 [m] Isa 10:7

[a] *2,3* Masoretic Text; one Dead Sea Scroll *Sidon, / who cross over the sea; / your envoys* [3]*are on the great waters. / The grain of the Shihor, / the harvest of the Nile,* [b] *10* Dead Sea Scrolls and some Septuagint manuscripts; Masoretic Text *Go through* [c] *11* Hebrew *Canaan* [d] *12* Hebrew *Kittim* [e] *13* Or *Chaldeans*

[14]Wail, you ships of Tarshish;[a]
your fortress is destroyed!

[15]At that time Tyre[b] will be forgotten for seventy years, the span
of a king's life. But at the end of these seventy years, it will happen to Tyre as in the song of the prostitute:

[16]"Take up a harp, walk through the city,
O prostitute forgotten;
play the harp well, sing many a song,
so that you will be remembered."

[17]At the end of seventy years, the LORD will deal with Tyre. She
will return to her hire as a prostitute[c] and will ply her trade with
all the kingdoms on the face of the earth. [18]Yet her profit and her
earnings will be set apart for the LORD;[d] they will not be stored
up or hoarded. Her profits will go to those who live before the
LORD,[e] for abundant food and fine clothes.

Chapter 24 Theme ____________________

24

See, the LORD is going to lay waste the earth[f]
and devastate it;
he will ruin its face
and scatter its inhabitants—
[2]it will be the same
for priest as for people,[g]
for master as for servant,
for mistress as for maid,
for seller as for buyer,[h]
for borrower as for lender,
for debtor as for creditor.[i]
[3]The earth will be completely laid waste
and totally plundered.[j]
The LORD has spoken this word.
[4]The earth dries up and withers,
the world languishes and withers,
the exalted[k] of the earth languish.
[5]The earth is defiled[l] by its people;
they have disobeyed[m] the laws,
violated the statutes
and broken the everlasting covenant.
[6]Therefore a curse consumes the earth;
its people must bear their guilt.
Therefore earth's inhabitants are burned up,[n]
and very few are left.
[7]The new wine dries up and the vine withers;[o]
all the merrymakers groan.[p]

23:14 [a]Isa 2:16*fn*

23:15 [b]Jer 25:22

23:17 [c]Eze 16:26; Na 3:4; Rev 17:1

23:18 [d]Ex 28:36; Ps 72:10 [e]Isa 60:5-9; Mic 4:13

24:1 [f]ver 20; Isa 2:19-21; 33:9

24:2 [g]Hos 4:9 [h]Eze 7:12 [i]Lev 25:35-37; Dt 23:19-20

24:3 [j]Isa 6:11-12

24:4 [k]Isa 2:12

24:5 [l]Ge 3:17; Nu 35:33 [m]Isa 10:6; 59:12

24:6 [n]Isa 1:31

24:7 [o]Joel 1:10-12 [p]Isa 16:8-10

24:8 [a] Isa 5:12 [b] Jer 7:34; 16:9; 25:10; Hos 2:11 [c] Rev 18:22 [d] Eze 26:13
24:9 [e] Isa 5:11,22 [f] Isa 5:20
24:11 [g] Isa 16:10; 32:13; Jer 14:3
24:13 [h] Isa 17:6
24:14 [i] Isa 12:6
24:15 [j] Isa 66:19 [k] Isa 25:3; Mal 1:11
24:16 [l] Isa 28:5 [m] Isa 21:2; Jer 5:11
24:17 [n] Jer 48:43
24:18 [o] Ge 7:11 [p] Ps 18:7
24:19 [q] Dt 11:6
24:20 [r] Isa 19:14 [s] Isa 1:2,28; 43:27

8 The gaiety of the tambourines[a] is stilled,
the noise[b] of the revelers has stopped,
the joyful harp[c] is silent.[d]
9 No longer do they drink wine[e] with a song;
the beer is bitter[f] to its drinkers.
10 The ruined city lies desolate;
the entrance to every house is barred.
11 In the streets they cry out for wine;
all joy turns to gloom,[g]
all gaiety is banished from the earth.
12 The city is left in ruins,
its gate is battered to pieces.
13 So will it be on the earth
and among the nations,
as when an olive tree is beaten,[h]
or as when gleanings are left after the grape harvest.

14 They raise their voices, they shout for joy;[i]
from the west they acclaim the LORD's majesty.
15 Therefore in the east give glory[j] to the LORD;
exalt[k] the name of the LORD, the God of Israel,
in the islands of the sea.
16 From the ends of the earth we hear singing:
"Glory[l] to the Righteous One."

But I said, "I waste away, I waste away!
Woe to me!
The treacherous betray!
With treachery the treacherous betray![m]"
17 Terror and pit and snare[n] await you,
O people of the earth.
18 Whoever flees at the sound of terror
will fall into a pit;
whoever climbs out of the pit
will be caught in a snare.

The floodgates of the heavens[o] are opened,
the foundations of the earth shake.[p]
19 The earth is broken up,
the earth is split asunder,[q]
the earth is thoroughly shaken.
20 The earth reels like a drunkard,[r]
it sways like a hut in the wind;
so heavy upon it is the guilt of its rebellion[s]
that it falls—never to rise again.

[21]In that day the LORD will punish[a]
the powers in the heavens above
and the kings on the earth below.
[22]They will be herded together
like prisoners[b] bound in a dungeon;[c]
they will be shut up in prison
and be punished[a] after many days.[d]
[23]The moon will be abashed, the sun[e] ashamed;
for the LORD Almighty will reign[f]
on Mount Zion[g] and in Jerusalem,
and before its elders, gloriously.[h]

Chapter 25 Theme ______________________

25 O LORD, you are my God;
I will exalt you and praise your name,
for in perfect faithfulness
you have done marvelous things,[i]
things planned[j] long ago.
[2]You have made the city a heap of rubble,[k]
the fortified[l] town a ruin,
the foreigners' stronghold[m] a city no more;
it will never be rebuilt.
[3]Therefore strong peoples will honor you;
cities of ruthless[n] nations will revere you.
[4]You have been a refuge[o] for the poor,
a refuge for the needy in his distress,
a shelter from the storm
and a shade from the heat.
For the breath of the ruthless[p]
is like a storm driving against a wall
5 and like the heat of the desert.
You silence[q] the uproar of foreigners;
as heat is reduced by the shadow of a cloud,
so the song of the ruthless is stilled.

[6]On this mountain[r] the LORD Almighty will prepare
a feast[s] of rich food for all peoples,
a banquet of aged wine—
the best of meats and the finest of wines.[t]
[7]On this mountain he will destroy
the shroud[u] that enfolds all peoples,
the sheet that covers all nations;
8 he will swallow up death[v] forever.
The Sovereign LORD will wipe away the tears[w]
from all faces;

a 22 Or *released*

24:21
a Isa 10:12

24:22
b Isa 10:4
c Isa 42:7,22
d Eze 38:8

24:23
e Isa 13:10
f Rev 22:5
g Heb 12:22
h Isa 60:19

25:1
i Ps 98:1
j Nu 23:19

25:2
k Isa 17:1
l Isa 17:3
m Isa 13:22

25:3
n Isa 13:11

25:4
o Isa 4:6; 17:10; 27:5; 33:16
p Isa 29:5; 49:25

25:5
q Jer 51:55

25:6
r Isa 2:2
s Isa 1:19; Mt 8:11; 22:4
t Pr 9:2

25:7
u 2Co 3:15-16; Eph 4:18

25:8
v Hos 13:14; 1Co 15:54-55*
w Isa 30:19; 35:10; 51:11; 65:19; Rev 7:17; 21:4

25:8 [a]Mt 5:11; 1Pe 4:14

he will remove the disgrace[a] of his people
from all the earth.
The LORD has spoken.

9 In that day they will say,

"Surely this is our God;[b]
we trusted in him, and he saved[c] us.
This is the LORD, we trusted in him;
let us rejoice[d] and be glad in his salvation."

25:9 [b]Isa 40:9 [c]Ps 20:5; Isa 33:22; 35:4; 49:25-26; 60:16 [d]Isa 35:2,10

10 The hand of the LORD will rest on this mountain;
but Moab[e] will be trampled under him
as straw is trampled down in the manure.
11 They will spread out their hands in it,
as a swimmer spreads out his hands to swim.
God will bring down[f] their pride[g]
despite the cleverness[a] of their hands.
12 He will bring down your high fortified walls
and lay them low;[h]
he will bring them down to the ground,
to the very dust.

25:10 [e]Am 2:1-3

25:11 [f]Isa 5:25; 14:26; 16:14 [g]Job 40:12

25:12 [h]Isa 15:1

Chapter 26 Theme ____________________

26

In that day this song will be sung in the land of Judah:

We have a strong city;[i]
God makes salvation
its walls[j] and ramparts.
2 Open the gates
that the righteous[k] nation may enter,
the nation that keeps faith.
3 You will keep in perfect peace
him whose mind is steadfast,
because he trusts in you.
4 Trust[l] in the LORD forever,
for the LORD, the LORD, is the Rock eternal.
5 He humbles those who dwell on high,
he lays the lofty city low;
he levels it to the ground[m]
and casts it down to the dust.
6 Feet trample it down—
the feet of the oppressed,
the footsteps of the poor.[n]

26:1 [i]Isa 14:32 [j]Isa 60:18

26:2 [k]Isa 54:14; 58:8; 62:2

26:4 [l]Isa 12:2; 50:10

26:5 [m]Isa 25:12

26:6 [n]Isa 3:15

[a] *11* The meaning of the Hebrew for this word is uncertain.

7The path of the righteous is level;
O upright One, you make the way of the
righteous smooth.[a]
8Yes, LORD, walking in the way of your laws,[a][b]
we wait for you;
your name[c] and renown
are the desire of our hearts.
9My soul yearns for you in the night;
in the morning my spirit longs[d] for you.
When your judgments come upon the earth,
the people of the world learn righteousness.[e]
10Though grace is shown to the wicked,
they do not learn righteousness;
even in a land of uprightness they go on doing evil[f]
and regard[g] not the majesty of the LORD.
11O LORD, your hand is lifted high,
but they do not see[h] it.
Let them see your zeal for your people and be put to
shame;
let the fire[i] reserved for your enemies consume them.

12LORD, you establish peace for us;
all that we have accomplished you have done for us.
13O LORD, our God, other lords[j] besides you have ruled
over us,
but your name alone do we honor.[k]
14They are now dead,[l] they live no more;
those departed spirits do not rise.
You punished them and brought them to ruin;[m]
you wiped out all memory of them.
15You have enlarged the nation, O LORD;
you have enlarged the nation.
You have gained glory for yourself;
you have extended all the borders[n] of the land.

16LORD, they came to you in their distress;[o]
when you disciplined them,
they could barely whisper a prayer.[b]
17As a woman with child and about to give birth[p]
writhes and cries out in her pain,
so were we in your presence, O LORD.
18We were with child, we writhed in pain,
but we gave birth[q] to wind.
We have not brought salvation[r] to the earth;
we have not given birth to people of the world.

a8 Or *judgments* b16 The meaning of the Hebrew for this clause is uncertain.

26:7 [a]Isa 42:16
26:8 [b]Isa 56:1 [c]Isa 12:4
26:9 [d]Ps 63:1; 78:34; Isa 55:6 [e]Mt 6:33
26:10 [f]Isa 32:6 [g]Isa 22:12-13; Hos 11:7; Jn 5:37-38; Ro 2:4
26:11 [h]Isa 44:9,18 [i]Heb 10:27
26:13 [j]Isa 2:8; 10:5,11 [k]Isa 63:7
26:14 [l]Dt 4:28 [m]Isa 10:3
26:15 [n]Isa 33:17
26:16 [o]Hos 5:15
26:17 [p]Jn 16:21
26:18 [q]Isa 33:11; 59:4 [r]Ps 17:14

26:19 [a]Isa 25:8; Eph 5:14 [b]Eze 37:1-14; Da 12:2

19 But your dead[a] will live;
their bodies will rise.
You who dwell in the dust,
wake up and shout for joy.
Your dew is like the dew of the morning;
the earth will give birth to her dead.[b]

26:20 [c]Ex 12:23 [d]Ps 91:1,4 [e]Ps 30:5; Isa 54:7-8

20 Go, my people, enter your rooms
and shut the doors[c] behind you;
hide[d] yourselves for a little while
until his wrath has passed by.[e]

26:21 [f]Jude 14 [g]Mic 1:3 [h]Isa 13:9,11; 30:12-14 [i]Job 16:18; Lk 11:50-51

21 See, the LORD is coming[f] out of his dwelling[g]
to punish[h] the people of the earth for their sins.
The earth will disclose the blood[i] shed upon her;
she will conceal her slain no longer.

Chapter 27 Theme ____________________

27:1 [j]Isa 34:6; 66:16 [k]Job 3:8 [l]Ps 74:13

27

In that day,
the LORD will punish with his sword,[j]
his fierce, great and powerful sword,
Leviathan[k] the gliding serpent,
Leviathan the coiling serpent;
he will slay the monster[l] of the sea.

27:2 [m]Jer 2:21

2 In that day—

"Sing about a fruitful vineyard:[m]

27:3 [n]Isa 58:11

3 I, the LORD, watch over it;
I water[n] it continually.
I guard it day and night
so that no one may harm it.

27:4 [o]Isa 10:17; Mt 3:12; Heb 6:8

4 I am not angry.
If only there were briers and thorns confronting me!
I would march against them in battle;
I would set them all on fire.[o]

27:5 [p]Isa 25:4 [q]Job 22:21; Ro 5:1; 2Co 5:20

5 Or else let them come to me for refuge;[p]
let them make peace[q] with me,
yes, let them make peace with me."

27:6 [r]Hos 14:5-6 [s]Isa 37:31

6 In days to come Jacob will take root,
Israel will bud and blossom[r]
and fill all the world with fruit.[s]

27:7 [t]Isa 37:36-38

7 Has ⌊the LORD⌋ struck her
as he struck[t] down those who struck her?
Has she been killed
as those were killed who killed her?

8By warfare[a] and exile[a] you contend with her—
with his fierce blast he drives her out,
as on a day the east wind blows.
9By this, then, will Jacob's guilt be atoned for,
and this will be the full fruitage of the removal of
his sin:[b]
When he makes all the altar stones
to be like chalk stones crushed to pieces,
no Asherah poles[b][c] or incense altars
will be left standing.
10The fortified city stands desolate,[d]
an abandoned settlement, forsaken like the desert;
there the calves graze,
there they lie down;[e]
they strip its branches bare.
11When its twigs are dry, they are broken off
and women come and make fires with them.
For this is a people without understanding;[f]
so their Maker has no compassion on them,
and their Creator[g] shows them no favor.[h]

12In that day the LORD will thresh from the flowing Euphrates[c] to
the Wadi of Egypt,[i] and you, O Israelites, will be gathered[j] up one
by one. 13And in that day a great trumpet[k] will sound. Those who
were perishing in Assyria and those who were exiled in Egypt[l] will
come and worship the LORD on the holy mountain in Jerusalem.

Chapter 28 Theme ________________________

28

Woe to that wreath, the pride of Ephraim's[m] drunkards,
to the fading flower, his glorious beauty,
set on the head of a fertile valley[n]—
to that city, the pride of those laid low by wine![o]
2See, the Lord has one who is powerful[p] and strong.
Like a hailstorm[q] and a destructive wind,[r]
like a driving rain and a flooding[s] downpour,
he will throw it forcefully to the ground.
3That wreath, the pride of Ephraim's[t] drunkards,
will be trampled underfoot.
4That fading flower, his glorious beauty,
set on the head of a fertile valley,[u]
will be like a fig[v] ripe before harvest—
as soon as someone sees it and takes it in his hand,
he swallows it.

a8 See Septuagint; the meaning of the Hebrew for this word is uncertain. b9 That is, symbols of the goddess Asherah c12 Hebrew *River*

27:8
a Isa 50:1; 54:7

27:9
b Ro 11:27*
c Ex 34:13

27:10
d Isa 32:14; Jer 26:6
e Isa 17:2

27:11
f Dt 32:28; Isa 1:3; Jer 8:7
g Dt 32:18; Isa 43:1,7,15; 44:1-2,21,24
h Isa 9:17

27:12
i Ge 15:18
j Dt 30:4; Isa 11:12; 17:6

27:13
k Lev 25:9; Mt 24:31
l Isa 19:21,25

28:1
m ver 3; Isa 9:9
n ver 4
o Hos 7:5

28:2
p Isa 40:10
q Isa 30:30; Eze 13:11
r Isa 29:6
s Isa 8:7

28:3
t ver 1

28:4
u ver 1
v Hos 9:10; Na 3:12

28:5 [a]Isa 62:3

[5]In that day the LORD Almighty
will be a glorious crown,[a]
a beautiful wreath
for the remnant of his people.

28:6 [b]Isa 11:2-4; 32:1,16 [c]Jn 5:30 [d]2Ch 32:8

[6]He will be a spirit of justice[b]
to him who sits in judgment,[c]
a source of strength
to those who turn back the battle[d] at the gate.

28:7 [e]Isa 22:13 [f]Isa 56:10-12 [g]Isa 24:2 [h]Isa 9:15 [i]Isa 29:11; Hos 4:11

[7]And these also stagger from wine[e]
and reel[f] from beer:
Priests[g] and prophets[h] stagger from beer
and are befuddled with wine;
they reel from beer,
they stagger when seeing visions,[i]
they stumble when rendering decisions.

28:8 [j]Jer 48:26

[8]All the tables are covered with vomit[j]
and there is not a spot without filth.

28:9 [k]ver 26; Isa 30:20; 48:17; 50:4; 54:13 [l]Ps 131:2 [m]Heb 5:12-13

[9]"Who is it he is trying to teach?[k]
To whom is he explaining his message?
To children weaned[l] from their milk,[m]
to those just taken from the breast?
[10]For it is:
Do and do, do and do,
rule on rule, rule on rule[a];
a little here, a little there."

28:11 [n]Isa 33:19 [o]1Co 14:21*

[11]Very well then, with foreign lips and strange tongues[n]
God will speak to this people,[o]
[12]to whom he said,
"This is the resting place, let the weary rest";[p]
and, "This is the place of repose"—
but they would not listen.

28:12 [p]Isa 11:10; Mt 11:28-29

[13]So then, the word of the LORD to them will become:
Do and do, do and do,
rule on rule, rule on rule;
a little here, a little there—
so that they will go and fall backward,
be injured[q] and snared and captured.[r]

28:13 [q]Mt 21:44 [r]Isa 8:15

[14]Therefore hear the word of the LORD,[s] you scoffers
who rule this people in Jerusalem.
[15]You boast, "We have entered into a covenant with death,
with the grave[b] we have made an agreement.

28:14 [s]Isa 1:10

[a] *10* Hebrew / *sav lasav sav lasav* / *kav lakav kav lakav* (possibly meaningless sounds; perhaps a mimicking of the prophet's words); also in verse 13 [b] *15* Hebrew *Sheol*; also in verse 18

When an overwhelming scourge sweeps by,[a]
it cannot touch us,
for we have made a lie[b] our refuge
and falsehood[a] our hiding place.[c]"

16So this is what the Sovereign LORD says:

"See, I lay a stone in Zion,
a tested stone,[d]
a precious cornerstone for a sure foundation;
the one who trusts will never be dismayed.[e]
17I will make justice[f] the measuring line
and righteousness the plumb line;[g]
hail will sweep away your refuge, the lie,
and water will overflow your hiding place.
18Your covenant with death will be annulled;
your agreement with the grave will not stand.[h]
When the overwhelming scourge sweeps by,[i]
you will be beaten down[j] by it.
19As often as it comes it will carry you away;[k]
morning after morning, by day and by night,
it will sweep through."

The understanding of this message
will bring sheer terror.[l]
20The bed is too short to stretch out on,
the blanket too narrow to wrap around you.[m]
21The LORD will rise up as he did at Mount Perazim,[n]
he will rouse himself as in the Valley of Gibeon[o]—
to do his work,[p] his strange work,
and perform his task, his alien task.
22Now stop your mocking,
or your chains will become heavier;
the Lord, the LORD Almighty, has told me
of the destruction decreed[q] against the whole land.[r]

23Listen and hear my voice;
pay attention and hear what I say.
24When a farmer plows for planting, does he plow
continually?
Does he keep on breaking up and harrowing the soil?
25When he has leveled the surface,
does he not sow caraway and scatter cummin?[s]
Does he not plant wheat in its place,[b]
barley in its plot,[b]
and spelt[t] in its field?

a 15 Or *false gods*   b 25 The meaning of the Hebrew for this word is uncertain.

28:15 [a] ver 2,18; Isa 8:7-8; 30:28; Da 11:22 [b] Isa 9:15 [c] Isa 29:15
28:16 [d] Ps 118:22; Isa 8:14-15; Mt 21:42; Ac 4:11; Eph 2:20 [e] Ro 9:33*; 10:11*; 1Pe 2:6*
28:17 [f] Isa 5:16 [g] 2Ki 21:13
28:18 [h] Isa 7:7 [i] ver 15 [j] Da 8:13
28:19 [k] 2Ki 24:2 [l] Job 18:11
28:20 [m] Isa 59:6
28:21 [n] 1Ch 14:11 [o] Jos 10:10,12; 1Ch 14:16 [p] Isa 10:12; Lk 19:41-44
28:22 [q] Isa 10:22 [r] Isa 10:23
28:25 [s] Mt 23:23 [t] Ex 9:32

26 His God instructs him
and teaches him the right way.

27 Caraway is not threshed with a sledge,
nor is a cartwheel rolled over cummin;
caraway is beaten out with a rod,
and cummin with a stick.
28 Grain must be ground to make bread;
so one does not go on threshing it forever.
Though he drives the wheels of his threshing cart over it,
his horses do not grind it.
29 All this also comes from the LORD Almighty,
wonderful in counsel[a] and magnificent in wisdom.[b]

Chapter 29 Theme ________________________________

29

Woe[c] to you, Ariel, Ariel,[d]
the city where David settled!
Add year to year
and let your cycle of festivals[e] go on.
2 Yet I will besiege Ariel;
she will mourn and lament,[f]
she will be to me like an altar hearth.[a]
3 I will encamp against you all around;
I will encircle[g] you with towers
and set up my siege works against you.
4 Brought low, you will speak from the ground;
your speech will mumble[h] out of the dust.
Your voice will come ghostlike from the earth;
out of the dust your speech will whisper.

5 But your many enemies will become like fine dust,
the ruthless hordes like blown chaff.[i]
Suddenly,[j] in an instant,
6 the LORD Almighty will come
with thunder and earthquake[k] and great noise,
with windstorm and tempest and flames of a
devouring fire.
7 Then the hordes of all the nations[l] that fight against Ariel,
that attack her and her fortress and besiege her,
will be as it is with a dream,[m]
with a vision in the night—
8 as when a hungry man dreams that he is eating,
but he awakens,[n] and his hunger remains;
as when a thirsty man dreams that he is drinking,
but he awakens faint, with his thirst unquenched.

28:29 [a]Isa 9:6 [b]Ro 11:33
29:1 [c]Isa 22:12-13 [d]2Sa 5:9 [e]Isa 1:14
29:2 [f]Isa 3:26; La 2:5
29:3 [g]Lk 19:43-44
29:4 [h]Isa 8:19
29:5 [i]Isa 17:13 [j]Isa 17:14; 1Th 5:3
29:6 [k]Mt 24:7; Mk 13:8; Lk 21:11; Rev 11:19
29:7 [l]Mic 4:11-12; Zec 12:9 [m]Job 20:8
29:8 [n]Ps 73:20

[a] 2 The Hebrew for *altar hearth* sounds like the Hebrew for *Ariel.*

So will it be with the hordes of all the nations
that fight against Mount Zion.

9Be stunned and amazed,
blind yourselves and be sightless;
be drunk,[a] but not from wine,[b]
stagger, but not from beer.
10The LORD has brought over you a deep sleep:
He has sealed your eyes[c] (the prophets);[d]
he has covered your heads (the seers).[e]

11For you this whole vision is nothing but words sealed[f] in a
scroll. And if you give the scroll to someone who can read, and say
to him, "Read this, please," he will answer, "I can't; it is sealed."
12Or if you give the scroll to someone who cannot read, and say,
"Read this, please," he will answer, "I don't know how to read."

13The Lord says:

"These people come near to me with their mouth
and honor me with their lips,
but their hearts are far from me.[g]
Their worship of me
is made up only of rules taught by men.[a] [h]
14Therefore once more I will astound these people
with wonder upon wonder;[i]
the wisdom of the wise[j] will perish,
the intelligence of the intelligent will vanish.[k]"
15Woe to those who go to great depths
to hide their plans from the LORD,
who do their work in darkness and think,
"Who sees us?[l] Who will know?"[m]
16You turn things upside down,
as if the potter were thought to be like the clay!
Shall what is formed say to him who formed it,
"He did not make me"?
Can the pot say of the potter,[n]
"He knows nothing"?

17In a very short time, will not Lebanon be turned into a
fertile field[o]
and the fertile field seem like a forest?[p]
18In that day the deaf[q] will hear the words of the scroll,
and out of gloom and darkness
the eyes of the blind will see.[r]
19Once more the humble[s] will rejoice in the LORD;
the needy[t] will rejoice in the Holy One of Israel.

29:9 [a]Isa 51:17 [b]Isa 51:21-22

29:10 [c]Ps 69:23; Isa 6:9-10; Ro 11:8* [d]Mic 3:6 [e]1Sa 9:9

29:11 [f]Isa 8:16; Mt 13:11; Rev 5:1-2

29:13 [g]Eze 33:31 [h]Mt 15:8-9*; Mk 7:6-7*; Col 2:22

29:14 [i]Hab 1:5 [j]Jer 8:9; 49:7 [k]Isa 6:9-10; 1Co 1:19*

29:15 [l]Ps 10:11-13; 94:7; Isa 57:12 [m]Job 22:13

29:16 [n]Isa 45:9; 64:8; Ro 9:20-21*

29:17 [o]Ps 84:6 [p]Isa 32:15

29:18 [q]Mk 7:37 [r]Isa 32:3; 35:5; Mt 11:5

29:19 [s]Isa 61:1; Mt 5:5; 11:29 [t]Isa 14:30; Mt 11:5; Jas 1:9; 2:5

a *13* Hebrew; Septuagint *They worship me in vain; / their teachings are but rules taught by men*

20 The ruthless will vanish,
the mockers[a] will disappear,
and all who have an eye for evil[b] will be cut down—
21 those who with a word make a man out to be guilty,
who ensnare the defender in court[c]
and with false testimony deprive the innocent
of justice.[d]

22 Therefore this is what the LORD, who redeemed Abraham,[e] says
to the house of Jacob:

"No longer will Jacob be ashamed;[f]
no longer will their faces grow pale.
23 When they see among them their children,[g]
the work of my hands,[h]
they will keep my name holy;
they will acknowledge the holiness of the Holy One
of Jacob,
and will stand in awe of the God of Israel.
24 Those who are wayward[i] in spirit will gain
understanding;[j]
those who complain will accept instruction."[k]

Chapter 30 Theme ______________________

30

"Woe[l] to the obstinate children,"[m]
declares the LORD,
"to those who carry out plans that are not mine,
forming an alliance,[n] but not by my Spirit,
heaping sin upon sin;
2 who go down to Egypt[o]
without consulting[p] me;
who look for help to Pharaoh's protection,[q]
to Egypt's shade for refuge.
3 But Pharaoh's protection will be to your shame,
Egypt's shade will bring you disgrace.[r]
4 Though they have officials in Zoan[s]
and their envoys have arrived in Hanes,
5 everyone will be put to shame
because of a people[t] useless to them,
who bring neither help nor advantage,
but only shame and disgrace."

6 An oracle concerning the animals of the Negev:

Through a land of hardship and distress,[u]
of lions and lionesses,
of adders and darting snakes,[v]

29:20 [a] Isa 28:22 [b] Isa 59:4; Mic 2:1
29:21 [c] Am 5:10,15 [d] Isa 32:7
29:22 [e] Isa 41:8; 63:16 [f] Isa 49:23
29:23 [g] Isa 49:20-26 [h] Isa 19:25
29:24 [i] Isa 28:7; Heb 5:2 [j] Isa 41:20; 60:16 [k] Isa 30:21
30:1 [l] Isa 29:15 [m] Isa 1:2 [n] Isa 8:12
30:2 [o] Isa 31:1 [p] Nu 27:21 [q] Isa 36:9
30:3 [r] Isa 20:4-5; 36:6
30:4 [s] Isa 19:11
30:5 [t] ver 7
30:6 [u] Ex 5:10,21; Isa 8:22; Jer 11:4 [v] Dt 8:15

the envoys carry their riches on donkeys' backs,
their treasures[a] on the humps of camels,
to that unprofitable nation,
7 to Egypt, whose help is utterly useless.
Therefore I call her
Rahab the Do-Nothing.

8 Go now, write it on a tablet for them,
inscribe it on a scroll,[b]
that for the days to come
it may be an everlasting witness.
9 These are rebellious people, deceitful[c] children,
children unwilling to listen to the LORD's instruction.[d]
10 They say to the seers,
"See no more visions[e]!"
and to the prophets,
"Give us no more visions of what is right!
Tell us pleasant things,[f]
prophesy illusions.[g]
11 Leave this way,
get off this path,
and stop confronting[h] us
with the Holy One of Israel!"

12 Therefore, this is what the Holy One of Israel says:

"Because you have rejected this message,[i]
relied on oppression[j]
and depended on deceit,
13 this sin will become for you
like a high wall,[k] cracked and bulging,
that collapses[l] suddenly,[m] in an instant.
14 It will break in pieces like pottery,[n]
shattered so mercilessly
that among its pieces not a fragment will be found
for taking coals from a hearth
or scooping water out of a cistern."

15 This is what the Sovereign LORD, the Holy One of Israel, says:

"In repentance and rest is your salvation,
in quietness and trust[o] is your strength,
but you would have none of it.
16 You said, 'No, we will flee on horses.'[p]
Therefore you will flee!
You said, 'We will ride off on swift horses.'
Therefore your pursuers will be swift!

30:6 [a] Isa 15:7
30:8 [b] Isa 8:1; Hab 2:2
30:9 [c] Isa 28:15; 59:3-4 [d] Isa 1:10
30:10 [e] Jer 11:21; Am 7:13 [f] 1Ki 22:8 [g] Eze 13:7; Ro 16:18
30:11 [h] Job 21:14
30:12 [i] Isa 5:24 [j] Isa 5:7
30:13 [k] Ps 62:3 [l] 1Ki 20:30 [m] Isa 29:5
30:14 [n] Ps 2:9; Jer 19:10-11
30:15 [o] Isa 32:17
30:16 [p] Isa 31:1,3

17A thousand will flee
at the threat of one;
at the threat of five[a]
you will all flee[b] away,
till you are left
like a flagstaff on a mountaintop,
like a banner on a hill."

18Yet the LORD longs[c] to be gracious to you;
he rises to show you compassion.
For the LORD is a God of justice.[d]
Blessed are all who wait for him![e]

19O people of Zion, who live in Jerusalem, you will weep no
more.[f] How gracious he will be when you cry for help! As soon as
he hears, he will answer[g] you. 20Although the Lord gives you the
bread[h] of adversity and the water of affliction, your teachers will be
hidden[i] no more; with your own eyes you will see them. 21Whether
you turn to the right or to the left, your ears will hear a voice[j]
behind you, saying, "This is the way; walk in it." 22Then you will
defile your idols[k] overlaid with silver and your images covered with
gold; you will throw them away like a menstrual cloth and say to
them, "Away with you!"

23He will also send you rain[l] for the seed you sow in the ground,
and the food that comes from the land will be rich and plentiful. In
that day your cattle will graze in broad meadows.[m] 24The oxen and
donkeys that work the soil will eat fodder and mash, spread out
with fork[n] and shovel. 25In the day of great slaughter, when the
towers[o] fall, streams of water will flow[p] on every high mountain
and every lofty hill. 26The moon will shine like the sun,[q] and the
sunlight will be seven times brighter, like the light of seven full
days, when the LORD binds up the bruises of his people and heals[r]
the wounds he inflicted.

27See, the Name[s] of the LORD comes from afar,
with burning anger[t] and dense clouds of smoke;
his lips are full of wrath,[u]
and his tongue is a consuming fire.
28His breath[v] is like a rushing torrent,
rising up to the neck.[w]
He shakes the nations in the sieve[x] of destruction;
he places in the jaws of the peoples
a bit[y] that leads them astray.
29And you will sing
as on the night you celebrate a holy festival;
your hearts will rejoice
as when people go up with flutes

30:17 [a]Lev 26:8; Jos 23:10 [b]Lev 26:36; Dt 28:25
30:18 [c]Isa 42:14; 2Pe 3:9,15 [d]Isa 5:16 [e]Isa 25:9
30:19 [f]Isa 60:20; 61:3 [g]Ps 50:15; Isa 58:9; 65:24; Mt 7:7-11
30:20 [h]1Ki 22:27 [i]Ps 74:9; Am 8:11
30:21 [j]Isa 29:24
30:22 [k]Ex 32:4
30:23 [l]Isa 65:21-22 [m]Ps 65:13
30:24 [n]Mt 3:12; Lk 3:17
30:25 [o]Isa 2:15 [p]Isa 41:18
30:26 [q]Isa 24:23; 60:19-20; Rev 21:23; 22:5 [r]Dt 32:39; Isa 1:5
30:27 [s]Isa 59:19 [t]Isa 66:14 [u]Isa 10:5
30:28 [v]Isa 11:4 [w]Isa 8:8 [x]Am 9:9 [y]2Ki 19:28; Isa 37:29

to the mountain[a] of the LORD,
to the Rock of Israel.
30 The LORD will cause men to hear his majestic voice
and will make them see his arm coming down
with raging anger and consuming fire,
with cloudburst, thunderstorm and hail.
31 The voice of the LORD will shatter Assyria;[b]
with his scepter he will strike[c] them down.
32 Every stroke the LORD lays on them
with his punishing rod
will be to the music of tambourines and harps,
as he fights them in battle with the blows of his arm.[d]
33 Topheth[e] has long been prepared;
it has been made ready for the king.
Its fire pit has been made deep and wide,
with an abundance of fire and wood;
the breath of the LORD,
like a stream of burning sulfur,[f]
sets it ablaze.

Chapter 31 Theme ______________________________

31

Woe to those who go down to Egypt[g] for help,
who rely on horses,
who trust in the multitude of their chariots[h]
and in the great strength of their horsemen,
but do not look to the Holy One of Israel,
or seek help from the LORD.[i]
2 Yet he too is wise[j] and can bring disaster;[k]
he does not take back his words.[l]
He will rise up against the house of the wicked,[m]
against those who help evildoers.
3 But the Egyptians[n] are men and not God;[o]
their horses are flesh and not spirit.
When the LORD stretches out his hand,[p]
he who helps will stumble,
he who is helped[q] will fall;
both will perish together.

4 This is what the LORD says to me:

"As a lion[r] growls,
a great lion over his prey—
and though a whole band of shepherds
is called together against him,
he is not frightened by their shouts
or disturbed by their clamor—

30:29 [a] Ps 42:4

30:31 [b] Isa 10:5,12 [c] Isa 11:4

30:32 [d] Isa 11:15; Eze 32:10

30:33 [e] 2Ki 23:10 [f] Ge 19:24

31:1 [g] Dt 17:16; Isa 30:2,5 [h] Isa 2:7 [i] Ps 20:7; Da 9:13

31:2 [j] Ro 16:27 [k] Isa 45:7 [l] Nu 23:19 [m] Isa 32:6

31:3 [n] Isa 36:9 [o] Eze 28:9; 2Th 2:4 [p] Isa 9:17,21 [q] Isa 30:5-7

31:4 [r] Nu 24:9; Hos 11:10; Am 3:8

so the LORD Almighty will come down[a]
to do battle on Mount Zion and on its heights.
5 Like birds hovering overhead,
the LORD Almighty will shield[b] Jerusalem;
he will shield it and deliver[c] it,
he will 'pass over' it and will rescue it."

6 Return to him you have so greatly revolted against, O Israelites.
7 For in that day every one of you will reject the idols of silver and
gold[d] your sinful hands have made.

8 "Assyria[e] will fall by a sword that is not of man;
a sword, not of mortals, will devour[f] them.
They will flee before the sword
and their young men will be put to forced labor.[g]
9 Their stronghold[h] will fall because of terror;
at sight of the battle standard their commanders
will panic,"
declares the LORD,
whose fire[i] is in Zion,
whose furnace is in Jerusalem.

Chapter 32 Theme ______________________________

32

See, a king[j] will reign in righteousness
and rulers will rule with justice.[k]
2 Each man will be like a shelter[l] from the wind
and a refuge from the storm,
like streams of water in the desert
and the shadow of a great rock in a thirsty land.

3 Then the eyes of those who see will no longer be closed,[m]
and the ears of those who hear will listen.
4 The mind of the rash will know and understand,[n]
and the stammering tongue will be fluent and clear.
5 No longer will the fool[o] be called noble
nor the scoundrel be highly respected.
6 For the fool speaks folly,[p]
his mind is busy with evil:
He practices ungodliness[q]
and spreads error[r] concerning the LORD;
the hungry he leaves empty[s]
and from the thirsty he withholds water.
7 The scoundrel's methods are wicked,[t]
he makes up evil schemes[u]
to destroy the poor with lies,
even when the plea of the needy[v] is just.

31:4 [a] Isa 42:13
31:5 [b] Ps 91:4 [c] Isa 37:35; 38:6
31:7 [d] Isa 2:20; 30:22
31:8 [e] Isa 10:12 [f] Isa 14:25; 37:7 [g] Ge 49:15
31:9 [h] Dt 32:31,37 [i] Isa 10:17
32:1 [j] Eze 37:24 [k] Ps 72:1-4; Isa 9:7
32:2 [l] Isa 4:6
32:3 [m] Isa 29:18
32:4 [n] Isa 29:24
32:5 [o] 1Sa 25:25
32:6 [p] Pr 19:3 [q] Isa 9:17 [r] Isa 9:16 [s] Isa 3:15
32:7 [t] Jer 5:26-28 [u] Mic 7:3 [v] Isa 61:1

8But the noble man makes noble plans,
and by noble deeds[a] he stands.

9You women who are so complacent,
rise up and listen[b] to me;
you daughters who feel secure,[c]
hear what I have to say!
10In little more than a year
you who feel secure will tremble;
the grape harvest will fail,[d]
and the harvest of fruit will not come.
11Tremble, you complacent women;
shudder, you daughters who feel secure!
Strip off your clothes,[e]
put sackcloth around your waists.
12Beat your breasts[f] for the pleasant fields,
for the fruitful vines
13and for the land of my people,
a land overgrown with thorns and briers[g]—
yes, mourn for all houses of merriment
and for this city of revelry.[h]
14The fortress[i] will be abandoned,
the noisy city deserted;[j]
citadel and watchtower[k] will become a wasteland forever,
the delight of donkeys,[l] a pasture for flocks,
15till the Spirit[m] is poured upon us from on high,
and the desert becomes a fertile field,[n]
and the fertile field seems like a forest.[o]
16Justice will dwell in the desert
and righteousness live in the fertile field.
17The fruit of righteousness will be peace;[p]
the effect of righteousness will be quietness and
confidence[q] forever.
18My people will live in peaceful dwelling places,
in secure homes,
in undisturbed places of rest.[r]
19Though hail[s] flattens the forest[t]
and the city is leveled[u] completely,
20how blessed you will be,
sowing[v] your seed by every stream,
and letting your cattle and donkeys range free.[w]

32:8
[a]Pr 11:25

32:9
[b]Isa 28:23
[c]Isa 47:8; Am 6:1; Zep 2:15

32:10
[d]Isa 5:5-6; 24:7

32:11
[e]Isa 47:2

32:12
[f]Na 2:7

32:13
[g]Isa 5:6
[h]Isa 22:2

32:14
[i]Isa 13:22
[j]Isa 6:11; 27:10
[k]Isa 34:13
[l]Ps 104:11

32:15
[m]Isa 11:2; Joel 2:28
[n]Ps 107:35; Isa 35:1-2
[o]Isa 29:17

32:17
[p]Ps 119:165; Ro 14:17; Jas 3:18
[q]Isa 30:15

32:18
[r]Hos 2:18-23

32:19
[s]Isa 28:17; 30:30
[t]Isa 10:19; Zec 11:2
[u]Isa 24:10; 27:10

32:20
[v]Ecc 11:1
[w]Isa 30:24

Chapter 33 Theme ____________________

33 Woe to you, O destroyer,
you who have not been destroyed!
Woe to you, O traitor,
you who have not been betrayed!

When you stop destroying,
you will be destroyed;[a]
when you stop betraying,
you will be betrayed.[b]

2 O LORD, be gracious to us;
we long for you.
Be our strength[c] every morning,
our salvation[d] in time of distress.
3 At the thunder of your voice, the peoples flee;
when you rise up,[e] the nations scatter.
4 Your plunder, O nations, is harvested as by young locusts;
like a swarm of locusts men pounce on it.

5 The LORD is exalted,[f] for he dwells on high;
he will fill Zion with justice[g] and righteousness.[h]
6 He will be the sure foundation for your times,
a rich store of salvation[i] and wisdom and knowledge;
the fear[j] of the LORD is the key to this treasure.[a]

7 Look, their brave men cry aloud in the streets;
the envoys[k] of peace weep bitterly.
8 The highways are deserted,
no travelers are on the roads.[l]
The treaty is broken,
its witnesses[b] are despised,
no one is respected.
9 The land mourns[c] [m] and wastes away,
Lebanon[n] is ashamed and withers;[o]
Sharon is like the Arabah,
and Bashan and Carmel drop their leaves.

10 "Now will I arise,[p]" says the LORD.
"Now will I be exalted;
now will I be lifted up.
11 You conceive[q] chaff,
you give birth[r] to straw;
your breath is a fire[s] that consumes you.
12 The peoples will be burned as if to lime;
like cut thornbushes they will be set ablaze.[t]"

13 You who are far away,[u] hear[v] what I have done;
you who are near, acknowledge my power!
14 The sinners in Zion are terrified;
trembling[w] grips the godless:
"Who of us can dwell with the consuming fire?[x]
Who of us can dwell with everlasting burning?"

33:1 [a]Hab 2:8; Mt 7:2 [b]Isa 21:2
33:2 [c]Isa 40:10; 51:9; 59:16 [d]Isa 25:9
33:3 [e]Isa 59:16-18
33:5 [f]Ps 97:9 [g]Isa 28:6 [h]Isa 1:26
33:6 [i]Isa 51:6 [j]Isa 11:2-3; Mt 6:33
33:7 [k]2Ki 18:37
33:8 [l]Jdg 5:6; Isa 35:8
33:9 [m]Isa 3:26 [n]Isa 2:13; 35:2 [o]Isa 24:4
33:10 [p]Ps 12:5; Isa 2:21
33:11 [q]Ps 7:14; Isa 59:4; Jas 1:15 [r]Isa 26:18 [s]Isa 1:31
33:12 [t]Isa 10:17
33:13 [u]Ps 48:10; 49:1 [v]Isa 49:1
33:14 [w]Isa 32:11 [x]Isa 30:30; Heb 12:29

[a]6 Or *is a treasure from him* [b]8 Dead Sea Scrolls; Masoretic Text / *the cities* [c]9 Or *dries up*

15He who walks righteously[a]
and speaks what is right,[b]
who rejects gain from extortion
and keeps his hand from accepting bribes,
who stops his ears against plots of murder
and shuts his eyes[c] against contemplating evil—
16this is the man who will dwell on the heights,
whose refuge[d] will be the mountain fortress.[e]
His bread will be supplied,
and water will not fail[f] him.

17Your eyes will see the king[g] in his beauty
and view a land that stretches afar.[h]
18In your thoughts you will ponder the former terror:[i]
"Where is that chief officer?
Where is the one who took the revenue?
Where is the officer in charge of the towers?"
19You will see those arrogant people no more,
those people of an obscure speech,
with their strange, incomprehensible tongue.[j]

20Look upon Zion, the city of our festivals;
your eyes will see Jerusalem,
a peaceful abode,[k] a tent that will not be moved;[l]
its stakes will never be pulled up,
nor any of its ropes broken.
21There the LORD will be our Mighty One.
It will be like a place of broad rivers and streams.[m]
No galley with oars will ride them,
no mighty ship will sail them.
22For the LORD is our judge,[n]
the LORD is our lawgiver,[o]
the LORD is our king;[p]
it is he who will save[q] us.

23Your rigging hangs loose:
The mast is not held secure,
the sail is not spread.
Then an abundance of spoils will be divided
and even the lame[r] will carry off plunder.[s]
24No one living in Zion will say, "I am ill";[t]
and the sins of those who dwell there will be forgiven.[u]

Chapter 34 Theme ______________________

34 Come near, you nations, and listen;
pay attention, you peoples![v]

33:15
[a]Isa 58:8
[b]Ps 15:2; 24:4
[c]Ps 119:37

33:16
[d]Isa 25:4
[e]Isa 26:1
[f]Isa 49:10

33:17
[g]Isa 6:5
[h]Isa 26:15

33:18
[i]Isa 17:14

33:19
[j]Isa 28:11; Jer 5:15

33:20
[k]Isa 32:18
[l]Ps 46:5; 125:1-2

33:21
[m]Isa 41:18; 48:18; 66:12

33:22
[n]Isa 11:4
[o]Isa 2:3; Jas 4:12
[p]Ps 89:18
[q]Isa 25:9

33:23
[r]2Ki 7:8
[s]2Ki 7:16

33:24
[t]Isa 30:26
[u]Jer 50:20; 1Jn 1:7-9

34:1
[v]Isa 41:1; 43:9

Let the earth[a] hear, and all that is in it,
the world, and all that comes out of it![b]
2 The LORD is angry with all nations;
his wrath is upon all their armies.
He will totally destroy[a][c] them,
he will give them over to slaughter.[d]
3 Their slain will be thrown out,
their dead bodies will send up a stench;[e]
the mountains will be soaked with their blood.[f]
4 All the stars of the heavens will be dissolved[g]
and the sky rolled up[h] like a scroll;
all the starry host will fall[i]
like withered leaves from the vine,
like shriveled figs from the fig tree.

5 My sword[j] has drunk its fill in the heavens;
see, it descends in judgment on Edom,[k]
the people I have totally destroyed.[l]
6 The sword of the LORD is bathed in blood,
it is covered with fat—
the blood of lambs and goats,
fat from the kidneys of rams.
For the LORD has a sacrifice in Bozrah
and a great slaughter in Edom.
7 And the wild oxen will fall with them,
the bull calves and the great bulls.[m]
Their land will be drenched with blood,
and the dust will be soaked with fat.

8 For the LORD has a day of vengeance,[n]
a year of retribution, to uphold Zion's cause.
9 Edom's streams will be turned into pitch,
her dust into burning sulfur;
her land will become blazing pitch!
10 It will not be quenched night and day;
its smoke will rise forever.[o]
From generation to generation it will lie desolate;[p]
no one will ever pass through it again.
11 The desert owl[b][q] and screech owl[b] will possess it;
the great owl[b] and the raven will nest there.
God will stretch out over Edom
the measuring line of chaos
and the plumb line[r] of desolation.

34:1 [a]Ps 49:1 [b]Dt 32:1
34:2 [c]Isa 13:5 [d]Isa 30:25
34:3 [e]Joel 2:20; Am 4:10 [f]ver 7; Eze 14:19; 35:6; 38:22
34:4 [g]Isa 13:13; 2Pe 3:10 [h]Eze 32:7-8 [i]Joel 2:31; Mt 24:29*; Rev 6:13
34:5 [j]Dt 32:41-42; Jer 46:10; Eze 21:5 [k]Am 1:11-12 [l]Isa 24:6; Mal 1:4
34:7 [m]Ps 68:30
34:8 [n]Isa 63:4
34:10 [o]Rev 14:10-11; 19:3 [p]Isa 13:20; 24:1; Eze 29:12; Mal 1:3
34:11 [q]Zep 2:14; Rev 18:2 [r]2Ki 21:13; La 2:8

a *2* The Hebrew term refers to the irrevocable giving over of things or persons to the LORD, often by totally destroying them; also in verse 5. b *11* The precise identification of these birds is uncertain.

[12]Her nobles will have nothing there to be called
a kingdom,
all her princes[a] will vanish[b] away.
[13]Thorns will overrun her citadels,
nettles and brambles her strongholds.[c]
She will become a haunt for jackals,[d]
a home for owls.
[14]Desert creatures will meet with hyenas,[e]
and wild goats will bleat to each other;
there the night creatures will also repose
and find for themselves places of rest.
[15]The owl will nest there and lay eggs,
she will hatch them, and care for her young under the
shadow of her wings;
there also the falcons[f] will gather,
each with its mate.

[16]Look in the scroll[g] of the LORD and read:

None of these will be missing,
not one will lack her mate.
For it is his mouth[h] that has given the order,
and his Spirit will gather them together.
[17]He allots their portions;[i]
his hand distributes them by measure.
They will possess it forever
and dwell there from generation to generation.[j]

Chapter 35 Theme ________________________________

35

The desert[k] and the parched land will be glad;
the wilderness will rejoice and blossom.[l]
Like the crocus, [2]it will burst into bloom;
it will rejoice greatly and shout for joy.[m]
The glory of Lebanon[n] will be given to it,
the splendor of Carmel[o] and Sharon;
they will see the glory of the LORD,
the splendor of our God.[p]

[3]Strengthen the feeble hands,
steady the knees[q] that give way;
[4]say to those with fearful hearts,
"Be strong, do not fear;
your God will come,
he will come with vengeance;[r]
with divine retribution
he will come to save you."

34:12 [a]Jer 27:20; 39:6 [b]Isa 41:11-12
34:13 [c]Isa 13:22; 32:13 [d]Ps 44:19; Jer 9:11; 10:22
34:14 [e]Isa 13:22
34:15 [f]Dt 14:13
34:16 [g]Isa 30:8 [h]Isa 1:20; 58:14
34:17 [i]Isa 17:14; Jer 13:25 [j]ver 10
35:1 [k]Isa 27:10; 41:18-19 [l]Isa 51:3
35:2 [m]Isa 25:9; 55:12 [n]Isa 32:15 [o]SS 7:5 [p]Isa 25:9
35:3 [q]Job 4:4; Heb 12:12
35:4 [r]Isa 1:24; 34:8

5 Then will the eyes of the blind be opened[a]
and the ears of the deaf[b] unstopped.
6 Then will the lame[c] leap like a deer,
and the mute tongue[d] shout for joy.
Water will gush forth in the wilderness
and streams[e] in the desert.
7 The burning sand will become a pool,
the thirsty ground bubbling springs.[f]
In the haunts where jackals[g] once lay,
grass and reeds and papyrus will grow.

8 And a highway[h] will be there;
it will be called the Way of Holiness.[i]
The unclean[j] will not journey on it;
it will be for those who walk in that Way;
wicked fools will not go about on it.[a]
9 No lion[k] will be there,
nor will any ferocious beast[l] get up on it;
they will not be found there.
But only the redeemed[m] will walk there,
10 and the ransomed of the LORD will return.
They will enter Zion with singing;
everlasting joy[n] will crown their heads.
Gladness and joy will overtake them,
and sorrow and sighing will flee away.[o]

Chapter 36 Theme

36 In the fourteenth year of King Hezekiah's reign, Sennacherib[p] king of Assyria attacked all the fortified cities of
Judah and captured them. 2 Then the king of Assyria sent his field
commander with a large army from Lachish to King Hezekiah at
Jerusalem. When the commander stopped at the aqueduct of the
Upper Pool, on the road to the Washerman's Field,[q] 3 Eliakim[r] son
of Hilkiah the palace administrator, Shebna[s] the secretary, and
Joah son of Asaph the recorder went out to him.
4 The field commander said to them, "Tell Hezekiah,

" 'This is what the great king, the king of Assyria, says: On
what are you basing this confidence of yours? 5 You say you have
strategy and military strength—but you speak only empty
words. On whom are you depending, that you rebel[t] against
me? 6 Look now, you are depending on Egypt,[u] that splintered
reed[v] of a staff, which pierces a man's hand and wounds him if
he leans on it! Such is Pharaoh king of Egypt to all who depend

[a] 8 Or / *the simple will not stray from it*

35:5 [a] Mt 11:5; Jn 9:6-7 [b] Isa 29:18; 50:4
35:6 [c] Mt 15:30; Jn 5:8-9; Ac 3:8 [d] Isa 32:4; Mt 9:32-33; 12:22; Lk 11:14 [e] Isa 41:18; Jn 7:38
35:7 [f] Isa 49:10 [g] Isa 13:22
35:8 [h] Isa 11:16; 33:8; Mt 7:13-14 [i] Isa 4:3; 1Pe 1:15 [j] Isa 52:1
35:9 [k] Isa 30:6 [l] Isa 34:14 [m] Isa 51:11; 62:12; 63:4
35:10 [n] Isa 25:9 [o] Isa 30:19; 51:11; Rev 7:17; 21:4
36:1 [p] 2Ch 32:1
36:2 [q] Isa 7:3
36:3 [r] Isa 22:20-21 [s] 2Ki 18:18
36:5 [t] 2Ki 18:7
36:6 [u] Isa 30:2,5 [v] Eze 29:6-7

on him. 7And if you say to me, "We are depending on the LORD
our God"—isn't he the one whose high places and altars
Hezekiah removed,[a] saying to Judah and Jerusalem, "You must
worship before this altar"?[b]
8" 'Come now, make a bargain with my master, the king of
Assyria: I will give you two thousand horses—if you can put
riders on them! 9How then can you repulse one officer of the
least of my master's officials, even though you are depending
on Egypt[c] for chariots and horsemen?[d] 10Furthermore, have I
come to attack and destroy this land without the LORD? The
LORD himself told[e] me to march against this country and
destroy it.' "

11Then Eliakim, Shebna and Joah said to the field commander,
"Please speak to your servants in Aramaic,[f] since we understand
it. Don't speak to us in Hebrew in the hearing of the people on the
wall."
12But the commander replied, "Was it only to your master and
you that my master sent me to say these things, and not to the men
sitting on the wall—who, like you, will have to eat their own filth
and drink their own urine?"
13Then the commander stood and called out in Hebrew,[g] "Hear
the words of the great king, the king of Assyria! 14This is what the
king says: Do not let Hezekiah deceive you. He cannot deliver you!
15Do not let Hezekiah persuade you to trust in the LORD when he
says, 'The LORD will surely deliver us; this city will not be given into
the hand of the king of Assyria.'[h]
16"Do not listen to Hezekiah. This is what the king of Assyria
says: Make peace with me and come out to me. Then every one of
you will eat from his own vine and fig tree[i] and drink water from
his own cistern,[j] 17until I come and take you to a land like your
own—a land of grain and new wine, a land of bread and vineyards.
18"Do not let Hezekiah mislead you when he says, 'The LORD will
deliver us.' Has the god of any nation ever delivered his land from
the hand of the king of Assyria? 19Where are the gods of Hamath
and Arpad? Where are the gods of Sepharvaim? Have they rescued
Samaria from my hand? 20Who of all the gods[k] of these countries
has been able to save his land from me? How then can the LORD
deliver Jerusalem from my hand?"
21But the people remained silent and said nothing in reply, because the king had commanded, "Do not answer him."[l]
22Then Eliakim son of Hilkiah the palace administrator, Shebna
the secretary, and Joah son of Asaph the recorder went to Hezekiah,
with their clothes torn, and told him what the field commander
had said.

36:7 [a] 2Ki 18:4 [b] Dt 12:2-5
36:9 [c] Isa 31:3 [d] Isa 30:2-5
36:10 [e] 1Ki 13:18
36:11 [f] Ezr 4:7
36:13 [g] 2Ch 32:18
36:15 [h] Isa 37:10
36:16 [i] 1Ki 4:25; Zec 3:10 [j] Pr 5:15
36:20 [k] 1Ki 20:23
36:21 [l] Pr 9:7-8; 26:4

Chapter 37 Theme ____________________

37 When King Hezekiah heard this, he tore his clothes and
put on sackcloth and went into the temple of the LORD.
2He sent Eliakim the palace administrator, Shebna the secretary,
and the leading priests, all wearing sackcloth, to the prophet Isaiah
son of Amoz.[a] 3They told him, "This is what Hezekiah says: This
day is a day of distress and rebuke and disgrace, as when children
come to the point of birth[b] and there is no strength to deliver
them. 4It may be that the LORD your God will hear the words of
the field commander, whom his master, the king of Assyria, has
sent to ridicule the living God, and that he will rebuke him for
the words the LORD your God has heard.[c] Therefore pray for the
remnant[d] that still survives."

5When King Hezekiah's officials came to Isaiah, 6Isaiah said to
them, "Tell your master, 'This is what the LORD says: Do not be
afraid[e] of what you have heard—those words with which the
underlings of the king of Assyria have blasphemed me. 7Listen! I
am going to put a spirit in him so that when he hears a certain
report,[f] he will return to his own country, and there I will have
him cut down with the sword.'"

8When the field commander heard that the king of Assyria had
left Lachish, he withdrew and found the king fighting against
Libnah.[g]

9Now Sennacherib received a report[h] that Tirhakah, the Cushite[a]
king ⌊of Egypt⌋, was marching out to fight against him. When he
heard it, he sent messengers to Hezekiah with this word: 10"Say to
Hezekiah king of Judah: Do not let the god you depend on deceive
you when he says, 'Jerusalem will not be handed over to the king of
Assyria.'[i] 11Surely you have heard what the kings of Assyria have
done to all the countries, destroying them completely. And will
you be delivered?[j] 12Did the gods of the nations that were destroyed
by my forefathers[k] deliver them—the gods of Gozan, Haran,[l]
Rezeph and the people of Eden who were in Tel Assar? 13Where is
the king of Hamath, the king of Arpad, the king of the city of
Sepharvaim, or of Hena or Ivvah?"

14Hezekiah received the letter from the messengers and read it.
Then he went up to the temple of the LORD and spread it out before
the LORD. 15And Hezekiah prayed to the LORD: 16"O LORD Almighty,
God of Israel, enthroned between the cherubim, you alone are
God[m] over all the kingdoms of the earth. You have made heaven
and earth. 17Give ear, O LORD, and hear;[n] open your eyes, O LORD,
and see;[o] listen to all the words Sennacherib has sent to insult the
living God.

a9 That is, from the upper Nile region

37:2 [a]Isa 1:1
37:3 [b]Isa 26:18; 66:9; Hos 13:13
37:4 [c]Isa 36:13, 18-20 [d]Isa 1:9
37:6 [e]Isa 7:4
37:7 [f]ver 9
37:8 [g]Nu 33:20
37:9 [h]ver 7
37:10 [i]Isa 36:15
37:11 [j]Isa 36:18-20
37:12 [k]2Ki 18:11 [l]Ge 11:31; 12:1-4; Ac 7:2
37:16 [m]Dt 10:17; Ps 86:10; 136:2-3
37:17 [n]2Ch 6:40 [o]Da 9:18

18"It is true, O LORD, that the Assyrian kings have laid waste all
these peoples and their lands.[a] 19They have thrown their gods into
the fire and destroyed them,[b] for they were not gods[c] but only
wood and stone, fashioned by human hands. 20Now, O LORD our
God, deliver us from his hand, so that all kingdoms on earth may
know that you alone, O LORD, are God.[a][d]"
21Then Isaiah son of Amoz[e] sent a message to Hezekiah: "This is
what the LORD, the God of Israel, says: Because you have prayed to
me concerning Sennacherib king of Assyria, 22this is the word the
LORD has spoken against him:

"The Virgin Daughter of Zion
despises and mocks you.
The Daughter of Jerusalem
tosses her head[f] as you flee.
23Who is it you have insulted and blasphemed?[g]
Against whom have you raised your voice
and lifted your eyes in pride?[h]
Against the Holy One of Israel!
24By your messengers
you have heaped insults on the Lord.
And you have said,
'With my many chariots
I have ascended the heights of the mountains,
the utmost heights of Lebanon.[i]
I have cut down its tallest cedars,
the choicest of its pines.
I have reached its remotest heights,
the finest of its forests.
25I have dug wells in foreign lands[b]
and drunk the water there.
With the soles of my feet
I have dried up all the streams of Egypt.[j]'

26"Have you not heard?
Long ago I ordained[k] it.
In days of old I planned[l] it;
now I have brought it to pass,
that you have turned fortified cities
into piles of stone.[m]
27Their people, drained of power,
are dismayed and put to shame.
They are like plants in the field,
like tender green shoots,

a 20 Dead Sea Scrolls (see also 2 Kings 19:19); Masoretic Text *alone are the LORD* b 25 Dead Sea Scrolls (see also 2 Kings 19:24); Masoretic Text does not have *in foreign lands.*

37:18 [a] 2Ki 15:29; Na 2:11-12
37:19 [b] Isa 26:14 [c] Isa 41:24,29
37:20 [d] Ps 46:10
37:21 [e] ver 2
37:22 [f] Job 16:4
37:23 [g] ver 4 [h] Isa 2:11
37:24 [i] Isa 14:8
37:25 [j] Dt 11:10
37:26 [k] Ac 2:23; 4:27-28; 1Pe 2:8 [l] Isa 10:6; 25:1 [m] Isa 25:2

like grass sprouting on the roof,[a]
scorched[a] before it grows up.

[28]"But I know where you stay
and when you come and go[b]
and how you rage[c] against me.
[29]Because you rage against me
and because your insolence[d] has reached my ears,
I will put my hook in your nose[e]
and my bit in your mouth,
and I will make you return
by the way you came.[f]

[30]"This will be the sign for you, O Hezekiah:

"This year you will eat what grows by itself,
and the second year what springs from that.
But in the third year sow and reap,
plant vineyards and eat their fruit.
[31]Once more a remnant of the house of Judah
will take root below and bear fruit[g] above.
[32]For out of Jerusalem will come a remnant,
and out of Mount Zion a band of survivors.
The zeal[h] of the LORD Almighty
will accomplish this.

[33]"Therefore this is what the LORD says concerning the king of
Assyria:

"He will not enter this city
or shoot an arrow here.
He will not come before it with shield
or build a siege ramp against it.
[34]By the way that he came he will return;[i]
he will not enter this city,"
declares the LORD.
[35]"I will defend[j] this city and save it,
for my sake[k] and for the sake of David[l] my servant!"

[36]Then the angel of the LORD went out and put to death a hundred and eighty-five thousand men in the Assyrian[m] camp.
When the people got up the next morning—there were all the
dead bodies! [37]So Sennacherib king of Assyria broke camp and
withdrew. He returned to Nineveh[n] and stayed there.
[38]One day, while he was worshiping in the temple of his god
Nisroch, his sons Adrammelech and Sharezer cut him down with

37:27 [a]Ps 129:6
37:28 [b]Ps 139:1-3 [c]Ps 2:1
37:29 [d]Isa 10:12 [e]Isa 30:28; Eze 38:4 [f]ver 34
37:31 [g]Isa 27:6
37:32 [h]Isa 9:7
37:34 [i]ver 29
37:35 [j]Isa 31:5; 38:6 [k]Isa 43:25; 48:9,11 [l]2Ki 20:6
37:36 [m]Isa 10:12
37:37 [n]Ge 10:11

[a]*27* Some manuscripts of the Masoretic Text, Dead Sea Scrolls and some Septuagint manuscripts (see also 2 Kings 19:26); most manuscripts of the Masoretic Text *roof / and terraced fields*

the sword, and they escaped to the land of Ararat.[a] And Esarhaddon his son succeeded him as king.

Chapter 38 Theme ______________________

38 In those days Hezekiah became ill and was at the point of
death. The prophet Isaiah son of Amoz[b] went to him and
said, "This is what the LORD says: Put your house in order,[c] because
you are going to die; you will not recover."
2Hezekiah turned his face to the wall and prayed to the LORD,
3"Remember, O LORD, how I have walked[d] before you faithfully
and with wholehearted devotion[e] and have done what is good in
your eyes.[f]" And Hezekiah wept[g] bitterly.
4Then the word of the LORD came to Isaiah: 5"Go and tell Hezekiah, 'This is what the LORD, the God of your father David, says: I
have heard your prayer and seen your tears; I will add fifteen years[h]
to your life. 6And I will deliver you and this city from the hand of
the king of Assyria. I will defend[i] this city.
7" 'This is the LORD's sign[j] to you that the LORD will do what he
has promised: 8I will make the shadow cast by the sun go back the
ten steps it has gone down on the stairway of Ahaz.' " So the sunlight went back the ten steps it had gone down.[k]

9A writing of Hezekiah king of Judah after his illness and
recovery:

10I said, "In the prime of my life[l]
must I go through the gates of death[a][m]
and be robbed of the rest of my years?[n]"
11I said, "I will not again see the LORD,
the LORD, in the land of the living;[o]
no longer will I look on mankind,
or be with those who now dwell in this world.[b]
12Like a shepherd's tent[p] my house
has been pulled down[q] and taken from me.
Like a weaver I have rolled[r] up my life,
and he has cut me off from the loom;[s]
day and night[t] you made an end of me.
13I waited patiently till dawn,
but like a lion he broke[u] all my bones;[v]
day and night you made an end of me.
14I cried like a swift or thrush,
I moaned like a mourning dove.[w]
My eyes grew weak as I looked to the heavens.
I am troubled; O Lord, come to my aid!"[x]

[a] *10* Hebrew *Sheol* [b] *11* A few Hebrew manuscripts; most Hebrew manuscripts *in the place of cessation*

37:38 [a] Ge 8:4; Jer 51:27
38:1 [b] Isa 37:2 [c] 2Sa 17:23
38:3 [d] Ne 13:14; Ps 26:3 [e] 1Ch 29:19 [f] Dt 6:18 [g] Ps 6:8
38:5 [h] 2Ki 18:2
38:6 [i] Isa 31:5; 37:35
38:7 [j] Isa 7:11,14
38:8 [k] Jos 10:13
38:10 [l] Ps 102:24 [m] Ps 107:18; 2Co 1:9 [n] Job 17:11
38:11 [o] Ps 27:13; 116:9
38:12 [p] 2Co 5:1,4; 2Pe 1:13-14 [q] Job 4:21 [r] Heb 1:12 [s] Job 7:6 [t] Ps 73:14
38:13 [u] Ps 51:8 [v] Job 10:16; Da 6:24
38:14 [w] Isa 59:11 [x] Job 17:3

15But what can I say?
He has spoken to me, and he himself has done this.[a]
I will walk humbly[b] all my years
because of this anguish of my soul.[c]
16Lord, by such things men live;
and my spirit finds life in them too.
You restored me to health
and let me live.[d]
17Surely it was for my benefit
that I suffered such anguish.
In your love you kept me
from the pit[e] of destruction;
you have put all my sins[f]
behind your back.[g]
18For the grave[a] [h] cannot praise you,
death cannot sing your praise;[i]
those who go down to the pit[j]
cannot hope for your faithfulness.
19The living, the living—they praise[k] you,
as I am doing today;
fathers tell their children[l]
about your faithfulness.

20The LORD will save me,
and we will sing[m] with stringed instruments[n]
all the days of our lives[o]
in the temple[p] of the LORD.

21Isaiah had said, "Prepare a poultice of figs and apply it to the boil, and he will recover."

22Hezekiah had asked, "What will be the sign that I will go up to the temple of the LORD?"

Chapter 39 Theme ______________________

39 At that time Merodach-Baladan son of Baladan king of
Babylon[q] sent Hezekiah letters and a gift, because he had
heard of his illness and recovery. 2Hezekiah received the envoys[r]
gladly and showed them what was in his storehouses—the silver,
the gold,[s] the spices, the fine oil, his entire armory and everything
found among his treasures. There was nothing in his palace or in
all his kingdom that Hezekiah did not show them.
3Then Isaiah the prophet went to King Hezekiah and asked,
"What did those men say, and where did they come from?"
"From a distant land,[t]" Hezekiah replied. "They came to me
from Babylon."

38:15 [a]Ps 39:9 [b]1Ki 21:27 [c]Job 7:11
38:16 [d]Ps 119:25
38:17 [e]Ps 30:3 [f]Jer 31:34 [g]Isa 43:25; Mic 7:19
38:18 [h]Ecc 9:10 [i]Ps 6:5; 88:10-11; 115:17 [j]Ps 30:9
38:19 [k]Dt 6:7; Ps 118:17; 119:175 [l]Dt 11:19
38:20 [m]Ps 68:25 [n]Ps 33:2 [o]Ps 116:2 [p]Ps 116:17-19
39:1 [q]2Ch 32:31
39:2 [r]2Ch 32:31 [s]2Ki 18:15
39:3 [t]Dt 28:49

a *18* Hebrew *Sheol*

[4]The prophet asked, "What did they see in your palace?"
"They saw everything in my palace," Hezekiah said. "There is
nothing among my treasures that I did not show them."
[5]Then Isaiah said to Hezekiah, "Hear the word of the LORD
Almighty: [6]The time will surely come when everything in your
palace, and all that your fathers have stored up until this day, will
be carried off to Babylon.[a] Nothing will be left, says the LORD. [7]And
some of your descendants, your own flesh and blood who will be
born to you, will be taken away, and they will become eunuchs in
the palace of the king of Babylon.[b]"
[8]"The word of the LORD you have spoken is good," Hezekiah
replied. For he thought, "There will be peace and security in my
lifetime.[c]"

Chapter 40 Theme ______________________

40 Comfort, comfort[d] my people,
says your God.
[2]Speak tenderly[e] to Jerusalem,
and proclaim to her
that her hard service has been completed,[f]
that her sin has been paid for,
that she has received from the LORD's hand
double[g] for all her sins.

[3]A voice of one calling:
"In the desert prepare
the way[h] for the LORD[a];
make straight in the wilderness
a highway for our God.[b][i]
[4]Every valley shall be raised up,
every mountain and hill made low;
the rough ground shall become level,[j]
the rugged places a plain.
[5]And the glory of the LORD will be revealed,
and all mankind together will see it.[k]
For the mouth of the LORD has spoken."[l]

[6]A voice says, "Cry out."
And I said, "What shall I cry?"

"All men are like grass,[m]
and all their glory is like the flowers of the field.
[7]The grass withers and the flowers fall,
because the breath[n] of the LORD blows on them.
Surely the people are grass.

a3 Or *A voice of one calling in the desert: / "Prepare the way for the LORD* b3 Hebrew; Septuagint *make straight the paths of our God*

39:6 [a]2Ki 24:13; Jer 20:5
39:7 [b]2Ki 24:15; Da 1:1-7
39:8 [c]2Ch 32:26
40:1 [d]Isa 12:1; 49:13; 51:3,12; 52:9; 61:2; 66:13; Jer 31:13; Zep 3:14-17; 2Co 1:3
40:2 [e]Isa 35:4 [f]Isa 41:11-13; 49:25 [g]Isa 61:7; Jer 16:18; Zec 9:12; Rev 18:6
40:3 [h]Mal 3:1 [i]Mt 3:3*; Mk 1:3*; Jn 1:23*
40:4 [j]Isa 45:2,13
40:5 [k]Isa 52:10; Lk 3:4-6* [l]Isa 1:20; 58:14
40:6 [m]Job 14:2
40:7 [n]Job 41:21

40:8 [a]Isa 55:11; 59:21 [b]Mt 5:18; 1Pe 1:24-25*

8 The grass withers and the flowers fall,
but the word[a] of our God stands forever.[b]"

40:9 [c]Isa 52:7-10; 61:1; Ro 10:15 [d]Isa 25:9

9 You who bring good tidings[c] to Zion,
go up on a high mountain.
You who bring good tidings to Jerusalem,[a]
lift up your voice with a shout,
lift it up, do not be afraid;
say to the towns of Judah,
"Here is your God!"[d]

40:10 [e]Rev 22:7 [f]Isa 59:16 [g]Isa 9:6-7 [h]Isa 62:11; Rev 22:12

10 See, the Sovereign LORD comes[e] with power,
and his arm[f] rules[g] for him.
See, his reward[h] is with him,
and his recompense accompanies him.

40:11 [i]Eze 34:23; Mic 5:4; Jn 10:11

11 He tends his flock like a shepherd:[i]
He gathers the lambs in his arms
and carries them close to his heart;
he gently leads those that have young.

40:12 [j]Job 38:10 [k]Pr 30:4 [l]Heb 1:10-12

12 Who has measured the waters[j] in the hollow of his hand,[k]
or with the breadth of his hand marked off the heavens?[l]
Who has held the dust of the earth in a basket,
or weighed the mountains on the scales
and the hills in a balance?

40:13 [m]Ro 11:34*; 1Co 2:16*

13 Who has understood the mind[b] of the LORD,
or instructed him as his counselor?[m]

40:14 [n]Job 21:22; Col 2:3

14 Whom did the LORD consult to enlighten him,
and who taught him the right way?
Who was it that taught him knowledge[n]
or showed him the path of understanding?

40:16 [o]Ps 50:9-11; Mic 6:7; Heb 10:5-9

15 Surely the nations are like a drop in a bucket;
they are regarded as dust on the scales;
he weighs the islands as though they were fine dust.
16 Lebanon is not sufficient for altar fires,
nor its animals[o] enough for burnt offerings.

40:17 [p]Isa 30:28 [q]Isa 29:7 [r]Da 4:35

17 Before him all the nations[p] are as nothing;[q]
they are regarded by him as worthless
and less than nothing.[r]

40:18 [s]Ex 8:10; 1Sa 2:2; Isa 46:5 [t]Ac 17:29

18 To whom, then, will you compare God?[s]
What image[t] will you compare him to?

40:19 [u]Ps 115:4 [v]Isa 41:7; Jer 10:3 [w]Isa 2:20

19 As for an idol,[u] a craftsman casts it,
and a goldsmith[v] overlays it with gold[w]
and fashions silver chains for it.

a 9 Or *O Zion, bringer of good tidings, / go up on a high mountain. / O Jerusalem, bringer of good tidings* b 13 Or *Spirit*; or *spirit*

[20]A man too poor to present such an offering
selects wood that will not rot.
He looks for a skilled craftsman
to set up an idol that will not topple.[a]

[21]Do you not know?
Have you not heard?
Has it not been told[b] you from the beginning?
Have you not understood[c] since the earth was founded?[d]
[22]He sits enthroned above the circle of the earth,
and its people are like grasshoppers.[e]
He stretches out the heavens like a canopy,[f]
and spreads them out like a tent[g] to live in.
[23]He brings princes[h] to naught
and reduces the rulers of this world to nothing.[i]
[24]No sooner are they planted,
no sooner are they sown,
no sooner do they take root in the ground,
than he blows[j] on them and they wither,
and a whirlwind sweeps them away like chaff.

[25]"To whom will you compare me?[k]
Or who is my equal?" says the Holy One.
[26]Lift your eyes and look to the heavens:[l]
Who created[m] all these?
He who brings out the starry host[n] one by one,
and calls them each by name.
Because of his great power and mighty strength,
not one of them is missing.[o]

[27]Why do you say, O Jacob,
and complain, O Israel,
"My way is hidden from the LORD;
my cause is disregarded by my God"?[p]
[28]Do you not know?
Have you not heard?[q]
The LORD is the everlasting[r] God,
the Creator of the ends of the earth.
He will not grow tired or weary,
and his understanding no one can fathom.[s]
[29]He gives strength to the weary[t]
and increases the power of the weak.
[30]Even youths grow tired and weary,
and young men[u] stumble and fall;
[31]but those who hope[v] in the LORD
will renew their strength.[w]

40:20
[a] 1Sa 5:3

40:21
[b] Ps 19:1; 50:6; Ac 14:17
[c] Ro 1:19
[d] Isa 48:13; 51:13

40:22
[e] Nu 13:33; Ps 104:2; Isa 42:5
[f] Job 22:14
[g] Job 36:29

40:23
[h] Isa 34:12
[i] Job 12:21; Ps 107:40

40:24
[j] Isa 41:16

40:25
[k] ver 18

40:26
[l] Isa 51:6
[m] Ps 89:11-13; Isa 42:5
[n] Ps 147:4
[o] Isa 34:16

40:27
[p] Job 27:2; Lk 18:7-8

40:28
[q] ver 21
[r] Ps 90:2
[s] Ps 147:5; Ro 11:33

40:29
[t] Isa 50:4; Jer 31:25

40:30
[u] Isa 9:17; Jer 6:11; 9:21

40:31
[v] Lk 18:1
[w] 2Co 4:16

40:31 [a]Ex 19:4; Ps 103:5 [b]2Co 4:1; Heb 12:1-3

They will soar on wings like eagles;[a]
they will run and not grow weary,
they will walk and not be faint.[b]

Chapter 41 Theme ______________________________

41:1 [c]Hab 2:20; Zec 2:13 [d]Isa 11:11 [e]Isa 48:16 [f]Isa 1:18; 34:1; 50:8

41

"Be silent[c] before me, you islands![d]
Let the nations renew their strength!
Let them come forward[e] and speak;
let us meet together[f] at the place of judgment.

41:2 [g]Ezr 1:2 [h]ver 25; Isa 45:1,13 [i]2Sa 22:43 [j]Isa 40:24

2"Who has stirred[g] up one from the east,[h]
calling him in righteousness to his service[a]
He hands nations over to him
and subdues kings before him.
He turns them to dust[i] with his sword,
to windblown chaff[j] with his bow.
3He pursues them and moves on unscathed,
by a path his feet have not traveled before.
4Who has done this and carried it through,
calling forth the generations from the beginning?[k]
I, the LORD—with the first of them
and with the last[l]—I am he."

41:4 [k]ver 26; Isa 46:10 [l]Isa 44:6; 48:12; Rev 1:8,17; 22:13

5The islands[m] have seen it and fear;
the ends of the earth tremble.
They approach and come forward;
6 each helps the other
and says to his brother, "Be strong!"
7The craftsman encourages the goldsmith,[n]
and he who smooths with the hammer
spurs on him who strikes the anvil.
He says of the welding, "It is good."
He nails down the idol so it will not topple.

41:5 [m]Eze 26:17-18

41:7 [n]Isa 40:19

8"But you, O Israel, my servant,
Jacob, whom I have chosen,
you descendants of Abraham[o] my friend,[p]
9I took you from the ends of the earth,[q]
from its farthest corners I called you.
I said, 'You are my servant';
I have chosen[r] you and have not rejected you.
10So do not fear, for I am with you;[s]
do not be dismayed, for I am your God.
I will strengthen you and help[t] you;
I will uphold you with my righteous right hand.

41:8 [o]Isa 29:22; 51:2; 63:16 [p]2Ch 20:7; Jas 2:23

41:9 [q]Isa 11:12 [r]Dt 7:6

41:10 [s]Jos 1:9; Isa 43:2,5; Ro 8:31 [t]ver 13-14; Isa 44:2; 49:8

a 2 Or / *whom victory meets at every step*

11"All who rage[a] against you
will surely be ashamed and disgraced;[b]
those who oppose[c] you
will be as nothing and perish.[d]
12Though you search for your enemies,
you will not find them.[e]
Those who wage war against you
will be as nothing[f] at all.
13For I am the LORD, your God,
who takes hold of your right hand[g]
and says to you, Do not fear;
I will help[h] you.
14Do not be afraid, O worm Jacob,
O little Israel,
for I myself will help you," declares the LORD,
your Redeemer, the Holy One of Israel.
15"See, I will make you into a threshing sledge,[i]
new and sharp, with many teeth.
You will thresh the mountains and crush them,
and reduce the hills to chaff.
16You will winnow[j] them, the wind will pick them up,
and a gale will blow them away.
But you will rejoice in the LORD
and glory[k] in the Holy One of Israel.

17"The poor and needy search for water,[l]
but there is none;
their tongues are parched with thirst.
But I the LORD will answer[m] them;
I, the God of Israel, will not forsake them.
18I will make rivers flow[n] on barren heights,
and springs within the valleys.
I will turn the desert[o] into pools of water,
and the parched ground into springs.[p]
19I will put in the desert
the cedar and the acacia, the myrtle and the olive.
I will set pines in the wasteland,
the fir and the cypress together,[q]
20so that people may see and know,
may consider and understand,
that the hand of the LORD has done this,
that the Holy One of Israel has created[r] it.

21"Present your case," says the LORD.
"Set forth your arguments," says Jacob's King.[s]
22"Bring in ⌊your idols⌋ to tell us
what is going to happen.[t]

41:11 [a]Isa 17:12 [b]Isa 45:24 [c]Ex 23:22 [d]Isa 29:8
41:12 [e]Ps 37:35-36 [f]Isa 17:14
41:13 [g]Isa 42:6; 45:1 [h]ver 10
41:15 [i]Mic 4:13
41:16 [j]Jer 51:2 [k]Isa 45:25
41:17 [l]Isa 43:20 [m]Isa 30:19
41:18 [n]Isa 30:25 [o]Isa 43:19 [p]Isa 35:7
41:19 [q]Isa 60:13
41:20 [r]Job 12:9
41:21 [s]Isa 43:15
41:22 [t]Isa 43:9; 45:21

Tell us what the former things were,
so that we may consider them
and know their final outcome.
Or declare to us the things to come,[a]
23 tell us what the future holds,
so we may know[b] that you are gods.
Do something, whether good or bad,[c]
so that we will be dismayed and filled with fear.
24But you are less than nothing[d]
and your works are utterly worthless;
he who chooses you is detestable.[e]

25"I have stirred up one from the north,[f] and he comes—
one from the rising sun who calls on my name.
He treads[g] on rulers as if they were mortar,
as if he were a potter treading the clay.
26Who told of this from the beginning, so we could know,
or beforehand, so we could say, 'He was right'?
No one told of this,
no one foretold it,
no one heard any words[h] from you.
27I was the first to tell[i] Zion, 'Look, here they are!'
I gave to Jerusalem a messenger of good tidings.[j]
28I look but there is no one[k]—
no one among them to give counsel,[l]
no one to give answer when I ask them.
29See, they are all false!
Their deeds amount to nothing;[m]
their images are but wind[n] and confusion.

Chapter 42 Theme ____________________________________

42 "Here is my servant, whom I uphold,
my chosen one[o] in whom I delight;
I will put my Spirit[p] on him
and he will bring justice to the nations.
2He will not shout or cry out,
or raise his voice in the streets.
3A bruised reed he will not break,
and a smoldering wick he will not snuff out.
In faithfulness he will bring forth justice;[q]
4 he will not falter or be discouraged
till he establishes justice on earth.
In his law the islands will put their hope."[r]

5This is what God the LORD says—
he who created the heavens and stretched them out,
who spread out the earth and all that comes out of it,[s]

41:22 [a]Isa 46:10
41:23 [b]Isa 42:9; 44:7-8; 45:3 [c]Jer 10:5
41:24 [d]Isa 37:19; 44:9; 1Co 8:4 [e]Ps 115:8
41:25 [f]ver 2 [g]2Sa 22:43
41:26 [h]Hab 2:18-19
41:27 [i]Isa 48:3,16 [j]Isa 40:9
41:28 [k]Isa 50:2; 59:16; 63:5 [l]Isa 40:13-14
41:29 [m]ver 24 [n]Jer 5:13
42:1 [o]Isa 43:10; Lk 9:35; 1Pe 2:4,6 [p]Isa 11:2; Mt 3:16-17; Jn 3:34
42:3 [q]Ps 72:2
42:4 [r]Ge 49:10; Mt 12:18-21*
42:5 [s]Ps 24:2

who gives breath[a] to its people,
and life to those who walk on it:
6"I, the LORD, have called[b] you in righteousness;[c]
I will take hold of your hand.
I will keep[d] you and will make you
to be a covenant[e] for the people
and a light for the Gentiles,[f]
7to open eyes that are blind,[g]
to free[h] captives from prison[i]
and to release from the dungeon those who sit
in darkness.

8"I am the LORD; that is my name![j]
I will not give my glory to another[k]
or my praise to idols.
9See, the former things have taken place,
and new things I declare;
before they spring into being
I announce them to you."

10Sing to the LORD a new song,[l]
his praise from the ends of the earth,[m]
you who go down to the sea, and all that is in it,[n]
you islands, and all who live in them.
11Let the desert[o] and its towns raise their voices;
let the settlements where Kedar[p] lives rejoice.
Let the people of Sela sing for joy;
let them shout from the mountaintops.[q]
12Let them give glory[r] to the LORD
and proclaim his praise in the islands.
13The LORD will march out like a mighty[s] man,
like a warrior he will stir up his zeal;[t]
with a shout[u] he will raise the battle cry
and will triumph over his enemies.[v]

14"For a long time I have kept silent,
I have been quiet and held myself back.
But now, like a woman in childbirth,
I cry out, I gasp and pant.
15I will lay waste[w] the mountains and hills
and dry up all their vegetation;
I will turn rivers into islands
and dry up[x] the pools.
16I will lead[y] the blind[z] by ways they have not known,
along unfamiliar paths I will guide them;
I will turn the darkness into light before them
and make the rough places smooth.[a]

42:5
[a]Ac 17:25

42:6
[b]Isa 43:1
[c]Jer 23:6
[d]Isa 26:3
[e]Isa 49:8
[f]Lk 2:32; Ac 13:47

42:7
[g]Isa 35:5
[h]Isa 49:9; 61:1
[i]Lk 4:19; 2Ti 2:26; Heb 2:14-15

42:8
[j]Ex 3:15
[k]Isa 48:11

42:10
[l]Ps 33:3; 40:3; 98:1
[m]Isa 49:6
[n]1Ch 16:32; Ps 96:11

42:11
[o]Isa 32:16
[p]Isa 60:7
[q]Isa 52:7; Na 1:15

42:12
[r]Isa 24:15

42:13
[s]Isa 9:6
[t]Isa 26:11
[u]Hos 11:10
[v]Isa 66:14

42:15
[w]Eze 38:20
[x]Isa 50:2; Na 1:4-6

42:16
[y]Lk 1:78-79
[z]Isa 32:3
[a]Lk 3:5

These are the things I will do;
I will not forsake[a] them.
17 But those who trust in idols,
who say to images, 'You are our gods,'
will be turned back in utter shame.[b]

18 "Hear, you deaf;[c]
look, you blind, and see!
19 Who is blind[d] but my servant,[e]
and deaf like the messenger[f] I send?
Who is blind like the one committed[g] to me,
blind like the servant of the LORD?
20 You have seen many things, but have paid no attention;
your ears are open, but you hear nothing."[h]
21 It pleased the LORD
for the sake of his righteousness
to make his law[i] great and glorious.
22 But this is a people plundered and looted,
all of them trapped in pits[j]
or hidden away in prisons.[k]
They have become plunder,
with no one to rescue them;
they have been made loot,
with no one to say, "Send them back."

23 Which of you will listen to this
or pay close attention[l] in time to come?
24 Who handed Jacob over to become loot,
and Israel to the plunderers?
Was it not the LORD,
against whom we have sinned?
For they would not follow[m] his ways;
they did not obey his law.
25 So he poured out on them his burning anger,
the violence of war.
It enveloped them in flames,[n] yet they did not understand;
it consumed them, but they did not take it to heart.[o]

Chapter 43 Theme ______________________________

43 But now, this is what the LORD says—
he who created you, O Jacob,
he who formed[p] you, O Israel:[q]
"Fear not, for I have redeemed[r] you;
I have summoned you by name;[s] you are mine.
2 When you pass through the waters,[t]
I will be with you;[u]

42:16 [a]Heb 13:5
42:17 [b]Ps 97:7; Isa 1:29; 44:11; 45:16
42:18 [c]Isa 35:5
42:19 [d]Isa 43:8; Eze 12:2 [e]Isa 41:8-9 [f]Isa 44:26 [g]Isa 26:3
42:20 [h]Jer 6:10
42:21 [i]ver 4
42:22 [j]Isa 24:18 [k]Isa 24:22
42:23 [l]Isa 48:18
42:24 [m]Isa 30:15
42:25 [n]2Ki 25:9 [o]Isa 29:13; 47:7; 57:1,11; Hos 7:9
43:1 [p]ver 7 [q]Ge 32:28; Isa 44:21 [r]Isa 44:2,6 [s]Isa 42:6; 45:3-4
43:2 [t]Isa 8:7 [u]Dt 31:6,8

and when you pass through the rivers,
they will not sweep over you.
When you walk through the fire,[a]
you will not be burned;
the flames will not set you ablaze.[b]
3For I am the LORD, your God,[c]
the Holy One of Israel, your Savior;
I give Egypt for your ransom,
Cush[a] [d] and Seba in your stead.[e]
4Since you are precious and honored in my sight,
and because I love[f] you,
I will give men in exchange for you,
and people in exchange for your life.
5Do not be afraid,[g] for I am with you;[h]
I will bring your children[i] from the east
and gather you from the west.
6I will say to the north, 'Give them up!'
and to the south,[j] 'Do not hold them back.'
Bring my sons from afar
and my daughters[k] from the ends of the earth—
7everyone who is called by my name,[l]
whom I created for my glory,
whom I formed and made.[m]"

8Lead out those who have eyes but are blind,[n]
who have ears but are deaf.[o]
9All the nations gather together[p]
and the peoples assemble.
Which of them foretold[q] this
and proclaimed to us the former things?
Let them bring in their witnesses to prove they were right,
so that others may hear and say, "It is true."
10"You are my witnesses," declares the LORD,
"and my servant[r] whom I have chosen,
so that you may know and believe me
and understand that I am he.
Before me no god[s] was formed,
nor will there be one after me.
11I, even I, am the LORD,
and apart from me there is no savior.[t]
12I have revealed and saved and proclaimed—
I, and not some foreign god[u] among you.
You are my witnesses,[v]" declares the LORD, "that I am God.

a 3 That is, the upper Nile region

43:2 [a]Isa 29:6; 30:27 [b]Ps 66:12; Da 3:25-27
43:3 [c]Ex 20:2 [d]Isa 20:3 [e]Pr 21:18
43:4 [f]Isa 63:9
43:5 [g]Isa 44:2 [h]Jer 30:10-11 [i]Isa 41:8
43:6 [j]Ps 107:3 [k]2Co 6:18
43:7 [l]Isa 56:5; 63:19; Jas 2:7 [m]ver 1,21; Ps 100:3; Eph 2:10
43:8 [n]Isa 6:9-10 [o]Isa 42:20; Eze 12:2
43:9 [p]Isa 41:1 [q]Isa 41:26
43:10 [r]Isa 41:8-9 [s]Isa 44:6,8
43:11 [t]Isa 45:21
43:12 [u]Dt 32:12; Ps 81:9 [v]Isa 44:8

13 Yes, and from ancient days[a] I am he.
No one can deliver out of my hand.
When I act, who can reverse it?"[b]

14This is what the LORD says—
your Redeemer, the Holy One of Israel:
"For your sake I will send to Babylon
and bring down as fugitives[c] all the
Babylonians,[a d]
in the ships in which they took pride.
15I am the LORD, your Holy One,
Israel's Creator, your King."

16This is what the LORD says—
he who made a way through the sea,
a path through the mighty waters,[e]
17who drew out[f] the chariots and horses,
the army and reinforcements together,[g]
and they lay there, never to rise again,
extinguished, snuffed out like a wick:
18"Forget the former things;
do not dwell on the past.
19See, I am doing a new thing![h]
Now it springs up; do you not perceive it?
I am making a way in the desert[i]
and streams in the wasteland.
20The wild animals honor me,
the jackals[j] and the owls,
because I provide water[k] in the desert
and streams in the wasteland,
to give drink to my people, my chosen,
21 the people I formed for myself
that they may proclaim my praise.[l]

22"Yet you have not called upon me, O Jacob,
you have not wearied yourselves for me, O Israel.[m]
23You have not brought me sheep for burnt offerings,
nor honored[n] me with your sacrifices.[o]
I have not burdened you with grain offerings
nor wearied you with demands[p] for incense.[q]
24You have not bought any fragrant calamus[r] for me,
or lavished on me the fat of your sacrifices.
But you have burdened me with your sins
and wearied[s] me with your offenses.[t]

43:13 [a]Ps 90:2 [b]Job 9:12; Isa 14:27
43:14 [c]Isa 13:14-15 [d]Isa 23:13
43:16 [e]Ps 77:19; Isa 11:15; 51:10
43:17 [f]Ps 118:12; Isa 1:31 [g]Ex 14:9
43:19 [h]2Co 5:17; Rev 21:5 [i]Ex 17:6; Nu 20:11
43:20 [j]Isa 13:22 [k]Isa 48:21
43:21 [l]Ps 102:18; 1Pe 2:9
43:22 [m]Isa 30:11
43:23 [n]Zec 7:5-6; Mal 1:6-8 [o]Am 5:25 [p]Jer 7:22 [q]Ex 30:35; Lev 2:1
43:24 [r]Ex 30:23 [s]Isa 1:14; 7:13 [t]Mal 2:17

a *14* Or *Chaldeans*

25"I, even I, am he who blots out
your transgressions,[a] for my own sake,[b]
and remembers your sins no more.[c]
26Review the past for me,
let us argue the matter together;[d]
state the case[e] for your innocence.
27Your first father sinned;
your spokesmen[f] rebelled against me.
28So I will disgrace the dignitaries of your temple,
and I will consign Jacob to destruction[a]
and Israel to scorn.[g]

Chapter 44 Theme ________________________

44 "But now listen, O Jacob, my servant,[h]
Israel, whom I have chosen.
2This is what the LORD says—
he who made you, who formed you in the womb,
and who will help[i] you:
Do not be afraid, O Jacob, my servant,
Jeshurun,[j] whom I have chosen.
3For I will pour water[k] on the thirsty land,
and streams on the dry ground;
I will pour out my Spirit[l] on your offspring,
and my blessing on your descendants.[m]
4They will spring up like grass in a meadow,
like poplar trees[n] by flowing streams.[o]
5One will say, 'I belong to the LORD';
another will call himself by the name of Jacob;
still another will write on his hand,[p] 'The LORD's,'[q]
and will take the name Israel.

6"This is what the LORD says—
Israel's King[r] and Redeemer,[s] the LORD Almighty:
I am the first and I am the last;[t]
apart from me there is no God.
7Who then is like me? Let him proclaim it.
Let him declare and lay out before me
what has happened since I established my ancient people,
and what is yet to come—
yes, let him foretell[u] what will come.
8Do not tremble, do not be afraid.
Did I not proclaim this and foretell it long ago?

a *28* The Hebrew term refers to the irrevocable giving over of things or persons to the LORD, often by totally destroying them.

43:25
[a] Ac 3:19
[b] Isa 37:35; Eze 36:22
[c] Isa 38:17; Jer 31:34

43:26
[d] Isa 1:18
[e] Isa 41:1; 50:8

43:27
[f] Isa 9:15; 28:7; Jer 5:31

43:28
[g] Jer 24:9; Eze 5:15

44:1
[h] ver 21; Jer 30:10; 46:27-28

44:2
[i] Isa 41:10
[j] Dt 32:15

44:3
[k] Joel 3:18
[l] Joel 2:28; Ac 2:17
[m] Isa 61:9; 65:23

44:4
[n] Lev 23:40
[o] Job 40:22

44:5
[p] Ex 13:9
[q] Zec 8:20-22

44:6
[r] Isa 41:21
[s] Isa 43:1
[t] Isa 41:4; Rev 1:8,17; 22:13

44:7
[u] Isa 41:22,26

You are my witnesses. Is there any God[a] besides me?
No, there is no other Rock;[b] I know not one."

9 All who make idols are nothing,
and the things they treasure are worthless.[c]
Those who would speak up for them are blind;
they are ignorant, to their own shame.
10 Who shapes a god and casts an idol,
which can profit him nothing?[d]
11 He and his kind will be put to shame;[e]
craftsmen are nothing but men.
Let them all come together and take their stand;
they will be brought down to terror and infamy.[f]

12 The blacksmith[g] takes a tool
and works with it in the coals;
he shapes an idol with hammers,
he forges it with the might of his arm.[h]
He gets hungry and loses his strength;
he drinks no water and grows faint.
13 The carpenter[i] measures with a line
and makes an outline with a marker;
he roughs it out with chisels
and marks it with compasses.
He shapes it in the form of man,[j]
of man in all his glory,
that it may dwell in a shrine.[k]
14 He cut down cedars,
or perhaps took a cypress or oak.
He let it grow among the trees of the forest,
or planted a pine, and the rain made it grow.
15 It is man's fuel[l] for burning;
some of it he takes and warms himself,
he kindles a fire and bakes bread.
But he also fashions a god and worships it;
he makes an idol and bows[m] down to it.
16 Half of the wood he burns in the fire;
over it he prepares his meal,
he roasts his meat and eats his fill.
He also warms himself and says,
"Ah! I am warm; I see the fire."
17 From the rest he makes a god, his idol;
he bows down to it and worships.
He prays[n] to it and says,
"Save[o] me; you are my god."
18 They know nothing, they understand[p] nothing;
their eyes[q] are plastered over so they cannot see,

44:8 [a] Isa 43:10 [b] Dt 4:35; 1Sa 2:2
44:9 [c] Isa 41:24
44:10 [d] Isa 41:29; Jer 10:5; Ac 19:26
44:11 [e] Isa 1:29 [f] Isa 42:17
44:12 [g] Isa 40:19; 41:6-7 [h] Jer 10:3-5; Ac 17:29
44:13 [i] Isa 41:7 [j] Ps 115:4-7 [k] Jdg 17:4-5
44:15 [l] ver 19 [m] 2Ch 25:14
44:17 [n] 1Ki 18:26 [o] Isa 45:20
44:18 [p] Isa 1:3 [q] Isa 6:9-10

and their minds closed so they cannot understand.
19No one stops to think,
no one has the knowledge or understanding[a] to say,
"Half of it I used for fuel;
I even baked bread over its coals,
I roasted meat and I ate.
Shall I make a detestable[b] thing from what is left?
Shall I bow down to a block of wood?"
20He feeds on ashes,[c] a deluded[d] heart misleads him;
he cannot save himself, or say,
"Is not this thing in my right hand a lie?[e]"

21"Remember[f] these things, O Jacob,
for you are my servant, O Israel.
I have made you, you are my servant;[g]
O Israel, I will not forget you.[h]
22I have swept away[i] your offenses like a cloud,
your sins like the morning mist.
Return[j] to me,
for I have redeemed[k] you."

23Sing for joy,[l] O heavens, for the LORD has done this;
shout aloud, O earth[m] beneath.
Burst into song, you mountains,[n]
you forests and all your trees,
for the LORD has redeemed Jacob,
he displays his glory[o] in Israel.

24"This is what the LORD says—
your Redeemer,[p] who formed you in the womb:

I am the LORD,
who has made all things,
who alone stretched out the heavens,[q]
who spread out the earth by myself,

25who foils[r] the signs of false prophets
and makes fools of diviners,[s]
who overthrows the learning of the wise[t]
and turns it into nonsense,[u]
26who carries out the words[v] of his servants
and fulfills[w] the predictions of his messengers,

who says of Jerusalem, 'It shall be inhabited,'
of the towns of Judah, 'They shall be built,'
and of their ruins, 'I will restore them,'[x]
27who says to the watery deep, 'Be dry,
and I will dry up your streams,'

44:19
[a] Isa 5:13; 27:11; 45:20
[b] Dt 27:15

44:20
[c] Ps 102:9
[d] Job 15:31; Ro 1:21-23,28; 2Th 2:11; 2Ti 3:13
[e] Isa 59:3,4,13; Ro 1:25

44:21
[f] Isa 46:8; Zec 10:9
[g] ver 1-2
[h] Isa 49:15

44:22
[i] Isa 43:25; Ac 3:19
[j] Isa 55:7
[k] 1Co 6:20

44:23
[l] Isa 42:10
[m] Ps 148:7
[n] Ps 98:8
[o] Isa 61:3

44:24
[p] Isa 43:14
[q] Isa 42:5

44:25
[r] Ps 33:10
[s] Isa 47:13
[t] 1Co 1:27
[u] 2Sa 15:31; 1Co 1:19-20

44:26
[v] Zec 1:6
[w] Isa 55:11; Mt 5:18
[x] Isa 49:8-21

44:28
[a] 2Ch 36:22
[b] Isa 14:32
[c] Ezr 1:2-4

28 who says of Cyrus,[a] 'He is my shepherd
and will accomplish all that I please;
he will say of Jerusalem,[b] "Let it be rebuilt,"
and of the temple,[c] "Let its foundations be laid." '

Chapter 45 Theme ______________________________

45:1
[d] Ps 73:23; Isa 41:13; 42:6
[e] Jer 50:35

45:2
[f] Isa 40:4
[g] Ps 107:16; Jer 51:30

45:3
[h] Jer 50:37
[i] Jer 41:8
[j] Isa 41:23
[k] Ex 33:12; Isa 43:1

45:4
[l] Isa 41:8-9
[m] Ac 17:23

45:5
[n] Isa 44:8
[o] Ps 18:31
[p] Ps 18:39

45:6
[q] Isa 43:5; Mal 1:11
[r] ver 5,18

45:7
[s] Isa 31:2; Am 3:6

45:8
[t] Ps 72:6; Joel 3:18
[u] Ps 85:11; Isa 60:21; 61:10,11; Hos 10:12
[v] Isa 12:3

45

"This is what the LORD says to his anointed,
to Cyrus, whose right hand I take hold[d] of
to subdue nations[e] before him
and to strip kings of their armor,
to open doors before him
so that gates will not be shut:
2 I will go before you
and will level[f] the mountains[a];
I will break down gates of bronze
and cut through bars of iron.[g]
3 I will give you the treasures[h] of darkness,
riches stored in secret places,[i]
so that you may know[j] that I am the LORD,
the God of Israel, who summons you by name.[k]
4 For the sake of Jacob my servant,[l]
of Israel my chosen,
I summon you by name
and bestow on you a title of honor,
though you do not acknowledge[m] me.
5 I am the LORD, and there is no other;[n]
apart from me there is no God.[o]
I will strengthen you,[p]
though you have not acknowledged me,
6 so that from the rising of the sun
to the place of its setting[q]
men may know there is none besides me.[r]
I am the LORD, and there is no other.
7 I form the light and create darkness,
I bring prosperity and create disaster;[s]
I, the LORD, do all these things.

8 "You heavens above, rain[t] down righteousness;[u]
let the clouds shower it down.
Let the earth open wide,
let salvation[v] spring up,
let righteousness grow with it;
I, the LORD, have created it.

INSIGHT

This prophecy regarding Cyrus was given 175 years before his birth. In 539 B.C. Babylon was conquered by Cyrus and Darius of the Medo-Persian Empire.

[a] *2* Dead Sea Scrolls and Septuagint; the meaning of the word in the Masoretic Text is uncertain.

9"Woe to him who quarrels[a] with his Maker,
to him who is but a potsherd among the potsherds on the ground.
Does the clay say to the potter,[b]
'What are you making?'
Does your work say,
'He has no hands'?
10Woe to him who says to his father,
'What have you begotten?'
or to his mother,
'What have you brought to birth?'

11"This is what the LORD says—
the Holy One of Israel, and its Maker:
Concerning things to come,
do you question me about my children,
or give me orders about the work of my hands?[c]
12It is I who made the earth
and created mankind upon it.
My own hands stretched out the heavens;[d]
I marshaled their starry hosts.[e]
13I will raise up Cyrus[a] [f] in my righteousness:
I will make all his ways straight.
He will rebuild my city
and set my exiles free,
but not for a price or reward,[g]
says the LORD Almighty."

14This is what the LORD says:

"The products of Egypt and the merchandise of Cush,[b]
and those tall Sabeans—
they will come over to you
and will be yours;
they will trudge behind you,
coming over to you in chains.[h]
They will bow down before you
and plead[i] with you, saying,
'Surely God is with you,[j] and there is no other;
there is no other god.'"

15Truly you are a God who hides[k] himself,
O God and Savior of Israel.
16All the makers of idols will be put to shame
and disgraced;[l]
they will go off into disgrace together.

a 13 Hebrew *him* b 14 That is, the upper Nile region

45:9 [a] Job 15:25 [b] Isa 29:16; Ro 9:20-21*
45:11 [c] Isa 19:25
45:12 [d] Ge 2:1; Isa 42:5 [e] Ne 9:6
45:13 [f] 2Ch 36:22; Isa 41:2 [g] Isa 52:3
45:14 [h] Isa 14:1-2 [i] Jer 16:19; Zec 8:20-23 [j] 1Co 14:25
45:15 [k] Ps 44:24
45:16 [l] Isa 44:9,11

17But Israel will be saved[a] by the LORD
with an everlasting salvation;[b]
you will never be put to shame or disgraced,
to ages everlasting.

18For this is what the LORD says—
he who created the heavens,
he is God;
he who fashioned and made the earth,
he founded it;
he did not create it to be empty,[c]
but formed it to be inhabited[d]—
he says:
"I am the LORD,
and there is no other.[e]
19I have not spoken in secret,[f]
from somewhere in a land of darkness;
I have not said to Jacob's descendants,[g]
'Seek me in vain.'
I, the LORD, speak the truth;
I declare what is right.[h]

20"Gather together[i] and come;
assemble, you fugitives from the nations.
Ignorant[j] are those who carry[k] about idols of wood,
who pray to gods that cannot save.[l]
21Declare what is to be, present it—
let them take counsel together.
Who foretold[m] this long ago,
who declared it from the distant past?
Was it not I, the LORD?
And there is no God apart from me,[n]
a righteous God and a Savior;
there is none but me.

22"Turn[o] to me and be saved,[p]
all you ends of the earth;[q]
for I am God, and there is no other.
23By myself I have sworn,[r]
my mouth has uttered in all integrity[s]
a word that will not be revoked:[t]
Before me every knee will bow;
by me every tongue will swear.[u]
24They will say of me, 'In the LORD alone
are righteousness[v] and strength.'"
All who have raged against him
will come to him and be put to shame.[w]

45:17
[a]Ro 11:26
[b]Isa 26:4

45:18
[c]Ge 1:2
[d]Ge 1:26; Isa 42:5
[e]ver 5

45:19
[f]Isa 48:16
[g]Isa 41:8
[h]Dt 30:11

45:20
[i]Isa 43:9
[j]Isa 44:19
[k]Isa 46:1; Jer 10:5
[l]Isa 44:17; 46:6-7

45:21
[m]Isa 41:22
[n]ver 5

45:22
[o]Zec 12:10
[p]Nu 21:8-9; 2Ch 20:12
[q]Isa 49:6,12

45:23
[r]Ge 22:16
[s]Heb 6:13
[t]Isa 55:11
[u]Ps 63:11; Isa 19:18; Ro 14:11*; Php 2:10-11

45:24
[v]Jer 33:16
[w]Isa 41:11

[25]But in the LORD all the descendants of Israel
will be found righteous and will exult.[a]

Chapter 46 Theme ________________________

46

Bel[b] bows down, Nebo stoops low;
their idols are borne by beasts of burden.[a]
The images that are carried[c] about are burdensome,
a burden for the weary.
[2]They stoop and bow down together;
unable to rescue the burden,
they themselves go off into captivity.[d]

[3]"Listen[e] to me, O house of Jacob,
all you who remain of the house of Israel,
you whom I have upheld since you were conceived,
and have carried since your birth.
[4]Even to your old age and gray hairs[f]
I am he,[g] I am he who will sustain you.
I have made you and I will carry you;
I will sustain you and I will rescue you.

[5]"To whom will you compare me or count me equal?
To whom will you liken me that we may be compared?[h]
[6]Some pour out gold from their bags
and weigh out silver on the scales;
they hire a goldsmith[i] to make it into a god,
and they bow down and worship it.[j]
[7]They lift it to their shoulders and carry[k] it;
they set it up in its place, and there it stands.
From that spot it cannot move.
Though one cries out to it, it does not answer;
it cannot save[l] him from his troubles.

[8]"Remember[m] this, fix it in mind,
take it to heart, you rebels.
[9]Remember the former things, those of long ago;[n]
I am God, and there is no other;
I am God, and there is none like me.[o]
[10]I make known the end from the beginning,
from ancient times,[p] what is still to come.
I say: My purpose will stand,[q]
and I will do all that I please.
[11]From the east I summon a bird of prey;
from a far-off land, a man to fulfill my purpose.
What I have said, that will I bring about;
what I have planned, that will I do.

a *1* Or *are but beasts and cattle*

45:25
[a]Isa 41:16

46:1
[b]Isa 21:9; Jer 50:2; 51:44
[c]Isa 45:20

46:2
[d]Jdg 18:17-18; 2Sa 5:21

46:3
[e]ver 12

46:4
[f]Ps 71:18
[g]Isa 43:13

46:5
[h]Isa 40:18,25

46:6
[i]Isa 40:19
[j]Isa 44:17

46:7
[k]ver 1
[l]Isa 44:17; Isa 45:20

46:8
[m]Isa 44:21

46:9
[n]Dt 32:7
[o]Isa 45:5,21

46:10
[p]Isa 45:21
[q]Pr 19:21; Ac 5:39

46:12 [a]ver 3 [b]Ps 119:150; Isa 48:1; Jer 2:5
46:13 [c]Isa 44:23
47:1 [d]Isa 23:12 [e]Ps 137:8; Jer 50:42; 51:33; Zec 2:7 [f]Dt 28:56
47:2 [g]Ex 11:5; Mt 24:41 [h]Jdg 16:21 [i]Ge 24:65 [j]Isa 32:11
47:3 [k]Eze 16:37; Na 3:5 [l]Isa 20:4 [m]Isa 34:8
47:4 [n]Jer 50:34
47:5 [o]Isa 13:10 [p]Isa 13:19
47:6 [q]2Ch 28:9 [r]Isa 10:13
47:7 [s]ver 5; Rev 18:7 [t]Isa 42:23,25 [u]Dt 32:29
47:8 [v]Isa 32:9 [w]Isa 45:6; Zep 2:15

12 Listen[a] to me, you stubborn-hearted,
you who are far from righteousness.[b]
13 I am bringing my righteousness near,
it is not far away;
and my salvation will not be delayed.
I will grant salvation to Zion,
my splendor[c] to Israel.

Chapter 47 Theme ____________________

47

"Go down, sit in the dust,
Virgin Daughter[d] of Babylon;
sit on the ground without a throne,
Daughter of the Babylonians.[a] [e]
No more will you be called
tender or delicate.[f]
2 Take millstones[g] and grind[h] flour;
take off your veil.[i]
Lift up your skirts,[j] bare your legs,
and wade through the streams.
3 Your nakedness[k] will be exposed
and your shame[l] uncovered.
I will take vengeance;[m]
I will spare no one."

4 Our Redeemer—the LORD Almighty is his name[n]—
is the Holy One of Israel.

5 "Sit in silence, go into darkness,[o]
Daughter of the Babylonians;
no more will you be called
queen of kingdoms.[p]
6 I was angry[q] with my people
and desecrated my inheritance;
I gave them into your hand,[r]
and you showed them no mercy.
Even on the aged
you laid a very heavy yoke.
7 You said, 'I will continue forever—
the eternal queen!'[s]
But you did not consider these things
or reflect[t] on what might happen.[u]

8 "Now then, listen, you wanton creature,
lounging in your security[v]
and saying to yourself,
'I am, and there is none besides me.[w]

[a] *1* Or *Chaldeans*; also in verse 5

I will never be a widow[a]
or suffer the loss of children.'
9Both of these will overtake you
in a moment,[b] on a single day:
loss of children[c] and widowhood.
They will come upon you in full measure,
in spite of your many sorceries[d]
and all your potent spells.[e]
10You have trusted[f] in your wickedness
and have said, 'No one sees me.'[g]
Your wisdom[h] and knowledge mislead[i] you
when you say to yourself,
'I am, and there is none besides me.'
11Disaster will come upon you,
and you will not know how to conjure it away.
A calamity will fall upon you
that you cannot ward off with a ransom;
a catastrophe you cannot foresee
will suddenly[j] come upon you.

12"Keep on, then, with your magic spells
and with your many sorceries,[k]
which you have labored at since childhood.
Perhaps you will succeed,
perhaps you will cause terror.
13All the counsel you have received has only worn you out![l]
Let your astrologers[m] come forward,
those stargazers who make predictions month by month,
let them save[n] you from what is coming upon you.
14Surely they are like stubble;[o]
the fire will burn them up.
They cannot even save themselves
from the power of the flame.[p]
Here are no coals to warm anyone;
here is no fire to sit by.
15That is all they can do for you—
these you have labored with
and trafficked[q] with since childhood.
Each of them goes on in his error;
there is not one that can save you.

Chapter 48 Theme ______________________

48 "Listen to this, O house of Jacob,
you who are called by the name of Israel
and come from the line of Judah,

47:8
[a]Rev 18:7

47:9
[b]Ps 73:19; 1Th 5:3; Rev 18:8-10
[c]Isa 13:18
[d]Na 3:4
[e]Rev 18:23

47:10
[f]Ps 52:7; 62:10
[g]Isa 29:15
[h]Isa 5:21
[i]Isa 44:20

47:11
[j]1Th 5:3

47:12
[k]ver 9

47:13
[l]Isa 57:10; Jer 51:58
[m]Isa 44:25
[n]ver 15

47:14
[o]Isa 5:24; Na 1:10
[p]Isa 10:17; Jer 51:30,32,58

47:15
[q]Rev 18:11

you who take oaths in the name of the LORD
and invoke[a] the God of Israel—
but not in truth[b] or righteousness—
2 you who call yourselves citizens of the holy city[c]
and rely[d] on the God of Israel—
the LORD Almighty is his name:
3 I foretold the former things[e] long ago,
my mouth announced[f] them and I made them known;
then suddenly I acted, and they came to pass.
4 For I knew how stubborn[g] you were;
the sinews of your neck[h] were iron,
your forehead[i] was bronze.
5 Therefore I told you these things long ago;
before they happened I announced them to you
so that you could not say,
'My idols did them;[j]
my wooden image and metal god ordained them.'
6 You have heard these things; look at them all.
Will you not admit them?

"From now on I will tell you of new things,
of hidden things unknown to you.
7 They are created now, and not long ago;
you have not heard of them before today.
So you cannot say,
'Yes, I knew of them.'
8 You have neither heard nor understood;
from of old your ear has not been open.
Well do I know how treacherous you are;
you were called a rebel[k] from birth.
9 For my own name's sake I delay my wrath;[l]
for the sake of my praise I hold it back from you,
so as not to cut you off.[m]
10 See, I have refined you, though not as silver;
I have tested you in the furnace[n] of affliction.
11 For my own sake,[o] for my own sake, I do this.
How can I let myself be defamed?[p]
I will not yield my glory to another.[q]

12 "Listen[r] to me, O Jacob,
Israel, whom I have called:
I am he;
I am the first and I am the last.[s]
13 My own hand laid the foundations of the earth,[t]
and my right hand spread out the heavens;[u]
when I summon them,
they all stand up together.[v]

48:1 [a]Isa 58:2 [b]Jer 4:2
48:2 [c]Isa 52:1 [d]Isa 10:20; Mic 3:11; Ro 2:17
48:3 [e]Isa 41:22 [f]Isa 45:21
48:4 [g]Dt 31:27 [h]Ex 32:9; Ac 7:51 [i]Eze 3:9
48:5 [j]Jer 44:15-18
48:8 [k]Dt 9:7,24; Ps 58:3
48:9 [l]Ps 78:38; Isa 30:18 [m]Ne 9:31
48:10 [n]1Ki 8:51
48:11 [o]1Sa 12:22; Isa 37:35 [p]Dt 32:27; Jer 14:7,21; Eze 20:9,14,22,44 [q]Isa 42:8
48:12 [r]Isa 46:3 [s]Isa 41:4; Rev 1:17; 22:13
48:13 [t]Heb 1:10-12 [u]Ex 20:11 [v]Isa 40:26

14"Come together,[a] all of you, and listen:
Which of ⌊the idols⌋ has foretold these things?
The LORD's chosen ally
will carry out his purpose[b] against Babylon;
his arm will be against the Babylonians.[a]
15I, even I, have spoken;
yes, I have called[c] him.
I will bring him,
and he will succeed in his mission.

16"Come near[d] me and listen to this:

"From the first announcement I have not spoken
in secret;[e]
at the time it happens, I am there."

And now the Sovereign LORD has sent[f] me,
with his Spirit.

17This is what the LORD says—
your Redeemer,[g] the Holy One[h] of Israel:
"I am the LORD your God,
who teaches you what is best for you,
who directs[i] you in the way[j] you should go.
18If only you had paid attention[k] to my commands,
your peace[l] would have been like a river,
your righteousness[m] like the waves of the sea.
19Your descendants would have been like the sand,
your children like its numberless grains;[n]
their name would never be cut off[o]
nor destroyed from before me."
20Leave Babylon,
flee[p] from the Babylonians!
Announce this with shouts of joy[q]
and proclaim it.
Send it out to the ends of the earth;
say, "The LORD has redeemed[r] his servant Jacob."
21They did not thirst[s] when he led them through
the deserts;
he made water flow[t] for them from the rock;
he split the rock
and water gushed out.[u]

22"There is no peace," says the LORD, "for the wicked."[v]

a *14* Or *Chaldeans*; also in verse 20

48:14
[a]Isa 43:9
[b]Isa 46:10-11

48:15
[c]Isa 45:1

48:16
[d]Isa 41:1
[e]Isa 45:19
[f]Zec 2:9,11

48:17
[g]Isa 49:7
[h]Isa 43:14
[i]Isa 49:10
[j]Ps 32:8

48:18
[k]Dt 32:29
[l]Ps 119:165; Isa 66:12
[m]Isa 45:8

48:19
[n]Ge 22:17
[o]Isa 56:5; 66:22

48:20
[p]Jer 50:8; 51:6,45; Zec 2:6-7; Rev 18:4
[q]Isa 49:13
[r]Isa 52:9; 63:9

48:21
[s]Isa 41:17
[t]Isa 30:25
[u]Ex 17:6; Nu 20:11; Ps 105:41; Isa 35:6

48:22
[v]Isa 57:21

Chapter 49 Theme ______________________________

49

Listen to me, you islands;
hear this, you distant nations:
Before I was born[a] the LORD called[b] me;
from my birth he has made mention of my name.
2He made my mouth like a sharpened sword,[c]
in the shadow of his hand he hid me;
he made me into a polished arrow
and concealed me in his quiver.
3He said to me, "You are my servant,[d]
Israel, in whom I will display my splendor.[e]"
4But I said, "I have labored to no purpose;
I have spent my strength in vain[f] and for nothing.
Yet what is due me is in the LORD's hand,
and my reward[g] is with my God."

5And now the LORD says—
he who formed me in the womb to be his servant
to bring Jacob back to him
and gather Israel[h] to himself,
for I am honored[i] in the eyes of the LORD
and my God has been my strength—
6he says:
"It is too small a thing for you to be my servant
to restore the tribes of Jacob
and bring back those of Israel I have kept.
I will also make you a light for the Gentiles,[j]
that you may bring my salvation to the ends of
the earth."[k]

7This is what the LORD says—
the Redeemer and Holy One of Israel[l]—
to him who was despised[m] and abhorred by
the nation,
to the servant of rulers:
"Kings[n] will see you and rise up,
princes will see and bow down,
because of the LORD, who is faithful,
the Holy One of Israel, who has chosen you

8This is what the LORD says:

"In the time of my favor[o] I will answer yo
and in the day of salvation I will help
I will keep[q] you and will make you
to be a covenant for the people,[r]

49:1 [a] Isa 44:24; 46:3; Mt 1:20 [b] Isa 7:14; 9:6; 44:2; Jer 1:5; Gal 1:15
49:2 [c] Isa 11:4; Rev 1:16
49:3 [d] Zec 3:8 [e] Isa 44:23
49:4 [f] Isa 65:23 [g] Isa 35:4
49:5 [h] Isa 11:12 [i] Isa 43:4
49:6 [j] Lk 2:32 [k] Ac 13:47*
49:7 [l] Isa 48:17 [m] Ps 22:6; 69:7-9 [n] Isa 52:15
49:8 [o] Ps 69:13 [p] 2Co 6:2* [q] Isa 26:3 [r] Isa 42:6

to restore the land[a]
and to reassign its desolate inheritances,
9to say to the captives,[b] 'Come out,'
and to those in darkness, 'Be free!'

"They will feed beside the roads
and find pasture on every barren hill.[c]
10They will neither hunger nor thirst,[d]
nor will the desert heat or the sun beat upon them.[e]
He who has compassion[f] on them will guide them
and lead them beside springs[g] of water.
11I will turn all my mountains into roads,
and my highways[h] will be raised up.[i]
12See, they will come from afar[j]—
some from the north, some from the west,
some from the region of Aswan.[a]"

13Shout for joy, O heavens;
rejoice, O earth;
burst into song, O mountains![k]
For the LORD comforts[l] his people
and will have compassion on his afflicted ones.

14But Zion said, "The LORD has forsaken me,
the Lord has forgotten me."
15"Can a mother forget the baby at her breast
and have no compassion on the child she has borne?
Though she may forget,
I will not forget you![m]
16See, I have engraved[n] you on the palms of my hands;
your walls[o] are ever before me.
17Your sons hasten back,
and those who laid you waste[p] depart from you.
18Lift up your eyes and look around;
all your sons gather[q] and come to you.
As surely as I live,[r]" declares the LORD,
"you will wear[s] them all as ornaments;
you will put them on, like a bride.

"Though you were ruined and made desolate[t]
and your land laid waste,[u]
v you will be too small for your people,[v]
20T d those who devoured you will be far away.
ildren born during your bereavement
t say in your hearing,

a 12 Dead Sea Scro... retic Text *Sinim*

49:8 [a]Isa 44:26
49:9 [b]Isa 42:7; 61:1; Lk 4:19 [c]Isa 41:18
49:10 [d]Isa 33:16 [e]Ps 121:6; Rev 7:16 [f]Isa 14:1 [g]Isa 35:7
49:11 [h]Isa 11:16 [i]Isa 40:4
49:12 [j]Isa 43:5-6
49:13 [k]Isa 44:23 [l]Isa 40:1
49:15 [m]Isa 44:21
49:16 [n]SS 8:6 [o]Ps 48:12-13; Isa 62:6
49:17 [p]Isa 10:6
49:18 [q]Isa 43:5; 54:7; Isa 60:4 [r]Isa 45:23 [s]Isa 52:1
49:19 [t]Isa 54:1,3 [u]Isa 5:6 [v]Zec 10:10

'This place is too small for us;
give us more space to live in.'[a]
21 Then you will say in your heart,
'Who bore me these?
I was bereaved and barren;
I was exiled and rejected.[b]
Who brought these up?
I was left[c] all alone,
but these—where have they come from?'"

22 This is what the Sovereign LORD says:

"See, I will beckon to the Gentiles,
I will lift up my banner[d] to the peoples;
they will bring your sons in their arms
and carry your daughters on their shoulders.[e]
23 Kings[f] will be your foster fathers,
and their queens your nursing mothers.[g]
They will bow down before you with their faces to the
ground;
they will lick the dust[h] at your feet.
Then you will know that I am the LORD;[i]
those who hope in me will not be disappointed."

24 Can plunder be taken from warriors,[j]
or captives rescued from the fierce[a]?

25 But this is what the LORD says:

"Yes, captives[k] will be taken from warriors,[l]
and plunder retrieved from the fierce;
I will contend with those who contend with you,
and your children I will save.[m]
26 I will make your oppressors[n] eat[o] their own flesh;
they will be drunk on their own blood,[p] as with wine.
Then all mankind will know[q]
that I, the LORD, am your Savior,
your Redeemer, the Mighty One of Jacob."

Chapter 50 Theme ____________________

50

This is what the LORD says:

"Where is your mother's certificate of divorce[r]
with which I sent her away?
Or to which of my creditors
did I sell[s] you?

49:20 [a] Isa 54:1-3
49:21 [b] Isa 5:13 [c] Isa 1:8
49:22 [d] Isa 11:10 [e] Isa 60:4
49:23 [f] Isa 60:3,10-11 [g] Isa 60:16 [h] Ps 72:9 [i] Mic 7:17
49:24 [j] Mt 12:29; Lk 11:21
49:25 [k] Isa 14:2 [l] Jer 50:33-34 [m] Isa 25:9; 35:4
49:26 [n] Isa 9:4 [o] Isa 9:20 [p] Rev 16:6 [q] Eze 39:7
50:1 [r] Dt 24:1; Jer 3:8; Hos 2:2 [s] Ne 5:5; Mt 18:25

a *24* Dead Sea Scrolls, Vulgate and Syriac (see also Septuagint and verse 25); Masoretic Text *righteous*

Because of your sins you were sold;[a]
because of your transgressions your mother was sent away.
2When I came, why was there no one?
When I called, why was there no one to answer?[b]
Was my arm too short[c] to ransom you?
Do I lack the strength[d] to rescue you?
By a mere rebuke I dry up the sea,[e]
I turn rivers into a desert;
their fish rot for lack of water
and die of thirst.
3I clothe the sky with darkness
and make sackcloth[f] its covering."

4The Sovereign LORD has given me an instructed tongue,[g]
to know the word that sustains the weary.[h]
He wakens me morning by morning,[i]
wakens my ear to listen like one being taught.
5The Sovereign LORD has opened my ears,[j]
and I have not been rebellious;[k]
I have not drawn back.
6I offered my back to those who beat[l] me,
my cheeks to those who pulled out my beard;
I did not hide my face
from mocking and spitting.[m]
7Because the Sovereign LORD helps[n] me,
I will not be disgraced.
Therefore have I set my face like flint,[o]
and I know I will not be put to shame.
8He who vindicates me is near.
Who then will bring charges against me?[p]
Let us face each other![q]
Who is my accuser?
Let him confront me!
9It is the Sovereign LORD who helps[r] me.
Who is he that will condemn me?
They will all wear out like a garment;
the moths[s] will eat them up.

10Who among you fears the LORD
and obeys the word of his servant?[t]
Let him who walks in the dark,
who has no light,
trust[u] in the name of the LORD
and rely on his God.
11But now, all you who light fires
and provide yourselves with flaming torches,[v]

50:1 [a] Dt 32:30; Isa 52:3
50:2 [b] Isa 41:28 [c] Nu 11:23; Isa 59:1 [d] Ge 18:14 [e] Ex 14:22; Jos 3:16
50:3 [f] Rev 6:12
50:4 [g] Ex 4:12 [h] Mt 11:28 [i] Ps 5:3; 119:147; 143:8
50:5 [j] Isa 35:5 [k] Mt 26:39; Jn 8:29; 14:31; 15:10; Ac 26:19; Heb 5:8
50:6 [l] Isa 53:5; Mt 27:30; Mk 14:65; 15:19; Lk 22:63 [m] La 3:30; Mt 26:67
50:7 [n] Isa 42:1 [o] Eze 3:8-9
50:8 [p] Isa 43:26; Ro 8:32-34 [q] Isa 41:1
50:9 [r] Isa 41:10 [s] Job 13:28; Isa 51:8
50:10 [t] Isa 49:3 [u] Isa 26:4
50:11 [v] Pr 26:18

50:11 [a]Jas 3:6 [b]Isa 65:13-15

go, walk in the light of your fires[a]
  and of the torches you have set ablaze.
This is what you shall receive from my hand:
  You will lie down in torment.[b]

Chapter 51 Theme

51:1 [c]Isa 46:3 [d]ver 7; Ps 94:15; Ro 9:30-31
51:2 [e]Isa 29:22; Ro 4:16; Heb 11:11 [f]Ge 12:2
51:3 [g]Isa 40:1 [h]Isa 52:9 [i]Ge 2:8 [j]Isa 25:9; 66:10
51:4 [k]Ps 50:7 [l]Isa 2:4 [m]Isa 42:4,6
51:5 [n]Isa 46:13 [o]Isa 40:10; 63:1,5
51:6 [p]Mt 24:35; 2Pe 3:10 [q]Ps 102:25-26
51:7 [r]ver 1 [s]Ps 37:31 [t]Mt 5:11; Ac 5:41
51:8 [u]Isa 50:9 [v]ver 6

51 "Listen[c] to me, you who pursue righteousness[d]
  and who seek the LORD:
Look to the rock from which you were cut
  and to the quarry from which you were hewn;
2 look to Abraham,[e] your father,
  and to Sarah, who gave you birth.
When I called him he was but one,
  and I blessed him and made him many.[f]
3 The LORD will surely comfort[g] Zion
  and will look with compassion on all her ruins;[h]
he will make her deserts like Eden,[i]
  her wastelands like the garden of the LORD.
Joy and gladness[j] will be found in her,
  thanksgiving and the sound of singing.

4 "Listen to me, my people;[k]
  hear me, my nation:
The law will go out from me;
  my justice[l] will become a light to the nations.[m]
5 My righteousness draws near speedily,
  my salvation is on the way,[n]
  and my arm[o] will bring justice to the nations.
The islands will look to me
  and wait in hope for my arm.
6 Lift up your eyes to the heavens,
  look at the earth beneath;
the heavens will vanish like smoke,[p]
  the earth will wear out like a garment[q]
  and its inhabitants die like flies.
But my salvation will last forever,
  my righteousness will never fail.

7 "Hear me, you who know what is right,[r]
  you people who have my law in your hearts:[s]
Do not fear the reproach of men
  or be terrified by their insults.[t]
8 For the moth will eat them up like a garment;[u]
  the worm will devour them like wool.
But my righteousness will last forever,[v]
  my salvation through all generations."

9 Awake, awake! Clothe yourself with strength,[a]
O arm of the LORD;
awake, as in days gone by,
as in generations of old.[b]
Was it not you who cut Rahab to pieces,
who pierced that monster[c] through?
10 Was it not you who dried up the sea,[d]
the waters of the great deep,
who made a road in the depths of the sea
so that the redeemed might cross over?
11 The ransomed[e] of the LORD will return.
They will enter Zion with singing;
everlasting joy will crown their heads.
Gladness and joy[f] will overtake them,
and sorrow and sighing will flee away.[g]

12 "I, even I, am he who comforts[h] you.
Who are you that you fear mortal men,[i]
the sons of men, who are but grass,[j]
13 that you forget[k] the LORD your Maker,[l]
who stretched out the heavens[m]
and laid the foundations of the earth,
that you live in constant terror[n] every day
because of the wrath of the oppressor,
who is bent on destruction?
For where is the wrath of the oppressor?
14 The cowering prisoners will soon be set free;
they will not die in their dungeon,
nor will they lack bread.[o]
15 For I am the LORD your God,
who churns up the sea[p] so that its waves roar—
the LORD Almighty is his name.
16 I have put my words in your mouth[q]
and covered you with the shadow of my hand[r]—
I who set the heavens in place,
who laid the foundations of the earth,
and who say to Zion, 'You are my people.' "

17 Awake, awake![s]
Rise up, O Jerusalem,
you who have drunk from the hand of the LORD
the cup of his wrath,[t]
you who have drained to its dregs
the goblet that makes men stagger.[u]
18 Of all the sons[v] she bore
there was none to guide her;[w]
of all the sons she reared
there was none to take her by the hand.

51:9 [a] Isa 52:1 [b] Dt 4:34 [c] Ps 74:13
51:10 [d] Ex 14:22
51:11 [e] Isa 35:9 [f] Jer 33:11 [g] Rev 7:17
51:12 [h] 2Co 1:4 [i] Ps 118:6; Isa 2:22 [j] Isa 40:6-7; 1Pe 1:24
51:13 [k] Isa 17:10 [l] Isa 45:11 [m] Ps 104:2; Isa 48:13 [n] Isa 7:4
51:14 [o] Isa 49:10
51:15 [p] Jer 31:35
51:16 [q] Dt 18:18; Isa 59:21 [r] Ex 33:22
51:17 [s] Isa 52:1 [t] Job 21:20; Rev 14:10; 16:19 [u] Ps 60:3
51:18 [v] Ps 88:18 [w] Isa 49:21

51:19 [a]Isa 47:9 [b]Isa 14:30

[19]These double calamities[a] have come upon you—
who can comfort you?—
ruin and destruction, famine[b] and sword—
who can[a] console you?
[20]Your sons have fainted;
they lie at the head of every street,[c]
like antelope caught in a net.
They are filled with the wrath of the LORD
and the rebuke of your God.

51:20 [c]Isa 5:25; Jer 14:16

[21]Therefore hear this, you afflicted one,
made drunk,[d] but not with wine.
[22]This is what your Sovereign LORD says,
your God, who defends[e] his people:
"See, I have taken out of your hand
the cup[f] that made you stagger;
from that cup, the goblet of my wrath,
you will never drink again.
[23]I will put it into the hands of your tormentors,[g]
who said to you,
'Fall prostrate[h] that we may walk[i] over you.'
And you made your back like the ground,
like a street to be walked over."

51:21 [d]ver 17; Isa 29:9

51:22 [e]Isa 49:25 [f]ver 17

51:23 [g]Isa 49:26; Jer 25:15-17, 26,28; 49:12 [h]Zec 12:2 [i]Jos 10:24

Chapter 52 Theme ______________________

52

Awake, awake,[j] O Zion,
clothe yourself with strength.[k]
Put on your garments of splendor,[l]
O Jerusalem, the holy city.[m]
The uncircumcised and defiled
will not enter you again.[n]
[2]Shake off your dust;[o]
rise up, sit enthroned, O Jerusalem.
Free yourself from the chains on your neck,
O captive Daughter of Zion.

52:1 [j]Isa 51:17 [k]Isa 51:9 [l]Ex 28:2,40; Ps 110:3; Zec 3:4 [m]Ne 11:1; Mt 4:5; Rev 21:2 [n]Na 1:15; Rev 21:27

[3]For this is what the LORD says:

"You were sold for nothing,[p]
and without money[q] you will be redeemed."

52:2 [o]Isa 29:4

[4]For this is what the Sovereign LORD says:

"At first my people went down to Egypt[r] to live;
lately, Assyria has oppressed them.

52:3 [p]Ps 44:12 [q]Isa 45:13

[5]"And now what do I have here?" declares the LORD.

52:4 [r]Ge 46:6

a *19* Dead Sea Scrolls, Septuagint, Vulgate and Syriac; Masoretic Text / *how can I*

"For my people have been taken away for nothing,
and those who rule them mock,[a]"
declares the LORD.
"And all day long
my name is constantly blasphemed.[a]
6 Therefore my people will know[b] my name;
therefore in that day they will know
that it is I who foretold it.
Yes, it is I."

7 How beautiful on the mountains
are the feet of those who bring good news,[c]
who proclaim peace,[d]
who bring good tidings,
who proclaim salvation,
who say to Zion,
"Your God reigns!"[e]
8 Listen! Your watchmen[f] lift up their voices;
together they shout for joy.
When the LORD returns to Zion,
they will see it with their own eyes.
9 Burst into songs of joy[g] together,
you ruins[h] of Jerusalem,
for the LORD has comforted his people,
he has redeemed Jerusalem.[i]
10 The LORD will lay bare his holy arm
in the sight of all the nations,[j]
and all the ends of the earth will see
the salvation[k] of our God.

11 Depart,[l] depart, go out from there!
Touch no unclean thing![m]
Come out from it and be pure,[n]
you who carry the vessels of the LORD.
12 But you will not leave in haste[o]
or go in flight;
for the LORD will go before you,[p]
the God of Israel will be your rear guard.[q]

13 See, my servant[r] will act wisely[b];
he will be raised and lifted up and highly exalted.[s]
14 Just as there were many who were appalled at him[c]—
his appearance was so disfigured beyond that of
any man
and his form marred beyond human likeness—

[a]5 Dead Sea Scrolls and Vulgate; Masoretic Text *wail* [b]13 Or *will prosper* [c]14 Hebrew *you*

52:5
[a] Eze 36:20; Ro 2:24*

52:6
[b] Isa 49:23

52:7
[c] Isa 40:9; Ro 10:15*
[d] Na 1:15; Eph 6:15
[e] Ps 93:1

52:8
[f] Isa 62:6

52:9
[g] Ps 98:4
[h] Isa 51:3
[i] Isa 48:20

52:10
[j] Isa 66:18
[k] Ps 98:2-3; Lk 3:6

52:11
[l] Isa 48:20
[m] Isa 1:16; 2Co 6:17*
[n] 2Ti 2:19

52:12
[o] Ex 12:11
[p] Mic 2:13
[q] Ex 14:19

52:13
[r] Isa 42:1
[s] Isa 57:15; Php 2:9

15 so will he sprinkle many nations,[a]
and kings will shut their mouths because of him.
For what they were not told, they will see,
and what they have not heard, they will understand.[a]

Chapter 53 Theme ______________________

53 Who has believed our message[b]
and to whom has the arm of the LORD been revealed?[c]
2 He grew up before him like a tender shoot,
and like a root out of dry ground.
He had no beauty or majesty to attract us to him,
nothing in his appearance[d] that we should desire him.
3 He was despised and rejected by men,
a man of sorrows, and familiar with suffering.[e]
Like one from whom men hide their faces
he was despised,[f] and we esteemed him not.

4 Surely he took up our infirmities
and carried our sorrows,[g]
yet we considered him stricken by God,[h]
smitten by him, and afflicted.
5 But he was pierced for our transgressions,[i]
he was crushed for our iniquities;
the punishment that brought us peace was upon him,
and by his wounds we are healed.[j]
6 We all, like sheep, have gone astray,
each of us has turned to his own way;
and the LORD has laid on him
the iniquity of us all.

7 He was oppressed and afflicted,
yet he did not open his mouth;[k]
he was led like a lamb to the slaughter,
and as a sheep before her shearers is silent,
so he did not open his mouth.
8 By oppression[b] and judgment he was taken away.
And who can speak of his descendants?
For he was cut off from the land of the living;[l]
for the transgression[m] of my people he was stricken.[c]
9 He was assigned a grave with the wicked,
and with the rich[n] in his death,
though he had done no violence,[o]
nor was any deceit in his mouth.[p]

52:15 [a] Ro 15:21*; Eph 3:4-5
53:1 [b] Ro 10:16* [c] Jn 12:38*
53:2 [d] Isa 52:14
53:3 [e] ver 4,10; Lk 18:31-33 [f] Ps 22:6; Jn 1:10-11
53:4 [g] Mt 8:17* [h] Jn 19:7
53:5 [i] Ro 4:25; 1Co 15:3; Heb 9:28 [j] 1Pe 2:24-25
53:7 [k] Mk 14:61
53:8 [l] Da 9:26; Ac 8:32-33* [m] ver 12
53:9 [n] Mt 27:57-60 [o] Isa 42:1-3 [p] 1Pe 2:22*

[a] *15* Hebrew; Septuagint *so will many nations marvel at him* [b] *8* Or *From arrest* [c] *8* Or *away. / Yet who of his generation considered / that he was cut off from the land of the living / for the transgression of my people, / to whom the blow was due?*

[10]Yet it was the LORD's will[a] to crush[b] him and cause him
to suffer,[c]
and though the LORD makes[a] his life a guilt offering,
he will see his offspring[d] and prolong his days,
and the will of the LORD will prosper in his hand.
[11]After the suffering[e] of his soul,
he will see the light ⌊of life⌋[b] and be satisfied[c];
by his knowledge[d] my righteous servant will justify[f] many,
and he will bear their iniquities.
[12]Therefore I will give him a portion among the great,[e] [g]
and he will divide the spoils with the strong,[f]
because he poured out his life unto death,[h]
and was numbered with the transgressors.[i]
For he bore the sin of many,
and made intercession for the transgressors.

53:10 [a]Isa 46:10 [b]ver 5 [c]ver 3 [d]Ps 22:30
53:11 [e]Jn 10:14-18 [f]Ro 5:18-19
53:12 [g]Php 2:9 [h]Mt 26:28, 38,39,42 [i]Mk 15:27*; Lk 22:37*; 23:32

Chapter 54 Theme ______________________

54

"Sing, O barren woman,
you who never bore a child;
burst into song, shout for joy,
you who were never in labor;
because more are the children[j] of the desolate woman
than of her who has a husband,[k]"
says the LORD.

[2]"Enlarge the place of your tent,[l]
stretch your tent curtains wide,
do not hold back;
lengthen your cords,
strengthen your stakes.[m]
[3]For you will spread out to the right and to the left;
your descendants will dispossess nations
and settle in their desolate[n] cities.

[4]"Do not be afraid; you will not suffer shame.
Do not fear disgrace; you will not be humiliated.
You will forget the shame of your youth
and remember no more the reproach[o] of your
widowhood.
[5]For your Maker is your husband[p]—
the LORD Almighty is his name—
the Holy One of Israel is your Redeemer;[q]
he is called the God of all the earth.[r]

54:1 [j]Isa 49:20 [k]1Sa 2:5; Gal 4:27*
54:2 [l]Isa 49:19-20 [m]Ex 35:18; 39:40
54:3 [n]Isa 49:19
54:4 [o]Isa 51:7
54:5 [p]Jer 3:14 [q]Isa 48:17 [r]Isa 6:3

[a]*10* Hebrew *though you make* [b]*11* Dead Sea Scrolls (see also Septuagint); Masoretic Text does not have *the light ⌊of life⌋*. [c]*11* Or (with Masoretic Text) *[11]He will see the result of the suffering of his soul / and be satisfied* [d]*11* Or *by knowledge of him* [e]*12* Or *many* [f]*12* Or *numerous*

6 The LORD will call you back[a]
as if you were a wife deserted[b] and distressed in spirit—
a wife who married young,
only to be rejected," says your God.
7 "For a brief moment[c] I abandoned you,
but with deep compassion I will bring you back.[d]
8 In a surge of anger[e]
I hid my face from you for a moment,
but with everlasting kindness[f]
I will have compassion on you,"
says the LORD your Redeemer.

9 "To me this is like the days of Noah,
when I swore that the waters of Noah would never
again cover the earth.[g]
So now I have sworn not to be angry[h] with you,
never to rebuke you again.
10 Though the mountains be shaken[i]
and the hills be removed,
yet my unfailing love for you will not be shaken[j]
nor my covenant[k] of peace be removed,"
says the LORD, who has compassion[l] on you.

11 "O afflicted[m] city, lashed by storms[n] and not comforted,[o]
I will build you with stones of turquoise,[a][p]
your foundations[q] with sapphires.[b]
12 I will make your battlements of rubies,
your gates of sparkling jewels,
and all your walls of precious stones.
13 All your sons will be taught by the LORD,[r]
and great will be your children's peace.[s]
14 In righteousness you will be established:
Tyranny[t] will be far from you;
you will have nothing to fear.
Terror will be far removed;
it will not come near you.
15 If anyone does attack you, it will not be my doing;
whoever attacks you will surrender[u] to you.

16 "See, it is I who created the blacksmith
who fans the coals into flame
and forges a weapon fit for its work.
And it is I who have created the destroyer to work havoc;
17 no weapon forged against you will prevail,[v]
and you will refute[w] every tongue that accuses you.

54:6 [a] Isa 49:14-21 [b] Isa 50:1-2; 62:4,12
54:7 [c] Isa 26:20 [d] Isa 49:18
54:8 [e] Isa 60:10 [f] ver 10
54:9 [g] Ge 8:21 [h] Isa 12:1
54:10 [i] Ps 46:2 [j] Isa 51:6 [k] Ps 89:34 [l] ver 8
54:11 [m] Isa 14:32 [n] Isa 28:2; 29:6 [o] Isa 51:19 [p] 1Ch 29:2; Rev 21:18 [q] Isa 28:16; Rev 21:19-20
54:13 [r] Jn 6:45* [s] Isa 48:18
54:14 [t] Isa 9:4
54:15 [u] Isa 41:11-16
54:17 [v] Isa 29:8 [w] Isa 45:24-25

[a] *11* The meaning of the Hebrew for this word is uncertain. [b] *11* Or *lapis lazuli*

This is the heritage of the servants of the LORD,
and this is their vindication from me,"
declares the LORD.

Chapter 55 Theme

55

"Come, all you who are thirsty,[a]
come to the waters;
and you who have no money,
come, buy[b] and eat!
Come, buy wine and milk[c]
without money and without cost.[d]
2Why spend money on what is not bread,
and your labor on what does not satisfy?[e]
Listen, listen to me, and eat what is good,[f]
and your soul will delight in the richest of fare.
3Give ear and come to me;
hear me, that your soul may live.[g]
I will make an everlasting covenant[h] with you,
my faithful love[i] promised to David.[j]
4See, I have made him a witness to the peoples,
a leader and commander[k] of the peoples.
5Surely you will summon nations[l] you know not,
and nations that do not know you will hasten to you,
because of the LORD your God,
the Holy One of Israel,
for he has endowed you with splendor."[m]

6Seek the LORD while he may be found;[n]
call[o] on him while he is near.
7Let the wicked forsake his way
and the evil man his thoughts.[p]
Let him turn[q] to the LORD, and he will have mercy[r] on him,
and to our God, for he will freely pardon.[s]

8"For my thoughts are not your thoughts,
neither are your ways my ways,"[t]
declares the LORD.
9"As the heavens are higher than the earth,[u]
so are my ways higher than your ways
and my thoughts than your thoughts.
10As the rain[v] and the snow
come down from heaven,
and do not return to it
without watering the earth
and making it bud and flourish,
so that it yields seed for the sower and bread for
the eater,[w]

55:1
[a] Jn 4:14; 7:37
[b] La 5:4; Mt 13:44; Rev 3:18
[c] SS 5:1
[d] Hos 14:4; Mt 10:8; Rev 21:6

55:2
[e] Ps 22:26; Ecc 6:2; Hos 8:7
[f] Isa 1:19

55:3
[g] Lev 18:5; Ro 10:5
[h] Isa 61:8
[i] Isa 54:8
[j] Ac 13:34*

55:4
[k] Jer 30:9; Eze 34:23-24

55:5
[l] Isa 49:6
[m] Isa 60:9

55:6
[n] Ps 32:6; Isa 49:8; 2Co 6:1-2
[o] Isa 65:24

55:7
[p] Isa 32:7; 59:7
[q] Isa 44:22
[r] Isa 54:10
[s] Isa 1:18; 40:2

55:8
[t] Isa 53:6

55:9
[u] Ps 103:11

55:10
[v] Isa 30:23
[w] 2Co 9:10

55:11
[a] Isa 45:23
[b] Isa 44:26

11 so is my word that goes out from my mouth:
It will not return to me empty,[a]
but will accomplish what I desire
and achieve the purpose[b] for which I sent it.
12 You will go out in joy
and be led forth in peace;[c]
the mountains and hills
will burst into song before you,
and all the trees[d] of the field
will clap their hands.[e]

55:12
[c] Isa 54:10,13
[d] 1Ch 16:33
[e] Ps 98:8

13 Instead of the thornbush will grow the pine tree,
and instead of briers[f] the myrtle[g] will grow.
This will be for the LORD's renown,[h]
for an everlasting sign,
which will not be destroyed."

55:13
[f] Isa 5:6
[g] Isa 41:19
[h] Isa 63:12

Chapter 56 Theme ____________________

56

This is what the LORD says:
"Maintain justice[i]
and do what is right,
for my salvation[j] is close at hand
and my righteousness will soon be revealed.

56:1
[i] Isa 1:17
[j] Ps 85:9

2 Blessed[k] is the man who does this,
the man who holds it fast,
who keeps the Sabbath[l] without desecrating it,
and keeps his hand from doing any evil."

56:2
[k] Ps 119:2
[l] Ex 20:8,10; Isa 58:13

3 Let no foreigner who has bound himself to the LORD say,
"The LORD will surely exclude me from his people."
And let not any eunuch[m] complain,
"I am only a dry tree."

56:3
[m] Jer 38:7*fn*; Ac 8:27

4 For this is what the LORD says:

"To the eunuchs who keep my Sabbaths,
who choose what pleases me
and hold fast to my covenant—
5 to them I will give within my temple and its walls[n]
a memorial and a name
better than sons and daughters;
I will give them an everlasting name
that will not be cut off.[o]

56:5
[n] Isa 26:1; 60:18
[o] Isa 48:19; 55:13

6 And foreigners who bind themselves to the LORD
to serve[p] him,
to love the name of the LORD,
and to worship him,

56:6
[p] Isa 60:7,10; 61:5

all who keep the Sabbath[a] without desecrating it
and who hold fast to my covenant—
[7]these I will bring to my holy mountain[b]
and give them joy in my house of prayer.
Their burnt offerings and sacrifices[c]
will be accepted on my altar;
for my house will be called
a house of prayer for all nations.[d]"[e]
[8]The Sovereign LORD declares—
he who gathers the exiles of Israel:
"I will gather[f] still others to them
besides those already gathered."

[9]Come, all you beasts of the field,[g]
come and devour, all you beasts of the forest!
[10]Israel's watchmen[h] are blind,
they all lack knowledge;
they are all mute dogs,
they cannot bark;
they lie around and dream,
they love to sleep.[i]
[11]They are dogs with mighty appetites;
they never have enough.
They are shepherds[j] who lack understanding;[k]
they all turn to their own way,
each seeks his own gain.[l]
[12]"Come," each one cries, "let me get wine!
Let us drink our fill of beer!
And tomorrow will be like today,
or even far better."[m]

Chapter 57 Theme ______________________

57 The righteous perish,[n]
and no one ponders it in his heart;[o]
devout men are taken away,
and no one understands
that the righteous are taken away
to be spared from evil.[p]
[2]Those who walk uprightly[q]
enter into peace;
they find rest as they lie in death.

[3]"But you—come here, you sons of a sorceress,
you offspring of adulterers[r] and prostitutes![s]
[4]Whom are you mocking?
At whom do you sneer
and stick out your tongue?

56:6 [a]ver 2,4
56:7 [b]Isa 2:2 [c]Ro 12:1; Heb 13:15 [d]Mt 21:13*; Lk 19:46* [e]Mk 11:17*
56:8 [f]Isa 11:12; 60:3-11; Jn 10:16
56:9 [g]Isa 18:6; Jer 12:9
56:10 [h]Eze 3:17 [i]Na 3:18
56:11 [j]Eze 34:2 [k]Isa 1:3 [l]Isa 57:17; Eze 13:19; Mic 3:11
56:12 [m]Ps 10:6; Lk 12:18-19
57:1 [n]Ps 12:1 [o]Isa 42:25 [p]2Ki 22:20
57:2 [q]Isa 26:7
57:3 [r]Mt 16:4 [s]Isa 1:21

Are you not a brood of rebels,
the offspring of liars?
5You burn with lust among the oaks
and under every spreading tree;[a]
you sacrifice your children[b] in the ravines
and under the overhanging crags.
6⌊The idols⌋[c] among the smooth stones of the ravines
are your portion;
they, they are your lot.
Yes, to them you have poured out drink offerings[d]
and offered grain offerings.
In the light of these things, should I relent?[e]
7You have made your bed on a high and lofty hill;[f]
there you went up to offer your sacrifices.
8Behind your doors and your doorposts
you have put your pagan symbols.
Forsaking me, you uncovered your bed,
you climbed into it and opened it wide;
you made a pact with those whose beds you love,[g]
and you looked on their nakedness.[h]
9You went to Molech[a] with olive oil
and increased your perfumes.
You sent your ambassadors[b][i] far away;
you descended to the grave[c] itself!
10You were wearied by all your ways,
but you would not say, 'It is hopeless.'[j]
You found renewal of your strength,
and so you did not faint.

11"Whom have you so dreaded and feared[k]
that you have been false to me,
and have neither remembered[l] me
nor pondered this in your hearts?
Is it not because I have long been silent[m]
that you do not fear me?
12I will expose your righteousness and your works,[n]
and they will not benefit you.
13When you cry out[o] for help,
let your collection ⌊of idols⌋ save you!
The wind will carry all of them off,
a mere breath will blow them away.
But the man who makes me his refuge
will inherit the land[p]
and possess my holy mountain."[q]

57:5 [a] 2Ki 16:4 [b] Lev 18:21; Ps 106:37-38; Eze 16:20
57:6 [c] Jer 3:9 [d] Jer 7:18 [e] Jer 5:9,29; 9:9
57:7 [f] Jer 3:6; Eze 16:16
57:8 [g] Eze 16:26; 23:7 [h] Eze 23:18
57:9 [i] Eze 23:16,40
57:10 [j] Jer 2:25; 18:12
57:11 [k] Pr 29:25 [l] Jer 2:32; 3:21 [m] Ps 50:21
57:12 [n] Isa 29:15; Mic 3:2-4,8
57:13 [o] Jer 22:20; 30:15 [p] Ps 37:9 [q] Isa 65:9-11

[a] 9 Or *to the king* [b] 9 Or *idols* [c] 9 Hebrew *Sheol*

14And it will be said:

"Build up, build up, prepare the road!
Remove the obstacles out of the way of my people."[a]
15For this is what the high and lofty[b] One says—
he who lives forever,[c] whose name is holy:
"I live in a high and holy place,
but also with him who is contrite[d] and lowly in spirit,[e]
to revive the spirit of the lowly
and to revive the heart of the contrite.[f]
16I will not accuse forever,
nor will I always be angry,[g]
for then the spirit of man would grow faint before me—
the breath of man that I have created.
17I was enraged by his sinful greed;[h]
I punished him, and hid my face in anger,
yet he kept on in his willful ways.[i]
18I have seen his ways, but I will heal[j] him;
I will guide him and restore comfort[k] to him,
19 creating praise on the lips[l] of the mourners in Israel.
Peace, peace,[m] to those far and near,"[n]
says the LORD. "And I will heal them."
20But the wicked[o] are like the tossing sea,
which cannot rest,
whose waves cast up mire and mud.
21"There is no peace,"[p] says my God, "for the wicked."[q]

Chapter 58 Theme ______________________

58

"Shout it aloud,[r] do not hold back.
Raise your voice like a trumpet.
Declare to my people their rebellion[s]
and to the house of Jacob their sins.
2For day after day they seek[t] me out;
they seem eager to know my ways,
as if they were a nation that does what is right
and has not forsaken the commands of its God.
They ask me for just decisions
and seem eager for God to come near[u] them.
3'Why have we fasted,'[v] they say,
'and you have not seen it?
Why have we humbled ourselves,
and you have not noticed?'[w]

"Yet on the day of your fasting, you do as you please[x]
and exploit all your workers.
4Your fasting ends in quarreling and strife,[y]
and in striking each other with wicked fists.

57:14 [a]Isa 62:10; Jer 18:15
57:15 [b]Isa 52:13 [c]Dt 33:27 [d]Ps 147:3 [e]Ps 34:18; 51:17; Isa 66:2 [f]Isa 61:1
57:16 [g]Ps 85:5; 103:9; Mic 7:18
57:17 [h]Isa 56:11 [i]Isa 1:4
57:18 [j]Isa 30:26 [k]Isa 61:1-3
57:19 [l]Isa 6:7; Heb 13:15 [m]Eph 2:17 [n]Ac 2:39
57:20 [o]Job 18:5-21
57:21 [p]Isa 59:8 [q]Isa 48:22
58:1 [r]Isa 40:6 [s]Isa 48:8
58:2 [t]Isa 48:1; Tit 1:16; Jas 4:8 [u]Isa 29:13
58:3 [v]Lev 16:29 [w]Mal 3:14 [x]Isa 22:13; Zec 7:5-6
58:4 [y]1Ki 21:9-13; Isa 59:6

You cannot fast as you do today
and expect your voice to be heard[a] on high.
5 Is this the kind of fast[b] I have chosen,
only a day for a man to humble[c] himself?
Is it only for bowing one's head like a reed
and for lying on sackcloth and ashes?[d]
Is that what you call a fast,
a day acceptable to the LORD?

6 "Is not this the kind of fasting I have chosen:
to loose the chains of injustice[e]
and untie the cords of the yoke,
to set the oppressed[f] free
and break every yoke?
7 Is it not to share your food with the hungry[g]
and to provide the poor wanderer with shelter[h]—
when you see the naked, to clothe[i] him,
and not to turn away from your own flesh and blood?[j]
8 Then your light will break forth like the dawn,[k]
and your healing[l] will quickly appear;
then your righteousness[a] will go before you,
and the glory of the LORD will be your rear guard.[m]
9 Then you will call,[n] and the LORD will answer;
you will cry for help, and he will say: Here am I.

"If you do away with the yoke of oppression,
with the pointing finger[o] and malicious talk,[p]
10 and if you spend yourselves in behalf of the hungry
and satisfy the needs of the oppressed,[q]
then your light[r] will rise in the darkness,
and your night will become like the noonday.[s]
11 The LORD will guide you always;
he will satisfy your needs[t] in a sun-scorched land
and will strengthen your frame.
You will be like a well-watered garden,[u]
like a spring[v] whose waters never fail.
12 Your people will rebuild the ancient ruins[w]
and will raise up the age-old foundations;[x]
you will be called Repairer of Broken Walls,
Restorer of Streets with Dwellings.

13 "If you keep your feet from breaking the Sabbath[y]
and from doing as you please on my holy day,
if you call the Sabbath a delight[z]
and the LORD's holy day honorable,

58:4 [a] Isa 59:2
58:5 [b] Zec 7:5 [c] 1Ki 21:27 [d] Job 2:8
58:6 [e] Ne 5:10-11 [f] Jer 34:9
58:7 [g] Eze 18:16; Lk 3:11 [h] Isa 16:4; Heb 13:2 [i] Job 31:19-20; Mt 25:36 [j] Ge 29:14; Lk 10:31-32
58:8 [k] Job 11:17 [l] Isa 30:26 [m] Ex 14:19
58:9 [n] Ps 50:15 [o] Pr 6:13 [p] Ps 12:2; Isa 59:13
58:10 [q] Dt 15:7-8 [r] Isa 42:16 [s] Job 11:17
58:11 [t] Ps 107:9 [u] SS 4:15 [v] Jn 4:14
58:12 [w] Isa 49:8 [x] Isa 44:28
58:13 [y] Isa 56:2 [z] Ps 84:2,10

a 8 Or *your righteous One*

and if you honor it by not going your own way
and not doing as you please or speaking idle words,
14then you will find your joy[a] in the LORD,
and I will cause you to ride on the heights[b] of the land
and to feast on the inheritance of your father Jacob."
The mouth of the LORD has spoken.[c]

Chapter 59 Theme ____________________

59 Surely the arm of the LORD is not too short[d] to save,
nor his ear too dull to hear.[e]
2But your iniquities have separated
you from your God;
your sins have hidden his face from you,
so that he will not hear.[f]
3For your hands are stained with blood,[g]
your fingers with guilt.
Your lips have spoken lies,
and your tongue mutters wicked things.
4No one calls for justice;
no one pleads his case with integrity.
They rely on empty arguments and speak lies;
they conceive trouble and give birth to evil.[h]
5They hatch the eggs of vipers
and spin a spider's web.[i]
Whoever eats their eggs will die,
and when one is broken, an adder is hatched.
6Their cobwebs are useless for clothing;
they cannot cover themselves with what they make.[j]
Their deeds are evil deeds,
and acts of violence[k] are in their hands.
7Their feet rush into sin;
they are swift to shed innocent blood.[l]
Their thoughts are evil thoughts;[m]
ruin and destruction mark their ways.[n]
8The way of peace they do not know;
there is no justice in their paths.
They have turned them into crooked roads;
no one who walks in them will know peace.[o]

9So justice is far from us,
and righteousness does not reach us.
We look for light, but all is darkness;[p]
for brightness, but we walk in deep shadows.
10Like the blind[q] we grope along the wall,
feeling our way like men without eyes.
At midday we stumble[r] as if it were twilight;
among the strong, we are like the dead.[s]

58:14 [a]Job 22:26 [b]Dt 32:13 [c]Isa 1:20
59:1 [d]Nu 11:23; Isa 50:2 [e]Isa 58:9; 65:24
59:2 [f]Isa 1:15; 58:4
59:3 [g]Isa 1:15
59:4 [h]Job 15:35; Ps 7:14
59:5 [i]Job 8:14
59:6 [j]Isa 28:20 [k]Isa 58:4
59:7 [l]Pr 6:17 [m]Mk 7:21-22 [n]Ro 3:15-17*
59:8 [o]Isa 57:21; Lk 1:79
59:9 [p]Isa 5:30; 8:20
59:10 [q]Dt 28:29 [r]Isa 8:15 [s]La 3:6

59:11
[a] Isa 38:14; Eze 7:16

11 We all growl like bears;
we moan mournfully like doves.[a]
We look for justice, but find none;
for deliverance, but it is far away.

59:12
[b] Ezr 9:6
[c] Isa 3:9

12 For our offenses[b] are many in your sight,
and our sins testify[c] against us.
Our offenses are ever with us,
and we acknowledge our iniquities:
13 rebellion and treachery against the LORD,
turning our backs[d] on our God,

59:13
[d] Pr 30:9; Mt 10:33; Tit 1:16
[e] Isa 5:7
[f] Mk 7:21-22

fomenting oppression[e] and revolt,
uttering lies[f] our hearts have conceived.
14 So justice is driven back,
and righteousness[g] stands at a distance;
truth[h] has stumbled in the streets,
honesty cannot enter.
15 Truth is nowhere to be found,
and whoever shuns evil becomes a prey.

59:14
[g] Isa 1:21
[h] Isa 48:1

The LORD looked and was displeased
that there was no justice.
16 He saw that there was no one,[i]
he was appalled that there was no one to intervene;
so his own arm worked salvation[j] for him,
and his own righteousness sustained him.

59:16
[i] Isa 41:28
[j] Ps 98:1; Isa 63:5

17 He put on righteousness as his breastplate,[k]
and the helmet[l] of salvation on his head;
he put on the garments[m] of vengeance
and wrapped himself in zeal[n] as in a cloak.

59:17
[k] Eph 6:14
[l] Eph 6:17; 1Th 5:8
[m] Isa 63:3
[n] Isa 9:7

18 According to what they have done,
so will he repay
wrath to his enemies
and retribution to his foes;
he will repay the islands their due.
19 From the west,[o] men will fear the name of the LORD,
and from the rising of the sun,[p] they will revere
his glory.

59:19
[o] Isa 49:12
[p] Ps 113:3

For he will come like a pent-up flood
that the breath of the LORD drives along.[a]

20 "The Redeemer will come to Zion,
to those in Jacob who repent of their sins,"[q]
declares the LORD.

59:20
[q] Ac 2:38-39; Ro 11:26-27*

21 "As for me, this is my covenant with them," says the LORD.
"My Spirit,[r] who is on you, and my words that I have put in your

59:21
[r] Isa 11:2; 44:3

[a] 19 Or *When the enemy comes in like a flood, / the Spirit of the LORD will put him to flight*

mouth will not depart from your mouth, or from the mouths of your children, or from the mouths of their descendants from this time on and forever," says the LORD.

Chapter 60 Theme ____________________

60 "Arise,[a] shine, for your light[b] has come,
and the glory of the LORD rises upon you.
2See, darkness covers the earth
and thick darkness[c] is over the peoples,
but the LORD rises upon you
and his glory appears over you.
3Nations[d] will come to your light,
and kings[e] to the brightness of your dawn.

4"Lift up your eyes and look about you:
All assemble[f] and come to you;
your sons come from afar,
and your daughters[g] are carried on the arm.[h]
5Then you will look and be radiant,
your heart will throb and swell with joy;
the wealth on the seas will be brought to you,
to you the riches of the nations will come.
6Herds of camels will cover your land,
young camels of Midian[i] and Ephah.[j]
And all from Sheba[k] will come,
bearing gold and incense[l]
and proclaiming the praise[m] of the LORD.
7All Kedar's[n] flocks will be gathered to you,
the rams of Nebaioth will serve you;
they will be accepted as offerings on my altar,
and I will adorn my glorious temple.[o]

8"Who are these[p] that fly along like clouds,
like doves to their nests?
9Surely the islands[q] look to me;
in the lead are the ships of Tarshish,[a][r]
bringing[s] your sons from afar,
with their silver and gold,
to the honor of the LORD your God,
the Holy One of Israel,
for he has endowed you with splendor.[t]

10"Foreigners[u] will rebuild your walls,
and their kings[v] will serve you.

[a]9 Or *the trading ships*

60:1 [a]Isa 52:2 [b]Eph 5:14
60:2 [c]Jer 13:16; Col 1:13
60:3 [d]Isa 45:14; Rev 21:24 [e]Isa 49:23
60:4 [f]Isa 11:12 [g]Isa 43:6 [h]Isa 49:20-22
60:6 [i]Ge 25:2 [j]Ge 25:4 [k]Ps 72:10 [l]Isa 43:23; Mt 2:11 [m]Isa 42:10
60:7 [n]Ge 25:13 [o]ver 13; Hag 2:3,7,9
60:8 [p]Isa 49:21
60:9 [q]Isa 11:11 [r]Isa 2:16*fn* [s]Isa 14:2; 43:6 [t]Isa 55:5
60:10 [u]Isa 14:1-2 [v]Isa 49:23; Rev 21:24

Though in anger I struck you,
in favor I will show you compassion.[a]
11Your gates[b] will always stand open,
they will never be shut, day or night,
so that men may bring you the wealth of the nations[c]—
their kings[d] led in triumphal procession.
12For the nation or kingdom that will not serve[e] you
will perish;
it will be utterly ruined.

13"The glory of Lebanon[f] will come to you,
the pine, the fir and the cypress together,[g]
to adorn the place of my sanctuary;
and I will glorify the place of my feet.[h]
14The sons of your oppressors[i] will come bowing
before you;
all who despise you will bow down[j] at your feet
and will call you the City of the LORD,
Zion[k] of the Holy One of Israel.

15"Although you have been forsaken[l] and hated,
with no one traveling[m] through,
I will make you the everlasting pride[n]
and the joy[o] of all generations.
16You will drink the milk of nations
and be nursed[p] at royal breasts.
Then you will know that I, the LORD, am your Savior,
your Redeemer,[q] the Mighty One of Jacob.
17Instead of bronze I will bring you gold,
and silver in place of iron.
Instead of wood I will bring you bronze,
and iron in place of stones.
I will make peace your governor
and righteousness your ruler.
18No longer will violence be heard in your land,
nor ruin or destruction within your borders,
but you will call your walls Salvation[r]
and your gates Praise.
19The sun will no more be your light by day,
nor will the brightness of the moon shine on you,
for the LORD will be your everlasting light,[s]
and your God will be your glory.[t]
20Your sun[u] will never set again,
and your moon will wane no more;
the LORD will be your everlasting light,
and your days of sorrow[v] will end.

60:10
[a] Isa 54:8

60:11
[b] ver 18; Isa 62:10; Rev 21:25
[c] ver 5; Rev 21:26
[d] Ps 149:8

60:12
[e] Isa 14:2

60:13
[f] Isa 35:2
[g] Isa 41:19
[h] 1Ch 28:2; Ps 132:7

60:14
[i] Isa 14:2
[j] Isa 49:23; Rev 3:9
[k] Heb 12:22

60:15
[l] Isa 1:7-9; 6:12
[m] Isa 33:8
[n] Isa 4:2
[o] Isa 65:18

60:16
[p] Isa 49:23; 66:11,12
[q] Isa 59:20

60:18
[r] Isa 26:1

60:19
[s] Rev 22:5
[t] Zec 2:5; Rev 21:23

60:20
[u] Isa 30:26
[v] Isa 35:10

[21]Then will all your people be righteous[a]
and they will possess[b] the land forever.
They are the shoot I have planted,[c]
the work of my hands,[d]
for the display of my splendor.[e]
[22]The least of you will become a thousand,
the smallest a mighty nation.
I am the LORD;
in its time I will do this swiftly."

60:21
[a]Rev 21:27
[b]Ps 37:11,22; Isa 57:13; 61:7
[c]Mt 15:13
[d]Isa 19:25; 29:23; Eph 2:10
[e]Isa 52:1

Chapter 61 Theme ______________________

61

The Spirit[f] of the Sovereign LORD is on me,
because the LORD has anointed[g] me
to preach good news to the poor.[h]
He has sent me to bind up[i] the brokenhearted,
to proclaim freedom for the captives[j]
and release from darkness for the prisoners,[a]
[2]to proclaim the year of the LORD's favor[k]
and the day of vengeance[l] of our God,
to comfort[m] all who mourn,
[3] and provide for those who grieve in Zion—
to bestow on them a crown of beauty
instead of ashes,
the oil of gladness
instead of mourning,
and a garment of praise
instead of a spirit of despair.
They will be called oaks of righteousness,
a planting of the LORD
for the display of his splendor.[n]

[4]They will rebuild the ancient ruins[o]
and restore the places long devastated;
they will renew the ruined cities
that have been devastated for generations.
[5]Aliens[p] will shepherd your flocks;
foreigners will work your fields and vineyards.
[6]And you will be called priests[q] of the LORD,
you will be named ministers of our God.
You will feed on the wealth[r] of nations,
and in their riches you will boast.

[7]Instead of their shame
my people will receive a double[s] portion,

61:1
[f]Isa 11:2
[g]Ps 45:7
[h]Mt 11:5; Lk 7:22
[i]Isa 57:15
[j]Isa 42:7; 49:9

61:2
[k]Isa 49:8; Lk 4:18-19*
[l]Isa 34:8
[m]Isa 57:18; Mt 5:4

61:3
[n]Isa 60:20-21

61:4
[o]Isa 49:8; Eze 36:33; Am 9:14

61:5
[p]Isa 14:1-2

61:6
[q]Ex 19:6; 1Pe 2:5
[r]Isa 60:11

61:7
[s]Isa 40:2; Zec 9:12

[a]*1* Hebrew; Septuagint *the blind*

61:8 [a]Ps 11:7; Isa 5:16 [b]Isa 55:3
61:10 [c]Isa 25:9; Hab 3:18 [d]Ps 132:9; Isa 52:1 [e]Isa 49:18; Rev 21:2
61:11 [f]Ps 85:11
62:1 [g]Isa 1:26
62:2 [h]Isa 52:10; 60:3 [i]ver 4,12
62:3 [j]Isa 28:5; Zec 9:16; 1Th 2:19
62:4 [k]Isa 54:6 [l]Jer 32:41; Zep 3:17 [m]Jer 3:14; Hos 2:19

and instead of disgrace
  they will rejoice in their inheritance;
and so they will inherit a double portion in their land,
  and everlasting joy will be theirs.

8 “For I, the LORD, love justice;[a]
  I hate robbery and iniquity.
In my faithfulness I will reward them
  and make an everlasting covenant[b] with them.
9 Their descendants will be known among the nations
  and their offspring among the peoples.
All who see them will acknowledge
  that they are a people the LORD has blessed.”

10 I delight greatly in the LORD;
  my soul rejoices[c] in my God.
For he has clothed me with garments of salvation
  and arrayed me in a robe of righteousness,[d]
as a bridegroom adorns his head like a priest,
  and as a bride[e] adorns herself with her jewels.
11 For as the soil makes the sprout come up
  and a garden causes seeds to grow,
so the Sovereign LORD will make righteousness[f]
    and praise
  spring up before all nations.

Chapter 62 Theme ____________________

62 For Zion's sake I will not keep silent,
  for Jerusalem's sake I will not remain quiet,
till her righteousness[g] shines out like the dawn,
  her salvation like a blazing torch.
2 The nations[h] will see your righteousness,
  and all kings your glory;
you will be called by a new name[i]
  that the mouth of the LORD will bestow.
3 You will be a crown[j] of splendor in the LORD's hand,
  a royal diadem in the hand of your God.
4 No longer will they call you Deserted,[k]
  or name your land Desolate.
But you will be called Hephzibah,[a]
  and your land Beulah[b];
for the LORD will take delight[l] in you,
  and your land will be married.[m]
5 As a young man marries a maiden,
  so will your sons[c] marry you;

[a]4 *Hephzibah* means *my delight is in her.* [b]4 *Beulah* means *married.* [c]5 Or *Builder*

as a bridegroom rejoices over his bride,
so will your God rejoice[a] over you.

6I have posted watchmen[b] on your walls, O Jerusalem;
they will never be silent day or night.
You who call on the LORD,
give yourselves no rest,
7and give him no rest[c] till he establishes Jerusalem
and makes her the praise of the earth.

8The LORD has sworn by his right hand
and by his mighty arm:
"Never again will I give your grain[d]
as food for your enemies,
and never again will foreigners drink the new wine
for which you have toiled;
9but those who harvest it will eat it
and praise the LORD,
and those who gather the grapes will drink it
in the courts of my sanctuary."

10Pass through, pass through the gates![e]
Prepare the way for the people.
Build up, build up the highway![f g]
Remove the stones.
Raise a banner[h] for the nations.

11The LORD has made proclamation
to the ends of the earth:
"Say to the Daughter of Zion,[i]
'See, your Savior comes![j]
See, his reward is with him,
and his recompense accompanies him.' "[k]
12They will be called[l] the Holy People,[m]
the Redeemed[n] of the LORD;
and you will be called Sought After,
the City No Longer Deserted.[o]

Chapter 63 Theme ______________________

63 Who is this coming from Edom,
from Bozrah,[p] with his garments stained crimson?
Who is this, robed in splendor,
striding forward in the greatness of his strength?

"It is I, speaking in righteousness,
mighty to save."[q]

2Why are your garments red,
like those of one treading the winepress?

62:5 [a]Isa 65:19
62:6 [b]Isa 52:8; Eze 3:17
62:7 [c]Mt 15:21-28; Lk 18:1-8
62:8 [d]Dt 28:30-33; Isa 1:7; Jer 5:17
62:10 [e]Isa 60:11 [f]Isa 57:14 [g]Isa 11:16 [h]Isa 11:10
62:11 [i]Zec 9:9; Mt 21:5 [j]Rev 22:12 [k]Isa 40:10
62:12 [l]ver 4 [m]1Pe 2:9 [n]Isa 35:9 [o]Isa 42:16
63:1 [p]Am 1:12 [q]Zep 3:17

3 “I have trodden the winepress[a] alone;
from the nations no one was with me.
I trampled them in my anger
and trod them down in my wrath;[b]
their blood spattered my garments,[c]
and I stained all my clothing.
4 For the day of vengeance was in my heart,
and the year of my redemption has come.
5 I looked, but there was no one[d] to help,
I was appalled that no one gave support;
so my own arm[e] worked salvation for me,
and my own wrath sustained me.[f]
6 I trampled the nations in my anger;
in my wrath I made them drunk[g]
and poured their blood[h] on the ground.”

7 I will tell of the kindnesses[i] of the LORD,
the deeds for which he is to be praised,
according to all the LORD has done for us—
yes, the many good things he has done
for the house of Israel,
according to his compassion[j] and many kindnesses.
8 He said, “Surely they are my people,[k]
sons who will not be false to me”;
and so he became their Savior.
9 In all their distress he too was distressed,
and the angel of his presence[l] saved them.
In his love and mercy he redeemed[m] them;
he lifted them up and carried[n] them
all the days of old.
10 Yet they rebelled[o]
and grieved his Holy Spirit.[p]
So he turned and became their enemy[q]
and he himself fought against them.
11 Then his people recalled[a] the days of old,
the days of Moses and his people—
where is he who brought them through the sea,[r]
with the shepherd of his flock?
Where is he who set
his Holy Spirit[s] among them,
12 who sent his glorious arm of power
to be at Moses’ right hand,
who divided the waters[t] before them,
to gain for himself everlasting renown,

63:3 [a] Rev 14:20; 19:15 [b] Isa 22:5 [c] Rev 19:13
63:5 [d] Isa 41:28 [e] Ps 44:3; 98:1 [f] Isa 59:16
63:6 [g] Isa 29:9 [h] Isa 34:3
63:7 [i] Isa 54:8 [j] Ps 51:1; Eph 2:4
63:8 [k] Isa 51:4
63:9 [l] Ex 33:14 [m] Dt 7:7-8 [n] Dt 1:31
63:10 [o] Ps 78:40 [p] Ps 51:11; Ac 7:51; Eph 4:30 [q] Ps 106:40
63:11 [r] Ex 14:22,30 [s] Nu 11:17
63:12 [t] Ex 14:21-22; Isa 11:15

a *11* Or *But may he recall*

13who led[a] them through the depths?
Like a horse in open country,
they did not stumble;[b]
14like cattle that go down to the plain,
they were given rest by the Spirit of the LORD.
This is how you guided your people
to make for yourself a glorious name.

15Look down from heaven[c] and see
from your lofty throne,[d] holy and glorious.
Where are your zeal[e] and your might?
Your tenderness and compassion[f] are withheld from us.
16But you are our Father,
though Abraham does not know us
or Israel acknowledge[g] us;
you, O LORD, are our Father,
our Redeemer[h] from of old is your name.
17Why, O LORD, do you make us wander from your ways
and harden our hearts so we do not revere[i] you?
Return[j] for the sake of your servants,
the tribes that are your inheritance.
18For a little while your people possessed your holy place,
but now our enemies have trampled down your
sanctuary.[k]
19We are yours from of old;
but you have not ruled over them,
they have not been called by your name.[a]

Chapter 64 Theme

64 Oh, that you would rend the heavens[l] and come down,[m]
that the mountains[n] would tremble before you!
2As when fire sets twigs ablaze
and causes water to boil,
come down to make your name known to your enemies
and cause the nations to quake[o] before you!
3For when you did awesome[p] things that we
did not expect,
you came down, and the mountains trembled
before you.
4Since ancient times no one has heard,
no ear has perceived,
no eye has seen any God besides you,
who acts on behalf of those who wait for him.[q]
5You come to the help of those who gladly do right,[r]
who remember your ways.

a 19 Or *We are like those you have never ruled, / like those never called by your name*

63:13
a Dt 32:12
b Jer 31:9

63:15
c Dt 26:15; Ps 80:14
d Ps 123:1
e Isa 9:7; 26:11
f Jer 31:20; Hos 11:8

63:16
g Job 14:21
h Isa 41:14; 44:6

63:17
i Isa 29:13
j Nu 10:36

63:18
k Ps 74:3-8

64:1
l Ps 18:9; 144:5
m Mic 1:3
n Ex 19:18

64:2
o Ps 99:1; Jer 5:22; 33:9

64:3
p Ps 65:5

64:4
q Isa 30:18; 1Co 2:9*

64:5
r Isa 26:8

But when we continued to sin against them,
you were angry.
How then can we be saved?
6 All of us have become like one who is unclean,
and all our righteous[a] acts are like filthy rags;
we all shrivel up like a leaf,[b]
and like the wind our sins sweep us away.
7 No one[c] calls on your name
or strives to lay hold of you;
for you have hidden[d] your face from us
and made us waste away[e] because of our sins.
8 Yet, O LORD, you are our Father.[f]
We are the clay, you are the potter;[g]
we are all the work of your hand.
9 Do not be angry[h] beyond measure, O LORD;
do not remember our sins[i] forever.
Oh, look upon us, we pray,
for we are all your people.
10 Your sacred cities have become a desert;
even Zion is a desert, Jerusalem a desolation.
11 Our holy and glorious temple,[j] where our fathers
praised you,
has been burned with fire,
and all that we treasured[k] lies in ruins.
12 After all this, O LORD, will you hold yourself back?[l]
Will you keep silent[m] and punish us beyond measure?

Chapter 65 Theme ________________________

65 "I revealed myself to those who did not ask for me;
I was found by those who did not seek me.[n]
To a nation[o] that did not call on my name,
I said, 'Here am I, here am I.'
2 All day long I have held out my hands
to an obstinate people,[p]
who walk in ways not good,
pursuing their own imaginations[q]—
3 a people who continually provoke me
to my very face,[r]
offering sacrifices in gardens[s]
and burning incense on altars of brick;
4 who sit among the graves
and spend their nights keeping secret vigil;
who eat the flesh of pigs,[t]
and whose pots hold broth of unclean meat;
5 who say, 'Keep away; don't come near me,
for I am too sacred[u] for you!'

64:6 [a] Isa 46:12; 48:1 [b] Ps 90:5-6
64:7 [c] Isa 59:4 [d] Dt 31:18; Isa 1:15; 54:8 [e] Isa 9:18
64:8 [f] Isa 63:16 [g] Isa 29:16
64:9 [h] Isa 57:17; 60:10 [i] Isa 43:25
64:11 [j] Ps 74:3-7 [k] La 1:7,10
64:12 [l] Ps 74:10-11; Isa 42:14 [m] Ps 83:1
65:1 [n] Hos 1:10; Ro 9:24-26; 10:20* [o] Eph 2:12
65:2 [p] Isa 1:2,23; Ro 10:21* [q] Ps 81:11-12; Isa 66:18
65:3 [r] Job 1:11 [s] Isa 1:29
65:4 [t] Lev 11:7
65:5 [u] Mt 9:11; Lk 7:39; 18:9-12

Such people are smoke in my nostrils,
a fire that keeps burning all day.

6"See, it stands written before me:
I will not keep silent[a] but will pay back[b] in full;
I will pay it back into their laps[c]—
7both your sins[d] and the sins of your fathers,"[e]
says the LORD.
"Because they burned sacrifices on the mountains
and defied me on the hills,[f]
I will measure into their laps
the full payment for their former deeds."

8This is what the LORD says:

"As when juice is still found in a cluster of grapes
and men say, 'Don't destroy it,
there is yet some good in it,'
so will I do in behalf of my servants;
I will not destroy them all.
9I will bring forth descendants[g] from Jacob,
and from Judah those who will possess[h] my mountains;
my chosen people will inherit them,
and there will my servants live.[i]
10Sharon[j] will become a pasture for flocks,
and the Valley of Achor[k] a resting place for herds,
for my people who seek[l] me.
11"But as for you who forsake[m] the LORD
and forget my holy mountain,
who spread a table for Fortune
and fill bowls of mixed wine for Destiny,
12I will destine you for the sword,[n]
and you will all bend down for the slaughter;
for I called but you did not answer,[o]
I spoke but you did not listen.[p]
You did evil in my sight
and chose what displeases me."

13Therefore this is what the Sovereign LORD says:

"My servants will eat,[q]
but you will go hungry;
my servants will drink,
but you will go thirsty;[r]
my servants will rejoice,
but you will be put to shame.[s]
14My servants will sing
out of the joy of their hearts,

65:6
[a] Ps 50:3
[b] Jer 16:18
[c] Ps 79:12

65:7
[d] Isa 22:14
[e] Ex 20:5
[f] Isa 57:7

65:9
[g] Isa 45:19
[h] Am 9:11-15
[i] Isa 32:18

65:10
[j] Isa 35:2
[k] Jos 7:26
[l] Isa 51:1

65:11
[m] Dt 29:24-25; Isa 1:28

65:12
[n] Isa 27:1
[o] Pr 1:24-25; Isa 41:28; 66:4
[p] 2Ch 36:15-16; Jer 7:13

65:13
[q] Isa 1:19
[r] Isa 41:17
[s] Isa 44:9

but you will cry out[a]
from anguish of heart
and wail in brokenness of spirit.
15You will leave your name
to my chosen ones as a curse;[b]
the Sovereign LORD will put you to death,
but to his servants he will give another name.
16Whoever invokes a blessing in the land
will do so by the God of truth;[c]
he who takes an oath in the land
will swear[d] by the God of truth.
For the past troubles will be forgotten
and hidden from my eyes.

17"Behold, I will create
new heavens and a new earth.[e]
The former things will not be remembered,[f]
nor will they come to mind.
18But be glad and rejoice[g] forever
in what I will create,
for I will create Jerusalem to be a delight
and its people a joy.
19I will rejoice[h] over Jerusalem
and take delight in my people;
the sound of weeping and of crying[i]
will be heard in it no more.

20"Never again will there be in it
an infant who lives but a few days,
or an old man who does not live out his years;[j]
he who dies at a hundred
will be thought a mere youth;
he who fails to reach[a] a hundred
will be considered accursed.
21They will build houses[k] and dwell in them;
they will plant vineyards and eat their fruit.[l]
22No longer will they build houses and others live in them,
or plant and others eat.
For as the days of a tree,[m]
so will be the days[n] of my people;
my chosen ones will long enjoy
the works of their hands.
23They will not toil in vain
or bear children doomed to misfortune;
for they will be a people blessed[o] by the LORD,
they and their descendants[p] with them.

65:14 [a]Mt 8:12; Lk 13:28
65:15 [b]Zec 8:13
65:16 [c]Ps 31:5 [d]Isa 19:18
65:17 [e]Isa 66:22; 2Pe 3:13 [f]Isa 43:18; Jer 3:16
65:18 [g]Ps 98:1-9; Isa 25:9
65:19 [h]Isa 35:10; 62:5 [i]Isa 25:8; Rev 7:17
65:20 [j]Ecc 8:13
65:21 [k]Isa 32:18 [l]Isa 37:30; Am 9:14
65:22 [m]Ps 92:12-14 [n]Ps 21:4; 91:16
65:23 [o]Dt 28:3-12; Isa 61:9 [p]Ac 2:39

a *20* Or / *the sinner who reaches*

[24]Before they call[a] I will answer;
while they are still speaking[b] I will hear.
[25]The wolf and the lamb[c] will feed together,
and the lion will eat straw like the ox,
but dust will be the serpent's[d] food.
They will neither harm nor destroy
on all my holy mountain,"
says the LORD.

65:24
[a]Isa 55:6
[b]Da 9:20-23; 10:12

65:25
[c]Isa 11:6
[d]Ge 3:14; Mic 7:17

Chapter 66 Theme ______________________

66

This is what the LORD says:

"Heaven is my throne,[e]
and the earth is my footstool.[f]
Where is the house[g] you will build for me?
Where will my resting place be?
[2]Has not my hand made all these things,[h]
and so they came into being?"
declares the LORD.

"This is the one I esteem:
he who is humble and contrite in spirit,[i]
and trembles at my word.[j]
[3]But whoever sacrifices a bull[k]
is like one who kills a man,
and whoever offers a lamb,
like one who breaks a dog's neck;
whoever makes a grain offering
is like one who presents pig's blood,
and whoever burns memorial incense,[l]
like one who worships an idol.
They have chosen their own ways,[m]
and their souls delight in their abominations;
[4]so I also will choose harsh treatment for them
and will bring upon them what they dread.[n]
For when I called, no one answered,[o]
when I spoke, no one listened.
They did evil[p] in my sight
and chose what displeases me."[q]

[5]Hear the word of the LORD,
you who tremble at his word:
"Your brothers who hate[r] you,
and exclude you because of my name, have said,
'Let the LORD be glorified,
that we may see your joy!'

66:1
[e]Mt 23:22
[f]1Ki 8:27; Mt 5:34-35
[g]2Sa 7:7; Jn 4:20-21; Ac 7:49*; 17:24

66:2
[h]Isa 40:26; Ac 7:50*
[i]Isa 57:15; Mt 5:3-4; Lk 18:13-14
[j]Ezr 9:4

66:3
[k]Isa 1:11
[l]Lev 2:2
[m]Isa 57:17

66:4
[n]Pr 10:24
[o]Pr 1:24; Jer 7:13
[p]2Ki 21:2,4,6
[q]Isa 65:12

66:5
[r]Ps 38:20; Isa 60:15

Yet they will be put to shame.[a]
6Hear that uproar from the city,
hear that noise from the temple!
It is the sound of the LORD
repaying[b] his enemies all they deserve.

7"Before she goes into labor,[c]
she gives birth;
before the pains come upon her,
she delivers a son.[d]
8Who has ever heard of such a thing?
Who has ever seen[e] such things?
Can a country be born in a day
or a nation be brought forth in a moment?
Yet no sooner is Zion in labor
than she gives birth to her children.
9Do I bring to the moment of birth[f]
and not give delivery?" says the LORD.
"Do I close up the womb
when I bring to delivery?" says your God.
10"Rejoice[g] with Jerusalem and be glad for her,
all you who love[h] her;
rejoice greatly with her,
all you who mourn over her.
11For you will nurse[i] and be satisfied
at her comforting breasts;
you will drink deeply
and delight in her overflowing abundance."

12For this is what the LORD says:

"I will extend peace to her like a river,[j]
and the wealth[k] of nations like a flooding stream;
you will nurse and be carried[l] on her arm
and dandled on her knees.
13As a mother comforts her child,
so will I comfort[m] you;
and you will be comforted over Jerusalem."

14When you see this, your heart will rejoice
and you will flourish like grass;
the hand of the LORD will be made known to his servants,
but his fury[n] will be shown to his foes.
15See, the LORD is coming with fire,
and his chariots[o] are like a whirlwind;
he will bring down his anger with fury,
and his rebuke[p] with flames of fire.

66:5
[a] Lk 13:17

66:6
[b] Isa 65:6; Joel 3:7

66:7
[c] Isa 54:1
[d] Rev 12:5

66:8
[e] Isa 64:4

66:9
[f] Isa 37:3

66:10
[g] Dt 32:43; Ro 15:10
[h] Ps 26:8

66:11
[i] Isa 60:16

66:12
[j] Isa 48:18
[k] Ps 72:3; Isa 60:5; 61:6
[l] Isa 60:4

66:13
[m] Isa 40:1; 2Co 1:4

66:14
[n] Isa 10:5

66:15
[o] Ps 68:17
[p] Ps 9:5

16For with fire[a] and with his sword[b]
the LORD will execute judgment upon all men,
and many will be those slain by the LORD.

17"Those who consecrate and purify themselves to go into the
gardens,[c] following the one in the midst of[a] those who eat the flesh
of pigs[d] and rats and other abominable things—they will meet
their end[e] together," declares the LORD.
18"And I, because of their actions and their imaginations, am
about to come[b] and gather all nations and tongues, and they will
come and see my glory.
19"I will set a sign[f] among them, and I will send some of those
who survive to the nations—to Tarshish,[g] to the Libyans[c] and
Lydians[h] (famous as archers), to Tubal[i] and Greece, and to the
distant islands[j] that have not heard of my fame or seen my glory.[k]
They will proclaim my glory among the nations. 20And they will
bring all your brothers, from all the nations, to my holy mountain
in Jerusalem as an offering to the LORD—on horses, in chariots
and wagons, and on mules and camels," says the LORD. "They will
bring them, as the Israelites bring their grain offerings, to the temple of the LORD in ceremonially clean vessels.[l] 21And I will select
some of them also to be priests[m] and Levites," says the LORD.

22"As the new heavens and the new earth[n] that I make will endure
before me," declares the LORD, "so will your name and descendants endure.[o] 23From one New Moon to another and from one
Sabbath[p] to another, all mankind will come and bow down[q]
before me," says the LORD. 24"And they will go out and look upon
the dead bodies of those who rebelled against me; their worm[r] will
not die, nor will their fire be quenched,[s] and they will be loathsome to all mankind."

a 17 Or *gardens behind one of your temples, and* b 18 The meaning of the Hebrew for this clause is uncertain. c 19 Some Septuagint manuscripts *Put* (Libyans); Hebrew *Pul*

66:16
a Isa 30:30
b Isa 27:1

66:17
c Isa 1:29
d Lev 11:7
e Ps 37:20; Isa 1:28

66:19
f Isa 11:10; 49:22
g Isa 2:16
h Eze 27:10
i Ge 10:2
j Isa 11:11
k 1Ch 16:24; Isa 24:15

66:20
l Isa 52:11

66:21
m Ex 19:6; Isa 61:6; 1Pe 2:5,9

66:22
n Isa 65:17; Heb 12:26-27; 2Pe 3:13; Rev 21:1
o Jn 10:27-29; 1Pe 1:4-5

66:23
p Eze 46:1-3
q Isa 19:21

66:24
r Isa 14:11
s Isa 1:31; Mk 9:48*

Isaiah at a Glance

Theme of Isaiah:

Author:

Date:

Purpose:

Key Words:

Segment Divisions

			Chapter Themes
	Discourses Regarding Jerusalem	God's Character and Judgment	1
			2
			3
			4
			5
			6
			7
			8
			9
			10
			11
			12
	Oracles		13
			14
			15
			16
			17
			18
			19
			20
			21
			22
			23
	Discourses Regarding That Day		24
			25
			26
			27
	Woes		28
			29
			30
			31
			32
			33

SEGMENT DIVISIONS

				CHAPTER THEMES
	GOD'S RANSOM	GOD'S CHARACTER AND JUDGMENT	34	
			35	
	HISTORICAL INTERLUDE		36	
			37	
			38	
			39	
	DISCOURSES REGARDING:	GOD'S COMFORT AND REDEMPTION	40	
			41	
			42	
			43	
			44	
			45	
			46	
			47	
			48	
	DISCOURSES REGARDING:		49	
			50	
			51	
			52	
			53	
			54	
			55	
			56	
			57	
	DISCOURSES REGARDING:		58	
			59	
			60	
			61	
			62	
			63	
			64	
			65	
			66	

JEREMIAH

Isaiah lived and prophesied one hundred years before the Babylonian captivity; Jeremiah prophesied just before and during Babylon's three sieges of Judah. Between these two great prophets there was about a 30-year period when God didn't speak. True prophets were silent, but false prophets were very vocal, proclaiming peace rather than judgment—and the people loved it. This occurred during Manasseh's reign, a reign noted for its blasphemy and bloodshed.

Jeremiah was born at this time. However, Jeremiah's ministry as a prophet didn't begin until about 627 B.C., the same time that Nabopolassar began his rule of the Neo-Babylonian Empire. Josiah succeeded Manasseh as ruler over Judah. Revival came when the Word of the Lord was found in the house of God and Josiah called the people to repentance.

Then, in 612 B.C., Nineveh, the capital of Assyria, fell to the Babylonians. In 605 B.C., as Egypt went to engage Babylon in battle at Carchemish, Josiah intercepted Neco, king of Egypt, on the plain of Megiddo. Although Neco had warned Josiah not to try to stop him, Josiah tried anyway, and as a result he was killed in battle (see 2 Chronicles 35:20-27).

The revival came to an end, and like her sister Israel, Judah played the harlot again. Egypt was defeated by Babylon at Carchemish, leaving Babylon the predominant world power, God's rod of judgment for his adulterous wife. And Jeremiah the prophet wept.

Things to Do

Chapter 1: Understanding Jeremiah's Message

To understand Jeremiah's message you must understand Jeremiah's call and commission from the Lord. To do so, become thoroughly familiar with Jeremiah 1 before reading the instructions for Jeremiah 2 through 38.

1. Read the chapter, asking God for insight and understanding. Then read the chapter one more time to become familiar with it as a whole.
2. The first three verses give the historical setting of Jeremiah.
   a. Examine the historical chart at the beginning of Jeremiah on page 1283 in the light of these verses. "When the people of Jerusalem went into exile" (1:3) refers to the final siege and destruction of Jerusalem by Nebuchadnezzar, king of Babylon, in 586 B.C.
   b. Jeremiah contains many references to time, such as in Jeremiah 1:1-3. When you encounter one, consult the chart to see who was reigning at the time and what his relationship was to the other kings. The book of Jeremiah is not strictly chronological, so this will help you keep the timing of events in perspective. Mark every reference to time in a distinctive way.
   c. Fill in "Author" and "Date" on the JEREMIAH AT A GLANCE chart on page 1394.
3. Read Jeremiah 1 again. As you do, ask the five W's and an H. Ask questions such as: Who was Jeremiah? What was Jeremiah called to do or be? To whom was he appointed and by whom? When was he called and why? How did he respond? How will he be able to fulfill his appointment? What was he to say? How would the people respond? What was Jeremiah to do? What if the people didn't respond? What would God do?
   a. On a piece of paper, jot down your answers to these questions and any others you think of while observing the text. Don't read anything into the text, but simply let it speak for itself.

b. In the margin of Jeremiah 1, list all you learn about Jeremiah, his call, and the specifics of his commission. Record what you observed from examining the chapter in light of the five W's and an H. Be as specific as possible. Read the chapter through several more times.

4. Record the theme of this chapter on JEREMIAH AT A GLANCE and in the text next to the chapter number.

5. The rest of Jeremiah revolves around Jeremiah's call and commission. Everything Jeremiah says and does is rooted in chapter 1. Remember this as you study!

Jeremiah's critical and passionate message consists of discourses and narrative accounts of events in Jeremiah's life and in the history of Israel, Judah, and the nations.

Chapters 2-38: Judah's Sin and God's Warning to Return

Read all the instructions before you begin. Every now and then refresh your memory, since Jeremiah is a long book.

1. Study this segment chapter by chapter doing the following:
   a. When Jeremiah spoke he was to do two things, one negative and one positive, in that order. First, he was to uproot, tear down, destroy, and overthrow. Second, he was to build and plant. As you read, observe how Jeremiah does these two things in regard to Judah.
      1) List their sins, their "wickedness" (1:16), which God has to deal with by uprooting, tearing down, destroying, and overthrowing. Note their sins by writing them in the margin.
      2) Also note any promise of building and planting—restoration. Record in the margin what God will do on their behalf, when he will do it, and why.
   b. Jeremiah had the assurance that God would fulfill his word (1:12). As you read, note in the margin what God says will happen to Judah in the way of judgment.
      1) Watch for how God will bring about this judgment. In several places God has Jeremiah do some symbolic acts in order to get his point across to the people. Watch for these.
      2) Watch for any verse which shows that God fulfilled (accomplished or carried out) what he said he would do. Also note what God has to do because of the covenant (the law) he made with them.
   c. Mark all references to time with a symbol in the margin.

2. Jeremiah was told to speak all God commanded him and that he would be opposed by kings, officials, priests, and people.
   a. Note in the margin any opposition that comes Jeremiah's way. You may want to put it under the heading "Opposition." Observe Jeremiah's struggles and how he handles these. Also note how God rescues Jeremiah as he said he would in 1:8, 18, 19. (The height of Jeremiah's physical suffering is described in chapters 37 through 38.)
   b. Also note what you learn about the leaders, the shepherds (spiritual), and the prophets.

3. In chapter 21 Nebuchadnezzar, king of Babylon, appears on the scene, for "from the north disaster will be poured out on all who live in the land" (1:14). From this point on, Babylon and Nebuchadnezzar are prominent. You might want to summarize your insights about them in the margin under the heading "Babylon."

4. There are many key repeated words. The following list contains suggestions about which words to mark, though you may want to add to or delete from it. Marking key words is helpful as long as you think about how they contribute to the text and what you learn from their occurrence.
   a. Mark every reference to *nation, people,* or *nations*. Observe which nation it is and make a list in the margin of what you learn about it.

b. Watch for any words or synonyms that have to do with uprooting, destroying, building, planting, or restoring. Mark these in a distinctive way or underline them in the text.

c. You also might want to mark the following words and their synonyms in a distinctive way so you can easily recognize their occurrence in the text: *listen (hear, obey, listened, pay any attention), return (repent, come back, go back, send me back, turn, restrain, turns, stop, changed, relent), prostitute (adultery, adulteries), wickedness (disaster, evil, wicked, calamity, worst, guilt, sin, sins, sinning, crimes, wrong), heart (hearts, to themselves, cares, yourself, heart's, minds), forsaken (forsake, deserted, abandoned, rejected, forsook, desert, vanish from), heal (dress the wound, cure, healing, healed, Comforter, incurable),* and *covenant.* Write these on an index card, color code them as you want to mark them in your Bible, and use the card as a bookmark as you study Jeremiah.

5. As you finish observing each chapter, marking its key words, and putting notes in the margin, record the theme of that chapter on JEREMIAH AT A GLANCE. Also record it in the text on the line next to the chapter number.

Chapters 39-45: Jerusalem's Fall and Judah's Uprooting

1. Except for chapter 45, this section is narrative. Therefore as you read each chapter:

a. Note what happens, when it happens (mark references to time), where it happens, and why.

b. Note who is involved. Mark in a distinctive way the main characters in each chapter, and then in the margin list who they are and anything significant you want to remember about them.

c. Mark the key word *listen (obey, hear)* and any other words which are distinctive to each chapter.

2. Record the theme of each chapter as you have done before.

Chapters 46-51: Jeremiah's Prophecy Concerning the Nations

1. As you read, note what the Lord says will happen and why. Also note the end result and if the Lord gives any hope for the future. Watch for and mark time phrases.

2. Mark the key words: *concerning (against), nations (nations'), Medes,* and *north.* Also observe what you learn about Israel from these chapters.

3. These chapters contain critical information about Babylon which will help when you study prophecy and/or the book of Revelation. In the margin list what you learn about Babylon. Also list your insights on the chart WHAT THE BIBLE TEACHES ABOUT BABYLON beginning on page 2176. (Note the book, chapter, and verse from which you gain insights.)

Chapter 52: Judah's Final Days of Exile

1. As you observe this chapter, mark the time phrases and list in the margin what was done to the kings, the city, the temple vessels, and who did it.

2. Record the theme of this chapter on JEREMIAH AT A GLANCE and then complete the chart. Record the segment divisions of Jeremiah.

THINGS TO THINK ABOUT

1. Judah lived like a prostitute. How have you behaved as the bride of Christ? Do you relate to any of Judah's sins? In James 4:4 God calls those who are friends with the world adulteresses. What would he call you?

2. How faithful are you to proclaim God's Word to others? What can you learn from Jeremiah's life in this respect? Do you hesitate to share God's Word with others because of fear or because you think they wouldn't listen? Are you dismayed by their faces? What should you do? Think about all the times you marked *listen* (*hear, obey, listened*) in Jeremiah. Judah didn't listen to God—only to those prophets who tickled her ears. How carefully do you listen to God's Word?

3. Would God have relented of the calamity he was about to bring on Judah? Why? What do you learn from this?

4. God uses nations as his rod of judgment and yet he holds them accountable for their actions. What does this tell you about God and about your accountability before him?

Chapter 1 Theme ________________

1 The words of Jeremiah son of Hilkiah, one of the priests at
Anathoth[a] in the territory of Benjamin. 2The word of the LORD
came to him in the thirteenth year of the reign of Josiah son of
Amon king of Judah, 3and through the reign of Jehoiakim[b] son of
Josiah king of Judah, down to the fifth month of the eleventh year
of Zedekiah[c] son of Josiah king of Judah, when the people of
Jerusalem went into exile.[d]

4The word of the LORD came to me, saying,

5"Before I formed you in the womb I knew[a][e] you,
before you were born[f] I set you apart;
I appointed you as a prophet to the nations.[g]"

6"Ah, Sovereign LORD," I said, "I do not know how to speak;[h] I
am only a child."[i]
7But the LORD said to me, "Do not say, 'I am only a child.' You
must go to everyone I send you to and say whatever I command
you. 8Do not be afraid[j] of them, for I am with you[k] and will rescue
you," declares the LORD.
9Then the LORD reached out his hand and touched[l] my mouth
and said to me, "Now, I have put my words in your mouth.[m] 10See,
today I appoint you over nations and kingdoms to uproot and
tear down, to destroy and overthrow, to build and to plant."[n]
11The word of the LORD came to me: "What do you see, Jeremiah?"[o]
"I see the branch of an almond tree," I replied.
12The LORD said to me, "You have seen correctly, for I am watching[b] to see that my word is fulfilled."
13The word of the LORD came to me again: "What do you see?"[p]
"I see a boiling pot, tilting away from the north," I answered.
14The LORD said to me, "From the north disaster will be poured
out on all who live in the land. 15I am about to summon all the
peoples of the northern kingdoms," declares the LORD.

"Their kings will come and set up their thrones
in the entrance of the gates of Jerusalem;
they will come against all her surrounding walls
and against all the towns of Judah.[q]

INSIGHT

The Last Kings of Judah

Josiah
640-609 B.C.

Jehoahaz
(also called Joahaz or Shallum)
609 B.C.

Jehoiakim
(also called Eliakim)
609-597 B.C.

Jehoiachin
(also called Coniah or Jeconiah)
597 B.C.

Zedekiah
(also called Mattaniah)
597-586 B.C.

1:1
[a] Jos 21:18; 1Ch 6:60; Jer 32:7-9

1:3
[b] 2Ki 23:34
[c] 2Ki 24:17; Jer 39:2
[d] Jer 52:15

1:5
[e] Ps 139:16
[f] Isa 49:1
[g] ver 10; Jer 25:15-26

1:6
[h] Ex 4:10; 6:12
[i] 1Ki 3:7

1:8
[j] Eze 2:6
[k] Jos 1:5; Jer 15:20

1:9
[l] Isa 6:7
[m] Ex 4:12

1:10
[n] Jer 18:7-10; 24:6; 31:4,28

1:11
[o] Jer 24:3; Am 7:8

1:13
[p] Zec 4:2

1:15
[q] Jer 4:16; 9:11

[a] 5 Or *chose* [b] *12* The Hebrew for *watching* sounds like the Hebrew for *almond tree.*

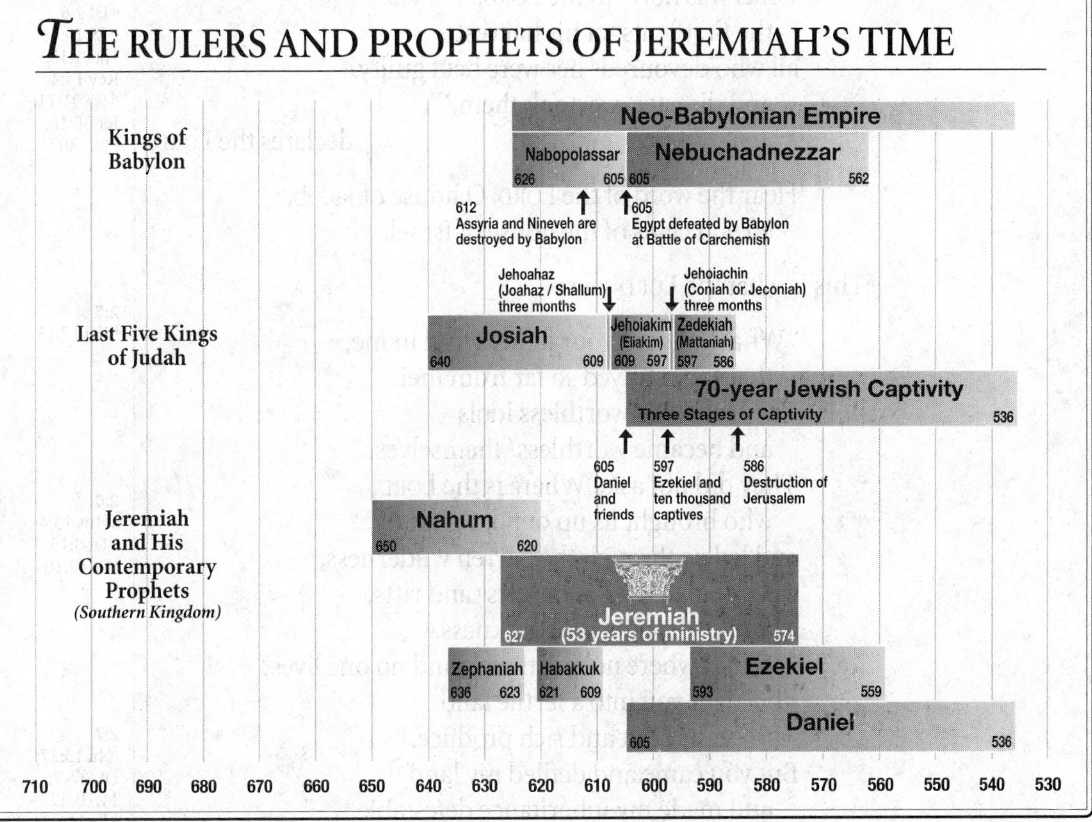

1:16 [a]Dt 28:20 [b]Jer 17:13 [c]Jer 7:9; 19:4

16 I will pronounce my judgments on my people
because of their wickedness[a] in forsaking me,[b]
in burning incense to other gods[c]
and in worshiping what their hands have made.

1:17 [d]Eze 2:6

1:18 [e]Isa 50:7

17 "Get yourself ready! Stand up and say to them whatever I command you. Do not be terrified[d] by them, or I will terrify you before
them. 18 Today I have made you[e] a fortified city, an iron pillar and
a bronze wall to stand against the whole land—against the kings
of Judah, its officials, its priests and the people of the land. 19 They
will fight against you but will not overcome you, for I am with
you[f] and will rescue[g] you," declares the LORD.

1:19 [f]Jer 20:11 [g]ver 8

Chapter 2 Theme ______________________

2 The word of the LORD came to me: 2 "Go and proclaim in the hearing of Jerusalem:

2:2 [h]Eze 16:8-14, 60; Hos 2:15 [i]Dt 2:7

"'I remember the devotion of your youth,[h]
how as a bride you loved me
and followed me through the desert,[i]
through a land not sown.

3Israel was holy[a] to the LORD,[b]
the firstfruits[c] of his harvest;
all who devoured[d] her were held guilty,[e]
and disaster overtook them,' "
declares the LORD.

4Hear the word of the LORD, O house of Jacob,
all you clans of the house of Israel.

5This is what the LORD says:

"What fault did your fathers find in me,
that they strayed so far from me?
They followed worthless idols
and became worthless[f] themselves.
6They did not ask, 'Where is the LORD,
who brought us up out of Egypt[g]
and led us through the barren wilderness,
through a land of deserts[h] and rifts,[i]
a land of drought and darkness,[a]
a land where no one travels and no one lives?'
7I brought you into a fertile land
to eat its fruit and rich produce.[j]
But you came and defiled my land
and made my inheritance detestable.[k]
8The priests did not ask,
'Where is the LORD?'
Those who deal with the law did not know me;[l]
the leaders rebelled against me.
The prophets prophesied by Baal,[m]
following worthless idols.[n]
9"Therefore I bring charges[o] against you again,"
declares the LORD.
"And I will bring charges against your children's
children.
10Cross over to the coasts of Kittim[b] and look,
send to Kedar[c] and observe closely;
see if there has ever been anything like this:
11Has a nation ever changed its gods?
(Yet they are not gods[p] at all.)
But my people have exchanged their[d] Glory[q]
for worthless idols.

[a]6 Or *and the shadow of death* [b]10 That is, Cyprus and western coastlands [c]10 The home of Bedouin tribes in the Syro-Arabian desert [d]11 Masoretic Text; an ancient Hebrew scribal tradition *my*

2:3 [a]Dt 7:6 [b]Ex 19:6 [c]Jas 1:18; Rev 14:4 [d]Isa 41:11; Jer 30:16 [e]Jer 50:7
2:5 [f]2Ki 17:15
2:6 [g]Hos 13:4 [h]Dt 8:15 [i]Dt 32:10
2:7 [j]Nu 13:27; Dt 8:7-9; 11:10-12 [k]Ps 106:34-39; Jer 16:18
2:8 [l]Jer 4:22 [m]Jer 23:13 [n]Jer 16:19
2:9 [o]Eze 20:35-36; Mic 6:2
2:11 [p]Isa 37:19; Jer 16:20 [q]Ps 106:20; Ro 1:23

12 Be appalled at this, O heavens,
  and shudder with great horror,"
    declares the LORD.

13 "My people have committed two sins:
They have forsaken me,
  the spring of living water,[a]
and have dug their own cisterns,
  broken cisterns that cannot hold water.
14 Is Israel a servant, a slave[b] by birth?
  Why then has he become plunder?
15 Lions[c] have roared;
  they have growled at him.
They have laid waste[d] his land;
  his towns are burned and deserted.
16 Also, the men of Memphis[a][e] and Tahpanhes[f]
  have shaved the crown of your head.[b]
17 Have you not brought this on yourselves[g]
  by forsaking the LORD your God
  when he led you in the way?
18 Now why go to Egypt[h]
  to drink water from the Shihor[c]?[i]
And why go to Assyria
  to drink water from the River[d]?
19 Your wickedness will punish you;
  your backsliding[j] will rebuke[k] you.
Consider then and realize
  how evil and bitter[l] it is for you
when you forsake the LORD your God
  and have no awe[m] of me,"
    declares the Lord, the LORD Almighty.

20 "Long ago you broke off your yoke[n]
  and tore off your bonds;
  you said, 'I will not serve you!'
Indeed, on every high hill[o]
  and under every spreading tree[p]
  you lay down as a prostitute.
21 I had planted[q] you like a choice vine[r]
  of sound and reliable stock.
How then did you turn against me
  into a corrupt,[s] wild vine?
22 Although you wash yourself with soda
  and use an abundance of soap,

2:13 [a] Ps 36:9; Jn 4:14
2:14 [b] Ex 4:22
2:15 [c] Jer 4:7; 50:17 [d] Isa 1:7
2:16 [e] Isa 19:13 [f] Jer 43:7-9
2:17 [g] Jer 4:18
2:18 [h] Isa 30:2 [i] Jos 13:3
2:19 [j] Jer 3:11,22 [k] Isa 3:9; Hos 5:5 [l] Job 20:14; Am 8:10 [m] Ps 36:1
2:20 [n] Lev 26:13 [o] Isa 57:7; Jer 17:2 [p] Dt 12:2
2:21 [q] Ex 15:17 [r] Ps 80:8 [s] Isa 5:4

a *16* Hebrew *Noph* b *16* Or *have cracked your skull* c *18* That is, a branch of the Nile
d *18* That is, the Euphrates

the stain of your guilt is still before me,"
declares the Sovereign LORD.
23"How can you say, 'I am not defiled;[a]
I have not run after the Baals'?[b]
See how you behaved in the valley;[c]
consider what you have done.
You are a swift she-camel
running[d] here and there,
24a wild donkey[e] accustomed to the desert,
sniffing the wind in her craving—
in her heat who can restrain her?
Any males that pursue her need not tire themselves;
at mating time they will find her.
25Do not run until your feet are bare
and your throat is dry.
But you said, 'It's no use!
I love foreign gods,[f]
and I must go after them.'

26"As a thief is disgraced[g] when he is caught,
so the house of Israel is disgraced—
they, their kings and their officials,
their priests and their prophets.
27They say to wood, 'You are my father,'
and to stone,[h] 'You gave me birth.'
They have turned their backs to me
and not their faces;[i]
yet when they are in trouble,[j] they say,
'Come and save us!'
28Where then are the gods[k] you made for yourselves?
Let them come if they can save you
when you are in trouble![l]
For you have as many gods
as you have towns,[m] O Judah.

29"Why do you bring charges against me?
You have all[n] rebelled against me,"
declares the LORD.
30"In vain I punished your people;
they did not respond to correction.
Your sword has devoured your prophets[o]
like a ravening lion.

31"You of this generation, consider the word of the LORD:

"Have I been a desert to Israel
or a land of great darkness?[p]

2:23 [a]Pr 30:12 [b]Jer 9:14 [c]Jer 7:31 [d]ver 33; Jer 31:22
2:24 [e]Jer 14:6
2:25 [f]Dt 32:16; Jer 3:13; 14:10
2:26 [g]Jer 48:27
2:27 [h]Jer 3:9 [i]Jer 18:17; 32:33 [j]Jdg 10:10; Isa 26:16
2:28 [k]Isa 45:20 [l]Dt 32:37 [m]2Ki 17:29; Jer 11:13
2:29 [n]Jer 5:1; 6:13; Da 9:11
2:30 [o]Ne 9:26; Ac 7:52; 1Th 2:15
2:31 [p]Isa 45:19

Why do my people say, 'We are free to roam;
we will come to you no more'?
32Does a maiden forget her jewelry,
a bride her wedding ornaments?
Yet my people have forgotten me,
days without number.
33How skilled you are at pursuing love!
Even the worst of women can learn from your ways.
34On your clothes men find
the lifeblood[a] of the innocent poor,
though you did not catch them breaking in.[b]
Yet in spite of all this
35 you say, 'I am innocent;
he is not angry with me.'
But I will pass judgment[c] on you
because you say, 'I have not sinned.'[d]
36Why do you go about so much,
changing[e] your ways?
You will be disappointed by Egypt[f]
as you were by Assyria.
37You will also leave that place
with your hands on your head,[g]
for the LORD has rejected those you trust;
you will not be helped[h] by them.

Chapter 3 Theme ______________________

3

"If a man divorces[i] his wife
and she leaves him and marries another man,
should he return to her again?
Would not the land be completely defiled?
But you have lived as a prostitute with many lovers[j]—
would you now return to me?"
declares the LORD.

2"Look up to the barren heights and see.
Is there any place where you have not been ravished?
By the roadside[k] you sat waiting for lovers,
sat like a nomad[a] in the desert.
You have defiled the land[l]
with your prostitution and wickedness.
3Therefore the showers have been withheld,[m]
and no spring rains[n] have fallen.
Yet you have the brazen look of a prostitute;
you refuse to blush with shame.[o]

a2 Or *an Arab*

2:34 [a]2Ki 21:16 [b]Ex 22:2
2:35 [c]Jer 25:31 [d]1Jn 1:8,10
2:36 [e]Jer 31:22 [f]Isa 30:2,3,7
2:37 [g]2Sa 13:19 [h]Jer 37:7
3:1 [i]Dt 24:1-4 [j]Jer 2:20,25; Eze 16:26,29
3:2 [k]Ge 38:14; Eze 16:25 [l]Jer 2:7
3:3 [m]Lev 26:19 [n]Jer 14:4 [o]Jer 6:15; 8:12; Zep 3:5

4Have you not just called to me:
'My Father,[a] my friend from my youth,[b]
5will you always be angry?[c]
Will your wrath continue forever?'
This is how you talk,
but you do all the evil you can."

6During the reign of King Josiah, the LORD said to me, "Have you
seen what faithless Israel has done? She has gone up on every high
hill and under every spreading tree[d] and has committed adultery[e]
there. 7I thought that after she had done all this she would return
to me but she did not, and her unfaithful sister[f] Judah saw it. 8I
gave faithless Israel her certificate of divorce and sent her away
because of all her adulteries. Yet I saw that her unfaithful sister
Judah had no fear;[g] she also went out and committed adultery.
9Because Israel's immorality mattered so little to her, she defiled
the land[h] and committed adultery with stone[i] and wood.[j] 10In
spite of all this, her unfaithful sister Judah did not return to me
with all her heart, but only in pretense,[k]" declares the LORD.
11The LORD said to me, "Faithless Israel is more righteous[l] than
unfaithful[m] Judah. 12Go, proclaim this message toward the north:[n]

"'Return,[o] faithless Israel,' declares the LORD,
'I will frown on you no longer,
for I am merciful,' declares the LORD,
'I will not be angry[p] forever.
13Only acknowledge[q] your guilt—
you have rebelled against the LORD your God,
you have scattered your favors to foreign gods[r]
under every spreading tree,[s]
and have not obeyed[t] me,'"
declares the LORD.

14"Return,[u] faithless people," declares the LORD, "for I am your
husband. I will choose you—one from a town and two from a
clan—and bring you to Zion. 15Then I will give you shepherds[v]
after my own heart, who will lead you with knowledge and understanding. 16In those days, when your numbers have increased
greatly in the land," declares the LORD, "men will no longer say,
'The ark of the covenant of the LORD.' It will never enter their
minds or be remembered;[w] it will not be missed, nor will another
one be made. 17At that time they will call Jerusalem The Throne[x]
of the LORD, and all nations will gather in Jerusalem to honor[y] the
name of the LORD. No longer will they follow the stubbornness of
their evil hearts.[z] 18In those days the house of Judah will join the
house of Israel,[a] and together[b] they will come from a northern[c]
land to the land[d] I gave your forefathers as an inheritance.

3:4 [a]ver 19 [b]Jer 2:2
3:5 [c]Ps 103:9; Isa 57:16
3:6 [d]Jer 17:2 [e]Jer 2:20
3:7 [f]Eze 16:46
3:8 [g]Eze 16:47; 23:11
3:9 [h]ver 2 [i]Isa 57:6 [j]Jer 2:27
3:10 [k]Jer 12:2
3:11 [l]Eze 16:52; 23:11 [m]ver 7
3:12 [n]2Ki 17:3-6 [o]ver 14; Jer 31:21,22; Eze 33:11 [p]Ps 86:15
3:13 [q]Dt 30:1-3; Jer 14:20; 1Jn 1:9 [r]Jer 2:25 [s]Dt 12:2 [t]ver 25
3:14 [u]Hos 2:19
3:15 [v]Ac 20:28
3:16 [w]Isa 65:17
3:17 [x]Jer 17:12; Eze 43:7 [y]Isa 60:9 [z]Jer 11:8
3:18 [a]Hos 1:11 [b]Isa 11:13; Jer 50:4 [c]Jer 16:15; 31:8 [d]Am 9:15

3:19 [a]ver 4; Isa 63:16
3:21 [b]ver 2
3:22 [c]Hos 14:4 [d]Jer 33:6; Hos 6:1
3:23 [e]Ps 3:8; Jer 17:14
3:24 [f]Hos 9:10
3:25 [g]Ezr 9:6 [h]Jer 22:21
4:1 [i]Jer 3:1,22; Joel 2:12 [j]Jer 35:15
4:2 [k]Dt 10:20; Isa 65:16 [l]Jer 12:16 [m]Ge 22:18; Gal 3:8

19"I myself said,

"'How gladly would I treat you like sons
and give you a desirable land,
the most beautiful inheritance of any nation.'
I thought you would call me 'Father'[a]
and not turn away from following me.
20But like a woman unfaithful to her husband,
so you have been unfaithful to me, O house of Israel,"
declares the LORD.

21A cry is heard on the barren heights,[b]
the weeping and pleading of the people of Israel,
because they have perverted their ways
and have forgotten the LORD their God.

22"Return,[c] faithless people;
I will cure[d] you of backsliding."

"Yes, we will come to you,
for you are the LORD our God.
23Surely the ⌊idolatrous⌋ commotion on the hills
and mountains is a deception;
surely in the LORD our God
is the salvation[e] of Israel.
24From our youth shameful[f] gods have consumed
the fruits of our fathers' labor—
their flocks and herds,
their sons and daughters.
25Let us lie down in our shame,[g]
and let our disgrace cover us.
We have sinned against the LORD our God,
both we and our fathers;
from our youth[h] till this day
we have not obeyed the LORD our God."

INSIGHT

The people set up their idols on hills (see 1 Kings 14:23).

Chapter 4 Theme ____________

4 "If you will return[i], O Israel,
return to me,"
declares the LORD.
"If you put your detestable idols[j] out of my sight
and no longer go astray,
2and if in a truthful, just and righteous way
you swear,[k] 'As surely as the LORD lives,'[l]
then the nations will be blessed[m] by him
and in him they will glory."

3This is what the LORD says to the men of Judah and to Jerusalem:

"Break up your unplowed ground[a]
and do not sow among thorns.[b]
4Circumcise yourselves to the LORD,
circumcise your hearts,[c]
you men of Judah and people of Jerusalem,
or my wrath[d] will break out and burn like fire
because of the evil you have done—
burn with no one to quench[e] it.

5"Announce in Judah and proclaim in Jerusalem and say:
'Sound the trumpet throughout the land!'
Cry aloud and say:
'Gather together!
Let us flee to the fortified cities!'[f]
6Raise the signal to go to Zion!
Flee for safety without delay!
For I am bringing disaster from the north,[g]
even terrible destruction."

7A lion[h] has come out of his lair;
a destroyer of nations has set out.
He has left his place
to lay waste[i] your land.
Your towns will lie in ruins[j]
without inhabitant.
8So put on sackcloth,[k]
lament and wail,
for the fierce anger[l] of the LORD
has not turned away from us.

9"In that day," declares the LORD,
"the king and the officials will lose heart,
the priests will be horrified,
and the prophets will be appalled."[m]

10Then I said, "Ah, Sovereign LORD, how completely you have
deceived[n] this people and Jerusalem by saying, 'You will have
peace,'[o] when the sword is at our throats."
11At that time this people and Jerusalem will be told, "A scorching wind[p] from the barren heights in the desert blows toward my
people, but not to winnow or cleanse; 12a wind too strong for that
comes from me.[a] Now I pronounce my judgments[q] against them."

13Look! He advances like the clouds,[r]
his chariots[s] come like a whirlwind,[t]

[a] *12* Or *comes at my command*

4:3 [a]Hos 10:12 [b]Mk 4:18
4:4 [c]Dt 10:16; Jer 9:26; Ro 2:28-29 [d]Zep 2:2 [e]Am 5:6
4:5 [f]Jos 10:20; Jer 8:14
4:6 [g]Jer 1:13-15; 50:3
4:7 [h]2Ki 24:1; Jer 2:15 [i]Isa 1:7 [j]Jer 25:9
4:8 [k]Isa 22:12; Jer 6:26 [l]Jer 30:24
4:9 [m]Isa 29:9
4:10 [n]2Th 2:11 [o]Jer 14:13
4:11 [p]Eze 17:10; Hos 13:15
4:12 [q]Jer 1:16
4:13 [r]Isa 19:1 [s]Isa 66:15 [t]Isa 5:28

his horses are swifter than eagles.[a]
Woe to us! We are ruined!
14O Jerusalem, wash[b] the evil from your heart and be saved.
How long will you harbor wicked thoughts?
15A voice is announcing from Dan,[c]
proclaiming disaster from the hills of Ephraim.
16"Tell this to the nations,
proclaim it to Jerusalem:
'A besieging army is coming from a distant land,
raising a war cry[d] against the cities of Judah.
17They surround[e] her like men guarding a field,
because she has rebelled[f] against me,'"
declares the LORD.

18"Your own conduct and actions[g]
have brought this upon you.[h]
This is your punishment.
How bitter[i] it is!
How it pierces to the heart!"

19Oh, my anguish, my anguish![j]
I writhe in pain.
Oh, the agony of my heart!
My heart pounds within me,
I cannot keep silent.[k]
For I have heard the sound of the trumpet;
I have heard the battle cry.[l]
20Disaster follows disaster;[m]
the whole land lies in ruins.
In an instant my tents[n] are destroyed,
my shelter in a moment.
21How long must I see the battle standard
and hear the sound of the trumpet?

22"My people are fools;[o]
they do not know me.[p]
They are senseless children;
they have no understanding.
They are skilled in doing evil;[q]
they know not how to do good."[r]

23I looked at the earth,
and it was formless and empty;[s]
and at the heavens,
and their light was gone.
24I looked at the mountains,
and they were quaking;[t]
all the hills were swaying.

4:13 [a] Dt 28:49; Hab 1:8
4:14 [b] Jas 4:8
4:15 [c] Jer 8:16
4:16 [d] Eze 21:22
4:17 [e] 2Ki 25:1,4 [f] Jer 5:23
4:18 [g] Ps 107:17; Isa 50:1 [h] Jer 2:17 [i] Jer 2:19
4:19 [j] Isa 16:11; 22:4; Jer 9:10 [k] Jer 20:9 [l] Nu 10:9
4:20 [m] Ps 42:7; Eze 7:26 [n] Jer 10:20
4:22 [o] Jer 10:8 [p] Jer 2:8 [q] Jer 13:23; 1Co 14:20 [r] Ro 16:19
4:23 [s] Ge 1:2
4:24 [t] Isa 5:25; Eze 38:20

25I looked, and there were no people;
every bird in the sky had flown away.[a]
26I looked, and the fruitful land was a desert;
all its towns lay in ruins
before the LORD, before his fierce anger.

27This is what the LORD says:

"The whole land will be ruined,
though I will not destroy[b] it completely.
28Therefore the earth will mourn[c]
and the heavens above grow dark,[d]
because I have spoken and will not relent,[e]
I have decided and will not turn back.[f]"

29At the sound of horsemen and archers[g]
every town takes to flight.[h]
Some go into the thickets;
some climb up among the rocks.
All the towns are deserted;[i]
no one lives in them.

30What are you doing,[j] O devastated one?
Why dress yourself in scarlet
and put on jewels[k] of gold?
Why shade your eyes with paint?[l]
You adorn yourself in vain.
Your lovers[m] despise you;
they seek your life.

31I hear a cry as of a woman in labor,[n]
a groan as of one bearing her first child—
the cry of the Daughter of Zion gasping for breath,[o]
stretching out her hands[p] and saying,
"Alas! I am fainting;
my life is given over to murderers."

Chapter 5 Theme ______________________

5

"Go up and down[q] the streets of Jerusalem,
look around and consider,
search through her squares.
If you can find but one person[r]
who deals honestly and seeks the truth,
I will forgive[s] this city.
2Although they say, 'As surely as the LORD lives,'[t]
still they are swearing falsely."

4:25 [a]Jer 9:10; 12:4; Zep 1:3
4:27 [b]Jer 5:10,18; 12:12; 30:11; 46:28
4:28 [c]Jer 12:4,11; 14:2; Hos 4:3 [d]Isa 5:30; 50:3 [e]Nu 23:19 [f]Jer 23:20; 30:24
4:29 [g]Jer 6:23 [h]2Ki 25:4 [i]ver 7
4:30 [j]Isa 10:3-4 [k]Eze 23:40 [l]2Ki 9:30 [m]La 1:2; Eze 23:9,22
4:31 [n]Jer 13:21 [o]Isa 42:14 [p]Isa 1:15; La 1:17
5:1 [q]2Ch 16:9; Eze 22:30 [r]Ge 18:32 [s]Ge 18:24
5:2 [t]Jer 4:2

3 O LORD, do not your eyes[a] look for truth?
You struck[b] them, but they felt no pain;
you crushed them, but they refused correction.[c]
They made their faces harder than stone[d]
and refused to repent.
4 I thought, "These are only the poor;
they are foolish,
for they do not know[e] the way of the LORD,
the requirements of their God.
5 So I will go to the leaders[f]
and speak to them;
surely they know the way of the LORD,
the requirements of their God."
But with one accord they too had broken off the yoke
and torn off the bonds.[g]
6 Therefore a lion from the forest will attack them,
a wolf from the desert will ravage them,
a leopard[h] will lie in wait near their towns
to tear to pieces any who venture out,
for their rebellion is great
and their backslidings many.[i]

7 "Why should I forgive you?
Your children have forsaken me
and sworn[j] by gods that are not gods.[k]
I supplied all their needs,
yet they committed adultery[l]
and thronged to the houses of prostitutes.
8 They are well-fed, lusty stallions,
each neighing for another man's wife.[m]
9 Should I not punish them for this?"[n]
declares the LORD.
"Should I not avenge myself
on such a nation as this?

10 "Go through her vineyards and ravage them,
but do not destroy them completely.[o]
Strip off her branches,
for these people do not belong to the LORD.
11 The house of Israel and the house of Judah
have been utterly unfaithful[p] to me,"
declares the LORD.

12 They have lied about the LORD;
they said, "He will do nothing!
No harm will come to us;[q]
we will never see sword or famine.[r]

5:3 [a] 2Ch 16:9 [b] Isa 9:13 [c] Jer 2:30; Zep 3:2 [d] Jer 7:26; 19:15; Eze 3:8-9
5:4 [e] Jer 8:7
5:5 [f] Mic 3:1,9 [g] Ps 2:3; Jer 2:20
5:6 [h] Hos 13:7 [i] Jer 30:14
5:7 [j] Jos 23:7; Zep 1:5 [k] Dt 32:21; Jer 2:11; Gal 4:8 [l] Nu 25:1
5:8 [m] Jer 29:23; Eze 22:11
5:9 [n] ver 29; Jer 9:9
5:10 [o] Jer 4:27
5:11 [p] Jer 3:20
5:12 [q] Jer 23:17 [r] 2Ch 36:16; Jer 14:13

13The prophets[a] are but wind
and the word is not in them;
so let what they say be done to them."

14Therefore this is what the LORD God Almighty says:

"Because the people have spoken these words,
I will make my words in your mouth[b] a fire[c]
and these people the wood it consumes.
15O house of Israel," declares the LORD,
"I am bringing a distant nation[d] against you—
an ancient and enduring nation,
a people whose language[e] you do not know,
whose speech you do not understand.
16Their quivers are like an open grave;
all of them are mighty warriors.
17They will devour[f g] your harvests and food,
devour[h i] your sons and daughters;
they will devour[j] your flocks and herds,
devour your vines and fig trees.
With the sword they will destroy
the fortified cities in which you trust.[k]

18"Yet even in those days," declares the LORD, "I will not destroy[l]
you completely. 19And when the people ask,[m] 'Why has the LORD
our God done all this to us?' you will tell them, 'As you have forsaken me and served foreign gods[n] in your own land, so now you
will serve foreigners[o] in a land not your own.'

20"Announce this to the house of Jacob
and proclaim it in Judah:
21Hear this, you foolish and senseless people,
who have eyes[p] but do not see,
who have ears but do not hear:[q]
22Should you not fear[r] me?" declares the LORD.
"Should you not tremble in my presence?
I made the sand a boundary for the sea,
an everlasting barrier it cannot cross.
The waves may roll, but they cannot prevail;
they may roar, but they cannot cross it.
23But these people have stubborn and rebellious[s] hearts;
they have turned aside and gone away.
24They do not say to themselves,
'Let us fear the LORD our God,
who gives autumn and spring rains[t] in season,
who assures us of the regular weeks of harvest.'[u]
25Your wrongdoings have kept these away;
your sins have deprived you of good.

5:13 [a]Jer 14:15
5:14 [b]Jer 1:9; Hos 6:5 [c]Jer 23:29
5:15 [d]Dt 28:49; Isa 5:26; Jer 4:16 [e]Isa 28:11
5:17 [f]Jer 8:16 [g]Lev 26:16 [h]Jer 50:7,17 [i]Dt 28:32 [j]Dt 28:31 [k]Dt 28:33
5:18 [l]Jer 4:27
5:19 [m]Dt 29:24-26; 1Ki 9:9 [n]Jer 16:13 [o]Dt 28:48
5:21 [p]Isa 6:10; Eze 12:2 [q]Mt 13:15; Mk 8:18
5:22 [r]Dt 28:58
5:23 [s]Dt 21:18
5:24 [t]Ps 147:8; Joel 2:23 [u]Ge 8:22; Ac 14:17

26"Among my people are wicked men
who lie in wait[a] like men who snare birds
and like those who set traps to catch men.
27Like cages full of birds,
their houses are full of deceit;[b]
they have become rich[c] and powerful
28 and have grown fat[d] and sleek.
Their evil deeds have no limit;
they do not plead the case of the fatherless[e] to win it,
they do not defend the rights of the poor.[f]
29Should I not punish them for this?"
declares the LORD.
"Should I not avenge myself
on such a nation as this?

30"A horrible[g] and shocking thing
has happened in the land:
31The prophets prophesy lies,[h]
the priests rule by their own authority,
and my people love it this way.
But what will you do in the end?

Chapter 6 Theme ______________________

6

"Flee for safety, people of Benjamin!
Flee from Jerusalem!
Sound the trumpet in Tekoa![i]
Raise the signal over Beth Hakkerem![j]
For disaster looms out of the north,[k]
even terrible destruction.
2I will destroy the Daughter of Zion,
so beautiful and delicate.
3Shepherds[l] with their flocks will come against her;
they will pitch their tents around[m] her,
each tending his own portion."

4"Prepare for battle against her!
Arise, let us attack at noon![n]
But, alas, the daylight is fading,
and the shadows of evening grow long.
5So arise, let us attack at night
and destroy her fortresses!"

6This is what the LORD Almighty says:

"Cut down the trees[o]
and build siege ramps[p] against Jerusalem.
This city must be punished;
it is filled with oppression.

5:26 [a]Ps 10:8; Pr 1:11
5:27 [b]Jer 9:6 [c]Jer 12:1
5:28 [d]Dt 32:15 [e]Zec 7:10 [f]Isa 1:23; Jer 7:6
5:30 [g]Jer 23:14; Hos 6:10
5:31 [h]Eze 13:6; Mic 2:11
6:1 [i]2Ch 11:6 [j]Ne 3:14 [k]Jer 4:6
6:3 [l]Jer 12:10 [m]2Ki 25:4; Lk 19:43
6:4 [n]Jer 15:8
6:6 [o]Dt 20:19-20 [p]Jer 32:24

7As a well pours out its water,
so she pours out her wickedness.
Violence[a] and destruction[b] resound in her;
her sickness and wounds are ever before me.
8Take warning, O Jerusalem,
or I will turn away[c] from you
and make your land desolate
so no one can live in it."

9This is what the LORD Almighty says:

"Let them glean the remnant of Israel
as thoroughly as a vine;
pass your hand over the branches again,
like one gathering grapes."

10To whom can I speak and give warning?
Who will listen to me?
Their ears are closed[a] [d]
so they cannot hear.
The word[e] of the LORD is offensive to them;
they find no pleasure in it.
11But I am full of the wrath[f] of the LORD,
and I cannot hold it in.[g]

"Pour it out on the children in the street
and on the young men[h] gathered together;
both husband and wife will be caught in it,
and the old, those weighed down with years.
12Their houses will be turned over to others,[i]
together with their fields and their wives,[j]
when I stretch out my hand[k]
against those who live in the land,"
declares the LORD.
13"From the least to the greatest,
all are greedy for gain;[l]
prophets and priests alike,
all practice deceit.[m]
14They dress the wound of my people
as though it were not serious.
'Peace, peace,' they say,
when there is no peace.[n]
15Are they ashamed of their loathsome conduct?
No, they have no shame at all;
they do not even know how to blush.[o]

a 10 Hebrew *uncircumcised*

6:7 [a] Ps 55:9; Eze 7:11,23 [b] Jer 20:8
6:8 [c] Eze 23:18; Hos 9:12
6:10 [d] Ac 7:51 [e] Jer 20:8
6:11 [f] Jer 7:20 [g] Job 32:20; Jer 20:9 [h] Jer 9:21
6:12 [i] Dt 28:30 [j] Jer 8:10; 38:22 [k] Isa 5:25
6:13 [l] Isa 56:11 [m] Jer 8:10
6:14 [n] Jer 4:10; 8:11; Eze 13:10
6:15 [o] Jer 3:3; 8:10-12

6:16
[a]Jer 18:15
[b]Ps 119:3
[c]Mt 11:29

6:17
[d]Eze 3:17
[e]Jer 11:7-8; 25:4

6:19
[f]Isa 1:2; Jer 22:29
[g]Pr 1:31
[h]Jer 8:9

6:20
[i]Ex 30:23
[j]Am 5:22
[k]Ps 50:8-10; Jer 7:21; Mic 6:7-8
[l]Isa 1:11

6:21
[m]Isa 8:14

6:22
[n]Jer 1:15; 10:22

6:23
[o]Isa 13:18
[p]Jer 4:29

6:24
[q]Jer 4:19
[r]Jer 4:31; 50:41-43

So they will fall among the fallen;
they will be brought down when I punish them,"
says the LORD.

16This is what the LORD says:

"Stand at the crossroads and look;
ask for the ancient paths,[a]
ask where the good way[b] is, and walk in it,
and you will find rest[c] for your souls.
But you said, 'We will not walk in it.'
17I appointed watchmen[d] over you and said,
'Listen to the sound of the trumpet!'
But you said, 'We will not listen.'[e]
18Therefore hear, O nations;
observe, O witnesses,
what will happen to them.
19Hear, O earth:[f]
I am bringing disaster on this people,
the fruit of their schemes,[g]
because they have not listened to my words
and have rejected my law.[h]
20What do I care about incense from Sheba
or sweet calamus[i] from a distant land?
Your burnt offerings are not acceptable;[j]
your sacrifices[k] do not please me."[l]

21Therefore this is what the LORD says:

"I will put obstacles before this people.
Fathers and sons alike will stumble[m] over them;
neighbors and friends will perish."

22This is what the LORD says:

"Look, an army is coming
from the land of the north;[n]
a great nation is being stirred up
from the ends of the earth.
23They are armed with bow and spear;
they are cruel and show no mercy.[o]
They sound like the roaring sea
as they ride on their horses;[p]
they come like men in battle formation
to attack you, O Daughter of Zion."

24We have heard reports about them,
and our hands hang limp.
Anguish[q] has gripped us,
pain like that of a woman in labor.[r]

25 Do not go out to the fields
  or walk on the roads,
for the enemy has a sword,
  and there is terror on every side.[a]
26 O my people, put on sackcloth[b]
  and roll in ashes;[c]
mourn with bitter wailing
  as for an only son,[d]
for suddenly the destroyer
  will come upon us.

27 "I have made you a tester[e] of metals
  and my people the ore,
that you may observe
  and test their ways.
28 They are all hardened rebels,[f]
  going about to slander.[g]
They are bronze and iron;[h]
  they all act corruptly.
29 The bellows blow fiercely
  to burn away the lead with fire,
but the refining goes on in vain;
  the wicked are not purged out.
30 They are called rejected silver,
  because the LORD has rejected them."[i]

Chapter 7 Theme ______________________________

7 This is the word that came to Jeremiah from the LORD:
2 "Stand[j] at the gate of the LORD's house and there proclaim
this message:

"'Hear the word of the LORD, all you people of Judah who come
through these gates to worship the LORD. 3 This is what the LORD
Almighty, the God of Israel, says: Reform your ways[k] and your
actions, and I will let you live in this place. 4 Do not trust in deceptive[l] words and say, "This is the temple of the LORD, the temple of
the LORD, the temple of the LORD!" 5 If you really change your ways
and your actions and deal with each other justly,[m] 6 if you do not
oppress the alien, the fatherless or the widow and do not shed
innocent blood[n] in this place, and if you do not follow other gods[o]
to your own harm, 7 then I will let you live in this place, in the land[p]
I gave your forefathers for ever and ever. 8 But look, you are trusting
in deceptive words that are worthless.

9 "'Will you steal and murder, commit adultery and perjury,[a]
burn incense to Baal[q] and follow other gods[r] you have not known,

[a] 9 Or *and swear by false gods*

6:25 [a] Jer 49:29
6:26 [b] Jer 4:8 [c] Jer 25:34; Mic 1:10 [d] Zec 12:10
6:27 [e] Jer 9:7
6:28 [f] Jer 5:23 [g] Jer 9:4 [h] Eze 22:18
6:30 [i] Ps 119:119; Jer 7:29; Hos 9:17
7:2 [j] Jer 17:19
7:3 [k] Jer 18:11; 26:13
7:4 [l] Mic 3:11
7:5 [m] Jer 22:3
7:6 [n] Jer 2:34; 19:4 [o] Dt 8:19
7:7 [p] Dt 4:40
7:9 [q] Jer 11:13,17 [r] Ex 20:3

10 and then come and stand before me in this house,[a] which bears
my Name, and say, "We are safe"—safe to do all these detestable
things? 11 Has this house,[b] which bears my Name, become a den of
robbers[c] to you? But I have been watching![d] declares the LORD.
12 "'Go now to the place in Shiloh[e] where I first made a dwelling
for my Name, and see what I did[f] to it because of the wickedness of
my people Israel. 13 While you were doing all these things, declares
the LORD, I spoke to you again and again,[g] but you did not listen;[h]
I called you, but you did not answer.[i] 14 Therefore, what I did to
Shiloh I will now do to the house that bears my Name,[j] the temple
you trust in, the place I gave to you and your fathers. 15 I will thrust
you from my presence, just as I did all your brothers, the people of
Ephraim.'[k]
16 "So do not pray for this people nor offer any plea[l] or petition
for them; do not plead with me, for I will not listen to you. 17 Do
you not see what they are doing in the towns of Judah and in the
streets of Jerusalem? 18 The children gather wood, the fathers light
the fire, and the women knead the dough and make cakes of bread
for the Queen of Heaven.[m] They pour out drink offerings[n] to other
gods to provoke[o] me to anger. 19 But am I the one they are provoking? declares the LORD. Are they not rather harming themselves,
to their own shame?[p]
20 "'Therefore this is what the Sovereign LORD says: My anger[q]
and my wrath will be poured out on this place, on man and beast,
on the trees of the field and on the fruit of the ground, and it will
burn and not be quenched.
21 "'This is what the LORD Almighty, the God of Israel, says: Go
ahead, add your burnt offerings to your other sacrifices[r] and eat[s]
the meat yourselves! 22 For when I brought your forefathers out of
Egypt and spoke to them, I did not just give them commands about
burnt offerings and sacrifices,[t] 23 but I gave them this command:
Obey[u] me, and I will be your God and you will be my people.[v]
Walk in all the ways I command you, that it may go well[w] with you.
24 But they did not listen or pay attention;[x] instead, they followed
the stubborn inclinations of their evil hearts. They went backward
and not forward. 25 From the time your forefathers left Egypt until
now, day after day, again and again I sent you my servants the
prophets.[y] 26 But they did not listen to me or pay attention. They
were stiff-necked and did more evil than their forefathers.'[z]
27 "When you tell[a] them all this, they will not listen[b] to you;
when you call to them, they will not answer. 28 Therefore say to
them, 'This is the nation that has not obeyed the LORD its God or
responded to correction. Truth has perished; it has vanished from
their lips. 29 Cut off[c] your hair and throw it away; take up a lament

7:10 [a] Jer 32:34; Eze 23:38-39
7:11 [b] Isa 56:7 [c] Mt 21:13*; Mk 11:17*; Lk 19:46* [d] Jer 29:23
7:12 [e] Jos 18:1 [f] 1Sa 4:10-11,22; Ps 78:60-64
7:13 [g] 2Ch 36:15 [h] Isa 65:12 [i] Jer 35:17
7:14 [j] 1Ki 9:7
7:15 [k] Ps 78:67
7:16 [l] Ex 32:10; Dt 9:14; Jer 15:1
7:18 [m] Jer 44:17-19 [n] Jer 19:13 [o] 1Ki 14:9
7:19 [p] Jer 9:19
7:20 [q] Jer 42:18; La 2:3-5
7:21 [r] Isa 1:11; Am 5:21-22 [s] Hos 8:13
7:22 [t] 1Sa 15:22; Ps 51:16; Hos 6:6
7:23 [u] Ex 19:5 [v] Lev 26:12 [w] Ex 15:26
7:24 [x] Ps 81:11-12; Jer 11:8
7:25 [y] Jer 25:4
7:26 [z] Jer 16:12
7:27 [a] Eze 2:7 [b] Eze 3:7
7:29 [c] Job 1:20; Isa 15:2; Mic 1:16

INSIGHT

Shiloh, the home of the tabernacle, was Israel's religious center for over a century after the conquest of Canaan under Joshua. When they took the ark of the covenant from Shiloh, the Philistines slaughtered 30,000 of Israel's foot soldiers (1 Samuel 4:1-11).

on the barren heights, for the LORD has rejected and abandoned[a]
this generation that is under his wrath.

30“‘The people of Judah have done evil in my eyes, declares the
LORD. They have set up their detestable idols[b] in the house that
bears my Name and have defiled[c] it. 31They have built the high
places of Topheth[d] in the Valley of Ben Hinnom to burn their sons
and daughters[e] in the fire—something I did not command, nor
did it enter my mind.[f] 32So beware, the days are coming, declares
the LORD, when people will no longer call it Topheth or the Valley
of Ben Hinnom, but the Valley of Slaughter,[g] for they will bury[h]
the dead in Topheth until there is no more room. 33Then the carcasses of this people will become food[i] for the birds of the air and
the beasts of the earth, and there will be no one to frighten them
away. 34I will bring an end to the sounds[j] of joy and gladness and
to the voices of bride and bridegroom[k] in the towns of Judah and
the streets of Jerusalem, for the land will become desolate.[l]

Chapter 8 Theme ______________________________

8 “‘At that time, declares the LORD, the bones of the kings and
officials of Judah, the bones of the priests and prophets, and
the bones of the people of Jerusalem will be removed from their
graves. 2They will be exposed to the sun and the moon and all the
stars of the heavens, which they have loved and served[m] and which
they have followed and consulted and worshiped. They will not be
gathered up or buried, but will be like refuse lying on the ground.
3Wherever I banish them, all the survivors of this evil nation will
prefer death to life,[n] declares the LORD Almighty.’

4“Say to them, ‘This is what the LORD says:

“‘When men fall down, do they not get up?[o]
  When a man turns away, does he not return?
5Why then have these people turned away?
  Why does Jerusalem always turn away?
They cling to deceit;[p]
  they refuse to return.[q]
6I have listened attentively,
  but they do not say what is right.
No one repents[r] of his wickedness,
  saying, “What have I done?”
Each pursues his own course[s]
  like a horse charging into battle.
7Even the stork in the sky
  knows her appointed seasons,
and the dove, the swift and the thrush
  observe the time of their migration.

7:29 [a] Jer 6:30
7:30 [b] Eze 7:20-22 [c] Jer 32:34
7:31 [d] 2Ki 23:10 [e] Ps 106:38 [f] Jer 19:5
7:32 [g] Jer 19:6 [h] Jer 19:11
7:33 [i] Dt 28:26
7:34 [j] Isa 24:8; Eze 26:13 [k] Rev 18:23 [l] Lev 26:34
8:2 [m] 2Ki 23:5; Ac 7:42
8:3 [n] Job 3:22; Rev 9:6
8:4 [o] Pr 24:16
8:5 [p] Jer 5:27 [q] Jer 7:24; 9:6
8:6 [r] Rev 9:20 [s] Ps 14:1-3

But my people do not know[a]
the requirements of the LORD.

8"'How can you say, "We are wise,
for we have the law[b] of the LORD,"
when actually the lying pen of the scribes
has handled it falsely?
9The wise[c] will be put to shame;
they will be dismayed and trapped.
Since they have rejected the word[d] of the LORD,
what kind of wisdom do they have?
10Therefore I will give their wives to other men
and their fields to new owners.[e]
From the least to the greatest,
all are greedy for gain;[f]
prophets and priests alike,
all practice deceit.
11They dress the wound of my people
as though it were not serious.
"Peace, peace," they say,
when there is no peace.[g]
12Are they ashamed of their loathsome conduct?
No, they have no shame[h] at all;
they do not even know how to blush.
So they will fall among the fallen;
they will be brought down when they are punished,[i]
says the LORD.[j]

13"'I will take away their harvest,
declares the Lord.
There will be no grapes on the vine.[k]
There will be no figs[l] on the tree,
and their leaves will wither.[m]
What I have given them
will be taken[n] from them.[a]'"

14"Why are we sitting here?
Gather together!
Let us flee to the fortified cities[o]
and perish there!
For the LORD our God has doomed us to perish
and given us poisoned water[p] to drink,
because we have sinned[q] against him.
15We hoped for peace[r]
but no good has come,
for a time of healing
but there was only terror.[s]

8:7 [a]Isa 1:3; Jer 5:4-5
8:8 [b]Ro 2:17
8:9 [c]Jer 6:15 [d]Jer 6:19
8:10 [e]Jer 6:12 [f]Isa 56:11
8:11 [g]Jer 6:14
8:12 [h]Jer 3:3 [i]Ps 52:5-7; Isa 3:9 [j]Jer 6:15
8:13 [k]Joel 1:7 [l]Lk 13:6 [m]Mt 21:19 [n]Jer 5:17
8:14 [o]Jer 4:5; Jer 35:11 [p]Dt 29:18; Jer 9:15; 23:15 [q]Jer 14:7,20
8:15 [r]ver 11 [s]Jer 14:19

a *13* The meaning of the Hebrew for this sentence is uncertain.

16The snorting of the enemy's horses
is heard from Dan;[a]
at the neighing of their stallions
the whole land trembles.
They have come to devour
the land and everything in it,
the city and all who live there."

17"See, I will send venomous snakes[b] among you,
vipers that cannot be charmed,[c]
and they will bite you,"
declares the LORD.

18O my Comforter[a] in sorrow,
my heart is faint[d] within me.
19Listen to the cry of my people
from a land far away:[e]
"Is the LORD not in Zion?
Is her King no longer there?"

"Why have they provoked me to anger with their images,
with their worthless foreign idols?"[f]

20"The harvest is past,
the summer has ended,
and we are not saved."

21Since my people are crushed, I am crushed;
I mourn,[g] and horror grips me.
22Is there no balm in Gilead?[h]
Is there no physician there?
Why then is there no healing[i]
for the wound of my people?

Chapter 9 Theme ______________________________

9

Oh, that my head were a spring of water
and my eyes a fountain of tears!
I would weep[j] day and night
for the slain of my people.[k]
2Oh, that I had in the desert
a lodging place for travelers,
so that I might leave my people
and go away from them;
for they are all adulterers,[l]
a crowd of unfaithful people.

3"They make ready their tongue
like a bow, to shoot lies;[m]

a *18* The meaning of the Hebrew for this word is uncertain.

8:16 [a]Jer 4:15
8:17 [b]Nu 21:6; Dt 32:24 [c]Ps 58:5
8:18 [d]La 5:17
8:19 [e]Jer 9:16 [f]Dt 32:21
8:21 [g]Jer 14:17
8:22 [h]Ge 37:25 [i]Jer 30:12
9:1 [j]Jer 13:17; La 2:11,18 [k]Isa 22:4
9:2 [l]Jer 5:7-8; 23:10; Hos 4:2
9:3 [m]Ps 64:3

it is not by truth
that they triumph[a] in the land.
They go from one sin to another;
they do not acknowledge me,”
declares the LORD.

4“Beware of your friends;
do not trust your brothers.[a]
For every brother is a deceiver,[b][b]
and every friend a slanderer.
5Friend deceives friend,
and no one speaks the truth.
They have taught their tongues to lie;
they weary themselves with sinning.
6You[c] live in the midst of deception;[c]
in their deceit they refuse to acknowledge me,”
declares the LORD.

7Therefore this is what the LORD Almighty says:

“See, I will refine[d] and test[e] them,
for what else can I do
because of the sin of my people?
8Their tongue[f] is a deadly arrow;
it speaks with deceit.
With his mouth each speaks cordially to his neighbor,
but in his heart he sets a trap[g] for him.
9Should I not punish them for this?”
declares the LORD.
“Should I not avenge[h] myself
on such a nation as this?”

10I will weep and wail for the mountains
and take up a lament concerning the desert pastures.
They are desolate and untraveled,
and the lowing of cattle is not heard.
The birds of the air[i] have fled
and the animals are gone.

11“I will make Jerusalem a heap of ruins,
a haunt of jackals;[j]
and I will lay waste the towns of Judah
so no one can live there.”[k]

12What man is wise[l] enough to understand this? Who has been instructed by the LORD and can explain it? Why has the land been ruined and laid waste like a desert that no one can cross?

9:4 [a]Mic 7:5-6 [b]Ge 27:35
9:6 [c]Jer 5:27
9:7 [d]Isa 1:25 [e]Jer 6:27
9:8 [f]ver 3 [g]Jer 5:26
9:9 [h]Jer 5:9, 29
9:10 [i]Jer 4:25; 12:4; Hos 4:3
9:11 [j]Isa 34:13 [k]Isa 25:2; Jer 26:9
9:12 [l]Ps 107:43; Hos 14:9

[a]3 Or *lies; / they are not valiant for truth* [b]4 Or *a deceiving Jacob* [c]6 That is, Jeremiah (the Hebrew is singular)

13 The LORD said, "It is because they have forsaken my law, which
I set before them; they have not obeyed me or followed my law.[a]
14 Instead, they have followed[b] the stubbornness of their hearts;[c]
they have followed the Baals, as their fathers taught them."
15 Therefore, this is what the LORD Almighty, the God of Israel, says:
"See, I will make this people eat bitter food[d] and drink poisoned
water.[e] 16 I will scatter them among nations[f] that neither they nor
their fathers have known,[g] and I will pursue them with the sword[h]
until I have destroyed them."[i]

17 This is what the LORD Almighty says:

"Consider now! Call for the wailing women[j] to come;
  send for the most skillful of them.
18 Let them come quickly
  and wail over us
till our eyes overflow with tears
  and water streams from our eyelids.[k]
19 The sound of wailing is heard from Zion:
  'How ruined[l] we are!
  How great is our shame!
We must leave our land
  because our houses are in ruins.'"

20 Now, O women, hear the word of the LORD;
  open your ears to the words of his mouth.
Teach your daughters how to wail;
  teach one another a lament.[m]
21 Death has climbed in through our windows
  and has entered our fortresses;
it has cut off the children from the streets
  and the young men[n] from the public squares.

22 Say, "This is what the LORD declares:

"'The dead bodies of men will lie
  like refuse[o] on the open field,
like cut grain behind the reaper,
  with no one to gather them.'"

23 This is what the LORD says:

"Let not the wise man boast of his wisdom[p]
  or the strong man boast of his strength[q]
  or the rich man boast of his riches,[r]
24 but let him who boasts boast[s] about this:
  that he understands and knows me,

9:13 [a] 2Ch 7:19; Ps 89:30-32
9:14 [b] Jer 2:8,23 [c] Jer 7:24
9:15 [d] La 3:15 [e] Jer 8:14
9:16 [f] Lev 26:33 [g] Dt 28:64 [h] Eze 5:2 [i] Jer 44:27; Eze 5:12
9:17 [j] 2Ch 35:25; Ecc 12:5; Am 5:16
9:18 [k] Jer 14:17
9:19 [l] Jer 4:13
9:20 [m] Isa 32:9-13
9:21 [n] 2Ch 36:17
9:22 [o] Jer 8:2
9:23 [p] Ecc 9:11 [q] 1Ki 20:11 [r] Eze 28:4-5
9:24 [s] 1Co 1:31*; Gal 6:14

that I am the LORD,[a] who exercises kindness,[b]
justice and righteousness[c] on earth,
for in these I delight,"
declares the LORD.

25"The days are coming," declares the LORD, "when I will punish
all who are circumcised only in the flesh[d]— 26Egypt, Judah, Edom,
Ammon, Moab and all who live in the desert in distant places.[a][e]
For all these nations are really uncircumcised, and even the whole
house of Israel is uncircumcised in heart.[f]"

Chapter 10 Theme ____________________

10 Hear what the LORD says to you, O house of Israel. 2This is
what the LORD says:

"Do not learn the ways of the nations[g]
or be terrified by signs in the sky,
though the nations are terrified by them.
3For the customs of the peoples are worthless;
they cut a tree out of the forest,
and a craftsman[h] shapes it with his chisel.
4They adorn it with silver and gold;
they fasten it with hammer and nails
so it will not totter.[i]
5Like a scarecrow in a melon patch,
their idols cannot speak;[j]
they must be carried
because they cannot walk.[k]
Do not fear them;
they can do no harm
nor can they do any good."[l]

6No one is like you, O LORD;
you are great,[m]
and your name is mighty in power.
7Who should not revere you,
O King of the nations?[n]
This is your due.
Among all the wise men of the nations
and in all their kingdoms,
there is no one like you.
8They are all senseless and foolish;[o]
they are taught by worthless wooden idols.
9Hammered silver is brought from Tarshish
and gold from Uphaz.

9:24 [a]2Co 10:17* [b]Ps 51:1; Mic 7:18 [c]Ps 36:6
9:25 [d]Ro 2:8-9
9:26 [e]Jer 25:23 [f]Lev 26:41; Ac 7:51; Ro 2:28
10:2 [g]Lev 20:23
10:3 [h]Isa 40:19
10:4 [i]Isa 41:7
10:5 [j]1Co 12:2 [k]Ps 115:5,7 [l]Isa 41:24; 46:7
10:6 [m]Ps 48:1
10:7 [n]Ps 22:28; Rev 15:4
10:8 [o]Isa 40:19; Jer 4:22

[a]26 Or *desert and who clip the hair by their foreheads*

What the craftsman and goldsmith have made[a]
is then dressed in blue and purple—
all made by skilled workers.
10But the LORD is the true God;
he is the living God, the eternal King.
When he is angry, the earth trembles;
the nations cannot endure his wrath.[b]

11"Tell them this: 'These gods, who did not make the heavens
and the earth, will perish[c] from the earth and from under the
heavens.' "[a]

12But God made the earth by his power;
he founded the world by his wisdom
and stretched out the heavens[d] by his understanding.
13When he thunders,[e] the waters in the heavens roar;
he makes clouds rise from the ends of the earth.
He sends lightning with the rain[f]
and brings out the wind from his storehouses.

14Everyone is senseless and without knowledge;
every goldsmith is shamed by his idols.
His images are a fraud;
they have no breath in them.
15They are worthless,[g] the objects of mockery;
when their judgment comes, they will perish.
16He who is the Portion[h] of Jacob is not like these,
for he is the Maker of all things,[i]
including Israel, the tribe of his inheritance[j]—
the LORD Almighty is his name.[k]

17Gather up your belongings[l] to leave the land,
you who live under siege.
18For this is what the LORD says:
"At this time I will hurl[m] out
those who live in this land;
I will bring distress on them
so that they may be captured."

19Woe to me because of my injury!
My wound[n] is incurable!
Yet I said to myself,
"This is my sickness, and I must endure[o] it."
20My tent[p] is destroyed;
all its ropes are snapped.

10:9 [a]Ps 115:4; Isa 40:19
10:10 [b]Ps 76:7
10:11 [c]Ps 96:5; Isa 2:18
10:12 [d]Ge 1:1,8; Job 9:8; Isa 40:22
10:13 [e]Job 36:29 [f]Ps 135:7
10:15 [g]Isa 41:24; Jer 14:22
10:16 [h]Dt 32:9; Ps 119:57 [i]ver 12 [j]Ps 74:2 [k]Jer 31:35; 32:18
10:17 [l]Eze 12:3-12
10:18 [m]1Sa 25:29
10:19 [n]Jer 14:17 [o]Mic 7:9
10:20 [p]Jer 4:20

a *11* The text of this verse is in Aramaic.

My sons are gone from me and are no more;[a]
no one is left now to pitch my tent
or to set up my shelter.
21 The shepherds are senseless
and do not inquire of the LORD;
so they do not prosper
and all their flock is scattered.[b]
22 Listen! The report is coming—
a great commotion from the land of the north!
It will make the towns of Judah desolate,
a haunt of jackals.[c]

23 I know, O LORD, that a man's life is not his own;
it is not for man to direct his steps.[d]
24 Correct me, LORD, but only with justice—
not in your anger,[e]
lest you reduce me to nothing.[f]
25 Pour out your wrath on the nations[g]
that do not acknowledge you,
on the peoples who do not call on your name.[h]
For they have devoured[i] Jacob;
they have devoured him completely
and destroyed his homeland.[j]

Chapter 11 Theme ______________________

11 This is the word that came to Jeremiah from the LORD:
2 "Listen to the terms of this covenant and tell them to the
people of Judah and to those who live in Jerusalem. 3 Tell them that
this is what the LORD, the God of Israel, says: 'Cursed[k] is the man
who does not obey the terms of this covenant— 4 the terms I
commanded your forefathers when I brought them out of Egypt,
out of the iron-smelting furnace.[l] I said, 'Obey[m] me and do everything I command you, and you will be my people,[n] and I will be
your God. 5 Then I will fulfill the oath I swore[o] to your forefathers,
to give them a land flowing with milk and honey'—the land you
possess today."

I answered, "Amen, LORD."

6 The LORD said to me, "Proclaim all these words in the towns of
Judah and in the streets of Jerusalem: 'Listen to the terms of this
covenant and follow[p] them. 7 From the time I brought your forefathers up from Egypt until today, I warned them again and again,[q]
saying, "Obey me." 8 But they did not listen or pay attention;[r]
instead, they followed the stubbornness of their evil hearts. So I
brought on them all the curses[s] of the covenant I had commanded
them to follow but that they did not keep.'"

10:20 [a] Jer 31:15; La 1:5
10:21 [b] Jer 23:2
10:22 [c] Jer 9:11
10:23 [d] Pr 20:24
10:24 [e] Ps 6:1; 38:1 [f] Jer 30:11
10:25 [g] Zep 3:8 [h] Job 18:21; Ps 14:4 [i] Ps 79:7; Jer 8:16 [j] Ps 79:6-7
11:3 [k] Dt 27:26; Gal 3:10
11:4 [l] Dt 4:20; 1Ki 8:51 [m] Ex 24:8 [n] Jer 7:23; 31:33
11:5 [o] Ex 13:5; Dt 7:12; Ps 105:8-11
11:6 [p] Dt 15:5; Ro 2:13; Jas 1:22
11:7 [q] 2Ch 36:15
11:8 [r] Jer 7:26 [s] Lev 26:14-43

9 Then the LORD said to me, "There is a conspiracy[a] among the
people of Judah and those who live in Jerusalem. 10 They have
returned to the sins of their forefathers,[b] who refused to listen to
my words. They have followed other gods[c] to serve them. Both the
house of Israel and the house of Judah have broken the covenant
I made with their forefathers. 11 Therefore this is what the LORD
says: 'I will bring on them a disaster[d] they cannot escape. Although
they cry[e] out to me, I will not listen[f] to them. 12 The towns of
Judah and the people of Jerusalem will go and cry out to the gods
to whom they burn incense,[g] but they will not help them at all
when disaster[h] strikes. 13 You have as many gods as you have
towns, O Judah; and the altars you have set up to burn incense[i] to
that shameful[j] god Baal are as many as the streets of Jerusalem.'
14 "Do not pray[k] for this people nor offer any plea or petition for
them, because I will not listen[l] when they call to me in the time of
their distress.

15 "What is my beloved doing in my temple
as she works out her evil schemes with many?
Can consecrated meat avert ⌊your punishment⌋?
When you engage in your wickedness,
then you rejoice.[a]"

16 The LORD called you a thriving olive tree
with fruit beautiful in form.
But with the roar of a mighty storm
he will set it on fire,[m]
and its branches will be broken.[n]

17 The LORD Almighty, who planted[o] you, has decreed disaster for
you, because the house of Israel and the house of Judah have
done evil and provoked me to anger by burning incense to Baal.[p]
18 Because the LORD revealed their plot to me, I knew it, for at that
time he showed me what they were doing. 19 I had been like a gentle
lamb led to the slaughter; I did not realize that they had plotted[q]
against me, saying,

"Let us destroy the tree and its fruit;
let us cut him off from the land of the living,[r]
that his name be remembered[s] no more."
20 But, O LORD Almighty, you who judge righteously
and test the heart and mind,[t]
let me see your vengeance upon them,
for to you I have committed my cause.

21 "Therefore this is what the LORD says about the men of Anathoth who are seeking your life[u] and saying, 'Do not prophesy in the

[a] 15 Or *Could consecrated meat avert your punishment? / Then you would rejoice*

11:9 [a]Eze 22:25
11:10 [b]Dt 9:7 [c]Jdg 2:12-13
11:11 [d]2Ki 22:16 [e]Jer 14:12; Eze 8:18 [f]ver 14; Pr 1:28; Isa 1:15; Zec 7:13
11:12 [g]Jer 44:17 [h]Dt 32:37
11:13 [i]Jer 7:9 [j]Jer 3:24
11:14 [k]Ex 32:10 [l]ver 11
11:16 [m]Jer 21:14 [n]Isa 27:11; Ro 11:17-24
11:17 [o]Isa 5:2; Jer 12:2 [p]Jer 7:9
11:19 [q]Jer 18:18; 20:10 [r]Job 28:13; Isa 53:8 [s]Ps 83:4
11:20 [t]Ps 7:9
11:21 [u]Jer 12:6

name of the LORD or you will die[a] by our hands'— 22therefore this
is what the LORD Almighty says: 'I will punish them. Their young
men[b] will die by the sword, their sons and daughters by famine.
23Not even a remnant[c] will be left to them, because I will bring disaster on the men of Anathoth in the year of their punishment.[d]'"

Chapter 12 Theme ______________________

12

You are always righteous,[e] O LORD,
  when I bring a case before you.
Yet I would speak with you about your justice:
  Why does the way of the wicked prosper?[f]
  Why do all the faithless live at ease?
2You have planted[g] them, and they have taken root;
  they grow and bear fruit.
You are always on their lips
  but far from their hearts.[h]
3Yet you know me, O LORD;
  you see me and test[i] my thoughts about you.
Drag them off like sheep to be butchered!
  Set them apart for the day of slaughter![j]
4How long will the land lie parched[a][k]
  and the grass in every field be withered?[l]
Because those who live in it are wicked,
  the animals and birds have perished.[m]
Moreover, the people are saying,
  "He will not see what happens to us."

5"If you have raced with men on foot
  and they have worn you out,
  how can you compete with horses?
If you stumble in safe country,[b]
  how will you manage in the thickets[n] by[c] the Jordan?
6Your brothers, your own family—
  even they have betrayed you;
  they have raised a loud cry against you.[o]
Do not trust them,
  though they speak well of you.[p]

7"I will forsake my house,
  abandon[q] my inheritance;
I will give the one I love
  into the hands of her enemies.
8My inheritance has become to me
  like a lion in the forest.

a4 Or *land mourn* b5 Or *If you put your trust in a land of safety* c5 Or *the flooding of*

11:21 [a]Jer 26:8,11; 38:4
11:22 [b]Jer 18:21
11:23 [c]Jer 6:9 [d]Jer 23:12
12:1 [e]Ezr 9:15 [f]Jer 5:27-28
12:2 [g]Jer 11:17 [h]Isa 29:13; Jer 3:10; Mt 15:8; Tit 1:16
12:3 [i]Ps 7:9; 11:5; 139:1-4; Jer 11:20 [j]Jer 17:18
12:4 [k]Jer 4:28 [l]Joel 1:10-12 [m]Jer 4:25; 9:10
12:5 [n]Jer 49:19; 50:44
12:6 [o]Pr 26:24-25; Jer 9:4 [p]Ps 12:2
12:7 [q]Jer 7:29

She roars at me;
therefore I hate her.[a]
9Has not my inheritance become to me
like a speckled bird of prey
that other birds of prey surround and attack?
Go and gather all the wild beasts;
bring them to devour.[b]
10Many shepherds[c] will ruin my vineyard
and trample down my field;
they will turn my pleasant field
into a desolate wasteland.[d]
11It will be made a wasteland,
parched and desolate before me;[e]
the whole land will be laid waste
because there is no one who cares.
12Over all the barren heights in the desert
destroyers will swarm,
for the sword of the LORD[f] will devour
from one end of the land to the other;[g]
no one will be safe.
13They will sow wheat but reap thorns;
they will wear themselves out but gain nothing.[h]
So bear the shame of your harvest
because of the LORD's fierce anger."[i]

14This is what the LORD says: "As for all my wicked neighbors
who seize the inheritance I gave my people Israel, I will uproot[j]
them from their lands and I will uproot the house of Judah from
among them. 15But after I uproot them, I will again have compassion and will bring[k] each of them back to his own inheritance and
his own country. 16And if they learn well the ways of my people
and swear by my name, saying, 'As surely as the LORD lives'[l]—
even as they once taught my people to swear by Baal[m]—then they
will be established among my people.[n] 17But if any nation does not
listen, I will completely uproot and destroy[o] it," declares the LORD.

Chapter 13 Theme ______________________________

13 This is what the LORD said to me: "Go and buy a linen belt
and put it around your waist, but do not let it touch water."
2So I bought a belt, as the LORD directed, and put it around my
waist.
3Then the word of the LORD came to me a second time: 4"Take
the belt you bought and are wearing around your waist, and go
now to Perath[a] and hide it there in a crevice in the rocks." 5So I
went and hid it at Perath, as the LORD told me.[p]

[a]4 Or possibly *the Euphrates*; also in verses 5-7

12:8 [a]Hos 9:15; Am 6:8
12:9 [b]Isa 56:9; Jer 15:3; Eze 23:25
12:10 [c]Jer 23:1 [d]Isa 5:1-7
12:11 [e]ver 4; Isa 42:25; Jer 23:10
12:12 [f]Jer 47:6 [g]Jer 3:2
12:13 [h]Lev 26:20; Dt 28:38; Mic 6:15; Hag 1:6 [i]Jer 4:26
12:14 [j]Zec 2:7-9
12:15 [k]Am 9:14-15
12:16 [l]Jer 4:2 [m]Jos 23:7 [n]Isa 49:6; Jer 3:17
12:17 [o]Isa 60:12
13:5 [p]Ex 40:16

6Many days later the LORD said to me, "Go now to Perath and get
the belt I told you to hide there." 7So I went to Perath and dug up
the belt and took it from the place where I had hidden it, but now it
was ruined and completely useless.

8Then the word of the LORD came to me: 9"This is what the LORD
says: 'In the same way I will ruin the pride of Judah and the great
pride[a] of Jerusalem. 10These wicked people, who refuse to listen
to my words, who follow the stubbornness of their hearts[b] and go
after other gods[c] to serve and worship them, will be like this
belt—completely useless! 11For as a belt is bound around a man's
waist, so I bound the whole house of Israel and the whole house of
Judah to me,' declares the LORD, 'to be my people for my renown[d]
and praise and honor.[e] But they have not listened.'[f]

12"Say to them: 'This is what the LORD, the God of Israel, says:
Every wineskin should be filled with wine.' And if they say to you,
'Don't we know that every wineskin should be filled with wine?'
13then tell them, 'This is what the LORD says: I am going to fill with
drunkenness[g] all who live in this land, including the kings who sit
on David's throne, the priests, the prophets and all those living in
Jerusalem. 14I will smash them one against the other, fathers and
sons alike, declares the LORD. I will allow no pity or mercy or compassion[h] to keep me from destroying[i] them.'"

15Hear and pay attention,
do not be arrogant,
for the LORD has spoken.
16Give glory[j] to the LORD your God
before he brings the darkness,
before your feet stumble[k]
on the darkening hills.
You hope for light,
but he will turn it to thick darkness
and change it to deep gloom.[l]
17But if you do not listen,[m]
I will weep in secret
because of your pride;
my eyes will weep bitterly,
overflowing with tears,[n]
because the LORD's flock[o] will be taken captive.[p]

18Say to the king and to the queen mother,
"Come down from your thrones,
for your glorious crowns
will fall from your heads."
19The cities in the Negev will be shut up,
and there will be no one to open them.

13:9 [a]Lev 26:19
13:10 [b]Jer 11:8; 16:12 [c]Jer 9:14
13:11 [d]Jer 32:20; 33:9 [e]Ex 19:5-6 [f]Jer 7:26
13:13 [g]Ps 60:3; 75:8; Isa 51:17; 63:6; Jer 51:57
13:14 [h]Jer 16:5 [i]Dt 29:20; Eze 5:10
13:16 [j]Jos 7:19 [k]Jer 23:12 [l]Isa 59:9
13:17 [m]Mal 2:2 [n]Jer 9:1 [o]Ps 80:1; Jer 23:1 [p]Jer 14:18

All Judah[a] will be carried into exile,
carried completely away.

[20]Lift up your eyes and see
those who are coming from the north.[b]
Where is the flock[c] that was entrusted to you,
the sheep of which you boasted?
[21]What will you say when ⌊the LORD⌋ sets over you
those you cultivated as your special allies?[d]
Will not pain grip you
like that of a woman in labor?[e]
[22]And if you ask yourself,
"Why has this happened to me?"—
it is because of your many sins[f]
that your skirts have been torn off
and your body mistreated.[g]
[23]Can the Ethiopian[a] change his skin
or the leopard its spots?
Neither can you do good
who are accustomed to doing evil.

[24]"I will scatter you like chaff[h]
driven by the desert wind.[i]
[25]This is your lot,
the portion[j] I have decreed for you,"
declares the LORD,
"because you have forgotten me
and trusted in false gods.
[26]I will pull up your skirts over your face
that your shame may be seen[k]—
[27]your adulteries and lustful neighings,
your shameless prostitution![l]
I have seen your detestable acts
on the hills and in the fields.[m]
Woe to you, O Jerusalem!
How long will you be unclean?"[n]

Chapter 14 Theme ______________________________

14

This is the word of the LORD to Jeremiah concerning the drought:

[2]"Judah mourns,[o]
her cities languish;
they wail for the land,
and a cry goes up from Jerusalem.

a 23 Hebrew *Cushite* (probably a person from the upper Nile region)

13:19
[a] Jer 20:4; 52:30

13:20
[b] Jer 6:22; Hab 1:6
[c] Jer 23:2

13:21
[d] Jer 38:22
[e] Jer 4:31

13:22
[f] Jer 9:2-6; 16:10-12
[g] Eze 16:37; Na 3:5-6

13:24
[h] Ps 1:4
[i] Lev 26:33

13:25
[j] Job 20:29; Mt 24:51

13:26
[k] La 1:8; Eze 16:37; Hos 2:10

13:27
[l] Jer 2:20
[m] Eze 6:13
[n] Hos 8:5

14:2
[o] Isa 3:26; Jer 8:21

3 The nobles send their servants for water;
  they go to the cisterns
  but find no water.[a]
They return with their jars unfilled;
  dismayed and despairing,
  they cover their heads.[b]
4 The ground is cracked
  because there is no rain in the land;[c]
the farmers are dismayed
  and cover their heads.
5 Even the doe in the field
  deserts her newborn fawn
  because there is no grass.[d]
6 Wild donkeys stand on the barren heights[e]
  and pant like jackals;
their eyesight fails
  for lack of pasture."

7 Although our sins testify[f] against us,
  O LORD, do something for the sake of your name.
For our backsliding[g] is great;
  we have sinned[h] against you.
8 O Hope[i] of Israel,
  its Savior in times of distress,
why are you like a stranger in the land,
  like a traveler who stays only a night?
9 Why are you like a man taken by surprise,
  like a warrior powerless to save?[j]
You are among[k] us, O LORD,
  and we bear your name;[l]
  do not forsake us!

10 This is what the LORD says about this people:

"They greatly love to wander;
  they do not restrain their feet.[m]
So the LORD does not accept[n] them;
  he will now remember[o] their wickedness
  and punish them for their sins."[p]

11 Then the LORD said to me, "Do not pray[q] for the well-being of
this people. 12 Although they fast, I will not listen to their cry;[r]
though they offer burnt offerings[s] and grain offerings, I will not
accept[t] them. Instead, I will destroy them with the sword, famine
and plague."
13 But I said, "Ah, Sovereign LORD, the prophets keep telling them,
'You will not see the sword or suffer famine.[u] Indeed, I will give
you lasting peace in this place.'"

14:3 [a] 2Ki 18:31; Job 6:19-20 [b] 2Sa 15:30
14:4 [c] Jer 3:3
14:5 [d] Isa 15:6
14:6 [e] Job 39:5-6; Jer 2:24
14:7 [f] Hos 5:5 [g] Jer 5:6 [h] Jer 8:14
14:8 [i] Jer 17:13
14:9 [j] Isa 50:2 [k] Jer 8:19 [l] Isa 63:19; Jer 15:16
14:10 [m] Ps 119:101; Jer 2:25 [n] Jer 6:20; Am 5:22 [o] Hos 9:9 [p] Jer 44:21-23; Hos 8:13
14:11 [q] Ex 32:10
14:12 [r] Isa 1:15; Jer 11:11 [s] Jer 7:21 [t] Jer 6:20
14:13 [u] Jer 5:12

14Then the LORD said to me, "The prophets are prophesying lies[a]
in my name. I have not sent[b] them or appointed them or spoken
to them. They are prophesying to you false visions,[c] divinations,[d]
idolatries[a] and the delusions of their own minds. 15Therefore, this
is what the LORD says about the prophets who are prophesying in
my name: I did not send them, yet they are saying, 'No sword or
famine will touch this land.' Those same prophets will perish[e] by
sword and famine.[f] 16And the people they are prophesying to will
be thrown out into the streets of Jerusalem because of the famine
and sword. There will be no one to bury[g] them or their wives, their
sons or their daughters.[h] I will pour out on them the calamity they
deserve.[i]

17"Speak this word to them:

"'Let my eyes overflow with tears[j]
night and day without ceasing;
for my virgin daughter—my people—
has suffered a grievous wound,
a crushing blow.[k]
18If I go into the country,
I see those slain by the sword;
if I go into the city,
I see the ravages of famine.[l]
Both prophet and priest
have gone to a land they know not.'"

19Have you rejected Judah completely?[m]
Do you despise Zion?
Why have you afflicted us
so that we cannot be healed?[n]
We hoped for peace
but no good has come,
for a time of healing
but there is only terror.[o]
20O LORD, we acknowledge our wickedness
and the guilt of our fathers;
we have indeed sinned[p] against you.
21For the sake of your name[q] do not despise us;
do not dishonor your glorious throne.[r]
Remember your covenant with us
and do not break it.
22Do any of the worthless idols of the nations bring rain?[s]
Do the skies themselves send down showers?

a 14 Or *visions, worthless divinations*

14:14
[a] Jer 27:14
[b] Jer 23:21,32
[c] Jer 23:16
[d] Eze 12:24

14:15
[e] Eze 14:9
[f] Jer 5:12-13

14:16
[g] Ps 79:3
[h] Jer 7:33
[i] Pr 1:31

14:17
[j] Jer 9:1
[k] Jer 8:21

14:18
[l] Eze 7:15

14:19
[m] Jer 7:29
[n] Jer 30:12-13
[o] Jer 8:15

14:20
[p] Da 9:7-8

14:21
[q] ver 7
[r] Jer 3:17

14:22
[s] Ps 135:7

No, it is you, O LORD our God.
  Therefore our hope is in you,
  for you are the one who does all this.

Chapter 15 Theme ______________________________

15 Then the LORD said to me: "Even if Moses[a] and Samuel[b]
were to stand before me, my heart would not go out to this
people.[c] Send them away from my presence![d] Let them go! 2And if
they ask you, 'Where shall we go?' tell them, 'This is what the LORD
says:

"'Those destined for death, to death;
those for the sword, to the sword;[e]
those for starvation, to starvation;[f]
those for captivity, to captivity.'[g]

3"I will send four kinds of destroyers[h] against them," declares the
LORD, "the sword to kill and the dogs to drag away and the birds[i] of
the air and the beasts of the earth to devour and destroy.[j] 4I will
make them abhorrent[k] to all the kingdoms of the earth[l] because of
what Manasseh[m] son of Hezekiah king of Judah did in Jerusalem.

5"Who will have pity[n] on you, O Jerusalem?
  Who will mourn for you?
  Who will stop to ask how you are?
6You have rejected[o] me," declares the LORD.
  "You keep on backsliding.
So I will lay hands[p] on you and destroy you;
  I can no longer show compassion.
7I will winnow them with a winnowing fork
  at the city gates of the land.
I will bring bereavement and destruction on my people,[q]
  for they have not changed their ways.
8I will make their widows more numerous
  than the sand of the sea.
At midday I will bring a destroyer[r]
  against the mothers of their young men;
suddenly I will bring down on them
  anguish and terror.
9The mother of seven will grow faint[s]
  and breathe her last.
Her sun will set while it is still day;
  she will be disgraced and humiliated.
I will put the survivors to the sword[t]
  before their enemies,"
declares the LORD.

INSIGHT

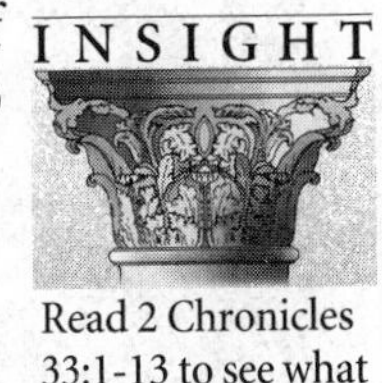

Read 2 Chronicles 33:1-13 to see what Manasseh did.

15:1 [a]Ex 32:11; Nu 14:13-20 [b]1Sa 7:9 [c]Jer 7:16; Eze 14:14,20 [d]2Ki 17:20
15:2 [e]Jer 43:11 [f]Jer 14:12 [g]Rev 13:10
15:3 [h]Lev 26:16 [i]Dt 28:26 [j]Lev 26:22; Eze 14:21
15:4 [k]Jer 24:9; 29:18 [l]Dt 28:25 [m]2Ki 21:2; 23:26-27
15:5 [n]Isa 51:19; Jer 13:14; 21:7; Na 3:7
15:6 [o]Jer 6:19; 7:24 [p]Zep 1:4
15:7 [q]Jer 18:21
15:8 [r]Jer 6:4
15:9 [s]1Sa 2:5 [t]Jer 21:7

[10]Alas, my mother, that you gave me birth,[a]
a man with whom the whole land strives and contends![b]
I have neither lent[c] nor borrowed,
yet everyone curses me.

[11]The LORD said,

"Surely I will deliver you[d] for a good purpose;
surely I will make your enemies plead[e] with you
in times of disaster and times of distress.

[12]"Can a man break iron—
iron from the north[f]—or bronze?
[13]Your wealth and your treasures
I will give as plunder, without charge,[g]
because of all your sins
throughout your country.[h]
[14]I will enslave you to your enemies
in[a] a land you do not know,[i]
for my anger will kindle a fire[j]
that will burn against you."
[15]You understand, O LORD;
remember me and care for me.
Avenge me on my persecutors.[k]
You are long-suffering—do not take me away;
think of how I suffer reproach for your sake.[l]
[16]When your words came, I ate[m] them;
they were my joy and my heart's delight,[n]
for I bear your name,[o]
O LORD God Almighty.
[17]I never sat[p] in the company of revelers,
never made merry with them;
I sat alone because your hand was on me
and you had filled me with indignation.
[18]Why is my pain unending
and my wound grievous and incurable?[q]
Will you be to me like a deceptive brook,
like a spring that fails?[r]

[19]Therefore this is what the LORD says:

"If you repent, I will restore you
that you may serve[s] me;
if you utter worthy, not worthless, words,
you will be my spokesman.

a *14* Some Hebrew manuscripts, Septuagint and Syriac (see also Jer. 17:4); most Hebrew manuscripts *I will cause your enemies to bring you / into*

15:10
[a]Job 3:1
[b]Jer 1:19
[c]Lev 25:36

15:11
[d]Jer 40:4
[e]Jer 21:1-2; 37:3; 42:1-3

15:12
[f]Jer 28:14

15:13
[g]Ps 44:12
[h]Jer 17:3

15:14
[i]Dt 28:36; Jer 16:13
[j]Dt 32:22; Ps 21:9

15:15
[k]Jer 12:3
[l]Ps 69:7-9

15:16
[m]Eze 3:3; Rev 10:10
[n]Ps 119:72,103
[o]Jer 14:9

15:17
[p]Ps 1:1; 26:4-5; Jer 16:8

15:18
[q]Jer 30:15; Mic 1:9
[r]Job 6:15

15:19
[s]Zec 3:7

Let this people turn to you,
but you must not turn to them.
20 I will make you a wall to this people,
a fortified wall of bronze;
they will fight against you
but will not overcome you,
for I am with you
to rescue and save you,"[a]
declares the LORD.
21 "I will save you from the hands of the wicked
and redeem[b] you from the grasp of the cruel."[c]

Chapter 16 Theme

16 Then the word of the LORD came to me: 2 "You must not
marry[d] and have sons or daughters in this place." 3 For this
is what the LORD says about the sons and daughters born in this
land and about the women who are their mothers and the men
who are their fathers:[e] 4 "They will die of deadly diseases. They
will not be mourned or buried[f] but will be like refuse lying on the
ground.[g] They will perish by sword and famine, and their dead
bodies will become food for the birds of the air and the beasts of
the earth."[h]

5 For this is what the LORD says: "Do not enter a house where
there is a funeral meal; do not go to mourn or show sympathy,
because I have withdrawn my blessing, my love and my pity from
this people," declares the LORD. 6 "Both high and low will die in
this land.[i] They will not be buried or mourned, and no one will
cut[j] himself or shave[k] his head for them. 7 No one will offer food to
comfort those who mourn[l] for the dead—not even for a father or
a mother—nor will anyone give them a drink to console them.

8 "And do not enter a house where there is feasting and sit down
to eat and drink.[m] 9 For this is what the LORD Almighty, the God
of Israel, says: Before your eyes and in your days I will bring an
end to the sounds[n] of joy and gladness and to the voices of bride
and bridegroom in this place.[o]

10 "When you tell these people all this and they ask you, 'Why has
the LORD decreed such a great disaster against us? What wrong
have we done? What sin have we committed against the LORD our
God?'[p] 11 then say to them, 'It is because your fathers forsook me,'
declares the LORD, 'and followed other gods and served and worshiped them. They forsook me and did not keep my law.[q] 12 But you
have behaved more wickedly than your fathers.[r] See how each of
you is following the stubbornness of his evil heart[s] instead of
obeying me. 13 So I will throw you out of this land into a land neither your nor your fathers have known,[t] and there you will serve
other gods[u] day and night, for I will show you no favor.'[v]

15:20 [a] Jer 20:11; Eze 3:8
15:21 [b] Jer 50:34 [c] Ge 48:16
16:2 [d] 1Co 7:26-27
16:3 [e] Jer 6:21
16:4 [f] Jer 25:33 [g] Ps 83:10; Jer 9:22 [h] Ps 79:1-3; Jer 15:3; 34:20
16:6 [i] Eze 9:5-6 [j] Lev 19:28 [k] Jer 41:5; 47:5
16:7 [l] Eze 24:17; Hos 9:4
16:8 [m] Ecc 7:2-4; Jer 15:17
16:9 [n] Isa 24:8; Eze 26:13; Hos 2:11 [o] Rev 18:23
16:10 [p] Dt 29:24; Jer 5:19
16:11 [q] Dt 29:25-26; 1Ki 9:9; Ps 106:35-43; Jer 22:9
16:12 [r] Jer 7:26 [s] Ecc 9:3; Jer 13:10
16:13 [t] Dt 28:36; Jer 5:19 [u] Dt 4:28 [v] Jer 15:5

14“However, the days are coming,” declares the LORD, “when
men will no longer say, ‘As surely as the LORD lives, who brought
the Israelites up out of Egypt,’[a] 15but they will say, ‘As surely as the
LORD lives, who brought the Israelites up out of the land of the
north and out of all the countries where he had banished them.’[b]
For I will restore[c] them to the land I gave their forefathers.

16“But now I will send for many fishermen,” declares the LORD,
“and they will catch them.[d] After that I will send for many
hunters, and they will hunt[e] them down on every mountain and
hill and from the crevices of the rocks.[f] 17My eyes are on all their
ways; they are not hidden[g] from me, nor is their sin concealed
from my eyes.[h] 18I will repay them double[i] for their wickedness
and their sin, because they have defiled my land[j] with the lifeless
forms of their vile images and have filled my inheritance with
their detestable idols.”

19O LORD, my strength and my fortress,
my refuge in time of distress,
to you the nations will come[k]
from the ends of the earth and say,
“Our fathers possessed nothing but false gods,[l]
worthless idols that did them no good.
20Do men make their own gods?
Yes, but they are not gods!”[m]

21“Therefore I will teach them—
this time I will teach them
my power and might.
Then they will know
that my name is the LORD.

Chapter 17 Theme

17 “Judah’s sin is engraved with an iron tool,[n]
inscribed with a flint point,
on the tablets of their hearts[o]
and on the horns of their altars.
2Even their children remember
their altars and Asherah poles[a] [p]
beside the spreading trees
and on the high hills.[q]
3My mountain in the land
and your[b] wealth and all your treasures
I will give away as plunder,[r]
together with your high places,[s]
because of sin throughout your country.[t]

[a]2 That is, symbols of the goddess Asherah [b]2,3 *Or hills / [3]and the mountains of the land. / Your*

16:14 [a]Dt 15:15; Jer 23:7-8
16:15 [b]Isa 11:11; Jer 23:8 [c]Jer 24:6
16:16 [d]Am 4:2; Hab 1:14-15 [e]Am 9:3; Mic 7:2 [f]1Sa 26:20
16:17 [g]1Co 4:5; Heb 4:13 [h]Pr 15:3
16:18 [i]Isa 40:2; Rev 18:6 [j]Nu 35:34; Jer 2:7
16:19 [k]Isa 2:2; Jer 3:17 [l]Ps 4:2
16:20 [m]Ps 115:4-7; Isa 37:19; Jer 2:11
17:1 [n]Job 19:24 [o]Pr 3:3; 2Co 3:3
17:2 [p]2Ch 24:18 [q]Jer 2:20
17:3 [r]2Ki 24:13 [s]Jer 26:18; Mic 3:12 [t]Jer 15:13

17:4
[a] La 5:2
[b] Dt 28:48; Jer 12:7
[c] Jer 16:13
[d] Jer 7:20; 15:14

17:5
[e] Isa 2:22; 30:1-3

17:6
[f] Dt 29:23; Job 39:6

17:7
[g] Ps 34:8; 40:4; Pr 16:20

17:8
[h] Jer 14:1-6
[i] Ps 1:3; 92:12-14

17:9
[j] Ecc 9:3; Mt 13:15; Mk 7:21-22

17:10
[k] 1Sa 16:7; Rev 2:23
[l] Ps 17:3; 139:23; Jer 11:20; 20:12; Ro 8:27
[m] Ps 62:12; Jer 32:19
[n] Ro 2:6

17:11
[o] Lk 12:20

17:12
[p] Jer 3:17

17:13
[q] Jer 14:8
[r] Isa 1:28; Jer 2:17

17:14
[s] Ps 109:1

4 Through your own fault you will lose
the inheritance[a] I gave you.
I will enslave you to your enemies[b]
in a land[c] you do not know,
for you have kindled my anger,
and it will burn[d] forever."

5 This is what the LORD says:

"Cursed is the one who trusts in man,[e]
who depends on flesh for his strength
and whose heart turns away from the LORD.
6 He will be like a bush in the wastelands;
he will not see prosperity when it comes.
He will dwell in the parched places of the desert,
in a salt[f] land where no one lives.

7 "But blessed is the man who trusts[g] in the LORD,
whose confidence is in him.
8 He will be like a tree planted by the water
that sends out its roots by the stream.
It does not fear when heat comes;
its leaves are always green.
It has no worries in a year of drought[h]
and never fails to bear fruit."[i]

9 The heart[j] is deceitful above all things
and beyond cure.
Who can understand it?

10 "I the LORD search the heart[k]
and examine the mind,[l]
to reward[m] a man according to his conduct,
according to what his deeds deserve."[n]

11 Like a partridge that hatches eggs it did not lay
is the man who gains riches by unjust means.
When his life is half gone, they will desert him,
and in the end he will prove to be a fool.[o]

12 A glorious throne,[p] exalted from the beginning,
is the place of our sanctuary.
13 O LORD, the hope[q] of Israel,
all who forsake[r] you will be put to shame.
Those who turn away from you will be written in the dust
because they have forsaken the LORD,
the spring of living water.

14 Heal me, O LORD, and I will be healed;
save me and I will be saved,
for you are the one I praise.[s]

[15]They keep saying to me,
"Where is the word of the LORD?
Let it now be fulfilled!"[a]
[16]I have not run away from being your shepherd;
you know I have not desired the day of despair.
What passes my lips is open before you.
[17]Do not be a terror[b] to me;
you are my refuge[c] in the day of disaster.
[18]Let my persecutors be put to shame,
but keep me from shame;
let them be terrified,
but keep me from terror.
Bring on them the day of disaster;
destroy them with double destruction.[d]

[19]This is what the LORD said to me: "Go and stand at the gate of
the people, through which the kings of Judah go in and out; stand
also at all the other gates of Jerusalem.[e] [20]Say to them, 'Hear the
word of the LORD, O kings of Judah and all people of Judah and
everyone living in Jerusalem[f] who come through these gates.[g]
[21]This is what the LORD says: Be careful not to carry a load on the
Sabbath[h] day or bring it through the gates of Jerusalem. [22]Do not
bring a load out of your houses or do any work on the Sabbath,
but keep the Sabbath day holy, as I commanded your forefathers.[i]
[23]Yet they did not listen or pay attention;[j] they were stiff-necked[k]
and would not listen or respond to discipline.[l] [24]But if you are
careful to obey me, declares the LORD, and bring no load through
the gates of this city on the Sabbath, but keep the Sabbath day
holy by not doing any work on it, [25]then kings who sit on David's
throne[m] will come through the gates of this city with their officials.
They and their officials will come riding in chariots and on horses,
accompanied by the men of Judah and those living in Jerusalem,
and this city will be inhabited forever. [26]People will come from the
towns of Judah and the villages around Jerusalem, from the territory of Benjamin and the western foothills, from the hill country
and the Negev,[n] bringing burnt offerings and sacrifices, grain
offerings, incense and thank offerings to the house of the LORD.
[27]But if you do not obey[o] me to keep the Sabbath day holy by not
carrying any load as you come through the gates of Jerusalem on
the Sabbath day, then I will kindle an unquenchable fire[p] in the
gates of Jerusalem that will consume her fortresses.'"[q]

Chapter 18 Theme ______________________

18 This is the word that came to Jeremiah from the LORD: [2]"Go
down to the potter's house, and there I will give you my
message." [3]So I went down to the potter's house, and I saw him

17:15 [a]Isa 5:19; 2Pe 3:4
17:17 [b]Ps 88:15-16 [c]Jer 16:19; Na 1:7
17:18 [d]Ps 35:1-8
17:19 [e]Jer 7:2; 26:2
17:20 [f]Jer 19:3 [g]Jer 22:2
17:21 [h]Nu 15:32-36; Ne 13:15-21; Jn 5:10
17:22 [i]Ex 20:8; 31:13; Isa 56:2-6; Eze 20:12
17:23 [j]Jer 7:26 [k]Jer 19:15 [l]Jer 7:28
17:25 [m]2Sa 7:13; Isa 9:7; Jer 22:2,4; Lk 1:32
17:26 [n]Jer 32:44; 33:13; Zec 7:7
17:27 [o]Jer 22:5 [p]Jer 7:20 [q]2Ki 25:9; Am 2:5

working at the wheel. [4]But the pot he was shaping from the clay
was marred in his hands; so the potter formed it into another pot,
shaping it as seemed best to him.

[5]Then the word of the LORD came to me: [6]"O house of Israel, can
I not do with you as this potter does?" declares the LORD. "Like
clay[a] in the hand of the potter, so are you in my hand, O house of
Israel. [7]If at any time I announce that a nation or kingdom is to be
uprooted,[b] torn down and destroyed, [8]and if that nation I warned
repents of its evil, then I will relent[c] and not inflict on it the disaster[d] I had planned. [9]And if at another time I announce that a
nation or kingdom is to be built[e] up and planted, [10]and if it does
evil[f] in my sight and does not obey me, then I will reconsider[g] the
good I had intended to do for it.

[11]"Now therefore say to the people of Judah and those living in
Jerusalem, 'This is what the LORD says: Look! I am preparing a
disaster[h] for you and devising a plan against you. So turn[i] from
your evil ways,[j] each one of you, and reform your ways and your
actions.' [12]But they will reply, 'It's no use.[k] We will continue with
our own plans; each of us will follow the stubbornness of his evil
heart.' "

[13]Therefore this is what the LORD says:

"Inquire among the nations:
 Who has ever heard anything like this?[l]
A most horrible[m] thing has been done
 by Virgin Israel.
[14]Does the snow of Lebanon
 ever vanish from its rocky slopes?
Do its cool waters from distant sources
 ever cease to flow?[a]
[15]Yet my people have forgotten me;
 they burn incense to worthless idols,[n]
which made them stumble in their ways
 and in the ancient paths.[o]
They made them walk in bypaths
 and on roads not built up.[p]
[16]Their land will be laid waste,[q]
 an object of lasting scorn;[r]
all who pass by will be appalled
 and will shake their heads.[s]
[17]Like a wind[t] from the east,
 I will scatter them before their enemies;
I will show them my back and not my face[u]
 in the day of their disaster."

a *14* The meaning of the Hebrew for this sentence is uncertain.

18:6 [a]Isa 45:9; Ro 9:20-21
18:7 [b]Jer 1:10
18:8 [c]Jer 26:13; Jnh 3:8-10 [d]Eze 18:21; Hos 11:8-9
18:9 [e]Jer 1:10; 31:28
18:10 [f]Eze 33:18 [g]1Sa 2:29-30
18:11 [h]Jer 4:6 [i]2Ki 17:13; Isa 1:16-19 [j]Jer 7:3
18:12 [k]Isa 57:10; Jer 2:25
18:13 [l]Isa 66:8; Jer 2:10 [m]Jer 5:30
18:15 [n]Jer 10:15 [o]Jer 6:16 [p]Isa 57:14; 62:10
18:16 [q]Jer 25:9 [r]Jer 19:8 [s]Ps 22:7
18:17 [t]Jer 13:24 [u]Jer 2:27

18They said, "Come, let's make plans[a] against Jeremiah; for the
teaching of the law by the priest[b] will not be lost, nor will counsel
from the wise, nor the word from the prophets.[c] So come, let's
attack him with our tongues[d] and pay no attention to anything
he says."

19Listen to me, O LORD;
  hear what my accusers are saying!
20Should good be repaid with evil?
  Yet they have dug a pit[e] for me.
Remember that I stood before you
  and spoke in their behalf[f]
  to turn your wrath away from them.
21So give their children over to famine;[g]
  hand them over to the power of the sword.
Let their wives be made childless and widows;[h]
  let their men be put to death,
  their young men slain by the sword in battle.
22Let a cry[i] be heard from their houses
  when you suddenly bring invaders against them,
for they have dug a pit to capture me
  and have hidden snares[j] for my feet.
23But you know, O LORD,
  all their plots to kill[k] me.
Do not forgive[l] their crimes
  or blot out their sins from your sight.
Let them be overthrown before you;
  deal with them in the time of your anger.

Chapter 19 Theme ______________________________

19 This is what the LORD says: "Go and buy a clay jar from a
potter.[m] Take along some of the elders[n] of the people and of
the priests 2and go out to the Valley of Ben Hinnom,[o] near the
entrance of the Potsherd Gate. There proclaim the words I tell you,
3and say, 'Hear the word of the LORD, O kings[p] of Judah and people
of Jerusalem. This is what the LORD Almighty, the God of Israel,
says: Listen! I am going to bring a disaster[q] on this place that will
make the ears of everyone who hears of it tingle.[r] 4For they have
forsaken[s] me and made this a place of foreign gods; they have
burned sacrifices[t] in it to gods that neither they nor their fathers
nor the kings of Judah ever knew, and they have filled this place
with the blood of the innocent.[u] 5They have built the high places
of Baal to burn their sons[v] in the fire as offerings to Baal—something I did not command or mention, nor did it enter my mind.[w]
6So beware, the days are coming, declares the LORD, when people

18:18 [a]Jer 11:19 [b]Mal 2:7 [c]Jer 5:13 [d]Ps 52:2
18:20 [e]Ps 35:7; 57:6 [f]Ps 106:23
18:21 [g]Jer 11:22 [h]Ps 109:9
18:22 [i]Jer 6:26 [j]Ps 140:5
18:23 [k]Jer 11:21 [l]Ps 109:14
19:1 [m]Jer 18:2 [n]Nu 11:17
19:2 [o]Jos 15:8
19:3 [p]Jer 17:20 [q]Jer 6:19 [r]1Sa 3:11
19:4 [s]Dt 28:20; Isa 65:11 [t]Lev 18:21 [u]2Ki 21:16; Jer 2:34
19:5 [v]Lev 18:21; Ps 106:37-38 [w]Jer 7:31; 32:35

will no longer call this place Topheth or the Valley of Ben Hinnom,[a] but the Valley of Slaughter.[b]
7"'In this place I will ruin[a] the plans of Judah and Jerusalem. I
will make them fall by the sword before their enemies,[c] at the
hands of those who seek their lives, and I will give their carcasses[d]
as food[e] to the birds of the air and the beasts of the earth. 8I will
devastate this city and make it an object of scorn;[f] all who pass by
will be appalled and will scoff because of all its wounds. 9I will
make them eat[g] the flesh of their sons and daughters, and they
will eat one another's flesh during the stress of the siege imposed
on them by the enemies[h] who seek their lives.'
10"Then break the jar[i] while those who go with you are watching, 11and say to them, 'This is what the LORD Almighty says: I will
smash[j] this nation and this city just as this potter's jar is smashed
and cannot be repaired. They will bury[k] the dead in Topheth until
there is no more room. 12This is what I will do to this place and to
those who live here, declares the LORD. I will make this city like
Topheth. 13The houses[l] in Jerusalem and those of the kings of
Judah will be defiled like this place, Topheth—all the houses
where they burned incense on the roofs to all the starry hosts[m]
and poured out drink offerings[n] to other gods.'"
14Jeremiah then returned from Topheth, where the LORD had
sent him to prophesy, and stood in the court[o] of the LORD's temple
and said to all the people, 15"This is what the LORD Almighty, the
God of Israel, says: 'Listen! I am going to bring on this city and
the villages around it every disaster I pronounced against them,
because they were stiff-necked[p] and would not listen to my
words.'"

Chapter 20 Theme ____________________

20 When the priest Pashhur son of Immer,[q] the chief officer[r]
in the temple of the LORD, heard Jeremiah prophesying
these things, 2he had Jeremiah the prophet beaten[s] and put in the
stocks[t] at the Upper Gate of Benjamin[u] at the LORD's temple. 3The
next day, when Pashhur released him from the stocks, Jeremiah
said to him, "The LORD's name for you is not Pashhur, but Magor-
Missabib.[b][v] 4For this is what the LORD says: 'I will make you a terror
to yourself and to all your friends; with your own eyes[w] you will
see them fall by the sword of their enemies. I will hand[x] all Judah
over to the king of Babylon, who will carry[y] them away to Babylon
or put them to the sword. 5I will hand over to their enemies all the
wealth[z] of this city—all its products, all its valuables and all the
treasures of the kings of Judah. They will take it away[a] as plunder

a7 The Hebrew for *ruin* sounds like the Hebrew for *jar* (see verses 1 and 10).
b3 *Magor-Missabib* means *terror on every side.*

19:6 [a]Jos 15:8 [b]Jer 7:32
19:7 [c]Lev 26:17; Dt 28:25 [d]Jer 16:4; 34:20 [e]Ps 79:2
19:8 [f]Jer 18:16
19:9 [g]Lev 26:29; Dt 28:49-57; La 4:10 [h]Isa 9:20
19:10 [i]ver 1
19:11 [j]Ps 2:9; Isa 30:14 [k]Jer 7:32
19:13 [l]Jer 32:29; 52:13 [m]Dt 4:19; Ac 7:42 [n]Jer 7:18; Eze 20:28
19:14 [o]2Ch 20:5; Jer 26:2
19:15 [p]Ne 9:16; Jer 7:26; 17:23
20:1 [q]1Ch 24:14 [r]2Ki 25:18
20:2 [s]Jer 1:19 [t]Job 13:27 [u]Jer 37:13; 38:7; Zec 14:10
20:3 [v]ver 10
20:4 [w]Jer 29:21 [x]Jer 21:10 [y]Jer 52:27
20:5 [z]Jer 17:3 [a]2Ki 20:17

and carry it off to Babylon. 6And you, Pashhur, and all who live in
your house will go into exile to Babylon. There you will die and be
buried, you and all your friends to whom you have prophesied[a]
lies.'"

7O LORD, you deceived[a] me, and I was deceived[a];
you overpowered me and prevailed.
I am ridiculed all day long;
everyone mocks me.
8Whenever I speak, I cry out
proclaiming violence and destruction.[b]
So the word of the LORD has brought me
insult and reproach[c] all day long.
9But if I say, "I will not mention him
or speak any more in his name,"
his word is in my heart like a fire,[d]
a fire shut up in my bones.
I am weary of holding it in;[e]
indeed, I cannot.
10I hear many whispering,
"Terror[f] on every side!
Report[g] him! Let's report him!"
All my friends[h]
are waiting for me to slip,[i] saying,
"Perhaps he will be deceived;
then we will prevail[j] over him
and take our revenge on him."
11But the LORD[k] is with me like a mighty warrior;
so my persecutors[l] will stumble and not prevail.[m]
They will fail and be thoroughly disgraced;[n]
their dishonor will never be forgotten.
12O LORD Almighty, you who examine the righteous
and probe the heart and mind,[o]
let me see your vengeance[p] upon them,
for to you I have committed[q] my cause.
13Sing to the LORD!
Give praise to the LORD!
He rescues[r] the life of the needy
from the hands of the wicked.
14Cursed be the day I was born![s]
May the day my mother bore me not be blessed!
15Cursed be the man who brought my father the news,
who made him very glad, saying,
"A child is born to you—a son!"

a 7 Or *persuaded*

20:6 [a] Jer 14:15; La 2:14
20:8 [b] Jer 6:7 [c] 2Ch 36:16; Jer 6:10
20:9 [d] Ps 39:3 [e] Job 32:18-20; Ac 4:20
20:10 [f] Ps 31:13; Jer 6:25 [g] Isa 29:21 [h] Ps 41:9 [i] Lk 11:53-54 [j] 1Ki 19:2
20:11 [k] Jer 1:8; Ro 8:31 [l] Jer 17:18 [m] Jer 15:20 [n] Jer 23:40
20:12 [o] Jer 17:10 [p] Ps 54:7; 59:10 [q] Ps 62:8; Jer 11:20
20:13 [r] Ps 35:10
20:14 [s] Job 3:3; Jer 15:10

[16]May that man be like the towns[a]
the LORD overthrew without pity.
May he hear wailing in the morning,
a battle cry at noon.
[17]For he did not kill me in the womb,[b]
with my mother as my grave,
her womb enlarged forever.
[18]Why did I ever come out of the womb
to see trouble and sorrow
and to end my days in shame?[c]

Chapter 21 Theme ______________________

21 The word came to Jeremiah from the LORD when King
Zedekiah[d] sent to him Pashhur[e] son of Malkijah and the
priest Zephaniah[f] son of Maaseiah. They said: [2]"Inquire[g] now of
the LORD for us because Nebuchadnezzar[a][h] king of Babylon is
attacking us. Perhaps the LORD will perform wonders[i] for us as in
times past so that he will withdraw from us."
[3]But Jeremiah answered them, "Tell Zedekiah, [4]'This is what
the LORD, the God of Israel, says: I am about to turn[j] against you
the weapons of war that are in your hands, which you are using
to fight the king of Babylon and the Babylonians[b] who are outside the wall besieging[k] you. And I will gather them inside this
city. [5]I myself will fight against you with an outstretched hand[l]
and a mighty arm in anger and fury and great wrath. [6]I will strike
down those who live in this city—both men and animals—and
they will die of a terrible plague.[m] [7]After that, declares the LORD, I
will hand over Zedekiah[n] king of Judah, his officials and the people in this city who survive the plague, sword and famine, to
Nebuchadnezzar king of Babylon[o] and to their enemies who seek
their lives. He will put them to the sword; he will show them no
mercy or pity or compassion.'[p]
[8]"Furthermore, tell the people, 'This is what the LORD says: See,
I am setting before you the way of life and the way of death.
[9]Whoever stays in this city will die by the sword, famine or
plague.[q] But whoever goes out and surrenders to the Babylonians
who are besieging you will live; he will escape with his life.[r] [10]I
have determined to do this city harm[s] and not good, declares the
LORD. It will be given into the hands[t] of the king of Babylon, and
he will destroy it with fire.'[u]
[11]"Moreover, say to the royal house[v] of Judah, 'Hear the word of
the LORD; [12]O house of David, this is what the LORD says:

[a]2 Hebrew *Nebuchadrezzar,* of which *Nebuchadnezzar* is a variant; here and often in Jeremiah and Ezekiel [b]4 Or *Chaldeans;* also in verse 9

20:16 [a]Ge 19:25
20:17 [b]Job 10:18-19
20:18 [c]Ps 90:9
21:1 [d]2Ki 24:18; Jer 52:1 [e]Jer 38:1 [f]2Ki 25:18; Jer 29:25; 37:3
21:2 [g]Jer 37:3,7 [h]2Ki 25:1 [i]Ps 44:1-4; Jer 32:17
21:4 [j]Jer 32:5 [k]Jer 37:8-10
21:5 [l]Jer 6:12
21:6 [m]Jer 14:12
21:7 [n]2Ki 25:7; Jer 52:9 [o]Jer 37:17; 39:5 [p]2Ch 36:17; Eze 7:9; Hab 1:6
21:9 [q]Jer 14:12 [r]Jer 38:2,17; 39:18; 45:5
21:10 [s]Jer 44:11,27; Am 9:4 [t]Jer 32:28; 38:2-3 [u]Jer 52:13
21:11 [v]Jer 13:18

"'Administer justice[a] every morning;
rescue from the hand of his oppressor
the one who has been robbed,
or my wrath will break out and burn like fire
because of the evil you have done—
burn with no one to quench[b] it.
13I am against[c] you, ⌊Jerusalem,⌋
you who live above this valley[d]
on the rocky plateau,
declares the LORD—
you who say, "Who can come against us?
Who can enter our refuge?"[e]
14I will punish you as your deeds[f] deserve,
declares the LORD.
I will kindle a fire[g] in your forests[h]
that will consume everything around you.'"

Chapter 22 Theme ______________________

22 This is what the LORD says: "Go down to the palace of the
king of Judah and proclaim this message there: 2'Hear the
word of the LORD, O king of Judah, you who sit on David's
throne[i]—you, your officials and your people who come through
these gates.[j] 3This is what the LORD says: Do what is just[k] and
right. Rescue from the hand of his oppressor[l] the one who has
been robbed. Do no wrong or violence to the alien, the fatherless
or the widow,[m] and do not shed innocent blood in this place. 4For
if you are careful to carry out these commands, then kings[n] who sit
on David's throne will come through the gates of this palace, riding in chariots and on horses, accompanied by their officials and
their people. 5But if you do not obey[o] these commands, declares
the LORD, I swear[p] by myself that this palace will become a ruin.'"
6For this is what the LORD says about the palace of the king of
Judah:

"Though you are like Gilead to me,
like the summit of Lebanon,
I will surely make you like a desert,[q]
like towns not inhabited.
7I will send destroyers[r] against you,
each man with his weapons,
and they will cut[s] up your fine cedar beams
and throw them into the fire.

8"People from many nations will pass by this city and will ask
one another, 'Why has the LORD done such a thing to this great

21:12 [a]Jer 22:3 [b]Isa 1:31
21:13 [c]Eze 13:8 [d]Ps 125:2 [e]Jer 49:4; Ob 3-4
21:14 [f]Isa 3:10-11 [g]2Ch 36:19; Jer 52:13 [h]Eze 20:47
22:2 [i]Jer 17:25; Lk 1:32 [j]Jer 17:20
22:3 [k]Mic 6:8; Zec 7:9 [l]Ps 72:4; Jer 21:12 [m]Ex 22:22
22:4 [n]Jer 17:25
22:5 [o]Jer 17:27 [p]Heb 6:13
22:6 [q]Mic 3:12
22:7 [r]Jer 4:7 [s]Isa 10:34

city?'[a] 9And the answer will be: 'Because they have forsaken the
covenant of the LORD their God and have worshiped and served
other gods.[b]'"

10Do not weep for the dead[c] ⌊king⌋ or mourn[d] his loss;
rather, weep bitterly for him who is exiled,
because he will never return
nor see his native land again.

11For this is what the LORD says about Shallum[a][e] son of Josiah,
who succeeded his father as king of Judah but has gone from this
place: "He will never return. 12He will die[f] in the place where they
have led him captive; he will not see this land again."

13"Woe to him who builds[g] his palace by unrighteousness,
his upper rooms by injustice,
making his countrymen work for nothing,
not paying[h] them for their labor.
14He says, 'I will build myself a great palace[i]
with spacious upper rooms.'
So he makes large windows in it,
panels it with cedar[j]
and decorates it in red.

15"Does it make you a king
to have more and more cedar?
Did not your father have food and drink?
He did what was right and just,[k]
so all went well[l] with him.
16He defended the cause of the poor and needy,[m]
and so all went well.
Is that not what it means to know me?"
declares the LORD.
17"But your eyes and your heart
are set only on dishonest gain,
on shedding innocent blood[n]
and on oppression and extortion."

18Therefore this is what the LORD says about Jehoiakim son of
Josiah king of Judah:

"They will not mourn for him:
'Alas, my brother! Alas, my sister!'
They will not mourn for him:
'Alas, my master! Alas, his splendor!'
19He will have the burial of a donkey—
dragged away and thrown[o]
outside the gates of Jerusalem."

22:8 [a] Dt 29:25-26; 1Ki 9:8-9; Jer 16:10-11
22:9 [b] 2Ki 22:17; 2Ch 34:25
22:10 [c] Ecc 4:2 [d] ver 18
22:11 [e] 2Ki 23:31
22:12 [f] 2Ki 23:34
22:13 [g] Mic 3:10; Hab 2:9 [h] Lev 19:13; Jas 5:4
22:14 [i] Isa 5:8-9 [j] 2Sa 7:2
22:15 [k] 2Ki 23:25 [l] Ps 128:2; Isa 3:10
22:16 [m] Ps 72:1-4, 12-13
22:17 [n] 2Ki 24:4
22:19 [o] Jer 36:30

a 11 Also called *Jehoahaz*

20"Go up to Lebanon and cry out,
let your voice be heard in Bashan,
cry out from Abarim,[a]
for all your allies are crushed.
21I warned you when you felt secure,
but you said, 'I will not listen!'
This has been your way from your youth;[b]
you have not obeyed[c] me.
22The wind will drive all your shepherds away,
and your allies will go into exile.
Then you will be ashamed and disgraced
because of all your wickedness.
23You who live in 'Lebanon,[a]'
who are nestled in cedar buildings,
how you will groan when pangs come upon you,
pain[d] like that of a woman in labor!

24"As surely as I live," declares the LORD, "even if you, Jehoiachin[b][e] son of Jehoiakim king of Judah, were a signet ring on my
right hand, I would still pull you off. 25I will hand you over[f] to
those who seek your life, those you fear—to Nebuchadnezzar
king of Babylon and to the Babylonians.[c] 26I will hurl[g] you and
the mother who gave you birth into another country, where neither of you was born, and there you both will die. 27You will never come back to the land you long to return to."

28Is this man Jehoiachin a despised, broken pot,[h]
an object no one wants?
Why will he and his children be hurled[i] out,
cast into a land[j] they do not know?
29O land,[k] land, land,
hear the word of the LORD!
30This is what the LORD says:
"Record this man as if childless,[l]
a man who will not prosper[m] in his lifetime,
for none of his offspring will prosper,
none will sit on the throne[n] of David
or rule anymore in Judah."

Chapter 23 Theme ______________________

23 "Woe to the shepherds[o] who are destroying and scattering[p]
the sheep of my pasture!"[q] declares the LORD. 2Therefore
this is what the LORD, the God of Israel, says to the shepherds who

22:20 [a]Nu 27:12
22:21 [b]Jer 3:25; 32:30 [c]Jer 7:23-28
22:23 [d]Jer 4:31
22:24 [e]2Ki 24:6,8; Jer 37:1
22:25 [f]2Ki 24:16; Jer 34:20
22:26 [g]2Ki 24:8; 2Ch 36:10
22:28 [h]Ps 31:12; Jer 48:38; Hos 8:8 [i]Jer 15:1 [j]Jer 17:4
22:29 [k]Jer 6:19; Mic 1:2
22:30 [l]1Ch 3:18; Mt 1:12 [m]Jer 10:21 [n]Ps 94:20
23:1 [o]Jer 10:21; Eze 34:1-10; Zec 11:15-17 [p]Isa 56:11 [q]Eze 34:31

[a]23 That is, the palace in Jerusalem (see 1Kings 7:2) [b]24 Hebrew *Coniah*, a variant of *Jehoiachin*; also in verse 28 [c]25 Or *Chaldeans*

tend my people: "Because you have scattered my flock and driven
them away and have not bestowed care on them, I will bestow
punishment on you for the evil[a] you have done," declares the
LORD. 3"I myself will gather the remnant[b] of my flock out of all the
countries where I have driven them and will bring them back to
their pasture, where they will be fruitful and increase in number.
4I will place shepherds[c] over them who will tend them, and they
will no longer be afraid[d] or terrified, nor will any be missing,[e]"
declares the LORD.

5"The days are coming," declares the LORD,
"when I will raise up to David[a] a righteous Branch,[f]
a King who will reign[g] wisely
and do what is just and right[h] in the land.
6In his days Judah will be saved
and Israel will live in safety.
This is the name[i] by which he will be called:
The LORD Our Righteousness.[j]

7"So then, the days are coming," declares the LORD, "when people
will no longer say, 'As surely as the LORD lives, who brought the
Israelites up out of Egypt,'[k] 8but they will say, 'As surely as the LORD
lives, who brought the descendants of Israel up out of the land of
the north and out of all the countries where he had banished
them.' Then they will live in their own land."[l]

9Concerning the prophets:

My heart is broken within me;
all my bones tremble.
I am like a drunken man,
like a man overcome by wine,
because of the LORD
and his holy words.[m]
10The land is full of adulterers;[n]
because of the curse[b] the land lies parched[c]
and the pastures[o] in the desert are withered.[p]
The ⌊prophets⌋ follow an evil course
and use their power unjustly.

11"Both prophet and priest are godless;[q]
even in my temple[r] I find their wickedness,"
declares the LORD.
12"Therefore their path will become slippery;[s]
they will be banished to darkness
and there they will fall.

23:2 [a] Jer 21:12
23:3 [b] Isa 11:10-12; Jer 32:37; Eze 34:11-16
23:4 [c] Jer 3:15; 31:10; Eze 34:23 [d] Jer 30:10; 46:27-28 [e] Jn 6:39
23:5 [f] Isa 4:2 [g] Isa 9:7 [h] Isa 11:1; Zec 6:12
23:6 [i] Jer 33:16; Mt 1:21-23 [j] Ro 3:21-22; 1Co 1:30
23:7 [k] Jer 16:14
23:8 [l] Isa 43:5-6; Am 9:14-15
23:9 [m] Jer 20:8-9
23:10 [n] Jer 9:2 [o] Ps 107:34; Jer 9:10 [p] Hos 4:2-3
23:11 [q] Jer 6:13; 8:10; Zep 3:4 [r] Jer 7:10
23:12 [s] Ps 35:6; Jer 13:16

[a]5 Or *up from David's line* [b]10 Or *because of these things* [c]10 Or *land mourns*

I will bring disaster on them
in the year they are punished,[a]"
declares the LORD.

13"Among the prophets of Samaria
I saw this repulsive thing:
They prophesied by Baal[b]
and led my people Israel astray.
14And among the prophets of Jerusalem
I have seen something horrible:[c]
They commit adultery and live a lie.[d]
They strengthen the hands of evildoers,[e]
so that no one turns from his wickedness.
They are all like Sodom[f] to me;
the people of Jerusalem are like Gomorrah."[g]

15Therefore, this is what the LORD Almighty says concerning the prophets:

"I will make them eat bitter food
and drink poisoned water,[h]
because from the prophets of Jerusalem
ungodliness has spread throughout the land."

16This is what the LORD Almighty says:

"Do not listen[i] to what the prophets are prophesying
to you;
they fill you with false hopes.
They speak visions[j] from their own minds,
not from the mouth[k] of the LORD.
17They keep saying to those who despise me,
'The LORD says: You will have peace.'[l]
And to all who follow the stubbornness[m] of their hearts
they say, 'No harm[n] will come to you.'
18But which of them has stood in the council of the LORD
to see or to hear his word?
Who has listened and heard his word?
19See, the storm[o] of the LORD
will burst out in wrath,
a whirlwind swirling down
on the heads of the wicked.
20The anger[p] of the LORD will not turn back[q]
until he fully accomplishes
the purposes of his heart.
In days to come
you will understand it clearly.

23:12 [a]Jer 11:23
23:13 [b]Jer 2:8
23:14 [c]Jer 5:30 [d]Jer 29:23 [e]Eze 13:22 [f]Ge 18:20 [g]Isa 1:9-10; Jer 20:16
23:15 [h]Jer 8:14; 9:15
23:16 [i]Jer 27:9-10,14; Mt 7:15 [j]Jer 14:14 [k]Jer 9:20
23:17 [l]Jer 8:11 [m]Jer 13:10 [n]Jer 5:12; Am 9:10; Mic 3:11
23:19 [o]Jer 25:32; 30:23
23:20 [p]2Ki 23:26 [q]Jer 30:24

21 I did not send[a] these prophets,
yet they have run with their message;
I did not speak to them,
yet they have prophesied.
22 But if they had stood in my council,
they would have proclaimed my words to my people
and would have turned[b] them from their evil ways
and from their evil deeds.

23 "Am I only a God nearby,[c]"
declares the LORD,
"and not a God far away?
24 Can anyone hide[d] in secret places
so that I cannot see him?"
declares the LORD.
"Do not I fill heaven and earth?"[e]
declares the LORD.

25 "I have heard what the prophets say who prophesy lies[f] in my
name. They say, 'I had a dream![g] I had a dream!' 26 How long will
this continue in the hearts of these lying prophets, who prophesy
the delusions[h] of their own minds? 27 They think the dreams they
tell one another will make my people forget[i] my name, just as their
fathers forgot[j] my name through Baal worship. 28 Let the prophet
who has a dream tell his dream, but let the one who has my word
speak it faithfully. For what has straw to do with grain?" declares
the LORD. 29 "Is not my word like fire,"[k] declares the LORD, "and like
a hammer that breaks a rock in pieces?
30 "Therefore," declares the LORD, "I am against[l] the prophets[m]
who steal from one another words supposedly from me. 31 Yes,"
declares the LORD, "I am against the prophets who wag their own
tongues and yet declare, 'The LORD declares.'[n] 32 Indeed, I am
against those who prophesy false dreams,[o]" declares the LORD.
"They tell them and lead my people astray with their reckless lies,
yet I did not send or appoint them. They do not benefit[p] these
people in the least," declares the LORD.
33 "When these people, or a prophet or a priest, ask you, 'What is
the oracle[a][q] of the LORD?' say to them, 'What oracle?[b] I will forsake[r]
you, declares the LORD.' 34 If a prophet or a priest or anyone else
claims, 'This is the oracle[s] of the LORD,' I will punish[t] that man and
his household. 35 This is what each of you keeps on saying to his
friend or relative: 'What is the LORD's answer?'[u] or 'What has the
LORD spoken?' 36 But you must not mention 'the oracle of the LORD'
again, because every man's own word becomes his oracle and so

a 33 Or *burden* (see Septuagint and Vulgate) b 33 Hebrew; Septuagint and Vulgate *'You are the burden.* (The Hebrew for *oracle* and *burden* is the same.)

23:21 a Jer 14:14; 27:15
23:22 b Jer 25:5; Zec 1:4
23:23 c Ps 139:1-10
23:24 d Job 22:12-14 e 1Ki 8:27
23:25 f Jer 14:14 g ver 28,32; Jer 29:8
23:26 h 1Ti 4:1-2
23:27 i Dt 13:1-3; Jer 29:8 j Jdg 3:7; 8:33-34
23:29 k Jer 5:14
23:30 l Ps 34:16 m Dt 18:20; Jer 14:15
23:31 n ver 17
23:32 o ver 25 p Jer 7:8; La 2:14
23:33 q Mal 1:1 r ver 39
23:34 s La 2:14 t Zec 13:3
23:35 u Jer 33:3; 42:4

you distort[a] the words of the living God, the LORD Almighty, our
God. 37This is what you keep saying to a prophet: 'What is the
LORD's answer to you?' or 'What has the LORD spoken?' 38Although
you claim, 'This is the oracle of the LORD,' this is what the LORD
says: You used the words, 'This is the oracle of the LORD,' even
though I told you that you must not claim, 'This is the oracle of the
LORD.' 39Therefore, I will surely forget you and cast[b] you out of my
presence along with the city I gave to you and your fathers. 40I will
bring upon you everlasting disgrace[c]—everlasting shame that will
not be forgotten."

Chapter 24 Theme ______________________________

24 After Jehoiachin[a][d] son of Jehoiakim king of Judah and
the officials, the craftsmen and the artisans of Judah were
carried into exile from Jerusalem to Babylon by Nebuchadnezzar
king of Babylon, the LORD showed me two baskets of figs[e] placed
in front of the temple of the LORD. 2One basket had very good figs,
like those that ripen early; the other basket had very poor[f] figs, so
bad they could not be eaten.
3Then the LORD asked me, "What do you see,[g] Jeremiah?"
"Figs," I answered. "The good ones are very good, but the poor
ones are so bad they cannot be eaten."
4Then the word of the LORD came to me: 5"This is what the LORD,
the God of Israel, says: 'Like these good figs, I regard as good the
exiles from Judah, whom I sent away from this place to the land of
the Babylonians.[b] 6My eyes will watch over them for their good,
and I will bring them back[h] to this land. I will build[i] them up and
not tear them down; I will plant them and not uproot them. 7I will
give them a heart to know me, that I am the LORD. They will be my
people,[j] and I will be their God, for they will return[k] to me with all
their heart.[l]
8" 'But like the poor[m] figs, which are so bad they cannot be eat-
en,' says the LORD, 'so will I deal with Zedekiah king of Judah, his
officials[n] and the survivors[o] from Jerusalem, whether they remain
in this land or live in Egypt.[p] 9I will make them abhorrent[q] and
an offense to all the kingdoms of the earth, a reproach and a
byword,[r] an object of ridicule and cursing,[s] wherever I banish[t]
them. 10I will send the sword,[u] famine and plague[v] against them
until they are destroyed from the land I gave to them and their
fathers.' "

Chapter 25 Theme ______________________________

25 The word came to Jeremiah concerning all the people of
Judah in the fourth year of Jehoiakim[w] son of Josiah king

INSIGHT

Read 2 Kings 24:10-17 for the historical account of this time. Jehoiachin is also called Jeconiah.

23:36 [a]Gal 1:7-8; 2Pe 3:16
23:39 [b]Jer 7:15
23:40 [c]Jer 20:11; Eze 5:14-15
24:1 [d]2Ki 24:16; 2Ch 36:9; Jer 29:2 [e]Am 8:1-2
24:2 [f]Isa 5:4
24:3 [g]Jer 1:11; Am 8:2
24:6 [h]Jer 29:10; Eze 11:17 [i]Jer 33:7; 42:10
24:7 [j]Isa 51:16; Jer 31:33; Heb 8:10 [k]Jer 32:40 [l]Eze 11:19
24:8 [m]Jer 29:17 [n]Jer 39:6 [o]Jer 39:9 [p]Jer 44:1,26
24:9 [q]Jer 15:4; 34:17 [r]Dt 28:25; 1Ki 9:7 [s]Jer 29:18 [t]Dt 28:37
24:10 [u]Isa 51:19 [v]Jer 27:8
25:1 [w]2Ki 24:2; Jer 36:1

a *1* Hebrew *Jeconiah,* a variant of *Jehoiachin* b *5* Or *Chaldeans*

and put it on your neck. 3 Then send word to the kings of Edom,
Moab, Ammon,[a] Tyre and Sidon through the envoys who have
come to Jerusalem to Zedekiah king of Judah. 4 Give them a message for their masters and say, 'This is what the LORD Almighty,
the God of Israel, says: "Tell this to your masters: 5 With my great
power and outstretched arm[b] I made the earth and its people and
the animals that are on it, and I give[c] it to anyone I please. 6 Now I
will hand all your countries over to my servant[d] Nebuchadnezzar[e]
king of Babylon; I will make even the wild animals subject to him.[f]
7 All nations will serve[g] him and his son and his grandson until the
time[h] for his land comes; then many nations and great kings will
subjugate[i] him.

8 " ' "If, however, any nation or kingdom will not serve Nebuchadnezzar king of Babylon or bow its neck under his yoke, I will
punish that nation with the sword, famine and plague, declares
the LORD, until I destroy it by his hand. 9 So do not listen to your
prophets, your diviners, your interpreters of dreams, your mediums[j] or your sorcerers who tell you, 'You will not serve the king
of Babylon.' 10 They prophesy lies[k] to you that will only serve to
remove you far from your lands; I will banish you and you will
perish. 11 But if any nation will bow its neck under the yoke[l] of the
king of Babylon and serve him, I will let that nation remain in its
own land to till it and to live there, declares the LORD." ' "

12 I gave the same message to Zedekiah king of Judah. I said,
"Bow your neck under the yoke of the king of Babylon; serve him
and his people, and you will live. 13 Why will you and your people
die[m] by the sword, famine and plague with which the LORD has
threatened any nation that will not serve the king of Babylon? 14 Do
not listen to the words of the prophets who say to you, 'You will not
serve the king of Babylon,' for they are prophesying lies[n] to you.
15 'I have not sent[o] them,' declares the LORD. 'They are prophesying
lies in my name.[p] Therefore, I will banish you and you will perish,[q]
both you and the prophets who prophesy to you.' "

16 Then I said to the priests and all these people, "This is what
the LORD says: Do not listen to the prophets who say, 'Very soon
now the articles[r] from the LORD's house will be brought back
from Babylon.' They are prophesying lies to you. 17 Do not listen
to them. Serve the king of Babylon, and you will live. Why should
this city become a ruin? 18 If they are prophets and have the word
of the LORD, let them plead[s] with the LORD Almighty that the furnishings remaining in the house of the LORD and in the palace of
the king of Judah and in Jerusalem not be taken to Babylon. 19 For
this is what the LORD Almighty says about the pillars, the Sea,[t] the
movable stands and the other furnishings[u] that are left in this city,
20 which Nebuchadnezzar king of Babylon did not take away when

27:3 [a] Jer 25:21
27:5 [b] Dt 9:29 [c] Ps 115:16
27:6 [d] Jer 25:9 [e] Jer 21:7; Eze 29:18-20 [f] Jer 28:14; Da 2:37-38
27:7 [g] 2Ch 36:20 [h] Jer 25:12 [i] Jer 25:14; Da 5:28
27:9 [j] Dt 18:11
27:10 [k] Jer 23:25
27:11 [l] Jer 21:9
27:13 [m] Eze 18:31
27:14 [n] Jer 14:14
27:15 [o] Jer 23:21 [p] Jer 29:9 [q] Jer 6:15
27:16 [r] 2Ki 24:13; 2Ch 36:7,10; Jer 28:3; Da 1:2
27:18 [s] 1Sa 7:8
27:19 [t] 2Ki 25:13 [u] Jer 52:17-23

he carried[a] Jehoiachin[a][b] son of Jehoiakim king of Judah into exile
from Jerusalem to Babylon, along with all the nobles of Judah and
Jerusalem— 21yes, this is what the LORD Almighty, the God of
Israel, says about the things that are left in the house of the LORD
and in the palace of the king of Judah and in Jerusalem: 22'They
will be taken[c] to Babylon and there they will remain until the day[d]
I come for them,' declares the LORD. 'Then I will bring[e] them back
and restore them to this place.'"

Chapter 28 Theme ____________________

28 In the fifth month of that same year, the fourth year, early
in the reign of Zedekiah[f] king of Judah, the prophet Hananiah son of Azzur, who was from Gibeon,[g] said to me in the
house of the LORD in the presence of the priests and all the people: 2"This is what the LORD Almighty, the God of Israel, says: 'I
will break the yoke[h] of the king of Babylon. 3Within two years I
will bring back to this place all the articles[i] of the LORD's house
that Nebuchadnezzar king of Babylon removed from here and
took to Babylon. 4I will also bring back to this place Jehoiachin[a][j]
son of Jehoiakim king of Judah and all the other exiles from
Judah who went to Babylon,' declares the LORD, 'for I will break
the yoke of the king of Babylon.'"

5Then the prophet Jeremiah replied to the prophet Hananiah
before the priests and all the people who were standing in the
house of the LORD. 6He said, "Amen! May the LORD do so! May
the LORD fulfill the words you have prophesied by bringing the
articles of the LORD's house and all the exiles back to this place
from Babylon. 7Nevertheless, listen to what I have to say in your
hearing and in the hearing of all the people: 8From early times
the prophets who preceded you and me have prophesied war,
disaster and plague[k] against many countries and great kingdoms.
9But the prophet who prophesies peace will be recognized as one
truly sent by the LORD only if his prediction comes true.[l]"

10Then the prophet Hananiah took the yoke[m] off the neck of the
prophet Jeremiah and broke it, 11and he said[n] before all the people, "This is what the LORD says: 'In the same way will I break the
yoke of Nebuchadnezzar king of Babylon off the neck of all the
nations within two years.'" At this, the prophet Jeremiah went on
his way.

12Shortly after the prophet Hananiah had broken the yoke off
the neck of the prophet Jeremiah, the word of the LORD came to
Jeremiah: 13"Go and tell Hananiah, 'This is what the LORD says:
You have broken a wooden yoke, but in its place you will get a
yoke of iron. 14This is what the LORD Almighty, the God of Israel,

INSIGHT

Read 2 Chronicles 36:11-13 and 2 Kings 24:18–25:7 to see whose prophecy came to pass.

27:20 [a]2Ch 36:10; Jer 24:1 [b]Jer 22:24
27:22 [c]2Ki 25:13 [d]2Ch 36:21 [e]Ezr 1:7; 7:19
28:1 [f]Jer 27:1,3 [g]Jos 9:3
28:2 [h]Jer 27:12
28:3 [i]2Ki 24:13
28:4 [j]Jer 22:24-27
28:8 [k]Lev 26:14-17; Isa 5:5-7
28:9 [l]Dt 18:22
28:10 [m]Jer 27:2
28:11 [n]Jer 14:14; 27:10

[a] 20,4 Hebrew *Jeconiah,* a variant of *Jehoiachin*

says: I will put an iron yoke[a] on the necks of all these nations to
make them serve[b] Nebuchadnezzar king of Babylon, and they will
serve him. I will even give him control over the wild animals.[c]'"

15Then the prophet Jeremiah said to Hananiah the prophet,
"Listen, Hananiah! The LORD has not sent[d] you, yet you have per-
suaded this nation to trust in lies.[e] 16Therefore, this is what the
LORD says: 'I am about to remove you from the face of the earth.[f]
This very year you are going to die, because you have preached
rebellion[g] against the LORD.'"

17In the seventh month of that same year, Hananiah the prophet
died.

Chapter 29 Theme ______________________

29 This is the text of the letter that the prophet Jeremiah sent
from Jerusalem to the surviving elders among the exiles
and to the priests, the prophets and all the other people Nebuchadnezzar had carried into exile from Jerusalem to Babylon.[h] 2(This
was after King Jehoiachin[a][i] and the queen mother, the court officials and the leaders of Judah and Jerusalem, the craftsmen and
the artisans had gone into exile from Jerusalem.) 3He entrusted the
letter to Elasah son of Shaphan and to Gemariah son of Hilkiah,
whom Zedekiah king of Judah sent to King Nebuchadnezzar in
Babylon. It said:

> 4This is what the LORD Almighty, the God of Israel, says to
> all those I carried[j] into exile from Jerusalem to Babylon:
> 5"Build[k] houses and settle down; plant gardens and eat what
> they produce. 6Marry and have sons and daughters; find wives
> for your sons and give your daughters in marriage, so that
> they too may have sons and daughters. Increase in number
> there; do not decrease. 7Also, seek the peace and prosperity
> of the city to which I have carried you into exile. Pray[l] to the
> LORD for it, because if it prospers, you too will prosper." 8Yes,
> this is what the LORD Almighty, the God of Israel, says: "Do
> not let the prophets and diviners among you deceive[m] you. Do
> not listen to the dreams you encourage them to have.[n] 9They
> are prophesying lies[o] to you in my name. I have not sent
> them," declares the LORD.
>
> 10This is what the LORD says: "When seventy years[p] are com-
> pleted for Babylon, I will come to you and fulfill my gracious
> promise to bring you back[q] to this place. 11For I know the
> plans[r] I have for you," declares the LORD, "plans to prosper
> you and not to harm you, plans to give you hope and a future.
> 12Then you will call upon me and come and pray to me, and I

INSIGHT

Why 70 years of captivity? Because for 490 years Israel had not given the land its Sabbath rest. See Leviticus 25:1-7; 26:27-35, 40-43; 2 Chronicles 36:20, 21.

28:14 [a]Dt 28:48 [b]Jer 25:11 [c]Jer 27:6
28:15 [d]Jer 29:31 [e]Jer 20:6; 29:21; La 2:14; Eze 13:6
28:16 [f]Ge 7:4 [g]Dt 13:5; Jer 29:32
29:1 [h]2Ch 36:10
29:2 [i]2Ki 24:12; Jer 22:24-28
29:4 [j]Jer 24:5
29:5 [k]ver 28
29:7 [l]Ezr 6:10; 1Ti 2:1-2
29:8 [m]Jer 37:9 [n]Jer 23:27
29:9 [o]Jer 14:14; 27:15
29:10 [p]2Ch 36:21; Jer 25:12; Da 9:2 [q]Jer 21:22
29:11 [r]Ps 40:5

[a]2 Hebrew *Jeconiah,* a variant of *Jehoiachin*

will listen[a] to you. 13You will seek[b] me and find me when you
seek me with all your heart.[c] 14I will be found by you," declares
the LORD, "and will bring you back[d] from captivity.[a] I will
gather you from all the nations and places where I have banished you," declares the LORD, "and will bring you back to the
place from which I carried you into exile."[e]

15You may say, "The LORD has raised up prophets for us in
Babylon," 16but this is what the LORD says about the king who
sits on David's throne and all the people who remain in this
city, your countrymen who did not go with you into exile—
17yes, this is what the LORD Almighty says: "I will send the
sword, famine and plague[f] against them and I will make them
like poor figs[g] that are so bad they cannot be eaten. 18I will pursue them with the sword, famine and plague and will make
them abhorrent[h] to all the kingdoms of the earth and an object
of cursing and horror,[i] of scorn and reproach, among all the
nations where I drive them. 19For they have not listened to my
words,"[j] declares the LORD, "words that I sent to them again
and again by my servants the prophets.[k] And you exiles have
not listened either," declares the LORD.

20Therefore, hear the word of the LORD, all you exiles whom I
have sent[l] away from Jerusalem to Babylon. 21This is what the
LORD Almighty, the God of Israel, says about Ahab son of Kolaiah and Zedekiah son of Maaseiah, who are prophesying lies[m]
to you in my name: "I will hand them over to Nebuchadnezzar
king of Babylon, and he will put them to death before your
very eyes. 22Because of them, all the exiles from Judah who are
in Babylon will use this curse: 'The LORD treat you like Zedekiah and Ahab, whom the king of Babylon burned[n] in the fire.'
23For they have done outrageous things in Israel; they have
committed adultery[o] with their neighbors' wives and in my
name have spoken lies, which I did not tell them to do. I know[p]
it and am a witness to it," declares the LORD.

24Tell Shemaiah the Nehelamite, 25"This is what the LORD
Almighty, the God of Israel, says: You sent letters in your own
name to all the people in Jerusalem, to Zephaniah[q] son of Maaseiah the priest, and to all the other priests. You said to Zephaniah,
26'The LORD has appointed you priest in place of Jehoiada to be in
charge of the house of the LORD; you should put any madman[r]
who acts like a prophet into the stocks[s] and neck-irons. 27So why
have you not reprimanded Jeremiah from Anathoth, who poses as
a prophet among you? 28He has sent this message[t] to us in Babylon: It will be a long time.[u] Therefore build[v] houses and settle
down; plant gardens and eat what they produce.'"

[a] 14 Or *will restore your fortunes*

29:12 [a]Ps 145:19
29:13 [b]Mt 7:7 [c]Dt 4:29; Jer 24:7
29:14 [d]Dt 30:3; Jer 30:3 [e]Jer 23:3-4
29:17 [f]Jer 27:8 [g]Jer 24:8-10
29:18 [h]Jer 15:4 [i]Dt 28:25; Jer 42:18
29:19 [j]Jer 6:19 [k]Jer 25:4
29:20 [l]Jer 24:5
29:21 [m]ver 9; Jer 14:14
29:22 [n]Da 3:6
29:23 [o]Jer 23:14 [p]Heb 4:13
29:25 [q]2Ki 25:18; Jer 21:1
29:26 [r]2Ki 9:11; Hos 9:7; Jn 10:20 [s]Jer 20:2
29:28 [t]ver 1 [u]ver 10 [v]ver 5

29 Zephaniah the priest, however, read the letter to Jeremiah the
prophet. 30 Then the word of the LORD came to Jeremiah: 31 "Send
this message to all the exiles: 'This is what the LORD says about
Shemaiah[a] the Nehelamite: Because Shemaiah has prophesied to
you, even though I did not send[b] him, and has led you to believe
a lie, 32 this is what the LORD says: I will surely punish Shemaiah
the Nehelamite and his descendants.[c] He will have no one left
among this people, nor will he see the good[d] things I will do for
my people, declares the LORD, because he has preached rebellion[e]
against me.' "

Chapter 30 Theme ______________________

30 This is the word that came to Jeremiah from the LORD:
2 "This is what the LORD, the God of Israel, says: 'Write[f] in
a book all the words I have spoken to you. 3 The days are coming,'
declares the LORD, 'when I will bring[g] my people Israel and Judah
back from captivity[a] and restore[h] them to the land I gave their
forefathers to possess,' says the LORD."
4 These are the words the LORD spoke concerning Israel and
Judah: 5 "This is what the LORD says:

" 'Cries of fear[i] are heard—
  terror, not peace.
6 Ask and see:
  Can a man bear children?
Then why do I see every strong man
  with his hands on his stomach like a woman in labor,[j]
  every face turned deathly pale?
7 How awful that day[k] will be!
  None will be like it.
It will be a time of trouble[l] for Jacob,
  but he will be saved[m] out of it.

8 " 'In that day,' declares the LORD Almighty,
  'I will break the yoke[n] off their necks
and will tear off their bonds;
  no longer will foreigners enslave them.[o]
9 Instead, they will serve the LORD their God
  and David[p] their king,[q]
  whom I will raise up for them.

10 " 'So do not fear,[r] O Jacob my servant;[s]
  do not be dismayed, O Israel,'
    declares the LORD.
'I will surely save[t] you out of a distant place,
  your descendants from the land of their exile.

[a] 3 Or *will restore the fortunes of my people Israel and Judah*

29:31 [a] ver 24 [b] Jer 14:14; 28:15
29:32 [c] 1Sa 2:30-33 [d] ver 10 [e] Jer 28:16
30:2 [f] Isa 30:8
30:3 [g] Jer 29:14 [h] Jer 16:15
30:5 [i] Jer 6:25
30:6 [j] Jer 4:31
30:7 [k] Isa 2:12; Joel 2:11 [l] Zep 1:15 [m] ver 10
30:8 [n] Isa 9:4 [o] Eze 34:27
30:9 [p] Isa 55:3-4; Lk 1:69; Ac 2:30; 13:23 [q] Eze 34:23-24; 37:24; Hos 3:5
30:10 [r] Isa 43:5; Jer 46:27-28 [s] Isa 44:2 [t] Jer 29:14

Jacob will again have peace and security,[a]
and no one will make him afraid.
11 I am with you and will save you,'
declares the LORD.
'Though I completely destroy all the nations
among which I scatter you,
I will not completely destroy[b] you.
I will discipline[c] you but only with justice;
I will not let you go entirely unpunished.'[d]

12 "This is what the LORD says:

"'Your wound is incurable,
your injury beyond healing.[e]
13 There is no one to plead your cause,
no remedy for your sore,
no healing[f] for you.
14 All your allies[g] have forgotten you;
they care nothing for you.
I have struck you as an enemy[h] would
and punished you as would the cruel,[i]
because your guilt is so great
and your sins[j] so many.
15 Why do you cry out over your wound,
your pain that has no cure?
Because of your great guilt and many sins
I have done these things to you.

16 "'But all who devour[k] you will be devoured;
all your enemies will go into exile.[l]
Those who plunder[m] you will be plundered;
all who make spoil of you I will despoil.
17 But I will restore you to health
and heal your wounds,'
declares the LORD,
'because you are called an outcast,[n]
Zion for whom no one cares.'

18 "This is what the LORD says:

"'I will restore the fortunes[o] of Jacob's tents
and have compassion[p] on his dwellings;
the city will be rebuilt[q] on her ruins,
and the palace will stand in its proper place.
19 From them will come songs[r] of thanksgiving[s]
and the sound of rejoicing.[t]
I will add to their numbers,[u]
and they will not be decreased;

30:10 [a] Isa 35:9
30:11 [b] Jer 4:27; 46:28 [c] Jer 10:24 [d] Am 9:8
30:12 [e] Jer 15:18
30:13 [f] Jer 8:22; 14:19; 46:11
30:14 [g] Jer 22:20; La 1:2 [h] Job 13:24 [i] Job 30:21 [j] Jer 5:6
30:16 [k] Isa 33:1; Jer 2:3; 10:25 [l] Isa 14:2; Joel 3:4-8 [m] Jer 50:10
30:17 [n] Jer 33:24
30:18 [o] ver 3; Jer 31:23 [p] Ps 102:13 [q] Jer 31:4,24,38
30:19 [r] Isa 35:10; 51:11 [s] Isa 51:3 [t] Ps 126:1-2; Jer 31:4 [u] Jer 33:22

I will bring them honor,[a]
and they will not be disdained.
20 Their children[b] will be as in days of old,
and their community will be established[c] before me;
I will punish all who oppress them.
21 Their leader[d] will be one of their own;
their ruler will arise from among them.
I will bring him near[e] and he will come close to me,
for who is he who will devote himself
to be close to me?'
declares the LORD.

22 "'So you will be my people,
and I will be your God.'"

23 See, the storm[f] of the LORD
will burst out in wrath,
a driving wind swirling down
on the heads of the wicked.
24 The fierce anger[g] of the LORD will not turn back[h]
until he fully accomplishes
the purposes of his heart.
In days to come
you will understand[i] this.

Chapter 31 Theme ______________________________

31

"At that time," declares the LORD, "I will be the God[j] of all
the clans of Israel, and they will be my people."
2 This is what the LORD says:

"The people who survive the sword
will find favor[k] in the desert;
I will come to give rest[l] to Israel."

3 The LORD appeared to us in the past,[a] saying:

"I have loved[m] you with an everlasting love;
I have drawn[n] you with loving-kindness.
4 I will build you up again
and you will be rebuilt, O Virgin Israel.
Again you will take up your tambourines
and go out to dance with the joyful.[o]
5 Again you will plant vineyards
on the hills of Samaria;[p]
the farmers will plant them
and enjoy their fruit.[q]

30:19 [a]Isa 60:9
30:20 [b]Isa 54:13; Jer 31:17 [c]Isa 54:14
30:21 [d]ver 9 [e]Nu 16:5
30:23 [f]Jer 23:19
30:24 [g]Jer 4:8 [h]Jer 4:28 [i]Jer 23:19-20
31:1 [j]Jer 30:22
31:2 [k]Nu 14:20 [l]Ex 33:14
31:3 [m]Dt 4:37 [n]Hos 11:4
31:4 [o]Jer 30:19
31:5 [p]Jer 50:19 [q]Isa 65:21; Am 9:14

a 3 Or *Lord has appeared to us from afar*

[6]There will be a day when watchmen cry out
on the hills of Ephraim,
'Come, let us go up to Zion,
to the LORD our God.'"[a]

[7]This is what the LORD says:

"Sing with joy for Jacob;
shout for the foremost[b] of the nations.
Make your praises heard, and say,
'O LORD, save[c] your people,
the remnant[d] of Israel.'
[8]See, I will bring them from the land of the north[e]
and gather[f] them from the ends of the earth.
Among them will be the blind[g] and the lame,[h]
expectant mothers and women in labor;
a great throng will return.
[9]They will come with weeping;[i]
they will pray as I bring them back.
I will lead[j] them beside streams of water
on a level[k] path where they will not stumble,
because I am Israel's father,[l]
and Ephraim is my firstborn son.

[10]"Hear the word of the LORD, O nations;
proclaim it in distant coastlands:[m]
'He who scattered Israel will gather[n] them
and will watch over his flock like a shepherd.'[o]
[11]For the LORD will ransom Jacob
and redeem[p] them from the hand of those stronger[q]
than they.
[12]They will come and shout for joy on the heights[r]
of Zion;
they will rejoice in the bounty[s] of the LORD—
the grain, the new wine and the oil,[t]
the young of the flocks and herds.
They will be like a well-watered garden,[u]
and they will sorrow[v] no more.
[13]Then maidens will dance and be glad,
young men and old as well.
I will turn their mourning[w] into gladness;
I will give them comfort and joy[x] instead
of sorrow.
[14]I will satisfy[y] the priests with abundance,
and my people will be filled with my bounty,"
declares the LORD.

31:6
[a]Isa 2:3; Jer 50:4-5; Mic 4:2

31:7
[b]Dt 28:13; Isa 61:9
[c]Ps 14:7; 28:9
[d]Isa 37:31

31:8
[e]Jer 3:18; 23:8
[f]Dt 30:4; Eze 34:12-14
[g]Isa 42:16
[h]Eze 34:16; Mic 4:6

31:9
[i]Ps 126:5
[j]Isa 63:13
[k]Isa 49:11
[l]Ex 4:22; Jer 3:4

31:10
[m]Isa 66:19; Jer 25:22
[n]Jer 50:19
[o]Isa 40:11; Eze 34:12

31:11
[p]Isa 44:23; 48:20
[q]Ps 142:6

31:12
[r]Eze 17:23; Mic 4:1
[s]Joel 3:18
[t]Hos 2:21-22
[u]Isa 58:11
[v]Isa 65:19; Jn 16:22; Rev 7:17

31:13
[w]Isa 61:3
[x]Ps 30:11; Isa 51:11

31:14
[y]ver 25

31:15 [a]Jos 18:25 [b]Ge 37:35 [c]Jer 10:20; Mt 2:17-18*

15 This is what the LORD says:

"A voice is heard in Ramah,[a]
mourning and great weeping,
Rachel weeping for her children
and refusing to be comforted,[b]
because her children are no more."[c]

31:16 [d]Isa 25:8; 30:19 [e]Ru 2:12 [f]Jer 30:3; Eze 11:17

16 This is what the LORD says:

"Restrain your voice from weeping
and your eyes from tears,[d]
for your work will be rewarded,[e]"
declares the LORD.
"They will return[f] from the land of the enemy.
17 So there is hope for your future,"
declares the LORD.
"Your children will return to their own land.

31:18 [g]Job 5:17 [h]Hos 4:16 [i]Ps 80:3

18 "I have surely heard Ephraim's moaning:
'You disciplined[g] me like an unruly calf,[h]
and I have been disciplined.
Restore[i] me, and I will return,
because you are the LORD my God.

31:19 [j]Eze 36:31 [k]Eze 21:12; Lk 18:13

19 After I strayed,[j]
I repented;
after I came to understand,
I beat[k] my breast.
I was ashamed and humiliated
because I bore the disgrace of my youth.'

31:20 [l]Hos 4:4; 11:8 [m]Isa 55:7; 63:15; Mic 7:18

20 Is not Ephraim my dear son,
the child in whom I delight?
Though I often speak against him,
I still remember[l] him.
Therefore my heart yearns for him;
I have great compassion[m] for him,"
declares the LORD.

31:21 [n]Jer 50:5 [o]Isa 52:11 [p]ver 4

21 "Set up road signs;
put up guideposts.
Take note of the highway,[n]
the road that you take.
Return,[o] O Virgin[p] Israel,
return to your towns.

31:22 [q]Jer 2:23 [r]Jer 3:6

22 How long will you wander,[q]
O unfaithful[r] daughter?

The LORD will create a new thing on earth—
a woman will surround[a] a man."

23This is what the LORD Almighty, the God of Israel, says: "When
I bring them back from captivity,[b][a] the people in the land of Judah
and in its towns will once again use these words: 'The LORD bless
you, O righteous dwelling,[b] O sacred mountain.'[c] 24People will
live[d] together in Judah and all its towns—farmers and those who
move about with their flocks. 25I will refresh the weary and satisfy
the faint."[e]

26At this I awoke[f] and looked around. My sleep had been pleasant
to me.

27"The days are coming," declares the LORD, "when I will plant[g]
the house of Israel and the house of Judah with the offspring of
men and of animals. 28Just as I watched over them to uproot and
tear down, and to overthrow, destroy and bring disaster,[h] so I will
watch over them to build and to plant,"[i] declares the LORD. 29"In
those days people will no longer say,

'The fathers[j] have eaten sour grapes,
and the children's teeth are set on edge.'[k]

30Instead, everyone will die for his own sin;[l] whoever eats sour
grapes—his own teeth will be set on edge.

31"The time is coming," declares the LORD,
"when I will make a new covenant[m]
with the house of Israel
and with the house of Judah.
32It will not be like the covenant[n]
I made with their forefathers[o]
when I took them by the hand
to lead them out of Egypt,
because they broke my covenant,
though I was a husband to[c] them,[d]"
declares the LORD.
33"This is the covenant I will make with the house of Israel
after that time," declares the LORD.
"I will put my law in their minds
and write it on their hearts.[p]
I will be their God,
and they will be my people.[q]
34No longer will a man teach[r] his neighbor,
or a man his brother, saying, 'Know the LORD,'

[a]22 Or *will go about ⌊seeking⌋*; or *will protect* [b]23 Or *I restore their fortunes* [c]32 Hebrew; Septuagint and Syriac / *and I turned away from* [d]32 Or *was their master*

31:23 [a]Jer 30:18 [b]Isa 1:26 [c]Ps 48:1; Zec 8:3
31:24 [d]Zec 8:4-8
31:25 [e]Jn 4:14
31:26 [f]Zec 4:1
31:27 [g]Eze 36:9-11; Hos 2:23
31:28 [h]Jer 18:8; 44:27 [i]Jer 1:10
31:29 [j]La 5:7 [k]Eze 18:2
31:30 [l]Isa 3:11; Gal 6:7
31:31 [m]Jer 32:40; Eze 37:26; Lk 22:20; Heb 8:8-12*; 10:16-17
31:32 [n]Ex 24:8 [o]Dt 5:3
31:33 [p]2Co 3:3 [q]Jer 24:7; Heb 10:16
31:34 [r]1Jn 2:27

because they will all know[a] me,
  from the least of them to the greatest,"
    declares the LORD.
"For I will forgive[b] their wickedness
  and will remember their sins[c] no more."

35This is what the LORD says,

he who appoints[d] the sun
  to shine by day,
who decrees the moon and stars
  to shine by night,[e]
who stirs up the sea
  so that its waves roar—
  the LORD Almighty is his name:[f]
36"Only if these decrees[g] vanish from my sight,"
  declares the LORD,
"will the descendants[h] of Israel ever cease
  to be a nation before me."

37This is what the LORD says:

"Only if the heavens above can be measured[i]
  and the foundations of the earth below be searched out
will I reject[j] all the descendants of Israel
  because of all they have done,"
    declares the LORD.

38"The days are coming," declares the LORD, "when this city
will be rebuilt[k] for me from the Tower of Hananel[l] to the Corner
Gate.[m] 39The measuring line will stretch from there straight to the
hill of Gareb and then turn to Goah. 40The whole valley[n] where
dead bodies[o] and ashes are thrown, and all the terraces out to the
Kidron Valley[p] on the east as far as the corner of the Horse Gate,[q]
will be holy[r] to the LORD. The city will never again be uprooted or
demolished."

Chapter 32 Theme ______________________________

32 This is the word that came to Jeremiah from the LORD in the
tenth[s] year of Zedekiah king of Judah, which was the eighteenth[t] year of Nebuchadnezzar. 2The army of the king of Babylon
was then besieging Jerusalem, and Jeremiah the prophet was confined in the courtyard of the guard[u] in the royal palace of Judah.
3Now Zedekiah king of Judah had imprisoned him there, saying,
"Why do you prophesy[v] as you do? You say, 'This is what the LORD
says: I am about to hand this city over to the king of Babylon, and
he will capture[w] it. 4Zedekiah king of Judah will not escape[x] out of

31:34 [a]Jn 6:45 [b]Isa 54:13; Jer 33:8; 50:20 [c]Ro 11:27; Mic 7:19; Heb 10:17*
31:35 [d]Ps 136:7-9 [e]Ge 1:16 [f]Jer 10:16
31:36 [g]Isa 54:9-10; Jer 33:20-26 [h]Ps 89:36-37
31:37 [i]Jer 33:22 [j]Jer 33:24-26; Ro 11:1-5
31:38 [k]Jer 30:18 [l]Ne 3:1 [m]2Ki 14:13; Zec 14:10
31:40 [n]Jer 7:31-32 [o]Jer 8:2 [p]2Sa 15:23; Jn 18:1 [q]2Ki 11:16 [r]Joel 3:17; Zec 14:21
32:1 [s]2Ki 25:1 [t]Jer 25:1; 39:1
32:2 [u]Ne 3:25; Jer 37:21
32:3 [v]Jer 26:8-9 [w]ver 28; Jer 34:2-3
32:4 [x]Jer 38:18,23; 39:5-7; 52:9

the hands of the Babylonians[a] but will certainly be handed over
to the king of Babylon, and will speak with him face to face and
see him with his own eyes. 5He will take[a] Zedekiah to Babylon,
where he will remain until I deal with him, declares the LORD. If
you fight against the Babylonians, you will not succeed.'"[b]
6Jeremiah said, "The word of the LORD came to me: 7Hanamel
son of Shallum your uncle is going to come to you and say, 'Buy
my field at Anathoth, because as nearest relative it is your right
and duty[c] to buy it.'
8"Then, just as the LORD had said, my cousin Hanamel came to
me in the courtyard of the guard and said, 'Buy my field at
Anathoth in the territory of Benjamin. Since it is your right to
redeem it and possess it, buy it for yourself.'
"I knew that this was the word of the LORD; 9so I bought the
field at Anathoth from my cousin Hanamel and weighed out for
him seventeen shekels[b] of silver.[d] 10I signed and sealed the deed,
had it witnessed,[e] and weighed out the silver on the scales. 11I
took the deed of purchase—the sealed copy containing the terms
and conditions, as well as the unsealed copy— 12and I gave this
deed to Baruch[f] son of Neriah,[g] the son of Mahseiah, in the presence of my cousin Hanamel and of the witnesses who had signed
the deed and of all the Jews sitting in the courtyard of the guard.
13"In their presence I gave Baruch these instructions: 14'This is
what the LORD Almighty, the God of Israel, says: Take these documents, both the sealed and unsealed copies of the deed of purchase, and put them in a clay jar so they will last a long time.
15For this is what the LORD Almighty, the God of Israel, says:
Houses, fields and vineyards will again be bought in this land.'[h]
16"After I had given the deed of purchase to Baruch son of Neriah, I prayed to the LORD:

17"Ah, Sovereign LORD,[i] you have made the heavens and the
earth by your great power and outstretched arm.[j] Nothing is
too hard[k] for you. 18You show love[l] to thousands but bring the
punishment for the fathers' sins into the laps of their children[m]
after them. O great and powerful God, whose name is the LORD
Almighty,[n] 19great are your purposes and mighty are your
deeds.[o] Your eyes are open to all the ways of men;[p] you reward
everyone according to his conduct and as his deeds deserve.[q]
20You performed miraculous signs and wonders in Egypt[r] and
have continued them to this day, both in Israel and among all
mankind, and have gained the renown that is still yours. 21You
brought your people Israel out of Egypt with signs and wonders, by a mighty hand[s] and an outstretched arm and with

INSIGHT

Read Leviticus 25:23-28 in regard to redeeming the land.

32:5 [a]Jer 39:7; Eze 12:13 [b]Jer 21:4
32:7 [c]Lev 25:24-25; Ru 4:3-4; Mt 27:10*
32:9 [d]Ge 23:16
32:10 [e]Ru 4:9
32:12 [f]ver 16; Jer 36:4; 43:3,6; 45:1 [g]Jer 51:59
32:15 [h]ver 43-44; Jer 30:18; Am 9:14-15
32:17 [i]Jer 1:6 [j]2Ki 19:15; Ps 102:25 [k]Mt 19:26
32:18 [l]Dt 5:10 [m]Ex 20:5 [n]Jer 10:16
32:19 [o]Isa 28:29 [p]Pr 5:21; Jer 16:17 [q]Jer 17:10; Mt 16:27
32:20 [r]Ex 9:16
32:21 [s]Ex 6:6; 1Ch 17:21; Da 9:15

[a]4 Or *Chaldeans*; also in verses 5, 24, 25, 28, 29 and 43 [b]9 That is, about 7 ounces (about 200 grams)

great terror.[a] 22You gave them this land you had sworn to give
their forefathers, a land flowing with milk and honey.[b] 23They
came in and took possession[c] of it, but they did not obey you
or follow your law;[d] they did not do what you commanded
them to do. So you brought all this disaster[e] upon them.

24"See how the siege ramps are built up to take the city.
Because of the sword, famine and plague,[f] the city will be
handed over to the Babylonians who are attacking it. What
you said[g] has happened, as you now see. 25And though the
city will be handed over to the Babylonians, you, O Sovereign
LORD, say to me, 'Buy the field with silver and have the trans-
action witnessed.'"

26Then the word of the LORD came to Jeremiah: 27"I am the LORD,
the God of all mankind.[h] Is anything too hard for me? 28Therefore,
this is what the LORD says: I am about to hand this city over to the
Babylonians and to Nebuchadnezzar[i] king of Babylon, who will
capture it.[j] 29The Babylonians who are attacking this city will come
in and set it on fire; they will burn it down,[k] along with the houses[l]
where the people provoked me to anger by burning incense on the
roofs to Baal and by pouring out drink offerings[m] to other gods.

30"The people of Israel and Judah have done nothing but evil in
my sight from their youth;[n] indeed, the people of Israel have done
nothing but provoke[o] me with what their hands have made,[p]
declares the LORD. 31From the day it was built until now, this city
has so aroused my anger and wrath that I must remove[q] it from my
sight. 32The people of Israel and Judah have provoked me by all the
evil[r] they have done—they, their kings and officials, their priests
and prophets, the men of Judah and the people of Jerusalem.
33They turned their backs[s] to me and not their faces; though I
taught[t] them again and again, they would not listen or respond to
discipline. 34They set up their abominable idols in the house that
bears my Name and defiled[u] it. 35They built high places for Baal in
the Valley of Ben Hinnom to sacrifice their sons and daughters[a] to
Molech,[v] though I never commanded, nor did it enter my mind,[w]
that they should do such a detestable thing and so make Judah sin.

36"You are saying about this city, 'By the sword, famine and
plague[x] it will be handed over to the king of Babylon'; but this is
what the LORD, the God of Israel, says: 37I will surely gather[y] them
from all the lands where I banish them in my furious anger and
great wrath; I will bring them back to this place and let them live in
safety.[z] 38They will be my people,[a] and I will be their God. 39I will
give them singleness[b] of heart and action, so that they will always
fear me for their own good and the good of their children after

32:21 [a]Dt 26:8
32:22 [b]Ex 3:8; Jer 11:5
32:23 [c]Ps 44:2; 78:54-55 [d]Ne 9:26; Jer 11:8 [e]Da 9:14
32:24 [f]Jer 14:12 [g]Dt 4:25-26; Jos 23:15-16
32:27 [h]Nu 16:22
32:28 [i]2Ch 36:17 [j]ver 3
32:29 [k]2Ch 36:19; Jer 21:10; 37:8,10; 52:13 [l]Jer 19:13 [m]Jer 44:18
32:30 [n]Jer 22:21 [o]Jer 8:19 [p]Jer 25:7
32:31 [q]2Ki 23:27; 24:3
32:32 [r]Isa 1:4-6; Da 9:8
32:33 [s]Jer 2:27; Eze 8:16 [t]Jer 7:13
32:34 [u]Jer 7:30
32:35 [v]Lev 18:21 [w]Jer 7:31; 19:5
32:36 [x]ver 24
32:37 [y]Jer 23:3,6 [z]Dt 30:3; Eze 34:28
32:38 [a]Jer 24:7; 2Co 6:16*
32:39 [b]Eze 11:19

a 35 Or *to make their sons and daughters pass through* ⌊*the fire*⌋

them. 40I will make an everlasting covenant[a] with them: I will never stop doing good to them, and I will inspire them to fear me, so that they will never turn away from me.[b] 41I will rejoice in doing them good[c] and will assuredly plant[d] them in this land with all my heart and soul.

42"This is what the LORD says: As I have brought all this great calamity on this people, so I will give them all the prosperity I have promised[e] them. 43Once more fields will be bought[f] in this land of which you say, 'It is a desolate waste, without men or animals, for it has been handed over to the Babylonians.' 44Fields will be bought for silver, and deeds[g] will be signed, sealed and witnessed in the territory of Benjamin, in the villages around Jerusalem, in the towns of Judah and in the towns of the hill country, of the western foothills and of the Negev,[h] because I will restore[i] their fortunes,[a] declares the LORD."

Chapter 33 Theme ______________________________

33 While Jeremiah was still confined in the courtyard[j] of the guard, the word of the LORD came to him a second time: 2"This is what the LORD says, he who made the earth,[k] the LORD who formed it and established it—the LORD is his name:[l] 3'Call[m] to me and I will answer you and tell you great and unsearchable things you do not know.' 4For this is what the LORD, the God of Israel, says about the houses in this city and the royal palaces of Judah that have been torn down to be used against the siege[n] ramps[o] and the sword 5in the fight with the Babylonians[b]: 'They will be filled with the dead bodies of the men I will slay in my anger and wrath.[p] I will hide my face[q] from this city because of all its wickedness.

6"'Nevertheless, I will bring health and healing to it; I will heal my people and will let them enjoy abundant peace and security. 7I will bring Judah[r] and Israel back from captivity[c][s] and will rebuild them as they were before.[t] 8I will cleanse[u] them from all the sin they have committed against me and will forgive[v] all their sins of rebellion against me. 9Then this city will bring me renown, joy, praise[w] and honor[x] before all nations on earth that hear of all the good things I do for it; and they will be in awe and will tremble at the abundant prosperity and peace I provide for it.'

10"This is what the LORD says: 'You say about this place, "It is a desolate waste, without men or animals."[y] Yet in the towns of Judah and the streets of Jerusalem that are deserted, inhabited by neither men nor animals, there will be heard once more 11the sounds of joy

a44 Or *will bring them back from captivity* b5 Or *Chaldeans* c7 Or *will restore the fortunes of Judah and Israel*

32:40 [a]Isa 55:3 [b]Jer 24:7
32:41 [c]Dt 30:9 [d]Jer 24:6; 31:28; Am 9:15
32:42 [e]Jer 31:28
32:43 [f]ver 15
32:44 [g]ver 10 [h]Jer 17:26 [i]Jer 33:7,11,26
33:1 [j]Jer 32:2-3; 37:21; 38:28
33:2 [k]Jer 10:16 [l]Ex 3:15; 15:3
33:3 [m]Isa 55:6; Jer 29:12
33:4 [n]Eze 4:2 [o]Jer 32:24; Hab 1:10
33:5 [p]Jer 21:4-7 [q]Isa 8:17
33:7 [r]Jer 32:44 [s]Jer 30:3; Am 9:14 [t]Isa 1:26
33:8 [u]Heb 9:13-14 [v]Jer 31:34; Mic 7:18; Zec 13:1
33:9 [w]Jer 13:11 [x]Isa 62:7; Jer 3:17
33:10 [y]Jer 32:43

and gladness,[a] the voices of bride and bridegroom, and the voices
of those who bring thank offerings[b] to the house of the LORD, saying,

> "Give thanks to the LORD Almighty,
> for the LORD is good;[c]
> his love endures forever."[d]

For I will restore the fortunes of the land as they were before,' says
the LORD.

12"This is what the LORD Almighty says: 'In this place, desolate[e]
and without men or animals—in all its towns there will again be
pastures for shepherds to rest their flocks.[f] 13In the towns of the
hill country, of the western foothills and of the Negev,[g] in the territory of Benjamin, in the villages around Jerusalem and in the
towns of Judah, flocks will again pass under the hand[h] of the one
who counts them,' says the LORD.

14"'The days are coming,' declares the LORD, 'when I will fulfill
the gracious promise[i] I made to the house of Israel and to the
house of Judah.

> 15"'In those days and at that time
> I will make a righteous[j] Branch[k] sprout from
> David's line;
> he will do what is just and right in the land.
> 16In those days Judah will be saved[l]
> and Jerusalem will live in safety.
> This is the name by which it[a] will be called:
> The LORD Our Righteousness.'[m]

17For this is what the LORD says: 'David will never fail[n] to have a
man to sit on the throne of the house of Israel, 18nor will the priests,
who are Levites,[o] ever fail to have a man to stand before me continually to offer burnt offerings, to burn grain offerings and to
present sacrifices.[p]'"

19The word of the LORD came to Jeremiah: 20"This is what the
LORD says: 'If you can break my covenant with the day[q] and my
covenant with the night, so that day and night no longer come at
their appointed time, 21then my covenant[r] with David my servant—and my covenant with the Levites who are priests ministering before me—can be broken and David will no longer have a
descendant to reign on his throne.[s] 22I will make the descendants
of David my servant and the Levites who minister before me as
countless[t] as the stars of the sky and as measureless as the sand on
the seashore.'"

23The word of the LORD came to Jeremiah: 24"Have you not
noticed that these people are saying, 'The LORD has rejected the two

33:11 [a]Isa 51:3 [b]Lev 7:12 [c]1Ch 16:8; Ps 136:1 [d]1Ch 16:34; 2Ch 5:13; Ps 100:4-5
33:12 [e]Jer 32:43 [f]Isa 65:10; Eze 34:11-15
33:13 [g]Jer 17:26 [h]Lev 27:32
33:14 [i]Jer 29:10
33:15 [j]Ps 72:2 [k]Isa 4:2; 11:1; Jer 23:5
33:16 [l]Isa 45:17 [m]1Co 1:30
33:17 [n]2Sa 7:13; 1Ki 2:4; Ps 89:29-37; Lk 1:33
33:18 [o]Dt 18:1 [p]Heb 13:15
33:20 [q]Ps 89:36
33:21 [r]Ps 89:34 [s]2Ch 7:18
33:22 [t]Ge 15:5

[a]16 Or *he*

kingdoms[a][a] he chose'? So they despise[b] my people and no longer
regard them as a nation.[c] [25]This is what the LORD says: 'If I have not
established my covenant with day and night[d] and the fixed laws of
heaven and earth,[e] [26]then I will reject[f] the descendants of Jacob[g]
and David my servant and will not choose one of his sons to rule
over the descendants of Abraham, Isaac and Jacob. For I will
restore their fortunes[b][h] and have compassion on them.'"

Chapter 34 Theme ____________________

34 While Nebuchadnezzar king of Babylon and all his army
and all the kingdoms and peoples[i] in the empire he ruled
were fighting against Jerusalem[j] and all its surrounding towns, this
word came to Jeremiah from the LORD: [2]"This is what the LORD, the
God of Israel, says: Go to Zedekiah[k] king of Judah and tell him,
'This is what the LORD says: I am about to hand this city over to the
king of Babylon, and he will burn it down.[l] [3]You will not escape
from his grasp but will surely be captured and handed over[m] to
him. You will see the king of Babylon with your own eyes, and he
will speak with you face to face. And you will go to Babylon.

[4]"'Yet hear the promise of the LORD, O Zedekiah king of Judah.
This is what the LORD says concerning you: You will not die by
the sword; [5]you will die peacefully. As people made a funeral fire[n]
in honor of your fathers, the former kings who preceded you, so
they will make a fire in your honor and lament, "Alas,[o] O master!" I myself make this promise, declares the LORD.'"

[6]Then Jeremiah the prophet told all this to Zedekiah king of
Judah, in Jerusalem, [7]while the army of the king of Babylon was
fighting against Jerusalem and the other cities of Judah that were
still holding out—Lachish[p] and Azekah.[q] These were the only
fortified cities left in Judah.

[8]The word came to Jeremiah from the LORD after King Zedekiah
had made a covenant with all the people[r] in Jerusalem to proclaim
freedom[s] for the slaves. [9]Everyone was to free his Hebrew slaves,
both male and female; no one was to hold a fellow Jew in bondage.[t] [10]So all the officials and people who entered into this
covenant agreed that they would free their male and female slaves
and no longer hold them in bondage. They agreed, and set them
free. [11]But afterward they changed their minds and took back the
slaves they had freed and enslaved them again.

[12]Then the word of the LORD came to Jeremiah: [13]"This is what
the LORD, the God of Israel, says: I made a covenant with your
forefathers[u] when I brought them out of Egypt, out of the land of
slavery. I said, [14]'Every seventh year each of you must free any fellow

[a]24 Or *families* [b]26 Or *will bring them back from captivity*

33:24 [a]Eze 37:22 [b]Ne 4:4 [c]Jer 30:17
33:25 [d]Jer 31:35-36 [e]Ps 74:16-17
33:26 [f]Jer 31:37 [g]Isa 14:1 [h]ver 7
34:1 [i]Jer 27:7 [j]2Ki 25:1; Jer 39:1
34:2 [k]2Ch 36:11 [l]ver 22; Jer 32:29; 37:8
34:3 [m]2Ki 25:7; Jer 21:7; 32:4
34:5 [n]2Ch 16:14; 21:19 [o]Jer 22:18
34:7 [p]Jos 10:3 [q]Jos 10:10; 2Ch 11:9
34:8 [r]2Ki 11:17 [s]Ex 21:2; Lev 25:10, 39-41; Ne 5:5-8
34:9 [t]Lev 25:39-46
34:13 [u]Ex 24:8

Hebrew who has sold himself to you. After he has served you six
years, you must let him go free.'[a] [a] Your fathers, however, did not
listen to me or pay attention[b] to me. 15 Recently you repented and
did what is right in my sight: Each of you proclaimed freedom to
his countrymen.[c] You even made a covenant before me in the
house that bears my Name.[d] 16 But now you have turned around[e]
and profaned[f] my name; each of you has taken back the male and
female slaves you had set free to go where they wished. You have
forced them to become your slaves again.

17 "Therefore, this is what the LORD says: You have not obeyed
me; you have not proclaimed freedom for your fellow countrymen. So I now proclaim 'freedom' for you,[g] declares the LORD—
'freedom' to fall by the sword, plague and famine. I will make you
abhorrent to all the kingdoms of the earth.[h] 18 The men who have
violated my covenant and have not fulfilled the terms of the covenant they made before me, I will treat like the calf they cut in two
and then walked between its pieces.[i] 19 The leaders of Judah and
Jerusalem, the court officials,[j] the priests and all the people of the
land who walked between the pieces of the calf, 20 I will hand over[k]
to their enemies who seek their lives.[l] Their dead bodies will
become food for the birds of the air and the beasts of the earth.[m]

21 "I will hand Zedekiah[n] king of Judah and his officials[o] over to
their enemies who seek their lives, to the army of the king of Babylon, which has withdrawn[p] from you. 22 I am going to give the
order, declares the LORD, and I will bring them back to this city.
They will fight against it, take[q] it and burn[r] it down. And I will lay
waste the towns of Judah so no one can live there."

Chapter 35 Theme ______________________

35 This is the word that came to Jeremiah from the LORD during
the reign of Jehoiakim[s] son of Josiah king of Judah: 2 "Go
to the Recabite[t] family and invite them to come to one of the side
rooms[u] of the house of the LORD and give them wine to drink."

3 So I went to get Jaazaniah son of Jeremiah, the son of Habaz-
ziniah, and his brothers and all his sons—the whole family of the
Recabites. 4 I brought them into the house of the LORD, into the
room of the sons of Hanan son of Igdaliah the man of God.[v] It was
next to the room of the officials, which was over that of Maaseiah
son of Shallum[w] the doorkeeper.[x] 5 Then I set bowls full of wine
and some cups before the men of the Recabite family and said to
them, "Drink some wine."

6 But they replied, "We do not drink wine, because our forefather
Jonadab[y] son of Recab gave us this command: 'Neither you nor
your descendants must ever drink wine.[z] 7 Also you must never

34:14 [a] Ex 21:2 [b] Dt 15:12; 2Ki 17:14
34:15 [c] ver 8 [d] Jer 7:10-11; 32:34
34:16 [e] Eze 3:20; 18:24 [f] Ex 20:7; Lev 19:12
34:17 [g] Mt 7:2; Gal 6:7 [h] Dt 28:25,64; Jer 29:18
34:18 [i] Ge 15:10
34:19 [j] Zep 3:3-4
34:20 [k] Jer 21:7 [l] Jer 11:21 [m] Dt 28:26; Jer 7:33; 19:7
34:21 [n] Jer 32:4 [o] Jer 39:6; 52:24-27 [p] Jer 37:5
34:22 [q] Jer 39:1-2 [r] Jer 39:8
35:1 [s] 2Ch 36:5
35:2 [t] 2Ki 10:15; 1Ch 2:55 [u] 1Ki 6:5
35:4 [v] Dt 33:1 [w] 1Ch 9:19 [x] 2Ki 12:9
35:6 [y] 2Ki 10:15 [z] Lev 10:9; Nu 6:2-4; Lk 1:15

[a] *14* Deut. 15:12

build houses, sow seed or plant vineyards; you must never have
any of these things, but must always live in tents.[a] Then you will
live a long time in the land[b] where you are nomads.' 8We have
obeyed everything our forefather[c] Jonadab son of Recab commanded us. Neither we nor our wives nor our sons and daughters
have ever drunk wine 9or built houses to live in or had vineyards,
fields or crops.[d] 10We have lived in tents and have fully obeyed
everything our forefather Jonadab commanded us. 11But when
Nebuchadnezzar king of Babylon invaded[e] this land, we said,
'Come, we must go to Jerusalem[f] to escape the Babylonian[a] and
Aramean armies.' So we have remained in Jerusalem."

12Then the word of the LORD came to Jeremiah, saying: 13"This
is what the LORD Almighty, the God of Israel, says: Go and tell the
men of Judah and the people of Jerusalem, 'Will you not learn a
lesson[g] and obey my words?' declares the LORD. 14'Jonadab son of
Recab ordered his sons not to drink wine and this command has
been kept. To this day they do not drink wine, because they obey
their forefather's command. But I have spoken to you again and
again,[h] yet you have not obeyed[i] me. 15Again and again I sent all
my servants the prophets[j] to you. They said, "Each of you must
turn[k] from your wicked ways and reform[l] your actions; do not
follow other gods to serve them. Then you will live in the land[m] I
have given to you and your fathers." But you have not paid attention or listened[n] to me. 16The descendants of Jonadab son of Recab
have carried out the command their forefather[o] gave them, but
these people have not obeyed me.'

17"Therefore, this is what the LORD God Almighty, the God of
Israel, says: 'Listen! I am going to bring on Judah and on everyone
living in Jerusalem every disaster[p] I pronounced against them. I
spoke to them, but they did not listen;[q] I called to them, but they
did not answer.'"[r]

18Then Jeremiah said to the family of the Recabites, "This is what
the LORD Almighty, the God of Israel, says: 'You have obeyed the
command of your forefather Jonadab and have followed all his
instructions and have done everything he ordered.' 19Therefore,
this is what the LORD Almighty, the God of Israel, says: 'Jonadab
son of Recab will never fail[s] to have a man to serve[t] me.'"

Chapter 36 Theme ______________________

36 In the fourth year of Jehoiakim[u] son of Josiah king of
Judah, this word came to Jeremiah from the LORD: 2"Take a
scroll[v] and write on it all the words I have spoken to you concerning Israel, Judah and all the other nations from the time I began

[a]11 Or *Chaldean*

35:7 [a]Heb 11:9 [b]Ex 20:12; Eph 6:2-3
35:8 [c]Pr 1:8; Col 3:20
35:9 [d]1Ti 6:6
35:11 [e]2Ki 24:1 [f]Jer 8:14
35:13 [g]Jer 6:10; 32:33
35:14 [h]Jer 7:13; 25:3 [i]Isa 30:9
35:15 [j]Jer 7:25 [k]Jer 26:3 [l]Isa 1:16-17; Jer 4:1; 18:11; Eze 18:30 [m]Jer 25:5 [n]Jer 7:26
35:16 [o]Mal 1:6
35:17 [p]Jos 23:15; Jer 21:4-7 [q]Pr 1:24; Ro 10:21 [r]Isa 65:12; 66:4; Jer 7:13
35:19 [s]Jer 33:17 [t]Jer 15:19
36:1 [u]2Ch 36:5
36:2 [v]Ex 17:14; Jer 30:2; Hab 2:2

speaking to you in the reign of Josiah[a] till now. 3 Perhaps[b] when the
people of Judah hear[c] about every disaster I plan to inflict on them,
each of them will turn[d] from his wicked way; then I will forgive[e]
their wickedness and their sin."
4 So Jeremiah called Baruch[f] son of Neriah, and while Jeremiah
dictated[g] all the words the LORD had spoken to him, Baruch wrote
them on the scroll.[h] 5 Then Jeremiah told Baruch, "I am restricted;
I cannot go to the LORD's temple. 6 So you go to the house of the
LORD on a day of fasting[i] and read to the people from the scroll
the words of the LORD that you wrote as I dictated. Read them to
all the people of Judah who come in from their towns. 7 Perhaps
they will bring their petition before the LORD, and each will turn[j]
from his wicked ways, for the anger[k] and wrath pronounced
against this people by the LORD are great."
8 Baruch son of Neriah did everything Jeremiah the prophet told
him to do; at the LORD's temple he read the words of the LORD
from the scroll. 9 In the ninth month[l] of the fifth year of Jehoiakim
son of Josiah king of Judah, a time of fasting[m] before the LORD was
proclaimed for all the people in Jerusalem and those who had
come from the towns of Judah. 10 From the room of Gemariah son
of Shaphan the secretary,[n] which was in the upper courtyard at
the entrance of the New Gate[o] of the temple, Baruch read to all the
people at the LORD's temple the words of Jeremiah from the scroll.
11 When Micaiah son of Gemariah, the son of Shaphan, heard all
the words of the LORD from the scroll, 12 he went down to the secretary's room in the royal palace, where all the officials were sitting:
Elishama the secretary, Delaiah son of Shemaiah, Elnathan[p] son of
Acbor, Gemariah son of Shaphan, Zedekiah son of Hananiah, and
all the other officials. 13 After Micaiah told them everything he
had heard Baruch read to the people from the scroll, 14 all the officials sent Jehudi[q] son of Nethaniah, the son of Shelemiah, the son
of Cushi, to say to Baruch, "Bring the scroll from which you have
read to the people and come." So Baruch son of Neriah went to
them with the scroll in his hand. 15 They said to him, "Sit down,
please, and read it to us."
So Baruch read it to them. 16 When they heard all these words,
they looked at each other in fear and said to Baruch, "We must
report all these words to the king." 17 Then they asked Baruch, "Tell
us, how did you come to write all this? Did Jeremiah dictate it?"
18 "Yes," Baruch replied, "he dictated[r] all these words to me, and
I wrote them in ink on the scroll."
19 Then the officials said to Baruch, "You and Jeremiah, go and
hide.[s] Don't let anyone know where you are."
20 After they put the scroll in the room of Elishama the secretary,
they went to the king in the courtyard and reported everything
to him. 21 The king sent Jehudi[t] to get the scroll, and Jehudi brought

36:2 [a] Jer 1:2; 25:3
36:3 [b] ver 7; Eze 12:3 [c] Mk 4:12 [d] Jer 26:3; Jnh 3:8; Ac 3:19 [e] Jer 18:8
36:4 [f] Jer 32:12 [g] ver 18 [h] Eze 2:9
36:6 [i] ver 9
36:7 [j] Jer 26:3 [k] Dt 31:17
36:9 [l] ver 22 [m] 2Ch 20:3
36:10 [n] Jer 52:25 [o] Jer 26:10
36:12 [p] Jer 26:22
36:14 [q] ver 21
36:18 [r] ver 4
36:19 [s] 1Ki 17:3
36:21 [t] ver 14

it from the room of Elishama the secretary and read it to the king[a] and all the officials standing beside him. 22It was the ninth month and the king was sitting in the winter apartment,[b] with a fire burning in the firepot in front of him. 23Whenever Jehudi had read three or four columns of the scroll, the king cut them off with a scribe's knife and threw them into the firepot, until the entire scroll was burned in the fire.[c] 24The king and all his attendants who heard all these words showed no fear,[d] nor did they tear their clothes.[e] 25Even though Elnathan, Delaiah and Gemariah urged the king not to burn the scroll, he would not listen to them. 26Instead, the king commanded Jerahmeel, a son of the king, Seraiah son of Azriel and Shelemiah son of Abdeel to arrest[f] Baruch the scribe and Jeremiah the prophet. But the LORD had hidden[g] them.

27After the king burned the scroll containing the words that Baruch had written at Jeremiah's dictation,[h] the word of the LORD came to Jeremiah: 28"Take another scroll and write on it all the words that were on the first scroll, which Jehoiakim king of Judah burned up. 29Also tell Jehoiakim king of Judah, 'This is what the LORD says: You burned that scroll and said, "Why did you write on it that the king of Babylon would certainly come and destroy this land and cut off both men and animals from it?"[i] 30Therefore, this is what the LORD says about Jehoiakim king of Judah: He will have no one to sit on the throne of David; his body will be thrown out[j] and exposed to the heat by day and the frost by night. 31I will punish him and his children and his attendants for their wickedness; I will bring on them and those living in Jerusalem and the people of Judah every disaster[k] I pronounced against them, because they have not listened.'"

32So Jeremiah took another scroll and gave it to the scribe Baruch son of Neriah, and as Jeremiah dictated,[l] Baruch wrote[m] on it all the words of the scroll that Jehoiakim king of Judah had burned[n] in the fire. And many similar words were added to them.

Chapter 37 Theme ______________________

37 Zedekiah[o] son of Josiah was made king[p] of Judah by Nebuchadnezzar king of Babylon; he reigned in place of Jehoiachin[a][q] son of Jehoiakim. 2Neither he nor his attendants nor the people of the land paid any attention[r] to the words the LORD had spoken through Jeremiah the prophet.

3King Zedekiah, however, sent Jehucal son of Shelemiah with the priest Zephaniah[s] son of Maaseiah to Jeremiah the prophet with this message: "Please pray[t] to the LORD our God for us."

4Now Jeremiah was free to come and go among the people, for he had not yet been put in prison.[u] 5Pharaoh's army had marched

a 1 Hebrew *Coniah,* a variant of *Jehoiachin*

36:21 [a] 2Ki 22:10
36:22 [b] Am 3:15
36:23 [c] 1Ki 22:8
36:24 [d] Ps 36:1 [e] Ge 37:29; 2Ki 22:11; Isa 37:1
36:26 [f] Mt 23:34 [g] Jer 15:21
36:27 [h] ver 4
36:29 [i] Isa 30:10
36:30 [j] Jer 22:19
36:31 [k] Pr 29:1
36:32 [l] ver 4 [m] Ex 34:1 [n] ver 23
37:1 [o] 2Ki 24:17 [p] Eze 17:13 [q] 2Ki 24:8,12; 2Ch 36:10; Jer 22:24
37:2 [r] 2Ki 24:19; 2Ch 36:12,14
37:3 [s] Jer 29:25; 52:24 [t] 1Ki 13:6; Jer 21:1-2; 42:2
37:4 [u] ver 15; Jer 32:2

out of Egypt,[a] and when the Babylonians[a] who were besieging
Jerusalem heard the report about them, they withdrew[b] from
Jerusalem.[c]
6Then the word of the LORD came to Jeremiah the prophet: 7"This
is what the LORD, the God of Israel, says: Tell the king of Judah, who
sent you to inquire[d] of me, 'Pharaoh's army, which has marched
out to support you, will go back to its own land, to Egypt.[e] 8Then
the Babylonians will return and attack this city; they will capture
it and burn[f] it down.'
9"This is what the LORD says: Do not deceive[g] yourselves, thinking, 'The Babylonians will surely leave us.' They will not! 10Even if
you were to defeat the entire Babylonian[b] army that is attacking
you and only wounded men were left in their tents, they would
come out and burn this city down."
11After the Babylonian army had withdrawn[h] from Jerusalem
because of Pharaoh's army, 12Jeremiah started to leave the city to
go to the territory of Benjamin to get his share of the property[i]
among the people there. 13But when he reached the Benjamin
Gate, the captain of the guard, whose name was Irijah son of
Shelemiah, the son of Hananiah, arrested him and said, "You are
deserting to the Babylonians!"
14"That's not true!" Jeremiah said. "I am not deserting to the
Babylonians." But Irijah would not listen to him; instead, he arrested[j] Jeremiah and brought him to the officials. 15They were angry
with Jeremiah and had him beaten[k] and imprisoned in the house[l]
of Jonathan the secretary, which they had made into a prison.
16Jeremiah was put into a vaulted cell in a dungeon, where he
remained a long time. 17Then King Zedekiah sent for him and had
him brought to the palace, where he asked[m] him privately,[n] "Is there
any word from the LORD?"
"Yes," Jeremiah replied, "you will be handed over[o] to the king
of Babylon."
18Then Jeremiah said to King Zedekiah, "What crime[p] have I
committed against you or your officials or this people, that you
have put me in prison? 19Where are your prophets who prophesied
to you, 'The king of Babylon will not attack you or this land'? 20But
now, my lord the king, please listen. Let me bring my petition
before you: Do not send me back to the house of Jonathan the
secretary, or I will die there."
21King Zedekiah then gave orders for Jeremiah to be placed in
the courtyard of the guard and given bread from the street of the
bakers each day until all the bread[q] in the city was gone.[r] So Jeremiah remained in the courtyard of the guard.[s]

37:5 [a] Eze 17:15 [b] Jer 34:21 [c] 2Ki 24:7
37:7 [d] 2Ki 22:18 [e] Jer 2:36; La 4:17
37:8 [f] Jer 34:22; 39:8
37:9 [g] Jer 29:8
37:11 [h] ver 5
37:12 [i] Jer 32:9
37:14 [j] Jer 40:4
37:15 [k] Jer 20:2 [l] Jer 38:26
37:17 [m] Jer 15:11 [n] Jer 38:16 [o] Jer 21:7
37:18 [p] 1Sa 26:18; Jn 10:32; Ac 25:8
37:21 [q] Isa 33:16; Jer 38:9 [r] 2Ki 25:3; Jer 52:6 [s] Jer 32:2; 38:6,13,28

a *5* Or *Chaldeans*; also in verses 8, 9, 13 and 14 b *10* Or *Chaldean*; also in verse 11

Chapter 38 Theme ______________________

38 Shephatiah son of Mattan, Gedaliah son of Pashhur, Jehucal[a][a] son of Shelemiah, and Pashhur son of Malkijah
heard what Jeremiah was telling all the people when he said,
2“This is what the LORD says: ‘Whoever stays in this city will die
by the sword, famine or plague,[b] but whoever goes over to the
Babylonians[b] will live. He will escape with his life; he will live.’[c]
3And this is what the LORD says: ‘This city will certainly be handed over to the army of the king of Babylon, who will capture it.’ ”[d]
4Then the officials[e] said to the king, “This man should be put to
death.[f] He is discouraging the soldiers who are left in this city, as
well as all the people, by the things he is saying to them. This man
is not seeking the good of these people but their ruin.”
5“He is in your hands,” King Zedekiah answered. “The king can
do nothing to oppose you.”
6So they took Jeremiah and put him into the cistern of Malkijah,
the king’s son, which was in the courtyard of the guard.[g] They lowered Jeremiah by ropes into the cistern; it had no water in it, only
mud, and Jeremiah sank down into the mud.
7But Ebed-Melech,[h] a Cushite,[c] an official[d][i] in the royal palace,
heard that they had put Jeremiah into the cistern. While the king
was sitting in the Benjamin Gate,[j] 8Ebed-Melech went out of the
palace and said to him, 9“My lord the king, these men have acted
wickedly in all they have done to Jeremiah the prophet. They have
thrown him into a cistern, where he will starve to death when there
is no longer any bread[k] in the city.”
10Then the king commanded Ebed-Melech the Cushite, “Take
thirty men from here with you and lift Jeremiah the prophet out of
the cistern before he dies.”
11So Ebed-Melech took the men with him and went to a room
under the treasury in the palace. He took some old rags and worn-
out clothes from there and let them down with ropes to Jeremiah
in the cistern. 12Ebed-Melech the Cushite said to Jeremiah, “Put
these old rags and worn-out clothes under your arms to pad the
ropes.” Jeremiah did so, 13and they pulled him up with the ropes
and lifted him out of the cistern. And Jeremiah remained in the
courtyard of the guard.[l]
14Then King Zedekiah sent for Jeremiah the prophet and had
him brought to the third entrance to the temple of the LORD. “I am
going to ask you something,” the king said to Jeremiah. “Do not
hide[m] anything from me.”

a *1* Hebrew *Jucal,* a variant of *Jehucal* b *2* Or *Chaldeans*; also in verses 18, 19 and 23
c *7* Probably from the upper Nile region d *7* Or *a eunuch*

38:1 [a]Jer 37:3
38:2 [b]Jer 34:17 [c]Jer 21:9; 39:18; 45:5
38:3 [d]Jer 21:4,10; 32:3
38:4 [e]Jer 36:12 [f]Jer 26:11
38:6 [g]Jer 37:21
38:7 [h]Jer 39:16 [i]Ac 8:27 [j]Job 29:7
38:9 [k]Jer 37:21
38:13 [l]Jer 37:21
38:14 [m]1Sa 3:17

15 Jeremiah said to Zedekiah, "If I give you an answer, will you not kill me? Even if I did give you counsel, you would not listen to me."

16 But King Zedekiah swore this oath secretly[a] to Jeremiah: "As surely as the LORD lives, who has given us breath,[b] I will neither kill you nor hand you over to those who are seeking your life."[c]

17 Then Jeremiah said to Zedekiah, "This is what the LORD God Almighty, the God of Israel, says: 'If you surrender to the officers of the king of Babylon, your life will be spared and this city will not be burned down; you and your family will live.[d] 18 But if you will not surrender to the officers of the king of Babylon, this city will be handed over[e] to the Babylonians and they will burn[f] it down; you yourself will not escape[g] from their hands.' "

19 King Zedekiah said to Jeremiah, "I am afraid[h] of the Jews who have gone over[i] to the Babylonians, for the Babylonians may hand me over to them and they will mistreat me."

20 "They will not hand you over," Jeremiah replied. "Obey[j] the LORD by doing what I tell you. Then it will go well with you, and your life[k] will be spared. 21 But if you refuse to surrender, this is what the LORD has revealed to me: 22 All the women[l] left in the palace of the king of Judah will be brought out to the officials of the king of Babylon. Those women will say to you:

" 'They misled you and overcame you—
those trusted friends of yours.
Your feet are sunk in the mud;
your friends have deserted you.'

23 "All your wives and children[m] will be brought out to the Babylonians. You yourself will not escape from their hands but will be captured[n] by the king of Babylon; and this city will[a] be burned down."

24 Then Zedekiah said to Jeremiah, "Do not let anyone know about this conversation, or you may die. 25 If the officials hear that I talked with you, and they come to you and say, 'Tell us what you said to the king and what the king said to you; do not hide it from us or we will kill you,' 26 then tell them, 'I was pleading with the king not to send me back to Jonathan's house[o] to die there.' "

27 All the officials did come to Jeremiah and question him, and he told them everything the king had ordered him to say. So they said no more to him, for no one had heard his conversation with the king.

28 And Jeremiah remained in the courtyard of the guard[p] until the day Jerusalem was captured.

38:16 [a]Jer 37:17 [b]Isa 42:5; 57:16 [c]ver 4
38:17 [d]2Ki 24:12; Jer 21:9
38:18 [e]ver 3; Jer 34:3 [f]Jer 37:8 [g]Jer 24:8; 32:4
38:19 [h]Isa 51:12; Jn 12:42 [i]Jer 39:9
38:20 [j]Jer 11:4 [k]Isa 55:3
38:22 [l]Jer 6:12
38:23 [m]2Ki 25:6 [n]Jer 41:10
38:26 [o]Jer 37:15
38:28 [p]Jer 37:21; 39:14

[a] 23 Or *and you will cause this city to*

Chapter 39 Theme ______________________

39 This is how Jerusalem was taken: 1In the ninth year of
Zedekiah king of Judah, in the tenth month, Nebuchadnezzar king of Babylon marched against Jerusalem with his whole
army and laid siege[a] to it. 2And on the ninth day of the fourth
month of Zedekiah's eleventh year, the city wall was broken
through. 3Then all the officials[b] of the king of Babylon came and
took seats in the Middle Gate: Nergal-Sharezer of Samgar, Nebo-
Sarsekim[a] a chief officer, Nergal-Sharezer a high official and all the
other officials of the king of Babylon. 4When Zedekiah king of
Judah and all the soldiers saw them, they fled; they left the city at
night by way of the king's garden, through the gate between the
two walls, and headed toward the Arabah.[b]

5But the Babylonian[c] army pursued them and overtook Zedekiah[c] in the plains of Jericho. They captured him and took him to
Nebuchadnezzar king of Babylon at Riblah[d] in the land of Hamath, where he pronounced sentence on him. 6There at Riblah
the king of Babylon slaughtered the sons of Zedekiah before his
eyes and also killed all the nobles of Judah. 7Then he put out Zedekiah's eyes[e] and bound him with bronze shackles to take him to
Babylon.[f]

8The Babylonians[d] set fire[g] to the royal palace and the houses of
the people and broke down the walls[h] of Jerusalem. 9Nebuzaradan
commander of the imperial guard carried into exile to Babylon the
people who remained in the city, along with those who had gone
over to him, and the rest of the people.[i] 10But Nebuzaradan the
commander of the guard left behind in the land of Judah some of
the poor people, who owned nothing; and at that time he gave
them vineyards and fields.

11Now Nebuchadnezzar king of Babylon had given these orders
about Jeremiah through Nebuzaradan commander of the imperial
guard: 12"Take him and look after him; don't harm[j] him but do for
him whatever he asks." 13So Nebuzaradan the commander of the
guard, Nebushazban a chief officer, Nergal-Sharezer a high official
and all the other officers of the king of Babylon 14sent and had
Jeremiah taken out of the courtyard of the guard.[k] They turned
him over to Gedaliah son of Ahikam,[l] the son of Shaphan, to take
him back to his home. So he remained among his own people.[m]

15While Jeremiah had been confined in the courtyard of the
guard, the word of the LORD came to him: 16"Go and tell Ebed-
Melech[n] the Cushite, 'This is what the LORD Almighty, the God of
Israel, says: I am about to fulfill my words against this city through
disaster,[o] not prosperity. At that time they will be fulfilled before

[a]3 Or *Nergal-Sharezer, Samgar-Nebo, Sarsekim* [b]4 Or *the Jordan Valley* [c]5 Or *Chaldean*
[d]8 Or *Chaldeans*

39:1 [a]2Ki 25:1; Jer 52:4; Eze 24:2
39:3 [b]Jer 21:4
39:5 [c]Jer 32:4 [d]2Ki 23:33
39:7 [e]Eze 12:13 [f]Jer 32:5
39:8 [g]Jer 38:18 [h]Ne 1:3
39:9 [i]Jer 40:1
39:12 [j]Pr 16:7; 1Pe 3:13
39:14 [k]Jer 38:28 [l]2Ki 22:12 [m]Jer 40:5
39:16 [n]Jer 38:7 [o]Jer 21:10; Da 9:12

39:17 your eyes. [17]But I will rescue[a] you on that day, declares the LORD;
[a]Ps 41:1-2 you will not be handed over to those you fear. [18]I will save you;
you will not fall by the sword[b] but will escape with your life,[c]
39:18 because you trust[d] in me, declares the LORD.'"

[b]Jer 45:5 [c]Jer 21:9; 38:2 [d]Jer 17:7

Chapter 40 Theme ____________________

40 The word came to Jeremiah from the LORD after Nebuzaradan commander of the imperial guard had released him
40:2 at Ramah. He had found Jeremiah bound in chains among all the
[e]Jer 50:7 captives from Jerusalem and Judah who were being carried into
exile to Babylon. [2]When the commander of the guard found Jeremiah, he said to him, "The LORD your God decreed this disaster for
40:3 this place.[e] [3]And now the LORD has brought it about; he has done
[f]Da 9:11 [g]Dt 29:24-28; just as he said he would. All this happened because you people
Ro 2:5-9 sinned[f] against the LORD and did not obey[g] him. [4]But today I am
freeing you from the chains on your wrists. Come with me to
Babylon, if you like, and I will look after you; but if you do not
40:4 [h]Ge 13:9; want to, then don't come. Look, the whole country lies before you;
Jer 39:11-12 go wherever you please."[h] [5]However, before Jeremiah turned to
go,[a] Nebuzaradan added, "Go back to Gedaliah[i] son of Ahikam,
the son of Shaphan, whom the king of Babylon has appointed over
40:5 the towns of Judah, and live with him among the people, or go
[i]2Ki 25:22 [j]Jer 39:14 anywhere else you please."[j]

Then the commander gave him provisions and a present and let
him go. [6]So Jeremiah went to Gedaliah son of Ahikam at Mizpah[k]
40:6 and stayed with him among the people who were left behind in
[k]Jdg 20:1; 1Sa 7:5-17 the land.

[7]When all the army officers and their men who were still in the
open country heard that the king of Babylon had appointed
40:7 Gedaliah son of Ahikam as governor over the land and had put
[l]Jer 39:10 him in charge of the men, women and children who were the
poorest[l] in the land and who had not been carried into exile to
Babylon, [8]they came to Gedaliah at Mizpah[m]—Ishmael[n] son of
40:8 Nethaniah, Johanan and Jonathan the sons of Kareah, Seraiah
[m]ver 13 [n]ver 14; son of Tanhumeth, the sons of Ephai the Netophathite,[o] and
Jer 41:1,2 [o]2Sa 23:28 Jaazaniah[b] the son of the Maacathite,[p] and their men. [9]Gedaliah
[p]Dt 3:14 son of Ahikam, the son of Shaphan, took an oath to reassure them
and their men. "Do not be afraid to serve[q] the Babylonians,[c]" he
said. "Settle down in the land and serve the king of Babylon, and it
40:9 will go well with you.[r] [10]I myself will stay at Mizpah[s] to represent
[q]Jer 27:11 [r]Jer 38:20 you before the Babylonians who come to us, but you are to harvest
the wine, summer fruit and oil, and put them in your storage jars,
and live in the towns you have taken over."[t]

40:10 [s]ver 6 [t]Dt 1:39

[a]5 Or *Jeremiah answered* [b]8 Hebrew *Jezaniah,* a variant of *Jaazaniah* [c]9 Or *Chaldeans;* also in verse 10

[11]When all the Jews in Moab,[a] Ammon, Edom and all the other
countries heard that the king of Babylon had left a remnant in
Judah and had appointed Gedaliah son of Ahikam, the son of
Shaphan, as governor over them, [12]they all came back to the land
of Judah, to Gedaliah at Mizpah, from all the countries where they
had been scattered.[b] And they harvested an abundance of wine
and summer fruit.

[13]Johanan son of Kareah and all the army officers still in the open
country came to Gedaliah at Mizpah[c] [14]and said to him, "Don't
you know that Baalis king of the Ammonites[d] has sent Ishmael
son of Nethaniah to take your life?" But Gedaliah son of Ahikam
did not believe them.

[15]Then Johanan son of Kareah said privately to Gedaliah in Mizpah, "Let me go and kill Ishmael son of Nethaniah, and no one
will know it. Why should he take your life and cause all the Jews
who are gathered around you to be scattered and the remnant of
Judah to perish?"

[16]But Gedaliah son of Ahikam said to Johanan son of Kareah,
"Don't do such a thing! What you are saying about Ishmael is not
true."

Chapter 41 Theme ______________________

41 In the seventh month Ishmael[e] son of Nethaniah, the son of
Elishama, who was of royal blood and had been one of the
king's officers, came with ten men to Gedaliah son of Ahikam at
Mizpah. While they were eating together there, [2]Ishmael[f] son of
Nethaniah and the ten men who were with him got up and struck
down Gedaliah son of Ahikam, the son of Shaphan, with the
sword, killing the one whom the king of Babylon had appointed[g]
as governor over the land.[h] [3]Ishmael also killed all the Jews who
were with Gedaliah at Mizpah, as well as the Babylonian[a] soldiers
who were there.

[4]The day after Gedaliah's assassination, before anyone knew
about it, [5]eighty men who had shaved off their beards,[i] torn their
clothes and cut themselves came from Shechem,[j] Shiloh[k] and
Samaria,[l] bringing grain offerings and incense with them to the
house of the LORD.[m] [6]Ishmael son of Nethaniah went out from
Mizpah to meet them, weeping[n] as he went. When he met them,
he said, "Come to Gedaliah son of Ahikam." [7]When they went
into the city, Ishmael son of Nethaniah and the men who were
with him slaughtered them and threw them into a cistern. [8]But
ten of them said to Ishmael, "Don't kill us! We have wheat and
barley, oil and honey, hidden in a field."[o] So he let them alone and

[a]3 Or *Chaldean*

40:11 [a]Nu 25:1
40:12 [b]Jer 43:5
40:13 [c]ver 8
40:14 [d]2Sa 10:1-19; Jer 25:21; 41:10
41:1 [e]Jer 40:8
41:2 [f]Ps 41:9; 109:5 [g]Jer 40:5 [h]2Sa 3:27; 20:9-10
41:5 [i]Lev 19:27 [j]Ge 33:18; Jdg 9:1-57; 1Ki 12:1 [k]Jos 18:1 [l]1Ki 16:24 [m]2Ki 25:9
41:6 [n]2Sa 3:16
41:8 [o]Isa 45:3

did not kill them with the others. 9Now the cistern where he threw
all the bodies of the men he had killed along with Gedaliah was the
one King Asa[a] had made as part of his defense[b] against Baasha[c]
king of Israel. Ishmael son of Nethaniah filled it with the dead.
10Ishmael made captives of all the rest of the people[d] who were in
Mizpah—the king's daughters along with all the others who were
left there, over whom Nebuzaradan commander of the imperial
guard had appointed Gedaliah son of Ahikam. Ishmael son of
Nethaniah took them captive and set out to cross over to the
Ammonites.[e]
11When Johanan[f] son of Kareah and all the army officers who
were with him heard about all the crimes Ishmael son of Nethaniah
had committed, 12they took all their men and went to fight Ishmael
son of Nethaniah. They caught up with him near the great pool[g] in
Gibeon. 13When all the people[h] Ishmael had with him saw Johanan
son of Kareah and the army officers who were with him, they were
glad. 14All the people Ishmael had taken captive at Mizpah turned
and went over to Johanan son of Kareah. 15But Ishmael son of
Nethaniah and eight of his men escaped[i] from Johanan and fled
to the Ammonites.
16Then Johanan son of Kareah and all the army officers who were
with him led away all the survivors[j] from Mizpah whom he had
recovered from Ishmael son of Nethaniah after he had assassinated
Gedaliah son of Ahikam: the soldiers, women, children and court
officials he had brought from Gibeon. 17And they went on, stopping
at Geruth Kimham[k] near Bethlehem on their way to Egypt[l] 18to
escape the Babylonians.[a] They were afraid[m] of them because Ishmael son of Nethaniah had killed Gedaliah[n] son of Ahikam, whom
the king of Babylon had appointed as governor over the land.

Chapter 42 Theme ______________________

42 Then all the army officers, including Johanan[o] son of
Kareah and Jezaniah[b] son of Hoshaiah, and all the people
from the least to the greatest[p] approached 2Jeremiah the prophet
and said to him, "Please hear our petition and pray[q] to the LORD
your God for this entire remnant.[r] For as you now see, though we
were once many, now only a few[s] are left. 3Pray that the LORD your
God will tell us where we should go and what we should do."[t]
4"I have heard you," replied Jeremiah the prophet. "I will certainly pray[u] to the LORD your God as you have requested; I will tell you
everything the LORD says and will keep nothing back from you."[v]
5Then they said to Jeremiah, "May the LORD be a true and faithful
witness[w] against us if we do not act in accordance with everything
the LORD your God sends you to tell us. 6Whether it is favorable or

41:9 [a] 1Ki 15:22; 2Ch 16:6 [b] Jdg 6:2 [c] 2Ch 16:1
41:10 [d] Jer 40:7,12 [e] Jer 40:14
41:11 [f] Jer 40:8
41:12 [g] 2Sa 2:13
41:13 [h] ver 10
41:15 [i] Job 21:30; Pr 28:17
41:16 [j] Jer 43:4
41:17 [k] 2Sa 19:37 [l] Jer 42:14
41:18 [m] Isa 51:12; Jer 42:16; Lk 12:4-5 [n] Jer 40:5
42:1 [o] Jer 40:13; 41:11 [p] Jer 6:13; 44:12
42:2 [q] Jer 36:7; Ac 8:24; Jas 5:16 [r] Isa 1:9 [s] Lev 26:22; La 1:1
42:3 [t] Ps 86:11; Pr 3:6
42:4 [u] Ex 8:29; 1Sa 12:23 [v] 1Ki 22:14; 1Sa 3:17
42:5 [w] Ge 31:50

[a] *18* Or *Chaldeans* [b] *1* Hebrew; Septuagint (see also 43:2) *Azariah*

unfavorable, we will obey the LORD our God, to whom we are sending you, so that it will go well[a] with us, for we will obey[b] the LORD
our God."
7Ten days later the word of the LORD came to Jeremiah. 8So he
called together Johanan son of Kareah and all the army officers[c]
who were with him and all the people from the least to the greatest. 9He said to them, "This is what the LORD, the God of Israel, to
whom you sent me to present your petition, says:[d] 10'If you stay in
this land, I will build[e] you up and not tear you down; I will plant[f]
you and not uproot you,[g] for I am grieved over the disaster I have
inflicted on you.[h] 11Do not be afraid of the king of Babylon,[i] whom
you now fear.[j] Do not be afraid of him, declares the LORD, for I am
with you and will save[k] you and deliver you from his hands.[l] 12I
will show you compassion so that he will have compassion on you
and restore you to your land.'[m]
13"However, if you say, 'We will not stay in this land,' and so disobey[n] the LORD your God, 14and if you say, 'No, we will go and live
in Egypt,[o] where we will not see war or hear the trumpet or be
hungry for bread,' 15then hear the word of the LORD, O remnant of
Judah. This is what the LORD Almighty, the God of Israel, says: 'If
you are determined to go to Egypt and you do go to settle there,
16then the sword[p] you fear will overtake you there, and the famine
you dread will follow you into Egypt, and there you will die. 17In-
deed, all who are determined to go to Egypt to settle there will die
by the sword, famine and plague;[q] not one of them will survive or
escape the disaster I will bring on them.' 18This is what the LORD
Almighty, the God of Israel, says: 'As my anger and wrath[r] have
been poured out on those who lived in Jerusalem,[s] so will my
wrath be poured out on you when you go to Egypt. You will be an
object of cursing and horror,[t] of condemnation and reproach; you
will never see this place again.'[u]
19"O remnant of Judah, the LORD has told you, 'Do not go to
Egypt.'[v] Be sure of this: I warn you today 20that you made a fatal
mistake[a] when you sent me to the LORD your God and said, 'Pray
to the LORD our God for us; tell us everything he says and we will
do it.'[w] 21I have told you today, but you still have not obeyed the
LORD your God in all he sent me to tell you.[x] 22So now, be sure of
this: You will die by the sword, famine and plague[y] in the place
where you want to go to settle."[z]

Chapter 43 Theme ______________________________

43 When Jeremiah finished telling the people all the words of
the LORD their God—everything the LORD had sent him
to tell them[a]— 2Azariah son of Hoshaiah and Johanan[b] son of

[a] 20 Or *you erred in your hearts*

42:6 [a] Dt 5:29; 6:3; Jer 7:23 [b] Ex 24:7; Jos 24:24
42:8 [c] ver 1
42:9 [d] 2Ki 22:15
42:10 [e] Jer 24:6 [f] Jer 31:28 [g] Eze 36:36 [h] Jer 18:8
42:11 [i] Jer 27:11 [j] Nu 14:9 [k] Isa 43:5 [l] Jer 1:8; Ro 8:31
42:12 [m] Ps 106:44-46
42:13 [n] Jer 44:16
42:14 [o] Nu 11:4-5
42:16 [p] Eze 11:8
42:17 [q] ver 22; Jer 44:13
42:18 [r] Dt 29:18-20; Jer 7:20 [s] 2Ch 36:19; Jer 39:1-9 [t] Jer 29:18 [u] Jer 22:10
42:19 [v] Dt 17:16; Isa 30:7
42:20 [w] ver 2
42:21 [x] Eze 2:7; Zec 7:11-12
42:22 [y] ver 17; Eze 6:11 [z] Hos 9:6
43:1 [a] Jer 26:8; 42:9-22
43:2 [b] Jer 42:1

Kareah and all the arrogant men said to Jeremiah, "You are lying!
The LORD our God has not sent you to say, 'You must not go to
Egypt to settle there.' 3But Baruch son of Neriah is inciting you
against us to hand us over to the Babylonians,[a] so they may kill us
or carry us into exile to Babylon."[a]
4So Johanan son of Kareah and all the army officers and all the
people disobeyed the LORD's command[b] to stay in the land of
Judah.[c] 5Instead, Johanan son of Kareah and all the army officers
led away all the remnant of Judah who had come back to live in
the land of Judah from all the nations where they had been scattered.[d] 6They also led away all the men, women and children and
the king's daughters whom Nebuzaradan commander of the
imperial guard had left with Gedaliah son of Ahikam, the son of
Shaphan, and Jeremiah the prophet and Baruch son of Neriah.
7So they entered Egypt in disobedience to the LORD and went as
far as Tahpanhes.[e]
8In Tahpanhes[f] the word of the LORD came to Jeremiah: 9"While
the Jews are watching, take some large stones with you and bury
them in clay in the brick pavement at the entrance to Pharaoh's
palace in Tahpanhes. 10Then say to them, 'This is what the LORD
Almighty, the God of Israel, says: I will send for my servant[g] Nebuchadnezzar king of Babylon, and I will set his throne over these
stones I have buried here; he will spread his royal canopy above
them. 11He will come and attack Egypt,[h] bringing death to those
destined for death, captivity to those destined for captivity, and the
sword to those destined for the sword.[i] 12He[b] will set fire to the
temples of the gods[j] of Egypt; he will burn their temples and take
their gods captive. As a shepherd wraps[k] his garment around him,
so will he wrap Egypt around himself and depart from there unscathed. 13There in the temple of the sun[c] in Egypt he will demolish the sacred pillars and will burn down the temples of the gods
of Egypt.'"

Chapter 44 Theme ____________________

44 This word came to Jeremiah concerning all the Jews living in Lower Egypt—in Migdol,[l] Tahpanhes[m] and Memphis[d][n]—and in Upper Egypt[e]:[o] 2"This is what the LORD Almighty,
the God of Israel, says: You saw the great disaster I brought on
Jerusalem and on all the towns of Judah. Today they lie deserted
and in ruins[p] 3because of the evil they have done. They provoked
me to anger by burning incense and by worshiping other gods[q]
that neither they nor you nor your fathers[r] ever knew. 4Again and
again[s] I sent my servants the prophets,[t] who said, 'Do not do this

INSIGHT

Jeremiah's ministry ended sometime after 586 B.C., possibly about 574 B.C., when, according to tradition, he was stoned to death in Egypt. Jeremiah 43:6, 7 tells us that Jeremiah's last days were spent in Egypt.

43:3 [a]Jer 38:4
43:4 [b]Jer 42:5-6 [c]Jer 42:10
43:5 [d]Jer 40:12
43:7 [e]Jer 2:16; 44:1
43:8 [f]Jer 2:16
43:10 [g]Isa 44:28; Jer 25:9; 27:6
43:11 [h]Jer 46:13-26; Eze 29:19-20 [i]Jer 15:2; 44:13; Zec 11:9
43:12 [j]Jer 46:25; Eze 30:13 [k]Ps 104:2; 109:18-19
44:1 [l]Ex 14:2 [m]Jer 43:7,8 [n]Isa 19:13 [o]Isa 11:11; Jer 46:14
44:2 [p]Isa 6:11; Jer 9:11; 34:22
44:3 [q]ver 8; Dt 13:6-11; 29:26 [r]Dt 32:17; Jer 19:4
44:4 [s]Jer 7:13 [t]Jer 7:25; 25:4; 26:5

[a]3 Or *Chaldeans* [b]12 Or *I* [c]13 Or *in Heliopolis* [d]1 Hebrew *Noph* [e]1 Hebrew *in Pathros*

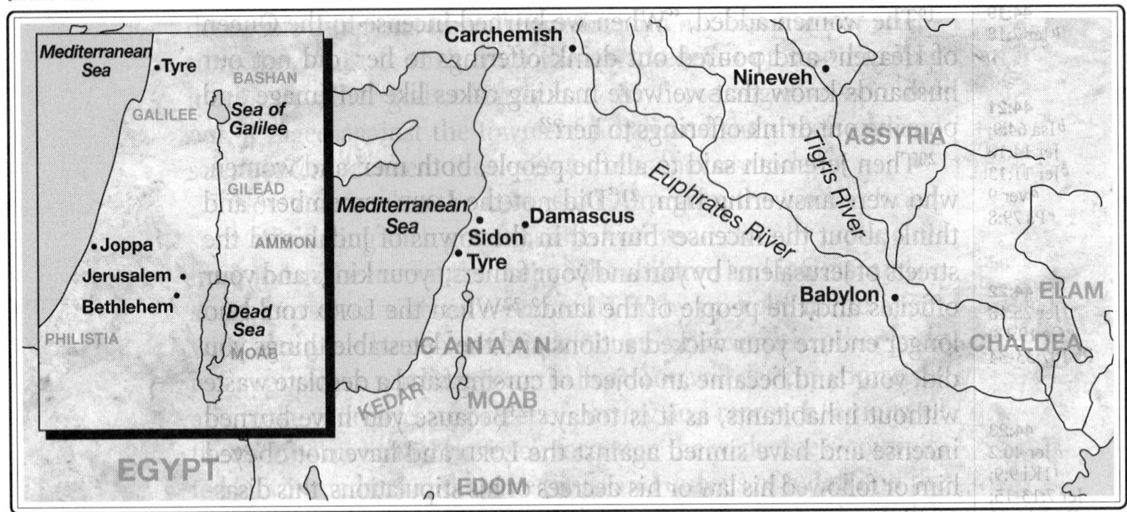

The Nations of Jeremiah's Prophecy

to you, Baruch: 3You said, 'Woe to me! The LORD has added sorrow to my pain; I am worn out with groaning[a] and find no rest.'"
4⌊The LORD said,⌋ "Say this to him: 'This is what the LORD says: I
will overthrow what I have built and uproot what I have planted,[b]
throughout the land.[c] 5Should you then seek great things for
yourself? Seek them not.[d] For I will bring disaster on all people,
declares the LORD, but wherever you go I will let you escape with
your life.'"[e]

Chapter 46 Theme ________________

46 This is the word of the LORD that came to Jeremiah the
prophet concerning the nations:[f]

2Concerning Egypt:

This is the message against the army of Pharaoh Neco[g] king of
Egypt, which was defeated at Carchemish[h] on the Euphrates River
by Nebuchadnezzar king of Babylon in the fourth year of Jehoiakim[i] son of Josiah king of Judah:

3"Prepare your shields,[j] both large and small,
and march out for battle!
4Harness the horses,
mount the steeds!
Take your positions
with helmets on!
Polish[k] your spears,
put on your armor![l]
5What do I see?
They are terrified,

45:3 [a]Ps 69:3
45:4 [b]Jer 11:17 [c]Isa 5:5-7; Jer 18:7-10
45:5 [d]Mt 6:25-27,33 [e]Jer 21:9; 38:2; 39:18
46:1 [f]Jer 1:10; 25:15-38
46:2 [g]2Ki 23:29 [h]2Ch 35:20 [i]Jer 45:1
46:3 [j]Isa 21:5; Jer 51:11-12
46:4 [k]Eze 21:9-11 [l]1Sa 17:5,38; 2Ch 26:14; Ne 4:16

they are retreating,
their warriors are defeated.
They flee[a] in haste
without looking back,
and there is terror[b] on every side,"
declares the LORD.
6"The swift cannot flee[c]
nor the strong escape.
In the north by the River Euphrates
they stumble and fall.[d]

7"Who is this that rises like the Nile,
like rivers of surging waters?[e]
8Egypt rises like the Nile,
like rivers of surging waters.
She says, 'I will rise and cover the earth;
I will destroy cities and their people.'
9Charge, O horses!
Drive furiously, O charioteers![f]
March on, O warriors—
men of Cush[a] and Put who carry shields,
men of Lydia[g] who draw the bow.
10But that day[h] belongs to the Lord, the LORD Almighty—
a day of vengeance, for vengeance on his foes.
The sword will devour[i] till it is satisfied,
till it has quenched its thirst with blood.
For the Lord, the LORD Almighty, will offer sacrifice[j]
in the land of the north by the River Euphrates.

11"Go up to Gilead and get balm,[k]
O Virgin[l] Daughter of Egypt.
But you multiply remedies in vain;
there is no healing[m] for you.
12The nations will hear of your shame;
your cries will fill the earth.
One warrior will stumble over another;
both will fall[n] down together."

13This is the message the LORD spoke to Jeremiah the prophet
about the coming of Nebuchadnezzar king of Babylon to attack
Egypt:[o]

14"Announce this in Egypt, and proclaim it in Migdol;
proclaim it also in Memphis[b] and Tahpanhes:[p]
'Take your positions and get ready,
for the sword devours those around you.'

46:5 [a] ver 21 [b] Jer 49:29
46:6 [c] Isa 30:16 [d] ver 12,16; Da 11:19
46:7 [e] Jer 47:2
46:9 [f] Jer 47:3 [g] Isa 66:19
46:10 [h] Joel 1:15 [i] Dt 32:42 [j] Zep 1:7
46:11 [k] Jer 8:22 [l] Isa 47:1 [m] Jer 30:13; Mic 1:9
46:12 [n] Isa 19:4; Na 3:8-10
46:13 [o] Isa 19:1
46:14 [p] Jer 43:8

a 9 That is, the upper Nile region b 14 Hebrew *Noph*; also in verse 19

[6]"'Ah, sword[a] of the LORD,' ⌊you cry,⌋
'how long till you rest?
Return to your scabbard;
cease and be still.'
[7]But how can it rest
when the LORD has commanded it,
when he has ordered it
to attack Ashkelon and the coast?"

Chapter 48 Theme ______________________

48

Concerning Moab:

This is what the LORD Almighty, the God of Israel, says:

"Woe to Nebo,[b] for it will be ruined.
Kiriathaim[c] will be disgraced and captured;
the stronghold[a] will be disgraced and shattered.
[2]Moab will be praised[d] no more;
in Heshbon[b][e] men will plot her downfall:
'Come, let us put an end to that nation.'
You too, O Madmen,[c] will be silenced;
the sword will pursue you.
[3]Listen to the cries from Horonaim,[f]
cries of great havoc and destruction.
[4]Moab will be broken;
her little ones will cry out.[d]
[5]They go up the way to Luhith,[g]
weeping bitterly as they go;
on the road down to Horonaim
anguished cries over the destruction are heard.
[6]Flee! Run for your lives;
become like a bush[e] in the desert.[h]
[7]Since you trust in your deeds and riches,
you too will be taken captive,
and Chemosh[i] will go into exile,[j]
together with his priests and officials.
[8]The destroyer will come against every town,
and not a town will escape.
The valley will be ruined
and the plateau destroyed,
because the LORD has spoken.
[9]Put salt on Moab,
for she will be laid waste[f];

[a]*1* Or / *Misgab* [b]*2* The Hebrew for *Heshbon* sounds like the Hebrew for *plot.* [c]*2* The name of the Moabite town Madmen sounds like the Hebrew for *be silenced.* [d]*4* Hebrew; Septuagint / *proclaim it to Zoar* [e]*6* Or *like Aroer* [f]*9* Or *Give wings to Moab, / for she will fly away*

47:6 [a]Jer 12:12
48:1 [b]Nu 32:38 [c]Nu 32:37
48:2 [d]Isa 16:14 [e]Nu 21:25
48:3 [f]Isa 15:5
48:5 [g]Isa 15:5
48:6 [h]Jer 17:6
48:7 [i]Nu 21:29 [j]Isa 46:1-2; Jer 49:3

her towns will become desolate,
with no one to live in them.

10"A curse on him who is lax in doing the LORD's work!
A curse on him who keeps his sword[a] from bloodshed![b]

11"Moab has been at rest[c] from youth,
like wine left on its dregs,[d]
not poured from one jar to another—
she has not gone into exile.
So she tastes as she did,
and her aroma is unchanged.
12But days are coming,"
declares the LORD,
"when I will send men who pour from jars,
and they will pour her out;
they will empty her jars
and smash her jugs.
13Then Moab will be ashamed[e] of Chemosh,
as the house of Israel was ashamed
when they trusted in Bethel.

14"How can you say, 'We are warriors,[f]
men valiant in battle'?
15Moab will be destroyed and her towns invaded;
her finest young men will go down in the slaughter,[g]"
declares the King,[h] whose name is the LORD Almighty.[i]
16"The fall of Moab is at hand;[j]
her calamity will come quickly.
17Mourn for her, all who live around her,
all who know her fame;
say, 'How broken is the mighty scepter,
how broken the glorious staff!'

18"Come down from your glory
and sit on the parched ground,[k]
O inhabitants of the Daughter of Dibon,[l]
for he who destroys Moab
will come up against you
and ruin your fortified cities.[m]
19Stand by the road and watch,
you who live in Aroer.[n]
Ask the man fleeing and the woman escaping,
ask them, 'What has happened?'
20Moab is disgraced, for she is shattered.
Wail[o] and cry out!

48:10 [a]Jer 47:6 [b]1Ki 20:42; 2Ki 13:15-19
48:11 [c]Zec 1:15 [d]Zep 1:12
48:13 [e]Hos 10:6
48:14 [f]Ps 33:16
48:15 [g]Jer 50:27 [h]Jer 46:18 [i]Jer 51:57
48:16 [j]Isa 13:22
48:18 [k]Isa 47:1 [l]Nu 21:30; Jos 13:9 [m]ver 8
48:19 [n]Dt 2:36
48:20 [o]Isa 16:7

INSIGHT

Chemosh was a Moabite god who was believed to provide the people with land. During his reforms King Josiah desecrated a temple built by Solomon for Chemosh (2 Kings 23:13).

Announce by the Arnon[a]
that Moab is destroyed.
21 Judgment has come to the plateau—
to Holon, Jahzah[b] and Mephaath,[c]
22 to Dibon,[d] Nebo and Beth Diblathaim,
23 to Kiriathaim, Beth Gamul and Beth Meon,[e]
24 to Kerioth[f] and Bozrah—
to all the towns of Moab, far and near.
25 Moab's horn[a][g] is cut off;
her arm[h] is broken,"
declares the LORD.

26 "Make her drunk,[i]
for she has defied the LORD.
Let Moab wallow in her vomit;
let her be an object of ridicule.
27 Was not Israel the object of your ridicule?[j]
Was she caught among thieves,
that you shake your head[k] in scorn[l]
whenever you speak of her?
28 Abandon your towns and dwell among the rocks,
you who live in Moab.
Be like a dove[m] that makes its nest
at the mouth of a cave.[n]

29 "We have heard of Moab's pride[o]—
her overweening pride and conceit,
her pride and arrogance
and the haughtiness of her heart.
30 I know her insolence but it is futile,"
declares the LORD,
"and her boasts accomplish nothing.
31 Therefore I wail[p] over Moab,
for all Moab I cry out,
I moan for the men of Kir Hareseth.[q]
32 I weep for you, as Jazer weeps,
O vines of Sibmah.[r]
Your branches spread as far as the sea;
they reached as far as the sea of Jazer.
The destroyer has fallen
on your ripened fruit and grapes.
33 Joy and gladness are gone
from the orchards and fields of Moab.
I have stopped the flow of wine[s] from the presses;
no one treads them with shouts of joy.[t]

a 25 *Horn* here symbolizes strength.

48:20
[a] Nu 21:13

48:21
[b] Nu 21:23; Isa 15:4
[c] Jos 13:18

48:22
[d] Jos 13:9,17

48:23
[e] Jos 13:17

48:24
[f] Am 2:2

48:25
[g] Ps 75:10
[h] Ps 10:15; Eze 30:21

48:26
[i] Jer 25:16,27

48:27
[j] Jer 2:26
[k] Job 16:4; Jer 18:16
[l] Mic 7:8-10

48:28
[m] Ps 55:6-7
[n] Jdg 6:2

48:29
[o] Job 40:12; Isa 16:6

48:31
[p] Isa 15:5-8
[q] 2Ki 3:25

48:32
[r] Isa 16:8-9

48:33
[s] Isa 16:10
[t] Joel 1:12

48:34 [a]Nu 32:3 [b]Isa 15:4 [c]Ge 13:10 [d]Isa 15:5 [e]Isa 15:6
48:35 [f]Isa 15:2; 16:12 [g]Jer 11:13
48:36 [h]Isa 16:11 [i]Isa 15:7
48:37 [j]Isa 15:2; Jer 41:5 [k]Ge 37:34
48:38 [l]Jer 22:28
48:40 [m]Dt 28:49; Hab 1:8 [n]Isa 8:8
48:41 [o]Isa 21:3
48:42 [p]Ps 83:4; Isa 16:14 [q]ver 2 [r]ver 26
48:43 [s]Isa 24:17
48:44 [t]1Ki 19:17; Isa 24:18

Although there are shouts,
they are not shouts of joy.

34 “The sound of their cry rises
from Heshbon to Elealeh[a] and Jahaz,[b]
from Zoar[c] as far as Horonaim[d] and Eglath Shelishiyah,
for even the waters of Nimrim are dried up.[e]
35 In Moab I will put an end
to those who make offerings on the high places[f]
and burn incense[g] to their gods,”
declares the LORD.
36 “So my heart laments[h] for Moab like a flute;
it laments like a flute for the men of Kir Hareseth.
The wealth they acquired[i] is gone.
37 Every head is shaved[j]
and every beard cut off;
every hand is slashed
and every waist is covered with sackcloth.[k]
38 On all the roofs in Moab
and in the public squares
there is nothing but mourning,
for I have broken Moab
like a jar[l] that no one wants,”
declares the LORD.
39 “How shattered she is! How they wail!
How Moab turns her back in shame!
Moab has become an object of ridicule,
an object of horror to all those around her.”

40 This is what the LORD says:

“Look! An eagle is swooping[m] down,
spreading its wings[n] over Moab.
41 Kerioth[a] will be captured
and the strongholds taken.
In that day the hearts of Moab's warriors
will be like the heart of a woman in labor.[o]
42 Moab will be destroyed[p] as a nation[q]
because she defied[r] the LORD.
43 Terror and pit and snare[s] await you,
O people of Moab,”
declares the LORD.
44 “Whoever flees[t] from the terror
will fall into a pit,
whoever climbs out of the pit
will be caught in a snare;

a *41* Or *The cities*

for I will bring upon Moab
the year[a] of her punishment,"
declares the LORD.

45"In the shadow of Heshbon
the fugitives stand helpless,
for a fire has gone out from Heshbon,
a blaze from the midst of Sihon;[b]
it burns the foreheads of Moab,
the skulls[c] of the noisy boasters.
46Woe to you, O Moab![d]
The people of Chemosh are destroyed;
your sons are taken into exile
and your daughters into captivity.

47"Yet I will restore[e] the fortunes of Moab
in days to come,"
declares the LORD.

Here ends the judgment on Moab.

Chapter 49 Theme ______________________

49

Concerning the Ammonites:[f]
This is what the LORD says:

"Has Israel no sons?
Has she no heirs?
Why then has Molech[a] taken possession of Gad?
Why do his people live in its towns?
2But the days are coming,"
declares the LORD,
"when I will sound the battle cry[g]
against Rabbah[h] of the Ammonites;
it will become a mound of ruins,
and its surrounding villages will be set on fire.
Then Israel will drive out
those who drove her out,[i]"
says the LORD.

3"Wail, O Heshbon, for Ai[j] is destroyed!
Cry out, O inhabitants of Rabbah!
Put on sackcloth and mourn;
rush here and there inside the walls,
for Molech will go into exile,[k]
together with his priests and officials.
4Why do you boast of your valleys,
boast of your valleys so fruitful?

INSIGHT

Molech was the national god of Ammon. When King Solomon was old he worshiped Molech on the high places he built just outside Jerusalem. King Josiah desecrated these high places during his reforms. Molech is also called *Milcom* or *Malcam.* (1 Kings 11:1-8, 33; 2 Kings 23:13).

48:44 [a]Jer 11:23
48:45 [b]Nu 21:21, 26-28 [c]Nu 24:17
48:46 [d]Nu 21:29
48:47 [e]Jer 12:15; 49:6,39
49:1 [f]Am 1:13; Zep 2:8-9
49:2 [g]Jer 4:19 [h]Dt 3:11 [i]Isa 14:2; Eze 21:28-32; 25:2-11
49:3 [j]Jos 8:28 [k]Jer 48:7

a *1* Or *their king;* Hebrew *malcam;* also in verse 3

O unfaithful daughter,
you trust in your riches[a] and say,
'Who will attack me?'[b]
5 I will bring terror on you
from all those around you,"
declares the Lord, the LORD Almighty.
"Every one of you will be driven away,
and no one will gather the fugitives.

6 "Yet afterward, I will restore[c] the fortunes of
the Ammonites,"
declares the LORD.

7 Concerning Edom:[d]

This is what the LORD Almighty says:

"Is there no longer wisdom in Teman?[e]
Has counsel perished from the prudent?
Has their wisdom decayed?
8 Turn and flee, hide in deep caves,
you who live in Dedan,[f]
for I will bring disaster on Esau
at the time I punish him.
9 If grape pickers came to you,
would they not leave a few grapes?
If thieves came during the night,
would they not steal only as much as they wanted?
10 But I will strip Esau bare;
I will uncover his hiding places,
so that he cannot conceal himself.
His children, relatives and neighbors will perish,
and he will be no more.[g]
11 Leave your orphans;[h] I will protect their lives.
Your widows too can trust in me."

12 This is what the LORD says: "If those who do not deserve to
drink the cup[i] must drink it, why should you go unpunished?[j] You
will not go unpunished, but must drink it. 13 I swear[k] by myself,"
declares the LORD, "that Bozrah[l] will become a ruin and an object
of horror, of reproach and of cursing; and all its towns will be in
ruins forever."

14 I have heard a message from the LORD:
An envoy was sent to the nations to say,
"Assemble yourselves to attack it!
Rise up for battle!"

49:4 [a] Jer 9:23; 1Ti 6:17 [b] Jer 21:13
49:6 [c] ver 39; Jer 48:47
49:7 [d] Ge 25:30; Eze 25:12 [e] Ge 36:11,15,34
49:8 [f] Jer 25:23
49:10 [g] Mal 1:2-5
49:11 [h] Hos 14:3
49:12 [i] Jer 25:15 [j] Jer 25:28-29
49:13 [k] Ge 22:16 [l] Ge 36:33; Isa 34:6

15"Now I will make you small among the nations,
despised among men.
16The terror you inspire
and the pride of your heart have deceived you,
you who live in the clefts of the rocks,
who occupy the heights of the hill.
Though you build your nest[a] as high as the eagle's,
from there I will bring you down,"
declares the LORD.
17"Edom will become an object of horror;[b]
all who pass by will be appalled and will scoff
because of all its wounds.[c]
18As Sodom and Gomorrah[d] were overthrown,
along with their neighboring towns,"
says the LORD,
"so no one will live there;
no man will dwell[e] in it.
19"Like a lion coming up from Jordan's thickets[f]
to a rich pastureland,
I will chase Edom from its land in an instant.
Who is the chosen one I will appoint for this?
Who is like me and who can challenge me?[g]
And what shepherd can stand against me?"
20Therefore, hear what the LORD has planned against Edom,
what he has purposed[h] against those who live in Teman:
The young of the flock[i] will be dragged away;
he will completely destroy[j] their pasture because of them.
21At the sound of their fall the earth will tremble;[k]
their cry[l] will resound to the Red Sea.[a]
22Look! An eagle will soar and swoop[m] down,
spreading its wings over Bozrah.
In that day the hearts of Edom's warriors
will be like the heart of a woman in labor.[n]

23Concerning Damascus:[o]

"Hamath[p] and Arpad[q] are dismayed,
for they have heard bad news.
They are disheartened,
troubled like[b] the restless sea.[r]
24Damascus has become feeble,
she has turned to flee
and panic has gripped her;
anguish and pain have seized her,
pain like that of a woman in labor.

a 21 Hebrew *Yam Suph*; that is, Sea of Reeds b 23 Hebrew *on* or *by*

49:16 [a] Job 39:27; Am 9:2
49:17 [b] ver 13 [c] Jer 50:13; Eze 35:7
49:18 [d] Ge 19:24; Dt 29:23 [e] ver 33
49:19 [f] Jer 12:5 [g] Jer 50:44
49:20 [h] Isa 14:27 [i] Jer 50:45 [j] Mal 1:3-4
49:21 [k] Eze 26:15 [l] Jer 50:46; Eze 26:18
49:22 [m] Hos 8:1 [n] Isa 13:8; Jer 48:40-41
49:23 [o] Ge 14:15; 2Ch 16:2; Ac 9:2 [p] Isa 10:9; Am 6:2; Zec 9:2 [q] 2Ki 18:34 [r] Ge 49:4; Isa 57:20

25Why has the city of renown not been abandoned,
the town in which I delight?
26Surely, her young men will fall in the streets;
all her soldiers will be silenced[a] in that day,"
declares the LORD Almighty.
27"I will set fire[b] to the walls of Damascus;
it will consume the fortresses of Ben-Hadad.[c]"

28Concerning Kedar[d] and the kingdoms of Hazor, which Nebuchadnezzar king of Babylon attacked:

This is what the LORD says:

"Arise, and attack Kedar
and destroy the people of the East.[e]
29Their tents and their flocks will be taken;
their shelters will be carried off
with all their goods and camels.
Men will shout to them,
'Terror[f] on every side!'

30"Flee quickly away!
Stay in deep caves, you who live in Hazor,"
declares the LORD.
"Nebuchadnezzar king of Babylon has plotted against you;
he has devised a plan against you.

31"Arise and attack a nation at ease,
which lives in confidence,"
declares the LORD,
"a nation that has neither gates nor bars;[g]
its people live alone.
32Their camels will become plunder,
and their large herds will be booty.
I will scatter to the winds those who are in distant places[a] [h]
and will bring disaster on them from every side,"
declares the LORD.
33"Hazor will become a haunt of jackals,
a desolate[i] place forever.
No one will live there;
no man will dwell[j] in it."

34This is the word of the LORD that came to Jeremiah the prophet
concerning Elam,[k] early in the reign of Zedekiah[l] king of Judah:
35This is what the LORD Almighty says:

"See, I will break the bow[m] of Elam,
the mainstay of their might.

49:26 [a]Jer 50:30
49:27 [b]Jer 43:12; Am 1:4 [c]1Ki 15:18
49:28 [d]Ge 25:13 [e]Jdg 6:3
49:29 [f]Jer 6:25; 46:5
49:31 [g]Eze 38:11
49:32 [h]Jer 9:26
49:33 [i]Jer 10:22 [j]ver 18; Jer 51:37
49:34 [k]Ge 10:22 [l]2Ki 24:18
49:35 [m]Isa 22:6

a 32 Or *who clip the hair by their foreheads*

36I will bring against Elam the four winds[a]
from the four quarters of the heavens;
I will scatter them to the four winds,
and there will not be a nation
where Elam's exiles do not go.
37I will shatter Elam before their foes,
before those who seek their lives;
I will bring disaster upon them,
even my fierce anger,"[b]
declares the LORD.
"I will pursue them with the sword[c]
until I have made an end of them.
38I will set my throne in Elam
and destroy her king and officials,"
declares the LORD.

39"Yet I will restore[d] the fortunes of Elam
in days to come,"
declares the LORD.

Chapter 50 Theme ______________________________

INSIGHT

Marduk and ***Bel*** were Babylonian deities. Bel was the Babylonian equivalent of Baal, acknowledged as the lord of heaven.

50 This is the word the LORD spoke through Jeremiah the prophet concerning Babylon[e] and the land of the Babylonians[a]:

2"Announce and proclaim[f] among the nations,
lift up a banner and proclaim it;
keep nothing back, but say,
'Babylon will be captured;[g]
Bel[h] will be put to shame,
Marduk[i] filled with terror.
Her images will be put to shame
and her idols filled with terror.'
3A nation from the north will attack her
and lay waste her land.
No one will live[j] in it;
both men and animals[k] will flee away.

4"In those days, at that time,"
declares the LORD,
"the people of Israel and the people of Judah together[l]
will go in tears[m] to seek[n] the LORD their God.
5They will ask the way to Zion
and turn their faces toward it.

[a] *1* Or *Chaldeans;* also in verses 8, 25, 35 and 45

49:36 [a]ver 32
49:37 [b]Jer 30:24 [c]Jer 9:16
49:39 [d]Jer 48:47
50:1 [e]Ge 10:10; Isa 13:1
50:2 [f]Jer 4:16 [g]Jer 51:31 [h]Isa 46:1 [i]Jer 51:47
50:3 [j]ver 13; Isa 14:22-23 [k]Zep 1:3
50:4 [l]Jer 3:18; Hos 1:11 [m]Ezr 3:12; Jer 31:9 [n]Hos 3:5

They will come[a] and bind themselves to the LORD
in an everlasting covenant[b]
that will not be forgotten.

6 "My people have been lost sheep;[c]
their shepherds have led them astray
and caused them to roam on the mountains.
They wandered over mountain and hill[d]
and forgot their own resting place.[e]
7 Whoever found them devoured them;
their enemies said, 'We are not guilty,[f]
for they sinned against the LORD, their true pasture,
the LORD, the hope[g] of their fathers.'

8 "Flee[h] out of Babylon;
leave the land of the Babylonians,
and be like the goats that lead the flock.
9 For I will stir up and bring against Babylon
an alliance of great nations from the land of the north.
They will take up their positions against her,
and from the north she will be captured.
Their arrows will be like skilled warriors
who do not return empty-handed.
10 So Babylonia[a] will be plundered;
all who plunder her will have their fill,"
declares the LORD.

11 "Because you rejoice and are glad,
you who pillage my inheritance,[i]
because you frolic like a heifer threshing grain
and neigh like stallions,
12 your mother will be greatly ashamed;
she who gave you birth will be disgraced.
She will be the least of the nations—
a wilderness, a dry land, a desert.
13 Because of the LORD's anger she will not be inhabited
but will be completely desolate.
All who pass Babylon will be horrified and scoff[j]
because of all her wounds.[k]

14 "Take up your positions around Babylon,
all you who draw the bow.[l]
Shoot at her! Spare no arrows,
for she has sinned against the LORD.
15 Shout[m] against her on every side!
She surrenders, her towers fall,
her walls[n] are torn down.

50:5 [a] Jer 33:7 [b] Isa 55:3; Jer 32:40; Heb 8:6-10
50:6 [c] Isa 53:6; Mt 9:36; 10:6 [d] Jer 3:6; Eze 34:6 [e] ver 19
50:7 [f] Jer 2:3 [g] Jer 14:8
50:8 [h] Isa 48:20; Jer 51:6; Rev 18:4
50:11 [i] Isa 47:6
50:13 [j] Jer 18:16 [k] Jer 49:17
50:14 [l] ver 29,42
50:15 [m] Jer 51:14 [n] Jer 51:44,58

a *10* Or *Chaldea*

Since this is the vengeance[a] of the LORD,
take vengeance on her;
do to her[b] as she has done to others.
16Cut off from Babylon the sower,
and the reaper with his sickle at harvest.
Because of the sword[c] of the oppressor
let everyone return to his own people,[d]
let everyone flee to his own land.[e]

17"Israel is a scattered flock
that lions[f] have chased away.
The first to devour him
was the king[g] of Assyria;
the last to crush his bones
was Nebuchadnezzar[h] king[i] of Babylon."

18Therefore this is what the LORD Almighty, the God of Israel, says:

"I will punish the king of Babylon and his land
as I punished the king[j] of Assyria.[k]
19But I will bring[l] Israel back to his own pasture
and he will graze on Carmel and Bashan;
his appetite will be satisfied
on the hills[m] of Ephraim and Gilead.
20In those days, at that time,"
declares the LORD,
"search will be made for Israel's guilt,
but there will be none,
and for the sins[n] of Judah,
but none will be found,
for I will forgive[o] the remnant[p] I spare.

21"Attack the land of Merathaim
and those who live in Pekod.[q]
Pursue, kill and completely destroy[a] them,"
declares the LORD.
"Do everything I have commanded you.
22The noise[r] of battle is in the land,
the noise of great destruction!
23How broken and shattered
is the hammer of the whole earth!
How desolate[s] is Babylon
among the nations!
24I set a trap[t] for you, O Babylon,
and you were caught before you knew it;

a *21* The Hebrew term refers to the irrevocable giving over of things or persons to the LORD, often by totally destroying them; also in verse 26.

50:15 [a] Jer 51:6 [b] Ps 137:8; Rev 18:6
50:16 [c] Jer 25:38 [d] Isa 13:14 [e] Jer 51:9
50:17 [f] Jer 2:15 [g] 2Ki 17:6 [h] 2Ki 24:10,14 [i] 2Ki 25:7
50:18 [j] Isa 10:12 [k] Eze 31:3
50:19 [l] Jer 31:10; Eze 34:13 [m] Jer 31:5; 33:12
50:20 [n] Mic 7:18,19 [o] Jer 31:34 [p] Isa 1:9
50:21 [q] Eze 23:23
50:22 [r] Jer 4:19-21; 51:54
50:23 [s] Isa 14:16
50:24 [t] Da 5:30-31

you were found and captured[a]
because you opposed[b] the LORD.
25 The LORD has opened his arsenal
and brought out the weapons[c] of his wrath,
for the Sovereign LORD Almighty has work to do
in the land of the Babylonians.[d]
26 Come against her from afar.
Break open her granaries;
pile her up like heaps of grain.
Completely destroy[e] her
and leave her no remnant.
27 Kill all her young bulls;
let them go down to the slaughter!
Woe to them! For their day has come,
the time for them to be punished.
28 Listen to the fugitives and refugees from Babylon
declaring in Zion[f]
how the LORD our God has taken vengeance,[g]
vengeance for his temple.

29 "Summon archers against Babylon,
all those who draw the bow.[h]
Encamp all around her;
let no one escape.
Repay[i] her for her deeds;[j]
do to her as she has done.
For she has defied[k] the LORD,
the Holy One of Israel.
30 Therefore, her young men[l] will fall in the streets;
all her soldiers will be silenced in that day,"
declares the LORD.
31 "See, I am against[m] you, O arrogant one,"
declares the Lord, the LORD Almighty,
"for your day has come,
the time for you to be punished.
32 The arrogant one will stumble and fall
and no one will help her up;
I will kindle a fire[n] in her towns
that will consume all who are around her."

33 This is what the LORD Almighty says:

"The people of Israel are oppressed,[o]
and the people of Judah as well.
All their captors hold them fast,
refusing to let them go.[p]
34 Yet their Redeemer is strong;
the LORD Almighty[q] is his name.

50:24 [a] Jer 51:31 [b] Job 9:4
50:25 [c] Isa 13:5 [d] Jer 51:25,55
50:26 [e] Isa 14:22-23
50:28 [f] Isa 48:20; Jer 51:10 [g] ver 15
50:29 [h] ver 14 [i] Rev 18:6 [j] Jer 51:56 [k] Isa 47:10
50:30 [l] Isa 13:18; Jer 49:26
50:31 [m] Jer 21:13
50:32 [n] Jer 21:14; 49:27
50:33 [o] Isa 58:6 [p] Isa 14:17
50:34 [q] Jer 51:19

He will vigorously defend their cause[a]
so that he may bring rest[b] to their land,
but unrest to those who live in Babylon.

35"A sword[c] against the Babylonians!"
declares the LORD—
"against those who live in Babylon
and against her officials and wise[d] men!
36A sword against her false prophets!
They will become fools.
A sword against her warriors![e]
They will be filled with terror.
37A sword against her horses and chariots[f]
and all the foreigners in her ranks!
They will become women.[g]
A sword against her treasures!
They will be plundered.
38A drought on[a] her waters!
They will dry[h] up.
For it is a land of idols,[i]
idols that will go mad with terror.

39"So desert creatures and hyenas will live there,
and there the owl will dwell.
It will never again be inhabited
or lived in from generation to generation.[j]
40As God overthrew Sodom and Gomorrah[k]
along with their neighboring towns,"
declares the LORD,
"so no one will live there;
no man will dwell in it.

41"Look! An army is coming from the north;[l]
a great nation and many kings
are being stirred up from the ends of the earth.[m]
42They are armed with bows[n] and spears;
they are cruel and without mercy.[o]
They sound like the roaring sea[p]
as they ride on their horses;
they come like men in battle formation
to attack you, O Daughter of Babylon.[q]
43The king of Babylon has heard reports about them,
and his hands hang limp.
Anguish has gripped him,
pain like that of a woman in labor.

a38 Or *A sword against*

50:34 [a]Jer 15:21; 51:36 [b]Isa 14:7
50:35 [c]Jer 47:6 [d]Da 5:7
50:36 [e]Jer 49:22
50:37 [f]Jer 51:21 [g]Jer 51:30; Na 3:13
50:38 [h]Jer 51:36 [i]ver 2
50:39 [j]Isa 13:19-22; 34:13-15; Jer 51:37; Rev 18:2
50:40 [k]Ge 19:24
50:41 [l]Jer 6:22 [m]Isa 13:4; Jer 51:22-28
50:42 [n]ver 14 [o]Isa 13:18 [p]Isa 5:30 [q]Jer 6:23

44 Like a lion coming up from Jordan's thickets
to a rich pastureland,
I will chase Babylon from its land in an instant.
Who is the chosen[a] one I will appoint for this?
Who is like me and who can challenge me?[b]
And what shepherd can stand against me?"
45 Therefore, hear what the LORD has planned against
Babylon,
what he has purposed[c] against the land of the
Babylonians:
The young of the flock will be dragged away;
he will completely destroy their pasture because of
them.
46 At the sound of Babylon's capture the earth will tremble;
its cry[d] will resound among the nations.

Chapter 51 Theme ________________________

51 This is what the LORD says:
"See, I will stir up the spirit of a destroyer
against Babylon and the people of Leb Kamai.[a]
2 I will send foreigners to Babylon
to winnow[e] her and to devastate her land;
they will oppose her on every side
in the day of her disaster.
3 Let not the archer string his bow,[f]
nor let him put on his armor.[g]
Do not spare her young men;
completely destroy[b] her army.
4 They will fall[h] down slain in Babylon,[c]
fatally wounded in her streets.[i]
5 For Israel and Judah have not been forsaken[j]
by their God, the LORD Almighty,
though their land[d] is full of guilt[k]
before the Holy One of Israel.

6 "Flee[l] from Babylon!
Run for your lives!
Do not be destroyed because of her sins.[m]
It is time for the LORD's vengeance;[n]
he will pay[o] her what she deserves.
7 Babylon was a gold cup[p] in the LORD's hand;
she made the whole earth drunk.

50:44 [a]Nu 16:5 [b]Job 41:10; Isa 46:9; Jer 49:19
50:45 [c]Ps 33:11; Isa 14:24; Jer 51:11
50:46 [d]Rev 18:9-10
51:2 [e]Isa 41:16; Jer 15:7; Mt 3:12
51:3 [f]Jer 50:29 [g]Jer 46:4
51:4 [h]Isa 13:15 [i]Jer 49:26; 50:30
51:5 [j]Isa 54:6-8 [k]Hos 4:1
51:6 [l]Jer 50:8 [m]Nu 16:26; Rev 18:4 [n]Jer 50:15 [o]Jer 25:14
51:7 [p]Jer 25:15-16; Rev 14:8-10; 17:4

[a] *1 Leb Kamai* is a cryptogram for Chaldea, that is, Babylonia. [b] 3 The Hebrew term refers to the irrevocable giving over of things or persons to the LORD, often by totally destroying them. [c] 4 Or *Chaldea* [d] 5 Or / *and the land* ⌊*of the Babylonians*⌋

The nations drank her wine;
therefore they have now gone mad.
8 Babylon will suddenly fall[a] and be broken.
Wail over her!
Get balm[b] for her pain;
perhaps she can be healed.

9 " 'We would have healed Babylon,
but she cannot be healed;
let us leave[c] her and each go to his own land,
for her judgment[d] reaches to the skies,
it rises as high as the clouds.'
10 " 'The LORD has vindicated[e] us;
come, let us tell in Zion
what the LORD our God has done.'[f]

11 "Sharpen the arrows,[g]
take up the shields![h]
The LORD has stirred up the kings of the Medes,[i]
because his purpose[j] is to destroy Babylon.
The LORD will take vengeance,
vengeance for his temple.[k]
12 Lift up a banner against the walls of Babylon!
Reinforce the guard,
station the watchmen,
prepare an ambush!
The LORD will carry out his purpose,
his decree against the people of Babylon.
13 You who live by many waters[l]
and are rich in treasures,[m]
your end has come,
the time for you to be cut off.
14 The LORD Almighty has sworn by himself:[n]
I will surely fill you with men, as with a swarm of locusts,[o]
and they will shout[p] in triumph over you.

15 "He made the earth by his power;
he founded the world by his wisdom
and stretched[q] out the heavens by his understanding.
16 When he thunders,[r] the waters in the heavens roar;
he makes clouds rise from the ends of the earth.
He sends lightning with the rain
and brings out the wind from his storehouses.[s]

17 "Every man is senseless and without knowledge;
every goldsmith is shamed by his idols.

51:8 [a] Isa 21:9; Rev 14:8 [b] Jer 46:11
51:9 [c] Isa 13:14; Jer 50:16 [d] Rev 18:4-5
51:10 [e] Mic 7:9 [f] Jer 50:28
51:11 [g] Jer 50:9 [h] Jer 46:4 [i] ver 28 [j] Jer 50:45 [k] Jer 50:28
51:13 [l] Rev 17:1,15 [m] Isa 45:3; Hab 2:9
51:14 [n] Am 6:8 [o] ver 27; Na 3:15 [p] Jer 50:15
51:15 [q] Ge 1:1; Job 9:8; Ps 104:2
51:16 [r] Ps 18:11-13 [s] Ps 135:7; Jnh 1:4

His images are a fraud;[a]
  they have no breath in them.
18 They are worthless,[b] the objects of mockery;
  when their judgment comes, they will perish.
19 He who is the Portion of Jacob is not like these,
  for he is the Maker of all things,
including the tribe of his inheritance—
  the LORD Almighty is his name.

20 "You are my war club,[c]
  my weapon for battle—
with you I shatter[d] nations,
  with you I destroy kingdoms,
21 with you I shatter horse and rider,[e]
  with you I shatter chariot and driver,
22 with you I shatter man and woman,
  with you I shatter old man and youth,
  with you I shatter young man and maiden,[f]
23 with you I shatter shepherd and flock,
  with you I shatter farmer and oxen,
  with you I shatter governors and officials.[g]

24 "Before your eyes I will repay[h] Babylon and all who live in Babylonia[a] for all the wrong they have done in Zion," declares the LORD.

25 "I am against you, O destroying mountain,
  you who destroy the whole earth,"
declares the LORD.
"I will stretch out my hand against you,
  roll you off the cliffs,
  and make you a burned-out mountain.[i]
26 No rock will be taken from you for a cornerstone,
  nor any stone for a foundation,
  for you will be desolate[j] forever,"
declares the LORD.

27 "Lift up a banner[k] in the land!
  Blow the trumpet among the nations!
Prepare the nations for battle against her;
  summon against her these kingdoms:[l]
  Ararat,[m] Minni and Ashkenaz.[n]
Appoint a commander against her;
  send up horses like a swarm of locusts.
28 Prepare the nations for battle against her—
  the kings of the Medes,[o]
their governors and all their officials,
  and all the countries they rule.

51:17 [a] Isa 44:20; Hab 2:18-19
51:18 [b] Jer 18:15
51:20 [c] Isa 10:5 [d] Mic 4:13
51:21 [e] Ex 15:1
51:22 [f] 2Ch 36:17; Isa 13:17-18
51:23 [g] ver 57
51:24 [h] Jer 50:15
51:25 [i] Zec 4:7
51:26 [j] ver 29; Isa 13:19-22; Jer 50:12
51:27 [k] Isa 13:2; Jer 50:2 [l] Jer 25:14 [m] Ge 8:4 [n] Ge 10:3
51:28 [o] ver 11

a 24 Or *Chaldea*; also in verse 35

29The land trembles and writhes,
for the LORD's purposes against Babylon stand—
to lay waste the land of Babylon
so that no one will live there.[a]
30Babylon's warriors[b] have stopped fighting;
they remain in their strongholds.
Their strength is exhausted;
they have become like women.[c]
Her dwellings are set on fire;
the bars[d] of her gates are broken.
31One courier[e] follows another
and messenger follows messenger
to announce to the king of Babylon
that his entire city is captured,
32the river crossings seized,
the marshes set on fire,
and the soldiers terrified.[f]"

33This is what the LORD Almighty, the God of Israel, says:

"The Daughter of Babylon is like a threshing floor[g]
at the time it is trampled;
the time to harvest[h] her will soon come."
34"Nebuchadnezzar[i] king of Babylon has devoured us,
he has thrown us into confusion,
he has made us an empty jar.
Like a serpent he has swallowed us
and filled his stomach with our delicacies,
and then has spewed us out.
35May the violence done to our flesh[a] be upon Babylon,"
say the inhabitants of Zion.
"May our blood be on those who live in Babylonia,"
says Jerusalem.[j]

36Therefore, this is what the LORD says:

"See, I will defend your cause[k]
and avenge[l] you;
I will dry up[m] her sea
and make her springs dry.
37Babylon will be a heap of ruins,
a haunt[n] of jackals,
an object of horror and scorn,
a place where no one lives.[o]
38Her people all roar like young lions,
they growl like lion cubs.

a 35 Or *done to us and to our children*

51:29 [a] ver 43; Isa 13:20
51:30 [b] Jer 50:36 [c] Isa 19:16 [d] Isa 45:2; La 2:9; Na 3:13
51:31 [e] 2Sa 18:19-31
51:32 [f] Jer 50:36
51:33 [g] Isa 21:10 [h] Isa 17:5; Hos 6:11
51:34 [i] Jer 50:17
51:35 [j] ver 24; Ps 137:8
51:36 [k] Ps 140:12; Jer 50:34; La 3:58 [l] ver 6; Ro 12:19 [m] Jer 50:38
51:37 [n] Isa 13:22; Rev 18:2 [o] Jer 50:13,39

39 But while they are aroused,
I will set out a feast for them
and make them drunk,
so that they shout with laughter—
then sleep forever and not awake,"
declares the LORD.[a]

40 "I will bring them down
like lambs to the slaughter,
like rams and goats.

41 "How Sheshach[a][b] will be captured,[c]
the boast of the whole earth seized!
What a horror Babylon will be
among the nations!
42 The sea will rise over Babylon;
its roaring waves[d] will cover her.
43 Her towns will be desolate,
a dry and desert land,
a land where no one lives,
through which no man travels.[e]
44 I will punish Bel[f] in Babylon
and make him spew out[g] what he has swallowed.
The nations will no longer stream to him.
And the wall[h] of Babylon will fall.

45 "Come out[i] of her, my people!
Run[j] for your lives!
Run from the fierce anger of the LORD.
46 Do not lose heart or be afraid[k]
when rumors[l] are heard in the land;
one rumor comes this year, another the next,
rumors of violence in the land
and of ruler against ruler.
47 For the time will surely come
when I will punish the idols[m] of Babylon;
her whole land will be disgraced[n]
and her slain will all lie fallen within her.
48 Then heaven and earth and all that is in them
will shout[o] for joy over Babylon,
for out of the north[p]
destroyers will attack her,"
declares the LORD.

49 "Babylon must fall because of Israel's slain,
just as the slain in all the earth
have fallen because of Babylon.[q]

51:39 [a] ver 57
51:41 [b] Jer 25:26 [c] Isa 13:19
51:42 [d] Isa 8:7
51:43 [e] ver 29,62; Isa 13:20; Jer 2:6
51:44 [f] Isa 46:1 [g] ver 34 [h] ver 58; Jer 50:15
51:45 [i] Rev 18:4 [j] ver 6; Isa 48:20; Jer 50:8
51:46 [k] Jer 46:27 [l] 2Ki 19:7
51:47 [m] ver 52; Isa 46:1-2; Jer 50:2 [n] Jer 50:12
51:48 [o] Isa 44:23; Rev 18:20 [p] ver 11
51:49 [q] Ps 137:8; Jer 50:29

a 41 *Sheshach* is a cryptogram for Babylon.

50You who have escaped the sword,
leave[a] and do not linger!
Remember[b] the LORD in a distant land,
and think on Jerusalem."

51"We are disgraced,[c]
for we have been insulted
and shame covers our faces,
because foreigners have entered
the holy places of the LORD's house."[d]

52"But days are coming," declares the LORD,
"when I will punish her idols,[e]
and throughout her land
the wounded will groan.
53Even if Babylon reaches the sky[f]
and fortifies her lofty stronghold,
I will send destroyers[g] against her,"
declares the LORD.

54"The sound of a cry comes from Babylon,
the sound of great destruction[h]
from the land of the Babylonians.[a]
55The LORD will destroy Babylon;
he will silence her noisy din.
Waves[i] ⌊of enemies⌋ will rage like great waters;
the roar of their voices will resound.
56A destroyer[j] will come against Babylon;
her warriors will be captured,
and their bows will be broken.[k]
For the LORD is a God of retribution;
he will repay[l] in full.
57I will make her officials and wise men drunk,
her governors, officers and warriors as well;
they will sleep[m] forever and not awake,"
declares the King,[n] whose name is the LORD Almighty.

58This is what the LORD Almighty says:

"Babylon's thick wall[o] will be leveled
and her high gates set on fire;
the peoples[p] exhaust themselves for nothing,
the nations' labor is only fuel for the flames."[q]

59This is the message Jeremiah gave to the staff officer Seraiah son
of Neriah,[r] the son of Mahseiah, when he went to Babylon with
Zedekiah[s] king of Judah in the fourth[t] year of his reign. 60Jeremiah

51:50 [a] ver 45 [b] Ps 137:6

51:51 [c] Ps 44:13-16; 79:4 [d] La 1:10

51:52 [e] ver 47

51:53 [f] Ge 11:4; Isa 14:13-14 [g] Jer 49:16

51:54 [h] Jer 50:22

51:55 [i] Ps 18:4

51:56 [j] ver 48 [k] Ps 46:9 [l] ver 6; Ps 94:1-2; Hab 2:8

51:57 [m] Ps 76:5; Jer 25:27 [n] Jer 46:18; 48:15

51:58 [o] ver 44 [p] ver 64 [q] Hab 2:13

51:59 [r] Jer 36:4 [s] Jer 52:1 [t] Jer 28:1

[a] 54 Or *Chaldeans*

had written on a scroll[a] about all the disasters that would come
upon Babylon—all that had been recorded concerning Babylon.
61 He said to Seraiah, "When you get to Babylon, see that you read
all these words aloud. 62 Then say, 'O LORD, you have said you will
destroy this place, so that neither man nor animal will live in it; it
will be desolate[b] forever.' 63 When you finish reading this scroll, tie
a stone to it and throw it into the Euphrates. 64 Then say, 'So will
Babylon sink to rise no more because of the disaster I will bring
upon her. And her people[c] will fall.' "

The words of Jeremiah end[d] here.

Chapter 52 Theme ____________________

52 Zedekiah[e] was twenty-one years old when he became king,
and he reigned in Jerusalem eleven years. His mother's
name was Hamutal daughter of Jeremiah; she was from Libnah.[f]
2 He did evil in the eyes of the LORD, just as Jehoiakim[g] had done.
3 It was because of the LORD's anger that all this happened to
Jerusalem and Judah,[h] and in the end he thrust them from his
presence.

Now Zedekiah rebelled[i] against the king of Babylon.

4 So in the ninth year of Zedekiah's reign, on the tenth[j] day of the
tenth month, Nebuchadnezzar king of Babylon marched against
Jerusalem[k] with his whole army. They camped outside the city and
built siege works all around it.[l] 5 The city was kept under siege until
the eleventh year of King Zedekiah.

6 By the ninth day of the fourth month the famine in the city had
become so severe that there was no food for the people to eat.[m]
7 Then the city wall was broken through, and the whole army fled.
They left the city at night through the gate between the two walls
near the king's garden, though the Babylonians[a] were surrounding
the city. They fled toward the Arabah,[b] 8 but the Babylonian[c] army
pursued King Zedekiah and overtook him in the plains of Jericho.
All his soldiers were separated from him and scattered, 9 and he
was captured.[n]

He was taken to the king of Babylon at Riblah[o] in the land of
Hamath,[p] where he pronounced sentence on him. 10 There at Riblah
the king of Babylon slaughtered the sons[q] of Zedekiah before his
eyes; he also killed all the officials of Judah. 11 Then he put out
Zedekiah's eyes, bound him with bronze shackles and took him to
Babylon, where he put him in prison till the day of his death.[r]

12 On the tenth day of the fifth[s] month, in the nineteenth year of
Nebuchadnezzar king of Babylon, Nebuzaradan[t] commander of
the imperial guard, who served the king of Babylon, came to

51:60 [a] Jer 30:2; 36:2
51:62 [b] Isa 13:20; Jer 50:13,39
51:64 [c] ver 58 [d] Job 31:40
52:1 [e] 2Ki 24:17 [f] Jos 10:29; 2Ki 8:22
52:2 [g] Jer 36:30
52:3 [h] Isa 3:1 [i] Eze 17:12-16
52:4 [j] Zec 8:19 [k] 2Ki 25:1-7; Jer 39:1 [l] Eze 24:1-2
52:6 [m] Isa 3:1
52:9 [n] Jer 32:4 [o] Nu 34:11 [p] Nu 13:21
52:10 [q] Jer 22:30
52:11 [r] Eze 12:13
52:12 [s] Zec 7:5; 8:19 [t] Jer 39:9

[a] 7 Or *Chaldeans*; also in verse 17 [b] 7 Or *the Jordan Valley* [c] 8 Or *Chaldean*; also in verse 14

Jerusalem. 13 He set fire[a] to the temple[b] of the LORD, the royal
palace and all the houses of Jerusalem. Every important building
he burned down. 14 The whole Babylonian army under the commander of the imperial guard broke down all the walls[c] around
Jerusalem. 15 Nebuzaradan the commander of the guard carried
into exile some of the poorest people and those who remained in
the city, along with the rest of the craftsmen[a] and those who had
gone over to the king of Babylon. 16 But Nebuzaradan left behind[d]
the rest of the poorest people of the land to work the vineyards
and fields.

17 The Babylonians broke up the bronze pillars,[e] the movable
stands[f] and the bronze Sea[g] that were at the temple of the LORD
and they carried all the bronze to Babylon.[h] 18 They also took away
the pots, shovels, wick trimmers, sprinkling bowls, dishes and all
the bronze articles used in the temple service.[i] 19 The commander
of the imperial guard took away the basins, censers,[j] sprinkling
bowls, pots, lampstands, dishes and bowls used for drink offerings—all that were made of pure gold or silver.

20 The bronze from the two pillars, the Sea and the twelve bronze
bulls under it, and the movable stands, which King Solomon had
made for the temple of the LORD, was more than could be
weighed.[k] 21 Each of the pillars was eighteen cubits high and twelve
cubits in circumference[b]; each was four fingers thick, and hollow.[l]
22 The bronze capital[m] on top of the one pillar was five cubits[c]
high and was decorated with a network and pomegranates of
bronze all around. The other pillar, with its pomegranates, was
similar. 23 There were ninety-six pomegranates on the sides; the
total number of pomegranates[n] above the surrounding network
was a hundred.

24 The commander of the guard took as prisoners Seraiah[o] the
chief priest, Zephaniah[p] the priest next in rank and the three doorkeepers. 25 Of those still in the city, he took the officer in charge of
the fighting men, and seven royal advisers. He also took the secretary who was chief officer in charge of conscripting the people of
the land and sixty of his men who were found in the city. 26 Nebuzaradan[q] the commander took them all and brought them to the
king of Babylon at Riblah. 27 There at Riblah, in the land of Hamath,
the king had them executed.

So Judah went into captivity, away[r] from her land. 28 This is the
number of the people Nebuchadnezzar carried into exile:[s]

in the seventh year, 3,023 Jews;
29 in Nebuchadnezzar's eighteenth year,
832 people from Jerusalem;

[a] *15* Or *populace* [b] *21* That is, about 27 feet (about 8.1 meters) high and 18 feet (about 5.4 meters) in circumference [c] *22* That is, about 7 1/2 feet (about 2.3 meters)

52:13 [a] 2Ch 36:19; Ps 74:8; La 2:6 [b] Ps 79:1; Mic 3:12
52:14 [c] Ne 1:3
52:16 [d] Jer 40:6
52:17 [e] 1Ki 7:15 [f] 1Ki 7:27-37 [g] 1Ki 7:23 [h] Jer 27:19-22
52:18 [i] Ex 27:3; 1Ki 7:45
52:19 [j] 1Ki 7:50
52:20 [k] 1Ki 7:47
52:21 [l] 1Ki 7:15
52:22 [m] 1Ki 7:16
52:23 [n] 1Ki 7:20
52:24 [o] 2Ki 25:18 [p] Jer 21:1; 37:3
52:26 [q] ver 12
52:27 [r] Jer 20:4
52:28 [s] 2Ki 24:14-16; 2Ch 36:20

52:33 [a]2Sa 9:7

[30]in his twenty-third year,
745 Jews taken into exile by Nebuzaradan the commander
of the imperial guard.
There were 4,600 people in all.

[31]In the thirty-seventh year of the exile of Jehoiachin king of
Judah, in the year Evil-Merodach[a] became king of Babylon, he
released Jehoiachin king of Judah and freed him from prison on
the twenty-fifth day of the twelfth month. [32]He spoke kindly to
him and gave him a seat of honor higher than those of the other
kings who were with him in Babylon. [33]So Jehoiachin put aside
his prison clothes and for the rest of his life ate regularly at the
king's table.[a] [34]Day by day the king of Babylon gave Jehoiachin a
regular allowance[b] as long as he lived, till the day of his death.

52:34 [b]2Sa 9:10

[a]*31* Also called *Amel-Marduk*

Theme of Jeremiah:

SEGMENT DIVISIONS

		CHAPTER THEMES
		1
		2
		3
		4
		5
		6
		7
		8
		9
		10
		11
		12
		13
		14
		15
		16
		17
		18
		19
		20
		21
		22
		23
		24
		25
		26

Author:

Date:

Purpose:

Key Words:

EGMENT DIVISIONS

		CHAPTER THEMES
		27
		28
		29
		30
		31
		32
		33
		34
		35
		36
		37
		38
		39
		40
		41
		42
		43
		44
		45
		46
		47
		48
		49
		50
		51
		52

LAMENTATIONS

Lamentations is a book of wailings that were read annually by the Jews as a reminder of the fall of Jerusalem and destruction of the temple. They were a reminder of an avoidable tragedy caused by sin—a reminder of a God who judges but who keeps his covenant forever.

These expressions of grief were written sometime between the destruction of Jerusalem and the return of the remnant after 70 years of captivity. Judah's plight is desperate but not hopeless when the people remember, "Because of the LORD's great love we are not consumed, for his compassions never fail. They are new every morning; great is your faithfulness" (3:22, 23).

THINGS TO DO

1. There are five laments in this book; each begins a new chapter. Lamentations is written as poetry. Each chapter, except chapter 3, is 22 verses long—a verse for every letter of the Hebrew alphabet. As you read chapter by chapter note how each lament begins and who or what the lament centers on.

2. Mark the key words listed on LAMENTATIONS AT A GLANCE on page 1411.

3. Note the personification of Jerusalem and Judah. Jerusalem is personified as a woman. The personification is seen in the first lines of Lamentations: "How deserted lies the city... like a widow is she." List what happened to Jerusalem and why; this is key. Note her emotions, the anguish because of her children, the thoughts and memories she has to deal with.

4. Carefully observe and list what you learn about God, his character, his judgments, and why he acts as he does. For example, 1:5 states that God caused Judah grief because of Judah's sin. God brought about Judah's captivity because of Judah's transgressions.

5. Lamentations gives a more definitive understanding of what took place during the Babylonian siege of Jerusalem. In the margin of the text, list what you learn. For example, 1:10 says the nations entered the sanctuary, the house of God where only Jewish priests were to go. Verse 11 reveals there was a famine—people were seeking bread and giving away their treasures in order to get it.

6. Determine the theme of each chapter. Write the theme next to each chapter number and on LAMENTATIONS AT A GLANCE.

7. Complete LAMENTATIONS AT A GLANCE.

THINGS TO THINK ABOUT

1. Have you become more aware of the consequences of sin?

2. God's judgment can take many forms. The sovereign God rules. None can stay his hand or say to him, "What have you done?" for he does according to his will in the army of heaven and among the inhabitants of the earth (Daniel 4:34, 35). Do you think you can sin and go unchastened by God? Judgment must begin at the house of God. Look at 1 Corinthians 11:31, 32.

3. Why do you think God deals with sin as he does? How should you respond? Read chapter 3 on your knees, so your "dancing" need not be turned into "mourning."

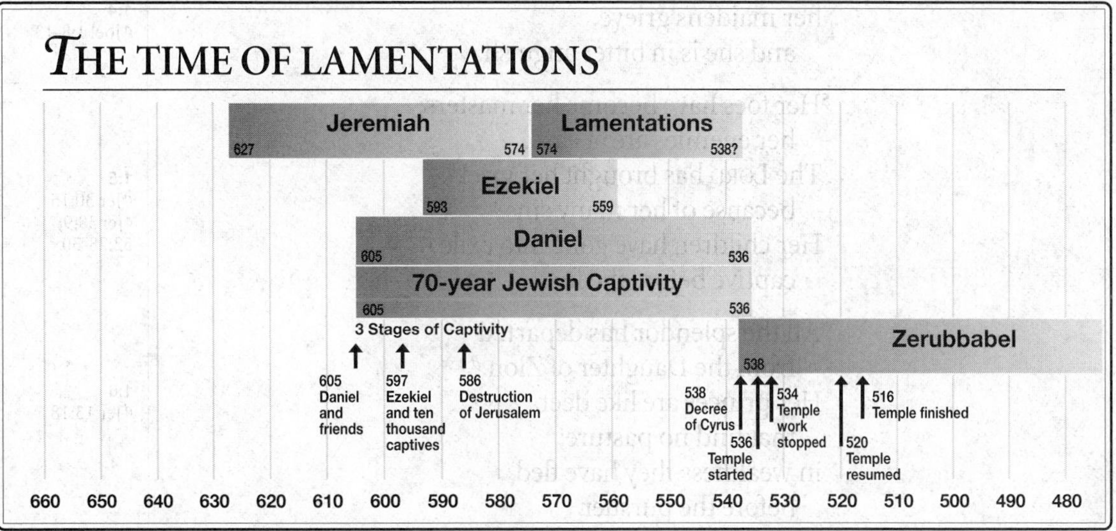

Chapter 1 Theme ____________________

1:1 [a]Isa 47:8 [b]1Ki 4:21 [c]Isa 3:26; Jer 40:9

1[a] How deserted lies the city,
once so full of people!
How like a widow[a] is she,
who once was great[b] among the nations!
She who was queen among the provinces
has now become a slave.[c]

1:2 [d]Ps 6:6 [e]Jer 3:1 [f]Jer 4:30; Mic 7:5 [g]ver 16

2 Bitterly she weeps[d] at night,
tears are upon her cheeks.
Among all her lovers[e]
there is none to comfort her.
All her friends have betrayed[f] her;
they have become her enemies.[g]

1:3 [h]Jer 13:19 [i]Dt 28:65

3 After affliction and harsh labor,
Judah has gone into exile.[h]
She dwells among the nations;
she finds no resting place.[i]
All who pursue her have overtaken her
in the midst of her distress.

1:4 [j]Jer 9:11

4 The roads to Zion mourn,
for no one comes to her appointed feasts.
All her gateways are desolate,[j]
her priests groan,

[a] This chapter is an acrostic poem, the verses of which begin with the successive letters of the Hebrew alphabet.

her maidens grieve,
and she is in bitter anguish.[a]

5 Her foes have become her masters;
her enemies are at ease.
The LORD has brought her grief[b]
because of her many sins.
Her children have gone into exile,[c]
captive before the foe.

6 All the splendor has departed
from the Daughter of Zion.[d]
Her princes are like deer
that find no pasture;
in weakness they have fled
before the pursuer.

7 In the days of her affliction and wandering
Jerusalem remembers all the treasures
that were hers in days of old.
When her people fell into enemy hands,
there was no one to help her.[e]
Her enemies looked at her
and laughed at her destruction.

8 Jerusalem has sinned[f] greatly
and so has become unclean.
All who honored her despise her,
for they have seen her nakedness;[g]
she herself groans[h]
and turns away.

9 Her filthiness clung to her skirts;
she did not consider her future.[i]
Her fall[j] was astounding;
there was none to comfort[k] her.
"Look, O LORD, on my affliction,[l]
for the enemy has triumphed."

10 The enemy laid hands
on all her treasures;[m]
she saw pagan nations
enter her sanctuary[n]—
those you had forbidden[o]
to enter your assembly.

11 All her people groan[p]
as they search for bread;[q]

1:4 [a] Joel 1:8-13
1:5 [b] Jer 30:15 [c] Jer 39:9; 52:28-30
1:6 [d] Jer 13:18
1:7 [e] Jer 37:7; La 4:17
1:8 [f] ver 20; Isa 59:2-13 [g] Jer 13:22,26 [h] ver 21,22
1:9 [i] Dt 32:28-29; Isa 47:7; Eze 24:13 [j] Jer 13:18 [k] Ecc 4:1; Jer 16:7 [l] Ps 25:18
1:10 [m] Isa 64:11 [n] Ps 74:7-8; Jer 51:51 [o] Dt 23:3
1:11 [p] Ps 38:8 [q] Jer 52:6

they barter their treasures for food
to keep themselves alive.
"Look, O LORD, and consider,
for I am despised."

12"Is it nothing to you, all you who pass by?[a]
Look around and see.
Is any suffering like my suffering[b]
that was inflicted on me,
that the LORD brought on me
in the day of his fierce anger?[c]

13"From on high he sent fire,
sent it down into my bones.[d]
He spread a net for my feet
and turned me back.
He made me desolate,[e]
faint[f] all the day long.

14"My sins have been bound into a yoke[a];[g]
by his hands they were woven together.
They have come upon my neck
and the Lord has sapped my strength.
He has handed me over[h]
to those I cannot withstand.

15"The Lord has rejected
all the warriors in my midst;[i]
he has summoned an army[j] against me
to[b] crush my young men.[k]
In his winepress the Lord has trampled
the Virgin Daughter of Judah.

16"This is why I weep
and my eyes overflow with tears.[l]
No one is near to comfort[m] me,
no one to restore my spirit.
My children are destitute
because the enemy has prevailed."[n]

17Zion stretches out her hands,[o]
but there is no one to comfort her.
The LORD has decreed for Jacob
that his neighbors become his foes;
Jerusalem has become
an unclean thing among them.

1:12 [a]Jer 18:16 [b]ver 18 [c]Isa 13:13; Jer 30:24
1:13 [d]Job 30:30 [e]Jer 44:6 [f]Hab 3:16
1:14 [g]Dt 28:48; Isa 47:6 [h]Jer 32:5
1:15 [i]Jer 37:10 [j]Isa 41:2 [k]Isa 28:18; Jer 18:21
1:16 [l]La 2:11,18; 3:48-49 [m]Ps 69:20; Ecc 4:1 [n]ver 2; Jer 13:17; 14:17
1:17 [o]Jer 4:31

a *14* Most Hebrew manuscripts; Septuagint *He kept watch over my sins* b *15* Or *has set a time for me / when he will*

18"The LORD is righteous,
yet I rebelled[a] against his command.
Listen, all you peoples;
look upon my suffering.[b]
My young men and maidens
have gone into exile.[c]

19"I called to my allies
but they betrayed me.
My priests and my elders
perished[d] in the city
while they searched for food
to keep themselves alive.

20"See, O LORD, how distressed[e] I am!
I am in torment[f] within,
and in my heart I am disturbed,
for I have been most rebellious.
Outside, the sword bereaves;
inside, there is only death.[g]

21"People have heard my groaning,[h]
but there is no one to comfort me.[i]
All my enemies have heard of my distress;
they rejoice[j] at what you have done.
May you bring the day[k] you have announced
so they may become like me.

22"Let all their wickedness come before you;
deal with them
as you have dealt with me
because of all my sins.[l]
My groans are many
and my heart is faint."

Chapter 2 Theme ______________________

2[a]

How the Lord has covered the Daughter of Zion
with the cloud of his anger[b]![m]
He has hurled down the splendor of Israel
from heaven to earth;
he has not remembered his footstool[n]
in the day of his anger.

2Without pity[o] the Lord has swallowed[p] up
all the dwellings of Jacob;

[a] This chapter is an acrostic poem, the verses of which begin with the successive letters of the Hebrew alphabet. [b] *1* Or *How the Lord in his anger / has treated the Daughter of Zion with contempt*

1:18 [a] 1Sa 12:14 [b] ver 12 [c] Dt 28:32,41

1:19 [d] Jer 14:15; La 2:20

1:20 [e] Jer 4:19 [f] La 2:11 [g] Dt 32:25; Eze 7:15

1:21 [h] ver 8 [i] ver 4 [j] La 2:15 [k] Isa 47:11; Jer 30:16

1:22 [l] Ne 4:5

2:1 [m] La 3:44 [n] Ps 99:5; 132:7

2:2 [o] La 3:43 [p] Ps 21:9

in his wrath he has torn down
the strongholds[a] of the Daughter of Judah.
He has brought her kingdom and its princes
down to the ground[b] in dishonor.

3 In fierce anger he has cut off
every horn[a][c] of Israel.
He has withdrawn his right hand[d]
at the approach of the enemy.
He has burned in Jacob like a flaming fire
that consumes everything around it.[e]

4 Like an enemy he has strung his bow;[f]
his right hand is ready.
Like a foe he has slain
all who were pleasing to the eye;[g]
he has poured out his wrath like fire[h]
on the tent of the Daughter of Zion.

5 The Lord is like an enemy;[i]
he has swallowed up Israel.
He has swallowed up all her palaces
and destroyed her strongholds.[j]
He has multiplied mourning and lamentation
for the Daughter of Judah.[k]

6 He has laid waste his dwelling like a garden;
he has destroyed his place of meeting.[l]
The LORD has made Zion forget
her appointed feasts and her Sabbaths;[m]
in his fierce anger he has spurned
both king and priest.[n]

7 The Lord has rejected his altar
and abandoned his sanctuary.
He has handed over to the enemy
the walls of her palaces;[o]
they have raised a shout in the house of the LORD
as on the day of an appointed feast.

8 The LORD determined to tear down
the wall around the Daughter of Zion.
He stretched out a measuring line[p]
and did not withhold his hand from destroying.
He made ramparts and walls lament;
together they wasted away.[q]

2:2 [a] Ps 89:39-40; Mic 5:11 [b] Isa 25:12
2:3 [c] Ps 75:5,10 [d] Ps 74:11 [e] Isa 42:25; Jer 21:4-5,14
2:4 [f] Job 16:13; La 3:12-13 [g] Eze 24:16,25 [h] Isa 42:25; Jer 7:20
2:5 [i] Jer 30:14 [j] ver 2 [k] Jer 9:17-20
2:6 [l] Jer 52:13 [m] La 1:4; Zep 3:18 [n] La 4:16
2:7 [o] Ps 74:7-8; Isa 64:11; Jer 33:4-5
2:8 [p] 2Ki 21:13; Isa 34:11 [q] Isa 3:26

[a] 3 Or / *all the strength*; or *every king*; *horn* here symbolizes strength.

9 Her gates[a] have sunk into the ground;
their bars he has broken and destroyed.
Her king and her princes are exiled[b] among the nations,
the law[c] is no more,
and her prophets no longer find
visions[d] from the LORD.

10 The elders of the Daughter of Zion
sit on the ground in silence;
they have sprinkled dust on their heads[e]
and put on sackcloth.[f]
The young women of Jerusalem
have bowed their heads to the ground.[g]

11 My eyes fail from weeping,[h]
I am in torment within,[i]
my heart is poured out[j] on the ground
because my people are destroyed,
because children and infants faint[k]
in the streets of the city.

12 They say to their mothers,
"Where is bread and wine?"
as they faint like wounded men
in the streets of the city,
as their lives ebb away
in their mothers' arms.[l]

13 What can I say for you?
With what can I compare you,
O Daughter of Jerusalem?
To what can I liken you,
that I may comfort you,
O Virgin Daughter of Zion?[m]
Your wound is as deep as the sea.[n]
Who can heal you?

14 The visions of your prophets
were false and worthless;
they did not expose your sin
to ward off your captivity.[o]
The oracles they gave you
were false and misleading.[p]

15 All who pass your way
clap their hands at you;[q]
they scoff[r] and shake their heads
at the Daughter of Jerusalem:

2:9 [a] Ne 1:3 [b] Dt 28:36; 2Ki 24:15 [c] 2Ch 15:3 [d] Jer 14:14

2:10 [e] Job 2:12 [f] Isa 15:3 [g] Job 2:13; Isa 3:26

2:11 [h] La 1:16; 3:48-51 [i] La 1:20 [j] ver 19; Ps 22:14 [k] La 4:4

2:12 [l] La 4:4

2:13 [m] Isa 37:22 [n] Jer 14:17; La 1:12

2:14 [o] Isa 58:1 [p] Jer 2:8; 23:25-32, 33-40; 29:9; Eze 13:3; 22:28

2:15 [q] Eze 25:6 [r] Jer 19:8

"Is this the city that was called
the perfection of beauty,[a]
the joy of the whole earth?"[b]

16All your enemies open their mouths
wide against you;[c]
they scoff and gnash their teeth[d]
and say, "We have swallowed her up.[e]
This is the day we have waited for;
we have lived to see it."

17The LORD has done what he planned;
he has fulfilled his word,
which he decreed long ago.[f]
He has overthrown you without pity,[g]
he has let the enemy gloat over you,
he has exalted the horn[a] of your foes.[h]

18The hearts of the people
cry out to the Lord.[i]
O wall of the Daughter of Zion,
let your tears[j] flow like a river
day and night;[k]
give yourself no relief,
your eyes no rest.[l]

19Arise, cry out in the night,
as the watches of the night begin;
pour out your heart[m] like water
in the presence of the Lord.[n]
Lift up your hands to him
for the lives of your children,
who faint[o] from hunger
at the head of every street.

20"Look, O LORD, and consider:
Whom have you ever treated like this?
Should women eat their offspring,[p]
the children they have cared for?[q]
Should priest and prophet be killed[r]
in the sanctuary of the Lord?

21"Young and old lie together
in the dust of the streets;
my young men and maidens
have fallen by the sword.[s]

2:15 [a]Ps 50:2 [b]Ps 48:2
2:16 [c]Ps 56:2; La 3:46 [d]Job 16:9 [e]Ps 35:25
2:17 [f]Dt 28:15-45 [g]ver 2; Eze 5:11 [h]Ps 89:42
2:18 [i]Ps 119:145 [j]La 1:16 [k]Jer 9:1 [l]La 3:49
2:19 [m]1Sa 1:15; Ps 62:8 [n]Isa 26:9 [o]Isa 51:20
2:20 [p]Dt 28:53; Jer 19:9 [q]La 4:10 [r]Ps 78:64; Jer 14:15
2:21 [s]2Ch 36:17; Ps 78:62-63; Jer 6:11

[a] *17 Horn* here symbolizes strength.

You have slain them in the day of your anger;
you have slaughtered them without pity.[a]

22"As you summon to a feast day,
so you summoned against me terrors[b] on every side.
In the day of the LORD's anger
no one escaped or survived;
those I cared for and reared,[c]
my enemy has destroyed."

Chapter 3 Theme ____________________

3[a]

I am the man who has seen affliction
by the rod of his wrath.[d]
2He has driven me away and made me walk
in darkness[e] rather than light;
3indeed, he has turned his hand against me[f]
again and again, all day long.

4He has made my skin and my flesh grow old
and has broken my bones.[g]
5He has besieged me and surrounded me
with bitterness[h] and hardship.[i]
6He has made me dwell in darkness
like those long dead.[j]

7He has walled me in so I cannot escape;[k]
he has weighed me down with chains.[l]
8Even when I call out or cry for help,
he shuts out my prayer.[m]
9He has barred my way with blocks of stone;
he has made my paths crooked.[n]

10Like a bear lying in wait,
like a lion in hiding,
11he dragged me from the path and mangled[o] me
and left me without help.
12He drew his bow[p]
and made me the target[q] for his arrows.[r]
13He pierced my heart
with arrows from his quiver.[s]
14I became the laughingstock[t] of all my people;
they mock me in song[u] all day long.
15He has filled me with bitter herbs
and sated me with gall.[v]

[a] This chapter is an acrostic poem; the verses of each stanza begin with the successive letters of the Hebrew alphabet, and the verses within each stanza begin with the same letter.

2:21 [a] Jer 13:14; La 3:43; Zec 11:6
2:22 [b] Ps 31:13; Jer 6:25 [c] Hos 9:13
3:1 [d] Job 19:21; Ps 88:7
3:2 [e] Jer 4:23
3:3 [f] Isa 5:25
3:4 [g] Ps 51:8; Isa 38:13; Jer 50:17
3:5 [h] ver 19 [i] Jer 23:15
3:6 [j] Ps 88:5-6
3:7 [k] Job 3:23 [l] Jer 40:4
3:8 [m] Job 30:20; Ps 22:2
3:9 [n] Isa 63:17; Hos 2:6
3:11 [o] Hos 6:1
3:12 [p] La 2:4 [q] Job 7:20 [r] Ps 7:12-13; 38:2
3:13 [s] Job 6:4
3:14 [t] Jer 20:7 [u] Job 30:9
3:15 [v] Jer 9:15

16 He has broken my teeth with gravel;[a]
he has trampled me in the dust.
17 I have been deprived of peace;
I have forgotten what prosperity is.
18 So I say, "My splendor is gone
and all that I had hoped from the LORD."[b]

19 I remember my affliction and my wandering,
the bitterness and the gall.
20 I well remember them,
and my soul is downcast[c] within me.[d]
21 Yet this I call to mind
and therefore I have hope:

22 Because of the LORD's great love we are not consumed,
for his compassions never fail.[e]
23 They are new every morning;
great is your faithfulness.[f]
24 I say to myself, "The LORD is my portion;[g]
therefore I will wait for him."

25 The LORD is good to those whose hope is in him,
to the one who seeks him;[h]
26 it is good to wait quietly
for the salvation of the LORD.[i]
27 It is good for a man to bear the yoke
while he is young.

28 Let him sit alone in silence,[j]
for the LORD has laid it on him.
29 Let him bury his face in the dust—
there may yet be hope.[k]
30 Let him offer his cheek to one who would strike him,[l]
and let him be filled with disgrace.

31 For men are not cast off
by the Lord forever.[m]
32 Though he brings grief, he will show compassion,
so great is his unfailing love.[n]
33 For he does not willingly bring affliction
or grief to the children of men.[o]

34 To crush underfoot
all prisoners in the land,
35 to deny a man his rights
before the Most High,
36 to deprive a man of justice—
would not the Lord see such things?[p]

3:16 [a] Pr 20:17
3:18 [b] Job 17:15
3:20 [c] Ps 42:5 [d] Ps 42:11
3:22 [e] Ps 78:38; Mal 3:6
3:23 [f] Zep 3:5
3:24 [g] Ps 16:5
3:25 [h] Isa 25:9; 30:18
3:26 [i] Ps 37:7; 40:1
3:28 [j] Jer 15:17
3:29 [k] Jer 31:17
3:30 [l] Job 16:10; Isa 50:6
3:31 [m] Ps 94:14; Isa 54:7
3:32 [n] Ps 78:38; Hos 11:8
3:33 [o] Eze 33:11
3:36 [p] Jer 22:3; Hab 1:13

37Who can speak and have it happen
if the Lord has not decreed it?[a]
38Is it not from the mouth of the Most High
that both calamities and good things come?[b]
39Why should any living man complain
when punished for his sins?[c]

40Let us examine our ways and test them,[d]
and let us return to the LORD.[e]
41Let us lift up our hearts and our hands
to God in heaven,[f] and say:
42"We have sinned and rebelled[g]
and you have not forgiven.[h]

43"You have covered yourself with anger and pursued us;
you have slain without pity.[i]
44You have covered yourself with a cloud[j]
so that no prayer[k] can get through.
45You have made us scum[l] and refuse
among the nations.

46"All our enemies have opened their mouths
wide against us.[m]
47We have suffered terror and pitfalls,[n]
ruin and destruction.[o]"
48Streams of tears flow from my eyes[p]
because my people are destroyed.[q]

49My eyes will flow unceasingly,
without relief,[r]
50until the LORD looks down
from heaven and sees.[s]
51What I see brings grief to my soul
because of all the women of my city.

52Those who were my enemies without cause
hunted me like a bird.[t]
53They tried to end my life in a pit[u]
and threw stones at me;
54the waters closed over my head,[v]
and I thought I was about to be cut off.

55I called on your name, O LORD,
from the depths of the pit.[w]
56You heard my plea:[x] "Do not close your ears
to my cry for relief."
57You came near when I called you,
and you said, "Do not fear."[y]

3:37 [a] Ps 33:9-11
3:38 [b] Job 2:10; Isa 45:7; Jer 32:42
3:39 [c] Jer 30:15; Mic 7:9
3:40 [d] 2Co 13:5 [e] Ps 119:59; 139:23-24
3:41 [f] Ps 25:1; 28:2
3:42 [g] Da 9:5 [h] Jer 5:7-9
3:43 [i] La 2:2,17,21
3:44 [j] Ps 97:2 [k] ver 8
3:45 [l] 1Co 4:13
3:46 [m] La 2:16
3:47 [n] Jer 48:43 [o] Isa 24:17-18; 51:19
3:48 [p] La 1:16, [q] La 2:11
3:49 [r] Jer 14:17
3:50 [s] Isa 63:15
3:52 [t] Ps 35:7
3:53 [u] Jer 37:16
3:54 [v] Ps 69:2; Jnh 2:3-5
3:55 [w] Ps 130:1; Jnh 2:2
3:56 [x] Ps 55:1
3:57 [y] Isa 41:10

58 O Lord, you took up my case;[a]
   you redeemed my life.[b]
59 You have seen, O LORD, the wrong done to me.[c]
   Uphold my cause!
60 You have seen the depth of their vengeance,
   all their plots against me.[d]

61 O LORD, you have heard their insults,
   all their plots against me—
62 what my enemies whisper and mutter
   against me all day long.[e]
63 Look at them! Sitting or standing,
   they mock me in their songs.

64 Pay them back what they deserve, O LORD,
   for what their hands have done.[f]
65 Put a veil over their hearts,[g]
   and may your curse be on them!
66 Pursue them in anger and destroy them
   from under the heavens of the LORD.

Chapter 4 Theme ____________________________

4[a] How the gold has lost its luster,
   the fine gold become dull!
The sacred gems are scattered
   at the head of every street.[h]

2 How the precious sons of Zion,
   once worth their weight in gold,
are now considered as pots of clay,
   the work of a potter's hands!

3 Even jackals offer their breasts
   to nurse their young,
but my people have become heartless
   like ostriches in the desert.[i]

4 Because of thirst the infant's tongue
   sticks to the roof of its mouth;[j]
the children beg for bread,
   but no one gives it to them.[k]

5 Those who once ate delicacies
   are destitute in the streets.
Those nurtured in purple[l]
   now lie on ash heaps.[m]

3:58 [a] Jer 51:36 [b] Ps 34:22; Jer 50:34
3:59 [c] Jer 18:19-20
3:60 [d] Jer 11:20; 18:18
3:62 [e] Eze 36:3
3:64 [f] Ps 28:4
3:65 [g] Isa 6:10
4:1 [h] Eze 7:19
4:3 [i] Job 39:16
4:4 [j] Ps 22:15 [k] La 2:11,12
4:5 [l] Jer 6:2 [m] Am 6:3-7

[a] This chapter is an acrostic poem, the verses of which begin with the successive letters of the Hebrew alphabet.

[6]The punishment of my people
is greater than that of Sodom,[a]
which was overthrown in a moment
without a hand turned to help her.

[7]Their princes were brighter than snow
and whiter than milk,
their bodies more ruddy than rubies,
their appearance like sapphires.[a]

[8]But now they are blacker[b] than soot;
they are not recognized in the streets.
Their skin has shriveled on their bones;[c]
it has become as dry as a stick.

[9]Those killed by the sword are better off
than those who die of famine;
racked with hunger, they waste away
for lack of food from the field.[d]

[10]With their own hands compassionate women
have cooked their own children,[e]
who became their food
when my people were destroyed.

[11]The LORD has given full vent to his wrath;
he has poured out his fierce anger.
He kindled a fire[f] in Zion
that consumed her foundations.[g]

[12]The kings of the earth did not believe,
nor did any of the world's people,
that enemies and foes could enter
the gates of Jerusalem.[h]

[13]But it happened because of the sins of her prophets
and the iniquities of her priests,[i]
who shed within her
the blood of the righteous.

[14]Now they grope through the streets
like men who are blind.[j]
They are so defiled with blood[k]
that no one dares to touch their garments.

[15]"Go away! You are unclean!" men cry to them.
"Away! Away! Don't touch us!"
When they flee and wander about,

4:6 [a]Ge 19:25
4:8 [b]Job 30:28 [c]Ps 102:3-5
4:9 [d]Jer 15:2; 16:4
4:10 [e]Lev 26:29; Dt 28:53-57; Jer 19:9; La 2:20; Eze 5:10
4:11 [f]Jer 17:27 [g]Dt 32:22; Jer 7:20; Eze 22:31
4:12 [h]1Ki 9:9; Jer 21:13
4:13 [i]Jer 5:31; 6:13; Eze 22:28; Mic 3:11
4:14 [j]Isa 59:10 [k]Jer 2:34; 19:4

[a]7 Or *lapis lazuli*

4:15
[a]Lev 13:46

4:16
[b]Isa 9:14-16
[c]La 5:12

4:17
[d]Isa 20:5; Eze 29:16
[e]La 1:7
[f]Jer 37:7

4:18
[g]Eze 7:2-12; Am 8:2

4:19
[h]Dt 28:49
[i]Isa 5:26-28

4:20
[j]2Sa 19:21
[k]Jer 39:5; Eze 12:12-13; 19:4,8

4:21
[l]Jer 25:15
[m]Isa 34:6-10; Am 1:11-12; Ob 16

4:22
[n]Isa 40:2; Jer 33:8
[o]Ps 137:7; Mal 1:4

5:1
[p]Ps 44:13-16; 89:50

5:2
[q]Ps 79:1
[r]Zep 1:13

5:3
[s]Jer 15:8; 18:21

5:4
[t]Isa 3:1

people among the nations say,
"They can stay here no longer."[a]

16The LORD himself has scattered them;
he no longer watches over them.[b]
The priests are shown no honor,
the elders[c] no favor.

17Moreover, our eyes failed,
looking in vain[d] for help;[e]
from our towers we watched
for a nation[f] that could not save us.

18Men stalked us at every step,
so we could not walk in our streets.
Our end was near, our days were numbered,
for our end had come.[g]

19Our pursuers were swifter
than eagles[h] in the sky;
they chased us[i] over the mountains
and lay in wait for us in the desert.

20The LORD's anointed,[j] our very life breath,
was caught in their traps.[k]
We thought that under his shadow
we would live among the nations.

21Rejoice and be glad, O Daughter of Edom,
you who live in the land of Uz.
But to you also the cup[l] will be passed;
you will be drunk and stripped naked.[m]

22O Daughter of Zion, your punishment will end;[n]
he will not prolong your exile.
But, O Daughter of Edom, he will punish your sin
and expose your wickedness.[o]

Chapter 5 Theme ______________________________

5

Remember, O LORD, what has happened to us;
look, and see our disgrace.[p]
2Our inheritance[q] has been turned over to aliens,
our homes[r] to foreigners.
3We have become orphans and fatherless,
our mothers like widows.[s]
4We must buy the water we drink;
our wood can be had only at a price.[t]

5Those who pursue us are at our heels;
we are weary[a] and find no rest.
6We submitted to Egypt and Assyria[b]
to get enough bread.
7Our fathers sinned and are no more,
and we bear their punishment.[c]
8Slaves[d] rule over us,
and there is none to free us from their hands.[e]
9We get our bread at the risk of our lives
because of the sword in the desert.
10Our skin is hot as an oven,
feverish from hunger.[f]
11Women have been ravished[g] in Zion,
and virgins in the towns of Judah.
12Princes have been hung up by their hands;
elders are shown no respect.[h]
13Young men toil at the millstones;
boys stagger under loads of wood.
14The elders are gone from the city gate;
the young men have stopped their music.[i]
15Joy is gone from our hearts;
our dancing has turned to mourning.[j]
16The crown[k] has fallen from our head.
Woe to us, for we have sinned![l]
17Because of this our hearts[m] are faint,
because of these things our eyes[n] grow dim
18for Mount Zion, which lies desolate,[o]
with jackals prowling over it.

19You, O LORD, reign forever;
your throne endures[p] from generation to generation.
20Why do you always forget us?[q]
Why do you forsake us so long?
21Restore[r] us to yourself, O LORD, that we may return;
renew our days as of old
22unless you have utterly rejected us
and are angry with us beyond measure.[s]

5:5 [a]Ne 9:37
5:6 [b]Hos 9:3
5:7 [c]Jer 14:20; 16:12
5:8 [d]Ne 5:15 [e]Zec 11:6
5:10 [f]La 4:8-9
5:11 [g]Zec 14:2
5:12 [h]La 4:16
5:14 [i]Isa 24:8; Jer 7:34
5:15 [j]Jer 25:10
5:16 [k]Ps 89:39 [l]Isa 3:11
5:17 [m]Isa 1:5, [n]Ps 6:7
5:18 [o]Mic 3:12
5:19 [p]Ps 45:6; 102:12,24-27
5:20 [q]Ps 13:1; 44:24
5:21 [r]Ps 80:3
5:22 [s]Isa 64:9

Theme of Lamentations:

uthor:

ate:

urpose:

ey Words:

- how, what
- Zion (Jerusalem, the city)
- anger (wrath)
- sin, punishment (wickedness)
- destroy, tear down (destroyed, destruction)
- affliction
- desolate (destitute, without help)

SEGMENT DIVISIONS		CHAPTER THEMES
		1
		2
		3
		4
		5

ƐZEKIEL

In 622 B.C. the book of the law was found in the house of the Lord. When it was brought to King Josiah, he wept, for he saw the awfulness of Judah's sin and knew that God's wrath burned against them. Although Josiah was determined that Judah would walk after the Lord and keep his commandments, the prophetess Huldah told him that after his death God would have to bring judgment upon Judah, for they had forsaken God and burned incense to other gods (see 2 Kings 22).

God's judgment on Judah began when King Josiah tried to stop Pharaoh Neco, king of Egypt, on his way to Carchemish on the Euphrates in 609 B.C. (see 2 Chronicles 35:20-27). Neco killed Josiah on the plain of Megiddo. Then four years later, in 605 B.C., Neco was defeated at Carchemish by Nebuchadnezzar, king of Babylon (see Jeremiah 46:2).

Ezekiel was eighteen years old when a handful of the nobles and princes were captured by King Nebuchadnezzar and taken from Judah to Babylon. Among them was a fifteen-year-old boy named Daniel, and his three friends, Hananiah, Mishael, and Azariah. Ezekiel, however, was left behind. At age 30 he would be eligible for the priesthood and would spend his life in service to God in the temple at Jerusalem. Or so it seemed.

For over ten years things were relatively quiet in Judah. The prophets were bringing good news prophesying peace. The people loved it and continued in their sin. Only one lonely voice disturbed their peace—the voice of Jeremiah.

Then Jehoiakim, king of Judah, rebelled against Nebuchadnezzar (2 Kings 23:36–24:4). When Jehoiakim died, Jehoiachin became king, and in 597 B.C. Nebuchadnezzar once again besieged Jerusalem. This time 10,000 people were taken captive into Babylon and Ezekiel, who would soon have been eligible for the priesthood, was among them. Never again would he see Jerusalem or the temple where he was to serve. Both would be destroyed by Nebuchadnezzar in 586 B.C.

But Ezekiel would see another temple and another Jerusalem—one which would be called Jehovah-shammah, the Lord is there! At age 30, Ezekiel had a vision.

~ Things to Do

In order to understand the depth and magnitude of the book of Ezekiel, you need to study it again and again. However, if you do the following, you will gain a good understanding of the message of Ezekiel.

General Instructions

1. Ezekiel has many references to time. These are important and need to be marked in a distinctive way with a color and/or symbol. Ezekiel 1:1, 2 establishes the historical setting of Ezekiel's ministry. The other references to time give you the historical timing of his visions and prophecies.
   a. Every time you mark references to time look at the calendar on page 1416 at the beginning of Ezekiel 1 to see what month Ezekiel is referring to. (Follow the sacred calendar highlighted in black.)
   b. Ezekiel 1:2 is a parenthesis and serves as an explanation of the timing of verse 2. Read 2 Kings 24:8 through 25:21 for a good overview of the historical setting. This will help you understand the timing of Ezekiel's prophecies.
      1) As you read, look for Jehoiachin's name, mark it in a distinctive way, and watch when he goes into exile. Also note who is made king when Jehoiachin goes into exile.
      2) In the margins of 2 Kings 24, 25, record the dates of Jerusalem's first, second, and third sieges. (Jehoiachin was taken captive when Nebuchadnezzar besieged Jerusalem the second time.) The first siege is recorded in 2 Kings 24:1-7 and occurred in 605 B.C. The second siege is recorded

in 2 Kings 24:10-16 and occurred in 597 B.C. (Ezekiel was taken captive during the second siege.) The third and final siege is recorded in 2 Kings 25:1-21. It began in 588 B.C. and in 586 B.C. the city was captured and destroyed.

3) Read Ezekiel 1:1-3 and record what you learn about Ezekiel under "Author" on the EZEKIEL AT A GLANCE chart on page 1498.

4) Now read Numbers 4:3 and observe at what age a man began his priestly service. Then look at Ezekiel 1 and compare this with the way Ezekiel is described and the year he had his first visions from God. Verse 2 tells you what year it was in relationship to the second siege of Jerusalem, the year when Jehoiachin went into exile.

2. Now that you have the historical setting, as you read the dates of all the other visions or prophecies in Ezekiel, you can know that the dates are calculated from the time of Jehoiachin's and Ezekiel's exile in 597 B.C.

3. Key repeated words and phrases to mark throughout the book are listed on EZEKIEL AT A GLANCE. Write them on an index card, color code each in a distinctive way, and then use the card as a bookmark while you study Ezekiel.

Chapters 1-3: Ezekiel's Call

1. Read chapters 1 through 3 and mark the key repeated words.

2. As you go through these chapters one at a time, interrogate the text with the five W's and an H. Ask questions such as: What does Ezekiel see? How are they described? Where are they? Where is Ezekiel? What is he told to do? Why is he told to do it? When is Ezekiel to speak?

3. In the margin of each chapter record your observations. Note what Ezekiel is called to do and how he is to do it. Also note to whom he is sent and why.

4. In summary form list everything you observe from the text about Ezekiel, the people to whom he was sent, and the glory of the Lord.

5. Record the theme of each chapter on EZEKIEL AT A GLANCE and in the text next to the chapter number.

Chapters 4-24: Prophecies about Judah and Jerusalem

1. Read through this segment one chapter at a time. On the first reading of a chapter, mark every reference to the time of a vision. Also mark the key words that are on your bookmark.
    a. Watch for and mark the phrase *know that I am the Lord (know that I the Lord made them)*. This is a key phrase used throughout the remainder of Ezekiel, so add this to your bookmark. Every time you see this phrase, in the margin note who is going to know and how they will know it.
    b. When you mark *Spirit, heart (hearts, courage),* and *the glory of the God of Israel (the glory of the Lord),* list in the margin what you learn about each from that chapter.
    c. Add *covenant (treaty)* to your list of key words. When they are used in a chapter, list what you learn about them in the margin. Also watch for additional key repeated words.

2. Now read through each chapter again. Watch for every reference to the *son of man.* In the margin note God's instructions to Ezekiel, the son of man. Note to whom or to what he was to speak and how. Note whether it was by symbolic acts, messages, visions, parables, or signs. Also note why he was to speak in that way and the significance of his action. Also notice when Ezekiel's mouth is shut and then later opened. This is important.

3. Record the theme of each chapter as you have done previously.

Chapters 25-32: Prophecies about the Nations

1. Read through this segment one chapter at a time. On the first reading mark the key words. When you mark the phrases *know that I am the Lord* and *know that I am the Sovereign Lord,* note in the margin who is going to know and how they will know it.

2. On the second reading of the chapter, identify and record in the margin the nation to whom the prophecy is given and the ruler—if he is mentioned. Also observe and note what will happen to the nation and why.

3. Make sure you note or mark *when* the word of the Lord came to Ezekiel.

4. Record the theme of each chapter as you have done previously.

Chapters 33-39: Prophecies about Israel's Restoration

1. Read each chapter and once again:

   a. Mark every reference to time. Do not miss when the visions or prophecies were given to Ezekiel.

   b. Mark every key word. In the margin list what you learn from marking *covenant* and then compare it with what you observed about covenant in Ezekiel 16 and 17.

   c. Continue noting the same observations from marking every occurrence of *know that I am the Lord* or *know that I the Lord am the Holy One.* Also list what you learn about the *Spirit, heart (hearts, courage),* and *the glory of the God of Israel (the glory of the Lord).*

2. Read the chapter again. List God's instructions to Ezekiel ("the son of man"). Note to whom or to what he was to speak and what the message was to be. As you look at the prophecy, list what is going to happen, to whom or what it will happen, and when it will happen. Put a symbol next to any indication of timing. Also note any symbolic acts he was to perform and why.

3. List the theme of each chapter as before.

Chapters 40-48: Prophecies about the Temple

1. As you begin observing this final segment, read 40:1-5. In a distinctive way, mark when this final vision is given. Then in the margin list who gives it, how, where, and what Ezekiel is to do.

2. Read each chapter carefully and do the following:

   a. Mark key words as before; however, add to your list *temple (sanctuary, house, wall), holy (sacred), offering (offerings, special gift),* and *gate (gateways, entrance, gateposts).* The phrase "know that I am the Lord" is not used in this final segment.

   b. Watch for and record the reason for the vision of the temple and its measurements. Also note what you learn about *the glory of the Lord* and *the Spirit,* and their relationship to the temple or sanctuary. Compare this with what you saw in Ezekiel 8 through 11.

   c. Warning: This last segment of Ezekiel may seem a little boring after the first 39 chapters. Don't get bogged down in all the temple measurements. Don't miss the last verse of Ezekiel, since it names the city.

   d. In the margin list the main points, instructions, or events of each chapter.

3. Record the theme of these chapters as you have done before. Then complete EZEKIEL AT A GLANCE. Go back to each vision Ezekiel had, note the year when it occurred, and from your calendar on page 1416 record the name of the month and the day. (Follow the sacred calendar highlighted in black.) Then transfer this information to the segment division portion of EZEKIEL AT A GLANCE.

Things to Think About

1. As you think about God's call upon Ezekiel's life, what do you see about Ezekiel's responsibility as a watchman that you could apply to your own life? If the people wouldn't listen, was Ezekiel still to

speak (Ezekiel 2, 3, 33)? Remember that the things in the Old Testament were written for our example, encouragement, and endurance (1 Corinthians 10:6, 11 and Romans 15:4).

2. Before Ezekiel ever shared God's message he was told to eat it, to take it to heart, and to listen closely to the Lord (Ezekiel 3). What lessons can you learn from his example? How would what you are doing in this inductive study Bible help you? What do you need to remember as you work your way through the Bible?

3. What have you learned about God and his ways from studying Ezekiel? God took Israel as his wife. Christians are espoused to Jesus Christ, their heavenly Bridegroom (2 Corinthians 11:2, 3). Have you, like Israel, played the prostitute spiritually and grieved God's heart (Ezekiel 6:9; James 4:4)? If so, what do you need to do? If not, what should you do so that you never do?

4. In Ezekiel 20:33 God tells Israel, "As surely as I live, I will rule over you with a mighty hand and an outstretched arm and with outpoured wrath." Think about this verse in the light of the character and position of God and in the light of Philippians 2:5-11. Have you genuinely confessed Jesus Christ as your Lord, your King who has a right to rule over you?

5. Think about what you have observed from marking the word *covenant*. What have you learned about the heart of stone and the Spirit dwelling within (Ezekiel 36)? Read 2 Corinthians 3 and see how this parallels what Ezekiel says. Do you have a heart of stone or a heart of flesh? Where is the Spirit of God in relationship to you? Is he within? Read Ezekiel 36:26, 27.

6. What have you learned about prophecy from Ezekiel that you could use in sharing God's Word with the Jews? What about the prophecies of Ezekiel 36 and 37 and the way they already are being fulfilled? And what do you learn about Israel's future in respect to Ezekiel 38 through 39? This is of great interest to Jews.

7. What have you learned about the holiness of God? What effect will it have on your life?

1:1 [a]Eze 11:24-25 — *Chapter 1 Theme* ____________

[b]Mt 3:16; 1 In the[a] thirtieth year, in the fourth month on the fifth day,
Ac 7:56 [c]Ex 24:10 while I was among the exiles[a] by the Kebar River, the heavens
1:2 were opened[b] and I saw visions[c] of God.
[d]2Ki 24:15 2On the fifth of the month—it was the fifth year of the exile of
1:3 King Jehoiachin[d]— 3the word of the LORD came to Ezekiel the
[e]2Ki 3:15; Eze 3:14,22 priest, the son of Buzi,[b] by the Kebar River in the land of the Bab-
1:4 ylonians.[c] There the hand of the LORD was upon him.[e]
[f]Jer 1:14 4I looked, and I saw a windstorm coming out of the north[f]—an
[g]Eze 8:2 immense cloud with flashing lightning and surrounded by bril-
1:5 [h]Rev 4:6 liant light. The center of the fire looked like glowing metal,[g] 5and in
[i]ver 26 the fire was what looked like four living creatures.[h] In appearance
1:6 their form was that of a man,[i] 6but each of them had four faces[j]
[j]Eze 10:14 and four wings. 7Their legs were straight; their feet were like those
1:7 [k]Da 10:6; of a calf and gleamed like burnished bronze.[k] 8Under their wings
Rev 1:15 on their four sides they had the hands of a man.[l] All four of them
1:8 had faces and wings, 9and their wings touched one another. Each
[l]Eze 10:8 one went straight ahead; they did not turn as they moved.[m]

1:9 [m]Eze 10:22

593 B.C.

INSIGHT

According to Numbers 4:3, men entered the priestly service at the age of thirty.

[a]*1* Or ⌊*my*⌋ [b]*3* Or *Ezekiel son of Buzi the priest* [c]*3* Or *Chaldeans*

The Jewish Calendar

Babylonian names (B) for the months are still used today for the Jewish calendar. Canaanite names (C) were used prior to the Babylonian captivity in 586 B.C. Four are mentioned in the Old Testament. **Adar-Sheni** is an intercalary month used every two to three years or seven times in 19 years.

1st month	**2nd month**	**3rd month**	**4th month**
Nisan (B) Abib (C) March-April	Iyyar (B) Ziv (C) April-May	Sivan (B) May-June	Tammuz (B) June-July
7th month	*8th month*	*9th month*	*10th month*
5th month	**6th month**	**7th month**	**8th month**
Ab (B) July-August	Elul (B) August-September	Tishri (B) Ethanim (C) September-October	Marcheshvan (B) Bul (C) October-November
11th month	*12th month*	*1st month*	*2nd month*
9th month	**10th month**	**11th month**	**12th month**
Chislev (B) November-December	Tebeth (B) December-January	Shebat (B) January-February	Adar (B) February-March
3rd month	*4th month*	*5th month*	*6th month*

Sacred calendar appears in black • Civil calendar appears in gray

10Their faces looked like this: Each of the four had the face of a
man, and on the right side each had the face of a lion, and on the
left the face of an ox; each also had the face of an eagle.[a] 11Such
were their faces. Their wings[b] were spread out upward; each had
two wings, one touching the wing of another creature on either
side, and two wings covering its body. 12Each one went straight
ahead. Wherever the spirit would go, they would go, without turning as they went. 13The appearance of the living creatures was like
burning coals of fire or like torches. Fire moved back and forth
among the creatures; it was bright, and lightning[c] flashed out of
it. 14The creatures sped back and forth like flashes of lightning.[d]
15As I looked at the living creatures, I saw a wheel on the ground
beside each creature with its four faces. 16This was the appearance
and structure of the wheels: They sparkled like chrysolite,[e] and all
four looked alike. Each appeared to be made like a wheel intersecting a wheel. 17As they moved, they would go in any one of the four
directions the creatures faced; the wheels did not turn[f] about[a] as
the creatures went. 18Their rims were high and awesome, and all
four rims were full of eyes[g] all around.
19When the living creatures moved, the wheels beside them
moved; and when the living creatures rose from the ground, the
wheels also rose. 20Wherever the spirit would go, they would go,[h]
and the wheels would rise along with them, because the spirit of the
living creatures was in the wheels. 21When the creatures moved,
they also moved; when the creatures stood still, they also stood
still; and when the creatures rose from the ground, the wheels rose
along with them, because the spirit of the living creatures was in
the wheels.[i]

a 17 Or *aside*

1:10 [a] Eze 10:14; Rev 4:7
1:11 [b] Isa 6:2
1:13 [c] Rev 4:5
1:14 [d] Ps 29:7
1:16 [e] Eze 10:9-11; Da 10:6
1:17 [f] ver 9
1:18 [g] Eze 10:12; Rev 4:6
1:20 [h] ver 12
1:21 [i] Eze 10:17

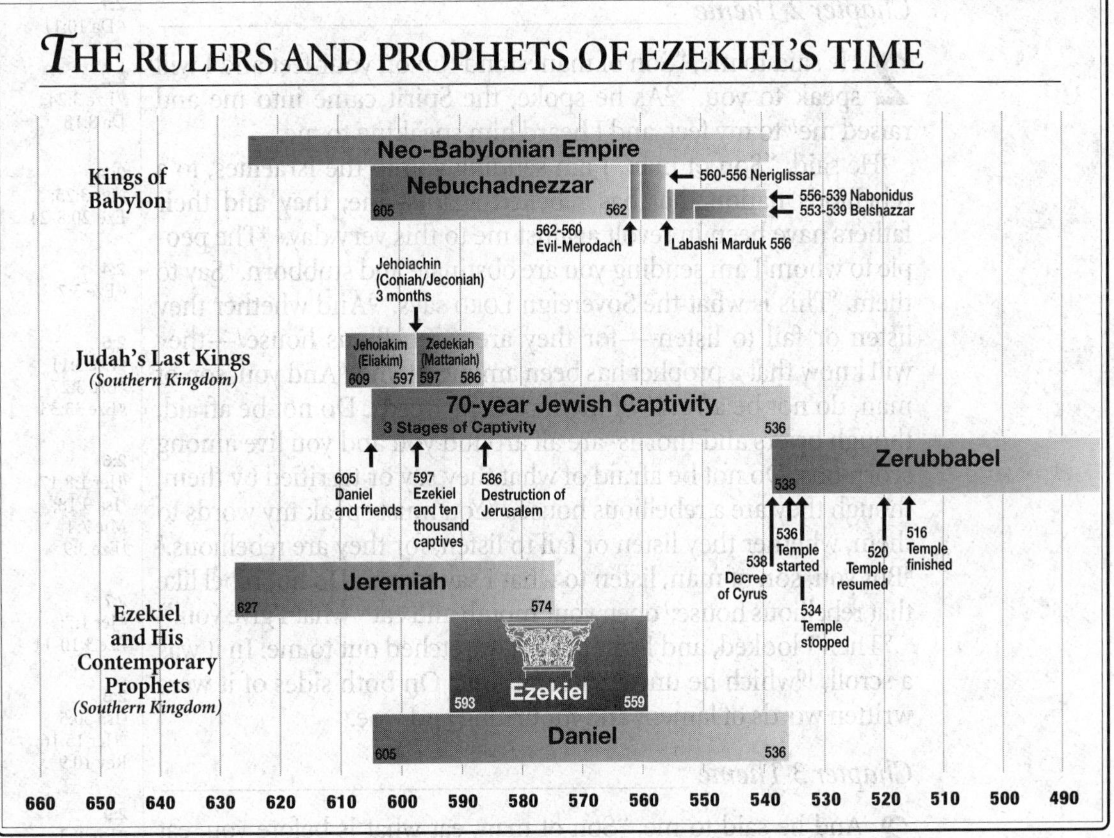

22 Spread out above the heads of the living creatures was what
looked like an expanse,[a] sparkling like ice, and awesome. 23 Under
the expanse their wings were stretched out one toward the other,
and each had two wings covering its body. 24 When the creatures
moved, I heard the sound of their wings, like the roar of rushing
waters, like the voice[b] of the Almighty,[a] like the tumult of an army.[c]
When they stood still, they lowered their wings.

25 Then there came a voice from above the expanse over their
heads as they stood with lowered wings. 26 Above the expanse over
their heads was what looked like a throne of sapphire,[b][d] and high
above on the throne was a figure like that of a man.[e] 27 I saw that
from what appeared to be his waist up he looked like glowing
metal, as if full of fire, and that from there down he looked like
fire; and brilliant light surrounded him.[f] 28 Like the appearance of
a rainbow[g] in the clouds on a rainy day, so was the radiance
around him.[h]

This was the appearance of the likeness of the glory[i] of the
LORD. When I saw it, I fell facedown,[j] and I heard the voice of one
speaking.

1:22 [a] Eze 10:1
1:24 [b] Eze 10:5; 43:2; Da 10:6; Rev 1:15; 19:6 [c] 2Ki 7:6
1:26 [d] Ex 24:10; Eze 10:1 [e] Rev 1:13
1:27 [f] Eze 8:2
1:28 [g] Ge 9:13; Rev 10:1 [h] Rev 4:2 [i] Eze 8:4 [j] Eze 3:23; Da 8:17; Rev 1:17

[a] 24 Hebrew *Shaddai* [b] 26 Or *lapis lazuli*

Chapter 2 Theme ____________________________

2 He said to me, "Son of man, stand[a] up on your feet and I will speak to you." 2As he spoke, the Spirit came into me and raised me[b] to my feet, and I heard him speaking to me.

3He said: "Son of man, I am sending you to the Israelites, to a rebellious nation that has rebelled against me; they and their fathers have been in revolt against me to this very day.[c] 4The people to whom I am sending you are obstinate and stubborn.[d] Say to them, 'This is what the Sovereign LORD says.' 5And whether they listen or fail to listen[e]—for they are a rebellious house[f]—they will know that a prophet has been among them.[g] 6And you, son of man, do not be afraid[h] of them or their words. Do not be afraid, though briers and thorns[i] are all around you and you live among scorpions. Do not be afraid of what they say or terrified by them, though they are a rebellious house.[j] 7You must speak my words to them, whether they listen or fail to listen, for they are rebellious.[k] 8But you, son of man, listen to what I say to you. Do not rebel like that rebellious house;[l] open your mouth and eat[m] what I give you."

9Then I looked, and I saw a hand[n] stretched out to me. In it was a scroll, 10which he unrolled before me. On both sides of it were written words of lament and mourning and woe.[o]

Chapter 3 Theme ____________________________

3 And he said to me, "Son of man, eat what is before you, eat this scroll; then go and speak to the house of Israel." 2So I opened my mouth, and he gave me the scroll to eat.

3Then he said to me, "Son of man, eat this scroll I am giving you and fill your stomach with it." So I ate[p] it, and it tasted as sweet as honey[q] in my mouth.

4He then said to me: "Son of man, go now to the house of Israel and speak my words to them. 5You are not being sent to a people of obscure speech and difficult language,[r] but to the house of Israel—6not to many peoples of obscure speech and difficult language, whose words you cannot understand. Surely if I had sent you to them, they would have listened to you.[s] 7But the house of Israel is not willing to listen to you because they are not willing to listen to me, for the whole house of Israel is hardened and obstinate.[t] 8But I will make you as unyielding and hardened as they are.[u] 9I will make your forehead like the hardest stone, harder than flint. Do not be afraid of them or terrified by them, though they are a rebellious house.[v]"

10And he said to me, "Son of man, listen carefully and take to heart all the words I speak to you. 11Go now to your countrymen in exile and speak to them. Say to them, 'This is what the Sovereign LORD says,' whether they listen or fail to listen.[w]"

2:1 [a] Da 10:11
2:2 [b] Eze 3:24; Da 8:18
2:3 [c] Jer 3:25; Eze 20:8-24
2:4 [d] Eze 3:7
2:5 [e] Eze 3:11 [f] Eze 3:27 [g] Eze 33:33
2:6 [h] Jer 1:8,17 [i] Isa 9:18; Mic 7:4 [j] Eze 3:9
2:7 [k] Jer 1:7; Eze 3:10-11
2:8 [l] Isa 50:5 [m] Jer 15:16; Rev 10:9
2:9 [n] Eze 8:3
2:10 [o] Rev 8:13
3:3 [p] Jer 15:16 [q] Ps 19:10; Ps 119:103; Rev 10:9-10
3:5 [r] Isa 28:11; Jnh 1:2
3:6 [s] Mt 11:21-23
3:7 [t] Eze 2:4; Jn 15:20-23
3:8 [u] Jer 1:18
3:9 [v] Isa 50:7; Eze 2:6; Mic 3:8
3:11 [w] Eze 2:4-5,7

12 Then the Spirit lifted me up,[a] and I heard behind me a loud
rumbling sound—May the glory of the LORD be praised in his
dwelling place!— 13 the sound of the wings of the living creatures
brushing against each other and the sound of the wheels beside
them, a loud rumbling sound.[b] 14 The Spirit then lifted me up and
took me away, and I went in bitterness and in the anger of my spirit, with the strong hand of the LORD upon me. 15 I came to the exiles
who lived at Tel Abib near the Kebar River.[c] And there, where they
were living, I sat among them for seven days[d]—overwhelmed.
16 At the end of seven days the word of the LORD came to me:[e]
17 "Son of man, I have made you a watchman[f] for the house of
Israel; so hear the word I speak and give them warning from me.
18 When I say to a wicked man, 'You will surely die,' and you do not
warn him or speak out to dissuade him from his evil ways in order
to save his life, that wicked man will die for[a] his sin, and I will hold
you accountable for his blood.[g] 19 But if you do warn the wicked
man and he does not turn from his wickedness or from his evil
ways, he will die for his sin; but you will have saved yourself.[h]
20 "Again, when a righteous man turns from his righteousness
and does evil, and I put a stumbling block before him, he will die.
Since you did not warn him, he will die for his sin. The righteous
things he did will not be remembered, and I will hold you accountable for his blood.[i] 21 But if you do warn the righteous man not to
sin and he does not sin, he will surely live because he took warning,
and you will have saved yourself.[j]"
22 The hand of the LORD[k] was upon me there, and he said to me,
"Get up and go[l] out to the plain,[m] and there I will speak to you."
23 So I got up and went out to the plain. And the glory of the LORD
was standing there, like the glory I had seen by the Kebar River,[n]
and I fell facedown.[o]
24 Then the Spirit came into me and raised me[p] to my feet. He
spoke to me and said: "Go, shut yourself inside your house. 25 And
you, son of man, they will tie with ropes; you will be bound so that
you cannot go out among the people.[q] 26 I will make your tongue
stick to the roof of your mouth so that you will be silent and unable
to rebuke them, though they are a rebellious house.[r] 27 But when I
speak to you, I will open your mouth and you shall say to them,
'This is what the Sovereign LORD says.'[s] Whoever will listen let him
listen, and whoever will refuse let him refuse; for they are a rebellious house.[t]

Chapter 4 Theme ______________________

4

"Now, son of man, take a clay tablet, put it in front of you and
draw the city of Jerusalem on it. 2 Then lay siege to it: Erect siege
works against it, build a ramp[u] up to it, set up camps against it and

3:12 [a] Eze 8:3; Ac 8:39
3:13 [b] Eze 1:24; 10:5,16-17
3:15 [c] Ps 137:1 [d] Job 2:13
3:16 [e] Jer 42:7
3:17 [f] Isa 52:8; Jer 6:17; Eze 33:7-9
3:18 [g] ver 20; Eze 33:6
3:19 [h] 2Ki 17:13; Eze 14:14,20; Ac 18:6; 20:26; 1Ti 4:14-16
3:20 [i] Ps 125:5; Eze 18:24; 33:12,18
3:21 [j] Ac 20:31
3:22 [k] Eze 1:3 [l] Ac 9:6 [m] Eze 8:4
3:23 [n] Eze 1:1 [o] Eze 1:28
3:24 [p] Eze 2:2
3:25 [q] Eze 4:8
3:26 [r] Eze 2:5; 24:27; 33:22
3:27 [s] ver 11 [t] Eze 12:3; 24:27; 33:22
4:2 [u] Jer 6:6

[a] *18* Or *in*; also in verses 19 and 20

put battering rams around it.[a] 3Then take an iron pan, place it as
an iron wall between you and the city and turn your face toward it.
It will be under siege, and you shall besiege it. This will be a sign[b]
to the house of Israel.[c]
4"Then lie on your left side and put the sin of the house of Israel
upon yourself.[a] You are to bear their sin for the number of days
you lie on your side. 5I have assigned you the same number of days
as the years of their sin. So for 390 days you will bear the sin of the
house of Israel.
6"After you have finished this, lie down again, this time on your
right side, and bear the sin of the house of Judah. I have assigned
you 40 days, a day for each year.[d] 7Turn your face toward the siege
of Jerusalem and with bared arm prophesy against her. 8I will tie
you up with ropes so that you cannot turn from one side to the
other until you have finished the days of your siege.[e]
9"Take wheat and barley, beans and lentils, millet and spelt;[f] put
them in a storage jar and use them to make bread for yourself. You
are to eat it during the 390 days you lie on your side. 10Weigh out
twenty shekels[b] of food to eat each day and eat it at set times.
11Also measure out a sixth of a hin[c] of water and drink it at set
times. 12Eat the food as you would a barley cake; bake it in the
sight of the people, using human excrement[g] for fuel." 13The LORD
said, "In this way the people of Israel will eat defiled food among
the nations where I will drive them."[h]
14Then I said, "Not so, Sovereign LORD![i] I have never defiled
myself. From my youth until now I have never eaten anything
found dead[j] or torn by wild animals. No unclean meat has ever
entered my mouth.[k]"
15"Very well," he said, "I will let you bake your bread over cow
manure instead of human excrement."
16He then said to me: "Son of man, I will cut off[l] the supply of
food in Jerusalem. The people will eat rationed food in anxiety
and drink rationed water in despair,[m] 17for food and water will be
scarce. They will be appalled at the sight of each other and will
waste away because of[d] their sin.[n]

Chapter 5 Theme ______________________

5 "Now, son of man, take a sharp sword and use it as a barber's
razor[o] to shave[p] your head and your beard.[q] Then take a set
of scales and divide up the hair. 2When the days of your siege
come to an end, burn a third of the hair with fire inside the city.
Take a third and strike it with the sword all around the city. And
scatter a third to the wind. For I will pursue them with drawn
sword.[r] 3But take a few strands of hair and tuck them away in the

a4 Or *your side* b10 That is, about 8 ounces (about 0.2 kilogram) c11 That is, about 2/3 quart (about 0.6 liter) d17 Or *away in*

4:2 [a]Eze 21:22
4:3 [b]Isa 8:18; 20:3; Eze 12:3-6; 24:24,27 [c]Jer 39:1
4:6 [d]Nu 14:34; Da 9:24-26; 12:11-12
4:8 [e]Eze 3:25
4:9 [f]Isa 28:25
4:12 [g]Isa 36:12
4:13 [h]Hos 9:3
4:14 [i]Jer 1:6; Eze 9:8; 20:49 [j]Lev 11:39 [k]Ex 22:31; Dt 14:3; Ac 10:14
4:16 [l]Ps 105:16; Eze 5:16 [m]ver 10-11; Lev 26:26; Isa 3:1; Eze 12:19
4:17 [n]Lev 26:39; Eze 24:23; 33:10
5:1 [o]Isa 7:20 [p]Eze 44:20 [q]Lev 21:5
5:2 [r]ver 12; Lev 26:33

folds of your garment.[a] 4Again, take a few of these and throw them
into the fire and burn them up. A fire will spread from there to
the whole house of Israel.
5"This is what the Sovereign LORD says: This is Jerusalem, which
I have set in the center of the nations, with countries all around
her. 6Yet in her wickedness she has rebelled against my laws and
decrees more than the nations and countries around her. She has
rejected my laws and has not followed my decrees.[b]
7"Therefore this is what the Sovereign LORD says: You have been
more unruly than the nations around you and have not followed
my decrees or kept my laws. You have not even[a] conformed to the
standards of the nations around you.[c]
8"Therefore this is what the Sovereign LORD says: I myself am
against you, Jerusalem, and I will inflict punishment on you in the
sight of the nations.[d] 9Because of all your detestable idols, I will do
to you what I have never done before and will never do again.[e]
10Therefore in your midst fathers will eat their children, and children will eat their fathers.[f] I will inflict punishment on you and will
scatter all your survivors to the winds.[g] 11Therefore as surely as I
live, declares the Sovereign LORD, because you have defiled my sanctuary with all your vile images[h] and detestable practices,[i] I myself
will withdraw my favor; I will not look on you with pity or spare
you.[j] 12A third of your people will die of the plague or perish by
famine inside you; a third will fall by the sword outside your walls;
and a third I will scatter to the winds and pursue with drawn
sword.[k]
13"Then my anger will cease and my wrath[l] against them will
subside, and I will be avenged.[m] And when I have spent my wrath
upon them, they will know that I the LORD have spoken in my zeal.
14"I will make you a ruin and a reproach among the nations
around you, in the sight of all who pass by.[n] 15You will be a
reproach and a taunt, a warning and an object of horror to the
nations around you when I inflict punishment on you in anger
and in wrath and with stinging rebuke.[o] I the LORD have spoken.[p]
16When I shoot at you with my deadly and destructive arrows of
famine, I will shoot to destroy you. I will bring more and more
famine upon you and cut off your supply of food.[q] 17I will send
famine and wild beasts against you, and they will leave you childless. Plague and bloodshed[r] will sweep through you, and I will
bring the sword against you. I the LORD have spoken.[s]"

Chapter 6 Theme

6 The word of the LORD came to me: 2"Son of man, set your
face against the mountains[t] of Israel; prophesy against them
3and say: 'O mountains of Israel, hear the word of the Sovereign

5:3 [a] Jer 39:10
5:6 [b] Jer 11:10; Eze 16:47-51; Zec 7:11
5:7 [c] 2Ch 33:9; Jer 2:10-11; Eze 16:47
5:8 [d] Eze 15:7
5:9 [e] Da 9:12; Mt 24:21
5:10 [f] Lev 26:29; La 2:20 [g] Lev 26:33; Ps 44:11; Eze 12:14; Zec 2:6
5:11 [h] Eze 7:20 [i] 2Ch 36:14; Eze 8:6 [j] Eze 7:4,9
5:12 [k] ver 2,17; Jer 15:2; 21:9; Eze 6:11-12; 12:14
5:13 [l] Eze 21:17; 36:6 [m] Isa 1:24
5:14 [n] Lev 26:32; Ne 2:17; Ps 74:3-10; 79:1-4
5:15 [o] 1Ki 9:7; Jer 22:8-9; 24:9 [p] Eze 25:17
5:16 [q] Dt 32:24
5:17 [r] Eze 38:22 [s] Eze 14:21
6:2 [t] Eze 36:1

a 7 Most Hebrew manuscripts; some Hebrew manuscripts and Syriac *You have*

LORD. This is what the Sovereign LORD says to the mountains and
hills, to the ravines and valleys:[a] I am about to bring a sword
against you, and I will destroy your high places.[b] 4Your altars will
be demolished and your incense altars[c] will be smashed; and I will
slay your people in front of your idols. 5I will lay the dead bodies of
the Israelites in front of their idols, and I will scatter your bones[d]
around your altars. 6Wherever you live, the towns will be laid waste
and the high places demolished, so that your altars will be laid
waste and devastated, your idols[e] smashed and ruined, your incense altars[f] broken down, and what you have made wiped out.[g]
7Your people will fall slain among you, and you will know that I am
the LORD.

8"'But I will spare some, for some of you will escape[h] the sword
when you are scattered among the lands and nations.[i] 9Then in the
nations where they have been carried captive, those who escape
will remember me—how I have been grieved[j] by their adulterous
hearts, which have turned away from me, and by their eyes, which
have lusted after their idols.[k] They will loathe themselves for the
evil they have done and for all their detestable practices.[l] 10And
they will know that I am the LORD; I did not threaten in vain to
bring this calamity on them.

11"'This is what the Sovereign LORD says: Strike your hands
together and stamp your feet and cry out "Alas!" because of all the
wicked and detestable practices of the house of Israel, for they will
fall by the sword, famine and plague.[m] 12He that is far away will
die of the plague, and he that is near will fall by the sword, and he
that survives and is spared will die of famine. So will I spend my
wrath upon them.[n] 13And they will know that I am the LORD,
when their people lie slain among their idols around their altars,
on every high hill and on all the mountaintops, under every
spreading tree and every leafy oak[o]—places where they offered fragrant incense to all their idols.[p] 14And I will stretch out my hand[q]
against them and make the land a desolate waste from the desert
to Diblah[a]—wherever they live. Then they will know that I am
the LORD.[r]'"

Chapter 7 Theme ______________________

7

The word of the LORD came to me: 2"Son of man, this is what
the Sovereign LORD says to the land of Israel: The end![s] The
end has come upon the four corners[t] of the land. 3The end is now
upon you and I will unleash my anger against you. I will judge you
according to your conduct and repay you for all your detestable
practices. 4I will not look on you with pity[u] or spare you; I will
surely repay you for your conduct and the detestable practices

a *14* Most Hebrew manuscripts; a few Hebrew manuscripts *Riblah*

6:3 [a] Eze 36:4 [b] Lev 26:30
6:4 [c] 2Ch 14:5
6:5 [d] Jer 8:1-2
6:6 [e] Mic 1:7; Zec 13:2 [f] Lev 26:30 [g] Isa 6:11; Eze 5:14
6:8 [h] Jer 44:28 [i] Isa 6:13; Jer 44:14; Eze 12:16; 14:22
6:9 [j] Ps 78:40; Isa 7:13 [k] Eze 20:7,24 [l] Eze 20:43; 36:31
6:11 [m] Eze 5:12; 21:14,17; 25:6
6:12 [n] Eze 5:12
6:13 [o] Isa 57:5 [p] 1Ki 14:23; Jer 2:20; Eze 20:28; Hos 4:13
6:14 [q] Isa 5:25 [r] Eze 14:13
7:2 [s] Am 8:2,10 [t] Rev 7:1; 20:8
7:4 [u] Eze 5:11

among you. Then you will know that I am the LORD.

5“This is what the Sovereign LORD says: Disaster![a] An unheard-of[a] disaster is coming. 6The end has come! The end has come! It has roused itself against you. It has come! 7Doom has come upon you—you who dwell in the land. The time has come, the day is near;[b] there is panic, not joy, upon the mountains. 8I am about to pour out my wrath[c] on you and spend my anger against you; I will judge you according to your conduct and repay you for all your detestable practices.[d] 9I will not look on you with pity or spare you; I will repay you in accordance with your conduct and the detestable practices among you. Then you will know that it is I the LORD who strikes the blow.

10“The day is here! It has come! Doom has burst forth, the rod[e] has budded, arrogance has blossomed! 11Violence has grown into[b] a rod to punish wickedness; none of the people will be left, none of that crowd—no wealth, nothing of value.[f] 12The time has come, the day has arrived. Let not the buyer rejoice nor the seller grieve, for wrath is upon the whole crowd.[g] 13The seller will not recover the land he has sold as long as both of them live, for the vision concerning the whole crowd will not be reversed. Because of their sins, not one of them will preserve his life.[h] 14Though they blow the trumpet and get everything ready, no one will go into battle, for my wrath is upon the whole crowd.

15“Outside is the sword, inside are plague and famine; those in the country will die by the sword, and those in the city will be devoured by famine and plague.[i] 16All who survive and escape will be in the mountains, moaning like doves[j] of the valleys, each because of his sins.[k] 17Every hand will go limp,[l] and every knee will become as weak as water. 18They will put on sackcloth and be clothed with terror.[m] Their faces will be covered with shame and their heads will be shaved.[n] 19They will throw their silver into the streets, and their gold will be an unclean thing. Their silver and gold will not be able to save them in the day of the LORD’s wrath.[o] They will not satisfy their hunger or fill their stomachs with it, for it has made them stumble[p] into sin.[q] 20They were proud of their beautiful jewelry and used it to make their detestable idols and vile images.[r] Therefore I will turn these into an unclean thing for them. 21I will hand it all over as plunder to foreigners and as loot to the wicked of the earth, and they will defile it.[s] 22I will turn my face[t] away from them, and they will desecrate my treasured place; robbers will enter it and desecrate it.

23“Prepare chains, because the land is full of bloodshed[u] and the city is full of violence. 24I will bring the most wicked of the nations

a5 Most Hebrew manuscripts; some Hebrew manuscripts and Syriac *Disaster after*
b11 Or *The violent one has become*

7:5 [a]2Ki 21:12
7:7 [b]Eze 12:23; Zep 1:14
7:8 [c]Isa 42:25; Eze 9:8; 14:19; Na 1:6 [d]Eze 20:8,21; 36:19
7:10 [e]Ps 89:32; Isa 10:5
7:11 [f]Jer 16:6; Zep 1:18
7:12 [g]ver 7; Isa 5:13-14; Eze 30:3
7:13 [h]Lev 25:24-28
7:15 [i]Dt 32:25; Jer 14:18; La 1:20; Eze 5:12
7:16 [j]Isa 59:11 [k]Ezr 9:15; Eze 6:8
7:17 [l]Isa 13:7; Eze 21:7; 22:14
7:18 [m]Ps 55:5 [n]Isa 15:2-3; Eze 27:31; Am 8:10
7:19 [o]Eze 13:5; Zep 1:7,18 [p]Eze 14:3 [q]Pr 11:4
7:20 [r]Jer 7:30
7:21 [s]2Ki 24:13
7:22 [t]Eze 39:23-24
7:23 [u]2Ki 21:16

to take possession of their houses; I will put an end to the pride
of the mighty, and their sanctuaries[a] will be desecrated.[b] 25When
terror comes, they will seek peace, but there will be none.[c]
26Calamity upon calamity[d] will come, and rumor upon rumor.
They will try to get a vision from the prophet; the teaching of the
law by the priest will be lost, as will the counsel of the elders.[e] 27The
king will mourn, the prince will be clothed with despair,[f] and the
hands of the people of the land will tremble. I will deal with them
according to their conduct,[g] and by their own standards I will
judge them. Then they will know that I am the LORD.[h]"

Chapter 8 Theme ______________________________

592 B.C.

8 In the sixth year, in the sixth month on the fifth day, while I
was sitting in my house and the elders[i] of Judah were sitting
before[j] me, the hand of the Sovereign LORD came upon me there.[k]
2I looked, and I saw a figure like that of a man.[a] From what
appeared to be his waist down he was like fire, and from there up
his appearance was as bright as glowing metal.[l] 3He stretched out
what looked like a hand and took me by the hair of my head. The
Spirit lifted me up[m] between earth and heaven and in visions of
God he took me to Jerusalem, to the entrance to the north gate of
the inner court, where the idol that provokes to jealousy[n] stood.
4And there before me was the glory[o] of the God of Israel, as in the
vision I had seen in the plain.[p]

5Then he said to me, "Son of man, look toward the north." So I
looked, and in the entrance north of the gate of the altar I saw this
idol[q] of jealousy.

6And he said to me, "Son of man, do you see what they are
doing—the utterly detestable[r] things the house of Israel is doing
here, things that will drive me far from my sanctuary? But you will
see things that are even more detestable."

7Then he brought me to the entrance to the court. I looked, and
I saw a hole in the wall. 8He said to me, "Son of man, now dig into
the wall." So I dug into the wall and saw a doorway there.

9And he said to me, "Go in and see the wicked and detestable
things they are doing here." 10So I went in and looked, and I saw
portrayed all over the walls all kinds of crawling things and
detestable animals and all the idols of the house of Israel.[s] 11In
front of them stood seventy elders of the house of Israel, and Jaazaniah son of Shaphan was standing among them. Each had a censer[t]
in his hand, and a fragrant cloud of incense[u] was rising.

12He said to me, "Son of man, have you seen what the elders of
the house of Israel are doing in the darkness, each at the shrine of
his own idol? They say, 'The LORD does not see[v] us; the LORD has

a 2 Or *saw a fiery figure*

7:24 [a] Eze 24:21 [b] 2Ch 7:20; Eze 28:7
7:25 [c] Eze 13:10,16
7:26 [d] Jer 4:20 [e] Isa 47:11; Eze 20:1-3; Mic 3:6
7:27 [f] Ps 109:19; Eze 26:16 [g] Eze 18:20 [h] ver 4
8:1 [i] Eze 14:1 [j] Eze 33:31 [k] Eze 1:1-3
8:2 [l] Eze 1:4,26-27
8:3 [m] Eze 3:12; 11:1 [n] Ex 20:5; Dt 32:16
8:4 [o] Eze 1:28 [p] Eze 3:22
8:5 [q] Ps 78:58; Jer 32:34
8:6 [r] Eze 5:11
8:10 [s] Ex 20:4
8:11 [t] Nu 16:17 [u] Nu 16:35
8:12 [v] Ps 10:11; Isa 29:15; Eze 9:9

forsaken the land.'" 13 Again, he said, "You will see them doing things that are even more detestable."

14 Then he brought me to the entrance to the north gate of the house of the LORD, and I saw women sitting there, mourning for Tammuz. 15 He said to me, "Do you see this, son of man? You will see things that are even more detestable than this."

16 He then brought me into the inner court of the house of the LORD, and there at the entrance to the temple, between the portico and the altar,[a] were about twenty-five men. With their backs toward the temple of the LORD and their faces toward the east, they were bowing down to the sun in the east.[b]

17 He said to me, "Have you seen this, son of man? Is it a trivial matter for the house of Judah to do the detestable things they are doing here? Must they also fill the land with violence[c] and continually provoke me to anger?[d] Look at them putting the branch to their nose! 18 Therefore I will deal with them in anger; I will not look on them with pity[e] or spare them. Although they shout in my ears, I will not listen[f] to them."

Chapter 9 Theme ________________________________

9 Then I heard him call out in a loud voice, "Bring the guards of the city here, each with a weapon in his hand." 2 And I saw six men coming from the direction of the upper gate, which faces north, each with a deadly weapon in his hand. With them was a man clothed in linen[g] who had a writing kit at his side. They came in and stood beside the bronze altar.

3 Now the glory[h] of the God of Israel went up from above the cherubim,[i] where it had been, and moved to the threshold of the temple. Then the LORD called to the man clothed in linen who had the writing kit at his side 4 and said to him, "Go throughout the city of Jerusalem and put a mark[j] on the foreheads of those who grieve and lament[k] over all the detestable things that are done in it.[l]"

5 As I listened, he said to the others, "Follow him through the city and kill, without showing pity[m] or compassion. 6 Slaughter old men, young men and maidens, women and children, but do not touch anyone who has the mark. Begin at my sanctuary." So they began with the elders[n] who were in front of the temple.[o]

7 Then he said to them, "Defile the temple and fill the courts with the slain. Go!" So they went out and began killing throughout the city. 8 While they were killing and I was left alone, I fell facedown,[p] crying out, "Ah, Sovereign LORD! Are you going to destroy the entire remnant of Israel in this outpouring of your wrath on Jerusalem?[q]"

9 He answered me, "The sin of the house of Israel and Judah is exceedingly great; the land is full of bloodshed and the city is full of injustice.[r] They say, 'The LORD has forsaken the land; the LORD

8:16 [a] Joel 2:17 [b] Dt 4:19; 17:3; Job 31:28; Jer 2:27; Eze 11:1,12
8:17 [c] Eze 9:9 [d] Eze 16:26
8:18 [e] Eze 9:10; 24:14 [f] Isa 1:15; Jer 11:11; Mic 3:4; Zec 7:13
9:2 [g] Lev 16:4; Eze 10:2; Rev 15:6
9:3 [h] Eze 10:4 [i] Eze 11:22
9:4 [j] Ex 12:7; 2Co 1:22; Rev 7:3; 9:4 [k] Ps 119:136; Jer 13:17; Eze 21:6 [l] Ps 119:53
9:5 [m] Eze 5:11
9:6 [n] Eze 8:11-13,16 [o] 2Ch 36:17; Jer 25:29; 1Pe 4:17
9:8 [p] Jos 7:6 [q] Eze 11:13; Am 7:1-6
9:9 [r] Eze 22:29

does not see.'[a] 10So I will not look on them with pity[b] or spare them,
but I will bring down on their own heads what they have done.[c]"
11Then the man in linen with the writing kit at his side brought
back word, saying, "I have done as you commanded."

Chapter 10 Theme ______________________________

10 I looked, and I saw the likeness of a throne[d] of sapphire[a][e]
above the expanse[f] that was over the heads of the cherubim.
2The LORD said to the man clothed in linen,[g] "Go in among the
wheels[h] beneath the cherubim. Fill[i] your hands with burning coals
from among the cherubim and scatter them over the city." And as
I watched, he went in.
3Now the cherubim were standing on the south side of the temple when the man went in, and a cloud filled the inner court. 4Then
the glory of the LORD[j] rose from above the cherubim and moved
to the threshold of the temple. The cloud filled the temple, and the
court was full of the radiance of the glory of the LORD. 5The sound
of the wings of the cherubim could be heard as far away as the
outer court, like the voice[k] of God Almighty[b] when he speaks.
6When the LORD commanded the man in linen, "Take fire from
among the wheels, from among the cherubim," the man went in
and stood beside a wheel. 7Then one of the cherubim reached out
his hand to the fire that was among them. He took up some of it
and put it into the hands of the man in linen, who took it and went
out. 8 (Under the wings of the cherubim could be seen what looked
like the hands of a man.)[l]
9I looked, and I saw beside the cherubim four wheels, one beside
each of the cherubim; the wheels sparkled like chrysolite.[m] 10As
for their appearance, the four of them looked alike; each was like
a wheel intersecting a wheel. 11As they moved, they would go in
any one of the four directions the cherubim faced; the wheels did
not turn about[c] as the cherubim went. The cherubim went in
whatever direction the head faced, without turning as they went.
12Their entire bodies, including their backs, their hands and their
wings, were completely full of eyes,[n] as were their four wheels.[o]
13I heard the wheels being called "the whirling wheels." 14Each of
the cherubim[p] had four faces:[q] One face was that of a cherub, the
second the face of a man, the third the face of a lion, and the
fourth the face of an eagle.[r]
15Then the cherubim rose upward. These were the living creatures[s] I had seen by the Kebar River. 16When the cherubim moved,
the wheels beside them moved; and when the cherubim spread
their wings to rise from the ground, the wheels did not leave their
side. 17When the cherubim stood still, they also stood still; and

a *1* Or *lapis lazuli* b *5* Hebrew *El-Shaddai* c *11* Or *aside*

9:9 [a]Job 22:13; Eze 8:12
9:10 [b]Eze 7:4; 8:18 [c]Isa 65:6; Eze 11:21
10:1 [d]Rev 4:2 [e]Ex 24:10 [f]Eze 1:22
10:2 [g]Eze 9:2 [h]Eze 1:15 [i]Rev 8:5
10:4 [j]Eze 1:28; 9:3
10:5 [k]Job 40:9; Eze 1:24
10:8 [l]Eze 1:8
10:9 [m]Eze 1:15-16; Rev 21:20
10:12 [n]Rev 4:6-8 [o]Eze 1:15-21
10:14 [p]1Ki 7:36 [q]Eze 1:6 [r]Eze 1:10; Rev 4:7
10:15 [s]Eze 1:3,5

when the cherubim rose, they rose with them, because the spirit of
the living creatures was in them.[a]
18 Then the glory of the LORD departed from over the threshold of
the temple and stopped above the cherubim.[b] 19 While I watched,
the cherubim spread their wings and rose from the ground, and
as they went, the wheels went with them.[c] They stopped at the
entrance to the east gate of the LORD's house, and the glory of the
God of Israel was above them.
20 These were the living creatures I had seen beneath the God of
Israel by the Kebar River,[d] and I realized that they were cherubim.
21 Each had four faces[e] and four wings,[f] and under their wings was
what looked like the hands of a man. 22 Their faces had the same
appearance as those I had seen by the Kebar River. Each one went
straight ahead.

Chapter 11 Theme ______________________

11 Then the Spirit lifted me up and brought me to the gate of
the house of the LORD that faces east. There at the entrance
to the gate were twenty-five men, and I saw among them Jaazaniah
son of Azzur and Pelatiah son of Benaiah, leaders of the people.[g]
2 The LORD said to me, "Son of man, these are the men who are
plotting evil and giving wicked advice in this city. 3 They say, 'Will
it not soon be time to build houses?[a] This city is a cooking pot,[h]
and we are the meat.'[i] 4 Therefore prophesy[j] against them; prophesy, son of man."
5 Then the Spirit of the LORD came upon me, and he told me to
say: "This is what the LORD says: That is what you are saying, O
house of Israel, but I know what is going through your mind.[k] 6 You
have killed many people in this city and filled its streets with the
dead.[l]
7 "Therefore this is what the Sovereign LORD says: The bodies you
have thrown there are the meat and this city is the pot, but I will
drive you out of it.[m] 8 You fear the sword, and the sword is what I
will bring against you, declares the Sovereign LORD.[n] 9 I will drive
you out of the city and hand you over[o] to foreigners and inflict
punishment on you.[p] 10 You will fall by the sword, and I will execute
judgment on you at the borders of Israel.[q] Then you will know that
I am the LORD. 11 This city will not be a pot[r] for you, nor will you
be the meat in it; I will execute judgment on you at the borders of
Israel. 12 And you will know that I am the LORD, for you have not
followed my decrees[s] or kept my laws but have conformed to the
standards of the nations around you.[t]"

10:17 [a]Eze 1:20-21
10:18 [b]Ps 18:10
10:19 [c]Eze 11:1,22
10:20 [d]Eze 1:1
10:21 [e]Eze 41:18 [f]Eze 1:6
11:1 [g]Eze 8:16; 10:19; 43:4-5
11:3 [h]Jer 1:13; Eze 24:3 [i]ver 7,11
11:4 [j]Eze 3:4,17
11:5 [k]Jer 17:10
11:6 [l]Eze 7:23; 22:6
11:7 [m]Eze 24:3-13; Mic 3:2-3
11:8 [n]Pr 10:24
11:9 [o]Ps 106:41 [p]Dt 28:36; Eze 5:8
11:10 [q]2Ki 14:25
11:11 [r]ver 3
11:12 [s]Lev 18:4; Eze 18:9 [t]Eze 8:10

a3 Or *This is not the time to build houses.*

13 Now as I was prophesying, Pelatiah[a] son of Benaiah died. Then
I fell facedown and cried out in a loud voice, "Ah, Sovereign LORD!
Will you completely destroy the remnant of Israel?[b]"
14 The word of the LORD came to me: 15 "Son of man, your brothers—your brothers who are your blood relatives[a] and the whole
house of Israel—are those of whom the people of Jerusalem have
said, 'They are[b] far away from the LORD; this land was given to us
as our possession.'[c]
16 "Therefore say: 'This is what the Sovereign LORD says: Although
I sent them far away among the nations and scattered them among
the countries, yet for a little while I have been a sanctuary[d] for them
in the countries where they have gone.'
17 "Therefore say: 'This is what the Sovereign LORD says: I will
gather you from the nations and bring you back from the countries
where you have been scattered, and I will give you back the land of
Israel again.'[e]
18 "They will return to it and remove all its vile images[f] and
detestable idols.[g] 19 I will give them an undivided heart[h] and put a
new spirit in them; I will remove from them their heart of stone[i]
and give them a heart of flesh.[j] 20 Then they will follow my decrees
and be careful to keep my laws.[k] They will be my people, and I
will be their God.[l] 21 But as for those whose hearts are devoted to
their vile images and detestable idols, I will bring down on their
own heads what they have done, declares the Sovereign LORD.[m]"
22 Then the cherubim, with the wheels beside them, spread their
wings, and the glory of the God of Israel was above them.[n] 23 The
glory[o] of the LORD went up from within the city and stopped above
the mountain[p] east of it. 24 The Spirit[q] lifted me up and brought me
to the exiles in Babylonia[c] in the vision[r] given by the Spirit of God.
Then the vision I had seen went up from me, 25 and I told the
exiles everything the LORD had shown me.[s]

Chapter 12 Theme

12 The word of the LORD came to me: 2 "Son of man, you are
living among a rebellious people. They have eyes to see but
do not see and ears to hear but do not hear, for they are a rebellious
people.[t]
3 "Therefore, son of man, pack your belongings for exile and in
the daytime, as they watch, set out and go from where you are to
another place. Perhaps[u] they will understand,[v] though they are a
rebellious house.[w] 4 During the daytime, while they watch, bring
out your belongings packed for exile. Then in the evening, while
they are watching, go out like those who go into exile.[x] 5 While

[a] 15 Or *are in exile with you* (see Septuagint and Syriac) [b] 15 Or *those to whom the people of Jerusalem have said, 'Stay* [c] 24 Or *Chaldea*

11:13 [a] ver 1 [b] Eze 9:8
11:15 [c] Eze 33:24
11:16 [d] Ps 90:1; 91:9; Isa 8:14
11:17 [e] Jer 3:18; 24:5-6; Eze 28:25; 34:13
11:18 [f] Eze 5:11 [g] Eze 37:23
11:19 [h] Jer 32:39 [i] Zec 7:12 [j] Eze 18:31; 36:26; 2Co 3:3
11:20 [k] Ps 105:45 [l] Eze 14:11; 36:26-28
11:21 [m] Eze 9:10; 16:43
11:22 [n] Eze 10:19
11:23 [o] Eze 8:4; 10:4 [p] Zec 14:4
11:24 [q] Eze 8:3 [r] 2Co 12:2-4
11:25 [s] Eze 3:4,11
12:2 [t] Isa 6:10; Eze 2:6-8; Mt 13:15
12:3 [u] Jer 36:3 [v] Jer 26:3 [w] 2Ti 2:25-26
12:4 [x] ver 12; Jer 39:4

they watch, dig through the wall and take your belongings out
through it. 6 Put them on your shoulder as they are watching and
carry them out at dusk. Cover your face so that you cannot see the
land, for I have made you a sign[a] to the house of Israel."

7 So I did as I was commanded.[b] During the day I brought out my
things packed for exile. Then in the evening I dug through the wall
with my hands. I took my belongings out at dusk, carrying them
on my shoulders while they watched.

8 In the morning the word of the LORD came to me: 9 "Son of
man, did not that rebellious house of Israel ask you, 'What are
you doing?'[c]

10 "Say to them, 'This is what the Sovereign LORD says: This oracle
concerns the prince in Jerusalem and the whole house of Israel who
are there.' 11 Say to them, 'I am a sign to you.'

"As I have done, so it will be done to them. They will go into exile
as captives.[d]

12 "The prince among them will put his things on his shoulder
at dusk[e] and leave, and a hole will be dug in the wall for him to go
through. He will cover his face so that he cannot see the land.[f] 13 I
will spread my net[g] for him, and he will be caught in my snare;[h] I
will bring him to Babylonia, the land of the Chaldeans, but he will
not see[i] it, and there he will die.[j] 14 I will scatter to the winds all
those around him—his staff and all his troops—and I will pursue
them with drawn sword.[k]

15 "They will know that I am the LORD, when I disperse them
among the nations and scatter them through the countries. 16 But
I will spare a few of them from the sword, famine and plague, so
that in the nations where they go they may acknowledge all their
detestable practices. Then they will know that I am the LORD.[l]"

17 The word of the LORD came to me: 18 "Son of man, tremble as
you eat your food,[m] and shudder in fear as you drink your water.
19 Say to the people of the land: 'This is what the Sovereign LORD
says about those living in Jerusalem and in the land of Israel: They
will eat their food in anxiety and drink their water in despair, for
their land will be stripped of everything[n] in it because of the violence of all who live there.[o] 20 The inhabited towns will be laid
waste and the land will be desolate. Then you will know that I am
the LORD.[p]'"

21 The word of the LORD came to me: 22 "Son of man, what is this
proverb you have in the land of Israel: 'The days go by and every
vision comes to nothing'?[q] 23 Say to them, 'This is what the Sovereign LORD says: I am going to put an end to this proverb, and they
will no longer quote it in Israel.' Say to them, 'The days are near
when every vision will be fulfilled.[r] 24 For there will be no more
false visions or flattering divinations[s] among the people of Israel.

12:6 [a] ver 12; Isa 8:18; 20:3; Eze 4:3; 24:24
12:7 [b] Eze 24:18; 37:10
12:9 [c] Eze 17:12; 20:49; 24:19
12:11 [d] 2Ki 25:7; Jer 15:2; 52:15
12:12 [e] Jer 39:4 [f] Jer 52:7
12:13 [g] Eze 17:20; 19:8; Hos 7:12 [h] Isa 24:17-18 [i] Jer 39:7 [j] Jer 52:11; Eze 17:16
12:14 [k] 2Ki 25:5; Eze 5:10,12
12:16 [l] Jer 22:8-9; Eze 6:8-10; 14:22
12:18 [m] La 5:9; Eze 4:16
12:19 [n] Eze 6:6-14; Mic 7:13; Zec 7:14 [o] Eze 4:16; 23:33
12:20 [p] Isa 7:23-24; Jer 4:7
12:22 [q] Eze 11:3; Am 6:3; 2Pe 3:4
12:23 [r] Ps 37:13; Joel 2:1; Zep 1:14
12:24 [s] Jer 14:14; Eze 13:23; Zec 13:2-4

25 But I the LORD will speak what I will, and it shall be fulfilled
without delay. For in your days, you rebellious house, I will fulfill
whatever I say, declares the Sovereign LORD.[a]'"
26 The word of the LORD came to me: 27 "Son of man, the house of
Israel is saying, 'The vision he sees is for many years from now, and
he prophesies about the distant future.'[b]
28 "Therefore say to them, 'This is what the Sovereign LORD says:
None of my words will be delayed any longer; whatever I say will
be fulfilled, declares the Sovereign LORD.'"

Chapter 13 Theme ______________________________

13 The word of the LORD came to me: 2 "Son of man, prophesy
against the prophets of Israel who are now prophesying.
Say to those who prophesy out of their own imagination: 'Hear the
word of the LORD![c] 3 This is what the Sovereign LORD says: Woe to
the foolish[a] prophets[d] who follow their own spirit and have seen
nothing![e] 4 Your prophets, O Israel, are like jackals among ruins.
5 You have not gone up to the breaks in the wall to repair[f] it for the
house of Israel so that it will stand firm in the battle on the day of
the LORD.[g] 6 Their visions are false and their divinations a lie. They
say, "The LORD declares," when the LORD has not sent them; yet
they expect their words to be fulfilled.[h] 7 Have you not seen false
visions and uttered lying divinations when you say, "The LORD
declares," though I have not spoken?
8 "'Therefore this is what the Sovereign LORD says: Because of
your false words and lying visions, I am against you, declares the
Sovereign LORD. 9 My hand will be against the prophets who see
false visions and utter lying divinations. They will not belong to
the council of my people or be listed in the records[i] of the house
of Israel, nor will they enter the land of Israel. Then you will know
that I am the Sovereign LORD.[j]
10 "'Because they lead my people astray,[k] saying, "Peace," when
there is no peace, and because, when a flimsy wall is built, they
cover it with whitewash,[l] 11 therefore tell those who cover it with
whitewash that it is going to fall. Rain will come in torrents, and I
will send hailstones hurtling down, and violent winds will burst
forth.[m] 12 When the wall collapses, will people not ask you,
"Where is the whitewash you covered it with?"
13 "'Therefore this is what the Sovereign LORD says: In my wrath
I will unleash a violent wind, and in my anger hailstones[n] and torrents of rain will fall with destructive fury.[o] 14 I will tear down the
wall you have covered with whitewash and will level it to the ground
so that its foundation[p] will be laid bare. When it[b] falls,[q] you will

[a]3 Or *wicked* [b]14 Or *the city*

12:25 [a] Isa 14:24; Hab 1:5
12:27 [b] Da 10:14
13:2 [c] ver 17; Jer 23:16; 37:19
13:3 [d] La 2:14 [e] Jer 23:25-32
13:5 [f] Isa 58:12; Eze 22:30 [g] Eze 7:19
13:6 [h] Jer 28:15; Eze 22:28
13:9 [i] Jer 17:13 [j] Eze 20:38
13:10 [k] Jer 50:6 [l] Eze 7:25; 22:28
13:11 [m] Eze 38:22
13:13 [n] Rev 11:19; 16:21 [o] Ex 9:25; Isa 30:30
13:14 [p] Mic 1:6 [q] Jer 6:15

be destroyed in it; and you will know that I am the LORD. 15 So I will spend my wrath against the wall and against those who covered it with whitewash. I will say to you, "The wall is gone and so are those who whitewashed it, 16 those prophets of Israel who prophesied to Jerusalem and saw visions of peace for her when there was no peace, declares the Sovereign LORD.[a]" '

17 "Now, son of man, set your face against the daughters[b] of your people who prophesy out of their own imagination. Prophesy against them[c] 18 and say, 'This is what the Sovereign LORD says: Woe to the women who sew magic charms on all their wrists and make veils of various lengths for their heads in order to ensnare people. Will you ensnare the lives of my people but preserve your own? 19 You have profaned[d] me among my people for a few handfuls of barley and scraps of bread. By lying to my people, who listen to lies, you have killed those who should not have died and have spared those who should not live.[e]

20 " 'Therefore this is what the Sovereign LORD says: I am against your magic charms with which you ensnare people like birds and I will tear them from your arms; I will set free the people that you ensnare like birds. 21 I will tear off your veils and save my people from your hands, and they will no longer fall prey to your power. Then you will know that I am the LORD.[f] 22 Because you disheartened the righteous with your lies, when I had brought them no grief, and because you encouraged the wicked not to turn from their evil ways and so save their lives,[g] 23 therefore you will no longer see false visions or practice divination.[h] I will save my people from your hands. And then you will know that I am the LORD.[i] ' "

Chapter 14 Theme ____________________________

14 Some of the elders of Israel came to me and sat down in front of me.[j] 2 Then the word of the LORD came to me: 3 "Son of man, these men have set up idols in their hearts and put wicked stumbling blocks[k] before their faces. Should I let them inquire of me at all?[l] 4 Therefore speak to them and tell them, 'This is what the Sovereign LORD says: When any Israelite sets up idols in his heart and puts a wicked stumbling block before his face and then goes to a prophet, I the LORD will answer him myself in keeping with his great idolatry. 5 I will do this to recapture the hearts of the people of Israel, who have all deserted[m] me for their idols.'[n]

6 "Therefore say to the house of Israel, 'This is what the Sovereign LORD says: Repent! Turn from your idols and renounce all your detestable practices![o]

7 " 'When any Israelite or any alien[p] living in Israel separates himself from me and sets up idols in his heart and puts a wicked stumbling block before his face and then goes to a prophet to

13:16 [a]Isa 57:21; Jer 6:14
13:17 [b]Rev 2:20 [c]ver 2
13:19 [d]Eze 20:39; 22:26 [e]Pr 28:21
13:21 [f]Ps 91:3
13:22 [g]Jer 23:14; Eze 33:14-16
13:23 [h]ver 6; Eze 12:24 [i]Mic 3:6
14:1 [j]Eze 8:1; 20:1
14:3 [k]ver 7; Eze 7:19 [l]Isa 1:15; Eze 20:31
14:5 [m]Zec 11:8 [n]Jer 2:11
14:6 [o]Isa 2:20; 30:22
14:7 [p]Ex 12:48; 20:10

inquire of me, I the LORD will answer him myself. 8 I will set my face
against[a] that man and make him an example and a byword.[b] I will
cut him off from my people. Then you will know that I am the
LORD.

9 "'And if the prophet[c] is enticed[d] to utter a prophecy, I the
LORD have enticed that prophet, and I will stretch out my hand
against him and destroy him from among my people Israel.[e]
10 They will bear their guilt—the prophet will be as guilty as the
one who consults him. 11 Then the people of Israel will no longer
stray[f] from me, nor will they defile themselves anymore with all
their sins. They will be my people, and I will be their God,
declares the Sovereign LORD.[g]'"

12 The word of the LORD came to me: 13 "Son of man, if a country
sins against me by being unfaithful and I stretch out my hand
against it to cut off its food supply[h] and send famine upon it and
kill its men and their animals,[i] 14 even if these three men—Noah,[j]
Daniel[a][k] and Job[l]—were in it, they could save only themselves
by their righteousness,[m] declares the Sovereign LORD.

15 "Or if I send wild beasts[n] through that country and they leave it
childless and it becomes desolate so that no one can pass through
it because of the beasts,[o] 16 as surely as I live, declares the Sovereign
LORD, even if these three men were in it, they could not save their
own sons or daughters. They alone would be saved, but the land
would be desolate.[p]

17 "Or if I bring a sword[q] against that country and say, 'Let the
sword pass throughout the land,' and I kill its men and their animals,[r] 18 as surely as I live, declares the Sovereign LORD, even if
these three men were in it, they could not save their own sons or
daughters. They alone would be saved.

19 "Or if I send a plague into that land and pour out my wrath[s]
upon it through bloodshed, killing its men and their animals,[t] 20 as
surely as I live, declares the Sovereign LORD, even if Noah, Daniel
and Job were in it, they could save neither son nor daughter. They
would save only themselves by their righteousness.[u]

21 "For this is what the Sovereign LORD says: How much worse will
it be when I send against Jerusalem my four dreadful judgments—
sword and famine and wild beasts and plague—to kill its men
and their animals![v] 22 Yet there will be some survivors—sons and
daughters who will be brought out of it.[w] They will come to you,
and when you see their conduct[x] and their actions, you will be consoled regarding the disaster I have brought upon Jerusalem—every
disaster I have brought upon it. 23 You will be consoled when you
see their conduct and their actions, for you will know that I have
done nothing in it without cause, declares the Sovereign LORD.[y]"

a *14* Or *Danel*; the Hebrew spelling may suggest a person other than the prophet Daniel; also in verse 20.

14:8
[a] Eze 15:7
[b] Eze 5:15

14:9
[c] Jer 14:15
[d] Jer 4:10
[e] 1Ki 22:23

14:11
[f] Eze 48:11
[g] Eze 11:19-20; 37:23

14:13
[h] Lev 26:26
[i] Eze 5:16; 6:14; 15:8

14:14
[j] Ge 6:8
[k] ver 20; Eze 28:3; Da 1:6; 6:13
[l] Job 1:1
[m] Job 42:9; Jer 15:1; Eze 18:20

14:15
[n] Eze 5:17
[o] Lev 26:22

14:16
[p] Eze 18:20

14:17
[q] Lev 26:25; Eze 5:12; 21:3-4
[r] Eze 25:13; Zep 1:3

14:19
[s] Eze 7:8
[t] Eze 38:22

14:20
[u] ver 14

14:21
[v] Jer 15:3; Eze 5:17; 33:27; Am 4:6-10; Rev 6:8

14:22
[w] Eze 12:16
[x] Eze 20:43

14:23
[y] Jer 22:8-9

Chapter 15 Theme ______________________________

15 The word of the LORD came to me: 2"Son of man, how is the wood of a vine[a] better than that of a branch on any of the trees in the forest? 3Is wood ever taken from it to make anything useful? Do they make pegs from it to hang things on? 4And after it is thrown on the fire as fuel and the fire burns both ends and chars the middle, is it then useful for anything?[b] 5If it was not useful for anything when it was whole, how much less can it be made into something useful when the fire has burned it and it is charred?

6"Therefore this is what the Sovereign LORD says: As I have given the wood of the vine among the trees of the forest as fuel for the fire, so will I treat the people living in Jerusalem. 7I will set my face against[c] them. Although they have come out of the fire, the fire will yet consume them. And when I set my face against them, you will know that I am the LORD.[d] 8I will make the land desolate[e] because they have been unfaithful,[f] declares the Sovereign LORD."

Chapter 16 Theme ______________________________

16 The word of the LORD came to me: 2"Son of man, confront Jerusalem with her detestable practices[g] 3and say, 'This is what the Sovereign LORD says to Jerusalem: Your ancestry[h] and birth were in the land of the Canaanites; your father was an Amorite and your mother a Hittite.[i] 4On the day you were born[j] your cord was not cut, nor were you washed with water to make you clean, nor were you rubbed with salt or wrapped in cloths. 5No one looked on you with pity or had compassion enough to do any of these things for you. Rather, you were thrown out into the open field, for on the day you were born you were despised.

6" 'Then I passed by and saw you kicking about in your blood, and as you lay there in your blood I said to you, "Live!"[a][k] 7I made you grow[l] like a plant of the field. You grew up and developed and became the most beautiful of jewels.[b] Your breasts were formed and your hair grew, you who were naked and bare.[m]

8" 'Later I passed by, and when I looked at you and saw that you were old enough for love, I spread the corner of my garment[n] over you and covered your nakedness. I gave you my solemn oath and entered into a covenant with you, declares the Sovereign LORD, and you became mine.[o]

9" 'I bathed[c] you with water and washed[p] the blood from you and put ointments on you. 10I clothed you with an embroidered[q] dress and put leather sandals on you. I dressed you in fine linen[r] and covered you with costly garments.[s] 11I adorned you with jewelry:[t]

[a]6 A few Hebrew manuscripts, Septuagint and Syriac; most Hebrew manuscripts *"Live!" And as you lay there in your blood I said to you, "Live!"* [b]7 Or *became mature* [c]9 Or *I had bathed*

15:2 [a]Isa 5:1-7; Jer 2:21; Hos 10:1
15:4 [b]Eze 19:14; Jn 15:6
15:7 [c]Ps 34:16; Eze 14:8 [d]Isa 24:18; Am 9:1-4
15:8 [e]Eze 14:13 [f]Eze 17:20
16:2 [g]Eze 20:4; 22:2
16:3 [h]Eze 21:30 [i]ver 45
16:4 [j]Hos 2:3
16:6 [k]Ex 19:4
16:7 [l]Dt 1:10 [m]Ex 1:7
16:8 [n]Ru 3:9 [o]Jer 2:2; Hos 2:7,19-20
16:9 [p]Ru 3:3
16:10 [q]Ex 26:36 [r]Eze 27:16 [s]ver 18
16:11 [t]Eze 23:40

I put bracelets[a] on your arms and a necklace[b] around your neck,
12and I put a ring on your nose,[c] earrings on your ears and a beautiful crown[d] on your head. 13So you were adorned with gold and
silver; your clothes were of fine linen and costly fabric and embroidered cloth. Your food was fine flour, honey and olive oil.[e] You
became very beautiful and rose to be a queen.[f] 14And your fame[g]
spread among the nations on account of your beauty,[h] because the
splendor I had given you made your beauty perfect, declares the
Sovereign LORD.

15" 'But you trusted in your beauty and used your fame to
become a prostitute. You lavished your favors on anyone who
passed by[i] and your beauty became his.[a] [j] 16You took some of your
garments to make gaudy high places, where you carried on your
prostitution.[k] Such things should not happen, nor should they ever
occur. 17You also took the fine jewelry I gave you, the jewelry made
of my gold and silver, and you made for yourself male idols and
engaged in prostitution with them.[l] 18And you took your embroidered clothes to put on them, and you offered my oil and incense
before them. 19Also the food I provided for you—the fine flour,
olive oil and honey I gave you to eat—you offered as fragrant
incense before them. That is what happened, declares the Sovereign LORD.[m]

20" 'And you took your sons and daughters[n] whom you bore to
me[o] and sacrificed them as food to the idols. Was your prostitution
not enough?[p] 21You slaughtered my children and sacrificed
them[b] to the idols.[q] 22In all your detestable practices and your
prostitution you did not remember the days of your youth,[r] when
you were naked and bare, kicking about in your blood.[s]

23" 'Woe! Woe to you, declares the Sovereign LORD. In addition to
all your other wickedness, 24you built a mound for yourself and
made a lofty shrine[t] in every public square.[u] 25At the head of every
street you built your lofty shrines and degraded your beauty, offering your body with increasing promiscuity to anyone who passed
by.[v] 26You engaged in prostitution with the Egyptians, your lustful neighbors, and provoked[w] me to anger with your increasing
promiscuity.[x] 27So I stretched out my hand[y] against you and
reduced your territory; I gave you over to the greed of your enemies, the daughters of the Philistines,[z] who were shocked by your
lewd conduct. 28You engaged in prostitution with the Assyrians[a]
too, because you were insatiable; and even after that, you still were
not satisfied. 29Then you increased your promiscuity to include
Babylonia,[c] [b] a land of merchants, but even with this you were
not satisfied.

[a] *15* Most Hebrew manuscripts; one Hebrew manuscript (see some Septuagint manuscripts) *by. Such a thing should not happen* [b] *21* Or *and made them pass through ⌞the fire⌟* [c] *29* Or *Chaldea*

16:11 [a] Isa 3:19; Eze 23:42 [b] Ge 41:42
16:12 [c] Isa 3:21 [d] Isa 28:5; Jer 13:18
16:13 [e] 1Sa 10:1 [f] Dt 32:13-14; 1Ki 4:21
16:14 [g] 1Ki 10:24 [h] La 2:15
16:15 [i] ver 25 [j] Isa 57:8; Jer 2:20; Eze 23:3; 27:3
16:16 [k] 2Ki 23:7
16:17 [l] Eze 7:20
16:19 [m] Hos 2:8
16:20 [n] Jer 7:31 [o] Ex 13:2 [p] Ps 106:37-38; Isa 57:5; Eze 23:37
16:21 [q] 2Ki 17:17; Jer 19:5
16:22 [r] Jer 2:2; Hos 11:1 [s] ver 6
16:24 [t] ver 31; Isa 57:7 [u] Ps 78:58; Jer 2:20; 3:2; Eze 20:28
16:25 [v] ver 15; Pr 9:14
16:26 [w] Eze 8:17 [x] Eze 20:8; 23:19-21
16:27 [y] Eze 20:33 [z] 2Ch 28:18
16:28 [a] 2Ki 16:7
16:29 [b] Eze 23:14-17

30 “ ‘How weak-willed you are, declares the Sovereign LORD, when
you do all these things, acting like a brazen prostitute![a] 31 When
you built your mounds at the head of every street and made your
lofty shrines[b] in every public square, you were unlike a prostitute,
because you scorned payment.

32 “ ‘You adulterous wife! You prefer strangers to your own husband! 33 Every prostitute receives a fee, but you give gifts[c] to all your
lovers, bribing them to come to you from everywhere for your illicit
favors.[d] 34 So in your prostitution you are the opposite of others; no
one runs after you for your favors. You are the very opposite, for
you give payment and none is given to you.

35 “ ‘Therefore, you prostitute, hear the word of the LORD! 36 This
is what the Sovereign LORD says: Because you poured out your
wealth[a] and exposed your nakedness in your promiscuity with
your lovers, and because of all your detestable idols, and because
you gave them your children’s blood,[e] 37 therefore I am going to
gather all your lovers, with whom you found pleasure, those you
loved as well as those you hated. I will gather them against you
from all around and will strip you in front of them, and they will
see all your nakedness.[f] 38 I will sentence you to the punishment of
women who commit adultery and who shed blood;[g] I will bring
upon you the blood vengeance of my wrath and jealous anger.[h]
39 Then I will hand you over to your lovers, and they will tear down
your mounds and destroy your lofty shrines. They will strip you of
your clothes and take your fine jewelry and leave you naked and
bare.[i] 40 They will bring a mob against you, who will stone[j] you
and hack you to pieces with their swords. 41 They will burn down[k]
your houses and inflict punishment on you in the sight of many
women.[l] I will put a stop[m] to your prostitution, and you will no
longer pay your lovers. 42 Then my wrath against you will subside
and my jealous anger will turn away from you; I will be calm and
no longer angry.[n]

43 “ ‘Because you did not remember[o] the days of your youth but
enraged me with all these things, I will surely bring down[p] on your
head what you have done, declares the Sovereign LORD. Did you
not add lewdness to all your other detestable practices?[q]

44 “ ‘Everyone who quotes proverbs will quote this proverb about
you: “Like mother, like daughter.” 45 You are a true daughter of your
mother, who despised her husband and her children; and you are
a true sister of your sisters, who despised their husbands and their
children. Your mother was a Hittite and your father an Amorite.[r]
46 Your older sister was Samaria, who lived to the north of you with
her daughters; and your younger sister, who lived to the south of
you with her daughters, was Sodom.[s] 47 You not only walked in
their ways and copied their detestable practices, but in all your

a 36 Or *lust*

16:30 [a] Jer 3:3
16:31 [b] ver 24
16:33 [c] Isa 30:6; 57:9 [d] Hos 8:9-10
16:36 [e] Jer 19:5; Eze 23:10
16:37 [f] Jer 13:22
16:38 [g] Eze 23:45 [h] Lev 20:10; Eze 23:25
16:39 [i] Eze 23:26; Hos 2:3
16:40 [j] Jn 8:5,7
16:41 [k] Dt 13:16 [l] Eze 23:10 [m] Eze 23:27,48
16:42 [n] Isa 54:9; Eze 5:13; 39:29
16:43 [o] Ps 78:42 [p] Eze 22:31 [q] ver 22; Eze 11:21
16:45 [r] Eze 23:2
16:46 [s] Ge 13:10-13; Eze 23:4

ways you soon became more depraved than they.[a] 48As surely as I
live, declares the Sovereign LORD, your sister Sodom and her
daughters never did what you and your daughters have done.[b]
49"'Now this was the sin of your sister Sodom:[c] She and her
daughters were arrogant,[d] overfed and unconcerned; they did not
help the poor and needy.[e] 50They were haughty and did detestable
things before me. Therefore I did away with them as you have
seen.[f] 51Samaria did not commit half the sins you did. You have
done more detestable things than they, and have made your sisters
seem righteous by all these things you have done.[g] 52Bear your disgrace, for you have furnished some justification for your sisters.
Because your sins were more vile than theirs, they appear more
righteous than you. So then, be ashamed and bear your disgrace,
for you have made your sisters appear righteous.
53"'However, I will restore[h] the fortunes of Sodom and her
daughters and of Samaria and her daughters, and your fortunes
along with them, 54so that you may bear your disgrace[i] and be
ashamed of all you have done in giving them comfort. 55And
your sisters, Sodom with her daughters and Samaria with her
daughters, will return to what they were before; and you and
your daughters will return to what you were before.[j] 56You would
not even mention your sister Sodom in the day of your pride,
57before your wickedness was uncovered. Even so, you are now
scorned by the daughters of Edom[a] [k] and all her neighbors and
the daughters of the Philistines—all those around you who despise you. 58You will bear the consequences of your lewdness and
your detestable practices, declares the LORD.[l]
59"'This is what the Sovereign LORD says: I will deal with you as
you deserve, because you have despised my oath by breaking the
covenant.[m] 60Yet I will remember the covenant I made with you in
the days of your youth, and I will establish an everlasting covenant[n]
with you. 61Then you will remember your ways and be ashamed[o]
when you receive your sisters, both those who are older than you
and those who are younger. I will give them to you as daughters, but
not on the basis of my covenant with you. 62So I will establish my
covenant with you, and you will know that I am the LORD.[p] 63Then,
when I make atonement[q] for you for all you have done, you will
remember and be ashamed and never again open your mouth[r]
because of your humiliation, declares the Sovereign LORD.[s]'"

Chapter 17 Theme

17 The word of the LORD came to me: 2"Son of man, set forth
an allegory and tell the house of Israel a parable.[t] 3Say to
them, 'This is what the Sovereign LORD says: A great eagle[u] with

[a]57 Many Hebrew manuscripts and Syriac; most Hebrew manuscripts, Septuagint and Vulgate *Aram*

16:47 [a]2Ki 21:9; Eze 5:7
16:48 [b]Mt 10:15; 11:23-24
16:49 [c]Ge 13:13 [d]Ps 138:6 [e]Eze 18:7,12,16; Lk 12:16-20
16:50 [f]Ge 18:20-21; 19:5
16:51 [g]Jer 3:8-11
16:53 [h]Isa 19:24-25
16:54 [i]Jer 2:26; Eze 14:22
16:55 [j]Mal 3:4
16:57 [k]2Ki 16:6
16:58 [l]Eze 23:49
16:59 [m]Eze 17:19
16:60 [n]Jer 32:40; Eze 37:26
16:61 [o]Eze 20:43
16:62 [p]Jer 24:7; Eze 20:37, 43-44; Hos 2:19-20
16:63 [q]Ps 65:3; 79:9 [r]Ro 3:19 [s]Ps 39:9; Da 9:7-8
17:2 [t]Eze 20:49
17:3 [u]Hos 8:1

powerful wings, long feathers and full plumage of varied colors
came to Lebanon.[a] Taking hold of the top of a cedar, 4he broke off
its topmost shoot and carried it away to a land of merchants, where
he planted it in a city of traders.
5"'He took some of the seed of your land and put it in fertile
soil. He planted it like a willow by abundant water,[b] 6and it
sprouted and became a low, spreading vine. Its branches turned
toward him, but its roots remained under it. So it became a vine
and produced branches and put out leafy boughs.
7"'But there was another great eagle with powerful wings and
full plumage. The vine now sent out its roots toward him from the
plot where it was planted and stretched out its branches to him for
water.[c] 8It had been planted in good soil by abundant water so that
it would produce branches, bear fruit and become a splendid vine.'
9"Say to them, 'This is what the Sovereign LORD says: Will it
thrive? Will it not be uprooted and stripped of its fruit so that it
withers? All its new growth will wither. It will not take a strong
arm or many people to pull it up by the roots. 10Even if it[d] is trans-
planted, will it thrive? Will it not wither completely when the east
wind strikes it—wither away in the plot where it grew?'"
11Then the word of the LORD came to me: 12"Say to this rebellious
house, 'Do you not know what these things mean?[e]' Say to them:
'The king of Babylon went to Jerusalem and carried off her king
and her nobles,[f] bringing them back with him to Babylon.[g] 13Then
he took a member of the royal family and made a treaty with him,
putting him under oath.[h] He also carried away the leading men of
the land, 14so that the kingdom would be brought low,[i] unable to
rise again, surviving only by keeping his treaty. 15But the king
rebelled[j] against him by sending his envoys to Egypt to get horses
and a large army.[k] Will he succeed? Will he who does such things
escape? Will he break the treaty and yet escape?[l]
16"'As surely as I live, declares the Sovereign LORD, he shall die[m]
in Babylon, in the land of the king who put him on the throne,
whose oath he despised and whose treaty he broke.[n] 17Pharaoh[o]
with his mighty army and great horde will be of no help to him in
war, when ramps[p] are built and siege works erected to destroy
many lives.[q] 18He despised the oath by breaking the covenant. Because he had given his hand in pledge[r] and yet did all these
things, he shall not escape.
19"'Therefore this is what the Sovereign LORD says: As surely as I
live, I will bring down on his head my oath that he despised and
my covenant that he broke.[s] 20I will spread my net[t] for him, and he
will be caught in my snare. I will bring him to Babylon and execute
judgment[u] upon him there because he was unfaithful to me. 21All
his fleeing troops will fall by the sword,[v] and the survivors[w] will

17:3 [a]Jer 22:23
17:5 [b]Dt 8:7-9; Isa 44:4
17:7 [c]Eze 31:4
17:10 [d]Hos 13:15
17:12 [e]Eze 12:9 [f]2Ki 24:15 [g]Eze 24:19
17:13 [h]2Ch 36:13
17:14 [i]Eze 29:14
17:15 [j]Jer 52:3 [k]Dt 17:16 [l]Jer 34:3; 38:18
17:16 [m]Jer 52:11; Eze 12:13 [n]2Ki 24:17
17:17 [o]Jer 37:7 [p]Eze 4:2 [q]Isa 36:6; Jer 37:5; Eze 29:6-7
17:18 [r]1Ch 29:24
17:19 [s]Eze 16:59
17:20 [t]Eze 12:13; 32:3 [u]Jer 2:35; Eze 20:36
17:21 [v]Eze 12:14 [w]2Ki 25:11

be scattered to the winds.[a] Then you will know that I the LORD
have spoken.

22"'This is what the Sovereign LORD says: I myself will take a
shoot from the very top of a cedar and plant it; I will break off a
tender sprig from its topmost shoots and plant it on a high and
lofty mountain.[b] 23On the mountain heights of Israel I will plant
it; it will produce branches and bear fruit and become a splendid
cedar. Birds of every kind will nest in it; they will find shelter in the
shade of its branches.[c] 24All the trees of the field[d] will know that I
the LORD bring down the tall tree and make the low tree grow tall.
I dry up the green tree and make the dry tree flourish.

"'I the LORD have spoken, and I will do it.[e]'"

Chapter 18 Theme

18 The word of the LORD came to me: 2"What do you people
mean by quoting this proverb about the land of Israel:

"'The fathers eat sour grapes,
and the children's teeth are set on edge'?[f]

3"As surely as I live, declares the Sovereign LORD, you will no
longer quote this proverb in Israel. 4For every living soul belongs
to me, the father as well as the son—both alike belong to me. The
soul who sins is the one who will die.[g]

5"Suppose there is a righteous man
who does what is just and right.
6He does not eat at the mountain[h] shrines
or look to the idols[i] of the house of Israel.
He does not defile his neighbor's wife
or lie with a woman during her period.
7He does not oppress[j] anyone,
but returns what he took in pledge[k] for a loan.
He does not commit robbery
but gives his food to the hungry
and provides clothing for the naked.[l]
8He does not lend at usury
or take excessive interest.[a][m]
He withholds his hand from doing wrong
and judges fairly[n] between man and man.
9He follows my decrees
and faithfully keeps my laws.
That man is righteous;[o]
he will surely live,[p]
declares the Sovereign LORD.

[a]8 Or *take interest*; similarly in verses 13 and 17

17:21 [a] 2Ki 25:5
17:22 [b] Jer 23:5; Eze 20:40; 36:1,36; 37:22
17:23 [c] Ps 92:12; Isa 2:2; Eze 31:6; Da 4:12; Hos 14:5-7; Mt 13:32
17:24 [d] Ps 96:12 [e] Eze 19:12; 21:26; 22:14; Am 9:11
18:2 [f] Isa 3:15; Jer 31:29; La 5:7
18:4 [g] ver 20; Isa 42:5; Ro 6:23
18:6 [h] Eze 22:9 [i] Dt 4:19; Eze 6:13; 20:24
18:7 [j] Ex 22:21 [k] Ex 22:26; Dt 24:12 [l] Dt 15:11; Mt 25:36
18:8 [m] Ex 22:25; Lev 25:35-37; Dt 23:19-20 [n] Zec 8:16
18:9 [o] Hab 2:4 [p] Lev 18:5; Eze 20:11; Am 5:4

18:10 [a]Ex 21:12

10“Suppose he has a violent son, who sheds blood[a] or does any of
these other things[a] 11(though the father has done none of them):

“He eats at the mountain shrines.
He defiles his neighbor’s wife.

18:12 [b]Am 4:1 [c]2Ki 21:11; Isa 59:6-7; Jer 22:17; Eze 8:6,17

12He oppresses the poor[b] and needy.
He commits robbery.
He does not return what he took in pledge.
He looks to the idols.
He does detestable things.[c]
13He lends at usury and takes excessive interest.[d]

18:13 [d]Ex 22:25 [e]Eze 33:4-5

Will such a man live? He will not! Because he has done all these
detestable things, he will surely be put to death and his blood will
be on his own head.[e]
14“But suppose this son has a son who sees all the sins his father
commits, and though he sees them, he does not do such things:[f]

18:14 [f]2Ch 34:21; Pr 23:24

15“He does not eat at the mountain shrines
or look to the idols of the house of Israel.
He does not defile his neighbor’s wife.
16He does not oppress anyone
or require a pledge for a loan.

18:16 [g]Ps 41:1; Isa 58:10

He does not commit robbery
but gives his food to the hungry
and provides clothing for the naked.[g]
17He withholds his hand from sin[b]
and takes no usury or excessive interest.
He keeps my laws and follows my decrees.

18:19 [h]Ex 20:5; Dt 5:9; Jer 15:4; Zec 1:3-6

He will not die for his father’s sin; he will surely live. 18But his father
will die for his own sin, because he practiced extortion, robbed his
brother and did what was wrong among his people.
19“Yet you ask, ‘Why does the son not share the guilt of his
father?’ Since the son has done what is just and right and has been
careful to keep all my decrees, he will surely live.[h] 20The soul who
sins is the one who will die. The son will not share the guilt of the
father, nor will the father share the guilt of the son. The righteousness of the righteous man will be credited to him, and the wickedness of the wicked will be charged against him.[i]

18:20 [i]Dt 24:16; 1Ki 8:32; 2Ki 14:6; Isa 3:11; Mt 16:27; Ro 2:9

21“But if a wicked man turns away from all the sins he has
committed and keeps all my decrees and does what is just and right,
he will surely live; he will not die.[j] 22None of the offenses he has
committed will be remembered against him. Because of the righteous things he has done, he will live.[k] 23Do I take any pleasure in

18:21 [j]Eze 33:12,19

18:22 [k]Ps 18:20-24; Isa 43:25; Mic 7:19

[a] 10 Or *things to a brother* [b] 17 Septuagint (see also verse 8); Hebrew *from the poor*

the death of the wicked? declares the Sovereign LORD. Rather, am I
not pleased[a] when they turn from their ways and live?[b]
24"But if a righteous man turns from his righteousness and
commits sin and does the same detestable things the wicked man
does, will he live? None of the righteous things he has done will
be remembered. Because of the unfaithfulness he is guilty of and
because of the sins he has committed, he will die.[c]
25"Yet you say, 'The way of the Lord is not just.' Hear, O house of
Israel: Is my way unjust?[d] Is it not your ways that are unjust? 26If a
righteous man turns from his righteousness and commits sin, he
will die for it; because of the sin he has committed he will die. 27But
if a wicked man turns away from the wickedness he has committed
and does what is just and right, he will save his life.[e] 28Because he
considers all the offenses he has committed and turns away from
them, he will surely live; he will not die. 29Yet the house of Israel
says, 'The way of the Lord is not just.' Are my ways unjust, O house
of Israel? Is it not your ways that are unjust?
30"Therefore, O house of Israel, I will judge you, each one according to his ways, declares the Sovereign LORD. Repent![f] Turn away
from all your offenses; then sin will not be your downfall.[g] 31Rid
yourselves of all the offenses you have committed, and get a new
heart[h] and a new spirit. Why will you die, O house of Israel?[i]
32For I take no pleasure in the death of anyone, declares the Sovereign LORD. Repent and live![j]

Chapter 19 Theme ________________________

19 "Take up a lament[k] concerning the princes[l] of Israel 2and
say:

"'What a lioness was your mother
among the lions!
She lay down among the young lions
and reared her cubs.
3She brought up one of her cubs,
and he became a strong lion.
He learned to tear the prey
and he devoured men.
4The nations heard about him,
and he was trapped in their pit.
They led him with hooks
to the land of Egypt.[m]
5"'When she saw her hope unfulfilled,
her expectation gone,
she took another of her cubs

18:23 [a]Ps 147:11 [b]Eze 33:11; 1Ti 2:4
18:24 [c]1Sa 15:11; 2Ch 24:17-20; Eze 3:20; 20:27; 2Pe 2:20-22
18:25 [d]Ge 18:25; Jer 12:1; Eze 33:17; Zep 3:5; Mal 2:17; 3:13-15
18:27 [e]Isa 1:18
18:30 [f]Mt 3:2 [g]Eze 7:3; 33:20; Hos 12:6
18:31 [h]Ps 51:10 [i]Isa 1:16-17; Eze 11:19; 36:26
18:32 [j]Eze 33:11
19:1 [k]Eze 26:17; 27:2,32 [l]2Ki 24:6
19:4 [m]2Ki 23:33-34; 2Ch 36:4

and made him a strong lion.[a]
[6]He prowled among the lions,
for he was now a strong lion.
He learned to tear the prey
and he devoured men.[b]
[7]He broke down[a] their strongholds
and devastated[c] their towns.
The land and all who were in it
were terrified by his roaring.
[8]Then the nations[d] came against him,
those from regions round about.
They spread their net for him,
and he was trapped in their pit.[e]
[9]With hooks they pulled him into a cage
and brought him to the king of Babylon.[f]
They put him in prison,
so his roar was heard no longer
on the mountains of Israel.[g]

[10]" 'Your mother was like a vine in your vineyard[b]
planted by the water;
it was fruitful and full of branches
because of abundant water.[h]
[11]Its branches were strong,
fit for a ruler's scepter.
It towered high
above the thick foliage,
conspicuous for its height
and for its many branches.[i]
[12]But it was uprooted[j] in fury
and thrown to the ground.
The east wind made it shrivel,
it was stripped of its fruit;
its strong branches withered
and fire consumed them.[k]
[13]Now it is planted in the desert,[l]
in a dry and thirsty land.[m]
[14]Fire spread from one of its main[c] branches
and consumed[n] its fruit.
No strong branch is left on it
fit for a ruler's scepter.'[o]
This is a lament and is to be used as a lament."

19:5 *a* 2Ki 23:34
19:6 *b* 2Ki 24:9; 2Ch 36:9
19:7 *c* Eze 30:12
19:8 *d* 2Ki 24:2 *e* 2Ki 24:11
19:9 *f* 2Ch 36:6 *g* 2Ki 24:15
19:10 *h* Ps 80:8-11
19:11 *i* Eze 31:3; Da 4:11
19:12 *j* Eze 17:10 *k* Isa 27:11; Eze 28:17; Hos 13:15
19:13 *l* Eze 20:35 *m* Hos 2:3
19:14 *n* Eze 20:47 *o* Eze 15:4

a *7* Targum (see Septuagint); Hebrew *He knew* b *10* Two Hebrew manuscripts; most Hebrew manuscripts *your blood* c *14* Or *from under its*

Chapter 20 Theme ______________________________

591 B.C. **20** In the seventh year, in the fifth month on the tenth day,
some of the elders of Israel came to inquire of the LORD,
and they sat down in front of me.[a]
2 Then the word of the LORD came to me: 3 "Son of man, speak
to the elders of Israel and say to them, 'This is what the Sovereign
LORD says: Have you come to inquire[b] of me? As surely as I live, I
will not let you inquire of me, declares the Sovereign LORD.[c]'
4 "Will you judge them? Will you judge them, son of man? Then
confront them with the detestable practices of their fathers[d] 5 and
say to them: 'This is what the Sovereign LORD says: On the day I
chose[e] Israel, I swore with uplifted hand to the descendants of the
house of Jacob and revealed myself to them in Egypt. With uplifted
hand I said to them, "I am the LORD your God.[f]" 6 On that day I
swore to them that I would bring them out of Egypt into a land I
had searched out for them, a land flowing with milk and honey,[g]
the most beautiful of all lands.[h] 7 And I said to them, "Each of you,
get rid of the vile images[i] you have set your eyes on, and do not
defile yourselves with the idols of Egypt. I am the LORD your God.[j]"
8 " 'But they rebelled against me and would not listen to me; they
did not get rid of the vile images they had set their eyes on, nor
did they forsake the idols of Egypt.[k] So I said I would pour out my
wrath on them and spend my anger against them in Egypt.[l] 9 But
for the sake of my name I did what would keep it from being profaned in the eyes of the nations they lived among and in whose
sight I had revealed myself to the Israelites by bringing them out of
Egypt.[m] 10 Therefore I led them out of Egypt and brought them into
the desert.[n] 11 I gave them my decrees and made known to them
my laws, for the man who obeys them will live by them.[o] 12 Also I
gave them my Sabbaths as a sign[p] between us, so they would
know that I the LORD made them holy.
13 " 'Yet the people of Israel rebelled[q] against me in the desert.
They did not follow my decrees but rejected my laws—although
the man who obeys them will live by them—and they utterly
desecrated my Sabbaths. So I said I would pour out my wrath[r] on
them and destroy them in the desert.[s] 14 But for the sake of my
name I did what would keep it from being profaned in the eyes of
the nations in whose sight I had brought them out.[t] 15 Also with
uplifted hand I swore to them in the desert that I would not bring
them into the land I had given them—a land flowing with milk
and honey, most beautiful of all lands[u]— 16 because they rejected
my laws and did not follow my decrees and desecrated my Sabbaths. For their hearts[v] were devoted to their idols.[w] 17 Yet I
looked on them with pity and did not destroy them or put an end
to them in the desert. 18 I said to their children in the desert, "Do

20:1 [a] Eze 8:1
20:3 [b] Eze 14:3 [c] Mic 3:7
20:4 [d] Eze 16:2; 22:2; Mt 23:32
20:5 [e] Dt 7:6 [f] Ex 6:7
20:6 [g] Ex 3:8; Jer 32:22 [h] Dt 8:7; Ps 48:2; Da 8:9
20:7 [i] Ex 20:4 [j] Ex 20:2; Lev 18:3; Dt 29:18
20:8 [k] Eze 7:8 [l] Isa 63:10
20:9 [m] Eze 36:22; 39:7
20:10 [n] Ex 13:18
20:11 [o] Lev 18:5; Dt 4:7-8; Ro 10:5
20:12 [p] Ex 31:13
20:13 [q] Ps 78:40 [r] Dt 9:8 [s] Nu 14:29; Ps 95:8-10; Isa 56:6
20:14 [t] Eze 36:23
20:15 [u] Ps 95:11; 106:26
20:16 [v] Nu 15:39 [w] Am 5:26

not follow the statutes of your fathers[a] or keep their laws or defile
yourselves with their idols. 19I am the LORD your God;[b] follow my
decrees and be careful to keep my laws.[c] 20Keep my Sabbaths holy,
that they may be a sign between us. Then you will know that I am
the LORD your God.[d]"

21"'But the children rebelled against me: They did not follow my
decrees, they were not careful to keep my laws—although the man
who obeys them will live by them—and they desecrated my Sabbaths. So I said I would pour out my wrath on them and spend
my anger against them in the desert. 22But I withheld[e] my hand,
and for the sake of my name I did what would keep it from being
profaned in the eyes of the nations in whose sight I had brought
them out. 23Also with uplifted hand I swore to them in the desert
that I would disperse them among the nations and scatter[f] them
through the countries, 24because they had not obeyed my laws but
had rejected my decrees and desecrated my Sabbaths,[g] and their
eyes ⌊lusted⌋ after[h] their fathers' idols.[i] 25I also gave them over[j] to
statutes that were not good and laws they could not live by;[k] 26I let
them become defiled through their gifts—the sacrifice of every
firstborn[a]—that I might fill them with horror so they would know
that I am the LORD.[l]'

27"Therefore, son of man, speak to the people of Israel and say
to them, 'This is what the Sovereign LORD says: In this also your
fathers blasphemed[m] me by forsaking me:[n] 28When I brought them
into the land[o] I had sworn to give them and they saw any high hill
or any leafy tree, there they offered their sacrifices, made offerings
that provoked me to anger, presented their fragrant incense and
poured out their drink offerings.[p] 29Then I said to them: What is
this high place you go to?'" (It is called Bamah[b] to this day.)

30"Therefore say to the house of Israel: 'This is what the Sovereign LORD says: Will you defile yourselves[q] the way your fathers did
and lust after their vile images?[r] 31When you offer your gifts—the
sacrifice of your sons[s] in[c] the fire—you continue to defile yourselves with all your idols to this day. Am I to let you inquire of me,
O house of Israel? As surely as I live, declares the Sovereign LORD, I
will not let you inquire of me.[t]

32"'You say, "We want to be like the nations, like the peoples of
the world, who serve wood and stone." But what you have in mind
will never happen. 33As surely as I live, declares the Sovereign
LORD, I will rule over you with a mighty hand and an outstretched
arm and with outpoured wrath.[u] 34I will bring you from the
nations[v] and gather you from the countries where you have been
scattered—with a mighty hand and an outstretched arm and with

20:18 [a] Zec 1:4
20:19 [b] Ex 20:2 [c] Dt 5:32-33; 6:1-2; 8:1; 11:1; 12:1
20:20 [d] Jer 17:22
20:22 [e] Ps 78:38
20:23 [f] Lev 26:33; Dt 28:64
20:24 [g] ver 13 [h] Eze 6:9 [i] ver 16
20:25 [j] Ps 81:12 [k] 2Th 2:11
20:26 [l] 2Ki 17:17
20:27 [m] Ro 2:24 [n] Eze 18:24
20:28 [o] Ps 78:55,58 [p] Eze 6:13
20:30 [q] ver 43 [r] Jer 16:12
20:31 [s] Eze 16:20 [t] Ps 106:37-39; Jer 7:31
20:33 [u] Jer 21:5
20:34 [v] 2Co 6:17*

[a] 26 Or *—making every firstborn pass through ⌊the fire⌋* [b] 29 *Bamah* means *high place.*
[c] 31 Or *—making your sons pass through*

outpoured wrath.[a] 35I will bring you into the desert of the nations
and there, face to face, I will execute judgment[b] upon you. 36As I
judged your fathers in the desert of the land of Egypt, so I will
judge you, declares the Sovereign LORD.[c] 37I will take note of you
as you pass under my rod,[d] and I will bring you into the bond of
the covenant.[e] 38I will purge[f] you of those who revolt and rebel
against me. Although I will bring them out of the land where they
are living, yet they will not enter the land of Israel. Then you will
know that I am the LORD.[g]

39"'As for you, O house of Israel, this is what the Sovereign LORD
says: Go and serve your idols,[h] every one of you! But afterward you
will surely listen to me and no longer profane my holy name with
your gifts and idols.[i] 40For on my holy mountain, the high mountain of Israel, declares the Sovereign LORD, there in the land the
entire house of Israel will serve me, and there I will accept them.
There I will require your offerings[j] and your choice gifts,[a] along
with all your holy sacrifices.[k] 41I will accept you as fragrant incense
when I bring you out from the nations and gather you from the
countries where you have been scattered, and I will show myself
holy[l] among you in the sight of the nations.[m] 42Then you will know
that I am the LORD,[n] when I bring you into the land of Israel,[o] the
land I had sworn with uplifted hand to give to your fathers. 43There
you will remember your conduct and all the actions by which you
have defiled yourselves, and you will loathe yourselves for all the
evil you have done.[p] 44You will know that I am the LORD, when I
deal with you for my name's sake[q] and not according to your evil
ways and your corrupt practices, O house of Israel, declares the
Sovereign LORD.[r]'"

45The word of the LORD came to me: 46"Son of man, set your face
toward the south; preach against the south and prophesy against[s]
the forest of the southland.[t] 47Say to the southern forest: 'Hear the
word of the LORD. This is what the Sovereign LORD says: I am about
to set fire to you, and it will consume all your trees, both green and
dry. The blazing flame will not be quenched, and every face from
south to north will be scorched by it.[u] 48Everyone will see that I the
LORD have kindled it; it will not be quenched.[v]'"

49Then I said, "Ah, Sovereign LORD! They are saying of me, 'Isn't
he just telling parables?[w]'"

Chapter 21 Theme ____________________

21 The word of the LORD came to me: 2"Son of man, set your
face against Jerusalem and preach against the sanctuary.
Prophesy against[x] the land of Israel 3and say to her: 'This is what

a 40 Or *and the gifts of your firstfruits*

20:34 [a]Isa 27:12-13; Jer 44:6; La 2:4
20:35 [b]Jer 2:35
20:36 [c]Nu 11:1-35; 1Co 10:5-10
20:37 [d]Lev 27:32; Jer 33:13 [e]Eze 16:62
20:38 [f]Eze 34:17-22; Am 9:9-10 [g]Ps 95:11; Jer 44:14; Eze 13:9; Mal 3:3; Heb 4:3
20:39 [h]Jer 44:25 [i]Isa 1:13; Eze 43:7; Am 4:4
20:40 [j]Isa 60:7 [k]Isa 56:7; Mal 3:4
20:41 [l]Eze 28:25; 36:23 [m]Eze 11:17
20:42 [n]Eze 38:23 [o]Eze 34:13; 36:24
20:43 [p]Eze 6:9; 16:61; Hos 5:15
20:44 [q]Eze 36:22 [r]Eze 24:24
20:46 [s]Eze 21:2; Am 7:16 [t]Isa 30:6; Jer 13:19
20:47 [u]Isa 9:18-19; 13:8; Jer 21:14
20:48 [v]Jer 7:20
20:49 [w]Mt 13:13; Jn 16:25
21:2 [x]Eze 20:46

the LORD says: I am against you.[a] I will draw my sword from its
scabbard and cut off from you both the righteous and the wicked.[b]
4 Because I am going to cut off the righteous and the wicked, my
sword will be unsheathed against everyone from south to north.[c]
5 Then all people will know that I the LORD have drawn my sword
from its scabbard; it will not return[d] again.'[e]

6 "Therefore groan, son of man! Groan before them with broken
heart and bitter grief.[f] 7 And when they ask you, 'Why are you
groaning?' you shall say, 'Because of the news that is coming. Every
heart will melt and every hand go limp;[g] every spirit will become
faint and every knee become as weak as water.' It is coming! It will
surely take place, declares the Sovereign LORD."

8 The word of the LORD came to me: 9 "Son of man, prophesy and
say, 'This is what the Lord says:

"'A sword, a sword,
sharpened and polished—
10 sharpened for the slaughter,[h]
polished to flash like lightning!

"'Shall we rejoice in the scepter of my son ⌊Judah⌋? The sword
despises every such stick.

11 "'The sword is appointed to be polished,[i]
to be grasped with the hand;
it is sharpened and polished,
made ready for the hand of the slayer.
12 Cry out and wail, son of man,
for it is against my people;
it is against all the princes of Israel.
They are thrown to the sword
along with my people.
Therefore beat your breast.[j]

13 "'Testing will surely come. And what if the scepter ⌊of Judah⌋,
which the sword despises, does not continue? declares the Sovereign LORD.'

14 "So then, son of man, prophesy
and strike your hands[k] together.
Let the sword strike twice,
even three times.
It is a sword for slaughter—
a sword for great slaughter,
closing in on them from every side.[l]
15 So that hearts may melt[m]
and the fallen be many,

21:3 [a]Jer 21:13 [b]ver 9-11; Job 9:22
21:4 [c]Eze 20:47
21:5 [d]ver 30 [e]Na 1:9
21:6 [f]Isa 22:4
21:7 [g]Eze 22:14; 7:17
21:10 [h]Ps 110:5-6; Isa 34:5-6
21:11 [i]Jer 46:4
21:12 [j]Jer 31:19
21:14 [k]Nu 24:10
21:14 [l]Eze 6:11; 30:24
21:15 [m]2Sa 17:10

I have stationed the sword for slaughter[a]
at all their gates.
Oh! It is made to flash like lightning,
it is grasped for slaughter.[a]
16O sword, slash to the right,
then to the left,
wherever your blade is turned.
17I too will strike my hands[b] together,
and my wrath[c] will subside.
I the LORD have spoken."

18The word of the LORD came to me: 19"Son of man, mark out
two roads for the sword of the king of Babylon to take, both starting from the same country. Make a signpost where the road
branches off to the city. 20Mark out one road for the sword to come
against Rabbah of the Ammonites[d] and another against Judah
and fortified Jerusalem. 21For the king of Babylon will stop at the
fork in the road, at the junction of the two roads, to seek an omen:
He will cast lots[e] with arrows, he will consult his idols, he will
examine the liver.[f] 22Into his right hand will come the lot for Jerusalem, where he is to set up battering rams, to give the command
to slaughter, to sound the battle cry, to set battering rams against
the gates, to build a ramp and to erect siege works.[g] 23It will seem
like a false omen to those who have sworn allegiance to him, but
he will remind[h] them of their guilt and take them captive.
24"Therefore this is what the Sovereign LORD says: 'Because you
people have brought to mind your guilt by your open rebellion,
revealing your sins in all that you do—because you have done this,
you will be taken captive.
25"'O profane and wicked prince of Israel, whose day has come,
whose time of punishment has reached its climax,[i] 26this is what
the Sovereign LORD says: Take off the turban, remove the crown.[j] It
will not be as it was: The lowly will be exalted and the exalted will
be brought low.[k] 27A ruin! A ruin! I will make it a ruin! It will not
be restored until he comes to whom it rightfully belongs; to him I
will give it.'[l]
28"And you, son of man, prophesy and say, 'This is what the
Sovereign LORD says about the Ammonites[m] and their insults:

"'A sword,[n] a sword,
drawn for the slaughter,
polished to consume
and to flash like lightning!
29Despite false visions concerning you
and lying divinations about you,

a *15* Septuagint; the meaning of the Hebrew for this word is uncertain.

21:15 [a]Ps 22:14
21:17 [b]ver 14; Eze 22:13 [c]Eze 5:13
21:20 [d]Dt 3:11; Jer 49:2; Am 1:14
21:21 [e]Pr 16:33 [f]Nu 22:7; 23:23
21:22 [g]Eze 4:2; 26:9
21:23 [h]Nu 5:15
21:25 [i]Eze 35:5
21:26 [j]Jer 13:18 [k]Ps 75:7; Eze 17:24
21:27 [l]Ps 2:6; Jer 23:5-6; Eze 37:24; Hag 2:21-22
21:28 [m]Zep 2:8 [n]Jer 12:12

it will be laid on the necks
of the wicked who are to be slain,
whose day has come,
whose time of punishment has reached its climax.[a]
30 Return the sword to its scabbard.[b]
In the place where you were created,
in the land of your ancestry,[c]
I will judge you.
31 I will pour out my wrath upon you
and breathe out my fiery anger[d] against you;
I will hand you over to brutal men,
men skilled in destruction.[e]
32 You will be fuel for the fire,[f]
your blood will be shed in your land,
you will be remembered[g] no more;
for I the LORD have spoken.'"

Chapter 22 Theme ____________________

22 The word of the LORD came to me: 2 "Son of man, will you judge her? Will you judge this city of bloodshed?[h] Then confront her with all her detestable practices[i] 3 and say: 'This is what the Sovereign LORD says: O city that brings on herself doom by shedding blood[j] in her midst and defiles herself by making idols, 4 you have become guilty because of the blood you have shed[k] and have become defiled by the idols you have made. You have brought your days to a close, and the end of your years has come.[l] Therefore I will make you an object of scorn to the nations and a laughingstock to all the countries.[m] 5 Those who are near and those who are far away will mock you, O infamous city, full of turmoil.

6 "'See how each of the princes of Israel who are in you uses his power to shed blood.[n] 7 In you they have treated father and mother with contempt;[o] in you they have oppressed the alien and mistreated the fatherless and the widow.[p] 8 You have despised my holy things and desecrated my Sabbaths.[q] 9 In you are slanderous men[r] bent on shedding blood; in you are those who eat at the mountain shrines[s] and commit lewd acts.[t] 10 In you are those who dishonor their fathers' bed; in you are those who violate women during their period, when they are ceremonially unclean.[u] 11 In you one man commits a detestable offense with his neighbor's wife, another shamefully defiles his daughter-in-law,[v] and another violates his sister,[w] his own father's daughter. 12 In you men accept bribes[x] to shed blood; you take usury and excessive interest[a] and make unjust gain from your neighbors[y] by extortion. And you have forgotten me, declares the Sovereign LORD.

21:29 [a] ver 25; Eze 22:28; 35:5
21:30 [b] Jer 47:6 [c] Eze 16:3
21:31 [d] Eze 22:20-21 [e] Jer 51:20-23
21:32 [f] Mal 4:1 [g] Eze 25:10
22:2 [h] Eze 24:6,9; Na 3:1 [i] Eze 16:2
22:3 [j] ver 6,13,27; Eze 23:37,45
22:4 [k] 2Ki 21:16 [l] Eze 21:25 [m] Eze 5:14
22:6 [n] Isa 1:23
22:7 [o] Dt 5:16; 27:16 [p] Ex 22:21-22
22:8 [q] Eze 23:38-39
22:9 [r] Lev 19:16 [s] Eze 18:11 [t] Hos 4:10,14
22:10 [u] Lev 18:8,19
22:11 [v] Lev 18:15 [w] Lev 18:9; 2Sa 13:14
22:12 [x] Dt 27:25; Mic 7:3 [y] Lev 19:13

a *12* Or *usury and interest*

13"'I will surely strike my hands[a] together at the unjust gain[b]
you have made and at the blood[c] you have shed in your midst.
14Will your courage endure or your hands be strong in the day I
deal with you? I the LORD have spoken,[d] and I will do it.[e] 15I will
disperse you among the nations and scatter[f] you through the
countries; and I will put an end to your uncleanness.[g] 16When you
have been defiled[a] in the eyes of the nations, you will know that I
am the LORD.'"

17Then the word of the LORD came to me: 18"Son of man, the
house of Israel has become dross[h] to me; all of them are the copper,
tin, iron and lead left inside a furnace. They are but the dross of
silver.[i] 19Therefore this is what the Sovereign LORD says: 'Because
you have all become dross, I will gather you into Jerusalem. 20As
men gather silver, copper, iron, lead and tin into a furnace to melt
it with a fiery blast, so will I gather you in my anger and my wrath
and put you inside the city and melt you.[j] 21I will gather you and
I will blow on you with my fiery wrath, and you will be melted
inside her. 22As silver is melted[k] in a furnace, so you will be melted
inside her, and you will know that I the LORD have poured out my
wrath upon you.'"[l]

23Again the word of the LORD came to me: 24"Son of man, say to
the land, 'You are a land that has had no rain or showers[b] in the
day of wrath.'[m] 25There is a conspiracy[n] of her princes[c] within her
like a roaring lion tearing its prey; they devour people,[o] take treasures and precious things and make many widows[p] within her.
26Her priests do violence to my law[q] and profane my holy things;
they do not distinguish between the holy and the common;[r] they
teach that there is no difference between the unclean and the
clean;[s] and they shut their eyes to the keeping of my Sabbaths, so
that I am profaned among them.[t] 27Her officials within her are
like wolves tearing their prey; they shed blood and kill people to
make unjust gain.[u] 28Her prophets whitewash[v] these deeds for
them by false visions and lying divinations. They say, 'This is what
the Sovereign LORD says'—when the LORD has not spoken.[w]
29The people of the land practice extortion and commit robbery;
they oppress the poor and needy and mistreat the alien,[x] denying
them justice.[y]

30"I looked for a man among them who would build up the wall[z]
and stand before me in the gap on behalf of the land so I would not
have to destroy it, but I found none.[a] 31So I will pour out my wrath
on them and consume them with my fiery anger, bringing down[b]
on their own heads all they have done, declares the Sovereign
LORD.[c]"

22:13 [a]Eze 21:17 [b]Isa 33:15 [c]ver 3
22:14 [d]Eze 24:14 [e]Eze 17:24; 21:7
22:15 [f]Dt 4:27; Zec 7:14 [g]Eze 23:27
22:18 [h]Ps 119:119; Isa 1:22 [i]Jer 6:28-30
22:20 [j]Mal 3:2
22:22 [k]Isa 1:25 [l]Eze 20:8,33
22:24 [m]Eze 24:13
22:25 [n]Jer 11:9 [o]Hos 6:9 [p]Jer 15:8
22:26 [q]Mal 2:7-8 [r]Eze 44:23 [s]Lev 10:10 [t]1Sa 2:12-17; Jer 2:8,26; Hag 2:11-14
22:27 [u]Isa 1:23
22:28 [v]Eze 13:10 [w]Eze 13:2,6-7
22:29 [x]Ex 22:21; 23:9 [y]Isa 5:7
22:30 [z]Eze 13:5 [a]Ps 106:23; Jer 5:1
22:31 [b]Eze 16:43 [c]Eze 7:8-9; 9:10; Ro 2:8

[a] *16* Or *When I have allotted you your inheritance* [b] *24* Septuagint; Hebrew *has not been cleansed or rained on* [c] *25* Septuagint; Hebrew *prophets*

Chapter 23 Theme ______________________________

23 The word of the LORD came to me: 2“Son of man, there were
two women, daughters of the same mother.[a] 3They became
prostitutes in Egypt,[b] engaging in prostitution[c] from their youth.
In that land their breasts were fondled and their virgin bosoms
caressed. 4The older was named Oholah, and her sister was
Oholibah. They were mine and gave birth to sons and daughters.
Oholah is Samaria, and Oholibah is Jerusalem.

5“Oholah engaged in prostitution while she was still mine; and
she lusted after her lovers, the Assyrians[d]—warriors[e] 6clothed in
blue, governors and commanders, all of them handsome young
men, and mounted horsemen. 7She gave herself as a prostitute to
all the elite of the Assyrians and defiled herself with all the idols of
everyone she lusted after.[f] 8She did not give up the prostitution
she began in Egypt,[g] when during her youth men slept with her,
caressed her virgin bosom and poured out their lust upon her.[h]

9“Therefore I handed her over[i] to her lovers, the Assyrians, for
whom she lusted.[j] 10They stripped[k] her naked, took away her sons
and daughters and killed her with the sword. She became a byword among women,[l] and punishment was inflicted on her.[m]

11“Her sister Oholibah saw this, yet in her lust and prostitution
she was more depraved than her sister.[n] 12She too lusted after the
Assyrians—governors and commanders, warriors in full dress,
mounted horsemen, all handsome young men.[o] 13I saw that she
too defiled herself; both of them went the same way.

14“But she carried her prostitution still further. She saw men
portrayed on a wall,[p] figures of Chaldeans[a] portrayed in red,[q]
15with belts around their waists and flowing turbans on their
heads; all of them looked like Babylonian chariot officers, natives
of Chaldea.[b] 16As soon as she saw them, she lusted after them and
sent messengers to them in Chaldea. 17Then the Babylonians came
to her, to the bed of love, and in their lust they defiled her. After
she had been defiled by them, she turned away from them in disgust. 18When she carried on her prostitution openly and exposed
her nakedness, I turned away[r] from her in disgust, just as I had
turned away from her sister.[s] 19Yet she became more and more
promiscuous as she recalled the days of her youth, when she was
a prostitute in Egypt. 20There she lusted after her lovers, whose
genitals were like those of donkeys and whose emission was like
that of horses. 21So you longed for the lewdness of your youth,
when in Egypt your bosom was caressed and your young breasts
fondled.[c][t]

[a] *14* Or *Babylonians* [b] *15* Or *Babylonia*; also in verse 16 [c] *21* Syriac (see also verse 3); Hebrew *caressed because of your young breasts*

23:2 [a] Jer 3:7; Eze 16:45
23:3 [b] Jos 24:14 [c] Lev 17:7
23:5 [d] 2Ki 16:7; Hos 5:13 [e] Hos 8:9
23:7 [f] Hos 5:3; 6:10
23:8 [g] Ex 32:4 [h] Eze 16:15
23:9 [i] 2Ki 18:11 [j] Hos 11:5
23:10 [k] Hos 2:10 [l] Eze 16:41 [m] Eze 16:36
23:11 [n] Jer 3:8-11; Eze 16:51
23:12 [o] 2Ki 16:7-15; 2Ch 28:16
23:14 [p] Eze 8:10 [q] Jer 22:14
23:18 [r] Ps 78:59; 106:40; Jer 6:8 [s] Jer 12:8; Am 5:21
23:21 [t] Eze 16:26

22“Therefore, Oholibah, this is what the Sovereign LORD says: I
will stir up your lovers against you, those you turned away from in
disgust, and I will bring them against you from every side[a]— 23the
Babylonians[b] and all the Chaldeans, the men of Pekod[c] and Shoa
and Koa, and all the Assyrians with them, handsome young men,
all of them governors and commanders, chariot officers and men
of high rank, all mounted on horses.[d] 24They will come against you
with weapons,[a] chariots and wagons[e] and with a throng of people;
they will take up positions against you on every side with large and
small shields and with helmets. I will turn you over to them for
punishment,[f] and they will punish you according to their standards. 25I will direct my jealous anger against you, and they will
deal with you in fury. They will cut off your noses and your ears,
and those of you who are left will fall by the sword. They will take
away your sons and daughters,[g] and those of you who are left will
be consumed by fire.[h] 26They will also strip[i] you of your clothes
and take your fine jewelry.[j] 27So I will put a stop[k] to the lewdness
and prostitution you began in Egypt. You will not look on these
things with longing or remember Egypt anymore.

28“For this is what the Sovereign LORD says: I am about to hand
you over[l] to those you hate, to those you turned away from in disgust. 29They will deal with you in hatred and take away everything
you have worked for. They will leave you naked and bare, and the
shame of your prostitution will be exposed. Your lewdness and
promiscuity[m] 30have brought this upon you, because you lusted
after the nations and defiled yourself with their idols.[n] 31You have
gone the way of your sister; so I will put her cup[o] into your hand.[p]

32“This is what the Sovereign LORD says:

“You will drink your sister’s cup,
 a cup large and deep;
it will bring scorn and derision,
 for it holds so much.[q]
33You will be filled with drunkenness and sorrow,
 the cup of ruin and desolation,
 the cup of your sister Samaria.[r]
34You will drink it[s] and drain it dry;
 you will dash it to pieces
 and tear your breasts.

I have spoken, declares the Sovereign LORD.

35“Therefore this is what the Sovereign LORD says: Since you have
forgotten[t] me and thrust me behind your back,[u] you must bear the
consequences of your lewdness and prostitution.”

a *24* The meaning of the Hebrew for this word is uncertain.

23:22 [a]Eze 16:37
23:23 [b]2Ki 20:14-18 [c]Jer 50:21 [d]2Ki 24:2
23:24 [e]Jer 47:3; Eze 26:7,10; Na 2:4 [f]Jer 39:5-6
23:25 [g]ver 47 [h]Eze 20:47-48
23:26 [i]Jer 13:22 [j]Isa 3:18-23; Eze 16:39
23:27 [k]Eze 16:41
23:28 [l]Jer 34:20
23:29 [m]Dt 28:48
23:30 [n]Eze 6:9
23:31 [o]Jer 25:15 [p]2Ki 21:13
23:32 [q]Ps 60:3; Isa 51:17; Jer 25:15
23:33 [r]Jer 25:15-16
23:34 [s]Ps 75:8; Isa 51:17
23:35 [t]Isa 17:10; Jer 3:21 [u]1Ki 14:9

36The LORD said to me: "Son of man, will you judge Oholah and
Oholibah? Then confront[a] them with their detestable practices,[b]
37for they have committed adultery and blood is on their hands.
They committed adultery with their idols; they even sacrificed their
children, whom they bore to me,[a] as food for them.[c] 38They have
also done this to me: At that same time they defiled my sanctuary
and desecrated my Sabbaths. 39On the very day they sacrificed their
children to their idols, they entered my sanctuary and desecrated[d]
it. That is what they did in my house.[e]

40"They even sent messengers for men who came from far away,[f]
and when they arrived you bathed yourself for them, painted your
eyes[g] and put on your jewelry.[h] 41You sat on an elegant couch,[i] with
a table[j] spread before it on which you had placed the incense and
oil that belonged to me.

42"The noise of a carefree crowd was around her; Sabeans[b] were
brought from the desert along with men from the rabble, and they
put bracelets[k] on the arms of the woman and her sister and beautiful crowns on their heads.[l] 43Then I said about the one worn out
by adultery, 'Now let them use her as a prostitute,[m] for that is all
she is.' 44And they slept with her. As men sleep with a prostitute,
so they slept with those lewd women, Oholah and Oholibah. 45But
righteous men will sentence them to the punishment of women
who commit adultery and shed blood, because they are adulterous
and blood is on their hands.[n]

46"This is what the Sovereign LORD says: Bring a mob[o] against
them and give them over to terror and plunder. 47The mob will
stone them and cut them down with their swords; they will kill
their sons and daughters and burn[p] down their houses.[q]

48"So I will put an end to lewdness in the land, that all women
may take warning and not imitate you.[r] 49You will suffer the penalty
for your lewdness and bear the consequences of your sins of idolatry. Then you will know that I am the Sovereign LORD.[s]"

Chapter 24 Theme ______________________________

588 B.C.

24

In the ninth year, in the tenth month on the tenth day, the
word of the LORD came to me:[t] 2"Son of man, record this
date, this very date, because the king of Babylon has laid siege to
Jerusalem this very day.[u] 3Tell this rebellious house[v] a parable[w] and
say to them: 'This is what the Sovereign LORD says:

"'Put on the cooking pot;[x] put it on
and pour water into it.
4Put into it the pieces of meat,
all the choice pieces—the leg and the shoulder.

[a]37 Or *even made the children they bore to me pass through* ⌊*the fire*⌋ [b]42 Or *drunkards*

23:36 [a]Eze 16:2 [b]Isa 58:1; Eze 22:2; Mic 3:8
23:37 [c]Eze 16:36
23:39 [d]2Ki 21:4 [e]Jer 7:10
23:40 [f]Isa 57:9 [g]2Ki 9:30 [h]Jer 4:30; Eze 16:13-19
23:41 [i]Est 1:6; Pr 7:17; Am 6:4 [j]Isa 65:11; Eze 44:16
23:42 [k]Ge 24:30 [l]Eze 16:11-12
23:43 [m]ver 3
23:45 [n]Lev 20:10; Eze 16:38; Hos 6:5
23:46 [o]Eze 16:40
23:47 [p]2Ch 36:19 [q]2Ch 36:17; Eze 16:40-41
23:48 [r]2Pe 2:6
23:49 [s]Eze 7:4; 9:10; 20:38
24:1 [t]Eze 8:1
24:2 [u]2Ki 25:1; Jer 39:1; 52:4
24:3 [v]Isa 1:2; Eze 2:3,6 [w]Eze 17:2; 20:49 [x]Jer 1:13; Eze 11:3

Fill it with the best of these bones;
5 take the pick of the flock.[a]
Pile wood beneath it for the bones;
bring it to a boil
and cook the bones in it.[b]

6"'For this is what the Sovereign LORD says:

"'Woe to the city of bloodshed,[c]
to the pot now encrusted,
whose deposit will not go away!
Empty it piece by piece
without casting lots[d] for them.

7"'For the blood she shed is in her midst:
She poured it on the bare rock;
she did not pour it on the ground,
where the dust would cover it.[e]
8To stir up wrath and take revenge
I put her blood on the bare rock,
so that it would not be covered.

9"'Therefore this is what the Sovereign LORD says:

"'Woe to the city of bloodshed!
I, too, will pile the wood high.
10So heap on the wood
and kindle the fire.
Cook the meat well,
mixing in the spices;
and let the bones be charred.
11Then set the empty pot on the coals
till it becomes hot and its copper glows
so its impurities may be melted
and its deposit burned away.[f]
12It has frustrated all efforts;
its heavy deposit has not been removed,
not even by fire.

13"'Now your impurity is lewdness. Because I tried to cleanse you
but you would not be cleansed from your impurity, you will not be
clean again until my wrath against you has subsided.[g]

14"'I the LORD have spoken. The time has come for me to act. I
will not hold back; I will not have pity, nor will I relent. You will be
judged according to your conduct and your actions,[h] declares the
Sovereign LORD.[i]'"

15The word of the LORD came to me: 16"Son of man, with one
blow I am about to take away from you the delight of your eyes. Yet

24:5
[a] Jer 52:10
[b] Jer 52:24-27

24:6
[c] Eze 22:2
[d] Ob 1:11; Na 3:10

24:7
[e] Lev 17:13

24:11
[f] Jer 21:10; Eze 22:15

24:13
[g] Jer 6:28-30; Eze 16:42; 22:24

24:14
[h] Eze 36:19
[i] Eze 18:30

do not lament or weep or shed any tears.[a] 17 Groan quietly; do not
mourn for the dead. Keep your turban fastened and your sandals
on your feet; do not cover the lower part of your face or eat the
customary food ⌊of mourners⌋.[b]"
18 So I spoke to the people in the morning, and in the evening my
wife died. The next morning I did as I had been commanded.
19 Then the people asked me, "Won't you tell us what these things
have to do with us?[c]"
20 So I said to them, "The word of the LORD came to me: 21 Say to
the house of Israel, 'This is what the Sovereign LORD says: I am
about to desecrate my sanctuary—the stronghold in which you
take pride, the delight of your eyes,[d] the object of your affection.
The sons and daughters[e] you left behind will fall by the sword.[f]
22 And you will do as I have done. You will not cover the lower part
of your face or eat the customary food ⌊of mourners⌋.[g] 23 You will
keep your turbans on your heads and your sandals on your feet.
You will not mourn[h] or weep but will waste away because of[a] your
sins and groan among yourselves.[i] 24 Ezekiel will be a sign[j] to you;
you will do just as he has done. When this happens, you will know
that I am the Sovereign LORD.'
25 "And you, son of man, on the day I take away their stronghold,
their joy and glory, the delight of their eyes, their heart's desire,
and their sons and daughters[k] as well— 26 on that day a fugitive

a 23 Or *away in*

24:16 [a] Jer 13:17; 16:5; 22:10
24:17 [b] Jer 16:7
24:19 [c] Eze 12:9; 37:18
24:21 [d] Ps 27:4 [e] Eze 23:25 [f] Jer 7:14,15; Eze 23:47
24:22 [g] Jer 16:7
24:23 [h] Job 27:15 [i] Ps 78:64
24:24 [j] Isa 20:3; Eze 4:3; 12:11
24:25 [k] Jer 11:22

The Nations of Ezekiel's Prophecies

will come to tell you[a] the news. 27At that time your mouth will be
opened; you will speak with him and will no longer be silent. So
you will be a sign to them, and they will know that I am the LORD.[b]"

Chapter 25 Theme ____________________________

25 The word of the LORD came to me: 2"Son of man, set your
face against the Ammonites[c] and prophesy against them.[d]
3Say to them, 'Hear the word of the Sovereign LORD. This is what
the Sovereign LORD says: Because you said "Aha![e]" over my sanctuary when it was desecrated and over the land of Israel when it
was laid waste and over the people of Judah when they went into
exile,[f] 4therefore I am going to give you to the people of the East[g]
as a possession. They will set up their camps and pitch their tents
among you; they will eat your fruit and drink your milk.[h] 5I will
turn Rabbah[i] into a pasture for camels and Ammon into a resting
place for sheep.[j] Then you will know that I am the LORD. 6For this
is what the Sovereign LORD says: Because you have clapped your
hands and stamped your feet, rejoicing with all the malice of your
heart against the land of Israel,[k] 7therefore I will stretch out my
hand[l] against you and give you as plunder to the nations. I will cut
you off from the nations and exterminate you from the countries.
I will destroy[m] you, and you will know that I am the LORD.[n]' "
8"This is what the Sovereign LORD says: 'Because Moab[o] and
Seir said, "Look, the house of Judah has become like all the other
nations," 9therefore I will expose the flank of Moab, beginning at its
frontier towns—Beth Jeshimoth[p], Baal Meon[q] and Kiriathaim[r]—
the glory of that land. 10I will give Moab along with the Ammonites
to the people of the East as a possession, so that the Ammonites
will not be remembered[s] among the nations; 11and I will inflict
punishment on Moab. Then they will know that I am the LORD.' "
12"This is what the Sovereign LORD says: 'Because Edom[t] took
revenge on the house of Judah and became very guilty by doing so,
13therefore this is what the Sovereign LORD says: I will stretch out
my hand against Edom and kill its men and their animals.[u] I will lay
it waste, and from Teman to Dedan[v] they will fall by the sword. 14I
will take vengeance on Edom by the hand of my people Israel, and
they will deal with Edom in accordance with my anger[w] and my
wrath; they will know my vengeance, declares the Sovereign LORD.' "
15"This is what the Sovereign LORD says: 'Because the Philistines[x]
acted in vengeance and took revenge with malice in their hearts,
and with ancient hostility sought to destroy Judah, 16therefore this
is what the Sovereign LORD says: I am about to stretch out my hand
against the Philistines,[y] and I will cut off the Kerethites[z] and
destroy those remaining along the coast. 17I will carry out great
vengeance on them and punish them in my wrath. Then they will
know that I am the LORD, when I take vengeance on them.' "

24:26 [a] 1Sa 4:12; Job 1:15-19
24:27 [b] Eze 3:26; 33:22
25:2 [c] Eze 21:28; Zep 2:8-9 [d] Jer 49:1-6
25:3 [e] Eze 26:2; 36:2 [f] Pr 17:5
25:4 [g] Jdg 6:3 [h] Dt 28:33,51; Jdg 6:33
25:5 [i] Dt 3:11; Eze 21:20 [j] Isa 17:2
25:6 [k] Ob 1:12; Zep 2:8
25:7 [l] Zep 1:4 [m] Eze 21:31 [n] Am 1:14-15
25:8 [o] Jer 48:1; Am 2:1
25:9 [p] Nu 33:49 [q] Nu 32:3; Jos 13:17 [r] Nu 32:37; Jos 13:19
25:10 [s] Eze 21:32
25:12 [t] 2Ch 28:17
25:13 [u] Eze 29:8 [v] Jer 25:23
25:14 [w] Eze 35:11
25:15 [x] 2Ch 28:18
25:16 [y] Jer 47:1-7 [z] 1Sa 30:14; Zep 2:4-5

Chapter 26 Theme ________________________

587-586 B.C.

26 In the eleventh year, on the first day of the month, the word
of the LORD came to me: 2“Son of man, because Tyre[a] has
said of Jerusalem, ‘Aha![b] The gate to the nations is broken, and its
doors have swung open to me; now that she lies in ruins I will
prosper,’ 3therefore this is what the Sovereign LORD says: I am
against you, O Tyre, and I will bring many nations against you, like
the sea[c] casting up its waves. 4They will destroy[d] the walls of Tyre[e]
and pull down her towers; I will scrape away her rubble and make
her a bare rock. 5Out in the sea[f] she will become a place to spread
fishnets, for I have spoken, declares the Sovereign LORD. She will
become plunder[g] for the nations, 6and her settlements on the
mainland will be ravaged by the sword. Then they will know that
I am the LORD.

7“For this is what the Sovereign LORD says: From the north I am
going to bring against Tyre Nebuchadnezzar[a][h] king of Babylon,
king of kings,[i] with horses and chariots,[j] with horsemen and a
great army. 8He will ravage your settlements on the mainland with
the sword; he will set up siege works[k] against you, build a ramp[l]
up to your walls and raise his shields against you. 9He will direct
the blows of his battering rams against your walls and demolish
your towers with his weapons. 10His horses will be so many that
they will cover you with dust. Your walls will tremble at the noise
of the war horses, wagons and chariots[m] when he enters your
gates as men enter a city whose walls have been broken through.
11The hoofs[n] of his horses will trample all your streets; he will kill
your people with the sword, and your strong pillars[o] will fall to
the ground.[p] 12They will plunder your wealth and loot your merchandise; they will break down your walls and demolish your
fine houses and throw your stones, timber and rubble into the
sea.[q] 13I will put an end[r] to your noisy songs, and the music of
your harps[s] will be heard no more.[t] 14I will make you a bare rock,
and you will become a place to spread fishnets. You will never be
rebuilt,[u] for I the LORD have spoken, declares the Sovereign LORD.

15“This is what the Sovereign LORD says to Tyre: Will not the
coastlands[v] tremble[w] at the sound of your fall, when the wounded
groan and the slaughter takes place in you? 16Then all the princes of
the coast will step down from their thrones and lay aside their robes
and take off their embroidered garments. Clothed[x] with terror, they
will sit on the ground, trembling[y] every moment, appalled[z] at you.
17Then they will take up a lament[a] concerning you and say to you:

> “ ‘How you are destroyed, O city of renown,
> peopled by men of the sea!

a 7 Hebrew *Nebuchadrezzar,* of which *Nebuchadnezzar* is a variant; here and often in Ezekiel and Jeremiah

26:2 [a] 2Sa 5:11; Isa 23 [b] Eze 25:3
26:3 [c] Isa 5:30; Jer 50:42; 51:42
26:4 [d] Isa 23:1,11 [e] Am 1:10
26:5 [f] Eze 27:32 [g] Eze 29:19
26:7 [h] Jer 27:6 [i] Ezr 7:12; Da 2:37 [j] Eze 23:24; Na 2:3-4
26:8 [k] Jer 6:6 [l] Eze 21:22
26:10 [m] Jer 4:13
26:11 [n] Isa 5:28 [o] Jer 43:13 [p] Isa 26:5
26:12 [q] Isa 23:8; Eze 27:3-27; 28:8
26:13 [r] Jer 7:34 [s] Isa 14:11 [t] Jer 25:10; Rev 18:22
26:14 [u] Job 12:14; Mal 1:4
26:15 [v] Eze 27:35 [w] Jer 49:21
26:16 [x] Job 8:22 [y] Hos 11:10 [z] Eze 32:10
26:17 [a] Eze 19:1; 27:32

You were a power on the seas,
you and your citizens;
you put your terror
on all who lived there.[a]
18Now the coastlands tremble
on the day of your fall;
the islands in the sea
are terrified at your collapse.'[b]

19"This is what the Sovereign LORD says: When I make you a
desolate city, like cities no longer inhabited, and when I bring the
ocean depths over you and its vast waters cover you,[c] 20then I will
bring you down with those who go down to the pit,[d] to the people
of long ago. I will make you dwell in the earth below, as in ancient
ruins, with those who go down to the pit, and you will not return
or take your place[a] in the land of the living.[e] 21I will bring you to a
horrible end and you will be no more. You will be sought, but you
will never again be found, declares the Sovereign LORD."[f]

Chapter 27 Theme ______

27 The word of the LORD came to me: 2"Son of man, take up a
lament concerning Tyre. 3Say to Tyre, situated at the gateway to the sea,[g] merchant of peoples on many coasts, 'This is what
the Sovereign LORD says:

"'You say, O Tyre,
"I am perfect in beauty.[h]"
4Your domain was on the high seas;
your builders brought your beauty to perfection.
5They made all your timbers
of pine trees from Senir[b];[i]
they took a cedar from Lebanon
to make a mast for you.
6Of oaks[j] from Bashan
they made your oars;
of cypress wood[c] from the coasts of Cyprus[d] [k]
they made your deck, inlaid with ivory.
7Fine embroidered linen from Egypt was your sail
and served as your banner;
your awnings were of blue and purple[l]
from the coasts of Elishah.
8Men of Sidon and Arvad[m] were your oarsmen;
your skilled men, O Tyre, were aboard as your seamen.[n]
9Veteran craftsmen of Gebal[e] [o] were on board
as shipwrights to caulk your seams.

[a]20 Septuagint; Hebrew *return, and I will give glory* [b]5 That is, Hermon [c]6 Targum; the Masoretic Text has a different division of the consonants. [d]6 Hebrew *Kittim* [e]9 That is, Byblos

26:17 [a]Isa 14:12
26:18 [b]Isa 23:5; 41:5; Eze 27:35
26:19 [c]Isa 8:7-8
26:20 [d]Eze 32:18; Am 9:2; Jnh 2:2,6 [e]Eze 32:24,30
26:21 [f]Eze 27:36; 28:19; Rev 18:21
27:3 [g]ver 33 [h]Eze 28:2
27:5 [i]Dt 3:9
27:6 [j]Nu 21:33; Jer 22:20; Zec 11:2 [k]Ge 10:4; Isa 23:12
27:7 [l]Ex 25:4; Jer 10:9
27:8 [m]Ge 10:18 [n]1Ki 9:27
27:9 [o]Jos 13:5; 1Ki 5:18

All the ships of the sea and their sailors
came alongside to trade for your wares.

10 "'Men of Persia,[a] Lydia and Put[b]
served as soldiers in your army.
They hung their shields and helmets on your walls,
bringing you splendor.
11 Men of Arvad and Helech
manned your walls on every side;
men of Gammad
were in your towers.
They hung their shields around your walls;
they brought your beauty to perfection.

12 "'Tarshish[c] did business with you because of your great wealth
of goods;[d] they exchanged silver, iron, tin and lead for your merchandise.
13 "'Greece, Tubal and Meshech[e] traded with you; they exchanged
slaves[f] and articles of bronze for your wares.
14 "'Men of Beth Togarmah[g] exchanged work horses, war horses
and mules for your merchandise.
15 "'The men of Rhodes[a][h] traded with you, and many coastlands[i]
were your customers; they paid you with ivory[j] tusks and ebony.
16 "'Aram[b][k] did business with you because of your many products; they exchanged turquoise,[l] purple fabric, embroidered work,
fine linen, coral and rubies for your merchandise.
17 "'Judah and Israel traded with you; they exchanged wheat from
Minnith[m] and confections,[c] honey, oil and balm for your wares.
18 "'Damascus,[n] because of your many products and great wealth
of goods, did business with you in wine from Helbon and wool
from Zahar.
19 "'Danites and Greeks from Uzal bought your merchandise; they
exchanged wrought iron, cassia and calamus for your wares.
20 "'Dedan traded in saddle blankets with you.
21 "'Arabia and all the princes of Kedar[o] were your customers;
they did business with you in lambs, rams and goats.
22 "'The merchants of Sheba[p] and Raamah traded with you; for
your merchandise they exchanged the finest of all kinds of spices[q]
and precious stones, and gold.
23 "'Haran,[r] Canneh and Eden[s] and merchants of Sheba, Asshur
and Kilmad traded with you. 24 In your marketplace they traded
with you beautiful garments, blue fabric, embroidered work and
multicolored rugs with cords twisted and tightly knotted.

a *15* Septuagint; Hebrew *Dedan* b *16* Most Hebrew manuscripts; some Hebrew manuscripts and Syriac *Edom* c *17* The meaning of the Hebrew for this word is uncertain.

27:10 a Eze 38:5 b Eze 30:5
27:12 c Ge 10:4 d ver 18,33
27:13 e Ge 10:2; Isa 66:19; Eze 38:2 f Rev 18:13
27:14 g Ge 10:3; Eze 38:6
27:15 h Ge 10:7 i Jer 25:22 j 1Ki 10:22; Rev 18:12
27:16 k Jdg 10:6; Isa 7:1-8 l Eze 28:13
27:17 m Jdg 11:33
27:18 n Ge 14:15; Eze 47:16-18
27:21 o Ge 25:13; Isa 60:7
27:22 p Ge 10:7,28; 1Ki 10:1-2; Isa 60:6 q Ge 43:11
27:23 r 2Ki 19:12 s Isa 37:12

[25]"'The ships of Tarshish[a] serve
as carriers for your wares.
You are filled with heavy cargo
in the heart of the sea.
[26]Your oarsmen take you
out to the high seas.
But the east wind[b] will break you to pieces
in the heart of the sea.
[27]Your wealth,[c] merchandise and wares,
your mariners, seamen and shipwrights,
your merchants and all your soldiers,
and everyone else on board
will sink into the heart of the sea
on the day of your shipwreck.
[28]The shorelands will quake[d]
when your seamen cry out.
[29]All who handle the oars
will abandon their ships;
the mariners and all the seamen
will stand on the shore.
[30]They will raise their voice
and cry bitterly over you;
they will sprinkle dust[e] on their heads
and roll[f] in ashes.[g]
[31]They will shave their heads because of you
and will put on sackcloth.
They will weep[h] over you with anguish of soul
and with bitter mourning.[i]
[32]As they wail and mourn over you,
they will take up a lament[j] concerning you:
"Who was ever silenced like Tyre,
surrounded by the sea?"
[33]When your merchandise went out on the seas,
you satisfied many nations;
with your great wealth[k] and your wares
you enriched the kings of the earth.
[34]Now you are shattered by the sea
in the depths of the waters;
your wares and all your company
have gone down with you.[l]
[35]All who live in the coastlands[m]
are appalled at you;
their kings shudder with horror
and their faces are distorted with fear.

27:25 [a]Isa 2:16 *fn*
27:26 [b]Ps 48:7; Jer 18:17
27:27 [c]Pr 11:4
27:28 [d]Eze 26:15
27:30 [e]2Sa 1:2 [f]Jer 6:26 [g]Rev 18:18-19
27:31 [h]Isa 16:9 [i]Isa 22:12; Eze 7:18
27:32 [j]Eze 26:17
27:33 [k]ver 12; Eze 28:4-5
27:34 [l]Zec 9:4
27:35 [m]Eze 26:15

27:36
[a]Jer 18:16; 19:8; 49:17; 50:13; Zep 2:15
[b]Ps 37:10,36; Eze 26:21

36The merchants among the nations hiss at you;[a]
you have come to a horrible end
and will be no more.[b]' "

Chapter 28 Theme ______________________

28 The word of the LORD came to me: 2"Son of man, say to
the ruler of Tyre, 'This is what the Sovereign LORD says:

28:2
[c]Isa 14:13
[d]Ps 9:20; 82:6-7; Isa 31:3; 2Th 2:4

" 'In the pride of your heart
you say, "I am a god;
I sit on the throne[c] of a god
in the heart of the seas."
But you are a man and not a god,
though you think you are as wise as a god.[d]
3Are you wiser than Daniel[a]?[e]
Is no secret hidden from you?
4By your wisdom and understanding
you have gained wealth for yourself
and amassed gold and silver
in your treasuries.[f]
5By your great skill in trading
you have increased your wealth,
and because of your wealth
your heart has grown proud.[g]

28:3
[e]Da 1:20; 5:11-12

28:4
[f]Zec 9:3

28:5
[g]Job 31:25; Ps 52:7; 62:10; Hos 12:8; 13:6

6" 'Therefore this is what the Sovereign LORD says:

" 'Because you think you are wise,
as wise as a god,
7I am going to bring foreigners against you,
the most ruthless of nations;[h]
they will draw their swords against your beauty
and wisdom
and pierce your shining splendor.
8They will bring you down to the pit,[i]
and you will die a violent death
in the heart of the seas.[j]
9Will you then say, "I am a god,"
in the presence of those who kill you?
You will be but a man, not a god,
in the hands of those who slay you.
10You will die the death of the uncircumcised[k]
at the hands of foreigners.

I have spoken, declares the Sovereign LORD.' "

28:7
[h]Eze 30:11; 31:12; 32:12; Hab 1:6

28:8
[i]Eze 32:30
[j]Eze 27:27

28:10
[k]Eze 31:18; 32:19,24

a3 Or *Danel*; the Hebrew spelling may suggest a person other than the prophet Daniel.

[11]The word of the LORD came to me: [12]"Son of man, take up a
lament[a] concerning the king of Tyre and say to him: 'This is what
the Sovereign LORD says:

"'You were the model of perfection,
full of wisdom and perfect in beauty.[b]
[13]You were in Eden,[c]
the garden of God;[d]
every precious stone adorned you:
ruby, topaz and emerald,
chrysolite, onyx and jasper,
sapphire,[a] turquoise[e] and beryl.[b]
Your settings and mountings[c] were made of gold;
on the day you were created they were prepared.
[14]You were anointed[f] as a guardian cherub,[g]
for so I ordained you.
You were on the holy mount of God;
you walked among the fiery stones.
[15]You were blameless in your ways
from the day you were created
till wickedness was found in you.
[16]Through your widespread trade
you were filled with violence,[h]
and you sinned.
So I drove you in disgrace from the mount of God,
and I expelled you, O guardian cherub,[i]
from among the fiery stones.
[17]Your heart became proud[j]
on account of your beauty,
and you corrupted your wisdom
because of your splendor.
So I threw you to the earth;
I made a spectacle of you before kings.
[18]By your many sins and dishonest trade
you have desecrated your sanctuaries.
So I made a fire come out from you,
and it consumed you,
and I reduced you to ashes[k] on the ground
in the sight of all who were watching.
[19]All the nations who knew you
are appalled at you;
you have come to a horrible end
and will be no more.[l]'"

a 13 Or *lapis lazuli* b 13 The precise identification of some of these precious stones is uncertain. c 13 The meaning of the Hebrew for this phrase is uncertain.

28:12 [a]Eze 19:1 [b]Eze 27:2-4
28:13 [c]Ge 2:8 [d]Eze 31:8-9 [e]Eze 27:16
28:14 [f]Ex 30:26; 40:9 [g]Ex 25:17-20
28:16 [h]Hab 2:17 [i]Ge 3:24
28:17 [j]Eze 31:10
28:18 [k]Mal 4:3
28:19 [l]Jer 51:64; Eze 26:21; 27:36

20 The word of the LORD came to me: 21 "Son of man, set your face
against[a] Sidon;[b] prophesy against her 22 and say: 'This is what the
Sovereign LORD says:

"'I am against you, O Sidon,
and I will gain glory[c] within you.
They will know that I am the LORD,
when I inflict punishment[d] on her
and show myself holy within her.
23 I will send a plague upon her
and make blood flow in her streets.
The slain will fall within her,
with the sword against her on every side.
Then they will know that I am the LORD.[e]

24 "'No longer will the people of Israel have malicious neighbors
who are painful briers and sharp thorns.[f] Then they will know that
I am the Sovereign LORD.

25 "'This is what the Sovereign LORD says: When I gather[g] the
people of Israel from the nations where they have been scattered,[h]
I will show myself holy[i] among them in the sight of the nations.
Then they will live in their own land, which I gave to my servant
Jacob.[j] 26 They will live there in safety[k] and will build houses and
plant vineyards; they will live in safety when I inflict punishment
on all their neighbors who maligned them. Then they will know
that I am the LORD their God.[l]'"

Chapter 29 Theme ______________________

29

In the tenth year, in the tenth month on the twelfth day, the 587 B.C.
word of the LORD came to me:[m] 2 "Son of man, set your
face against Pharaoh king of Egypt[n] and prophesy against him
and against all Egypt.[o] 3 Speak to him and say: 'This is what the
Sovereign LORD says:

"'I am against you, Pharaoh[p] king of Egypt,
you great monster[q] lying among your streams.
You say, "The Nile is mine;
I made it for myself."
4 But I will put hooks[r] in your jaws
and make the fish of your streams stick to your scales.
I will pull you out from among your streams,
with all the fish sticking to your scales.[s]
5 I will leave you in the desert,
you and all the fish of your streams.
You will fall on the open field
and not be gathered or picked up.

28:21 [a] Eze 6:2 [b] Ge 10:15; Jer 25:22
28:22 [c] Eze 39:13 [d] Eze 30:19
28:23 [e] Eze 38:22
28:24 [f] Nu 33:55; Jos 23:13; Eze 2:6
28:25 [g] Ps 106:47; Jer 32:37 [h] Isa 11:12 [i] Eze 20:41 [j] Jer 23:8; Eze 11:17; 34:27; 37:25
28:26 [k] Jer 23:6 [l] Isa 65:21; Jer 32:15; Eze 38:8; Am 9:14-15
29:1 [m] ver 17; Eze 26:1
29:2 [n] Jer 25:19 [o] Isa 19:1-17; Jer 46:2; Eze 30:1-26; 31:1-18; 32:1-32
29:3 [p] Jer 44:30 [q] Ps 74:13; Isa 27:1; Eze 32:2
29:4 [r] 2Ki 19:28 [s] Eze 38:4

I will give you as food
to the beasts of the earth and the birds of the air.[a]

6 Then all who live in Egypt will know that I am the LORD.

"'You have been a staff of reed[b] for the house of Israel. 7 When
they grasped you with their hands, you splintered[c] and you tore
open their shoulders; when they leaned on you, you broke and
their backs were wrenched.[a] [d]
8 "'Therefore this is what the Sovereign LORD says: I will bring a
sword against you and kill your men and their animals.[e] 9 Egypt
will become a desolate wasteland. Then they will know that I am
the LORD.
"'Because you said, "The Nile is mine; I made it,[f]" 10 therefore I
am against you and against your streams, and I will make the land
of Egypt a ruin and a desolate waste from Migdol to Aswan,[g] as far
as the border of Cush.[b] 11 No foot of man or animal will pass through
it; no one will live there for forty years.[h] 12 I will make the land of
Egypt desolate among devastated lands, and her cities will lie desolate forty years among ruined cities. And I will disperse the Egyptians among the nations and scatter them through the countries.[i]
13 "'Yet this is what the Sovereign LORD says: At the end of forty
years I will gather the Egyptians from the nations where they were
scattered. 14 I will bring them back from captivity and return them
to Upper Egypt,[c] [j] the land of their ancestry. There they will be a
lowly[k] kingdom. 15 It will be the lowliest of kingdoms and will
never again exalt itself above the other nations.[l] I will make it so
weak that it will never again rule over the nations. 16 Egypt will no
longer be a source of confidence[m] for the people of Israel but will
be a reminder of their sin in turning to her for help. Then they
will know that I am the Sovereign LORD.[n]'"
571 B.C. 17 In the twenty-seventh year, in the first month on the first day, the
word of the LORD came to me:[o] 18 "Son of man, Nebuchadnezzar[p]
king of Babylon drove his army in a hard campaign against Tyre;
every head was rubbed bare[q] and every shoulder made raw. Yet
he and his army got no reward from the campaign he led against
Tyre. 19 Therefore this is what the Sovereign LORD says: I am going
to give Egypt to Nebuchadnezzar king of Babylon, and he will
carry off its wealth. He will loot and plunder the land as pay for
his army.[r] 20 I have given him Egypt as a reward for his efforts because he and his army did it for me, declares the Sovereign LORD.[s]
21 "On that day I will make a horn[d] [t] grow for the house of Israel,
and I will open your mouth[u] among them. Then they will know
that I am the LORD.[v]"

[a] 7 Syriac (see also Septuagint and Vulgate); Hebrew *and you caused their backs to stand*
[b] 10 That is, the upper Nile region [c] 14 Hebrew *to Pathros* [d] 21 *Horn* here symbolizes strength.

29:5 [a] Jer 7:33; 34:20; Eze 32:4-6; 39:4
29:6 [b] 2Ki 18:21; Isa 36:6
29:7 [c] Isa 36:6 [d] Eze 17:15-17
29:8 [e] Eze 14:17; 32:11-13
29:9 [f] Eze 30:7-8,13-19
29:10 [g] Eze 30:6
29:11 [h] Eze 32:13
29:12 [i] Jer 46:19; Eze 30:7,23,26
29:14 [j] Eze 30:14 [k] Eze 17:14
29:15 [l] Zec 10:11
29:16 [m] Isa 36:4,6 [n] Isa 30:2; Hos 8:13
29:17 [o] Eze 24:1
29:18 [p] Jer 27:6; Eze 26:7-8 [q] Jer 48:37
29:19 [r] Jer 43:10-13; Eze 30:4,10,24-25
29:20 [s] Isa 10:6-7; 45:1; Jer 25:9
29:21 [t] Ps 132:17 [u] Eze 33:22 [v] Eze 24:27

Chapter 30 Theme ______________________________

30 The word of the LORD came to me: 2"Son of man, prophesy
and say: 'This is what the Sovereign LORD says:

"'Wail[a] and say,
"Alas for that day!"
3For the day is near,[b]
the day of the LORD[c] is near—
a day of clouds,
a time of doom for the nations.
4A sword will come against Egypt,
and anguish will come upon Cush.[a]
When the slain fall in Egypt,
her wealth will be carried away
and her foundations torn down.[d]

5Cush and Put,[e] Lydia and all Arabia, Libya[b] and the people[f] of the
covenant land will fall by the sword along with Egypt.
6"'This is what the LORD says:

"'The allies of Egypt will fall
and her proud strength will fail.
From Migdol to Aswan[g]
they will fall by the sword within her,
declares the Sovereign LORD.

7"'They will be desolate
among desolate lands,
and their cities will lie
among ruined cities.[h]
8Then they will know that I am the LORD,
when I set fire to Egypt
and all her helpers are crushed.

9"'On that day messengers will go out from me in ships to fright-
en Cush[i] out of her complacency. Anguish[j] will take hold of them
on the day of Egypt's doom, for it is sure to come.[k]

10"'This is what the Sovereign LORD says:

"'I will put an end to the hordes of Egypt
by the hand of Nebuchadnezzar king of Babylon.[l]
11He and his army—the most ruthless of nations[m]—
will be brought in to destroy the land.
They will draw their swords against Egypt
and fill the land with the slain.
12I will dry up[n] the streams of the Nile[o]
and sell the land to evil men;

30:2 *a* Isa 13:6
30:3 *b* Eze 7:7; Joel 2:1,11; Ob 1:15 *c* ver 18; Eze 7:12,19
30:4 *d* Eze 29:19
30:5 *e* Eze 27:10 *f* Jer 25:20
30:6 *g* Eze 29:10
30:7 *h* Eze 29:12
30:9 *i* Isa 18:1-2 *j* Isa 23:5 *k* Eze 32:9-10
30:10 *l* Eze 29:19
30:11 *m* Eze 28:7
30:12 *n* Isa 19:6 *o* Eze 29:9

a4 That is, the upper Nile region; also in verses 5 and 9 b5 Hebrew *Cub*

by the hand of foreigners
I will lay waste the land and everything in it.
I the LORD have spoken.

13"'This is what the Sovereign LORD says:

"'I will destroy the idols[a]
and put an end to the images in Memphis.[a][b]
No longer will there be a prince in Egypt,[c]
and I will spread fear throughout the land.
14I will lay[d] waste Upper Egypt,[b]
set fire to Zoan[e]
and inflict punishment on Thebes.[c][f]
15I will pour out my wrath on Pelusium,[d]
the stronghold of Egypt,
and cut off the hordes of Thebes.
16I will set fire to Egypt;
Pelusium will writhe in agony.
Thebes will be taken by storm;
Memphis will be in constant distress.
17The young men of Heliopolis[e][g] and Bubastis[f]
will fall by the sword,
and the cities themselves will go into captivity.
18Dark will be the day at Tahpanhes
when I break the yoke of Egypt;[h]
there her proud strength will come to an end.
She will be covered with clouds,
and her villages will go into captivity.[i]
19So I will inflict punishment on Egypt,
and they will know that I am the LORD.'"

587 B.C. 20In the eleventh year, in the first month on the seventh day, the
word of the LORD came to me:[j] 21"Son of man, I have broken the
arm[k] of Pharaoh king of Egypt. It has not been bound up for
healing[l] or put in a splint so as to become strong enough to hold
a sword. 22Therefore this is what the Sovereign LORD says: I am
against Pharaoh king of Egypt.[m] I will break both his arms, the
good arm as well as the broken one, and make the sword fall from
his hand.[n] 23I will disperse the Egyptians among the nations and
scatter them through the countries.[o] 24I will strengthen[p] the arms
of the king of Babylon and put my sword[q] in his hand, but I will
break the arms of Pharaoh, and he will groan before him like a
mortally wounded man. 25I will strengthen the arms of the king of

a 13 Hebrew *Noph*; also in verse 16 b 14 Hebrew *waste Pathros* c 14 Hebrew *No*; also in verses 15 and 16 d 15 Hebrew *Sin*; also in verse 16 e 17 Hebrew *Awen* (or *On*) f 17 Hebrew *Pi Beseth*

30:13 [a]Jer 43:12 [b]Isa 19:13 [c]Zec 10:11
30:14 [d]Eze 29:14 [e]Ps 78:12,43 [f]Jer 46:25
30:17 [g]Ge 41:45
30:18 [h]Lev 26:13 [i]ver 3
30:20 [j]Eze 26:1; 29:17; 31:1
30:21 [k]Jer 48:25 [l]Jer 30:13; 46:11
30:22 [m]Jer 46:25 [n]Ps 37:17
30:23 [o]Eze 29:12
30:24 [p]Zec 10:6,12 [q]Eze 21:14; Zep 2:12

Babylon, but the arms of Pharaoh will fall limp. Then they will
know that I am the LORD, when I put my sword into the hand of the
king of Babylon and he brandishes it against Egypt. 26I will disperse the Egyptians among the nations and scatter them through
the countries. Then they will know that I am the LORD.[a]"

Chapter 31 Theme ______________________

587 B.C.

31 In the eleventh year,[b] in the third month on the first day, the
word of the LORD came to me:[c] 2"Son of man, say to Pharaoh
king of Egypt and to his hordes:

"'Who can be compared with you in majesty?
3Consider Assyria, once a cedar in Lebanon,
with beautiful branches overshadowing the forest;
it towered on high,
its top above the thick foliage.[d]
4The waters nourished it,
deep springs made it grow tall;
their streams flowed
all around its base
and sent their channels
to all the trees of the field.
5So it towered higher
than all the trees of the field;
its boughs increased
and its branches grew long,
spreading because of abundant waters.[e]
6All the birds of the air
nested in its boughs,
all the beasts of the field
gave birth under its branches;
all the great nations
lived in its shade.[f]
7It was majestic in beauty,
with its spreading boughs,
for its roots went down
to abundant waters.
8The cedars[g] in the garden of God
could not rival it,
nor could the pine trees
equal its boughs,
nor could the plane trees
compare with its branches—
no tree in the garden of God
could match its beauty.[h]

30:26 [a]Eze 29:12
31:1 [b]Jer 52:5 [c]Eze 30:20
31:3 [d]Isa 10:34
31:5 [e]Eze 17:5
31:6 [f]Eze 17:23; Mt 13:32
31:8 [g]Ps 80:10 [h]Ge 2:8-9

[9]I made it beautiful
with abundant branches,
the envy of all the trees of Eden[a]
in the garden of God.[b]

[10]"'Therefore this is what the Sovereign LORD says: Because it
towered on high, lifting its top above the thick foliage, and
because it was proud[c] of its height, [11]I handed it over to the ruler
of the nations, for him to deal with according to its wickedness. I
cast it aside,[d] [12]and the most ruthless of foreign nations[e] cut it
down and left it. Its boughs fell on the mountains and in all the
valleys;[f] its branches lay broken in all the ravines of the land. All
the nations of the earth came out from under its shade and left it.[g]
[13]All the birds of the air settled on the fallen tree, and all the beasts
of the field were among its branches.[h] [14]Therefore no other trees
by the waters are ever to tower proudly on high, lifting their tops
above the thick foliage. No other trees so well-watered are ever to
reach such a height; they are all destined for death,[i] for the earth
below, among mortal men, with those who go down to the pit.[j]
[15]"'This is what the Sovereign LORD says: On the day it was
brought down to the grave[a] I covered the deep springs with
mourning for it; I held back its streams, and its abundant waters
were restrained. Because of it I clothed Lebanon with gloom, and
all the trees of the field withered away. [16]I made the nations tremble[k] at the sound of its fall when I brought it down to the grave
with those who go down to the pit. Then all the trees[l] of Eden, the
choicest and best of Lebanon, all the trees that were well-watered,
were consoled[m] in the earth below.[n] [17]Those who lived in its
shade, its allies among the nations, had also gone down to the
grave with it, joining those killed by the sword.[o]
[18]"'Which of the trees of Eden can be compared with you in
splendor and majesty? Yet you, too, will be brought down with the
trees of Eden to the earth below; you will lie among the uncircumcised,[p] with those killed by the sword.

"'This is Pharaoh and all his hordes, declares the Sovereign
LORD.'"

Chapter 32 Theme ______________________

585 B.C.

32

In the twelfth year, in the twelfth month on the first day, the
word of the LORD came to me:[q] [2]"Son of man, take up a
lament[r] concerning Pharaoh king of Egypt and say to him:

"'You are like a lion[s] among the nations;
you are like a monster in the seas

[a] *15* Hebrew *Sheol*; also in verses 16 and 17

31:9 [a]Ge 2:8 [b]Ge 13:10; Eze 28:13
31:10 [c]Isa 14:13-14; Eze 28:17
31:11 [d]Da 5:20
31:12 [e]Eze 28:7 [f]Eze 32:5; 35:8 [g]Eze 32:11-12; Da 4:14
31:13 [h]Isa 18:6; Eze 29:5; 32:4
31:14 [i]Ps 82:7 [j]Ps 63:9; Eze 26:20; 32:24
31:16 [k]Eze 26:15 [l]Isa 14:8 [m]Eze 14:22; 32:31 [n]Isa 14:15; Eze 32:18
31:17 [o]Ps 9:17
31:18 [p]Jer 9:26; Eze 32:19,21
32:1 [q]Eze 31:1; 33:21
32:2 [r]Eze 19:1; 27:2 [s]Eze 19:3,6; Na 2:11-13

thrashing about in your streams,
churning the water with your feet
and muddying the streams.[a]

3"'This is what the Sovereign LORD says:

"'With a great throng of people
I will cast my net over you,
and they will haul you up in my net.[b]
4I will throw you on the land
and hurl you on the open field.
I will let all the birds of the air settle on you
and all the beasts of the earth gorge themselves on you.[c]
5I will spread your flesh on the mountains
and fill the valleys[d] with your remains.
6I will drench the land with your flowing blood[e]
all the way to the mountains,
and the ravines will be filled with your flesh.
7When I snuff you out, I will cover the heavens
and darken their stars;
I will cover the sun with a cloud,
and the moon will not give its light.[f]
8All the shining lights in the heavens
I will darken over you;
I will bring darkness over your land,
declares the Sovereign LORD.
9I will trouble the hearts of many peoples
when I bring about your destruction among the nations,
among[a] lands you have not known.
10I will cause many peoples to be appalled at you,
and their kings will shudder with horror because of you
when I brandish my sword before them.
On the day[g] of your downfall
each of them will tremble
every moment for his life.[h]

11"'For this is what the Sovereign LORD says:

"'The sword of the king of Babylon[i]
will come against you.
12I will cause your hordes to fall
by the swords of mighty men—
the most ruthless of all nations.[j]
They will shatter the pride of Egypt,
and all her hordes will be overthrown.[k]

a9 Hebrew; Septuagint *bring you into captivity among the nations, / to*

32:2 [a]Eze 29:3; 34:18
32:3 [b]Eze 12:13
32:4 [c]Isa 18:6; Eze 31:12-13
32:5 [d]Eze 31:12
32:6 [e]Isa 34:3
32:7 [f]Isa 13:10; 34:4; Eze 30:3; Joel 2:2,31; 3:15; Mt 24:29; Rev 8:12
32:10 [g]Jer 46:10 [h]Eze 26:16; 27:35
32:11 [i]Jer 46:26
32:12 [j]Eze 28:7 [k]Eze 31:11-12

13 I will destroy all her cattle
from beside abundant waters
no longer to be stirred by the foot of man
or muddied by the hoofs of cattle.[a]
14 Then I will let her waters settle
and make her streams flow like oil,
declares the Sovereign LORD.
15 When I make Egypt desolate
and strip the land of everything in it,
when I strike down all who live there,
then they will know that I am the LORD.[b]'

16 "This is the lament[c] they will chant for her. The daughters of
the nations will chant it; for Egypt and all her hordes they will
chant it, declares the Sovereign LORD."

586-585 B.C. 17 In the twelfth year, on the fifteenth day of the month, the word
of the LORD came to me:[d] 18 "Son of man, wail for the hordes of
Egypt and consign[e] to the earth below both her and the daughters
of mighty nations, with those who go down to the pit.[f] 19 Say to
them, 'Are you more favored than others? Go down and be laid
among the uncircumcised.'[g] 20 They will fall among those killed by
the sword. The sword is drawn; let her be dragged[h] off with all her
hordes. 21 From within the grave[a][i] the mighty leaders will say of
Egypt and her allies, 'They have come down and they lie with the
uncircumcised, with those killed by the sword.'

22 "Assyria is there with her whole army; she is surrounded by
the graves of all her slain, all who have fallen by the sword. 23 Their
graves are in the depths of the pit[j] and her army lies around her
grave. All who had spread terror in the land of the living are slain,
fallen by the sword.

24 "Elam[k] is there, with all her hordes around her grave. All of
them are slain, fallen by the sword.[l] All who had spread terror in
the land of the living[m] went down uncircumcised to the earth below.
They bear their shame with those who go down to the pit.[n] 25 A bed
is made for her among the slain, with all her hordes around her
grave. All of them are uncircumcised, killed by the sword. Because
their terror had spread in the land of the living, they bear their
shame with those who go down to the pit; they are laid among the
slain.

26 "Meshech and Tubal[o] are there, with all their hordes around
their graves. All of them are uncircumcised, killed by the sword
because they spread their terror in the land of the living. 27 Do they
not lie with the other uncircumcised warriors who have fallen,
who went down to the grave with their weapons of war, whose

a *21* Hebrew *Sheol*; also in verse 27

32:13 [a] Eze 29:8,11
32:15 [b] Ex 7:5; 14:4,18; Ps 107:33-34; Eze 6:7
32:16 [c] 2Sa 1:17; 2Ch 35:25; Eze 26:17
32:17 [d] ver 1
32:18 [e] Jer 1:10 [f] Eze 31:14,16; Mic 1:8
32:19 [g] ver 29-30; Eze 28:10; 31:18
32:20 [h] Ps 28:3
32:21 [i] Isa 14:9
32:23 [j] Isa 14:15
32:24 [k] Ge 10:22 [l] Jer 49:37 [m] Job 28:13 [n] Eze 26:20
32:26 [o] Ge 10:2; Eze 27:13

swords were placed under their heads? The punishment for their
sins rested on their bones, though the terror of these warriors had
stalked through the land of the living.
28“You too, O Pharaoh, will be broken and will lie among the
uncircumcised, with those killed by the sword.
29“Edom[a] is there, her kings and all her princes; despite their
power, they are laid with those killed by the sword. They lie with
the uncircumcised, with those who go down to the pit.[b]
30“All the princes of the north[c] and all the Sidonians[d] are there;
they went down with the slain in disgrace despite the terror caused
by their power. They lie uncircumcised with those killed by the
sword and bear their shame with those who go down to the pit.
31“Pharaoh—he and all his army—will see them and he will be
consoled[e] for all his hordes that were killed by the sword, declares
the Sovereign LORD. 32Although I had him spread terror in the land
of the living, Pharaoh and all his hordes will be laid among the uncircumcised, with those killed by the sword, declares the Sovereign
LORD.”

Chapter 33 Theme ______________________

33 The word of the LORD came to me: 2“Son of man, speak to
your countrymen and say to them: ‘When I bring the
sword[f] against a land, and the people of the land choose one of
their men and make him their watchman,[g] 3and he sees the sword
coming against the land and blows the trumpet[h] to warn the people, 4then if anyone hears the trumpet but does not take warning[i]
and the sword comes and takes his life, his blood will be on his
own head.[j] 5Since he heard the sound of the trumpet but did not
take warning, his blood will be on his own head. If he had taken
warning, he would have saved himself. 6But if the watchman sees
the sword coming and does not blow the trumpet to warn the
people and the sword comes and takes the life of one of them,
that man will be taken away because of his sin, but I will hold the
watchman accountable for his blood.’[k]

32:29 [a]Isa 34:5-15; Jer 49:7; Eze 35:15; Ob 1:1 [b]Eze 25:12-14
32:30 [c]Jer 25:26; Eze 38:6; 39:2 [d]Jer 25:22; Eze 28:21
32:31 [e]Eze 14:22; 31:16
33:2 [f]Jer 12:12 [g]Eze 3:11
33:3 [h]Hos 8:1
33:4 [i]2Ch 25:16 [j]Jer 6:17; Eze 18:13; Zec 1:4; Ac 18:6
33:6 [k]Eze 3:18

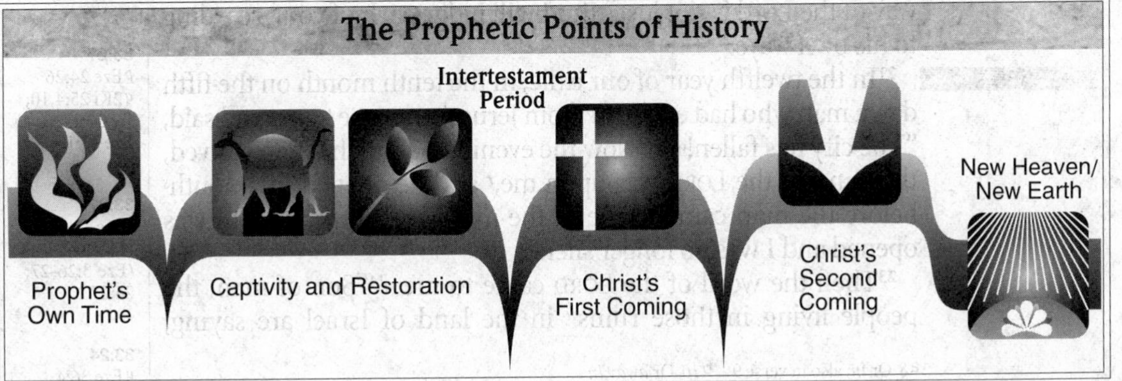

7“Son of man, I have made you a watchman for the house of
Israel; so hear the word I speak and give them warning from me.[a]
8When I say to the wicked, ‘O wicked man, you will surely die,[b]’
and you do not speak out to dissuade him from his ways, that
wicked man will die for[a] his sin, and I will hold you accountable
for his blood.[c] 9But if you do warn the wicked man to turn from
his ways and he does not do so, he will die for his sin, but you will
have saved yourself.[d]

10“Son of man, say to the house of Israel, ‘This is what you are
saying: “Our offenses and sins weigh us down, and we are wasting
away[e] because of[b] them. How then can we live?[f]” ’ 11Say to them,
‘As surely as I live, declares the Sovereign LORD, I take no pleasure
in the death of the wicked, but rather that they turn from their
ways and live.[g] Turn! Turn from your evil ways! Why will you die,
O house of Israel?’[h]

12“Therefore, son of man, say to your countrymen, ‘The righteousness of the righteous man will not save him when he dis-
obeys, and the wickedness of the wicked man will not cause him
to fall when he turns from it. The righteous man, if he sins, will
not be allowed to live because of his former righteousness.’[i] 13If I
tell the righteous man that he will surely live, but then he trusts in
his righteousness and does evil, none of the righteous things he
has done will be remembered; he will die for the evil he has done.[j]
14And if I say to the wicked man, ‘You will surely die,’ but he then
turns away from his sin and does what is just[k] and right— 15if he
gives back what he took in pledge for a loan, returns what he has
stolen,[l] follows the decrees that give life, and does no evil, he will
surely live; he will not die.[m] 16None of the sins he has committed
will be remembered against him. He has done what is just and
right; he will surely live.[n]

17“Yet your countrymen say, ‘The way of the Lord is not just.’ But
it is their way that is not just. 18If a righteous man turns from his
righteousness and does evil, he will die for it.[o] 19And if a wicked
man turns away from his wickedness and does what is just and
right, he will live by doing so. 20Yet, O house of Israel, you say, ‘The
way of the Lord is not just.’ But I will judge each of you according
to his own ways.”

585 B.C. 21In the twelfth year of our exile, in the tenth month on the fifth
day, a man who had escaped[p] from Jerusalem came to me and said,
“The city has fallen![q]” 22Now the evening before the man arrived,
the hand of the LORD was upon me,[r] and he opened my mouth[s]
before the man came to me in the morning. So my mouth was
opened and I was no longer silent.[t]

23Then the word of the LORD came to me: 24“Son of man, the
people living in those ruins[u] in the land of Israel are saying,

33:7 [a]Jer 26:2; Eze 3:17
33:8 [b]ver 14 [c]Eze 18:4
33:9 [d]Eze 3:17-19
33:10 [e]Eze 24:23 [f]Lev 26:39; Eze 4:17
33:11 [g]Eze 18:32; 2Pe 3:9 [h]Eze 18:23
33:12 [i]2Ch 7:14; Eze 3:20
33:13 [j]Eze 18:24; Heb 10:38; 2Pe 2:20-21
33:14 [k]Eze 18:27
33:15 [l]Ex 22:1-4; Lev 6:2-5 [m]Eze 20:11; Lk 19:8
33:16 [n]Isa 43:25; Eze 18:22
33:18 [o]Eze 3:20; Eze 18:26
33:21 [p]Eze 24:26 [q]2Ki 25:4,10; Jer 39:1-2; Eze 32:1
33:22 [r]Eze 1:3 [s]Lk 1:64 [t]Eze 3:26-27; 24:27
33:24 [u]Eze 36:4

[a]8 Or *in*; also in verse 9 [b]10 Or *away in*

'Abraham was only one man, yet he possessed the land. But we are
many; surely the land has been given to us as our possession.'[a]
25Therefore say to them, 'This is what the Sovereign LORD says:
Since you eat meat with the blood[b] still in it and look to your idols
and shed blood, should you then possess the land?[c] 26You rely on
your sword, you do detestable things, and each of you defiles his
neighbor's wife.[d] Should you then possess the land?'

27"Say this to them: 'This is what the Sovereign LORD says: As
surely as I live, those who are left in the ruins will fall by the sword,
those out in the country I will give to the wild animals to be
devoured, and those in strongholds and caves will die of a plague.[e]
28I will make the land a desolate waste, and her proud strength will
come to an end, and the mountains of Israel will become desolate
so that no one will cross them. 29Then they will know that I am the
LORD, when I have made the land a desolate waste because of all the
detestable things they have done.'

30"As for you, son of man, your countrymen are talking together
about you by the walls and at the doors of the houses, saying to
each other, 'Come and hear the message that has come from the
LORD.' 31My people come to you, as they usually do, and sit before[f]
you to listen to your words, but they do not put them into practice.
With their mouths they express devotion, but their hearts are
greedy for unjust gain.[g] 32Indeed, to them you are nothing more
than one who sings love songs with a beautiful voice and plays an
instrument well, for they hear your words but do not put them into
practice.[h]

33"When all this comes true—and it surely will—then they will
know that a prophet has been among them.[i]"

Chapter 34 Theme ______________________________

34 The word of the LORD came to me: 2"Son of man, prophesy
against the shepherds of Israel; prophesy and say to them:
'This is what the Sovereign LORD says: Woe to the shepherds of
Israel who only take care of themselves! Should not shepherds
take care of the flock?[j] 3You eat the curds, clothe yourselves with
the wool and slaughter the choice animals, but you do not take
care of the flock.[k] 4You have not strengthened the weak or healed
the sick or bound up the injured. You have not brought back the
strays or searched for the lost. You have ruled them harshly and
brutally.[l] 5So they were scattered because there was no shepherd,[m]
and when they were scattered they became food for all the wild
animals.[n] 6My sheep wandered over all the mountains and on
every high hill. They were scattered over the whole earth, and no
one searched or looked for them.[o]

7"'Therefore, you shepherds, hear the word of the LORD: 8As
surely as I live, declares the Sovereign LORD, because my flock lacks

33:24 [a] Isa 51:2; Jer 40:7; Eze 11:15; Ac 7:5
33:25 [b] Ge 9:4; Dt 12:16 [c] Jer 7:9-10; Eze 22:6,27
33:26 [d] Eze 22:11
33:27 [e] 1Sa 13:6; Isa 2:19; Jer 42:22; Eze 39:4
33:31 [f] Eze 8:1 [g] Ps 78:36-37; Isa 29:13; Eze 22:27; Mt 13:22; 1Jn 3:18
33:32 [h] Mk 6:20
33:33 [i] 1Sa 3:20; Jer 28:9; Eze 2:5
34:2 [j] Ps 78:70-72; Isa 40:11; Jer 3:15; 23:1; Mic 3:11; Jn 10:11; 21:15-17
34:3 [k] Isa 56:11; Eze 22:27; Zec 11:16
34:4 [l] Zec 11:15-17
34:5 [m] Nu 27:17 [n] ver 28; Isa 56:9
34:6 [o] Ps 142:4; 1Pe 2:25

a shepherd and so has been plundered and has become food for
all the wild animals, and because my shepherds did not search for
my flock but cared for themselves rather than for my flock, 9there-
fore, O shepherds, hear the word of the LORD: 10This is what the
Sovereign LORD says: I am against[a] the shepherds and will hold
them accountable for my flock. I will remove them from tending
the flock so that the shepherds can no longer feed themselves. I
will rescue[b] my flock from their mouths, and it will no longer be
food for them.[c]

11" 'For this is what the Sovereign LORD says: I myself will search
for my sheep and look after them. 12As a shepherd[d] looks after his
scattered flock when he is with them, so will I look after my sheep.
I will rescue them from all the places where they were scattered on
a day of clouds and darkness.[e] 13I will bring them out from the
nations and gather them from the countries, and I will bring them
into their own land. I will pasture them on the mountains of Israel,
in the ravines and in all the settlements in the land.[f] 14I will tend
them in a good pasture, and the mountain heights of Israel[g] will
be their grazing land. There they will lie down in good grazing
land, and there they will feed in a rich pasture[h] on the mountains
of Israel.[i] 15I myself will tend my sheep and have them lie down,
declares the Sovereign LORD.[j] 16I will search for the lost and bring
back the strays. I will bind up the injured and strengthen the
weak,[k] but the sleek and the strong I will destroy. I will shepherd
the flock with justice.[l]

17" 'As for you, my flock, this is what the Sovereign LORD says: I
will judge between one sheep and another, and between rams and
goats.[m] 18Is it not enough for you to feed on the good pasture? Must
you also trample the rest of your pasture with your feet? Is it not
enough for you to drink clear water? Must you also muddy the rest
with your feet? 19Must my flock feed on what you have trampled
and drink what you have muddied with your feet?

20" 'Therefore this is what the Sovereign LORD says to them: See,
I myself will judge between the fat sheep and the lean sheep.
21Because you shove with flank and shoulder, butting all the weak
sheep with your horns[n] until you have driven them away, 22I will
save my flock, and they will no longer be plundered. I will judge
between one sheep and another.[o] 23I will place over them one
shepherd, my servant David, and he will tend[p] them; he will tend
them and be their shepherd. 24I the LORD will be their God,[q] and
my servant David will be prince among them. I the LORD have
spoken.[r]

25" 'I will make a covenant of peace with them and rid the land
of wild beasts[s] so that they may live in the desert and sleep in the
forests in safety.[t] 26I will bless[u] them and the places surrounding

34:10 [a]Jer 21:13 [b]Ps 72:14 [c]1Sa 2:29-30; Zec 10:3
34:12 [d]Isa 40:11; Jer 31:10; Lk 19:10 [e]Eze 30:3
34:13 [f]Jer 23:3
34:14 [g]Eze 20:40 [h]Ps 23:2 [i]Eze 36:29-30
34:15 [j]Ps 23:1-2
34:16 [k]Mic 4:6 [l]Isa 10:16; Lk 5:32
34:17 [m]Mt 25:32-33
34:21 [n]Dt 33:17
34:22 [o]Ps 72:12-14; Jer 23:2-3
34:23 [p]Isa 40:11
34:24 [q]Eze 36:28 [r]Jer 30:9
34:25 [s]Lev 26:6 [t]Isa 11:6-9; Hos 2:18
34:26 [u]Ge 12:2

my hill.[a] I will send down showers in season;[a] there will be showers of blessing.[b] 27The trees of the field will yield their fruit and the ground will yield its crops; the people will be secure in their land. They will know that I am the LORD, when I break the bars of their yoke[c] and rescue them from the hands of those who enslaved them.[d] 28They will no longer be plundered by the nations, nor will wild animals devour them. They will live in safety, and no one will make them afraid.[e] 29I will provide for them a land renowned[f] for its crops, and they will no longer be victims of famine[g] in the land or bear the scorn[h] of the nations.[i] 30Then they will know that I, the LORD their God, am with them and that they, the house of Israel, are my people, declares the Sovereign LORD.[j] 31You my sheep, the sheep of my pasture,[k] are people, and I am your God, declares the Sovereign LORD.'"

Chapter 35 Theme

35 The word of the LORD came to me: 2"Son of man, set your face against Mount Seir; prophesy against it 3and say: 'This is what the Sovereign LORD says: I am against you, Mount Seir, and I will stretch out my hand[l] against you and make you a desolate waste.[m] 4I will turn your towns into ruins and you will be desolate. Then you will know that I am the LORD.[n]

5"'Because you harbored an ancient hostility and delivered the Israelites over to the sword at the time of their calamity, the time their punishment reached its climax,[o] 6therefore as surely as I live, declares the Sovereign LORD, I will give you over to bloodshed and it will pursue you.[p] Since you did not hate bloodshed, bloodshed will pursue you. 7I will make Mount Seir a desolate waste and cut off from it all who come and go. 8I will fill your mountains with the slain; those killed by the sword will fall on your hills and in your valleys and in all your ravines.[q] 9I will make you desolate forever; your towns will not be inhabited. Then you will know that I am the LORD.[r]

10"'Because you have said, "These two nations and countries will be ours and we will take possession[s] of them," even though I the LORD was there, 11therefore as surely as I live, declares the Sovereign LORD, I will treat you in accordance with the anger[t] and jealousy you showed in your hatred of them and I will make myself known among them when I judge you.[u] 12Then you will know that I the LORD have heard all the contemptible things you have said against the mountains of Israel. You said, "They have been laid waste and have been given over to us to devour.[v]" 13You boasted against me and spoke against me without restraint, and I

a26 Or *I will make them and the places surrounding my hill a blessing*

34:26 [a]Ps 68:9 [b]Dt 11:13-15; Isa 44:3
34:27 [c]Lev 26:13 [d]Jer 30:8
34:28 [e]Jer 30:10; Eze 39:26
34:29 [f]Isa 4:2 [g]Eze 36:29 [h]Eze 36:6 [i]Eze 36:15
34:30 [j]Eze 14:11; 37:27
34:31 [k]Ps 100:3; Jer 23:1
35:3 [l]Jer 6:12 [m]Eze 25:12-14
35:4 [n]ver 9
35:5 [o]Ps 137:7; Eze 21:29
35:6 [p]Isa 63:2-6
35:8 [q]Eze 31:12
35:9 [r]Jer 49:13
35:10 [s]Ps 83:12; Eze 36:2,5
35:11 [t]Eze 25:14 [u]Ps 9:16; Mt 7:2
35:12 [v]Jer 50:7

heard it.[a] 14This is what the Sovereign LORD says: While the whole
earth rejoices, I will make you desolate.[b] 15Because you rejoiced[c]
when the inheritance of the house of Israel became desolate, that
is how I will treat you. You will be desolate, O Mount Seir,[d] you
and all of Edom.[e] Then they will know that I am the LORD.'"

Chapter 36 Theme ____

36 "Son of man, prophesy to the mountains of Israel and say,
'O mountains of Israel, hear the word of the LORD. 2This is
what the Sovereign LORD says: The enemy said of you, "Aha![f] The
ancient heights[g] have become our possession."[h]' 3Therefore prophesy and say, 'This is what the Sovereign LORD says: Because they
ravaged and hounded you from every side so that you became
the possession of the rest of the nations and the object of people's
malicious talk and slander,[i] 4therefore, O mountains of Israel, hear
the word of the Sovereign LORD: This is what the Sovereign LORD
says to the mountains and hills, to the ravines and valleys,[j] to the
desolate ruins and the deserted towns that have been plundered
and ridiculed by the rest of the nations around you[k]— 5this is what
the Sovereign LORD says: In my burning zeal I have spoken against
the rest of the nations, and against all Edom, for with glee and with
malice in their hearts they made my land their own possession so
that they might plunder its pastureland.'[l] 6Therefore prophesy
concerning the land of Israel and say to the mountains and hills,
to the ravines and valleys: 'This is what the Sovereign LORD says: I
speak in my jealous wrath because you have suffered the scorn of
the nations.[m] 7Therefore this is what the Sovereign LORD says: I
swear with uplifted hand that the nations around you will also
suffer scorn.

8"'But you, O mountains of Israel, will produce branches and
fruit[n] for my people Israel, for they will soon come home. 9I am
concerned for you and will look on you with favor; you will be
plowed and sown, 10and I will multiply the number of people upon
you, even the whole house of Israel. The towns will be inhabited
and the ruins rebuilt.[o] 11I will increase the number of men and animals upon you, and they will be fruitful and become numerous. I
will settle people on you as in the past[p] and will make you prosper
more than before.[q] Then you will know that I am the LORD. 12I will
cause people, my people Israel, to walk upon you. They will possess you, and you will be their inheritance;[r] you will never again
deprive them of their children.

13"'This is what the Sovereign LORD says: Because people say to
you, "You devour men[s] and deprive your nation of its children,"
14therefore you will no longer devour men or make your nation
childless, declares the Sovereign LORD. 15No longer will I make you

35:13 [a]Da 11:36
35:14 [b]Jer 51:48
35:15 [c]Ob 1:12 [d]ver 3 [e]Isa 34:5-6,11; Jer 50:11-13; La 4:21
36:2 [f]Eze 25:3 [g]Dt 32:13 [h]Eze 35:10
36:3 [i]Ps 44:13-14
36:4 [j]Eze 6:3 [k]Dt 11:11; Ps 79:4; Eze 34:28
36:5 [l]Jer 50:11; Eze 25:12-14; 35:10,15
36:6 [m]Ps 123:3-4; Eze 34:29
36:8 [n]Isa 27:6
36:10 [o]ver 33; Isa 49:17-23
36:11 [p]Mic 7:14 [q]Jer 31:28; Eze 16:55
36:12 [r]Eze 47:14,22
36:13 [s]Nu 13:32

INSIGHT

See **Major Events in Israel's History** on page 2189. Notice the section from 1948 through modern times.

hear the taunts of the nations, and no longer will you suffer the
scorn of the peoples or cause your nation to fall, declares the Sovereign LORD.[a]'"
16Again the word of the LORD came to me: 17"Son of man, when
the people of Israel were living in their own land, they defiled it by
their conduct and their actions. Their conduct was like a woman's
monthly uncleanness in my sight.[b] 18So I poured out[c] my wrath
on them because they had shed blood in the land and because
they had defiled it with their idols. 19I dispersed them among the
nations, and they were scattered[d] through the countries; I judged
them according to their conduct and their actions.[e] 20And wherever they went among the nations they profaned[f] my holy name, for
it was said of them, 'These are the LORD's people, and yet they had
to leave his land.'[g] 21I had concern for my holy name, which the
house of Israel profaned among the nations where they had gone.[h]
22"Therefore say to the house of Israel, 'This is what the Sovereign LORD says: It is not for your sake, O house of Israel, that I am
going to do these things, but for the sake of my holy name, which
you have profaned[i] among the nations where you have gone.[j] 23I
will show the holiness of my great name, which has been profaned
among the nations, the name you have profaned among them.
Then the nations will know that I am the LORD, declares the Sovereign LORD, when I show myself holy[k] through you before their eyes.[l]
24" 'For I will take you out of the nations; I will gather you from
all the countries and bring you back into your own land.[m] 25I will
sprinkle[n] clean water on you, and you will be clean; I will cleanse[o]
you from all your impurities and from all your idols.[p] 26I will
give you a new heart[q] and put a new spirit in you; I will remove
from you your heart of stone and give you a heart of flesh.[r] 27And
I will put my Spirit[s] in you and move you to follow my decrees
and be careful to keep my laws. 28You will live in the land I gave
your forefathers; you will be my people,[t] and I will be your God.[u]
29I will save you from all your uncleanness. I will call for the grain
and make it plentiful and will not bring famine[v] upon you. 30I
will increase the fruit of the trees and the crops of the field, so
that you will no longer suffer disgrace among the nations because of famine.[w] 31Then you will remember your evil ways and
wicked deeds, and you will loathe yourselves for your sins and
detestable practices.[x] 32I want you to know that I am not doing
this for your sake, declares the Sovereign LORD. Be ashamed and
disgraced for your conduct, O house of Israel![y]
33" 'This is what the Sovereign LORD says: On the day I cleanse
you from all your sins, I will resettle your towns, and the ruins will
be rebuilt. 34The desolate land will be cultivated instead of lying
desolate in the sight of all who pass through it. 35They will say,

36:15 [a]Ps 89:50-51; Eze 34:29
36:17 [b]Jer 2:7
36:18 [c]2Ch 34:21
36:19 [d]Dt 28:64 [e]Eze 39:24
36:20 [f]Ro 2:24 [g]Isa 52:5; Jer 33:24; Eze 12:16
36:21 [h]Ps 74:18; Isa 48:9
36:22 [i]Ro 2:24* [j]Ps 106:8
36:23 [k]Eze 20:41 [l]Ps 126:2; Isa 5:16
36:24 [m]Eze 34:13; 37:21
36:25 [n]Heb 9:13; 10:22 [o]Ps 51:2,7 [p]Zec 13:2
36:26 [q]Jer 24:7 [r]Ps 51:10; Eze 11:19
36:27 [s]Eze 37:14
36:28 [t]Jer 30:22 [u]Eze 14:11; 37:14,27
36:29 [v]Eze 34:29
36:30 [w]Lev 26:4-5; Eze 34:27; Hos 2:21-22
36:31 [x]Eze 6:9; 20:43
36:32 [y]Dt 9:5

"This land that was laid waste has become like the garden of Eden;[a]
the cities that were lying in ruins, desolate and destroyed, are now
fortified and inhabited.[b]" 36Then the nations around you that
remain will know that I the LORD have rebuilt what was destroyed
and have replanted what was desolate. I the LORD have spoken, and
I will do it.'[c]
37"This is what the Sovereign LORD says: Once again I will yield
to the plea of the house of Israel and do this for them: I will make
their people as numerous as sheep, 38as numerous as the flocks for
offerings[d] at Jerusalem during her appointed feasts. So will the
ruined cities be filled with flocks of people. Then they will know
that I am the LORD."

Chapter 37 Theme ______________________

37 The hand of the LORD was upon me,[e] and he brought me
out by the Spirit[f] of the LORD and set me in the middle of
a valley;[g] it was full of bones.[h] 2He led me back and forth among
them, and I saw a great many bones on the floor of the valley,
bones that were very dry. 3He asked me, "Son of man, can these
bones live?"
I said, "O Sovereign LORD, you alone know.[i]"
4Then he said to me, "Prophesy to these bones and say to them,
'Dry bones, hear the word of the LORD![j] 5This is what the Sovereign LORD says to these bones: I will make breath[a] enter you, and
you will come to life.[k] 6I will attach tendons to you and make
flesh come upon you and cover you with skin; I will put breath in
you, and you will come to life. Then you will know that I am the
LORD.[l]'"
7So I prophesied as I was commanded. And as I was prophesying, there was a noise, a rattling sound, and the bones came
together, bone to bone. 8I looked, and tendons and flesh appeared
on them and skin covered them, but there was no breath in them.
9Then he said to me, "Prophesy to the breath;[m] prophesy, son of
man, and say to it, 'This is what the Sovereign LORD says: Come
from the four winds, O breath, and breathe into these slain, that
they may live.'" 10So I prophesied as he commanded me, and
breath entered them; they came to life and stood up on their feet—
a vast army.[n]
11Then he said to me: "Son of man, these bones are the whole
house of Israel. They say, 'Our bones are dried up and our hope is
gone; we are cut off.'[o] 12Therefore prophesy and say to them: 'This
is what the Sovereign LORD says: O my people, I am going to open
your graves and bring you up from them; I will bring you back to
the land of Israel.[p] 13Then you, my people, will know that I am the

[a]5 The Hebrew for this word can also mean *wind* or *spirit* (see verses 6-14).

36:35 [a]Joel 2:3 [b]Isa 51:3

36:36 [c]Eze 17:22; 22:14; 37:14; 39:27-28

36:38 [d]1Ki 8:63; 2Ch 35:7-9

37:1 [e]Eze 1:3; 8:3 [f]Eze 11:24; Lk 4:1; Ac 8:39 [g]Jer 7:32 [h]Jer 8:2; Eze 40:1

37:3 [i]Dt 32:39; 1Sa 2:6; Isa 26:19

37:4 [j]Jer 22:29

37:5 [k]Ge 2:7; Ps 104:29-30

37:6 [l]Eze 38:23; Joel 2:27; 3:17

37:9 [m]Ps 104:30

37:10 [n]Rev 11:11

37:11 [o]La 3:54

37:12 [p]Dt 32:39; 1Sa 2:6; Isa 26:19; Hos 13:14; Am 9:14-15

LORD, when I open your graves and bring you up from them. [14]I
will put my Spirit[a] in you and you will live, and I will settle you in
your own land. Then you will know that I the LORD have spoken,
and I have done it, declares the LORD.[b]'"
[15]The word of the LORD came to me: [16]"Son of man, take a stick
of wood and write on it, 'Belonging to Judah and the Israelites[c]
associated with him.[d]' Then take another stick of wood, and write
on it, 'Ephraim's stick, belonging to Joseph and all the house of
Israel associated with him.' [17]Join them together into one stick so
that they will become one in your hand.[e]
[18]"When your countrymen ask you, 'Won't you tell us what you
mean by this?'[f] [19]say to them, 'This is what the Sovereign LORD
says: I am going to take the stick of Joseph—which is in Ephraim's
hand—and of the Israelite tribes associated with him, and join it
to Judah's stick, making them a single stick of wood, and they will
become one in my hand.'[g] [20]Hold before their eyes the sticks you
have written on [21]and say to them, 'This is what the Sovereign
LORD says: I will take the Israelites out of the nations where they
have gone. I will gather them from all around and bring them
back into their own land.[h] [22]I will make them one nation in the
land, on the mountains of Israel. There will be one king over all of
them and they will never again be two nations or be divided into
two kingdoms.[i] [23]They will no longer defile[j] themselves with
their idols and vile images or with any of their offenses, for I will
save them from all their sinful backsliding,[a] and I will cleanse
them. They will be my people, and I will be their God.[k]
[24]"'My servant David[l] will be king over them, and they will all
have one shepherd.[m] They will follow my laws and be careful to
keep my decrees.[n] [25]They will live in the land I gave to my servant
Jacob, the land where your fathers lived.[o] They and their children
and their children's children will live there forever,[p] and David my
servant will be their prince forever.[q] [26]I will make a covenant of
peace[r] with them; it will be an everlasting covenant. I will establish
them and increase their numbers,[s] and I will put my sanctuary
among them forever.[t] [27]My dwelling place[u] will be with them; I will
be their God, and they will be my people.[v] [28]Then the nations will
know that I the LORD make Israel holy,[w] when my sanctuary is
among them forever.'"

Chapter 38 Theme

38 The word of the LORD came to me: [2]"Son of man, set your
face against Gog, of the land of Magog,[x] the chief prince
of[b] Meshech and Tubal;[y] prophesy against him [3]and say: 'This is
what the Sovereign LORD says: I am against you, O Gog, chief prince

[a]*23* Many Hebrew manuscripts (see also Septuagint); most Hebrew manuscripts *all their dwelling places where they sinned* [b]*2* Or *the prince of Rosh,*

37:14 [a]Joel 2:28-29 [b]Eze 36:27-28,36
37:16 [c]1Ki 12:20; 2Ch 10:17-19 [d]Nu 17:2-3; 2Ch 15:9
37:17 [e]ver 24; Isa 11:13; Jer 50:4; Hos 1:11
37:18 [f]Eze 24:19
37:19 [g]Zec 10:6
37:21 [h]Isa 43:5-6; Eze 36:24; 39:27
37:22 [i]Isa 11:13; Jer 3:18; Hos 1:11
37:23 [j]Eze 36:25; 43:7 [k]Eze 11:18; 36:28
37:24 [l]Hos 3:5 [m]Isa 40:11; Eze 34:23 [n]Ps 78:70-71
37:25 [o]Eze 28:25 [p]Am 9:15 [q]Isa 11:1
37:26 [r]Isa 55:3 [s]Jer 30:19 [t]Eze 16:62
37:27 [u]Lev 26:11; Jn 1:14 [v]2Co 6:16*
37:28 [w]Ex 31:13; Eze 20:12
38:2 [x]Ge 10:2 [y]Rev 20:8

of[a] Meshech and Tubal.[a] 4I will turn you around, put hooks[b] in
your jaws and bring you out with your whole army—your horses,
your horsemen fully armed, and a great horde with large and small
shields, all of them brandishing their swords.[c] 5Persia, Cush[b] [d] and
Put[e] will be with them, all with shields and helmets, 6also Gomer[f]
with all its troops, and Beth Togarmah[g] from the far north with all
its troops—the many nations with you.

7"'Get ready; be prepared,[h] you and all the hordes gathered
about you, and take command of them. 8After many days[i] you
will be called to arms. In future years you will invade a land that
has recovered from war, whose people were gathered from many
nations[j] to the mountains of Israel, which had long been desolate.
They had been brought out from the nations, and now all of them
live in safety.[k] 9You and all your troops and the many nations with
you will go up, advancing like a storm;[l] you will be like a cloud[m]
covering the land.

10"'This is what the Sovereign LORD says: On that day thoughts
will come into your mind and you will devise an evil scheme.[n] 11You
will say, "I will invade a land of unwalled villages; I will attack a
peaceful and unsuspecting people—all of them living without
walls and without gates and bars.[o] 12I will plunder and loot and
turn my hand against the resettled ruins and the people gathered
from the nations, rich in livestock and goods, living at the center of
the land." 13Sheba[p] and Dedan and the merchants of Tarshish and
all her villages[c] will say to you, "Have you come to plunder? Have
you gathered your hordes to loot, to carry off silver and gold, to
take away livestock and goods and to seize much plunder?[q]"'

14"Therefore, son of man, prophesy and say to Gog: 'This is what
the Sovereign LORD says: In that day, when my people Israel are living in safety,[r] will you not take notice of it? 15You will come from
your place in the far north, you and many nations with you, all of
them riding on horses, a great horde, a mighty army.[s] 16You will
advance against my people Israel like a cloud[t] that covers the land.
In days to come, O Gog, I will bring you against my land, so that
the nations may know me when I show myself holy through you
before their eyes.[u]

17"'This is what the Sovereign LORD says: Are you not the one I
spoke of in former days by my servants the prophets of Israel? At
that time they prophesied for years that I would bring you against
them. 18This is what will happen in that day: When Gog attacks the
land of Israel, my hot anger will be aroused, declares the Sovereign
LORD. 19In my zeal and fiery wrath I declare that at that time there
shall be a great earthquake in the land of Israel.[v] 20The fish of the
sea, the birds of the air, the beasts of the field, every creature that

a3 Or *Gog, prince of Rosh,* b5 That is, the upper Nile region c13 Or *her strong lions*

38:3 [a] Eze 39:1
38:4 [b] 2Ki 19:28 [c] Eze 29:4; Da 11:40
38:5 [d] Ge 10:6 [e] Eze 27:10
38:6 [f] Ge 10:2 [g] Eze 27:14
38:7 [h] Isa 8:9
38:8 [i] Isa 24:22 [j] Isa 11:11 [k] Jer 23:6
38:9 [l] Isa 28:2 [m] Jer 4:13; Joel 2:2
38:10 [n] Ps 36:4; Mic 2:1
38:11 [o] Jer 49:31; Zec 2:4
38:13 [p] Eze 27:22 [q] Isa 10:6; Jer 15:13
38:14 [r] ver 8; Zec 2:5
38:15 [s] Eze 39:2
38:16 [t] ver 9 [u] Isa 29:23; Eze 39:21
38:19 [v] Ps 18:7; Eze 5:13; Hag 2:6,21

moves along the ground, and all the people on the face of the earth
will tremble at my presence. The mountains will be overturned,
the cliffs will crumble and every wall will fall to the ground.[a] 21I
will summon a sword[b] against Gog on all my mountains, declares
the Sovereign LORD. Every man's sword will be against his brother.[c]
22I will execute judgment[d] upon him with plague and bloodshed; I
will pour down torrents of rain, hailstones[e] and burning sulfur on
him and on his troops and on the many nations with him. 23And
so I will show my greatness and my holiness, and I will make
myself known in the sight of many nations. Then they will know
that I am the LORD.[f]'

Chapter 39 Theme ____________________________

39 "Son of man, prophesy against Gog and say: 'This is what
the Sovereign LORD says: I am against you, O Gog, chief
prince of[a] Meshech and Tubal.[g] 2I will turn you around and drag
you along. I will bring you from the far north and send you against
the mountains of Israel. 3Then I will strike your bow[h] from your
left hand and make your arrows[i] drop from your right hand. 4On
the mountains of Israel you will fall, you and all your troops and
the nations with you. I will give you as food to all kinds of carrion
birds and to the wild animals.[j] 5You will fall in the open field, for
I have spoken, declares the Sovereign LORD. 6I will send fire[k] on
Magog and on those who live in safety in the coastlands,[l] and they
will know that I am the LORD.

7"'I will make known my holy name among my people Israel. I
will no longer let my holy name be profaned,[m] and the nations
will know that I the LORD am the Holy One in Israel.[n] 8It is coming! It will surely take place, declares the Sovereign LORD. This is
the day I have spoken of.

9"'Then those who live in the towns of Israel will go out and use
the weapons for fuel and burn them up—the small and large
shields, the bows and arrows, the war clubs and spears. For seven
years they will use them for fuel.[o] 10They will not need to gather
wood from the fields or cut it from the forests, because they will
use the weapons for fuel. And they will plunder those who plundered them and loot those who looted them, declares the Sovereign LORD.[p]

11"'On that day I will give Gog a burial place in Israel, in the valley of those who travel east toward[b] the Sea.[c] It will block the way
of travelers, because Gog and all his hordes will be buried there. So
it will be called the Valley of Hamon Gog.[d][q]

12"'For seven months the house of Israel will be burying them
in order to cleanse the land.[r] 13All the people of the land will bury

[a]1 Or *Gog, prince of Rosh,* [b]11 Or *of* [c]11 That is, the Dead Sea [d]11 *Hamon Gog* means *hordes of Gog.*

38:20 [a]Hos 4:3; Na 1:5
38:21 [b]Eze 14:17 [c]1Sa 14:20; 2Ch 20:23; Hag 2:22
38:22 [d]Isa 66:16; Jer 25:31 [e]Ps 18:12; Rev 16:21
38:23 [f]Eze 36:23
39:1 [g]Eze 38:2,3
39:3 [h]Hos 1:5 [i]Ps 76:3
39:4 [j]ver 17-20; Eze 29:5; 33:27
39:6 [k]Eze 30:8; Am 1:4 [l]Jer 25:22
39:7 [m]Ex 20:7 [n]Isa 12:6; Eze 36:16,23
39:9 [o]Ps 46:9
39:10 [p]Isa 14:2; 33:1; Hab 2:8
39:11 [q]Eze 38:2
39:12 [r]Dt 21:23

them, and the day I am glorified[a] will be a memorable day for
them, declares the Sovereign LORD.
14"'Men will be regularly employed to cleanse the land. Some
will go throughout the land and, in addition to them, others will
bury those that remain on the ground. At the end of the seven
months they will begin their search. 15As they go through the land
and one of them sees a human bone, he will set up a marker beside
it until the gravediggers have buried it in the Valley of Hamon Gog.
16(Also a town called Hamonah[a] will be there.) And so they will
cleanse the land.'
17"Son of man, this is what the Sovereign LORD says: Call out to
every kind of bird[b] and all the wild animals: 'Assemble and come
together from all around to the sacrifice I am preparing for you,
the great sacrifice on the mountains of Israel. There you will eat
flesh and drink blood. 18You will eat the flesh of mighty men and
drink the blood of the princes of the earth as if they were rams
and lambs, goats and bulls—all of them fattened animals from
Bashan.[c] 19At the sacrifice I am preparing for you, you will eat fat
till you are glutted and drink blood till you are drunk. 20At my
table you will eat your fill of horses and riders, mighty men and
soldiers of every kind,' declares the Sovereign LORD.[d]
21"I will display my glory among the nations, and all the nations
will see the punishment I inflict and the hand I lay upon them.[e]
22From that day forward the house of Israel will know that I am
the LORD their God. 23And the nations will know that the people
of Israel went into exile for their sin, because they were unfaithful
to me. So I hid my face from them and handed them over to their
enemies, and they all fell by the sword.[f] 24I dealt with them
according to their uncleanness and their offenses, and I hid my
face from them.[g]
25"Therefore this is what the Sovereign LORD says: I will now
bring Jacob back from captivity[b][h] and will have compassion[i] on
all the people of Israel, and I will be zealous for my holy name.[j]
26They will forget their shame and all the unfaithfulness they
showed toward me when they lived in safety[k] in their land with
no one to make them afraid.[l] 27When I have brought them back
from the nations and have gathered them from the countries of
their enemies, I will show myself holy through them in the sight
of many nations.[m] 28Then they will know that I am the LORD their
God, for though I sent them into exile among the nations, I will
gather them to their own land, not leaving any behind. 29I will no
longer hide my face from them, for I will pour out my Spirit[n] on
the house of Israel, declares the Sovereign LORD."

a 16 *Hamonah* means *horde.* b 25 Or *now restore the fortunes of Jacob*

39:13 [a] Eze 28:22
39:17 [b] Rev 19:17
39:18 [c] Ps 22:12; Jer 51:40
39:20 [d] Rev 19:17-18
39:21 [e] Ex 9:16; Isa 37:20; Eze 38:16
39:23 [f] Isa 1:15; 59:2; Jer 22:8-9; 44:23
39:24 [g] Jer 2:17,19; 4:18; Eze 36:19
39:25 [h] Jer 33:7; Eze 34:13 [i] Jer 30:18 [j] Isa 27:12-13
39:26 [k] 1Ki 4:25 [l] Isa 17:2; Eze 34:28; Mic 4:4
39:27 [m] Eze 36:23-24; 37:21; 38:16
39:29 [n] Joel 2:28; Ac 2:17

Chapter 40 Theme ______________________________

573 B.C.

40 In the twenty-fifth year of our exile, at the beginning of the year, on the tenth of the month, in the fourteenth year after the fall of the city[a]—on that very day the hand of the LORD was upon me[b] and he took me there. 2In visions[c] of God he took me to the land of Israel and set me on a very high mountain,[d] on whose south side were some buildings that looked like a city. 3He took me there, and I saw a man whose appearance was like bronze;[e] he was standing in the gateway with a linen cord and a measuring rod[f] in his hand. 4The man said to me, "Son of man, look with your eyes and hear with your ears and pay attention to everything I am going to show you, for that is why you have been brought here. Tell[g] the house of Israel everything you see.[h]"

5I saw a wall completely surrounding the temple area. The length of the measuring rod in the man's hand was six long cubits, each of which was a cubit[a] and a handbreadth.[b] He measured[i] the wall; it was one measuring rod thick and one rod high.

6Then he went to the gate facing east.[j] He climbed its steps and measured the threshold of the gate; it was one rod deep.[c] 7The alcoves[k] for the guards were one rod long and one rod wide, and the projecting walls between the alcoves were five cubits thick. And the threshold of the gate next to the portico facing the temple was one rod deep.

8Then he measured the portico of the gateway; 9it[d] was eight cubits deep and its jambs were two cubits thick. The portico of the gateway faced the temple.

10Inside the east gate were three alcoves on each side; the three had the same measurements, and the faces of the projecting walls on each side had the same measurements. 11Then he measured the width of the entrance to the gateway; it was ten cubits and its length was thirteen cubits. 12In front of each alcove was a wall one cubit high, and the alcoves were six cubits square. 13Then he measured the gateway from the top of the rear wall of one alcove to the top of the opposite one; the distance was twenty-five cubits from one parapet opening to the opposite one. 14He measured along the faces of the projecting walls all around the inside of the gateway—sixty cubits. The measurement was up to the portico[e] facing the courtyard.[f] [l] 15The distance from the entrance of the gateway to the far end of its portico was fifty cubits. 16The alcoves and the projecting walls inside the gateway were surmounted by narrow parapet openings all around, as was the portico; the openings all around

[a]5 The common cubit was about 1 1/2 feet (about 0.5 meter). [b]5 That is, about 3 inches (about 8 centimeters) [c]6 Septuagint; Hebrew *deep, the first threshold, one rod deep* [d]8,9 Many Hebrew manuscripts, Septuagint, Vulgate and Syriac; most Hebrew manuscripts *gateway facing the temple; it was one rod deep. 9Then he measured the portico of the gateway; it* [e]14 Septuagint; Hebrew *projecting wall* [f]14 The meaning of the Hebrew for this verse is uncertain.

40:1 [a]2Ki 25:7; Jer 39:1-10; 52:4-11; Eze 33:21 [b]Eze 1:3
40:2 [c]Da 7:1,7 [d]Eze 17:22; Rev 21:10
40:3 [e]Eze 1:7; Da 10:6; Rev 1:15 [f]Eze 47:3; Zec 2:1-2; Rev 11:1; 21:15
40:4 [g]Jer 26:2 [h]Eze 44:5
40:5 [i]Eze 42:20
40:6 [j]Eze 8:16
40:7 [k]ver 36
40:14 [l]Ex 27:9

faced inward. The faces of the projecting walls were decorated with
palm trees.[a]
17Then he brought me into the outer court.[b] There I saw some
rooms and a pavement that had been constructed all around the
court; there were thirty rooms[c] along the pavement.[d] 18It abutted
the sides of the gateways and was as wide as they were long; this
was the lower pavement. 19Then he measured the distance from
the inside of the lower gateway to the outside of the inner court;[e] it
was a hundred cubits[f] on the east side as well as on the north.
20Then he measured the length and width of the gate facing
north, leading into the outer court. 21Its alcoves[g]—three on each
side—its projecting walls and its portico had the same measurements as those of the first gateway. It was fifty cubits long and
twenty-five cubits wide. 22Its openings, its portico[h] and its palm
tree decorations had the same measurements as those of the gate
facing east. Seven steps led up to it, with its portico opposite them.
23There was a gate to the inner court facing the north gate, just as
there was on the east. He measured from one gate to the opposite
one; it was a hundred cubits.[i]
24Then he led me to the south side and I saw a gate facing south.
He measured its jambs and its portico, and they had the same
measurements as the others. 25The gateway and its portico had
narrow openings all around, like the openings of the others. It was
fifty cubits long and twenty-five cubits wide.[j] 26Seven steps led up
to it, with its portico opposite them; it had palm tree decorations
on the faces of the projecting walls on each side.[k] 27The inner
court[l] also had a gate facing south, and he measured from this gate
to the outer gate on the south side; it was a hundred cubits.
28Then he brought me into the inner court through the south
gate, and he measured the south gate; it had the same measurements[m] as the others. 29Its alcoves, its projecting walls and its portico had the same measurements as the others. The gateway and
its portico had openings all around. It was fifty cubits long and
twenty-five cubits wide. 30(The porticoes[n] of the gateways around
the inner court were twenty-five cubits wide and five cubits deep.)
31Its portico[o] faced the outer court; palm trees decorated its jambs,
and eight steps led up to it.
32Then he brought me to the inner court on the east side, and he
measured the gateway; it had the same measurements as the others.
33Its alcoves, its projecting walls and its portico had the same measurements as the others. The gateway and its portico had openings
all around. It was fifty cubits long and twenty-five cubits wide. 34Its
portico[p] faced the outer court; palm trees decorated the jambs
on either side, and eight steps led up to it.
35Then he brought me to the north gate[q] and measured it. It
had the same measurements as the others, 36as did its alcoves,[r] its

40:16 [a] ver 21-22; 2Ch 3:5; Eze 41:26
40:17 [b] Rev 11:2 [c] Eze 41:6 [d] Eze 42:1
40:19 [e] Eze 46:1 [f] ver 23,27
40:21 [g] ver 7
40:22 [h] ver 49
40:23 [i] ver 19
40:25 [j] ver 33
40:26 [k] ver 22
40:27 [l] ver 32
40:28 [m] ver 35
40:30 [n] ver 21
40:31 [o] ver 22
40:34 [p] ver 22
40:35 [q] Eze 44:4; 47:2
40:36 [r] ver 7

projecting walls and its portico, and it had openings all around.
It was fifty cubits long and twenty-five cubits wide. 37 Its portico[a]
faced the outer court; palm trees decorated the jambs on either
side, and eight steps led up to it.
38 A room with a doorway was by the portico in each of the inner
gateways, where the burnt offerings[a] were washed. 39 In the portico
of the gateway were two tables on each side, on which the burnt
offerings,[b] sin offerings[c] and guilt offerings[d] were slaughtered. 40 By
the outside wall of the portico of the gateway, near the steps at the
entrance to the north gateway were two tables, and on the other
side of the steps were two tables. 41 So there were four tables on
one side of the gateway and four on the other—eight tables in
all—on which the sacrifices were slaughtered. 42 There were also
four tables of dressed stone[e] for the burnt offerings, each a cubit
and a half long, a cubit and a half wide and a cubit high. On them
were placed the utensils for slaughtering the burnt offerings and
the other sacrifices.[f] 43 And double-pronged hooks, each a handbreadth long, were attached to the wall all around. The tables
were for the flesh of the offerings.
44 Outside the inner gate, within the inner court, were two rooms,
one[b] at the side of the north gate and facing south, and another at
the side of the south[c] gate and facing north. 45 He said to me, "The
room facing south is for the priests who have charge of the temple,[g]
46 and the room facing north[h] is for the priests who have charge of
the altar.[i] These are the sons of Zadok,[j] who are the only Levites
who may draw near to the LORD to minister before him.[k]"
47 Then he measured the court: It was square—a hundred cubits
long and a hundred cubits wide. And the altar was in front of the
temple.
48 He brought me to the portico of the temple[l] and measured the
jambs of the portico; they were five cubits wide on either side. The
width of the entrance was fourteen cubits and its projecting walls
were[d] three cubits wide on either side. 49 The portico[m] was twenty
cubits wide, and twelve[e] cubits from front to back. It was reached by
a flight of stairs,[f] and there were pillars[n] on each side of the jambs.

Chapter 41 Theme ____________________

41 Then the man brought me to the outer sanctuary[o] and measured the jambs; the width of the jambs was six cubits[g] on
each side.[h] 2 The entrance was ten cubits wide, and the projecting
walls on each side of it were five cubits wide. He also measured the
outer sanctuary; it was forty cubits long and twenty cubits wide.[p]

40:38 [a] 2Ch 4:6; Eze 42:13
40:39 [b] Eze 46:2 [c] Lev 4:3,28 [d] Lev 7:1
40:42 [e] Ex 20:25 [f] ver 39
40:45 [g] 1Ch 9:23
40:46 [h] Eze 42:13 [i] Nu 18:5 [j] 1Ki 2:35 [k] Nu 16:5; Eze 43:19; 44:15; 45:4; 48:11
40:48 [l] 1Ki 6:2
40:49 [m] ver 22; 1Ki 6:3 [n] 1Ki 7:15
41:1 [o] ver 23
41:2 [p] 2Ch 3:3

[a] *37* Septuagint (see also verses 31 and 34); Hebrew *jambs* [b] *44* Septuagint; Hebrew *were rooms for singers, which were* [c] *44* Septuagint; Hebrew *east* [d] *48* Septuagint; Hebrew *entrance was* [e] *49* Septuagint; Hebrew *eleven* [f] *49* Hebrew; Septuagint *Ten steps led up to it* [g] *1* The common cubit was about 1 1/2 feet (about 0.5 meter). [h] *1* One Hebrew manuscript and Septuagint; most Hebrew manuscripts *side, the width of the tent*

3Then he went into the inner sanctuary and measured the jambs
of the entrance; each was two cubits wide. The entrance was six
cubits wide, and the projecting walls on each side of it were seven
cubits wide. 4And he measured the length of the inner sanctuary;
it was twenty cubits, and its width was twenty cubits across the
end of the outer sanctuary.[a] He said to me, "This is the Most Holy
Place.[b]"

5Then he measured the wall of the temple; it was six cubits thick,
and each side room around the temple was four cubits wide. 6The
side rooms were on three levels, one above another, thirty[c] on each
level. There were ledges all around the wall of the temple to serve
as supports for the side rooms, so that the supports were not
inserted into the wall of the temple.[d] 7The side rooms all around
the temple were wider at each successive level. The structure surrounding the temple was built in ascending stages, so that the
rooms widened as one went upward. A stairway[e] went up from
the lowest floor to the top floor through the middle floor.

8I saw that the temple had a raised base all around it, forming the
foundation of the side rooms. It was the length of the rod, six long
cubits. 9The outer wall of the side rooms was five cubits thick.
The open area between the side rooms of the temple 10and the
⌊priests'⌋ rooms was twenty cubits wide all around the temple.
11There were entrances to the side rooms from the open area, one
on the north and another on the south; and the base adjoining
the open area was five cubits wide all around.

12The building facing the temple courtyard on the west side was
seventy cubits wide. The wall of the building was five cubits thick
all around, and its length was ninety cubits.

13Then he measured the temple; it was a hundred cubits long,
and the temple courtyard and the building with its walls were also
a hundred cubits long. 14The width of the temple courtyard on the
east, including the front of the temple, was a hundred cubits.[f]

15Then he measured the length of the building facing the courtyard at the rear of the temple, including its galleries[g] on each side;
it was a hundred cubits.

The outer sanctuary, the inner sanctuary and the portico facing
the court, 16as well as the thresholds and the narrow windows[h]
and galleries around the three of them—everything beyond and
including the threshold was covered with wood. The floor, the wall
up to the windows, and the windows were covered.[i] 17In the space
above the outside of the entrance to the inner sanctuary and on the
walls at regular intervals all around the inner and outer sanctuary
18were carved[j] cherubim[k] and palm trees.[l] Palm trees alternated
with cherubim. Each cherub had two faces:[m] 19the face of a man
toward the palm tree on one side and the face of a lion toward the

41:4 [a] 1Ki 6:20 [b] Ex 26:33; Heb 9:3-8
41:6 [c] Eze 40:17 [d] 1Ki 6:5
41:7 [e] 1Ki 6:8
41:14 [f] Eze 40:47
41:15 [g] Eze 42:3
41:16 [h] 1Ki 6:4 [i] ver 25-26; 1Ki 6:15; Eze 42:3
41:18 [j] 1Ki 6:18 [k] Ex 37:7; 2Ch 3:7 [l] 1Ki 6:29; 7:36 [m] Eze 10:21

palm tree on the other. They were carved all around the whole
temple.[a] 20From the floor to the area above the entrance, cherubim
and palm trees were carved on the wall of the outer sanctuary.
21The outer sanctuary[b] had a rectangular doorframe, and the
one at the front of the Most Holy Place was similar. 22There was a
wooden altar[c] three cubits high and two cubits square[a]; its corners,
its base[b] and its sides were of wood. The man said to me, "This is
the table[d] that is before the LORD." 23Both the outer sanctuary[e] and
the Most Holy Place had double doors.[f] 24Each door had two
leaves—two hinged leaves[g] for each door. 25And on the doors of
the outer sanctuary were carved cherubim and palm trees like
those carved on the walls, and there was a wooden overhang on
the front of the portico. 26On the sidewalls of the portico were
narrow windows with palm trees carved on each side. The side
rooms of the temple also had overhangs.[h]

Chapter 42 Theme

42 Then the man led me northward into the outer court and
brought me to the rooms[i] opposite the temple courtyard[j]
and opposite the outer wall on the north side.[k] 2The building
whose door faced north was a hundred cubits[c] long and fifty
cubits wide. 3Both in the section twenty cubits from the inner
court and in the section opposite the pavement of the outer court,
gallery[l] faced gallery at the three levels.[m] 4In front of the rooms was
an inner passageway ten cubits wide and a hundred cubits[d] long.
Their doors were on the north.[n] 5Now the upper rooms were nar-
rower, for the galleries took more space from them than from the
rooms on the lower and middle floors of the building. 6The rooms
on the third floor had no pillars, as the courts had; so they were
smaller in floor space than those on the lower and middle floors.
7There was an outer wall parallel to the rooms and the outer court;
it extended in front of the rooms for fifty cubits. 8While the row of
rooms on the side next to the outer court was fifty cubits long, the
row on the side nearest the sanctuary was a hundred cubits long.
9The lower rooms had an entrance[o] on the east side as one enters
them from the outer court.
10On the south side[e] along the length of the wall of the outer
court, adjoining the temple courtyard and opposite the outer wall,
were rooms[p] 11with a passageway in front of them. These were like
the rooms on the north; they had the same length and width, with
similar exits and dimensions. Similar to the doorways on the
north 12were the doorways of the rooms on the south. There was

41:19 [a]Eze 10:14
41:21 [b]ver 1
41:22 [c]Ex 30:1 [d]Ex 25:23; Eze 23:41; 44:16; Mal 1:7,12
41:23 [e]ver 1 [f]1Ki 6:32
41:24 [g]1Ki 6:34
41:26 [h]ver 15-16; Eze 40:16
42:1 [i]ver 13 [j]Eze 41:12-14 [k]Eze 40:17
42:3 [l]Eze 41:15 [m]Eze 41:16
42:4 [n]Eze 46:19
42:9 [o]Eze 44:5; 46:19
42:10 [p]ver 1

[a] *22* Septuagint; Hebrew *long* [b] *22* Septuagint; Hebrew *length* [c] *2* The common cubit was about 1 1/2 feet (about 0.5 meter). [d] *4* Septuagint and Syriac; Hebrew *and one cubit* [e] *10* Septuagint; Hebrew *Eastward*

a doorway at the beginning of the passageway that was parallel to
the corresponding wall extending eastward, by which one enters
the rooms.
13 Then he said to me, "The north[a] and south rooms facing the
temple courtyard are the priests' rooms, where the priests who
approach the LORD will eat the most holy offerings. There they will
put the most holy offerings—the grain offerings, the sin offerings[b]
and the guilt offerings[c]—for the place is holy.[d] 14 Once the priests
enter the holy precincts, they are not to go into the outer court
until they leave behind the garments[e] in which they minister, for
these are holy. They are to put on other clothes before they go near
the places that are for the people.[f]"
15 When he had finished measuring what was inside the temple
area, he led me out by the east gate[g] and measured the area all
around: 16 He measured the east side with the measuring rod; it
was five hundred cubits.[a] 17 He measured the north side; it was five
hundred cubits[b] by the measuring rod. 18 He measured the south
side; it was five hundred cubits by the measuring rod. 19 Then he
turned to the west side and measured; it was five hundred cubits
by the measuring rod. 20 So he measured[h] the area on all four sides.
It had a wall around it,[i] five hundred cubits long and five hundred
cubits wide,[j] to separate the holy from the common.[k]

Chapter 43 Theme

43 Then the man brought me to the gate facing east,[l] 2 and I
saw the glory of the God of Israel coming from the east. His
voice was like the roar of rushing waters,[m] and the land was radiant
with his glory.[n] 3 The vision I saw was like the vision I had seen
when he[c] came to destroy the city and like the visions I had seen
by the Kebar River, and I fell facedown. 4 The glory[o] of the LORD
entered the temple through the gate facing east.[p] 5 Then the Spirit[q]
lifted me up[r] and brought me into the inner court, and the glory
of the LORD filled the temple.
6 While the man was standing beside me, I heard someone
speaking to me from inside the temple. 7 He said: "Son of man, this
is the place of my throne and the place for the soles of my feet. This
is where I will live among the Israelites forever. The house of Israel
will never again defile my holy name—neither they nor their
kings—by their prostitution[d] and the lifeless idols[e] of their kings
at their high places.[s] 8 When they placed their threshold next to
my threshold and their doorposts beside my doorposts, with only
a wall between me and them, they defiled my holy name by their

a *16* See Septuagint of verse 17; Hebrew *rods*; also in verses 18 and 19. b *17* Septuagint; Hebrew *rods* c *3* Some Hebrew manuscripts and Vulgate; most Hebrew manuscripts *I*
d *7* Or *their spiritual adultery*; also in verse 9 e *7* Or *the corpses*; also in verse 9

42:13
a Eze 40:46
b Lev 10:17; 6:25
c Lev 14:13
d Ex 29:31; Lev 6:29; 7:6; 10:12-13; Nu 18:9-10

42:14
e Eze 44:19
f Ex 29:9; Lev 8:7-9

42:15
g Eze 43:1

42:20
h Eze 40:5
i Zec 2:5
j Eze 45:2; Rev 21:16
k Eze 22:26

43:1
l Eze 10:19; 42:15; 44:1; 46:1

43:2
m Rev 1:15
n Isa 6:3; Eze 11:23; Rev 18:1

43:4
o Eze 1:28
p Eze 10:19

43:5
q Eze 11:24
r Eze 3:12; 8:3

43:7
s Lev 26:30

detestable practices. So I destroyed them in my anger. 9Now let
them put away from me their prostitution and the lifeless idols of
their kings, and I will live among them forever.[a]
10"Son of man, describe the temple to the people of Israel, that
they may be ashamed[b] of their sins. Let them consider the plan,
11and if they are ashamed of all they have done, make known to
them the design of the temple—its arrangement, its exits and
entrances—its whole design and all its regulations[a] and laws.
Write these down before them so that they may be faithful to its
design and follow all its regulations.[c]
12"This is the law of the temple: All the surrounding area[d] on top
of the mountain will be most holy. Such is the law of the temple.
13"These are the measurements of the altar[e] in long cubits, that
cubit being a cubit[b] and a handbreadth[c]: Its gutter is a cubit deep
and a cubit wide, with a rim of one span[d] around the edge. And
this is the height of the altar: 14From the gutter on the ground up to
the lower ledge it is two cubits high and a cubit wide, and from the
smaller ledge up to the larger ledge it is four cubits high and a cubit
wide. 15The altar hearth is four cubits high, and four horns[f] project
upward from the hearth. 16The altar hearth is square, twelve cubits
long and twelve cubits wide. 17The upper ledge also is square, fourteen cubits long and fourteen cubits wide, with a rim of half a cubit
and a gutter of a cubit all around. The steps[g] of the altar face east."
18Then he said to me, "Son of man, this is what the Sovereign
LORD says: These will be the regulations for sacrificing burnt offerings[h] and sprinkling blood[i] upon the altar when it is built: 19You
are to give a young bull[j] as a sin offering to the priests, who are
Levites, of the family of Zadok,[k] who come near[l] to minister
before me, declares the Sovereign LORD. 20You are to take some of
its blood and put it on the four horns of the altar and on the four
corners of the upper ledge[m] and all around the rim, and so purify
the altar[n] and make atonement for it. 21You are to take the bull for
the sin offering and burn it in the designated part of the temple
area outside the sanctuary.[o]
22"On the second day you are to offer a male goat without defect
for a sin offering, and the altar is to be purified as it was purified
with the bull. 23When you have finished purifying it, you are to offer
a young bull and a ram from the flock, both without defect.[p] 24You
are to offer them before the LORD, and the priests are to sprinkle
salt[q] on them and sacrifice them as a burnt offering to the LORD.
25"For seven days[r] you are to provide a male goat daily for a sin
offering; you are also to provide a young bull and a ram from the

[a] *11* Some Hebrew manuscripts and Septuagint; most Hebrew manuscripts *regulations and its whole design* [b] *13* The common cubit was about 1 1/2 feet (about 0.5 meter). [c] *13* That is, about 3 inches (about 8 centimeters) [d] *13* That is, about 9 inches (about 22 centimeters)

43:9 *a* Eze 37:26-28
43:10 *b* Eze 16:61
43:11 *c* Eze 44:5
43:12 *d* Eze 40:2
43:13 *e* 2Ch 4:1
43:15 *f* Ex 27:2
43:17 *g* Ex 20:26
43:18 *h* Ex 40:29 *i* Lev 1:5,11; Heb 9:21-22
43:19 *j* Lev 4:3; Eze 45:18-19 *k* Eze 44:15 *l* Nu 16:40; Eze 40:46
43:20 *m* ver 17 *n* Lev 16:19
43:21 *o* Ex 29:14; Heb 13:11
43:23 *p* Ex 29:1
43:24 *q* Lev 2:13; Mk 9:49-50
43:25 *r* Lev 8:33

flock, both without defect.[a] 26For seven days they are to make
atonement for the altar and cleanse it; thus they will dedicate it.
27At the end of these days, from the eighth day[b] on, the priests are
to present your burnt offerings and fellowship offerings[a] [c] on the
altar. Then I will accept you, declares the Sovereign LORD."

Chapter 44 Theme

44 Then the man brought me back to the outer gate of the
sanctuary, the one facing east,[d] and it was shut. 2The LORD
said to me, "This gate is to remain shut. It must not be opened; no
one may enter through it.[e] It is to remain shut because the LORD,
the God of Israel, has entered through it. 3The prince himself is
the only one who may sit inside the gateway to eat in the presence[f]
of the LORD. He is to enter by way of the portico of the gateway and
go out the same way.[g]"

4Then the man brought me by way of the north gate to the front
of the temple. I looked and saw the glory of the LORD filling the
temple[h] of the LORD, and I fell facedown.[i]

5The LORD said to me, "Son of man, look carefully, listen closely
and give attention to everything I tell you concerning all the regulations regarding the temple of the LORD. Give attention to the
entrance of the temple and all the exits of the sanctuary.[j] 6Say to
the rebellious house[k] of Israel, 'This is what the Sovereign LORD
says: Enough of your detestable practices, O house of Israel! 7In
addition to all your other detestable practices, you brought foreigners uncircumcised in heart[l] and flesh into my sanctuary, desecrating my temple while you offered me food, fat and blood,
and you broke my covenant.[m] 8Instead of carrying out your duty
in regard to my holy things, you put others in charge of my sanctuary.[n] 9This is what the Sovereign LORD says: No foreigner uncircumcised in heart and flesh is to enter my sanctuary, not even the
foreigners who live among the Israelites.[o]

10"'The Levites who went far from me when Israel went astray[p]
and who wandered from me after their idols must bear the consequences of their sin.[q] 11They may serve in my sanctuary, having
charge of the gates of the temple and serving in it; they may
slaughter the burnt offerings[r] and sacrifices for the people and
stand before the people and serve them.[s] 12But because they
served them in the presence of their idols and made the house of
Israel fall into sin, therefore I have sworn with uplifted hand[t] that
they must bear the consequences of their sin, declares the Sovereign LORD.[u] 13They are not to come near to serve me as priests or
come near any of my holy things or my most holy offerings; they

a 27 Traditionally *peace offerings*

43:25
[a] Ex 29:37

43:27
[b] Lev 9:1
[c] Lev 17:5

44:1
[d] Eze 43:1

44:2
[e] Eze 43:4-5

44:3
[f] Ex 24:9-11
[g] Eze 46:2,8

44:4
[h] Isa 6:4; Rev 15:8
[i] Eze 1:28; 3:23

44:5
[j] Eze 40:4; 43:10-11

44:6
[k] Eze 3:9

44:7
[l] Lev 26:41
[m] Ge 17:14; Ex 12:48; Lev 22:25

44:8
[n] Lev 22:2; Nu 18:7

44:9
[o] Joel 3:17; Zec 14:21

44:10
[p] 2Ki 23:8
[q] Nu 18:23

44:11
[r] 2Ch 29:34
[s] Nu 3:5-37; 16:9; 1Ch 26:12-19

44:12
[t] Ps 106:26
[u] 2Ki 16:10-16

must bear the shame[a] of their detestable practices.[b] 14Yet I will put
them in charge of the duties of the temple and all the work that is
to be done in it.[c]

15"'But the priests, who are Levites and descendants of Zadok
and who faithfully carried out the duties of my sanctuary when the
Israelites went astray from me, are to come near to minister before
me; they are to stand before me to offer sacrifices of fat and blood,
declares the Sovereign LORD.[d] 16They alone are to enter my sanctuary; they alone are to come near my table[e] to minister before
me and perform my service.[f]

17"'When they enter the gates of the inner court, they are to wear
linen clothes;[g] they must not wear any woolen garment while
ministering at the gates of the inner court or inside the temple.
18They are to wear linen turbans[h] on their heads and linen undergarments[i] around their waists. They must not wear anything that
makes them perspire.[j] 19When they go out into the outer court
where the people are, they are to take off the clothes they have been
ministering in and are to leave them in the sacred rooms, and put
on other clothes, so that they do not consecrate[k] the people by
means of their garments.[l]

20"'They must not shave their heads or let their hair grow long,
but they are to keep the hair of their heads trimmed.[m] 21No priest
is to drink wine when he enters the inner court.[n] 22They must not
marry widows or divorced women; they may marry only virgins of
Israelite descent or widows of priests.[o] 23They are to teach my people the difference between the holy and the common[p] and show
them how to distinguish between the unclean and the clean.[q]

24"'In any dispute, the priests are to serve as judges[r] and decide
it according to my ordinances. They are to keep my laws and my
decrees for all my appointed feasts, and they are to keep my Sabbaths holy.[s]

25"'A priest must not defile himself by going near a dead person;
however, if the dead person was his father or mother, son or
daughter, brother or unmarried sister, then he may defile himself.[t] 26After he is cleansed, he must wait seven days.[u] 27On the day
he goes into the inner court of the sanctuary to minister in the
sanctuary, he is to offer a sin offering for himself, declares the
Sovereign LORD.

28"'I am to be the only inheritance[v] the priests have. You are to
give them no possession in Israel; I will be their possession. 29They
will eat the grain offerings, the sin offerings and the guilt offerings;
and everything in Israel devoted[a] to the LORD[w] will belong to
them.[x] 30The best of all the firstfruits[y] and of all your special gifts
will belong to the priests. You are to give them the first portion of

[a] 29 The Hebrew term refers to the irrevocable giving over of things or persons to the LORD.

44:13 [a] Eze 16:61 [b] Nu 18:3
44:14 [c] Nu 18:4; 1Ch 23:28-32
44:15 [d] Jer 33:18; Eze 40:46; Zec 3:7
44:16 [e] Eze 41:22 [f] Nu 18:5
44:17 [g] Ex 39:27-28; Rev 19:8
44:18 [h] Ex 28:39; Isa 3:20 [i] Ex 28:42 [j] Lev 16:4
44:19 [k] Lev 6:27; Eze 46:20 [l] Lev 6:10-11; Eze 42:14
44:20 [m] Lev 21:5; Nu 6:5
44:21 [n] Lev 10:9
44:22 [o] Lev 21:7
44:23 [p] Eze 22:26 [q] Mal 2:7
44:24 [r] Dt 17:8-9; 1Ch 23:4 [s] 2Ch 19:8
44:25 [t] Lev 21:1-4
44:26 [u] Nu 19:14
44:28 [v] Nu 18:20; Dt 10:9; 18:1-2; Jos 13:33
44:29 [w] Lev 27:21 [x] Nu 18:9,14
44:30 [y] Nu 18:12-13

your ground meal[a] so that a blessing[b] may rest on your household.[c] 31The priests must not eat anything, bird or animal, found dead or torn by wild animals.[d]

Chapter 45 Theme

45 "'When you allot the land as an inheritance,[e] you are to present to the LORD a portion of the land as a sacred district, 25,000 cubits long and 20,000[a] cubits wide; the entire area will be holy.[f] 2Of this, a section 500 cubits square[g] is to be for the sanctuary, with 50 cubits around it for open land. 3In the sacred district, measure off a section 25,000 cubits[b] long and 10,000 cubits[c] wide. In it will be the sanctuary, the Most Holy Place. 4It will be the sacred portion of the land for the priests,[h] who minister in the sanctuary and who draw near to minister before the LORD. It will be a place for their houses as well as a holy place for the sanctuary.[i] 5An area 25,000 cubits long and 10,000 cubits wide will belong to the Levites, who serve in the temple, as their possession for towns to live in.[d] [j]

6"'You are to give the city as its property an area 5,000 cubits wide and 25,000 cubits long, adjoining the sacred portion; it will belong to the whole house of Israel.[k]

7"'The prince will have the land bordering each side of the area formed by the sacred district and the property of the city. It will extend westward from the west side and eastward from the east side, running lengthwise from the western to the eastern border parallel to one of the tribal portions.[l] 8This land will be his possession in Israel. And my princes will no longer oppress my people but will allow the house of Israel to possess the land according to their tribes.[m]

9"'This is what the Sovereign LORD says: You have gone far enough, O princes of Israel! Give up your violence and oppression and do what is just and right.[n] Stop dispossessing my people, declares the Sovereign LORD. 10You are to use accurate scales,[o] an accurate ephah[e] [p] and an accurate bath.[f] 11The ephah[q] and the bath are to be the same size, the bath containing a tenth of a homer[g] and the ephah a tenth of a homer; the homer is to be the standard measure for both. 12The shekel[h] is to consist of twenty gerahs.[r] Twenty shekels plus twenty-five shekels plus fifteen shekels equal one mina.[i]

13"'This is the special gift you are to offer: a sixth of an ephah from each homer of wheat and a sixth of an ephah from each

[a] *1* Septuagint (see also verses 3 and 5 and 48:9); Hebrew *10,000* [b] *3* That is, about 7 miles (about 12 kilometers) [c] *3* That is, about 3 miles (about 5 kilometers) [d] *5* Septuagint; Hebrew *temple; they will have as their possession 20 rooms* [e] *10* An ephah was a dry measure. [f] *10* A bath was a liquid measure. [g] *11* A homer was a dry measure. [h] *12* A shekel weighed about 2/5 ounce (about 11.5 grams). [i] *12* That is, 60 shekels; the common mina was 50 shekels.

44:30 [a] Nu 15:18-21 [b] Mal 3:10 [c] Ne 10:35-37
44:31 [d] Ex 22:31; Lev 22:8
45:1 [e] Eze 47:21-22 [f] Eze 48:8-9,29
45:2 [g] Eze 42:20
45:4 [h] Eze 40:46 [i] Eze 48:10-11
45:5 [j] Eze 48:13
45:6 [k] Eze 48:15-18
45:7 [l] Eze 48:21
45:8 [m] Nu 26:53; Eze 46:18
45:9 [n] Jer 22:3; Zec 7:9-10; 8:16
45:10 [o] Dt 25:15; Pr 11:1; Am 8:4-6; Mic 6:10-11 [p] Lev 19:36
45:11 [q] Isa 5:10
45:12 [r] Ex 30:13; Lev 27:25; Nu 3:47

homer of barley. 14 The prescribed portion of oil, measured by the
bath, is a tenth of a bath from each cor (which consists of ten baths
or one homer, for ten baths are equivalent to a homer). 15 Also one
sheep is to be taken from every flock of two hundred from the
well-watered pastures of Israel. These will be used for the grain
offerings, burnt offerings[a] and fellowship offerings[a] to make atonement[b] for the people, declares the Sovereign LORD. 16 All the people
of the land will participate in this special gift for the use of the
prince in Israel. 17 It will be the duty of the prince to provide the
burnt offerings, grain offerings and drink offerings at the festivals,
the New Moons and the Sabbaths[c]—at all the appointed feasts of
the house of Israel. He will provide the sin offerings, grain offerings, burnt offerings and fellowship offerings to make atonement
for the house of Israel.[d]

18 " 'This is what the Sovereign LORD says: In the first month[e] on
the first day you are to take a young bull without defect[f] and purify the sanctuary.[g] 19 The priest is to take some of the blood of the
sin offering and put it on the doorposts of the temple, on the four
corners of the upper ledge[h] of the altar[i] and on the gateposts of
the inner court. 20 You are to do the same on the seventh day of
the month for anyone who sins unintentionally[j] or through ignorance; so you are to make atonement for the temple.

21 " 'In the first month on the fourteenth day you are to observe
the Passover,[k] a feast lasting seven days, during which you shall eat
bread made without yeast. 22 On that day the prince is to provide a
bull as a sin offering for himself and for all the people of the land.[l]
23 Every day during the seven days of the Feast he is to provide
seven bulls and seven rams[m] without defect as a burnt offering to
the LORD, and a male goat for a sin offering.[n] 24 He is to provide as a
grain offering[o] an ephah for each bull and an ephah for each ram,
along with a hin[b] of oil for each ephah.[p]

25 " 'During the seven days of the Feast,[q] which begins in the seventh month on the fifteenth day, he is to make the same provision
for sin offerings, burnt offerings, grain offerings and oil.[r]

Chapter 46 Theme ____________________

46 " 'This is what the Sovereign LORD says: The gate of the
inner court[s] facing east[t] is to be shut on the six working
days, but on the Sabbath day and on the day of the New Moon[u] it
is to be opened. 2 The prince is to enter from the outside through
the portico[v] of the gateway and stand by the gatepost. The priests
are to sacrifice his burnt offering and his fellowship offerings.[c] He
is to worship at the threshold of the gateway and then go out, but

45:15 [a] Lev 1:4 [b] Lev 6:30
45:17 [c] Lev 23:38; Isa 66:23 [d] 1Ki 8:62; 2Ch 31:3; Eze 46:4-12
45:18 [e] Ex 12:2 [f] Lev 22:20; Heb 9:14 [g] Lev 16:16,33
45:19 [h] Eze 43:17 [i] Lev 16:18-19; Eze 43:20
45:20 [j] Lev 4:27
45:21 [k] Ex 12:11; Lev 23:5-6
45:22 [l] Lev 4:14
45:23 [m] Job 42:8 [n] Nu 28:16-25
45:24 [o] Nu 28:12-13 [p] Eze 46:5-7
45:25 [q] Dt 16:13 [r] Lev 23:34-43; Nu 29:12-38
46:1 [s] Eze 40:19 [t] 1Ch 9:18 [u] ver 6; Isa 66:23
46:2 [v] ver 8

a *15* Traditionally *peace offerings*; also in verse 17 b *24* That is, probably about 4 quarts (about 4 liters) c *2* Traditionally *peace offerings*; also in verse 12

the gate will not be shut until evening.[a] 3On the Sabbaths and New
Moons the people of the land are to worship in the presence of the
LORD at the entrance to that gateway.[b] 4The burnt offering the prince
brings to the LORD on the Sabbath day is to be six male lambs and
a ram, all without defect. 5The grain offering given with the ram is
to be an ephah,[a] and the grain offering with the lambs is to be as
much as he pleases, along with a hin[b] of oil for each ephah.[c] 6On
the day of the New Moon[d] he is to offer a young bull, six lambs
and a ram, all without defect. 7He is to provide as a grain offering
one ephah with the bull, one ephah with the ram, and with the
lambs as much as he wants to give, along with a hin of oil with
each ephah.[e] 8When the prince enters, he is to go in through the
portico[f] of the gateway, and he is to come out the same way.[g]

9" 'When the people of the land come before the LORD at the
appointed feasts,[h] whoever enters by the north gate to worship is to
go out the south gate; and whoever enters by the south gate is to go
out the north gate. No one is to return through the gate by which
he entered, but each is to go out the opposite gate. 10The prince is
to be among them, going in when they go in and going out when
they go out.[i]

11" 'At the festivals and the appointed feasts, the grain offering
is to be an ephah with a bull, an ephah with a ram, and with the
lambs as much as one pleases, along with a hin of oil for each
ephah.[j] 12When the prince provides[k] a freewill offering[l] to the
LORD—whether a burnt offering or fellowship offerings—the gate
facing east is to be opened for him. He shall offer his burnt offering
or his fellowship offerings as he does on the Sabbath day. Then he
shall go out, and after he has gone out, the gate will be shut.[m]

13" 'Every day you are to provide a year-old lamb without defect
for a burnt offering to the LORD; morning by morning you shall
provide it.[n] 14You are also to provide with it morning by morning
a grain offering, consisting of a sixth of an ephah with a third of a
hin of oil to moisten the flour. The presenting of this grain offering
to the LORD is a lasting ordinance.[o] 15So the lamb and the grain
offering and the oil shall be provided morning by morning for a
regular[p] burnt offering.[q]

16" 'This is what the Sovereign LORD says: If the prince makes a
gift from his inheritance to one of his sons, it will also belong to his
descendants; it is to be their property by inheritance.[r] 17If, however, he makes a gift from his inheritance to one of his servants, the
servant may keep it until the year of freedom;[s] then it will revert
to the prince. His inheritance belongs to his sons only; it is theirs.
18The prince must not take any of the inheritance[t] of the people,

[a]5 That is, probably about 3/5 bushel (about 22 liters) [b]5 That is, probably about 4 quarts (about 4 liters)

46:2 [a]ver 12; Eze 44:3
46:3 [b]Lk 1:10
46:5 [c]ver 11; Eze 45:24
46:6 [d]ver 1; Nu 10:10
46:7 [e]Eze 45:24
46:8 [f]ver 2 [g]Eze 44:3
46:9 [h]Ex 23:14; 34:20
46:10 [i]2Sa 6:14-15; Ps 42:4
46:11 [j]ver 5
46:12 [k]Eze 45:17 [l]Lev 7:16 [m]ver 2
46:13 [n]Ex 29:38; Nu 28:3
46:14 [o]Da 8:11
46:15 [p]Ex 29:42 [q]Ex 29:38; Nu 28:5-6
46:16 [r]2Ch 21:3
46:17 [s]Lev 25:10
46:18 [t]Lev 25:23; Eze 45:8; Mic 2:1-2

46:19 driving them off their property. He is to give his sons their inher-
[a]Eze 42:9 itance out of his own property, so that none of my people will be
separated from his property.'"
19Then the man brought me through the entrance[a] at the side of
46:20 the gate to the sacred rooms facing north, which belonged to the
[b]Lev 6:27 priests, and showed me a place at the western end. 20He said to
[c]Zec 14:20 me, "This is the place where the priests will cook the guilt offering
and the sin offering and bake the grain offering, to avoid bringing
them into the outer court and consecrating[b] the people."[c]
21He then brought me to the outer court and led me around to its
47:1 four corners, and I saw in each corner another court. 22In the four
[d]Isa 55:1 corners of the outer court were enclosed[a] courts, forty cubits long
[e]Ps 46:4; Joel 3:18; Rev 22:1 and thirty cubits wide; each of the courts in the four corners was
the same size. 23Around the inside of each of the four courts was a
ledge of stone, with places for fire built all around under the ledge.
24He said to me, "These are the kitchens where those who minister
at the temple will cook the sacrifices of the people."

47:3 [f]Eze 40:3 *Chapter 47 Theme* ________________________

47 The man brought me back to the entrance of the temple,
and I saw water[d] coming out from under the threshold of
47:5 the temple toward the east (for the temple faced east). The water
[g]Isa 11:9; Hab 2:14 was coming down from under the south side of the temple, south
of the altar.[e] 2He then brought me out through the north gate and
led me around the outside to the outer gate facing east, and the
water was flowing from the south side.
3As the man went eastward with a measuring line[f] in his hand,
47:7 he measured off a thousand cubits[b] and then led me through water
[h]ver 12; Rev 22:2 that was ankle-deep. 4He measured off another thousand cubits
and led me through water that was knee-deep. He measured off
another thousand and led me through water that was up to the
waist. 5He measured off another thousand, but now it was a river
47:8 that I could not cross, because the water had risen and was deep
[i]Dt 3:17; Jos 3:16 enough to swim in—a river that no one could cross.[g] 6He asked
[j]Isa 41:18 me, "Son of man, do you see this?"
Then he led me back to the bank of the river. 7When I arrived
there, I saw a great number of trees on each side of the river.[h] 8He
said to me, "This water flows toward the eastern region and goes
47:9 down into the Arabah,[c][i] where it enters the Sea.[d] When it empties
[k]Isa 12:3; 55:1; Jn 4:14; 7:37-38 into the Sea,[d] the water there becomes fresh.[j] 9Swarms of living
creatures will live wherever the river flows. There will be large num-
bers of fish, because this water flows there and makes the salt water
fresh; so where the river flows everything will live.[k] 10Fishermen[l]

47:10 [a]22 The meaning of the Hebrew for this word is uncertain. [b]3 That is, about 1,500 feet
[l]Mt 4:19 (about 450 meters) [c]8 Or *the Jordan Valley* [d]8 That is, the Dead Sea

will stand along the shore; from En Gedi[a] to En Eglaim there will
be places for spreading nets.[b] The fish will be of many kinds[c]—
like the fish of the Great Sea.[a][d] 11But the swamps and marshes
will not become fresh; they will be left for salt.[e] 12Fruit trees of all
kinds will grow on both banks of the river.[f] Their leaves will not
wither, nor will their fruit[g] fail. Every month they will bear,
because the water from the sanctuary flows to them. Their fruit
will serve for food and their leaves for healing.[h]"

The Tribes, the Prince's Portion, the City, the Sanctuary

13This is what the Sover-
eign LORD says: "These are
the boundaries[i] by which
you are to divide the land for
an inheritance among the
twelve tribes of Israel, with
two portions for Joseph.[j]
14You are to divide it equally
among them. Because I
swore with uplifted hand to
give it to your forefathers,
this land will become your
inheritance.[k]

15"This is to be the boundary of the land:

"On the north side it will
run from the Great Sea
by the Hethlon road[l]
past Lebo[b] Hamath to Zedad, 16Berothah[c][m] and Sibraim
(which lies on the border between Damascus and Hamath),[n]
as far as Hazer Hatticon, which is on the border of Hauran.
17The boundary will extend from the sea to Hazar Enan,[d]
along the northern border of Damascus, with the border of
Hamath to the north. This will be the north boundary.[o]
18"On the east side the boundary will run between Hauran and
Damascus, along the Jordan between Gilead and the land of
Israel, to the eastern sea and as far as Tamar.[e] This will be the
east boundary.
19"On the south side it will run from Tamar as far as the waters of
Meribah Kadesh,[p] then along the Wadi ⌊of Egypt⌋[q] to the
Great Sea.[r] This will be the south boundary.
20"On the west side, the Great Sea will be the boundary to a point
opposite Lebo[f] Hamath.[s] This will be the west boundary.[t]

[a] *10* That is, the Mediterranean; also in verses 15, 19 and 20 [b] *15* Or *past the entrance to* [c] *15,16 See* Septuagint and Ezekiel 48:1; Hebrew *road to go into Zedad,* *16Hamath, Berothah* [d] *17* Hebrew *Enon,* a variant of *Enan* [e] *18* Septuagint and Syriac; Hebrew *Israel. You will measure to the eastern sea* [f] *20* Or *opposite the entrance to*

47:10 [a]Jos 15:62 [b]Eze 26:5 [c]Ps 104:25; Mt 13:47 [d]Nu 34:6

47:11 [e]Dt 29:23

47:12 [f]ver 7; Rev 22:2 [g]Ps 1:3 [h]Ge 2:9; Jer 17:8

47:13 [i]Nu 34:2-12 [j]Ge 48:5

47:14 [k]Ge 12:7; Dt 1:8; Eze 20:5-6

47:15 [l]Eze 48:1

47:16 [m]2Sa 8:8 [n]Nu 13:21; Eze 48:1

47:17 [o]Eze 48:1

47:19 [p]Dt 32:51 [q]Isa 27:12 [r]Eze 48:28

47:20 [s]Eze 48:1 [t]Nu 34:6

21"You are to distribute this land among yourselves according to
the tribes of Israel. 22You are to allot it as an inheritance for yourselves and for the aliens[a] who have settled among you and who
have children. You are to consider them as native-born Israelites;
along with you they are to be allotted an inheritance among the
tribes of Israel.[b] 23In whatever tribe the alien settles, there you are
to give him his inheritance," declares the Sovereign LORD.

Chapter 48 Theme

48 "These are the tribes, listed by name: At the northern frontier, Dan[c] will have one portion; it will follow the Hethlon
road[d] to Lebo[a] Hamath;[e] Hazar Enan and the northern border of
Damascus next to Hamath will be part of its border from the east
side to the west side.

2"Asher[f] will have one portion; it will border the territory of Dan
from east to west.

3"Naphtali[g] will have one portion; it will border the territory of
Asher from east to west.

4"Manasseh[h] will have one portion; it will border the territory of
Naphtali from east to west.

5"Ephraim[i] will have one portion; it will border the territory of
Manasseh[j] from east to west.[k]

6"Reuben[l] will have one portion; it will border the territory of
Ephraim from east to west.

7"Judah[m] will have one portion; it will border the territory of
Reuben from east to west.

8"Bordering the territory of Judah from east to west will be the
portion you are to present as a special gift. It will be 25,000 cubits[b]
wide, and its length from east to west will equal one of the tribal
portions; the sanctuary will be in the center of it.[n]

9"The special portion you are to offer to the LORD will be 25,000
cubits long and 10,000 cubits[c] wide.[o] 10This will be the sacred portion for the priests. It will be 25,000 cubits long on the north side,
10,000 cubits wide on the west side, 10,000 cubits wide on the east
side and 25,000 cubits long on the south side. In the center of it will
be the sanctuary of the LORD.[p] 11This will be for the consecrated
priests, the Zadokites,[q] who were faithful in serving me[r] and did
not go astray as the Levites did when the Israelites went astray.[s]
12It will be a special gift to them from the sacred portion of the
land, a most holy portion, bordering the territory of the Levites.

13"Alongside the territory of the priests, the Levites will have an
allotment 25,000 cubits long and 10,000 cubits wide. Its total
length will be 25,000 cubits and its width 10,000 cubits.[t] 14They

47:22 [a]Isa 14:1 [b]Nu 26:55-56; Isa 56:6-7; Ro 10:12; Eph 2:12-16; 3:6; Col 3:11
48:1 [c]Ge 30:6 [d]Eze 47:15-17 [e]Eze 47:20
48:2 [f]Jos 19:24-31
48:3 [g]Jos 19:32-39
48:4 [h]Jos 17:1-11
48:5 [i]Jos 16:5-9 [j]Jos 17:7-10 [k]Jos 17:17
48:6 [l]Jos 13:15-21
48:7 [m]Jos 15:1-63
48:8 [n]ver 21
48:9 [o]Eze 45:1
48:10 [p]ver 21; Eze 45:3-4
48:11 [q]2Sa 8:17 [r]Lev 8:35 [s]Eze 14:11; 44:15
48:13 [t]Eze 45:5

[a] *1* Or *to the entrance to* [b] *8* That is, about 7 miles (about 12 kilometers) [c] *9* That is, about 3 miles (about 5 kilometers)

must not sell or exchange any of it. This is the best of the land and
must not pass into other hands, because it is holy to the LORD.[a]
15"The remaining area, 5,000 cubits wide and 25,000 cubits long,
will be for the common use of the city, for houses and for pastureland. The city will be in the center of it 16and will have these measurements: the north side 4,500 cubits, the south side 4,500 cubits,
the east side 4,500 cubits, and the west side 4,500 cubits.[b] 17The
pastureland for the city will be 250 cubits on the north, 250 cubits
on the south, 250 cubits on the east, and 250 cubits on the west.
18What remains of the area, bordering on the sacred portion and
running the length of it, will be 10,000 cubits on the east side and
10,000 cubits on the west side. Its produce will supply food for the
workers of the city.[c] 19The workers from the city who farm it will
come from all the tribes of Israel. 20The entire portion will be a
square, 25,000 cubits on each side. As a special gift you will set
aside the sacred portion, along with the property of the city.
21"What remains on both sides of the area formed by the sacred
portion and the city property will belong to the prince. It will
extend eastward from the 25,000 cubits of the sacred portion to the
eastern border, and westward from the 25,000 cubits to the western
border. Both these areas running the length of the tribal portions
will belong to the prince, and the sacred portion with the temple
sanctuary will be in the center of them.[d] 22So the property of the
Levites and the property of the city will lie in the center of the area
that belongs to the prince. The area belonging to the prince will lie
between the border of Judah and the border of Benjamin.
23"As for the rest of the tribes: Benjamin[e] will have one portion;
it will extend from the east side to the west side.
24"Simeon[f] will have one portion; it will border the territory of
Benjamin from east to west.
25"Issachar[g] will have one portion; it will border the territory of
Simeon from east to west.
26"Zebulun[h] will have one portion; it will border the territory of
Issachar from east to west.
27"Gad[i] will have one portion; it will border the territory of
Zebulun from east to west.
28"The southern boundary of Gad will run south from Tamar[j] to
the waters of Meribah Kadesh, then along the Wadi ⌞of Egypt⌟ to the
Great Sea.[a][k]
29"This is the land you are to allot as an inheritance to the tribes of
Israel, and these will be their portions," declares the Sovereign LORD.
30"These will be the exits of the city: Beginning on the north side,
which is 4,500 cubits long, 31the gates of the city will be named after

a 28 That is, the Mediterranean

48:14 [a]Lev 25:34; 27:10,28
48:16 [b]Rev 21:16
48:18 [c]Eze 45:6
48:21 [d]ver 8,10; Eze 45:7
48:23 [e]Jos 18:11-28
48:24 [f]Ge 29:33; Jos 19:1-9
48:25 [g]Jos 19:17-23
48:26 [h]Jos 19:10-16
48:27 [i]Jos 13:24-28
48:28 [j]Ge 14:7 [k]Eze 47:19

48:35
[a] Isa 12:6; 24:23; Jer 3:17; 14:9; Jer 33:16; Joel 3:21; Zec 2:10; Rev 21:3

the tribes of Israel. The three gates on the north side will be the
gate of Reuben, the gate of Judah and the gate of Levi.
32 "On the east side, which is 4,500 cubits long, will be three gates:
the gate of Joseph, the gate of Benjamin and the gate of Dan.
33 "On the south side, which measures 4,500 cubits, will be three
gates: the gate of Simeon, the gate of Issachar and the gate of
Zebulun.
34 "On the west side, which is 4,500 cubits long, will be three gates:
the gate of Gad, the gate of Asher and the gate of Naphtali.
35 "The distance all around will be 18,000 cubits.

"And the name of the city from that time on will be:

THE LORD IS THERE.[a]"

Ezekiel at a Glance

Theme of Ezekiel:

Segment Divisions

		Chapter Themes
		1
		2
		3
		4
		5
		6
		7
		8
		9
		10
		11
		12
		13
		14
		15
		16
		17
		18
		19
		20
		21
		22
		23
		24

Author:

Date:

Purpose:

Key Words:

son of man

covenant

vision(s)

glory (most beautiful, splendor)

Spirit (spirit)

know that I am the Lord (know that I the Lord made them)

sin(s) (guilt[y], doing wrong, evil, wicked)

rebelled (rebel, rebellious)

wrath (anger, fury)

heart(s) (courage, think wise)

prostitute(s), prostitution (promiscuous, promiscuity, illicit favors, favors, adultery adulterous)

SEGMENT DIVISIONS

		CHAPTER THEMES
		25
		26
		27
		28
		29
		30
		31
		32
		33
		34
		35
		36
		37
		38
		39
		40
		41
		42
		43
		44
		45
		46
		47
		48

DANIEL

Daniel's prophetic ministry began and ended in Babylon. When Nebuchadnezzar first besieged Jerusalem in 605 B.C., Daniel, who was about fifteen years old, was among the captives taken to Babylon.

As Moses predicted, Israel lost her place of supremacy among the nations because she did not obey God. Instead of being the head, Israel became the tail to be wagged by the Gentiles (Deuteronomy 28). Yet, because the gifts and calling of God are irrevocable, when the fullness of the Gentiles is complete, then all Israel will be saved, for the deliverer will come out of Zion and take away Israel's sin (see Romans 11:25-30). All this becomes evident as the prophecies of Daniel unfold.

Things to Do

What the skeleton is to the body, Daniel is to prophecy. All the other prophecies in the Old and New Testament add flesh to Daniel's bones. If you carefully and thoroughly observe Daniel and discover exactly what the text says, you will find that Daniel's prophecies will become increasingly clear and more exciting with every new observation.

General Instructions

Read through Daniel one chapter at a time. Don't hurry. Simply do the following assignment on each chapter. Record all your notes in the margin of the chapter. As you read, answer the following questions and record the answers in the margin of the text:

1. When do the events of this chapter occur? Mark every reference to time with a symbol or with a distinctive color so you can see it immediately.
2. What king/kingdom is ruling at the time? Record this in the margin along with a notation of the "when" of the chapter. For instance, in the margin of chapter 1 you would put the following:

    Third year of Jehoiakim, king of Judah
    Nebuchadnezzar was king of Babylon
3. Who are the main characters in the chapter?
4. What, in general, is the chapter about?
5. Record the theme or event of the chapter on the DANIEL AT A GLANCE chart on page 1530 and on the line in the text next to the chapter number. Then in the margin list the key points or happenings connected with the main event of the chapter.
6. If a vision or dream is recorded, note in the margin who had the vision or dream and what the vision or dream was about. Also, sketch or draw on another piece of paper so you will better remember and understand the dream or vision.
7. When you finish the above, read "From 931 B.C. Until the Birth of Christ" beginning on page 2191 in the section called "Major Events in Israel's History."

Chapters 1-6

1. Read Daniel 1 through 6 again chapter by chapter. This time do the following:
    a. Mark every reference to God in a distinctive way. Watch for the repeated reference to God as the "Most High" and mark this. Then in the margin list what you learn about God from marking those references to him. Note what he is called or how he is referred to. Then meditate on what you have learned about God and how you can apply these truths to your own life.

b. In the margins list everything you learn about Daniel: his character, his relationship to God and to others, and how he handles and responds to various situations.

c. Mark in a distinctive way the following key repeated words: *kingdom (dominion, reign), rules (ruler, sovereign), dream, mystery (mysteries),* and *Nebuchadnezzar* (including pronouns). Put these on an index card and use it as a bookmark. Also watch for and mark key repeated words which appear in individual chapters. If there is room in the margin, summarize what you learn about Nebuchadnezzar.

2. Study the historical chart on page 1504. In the light of what you have observed in the text and on the chart, see if the first six chapters of Daniel come in chronological order.

Chapters 7-12

1. As you prepare to go through these final chapters of Daniel, review what you have observed in chapters 7 through 12 and what you recorded on DANIEL AT A GLANCE. Do you see any difference between the first six chapters of Daniel and the last six?

   a. Are the last six chapters chronological?

   b. Who had the dreams/visions in each of these major segments?

   c. Record your insights to these two questions on DANIEL AT A GLANCE under "Segment Divisions." Show the chronology or lack of it on one line, and then on the other write the main theme or emphasis of these two major divisions of Daniel.

2. Read Daniel 7 through 12 again chapter by chapter. Do the following:

   a. As you read each chapter mark the following key words: *vision, kingdom (sovereign power, king, empire, dominion, authority, power), horn (horns, two-horned), saints, you who are highly esteemed (man highly esteemed), end (fulfilled, appointed time, time of the end), covenant, Michael,* and *Gabriel.* Write these on an index card you can use as a bookmark.

   b. Mark every reference to God in a distinctive way. Then make a list in the margin of everything you learn about him.

   c. List everything you learn about Daniel from observing the text.

Understanding the Visions and Dreams in Daniel

1. When you come to a vision, observe the details of the vision carefully. See if the text interprets the vision. Read it over and over until you see exactly what the text is saying.

2. After you observe chapter 7, compare it with chapter 2.

   a. If you didn't do a sketch of the vision in chapter 2, stop and do it. Then do a sketch of the vision in chapter 7. What parallels do you see? Which chapter gives more details of the events encompassed in the vision? Pay attention to those details when you sketch out the vision.

   b. Mark any references to time with a symbol. In Jewish reckoning "time, times and half a time" is the equivalent of 3 1/2 years. Note what precedes a period of time and what brings it to an end.

3. When you observe chapter 8, list in the margin everything you learn about the ram and the goat. In a distinctive way mark every pronoun which refers to "another horn, which started small" of 8:9. Then list everything you observe from the text about this horn. Ask the five W's and an H: Where did it come from? What does it do and where? When does it happen? How long does it last?

4. When you observe Daniel 9:24-27, follow those verses chronologically.

   a. Number from 1 to 6 in the text the six things in Daniel 9:24 which will be accomplished, or list them in the margin.

   b. Observe who the 70 weeks pertain to. Read the reference note regarding *sevens.* Then on a piece of paper draw a line and put in the sequence of events. For example:

|Seven sevens|__________________________ (you complete the drawing).
Decree

Note when the prophecy begins (what starts it) and what happens at each interval of time. Note what happens after the seven sevens and 62 sevens and what happens during the last seven (the seventieth seven) mentioned in 9:27.

c. Observe who destroys the city and the sanctuary, and their relationship to the prince who is to come in 9:27. A historical fact that might help is that Jerusalem was destroyed in A.D. 70 by Titus, a Roman general.

5. Read chapters 10 through 12 as one unit and then concentrate on the message and vision of chapters 11 through 12.

   a. Mark every reference to time, including the word *then,* which shows the sequence of events.

   b. Chapter 11 is not an easy chapter to understand apart from a grasp of history. It was written years before the fact, but many people are not familiar with this period of time. When you read of the kings of the south and the north, keep in mind that they are so named because of their geographical relationship to Israel, the Beautiful Land.

   c. As you read through the chapter, consult the chart HISTORY OF ISRAEL'S RELATIONSHIP TO THE KINGS OF DANIEL 11 on page 1524. In 11:1-35 there are approximately 135 prophetic statements which have all been fulfilled. The accuracy of Daniel's prophecies regarding the Gentile nations and their relationship to Israel has staggered the minds of some theologians. Many even say that because of its historical accuracy, Daniel had to be written sometime after the Maccabean period in the second century B.C. However, the book of Daniel clearly refers to Daniel as the author, and so does our Lord Jesus Christ (see Matthew 24:15).

   d. If you have not done so, make a list in the margin of everything you learned about the contemptible person in Daniel 11:22-35. Then list the similarities between the description of the contemptible person of 11:22-35 and Antiochus IV Epiphanes (see history section on pages 2193, 2194 for information on Antiochus IV Epiphanes). To date, no person in history has yet fulfilled the description given in 11:36-45.

   e. Reading *Josephus, the Essential Writings* (Kregel, 1988) will help you understand the intertestament period, the 400 silent years from Malachi to Matthew. It also gives insight into Rome's role in Israel's history and tells more about the various kings mentioned in Daniel 11:1-35, especially Antiochus IV Epiphanes.

   f. In chapter 12 observe the transition from 11:45 to 12:1 chronologically. Mark all references to time and the events connected with them. Observe this chapter very carefully.

6. When you study the dreams and visions in Daniel, remember that Nebuchadnezzar's dream in chapter 2 gives a broad overview and that every vision which follows begins to fill in the details. Now that you have finished observing Daniel, you might want to study the chart PROPHETIC OVERVIEW OF DANIEL on page 1529 and see how it compares with the text and your understanding of it.

7. Finally, determine how the book of Daniel can be segmented. Note these under "Segment Divisions" on DANIEL AT A GLANCE. Then complete the chart.

Things to Think About

1. Keeping in mind the meaning of Daniel's name, "God is my judge," think about how Daniel lived. Review what you observed of his life and character and determine to be a Daniel. You have God's Spirit; you have his grace (John 14:17; 1 Corinthians 15:10).

2. What did Daniel know about God that would help him accept what happened to him? How does this understanding of God help you deal with the situations and circumstances of your life?

3. How does your understanding of future events help you understand and deal with what is happening in history? Have you thought about using Daniel as a tool in sharing the gospel with others? Many times prophecy will open the door when nothing else will.

Chapter 1 Theme ____________________

1 In the third year of the reign of Jehoiakim king of Judah, Nebuchadnezzar[a] king of Babylon came to Jerusalem and besieged
it.[b] 2And the Lord delivered Jehoiakim king of Judah into his hand,
along with some of the articles from the temple of God. These he
carried off to the temple of his god in Babylonia[a] and put in the
treasure house of his god.[c]
3Then the king ordered Ashpenaz, chief of his court officials, to
bring in some of the Israelites from the royal family and the
nobility[d]— 4young men without any physical defect, handsome,
showing aptitude for every kind of learning, well informed, quick
to understand, and qualified to serve in the king's palace. He was to
teach them the language and literature of the Babylonians.[b] 5The
king assigned them a daily amount of food and wine[e] from the
king's table. They were to be trained for three years, and after
that they were to enter the king's service.[f]
6Among these were some from Judah: Daniel,[g] Hananiah,
Mishael and Azariah. 7The chief official gave them new names: to
Daniel, the name Belteshazzar;[h] to Hananiah, Shadrach; to Mishael, Meshach; and to Azariah, Abednego.[i]
8But Daniel resolved not to defile[j] himself with the royal food
and wine, and he asked the chief official for permission not to
defile himself this way. 9Now God had caused the official to show
favor[k] and sympathy[l] to Daniel, 10but the official told Daniel, "I am
afraid of my lord the king, who has assigned your[c] food and
drink. Why should he see you looking worse than the other young
men your age? The king would then have my head because of you."
11Daniel then said to the guard whom the chief official had
appointed over Daniel, Hananiah, Mishael and Azariah, 12"Please
test your servants for ten days: Give us nothing but vegetables to
eat and water to drink. 13Then compare our appearance with that
of the young men who eat the royal food, and treat your servants
in accordance with what you see." 14So he agreed to this and tested them for ten days.
15At the end of the ten days they looked healthier and better
nourished than any of the young men who ate the royal food.[m]
16So the guard took away their choice food and the wine they
were to drink and gave them vegetables instead.[n]

1:1 [a]2Ki 24:1 [b]2Ch 36:6
1:2 [c]2Ch 36:7; Jer 27:19-20; Zec 5:5-11
1:3 [d]2Ki 20:18; 24:15; Isa 39:7
1:5 [e]ver 8,10 [f]ver 19
1:6 [g]Eze 14:14
1:7 [h]Da 4:8; 5:12 [i]Da 2:49; 3:12
1:8 [j]Eze 4:13-14
1:9 [k]Ge 39:21; Pr 16:7 [l]1Ki 8:50; Ps 106:46
1:15 [m]Ex 23:25
1:16 [n]ver 12-13

[a]2 Hebrew *Shinar* [b]4 Or *Chaldeans* [c]10 The Hebrew for *your* and *you* in this verse is plural.

[17]To these four young men God gave knowledge and understanding[a] of all kinds of literature and learning.[b] And Daniel could
understand visions and dreams of all kinds.[c]
[18]At the end of the time[d] set by the king to bring them in, the
chief official presented them to Nebuchadnezzar. [19]The king talked
with them, and he found none equal to Daniel, Hananiah, Mishael
and Azariah; so they entered the king's service.[e] [20]In every matter
of wisdom and understanding about which the king questioned
them, he found them ten times better than all the magicians and
enchanters in his whole kingdom.[f]
[21]And Daniel remained there until the first year of King Cyrus.[g]

Chapter 2 Theme ______________________

2 In the second year of his reign, Nebuchadnezzar had dreams;[h]
his mind was troubled[i] and he could not sleep.[j] [2]So the king
summoned the magicians,[k] enchanters, sorcerers[l] and astrologers[a][m] to tell him what he had dreamed.[n] When they came in and
stood before the king, [3]he said to them, "I have had a dream that
troubles[o] me and I want to know what it means.[b]"

a2 Or *Chaldeans*; also in verses 4, 5 and 10 b3 Or *was*

1:17 [a]1Ki 3:12 [b]Da 2:23; Jas 1:5 [c]Da 2:19,30; 7:1; 8:1
1:18 [d]ver 5
1:19 [e]Ge 41:46
1:20 [f]1Ki 4:30; Da 2:13,28
1:21 [g]Da 6:28; 10:1
2:1 [h]Job 33:15,18; Da 4:5 [i]Ge 41:8 [j]Est 6:1; Da 6:18
2:2 [k]Ge 41:8 [l]Ex 7:11 [m]ver 10; Da 5:7 [n]Da 4:6
2:3 [o]Da 4:5

THE RULERS AND PROPHETS OF DANIEL'S TIME

Babylonian and Medo-Persian Kings
Neo-Babylonian Empire
Medo-Persian Empire
Nabopolassar 626 605
Nebuchadnezzar 605 562
Nabonidus 556 539
Cyrus
Cam-byses
Darius I Hystaspes 521 486
Ahasuerus (Xerxes) 486
562-560 Evil-Merodach
560-556 Neriglissar
556 Labashi Marduk
553-539 Belshazzar
539-525 Darius the Mede
Smerdis
483 Vashti deposed
478 Esther queen
Jehoiachin (Coniah/Jeconiah) three months
Judah's Last Kings (*Southern Kingdom*)
Jehoiakim (Eliakim) 609 597
Zedekiah (Mattaniah) 597 586
Judah taken captive to Babylon by Nebuchadnezzar
538 Decree of Cyrus
536 Temple started
70-year Jewish Captivity
Three Stages of Captivity
536
605 Daniel and friends
597 Ezekiel and ten thousand captives
586 Destruction of Jerusalem
Zerubbabel 538
534 Temple stopped
520 Temple resumed
516 Temple finished
Daniel and His Contemporary Prophets (*Southern Kingdom*)
Daniel 605 536
Jeremiah 627 574
Ezekiel 593 559
650 640 630 620 610 600 590 580 570 560 550 540 530 520 510 500 490 480 470

4 Then the astrologers answered the king in Aramaic,[a][a] "O king,
live forever![b] Tell your servants the dream, and we will interpret it."
5 The king replied to the astrologers, "This is what I have firmly
decided: If you do not tell me what my dream was and interpret it,
I will have you cut into pieces[c] and your houses turned into piles of
rubble.[d] 6 But if you tell me the dream and explain it, you will
receive from me gifts and rewards and great honor.[e] So tell me the
dream and interpret it for me."
7 Once more they replied, "Let the king tell his servants the
dream, and we will interpret it."
8 Then the king answered, "I am certain that you are trying to
gain time, because you realize that this is what I have firmly
decided: 9 If you do not tell me the dream, there is just one penalty[f]
for you. You have conspired to tell me misleading and wicked things,
hoping the situation will change. So then, tell me the dream, and
I will know that you can interpret it for me."[g]
10 The astrologers answered the king, "There is not a man on
earth who can do what the king asks! No king, however great and
mighty, has ever asked such a thing of any magician or enchanter
or astrologer.[h] 11 What the king asks is too difficult. No one can
reveal it to the king except the gods,[i] and they do not live among
men."
12 This made the king so angry and furious[j] that he ordered the
execution[k] of all the wise men of Babylon. 13 So the decree was
issued to put the wise men to death, and men were sent to look for
Daniel and his friends to put them to death.[l]
14 When Arioch, the commander of the king's guard, had gone
out to put to death the wise men of Babylon, Daniel spoke to him
with wisdom and tact. 15 He asked the king's officer, "Why did the
king issue such a harsh decree?" Arioch then explained the matter
to Daniel. 16 At this, Daniel went in to the king and asked for time,
so that he might interpret the dream for him.
17 Then Daniel returned to his house and explained the matter to
his friends Hananiah, Mishael and Azariah.[m] 18 He urged them to
plead for mercy[n] from the God of heaven concerning this mystery,[o] so that he and his friends might not be executed with the rest
of the wise men of Babylon. 19 During the night the mystery[p] was
revealed to Daniel in a vision.[q] Then Daniel praised the God of
heaven 20 and said:

"Praise be to the name of God for ever and ever;[r]
wisdom and power[s] are his.
21 He changes times and seasons;[t]
he sets up kings and deposes[u] them.

INSIGHT

Daniel was written in Aramaic and Hebrew. The Aramaic portion was from 2:4 through 7:28.

2:4 [a]Ezr 4:7 [b]Da 3:9; 5:10
2:5 [c]ver 12 [d]Ezr 6:11; Da 3:29
2:6 [e]ver 48; Da 5:7,16
2:9 [f]Est 4:11 [g]Isa 41:22-24
2:10 [h]ver 27
2:11 [i]Da 5:11
2:12 [j]Da 3:13,19 [k]ver 5
2:13 [l]Da 1:20
2:17 [m]Da 1:6
2:18 [n]Isa 37:4 [o]Jer 33:3
2:19 [p]ver 28 [q]Job 33:15; Da 1:17
2:20 [r]Ps 113:2; 145:1-2 [s]Jer 32:19
2:21 [t]Da 7:25 [u]Job 12:19; Ps 75:6-7

[a]4 The text from here through chapter 7 is in Aramaic.

He gives wisdom[a] to the wise
and knowledge to the discerning.
22He reveals deep and hidden things;[b]
he knows what lies in darkness,[c]
and light[d] dwells with him.
23I thank and praise you, O God of my fathers:[e]
You have given me wisdom[f] and power,
you have made known to me what we asked of you,
you have made known to us the dream of the king."

24Then Daniel went to Arioch,[g] whom the king had appointed
to execute the wise men of Babylon, and said to him, "Do not execute the wise men of Babylon. Take me to the king, and I will interpret his dream for him."
25Arioch took Daniel to the king at once and said, "I have found a
man among the exiles from Judah[h] who can tell the king what his
dream means."
26The king asked Daniel (also called Belteshazzar),[i] "Are you
able to tell me what I saw in my dream and interpret it?"
27Daniel replied, "No wise man, enchanter, magician or diviner
can explain to the king the mystery he has asked about,[j] 28but
there is a God in heaven who reveals mysteries.[k] He has shown
King Nebuchadnezzar what will happen in days to come.[l] Your
dream and the visions that passed through your mind[m] as you
lay on your bed are these:
29"As you were lying there, O king, your mind turned to things
to come, and the revealer of mysteries showed you what is going to
happen. 30As for me, this mystery has been revealed[n] to me, not
because I have greater wisdom than other living men, but so that
you, O king, may know the interpretation and that you may
understand what went through your mind.
31"You looked, O king, and there before you stood a large statue—an enormous, dazzling statue,[o] awesome in appearance.
32The head of the statue was made of pure gold, its chest and arms
of silver, its belly and thighs of bronze, 33its legs of iron, its feet
partly of iron and partly of baked clay. 34While you were watching, a
rock was cut out, but not by human hands.[p] It struck the statue on
its feet of iron and clay and smashed them.[q] 35Then the iron, the
clay, the bronze, the silver and the gold were broken to pieces at the
same time and became like chaff on a threshing floor in the summer. The wind swept them away[r] without leaving a trace. But the
rock that struck the statue became a huge mountain[s] and filled the
whole earth.
36"This was the dream, and now we will interpret it to the king.
37You, O king, are the king of kings.[t] The God of heaven has given
you dominion[u] and power and might and glory; 38in your hands

2:21 [a]Jas 1:5
2:22 [b]Job 12:22; Ps 25:14; Da 5:11 [c]Ps 139:11-12; Jer 23:24; Heb 4:13 [d]Isa 45:7; Jas 1:17
2:23 [e]Ex 3:15 [f]Da 1:17
2:24 [g]ver 14
2:25 [h]Da 1:6; 5:13; 6:13
2:26 [i]Da 1:7
2:27 [j]ver 10
2:28 [k]Ge 40:8; Am 4:13 [l]Ge 49:1; Da 10:14 [m]Da 4:5
2:30 [n]Isa 45:3; Da 1:17; Am 4:13
2:31 [o]Hab 1:7
2:34 [p]Zec 4:6 [q]ver 44-45; Ps 2:9; Isa 60:12; Da 8:25
2:35 [r]Ps 1:4; 37:10; Isa 17:13 [s]Isa 2:3; Mic 4:1
2:37 [t]Eze 26:7 [u]Jer 27:7

he has placed mankind and the beasts of the field and the birds of
the air. Wherever they live, he has made you ruler over them all.[a]
You are that head of gold.
39 “After you, another kingdom will rise, inferior to yours. Next, a
third kingdom, one of bronze, will rule over the whole earth.
40 Finally, there will be a fourth kingdom, strong as iron—for iron
breaks and smashes everything—and as iron breaks things to
pieces, so it will crush and break all the others.[b] 41 Just as you saw
that the feet and toes were partly of baked clay and partly of iron,
so this will be a divided kingdom; yet it will have some of the
strength of iron in it, even as you saw iron mixed with clay. 42 As the
toes were partly iron and partly clay, so this kingdom will be partly
strong and partly brittle. 43 And just as you saw the iron mixed with
baked clay, so the people will be a mixture and will not remain
united, any more than iron mixes with clay.
44 “In the time of those kings, the God of heaven will set up a
kingdom that will never be destroyed, nor will it be left to another
people. It will crush[c] all those kingdoms[d] and bring them to an
end, but it will itself endure forever.[e] 45 This is the meaning of the
vision of the rock[f] cut out of a mountain, but not by human
hands[g]—a rock that broke the iron, the bronze, the clay, the silver
and the gold to pieces.
“The great God has shown the king what will take place in the
future. The dream is true and the interpretation is trustworthy.”
46 Then King Nebuchadnezzar fell prostrate[h] before Daniel and
paid him honor and ordered that an offering[i] and incense be presented to him. 47 The king said to Daniel, “Surely your God is the
God of gods[j] and the Lord of kings[k] and a revealer of mysteries,[l]
for you were able to reveal this mystery.”
48 Then the king placed Daniel in a high position and lavished
many gifts on him. He made him ruler over the entire province of
Babylon and placed him in charge of all its wise men.[m] 49 Moreover, at Daniel’s request the king appointed Shadrach, Meshach
and Abednego administrators over the province of Babylon,[n] while
Daniel himself remained at the royal court.

Chapter 3 Theme ______________________________

3 King Nebuchadnezzar made an image[o] of gold, ninety feet
high and nine feet[a] wide, and set it up on the plain of Dura in
the province of Babylon. 2 He then summoned the satraps, prefects,
governors, advisers, treasurers, judges, magistrates and all the other
provincial officials[p] to come to the dedication of the image he had
set up. 3 So the satraps, prefects, governors, advisers, treasurers,
judges, magistrates and all the other provincial officials assembled

a *1* Aramaic *sixty cubits high and six cubits wide* (about 27 meters high and 2.7 meters wide)

2:38 [a] Jer 27:6; Da 4:21-22
2:40 [b] Da 7:7,23
2:44 [c] Ps 2:9; 1Co 15:24 [d] Isa 60:12 [e] Ps 145:13; Isa 9:7; Da 4:34; 6:26; 7:14,27; Mic 4:7,13; Lk 1:33
2:45 [f] Isa 28:16 [g] Da 8:25
2:46 [h] Da 8:17; Ac 10:25 [i] Ac 14:13
2:47 [j] Da 11:36 [k] Da 4:25 [l] ver 22,28
2:48 [m] ver 6; Da 4:9; 5:11
2:49 [n] Da 1:7
3:1 [o] Isa 46:6; Jer 16:20; Hab 2:19
3:2 [p] ver 27; Da 6:7

For a clear understanding of the empires represented in the statue, consult the timeline on pages IISB-45 through IISB-48, and the historical account on pages 2191 through 2198.

for the dedication of the image that King Nebuchadnezzar had set
up, and they stood before it.
4Then the herald loudly proclaimed, "This is what you are commanded to do, O peoples, nations and men of every language:[a] 5As
soon as you hear the sound of the horn, flute, zither, lyre, harp, pipes
and all kinds of music, you must fall down and worship the image
of gold that King Nebuchadnezzar has set up.[b] 6Whoever does not
fall down and worship will immediately be thrown into a blazing
furnace."[c]

7Therefore, as soon as they heard the sound of the horn, flute,
zither, lyre, harp and all kinds of music, all the peoples, nations
and men of every language fell down and worshiped the image of
gold that King Nebuchadnezzar had set up.[d]
8At this time some astrologers[a][e] came forward and denounced
the Jews. 9They said to King Nebuchadnezzar, "O king, live forever![f]
10You have issued a decree,[g] O king, that everyone who hears the
sound of the horn, flute, zither, lyre, harp, pipes and all kinds of
music must fall down and worship the image of gold,[h] 11and that
whoever does not fall down and worship will be thrown into a
blazing furnace. 12But there are some Jews whom you have set over
the affairs of the province of Babylon—Shadrach, Meshach and
Abednego[i]—who pay no attention[j] to you, O king. They neither
serve your gods nor worship the image of gold you have set up."[k]
13Furious[l] with rage, Nebuchadnezzar summoned Shadrach,
Meshach and Abednego. So these men were brought before the
king, 14and Nebuchadnezzar said to them, "Is it true, Shadrach,
Meshach and Abednego, that you do not serve my gods[m] or worship the image[n] of gold I have set up? 15Now when you hear the

[a]8 Or *Chaldeans*

3:4 [a]Da 4:1; 6:25
3:5 [b]ver 10,15
3:6 [c]ver 11,15,21; Jer 29:22; Da 6:7; Mt 13:42,50; Rev 13:15
3:7 [d]ver 5
3:8 [e]Da 2:10
3:9 [f]Ne 2:3; Da 5:10; 6:6
3:10 [g]Da 6:12 [h]ver 4-6
3:12 [i]Da 2:49 [j]Da 6:13 [k]Est 3:3
3:13 [l]Da 2:12
3:14 [m]Isa 46:1; Jer 50:2 [n]ver 1

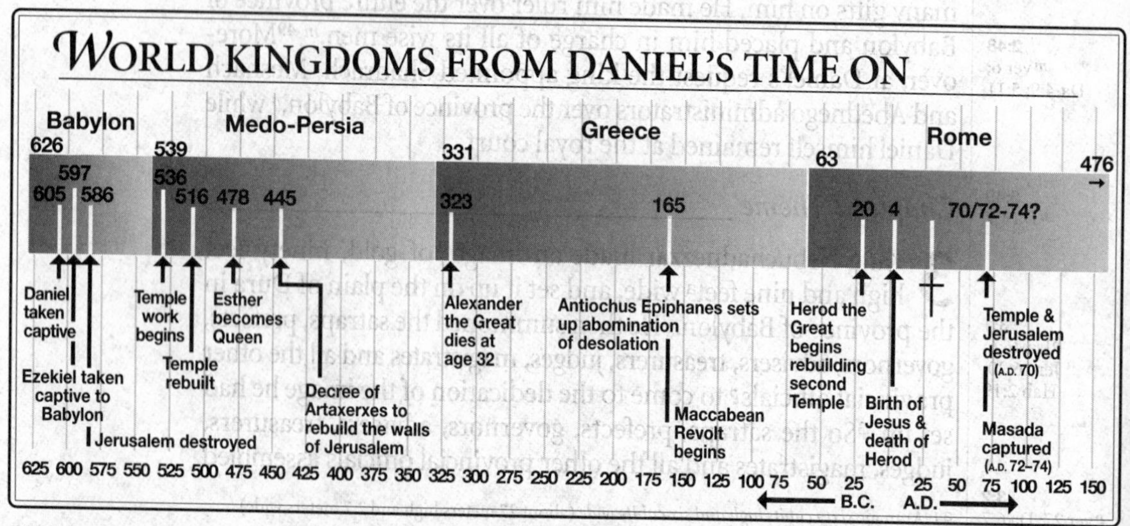

sound of the horn, flute, zither, lyre, harp, pipes and all kinds of music, if you are ready to fall down and worship the image I made, very good. But if you do not worship it, you will be thrown immediately into a blazing furnace. Then what god[a] will be able to rescue[b] you from my hand?"

16 Shadrach, Meshach and Abednego[c] replied to the king, "O Nebuchadnezzar, we do not need to defend ourselves before you in this matter. 17 If we are thrown into the blazing furnace, the God we serve is able to save[d] us from it, and he will rescue[e] us from your hand, O king. 18 But even if he does not, we want you to know, O king, that we will not serve your gods or worship the image of gold you have set up.[f]"

19 Then Nebuchadnezzar was furious with Shadrach, Meshach and Abednego, and his attitude toward them changed. He ordered the furnace heated seven[g] times hotter than usual 20 and commanded some of the strongest soldiers in his army to tie up Shadrach, Meshach and Abednego and throw them into the blazing furnace. 21 So these men, wearing their robes, trousers, turbans and other clothes, were bound and thrown into the blazing furnace. 22 The king's command was so urgent and the furnace so hot that the flames of the fire killed the soldiers who took up Shadrach, Meshach and Abednego,[h] 23 and these three men, firmly tied, fell into the blazing furnace.

24 Then King Nebuchadnezzar leaped to his feet in amazement and asked his advisers, "Weren't there three men that we tied up and threw into the fire?"

They replied, "Certainly, O king."

25 He said, "Look! I see four men walking around in the fire, unbound and unharmed, and the fourth looks like a son of the gods."

26 Nebuchadnezzar then approached the opening of the blazing furnace and shouted, "Shadrach, Meshach and Abednego, servants of the Most High God,[i] come out! Come here!"

So Shadrach, Meshach and Abednego came out of the fire, 27 and the satraps, prefects, governors and royal advisers[j] crowded around them.[k] They saw that the fire[l] had not harmed their bodies, nor was a hair of their heads singed; their robes were not scorched, and there was no smell of fire on them.

28 Then Nebuchadnezzar said, "Praise be to the God of Shadrach, Meshach and Abednego, who has sent his angel[m] and rescued his servants! They trusted[n] in him and defied the king's command and were willing to give up their lives rather than serve or worship any god except their own God.[o] 29 Therefore I decree[p] that the people of any nation or language who say anything against the God of Shadrach, Meshach and Abednego be cut into pieces and

3:15 [a] Isa 36:18-20 [b] Ex 5:2; 2Ch 32:15
3:16 [c] Da 1:7
3:17 [d] Ps 27:1-2 [e] Job 5:19; Jer 1:8
3:18 [f] ver 28; Jos 24:15
3:19 [g] Lev 26:18-28
3:22 [h] Da 1:7
3:26 [i] Da 4:2,34
3:27 [j] ver 2 [k] Isa 43:2; Heb 11:32-34 [l] Da 6:23
3:28 [m] Ps 34:7; Da 6:22; Ac 5:19 [n] Job 13:15; Ps 26:1; 84:12; Jer 17:7 [o] ver 18
3:29 [p] Da 6:26

their houses be turned into piles of rubble,[a] for no other god can
save[b] in this way."
30Then the king promoted Shadrach, Meshach and Abednego
in the province of Babylon.[c]

Chapter 4 Theme

4 King Nebuchadnezzar,

To the peoples, nations and men of every language,[d] who
live in all the world:

May you prosper greatly![e]

2It is my pleasure to tell you about the miraculous signs[f]
and wonders that the Most High God[g] has performed for me.

3How great are his signs,
how mighty his wonders![h]
His kingdom is an eternal kingdom;
his dominion endures[i] from generation
to generation.

4I, Nebuchadnezzar, was at home in my palace, contented[j]
and prosperous. 5I had a dream[k] that made me afraid. As I was
lying in my bed, the images and visions that passed through
my mind[l] terrified me. 6So I commanded that all the wise men
of Babylon be brought before me to interpret[m] the dream for
me. 7When the magicians,[n] enchanters, astrologers[a] and diviners[o] came, I told them the dream, but they could not interpret
it for me.[p] 8Finally, Daniel came into my presence and I told
him the dream. (He is called Belteshazzar,[q] after the name of
my god, and the spirit of the holy gods[r] is in him.)
9I said, "Belteshazzar, chief[s] of the magicians, I know that the
spirit of the holy gods[t] is in you, and no mystery is too difficult
for you. Here is my dream; interpret it for me. 10These are the
visions I saw while lying in my bed:[u] I looked, and there before
me stood a tree in the middle of the land. Its height was enormous.[v] 11The tree grew large and strong and its top touched
the sky; it was visible to the ends of the earth. 12Its leaves were
beautiful, its fruit abundant, and on it was food for all. Under
it the beasts of the field found shelter, and the birds of the air
lived in its branches;[w] from it every creature was fed.
13"In the visions I saw while lying in my bed,[x] I looked, and
there before me was a messenger,[b] a holy one,[y] coming down
from heaven. 14He called in a loud voice: 'Cut down the tree
and trim off its branches; strip off its leaves and scatter its

[a]7 Or *Chaldeans* [b]13 Or *watchman*; also in verses 17 and 23

3:29 [a]Ezr 6:11 [b]Da 6:27
3:30 [c]Da 2:49
4:1 [d]Da 3:4 [e]Da 6:25
4:2 [f]Ps 74:9 [g]Da 3:26
4:3 [h]Ps 105:27; Da 6:27 [i]Da 2:44
4:4 [j]Ps 30:6
4:5 [k]Da 2:1 [l]Da 2:28
4:6 [m]Da 2:2
4:7 [n]Ge 41:8 [o]Isa 44:25; Da 2:2 [p]Da 2:10
4:8 [q]Da 1:7 [r]Da 5:11,14
4:9 [s]Da 2:48 [t]Da 5:11-12
4:10 [u]ver 5 [v]Eze 31:3-4
4:12 [w]Eze 17:23; Mt 13:32
4:13 [x]Da 7:1 [y]ver 23; Dt 33:2; Da 8:13

fruit. Let the animals flee from under it and the birds from its
branches.[a] 15But let the stump and its roots, bound with iron
and bronze, remain in the ground, in the grass of the field.
"'Let him be drenched with the dew of heaven, and let him
live with the animals among the plants of the earth. 16Let his
mind be changed from that of a man and let him be given the
mind of an animal, till seven times[a] pass by for him.[b]
17"'The decision is announced by messengers, the holy ones
declare the verdict, so that the living may know that the Most
High[c] is sovereign[d] over the kingdoms of men and gives them
to anyone he wishes and sets over them the lowliest[e] of men.'
18"This is the dream that I, King Nebuchadnezzar, had. Now,
Belteshazzar, tell me what it means, for none of the wise men in
my kingdom can interpret it for me.[f] But you can,[g] because the
spirit of the holy gods is in you."[h]

19Then Daniel (also called Belteshazzar) was greatly perplexed
for a time, and his thoughts terrified[i] him. So the king said,
"Belteshazzar, do not let the dream or its meaning alarm you."
Belteshazzar answered, "My lord, if only the dream applied
to your enemies and its meaning to your adversaries! 20The
tree you saw, which grew large and strong, with its top touching the sky, visible to the whole earth, 21with beautiful leaves
and abundant fruit, providing food for all, giving shelter to the
beasts of the field, and having nesting places in its branches for
the birds of the air— 22you, O king, are that tree![j] You have
become great and strong; your greatness has grown until it
reaches the sky, and your dominion extends to distant parts of
the earth.[k]
23"You, O king, saw a messenger, a holy one,[l] coming down
from heaven and saying, 'Cut down the tree and destroy it, but
leave the stump, bound with iron and bronze, in the grass of
the field, while its roots remain in the ground. Let him be
drenched with the dew of heaven; let him live like the wild animals, until seven times pass by for him.'[m]
24"This is the interpretation, O king, and this is the decree[n]
the Most High has issued against my lord the king: 25You will be
driven away from people and will live with the wild animals;
you will eat grass like cattle and be drenched with the dew of
heaven. Seven times will pass by for you until you acknowledge
that the Most High[o] is sovereign over the kingdoms of men and
gives them to anyone he wishes.[p] 26The command to leave the
stump of the tree with its roots[q] means that your kingdom will
be restored to you when you acknowledge that Heaven rules.[r]

4:14 [a]Eze 31:12; Mt 3:10
4:16 [b]ver 23,32
4:17 [c]ver 2,25; Ps 83:18 [d]Jer 27:5-7; Da 2:21; 5:18-21 [e]Da 11:21
4:18 [f]Ge 41:8; Da 5:8,15 [g]Ge 41:15 [h]ver 7-9
4:19 [i]Da 7:15,28; 8:27; 10:16-17
4:22 [j]2Sa 12:7 [k]Jer 27:7; Da 2:37-38; 5:18-19
4:23 [l]ver 13 [m]Da 5:21
4:24 [n]Job 40:12; Ps 107:40
4:25 [o]ver 17; Ps 83:18 [p]Jer 27:5; Da 5:21
4:26 [q]ver 15 [r]Da 2:37

a *16* Or *years;* also in verses 23, 25 and 32

27 Therefore, O king, be pleased to accept my advice: Renounce
your sins by doing what is right, and your wickedness by being
kind to the oppressed.[a] It may be that then your prosperity will
continue.[b]"

28 All this happened[c] to King Nebuchadnezzar. 29 Twelve
months later, as the king was walking on the roof of the royal
palace of Babylon, 30 he said, "Is not this the great Babylon I
have built as the royal residence, by my mighty power and for
the glory of my majesty?"[d]
31 The words were still on his lips when a voice came from
heaven, "This is what is decreed for you, King Nebuchadnezzar: Your royal authority has been taken from you. 32 You will
be driven away from people and will live with the wild animals;
you will eat grass like cattle. Seven times will pass by for you
until you acknowledge that the Most High is sovereign over the
kingdoms of men and gives them to anyone he wishes."
33 Immediately what had been said about Nebuchadnezzar
was fulfilled. He was driven away from people and ate grass
like cattle. His body was drenched with the dew of heaven until
his hair grew like the feathers of an eagle and his nails like the
claws of a bird.[e]

34 At the end of that time, I, Nebuchadnezzar, raised my eyes
toward heaven, and my sanity was restored. Then I praised the
Most High; I honored and glorified him who lives forever.[f]

His dominion is an eternal dominion;
his kingdom endures from generation to generation.[g]
35 All the peoples of the earth
are regarded as nothing.[h]
He does as he pleases[i]
with the powers of heaven
and the peoples of the earth.
No one can hold back his hand
or say to him: "What have you done?"[j]

36 At the same time that my sanity was restored, my honor
and splendor were returned to me for the glory of my kingdom.[k] My advisers and nobles sought me out, and I was restored to my throne and became even greater than before.
37 Now I, Nebuchadnezzar, praise and exalt and glorify the King
of heaven, because everything he does is right and all his ways
are just.[l] And those who walk in pride he is able to humble.[m]

Chapter 5 Theme ____________________

5 King Belshazzar gave a great banquet[n] for a thousand of his
nobles and drank wine with them. 2 While Belshazzar was

4:27
[a] Isa 55:6-7
[b] 1Ki 21:29; Ps 41:3; Eze 18:22

4:28
[c] Nu 23:19

4:30
[d] Isa 37:24-25; Da 5:20; Hab 2:4

4:33
[e] Da 5:20-21

4:34
[f] Da 12:7; Rev 4:10
[g] Ps 145:13; Da 2:44; 5:21; 6:26; Lk 1:33

4:35
[h] Isa 40:17
[i] Ps 115:3; 135:6
[j] Isa 45:9; Ro 9:20

4:36
[k] Pr 22:4

4:37
[l] Dt 32:4; Ps 33:4-5
[m] Ex 18:11; Job 40:11-12; Da 5:20,23

5:1
[n] Est 1:3

drinking his wine, he gave orders to bring in the gold and silver
goblets[a] that Nebuchadnezzar his father[a] had taken from the
temple in Jerusalem, so that the king and his nobles, his wives and
his concubines might drink from them.[b] 3So they brought in the
gold goblets that had been taken from the temple of God in
Jerusalem, and the king and his nobles, his wives and his concubines drank from them. 4As they drank the wine, they praised the
gods of gold and silver, of bronze, iron, wood and stone.[c]
5Suddenly the fingers of a human hand appeared and wrote on
the plaster of the wall, near the lampstand in the royal palace.
The king watched the hand as it wrote. 6His face turned pale and
he was so frightened[d] that his knees knocked together and his
legs gave way.[e]
7The king called out for the enchanters, astrologers[b] and diviners[f]
to be brought and said to these wise[g] men of Babylon, "Whoever
reads this writing and tells me what it means will be clothed in
purple and have a gold chain placed around his neck,[h] and he will
be made the third highest ruler in the kingdom."[i]
8Then all the king's wise men came in, but they could not read
the writing or tell the king what it meant.[j] 9So King Belshazzar
became even more terrified[k] and his face grew more pale. His
nobles were baffled.
10The queen,[c] hearing the voices of the king and his nobles, came
into the banquet hall. "O king, live forever!"[l] she said. "Don't be
alarmed! Don't look so pale! 11There is a man in your kingdom
who has the spirit of the holy gods[m] in him. In the time of your
father he was found to have insight and intelligence and wisdom[n]
like that of the gods. King Nebuchadnezzar your father—your
father the king, I say—appointed him chief of the magicians,
enchanters, astrologers and diviners.[o] 12This man Daniel, whom
the king called Belteshazzar,[p] was found to have a keen mind and
knowledge and understanding, and also the ability to interpret
dreams, explain riddles and solve difficult problems.[q] Call for
Daniel, and he will tell you what the writing means."
13So Daniel was brought before the king, and the king said to
him, "Are you Daniel, one of the exiles my father the king brought
from Judah?[r] 14I have heard that the spirit of the gods is in you and
that you have insight, intelligence and outstanding wisdom. 15The
wise men and enchanters were brought before me to read this
writing and tell me what it means, but they could not explain it.
16Now I have heard that you are able to give interpretations and to
solve difficult problems. If you can read this writing and tell me what
it means, you will be clothed in purple and have a gold chain

5:2 [a]2Ki 24:13; Jer 52:19 [b]Est 1:7; Da 1:2
5:4 [c]Ps 135:15-18; Hab 2:19; Rev 9:20
5:6 [d]Da 4:5 [e]Eze 7:17
5:7 [f]Isa 44:25 [g]Da 4:6-7 [h]Ge 41:42 [i]Da 2:5-6,48; 6:2-3
5:8 [j]Da 2:10,27
5:9 [k]Isa 21:4
5:10 [l]Da 3:9
5:11 [m]Da 4:8-9,19 [n]ver 14; Da 1:17 [o]Da 2:47-48
5:12 [p]Da 1:7 [q]ver 14-16; Da 6:3
5:13 [r]Da 6:13

[a]2 Or *ancestor;* or *predecessor;* also in verses 11, 13 and 18 [b]7 Or *Chaldeans;* also in verse 11
[c]10 Or *queen mother*

placed around your neck, and you will be made the third highest
ruler in the kingdom."
17 Then Daniel answered the king, "You may keep your gifts for
yourself and give your rewards to someone else.[a] Nevertheless, I
will read the writing for the king and tell him what it means.
18 "O king, the Most High God gave your father Nebuchadnezzar
sovereignty and greatness and glory and splendor.[b] 19 Because of
the high position he gave him, all the peoples and nations and men
of every language dreaded and feared him. Those the king wanted
to put to death, he put to death;[c] those he wanted to spare, he
spared; those he wanted to promote, he promoted; and those he
wanted to humble, he humbled. 20 But when his heart became
arrogant and hardened with pride,[d] he was deposed from his royal
throne and stripped[e] of his glory.[f] 21 He was driven away from people and given the mind of an animal; he lived with the wild donkeys and ate grass like cattle; and his body was drenched with the
dew of heaven, until he acknowledged that the Most High God is
sovereign[g] over the kingdoms of men and sets over them anyone
he wishes.[h]
22 "But you his son,[a] O Belshazzar, have not humbled[i] yourself,
though you knew all this. 23 Instead, you have set yourself up
against[j] the Lord of heaven. You had the goblets from his temple
brought to you, and you and your nobles, your wives and your
concubines drank wine from them. You praised the gods of silver
and gold, of bronze, iron, wood and stone, which cannot see or
hear or understand.[k] But you did not honor the God who holds in
his hand your life[l] and all your ways.[m] 24 Therefore he sent the hand
that wrote the inscription.
25 "This is the inscription that was written:

MENE, MENE, TEKEL, PARSIN[b]

26 "This is what these words mean:

Mene[c]: God has numbered the days[n] of your reign and
brought it to an end.[o]
27 *Tekel*[d]: You have been weighed on the scales and found
wanting.[p]
28 *Peres*[e]: Your kingdom is divided and given to the Medes[q]
and Persians."[r]

29 Then at Belshazzar's command, Daniel was clothed in purple, a
gold chain was placed around his neck, and he was proclaimed the
third highest ruler in the kingdom.

[a] 22 Or *descendant*; or *successor* [b] 25 Aramaic *UPARSIN* (that is, *AND PARSIN*) [c] 26 *Mene* can mean *numbered* or *mina* (a unit of money). [d] 27 *Tekel* can mean *weighed* or *shekel*. [e] 28 *Peres* (the singular of *Parsin*) can mean *divided* or *Persia* or *a half mina* or *a half shekel*.

5:17 [a] 2Ki 5:16
5:18 [b] Jer 27:7; Da 2:37-38
5:19 [c] Da 2:12-13; 3:6
5:20 [d] Da 4:30 [e] Jer 13:18 [f] Job 40:12; Isa 14:13-15
5:21 [g] Eze 17:24 [h] Da 4:16-17,35
5:22 [i] Ex 10:3; 2Ch 33:23
5:23 [j] Jer 50:29 [k] Ps 115:4-8; Hab 2:19 [l] Job 12:10 [m] Job 31:4; Jer 10:23
5:26 [n] Jer 27:7 [o] Isa 13:6
5:27 [p] Ps 62:9
5:28 [q] Isa 13:17 [r] Da 6:28

30 That very night Belshazzar,[a] king of the Babylonians,[a] was
slain,[b] 31 and Darius[c] the Mede took over the kingdom, at the age of
sixty-two.

Chapter 6 Theme

6 It pleased Darius[d] to appoint 120 satraps[e] to rule throughout
the kingdom, 2 with three administrators over them, one of
whom was Daniel.[f] The satraps were made accountable[g] to them
so that the king might not suffer loss. 3 Now Daniel so distinguished himself among the administrators and the satraps by his
exceptional qualities that the king planned to set him over the
whole kingdom.[h] 4 At this, the administrators and the satraps tried
to find grounds for charges against Daniel in his conduct of government affairs, but they were unable to do so. They could find no
corruption in him, because he was trustworthy and neither corrupt nor negligent. 5 Finally these men said, "We will never find any
basis for charges against this man Daniel unless it has something
to do with the law of his God."[i]

6 So the administrators and the satraps went as a group to the
king and said: "O King Darius, live forever![j] 7 The royal administrators, prefects, satraps, advisers and governors[k] have all agreed
that the king should issue an edict and enforce the decree that
anyone who prays to any god or man during the next thirty days,
except to you, O king, shall be thrown into the lions' den.[l] 8 Now, O
king, issue the decree and put it in writing so that it cannot be
altered—in accordance with the laws of the Medes and Persians,
which cannot be repealed."[m] 9 So King Darius put the decree in
writing.

10 Now when Daniel learned that the decree had been published,
he went home to his upstairs room where the windows opened
toward[n] Jerusalem. Three times a day he got down on his knees[o]
and prayed, giving thanks to his God, just as he had done before.[p]
11 Then these men went as a group and found Daniel praying and
asking God for help. 12 So they went to the king and spoke to him
about his royal decree: "Did you not publish a decree that during
the next thirty days anyone who prays to any god or man except to
you, O king, would be thrown into the lions' den?"

The king answered, "The decree stands—in accordance with the
laws of the Medes and Persians, which cannot be repealed."[q]

13 Then they said to the king, "Daniel, who is one of the exiles
from Judah,[r] pays no attention[s] to you, O king, or to the decree
you put in writing. He still prays three times a day." 14 When the
king heard this, he was greatly distressed;[t] he was determined to
rescue Daniel and made every effort until sundown to save him.

a 30 Or *Chaldeans*

5:30 [a] ver 1 [b] Isa 21:9; Jer 51:31
5:31 [c] Da 6:1; 9:1
6:1 [d] Da 5:31 [e] Est 1:1
6:2 [f] Da 2:48-49 [g] Ezr 4:22
6:3 [h] Ge 41:41; Est 10:3; Da 5:12-14
6:5 [i] Ac 24:13-16
6:6 [j] Ne 2:3; Da 2:4
6:7 [k] Da 3:2 [l] Ps 59:3; 64:2-6; Da 3:6
6:8 [m] Est 1:19
6:10 [n] 1Ki 8:48-49 [o] Ps 95:6 [p] Ac 5:29
6:12 [q] Est 1:19; Da 3:8-12
6:13 [r] Da 2:25; 5:13 [s] Est 3:8; Da 3:12
6:14 [t] Mk 6:26

15 Then the men went as a group to the king and said to him,
"Remember, O king, that according to the law of the Medes and
Persians no decree or edict that the king issues can be changed."[a]
16 So the king gave the order, and they brought Daniel and threw
him into the lions' den.[b] The king said to Daniel, "May your God,
whom you serve continually, rescue[c] you!"
17 A stone was brought and placed over the mouth of the den,
and the king sealed[d] it with his own signet ring and with the rings
of his nobles, so that Daniel's situation might not be changed.
18 Then the king returned to his palace and spent the night without eating[e] and without any entertainment being brought to him.
And he could not sleep.[f]
19 At the first light of dawn, the king got up and hurried to the
lions' den. 20 When he came near the den, he called to Daniel in an
anguished voice, "Daniel, servant of the living God, has your God,
whom you serve continually, been able to rescue you from the
lions?"[g]
21 Daniel answered, "O king, live forever![h] 22 My God sent his
angel,[i] and he shut the mouths of the lions.[j] They have not hurt
me, because I was found innocent in his sight.[k] Nor have I ever
done any wrong before you, O king."
23 The king was overjoyed and gave orders to lift Daniel out of the
den. And when Daniel was lifted from the den, no wound[l] was
found on him, because he had trusted[m] in his God.
24 At the king's command, the men who had falsely accused
Daniel were brought in and thrown into the lions' den,[n] along with
their wives and children.[o] And before they reached the floor of the
den, the lions overpowered them and crushed all their bones.[p]
25 Then King Darius wrote to all the peoples, nations and men
of every language throughout the land:

"May you prosper greatly![q]

26 "I issue a decree that in every part of my kingdom people
must fear and reverence the God of Daniel.[r]

"For he is the living God
and he endures forever;
his kingdom will not be destroyed,
his dominion will never end.[s]
27 He rescues and he saves;
he performs signs and wonders[t]
in the heavens and on the earth.
He has rescued Daniel
from the power of the lions."[u]

6:15 [a] Est 8:8
6:16 [b] ver 7 [c] Job 5:19; Ps 37:39-40
6:17 [d] Mt 27:66
6:18 [e] 2Sa 12:17 [f] Est 6:1; Da 2:1
6:20 [g] Da 3:17
6:21 [h] Da 2:4
6:22 [i] Da 3:28 [j] Ps 91:11-13; Heb 11:33 [k] Ac 12:11; 2Ti 4:17
6:23 [l] Da 3:27 [m] 1Ch 5:20
6:24 [n] Dt 19:18-19; Est 7:9-10; Ps 54:5 [o] Dt 24:16; 2Ki 14:6 [p] Isa 38:13
6:25 [q] Da 4:1
6:26 [r] Ps 99:1-3; Da 3:29 [s] Da 2:44; 4:34
6:27 [t] Da 4:3 [u] ver 22

28 So Daniel prospered during the reign of Darius and the reign
of Cyrus[a][a] the Persian.

Chapter 7 Theme

7 In the first year of Belshazzar[b] king of Babylon, Daniel had a
dream, and visions passed through his mind[c] as he was lying
on his bed. He wrote[d] down the substance of his dream.
2 Daniel said: "In my vision at night I looked, and there before me
were the four winds of heaven[e] churning up the great sea. 3 Four
great beasts,[f] each different from the others, came up out of the sea.
4 "The first was like a lion,[g] and it had the wings of an eagle.[h] I
watched until its wings were torn off and it was lifted from the
ground so that it stood on two feet like a man, and the heart of a
man was given to it.
5 "And there before me was a second beast, which looked like a
bear. It was raised up on one of its sides, and it had three ribs in its
mouth between its teeth. It was told, 'Get up and eat your fill of
flesh!'[i]
6 "After that, I looked, and there before me was another beast,
one that looked like a leopard.[j] And on its back it had four wings
like those of a bird. This beast had four heads, and it was given
authority to rule.
7 "After that, in my vision at night I looked, and there before me
was a fourth beast—terrifying and frightening and very powerful.
It had large iron[k] teeth; it crushed and devoured its victims and
trampled underfoot whatever was left. It was different from all the
former beasts, and it had ten horns.[l]
8 "While I was thinking about the horns, there before me was
another horn, a little[m] one, which came up among them; and
three of the first horns were uprooted before it. This horn had
eyes like the eyes of a man[n] and a mouth that spoke boastfully.[o]
9 "As I looked,

"thrones were set in place,
  and the Ancient of Days took his seat.
His clothing was as white as snow;
  the hair of his head was white like wool.[p]
His throne was flaming with fire,
  and its wheels[q] were all ablaze.
10 A river of fire[r] was flowing,
  coming out from before him.[s]
Thousands upon thousands attended him;
  ten thousand times ten thousand stood before him.
The court was seated,
  and the books[t] were opened.

6:28 [a] 2Ch 36:22; Da 1:21
7:1 [b] Da 5:1 [c] Da 1:17 [d] Jer 36:4
7:2 [e] Rev 7:1
7:3 [f] Rev 13:1
7:4 [g] Jer 4:7 [h] Eze 17:3
7:5 [i] Da 2:39
7:6 [j] Rev 13:2
7:7 [k] Da 2:40 [l] Rev 12:3
7:8 [m] Da 8:9 [n] Rev 9:7 [o] Ps 12:3; Rev 13:5-6
7:9 [p] Rev 1:14 [q] Eze 1:15; 10:6
7:10 [r] Ps 50:3; 97:3; Isa 30:27 [s] Dt 33:2; Ps 68:17; Rev 5:11 [t] Rev 20:11-15

a 28 Or *Darius, that is, the reign of Cyrus*

11“Then I continued to watch because of the boastful words the
horn was speaking. I kept looking until the beast was slain and its
body destroyed and thrown into the blazing fire.[a] 12(The other
beasts had been stripped of their authority, but were allowed to live
for a period of time.)

13“In my vision at night I looked, and there before me was one
like a son of man,[b] coming with the clouds of heaven.[c] He
approached the Ancient of Days and was led into his presence.
14He was given authority,[d] glory and sovereign power; all peoples,
nations and men of every language worshiped him.[e] His dominion
is an everlasting dominion that will not pass away, and his kingdom
is one that will never be destroyed.[f]

15“I, Daniel, was troubled in spirit, and the visions that passed
through my mind disturbed me.[g] 16I approached one of those
standing there and asked him the true meaning of all this.

“So he told me and gave me the interpretation[h] of these things:
17‘The four great beasts are four kingdoms that will rise from the
earth. 18But the saints of the Most High will receive the kingdom
and will possess it forever—yes, for ever and ever.’[i]

19“Then I wanted to know the true meaning of the fourth beast,
which was different from all the others and most terrifying, with its
iron teeth and bronze claws—the beast that crushed and devoured
its victims and trampled underfoot whatever was left. 20I also
wanted to know about the ten horns on its head and about the other horn that came up, before which three of them fell—the horn
that looked more imposing than the others and that had eyes and a
mouth that spoke boastfully. 21As I watched, this horn was waging
war against the saints and defeating them,[j] 22until the Ancient of
Days came and pronounced judgment in favor of the saints of the
Most High, and the time came when they possessed the kingdom.

23“He gave me this explanation: ‘The fourth beast is a fourth
kingdom that will appear on earth. It will be different from all the
other kingdoms and will devour the whole earth, trampling it
down and crushing it.[k] 24The ten horns[l] are ten kings who will
come from this kingdom. After them another king will arise, different from the earlier ones; he will subdue three kings. 25He will
speak against the Most High[m] and oppress his saints and try to
change the set times[n] and the laws. The saints will be handed over
to him for a time, times and half a time.[a][o]

26“‘But the court will sit, and his power will be taken away and
completely destroyed forever. 27Then the sovereignty, power and
greatness of the kingdoms under the whole heaven will be handed
over to the saints, the people of the Most High. His kingdom will be
an everlasting[p] kingdom, and all rulers will worship[q] and obey him.’

[a] 25 Or *for a year, two years and half a year*

7:11 [a] Rev 19:20

7:13 [b] Mt 8:20*; Rev 1:13* [c] Mt 24:30; Rev 1:7

7:14 [d] Mt 28:18 [e] Ps 72:11; 102:22; 1Co 15:27; Eph 1:22 [f] Da 2:44; Heb 12:28; Rev 11:15

7:15 [g] Da 4:19

7:16 [h] Da 8:16; 9:22; Zec 1:9

7:18 [i] Isa 60:12-14; Rev 2:26; 20:4

7:21 [j] Rev 13:7

7:23 [k] Da 2:40

7:24 [l] Rev 17:12

7:25 [m] Isa 37:23; Da 11:36 [n] Da 2:21 [o] Da 8:24; 12:7; Rev 12:14

7:27 [p] Da 2:44; 4:34; Lk 1:33; Rev 11:15; 22:5 [q] Ps 22:27; 72:11; 86:9

28"This is the end of the matter. I, Daniel, was deeply troubled[a]
by my thoughts, and my face turned pale, but I kept the matter to
myself."

Chapter 8 Theme ________________

8 In the third year of King Belshazzar's reign, I, Daniel, had a
vision, after the one that had already appeared to me. 2In my
vision I saw myself in the citadel of Susa[b] in the province of Elam;[c]
in the vision I was beside the Ulai Canal. 3I looked up,[d] and there
before me was a ram with two horns, standing beside the canal,
and the horns were long. One of the horns was longer than the
other but grew up later. 4I watched the ram as he charged toward
the west and the north and the south. No animal could stand
against him, and none could rescue from his power. He did as he
pleased[e] and became great.

5As I was thinking about this, suddenly a goat with a prominent
horn between his eyes came from the west, crossing the whole earth
without touching the ground. 6He came toward the two-horned
ram I had seen standing beside the canal and charged at him in
great rage. 7I saw him attack the ram furiously, striking the ram
and shattering his two horns. The ram was powerless to stand
against him; the goat knocked him to the ground and trampled on
him,[f] and none could rescue the ram from his power. 8The goat
became very great, but at the height of his power his large horn
was broken off,[g] and in its place four prominent horns grew up
toward the four winds of heaven.[h]

9Out of one of them came another horn, which started small but
grew in power to the south and to the east and toward the Beautiful Land.[i] 10It grew until it reached[j] the host of the heavens, and it
threw some of the starry host down to the earth[k] and trampled[l] on
them. 11It set itself up to be as great as the Prince of the host;[m] it
took away the daily sacrifice[n] from him, and the place of his sanctuary was brought low.[o] 12Because of rebellion, the host ⌊of the
saints⌋[a] and the daily sacrifice were given over to it. It prospered in
everything it did, and truth was thrown to the ground.

13Then I heard a holy one[p] speaking, and another holy one said
to him, "How long will it take for the vision to be fulfilled[q]—the
vision concerning the daily sacrifice, the rebellion that causes
desolation, and the surrender of the sanctuary and of the host that
will be trampled[r] underfoot?"

14He said to me, "It will take 2,300 evenings and mornings; then
the sanctuary will be reconsecrated."[s]

15While I, Daniel, was watching the vision[t] and trying to understand it, there before me stood one who looked like a man.[u]

[a] 12 Or *rebellion, the armies*

7:28 [a] Da 4:19
8:2 [b] Est 1:2 [c] Ge 10:22
8:3 [d] Da 10:5
8:4 [e] Da 11:3,16
8:7 [f] Da 7:7
8:8 [g] 2Ch 26:16-21; Da 5:20 [h] Da 7:2; Rev 7:1
8:9 [i] Da 11:16
8:10 [j] Isa 14:13 [k] Rev 12:4 [l] Da 7:7
8:11 [m] Da 11:36-37 [n] Eze 46:13-14 [o] Da 11:31; 12:11
8:13 [p] Da 4:23 [q] Da 12:6 [r] Lk 21:24; Rev 11:2
8:14 [s] Da 12:11-12
8:15 [t] ver 1 [u] Da 10:16-18

INSIGHT

The maps on pages 2310, 2311 show the boundaries of the Babylonian, Persian, Greek, and Roman Empires as they relate to the nations today.

16 And I heard a man's voice from the Ulai calling, "Gabriel,[a] tell
this man the meaning of the vision."
17 As he came near the place where I was standing, I was terrified and fell prostrate.[b] "Son of man," he said to me, "understand
that the vision concerns the time of the end."[c]
18 While he was speaking to me, I was in a deep sleep, with my face
to the ground.[d] Then he touched me and raised me to my feet.[e]
19 He said: "I am going to tell you what will happen later in the
time of wrath, because the vision concerns the appointed time of
the end.[a][f] 20 The two-horned ram that you saw represents the
kings of Media and Persia. 21 The shaggy goat is the king of
Greece,[g] and the large horn between his eyes is the first king.[h]
22 The four horns that replaced the one that was broken off represent four kingdoms that will emerge from his nation but will not
have the same power.
23 "In the latter part of their reign, when rebels have become
completely wicked, a stern-faced king, a master of intrigue, will
arise. 24 He will become very strong, but not by his own power. He
will cause astounding devastation and will succeed in whatever he
does. He will destroy the mighty men and the holy people.[i] 25 He
will cause deceit to prosper, and he will consider himself superior.
When they feel secure, he will destroy many and take his stand
against the Prince of princes.[j] Yet he will be destroyed, but not by
human power.[k]
26 "The vision of the evenings and mornings that has been given
you is true,[l] but seal[m] up the vision, for it concerns the distant
future."[n]
27 I, Daniel, was exhausted and lay ill for several days. Then I got
up and went about the king's business.[o] I was appalled[p] by the
vision; it was beyond understanding.

Chapter 9 Theme ____________________

9 In the first year of Darius[q] son of Xerxes[b] (a Mede by descent),
who was made ruler over the Babylonian[c] kingdom— 2 in the
first year of his reign, I, Daniel, understood from the Scriptures,
according to the word of the LORD given to Jeremiah the prophet,
that the desolation of Jerusalem would last seventy[r] years. 3 So I
turned to the Lord God and pleaded with him in prayer and petition, in fasting, and in sackcloth and ashes.[s]
4 I prayed to the LORD my God and confessed:

"O Lord, the great and awesome God,[t] who keeps his
covenant of love[u] with all who love him and obey his commands, 5 we have sinned and done wrong.[v] We have been
wicked and have rebelled; we have turned away[w] from your

a 19 Or *because the end will be at the appointed time* b 1 Hebrew *Ahasuerus* c 1 Or *Chaldean*

8:16 [a] Da 9:21; Lk 1:19
8:17 [b] Eze 1:28; Da 2:46; Rev 1:17 [c] Hab 2:3
8:18 [d] Da 10:9 [e] Eze 2:2; Da 10:16-18
8:19 [f] Hab 2:3
8:21 [g] Da 10:20 [h] Da 11:3
8:24 [i] Da 7:25; 11:36
8:25 [j] Da 11:36 [k] Da 2:34; 11:21
8:26 [l] Da 10:1 [m] Rev 22:10 [n] Da 10:14
8:27 [o] Da 2:48 [p] Da 7:28
9:1 [q] Da 5:31
9:2 [r] 2Ch 36:21; Jer 29:10; Zec 7:5
9:3 [s] Ne 1:4; Jer 29:12
9:4 [t] Dt 7:21 [u] Dt 7:9
9:5 [v] Ps 106:6 [w] Isa 53:6

commands and laws.[a] 6We have not listened to your servants
the prophets,[b] who spoke in your name to our kings, our
princes and our fathers, and to all the people of the land.
7"Lord, you are righteous, but this day we are covered with
shame[c]—the men of Judah and people of Jerusalem and all
Israel, both near and far, in all the countries where you have
scattered[d] us because of our unfaithfulness to you.[e] 8O LORD,
we and our kings, our princes and our fathers are covered with
shame because we have sinned against you. 9The Lord our
God is merciful and forgiving,[f] even though we have rebelled
against him;[g] 10we have not obeyed the LORD our God or kept
the laws he gave us through his servants the prophets.[h] 11All
Israel has transgressed your law and turned away, refusing to
obey you.

"Therefore the curses and sworn judgments written in the
Law of Moses, the servant of God, have been poured out on us,
because we have sinned[i] against you. 12You have fulfilled[j] the
words spoken against us and against our rulers by bringing
upon us great disaster. Under the whole heaven nothing has
ever been done like what has been done to Jerusalem.[k] 13Just as
it is written in the Law of Moses, all this disaster has come
upon us, yet we have not sought the favor of the LORD our God
by turning from our sins and giving attention to your truth.[l]
14The LORD did not hesitate to bring the disaster[m] upon us,
for the LORD our God is righteous in everything he does; yet
we have not obeyed him.[n]

15"Now, O Lord our God, who brought your people out of
Egypt with a mighty hand[o] and who made for yourself a
name[p] that endures to this day, we have sinned, we have done
wrong. 16O Lord, in keeping with all your righteous acts,[q] turn
away your anger and your wrath from Jerusalem,[r] your city,
your holy hill.[s] Our sins and the iniquities of our fathers have
made Jerusalem and your people an object of scorn[t] to all
those around us.

17"Now, our God, hear the prayers and petitions of your
servant. For your sake, O Lord, look with favor[u] on your desolate sanctuary. 18Give ear, O God, and hear; open your eyes
and see[v] the desolation of the city that bears your Name.[w] We
do not make requests of you because we are righteous, but
because of your great mercy. 19O Lord, listen! O Lord, forgive![x]
O Lord, hear and act! For your sake, O my God, do not delay,
because your city and your people bear your Name."

20While I was speaking and praying, confessing my sin and the
sin of my people Israel and making my request to the LORD my
God for his holy hill[y]— 21while I was still in prayer, Gabriel,[z] the

9:5 [a] ver 11; La 1:20
9:6 [b] 2Ch 36:16; Jer 44:5
9:7 [c] Ps 44:15 [d] Dt 4:27; Am 9:9 [e] Jer 3:25
9:9 [f] Ps 130:4 [g] Ne 9:17; Jer 14:7
9:10 [h] 2Ki 17:13-15; 18:12
9:11 [i] Isa 1:4-6; Jer 8:5-10
9:12 [j] Isa 44:26; Zec 1:6 [k] Jer 44:2-6; Eze 5:9
9:13 [l] Isa 9:13; Jer 2:30
9:14 [m] Jer 44:27 [n] Ne 9:33
9:15 [o] Jer 32:21 [p] Ne 9:10
9:16 [q] Ps 31:1 [r] Jer 32:32 [s] Zec 8:3 [t] Eze 5:14
9:17 [u] Nu 6:24-26; Ps 80:19
9:18 [v] Ps 80:14 [w] Isa 37:17; Jer 7:10-12; 25:29
9:19 [x] Ps 44:23
9:20 [y] ver 3; Ps 145:18; Isa 58:9
9:21 [z] Da 8:16; Lk 1:19

man I had seen in the earlier vision, came to me in swift flight
about the time of the evening sacrifice.[a] 22He instructed me and
said to me, "Daniel, I have now come to give you insight and
understanding. 23As soon as you began to pray, an answer was giv-
en, which I have come to tell you, for you are highly esteemed.[b]
Therefore, consider the message and understand the vision:[c]
24"Seventy 'sevens'[a] are decreed for your people and your holy
city to finish[b] transgression, to put an end to sin, to atone[d] for
wickedness, to bring in everlasting righteousness,[e] to seal up
vision and prophecy and to anoint the most holy.[c]
25"Know and understand this: From the issuing of the decree[d] to
restore and rebuild[f] Jerusalem until the Anointed One,[e][g] the
ruler, comes, there will be seven 'sevens,' and sixty-two 'sevens.' It
will be rebuilt with streets and a trench, but in times of trouble.
26After the sixty-two 'sevens,' the Anointed One will be cut off[h]
and will have nothing.[f] The people of the ruler who will come
will destroy the city and the sanctuary. The end will come like a
flood:[i] War will continue until the end, and desolations have been
decreed. 27He will confirm a covenant with many for one 'seven.'[g]
In the middle of the 'seven'[g] he will put an end to sacrifice and
offering. And on a wing ⌊of the temple⌋ he will set up an abomination that causes desolation, until the end that is decreed[j] is
poured out on him.[h]"[i]

INSIGHT

The word *sevens* in Hebrew is *sāvûōt*. There is no indication whether the "sevens" refer to seven days, weeks, months, or years. Seventy sevens (or weeks) is 490. So, if the six things of Daniel 9:24 were not completed within 490 days, weeks, or months, it would be logical to assume that the *sevens* refers to sevens of years. A decree to rebuild and restore Jerusalem was issued by King Artaxerxes of Medo-Persia in 445 B.C. (see Nehemiah 1:1–2:8). This began the 490 years.

Chapter 10 Theme ____________________

10 In the third year of Cyrus[k] king of Persia, a revelation was
given to Daniel (who was called Belteshazzar).[l] Its message
was true[m] and it concerned a great war.[j] The understanding of
the message came to him in a vision.
2At that time I, Daniel, mourned[n] for three weeks. 3I ate no
choice food; no meat or wine touched my lips; and I used no
lotions at all until the three weeks were over.
4On the twenty-fourth day of the first month, as I was standing
on the bank of the great river, the Tigris,[o] 5I looked up and there
before me was a man dressed in linen,[p] with a belt of the finest
gold[q] around his waist. 6His body was like chrysolite, his face like
lightning,[r] his eyes like flaming torches,[s] his arms and legs like
the gleam of burnished bronze,[t] and his voice like the sound of a
multitude.
7I, Daniel, was the only one who saw the vision; the men with
me did not see it,[u] but such terror overwhelmed them that they

[a]24 Or '*weeks*'; also in verses 25 and 26 [b]24 Or *restrain* [c]24 Or *Most Holy Place*; or *most holy One* [d]25 Or *word* [e]25 Or *an anointed one*; also in verse 26 [f]26 Or *off and will have no one*; or *off, but not for himself* [g]27 Or *'week'* [h]27 Or *it* [i]27 Or *And one who causes desolation will come upon the pinnacle of the abominable ⌊temple⌋, until the end that is decreed is poured out on the desolated ⌊city⌋* [j]1 Or *true and burdensome*

9:21 [a]Ex 29:39
9:23 [b]Da 10:19; Lk 1:28 [c]Da 10:11-12; Mt 24:15
9:24 [d]Isa 53:10 [e]Isa 56:1
9:25 [f]Ezr 4:24 [g]Jn 4:25
9:26 [h]Isa 53:8 [i]Na 1:8
9:27 [j]Isa 10:22
10:1 [k]Da 1:21 [l]Da 1:7 [m]Da 8:26
10:2 [n]Ezr 9:4
10:4 [o]Ge 2:14
10:5 [p]Eze 9:2; Rev 15:6 [q]Jer 10:9
10:6 [r]Mt 17:2 [s]Rev 19:12 [t]Rev 1:15
10:7 [u]2Ki 6:17-20; Ac 9:7

fled and hid themselves. 8So I was left alone,[a] gazing at this great
vision; I had no strength left,[b] my face turned deathly pale and I
was helpless.[c] 9Then I heard him speaking, and as I listened to
him, I fell into a deep sleep, my face to the ground.[d]
10A hand touched me[e] and set me trembling on my hands and
knees.[f] 11He said, "Daniel, you who are highly esteemed,[g] consider
carefully the words I am about to speak to you, and stand up,[h] for I
have now been sent to you." And when he said this to me, I stood
up trembling.
12Then he continued, "Do not be afraid, Daniel. Since the first
day that you set your mind to gain understanding and to humble[i]
yourself before your God, your words were heard, and I have
come in response to them.[j] 13But the prince of the Persian kingdom resisted me twenty-one days. Then Michael,[k] one of the
chief princes, came to help me, because I was detained there with
the king of Persia. 14Now I have come to explain[l] to you what will
happen to your people in the future, for the vision concerns a
time yet to come.[m]"
15While he was saying this to me, I bowed with my face toward
the ground and was speechless.[n] 16Then one who looked like a
man[a] touched my lips, and I opened my mouth and began to
speak.[o] I said to the one standing before me, "I am overcome
with anguish[p] because of the vision, my lord, and I am helpless.
17How can I, your servant, talk with you, my lord? My strength is
gone and I can hardly breathe."[q]
18Again the one who looked like a man touched[r] me and gave me
strength. 19"Do not be afraid, O man highly esteemed," he said.
"Peace![s] Be strong now; be strong."[t]
When he spoke to me, I was strengthened and said, "Speak, my
lord, since you have given me strength."[u]
20So he said, "Do you know why I have come to you? Soon I
will return to fight against the prince of Persia, and when I go,
the prince of Greece[v] will come; 21but first I will tell you what is
written in the Book of Truth.[w] (No one supports me against them
except Michael,[x] your prince.

Chapter 11 Theme ____________________

11 And in the first year of Darius[y] the Mede, I took my stand
to support and protect him.)
2"Now then, I tell you the truth:[z] Three more kings will appear in
Persia, and then a fourth, who will be far richer than all the others.
When he has gained power by his wealth, he will stir up everyone
against the kingdom of Greece.[a] 3Then a mighty king will appear,

a *16* Most manuscripts of the Masoretic Text; one manuscript of the Masoretic Text, Dead Sea Scrolls and Septuagint *Then something that looked like a man's hand*

10:8 [a]Ge 32:24 [b]Da 8:27 [c]Hab 3:16
10:9 [d]Da 8:18
10:10 [e]Jer 1:9 [f]Rev 1:17
10:11 [g]Da 9:23 [h]Eze 2:1
10:12 [i]Da 9:3 [j]Da 9:20
10:13 [k]ver 21; Da 12:1; Jude 9
10:14 [l]Da 9:22 [m]Da 2:28; 8:26; Hab 2:3
10:15 [n]Eze 24:27; Lk 1:20
10:16 [o]Isa 6:7; Jer 1:9; Da 8:15-18 [p]Isa 21:3
10:17 [q]Da 4:19
10:18 [r]ver 16
10:19 [s]Jdg 6:23; Isa 35:4 [t]Jos 1:9 [u]Isa 6:1-8
10:20 [v]Da 8:21; 11:2
10:21 [w]Da 11:2 [x]ver 13; Jude 9
11:1 [y]Da 5:31
11:2 [z]Da 10:21 [a]Da 10:20

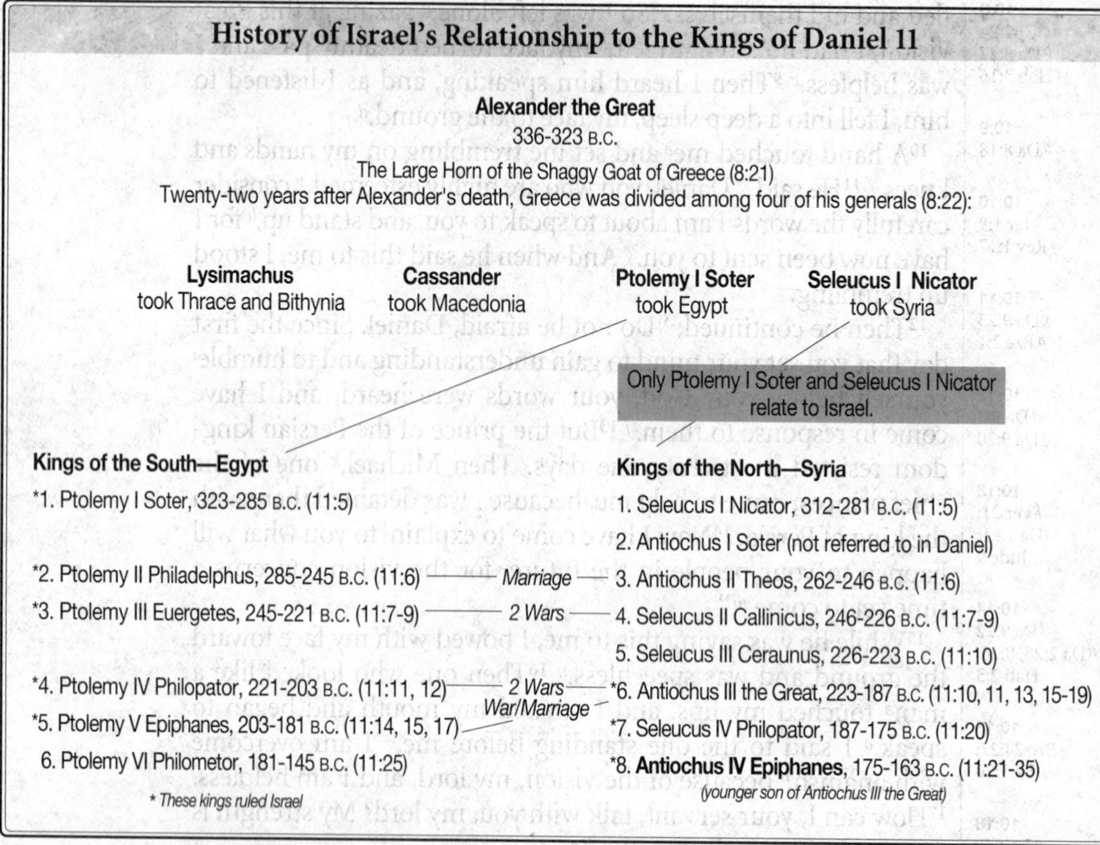

who will rule with great power and do as he pleases.[a] 4After he has
appeared, his empire will be broken up and parceled out toward
the four winds of heaven.[b] It will not go to his descendants, nor will
it have the power he exercised, because his empire will be uprooted
and given to others.

History of Israel's Relationship to the Kings of Daniel 11
Alexander the Great
336-323 B.C.
The Large Horn of the Shaggy Goat of Greece (8:21)
Twenty-two years after Alexander's death, Greece was divided among four of his generals (8:22):
Lysimachus
took Thrace and Bithynia
Cassander
took Macedonia
Ptolemy I Soter
took Egypt
Seleucus I Nicator
took Syria
Only Ptolemy I Soter and Seleucus I Nicator relate to Israel.
Kings of the South—Egypt
*1. Ptolemy I Soter, 323-285 B.C. (11:5)
*2. Ptolemy II Philadelphus, 285-245 B.C. (11:6)
*3. Ptolemy III Euergetes, 245-221 B.C. (11:7-9)
*4. Ptolemy IV Philopator, 221-203 B.C. (11:11, 12)
*5. Ptolemy V Epiphanes, 203-181 B.C. (11:14, 15, 17)
6. Ptolemy VI Philometor, 181-145 B.C. (11:25)
* These kings ruled Israel
Marriage
2 Wars
2 Wars
War/Marriage
Kings of the North—Syria
1. Seleucus I Nicator, 312-281 B.C. (11:5)
2. Antiochus I Soter (not referred to in Daniel)
3. Antiochus II Theos, 262-246 B.C. (11:6)
4. Seleucus II Callinicus, 246-226 B.C. (11:7-9)
5. Seleucus III Ceraunus, 226-223 B.C. (11:10)
*6. Antiochus III the Great, 223-187 B.C. (11:10, 11, 13, 15-19)
*7. Seleucus IV Philopator, 187-175 B.C. (11:20)
*8. Antiochus IV Epiphanes, 175-163 B.C. (11:21-35)
(younger son of Antiochus III the Great)

5"The king of the South will become strong, but one of his commanders will become even stronger than he and will rule his own
kingdom with great power. 6After some years, they will become
allies. The daughter of the king of the South will go to the king of
the North to make an alliance, but she will not retain her power,
and he and his power[a] will not last. In those days she will be
handed over, together with her royal escort and her father[b] and the
one who supported her.

7"One from her family line will arise to take her place. He will
attack the forces of the king of the North[c] and enter his fortress; he
will fight against them and be victorious. 8He will also seize their
gods,[d] their metal images and their valuable articles of silver and
gold and carry them off to Egypt.[e] For some years he will leave the

[a]6 Or *offspring* [b]6 Or *child* (see Vulgate and Syriac)

11:3 [a]Da 8:4,21

11:4 [b]Da 7:2; 8:22

11:7 [c]ver 6

11:8 [d]Isa 37:19; 46:1-2 [e]Jer 43:12

king of the North alone. 9Then the king of the North will invade
the realm of the king of the South but will retreat to his own country. 10His sons will prepare for war and assemble a great army,
which will sweep on like an irresistible flood[a] and carry the battle
as far as his fortress.
11"Then the king of the South will march out in a rage and fight
against the king of the North, who will raise a large army, but it
will be defeated.[b] 12When the army is carried off, the king of the
South will be filled with pride and will slaughter many thousands, yet he will not remain triumphant. 13For the king of the
North will muster another army, larger than the first; and after
several years, he will advance with a huge army fully equipped.
14"In those times many will rise against the king of the South.
The violent men among your own people will rebel in fulfillment
of the vision, but without success. 15Then the king of the North
will come and build up siege ramps[c] and will capture a fortified
city. The forces of the South will be powerless to resist; even their
best troops will not have the strength to stand. 16The invader will
do as he pleases;[d] no one will be able to stand against him.[e] He
will establish himself in the Beautiful Land and will have the
power to destroy it.[f] 17He will determine to come with the might
of his entire kingdom and will make an alliance with the king of
the South. And he will give him a daughter in marriage in order
to overthrow the kingdom, but his plans[a] will not succeed[g] or
help him. 18Then he will turn his attention to the coastlands[h] and
will take many of them, but a commander will put an end to his
insolence and will turn his insolence back upon him.[i] 19After
this, he will turn back toward the fortresses of his own country
but will stumble and fall,[j] to be seen no more.[k]
20"His successor will send out a tax collector to maintain the
royal splendor.[l] In a few years, however, he will be destroyed, yet
not in anger or in battle.
21"He will be succeeded by a contemptible[m] person who has
not been given the honor of royalty.[n] He will invade the kingdom
when its people feel secure, and he will seize it through intrigue.
22Then an overwhelming army will be swept away before him;
both it and a prince of the covenant will be destroyed.[o] 23After
coming to an agreement with him, he will act deceitfully,[p] and
with only a few people he will rise to power. 24When the richest
provinces feel secure, he will invade them and will achieve what
neither his fathers nor his forefathers did. He will distribute
plunder, loot and wealth among his followers.[q] He will plot the
overthrow of fortresses—but only for a time.

11:10 [a] Isa 8:8; Jer 46:8; Da 9:26
11:11 [b] Da 8:7-8
11:15 [c] Eze 4:2
11:16 [d] Da 8:4 [e] Jos 1:5; Da 8:7 [f] Da 8:9
11:17 [g] Ps 20:4
11:18 [h] Isa 66:19; Jer 25:22 [i] Hos 12:14
11:19 [j] Ps 27:2 [k] Ps 37:36; Eze 26:21
11:20 [l] Isa 60:17
11:21 [m] Da 4:17 [n] Da 8:25
11:22 [o] Da 8:10-11
11:23 [p] Da 8:25
11:24 [q] Ne 9:25

a *17* Or *but she*

25“With a large army he will stir up his strength and courage
against the king of the South. The king of the South will wage war
with a large and very powerful army, but he will not be able to
stand because of the plots devised against him. 26Those who eat
from the king’s provisions will try to destroy him; his army will be
swept away, and many will fall in battle. 27The two kings, with
their hearts bent on evil,[a] will sit at the same table and lie[b] to each
other, but to no avail, because an end will still come at the appointed time.[c] 28The king of the North will return to his own country
with great wealth, but his heart will be set against the holy covenant.
He will take action against it and then return to his own country.
29“At the appointed time he will invade the South again, but
this time the outcome will be different from what it was before.
30Ships of the western coastlands[a][d] will oppose him, and he will
lose heart. Then he will turn back and vent his fury against the
holy covenant. He will return and show favor to those who forsake the holy covenant.
31“His armed forces will rise up to desecrate the temple fortress
and will abolish the daily sacrifice. Then they will set up the
abomination that causes desolation.[e] 32With flattery he will corrupt those who have violated the covenant, but the people who
know their God will firmly resist[f] him.
33“Those who are wise will instruct[g] many, though for a time
they will fall by the sword or be burned or captured or plundered.[h]
34When they fall, they will receive a little help, and many who are
not sincere[i] will join them. 35Some of the wise will stumble, so that
they may be refined,[j] purified and made spotless until the time
of the end, for it will still come at the appointed time.
36“The king will do as he pleases. He will exalt and magnify
himself above every god and will say unheard-of things[k] against
the God of gods.[l] He will be successful until the time of wrath[m] is
completed, for what has been determined must take place. 37He
will show no regard for the gods of his fathers or for the one
desired by women, nor will he regard any god, but will exalt himself above them all. 38Instead of them, he will honor a god of
fortresses; a god unknown to his fathers he will honor with gold
and silver, with precious stones and costly gifts. 39He will attack the
mightiest fortresses with the help of a foreign god and will greatly
honor those who acknowledge him. He will make them rulers
over many people and will distribute the land at a price.[b]
40“At the time of the end the king of the South[n] will engage him
in battle, and the king of the North will storm[o] out against him
with chariots and cavalry and a great fleet of ships. He will invade
many countries and sweep through them like a flood.[p] 41He will

[a] 30 Hebrew *of Kittim* [b] 39 Or *land for a reward*

11:27 [a]Ps 64:6 [b]Ps 12:2; Jer 9:5 [c]Hab 2:3
11:30 [d]Ge 10:4
11:31 [e]Da 8:11-13; 9:27; Mt 24:15*; Mk 13:14*
11:32 [f]Mic 5:7-9
11:33 [g]Mal 2:7 [h]Mt 24:9; Jn 16:2; Heb 11:32-38
11:34 [i]Mt 7:15; Ro 16:18
11:35 [j]Ps 78:38; Da 12:10; Zec 13:9; Jn 15:2
11:36 [k]Rev 13:5-6 [l]Dt 10:17; Isa 14:13-14; Da 7:25; 8:11-12,25; 2Th 2:4 [m]Isa 10:25; 26:20
11:40 [n]Isa 21:1 [o]Isa 5:28 [p]Eze 38:4

also invade the Beautiful Land. Many countries will fall, but
Edom,[a] Moab[b] and the leaders of Ammon will be delivered from
his hand. 42He will extend his power over many countries; Egypt
will not escape. 43He will gain control of the treasures of gold and
silver and all the riches of Egypt,[c] with the Libyans[d] and Nubians
in submission. 44But reports from the east and the north will
alarm him, and he will set out in a great rage to destroy and
annihilate many. 45He will pitch his royal tents between the seas
at[a] the beautiful holy mountain. Yet he will come to his end, and no
one will help him.

Chapter 12 Theme ______________________________

12 "At that time Michael,[e] the great prince who protects your
people, will arise. There will be a time of distress[f] such as
has not happened from the beginning of nations until then. But at
that time your people—everyone whose name is found written in
the book[g]—will be delivered.[h] 2Multitudes who sleep in the dust of
the earth will awake: some to everlasting life, others to shame and
everlasting contempt.[i] 3Those who are wise[b][j] will shine[k] like the
brightness of the heavens, and those who lead many to righteousness, like the stars for ever and ever.[l] 4But you, Daniel, close up
and seal[m] the words of the scroll until the time of the end.[n] Many
will go here and there to increase knowledge."

5Then I, Daniel, looked, and there before me stood two others,
one on this bank of the river and one on the opposite bank.[o] 6One
of them said to the man clothed in linen,[p] who was above the waters of the river, "How long will it be before these astonishing
things are fulfilled?"[q]

7The man clothed in linen, who was above the waters of the river,
lifted his right hand and his left hand toward heaven, and I heard
him swear by him who lives forever,[r] saying, "It will be for a time,
times and half a time.[c][s] When the power of the holy people[t] has
been finally broken, all these things will be completed.[u]"

8I heard, but I did not understand. So I asked, "My lord, what
will the outcome of all this be?"

9He replied, "Go your way, Daniel, because the words are closed
up and sealed until the time of the end.[v] 10Many will be purified,
made spotless and refined,[w] but the wicked will continue to be
wicked.[x] None of the wicked will understand, but those who are
wise will understand.[y]

11"From the time that the daily sacrifice is abolished and the
abomination that causes desolation[z] is set up, there will be 1,290

11:41 [a]Isa 11:14 [b]Jer 48:47
11:43 [c]Eze 30:4 [d]2Ch 12:3; Na 3:9
12:1 [e]Da 10:13 [f]Da 9:12; Mt 24:21; Mk 13:19; Rev 16:18 [g]Ex 32:32; Ps 56:8 [h]Jer 30:7
12:2 [i]Isa 26:19; Mt 25:46; Jn 5:28-29
12:3 [j]Da 11:33 [k]Mt 13:43; Jn 5:35 [l]1Co 15:42
12:4 [m]Isa 8:16 [n]ver 9,13; Rev 22:10
12:5 [o]Da 10:4
12:6 [p]Eze 9:2 [q]Da 8:13
12:7 [r]Rev 10:5-6 [s]Da 7:25 [t]Da 8:24 [u]Lk 21:24; Rev 10:7
12:9 [v]ver 4
12:10 [w]Da 11:35 [x]Isa 32:7; Rev 22:11 [y]Hos 14:9
12:11 [z]Da 8:11; 9:27; Mt 24:15*; Mk 13:14*

[a]45 Or *the sea and* [b]3 Or *who impart wisdom* [c]7 Or *a year, two years and half a year*

days. [12]Blessed is the one who waits[a] for and reaches the end of
the 1,335 days.[b]

[13]"As for you, go your way till the end. You will rest,[c] and then at
the end of the days you will rise to receive your allotted inheritance.[d]"

12:12
[a]Isa 30:18
[b]Da 8:14

12:13
[c]Isa 57:2
[d]Ps 16:5;
Rev 14:13

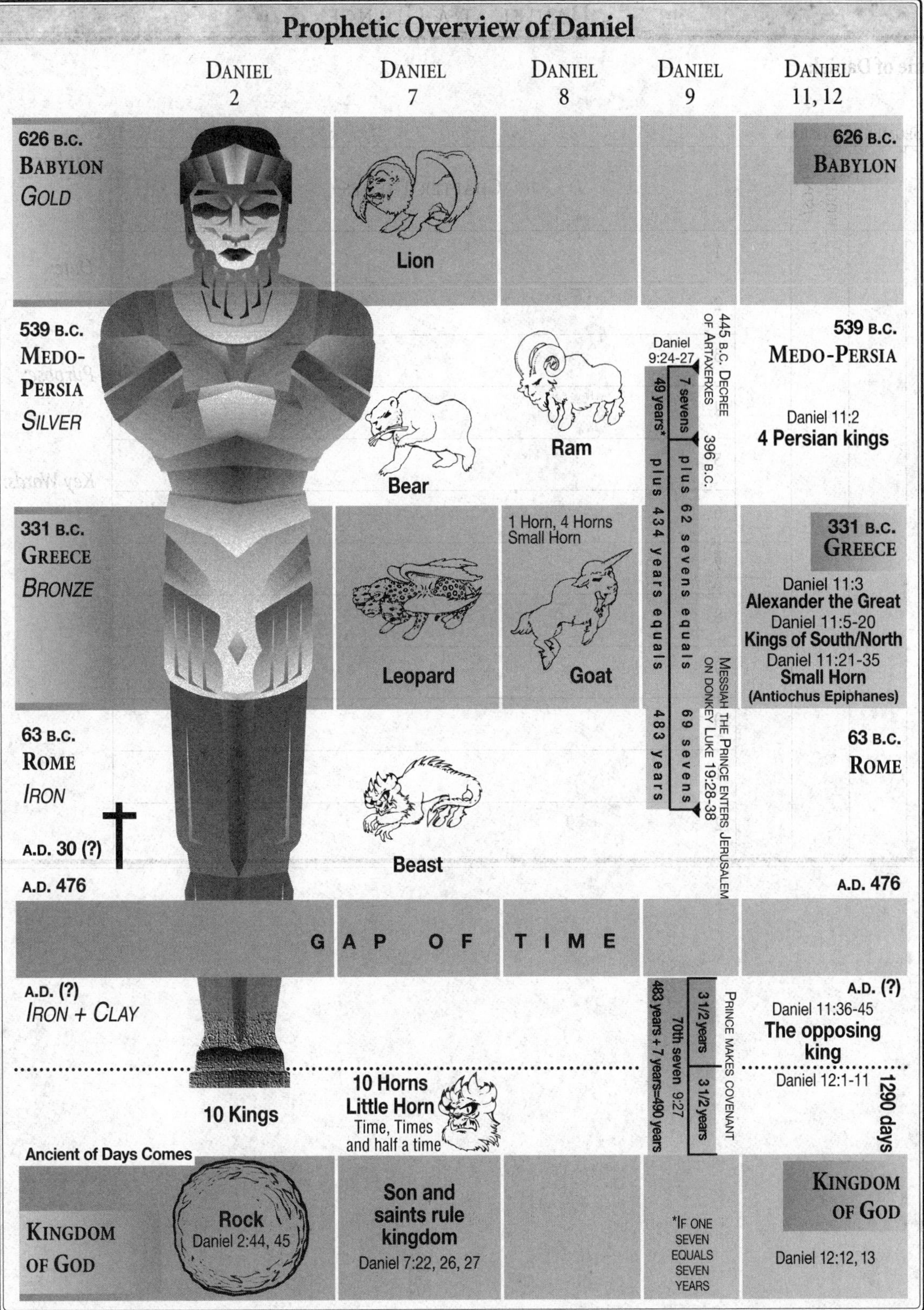

Prophetic Overview of Daniel
Daniel 2
Daniel 7
Daniel 8
Daniel 9
Daniel 11, 12
626 B.C.
Babylon
Gold
Lion
626 B.C.
Babylon
539 B.C.
Medo-Persia
Silver
Bear
Ram
Daniel 9:24-27
445 B.C. Decree of Artaxerxes
7 sevens
49 years*
396 B.C.
539 B.C.
Medo-Persia
Daniel 11:2
4 Persian kings
331 B.C.
Greece
Bronze
Leopard
1 Horn, 4 Horns
Small Horn
Goat
plus 62 sevens equals
plus 434 years equals
69 sevens
483 years
Messiah the Prince enters Jerusalem on donkey Luke 19:28-38
331 B.C.
Greece
Daniel 11:3
Alexander the Great
Daniel 11:5-20
Kings of South/North
Daniel 11:21-35
Small Horn
(Antiochus Epiphanes)
63 B.C.
Rome
Iron
A.D. 30 (?)
A.D. 476
Beast
63 B.C.
Rome
A.D. 476
GAP OF TIME
A.D. (?)
Iron + Clay
10 Kings
10 Horns
Little Horn
Time, Times
and half a time
Prince makes covenant
3 1/2 years
3 1/2 years
70th seven 9:27
483 years + 7 years=490 years
A.D. (?)
Daniel 11:36-45
The opposing
king
Daniel 12:1-11
1290 days
Ancient of Days Comes
Kingdom
of God
Rock
Daniel 2:44, 45
Son and
saints rule
kingdom
Daniel 7:22, 26, 27
*If one
seven
equals
seven
years
Kingdom
of God
Daniel 12:12, 13

Theme of Daniel:

SEGMENT DIVISIONS

		KINGS/ KINGDOM			CHAPTER THEMES
				1	
				2	
				3	
				4	
				5	
				6	
				7	
				8	
				9	
				10	
				11	
				12	

Author:

Date:

Purpose:

Key Words:

HOSEA

God had entered into a covenant with Israel. Yet from the time of Jeroboam's reign of the northern kingdom through Jeroboam II's reign, Israel continued to play the prostitute. God begged her to return to him, but she would not listen. God's heart hurt. If only Israel could understand, if only she could see what she was doing to the one who had betrothed her to himself. If only she could see what her infidelity was doing to her children! Then the word of the Lord came to Hosea: "Go, take to yourself an adulterous wife and children of unfaithfulness."

THINGS TO DO

Chapters 1-3

1. The first three chapters of Hosea provide the setting for Hosea's prophetic message to the northern kingdom of Israel. Read these three chapters as you would a story, but remember that it is a true story.
2. Read through Hosea 1 again. As you read:
   a. Mark every occurrence of the word *adulterous (adultery, unfaithfulness)*.
   b. In the margin, draw a simple family tree which shows whom Hosea married and the names of their children. Under each family member write a brief description of what the person was like or what his or her name meant. Consult the reference notes in the margin if you have problems discerning the meanings of the children's names.
   c. In the margin, list what this chapter teaches about the sons of Israel and the sons of Judah.
3. Now go back and read the introduction which precedes "Things to Do." Then:
   a. Read 1 Kings 11:26-40, where God tells Jeroboam what he will do after King Solomon's death. Notice why God does what he does.
   b. Read 1 Kings 12, which tells of the fulfillment of God's word to Jeroboam. This chapter describes how the kingdom of Israel was divided into the northern kingdom, consisting of ten tribes, and the southern kingdom, consisting of two tribes. Pay attention to what Jeroboam does, since the northern kingdom no longer has access to Jerusalem and the temple, where they were to worship God.
   c. Read Hosea 1:2 again, and then Hosea 3:1. Watch the word *as* in 3:1.
   d. In the margin of chapter 1 write why Hosea was told by God to marry Gomer. This will help you see why chapters 1 through 3 provide the setting for Hosea's message to the northern kingdom of Israel.
4. Keeping in mind what you have seen thus far, read Hosea 2 and do the following:
   a. Mark every occurrence of the words *adulterous* and *adultery* and the phrase *in that day.*
   b. Carefully observe what the children are to say to their mother and why.
   c. Read chapters 1 and 2 and underline every occurrence of *the Lord said* or *declares the Lord.* Then highlight or mark in a distinctive way every occurrence of *I will.* Then decide who is speaking throughout chapter 2 and who the *her* and *she* refer to.
   d. Finally, read each *I will* in chapter 2. Watch the sequence of events and summarize the type of action taken in these "I wills." Also watch what happens to *her.* Record your insights in the margin of chapter 2.
   e. When you come to 2:23 read the reference notes on this verse and compare this with 1:6, 9; 2:1.
5. In the light of all you have seen in chapters 1 and 2, read chapter 3 and do the following:

a. In a distinctive way mark the word *love.*

b. In the margin, summarize what God tells Hosea to do and why.

c. Read 3:5 and mark the reference to *in the last days,* but before you choose how to mark it, see if you notice any parallel to *in that day* in chapter 2. If you think any of these references pertain to the day of the Lord, record your insights on the chart THE DAY OF THE LORD beginning on page 2178.

6. Write the themes of each of the first three chapters on the HOSEA AT A GLANCE chart on page 1553. Then record the chapter theme next to the chapter number in the text.

Chapters 4-14

1. Keeping in mind the setting of Hosea 1 through 3, read through Hosea chapter by chapter. As you do:

a. Mark in a distinctive way the following key words (with their synonyms or pronouns): *prostitution (commit adultery, been unfaithful), knowledge (acknowledgment), covenant (treaty), return (go back, repent), iniquity (sin, sins, guilt, wicked, wickedness, evildoers).* Also mark the phrases *I will, from me,* and *against me (unfaithful to me* [the Lord]). Write these words on an index card and use it as a bookmark.

b. Also mark *Judah (Judah's), Israel (Israel's, Israelites),* and *Ephraim (Ephraim's)* each in its own distinctive way. As you do, remember that Ephraim was one of the ten tribes which comprised the northern kingdom of Israel. After Pekah took the throne in Israel, Tiglath-Pileser, king of Assyria, came against him and took all of the kingdom captive in 733 B.C. except Ephraim and western Manasseh. Ten years later the remainder of the northern kingdom was completely destroyed by the Assyrians in 722 B.C. Thus Ephraim refers to what remained of Israel in those last ten years.

2. After you read a chapter and mark key words and the references to Judah, Israel, and Ephraim, compile your insights on the chart GOD'S RESPONSE TO ISRAEL'S SIN on page 1552.

3. As you read through the remainder of Hosea, remember that this is a passionate discourse because of God's relationship to Israel, the relationship of a husband to his wife (Ezekiel 16; Jeremiah 3:6-8), and of a father to his children (Hosea 11:1-3; Jeremiah 31:20). Remember also that because it is passionate, there is quite a bit of repetition, but not without purpose.

4. As you finish reading each chapter, summarize the theme of each one and record it on HOSEA AT A GLANCE and in the text. Also, when you finish the book, decide on its theme and record it on the chart. Then fill in the remainder of the chart.

THINGS TO THINK ABOUT

In 2 Corinthians 11:2 Paul wrote, "I am jealous for you with a godly jealousy. I promised you to one husband, to Christ, so that I might present you as a pure virgin to him."

1. Are there any similarities between your relationship to Jesus Christ and Israel's relationship to God? How are you pleasing your heavenly Bridegroom? Are you breaking God's heart in any way?

2. What do you need to do?

3. How do you think God will respond, and why?

Chapter 1 Theme ____________________

1 The word of the LORD that came to Hosea son of Beeri during the
reigns of Uzziah, Jotham, Ahaz and Hezekiah, kings of Judah,[a]
and during the reign of Jeroboam[b] son of Jehoash[a] king of Israel:[c]

[a] *1* Hebrew *Joash,* a variant of *Jehoash*

1:1
[a]Isa 1:1; Mic 1:1
[b]2Ki 13:13
[c]Am 1:1

THE RULERS AND PROPHETS OF HOSEA'S TIME

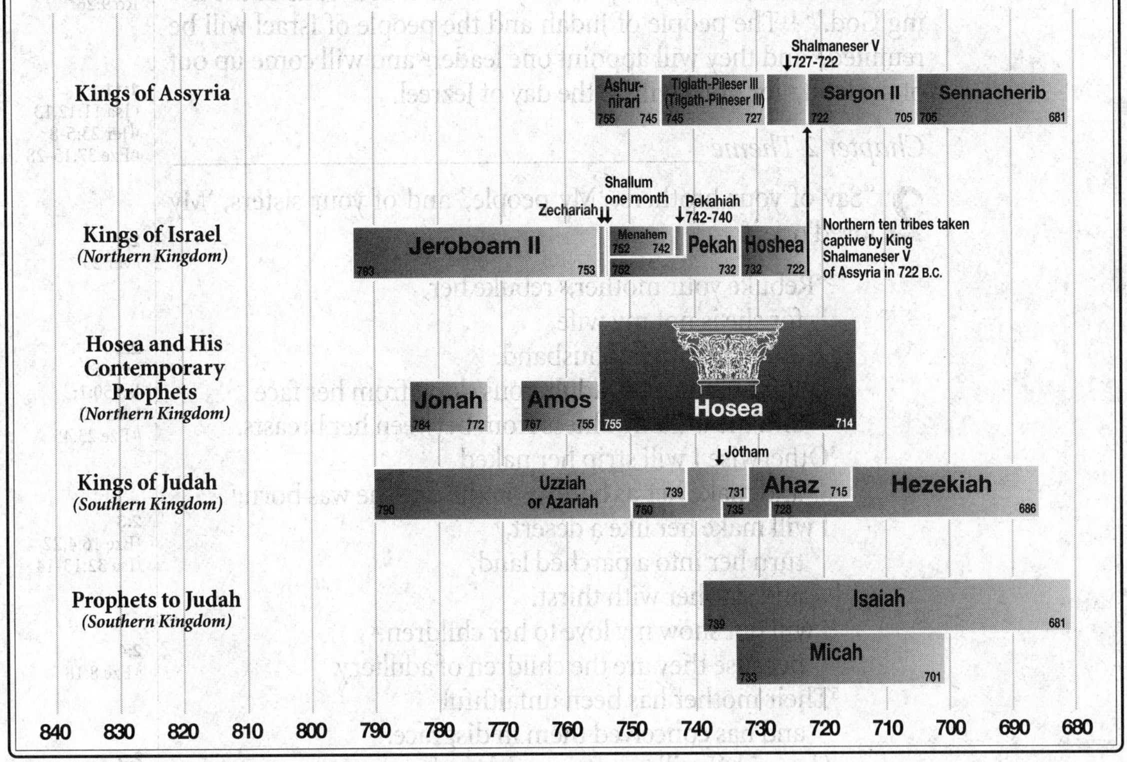

Kings of Assyria
Ashur-nirari 755–745
Tiglath-Pileser III (Tilgath-Pilneser III) 745–727
Shalmaneser V 727-722
Sargon II 722–705
Sennacherib 705–681

Kings of Israel *(Northern Kingdom)*
Jeroboam II 793–753
Zechariah
Shallum one month
Menahem 752–742
Pekahiah 742-740
Pekah 752–732
Hoshea 732–722
Northern ten tribes taken captive by King Shalmaneser V of Assyria in 722 B.C.

Hosea and His Contemporary Prophets *(Northern Kingdom)*
Jonah 784–772
Amos 767–755
Hosea 755–714

Kings of Judah *(Southern Kingdom)*
Uzziah or Azariah 790–739
Jotham 750–731
Ahaz 735–715
Hezekiah 728–686

Prophets to Judah *(Southern Kingdom)*
Isaiah 739–681
Micah 733–701

840 830 820 810 800 790 780 770 760 750 740 730 720 710 700 690 680

1:2 [a]Jer 3:1; Hos 2:2,5; 3:1 [b]Dt 31:16; Jer 3:14; Eze 23:3-21; Hos 5:3
1:4 [c]2Ki 10:1-14; Hos 2:22
1:5 [d]2Ki 15:29
1:6 [e]ver 3 [f]Hos 2:4
1:7 [g]Ps 44:6 [h]Zec 4:6

2When the LORD began to speak through Hosea, the LORD said
to him, "Go, take to yourself an adulterous[a] wife and children of
unfaithfulness, because the land is guilty of the vilest adultery[b] in
departing from the LORD." 3So he married Gomer daughter of
Diblaim, and she conceived and bore him a son.
4Then the LORD said to Hosea, "Call him Jezreel,[c] because I will
soon punish the house of Jehu for the massacre at Jezreel, and I
will put an end to the kingdom of Israel. 5In that day I will break
Israel's bow in the Valley of Jezreel.[d]"
6Gomer[e] conceived again and gave birth to a daughter. Then the
LORD said to Hosea, "Call her Lo-Ruhamah,[a] for I will no longer
show love to the house of Israel,[f] that I should at all forgive them.
7Yet I will show love to the house of Judah; and I will save them—
not by bow,[g] sword or battle, or by horses and horsemen, but by
the LORD their God.[h]"
8After she had weaned Lo-Ruhamah, Gomer had another son.
9Then the LORD said, "Call him Lo-Ammi,[b] for you are not my
people, and I am not your God.

[a]6 *Lo-Ruhamah* means *not loved.* [b]9 *Lo-Ammi* means *not my people.*

INSIGHT

Only one Israelite king, Jeroboam (often referred to as Jeroboam II), is mentioned in Hosea 1:1. Because Hosea mentions the names of the kings of Judah, we can know the other kings who ruled Israel during Hosea's ministry.

10"Yet the Israelites will be like the sand on the seashore, which
cannot be measured or counted.[a] In the place where it was said to
them, 'You are not my people,' they will be called 'sons of the living God.'[b] 11The people of Judah and the people of Israel will be
reunited,[c] and they will appoint one leader[d] and will come up out
of the land,[e] for great will be the day of Jezreel.

Chapter 2 Theme ______________________________

2 "Say of your brothers, 'My people,' and of your sisters, 'My loved one.'[f]

2"Rebuke your mother,[g] rebuke her,
for she is not my wife,
and I am not her husband.
Let her remove the adulterous[h] look from her face
and the unfaithfulness from between her breasts.
3Otherwise I will strip her naked
and make her as bare as on the day she was born;[i]
I will make her like a desert,[j]
turn her into a parched land,
and slay her with thirst.
4I will not show my love to her children,[k]
because they are the children of adultery.
5Their mother has been unfaithful
and has conceived them in disgrace.
She said, 'I will go after my lovers,[l]
who give me my food and my water,
my wool and my linen, my oil and my drink.'[m]
6Therefore I will block her path with thornbushes;
I will wall her in so that she cannot find her way.[n]
7She will chase after her lovers but not catch them;
she will look for them but not find them.[o]
Then she will say,
'I will go back to my husband as at first,[p]
for then I was better off[q] than now.'
8She has not acknowledged[r] that I was the one
who gave her the grain, the new wine and oil,
who lavished on her the silver and gold—
which they used for Baal.[s]
9"Therefore I will take away my grain[t] when it ripens,
and my new wine[u] when it is ready.
I will take back my wool and my linen,
intended to cover her nakedness.
10So now I will expose her lewdness
before the eyes of her lovers;
no one will take her out of my hands.[v]

INSIGHT

Baal, which meant "lord, owner, possessor," or "husband," was the Canaanite god of fertility. ***Baal*** was part of several compound names for locations where Canaanite deities were worshiped, such as Baal Peor.

1:10 [a]Ge 22:17; Jer 33:22 [b]ver 9; Ro 9:26*
1:11 [c]Isa 11:12,13 [d]Jer 23:5-8 [e]Eze 37:15-28
2:1 [f]ver 23
2:2 [g]ver 5; Isa 50:1; Hos 1:2 [h]Eze 23:45
2:3 [i]Eze 16:4,22 [j]Isa 32:13-14
2:4 [k]Eze 8:18
2:5 [l]Jer 3:6 [m]Jer 44:17-18
2:6 [n]Job 3:23; 19:8; La 3:9
2:7 [o]Hos 5:13 [p]Jer 2:2; 3:1 [q]Eze 16:8
2:8 [r]Isa 1:3 [s]Eze 16:15-19; Hos 8:4
2:9 [t]Hos 8:7 [u]Hos 9:2
2:10 [v]Eze 16:37

11 I will stop[a] all her celebrations:
her yearly festivals, her New Moons,
her Sabbath days—all her appointed feasts.[b]
12 I will ruin her vines[c] and her fig trees,
which she said were her pay from her lovers;
I will make them a thicket,[d]
and wild animals will devour them.[e]
13 I will punish her for the days
she burned incense to the Baals;[f]
she decked herself with rings and jewelry,[g]
and went after her lovers,[h]
but me she forgot,[i]"
declares the LORD.

14 "Therefore I am now going to allure her;
I will lead her into the desert
and speak tenderly to her.
15 There I will give her back her vineyards,
and will make the Valley of Achor[a][j] a door of hope.
There she will sing[b][k] as in the days of her youth,[l]
as in the day she came up out of Egypt.[m]

16 "In that day," declares the LORD,
"you will call me 'my husband';
you will no longer call me 'my master.[c]'
17 I will remove the names of the Baals from her lips;[n]
no longer will their names be invoked.[o]
18 In that day I will make a covenant for them
with the beasts of the field and the birds of the air
and the creatures that move along the ground.[p]
Bow and sword and battle
I will abolish[q] from the land,
so that all may lie down in safety.[r]
19 I will betroth[s] you to me forever;
I will betroth you in[d] righteousness and justice,[t]
in[e] love and compassion.
20 I will betroth you in faithfulness,
and you will acknowledge[u] the LORD.

21 "In that day I will respond,"
declares the LORD—
"I will respond[v] to the skies,
and they will respond to the earth;
22 and the earth will respond to the grain,
the new wine and oil,[w]

2:11 [a] Jer 7:34 [b] Isa 1:14; Jer 16:9; Hos 3:4; Am 8:10
2:12 [c] Isa 7:23; Jer 8:13 [d] Isa 5:6 [e] Hos 13:8
2:13 [f] Hos 11:2 [g] Eze 16:17 [h] Hos 4:13 [i] Hos 4:6; 8:14; 13:6
2:15 [j] Jos 7:24,26 [k] Ex 15:1-18 [l] Jer 2:2 [m] Hos 12:9
2:17 [n] Ex 23:13; Ps 16:4 [o] Jos 23:7
2:18 [p] Job 5:22 [q] Isa 2:4 [r] Jer 23:6; Eze 34:25
2:19 [s] Isa 62:4 [t] Isa 1:27
2:20 [u] Jer 31:34; Hos 6:6; 13:4
2:21 [v] Isa 55:10; Zec 8:12
2:22 [w] Jer 31:12; Joel 2:19

a 15 *Achor* means *trouble.* b 15 Or *respond* c 16 Hebrew *baal* d 19 Or *with*; also in verse 20 e 19 Or *with*

and they will respond to Jezreel.[a]
23 I will plant[a] her for myself in the land;
I will show my love to the one I called 'Not
my loved one.[b][b]'
I will say to those called 'Not my people,[c]' 'You are
my people';[c]
and they will say, 'You are my God.[d]'"

Chapter 3 Theme ________________________

3 The LORD said to me, "Go, show your love to your wife again,
though she is loved by another and is an adulteress.[e] Love her
as the LORD loves the Israelites, though they turn to other gods
and love the sacred raisin cakes.[f]"
2 So I bought her for fifteen shekels[d] of silver and about a homer
and a lethek[e] of barley. 3 Then I told her, "You are to live with[f] me
many days; you must not be a prostitute or be intimate with any
man, and I will live with[f] you."
4 For the Israelites will live many days without king or prince,[g]
without sacrifice[h] or sacred stones, without ephod or idol.[i] 5 Afterward the Israelites will return and seek the LORD their God and
David their king.[j] They will come trembling to the LORD and to
his blessings in the last days.[k]

Chapter 4 Theme ________________________

4 Hear the word of the LORD, you Israelites,
because the LORD has a charge to bring
against you who live in the land:
"There is no faithfulness, no love,
no acknowledgment[l] of God in the land.
2 There is only cursing,[g] lying[m] and murder,[n]
stealing[o] and adultery;
they break all bounds,
and bloodshed follows bloodshed.
3 Because of this the land mourns,[h][p]
and all who live in it waste away;[q]
the beasts of the field and the birds of the air
and the fish of the sea are dying.[r]

4 "But let no man bring a charge,
let no man accuse another,
for your people are like those
who bring charges against a priest.[s]

[a] 22 *Jezreel* means *God plants.* [b] 23 Hebrew *Lo-Ruhamah* [c] 23 Hebrew *Lo-Ammi*
[d] 2 That is, about 6 ounces (about 170 grams) [e] 2 That is, probably about 10 bushels (about 330 liters) [f] 3 Or *wait for* [g] 2 That is, to pronounce a curse upon [h] 3 Or *dries up*

2:23 [a] Jer 31:27 [b] Hos 1:6 [c] Hos 1:10 [d] Ro 9:25*; 1Pe 2:10
3:1 [e] Hos 1:2 [f] 2Sa 6:19
3:4 [g] Hos 13:11 [h] Da 11:31; Hos 2:11 [i] Jdg 17:5-6; Zec 10:2
3:5 [j] Eze 34:23-24 [k] Jer 50:4-5
4:1 [l] Jer 7:28
4:2 [m] Hos 7:3; 10:4 [n] Hos 6:9 [o] Hos 7:1
4:3 [p] Jer 4:28 [q] Isa 33:9 [r] Jer 4:25; Zep 1:3
4:4 [s] Dt 17:12; Eze 3:26

[5]You stumble[a] day and night,
  and the prophets stumble with you.
So I will destroy your mother[b]—
[6] my people are destroyed from lack of knowledge.[c]

"Because you have rejected knowledge,
  I also reject you as my priests;
because you have ignored the law[d] of your God,
  I also will ignore your children.
[7]The more the priests increased,
  the more they sinned against me;
  they exchanged[a] their[b] Glory[e] for something
    disgraceful.[f]
[8]They feed on the sins of my people
  and relish their wickedness.[g]
[9]And it will be: Like people, like priests.[h]
  I will punish both of them for their ways
  and repay them for their deeds.[i]

[10]"They will eat but not have enough;[j]
  they will engage in prostitution but not increase,
because they have deserted[k] the LORD
  to give themselves [11]to prostitution,[l]
to old wine and new,
  which take away the understanding[m] [12]of my people.
They consult a wooden idol[n]
  and are answered by a stick of wood.[o]
A spirit of prostitution leads them astray;[p]
  they are unfaithful to their God.
[13]They sacrifice on the mountaintops
  and burn offerings on the hills,
under oak,[q] poplar and terebinth,
  where the shade is pleasant.[r]
Therefore your daughters turn to prostitution[s]
  and your daughters-in-law to adultery.[t]

[14]"I will not punish your daughters
  when they turn to prostitution,
nor your daughters-in-law
  when they commit adultery,
because the men themselves consort with harlots[u]
  and sacrifice with shrine prostitutes—
  a people without understanding will come to ruin!

[15]"Though you commit adultery, O Israel,
  let not Judah become guilty.

4:5 [a]Eze 14:7 [b]Hos 2:2
4:6 [c]Hos 2:13; Mal 2:7-8 [d]Hos 8:1,12
4:7 [e]Hab 2:16 [f]Hos 10:1,6; 13:6
4:8 [g]Isa 56:11; Mic 3:11
4:9 [h]Isa 24:2 [i]Jer 5:31; Hos 8:13; 9:9,15
4:10 [j]Lev 26:26; Mic 6:14 [k]Hos 7:14; 9:17
4:11 [l]Hos 5:4 [m]Pr 20:1
4:12 [n]Jer 2:27 [o]Hab 2:19 [p]Isa 44:20
4:13 [q]Isa 1:29 [r]Jer 3:6; Hos 11:2 [s]Jer 2:20; Am 7:17 [t]Hos 2:13
4:14 [u]ver 11

a 7 Syriac and an ancient Hebrew scribal tradition; Masoretic Text *I will exchange*
b 7 Masoretic Text; an ancient Hebrew scribal tradition *my*

"Do not go to Gilgal;[a]
do not go up to Beth Aven.[a]
And do not swear, 'As surely as the LORD lives!'
16The Israelites are stubborn,
like a stubborn heifer.
How then can the LORD pasture them
like lambs[b] in a meadow?
17Ephraim is joined to idols;
leave him alone!
18Even when their drinks are gone,
they continue their prostitution;
their rulers dearly love shameful ways.
19A whirlwind[c] will sweep them away,
and their sacrifices will bring them shame.[d]

INSIGHT

After Pekah took the throne in Israel, Tiglath-Pileser, king of Assyria, came against him in 733 B.C. and took captive all of the kingdom except Ephraim and western Manasseh. Ten years later the remainder of the northern kingdom was completely destroyed by the Assyrians in 722 B.C. Thus Ephraim is a reference to what remained of Israel in those last ten years.

Chapter 5 Theme

5 "Hear this, you priests!
Pay attention, you Israelites!
Listen, O royal house!
This judgment is against you:
You have been a snare[e] at Mizpah,
a net spread out on Tabor.
2The rebels are deep in slaughter.[f]
I will discipline all of them.[g]
3I know all about Ephraim;
Israel is not hidden from me.
Ephraim, you have now turned to prostitution;
Israel is corrupt.[h]

4"Their deeds do not permit them
to return to their God.
A spirit of prostitution[i] is in their heart;
they do not acknowledge[j] the LORD.
5Israel's arrogance testifies[k] against them;
the Israelites, even Ephraim, stumble in their sin;
Judah also stumbles with them.
6When they go with their flocks and herds
to seek the LORD,[l]
they will not find him;
he has withdrawn[m] himself from them.
7They are unfaithful[n] to the LORD;
they give birth to illegitimate[o] children.
Now their New Moon festivals
will devour[p] them and their fields.

a 15 *Beth Aven* means *house of wickedness* (a name for Bethel, which means *house of God*).

4:15 [a]Hos 9:15; 12:11; Am 4:4
4:16 [b]Isa 5:17; 7:25
4:19 [c]Hos 12:1; 13:15 [d]Isa 1:29
5:1 [e]Hos 6:9; 9:8
5:2 [f]Hos 4:2 [g]Hos 9:15
5:3 [h]Hos 6:10
5:4 [i]Hos 4:11 [j]Hos 4:6
5:5 [k]Hos 7:10
5:6 [l]Mic 6:6-7 [m]Pr 1:28; Isa 1:15; Eze 8:6
5:7 [n]Hos 6:7 [o]Hos 2:4 [p]Hos 2:11-12

8"Sound the trumpet in Gibeah,[a]
the horn in Ramah.[b]
Raise the battle cry in Beth Aven[a];[c]
lead on, O Benjamin.
9Ephraim will be laid waste
on the day of reckoning.[d]
Among the tribes of Israel
I proclaim what is certain.[e]
10Judah's leaders are like those
who move boundary stones.[f]
I will pour out my wrath[g] on them
like a flood of water.
11Ephraim is oppressed,
trampled in judgment,
intent on pursuing idols.[b][h]
12I am like a moth[i] to Ephraim,
like rot to the people of Judah.

13"When Ephraim saw his sickness,
and Judah his sores,
then Ephraim turned to Assyria,[j]
and sent to the great king for help.[k]
But he is not able to cure[l] you,
not able to heal your sores.[m]
14For I will be like a lion[n] to Ephraim,
like a great lion to Judah.
I will tear them to pieces and go away;
I will carry them off, with no one to rescue them.[o]
15Then I will go back to my place
until they admit their guilt.
And they will seek my face;[p]
in their misery[q] they will earnestly seek me.[r]"

Chapter 6 Theme

6 "Come, let us return to the LORD.
He has torn us to pieces[s]
but he will heal us;
he has injured us
but he will bind up our wounds.[t]
2After two days he will revive us;[u]
on the third day he will restore us,
that we may live in his presence.
3Let us acknowledge the LORD;
let us press on to acknowledge him.

5:8 [a]Hos 9:9; 10:9 [b]Isa 10:29 [c]Hos 4:15
5:9 [d]Isa 37:3; Hos 9:11-17 [e]Isa 46:10; Zec 1:6
5:10 [f]Dt 19:14 [g]Eze 7:8
5:11 [h]Hos 9:16; Mic 6:16
5:12 [i]Isa 51:8
5:13 [j]Hos 7:11; 8:9 [k]Hos 10:6 [l]Hos 14:3 [m]Jer 30:12
5:14 [n]Am 3:4 [o]Mic 5:8
5:15 [p]Hos 3:5 [q]Jer 2:27 [r]Isa 64:9
6:1 [s]Hos 5:14 [t]Dt 32:39; Jer 30:17; Hos 14:4
6:2 [u]Ps 30:5

a *8* *Beth Aven* means *house of wickedness* (a name for Bethel, which means *house of God*).
b *11* The meaning of the Hebrew for this word is uncertain.

As surely as the sun rises,
he will appear;
he will come to us like the winter rains,[a]
like the spring rains that water the earth.[b]"

4"What can I do with you, Ephraim?[c]
What can I do with you, Judah?
Your love is like the morning mist,
like the early dew that disappears.[d]
5Therefore I cut you in pieces with my prophets,
I killed you with the words of my mouth;[e]
my judgments flashed like lightning upon you.[f]
6For I desire mercy, not sacrifice,[g]
and acknowledgment[h] of God rather
than burnt offerings.
7Like Adam,[a] they have broken the covenant[i]—
they were unfaithful[j] to me there.
8Gilead is a city of wicked men,
stained with footprints of blood.
9As marauders lie in ambush for a man,
so do bands of priests;
they murder on the road to Shechem,
committing shameful crimes.[k]
10I have seen a horrible[l] thing
in the house of Israel.
There Ephraim is given to prostitution
and Israel is defiled.[m]

11"Also for you, Judah,
a harvest[n] is appointed.

Chapter 7 Theme ______________________

7

"Whenever I would restore the fortunes of my people,
whenever I would heal Israel,
the sins of Ephraim are exposed
and the crimes of Samaria revealed.[o]
They practice deceit,[p]
thieves break into houses,[q]
bandits rob in the streets;
2but they do not realize
that I remember[r] all their evil deeds.
Their sins engulf them;[s]
they are always before me.

6:3 [a]Joel 2:23 [b]Ps 72:6
6:4 [c]Hos 11:8 [d]Hos 7:1; 13:3
6:5 [e]Jer 1:9-10; 23:29 [f]Heb 4:12
6:6 [g]Isa 1:11; Mt 9:13*; 12:7* [h]Hos 2:20
6:7 [i]Hos 8:1 [j]Hos 5:7
6:9 [k]Jer 7:9-10; Eze 22:9; Hos 7:1
6:10 [l]Jer 5:30 [m]Hos 5:3
6:11 [n]Jer 51:33; Joel 3:13
7:1 [o]Hos 6:4 [p]ver 13 [q]Hos 4:2
7:2 [r]Jer 14:10; Hos 8:13 [s]Jer 2:19

[a]7 Or *As at Adam*; or *Like men*

3 "They delight the king with their wickedness,
 the princes with their lies.[a]
4 They are all adulterers,[b]
 burning like an oven
whose fire the baker need not stir
 from the kneading of the dough till it rises.
5 On the day of the festival of our king
 the princes become inflamed with wine,[c]
 and he joins hands with the mockers.
6 Their hearts are like an oven;[d]
 they approach him with intrigue.
Their passion smolders all night;
 in the morning it blazes like a flaming fire.
7 All of them are hot as an oven;
 they devour their rulers.
All their kings fall,
 and none of them calls[e] on me.

8 "Ephraim mixes[f] with the nations;
 Ephraim is a flat cake not turned over.
9 Foreigners sap his strength,[g]
 but he does not realize it.
His hair is sprinkled with gray,
 but he does not notice.
10 Israel's arrogance testifies against him,[h]
 but despite all this
he does not return to the LORD his God
 or search[i] for him.

11 "Ephraim is like a dove,[j]
 easily deceived and senseless—
now calling to Egypt,
 now turning to Assyria.[k]
12 When they go, I will throw my net[l]
 over them;
 I will pull them down like birds of the air.
When I hear them flocking together,
 I will catch them.
13 Woe[m] to them,
 because they have strayed[n] from me!
Destruction to them,
 because they have rebelled against me!
I long to redeem them
 but they speak lies against me.[o]
14 They do not cry out to me from their hearts[p]
 but wail upon their beds.

7:3 [a] Hos 4:2; Mic 7:3
7:4 [b] Jer 9:2
7:5 [c] Isa 28:1,7
7:6 [d] Ps 21:9
7:7 [e] ver 16
7:8 [f] ver 11; Ps 106:35; Hos 5:13
7:9 [g] Isa 1:7; Hos 8:7
7:10 [h] Hos 5:5 [i] Isa 9:13
7:11 [j] Hos 11:11 [k] Hos 5:13; 12:1
7:12 [l] Eze 12:13
7:13 [m] Hos 9:12 [n] Jer 14:10; Eze 34:4-6; Hos 9:17 [o] ver 1; Mt 23:37
7:14 [p] Jer 3:10

They gather together[a] for grain and new wine[a]
but turn away from me.[b]
15I trained them and strengthened them,
but they plot evil[c] against me.
16They do not turn to the Most High;
they are like a faulty bow.[d]
Their leaders will fall by the sword
because of their insolent words.
For this they will be ridiculed[e]
in the land of Egypt.[f]

Chapter 8 Theme ______________________

8 "Put the trumpet to your lips!
An eagle[g] is over the house of the LORD
because the people have broken my covenant
and rebelled against my law.[h]
2Israel cries out to me,
'O our God, we acknowledge you!'
3But Israel has rejected what is good;
an enemy will pursue him.
4They set up kings without my consent;
they choose princes without my approval.[i]
With their silver and gold
they make idols[j] for themselves
to their own destruction.
5Throw out your calf-idol, O Samaria![k]
My anger burns against them.
How long will they be incapable of purity?[l]
6 They are from Israel!
This calf—a craftsman has made it;
it is not God.
It will be broken in pieces,
that calf of Samaria.

7"They sow the wind
and reap the whirlwind.[m]
The stalk has no head;
it will produce no flour.
Were it to yield grain,
foreigners would swallow it up.[n]
8Israel is swallowed up;[o]
now she is among the nations
like a worthless[p] thing.

a *14* Most Hebrew manuscripts; some Hebrew manuscripts and Septuagint *They slash themselves*

7:14 [a]Am 2:8 [b]Hos 13:16
7:15 [c]Na 1:9,11
7:16 [d]Ps 78:9,57 [e]Eze 23:32 [f]Hos 9:3
8:1 [g]Dt 28:49; Jer 4:13 [h]Hos 4:6; 6:7
8:4 [i]Hos 13:10 [j]Hos 2:8
8:5 [k]Hos 10:5 [l]Jer 13:27
8:7 [m]Pr 22:8; Isa 66:15; Hos 10:12-13; Na 1:3 [n]Hos 2:9
8:8 [o]Jer 51:34 [p]Jer 22:28

8:10 [a] Eze 16:37; 22:20 [b] Jer 42:2

[9]For they have gone up to Assyria
like a wild donkey wandering alone.
Ephraim has sold herself to lovers.
[10]Although they have sold themselves among the nations,
I will now gather them together.[a]
They will begin to waste away[b]
under the oppression of the mighty king.

8:11 [c] Hos 10:1; 12:11

[11]"Though Ephraim built many altars for sin offerings,
these have become altars for sinning.[c]
[12]I wrote for them the many things of my law,
but they regarded them as something alien.

8:13 [d] Jer 7:21 [e] Hos 7:2 [f] Hos 4:9 [g] Hos 9:3,6

[13]They offer sacrifices given to me
and they eat[d] the meat,
but the LORD is not pleased with them.
Now he will remember[e] their wickedness
and punish their sins:[f]
They will return to Egypt.[g]

8:14 [h] Dt 32:18; Hos 2:13 [i] Jer 17:27

[14]Israel has forgotten[h] his Maker
and built palaces;
Judah has fortified many towns.
But I will send fire upon their cities
that will consume their fortresses."[i]

Chapter 9 Theme ______________________

9:1 [j] Isa 22:12-13 [k] Hos 10:5

9 Do not rejoice, O Israel;
do not be jubilant[j] like the other nations.
For you have been unfaithful[k] to your God;
you love the wages of a prostitute
at every threshing floor.

9:2 [l] Hos 2:9

[2]Threshing floors and winepresses will not feed the people;
the new wine[l] will fail them.

9:3 [m] Lev 25:23 [n] Hos 8:13 [o] Eze 4:13; Hos 7:11

[3]They will not remain[m] in the LORD's land;
Ephraim will return to Egypt[n]
and eat unclean[a] food in Assyria.[o]
[4]They will not pour out wine offerings to the LORD,
nor will their sacrifices please[p] him.

9:4 [p] Jer 6:20; Hos 8:13 [q] Hag 2:13-14

Such sacrifices will be to them like the bread of mourners;
all who eat them will be unclean.[q]
This food will be for themselves;
it will not come into the temple of the LORD.

9:5 [r] Isa 10:3; Jer 5:31 [s] Hos 2:11

[5]What will you do[r] on the day of your appointed feasts,[s]
on the festival days of the LORD?

a 3 That is, ceremonially unclean

[6]Even if they escape from destruction,
Egypt will gather them,
and Memphis[a] will bury them.
Their treasures of silver will be taken over by briers,
and thorns[b] will overrun their tents.
[7]The days of punishment[c] are coming,
the days of reckoning are at hand.
Let Israel know this.
Because your sins[d] are so many
and your hostility so great,
the prophet is considered a fool,[e]
the inspired man a maniac.
[8]The prophet, along with my God,
is the watchman over Ephraim,[a]
yet snares[f] await him on all his paths,
and hostility in the house of his God.
[9]They have sunk deep into corruption,
as in the days of Gibeah.[g]
God will remember[h] their wickedness
and punish them for their sins.

[10]"When I found Israel,
it was like finding grapes in the desert;
when I saw your fathers,
it was like seeing the early fruit on the fig tree.
But when they came to Baal Peor,[i]
they consecrated themselves to that
shameful idol[j]
and became as vile as the thing they loved.
[11]Ephraim's glory will fly away like a bird[k]—
no birth, no pregnancy, no conception.[l]
[12]Even if they rear children,
I will bereave them of every one.
Woe[m] to them
when I turn away from them![n]
[13]I have seen Ephraim, like Tyre,
planted in a pleasant place.[o]
But Ephraim will bring out
their children to the slayer."

[14]Give them, O LORD—
what will you give them?
Give them wombs that miscarry
and breasts that are dry.[p]

[a]8 Or *The prophet is the watchman over Ephraim, / the people of my God*

9:6
[a]Isa 19:13
[b]Isa 5:6; Hos 10:8

9:7
[c]Isa 34:8; Jer 10:15; Mic 7:4
[d]Jer 16:18
[e]Isa 44:25; La 2:14; Eze 14:9-10

9:8
[f]Hos 5:1

9:9
[g]Jdg 19:16-30; Hos 5:8; 10:9
[h]Hos 8:13

9:10
[i]Nu 25:1-5; Ps 106:28-29
[j]Jer 11:13; Hos 4:14

9:11
[k]Hos 4:7; 10:5
[l]ver 14

9:12
[m]Hos 7:13
[n]Dt 31:17

9:13
[o]Eze 27:3

9:14
[p]ver 11; Lk 23:29

9:15
[a] Hos 4:15
[b] Hos 7:2
[c] Isa 1:23; Hos 4:9; 5:2

9:16
[d] Hos 5:11
[e] Hos 8:7
[f] ver 12

9:17
[g] Hos 4:10
[h] Dt 28:65; Hos 7:13

10:1
[i] Eze 15:2
[j] 1Ki 14:23
[k] Hos 8:11; 12:11

10:2
[l] 1Ki 18:21
[m] Hos 13:16
[n] ver 8
[o] Mic 5:13

10:4
[p] Hos 4:2
[q] Eze 17:19; Am 5:7

10:5
[r] Hos 5:8
[s] 2Ki 23:5
[t] Hos 8:5; 9:1,3,11

10:6
[u] Hos 11:5
[v] Hos 5:13

15"Because of all their wickedness in Gilgal,[a]
I hated them there.
Because of their sinful deeds,[b]
I will drive them out of my house.
I will no longer love them;
all their leaders are rebellious.[c]
16Ephraim[d] is blighted,
their root is withered,
they yield no fruit.[e]
Even if they bear children,
I will slay[f] their cherished offspring."
17My God will reject them
because they have not obeyed[g] him;
they will be wanderers among the nations.[h]

Chapter 10 Theme

10 Israel was a spreading vine;[i]
he brought forth fruit for himself.
As his fruit increased,
he built more altars;[j]
as his land prospered,
he adorned his sacred stones.[k]
2Their heart is deceitful,[l]
and now they must bear their guilt.[m]
The LORD will demolish their altars[n]
and destroy their sacred stones.[o]
3Then they will say, "We have no king
because we did not revere the LORD.
But even if we had a king,
what could he do for us?"
4They make many promises,
take false oaths[p]
and make agreements;[q]
therefore lawsuits spring up
like poisonous weeds in a plowed field.
5The people who live in Samaria fear
for the calf-idol of Beth Aven.[a] [r]
Its people will mourn over it,
and so will its idolatrous priests,[s]
those who had rejoiced over its splendor,
because it is taken from them into exile.[t]
6It will be carried to Assyria[u]
as tribute for the great king.[v]

[a] 5 *Beth Aven* means *house of wickedness* (a name for Bethel, which means *house of God*).

Ephraim will be disgraced;[a]
Israel will be ashamed of its wooden idols.[a]
7Samaria and its king will float away[b]
like a twig on the surface of the waters.
8The high places of wickedness[b] [c] will be destroyed—
it is the sin of Israel.
Thorns[d] and thistles will grow up
and cover their altars.[e]
Then they will say to the mountains, "Cover us!"
and to the hills, "Fall on us!"[f]

9"Since the days of Gibeah,[g] you have sinned, O Israel,
and there you have remained.[c]
Did not war overtake
the evildoers in Gibeah?
10When I please, I will punish[h] them;
nations will be gathered against them
to put them in bonds for their double sin.
11Ephraim is a trained heifer
that loves to thresh;
so I will put a yoke
on her fair neck.
I will drive Ephraim,
Judah must plow,
and Jacob must break up the ground.
12Sow for yourselves righteousness,[i]
reap the fruit of unfailing love,
and break up your unplowed ground;[j]
for it is time to seek[k] the LORD,
until he comes
and showers righteousness[l] on you.
13But you have planted wickedness,
you have reaped evil,[m]
you have eaten the fruit of deception.
Because you have depended on your own strength
and on your many warriors,[n]
14the roar of battle will rise against your people,
so that all your fortresses will be devastated[o]—
as Shalman devastated Beth Arbel on the day of battle,
when mothers were dashed to the ground with
their children.[p]
15Thus will it happen to you, O Bethel,
because your wickedness is great.

a6 Or *its counsel* b8 Hebrew *aven,* a reference to Beth Aven (a derogatory name for Bethel)
c9 Or *there a stand was taken*

10:6
[a]Isa 30:3; Hos 4:7
10:7
[b]Hos 13:11
10:8
[c]1Ki 12:28-30; Hos 4:13
[d]Hos 9:6
[e]ver 2; Isa 32:13
[f]Lk 23:30*; Rev 6:16
10:9
[g]Hos 5:8
10:10
[h]Eze 5:13; Hos 4:9
10:12
[i]Pr 11:18
[j]Jer 4:3
[k]Hos 12:6
[l]Isa 45:8
10:13
[m]Job 4:8; Hos 7:3; 11:12; Gal 6:7-8
[n]Ps 33:16
10:14
[o]Isa 17:3
[p]Hos 13:16

When that day dawns,
the king of Israel will be completely destroyed.[a]

Chapter 11 Theme ____________________

11 "When Israel was a child, I loved him,
and out of Egypt I called my son.[b]
2But the more I[a] called Israel,
the further they went from me.[b]
They sacrificed to the Baals[c]
and they burned incense to images.[d]
3It was I who taught Ephraim to walk,
taking them by the arms;[e]
but they did not realize
it was I who healed[f] them.
4I led them with cords of human kindness,
with ties of love;[g]
I lifted the yoke[h] from their neck
and bent down to feed[i] them.

5"Will they not return to Egypt[j]
and will not Assyria[k] rule over them
because they refuse to repent?
6Swords[l] will flash in their cities,
will destroy the bars of their gates
and put an end to their plans.
7My people are determined to turn from me.[m]
Even if they call to the Most High,
he will by no means exalt them.

8"How can I give you up, Ephraim?[n]
How can I hand you over, Israel?
How can I treat you like Admah?
How can I make you like Zeboiim?[o]
My heart is changed within me;
all my compassion is aroused.
9I will not carry out my fierce anger,[p]
nor will I turn and devastate[q] Ephraim.
For I am God, and not man[r]—
the Holy One among you.
I will not come in wrath.[c]
10They will follow the LORD;
he will roar like a lion.
When he roars,
his children will come trembling from the west.[s]

10:15 [a]ver 7
11:1 [b]Ex 4:22; Hos 12:9,13; 13:4; Mt 2:15*
11:2 [c]Hos 2:13 [d]2Ki 17:15; Isa 65:7; Jer 18:15
11:3 [e]Dt 1:31; Hos 7:15 [f]Jer 30:17
11:4 [g]Jer 31:2-3 [h]Lev 26:13 [i]Ex 16:32; Ps 78:25
11:5 [j]Hos 7:16 [k]Hos 10:6
11:6 [l]Hos 13:16
11:7 [m]Jer 3:6-7; 8:5
11:8 [n]Hos 6:4 [o]Ge 14:8
11:9 [p]Dt 13:17; Jer 30:11 [q]Mal 3:6 [r]Nu 23:19
11:10 [s]Hos 6:1-3

[a] *2* Some Septuagint manuscripts; Hebrew *they* [b] *2* Septuagint; Hebrew *them* [c] *9* Or *come against any city*

[11]They will come trembling
like birds from Egypt,
like doves from Assyria.[a]
I will settle them in their homes,"[b]
declares the LORD.

[12]Ephraim has surrounded me with lies,[c]
the house of Israel with deceit.
And Judah is unruly against God,
even against the faithful Holy One.

Chapter 12 Theme ____________________

12

Ephraim feeds on the wind;[d]
he pursues the east wind all day
and multiplies lies and violence.
He makes a treaty with Assyria
and sends olive oil to Egypt.[e]
[2]The LORD has a charge[f] to bring against Judah;
he will punish Jacob[a] according to his ways
and repay him according to his deeds.[g]
[3]In the womb he grasped his brother's heel;[h]
as a man he struggled[i] with God.
[4]He struggled with the angel and overcame him;
he wept and begged for his favor.
He found him at Bethel[j]
and talked with him there—
[5]the LORD God Almighty,
the LORD is his name[k] of renown!
[6]But you must return to your God;
maintain love and justice,[l]
and wait for your God always.[m]

[7]The merchant uses dishonest scales;[n]
he loves to defraud.
[8]Ephraim boasts,
"I am very rich; I have become wealthy.[o]
With all my wealth they will not find in me
any iniquity or sin."

[9]"I am the LORD your God,
⌊who brought you⌋ out of[b] Egypt;[p]
I will make you live in tents[q] again,
as in the days of your appointed feasts.
[10]I spoke to the prophets,
gave them many visions
and told parables[r] through them."[s]

[a]2 *Jacob* means *he grasps the heel* (figuratively, *he deceives*). [b]9 Or *God / ever since you were in*

11:11 [a]Isa 11:11 [b]Eze 28:26
11:12 [c]Hos 4:2
12:1 [d]Eze 17:10 [e]2Ki 17:4
12:2 [f]Mic 6:2 [g]Hos 4:9
12:3 [h]Ge 25:26 [i]Ge 32:24-29
12:4 [j]Ge 28:12-15; 35:15
12:5 [k]Ex 3:15
12:6 [l]Mic 6:8 [m]Hos 6:1-3; 10:12; Mic 7:7
12:7 [n]Am 8:5
12:8 [o]Ps 62:10; Rev 3:17
12:9 [p]Lev 23:43; Hos 11:1 [q]Ne 8:17
12:10 [r]Eze 20:49 [s]2Ki 17:13; Jer 7:25

12:11 [a]Hos 6:8 [b]Hos 4:15 [c]Hos 8:11

11 Is Gilead wicked?[a]
Its people are worthless!
Do they sacrifice bulls in Gilgal?[b]
Their altars will be like piles of stones
on a plowed field.[c]

12:12 [d]Ge 28:5 [e]Ge 29:18

12 Jacob fled to the country of Aram[a];[d]
Israel served to get a wife,
and to pay for her he tended sheep.[e]

12:13 [f]Ex 13:3; Isa 63:11-14

13 The LORD used a prophet to bring Israel up from Egypt,
by a prophet he cared for him.[f]
14 But Ephraim has bitterly provoked him to anger;
his Lord will leave upon him the guilt of
his bloodshed[g]
and will repay him for his contempt.[h]

12:14 [g]Eze 18:13 [h]Da 11:18

Chapter 13 Theme ______________________

13

When Ephraim spoke, men trembled;[i]
he was exalted[j] in Israel.
But he became guilty of Baal worship[k] and died.

13:1 [i]Jdg 12:1 [j]Jdg 8:1 [k]Hos 11:2

2 Now they sin more and more;
they make idols for themselves from their silver,[l]
cleverly fashioned images,
all of them the work of craftsmen.
It is said of these people,
"They offer human sacrifice
and kiss[b] the calf-idols.[m]"

13:2 [l]Isa 46:6; Jer 10:4 [m]Isa 44:17-20

3 Therefore they will be like the morning mist,
like the early dew that disappears,[n]
like chaff[o] swirling from a threshing floor,[p]
like smoke[q] escaping through a window.

13:3 [n]Hos 6:4 [o]Isa 17:13 [p]Da 2:35 [q]Ps 68:2

4 "But I am the LORD your God,
⌊who brought you⌋ out of[c] Egypt.[r]
You shall acknowledge no God but me,[s]
no Savior[t] except me.

13:4 [r]Hos 12:9 [s]Ex 20:3 [t]Isa 43:11; 45:21-22

5 I cared for you in the desert,
in the land of burning heat.
6 When I fed them, they were satisfied;
when they were satisfied, they became proud;
then they forgot me.[u]

13:6 [u]Dt 32:12-15; Hos 2:13

7 So I will come upon them like a lion,
like a leopard I will lurk by the path.
8 Like a bear robbed of her cubs,[v]
I will attack them and rip them open.

13:8 [v]2Sa 17:8

a 12 That is, Northwest Mesopotamia b 2 Or *"Men who sacrifice / kiss* c 4 Or *God / ever since you were in*

Like a lion I will devour them;
a wild animal will tear them apart.[a]

9"You are destroyed, O Israel,
because you are against me,[b] against your helper.[c]
10Where is your king,[d] that he may save you?
Where are your rulers in all your towns,
of whom you said,
'Give me a king and princes'?[e]
11So in my anger I gave you a king,
and in my wrath I took him away.[f]
12The guilt of Ephraim is stored up,
his sins are kept on record.[g]
13Pains as of a woman in childbirth[h] come to him,
but he is a child without wisdom;
when the time arrives,
he does not come to the opening of the womb.[i]

14"I will ransom them from the power of the grave[a];[j]
I will redeem them from death.
Where, O death, are your plagues?
Where, O grave,[a] is your destruction?[k]

"I will have no compassion,
15 even though he thrives[l] among his brothers.
An east wind[m] from the LORD will come,
blowing in from the desert;
his spring will fail
and his well dry up.[n]
His storehouse will be plundered[o]
of all its treasures.
16The people of Samaria must bear their guilt,[p]
because they have rebelled[q] against their God.
They will fall by the sword;[r]
their little ones will be dashed[s] to the ground,
their pregnant women[t] ripped open."

Chapter 14 Theme ____________________

14

Return, O Israel, to the LORD your God.
Your sins have been your downfall![u]
2Take words with you
and return to the LORD.
Say to him:
"Forgive all our sins
and receive us graciously,[v]
that we may offer the fruit of our lips.[b][w]

[a] 14 Hebrew *Sheol* [b] 2 Or *offer our lips as sacrifices of bulls*

13:8 [a] Ps 50:22
13:9 [b] Jer 2:17-19 [c] Dt 33:29
13:10 [d] 2Ki 17:4 [e] 1Sa 8:6; Hos 8:4
13:11 [f] 1Ki 14:10; Hos 10:7
13:12 [g] Dt 32:34
13:13 [h] Isa 13:8; Mic 4:9-10 [i] Isa 66:9
13:14 [j] Ps 49:15; Eze 37:12-13 [k] 1Co 15:55*
13:15 [l] Hos 10:1 [m] Eze 19:12 [n] Jer 51:36 [o] Jer 20:5
13:16 [p] Hos 10:2 [q] Hos 7:14 [r] Hos 11:6 [s] 2Ki 8:12; Hos 10:14 [t] 2Ki 15:16; Isa 13:16
14:1 [u] Hos 5:5
14:2 [v] Mic 7:18-19 [w] Heb 13:15

14:3
[a]Ps 33:17; Isa 31:1
[b]Hos 8:6
[c]Ps 10:14; 68:5

14:4
[d]Hos 6:1
[e]Zep 3:17

14:5
[f]SS 2:1
[g]Isa 35:2
[h]Job 29:19

14:6
[i]Ps 52:8; Jer 11:16
[j]SS 4:11

14:7
[k]Ps 91:1-4
[l]Hos 2:22
[m]Eze 17:23

14:8
[n]ver 3

14:9
[o]Ps 107:43
[p]Pr 10:29; Isa 1:28
[q]Ps 111:7-8; Zep 3:5; Ac 13:10
[r]Isa 26:7

3 Assyria cannot save us;
we will not mount war-horses.[a]
We will never again say 'Our gods'[b]
to what our own hands have made,
for in you the fatherless[c] find compassion."

4 "I will heal[d] their waywardness
and love them freely,[e]
for my anger has turned away from them.
5 I will be like the dew to Israel;
he will blossom like a lily.[f]
Like a cedar of Lebanon[g]
he will send down his roots;[h]
6 his young shoots will grow.
His splendor will be like an olive tree,[i]
his fragrance like a cedar of Lebanon.[j]
7 Men will dwell again in his shade.[k]
He will flourish like the grain.
He will blossom like a vine,
and his fame will be like the wine[l] from Lebanon.[m]
8 O Ephraim, what more have I[a] to do with idols?[n]
I will answer him and care for him.
I am like a green pine tree;
your fruitfulness comes from me."

9 Who is wise?[o] He will realize these things.
Who is discerning? He will understand them.[p]
The ways of the LORD are right;[q]
the righteous walk[r] in them,
but the rebellious stumble in them.

[a] 8 Or *What more has Ephraim*

God's Response to Israel's Sin

Their Sin (Iniquity)	The Immediate or Long-Range Consequences

Their Future or Hope

Hosea at a Glance

heme of Hosea:

uthor:

ate:

rpose:

y Words:

Segment Divisions		Chapter Themes
		1
		2
		3
		4
		5
		6
		7
		8
		9
		10
		11
		12
		13
		14

JOEL

Although we know nothing about Joel, nor the exact time of his writing other than what we read in this short prophetic book, Joel's message is significant. When Peter preached on Pentecost, he explained Pentecost in the light of a prophecy in Joel (Acts 2:14-21; Joel 2:28-32).

Joel uses a present-day plague to call God's people to repentance. As he does this, Joel, like the other prophets, warns them of the coming day of the Lord—a day that is as sure as the promises of God.

Things to Do

1. Read through Joel and mark the key words listed on the JOEL AT A GLANCE chart on page 1562.
2. To correctly interpret Joel, you must pay attention to the time when certain events occur. Joel switches from the present to the future. To pick this up, watch for and mark the words *then* and *now.* Put a symbol next to any references to time. Also, watch the sequence of events.
3. As you read through Joel, note the following and record what you learn in the appropriate section on the JOEL OBSERVATIONS CHART on page 1563:
   a. What is going to happen to the people, the land, the nations, and the animals and who or what is going to do it.
   b. What the people are to do and why.
   c. How God will respond and the effect it will have on the people.
   d. When applicable, note when any of the above will happen.
4. Record the theme of each chapter on JOEL AT A GLANCE as well as in the text next to the chapter number. Then fill in the rest of the chart. Be sure to record the theme or message of Joel.
5. The day of the Lord is an important day prophetically. Beginning on page 2178 you will find the chart THE DAY OF THE LORD. Record your insights from Joel on the day of the Lord. As you do so, note the reference (book, chapter, and verse) that you took your information from so you can find it later.

Things to Think About

1. What do you see happening in the world, in your nation? Could it be the judgment of the Lord? What could you and others learn from Joel's exhortations? What could you do?
2. Have you failed God in any way? According to what you have seen in Joel, is there a chance to return to him? What could you do? How can you apply the message of Joel to your life? What do you think would happen if your church collectively repented and returned to the Lord in this manner? Think about it and ask God what to do.

Chapter 1 Theme ______________________________

1 The word of the LORD that came[a] to Joel[b] son of Pethuel.

2 Hear this,[c] you elders;
  listen, all who live in the land.[d]
Has anything like this ever happened in your days
  or in the days of your forefathers?[e]
3 Tell it to your children,[f]
  and let your children tell it to their children,
  and their children to the next generation.

1:1 [a] Jer 1:2 [b] Ac 2:16
1:2 [c] Hos 5:1 [d] Hos 4:1 [e] Joel 2:2
1:3 [f] Ex 10:2; Ps 78:4

1:4 [a]Dt 28:39; Na 3:15

4 What the locust swarm has left
the great locusts have eaten;
what the great locusts have left
the young locusts have eaten;
what the young locusts have left
other locusts[a] have eaten.[a]

1:5 [b]Joel 3:3

5 Wake up, you drunkards, and weep!
Wail, all you drinkers of wine;[b]
wail because of the new wine,
for it has been snatched from your lips.

1:6 [c]Joel 2:2,11,25 [d]Rev 9:8

6 A nation has invaded my land,
powerful and without number;[c]
it has the teeth[d] of a lion,
the fangs of a lioness.

1:7 [e]Isa 5:6 [f]Am 4:9

7 It has laid waste[e] my vines
and ruined my fig trees.[f]
It has stripped off their bark
and thrown it away,
leaving their branches white.

1:8 [g]ver 13; Isa 22:12; Am 8:10

8 Mourn like a virgin[b] in sackcloth[g]
grieving for the husband[c] of her youth.
9 Grain offerings and drink offerings[h]
are cut off from the house of the LORD.

1:9 [h]Hos 9:4; Joel 2:14,17

a *4* The precise meaning of the four Hebrew words used here for locusts is uncertain.
b *8* Or *young woman* c *8* Or *betrothed*

THE RULERS AND PROPHETS OF JOEL'S TIME

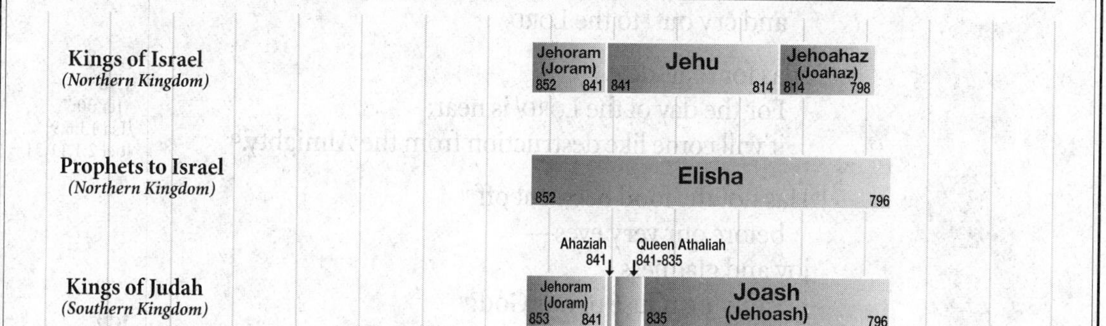

Kings of Israel *(Northern Kingdom)*
Jehoram (Joram) 852 841
Jehu 841 814
Jehoahaz (Joahaz) 814 798

Prophets to Israel *(Northern Kingdom)*
Elisha 852 796

Kings of Judah *(Southern Kingdom)*
Jehoram (Joram) 853 841
Ahaziah 841
Queen Athaliah 841-835
Joash (Jehoash) 835 796

Joel and His Contemporary Prophets *(Southern Kingdom)*
Obadiah 841 825
Joel 825 809
Jahaziel 865 835

930 920 910 900 890 880 870 860 850 840 830 820 810 800 790 780 770

The priests are in mourning,
those who minister before the LORD.
10The fields are ruined,
the ground is dried up[a];[a]
the grain is destroyed,
the new wine[b] is dried up,
the oil fails.
11Despair, you farmers,[c]
wail, you vine growers;
grieve for the wheat and the barley,
because the harvest of the field is destroyed.[d]
12The vine is dried up
and the fig tree is withered;
the pomegranate, the palm and the apple tree—
all the trees of the field—are dried up.[e]
Surely the joy of mankind
is withered away.

13Put on sackcloth,[f] O priests, and mourn;
wail, you who minister[g] before the altar.
Come, spend the night in sackcloth,
you who minister before my God;
for the grain offerings and drink offerings[h]
are withheld from the house of your God.
14Declare a holy fast;[i]
call a sacred assembly.
Summon the elders
and all who live in the land
to the house of the LORD your God,
and cry out[j] to the LORD.

15Alas for that[k] day!
For the day of the LORD[l] is near;
it will come like destruction from the Almighty.[b]

16Has not the food been cut off[m]
before our very eyes—
joy and gladness
from the house of our God?[n]
17The seeds are shriveled
beneath the clods.[c][o]
The storehouses are in ruins,
the granaries have been broken down,
for the grain has dried up.

1:10 [a] Isa 24:4 [b] Hos 9:2
1:11 [c] Jer 14:3-4; Am 5:16 [d] Isa 17:11
1:12 [e] Hag 2:19
1:13 [f] Jer 4:8 [g] Joel 2:17 [h] ver 9
1:14 [i] 2Ch 20:3 [j] Jnh 3:8
1:15 [k] Jer 30:7 [l] Isa 13:6,9; Joel 2:1,11,31
1:16 [m] Isa 3:7 [n] Dt 12:7
1:17 [o] Isa 17:10-11

a *10* Or *ground mourns* b *15* Hebrew *Shaddai* c *17* The meaning of the Hebrew for this word is uncertain.

1:19
[a] Ps 50:15
[b] Am 7:4
[c] Jer 9:10

[18]How the cattle moan!
The herds mill about
because they have no pasture;
even the flocks of sheep are suffering.

[19]To you, O LORD, I call,[a]
for fire[b] has devoured the open pastures[c]
and flames have burned up all the trees of the field.

1:20
[d] Ps 104:21
[e] 1Ki 17:7

[20]Even the wild animals pant for you;[d]
the streams of water have dried up[e]
and fire has devoured the open pastures.

2:1
[f] Jer 4:5
[g] ver 15
[h] Joel 1:15; Zep 1:14-16
[i] Ob 1:15

Chapter 2 Theme ______________________________

2

Blow the trumpet[f] in Zion;[g]
sound the alarm on my holy hill.
Let all who live in the land tremble,
for the day of the LORD[h] is coming.
It is close at hand[i]—

2:2
[j] Am 5:18
[k] Da 9:12
[l] Joel 1:6
[m] Joel 1:2

2 a day of darkness[j] and gloom,[k]
a day of clouds and blackness.
Like dawn spreading across the mountains
a large and mighty army[l] comes,
such as never was of old[m]
nor ever will be in ages to come.

2:3
[n] Ge 2:8
[o] Ps 105:34-35

[3]Before them fire devours,
behind them a flame blazes.
Before them the land is like the garden of Eden,[n]
behind them, a desert waste[o]—
nothing escapes them.

2:4
[p] Rev 9:7

[4]They have the appearance of horses;[p]
they gallop along like cavalry.

2:5
[q] Rev 9:9
[r] Isa 5:24; 30:30

[5]With a noise like that of chariots[q]
they leap over the mountaintops,
like a crackling fire[r] consuming stubble,
like a mighty army drawn up for battle.

2:6
[s] Isa 13:8
[t] Na 2:10

[6]At the sight of them, nations are in anguish;[s]
every face turns pale.[t]
[7]They charge like warriors;
they scale walls like soldiers.
They all march in line,
not swerving[u] from their course.
[8]They do not jostle each other;
each marches straight ahead.
They plunge through defenses
without breaking ranks.

2:7
[u] Isa 5:27

[9]They rush upon the city;
they run along the wall.
They climb into the houses;
like thieves they enter through the windows.[a]

[10]Before them the earth shakes,[b]
the sky trembles,
the sun and moon are darkened,[c]
and the stars no longer shine.[d]
[11]The LORD[e] thunders
at the head of his army;
his forces are beyond number,
and mighty are those who obey his command.
The day of the LORD is great;[f]
it is dreadful.
Who can endure it?[g]

[12]"Even now," declares the LORD,
"return[h] to me with all your heart,
with fasting and weeping and mourning."

[13]Rend your heart[i]
and not your garments.[j]
Return to the LORD your God,
for he is gracious and compassionate,
slow to anger and abounding in love,[k]
and he relents from sending calamity.[l]
[14]Who knows? He may turn[m] and have pity
and leave behind a blessing[n]—
grain offerings and drink offerings[o]
for the LORD your God.

[15]Blow the trumpet[p] in Zion,
declare a holy fast,[q]
call a sacred assembly.[r]
[16]Gather the people,
consecrate[s] the assembly;
bring together the elders,
gather the children,
those nursing at the breast.
Let the bridegroom[t] leave his room
and the bride her chamber.
[17]Let the priests, who minister before the LORD,
weep between the temple porch and the altar.[u]
Let them say, "Spare your people, O LORD.
Do not make your inheritance an object of scorn,[v]
a byword among the nations.

2:9
[a] Jer 9:21

2:10
[b] Ps 18:7
[c] Mt 24:29
[d] Isa 13:10; Eze 32:8

2:11
[e] Joel 1:15
[f] Zep 1:14; Rev 18:8
[g] Eze 22:14

2:12
[h] Jer 4:1; Hos 12:6

2:13
[i] Ps 34:18; Isa 57:15
[j] Job 1:20
[k] Ex 34:6
[l] Jer 18:8

2:14
[m] Jer 26:3
[n] Hag 2:19
[o] Joel 1:13

2:15
[p] Nu 10:2
[q] Jer 36:9
[r] Joel 1:14

2:16
[s] Ex 19:10,22
[t] Ps 19:5

2:17
[u] Eze 8:16; Mt 23:35
[v] Dt 9:26-29; Ps 44:13

Why should they say among the peoples,
'Where is their God?[a]'"

18Then the LORD will be jealous[b] for his land
and take pity on his people.

19The LORD will reply[a] to them:

"I am sending you grain, new wine and oil,[c]
enough to satisfy you fully;
never again will I make you
an object of scorn[d] to the nations.

20"I will drive the northern army[e] far from you,
pushing it into a parched and barren land,
with its front columns going into the eastern[f] sea[b]
and those in the rear into the western sea.[c]
And its stench[g] will go up;
its smell will rise."

Surely he has done great things.[d]
21 Be not afraid,[h] O land;
be glad and rejoice.
Surely the LORD has done great things.[i]
22 Be not afraid, O wild animals,
for the open pastures are becoming green.[j]
The trees are bearing their fruit;
the fig tree and the vine yield their riches.[k]
23Be glad, O people of Zion,
rejoice[l] in the LORD your God,
for he has given you
the autumn rains in righteousness.[e]
He sends you abundant showers,
both autumn and spring rains,[m] as before.
24The threshing floors will be filled with grain;
the vats will overflow[n] with new wine[o] and oil.

25"I will repay you for the years the locusts have eaten—
the great locust and the young locust,
the other locusts and the locust swarm[f]—
my great army that I sent among you.
26You will have plenty to eat, until you are full,[p]
and you will praise[q] the name of the LORD your God,
who has worked wonders[r] for you;
never again will my people be shamed.

2:17 [a] Ps 42:3
2:18 [b] Zec 1:14
2:19 [c] Jer 31:12 [d] Eze 34:29
2:20 [e] Jer 1:14-15 [f] Zec 14:8 [g] Isa 34:3
2:21 [h] Isa 54:4; Zep 3:16-17 [i] Ps 126:3
2:22 [j] Ps 65:12 [k] Joel 1:18-20
2:23 [l] Ps 149:2; Isa 12:6; 41:16; Hab 3:18; Zec 10:7 [m] Lev 26:4
2:24 [n] Lev 26:10; Mal 3:10 [o] Am 9:13
2:26 [p] Lev 26:5 [q] Isa 62:9 [r] Ps 126:3; Isa 25:1

[a] *18,19* Or *LORD was jealous . . . / and took pity . . . / 19The LORD replied* [b] *20* That is, the Dead Sea [c] *20* That is, the Mediterranean [d] *20* Or *rise. / Surely it has done great things."* [e] *23* Or / *the teacher for righteousness:* [f] *25* The precise meaning of the four Hebrew words used here for locusts is uncertain.

27 Then you will know that I am in Israel,
that I am the LORD[a] your God,
and that there is no other;
never again will my people be shamed.

28 "And afterward,
I will pour out my Spirit[b] on all people.
Your sons and daughters will prophesy,
your old men will dream dreams,
your young men will see visions.
29 Even on my servants,[c] both men and women,
I will pour out my Spirit in those days.
30 I will show wonders in the heavens[d]
and on the earth,[e]
blood and fire and billows of smoke.
31 The sun will be turned to darkness[f]
and the moon to blood
before the coming of the great and dreadful day of
the LORD.[g]
32 And everyone who calls
on the name of the LORD will be saved;[h]
for on Mount Zion[i] and in Jerusalem
there will be deliverance,[j]
as the LORD has said,
among the survivors[k]
whom the LORD calls.

Chapter 3 Theme ______________________________

The Valley of Jehoshaphat

3

"In those days and at that time,
when I restore the fortunes[l] of Judah and Jerusalem,
2 I will gather all nations
and bring them down to the Valley
of Jehoshaphat.[a]
There I will enter into judgment[m] against them
concerning my inheritance, my people Israel,
for they scattered my people among the nations
and divided up my land.
3 They cast lots for my people
and traded boys for prostitutes;
they sold girls for wine[n]
that they might drink.

4 "Now what have you against me, O Tyre and Sidon[o]
and all you regions of Philistia? Are you repaying me
for something I have done? If you are paying me back,
I will swiftly and speedily return on your own heads

[a] 2 *Jehoshaphat* means *the LORD judges*; also in verse 12.

2:27 [a] Joel 3:17
2:28 [b] Eze 39:29
2:29 [c] 1Co 12:13; Gal 3:28
2:30 [d] Lk 21:11 [e] Mk 13:24-25
2:31 [f] Mt 24:29 [g] Isa 13:9-10; Mal 4:1,5
2:32 [h] Ac 2:17-21*; Ro 10:13* [i] Isa 46:13 [j] Ob 1:17 [k] Isa 11:11; Mic 4:7; Ro 9:27
3:1 [l] Jer 16:15
3:2 [m] Eze 36:5
3:3 [n] Am 2:6
3:4 [o] Mt 11:21

what you have done.[a] 5For you took my silver and my gold and carried off my finest treasures to your temples.[b] 6You sold the people
of Judah and Jerusalem to the Greeks, that you might send them
far from their homeland.

7"See, I am going to rouse them out of the places to which you
sold them,[c] and I will return on your own heads what you have
done. 8I will sell your sons[d] and daughters to the people of Judah,[e]
and they will sell them to the Sabeans, a nation far away." The
LORD has spoken.

9Proclaim this among the nations:
  Prepare for war![f]
Rouse the warriors![g]
  Let all the fighting men draw near and attack.
10Beat your plowshares into swords
  and your pruning hooks[h] into spears.
Let the weakling[i] say,
  "I am strong!"
11Come quickly, all you nations from every side,
  and assemble[j] there.

Bring down your warriors,[k] O LORD!

12"Let the nations be roused;
  let them advance into the Valley of Jehoshaphat,
for there I will sit
  to judge[l] all the nations on every side.
13Swing the sickle,
  for the harvest[m] is ripe.
Come, trample the grapes,
  for the winepress[n] is full
  and the vats overflow—
so great is their wickedness!"

14Multitudes, multitudes
  in the valley of decision!
For the day of the LORD[o] is near
  in the valley of decision.
15The sun and moon will be darkened,
  and the stars no longer shine.
16The LORD will roar from Zion
  and thunder from Jerusalem;[p]
  the earth and the sky will tremble.[q]
But the LORD will be a refuge for his people,
  a stronghold[r] for the people of Israel.

17"Then you will know that I, the LORD your God,[s]
  dwell in Zion,[t] my holy hill.
Jerusalem will be holy;
  never again will foreigners invade her.

3:4 [a] Isa 34:8
3:5 [b] 2Ch 21:16-17
3:7 [c] Isa 43:5-6; Jer 23:8
3:8 [d] Isa 60:14 [e] Isa 14:2
3:9 [f] Isa 8:9 [g] Jer 46:4
3:10 [h] Isa 2:4; Mic 4:3 [i] Zec 12:8
3:11 [j] Eze 38:15-16; Zep 3:8 [k] Isa 13:3
3:12 [l] Isa 2:4
3:13 [m] Hos 6:11; Mt 13:39; Rev 14:15-19 [n] Rev 14:20
3:14 [o] Isa 34:2-8; Joel 1:15
3:16 [p] Am 1:2 [q] Eze 38:19 [r] Jer 16:19
3:17 [s] Joel 2:27 [t] Isa 4:3

INSIGHT

Sabeans are the descendants of Seba, the son of Cush or possibly of Sheba, the son of Raamah (see Genesis 10:7). Sabeans destroyed Job's flocks, herds, and servants. They were known as traveling merchants. The term *Sabeans* could have been adapted to refer to foreign or nomadic merchants.

[18]"In that day the mountains will drip new wine,
and the hills will flow with milk;[a]
all the ravines of Judah will run with water.[b]
A fountain will flow out of the LORD's house[c]
and will water the valley of acacias.[a] [d]
[19]But Egypt will be desolate,
Edom a desert waste,
because of violence[e] done to the people of Judah,
in whose land they shed innocent blood.
[20]Judah will be inhabited forever[f]
and Jerusalem through all generations.
[21]Their bloodguilt, which I have not pardoned,
I will pardon.[g]"

The LORD dwells in Zion!

a *18* Or *Valley of Shittim*

3:18
a Ex 3:8
b Isa 30:25; 35:6
c Rev 22:1-2
d Eze 47:1; Am 9:13

3:19
e Ob 1:10

3:20
f Am 9:15

3:21
g Eze 36:25

JOEL AT A GLANCE

Theme of Joel:

SEGMENT DIVISIONS

		CHAPTER THEMES
		1
		2
		3

Author:

Date:

Purpose:

Key Word
locust(s)
Zion
day of th
(in that
those da
return
I will (wi
never ag
then
now
nations
(nation
its pron

Joel Observations Chart

What Happens to the People | What the People Are to Do | What Is the Effect on People

What Happens to the Land Before and During Judgment | What Happens to the Land After Judgment

What Happens to the Animals

What Happens to the Nations and Why

How Will God Respond

AMOS

While the cows of Bashan (the best of breeds raised in Canaan) grazed and were pampered in the northern Transjordan region, the Israelites of the northern kingdom went up to worship at Bethel. There at Bethel the higher echelon would burn incense and present their sacrifices at the altar.

Bethel was the place where Jeroboam I, the first king of Israel (the northern kingdom), had set up the golden calves (see 1 Kings 12-13). He felt he had to. When the twelve tribes divided into two kingdoms, those of the northern kingdom were cut off from Jerusalem. Jerusalem now belonged to the two tribes of the southern kingdom, Judah and Benjamin. If Jeroboam's people went to celebrate the feasts in Jerusalem at the temple as God commanded, they might defect to the southern kingdom.

So Jeroboam commissioned his own priests and instituted his own feast. The people would worship as they pleased, where they pleased. Those who did not go to Bethel could go to Gilgal, another principal place of worship. In Gilgal they could present their thank offerings with leaven, proclaim their freewill offerings, and even worship other gods.

Israel became prosperous and politically secure. Jeroboam died, and later Jeroboam II reigned. It was a golden era. Surely God was pleased with Israel—or that is what they supposed until a shepherd from the small city of Tekoa, just ten miles south of Jerusalem, appeared on the scene.

Then the word of the Lord came.

THINGS TO DO

General Instructions

In order to understand the historical setting of Amos, do the following:

1. Read Amos 1:1 and then record what you learn about Amos on the AMOS AT A GLANCE chart on page 1581 under "Author." Then under "Date" record the information that gives you a clue as to the time of these visions (see Zechariah 14:5). Under "Purpose" fill in Amos's reason for writing (see Amos 1:1).

2. Study the historical chart on page 1566 which shows Amos's relationship to the kings of Israel and Judah. Remember, Amos is a prophet to the northern kingdom.

3. Read 2 Chronicles 26:1-23 and 2 Kings 14:23 through 15:7. When you come across Azariah, remember that this is another name for King Uzziah, who ruled over the southern kingdom.

As you read through Amos, you will find three key phrases which divide the book into three segments. Therefore your instructions will be divided accordingly.

Chapters 1, 2

1. Read Amos 1 and 2 and mark each occurrence of the phrase *This is what the Lord says, for three sins of __________ even for four*. Note whose transgressions God is going to deal with in each incident.

2. Read what follows each of the statements you have marked. Look for another key repeated phrase, then mark or color it in a distinctive way.

3. Then observe why God will not revoke their punishment, and what the punishment will be. Note their punishment by marking each occurrence of *I will*.

4. In 2:4, 6 God deals with the southern kingdom, Judah, and with the northern kingdom, Israel. To understand why God speaks to them separately, look at Amos 1:1 and notice to whom Amos was sent as a prophet. (This information is also on the historical chart on page 1566.) It is important to keep this in mind as you study the rest of Amos.

5. Record the theme of the first two chapters on AMOS AT A GLANCE and in the text next to the chapter numbers.

Chapters 3-6

1. The second key repeated phrase is *hear this word*. Read Amos 3 through 6 and distinctively mark each occurrence of this phrase. Also mark every *Israel (Israelites)* (and every reference to Israel throughout Amos). Then list in the margin all you learn from marking *Israel*.
2. Read Amos 3 through 6 a second time, chapter by chapter. As you read these messages from the Lord, ask the five W's and an H. Ask questions such as: Who is speaking? To whom? What is being said? What is going to happen? When will it happen? Where will it take place? Why will it happen? How will it happen? (Remember, you won't always find answers to every question.)
3. Mark in a distinctive way key repeated words or phrases. For instance, marking every *I will* as it refers to God and asking the five W's and an H will help you see what God is going to do. Watch for *yet* in chapter 4 and *seek* in chapter 5. Mark every reference to *the day of the Lord*. Then in the margin list everything you learn about this day.
4. In the margin list important insights about God, Israel, what the people are doing wrong, and what they don't like.
5. When you finish studying a chapter, decide on the theme or topic of that chapter and record it on AMOS AT A GLANCE and in the text next to the chapter number.

Chapters 7-9

1. The key repeated phrase which sets off the last segment of Amos is *This is what the Sovereign Lord showed me*. Read these last three chapters and distinctively mark each occurrence of this phrase.
2. As you read through this final segment of Amos, watch what Amos was shown, and how he responds. Also observe the response to Amos's prophecy and how Amos deals with this.
3. In chapter 8 you see one final *hear this*. Pay careful attention to what God is going to do. Compare 8:8 with 1:1.
4. Although the phrase *This is what the Sovereign Lord showed me* is not used in 9:1, can you see that *I saw the Lord...and he said* could be Amos's fifth vision, which parallels those you marked in chapters 7 and 8? If so, mark it as you did the others.
5. Mark the *I will's* of God and any other key words or phrases.
6. In the chapter margins record your insights about God and Israel.
7. Record the chapter themes as you did before and complete AMOS AT A GLANCE. Make sure you also record the theme of Amos.
8. Beginning on page 2178 you will find the chart called THE DAY OF THE LORD. Record your insights from Amos on the day of the Lord on this chart. As you do, note the reference (book, chapter, and verse) from which you took your information so you can find it later.
9. Finally, watch the closing words of Amos. What is God's promise? Remember any reference to the land. Has this promise regarding the land of Israel been fulfilled? Think of Israel's history. Read the section called "Major Events in Israel's History" on page 2189. Then answer the question.

Things to Think About

1. Has wealth, the ease of life, the possession of things, the pursuit of happiness led to complacency in your worship? Are you worshiping God his way or your way?
2. As you review the list of Israel's sins, are you guilty of any of these? According to what you read in Amos, could Israel or the other nations sin and not reap the consequences? Can you?
3. What is the purpose of God's judgments? When God decides to judge, what can we do? What can we expect?

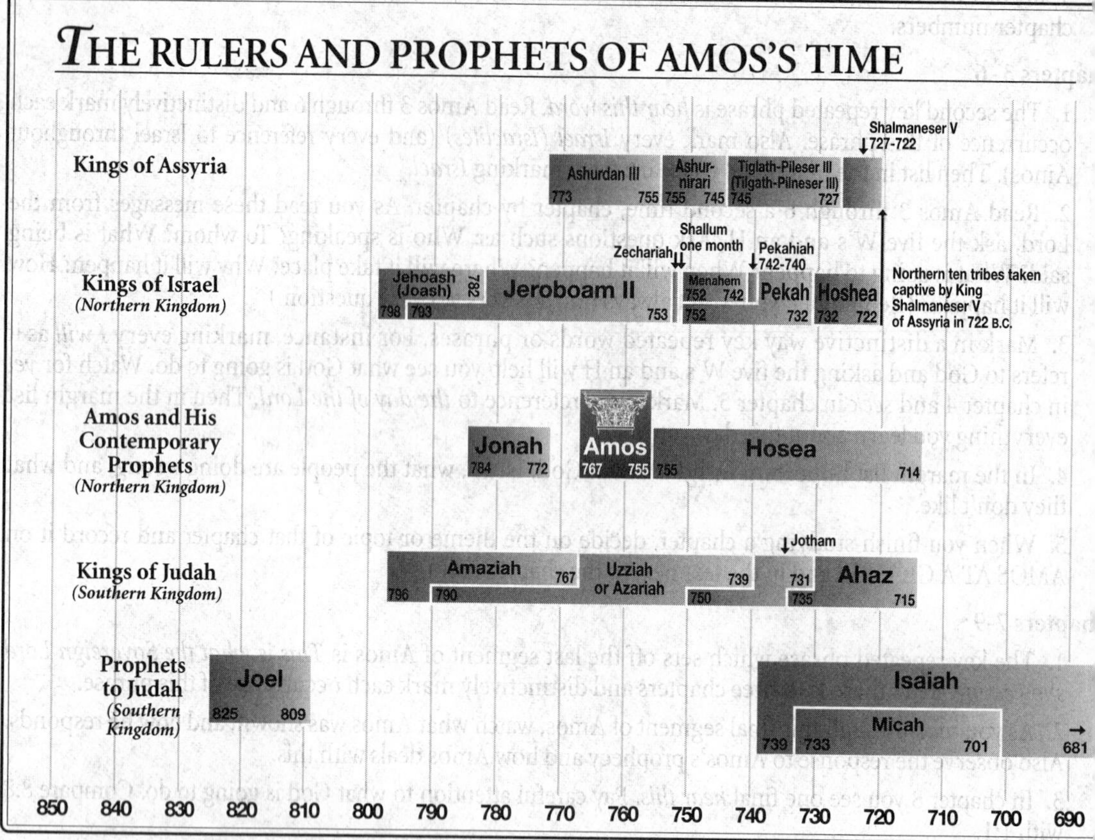

Chapter 1 Theme ______________________

1 The words of Amos, one of the shepherds of Tekoa[a]—what he
saw concerning Israel two years before the earthquake,[b] when
Uzziah[c] was king of Judah and Jeroboam[d] son of Jehoash[a] was
king of Israel.[e]
2 He said:

"The LORD roars[f] from Zion
and thunders from Jerusalem;[g]
the pastures of the shepherds dry up,[b]
and the top of Carmel[h] withers."[i]

3 This is what the LORD says:

"For three sins of Damascus,[j]
even for four, I will not turn back ⌊my wrath⌋.[k]
Because she threshed Gilead
with sledges having iron teeth,

INSIGHT

There are two Zions referred to in the Scriptures: the earthly Zion, Jerusalem, and the heavenly Zion, where God's throne is. Zion is also referred to as the city of God.

a 1 Hebrew *Joash*, a variant of *Jehoash*   b 2 Or *shepherds mourn*

1:1 [a] 2Sa 14:2 [b] Zec 14:5 [c] 2Ch 26:23 [d] 2Ki 14:23 [e] Hos 1:1

1:2 [f] Isa 42:13 [g] Joel 3:16 [h] Am 9:3 [i] Jer 12:4

1:3 [j] Isa 8:4; 17:1-3 [k] Am 2:6

4 I will send fire[a] upon the house of Hazael
that will consume the fortresses[b] of Ben-Hadad.[c]
5 I will break down the gate[d] of Damascus;
I will destroy the king who is in[a] the Valley of Aven[b]
and the one who holds the scepter in Beth Eden.
The people of Aram will go into exile to Kir,[e]"
says the LORD.

6 This is what the LORD says:

"For three sins of Gaza,[f]
even for four, I will not turn back ⌊my wrath⌋.
Because she took captive whole communities
and sold them to Edom,[g]
7 I will send fire upon the walls of Gaza
that will consume her fortresses.
8 I will destroy the king[c] of Ashdod[h]
and the one who holds the scepter in Ashkelon.
I will turn my hand[i] against Ekron,
till the last of the Philistines[j] is dead,"
says the Sovereign LORD.[k]

9 This is what the LORD says:

"For three sins of Tyre,[l]
even for four, I will not turn back
⌊my wrath⌋.
Because she sold whole communities of
captives to Edom,
disregarding a treaty of brotherhood,
10 I will send fire upon the walls of Tyre
that will consume her fortresses.[m]"

11 This is what the LORD says:

"For three sins of Edom,[n]
even for four, I will not turn back
⌊my wrath⌋.
Because he pursued his brother with a sword,
stifling all compassion,[d]
because his anger raged continually
and his fury flamed unchecked,[o]
12 I will send fire upon Teman[p]
that will consume the fortresses of Bozrah."

13 This is what the LORD says:

"For three sins of Ammon,[q]
even for four, I will not turn back ⌊my wrath⌋.

This Is What the Lord Says

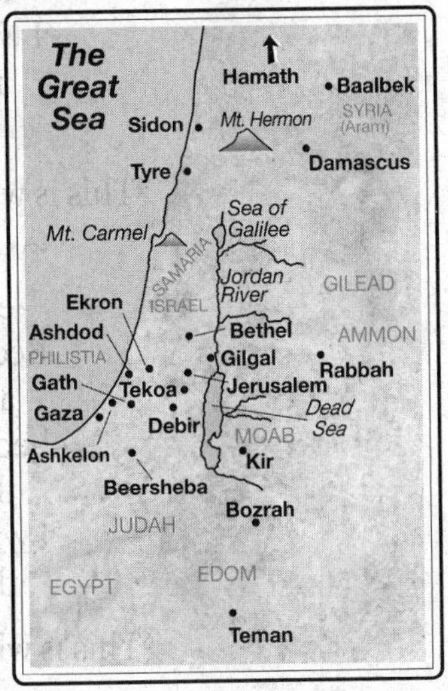

1:4 [a] Jer 49:27 [b] Jer 17:27 [c] 1Ki 20:1; 2Ki 6:24
1:5 [d] Jer 51:30 [e] 2Ki 16:9
1:6 [f] 1Sa 6:17; Zep 2:4 [g] Ob 11
1:8 [h] 2Ch 26:6 [i] Ps 81:14 [j] Eze 25:16 [k] Isa 14:28-32; Zep 2:4-7
1:9 [l] 1Ki 5:1; 9:11-14; Isa 23:1-18; Jer 25:22; Joel 3:4; Mt 11:21
1:10 [m] Zec 9:1-4
1:11 [n] Nu 20:14-21; 2Ch 28:17; Jer 49:7-22 [o] Eze 25:12-14
1:12 [p] Ob 9-10
1:13 [q] Jer 49:1-6; Eze 21:28; 25:2-7

[a] 5 Or *the inhabitants of* [b] 5 *Aven* means *wickedness.* [c] 8 Or *inhabitants* [d] 11 Or *sword / and destroyed his allies*

Because he ripped open the pregnant women[a] of Gilead
in order to extend his borders,
[14]I will set fire to the walls of Rabbah[b]
that will consume her fortresses
amid war cries[c] on the day of battle,
amid violent winds on a stormy day.
[15]Her king[a] will go into exile,
he and his officials together,"
says the LORD.

Chapter 2 Theme ____________________

2

This is what the LORD says:

"For three sins of Moab,
even for four, I will not turn back ⌊my wrath⌋.
Because he burned, as if to lime,
the bones of Edom's king,
[2]I will send fire upon Moab
that will consume the fortresses of Kerioth.[b]
Moab will go down in great tumult
amid war cries and the blast of the trumpet.
[3]I will destroy her ruler[d]
and kill all her officials with him,"[e]
says the LORD.

[4]This is what the LORD says:

"For three sins of Judah,[f]
even for four, I will not turn back ⌊my wrath⌋.
Because they have rejected the law[g] of the LORD
and have not kept his decrees,[h]
because they have been led astray[i] by false gods,[c][j]
the gods[d] their ancestors followed,[k]
[5]I will send fire upon Judah
that will consume the fortresses of Jerusalem.[l]"

[6]This is what the LORD says:

"For three sins of Israel,
even for four, I will not turn back ⌊my wrath⌋.
They sell the righteous for silver,
and the needy for a pair of sandals.[m]
[7]They trample on the heads of the poor
as upon the dust of the ground
and deny justice to the oppressed.
Father and son use the same girl
and so profane my holy name.[n]

1:13 [a]Hos 13:16
1:14 [b]Dt 3:11 [c]Am 2:2
2:3 [d]Ps 2:10 [e]Isa 40:23
2:4 [f]2Ki 17:19; Hos 12:2 [g]Jer 6:19 [h]Eze 20:24 [i]Isa 9:16 [j]Isa 28:15 [k]2Ki 22:13; Jer 16:12
2:5 [l]Jer 17:27; Hos 8:14
2:6 [m]Joel 3:3; Am 8:6
2:7 [n]Am 5:11-12; 8:4

[a]15 Or / *Molech*; Hebrew *malcam* [b]2 Or *of her cities* [c]4 Or *by lies* [d]4 Or *lies*

2:8
[a]Ex 22:26
[b]Am 4:1; 6:6

2:9
[c]Nu 21:23-26; Jos 10:12
[d]Eze 17:9; Mal 4:1

2:10
[e]Ex 20:2; Am 3:1
[f]Dt 2:7
[g]Ex 3:8; Am 9:7

2:11
[h]Dt 18:18; Jer 7:25
[i]Nu 6:2-3; Jdg 13:5

2:12
[j]Isa 30:10; Jer 11:21; Am 7:12-13; Mic 2:6

2:14
[k]Jer 9:23
[l]Ps 33:16; Isa 30:16-17

2:15
[m]Eze 39:3

2:16
[n]Jer 48:41

3:1
[o]Am 2:10

3:2
[p]Dt 7:6; Lk 12:47
[q]Jer 14:10

3:4
[r]Ps 104:21; Hos 5:14

8They lie down beside every altar
on garments taken in pledge.[a]
In the house of their god
they drink wine[b] taken as fines.

9"I destroyed the Amorite[c] before them,
though he was tall as the cedars
and strong as the oaks.
I destroyed his fruit above
and his roots[d] below.

10"I brought you up out of Egypt,[e]
and I led you forty years in the desert[f]
to give you the land of the Amorites.[g]
11I also raised up prophets[h] from among your sons
and Nazirites[i] from among your young men.
Is this not true, people of Israel?"
declares the LORD.

12"But you made the Nazirites drink wine
and commanded the prophets not to prophesy.[j]

13"Now then, I will crush you
as a cart crushes when loaded with grain.
14The swift will not escape,
the strong[k] will not muster their strength,
and the warrior will not save his life.[l]
15The archer[m] will not stand his ground,
the fleet-footed soldier will not get away,
and the horseman will not save his life.
16Even the bravest warriors[n]
will flee naked on that day,"
declares the LORD.

Chapter 3 Theme ____________________

3 Hear this word the LORD has spoken against you, O people of Israel—against the whole family I brought up out of Egypt:[o]

2"You only have I chosen[p]
of all the families of the earth;
therefore I will punish you
for all your sins.[q]"

3Do two walk together
unless they have agreed to do so?
4Does a lion roar in the thicket
when he has no prey?[r]
Does he growl in his den
when he has caught nothing?

[5]Does a bird fall into a trap on the ground
where no snare has been set?
Does a trap spring up from the earth
when there is nothing to catch?
[6]When a trumpet sounds in a city,
do not the people tremble?
When disaster comes to a city,
has not the LORD caused it?[a]

[7]Surely the Sovereign LORD does nothing
without revealing his plan[b]
to his servants the prophets.[c]

[8]The lion has roared—
who will not fear?
The Sovereign LORD has spoken—
who can but prophesy?[d]

[9]Proclaim to the fortresses of Ashdod
and to the fortresses of Egypt:
"Assemble yourselves on the mountains of Samaria;[e]
see the great unrest within her
and the oppression among her people."

[10]"They do not know how to do right,[f]" declares the LORD,
"who hoard plunder[g] and loot in their fortresses."[h]
[11]Therefore this is what the Sovereign LORD says:

"An enemy will overrun the land;
he will pull down your strongholds
and plunder your fortresses.[i]"

[12]This is what the LORD says:

"As a shepherd saves from the lion's[j] mouth
only two leg bones or a piece of an ear,
so will the Israelites be saved,
those who sit in Samaria
on the edge of their beds
and in Damascus on their couches.[a][k]"

[13]"Hear this and testify[l] against the house of Jacob," declares
the Lord, the LORD God Almighty.

[14]"On the day I punish Israel for her sins,
I will destroy the altars of Bethel;[m]
the horns of the altar will be cut off
and fall to the ground.

[a] *12* The meaning of the Hebrew for this line is uncertain.

3:6 [a]Isa 14:24-27; 45:7
3:7 [b]Ge 18:17; Da 9:22; Jn 15:15; Rev 10:7 [c]Jer 23:22
3:8 [d]Jer 20:9; Jnh 1:1-3; 3:1-3; Ac 4:20
3:9 [e]Am 4:1; 6:1
3:10 [f]Jer 4:22; Am 5:7; 6:12 [g]Hab 2:8 [h]Zep 1:9
3:11 [i]Am 2:5; 6:14
3:12 [j]1Sa 17:34 [k]Am 6:4
3:13 [l]Eze 2:7
3:14 [m]Am 5:5-6

3:15 [a]Jer 36:22 [b]Jdg 3:20 [c]1Ki 22:39

15 I will tear down the winter house[a]
along with the summer house;[b]
the houses adorned with ivory[c] will be destroyed
and the mansions will be demolished,"
declares the LORD.

4:1 [d]Ps 22:12; Eze 39:18 [e]Am 3:9 [f]Am 2:8; 5:11; 8:6

Chapter 4 Theme ______________________________

4 Hear this word, you cows of Bashan[d] on Mount Samaria,[e]
you women who oppress the poor and crush the needy
and say to your husbands, "Bring us some drinks![f]"
2 The Sovereign LORD has sworn by his holiness:
"The time will surely come
when you will be taken away[g] with hooks,
the last of you with fishhooks.
3 You will each go straight out
through breaks in the wall,[h]
and you will be cast out toward Harmon,[a]"
declares the LORD.

4:2 [g]Am 6:8

4:3 [h]Eze 12:5

4 "Go to Bethel and sin;
go to Gilgal[i] and sin yet more.
Bring your sacrifices every morning,[j]
your tithes[k] every three years.[b][l]
5 Burn leavened bread[m] as a thank offering
and brag about your freewill offerings[n]—
boast about them, you Israelites,
for this is what you love to do,"
declares the Sovereign LORD.

4:4 [i]Hos 4:15 [j]Nu 28:3 [k]Dt 14:28 [l]Eze 20:39; Am 5:21-22

4:5 [m]Lev 7:13 [n]Lev 22:18-21

6 "I gave you empty stomachs[c] in every city
and lack of bread in every town,
yet you have not returned to me,"
declares the LORD.[o]

4:6 [o]Isa 3:1; Jer 5:3; Hag 2:17

7 "I also withheld rain from you
when the harvest was still three months away.
I sent rain on one town,
but withheld it from another.[p]
One field had rain;
another had none and dried up.
8 People staggered from town to town for water[q]
but did not get enough to drink,
yet you have not returned[r] to me,"
declares the LORD.[s]

4:7 [p]Ex 9:4,26; Dt 11:17; 2Ch 7:13

4:8 [q]Eze 4:16-17 [r]Jer 3:7 [s]Jer 14:4

[a] 3 Masoretic Text; with a different word division of the Hebrew (see Septuagint) *out, O mountain of oppression* [b] 4 Or *tithes on the third day* [c] 6 Hebrew *you cleanness of teeth*

9"Many times I struck your gardens and vineyards,
I struck them with blight and mildew.[a]
Locusts devoured your fig and olive trees,[b]
yet you have not returned[c] to me,"
declares the LORD.

10"I sent plagues[d] among you
as I did to Egypt.
I killed your young men with the sword,
along with your captured horses.
I filled your nostrils with the stench of your camps,
yet you have not returned to me,"
declares the LORD.[e]

11"I overthrew some of you
as I[a] overthrew Sodom and Gomorrah.[f]
You were like a burning stick snatched from the fire,
yet you have not returned to me,"
declares the LORD.

12"Therefore this is what I will do to you, Israel,
and because I will do this to you,
prepare to meet your God, O Israel."

13He who forms the mountains,[g]
creates the wind,
and reveals his thoughts[h] to man,
he who turns dawn to darkness,
and treads the high places of the earth[i]—
the LORD God Almighty is his name.[j]

Chapter 5 Theme ____________________

5 Hear this word, O house of Israel, this lament[k] I take up concerning you:

2"Fallen is Virgin[l] Israel,
never to rise again,
deserted in her own land,
with no one to lift her up.[m]"

3This is what the Sovereign LORD says:

"The city that marches out a thousand strong for Israel
will have only a hundred left;
the town that marches out a hundred strong
will have only ten left.[n]"

4This is what the LORD says to the house of Israel:

[a] 11 Hebrew *God*

4:9 [a]Dt 28:22 [b]Joel 1:7 [c]Jer 3:10; Hag 2:17

4:10 [d]Ex 9:3; Dt 28:27 [e]Isa 9:13

4:11 [f]Ge 19:24; Jer 23:14

4:13 [g]Ps 65:6 [h]Da 2:28 [i]Mic 1:3 [j]Isa 47:4; Am 5:8,27; 9:6

5:1 [k]Eze 19:1

5:2 [l]Jer 14:17 [m]Jer 50:32; Am 8:14

5:3 [n]Isa 6:13; Am 6:9

"Seek me and live;[a]
5 do not seek Bethel,
do not go to Gilgal,[b]
do not journey to Beersheba.[c]
For Gilgal will surely go into exile,
and Bethel will be reduced to nothing.[a][d]"
6Seek[e] the LORD and live,[f]
or he will sweep through the house of Joseph like a fire;[g]
it will devour,
and Bethel[h] will have no one to quench it.

7You who turn justice into bitterness[i]
and cast righteousness to the ground
8(he who made the Pleiades and Orion,[j]
who turns blackness into dawn[k]
and darkens day into night,[l]
who calls for the waters of the sea
and pours them out over the face of the land—
the LORD is his name[m]—
9he flashes destruction on the stronghold
and brings the fortified city to ruin),[n]
10you hate the one who reproves in court[o]
and despise him who tells the truth.[p]

11You trample on the poor[q]
and force him to give you grain.
Therefore, though you have built stone mansions,[r]
you will not live in them;
though you have planted lush vineyards,
you will not drink their wine.[s]
12For I know how many are your offenses
and how great your sins.

You oppress the righteous and take bribes
and you deprive the poor of justice in the courts.[t]
13Therefore the prudent man keeps quiet in such times,
for the times are evil.

14Seek good, not evil,
that you may live.
Then the LORD God Almighty will be with you,
just as you say he is.
15Hate evil,[u] love good;
maintain justice in the courts.
Perhaps the LORD God Almighty will have mercy[v]
on the remnant[w] of Joseph.

5:4 [a]Isa 55:3; Jer 29:13
5:5 [b]1Sa 11:14; Am 4:4 [c]Am 8:14 [d]1Sa 7:16
5:6 [e]Isa 55:6 [f]ver 14 [g]Dt 4:24 [h]Am 3:14
5:7 [i]Am 6:12
5:8 [j]Job 9:9 [k]Isa 42:16 [l]Ps 104:20; Am 8:9 [m]Ps 104:6-9; Am 4:13
5:9 [n]Mic 5:11
5:10 [o]Isa 29:21 [p]1Ki 22:8
5:11 [q]Am 8:6 [r]Am 3:15 [s]Mic 6:15
5:12 [t]Isa 5:23; Am 2:6-7
5:15 [u]Ps 97:10; Ro 12:9 [v]Joel 2:14 [w]Mic 5:7,8

[a]5 Or *grief*; or *wickedness*; Hebrew *aven*, a reference to Beth Aven (a derogatory name for Bethel)

16Therefore this is what the Lord, the LORD God Almighty, says:

"There will be wailing[a] in all the streets
and cries of anguish in every public square.
The farmers[b] will be summoned to weep
and the mourners to wail.
17There will be wailing in all the vineyards,
for I will pass through[c] your midst,"
says the LORD.[d]

18Woe to you who long
for the day of the LORD![e]
Why do you long for the day of the LORD?
That day will be darkness,[f] not light.[g]
19It will be as though a man fled from a lion
only to meet a bear,
as though he entered his house
and rested his hand on the wall
only to have a snake bite him.[h]
20Will not the day of the LORD be darkness, not light—
pitch-dark, without a ray of brightness?[i]

21"I hate, I despise your religious feasts;[j]
I cannot stand your assemblies.[k]
22Even though you bring me burnt offerings and
grain offerings,
I will not accept them.
Though you bring choice fellowship offerings,[a]
I will have no regard for them.[l m]
23Away with the noise of your songs!
I will not listen to the music of your harps.[n]
24But let justice[o] roll on like a river,
righteousness like a never-failing stream![p]

25"Did you bring me sacrifices[q] and offerings
forty years[r] in the desert, O house of Israel?
26You have lifted up the shrine of your king,
the pedestal of your idols,
the star of your god[b]—
which you made for yourselves.
27Therefore I will send you into exile beyond Damascus,"
says the LORD, whose name is God Almighty.[s]

Chapter 6 Theme ________________________

6

Woe to you[t] who are complacent in Zion,
and to you who feel secure on Mount Samaria,

a 22 Traditionally *peace offerings* b 26 Or *lifted up Sakkuth your king / and Kaiwan your idols, / your star-gods*; Septuagint *lifted up the shrine of Molech / and the star of your god Rephan, / their idols*

5:16
[a]Jer 9:17
[b]Joel 1:11

5:17
[c]Ex 12:12
[d]Isa 16:10; Jer 48:33

5:18
[e]Joel 1:15
[f]Joel 2:2
[g]Isa 5:19,30; Jer 30:7

5:19
[h]Job 20:24; Isa 24:17-18; Jer 15:2-3; 48:44

5:20
[i]Isa 13:10; Zep 1:15

5:21
[j]Lev 26:31
[k]Isa 1:11-16

5:22
[l]Am 4:4; Mic 6:6-7
[m]Isa 66:3

5:23
[n]Am 6:5

5:24
[o]Jer 22:3
[p]Mic 6:8

5:25
[q]Isa 43:23
[r]Dt 32:17

5:27
[s]Am 4:13; Ac 7:42-43*

6:1
[t]Lk 6:24

14For the LORD God Almighty declares,
"I will stir up a nation[a] against you, O house of Israel,
that will oppress you all the way
from Lebo[a] Hamath[b] to the valley of the Arabah.[c]"

Chapter 7 Theme ____________

7 This is what the Sovereign LORD showed me:[d] He was preparing
swarms of locusts[e] after the king's share had been harvested and
just as the second crop was coming up. 2When they had stripped
the land clean,[f] I cried out, "Sovereign LORD, forgive! How can
Jacob survive?[g] He is so small![h]"
3So the LORD relented.[i]
"This will not happen," the LORD said.[j]
4This is what the Sovereign LORD showed me: The Sovereign
LORD was calling for judgment by fire;[k] it dried up the great deep
and devoured[l] the land. 5Then I cried out, "Sovereign LORD, I beg
you, stop! How can Jacob survive? He is so small![m]"
6So the LORD relented.[n]
"This will not happen either," the Sovereign LORD said.

7This is what he showed me: The Lord was standing by a wall
that had been built true to plumb, with a plumb line in his hand.
8And the LORD asked me, "What do you see,[o] Amos?[p]"
"A plumb line,[q]" I replied.
Then the Lord said, "Look, I am setting a plumb line among
my people Israel; I will spare them no longer.[r]

9"The high places of Isaac will be destroyed
and the sanctuaries[s] of Israel will be ruined;
with my sword I will rise against the house of
Jeroboam.[t]"

10Then Amaziah the priest of Bethel[u] sent a message to Jeroboam[v] king of Israel: "Amos is raising a conspiracy[w] against you
in the very heart of Israel. The land cannot bear all his words.[x]
11For this is what Amos is saying:

"'Jeroboam will die by the sword,
and Israel will surely go into exile,
away from their native land.'"

12Then Amaziah said to Amos, "Get out, you seer! Go back to
the land of Judah. Earn your bread there and do your prophesying there.[y] 13Don't prophesy anymore at Bethel, because this is
the king's sanctuary and the temple of the kingdom.[z]"
14Amos answered Amaziah, "I was neither a prophet[a] nor a

a 14 Or *from the entrance to*

6:14 [a] Jer 5:15 [b] 1Ki 8:65 [c] Am 3:11

7:1 [d] Am 8:1 [e] Joel 1:4

7:2 [f] Ex 10:15 [g] Isa 37:4 [h] Eze 11:13

7:3 [i] Dt 32:36; Jer 26:19; Jnh 3:10 [j] Hos 11:8

7:4 [k] Isa 66:16 [l] Dt 32:22

7:5 [m] ver 1-2; Joel 2:17

7:6 [n] Jnh 3:10

7:8 [o] Jer 1:11,13 [p] Isa 28:17; La 2:8; Am 8:2 [q] 2Ki 21:13 [r] Jer 15:6; Eze 7:2-9

7:9 [s] Lev 26:31 [t] 2Ki 15:9; Isa 63:18; Hos 10:8

7:10 [u] 1Ki 12:32 [v] 2Ki 14:23 [w] Jer 38:4 [x] Jer 26:8-11

7:12 [y] Mt 8:34

7:13 [z] Am 2:12; Ac 4:18

7:14 [a] 2Ki 2:5; 4:38

you notable men of the foremost nation,
to whom the people of Israel come![a]
2 Go to Calneh[b] and look at it;
go from there to great Hamath,[c]
and then go down to Gath[d] in Philistia.
Are they better off than[e] your two kingdoms?
Is their land larger than yours?
3 You put off the evil day
and bring near a reign of terror.[f]
4 You lie on beds inlaid with ivory
and lounge on your couches.
You dine on choice lambs
and fattened calves.[g]
5 You strum away on your harps[h] like David
and improvise on musical instruments.[i]
6 You drink wine[j] by the bowlful
and use the finest lotions,
but you do not grieve[k] over the ruin of Joseph.
7 Therefore you will be among the first to go into exile;
your feasting and lounging will end.

8 The Sovereign LORD has sworn by himself[l]—the LORD God
Almighty declares:

"I abhor[m] the pride of Jacob[n]
and detest his fortresses;
I will deliver up[o] the city
and everything in it.[p]"

9 If ten[q] men are left in one house, they too will die. 10 And if a
relative who is to burn the bodies[r] comes to carry them out of the
house and asks anyone still hiding there, "Is anyone with you?"
and he says, "No," then he will say, "Hush![s] We must not mention
the name of the LORD."

11 For the LORD has given the command,
and he will smash the great house[t] into pieces
and the small house into bits.[u]

12 Do horses run on the rocky crags?
Does one plow there with oxen?
But you have turned justice into poison[v]
and the fruit of righteousness into bitterness[w]—
13 you who rejoice in the conquest of Lo Debar[a]
and say, "Did we not take Karnaim[b] by our own
strength?[x]"

[a] 13 *Lo Debar* means *nothing.* [b] 13 *Karnaim* means *horns*; *horn* here symbolizes strength.

6:1 [a] Isa 32:9-11
6:2 [b] Ge 10:10 [c] 2Ki 18:34 [d] 2Ch 26:6 [e] Na 3:8
6:3 [f] Isa 56:12; Am 9:10
6:4 [g] Eze 34:2-3; Am 3:12
6:5 [h] Isa 5:12; Am 5:23 [i] 1Ch 15:16
6:6 [j] Am 2:8 [k] Eze 9:4
6:8 [l] Ge 22:16; Heb 6:13 [m] Lev 26:30 [n] Ps 47:4 [o] Am 4:2 [p] Dt 32:19
6:9 [q] Am 5:3
6:10 [r] 1Sa 31:12 [s] Am 8:3
6:11 [t] Am 3:15 [u] Isa 55:11
6:12 [v] Hos 10:4 [w] Am 5:7
6:13 [x] Job 8:15; Isa 28:14-15

7:15 [a]2Sa 7:8 prophet's son, but I was a shepherd, and I also took care of syc-
[b]Jer 7:1-2; amore-fig trees. 15But the LORD took me from tending the flock[a]
Eze 2:3-4 and said to me, 'Go, prophesy to my people Israel.'[b] 16Now then,
hear the word of the LORD. You say,

"'Do not prophesy against[c] Israel,
7:16 [c]Eze 20:46; and stop preaching against the house of Isaac.'
Mic 2:6

17"Therefore this is what the LORD says:

"'Your wife will become a prostitute[d] in the city,
7:17 and your sons and daughters will fall by the sword.
[d]Hos 4:13 [e]2Ki 17:6; Your land will be measured and divided up,
Eze 4:13; and you yourself will die in a pagan[a] country.
Hos 9:3 And Israel will certainly go into exile,
away from their native land.[e]'"

Chapter 8 Theme ____________________

8:2 [f]Jer 24:3 **8** This is what the Sovereign LORD showed me: a basket of ripe
[g]Am 7:8 [h]Eze 7:2-9 fruit. 2"What do you see,[f] Amos?[g]" he asked.
"A basket of ripe fruit," I answered.
Then the LORD said to me, "The time is ripe for my people Israel;
8:3 [i]Am 5:16 I will spare them no longer.[h]
[j]Am 5:23; 6:10 3"In that day," declares the Sovereign LORD, "the songs in the
temple will turn to wailing.[b][i] Many, many bodies—flung everywhere! Silence![j]"

8:4 [k]Pr 30:14 4Hear this, you who trample the needy
[l]Ps 14:4; Am 2:7 and do away with the poor[k] of the land,[l]

5saying,

"When will the New Moon be over
8:5 that we may sell grain,
[m]2Ki 4:23; Ne 13:15-16; and the Sabbath be ended
Hos 12:7; Mic 6:10-11 that we may market wheat?"—
skimping the measure,
boosting the price
and cheating with dishonest scales,[m]
8:6 [n]Am 2:6 6buying the poor with silver
and the needy for a pair of sandals,
selling even the sweepings with the wheat.[n]

8:7 [o]Am 6:8 7The LORD has sworn by the Pride of Jacob:[o] "I will never forget[p]
[p]Hos 8:13 anything they have done.

8"Will not the land tremble[q] for this,
and all who live in it mourn?

8:8 [q]Hos 4:3

[a]17 Hebrew *an unclean* [b]3 Or *"the temple singers will wail*

The whole land will rise like the Nile;
it will be stirred up and then sink
like the river of Egypt.[a]

9"In that day," declares the Sovereign LORD,

"I will make the sun go down at noon
and darken the earth in broad daylight.[b]
10I will turn your religious feasts into mourning
and all your singing into weeping.
I will make all of you wear sackcloth[c]
and shave your heads.
I will make that time like mourning for an only son[d]
and the end of it like a bitter day.[e]

11"The days are coming," declares the Sovereign LORD,
"when I will send a famine through the land—
not a famine of food or a thirst for water,
but a famine of hearing the words of the LORD.[f]
12Men will stagger from sea to sea
and wander from north to east,
searching for the word of the LORD,
but they will not find it.[g]

13"In that day

"the lovely young women and strong young men
will faint because of thirst.[h]
14They who swear by the shame[a] of Samaria,
or say, 'As surely as your god lives, O Dan,'[i]
or, 'As surely as the god[b] of Beersheba[j] lives'—
they will fall,
never to rise again.[k]"

Chapter 9 Theme

9 I saw the Lord standing by the altar, and he said:

"Strike the tops of the pillars
so that the thresholds shake.
Bring them down on the heads[l] of all the people;
those who are left I will kill with the sword.
Not one will get away,
none will escape.
2Though they dig down to the depths of the grave,[c][m]
from there my hand will take them.
Though they climb up to the heavens,[n]
from there I will bring them down.[o]

8:8 [a]Ps 18:7; Jer 46:8; Am 9:5
8:9 [b]Job 5:14; Isa 59:9-10; Jer 15:9; Am 5:8; Mic 3:6
8:10 [c]Jer 48:37 [d]Jer 6:26; Zec 12:10 [e]Eze 7:18
8:11 [f]1Sa 3:1; 2Ch 15:3; Eze 7:26
8:12 [g]Eze 20:3,31
8:13 [h]Isa 41:17; Hos 2:3
8:14 [i]1Ki 12:29 [j]Am 5:5 [k]Am 5:2
9:1 [l]Ps 68:21
9:2 [m]Ps 139:8 [n]Jer 51:53 [o]Ob 4

[a]14 Or *by Ashima*; or *by the idol* [b]14 Or *power* [c]2 Hebrew *to Sheol*

3 Though they hide themselves on the top of Carmel,[a]
there I will hunt them down and seize them.[b]
Though they hide from me at the bottom of the sea,
there I will command the serpent to bite them.[c]
4 Though they are driven into exile by their enemies,
there I will command the sword[d] to slay them.
I will fix my eyes upon them
for evil[e] and not for good.[f]"[g]

5 The Lord, the LORD Almighty,
he who touches the earth and it melts,[h]
and all who live in it mourn—
the whole land rises like the Nile,
then sinks like the river of Egypt[i]—
6 he who builds his lofty palace[a] in the heavens
and sets its foundation[b] on the earth,
who calls for the waters of the sea
and pours them out over the face of the land—
the LORD is his name.[j]

7 "Are not you Israelites
the same to me as the Cushites[c]?"[k]
declares the LORD.

"Did I not bring Israel up from Egypt,
the Philistines from Caphtor[d][l]
and the Arameans from Kir?[m]

8 "Surely the eyes of the Sovereign LORD
are on the sinful kingdom.
I will destroy it
from the face of the earth—
yet I will not totally destroy
the house of Jacob,"
declares the LORD.[n]

9 "For I will give the command,
and I will shake the house of Israel
among all the nations
as grain[o] is shaken in a sieve,[p]
and not a pebble will reach the ground.
10 All the sinners among my people
will die by the sword,
all those who say,
'Disaster will not overtake or meet us.'[q]

11 "In that day I will restore
David's fallen tent.

9:3 [a] Am 1:2 [b] Ps 139:8-10 [c] Jer 16:16-17
9:4 [d] Lev 26:33; Eze 5:12 [e] Jer 21:10 [f] Jer 39:16 [g] Jer 44:11
9:5 [h] Ps 46:2; Mic 1:4 [i] Am 8:8
9:6 [j] Ps 104:1-3, 5-6,13; Am 5:8
9:7 [k] Isa 20:4; 43:3 [l] Dt 2:23; Jer 47:4 [m] 2Ki 16:9; Isa 22:6; Am 1:5; 2:10
9:8 [n] Jer 44:27
9:9 [o] Lk 22:31 [p] Isa 30:28
9:10 [q] Am 6:3

[a] 6 The meaning of the Hebrew for this phrase is uncertain. [b] 6 The meaning of the Hebrew for this word is uncertain. [c] 7 That is, people from the upper Nile region [d] 7 That is, Crete

I will repair its broken places,
restore its ruins,
and build it as it used to be,[a]
12so that they may possess the remnant of Edom[b]
and all the nations that bear my name,[a][c]"
declares the LORD, who will do these things.[d]

13"The days are coming," declares the LORD,

"when the reaper will be overtaken by the plowman[e]
and the planter by the one treading grapes.
New wine will drip from the mountains
and flow from all the hills.[f]
14I will bring back my exiled[b] people Israel;
they will rebuild the ruined cities[g] and live in them.
They will plant vineyards and drink their wine;
they will make gardens and eat their fruit.[h]
15I will plant[i] Israel in their own land,
never again to be uprooted
from the land I have given them,"

says the LORD your God.[j]

a *12* Hebrew; Septuagint *so that the remnant of men / and all the nations that bear my name may seek ⌊the Lord⌋* b *14* Or *will restore the fortunes of my*

9:11 [a]Ps 80:12

9:12 [b]Nu 24:18 [c]Isa 43:7 [d]Ac 15:16-17*

9:13 [e]Lev 26:5 [f]Joel 3:18

9:14 [g]Isa 61:4 [h]Jer 30:18; 31:28; Eze 28:25-26

9:15 [i]Isa 60:21 [j]Jer 24:6; Eze 34:25-28; 37:12,25

eme of Amos:

thor:

te:

rpose:

y Words:

SEGMENT DIVISIONS		CHAPTER THEMES
		1
		2
		3
		4
		5
		6
		7
		8
		9

OBADIAH

God said that whoever touched Israel touched the apple (pupil) of his eye. According to Obadiah 1:10-14, Edom had touched God's eye.

Scholars are divided about whether the incident referred to in these verses occurred during the reign of Jehoram (853-841 B.C.), when the Philistines and the Arabs invaded Jerusalem or during Babylon's sieges of Jerusalem (between 605 and 586 B.C.). However, the exact date is not critical to the message of the book. What we do know is that in both instances Edom did not respond as God wanted, and thus comes this report from the Lord. It came as a word through "the Lord's servant," which is the meaning of Obadiah's name.

THINGS TO DO

1. Read this book once without stopping in order to get an overview of Obadiah's message.

2. Read through Obadiah, and in a distinctive way mark the key words listed on the OBADIAH AT A GLANCE chart on page 1586.

3. Remember that Jacob and Esau were brothers, born to Rebekah and Isaac. If you want to refresh your memory, read Genesis 27:1–28:9 and 32:1–33:20; Romans 9:10-13; and Numbers 20:14-21. Genesis 36 gives the genealogy of Esau and says, "Esau (that is, Edom)." It also names Esau as the father of the Edomites.

   Although the people of Edom (descendants of Esau) and Israel (descendants of Jacob) are related (Amos 1:11, 12), biblical history records many conflicts between them. Look at the map on page 1584 and notice the proximity of Edom to Israel. Edom was a constant threat to Israel, repeatedly thwarting the nation and blocking Judean access to the Gulf of Aqaba.

4. Now read through Obadiah again, asking the five W's and an H. Ask questions such as: Who is writing? To whom? Why? What is being written about? What is going to happen? To whom? How? Summarize your observations in the margin of the text.

5. Look at the map and find the Negev and the other places mentioned at the end of Obadiah. These are real lands and real people, and what God says will happen to them *will* happen.

6. Since Obadiah is just one chapter, record the theme (subject) of each paragraph on OBADIAH AT A GLANCE and then fill in the rest of the chart, including the theme of Obadiah.

7. The day of the Lord is an important day prophetically. Beginning on page 2178 you will find a chart titled THE DAY OF THE LORD. Record your insights on the day of the Lord on this chart. As you do so, note the reference (book, chapter, and verse) that you took your information from so you can find it later.

THINGS TO THINK ABOUT

1. Sometimes when tragic and unjust things happen, we wonder where God is. If he is righteous, just, and omnipotent, why doesn't he intervene? What do you learn from Obadiah that helps answer these questions? What do you learn from this for your own life?

2. How should we respond to the tragedies of others, the dark hours of our enemies? What does God think when we use their tragedy to our advantage?

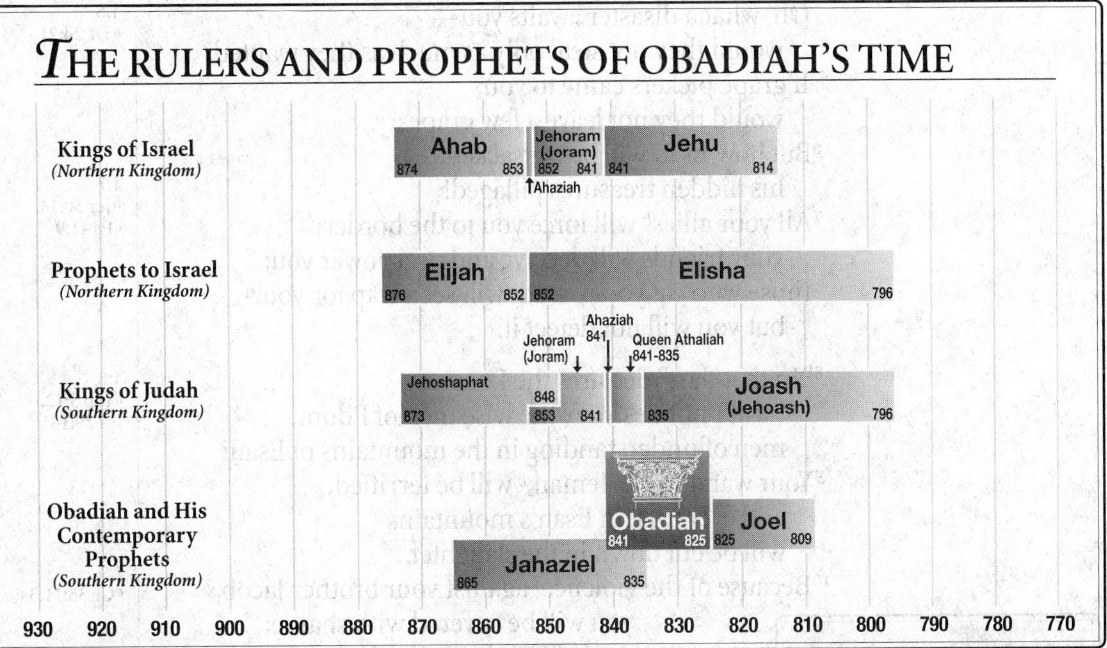

1:1
[a]Isa 63:1-6;
Jer 49:7-22;
Eze 25:12-14;
Am 1:11-12
[b]Isa 18:2
[c]Jer 6:4-5

1:3
[d]Isa 16:6
[e]Isa 14:13-15;
Rev 18:7

1:4
[f]Hab 2:9
[g]Isa 14:13
[h]Job 20:6

Chapter Theme ____________________

1 The vision of Obadiah.

This is what the Sovereign LORD says about Edom[a]—

We have heard a message from the LORD:
An envoy[b] was sent to the nations to say,
"Rise, and let us go against her for battle"[c]—

2 "See, I will make you small among the nations;
you will be utterly despised.
3 The pride[d] of your heart has deceived you,
you who live in the clefts of the rocks[a]
and make your home on the heights,
you who say to yourself,
'Who can bring me down to the ground?'[e]
4 Though you soar like the eagle
and make your nest[f] among the stars,
from there I will bring you down,"[g]
declares the LORD.[h]

5 "If thieves came to you,
if robbers in the night—

[a]3 Or *of Sela*

Oh, what a disaster awaits you—
would they not steal only as much as they wanted?
If grape pickers came to you,
would they not leave a few grapes?[a]
6But how Esau will be ransacked,
his hidden treasures pillaged!
7All your allies[b] will force you to the border;
your friends will deceive and overpower you;
those who eat your bread[c] will set a trap for you,[a]
but you will not detect it.

8"In that day," declares the LORD,
"will I not destroy[d] the wise men of Edom,
men of understanding in the mountains of Esau?
9Your warriors, O Teman,[e] will be terrified,
and everyone in Esau's mountains
will be cut down in the slaughter.
10Because of the violence[f] against your brother Jacob,[g]
you will be covered with shame;
you will be destroyed forever.[h]
11On the day you stood aloof
while strangers carried off his wealth
and foreigners entered his gates
and cast lots[i] for Jerusalem,
you were like one of them.
12You should not look down on your brother
in the day of his misfortune,
nor rejoice[j] over the people of Judah
in the day of their destruction,[k]
nor boast so much
in the day of their trouble.[l]
13You should not march through the gates of
my people
in the day of their disaster,
nor look down on them in their calamity[m]
in the day of their disaster,
nor seize their wealth
in the day of their disaster.
14You should not wait at the crossroads
to cut down their fugitives,
nor hand over their survivors
in the day of their trouble.

15"The day of the LORD is near[n]
for all nations.

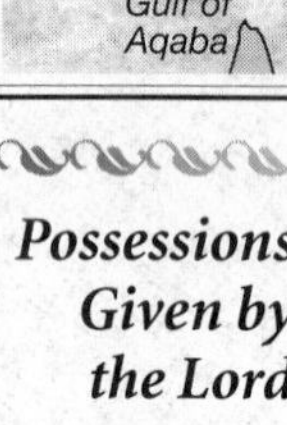

Possessions Given by the Lord

1:5 [a]Dt 24:21
1:7 [b]Jer 30:14 [c]Ps 41:9
1:8 [d]Job 5:12; Isa 29:14
1:9 [e]Ge 36:11,34
1:10 [f]Joel 3:19 [g]Ps 137:7; Am 1:11-12 [h]Eze 35:9
1:11 [i]Na 3:10
1:12 [j]Eze 35:15 [k]Pr 17:5 [l]Mic 4:11
1:13 [m]Eze 35:5
1:15 [n]Eze 30:3

a7 The meaning of the Hebrew for this clause is uncertain.

1:15 [a] Jer 50:29; Hab 2:8

As you have done, it will be done to you;
your deeds[a] will return upon your own head.
16 Just as you drank on my holy hill,
so all the nations will drink[b] continually;
they will drink and drink
and be as if they had never been.

1:16 [b] Jer 25:15; 49:12

17 But on Mount Zion will be deliverance;[c]
it will be holy,[d]
and the house of Jacob
will possess its inheritance.

1:17 [c] Am 9:11-15 [d] Isa 4:3

18 The house of Jacob will be a fire
and the house of Joseph a flame;
the house of Esau will be stubble,
and they will set it on fire and consume[e] it.
There will be no survivors
from the house of Esau."
The LORD has spoken.

1:18 [e] Zec 12:6

19 People from the Negev will occupy
the mountains of Esau,
and people from the foothills will possess
the land of the Philistines.[f]
They will occupy the fields of Ephraim and Samaria,[g]
and Benjamin will possess Gilead.

1:19 [f] Isa 11:14 [g] Jer 31:5

20 This company of Israelite exiles who are in Canaan
will possess ⌊the land⌋ as far as Zarephath;[h]
the exiles from Jerusalem who are in Sepharad
will possess the towns of the Negev.[i]

1:20 [h] 1Ki 17:9-10 [i] Jer 33:13

21 Deliverers will go up on[a] Mount Zion
to govern the mountains of Esau.
And the kingdom will be the LORD's.[j]

1:21 [j] Ps 22:28; Zec 14:9,16; Rev 11:15

[a] *21* Or *from*

Obadiah at a Glance

Theme of Obadiah:

Segment Divisions

		Paragraph Themes
		Verses 1-9
		Verses 10-14
		Verses 15-21

Author:

Date:

Purpose:

Key Words:

the day

Esau, Esau's (Edom)

Jacob (Judah

the nations (all nations)

Mount Zion (my holy hill

declares the Lord (or any phrase havin to do with th Lord speakin or reporting)

JONAH

Just before God commissioned Amos and then Hosea as prophets to the northern kingdom to warn Israel of the impending invasion by the Assyrians, he appointed the prophet Jonah to go to Nineveh, the capital of Assyria. Fifty years later, in 722 B.C., Assyria would take the northern kingdom into captivity.

God knew what Assyria would do. Why then did he bother to send Jonah to the wicked city of Nineveh? Because of who God is. The focus of Jonah is not a man trapped in the belly of a great fish; the focus is people engraved on the heart of God.

Things to Do

1. Before you read through Jonah, look up 2 Kings 14:23-27, which mentions Jonah and his ministry during the reign of Jeroboam II, king of Israel. At that time Shalmaneser IV was king of Assyria.
2. In the margin of each chapter list everything you learn about God. Note his character and ways as well as his response to a sinful people and a "wrong-way" prophet.
3. In a distinctive way mark the key words listed on the JONAH AT A GLANCE chart on page 1591.
4. Record the theme of each chapter on JONAH AT A GLANCE and in the text next to the chapter number. Then fill in the rest of the chart.
5. Contrast Jonah's heart with God's heart. Record your insights in the margin of chapter 4.

Things to Think About

1. What or who evokes compassion in your heart? How does your heart compare with God's? Does it long for the same things? Why?
2. Is there something that you know God wants you to do that you haven't done? What can you learn from Jonah's life?
3. How did Jesus view the story of Jonah? Read Matthew 12:39-41; 16:4. Will you accept as truth what Jesus accepted as fact—or did Jesus compare his resurrection to a mythological tale?

Chapter 1 Theme ____________________

1:1 [a]Mt 12:39-41 [b]2Ki 14:25

1 The word of the LORD came to Jonah[a] son of Amittai:[b] 2"Go to
the great city of Nineveh[c] and preach against it, because its
wickedness has come up before me."

1:2 [c]Ge 10:11

3But Jonah ran[d] away from the LORD and headed for Tarshish. He
went down to Joppa,[e] where he found a ship bound for that port.
After paying the fare, he went aboard and sailed for Tarshish to flee
from the LORD.

1:3 [d]Ps 139:7 [e]Jos 19:46; Ac 9:36,43

4Then the LORD sent a great wind on the sea, and such a violent
storm arose that the ship threatened to break up.[f] 5All the sailors
were afraid and each cried out to his own god. And they threw the
cargo into the sea to lighten the ship.[g]
But Jonah had gone below deck, where he lay down and fell into
a deep sleep. 6The captain went to him and said, "How can you

1:4 [f]Ps 107:23-26

1:5 [g]Ac 27:18-19

sleep? Get up and call[a] on your god! Maybe he will take notice of
us, and we will not perish."[b]
7Then the sailors said to each other, "Come, let us cast lots to
find out who is responsible for this calamity."[c] They cast lots and
the lot fell on Jonah.
8So they asked him, "Tell
us, who is responsible for
making all this trouble for
us? What do you do? Where
do you come from? What is
your country? From what
people are you?"
9He answered, "I am a
Hebrew and I worship the
LORD, the God of heaven,[d]
who made the sea and the
land.[e]"

Mediterranean Sea
Tarshish
Gath Hepher
Joppa
ISRAEL
JUDAH
Dead Sea
Nile River
Red Sea
Nineveh
Tigris River
Euphrates River
Persian Gulf (Lower Sea)

Jonah's Journey

10This terrified them and they asked, "What have you done?"
(They knew he was running away from the LORD, because he had
already told them so.)
11The sea was getting rougher and rougher. So they asked him,
"What should we do to you to make the sea calm down for us?"
12"Pick me up and throw me into the sea," he replied, "and it
will become calm. I know that it is my fault that this great storm
has come upon you."[f]
13Instead, the men did their best to row back to land. But they
could not, for the sea grew even wilder than before.[g] 14Then they
cried to the LORD, "O LORD, please do not let us die for taking this
man's life. Do not hold us accountable for killing an innocent
man,[h] for you, O LORD, have done as you pleased."[i] 15Then they
took Jonah and threw him overboard, and the raging sea grew
calm.[j] 16At this the men greatly feared[k] the LORD, and they offered a
sacrifice to the LORD and made vows to him.
17But the LORD provided a great fish to swallow Jonah,[l] and Jonah
was inside the fish three days and three nights.

Chapter 2 Theme ______________________

2 From inside the fish Jonah prayed to the LORD his God. 2He
said:

"In my distress I called to the LORD,[m]
 and he answered me.
From the depths of the grave[a] I called for help,
 and you listened to my cry.

[a]2 Hebrew *Sheol*

1:6 [a]Jnh 3:8 [b]Ps 107:28
1:7 [c]Jos 7:10-18; 1Sa 14:42
1:9 [d]Ac 17:24 [e]Ps 146:6
1:12 [f]2Sa 24:17; 1Ch 21:17
1:13 [g]Pr 21:30
1:14 [h]Dt 21:8 [i]Ps 115:3
1:15 [j]Ps 107:29; Lk 8:24
1:16 [k]Mk 4:41
1:17 [l]Mt 12:40; 16:4; Lk 11:30
2:2 [m]Ps 18:6; 120:1

2:3
[a]Ps 88:6
[b]Ps 42:7

2:4
[c]Ps 31:22

2:5
[d]Ps 69:1-2

2:7
[e]Ps 77:11-12

3You hurled me into the deep,[a]
into the very heart of the seas,
and the currents swirled about me;
all your waves and breakers
swept over me.[b]
4I said, 'I have been banished
from your sight;[c]
yet I will look again
toward your holy temple.'
5The engulfing waters threatened me,[a]
the deep surrounded me;
seaweed was wrapped around my head.[d]
6To the roots of the mountains I sank down;
the earth beneath barred me in forever.
But you brought my life up from the pit,
O LORD my God.

7"When my life was ebbing away,
I remembered[e] you, LORD,

[a]5 Or *waters were at my throat*

THE RULERS AND PROPHETS OF JONAH'S TIME

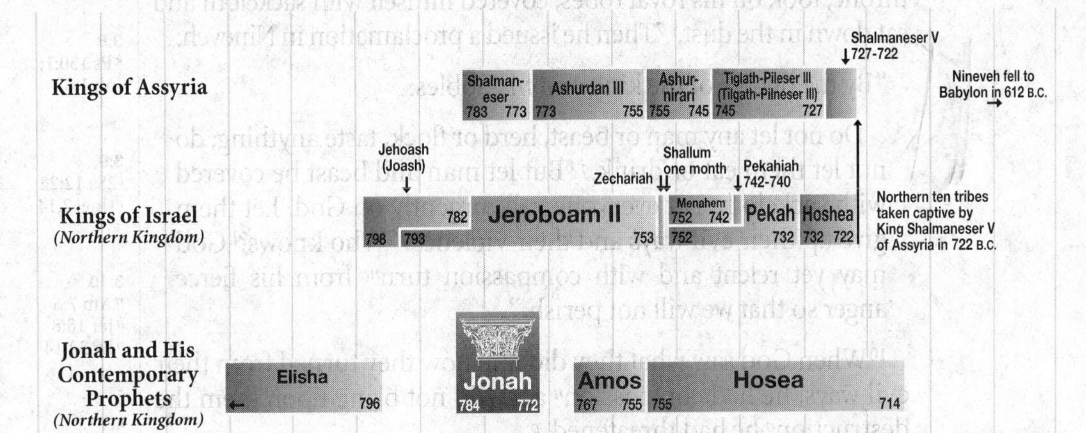

Kings of Assyria
Shalmaneser 783 773; Ashurdan III 773 755; Ashurnirari 755 745; Tiglath-Pileser III (Tilgath-Pilneser III) 745 727; Shalmaneser V 727-722
Nineveh fell to Babylon in 612 B.C.

Kings of Israel *(Northern Kingdom)*
Jehoash (Joash) 798; Jeroboam II 793 782 753; Zechariah; Shallum one month; Menahem 752 742; Pekahiah 742-740; Pekah 752 732; Hoshea 732 722
Northern ten tribes taken captive by King Shalmaneser V of Assyria in 722 B.C.

Jonah and His Contemporary Prophets *(Northern Kingdom)*
Elisha 796; Jonah 784 772; Amos 767 755; Hosea 755 714

Kings of Judah *(Southern Kingdom)*
Amaziah 796 767; Uzziah or Azariah 790 739; Jotham 750 731; Ahaz 735 715

Prophets to Judah *(Southern Kingdom)*
Joel 825 809; Isaiah 739 681; Micah 733 701

850 840 830 820 810 800 790 780 770 760 750 740 730 720 710 700 690

and my prayer[a] rose to you,
to your holy temple.[b]

8“Those who cling to worthless idols[c]
forfeit the grace that could be theirs.
9But I, with a song of thanksgiving,
will sacrifice[d] to you.
What I have vowed[e] I will make good.
Salvation[f] comes from the LORD.”

10And the LORD commanded the fish, and it vomited Jonah onto
dry land.

Chapter 3 Theme ______________________

3 Then the word of the LORD came to Jonah[g] a second time: 2“Go
to the great city of Nineveh and proclaim to it the message I
give you.”
3Jonah obeyed the word of the LORD and went to Nineveh. Now
Nineveh was a very important city—a visit required three days.
4On the first day, Jonah started into the city. He proclaimed: “Forty
more days and Nineveh will be overturned.” 5The Ninevites
believed God. They declared a fast, and all of them, from the greatest to the least, put on sackcloth.[h]
6When the news reached the king of Nineveh, he rose from his
throne, took off his royal robes, covered himself with sackcloth and
sat down in the dust.[i] 7Then he issued a proclamation in Nineveh:

“By the decree of the king and his nobles:

Do not let any man or beast, herd or flock, taste anything; do
not let them eat or drink.[j] 8But let man and beast be covered
with sackcloth. Let everyone call[k] urgently on God. Let them
give up their evil ways and their violence. 9Who knows?[l] God
may yet relent and with compassion turn[m] from his fierce
anger so that we will not perish.”

10When God saw what they did and how they turned from their
evil ways, he had compassion[n] and did not bring upon them the
destruction[o] he had threatened.[p]

Chapter 4 Theme ______________________

4 But Jonah was greatly displeased and became angry.[q] 2He
prayed to the LORD, “O LORD, is this not what I said when I was
still at home? That is why I was so quick to flee to Tarshish. I knew[r]
that you are a gracious and compassionate God, slow to anger and
abounding in love,[s] a God who relents from sending calamity.[t]
3Now, O LORD, take away my life,[u] for it is better for me to die[v] than
to live.”

2:7 [a]2Ch 30:27 [b]Ps 11:4; 18:6
2:8 [c]2Ki 17:15; Jer 10:8
2:9 [d]Ps 50:14,23; Hos 14:2 [e]Ecc 5:4-5 [f]Ps 3:8
3:1 [g]Jnh 1:1
3:5 [h]Da 9:3; Lk 11:32
3:6 [i]Job 2:8,13; Eze 27:30-31
3:7 [j]2Ch 20:3
3:8 [k]Ps 130:1; Jnh 1:6
3:9 [l]2Sa 12:22 [m]Joel 2:14
3:10 [n]Am 7:6 [o]Jer 18:8 [p]Ex 32:14
4:1 [q]ver 4; Lk 15:28
4:2 [r]Jer 20:7-8 [s]Ex 34:6; Ps 86:5,15 [t]Joel 2:13
4:3 [u]1Ki 19:4 [v]Job 7:15

4:4 [a] Mt 20:11-15 4But the LORD replied, "Have you any right to be angry?"[a]
5Jonah went out and sat down at a place east of the city. There he
made himself a shelter, sat in its shade and waited to see what
would happen to the city. 6Then the LORD God provided a vine
and made it grow up over Jonah to give shade for his head to ease
his discomfort, and Jonah was very happy about the vine. 7But at
dawn the next day God provided a worm, which chewed the vine
so that it withered.[b] 8When the sun rose, God provided a scorching
east wind, and the sun blazed on Jonah's head so that he grew
4:7 [b] Joel 1:12 faint. He wanted to die, and said, "It would be better for me to die
than to live."
9But God said to Jonah, "Do you have a right to be angry about
the vine?"
"I do," he said. "I am angry enough to die."
10But the LORD said, "You have been concerned about this vine,
though you did not tend it or make it grow. It sprang up overnight
and died overnight. 11But Nineveh[c] has more than a hundred and
twenty thousand people who cannot tell their right hand from
4:11 [c] Jnh 1:2; 3:2 their left, and many cattle as well. Should I not be concerned[d]
[d] Jnh 3:10 about that great city?"

JONAH AT A GLANCE

eme of Jonah:

SEGMENT DIVISIONS

		CHAPTER THEMES
		1
		2
		3
		4

thor:

te:

rpose:

y Words:

concerned (compassionate)
elent(s)
urn, give up (turned)
rayer (prayed)
erish (die)
ord
ried to the ord
called to the ord)

MICAH

Micah knew his calling and was ready to fulfill it, for Micah knew his God. What a contrast he is to the prophet Jonah! Micah, whose name means "who is like Jehovah," reminds a rebellious people that "the Lord is coming from his dwelling place."

Things to Do

1. Micah 1:1 gives the historical setting of Micah. Read it carefully and answer as many of the five W's and an H as you can concerning the who, when, where, why, what, and how of this book. Consult the historical chart at the beginning of Micah to see the book in context.

You will note that the reign of the three kings of Judah covers the years 750-686 B.C. Remember that Assyria conquered the northern kingdom in 722 B.C. and Babylon conquered the southern kingdom in 586 B.C.

2. For the historical background of the kings of Judah mentioned in Micah 1:1, read 2 Kings 15:32 through 20:21 and 2 Chronicles 27:1 through 33:20.

3. Read one chapter at a time. As you observe the text of each chapter:

   a. Mark the key words listed on the MICAH AT A GLANCE chart on page 1605. You will find it helpful to record these on an index card that you can use as a bookmark while you study Micah.

   b. Watch for references to time, such as *when, then, in that day, in the last days.* You might want to draw a symbol or note in some other way the references to time.

   c. Since Micah's prophecy concerns Samaria (representing the northern kingdom of Israel) and Jerusalem (representing the southern kingdom of Judah), next to the word *Samaria* in Micah 1:1 put "NK" for northern kingdom. Next to the word *Jerusalem* put "SK" for southern kingdom.

   As you observe the text, watch which kingdom Micah is referring to. Observe what is said regarding their sins, the consequences of their sin, their future, and the remnant. If it will help, list your insights in the margin.

   d. Watch what God is going to do and to whom. Always note to whom Micah is referring.

   e. In the margin list everything you learn about Micah and what he is to do.

   f. Record the theme or subject of each chapter on the line next to the chapter number in the text and on MICAH AT A GLANCE. When you finish the last chapter of Micah, complete the chart.

4. Beginning on page 2178 you will find a chart titled THE DAY OF THE LORD. Record your insights from Micah on the last days if you think these pertain to the day of the Lord. As you do so, note the reference (book, chapter, and verse) from which you took your information so you can find it later.

Things to Think About

1. Review what you have learned about God the Father and the Son in this book. Meditate on these truths. Tell God you want to know him more intimately and ask him to open the eyes of your understanding. Ask him to show you how to live in light of who he is.

2. Micah 4:12 says the nations do not know the thoughts of the Lord, nor do they understand his plan. Yet the child of God can know these things through studying his Word. Amos said, "Surely the Sovereign LORD does nothing without revealing his plan to his servants the prophets" (3:7). God's

secret counsel and his plan for the future is in the Word of God. Are you ordering your life in such a way that you take time to study his Word?

3. What have you learned about the unchanging love and compassion of God in pardoning your sins? Are you living accordingly?

4. Although you may not be able to trust in others, can you trust in God? Are you? Can he trust you? In Micah 6:6-8 God tells you how to approach him and what he requires. Will you live accordingly?

Chapter 1 Theme ______________________________

1 The word of the LORD that came to Micah of Moresheth[a] during
the reigns of Jotham,[b] Ahaz[c] and Hezekiah, kings of Judah[d]—
the vision[e] he saw concerning Samaria and Jerusalem.

2Hear, O peoples, all of you,[f]
listen, O earth[g] and all who are in it,
that the Sovereign LORD may witness[h] against you,
the Lord from his holy temple.[i]
3Look! The LORD is coming from his dwelling[j] place;
he comes down and treads the
high places of the earth.[k]
4The mountains melt[l] beneath him
and the valleys split apart,[m]
like wax before the fire,
like water rushing down a slope.
5All this is because of Jacob's transgression,
because of the sins of the house of Israel.
What is Jacob's transgression?
Is it not Samaria?[n]
What is Judah's high place?
Is it not Jerusalem?

6"Therefore I will make Samaria a heap of rubble,
a place for planting vineyards.
I will pour her stones[o] into the valley
and lay bare her foundations.[p]
7All her idols[q] will be broken to pieces;
all her temple gifts will be burned with fire;
I will destroy all her images.[r]
Since she gathered her gifts from the wages of prostitutes,[s]
as the wages of prostitutes they will again be used."

8Because of this I will weep[t] and wail;
I will go about barefoot and naked.
I will howl like a jackal
and moan like an owl.

1:1 [a]Jer 26:18 [b]1Ch 3:12 [c]1Ch 3:13 [d]Hos 1:1 [e]Isa 1:1

1:2 [f]Ps 50:7 [g]Jer 6:19 [h]Ge 31:50; Dt 4:26; Isa 1:2 [i]Ps 11:4

1:3 [j]Isa 18:4 [k]Am 4:13

1:4 [l]Ps 46:2,6 [m]Nu 16:31; Na 1:5

1:5 [n]Am 8:14

1:6 [o]Am 5:11 [p]Eze 13:14

1:7 [q]Eze 6:6 [r]Dt 9:21 [s]Dt 23:17-18

1:8 [t]Isa 15:3

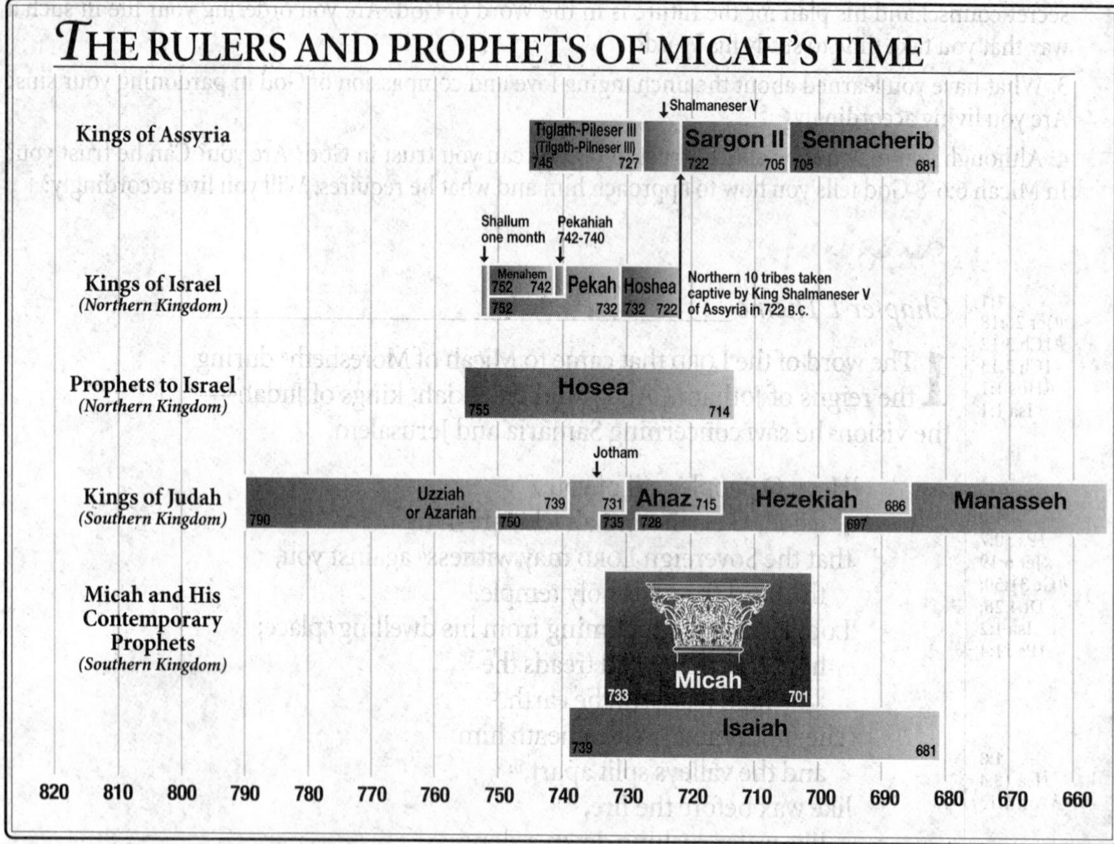

[9]For her wound[a] is incurable;
it has come to Judah.[b]
It[a] has reached the very gate[c] of my people,
even to Jerusalem itself.
[10]Tell it not in Gath[b];
weep not at all.[c]
In Beth Ophrah[d]
roll in the dust.
[11]Pass on in nakedness[d] and shame,
you who live in Shaphir.[e]
Those who live in Zaanan[f]
will not come out.
Beth Ezel is in mourning;
its protection is taken from you.
[12]Those who live in Maroth[g] writhe in pain,
waiting for relief,[e]

1:9 [a]Jer 46:11 [b]2Ki 18:13 [c]Isa 3:26
1:11 [d]Eze 23:29
1:12 [e]Jer 14:19

[a]9 Or *He* [b]10 *Gath* sounds like the Hebrew for *tell.* [c]10 Hebrew; Septuagint may suggest *not in Acco.* The Hebrew for *in Acco* sounds like the Hebrew for *weep.* [d]10 *Beth Ophrah* means *house of dust.* [e]11 *Shaphir* means *pleasant.* [f]11 *Zaanan* sounds like the Hebrew for *come out.* [g]12 *Maroth* sounds like the Hebrew for *bitter.*

1:13 [a]Jos 10:3

because disaster has come from the LORD,
even to the gate of Jerusalem.
13You who live in Lachish,[a] [a]
harness the team to the chariot.
You were the beginning of sin

1:14 [b]2Ki 16:8 [c]Jos 15:44 [d]Jer 15:18

to the Daughter of Zion,
for the transgressions of Israel
were found in you.
14Therefore you will give parting gifts[b]
to Moresheth Gath.
The town of Aczib[b] [c] will prove deceptive[d]
to the kings of Israel.
15I will bring a conqueror against you

1:15 [e]Jos 15:44 [f]Jos 12:15

who live in Mareshah.[c] [e]
He who is the glory of Israel
will come to Adullam.[f]
16Shave[g] your heads in mourning
for the children in whom you delight;
make yourselves as bald as the vulture,

1:16 [g]Job 1:20

for they will go from you into exile.

Chapter 2 Theme ______________________________

2

Woe to those who plan iniquity,
to those who plot evil on their beds![h]

2:1 [h]Ps 36:4

At morning's light they carry it out
because it is in their power to do it.
2They covet fields[i] and seize them,
and houses, and take them.
They defraud[j] a man of his home,
a fellowman of his inheritance.

2:2 [i]Isa 5:8 [j]Jer 22:17

3Therefore, the LORD says:
"I am planning disaster[k] against this people,
from which you cannot save yourselves.
You will no longer walk proudly,[l]
for it will be a time of calamity.

2:3 [k]Jer 18:11; Am 3:1-2 [l]Isa 2:12

4In that day men will ridicule you;
they will taunt you with this mournful song:
'We are utterly ruined;[m]
my people's possession is divided up.
He takes it from me!
He assigns our fields to traitors.' "

2:4 [m]Jer 4:13

a *13 Lachish* sounds like the Hebrew for *team.* b *14 Aczib* means *deception.* c *15 Mareshah* sounds like the Hebrew for *conqueror.*

5Therefore you will have no one in the assembly of the LORD
to divide the land[a] by lot.

6"Do not prophesy," their prophets say.
"Do not prophesy about these things;
disgrace[b] will not overtake us.[c]"
7Should it be said, O house of Jacob:
"Is the Spirit of the LORD angry?
Does he do such things?"

"Do not my words do good[d]
to him whose ways are upright?[e]
8Lately my people have risen up
like an enemy.
You strip off the rich robe
from those who pass by without a care,
like men returning from battle.
9You drive the women of my people
from their pleasant homes.[f]
You take away my blessing
from their children forever.
10Get up, go away!
For this is not your resting place,[g]
because it is defiled,[h]
it is ruined, beyond all remedy.
11If a liar and deceiver[i] comes and says,
'I will prophesy for you plenty of wine and beer,'
he would be just the prophet for this people![j]

12"I will surely gather all of you, O Jacob;
I will surely bring together the remnant[k] of Israel.
I will bring them together like sheep in a pen,
like a flock in its pasture;
the place will throng with people.
13One who breaks open the way will go up before[l] them;
they will break through the gate and go out.
Their king will pass through before them,
the LORD at their head."

Chapter 3 Theme ______________________

3

Then I said,

"Listen, you leaders[m] of Jacob,
you rulers of the house of Israel.
Should you not know justice,
2 you who hate good and love evil;
who tear the skin from my people
and the flesh from their bones;[n]

2:5 [a]Jos 18:4
2:6 [b]Mic 6:16 [c]Am 2:12
2:7 [d]Ps 119:65 [e]Ps 15:2; 84:11
2:9 [f]Jer 10:20
2:10 [g]Dt 12:9 [h]Lev 18:25-29; Ps 106:38-39
2:11 [i]Jer 5:31 [j]Isa 30:10
2:12 [k]Mic 4:7; 5:7; 7:18
2:13 [l]Isa 52:12
3:1 [m]Jer 5:5
3:2 [n]Ps 53:4; Eze 22:27

3:3
[a]Ps 14:4
[b]Zep 3:3
[c]Eze 11:7

3 who eat my people's flesh,[a]
strip off their skin
and break their bones in pieces;[b]
who chop them up like meat for the pan,
like flesh for the pot?[c]"

3:4
[d]Ps 18:41; Isa 1:15
[e]Dt 31:17

4 Then they will cry out to the LORD,
but he will not answer them.[d]
At that time he will hide his face[e] from them
because of the evil they have done.

5 This is what the LORD says:

3:5
[f]Isa 3:12; 9:16

"As for the prophets
who lead my people astray,[f]
if one feeds them,
they proclaim 'peace';
if he does not,
they prepare to wage war against him.

3:6
[g]Isa 8:19-22
[h]Isa 29:10

6 Therefore night will come over you, without visions,
and darkness, without divination.[g]
The sun will set for the prophets,[h]
and the day will go dark for them.

3:7
[i]Mic 7:16
[j]Isa 44:25

7 The seers will be ashamed[i]
and the diviners disgraced.[j]
They will all cover their faces
because there is no answer from God."

3:8
[k]Isa 58:1

8 But as for me, I am filled with power,
with the Spirit of the LORD,
and with justice and might,
to declare to Jacob his transgression,
to Israel his sin.[k]

3:9
[l]Ps 58:1-2; Isa 1:23

9 Hear this, you leaders of the house of Jacob,
you rulers of the house of Israel,
who despise justice
and distort all that is right;[l]

3:10
[m]Jer 22:13
[n]Hab 2:12
[o]Eze 22:27

10 who build[m] Zion with bloodshed,[n]
and Jerusalem with wickedness.[o]

3:11
[p]Isa 1:23; Jer 6:13; Hos 4:8,18
[q]Jer 7:4

11 Her leaders judge for a bribe,
her priests teach for a price,
and her prophets tell fortunes for money.[p]
Yet they lean upon the LORD and say,
"Is not the LORD among us?
No disaster will come upon us."[q]
12 Therefore because of you,
Zion will be plowed like a field,

Jerusalem will become a heap of rubble,[a]
the temple hill a mound overgrown with thickets.

Chapter 4 Theme ____________________

4

In the last days

the mountain[b] of the Lord's temple will be established
as chief among the mountains;
it will be raised above the hills,[c]
and peoples will stream to it.[d]

2Many nations will come and say,

"Come, let us go up to the mountain of the LORD,[e]
to the house of the God of Jacob.[f]
He will teach us his ways,[g]
so that we may walk in his paths."
The law will go out from Zion,
the word of the LORD from Jerusalem.
3He will judge between many peoples
and will settle disputes for strong nations far and wide.[h]
They will beat their swords into plowshares
and their spears into pruning hooks.[i]
Nation will not take up sword against nation,
nor will they train for war anymore.[j]
4Every man will sit under his own vine
and under his own fig tree,[k]
and no one will make them afraid,[l]
for the LORD Almighty has spoken.[m]
5All the nations may walk
in the name of their gods;[n]
we will walk in the name of the LORD
our God for ever and ever.[o]

6"In that day," declares the LORD,

"I will gather the lame;
I will assemble the exiles[p]
and those I have brought to grief.[q]
7I will make the lame a remnant,[r]
those driven away a strong nation.
The LORD will rule over them in Mount Zion
from that day and forever.[s]
8As for you, O watchtower of the flock,
O stronghold[a] of the Daughter of Zion,

a8 Or *hill*

3:12
aJer 26:18

4:1
bZec 8:3
cEze 17:22
dPs 22:27; 86:9; Jer 3:17

4:2
eJer 31:6
fZec 2:11; 14:16
gPs 25:8-9; Isa 54:13

4:3
hIsa 11:4
iJoel 3:10
jIsa 2:4

4:4
k1Ki 4:25
lLev 26:6
mIsa 1:20; Zec 3:10

4:5
n2Ki 17:29
oJos 24:14-15; Isa 26:8; Zec 10:12

4:6
pPs 147:2
qEze 34:13,16; 37:21; Zep 3:19

4:7
rMic 2:12
sDa 7:14; Lk 1:33; Rev 11:15

the former dominion will be restored[a] to you;
kingship will come to the Daughter of Jerusalem."

9Why do you now cry aloud—
have you no king?[b]
Has your counselor perished,
that pain seizes you like that of a woman in labor?[c]
10Writhe in agony, O Daughter of Zion,
like a woman in labor,
for now you must leave the city
to camp in the open field.
You will go to Babylon;[d]
there you will be rescued.
There the LORD will redeem[e] you
out of the hand of your enemies.

11But now many nations
are gathered against you.
They say, "Let her be defiled,
let our eyes gloat[f] over Zion!"
12But they do not know
the thoughts of the LORD;
they do not understand his plan,[g]
he who gathers them like sheaves to the threshing floor.

13"Rise and thresh, O Daughter of Zion,
for I will give you horns of iron;
I will give you hoofs of bronze
and you will break to pieces many nations."[h]

You will devote their ill-gotten gains to the LORD,
their wealth to the Lord of all the earth.

Chapter 5 Theme ________________________

5 Marshal your troops, O city of troops,[a]
for a siege is laid against us.
They will strike Israel's ruler
on the cheek[i] with a rod.

2"But you, Bethlehem[j] Ephrathah,[k]
though you are small among the clans[b] of Judah,
out of you will come for me
one who will be ruler over Israel,
whose origins[c] are from of old,[l]
from ancient times.[d]"[m]

4:8 [a]Isa 1:26
4:9 [b]Jer 8:19 [c]Jer 30:6
4:10 [d]2Ki 20:18; Isa 43:14 [e]Isa 48:20
4:11 [f]La 2:16; Ob 1:12
4:12 [g]Isa 55:8; Ro 11:33-34
4:13 [h]Da 2:44
5:1 [i]La 3:30
5:2 [j]Jn 7:42 [k]Ge 48:7 [l]Ps 102:25 [m]Mt 2:6*

a *1* Or *Strengthen your walls, O walled city* b *2* Or *rulers* c *2* Hebrew *goings out*
d *2* Or *from days of eternity*

[3]Therefore Israel will be abandoned
until the time when she who is in labor gives birth
and the rest of his brothers return
to join the Israelites.

[4]He will stand and shepherd his flock[a]
in the strength of the LORD,
in the majesty of the name of the LORD his God.
And they will live securely, for then his greatness[b]
will reach to the ends of the earth.
5 And he will be their peace.[c]

When the Assyrian invades[d] our land
and marches through our fortresses,
we will raise against him seven shepherds,
even eight leaders of men.[e]
[6]They will rule[a] the land of Assyria with the sword,
the land of Nimrod[f] with drawn sword.[b][g]
He will deliver us from the Assyrian
when he invades our land
and marches into our borders.[h]

[7]The remnant[i] of Jacob will be
in the midst of many peoples
like dew from the LORD,
like showers on the grass,[j]
which do not wait for man
or linger for mankind.
[8]The remnant of Jacob will be among the nations,
in the midst of many peoples,
like a lion among the beasts of the forest,[k]
like a young lion among flocks of sheep,
which mauls and mangles[l] as it goes,
and no one can rescue.[m]
[9]Your hand will be lifted up[n] in triumph
over your enemies,
and all your foes will be destroyed.

[10]"In that day," declares the LORD,

"I will destroy your horses from among you
and demolish your chariots.[o]
[11]I will destroy the cities[p] of your land
and tear down all your strongholds.[q]
[12]I will destroy your witchcraft
and you will no longer cast spells.[r]

5:4 [a]Isa 40:11; 49:9; Eze 34:11-15,23; Mic 7:14 [b]Isa 52:13; Lk 1:32
5:5 [c]Isa 9:6; Lk 2:14; Col 1:19-20 [d]Isa 8:7 [e]Isa 10:24-27
5:6 [f]Ge 10:8 [g]Zep 2:13 [h]Na 2:11-13
5:7 [i]Mic 2:12 [j]Isa 44:4
5:8 [k]Ge 49:9 [l]Mic 4:13; Zec 10:5 [m]Ps 50:22; Hos 5:14
5:9 [n]Ps 10:12
5:10 [o]Hos 14:3; Zec 9:10
5:11 [p]Isa 6:11 [q]Hos 10:14; Am 5:9
5:12 [r]Dt 18:10-12; Isa 2:6; 8:19

[a]6 Or *crush* [b]6 Or *Nimrod in its gates*

5:13 [a]Eze 6:9; Zec 13:2
5:14 [b]Ex 34:13
5:15 [c]Isa 65:12

13I will destroy your carved images
and your sacred stones from among you;
you will no longer bow down
to the work of your hands.[a]
14I will uproot from among you your Asherah poles[a][b]
and demolish your cities.
15I will take vengeance[c] in anger and wrath
upon the nations that have not obeyed me."

Chapter 6 Theme ____________________

6:1 [d]Ps 50:1; Eze 6:2
6:2 [e]Dt 32:1 [f]Hos 12:2 [g]Ps 50:7
6:3 [h]Jer 2:5
6:4 [i]Dt 7:8 [j]Ex 4:16 [k]Ps 77:20 [l]Ex 15:20
6:5 [m]Nu 22:5-6 [n]Nu 25:1 [o]Jos 5:9-10 [p]Jdg 5:11; 1Sa 12:7
6:6 [q]Ps 40:6-8; 51:16-17
6:7 [r]Isa 40:16 [s]Ps 50:8-10 [t]Lev 18:21 [u]2Ki 16:3
6:8 [v]Isa 1:17; Jer 22:3 [w]Isa 57:15 [x]Dt 10:12-13; 1Sa 15:22; Hos 6:6

6

Listen to what the LORD says:

"Stand up, plead your case before the mountains;[d]
let the hills hear what you have to say.
2Hear,[e] O mountains, the LORD's accusation;[f]
listen, you everlasting foundations of the earth.
For the LORD has a case against his people;
he is lodging a charge[g] against Israel.

3"My people, what have I done to you?
How have I burdened[h] you? Answer me.
4I brought you up out of Egypt
and redeemed you from the land of slavery.[i]
I sent Moses[j] to lead you,
also Aaron[k] and Miriam.[l]
5My people, remember
what Balak[m] king of Moab counseled
and what Balaam son of Beor answered.
Remember ⌊your journey⌋ from Shittim[n] to Gilgal,[o]
that you may know the righteous acts[p] of the LORD."

6With what shall I come before the LORD
and bow down before the exalted God?
Shall I come before him with burnt offerings,
with calves a year old?[q]
7Will the LORD be pleased with thousands of rams,[r]
with ten thousand rivers of oil?[s]
Shall I offer my firstborn[t] for my transgression,
the fruit of my body for the sin of my soul?[u]
8He has showed you, O man, what is good.
And what does the LORD require of you?
To act justly[v] and to love mercy
and to walk humbly[w] with your God.[x]

9Listen! The LORD is calling to the city—
and to fear your name is wisdom—

a *14* That is, symbols of the goddess Asherah

"Heed the rod and the One who appointed it.[a]
[10]Am I still to forget, O wicked house,
your ill-gotten treasures
and the short ephah,[b] which is accursed?[a]
[11]Shall I acquit a man with dishonest scales,[b]
with a bag of false weights?
[12]Her rich men are violent;[c]
her people are liars[d]
and their tongues speak deceitfully.[e]
[13]Therefore, I have begun to destroy[f] you,
to ruin you because of your sins.
[14]You will eat but not be satisfied;[g]
your stomach will still be empty.[c]
You will store up but save nothing,[h]
because what you save I will give to the sword.
[15]You will plant but not harvest;[i]
you will press olives but not use the oil on yourselves,
you will crush grapes but not drink the wine.[j]
[16]You have observed the statutes of Omri[k]
and all the practices of Ahab's[l] house,
and you have followed their traditions.[m]
Therefore I will give you over to ruin[n]
and your people to derision;
you will bear the scorn[o] of the nations.[d]"

Chapter 7 Theme ____________________

7 What misery is mine!
I am like one who gathers summer fruit
at the gleaning of the vineyard;
there is no cluster of grapes to eat,
none of the early figs that I crave.
[2]The godly have been swept from the land;[p]
not one upright man remains.
All men lie in wait to shed blood;[q]
each hunts his brother with a net.[r]
[3]Both hands are skilled in doing evil;[s]
the ruler demands gifts,
the judge accepts bribes,
the powerful dictate what they desire—
they all conspire together.
[4]The best of them is like a brier,[t]
the most upright worse than a thorn hedge.

[a]*9* The meaning of the Hebrew for this line is uncertain. [b]*10* An ephah was a dry measure.
[c]*14* The meaning of the Hebrew for this word is uncertain. [d]*16* Septuagint; Hebrew *scorn due my people*

6:10 [a]Eze 45:9-10; Am 3:10; 8:4-6
6:11 [b]Lev 19:36; Hos 12:7
6:12 [c]Isa 1:23 [d]Isa 3:8 [e]Jer 9:3
6:13 [f]Isa 1:7; 6:11
6:14 [g]Isa 9:20 [h]Isa 30:6
6:15 [i]Dt 28:38; Jer 12:13 [j]Am 5:11; Zep 1:13
6:16 [k]1Ki 16:25 [l]1Ki 16:29-33 [m]Jer 7:24 [n]Jer 25:9 [o]Jer 51:51
7:2 [p]Ps 12:1 [q]Mic 3:10 [r]Jer 5:26
7:3 [s]Pr 4:16
7:4 [t]Eze 2:6

The day of your watchmen has come,
the day God visits you.
Now is the time of their confusion.[a]
5 Do not trust a neighbor;
put no confidence in a friend.[b]
Even with her who lies in your embrace
be careful of your words.
6 For a son dishonors his father,
a daughter rises up against her mother,[c]
a daughter-in-law against her mother-in-law—
a man's enemies are the members
of his own household.[d]

7 But as for me, I watch in hope[e] for the LORD,
I wait for God my Savior;
my God will hear[f] me.

8 Do not gloat over me,[g] my enemy!
Though I have fallen, I will rise.[h]
Though I sit in darkness,
the LORD will be my light.[i]
9 Because I have sinned against him,
I will bear the LORD's wrath,[j]
until he pleads my case
and establishes my right.
He will bring me out into the light;
I will see his righteousness.[k]
10 Then my enemy will see it
and will be covered with shame,[l]
she who said to me,
"Where is the LORD your God?"
My eyes will see her downfall;[m]
even now she will be trampled[n] underfoot
like mire in the streets.

11 The day for building your walls[o] will come,
the day for extending your boundaries.
12 In that day people will come to you
from Assyria and the cities of Egypt,
even from Egypt to the Euphrates
and from sea to sea
and from mountain to mountain.[p]
13 The earth will become desolate because
of its inhabitants,
as the result of their deeds.[q]

14 Shepherd[r] your people with your staff,[s]
the flock of your inheritance,

7:4 [a] Isa 22:5; Hos 9:7
7:5 [b] Jer 9:4
7:6 [c] Eze 22:7 [d] Mt 10:35-36*
7:7 [e] Ps 130:5; Isa 25:9 [f] Ps 4:3
7:8 [g] Pr 24:17 [h] Ps 37:24; Am 9:11 [i] Isa 9:2
7:9 [j] La 3:39-40 [k] Isa 46:13
7:10 [l] Ps 35:26 [m] Isa 51:23 [n] Zec 10:5
7:11 [o] Isa 54:11
7:12 [p] Isa 19:23-25
7:13 [q] Isa 3:10-11
7:14 [r] Mic 5:4 [s] Ps 23:4

which lives by itself in a forest,
in fertile pasturelands.[a]
Let them feed in Bashan and Gilead[a]
as in days long ago.

15"As in the days when you came out of Egypt,
I will show them my wonders.[b]"

16Nations will see and be ashamed,[c]
deprived of all their power.
They will lay their hands on their mouths
and their ears will become deaf.
17They will lick dust like a snake,
like creatures that crawl on the ground.
They will come trembling out of their dens;
they will turn in fear[d] to the LORD our God
and will be afraid of you.
18Who is a God like you,
who pardons sin[e] and forgives[f] the transgression
of the remnant[g] of his inheritance?[h]
You do not stay angry[i] forever
but delight to show mercy.[j]
19You will again have compassion on us;
you will tread our sins underfoot
and hurl all our iniquities[k] into the depths of the sea.[l]
20You will be true to Jacob,
and show mercy to Abraham,
as you pledged on oath to our fathers[m]
in days long ago.

a 14 Or *in the middle of Carmel*

7:14
[a] Jer 50:19

7:15
[b] Ex 3:20; Ps 78:12

7:16
[c] Isa 26:11

7:17
[d] Isa 25:3; 49:23; 59:19

7:18
[e] Isa 43:25; Jer 50:20
[f] Ps 103:8-13
[g] Mic 2:12
[h] Ex 34:9
[i] Ps 103:9
[j] Jer 32:41

7:19
[k] Isa 43:25
[l] Jer 31:34

7:20
[m] Dt 7:8; Lk 1:72

MICAH AT A GLANCE

heme of Micah:

thor:

te:

rpose:

y Words:

Samaria

Jerusalem

Jacob (Jacob's)

Israel (Israel's)

Judah (Judah's)

Zion

Assyrian

demolish (destroy, ruin, ruined)

remnant

in that day (in the last days)

my (his, your) people('s) (mark these phrases only when they are referring to God)

Segment Divisions		Chapter Themes
		1
		2
		3
		4
		5
		6
		7

NAHUM

One hundred years had passed since Jonah went to Nineveh to proclaim its destruction. Now another prophet, Nahum, proclaims his vision from God regarding Nineveh, the capital of Assyria. What a sharp contrast between Nahum's prophetic message and the meaning of his name—comforter!

Assyria sat smugly on her throne. Under Shalmaneser V, Assyria had conquered Israel in 722 B.C. In 701 B.C. under Sennacherib's rule the Assyrians had invaded Judah. Sennacherib's field commander (Rabshakeh) had boasted to Judah that no gods of the nations they had conquered had been able to deliver their people. To Hezekiah, king of Judah, he proclaimed, "Do not let the god you depend on deceive you when he says, 'Jerusalem will not be handed over to the king of Assyria.' Surely you have heard what the kings of Assyria have done to all the countries, destroying them completely. And will you be delivered?" (2 Kings 19:10, 11).

But God did spare Judah. Sennacherib, king of Assyria, returned to Nineveh and died there.

Yet that wasn't the end of the story. God had a message for Nineveh, the capital of Assyria, who at the time of Nahum's prophecy sat at the pinnacle of wealth and power, secure behind her impregnable walls. Or so she thought.

Things to Do

1. If you have time, read Jonah to see what God said to the people of Nineveh 100 years earlier and how they responded.
2. Read Nahum and mark the key words listed on the NAHUM AT A GLANCE chart on page 1612.
3. Study the historical chart on page 1607 to see the context of the book.
4. Now read Nahum chapter by chapter and do the following:
   a. Nahum tells us much about God. Carefully observe the text and then in the margin summarize what you learn about God. For instance, in 1:4 it says that God rules over nature. Write that in your list in the margin under the title "God" (△).
   b. Observe all you can about Nineveh. Watch for the repeated use of *Nineveh* and the pronouns which refer to Nineveh, such as *you* and *your*. Mark any reference to Nineveh that you missed. Then in the margin list what you learn about "Nineveh's Sin."
   c. Make a third list in the margin, "What Will Happen to Nineveh?"
5. Record the theme or subject of each chapter on NAHUM AT A GLANCE and in the text on the line next to the chapter number. Also record the theme of the book and complete any other information requested on the chart.

Things to Think About

1. What do you learn about the justice of God and the certainty of his Word from this book? Is this the kind of God you can trust? Why?
2. Is there anything that can stop God from doing what he says or plans?
3. Can compassionate people deliver this kind of a message? What if you were impressed by God to bring this kind of warning to others? Would you? What would motivate you or hinder you? By the way, remember the meaning of Nahum's name.

THE RULERS AND PROPHETS OF NAHUM'S TIME

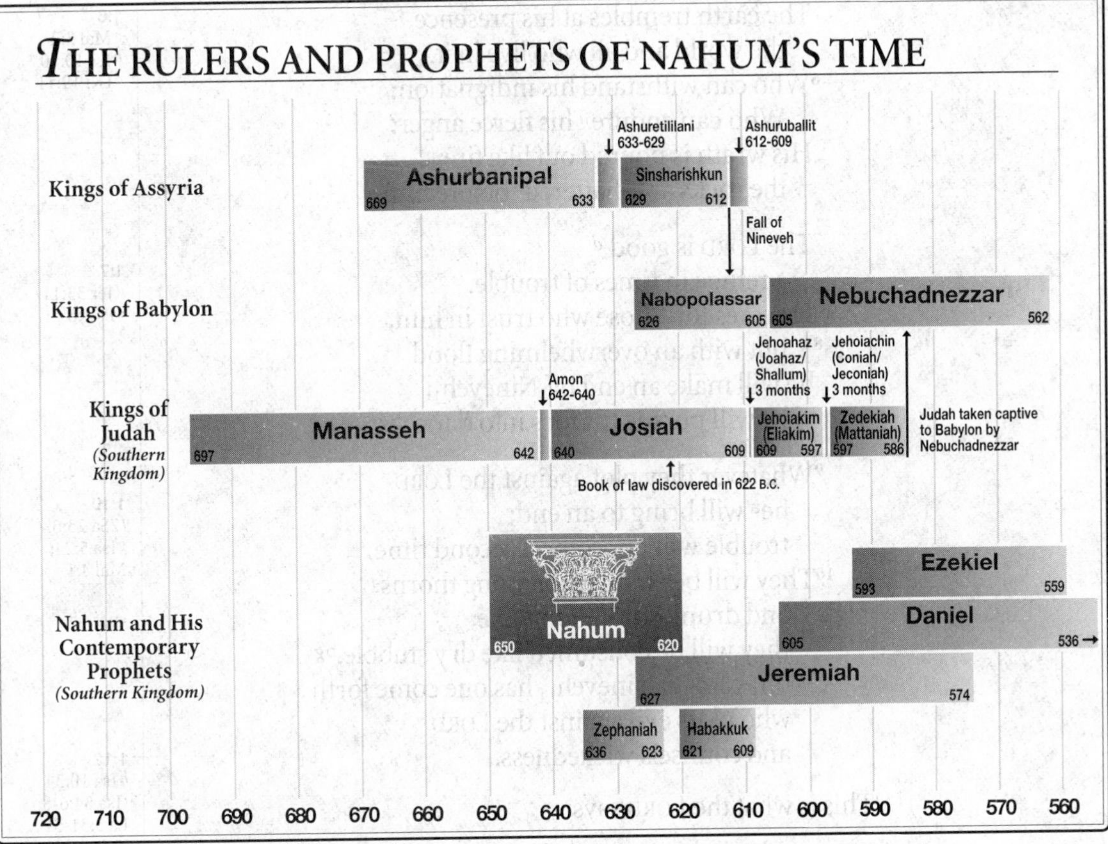

Chapter 1 Theme ______________________

1 An oracle[a] concerning Nineveh.[b] The book of the vision of Nahum the Elkoshite.

2The LORD is a jealous[c] and avenging God;
the LORD takes vengeance[d] and is filled with wrath.
The LORD takes vengeance on his foes
and maintains his wrath against his enemies.
3The LORD is slow to anger[e] and great in power;
the LORD will not leave the guilty unpunished.[f]
His way is in the whirlwind and the storm,
and clouds[g] are the dust of his feet.
4He rebukes the sea and dries it up;
he makes all the rivers run dry.
Bashan and Carmel[h] wither
and the blossoms of Lebanon fade.
5The mountains quake[i] before him
and the hills melt away.[j]

1:1 [a]Isa 13:1; 19:1; Jer 23:33-34 [b]Jnh 1:2; Na 2:8; Zep 2:13
1:2 [c]Ex 20:5 [d]Dt 32:41; Ps 94:1
1:3 [e]Ne 9:17 [f]Ex 34:7 [g]Ps 104:3
1:4 [h]Isa 33:9
1:5 [i]Ex 19:18 [j]Mic 1:4

The earth trembles at his presence,
the world and all who live in it.
6Who can withstand his indignation?
Who can endure[a] his fierce anger?
His wrath is poured out like fire;[b]
the rocks are shattered[c] before him.

7The LORD is good,[d]
a refuge in times of trouble.
He cares for[e] those who trust in him,
8 but with an overwhelming flood
he will make an end of ⌊Nineveh⌋;
he will pursue his foes into darkness.

9Whatever they plot against the LORD
he[a] will bring to an end;
trouble will not come a second time.
10They will be entangled among thorns[f]
and drunk from their wine;
they will be consumed like dry stubble.[b][g]
11From you, ⌊O Nineveh,⌋ has one come forth
who plots evil against the LORD
and counsels wickedness.

12This is what the LORD says:

"Although they have allies and are numerous,
they will be cut off[h] and pass away.
Although I have afflicted you, ⌊O Judah,⌋
I will afflict you no more.[i]
13Now I will break their yoke[j] from your neck
and tear your shackles away."

14The LORD has given a command concerning you,
⌊Nineveh⌋:
"You will have no descendants to bear your name.[k]
I will destroy the carved images[l] and cast idols
that are in the temple of your gods.
I will prepare your grave,[m]
for you are vile."

15Look, there on the mountains,
the feet of one who brings good news,[n]
who proclaims peace![o]
Celebrate your festivals,[p] O Judah,
and fulfill your vows.

a9 Or *What do you foes plot against the LORD? / He* b10 The meaning of the Hebrew for this verse is uncertain.

1:6 [a]Mal 3:2 [b]Jer 10:10 [c]1Ki 19:11
1:7 [d]Jer 33:11 [e]Ps 1:6
1:10 [f]2Sa 23:6 [g]Isa 5:24; Mal 4:1
1:12 [h]Isa 10:34 [i]Isa 54:6-8; La 3:31-32
1:13 [j]Isa 9:4
1:14 [k]Isa 14:22 [l]Mic 5:13 [m]Eze 32:22-23
1:15 [n]Isa 40:9; Ro 10:15 [o]Isa 52:7 [p]Lev 23:2-4

No more will the wicked invade you;[a]
they will be completely destroyed.

Chapter 2 Theme ____________________

2

An attacker[b] advances against you, ⌊Nineveh⌋.
Guard the fortress,
watch the road,
brace yourselves,
marshal all your strength!

2 The LORD will restore[c] the splendor[d] of Jacob
like the splendor of Israel,
though destroyers have laid them waste
and have ruined their vines.

3 The shields of his soldiers are red;
the warriors are clad in scarlet.[e]
The metal on the chariots flashes
on the day they are made ready;
the spears of pine are brandished.[a]
4 The chariots[f] storm through the streets,
rushing back and forth through the squares.
They look like flaming torches;
they dart about like lightning.

5 He summons his picked troops,
yet they stumble[g] on their way.
They dash to the city wall;
the protective shield is put in place.
6 The river gates[h] are thrown open
and the palace collapses.
7 It is decreed[b] that ⌊the city⌋
be exiled and carried away.
Its slave girls moan[i] like doves
and beat upon their breasts.[j]
8 Nineveh is like a pool,
and its water is draining away.
"Stop! Stop!" they cry,
but no one turns back.
9 Plunder the silver!
Plunder the gold!
The supply is endless,
the wealth from all its treasures!

1:15 [a] Isa 52:1
2:1 [b] Jer 51:20
2:2 [c] Eze 37:23 [d] Isa 60:15
2:3 [e] Eze 23:14-15
2:4 [f] Jer 4:13
2:5 [g] Jer 46:12
2:6 [h] Na 3:13
2:7 [i] Isa 59:11 [j] Isa 32:12

a 3 Hebrew; Septuagint and Syriac / *the horsemen rush to and fro* b 7 The meaning of the Hebrew for this word is uncertain.

[10]She is pillaged, plundered, stripped!
Hearts melt, knees give way,
bodies tremble, every face grows pale.[a]

[11]Where now is the lions' den,[b]
the place where they fed their young,
where the lion and lioness went,
and the cubs, with nothing to fear?
[12]The lion killed[c] enough for his cubs
and strangled the prey for his mate,
filling his lairs with the kill
and his dens with the prey.

[13]"I am against[d] you,"
declares the LORD Almighty.
"I will burn up your chariots in smoke,[e]
and the sword will devour your young lions.
I will leave you no prey on the earth.
The voices of your messengers
will no longer be heard."

Chapter 3 Theme ____________________

3

Woe to the city of blood,[f]
full of lies,
full of plunder,
never without victims!
[2]The crack of whips,
the clatter of wheels,
galloping horses
and jolting chariots!
[3]Charging cavalry,
flashing swords
and glittering spears!
Many casualties,
piles of dead,
bodies without number,
people stumbling over the corpses[g]—
[4]all because of the wanton lust of a harlot,
alluring, the mistress of sorceries,[h]
who enslaved nations by her prostitution[i]
and peoples by her witchcraft.

[5]"I am against[j] you," declares the LORD Almighty.
"I will lift your skirts[k] over your face.
I will show the nations your nakedness[l]
and the kingdoms your shame.

2:10 [a]Isa 29:22
2:11 [b]Isa 5:29
2:12 [c]Jer 51:34
2:13 [d]Jer 21:13; Na 3:5 [e]Ps 46:9
3:1 [f]Eze 22:2; Mic 3:10
3:3 [g]2Ki 19:35; Isa 34:3
3:4 [h]Isa 47:9 [i]Isa 23:17; Eze 16:25-29
3:5 [j]Na 2:13 [k]Jer 13:22 [l]Isa 47:3

6I will pelt you with filth,[a]
I will treat you with contempt[b]
and make you a spectacle.[c]
7All who see you will flee from you and say,
'Nineveh[d] is in ruins—who will mourn for her?'[e]
Where can I find anyone to comfort[f] you?"

8Are you better than[g] Thebes,[a][h]
situated on the Nile,[i]
with water around her?
The river was her defense,
the waters her wall.
9Cush[b][j] and Egypt were her boundless strength;
Put[k] and Libya[l] were among her allies.
10Yet she was taken captive[m]
and went into exile.
Her infants were dashed[n] to pieces
at the head of every street.
Lots were cast for her nobles,
and all her great men were put in chains.
11You too will become drunk;[o]
you will go into hiding[p]
and seek refuge from the enemy.

12All your fortresses are like fig trees
with their first ripe fruit;
when they are shaken,
the figs[q] fall into the mouth of the eater.
13Look at your troops—
they are all women![r]
The gates[s] of your land
are wide open to your enemies;
fire has consumed their bars.[t]

14Draw water for the siege,[u]
strengthen your defenses![v]
Work the clay,
tread the mortar,
repair the brickwork!
15There the fire will devour you;
the sword will cut you down
and, like grasshoppers, consume you.
Multiply like grasshoppers,
multiply like locusts![w]
16You have increased the number of your merchants
till they are more than the stars of the sky,

3:6 [a]Job 9:31 [b]1Sa 2:30; Jer 51:37 [c]Isa 14:16
3:7 [d]Na 1:1 [e]Jer 15:5 [f]Isa 51:19
3:8 [g]Am 6:2 [h]Jer 46:25 [i]Isa 19:6-9
3:9 [j]2Ch 12:3 [k]Eze 27:10 [l]Eze 30:5
3:10 [m]Isa 20:4 [n]Isa 13:16; Hos 13:16
3:11 [o]Isa 49:26 [p]Isa 2:10
3:12 [q]Isa 28:4
3:13 [r]Isa 19:16; Jer 50:37 [s]Na 2:6 [t]Isa 45:2
3:14 [u]2Ch 32:4 [v]Na 2:1
3:15 [w]Joel 1:4

INSIGHT

Thebes refers to ***No Amon***, the Hebrew name for No, the capital of Egypt. Since Nahum reminds Nineveh of the fall of Thebes (No Amon), his prophecy had to come after 661 B.C. and before Nineveh was destroyed in 612 B.C. by the Babylonians, Medes, and Scythians.

a8 Hebrew *No Amon* b9 That is, the upper Nile region

but like locusts they strip the land
  and then fly away.
17Your guards are like locusts,[a]
  your officials like swarms of locusts
  that settle in the walls on a cold day—
but when the sun appears they fly away,
  and no one knows where.

18O king of Assyria, your shepherds[a] slumber;[b]
  your nobles lie down to rest.[c]
Your people are scattered[d] on the mountains
  with no one to gather them.
19Nothing can heal your wound;[e]
  your injury is fatal.
Everyone who hears the news about you
  claps his hands[f] at your fall,
for who has not felt
  your endless cruelty?

a *18* Or *rulers*

3:17
a Jer 51:27

3:18
b Ps 76:5-6
c Isa 56:10
d 1Ki 22:17

3:19
e Jer 30:13; Mic 1:9
f Job 27:23; La 2:15; Zep 2:15

Nahum at a Glance

Theme of Nahum:

Segment Divisions		Chapter Themes
	1	
	2	
	3	

Author:

Date:

Purpose:

Key Words:

I am against you

I will

Nineveh (Assyria)

Judah (Jacob, Israel)

HABAKKUK

"The righteous will live by his faith." This verse, which pierced Martin Luther's heart and as a result brought about a reformation, is from Habakkuk 2:4. Paul echoed it in Romans and Galatians, but its roots are in the Old Testament, where God affirms that salvation has always been by faith and faith alone.

And what is the setting of the verse that unshackled Luther and brought him into a vital relationship with the living God? You will discover this as you study Habakkuk, a book which ends with a crescendo of faith in anticipation of Judah's darkest of hours.

THINGS TO DO

General Instructions

As you read Habakkuk it is critical for you to know whether God is speaking or Habakkuk is speaking. Since the book is only three chapters long, read through Habakkuk and note in the margin when God speaks or when Habakkuk speaks. Try it on your own, then look at the HABAKKUK AT A GLANCE chart on page 1620 for the segment divisions which show who is speaking when.

Chapter 1

1. An "oracle" can be translated "a burden." What is Habakkuk's burden; what is bothering him? Note this in the margin of chapter 1 where it is described.

2. Read through Habakkuk 1 and mark every reference to *God (God, the Holy One, Lord,* etc.) and every personal pronoun which refers to him. Then in the margin list everything you learn about God as a personality and note what he is going to do.

3. The Chaldeans, another name for the Babylonians, invaded the southern kingdom of Judah three times. In 605 B.C., Daniel and many nobles were taken captive. Then in 597 B.C., Ezekiel was taken captive. The third and final siege occurred in 586 B.C., when Jerusalem and the temple were destroyed. List in the margin everything you learn about the Chaldeans—what they will do and what will happen to them.

4. Study the historical chart on page 1615 and notice the relationship between the time of Habakkuk's writing and the Babylonian invasion.

Chapter 2

1. Mark every word that describes a proud man (e.g., *puffed up, arrogant, greedy,* etc). Also mark the pronouns. Then in the margin list what he is like and with whom he is contrasted.

2. Mark each use of the word *woe* and then observe to whom the woe is going to come, why it will come, and what will happen when it comes. If you want to, summarize this in the margin.

3. List in the margin what you learn about God.

Chapter 3

1. Habakkuk's prayer is written in a poetic form which is intensely emotional. A statement is made and then is followed by a similar statement which heightens the meaning or repeats the truth in another way. Read the prayer again, keeping its form in mind.

2. As you read, ask the five W's and an H: Who is doing what? To whom or what? When will it be done? Why will it be done? What specifically is going to happen? How? In the margin, list everything you learn about God from this chapter.

3. What does this chapter say about Habakkuk and his relationship to God? List it in the margin. Then compare what you write with 2:4. How is Habakkuk going to live? Have his circumstances changed?

4. Fill in the appropriate sections of HABAKKUK AT A GLANCE, recording the theme of each paragraph, each chapter, and the book itself. Fill in any other information asked for on the chart. Also record the theme of each chapter on the line in the text next to the chapter number.

Things to Think About

1. What do you learn about God? His ways, his Word, his character? If he is the same yesterday, today, and forever, how would such insight into God influence your relationship to him and to his Word? How would this affect your response to your circumstances?

2. What have you learned about the haughty or proud? God says in James 4 that he opposes the proud. Can you understand why? Can you see any element of pride or haughtiness in your life which you need to deal with?

3. Review what you learned about the woes pronounced by God. Ask God to search your heart. Would these woes be applicable to you because of your lifestyle? Do you need to confess anything to God and receive his forgiveness and cleansing (see 1 John 1:9)?

4. As you look at how Habakkuk begins and ends, think about what produced the difference in Habakkuk and then apply it to your own life. Are you questioning, doubting God and his ways, and is it causing despair? What do you need to do?

Chapter 1 Theme ________________________

1

The oracle[a] that Habakkuk the prophet received.

[2]How long, O LORD, must I call for help,
but you do not listen?[b]
Or cry out to you, "Violence!"
but you do not save?[c]
[3]Why do you make me look at injustice?
Why do you tolerate[d] wrong?
Destruction and violence[e] are before me;
there is strife,[f] and conflict abounds.
[4]Therefore the law[g] is paralyzed,
and justice never prevails.
The wicked hem in the righteous,
so that justice is perverted.[h]

[5]"Look at the nations and watch—
and be utterly amazed.[i]
For I am going to do something in your days
that you would not believe,
even if you were told.[j]
[6]I am raising up the Babylonians,[a][k]
that ruthless and impetuous people,

a6 Or *Chaldeans*

1:1 [a]Na 1:1
1:2 [b]Ps 13:1-2; 22:1-2 [c]Jer 14:9
1:3 [d]ver 13 [e]Jer 20:8 [f]Ps 55:9
1:4 [g]Ps 119:126 [h]Job 19:7; Isa 1:23; 5:20; Eze 9:9
1:5 [i]Isa 29:9 [j]Ac 13:41*
1:6 [k]2Ki 24:2

who sweep across the whole earth
to seize dwelling places not their own.[a]
7 They are a feared and dreaded people;[b]
they are a law to themselves
and promote their own honor.
8 Their horses are swifter[c] than leopards,
fiercer than wolves at dusk.
Their cavalry gallops headlong;
their horsemen come from afar.
They fly like a vulture swooping to devour;
9 they all come bent on violence.
Their hordes[a] advance like a desert wind
and gather prisoners[d] like sand.
10 They deride kings
and scoff at rulers.[e]
They laugh at all fortified cities;
they build earthen ramps and capture them.
11 Then they sweep past like the wind[f] and go on—
guilty men, whose own strength is their god."[g]

1:6 [a] Jer 13:20
1:7 [b] Isa 18:7; Jer 39:5-9
1:8 [c] Jer 4:13
1:9 [d] Hab 2:5
1:10 [e] 2Ch 36:6
1:11 [f] Jer 4:11-12 [g] Da 4:30

[a] 9 The meaning of the Hebrew for this word is uncertain.

THE RULERS AND PROPHETS OF HABAKKUK'S TIME

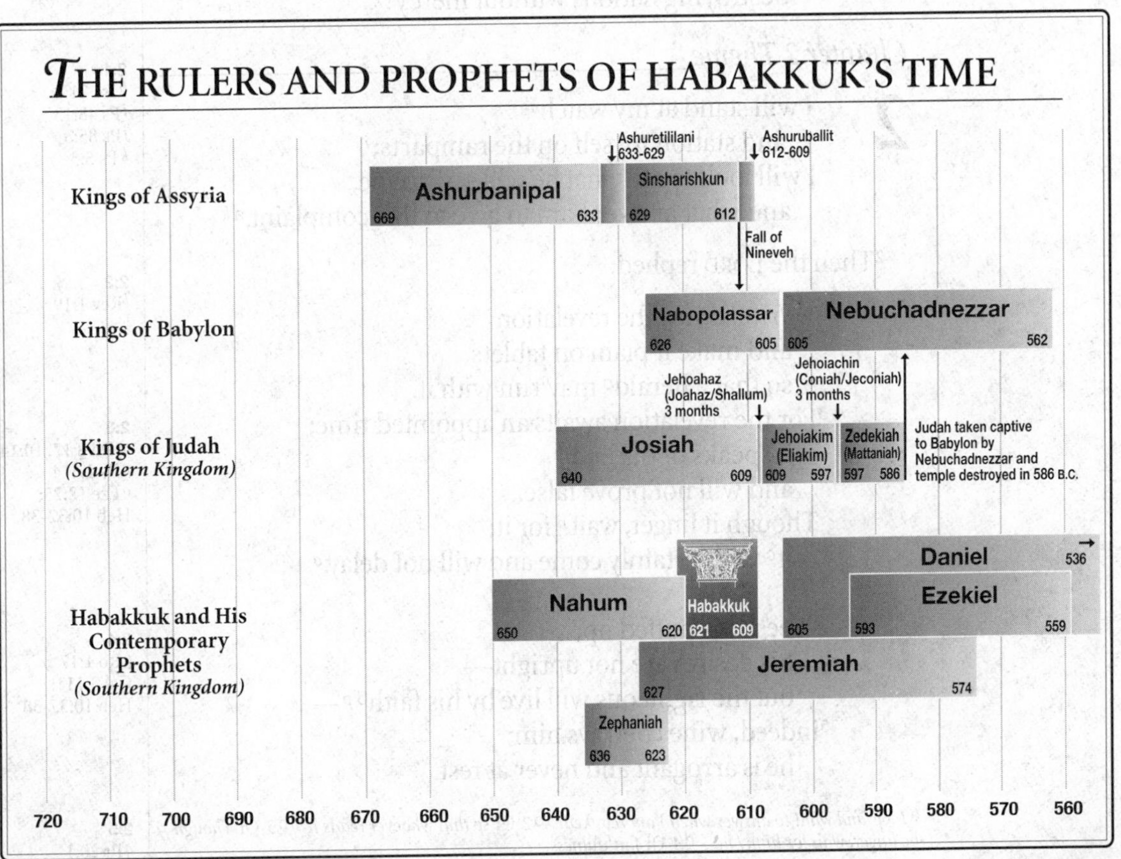

[12]O LORD, are you not from everlasting?
My God, my Holy One,[a] we will not die.
O LORD, you have appointed[b] them to execute judgment;
O Rock, you have ordained them to punish.
[13]Your eyes are too pure to look on evil;
you cannot tolerate wrong.[c]
Why then do you tolerate the treacherous?
Why are you silent while the wicked
swallow up those more righteous than themselves?
[14]You have made men like fish in the sea,
like sea creatures that have no ruler.
[15]The wicked foe pulls all of them up with hooks,[d]
he catches them in his net,[e]
he gathers them up in his dragnet;
and so he rejoices and is glad.
[16]Therefore he sacrifices to his net
and burns incense[f] to his dragnet,
for by his net he lives in luxury
and enjoys the choicest food.
[17]Is he to keep on emptying his net,
destroying nations without mercy?[g]

Chapter 2 Theme

2

I will stand at my watch[h]
and station myself on the ramparts;[i]
I will look to see what he will say[j] to me,
and what answer I am to give to this complaint.[a] [k]

[2]Then the LORD replied:

"Write[l] down the revelation
and make it plain on tablets
so that a herald[b] may run with it.
[3]For the revelation awaits an appointed time;
it speaks of the end[m]
and will not prove false.
Though it linger, wait[n] for it;
it[c] will certainly come and will not delay.[o]

[4]"See, he is puffed up;
his desires are not upright—
but the righteous will live by his faith[d] [p]—
[5]indeed, wine[q] betrays him;
he is arrogant and never at rest.

1:12 [a]Isa 31:1 [b]Isa 10:6
1:13 [c]La 3:34-36
1:15 [d]Isa 19:8 [e]Jer 16:16
1:16 [f]Jer 44:8
1:17 [g]Isa 14:6; 19:8
2:1 [h]Isa 21:8 [i]Ps 48:13 [j]Ps 85:8 [k]Ps 5:3
2:2 [l]Rev 1:19
2:3 [m]Da 8:17; 10:14 [n]Ps 27:14 [o]Eze 12:25; Heb 10:37-38
2:4 [p]Ro 1:17*; Gal 3:11*; Heb 10:37-38*
2:5 [q]Pr 20:1

a *1* Or *and what to answer when I am rebuked* b *2* Or *so that whoever reads it* c *3* Or *Though he linger, wait for him; / he* d *4* Or *faithfulness*

2:5 [a]Pr 27:20; 30:15-16

Because he is as greedy as the grave[a]
and like death is never satisfied,[a]
he gathers to himself all the nations
and takes captive all the peoples.

2:6 [b]Isa 14:4 [c]Am 2:8

6"Will not all of them taunt[b] him with ridicule and scorn, saying,

"'Woe to him who piles up stolen goods
and makes himself wealthy by extortion![c]
How long must this go on?'

2:7 [d]Pr 29:1

7Will not your debtors[b] suddenly arise?
Will they not wake up and make you tremble?
Then you will become their victim.[d]

2:8 [e]Isa 33:1; Zec 2:8-9 [f]ver 17

8Because you have plundered many nations,
the peoples who are left will plunder you.[e]
For you have shed man's blood;[f]
you have destroyed lands and cities and
everyone in them.

2:9 [g]Jer 22:13

9"Woe to him who builds[g] his realm by unjust gain
to set his nest on high,
to escape the clutches of ruin!

2:10 [h]Jer 26:19 [i]ver 16

10You have plotted the ruin[h] of many peoples,
shaming[i] your own house and forfeiting your life.

2:11 [j]Jos 24:27; Lk 19:40

11The stones[j] of the wall will cry out,
and the beams of the woodwork will echo it.

2:12 [k]Mic 3:10

12"Woe to him who builds a city with bloodshed[k]
and establishes a town by crime!

2:13 [l]Isa 50:11 [m]Isa 47:13

13Has not the LORD Almighty determined
that the people's labor is only fuel for the fire,[l]
that the nations exhaust themselves for nothing?[m]

2:14 [n]Nu 14:21 [o]Isa 11:9

14For the earth will be filled with the knowledge of the
glory[n] of the LORD,
as the waters cover the sea.[o]

15"Woe to him who gives drink to his neighbors,
pouring it from the wineskin till they are drunk,
so that he can gaze on their naked bodies.

2:16 [p]ver 10 [q]La 4:21 [r]Isa 51:22

16You will be filled with shame[p] instead of glory.
Now it is your turn! Drink and be exposed[c]![q]
The cup[r] from the LORD's right hand is coming
around to you,
and disgrace will cover your glory.

2:17 [s]Jer 51:35 [t]Jer 50:15

17The violence[s] you have done to Lebanon will
overwhelm you,
and your destruction of animals will terrify you.[t]

[a]5 Hebrew *Sheol* [b]7 Or *creditors* [c]16 Masoretic Text; Dead Sea Scrolls, Aquila, Vulgate and Syriac (see also Septuagint) *and stagger*

For you have shed man's blood;[a]
you have destroyed lands and cities and
everyone in them.

18"Of what value is an idol,[b] since a man has carved it?
Or an image that teaches lies?
For he who makes it trusts in his own creation;
he makes idols that cannot speak.[c]
19Woe to him who says to wood, 'Come to life!'
Or to lifeless stone, 'Wake up!'[d]
Can it give guidance?
It is covered with gold and silver;[e]
there is no breath in it.
20But the LORD is in his holy temple;[f]
let all the earth be silent[g] before him."

Chapter 3 Theme ____________________

3

A prayer of Habakkuk the prophet. On *shigionoth.*[a]

2LORD, I have heard[h] of your fame;
I stand in awe[i] of your deeds, O LORD.
Renew[j] them in our day,
in our time make them known;
in wrath remember mercy.[k]

3God came from Teman,
the Holy One from Mount Paran. *Selah*[b]
His glory covered the heavens
and his praise filled the earth.[l]
4His splendor was like the sunrise;
rays flashed from his hand,
where his power was hidden.
5Plague went before him;
pestilence followed his steps.
6He stood, and shook the earth;
he looked, and made the nations tremble.
The ancient mountains crumbled
and the age-old hills collapsed.[m]
His ways are eternal.
7I saw the tents of Cushan in distress,
the dwellings of Midian[n] in anguish.[o]

8Were you angry with the rivers,[p] O LORD?
Was your wrath against the streams?

2:17
[a]ver 8

2:18
[b]Jer 5:21
[c]Ps 115:4-5; Jer 10:14

2:19
[d]1Ki 18:27
[e]Jer 10:4

2:20
[f]Ps 11:4
[g]Isa 41:1

3:2
[h]Ps 44:1
[i]Ps 119:120
[j]Ps 85:6
[k]Isa 54:8

3:3
[l]Ps 48:10

3:6
[m]Ps 114:1-6

3:7
[n]Jdg 7:24-25
[o]Ex 15:14

3:8
[p]Ex 7:20

a *1* Probably a literary or musical term b *3* A word of uncertain meaning; possibly a musical term; also in verses 9 and 13

Did you rage against the sea
  when you rode with your horses
  and your victorious chariots?[a]
9 You uncovered your bow,
  you called for many arrows.[b] *Selah*
You split the earth with rivers;
10 the mountains saw you and writhed.
Torrents of water swept by;
  the deep roared[c]
  and lifted its waves[d] on high.

11 Sun and moon stood still[e] in the heavens
  at the glint of your flying arrows,[f]
  at the lightning of your flashing spear.
12 In wrath you strode through the earth
  and in anger you threshed[g] the nations.
13 You came out to deliver[h] your people,
  to save your anointed one.
You crushed[i] the leader of the land of wickedness,
  you stripped him from head to foot. *Selah*
14 With his own spear you pierced his head
  when his warriors stormed out to scatter us,[j]
gloating as though about to devour
  the wretched[k] who were in hiding.
15 You trampled the sea with your horses,
  churning the great waters.[l]

16 I heard and my heart pounded,
  my lips quivered at the sound;
decay crept into my bones,
  and my legs trembled.
Yet I will wait patiently for the day of calamity
  to come on the nation invading us.
17 Though the fig tree does not bud
  and there are no grapes on the vines,
though the olive crop fails
  and the fields produce no food,[m]
though there are no sheep in the pen
  and no cattle in the stalls,[n]
18 yet I will rejoice in the LORD,[o]
  I will be joyful in God my Savior.
19 The Sovereign LORD is my strength;[p]
  he makes my feet like the feet of a deer,
  he enables me to go on the heights.[q]

For the director of music. On my stringed instruments.

3:8 [a] Ps 68:17
3:9 [b] Ps 7:12-13
3:10 [c] Ps 98:7 [d] Ps 93:3
3:11 [e] Jos 10:13 [f] Ps 18:14
3:12 [g] Isa 41:15
3:13 [h] Ps 20:6; 28:8 [i] Ps 68:21; 110:6
3:14 [j] Jdg 7:22 [k] Ps 64:2-5
3:15 [l] Ex 15:8; Ps 77:19
3:17 [m] Joel 1:10-12,18 [n] Jer 5:17
3:18 [o] Isa 61:10; Php 4:4
3:19 [p] Dt 33:29; Ps 46:1-5 [q] Dt 32:13; 2Sa 22:34; Ps 18:33

Theme of Habakkuk:

SEGMENT DIVISIONS

	WHO IS SPEAKING	PARAGRAPH THEMES	CHAPTER THEMES
	HABAKKUK SPEAKS	1:1-4	1
	GOD SPEAKS	1:5-11	
	HABAKKUK SPEAKS	1:12-17	
	GOD SPEAKS	2:1-3	2
		2:4, 5	
		2:6-8	
		2:9-11	
		2:12-14	
		2:15-17	
		2:18-20	
	HABAKKUK PRAYS	3:1, 2	3
		3:3-7	
		3:8-15	
		3:16-19	

Author:

Date:

Purpose:

Key Words:

ZEPHANIAH

During the latter years of King Josiah's reign, Israel was a spiritual oasis which was surrounded by apostasy—an abandonment of faith.

We do not know exactly when Zephaniah's prophecy came, although it was during Josiah's reign (640-609 B.C.). However, some argument can be made from the text that Zephaniah prophesied before the reforms Josiah made sometime between 622 and 621 B.C. Whenever it came, it came full gale, a stormy blast calling God's people to humility and righteousness in the face of the day of the Lord's anger.

Things to Do

1. Zephaniah 1:1 gives the genealogy of Zephaniah and also the historical setting of the book. Record your insights about the author on the ZEPHANIAH AT A GLANCE chart on page 1629. If you want a more thorough picture of the historical setting of Zephaniah, read 2 Kings 22:1 through 23:30 and 2 Chronicles 34:1–35:27.

2. Consult the historical chart on page 1622 to see the relationship of his prophecy to the Babylonian captivity and the destruction of Nineveh.

3. Read Zephaniah paragraph by paragraph, watching carefully for the references to the different peoples and places. Mark these references and note what is said about each one.

   a. Be careful to note when there is a change of subject. Watch carefully what happens in 3:1. Although Jerusalem is not mentioned by name at the beginning of chapter 3, the prophecy changes from Nineveh (the Assyrian capital) to Jerusalem.

   b. Decide on the theme or subject covered in each paragraph and record this under "Paragraph Themes" on ZEPHANIAH AT A GLANCE.

4. Now read Zephaniah chapter by chapter and mark the key words listed on ZEPHANIAH AT A GLANCE.

   a. Watch for any other key words as you read chapter by chapter and mark these.

   b. As you mark *the day* or *that day* notice what will happen in that day and how it relates, if at all, to the day of the Lord. (Remember, prophecy can have a near and a distant fulfillment. If you are not familiar with interpreting prophecy, you can read "Guidelines for Interpreting Predictive Prophecy" on page 2205.)

   c. In the margin of each chapter list what you learn from the key words you marked. Note what God will do, to whom, and why. Also note what effect it will have on Israel.

5. Beginning on page 2178 is the chart titled THE DAY OF THE LORD on which you can record what you learn about the day of the Lord. Note the reference (book, chapter, and verse) that you took your information from so you can find it later.

6. Fill in ZEPHANIAH AT A GLANCE. Record the theme of each chapter and of the book in the designated spaces. Then record the chapter theme in the text next to the chapter number.

Things to Think About

1. The day of the Lord is also mentioned in the New Testament. One such reference is in 1 Thessalonians 5:1-11. If the day of the Lord is yet future, what should you be doing to prepare for the time of its approaching?

2. What do you learn about the nation of Israel and its future? Are you using these truths in sharing the good news of Jesus Christ with God's people, the Jews?

3. Think about what you have learned about God from Zephaniah and how such knowledge should affect the way you live.

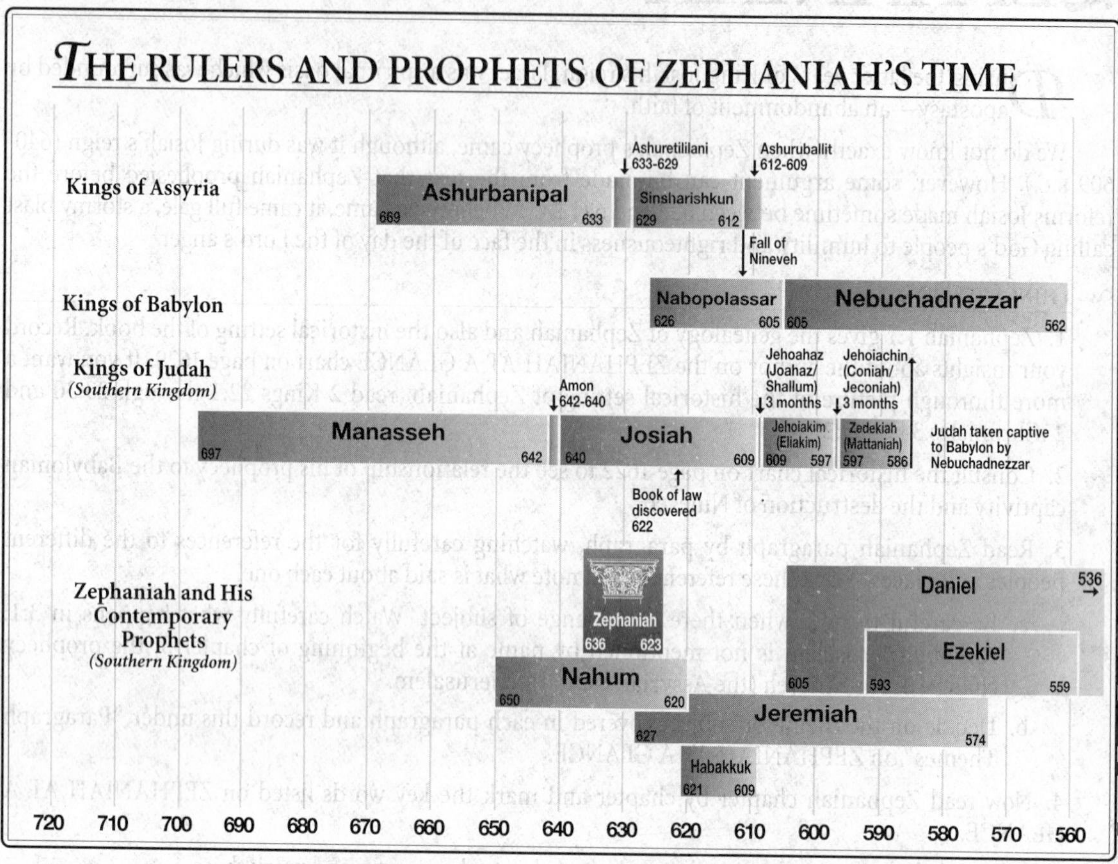

Chapter 1 Theme ________________________

1 The word of the LORD that came to Zephaniah son of Cushi,
the son of Gedaliah, the son of Amariah, the son of Hezekiah,
during the reign of Josiah[a] son of Amon king of Judah:

2"I will sweep away everything
from the face of the earth,"[b]
declares the LORD.

3"I will sweep away both men and animals;
I will sweep away the birds of the air[c]
and the fish of the sea.
The wicked will have only heaps of rubble[a]
when I cut off man from the face of the earth,"[d]
declares the LORD.

1:1 [a]2Ki 22:1; 2Ch 34:1–35:25

1:2 [b]Ge 6:7

1:3 [c]Jer 4:25 [d]Hos 4:3

[a]3 The meaning of the Hebrew for this line is uncertain.

4“I will stretch out my hand[a] against Judah
and against all who live in Jerusalem.
I will cut off from this place every remnant of Baal,[b]
the names of the pagan and the idolatrous priests[c]—
5those who bow down on the roofs
to worship the starry host,
those who bow down and swear by the LORD
and who also swear by Molech,[a][d]
6those who turn back from following[e] the LORD
and neither seek[f] the LORD nor inquire[g] of him.
7Be silent[h] before the Sovereign LORD,
for the day of the LORD[i] is near.
The LORD has prepared a sacrifice;[j]
he has consecrated those he has invited.
8On the day of the LORD's sacrifice
I will punish[k] the princes
and the king's sons[l]
and all those clad
in foreign clothes.
9On that day I will punish
all who avoid stepping on the threshold,[b]
who fill the temple of their gods
with violence and deceit.[m]

10“On that day,” declares the LORD,
“a cry will go up from the Fish Gate,[n]
wailing from the New Quarter,
and a loud crash from the hills.
11Wail,[o] you who live in the market district[c];
all your merchants will be wiped out,
all who trade with[d] silver will be ruined.[p]
12At that time I will search Jerusalem with lamps
and punish those who are complacent,[q]
who are like wine left on its dregs,[r]
who think, ‘The LORD will do nothing,[s]
either good or bad.’
13Their wealth will be plundered,[t]
their houses demolished.
They will build houses
but not live in them;
they will plant vineyards
but not drink the wine.[u]

14“The great day of the LORD[v] is near[w]—
near and coming quickly.

1:4 [a]Jer 6:12 [b]Mic 5:13 [c]Hos 10:5
1:5 [d]Jer 5:7
1:6 [e]Isa 1:4; Jer 2:13 [f]Isa 9:13 [g]Hos 7:7
1:7 [h]Hab 2:20; Zec 2:13 [i]ver 14; Isa 13:6 [j]Isa 34:6; Jer 46:10
1:8 [k]Isa 24:21 [l]Jer 39:6
1:9 [m]Am 3:10
1:10 [n]2Ch 33:14
1:11 [o]Jas 5:1 [p]Hos 9:6
1:12 [q]Am 6:1 [r]Jer 48:11 [s]Eze 8:12
1:13 [t]Jer 15:13 [u]Dt 28:30,39; Am 5:11; Mic 6:15
1:14 [v]ver 7; Joel 1:15 [w]Eze 7:7

[a]*5* Hebrew *Malcam,* that is, Milcom [b]*9* See 1 Samuel 5:5. [c]*11* Or *the Mortar* [d]*11* Or *in*

Listen! The cry on the day of the LORD will be bitter,
the shouting of the warrior there.
15That day will be a day of wrath,
a day of distress and anguish,
a day of trouble and ruin,
a day of darkness and gloom,
a day of clouds and blackness,[a]
16a day of trumpet and battle cry[b]
against the fortified cities
and against the corner towers.[c]
17I will bring distress on the people
and they will walk like blind[d] men,
because they have sinned against the LORD.
Their blood will be poured out[e] like dust
and their entrails like filth.[f]
18Neither their silver nor their gold
will be able to save them
on the day of the LORD's wrath.[g]
In the fire of his jealousy
the whole world will be consumed,[h]
for he will make a sudden end
of all who live in the earth.[i]"

1:15
[a]Isa 22:5; Joel 2:2

1:16
[b]Jer 4:19
[c]Isa 2:15

1:17
[d]Isa 59:10
[e]Ps 79:3
[f]Jer 9:22

1:18
[g]Eze 7:19
[h]ver 2-3; Zep 3:8
[i]Ge 6:7

The Nations of the Lord's Anger

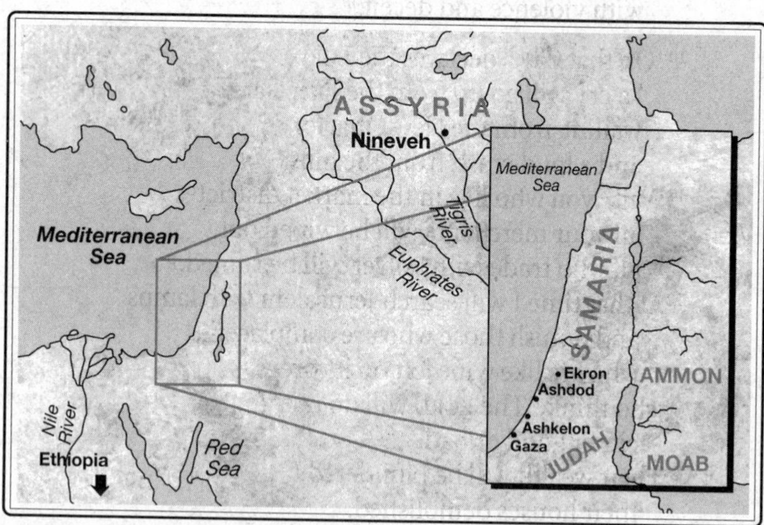

Chapter 2 Theme ____________________

2

Gather together,[j] gather together,
O shameful[k] nation,
2before the appointed time arrives
and that day sweeps on like chaff,[l]
before the fierce anger[m] of the LORD comes upon you,
before the day of the LORD's wrath comes upon you.

2:1
[j]2Ch 20:4; Joel 1:14
[k]Jer 3:3; 6:15

2:2
[l]Isa 17:13; Hos 13:3
[m]La 4:11

2:3 [a]Am 5:6 [b]Ps 45:4; Am 5:14-15 [c]Ps 57:1

[3]Seek[a] the LORD, all you humble of the land,
you who do what he commands.
Seek righteousness, seek humility;[b]
perhaps you will be sheltered[c]
on the day of the LORD's anger.

2:4 [d]Am 1:6,7-8; Zec 9:5-7

[4]Gaza[d] will be abandoned
and Ashkelon left in ruins.
At midday Ashdod will be emptied
and Ekron uprooted.
[5]Woe to you who live by the sea,
O Kerethite[e] people;

2:5 [e]Eze 25:16 [f]Am 3:1 [g]Isa 14:30

the word of the LORD is against you,[f]
O Canaan, land of the Philistines.

"I will destroy you,
and none will be left."[g]

2:6 [h]Isa 5:17

[6]The land by the sea, where the Kerethites[a] dwell,
will be a place for shepherds and sheep pens.[h]
[7]It will belong to the remnant of the house of Judah;
there they will find pasture.

2:7 [i]Ps 126:4; Jer 32:44

In the evening they will lie down
in the houses of Ashkelon.
The LORD their God will care for them;
he will restore their fortunes.[b][i]

2:8 [j]Jer 48:27 [k]Eze 25:3

[8]"I have heard the insults[j] of Moab
and the taunts of the Ammonites,
who insulted[k] my people
and made threats against their land.
[9]Therefore, as surely as I live,"

2:9 [l]Isa 15:1-16:14; Jer 48:1-47 [m]Dt 29:23 [n]Jer 49:1-6; Eze 25:1-7 [o]Isa 11:14 [p]Am 2:1-3

declares the LORD Almighty, the God of Israel,
"surely Moab[l] will become like Sodom,[m]
the Ammonites[n] like Gomorrah—
a place of weeds and salt pits,
a wasteland forever.
The remnant of my people will plunder[o] them;
the survivors of my nation will inherit their land.[p]"

2:10 [q]Isa 16:6 [r]Jer 48:27

[10]This is what they will get in return for their pride,[q]
for insulting[r] and mocking the people of the
LORD Almighty.
[11]The LORD will be awesome[s] to them
when he destroys all the gods[t] of the land.
The nations on every shore will worship him,[u]

2:11 [s]Joel 2:11 [t]Zep 1:4 [u]Zep 3:9

every one in its own land.

[a]6 The meaning of the Hebrew for this word is uncertain. [b]7 Or *will bring back their captives*

INSIGHT

The ***Kerethites*** were probably paid soldiers of the Philistines. David used some of these soldiers as personal bodyguards. Both Ezekiel and Zephaniah pronounced judgment on them.

12 “You too, O Cushites,[a][a]
will be slain by my sword.[b]”

13 He will stretch out his hand against the north
and destroy Assyria,
leaving Nineveh[c] utterly desolate
and dry as the desert.[d]
14 Flocks and herds will lie down there,
creatures of every kind.
The desert owl[e] and the screech owl
will roost on her columns.
Their calls will echo through the windows,
rubble will be in the doorways,
the beams of cedar will be exposed.
15 This is the carefree[f] city
that lived in safety.[g]
She said to herself,
“I am, and there is none besides me.”[h]
What a ruin she has become,
a lair for wild beasts!
All who pass by her scoff[i]
and shake their fists.

Chapter 3 Theme ______________________

3

Woe to the city of oppressors,[j]
rebellious and defiled![k]
2 She obeys[l] no one,
she accepts no correction.[m]
She does not trust in the LORD,
she does not draw near[n] to her God.
3 Her officials are roaring lions,
her rulers are evening wolves,[o]
who leave nothing for the morning.
4 Her prophets are arrogant;
they are treacherous[p] men.
Her priests profane the sanctuary
and do violence to the law.[q]
5 The LORD within her is righteous;
he does no wrong.[r]
Morning by morning he dispenses his justice,
and every new day he does not fail,
yet the unrighteous know no shame.

6 “I have cut off nations;
their strongholds are demolished.
I have left their streets deserted,

[a] *12* That is, people from the upper Nile region

2:12
[a] Isa 18:1; 20:4
[b] Jer 46:10

2:13
[c] Na 1:1
[d] Mic 5:6

2:14
[e] Isa 14:23

2:15
[f] Isa 32:9
[g] Isa 47:8
[h] Eze 28:2
[i] Na 3:19

3:1
[j] Jer 6:6
[k] Eze 23:30

3:2
[l] Jer 22:21
[m] Jer 7:28
[n] Ps 73:28; Jer 5:3

3:3
[o] Eze 22:27

3:4
[p] Jer 9:4
[q] Eze 22:26

3:5
[r] Dt 32:4

with no one passing through.
Their cities are destroyed;[a]
no one will be left—no one at all.
7 I said to the city,
'Surely you will fear me
and accept correction!'
Then her dwelling would not be cut off,
nor all my punishments come upon her.
But they were still eager
to act corruptly[b] in all they did.
8 Therefore wait[c] for me," declares the LORD,
"for the day I will stand up to testify.[a]
I have decided to assemble the nations,[d]
to gather the kingdoms
and to pour out my wrath on them—
all my fierce anger.
The whole world will be consumed[e]
by the fire of my jealous anger.

9 "Then will I purify the lips of the peoples,
that all of them may call[f] on the name of the LORD
and serve[g] him shoulder to shoulder.
10 From beyond the rivers of Cush[b][h]
my worshipers, my scattered people,
will bring me offerings.[i]
11 On that day you will not be put to shame[j]
for all the wrongs you have done to me,
because I will remove from this city
those who rejoice in their pride.
Never again will you be haughty
on my holy hill.
12 But I will leave within you
the meek[k] and humble,
who trust[l] in the name of the LORD.
13 The remnant[m] of Israel will do no wrong;[n]
they will speak no lies,[o]
nor will deceit be found in their mouths.
They will eat and lie down[p]
and no one will make them afraid.[q]"

14 Sing, O Daughter of Zion;[r]
shout aloud,[s] O Israel!
Be glad and rejoice with all your heart,
O Daughter of Jerusalem!
15 The LORD has taken away your punishment,
he has turned back your enemy.

3:6 [a] Lev 26:31
3:7 [b] Hos 9:9
3:8 [c] Ps 27:14 [d] Joel 3:2 [e] Zep 1:18
3:9 [f] Zep 2:11 [g] Isa 19:18
3:10 [h] Ps 68:31 [i] Isa 60:7
3:11 [j] Joel 2:26-27
3:12 [k] Isa 14:32 [l] Na 1:7
3:13 [m] Isa 10:21; Mic 4:7 [n] Ps 119:3 [o] Rev 14:5 [p] Eze 34:15; Zep 2:7 [q] Eze 34:25-28
3:14 [r] Zec 2:10 [s] Isa 12:6

[a] 8 Septuagint and Syriac; Hebrew *will rise up to plunder* [b] 10 That is, the upper Nile region

The LORD, the King of Israel, is with you;[a]
never again will you fear[b] any harm.
16 On that day they will say to Jerusalem,
"Do not fear, O Zion;
do not let your hands hang limp.[c]
17 The LORD your God is with you,
he is mighty to save.[d]
He will take great delight[e] in you,
he will quiet you with his love,
he will rejoice over you with singing."

18 "The sorrows for the appointed feasts
I will remove from you;
they are a burden and a reproach to you.[a]
19 At that time I will deal
with all who oppressed you;
I will rescue the lame
and gather those who have been scattered.[f]
I will give them praise[g] and honor
in every land where they were put to shame.
20 At that time I will gather you;
at that time I will bring[h] you home.
I will give you honor[i] and praise
among all the peoples of the earth
when I restore your fortunes[b][j]
before your very eyes,"

says the LORD.

a 18 Or *"I will gather you who mourn for the appointed feasts; / your reproach is a burden to you*
b 20 Or *I bring back your captives*

3:15 [a] Eze 37:26-28 [b] Isa 54:14
3:16 [c] Job 4:3; Isa 35:3-4; Heb 12:12
3:17 [d] Isa 63:1 [e] Isa 62:4
3:19 [f] Eze 34:16; Mic 4:6 [g] Isa 60:18
3:20 [h] Jer 29:14; Eze 37:12 [i] Isa 56:5; 66:22 [j] Joel 3:1

ZEPHANIAH AT A GLANCE

me of Zephaniah:

hor:

e:

pose:

Words:
will (will I)
he Lord will,
e will, he does)

ne day of
ne Lord
the day, in or
n that day)

emnant

SEGMENT DIVISIONS	PARAGRAPH THEMES	CHAPTER THEMES
	1:1-6	1
	1:7-13	
	1:14-18	
	2:1-3	2
	2:4-7	
	2:8-11	
	2:12-15	
	3:1-7	3
	3:8-13	
	3:14-20	

HAGGAI

Discouragement reigned. Only a remnant returned to Jerusalem after the 70 years of exile—a small remnant in comparison to the number of people taken captive. Many Jews were reluctant to leave Babylon to return to Jerusalem. The land of their captors had become home. The Babylonians had allowed them to establish businesses. They had built their houses. Their children, while born in captivity, were secure. Why should they leave?

A small remnant returned to rebuild the temple, soon to become a discouraging task. Their zeal dwindled. What was enthusiastically begun was forgotten before God's house was completed. For about sixteen years the temple stood unfinished and ignored.

Then around 520 B.C. the word of the Lord came to Haggai.

Things to Do

1. Read Haggai in one sitting in order to familiarize yourself with the pattern of the book. Then do the following:
   a. In a distinctive way, mark every reference to time throughout the book so you can spot it immediately. Also mark every use of the phrase *the word of the Lord came through the prophet Haggai.* Each occurrence of this phrase begins a message and will help you see the structure of Haggai.
   b. To get the historical setting of Haggai, read Ezra 4:24–6:22. Then study the two charts at the beginning of Haggai on pages 1631 and 1632. The first gives the historical setting of Haggai. Note who Darius is and also note Darius is mentioned in Haggai. Also note when the temple work started and stopped under Ezra and then when it resumed under Haggai.

      The second chart is a Jewish calendar which will help you discern when Haggai received his message from the Lord. (Follow the sacred calendar.)
2. As you read Haggai a second time, concentrate on one message at a time and do the following:
   a. As you read chapter 1, mark 1:13 the same way you marked the other phrases saying that the word of the Lord came by Haggai the prophet. Scholars debate whether this should be considered a separate message from the first part of the chapter. If so, the book would contain five messages rather than four. See what you think.
   b. As you study each message (which begins with "the word of the LORD came"), watch for and mark in a distinctive way the key repeated words used throughout Haggai. These are listed on the HAGGAI AT A GLANCE chart on page 1634. Mark any other key words you observe.
   c. After you have read each message and marked key words, observe the content of each message by asking the five W's and an H. Ask: What is the specific message and to whom was it given? What has happened? To whom? Why? What is going to happen? What are they to believe or do? Summarize and record what you learn about each message in the section for "Paragraph Themes" on HAGGAI AT A GLANCE.
3. Now go back through Haggai and list the truths you learned about God, the people, and the temple. You may want to record these lists in the margins of Haggai.
4. Complete HAGGAI AT A GLANCE. Record the theme of each chapter in the appropriate places. Then record the chapter theme in the text next to the chapter number. Finally, write out the theme of the book and fill in any other information needed.

Things to Think About

1. Have you given too much attention and time to your personal affairs and needs but neglected the things of God that are important for the spreading of the gospel or the furtherance of his work?

2. What might God be trying to say when cataclysmic events take place? Do you take advantage of these things to turn people's attention and thoughts to God?

3. When discouraged in your service to God, do you quit, or do you courageously persevere, determined to be faithful and to leave the outcome to God?

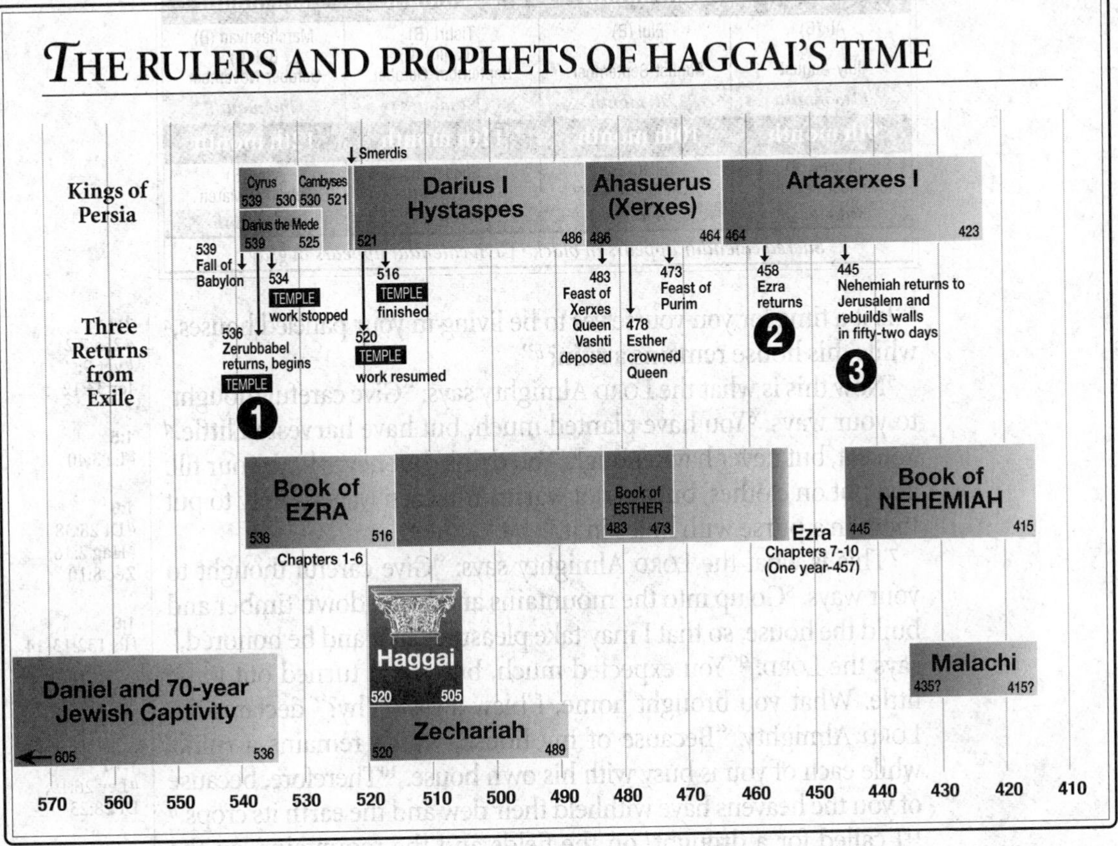

1:1
[a] Ezr 4:24
[b] Ezr 5:1
[c] Mt 1:12-13
[d] Ezr 5:3
[e] Ezr 2:2
[f] 1Ch 6:15; Ezr 3:2
1:3
[g] Ezr 5:1

Chapter 1 Theme

1 In the second year of King Darius,[a] on the first day of the sixth
month, the word of the LORD came through the prophet Haggai[b] to Zerubbabel[c] son of Shealtiel, governor[d] of Judah, and to
Joshua[a] [e] son of Jehozadak,[f] the high priest:
2This is what the LORD Almighty says: "These people say, 'The
time has not yet come for the LORD's house to be built.'"
3Then the word of the LORD came through the prophet Haggai:[g]

a *1* A variant of *Jeshua*; here and elsewhere in Haggai

The Jewish Calendar

Babylonian names (B) for the months are still used today for the Jewish calendar. Canaanite names (C) were used prior to the Babylonian captivity in 586 B.C. Four are mentioned in the Old Testament. **Adar-Sheni** is an intercalary month used every two to three years or seven times in 19 years.

1st month	2nd month	3rd month	4th month
Nisan (B) Abib (C) March-April	Iyyar (B) Ziv (C) April-May	Sivan (B) May-June	Tammuz (B) June-July
7th month	*8th month*	*9th month*	*10th month*
5th month	**6th month**	**7th month**	**8th month**
Ab (B) July-August	Elul (B) August-September	Tishri (B) Ethanim (C) September-October	Marcheshvan (B) Bul (C) October-November
11th month	*12th month*	*1st month*	*2nd month*
9th month	**10th month**	**11th month**	**12th month**
Chislev (B) November-December	Tebeth (B) December-January	Shebat (B) January-February	Adar (B) February-March
3rd month	*4th month*	*5th month*	*6th month*

Sacred calendar appears in black • Civil calendar appears in gray

4"Is it a time for you yourselves to be living in your paneled houses,[a]
while this house remains a ruin?[b]"
5Now this is what the LORD Almighty says: "Give careful thought[c]
to your ways. 6You have planted much, but have harvested little.[d]
You eat, but never have enough. You drink, but never have your fill.
You put on clothes, but are not warm. You earn wages,[e] only to put
them in a purse with holes in it."
7This is what the LORD Almighty says: "Give careful thought to
your ways. 8Go up into the mountains and bring down timber and
build the house, so that I may take pleasure[f] in it and be honored,"
says the LORD. 9"You expected much, but see, it turned out to be
little. What you brought home, I blew away. Why?" declares the
LORD Almighty. "Because of my house, which remains a ruin,[g]
while each of you is busy with his own house. 10Therefore, because
of you the heavens have withheld their dew and the earth its crops.[h]
11I called for a drought[i] on the fields and the mountains, on the
grain, the new wine, the oil and whatever the ground produces,
on men and cattle, and on the labor of your hands.[j]"

12Then Zerubbabel[k] son of Shealtiel, Joshua son of Jehozadak,
the high priest, and the whole remnant[l] of the people obeyed[m] the
voice of the LORD their God and the message of the prophet Haggai, because the LORD their God had sent him. And the people
feared[n] the LORD.
13Then Haggai, the LORD's messenger, gave this message of the
LORD to the people: "I am with[o] you," declares the LORD. 14So the
LORD stirred up the spirit of Zerubbabel[p] son of Shealtiel, governor
of Judah, and the spirit of Joshua son of Jehozadak, the high priest,
and the spirit of the whole remnant[q] of the people. They came and

1:4 [a] 2Sa 7:2 [b] ver 9; Jer 33:12
1:5 [c] La 3:40
1:6 [d] Dt 28:38 [e] Hag 2:16; Zec 8:10
1:8 [f] Ps 132:13-14
1:9 [g] ver 4
1:10 [h] Lev 26:19; Dt 28:23
1:11 [i] Dt 28:22; 1Ki 17:1 [j] Hag 2:17
1:12 [k] ver 1 [l] ver 14; Isa 1:9; Hag 2:2 [m] Isa 50:10 [n] Dt 31:12
1:13 [o] Mt 28:20; Ro 8:31
1:14 [p] Ezr 5:2 [q] ver 12

began to work on the house of the LORD Almighty, their God, 15on
the twenty-fourth day of the sixth month[a] in the second year of
King Darius.

Chapter 2 Theme ________________________________

2 On the twenty-first day of the seventh month, the word of
the LORD came through the prophet Haggai: 2"Speak to
Zerubbabel son of Shealtiel, governor of Judah, to Joshua son of
Jehozadak, the high priest, and to the remnant of the people. Ask
them, 3'Who of you is left who saw this house[b] in its former glory?
How does it look to you now? Does it not seem to you like nothing?[c] 4But now be strong, O Zerubbabel,' declares the LORD. 'Be
strong,[d] O Joshua son of Jehozadak, the high priest. Be strong, all
you people of the land,' declares the LORD, 'and work. For I am
with[e] you,' declares the LORD Almighty. 5'This is what I covenanted
with you when you came out of Egypt.[f] And my Spirit[g] remains
among you. Do not fear.'
6"This is what the LORD Almighty says: 'In a little while[h] I will
once more shake the heavens and the earth,[i] the sea and the dry
land. 7I will shake all nations, and the desired of all nations will
come, and I will fill this house[j] with glory,' says the LORD
Almighty. 8'The silver is mine and the gold is mine,' declares the
LORD Almighty. 9'The glory[k] of this present house will be greater
than the glory of the former house,' says the LORD Almighty. 'And
in this place I will grant peace,' declares the LORD Almighty."
10On the twenty-fourth day of the ninth month,[l] in the second
year of Darius, the word of the LORD came to the prophet Haggai:
11"This is what the LORD Almighty says: 'Ask the priests[m] what
the law says: 12If a person carries consecrated meat in the fold of
his garment, and that fold touches some bread or stew, some
wine, oil or other food, does it become consecrated?[n]' "
The priests answered, "No."
13Then Haggai said, "If a person defiled by contact with a dead
body touches one of these things, does it become defiled?"
"Yes," the priests replied, "it becomes defiled.[o]"
14Then Haggai said, " 'So it is with this people and this nation in
my sight,' declares the LORD. 'Whatever they do and whatever they
offer[p] there is defiled.
15" 'Now give careful thought[q] to this from this day on[a]—consider how things were before one stone was laid[r] on another in the
LORD's temple.[s] 16When anyone came to a heap of twenty measures,
there were only ten. When anyone went to a wine vat to draw fifty
measures, there were only twenty.[t] 17I struck all the work of your
hands[u] with blight,[v] mildew and hail, yet you did not turn to me,'

1:15 [a]ver 1
2:3 [b]Ezr 3:12 [c]Zec 4:10
2:4 [d]1Ch 28:20; Zec 8:9; Eph 6:10 [e]2Sa 5:10; Ac 7:9
2:5 [f]Ex 29:46 [g]Ne 9:20; Isa 63:11
2:6 [h]Isa 10:25 [i]Heb 12:26*
2:7 [j]Isa 60:7
2:9 [k]Ps 85:9
2:10 [l]ver 1
2:11 [m]Lev 10:10-11; Dt 17:8-11; Mal 2:7
2:12 [n]Lev 6:27; Mt 23:19
2:13 [o]Lev 22:4-6
2:14 [p]Isa 1:13
2:15 [q]Hag 1:5 [r]Ezr 3:10 [s]Ezr 4:24
2:16 [t]Hag 1:6
2:17 [u]Hag 1:11 [v]Dt 28:22; 1Ki 8:37; Am 4:9

[a]15 *Or to the days past*

declares the LORD.[a] 18'From this day on, from this twenty-fourth
day of the ninth month, give careful thought to the day when the
foundation[b] of the LORD's temple was laid. Give careful thought:
19Is there yet any seed left in the barn? Until now, the vine and the
fig tree, the pomegranate and the olive tree have not borne fruit.
"'From this day on I will bless you.'"
20The word of the LORD came to Haggai a second time on the
twenty-fourth day of the month: 21"Tell Zerubbabel[c] governor of
Judah that I will shake the heavens and the earth. 22I will over-
turn royal thrones and shatter the power of the foreign kingdoms.[d] I will overthrow chariots[e] and their drivers; horses and
their riders will fall, each by the sword of his brother.[f]
23"'On that day,' declares the LORD Almighty, 'I will take you,
my servant[g] Zerubbabel son of Shealtiel,' declares the LORD, 'and
I will make you like my signet ring, for I have chosen you,' declares
the LORD Almighty."

2:17 [a] Am 4:6
2:18 [b] Zec 8:9
2:21 [c] Ezr 5:2
2:22 [d] Da 2:44 [e] Mic 5:10 [f] Jdg 7:22
2:23 [g] Isa 43:10

HAGGAI AT A GLANCE

Theme of Haggai:

SEGMENT DIVISIONS

		PARAGRAPH THEMES	CHAPTER THEMES
	1:1-12		1
	1:13-15		
	2:1-9		2
	2:10-19		
	2:20-23		

Author:

Date:

Purpose:

Key Words:

- day of the month
- the word of th Lord came
- house (templ
- people (and pronouns)
- give careful thought
- shake

ZECHARIAH

The earth was peaceful and quiet. All the nations, except for Israel, were at rest. From Israel's perspective, it looked as if God had abandoned his people and forgotten his holy city, Jerusalem. Jerusalem's walls were torn down, Solomon's temple had been destroyed, and now a partially rebuilt temple stood on its site. Even if this temple were completed, it would not begin to equal Solomon's.

The majority of God's people had settled in their land of exile and were reluctant to return to Jerusalem. Only a remnant had come back, and they were a discouraged lot who soon abandoned the rebuilding of the house of God until the word of the Lord first came through Haggai and then Zechariah.

Born in Babylon, Zechariah was among the remnant who returned to Jerusalem under the leadership of Zerubbabel and Joshua. Although Zechariah belonged to the priestly line, he, like Haggai his predecessor, was to be God's prophet to the returned and discouraged remnant.

And so, about 520 to 519 B.C., the word of the Lord came to Zechariah—a needed word, an encouraging word.

Things to Do

General Instructions

If you are going to have a good understanding of Zechariah, it will help to put the book into its historical context. Although this will take extra study, it will be worthwhile.

Ezra gives the historical setting of Zechariah; therefore if you have not studied Ezra, read it before you start Zechariah. Ezra, like Zechariah, is a post-exilic book, which simply means it was written after the Jews were sent into exile under the Babylonians (Chaldeans) in 586 B.C. Ezra records the return of a remnant to Jerusalem under the reign and decree of Cyrus, a Persian king who ruled from 539 to 530 B.C. The Babylonians conquered Judah, then the Medes and Persians conquered the Babylonians.

1. As you read Ezra, observe what is said regarding rebuilding the temple, since the temple plays a key role in Ezra and in Zechariah. Also watch for any reference to Zerubbabel and to Jeshua, who is called Joshua in Zechariah. Joshua is also called Jeshua in Nehemiah, another post-exilic book which focuses on rebuilding the walls of Jerusalem.

2. If you have not studied Haggai, study it next, since Haggai and Zechariah are contemporaries.

Chapters 1-8

1. The book of Zechariah divides into two segments: chapters 1 through 8 and chapters 9 through 14. As you read the first segment, mark every occurrence of the phrase *the word of the Lord came.* There will be slight variations to the wording (e.g. *the word of the Lord Almighty came).* However, mark each occurrence the same way. Then in the margin, note the main point of the Lord's message. Also, if the text tells you when the word came, draw a time symbol in the text. Consult the historical chart on page 1637 for the chronological setting of these messages.

2. As you read, also watch for the phrases, *what do you see?, the Lord showed me, I had,* or *I lifted up* or *I looked.* In the margin write "Vision," and then note briefly what the vision was. As you do this, you will see many correlations between the *word of the Lord* and the vision.

3. Watch for and mark in a distinctive way the following key words or phrases, along with their synonyms or pronouns: *listen (stopped up their ears), return (turn), again (further, added), temple (house,*

house of the Lord), nations, Judah, Jerusalem, I will live among you (I will be its glory within or reference to the Lord's coming), and *seventy years.*

Record these key words and phrases on an index card and use it as a bookmark as you study Zechariah. You will find it helpful to color or mark these phrases in the same way you mark them in the text.

4. Zechariah contains many prophecies regarding the Messiah's first and final comings, the nation of Israel and Jerusalem, and the future of the nations. Therefore, as you read Zechariah chapter by chapter, watch for these prophecies and note them under the appropriate columns on the chart ZECHARIAH'S PROPHETIC REVELATIONS on page 1653.

5. God's name, Jehovah-sabaoth, Lord of hosts, is used repeatedly. Mark these occurrences. Then as you study Zechariah, on a separate piece of paper keep a list of all you learn about God. When you finish Zechariah, record this list in the margin of Zechariah.

6. After you study each chapter, record its theme (subject) on the ZECHARIAH AT A GLANCE chart on page 1654 under the appropriate chapter number and then in the text next to the chapter number.

Chapters 9-14

1. As you read through this segment, watch for the same key words and/or phrases you marked in chapters 1 through 8, but add to your list *in that day* and any reference to the Lord as *King.*

2. Also mark the phrase *this is the word of the Lord.* The occurrences of this phrase divide these final chapters of Zechariah into segments.

3. After you mark the key words and phrases in this segment, list in the margin or on the chart ZECHARIAH'S PROPHETIC REVELATIONS what you learn about each. If you believe *that day* refers to the day of the Lord, also record your insights on the chart THE DAY OF THE LORD beginning on page 2178.

4. When you read chapter 13, watch what will happen to the two parts and the *third (one-third).* Watch the pronouns *they* and *them,* and then list in the margin all you learn about the *third (one-third)*—the remnant that survives.

5. In chapter 14 you will see a reference to the Feast of Booths. On pages 210 and 211, you will find a chart called THE FEASTS OF ISRAEL. As you look at the chart, note the significance of the Feast of Booths (or Tabernacles, as it is sometimes referred to).

6. Record the theme of each chapter as you did previously. Then when you finish, write the theme of Zechariah on ZECHARIAH AT A GLANCE. Record the main theme of the two major segment divisions and fill in the other information called for on the chart.

7. Since Haggai and Zechariah were contemporaries, it would be interesting to note how the messages given by the Lord to these two prophets correlate in time. After you have studied both books, look at the "time symbols" in both books and note when the messages came in relationship to each other. List the messages in the order of their occurrence, using the space at the end of Zechariah 14.

Things to Think About

1. As you have studied Zechariah, have you been touched by the awesomeness of God's sovereignty? What does it mean to you personally to realize that God reigns supreme over the nations? That he has declared things before they have come to pass, and that as he has purposed, so it shall be? If he can handle nations, can he handle your life?

2. Do you take time to listen—really listen—to what God says in his Word? If you have not listened, God's invitation to return to him is still there in Zechariah for you. Believe him . . . and return.

3. How can you apply the truth of Zechariah 4:6, 7 to your own life? Remember the things that were written in the Old Testament were written for our encouragement and perseverance. They are not simply historical records; they are the bread of life by which we live.

4. God said, "I am coming, and I will live among you." Are you prepared? According to 1 John 3:2, 3 the coming of the Lord is a purifying hope. What do you need to do in order not to be ashamed at his coming?

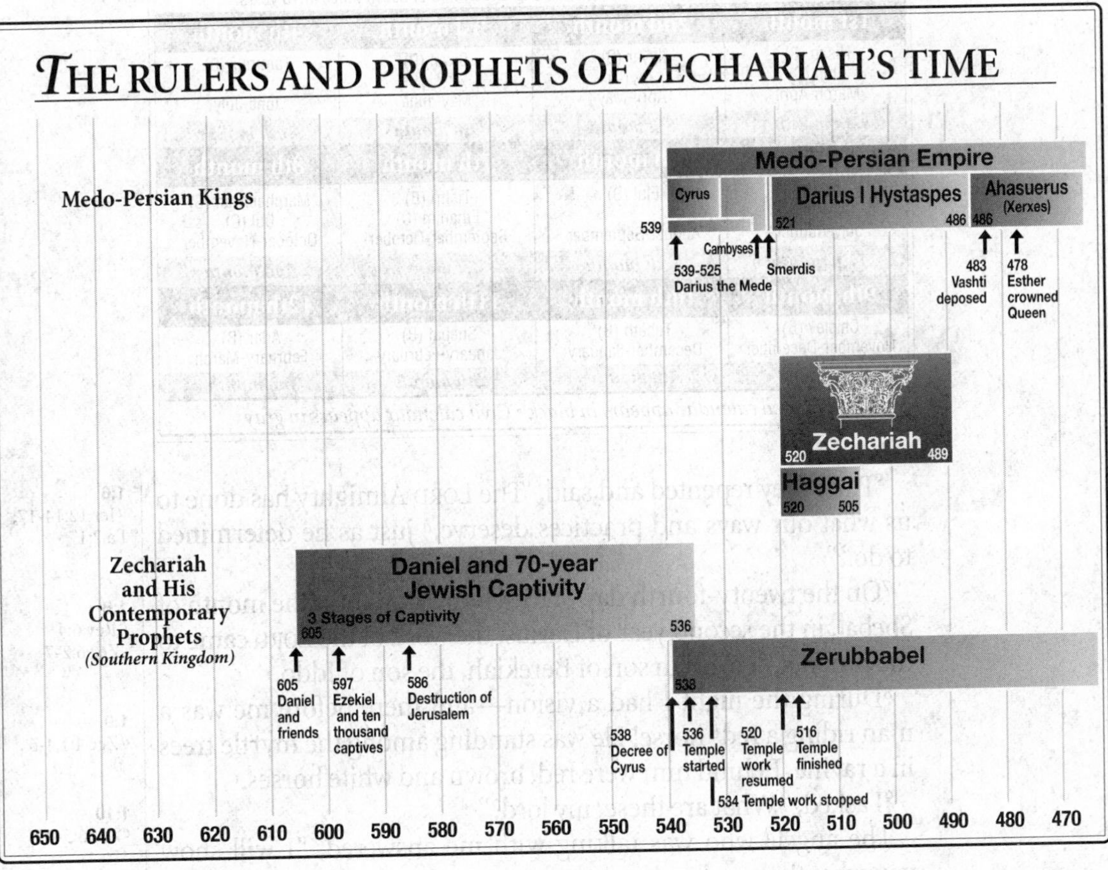

Chapter 1 Theme ______________________

1:1 [a]Ezr 4:24; 6:15 [b]Ezr 5:1 [c]Mt 23:35; Lk 11:51 [d]ver 7; Ne 12:4
1:2 [e]2Ch 36:16
1:3 [f]Mal 3:7; Jas 4:8
1:4 [g]2Ch 36:15 [h]Ps 106:6 [i]2Ch 24:19; Ps 78:8; Jer 6:17

1 In the eighth month of the second year of Darius,[a] the word of
the LORD came to the prophet Zechariah[b] son of Berekiah,[c] the
son of Iddo:[d]
2"The LORD was very angry[e] with your forefathers. 3Therefore
tell the people: This is what the LORD Almighty says: 'Return to me,'
declares the LORD Almighty, 'and I will return to you,'[f] says the
LORD Almighty. 4Do not be like your forefathers,[g] to whom the
earlier prophets proclaimed: This is what the LORD Almighty says:
'Turn from your evil ways[h] and your evil practices.' But they would
not listen or pay attention to me,[i] declares the LORD. 5Where are
your forefathers now? And the prophets, do they live forever? 6But
did not my words and my decrees, which I commanded my servants the prophets, overtake your forefathers?

The Jewish Calendar

Babylonian names (B) for the months are still used today for the Jewish calendar. Canaanite names (C) were used prior to the Babylonian captivity in 586 B.C. Four are mentioned in the Old Testament. **Adar-Sheni** is an intercalary month used every two to three years or seven times in 19 years.

1st month	2nd month	3rd month	4th month
Nisan (B) Abib (C) March-April	Iyyar (B) Ziv (C) April-May	Sivan (B) May-June	Tammuz (B) June-July
7th month	*8th month*	*9th month*	*10th month*
5th month	**6th month**	**7th month**	**8th month**
Ab (B) July-August	Elul (B) August-September	Tishri (B) Ethanim (C) September-October	Marcheshvan (B) Bul (C) October-November
11th month	*12th month*	*1st month*	*2nd month*
9th month	**10th month**	**11th month**	**12th month**
Chislev (B) November-December	Tebeth (B) December-January	Shebat (B) January-February	Adar (B) February-March
3rd month	*4th month*	*5th month*	*6th month*

Sacred calendar appears in black • Civil calendar appears in gray

"Then they repented and said, 'The LORD Almighty has done to
us what our ways and practices deserve,[a] just as he determined
to do.'"
7On the twenty-fourth day of the eleventh month, the month of
Shebat, in the second year of Darius, the word of the LORD came to
the prophet Zechariah son of Berekiah, the son of Iddo.
8During the night I had a vision—and there before me was a
man riding a red[b] horse! He was standing among the myrtle trees
in a ravine. Behind him were red, brown and white horses.[c]
9I asked, "What are these, my lord?"
The angel[d] who was talking with me answered, "I will show
you what they are."
10Then the man standing among the myrtle trees explained,
"They are the ones the LORD has sent to go throughout the earth."[e]
11And they reported to the angel of the LORD, who was standing
among the myrtle trees, "We have gone throughout the earth and
found the whole world at rest and in peace."[f]
12Then the angel of the LORD said, "LORD Almighty, how long will
you withhold mercy from Jerusalem and from the towns of
Judah, which you have been angry with these seventy[g] years?"
13So the LORD spoke kind and comforting words to the angel who
talked with me.[h]
14Then the angel who was speaking to me said, "Proclaim this
word: This is what the LORD Almighty says: 'I am very jealous[i] for
Jerusalem and Zion, 15but I am very angry with the nations that feel
secure.[j] I was only a little angry, but they added to the calamity.'[k]
16"Therefore, this is what the LORD says: 'I will return[l] to Jerusalem with mercy, and there my house will be rebuilt. And the

1:6 [a]Jer 12:14-17; La 2:17
1:8 [b]Rev 6:4 [c]Zec 6:2-7
1:9 [d]Zec 4:1,4-5
1:10 [e]Zec 6:5-8
1:11 [f]Isa 14:7
1:12 [g]Da 9:2
1:13 [h]Zec 4:1
1:14 [i]Joel 2:18; Zec 8:2
1:15 [j]Jer 48:11 [k]Ps 123:3-4; Am 1:11
1:16 [l]Zec 8:3

measuring line[a] will be stretched out over Jerusalem,' declares the LORD Almighty.

17 "Proclaim further: This is what the LORD Almighty says: 'My towns will again overflow with prosperity, and the LORD will again comfort[b] Zion and choose[c] Jerusalem.'"[d]

18 Then I looked up—and there before me were four horns! 19 I asked the angel who was speaking to me, "What are these?"

He answered me, "These are the horns[e] that scattered Judah, Israel and Jerusalem."

20 Then the LORD showed me four craftsmen. 21 I asked, "What are these coming to do?"

He answered, "These are the horns that scattered Judah so that no one could raise his head, but the craftsmen have come to terrify them and throw down these horns of the nations who lifted up their horns[f] against the land of Judah to scatter its people."[g]

Chapter 2 Theme ________________________

2 Then I looked up—and there before me was a man with a measuring line in his hand! 2 I asked, "Where are you going?"

He answered me, "To measure Jerusalem, to find out how wide and how long it is."[h]

3 Then the angel who was speaking to me left, and another angel came to meet him 4 and said to him: "Run, tell that young man, 'Jerusalem will be a city without walls[i] because of the great number[j] of men and livestock in it. 5 And I myself will be a wall[k] of fire around it,' declares the LORD, 'and I will be its glory[l] within.'

6 "Come! Come! Flee from the land of the north," declares the LORD, "for I have scattered you to the four winds of heaven,"[m] declares the LORD.

7 "Come, O Zion! Escape, you who live in the Daughter of Babylon!"[n] 8 For this is what the LORD Almighty says: "After he has honored me and has sent me against the nations that have plundered you—for whoever touches you touches the apple of his eye[o]— 9 I will surely raise my hand against them so that their slaves will plunder them.[a][p] Then you will know that the LORD Almighty has sent me.[q]

10 "Shout and be glad, O Daughter of Zion.[r] For I am coming,[s] and I will live among you,"[t] declares the LORD. 11 "Many nations will be joined with the LORD in that day and will become my people. I will live among you and you will know that the LORD Almighty has sent me to you. 12 The LORD will inherit[u] Judah as his portion in the holy land and will again choose[v] Jerusalem. 13 Be still[w] before the LORD, all mankind, because he has roused himself from his holy dwelling."

1:16 [a]Zec 2:1-2
1:17 [b]Isa 51:3 [c]Isa 14:1 [d]Zec 2:12
1:19 [e]Am 6:13
1:21 [f]Ps 75:4 [g]Ps 75:10
2:2 [h]Eze 40:3; Rev 21:15
2:4 [i]Eze 38:11 [j]Isa 49:20; Jer 30:19; 33:22
2:5 [k]Isa 26:1 [l]Rev 21:23
2:6 [m]Eze 17:21
2:7 [n]Isa 48:20
2:8 [o]Dt 32:10
2:9 [p]Isa 14:2 [q]Zec 4:9
2:10 [r]Zep 3:14 [s]Zec 9:9 [t]Lev 26:12; Zec 8:3
2:12 [u]Dt 32:9; Ps 33:12; Jer 10:16 [v]Zec 1:17
2:13 [w]Hab 2:20

a 8,9 Or *says after . . . eye:* 9 *"I . . . plunder them."*

Chapter 3 Theme ________________________________

3 Then he showed me Joshua[a] [a] the high priest standing before
the angel of the LORD, and Satan[b] [b] standing at his right side to
accuse him. 2The LORD said to Satan, "The LORD rebuke you,[c]
Satan! The LORD, who has chosen[d] Jerusalem, rebuke you! Is not
this man a burning stick snatched from the fire?"[e]
3Now Joshua was dressed in filthy clothes as he stood before the
angel. 4The angel said to those who were standing before him,
"Take off his filthy clothes."
Then he said to Joshua, "See, I have taken away your sin,[f] and I
will put rich garments[g] on you."
5Then I said, "Put a clean turban[h] on his head." So they put a
clean turban on his head and clothed him, while the angel of the
LORD stood by.
6The angel of the LORD gave this charge to Joshua: 7"This is what
the LORD Almighty says: 'If you will walk in my ways and keep
my requirements, then you will govern my house[i] and have charge
of my courts, and I will give you a place among these standing
here.
8"'Listen, O high priest Joshua and your associates seated
before you, who are men symbolic[j] of things to come: I am going
to bring my servant, the Branch.[k] 9See, the stone I have set in front
of Joshua! There are seven eyes[c] on that one stone,[l] and I will
engrave an inscription on it,' says the LORD Almighty, 'and I will
remove the sin[m] of this land in a single day.
10"'In that day each of you will invite his neighbor to sit under
his vine and fig tree,[n]' declares the LORD Almighty."

Chapter 4 Theme ________________________________

4 Then the angel who talked with me returned and wakened[o]
me, as a man is wakened from his sleep.[p] 2He asked me, "What
do you see?"[q]
I answered, "I see a solid gold lampstand[r] with a bowl at the top
and seven lights[s] on it, with seven channels to the lights. 3Also
there are two olive trees[t] by it, one on the right of the bowl and the
other on its left."
4I asked the angel who talked with me, "What are these, my
lord?"
5He answered, "Do you not know what these are?"
"No, my lord," I replied.[u]
6So he said to me, "This is the word of the LORD to Zerubbabel:[v]
'Not by might nor by power, but by my Spirit,'[w] says the LORD
Almighty.

[a] *1* A variant of *Jeshua*; here and elsewhere in Zechariah [b] *1* *Satan* means *accuser.* [c] *9* Or *facets*

3:1 [a] Hag 1:1; Zec 6:11 [b] Ps 109:6
3:2 [c] Jude 9 [d] Isa 14:1 [e] Am 4:11; Jude 23
3:4 [f] Eze 36:25; Mic 7:18 [g] Isa 52:1; Rev 19:8
3:5 [h] Ex 29:6
3:7 [i] Dt 17:8-11; Eze 44:15-16
3:8 [j] Eze 12:11 [k] Isa 4:2
3:9 [l] Isa 28:16 [m] Jer 50:20
3:10 [n] 1Ki 4:25; Mic 4:4
4:1 [o] Da 8:18 [p] Jer 31:26
4:2 [q] Jer 1:13 [r] Ex 25:31; Rev 1:12 [s] Rev 4:5
4:3 [t] ver 11; Rev 11:4
4:5 [u] Zec 1:9
4:6 [v] Ezr 5:2 [w] Isa 11:2-4; Hos 1:7

7“What[a] are you, O mighty mountain? Before Zerubbabel you
will become level ground.[a] Then he will bring out the capstone[b]
to shouts of ‘God bless it! God bless it!’ ”
8Then the word of the LORD came to me: 9“The hands of Zerubbabel have laid the foundation[c] of this temple; his hands will also
complete it.[d] Then you will know that the LORD Almighty has sent
me[e] to you.
10“Who despises the day of small things?[f] Men will rejoice when
they see the plumb line in the hand of Zerubbabel.
“(These seven are the eyes[g] of the LORD, which range throughout
the earth.)”
11Then I asked the angel, “What are these two olive trees[h] on the
right and the left of the lampstand?”
12Again I asked him, “What are these two olive branches beside
the two gold pipes that pour out golden oil?”
13He replied, “Do you not know what these are?”
“No, my lord,” I said.
14So he said, “These are the two who are anointed[i] to[b] serve the
Lord of all the earth.”

Chapter 5 Theme ______________________

5 I looked again—and there before me was a flying scroll![j]
2He asked me, “What do you see?”
I answered, “I see a flying scroll, thirty feet long and fifteen feet
wide.[c]”
3And he said to me, “This is the curse[k] that is going out over the
whole land; for according to what it says on one side, every thief[l]
will be banished, and according to what it says on the other, everyone who swears falsely[m] will be banished. 4The LORD Almighty
declares, ‘I will send it out, and it will enter the house of the thief
and the house of him who swears falsely by my name. It will remain
in his house and destroy it, both its timbers and its stones.[n]’ ”
5Then the angel who was speaking to me came forward and
said to me, “Look up and see what this is that is appearing.”
6I asked, “What is it?”
He replied, “It is a measuring basket.[d]” And he added, “This is
the iniquity[e] of the people throughout the land.”
7Then the cover of lead was raised, and there in the basket sat a
woman! 8He said, “This is wickedness,” and he pushed her back
into the basket and pushed the lead cover down over its mouth.[o]
9Then I looked up—and there before me were two women, with
the wind in their wings! They had wings like those of a stork,[p] and
they lifted up the basket between heaven and earth.

4:7 [a]Jer 51:25 [b]Ps 118:22
4:9 [c]Ezr 3:11 [d]Ezr 3:8; 6:15; Zec 6:12 [e]Zec 2:9
4:10 [f]Hag 2:3 [g]Zec 3:9; Rev 5:6
4:11 [h]ver 3; Rev 11:4
4:14 [i]Ex 29:7; 40:15; Da 9:24-26; Zec 3:1-7
5:1 [j]Eze 2:9; Rev 5:1
5:3 [k]Isa 24:6; 43:28; Mal 3:9; 4:6 [l]Ex 20:15; Mal 3:8 [m]Isa 48:1
5:4 [n]Lev 14:34-45; Hab 2:9-11; Mal 3:5
5:8 [o]Mic 6:11
5:9 [p]Lev 11:19

a 7 Or *Who* b 14 Or *two who bring oil and* c 2 Hebrew *twenty cubits long and ten cubits wide* (about 9 meters long and 4.5 meters wide) d 6 Hebrew *an ephah*; also in verses 7-11 e 6 Or *appearance*

10“Where are they taking the basket?” I asked the angel who was
speaking to me.
11He replied, “To the country of Babylonia[a][a] to build a house[b] for
it. When it is ready, the basket will be set there in its place.”[c]

Chapter 6 Theme ____

6 I looked up again—and there before me were four chariots[d]
coming out from between two mountains—mountains of
bronze! 2The first chariot had red horses, the second black,[e] 3the
third white,[f] and the fourth dappled—all of them powerful. 4I
asked the angel who was speaking to me, “What are these, my
lord?”
5The angel answered me, “These are the four spirits[b][g] of heaven,
going out from standing in the presence of the Lord of the whole
world. 6The one with the black horses is going toward the north
country, the one with the white horses toward the west,[c] and the
one with the dappled horses toward the south.”
7When the powerful horses went out, they were straining to go
throughout the earth.[h] And he said, “Go throughout the earth!”
So they went throughout the earth.
8Then he called to me, “Look, those going toward the north
country have given my Spirit[d] rest[i] in the land of the north.”
9The word of the LORD came to me: 10“Take ⌞silver and gold⌟
from the exiles Heldai, Tobijah and Jedaiah, who have arrived from
Babylon.[j] Go the same day to the house of Josiah son of Zephaniah. 11Take the silver and gold and make a crown,[k] and set it on the
head of the high priest, Joshua[l] son of Jehozadak.[m] 12Tell him this
is what the LORD Almighty says: ‘Here is the man whose name is
the Branch,[n] and he will branch out from his place and build the
temple of the LORD.[o] 13It is he who will build the temple of the
LORD, and he will be clothed with majesty and will sit and rule on
his throne. And he will be a priest[p] on his throne. And there will
be harmony between the two.’ 14The crown will be given to
Heldai,[e] Tobijah, Jedaiah and Hen[f] son of Zephaniah as a memorial in the temple of the LORD. 15Those who are far away will come
and help to build the temple of the LORD,[q] and you will know that
the LORD Almighty has sent me to you.[r] This will happen if you
diligently obey[s] the LORD your God.”

Chapter 7 Theme ____

7 In the fourth year of King Darius, the word of the LORD came
to Zechariah on the fourth day of the ninth month, the
month of Kislev.[t] 2The people of Bethel had sent Sharezer and

[a] *11* Hebrew *Shinar* [b] *5* Or *winds* [c] *6* Or *horses after them* [d] *8* Or *spirit* [e] *14* Syriac; Hebrew *Helem* [f] *14* Or *and the gracious one, the*

5:11 [a] Ge 10:10 [b] Jer 29:5,28 [c] Da 1:2
6:1 [d] ver 5
6:2 [e] Rev 6:5
6:3 [f] Rev 6:2
6:5 [g] Eze 37:9; Mt 24:31; Rev 7:1
6:7 [h] Zec 1:10
6:8 [i] Eze 5:13; 24:13
6:10 [j] Ezr 7:14-16; Jer 28:6
6:11 [k] Ps 21:3 [l] Zec 3:1 [m] Ezr 3:2
6:12 [n] Isa 4:2; Zec 3:8 [o] Ezr 3:8-10; Zec 4:6-9
6:13 [p] Ps 110:4
6:15 [q] Isa 60:10 [r] Zec 2:9-11 [s] Isa 58:12; Jer 7:23; Zec 3:7
7:1 [t] Ne 1:1

Regem-Melech, together with their men, to entreat[a] the LORD 3by
asking the priests of the house of the LORD Almighty and the
prophets, "Should I mourn[b] and fast in the fifth[c] month, as I have
done for so many years?"
4Then the word of the LORD Almighty came to me: 5"Ask all the
people of the land and the priests, 'When you fasted[d] and mourned
in the fifth and seventh months for the past seventy years, was it
really for me that you fasted? 6And when you were eating and
drinking, were you not just feasting for yourselves? 7Are these not
the words the LORD proclaimed through the earlier prophets[e] when
Jerusalem and its surrounding towns were at rest[f] and prosperous,
and the Negev and the western foothills[g] were settled?'"
8And the word of the LORD came again to Zechariah: 9"This is
what the LORD Almighty says: 'Administer true justice;[h] show mercy and compassion to one another. 10Do not oppress the widow or
the fatherless, the alien[i] or the poor. In your hearts do not think
evil of each other.'[j]
11"But they refused to pay attention; stubbornly they turned
their backs and stopped up their ears.[k] 12They made their hearts
as hard as flint[l] and would not listen to the law or to the words that
the LORD Almighty had sent by his Spirit through the earlier
prophets.[m] So the LORD Almighty was very angry.[n]
13"'When I called, they did not listen;[o] so when they called, I
would not listen,'[p] says the LORD Almighty.[q] 14'I scattered[r] them
with a whirlwind[s] among all the nations, where they were strangers. The land was left so desolate behind them that no one could
come or go. This is how they made the pleasant land desolate.[t]'"

Chapter 8 Theme ____________________________

8 Again the word of the LORD Almighty came to me. 2This is
what the LORD Almighty says: "I am very jealous for Zion; I
am burning with jealousy for her."
3This is what the LORD says: "I will return[u] to Zion and dwell in
Jerusalem.[v] Then Jerusalem will be called the City of Truth, and the
mountain of the LORD Almighty will be called the Holy Mountain."
4This is what the LORD Almighty says: "Once again men and
women of ripe old age will sit in the streets of Jerusalem,[w] each
with cane in hand because of his age. 5The city streets will be filled
with boys and girls playing there.[x]"
6This is what the LORD Almighty says: "It may seem marvelous to
the remnant of this people at that time,[y] but will it seem marvelous
to me?[z]" declares the LORD Almighty.
7This is what the LORD Almighty says: "I will save my people
from the countries of the east and the west.[a] 8I will bring them
back[b] to live in Jerusalem; they will be my people,[c] and I will be
faithful and righteous to them as their God."

7:2 [a]Jer 26:19; Zec 8:21
7:3 [b]Zec 12:12-14 [c]Jer 52:12-14; Zec 8:19
7:5 [d]Isa 58:5
7:7 [e]Zec 1:4 [f]Jer 22:21 [g]Jer 17:26
7:9 [h]Zec 8:16
7:10 [i]Ex 22:21 [j]Ex 22:22; Isa 1:17
7:11 [k]Jer 8:5; 11:10; 17:23
7:12 [l]Jer 17:1; Eze 11:19 [m]Ne 9:29 [n]Da 9:12
7:13 [o]Pr 1:24 [p]Isa 1:15; Jer 11:11; 14:12; Mic 3:4 [q]Pr 1:28
7:14 [r]Dt 4:27; 28:64-67 [s]Jer 23:19 [t]Jer 44:6
8:3 [u]Zec 1:16 [v]Zec 2:10
8:4 [w]Isa 65:20
8:5 [x]Jer 30:20; 31:13
8:6 [y]Ps 118:23; 126:1-3 [z]Jer 32:17,27
8:7 [a]Ps 107:3; Isa 11:11; 43:5
8:8 [b]Zec 10:10 [c]Eze 11:19-20; 36:28; Zec 2:11

9This is what the LORD Almighty says: "You who now hear these
words spoken by the prophets[a] who were there when the foundation was laid for the house of the LORD Almighty, let your hands be
strong[b] so that the temple may be built. 10Before that time there
were no wages[c] for man or beast. No one could go about his business safely because of his enemy, for I had turned every man
against his neighbor. 11But now I will not deal with the remnant
of this people as I did in the past,"[d] declares the LORD Almighty.
12"The seed will grow well, the vine will yield its fruit,[e] the
ground will produce its crops,[f] and the heavens will drop their
dew.[g] I will give all these things as an inheritance[h] to the remnant
of this people. 13As you have been an object of cursing[i] among the
nations, O Judah and Israel, so will I save you, and you will be a
blessing.[j] Do not be afraid, but let your hands be strong."
14This is what the LORD Almighty says: "Just as I had determined to bring disaster[k] upon you and showed no pity when your
fathers angered me," says the LORD Almighty, 15"so now I have
determined to do good[l] again to Jerusalem and Judah. Do not be
afraid. 16These are the things you are to do: Speak the truth[m] to
each other, and render true and sound judgment in your courts;[n]
17do not plot evil[o] against your neighbor, and do not love to swear
falsely.[p] I hate all this," declares the LORD.
18Again the word of the LORD Almighty came to me. 19This is what
the LORD Almighty says: "The fasts of the fourth,[q] fifth,[r] seventh[s]
and tenth[t] months will become joyful[u] and glad occasions and
happy festivals for Judah. Therefore love truth[v] and peace."
20This is what the LORD Almighty says: "Many peoples and the
inhabitants of many cities will yet come, 21and the inhabitants of
one city will go to another and say, 'Let us go at once to entreat[w]
the LORD and seek the LORD Almighty. I myself am going.' 22And
many peoples and powerful nations will come to Jerusalem to seek
the LORD Almighty and to entreat him."[x]
23This is what the LORD Almighty says: "In those days ten men
from all languages and nations will take firm hold of one Jew by
the hem of his robe and say, 'Let us go with you, because we have
heard that God is with you.'"[y]

Chapter 9 Theme ____________________

An Oracle

The word of the LORD is against the land of Hadrach
and will rest upon Damascus[z]—
for the eyes of men and all the tribes of Israel
are on the LORD—[a]

[a] 1 Or *Damascus. / For the eye of the LORD is on all mankind, / as well as on the tribes of Israel,*

8:9 [a] Ezr 5:1 [b] Hag 2:4
8:10 [c] Hag 1:6
8:11 [d] Isa 12:1
8:12 [e] Joel 2:22 [f] Ps 67:6 [g] Ge 27:28 [h] Ob 1:17
8:13 [i] Jer 42:18 [j] Ge 12:2
8:14 [k] Jer 31:28; Eze 24:14
8:15 [l] ver 13; Jer 29:11; Mic 7:18-20
8:16 [m] Ps 15:2; Eph 4:25 [n] Zec 7:9
8:17 [o] Pr 3:29 [p] Pr 6:16-19
8:19 [q] Jer 39:2 [r] Jer 52:12 [s] 2Ki 25:25 [t] Jer 52:4 [u] Ps 30:11 [v] ver 16
8:21 [w] Zec 7:2
8:22 [x] Ps 117:1; Isa 60:3; Zec 2:11
8:23 [y] Isa 45:14; 1Co 14:25
9:1 [z] Isa 17:1

God's Judgment Pronounced

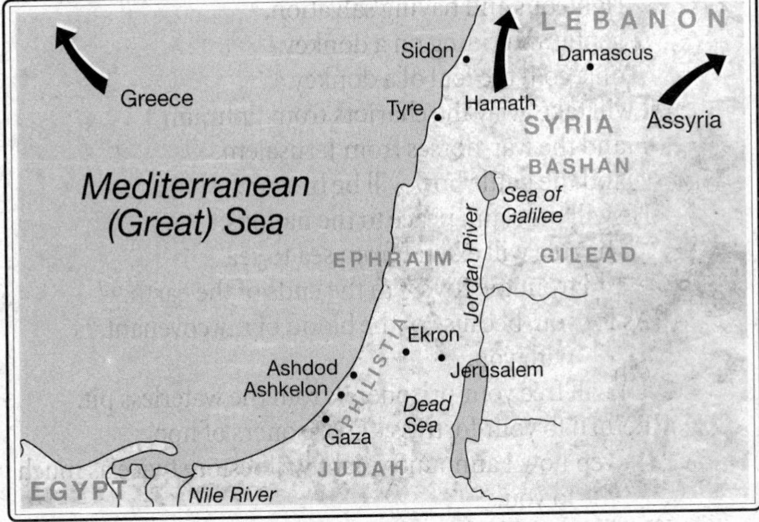

9:2
[a] Jer 49:23
[b] Eze 28:1-19

9:3
[c] Job 27:16; Eze 28:4

9:4
[d] Isa 23:1; Eze 26:3-5; 28:18

9:8
[e] Isa 52:1; 54:14

2 and upon Hamath[a] too, which borders on it,
and upon Tyre[b] and Sidon, though they are
very skillful.
3 Tyre has built herself a stronghold;
she has heaped up silver like dust,
and gold like the dirt of the streets.[c]
4 But the Lord will take away her possessions
and destroy her power on the sea,
and she will be consumed by fire.[d]
5 Ashkelon will see it and fear;
Gaza will writhe in agony,
and Ekron too, for her hope will wither.
Gaza will lose her king
and Ashkelon will be deserted.
6 Foreigners will occupy Ashdod,
and I will cut off the pride of the Philistines.
7 I will take the blood from their mouths,
the forbidden food from between their teeth.
Those who are left will belong to our God
and become leaders in Judah,
and Ekron will be like the Jebusites.
8 But I will defend my house
against marauding forces.
Never again will an oppressor overrun my people,
for now I am keeping watch.[e]

9 Rejoice greatly, O Daughter of Zion!
Shout, Daughter of Jerusalem!
See, your king[a] comes to you,

[a] 9 Or *King*

righteous and having salvation,[a]
gentle and riding on a donkey,
on a colt, the foal of a donkey.[b]
10 I will take away the chariots from Ephraim
and the war-horses from Jerusalem,
and the battle bow will be broken.[c]
He will proclaim peace to the nations.
His rule will extend from sea to sea
and from the River[a] to the ends of the earth.[b][d]
11 As for you, because of the blood of my covenant[e]
with you,
I will free your prisoners[f] from the waterless pit.
12 Return to your fortress,[g] O prisoners of hope;
even now I announce that I will restore twice as much
to you.
13 I will bend Judah as I bend my bow
and fill it with Ephraim.[h]
I will rouse your sons, O Zion,
against your sons, O Greece,[i]
and make you like a warrior's sword.[j]
14 Then the LORD will appear over them;[k]
his arrow will flash like lightning.[l]
The Sovereign LORD will sound the trumpet;
he will march in the storms[m] of the south,
15 and the LORD Almighty will shield[n] them.
They will destroy
and overcome with slingstones.
They will drink and roar as with wine;
they will be full like a bowl
used for sprinkling[c] the corners[o] of the altar.
16 The LORD their God will save them on that day
as the flock of his people.
They will sparkle in his land
like jewels in a crown.[p]
17 How attractive and beautiful they will be!
Grain will make the young men thrive,
and new wine the young women.

Chapter 10 Theme

10 Ask the LORD for rain in the springtime;
it is the LORD who makes the storm clouds.
He gives showers of rain to men,
and plants of the field to everyone.

[a] *10* That is, the Euphrates [b] *10* Or *the end of the land* [c] *15* Or *bowl, / like*

9:9 [a] Isa 9:6-7; 43:3-11; Jer 23:5-6; Zep 3:14-15; Zec 2:10 [b] Mt 21:5*; Jn 12:15*
9:10 [c] Hos 1:7; 2:18; Mic 4:3; 5:10; Zec 10:4 [d] Ps 72:8
9:11 [e] Ex 24:8 [f] Isa 42:7
9:12 [g] Joel 3:16
9:13 [h] Isa 49:2 [i] Joel 3:6 [j] Jer 51:20
9:14 [k] Isa 31:5 [l] Ps 18:14; Hab 3:11 [m] Isa 21:1; 66:15
9:15 [n] Isa 37:35; Zec 12:8 [o] Ex 27:2
9:16 [p] Isa 62:3; Jer 31:11

10:2
[a]Eze 21:21
[b]Eze 34:5; Hos 3:4; Mt 9:36

[2]The idols[a] speak deceit,
diviners see visions that lie;
they tell dreams that are false,
they give comfort in vain.
Therefore the people wander like sheep
oppressed for lack of a shepherd.[b]

10:3
[c]Jer 25:34

[3]"My anger burns against the shepherds,
and I will punish the leaders;[c]
for the LORD Almighty will care
for his flock, the house of Judah,
and make them like a proud horse in battle.

10:4
[d]Isa 22:23
[e]Zec 9:10

[4]From Judah will come the cornerstone,
from him the tent peg,[d]
from him the battle bow,[e]
from him every ruler.
[5]Together they[a] will be like mighty men

10:5
[f]2Sa 22:43
[g]Am 2:15; Hag 2:22

trampling the muddy streets in battle.[f]
Because the LORD is with them,
they will fight and overthrow the horsemen.[g]

[6]"I will strengthen the house of Judah
and save the house of Joseph.
I will restore them

10:6
[h]Zec 8:7-8
[i]Zec 13:9

because I have compassion on them.[h]
They will be as though
I had not rejected them,
for I am the LORD their God
and I will answer[i] them.

10:7
[j]Zec 9:15

[7]The Ephraimites will become like mighty men,
and their hearts will be glad as with wine.[j]
Their children will see it and be joyful;
their hearts will rejoice in the LORD.

10:8
[k]Isa 5:26
[l]Jer 33:22; Eze 36:11

[8]I will signal[k] for them
and gather them in.
Surely I will redeem them;
they will be as numerous[l] as before.
[9]Though I scatter them among the peoples,
yet in distant lands they will remember me.[m]

10:9
[m]Eze 6:9

They and their children will survive,
and they will return.
[10]I will bring them back from Egypt
and gather them from Assyria.[n]
I will bring them to Gilead[o] and Lebanon,

10:10
[n]Isa 11:11
[o]Jer 50:19
[p]Isa 49:19

and there will not be room[p] enough for them.

[a]4,5 Or *ruler, all of them together.* / [5]*They*

[11]They will pass through the sea of trouble;
the surging sea will be subdued
and all the depths of the Nile will dry up.[a]
Assyria's pride[b] will be brought down
and Egypt's scepter[c] will pass away.
[12]I will strengthen them in the LORD
and in his name they will walk,[d]"
declares the LORD.

Chapter 11 Theme

11

Open your doors, O Lebanon,[e]
so that fire may devour your cedars!
[2]Wail, O pine tree, for the cedar has fallen;
the stately trees are ruined!
Wail, oaks of Bashan;
the dense forest[f] has been cut down!
[3]Listen to the wail of the shepherds;
their rich pastures are destroyed!
Listen to the roar of the lions;
the lush thicket of the Jordan is ruined![g]

[4]This is what the LORD my God says: "Pasture the flock marked
for slaughter. [5]Their buyers slaughter them and go unpunished.
Those who sell them say, 'Praise the LORD, I am rich!' Their own
shepherds do not spare them.[h] [6]For I will no longer have pity on
the people of the land," declares the LORD. "I will hand everyone
over to his neighbor[i] and his king. They will oppress the land, and
I will not rescue them from their hands."[j]

[7]So I pastured the flock marked for slaughter, particularly the
oppressed of the flock. Then I took two staffs and called one Favor
and the other Union, and I pastured the flock. [8]In one month I got
rid of the three shepherds.

The flock detested me, and I grew weary of them [9]and said, "I
will not be your shepherd. Let the dying die, and the perishing perish.[k] Let those who are left eat one another's flesh."

[10]Then I took my staff called Favor[l] and broke it, revoking[m] the
covenant I had made with all the nations. [11]It was revoked on that
day, and so the afflicted of the flock who were watching me knew it
was the word of the LORD.

[12]I told them, "If you think it best, give me my pay; but if not,
keep it." So they paid me thirty pieces of silver.[n]

[13]And the LORD said to me, "Throw it to the potter"—the handsome price at which they priced me! So I took the thirty pieces of
silver and threw them into the house of the LORD to the potter.[o]

[14]Then I broke my second staff called Union, breaking the brotherhood between Judah and Israel.

10:11 [a]Isa 19:5-7; 51:10 [b]Zep 2:13 [c]Eze 30:13
10:12 [d]Mic 4:5
11:1 [e]Eze 31:3
11:2 [f]Isa 32:19
11:3 [g]Jer 2:15; 50:44
11:5 [h]Jer 50:7; Eze 34:2-3
11:6 [i]Zec 14:13 [j]Isa 9:19-21; Jer 13:14; Mic 5:8; 7:2-6
11:9 [k]Jer 15:2; 43:11
11:10 [l]ver 7 [m]Ps 89:39; Jer 14:21
11:12 [n]Ex 21:32; Mt 26:15
11:13 [o]Mt 27:9-10*; Ac 1:18-19

15 Then the LORD said to me, "Take again the equipment of a
foolish shepherd. 16 For I am going to raise up a shepherd over the
land who will not care for the lost, or seek the young, or heal the
injured, or feed the healthy, but will eat the meat of the choice
sheep, tearing off their hoofs.

17 "Woe to the worthless shepherd,[a]
who deserts the flock!
May the sword strike his arm[b] and his right eye!
May his arm be completely withered,
his right eye totally blinded!"[c]

Chapter 12 Theme

An Oracle

12 This is the word of the LORD concerning Israel. The LORD,
who stretches out the heavens,[d] who lays the foundation of
the earth,[e] and who forms the spirit of man[f] within him, declares:
2 "I am going to make Jerusalem a cup[g] that sends all the surrounding peoples reeling.[h] Judah[i] will be besieged as well as Jerusalem.
3 On that day, when all the nations[j] of the earth are gathered against
her, I will make Jerusalem an immovable rock[k] for all the nations.
All who try to move it will injure[l] themselves. 4 On that day I will
strike every horse with panic and its rider with madness," declares
the LORD. "I will keep a watchful eye over the house of Judah, but
I will blind all the horses of the nations.[m] 5 Then the leaders of
Judah will say in their hearts, 'The people of Jerusalem are strong,
because the LORD Almighty is their God.'

6 "On that day I will make the leaders of Judah like a firepot[n] in a
woodpile, like a flaming torch among sheaves. They will consume[o]
right and left all the surrounding peoples, but Jerusalem will remain intact in her place.

7 "The LORD will save the dwellings of Judah first, so that the hon-
or of the house of David and of Jerusalem's inhabitants may not
be greater than that of Judah.[p] 8 On that day the LORD will shield[q]
those who live in Jerusalem, so that the feeblest among them will
be like David, and the house of David will be like God,[r] like the
Angel of the LORD going before[s] them. 9 On that day I will set out to
destroy all the nations that attack Jerusalem.[t]

10 "And I will pour out on the house of David and the inhabitants
of Jerusalem a spirit[a] of grace and supplication.[u] They will look
on[b] me, the one they have pierced,[v] and they will mourn for him as
one mourns for an only child, and grieve bitterly for him as one
grieves for a firstborn son. 11 On that day the weeping in Jerusalem

11:17 [a] Jer 23:1 [b] Eze 30:21-22 [c] Jer 23:1
12:1 [d] Isa 42:5; Jer 51:15 [e] Ps 102:25; Heb 1:10 [f] Isa 57:16
12:2 [g] Ps 75:8 [h] Isa 51:23 [i] Zec 14:14
12:3 [j] Zec 14:2 [k] Da 2:34-35 [l] Mt 21:44
12:4 [m] Ps 76:6
12:6 [n] Isa 10:17-18; Zec 11:1 [o] Ob 1:18
12:7 [p] Jer 30:18; Am 9:11
12:8 [q] Joel 3:16; Zec 9:15 [r] Ps 82:6 [s] Mic 7:8
12:9 [t] Zec 14:2-3
12:10 [u] Isa 44:3; Eze 39:29; Joel 2:28-29 [v] Jn 19:34,37*; Rev 1:7

a 10 Or *the Spirit* b 10 Or *to*

will be great, like the weeping of Hadad Rimmon in the plain of
Megiddo.[a] 12The land will mourn,[b] each clan by itself, with their
wives by themselves: the clan of the house of David and their
wives, the clan of the house of Nathan and their wives, 13the clan of
the house of Levi and their wives, the clan of Shimei and their
wives, 14and all the rest of the clans and their wives.

Chapter 13 Theme ______________________

13 "On that day a fountain[c] will be opened to the house of
David and the inhabitants of Jerusalem, to cleanse[d] them
from sin and impurity.

2"On that day, I will banish the names of the idols[e] from the
land, and they will be remembered no more," declares the LORD
Almighty. "I will remove both the prophets[f] and the spirit of impurity from the land. 3And if anyone still prophesies, his father and
mother, to whom he was born, will say to him, 'You must die, because you have told lies in the LORD's name.' When he prophesies,
his own parents will stab him.[g]

4"On that day every prophet will be ashamed[h] of his prophetic
vision. He will not put on a prophet's garment[i] of hair[j] in order to
deceive. 5He will say, 'I am not a prophet. I am a farmer; the land
has been my livelihood since my youth.[a][k] 6If someone asks him,
'What are these wounds on your body[b]?' he will answer, 'The
wounds I was given at the house of my friends.'

7"Awake, O sword,[l] against my shepherd,[m]
against the man who is close to me!"
declares the LORD Almighty.
"Strike the shepherd,
and the sheep will be scattered,[n]
and I will turn my hand against the little ones.
8In the whole land," declares the LORD,
"two-thirds will be struck down and perish;
yet one-third will be left in it.[o]
9This third I will bring into the fire;[p]
I will refine them like silver[q]
and test them like gold.
They will call[r] on my name
and I will answer[s] them;
I will say, 'They are my people,'[t]
and they will say, 'The LORD is our God.[u]'"

Chapter 14 Theme ______________________

14 A day of the LORD[v] is coming when your plunder will be
divided among you.

a5 Or *farmer; a man sold me in my youth* b6 Or *wounds between your hands*

12:11 [a]2Ki 23:29
12:12 [b]Mt 24:30; Rev 1:7
13:1 [c]Jer 17:13 [d]Ps 51:2; Heb 9:14
13:2 [e]Ex 23:13; Eze 36:25; Hos 2:17 [f]1Ki 22:22; Jer 23:14-15
13:3 [g]Dt 13:6-11; 18:20; Jer 23:34; Eze 14:9
13:4 [h]Jer 6:15; Mic 3:6-7 [i]Mt 3:4 [j]2Ki 1:8; Isa 20:2
13:5 [k]Am 7:14
13:7 [l]Jer 47:6 [m]Isa 40:11; 53:4; Eze 37:24 [n]Mt 26:31*; Mk 14:27*
13:8 [o]Eze 5:2-4,12
13:9 [p]Mal 3:2 [q]Isa 48:10; 1Pe 1:6-7 [r]Ps 50:15 [s]Zec 10:6 [t]Jer 30:22 [u]Jer 29:12
14:1 [v]Isa 13:9; Mal 4:1

2I will gather all the nations to Jerusalem to fight against it; the
city will be captured, the houses ransacked, and the women raped.
Half of the city will go into exile, but the rest of the people will not
be taken from the city.[a]
3Then the LORD will go out and fight[b] against those nations, as he
fights in the day of battle. 4On that day his feet will stand on the
Mount of Olives,[c] east of Jerusalem, and the Mount of Olives will
be split in two from east to west, forming a great valley, with half of
the mountain moving north and half moving south. 5You will
flee by my mountain valley, for it will extend to Azel. You will flee
as you fled from the earthquake[a][d] in the days of Uzziah king of
Judah. Then the LORD my God will come,[e] and all the holy ones
with him.[f]
6On that day there will be no light,[g] no cold or frost. 7It will be a
unique[h] day, without daytime or nighttime[i]—a day known to the
LORD. When evening comes, there will be light.[j]
8On that day living water[k] will flow out from Jerusalem, half to
the eastern[l] sea[b] and half to the western sea,[c] in summer and in
winter.
9The LORD will be king over the whole earth.[m] On that day there
will be one LORD, and his name the only name.[n]
10The whole land, from Geba[o] to Rimmon, south of Jerusalem,
will become like the Arabah. But Jerusalem will be raised up[p] and
remain in its place,[q] from the Benjamin Gate to the site of the First
Gate, to the Corner Gate, and from the Tower of Hananel to the
royal winepresses. 11It will be inhabited; never again will it be
destroyed. Jerusalem will be secure.[r]
12This is the plague with which the LORD will strike all the
nations that fought against Jerusalem: Their flesh will rot while
they are still standing on their feet, their eyes will rot in their sockets, and their tongues will rot in their mouths.[s] 13On that day men
will be stricken by the LORD with great panic. Each man will seize
the hand of another, and they will attack each other.[t] 14Judah[u] too
will fight at Jerusalem. The wealth of all the surrounding nations
will be collected[v]—great quantities of gold and silver and clothing.
15A similar plague[w] will strike the horses and mules, the camels and
donkeys, and all the animals in those camps.
16Then the survivors from all the nations that have attacked Jerusalem will go up year after year to worship the King, the LORD
Almighty, and to celebrate the Feast of Tabernacles.[x] 17If any of the
peoples of the earth do not go up to Jerusalem to worship the King,
the LORD Almighty, they will have no rain.[y] 18If the Egyptian people do not go up and take part, they will have no rain. The LORD[d]

14:2 [a] Isa 13:6; Zec 13:8
14:3 [b] Zec 9:14-15
14:4 [c] Eze 11:23
14:5 [d] Am 1:1 [e] Isa 29:6; 66:15-16 [f] Mt 16:27; 25:31
14:6 [g] Isa 13:10; Jer 4:23
14:7 [h] Jer 30:7 [i] Rev 21:23-25; 22:5 [j] Isa 30:26
14:8 [k] Eze 47:1-12; Jn 7:38; Rev 22:1-2 [l] Joel 2:20
14:9 [m] Dt 6:4; Isa 45:24; Rev 11:15 [n] Eph 4:5-6
14:10 [o] 1Ki 15:22 [p] Jer 30:18; Am 9:11 [q] Zec 12:6
14:11 [r] Eze 34:25-28
14:12 [s] Lev 26:16; Dt 28:22
14:13 [t] Zec 11:6
14:14 [u] Zec 12:2 [v] Isa 23:18
14:15 [w] ver 12
14:16 [x] Isa 60:6-9
14:17 [y] Jer 14:4; Am 4:7

a5 Or *5My mountain valley will be blocked and will extend to Azel. It will be blocked as it was blocked because of the earthquake* b8 That is, the Dead Sea c8 That is, the Mediterranean d18 Or *part, then the LORD*

will bring on them the plague he inflicts on the nations that do
not go up to celebrate the Feast of Tabernacles.[a] 19This will be the
punishment of Egypt and the punishment of all the nations that
do not go up to celebrate the Feast of Tabernacles.

20On that day HOLY TO THE LORD will be inscribed on the bells of
the horses, and the cooking pots[b] in the LORD's house will be like
the sacred bowls[c] in front of the altar. 21Every pot in Jerusalem
and Judah will be holy[d] to the LORD Almighty, and all who come
to sacrifice will take some of the pots and cook in them. And on
that day[e] there will no longer be a Canaanite[a][f] in the house of the
LORD Almighty.[g]

a 21 Or *merchant*

14:18
[a] ver 12

14:20
[b] Eze 46:20
[c] Zec 9:15

14:21
[d] Ro 14:6-7; 1Co 10:31
[e] Ne 8:10
[f] Zec 9:8
[g] Eze 44:9

Zechariah's Prophetic Revelations

Concerning Messiah, Judah, and Jerusalem	Concerning the Nations	Concerning Messiah, the Savior and King

Theme of Zechariah:

SEGMENT DIVISIONS

		CHAPTER THEMES
		1
		2
		3
		4
		5
		6
		7
		8
		9
		10
		11
		12
		13
		14

Author:

Date:

Purpose:

Key Words:

MALACHI

Because they had not obeyed the word of the Lord, in 586 B.C. the children of Israel were taken into captivity. The nation that was once the head became the tail, just as God had spoken through his prophet Moses. And just as God had spoken through Jeremiah the prophet, the children of Israel's captivity lasted for 70 years.

In 538 B.C. Cyrus, king of Persia, issued a decree allowing the children of Israel to return to Jerusalem and rebuild their temple. It was just as God had said when Isaiah gave this prophecy 175 years before Cyrus was born. In 516 B.C. Zerubbabel finished the temple, just as God promised. In 445 B.C. the Persian King Artaxerxes permitted Nehemiah to return to Jerusalem and rebuild its walls, just as Daniel had prophesied.

Over and over the children of Israel saw that God stood by his word. Just as Solomon wrote in Proverbs, the hearts of kings were in God's hands and he could turn them wherever he wanted. Why then did the remnant of Israel think that they could live and worship any way they wanted once they had returned from their 70 years of exile and had settled again in Israel? Had they grown tired of waiting for the fulfillment of the prophecies which promised that the Messiah would reign as King over all the earth? Had God abandoned them as he had Esau's descendants? Did they think he would allow the heathen nations who had come against them to go unpunished? Or were they entertaining thoughts that God really did not love them, that he would not keep his covenant promises?

Whatever it was, once again the remnant became apathetic in their relationship with God. So he spoke one more time through Malachi, whose name means "my messenger." It was sometime around 433 B.C.

Things to Do

1. Since Malachi is a short book, read it without interruption so you can get a perspective of the book before you observe it chapter by chapter. As you read, catch the atmosphere of this book. Remember, this was written to people who had been sent into exile because of disobedience and then had returned to their land just as God had promised.

2. Now read through Malachi one chapter at a time, doing the following:
   a. In a distinctive way or color mark the key words listed on the MALACHI AT A GLANCE chart on page 1661. Write these key words on an index card you can use as a bookmark while you study Malachi.
   b. As you mark every reference to *you say, you ask, saying* or *said,* watch what the priests and/or the people say and how God answers.
   c. Note in the margin with whom God is upset, why he is upset, and what he tells them to do or what he is going to do as a result.
   d. Take note of what will happen to those who fear his name and to those who do not. Record your insights in the margin.
   e. Note God's call to return to him, how they are to return, and what will happen if they do.

3. When you finish each chapter, decide what the main subject or theme of that chapter is and then record it on MALACHI AT A GLANCE and next to the chapter number in the text.

4. As you read the final chapter of Malachi, read Deuteronomy 28-30 which speaks of the blessings or curses upon those who obey or disobey the law given by Moses.

5. God was silent for 400 years after he spoke through his prophet Malachi. His silence was broken when an angel appeared to Zacharias with the news that he and Elizabeth would give birth to a son.

Read Luke 1:5-17 and Matthew 11:2-15 and see how these passages relate to God's final promise in Malachi. Record the essence of that promise in the margin of Malachi 4 and then write next to it the cross-references in Luke and Matthew.

6. Beginning on page 2178 is a chart called THE DAY OF THE LORD. Record on it what you learn from Malachi about that day. Note the reference (book, chapter, and verse) that you took your information from so you can find it later.

Things to Think About

1. What do you learn from God's word to the priests that you can apply to your own life? Read through the list you compiled on "the priests" and remember that if you belong to the Lord Jesus Christ you are part of a kingdom of priests unto God. What kind of a priest are you? In principle do you think God expects anything less of you as a Christian? For instance, what do you offer the Lord of your time and talents, your tithe and offering? Do you give others instructions according to the Word of the Lord or according to the current philosophy of the world? What about your covenant relationship with your mate?

2. Are you tired of serving God? Do you fear him? If so, what is God's promise to you?

Chapter 1 Theme ______________________________

1 An oracle:[a] The word[b] of the LORD to Israel through Malachi.[a]

2 "I have loved[c] you," says the LORD.
"But you ask, 'How have you loved us?'
"Was not Esau Jacob's brother?" the LORD says. "Yet I have loved
Jacob,[d] 3 but Esau I have hated, and I have turned his mountains
into a wasteland[e] and left his inheritance to the desert jackals.[f]"
4 Edom may say, "Though we have been crushed, we will rebuild[g]
the ruins."
But this is what the LORD Almighty says: "They may build, but I
will demolish. They will be called the Wicked Land, a people always
under the wrath of the LORD.[h] 5 You will see it with your own eyes
and say, 'Great[i] is the LORD—even beyond the borders of Israel!'[j]
6 "A son honors his father, and a servant his master. If I am a
father, where is the honor due me? If I am a master, where is the
respect[k] due me?" says the LORD Almighty.[l] "It is you, O priests,
who show contempt for my name.
"But you ask, 'How have we shown contempt for your name?'
7 "You place defiled food[m] on my altar.
"But you ask, 'How have we defiled you?'
"By saying that the LORD's table is contemptible. 8 When you
bring blind animals for sacrifice, is that not wrong? When you
sacrifice crippled or diseased animals,[n] is that not wrong? Try
offering them to your governor! Would he be pleased with you?
Would he accept you?" says the LORD Almighty.[o]
9 "Now implore God to be gracious to us. With such offerings[p]
from your hands, will he accept you?"—says the LORD Almighty.

1:1 [a] Na 1:1 [b] 1Pe 4:11
1:2 [c] Dt 4:37 [d] Ro 9:13*
1:3 [e] Isa 34:10 [f] Eze 35:3-9
1:4 [g] Isa 9:10 [h] Eze 25:12-14
1:5 [i] Ps 35:27; Mic 5:4 [j] Am 1:11-12
1:6 [k] Isa 1:2 [l] Job 5:17
1:7 [m] ver 12; Lev 21:6
1:8 [n] Lev 22:22; Dt 15:21 [o] Isa 43:23
1:9 [p] Lev 23:33-44

[a] 1 *Malachi* means *my messenger.*

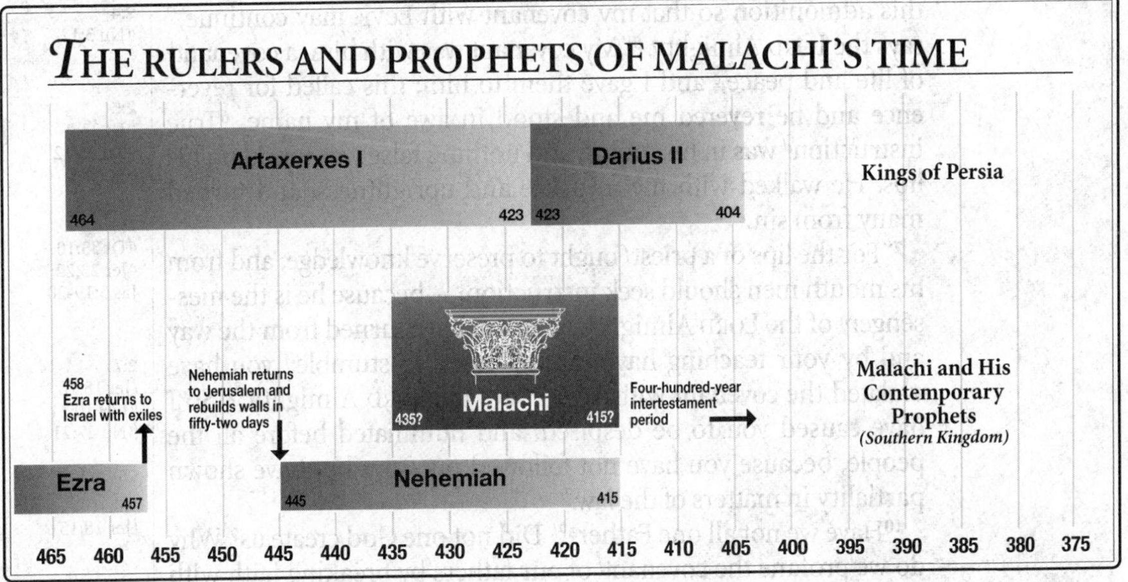

1:10 [a]Hos 5:6 [b]Isa 1:11-14; Jer 14:12
1:11 [c]Isa 60:6-7; Rev 8:3
1:12 [d]ver 7
1:13 [e]Isa 43:22-24
1:14 [f]Lev 22:18-21 [g]1Ti 6:15
2:1 [h]ver 7
2:2 [i]Dt 28:20
2:3 [j]Ex 29:14 [k]1Ki 14:10

10"Oh, that one of you would shut the temple doors, so that you
would not light useless fires on my altar! I am not pleased[a] with
you," says the LORD Almighty, "and I will accept no offering[b] from
your hands. 11My name will be great among the nations, from the
rising to the setting of the sun. In every place incense[c] and pure
offerings will be brought to my name, because my name will be
great among the nations," says the LORD Almighty.
12"But you profane it by saying of the Lord's table, 'It is defiled,'
and of its food,[d] 'It is contemptible.' 13And you say, 'What a burden!'[e] and you sniff at it contemptuously," says the LORD Almighty.
"When you bring injured, crippled or diseased animals and offer
them as sacrifices, should I accept them from your hands?" says the
LORD. 14"Cursed is the cheat who has an acceptable male in his
flock and vows to give it, but then sacrifices a blemished animal[f]
to the Lord. For I am a great king,[g]" says the LORD Almighty,
"and my name is to be feared among the nations.

Chapter 2 Theme ________________

2 "And now this admonition is for you, O priests.[h] 2If you do
not listen, and if you do not set your heart to honor my name,"
says the LORD Almighty, "I will send a curse[i] upon you, and I will
curse your blessings. Yes, I have already cursed them, because
you have not set your heart to honor me.
3"Because of you I will rebuke[a] your descendants[b]; I will spread
on your faces the offal[j] from your festival sacrifices, and you will
be carried off with it.[k] 4And you will know that I have sent you

a3 Or *cut off* (see Septuagint) b3 Or *will blight your grain*

this admonition so that my covenant with Levi[a] may continue,"
says the LORD Almighty. 5"My covenant was with him, a covenant[b]
of life and peace,[c] and I gave them to him; this called for reverence and he revered me and stood in awe of my name. 6True
instruction[d] was in his mouth and nothing false was found on his
lips. He walked with me in peace and uprightness, and turned
many from sin.[e]

7"For the lips of a priest[f] ought to preserve knowledge, and from
his mouth men should seek instruction[g]—because he is the messenger[h] of the LORD Almighty. 8But you have turned from the way
and by your teaching have caused many to stumble;[i] you have
violated the covenant with Levi," says the LORD Almighty. 9"So I
have caused you to be despised[j] and humiliated before all the
people, because you have not followed my ways but have shown
partiality in matters of the law."

10Have we not all one Father[a]?[k] Did not one God create us? Why
do we profane the covenant[l] of our fathers by breaking faith with
one another?

11Judah has broken faith. A detestable thing has been committed in Israel and in Jerusalem: Judah has desecrated the sanctuary the LORD loves, by marrying[m] the daughter of a foreign god.[n]
12As for the man who does this, whoever he may be, may the LORD
cut him off[o] from the tents of Jacob[b]—even though he brings
offerings[p] to the LORD Almighty.

13Another thing you do: You flood the LORD's altar with tears. You
weep and wail because he no longer pays attention[q] to your offerings or accepts them with pleasure from your hands. 14You ask,
"Why?" It is because the LORD is acting as the witness between you
and the wife of your youth,[r] because you have broken faith with her,
though she is your partner, the wife of your marriage covenant.

15Has not ⌊the LORD⌋ made them one?[s] In flesh and spirit they
are his. And why one? Because he was seeking godly offspring.[c][t]
So guard yourself in your spirit, and do not break faith with the
wife of your youth.

16"I hate divorce,[u]" says the LORD God of Israel, "and I hate a
man's covering himself[d] with violence as well as with his garment," says the LORD Almighty.

So guard yourself in your spirit, and do not break faith.

17You have wearied[v] the LORD with your words.

"How have we wearied him?" you ask.

By saying, "All who do evil are good in the eyes of the LORD,
and he is pleased with them" or "Where is the God of justice?"

a *10* Or *father* b *12* Or *12May the LORD cut off from the tents of Jacob anyone who gives testimony in behalf of the man who does this* c *15* Or *15But the one ⌊who is our father⌋ did not do this, not as long as life remained in him. And what was he seeking? An offspring from God*
d *16* Or *his wife*

2:4 [a]Nu 3:12
2:5 [b]Dt 33:9 [c]Nu 25:12
2:6 [d]Dt 33:10 [e]Jer 23:22; Jas 5:19-20
2:7 [f]Jer 18:18 [g]Lev 10:11 [h]Nu 27:21
2:8 [i]Jer 18:15
2:9 [j]1Sa 2:30
2:10 [k]1Co 8:6 [l]Ex 19:5
2:11 [m]Ne 13:23 [n]Ezr 9:1; Jer 3:7-9
2:12 [o]Eze 24:21 [p]Mal 1:10
2:13 [q]Jer 14:12
2:14 [r]Pr 5:18
2:15 [s]Ge 2:24; Mt 19:4-6 [t]1Co 7:14
2:16 [u]Dt 24:1; Mt 5:31-32; 19:4-9
2:17 [v]Isa 43:24

Chapter 3 Theme ____________________________

3 "See, I will send my messenger, who will prepare the way
before me.[a] Then suddenly the Lord you are seeking will
come to his temple; the messenger of the covenant, whom you
desire, will come," says the LORD Almighty.
2But who can endure[b] the day of his coming? Who can stand
when he appears? For he will be like a refiner's fire[c] or a launderer's
soap. 3He will sit as a refiner and purifier of silver;[d] he will purify[e]
the Levites and refine them like gold and silver. Then the LORD
will have men who will bring offerings in righteousness, 4and the
offerings[f] of Judah and Jerusalem will be acceptable to the LORD,
as in days gone by, as in former years.[g]
5"So I will come near to you for judgment. I will be quick to testify against sorcerers, adulterers and perjurers,[h] against those who
defraud laborers of their wages,[i] who oppress the widows[j] and the
fatherless, and deprive aliens of justice, but do not fear me," says
the LORD Almighty.
6"I the LORD do not change.[k] So you, O descendants of Jacob, are
not destroyed. 7Ever since the time of your forefathers you have
turned away[l] from my decrees and have not kept them. Return to
me, and I will return to you,"[m] says the LORD Almighty.
"But you ask, 'How are we to return?'
8"Will a man rob God? Yet you rob me.
"But you ask, 'How do we rob you?'
"In tithes[n] and offerings. 9You are under a curse—the whole
nation of you—because you are robbing me. 10Bring the whole
tithe into the storehouse,[o] that there may be food in my house.
Test me in this," says the LORD Almighty, "and see if I will not throw
open the floodgates[p] of heaven and pour out so much blessing
that you will not have room enough for it. 11I will prevent pests
from devouring your crops, and the vines in your fields will not
cast their fruit," says the LORD Almighty. 12"Then all the nations
will call you blessed,[q] for yours will be a delightful land,"[r] says
the LORD Almighty.
13"You have said harsh things[s] against me," says the LORD.
"Yet you ask, 'What have we said against you?'
14"You have said, 'It is futile[t] to serve God. What did we gain by
carrying out his requirements and going about like mourners[u]
before the LORD Almighty? 15But now we call the arrogant blessed.
Certainly the evildoers[v] prosper, and even those who challenge
God escape.'"
16Then those who feared the LORD talked with each other, and
the LORD listened and heard.[w] A scroll[x] of remembrance was written in his presence concerning those who feared the LORD and
honored his name.

3:1 [a]Isa 40:3; Mt 11:10*; Mk 1:2*; Lk 7:27*
3:2 [b]Eze 22:14; Rev 6:17 [c]Zec 13:9; Mt 3:10-12
3:3 [d]Da 12:10 [e]Isa 1:25
3:4 [f]2Ch 7:12; Ps 51:19; Mal 1:11 [g]2Ch 7:3
3:5 [h]Jer 7:9 [i]Lev 19:13; Jas 5:4 [j]Ex 22:22
3:6 [k]Nu 23:19; Jas 1:17
3:7 [l]Jer 7:26; Ac 7:51 [m]Zec 1:3
3:8 [n]Ne 13:10-12
3:10 [o]Ne 13:12 [p]2Ki 7:2
3:12 [q]Isa 61:9 [r]Isa 62:4
3:13 [s]Mal 2:17
3:14 [t]Ps 73:13 [u]Isa 58:3
3:15 [v]Jer 7:10
3:16 [w]Ps 34:15 [x]Ps 56:8

17"They will be mine," says the LORD Almighty, "in the day when
I make up my treasured possession.[a][a] I will spare[b] them, just as
in compassion a man spares his son who serves him. 18And you
will again see the distinction between the righteous[c] and the
wicked, between those who serve God and those who do not.

Chapter 4 Theme ______________

4 "Surely the day is coming;[d] it will burn like a furnace. All the
arrogant and every evildoer will be stubble,[e] and that day
that is coming will set them on fire," says the LORD Almighty.
"Not a root or a branch will be left to them. 2But for you who
revere my name, the sun of righteousness[f] will rise with healing[g]
in its wings. And you will go out and leap[h] like calves released
from the stall. 3Then you will trample[i] down the wicked; they will
be ashes[j] under the soles of your feet on the day when I do these
things," says the LORD Almighty.
4"Remember the law[k] of my servant Moses, the decrees and
laws I gave him at Horeb for all Israel.
5"See, I will send you the prophet Elijah[l] before that great and
dreadful day of the LORD comes.[m] 6He will turn the hearts of the
fathers to their children,[n] and the hearts of the children to their
fathers; or else I will come and strike[o] the land with a curse."[p]

a 17 Or *Almighty, "my treasured possession, in the day when I act*

3:17
[a] Dt 7:6
[b] Ps 103:13; Isa 26:20

3:18
[c] Ge 18:25

4:1
[d] Joel 2:31
[e] Isa 5:24; Ob 18

4:2
[f] Lk 1:78; Eph 5:14
[g] Isa 30:26
[h] Isa 35:6

4:3
[i] Job 40:12
[j] Eze 28:18

4:4
[k] Ps 147:19

4:5
[l] Mt 11:14; Lk 1:17
[m] Joel 2:31

4:6
[n] Lk 1:17
[o] Isa 11:4; Rev 19:15
[p] Zec 5:3

eme of Malachi:

thor:

te:

rpose:

y Words:

Lord Almighty

you say, you ask, saying (said)

profane (desecrated)

my name (or your name)

priest(s)

sacrifice(s) (offering[s], offer them as sacrifices)

curse

covenant

SEGMENT DIVISIONS	CHAPTER THEMES
	1
	2
	3
	4

THE NEW TESTAMENT

ITSB

The Genealogy of Jesus the Christ

As proof of his right to the throne of David through Mary

For the generations from Adam to Abraham, see Luke 3:34-38

Abraham
Isaac
Jacob
Judah
Perez
Hezron
Ram
Admin
Amminadab
Nahshon
Salmon—Rahab
Boaz—Ruth
Obed
Jesse

David

Nathan
Mattatha
Menna
Melea
Eliakim
Jonam
Joseph
Judah
Simeon
Levi
Matthat
Jorim
Eliezer
Joshua
Er
Elmadam
Cosam
Addi
Melki
Neri
Shealtiel
Zerubbabel
Rhesa
Joanan
Joda
Josech
Semein
Mattathias
Maath
Naggai
Esli
Nahum
Amos
Mattathias
Joseph
Jannai
Melki
Levi
Matthat
Heli
Mary

Solomon
Rehoboam
Abijah
Asa
Jehoshaphat
Joram (Jehoram)
Ahaziah
Joash
Amaziah
Uzziah (Azariah)
Jotham
Ahaz
Hezekiah
Manasseh
Amon
Josiah
Jehoiakim
Jeconiah (Jehoiachin)
Shealtiel
Zerubbabel
Abiud
Eliakim
Azor
Zadok
Akim
Eliud
Eleazar
Matthan
Jacob
Joseph

The Holy Spirit
Luke 1:35

Jesus
("He was the son, so it was thought, of Joseph" [Luke 3:23])

This information is taken from
1 Chronicles 3
Matthew 1
Luke 3

Mediterranean (Great) Sea
Sidon
Mt. Lebanon
SYRIA
ABILENE
Mt. Hermon
Tyre
PHOENICIA
Caesarea Philippi
Kedesh
GALILEE
Acco (Ptolemais)
Chorazin
Bethsaida
Gennesaret
Capernaum
Magdala
Cana
Tiberias
Yarmuk River
Mt. Tabor
Sea of Galilee
Nazareth
Japhia
Gadara
Dora
Nain
Beth Shan
Jordan River
Caesarea
SAMARIA
Aenon
DECAPOLIS
Plain of Sharon
Samaria
Mt.Ebal
Sychar
Shechem
Mt. Gerizim
Jabbok River
Antipatris
Joppa
PEREA
Lydda (Lod)
Ephraim
Emmaus
Ramah
Jericho
Mt. of Olives
Jerusalem
Bethany
Qumran
(Essene community)
Medeba
Bethlehem
JUDEA
Herodium
Tekoa
Gaza
Hebron
Dibon
En Gedi
Arnon River
Dead (Salt) Sea
Masada
IDUMEA
Arad
NABATEANS
Beersheba
Zoar
Zered Brook

Bible Cities in the Time of Jesus

MATTHEW

God promised Abraham that through his seed all the nations of the earth would be blessed (Genesis 12:3; 15:1-6). Where was this son of Abraham?

God promised Isaiah that a child would be born, a son would be given, and the government would rest on his shoulders. His name would be Wonderful Counselor, Mighty God, Everlasting Father, Prince of Peace. There would be no end to the increase of his government or of peace. He would occupy the throne of David (Isaiah 9:6, 7). Where was this son of David?

No one knew until a baby's cry went up from Bethlehem Ephrathah. The Magi from the East arrived in Jerusalem saying, "Where is the one who has been born king of the Jews?" The one who was to be ruler in Israel (Micah 5:2), the son of David, the son of Abraham, had been born. Matthew tells us about him, the king of the Jews.

Things to Do

1. From the first verse Matthew's purpose is clear: to show that Jesus was the long-awaited king, the son of David, the Messiah whose coming was prophesied throughout the Old Testament.

   There is a pattern to Matthew that repeats itself and divides the Gospel into six segments. Matthew presents certain facts concerning the person and work of Jesus which he then follows with an account of Jesus' teaching. Each teaching account is brought to a conclusion with one of the following phrases: "When Jesus had finished saying these things," "finished instructing," "finished these parables," "when Jesus had finished saying these things," or "when Jesus had finished saying all these things."

   Therefore before you read through Matthew chapter by chapter, mark in a distinctive way each occurrence of a dividing phrase in 7:28; 11:1; 13:53; 19:1; and 26:1. Remember, these phrases conclude that particular teaching. Then the cycle begins again.

2. Now read Matthew chapter by chapter, keeping in mind these six segments. As you read:

   a. In a distinctive way mark in the text the key words listed on the MATTHEW AT A GLANCE chart on page 1722.

      1) List in the margin what you learn about the kingdom from the references where you marked the key words *king* and the *kingdom of heaven/God.*

      2) In addition to these key words, watch for other key words or phrases. Reread the observation section in "How to Use The International Inductive Study Bible" on page IISB-15.

   b. Using the same color pen each time, underline each reference to or quotation from an Old Testament prophecy which shows Jesus as the promised king. Then note in the margin how Jesus fulfills that prophecy. (You can recognize Old Testament quotes easily because the NIV text is indented on both sides.)

   c. Watch for the events, works, or facts which demonstrate who Jesus Christ is. You may want to note these in the margin.

   d. When you read Jesus' teaching on a particular subject, in the margin make a list of the main points covered in his teaching. If it is a prophetic teaching, pay attention to time phrases or indicators, including *then, therefore, at that time, when, after, as soon as, while, if, now, as,* and *before.* Watch for the progression of events.

   e. Record the main theme or event of each chapter in the text next to the chapter number and on MATTHEW AT A GLANCE.

3. Chapters 26 through 28 give an account of the final events in the life of Jesus. Record the progression of events on the charts titled THE ARREST, TRIAL, AND CRUCIFIXION OF JESUS CHRIST on

page 1862 and/or THE ACCOUNT OF JESUS' RESURRECTION on page 1863. You may want to first record these insights on notebook paper and then transfer them to the charts. Note the chapter and verse of each insight for future reference.

a. When you record the circumstances surrounding the resurrection of Jesus Christ, also note any postresurrection appearances which are recorded in Matthew. After you do this for all four Gospels you will have comprehensive notes on all that took place.

b. As you do this, remember that Luke gives the consecutive order of events, and therefore, Luke becomes a plumb line for the other Gospel records.

4. A chart titled WHAT THE GOSPELS TEACH ABOUT THE KINGDOM OF GOD/THE KINGDOM OF HEAVEN is on pages 1864 and 1865. List and consolidate everything you learn from Matthew about the kingdom on a piece of notebook paper. Then transfer this to the chart. Be sure to note the chapter and verse for future reference.

5. Complete MATTHEW AT A GLANCE. Under "Segment Divisions," record the theme of each segment of Matthew. There is also a blank column for any other segment divisions you might see.

Things to Think About

1. Have you bowed your knee to Jesus as king in your life? Read Matthew 7:21-27 and think about the difference between *merely hearing* something and *hearing and living accordingly.* Which best describes you?

2. Can you explain from Scripture to another person why Jesus is the king of the promised kingdom?

3. Do you realize that Jesus' final words to his disciples in Matthew 28:19, 20 are your responsibility also? What are you doing in order to fulfill his Great Commission? As you go, are you making disciples? Are you teaching them to observe all that he has commanded?

Chapter 1 Theme ____________________

1 A record of the genealogy of Jesus Christ the son of David,[a]
the son of Abraham:[b]

2 Abraham was the father of Isaac,[c]
Isaac the father of Jacob,[d]
Jacob the father of Judah and his brothers,[e]
3 Judah the father of Perez and Zerah, whose mother was Tamar,[f]
Perez the father of Hezron,
Hezron the father of Ram,
4 Ram the father of Amminadab,
Amminadab the father of Nahshon,
Nahshon the father of Salmon,
5 Salmon the father of Boaz, whose mother was Rahab,
Boaz the father of Obed, whose mother was Ruth,
Obed the father of Jesse,
6 and Jesse the father of King David.[g]

David was the father of Solomon, whose mother had been Uriah's wife,[h]

INSIGHT

See **The Genealogy of Jesus the Christ** on page 1665.

1:1 [a] 2Sa 7:12-16; Isa 9:6,7; 11:1; Jer 23:5,6; Mt 9:27; Lk 1:32,69; Ro 1:3; Rev 22:16 [b] Ge 22:18; Gal 3:16

1:2 [c] Ge 21:3,12 [d] Ge 25:26 [e] Ge 29:35

1:3 [f] Ge 38:27-30

1:6 [g] 1Sa 16:1; 17:12 [h] 2Sa 12:24

1:10 a2Ki 20:21 7 Solomon the father of Rehoboam,
Rehoboam the father of Abijah,
Abijah the father of Asa,
8 Asa the father of Jehoshaphat,
Jehoshaphat the father of Jehoram,
Jehoram the father of Uzziah,
9 Uzziah the father of Jotham,
1:11 b2Ki 24:14-16; Jer 27:20; Da 1:1,2 Jotham the father of Ahaz,
Ahaz the father of Hezekiah,
10 Hezekiah the father of Manasseh,[a]
Manasseh the father of Amon,
Amon the father of Josiah,
11 and Josiah the father of Jeconiah[a] and his brothers at the time of the exile to Babylon.[b]

1:12 c1Ch 3:17 d1Ch 3:19; Ezr 3:2 12 After the exile to Babylon:
Jeconiah was the father of Shealtiel,[c]
Shealtiel the father of Zerubbabel,[d]
13 Zerubbabel the father of Abiud,
Abiud the father of Eliakim,
Eliakim the father of Azor,
14 Azor the father of Zadok,
Zadok the father of Akim,
1:16 eLk 1:27 fMt 27:17 Akim the father of Eliud,
15 Eliud the father of Eleazar,
Eleazar the father of Matthan,
Matthan the father of Jacob,
16 and Jacob the father of Joseph, the husband of Mary,[e] of whom was born Jesus, who is called Christ.[f]

17 Thus there were fourteen generations in all from Abraham to
1:18 gLk 1:35 David, fourteen from David to the exile to Babylon, and fourteen
from the exile to the Christ.[b]
18 This is how the birth of Jesus Christ came about: His mother
Mary was pledged to be married to Joseph, but before they came
together, she was found to be with child through the Holy Spirit.[g]
19 Because Joseph her husband was a righteous man and did not
want to expose her to public disgrace, he had in mind to divorce[h]
1:19 hDt 24:1 her quietly.
20 But after he had considered this, an angel of the Lord appeared
to him in a dream and said, "Joseph son of David, do not be afraid
to take Mary home as your wife, because what is conceived in her
is from the Holy Spirit. 21 She will give birth to a son, and you are
to give him the name Jesus,[c][i] because he will save his people from
1:21 iLk 1:31 jLk 2:11; Ac 5:31; 13:23,28 their sins."[j]

[a] *11* That is, Jehoiachin; also in verse 12 [b] *17* Or *Messiah.* "The Christ" (Greek) and "the Messiah" (Hebrew) both mean "the Anointed One." [c] *21* *Jesus* is the Greek form of *Joshua,* which means *the LORD saves.*

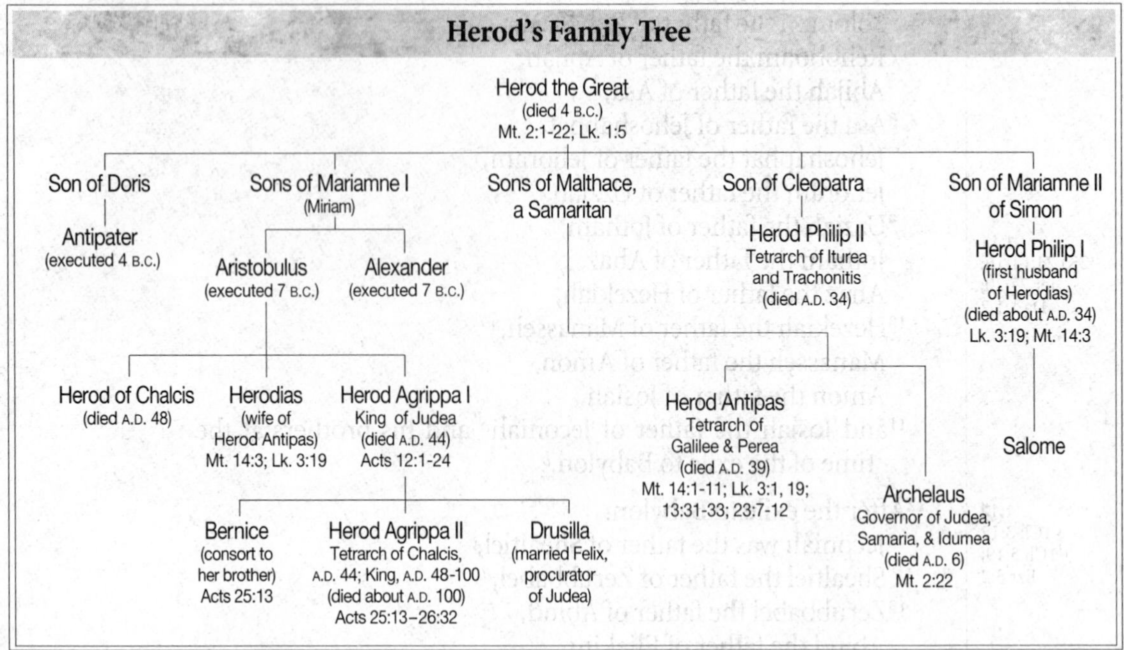

22 All this took place to fulfill what the Lord had said through the
prophet: 23 “The virgin will be with child and will give birth to a
son, and they will call him Immanuel”[a] [a]—which means, “God
with us.”

24 When Joseph woke up, he did what the angel of the Lord had
commanded him and took Mary home as his wife. 25 But he had
no union with her until she gave birth to a son. And he gave him
the name Jesus.[b]

Chapter 2 Theme ____________________

2 After Jesus was born in Bethlehem in Judea,[c] during the time
of King Herod,[d] Magi[b] from the east came to Jerusalem 2 and
asked, “Where is the one who has been born king of the Jews?[e]
We saw his star[f] in the east[c] and have come to worship him.”

3 When King Herod heard this he was disturbed, and all Jerusalem with him. 4 When he had called together all the people's chief
priests and teachers of the law, he asked them where the Christ[d]
was to be born. 5 “In Bethlehem[g] in Judea,” they replied, “for this is
what the prophet has written:

> 6 “ ‘But you, Bethlehem, in the land of Judah,
> are by no means least among the rulers of Judah;
> for out of you will come a ruler
> who will be the shepherd of my people Israel.’[e]”[h]

1:23 [a] Isa 7:14; 8:8,10
1:25 [b] ver 21
2:1 [c] Lk 2:4-7 [d] Lk 1:5
2:2 [e] Jer 23:5; Mt 27:11; Mk 15:2; Jn 1:49; 18:33-37 [f] Nu 24:17
2:5 [g] Jn 7:42
2:6 [h] Mic 5:2; 2Sa 5:2

[a] *23* Isaiah 7:14 [b] *1* Traditionally *Wise Men* [c] *2* Or *star when it rose* [d] *4* Or *Messiah*
[e] *6* Micah 5:2

7Then Herod called the Magi secretly and found out from them the exact time the star had appeared. 8He sent them to Bethlehem and said, "Go and make a careful search for the child. As soon as you find him, report to me, so that I too may go and worship him."

9After they had heard the king, they went on their way, and the star they had seen in the east[a] went ahead of them until it stopped over the place where the child was. 10When they saw the star, they were overjoyed. 11On coming to the house, they saw the child with his mother Mary, and they bowed down and worshiped him.[a] Then they opened their treasures and presented him with gifts[b] of gold and of incense and of myrrh. 12And having been warned[c] in a dream[d] not to go back to Herod, they returned to their country by another route.

13When they had gone, an angel[e] of the Lord appeared to Joseph in a dream.[f] "Get up," he said, "take the child and his mother and escape to Egypt. Stay there until I tell you, for Herod is going to search for the child to kill him."

14So he got up, took the child and his mother during the night and left for Egypt, 15where he stayed until the death of Herod. And so was fulfilled what the Lord had said through the prophet: "Out of Egypt I called my son."[b][g]

16When Herod realized that he had been outwitted by the Magi, he was furious, and he gave orders to kill all the boys in Bethlehem and its vicinity who were two years old and under, in accordance with the time he had learned from the Magi. 17Then what was said through the prophet Jeremiah was fulfilled:

> 18"A voice is heard in Ramah,
> weeping and great mourning,
> Rachel weeping for her children
> and refusing to be comforted,
> because they are no more."[c][h]

19After Herod died, an angel of the Lord appeared in a dream[i] to Joseph in Egypt 20and said, "Get up, take the child and his mother and go to the land of Israel, for those who were trying to take the child's life are dead."

21So he got up, took the child and his mother and went to the land of Israel. 22But when he heard that Archelaus was reigning in Judea in place of his father Herod, he was afraid to go there. Having been warned in a dream,[j] he withdrew to the district of Galilee,[k] 23and he went and lived in a town called Nazareth.[l] So was fulfilled[m] what was said through the prophets: "He will be called a Nazarene."[n]

2:11 [a]Isa 60:3 [b]Ps 72:10
2:12 [c]Heb 11:7 [d]ver 13,19,22; Mt 27:19
2:13 [e]Ac 5:19 [f]ver 12,19,22
2:15 [g]Hos 11:1; Ex 4:22,23
2:18 [h]Jer 31:15
2:19 [i]ver 12,13,22
2:22 [j]ver 12,13,19; Mt 27:19 [k]Lk 2:39
2:23 [l]Lk 1:26; Jn 1:45,46 [m]Mt 1:22 [n]Mk 1:24

[a]9 Or *seen when it rose* [b]15 Hosea 11:1 [c]18 Jer. 31:15

Chapter 3 Theme ______________________

3 In those days John the Baptist[a] came, preaching in the Desert
of Judea [2]and saying, "Repent, for the kingdom of heaven[b] is
near." [3]This is he who was spoken of through the prophet Isaiah:

"A voice of one calling in the desert,
'Prepare the way for the Lord,
make straight paths for him.'"[a] [c]

[4]John's clothes were made of camel's hair, and he had a leather
belt around his waist.[d] His food was locusts[e] and wild honey.
[5]People went out to him from Jerusalem and all Judea and the
whole region of the Jordan. [6]Confessing their sins, they were baptized by him in the Jordan River.
[7]But when he saw many of the Pharisees and Sadducees coming
to where he was baptizing, he said to them: "You brood of vipers![f]
Who warned you to flee from the coming wrath?[g] [8]Produce fruit
in keeping with repentance.[h] [9]And do not think you can say to
yourselves, 'We have Abraham as our father.' I tell you that out of
these stones God can raise up children for Abraham. [10]The ax is
already at the root of the trees, and every tree that does not produce good fruit will be cut down and thrown into the fire.[i]
[11]"I baptize you with[b] water for repentance. But after me will
come one who is more powerful than I, whose sandals I am not
fit to carry. He will baptize you with the Holy Spirit[j] and with
fire.[k] [12]His winnowing fork is in his hand, and he will clear his
threshing floor, gathering his wheat into the barn and burning
up the chaff with unquenchable fire."[l]
[13]Then Jesus came from Galilee to the Jordan to be baptized by
John.[m] [14]But John tried to deter him, saying, "I need to be baptized by you, and do you come to me?"
[15]Jesus replied, "Let it be so now; it is proper for us to do this to
fulfill all righteousness." Then John consented.
[16]As soon as Jesus was baptized, he went up out of the water. At
that moment heaven was opened, and he saw the Spirit of God[n]
descending like a dove and lighting on him. [17]And a voice from
heaven[o] said, "This is my Son,[p] whom I love; with him I am well
pleased."[q]

Chapter 4 Theme ______________________

4 Then Jesus was led by the Spirit into the desert to be tempted
by the devil. [2]After fasting forty days and forty nights,[r] he
was hungry. [3]The tempter[s] came to him and said, "If you are the
Son of God,[t] tell these stones to become bread."

3:1 [a]Lk 1:13,57-66; 3:2-19

3:2 [b]Da 2:44; Mt 4:17; 6:10; Lk 11:20; 21:31; Jn 3:3,5; Ac 1:3,6

3:3 [c]Isa 40:3; Mal 3:1; Lk 1:76; Jn 1:23

3:4 [d]2Ki 1:8 [e]Lev 11:22

3:7 [f]Mt 12:34; 23:33 [g]Ro 1:18; 1Th 1:10

3:8 [h]Ac 26:20

3:10 [i]Mt 7:19; Lk 13:6-9; Jn 15:2,6

3:11 [j]Mk 1:8 [k]Isa 4:4; Ac 2:3,4

3:12 [l]Mt 13:30

3:13 [m]Mk 1:4

3:16 [n]Isa 11:2; 42:1

3:17 [o]Mt 17:5; Jn 12:28 [p]Ps 2:7; 2Pe 1:17,18 [q]Isa 42:1; Mt 12:18; 17:5; Mk 1:11; 9:7; Lk 9:35

4:2 [r]Ex 34:28; 1Ki 19:8

4:3 [s]1Th 3:5 [t]Mt 3:17; Jn 5:25; Ac 9:20

[a] *3* Isaiah 40:3 [b] *11* Or *in*

4 Jesus answered, "It is written: 'Man does not live on bread
alone, but on every word that comes from the mouth of God.'[a]"[a]
5 Then the devil took him to the holy city[b] and had him stand
on the highest point of the temple. 6 "If you are the Son of God,"
he said, "throw yourself down. For it is written:

> "'He will command his angels concerning you,
> and they will lift you up in their hands,
> so that you will not strike your foot against a stone.'[b]"[c]

7 Jesus answered him, "It is also written: 'Do not put the Lord
your God to the test.'[c]"[d]
8 Again, the devil took him to a very high mountain and
showed him all the kingdoms of the world and their splendor.
9 "All this I will give you," he said, "if you will bow down and
worship me."
10 Jesus said to him, "Away from me, Satan![e] For it is written:
'Worship the Lord your God, and serve him only.'[d]"[f]
11 Then the devil left him, and angels came and attended him.[g]
12 When Jesus heard that John had been put in prison,[h] he
returned to Galilee.[i] 13 Leaving Nazareth, he went and lived in
Capernaum,[j] which was by the lake in the area of Zebulun and
Naphtali— 14 to fulfill what was said through the prophet Isaiah:

> 15 "Land of Zebulun and land of Naphtali,
> the way to the sea, along the Jordan,
> Galilee of the Gentiles—
> 16 the people living in darkness
> have seen a great light;
> on those living in the land of the shadow of death
> a light has dawned."[e][k]

17 From that time on Jesus began to
preach, "Repent, for the kingdom of
heaven[l] is near."
18 As Jesus was walking beside the
Sea of Galilee,[m] he saw two brothers,
Simon called Peter[n] and his brother
Andrew. They were casting a net into
the lake, for they were fishermen.
19 "Come, follow me,"[o] Jesus said,
"and I will make you fishers of
men." 20 At once they left their nets
and followed him.
21 Going on from there, he saw two
other brothers, James son of Zebedee
and his brother John.[p] They were in

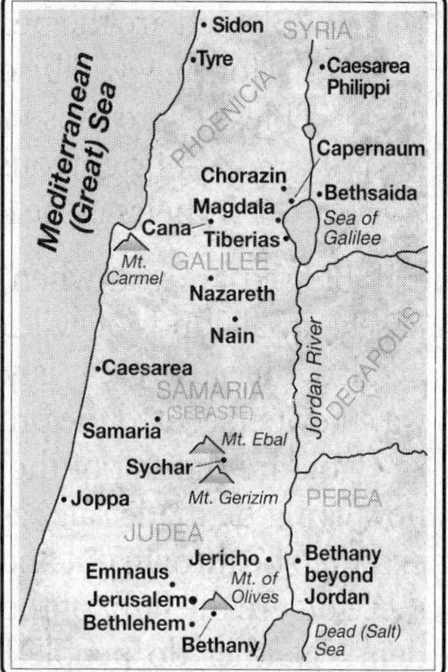

Israel in the Time of Christ

Cross-references:
4:4 [a]Dt 8:3
4:5 [b]Ne 11:1; Da 9:24; Mt 27:53
4:6 [c]Ps 91:11,12
4:7 [d]Dt 6:16
4:10 [e]1Ch 21:1 [f]Dt 6:13
4:11 [g]Mt 26:53; Lk 22:43; Heb 1:14
4:12 [h]Mt 14:3 [i]Mk 1:14
4:13 [j]Mk 1:21; Lk 4:23,31; Jn 2:12; 4:46,47
4:16 [k]Isa 9:1,2; Lk 2:32
4:17 [l]Mt 3:2
4:18 [m]Mt 15:29; Mk 7:31; Jn 6:1 [n]Mt 16:17,18
4:19 [o]Mk 10:21, 28,52
4:21 [p]Mt 20:20

[a]4 Deut. 8:3 [b]6 Psalm 91:11,12 [c]7 Deut. 6:16 [d]10 Deut. 6:13 [e]16 Isaiah 9:1,2

a boat with their father Zebedee, preparing their nets. Jesus called
them, 22and immediately they left the boat and their father and followed him.

23Jesus went throughout Galilee,[a] teaching in their synagogues,[b]
preaching the good news[c] of the kingdom,[d] and healing every disease and sickness among the people.[e] 24News about him spread all
over Syria,[f] and people brought to him all who were ill with various diseases, those suffering severe pain, the demon-possessed,[g]
those having seizures,[h] and the paralyzed,[i] and he healed them.
25Large crowds from Galilee, the Decapolis,[a] Jerusalem, Judea and
the region across the Jordan followed him.[j]

Chapter 5 Theme ______________________________

5 Now when he saw the crowds, he went up on a mountainside
and sat down. His disciples came to him, 2and he began to
teach them, saying:

3"Blessed are the poor in spirit,
for theirs is the kingdom of heaven.[k]
4Blessed are those who mourn,
for they will be comforted.[l]
5Blessed are the meek,
for they will inherit the earth.[m]
6Blessed are those who hunger and thirst
for righteousness,
for they will be filled.[n]
7Blessed are the merciful,
for they will be shown mercy.
8Blessed are the pure in heart,[o]
for they will see God.[p]
9Blessed are the peacemakers,
for they will be called sons of God.[q]
10Blessed are those who are persecuted because
of righteousness,[r]
for theirs is the kingdom of heaven.

11"Blessed are you when people insult you,[s] persecute you and
falsely say all kinds of evil against you because of me. 12Rejoice and
be glad,[t] because great is your reward in heaven, for in the same
way they persecuted the prophets who were before you.[u]

13"You are the salt of the earth. But if the salt loses its saltiness,
how can it be made salty again? It is no longer good for anything,
except to be thrown out and trampled by men.[v]

14"You are the light of the world.[w] A city on a hill cannot be hidden. 15Neither do people light a lamp and put it under a bowl.

4:23 [a]Mk 1:39; Lk 4:15,44 [b]Mt 9:35; 13:54; Mk 1:21; Lk 4:15; Jn 6:59 [c]Mk 1:14 [d]Mt 3:2; Ac 20:25 [e]Mt 8:16; 15:30; Ac 10:38

4:24 [f]Lk 2:2 [g]Mt 8:16,28; 9:32; 15:22; Mk 1:32; 5:15,16,18 [h]Mt 17:15 [i]Mt 8:6; 9:2; Mk 2:3

4:25 [j]Mk 3:7,8; Lk 6:17

5:3 [k]ver 10,19; Mt 25:34

5:4 [l]Isa 61:2,3; Rev 7:17

5:5 [m]Ps 37:11; Ro 4:13

5:6 [n]Isa 55:1,2

5:8 [o]Ps 24:3,4 [p]Heb 12:14; Rev 22:4

5:9 [q]ver 44,45; Ro 8:14

5:10 [r]1Pe 3:14

5:11 [s]1Pe 4:14

5:12 [t]Ac 5:41; 1Pe 4:13,16 [u]Mt 23:31,37; Ac 7:52; 1Th 2:15

5:13 [v]Mk 9:50; Lk 14:34,35

5:14 [w]Jn 8:12

[a]25 That is, the Ten Cities

5:15 [a]Mk 4:21; Instead they put it on its stand, and it gives light to everyone in the
Lk 8:16 house.[a] 16 In the same way, let your light shine before men, that
they may see your good deeds and praise[b] your Father in heaven.
17 "Do not think that I have come to abolish the Law or the
5:16 [b]Mt 9:8 Prophets; I have not come to abolish them but to fulfill them.[c] 18 I
tell you the truth, until heaven and earth disappear, not the smallest letter, not the least stroke of a pen, will by any means disappear
5:17 from the Law until everything is accomplished.[d] 19 Anyone who
[c]Ro 3:31 breaks one of the least of these commandments[e] and teaches others to do the same will be called least in the kingdom of heaven,
but whoever practices and teaches these commands will be called
5:18 [d]Lk 16:17 great in the kingdom of heaven. 20 For I tell you that unless your
righteousness surpasses that of the Pharisees and the teachers of
the law, you will certainly not enter the kingdom of heaven.
5:19 21 "You have heard that it was said to the people long ago, 'Do
[e]Jas 2:10 not murder,[a][f] and anyone who murders will be subject to judgment.' 22 But I tell you that anyone who is angry with his brother[b]
5:21 will be subject to judgment.[g] Again, anyone who says to his broth-
[f]Ex 20:13; er, 'Raca,[c]' is answerable to the Sanhedrin.[h] But anyone who says,
Dt 5:17 'You fool!' will be in danger of the fire of hell.[i]
23 "Therefore, if you are offering your gift at the altar and there
remember that your brother has something against you, 24 leave
5:22 [g]1Jn 3:15 your gift there in front of the altar. First go and be reconciled to
[h]Mt 26:59 your brother; then come and offer your gift.
[i]Jas 3:6 25 "Settle matters quickly with your adversary who is taking you
to court. Do it while you are still with him on the way, or he may
5:27 hand you over to the judge, and the judge may hand you over to
[j]Ex 20:14; the officer, and you may be thrown into prison. 26 I tell you the
Dt 5:18 truth, you will not get out until you have paid the last penny.[d]
27 "You have heard that it was said, 'Do not commit adultery.'[e][j]
5:28 28 But I tell you that anyone who looks at a woman lustfully has
[k]Pr 6:25 already committed adultery with her in his heart.[k] 29 If your right
eye causes you to sin,[l] gouge it out and throw it away. It is better
for you to lose one part of your body than for your whole body to
5:29 be thrown into hell. 30 And if your right hand causes you to sin,
[l]Mt 18:6,8,9; Mk 9:42-47 cut it off and throw it away. It is better for you to lose one part of
your body than for your whole body to go into hell.
31 "It has been said, 'Anyone who divorces his wife must give
5:31 her a certificate of divorce.'[f][m] 32 But I tell you that anyone who
[m]Dt 24:1-4 divorces his wife, except for marital unfaithfulness, causes her to
become an adulteress, and anyone who marries the divorced
5:32 woman commits adultery.[n]
[n]Lk 16:18 33 "Again, you have heard that it was said to the people long ago,
'Do not break your oath,[o] but keep the oaths you have made to

5:33 [o]Lev 19:12 [a]21 Exodus 20:13 [b]22 Some manuscripts *brother without cause* [c]22 An Aramaic term of contempt [d]26 Greek *kodrantes* [e]27 Exodus 20:14 [f]31 Deut. 24:1

the Lord.'[a] 34But I tell you, Do not swear at all:[b] either by heaven,
for it is God's throne;[c] 35or by the earth, for it is his footstool; or by
Jerusalem, for it is the city of the Great King.[d] 36And do not swear
by your head, for you cannot make even one hair white or black.
37Simply let your 'Yes' be 'Yes,' and your 'No,' 'No';[e] anything
beyond this comes from the evil one.[f]

38"You have heard that it was said, 'Eye for eye, and tooth for
tooth.'[a][g] 39But I tell you, Do not resist an evil person. If someone
strikes you on the right cheek, turn to him the other also.[h] 40And
if someone wants to sue you and take your tunic, let him have
your cloak as well. 41If someone forces you to go one mile, go
with him two miles. 42Give to the one who asks you, and do not
turn away from the one who wants to borrow from you.[i]

43"You have heard that it was said, 'Love your neighbor[b][j] and
hate your enemy.'[k] 44But I tell you: Love your enemies[c] and pray
for those who persecute you,[l] 45that you may be sons[m] of your
Father in heaven. He causes his sun to rise on the evil and the
good, and sends rain on the righteous and the unrighteous.[n] 46If
you love those who love you, what reward will you get?[o] Are not
even the tax collectors doing that? 47And if you greet only your
brothers, what are you doing more than others? Do not even
pagans do that? 48Be perfect, therefore, as your heavenly Father is
perfect.[p]

Chapter 6 Theme ______________________

6 "Be careful not to do your 'acts of righteousness' before men,
to be seen by them.[q] If you do, you will have no reward from
your Father in heaven.

2"So when you give to the needy, do not announce it with trumpets, as the hypocrites do in the synagogues and on the streets, to
be honored by men. I tell you the truth, they have received their
reward in full. 3But when you give to the needy, do not let your left
hand know what your right hand is doing, 4so that your giving
may be in secret. Then your Father, who sees what is done in
secret, will reward you.[r]

5"And when you pray, do not be like the hypocrites, for they
love to pray standing[s] in the synagogues and on the street corners
to be seen by men. I tell you the truth, they have received their
reward in full. 6But when you pray, go into your room, close the
door and pray to your Father,[t] who is unseen. Then your Father,
who sees what is done in secret, will reward you. 7And when you
pray, do not keep on babbling[u] like pagans, for they think they

5:33 [a] Nu 30:2; Dt 23:21; Mt 23:16-22
5:34 [b] Jas 5:12 [c] Isa 66:1; Mt 23:22
5:35 [d] Ps 48:2
5:37 [e] Jas 5:12 [f] Mt 6:13; 13:19,38; Jn 17:15; 2Th 3:3; 1Jn 2:13,14; 3:12; 5:18,19
5:38 [g] Ex 21:24; Lev 24:20; Dt 19:21
5:39 [h] Lk 6:29; Ro 12:17,19; 1Co 6:7; 1Pe 3:9
5:42 [i] Dt 15:8; Lk 6:30
5:43 [j] Lev 19:18 [k] Dt 23:6
5:44 [l] Lk 6:27,28; 23:34; Ac 7:60; Ro 12:14; 1Co 4:12; 1Pe 2:23
5:45 [m] ver 9 [n] Job 25:3
5:46 [o] Lk 6:32
5:48 [p] Lev 19:2; 1Pe 1:16
6:1 [q] Mt 23:5
6:4 [r] ver 6,18; Col 3:23,24
6:5 [s] Mk 11:25; Lk 18:10-14
6:6 [t] 2Ki 4:33
6:7 [u] Ecc 5:2

[a] *38* Exodus 21:24; Lev. 24:20; Deut. 19:21 [b] *43* Lev. 19:18 [c] *44* Some late manuscripts *enemies, bless those who curse you, do good to those who hate you*

will be heard because of their many words.[a] 8 Do not be like them,
for your Father knows what you need[b] before you ask him.
9 "This, then, is how you should pray:

"'Our Father in heaven,
hallowed be your name,
10 your kingdom[c] come,
your will be done[d]
on earth as it is in heaven.
11 Give us today our daily bread.[e]
12 Forgive us our debts,
as we also have forgiven our debtors.[f]
13 And lead us not into temptation,[g]
but deliver us from the evil one.[a]'[h]

14 For if you forgive men when they sin against you, your heavenly
Father will also forgive you.[i] 15 But if you do not forgive men their
sins, your Father will not forgive your sins.[j]
16 "When you fast, do not look somber[k] as the hypocrites do, for they
disfigure their faces to show men they are fasting. I tell you the
truth, they have received their reward in full. 17 But when you fast,
put oil on your head and wash your face, 18 so that it will not be
obvious to men that you are fasting, but only to your Father, who
is unseen; and your Father, who sees what is done in secret, will
reward you.[l]
19 "Do not store up for yourselves treasures on earth,[m] where
moth and rust destroy,[n] and where thieves break in and steal.
20 But store up for yourselves treasures in heaven,[o] where moth
and rust do not destroy, and where thieves do not break in and
steal.[p] 21 For where your treasure is, there your heart will be also.[q]
22 "The eye is the lamp of the body. If your eyes are good, your
whole body will be full of light. 23 But if your eyes are bad, your
whole body will be full of darkness. If then the light within you is
darkness, how great is that darkness!
24 "No one can serve two masters. Either he will hate the one
and love the other, or he will be devoted to the one and despise
the other. You cannot serve both God and Money.[r]
25 "Therefore I tell you, do not worry[s] about your life, what you
will eat or drink; or about your body, what you will wear. Is not
life more important than food, and the body more important
than clothes? 26 Look at the birds of the air; they do not sow or
reap or store away in barns, and yet your heavenly Father feeds
them.[t] Are you not much more valuable than they?[u] 27 Who of
you by worrying can add a single hour to his life[b]?[v]

6:7 [a] 1Ki 18:26-29
6:8 [b] ver 32
6:10 [c] Mt 3:2 [d] Mt 26:39
6:11 [e] Pr 30:8
6:12 [f] Mt 18:21-35
6:13 [g] Jas 1:13 [h] Mt 5:37
6:14 [i] Mt 18:21-35; Mk 11:25,26; Eph 4:32; Col 3:13
6:15 [j] Mt 18:35
6:16 [k] Isa 58:5
6:18 [l] ver 4,6
6:19 [m] Pr 23:4; Heb 13:5 [n] Jas 5:2,3
6:20 [o] Mt 19:21; Lk 12:33; 18:22; 1Ti 6:19 [p] Lk 12:33
6:21 [q] Lk 12:34
6:24 [r] Lk 16:13
6:25 [s] ver 27,28,31,34; Lk 10:41; 12:11,22; Php 4:6; 1Pe 5:7
6:26 [t] Job 38:41; Ps 147:9 [u] Mt 10:29-31
6:27 [v] Ps 39:5

[a] *13* Or *from evil;* some late manuscripts *one, / for yours is the kingdom and the power and the glory forever. Amen.* [b] *27* Or *single cubit to his height*

28 “And why do you worry about clothes? See how the lilies of the
field grow. They do not labor or spin. 29 Yet I tell you that not even
Solomon in all his splendor[a] was dressed like one of these. 30 If that
is how God clothes the grass of the field, which is here today and
tomorrow is thrown into the fire, will he not much more clothe
you, O you of little faith?[b] 31 So do not worry, saying, ‘What shall we
eat?’ or ‘What shall we drink?’ or ‘What shall we wear?’ 32 For the
pagans run after all these things, and your heavenly Father knows
that you need them.[c] 33 But seek first his kingdom and his righteousness, and all these things will be given to you as well.[d] 34 Therefore do not worry about tomorrow, for tomorrow will worry about
itself. Each day has enough trouble of its own.

Chapter 7 Theme ______________________

7 “Do not judge, or you too will be judged.[e] 2 For in the same
way you judge others, you will be judged, and with the measure you use, it will be measured to you.[f]
3 “Why do you look at the speck of sawdust in your brother’s
eye and pay no attention to the plank in your own eye? 4 How can
you say to your brother, ‘Let me take the speck out of your eye,’
when all the time there is a plank in your own eye? 5 You hypocrite, first take the plank out of your own eye, and then you will
see clearly to remove the speck from your brother’s eye.
6 “Do not give dogs what is sacred; do not throw your pearls to
pigs. If you do, they may trample them under their feet, and then
turn and tear you to pieces.
7 “Ask and it will be given to you;[g] seek and you will find; knock
and the door will be opened to you. 8 For everyone who asks
receives; he who seeks finds;[h] and to him who knocks, the door
will be opened.
9 “Which of you, if his son asks for bread, will give him a stone?
10 Or if he asks for a fish, will give him a snake? 11 If you, then,
though you are evil, know how to give good gifts to your children,
how much more will your Father in heaven give good gifts to those
who ask him! 12 So in everything, do to others what you would have
them do to you,[i] for this sums up the Law and the Prophets.[j]
13 “Enter through the narrow gate.[k] For wide is the gate and
broad is the road that leads to destruction, and many enter
through it. 14 But small is the gate and narrow the road that leads
to life, and only a few find it.
15 “Watch out for false prophets.[l] They come to you in sheep’s
clothing, but inwardly they are ferocious wolves.[m] 16 By their fruit
you will recognize them.[n] Do people pick grapes from thornbushes, or figs from thistles?[o] 17 Likewise every good tree bears
good fruit, but a bad tree bears bad fruit. 18 A good tree cannot

6:29 [a] 1Ki 10:4-7
6:30 [b] Mt 8:26; 14:31; 16:8
6:32 [c] ver 8
6:33 [d] Mt 19:29; Mk 10:29-30
7:1 [e] Lk 6:37; Ro 14:4,10,13; 1Co 4:5; Jas 4:11,12
7:2 [f] Mk 4:24; Lk 6:38
7:7 [g] Mt 21:22; Mk 11:24; Jn 14:13,14; 15:7,16; 16:23,24; Jas 1:5-8; 4:2,3; 1Jn 3:22; 5:14,15
7:8 [h] Pr 8:17; Jer 29:12,13
7:12 [i] Lk 6:31 [j] Ro 13:8-10; Gal 5:14
7:13 [k] Lk 13:24
7:15 [l] Jer 23:16; Mt 24:24; Mk 13:22; Lk 6:26; 2Pe 2:1; 1Jn 4:1; Rev 16:13 [m] Ac 20:29
7:16 [n] Mt 12:33; Lk 6:44 [o] Jas 3:12

bear bad fruit, and a bad tree cannot bear good fruit. 19 Every tree
that does not bear good fruit is cut down and thrown into the
fire.[a] 20 Thus, by their fruit you will recognize them.

21 "Not everyone who says to me, 'Lord, Lord,'[b] will enter the
kingdom of heaven, but only he who does the will of my Father
who is in heaven.[c] 22 Many will say to me on that day,[d] 'Lord,
Lord, did we not prophesy in your name, and in your name drive
out demons and perform many miracles?'[e] 23 Then I will tell them
plainly, 'I never knew you. Away from me, you evildoers!'[f]

24 "Therefore everyone who hears these words of mine and puts
them into practice[g] is like a wise man who built his house on the
rock. 25 The rain came down, the streams rose, and the winds blew
and beat against that house; yet it did not fall, because it had its
foundation on the rock. 26 But everyone who hears these words of
mine and does not put them into practice is like a foolish man who
built his house on sand. 27 The rain came down, the streams rose,
and the winds blew and beat against that house, and it fell with a
great crash."

28 When Jesus had finished saying these things,[h] the crowds
were amazed at his teaching,[i] 29 because he taught as one who had
authority, and not as their teachers of the law.

Chapter 8 Theme

8 When he came down from the mountainside, large crowds
followed him. 2 A man with leprosy[a][j] came and knelt before
him[k] and said, "Lord, if you are willing, you can make me clean."
3 Jesus reached out his hand and touched the man. "I am willing," he said. "Be clean!" Immediately he was cured[b] of his leprosy. 4 Then Jesus said to him, "See that you don't tell anyone.[l] But
go, show yourself to the priest and offer the gift Moses commanded,[m] as a testimony to them."
5 When Jesus had entered Capernaum, a centurion came to
him, asking for help. 6 "Lord," he said, "my servant lies at home
paralyzed and in terrible suffering."
7 Jesus said to him, "I will go and heal him."
8 The centurion replied, "Lord, I do not deserve to have you come
under my roof. But just say the word, and my servant will be
healed.[n] 9 For I myself am a man under authority, with soldiers
under me. I tell this one, 'Go,' and he goes; and that one, 'Come,'
and he comes. I say to my servant, 'Do this,' and he does it."
10 When Jesus heard this, he was astonished and said to those
following him, "I tell you the truth, I have not found anyone in
Israel with such great faith.[o] 11 I say to you that many will come

7:19 [a]Mt 3:10
7:21 [b]Hos 8:2; Mt 25:11 [c]Ro 2:13; Jas 1:22
7:22 [d]Mt 10:15 [e]1Co 13:1-3
7:23 [f]Ps 6:8; Mt 25:12,41; Lk 13:25-27
7:24 [g]Jas 1:22-25
7:28 [h]Mt 11:1; 13:53; 19:1; 26:1 [i]Mt 13:54; Mk 1:22; 6:2; Lk 4:32; Jn 7:46
8:2 [j]Lk 5:12 [k]Mt 9:18; 15:25; 18:26; 20:20
8:4 [l]Mt 9:30; Mk 5:43; 7:36; 8:30 [m]Lev 14:2-32
8:8 [n]Ps 107:20
8:10 [o]Mt 15:28

[a] *2* The Greek word was used for various diseases affecting the skin—not necessarily leprosy.
[b] *3* Greek *made clean*

from the east and the west,[a] and will take their places at the feast
with Abraham, Isaac and Jacob in the kingdom of heaven.[b] 12But
the subjects of the kingdom[c] will be thrown outside, into the
darkness, where there will be weeping and gnashing of teeth."[d]
13Then Jesus said to the centurion, "Go! It will be done just as you
believed it would."[e] And his servant was healed at that very hour.
14When Jesus came into Peter's house, he saw Peter's mother-
in-law lying in bed with a fever. 15He touched her hand and the
fever left her, and she got up and began to wait on him.
16When evening came, many who were demon-possessed were
brought to him, and he drove out the spirits with a word and
healed all the sick.[f] 17This was to fulfill[g] what was spoken
through the prophet Isaiah:

> "He took up our infirmities
> and carried our diseases."[a][h]

18When Jesus saw the crowd around him, he gave orders to cross
to the other side of the lake.[i] 19Then a teacher of the law came to
him and said, "Teacher, I will follow you wherever you go."
20Jesus replied, "Foxes have holes and birds of the air have
nests, but the Son of Man[j] has no place to lay his head."
21Another disciple said to him, "Lord, first let me go and bury
my father."
22But Jesus told him, "Follow me,[k] and let the dead bury their
own dead."
23Then he got into the boat and his disciples followed him.
24Without warning, a furious storm came up on the lake, so that the
waves swept over the boat. But Jesus was sleeping. 25The disciples
went and woke him, saying, "Lord,
save us! We're going to drown!"
26He replied, "You of little faith,[l]
why are you so afraid?" Then he got
up and rebuked the winds and the
waves, and it was completely calm.[m]
27The men were amazed and
asked, "What kind of man is this?
Even the winds and the waves obey
him!"
28When he arrived at the other
side in the region of the Gadarenes,[b]
two demon-possessed[n] men coming from the tombs met him. They
were so violent that no one could
pass that way. 29"What do you want

Galilee

8:11 [a]Ps 107:3; Isa 49:12; 59:19; Mal 1:11 [b]Lk 13:29
8:12 [c]Mt 13:38 [d]Mt 13:42,50; 22:13; 24:51; 25:30; Lk 13:28
8:13 [e]Mt 9:22
8:16 [f]Mt 4:23,24
8:17 [g]Mt 1:22 [h]Isa 53:4
8:18 [i]Mk 4:35
8:20 [j]Da 7:13; Mt 12:8,32,40; 16:13,27,28; 17:9; 19:28; Mk 2:10; 8:31
8:22 [k]Mt 4:19
8:26 [l]Mt 6:30 [m]Ps 65:7; 89:9; 107:29
8:28 [n]Mt 4:24

a *17* Isaiah 53:4 b *28* Some manuscripts *Gergesenes*; others *Gerasenes*

with us,[a] Son of God?" they shouted. "Have you come here to torture us before the appointed time?"[b]
30Some distance from them a large herd of pigs was feeding.
31The demons begged Jesus, "If you drive us out, send us into the
herd of pigs."
32He said to them, "Go!" So they came out and went into the
pigs, and the whole herd rushed down the steep bank into the
lake and died in the water. 33Those tending the pigs ran off, went
into the town and reported all this, including what had happened
to the demon-possessed men. 34Then the whole town went out to
meet Jesus. And when they saw him, they pleaded with him to
leave their region.[c]

Chapter 9 Theme

9 Jesus stepped into a boat, crossed over and came to his own
town.[d] 2Some men brought to him a paralytic,[e] lying on a
mat. When Jesus saw their faith,[f] he said to the paralytic, "Take
heart,[g] son; your sins are forgiven."[h]
3At this, some of the teachers of the law said to themselves,
"This fellow is blaspheming!"[i]
4Knowing their thoughts,[j] Jesus said, "Why do you entertain
evil thoughts in your hearts? 5Which is easier: to say, 'Your sins are
forgiven,' or to say, 'Get up and walk'? 6But so that you may know
that the Son of Man[k] has authority on earth to forgive sins. . . ."
Then he said to the paralytic, "Get up, take your mat and go
home." 7And the man got up and went home. 8When the crowd
saw this, they were filled with awe; and they praised God,[l] who
had given such authority to men.
9As Jesus went on from there, he saw a man named Matthew
sitting at the tax collector's booth. "Follow me," he told him, and
Matthew got up and followed him.
10While Jesus was having dinner at Matthew's house, many tax
collectors and "sinners" came and ate with him and his disciples.
11When the Pharisees saw this, they asked his disciples, "Why
does your teacher eat with tax collectors and 'sinners'?"[m]
12On hearing this, Jesus said, "It is not the healthy who need a
doctor, but the sick. 13But go and learn what this means: 'I desire
mercy, not sacrifice.'[a][n] For I have not come to call the righteous,
but sinners."[o]
14Then John's disciples came and asked him, "How is it that we
and the Pharisees fast,[p] but your disciples do not fast?"
15Jesus answered, "How can the guests of the bridegroom mourn
while he is with them?[q] The time will come when the bridegroom
will be taken from them; then they will fast.[r]

a *13* Hosea 6:6

8:29 [a] Jdg 11:12; 2Sa 16:10; 1Ki 17:18; Mk 1:24; Lk 4:34; Jn 2:4 [b] 2Pe 2:4
8:34 [c] Lk 5:8; Ac 16:39
9:1 [d] Mt 4:13
9:2 [e] Mt 4:24 [f] ver 22 [g] Jn 16:33 [h] Lk 7:48
9:3 [i] Mt 26:65; Jn 10:33
9:4 [j] Ps 94:11; Mt 12:25; Lk 6:8; 9:47; 11:17
9:6 [k] Mt 8:20
9:8 [l] Mt 5:16; 15:31; Lk 7:16; 13:13; 17:15; 23:47; Jn 15:8; Ac 4:21; 11:18; 21:20
9:11 [m] Mt 11:19; Lk 5:30; 15:2; Gal 2:15
9:13 [n] Hos 6:6; Mic 6:6-8; Mt 12:7 [o] 1Ti 1:15
9:14 [p] Lk 18:12
9:15 [q] Jn 3:29 [r] Ac 13:2,3; 14:23

16“No one sews a patch of unshrunk cloth on an old garment,
for the patch will pull away from the garment, making the tear
worse. 17Neither do men pour new wine into old wineskins. If
they do, the skins will burst, the wine will run out and the wineskins will be ruined. No, they pour new wine into new wineskins,
and both are preserved.”
18While he was saying this, a ruler came and knelt before him[a]
and said, “My daughter has just died. But come and put your
hand on her,[b] and she will live.” 19Jesus got up and went with
him, and so did his disciples.
20Just then a woman who had been subject to bleeding for twelve
years came up behind him and touched the edge of his cloak.[c]
21She said to herself, “If I only touch his cloak, I will be healed.”
22Jesus turned and saw her. “Take heart, daughter,” he said,
“your faith has healed you.”[d] And the woman was healed from
that moment.[e]
23When Jesus entered the ruler’s house and saw the flute players and the noisy crowd,[f] 24he said, “Go away. The girl is not
dead[g] but asleep.”[h] But they laughed at him. 25After the crowd
had been put outside, he went in and took the girl by the hand,
and she got up. 26News of this spread through all that region.[i]
27As Jesus went on from there, two blind men followed him,
calling out, “Have mercy on us, Son of David!”[j]
28When he had gone indoors, the blind men came to him, and
he asked them, “Do you believe that I am able to do this?”
“Yes, Lord,” they replied.
29Then he touched their eyes and said, “According to your faith
will it be done to you”;[k] 30and their sight was restored. Jesus
warned them sternly, “See that no one knows about this.”[l] 31But
they went out and spread the news about him all over that region.[m]
32While they were going out, a man who was demon-possessed[n]
and could not talk[o] was brought to Jesus. 33And when the demon
was driven out, the man who had been mute spoke. The crowd was
amazed and said, “Nothing like this has ever been seen in Israel.”[p]
34But the Pharisees said, “It is by the prince of demons that he
drives out demons.”[q]
35Jesus went through all the towns and villages, teaching in
their synagogues, preaching the good news of the kingdom and
healing every disease and sickness.[r] 36When he saw the crowds,
he had compassion on them,[s] because they were harassed and
helpless, like sheep without a shepherd.[t] 37Then he said to his disciples, “The harvest[u] is plentiful but the workers are few.[v] 38Ask
the Lord of the harvest, therefore, to send out workers into his
harvest field.”

9:18 [a] Mt 8:2 [b] Mk 5:23
9:20 [c] Mt 14:36; Mk 3:10
9:22 [d] Mk 10:52; Lk 7:50; 17:19; 18:42 [e] Mt 15:28
9:23 [f] 2Ch 35:25; Jer 9:17,18
9:24 [g] Ac 20:10 [h] Jn 11:11-14
9:26 [i] Mt 4:24
9:27 [j] Mt 15:22; Mk 10:47; Lk 18:38-39
9:29 [k] ver 22
9:30 [l] Mt 8:4
9:31 [m] ver 26; Mk 7:36
9:32 [n] Mt 4:24 [o] Mt 12:22-24
9:33 [p] Mk 2:12
9:34 [q] Mt 12:24; Lk 11:15
9:35 [r] Mt 4:23
9:36 [s] Mt 14:14 [t] Nu 27:17; Eze 34:5,6; Zec 10:2; Mk 6:34
9:37 [u] Jn 4:35 [v] Lk 10:2

Chapter 10 Theme

10 He called his twelve disciples to him and gave them authority to drive out evil[a] spirits[a] and to heal every disease and sickness.

2These are the names of the twelve apostles: first, Simon (who is called Peter) and his brother Andrew; James son of Zebedee, and his brother John; 3Philip and Bartholomew; Thomas and Matthew the tax collector; James son of Alphaeus, and Thaddaeus; 4Simon the Zealot and Judas Iscariot, who betrayed him.[b]

5These twelve Jesus sent out with the following instructions: "Do not go among the Gentiles or enter any town of the Samaritans.[c] 6Go rather to the lost sheep of Israel.[d] 7As you go, preach this message: 'The kingdom of heaven[e] is near.' 8Heal the sick, raise the dead, cleanse those who have leprosy,[b] drive out demons. Freely you have received, freely give. 9Do not take along any gold or silver or copper in your belts;[f] 10take no bag for the journey, or extra tunic, or sandals or a staff; for the worker is worth his keep.[g]

11"Whatever town or village you enter, search for some worthy person there and stay at his house until you leave. 12As you enter the home, give it your greeting.[h] 13If the home is deserving, let your peace rest on it; if it is not, let your peace return to you. 14If anyone will not welcome you or listen to your words, shake the dust off your feet[i] when you leave that home or town. 15I tell you the truth, it will be more bearable for Sodom and Gomorrah[j] on the day of judgment[k] than for that town.[l] 16I am sending you out like sheep among wolves.[m] Therefore be as shrewd as snakes and as innocent as doves.[n]

17"Be on your guard against men; they will hand you over to the local councils[o] and flog you in their synagogues.[p] 18On my account you will be brought before governors and kings[q] as witnesses to them and to the Gentiles. 19But when they arrest you, do not worry about what to say or how to say it.[r] At that time you will be given what to say, 20for it will not be you speaking, but the Spirit of your Father[s] speaking through you.

21"Brother will betray brother to death, and a father his child; children will rebel against their parents[t] and have them put to death. 22All men will hate you because of me, but he who stands firm to the end will be saved.[u] 23When you are persecuted in one place, flee to another. I tell you the truth, you will not finish going through the cities of Israel before the Son of Man comes.

24"A student is not above his teacher, nor a servant above his master.[v] 25It is enough for the student to be like his teacher, and

10:1 [a]Mk 3:13-15; Lk 9:1
10:4 [b]Mt 26:14-16, 25,47; Jn 13:2,26,27
10:5 [c]2Ki 17:24; Lk 9:52; Jn 4:4-26,39,40; Ac 8:5,25
10:6 [d]Jer 50:6; Mt 15:24
10:7 [e]Mt 3:2
10:9 [f]Lk 22:35
10:10 [g]1Ti 5:18
10:12 [h]1Sa 25:6
10:14 [i]Ne 5:13; Lk 10:11; Ac 13:51
10:15 [j]2Pe 2:6 [k]Mt 12:36; 2Pe 2:9; 1Jn 4:17 [l]Mt 11:22,24
10:16 [m]Lk 10:3 [n]Ro 16:19
10:17 [o]Mt 5:22 [p]Mt 23:34; Mk 13:9; Ac 5:40; 26:11
10:18 [q]Ac 25:24-26
10:19 [r]Ex 4:12
10:20 [s]Ac 4:8
10:21 [t]ver 35,36; Mic 7:6
10:22 [u]Mt 24:13; Mk 13:13
10:24 [v]Lk 6:40; Jn 13:16; 15:20

a *1* Greek *unclean* b *8* The Greek word was used for various diseases affecting the skin—not necessarily leprosy.

the servant like his master. If the head of the house has been called
Beelzebub,[a][a] how much more the members of his household!
26"So do not be afraid of them. There is nothing concealed that
will not be disclosed, or hidden that will not be made known.[b]
27What I tell you in the dark, speak in the daylight; what is whispered in your ear, proclaim from the roofs. 28Do not be afraid of
those who kill the body but cannot kill the soul. Rather, be afraid
of the One[c] who can destroy both soul and body in hell. 29Are not
two sparrows sold for a penny[b]? Yet not one of them will fall to
the ground apart from the will of your Father. 30And even the
very hairs of your head are all numbered.[d] 31So don't be afraid;
you are worth more than many sparrows.[e]
32"Whoever acknowledges me before men,[f] I will also acknowledge him before my Father in heaven. 33But whoever disowns me
before men, I will disown him before my Father in heaven.[g]
34"Do not suppose that I have come to bring peace to the earth. I
did not come to bring peace, but a sword. 35For I have come to turn

> "'a man against his father,
> a daughter against her mother,
> a daughter-in-law against her mother-in-law[h]—
> 36 a man's enemies will be the members of
> his own household.'[c][i]

37"Anyone who loves his father or mother more than me is not
worthy of me; anyone who loves his son or daughter more than
me is not worthy of me;[j] 38and anyone who does not take his
cross and follow me is not worthy of me.[k] 39Whoever finds his life
will lose it, and whoever loses his life for my sake will find it.[l]
40"He who receives you receives me,[m] and he who receives me
receives the one who sent me.[n] 41Anyone who receives a prophet
because he is a prophet will receive a prophet's reward, and anyone who receives a righteous man because he is a righteous man
will receive a righteous man's reward. 42And if anyone gives even
a cup of cold water to one of these little ones because he is my disciple, I tell you the truth, he will certainly not lose his reward."[o]

Chapter 11 Theme

11 After Jesus had finished instructing his twelve disciples,[p] he
went on from there to teach and preach in the towns of
Galilee.[d]
2When John heard in prison[q] what Christ was doing, he sent
his disciples 3to ask him, "Are you the one who was to come,[r] or
should we expect someone else?"

[a] 25 Greek *Beezeboul* or *Beelzeboul* [b] 29 Greek *an assarion* [c] 36 Micah 7:6 [d] 1 Greek *in their towns*

10:25 *a* Mk 3:22
10:26 *b* Mk 4:22; Lk 8:17
10:28 *c* Isa 8:12,13; Heb 10:31
10:30 *d* 1Sa 14:45; 2Sa 14:11; Lk 21:18; Ac 27:34
10:31 *e* Mt 12:12
10:32 *f* Ro 10:9
10:33 *g* Mk 8:38; 2Ti 2:12
10:35 *h* ver 21
10:36 *i* Mic 7:6
10:37 *j* Lk 14:26
10:38 *k* Mt 16:24; Lk 14:27
10:39 *l* Lk 17:33; Jn 12:25
10:40 *m* Mt 18:5; Gal 4:14 *n* Lk 9:48; Jn 12:44; 13:20
10:42 *o* Mt 25:40; Mk 9:41; Heb 6:10
11:1 *p* Mt 7:28
11:2 *q* Mt 14:3
11:3 *r* Ps 118:26; Jn 11:27; Heb 10:37

[4]Jesus replied, "Go back and report to John what you hear and
see: [5]The blind receive sight, the lame walk, those who have leprosy[a] are cured, the deaf hear, the dead are raised, and the good
news is preached to the poor.[a] [6]Blessed is the man who does not
fall away on account of me."[b]

[7]As John's[c] disciples were leaving, Jesus began to speak to the
crowd about John: "What did you go out into the desert to see? A
reed swayed by the wind? [8]If not, what did you go out to see? A
man dressed in fine clothes? No, those who wear fine clothes are
in kings' palaces. [9]Then what did you go out to see? A prophet?[d]
Yes, I tell you, and more than a prophet. [10]This is the one about
whom it is written:

> "'I will send my messenger ahead of you,
> who will prepare your way before you.'[b][e]

[11]I tell you the truth: Among those born of women there has not
risen anyone greater than John the Baptist; yet he who is least in
the kingdom of heaven is greater than he. [12]From the days of John
the Baptist until now, the kingdom of heaven has been forcefully
advancing, and forceful men lay hold of it. [13]For all the Prophets
and the Law prophesied until John. [14]And if you are willing to
accept it, he is the Elijah who was to come.[f] [15]He who has ears, let
him hear.[g]

[16]"To what can I compare this generation? They are like children sitting in the marketplaces and calling out to others:

> [17]"'We played the flute for you,
> and you did not dance;
> we sang a dirge,
> and you did not mourn.'

[18]For John came neither eating[h] nor drinking,[i] and they say, 'He
has a demon.' [19]The Son of Man came eating and drinking, and
they say, 'Here is a glutton and a drunkard, a friend of tax collectors and "sinners."'[j] But wisdom is proved right by her actions."

[20]Then Jesus began to denounce the cities in which most of his
miracles had been performed, because they did not repent.
[21]"Woe to you, Korazin! Woe to you, Bethsaida![k] If the miracles
that were performed in you had been performed in Tyre and
Sidon,[l] they would have repented long ago in sackcloth and ashes.[m] [22]But I tell you, it will be more bearable for Tyre and Sidon
on the day of judgment than for you.[n] [23]And you, Capernaum,[o]
will you be lifted up to the skies? No, you will go down to the
depths.[c][p] If the miracles that were performed in you had been

11:5 [a]Isa 35:4-6; 61:1; Lk 4:18,19
11:6 [b]Mt 13:21
11:7 [c]Mt 3:1
11:9 [d]Mt 21:26; Lk 1:76
11:10 [e]Mal 3:1; Mk 1:2
11:14 [f]Mal 4:5; Mt 17:10-13; Mk 9:11-13; Lk 1:17; Jn 1:21
11:15 [g]Mt 13:9,43; Mk 4:23; Lk 14:35; Rev 2:7
11:18 [h]Mt 3:4 [i]Lk 1:15
11:19 [j]Mt 9:11
11:21 [k]Mk 6:45; Lk 9:10; Jn 12:21 [l]Mt 15:21; Lk 6:17; Ac 12:20 [m]Jnh 3:5-9
11:22 [n]ver 24; Mt 10:15
11:23 [o]Mt 4:13 [p]Isa 14:13-15

[a] *5* The Greek word was used for various diseases affecting the skin—not necessarily leprosy.
[b] *10* Mal. 3:1 [c] *23* Greek *Hades*

performed in Sodom, it would have remained to this day. 24 But I
tell you that it will be more bearable for Sodom on the day of
judgment than for you."[a]
25 At that time Jesus said, "I praise you, Father,[b] Lord of heaven
and earth, because you have hidden these things from the wise
and learned, and revealed them to little children.[c] 26 Yes, Father,
for this was your good pleasure.
27 "All things have been committed to me[d] by my Father.[e] No
one knows the Son except the Father, and no one knows the
Father except the Son and those to whom the Son chooses to
reveal him.[f]
28 "Come to me,[g] all you who are weary and burdened, and I
will give you rest. 29 Take my yoke upon you and learn from me,[h]
for I am gentle and humble in heart, and you will find rest for
your souls.[i] 30 For my yoke is easy and my burden is light."[j]

Chapter 12 Theme ____________________

12 At that time Jesus went through the grainfields on the Sabbath. His disciples were hungry and began to pick some
heads of grain[k] and eat them. 2 When the Pharisees saw this, they
said to him, "Look! Your disciples are doing what is unlawful on
the Sabbath."[l]
3 He answered, "Haven't you read what David did when he and
his companions were hungry?[m] 4 He entered the house of God,
and he and his companions ate the consecrated bread—which was
not lawful for them to do, but only for the priests.[n] 5 Or haven't
you read in the Law that on the Sabbath the priests in the temple
desecrate the day[o] and yet are innocent? 6 I tell you that one[a]
greater than the temple is here.[p] 7 If you had known what these
words mean, 'I desire mercy, not sacrifice,'[b][q] you would not have
condemned the innocent. 8 For the Son of Man[r] is Lord of the
Sabbath."
9 Going on from that place, he went into their synagogue, 10 and a
man with a shriveled hand was there. Looking for a reason to
accuse Jesus, they asked him, "Is it lawful to heal on the Sabbath?"[s]
11 He said to them, "If any of you has a sheep and it falls into a
pit on the Sabbath, will you not take hold of it and lift it out?[t]
12 How much more valuable is a man than a sheep![u] Therefore it
is lawful to do good on the Sabbath."
13 Then he said to the man, "Stretch out your hand." So he
stretched it out and it was completely restored, just as sound as
the other. 14 But the Pharisees went out and plotted how they
might kill Jesus.[v]

a6 Or *something*; also in verses 41 and 42 b7 Hosea 6:6

11:24 [a]Mt 10:15
11:25 [b]Lk 22:42; Jn 11:41 [c]1Co 1:26-29
11:27 [d]Mt 28:18 [e]Jn 3:35; 13:3; 17:2 [f]Jn 10:15
11:28 [g]Jn 7:37
11:29 [h]Jn 13:15; Php 2:5; 1Pe 2:21; 1Jn 2:6 [i]Jer 6:16
11:30 [j]1Jn 5:3
12:1 [k]Dt 23:25
12:2 [l]ver 10; Lk 13:14; 14:3; Jn 5:10; 7:23; 9:16
12:3 [m]1Sa 21:6
12:4 [n]Lev 24:5,9
12:5 [o]Nu 28:9,10; Jn 7:22,23
12:6 [p]ver 41,42
12:7 [q]Hos 6:6; Mic 6:6-8; Mt 9:13
12:8 [r]Mt 8:20
12:10 [s]ver 2; Lk 13:14; 14:3; Jn 9:16
12:11 [t]Lk 14:5
12:12 [u]Mt 10:31
12:14 [v]Mt 26:4; 27:1; Mk 3:6; Lk 6:11; Jn 5:18; 11:53

15 Aware of this, Jesus withdrew from that place. Many followed him, and he healed all their sick,[a] 16 warning them not to tell who he was.[b] 17 This was to fulfill what was spoken through the prophet Isaiah:

> 18 "Here is my servant whom I have chosen,
> the one I love, in whom I delight;[c]
> I will put my Spirit on him,
> and he will proclaim justice to the nations.
> 19 He will not quarrel or cry out;
> no one will hear his voice in the streets.
> 20 A bruised reed he will not break,
> and a smoldering wick he will not snuff out,
> till he leads justice to victory.
> 21 In his name the nations will put their hope."[a][d]

22 Then they brought him a demon-possessed man who was blind and mute, and Jesus healed him, so that he could both talk and see.[e] 23 All the people were astonished and said, "Could this be the Son of David?"[f]

24 But when the Pharisees heard this, they said, "It is only by Beelzebub,[b][g] the prince of demons, that this fellow drives out demons."[h]

25 Jesus knew their thoughts[i] and said to them, "Every kingdom divided against itself will be ruined, and every city or household divided against itself will not stand. 26 If Satan[j] drives out Satan, he is divided against himself. How then can his kingdom stand? 27 And if I drive out demons by Beelzebub, by whom do your people[k] drive them out? So then, they will be your judges. 28 But if I drive out demons by the Spirit of God, then the kingdom of God has come upon you.

29 "Or again, how can anyone enter a strong man's house and carry off his possessions unless he first ties up the strong man? Then he can rob his house.

30 "He who is not with me is against me, and he who does not gather with me scatters.[l] 31 And so I tell you, every sin and blasphemy will be forgiven men, but the blasphemy against the Spirit will not be forgiven.[m] 32 Anyone who speaks a word against the Son of Man will be forgiven, but anyone who speaks against the Holy Spirit will not be forgiven, either in this age[n] or in the age to come.[o]

33 "Make a tree good and its fruit will be good, or make a tree bad and its fruit will be bad, for a tree is recognized by its fruit.[p] 34 You brood of vipers,[q] how can you who are evil say anything good? For out of the overflow of the heart the mouth speaks.[r] 35 The good man brings good things out of the good stored up in

12:15 [a] Mt 4:23
12:16 [b] Mt 8:4
12:18 [c] Mt 3:17
12:21 [d] Isa 42:1-4
12:22 [e] Mt 4:24; 9:32-33
12:23 [f] Mt 9:27
12:24 [g] Mk 3:22 [h] Mt 9:34
12:25 [i] Mt 9:4
12:26 [j] Mt 4:10
12:27 [k] Ac 19:13
12:30 [l] Mk 9:40; Lk 11:23
12:31 [m] Mk 3:28,29; Lk 12:10
12:32 [n] Tit 2:12 [o] Mk 10:30; Lk 20:34,35; Eph 1:21; Heb 6:5
12:33 [p] Mt 7:16,17; Lk 6:43,44
12:34 [q] Mt 3:7; 23:33 [r] Mt 15:18; Lk 6:45

a *21* Isaiah 42:1-4 b *24* Greek *Beezeboul* or *Beelzeboul*; also in verse 27

him, and the evil man brings evil things out of the evil stored up
in him. 36But I tell you that men will have to give account on the
day of judgment for every careless word they have spoken. 37For
by your words you will be acquitted, and by your words you will
be condemned."

38Then some of the Pharisees and teachers of the law said to
him, "Teacher, we want to see a miraculous sign from you."[a]

39He answered, "A wicked and adulterous generation asks for a
miraculous sign! But none will be given it except the sign of the
prophet Jonah.[b] 40For as Jonah was three days and three nights in
the belly of a huge fish,[c] so the Son of Man[d] will be three days and
three nights in the heart of the earth.[e] 41The men of Nineveh[f] will
stand up at the judgment with this generation and condemn it;
for they repented at the preaching of Jonah,[g] and now one[a]
greater than Jonah is here. 42The Queen of the South will rise at
the judgment with this generation and condemn it; for she came[h]
from the ends of the earth to listen to Solomon's wisdom, and
now one greater than Solomon is here.

43"When an evil[b] spirit comes out of a man, it goes through arid
places seeking rest and does not find it. 44Then it says, 'I will return
to the house I left.' When it arrives, it finds the house unoccupied,
swept clean and put in order. 45Then it goes and takes with it seven
other spirits more wicked than itself, and they go in and live there.
And the final condition of that man is worse than the first.[i] That is
how it will be with this wicked generation."

46While Jesus was still talking to the crowd, his mother[j] and
brothers[k] stood outside, wanting to speak to him. 47Someone
told him, "Your mother and brothers are standing outside, wanting to speak to you."[c]

48He replied to him, "Who is my mother, and who are my
brothers?" 49Pointing to his disciples, he said, "Here are my mother and my brothers. 50For whoever does the will of my Father in
heaven[l] is my brother and sister and mother."

INSIGHT

See the section on *Parables*, under **Figures of Speech**, on page 2209.

Chapter 13 Theme ______________________

13 That same day Jesus went out of the house[m] and sat by the
lake. 2Such large crowds gathered around him that he got
into a boat[n] and sat in it, while all the people stood on the shore.
3Then he told them many things in parables, saying: "A farmer
went out to sow his seed. 4As he was scattering the seed, some fell
along the path, and the birds came and ate it up. 5Some fell on
rocky places, where it did not have much soil. It sprang up quickly, because the soil was shallow. 6But when the sun came up, the

[a] *41* Or *something;* also in verse 42 [b] *43* Greek *unclean* [c] *47* Some manuscripts do not have verse 47.

12:38 [a]Mt 16:1; Mk 8:11,12; Lk 11:16; Jn 2:18; 6:30; 1Co 1:22

12:39 [b]Mt 16:4; Lk 11:29

12:40 [c]Jnh 1:17 [d]Mt 8:20 [e]Mt 16:21

12:41 [f]Jnh 1:2 [g]Jnh 3:5

12:42 [h]1Ki 10:1; 2Ch 9:1

12:45 [i]2Pe 2:20

12:46 [j]Mt 1:18; 2:11,13,14,20; Lk 1:43; 2:33,34,48,51; Jn 2:1,5; 19:25,26 [k]Mt 13:55; Jn 2:12; 7:3,5; Ac 1:14; 1Co 9:5; Gal 1:19

12:50 [l]Jn 15:14

13:1 [m]ver 36; Mt 9:28

13:2 [n]Lk 5:3

plants were scorched, and they withered because they had no
root. 7Other seed fell among thorns, which grew up and choked
the plants. 8Still other seed fell on good soil, where it produced a
crop—a hundred,[a] sixty or thirty times what was sown. 9He who
has ears, let him hear."[b]

10The disciples came to him and asked, "Why do you speak to
the people in parables?"

11He replied, "The knowledge of the secrets of the kingdom of
heaven has been given to you,[c] but not to them. 12Whoever has
will be given more, and he will have an abundance. Whoever
does not have, even what he has will be taken from him.[d] 13This is
why I speak to them in parables:

> "Though seeing, they do not see;
> though hearing, they do not hear or understand.[e]

14In them is fulfilled the prophecy of Isaiah:

> " 'You will be ever hearing but never understanding;
> you will be ever seeing but never perceiving.
> 15For this people's heart has become calloused;
> they hardly hear with their ears,
> and they have closed their eyes.
> Otherwise they might see with their eyes,
> hear with their ears,
> understand with their hearts
> and turn, and I would heal them.'[a][f]

16But blessed are your eyes because they see, and your ears
because they hear.[g] 17For I tell you the truth, many prophets and
righteous men longed to see what you see[h] but did not see it, and
to hear what you hear but did not hear it.

18"Listen then to what the parable of the sower means: 19When
anyone hears the message about the kingdom[i] and does not
understand it, the evil one[j] comes and snatches away what was
sown in his heart. This is the seed sown along the path. 20The one
who received the seed that fell on rocky places is the man who
hears the word and at once receives it with joy. 21But since he has
no root, he lasts only a short time. When trouble or persecution
comes because of the word, he quickly falls away.[k] 22The one who
received the seed that fell among the thorns is the man who hears
the word, but the worries of this life and the deceitfulness of
wealth[l] choke it, making it unfruitful. 23But the one who received
the seed that fell on good soil is the man who hears the word and
understands it. He produces a crop, yielding a hundred, sixty or
thirty times what was sown."[m]

13:8 [a]Ge 26:12
13:9 [b]Mt 11:15
13:11 [c]Mt 11:25; 16:17; 19:11; Jn 6:65; 1Co 2:10,14; Col 1:27; 1Jn 2:20,27
13:12 [d]Mt 25:29; Lk 19:26
13:13 [e]Dt 29:4; Jer 5:21; Eze 12:2
13:15 [f]Isa 6:9,10; Jn 12:40; Ac 28:26,27; Ro 11:8
13:16 [g]Mt 16:17
13:17 [h]Jn 8:56; Heb 11:13; 1Pe 1:10-12
13:19 [i]Mt 4:23 [j]Mt 5:37
13:21 [k]Mt 11:6
13:22 [l]Mt 19:23; 1Ti 6:9,10,17
13:23 [m]ver 8

[a] *15* Isaiah 6:9,10

24 Jesus told them another parable: "The kingdom of heaven is
like[a] a man who sowed good seed in his field. 25 But while everyone was sleeping, his enemy came and sowed weeds among the
wheat, and went away. 26 When the wheat sprouted and formed
heads, then the weeds also appeared.

27 "The owner's servants came to him and said, 'Sir, didn't you
sow good seed in your field? Where then did the weeds come
from?'

28 " 'An enemy did this,' he replied.

"The servants asked him, 'Do you want us to go and pull
them up?'

29 " 'No,' he answered, 'because while you are pulling the weeds,
you may root up the wheat with them. 30 Let both grow together
until the harvest. At that time I will tell the harvesters: First collect the weeds and tie them in bundles to be burned; then gather
the wheat and bring it into my barn.' "[b]

31 He told them another parable: "The kingdom of heaven is
like[c] a mustard seed,[d] which a man took and planted in his field.
32 Though it is the smallest of all your seeds, yet when it grows, it
is the largest of garden plants and becomes a tree, so that the
birds of the air come and perch in its branches."[e]

33 He told them still another parable: "The kingdom of heaven
is like[f] yeast that a woman took and mixed into a large amount[a]
of flour[g] until it worked all through the dough."[h]

34 Jesus spoke all these things to the crowd in parables; he did
not say anything to them without using a parable.[i] 35 So was fulfilled what was spoken through the prophet:

> "I will open my mouth in parables,
> I will utter things hidden since the creation
> of the world."[b][j]

36 Then he left the crowd and went into the house. His disciples
came to him and said, "Explain to us the parable[k] of the weeds in
the field."

37 He answered, "The one who sowed the good seed is the Son
of Man.[l] 38 The field is the world, and the good seed stands for the
sons of the kingdom. The weeds are the sons of the evil one,[m]
39 and the enemy who sows them is the devil. The harvest[n] is the
end of the age,[o] and the harvesters are angels.[p]

40 "As the weeds are pulled up and burned in the fire, so it will
be at the end of the age. 41 The Son of Man[q] will send out his
angels,[r] and they will weed out of his kingdom everything that
causes sin and all who do evil. 42 They will throw them into the
fiery furnace, where there will be weeping and gnashing of teeth.[s]

[a] 33 Greek *three satas* (probably about 1/2 bushel or 22 liters) [b] 35 Psalm 78:2

13:24 [a] ver 31,33,45,47; Mt 18:23; 20:1; 22:2; 25:1; Mk 4:26,30
13:30 [b] Mt 3:12
13:31 [c] ver 24 [d] Mt 17:20; Lk 17:6
13:32 [e] Ps 104:12; Eze 17:23; 31:6; Da 4:12
13:33 [f] ver 24 [g] Ge 18:6 [h] Gal 5:9
13:34 [i] Mk 4:33; Jn 16:25
13:35 [j] Ps 78:2; Ro 16:25,26; 1Co 2:7; Eph 3:9; Col 1:26
13:36 [k] Mt 15:15
13:37 [l] Mt 8:20
13:38 [m] Jn 8:44,45; 1Jn 3:10
13:39 [n] Joel 3:13 [o] Mt 24:3; 28:20 [p] Rev 14:15
13:41 [q] Mt 8:20 [r] Mt 24:31
13:42 [s] ver 50; Mt 8:12

43Then the righteous will shine like the sun[a] in the kingdom of
their Father. He who has ears, let him hear.[b]
44"The kingdom of heaven is like[c] treasure hidden in a field.
When a man found it, he hid it again, and then in his joy went
and sold all he had and bought that field.[d]
45"Again, the kingdom of heaven is like[e] a merchant looking for
fine pearls. 46When he found one of great value, he went away
and sold everything he had and bought it.
47"Once again, the kingdom of heaven is like[f] a net that was let
down into the lake and caught all kinds[g] of fish. 48When it was full,
the fishermen pulled it up on the shore. Then they sat down and
collected the good fish in baskets, but threw the bad away. 49This is
how it will be at the end of the age. The angels will come and separate the wicked from the righteous[h] 50and throw them into the
fiery furnace, where there will be weeping and gnashing of teeth.[i]
51"Have you understood all these things?" Jesus asked.
"Yes," they replied.
52He said to them, "Therefore every teacher of the law who has
been instructed about the kingdom of heaven is like the owner of
a house who brings out of his storeroom new treasures as well as
old."
53When Jesus had finished these parables,[j] he moved on from
there. 54Coming to his hometown, he began teaching the people in
their synagogue,[k] and they were amazed.[l] "Where did this man get
this wisdom and these miraculous powers?" they asked. 55"Isn't
this the carpenter's son?[m] Isn't his mother's[n] name Mary, and aren't
his brothers James, Joseph, Simon and Judas? 56Aren't all his sisters with us? Where then did this man get all these things?"
57And they took offense[o] at him.
But Jesus said to them, "Only in his hometown and in his own
house is a prophet without honor."[p]
58And he did not do many miracles there because of their lack
of faith.

Chapter 14 Theme

14 At that time Herod[q] the tetrarch heard the reports about
Jesus,[r] 2and he said to his attendants, "This is John the Baptist;[s] he has risen from the dead! That is why miraculous powers
are at work in him."
3Now Herod had arrested John and bound him and put him in
prison[t] because of Herodias, his brother Philip's wife,[u] 4for John
had been saying to him: "It is not lawful for you to have her."[v]
5Herod wanted to kill John, but he was afraid of the people, because
they considered him a prophet.[w]

13:43 [a]Da 12:3 [b]Mt 11:15
13:44 [c]ver 24 [d]Isa 55:1; Php 3:7,8
13:45 [e]ver 24
13:47 [f]ver 24 [g]Mt 22:10
13:49 [h]Mt 25:32
13:50 [i]Mt 8:12
13:53 [j]Mt 7:28
13:54 [k]Mt 4:23 [l]Mt 7:28
13:55 [m]Lk 3:23; Jn 6:42 [n]Mt 12:46
13:57 [o]Jn 6:61 [p]Lk 4:24; Jn 4:44
14:1 [q]Mk 8:15; Lk 3:1,19; 13:31; 23:7,8; Ac 4:27; 12:1 [r]Lk 9:7-9
14:2 [s]Mt 3:1
14:3 [t]Mt 4:12; 11:2 [u]Lk 3:19,20
14:4 [v]Lev 18:16; 20:21
14:5 [w]Mt 11:9

6On Herod's birthday the daughter of Herodias danced for them
and pleased Herod so much 7that he promised with an oath to give
her whatever she asked. 8Prompted by her mother, she said, "Give
me here on a platter the head of John the Baptist." 9The king was
distressed, but because of his oaths and his dinner guests, he
ordered that her request be granted 10and had John beheaded[a] in
the prison. 11His head was brought in on a platter and given to the
girl, who carried it to her mother. 12John's disciples came and took
his body and buried it.[b] Then they went and told Jesus.

13When Jesus heard what had happened, he withdrew by boat
privately to a solitary place. Hearing of this, the crowds followed
him on foot from the towns. 14When Jesus landed and saw a large
crowd, he had compassion on them[c] and healed their sick.[d]

15As evening approached, the disciples came to him and said,
"This is a remote place, and it's already getting late. Send the
crowds away, so they can go to the villages and buy themselves
some food."

16Jesus replied, "They do not need to go away. You give them
something to eat."

17"We have here only five loaves[e] of bread and two fish," they
answered.

18"Bring them here to me," he said. 19And he directed the people to sit down on the grass. Taking the five loaves and the two
fish and looking up to heaven, he gave thanks and broke the
loaves.[f] Then he gave them to the disciples, and the disciples gave
them to the people. 20They all ate and were satisfied, and the disciples picked up twelve basketfuls of broken pieces that were left
over. 21The number of those who ate was about five thousand
men, besides women and children.

22Immediately Jesus made the disciples get into the boat and go
on ahead of him to the other side, while he dismissed the crowd.
23After he had dismissed them, he went up on a mountainside by
himself to pray.[g] When evening came, he was there alone, 24but
the boat was already a considerable distance[a] from land, buffeted
by the waves because the wind was against it.

25During the fourth watch of the night Jesus went out to them,
walking on the lake. 26When the disciples saw him walking on
the lake, they were terrified. "It's a ghost,"[h] they said, and cried
out in fear.

27But Jesus immediately said to them: "Take courage![i] It is I.
Don't be afraid."[j]

28"Lord, if it's you," Peter replied, "tell me to come to you on
the water."

29"Come," he said.

14:10 [a] Mt 17:12
14:12 [b] Ac 8:2
14:14 [c] Mt 9:36 [d] Mt 4:23
14:17 [e] Mt 16:9
14:19 [f] 1Sa 9:13; Mt 26:26; Mk 8:6; Lk 24:30; Ac 2:42; 27:35; 1Ti 4:4
14:23 [g] Lk 3:21
14:26 [h] Lk 24:37
14:27 [i] Mt 9:2; Ac 23:11 [j] Da 10:12; Mt 17:7; 28:10; Lk 1:13,30; 2:10; Ac 18:9; 23:11; Rev 1:17

a 24 Greek *many stadia*

Then Peter got down out of the boat, walked on the water and
came toward Jesus. 30But when he saw the wind, he was afraid and,
beginning to sink, cried out, "Lord, save me!"
31Immediately Jesus reached out his hand and caught him. "You
of little faith,"[a] he said, "why did you doubt?"
32And when they climbed into the boat, the wind died down.
33Then those who were in the boat worshiped him, saying, "Truly
you are the Son of God."[b]
34When they had crossed over, they landed at Gennesaret. 35And
when the men of that place recognized Jesus, they sent word to
all the surrounding country. People brought all their sick to him
36and begged him to let the sick just touch the edge of his cloak,[c]
and all who touched him were healed.

Chapter 15 Theme ______________________

15 Then some Pharisees and teachers of the law came to Jesus
from Jerusalem and asked, 2"Why do your disciples break
the tradition of the elders? They don't wash their hands before
they eat!"[d]
3Jesus replied, "And why do you break the command of God for
the sake of your tradition? 4For God said, 'Honor your father and
mother'[a][e] and 'Anyone who curses his father or mother must be
put to death.'[b][f] 5But you say that if a man says to his father or
mother, 'Whatever help you might otherwise have received from
me is a gift devoted to God,' 6he is not to 'honor his father[c]' with it.
Thus you nullify the word of God for the sake of your tradition.
7You hypocrites! Isaiah was right when he prophesied about you:

> 8"'These people honor me with their lips,
> but their hearts are far from me.
> 9They worship me in vain;
> their teachings are but rules taught by men.[g]'[d][h]"

10Jesus called the crowd to him and said, "Listen and understand.
11What goes into a man's mouth does not make him 'unclean,'[i]
but what comes out of his mouth, that is what makes him
'unclean.'"[j]
12Then the disciples came to him and asked, "Do you know that
the Pharisees were offended when they heard this?"
13He replied, "Every plant that my heavenly Father has not
planted[k] will be pulled up by the roots. 14Leave them; they are
blind guides.[e][l] If a blind man leads a blind man, both will fall into
a pit."[m]
15Peter said, "Explain the parable to us."[n]

14:31 [a]Mt 6:30
14:33 [b]Ps 2:7; Mt 4:3
14:36 [c]Mt 9:20
15:2 [d]Lk 11:38
15:4 [e]Ex 20:12; Dt 5:16; Eph 6:2 [f]Ex 21:17; Lev 20:9
15:9 [g]Col 2:20-22 [h]Isa 29:13; Mal 2:2
15:11 [i]Ac 10:14,15 [j]ver 18
15:13 [k]Isa 60:21; 61:3; Jn 15:2
15:14 [l]Mt 23:16,24; Ro 2:19 [m]Lk 6:39
15:15 [n]Mt 13:36

[a] *4* Exodus 20:12; Deut. 5:16 [b] *4* Exodus 21:17; Lev. 20:9 [c] *6* Some manuscripts *father or his mother* [d] *9* Isaiah 29:13 [e] *14* Some manuscripts *guides of the blind*

16“Are you still so dull?”[a] Jesus asked them. 17“Don’t you see that
whatever enters the mouth goes into the stomach and then out of
the body? 18But the things that come out of the mouth come from
the heart,[b] and these make a man ‘unclean.’ 19For out of the heart
come evil thoughts, murder, adultery, sexual immorality, theft, false
testimony, slander.[c] 20These are what make a man ‘unclean’;[d] but
eating with unwashed hands does not make him ‘unclean.’”

21Leaving that place, Jesus withdrew to the region of Tyre and
Sidon.[e] 22A Canaanite woman from that vicinity came to him,
crying out, “Lord, Son of David,[f] have mercy on me! My daughter is suffering terribly from demon-possession.”[g]

23Jesus did not answer a word. So his disciples came to him and
urged him, “Send her away, for she keeps crying out after us.”

24He answered, “I was sent only to the lost sheep of Israel.”[h]

25The woman came and knelt before him.[i] “Lord, help me!” she
said.

26He replied, “It is not right to take the children’s bread and toss
it to their dogs.”

27“Yes, Lord,” she said, “but even the dogs eat the crumbs that
fall from their masters’ table.”

28Then Jesus answered, “Woman, you have great faith![j] Your
request is granted.” And her daughter was healed from that very
hour.

29Jesus left there and went along the Sea of Galilee. Then he went
up on a mountainside and sat down. 30Great crowds came to him,
bringing the lame, the blind, the crippled, the mute and many
others, and laid them at his feet; and he healed them.[k] 31The people were amazed when they saw the mute speaking, the crippled
made well, the lame walking and the blind seeing. And they
praised the God of Israel.[l]

32Jesus called his disciples to him and said, “I have compassion
for these people;[m] they have already been with me three days and
have nothing to eat. I do not want to send them away hungry, or
they may collapse on the way.”

33His disciples answered, “Where could we get enough bread in
this remote place to feed such a crowd?”

34“How many loaves do you have?” Jesus asked.

“Seven,” they replied, “and a few small fish.”

35He told the crowd to sit down on the ground. 36Then he took
the seven loaves and the fish, and when he had given thanks, he
broke them[n] and gave them to the disciples, and they in turn to
the people. 37They all ate and were satisfied. Afterward the disciples picked up seven basketfuls of broken pieces that were left
over.[o] 38The number of those who ate was four thousand, besides
women and children. 39After Jesus had sent the crowd away, he
got into the boat and went to the vicinity of Magadan.

15:16 [a] Mt 16:9
15:18 [b] Mt 12:34; Lk 6:45; Jas 3:6
15:19 [c] Gal 5:19-21
15:20 [d] Ro 14:14
15:21 [e] Mt 11:21
15:22 [f] Mt 9:27 [g] Mt 4:24
15:24 [h] Mt 10:6,23; Ro 15:8
15:25 [i] Mt 8:2
15:28 [j] Mt 9:22
15:30 [k] Mt 4:23
15:31 [l] Mt 9:8
15:32 [m] Mt 9:36
15:36 [n] Mt 14:19
15:37 [o] Mt 16:10

Chapter 16 Theme ______________________

16 The Pharisees and Sadducees[a] came to Jesus and tested him
by asking him to show them a sign from heaven.[b]
2 He replied,[a] "When evening comes, you say, 'It will be fair
weather, for the sky is red,' 3 and in the morning, 'Today it will be
stormy, for the sky is red and overcast.' You know how to interpret the appearance of the sky, but you cannot interpret the signs
of the times.[c] 4 A wicked and adulterous generation looks for a
miraculous sign, but none will be given it except the sign of Jonah."[d] Jesus then left them and went away.
5 When they went across the lake, the disciples forgot to take
bread. 6 "Be careful," Jesus said to them. "Be on your guard against
the yeast of the Pharisees and Sadducees."[e]
7 They discussed this among themselves and said, "It is because
we didn't bring any bread."
8 Aware of their discussion, Jesus asked, "You of little faith,[f] why
are you talking among yourselves about having no bread? 9 Do
you still not understand? Don't you remember the five loaves for
the five thousand, and how many basketfuls you gathered?[g] 10 Or
the seven loaves for the four thousand, and how many basketfuls
you gathered?[h] 11 How is it you don't understand that I was not
talking to you about bread? But be on your guard against the
yeast of the Pharisees and Sadducees." 12 Then they understood that
he was not telling them to guard against the yeast used in bread,
but against the teaching of the Pharisees and Sadducees.[i]
13 When Jesus came to the region of Caesarea Philippi, he asked
his disciples, "Who do people say the Son of Man is?"
14 They replied, "Some say John the Baptist;[j] others say Elijah;
and still others, Jeremiah or one of the prophets."[k]
15 "But what about you?" he asked. "Who do you say I am?"
16 Simon Peter answered, "You are the Christ,[b] the Son of the
living God."[l]
17 Jesus replied, "Blessed are you, Simon son of Jonah, for this
was not revealed to you by man,[m] but by my Father in heaven.
18 And I tell you that you are Peter,[c][n] and on this rock I will build
my church,[o] and the gates of Hades[d] will not overcome it.[e] 19 I
will give you the keys[p] of the kingdom of heaven; whatever you
bind on earth will be[f] bound in heaven, and whatever you loose
on earth will be[f] loosed in heaven."[q] 20 Then he warned his disciples not to tell anyone[r] that he was the Christ.
21 From that time on Jesus began to explain to his disciples that
he must go to Jerusalem and suffer many things[s] at the hands of

16:1 [a]Ac 4:1 [b]Mt 12:38
16:3 [c]Lk 12:54-56
16:4 [d]Mt 12:39
16:6 [e]Lk 12:1
16:8 [f]Mt 6:30
16:9 [g]Mt 14:17-21
16:10 [h]Mt 15:34-38
16:12 [i]Ac 4:1
16:14 [j]Mt 3:1; 14:2 [k]Mk 6:15; Jn 1:21
16:16 [l]Mt 4:3; Ps 42:2; Jn 11:27; Ac 14:15; 2Co 6:16; 1Th 1:9; 1Ti 3:15; Heb 10:31; 12:22
16:17 [m]1Co 15:50; Gal 1:16; Eph 6:12; Heb 2:14
16:18 [n]Jn 1:42 [o]Eph 2:20
16:19 [p]Isa 22:22; Rev 3:7 [q]Mt 18:18; Jn 20:23
16:20 [r]Mk 8:30
16:21 [s]Mk 10:34; Lk 17:25

[a] *2* Some early manuscripts do not have the rest of verse 2 and all of verse 3. [b] *16* Or *Messiah;* also in verse 20 [c] *18* *Peter* means *rock.* [d] *18* Or *hell* [e] *18* Or *not prove stronger than it* [f] *19* Or *have been*

the elders, chief priests and teachers of the law, and that he must be killed and on the third day[a] be raised to life.[b]

22Peter took him aside and began to rebuke him. "Never, Lord!" he said. "This shall never happen to you!"

23Jesus turned and said to Peter, "Get behind me, Satan![c] You are a stumbling block to me; you do not have in mind the things of God, but the things of men."

24Then Jesus said to his disciples, "If anyone would come after me, he must deny himself and take up his cross and follow me.[d] 25For whoever wants to save his life[a] will lose it, but whoever loses his life for me will find it.[e] 26What good will it be for a man if he gains the whole world, yet forfeits his soul? Or what can a man give in exchange for his soul? 27For the Son of Man[f] is going to come[g] in his Father's glory with his angels, and then he will reward each person according to what he has done.[h] 28I tell you the truth, some who are standing here will not taste death before they see the Son of Man coming in his kingdom."

Chapter 17 Theme

17 After six days Jesus took with him Peter, James and John the brother of James, and led them up a high mountain by themselves. 2There he was transfigured before them. His face shone like the sun, and his clothes became as white as the light. 3Just then there appeared before them Moses and Elijah, talking with Jesus.

4Peter said to Jesus, "Lord, it is good for us to be here. If you wish, I will put up three shelters—one for you, one for Moses and one for Elijah."

5While he was still speaking, a bright cloud enveloped them, and a voice from the cloud said, "This is my Son, whom I love; with him I am well pleased.[i] Listen to him!"[j]

6When the disciples heard this, they fell facedown to the ground, terrified. 7But Jesus came and touched them. "Get up," he said. "Don't be afraid."[k] 8When they looked up, they saw no one except Jesus.

9As they were coming down the mountain, Jesus instructed them, "Don't tell anyone[l] what you have seen, until the Son of Man[m] has been raised from the dead."[n]

10The disciples asked him, "Why then do the teachers of the law say that Elijah must come first?"

11Jesus replied, "To be sure, Elijah comes and will restore all things.[o] 12But I tell you, Elijah has already come,[p] and they did not recognize him, but have done to him everything they wished.[q] In the same way the Son of Man is going to suffer[r] at their hands."

a *25* The Greek word means either *life* or *soul*; also in verse 26.

16:21 [a] Jn 2:19 [b] Mt 17:22,23; Mk 9:31; Lk 9:22; 18:31-33; 24:6,7

16:23 [c] Mt 4:10

16:24 [d] Mt 10:38; Lk 14:27

16:25 [e] Jn 12:25

16:27 [f] Mt 8:20 [g] Ac 1:11 [h] Job 34:11; Ps 62:12; Jer 17:10; Ro 2:6; 2Co 5:10; Rev 22:12

17:5 [i] Mt 3:17; 2Pe 1:17 [j] Ac 3:22,23

17:7 [k] Mt 14:27

17:9 [l] Mk 8:30 [m] Mt 8:20 [n] Mt 16:21

17:11 [o] Mal 4:6; Lk 1:16,17

17:12 [p] Mt 11:14 [q] Mt 14:3,10 [r] Mt 16:21

17:15 [a]Mt 4:24
17:20 [b]Mt 21:21 [c]Mt 13:31; Mk 11:23; Lk 17:6 [d]1Co 13:2
17:22 [e]Mt 8:20
17:23 [f]Ac 2:23; 3:13 [g]Mt 16:21 [h]Mt 16:21
17:24 [i]Ex 30:13
17:25 [j]Mt 22:17-21; Ro 13:7
17:27 [k]Jn 6:61
18:3 [l]Mt 19:14; 1Pe 2:2 [m]Mt 3:2
18:4 [n]Mk 9:35

13 Then the disciples understood that he was talking to them about
John the Baptist.
14 When they came to the crowd, a man approached Jesus and
knelt before him. 15 "Lord, have mercy on my son," he said. "He
has seizures[a] and is suffering greatly. He often falls into the fire or
into the water. 16 I brought him to your disciples, but they could
not heal him."
17 "O unbelieving and perverse generation," Jesus replied, "how
long shall I stay with you? How long shall I put up with you? Bring
the boy here to me." 18 Jesus rebuked the demon, and it came out
of the boy, and he was healed from that moment.
19 Then the disciples came to Jesus in private and asked, "Why
couldn't we drive it out?"
20 He replied, "Because you have so little faith. I tell you the truth,
if you have faith[b] as small as a mustard seed,[c] you can say to this
mountain, 'Move from here to there' and it will move.[d] Nothing
will be impossible for you.[a]"
22 When they came together in Galilee, he said to them, "The
Son of Man[e] is going to be betrayed into the hands of men. 23 They
will kill him,[f] and on the third day[g] he will be raised to life."[h]
And the disciples were filled with grief.
24 After Jesus and his disciples arrived in Capernaum, the collectors of the two-drachma tax[i] came to Peter and asked, "Doesn't
your teacher pay the temple tax[b]?"
25 "Yes, he does," he replied.
When Peter came into the house, Jesus was the first to speak.
"What do you think, Simon?" he asked. "From whom do the kings
of the earth collect duty and taxes[j]—from their own sons or
from others?"
26 "From others," Peter answered.
"Then the sons are exempt," Jesus said to him. 27 "But so that we
may not offend[k] them, go to the lake and throw out your line. Take
the first fish you catch; open its mouth and you will find a four-
drachma coin. Take it and give it to them for my tax and yours."

Chapter 18 Theme ______________________________

18

At that time the disciples came to Jesus and asked, "Who is
the greatest in the kingdom of heaven?"
2 He called a little child and had him stand among them. 3 And
he said: "I tell you the truth, unless you change and become like
little children,[l] you will never enter the kingdom of heaven.[m]
4 Therefore, whoever humbles himself like this child is the greatest in the kingdom of heaven.[n]

a 20 Some manuscripts *you.* [21] *But this kind does not go out except by prayer and fasting.*
b 24 Greek *the two drachmas*

5"And whoever welcomes a little child like this in my name
welcomes me.[a] 6But if anyone causes one of these little ones who
believe in me to sin,[b] it would be better for him to have a large millstone hung around his neck and to be drowned in the depths of
the sea.[c]
7"Woe to the world because of the things that cause people to
sin! Such things must come, but woe to the man through whom
they come![d] 8If your hand or your foot causes you to sin,[e] cut it
off and throw it away. It is better for you to enter life maimed or
crippled than to have two hands or two feet and be thrown into
eternal fire. 9And if your eye causes you to sin,[f] gouge it out and
throw it away. It is better for you to enter life with one eye than to
have two eyes and be thrown into the fire of hell.[g]
10"See that you do not look down on one of these little ones.
For I tell you that their angels[h] in heaven always see the face of my
Father in heaven.[a]
12"What do you think? If a man owns a hundred sheep, and one
of them wanders away, will he not leave the ninety-nine on the
hills and go to look for the one that wandered off? 13And if he finds
it, I tell you the truth, he is happier about that one sheep than about
the ninety-nine that did not wander off. 14In the same way your
Father in heaven is not willing that any of these little ones should
be lost.
15"If your brother sins against you,[b] go and show him his fault,[i]
just between the two of you. If he listens to you, you have won
your brother over. 16But if he will not listen, take one or two others
along, so that 'every matter may be established by the testimony
of two or three witnesses.'[c][j] 17If he refuses to listen to them, tell it
to the church;[k] and if he refuses to listen even to the church, treat
him as you would a pagan or a tax collector.[l]
18"I tell you the truth, whatever you bind on earth will be[d]
bound in heaven, and whatever you loose on earth will be[d] loosed
in heaven.[m]
19"Again, I tell you that if two of you on earth agree about anything you ask for, it will be done for you[n] by my Father in heaven.
20For where two or three come together in my name, there am I
with them."
21Then Peter came to Jesus and asked, "Lord, how many times
shall I forgive my brother when he sins against me?[o] Up to seven
times?"[p]
22Jesus answered, "I tell you, not seven times, but seventy-seven
times.[e][q]

18:5 [a]Mt 10:40
18:6 [b]Mt 5:29 [c]Mk 9:42; Lk 17:2
18:7 [d]Lk 17:1
18:8 [e]Mt 5:29; Mk 9:43,45
18:9 [f]Mt 5:29 [g]Mt 5:22
18:10 [h]Ge 48:16; Ps 34:7; Ac 12:11,15; Heb 1:14
18:15 [i]Lev 19:17; Lk 17:3; Gal 6:1; Jas 5:19,20
18:16 [j]Nu 35:30; Dt 17:6; 19:15; Jn 8:17; 2Co 13:1; 1Ti 5:19; Heb 10:28
18:17 [k]1Co 6:1-6 [l]Ro 16:17; 2Th 3:6,14
18:18 [m]Mt 16:19; Jn 20:23
18:19 [n]Mt 7:7
18:21 [o]Mt 6:14 [p]Lk 17:4
18:22 [q]Ge 4:24

[a]10 Some manuscripts *heaven.* [11]*The Son of Man came to save what was lost.* [b]15 Some manuscripts do not have *against you.* [c]16 Deut. 19:15 [d]18 Or *have been* [e]22 Or *seventy times seven*

18:23 [a]Mt 13:24 [b]Mt 25:19

23"Therefore, the kingdom of heaven is like[a] a king who wanted
to settle accounts[b] with his servants. 24As he began the settlement,
a man who owed him ten thousand talents[a] was brought to him.
25Since he was not able to pay,[c] the master ordered that he and his
wife and his children and all that he had be sold[d] to repay the debt.
26"The servant fell on his knees before him.[e] 'Be patient with
me,' he begged, 'and I will pay back everything.' 27The servant's
master took pity on him, canceled the debt and let him go.
28"But when that servant went out, he found one of his fellow
servants who owed him a hundred denarii.[b] He grabbed him and
began to choke him. 'Pay back what you owe me!' he demanded.
29"His fellow servant fell to his knees and begged him, 'Be
patient with me, and I will pay you back.'
30"But he refused. Instead, he went off and had the man thrown
into prison until he could pay the debt. 31When the other servants saw what had happened, they were greatly distressed and
went and told their master everything that had happened.
32"Then the master called the servant in. 'You wicked servant,'
he said, 'I canceled all that debt of yours because you begged me
to. 33Shouldn't you have had mercy on your fellow servant just as
I had on you?' 34In anger his master turned him over to the jailers
to be tortured, until he should pay back all he owed.
35"This is how my heavenly Father will treat each of you unless
you forgive your brother from your heart."[f]

18:25 [c]Lk 7:42 [d]Lev 25:39; 2Ki 4:1; Ne 5:5,8

18:26 [e]Mt 8:2

18:35 [f]Mt 6:14; Jas 2:13

Chapter 19 Theme ______

19 When Jesus had finished saying these things,[g] he left Galilee
and went into the region of Judea to the other side of the
Jordan. 2Large crowds followed him,
and he healed them[h] there.
3Some Pharisees came to him to
test him. They asked, "Is it lawful for
a man to divorce his wife[i] for any
and every reason?"
4"Haven't you read," he replied,
"that at the beginning the Creator
'made them male and female,'[c][j] 5and
said, 'For this reason a man will leave
his father and mother and be united
to his wife, and the two will become
one flesh'[d]?[k] 6So they are no longer
two, but one. Therefore what God
has joined together, let man not separate."

19:1 [g]Mt 7:28

19:2 [h]Mt 4:23

19:3 [i]Mt 5:31

19:4 [j]Ge 1:27; 5:2

19:5 [k]Ge 2:24; 1Co 6:16; Eph 5:31

Samaria
Sychar
Mt. Ebal
Mt. Gerizim
Shechem
Jordan River
PEREA
Jericho
Bethany beyond Jordan
Emmaus
Mt. of Olives
Jerusalem
Bethany
Bethlehem
JUDEA
Dead (Salt) Sea

Judea

[a]24 That is, millions of dollars [b]28 That is, a few dollars [c]4 Gen. 1:27 [f]5 Gen. 2:24

7“Why then,” they asked, “did Moses command that a man give
his wife a certificate of divorce and send her away?”[a]
8Jesus replied, “Moses permitted you to divorce your wives
because your hearts were hard. But it was not this way from the
beginning. 9I tell you that anyone who divorces his wife, except
for marital unfaithfulness, and marries another woman commits
adultery.”[b]
10The disciples said to him, “If this is the situation between a husband and wife, it is better not to marry.”
11Jesus replied, “Not everyone can accept this word, but only
those to whom it has been given.[c] 12For some are eunuchs because
they were born that way; others were made that way by men; and
others have renounced marriage[a] because of the kingdom of heav-
en. The one who can accept this should accept it.”
13Then little children were brought to Jesus for him to place his
hands on them[d] and pray for them. But the disciples rebuked those
who brought them.
14Jesus said, “Let the little children come to me, and do not hinder them, for the kingdom of heaven belongs[e] to such as these.”[f]
15When he had placed his hands on them, he went on from there.
16Now a man came up to Jesus and asked, “Teacher, what good
thing must I do to get eternal life[g]?”[h]
17“Why do you ask me about what is good?” Jesus replied. “There
is only One who is good. If you want to enter life, obey the commandments.”[i]
18“Which ones?” the man inquired.
Jesus replied, “ ‘Do not murder, do not commit adultery,[j] do not
steal, do not give false testimony, 19honor your father and mother,’[b][k] and ‘love your neighbor as yourself.’[c]”[l]
20“All these I have kept,” the young man said. “What do I still
lack?”
21Jesus answered, “If you want to be perfect,[m] go, sell your possessions and give to the poor,[n] and you will have treasure in heav-
en.[o] Then come, follow me.”
22When the young man heard this, he went away sad, because
he had great wealth.
23Then Jesus said to his disciples, “I tell you the truth, it is hard
for a rich man[p] to enter the kingdom of heaven. 24Again I tell you,
it is easier for a camel to go through the eye of a needle than for a
rich man to enter the kingdom of God.”
25When the disciples heard this, they were greatly astonished
and asked, “Who then can be saved?”
26Jesus looked at them and said, “With man this is impossible,
but with God all things are possible.”[q]

[a] *12* Or *have made themselves eunuchs* [b] *19* Exodus 20:12-16; Deut. 5:16-20 [c] *19* Lev. 19:18

19:7 [a] Dt 24:1-4; Mt 5:31
19:9 [b] Mt 5:32; Lk 16:18
19:11 [c] Mt 13:11; 1Co 7:7-9,17
19:13 [d] Mk 5:23
19:14 [e] Mt 25:34 [f] Mt 18:3; 1Pe 2:2
19:16 [g] Mt 25:46 [h] Lk 10:25
19:17 [i] Lev 18:5
19:18 [j] Jas 2:11
19:19 [k] Ex 20:12-16; Dt 5:16-20 [l] Lev 19:18; Mt 5:43
19:21 [m] Mt 5:48 [n] Lk 12:33; Ac 2:45; 4:34-35 [o] Mt 6:20
19:23 [p] Mt 13:22; 1Ti 6:9,10
19:26 [q] Ge 18:14; Job 42:2; Jer 32:17; Zec 8:6; Lk 1:37; 18:27; Ro 4:21

27Peter answered him, "We have left everything to follow you![a] What then will there be for us?"

28Jesus said to them, "I tell you the truth, at the renewal of all things, when the Son of Man sits on his glorious throne,[b] you who have followed me will also sit on twelve thrones, judging the twelve tribes of Israel.[c] 29And everyone who has left houses or brothers or sisters or father or mother[a] or children or fields for my sake will receive a hundred times as much and will inherit eternal life.[d] 30But many who are first will be last, and many who are last will be first.[e]

Chapter 20 Theme ______________________

20

"For the kingdom of heaven is like[f] a landowner who went out early in the morning to hire men to work in his vineyard.[g] 2He agreed to pay them a denarius for the day and sent them into his vineyard.

3"About the third hour he went out and saw others standing in the marketplace doing nothing. 4He told them, 'You also go and work in my vineyard, and I will pay you whatever is right.' 5So they went.

"He went out again about the sixth hour and the ninth hour and did the same thing. 6About the eleventh hour he went out and found still others standing around. He asked them, 'Why have you been standing here all day long doing nothing?'

7"'Because no one has hired us,' they answered.

"He said to them, 'You also go and work in my vineyard.'

8"When evening came,[h] the owner of the vineyard said to his foreman, 'Call the workers and pay them their wages, beginning with the last ones hired and going on to the first.'

9"The workers who were hired about the eleventh hour came and each received a denarius. 10So when those came who were hired first, they expected to receive more. But each one of them also received a denarius. 11When they received it, they began to grumble[i] against the landowner. 12'These men who were hired last worked only one hour,' they said, 'and you have made them equal to us who have borne the burden of the work and the heat[j] of the day.'

13"But he answered one of them, 'Friend,[k] I am not being unfair to you. Didn't you agree to work for a denarius? 14Take your pay and go. I want to give the man who was hired last the same as I gave you. 15Don't I have the right to do what I want with my own money? Or are you envious because I am generous?'[l]

16"So the last will be first, and the first will be last."[m]

a 29 Some manuscripts *mother or wife*

19:27 a Mt 4:19
19:28 b Mt 20:21; 25:31 c Lk 22:28-30; Rev 3:21; 4:4; 20:4
19:29 d Mt 6:33; 25:46
19:30 e Mt 20:16; Mk 10:31; Lk 13:30
20:1 f Mt 13:24 g Mt 21:28,33
20:8 h Lev 19:13; Dt 24:15
20:11 i Jnh 4:1
20:12 j Jnh 4:8; Lk 12:55; Jas 1:11
20:13 k Mt 22:12; 26:50
20:15 l Dt 15:9; Mk 7:22
20:16 m Mt 19:30

17Now as Jesus was going up to Jerusalem, he took the twelve disciples aside and said to them, 18"We are going up to Jerusalem,[a]
and the Son of Man[b] will be betrayed to the chief priests and the
teachers of the law.[c] They will condemn him to death 19and will
turn him over to the Gentiles to be mocked and flogged[d] and
crucified.[e] On the third day[f] he will be raised to life!"[g]
20Then the mother of Zebedee's sons[h] came to Jesus with her
sons and, kneeling down,[i] asked a favor of him.
21"What is it you want?" he asked.
She said, "Grant that one of these two sons of mine may sit at
your right and the other at your left in your kingdom."[j]
22"You don't know what you are asking," Jesus said to them.
"Can you drink the cup[k] I am going to drink?"
"We can," they answered.
23Jesus said to them, "You will indeed drink from my cup,[l] but to
sit at my right or left is not for me to grant. These places belong to
those for whom they have been prepared by my Father."
24When the ten heard about this, they were indignant[m] with the
two brothers. 25Jesus called them together and said, "You know
that the rulers of the Gentiles lord it over them, and their high
officials exercise authority over them. 26Not so with you. Instead,
whoever wants to become great among you must be your servant,[n]
27and whoever wants to be first must be your slave— 28just as the
Son of Man[o] did not come to be served, but to serve,[p] and to give
his life as a ransom[q] for many."
29As Jesus and his disciples were leaving Jericho, a large crowd
followed him. 30Two blind men were sitting by the roadside, and
when they heard that Jesus was going by, they shouted, "Lord, Son
of David,[r] have mercy on us!"
31The crowd rebuked them and told them to be quiet, but they
shouted all the louder, "Lord, Son of David, have mercy on us!"
32Jesus stopped and called them. "What do you want me to do
for you?" he asked.
33"Lord," they answered, "we want our sight."
34Jesus had compassion on them and touched their eyes.
Immediately they received their sight and followed him.

Chapter 21 Theme ______________________

21 As they approached Jerusalem and came to Bethphage on
the Mount of Olives,[s] Jesus sent two disciples, 2saying to
them, "Go to the village ahead of you, and at once you will find a
donkey tied there, with her colt by her. Untie them and bring them
to me. 3If anyone says anything to you, tell him that the Lord needs
them, and he will send them right away."
4This took place to fulfill what was spoken through the prophet:

20:18 [a]Lk 9:51 [b]Mt 8:20 [c]Mt 16:21; 27:1,2

20:19 [d]Mt 16:21 [e]Ac 2:23 [f]Mt 16:21 [g]Mt 16:21

20:20 [h]Mt 4:21 [i]Mt 8:2

20:21 [j]Mt 19:28

20:22 [k]Isa 51:17,22; Jer 49:12; Mt 26:39,42; Mk 14:36; Lk 22:42; Jn 18:11

20:23 [l]Ac 12:2; Rev 1:9

20:24 [m]Lk 22:24,25

20:26 [n]Mt 23:11; Mk 9:35

20:28 [o]Mt 8:20 [p]Lk 22:27; Jn 13:13-16; 2Co 8:9; Php 2:7 [q]Isa 53:10; Mt 26:28; 1Ti 2:6; Tit 2:14; Heb 9:28; 1Pe 1:18,19

20:30 [r]Mt 9:27

21:1 [s]Mt 24:3; 26:30; Mk 14:26; Lk 19:37; 21:37; 22:39; Jn 8:1; Ac 1:12

21:5 [a]Zec 9:9; Isa 62:11 5"Say to the Daughter
of Zion,
'See, your king comes
to you,
21:8 [b]2Ki 9:13 gentle and riding on
a donkey,
on a colt, the foal of
a donkey.'"[a][a]

21:9 [c]ver 15; Mt 9:27 [d]Ps 118:26; Mt 23:39 [e]Lk 2:14 6The disciples went and did as
Jesus had instructed them. 7They
brought the donkey and the colt,
placed their cloaks on them, and
Jesus sat on them. 8A very large
crowd spread their cloaks[b] on the
21:11 [f]Lk 7:16,39; 24:19; Jn 1:21,25; 6:14; 7:40 road, while others cut branches
from the trees and spread them on the road. 9The crowds that
went ahead of him and those that followed shouted,

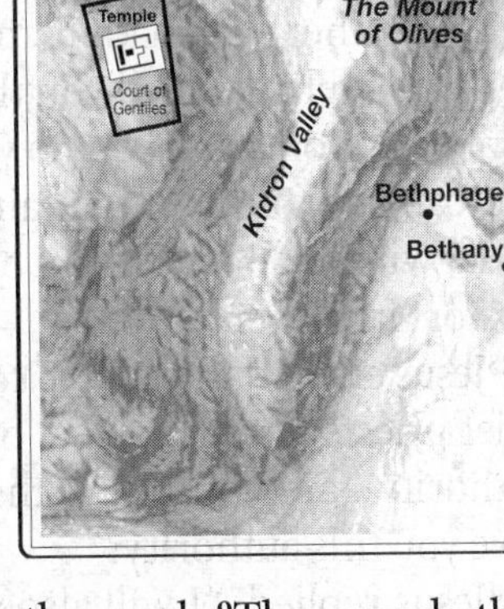

From Bethany, Bethphage across the Mount of Olives into Jerusalem

"Hosanna[b] to the Son of David!"[c]

"Blessed is he who comes in the name of the Lord!"[c][d]

21:12 [g]Dt 14:26 [h]Ex 30:13 [i]Lev 1:14 "Hosanna[b] in the highest!"[e]

10When Jesus entered Jerusalem, the whole city was stirred and
asked, "Who is this?"
11The crowds answered, "This is Jesus, the prophet[f] from
21:13 [j]Isa 56:7 [k]Jer 7:11 Nazareth in Galilee."
12Jesus entered the temple area and drove out all who were buying[g] and selling there. He overturned the tables of the money
changers[h] and the benches of those selling doves.[i] 13"It is writ-
21:14 [l]Mt 4:23 ten," he said to them, "'My house will be called a house of
prayer,'[d][j] but you are making it a 'den of robbers.'[e]"[k]
14The blind and the lame came to him at the temple, and he
healed them.[l] 15But when the chief priests and the teachers of the
21:15 [m]ver 9; Mt 9:27 [n]Lk 19:39 law saw the wonderful things he did and the children shouting in
the temple area, "Hosanna to the Son of David,"[m] they were
indignant.[n]
16"Do you hear what these children are saying?" they asked him.
"Yes," replied Jesus, "have you never read,

21:16 [o]Ps 8:2 "'From the lips of children and infants
you have ordained praise'[f]?"[o]

17And he left them and went out of the city to Bethany,[p] where
21:17 [p]Mt 26:6; Mk 11:1; Lk 24:50; Jn 11:1,18; 12:1 he spent the night.

[a]5 Zech. 9:9 [b]9 A Hebrew expression meaning "Save!" which became an exclamation of praise; also in verse 15 [c]9 Psalm 118:26 [d]13 Isaiah 56:7 [e]13 Jer. 7:11 [f]16 Psalm 8:2

18 Early in the morning, as he was on his way back to the city, he was hungry. 19 Seeing a fig tree by the road, he went up to it but found nothing on it except leaves. Then he said to it, "May you never bear fruit again!" Immediately the tree withered.[a]

20 When the disciples saw this, they were amazed. "How did the fig tree wither so quickly?" they asked.

21 Jesus replied, "I tell you the truth, if you have faith and do not doubt,[b] not only can you do what was done to the fig tree, but also you can say to this mountain, 'Go, throw yourself into the sea,' and it will be done. 22 If you believe, you will receive whatever you ask for[c] in prayer."

23 Jesus entered the temple courts, and, while he was teaching, the chief priests and the elders of the people came to him. "By what authority[d] are you doing these things?" they asked. "And who gave you this authority?"

24 Jesus replied, "I will also ask you one question. If you answer me, I will tell you by what authority I am doing these things. 25 John's baptism—where did it come from? Was it from heaven, or from men?"

They discussed it among themselves and said, "If we say, 'From heaven,' he will ask, 'Then why didn't you believe him?' 26 But if we say, 'From men'—we are afraid of the people, for they all hold that John was a prophet."[e]

27 So they answered Jesus, "We don't know."

Then he said, "Neither will I tell you by what authority I am doing these things.

28 "What do you think? There was a man who had two sons. He went to the first and said, 'Son, go and work today in the vineyard.'[f]

29 " 'I will not,' he answered, but later he changed his mind and went.

30 "Then the father went to the other son and said the same thing. He answered, 'I will, sir,' but he did not go.

31 "Which of the two did what his father wanted?"

"The first," they answered.

Jesus said to them, "I tell you the truth, the tax collectors[g] and the prostitutes[h] are entering the kingdom of God ahead of you. 32 For John came to you to show you the way of righteousness,[i] and you did not believe him, but the tax collectors[j] and the prostitutes[k] did. And even after you saw this, you did not repent[l] and believe him.

33 "Listen to another parable: There was a landowner who planted[m] a vineyard. He put a wall around it, dug a winepress in it and built a watchtower.[n] Then he rented the vineyard to some farmers and went away on a journey.[o] 34 When the harvest time approached, he sent his servants[p] to the tenants to collect his fruit.

21:19 [a] Isa 34:4; Jer 8:13
21:21 [b] Mt 17:20; Lk 17:6; 1Co 13:2; Jas 1:6
21:22 [c] Mt 7:7
21:23 [d] Ac 4:7; 7:27
21:26 [e] Mt 11:9; Mk 6:20
21:28 [f] ver 33; Mt 20:1
21:31 [g] Lk 7:29 [h] Lk 7:50
21:32 [i] Mt 3:1-12 [j] Lk 3:12,13; 7:29 [k] Lk 7:36-50 [l] Lk 7:30
21:33 [m] Ps 80:8 [n] Isa 5:1-7 [o] Mt 25:14,15
21:34 [p] Mt 22:3

35"The tenants seized his servants; they beat one, killed another,
and stoned a third.[a] 36Then he sent other servants[b] to them, more
than the first time, and the tenants treated them the same way.
37Last of all, he sent his son to them. 'They will respect my son,' he
said.

38"But when the tenants saw the son, they said to each other,
'This is the heir.[c] Come, let's kill him[d] and take his inheritance.'[e]
39So they took him and threw him out of the vineyard and killed
him.

40"Therefore, when the owner of the vineyard comes, what will
he do to those tenants?"

41"He will bring those wretches to a wretched end,"[f] they
replied, "and he will rent the vineyard to other tenants,[g] who will
give him his share of the crop at harvest time."

42Jesus said to them, "Have you never read in the Scriptures:

> " 'The stone the builders rejected
> has become the capstone[a];
> the Lord has done this,
> and it is marvelous in our eyes'[b]?[h]

43"Therefore I tell you that the kingdom of God will be taken
away from you[i] and given to a people who will produce its fruit.
44He who falls on this stone will be broken to pieces, but he on
whom it falls will be crushed."[c][j]

45When the chief priests and the Pharisees heard Jesus' parables, they knew he was talking about them. 46They looked for a
way to arrest him, but they were afraid of the crowd because the
people held that he was a prophet.[k]

Chapter 22 Theme ______________________

22 Jesus spoke to them again in parables, saying: 2"The kingdom of heaven is like[l] a king who prepared a wedding banquet for his son. 3He sent his servants[m] to those who had been
invited to the banquet to tell them to come, but they refused to
come.

4"Then he sent some more servants[n] and said, 'Tell those who
have been invited that I have prepared my dinner: My oxen and
fattened cattle have been butchered, and everything is ready.
Come to the wedding banquet.'

5"But they paid no attention and went off—one to his field,
another to his business. 6The rest seized his servants, mistreated
them and killed them. 7The king was enraged. He sent his army
and destroyed those murderers[o] and burned their city.

21:35 [a]2Ch 24:21; Mt 23:34,37; Heb 11:36,37
21:36 [b]Mt 22:4
21:38 [c]Heb 1:2 [d]Mt 12:14 [e]Ps 2:8
21:41 [f]Mt 8:11,12 [g]Ac 13:46; 18:6; 28:28
21:42 [h]Ps 118:22,23; Ac 4:11; 1Pe 2:7
21:43 [i]Mt 8:12
21:44 [j]Lk 2:34
21:46 [k]ver 11,26
22:2 [l]Mt 13:24
22:3 [m]Mt 21:34
22:4 [n]Mt 21:36
22:7 [o]Lk 19:27

[a] 42 Or *cornerstone* [b] 42 Psalm 118:22,23 [c] 44 Some manuscripts do not have verse 44.

8“Then he said to his servants, ‘The wedding banquet is ready,
but those I invited did not deserve to come. 9Go to the street corners[a] and invite to the banquet anyone you find.’ 10So the servants
went out into the streets and gathered all the people they could
find, both good and bad,[b] and the wedding hall was filled with
guests.

11“But when the king came in to see the guests, he noticed a
man there who was not wearing wedding clothes. 12‘Friend,’[c] he
asked, ‘how did you get in here without wedding clothes?’ The
man was speechless.

13“Then the king told the attendants, ‘Tie him hand and foot,
and throw him outside, into the darkness, where there will be
weeping and gnashing of teeth.’[d]

14“For many are invited, but few are chosen.”[e]

15Then the Pharisees went out and laid plans to trap him in his
words. 16They sent their disciples to him along with the Herodians.[f] “Teacher,” they said, “we know you are a man of integrity
and that you teach the way of God in accordance with the truth.
You aren’t swayed by men, because you pay no attention to who
they are. 17Tell us then, what is your opinion? Is it right to pay taxes[g] to Caesar or not?”

18But Jesus, knowing their evil intent, said, “You hypocrites,
why are you trying to trap me? 19Show me the coin used for paying
the tax.” They brought him a denarius, 20and he asked them,
“Whose portrait is this? And whose inscription?”

21“Caesar’s,” they replied.

Then he said to them, “Give to Caesar what is Caesar’s,[h] and to
God what is God’s.”

22When they heard this, they were amazed. So they left him
and went away.[i]

23That same day the Sadducees,[j] who say there is no resurrection,[k] came to him with a question. 24“Teacher,” they said,
“Moses told us that if a man dies without having children, his
brother must marry the widow and have children for him.[l] 25Now
there were seven brothers among us. The first one married and
died, and since he had no children, he left his wife to his brother.
26The same thing happened to the second and third brother,
right on down to the seventh. 27Finally, the woman died. 28Now
then, at the resurrection, whose wife will she be of the seven,
since all of them were married to her?”

29Jesus replied, “You are in error because you do not know the
Scriptures[m] or the power of God. 30At the resurrection people
will neither marry nor be given in marriage;[n] they will be like the
angels in heaven. 31But about the resurrection of the dead—have
you not read what God said to you, 32‘I am the God of Abraham,

22:9 [a] Eze 21:21
22:10 [b] Mt 13:47,48
22:12 [c] Mt 20:13; 26:50
22:13 [d] Mt 8:12
22:14 [e] Rev 17:14
22:16 [f] Mk 3:6
22:17 [g] Mt 17:25
22:21 [h] Ro 13:7
22:22 [i] Mk 12:12
22:23 [j] Ac 4:1 [k] Ac 23:8; 1Co 15:12
22:24 [l] Dt 25:5,6
22:29 [m] Jn 20:9
22:30 [n] Mt 24:38

the God of Isaac, and the God of Jacob'[a]?[a] He is not the God of
the dead but of the living."
33 When the crowds heard this, they were astonished at his
teaching.[b]
34 Hearing that Jesus had silenced the Sadducees,[c] the Pharisees
got together. 35 One of them, an expert in the law,[d] tested him with
this question: 36 "Teacher, which is the greatest commandment in
the Law?"
37 Jesus replied: "'Love the Lord your God with all your heart
and with all your soul and with all your mind.'[b][e] 38 This is the first
and greatest commandment. 39 And the second is like it: 'Love
your neighbor as yourself.'[c][f] 40 All the Law and the Prophets hang
on these two commandments."[g]
41 While the Pharisees were gathered together, Jesus asked
them, 42 "What do you think about the Christ[d]? Whose son
is he?"
"The son of David,"[h] they replied.
43 He said to them, "How is it then that David, speaking by the
Spirit, calls him 'Lord'? For he says,

44 "'The Lord said to my Lord:
"Sit at my right hand
until I put your enemies
under your feet."'[e][i]

45 If then David calls him 'Lord,' how can he be his son?" 46 No one
could say a word in reply, and from that day on no one dared to
ask him any more questions.[j]

Chapter 23 Theme ______________________

23 Then Jesus said to the crowds and to his disciples: 2 "The
teachers of the law[k] and the Pharisees sit in Moses' seat.
3 So you must obey them and do everything they tell you. But do
not do what they do, for they do not practice what they preach.
4 They tie up heavy loads and put them on men's shoulders, but
they themselves are not willing to lift a finger to move them.[l]
5 "Everything they do is done for men to see:[m] They make their
phylacteries[f][n] wide and the tassels on their garments[o] long; 6 they
love the place of honor at banquets and the most important seats
in the synagogues;[p] 7 they love to be greeted in the marketplaces
and to have men call them 'Rabbi.'[q]
8 "But you are not to be called 'Rabbi,' for you have only one
Master and you are all brothers. 9 And do not call anyone on earth

22:32 [a] Ex 3:6; Ac 7:32
22:33 [b] Mt 7:28
22:34 [c] Ac 4:1
22:35 [d] Lk 7:30; 10:25; 11:45; 14:3
22:37 [e] Dt 6:5
22:39 [f] Lev 19:18; Mt 5:43; 19:19; Gal 5:14
22:40 [g] Mt 7:12
22:42 [h] Mt 9:27
22:44 [i] Ps 110:1; Ac 2:34,35; 1Co 15:25; Heb 1:13; 10:13
22:46 [j] Mk 12:34; Lk 20:40
23:2 [k] Ezr 7:6,25; Ne 8:4
23:4 [l] Lk 11:46; Ac 15:10; Gal 6:13
23:5 [m] Mt 6:1,2,5,16 [n] Ex 13:9; Dt 6:8 [o] Nu 15:38; Dt 22:12
23:6 [p] Lk 11:43; 14:7; 20:46
23:7 [q] ver 8; Mk 9:5; 10:51; Jn 1:38,49

[a] 32 Exodus 3:6 [b] 37 Deut. 6:5 [c] 39 Lev. 19:18 [d] 42 Or *Messiah* [e] 44 Psalm 110:1
[f] 5 That is, boxes containing Scripture verses, worn on forehead and arm

'father,' for you have one Father,[a] and he is in heaven. 10 Nor are you
to be called 'teacher,' for you have one Teacher, the Christ.[a] 11 The
greatest among you will be your servant.[b] 12 For whoever exalts
himself will be humbled, and whoever humbles himself will be
exalted.[c]

13 "Woe to you, teachers of the law and Pharisees, you hypocrites![d]
You shut the kingdom of heaven in men's faces. You yourselves do
not enter, nor will you let those enter who are trying to.[b][e]

15 "Woe to you, teachers of the law and Pharisees, you hypocrites!
You travel over land and sea to win a single convert,[f] and when he
becomes one, you make him twice as much a son of hell[g] as you are.

16 "Woe to you, blind guides![h] You say, 'If anyone swears by the
temple, it means nothing; but if anyone swears by the gold of the
temple, he is bound by his oath.'[i] 17 You blind fools! Which is
greater: the gold, or the temple that makes the gold sacred?[j] 18 You
also say, 'If anyone swears by the altar, it means nothing; but if
anyone swears by the gift on it, he is bound by his oath.' 19 You
blind men! Which is greater: the gift, or the altar that makes the
gift sacred?[k] 20 Therefore, he who swears by the altar swears by it
and by everything on it. 21 And he who swears by the temple
swears by it and by the one who dwells[l] in it. 22 And he who swears
by heaven swears by God's throne and by the one who sits on it.[m]

23 "Woe to you, teachers of the law and Pharisees, you hypocrites! You give a tenth[n] of your spices—mint, dill and cummin.
But you have neglected the more important matters of the law—
justice, mercy and faithfulness.[o] You should have practiced the latter, without neglecting the former. 24 You blind guides![p] You strain
out a gnat but swallow a camel.

25 "Woe to you, teachers of the law and Pharisees, you hypocrites! You clean the outside of the cup and dish,[q] but inside
they are full of greed and self-indulgence.[r] 26 Blind Pharisee! First
clean the inside of the cup and dish, and then the outside also will
be clean.

27 "Woe to you, teachers of the law and Pharisees, you hypocrites!
You are like whitewashed tombs,[s] which look beautiful on the outside but on the inside are full of dead men's bones and everything unclean. 28 In the same way, on the outside you appear to
people as righteous but on the inside you are full of hypocrisy
and wickedness.

29 "Woe to you, teachers of the law and Pharisees, you hypocrites!
You build tombs for the prophets[t] and decorate the graves of the

[a] 10 Or *Messiah* [b] 13 Some manuscripts *to.* [14] *Woe to you, teachers of the law and Pharisees, you hypocrites! You devour widows' houses and for a show make lengthy prayers. Therefore you will be punished more severely.*

23:9 [a] Mal 1:6; Mt 7:11
23:11 [b] Mt 20:26; Mk 9:35
23:12 [c] Lk 14:11
23:13 [d] ver 15,23, 25,27,29 [e] Lk 11:52
23:15 [f] Ac 2:11; 6:5; 13:43 [g] Mt 5:22
23:16 [h] ver 24; Mt 15:14 [i] Mt 5:33-35
23:17 [j] Ex 30:29
23:19 [k] Ex 29:37
23:21 [l] 1Ki 8:13; Ps 26:8
23:22 [m] Ps 11:4; Mt 5:34
23:23 [n] Lev 27:30 [o] Mic 6:8; Lk 11:42
23:24 [p] ver 16
23:25 [q] Mk 7:4 [r] Lk 11:39
23:27 [s] Lk 11:44; Ac 23:3
23:29 [t] Lk 11:47,48

righteous. 30And you say, 'If we had lived in the days of our forefathers, we would not have taken part with them in shedding the
blood of the prophets.' 31So you testify against yourselves that you
are the descendants of those who murdered the prophets.[a] 32Fill
up, then, the measure[b] of the sin of your forefathers!

33"You snakes! You brood of vipers![c] How will you escape being
condemned to hell?[d] 34Therefore I am sending you prophets and
wise men and teachers. Some of them you will kill and crucify;[e]
others you will flog in your synagogues[f] and pursue from town to
town.[g] 35And so upon you will come all the righteous blood that
has been shed on earth, from the blood of righteous Abel[h] to the
blood of Zechariah son of Berekiah,[i] whom you murdered between
the temple and the altar.[j] 36I tell you the truth, all this will come
upon this generation.[k]

37"O Jerusalem, Jerusalem, you who kill the prophets and stone
those sent to you,[l] how often I have longed to gather your children
together, as a hen gathers her chicks under her wings, but you
were not willing. 38Look, your house is left to you desolate.[m] 39For
I tell you, you will not see me again until you say, 'Blessed is he
who comes in the name of the Lord.'[a]"[n]

Chapter 24 Theme

24 Jesus left the temple and was walking away when his disciples came up to him to call his attention to its buildings.
2"Do you see all these things?" he asked. "I tell you the truth, not
one stone here will be left on another;[o] every one will be thrown
down."

3As Jesus was sitting on the Mount of Olives,[p] the disciples came
to him privately. "Tell us," they said, "when will this happen, and
what will be the sign of your coming and of the end of the age?"

4Jesus answered: "Watch out that no one deceives you. 5For
many will come in my name, claiming, 'I am the Christ,[b]' and will
deceive many.[q] 6You will hear of wars and rumors of wars, but see
to it that you are not alarmed. Such things must happen, but the
end is still to come. 7Nation will rise against nation, and kingdom
against kingdom.[r] There will be famines[s] and earthquakes in various places. 8All these are the beginning of birth pains.

9"Then you will be handed over to be persecuted[t] and put to
death,[u] and you will be hated by all nations because of me. 10At
that time many will turn away from the faith and will betray and
hate each other, 11and many false prophets[v] will appear and
deceive many people. 12Because of the increase of wickedness,

INSIGHT

See the illustration of the temple mount on IISB-40.

23:31 [a]Ac 7:51-52
23:32 [b]1Th 2:16
23:33 [c]Mt 3:7; 12:34 [d]Mt 5:22
23:34 [e]2Ch 36:15,16; Lk 11:49 [f]Mt 10:17 [g]Mt 10:23
23:35 [h]Ge 4:8; Heb 11:4 [i]Zec 1:1 [j]2Ch 24:21
23:36 [k]Mt 10:23; 24:34
23:37 [l]2Ch 24:21; Mt 5:12
23:38 [m]1Ki 9:7,8; Jer 22:5
23:39 [n]Ps 118:26; Mt 21:9
24:2 [o]Lk 19:44
24:3 [p]Mt 21:1
24:5 [q]ver 11,23,24; 1Jn 2:18
24:7 [r]Isa 19:2 [s]Ac 11:28
24:9 [t]Mt 10:17 [u]Jn 16:2
24:11 [v]Mt 7:15

[a]39 Psalm 118:26 [b]5 Or *Messiah*; also in verse 23

the love of most will grow cold, 13but he who stands firm to the
end will be saved.[a] 14And this gospel of the kingdom[b] will be
preached in the whole world[c] as a testimony to all nations, and
then the end will come.

15"So when you see standing in the holy place[d] 'the abomination that causes desolation,'[a][e] spoken of through the prophet
Daniel—let the reader understand— 16then let those who are in
Judea flee to the mountains. 17Let no one on the roof of his house[f]
go down to take anything out of the house. 18Let no one in the
field go back to get his cloak. 19How dreadful it will be in those
days for pregnant women and nursing mothers![g] 20Pray that your
flight will not take place in winter or on the Sabbath. 21For then
there will be great distress, unequaled from the beginning of the
world until now—and never to be equaled again.[h] 22If those days
had not been cut short, no one would survive, but for the sake of
the elect[i] those days will be shortened. 23At that time if anyone
says to you, 'Look, here is the Christ!' or, 'There he is!' do not
believe it.[j] 24For false Christs and false prophets will appear and
perform great signs and miracles[k] to deceive even the elect—if
that were possible. 25See, I have told you ahead of time.

26"So if anyone tells you, 'There he is, out in the desert,' do not
go out; or, 'Here he is, in the inner rooms,' do not believe it. 27For
as lightning[l] that comes from the east is visible even in the west,
so will be the coming of the Son of Man.[m] 28Wherever there is a
carcass, there the vultures will gather.[n]

29"Immediately after the distress of those days

"'the sun will be darkened,
  and the moon will not give its light;
the stars will fall from the sky,
  and the heavenly bodies will be shaken.'[b][o]

30"At that time the sign of the Son of Man will appear in the
sky, and all the nations of the earth will mourn. They will see the
Son of Man coming on the clouds of the sky,[p] with power and
great glory. 31And he will send his angels[q] with a loud trumpet
call,[r] and they will gather his elect from the four winds, from one
end of the heavens to the other.

32"Now learn this lesson from the fig tree: As soon as its twigs
get tender and its leaves come out, you know that summer is
near. 33Even so, when you see all these things, you know that it[c] is
near, right at the door.[s] 34I tell you the truth, this generation[d] will
certainly not pass away until all these things have happened.[t]
35Heaven and earth will pass away, but my words will never pass
away.[u]

[a] *15* Daniel 9:27; 11:31; 12:11 [b] *29* Isaiah 13:10; 34:4 [c] *33* Or *he* [d] *34* Or *race*

24:13 [a] Mt 10:22
24:14 [b] Mt 4:23 [c] Ro 10:18; Col 1:6,23; Lk 2:1; 4:5; Ac 11:28; 17:6; Rev 3:10; 16:14
24:15 [d] Ac 6:13 [e] Da 9:27; 11:31; 12:11
24:17 [f] 1Sa 9:25; Mt 10:27; Lk 12:3; Ac 10:9
24:19 [g] Lk 23:29
24:21 [h] Da 12:1; Joel 2:2
24:22 [i] ver 24,31
24:23 [j] Lk 17:23; 21:8
24:24 [k] 2Th 2:9-11; Rev 13:13
24:27 [l] Lk 17:24 [m] Mt 8:20
24:28 [n] Lk 17:37
24:29 [o] Isa 13:10; 34:4; Eze 32:7; Joel 2:10,31; Zep 1:15; Rev 6:12,13; 8:12
24:30 [p] Da 7:13; Rev 1:7
24:31 [q] Mt 13:41 [r] Isa 27:13; Zec 9:14; 1Co 15:52; 1Th 4:16; Rev 8:2; 10:7; 11:15
24:33 [s] Jas 5:9
24:34 [t] Mt 16:28; 23:36
24:35 [u] Mt 5:18

36“No one knows about that day or hour, not even the angels in
heaven, nor the Son,[a] but only the Father.[a] 37As it was in the days of
Noah,[b] so it will be at the coming of the Son of Man. 38For in the
days before the flood, people were eating and drinking, marrying
and giving in marriage,[c] up to the day Noah entered the ark;
39and they knew nothing about what would happen until the
flood came and took them all away. That is how it will be at the
coming of the Son of Man. 40Two men will be in the field; one will
be taken and the other left.[d] 41Two women will be grinding with
a hand mill; one will be taken and the other left.[e]

42“Therefore keep watch, because you do not know on what day
your Lord will come.[f] 43But understand this: If the owner of the
house had known at what time of night the thief was coming,[g] he
would have kept watch and would not have let his house be broken
into. 44So you also must be ready,[h] because the Son of Man will
come at an hour when you do not expect him.

45“Who then is the faithful and wise servant,[i] whom the master
has put in charge of the servants in his household to give them
their food at the proper time? 46It will be good for that servant
whose master finds him doing so when he returns.[j] 47I tell you the
truth, he will put him in charge of all his possessions.[k] 48But suppose that servant is wicked and says to himself, ‘My master is
staying away a long time,’ 49and he then begins to beat his fellow
servants and to eat and drink with drunkards.[l] 50The master of
that servant will come on a day when he does not expect him and
at an hour he is not aware of. 51He will cut him to pieces and assign
him a place with the hypocrites, where there will be weeping and
gnashing of teeth.[m]

Chapter 25 Theme ____________________

25 “At that time the kingdom of heaven will be like[n] ten virgins who took their lamps[o] and went out to meet the bridegroom.[p] 2Five of them were foolish and five were wise.[q] 3The
foolish ones took their lamps but did not take any oil with them.
4The wise, however, took oil in jars along with their lamps. 5The
bridegroom was a long time in coming, and they all became
drowsy and fell asleep.[r]

6“At midnight the cry rang out: ‘Here’s the bridegroom! Come
out to meet him!’

7“Then all the virgins woke up and trimmed their lamps. 8The
foolish ones said to the wise, ‘Give us some of your oil; our lamps
are going out.’[s]

9“ ‘No,’ they replied, ‘there may not be enough for both us and
you. Instead, go to those who sell oil and buy some for yourselves.’

24:36 [a] Ac 1:7
24:37 [b] Ge 6:5; 7:6-23
24:38 [c] Mt 22:30
24:40 [d] Lk 17:34
24:41 [e] Lk 17:35
24:42 [f] Mt 25:13; Lk 12:40
24:43 [g] Lk 12:39
24:44 [h] 1Th 5:6
24:45 [i] Mt 25:21,23
24:46 [j] Rev 16:15
24:47 [k] Mt 25:21,23
24:49 [l] Lk 21:34
24:51 [m] Mt 8:12
25:1 [n] Mt 13:24 [o] Lk 12:35-38; Ac 20:8; Rev 4:5 [p] Rev 19:7; 21:2
25:2 [q] Mt 24:45
25:5 [r] 1Th 5:6
25:8 [s] Lk 12:35

[a] 36 Some manuscripts do not have *nor the Son.*

10“But while they were on their way to buy the oil, the bridegroom arrived. The virgins who were ready went in with him to
the wedding banquet.[a] And the door was shut.
11“Later the others also came. ‘Sir! Sir!’ they said. ‘Open the
door for us!’
12“But he replied, ‘I tell you the truth, I don’t know you.’
13“Therefore keep watch, because you do not know the day or
the hour.[b]
14“Again, it will be like a man going on a journey,[c] who called his
servants and entrusted his property to them. 15To one he gave
five talents[a] of money, to another two talents, and to another one
talent, each according to his ability.[d] Then he went on his journey.
16The man who had received the five talents went at once and put
his money to work and gained five more. 17So also, the one with
the two talents gained two more. 18But the man who had received
the one talent went off, dug a hole in the ground and hid his master’s money.
19“After a long time the master of those servants returned and
settled accounts with them.[e] 20The man who had received the five
talents brought the other five. ‘Master,’ he said, ‘you entrusted me
with five talents. See, I have gained five more.’
21“His master replied, ‘Well done, good and faithful servant!
You have been faithful with a few things; I will put you in charge of
many things.[f] Come and share your master’s happiness!’
22“The man with the two talents also came. ‘Master,’ he said,
‘you entrusted me with two talents; see, I have gained two more.’
23“His master replied, ‘Well done, good and faithful servant!
You have been faithful with a few things; I will put you in charge
of many things.[g] Come and share your master’s happiness!’
24“Then the man who had received the one talent came. ‘Master,’
he said, ‘I knew that you are a hard man, harvesting where you
have not sown and gathering where you have not scattered seed.
25So I was afraid and went out and hid your talent in the ground.
See, here is what belongs to you.’
26“His master replied, ‘You wicked, lazy servant! So you knew
that I harvest where I have not sown and gather where I have not
scattered seed? 27Well then, you should have put my money on
deposit with the bankers, so that when I returned I would have
received it back with interest.
28“ ‘Take the talent from him and give it to the one who has the ten
talents. 29For everyone who has will be given more, and he will have
an abundance. Whoever does not have, even what he has will be
taken from him.[h] 30And throw that worthless servant outside, into
the darkness, where there will be weeping and gnashing of teeth.’[i]

[a] *15* A talent was worth more than a thousand dollars.

25:10 [a] Rev 19:9
25:13 [b] Mt 24:42,44; Mk 13:35; Lk 12:40
25:14 [c] Mt 21:33; Lk 19:12
25:15 [d] Mt 18:24,25
25:19 [e] Mt 18:23
25:21 [f] ver 23; Mt 24:45,47; Lk 16:10
25:23 [g] ver 21
25:29 [h] Mt 13:12; Mk 4:25; Lk 8:18; 19:26
25:30 [i] Mt 8:12

31“When the Son of Man comes[a] in his glory, and all the angels
with him, he will sit on his throne[b] in heavenly glory. 32All the
nations will be gathered before him, and he will separate[c] the people one from another as a shepherd separates the sheep from the
goats.[d] 33He will put the sheep on his right and the goats on his left.

34“Then the King will say to those on his right, ‘Come, you who
are blessed by my Father; take your inheritance, the kingdom[e]
prepared for you since the creation of the world.[f] 35For I was hungry and you gave me something to eat, I was thirsty and you gave
me something to drink, I was a stranger and you invited me in,[g]
36I needed clothes and you clothed me,[h] I was sick and you looked
after me,[i] I was in prison and you came to visit me.’[j]

37“Then the righteous will answer him, ‘Lord, when did we see
you hungry and feed you, or thirsty and give you something to
drink? 38When did we see you a stranger and invite you in, or
needing clothes and clothe you? 39When did we see you sick or in
prison and go to visit you?’

40“The King will reply, ‘I tell you the truth, whatever you did for
one of the least of these brothers of mine, you did for me.’[k]

41“Then he will say to those on his left, ‘Depart from me,[l] you
who are cursed, into the eternal fire[m] prepared for the devil and his
angels.[n] 42For I was hungry and you gave me nothing to eat, I was
thirsty and you gave me nothing to drink, 43I was a stranger and
you did not invite me in, I needed clothes and you did not clothe
me, I was sick and in prison and you did not look after me.’

44“They also will answer, ‘Lord, when did we see you hungry or
thirsty or a stranger or needing clothes or sick or in prison, and
did not help you?’

45“He will reply, ‘I tell you the truth, whatever you did not do for
one of the least of these, you did not do for me.’[o]

46“Then they will go away to eternal punishment, but the righteous to eternal life.[p]”[q]

Chapter 26 Theme ____________________________

26 When Jesus had finished saying all these things,[r] he said to
his disciples, 2“As you know, the Passover[s] is two days
away—and the Son of Man will be handed over to be crucified.”

3Then the chief priests and the elders of the people assembled[t] in
the palace of the high priest, whose name was Caiaphas,[u] 4and
they plotted to arrest Jesus in some sly way and kill him.[v] 5“But not
during the Feast,” they said, “or there may be a riot[w] among the
people.”

6While Jesus was in Bethany[x] in the home of a man known as
Simon the Leper, 7a woman came to him with an alabaster jar of

INSIGHT

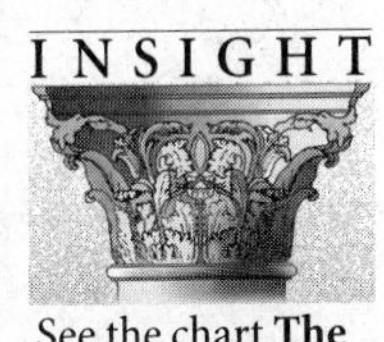

See the chart **The Feasts of Israel** located on pages 210, 211.

25:31 [a]Mt 16:27; Lk 17:30 [b]Mt 19:28
25:32 [c]Mal 3:18 [d]Eze 34:17,20
25:34 [e]Mt 3:2; 5:3,10,19; 19:14; Ac 20:32; 1Co 15:50; Gal 5:21; Jas 2:5 [f]Heb 4:3; 9:26; Rev 13:8; 17:8
25:35 [g]Job 31:32; Isa 58:7; Eze 18:7; Heb 13:2
25:36 [h]Isa 58:7; Eze 18:7; Jas 2:15,16 [i]Jas 1:27 [j]2Ti 1:16
25:40 [k]Pr 19:17; Mt 10:40,42; Heb 6:10; 13:2
25:41 [l]Mt 7:23 [m]Isa 66:24; Mt 3:12; 5:22; Mk 9:43,48; Lk 3:17; Jude 7 [n]2Pe 2:4
25:45 [o]Pr 14:31; 17:5
25:46 [p]Mt 19:29; Jn 3:15,16,36; 17:2,3; Ro 2:7; Gal 6:8; 5:11,13,20 [q]Da 12:2; Jn 5:29; Ac 24:15; Ro 2:7,8; Gal 6:8
26:1 [r]Mt 7:28
26:2 [s]Jn 11:55; 13:1
26:3 [t]Ps 2:2 [u]ver 57; Jn 11:47-53; 18:13,14,24,28
26:4 [v]Mt 12:14
26:5 [w]Mt 27:24
26:6 [x]Mt 21:17

very expensive perfume, which she poured on his head as he was
reclining at the table.
8When the disciples saw this, they were indignant. “Why this
waste?” they asked. 9“This perfume could have been sold at a high
price and the money given to the poor.”
10Aware of this, Jesus said to them, “Why are you bothering this
woman? She has done a beautiful thing to me. 11The poor you will
always have with you,[a] but you will not always have me. 12When
she poured this perfume on my body, she did it to prepare me for
burial.[b] 13I tell you the truth, wherever this gospel is preached
throughout the world, what she has done will also be told, in
memory of her.”
14Then one of the Twelve—the one called Judas Iscariot[c]—went
to the chief priests 15and asked, “What are you willing to give me if
I hand him over to you?” So they counted out for him thirty silver
coins.[d] 16From then on Judas watched for an opportunity to hand
him over.
17On the first day of the Feast of Unleavened Bread,[e] the disciples
came to Jesus and asked, “Where do you want us to make preparations for you to eat the Passover?”
18He replied, “Go into the city to a certain man and tell him,
‘The Teacher says: My appointed time[f] is near. I am going to celebrate the Passover with my disciples at your house.’ ” 19So the disciples did as Jesus had directed them and prepared the Passover.
20When evening came, Jesus was reclining at the table with the
Twelve. 21And while they were eating, he said, “I tell you the truth,
one of you will betray me.”[g]
22They were very sad and began to say to him one after the other,
“Surely not I, Lord?”
23Jesus replied, “The one who has dipped his hand into the
bowl with me will betray me.[h] 24The Son of Man will go just as it is
written about him.[i] But woe to that man who betrays the Son of
Man! It would be better for him if he had not been born.”
25Then Judas, the one who would betray him, said, “Surely not
I, Rabbi?”[j]
Jesus answered, “Yes, it is you.”[a]
26While they were eating, Jesus took bread, gave thanks and
broke it,[k] and gave it to his disciples, saying, “Take and eat; this is
my body.”
27Then he took the cup, gave thanks and offered it to them, saying, “Drink from it, all of you. 28This is my blood of the[b] covenant,[l]
which is poured out for many for the forgiveness of sins.[m] 29I tell
you, I will not drink of this fruit of the vine from now on until that
day when I drink it anew with you[n] in my Father’s kingdom.”

[a] 25 Or *“You yourself have said it”* [b] 28 Some manuscripts *the new*

26:11 [a] Dt 15:11
26:12 [b] Jn 19:40
26:14 [c] ver 25,47; Mt 10:4
26:15 [d] Ex 21:32; Zec 11:12
26:17 [e] Ex 12:18-20
26:18 [f] Jn 7:6,8,30; 12:23; 13:1; 17:1
26:21 [g] Lk 22:21-23; Jn 13:21
26:23 [h] Ps 41:9; Jn 13:18
26:24 [i] Isa 53; Da 9:26; Mk 9:12; Lk 24:25-27,46; Ac 17:2,3; 26:22,23
26:25 [j] Mt 23:7
26:26 [k] Mt 14:19; 1Co 10:16
26:28 [l] Ex 24:6-8; Heb 9:20 [m] Mt 20:28; Mk 1:4
26:29 [n] Ac 10:41

30 When they had sung a hymn, they went out to the Mount of
Olives.[a]
31 Then Jesus told them, "This very night you will all fall away
on account of me,[b] for it is written:

"'I will strike the shepherd,
and the sheep of the flock will be scattered.'[a][c]

32 But after I have risen, I will go ahead of you into Galilee."[d]
33 Peter replied, "Even if all fall away on account of you, I never
will."
34 "I tell you the truth," Jesus answered, "this very night, before
the rooster crows, you will disown me three times."[e]
35 But Peter declared, "Even if I have to die with you,[f] I will never
disown you." And all the other disciples said the same.
36 Then Jesus went with his disciples to a place called Gethsemane, and he said to them, "Sit here while I go over there and
pray." 37 He took Peter and the two sons of Zebedee[g] along with
him, and he began to be sorrowful and troubled. 38 Then he said
to them, "My soul is overwhelmed with sorrow[h] to the point of
death. Stay here and keep watch with me."[i]
39 Going a little farther, he fell with his face to the ground and
prayed, "My Father, if it is possible, may this cup[j] be taken from
me. Yet not as I will, but as you will."[k]
40 Then he returned to his disciples and found them sleeping.
"Could you men not keep watch with me[l] for one hour?" he
asked Peter. 41 "Watch and pray so that you will not fall into temptation.[m] The spirit is willing, but the body is weak."
42 He went away a second time and prayed, "My Father, if it is
not possible for this cup to be taken away unless I drink it, may
your will be done."
43 When he came back, he again found them sleeping, because
their eyes were heavy. 44 So he left them and went away once more
and prayed the third time, saying the same thing.
45 Then he returned to the disciples and said to them, "Are you
still sleeping and resting? Look, the hour[n] is near, and the Son of
Man is betrayed into the hands of sinners. 46 Rise, let us go! Here
comes my betrayer!"
47 While he was still speaking, Judas, one of the Twelve, arrived.
With him was a large crowd armed with swords and clubs, sent
from the chief priests and the elders of the people. 48 Now the
betrayer had arranged a signal with them: "The one I kiss is the
man; arrest him." 49 Going at once to Jesus, Judas said, "Greetings,
Rabbi!"[o] and kissed him.
50 Jesus replied, "Friend,[p] do what you came for."[b]
Then the men stepped forward, seized Jesus and arrested him.

26:30 [a] Mt 21:1; Mk 14:26
26:31 [b] Mt 11:6 [c] Zec 13:7; Jn 16:32
26:32 [d] Mt 28:7,10,16
26:34 [e] ver 75; Jn 13:38
26:35 [f] Jn 13:37
26:37 [g] Mt 4:21
26:38 [h] Jn 12:27 [i] ver 40,41
26:39 [j] Mt 20:22 [k] ver 42; Ps 40:6-8; Isa 50:5; Jn 5:30; 6:38
26:40 [l] ver 38
26:41 [m] Mt 6:13
26:45 [n] ver 18
26:49 [o] ver 25
26:50 [p] Mt 20:13; 22:12

a *31* Zech. 13:7 b *50* Or *"Friend, why have you come?"*

[51]With that, one of Jesus' companions reached for his sword,[a] drew
it out and struck the servant of the high priest, cutting off his ear.[b]

Jerusalem of the New Testament

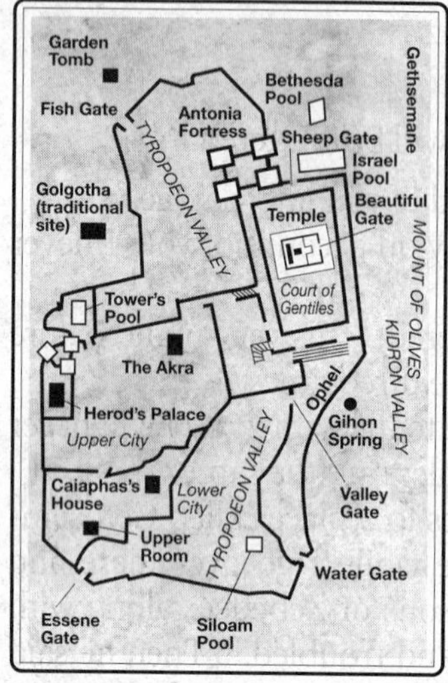

[52]"Put your sword back in its
place," Jesus said to him, "for all
who draw the sword will die by the
sword.[c] [53]Do you think I cannot call
on my Father, and he will at once
put at my disposal more than twelve
legions of angels?[d] [54]But how then
would the Scriptures be fulfilled[e]
that say it must happen in this way?"
[55]At that time Jesus said to the
crowd, "Am I leading a rebellion,
that you have come out with swords
and clubs to capture me? Every day
I sat in the temple courts teaching,[f]
and you did not arrest me. [56]But
this has all taken place that the
writings of the prophets might be fulfilled."[g] Then all the disciples deserted him and fled.
[57]Those who had arrested Jesus took him to Caiaphas,[h] the
high priest, where the teachers of the law and the elders had
assembled. [58]But Peter followed him at a distance, right up to the
courtyard of the high priest.[i] He entered and sat down with the
guards[j] to see the outcome.
[59]The chief priests and the whole Sanhedrin[k] were looking for
false evidence against Jesus so that they could put him to death.
[60]But they did not find any, though many false witnesses[l] came
forward.
Finally two[m] came forward [61]and declared, "This fellow said, 'I
am able to destroy the temple of God and rebuild it in three
days.'"[n]
[62]Then the high priest stood up and said to Jesus, "Are you not
going to answer? What is this testimony that these men are
bringing against you?" [63]But Jesus remained silent.[o]
The high priest said to him, "I charge you under oath[p] by the
living God:[q] Tell us if you are the Christ,[a] the Son of God."
[64]"Yes, it is as you say," Jesus replied. "But I say to all of you: In
the future you will see the Son of Man sitting at the right hand of
the Mighty One[r] and coming on the clouds of heaven."[s]
[65]Then the high priest tore his clothes[t] and said, "He has spoken blasphemy! Why do we need any more witnesses? Look, now
you have heard the blasphemy. [66]What do you think?"
"He is worthy of death,"[u] they answered.

[a] 63 Or *Messiah*; also in verse 68

26:51 [a] Lk 22:36,38 [b] Jn 18:10
26:52 [c] Ge 9:6; Rev 13:10
26:53 [d] 2Ki 6:17; Da 7:10; Mt 4:11
26:54 [e] ver 24
26:55 [f] Mk 12:35; Lk 21:37; Jn 7:14,28; 18:20
26:56 [g] ver 24
26:57 [h] ver 3
26:58 [i] Jn 18:15 [j] Jn 7:32,45,46
26:59 [k] Mt 5:22
26:60 [l] Ps 27:12; 35:11; Ac 6:13 [m] Dt 19:15
26:61 [n] Jn 2:19
26:63 [o] Mt 27:12,14 [p] Lev 5:1 [q] Mt 16:16
26:64 [r] Ps 110:1 [s] Da 7:13; Rev 1:7
26:65 [t] Mk 14:63
26:66 [u] Lev 24:16; Jn 19:7

67 Then they spit in his face and struck him with their fists.[a]
Others slapped him 68 and said, "Prophesy to us, Christ. Who hit
you?"[b]
69 Now Peter was sitting out in the courtyard, and a servant girl
came to him. "You also were with Jesus of Galilee," she said.
70 But he denied it before them all. "I don't know what you're
talking about," he said.
71 Then he went out to the gateway, where another girl saw him
and said to the people there, "This fellow was with Jesus of
Nazareth."
72 He denied it again, with an oath: "I don't know the man!"
73 After a little while, those standing there went up to Peter and
said, "Surely you are one of them, for your accent gives you away."
74 Then he began to call down curses on himself and he swore to
them, "I don't know the man!"
Immediately a rooster crowed. 75 Then Peter remembered the
word Jesus had spoken: "Before the rooster crows, you will disown me three times."[c] And he went outside and wept bitterly.

Chapter 27 Theme ____________________________

27 Early in the morning, all the chief priests and the elders
of the people came to the decision to put Jesus to death.[d]
2 They bound him, led him away and handed him over[e] to Pilate,
the governor.[f]
3 When Judas, who had betrayed him,[g] saw that Jesus was condemned, he was seized with remorse and returned the thirty silver
coins[h] to the chief priests and the elders. 4 "I have sinned," he said,
"for I have betrayed innocent blood."
"What is that to us?" they replied. "That's your responsibility."[i]
5 So Judas threw the money into the temple[j] and left. Then he
went away and hanged himself.[k]
6 The chief priests picked up the coins and said, "It is against the
law to put this into the treasury, since it is blood money." 7 So
they decided to use the money to buy the potter's field as a burial
place for foreigners. 8 That is why it has been called the Field of
Blood[l] to this day. 9 Then what was spoken by Jeremiah the prophet
was fulfilled:[m] "They took the thirty silver coins, the price set on
him by the people of Israel, 10 and they used them to buy the potter's field, as the Lord commanded me."[a][n]
11 Meanwhile Jesus stood before the governor, and the governor
asked him, "Are you the king of the Jews?"[o]
"Yes, it is as you say," Jesus replied.
12 When he was accused by the chief priests and the elders, he
gave no answer.[p] 13 Then Pilate asked him, "Don't you hear the

a *10* See Zech. 11:12, 13; Jer. 19:1-13; 32:6-9.

26:67 *a* Mt 16:21; 27:30
26:68 *b* Lk 22:63-65
26:75 *c* ver 34; Jn 13:38
27:1 *d* Mt 12:14; Mk 15:1; Lk 22:66
27:2 *e* Mt 20:19 *f* Mk 15:1; Lk 13:1; Ac 3:13; 1Ti 6:13
27:3 *g* Mt 10:4 *h* Mt 26:14,15
27:4 *i* ver 24
27:5 *j* Lk 1:9,21 *k* Ac 1:18
27:8 *l* Ac 1:19
27:9 *m* Mt 1:22
27:10 *n* Zec 11:12,13; Jer 32:6-9
27:11 *o* Mt 2:2
27:12 *p* Mt 26:63; Mk 14:61; Jn 19:9

testimony they are bringing against you?"[a] 14But Jesus made no
reply,[b] not even to a single charge—to the great amazement of the
governor.
15Now it was the governor's custom at the Feast to release a
prisoner[c] chosen by the crowd. 16At that time they had a notorious
prisoner, called Barabbas. 17So when the crowd had gathered,
Pilate asked them, "Which one do you want me to release to you:
Barabbas, or Jesus who is called Christ?"[d] 18For he knew it was out
of envy that they had handed Jesus over to him.
19While Pilate was sitting on the judge's seat,[e] his wife sent him
this message: "Don't have anything to do with that innocent[f]
man, for I have suffered a great deal today in a dream[g] because of
him."
20But the chief priests and the elders persuaded the crowd to ask
for Barabbas and to have Jesus executed.[h]
21"Which of the two do you want me to release to you?" asked
the governor.
"Barabbas," they answered.
22"What shall I do, then, with Jesus who is called Christ?"[i]
Pilate asked.
They all answered, "Crucify him!"
23"Why? What crime has he committed?" asked Pilate.
But they shouted all the louder, "Crucify him!"
24When Pilate saw that he was getting nowhere, but that instead
an uproar[j] was starting, he took water and washed his hands[k] in
front of the crowd. "I am innocent of this man's blood,"[l] he said.
"It is your responsibility!"[m]
25All the people answered, "Let his blood be on us and on our
children!"[n]
26Then he released Barabbas to them. But he had Jesus flogged,[o]
and handed him over to be crucified.
27Then the governor's soldiers took Jesus into the Praetorium[p]
and gathered the whole company of soldiers around him. 28They
stripped him and put a scarlet robe on him,[q] 29and then twisted
together a crown of thorns and set it on his head. They put a staff
in his right hand and knelt in front of him and mocked him.
"Hail, king of the Jews!" they said.[r] 30They spit on him, and took
the staff and struck him on the head again and again.[s] 31After they
had mocked him, they took off the robe and put his own clothes
on him. Then they led him away to crucify him.[t]
32As they were going out,[u] they met a man from Cyrene,[v] named
Simon, and they forced him to carry the cross.[w] 33They came to a
place called Golgotha (which means The Place of the Skull).[x]
34There they offered Jesus wine to drink, mixed with gall;[y] but
after tasting it, he refused to drink it. 35When they had crucified

INSIGHT

The palace of the Roman governor (the ***Praetorium***) was either a building next to Herod's palace or the Antonia Fortress beside the temple mount complex. See the map on page 1716 and the illustration of the temple mount on page IISB-40.

27:13 [a] Mt 26:62
27:14 [b] Mk 14:61
27:15 [c] Jn 18:39
27:17 [d] ver 22; Mt 1:16
27:19 [e] Jn 19:13 [f] ver 24 [g] Ge 20:6; Nu 12:6; 1Ki 3:5; Job 33:14-16; Mt 1:20; 2:12,13,19,22
27:20 [h] Ac 3:14
27:22 [i] Mt 1:16
27:24 [j] Mt 26:5 [k] Ps 26:6 [l] Dt 21:6-8 [m] ver 4
27:25 [n] Jos 2:19; Ac 5:28
27:26 [o] Isa 53:5; Jn 19:1
27:27 [p] Jn 18:28,33; 19:9
27:28 [q] Jn 19:2
27:29 [r] Isa 53:3; Jn 19:2,3
27:30 [s] Mt 16:21; 26:67
27:31 [t] Isa 53:7
27:32 [u] Heb 13:12 [v] Ac 2:10; 6:9; 11:20; 13:1 [w] Mk 15:21; Lk 23:26
27:33 [x] Jn 19:17
27:34 [y] ver 48; Ps 69:21

27:35 *a* Ps 22:18 him, they divided up his clothes by casting lots.[a][a] 36 And sitting
down, they kept watch[b] over him there. 37 Above his head they
27:36 placed the written charge against him: THIS IS JESUS, THE KING OF
b ver 54 THE JEWS. 38 Two robbers were crucified with him,[c] one on his right
and one on his left. 39 Those who passed by hurled insults at him,
27:38 *c* Isa 53:12 shaking their heads[d] 40 and saying, "You who are going to destroy
the temple and build it in three days,[e] save yourself![f] Come down
27:39 from the cross, if you are the Son of God!"[g]
d Ps 22:7; 109:25; 41 In the same way the chief priests, the teachers of the law and
La 2:15 the elders mocked him. 42 "He saved others," they said, "but he
can't save himself! He's the King of Israel![h] Let him come down
27:40 *e* Mt 26:61; now from the cross, and we will believe[i] in him. 43 He trusts in
Jn 2:19 *f* ver 42 God. Let God rescue him[j] now if he wants him, for he said, 'I am
g Mt 4:3,6 the Son of God.'" 44 In the same way the robbers who were crucified with him also heaped insults on him.
27:42 45 From the sixth hour until the ninth hour darkness[k] came
h Jn 1:49; 12:13 over all the land. 46 About the ninth hour Jesus cried out in a loud
i Jn 3:15 voice, *"Eloi, Eloi,*[b] *lama sabachthani?"*—which means, "My God,
27:43 my God, why have you forsaken me?"[c][l]
j Ps 22:8 47 When some of those standing there heard this, they said,
"He's calling Elijah."
27:45 *k* Am 8:9 48 Immediately one of them ran and got a sponge. He filled it with
wine vinegar,[m] put it on a stick, and offered it to Jesus to drink.
27:46 49 The rest said, "Now leave him alone. Let's see if Elijah comes to
l Ps 22:1 save him."
50 And when Jesus had cried out again in a loud voice, he gave up
27:48 *m* ver 34; his spirit.[n]
Ps 69:21 51 At that moment the curtain of the temple[o] was torn in two
from top to bottom. The earth shook and the rocks split.[p] 52 The
27:50 *n* Jn 19:30 tombs broke open and the bodies of many holy people who had
died were raised to life. 53 They came out of the tombs, and after
27:51 Jesus' resurrection they went into the holy city[q] and appeared to
o Ex 26:31-33; many people.
Heb 9:3,8 *p* ver 54 54 When the centurion and those with him who were guarding[r]
Jesus saw the earthquake and all that had happened, they were
27:53 *q* Mt 4:5 terrified, and exclaimed, "Surely he was the Son[d] of God!"[s]
55 Many women were there, watching from a distance. They had
27:54 followed Jesus from Galilee to care for his needs.[t] 56 Among them
r ver 36 were Mary Magdalene, Mary the mother of James and Joses, and
s Mt 4:3; 17:5 the mother of Zebedee's sons.[u]
57 As evening approached, there came a rich man from Arima-
27:55 *t* Lk 8:2,3 thea, named Joseph, who had himself become a disciple of Jesus.
58 Going to Pilate, he asked for Jesus' body, and Pilate ordered that

27:56 *u* Mk 15:47; Lk 24:10; Jn 19:25

[a] 35 A few late manuscripts *lots that the word spoken by the prophet might be fulfilled: "They divided my garments among themselves and cast lots for my clothing"* (Psalm 22:18) [b] 46 Some manuscripts *Eli, Eli* [c] 46 Psalm 22:1 [d] 54 Or *a son*

it be given to him. 59Joseph took the body, wrapped it in a clean
linen cloth, 60and placed it in his own new tomb[a] that he had cut
out of the rock. He rolled a big stone in front of the entrance to
the tomb and went away. 61Mary Magdalene and the other Mary
were sitting there opposite the tomb.

62The next day, the one after Preparation Day, the chief priests
and the Pharisees went to Pilate. 63"Sir," they said, "we remember
that while he was still alive that deceiver said, 'After three days I
will rise again.'[b] 64So give the order for the tomb to be made
secure until the third day. Otherwise, his disciples may come and
steal the body and tell the people that he has been raised from the
dead. This last deception will be worse than the first."

65"Take a guard,"[c] Pilate answered. "Go, make the tomb as secure
as you know how." 66So they went and made the tomb secure by
putting a seal[d] on the stone[e] and posting the guard.[f]

Chapter 28 Theme

28 After the Sabbath, at dawn on the first day of the week,
Mary Magdalene and the other Mary[g] went to look at the
tomb.

2There was a violent earthquake,[h] for an angel[i] of the Lord
came down from heaven and, going to the tomb, rolled back the
stone and sat on it. 3His appearance was like lightning, and his
clothes were white as snow.[j] 4The guards were so afraid of him
that they shook and became like dead men.

5The angel said to the women, "Do not be afraid,[k] for I know
that you are looking for Jesus, who was crucified. 6He is not here;
he has risen, just as he said.[l] Come and see the place where he lay.
7Then go quickly and tell his disciples: 'He has risen from the
dead and is going ahead of you into Galilee.[m] There you will see
him.' Now I have told you."

8So the women hurried away from the tomb, afraid yet filled
with joy, and ran to tell his disciples. 9Suddenly Jesus met them.[n]
"Greetings," he said. They came to him, clasped his feet and worshiped him. 10Then Jesus said to them, "Do not be afraid. Go and
tell my brothers[o] to go to Galilee; there they will see me."

11While the women were on their way, some of the guards[p]
went into the city and reported to the chief priests everything that
had happened. 12When the chief priests had met with the elders
and devised a plan, they gave the soldiers a large sum of money,
13telling them, "You are to say, 'His disciples came during the night
and stole him away while we were asleep.' 14If this report gets to the
governor,[q] we will satisfy him and keep you out of trouble." 15So
the soldiers took the money and did as they were instructed. And
this story has been widely circulated among the Jews to this very
day.

27:60 [a] Mt 27:66; 28:2; Mk 16:4

27:63 [b] Mt 16:21

27:65 [c] ver 66; Mt 28:11

27:66 [d] Da 6:17 [e] ver 60; Mt 28:2 [f] Mt 28:11

28:1 [g] Mt 27:56

28:2 [h] Mt 27:51 [i] Jn 20:12

28:3 [j] Da 10:6; Mk 9:3; Jn 20:12

28:5 [k] ver 10; Mt 14:27

28:6 [l] Mt 16:21

28:7 [m] ver 10,16; Mt 26:32

28:9 [n] Jn 20:14-18

28:10 [o] Jn 20:17; Ro 8:29; Heb 2:11-13,17

28:11 [p] Mt 27:65,66

28:14 [q] Mt 27:2

28:16
[a] ver 7,10; Mt 26:32
28:18
[b] Da 7:13,14; Lk 10:22; Jn 3:35; 17:2; 1Co 15:27; Eph 1:20-22; Php 2:9,10
28:19
[c] Mk 16:15,16; Lk 24:47; Ac 1:8; 14:21
[d] Ac 2:38; 8:16; Ro 6:3,4

16 Then the eleven disciples went to Galilee, to the mountain
where Jesus had told them to go.[a] 17 When they saw him, they
worshiped him; but some doubted. 18 Then Jesus came to them and
said, "All authority in heaven and on earth has been given to me.[b]
19 Therefore go and make disciples of all nations,[c] baptizing them
in[a] the name of the Father and of the Son and of the Holy Spirit,[d]
20 and teaching[e] them to obey everything I have commanded you.
And surely I am with you[f] always, to the very end of the age."[g]

[a] *19* Or *into*; see Acts 8:16; 19:5; Romans 6:3; 1Cor. 1:13; 10:2 and Gal. 3:27.

28:20 [e] Ac 2:42 [f] Mt 18:20; Ac 18:10 [g] Mt 13:39

Theme of Matthew:

SEGMENT DIVISIONS

		CHAPTER THEMES
		1
		2
		3
		4
		5
		6
		7
		8
		9
		10
		11
		12
		13
		14
		15
		16
		17
		18
		19
		20
		21
		22
		23
		24
		25
		26
		27
		28

Author:

Date:

Purpose:

Key Words:

king (mark only when referring to Jesus as king) (kingdom, kingdom of heaven, kingdom of God)

fulfill, fulfilled

mark every reference to the devil or demons

covenant

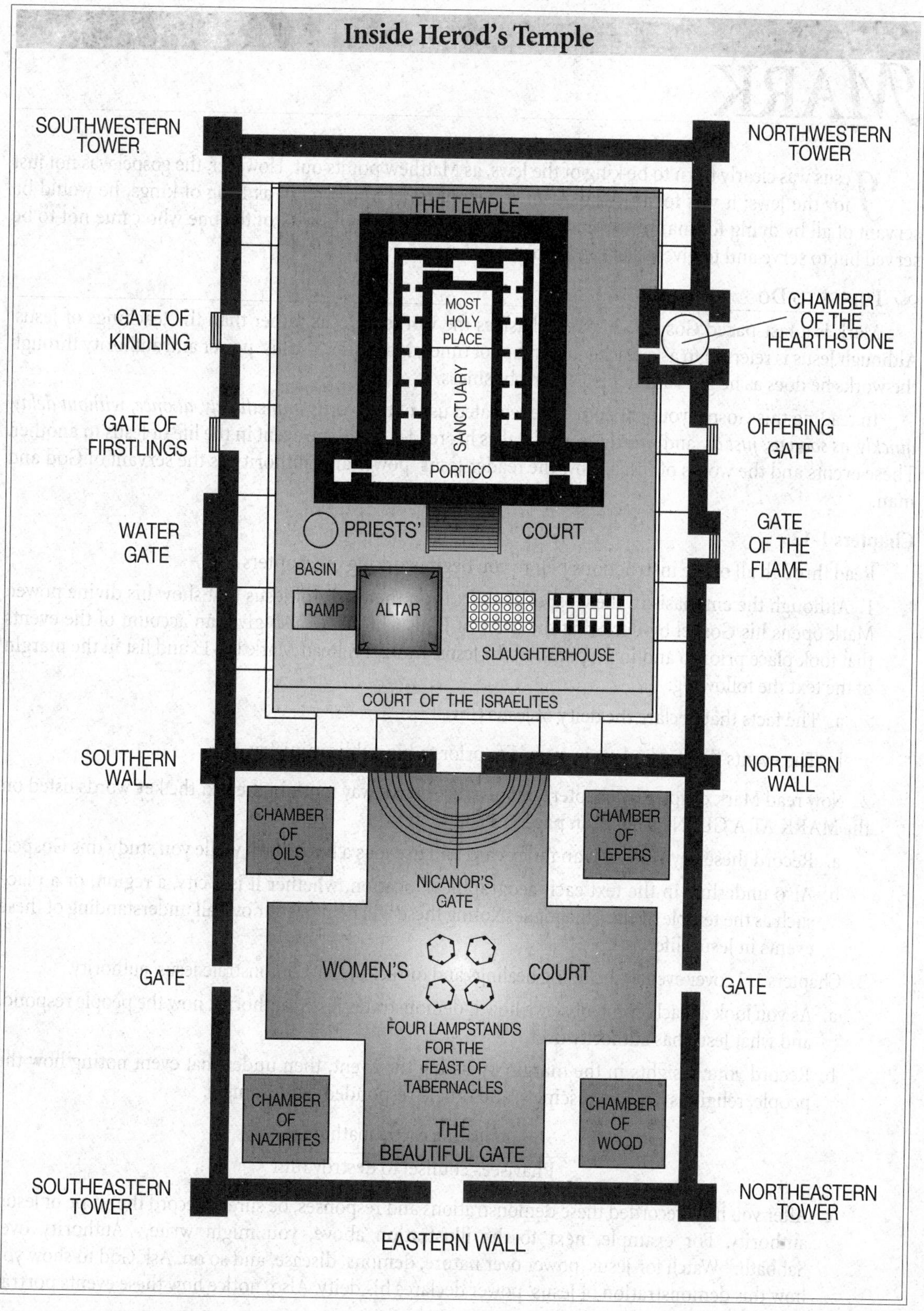
Inside Herod's Temple
SOUTHWESTERN TOWER
NORTHWESTERN TOWER
THE TEMPLE
MOST HOLY PLACE
SANCTUARY
PORTICO
CHAMBER OF THE HEARTHSTONE
GATE OF KINDLING
GATE OF FIRSTLINGS
OFFERING GATE
WATER GATE
PRIESTS' COURT
GATE OF THE FLAME
BASIN
RAMP
ALTAR
SLAUGHTERHOUSE
COURT OF THE ISRAELITES
SOUTHERN WALL
NORTHERN WALL
CHAMBER OF OILS
CHAMBER OF LEPERS
NICANOR'S GATE
WOMEN'S COURT
GATE
GATE
FOUR LAMPSTANDS FOR THE FEAST OF TABERNACLES
CHAMBER OF NAZIRITES
THE BEAUTIFUL GATE
CHAMBER OF WOOD
SOUTHEASTERN TOWER
NORTHEASTERN TOWER
EASTERN WALL

MARK

Jesus was clearly born to be king of the Jews, as Matthew points out. However, the gospel was not just for the Jews; it was for the whole world. Before Jesus would reign as King of kings, he would be servant of all by dying for mankind. Mark tells of the works and authority of the one who came not to be served but to serve and to give his life as a ransom for many.

THINGS TO DO

Mark is a fast-paced Gospel which emphasizes the works of Jesus rather than the teachings of Jesus. Although Jesus is referred to as a teacher a number of times, Mark shows Jesus' power and authority through the works he does as he goes about his Father's business.

In reading this Gospel you will notice the repeated use of the words *immediately, at once, without delay, quickly, as soon as, just as,* and *shortly* as Mark takes his reader from one event in the life of Jesus to another. These events and the works of Jesus show the reader Jesus' power and authority as the servant of God and man.

Chapters 1-13

Read through all of the instructions before you begin working on chapters 1-13.

1. Although the emphasis in the Gospel of Mark is on the works of Jesus that show his divine power, Mark opens his Gospel by declaring the deity of Jesus Christ. He also gives an account of the events that took place prior to and in preparation for Jesus' ministry. Read Mark 1:1-13 and list in the margin of the text the following:
   a. The facts that declare the deity of Jesus Christ.
   b. The events that took place in Jesus' life prior to his public ministry.
2. Now read Mark chapter by chapter, and in a distinctive way mark in the text the key words listed on the MARK AT A GLANCE chart on page 1758.
   a. Record these key words on an index card and use it as a bookmark while you study this Gospel.
   b. Also underline in the text each geographical location, whether it is a city, a region, or a place such as the temple or the synagogue. Noting these will help in your overall understanding of these events in Jesus' life.
3. Chapters 1-3 cover events (including healings and miracles) that demonstrate Jesus' authority.
   a. As you look at each event, observe how it demonstrates Jesus' authority, how the people respond, and what Jesus has authority over.
   b. Record your insights in the margin by listing the event, then under that event noting how the people, religious leaders, disciples, and others responded. For example:

      Healing on Sabbath

      Pharisees counsel to destroy him

   c. After you have recorded these demonstrations and responses, be sure to record the scope of Jesus' authority. For example, next to the illustration above, you might write, "Authority over Sabbath." Watch for Jesus' power over nature, demons, disease, and so on. Ask God to show you how this demonstration of Jesus' power declares his deity. Also, notice how these events portray Jesus as a servant.

d. Throughout these chapters, Jesus faces the accusations and rejection of the Jewish religious leaders of his day. Each time the scribes, Pharisees, or Sadducees accuse Jesus, he reasons with them. Note that conflict in the margin.

4. Also list in the margin the main points of Jesus' teachings, whether the teaching comes as a result of healing, casting out demons, working a miracle, or responding to a question from either the disciples or the multitude. Also note the response of those who hear the teaching.

5. Look at every reference you marked to the kingdom of God and do the following:

   a. Note in the margin when Jesus increases his emphasis on the kingdom of God.

   b. Underline every prediction of Jesus' death and resurrection and note how it coincides with Jesus' emphasis on the kingdom of God.

   c. Observe that in the first part of Mark, Jesus defines the kingdom of God, then at chapter 9 the emphasis shifts to how to enter the kingdom.

   d. Compile the *main* teachings from Mark about the kingdom of God on the chart titled WHAT THE GOSPELS TEACH ABOUT THE KINGDOM OF GOD/THE KINGDOM OF HEAVEN on pages 1864, 1865. It would be good to do this on notebook paper first and then consolidate your insights and transfer them to the chart. Note the chapter and verse beside each insight for future reference.

6. After you finish reading and marking each chapter, record the theme of that chapter on MARK AT A GLANCE. Also record it in the text on the line next to the chapter number.

Chapters 14-16

1. When you read Mark's account of the trial, death, burial, and resurrection of Jesus Christ, record the progression of events on the appropriate charts: THE ARREST, TRIAL, AND CRUCIFIXION OF JESUS CHRIST on page 1862 and THE ACCOUNT OF JESUS' RESURRECTION on page 1863. Once again, do this on notebook paper before transferring the information to the chart and note the chapter and verse beside each insight.

   a. When you record the circumstances surrounding the resurrection of Jesus Christ, also note any postresurrection appearances recorded in Mark. After you do this for all four Gospels you will have comprehensive notes on everything that took place at this time in our Lord's life.

   b. As you do this, remember that because Luke gives the consecutive order of events, it is a plumb line for the other Gospel records.

2. Complete MARK AT A GLANCE. Fill in any segment divisions you have seen from studying the book.

Things to Think About

1. People often say that Mark shows the servant aspect of Jesus' ministry. Although the word *servant* is used only seven times, Mark 10:45 says that Jesus "did not come to be served, but to serve, and to give his life as a ransom for many." How like your Lord are you in that respect? Would others regard you as a servant? Or do they see you as having to be "number one"? What is it to be "number one" in God's eyes?

2. Jesus talks about discipleship in this Gospel. According to Jesus, what is required of disciples? Can you consider yourself a true disciple of Jesus Christ? Why? Think about Mark 8:34-36 and 10:28-31.

3. Can you say with Peter, "You are the Christ, the Son of the living God"? And will you listen to Jesus as the Father commands?

Chapter 1 Theme ______________________________

1

The beginning of the gospel about Jesus Christ, the Son of
God.[a][a]

2It is written in Isaiah the prophet:

> "I will send my messenger ahead of you,
> who will prepare your way"[b][b]—
> 3"a voice of one calling in the desert,
> 'Prepare the way for the Lord,
> make straight paths for him.'"[c][c]

4And so John[d] came, baptizing in the desert region and preaching
a baptism of repentance[e] for the forgiveness of sins.[f] 5The whole
Judean countryside and all the people of Jerusalem went out to
him. Confessing their sins, they were baptized by him in the
Jordan River. 6John wore clothing made of camel's hair, with a
leather belt around his waist, and he ate locusts[g] and wild honey.
7And this was his message: "After me will come one more powerful than I, the thongs of whose sandals I am not worthy to stoop
down and untie.[h] 8I baptize you with[d] water, but he will baptize
you with the Holy Spirit."[i]

9At that time Jesus came from Nazareth[j] in Galilee and was
baptized by John in the Jordan. 10As Jesus was coming up out of
the water, he saw heaven being torn open and the Spirit descending on him like a dove.[k] 11And a voice came from heaven: "You are
my Son,[l] whom I love; with you I am well pleased."

12At once the Spirit sent him out into the desert, 13and he was in
the desert forty days, being tempted by Satan.[m] He was with the
wild animals, and angels attended him.

14After John was put in prison, Jesus went into Galilee,[n] proclaiming the good news of God.[o] 15"The time has come,"[p] he said.
"The kingdom of God is near. Repent and believe the good news!"[q]

16As Jesus walked beside the Sea of Galilee, he saw Simon and
his brother Andrew casting a net into the lake, for they were fishermen. 17"Come, follow me," Jesus said, "and I will make you fishers
of men." 18At once they left their nets and followed him.

19When he had gone a little farther, he saw James son of Zebedee
and his brother John in a boat, preparing their nets. 20Without
delay he called them, and they left their father Zebedee in the boat
with the hired men and followed him.

21They went to Capernaum, and when the Sabbath came, Jesus
went into the synagogue and began to teach.[r] 22The people were

1:1 [a]Mt 4:3
1:2 [b]Mal 3:1; Mt 11:10; Lk 7:27
1:3 [c]Isa 40:3; Jn 1:23
1:4 [d]Mt 3:1 [e]Ac 13:24 [f]Lk 1:77
1:6 [g]Lev 11:22
1:7 [h]Ac 13:25
1:8 [i]Isa 44:3; Joel 2:28; Ac 1:5; 2:4; 11:16; 19:4-6
1:9 [j]Mt 2:23
1:10 [k]Jn 1:32
1:11 [l]Mt 3:17
1:13 [m]Mt 4:10
1:14 [n]Mt 4:12 [o]Mt 4:23
1:15 [p]Gal 4:4; Eph 1:10 [q]Ac 20:21
1:21 [r]Mt 4:23; Mk 10:1

[a]*1* Some manuscripts do not have *the Son of God.* [b]*2* Mal. 3:1 [c]*3* Isaiah 40:3 [d]*8* Or *in*

amazed at his teaching, because he taught them as one who had
authority, not as the teachers of the law.[a] 23 Just then a man in their
synagogue who was possessed by an evil[a] spirit cried out, 24 "What
do you want with us,[b] Jesus of Nazareth?[c] Have you come to destroy
us? I know who you are—the Holy One of God!"[d]

25 "Be quiet!" said Jesus sternly. "Come out of him!"[e] 26 The evil
spirit shook the man violently and came out of him with a shriek.[f]

27 The people were all so amazed[g] that they asked each other,
"What is this? A new teaching—and with authority! He even gives
orders to evil spirits and they obey him." 28 News about him spread
quickly over the whole region[h] of Galilee.

29 As soon as they left the synagogue,[i] they went with James and
John to the home of Simon and Andrew. 30 Simon's mother-in-law
was in bed with a fever, and they told Jesus about her. 31 So he went
to her, took her hand and helped her up.[j] The fever left her and
she began to wait on them.

32 That evening after sunset the people brought to Jesus all the
sick and demon-possessed.[k] 33 The whole town gathered at the
door, 34 and Jesus healed many who had various diseases.[l] He also
drove out many demons, but he would not let the demons speak
because they knew who he was.[m]

35 Very early in the morning, while it was still dark, Jesus got up,
left the house and went off to a solitary place, where he prayed.[n]
36 Simon and his companions went to look for him, 37 and when
they found him, they exclaimed: "Everyone is looking for you!"

38 Jesus replied, "Let us go somewhere else—to the nearby villages—so I can preach there also. That is why I have come."[o] 39 So
he traveled throughout Galilee, preaching in their synagogues[p]
and driving out demons.[q]

40 A man with leprosy[b] came to him and begged him on his
knees,[r] "If you are willing, you can make me clean."

41 Filled with compassion, Jesus reached out his hand and touched
the man. "I am willing," he said. "Be clean!" 42 Immediately the leprosy left him and he was cured.

43 Jesus sent him away at once with a strong warning: 44 "See that
you don't tell this to anyone.[s] But go, show yourself to the priest[t]
and offer the sacrifices that Moses commanded for your cleansing,[u] as a testimony to them." 45 Instead he went out and began to
talk freely, spreading the news. As a result, Jesus could no longer
enter a town openly but stayed outside in lonely places.[v] Yet the
people still came to him from everywhere.[w]

1:22 [a] Mt 7:28,29
1:24 [b] Mt 8:29 [c] Mt 2:23; Lk 24:19; Ac 24:5 [d] Lk 1:35; Jn 6:69; Ac 3:14
1:25 [e] ver 34
1:26 [f] Mk 9:20
1:27 [g] Mk 10:24,32
1:28 [h] Mt 9:26
1:29 [i] ver 21,23
1:31 [j] Lk 7:14
1:32 [k] Mt 4:24
1:34 [l] Mt 4:23 [m] Mk 3:12; Ac 16:17,18
1:35 [n] Lk 3:21
1:38 [o] Isa 61:1
1:39 [p] Mt 4:23 [q] Mt 4:24
1:40 [r] Mk 10:17
1:44 [s] Mt 8:4 [t] Lev 13:49 [u] Lev 14:1-32
1:45 [v] Lk 5:15,16 [w] Mk 2:13; Lk 5:17; Jn 6:2

[a] *23* Greek *unclean;* also in verses 26 and 27 [b] *40* The Greek word was used for various diseases affecting the skin—not necessarily leprosy.

Chapter 2 Theme ______________________________

2 A few days later, when Jesus again entered Capernaum, the
people heard that he had come home. 2So many[a] gathered that
there was no room left, not even outside the door, and he preached
the word to them. 3Some men came, bringing to him a paralytic,[b]
carried by four of them. 4Since they could not get him to Jesus
because of the crowd, they made an opening in the roof above
Jesus and, after digging through it, lowered the mat the paralyzed
man was lying on. 5When Jesus saw their faith, he said to the paralytic, "Son, your sins are forgiven."[c]

6Now some teachers of the law were sitting there, thinking to
themselves, 7"Why does this fellow talk like that? He's blaspheming! Who can forgive sins but God alone?"[d]

8Immediately Jesus knew in his spirit that this was what they were
thinking in their hearts, and he said to them, "Why are you thinking these things? 9Which is easier: to say to the paralytic, 'Your sins
are forgiven,' or to say, 'Get up, take your mat and walk'? 10But
that you may know that the Son of Man[e] has authority on earth to
forgive sins. . . ." He said to the paralytic, 11"I tell you, get up, take
your mat and go home." 12He got up, took his mat and walked out
in full view of them all. This amazed everyone and they praised
God,[f] saying, "We have never seen anything like this!"[g]

13Once again Jesus went out beside the lake. A large crowd came
to him,[h] and he began to teach them. 14As he walked along, he saw
Levi son of Alphaeus sitting at the tax collector's booth. "Follow
me,"[i] Jesus told him, and Levi got up and followed him.

15While Jesus was having dinner at Levi's house, many tax collectors and "sinners" were eating with him and his disciples, for
there were many who followed him. 16When the teachers of the law
who were Pharisees[j] saw him eating with the "sinners" and tax
collectors, they asked his disciples: "Why does he eat with tax
collectors and 'sinners'?"[k]

17On hearing this, Jesus said to them, "It is not the healthy who
need a doctor, but the sick. I have not come to call the righteous,
but sinners."[l]

18Now John's disciples and the Pharisees were fasting.[m] Some
people came and asked Jesus, "How is it that John's disciples and
the disciples of the Pharisees are fasting, but yours are not?"

19Jesus answered, "How can the guests of the bridegroom fast
while he is with them? They cannot, so long as they have him with
them. 20But the time will come when the bridegroom will be taken
from them,[n] and on that day they will fast.

21"No one sews a patch of unshrunk cloth on an old garment. If
he does, the new piece will pull away from the old, making the

2:2 [a]ver 13; Mk 1:45
2:3 [b]Mt 4:24
2:5 [c]Lk 7:48
2:7 [d]Isa 43:25
2:10 [e]Mt 8:20
2:12 [f]Mt 9:8 [g]Mt 9:33
2:13 [h]Mk 1:45; Lk 5:15; Jn 6:2
2:14 [i]Mt 4:19
2:16 [j]Ac 23:9 [k]Mt 9:11
2:17 [l]Lk 19:10; 1Ti 1:15
2:18 [m]Mt 6:16-18; Ac 13:2
2:20 [n]Lk 17:22

tear worse. 22And no one pours new wine into old wineskins. If
he does, the wine will burst the skins, and both the wine and the
wineskins will be ruined. No, he pours new wine into new wineskins."

23One Sabbath Jesus was going through the grainfields, and as
his disciples walked along, they began to pick some heads of
grain.[a] 24The Pharisees said to him, "Look, why are they doing
what is unlawful on the Sabbath?"[b]

25He answered, "Have you never read what David did when he
and his companions were hungry and in need? 26In the days of
Abiathar the high priest,[c] he entered the house of God and ate the
consecrated bread, which is lawful only for priests to eat.[d] And he
also gave some to his companions."[e]

27Then he said to them, "The Sabbath was made for man,[f] not
man for the Sabbath.[g] 28So the Son of Man[h] is Lord even of the
Sabbath."

Chapter 3 Theme ______________________________________

3 Another time he went into the synagogue,[i] and a man with a
shriveled hand was there. 2Some of them were looking for a
reason to accuse Jesus, so they watched him closely[j] to see if he
would heal him on the Sabbath.[k] 3Jesus said to the man with the
shriveled hand, "Stand up in front of everyone."

4Then Jesus asked them, "Which is lawful on the Sabbath: to do
good or to do evil, to save life or to kill?" But they remained silent.

5He looked around at them in anger and, deeply distressed at
their stubborn hearts, said to the man, "Stretch out your hand."
He stretched it out, and his hand was completely restored. 6Then
the Pharisees went out and began to plot with the Herodians[l] how
they might kill Jesus.[m]

7Jesus withdrew with his disciples to the lake, and a large crowd
from Galilee followed.[n] 8When they heard all he was doing, many
people came to him from Judea, Jerusalem, Idumea, and the
regions across the Jordan and around Tyre and Sidon.[o] 9Because of
the crowd he told his disciples to have a small boat ready for him,
to keep the people from crowding him. 10For he had healed many,[p]
so that those with diseases were pushing forward to touch him.[q]
11Whenever the evil[a] spirits saw him, they fell down before him
and cried out, "You are the Son of God."[r] 12But he gave them strict
orders not to tell who he was.[s]

13Jesus went up on a mountainside and called to him those he
wanted, and they came to him.[t] 14He appointed twelve—designating them apostles[b][u]—that they might be with him and that he

[a] *11* Greek *unclean;* also in verse 30 [b] *14* Some manuscripts do not have *designating them apostles.*

2:23 [a]Dt 23:25
2:24 [b]Mt 12:2
2:26 [c]1Ch 24:6; 2Sa 8:17 [d]Lev 24:5-9 [e]1Sa 21:1-6
2:27 [f]Ex 23:12; Dt 5:14 [g]Col 2:16
2:28 [h]Mt 8:20
3:1 [i]Mt 4:23; Mk 1:21
3:2 [j]Mt 12:10 [k]Lk 14:1
3:6 [l]Mt 22:16; Mk 12:13 [m]Mt 12:14
3:7 [n]Mt 4:25
3:8 [o]Mt 11:21
3:10 [p]Mt 4:23 [q]Mt 9:20
3:11 [r]Mt 4:3; Mk 1:23,24
3:12 [s]Mt 8:4; Mk 1:24, 25,34; Ac 16:17,18
3:13 [t]Mt 5:1
3:14 [u]Mk 6:30

might send them out to preach 15and to have authority to drive out
demons.[a] 16These are the twelve he appointed: Simon (to whom
he gave the name Peter);[b] 17James son of Zebedee and his brother
John (to them he gave the name Boanerges, which means Sons of
Thunder); 18Andrew, Philip, Bartholomew, Matthew, Thomas,
James son of Alphaeus, Thaddaeus, Simon the Zealot 19and Judas
Iscariot, who betrayed him.

20Then Jesus entered a house, and again a crowd gathered,[c] so
that he and his disciples were not even able to eat.[d] 21When his
family heard about this, they went to take charge of him, for they
said, "He is out of his mind."[e]

22And the teachers of the law who came down from Jerusalem[f]
said, "He is possessed by Beelzebub[a]![g] By the prince of demons he
is driving out demons."[h]

23So Jesus called them and spoke to them in parables:[i] "How can
Satan[j] drive out Satan? 24If a kingdom is divided against itself,
that kingdom cannot stand. 25If a house is divided against itself,
that house cannot stand. 26And if Satan opposes himself and is
divided, he cannot stand; his end has come. 27In fact, no one can
enter a strong man's house
and carry off his possessions
unless he first ties up
the strong man. Then he
can rob his house.[k] 28I tell
you the truth, all the sins and
blasphemies of men will be
forgiven them. 29But whoever
blasphemes against the
Holy Spirit will never be forgiven;
he is guilty of an eternal
sin."[l]

30He said this because they
were saying, "He has an evil
spirit."

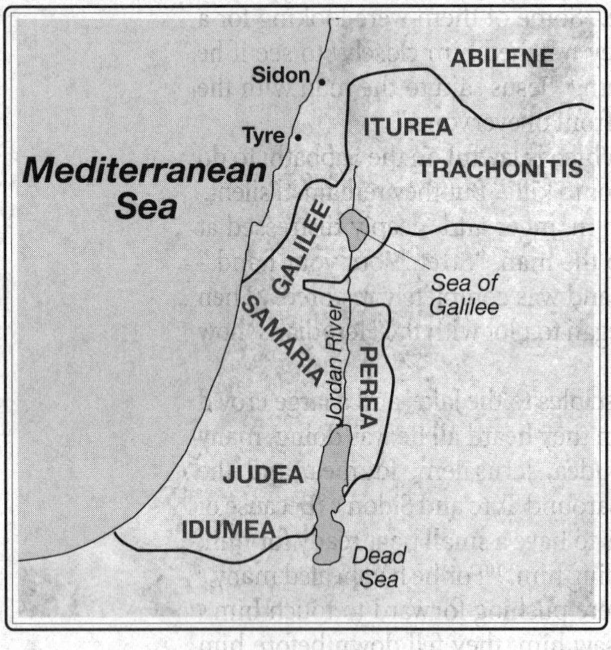

31Then Jesus' mother and
brothers arrived.[m] Standing
outside, they sent someone
in to call him. 32A crowd was
sitting around him, and they told him, "Your mother and brothers
are outside looking for you."

33"Who are my mother and my brothers?" he asked.

34Then he looked at those seated in a circle around him and said,
"Here are my mother and my brothers! 35Whoever does God's will
is my brother and sister and mother."

The Region of the Tetrarchs

[a]22 Greek *Beezeboul* or *Beelzeboul*

3:15 [a]Mt 10:1
3:16 [b]Jn 1:42
3:20 [c]ver 7 [d]Mk 6:31
3:21 [e]Jn 10:20; Ac 26:24
3:22 [f]Mt 15:1 [g]Mt 10:25; 11:18; 12:24; Jn 7:20; 8:48,52; 10:20 [h]Mt 9:34
3:23 [i]Mk 4:2 [j]Mt 4:10
3:27 [k]Isa 49:24,25
3:29 [l]Mt 12:31, 32; Lk 12:10
3:31 [m]ver 21

4:1 [a]Mk 2:13; 3:7
Chapter 4 Theme ____________________

4 Again Jesus began to teach by the lake.[a] The crowd that gath-
4:2 [b]ver 11; ered around him was so large that he got into a boat and sat in
Mk 3:23 it out on the lake, while all the people were along the shore at the
water's edge. 2He taught them many things by parables,[b] and in his
4:3 teaching said: 3"Listen! A farmer went out to sow his seed.[c] 4As he
[c]ver 26 was scattering the seed, some fell along the path, and the birds
came and ate it up. 5Some fell on rocky places, where it did not
4:8 have much soil. It sprang up quickly, because the soil was shallow.
[d]Jn 15:5; Col 1:6 6But when the sun came up, the plants were scorched, and they
withered because they had no root. 7Other seed fell among thorns,
4:9 which grew up and choked the plants, so that they did not bear
[e]ver 23; grain. 8Still other seed fell on good soil. It came up, grew and pro-
Mt 11:15 duced a crop, multiplying thirty, sixty, or even a hundred times."[d]
9Then Jesus said, "He who has ears to hear, let him hear."[e]
4:11 [f]Mt 3:2 10When he was alone, the Twelve and the others around him
[g]1Co 5:12,13; asked him about the parables. 11He told them, "The secret of the
Col 4:5; 1Th 4:12; kingdom of God[f] has been given to you. But to those on the out-
1Ti 3:7 side[g] everything is said in parables 12so that,

4:12 [h]Isa 6:9,10; Mt 13:13-15
"'they may be ever seeing but never perceiving,
and ever hearing but never understanding;
otherwise they might turn and be forgiven!'[a]"[h]

4:14 [i]Mk 16:20; 13Then Jesus said to them, "Don't you understand this parable?
Lk 1:2; How then will you understand any parable? 14The farmer sows
Ac 4:31; 8:4; 16:6; 17:11; the word.[i] 15Some people are like seed along the path, where the
Php 1:14 word is sown. As soon as they hear it, Satan[j] comes and takes
away the word that was sown in them. 16Others, like seed sown on
4:15 rocky places, hear the word and at once receive it with joy. 17But
[j]Mt 4:10 since they have no root, they last only a short time. When trouble
or persecution comes because of the word, they quickly fall away.
4:19 18Still others, like seed sown among thorns, hear the word; 19but
[k]Mt 19:23; 1Ti 6:9,10,17; the worries of this life, the deceitfulness of wealth[k] and the desires
1Jn 2:15-17 for other things come in and choke the word, making it unfruit-
ful. 20Others, like seed sown on good soil, hear the word, accept
4:21 [l]Mt 5:15 it, and produce a crop—thirty, sixty or even a hundred times
what was sown."
21He said to them, "Do you bring in a lamp to put it under a bowl
4:22 [m]Jer 16:17; or a bed? Instead, don't you put it on its stand?[l] 22For whatever is
Mt 10:26; Lk 8:17; 12:2 hidden is meant to be disclosed, and whatever is concealed is
meant to be brought out into the open.[m] 23If anyone has ears to
hear, let him hear."[n]

4:23 [n]ver 9; Mt 11:15

See the section on *Parables*, under **Figures of Speech**, on page 2209.

a *12* Isaiah 6:9,10

24“Consider carefully what you hear,” he continued. “With the
measure you use, it will be measured to you—and even more.[a]
25Whoever has will be given more; whoever does not have, even
what he has will be taken from him.”[b]

26He also said, “This is what the kingdom of God is like.[c] A man
scatters seed on the ground. 27Night and day, whether he sleeps
or gets up, the seed sprouts and grows, though he does not know
how. 28All by itself the soil produces grain—first the stalk, then the
head, then the full kernel in the head. 29As soon as the grain is ripe,
he puts the sickle to it, because the harvest has come.”[d]

30Again he said, “What shall we say the kingdom of God is like,[e]
or what parable shall we use to describe it? 31It is like a mustard
seed, which is the smallest seed you plant in the ground. 32Yet
when planted, it grows and becomes the largest of all garden
plants, with such big branches that the birds of the air can perch in
its shade.”

33With many similar parables Jesus spoke the word to them, as
much as they could understand.[f] 34He did not say anything to
them without using a parable.[g] But when he was alone with his
own disciples, he explained everything.

35That day when evening came, he said to his disciples, “Let us
go over to the other side.” 36Leaving the crowd behind, they took
him along, just as he was, in the boat.[h] There were also other
boats with him. 37A furious squall came up, and the waves broke
over the boat, so that it was nearly swamped. 38Jesus was in the
stern, sleeping on a cushion. The disciples woke him and said to
him, “Teacher, don’t you care if we drown?”

39He got up, rebuked the wind and said to the waves, “Quiet! Be
still!” Then the wind died down and it was completely calm.

40He said to his disciples, “Why are you so afraid? Do you still
have no faith?”[i]

41They were terrified and asked each other, “Who is this? Even
the wind and the waves obey him!”

Chapter 5 Theme ____________________

5 They went across the lake to the region of the Gerasenes.[a]
2When Jesus got out of the boat,[j] a man with an evil[b] spirit[k]
came from the tombs to meet him. 3This man lived in the tombs,
and no one could bind him any more, not even with a chain. 4For
he had often been chained hand and foot, but he tore the chains
apart and broke the irons on his feet. No one was strong enough to
subdue him. 5Night and day among the tombs and in the hills he
would cry out and cut himself with stones.

a *1* Some manuscripts *Gadarenes*; other manuscripts *Gergesenes* b *2* Greek *unclean*; also in verses 8 and 13

4:24 [a] Mt 7:2; Lk 6:38
4:25 [b] Mt 13:12; 25:29
4:26 [c] Mt 13:24
4:29 [d] Rev 14:15
4:30 [e] Mt 13:24
4:33 [f] Jn 16:12
4:34 [g] Jn 16:25
4:36 [h] ver 1; Mk 3:9; 5:2,21; 6:32,45
4:40 [i] Mt 14:31; Mk 16:14
5:2 [j] Mk 4:1 [k] Mk 1:23

6 When he saw Jesus from a distance, he ran and fell on his knees
in front of him. 7 He shouted at the top of his voice, "What do you
want with me,[a] Jesus, Son of the Most High God?[b] Swear to God
that you won't torture me!" 8 For Jesus had said to him, "Come out
of this man, you evil spirit!"
9 Then Jesus asked him, "What is your name?"
"My name is Legion,"[c] he replied, "for we are many." 10 And he
begged Jesus again and again not to send them out of the area.
11 A large herd of pigs was feeding on the nearby hillside. 12 The
demons begged Jesus, "Send us among the pigs; allow us to go into
them." 13 He gave them permission, and the evil spirits came out
and went into the pigs. The herd, about two thousand in number,
rushed down the steep bank into the lake and were drowned.
14 Those tending the pigs ran off and reported this in the town
and countryside, and the people went out to see what had happened. 15 When they came to Jesus, they saw the man who had
been possessed by the legion[d] of demons,[e] sitting there, dressed
and in his right mind; and they were afraid. 16 Those who had seen
it told the people what had happened to the demon-possessed
man—and told about the pigs as well. 17 Then the people began to
plead with Jesus to leave their region.
18 As Jesus was getting into the boat, the man who had been
demon-possessed begged to go with him. 19 Jesus did not let him,
but said, "Go home to your family and tell them[f] how much the
Lord has done for you, and how he has had mercy on you." 20 So
the man went away and began to tell in the Decapolis[a] [g] how much
Jesus had done for him. And all the people were amazed.
21 When Jesus had again crossed over by boat to the other side of
the lake,[h] a large crowd gathered around him while he was by the
lake.[i] 22 Then one of the synagogue rulers,[j] named Jairus, came
there. Seeing Jesus, he fell at his feet 23 and pleaded earnestly with
him, "My little daughter is dying. Please come and put your hands
on[k] her so that she will be healed and live." 24 So Jesus went with
him.
A large crowd followed and pressed around him. 25 And a woman
was there who had been subject to bleeding[l] for twelve years. 26 She
had suffered a great deal under the care of many doctors and had
spent all she had, yet instead of getting better she grew worse.
27 When she heard about Jesus, she came up behind him in the
crowd and touched his cloak, 28 because she thought, "If I just touch
his clothes,[m] I will be healed." 29 Immediately her bleeding stopped
and she felt in her body that she was freed from her suffering.[n]
30 At once Jesus realized that power[o] had gone out from him. He
turned around in the crowd and asked, "Who touched my clothes?"

5:7 [a] Mt 8:29 [b] Mt 4:3; Lk 1:32; 6:35; Ac 16:17; Heb 7:1
5:9 [c] ver 15
5:15 [d] ver 9 [e] ver 16,18; Mt 4:24
5:19 [f] Mt 8:4
5:20 [g] Mt 4:25; Mk 7:31
5:21 [h] Mt 9:1 [i] Mk 4:1
5:22 [j] ver 35,36,38; Lk 13:14; Ac 13:15; 18:8,17
5:23 [k] Mt 19:13; Mk 6:5; 7:32; 8:23; 16:18; Lk 4:40; 13:13; Ac 6:6
5:25 [l] Lev 15:25-30
5:28 [m] Mt 9:20
5:29 [n] ver 34
5:30 [o] Lk 5:17; 6:19

[a] *20* That is, the Ten Cities

31"You see the people crowding against you," his disciples
answered, "and yet you can ask, 'Who touched me?' "
32But Jesus kept looking around to see who had done it. 33Then
the woman, knowing what had happened to her, came and fell at
his feet and, trembling with fear, told him the whole truth. 34He said
to her, "Daughter, your faith has healed you.[a] Go in peace[b] and be
freed from your suffering."
35While Jesus was still speaking, some men came from the house
of Jairus, the synagogue ruler.[c] "Your daughter is dead," they said.
"Why bother the teacher any more?"
36Ignoring what they said, Jesus told the synagogue ruler, "Don't
be afraid; just believe."
37He did not let anyone follow him except Peter, James and
John the brother of James.[d] 38When they came to the home of the
synagogue ruler,[e] Jesus saw a commotion, with people crying and
wailing loudly. 39He went in and said to them, "Why all this commotion and wailing? The child is not dead but asleep."[f] 40But they
laughed at him.
After he put them all out, he took the child's father and mother
and the disciples who were with him, and went in where the child
was. 41He took her by the hand[g] and said to her, *"Talitha koum!"*
(which means, "Little girl, I say to you, get up!").[h] 42Immediately
the girl stood up and walked around (she was twelve years old).
At this they were completely astonished. 43He gave strict orders not
to let anyone know about this,[i] and told them to give her something to eat.

Chapter 6 Theme ______________________

6 Jesus left there and went to his hometown,[j] accompanied by
his disciples. 2When the Sabbath came,[k] he began to teach in
the synagogue,[l] and many who heard him were amazed.[m]
"Where did this man get these things?" they asked. "What's
this wisdom that has been given him, that he even does miracles!
3Isn't this the carpenter? Isn't this Mary's son and the brother of
James, Joseph,[a] Judas and Simon?[n] Aren't his sisters here with us?"
And they took offense at him.[o]
4Jesus said to them, "Only in his hometown, among his relatives and in his own house is a prophet without honor."[p] 5He could
not do any miracles there, except lay his hands on[q] a few sick
people and heal them. 6And he was amazed at their lack of faith.
Then Jesus went around teaching from village to village.[r] 7Call-
ing the Twelve to him,[s] he sent them out two by two[t] and gave
them authority over evil[b] spirits.[u]

5:34 [a]Mt 9:22 [b]Ac 15:33
5:35 [c]ver 22
5:37 [d]Mt 4:21
5:38 [e]ver 22
5:39 [f]Mt 9:24
5:41 [g]Mk 1:31 [h]Lk 7:14; Ac 9:40
5:43 [i]Mt 8:4
6:1 [j]Mt 2:23
6:2 [k]Mk 1:21 [l]Mt 4:23 [m]Mt 7:28
6:3 [n]Mt 12:46 [o]Mt 11:6; Jn 6:61
6:4 [p]Lk 4:24; Jn 4:44
6:5 [q]Mk 5:23
6:6 [r]Mt 9:35; Mk 1:39; Lk 13:22
6:7 [s]Mk 3:13 [t]Dt 17:6; Lk 10:1 [u]Mt 10:1

[a]3 Greek *Joses,* a variant of *Joseph* [b]7 Greek *unclean*

8These were his instructions: "Take nothing for the journey
except a staff—no bread, no bag, no money in your belts. 9Wear
sandals but not an extra tunic. 10Whenever you enter a house, stay
there until you leave that town. 11And if any place will not welcome
you or listen to you, shake the dust off your feet[a] when you leave,
as a testimony against them."

12They went out and preached that people should repent.[b] 13They
drove out many demons and anointed many sick people with oil[c]
and healed them.

14King Herod heard about this, for Jesus' name had become well
known. Some were saying,[a] "John the Baptist[d] has been raised from
the dead, and that is why miraculous powers are at work in him."

15Others said, "He is Elijah."[e]

And still others claimed, "He is a prophet,[f] like one of the
prophets of long ago."[g]

16But when Herod heard this, he said, "John, the man I beheaded,
has been raised from the dead!"

17For Herod himself had given orders to have John arrested, and
he had him bound and put in prison.[h] He did this because of
Herodias, his brother Philip's wife, whom he had married. 18For
John had been saying to Herod, "It is not lawful for you to have
your brother's wife."[i] 19So Herodias nursed a grudge against John
and wanted to kill him. But she was not able to, 20because Herod
feared John and protected him, knowing him to be a righteous and
holy man.[j] When Herod heard John, he was greatly puzzled[b]; yet
he liked to listen to him.

21Finally the opportune time came. On his birthday Herod gave
a banquet[k] for his high officials and military commanders and the
leading men of Galilee.[l] 22When the daughter of Herodias came in
and danced, she pleased Herod and his dinner guests.

The king said to the girl, "Ask me for anything you want, and
I'll give it to you." 23And he promised her with an oath, "Whatever
you ask I will give you, up to half my kingdom."[m]

24She went out and said to her mother, "What shall I ask for?"

"The head of John the Baptist," she answered.

25At once the girl hurried in to the king with the request: "I want
you to give me right now the head of John the Baptist on a platter."

26The king was greatly distressed, but because of his oaths and
his dinner guests, he did not want to refuse her. 27So he immediately sent an executioner with orders to bring John's head. The
man went, beheaded John in the prison, 28and brought back his
head on a platter. He presented it to the girl, and she gave it to her
mother. 29On hearing of this, John's disciples came and took his
body and laid it in a tomb.

6:11 [a]Mt 10:14
6:12 [b]Lk 9:6
6:13 [c]Jas 5:14
6:14 [d]Mt 3:1
6:15 [e]Mal 4:5 [f]Mt 21:11 [g]Mt 16:14; Mk 8:28
6:17 [h]Mt 4:12; 11:2; Lk 3:19,20
6:18 [i]Lev 18:16; 20:21
6:20 [j]Mt 11:9; 21:26
6:21 [k]Est 1:3; 2:18 [l]Lk 3:1
6:23 [m]Est 5:3,6; 7:2

a *14* Some early manuscripts *He was saying* b *20* Some early manuscripts *he did many things*

30 The apostles[a] gathered around Jesus and reported to him all
they had done and taught.[b] 31 Then, because so many people were
coming and going that they did not even have a chance to eat,[c] he
said to them, "Come with me by yourselves to a quiet place and get
some rest."

32 So they went away by themselves in a boat[d] to a solitary place.
33 But many who saw them leaving recognized them and ran on
foot from all the towns and got there ahead of them. 34 When Jesus
landed and saw a large crowd, he had compassion on them,
because they were like sheep without a shepherd.[e] So he began
teaching them many things.

35 By this time it was late in the day, so his disciples came to him.
"This is a remote place," they said, "and it's already very late.
36 Send the people away so they can go to the surrounding countryside and villages and buy themselves something to eat."

37 But he answered, "You give them something to eat."[f]

They said to him, "That would take eight months of a man's
wages[a]! Are we to go and spend that much on bread and give it to
them to eat?"

38 "How many loaves do you have?" he asked. "Go and see."

When they found out, they said, "Five—and two fish."[g]

39 Then Jesus directed them to have all the people sit down in
groups on the green grass. 40 So they sat down in groups of hundreds and fifties. 41 Taking the five loaves and the two fish and looking up to heaven, he gave thanks and broke the loaves.[h] Then he
gave them to his disciples to set before the people. He also divided
the two fish among them all. 42 They all ate and were satisfied,
43 and the disciples picked up twelve basketfuls of broken pieces of
bread and fish. 44 The number of the men who had eaten was five
thousand.

45 Immediately Jesus made his disciples get into the boat[i] and go
on ahead of him to Bethsaida,[j] while he dismissed the crowd.
46 After leaving them, he went up on a mountainside to pray.[k]

47 When evening came, the boat was in the middle of the lake,
and he was alone on land. 48 He saw the disciples straining at the
oars, because the wind was against them. About the fourth watch
of the night he went out to them, walking on the lake. He was
about to pass by them, 49 but when they saw him walking on the
lake, they thought he was a ghost.[l] They cried out, 50 because they
all saw him and were terrified.

Immediately he spoke to them and said, "Take courage! It is I.
Don't be afraid."[m] 51 Then he climbed into the boat[n] with them, and
the wind died down.[o] They were completely amazed, 52 for they had
not understood about the loaves; their hearts were hardened.[p]

6:30 [a] Mt 10:2; Lk 9:10; 17:5; 22:14; 24:10; Ac 1:2,26 [b] Lk 9:10
6:31 [c] Mk 3:20
6:32 [d] ver 45; Mk 4:36
6:34 [e] Mt 9:36
6:37 [f] 2Ki 4:42-44
6:38 [g] Mt 15:34; Mk 8:5
6:41 [h] Mt 14:19
6:45 [i] ver 32 [j] Mt 11:21
6:46 [k] Lk 3:21
6:49 [l] Lk 24:37
6:50 [m] Mt 14:27
6:51 [n] ver 32 [o] Mk 4:39
6:52 [p] Mk 8:17-21

a 37 Greek *take two hundred denarii*

6:53 [a]Jn 6:24,25 53When they had crossed over, they landed at Gennesaret and
anchored there.[a] 54As soon as they got out of the boat, people
recognized Jesus. 55They ran throughout that whole region and
6:56 carried the sick on mats to wherever they heard he was. 56And
[b]Mt 9:20 wherever he went—into villages, towns or countryside—they
placed the sick in the marketplaces. They begged him to let them
touch even the edge of his cloak,[b] and all who touched him were
7:2 [c]Ac 10:14,28; 11:8; Ro 14:14 healed.

Chapter 7 Theme ____

7 The Pharisees and some of the teachers of the law who had
7:3 [d]ver 5,8,9,13; Lk 11:38 come from Jerusalem gathered around Jesus and 2saw some
of his disciples eating food with hands that were "unclean,"[c] that
is, unwashed. 3(The Pharisees and all the Jews do not eat unless
they give their hands a ceremonial washing, holding to the tradi-
7:4 [e]Mt 23:25; Lk 11:39 tion of the elders.[d] 4When they come from the marketplace they do
not eat unless they wash. And they observe many other traditions,
such as the washing of cups, pitchers and kettles.[a])[e]

5So the Pharisees and teachers of the law asked Jesus, "Why
7:5 [f]ver 3; Gal 1:14; Col 2:8 don't your disciples live according to the tradition of the elders[f]
instead of eating their food with 'unclean' hands?"

6He replied, "Isaiah was right when he prophesied about you
hypocrites; as it is written:

7:7 [g]Isa 29:13 " 'These people honor me with their lips,
but their hearts are far from me.
7They worship me in vain;
their teachings are but rules taught by men.'[b][g]

7:8 [h]ver 3 8You have let go of the commands of God and are holding on to
the traditions of men."[h]

7:9 [i]ver 3 9And he said to them: "You have a fine way of setting aside the
commands of God in order to observe[c] your own traditions![i]
10For Moses said, 'Honor your father and your mother,'[d][j] and,
7:10 [j]Ex 20:12; Dt 5:16 [k]Ex 21:17; Lev 20:9 'Anyone who curses his father or mother must be put to death.'[e][k]
11But you say[l] that if a man says to his father or mother: 'Whatever
help you might otherwise have received from me is Corban' (that
is, a gift devoted to God), 12then you no longer let him do anything for his father or mother. 13Thus you nullify the word of God[m]
7:11 [l]Mt 23:16,18 by your tradition[n] that you have handed down. And you do many
things like that."

14Again Jesus called the crowd to him and said, "Listen to me,
everyone, and understand this. 15Nothing outside a man can make

7:13 [m]Heb 4:12 [n]ver 3

[a] *4* Some early manuscripts *pitchers, kettles and dining couches* [b] *6,7* Isaiah 29:13 [c] *9* Some manuscripts *set up* [d] *10* Exodus 20:12; Deut. 5:16 [e] *10* Exodus 21:17; Lev. 20:9

him 'unclean' by going into him. Rather, it is what comes out of a
man that makes him 'unclean.'[a]"
17After he had left the crowd and entered the house, his disciples
asked him[a] about this parable. 18"Are you so dull?" he asked.
"Don't you see that nothing that enters a man from the outside
can make him 'unclean'? 19For it doesn't go into his heart but into
his stomach, and then out of his body." (In saying this, Jesus
declared all foods[b] "clean.")[c]
20He went on: "What comes out of a man is what makes him
'unclean.' 21For from within, out of men's hearts, come evil
thoughts, sexual immorality, theft, murder, adultery, 22greed,[d]
malice, deceit, lewdness, envy, slander, arrogance and folly. 23All
these evils come from inside and make a man 'unclean.'"
24Jesus left that place and went to the vicinity of Tyre.[b][e] He
entered a house and did not want anyone to know it; yet he could
not keep his presence secret. 25In fact, as soon as she heard about
him, a woman whose little daughter was possessed by an evil[c]
spirit[f] came and fell at his feet. 26The woman was a Greek, born in
Syrian Phoenicia. She begged Jesus to drive the demon out of her
daughter.
27"First let the children eat all they want," he told her, "for it is
not right to take the children's bread and toss it to their dogs."
28"Yes, Lord," she replied, "but even the dogs under the table eat
the children's crumbs."
29Then he told her, "For such a reply, you may go; the demon has
left your daughter."
30She went home and found her child lying on the bed, and the
demon gone.
31Then Jesus left the vicinity of Tyre[g] and went through Sidon,
down to the Sea of Galilee[h] and into the region of the Decapolis.[d][i]
32There some people brought to him a man who was deaf and
could hardly talk,[j] and they begged him to place his hand on[k] the
man.
33After he took him aside, away from the crowd, Jesus put his
fingers into the man's ears. Then he spit[l] and touched the man's
tongue. 34He looked up to heaven[m] and with a deep sigh[n] said to
him, "*Ephphatha!*" (which means, "Be opened!"). 35At this, the
man's ears were opened, his tongue was loosened and he began to
speak plainly.[o]
36Jesus commanded them not to tell anyone.[p] But the more he
did so, the more they kept talking about it. 37People were overwhelmed with amazement. "He has done everything well," they
said. "He even makes the deaf hear and the mute speak."

[a]*15* Some early manuscripts *'unclean.' 16If anyone has ears to hear, let him hear.* [b]*24* Many early manuscripts *Tyre and Sidon* [c]*25* Greek *unclean* [d]*31* That is, the Ten Cities

7:17 [a]Mk 9:28
7:19 [b]Ro 14:1-12; Col 2:16; 1Ti 4:3-5 [c]Ac 10:15
7:22 [d]Mt 20:15
7:24 [e]Mt 11:21
7:25 [f]Mt 4:24
7:31 [g]ver 24; Mt 11:21 [h]Mt 4:18 [i]Mt 4:25; Mk 5:20
7:32 [j]Mt 9:32; Lk 11:14 [k]Mk 5:23
7:33 [l]Mk 8:23
7:34 [m]Mk 6:41; Jn 11:41 [n]Mk 8:12
7:35 [o]Isa 35:5,6
7:36 [p]Mt 8:4

8:2 [a]Mt 9:36
8:7 [b]Mt 14:19
8:8 [c]ver 20
8:11 [d]Mt 12:38
8:12 [e]Mk 7:34
8:15 [f]1Co 5:6-8 [g]Lk 12:1 [h]Mt 14:1; Mk 12:13
8:17 [i]Isa 6:9,10; Mk 6:52
8:19 [j]Mt 14:20; Mk 6:41-44; Lk 9:17; Jn 6:13
8:20 [k]ver 6-9; Mt 15:37
8:21 [l]Mk 6:52
8:22 [m]Mt 11:21 [n]Mk 10:46; Jn 9:1
8:23 [o]Mk 7:33

Chapter 8 Theme ______________________

8 During those days another large crowd gathered. Since they had nothing to eat, Jesus called his disciples to him and said, 2"I have compassion for these people;[a] they have already been with me three days and have nothing to eat. 3If I send them home hungry, they will collapse on the way, because some of them have come a long distance."

4His disciples answered, "But where in this remote place can anyone get enough bread to feed them?"

5"How many loaves do you have?" Jesus asked.

"Seven," they replied.

6He told the crowd to sit down on the ground. When he had taken the seven loaves and given thanks, he broke them and gave them to his disciples to set before the people, and they did so. 7They had a few small fish as well; he gave thanks for them also and told the disciples to distribute them.[b] 8The people ate and were satisfied. Afterward the disciples picked up seven basketfuls of broken pieces that were left over.[c] 9About four thousand men were present. And having sent them away, 10he got into the boat with his disciples and went to the region of Dalmanutha.

11The Pharisees came and began to question Jesus. To test him, they asked him for a sign from heaven.[d] 12He sighed deeply[e] and said, "Why does this generation ask for a miraculous sign? I tell you the truth, no sign will be given to it." 13Then he left them, got back into the boat and crossed to the other side.

14The disciples had forgotten to bring bread, except for one loaf they had with them in the boat. 15"Be careful," Jesus warned them. "Watch out for the yeast[f] of the Pharisees[g] and that of Herod."[h]

16They discussed this with one another and said, "It is because we have no bread."

17Aware of their discussion, Jesus asked them: "Why are you talking about having no bread? Do you still not see or understand? Are your hearts hardened?[i] 18Do you have eyes but fail to see, and ears but fail to hear? And don't you remember? 19When I broke the five loaves for the five thousand, how many basketfuls of pieces did you pick up?"

"Twelve,"[j] they replied.

20"And when I broke the seven loaves for the four thousand, how many basketfuls of pieces did you pick up?"

They answered, "Seven."[k]

21He said to them, "Do you still not understand?"[l]

22They came to Bethsaida,[m] and some people brought a blind man[n] and begged Jesus to touch him. 23He took the blind man by the hand and led him outside the village. When he had spit[o] on

INSIGHT

The exact location of ***Dalmanutha*** is unknown. However, it is believed to be another name for Magdala or the name for a nearby region.

Galilee

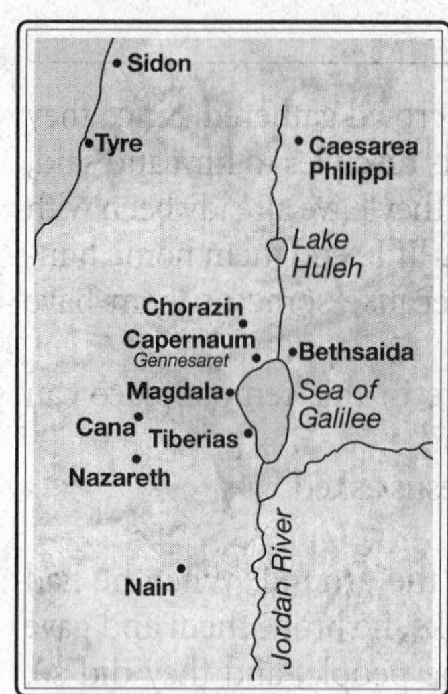

the man's eyes and put his hands on[a]
him, Jesus asked, "Do you see anything?"
24 He looked up and said, "I see
people; they look like trees walking
around."
25 Once more Jesus put his hands
on the man's eyes. Then his eyes
were opened, his sight was restored,
and he saw everything clearly. 26 Jesus
sent him home, saying, "Don't go
into the village.[a]"
27 Jesus and his disciples went on to
the villages around Caesarea Philippi.
On the way he asked them, "Who do
people say I am?"
28 They replied, "Some say John the Baptist;[b] others say Elijah;[c]
and still others, one of the prophets."
29 "But what about you?" he asked. "Who do you say I am?"
Peter answered, "You are the Christ.[b]"[d]
30 Jesus warned them not to tell anyone about him.[e]
31 He then began to teach them that the Son of Man[f] must suffer
many things[g] and be rejected by the elders, chief priests and
teachers of the law,[h] and that he must be killed[i] and after three
days[j] rise again.[k] 32 He spoke plainly[l] about this, and Peter took
him aside and began to rebuke him.
33 But when Jesus turned and looked at his disciples, he rebuked
Peter. "Get behind me, Satan!"[m] he said. "You do not have in
mind the things of God, but the things of men."
34 Then he called the crowd to him along with his disciples and
said: "If anyone would come after me, he must deny himself and
take up his cross and follow me.[n] 35 For whoever wants to save his
life[c] will lose it, but whoever loses his life for me and for the
gospel will save it.[o] 36 What good is it for a man to gain the whole
world, yet forfeit his soul? 37 Or what can a man give in exchange
for his soul? 38 If anyone is ashamed of me and my words in this
adulterous and sinful generation, the Son of Man[p] will be ashamed
of him[q] when he comes[r] in his Father's glory with the holy angels."

Chapter 9 Theme ________________________

9 And he said to them, "I tell you the truth, some who are
standing here will not taste death before they see the kingdom
of God come[s] with power."[t]

[a] 26 Some manuscripts *Don't go and tell anyone in the village* [b] 29 Or *Messiah.* "The Christ" (Greek) and "the Messiah" (Hebrew) both mean "the Anointed One." [c] 35 The Greek word means either *life* or *soul*; also in verse 36.

8:23 [a] Mk 5:23
8:28 [b] Mt 3:1 [c] Mal 4:5
8:29 [d] Jn 6:69; 11:27
8:30 [e] Mt 8:4; 16:20; 17:9; Mk 9:9; Lk 9:21
8:31 [f] Mt 8:20 [g] Mt 16:21 [h] Mt 27:1,2 [i] Ac 2:23; 3:13 [j] Mt 16:21 [k] Mt 16:21
8:32 [l] Jn 18:20
8:33 [m] Mt 4:10
8:34 [n] Mt 10:38; Lk 14:27
8:35 [o] Jn 12:25
8:38 [p] Mt 8:20 [q] Mt 10:33; Lk 12:9 [r] 1Th 2:19
9:1 [s] Mk 13:30; Lk 22:18 [t] Mt 24:30; 25:31

2 After six days Jesus took Peter, James and John[a] with him and
led them up a high mountain, where they were all alone. There
he was transfigured before them. 3 His clothes became dazzling
white,[b] whiter than anyone in the world could bleach them. 4 And
there appeared before them Elijah and Moses, who were talking
with Jesus.
5 Peter said to Jesus, "Rabbi,[c] it is good for us to be here. Let us
put up three shelters—one for you, one for Moses and one for
Elijah." 6 (He did not know what to say, they were so frightened.)
7 Then a cloud appeared and enveloped them, and a voice came
from the cloud:[d] "This is my Son, whom I love. Listen to him!"[e]
8 Suddenly, when they looked around, they no longer saw anyone with them except Jesus.
9 As they were coming down the mountain, Jesus gave them
orders not to tell anyone[f] what they had seen until the Son of
Man[g] had risen from the dead. 10 They kept the matter to themselves, discussing what "rising from the dead" meant.
11 And they asked him, "Why do the teachers of the law say that
Elijah must come first?"
12 Jesus replied, "To be sure, Elijah does come first, and restores
all things. Why then is it written that the Son of Man[h] must suffer
much[i] and be rejected?[j] 13 But I tell you, Elijah has come,[k] and
they have done to him everything they wished, just as it is written about him."
14 When they came to the other disciples, they saw a large crowd
around them and the teachers of the law arguing with them. 15 As
soon as all the people saw Jesus, they were overwhelmed with
wonder and ran to greet him.
16 "What are you arguing with them about?" he asked.
17 A man in the crowd answered, "Teacher, I brought you my
son, who is possessed by a spirit that has robbed him of speech.
18 Whenever it seizes him, it throws him to the ground. He foams
at the mouth, gnashes his teeth and becomes rigid. I asked your
disciples to drive out the spirit, but they could not."
19 "O unbelieving generation," Jesus replied, "how long shall I
stay with you? How long shall I put up with you? Bring the boy
to me."
20 So they brought him. When the spirit saw Jesus, it immediately threw the boy into a convulsion. He fell to the ground and
rolled around, foaming at the mouth.[l]
21 Jesus asked the boy's father, "How long has he been like this?"
"From childhood," he answered. 22 "It has often thrown him
into fire or water to kill him. But if you can do anything, take pity
on us and help us."
23 " 'If you can'?" said Jesus. "Everything is possible for him who
believes."[m]

9:2 [a]Mt 4:21
9:3 [b]Mt 28:3
9:5 [c]Mt 23:7
9:7 [d]Ex 24:16 [e]Mt 3:17
9:9 [f]Mk 8:30 [g]Mt 8:20
9:12 [h]Mt 8:20 [i]Mt 16:21 [j]Lk 23:11
9:13 [k]Mt 11:14
9:20 [l]Mk 1:26
9:23 [m]Mt 21:21; Mk 11:23; Jn 11:40

24 Immediately the boy's father exclaimed, "I do believe; help me
overcome my unbelief!"
25 When Jesus saw that a crowd was running to the scene,[a] he
rebuked the evil[a] spirit. "You deaf and mute spirit," he said, "I
command you, come out of him and never enter him again."
26 The spirit shrieked, convulsed him violently and came out.
The boy looked so much like a corpse that many said, "He's
dead." 27 But Jesus took him by the hand and lifted him to his
feet, and he stood up.
28 After Jesus had gone indoors, his disciples asked him privately,[b]
"Why couldn't we drive it out?"
29 He replied, "This kind can come out only by prayer.[b]"
30 They left that place and passed through Galilee. Jesus did not
want anyone to know where they were, 31 because he was teaching
his disciples. He said to them, "The Son of Man[c] is going to be
betrayed into the hands of men. They will kill him,[d] and after
three days[e] he will rise."[f] 32 But they did not understand what he
meant[g] and were afraid to ask him about it.
33 They came to Capernaum.[h] When he was in the house,[i] he
asked them, "What were you arguing about on the road?" 34 But
they kept quiet because on the way they had argued about who
was the greatest.[j]
35 Sitting down, Jesus called the Twelve and said, "If anyone
wants to be first, he must be the very last, and the servant of all."[k]
36 He took a little child and had him stand among them. Taking
him in his arms,[l] he said to them, 37 "Whoever welcomes one of
these little children in my name welcomes me; and whoever welcomes me does not welcome me but the one who sent me."[m]
38 "Teacher," said John, "we saw a man driving out demons in
your name and we told him to stop, because he was not one of us."[n]
39 "Do not stop him," Jesus said. "No one who does a miracle in
my name can in the next moment say anything bad about me,
40 for whoever is not against us is for us.[o] 41 I tell you the truth,
anyone who gives you a cup of water in my name because you
belong to Christ will certainly not lose his reward.[p]
42 "And if anyone causes one of these little ones who believe in
me to sin,[q] it would be better for him to be thrown into the sea
with a large millstone tied around his neck.[r] 43 If your hand causes
you to sin,[s] cut it off. It is better for you to enter life maimed than
with two hands to go into hell,[t] where the fire never goes out.[c] [u]
45 And if your foot causes you to sin,[v] cut it off. It is better for you to
enter life crippled than to have two feet and be thrown into hell.[d] [w]

[a] 25 Greek *unclean* [b] 29 Some manuscripts *prayer and fasting* [c] 43 Some manuscripts *out,* [44] *where / "'their worm does not die, / and the fire is not quenched.'* [d] 45 Some manuscripts *hell,* [46] *where / "'their worm does not die, / and the fire is not quenched.'*

9:25 [a] ver 15
9:28 [b] Mk 7:17
9:31 [c] Mt 8:20 [d] ver 12; Ac 2:23; 3:13 [e] Mt 16:21 [f] Mt 16:21
9:32 [g] Lk 2:50; 9:45; 18:34; Jn 12:16
9:33 [h] Mt 4:13 [i] Mk 1:29
9:34 [j] Lk 22:24
9:35 [k] Mt 18:4; 20:26; Mk 10:43; Lk 22:26
9:36 [l] Mk 10:16
9:37 [m] Mt 10:40
9:38 [n] Nu 11:27-29
9:40 [o] Mt 12:30; Lk 11:23
9:41 [p] Mt 10:42
9:42 [q] Mt 5:29 [r] Mt 18:6; Lk 17:2
9:43 [s] Mt 5:29 [t] Mt 5:30; 18:8 [u] Mt 25:41
9:45 [v] Mt 5:29 [w] Mt 18:8

47And if your eye causes you to sin,[a] pluck it out. It is better for you
to enter the kingdom of God with one eye than to have two eyes and
be thrown into hell,[b] 48where

> " 'their worm does not die,
> and the fire is not quenched.'[a] [c]

49Everyone will be salted[d] with fire.
50"Salt is good, but if it loses its saltiness, how can you make it
salty again?[e] Have salt in yourselves,[f] and be at peace with each
other."[g]

Chapter 10 Theme ______________________________

10 Jesus then left that place and went into the region of Judea
and across the Jordan.[h] Again crowds of people came to
him, and as was his custom, he taught them.[i]
2Some Pharisees[j] came and tested him by asking, "Is it lawful for
a man to divorce his wife?"
3"What did Moses command you?" he replied.
4They said, "Moses permitted a man to write a certificate of
divorce and send her away."[k]
5"It was because your hearts were hard[l] that Moses wrote you
this law," Jesus replied. 6"But at the beginning of creation God
'made them male and female.'[b] [m] 7'For this reason a man will leave
his father and mother and be united to his wife,[c] 8and the two will
become one flesh.'[d] [n] So they are no longer two, but one. 9Therefore
what God has joined together, let man not separate."
10When they were in the house again, the disciples asked Jesus
about this. 11He answered, "Anyone who divorces his wife and
marries another woman commits adultery against her.[o] 12And if
she divorces her husband and marries another man, she commits
adultery."[p]
13People were bringing little children to Jesus to have him touch
them, but the disciples rebuked them. 14When Jesus saw this, he
was indignant. He said to them, "Let the little children come to me,
and do not hinder them, for the kingdom of God belongs to such
as these.[q] 15I tell you the truth, anyone who will not receive the
kingdom of God like a little child will never enter it."[r] 16And he
took the children in his arms,[s] put his hands on them and blessed
them.
17As Jesus started on his way, a man ran up to him and fell on his
knees[t] before him. "Good teacher," he asked, "what must I do to
inherit eternal life?"[u]

9:47 [a]Mt 5:29 [b]Mt 5:29; 18:9
9:48 [c]Isa 66:24; Mt 25:41
9:49 [d]Lev 2:13
9:50 [e]Mt 5:13; Lk 14:34,35 [f]Col 4:6 [g]Ro 12:18; 2Co 13:11; 1Th 5:13
10:1 [h]Mk 1:5; Jn 10:40; 11:7 [i]Mt 4:23; Mk 2:13; 4:2; 6:6,34
10:2 [j]Mk 2:16
10:4 [k]Dt 24:1-4; Mt 5:31
10:5 [l]Ps 95:8; Heb 3:15
10:6 [m]Ge 1:27; 5:2
10:8 [n]Ge 2:24; 1Co 6:16
10:11 [o]Mt 5:32; Lk 16:18
10:12 [p]Ro 7:3; 1Co 7:10,11
10:14 [q]Mt 25:34
10:15 [r]Mt 18:3
10:16 [s]Mk 9:36
10:17 [t]Mk 1:40 [u]Lk 10:25; Ac 20:32

[a] *48* Isaiah 66:24 [b] *6* Gen. 1:27 [c] *7* Some early manuscripts do not have *and be united to his wife.* [d] *8* Gen. 2:24

18 “Why do you call me good?” Jesus answered. “No one is
good—except God alone. 19 You know the commandments: ‘Do
not murder, do not commit adultery, do not steal, do not give false
testimony, do not defraud, honor your father and mother.’[a]”[a]
20 “Teacher,” he declared, “all these I have kept since I was a boy.”
21 Jesus looked at him and loved him. “One thing you lack,” he
said. “Go, sell everything you have and give to the poor,[b] and you
will have treasure in heaven.[c] Then come, follow me.”[d]
22 At this the man’s face fell. He went away sad, because he had
great wealth.
23 Jesus looked around and said to his disciples, “How hard it is
for the rich[e] to enter the kingdom of God!”
24 The disciples were amazed at his words. But Jesus said again,
“Children, how hard it is[b] to enter the kingdom of God![f] 25 It is
easier for a camel to go through the eye of a needle than for a rich
man to enter the kingdom of God.”[g]
26 The disciples were even more amazed, and said to each other,
“Who then can be saved?”
27 Jesus looked at them and said, “With man this is impossible,
but not with God; all things are possible with God.”[h]
28 Peter said to him, “We have left everything to follow you!”[i]
29 “I tell you the truth,” Jesus replied, “no one who has left home
or brothers or sisters or mother or father or children or fields for
me and the gospel 30 will fail to receive a hundred times as much[j] in
this present age (homes, brothers, sisters, mothers, children and
fields—and with them, persecutions) and in the age to come,[k]
eternal life.[l] 31 But many who are first will be last, and the last
first.”[m]
32 They were on their way up to Jerusalem, with Jesus leading the
way, and the disciples were astonished, while those who followed
were afraid. Again he took the Twelve[n] aside and told them what
was going to happen to him. 33 “We are going up to Jerusalem,”[o]
he said, “and the Son of Man[p] will be betrayed to the chief priests
and teachers of the law.[q] They will condemn him to death and
will hand him over to the Gentiles, 34 who will mock him and spit
on him, flog him[r] and kill him.[s] Three days later[t] he will rise.”[u]
35 Then James and John, the sons of Zebedee, came to him.
“Teacher,” they said, “we want you to do for us whatever we ask.”
36 “What do you want me to do for you?” he asked.
37 They replied, “Let one of us sit at your right and the other at
your left in your glory.”[v]
38 “You don’t know what you are asking,”[w] Jesus said. “Can you
drink the cup[x] I drink or be baptized with the baptism I am baptized with?”[y]

a *19* Exodus 20:12-16; Deut. 5:16-20 b *24* Some manuscripts *is for those who trust in riches*

10:19 [a] Ex 20:12-16; Dt 5:16-20
10:21 [b] Ac 2:45 [c] Mt 6:20; Lk 12:33 [d] Mt 4:19
10:23 [e] Ps 52:7; 62:10; 1Ti 6:9,10,17
10:24 [f] Mt 7:13,14
10:25 [g] Lk 12:16-20
10:27 [h] Mt 19:26
10:28 [i] Mt 4:19
10:30 [j] Mt 6:33 [k] Mt 12:32 [l] Mt 25:46
10:31 [m] Mt 19:30
10:32 [n] Mk 3:16-19
10:33 [o] Lk 9:51 [p] Mt 8:20 [q] Mt 27:1,2
10:34 [r] Mt 16:21 [s] Ac 2:23; 3:13 [t] Mt 16:21 [u] Mt 16:21
10:37 [v] Mt 19:28
10:38 [w] Job 38:2 [x] Mt 20:22 [y] Lk 12:50

10:39 [a] Ac 12:2; 39"We can," they answered.
Rev 1:9 Jesus said to them, "You will drink the cup I drink and be baptized with the baptism I am baptized with,[a] 40but to sit at my right
or left is not for me to grant. These places belong to those for
whom they have been prepared."
10:43 41When the ten heard about this, they became indignant with
[b] Mk 9:35 James and John. 42Jesus called them together and said, "You know
that those who are regarded as rulers of the Gentiles lord it over
them, and their high officials exercise authority over them. 43Not
so with you. Instead, whoever wants to become great among you
10:45 must be your servant,[b] 44and whoever wants to be first must be
[c] Mt 20:28 slave of all. 45For even the Son of Man did not come to be served,
[d] Mt 20:28 but to serve,[c] and to give his life as a ransom for many."[d]
46Then they came to Jericho. As Jesus and his disciples, together
with a large crowd, were leaving the city, a blind man, Bartimaeus
(that is, the Son of Timaeus), was sitting by the roadside begging.
10:47 47When he heard that it was Jesus of Nazareth,[e] he began to shout,
[e] Mk 1:24
[f] Mt 9:27 "Jesus, Son of David,[f] have mercy on me!"
48Many rebuked him and told him to be quiet, but he shouted all
the more, "Son of David, have mercy on me!"
49Jesus stopped and said, "Call him."
10:51 So they called to the blind man, "Cheer up! On your feet! He's
[g] Mt 23:7 calling you." 50Throwing his cloak aside, he jumped to his feet and
came to Jesus.
51"What do you want me to do for you?" Jesus asked him.
The blind man said, "Rabbi,[g] I want to see."
10:52 52"Go," said Jesus, "your faith has healed you."[h] Immediately he
[h] Mt 9:22 received his sight and followed[i] Jesus along the road.
[i] Mt 4:19

Chapter 11 Theme ______________________

11 As they approached Jerusalem and came to Bethphage and
Bethany[j] at the Mount of Olives,[k] Jesus sent two of his disci-
11:1 ples, 2saying to them, "Go to the village ahead of you, and just as
[j] Mt 21:17
[k] Mt 21:1 you enter it, you will find a colt tied there, which no one has ever
ridden.[l] Untie it and bring it here. 3If anyone asks you, 'Why are
you doing this?' tell him, 'The Lord needs it and will send it back
here shortly.'"
11:2 4They went and found a colt outside in the street, tied at a
[l] Nu 19:2; doorway.[m] As they untied it, 5some people standing there asked,
Dt 21:3; "What are you doing, untying that colt?" 6They answered as Jesus
1Sa 6:7 had told them to, and the people let them go. 7When they brought
the colt to Jesus and threw their cloaks over it, he sat on it. 8Many
people spread their cloaks on the road, while others spread
branches they had cut in the fields. 9Those who went ahead and
11:4 [m] Mk 14:16 those who followed shouted,

> "Hosanna![a]"
>
> "Blessed is he who comes in the name of the Lord!"[b][a]
>
> 10"Blessed is the coming kingdom of our father David!"
>
> "Hosanna in the highest!"[b]

11Jesus entered Jerusalem and went to the temple. He looked
around at everything, but since it was already late, he went out to
Bethany with the Twelve.[c]

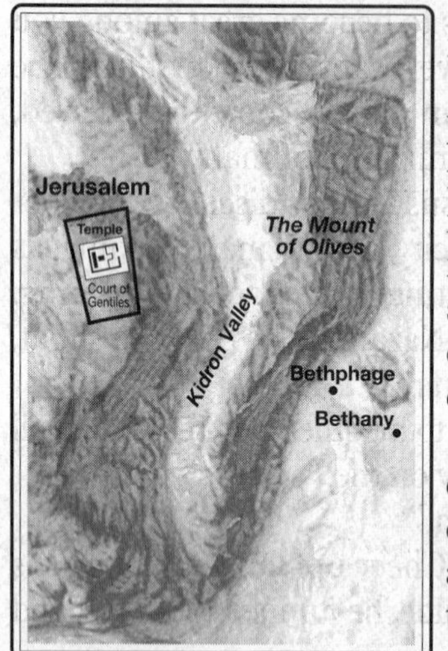

From Bethany, Bethphage across the Mount of Olives into Jerusalem

12The next day as they were leaving Bethany, Jesus was hungry.
13Seeing in the distance a fig tree in
leaf, he went to find out if it had any
fruit. When he reached it, he found
nothing but leaves, because it was
not the season for figs.[d] 14Then he
said to the tree, "May no one ever
eat fruit from you again." And his
disciples heard him say it.
15On reaching Jerusalem, Jesus
entered the temple area and began
driving out those who were buying
and selling there. He overturned the
tables of the money changers and
the benches of those selling doves,
16and would not allow anyone to carry merchandise through the
temple courts. 17And as he taught them, he said, "Is it not written:

> "'My house will be called
> a house of prayer for all nations'[c]?[e]

But you have made it 'a den of robbers.'[d]"[f]
18The chief priests and the teachers of the law heard this and
began looking for a way to kill him, for they feared him,[g] because
the whole crowd was amazed at his teaching.[h]
19When evening came, they[e] went out of the city.[i]
20In the morning, as they went along, they saw the fig tree
withered from the roots. 21Peter remembered and said to Jesus,
"Rabbi,[j] look! The fig tree you cursed has withered!"
22"Have[f] faith in God," Jesus answered. 23"I tell you the truth, if
anyone says to this mountain, 'Go, throw yourself into the sea,' and
does not doubt in his heart but believes that what he says will
happen, it will be done for him.[k] 24Therefore I tell you, whatever
you ask for in prayer, believe that you have received it, and it will be
yours.[l] 25And when you stand praying, if you hold anything

[a]9 A Hebrew expression meaning "Save!" which became an exclamation of praise; also in verse 10 [b]9 Psalm 118:25,26 [c]17 Isaiah 56:7 [d]17 Jer. 7:11 [e]19 Some early manuscripts *he* [f]22 Some early manuscripts *If you have*

11:9 [a]Ps 118:25,26; Mt 23:39
11:10 [b]Lk 2:14
11:11 [c]Mt 21:12,17
11:13 [d]Lk 13:6-9
11:17 [e]Isa 56:7 [f]Jer 7:11
11:18 [g]Mt 21:46; Mk 12:12; Lk 20:19 [h]Mt 7:28
11:19 [i]Lk 21:37
11:21 [j]Mt 23:7
11:23 [k]Mt 21:21
11:24 [l]Mt 7:7

11:25 [a]Mt 6:14 against anyone, forgive him, so that your Father in heaven may
forgive you your sins.[a]"[a]
27They arrived again in Jerusalem, and while Jesus was walking
in the temple courts, the chief priests, the teachers of the law and
the elders came to him. 28"By what authority are you doing these
things?" they asked. "And who gave you authority to do this?"
29Jesus replied, "I will ask you one question. Answer me, and I
11:32 will tell you by what authority I am doing these things. 30John's
[b]Mt 11:9 baptism—was it from heaven, or from men? Tell me!"
31They discussed it among themselves and said, "If we say,
'From heaven,' he will ask, 'Then why didn't you believe him?'
32But if we say, 'From men'. . . ." (They feared the people, for
everyone held that John really was a prophet.)[b]
33So they answered Jesus, "We don't know."
12:1 Jesus said, "Neither will I tell you by what authority I am doing
[c]Isa 5:1-7 these things."

Chapter 12 Theme ______________________________

12 He then began to speak to them in parables: "A man planted
a vineyard.[c] He put a wall around it, dug a pit for the winepress and built a watchtower. Then he rented the vineyard to some
farmers and went away on a journey. 2At harvest time he sent a
12:6 [d]Heb 1:1-3 servant to the tenants to collect from them some of the fruit of the
vineyard. 3But they seized him, beat him and sent him away empty-
handed. 4Then he sent another servant to them; they struck this
man on the head and treated him shamefully. 5He sent still another,
and that one they killed. He sent many others; some of them they
beat, others they killed.
6"He had one left to send, a son, whom he loved. He sent him
12:10 last of all,[d] saying, 'They will respect my son.'
[e]Ac 4:11 7"But the tenants said to one another, 'This is the heir. Come,
let's kill him, and the inheritance will be ours.' 8So they took him
and killed him, and threw him out of the vineyard.
9"What then will the owner of the vineyard do? He will come
and kill those tenants and give the vineyard to others. 10Haven't
you read this scripture:

12:11 " 'The stone the builders rejected
[f]Ps 118:22,23 has become the capstone[b];[e]
11the Lord has done this,
and it is marvelous in our eyes'[c]?"[f]

12Then they looked for a way to arrest him because they knew
he had spoken the parable against them. But they were afraid of
the crowd;[g] so they left him and went away.[h]

12:12
[g]Mk 11:18
[h]Mt 22:22

[a] *25* Some manuscripts *sins.* *26But if you do not forgive, neither will your Father who is in heaven forgive your sins.* [b] *10* Or *cornerstone* [c] *11* Psalm 118:22,23

13 Later they sent some of the Pharisees and Herodians[a] to Jesus
to catch him[b] in his words. 14 They came to him and said, "Teacher,
we know you are a man of integrity. You aren't swayed by men,
because you pay no attention to who they are; but you teach the
way of God in accordance with the truth. Is it right to pay taxes to
Caesar or not? 15 Should we pay or shouldn't we?"
But Jesus knew their hypocrisy. "Why are you trying to trap
me?" he asked. "Bring me a denarius and let me look at it." 16 They
brought the coin, and he asked them, "Whose portrait is this? And
whose inscription?"
"Caesar's," they replied.
17 Then Jesus said to them, "Give to Caesar what is Caesar's and
to God what is God's."[c]
And they were amazed at him.
18 Then the Sadducees,[d] who say there is no resurrection,[e] came
to him with a question. 19 "Teacher," they said, "Moses wrote for us
that if a man's brother dies and leaves a wife but no children, the
man must marry the widow and have children for his brother.[f]
20 Now there were seven brothers. The first one married and died
without leaving any children. 21 The second one married the widow, but he also died, leaving no child. It was the same with the
third. 22 In fact, none of the seven left any children. Last of all, the
woman died too. 23 At the resurrection[a] whose wife will she be,
since the seven were married to her?"
24 Jesus replied, "Are you not in error because you do not know
the Scriptures[g] or the power of God? 25 When the dead rise, they
will neither marry nor be given in marriage; they will be like the
angels in heaven.[h] 26 Now about the dead rising—have you not read
in the book of Moses, in the account of the bush, how God said to
him, 'I am the God of Abraham, the God of Isaac, and the God of
Jacob'[b]?[i] 27 He is not the God of the dead, but of the living. You are
badly mistaken!"
28 One of the teachers of the law[j] came and heard them debating.
Noticing that Jesus had given them a good answer, he asked him,
"Of all the commandments, which is the most important?"
29 "The most important one," answered Jesus, "is this: 'Hear, O
Israel, the Lord our God, the Lord is one.[c] 30 Love the Lord your
God with all your heart and with all your soul and with all your
mind and with all your strength.'[d][k] 31 The second is this: 'Love
your neighbor as yourself.'[e][l] There is no commandment greater
than these."
32 "Well said, teacher," the man replied. "You are right in saying
that God is one and there is no other but him.[m] 33 To love him with

12:13 [a]Mt 22:16; Mk 3:6 [b]Mt 12:10
12:17 [c]Ro 13:7
12:18 [d]Ac 4:1 [e]Ac 23:8; 1Co 15:12
12:19 [f]Dt 25:5
12:24 [g]2Ti 3:15-17
12:25 [h]1Co 15:42, 49,52
12:26 [i]Ex 3:6
12:28 [j]Lk 10:25-28; 20:39
12:30 [k]Dt 6:4,5
12:31 [l]Lev 19:18; Mt 5:43
12:32 [m]Dt 4:35,39; Isa 45:6,14; 46:9

[a] *23* Some manuscripts *resurrection, when men rise from the dead,* [b] *26* Exodus 3:6 [c] *29* Or *the Lord our God is one Lord* [d] *30* Deut. 6:4,5 [e] *31* Lev. 19:18

all your heart, with all your understanding and with all your strength, and to love your neighbor as yourself is more important than all burnt offerings and sacrifices."[a]

34When Jesus saw that he had answered wisely, he said to him, "You are not far from the kingdom of God."[b] And from then on no one dared ask him any more questions.[c]

35While Jesus was teaching in the temple courts,[d] he asked, "How is it that the teachers of the law say that the Christ[a] is the son of David?[e] 36David himself, speaking by the Holy Spirit,[f] declared:

" 'The Lord said to my Lord:
"Sit at my right hand
until I put your enemies
under your feet." '[b][g]

37David himself calls him 'Lord.' How then can he be his son?"

The large crowd[h] listened to him with delight.

38As he taught, Jesus said, "Watch out for the teachers of the law. They like to walk around in flowing robes and be greeted in the marketplaces, 39and have the most important seats in the synagogues and the places of honor at banquets.[i] 40They devour widows' houses and for a show make lengthy prayers. Such men will be punished most severely."

41Jesus sat down opposite the place where the offerings were put[j] and watched the crowd putting their money into the temple treasury. Many rich people threw in large amounts. 42But a poor widow came and put in two very small copper coins,[c] worth only a fraction of a penny.[d]

43Calling his disciples to him, Jesus said, "I tell you the truth, this poor widow has put more into the treasury than all the others. 44They all gave out of their wealth; but she, out of her poverty, put in everything—all she had to live on."[k]

Chapter 13 Theme ____________________

13

As he was leaving the temple, one of his disciples said to him, "Look, Teacher! What massive stones! What magnificent buildings!"

2"Do you see all these great buildings?" replied Jesus. "Not one stone here will be left on another; every one will be thrown down."[l]

3As Jesus was sitting on the Mount of Olives[m] opposite the temple, Peter, James, John[n] and Andrew asked him privately, 4"Tell us, when will these things happen? And what will be the sign that they are all about to be fulfilled?"

INSIGHT

The treasury was in the women's court of the temple, where there were thirteen trumpet-shaped offering receptacles. See the illustration of the floor plan of Herod's Temple on page 1723, and see the illustration of Herod's Temple on page IISB-38.

12:33 [a] 1Sa 15:22; Hos 6:6; Mic 6:6-8; Heb 10:8
12:34 [b] Mt 3:2 [c] Mt 22:46; Lk 20:40
12:35 [d] Mt 26:55 [e] Mt 9:27
12:36 [f] 2Sa 23:2 [g] Ps 110:1; Mt 22:44
12:37 [h] Jn 12:9
12:39 [i] Lk 11:43
12:41 [j] 2Ki 12:9; Jn 8:20
12:44 [k] 2Co 8:12
13:2 [l] Lk 19:44
13:3 [m] Mt 21:1 [n] Mt 4:21

[a] 35 Or *Messiah* [b] 36 Psalm 110:1 [c] 42 Greek *two lepta* [d] 42 Greek *kodrantes*

5 Jesus said to them: “Watch out that no one deceives you.[a]
6 Many will come in my name, claiming, ‘I am he,’ and will deceive
many. 7 When you hear of wars and rumors of wars, do not be
alarmed. Such things must happen, but the end is still to come.
8 Nation will rise against nation, and kingdom against kingdom.
There will be earthquakes in various places, and famines. These
are the beginning of birth pains.

9 “You must be on your guard. You will be handed over to the
local councils and flogged in the synagogues.[b] On account of me
you will stand before governors and kings as witnesses to them.
10 And the gospel must first be preached to all nations. 11 Whenever
you are arrested and brought to trial, do not worry beforehand
about what to say. Just say whatever is given you at the time, for it is
not you speaking, but the Holy Spirit.[c]

12 “Brother will betray brother to death, and a father his child.
Children will rebel against their parents and have them put to
death.[d] 13 All men will hate you because of me,[e] but he who stands
firm to the end will be saved.[f]

14 “When you see ‘the abomination that causes desolation’[a][g]
standing where it[b] does not belong—let the reader understand—
then let those who are in Judea flee to the mountains. 15 Let no one
on the roof of his house go down or enter the house to take anything
out. 16 Let no one in the field go back to get his cloak. 17 How dreadful it will be in those days for pregnant women and nursing mothers![h] 18 Pray that this will not take place in winter, 19 because those
will be days of distress unequaled from the beginning, when God
created the world,[i] until now—and never to be equaled again.[j]
20 If the Lord had not cut short those days, no one would survive.
But for the sake of the elect, whom he has chosen, he has shortened
them. 21 At that time if anyone says to you, ‘Look, here is the
Christ[c]!’ or, ‘Look, there he is!’ do not believe it.[k] 22 For false Christs
and false prophets[l] will appear and perform signs and miracles[m]
to deceive the elect—if that were possible. 23 So be on your guard;[n]
I have told you everything ahead of time.

24 “But in those days, following that distress,

> “ ‘the sun will be darkened,
> and the moon will not give its light;
> 25 the stars will fall from the sky,
> and the heavenly bodies will be shaken.’[d][o]

26 “At that time men will see the Son of Man coming in clouds[p]
with great power and glory. 27 And he will send his angels and gather his elect from the four winds, from the ends of the earth to the
ends of the heavens.[q]

a *14* Daniel 9:27; 11:31; 12:11 b *14* Or *he*; also in verse 29 c *21* Or *Messiah* d *25* Isaiah 13:10; 34:4

13:5 *a* ver 22; Jer 29:8; Eph 5:6; 2Th 2:3,10-12; 1Ti 4:1; 2Ti 3:13; 1Jn 4:6

13:9 *b* Mt 10:17

13:11 *c* Mt 10:19,20; Lk 12:11,12

13:12 *d* Mic 7:6; Mt 10:21; Lk 12:51-53

13:13 *e* Jn 15:21 *f* Mt 10:22

13:14 *g* Da 9:27; 11:31; 12:11

13:17 *h* Lk 23:29

13:19 *i* Mk 10:6 *j* Da 9:26; 12:1; Joel 2:2

13:21 *k* Lk 17:23; 21:8

13:22 *l* Mt 7:15 *m* Jn 4:48; 2Th 2:9,10

13:23 *n* 2Pe 3:17

13:25 *o* Isa 13:10; 34:4; Mt 24:29

13:26 *p* Da 7:13; Mt 16:27; Rev 1:7

13:27 *q* Zec 2:6

28“Now learn this lesson from the fig tree: As soon as its twigs get
tender and its leaves come out, you know that summer is near.
29Even so, when you see these things happening, you know that it
is near, right at the door. 30I tell you the truth, this generation[a][a] will
certainly not pass away until all these things have happened.[b]
31Heaven and earth will pass away, but my words will never pass
away.[c]

32“No one knows about that day or hour, not even the angels in
heaven, nor the Son, but only the Father.[d] 33Be on guard! Be alert[b]![e]
You do not know when that time will come. 34It’s like a man going
away: He leaves his house and puts his servants[f] in charge, each
with his assigned task, and tells the one at the door to keep watch.

35“Therefore keep watch because you do not know when the
owner of the house will come back—whether in the evening, or at
midnight, or when the rooster crows, or at dawn. 36If he comes
suddenly, do not let him find you sleeping. 37What I say to you, I
say to everyone: ‘Watch!’ ”[g]

Chapter 14 Theme ____________________

14 Now the Passover[h] and the Feast of Unleavened Bread were
only two days away, and the chief priests and the teachers
of the law were looking for some sly way to arrest Jesus and kill
him.[i] 2“But not during the Feast,” they said, “or the people may
riot.”

3While he was in Bethany,[j] reclining at the table in the home of a
man known as Simon the Leper, a woman came with an alabaster
jar of very expensive perfume, made of pure nard. She broke the
jar and poured the perfume on his head.[k]

4Some of those present were saying indignantly to one another,
“Why this waste of perfume? 5It could have been sold for more
than a year’s wages[c] and the money given to the poor.” And they
rebuked her harshly.

6“Leave her alone,” said Jesus. “Why are you bothering her?
She has done a beautiful thing to me. 7The poor you will always
have with you, and you can help them any time you want.[l] But
you will not always have me. 8She did what she could. She poured
perfume on my body beforehand to prepare for my burial.[m] 9I tell
you the truth, wherever the gospel is preached throughout the
world,[n] what she has done will also be told, in memory of her.”

10Then Judas Iscariot, one of the Twelve,[o] went to the chief
priests to betray Jesus to them.[p] 11They were delighted to hear this
and promised to give him money. So he watched for an opportunity to hand him over.

13:30 [a]Mk 9:1; [b]Lk 17:25
13:31 [c]Mt 5:18
13:32 [d]Ac 1:7; 1Th 5:1,2
13:33 [e]1Th 5:6
13:34 [f]Mt 25:14
13:37 [g]Lk 12:35-40
14:1 [h]Jn 11:55; 13:1; [i]Mt 12:14
14:3 [j]Mt 21:17; [k]Lk 7:37-39
14:7 [l]Dt 15:11
14:8 [m]Jn 19:40
14:9 [n]Mt 24:14; Mk 16:15
14:10 [o]Mk 3:16-19; [p]Mt 10:4

[a]30 Or *race* [b]33 Some manuscripts *alert and pray* [c]5 Greek *than three hundred denarii*

[12]On the first day of the Feast of Unleavened Bread, when it was
customary to sacrifice the Passover lamb,[a] Jesus' disciples asked
him, "Where do you want us to go and make preparations for you
to eat the Passover?"

[13]So he sent two of his disciples, telling them, "Go into the city,
and a man carrying a jar of water will meet you. Follow him.
[14]Say to the owner of the house he enters, 'The Teacher asks:
Where is my guest room, where I may eat the Passover with my
disciples?' [15]He will show you a large upper room,[b] furnished and
ready. Make preparations for us there."

[16]The disciples left, went into the city and found things just as
Jesus had told them. So they prepared the Passover.

[17]When evening came, Jesus arrived with the Twelve. [18]While
they were reclining at the table eating, he said, "I tell you the truth,
one of you will betray me—one who is eating with me."

[19]They were saddened, and one by one they said to him, "Surely
not I?"

[20]"It is one of the Twelve," he replied, "one who dips bread into
the bowl with me.[c] [21]The Son of Man[d] will go just as it is written
about him. But woe to that man who betrays the Son of Man! It
would be better for him if he had not been born."

[22]While they were eating, Jesus took bread, gave thanks and
broke it,[e] and gave it to his disciples, saying, "Take it; this is my
body."

[23]Then he took the cup, gave thanks and offered it to them, and
they all drank from it.[f]

[24]"This is my blood of the[a] covenant,[g] which is poured out for
many," he said to them. [25]"I tell you the truth, I will not drink
again of the fruit of the vine until that day when I drink it anew in
the kingdom of God."[h]

[26]When they had sung a hymn, they went out to the Mount of
Olives.[i]

[27]"You will all fall away," Jesus told them, "for it is written:

> " 'I will strike the shepherd,
> and the sheep will be scattered.'[b][j]

[28]But after I have risen, I will go ahead of you into Galilee."[k]

[29]Peter declared, "Even if all fall away, I will not."

[30]"I tell you the truth," Jesus answered, "today—yes, tonight—
before the rooster crows twice[c] you yourself will disown me three
times."[l]

[31]But Peter insisted emphatically, "Even if I have to die with
you,[m] I will never disown you." And all the others said the same.

[a]*24* Some manuscripts *the new* [b]*27* Zech. 13:7 [c]*30* Some early manuscripts do not have *twice.*

14:12 [a]Ex 12:1-11; Dt 16:1-4; 1Co 5:7
14:15 [b]Ac 1:13
14:20 [c]Jn 13:18-27
14:21 [d]Mt 8:20
14:22 [e]Mt 14:19
14:23 [f]1Co 10:16
14:24 [g]Mt 26:28
14:25 [h]Mt 3:2
14:26 [i]Mt 21:1
14:27 [j]Zec 13:7
14:28 [k]Mk 16:7
14:30 [l]ver 66-72; Lk 22:34; Jn 13:38
14:31 [m]Lk 22:33; Jn 13:37

32They went to a place called Gethsemane, and Jesus said to his
disciples, "Sit here while I pray." 33He took Peter, James and John[a]
along with him, and he began to be deeply distressed and troubled. 34"My soul is overwhelmed with sorrow to the point of
death,"[b] he said to them. "Stay here and keep watch."

35Going a little farther, he fell to the ground and prayed that if
possible the hour[c] might pass from him. 36"*Abba*,[a] Father,"[d] he
said, "everything is possible for you. Take this cup[e] from me. Yet
not what I will, but what you will."[f]

37Then he returned to his disciples and found them sleeping.
"Simon," he said to Peter, "are you asleep? Could you not keep
watch for one hour? 38Watch and pray so that you will not fall into
temptation.[g] The spirit is willing, but the body is weak."[h]

39Once more he went away and prayed the same thing. 40When
he came back, he again found them sleeping, because their eyes
were heavy. They did not know what to say to him.

41Returning the third time, he said to them, "Are you still sleeping and resting? Enough! The hour[i] has come. Look, the Son of
Man is betrayed into the hands of sinners. 42Rise! Let us go! Here
comes my betrayer!"

43Just as he was speaking, Judas,[j] one of the Twelve, appeared.
With him was a crowd armed with swords and clubs, sent from the
chief priests, the teachers of the law, and the elders.

44Now the betrayer had arranged a signal with them: "The one I
kiss is the man; arrest him and lead him away under guard."
45Going at once to Jesus, Judas said, "Rabbi!"[k] and kissed him.
46The men seized Jesus and arrested him. 47Then one of those
standing near drew his sword and struck the servant of the high
priest, cutting off his ear.

48"Am I leading a rebellion," said Jesus, "that you have come
out with swords and clubs to capture me? 49Every day I was with
you, teaching in the temple courts,[l] and you did not arrest me. But
the Scriptures must be fulfilled."[m] 50Then everyone deserted him
and fled.[n]

51A young man, wearing nothing but a linen garment, was following Jesus. When they seized him, 52he fled naked, leaving his
garment behind.

53They took Jesus to the high priest, and all the chief priests,
elders and teachers of the law came together. 54Peter followed him
at a distance, right into the courtyard of the high priest.[o] There he
sat with the guards and warmed himself at the fire.[p]

55The chief priests and the whole Sanhedrin[q] were looking for
evidence against Jesus so that they could put him to death, but they

14:33 [a]Mt 4:21
14:34 [b]Jn 12:27
14:35 [c]ver 41; Mt 26:18
14:36 [d]Ro 8:15; Gal 4:6 [e]Mt 20:22 [f]Mt 26:39
14:38 [g]Mt 6:13 [h]Ro 7:22,23
14:41 [i]ver 35; Mt 26:18
14:43 [j]Mt 10:4
14:45 [k]Mt 23:7
14:49 [l]Mt 26:55 [m]Isa 53:7-12; Mt 1:22
14:50 [n]ver 27
14:54 [o]Mt 26:3 [p]Jn 18:18
14:55 [q]Mt 5:22

a 36 Aramaic for *Father*

did not find any. 56 Many testified falsely against him, but their
statements did not agree.
57 Then some stood up and gave this false testimony against
him: 58 "We heard him say, 'I will destroy this man-made temple
and in three days will build another,[a] not made by man.'" 59 Yet
even then their testimony did not agree.
60 Then the high priest stood up before them and asked Jesus,
"Are you not going to answer? What is this testimony that these
men are bringing against you?" 61 But Jesus remained silent and
gave no answer.[b]
Again the high priest asked him, "Are you the Christ,[a] the Son
of the Blessed One?"[c]
62 "I am," said Jesus. "And you will see the Son of Man sitting at
the right hand of the Mighty One and coming on the clouds of
heaven."[d]
63 The high priest tore his clothes.[e] "Why do we need any more
witnesses?" he asked. 64 "You have heard the blasphemy. What do
you think?"
They all condemned him as worthy of death.[f] 65 Then some began
to spit at him; they blindfolded him, struck him with their fists,
and said, "Prophesy!" And the guards took him and beat him.[g]
66 While Peter was below in the courtyard,[h] one of the servant
girls of the high priest came by. 67 When she saw Peter warming
himself,[i] she looked closely at him.
"You also were with that Nazarene, Jesus,"[j] she said.
68 But he denied it. "I don't know or understand what you're
talking about,"[k] he said, and went out into the entryway.[b]
69 When the servant girl saw him there, she said again to those
standing around, "This fellow is one of them." 70 Again he
denied it.[l]
After a little while, those standing near said to Peter, "Surely
you are one of them, for you are a Galilean."[m]
71 He began to call down curses on himself, and he swore to
them, "I don't know this man you're talking about."[n]
72 Immediately the rooster crowed the second time.[c] Then Peter
remembered the word Jesus had spoken to him: "Before the rooster
crows twice[d] you will disown me three times."[o] And he broke
down and wept.

Chapter 15 Theme ____________________

15 Very early in the morning, the chief priests, with the elders,
the teachers of the law[p] and the whole Sanhedrin,[q] reached

[a] 61 Or *Messiah* [b] 68 Some early manuscripts *entryway and the rooster crowed* [c] 72 Some early manuscripts do not have *the second time.* [d] 72 Some early manuscripts do not have *twice.*

14:58 [a] Mk 15:29; Jn 2:19
14:61 [b] Isa 53:7; Mt 27:12,14; Mk 15:5; Lk 23:9; Jn 19:9 [c] Mt 16:16; Jn 4:25,26
14:62 [d] Rev 1:7
14:63 [e] Lev 10:6; 21:10; Nu 14:6; Ac 14:14
14:64 [f] Lev 24:16
14:65 [g] Mt 16:21
14:66 [h] ver 54
14:67 [i] ver 54 [j] Mk 1:24
14:68 [k] ver 30,72
14:70 [l] ver 30,68,72 [m] Ac 2:7
14:71 [n] ver 30,72
14:72 [o] ver 30,68
15:1 [p] Mt 27:1; Lk 22:66 [q] Mt 5:22

15:1 *a*Mt 27:2 a decision. They bound Jesus, led him away and handed him over
to Pilate.[a]
2“Are you the king of the Jews?”[b] asked Pilate.
15:2 “Yes, it is as you say,” Jesus replied.
*b*ver 9,12,18,26; 3The chief priests accused him of many things. 4So again Pilate
Mt 2:2 asked him, “Aren’t you going to answer? See how many things
they are accusing you of.”
5But Jesus still made no reply,[c] and Pilate was amazed.
15:5 6Now it was the custom at the
*c*Mk 14:61 Feast to release a prisoner whom the
people requested. 7A man called
15:9 Barabbas was in prison with the
*d*ver 2 insurrectionists who had committed murder in the uprising. 8The
crowd came up and asked Pilate to
15:11 do for them what he usually did.
*e*Ac 3:14 9“Do you want me to release to
you the king of the Jews?”[d] asked
Pilate, 10knowing it was out of envy
15:15 that the chief priests had handed
*f*Isa 53:6 Jesus over to him. 11But the chief
priests stirred up the crowd to have
15:16 Pilate release Barabbas[e] instead.
*g*Jn 18:28,33; 12“What shall I do, then, with the
19:9 one you call the king of the Jews?” Pilate asked them.
13“Crucify him!” they shouted.
14“Why? What crime has he committed?” asked Pilate.
15:18 But they shouted all the louder, “Crucify him!”
*h*ver 2 15Wanting to satisfy the crowd, Pilate released Barabbas to
them. He had Jesus flogged,[f] and handed him over to be crucified.
15:20 16The soldiers led Jesus away into the palace[g] (that is, the Prae-
*i*Heb 13:12 torium) and called together the whole company of soldiers.
17They put a purple robe on him, then twisted together a crown
of thorns and set it on him. 18And they began to call out to him,
15:21 “Hail, king of the Jews!”[h] 19Again and again they struck him on
*j*Mt 27:32 the head with a staff and spit on him. Falling on their knees, they
*k*Ro 16:13 paid homage to him. 20And when they had mocked him, they took
*l*Mt 27:32; off the purple robe and put his own clothes on him. Then they led
Lk 23:26 him out[i] to crucify him.
21A certain man from Cyrene,[j] Simon, the father of Alexander
15:23 and Rufus,[k] was passing by on his way in from the country, and
*m*ver 36; they forced him to carry the cross.[l] 22They brought Jesus to the
Ps 69:21; place called Golgotha (which means The Place of the Skull).
Pr 31:6 23Then they offered him wine mixed with myrrh,[m] but he did not
15:24 take it. 24And they crucified him. Dividing up his clothes, they cast
*n*Ps 22:18 lots[n] to see what each would get.

Jerusalem of the New Testament

INSIGHT

The palace of the Roman governor (the ***Praetorium***) was either a building next to Herod’s palace or the Antonia Fortress beside the temple mount complex. See the map above and the illustration of the temple mount on page IISB-40.

25 It was the third hour when they crucified him. 26 The written
notice of the charge against him read: THE KING OF THE JEWS.[a] 27 They
crucified two robbers with him, one on his right and one on his
left.[a] 29 Those who passed by hurled insults at him, shaking their
heads[b] and saying, "So! You who are going to destroy the temple
and build it in three days,[c] 30 come down from the cross and save
yourself!"
31 In the same way the chief priests and the teachers of the law
mocked him[d] among themselves. "He saved others," they said,
"but he can't save himself! 32 Let this Christ,[b][e] this King of Israel,[f]
come down now from the cross, that we may see and believe."
Those crucified with him also heaped insults on him.
33 At the sixth hour darkness came over the whole land until the
ninth hour.[g] 34 And at the ninth hour Jesus cried out in a loud
voice, *"Eloi, Eloi, lama sabachthani?"*—which means, "My God,
my God, why have you forsaken me?"[c][h]
35 When some of those standing near heard this, they said, "Listen, he's calling Elijah."
36 One man ran, filled a sponge with wine vinegar,[i] put it on a
stick, and offered it to Jesus to drink. "Now leave him alone. Let's
see if Elijah comes to take him down," he said.
37 With a loud cry, Jesus breathed his last.[j]
38 The curtain of the temple was torn in two from top to bottom.[k]
39 And when the centurion,[l] who stood there in front of Jesus,
heard his cry and[d] saw how he died, he said, "Surely this man
was the Son[e] of God!"[m]
40 Some women were watching from a distance.[n] Among them
were Mary Magdalene, Mary the mother of James the younger and
of Joses, and Salome.[o] 41 In Galilee these women had followed him
and cared for his needs. Many other women who had come up
with him to Jerusalem were also there.[p]
42 It was Preparation Day (that is, the day before the Sabbath).[q]
So as evening approached, 43 Joseph of Arimathea, a prominent
member of the Council,[r] who was himself waiting for the kingdom
of God,[s] went boldly to Pilate and asked for Jesus' body. 44 Pilate
was surprised to hear that he was already dead. Summoning the
centurion, he asked him if Jesus had already died. 45 When he
learned from the centurion[t] that it was so, he gave the body to
Joseph. 46 So Joseph bought some linen cloth, took down the body,
wrapped it in the linen, and placed it in a tomb cut out of rock.
Then he rolled a stone against the entrance of the tomb.[u] 47 Mary
Magdalene and Mary the mother of Joses[v] saw where he was laid.

a 27 Some manuscripts *left,* [28] *and the scripture was fulfilled which says, "He was counted with the lawless ones"* (Isaiah 53:12) b 32 Or *Messiah* c 34 Psalm 22:1 d 39 Some manuscripts do not have *heard his cry and.* e 39 Or *a son*

15:26 *a* ver 2
15:29 *b* Ps 22:7; 109:25 *c* Mk 14:58; Jn 2:19
15:31 *d* Ps 22:7
15:32 *e* Mk 14:61 *f* ver 2
15:33 *g* Am 8:9
15:34 *h* Ps 22:1
15:36 *i* ver 23; Ps 69:21
15:37 *j* Jn 19:30
15:38 *k* Heb 10:19,20
15:39 *l* ver 45 *m* Mk 1:1,11; 9:7; Mt 4:3
15:40 *n* Ps 38:11 *o* Mk 16:1; Lk 24:10; Jn 19:25
15:41 *p* Mt 27:55,56; Lk 8:2,3
15:42 *q* Mt 27:62; Jn 19:31
15:43 *r* Mt 5:22 *s* Mt 3:2; Lk 2:25,38
15:45 *t* ver 39
15:46 *u* Mk 16:3
15:47 *v* ver 40

Chapter 16 Theme ______________________________

16 When the Sabbath was over, Mary Magdalene, Mary the
mother of James, and Salome bought spices[a] so that they
might go to anoint Jesus' body. 2Very early on the first day of the
week, just after sunrise, they were on their way to the tomb 3and
they asked each other, "Who will roll the stone away from the
entrance of the tomb?"[b]

4But when they looked up, they saw that the stone, which was
very large, had been rolled away. 5As they entered the tomb, they
saw a young man dressed in a white robe[c] sitting on the right
side, and they were alarmed.

6"Don't be alarmed," he said. "You are looking for Jesus the
Nazarene,[d] who was crucified. He has risen! He is not here. See
the place where they laid him. 7But go, tell his disciples and Peter,
'He is going ahead of you into Galilee. There you will see him,[e]
just as he told you.'"[f]

8Trembling and bewildered, the women went out and fled from
the tomb. They said nothing to anyone, because they were afraid.

[The earliest manuscripts and some
other ancient witnesses do not
have Mark 16:9-20.]

9When Jesus rose early on the first day of the week, he appeared
first to Mary Magdalene,[g] out of whom he had driven seven
demons. 10She went and told those who had been with him and
who were mourning and weeping. 11When they heard that Jesus
was alive and that she had seen him, they did not believe it.[h]

12Afterward Jesus appeared in a different form to two of them
while they were walking in the country.[i] 13These returned and
reported it to the rest; but they did not believe them either.

14Later Jesus appeared to the Eleven as they were eating; he
rebuked them for their lack of faith and their stubborn refusal to
believe those who had seen him after he had risen.[j]

15He said to them, "Go into all the world and preach the good
news to all creation.[k] 16Whoever believes and is baptized will be
saved, but whoever does not believe will be condemned.[l] 17And
these signs will accompany those who believe: In my name they
will drive out demons;[m] they will speak in new tongues;[n] 18they
will pick up snakes[o] with their hands; and when they drink deadly poison, it will not hurt them at all; they will place their hands
on[p] sick people, and they will get well."

19After the Lord Jesus had spoken to them, he was taken up into
heaven[q] and he sat at the right hand of God.[r] 20Then the disciples
went out and preached everywhere, and the Lord worked with
them and confirmed his word by the signs that accompanied it.

16:1 [a]Lk 23:56; Jn 19:39,40
16:3 [b]Mk 15:46
16:5 [c]Jn 20:12
16:6 [d]Mk 1:24
16:7 [e]Jn 21:1-23 [f]Mk 14:28
16:9 [g]Jn 20:11-18
16:11 [h]ver 13,14; Lk 24:11
16:12 [i]Lk 24:13-32
16:14 [j]Lk 24:36-43
16:15 [k]Mt 28:18-20; Lk 24:47,48
16:16 [l]Jn 3:16,18,36; Ac 16:31
16:17 [m]Mk 9:38; Lk 10:17; Ac 5:16; 8:7; 16:18; 19:13-16 [n]Ac 2:4; 10:46; 19:6; 1Co 12:10, 28,30
16:18 [o]Lk 10:19; Ac 28:3-5 [p]Ac 6:6
16:19 [q]Lk 24:50,51; Jn 6:62; Ac 1:9-11 1Ti 3:16 [r]Ps 110:1; Ro 8:34; Col 3:1; Heb 1:3; 12:2

Mark at a Glance

Theme of Mark:

Segment Divisions

		Chapter Themes
		1
		2
		3
		4
		5
		6
		7
		8
		9
		10
		11
		12
		13
		14
		15
		16

Author:

Date:

Purpose:

Key Words:

immediately once, withou delay, quickl as soon as, shortly, just

authority

kingdom of God

mark every reference to Satan or demons

covenant

LUKE

In Matthew we see Jesus as king of the Jews. In Mark we see the servant who came to give his life a ransom for many. Then Luke takes us consecutively through the days of the Son of Man. In this book we see the fulfillment of the things written about him in the law of Moses, the Prophets, and the Psalms, things which no other Gospel tells us.

Things to Do

1. Luke's purpose in writing is stated in Luke 1:1-4. Read it and then record his purpose on the LUKE AT A GLANCE chart on page 1815.

2. As you read chapter by chapter, be sure to do the following:

   a. Mark in the text the key words listed on LUKE AT A GLANCE.

   b. Mark references to time with a symbol of your choice. The references will come in many different forms, from the mention of actual days or years to the naming of a Jewish feast, a chief priest, or a king. This part of your study will keep before you the timing and sequence of the events in Jesus' life. These are critical to Luke's purpose.

   c. It is also important to note where each event takes place. Underline every reference to places, cities, or regions. Locate these on the map on page 1770. Note in the margin *where* something occurs, along with *when* it occurs.

   d. List in the margin the main points covered in each chapter.

      1) As you list each event in the margin of the text, color code or mark it in a distinctive way so it can be recognized as an event. This will help you see at a glance the chronology of events in Luke. You can also consult the chart on page 1816.

      2) As you note each event or teaching, pay attention to the setting and the response of those who are listening or participating in what is happening. In the margin, note their response. Watch where Jesus is, his relationships to people, what social events he is involved in, and what he expects from people.

   e. If Jesus tells a parable or tells of an incident such as the rich man and Lazarus dying (Luke 16), note what provokes Jesus to do so.

   f. Record the theme of each chapter on the line next to the chapter number and on LUKE AT A GLANCE. Do the same for the theme of the book as you complete the chart.

3. Record the facts concerning Jesus' betrayal, arrest, trial, crucifixion, resurrection, postresurrection appearances, and ascension on the appropriate charts: THE ARREST, TRIAL, AND CRUCIFIXION OF JESUS CHRIST on page 1862 and/or THE ACCOUNT OF JESUS' RESURRECTION on page 1863. Note the chapter and verse for each insight. Do this on notebook paper before you write it in your Bible. After you do this for all four Gospels you will have comprehensive notes on what took place at this time in our Lord's life.

4. On pages 1864, 1865 you will find a chart titled WHAT THE GOSPELS TEACH ABOUT THE KINGDOM OF GOD/THE KINGDOM OF HEAVEN. Record on a piece of paper the information you glean from marking every reference to the *kingdom of God* in Luke. Then consolidate your findings and record them on the chart in your Bible. After you study all the Gospels, you will have an overview of what the Gospels teach about the kingdom of God.

Things to Think About

1. Have you been slow of heart to believe all that Moses and the prophets wrote about Jesus Christ? Do you see Jesus as the Son of Man, the fulfillment of prophecy, the Christ, the Son of God? Have you bowed to him as Lord of your life?

2. Jesus reached out to the hurting, the sinners, and the outcasts. He visited in their homes. He was available and accessible. What about you? Do you have compassion on these people? Are you wasting your life on self or are you investing in others? What did you learn from watching Christ's response to others that you can apply to your life?

3. If Jesus needed to withdraw often to a lonely place to pray, what about you? Is prayer a high priority in your life? Do you understand and incorporate the principles of prayer that Jesus taught in the Gospel of Luke?

Chapter 1 Theme ______________________

1 Many have undertaken to draw up an account of the things that
have been fulfilled[a] among us, 2 just as they were handed down
to us by those who from the first[a] were eyewitnesses[b] and servants
of the word.[c] 3 Therefore, since I myself have carefully investigated
everything from the beginning, it seemed good also to me to write
an orderly account[d] for you, most excellent[e] Theophilus,[f] 4 so that
you may know the certainty of the things you have been taught.[g]
5 In the time of Herod king of Judea[h] there was a priest named
Zechariah, who belonged to the priestly division of Abijah;[i] his
wife Elizabeth was also a descendant of Aaron. 6 Both of them were
upright in the sight of God, observing all the Lord's commandments and regulations blamelessly.[j] 7 But they had no children,
because Elizabeth was barren; and they were both well along in
years.
8 Once when Zechariah's division was on duty and he was serving as priest before God,[k] 9 he was chosen by lot, according to the
custom of the priesthood, to go into the temple of the Lord and
burn incense.[l] 10 And when the time for the burning of incense
came, all the assembled worshipers were praying outside.[m]
11 Then an angel[n] of the Lord appeared to him, standing at the
right side of the altar of incense.[o] 12 When Zechariah saw him, he
was startled and was gripped with fear.[p] 13 But the angel said to
him: "Do not be afraid,[q] Zechariah; your prayer has been heard.
Your wife Elizabeth will bear you a son, and you are to give him the
name John.[r] 14 He will be a joy and delight to you, and many will
rejoice because of his birth,[s] 15 for he will be great in the sight of the
Lord. He is never to take wine or other fermented drink,[t] and he
will be filled with the Holy Spirit even from birth.[b][u] 16 Many of the

1:2 [a] Mk 1:1; Jn 15:27; Ac 1:21,22 [b] Heb 2:3; 1Pe 5:1; 2Pe 1:16; 1Jn 1:1 [c] Mk 4:14
1:3 [d] Ac 11:4 [e] Ac 24:3; 26:25 [f] Ac 1:1
1:4 [g] Jn 20:31
1:5 [h] Mt 2:1 [i] 1Ch 24:10
1:6 [j] Ge 7:1; 1Ki 9:4
1:8 [k] 1Ch 24:19; 2Ch 8:14
1:9 [l] Ex 30:7,8; 1Ch 23:13; 2Ch 29:11
1:10 [m] Lev 16:17
1:11 [n] Ac 5:19 [o] Ex 30:1-10
1:12 [p] Jdg 6:22,23; 13:22
1:13 [q] ver 30; Mt 14:27 [r] ver 60,63
1:14 [s] ver 58
1:15 [t] Nu 6:3; Jdg 13:4; Lk 7:33 [u] Jer 1:5; Gal 1:15

a 1 *Or been surely believed* b 15 *Or from his mother's womb*

people of Israel will he bring back to the Lord their God. 17And he
will go on before the Lord,[a] in the spirit and power of Elijah,[b] to
turn the hearts of the fathers to their children[c] and the disobedient
to the wisdom of the righteous—to make ready a people prepared
for the Lord."
18Zechariah asked the angel, "How can I be sure of this? I am an
old man and my wife is well along in years."[d]
19The angel answered, "I am Gabriel.[e] I stand in the presence of
God, and I have been sent to speak to you and to tell you this good
news. 20And now you will be silent and not able to speak[f] until the
day this happens, because you did not believe my words, which
will come true at their proper time."
21Meanwhile, the people were waiting for Zechariah and wondering why he stayed so long in the temple. 22When he came out,
he could not speak to them. They realized he had seen a vision in
the temple, for he kept making signs[g] to them but remained
unable to speak.
23When his time of service was completed, he returned home.
24After this his wife Elizabeth became pregnant and for five
months remained in seclusion. 25"The Lord has done this for me,"
she said. "In these days he has shown his favor and taken away my
disgrace[h] among the people."
26In the sixth month, God sent the angel Gabriel[i] to Nazareth,[j]
a town in Galilee, 27to a virgin pledged to be married to a man
named Joseph,[k] a descendant of David. The virgin's name was
Mary. 28The angel went to her and said, "Greetings, you who are
highly favored! The Lord is with you."
29Mary was greatly troubled at his words and wondered what
kind of greeting this might be. 30But the angel said to her, "Do
not be afraid,[l] Mary, you have found favor with God. 31You will
be with child and give birth to a son, and you are to give him the
name Jesus.[m] 32He will be great and will be called the Son of the
Most High.[n] The Lord God will give him the throne of his father
David, 33and he will reign over the house of Jacob forever; his kingdom[o] will never end."[p]
34"How will this be," Mary asked the angel, "since I am a virgin?"
35The angel answered, "The Holy Spirit will come upon you,[q]
and the power of the Most High[r] will overshadow you. So the holy
one[s] to be born will be called[a] the Son of God.[t] 36Even Elizabeth
your relative is going to have a child in her old age, and she who
was said to be barren is in her sixth month. 37For nothing is impossible with God."[u]
38"I am the Lord's servant," Mary answered. "May it be to me as
you have said." Then the angel left her.

1:17 [a] ver 76 [b] Mt 11:14 [c] Mal 4:5,6
1:18 [d] ver 34; Ge 17:17
1:19 [e] ver 26; Mt 18:10; Da 8:16; 9:21
1:20 [f] Eze 3:26
1:22 [g] ver 62
1:25 [h] Ge 30:23; Isa 4:1
1:26 [i] ver 19 [j] Mt 2:23
1:27 [k] Mt 1:16,18,20; Lk 2:4
1:30 [l] ver 13; Mt 14:27
1:31 [m] Isa 7:14; Mt 1:21,25; Lk 2:21
1:32 [n] ver 35,76; Mk 5:7
1:33 [o] Mt 28:18 [p] Da 2:44; 7:14,27; Mic 4:7; Heb 1:8
1:35 [q] Mt 1:18 [r] ver 32,76 [s] Mk 1:24 [t] Mt 4:3
1:37 [u] Mt 19:26

a 35 Or *So the child to be born will be called holy,*

39At that time Mary got ready and hurried to a town in the hill
country of Judea,[a] 40where she entered Zechariah's home and
greeted Elizabeth. 41When Elizabeth heard Mary's greeting, the
baby leaped in her womb, and Elizabeth was filled with the Holy
Spirit. 42In a loud voice she exclaimed: "Blessed are you among
women,[b] and blessed is the child you will bear! 43But why am I so
favored, that the mother of my Lord should come to me? 44As soon
as the sound of your greeting reached my ears, the baby in my
womb leaped for joy. 45Blessed is she who has believed that what
the Lord has said to her will be accomplished!"
46And Mary said:

"My soul glorifies the Lord[c]
47 and my spirit rejoices in God my Savior,[d]
48for he has been mindful
of the humble state of his servant.[e]
From now on all generations will call me blessed,[f]
49 for the Mighty One has done great things[g] for me—
holy is his name.[h]
50His mercy extends to those who fear him,
from generation to generation.[i]
51He has performed mighty deeds with his arm;[j]
he has scattered those who are proud in their
inmost thoughts.
52He has brought down rulers from their thrones
but has lifted up the humble.
53He has filled the hungry with good things[k]
but has sent the rich away empty.
54He has helped his servant Israel,
remembering to be merciful[l]
55to Abraham and his descendants[m] forever,
even as he said to our fathers."

56Mary stayed with Elizabeth for about three months and then
returned home.
57When it was time for Elizabeth to have her baby, she gave birth
to a son. 58Her neighbors and relatives heard that the Lord had
shown her great mercy, and they shared her joy.
59On the eighth day they came to circumcise[n] the child, and they
were going to name him after his father Zechariah, 60but his
mother spoke up and said, "No! He is to be called John."[o]
61They said to her, "There is no one among your relatives who
has that name."
62Then they made signs[p] to his father, to find out what he would
like to name the child. 63He asked for a writing tablet, and to everyone's astonishment he wrote, "His name is John."[q] 64Immediately

1:39 [a] ver 65
1:42 [b] Jdg 5:24
1:46 [c] Ps 34:2,3
1:47 [d] 1Ti 1:1; 2:3
1:48 [e] Ps 138:6 [f] Lk 11:27
1:49 [g] Ps 71:19 [h] Ps 111:9
1:50 [i] Ex 20:6; Ps 103:17
1:51 [j] Ps 98:1; Isa 40:10
1:53 [k] Ps 107:9
1:54 [l] Ps 98:3
1:55 [m] Ge 17:19; Ps 132:11; Gal 3:16
1:59 [n] Ge 17:12; Lev 12:3; Lk 2:21; Php 3:5
1:60 [o] ver 13,63
1:62 [p] ver 22
1:63 [q] ver 13,60

his mouth was opened and his tongue was loosed, and he began to
speak,[a] praising God. 65The neighbors were all filled with awe, and
throughout the hill country of Judea[b] people were talking about
all these things. 66Everyone who heard this wondered about it,
asking, "What then is this child going to be?" For the Lord's hand
was with him.[c]

67His father Zechariah was filled with the Holy Spirit and prophesied:[d]

68"Praise be to the Lord, the God of Israel,[e]
because he has come and has redeemed his people.[f]
69He has raised up a horn[a][g] of salvation for us
in the house of his servant David[h]
70(as he said through his holy prophets of long ago),[i]
71salvation from our enemies
and from the hand of all who hate us—
72to show mercy to our fathers[j]
and to remember his holy covenant,[k]
73 the oath he swore to our father Abraham:[l]
74to rescue us from the hand of our enemies,
and to enable us to serve him[m] without fear
75 in holiness and righteousness[n] before him all our days.

76And you, my child, will be called a prophet[o] of the
Most High;[p]
for you will go on before the Lord to prepare the way
for him,[q]
77to give his people the knowledge of salvation
through the forgiveness of their sins,[r]
78because of the tender mercy of our God,
by which the rising sun[s] will come to us from heaven
79to shine on those living in darkness
and in the shadow of death,[t]
to guide our feet into the path of peace."

80And the child grew and became strong in spirit;[u] and he lived
in the desert until he appeared publicly to Israel.

Chapter 2 Theme

2 In those days Caesar Augustus[v] issued a decree that a census
should be taken of the entire Roman world.[w] 2(This was the
first census that took place while Quirinius was governor of Syria.)[x]
3And everyone went to his own town to register.
4So Joseph also went up from the town of Nazareth in Galilee to
Judea, to Bethlehem[y] the town of David, because he belonged to

1:64 [a]ver 20
1:65 [b]ver 39
1:66 [c]Ge 39:2; Ac 11:21
1:67 [d]Joel 2:28
1:68 [e]Ps 72:18 [f]Ps 111:9; Lk 7:16
1:69 [g]1Sa 2:1,10; Ps 18:2; 89:17; 132:17; Eze 29:21 [h]Mt 1:1
1:70 [i]Jer 23:5
1:72 [j]Mic 7:20 [k]Ps 105:8,9; 106:45; Eze 16:60
1:73 [l]Ge 22:16-18
1:74 [m]Heb 9:14
1:75 [n]Eph 4:24
1:76 [o]Mt 11:9 [p]ver 32,35 [q]ver 17; Mal 3:1
1:77 [r]Jer 31:34; Mk 1:4
1:78 [s]Mal 4:2
1:79 [t]Isa 9:2; 59:9; Mt 4:16; Ac 26:18
1:80 [u]Lk 2:40,52
2:1 [v]Lk 3:1; Mt 22:17 [w]Mt 24:14
2:2 [x]Mt 4:24
2:4 [y]Jn 7:42

a69 *Horn* here symbolizes strength.

the house and line of David. 5He went there to register with Mary,
who was pledged to be married to him and was expecting a child.
6While they were there, the time came for the baby to be born,
7and she gave birth to her firstborn, a son. She wrapped him in
cloths and placed him in a manger, because there was no room for
them in the inn.

8And there were shepherds living out in the fields nearby, keeping watch over their flocks at night. 9An angel[a] of the Lord appeared
to them, and the glory of the Lord shone around them, and they
were terrified. 10But the angel said to them, "Do not be afraid.[b] I
bring you good news of great joy that will be for all the people.
11Today in the town of David a Savior[c] has been born to you; he is
Christ[a][d] the Lord. 12This will be a sign[e] to you: You will find a
baby wrapped in cloths and lying in a manger."

13Suddenly a great company of the heavenly host appeared with
the angel, praising God and saying,

> 14"Glory to God in the highest,
> and on earth peace[f] to men on whom his favor rests."

15When the angels had left them and gone into heaven, the shepherds said to one another, "Let's go to Bethlehem and see this thing
that has happened, which the Lord has told us about."

16So they hurried off and found Mary and Joseph, and the baby,
who was lying in the manger. 17When they had seen him, they
spread the word concerning what had been told them about this
child, 18and all who heard it were amazed at what the shepherds
said to them. 19But Mary treasured up all these things and pondered them in her heart.[g] 20The shepherds returned, glorifying
and praising God[h] for all the things they had heard and seen,
which were just as they had been told.

21On the eighth day, when it was time to circumcise him,[i] he was
named Jesus, the name the angel had given him before he had
been conceived.[j]

22When the time of their purification according to the Law of
Moses[k] had been completed, Joseph and Mary took him to
Jerusalem to present him to the Lord 23(as it is written in the Law
of the Lord, "Every firstborn male is to be consecrated to the
Lord"[b]),[l] 24and to offer a sacrifice in keeping with what is said in
the Law of the Lord: "a pair of doves or two young pigeons."[c][m]

25Now there was a man in Jerusalem called Simeon, who was
righteous and devout.[n] He was waiting for the consolation of Israel,[o]
and the Holy Spirit was upon him. 26It had been revealed to him
by the Holy Spirit that he would not die before he had seen the

[a] *11* Or *Messiah.* "The Christ" (Greek) and "the Messiah" (Hebrew) both mean "the Anointed One"; also in verse 26. [b] *23* Exodus 13:2,12 [c] *24* Lev. 12:8

2:9 *a* Lk 1:11; Ac 5:19
2:10 *b* Mt 14:27
2:11 *c* Mt 1:21; Jn 4:42; Ac 5:31 *d* Mt 1:16; 16:16,20; Jn 11:27; Ac 2:36
2:12 *e* 1Sa 2:34; 2Ki 19:29; Isa 7:14
2:14 *f* Lk 1:79; Ro 5:1; Eph 2:14,17
2:19 *g* ver 51
2:20 *h* Mt 9:8
2:21 *i* Lk 1:59 *j* Lk 1:31
2:22 *k* Lev 12:2-8
2:23 *l* Ex 13:2,12,15; Nu 3:13
2:24 *m* Lev 12:8
2:25 *n* Lk 1:6 *o* ver 38; Isa 52:9; Lk 23:51

Lord's Christ. 27Moved by the Spirit, he went into the temple
courts. When the parents brought in the child Jesus to do for him
what the custom of the Law required,[a] 28Simeon took him in his
arms and praised God, saying:

> 29"Sovereign Lord, as you have promised,[b]
> you now dismiss[a] your servant in peace.[c]
> 30For my eyes have seen your salvation,[d]
> 31 which you have prepared in the sight of all people,
> 32a light for revelation to the Gentiles
> and for glory to your people Israel."[e]

33The child's father and mother marveled at what was said
about him. 34Then Simeon blessed them and said to Mary, his
mother:[f] "This child is destined to cause the falling[g] and rising of
many in Israel, and to be a sign that will be spoken against, 35so
that the thoughts of many hearts will be revealed. And a sword
will pierce your own soul too."

36There was also a prophetess,[h] Anna, the daughter of Phanuel,
of the tribe of Asher. She was very old; she had lived with her
husband seven years after her marriage, 37and then was a widow
until she was eighty-four.[b][i] She never left the temple but worshiped night and day, fasting and praying.[j] 38Coming up to them
at that very moment, she gave thanks to God and spoke about the
child to all who were looking forward to the redemption of
Jerusalem.[k]

39When Joseph and Mary had done everything required by the
Law of the Lord, they returned to Galilee to their own town of
Nazareth.[l] 40And the child grew and became strong; he was filled
with wisdom, and the grace of God was upon him.[m]

41Every year his parents went to Jerusalem for the Feast of the
Passover.[n] 42When he was twelve years old, they went up to the
Feast, according to the custom. 43After the Feast was over, while
his parents were returning home, the boy Jesus stayed behind in
Jerusalem, but they were unaware of it. 44Thinking he was in their
company, they traveled on for a day. Then they began looking for
him among their relatives and friends. 45When they did not find
him, they went back to Jerusalem to look for him. 46After three
days they found him in the temple courts, sitting among the
teachers, listening to them and asking them questions. 47Everyone
who heard him was amazed[o] at his understanding and his answers.
48When his parents saw him, they were astonished. His mother[p]
said to him, "Son, why have you treated us like this? Your father[q]
and I have been anxiously searching for you."

2:27 [a] ver 22
2:29 [b] ver 26 [c] Ac 2:24
2:30 [d] Isa 52:10; Lk 3:6
2:32 [e] Isa 42:6; 49:6; Ac 13:47; 26:23
2:34 [f] Mt 12:46 [g] Isa 8:14; Mt 21:44; 1Co 1:23; 2Co 2:16; 1Pe 2:7,8
2:36 [h] Ac 21:9
2:37 [i] 1Ti 5:9 [j] Ac 13:3; 14:23; 1Ti 5:5
2:38 [k] ver 25; Isa 40:2; Lk 1:68; 24:21
2:39 [l] ver 51; Mt 2:23
2:40 [m] ver 52; Lk 1:80
2:41 [n] Ex 23:15; Dt 16:1-8
2:47 [o] Mt 7:28
2:48 [p] Mt 12:46 [q] Lk 3:23; 4:22

[a] 29 Or *promised, / now dismiss* [b] 37 Or *widow for eighty-four years*

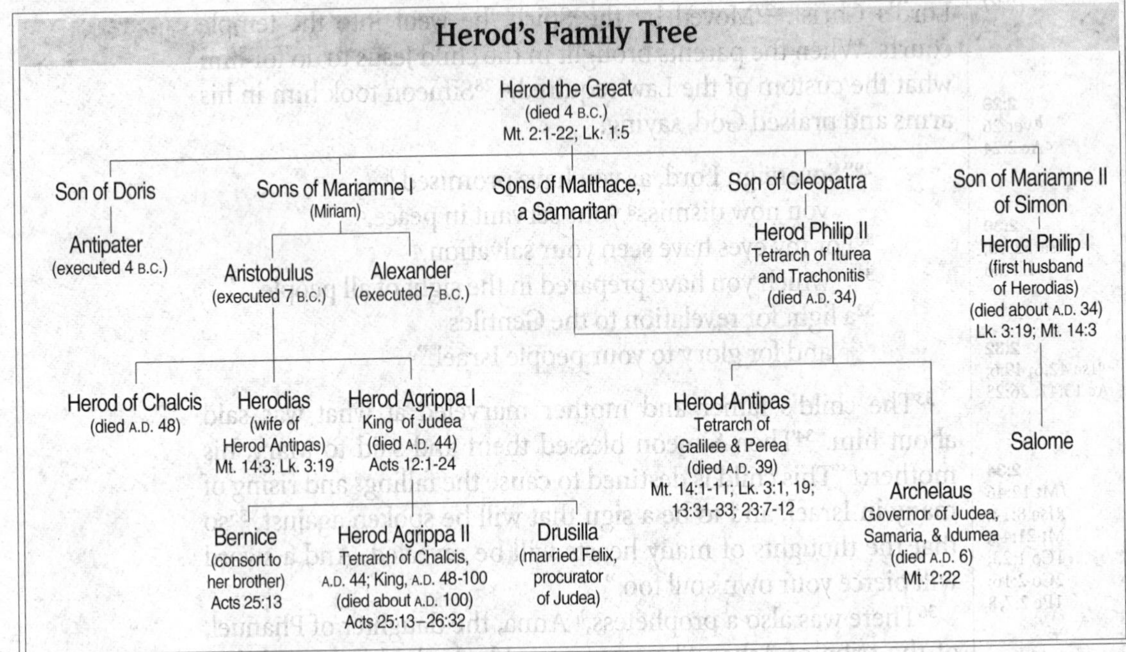

49"Why were you searching for me?" he asked. "Didn't you know I
had to be in my Father's house?"[a] 50But they did not understand
what he was saying to them.[b]
51Then he went down to Nazareth with them[c] and was obedient to
them. But his mother treasured all these things in her heart.[d] 52And
Jesus grew in wisdom and stature, and in favor with God and men.[e]

Chapter 3 Theme ____________________________________

3 In the fifteenth year of the reign of Tiberius Caesar—when
Pontius Pilate[f] was governor of Judea, Herod[g] tetrarch of
Galilee, his brother Philip tetrarch of Iturea and Traconitis, and
Lysanias tetrarch of Abilene—2during the high priesthood of Annas
and Caiaphas,[h] the word of God came to John[i] son of Zechariah[j] in
the desert. 3He went into all the country around the Jordan, preaching a baptism of repentance for the forgiveness of sins.[k] 4As is written in the book of the words of Isaiah the prophet:

"A voice of one calling in the desert,
'Prepare the way for the Lord,
make straight paths for him.
5Every valley shall be filled in,
every mountain and hill made low.
The crooked roads shall become straight,
the rough ways smooth.
6And all mankind will see God's salvation.'"[a][l]

[a]6 Isaiah 40:3-5

2:49
[a]Jn 2:16

2:50
[b]Mk 9:32

2:51
[c]ver 39; Mt 2:23
[d]ver 19

2:52
[e]ver 40;
1Sa 2:26;
Lk 1:80

3:1
[f]Mt 27:2
[g]Mt 14:1

3:2
[h]Mt 26:3;
Jn 18:13;
Ac 4:6
[i]Mt 3:1
[j]Lk 1:13

3:3
[k]ver 16;
Mk 1:4

3:6
[l]Isa 40:3-5;
Ps 98:2;
Isa 42:16; 52:10;
Lk 2:30

7 John said to the crowds coming out to be baptized by him,
"You brood of vipers![a] Who warned you to flee from the coming
wrath?[b] 8 Produce fruit in keeping with repentance. And do not
begin to say to yourselves, 'We have Abraham as our father.'[c] For
I tell you that out of these stones God can raise up children for
Abraham. 9 The ax is already at the root of the trees, and every tree
that does not produce good fruit will be cut down and thrown
into the fire."[d]
10 "What should we do then?"[e] the crowd asked.
11 John answered, "The man with two tunics should share with
him who has none, and the one who has food should do the
same."[f]
12 Tax collectors also came to be baptized.[g] "Teacher," they
asked, "what should we do?"
13 "Don't collect any more than you are required to,"[h] he told
them.
14 Then some soldiers asked him, "And what should we do?"
He replied, "Don't extort money and don't accuse people
falsely[i]—be content with your pay."
15 The people were waiting expectantly and were all wondering in their hearts if John[j]
might possibly be the
Christ.[a][k] 16 John answered
them all, "I baptize you
with[b] water.[l] But one more
powerful than I will come,
the thongs of whose san-
dals I am not worthy to
untie. He will baptize you
with the Holy Spirit and
with fire.[m] 17 His winnowing
fork[n] is in his hand to clear
his threshing floor and to
gather the wheat into his
barn, but he will burn up
the chaff with unquenchable
fire."[o] 18 And with many other words John exhorted the
people and preached the
good news to them.
19 But when John rebuked Herod[p] the tetrarch because of Herodias, his brother's wife, and all the other evil things he had done,
20 Herod added this to them all: He locked John up in prison.[q]

The Region of the Tetrarchs

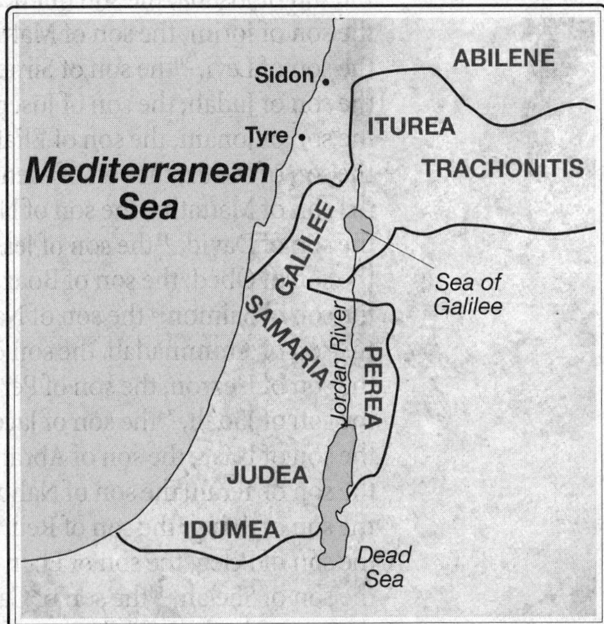

3:7 [a]Mt 12:34; 23:33 [b]Ro 1:18
3:8 [c]Isa 51:2; Lk 19:9; Jn 8:33,39; Ac 13:26; Ro 4:1,11,12,16, 17; Gal 3:7
3:9 [d]Mt 3:10
3:10 [e]ver 12,14; Ac 2:37; 16:30
3:11 [f]Isa 58:7
3:12 [g]Lk 7:29
3:13 [h]Lk 19:8
3:14 [i]Ex 23:1; Lev 19:11
3:15 [j]Mt 3:1 [k]Jn 1:19,20; Ac 13:25
3:16 [l]ver 3; Mk 1:4 [m]Jn 1:26,33; Ac 1:5; 11:16; 19:4
3:17 [n]Isa 30:24 [o]Mt 13:30; 25:41
3:19 [p]ver 1
3:20 [q]Mt 14:3,4; Mk 6:17-18

[a] 15 Or *Messiah* [b] 16 Or *in*

21When all the people were being baptized, Jesus was baptized
too. And as he was praying,[a] heaven was opened 22and the Holy
Spirit descended on him[b] in bodily form like a dove. And a voice
came from heaven: "You are my Son,[c] whom I love; with you I am
well pleased."[d]
23Now Jesus himself was about thirty years old when he began
his ministry.[e] He was the son, so it was thought, of Joseph,[f]

INSIGHT

See **The Genealogy of Jesus the Christ** on page 1665.

the son of Heli, 24the son of Matthat,
the son of Levi, the son of Melki,
the son of Jannai, the son of Joseph,
25the son of Mattathias, the son of Amos,
the son of Nahum, the son of Esli,
the son of Naggai, 26the son of Maath,
the son of Mattathias, the son of Semein,
the son of Josech, the son of Joda,
27the son of Joanan, the son of Rhesa,
the son of Zerubbabel,[g] the son of Shealtiel,
the son of Neri, 28the son of Melki,
the son of Addi, the son of Cosam,
the son of Elmadam, the son of Er,
29the son of Joshua, the son of Eliezer,
the son of Jorim, the son of Matthat,
the son of Levi, 30the son of Simeon,
the son of Judah, the son of Joseph,
the son of Jonam, the son of Eliakim,
31the son of Melea, the son of Menna,
the son of Mattatha, the son of Nathan,[h]
the son of David, 32the son of Jesse,
the son of Obed, the son of Boaz,
the son of Salmon,[a] the son of Nahshon,
33the son of Amminadab, the son of Ram,[b]
the son of Hezron, the son of Perez,[i]
the son of Judah, 34the son of Jacob,
the son of Isaac, the son of Abraham,
the son of Terah, the son of Nahor,[j]
35the son of Serug, the son of Reu,
the son of Peleg, the son of Eber,
the son of Shelah, 36the son of Cainan,
the son of Arphaxad,[k] the son of Shem,
the son of Noah, the son of Lamech,[l]
37the son of Methuselah, the son of Enoch,
the son of Jared, the son of Mahalalel,

[a] 32 Some early manuscripts *Sala* [b] 33 Some manuscripts *Amminadab, the son of Admin, the son of Arni*; other manuscripts vary widely.

3:21
[a] Mt 14:23; Mk 1:35; 6:46; Lk 5:16; 6:12; 9:18,28; 11:1

3:22
[b] Isa 42:1; Jn 1:32,33; Ac 10:38
[c] Mt 3:17
[d] Mt 3:17

3:23
[e] Mt 4:17; Ac 1:1
[f] Lk 1:27

3:27
[g] Mt 1:12

3:31
[h] 2Sa 5:14; 1Ch 3:5

3:33
[i] Ru 4:18-22; 1Ch 2:10-12

3:34
[j] Ge 11:24,26

3:36
[k] Ge 11:12
[l] Ge 5:28-32

3:38 [a]Ge 5:1,2,6-9 the son of Kenan, 38the son of Enosh,
the son of Seth, the son of Adam,
the son of God.[a]

4:1 [b]ver 14,18 [c]Lk 3:3,21 [d]Lk 2:27

Chapter 4 Theme ____________________

4 Jesus, full of the Holy Spirit,[b] returned from the Jordan[c] and
was led by the Spirit[d] in the desert, 2where for forty days[e] he
4:2 [e]Ex 34:28; 1Ki 19:8 was tempted by the devil. He ate nothing during those days, and
at the end of them he was hungry.
3The devil said to him, "If you are the Son of God, tell this stone
to become bread."
4:4 [f]Dt 8:3 4Jesus answered, "It is written: 'Man does not live on bread
alone.'[a]"[f]
4:5 [g]Mt 24:14 5The devil led him up to a high place and showed him in an
instant all the kingdoms of the world.[g] 6And he said to him, "I will
give you all their authority and splendor, for it has been given to
4:6 [h]Jn 12:31; 14:30; 1Jn 5:19 me,[h] and I can give it to anyone I want to. 7So if you worship me, it
will all be yours."
8Jesus answered, "It is written: 'Worship the Lord your God and
serve him only.'[b]"[i]
4:8 [i]Dt 6:13 9The devil led him to Jerusalem and had him stand on the highest
point of the temple. "If you are the Son of God," he said, "throw
yourself down from here. 10For it is written:

4:11 [j]Ps 91:11,12 " 'He will command his angels concerning you
to guard you carefully;
11they will lift you up in their hands,
4:12 [k]Dt 6:16 so that you will not strike your foot against a stone.'[c]"[j]

12Jesus answered, "It says: 'Do not put the Lord your God to the
4:13 [l]Heb 4:15 [m]Jn 14:30 test.'[d]"[k]
13When the devil had finished all this tempting,[l] he left him[m]
until an opportune time.
14Jesus returned to Galilee[n] in the power of the Spirit, and news
4:14 [n]Mt 4:12 [o]Mt 9:26 about him spread through the whole countryside.[o] 15He taught in
their synagogues,[p] and everyone praised him.
16He went to Nazareth,[q] where he had been brought up, and on
4:15 [p]Mt 4:23 the Sabbath day he went into the synagogue,[r] as was his custom.
And he stood up to read. 17The scroll of the prophet Isaiah was
handed to him. Unrolling it, he found the place where it is written:

4:16 [q]Mt 2:23 [r]Mt 13:54 18"The Spirit of the Lord is on me,[s]
because he has anointed me
to preach good news to the poor.

4:18 [s]Jn 3:34 [a]4 Deut. 8:3 [b]8 Deut. 6:13 [c]11 Psalm 91:11,12 [d]12 Deut. 6:16

He has sent me to proclaim freedom for the prisoners
and recovery of sight for the blind,
to release the oppressed,
19 to proclaim the year of the Lord's favor."[a] [a]

20 Then he rolled up the scroll, gave it back to the attendant and
sat down.[b] The eyes of everyone in the synagogue were fastened
on him, 21 and he began by saying to them, "Today this scripture is
fulfilled in your hearing."
22 All spoke well of him and were amazed at the gracious words
that came from his lips. "Isn't this Joseph's son?" they asked.[c]
23 Jesus said to them, "Surely you will quote this proverb to me:
'Physician, heal yourself! Do here in your hometown[d] what we
have heard that you did in Capernaum.' "[e]
24 "I tell you the truth," he continued, "no prophet is accepted
in his hometown.[f] 25 I assure you that there were many widows in
Israel in Elijah's time, when the sky was shut for three and a half
years and there was a severe famine throughout the land.[g] 26 Yet
Elijah was not sent to any of them, but to a widow in Zarephath
in the region of Sidon.[h] 27 And there were many in Israel with leprosy[b] in the time of Elisha the prophet, yet not one of them was
cleansed—only Naaman the Syrian."[i]
28 All the people in the synagogue were furious when they heard
this. 29 They got up, drove him out of the town,[j] and took him to
the brow of the hill on which the town was built, in order to throw
him down the cliff. 30 But he walked right through
the crowd and went on his way.[k]
31 Then he went down to Capernaum,[l] a town in
Galilee, and on the Sabbath began to teach the people. 32 They were amazed at his teaching,[m] because
his message had authority.[n]
33 In the synagogue there was a man possessed by
a demon, an evil[c] spirit. He cried out at the top of his
voice, 34 "Ha! What do you want with us,[o] Jesus of
Nazareth?[p] Have you come to destroy us? I know
who you are[q]—the Holy One of God!"[r]
35 "Be quiet!" Jesus said sternly.[s] "Come out of
him!" Then the demon threw the man down before
them all and came out without injuring him.
36 All the people were amazed[t] and said to each
other, "What is this teaching? With authority[u] and power he gives
orders to evil spirits and they come out!" 37 And the news about
him spread throughout the surrounding area.[v]

Israel in the Time of Christ

Sidon
SYRIA
Tyre
Caesarea Philippi
Mediterranean (Great) Sea
PHOENICIA
Capernaum
Chorazin
Bethsaida
Magdala
Cana
Tiberias
Sea of Galilee
Mt. Carmel
GALILEE
Nazareth
Nain
Jordan River
DECAPOLIS
Caesarea
SAMARIA
(SEBASTE)
Samaria
Mt. Ebal
Sychar
Joppa
Mt. Gerizim
PEREA
JUDEA
Jericho
Bethany beyond Jordan
Emmaus
Mt. of Olives
Jerusalem
Bethlehem
Bethany
Dead (Salt) Sea

[a] *19* Isaiah 61:1,2 [b] *27* The Greek word was used for various diseases affecting the skin—not necessarily leprosy. [c] *33* Greek *unclean*; also in verse 36

4:19 [a] Isa 61:1,2; Lev 25:10
4:20 [b] ver 17; Mt 26:55
4:22 [c] Mt 13:54,55; Jn 6:42; 7:15
4:23 [d] ver 16 [e] Mk 1:21-28; 2:1-12
4:24 [f] Mt 13:57; Jn 4:44
4:25 [g] 1Ki 17:1; 18:1; Jas 5:17,18
4:26 [h] 1Ki 17:8-16; Mt 11:21
4:27 [i] 2Ki 5:1-14
4:29 [j] Nu 15:35; Ac 7:58; Heb 13:12
4:30 [k] Jn 8:59; 10:39
4:31 [l] ver 23; Mt 4:13
4:32 [m] Mt 7:28 [n] ver 36; Mt 7:29
4:34 [o] Mt 8:29 [p] Mk 1:24 [q] Jas 2:19 [r] ver 41; Mk 1:24
4:35 [s] ver 39,41; Mt 8:26; Lk 8:24
4:36 [t] Mt 7:28 [u] ver 32; Mt 7:29; Mt 10:1
4:37 [v] ver 14; Mt 9:26

4:39 [a]ver 35,41 38 Jesus left the synagogue and went to the home of Simon. Now
Simon's mother-in-law was suffering from a high fever, and they
asked Jesus to help her. 39 So he bent over her and rebuked[a] the
4:40 [b]Mk 5:23 fever, and it left her. She got up at once and began to wait on them.
[c]Mt 4:23 40 When the sun was setting, the people brought to Jesus all who
had various kinds of sickness, and laying his hands on each one,[b]
4:41 he healed them.[c] 41 Moreover, demons came out of many people,
[d]Mt 4:3 shouting, "You are the Son of God!"[d] But he rebuked[e] them and
[e]ver 35 [f]Mt 8:4 would not allow them to speak,[f] because they knew he was the
Christ.[a]
42 At daybreak Jesus went out to a solitary place. The people were
4:43 [g]Mt 3:2 looking for him and when they came to where he was, they tried
to keep him from leaving them. 43 But he said, "I must preach the
good news of the kingdom of God[g] to the other towns also,
4:44 [h]Mt 4:23 because that is why I was sent." 44 And he kept on preaching in the
synagogues of Judea.[b][h]

5:1 [i]Mk 4:14; Heb 4:12 *Chapter 5 Theme* __________________________

5 One day as Jesus was standing by the Lake of Gennesaret,[c] with
the people crowding around him and listening to the word of
5:3 [j]Mt 13:2 God,[i] 2 he saw at the water's edge two boats, left there by the fishermen, who were washing their nets. 3 He got into one of the boats,
the one belonging to Simon, and asked him to put out a little from
5:4 [k]Jn 21:6 shore. Then he sat down and taught the people from the boat.[j]
4 When he had finished speaking, he said to Simon, "Put out
into deep water, and let down[d] the nets for a catch."[k]
5:5 [l]Lk 8:24,45; 9:33,49; 17:13 5 Simon answered, "Master,[l] we've worked hard all night and
[m]Jn 21:3 haven't caught anything.[m] But because you say so, I will let down
the nets."
6 When they had done so, they caught such a large number of fish
5:6 [n]Jn 21:11 that their nets began to break.[n] 7 So they signaled their partners in
the other boat to come and help them, and they came and filled
both boats so full that they began to sink.
5:8 [o]Ge 18:27; Job 42:6; Isa 6:5 8 When Simon Peter saw this, he fell at Jesus' knees and said, "Go
away from me, Lord; I am a sinful man!"[o] 9 For he and all his com-
panions were astonished at the catch of fish they had taken, 10 and
so were James and John, the sons of Zebedee, Simon's partners.
5:10 [p]Mt 14:27 Then Jesus said to Simon, "Don't be afraid;[p] from now on you
will catch men." 11 So they pulled their boats up on shore, left
everything and followed him.[q]
5:11 [q]ver 28; Mt 4:19 12 While Jesus was in one of the towns, a man came along who
was covered with leprosy.[e][r] When he saw Jesus, he fell with his face

[a]41 Or *Messiah* [b]44 Or *the land of the Jews*; some manuscripts *Galilee* [c]1 That is, Sea of Galilee [d]4 The Greek verb is plural. [e]12 The Greek word was used for various diseases affecting the skin—not necessarily leprosy.

5:12 [r]Mt 8:2

to the ground and begged him, “Lord, if you are willing, you can
make me clean.”
13 Jesus reached out his hand and touched the man. “I am willing,” he said. “Be clean!” And immediately the leprosy left him.
14 Then Jesus ordered him, “Don’t tell anyone,[a] but go, show yourself to the priest and offer the sacrifices that Moses commanded[b]
for your cleansing, as a testimony to them.”
15 Yet the news about him spread all the more,[c] so that crowds of
people came to hear him and to be healed of their sicknesses. 16 But
Jesus often withdrew to lonely places and prayed.[d]
17 One day as he was teaching, Pharisees and teachers of the
law,[e] who had come from every village of Galilee and from Judea
and Jerusalem, were sitting there. And the power of the Lord was
present for him to heal the sick.[f] 18 Some men came carrying a
paralytic on a mat and tried to take him into the house to lay him
before Jesus. 19 When they could not find a way to do this because
of the crowd, they went up on the roof and lowered him on his
mat through the tiles into the middle of the crowd, right in front
of Jesus.
20 When Jesus saw their faith, he said, “Friend, your sins are forgiven.”[g]
21 The Pharisees and the teachers of the law began thinking to
themselves, “Who is this fellow who speaks blasphemy? Who can
forgive sins but God alone?”[h]
22 Jesus knew what they were thinking and asked, “Why are you
thinking these things in your hearts? 23 Which is easier: to say,
‘Your sins are forgiven,’ or to say, ‘Get up and walk’? 24 But that you
may know that the Son of Man[i] has authority on earth to forgive
sins. . . .” He said to the paralyzed man, “I tell you, get up, take
your mat and go home.” 25 Immediately he stood up in front of
them, took what he had been lying on and went home praising
God. 26 Everyone was amazed and gave praise to God.[j] They were
filled with awe and said, “We have seen remarkable things today.”
27 After this, Jesus went out and saw a tax collector by the name
of Levi sitting at his tax booth. “Follow me,”[k] Jesus said to him,
28 and Levi got up, left everything and followed him.[l]
29 Then Levi held a great banquet for Jesus at his house, and a
large crowd of tax collectors[m] and others were eating with them.
30 But the Pharisees and the teachers of the law who belonged to
their sect[n] complained to his disciples, “Why do you eat and drink
with tax collectors and ‘sinners’?”[o]
31 Jesus answered them, “It is not the healthy who need a doctor,
but the sick. 32 I have not come to call the righteous, but sinners to
repentance.”[p]

5:14 [a]Mt 8:4 [b]Lev 14:2-32
5:15 [c]Mt 9:26
5:16 [d]Mt 14:23; Lk 3:21
5:17 [e]Mt 15:1; Lk 2:46 [f]Mk 5:30; Lk 6:19
5:20 [g]Lk 7:48,49
5:21 [h]Isa 43:25
5:24 [i]Mt 8:20
5:26 [j]Mt 9:8
5:27 [k]Mt 4:19
5:28 [l]ver 11; Mt 4:19
5:29 [m]Lk 15:1
5:30 [n]Ac 23:9 [o]Mt 9:11
5:32 [p]Jn 3:17

33They said to him, "John's disciples[a] often fast and pray, and
so do the disciples of the Pharisees, but yours go on eating and
drinking."
34Jesus answered, "Can you make the guests of the bridegroom[b]
fast while he is with them? 35But the time will come when the
bridegroom will be taken from them;[c] in those days they will fast."
36He told them this parable: "No one tears a patch from a new
garment and sews it on an old one. If he does, he will have torn the
new garment, and the patch from the new will not match the old.
37And no one pours new wine into old wineskins. If he does, the
new wine will burst the skins, the wine will run out and the wineskins will be ruined. 38No, new wine must be poured into new
wineskins. 39And no one after drinking old wine wants the new,
for he says, 'The old is better.' "

Chapter 6 Theme ____________________

6 One Sabbath Jesus was going through the grainfields, and
his disciples began to pick some heads of grain, rub them in
their hands and eat the kernels.[d] 2Some of the Pharisees asked,
"Why are you doing what is unlawful on the Sabbath?"[e]
3Jesus answered them, "Have you never read what David did
when he and his companions were hungry?[f] 4He entered the
house of God, and taking the consecrated bread, he ate what is
lawful only for priests to eat.[g] And he also gave some to his companions." 5Then Jesus said to them, "The Son of Man[h] is Lord of
the Sabbath."
6On another Sabbath[i] he went into the synagogue and was
teaching, and a man was there whose right hand was shriveled.
7The Pharisees and the teachers of the law were looking for a reason to accuse Jesus, so they watched him closely[j] to see if he would
heal on the Sabbath.[k] 8But Jesus knew what they were thinking[l]
and said to the man with the shriveled hand, "Get up and stand
in front of everyone." So he got up and stood there.
9Then Jesus said to them, "I ask you, which is lawful on the Sabbath: to do good or to do evil, to save life or to destroy it?"
10He looked around at them all, and then said to the man,
"Stretch out your hand." He did so, and his hand was completely
restored. 11But they were furious[m] and began to discuss with one
another what they might do to Jesus.
12One of those days Jesus went out to a mountainside to pray,
and spent the night praying to God.[n] 13When morning came, he
called his disciples to him and chose twelve of them, whom he also
designated apostles:[o] 14Simon (whom he named Peter), his brother
Andrew, James, John, Philip, Bartholomew, 15Matthew,[p] Thomas,

5:33 [a]Lk 7:18; Jn 1:35; 3:25,26
5:34 [b]Jn 3:29
5:35 [c]Lk 9:22; 17:22; Jn 16:5-7
6:1 [d]Dt 23:25
6:2 [e]Mt 12:2
6:3 [f]1Sa 21:6
6:4 [g]Lev 24:5,9
6:5 [h]Mt 8:20
6:6 [i]ver 1
6:7 [j]Mt 12:10 [k]Mt 12:2
6:8 [l]Mt 9:4
6:11 [m]Jn 5:18
6:12 [n]Lk 3:21
6:13 [o]Mk 6:30
6:15 [p]Mt 9:9

James son of Alphaeus, Simon who was called the Zealot, 16Judas
son of James, and Judas Iscariot, who became a traitor.
17He went down with them and stood on a level place. A large
crowd of his disciples was there and a great number of people from
all over Judea, from Jerusalem, and from the coast of Tyre and
Sidon,[a] 18who had come to hear him and to be healed of their
diseases. Those troubled by evil[a] spirits were cured, 19and the people all tried to touch him,[b] because power was coming from him
and healing them all.[c]
20Looking at his disciples, he said:

"Blessed are you who are poor,
for yours is the kingdom of God.[d]
21Blessed are you who hunger now,
for you will be satisfied.[e]
Blessed are you who weep now,
for you will laugh.[f]
22Blessed are you when men hate you,
when they exclude you[g] and insult you[h]
and reject your name as evil,
because of the Son of Man.[i]

23"Rejoice in that day and leap for joy,[j] because great is your
reward in heaven. For that is how their fathers treated the prophets.[k]

24"But woe to you who are rich,[l]
for you have already received your comfort.[m]
25Woe to you who are well fed now,
for you will go hungry.[n]
Woe to you who laugh now,
for you will mourn and weep.[o]
26Woe to you when all men speak well of you,
for that is how their fathers treated the false prophets.[p]

27"But I tell you who hear me: Love your enemies, do good to
those who hate you,[q] 28bless those who curse you, pray for those
who mistreat you.[r] 29If someone strikes you on one cheek, turn to
him the other also. If someone takes your cloak, do not stop him
from taking your tunic. 30Give to everyone who asks you, and if
anyone takes what belongs to you, do not demand it back.[s] 31Do
to others as you would have them do to you.[t]
32"If you love those who love you, what credit is that to you?[u]
Even 'sinners' love those who love them. 33And if you do good to
those who are good to you, what credit is that to you? Even 'sinners' do that. 34And if you lend to those from whom you expect
repayment, what credit is that to you?[v] Even 'sinners' lend to 'sinners,' expecting to be repaid in full. 35But love your enemies, do

a 18 Greek *unclean*

6:17 [a]Mt 4:25; Mt 11:21; Mk 3:7,8
6:19 [b]Mt 9:20 [c]Mt 14:36; Mk 5:30; Lk 5:17
6:20 [d]Mt 25:34
6:21 [e]Isa 55:1,2; Mt 5:6 [f]Isa 61:2,3; Mt 5:4; Rev 7:17
6:22 [g]Jn 9:22; 16:2 [h]Isa 51:7 [i]Jn 15:21
6:23 [j]Mt 5:12 [k]Mt 5:12
6:24 [l]Jas 5:1 [m]Lk 16:25
6:25 [n]Isa 65:13 [o]Pr 14:13
6:26 [p]Mt 7:15
6:27 [q]ver 35; Mt 5:44; Ro 12:20
6:28 [r]Mt 5:44
6:30 [s]Dt 15:7,8,10; Pr 21:26
6:31 [t]Mt 7:12
6:32 [u]Mt 5:46
6:34 [v]Mt 5:42

good to them,[a] and lend to them without expecting to get anything
back. Then your reward will be great, and you will be sons[b] of the
Most High,[c] because he is kind to the ungrateful and wicked. 36Be
merciful,[d] just as your Father[e] is merciful.
37"Do not judge, and you will not be judged.[f] Do not condemn,
and you will not be condemned. Forgive, and you will be forgiven.[g]
38Give, and it will be given to you. A good measure, pressed down,
shaken together and running over, will be poured into your lap.[h]
For with the measure you use, it will be measured to you."[i]
39He also told them this parable: "Can a blind man lead a blind
man? Will they not both fall into a pit?[j] 40A student is not above his
teacher, but everyone who is fully trained will be like his teacher.[k]
41"Why do you look at the speck of sawdust in your brother's eye
and pay no attention to the plank in your own eye? 42How can you
say to your brother, 'Brother, let me take the speck out of your eye,'
when you yourself fail to see the plank in your own eye? You hypocrite, first take the plank out of your eye, and then you will see
clearly to remove the speck from your brother's eye.
43"No good tree bears bad fruit, nor does a bad tree bear good
fruit. 44Each tree is recognized by its own fruit.[l] People do not pick
figs from thornbushes, or grapes from briers. 45The good man
brings good things out of the good stored up in his heart, and the
evil man brings evil things out of the evil stored up in his heart.
For out of the overflow of his heart his mouth speaks.[m]
46"Why do you call me, 'Lord, Lord,'[n] and do not do what I say?[o]
47I will show you what he is like who comes to me and hears my
words and puts them into practice.[p] 48He is like a man building a
house, who dug down deep and laid the foundation on rock. When
a flood came, the torrent struck that house but could not shake it,
because it was well built. 49But the one who hears my words and
does not put them into practice is like a man who built a house
on the ground without a foundation. The moment the torrent
struck that house, it collapsed and its destruction was complete."

Chapter 7 Theme ________________

7 When Jesus had finished saying all this[q] in the hearing of the
people, he entered Capernaum. 2There a centurion's servant,
whom his master valued highly, was sick and about to die. 3The
centurion heard of Jesus and sent some elders of the Jews to him,
asking him to come and heal his servant. 4When they came to
Jesus, they pleaded earnestly with him, "This man deserves to have
you do this, 5because he loves our nation and has built our synagogue." 6So Jesus went with them.
He was not far from the house when the centurion sent friends
to say to him: "Lord, don't trouble yourself, for I do not deserve to

6:35 [a]ver 27 [b]Ro 8:14 [c]Mk 5:7
6:36 [d]Jas 2:13 [e]Mt 5:48; 6:1; Lk 11:2; 12:32; Ro 8:15; Eph 4:6; 1Pe 1:17; 1Jn 1:3; 3:1
6:37 [f]Mt 7:1 [g]Mt 6:14
6:38 [h]Ps 79:12; Isa 65:6,7 [i]Mt 7:2; Mk 4:24
6:39 [j]Mt 15:14
6:40 [k]Mt 10:24; Jn 13:16
6:44 [l]Mt 12:33
6:45 [m]Pr 4:23; Mt 12:34,35; Mk 7:20
6:46 [n]Jn 13:13 [o]Mal 1:6; Mt 7:21
6:47 [p]Lk 8:21; 11:28; Jas 1:22-25
7:1 [q]Mt 7:28

have you come under my roof. 7That is why I did not even consider
myself worthy to come to you. But say the word, and my servant
will be healed.[a] 8For I myself am a man under authority, with soldiers under me. I tell this one, 'Go,' and he goes; and that one,
'Come,' and he comes. I say to my servant, 'Do this,' and he
does it."

9When Jesus heard this, he was amazed at him, and turning to
the crowd following him, he said, "I tell you, I have not found such
great faith even in Israel." 10Then the men who had been sent
returned to the house and found the servant well.

11Soon afterward, Jesus went to a town called Nain, and his disciples and a large crowd went along with him. 12As he approached
the town gate, a dead person was being carried out—the only son
of his mother, and she was a widow. And a large crowd from the
town was with her. 13When the Lord[b] saw her, his heart went out
to her and he said, "Don't cry."

14Then he went up and touched the coffin, and those carrying it
stood still. He said, "Young man, I say to you, get up!"[c] 15The dead
man sat up and began to talk, and Jesus gave him back to his
mother.

16They were all filled with awe[d] and praised God.[e] "A great
prophet[f] has appeared among us," they said. "God has come to
help his people."[g] 17This news about Jesus spread throughout
Judea[a] and the surrounding country.[h]

18John's[i] disciples[j] told him about all these things. Calling two of
them, 19he sent them to the Lord to ask, "Are you the one who was
to come, or should we expect someone else?"

20When the men came to Jesus, they said, "John the Baptist sent
us to you to ask, 'Are you the one who was to come, or should we
expect someone else?'"

21At that very time Jesus cured many who had diseases, sicknesses[k] and evil spirits, and gave sight to many who were blind.
22So he replied to the messengers, "Go back and report to John
what you have seen and heard: The blind receive sight, the lame
walk, those who have leprosy[b] are cured, the deaf hear, the dead
are raised, and the good news is preached to the poor.[l] 23Blessed
is the man who does not fall away on account of me."

24After John's messengers left, Jesus began to speak to the crowd
about John: "What did you go out into the desert to see? A reed
swayed by the wind? 25If not, what did you go out to see? A man
dressed in fine clothes? No, those who wear expensive clothes and
indulge in luxury are in palaces. 26But what did you go out to see?
A prophet?[m] Yes, I tell you, and more than a prophet. 27This is the
one about whom it is written:

[a] 17 Or *the land of the Jews* [b] 22 The Greek word was used for various diseases affecting the skin—not necessarily leprosy.

7:7 [a] Ps 107:20
7:13 [b] ver 19; Lk 10:1; 13:15; 17:5; 22:61; 24:34; Jn 11:2
7:14 [c] Mt 9:25; Mk 1:31; Lk 8:54; Jn 11:43; Ac 9:40
7:16 [d] Lk 1:65 [e] Mt 9:8 [f] ver 39; Mt 21:11 [g] Lk 1:68
7:17 [h] Mt 9:26
7:18 [i] Mt 3:1 [j] Lk 5:33
7:21 [k] Mt 4:23
7:22 [l] Isa 29:18,19; 35:5,6; 61:1,2; Lk 4:18
7:26 [m] Mt 11:9

> "'I will send my messenger ahead of you,
> who will prepare your way before you.'[a][a]

[28]I tell you, among those born of women there is no one greater than John; yet the one who is least in the kingdom of God[b] is greater than he."

[29](All the people, even the tax collectors, when they heard Jesus' words, acknowledged that God's way was right, because they had been baptized by John.[c] [30]But the Pharisees and experts in the law[d] rejected God's purpose for themselves, because they had not been baptized by John.)

[31]"To what, then, can I compare the people of this generation? What are they like? [32]They are like children sitting in the marketplace and calling out to each other:

> "'We played the flute for you,
> and you did not dance;
> we sang a dirge,
> and you did not cry.'

[33]For John the Baptist came neither eating bread nor drinking wine,[e] and you say, 'He has a demon.' [34]The Son of Man came eating and drinking, and you say, 'Here is a glutton and a drunkard, a friend of tax collectors and "sinners."'[f] [35]But wisdom is proved right by all her children."

[36]Now one of the Pharisees invited Jesus to have dinner with him, so he went to the Pharisee's house and reclined at the table. [37]When a woman who had lived a sinful life in that town learned that Jesus was eating at the Pharisee's house, she brought an alabaster jar of perfume, [38]and as she stood behind him at his feet weeping, she began to wet his feet with her tears. Then she wiped them with her hair, kissed them and poured perfume on them.

[39]When the Pharisee who had invited him saw this, he said to himself, "If this man were a prophet,[g] he would know who is touching him and what kind of woman she is—that she is a sinner."

[40]Jesus answered him, "Simon, I have something to tell you."

"Tell me, teacher," he said.

[41]"Two men owed money to a certain moneylender. One owed him five hundred denarii,[b] and the other fifty. [42]Neither of them had the money to pay him back, so he canceled the debts of both. Now which of them will love him more?"

[43]Simon replied, "I suppose the one who had the bigger debt canceled."

"You have judged correctly," Jesus said.

[44]Then he turned toward the woman and said to Simon, "Do you see this woman? I came into your house. You did not give me

7:27 *a*Mal 3:1; Mt 11:10; Mk 1:2
7:28 *b*Mt 3:2
7:29 *c*Mt 21:32; Mk 1:5; Lk 3:12
7:30 *d*Mt 22:35
7:33 *e*Lk 1:15
7:34 *f*Lk 5:29,30; 15:1,2
7:39 *g*ver 16; Mt 21:11

a *27* Mal. 3:1   b *41* A denarius was a coin worth about a day's wages.

any water for my feet,[a] but she wet my feet with her tears and
wiped them with her hair. 45You did not give me a kiss,[b] but this
woman, from the time I entered, has not stopped kissing my feet.
46You did not put oil on my head,[c] but she has poured perfume on
my feet. 47Therefore, I tell you, her many sins have been forgiven—
for she loved much. But he who has been forgiven little loves little."

48Then Jesus said to her, "Your sins are forgiven."[d]

49The other guests began to say among themselves, "Who is this
who even forgives sins?"

50Jesus said to the woman, "Your faith has saved you;[e] go in
peace."[f]

Chapter 8 Theme ______________________________

8 After this, Jesus traveled about from one town and village to
another, proclaiming the good news of the kingdom of God.[g]
The Twelve were with him, 2and also some women who had been
cured of evil spirits and diseases: Mary (called Magdalene)[h] from
whom seven demons had come out; 3Joanna the wife of Cuza, the
manager of Herod's[i] household; Susanna; and many others. These
women were helping to support them out of their own means.

4While a large crowd was gathering and people were coming to
Jesus from town after town, he told this parable: 5"A farmer went
out to sow his seed. As he was scattering the seed, some fell along
the path; it was trampled on, and the birds of the air ate it up.
6Some fell on rock, and when it came up, the plants withered
because they had no moisture. 7Other seed fell among thorns,
which grew up with it and choked the plants. 8Still other seed fell
on good soil. It came up and yielded a crop, a hundred times more
than was sown."

When he said this, he called out, "He who has ears to hear, let
him hear."[j]

9His disciples asked him what this parable meant. 10He said,
"The knowledge of the secrets of the kingdom of God has been
given to you,[k] but to others I speak in parables, so that,

> "'though seeing, they may not see;
> though hearing, they may not understand.'[a][l]

11"This is the meaning of the parable: The seed is the word of
God.[m] 12Those along the path are the ones who hear, and then the
devil comes and takes away the word from their hearts, so that
they may not believe and be saved. 13Those on the rock are the
ones who receive the word with joy when they hear it, but they
have no root. They believe for a while, but in the time of testing

[a] *10* Isaiah 6:9

7:44 [a]Ge 18:4; 19:2; 43:24; Jdg 19:21; Jn 13:4-14; 1Ti 5:10

7:45 [b]Lk 22:47,48; Ro 16:16

7:46 [c]Ps 23:5; Ecc 9:8

7:48 [d]Mt 9:2

7:50 [e]Mt 9:22; Mk 5:34; Lk 8:48 [f]Ac 15:33

8:1 [g]Mt 4:23

8:2 [h]Mt 27:55,56

8:3 [i]Mt 14:1

8:8 [j]Mt 11:15

8:10 [k]Mt 13:11 [l]Isa 6:9; Mt 13:13,14

8:11 [m]Heb 4:12

they fall away.[a] 14The seed that fell among thorns stands for those who hear, but as they go on their way they are choked by life's worries, riches[b] and pleasures, and they do not mature. 15But the seed on good soil stands for those with a noble and good heart, who hear the word, retain it, and by persevering produce a crop.

16"No one lights a lamp and hides it in a jar or puts it under a bed. Instead, he puts it on a stand, so that those who come in can see the light.[c] 17For there is nothing hidden that will not be disclosed, and nothing concealed that will not be known or brought out into the open.[d] 18Therefore consider carefully how you listen. Whoever has will be given more; whoever does not have, even what he thinks he has will be taken from him."[e]

19Now Jesus' mother and brothers came to see him, but they were not able to get near him because of the crowd. 20Someone told him, "Your mother and brothers[f] are standing outside, wanting to see you."

21He replied, "My mother and brothers are those who hear God's word and put it into practice."[g]

22One day Jesus said to his disciples, "Let's go over to the other side of the lake." So they got into a boat and set out. 23As they sailed, he fell asleep. A squall came down on the lake, so that the boat was being swamped, and they were in great danger.

24The disciples went and woke him, saying, "Master, Master,[h] we're going to drown!"

He got up and rebuked[i] the wind and the raging waters; the storm subsided, and all was calm.[j] 25"Where is your faith?" he asked his disciples.

In fear and amazement they asked one another, "Who is this? He commands even the winds and the water, and they obey him."

26They sailed to the region of the Gerasenes,[a] which is across the lake from Galilee. 27When Jesus stepped ashore, he was met by a demon-possessed man from the town. For a long time this man had not worn clothes or lived in a house, but had lived in the tombs. 28When he saw Jesus, he cried out and fell at his feet, shouting at the top of his voice, "What do you want with me,[k] Jesus, Son of the Most High God?[l] I beg you, don't torture me!" 29For Jesus had commanded the evil[b] spirit to come out of the man. Many times it had seized him, and though he was chained hand and foot and kept under guard, he had broken his chains and had been driven by the demon into solitary places.

30Jesus asked him, "What is your name?"

"Legion," he replied, because many demons had gone into him. 31And they begged him repeatedly not to order them to go into the Abyss.[m]

8:13 [a]Mt 11:6
8:14 [b]Mt 19:23; 1Ti 6:9,10,17
8:16 [c]Mt 5:15; Mk 4:21; Lk 11:33
8:17 [d]Mt 10:26; Mk 4:22; Lk 12:2
8:18 [e]Mt 13:12; 25:29; Lk 19:26
8:20 [f]Jn 7:5
8:21 [g]Lk 6:47; 11:28; Jn 14:21
8:24 [h]Lk 5:5 [i]Lk 4:35,39,41 [j]Ps 107:29; Jnh 1:15
8:28 [k]Mt 8:29 [l]Mk 5:7
8:31 [m]Rev 9:1,2,11; 11:7; 17:8; 20:1,3

[a] *26* Some manuscripts *Gadarenes;* other manuscripts *Gergesenes;* also in verse 37 [b] *29* Greek *unclean*

32A large herd of pigs was feeding there on the hillside. The
demons begged Jesus to let them go into them, and he gave them
permission. 33When the demons came out of the man, they went
into the pigs, and the herd rushed down the steep bank into the
lake[a] and was drowned.
34When those tending the pigs saw what had happened, they ran
off and reported this in the town and countryside, 35and the people
went out to see what had happened. When they came to Jesus, they
found the man from whom the demons had gone out, sitting at
Jesus' feet,[b] dressed and in his right mind; and they were afraid.
36Those who had seen it told the people how the demon-possessed[c]
man had been cured. 37Then all the people of the region of the
Gerasenes asked Jesus to leave them,[d] because they were overcome
with fear. So he got into the boat and left.
38The man from whom the demons had gone out begged to go
with him, but Jesus sent him away, saying, 39"Return home and tell
how much God has done for you." So the man went away and told
all over town how much Jesus had done for him.
40Now when Jesus returned, a crowd welcomed him, for they
were all expecting him. 41Then a man named Jairus, a ruler of the
synagogue,[e] came and fell at Jesus' feet, pleading with him to come
to his house 42because his only daughter, a girl of about twelve,
was dying.
As Jesus was on his way, the crowds almost crushed him. 43And
a woman was there who had been subject to bleeding[f] for twelve
years,[a] but no one could heal her. 44She came up behind him and
touched the edge of his cloak,[g] and immediately her bleeding
stopped.
45"Who touched me?" Jesus asked.
When they all denied it, Peter said, "Master,[h] the people are
crowding and pressing against you."
46But Jesus said, "Someone touched me;[i] I know that power has
gone out from me."[j]
47Then the woman, seeing that she could not go unnoticed, came
trembling and fell at his feet. In the presence of all the people, she
told why she had touched him and how she had been instantly
healed. 48Then he said to her, "Daughter, your faith has healed
you.[k] Go in peace."[l]
49While Jesus was still speaking, someone came from the house
of Jairus, the synagogue ruler.[m] "Your daughter is dead," he said.
"Don't bother the teacher any more."
50Hearing this, Jesus said to Jairus, "Don't be afraid; just believe,
and she will be healed."
51When he arrived at the house of Jairus, he did not let anyone
go in with him except Peter, John and James,[n] and the child's father

a 43 Many manuscripts *years, and she had spent all she had on doctors*

8:33 [a] ver 22,23
8:35 [b] Lk 10:39
8:36 [c] Mt 4:24
8:37 [d] Ac 16:39
8:41 [e] ver 49; Mk 5:22
8:43 [f] Lev 15:25-30
8:44 [g] Mt 9:20
8:45 [h] Lk 5:5
8:46 [i] Mt 14:36; Mk 3:10 [j] Lk 5:17; 6:19
8:48 [k] Mt 9:22 [l] Ac 15:33
8:49 [m] ver 41
8:51 [n] Mt 4:21

and mother. 52 Meanwhile, all the people were wailing and mourning[a] for her. "Stop wailing," Jesus said. "She is not dead but asleep."[b]
53 They laughed at him, knowing that she was dead. 54 But he
took her by the hand and said, "My child, get up!"[c] 55 Her spirit
returned, and at once she stood up. Then Jesus told them to give
her something to eat. 56 Her parents were astonished, but he
ordered them not to tell anyone what had happened.[d]

Chapter 9 Theme

9 When Jesus had called the Twelve together, he gave them
power and authority to drive out all demons[e] and to cure diseases,[f] 2 and he sent them out to preach the kingdom of God[g] and
to heal the sick. 3 He told them: "Take nothing for the journey—
no staff, no bag, no bread, no money, no extra tunic.[h] 4 Whatever
house you enter, stay there until you leave that town. 5 If people do
not welcome you, shake the dust off your feet when you leave their
town, as a testimony against them."[i] 6 So they set out and went
from village to village, preaching the gospel and healing people
everywhere.
7 Now Herod[j] the tetrarch heard about all that was going on. And
he was perplexed, because some were saying that John[k] had been
raised from the dead,[l] 8 others that Elijah had appeared,[m] and still
others that one of the prophets of long ago had come back to life.[n]
9 But Herod said, "I beheaded John. Who, then, is this I hear such
things about?" And he tried to see him.[o]
10 When the apostles[p] returned, they reported to Jesus what they
had done. Then he took them with him and they withdrew by
themselves to a town called Bethsaida,[q] 11 but the crowds learned
about it and followed him. He welcomed them and spoke to them
about the kingdom of God,[r] and healed those who needed healing.
12 Late in the afternoon the Twelve came to him and said, "Send
the crowd away so they can go to the surrounding villages and
countryside and find food and lodging, because we are in a remote
place here."
13 He replied, "You give them something to eat."
They answered, "We have only five loaves of bread and two
fish—unless we go and buy food for all this crowd." 14 (About five
thousand men were there.)
But he said to his disciples, "Have them sit down in groups of
about fifty each." 15 The disciples did so, and everybody sat down.
16 Taking the five loaves and the two fish and looking up to heav-
en, he gave thanks and broke them.[s] Then he gave them to the
disciples to set before the people. 17 They all ate and were satisfied,
and the disciples picked up twelve basketfuls of broken pieces that
were left over.

8:52 [a] Lk 23:27 [b] Mt 9:24; Jn 11:11,13
8:54 [c] Lk 7:14
8:56 [d] Mt 8:4
9:1 [e] Mt 10:1 [f] Mt 4:23; Lk 5:17
9:2 [g] Mt 3:2
9:3 [h] Lk 10:4; 22:35
9:5 [i] Mt 10:14
9:7 [j] Mt 14:1 [k] Mt 3:1 [l] ver 19
9:8 [m] Mt 11:14 [n] ver 19; Jn 1:21
9:9 [o] Lk 23:8
9:10 [p] Mk 6:30 [q] Mt 11:21
9:11 [r] ver 2; Mt 3:2
9:16 [s] Mt 14:19

18 Once when Jesus was praying[a] in private and his disciples were
with him, he asked them, "Who do the crowds say I am?"
19 They replied, "Some say John the Baptist;[b] others say Elijah;
and still others, that one of the prophets of long ago has come back
to life."[c]
20 "But what about you?" he asked. "Who do you say I am?"
Peter answered, "The Christ[a] of God."[d]
21 Jesus strictly warned them not to tell this to anyone.[e] 22 And he
said, "The Son of Man[f] must suffer many things[g] and be rejected
by the elders, chief priests and teachers of the law,[h] and he must be
killed[i] and on the third day[j] be raised to life."[k]
23 Then he said to them all: "If anyone would come after me, he
must deny himself and take up his cross daily and follow me.[l]
24 For whoever wants to save his life will lose it, but whoever loses
his life for me will save it.[m] 25 What good is it for a man to gain the
whole world, and yet lose or forfeit his very self? 26 If anyone is
ashamed of me and my words, the Son of Man will be ashamed
of him[n] when he comes in his glory and in the glory of the Father
and of the holy angels.[o] 27 I tell you the truth, some who are standing here will not taste death before they see the kingdom of God."
28 About eight days after Jesus said this, he took Peter, John and
James[p] with him and went up onto a mountain to pray.[q] 29 As he
was praying, the appearance of his face changed, and his clothes
became as bright as a flash of lightning. 30 Two men, Moses and
Elijah, 31 appeared in glorious splendor, talking with Jesus. They
spoke about his departure,[r] which he was about to bring to fulfillment at Jerusalem. 32 Peter and his companions were very sleepy,[s]
but when they became fully awake, they saw his glory and the two
men standing with him. 33 As the men were leaving Jesus, Peter
said to him, "Master,[t] it is good for us to be here. Let us put up
three shelters—one for you, one for Moses and one for Elijah."
(He did not know what he was saying.)
34 While he was speaking, a cloud appeared and enveloped them,
and they were afraid as they entered the cloud. 35 A voice came
from the cloud, saying, "This is my Son, whom I have chosen;[u] listen to him."[v] 36 When the voice had spoken, they found that Jesus
was alone. The disciples kept this to themselves, and told no one
at that time what they had seen.[w]
37 The next day, when they came down from the mountain, a large
crowd met him. 38 A man in the crowd called out, "Teacher, I beg
you to look at my son, for he is my only child. 39 A spirit seizes him
and he suddenly screams; it throws him into convulsions so that he
foams at the mouth. It scarcely ever leaves him and is destroying
him. 40 I begged your disciples to drive it out, but they could not."

a *20* Or *Messiah*

9:18 [a]Lk 3:21
9:19 [b]Mt 3:1 [c]ver 7,8
9:20 [d]Jn 1:49; 6:66-69; 11:27
9:21 [e]Mt 16:20; Mk 8:30
9:22 [f]Mt 8:20 [g]Mt 16:21 [h]Mt 27:1,2 [i]Ac 2:23; 3:13 [j]Mt 16:21 [k]Mt 16:21
9:23 [l]Mt 10:38; Lk 14:27
9:24 [m]Jn 12:25
9:26 [n]Mt 10:33; Lk 12:9; 2Ti 2:12 [o]Mt 16:27
9:28 [p]Mt 4:21 [q]Lk 3:21
9:31 [r]2Pe 1:15
9:32 [s]Mt 26:43
9:33 [t]Lk 5:5
9:35 [u]Isa 42:1 [v]Mt 3:17
9:36 [w]Mt 17:9

41"O unbelieving and perverse generation,"[a] Jesus replied, "how
long shall I stay with you and put up with you? Bring your son
here."
42Even while the boy was coming, the demon threw him to the
ground in a convulsion. But Jesus rebuked the evil[a] spirit, healed
the boy and gave him back to his father. 43And they were all
amazed at the greatness of God.
While everyone was marveling at all that Jesus did, he said to his
disciples, 44"Listen carefully to what I am about to tell you: The Son
of Man is going to be betrayed into the hands of men."[b] 45But they
did not understand what this meant. It was hidden from them, so
that they did not grasp it,[c] and they were afraid to ask him about it.
46An argument started among the disciples as to which of them
would be the greatest.[d] 47Jesus, knowing their thoughts,[e] took a
little child and had him stand beside him. 48Then he said to them,
"Whoever welcomes this little child in my name welcomes me; and
whoever welcomes me welcomes the one who sent me.[f] For he who
is least among you all—he is the greatest."[g]
49"Master,"[h] said John, "we saw a man driving out demons in
your name and we tried to stop him, because he is not one of us."
50"Do not stop him," Jesus said, "for whoever is not against you
is for you."[i]
51As the time approached for him to be taken up to heaven,[j]
Jesus resolutely set out for Jerusalem.[k] 52And he sent messengers
on ahead, who went into a Samaritan[l] village to get things ready
for him; 53but the people there did not welcome him, because he
was heading for Jerusalem. 54When the disciples James and John[m]
saw this, they asked, "Lord, do you want us to call fire down from
heaven to destroy them[b]?"[n] 55But Jesus turned and rebuked
them, 56and[c] they went to another village.
57As they were walking along the road,[o] a man said to him, "I
will follow you wherever you go."
58Jesus replied, "Foxes have holes and birds of the air have nests,
but the Son of Man[p] has no place to lay his head."
59He said to another man, "Follow me."[q]
But the man replied, "Lord, first let me go and bury my father."
60Jesus said to him, "Let the dead bury their own dead, but you
go and proclaim the kingdom of God."[r]
61Still another said, "I will follow you, Lord; but first let me go
back and say good-by to my family."[s]
62Jesus replied, "No one who puts his hand to the plow and looks
back is fit for service in the kingdom of God."

9:41 [a]Dt 32:5
9:44 [b]ver 22
9:45 [c]Mk 9:32
9:46 [d]Lk 22:24
9:47 [e]Mt 9:4
9:48 [f]Mt 10:40 [g]Mk 9:35
9:49 [h]Lk 5:5
9:50 [i]Mt 12:30; Lk 11:23
9:51 [j]Mk 16:19 [k]Lk 13:22; 17:11; 18:31; 19:28
9:52 [l]Mt 10:5
9:54 [m]Mt 4:21 [n]2Ki 1:10,12
9:57 [o]ver 51
9:58 [p]Mt 8:20
9:59 [q]Mt 4:19
9:60 [r]Mt 3:2
9:61 [s]1Ki 19:20

[a]42 Greek *unclean* [b]54 Some manuscripts *them, even as Elijah did* [c]55,56 Some manuscripts *them. And he said, "You do not know what kind of spirit you are of, for the Son of Man did not come to destroy men's lives, but to save them."* 56*And*

Chapter 10 Theme ____________________

10 After this the Lord[a] appointed seventy-two[a] others[b] and
sent them two by two[c] ahead of him to every town and place
where he was about to go.[d] 2He told them, "The harvest is plentiful,
but the workers are few. Ask the Lord of the harvest, therefore, to
send out workers into his harvest field.[e] 3Go! I am sending you out
like lambs among wolves.[f] 4Do not take a purse or bag or sandals;
and do not greet anyone on the road.

5"When you enter a house, first say, 'Peace to this house.' 6If a
man of peace is there, your peace will rest on him; if not, it will
return to you. 7Stay in that house, eating and drinking whatever
they give you, for the worker deserves his wages.[g] Do not move
around from house to house.

8"When you enter a town and are welcomed, eat what is set
before you.[h] 9Heal the sick who are there and tell them, 'The kingdom of God[i] is near you.' 10But when you enter a town and are not
welcomed, go into its streets and say, 11'Even the dust of your town
that sticks to our feet we wipe off against you.[j] Yet be sure of this:
The kingdom of God is near.'[k] 12I tell you, it will be more bearable
on that day for Sodom[l] than for that town.[m]

13"Woe to you,[n] Korazin! Woe to you, Bethsaida! For if the miracles that were performed in you had been performed in Tyre and
Sidon, they would have repented long ago, sitting in sackcloth[o]
and ashes. 14But it will be more bearable for Tyre and Sidon at the
judgment than for you. 15And you, Capernaum,[p] will you be lifted
up to the skies? No, you will go down to the depths.[b]

16"He who listens to you listens to me; he who rejects you rejects
me; but he who rejects me rejects him who sent me."[q]

17The seventy-two[r] returned with joy and said, "Lord, even the
demons submit to us in your name."[s]

18He replied, "I saw Satan[t] fall like lightning from heaven.[u] 19I
have given you authority to trample on snakes[v] and scorpions and
to overcome all the power of the enemy; nothing will harm you.
20However, do not rejoice that the spirits submit to you, but rejoice
that your names are written in heaven."[w]

21At that time Jesus, full of joy through the Holy Spirit, said, "I
praise you, Father, Lord of heaven and earth, because you have
hidden these things from the wise and learned, and revealed them
to little children.[x] Yes, Father, for this was your good pleasure.

22"All things have been committed to me by my Father.[y] No one
knows who the Son is except the Father, and no one knows who
the Father is except the Son and those to whom the Son chooses to
reveal him."[z]

[a] *1* Some manuscripts *seventy*; also in verse 17 [b] *15* Greek *Hades*

10:1 [a] Lk 7:13 [b] Lk 9:1,2,51,52 [c] Mk 6:7 [d] Mt 10:1
10:2 [e] Mt 9:37,38; Jn 4:35
10:3 [f] Mt 10:16
10:7 [g] Mt 10:10; 1Co 9:14; 1Ti 5:18
10:8 [h] 1Co 10:27
10:9 [i] Mt 3:2; 10:7
10:11 [j] Mt 10:14; Mk 6:11 [k] ver 9
10:12 [l] Mt 10:15 [m] Mt 11:24
10:13 [n] Lk 6:24-26 [o] Rev 11:3
10:15 [p] Mt 4:13
10:16 [q] Mt 10:40; Jn 13:20
10:17 [r] ver 1 [s] Mk 16:17
10:18 [t] Mt 4:10 [u] Isa 14:12; Rev 9:1; 12:8,9
10:19 [v] Mk 16:18; Ac 28:3-5
10:20 [w] Ex 32:32; Ps 69:28; Da 12:1; Php 4:3; Heb 12:23; Rev 13:8; 20:12; 21:27
10:21 [x] 1Co 1:26-29
10:22 [y] Mt 28:18 [z] Jn 1:18

23Then he turned to his disciples and said privately, "Blessed are
the eyes that see what you see. 24For I tell you that many prophets
and kings wanted to see what you see but did not see it, and to hear
what you hear but did not hear it."[a]
25On one occasion an expert in the law stood up to test Jesus.
"Teacher," he asked, "what must I do to inherit eternal life?"[b]
26"What is written in the Law?" he replied. "How do you read it?"
27He answered: "'Love the Lord your God with all your heart and
with all your soul and with all your strength and with all your
mind'[a];[c] and, 'Love your neighbor as yourself.'[b]"[d]
28"You have answered correctly," Jesus replied. "Do this and you
will live."[e]
29But he wanted to justify himself,[f] so he asked Jesus, "And who
is my neighbor?"
30In reply Jesus said: "A man was going down from Jerusalem to
Jericho, when he fell into the hands of robbers. They stripped him
of his clothes, beat him and went away, leaving him half dead. 31A
priest happened to be going down the same road, and when he
saw the man, he passed by on the other side.[g] 32So too, a Levite,
when he came to the place and saw him, passed by on the other
side. 33But a Samaritan,[h] as he traveled, came where the man was;
and when he saw him, he took pity on him. 34He went to him and
bandaged his wounds, pouring on oil and wine. Then he put the
man on his own donkey, took him to an inn and took care of him.
35The next day he took out two silver coins[c] and gave them to the
inn-keeper. 'Look after him,' he said, 'and when I return, I will
reimburse you for any extra expense you may have.'
36"Which of these three do you think was a neighbor to the man
who fell into the hands of robbers?"
37The expert in the law replied, "The one who had mercy on
him."
Jesus told him, "Go and do likewise."
38As Jesus and his disciples were on their way, he came to a village where a woman named Martha[i] opened her home to him.
39She had a sister called Mary,[j] who sat at the Lord's feet[k] listening
to what he said. 40But Martha was distracted by all the preparations that had to be made. She came to him and asked, "Lord,
don't you care[l] that my sister has left me to do the work by myself?
Tell her to help me!"
41"Martha, Martha," the Lord answered, "you are worried[m]
and upset about many things, 42but only one thing is needed.[d][n]
Mary has chosen what is better, and it will not be taken away
from her."

[a] 27 Deut. 6:5 [b] 27 Lev. 19:18 [c] 35 Greek *two denarii* [d] 42 Some manuscripts *but few things are needed—or only one*

10:24 [a] 1Pe 1:10-12
10:25 [b] Mt 19:16; Lk 18:18
10:27 [c] Dt 6:5 [d] Lev 19:18; Mt 5:43
10:28 [e] Lev 18:5; Ro 7:10
10:29 [f] Lk 16:15
10:31 [g] Lev 21:1-3
10:33 [h] Mt 10:5
10:38 [i] Jn 11:1; 12:2
10:39 [j] Jn 11:1; 12:3 [k] Lk 8:35
10:40 [l] Mk 4:38
10:41 [m] Mt 6:25-34; Lk 12:11,22
10:42 [n] Ps 27:4

Chapter 11 Theme ______________________________

11 One day Jesus was praying[a] in a certain place. When he finished, one of his disciples said to him, "Lord,[b] teach us to
pray, just as John taught his disciples."
2He said to them, "When you pray, say:

"'Father,[a]
hallowed be your name,
your kingdom[c] come.[b]
3Give us each day our daily bread.
4Forgive us our sins,
for we also forgive everyone who sins against us.[c][d]
And lead us not into temptation.[d]'"[e]

5Then he said to them, "Suppose one of you has a friend, and he
goes to him at midnight and says, 'Friend, lend me three loaves of
bread, 6because a friend of mine on a journey has come to me, and
I have nothing to set before him.'
7"Then the one inside answers, 'Don't bother me. The door is
already locked, and my children are with me in bed. I can't get up
and give you anything.' 8I tell you, though he will not get up and
give him the bread because he is his friend, yet because of the
man's boldness[e] he will get up and give him as much as he needs.[f]
9"So I say to you: Ask and it will be given to you;[g] seek and you
will find; knock and the door will be opened to you. 10For everyone
who asks receives; he who seeks finds; and to him who knocks, the
door will be opened.
11"Which of you fathers, if your son asks for[f] a fish, will give him
a snake instead? 12Or if he asks for an egg, will give him a scorpion?
13If you then, though you are evil, know how to give good gifts to
your children, how much more will your Father in heaven give the
Holy Spirit to those who ask him!"
14Jesus was driving out a demon that was mute. When the demon
left, the man who had been mute spoke, and the crowd was
amazed.[h] 15But some of them said, "By Beelzebub,[g][i] the prince of
demons, he is driving out demons."[j] 16Others tested him by asking
for a sign from heaven.[k]
17Jesus knew their thoughts[l] and said to them: "Any kingdom
divided against itself will be ruined, and a house divided against
itself will fall. 18If Satan[m] is divided against himself, how can his
kingdom stand? I say this because you claim that I drive out
demons by Beelzebub. 19Now if I drive out demons by Beelzebub,

a2 Some manuscripts *Our Father in heaven* b2 Some manuscripts *come. May your will be done on earth as it is in heaven.* c4 Greek *everyone who is indebted to us* d4 Some manuscripts *temptation but deliver us from the evil one* e8 Or *persistence* f11 Some manuscripts *for bread, will give him a stone; or if he asks for* g15 Greek *Beezeboul* or *Beelzeboul*; also in verses 18 and 19

11:1 *a*Lk 3:21 *b*Jn 13:13
11:2 *c*Mt 3:2
11:4 *d*Mt 18:35; Mk 11:25 *e*Mt 26:41; Jas 1:13
11:8 *f*Lk 18:1-6
11:9 *g*Mt 7:7
11:14 *h*Mt 9:32,33
11:15 *i*Mk 3:22 *j*Mt 9:34
11:16 *k*Mt 12:38
11:17 *l*Mt 9:4
11:18 *m*Mt 4:10

by whom do your followers drive them out? So then, they will be
your judges. 20 But if I drive out demons by the finger of God,[a] then
the kingdom of God[b] has come to you.

21 "When a strong man, fully armed, guards his own house, his
possessions are safe. 22 But when someone stronger attacks and
overpowers him, he takes away the armor in which the man trusted
and divides up the spoils.

23 "He who is not with me is against me, and he who does not
gather with me, scatters.[c]

24 "When an evil[a] spirit comes out of a man, it goes through arid
places seeking rest and does not find it. Then it says, 'I will return
to the house I left.' 25 When it arrives, it finds the house swept clean
and put in order. 26 Then it goes and takes seven other spirits more
wicked than itself, and they go in and live there. And the final condition of that man is worse than the first."[d]

27 As Jesus was saying these things, a woman in the crowd called
out, "Blessed is the mother who gave you birth and nursed you."[e]

28 He replied, "Blessed rather are those who hear the word of God[f]
and obey it."[g]

29 As the crowds increased, Jesus said, "This is a wicked generation. It asks for a miraculous sign,[h] but none will be given it except
the sign of Jonah.[i] 30 For as Jonah was a sign to the Ninevites, so
also will the Son of Man be to this generation. 31 The Queen of the
South will rise at the judgment with the men of this generation and
condemn them; for she came from the ends of the earth to listen
to Solomon's wisdom,[j] and now one[b] greater than Solomon is
here. 32 The men of Nineveh will stand up at the judgment with this
generation and condemn it; for they repented at the preaching of
Jonah,[k] and now one greater than Jonah is here.

33 "No one lights a lamp and puts it in a place where it will be hidden, or under a bowl. Instead he puts it on its stand, so that those
who come in may see the light.[l] 34 Your eye is the lamp of your body.
When your eyes are good, your whole body also is full of light. But
when they are bad, your body also is full of darkness. 35 See to it,
then, that the light within you is not darkness. 36 Therefore, if your
whole body is full of light, and no part of it dark, it will be completely lighted, as when the light of a lamp shines on you."

37 When Jesus had finished speaking, a Pharisee invited him to
eat with him; so he went in and reclined at the table.[m] 38 But the
Pharisee, noticing that Jesus did not first wash before the meal,[n]
was surprised.

39 Then the Lord[o] said to him, "Now then, you Pharisees clean
the outside of the cup and dish, but inside you are full of greed and
wickedness.[p] 40 You foolish people![q] Did not the one who made

11:20 [a]Ex 8:19 [b]Mt 3:2
11:23 [c]Mt 12:30; Mk 9:40; Lk 9:50
11:26 [d]2Pe 2:20
11:27 [e]Lk 23:29
11:28 [f]Heb 4:12 [g]Pr 8:32; Lk 6:47; 8:21; Jn 14:21
11:29 [h]ver 16; Mt 12:38 [i]Jnh 1:17; Mt 16:4
11:31 [j]1Ki 10:1; 2Ch 9:1
11:32 [k]Jnh 3:5
11:33 [l]Mt 5:15; Mk 4:21; Lk 8:16
11:37 [m]Lk 7:36; 14:1
11:38 [n]Mk 7:3,4
11:39 [o]Lk 7:13 [p]Mt 23:25,26; Mk 7:20-23
11:40 [q]Lk 12:20; 1Co 15:36

a *24* Greek *unclean* b *31* Or *something*; also in verse 32

the outside make the inside also? 41But give what is inside ⌊the
dish⌋[a] to the poor,[a] and everything will be clean for you.[b]
42"Woe to you Pharisees, because you give God a tenth[c] of your
mint, rue and all other kinds of garden herbs, but you neglect
justice and the love of God.[d] You should have practiced the latter
without leaving the former undone.[e]
43"Woe to you Pharisees, because you love the most important
seats in the synagogues and greetings in the marketplaces.[f]
44"Woe to you, because you are like unmarked graves,[g] which
men walk over without knowing it."
45One of the experts in the law[h] answered him, "Teacher, when
you say these things, you insult us also."
46Jesus replied, "And you experts in the law, woe to you, because
you load people down with burdens they can hardly carry, and you
yourselves will not lift one finger to help them.[i]
47"Woe to you, because you build tombs for the prophets, and it
was your forefathers who killed them. 48So you testify that you
approve of what your forefathers did; they killed the prophets, and
you build their tombs.[j] 49Because of this, God in his wisdom[k]
said, 'I will send them prophets and apostles, some of whom they
will kill and others they will persecute.'[l] 50Therefore this generation will be held responsible for the blood of all the prophets that
has been shed since the beginning of the world, 51from the blood
of Abel[m] to the blood of Zechariah,[n] who was killed between the
altar and the sanctuary. Yes, I tell you, this generation will be held
responsible for it all.[o]
52"Woe to you experts in the law, because you have taken away
the key to knowledge. You yourselves have not entered, and you
have hindered those who were entering."[p]
53When Jesus left there, the Pharisees and the teachers of the law
began to oppose him fiercely and to besiege him with questions,
54waiting to catch him in something he might say.[q]

Chapter 12 Theme

12 Meanwhile, when a crowd of many thousands had gathered, so that they were trampling on one another, Jesus
began to speak first to his disciples, saying: "Be on your guard
against the yeast of the Pharisees, which is hypocrisy.[r] 2There is
nothing concealed that will not be disclosed, or hidden that will
not be made known.[s] 3What you have said in the dark will be
heard in the daylight, and what you have whispered in the ear in
the inner rooms will be proclaimed from the roofs.
4"I tell you, my friends,[t] do not be afraid of those who kill the
body and after that can do no more. 5But I will show you whom

11:41 [a] Lk 12:33 [b] Ac 10:15

11:42 [c] Lk 18:12 [d] Dt 6:5; Mic 6:8 [e] Mt 23:23

11:43 [f] Mt 23:6,7; Mk 12:38-39; Lk 14:7; 20:46

11:44 [g] Mt 23:27

11:45 [h] Mt 22:35

11:46 [i] Mt 23:4

11:48 [j] Mt 23:29-32; Ac 7:51-53

11:49 [k] 1Co 1:24,30; Col 2:3 [l] Mt 23:34

11:51 [m] Ge 4:8 [n] 2Ch 24:20,21 [o] Mt 23:35,36

11:52 [p] Mt 23:13

11:54 [q] Mt 12:10; Mk 12:13

12:1 [r] Mt 16:6,11,12; Mk 8:15

12:2 [s] Mk 4:22; Lk 8:17

12:4 [t] Jn 15:14,15

[a] *41* Or *what you have*

you should fear: Fear him who, after the killing of the body, has
power to throw you into hell. Yes, I tell you, fear him.[a] 6 Are not five
sparrows sold for two pennies[a]? Yet not one of them is forgotten
by God. 7 Indeed, the very hairs of your head are all numbered.[b]
Don't be afraid; you are worth more than many sparrows.[c]

8 "I tell you, whoever acknowledges me before men, the Son of
Man will also acknowledge him before the angels of God.[d] 9 But he
who disowns me before men will be disowned[e] before the angels
of God. 10 And everyone who speaks a word against the Son of
Man[f] will be forgiven, but anyone who blasphemes against the
Holy Spirit will not be forgiven.[g]

11 "When you are brought before synagogues, rulers and authorities, do not worry about how you will defend yourselves or what
you will say,[h] 12 for the Holy Spirit will teach you at that time what
you should say."[i]

13 Someone in the crowd said to him, "Teacher, tell my brother to
divide the inheritance with me."

14 Jesus replied, "Man, who appointed me a judge or an arbiter
between you?" 15 Then he said to them, "Watch out! Be on your
guard against all kinds of greed; a man's life does not consist in
the abundance of his possessions."[j]

16 And he told them this parable: "The ground of a certain rich
man produced a good crop. 17 He thought to himself, 'What shall
I do? I have no place to store my crops.'

18 "Then he said, 'This is what I'll do. I will tear down my barns
and build bigger ones, and there I will store all my grain and my
goods. 19 And I'll say to myself, "You have plenty of good things laid
up for many years. Take life easy; eat, drink and be merry." '

20 "But God said to him, 'You fool![k] This very night your life will
be demanded from you.[l] Then who will get what you have prepared for yourself?'[m]

21 "This is how it will be with anyone who stores up things for
himself but is not rich toward God."[n]

22 Then Jesus said to his disciples: "Therefore I tell you, do not
worry about your life, what you will eat; or about your body, what
you will wear. 23 Life is more than food, and the body more than
clothes. 24 Consider the ravens: They do not sow or reap, they have
no storeroom or barn; yet God feeds them.[o] And how much more
valuable you are than birds! 25 Who of you by worrying can add a
single hour to his life[b]? 26 Since you cannot do this very little thing,
why do you worry about the rest?

27 "Consider how the lilies grow. They do not labor or spin. Yet I
tell you, not even Solomon in all his splendor[p] was dressed like one
of these. 28 If that is how God clothes the grass of the field, which

12:5 [a] Heb 10:31
12:7 [b] Mt 10:30 [c] Mt 12:12
12:8 [d] Lk 15:10
12:9 [e] Mk 8:38; 2Ti 2:12
12:10 [f] Mt 8:20 [g] Mt 12:31,32; Mk 3:28-29; 1Jn 5:16
12:11 [h] Mt 10:17,19; Mk 13:11; Lk 21:12,14
12:12 [i] Ex 4:12; Mt 10:20; Mk 13:11; Lk 21:15
12:15 [j] Job 20:20; 31:24; Ps 62:10
12:20 [k] Jer 17:11; Lk 11:40 [l] Job 27:8 [m] Ps 39:6; 49:10
12:21 [n] ver 33
12:24 [o] Job 38:41; Ps 147:9
12:27 [p] 1Ki 10:4-7

a *6* Greek *two assaria* b *25* Or *single cubit to his height*

is here today, and tomorrow is thrown into the fire, how much
more will he clothe you, O you of little faith![a] 29And do not set your
heart on what you will eat or drink; do not worry about it. 30For
the pagan world runs after all such things, and your Father[b] knows
that you need them.[c] 31But seek his kingdom,[d] and these things
will be given to you as well.[e]

32"Do not be afraid,[f] little flock, for your Father has been pleased
to give you the kingdom.[g] 33Sell your possessions and give to the
poor.[h] Provide purses for yourselves that will not wear out, a treasure in heaven[i] that will not be exhausted, where no thief comes
near and no moth destroys.[j] 34For where your treasure is, there
your heart will be also.[k]

35"Be dressed ready for service and keep your lamps burning,
36like men waiting for their master to return from a wedding banquet, so that when he comes and knocks they can immediately
open the door for him. 37It will be good for those servants whose
master finds them watching when he comes.[l] I tell you the truth,
he will dress himself to serve, will have them recline at the table and
will come and wait on them.[m] 38It will be good for those servants
whose master finds them ready, even if he comes in the second or
third watch of the night. 39But understand this: If the owner of the
house had known at what hour the thief[n] was coming, he would
not have let his house be broken into. 40You also must be ready,[o]
because the Son of Man will come at an hour when you do not
expect him."

41Peter asked, "Lord, are you telling this parable to us, or to
everyone?"

42The Lord[p] answered, "Who then is the faithful and wise manager, whom the master puts in charge of his servants to give them
their food allowance at the proper time? 43It will be good for that
servant whom the master finds doing so when he returns. 44I tell
you the truth, he will put him in charge of all his possessions. 45But
suppose the servant says to himself, 'My master is taking a long
time in coming,' and he then begins to beat the menservants and
maidservants and to eat and drink and get drunk. 46The master of
that servant will come on a day when he does not expect him and
at an hour he is not aware of.[q] He will cut him to pieces and assign
him a place with the unbelievers.

47"That servant who knows his master's will and does not get
ready or does not do what his master wants will be beaten with
many blows.[r] 48But the one who does not know and does things
deserving punishment will be beaten with few blows.[s] From
everyone who has been given much, much will be demanded; and
from the one who has been entrusted with much, much more will
be asked.

12:28 [a] Mt 6:30
12:30 [b] Lk 6:36 [c] Mt 6:8
12:31 [d] Mt 3:2 [e] Mt 19:29
12:32 [f] Mt 14:27 [g] Mt 25:34
12:33 [h] Mt 19:21; Ac 2:45 [i] Mt 6:20 [j] Jas 5:2
12:34 [k] Mt 6:21
12:37 [l] Mt 24:42,46; 25:13 [m] Mt 20:28
12:39 [n] Mt 6:19; 1Th 5:2; 2Pe 3:10; Rev 3:3; 16:15
12:40 [o] Mk 13:33; Lk 21:36
12:42 [p] Lk 7:13
12:46 [q] ver 40
12:47 [r] Dt 25:2
12:48 [s] Lev 5:17; Nu 15:27-30

12:50 [a]Mk 10:38 [49]"I have come to bring fire on the earth, and how I wish it were
[b]Jn 19:30 already kindled! [50]But I have a baptism[a] to undergo, and how distressed I am until it is completed![b] [51]Do you think I came to bring
12:53 peace on earth? No, I tell you, but division. [52]From now on there
[c]Mic 7:6; Mt 10:21 will be five in one family divided against each other, three against
two and two against three. [53]They will be divided, father against
son and son against father, mother against daughter and daugh-
12:54 ter against mother, mother-in-law against daughter-in-law and
[d]Mt 16:2 daughter-in-law against mother-in-law."[c]

[54]He said to the crowd: "When you see a cloud rising in the
12:56 west, immediately you say, 'It's going to rain,' and it does.[d] [55]And
[e]Mt 16:3 when the south wind blows, you say, 'It's going to be hot,' and it
is. [56]Hypocrites! You know how to interpret the appearance of the
12:58 earth and the sky. How is it that you don't know how to interpret
[f]Mt 5:25 this present time?[e]

[57]"Why don't you judge for yourselves what is right? [58]As you
12:59 are going with your adversary to the magistrate, try hard to be
[g]Mt 5:26; Mk 12:42 reconciled to him on the way, or he may drag you off to the judge,
and the judge turn you over to the officer, and the officer throw
you into prison.[f] [59]I tell you, you will not get out until you have
13:1 [h]Mt 27:2 paid the last penny.[a]"[g]

Chapter 13 Theme ____________________

13:2 [i]Jn 9:2,3 **13** Now there were some present at that time who told Jesus
about the Galileans whose blood Pilate[h] had mixed with
their sacrifices. [2]Jesus answered, "Do you think that these Galileans
13:4 were worse sinners than all the other Galileans because they suf-
[j]Jn 9:7,11 fered this way?[i] [3]I tell you, no! But unless you repent, you too will
all perish. [4]Or those eighteen who died when the tower in Siloam[j]
13:5 fell on them—do you think they were more guilty than all the
[k]Mt 3:2; Ac 2:38 others living in Jerusalem? [5]I tell you, no! But unless you repent,[k]
you too will all perish."

13:6 [6]Then he told this parable: "A man had a fig tree, planted in his
[l]Isa 5:2; Jer 8:13; vineyard, and he went to look for fruit on it, but did not find any.[l]
Mt 21:19 [7]So he said to the man who took care of the vineyard, 'For three
years now I've been coming to look for fruit on this fig tree and
haven't found any. Cut it down![m] Why should it use up the soil?'

13:7 [m]Mt 3:10 [8]" 'Sir,' the man replied, 'leave it alone for one more year, and I'll
dig around it and fertilize it. [9]If it bears fruit next year, fine! If not,
then cut it down.' "

13:10 [n]Mt 4:23 [10]On a Sabbath Jesus was teaching in one of the synagogues,[n]
[11]and a woman was there who had been crippled by a spirit for
eighteen years.[o] She was bent over and could not straighten up at

13:11 [o]ver 16

[a]59 Greek *lepton*

all. 12When Jesus saw her, he called her forward and said to her,
"Woman, you are set free from your infirmity." 13Then he put his
hands on her,[a] and immediately she straightened up and praised
God.
14Indignant because Jesus had healed on the Sabbath,[b] the synagogue ruler[c] said to the people, "There are six days for work.[d] So
come and be healed on those days, not on the Sabbath."
15The Lord answered him, "You hypocrites! Doesn't each of you
on the Sabbath untie his ox or donkey from the stall and lead it
out to give it water?[e] 16Then should not this woman, a daughter of
Abraham,[f] whom Satan[g] has kept bound for eighteen long years,
be set free on the Sabbath day from what bound her?"
17When he said this, all his opponents were humiliated,[h] but the
people were delighted with all the wonderful things he was doing.
18Then Jesus asked, "What is the kingdom of God[i] like?[j] What
shall I compare it to? 19It is like a mustard seed, which a man took
and planted in his garden. It grew and became a tree,[k] and the
birds of the air perched in its branches."[l]
20Again he asked, "What shall I compare the kingdom of God to?
21It is like yeast that a woman took and mixed into a large amount[a]
of flour until it worked all through the dough."[m]
22Then Jesus went through the towns and villages, teaching as he
made his way to Jerusalem.[n] 23Someone asked him, "Lord, are only
a few people going to be saved?"
He said to them, 24"Make every effort to enter through the narrow door,[o] because many, I tell you, will try to enter and will not be
able to. 25Once the owner of the house gets up and closes the door,
you will stand outside knocking and pleading, 'Sir, open the door
for us.'
"But he will answer, 'I don't know you or where you come from.'[p]
26"Then you will say, 'We ate and drank with you, and you taught
in our streets.'
27"But he will reply, 'I don't know you or where you come from.
Away from me, all you evildoers!'[q]
28"There will be weeping there, and gnashing of teeth,[r] when you
see Abraham, Isaac and Jacob and all the prophets in the kingdom
of God, but you yourselves thrown out. 29People will come from
east and west[s] and north and south, and will take their places at
the feast in the kingdom of God. 30Indeed there are those who are
last who will be first, and first who will be last."[t]
31At that time some Pharisees came to Jesus and said to him,
"Leave this place and go somewhere else. Herod[u] wants to kill you."
32He replied, "Go tell that fox, 'I will drive out demons and heal
people today and tomorrow, and on the third day I will reach my

a 21 Greek *three satas* (probably about 1/2 bushel or 22 liters)

13:13 [a] Mk 5:23
13:14 [b] Mt 12:2; Lk 14:3 [c] Mk 5:22 [d] Ex 20:9
13:15 [e] Lk 14:5
13:16 [f] Lk 3:8; 19:9 [g] Mt 4:10
13:17 [h] Isa 66:5
13:18 [i] Mt 3:2 [j] Mt 13:24
13:19 [k] Lk 17:6 [l] Mt 13:32
13:21 [m] 1Co 5:6
13:22 [n] Lk 9:51
13:24 [o] Mt 7:13
13:25 [p] Mt 7:23; 25:10-12
13:27 [q] Mt 7:23; 25:41
13:28 [r] Mt 8:12
13:29 [s] Mt 8:11
13:30 [t] Mt 19:30
13:31 [u] Mt 14:1

goal.'[a] 33In any case, I must keep going today and tomorrow and
the next day—for surely no prophet[b] can die outside Jerusalem!
34"O Jerusalem, Jerusalem, you who kill the prophets and stone
those sent to you, how often I have longed to gather your children
together, as a hen gathers her chicks under her wings,[c] but you
were not willing! 35Look, your house is left to you desolate.[d] I tell
you, you will not see me again until you say, 'Blessed is he who
comes in the name of the Lord.'[a]"[e]

Chapter 14 Theme ______________________________

14 One Sabbath, when Jesus went to eat in the house of a
prominent Pharisee,[f] he was being carefully watched.[g]
2There in front of him was a man suffering from dropsy. 3Jesus
asked the Pharisees and experts in the law,[h] "Is it lawful to heal on
the Sabbath or not?"[i] 4But they remained silent. So taking hold of
the man, he healed him and sent him away.
5Then he asked them, "If one of you has a son[b] or an ox that falls
into a well on the Sabbath day, will you not immediately pull him
out?"[j] 6And they had nothing to say.
7When he noticed how the guests picked the places of honor at
the table,[k] he told them this parable: 8"When someone invites you
to a wedding feast, do not take the place of honor, for a person
more distinguished than you may have been invited. 9If so, the
host who invited both of you will come and say to you, 'Give this
man your seat.' Then, humiliated, you will have to take the least
important place. 10But when you are invited, take the lowest place,
so that when your host comes, he will say to you, 'Friend, move up
to a better place.' Then you will be honored in the presence of all
your fellow guests. 11For everyone who exalts himself will be humbled, and he who humbles himself will be exalted."[l]
12Then Jesus said to his host, "When you give a luncheon or dinner, do not invite your friends, your brothers or relatives, or your
rich neighbors; if you do, they may invite you back and so you
will be repaid. 13But when you give a banquet, invite the poor, the
crippled, the lame, the blind,[m] 14and you will be blessed. Although
they cannot repay you, you will be repaid at the resurrection of
the righteous."[n]
15When one of those at the table with him heard this, he said to
Jesus, "Blessed is the man who will eat at the feast[o] in the kingdom
of God."[p]
16Jesus replied: "A certain man was preparing a great banquet
and invited many guests. 17At the time of the banquet he sent his
servant to tell those who had been invited, 'Come, for everything
is now ready.'

a35 Psalm 118:26 b5 Some manuscripts *donkey*

13:32 [a] Heb 2:10
13:33 [b] Mt 21:11
13:34 [c] Mt 23:37
13:35 [d] Jer 12:17; 22:5 [e] Ps 118:26; Mt 21:9; Lk 19:38
14:1 [f] Lk 7:36; 11:37 [g] Mt 12:10
14:3 [h] Mt 22:35 [i] Mt 12:2
14:5 [j] Lk 13:15
14:7 [k] Lk 11:43
14:11 [l] Mt 23:12; Lk 18:14
14:13 [m] ver 21
14:14 [n] Ac 24:15
14:15 [o] Isa 25:6; Mt 26:29; Lk 13:29; Rev 19:9 [p] Mt 3:2

18“But they all alike began to make excuses. The first said, ‘I have
just bought a field, and I must go and see it. Please excuse me.’
19“Another said, ‘I have just bought five yoke of oxen, and I’m on
my way to try them out. Please excuse me.’
20“Still another said, ‘I just got married, so I can’t come.’
21“The servant came back and reported this to his master. Then
the owner of the house became angry and ordered his servant, ‘Go
out quickly into the streets and alleys of the town and bring in the
poor, the crippled, the blind and the lame.’[a]
22“ ‘Sir,’ the servant said, ‘what you ordered has been done, but
there is still room.’
23“Then the master told his servant, ‘Go out to the roads and
country lanes and make them come in, so that my house will be
full. 24I tell you, not one of those men who were invited will get a
taste of my banquet.’ ”[b]
25Large crowds were traveling with Jesus, and turning to them
he said: 26“If anyone comes to me and does not hate his father and
mother, his wife and children, his brothers and sisters—yes, even
his own life—he cannot be my disciple.[c] 27And anyone who does
not carry his cross and follow me cannot be my disciple.[d]
28“Suppose one of you wants to build a tower. Will he not first sit
down and estimate the cost to see if he has enough money to complete it? 29For if he lays the foundation and is not able to finish it,
everyone who sees it will ridicule him, 30saying, ‘This fellow began
to build and was not able to finish.’
31“Or suppose a king is about to go to war against another king.
Will he not first sit down and consider whether he is able with ten
thousand men to oppose the one coming against him with twenty
thousand? 32If he is not able, he will send a delegation while the
other is still a long way off and will ask for terms of peace. 33In the
same way, any of you who does not give up everything he has cannot be my disciple.[e]
34“Salt is good, but if it loses its saltiness, how can it be made
salty again?[f] 35It is fit neither for the soil nor for the manure pile; it
is thrown out.[g]
“He who has ears to hear, let him hear.”[h]

Chapter 15 Theme ______________________________

15 Now the tax collectors[i] and “sinners” were all gathering
around to hear him. 2But the Pharisees and the teachers of
the law muttered, “This man welcomes sinners and eats with
them.”[j]
3Then Jesus told them this parable:[k] 4“Suppose one of you has a
hundred sheep and loses one of them. Does he not leave the ninety-
nine in the open country and go after the lost sheep until he finds

14:21 [a]ver 13
14:24 [b]Mt 21:43; Ac 13:46
14:26 [c]Mt 10:37; Jn 12:25
14:27 [d]Mt 10:38; Lk 9:23
14:33 [e]Php 3:7,8
14:34 [f]Mk 9:50
14:35 [g]Mt 5:13 [h]Mt 11:15
15:1 [i]Lk 5:29
15:2 [j]Mt 9:11
15:3 [k]Mt 13:3

it?[a] 5And when he finds it, he joyfully puts it on his shoulders 6and
goes home. Then he calls his friends and neighbors together and
says, 'Rejoice with me; I have found my lost sheep.'[b] 7I tell you that
in the same way there will be more rejoicing in heaven over one
sinner who repents than over ninety-nine righteous persons who
do not need to repent.[c]

8"Or suppose a woman has ten silver coins[a] and loses one. Does
she not light a lamp, sweep the house and search carefully until she
finds it? 9And when she finds it, she calls her friends and neighbors
together and says, 'Rejoice with me; I have found my lost coin.'[d]
10In the same way, I tell you, there is rejoicing in the presence of
the angels of God over one sinner who repents."[e]

11Jesus continued: "There was a man who had two sons.[f] 12The
younger one said to his father, 'Father, give me my share of the
estate.'[g] So he divided his property[h] between them.

13"Not long after that, the younger son got together all he had, set
off for a distant country and there squandered his wealth[i] in wild
living. 14After he had spent everything, there was a severe famine
in that whole country, and he began to be in need. 15So he went
and hired himself out to a citizen of that country, who sent him
to his fields to feed pigs.[j] 16He longed to fill his stomach with the
pods that the pigs were eating, but no one gave him anything.

17"When he came to his senses, he said, 'How many of my
father's hired men have food to spare, and here I am starving to
death! 18I will set out and go back to my father and say to him:
Father, I have sinned[k] against heaven and against you. 19I am no
longer worthy to be called your son; make me like one of your
hired men.' 20So he got up and went to his father.

"But while he was still a long way off, his father saw him and was
filled with compassion for him; he ran to his son, threw his arms
around him and kissed him.[l]

21"The son said to him, 'Father, I have sinned against heaven and
against you.[m] I am no longer worthy to be called your son.[b]'

22"But the father said to his servants, 'Quick! Bring the best robe[n]
and put it on him. Put a ring on his finger[o] and sandals on his feet.
23Bring the fattened calf and kill it. Let's have a feast and celebrate.
24For this son of mine was dead and is alive again;[p] he was lost and
is found.' So they began to celebrate.[q]

25"Meanwhile, the older son was in the field. When he came near
the house, he heard music and dancing. 26So he called one of the
servants and asked him what was going on. 27'Your brother has
come,' he replied, 'and your father has killed the fattened calf
because he has him back safe and sound.'

15:4 [a] Ps 23; 119:176; Jer 31:10; Eze 34:11-16; Lk 5:32; 19:10
15:6 [b] ver 9
15:7 [c] ver 10
15:9 [d] ver 6
15:10 [e] ver 7
15:11 [f] Mt 21:28
15:12 [g] Dt 21:17 [h] ver 30
15:13 [i] ver 30; Lk 16:1
15:15 [j] Lev 11:7
15:18 [k] Lev 26:40; Mt 3:2
15:20 [l] Ge 45:14,15; 46:29; Ac 20:37
15:21 [m] Ps 51:4
15:22 [n] Zec 3:4; Rev 6:11 [o] Ge 41:42
15:24 [p] Eph 2:1,5; 5:14; 1Ti 5:6 [q] ver 32

[a] *8* Greek *ten drachmas,* each worth about a day's wages [b] *21* Some early manuscripts *son. Make me like one of your hired men.*

28"The older brother became angry[a] and refused to go in. So
his father went out and pleaded with him. 29But he answered his
father, 'Look! All these years I've been slaving for you and never
disobeyed your orders. Yet you never gave me even a young goat
so I could celebrate with my friends. 30But when this son of yours
who has squandered your property[b] with prostitutes[c] comes home,
you kill the fattened calf for him!'

31"'My son,' the father said, 'you are always with me, and everything I have is yours. 32But we had to celebrate and be glad,
because this brother of yours was dead and is alive again; he was
lost and is found.'"[d]

Chapter 16 Theme ______________________________

16 Jesus told his disciples: "There was a rich man whose manager was accused of wasting his possessions.[e] 2So he called
him in and asked him, 'What is this I hear about you? Give an
account of your management, because you cannot be manager any
longer.'

3"The manager said to himself, 'What shall I do now? My master is taking away my job. I'm not strong enough to dig, and I'm
ashamed to beg— 4I know what I'll do so that, when I lose my job
here, people will welcome me into their houses.'

5"So he called in each one of his master's debtors. He asked the
first, 'How much do you owe my master?'

6"'Eight hundred gallons[a] of olive oil,' he replied.

"The manager told him, 'Take your bill, sit down quickly, and
make it four hundred.'

7"Then he asked the second, 'And how much do you owe?'

"'A thousand bushels[b] of wheat,' he replied.

"He told him, 'Take your bill and make it eight hundred.'

8"The master commended the dishonest manager because he
had acted shrewdly. For the people of this world[f] are more shrewd[g]
in dealing with their own kind than are the people of the light.[h] 9I
tell you, use worldly wealth[i] to gain friends for yourselves, so that
when it is gone, you will be welcomed into eternal dwellings.[j]

10"Whoever can be trusted with very little can also be trusted
with much,[k] and whoever is dishonest with very little will also be
dishonest with much. 11So if you have not been trustworthy in handling worldly wealth,[l] who will trust you with true riches? 12And if
you have not been trustworthy with someone else's property, who
will give you property of your own?

13"No servant can serve two masters. Either he will hate the one
and love the other, or he will be devoted to the one and despise the
other. You cannot serve both God and Money."[m]

[a]6 Greek *one hundred batous* (probably about 3 kiloliters) [b]7 Greek *one hundred korous* (probably about 35 kiloliters)

15:28 [a]Jnh 4:1
15:30 [b]ver 12,13 [c]Pr 29:3
15:32 [d]ver 24; Mal 3:17
16:1 [e]Lk 15:13,30
16:8 [f]Ps 17:14 [g]Ps 18:26 [h]Jn 12:36; Eph 5:8; 1Th 5:5
16:9 [i]ver 11,13 [j]Mt 19:21; Lk 12:33
16:10 [k]Mt 25:21,23; Lk 19:17
16:11 [l]ver 9,13
16:13 [m]ver 9,11; Mt 6:24

14 The Pharisees, who loved money,[a] heard all this and were sneer-
ing at Jesus.[b] 15 He said to them, "You are the ones who justify yourselves[c] in the eyes of men, but God knows your hearts.[d] What is
highly valued among men is detestable in God's sight.

16 "The Law and the Prophets were proclaimed until John.[e] Since
that time, the good news of the kingdom of God is being preached,[f]
and everyone is forcing his way into it. 17 It is easier for heaven and
earth to disappear than for the least stroke of a pen to drop out of
the Law.[g]

18 "Anyone who divorces his wife and marries another woman
commits adultery, and the man who marries a divorced woman
commits adultery.[h]

19 "There was a rich man who was dressed in purple and fine
linen and lived in luxury every day.[i] 20 At his gate was laid a beggar[j]
named Lazarus, covered with sores 21 and longing to eat what fell
from the rich man's table.[k] Even the dogs came and licked his sores.

22 "The time came when the beggar died and the angels carried
him to Abraham's side. The rich man also died and was buried.
23 In hell,[a] where he was in torment, he looked up and saw Abraham far away, with Lazarus by his side. 24 So he called to him,
'Father Abraham,[l] have pity on me and send Lazarus to dip the tip
of his finger in water and cool my tongue, because I am in agony
in this fire.'[m]

25 "But Abraham replied, 'Son, remember that in your lifetime
you received your good things, while Lazarus received bad things,[n]
but now he is comforted here and you are in agony.[o] 26 And besides
all this, between us and you a great chasm has been fixed, so that
those who want to go from here to you cannot, nor can anyone
cross over from there to us.'

27 "He answered, 'Then I beg you, father, send Lazarus to my
father's house, 28 for I have five brothers. Let him warn them,[p] so
that they will not also come to this place of torment.'

29 "Abraham replied, 'They have Moses[q] and the Prophets;[r] let
them listen to them.'

30 " 'No, father Abraham,'[s] he said, 'but if someone from the dead
goes to them, they will repent.'

31 "He said to him, 'If they do not listen to Moses and the Prophets, they will not be convinced even if someone rises from the
dead.' "

Chapter 17 Theme ______________________

17 Jesus said to his disciples: "Things that cause people to sin[t]
are bound to come, but woe to that person through whom
they come.[u] 2 It would be better for him to be thrown into the sea

[a] 23 Greek *Hades*

16:14 [a] 1Ti 3:3 [b] Lk 23:35
16:15 [c] Lk 10:29 [d] 1Sa 16:7; Rev 2:23
16:16 [e] Mt 11:12,13 [f] Mt 4:23
16:17 [g] Mt 5:18
16:18 [h] Mt 5:31,32; 19:9; Mk 10:11; Ro 7:2,3; 1Co 7:10,11
16:19 [i] Eze 16:49
16:20 [j] Ac 3:2
16:21 [k] Mt 15:27
16:24 [l] ver 30; Lk 3:8 [m] Mt 5:22
16:25 [n] Ps 17:14 [o] Lk 6:21,24, 25
16:28 [p] Ac 2:40; 20:23; 1Th 4:6
16:29 [q] Lk 24:27,44; Jn 5:45-47; Ac 15:21 [r] Lk 4:17; Jn 1:45
16:30 [s] ver 24; Lk 3:8
17:1 [t] Mt 5:29 [u] Mt 18:7

with a millstone tied around his neck than for him to cause one of
these little ones[a] to sin.[b] 3So watch yourselves.
"If your brother sins, rebuke him,[c] and if he repents, forgive
him.[d] 4If he sins against you seven times in a day, and seven times
comes back to you and says, 'I repent,' forgive him."[e]
5The apostles[f] said to the Lord,[g] "Increase our faith!"
6He replied, "If you have faith as small as a mustard seed,[h] you
can say to this mulberry tree, 'Be uprooted and planted in the sea,'
and it will obey you.[i]
7"Suppose one of you had a servant plowing or looking after the
sheep. Would he say to the servant when he comes in from the field,
'Come along now and sit down to eat'? 8Would he not rather say,
'Prepare my supper, get yourself ready and wait on me[j] while I eat
and drink; after that you may eat and drink'? 9Would he thank the
servant because he did what he was told to do? 10So you also, when
you have done everything you were told to do, should say, 'We are
unworthy servants; we have only done our duty.'"[k]
11Now on his way to Jerusalem,[l] Jesus traveled along the border
between Samaria and Galilee.[m] 12As he was going into a village, ten
men who had leprosy[a] [n] met him. They stood at a distance[o] 13and
called out in a loud voice, "Jesus, Master,[p] have pity on us!"
14When he saw them, he said, "Go, show yourselves to the
priests."[q] And as they went, they were cleansed.
15One of them, when he saw he was healed, came back, praising
God[r] in a loud voice. 16He threw himself at Jesus' feet and thanked
him—and he was a Samaritan.[s]
17Jesus asked, "Were not all ten cleansed? Where are the other
nine? 18Was no one found to return and give praise to God except
this foreigner?" 19Then he said to him, "Rise and go; your faith has
made you well."[t]
20Once, having been asked by the Pharisees when the kingdom
of God would come,[u] Jesus replied, "The kingdom of God does not
come with your careful observation, 21nor will people say, 'Here it
is,' or 'There it is,'[v] because the kingdom of God is within[b] you."
22Then he said to his disciples, "The time is coming when you
will long to see one of the days of the Son of Man,[w] but you will not
see it.[x] 23Men will tell you, 'There he is!' or 'Here he is!' Do not go
running off after them.[y] 24For the Son of Man in his day[c] will be
like the lightning,[z] which flashes and lights up the sky from one
end to the other. 25But first he must suffer many things[a] and be
rejected[b] by this generation.[c]
26"Just as it was in the days of Noah,[d] so also will it be in the days
of the Son of Man. 27People were eating, drinking, marrying and

[a] *12* The Greek word was used for various diseases affecting the skin—not necessarily leprosy.
[b] *21* Or *among* [c] *24* Some manuscripts do not have *in his day*.

17:2 [a] Mk 10:24; Lk 10:21 [b] Mt 5:29
17:3 [c] Mt 18:15 [d] Eph 4:32; Col 3:13
17:4 [e] Mt 18:21,22
17:5 [f] Mk 6:30 [g] Lk 7:13
17:6 [h] Mt 13:31; 17:20; Lk 13:19 [i] Mt 21:21; Mk 9:23
17:8 [j] Lk 12:37
17:10 [k] 1Co 9:16
17:11 [l] Lk 9:51 [m] Lk 9:51,52; Jn 4:3,4
17:12 [n] Mt 8:2 [o] Lev 13:45,46
17:13 [p] Lk 5:5
17:14 [q] Lev 14:2; Mt 8:4
17:15 [r] Mt 9:8
17:16 [s] Mt 10:5
17:19 [t] Mt 9:22
17:20 [u] Mt 3:2
17:21 [v] ver 23
17:22 [w] Mt 8:20 [x] Mt 9:15; Lk 5:35
17:23 [y] Mt 24:23; Mk 13:21; Lk 21:8
17:24 [z] Mt 24:27
17:25 [a] Mt 16:21 [b] Lk 9:22; 18:32 [c] Mk 13:30; Lk 21:32
17:26 [d] Ge 7:6-24

being given in marriage up to the day Noah entered the ark. Then
the flood came and destroyed them all.
28“It was the same in the days of Lot.[a] People were eating and
drinking, buying and selling, planting and building. 29But the
day Lot left Sodom, fire and sulfur rained down from heaven and
destroyed them all.
30“It will be just like this on the day the Son of Man is revealed.[b]
31On that day no one who is on the roof of his house, with his
goods inside, should go down to get them. Likewise, no one in
the field should go back for anything.[c] 32Remember Lot’s wife![d]
33Whoever tries to keep his life will lose it, and whoever loses his
life will preserve it.[e] 34I tell you, on that night two people will be in
one bed; one will be taken and the other left. 35Two women will be
grinding grain together; one will be taken and the other left.[a]”[f]
37“Where, Lord?” they asked.
He replied, “Where there is a dead body, there the vultures will
gather.”[g]

Chapter 18 Theme ________________________

18 Then Jesus told his disciples a parable to show them that
they should always pray and not give up.[h] 2He said: “In a
certain town there was a judge who neither feared God nor cared
about men. 3And there was a widow in that town who kept coming
to him with the plea, ‘Grant me justice[i] against my adversary.’
4“For some time he refused. But finally he said to himself, ‘Even
though I don’t fear God or care about men, 5yet because this widow
keeps bothering me, I will see that she gets justice, so that she won’t
eventually wear me out with her coming!’ ”[j]
6And the Lord[k] said, “Listen to what the unjust judge says. 7And
will not God bring about justice for his chosen ones, who cry out[l]
to him day and night? Will he keep putting them off? 8I tell you, he
will see that they get justice, and quickly. However, when the Son of
Man[m] comes,[n] will he find faith on the earth?”
9To some who were confident of their own righteousness[o] and
looked down on everybody else,[p] Jesus told this parable: 10“Two
men went up to the temple to pray,[q] one a Pharisee and the other a
tax collector. 11The Pharisee stood up[r] and prayed about[b] himself:
‘God, I thank you that I am not like other men—robbers, evildoers,
adulterers—or even like this tax collector. 12I fast[s] twice a week and
give a tenth[t] of all I get.’
13“But the tax collector stood at a distance. He would not even
look up to heaven, but beat his breast[u] and said, ‘God, have mercy
on me, a sinner.’[v]

17:28 [a]Ge 19:1-28
17:30 [b]Mt 10:23; 16:27; 24:3,27,37,39; 25:31; 1Co 1:7; 1Th 2:19; 2Th 1:7; 2:8; 2Pe 3:4; Rev 1:7
17:31 [c]Mt 24:17,18; Mk 13:15-16
17:32 [d]Ge 19:26
17:33 [e]Jn 12:25
17:35 [f]Mt 24:41
17:37 [g]Mt 24:28
18:1 [h]Isa 40:31; Lk 11:5-8; Ac 1:14; Ro 12:12; Eph 6:18; Col 4:2; 1Th 5:17
18:3 [i]Isa 1:17
18:5 [j]Lk 11:8
18:6 [k]Lk 7:13
18:7 [l]Ex 22:23; Ps 88:1; Rev 6:10
18:8 [m]Mt 8:20 [n]Mt 16:27
18:9 [o]Lk 16:15 [p]Isa 65:5
18:10 [q]Ac 3:1
18:11 [r]Mt 6:5; Mk 11:25
18:12 [s]Isa 58:3; Mt 9:14 [t]Mal 3:8; Lk 11:42
18:13 [u]Isa 66:2; Jer 31:19; Lk 23:48 [v]Lk 5:32; 1Ti 1:15

[a] *35* Some manuscripts *left.* [36]*Two men will be in the field; one will be taken and the other left.*
[b] *11* Or *to*

14"I tell you that this man, rather than the other, went home justified before God. For everyone who exalts himself will be humbled,
and he who humbles himself will be exalted."[a]
15People were also bringing babies to Jesus to have him touch
them. When the disciples saw this, they rebuked them. 16But Jesus
called the children to him and said, "Let the little children come
to me, and do not hinder them, for the kingdom of God belongs
to such as these. 17I tell you the truth, anyone who will not receive
the kingdom of God like a little child[b] will never enter it."
18A certain ruler asked him, "Good teacher, what must I do to
inherit eternal life?"[c]
19"Why do you call me good?" Jesus answered. "No one is
good—except God alone. 20You know the commandments: 'Do
not commit adultery, do not murder, do not steal, do not give false
testimony, honor your father and mother.'[a]"[d]
21"All these I have kept since I was a boy," he said.
22When Jesus heard this, he said to him, "You still lack one thing.
Sell everything you have and give to the poor,[e] and you will have
treasure in heaven.[f] Then come, follow me."
23When he heard this, he became very sad, because he was a
man of great wealth. 24Jesus looked at him and said, "How hard it
is for the rich to enter the kingdom of God![g] 25Indeed, it is easier
for a camel to go through the eye of a needle than for a rich man
to enter the kingdom of God."
26Those who heard this asked, "Who then can be saved?"
27Jesus replied, "What is impossible with men is possible with
God."[h]
28Peter said to him, "We have left all we had to follow you!"[i]
29"I tell you the truth," Jesus said to them, "no one who has left
home or wife or brothers or parents or children for the sake of the
kingdom of God 30will fail to receive many times as much in this
age and, in the age to come,[j] eternal life."[k]
31Jesus took the Twelve aside and told them, "We are going up to
Jerusalem,[l] and everything that is written by the prophets[m] about
the Son of Man[n] will be fulfilled. 32He will be handed over to the
Gentiles.[o] They will mock him, insult him, spit on him, flog him[p]
and kill him.[q] 33On the third day[r] he will rise again."[s]
34The disciples did not understand any of this. Its meaning was
hidden from them, and they did not know what he was talking
about.[t]
35As Jesus approached Jericho,[u] a blind man was sitting by the
roadside begging. 36When he heard the crowd going by, he asked
what was happening. 37They told him, "Jesus of Nazareth is passing by."[v]

a 20 Exodus 20:12-16; Deut. 5:16-20

18:14 [a] Mt 23:12; Lk 14:11
18:17 [b] Mt 11:25; 18:3
18:18 [c] Lk 10:25
18:20 [d] Ex 20:12-16; Dt 5:16-20; Ro 13:9
18:22 [e] Ac 2:45 [f] Mt 6:20
18:24 [g] Pr 11:28
18:27 [h] Mt 19:26
18:28 [i] Mt 4:19
18:30 [j] Mt 12:32 [k] Mt 25:46
18:31 [l] Lk 9:51 [m] Ps 22; Isa 53 [n] Mt 8:20
18:32 [o] Lk 23:1 [p] Mt 16:21 [q] Ac 2:23
18:33 [r] Mt 16:21 [s] Mt 16:21
18:34 [t] Mk 9:32; Lk 9:45
18:35 [u] Lk 19:1
18:37 [v] Lk 19:4

38He called out, "Jesus, Son of David,[a] have mercy[b] on me!"
39Those who led the way rebuked him and told him to be quiet,
but he shouted all the more, "Son of David, have mercy on me!"[c]
40Jesus stopped and ordered the man to be brought to him.
When he came near, Jesus asked him, 41"What do you want me to
do for you?"

"Lord, I want to see," he replied.

42Jesus said to him, "Receive your sight; your faith has healed
you."[d] 43Immediately he received his sight and followed Jesus,
praising God. When all the people saw it, they also praised God.[e]

Chapter 19 Theme

19 Jesus entered Jericho[f] and was passing through. 2A man was
there by the name of Zacchaeus; he was a chief tax collector and was wealthy. 3He wanted to see who Jesus was, but being a
short man he could not, because of the crowd. 4So he ran ahead
and climbed a sycamore-fig[g] tree to see him, since Jesus was coming that way.[h]

5When Jesus reached the spot, he looked up and said to him,
"Zacchaeus, come down immediately. I must stay at your house
today." 6So he came down at once and welcomed him gladly.

7All the people saw this and began to mutter, "He has gone to be
the guest of a 'sinner.'"[i]

8But Zacchaeus stood up and said to the Lord,[j] "Look, Lord!
Here and now I give half of my possessions to the poor, and if I
have cheated anybody out of anything,[k] I will pay back four times
the amount."[l]

9Jesus said to him, "Today salvation has come to this house,
because this man, too, is a son of Abraham.[m] 10For the Son of Man
came to seek and to save what was lost."[n]

11While they were listening to this, he went on to tell them a
parable, because he was near Jerusalem and the people thought
that the kingdom of God[o] was going to appear at once.[p] 12He said:
"A man of noble birth went to a distant country to have himself
appointed king and then to return. 13So he called ten of his servants[q] and gave them ten minas.[a] 'Put this money to work,' he said,
'until I come back.'

14"But his subjects hated him and sent a delegation after him to
say, 'We don't want this man to be our king.'

15"He was made king, however, and returned home. Then he
sent for the servants to whom he had given the money, in order to
find out what they had gained with it.

16"The first one came and said, 'Sir, your mina has earned ten
more.'

18:38 [a]ver 39; Mt 9:27 [b]Mt 17:15; Lk 18:13
18:39 [c]ver 38
18:42 [d]Mt 9:22
18:43 [e]Mt 9:8; Lk 13:17
19:1 [f]Lk 18:35
19:4 [g]1Ki 10:27; 1Ch 27:28; Isa 9:10 [h]Lk 18:37
19:7 [i]Mt 9:11
19:8 [j]Lk 7:13 [k]Lk 3:12,13 [l]Ex 22:1; Lev 6:4,5; Nu 5:7; 2Sa 12:6
19:9 [m]Lk 3:8; 13:16; Ro 4:16; Gal 3:7
19:10 [n]Eze 34:12,16; Jn 3:17
19:11 [o]Mt 3:2 [p]Lk 17:20; Ac 1:6
19:13 [q]Mk 13:34

a *13* A mina was about three months' wages.

17" 'Well done, my good servant!'[a] his master replied. 'Because
you have been trustworthy in a very small matter, take charge of
ten cities.'[b]
18"The second came and said, 'Sir, your mina has earned five
more.'
19"His master answered, 'You take charge of five cities.'
20"Then another servant came and said, 'Sir, here is your mina;
I have kept it laid away in a piece of cloth. 21I was afraid of you,
because you are a hard man. You take out what you did not put in
and reap what you did not sow.'[c]
22"His master replied, 'I will judge you by your own words,[d]
you wicked servant! You knew, did you, that I am a hard man,
taking out what I did not put in, and reaping what I did not sow?[e]
23Why then didn't you put my money on deposit, so that when I
came back, I could have collected it with interest?'
24"Then he said to those standing by, 'Take his mina away from
him and give it to the one who has ten minas.'
25" 'Sir,' they said, 'he already has
ten!'
26"He replied, 'I tell you that to
everyone who has, more will be giv-
en, but as for the one who has nothing, even what he has will be taken
away.[f] 27But those enemies of mine
who did not want me to be king
over them—bring them here and
kill them in front of me.' "
28After Jesus had said this, he went
on ahead, going up to Jerusalem.[g]
29As he approached Bethphage and
Bethany[h] at the hill called the Mount
of Olives,[i] he sent two of his disciples, saying to them, 30"Go to the vil-
lage ahead of you, and as you enter it, you will find a colt tied there,
which no one has ever ridden. Untie it and bring it here. 31If anyone
asks you, 'Why are you untying it?' tell him, 'The Lord needs it.' "
32Those who were sent ahead went and found it just as he had
told them.[j] 33As they were untying the colt, its owners asked
them, "Why are you untying the colt?"
34They replied, "The Lord needs it."
35They brought it to Jesus, threw their cloaks on the colt and
put Jesus on it. 36As he went along, people spread their cloaks[k] on
the road.
37When he came near the place where the road goes down the
Mount of Olives,[l] the whole crowd of disciples began joyfully to
praise God in loud voices for all the miracles they had seen:

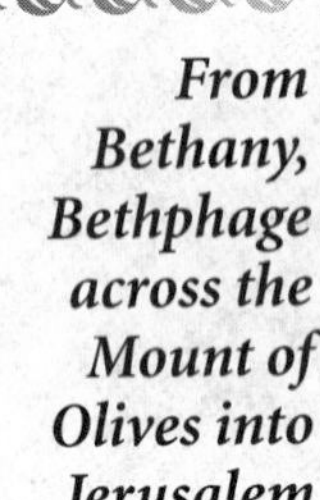

From Bethany, Bethphage across the Mount of Olives into Jerusalem

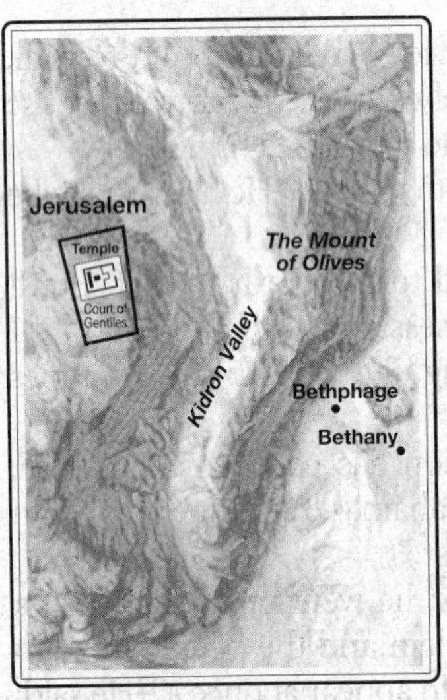

19:17 [a]Pr 27:18 [b]Lk 16:10
19:21 [c]Mt 25:24
19:22 [d]2Sa 1:16; Job 15:6 [e]Mt 25:26
19:26 [f]Mt 13:12; 25:29; Lk 8:18
19:28 [g]Mk 10:32; Lk 9:51
19:29 [h]Mt 21:17 [i]Mt 21:1
19:32 [j]Lk 22:13
19:36 [k]2Ki 9:13
19:37 [l]Mt 21:1

38"Blessed is the king who comes in the name of the Lord!"[a][a]

"Peace in heaven and glory in the highest!"[b]

39Some of the Pharisees in the crowd said to Jesus, "Teacher,
rebuke your disciples!"[c]
40"I tell you," he replied, "if they keep quiet, the stones will cry
out."[d]
41As he approached Jerusalem and saw the city, he wept over it[e]
42and said, "If you, even you, had only known on this day what
would bring you peace—but now it is hidden from your eyes.
43The days will come upon you when your enemies will build an
embankment against you and encircle you and hem you in on
every side.[f] 44They will dash you to the ground, you and the children within your walls.[g] They will not leave one stone on another,[h]
because you did not recognize the time of God's coming[i] to you."
45Then he entered the temple area and began driving out those
who were selling. 46"It is written," he said to them, "'My house will
be a house of prayer'[b];[j] but you have made it 'a den of robbers.'[c]"[k]
47Every day he was teaching at the temple.[l] But the chief priests,
the teachers of the law and the leaders among the people were trying to kill him.[m] 48Yet they could not find any way to do it, because
all the people hung on his words.

Chapter 20 Theme ______________________

20
One day as he was teaching the people in the temple courts[n]
and preaching the gospel,[o] the chief priests and the teachers of the law, together with the elders, came up to him. 2"Tell us
by what authority you are doing these things," they said. "Who
gave you this authority?"[p]
3He replied, "I will also ask you a question. Tell me, 4John's baptism[q]—was it from heaven, or from men?"
5They discussed it among themselves and said, "If we say, 'From
heaven,' he will ask, 'Why didn't you believe him?' 6But if we say,
'From men,' all the people[r] will stone us, because they are persuaded that John was a prophet."[s]
7So they answered, "We don't know where it was from."
8Jesus said, "Neither will I tell you by what authority I am doing
these things."
9He went on to tell the people this parable: "A man planted a
vineyard,[t] rented it to some farmers and went away for a long
time.[u] 10At harvest time he sent a servant to the tenants so they
would give him some of the fruit of the vineyard. But the tenants
beat him and sent him away empty-handed. 11He sent another
servant, but that one also they beat and treated shamefully and

19:38 [a]Ps 118:26; Lk 13:35 [b]Lk 2:14
19:39 [c]Mt 21:15,16
19:40 [d]Hab 2:11
19:41 [e]Isa 22:4; Lk 13:34,35
19:43 [f]Isa 29:3; Jer 6:6; Eze 4:2; 26:8; Lk 21:20
19:44 [g]Ps 137:9 [h]Mt 24:2; Mk 13:2; Lk 21:6 [i]1Pe 2:12
19:46 [j]Isa 56:7 [k]Jer 7:11
19:47 [l]Mt 26:55 [m]Mt 12:14; Mk 11:18
20:1 [n]Mt 26:55 [o]Lk 8:1
20:2 [p]Jn 2:18; Ac 4:7; 7:27
20:4 [q]Mk 1:4
20:6 [r]Lk 7:29 [s]Mt 11:9
20:9 [t]Isa 5:1-7 [u]Mt 25:14

[a]38 Psalm 118:26 [b]46 Isaiah 56:7 [c]46 Jer. 7:11

sent away empty-handed. 12He sent still a third, and they wounded
him and threw him out.

13“Then the owner of the vineyard said, ‘What shall I do? I will
send my son, whom I love;[a] perhaps they will respect him.’

14“But when the tenants saw him, they talked the matter over.
‘This is the heir,’ they said. ‘Let’s kill him, and the inheritance will
be ours.’ 15So they threw him out of the vineyard and killed him.

“What then will the owner of the vineyard do to them? 16He will
come and kill those tenants[b] and give the vineyard to others.”

When the people heard this, they said, “May this never be!”

17Jesus looked directly at them and asked, “Then what is the
meaning of that which is written:

> “ ‘The stone the builders rejected
> has become the capstone’[a]?”[b][c]

18Everyone who falls on that stone will be broken to pieces, but he
on whom it falls will be crushed.”[d]

19The teachers of the law and the chief priests looked for a way
to arrest him[e] immediately, because they knew he had spoken this
parable against them. But they were afraid of the people.[f]

20Keeping a close watch on him, they sent spies, who pretended
to be honest. They hoped to catch Jesus in something he said[g] so
that they might hand him over to the power and authority of the
governor.[h] 21So the spies questioned him: “Teacher, we know that
you speak and teach what is right, and that you do not show partiality but teach the way of God in accordance with the truth.[i] 22Is
it right for us to pay taxes to Caesar or not?”

23He saw through their duplicity and said to them, 24“Show me a
denarius. Whose portrait and inscription are on it?”

25“Caesar’s,” they replied.

He said to them, “Then give to Caesar what is Caesar’s,[j] and to
God what is God’s.”

26They were unable to trap him in what he had said there in
public. And astonished by his answer, they became silent.

27Some of the Sadducees,[k] who say there is no resurrection,[l]
came to Jesus with a question. 28“Teacher,” they said, “Moses
wrote for us that if a man’s brother dies and leaves a wife but no
children, the man must marry the widow and have children for his
brother.[m] 29Now there were seven brothers. The first one married a
woman and died childless. 30The second 31and then the third married her, and in the same way the seven died, leaving no children.
32Finally, the woman died too. 33Now then, at the resurrection
whose wife will she be, since the seven were married to her?”

[a] 17 Or *cornerstone* [b] 17 Psalm 118:22

20:13 [a] Mt 3:17
20:16 [b] Lk 19:27
20:17 [c] Ps 118:22; Ac 4:11
20:18 [d] Isa 8:14,15
20:19 [e] Lk 19:47 [f] Mk 11:18
20:20 [g] Mt 12:10 [h] Mt 27:2
20:21 [i] Jn 3:2
20:25 [j] Lk 23:2; Ro 13:7
20:27 [k] Ac 4:1 [l] Ac 23:8; 1Co 15:12
20:28 [m] Dt 25:5

34Jesus replied, "The people of this age marry and are given in
marriage. 35But those who are considered worthy of taking part
in that age[a] and in the resurrection from the dead will neither
marry nor be given in marriage, 36and they can no longer die; for
they are like the angels. They are God's children,[b] since they are
children of the resurrection. 37But in the account of the bush, even
Moses showed that the dead rise, for he calls the Lord 'the God of
Abraham, and the God of Isaac, and the God of Jacob.'[a][c] 38He is
not the God of the dead, but of the living, for to him all are alive."
39Some of the teachers of the law responded, "Well said, teacher!"
40And no one dared to ask him any more questions.[d]
41Then Jesus said to them, "How is it that they say the Christ[b] is
the Son of David?[e] 42David himself declares in the Book of Psalms:

"'The Lord said to my Lord:
"Sit at my right hand
43until I make your enemies
a footstool for your feet."'[c][f]

44David calls him 'Lord.' How then can he be his son?"
45While all the people were listening, Jesus said to his disciples,
46"Beware of the teachers of the law. They like to walk around in
flowing robes and love to be greeted in the marketplaces and have
the most important seats in the synagogues and the places of honor
at banquets.[g] 47They devour widows' houses and for a show make
lengthy prayers. Such men will be punished most severely."

Chapter 21 Theme ________________________

21
As he looked up, Jesus saw the rich putting their gifts into
the temple treasury.[h] 2He also saw a poor widow put in two
very small copper coins.[d] 3"I tell you the truth," he said, "this poor
widow has put in more than all the others. 4All these people gave
their gifts out of their wealth; but she out of her poverty put in all
she had to live on."[i]
5Some of his disciples were remarking about how the temple was
adorned with beautiful stones and with gifts dedicated to God. But
Jesus said, 6"As for what you see here, the time will come when
not one stone will be left on another;[j] every one of them will be
thrown down."
7"Teacher," they asked, "when will these things happen? And
what will be the sign that they are about to take place?"
8He replied: "Watch out that you are not deceived. For many will
come in my name, claiming, 'I am he,' and, 'The time is near.' Do
not follow them.[k] 9When you hear of wars and revolutions, do not

INSIGHT

The treasury was in the women's court of the temple, where there were thirteen trumpet-shaped offering receptacles. See the illustration of the floor plan of Herod's temple on page 1723, and see the illustration of Herod's temple on page IISB-38.

20:35 [a]Mt 12:32
20:36 [b]Jn 1:12; 1Jn 3:1-2
20:37 [c]Ex 3:6
20:40 [d]Mt 22:46; Mk 12:34
20:41 [e]Mt 1:1
20:43 [f]Ps 110:1; Mt 22:44
20:46 [g]Lk 11:43
21:1 [h]Mt 27:6; Jn 8:20
21:4 [i]2Co 8:12
21:6 [j]Lk 19:44
21:8 [k]Lk 17:23

[a] *37* Exodus 3:6 [b] *41* Or *Messiah* [c] *43* Psalm 110:1 [d] *2* Greek *two lepta*

be frightened. These things must happen first, but the end will not
come right away."
10 Then he said to them: "Nation will rise against nation, and kingdom against kingdom.[a] 11 There will be great earthquakes, famines
and pestilences in various places, and fearful events and great signs
from heaven.[b]
12 "But before all this, they will lay hands on you and persecute
you. They will deliver you to synagogues and prisons, and you will
be brought before kings and governors, and all on account of my
name. 13 This will result in your being witnesses to them.[c] 14 But
make up your mind not to worry beforehand how you will defend
yourselves.[d] 15 For I will give you[e] words and wisdom that none of
your adversaries will be able to resist or contradict. 16 You will be
betrayed even by parents, brothers, relatives and friends,[f] and they
will put some of you to death. 17 All men will hate you because of
me.[g] 18 But not a hair of your head will perish.[h] 19 By standing firm
you will gain life.[i]
20 "When you see Jerusalem being surrounded by armies,[j] you
will know that its desolation is near. 21 Then let those who are in
Judea flee to the mountains, let those in the city get out, and let
those in the country not enter the city.[k] 22 For this is the time of
punishment[l] in fulfillment[m] of all that has been written. 23 How
dreadful it will be in those days for pregnant women and nursing
mothers! There will be great distress in the land and wrath against
this people. 24 They will fall by the sword and will be taken as prisoners to all the nations. Jerusalem will be trampled[n] on by the
Gentiles until the times of the Gentiles are fulfilled.
25 "There will be signs in the sun, moon and stars. On the earth,
nations will be in anguish and perplexity at the roaring and tossing of the sea.[o] 26 Men will faint from terror, apprehensive of what is
coming on the world, for the heavenly bodies will be shaken.[p] 27 At
that time they will see the Son of Man[q] coming in a cloud[r] with
power and great glory. 28 When these things begin to take place,
stand up and lift up your heads, because your redemption is drawing near."[s]
29 He told them this parable: "Look at the fig tree and all the trees.
30 When they sprout leaves, you can see for yourselves and know
that summer is near. 31 Even so, when you see these things happening, you know that the kingdom of God[t] is near.
32 "I tell you the truth, this generation[a][u] will certainly not pass
away until all these things have happened. 33 Heaven and earth will
pass away, but my words will never pass away.[v]
34 "Be careful, or your hearts will be weighed down with dissipation, drunkenness and the anxieties of life,[w] and that day will close

[a] 32 Or *race*

21:10 [a] 2Ch 15:6; Isa 19:2
21:11 [b] Isa 29:6; Joel 2:30
21:13 [c] Php 1:12
21:14 [d] Lk 12:11
21:15 [e] Lk 12:12
21:16 [f] Lk 12:52,53
21:17 [g] Jn 15:21
21:18 [h] Mt 10:30
21:19 [i] Mt 10:22
21:20 [j] Lk 19:43
21:21 [k] Lk 17:31
21:22 [l] Isa 63:4; Da 9:24-27; Hos 9:7 [m] Mt 1:22
21:24 [n] Isa 5:5; 63:18; Da 8:13; Rev 11:2
21:25 [o] 2Pe 3:10,12
21:26 [p] Mt 24:29
21:27 [q] Mt 8:20 [r] Rev 1:7
21:28 [s] Lk 18:7
21:31 [t] Mt 3:2
21:32 [u] Lk 11:50; 17:25
21:33 [v] Mt 5:18
21:34 [w] Mk 4:19

on you unexpectedly[a] like a trap. 35 For it will come upon all those
who live on the face of the whole earth. 36 Be always on the watch,
and pray[b] that you may be able to escape all that is about to happen, and that you may be able to stand before the Son of Man."
37 Each day Jesus was teaching at the temple,[c] and each evening
he went out[d] to spend the night on the hill called the Mount of
Olives,[e] 38 and all the people came early in the morning to hear him
at the temple.[f]

Chapter 22 Theme ____

22 Now the Feast of Unleavened Bread, called the Passover,
was approaching,[g] 2 and the chief priests and the teachers of
the law were looking for some way to get rid of Jesus,[h] for they were
afraid of the people. 3 Then Satan[i] entered Judas, called Iscariot,[j]
one of the Twelve. 4 And Judas went to the chief priests and the officers of the temple guard[k] and discussed with them how he might
betray Jesus. 5 They were delighted and agreed to give him money.[l]
6 He consented, and watched for an opportunity to hand Jesus over
to them when no crowd was present.
7 Then came the day of Unleavened Bread on which the Passover
lamb had to be sacrificed.[m] 8 Jesus sent Peter and John,[n] saying, "Go
and make preparations for us to eat the Passover."
9 "Where do you want us to prepare for it?" they asked.
10 He replied, "As you enter the city, a man carrying a jar of water
will meet you. Follow him to the house that he enters, 11 and say to
the owner of the house, 'The Teacher asks: Where is the guest room,
where I may eat the Passover with my disciples?' 12 He will show
you a large upper room, all furnished. Make preparations there."
13 They left and found things just as Jesus had told them.[o] So they
prepared the Passover.
14 When the hour came, Jesus and his apostles[p] reclined at the
table.[q] 15 And he said to them, "I have eagerly desired to eat this
Passover with you before I suffer.[r] 16 For I tell you, I will not eat it
again until it finds fulfillment in the kingdom of God."[s]
17 After taking the cup, he gave thanks and said, "Take this and
divide it among you. 18 For I tell you I will not drink again of the
fruit of the vine until the kingdom of God comes."
19 And he took bread, gave thanks and broke it,[t] and gave it to
them, saying, "This is my body given for you; do this in remembrance of me."
20 In the same way, after the supper he took the cup, saying, "This
cup is the new covenant[u] in my blood, which is poured out for
you. 21 But the hand of him who is going to betray me is with mine
on the table.[v] 22 The Son of Man[w] will go as it has been decreed,[x]

21:34 [a] Lk 12:40,46; 1Th 5:2-7
21:36 [b] Mt 26:41
21:37 [c] Mt 26:55 [d] Mk 11:19 [e] Mt 21:1
21:38 [f] Jn 8:2
22:1 [g] Jn 11:55
22:2 [h] Mt 12:14
22:3 [i] Mt 4:10; Jn 13:2 [j] Mt 10:4
22:4 [k] ver 52; Ac 4:1; 5:24
22:5 [l] Zec 11:12
22:7 [m] Ex 12:18-20; Dt 16:5-8; Mk 14:12
22:8 [n] Ac 3:1,11; 4:13,19; 8:14
22:13 [o] Lk 19:32
22:14 [p] Mk 6:30 [q] Mt 26:20; Mk 14:17,18
22:15 [r] Mt 16:21
22:16 [s] Lk 14:15; Rev 19:9
22:19 [t] Mt 14:19
22:20 [u] Ex 24:8; Isa 42:6; Jer 31:31-34; Zec 9:11; 2Co 3:6; Heb 8:6; 9:15
22:21 [v] Ps 41:9
22:22 [w] Mt 8:20 [x] Ac 2:23; 4:28

but woe to that man who betrays him." 23They began to question
among themselves which of them it might be who would do this.
24Also a dispute arose among them as to which of them was
considered to be greatest.[a] 25Jesus said to them, "The kings of the
Gentiles lord it over them; and those who exercise authority over
them call themselves Benefactors. 26But you are not to be like that.
Instead, the greatest among you should be like the youngest,[b] and
the one who rules like the one who serves.[c] 27For who is greater,
the one who is at the table or the one who serves? Is it not the one
who is at the table? But I am among you as one who serves.[d] 28You
are those who have stood by me in my trials. 29And I confer on
you a kingdom,[e] just as my Father conferred one on me, 30so that
you may eat and drink at my table in my kingdom[f] and sit on
thrones, judging the twelve tribes of Israel.[g]
31"Simon, Simon, Satan has asked[h] to sift you[a] as wheat.[i] 32But I
have prayed for you,[j] Simon, that your faith may not fail. And
when you have turned back, strengthen your brothers."[k]
33But he replied, "Lord, I am ready to go with you to prison and
to death."[l]
34Jesus answered, "I tell you, Peter, before the rooster crows today,
you will deny three times that you know me."
35Then Jesus asked them, "When I sent you without purse, bag
or sandals,[m] did you lack anything?"
"Nothing," they answered.
36He said to them, "But now if you have a purse, take it, and also
a bag; and if you don't have a sword, sell your cloak and buy one.
37It is written: 'And he was numbered with the transgressors'[b];[n]
and I tell you that this must be fulfilled in me. Yes, what is written
about me is reaching its fulfillment."
38The disciples said, "See, Lord, here are two swords."
"That is enough," he replied.
39Jesus went out as usual[o] to the Mount of Olives,[p] and his disciples followed him. 40On reaching the place, he said to them, "Pray
that you will not fall into temptation."[q] 41He withdrew about a
stone's throw beyond them, knelt down[r] and prayed, 42"Father, if
you are willing, take this cup[s] from me; yet not my will, but yours
be done."[t] 43An angel from heaven appeared to him and strengthened him.[u] 44And being in anguish, he prayed more earnestly,
and his sweat was like drops of blood falling to the ground.[c]
45When he rose from prayer and went back to the disciples, he
found them asleep, exhausted from sorrow. 46"Why are you sleeping?" he asked them. "Get up and pray so that you will not fall into
temptation."[v]

[a] 31 The Greek is plural. [b] 37 Isaiah 53:12 [c] 44 Some early manuscripts do not have verses 43 and 44.

22:24 [a] Mk 9:34; Lk 9:46
22:26 [b] 1Pe 5:5 [c] Mk 9:35; Lk 9:48
22:27 [d] Mt 20:28; Lk 12:37
22:29 [e] Mt 25:34; 2Ti 2:12
22:30 [f] Lk 14:15 [g] Mt 19:28
22:31 [h] Job 1:6-12 [i] Am 9:9
22:32 [j] Jn 17:9,15; Ro 8:34 [k] Jn 21:15-17
22:33 [l] Jn 11:16
22:35 [m] Mt 10:9,10; Lk 9:3; 10:4
22:37 [n] Isa 53:12
22:39 [o] Lk 21:37 [p] Mt 21:1
22:40 [q] Mt 6:13
22:41 [r] Lk 18:11
22:42 [s] Mt 20:22 [t] Mt 26:39
22:43 [u] Mt 4:11; Mk 1:13
22:46 [v] ver 40

47While he was still speaking a crowd came up, and the man
who was called Judas, one of the Twelve, was leading them. He
approached Jesus to kiss him, 48but Jesus asked him, "Judas, are
you betraying the Son of Man with a kiss?"
49When Jesus' followers saw what was going to happen, they said,
"Lord, should we strike with our swords?"[a] 50And one of them
struck the servant of the high priest, cutting off his right ear.
51But Jesus answered, "No more of this!" And he touched the
man's ear and healed him.
52Then Jesus said to the chief priests, the officers of the temple
guard,[b] and the elders, who had come for him, "Am I leading a
rebellion, that you have come with swords and clubs? 53Every day
I was with you in the temple courts,[c] and you did not lay a hand
on me. But this is your hour[d]—when darkness reigns."[e]
54Then seizing him, they led him away and took him into the
house of the high priest.[f] Peter followed at a distance.[g] 55But when
they had kindled a fire in the middle of the courtyard and had sat
down together, Peter sat down with them. 56A servant girl saw him
seated there in the firelight. She looked closely at him and said,
"This man was with him."
57But he denied it. "Woman, I don't know him," he said.
58A little later someone else saw him and said, "You also are one
of them."
"Man, I am not!" Peter replied.
59About an hour later another asserted, "Certainly this fellow
was with him, for he is a Galilean."[h]
60Peter replied, "Man, I don't know what you're talking about!"
Just as he was speaking, the rooster crowed. 61The Lord[i] turned
and looked straight at Peter. Then Peter remembered the word the
Lord had spoken to him: "Before the rooster crows today, you will
disown me three times."[j] 62And he went outside and wept bitterly.
63The men who were guarding Jesus began mocking and beating
him. 64They blindfolded him and demanded, "Prophesy! Who hit
you?" 65And they said many other insulting things to him.[k]
66At daybreak the council[l] of the elders of the people, both the
chief priests and teachers of the law, met together,[m] and Jesus was
led before them. 67"If you are the Christ,[a]" they said, "tell us."
Jesus answered, "If I tell you, you will not believe me, 68and if I
asked you, you would not answer.[n] 69But from now on, the Son of
Man will be seated at the right hand of the mighty God."[o]
70They all asked, "Are you then the Son of God?"[p]
He replied, "You are right in saying I am."[q]
71Then they said, "Why do we need any more testimony? We
have heard it from his own lips."

[a] 67 Or *Messiah*

22:49 [a] ver 38
22:52 [b] ver 4
22:53 [c] Mt 26:55 [d] Jn 12:27 [e] Mt 8:12; Jn 1:5; 3:20
22:54 [f] Mt 26:57; Mk 14:53 [g] Mt 26:58; Mk 14:54; Jn 18:15
22:59 [h] Lk 23:6
22:61 [i] Lk 7:13 [j] ver 34
22:65 [k] Mt 16:21
22:66 [l] Mt 5:22 [m] Mt 27:1; Mk 15:1
22:68 [n] Lk 20:3-8
22:69 [o] Mk 16:19
22:70 [p] Mt 4:3 [q] Mt 27:11; Lk 23:3

Chapter 23 Theme ______________________

23 Then the whole assembly rose and led him off to Pilate.[a]
2And they began to accuse him, saying, "We have found
this man subverting our nation.[b] He opposes payment of taxes to
Caesar[c] and claims to be Christ,[a] a king."[d]
3So Pilate asked Jesus, "Are you the king of the Jews?"
"Yes, it is as you say," Jesus replied.
4Then Pilate announced to the chief priests and the crowd, "I
find no basis for a charge against this man."[e]
5But they insisted, "He stirs up the people all over Judea[b] by his
teaching. He started in Galilee[f] and has come all the way here."
6On hearing this, Pilate asked if the man was a Galilean.[g] 7When
he learned that Jesus was under Herod's jurisdiction, he sent him
to Herod,[h] who was also in Jerusalem at that time.
8When Herod saw Jesus, he was greatly pleased, because for a
long time he had been wanting to
see him.[i] From what he had heard
about him, he hoped to see him perform some miracle. 9He plied him
with many questions, but Jesus gave
him no answer.[j] 10The chief priests
and the teachers of the law were
standing there, vehemently accusing
him. 11Then Herod and his soldiers
ridiculed and mocked him. Dress-
ing him in an elegant robe,[k] they
sent him back to Pilate. 12That day
Herod and Pilate became friends[l]—
before this they had been enemies.
13Pilate called together the chief
priests, the rulers and the people,
14and said to them, "You brought me this man as one who was
inciting the people to rebellion. I have examined him in your
presence and have found no basis for your charges against him.[m]
15Neither has Herod, for he sent him back to us; as you can see,
he has done nothing to deserve death. 16Therefore, I will punish
him[n] and then release him.[c]"
18With one voice they cried out, "Away with this man! Release
Barabbas to us!"[o] 19(Barabbas had been thrown into prison for an
insurrection in the city, and for murder.)
20Wanting to release Jesus, Pilate appealed to them again. 21But
they kept shouting, "Crucify him! Crucify him!"

Jerusalem of the New Testament

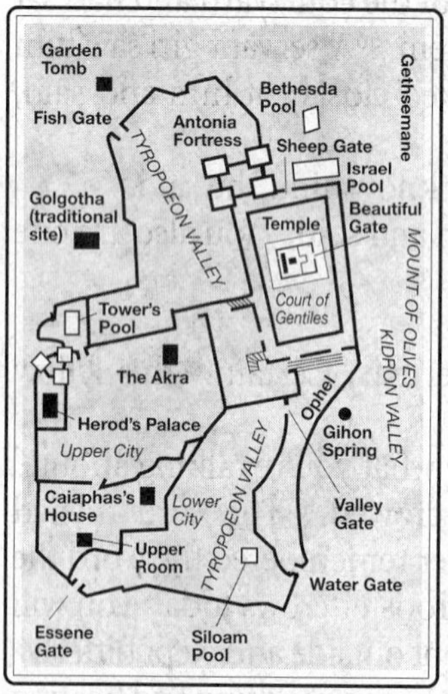

[a]2 Or *Messiah;* also in verses 35 and 39 [b]5 Or *over the land of the Jews* [c]16 Some manuscripts *him."* [17]*Now he was obliged to release one man to them at the Feast.*

23:1 [a]Mt 27:2; Mk 15:1; Jn 18:28

23:2 [b]ver 14 [c]Lk 20:22 [d]Jn 19:12

23:4 [e]ver 14,22,41; Mt 27:23; Jn 18:38; 1Ti 6:13; 2Co 5:21

23:5 [f]Mk 1:14

23:6 [g]Lk 22:59

23:7 [h]Mt 14:1; Lk 3:1

23:8 [i]Lk 9:9

23:9 [j]Mk 14:61

23:11 [k]Mk 15:17-19; Jn 19:2,3

23:12 [l]Ac 4:27

23:14 [m]ver 4

23:16 [n]ver 22; Mt 27:26; Jn 19:1; Ac 16:37; 2Co 11:23,24

23:18 [o]Ac 3:13,14

22For the third time he spoke to them: "Why? What crime has
this man committed? I have found in him no grounds for the death
penalty. Therefore I will have him punished and then release him."[a]
23But with loud shouts they insistently demanded that he be
crucified, and their shouts prevailed. 24So Pilate decided to grant
their demand. 25He released the man who had been thrown into
prison for insurrection and murder, the one they asked for, and
surrendered Jesus to their will.
26As they led him away, they seized Simon from Cyrene,[b] who
was on his way in from the country, and put the cross on him and
made him carry it behind Jesus.[c] 27A large number of people followed him, including women who mourned and wailed[d] for him.
28Jesus turned and said to them, "Daughters of Jerusalem, do not
weep for me; weep for yourselves and for your children.[e] 29For the
time will come when you will say, 'Blessed are the barren women,
the wombs that never bore and the breasts that never nursed!'[f]
30Then

> " 'they will say to the mountains, "Fall on us!"
> and to the hills, "Cover us!" '[a][g]

31For if men do these things when the tree is green, what will happen when it is dry?"[h]
32Two other men, both criminals, were also led out with him to
be executed.[i] 33When they came to the place called the Skull, there
they crucified him, along with the criminals—one on his right, the
other on his left. 34Jesus said, "Father,[j] forgive them, for they do
not know what they are doing."[b][k] And they divided up his clothes
by casting lots.[l]
35The people stood watching, and the rulers even sneered at
him.[m] They said, "He saved others; let him save himself if he is
the Christ of God, the Chosen One."[n]
36The soldiers also came up and mocked him.[o] They offered him
wine vinegar[p] 37and said, "If you are the king of the Jews,[q] save
yourself."
38There was a written notice above him, which read: THIS IS THE
KING OF THE JEWS.[r]
39One of the criminals who hung there hurled insults at him:
"Aren't you the Christ? Save yourself and us!"[s]
40But the other criminal rebuked him. "Don't you fear God," he
said, "since you are under the same sentence? 41We are punished
justly, for we are getting what our deeds deserve. But this man
has done nothing wrong."[t]

23:22 [a] ver 16
23:26 [b] Mt 27:32 [c] Mk 15:21; Jn 19:17
23:27 [d] Lk 8:52
23:28 [e] Lk 19:41-44; 21:23,24
23:29 [f] Mt 24:19
23:30 [g] Hos 10:8; Isa 2:19; Rev 6:16
23:31 [h] Eze 20:47
23:32 [i] Isa 53:12; Mt 27:38; Mk 15:27; Jn 19:18
23:34 [j] Mt 11:25 [k] Mt 5:44 [l] Ps 22:18
23:35 [m] Ps 22:17 [n] Isa 42:1
23:36 [o] Ps 22:7 [p] Ps 69:21; Mt 27:48
23:37 [q] Lk 4:3,9
23:38 [r] Mt 2:2
23:39 [s] ver 35,37
23:41 [t] ver 4

[a] *30* Hosea 10:8 [b] *34* Some early manuscripts do not have this sentence.

[42]Then he said, "Jesus, remember me when you come into your
kingdom.[a]"[a]
[43]Jesus answered him, "I tell you the truth, today you will be with
me in paradise."[b]
[44]It was now about the sixth hour, and darkness came over the
whole land until the ninth hour,[c] [45]for the sun stopped shining.
And the curtain of the temple[d] was torn in two.[e] [46]Jesus called out
with a loud voice,[f] "Father, into your hands I commit my spirit."[g]
When he had said this, he breathed his last.[h]
[47]The centurion, seeing what had happened, praised God[i] and
said, "Surely this was a righteous man." [48]When all the people
who had gathered to witness this sight saw what took place, they
beat their breasts[j] and went away. [49]But all those who knew him,
including the women who had followed him from Galilee,[k] stood
at a distance,[l] watching these things.
[50]Now there was a man named Joseph, a member of the Council,
a good and upright man, [51]who had not consented to their decision and action. He came from the Judean town of Arimathea
and he was waiting for the kingdom of God.[m] [52]Going to Pilate,
he asked for Jesus' body. [53]Then he took it down, wrapped it in
linen cloth and placed it in a tomb cut in the rock, one in which
no one had yet been laid. [54]It was Preparation Day,[n] and the Sabbath was about to begin.
[55]The women who had come with Jesus from Galilee[o] followed
Joseph and saw the tomb and how his body was laid in it. [56]Then
they went home and prepared spices and perfumes.[p] But they
rested on the Sabbath in obedience to the commandment.[q]

Chapter 24 Theme ______________________________________

24 On the first day of the week, very early in the morning, the
women took the spices they had prepared[r] and went to
the tomb. [2]They found the stone rolled away from the tomb, [3]but
when they entered, they did not find the body of the Lord Jesus.[s]
[4]While they were wondering about this, suddenly two men in
clothes that gleamed like lightning[t] stood beside them. [5]In their
fright the women bowed down with their faces to the ground, but
the men said to them, "Why do you look for the living among the
dead? [6]He is not here; he has risen! Remember how he told you,
while he was still with you in Galilee:[u] [7]'The Son of Man[v] must be
delivered into the hands of sinful men, be crucified and on the
third day be raised again.'"[w] [8]Then they remembered his words.[x]
[9]When they came back from the tomb, they told all these things
to the Eleven and to all the others. [10]It was Mary Magdalene, Joan-
na, Mary the mother of James, and the others with them[y] who told
this to the apostles.[z] [11]But they did not believe[a] the women, because

23:42 [a]Mt 16:27
23:43 [b]2Co 12:3,4; Rev 2:7
23:44 [c]Am 8:9
23:45 [d]Ex 26:31-33; Heb 9:3,8 [e]Heb 10:19,20
23:46 [f]Mt 27:50 [g]Ps 31:5; 1Pe 2:23 [h]Jn 19:30
23:47 [i]Mt 9:8
23:48 [j]Lk 18:13
23:49 [k]Lk 8:2 [l]Ps 38:11
23:51 [m]Lk 2:25,38
23:54 [n]Mt 27:62
23:55 [o]ver 49
23:56 [p]Mk 16:1; Lk 24:1 [q]Ex 12:16; 20:10
24:1 [r]Lk 23:56
24:3 [s]ver 23,24
24:4 [t]Jn 20:12
24:6 [u]Mt 17:22,23; Mk 9:30-31; Lk 9:22; 24:44
24:7 [v]Mt 8:20 [w]Mt 16:21
24:8 [x]Jn 2:22
24:10 [y]Lk 8:1-3 [z]Mk 6:30
24:11 [a]Mk 16:11

[a]42 Some manuscripts *come with your kingly power*

their words seemed to them like nonsense. 12Peter, however, got
up and ran to the tomb. Bending over, he saw the strips of linen
lying by themselves,[a] and he went away,[b] wondering to himself
what had happened.
13Now that same day two of them were going to a village called
Emmaus, about seven miles[a] from Jerusalem.[c] 14They were talking
with each other about everything that had happened. 15As they
talked and discussed these things with each other, Jesus himself
came up and walked along with them;[d] 16but they were kept from
recognizing him.[e]
17He asked them, "What are you discussing together as you walk
along?"
They stood still, their faces downcast. 18One of them, named
Cleopas,[f] asked him, "Are you only a visitor to Jerusalem and do
not know the things that have happened there in these days?"
19"What things?" he asked.
"About Jesus of Nazareth,"[g] they replied. "He was a prophet,[h]
powerful in word and deed before God and all the people. 20The
chief priests and our rulers[i] handed him over to be sentenced to
death, and they crucified him; 21but we had hoped that he was
the one who was going to redeem Israel.[j] And what is more, it is
the third day[k] since all this took place. 22In addition, some of our
women amazed us.[l] They went to the tomb early this morning
23but didn't find his body. They came and told us that they had
seen a vision of angels, who said he was alive. 24Then some of our
companions went to the tomb and found it just as the women had
said, but him they did not see."[m]
25He said to them, "How foolish you are, and how slow of heart
to believe all that the prophets have spoken! 26Did not the Christ[b]
have to suffer these things and then enter his glory?"[n] 27And beginning with Moses[o] and all the Prophets,[p] he explained to them what
was said in all the Scriptures concerning himself.[q]
28As they approached the village to which they were going, Jesus
acted as if he were going farther. 29But they urged him strongly,
"Stay with us, for it is nearly evening; the day is almost over." So
he went in to stay with them.
30When he was at the table with them, he took bread, gave
thanks, broke it[r] and began to give it to them. 31Then their eyes
were opened and they recognized him,[s] and he disappeared from
their sight. 32They asked each other, "Were not our hearts burning
within us[t] while he talked with us on the road and opened the
Scriptures[u] to us?"
33They got up and returned at once to Jerusalem. There they
found the Eleven and those with them, assembled together 34and

24:12 [a]Jn 20:3-7 [b]Jn 20:10
24:13 [c]Mk 16:12
24:15 [d]ver 36
24:16 [e]Jn 20:14; 21:4
24:18 [f]Jn 19:25
24:19 [g]Mk 1:24 [h]Mt 21:11
24:20 [i]Lk 23:13
24:21 [j]Lk 1:68; 2:38; 21:28 [k]Mt 16:21
24:22 [l]ver 1-10
24:24 [m]ver 12
24:26 [n]Heb 2:10; 1Pe 1:11
24:27 [o]Ge 3:15; Nu 21:9; Dt 18:15 [p]Isa 7:14; 9:6; 40:10,11; 53; Eze 34:23; Da 9:24; Mic 7:20; Mal 3:1 [q]Jn 1:45
24:30 [r]Mt 14:19
24:31 [s]ver 16
24:32 [t]Ps 39:3 [u]ver 27,45

[a]*13* Greek *sixty stadia* (about 11 kilometers) [b]*26* Or *Messiah;* also in verse 46

saying, "It is true! The Lord has risen and has appeared to Simon."[a]
35 Then the two told what had happened on the way, and how Jesus
was recognized by them when he broke the bread.[b]
36 While they were still talking about this, Jesus himself stood
among them and said to them, "Peace be with you."[c]
37 They were startled and frightened, thinking they saw a ghost.[d]
38 He said to them, "Why are you troubled, and why do doubts
rise in your minds? 39 Look at my hands and my feet. It is I myself!
Touch me and see;[e] a ghost does not have flesh and bones, as you
see I have."
40 When he had said this, he showed them his hands and feet.
41 And while they still did not believe it because of joy and amazement, he asked them, "Do you have anything here to eat?" 42 They
gave him a piece of broiled fish, 43 and he took it and ate it in their
presence.[f]
44 He said to them, "This is what I told you while I was still with
you:[g] Everything must be fulfilled[h] that is written about me in the
Law of Moses,[i] the Prophets and the Psalms."[j]
45 Then he opened their minds so they could understand the
Scriptures. 46 He told them, "This is what is written: The Christ will
suffer and rise from the dead on the third day, 47 and repentance and
forgiveness of sins will be preached in his name[k] to all nations,[l]
beginning at Jerusalem. 48 You are witnesses[m] of these things. 49 I am
going to send you what my Father has promised;[n] but stay in the
city until you have been clothed with power from on high."
50 When he had led them out to the vicinity of Bethany,[o] he lifted
up his hands and blessed them. 51 While he was blessing them, he
left them and was taken up into heaven.[p] 52 Then they worshiped
him and returned to Jerusalem with great joy. 53 And they stayed
continually at the temple,[q] praising God.

24:34
[a] 1Co 15:5
24:35
[b] ver 30,31
24:36
[c] Jn 20:19,21,26; 14:27
24:37
[d] Mk 6:49
24:39
[e] Jn 20:27; 1Jn 1:1
24:43
[f] Ac 10:41
24:44
[g] Lk 9:45; 18:34
[h] Mt 16:21; Lk 9:22,44; 18:31-33; 22:37
[i] ver 27
[j] Ps 2; 16; 22; 69; 72; 110; 118
24:47
[k] Ac 5:31; 10:43; 13:38
[l] Mt 28:19
24:48
[m] Ac 1:8; 2:32; 5:32; 13:31; 1 Pe 5:1
24:49
[n] Jn 14:16; Ac 1:4
24:50
[o] Mt 21:17
24:51
[p] 2Ki 2:11
24:53
[q] Ac 2:46

me of Luke:

:or:

::

•ose:

Words:

ngdom of
od

•n of Man

ark every
ference to
e devil or
emons

•venant

Segment Divisions		Chapter Themes
		1
		2
		3
		4
		5
		6
		7
		8
		9
		10
		11
		12
		13
		14
		15
		16
		17
		18
		19
		20
		21
		22
		23
		24

Life of Christ Showing Coverage by Luke (Shaded Area)

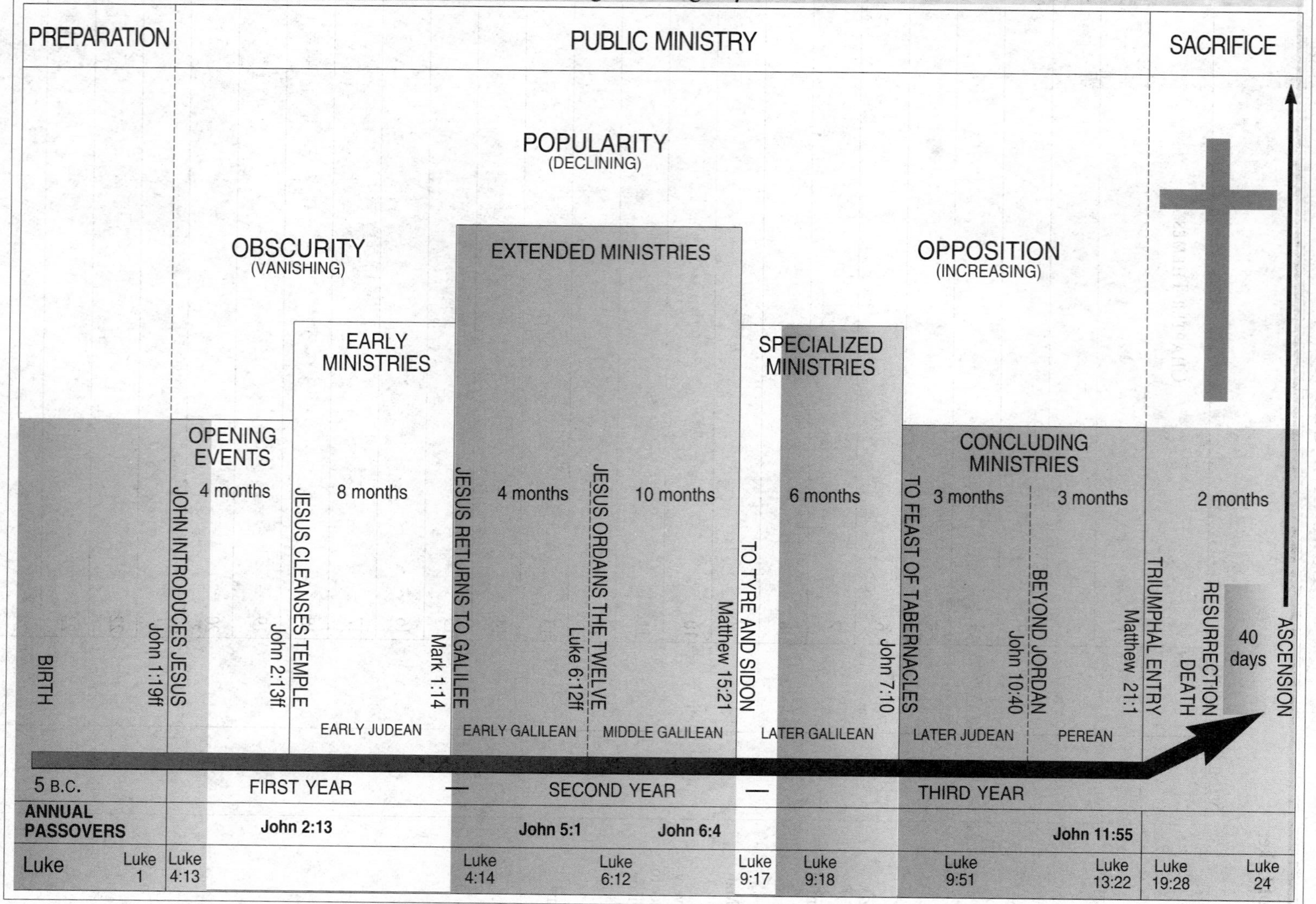

PREPARATION | PUBLIC MINISTRY | SACRIFICE

OBSCURITY (VANISHING)

POPULARITY (DECLINING)

OPPOSITION (INCREASING)

OPENING EVENTS — 4 months

EARLY MINISTRIES — 8 months — EARLY JUDEAN

EXTENDED MINISTRIES — 4 months — EARLY GALILEAN; 10 months — MIDDLE GALILEAN

SPECIALIZED MINISTRIES — 6 months — LATER GALILEAN

CONCLUDING MINISTRIES — 3 months — LATER JUDEAN; 3 months — PEREAN

2 months

BIRTH

JOHN INTRODUCES JESUS
John 1:19ff

JESUS CLEANSES TEMPLE
John 2:13ff

JESUS RETURNS TO GALILEE
Mark 1:14

JESUS ORDAINS THE TWELVE
Luke 6:12ff

TO TYRE AND SIDON
Matthew 15:21

TO FEAST OF TABERNACLES
John 7:10

BEYOND JORDAN
John 10:40

TRIUMPHAL ENTRY
Matthew 21:1

DEATH

RESURRECTION

40 days

ASCENSION

5 B.C.	FIRST YEAR	SECOND YEAR	THIRD YEAR
ANNUAL PASSOVERS	John 2:13	John 5:1; John 6:4	John 11:55

Luke: Luke 1 | Luke 4:13 | Luke 4:14 | Luke 6:12 | Luke 9:17 | Luke 9:18 | Luke 9:51 | Luke 13:22 | Luke 19:28 | Luke 24

Used by permission. Jensen, Irving L. *Luke: A Self-Study Guide*. Chicago: Moody Press, 1970.

JOHN

God in the flesh! What would he be like? What would he do? How would he live in relationship to the Father once he came to earth? How would people know he was God? Would he force people to believe in him? And what about those who refused to believe he was God?

And what of those who believed, who followed him? What would God in the flesh expect from them? And what if they failed?

God in the flesh. It would be hard for some to believe, but their belief or unbelief would be a matter of life or death.

Three other Gospels had been written, and years had passed. One more Gospel was needed, one which would answer these questions and more, one which would illuminate the shadows of doubt. So the apostle John answered God's call to write a fourth and final Gospel to explain the one who came to reveal the Father. It was about A.D. 85.

Things to Do

1. Although the author of John is not identified by name, tradition holds that it was the apostle John. Read John 21:20-25 and note how the author identifies himself. You might want to put this reference or information under "Author" on the JOHN AT A GLANCE chart on page 1861.

2. To understand the purpose of John read John 20:30, 31. Record John's purpose on JOHN AT A GLANCE.

Chapters 1-12

1. Carefully read this segment chapter by chapter, observing what the author includes to accomplish his purpose.

   a. As you read these chapters, look for and mark the following key words and their synonyms: *believe (believed, faith, trust), life (live), miraculous sign(s), judge (judging, judgment, condemn, verdict, condemned, decisions), witness (testify, testifies, testified, testimony, speak, spread the word), true (truth, truthful, valid, real, right, reliable, truly, surely),* and *king (kingdom).*

   b. You will find it helpful to write down the key words on an index card to use as a bookmark. Mark the words on the card in the same way you want to mark them in your Bible.

   c. Also mark any other repeated key words that are pertinent to the message of the chapter.

2. As you read each of the first twelve chapters, ask the five W's and an H: Who? What? Where? When? Why? and How? Look specifically for the following, recording whatever facts you find in each chapter in the margin. As you move your findings to the margin, use the headings set in italics below as your headings in the margins.

   a. *Events:* What is happening? For example, "Nicodemus came to Jesus at night."

   b. *Geographic locations:* Where is this event taking place? For example, John was baptizing at Bethany on the other side of the Jordan.

   c. *Timing of events:* When is this event taking place? For example, "on the third day," or "just before the Passover feast." In the margin next to the text, note these mentions of time by drawing an appropriate symbol. When you read of Jesus attending a feast, consult the chart THE FEASTS OF ISRAEL on pages 210, 211.

   d. *Portrayals of Jesus Christ:* How is Jesus pictured or described? For example: "the Word," "the Lamb of God," etc.

   e. *Signs and Miracles:* The signs that John recorded were for the purpose of leading people to believe that Jesus is the Christ, the Son of God. Look for these signs or miracles. For example, Jesus turned water into wine. The text says, "This, the first of his miraculous signs."

f. *References that show the deity of Jesus* (references that show that Jesus is God): Look for verses that show Jesus is God. For example, John 10:33 says, "'We are not stoning you for any of these,' replied the Jews, 'but for blasphemy, because you, a mere man, claim to be God.'"

g. *Witnesses:* Throughout his Gospel, John refers to those who bear witness to Jesus. Who are these witnesses and what is their witness? For example, John said, "I have seen and I testify that this is the Son of God" (John 1:34).

3. Determine the main subject or theme of each chapter and then record it next to the chapter number and on JOHN AT A GLANCE.

Chapters 13-17

1. This segment brings a change in Jesus' ministry as he draws away with the disciples in order to prepare them for what is to come. Make a new list of key words on a bookmark: *believe (trust), love (loved), work (miracles, things), command (commands), fruit (fruitful), remain, ask (prayer, pray, praying), truth (true, I tell you the truth),* and *devil (Satan, prince of this world).* (Go back to chapter 12 and mark the references to *prince of this world.*)

2. Mark in the text in a distinctive way all references, including pronouns, to God, Jesus, and the Holy Spirit. Then list in the margin everything you learn about the Holy Spirit. This is especially important in chapters 14 through 16.

3. List in the chapter margins any specific instructions or commandments that Jesus gives the disciples.

4. Record the main theme of each chapter as you did before.

Chapters 18-21

1. The final chapters of John give an account of the events surrounding the arrest, trial, crucifixion, resurrection, and the postresurrection appearances of Jesus Christ. As you read each chapter:

a. Mark the following key words and their synonyms: *testify (testifies, testimony), believe, love, truth (true), life,* and *king (kingdom).*

b. On pages 1862 and 1863 you will find two charts: THE ARREST, TRIAL, AND CRUCIFIXION OF JESUS CHRIST (page 1862) and THE ACCOUNT OF JESUS' RESURRECTION (page 1863). Record on the appropriate chart the progression of events from Jesus' arrest through his resurrection and postresurrection appearances. Note chapter and verse for future reference. (It would be good to do this on notebook paper before recording it on the chart.) Also remember that since Luke gives the consecutive order of events, it becomes a plumb line for the other Gospel records.

2. Once again determine the theme of each chapter and record it as you have done previously.

3. On pages 1864, 1865 you will find a chart WHAT THE GOSPELS TEACH ABOUT THE KINGDOM OF GOD/THE KINGDOM OF HEAVEN. Compile what John teaches about the king and the kingdom on this chart. John 3 contains the only two references to the kingdom. The other references to Jesus as the king are in the first and last segments of John. (Compile your information on notebook paper before you write it on the chart and note chapter and verse of insight.)

4. Complete JOHN AT A GLANCE by doing the following:

a. Review your chapter themes of John and determine the theme of the book. Record this in the appropriate place on JOHN AT A GLANCE.

b. You will notice a section titled "Segment Divisions" and two lines where you can record "Signs and Miracles" and "Portrayals of Jesus Christ." Review the information you have recorded in the margins. Record your observations on the appropriate segment division line. For example, in chapter 1 Jesus is referred to as "the Lamb of God." Record that fact at chapter 1 under "Portrayals of Jesus Christ." This will give you a visual picture of the structure of John.

Things to Think About

1. Do you really believe that Jesus is God? Do you live accordingly?
2. Do you know how to take another person through the Scriptures to show him that Jesus is God?
3. Do people know that you are a disciple of Jesus Christ because of your love for others and because you have continued in his Word?
4. Are you relying on the Spirit of God to comfort you, help you, bear witness through you, do the work of God through you, and guide you into all truth?
5. Do you look at other Christians and wonder why God deals differently with you than he does with them? Do you need to hear his words to Peter in John 21:22, "If I want him to remain alive until I return, what is that to you? You must follow me"? Are you willing to follow Jesus wherever he leads, even if you have to do it alone? Are you telling others about him?

Chapter 1 Theme ____________________

1 In the beginning was the Word,[a] and the Word was with God,[b]
and the Word was God.[c] 2 He was with God in the beginning.[d]
3 Through him all things were made; without him nothing was
made that has been made.[e] 4 In him was life,[f] and that life was the
light[g] of men. 5 The light shines in the darkness, but the darkness
has not understood[a] it.[h]
6 There came a man who was sent from God; his name was
John.[i] 7 He came as a witness to testify[j] concerning that light, so
that through him all men might believe.[k] 8 He himself was not the
light; he came only as a witness to the light. 9 The true light[l] that
gives light to every man[m] was coming into the world.[b]
10 He was in the world, and though the world was made through
him,[n] the world did not recognize him. 11 He came to that which
was his own, but his own did not receive him. 12 Yet to all who
received him, to those who believed[o] in his name,[p] he gave the
right to become children of God[q]— 13 children born not of natural
descent,[c] nor of human decision or a husband's will, but born
of God.[r]
14 The Word became flesh[s] and made his dwelling among us. We
have seen his glory, the glory of the One and Only,[d] who came
from the Father, full of grace and truth.[t]
15 John testifies[u] concerning him. He cries out, saying, "This was
he of whom I said, 'He who comes after me has surpassed me
because he was before me.'"[v] 16 From the fullness[w] of his grace we

1:1 [a] Rev 19:13 [b] Jn 17:5; 1Jn 1:2 [c] Php 2:6
1:2 [d] Ge 1:1
1:3 [e] 1Co 8:6; Col 1:16; Heb 1:2
1:4 [f] Jn 5:26; 11:25; 14:6 [g] Jn 8:12
1:5 [h] Jn 3:19
1:6 [i] Mt 3:1
1:7 [j] ver 15,19,32 [k] ver 12
1:9 [l] 1Jn 2:8 [m] Isa 49:6
1:10 [n] Heb 1:2
1:12 [o] ver 7 [p] 1Jn 3:23 [q] Gal 3:26
1:13 [r] Jn 3:6; Jas 1:18; 1Pe 1:23; 1Jn 3:9
1:14 [s] Gal 4:4; Php 2:7,8; 1Ti 3:16; Heb 2:14 [t] Jn 14:6
1:15 [u] ver 7 [v] ver 30; Mt 3:11
1:16 [w] Eph 1:23; Col 1:19

[a] 5 Or *darkness, and the darkness has not overcome* [b] 9 Or *This was the true light that gives light to every man who comes into the world* [c] 13 Greek *of bloods* [d] 14 Or *the Only Begotten*

have all received one blessing after another. 17For the law was giv-
en through Moses;[a] grace and truth came through Jesus Christ.[b]
18No one has ever seen God,[c] but God the One and Only,[a,b][d] who
is at the Father's side, has made him known.
19Now this was John's testimony when the Jews[e] of Jerusalem
sent priests and Levites to ask him who he was. 20He did not fail
to confess, but confessed freely, "I am not the Christ.[c]"[f]
21They asked him, "Then who are you? Are you Elijah?"[g]
He said, "I am not."
"Are you the Prophet?"[h]
He answered, "No."
22Finally they said, "Who are you? Give us an answer to take
back to those who sent us. What do you say about yourself?"
23John replied in the words of Isaiah the prophet, "I am the voice
of one calling in the desert,[i] 'Make straight the way for the Lord.'"[d][j]
24Now some Pharisees who had been sent 25questioned him,
"Why then do you baptize if you are not the Christ, nor Elijah,
nor the Prophet?"
26"I baptize with[e] water," John replied, "but among you stands
one you do not know. 27He is the one who comes after me,[k] the
thongs of whose sandals I am not worthy to untie."
28This all happened at Bethany on the other side of the Jordan,[l]
where John was baptizing.
29The next day John saw Jesus coming toward him and said,
"Look, the Lamb of God,[m] who takes away the sin of the world!
30This is the one I meant when I said, 'A man who comes after
me has surpassed me because he was before me.'[n] 31I myself did
not know him, but the reason I came baptizing with water was
that he might be revealed to Israel."
32Then John gave this testimony: "I saw the Spirit come down
from heaven as a dove and remain on him.[o] 33I would not have
known him, except that the one who sent me to baptize with
water[p] told me, 'The man on whom you see the Spirit come down
and remain is he who will baptize with the Holy Spirit.'[q] 34I have
seen and I testify that this is the Son of God."[r]
35The next day John[s] was there again with two of his disciples.
36When he saw Jesus passing by, he said, "Look, the Lamb of
God!"[t]
37When the two disciples heard him say this, they followed
Jesus. 38Turning around, Jesus saw them following and asked,
"What do you want?"
They said, "Rabbi"[u] (which means Teacher), "where are you
staying?"

[a] *18* Or *the Only Begotten* [b] *18* Some manuscripts *but the only* (or *only begotten*) *Son*
[c] *20* Or *Messiah.* "The Christ" (Greek) and "the Messiah" (Hebrew) both mean "the Anointed One"; also in verse 25. [d] *23* Isaiah 40:3 [e] *26* Or *in*; also in verses 31 and 33

1:17 [a] Jn 7:19 [b] ver 14
1:18 [c] Ex 33:20; Jn 6:46; Col 1:15; 1Ti 6:16 [d] Jn 3:16,18; 1Jn 4:9
1:19 [e] Jn 2:18; 5:10,16; 6:41,52
1:20 [f] Jn 3:28; Lk 3:15,16
1:21 [g] Mt 11:14 [h] Dt 18:15
1:23 [i] Mt 3:1 [j] Isa 40:3
1:27 [k] ver 15,30
1:28 [l] Jn 3:26; 10:40
1:29 [m] ver 36; Isa 53:7; 1Pe 1:19; Rev 5:6
1:30 [n] ver 15,27
1:32 [o] Mt 3:16; Mk 1:10
1:33 [p] Mk 1:4 [q] Mt 3:11; Mk 1:8
1:34 [r] ver 49; Mt 4:3
1:35 [s] Mt 3:1
1:36 [t] ver 29
1:38 [u] ver 49; Mt 23:7

39 “Come,” he replied, “and you will see.”

So they went and saw where he was staying, and spent that day with him. It was about the tenth hour.

40 Andrew, Simon Peter’s brother, was one of the two who heard what John had said and who had followed Jesus. 41 The first thing Andrew did was to find his brother Simon and tell him, “We have found the Messiah” (that is, the Christ).[a] 42 And he brought him to Jesus.

Jesus looked at him and said, “You are Simon son of John. You will be called[b] Cephas” (which, when translated, is Peter[a]).[c]

43 The next day Jesus decided to leave for Galilee. Finding Philip,[d] he said to him, “Follow me.”[e]

44 Philip, like Andrew and Peter, was from the town of Bethsaida.[f] 45 Philip found Nathanael[g] and told him, “We have found the one Moses wrote about in the Law,[h] and about whom the prophets also wrote[i]—Jesus of Nazareth,[j] the son of Joseph.”[k]

46 “Nazareth! Can anything good come from there?”[l] Nathanael asked.

“Come and see,” said Philip.

47 When Jesus saw Nathanael approaching, he said of him, “Here is a true Israelite,[m] in whom there is nothing false.”[n]

48 “How do you know me?” Nathanael asked.

Jesus answered, “I saw you while you were still under the fig tree before Philip called you.”

49 Then Nathanael declared, “Rabbi,[o] you are the Son of God;[p] you are the King of Israel.”[q]

50 Jesus said, “You believe[b] because I told you I saw you under the fig tree. You shall see greater things than that.” 51 He then added, “I tell you[c] the truth, you[c] shall see heaven open,[r] and the angels of God ascending and descending[s] on the Son of Man.”[t]

Chapter 2 Theme ____________________________

2 On the third day a wedding took place at Cana in Galilee.[u] Jesus’ mother[v] was there, 2 and Jesus and his disciples had also been invited to the wedding. 3 When the wine was gone, Jesus’ mother said to him, “They have no more wine.”

4 “Dear woman,[w] why do you involve me?”[x] Jesus replied. “My time[y] has not yet come.”

5 His mother said to the servants, “Do whatever he tells you.”[z]

6 Nearby stood six stone water jars, the kind used by the Jews for ceremonial washing,[a] each holding from twenty to thirty gallons.[d]

7 Jesus said to the servants, “Fill the jars with water”; so they filled them to the brim.

1:41 [a] Jn 4:25
1:42 [b] Ge 17:5,15 [c] Mt 16:18
1:43 [d] Mt 10:3; Jn 6:5-7; 12:21, 22; 14:8,9 [e] Mt 4:19
1:44 [f] Mt 11:21; Jn 12:21
1:45 [g] Jn 21:2 [h] Lk 24:27 [i] Lk 24:27 [j] Mt 2:23; Mk 1:24 [k] Lk 3:23
1:46 [l] Jn 7:41,42,52
1:47 [m] Ro 9:4,6 [n] Ps 32:2
1:49 [o] ver 38; Mt 23:7 [p] ver 34; Mt 4:3 [q] Mt 2:2; 27:42; Jn 12:13
1:51 [r] Mt 3:16 [s] Ge 28:12 [t] Mt 8:20
2:1 [u] Jn 4:46; 21:2 [v] Mt 12:46
2:4 [w] Jn 19:26 [x] Mt 8:29 [y] Mt 26:18; Jn 7:6
2:5 [z] Ge 41:55
2:6 [a] Mk 7:3,4; Jn 3:25

[a] *42* Both *Cephas* (Aramaic) and *Peter* (Greek) mean *rock.* [b] *50* Or *Do you believe . . . ?*
[c] *51* The Greek is plural. [d] *6* Greek *two to three metretes* (probably about 75 to 115 liters)

8Then he told them, "Now draw some out and take it to the
master of the banquet."
They did so, 9and the master of the banquet tasted the water that
had been turned into wine.[a] He did not realize where it had come
from, though the servants who had drawn the water knew. Then
he called the bridegroom aside 10and said, "Everyone brings out
the choice wine first and then the cheaper wine after the guests
have had too much to drink; but you have saved the best till now."
11This, the first of his miraculous signs,[b] Jesus performed at
Cana in Galilee. He thus revealed his glory,[c] and his disciples put
their faith in him.[d]
12After this he went down to Capernaum[e] with his mother and
brothers[f] and his disciples. There they stayed for a few days.
13When it was almost time for the Jewish Passover,[g] Jesus went

Jesus Ministers from Capernaum to Jerusalem

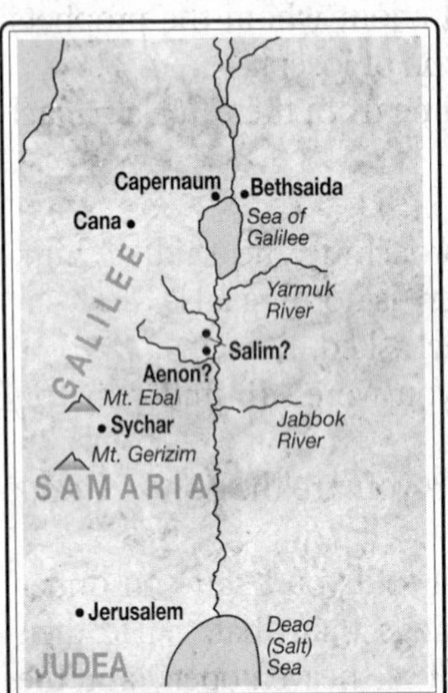

up to Jerusalem.[h] 14In the temple
courts he found men selling cattle,
sheep and doves, and others sitting
at tables exchanging money. 15So he
made a whip out of cords, and
drove all from the temple area, both
sheep and cattle; he scattered the
coins of the money changers and
overturned their tables. 16To those
who sold doves he said, "Get these
out of here! How dare you turn my
Father's house[i] into a market!"
17His disciples remembered that
it is written: "Zeal for your house
will consume me."[a][j]
18Then the Jews demanded of him,
"What miraculous sign can you show us to prove your authority to
do all this?"[k]
19Jesus answered them, "Destroy this temple, and I will raise it
again in three days."[l]
20The Jews replied, "It has taken forty-six years to build this
temple, and you are going to raise it in three days?" 21But the
temple he had spoken of was his body.[m] 22After he was raised
from the dead, his disciples recalled what he had said.[n] Then they
believed the Scripture and the words that Jesus had spoken.
23Now while he was in Jerusalem at the Passover Feast,[o] many
people saw the miraculous signs he was doing and believed in his
name.[b] 24But Jesus would not entrust himself to them, for he
knew all men. 25He did not need man's testimony about man, for
he knew what was in a man.[p]

[a] 17 Psalm 69:9 [b] 23 Or *and believed in him*

2:9 [a] Jn 4:46
2:11 [b] ver 23; Jn 3:2; 4:48; 6:2,14,26,30; 12:37; 20:30 [c] Jn 1:14 [d] Ex 14:31
2:12 [e] Mt 4:13 [f] Mt 12:46
2:13 [g] Jn 11:55 [h] Dt 16:1-6; Lk 2:41
2:16 [i] Lk 2:49
2:17 [j] Ps 69:9
2:18 [k] Mt 12:38
2:19 [l] Mt 26:61; 27:40; Mk 14:58; 15:29
2:21 [m] 1Co 6:19
2:22 [n] Lk 24:5-8; Jn 12:16; 14:26
2:23 [o] ver 13
2:25 [p] Mt 9:4; Jn 6:61,64; 13:11

Chapter 3 Theme ______________________________

3 Now there was a man of the Pharisees named Nicodemus,[a] a member of the Jewish ruling council.[b] 2He came to Jesus at night and said, "Rabbi, we know you are a teacher who has come from God. For no one could perform the miraculous signs[c] you are doing if God were not with him."[d]

3In reply Jesus declared, "I tell you the truth, no one can see the kingdom of God unless he is born again.[a]"[e]

4"How can a man be born when he is old?" Nicodemus asked. "Surely he cannot enter a second time into his mother's womb to be born!"

5Jesus answered, "I tell you the truth, no one can enter the kingdom of God unless he is born of water and the Spirit.[f] 6Flesh gives birth to flesh, but the Spirit[b] gives birth to spirit.[g] 7You should not be surprised at my saying, 'You[c] must be born again.' 8The wind blows wherever it pleases. You hear its sound, but you cannot tell where it comes from or where it is going. So it is with everyone born of the Spirit."

9"How can this be?"[h] Nicodemus asked.

10"You are Israel's teacher,"[i] said Jesus, "and do you not understand these things? 11I tell you the truth, we speak of what we know,[j] and we testify to what we have seen, but still you people do not accept our testimony.[k] 12I have spoken to you of earthly things and you do not believe; how then will you believe if I speak of heavenly things? 13No one has ever gone into heaven[l] except the one who came from heaven[m]—the Son of Man.[d] 14Just as Moses lifted up the snake in the desert,[n] so the Son of Man must be lifted up,[o] 15that everyone who believes[p] in him may have eternal life.[e]

16"For God so loved[q] the world that he gave his one and only Son,[f] that whoever believes in him shall not perish but have eternal life.[r] 17For God did not send his Son into the world[s] to condemn the world, but to save the world through him.[t] 18Whoever believes in him is not condemned,[u] but whoever does not believe stands condemned already because he has not believed in the name of God's one and only Son.[g][v] 19This is the verdict: Light[w] has come into the world, but men loved darkness instead of light because their deeds were evil. 20Everyone who does evil hates the light, and will not come into the light for fear that his deeds will be exposed.[x] 21But whoever lives by the truth comes into the light, so that it may be seen plainly that what he has done has been done through God."[h]

22After this, Jesus and his disciples went out into the Judean

[a]3 Or *born from above;* also in verse 7 [b]6 Or *but spirit* [c]7 The Greek is plural. [d]13 Some manuscripts *Man, who is in heaven* [e]15 Or *believes may have eternal life in him* [f]16 Or *his only begotten Son* [g]18 Or *God's only begotten Son* [h]21 Some interpreters end the quotation after verse 15.

3:1 [a]Jn 7:50; 19:39 [b]Lk 23:13
3:2 [c]Jn 9:16,33 [d]Ac 2:22; 10:38
3:3 [e]Jn 1:13; 1Pe 1:23
3:5 [f]Tit 3:5
3:6 [g]Jn 1:13; 1Co 15:50
3:9 [h]Jn 6:52,60
3:10 [i]Lk 2:46
3:11 [j]Jn 1:18; 7:16,17 [k]ver 32
3:13 [l]Pr 30:4; Ac 2:34; Eph 4:8-10 [m]Jn 6:38,42
3:14 [n]Nu 21:8,9 [o]Jn 8:28; 12:32
3:15 [p]ver 16,36
3:16 [q]Ro 5:8; Eph 2:4; 1Jn 4:9,10 [r]ver 36; Jn 6:29,40; 11:25,26
3:17 [s]Jn 6:29,57; 10:36; 11:42; 17:8,21; 20:21 [t]Jn 12:47; 1Jn 4:14
3:18 [u]Jn 5:24 [v]1Jn 4:9
3:19 [w]Jn 1:4; 8:12
3:20 [x]Eph 5:11,13

countryside, where he spent some time with them, and baptized.[a]
23Now John also was baptizing at Aenon near Salim, because there
was plenty of water, and people were constantly coming to be baptized. 24(This was before John was put in prison.)[b] 25An argument
developed between some of John's disciples and a certain Jew[a]
over the matter of ceremonial washing.[c] 26They came to John and
said to him, "Rabbi,[d] that man who was with you on the other side
of the Jordan—the one you testified[e] about—well, he is baptizing,
and everyone is going to him."

27To this John replied, "A man can receive only what is given him
from heaven. 28You yourselves can testify that I said, 'I am not the
Christ[b] but am sent ahead of him.'[f] 29The bride belongs to the
bridegroom.[g] The friend who attends the bridegroom waits and
listens for him, and is full of joy when he hears the bridegroom's
voice. That joy is mine, and it is now complete.[h] 30He must become
greater; I must become less.

31"The one who comes from above[i] is above all; the one who is
from the earth belongs to the earth, and speaks as one from the
earth.[j] The one who comes from heaven is above all. 32He testifies to what he has seen and heard,[k] but no one accepts his testimony.[l] 33The man who has accepted it has certified that God is
truthful. 34For the one whom God has sent[m] speaks the words of
God, for God[c] gives the Spirit[n] without limit. 35The Father loves
the Son and has placed everything in his hands.[o] 36Whoever
believes in the Son has eternal life,[p] but whoever rejects the Son
will not see life, for God's wrath remains on him."[d]

Chapter 4 Theme ________________________________

4 The Pharisees heard that Jesus was gaining and baptizing
more disciples than John,[q] 2although in fact it was not Jesus
who baptized, but his disciples. 3When the Lord learned of this,
he left Judea[r] and went back once more to Galilee.

4Now he had to go through Samaria. 5So he came to a town in
Samaria called Sychar, near the plot of ground Jacob had given to
his son Joseph.[s] 6Jacob's well was there, and Jesus, tired as he was
from the journey, sat down by the well. It was about the sixth hour.

7When a Samaritan woman came to draw water, Jesus said to
her, "Will you give me a drink?" 8(His disciples had gone into the
town[t] to buy food.)

9The Samaritan woman said to him, "You are a Jew and I am a
Samaritan[u] woman. How can you ask me for a drink?" (For Jews
do not associate with Samaritans.[e])

10Jesus answered her, "If you knew the gift of God and who it is

[a]25 Some manuscripts *and certain Jews* [b]28 Or *Messiah* [c]34 Greek *he* [d]36 Some interpreters end the quotation after verse 30. [e]9 Or *do not use dishes Samaritans have used*

INSIGHT

It is difficult to pinpoint who the ***Samaritans*** are racially. However, it is believed that after the Assyrians conquered the northern kingdom, they "imported" people into Samaria. Some of the Samaritan Jews married these importees. Their offspring were called Samaritans. When the Jews returned after the captivity, the Samaritans wanted a share in rebuilding the temple but were rejected because of their pagan practices. The enmity continued through the time of Jesus (see 2 Kings 17:33 and Ezra 4:2, 3).

3:22 [a]Jn 4:2
3:24 [b]Mt 4:12; 14:3
3:25 [c]Jn 2:6
3:26 [d]Mt 23:7 [e]Jn 1:7
3:28 [f]Jn 1:20,23
3:29 [g]Mt 9:15 [h]Jn 16:24; 17:13; Php 2:2; 1Jn 1:4; 2Jn 12
3:31 [i]ver 13 [j]Jn 8:23; 1Jn 4:5
3:32 [k]Jn 8:26; 15:15 [l]ver 11
3:34 [m]ver 17 [n]Mt 12:18; Lk 4:18; Ac 10:38
3:35 [o]Mt 28:18; Jn 5:20,22; 17:2
3:36 [p]ver 15; Jn 5:24; 6:47
4:1 [q]Jn 3:22,26
4:3 [r]Jn 3:22
4:5 [s]Ge 33:19; 48:22; Jos 24:32
4:8 [t]ver 5,39
4:9 [u]Mt 10:5; Lk 9:52,53

that asks you for a drink, you would have asked him and he
would have given you living water.”[a]
11 “Sir,” the woman said, “you have nothing to draw with and
the well is deep. Where can you get this living water? 12 Are you
greater than our father Jacob, who gave us the well[b] and drank
from it himself, as did also his sons and his flocks and herds?”
13 Jesus answered, “Everyone who drinks this water will be thirsty
again, 14 but whoever drinks the water I give him will never thirst.[c]
Indeed, the water I give him will become in him a spring of water[d]
welling up to eternal life.”[e]
15 The woman said to him, “Sir, give me this water so that I
won’t get thirsty[f] and have to keep coming here to draw water.”
16 He told her, “Go, call your husband and come back.”
17 “I have no husband,” she replied.
Jesus said to her, “You are right when you say you have no husband. 18 The fact is, you have had five husbands, and the man you
now have is not your husband. What you have just said is quite
true.”
19 “Sir,” the woman said, “I can see that you are a prophet.[g]
20 Our fathers worshiped on this mountain,[h] but you Jews claim
that the place where we must worship is in Jerusalem.”[i]
21 Jesus declared, “Believe me, woman, a time is coming[j] when
you will worship the Father neither on this mountain nor in
Jerusalem.[k] 22 You Samaritans worship what you do not know;[l] we
worship what we do know, for salvation is from the Jews.[m] 23 Yet a
time is coming and has now come[n] when the true worshipers will
worship the Father in spirit[o] and truth, for they are the kind of
worshipers the Father seeks. 24 God is spirit,[p] and his worshipers
must worship in spirit and in truth.”
25 The woman said, “I know that Messiah” (called Christ)[q] “is
coming. When he comes, he will explain everything to us.”
26 Then Jesus declared, “I who speak to you am he.”[r]
27 Just then his disciples returned[s] and were surprised to find
him talking with a woman. But no one asked, “What do you
want?” or “Why are you talking with her?”
28 Then, leaving her water jar, the woman went back to the town
and said to the people, 29 “Come, see a man who told me everything I ever did.[t] Could this be the Christ[a]?”[u] 30 They came out of
the town and made their way toward him.
31 Meanwhile his disciples urged him, “Rabbi,[v] eat something.”
32 But he said to them, “I have food to eat[w] that you know nothing about.”
33 Then his disciples said to each other, “Could someone have
brought him food?”

a 29 Or *Messiah*

4:10 [a] Isa 44:3; Jer 2:13; Zec 14:8; Jn 7:37,38; Rev 21:6; 22:1,17
4:12 [b] ver 6
4:14 [c] Jn 6:35 [d] Jn 7:38 [e] Mt 25:46
4:15 [f] Jn 6:34
4:19 [g] Mt 21:11
4:20 [h] Dt 11:29; Jos 8:33 [i] Lk 9:53
4:21 [j] Jn 5:28; 16:2 [k] Mal 1:11; 1Ti 2:8
4:22 [l] 2Ki 17:28-41 [m] Isa 2:3; Ro 3:1,2; 9:4,5
4:23 [n] Jn 5:25; 16:32 [o] Php 3:3
4:24 [p] Php 3:3
4:25 [q] Mt 1:16
4:26 [r] Jn 8:24; 9:35-37
4:27 [s] ver 8
4:29 [t] ver 17,18 [u] Mt 12:23; Jn 7:26,31
4:31 [v] Mt 23:7
4:32 [w] Job 23:12; Mt 4:4; Jn 6:27

34“My food,” said Jesus, “is to do the will[a] of him who sent me
and to finish his work.[b] 35Do you not say, ‘Four months more and
then the harvest’? I tell you, open your eyes and look at the fields!
They are ripe for harvest.[c] 36Even now the reaper draws his
wages, even now he harvests[d] the crop for eternal life,[e] so that the
sower and the reaper may be glad together. 37Thus the saying
‘One sows and another reaps’[f] is true. 38I sent you to reap what
you have not worked for. Others have done the hard work, and
you have reaped the benefits of their labor.”

39Many of the Samaritans from that town[g] believed in him
because of the woman’s testimony, “He told me everything I ever
did.”[h] 40So when the Samaritans came to him, they urged him to
stay with them, and he stayed two days. 41And because of his
words many more became believers.

42They said to the woman, “We no longer believe just because
of what you said; now we have heard for ourselves, and we know
that this man really is the Savior of the world.”[i]

43After the two days[j] he left for Galilee. 44(Now Jesus himself had
pointed out that a prophet has no honor in his own country.)[k]
45When he arrived in Galilee, the Galileans welcomed him. They
had seen all that he had done in Jerusalem at the Passover Feast,[l]
for they also had been there.

46Once more he visited Cana in Galilee, where he had turned
the water into wine.[m] And there was a certain royal official whose
son lay sick at Capernaum. 47When this man heard that Jesus had
arrived in Galilee from Judea,[n] he went to him and begged him to
come and heal his son, who was close to death.

48“Unless you people see miraculous signs and wonders,”[o]
Jesus told him, “you will never believe.”

49The royal official said, “Sir, come down before my child dies.”

50Jesus replied, “You may go. Your son will live.”

The man took Jesus at his word and departed. 51While he was
still on the way, his servants met him with the news that his boy
was living. 52When he inquired as to the time when his son got
better, they said to him, “The fever left him yesterday at the seventh hour.”

53Then the father realized that this was the exact time at which
Jesus had said to him, “Your son will live.” So he and all his
household[p] believed.

54This was the second miraculous sign[q] that Jesus performed,
having come from Judea to Galilee.

Chapter 5 Theme ______________________________

5 Some time later, Jesus went up to Jerusalem for a feast of the
Jews. 2Now there is in Jerusalem near the Sheep Gate[r] a pool,

4:34 [a] Mt 26:39; Jn 6:38; 17:4; 19:30 [b] Jn 19:30
4:35 [c] Mt 9:37; Lk 10:2
4:36 [d] Ro 1:13 [e] Mt 25:46
4:37 [f] Job 31:8; Mic 6:15
4:39 [g] ver 5 [h] ver 29
4:42 [i] Lk 2:11; 1Jn 4:14
4:43 [j] ver 40
4:44 [k] Mt 13:57; Lk 4:24
4:45 [l] Jn 2:23
4:46 [m] Jn 2:1-11
4:47 [n] ver 3,54
4:48 [o] Da 4:2,3; Jn 2:11; Ac 2:43; 14:3; Ro 15:19; 2Co 12:12; Heb 2:4
4:53 [p] Ac 11:14
4:54 [q] ver 48; Jn 2:11
5:2 [r] Ne 3:1; 12:39

which in Aramaic[a] is called Bethesda[a] and which is surrounded
by five covered colonnades. [3]Here a great number of disabled people used to lie—the blind, the lame, the paralyzed.[b] [5]One who was
there had been an invalid for thirty-eight years. [6]When Jesus saw
him lying there and learned that he had been in this condition for
a long time, he asked him, "Do you want to get well?"
[7]"Sir," the invalid replied, "I have no one to help me into the
pool when the water is stirred. While I am trying to get in, someone else goes down ahead of me."
[8]Then Jesus said to him, "Get up! Pick up your mat and walk."[b]
[9]At once the man was cured; he picked up his mat and walked.
The day on which this took place was a Sabbath,[c] [10]and so the
Jews[d] said to the man who had been healed, "It is the Sabbath;
the law forbids you to carry your mat."[e]
[11]But he replied, "The man who made me well said to me, 'Pick
up your mat and walk.'"
[12]So they asked him, "Who is this fellow who told you to pick it
up and walk?"
[13]The man who was healed had no idea who it was, for Jesus
had slipped away into the crowd that was there.
[14]Later Jesus found him at the temple and said to him, "See,
you are well again. Stop sinning[f] or something worse may happen to you." [15]The man went away and told the Jews[g] that it was
Jesus who had made him well.
[16]So, because Jesus was doing these things on the Sabbath, the
Jews persecuted him. [17]Jesus said to them, "My Father is always at
his work[h] to this very day, and I, too, am working." [18]For this reason the Jews tried all the harder to kill him;[i] not only was he
breaking the Sabbath, but he was even calling God his own
Father, making himself equal with God.[j]
[19]Jesus gave them this answer: "I tell you the truth, the Son can
do nothing by himself;[k] he can do only what he sees his Father
doing, because whatever the Father does the Son also does. [20]For
the Father loves the Son[l] and shows him all he does. Yes, to your
amazement he will show him even greater things than these.[m]
[21]For just as the Father raises the dead and gives them life,[n] even so
the Son gives life[o] to whom he is pleased to give it. [22]Moreover, the
Father judges no one, but has entrusted all judgment to the Son,[p]
[23]that all may honor the Son just as they honor the Father. He who
does not honor the Son does not honor the Father, who sent him.[q]
[24]"I tell you the truth, whoever hears my word and believes him

5:2 [a]Jn 19:13, 17,20; 20:16; Ac 21:40; 22:2; 26:14
5:8 [b]Mt 9:5,6; Mk 2:11; Lk 5:24
5:9 [c]Jn 9:14
5:10 [d]ver 16 [e]Ne 13:15-22; Jer 17:21; Mt 12:2
5:14 [f]Mk 2:5; Jn 8:11
5:15 [g]Jn 1:19
5:17 [h]Jn 9:4; 14:10
5:18 [i]Jn 7:1 [j]Jn 10:30,33; 19:7
5:19 [k]ver 30; Jn 8:28
5:20 [l]Jn 3:35 [m]Jn 14:12
5:21 [n]Ro 4:17; 8:11 [o]Jn 11:25
5:22 [p]ver 27; Jn 9:39; Ac 10:42; 17:31
5:23 [q]Lk 10:16; 1Jn 2:23

[a]2 Some manuscripts *Bethzatha*; other manuscripts *Bethsaida* [b]3 Some less important manuscripts *paralyzed—and they waited for the moving of the waters.* [4]*From time to time an angel of the Lord would come down and stir up the waters. The first one into the pool after each such disturbance would be cured of whatever disease he had.*

who sent me has eternal life and will not be condemned;[a] he has
crossed over from death to life.[b] 25I tell you the truth, a time is
coming and has now come[c] when the dead will hear[d] the voice of
the Son of God and those who hear will live. 26For as the Father
has life in himself, so he has granted the Son to have life in himself. 27And he has given him authority to judge[e] because he is the
Son of Man.

28"Do not be amazed at this, for a time is coming[f] when all who
are in their graves will hear his voice 29and come out—those
who have done good will rise to live, and those who have done
evil will rise to be condemned.[g] 30By myself I can do nothing;[h] I
judge only as I hear, and my judgment is just,[i] for I seek not to
please myself but him who sent me.[j]

31"If I testify about myself, my testimony is not valid.[k] 32There is
another who testifies in my favor,[l] and I know that his testimony
about me is valid.

33"You have sent to John and he has testified[m] to the truth.
34Not that I accept human testimony;[n] but I mention it that you
may be saved. 35John was a lamp that burned and gave light,[o] and
you chose for a time to enjoy his light.

36"I have testimony weightier than that of John.[p] For the very
work that the Father has given me to finish, and which I am
doing,[q] testifies that the Father has sent me.[r] 37And the Father
who sent me has himself testified concerning me.[s] You have never
heard his voice nor seen his form,[t] 38nor does his word dwell in
you,[u] for you do not believe the one he sent.[v] 39You diligently
study[a] the Scriptures[w] because you think that by them you possess eternal life. These are the Scriptures that testify about me,[x]
40yet you refuse to come to me to have life.

41"I do not accept praise from men,[y] 42but I know you. I know
that you do not have the love of God in your hearts. 43I have come
in my Father's name, and you do not accept me; but if someone
else comes in his own name, you will accept him. 44How can you
believe if you accept praise from one another, yet make no effort
to obtain the praise that comes from the only God[b]?[z]

45"But do not think I will accuse you before the Father. Your
accuser is Moses,[a] on whom your hopes are set.[b] 46If you believed
Moses, you would believe me, for he wrote about me.[c] 47But since
you do not believe what he wrote, how are you going to believe
what I say?"[d]

Chapter 6 Theme ____________________

6 Some time after this, Jesus crossed to the far shore of the Sea
of Galilee (that is, the Sea of Tiberias), 2and a great crowd of

a 39 Or *Study diligently* (the imperative) b 44 Some early manuscripts *the Only One*

5:24 [a]Jn 3:18 [b]1Jn 3:14
5:25 [c]Jn 4:23 [d]Jn 8:43,47
5:27 [e]ver 22; Ac 10:42; 17:31
5:28 [f]Jn 4:21
5:29 [g]Da 12:2; Mt 25:46
5:30 [h]ver 19 [i]Jn 8:16 [j]Mt 26:39; Jn 4:34; 6:38
5:31 [k]Jn 8:14
5:32 [l]ver 37; Jn 8:18
5:33 [m]Jn 1:7
5:34 [n]1Jn 5:9
5:35 [o]2Pe 1:19
5:36 [p]1Jn 5:9 [q]Jn 14:11; 15:24 [r]Jn 3:17; 10:25
5:37 [s]Jn 8:18 [t]Dt 4:12; 1Ti 1:17; Jn 1:18
5:38 [u]1Jn 2:14 [v]Jn 3:17
5:39 [w]Ro 2:17,18 [x]Lk 24:27,44; Ac 13:27
5:41 [y]ver 44
5:44 [z]Ro 2:29
5:45 [a]Jn 9:28 [b]Ro 2:17
5:46 [c]Ge 3:15; Lk 24:27,44; Ac 26:22
5:47 [d]Lk 16:29,31

people followed him because they saw the miraculous signs[a] he
had performed on the sick. 3Then Jesus went up on a mountainside[b] and sat down with his disciples. 4The Jewish Passover Feast[c]
was near.
5When Jesus looked up and saw a great crowd coming toward
him, he said to Philip,[d] "Where shall we buy bread for these people to eat?" 6He asked this only to test him, for he already had in
mind what he was going to do.
7Philip answered him, "Eight months' wages[a] would not buy
enough bread for each one to have a bite!"
8Another of his disciples, Andrew, Simon Peter's brother,[e]
spoke up, 9"Here is a boy with five small barley loaves and two
small fish, but how far will they go among so many?"[f]
10Jesus said, "Have the people sit down." There was plenty of
grass in that place, and the men sat down, about five thousand of
them. 11Jesus then took the loaves, gave thanks,[g] and distributed
to those who were seated as much as they wanted. He did the
same with the fish.
12When they had all had enough to eat, he said to his disciples,
"Gather the pieces that are left over. Let nothing be wasted." 13So
they gathered them and filled twelve baskets with the pieces of
the five barley loaves left over by those who had eaten.
14After the people saw the miraculous sign[h] that Jesus did, they
began to say, "Surely this is the Prophet who is to come into the
world."[i] 15Jesus, knowing that they intended to come and make
him king[j] by force, withdrew again to a mountain by himself.[k]
16When evening came, his disciples went down to the lake,
17where they got into a boat and set off across the lake for Capernaum. By now it was dark, and Jesus had not yet joined them. 18A
strong wind was blowing and the waters grew rough. 19When
they had rowed three or three and a half miles,[b] they saw Jesus
approaching the boat, walking on the water;[l] and they were terrified. 20But he said to them, "It is I; don't be afraid."[m] 21Then they
were willing to take him into the boat, and immediately the boat
reached the shore where they were heading.
22The next day the crowd that had stayed on the opposite shore
of the lake[n] realized that only one boat had been there, and that
Jesus had not entered it with his disciples, but that they had gone
away alone.[o] 23Then some boats from Tiberias[p] landed near the
place where the people had eaten the bread after the Lord had
given thanks.[q] 24Once the crowd realized that neither Jesus nor
his disciples were there, they got into the boats and went to
Capernaum in search of Jesus.

6:2 [a]Jn 2:11
6:3 [b]ver 15
6:4 [c]Jn 2:13; 11:55
6:5 [d]Jn 1:43
6:8 [e]Jn 1:40
6:9 [f]2Ki 4:43
6:11 [g]ver 23; Mt 14:19
6:14 [h]Jn 2:11 [i]Dt 18:15,18; Mt 11:3; 21:11
6:15 [j]Jn 18:36 [k]Mt 14:23; Mk 6:46
6:19 [l]Job 9:8
6:20 [m]Mt 14:27
6:22 [n]ver 2 [o]ver 15-21
6:23 [p]ver 1 [q]ver 11

INSIGHT

See the chart **The Feasts of Israel** located on pages 210, 211.

a 7 Greek *two hundred denarii* b 19 Greek *rowed twenty-five or thirty stadia* (about 5 or 6 kilometers)

25When they found him on the other side of the lake, they asked him, "Rabbi,[a] when did you get here?"

26Jesus answered, "I tell you the truth, you are looking for me,[b] not because you saw miraculous signs[c] but because you ate the loaves and had your fill. 27Do not work for food that spoils, but for food that endures[d] to eternal life,[e] which the Son of Man[f] will give you. On him God the Father has placed his seal[g] of approval."

28Then they asked him, "What must we do to do the works God requires?"

29Jesus answered, "The work of God is this: to believe[h] in the one he has sent."[i]

30So they asked him, "What miraculous sign[j] then will you give that we may see it and believe you?[k] What will you do? 31Our forefathers ate the manna[l] in the desert; as it is written: 'He gave them bread from heaven to eat.'[a]"[m]

32Jesus said to them, "I tell you the truth, it is not Moses who has given you the bread from heaven, but it is my Father who gives you the true bread from heaven. 33For the bread of God is he who comes down from heaven[n] and gives life to the world."

34"Sir," they said, "from now on give us this bread."[o]

35Then Jesus declared, "I am the bread of life.[p] He who comes to me will never go hungry, and he who believes in me will never be thirsty.[q] 36But as I told you, you have seen me and still you do not believe. 37All that the Father gives me[r] will come to me, and whoever comes to me I will never drive away. 38For I have come down from heaven not to do my will but to do the will of him who sent me.[s] 39And this is the will of him who sent me, that I shall lose none of all that he has given me,[t] but raise them up at the last day.[u] 40For my Father's will is that everyone who looks to the Son and believes in him shall have eternal life,[v] and I will raise him up at the last day."

41At this the Jews began to grumble about him because he said, "I am the bread that came down from heaven." 42They said, "Is this not Jesus, the son of Joseph,[w] whose father and mother we know?[x] How can he now say, 'I came down from heaven'?"[y]

43"Stop grumbling among yourselves," Jesus answered. 44"No one can come to me unless the Father who sent me draws him,[z] and I will raise him up at the last day. 45It is written in the Prophets: 'They will all be taught by God.'[b][a] Everyone who listens to the Father and learns from him comes to me. 46No one has seen the Father except the one who is from God;[b] only he has seen the Father. 47I tell you the truth, he who believes has everlasting life. 48I am the bread of life.[c] 49Your forefathers ate the manna in the desert, yet they died.[d] 50But here is the bread that

[a] 31 Exodus 16:4; Neh. 9:15; Psalm 78:24,25 [b] 45 Isaiah 54:13

6:25 [a] Mt 23:7
6:26 [b] ver 24 [c] ver 30; Jn 2:11
6:27 [d] Isa 55:2 [e] ver 54; Mt 25:46; Jn 4:14 [f] Mt 8:20 [g] Ro 4:11; 1Co 9:2; 2Co 1:22; Eph 1:13; 4:30; 2Ti 2:19; Rev 7:3
6:29 [h] 1Jn 3:23 [i] Jn 3:17
6:30 [j] Jn 2:11 [k] Mt 12:38
6:31 [l] Nu 11:7-9 [m] Ex 16:4,15; Ne 9:15; Ps 78:24; 105:40
6:33 [n] ver 50
6:34 [o] Jn 4:15
6:35 [p] ver 48,51 [q] Jn 4:14
6:37 [r] ver 39; Jn 17:2,6,9,24
6:38 [s] Jn 4:34; 5:30
6:39 [t] Jn 10:28; 17:12; 18:9 [u] ver 40,44,54
6:40 [v] Jn 3:15,16
6:42 [w] Lk 4:22 [x] Jn 7:27,28 [y] ver 38,62
6:44 [z] ver 65; Jer 31:3; Jn 12:32
6:45 [a] Isa 54:13; Jer 31:33,34; Heb 8:10,11; 10:16
6:46 [b] Jn 1:18; 5:37; 7:29
6:48 [c] ver 35,51
6:49 [d] ver 31,58

comes down from heaven,[a] which a man may eat and not die. 51 I
am the living bread that came down from heaven. If anyone eats
of this bread, he will live forever. This bread is my flesh, which I
will give for the life of the world."[b]

52 Then the Jews began to argue sharply among themselves,[c]
"How can this man give us his flesh to eat?"

53 Jesus said to them, "I tell you the truth, unless you eat the
flesh of the Son of Man[d] and drink his blood, you have no life in
you. 54 Whoever eats my flesh and drinks my blood has eternal
life, and I will raise him up at the last day.[e] 55 For my flesh is real
food and my blood is real drink. 56 Whoever eats my flesh and
drinks my blood remains in me, and I in him.[f] 57 Just as the living
Father sent me[g] and I live because of the Father, so the one who
feeds on me will live because of me. 58 This is the bread that came
down from heaven. Your forefathers ate manna and died, but he
who feeds on this bread will live forever."[h] 59 He said this while
teaching in the synagogue in Capernaum.

60 On hearing it, many of his disciples[i] said, "This is a hard
teaching. Who can accept it?"

61 Aware that his disciples were grumbling about this, Jesus said
to them, "Does this offend you?[j] 62 What if you see the Son of
Man ascend to where he was before![k] 63 The Spirit gives life;[l] the
flesh counts for nothing. The words I have spoken to you are
spirit[a] and they are life. 64 Yet there are some of you who do not
believe." For Jesus had known[m] from the beginning which of
them did not believe and who would betray him. 65 He went on to
say, "This is why I told you that no one can come to me unless the
Father has enabled him."[n]

66 From this time many of his disciples[o] turned back and no
longer followed him.

67 "You do not want to leave too, do you?" Jesus asked the
Twelve.[p]

68 Simon Peter answered him,[q] "Lord, to whom shall we go? You
have the words of eternal life. 69 We believe and know that you are
the Holy One of God."[r]

70 Then Jesus replied, "Have I not chosen you,[s] the Twelve? Yet
one of you is a devil!"[t] 71 (He meant Judas, the son of Simon Iscariot, who, though one of the Twelve, was later to betray him.)

Chapter 7 Theme ______________

7 After this, Jesus went around in Galilee, purposely staying
away from Judea because the Jews[u] there were waiting to
take his life.[v] 2 But when the Jewish Feast of Tabernacles[w] was

[a] 63 Or *Spirit*

6:50 [a] ver 33
6:51 [b] Heb 10:10
6:52 [c] Jn 7:43; 9:16; 10:19
6:53 [d] Mt 8:20
6:54 [e] ver 39
6:56 [f] Jn 15:4-7; 1Jn 3:24; 4:15
6:57 [g] Jn 3:17
6:58 [h] ver 49-51; Jn 3:36
6:60 [i] ver 66
6:61 [j] Mt 11:6
6:62 [k] Mk 16:19; Jn 3:13; 17:5
6:63 [l] 2Co 3:6
6:64 [m] Jn 2:25
6:65 [n] ver 37,44
6:66 [o] ver 60
6:67 [p] Mt 10:2
6:68 [q] Mt 16:16
6:69 [r] Mk 8:29; Lk 9:20
6:70 [s] Jn 15:16,19 [t] Jn 13:27
7:1 [u] Jn 1:19 [v] Jn 5:18
7:2 [w] Lev 23:34; Dt 16:16

near, 3Jesus' brothers[a] said to him, "You ought to leave here and
go to Judea, so that your disciples may see the miracles you do.
4No one who wants to become a public figure acts in secret. Since
you are doing these things, show yourself to the world." 5For even
his own brothers did not believe in him.[b]

6Therefore Jesus told them, "The right time[c] for me has not yet
come; for you any time is right. 7The world cannot hate you, but
it hates me[d] because I testify that what it does is evil.[e] 8You go to
the Feast. I am not yet[a] going up to this Feast, because for me the
right time[f] has not yet come." 9Having said this, he stayed in
Galilee.

10However, after his brothers had left for the Feast, he went also,
not publicly, but in secret. 11Now at the Feast the Jews were
watching for him[g] and asking, "Where is that man?"

12Among the crowds there was wide-spread whispering about
him. Some said, "He is a good man."

Others replied, "No, he deceives the people."[h] 13But no one
would say anything publicly about him for fear of the Jews.[i]

14Not until halfway through the Feast did Jesus go up to the
temple courts and begin to teach.[j] 15The Jews[k] were amazed and
asked, "How did this man get such learning[l] without having
studied?"[m]

16Jesus answered, "My teaching is not my own. It comes from
him who sent me.[n] 17If anyone chooses to do God's will, he will
find out[o] whether my teaching comes from God or whether I
speak on my own. 18He who speaks on his own does so to gain
honor for himself,[p] but he who works for the honor of the one
who sent him is a man of truth; there is nothing false about him.
19Has not Moses given you the law?[q] Yet not one of you keeps the
law. Why are you trying to kill me?"[r]

20"You are demon-possessed,"[s] the crowd answered. "Who is
trying to kill you?"

21Jesus said to them, "I did one miracle, and you are all astonished. 22Yet, because Moses gave you circumcision[t] (though actually it did not come from Moses, but from the patriarchs),[u] you
circumcise a child on the Sabbath. 23Now if a child can be circumcised on the Sabbath so that the law of Moses may not be
broken, why are you angry with me for healing the whole man on
the Sabbath? 24Stop judging by mere appearances, and make a
right judgment."[v]

25At that point some of the people of Jerusalem began to ask,
"Isn't this the man they are trying to kill? 26Here he is, speaking
publicly, and they are not saying a word to him. Have the authorities[w] really concluded that he is the Christ[b]? 27But we know

[a] 8 Some early manuscripts do not have *yet*. [b] 26 Or *Messiah*; also in verses 27, 31, 41 and 42

7:3 [a] Mt 12:46
7:5 [b] Mk 3:21
7:6 [c] Mt 26:18
7:7 [d] Jn 15:18,19 [e] Jn 3:19,20
7:8 [f] ver 6
7:11 [g] Jn 11:56
7:12 [h] ver 40,43
7:13 [i] Jn 9:22; 12:42; 19:38
7:14 [j] ver 28; Mt 26:55
7:15 [k] Jn 1:19 [l] Ac 26:24 [m] Mt 13:54
7:16 [n] Jn 3:11; 14:24
7:17 [o] Ps 25:14; Jn 8:43
7:18 [p] Jn 5:41; 8:50,54
7:19 [q] Jn 1:17 [r] ver 1; Mt 12:14
7:20 [s] Jn 8:48; 10:20
7:22 [t] Lev 12:3 [u] Ge 17:10-14
7:24 [v] Isa 11:3,4; Jn 8:15
7:26 [w] ver 48

where this man is from;[a] when the Christ comes, no one will
know where he is from."
28 Then Jesus, still teaching in the temple courts,[b] cried out,
"Yes, you know me, and you know where I am from.[c] I am not
here on my own, but he who sent me is true.[d] You do not know
him, 29 but I know him[e] because I am from him and he sent me."
30 At this they tried to seize him, but no one laid a hand on him,[f]
because his time had not yet come. 31 Still, many in the crowd put
their faith in him.[g] They said, "When the Christ comes, will he do
more miraculous signs[h] than this man?"
32 The Pharisees heard the crowd whispering such things about
him. Then the chief priests and the Pharisees sent temple guards
to arrest him.
33 Jesus said, "I am with you for only a short time,[i] and then I go
to the one who sent me.[j] 34 You will look for me, but you will not
find me; and where I am, you cannot come."[k]
35 The Jews said to one another, "Where does this man intend to
go that we cannot find him? Will he go where our people live
scattered[l] among the Greeks,[m] and teach the Greeks? 36 What
did he mean when he said, 'You will look for me, but you will not
find me,' and 'Where I am, you cannot come'?"
37 On the last and greatest day of the Feast,[n] Jesus stood and said
in a loud voice, "If anyone is thirsty, let him come to me and
drink.[o] 38 Whoever believes in me, as[a] the Scripture has said,[p]
streams of living water[q] will flow from within him."[r] 39 By this he
meant the Spirit,[s] whom those who believed in him were later to
receive.[t] Up to that time the Spirit had not been given, since Jesus
had not yet been glorified.[u]
40 On hearing his words, some of the people said, "Surely this
man is the Prophet."[v]
41 Others said, "He is the Christ."
Still others asked, "How can the Christ come from Galilee?[w]
42 Does not the Scripture say that the Christ will come from
David's family[b][x] and from Bethlehem,[y] the town where David
lived?" 43 Thus the people were divided[z] because of Jesus. 44 Some
wanted to seize him, but no one laid a hand on him.[a]
45 Finally the temple guards went back to the chief priests and
Pharisees, who asked them, "Why didn't you bring him in?"
46 "No one ever spoke the way this man does,"[b] the guards
declared.
47 "You mean he has deceived you also?"[c] the Pharisees retorted.
48 "Has any of the rulers or of the Pharisees believed in him?[d]
49 No! But this mob that knows nothing of the law—there is a
curse on them."

[a] 37,38 Or / *If anyone is thirsty, let him come to me. / And let him drink,* [38] *who believes in me. / As*
[b] 42 *Greek seed*

7:27 [a] Mt 13:55; Lk 4:22
7:28 [b] ver 14 [c] Jn 8:14 [d] Jn 8:26,42
7:29 [e] Mt 11:27
7:30 [f] ver 32,44; Jn 10:39
7:31 [g] Jn 8:30 [h] Jn 2:11
7:33 [i] Jn 13:33; 16:16 [j] Jn 16:5, 10,17,28
7:34 [k] Jn 8:21; 13:33
7:35 [l] Jas 1:1 [m] Jn 12:20; 1Pe 1:1
7:37 [n] Lev 23:36 [o] Isa 55:1; Rev 22:17
7:38 [p] Isa 58:11 [q] Jn 4:10 [r] Jn 4:14
7:39 [s] Joel 2:28; Ac 2:17,33 [t] Jn 20:22 [u] Jn 12:23; 13:31,32
7:40 [v] Mt 21:11; Jn 1:21
7:41 [w] ver 52; Jn 1:46
7:42 [x] Mt 1:1 [y] Mic 5:2; Mt 2:5,6; Lk 2:4
7:43 [z] Jn 9:16; 10:19
7:44 [a] ver 30
7:46 [b] Mt 7:28
7:47 [c] ver 12
7:48 [d] Jn 12:42

50 Nicodemus,[a] who had gone to Jesus earlier and who was one
of their own number, asked, 51 "Does our law condemn anyone
without first hearing him to find out what he is doing?"
52 They replied, "Are you from Galilee, too? Look into it, and
you will find that a prophet[a] does not come out of Galilee."[b]

[The earliest manuscripts and many
other ancient witnesses do not have
John 7:53–8:11.]

Chapter 8 Theme ______________________

53 Then each went to his own home.

8 But Jesus went to the Mount of Olives.[c] 2 At dawn he appeared
again in the temple courts, where all the people gathered
around him, and he sat down to teach them.[d] 3 The teachers of the
law and the Pharisees brought in a woman caught in adultery.
They made her stand before the group 4 and said to Jesus, "Teacher,
this woman was caught in the act of adultery. 5 In the Law Moses
commanded us to stone such women.[e] Now what do you say?"
6 They were using this question as a trap,[f] in order to have a basis
for accusing him.[g]
But Jesus bent down and started to write on the ground with his
finger. 7 When they kept on questioning him, he straightened up
and said to them, "If any one of you is without sin, let him be the
first to throw a stone[h] at her."[i] 8 Again he stooped down and wrote
on the ground.
9 At this, those who heard began to go away one at a time, the
older ones first, until only Jesus was left, with the woman still
standing there. 10 Jesus straightened up and asked her, "Woman,
where are they? Has no one condemned you?"
11 "No one, sir," she said.
"Then neither do I condemn you,"[j] Jesus declared. "Go now
and leave your life of sin."[k]

---

12 When Jesus spoke again to the people, he said, "I am[l] the
light of the world.[m] Whoever follows me will never walk in darkness, but will have the light of life."[n]
13 The Pharisees challenged him, "Here you are, appearing as
your own witness; your testimony is not valid."[o]

a 52 Two early manuscripts *the Prophet*

7:50 [a] Jn 3:1; 19:39
7:52 [b] ver 41
8:1 [c] Mt 21:1
8:2 [d] ver 20; Mt 26:55
8:5 [e] Lev 20:10; Dt 22:22
8:6 [f] Mt 22:15,18 [g] Mt 12:10
8:7 [h] Dt 17:7 [i] Ro 2:1,22
8:11 [j] Jn 3:17 [k] Jn 5:14
8:12 [l] Jn 6:35 [m] Jn 1:4; 12:35 [n] Pr 4:18; Mt 5:14
8:13 [o] Jn 5:31

14 Jesus answered, "Even if I testify on my own behalf, my testimony is valid, for I know where I came from and where I am
going.[a] But you have no idea where I come from[b] or where I am
going. 15 You judge by human standards;[c] I pass judgment on no
one.[d] 16 But if I do judge, my decisions are right, because I am not
alone. I stand with the Father, who sent me.[e] 17 In your own Law it
is written that the testimony of two men is valid.[f] 18 I am one who
testifies for myself; my other witness is the Father, who sent me."[g]
19 Then they asked him, "Where is your father?"
"You do not know me or my Father,"[h] Jesus replied. "If you
knew me, you would know my Father also."[i] 20 He spoke these
words while teaching[j] in the temple area near the place where the
offerings were put.[k] Yet no one seized him, because his time had
not yet come.[l]
21 Once more Jesus said to them, "I am going away, and you will
look for me, and you will die[m] in your sin. Where I go, you cannot come."[n]
22 This made the Jews ask, "Will he kill himself? Is that why he
says, 'Where I go, you cannot come'?"
23 But he continued, "You are from below; I am from above. You
are of this world; I am not of this world.[o] 24 I told you that you
would die in your sins; if you do not believe that I am ⌊the one I
claim to be⌋,[a][p] you will indeed die in your sins."
25 "Who are you?" they asked.
"Just what I have been claiming all along," Jesus replied. 26 "I
have much to say in judgment of you. But he who sent me is reliable,[q] and what I have heard from him I tell the world."[r]
27 They did not understand that he was telling them about his
Father. 28 So Jesus said, "When you have lifted up the Son of Man,[s]
then you will know that I am ⌊the one I claim to be⌋ and that I do
nothing on my own but speak just what the Father has taught
me. 29 The one who sent me is with me; he has not left me alone,[t]
for I always do what pleases him."[u] 30 Even as he spoke, many put
their faith in him.[v]
31 To the Jews who had believed him, Jesus said, "If you hold to
my teaching,[w] you are really my disciples. 32 Then you will know
the truth, and the truth will set you free."[x]
33 They answered him, "We are Abraham's descendants[b][y] and
have never been slaves of anyone. How can you say that we shall
be set free?"
34 Jesus replied, "I tell you the truth, everyone who sins is a slave
to sin.[z] 35 Now a slave has no permanent place in the family, but a
son belongs to it forever.[a] 36 So if the Son sets you free, you will be
free indeed. 37 I know you are Abraham's descendants. Yet you are

8:14 [a] Jn 13:3; 16:28 [b] Jn 7:28; 9:29
8:15 [c] Jn 7:24 [d] Jn 3:17
8:16 [e] Jn 5:30
8:17 [f] Dt 17:6; Mt 18:16
8:18 [g] Jn 5:37
8:19 [h] Jn 16:3 [i] Jn 14:7; 1Jn 2:23
8:20 [j] Mt 26:55 [k] Mk 12:41 [l] Mt 26:18; Jn 7:30
8:21 [m] Eze 3:18 [n] Jn 7:34; 13:33
8:23 [o] Jn 3:31; 17:14
8:24 [p] Jn 4:26; 13:19
8:26 [q] Jn 7:28 [r] Jn 3:32; 15:15
8:28 [s] Jn 3:14; 5:19; 12:32
8:29 [t] ver 16; Jn 16:32 [u] Jn 4:34; 5:30; 6:38
8:30 [v] Jn 7:31
8:31 [w] Jn 15:7; 2Jn 9
8:32 [x] Ro 8:2; Jas 2:12
8:33 [y] ver 37,39; Mt 3:9
8:34 [z] Ro 6:16; 2Pe 2:19
8:35 [a] Gal 4:30

INSIGHT

"The place" mentioned in verse 20 was in the women's court of the temple, where there were thirteen trumpet-shaped offering receptacles. See the illustration of the floor plan of Herod's Temple on page 1723, and see the illustration of Herod's Temple on page IISB-38.

[a] 24 Or *I am he*; also in verse 28 [b] 33 Greek *seed*; also in verse 37

ready to kill me,[a] because you have no room for my word. 38 I am
telling you what I have seen in the Father's presence,[b] and you do
what you have heard from your father.[a]"

39 "Abraham is our father," they answered.

"If you were Abraham's children,"[c] said Jesus, "then you
would[b] do the things Abraham did. 40 As it is, you are determined
to kill me, a man who has told you the truth that I heard from
God.[d] Abraham did not do such things. 41 You are doing the
things your own father does."[e]

"We are not illegitimate children," they protested. "The only
Father we have is God himself."[f]

42 Jesus said to them, "If God were your Father, you would love
me,[g] for I came from God[h] and now am here. I have not come on
my own;[i] but he sent me.[j] 43 Why is my language not clear to you?
Because you are unable to hear what I say. 44 You belong to your
father, the devil,[k] and you want to carry out your father's desire.[l]
He was a murderer from the beginning, not holding to the truth,
for there is no truth in him. When he lies, he speaks his native
language, for he is a liar and the father of lies.[m] 45 Yet because I tell
the truth,[n] you do not believe me! 46 Can any of you prove me
guilty of sin? If I am telling the truth, why don't you believe me?
47 He who belongs to God hears what God says.[o] The reason you
do not hear is that you do not belong to God."

48 The Jews answered him, "Aren't we right in saying that you
are a Samaritan[p] and demon-possessed?"[q]

49 "I am not possessed by a demon," said Jesus, "but I honor my
Father and you dishonor me. 50 I am not seeking glory for myself;[r]
but there is one who seeks it, and he is the judge. 51 I tell you the
truth, if anyone keeps my word, he will never see death."[s]

52 At this the Jews exclaimed, "Now we know that you are demon-
possessed! Abraham died and so did the prophets, yet you say that
if anyone keeps your word, he will never taste death. 53 Are you
greater than our father Abraham?[t] He died, and so did the
prophets. Who do you think you are?"

54 Jesus replied, "If I glorify myself,[u] my glory means nothing.
My Father, whom you claim as your God, is the one who glorifies
me.[v] 55 Though you do not know him,[w] I know him.[x] If I said I did
not, I would be a liar like you, but I do know him and keep his
word.[y] 56 Your father Abraham[z] rejoiced at the thought of seeing
my day; he saw it[a] and was glad."

57 "You are not yet fifty years old," the Jews said to him, "and
you have seen Abraham!"

58 "I tell you the truth," Jesus answered, "before Abraham was

[a] 38 Or *presence. Therefore do what you have heard from the Father.* [b] 39 Some early manuscripts *"If you are Abraham's children," said Jesus, "then*

8:37 [a] ver 39,40
8:38 [b] Jn 5:19,30; 14:10,24
8:39 [c] ver 37; Ro 9:7; Gal 3:7
8:40 [d] ver 26
8:41 [e] ver 38,44 [f] Isa 63:16; 64:8
8:42 [g] 1Jn 5:1 [h] Jn 16:27; 17:8 [i] Jn 7:28 [j] Jn 3:17
8:44 [k] 1Jn 3:8 [l] ver 38,41 [m] Ge 3:4
8:45 [n] Jn 18:37
8:47 [o] Jn 18:37; 1Jn 4:6
8:48 [p] Mt 10:5 [q] ver 52; Jn 7:20
8:50 [r] ver 54; Jn 5:41
8:51 [s] Jn 11:26
8:53 [t] Jn 4:12
8:54 [u] ver 50 [v] Jn 16:14; 17:1,5
8:55 [w] ver 19 [x] Jn 7:28,29 [y] Jn 15:10
8:56 [z] ver 37,39 [a] Mt 13:17; Heb 11:13

born,[a] I am!"[b] 59At this, they picked up stones to stone him,[c] but Jesus hid himself,[d] slipping away from the temple grounds.

Chapter 9 Theme ______________________

9 As he went along, he saw a man blind from birth. 2His disciples asked him, "Rabbi,[e] who sinned,[f] this man[g] or his parents,[h] that he was born blind?"

3"Neither this man nor his parents sinned," said Jesus, "but this happened so that the work of God might be displayed in his life.[i] 4As long as it is day,[j] we must do the work of him who sent me. Night is coming, when no one can work. 5While I am in the world, I am the light of the world."[k]

6Having said this, he spit[l] on the ground, made some mud with the saliva, and put it on the man's eyes. 7"Go," he told him, "wash in the Pool of Siloam"[m] (this word means Sent). So the man went and washed, and came home seeing.[n]

8His neighbors and those who had formerly seen him begging asked, "Isn't this the same man who used to sit and beg?"[o] 9Some claimed that he was.

Others said, "No, he only looks like him."

But he himself insisted, "I am the man."

10"How then were your eyes opened?" they demanded.

11He replied, "The man they call Jesus made some mud and put it on my eyes. He told me to go to Siloam and wash. So I went and washed, and then I could see."[p]

12"Where is this man?" they asked him.

"I don't know," he said.

13They brought to the Pharisees the man who had been blind. 14Now the day on which Jesus had made the mud and opened the man's eyes was a Sabbath.[q] 15Therefore the Pharisees also asked him how he had received his sight.[r] "He put mud on my eyes," the man replied, "and I washed, and now I see."

16Some of the Pharisees said, "This man is not from God, for he does not keep the Sabbath."[s]

But others asked, "How can a sinner do such miraculous signs?" So they were divided.[t]

17Finally they turned again to the blind man, "What have you to say about him? It was your eyes he opened."

The man replied, "He is a prophet."[u]

18The Jews[v] still did not believe that he had been blind and had received his sight until they sent for the man's parents. 19"Is this your son?" they asked. "Is this the one you say was born blind? How is it that now he can see?"

20"We know he is our son," the parents answered, "and we know he was born blind. 21But how he can see now, or who opened his

8:58 [a]Jn 1:2; 17:5,24 [b]Ex 3:14
8:59 [c]Lev 24:16; Jn 10:31; 11:8 [d]Jn 12:36
9:2 [e]Mt 23:7 [f]ver 34; Lk 13:2; Ac 28:4 [g]Eze 18:20 [h]Ex 20:5; Job 21:19
9:3 [i]Jn 11:4
9:4 [j]Jn 11:9; 12:35
9:5 [k]Jn 1:4; 8:12; 12:46
9:6 [l]Mk 7:33; 8:23
9:7 [m]ver 11; 2Ki 5:10; Lk 13:4 [n]Isa 35:5; Jn 11:37
9:8 [o]Ac 3:2,10
9:11 [p]ver 7
9:14 [q]Jn 5:9
9:15 [r]ver 10
9:16 [s]Mt 12:2 [t]Jn 6:52; 7:43; 10:19
9:17 [u]Mt 21:11
9:18 [v]Jn 1:19

eyes, we don't know. Ask him. He is of age; he will speak for himself." 22His parents said this because they were afraid of the Jews,[a] for
already the Jews had decided that anyone who acknowledged that
Jesus was the Christ[a] would be put out[b] of the synagogue.[c] 23That
was why his parents said, "He is of age; ask him."[d]
24A second time they summoned the man who had been blind.
"Give glory to God,[b]"[e] they said. "We know this man is a sinner."[f]
25He replied, "Whether he is a sinner or not, I don't know. One
thing I do know. I was blind but now I see!"
26Then they asked him, "What did he do to you? How did he
open your eyes?"
27He answered, "I have told you already[g] and you did not listen.
Why do you want to hear it again? Do you want to become his
disciples, too?"
28Then they hurled insults at him and said, "You are this fellow's disciple! We are disciples of Moses![h] 29We know that God
spoke to Moses, but as for this fellow, we don't even know where
he comes from."[i]
30The man answered, "Now that is remarkable! You don't know
where he comes from, yet he opened my eyes. 31We know that God
does not listen to sinners. He listens to the godly man who does his
will.[j] 32Nobody has ever heard of opening the eyes of a man born
blind. 33If this man were not from God,[k] he could do nothing."
34To this they replied, "You were steeped in sin at birth;[l] how dare
you lecture us!" And they threw him out.[m]
35Jesus heard that they had thrown him out, and when he
found him, he said, "Do you believe in the Son of Man?"
36"Who is he, sir?" the man asked. "Tell me so that I may
believe in him."[n]
37Jesus said, "You have now seen him; in fact, he is the one
speaking with you."[o]
38Then the man said, "Lord, I believe," and he worshiped him.[p]
39Jesus said, "For judgment[q] I have come into this world,[r] so
that the blind will see[s] and those who see will become blind."[t]
40Some Pharisees who were with him heard him say this and
asked, "What? Are we blind too?"[u]
41Jesus said, "If you were blind, you would not be guilty of sin;
but now that you claim you can see, your guilt remains.[v]

Chapter 10 Theme ______________________

10 "I tell you the truth, the man who does not enter the sheep
pen by the gate, but climbs in by some other way, is a thief
and a robber. 2The man who enters by the gate is the shepherd of

[a] 22 Or *Messiah* [b] 24 A solemn charge to tell the truth (see Joshua 7:19)

9:22
[a] Jn 7:13
[b] ver 34; Lk 6:22
[c] Jn 12:42; 16:2

9:23
[d] ver 21

9:24
[e] Jos 7:19
[f] ver 16

9:27
[g] ver 15

9:28
[h] Jn 5:45

9:29
[i] Jn 8:14

9:31
[j] Ge 18:23-32; Ps 34:15,16; 66:18;145:19,20; Pr 15:29; Isa 1:15; 59:1,2; Jn 15:7; Jas 5:16-18; 1Jn 5:14,15

9:33
[k] ver 16; Jn 3:2

9:34
[l] ver 2
[m] ver 22,35; Isa 66:5

9:36
[n] Ro 10:14

9:37
[o] Jn 4:26

9:38
[p] Mt 28:9

9:39
[q] Jn 5:22
[r] Jn 3:19
[s] Lk 4:18
[t] Mt 13:13

9:40
[u] Ro 2:19

9:41
[v] Jn 15:22,24

his sheep.[a] 3The watchman opens the gate for him, and the sheep
listen to his voice.[b] He calls his own sheep by name and leads
them out. 4When he has brought out all his own, he goes on
ahead of them, and his sheep follow him because they know his
voice. 5But they will never follow a stranger; in fact, they will run
away from him because they do not recognize a stranger's voice."
6Jesus used this figure of speech,[c] but they did not understand
what he was telling them.

7Therefore Jesus said again, "I tell you the truth, I am the gate
for the sheep. 8All who ever came before me[d] were thieves and
robbers, but the sheep did not listen to them. 9I am the gate;
whoever enters through me will be saved.[a] He will come in and
go out, and find pasture. 10The thief comes only to steal and kill
and destroy; I have come that they may have life, and have it to
the full.

11"I am the good shepherd.[e] The good shepherd lays down his
life for the sheep.[f] 12The hired hand is not the shepherd who owns
the sheep. So when he sees the wolf coming, he abandons the
sheep and runs away.[g] Then the wolf attacks the flock and scatters it. 13The man runs away because he is a hired hand and cares
nothing for the sheep.

14"I am the good shepherd;[h] I know my sheep[i] and my sheep
know me—15just as the Father knows me and I know the
Father[j]—and I lay down my life for the sheep. 16I have other
sheep[k] that are not of this sheep pen. I must bring them also.
They too will listen to my voice, and there shall be one flock[l] and
one shepherd.[m] 17The reason my Father loves me is that I lay
down my life[n]—only to take it up again. 18No one takes it from
me, but I lay it down of my own accord.[o] I have authority to lay it
down and authority to take it up again. This command I received
from my Father."[p]

19At these words the Jews were again divided.[q] 20Many of them
said, "He is demon-possessed[r] and raving mad.[s] Why listen to
him?"

21But others said, "These are not the sayings of a man possessed by a demon.[t] Can a demon open the eyes of the blind?"[u]

22Then came the Feast of Dedication[b] at Jerusalem. It was winter,
23and Jesus was in the temple area walking in Solomon's Colonnade.[v] 24The Jews[w] gathered around him, saying, "How long will
you keep us in suspense? If you are the Christ,[c] tell us plainly."[x]

25Jesus answered, "I did tell you,[y] but you do not believe. The
miracles I do in my Father's name speak for me,[z] 26but you do
not believe because you are not my sheep.[a] 27My sheep listen to

10:2 [a]ver 11,14
10:3 [b]ver 4,5,14, 16,27
10:6 [c]Jn 16:25
10:8 [d]Jer 23:1,2
10:11 [e]ver 14; Isa 40:11; Eze 34:11-16, 23; Heb 13:20; 1Pe 5:4; Rev 7:17 [f]Jn 15:13; 1Jn 3:16
10:12 [g]Zec 11:16,17
10:14 [h]ver 11 [i]ver 27
10:15 [j]Mt 11:27
10:16 [k]Isa 56:8 [l]Jn 11:52; Eph 2:11-19 [m]Eze 37:24; 1Pe 2:25
10:17 [n]ver 11,15,18
10:18 [o]Mt 26:53 [p]Jn 15:10; Php 2:8; Heb 5:8
10:19 [q]Jn 7:43; 9:16
10:20 [r]Jn 7:20 [s]Mk 3:21
10:21 [t]Mt 4:24 [u]Ex 4:11; Jn 9:32,33
10:23 [v]Ac 3:11; 5:12
10:24 [w]Jn 1:19 [x]Jn 16:25,29
10:25 [y]Jn 8:58 [z]Jn 5:36
10:26 [a]Jn 8:47

[a]9 Or *kept safe* [b]22 That is, Hanukkah [c]24 Or *Messiah*

my voice; I know them,[a] and they follow me.[b] 28I give them eternal life, and they shall never perish; no one can snatch them out
of my hand.[c] 29My Father, who has given them to me,[d] is greater
than all[a];[e] no one can snatch them out of my Father's hand. 30I
and the Father are one."[f]
31Again the Jews picked up stones to stone him,[g] 32but Jesus
said to them, "I have shown you many great miracles from the
Father. For which of these do you stone me?"
33"We are not stoning you for any of these," replied the Jews,
"but for blasphemy, because you, a mere man, claim to be God."[h]
34Jesus answered them, "Is it not written in your Law,[i] 'I have
said you are gods'[b]?[j] 35If he called them 'gods,' to whom the word
of God came—and the Scripture cannot be broken— 36what
about the one whom the Father set apart[k] as his very own[l] and
sent into the world?[m] Why then do you accuse me of blasphemy
because I said, 'I am God's Son'?[n] 37Do not believe me unless I do
what my Father does.[o] 38But if I do it, even though you do not
believe me, believe the miracles, that you may know and understand that the Father is in me, and I in the Father."[p] 39Again they
tried to seize him,[q] but he escaped their grasp.[r]
40Then Jesus went back across the Jordan[s] to the place where
John had been baptizing in the early days. Here he stayed 41and
many people came to him. They said, "Though John never performed a miraculous sign,[t] all that John said about this man was
true."[u] 42And in that place many believed in Jesus.[v]

Chapter 11 Theme

11 Now a man named Lazarus was sick. He was from Bethany,[w]
the village of Mary and her sister Martha.[x] 2This Mary, whose
brother Lazarus now lay sick, was the same one who poured perfume on the Lord and wiped his feet with her hair.[y] 3So the sisters
sent word to Jesus, "Lord, the one you love[z] is sick."
4When he heard this, Jesus said, "This sickness will not end in
death. No, it is for God's glory[a] so that God's Son may be glorified through it." 5Jesus loved Martha and her sister and Lazarus.
6Yet when he heard that Lazarus was sick, he stayed where he was
two more days.
7Then he said to his disciples, "Let us go back to Judea."[b]
8"But Rabbi,"[c] they said, "a short while ago the Jews tried to
stone you,[d] and yet you are going back there?"
9Jesus answered, "Are there not twelve hours of daylight? A man
who walks by day will not stumble, for he sees by this world's light.[e]
10It is when he walks by night that he stumbles, for he has no light."

10:27 [a]ver 14 [b]ver 4
10:28 [c]Jn 6:39
10:29 [d]Jn 17:2,6,24 [e]Jn 14:28
10:30 [f]Jn 17:21-23
10:31 [g]Jn 8:59
10:33 [h]Lev 24:16; Jn 5:18
10:34 [i]Jn 8:17; Ro 3:19 [j]Ps 82:6
10:36 [k]Jer 1:5 [l]Jn 6:69 [m]Jn 3:17 [n]Jn 5:17,18
10:37 [o]ver 25; Jn 15:24
10:38 [p]Jn 14:10, 11,20; 17:21
10:39 [q]Jn 7:30 [r]Lk 4:30; Jn 8:59
10:40 [s]Jn 1:28
10:41 [t]Jn 2:11; 3:30 [u]Jn 1:26,27, 30,34
10:42 [v]Jn 7:31
11:1 [w]Mt 21:17 [x]Lk 10:38
11:2 [y]Mk 14:3; Lk 7:38; Jn 12:3
11:3 [z]ver 5,36
11:4 [a]ver 40; Jn 9:3
11:7 [b]Jn 10:40
11:8 [c]Mt 23:7 [d]Jn 8:59; 10:31
11:9 [e]Jn 9:4; 12:35

[a]29 Many early manuscripts *What my Father has given me is greater than all* [b]34 Psalm 82:6

11After he had said this, he went on to tell them, "Our friend[a]
Lazarus has fallen asleep;[b] but I am going there to wake him up."
12His disciples replied, "Lord, if he sleeps, he will get better."
13Jesus had been speaking of his death, but his disciples thought
he meant natural sleep.[c]
14So then he told them plainly, "Lazarus is dead, 15and for your
sake I am glad I was not there, so that you may believe. But let us
go to him."
16Then Thomas[d] (called Didymus) said to the rest of the disciples, "Let us also go, that we may die with him."
17On his arrival, Jesus found that Lazarus had already been in
the tomb for four days.[e] 18Bethany[f] was less than two miles[a] from
Jerusalem, 19and many Jews had come to Martha and Mary to
comfort them in the loss of their brother.[g] 20When Martha heard
that Jesus was coming, she went out to meet him, but Mary
stayed at home.[h]
21"Lord," Martha said to Jesus, "if you had been here, my
brother would not have died.[i] 22But I know that even now God
will give you whatever you ask."[j]
23Jesus said to her, "Your brother will rise again."
24Martha answered, "I know he will rise again in the resurrection[k] at the last day."
25Jesus said to her, "I am the resurrection and the life.[l] He who
believes in me will live, even though he dies; 26and whoever lives
and believes in me will never die. Do you believe this?"
27"Yes, Lord," she told him, "I believe that you are the Christ,[b][m]
the Son of God,[n] who was to come into the world."[o]
28And after she had said this, she went back and called her sister
Mary aside. "The Teacher[p] is here," she said, "and is asking for
you." 29When Mary heard this, she got up quickly and went to
him. 30Now Jesus had not yet entered the village, but was still at the
place where Martha had met him.[q] 31When the Jews who had been
with Mary in the house, comforting her,[r] noticed how quickly she
got up and went out, they followed her, supposing she was going to
the tomb to mourn there.
32When Mary reached the place where Jesus was and saw him,
she fell at his feet and said, "Lord, if you had been here, my
brother would not have died."[s]
33When Jesus saw her weeping, and the Jews who had come
along with her also weeping, he was deeply moved[t] in spirit and
troubled.[u] 34"Where have you laid him?" he asked.
"Come and see, Lord," they replied.
35Jesus wept.[v]
36Then the Jews said, "See how he loved him!"[w]

11:11 [a] ver 3 [b] Ac 7:60
11:13 [c] Mt 9:24
11:16 [d] Mt 10:3; Jn 14:5; 20:24-28; 21:2; Ac 1:13
11:17 [e] ver 6,39
11:18 [f] ver 1
11:19 [g] ver 31; Job 2:11
11:20 [h] Lk 10:38-42
11:21 [i] ver 32,37
11:22 [j] ver 41,42; Jn 9:31
11:24 [k] Da 12:2; Jn 5:28,29; Ac 24:15
11:25 [l] Jn 1:4
11:27 [m] Lk 2:11 [n] Mt 16:16 [o] Jn 6:14
11:28 [p] Mt 26:18; Jn 13:13
11:30 [q] ver 20
11:31 [r] ver 19
11:32 [s] ver 21
11:33 [t] ver 38 [u] Jn 12:27
11:35 [v] Lk 19:41
11:36 [w] ver 3

[a] *18* Greek *fifteen stadia* (about 3 kilometers) [b] *27* Or *Messiah*

37 But some of them said, "Could not he who opened the eyes of
the blind man[a] have kept this man from dying?"[b]
38 Jesus, once more deeply moved,[c] came to the tomb. It was a
cave with a stone laid across the entrance.[d] 39 "Take away the
stone," he said.
"But, Lord," said Martha, the sister of the dead man, "by this
time there is a bad odor, for he has been there four days."[e]
40 Then Jesus said, "Did I not tell you that if you believed,[f] you
would see the glory of God?"[g]
41 So they took away the stone. Then Jesus looked up[h] and said,
"Father,[i] I thank you that you have heard me. 42 I knew that you
always hear me, but I said this for the benefit of the people standing here,[j] that they may believe that you sent me."[k]
43 When he had said this, Jesus called in a loud voice, "Lazarus,
come out!"[l] 44 The dead man came out, his hands and feet
wrapped with strips of linen,[m] and a cloth around his face.[n]
Jesus said to them, "Take off the grave clothes and let him go."
45 Therefore many of the Jews who had come to visit Mary,[o] and
had seen what Jesus did,[p] put their faith in him.[q] 46 But some of
them went to the Pharisees and told them what Jesus had done.
47 Then the chief priests and the Pharisees[r] called a meeting[s] of the
Sanhedrin.[t]
"What are we accomplishing?" they asked. "Here is this man
performing many miraculous signs.[u] 48 If we let him go on like
this, everyone will believe in him, and then the Romans will come
and take away both our place[a] and our nation."
49 Then one of them, named Caiaphas,[v] who was high priest
that year,[w] spoke up, "You know nothing at all! 50 You do not realize that it is better for you that one man die for the people than
that the whole nation perish."[x]
51 He did not say this on his own, but as high priest that year he
prophesied that Jesus would die for the Jewish nation, 52 and not
only for that nation but also for the scattered children of God, to
bring them together and make them one.[y] 53 So from that day on
they plotted to take his life.[z]
54 Therefore Jesus no longer moved about publicly among the
Jews.[a] Instead he withdrew to a region near the desert, to a village
called Ephraim, where he stayed with his disciples.
55 When it was almost time for the Jewish Passover,[b] many went
up from the country to Jerusalem for their ceremonial cleansing[c]
before the Passover. 56 They kept looking for Jesus,[d] and as they
stood in the temple area they asked one another, "What do you
think? Isn't he coming to the Feast at all?" 57 But the chief priests
and Pharisees had given orders that if anyone found out where
Jesus was, he should report it so that they might arrest him.

a48 Or *temple*

11:37 [a] Jn 9:6,7 [b] ver 21,32
11:38 [c] ver 33 [d] Mt 27:60; Lk 24:2; Jn 20:1
11:39 [e] ver 17
11:40 [f] ver 23-25 [g] ver 4
11:41 [h] Jn 17:1 [i] Mt 11:25
11:42 [j] Jn 12:30 [k] Jn 3:17
11:43 [l] Lk 7:14
11:44 [m] Jn 19:40 [n] Jn 20:7
11:45 [o] ver 19 [p] Jn 2:23 [q] Ex 14:31; Jn 7:31
11:47 [r] ver 57 [s] Mt 26:3 [t] Mt 5:22 [u] Jn 2:11
11:49 [v] Mt 26:3 [w] ver 51; Jn 18:13,14
11:50 [x] Jn 18:14
11:52 [y] Isa 49:6; Jn 10:16
11:53 [z] Mt 12:14
11:54 [a] Jn 7:1
11:55 [b] Ex 12:13,23,27; Mt 26:1,2; Mk 14:1; Jn 13:1 [c] 2Ch 30:17,18
11:56 [d] Jn 7:11

12:1 a Jn 11:55 *Chapter 12 Theme* ________________________
b Mt 21:17 **12** Six days before the Passover,[a] Jesus arrived at Bethany,[b]
where Lazarus lived, whom Jesus had raised from the
dead. 2Here a dinner was given in Jesus' honor. Martha served,[c]
12:2 while Lazarus was among those reclining at the table with him.
c Lk 10:38-42 3Then Mary took about a pint[a] of pure nard, an expensive perfume;[d] she poured it on Jesus' feet and wiped his feet with her
hair.[e] And the house was filled with the fragrance of the perfume.
12:3 4But one of his disciples, Judas Iscariot, who was later to betray
d Mk 14:3 him,[f] objected, 5"Why wasn't this perfume sold and the money
e Jn 11:2 given to the poor? It was worth a year's wages.[b]" 6He did not say
this because he cared about the poor but because he was a thief;
as keeper of the money bag,[g] he used to help himself to what was
12:4 put into it.
f Mt 10:4 7"Leave her alone," Jesus replied.
"⌊It was intended⌋ that she should
save this perfume for the day of my
12:6 burial.[h] 8You will always have the
g Jn 13:29 poor among you,[i] but you will not
always have me."
9Meanwhile a large crowd of Jews
12:7 found out that Jesus was there and
h Jn 19:40 came, not only because of him but
also to see Lazarus, whom he had
raised from the dead.[j] 10So the chief
12:8 priests made plans to kill Lazarus as
i Dt 15:11 well, 11for on account of him[k] many
of the Jews were going over to Jesus
and putting their faith in him.[l]
12The next day the great crowd that had come for the Feast
12:9 j Jn 11:43,44 heard that Jesus was on his way to Jerusalem. 13They took palm
branches and went out to meet him, shouting,

"Hosanna![c]"

12:11 k ver 17,18; Jn 11:45 "Blessed is he who comes in the name of the Lord!"[d] [m]

l Jn 7:31 "Blessed is the King of Israel!"[n]

14Jesus found a young donkey and sat upon it, as it is written,

12:13 m Ps 118:25,26 15"Do not be afraid, O Daughter of Zion;
n Jn 1:49 see, your king is coming,
seated on a donkey's colt."[e] [o]

From Bethany, Bethphage across the Mount of Olives into Jerusalem

a 3 Greek *a litra* (probably about 0.5 liter) b 5 Greek *three hundred denarii* c 13 A Hebrew
12:15 expression meaning "Save!" which became an exclamation of praise d 13 Psalm 118:25, 26
o Zec 9:9 e 15 Zech. 9:9

16At first his disciples did not understand all this.[a] Only after
Jesus was glorified[b] did they realize that these things had been
written about him and that they had done these things to him.
17Now the crowd that was with him[c] when he called Lazarus
from the tomb and raised him from the dead continued to spread
the word. 18Many people, because they had heard that he had giv-
en this miraculous sign,[d] went out to meet him. 19So the Pharisees
said to one another, "See, this is getting us nowhere. Look how the
whole world has gone after him!"[e]

20Now there were some Greeks[f] among those who went up to
worship at the Feast. 21They came to Philip, who was from Bethsaida[g] in Galilee, with a request. "Sir," they said, "we would like
to see Jesus." 22Philip went to tell Andrew; Andrew and Philip in
turn told Jesus.

23Jesus replied, "The hour has come for the Son of Man to be
glorified.[h] 24I tell you the truth, unless a kernel of wheat falls to the
ground and dies,[i] it remains only a single seed. But if it dies, it
produces many seeds. 25The man who loves his life will lose it,
while the man who hates his life in this world will keep it[j] for eternal life. 26Whoever serves me must follow me; and where I am, my
servant also will be.[k] My Father will honor the one who serves me.
27"Now my heart is troubled,[l] and what shall I say? 'Father,[m]
save me from this hour'?[n] No, it was for this very reason I came to
this hour. 28Father, glorify your name!"

Then a voice came from heaven,[o] "I have glorified it, and will
glorify it again." 29The crowd that was there and heard it said it
had thundered; others said an angel had spoken to him.
30Jesus said, "This voice was for your benefit,[p] not mine. 31Now
is the time for judgment on this world;[q] now the prince of this
world[r] will be driven out. 32But I, when I am lifted up from the
earth,[s] will draw all men to myself."[t] 33He said this to show the
kind of death he was going to die.[u]
34The crowd spoke up, "We have heard from the Law that the
Christ[a] will remain forever,[v] so how can you say, 'The Son of Man[w]
must be lifted up'?[x] Who is this 'Son of Man'?"
35Then Jesus told them, "You are going to have the light[y] just a
little while longer. Walk while you have the light,[z] before darkness
overtakes you.[a] The man who walks in the dark does not know
where he is going. 36Put your trust in the light while you have it, so
that you may become sons of light."[b] When he had finished
speaking, Jesus left and hid himself from them.[c]
37Even after Jesus had done all these miraculous signs[d] in their
presence, they still would not believe in him. 38This was to fulfill
the word of Isaiah the prophet:

[a] 34 Or *Messiah*

12:16 [a] Mk 9:32 [b] Jn 2:22; 7:39; 14:26
12:17 [c] Jn 11:42
12:18 [d] ver 11
12:19 [e] Jn 11:47,48
12:20 [f] Jn 7:35; Ac 11:20
12:21 [g] Mt 11:21; Jn 1:44
12:23 [h] Jn 13:32; 17:1
12:24 [i] 1Co 15:36
12:25 [j] Mt 10:39; Mk 8:35; Lk 14:26
12:26 [k] Jn 14:3; 17:24; 2Co 5:8; 1Th 4:17
12:27 [l] Mt 26:38,39; Jn 11:33,38; 13:21 [m] Mt 11:25 [n] ver 23
12:28 [o] Mt 3:17
12:30 [p] Jn 11:42
12:31 [q] Jn 16:11 [r] Jn 14:30; 16:11; 2Co 4:4; Eph 2:2; 1Jn 4:4
12:32 [s] ver 34; Jn 3:14; 8:28 [t] Jn 6:44
12:33 [u] Jn 18:32
12:34 [v] Ps 110:4; Isa 9:7; Eze 37:25; Da 7:14 [w] Mt 8:20 [x] Jn 3:14
12:35 [y] ver 46 [z] Eph 5:8 [a] 1Jn 2:11
12:36 [b] Lk 16:8 [c] Jn 8:59
12:37 [d] Jn 2:11

"Lord, who has believed our message
and to whom has the arm of the Lord been revealed?"[a][a]

39For this reason they could not believe, because, as Isaiah says
elsewhere:

40"He has blinded their eyes
and deadened their hearts,
so they can neither see with their eyes,
nor understand with their hearts,
nor turn—and I would heal them."[b][b]

41Isaiah said this because he saw Jesus' glory[c] and spoke about
him.[d]
42Yet at the same time many even among the leaders believed in
him.[e] But because of the Pharisees[f] they would not confess their
faith for fear they would be put out of the synagogue;[g] 43for they
loved praise from men more than praise from God.[h]
44Then Jesus cried out, "When a man believes in me, he does
not believe in me only, but in the one who sent me.[i] 45When he
looks at me, he sees the one who sent me.[j] 46I have come into the
world as a light,[k] so that no one who believes in me should stay in
darkness.
47"As for the person who hears my words but does not keep
them, I do not judge him. For I did not come to judge the world,
but to save it.[l] 48There is a judge for the one who rejects me and
does not accept my words; that very word which I spoke will condemn him[m] at the last day. 49For I did not speak of my own
accord, but the Father who sent me commanded me[n] what to say
and how to say it. 50I know that his command leads to eternal life.
So whatever I say is just what the Father has told me to say."

Chapter 13 Theme ______________________

13

It was just before the Passover Feast.[o] Jesus knew that the
time had come[p] for him to leave this world and go to the
Father.[q] Having loved his own who were in the world, he now
showed them the full extent of his love.[c]
2The evening meal was being served, and the devil had already
prompted Judas Iscariot, son of Simon, to betray Jesus. 3Jesus
knew that the Father had put all things under his power,[r] and that
he had come from God[s] and was returning to God; 4so he got up
from the meal, took off his outer clothing, and wrapped a towel
around his waist. 5After that, he poured water into a basin and
began to wash his disciples' feet,[t] drying them with the towel that
was wrapped around him.

12:38 [a]Isa 53:1; Ro 10:16
12:40 [b]Isa 6:10; Mt 13:13,15
12:41 [c]Isa 6:1-4 [d]Lk 24:27
12:42 [e]ver 11; Jn 7:48 [f]Jn 7:13 [g]Jn 9:22
12:43 [h]Jn 5:44
12:44 [i]Mt 10:40; Jn 5:24
12:45 [j]Jn 14:9
12:46 [k]Jn 1:4; 3:19; 8:12; 9:5
12:47 [l]Jn 3:17
12:48 [m]Jn 5:45
12:49 [n]Jn 14:31
13:1 [o]Jn 11:55 [p]Jn 12:23 [q]Jn 16:28
13:3 [r]Mt 28:18 [s]Jn 8:42; 16:27,28,30
13:5 [t]Lk 7:44

[a]*38* Isaiah 53:1 [b]*40* Isaiah 6:10 [c]*1* Or *he loved them to the last*

6He came to Simon Peter, who said to him, "Lord, are you going
to wash my feet?"
7Jesus replied, "You do not realize now what I am doing, but
later you will understand."[a]
8"No," said Peter, "you shall never wash my feet."
Jesus answered, "Unless I wash you, you have no part with me."
9"Then, Lord," Simon Peter replied, "not just my feet but my
hands and my head as well!"
10Jesus answered, "A person who has had a bath needs only to
wash his feet; his whole body is clean. And you are clean,[b] though
not every one of you." 11For he knew who was going to betray
him, and that was why he said not every one was clean.
12When he had finished washing their feet, he put on his clothes
and returned to his place. "Do you understand what I have done
for you?" he asked them. 13"You call me 'Teacher'[c] and 'Lord,'[d] and
rightly so, for that is what I am. 14Now that I, your Lord and Teacher,
have washed your feet, you also should wash one another's feet.[e]
15I have set you an example that you should do as I have done for
you.[f] 16I tell you the truth, no servant is greater than his master,[g]
nor is a messenger greater than the one who sent him. 17Now that
you know these things, you will be blessed if you do them.[h]
18"I am not referring to all of you;[i] I know those I have chosen.[j]
But this is to fulfill the scripture: 'He who shares my bread[k] has
lifted up his heel[l] against me.'[a][m]
19"I am telling you now before it happens, so that when it does
happen you will believe[n] that I am He.[o] 20I tell you the truth,
whoever accepts anyone I send accepts me; and whoever accepts
me accepts the one who sent me."[p]
21After he had said this, Jesus was troubled in spirit[q] and testified, "I tell you the truth, one of you is going to betray me."[r]
22His disciples stared at one another, at a loss to know which of
them he meant. 23One of them, the disciple whom Jesus loved,[s]
was reclining next to him. 24Simon Peter motioned to this disciple and said, "Ask him which one he means."
25Leaning back against Jesus, he asked him, "Lord, who is it?"[t]
26Jesus answered, "It is the one to whom I will give this piece of
bread when I have dipped it in the dish." Then, dipping the piece
of bread, he gave it to Judas Iscariot, son of Simon. 27As soon as
Judas took the bread, Satan entered into him.[u]
"What you are about to do, do quickly," Jesus told him, 28but
no one at the meal understood why Jesus said this to him. 29Since
Judas had charge of the money,[v] some thought Jesus was telling
him to buy what was needed for the Feast, or to give something
to the poor. 30As soon as Judas had taken the bread, he went out.
And it was night.[w]

[a] *18* Psalm 41:9

13:7 [a] ver 12
13:10 [b] Jn 15:3
13:13 [c] Jn 11:28 [d] Lk 6:46; 1Co 12:3; Php 2:11
13:14 [e] 1Pe 5:5
13:15 [f] Mt 11:29
13:16 [g] Mt 10:24; Lk 6:40; Jn 15:20
13:17 [h] Mt 7:24,25; Lk 11:28; Jas 1:25
13:18 [i] ver 10 [j] Jn 15:16,19 [k] Mt 26:23 [l] Jn 6:70 [m] Ps 41:9
13:19 [n] Jn 14:29; 16:4 [o] Jn 8:24
13:20 [p] Mt 10:40; Lk 10:16
13:21 [q] Jn 12:27 [r] Mt 26:21
13:23 [s] Jn 19:26; 20:2; 21:7,20
13:25 [t] Jn 21:20
13:27 [u] Lk 22:3
13:29 [v] Jn 12:6
13:30 [w] Lk 22:53

going to the Father. 13And I will do whatever you ask[a] in my name,
so that the Son may bring glory to the Father. 14You may ask me
for anything in my name, and I will do it.
15“If you love me, you will obey what I command.[b] 16And I will
ask the Father, and he will give you another Counselor[c] to be with
you forever— 17the Spirit of truth.[d] The world cannot accept
him,[e] because it neither sees him nor knows him. But you know
him, for he lives with you and will be[a] in you. 18I will not leave
you as orphans; I will come to you.[f] 19Before long, the world will
not see me anymore, but you will see me.[g] Because I live, you also
will live.[h] 20On that day you will realize that I am in my Father,[i]
and you are in me, and I am in you. 21Whoever has my commands and obeys them, he is the one who loves me.[j] He who loves
me will be loved by my Father,[k] and I too will love him and show
myself to him.”
22Then Judas[l] (not Judas Iscariot) said, “But, Lord, why do you
intend to show yourself to us and not to the world?”[m]
23Jesus replied, “If anyone loves me, he will obey my teaching.[n]
My Father will love him, and we will come to him and make our
home with him.[o] 24He who does not love me will not obey my
teaching. These words you hear are not my own; they belong to
the Father who sent me.[p]
25“All this I have spoken while still with you. 26But the Counselor,[q] the Holy Spirit, whom the Father will send in my name,[r]
will teach you all things[s] and will remind you of everything I have
said to you.[t] 27Peace I leave with you; my peace I give you.[u] I do
not give to you as the world gives. Do not let your hearts be troubled and do not be afraid.
28“You heard me say, ‘I am going away and I am coming back to
you.’[v] If you loved me, you would be glad that I am going to the
Father,[w] for the Father is greater than I.[x] 29I have told you now
before it happens, so that when it does happen you will believe.[y]
30I will not speak with you much longer, for the prince of this
world[z] is coming. He has no hold on me, 31but the world must
learn that I love the Father and that I do exactly what my Father
has commanded me.[a]
“Come now; let us leave.

Chapter 15 Theme ____________________

15

“I am the true vine,[b] and my Father is the gardener. 2He
cuts off every branch in me that bears no fruit, while every
branch that does bear fruit he prunes[b] so that it will be even more
fruitful. 3You are already clean because of the word I have spoken

a 17 Some early manuscripts *and is* b 2 The Greek for *prunes* also means *cleans.*

14:13 [a] Mt 7:7
14:15 [b] ver 21,23; Jn 15:10; 1Jn 5:3
14:16 [c] Jn 15:26; 16:7
14:17 [d] Jn 15:26; 16:13; 1Jn 4:6 [e] 1Co 2:14
14:18 [f] ver 3,28
14:19 [g] Jn 7:33,34; 16:16 [h] Jn 6:57
14:20 [i] Jn 10:38
14:21 [j] 1Jn 5:3 [k] 1Jn 2:5
14:22 [l] Lk 6:16; Ac 1:13 [m] Ac 10:41
14:23 [n] ver 15 [o] 1Jn 2:24; Rev 3:20
14:24 [p] Jn 7:16
14:26 [q] Jn 15:26; 16:7 [r] Ac 2:33 [s] Jn 16:13; 1Jn 2:20,27 [t] Jn 2:22
14:27 [u] Jn 16:33; Php 4:7; Col 3:15
14:28 [v] ver 2-4,18 [w] Jn 5:18 [x] Jn 10:29; Php 2:6
14:29 [y] Jn 13:19; 16:4
14:30 [z] Jn 12:31
14:31 [a] Jn 10:18; 12:49
15:1 [b] Isa 5:1-7

31When he was gone, Jesus said, "Now is the Son of Man glorified[a] and God is glorified in him.[b] 32If God is glorified in him,[a]
God will glorify the Son in himself,[c] and will glorify him at once.
33"My children, I will be with you only a little longer. You will
look for me, and just as I told the Jews, so I tell you now: Where I
am going, you cannot come.[d]
34"A new command[e] I give you: Love one another.[f] As I have
loved you, so you must love one another.[g] 35By this all men will
know that you are my disciples, if you love one another."[h]
36Simon Peter asked him, "Lord, where are you going?"
Jesus replied, "Where I am going, you cannot follow now,[i] but
you will follow later."[j]
37Peter asked, "Lord, why can't I follow you now? I will lay down
my life for you."
38Then Jesus answered, "Will you really lay down your life for
me? I tell you the truth, before the rooster crows, you will disown
me three times![k]

Chapter 14 Theme

14 "Do not let your hearts be troubled.[l] Trust in God[b]; trust
also in me. 2In my Father's house are many rooms; if it
were not so, I would have told you. I am going there[m] to prepare a
place for you. 3And if I go and prepare a place for you, I will come
back and take you to be with me that you also may be where I
am.[n] 4You know the way to the place where I am going."
5Thomas[o] said to him, "Lord, we don't know where you are
going, so how can we know the way?"
6Jesus answered, "I am the way[p] and the truth and the life.[q] No
one comes to the Father except through me. 7If you really knew
me, you would know[c] my Father as well.[r] From now on, you do
know him and have seen him."
8Philip said, "Lord, show us the Father and that will be enough
for us."
9Jesus answered: "Don't you know me, Philip, even after I have
been among you such a long time? Anyone who has seen me has
seen the Father.[s] How can you say, 'Show us the Father'? 10Don't
you believe that I am in the Father, and that the Father is in me?[t]
The words I say to you are not just my own.[u] Rather, it is the
Father, living in me, who is doing his work. 11Believe me when I
say that I am in the Father and the Father is in me; or at least
believe on the evidence of the miracles themselves.[v] 12I tell you
the truth, anyone who has faith[w] in me will do what I have been
doing.[x] He will do even greater things than these, because I am

a32 Many early manuscripts do not have *If God is glorified in him.* b1 Or *You trust in God*
c7 Some early manuscripts *If you really have known me, you will know*

13:31 [a]Jn 7:39 [b]Jn 14:13; 17:4; 1Pe 4:11
13:32 [c]Jn 17:1
13:33 [d]Jn 7:33,34
13:34 [e]1Jn 2:7-11; 3:11 [f]Lev 19:18; 1Th 4:9; 1Pe 1:22 [g]Jn 15:12; Eph 5:2; 1Jn 4:10,11
13:35 [h]1Jn 3:14; 4:20
13:36 [i]ver 33; Jn 14:2 [j]Jn 21:18,19; 2Pe 1:14
13:38 [k]Jn 18:27
14:1 [l]ver 27
14:2 [m]Jn 13:33,36
14:3 [n]Jn 12:26
14:5 [o]Jn 11:16
14:6 [p]Jn 10:9 [q]Jn 11:25
14:7 [r]Jn 8:19
14:9 [s]Jn 12:45; Col 1:15; Heb 1:3
14:10 [t]Jn 10:38 [u]Jn 5:19
14:11 [v]Jn 5:36; 10:38
14:12 [w]Mt 21:21 [x]Lk 10:17

to you.[a] 4Remain in me, and I will remain in you.[b] No branch can
bear fruit by itself; it must remain in the vine. Neither can you bear
fruit unless you remain in me.

5"I am the vine; you are the branches. If a man remains in me
and I in him, he will bear much fruit;[c] apart from me you can do
nothing. 6If anyone does not remain in me, he is like a branch
that is thrown away and withers; such branches are picked up,
thrown into the fire and burned.[d] 7If you remain in me and my
words remain in you, ask whatever you wish, and it will be given
you.[e] 8This is to my Father's glory,[f] that you bear much fruit,
showing yourselves to be my disciples.[g]

9"As the Father has loved me,[h] so have I loved you. Now remain
in my love. 10If you obey my commands,[i] you will remain in my
love, just as I have obeyed my Father's commands and remain in
his love. 11I have told you this so that my joy may be in you and
that your joy may be complete.[j] 12My command is this: Love each
other as I have loved you.[k] 13Greater love has no one than this,
that he lay down his life for his friends.[l] 14You are my friends[m] if
you do what I command.[n] 15I no longer call you servants, because
a servant does not know his master's business. Instead, I have
called you friends, for everything that I learned from my Father I
have made known to you.[o] 16You did not choose me, but I chose
you and appointed you[p] to go and bear fruit—fruit that will last.
Then the Father will give you whatever you ask in my name.
17This is my command: Love each other.[q]

18"If the world hates you,[r] keep in mind that it hated me first.
19If you belonged to the world, it would love you as its own. As it
is, you do not belong to the world, but I have chosen you[s] out of
the world. That is why the world hates you.[t] 20Remember the
words I spoke to you: 'No servant is greater than his master.'[a][u] If
they persecuted me, they will persecute you also.[v] If they obeyed
my teaching, they will obey yours also. 21They will treat you this
way because of my name,[w] for they do not know the One who
sent me.[x] 22If I had not come and spoken to them, they would not
be guilty of sin. Now, however, they have no excuse for their sin.[y]
23He who hates me hates my Father as well. 24If I had not done
among them what no one else did,[z] they would not be guilty of
sin. But now they have seen these miracles, and yet they have hated both me and my Father. 25But this is to fulfill what is written in
their Law: 'They hated me without reason.'[b][a]

26"When the Counselor[b] comes, whom I will send to you from
the Father,[c] the Spirit of truth[d] who goes out from the Father, he
will testify about me.[e] 27And you also must testify,[f] for you have
been with me from the beginning.[g]

15:3 [a] Jn 13:10; 17:17; Eph 5:26
15:4 [b] Jn 6:56; 1Jn 2:6
15:5 [c] ver 16
15:6 [d] ver 2
15:7 [e] Mt 7:7
15:8 [f] Mt 5:16 [g] Jn 8:31
15:9 [h] Jn 17:23, 24,26
15:10 [i] Jn 14:15
15:11 [j] Jn 17:13
15:12 [k] Jn 13:34
15:13 [l] Jn 10:11; Ro 5:7,8
15:14 [m] Lk 12:4 [n] Mt 12:50
15:15 [o] Jn 8:26
15:16 [p] Jn 6:70; 13:18
15:17 [q] ver 12
15:18 [r] 1Jn 3:13
15:19 [s] ver 16 [t] Jn 17:14
15:20 [u] Jn 13:16 [v] 2Ti 3:12
15:21 [w] Mt 10:22 [x] Jn 16:3
15:22 [y] Jn 9:41; Ro 1:20
15:24 [z] Jn 5:36
15:25 [a] Ps 35:19; 69:4
15:26 [b] Jn 14:16 [c] Jn 14:26 [d] Jn 14:17 [e] 1Jn 5:7
15:27 [f] Lk 24:48; 1Jn 1:2; 4:14 [g] Lk 1:2

a *20* John 13:16 b *25* Psalms 35:19; 69:4

Chapter 16 Theme ______________________________

16 “All this[a] I have told you so that you will not go astray.[b]
2They will put you out of the synagogue;[c] in fact, a time is
coming when anyone who kills you will think he is offering a service to God.[d] 3They will do such things because they have not
known the Father or me.[e] 4I have told you this, so that when the
time comes you will remember[f] that I warned you. I did not tell
you this at first because I was with you.
5“Now I am going to him who sent me,[g] yet none of you asks
me, ‘Where are you going?’[h] 6Because I have said these things,
you are filled with grief. 7But I tell you the truth: It is for your good
that I am going away. Unless I go away, the Counselor[i] will not
come to you; but if I go, I will send him to you.[j] 8When he comes,
he will convict the world of guilt[a] in regard to sin and righteousness and judgment: 9in regard to sin,[k] because men do not believe
in me; 10in regard to righteousness,[l] because I am going to the
Father, where you can see me no longer; 11and in regard to judgment, because the prince of this world[m] now stands condemned.
12“I have much more to say to you, more than you can now bear.[n]
13But when he, the Spirit of truth,[o] comes, he will guide you into
all truth.[p] He will not speak on his own; he will speak only what
he hears, and he will tell you what is yet to come. 14He will bring
glory to me by taking from what is mine and making it known to
you. 15All that belongs to the Father is mine.[q] That is why I said
the Spirit will take from what is mine and make it known to you.
16“In a little while[r] you will see me no more, and then after a little while you will see me.”[s]
17Some of his disciples said to one another, “What does he mean
by saying, ‘In a little while you will see me no more, and then after
a little while you will see me,’[t] and ‘Because I am going to the
Father’?”[u] 18They kept asking, “What does he mean by ‘a little
while’? We don’t understand what he is saying.”
19Jesus saw that they wanted to ask him about this, so he said to
them, “Are you asking one another what I meant when I said, ‘In
a little while you will see me no more, and then after a little while
you will see me’? 20I tell you the truth, you will weep and mourn[v]
while the world rejoices. You will grieve, but your grief will turn
to joy.[w] 21A woman giving birth to a child has pain[x] because her
time has come; but when her baby is born she forgets the anguish
because of her joy that a child is born into the world. 22So with
you: Now is your time of grief,[y] but I will see you again[z] and you
will rejoice, and no one will take away your joy. 23In that day you
will no longer ask me anything. I tell you the truth, my Father

[a]8 Or *will expose the guilt of the world*

16:1
[a] Jn 15:18-27
[b] Mt 11:6

16:2
[c] Jn 9:22
[d] Isa 66:5; Ac 26:9,10; Rev 6:9

16:3
[e] Jn 15:21; 17:25; 1Jn 3:1

16:4
[f] Jn 13:19

16:5
[g] Jn 7:33
[h] Jn 13:36; 14:5

16:7
[i] Jn 14:16,26; 15:26
[j] Jn 7:39

16:9
[k] Jn 15:22

16:10
[l] Ac 3:14; 7:52; 1Pe 3:18

16:11
[m] Jn 12:31

16:12
[n] Mk 4:33

16:13
[o] Jn 14:17
[p] Jn 14:26

16:15
[q] Jn 17:10

16:16
[r] Jn 7:33
[s] Jn 14:18-24

16:17
[t] ver 16
[u] ver 5

16:20
[v] Lk 23:27
[w] Jn 20:20

16:21
[x] Isa 26:17; 1Th 5:3

16:22
[y] ver 6
[z] ver 16

will give you whatever you ask in my name.[a] 24 Until now you have
not asked for anything in my name. Ask and you will receive, and
your joy will be complete.[b]
25 "Though I have been speaking figuratively,[c] a time is coming[d]
when I will no longer use this kind of language but will tell you
plainly about my Father. 26 In that day you will ask in my name.[e] I
am not saying that I will ask the Father on your behalf. 27 No, the
Father himself loves you because you have loved me[f] and have
believed that I came from God. 28 I came from the Father and
entered the world; now I am leaving the world and going back to
the Father."[g]
29 Then Jesus' disciples said, "Now you are speaking clearly and
without figures of speech.[h] 30 Now we can see that you know all
things and that you do not even need to have anyone ask you
questions. This makes us believe that you came from God."
31 "You believe at last!"[a] Jesus answered. 32 "But a time is coming,[i]
and has come, when you will be scattered,[j] each to his own home.
You will leave me all alone. Yet I am not alone, for my Father is
with me.[k]
33 "I have told you these things, so that in me you may have
peace.[l] In this world you will have trouble.[m] But take heart! I have
overcome[n] the world."

Chapter 17 Theme ______________________

17

After Jesus said this, he looked toward heaven[o] and prayed:
"Father, the time has come. Glorify your Son, that your Son
may glorify you.[p] 2 For you granted him authority over all
people that he might give eternal life to all those you have given
him.[q] 3 Now this is eternal life: that they may know you, the
only true God, and Jesus Christ, whom you have sent.[r] 4 I have
brought you glory[s] on earth by completing the work you gave
me to do.[t] 5 And now, Father, glorify me in your presence with
the glory I had with you[u] before the world began.[v]
6 "I have revealed you[b][w] to those whom you gave me[x] out of
the world. They were yours; you gave them to me and they
have obeyed your word. 7 Now they know that everything you
have given me comes from you. 8 For I gave them the words
you gave me[y] and they accepted them. They knew with certainty that I came from you,[z] and they believed that you sent
me.[a] 9 I pray for them.[b] I am not praying for the world, but for
those you have given me, for they are yours. 10 All I have is
yours, and all you have is mine.[c] And glory has come to me
through them. 11 I will remain in the world no longer, but they

16:23 [a]Mt 7:7; Jn 15:16
16:24 [b]Jn 3:29; 15:11
16:25 [c]Mt 13:34; Jn 10:6 [d]ver 2
16:26 [e]ver 23,24
16:27 [f]Jn 14:21,23
16:28 [g]Jn 13:3
16:29 [h]ver 25
16:32 [i]ver 2,25 [j]Mt 26:31 [k]Jn 8:16,29
16:33 [l]Jn 14:27 [m]Jn 15:18-21 [n]Ro 8:37; 1Jn 4:4
17:1 [o]Jn 11:41 [p]Jn 12:23; 13:31,32
17:2 [q]ver 6,9,24; Da 7:14; Jn 6:37,39
17:3 [r]ver 8,18,21, 23,25; Jn 3:17
17:4 [s]Jn 13:31 [t]Jn 4:34
17:5 [u]Php 2:6 [v]Jn 1:2
17:6 [w]ver 26 [x]ver 2; Jn 6:37,39
17:8 [y]ver 14,26 [z]Jn 16:27 [a]ver 3,18,21, 23,25; Jn 3:17
17:9 [b]Lk 22:32
17:10 [c]Jn 16:15

[a]31 Or *"Do you now believe?"* [b]6 Greek *your name*; also in verse 26

are still in the world,[a] and I am coming to you.[b] Holy Father,
protect them by the power of your name—the name you gave
me—so that they may be one[c] as we are one.[d] 12 While I was
with them, I protected them and kept them safe by that name
you gave me. None has been lost[e] except the one doomed to
destruction[f] so that Scripture would be fulfilled.

13 "I am coming to you now, but I say these things while I am
still in the world, so that they may have the full measure of
my joy[g] within them. 14 I have given them your word and the
world has hated them,[h] for they are not of the world any more
than I am of the world.[i] 15 My prayer is not that you take them
out of the world but that you protect them from the evil one.[j]
16 They are not of the world, even as I am not of it.[k] 17 Sanctify[a]
them by the truth; your word is truth.[l] 18 As you sent me into
the world,[m] I have sent them into the world.[n] 19 For them I
sanctify myself, that they too may be truly sanctified.

20 "My prayer is not for them alone. I pray also for those who
will believe in me through their message, 21 that all of them may
be one, Father, just as you are in me and I am in you.[o] May they
also be in us so that the world may believe that you have sent
me.[p] 22 I have given them the glory that you gave me, that they
may be one as we are one:[q] 23 I in
them and you in me. May they be
brought to complete unity to let
the world know that you sent
me[r] and have loved them[s] even
as you have loved me.

24 "Father, I want those you
have given me to be with me
where I am,[t] and to see my glory,[u]
the glory you have given me
because you loved me before the
creation of the world.[v]

25 "Righteous Father, though
the world does not know you,[w] I
know you, and they know that
you have sent me.[x] 26 I have made
you known to them,[y] and will continue to make you known
in order that the love you have for me may be in them[z] and
that I myself may be in them."

Jerusalem of the New Testament

Chapter 18 Theme ____________________

18 When he had finished praying, Jesus left with his disciples
and crossed the Kidron Valley.[a] On the other side there
was an olive grove,[b] and he and his disciples went into it.[c]

a 17 Greek *hagiazo (set apart for sacred use* or *make holy)*; also in verse 19

17:11 [a] Jn 13:1 [b] Jn 7:33 [c] ver 21-23 [d] Jn 10:30
17:12 [e] Jn 6:39 [f] Jn 6:70
17:13 [g] Jn 3:29
17:14 [h] Jn 15:19 [i] Jn 8:23
17:15 [j] Mt 5:37
17:16 [k] ver 14
17:17 [l] Jn 15:3
17:18 [m] ver 3,8,21, 23,25 [n] Jn 20:21
17:21 [o] Jn 10:38 [p] ver 3,8,18, 23,25; Jn 3:17
17:22 [q] Jn 14:20
17:23 [r] Jn 3:17 [s] Jn 16:27
17:24 [t] Jn 12:26 [u] Jn 1:14 [v] ver 5; Mt 25:34
17:25 [w] Jn 15:21; 16:3 [x] ver 3,8,18, 21,23; Jn 3:17; 7:29; 16:27
17:26 [y] ver 6 [z] Jn 15:9
18:1 [a] 2Sa 15:23 [b] ver 26 [c] Mt 26:36

2 Now Judas, who betrayed him, knew the place, because Jesus
had often met there with his disciples.[a] 3 So Judas came to the
grove, guiding[b] a detachment of soldiers and some officials from
the chief priests and Pharisees.[c] They were carrying torches,
lanterns and weapons.

4 Jesus, knowing all that was going to happen to him,[d] went out
and asked them, "Who is it you want?"[e]

5 "Jesus of Nazareth," they replied.

"I am he," Jesus said. (And Judas the traitor was standing there
with them.) 6 When Jesus said, "I am he," they drew back and fell
to the ground.

7 Again he asked them, "Who is it you want?"[f]

And they said, "Jesus of Nazareth."

8 "I told you that I am he," Jesus answered. "If you are looking
for me, then let these men go." 9 This happened so that the words
he had spoken would be fulfilled: "I have not lost one of those
you gave me."[a][g]

10 Then Simon Peter, who had a sword, drew it and struck the
high priest's servant, cutting off his right ear. (The servant's name
was Malchus.)

11 Jesus commanded Peter, "Put your sword away! Shall I not
drink the cup[h] the Father has given me?"

12 Then the detachment of soldiers with its commander and the
Jewish officials[i] arrested Jesus. They bound him 13 and brought
him first to Annas, who was the father-in-law of Caiaphas,[j] the
high priest that year. 14 Caiaphas was the one who had advised the
Jews that it would be good if one man died for the people.[k]

15 Simon Peter and another disciple were following Jesus. Because
this disciple was known to the high priest,[l] he went with Jesus
into the high priest's courtyard,[m] 16 but Peter had to wait outside
at the door. The other disciple, who was known to the high priest,
came back, spoke to the girl on duty there and brought Peter in.

17 "You are not one of his disciples, are you?" the girl at the door
asked Peter.

He replied, "I am not."[n]

18 It was cold, and the servants and officials stood around a fire[o]
they had made to keep warm. Peter also was standing with them,
warming himself.[p]

19 Meanwhile, the high priest questioned Jesus about his disciples and his teaching.

20 "I have spoken openly to the world," Jesus replied. "I always
taught in synagogues[q] or at the temple,[r] where all the Jews come
together. I said nothing in secret.[s] 21 Why question me? Ask those
who heard me. Surely they know what I said."

18:2 [a] Lk 21:37; 22:39
18:3 [b] Ac 1:16 [c] ver 12
18:4 [d] Jn 6:64; 13:1,11 [e] ver 7
18:7 [f] ver 4
18:9 [g] Jn 17:12
18:11 [h] Mt 20:22
18:12 [i] ver 3
18:13 [j] ver 24; Mt 26:3
18:14 [k] Jn 11:49-51
18:15 [l] Mt 26:3 [m] Mt 26:58; Mk 14:54; Lk 22:54
18:17 [n] ver 25
18:18 [o] Jn 21:9 [p] Mk 14:54,67
18:20 [q] Mt 4:23 [r] Mt 26:55 [s] Jn 7:26

a9 John 6:39

22When Jesus said this, one of the officials[a] nearby struck him
in the face.[b] "Is this the way you answer the high priest?" he
demanded.
23"If I said something wrong," Jesus replied, "testify as to what
is wrong. But if I spoke the truth, why did you strike me?"[c] 24Then
Annas sent him, still bound, to Caiaphas[d] the high priest.[a]
25As Simon Peter stood warming himself,[e] he was asked, "You
are not one of his disciples, are you?"
He denied it, saying, "I am not."[f]
26One of the high priest's servants, a relative of the man whose
ear Peter had cut off,[g] challenged him, "Didn't I see you with him
in the olive grove?"[h] 27Again Peter denied it, and at that moment
a rooster began to crow.[i]
28Then the Jews led Jesus from Caiaphas to the palace of the
Roman governor.[j] By now it was early morning, and to avoid ceremonial uncleanness the Jews did not enter the palace;[k] they
wanted to be able to eat the Passover.[l] 29So Pilate came out to them
and asked, "What charges are you bringing against this man?"
30"If he were not a criminal," they replied, "we would not have
handed him over to you."
31Pilate said, "Take him yourselves and judge him by your own
law."
"But we have no right to execute anyone," the Jews objected.
32This happened so that the words Jesus had spoken indicating
the kind of death he was going to die[m] would be fulfilled.
33Pilate then went back inside the palace,[n] summoned Jesus
and asked him, "Are you the king of the Jews?"[o]
34"Is that your own idea," Jesus asked, "or did others talk to you
about me?"
35"Am I a Jew?" Pilate replied. "It was your people and your chief
priests who handed you over to me. What is it you have done?"
36Jesus said, "My kingdom[p] is not of this world. If it were, my
servants would fight to prevent my arrest by the Jews.[q] But now
my kingdom is from another place."[r]
37"You are a king, then!" said Pilate.
Jesus answered, "You are right in saying I am a king. In fact, for
this reason I was born, and for this I came into the world, to testify
to the truth.[s] Everyone on the side of truth listens to me."[t]
38"What is truth?" Pilate asked. With this he went out again to
the Jews and said, "I find no basis for a charge against him.[u] 39But
it is your custom for me to release to you one prisoner at the time
of the Passover. Do you want me to release 'the king of the Jews'?"
40They shouted back, "No, not him! Give us Barabbas!" Now
Barabbas had taken part in a rebellion.[v]

INSIGHT

The palace of the Roman governor (the ***Praetorium***) was either a building next to Herod's palace or the Antonia Fortress beside the temple mount complex. See the map on page 1852 and the illustration of the temple mount on page IISB-40.

18:22 [a]ver 3 [b]Mt 16:21; Jn 19:3
18:23 [c]Mt 5:39; Ac 23:2-5
18:24 [d]ver 13; Mt 26:3
18:25 [e]ver 18 [f]ver 17
18:26 [g]ver 10 [h]ver 1
18:27 [i]Jn 13:38
18:28 [j]Mt 27:2; Mk 15:1; Lk 23:1 [k]ver 33; Jn 19:9 [l]Jn 11:55
18:32 [m]Mt 20:19; 26:2; Jn 3:14; 8:28; 12:32,33
18:33 [n]ver 28,29; Jn 19:9 [o]Lk 23:3; Mt 2:2
18:36 [p]Mt 3:2 [q]Mt 26:53 [r]Lk 17:21; Jn 6:15
18:37 [s]Jn 3:32 [t]Jn 8:47; 1Jn 4:6
18:38 [u]Lk 23:4; Jn 19:4,6
18:40 [v]Ac 3:14

[a] 24 Or *(Now Annas had sent him, still bound, to Caiaphas the high priest.)*

Chapter 19 Theme ______________________

19 Then Pilate took Jesus and had him flogged.[a] 2The soldiers
twisted together a crown of thorns and put it on his head.
They clothed him in a purple robe 3and went up to him again
and again, saying, "Hail, king of the Jews!"[b] And they struck him
in the face.[c]

4Once more Pilate came out and said to the Jews, "Look, I am
bringing him out[d] to you to let you know that I find no basis for a
charge against him."[e] 5When Jesus came out wearing the crown of
thorns and the purple robe,[f] Pilate said to them, "Here is the man!"

6As soon as the chief priests and their officials saw him, they
shouted, "Crucify! Crucify!"

But Pilate answered, "You take him and crucify him.[g] As for me,
I find no basis for a charge against him."[h]

7The Jews insisted, "We have a law, and according to that law he
must die,[i] because he claimed to be the Son of God."[j]

8When Pilate heard this, he was even more afraid, 9and he went
back inside the palace.[k] "Where do you come from?" he asked
Jesus, but Jesus gave him no answer.[l] 10"Do you refuse to speak to
me?" Pilate said. "Don't you realize I have power either to free
you or to crucify you?"

11Jesus answered, "You would have no power over me if it were
not given to you from above.[m] Therefore the one who handed me
over to you[n] is guilty of a greater sin."

12From then on, Pilate tried to set Jesus free, but the Jews kept
shouting, "If you let this man go, you are no friend of Caesar.
Anyone who claims to be a king[o] opposes Caesar."

13When Pilate heard this, he brought Jesus out and sat down on
the judge's seat[p] at a place known as the Stone Pavement (which
in Aramaic[q] is Gabbatha). 14It was the day of Preparation[r] of
Passover Week, about the sixth hour.[s]

"Here is your king,"[t] Pilate said to the Jews.

15But they shouted, "Take him away! Take him away! Crucify
him!"

"Shall I crucify your king?" Pilate asked.

"We have no king but Caesar," the chief priests answered.

16Finally Pilate handed him over to them to be crucified.[u]

So the soldiers took charge of Jesus. 17Carrying his own cross,[v]
he went out to the place of the Skull[w] (which in Aramaic[x] is called
Golgotha). 18Here they crucified him, and with him two others[y]—
one on each side and Jesus in the middle.

19Pilate had a notice prepared and fastened to the cross. It read:
JESUS OF NAZARETH,[z] THE KING OF THE JEWS.[a] 20Many of the Jews read
this sign, for the place where Jesus was crucified was near the

19:1 [a]Dt 25:3; Isa 50:6; 53:5; Mt 27:26
19:3 [b]Mt 27:29 [c]Jn 18:22
19:4 [d]Jn 18:38 [e]ver 6; Lk 23:4
19:5 [f]ver 2
19:6 [g]Ac 3:13 [h]ver 4; Lk 23:4
19:7 [i]Lev 24:16 [j]Mt 26:63-66; Jn 5:18; 10:33
19:9 [k]Jn 18:33 [l]Mk 14:61
19:11 [m]Ro 13:1 [n]Jn 18:28-30; Ac 3:13
19:12 [o]Lk 23:2
19:13 [p]Mt 27:19 [q]Jn 5:2
19:14 [r]Mt 27:62 [s]Mk 15:25 [t]ver 19,21
19:16 [u]Mt 27:26; Mk 15:15; Lk 23:25
19:17 [v]Ge 22:6; Lk 14:27; 23:26 [w]Lk 23:33 [x]Jn 5:2
19:18 [y]Lk 23:32
19:19 [z]Mk 1:24 [a]ver 14,21

city,[a] and the sign was written in Aramaic, Latin and Greek. 21 The
chief priests of the Jews protested to Pilate, "Do not write 'The King
of the Jews,' but that this man claimed to be king of the Jews."[b]
22 Pilate answered, "What I have written, I have written."
23 When the soldiers crucified Jesus, they took his clothes,
dividing them into four shares, one for each of them, with the
undergarment remaining. This garment was seamless, woven in
one piece from top to bottom.
24 "Let's not tear it," they said to one another. "Let's decide by
lot who will get it."

This happened that the scripture might be fulfilled[c] which said,

> "They divided my garments among them
> and cast lots for my clothing."[a][d]

So this is what the soldiers did.
25 Near the cross[e] of Jesus stood his mother,[f] his mother's sister,
Mary the wife of Clopas, and Mary Magdalene.[g] 26 When Jesus
saw his mother[h] there, and the disciple whom he loved[i] standing
nearby, he said to his mother, "Dear woman, here is your son,"
27 and to the disciple, "Here is your mother." From that time on,
this disciple took her into his home.
28 Later, knowing that all was now completed,[j] and so that the
Scripture would be fulfilled,[k] Jesus said, "I am thirsty." 29 A jar of
wine vinegar[l] was there, so they soaked a sponge in it, put the
sponge on a stalk of the hyssop plant, and lifted it to Jesus' lips.
30 When he had received the drink, Jesus said, "It is finished."[m]
With that, he bowed his head and gave up his spirit.
31 Now it was the day of Preparation,[n] and the next day was to be
a special Sabbath. Because the Jews did not want the bodies left
on the crosses[o] during the Sabbath, they asked Pilate to have the
legs broken and the bodies taken down. 32 The soldiers therefore
came and broke the legs of the first man who had been crucified
with Jesus, and then those of the other.[p] 33 But when they came to
Jesus and found that he was already dead, they did not break his
legs. 34 Instead, one of the soldiers pierced[q] Jesus' side with a spear,
bringing a sudden flow of blood and water.[r] 35 The man who saw
it[s] has given testimony, and his testimony is true.[t] He knows that
he tells the truth, and he testifies so that you also may believe.
36 These things happened so that the scripture would be fulfilled:[u]
"Not one of his bones will be broken,"[b][v] 37 and, as another scripture says, "They will look on the one they have pierced."[c][w]
38 Later, Joseph of Arimathea asked Pilate for the body of Jesus.
Now Joseph was a disciple of Jesus, but secretly because he feared
the Jews. With Pilate's permission, he came and took the body

[a] *24* Psalm 22:18 [b] *36* Exodus 12:46; Num. 9:12; Psalm 34:20 [c] *37* Zech. 12:10

19:20 [a] Heb 13:12
19:21 [b] ver 14
19:24 [c] ver 28,36,37; Mt 1:22 [d] Ps 22:18
19:25 [e] Mt 27:55,56; Mk 15:40,41; Lk 23:49 [f] Mt 12:46 [g] Lk 24:18
19:26 [h] Mt 12:46 [i] Jn 13:23
19:28 [j] ver 30; Jn 13:1 [k] ver 24,36,37
19:29 [l] Ps 69:21
19:30 [m] Lk 12:50; Jn 17:4
19:31 [n] ver 14,42 [o] Dt 21:23; Jos 8:29; 10:26,27
19:32 [p] ver 18
19:34 [q] Zec 12:10 [r] 1Jn 5:6,8
19:35 [s] Lk 24:48 [t] Jn 15:27; 21:24
19:36 [u] ver 24,28,37; Mt 1:22 [v] Ex 12:46; Nu 9:12; Ps 34:20
19:37 [w] Zec 12:10; Rev 1:7

away. 39He was accompanied by Nicodemus,[a] the man who earlier
had visited Jesus at night. Nicodemus brought a mixture of myrrh
and aloes, about seventy-five pounds.[a] 40Taking Jesus' body, the
two of them wrapped it, with the spices, in strips of linen.[b] This
was in accordance with Jewish burial customs.[c] 41At the place
where Jesus was crucified, there was a garden, and in the garden
a new tomb, in which no one had ever been laid. 42Because it was
the Jewish day of Preparation[d] and since the tomb was nearby,[e]
they laid Jesus there.

Chapter 20 Theme ______________________________

20 Early on the first day of the week, while it was still dark,
Mary Magdalene[f] went to the tomb and saw that the stone
had been removed from the entrance.[g] 2So she came running to
Simon Peter and the other disciple, the one Jesus loved,[h] and said,
"They have taken the Lord out of the tomb, and we don't know
where they have put him!"[i]
3So Peter and the other disciple started for the tomb.[j] 4Both were
running, but the other disciple outran Peter and reached the tomb
first. 5He bent over and looked in[k] at the strips of linen[l] lying
there but did not go in. 6Then Simon Peter, who was behind him,
arrived and went into the tomb. He saw the strips of linen lying
there, 7as well as the burial cloth that had been around Jesus'
head.[m] The cloth was folded up by itself, separate from the linen.
8Finally the other disciple, who had reached the tomb first,[n] also
went inside. He saw and believed. 9(They still did not understand
from Scripture[o] that Jesus had to rise from the dead.)[p]
10Then the disciples went back to their homes, 11but Mary
stood outside the tomb crying. As she wept, she bent over to look
into the tomb[q] 12and saw two angels in white,[r] seated where Jesus'
body had been, one at the head and the other at the foot.
13They asked her, "Woman, why are you crying?"[s]
"They have taken my Lord away," she said, "and I don't know
where they have put him."[t] 14At this, she turned around and saw
Jesus standing there,[u] but she did not realize that it was Jesus.[v]
15"Woman," he said, "why are you crying?[w] Who is it you are
looking for?"
Thinking he was the gardener, she said, "Sir, if you have carried
him away, tell me where you have put him, and I will get him."
16Jesus said to her, "Mary."
She turned toward him and cried out in Aramaic,[x] "Rabboni!"[y]
(which means Teacher).
17Jesus said, "Do not hold on to me, for I have not yet returned to

[a] 39 Greek *a hundred litrai* (about 34 kilograms)

19:39 [a]Jn 3:1; 7:50
19:40 [b]Lk 24:12; Jn 11:44; 20:5,7 [c]Mt 26:12
19:42 [d]ver 14,31 [e]ver 20,41
20:1 [f]ver 18; Jn 19:25 [g]Mt 27:60,66
20:2 [h]Jn 13:23 [i]ver 13
20:3 [j]Lk 24:12
20:5 [k]ver 11 [l]Jn 19:40
20:7 [m]Jn 11:44
20:8 [n]ver 4
20:9 [o]Mt 22:29; Jn 2:22 [p]Lk 24:26,46
20:11 [q]ver 5
20:12 [r]Mt 28:2,3; Mk 16:5; Lk 24:4; Ac 5:19
20:13 [s]ver 15 [t]ver 2
20:14 [u]Mt 28:9; Mk 16:9 [v]Lk 24:16; Jn 21:4
20:15 [w]ver 13
20:16 [x]Jn 5:2 [y]Mt 23:7

the Father. Go instead to my brothers[a] and tell them, 'I am returning to my Father[b] and your Father, to my God and your God.'"
18 Mary Magdalene[c] went to the disciples[d] with the news: "I have
seen the Lord!" And she told them that he had said these things
to her.
19 On the evening of that first day of the week, when the disciples were together, with the doors locked for fear of the Jews,[e]
Jesus came and stood among them and said, "Peace[f] be with
you!"[g] 20 After he said this, he showed them his hands and side.[h]
The disciples were overjoyed[i] when they saw the Lord.
21 Again Jesus said, "Peace be with you![j] As the Father has sent
me,[k] I am sending you."[l] 22 And with that he breathed on them and
said, "Receive the Holy Spirit.[m] 23 If you forgive anyone his sins, they
are forgiven; if you do not forgive them, they are not forgiven."[n]
24 Now Thomas[o] (called Didymus), one of the Twelve, was not
with the disciples when Jesus came. 25 So the other disciples told
him, "We have seen the Lord!"
But he said to them, "Unless I see the nail marks in his hands
and put my finger where the nails were, and put my hand into his
side,[p] I will not believe it."[q]
26 A week later his disciples were in the house again, and Thomas
was with them. Though the doors were locked, Jesus came and
stood among them and said, "Peace[r] be with you!"[s] 27 Then he
said to Thomas, "Put your finger here; see my hands. Reach out
your hand and put it into my side. Stop doubting and believe."[t]
28 Thomas said to him, "My Lord and my God!"
29 Then Jesus told him, "Because you have seen me, you have
believed;[u] blessed are those who have not seen and yet have
believed."[v]
30 Jesus did many other miraculous signs[w] in the presence of his
disciples, which are not recorded in this book.[x] 31 But these are
written that you may[a] believe[y] that Jesus is the Christ, the Son of
God,[z] and that by believing you may have life in his name.[a]

Chapter 21 Theme ____________________

21 Afterward Jesus appeared again to his disciples,[b] by the
Sea of Tiberias.[b][c] It happened this way: 2 Simon Peter,
Thomas[d] (called Didymus), Nathanael[e] from Cana in Galilee,[f]
the sons of Zebedee,[g] and two other disciples were together. 3 "I'm
going out to fish," Simon Peter told them, and they said, "We'll
go with you." So they went out and got into the boat, but that
night they caught nothing.[h]
4 Early in the morning, Jesus stood on the shore, but the disciples did not realize that it was Jesus.[i]

a *31* Some manuscripts *may continue to* b *1* That is, Sea of Galilee

20:17 [a] Mt 28:10 [b] Jn 7:33
20:18 [c] ver 1 [d] Lk 24:10,22,23
20:19 [e] Jn 7:13 [f] Jn 14:27 [g] ver 21,26; Lk 24:36-39
20:20 [h] Lk 24:39,40; Jn 19:34 [i] Jn 16:20,22
20:21 [j] ver 19 [k] Jn 3:17 [l] Mt 28:19; Jn 17:18
20:22 [m] Jn 7:39; Ac 2:38; 8:15-17; 19:2; Gal 3:2
20:23 [n] Mt 16:19; 18:18
20:24 [o] Jn 11:16
20:25 [p] ver 20 [q] Mk 16:11
20:26 [r] Jn 14:27 [s] ver 21
20:27 [t] ver 25; Lk 24:40
20:29 [u] Jn 3:15 [v] 1Pe 1:8
20:30 [w] Jn 2:11 [x] Jn 21:25
20:31 [y] Jn 3:15; 19:35 [z] Mt 4:3 [a] Mt 25:46
21:1 [b] Jn 20:19,26 [c] Jn 6:1
21:2 [d] Jn 11:16 [e] Jn 1:45 [f] Jn 2:1 [g] Mt 4:21
21:3 [h] Lk 5:5
21:4 [i] Lk 24:16; Jn 20:14

5He called out to them, "Friends, haven't you any fish?"
"No," they answered.
6He said, "Throw your net on the right side of the boat and you
will find some." When they did, they were unable to haul the net
in because of the large number of fish.[a]
7Then the disciple whom Jesus loved[b] said to Peter, "It is the
Lord!" As soon as Simon Peter heard him say, "It is the Lord," he
wrapped his outer garment around him (for he had taken it off)
and jumped into the water. 8The other disciples followed in the
boat, towing the net full of fish, for they were not far from shore,
about a hundred yards.[a] 9When they landed, they saw a fire[c] of
burning coals there with fish on it,[d] and some bread.
10Jesus said to them, "Bring some of the fish you have just
caught."
11Simon Peter climbed aboard and dragged the net ashore. It was
full of large fish, 153, but even with so many the net was not torn.
12Jesus said to them, "Come and have breakfast." None of the
disciples dared ask him, "Who are you?" They knew it was the
Lord. 13Jesus came, took the bread and gave it to them, and did
the same with the fish.[e] 14This was now the third time Jesus
appeared to his disciples[f] after he was raised from the dead.
15When they had finished eating, Jesus said to Simon Peter,
"Simon son of John, do you truly love me more than these?"
"Yes, Lord," he said, "you know that I love you."[g]
Jesus said, "Feed my lambs."[h]
16Again Jesus said, "Simon son of John, do you truly love me?"
He answered, "Yes, Lord, you know that I love you."
Jesus said, "Take care of my sheep."[i]
17The third time he said to him, "Simon son of John, do you
love me?"
Peter was hurt because Jesus asked him the third time, "Do you
love me?"[j] He said, "Lord, you know all things;[k] you know that I
love you."
Jesus said, "Feed my sheep.[l] 18I tell you the truth, when you
were younger you dressed yourself and went where you wanted;
but when you are old you will stretch out your hands, and someone else will dress you and lead you where you do not want to
go." 19Jesus said this to indicate the kind of death[m] by which Peter
would glorify God.[n] Then he said to him, "Follow me!"
20Peter turned and saw that the disciple whom Jesus loved[o] was
following them. (This was the one who had leaned back against
Jesus at the supper and had said, "Lord, who is going to betray
you?")[p] 21When Peter saw him, he asked, "Lord, what about him?"

21:6 [a]Lk 5:4-7
21:7 [b]Jn 13:23
21:9 [c]Jn 18:18 [d]ver 10,13
21:13 [e]ver 9
21:14 [f]Jn 20:19,26
21:15 [g]Mt 26:33,35; Jn 13:37 [h]Lk 12:32
21:16 [i]Mt 2:6; Ac 20:28; 1Pe 5:2,3
21:17 [j]Jn 13:38 [k]Jn 16:30 [l]ver 16
21:19 [m]Jn 12:33; 18:32 [n]2Pe 1:14
21:20 [o]ver 7; Jn 13:23 [p]Jn 13:25

[a]8 Greek *about two hundred cubits* (about 90 meters)

[22]Jesus answered, "If I want him to remain alive until I return,[a]
what is that to you? You must follow me."[b] [23]Because of this, the
rumor spread among the brothers[c] that this disciple would not
die. But Jesus did not say that he would not die; he only said, "If I
want him to remain alive until I return, what is that to you?"
[24]This is the disciple who testifies to these things[d] and who
wrote them down. We know that his testimony is true.[e]
[25]Jesus did many other things as well.[f] If every one of them were
written down, I suppose that even the whole world would not
have room for the books that would be written.

21:22 [a]Mt 16:27; 1Co 4:5; Rev 2:25 [b]ver 19

21:23 [c]Ac 1:16

21:24 [d]Jn 15:27 [e]Jn 19:35

21:25 [f]Jn 20:30

John at a Glance

…me of John:

…hor:

…e:

…pose:

Words:

Segment Divisions

	Portrayals of Jesus Christ	Signs and Miracles	Ministry		Chapter Themes
			To Israel	1	
				2	
				3	
				4	
				5	
				6	
				7	
				8	
				9	
				10	
				11	
			To Disciples	12	
				13	
				14	
				15	
				16	
				17	
			To All Mankind	18	
				19	
				20	
			To Disciples	21	

MATTHEW	MARK	LUKE	JOHN
		Luke gives consecutive	
		order of events in Jesus' life	
		(Luke 1:3)	

The Account of Jesus' Resurrection

Matthew	Mark	Luke	John
		Luke gives consecutive order of events in Jesus' life (Luke 1:3)	

Postresurrection Appearances

What the Gospels Teach about t

Matthew	Mark

INGDOM OF GOD/THE KINGDOM OF HEAVEN

LUKE	JOHN

ACTS

"I'm going away."

The eleven heard nothing else. The promise of another Helper, the Holy Spirit, fell on deaf ears. The thought that they could do the works that Jesus had done—and even greater—must have seemed preposterous to them.

Jesus had died and been buried. But he had also risen! For over 40 days the disciples saw, heard, and touched the Word of Life as he spoke with them of things concerning the kingdom of God.

And then once again he was gone, taken away before their very eyes! He left with the promise to send the Spirit and he commissioned his disciples to reach the world.

Then came Pentecost and the acts of the apostles. Luke wrote Theophilus all about it. It was probably about A.D. 63.

Things to Do

Chapters 1, 2

In the first two chapters of the book of Acts, Luke gives an account of Christ's ascension and the Holy Spirit's coming.

1. Read chapter 1, looking for Jesus' instructions and promises to the apostles.
   a. In a distinctive way mark in the text every occurrence of the key words (along with their synonyms and pronouns) listed on the ACTS AT A GLANCE chart on page 1923. Record these key words on an index card that you can use as a bookmark while studying Acts.
   b. In the chapter margin list everything you learn from the references to the Holy Spirit.
   c. In the margin list the instructions and the promises that Jesus gives to the apostles.
   d. Note the main events that occur in this chapter by either marking these events within the text or listing them in the margin.
2. The key verse for Acts is found in chapter 1. This verse also gives an outline for the book. See if you can identify it. When you do, put a box around it and in the margin write, "Key verse of Acts."
3. As you read chapter 2:
   a. Keep in mind that you can easily recognize Old Testament quotes because the NIV text indents the Scripture on both sides. Observe how much is taken from the Old Testament.
   b. List in the margin the main events that occur. As you note them, ask the five W's and an H: Who? What? When? Where? Why? and How? For example, ask: Who was present on the day of Pentecost? What happened? Whom did it affect? What was their response? Why did they respond as they did? How did they hear?
   c. Mark key words. Also mark every reference to the Holy Spirit and to Jesus, including their synonyms or pronouns. Then list in the margin what you learn about each from this chapter. Watch the words *promise* and *promised* and note their relationship to the Spirit. Compare this with Acts 1:4, 5.
   d. Mark every reference to time with a symbol. Do this throughout the book of Acts whether the time is indicated by an event (such as a feast or the death of Herod) or by mentioning a certain period of months or years.

e. List in the margin the main points in Peter's sermon on the day of Pentecost. Note what he emphasized in his sermon and the result.

4. Determine the theme of each of these chapters. Then record the themes on ACTS AT A GLANCE and on the line next to the chapter number in the text.

Chapters 3-7

1. As you study, do the following:
   a. Read each chapter in the light of the five W's and an H. Then in the margin note: What happens in that chapter? Where and when did it happen? Who is involved? How are things done or said?
   b. Mark every reference to the Holy Spirit and then list what you learn about the Holy Spirit, his ministry, and the results. Also mark in the text the other key words listed on ACTS AT A GLANCE. Remember to use your bookmark.
   c. If a message is proclaimed in these chapters, list in the margin the main points of that message. Also note the effect of the message on those who hear it.
2. Determine the theme of each chapter and then record the theme as before.

Chapters 8-12

1. Read Acts 8:1-8 and then Acts 1:8. What do you see happening in Acts 8 that is a change from the first seven chapters? Note this in the margin of chapter 8.
2. Read chapters 8 through 11 carefully, as significant events occur in these chapters. As you read:
   a. List the main events in each chapter. Who does what? When? Where is it done? What is said? What is the result? Who is affected? How does it happen? Don't add to the text, but simply observe it and list in the margin what you learn.
   b. Mark key words and list everything you learn about the Holy Spirit in the margin of each chapter. This is crucial to chapters 8, 10, and 11. Note to whom the Holy Spirit comes.
   c. Record the theme of each chapter in the text and on ACTS AT A GLANCE.
3. As you read and study chapter 12, keep in mind that this chapter is pivotal. At this point the focus of the book turns from Peter's ministry to that of Paul (Saul).

Chapters 13-28

1. Included in these chapters is an account of Paul's missionary journeys: Paul's first missionary journey in 13 through 14; Paul's second missionary journey in 15:36 through 18:22; and Paul's third missionary journey in 18:23 through 21:17.

   For easy reference, write and color code in the margin where each journey begins.
2. As you study these chapters, mark the key repeated words. Add the words *synagogue* and *congregation* to your list. Also keep in mind what you learned from Acts 1:8 and watch carefully the work of the Spirit throughout these chapters. In the margin note your insights.
   a. Examine each chapter with the five W's and an H. Note in the text who accompanies Paul, where they go, and what happens. On the maps provided you can trace each of Paul's journeys.
   b. Carefully observe each time the gospel is proclaimed, whether to an individual or a group. Watch how Paul reasons with Jews and Gentiles. Also note what their response is and how Paul handles it.
3. In several instances you will notice Paul giving his testimony. Compare each of these instances with Acts 9 and the account of Paul's conversion. This will give you a more complete picture of all that happened on that significant day.

4. Record the theme of each chapter on ACTS AT A GLANCE and in the text. Then determine the main subject for the book of Acts and record it. Then complete the chart. Record the ways you might segment the book of Acts according to its themes.

Things to Think About

1. What have you learned from Acts about the Holy Spirit and your responsibility to be a witness for the Lord Jesus Christ?

2. Based on what you saw in the sermons that were preached and the personal witnesses which were given, what would you include in your witness? Where would the emphasis be?

3. As you studied the lives of the early apostles and the commitment of the early church, how has God spoken to your heart? Stop and think about how they lived, and then think about how you are living. Do you have the Holy Spirit living inside you? Isn't he the same today, yesterday, and forever? If you are filled with the Holy Spirit and are not quenching him, what should be happening in your life?

Chapter 1 Theme ______________________

1 In my former book,[a] Theophilus, I wrote about all that Jesus
began to do and to teach[b] 2until the day he was taken up to
heaven,[c] after giving instructions[d] through the Holy Spirit to the
apostles[e] he had chosen.[f] 3After his suffering, he showed himself
to these men and gave many convincing proofs that he was alive.
He appeared to them[g] over a period of forty days and spoke about
the kingdom of God. 4On one occasion, while he was eating with
them, he gave them this command: "Do not leave Jerusalem, but
wait for the gift my Father promised, which you have heard me
speak about.[h] 5For John baptized with[a] water, but in a few days
you will be baptized with the Holy Spirit."

6So when they met together, they asked him, "Lord, are you at
this time going to restore[i] the kingdom to Israel?"

7He said to them: "It is not for you to know the times or dates the
Father has set by his own authority.[j] 8But you will receive power
when the Holy Spirit comes on you;[k] and you will be my witnesses[l]
in Jerusalem, and in all Judea and Samaria,[m] and to the ends of the
earth."[n]

9After he said this, he was taken up[o] before their very eyes, and a
cloud hid him from their sight.

10They were looking intently up into the sky as he was going,
when suddenly two men dressed in white[p] stood beside them.
11"Men of Galilee,"[q] they said, "why do you stand here looking
into the sky? This same Jesus, who has been taken from you into
heaven, will come back[r] in the same way you have seen him go
into heaven."

12Then they returned to Jerusalem[s] from the hill called the
Mount of Olives,[t] a Sabbath day's walk[b] from the city. 13When they

[a]5 Or *in* [b]*12* That is, about 3/4 mile (about 1,100 meters)

1:1 [a]Lk 1:1-4 [b]Lk 3:23
1:2 [c]ver 9,11; Mk 16:19 [d]Mt 28:19,20 [e]Mk 6:30 [f]Jn 13:18
1:3 [g]Mt 28:17; Lk 24:34,36; Jn 20:19,26; 21:1,14; 1Co 15:5-7
1:4 [h]Lk 24:49; Jn 14:16; Ac 2:33
1:6 [i]Mt 17:11
1:7 [j]Mt 24:36
1:8 [k]Ac 2:1-4 [l]Lk 24:48 [m]Ac 8:1-25 [n]Mt 28:19
1:9 [o]ver 2
1:10 [p]Lk 24:4; Jn 20:12
1:11 [q]Ac 2:7 [r]Mt 16:27
1:12 [s]Lk 24:52 [t]Mt 21:1

arrived, they went upstairs to the room[a] where they were staying.
Those present were Peter, John, James and Andrew; Philip and
Thomas, Bartholomew and Matthew; James son of Alphaeus and
Simon the Zealot, and Judas son of James.[b] 14They all joined
together constantly in prayer,[c] along with the women[d] and Mary
the mother of Jesus, and with his brothers.[e]
15In those days Peter stood up among the believers[a] (a group
numbering about a hundred and twenty) 16and said, "Brothers,
the Scripture had to be fulfilled[f] which the Holy Spirit spoke long
ago through the mouth of David concerning Judas,[g] who served
as guide for those who arrested Jesus— 17he was one of our number[h] and shared in this ministry."[i]
18(With the reward[j] he got for his wickedness, Judas bought a
field;[k] there he fell headlong, his body burst open and all his
intestines spilled out. 19Everyone in Jerusalem heard about this,
so they called that field in their language Akeldama, that is, Field
of Blood.)
20"For," said Peter, "it is written in the book of Psalms,

"'May his place be deserted;
let there be no one to dwell in it,'[b] [l]

and,

"'May another take his place of leadership.'[c] [m]

21Therefore it is necessary to choose one of the men who have
been with us the whole time the Lord Jesus went in and out
among us, 22beginning from John's baptism[n] to the time when
Jesus was taken up from us. For one of these must become a witness[o] with us of his resurrection."
23So they proposed two men: Joseph called Barsabbas (also
known as Justus) and Matthias. 24Then they prayed,[p] "Lord, you
know everyone's heart.[q] Show us which of these two you have
chosen 25to take over this apostolic ministry, which Judas left to
go where he belongs." 26Then they cast lots, and the lot fell to
Matthias; so he was added to the eleven apostles.[r]

Chapter 2 Theme ______________________

2 When the day of Pentecost[s] came, they were all together[t] in
one place. 2Suddenly a sound like the blowing of a violent
wind came from heaven and filled the whole house where they
were sitting.[u] 3They saw what seemed to be tongues of fire that
separated and came to rest on each of them. 4All of them were
filled with the Holy Spirit and began to speak in other tongues[d] [v]
as the Spirit enabled them.

1:13 [a] Ac 9:37; 20:8 [b] Mt 10:2-4; Mk 3:16-19; Lk 6:14-16
1:14 [c] Ac 2:42; 6:4 [d] Lk 23:49,55 [e] Mt 12:46
1:16 [f] ver 20 [g] Jn 13:18
1:17 [h] Jn 6:70,71 [i] ver 25
1:18 [j] Mt 26:14,15 [k] Mt 27:3-10
1:20 [l] Ps 69:25 [m] Ps 109:8
1:22 [n] Mk 1:4 [o] ver 8
1:24 [p] Ac 6:6; 14:23 [q] 1Sa 16:7; Jer 17:10; Ac 15:8; Rev 2:23
1:26 [r] Ac 2:14
2:1 [s] Lev 23:15,16; Ac 20:16 [t] Ac 1:14
2:2 [u] Ac 4:31
2:4 [v] Mk 16:17; 1Co 12:10

a *15* Greek *brothers* b *20* Psalm 69:25 c *20* Psalm 109:8 d *4* Or *languages*; also in verse 11

INSIGHT

There were 150 Jewish colonies in major population centers throughout the Roman Empire. Many Jews came from these centers to Jerusalem to celebrate the feasts. Jesus' followers who spoke in tongues (known dialects) were Galilean Jews, yet they spoke in the languages of the men attending the Feast of Pentecost.

INSIGHT

To understand the significance of Pentecost, see the chart **The Feasts of Israel** located on pages 210, 211.

5Now there were staying in Jerusalem God-fearing[a] Jews from
every nation under heaven. 6When they heard this sound, a crowd
came together in bewilderment, because each one heard them
speaking in his own language. 7Utterly amazed,[b] they asked: "Are
not all these men who are speaking Galileans?[c] 8Then how is it
that each of us hears them in his own native language? 9Parthians,
Medes and Elamites; residents of Mesopotamia, Judea and Cappadocia,[d] Pontus[e] and Asia,[f] 10Phrygia[g] and Pamphylia,[h] Egypt
and the parts of Libya near Cyrene;[i] visitors from Rome 11(both
Jews and converts to Judaism); Cretans and Arabs—we hear them
declaring the wonders of God in our own tongues!" 12Amazed
and perplexed, they asked one another, "What does this mean?"

2:5
[a]Ac 8:2

2:7
[b]ver 12
[c]Ac 1:11

2:9
[d]1Pe 1:1
[e]Ac 18:2
[f]Ac 16:6; Ro 16:5; 1Co 16:19; 2Co 1:8

2:10
[g]Ac 16:6; 18:23
[h]Ac 13:13; 15:38
[i]Mt 27:32

Men from Every Nation at Pentecost

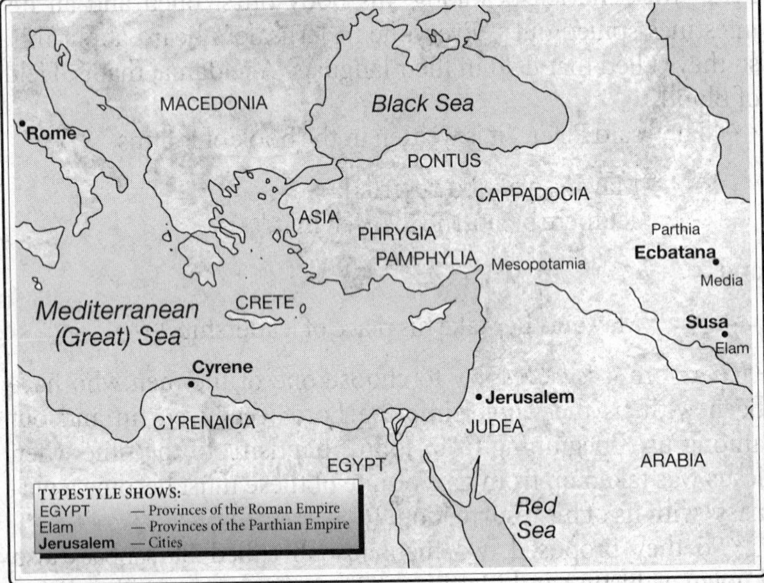

13Some, however, made fun of them and said, "They have had
too much wine.[a]"[j]

14Then Peter stood up with the Eleven, raised his voice and
addressed the crowd: "Fellow Jews and all of you who live in
Jerusalem, let me explain this to you; listen carefully to what I say.
15These men are not drunk, as you suppose. It's only nine in the
morning![k] 16No, this is what was spoken by the prophet Joel:

17" 'In the last days, God says,
I will pour out my Spirit on all people.[l]
Your sons and daughters will prophesy,[m]
your young men will see visions,
your old men will dream dreams.

2:13
[j]1Co 14:23

2:15
[k]1Th 5:7

2:17
[l]Isa 44:3; Jn 7:37-39; Ac 10:45
[m]Ac 21:9

[a]13 Or *sweet wine*

18 Even on my servants, both men and women,
I will pour out my Spirit in those days,
and they will prophesy.[a]
19 I will show wonders in the heaven above
and signs on the earth below,
blood and fire and billows of smoke.
20 The sun will be turned to darkness
and the moon to blood[b]
before the coming of the great and glorious day of the
Lord.
21 And everyone who calls
on the name of the Lord will be saved.'[a][c]

22 "Men of Israel, listen to this: Jesus of Nazareth was a man
accredited by God to you by miracles, wonders and signs,[d] which
God did among you through him,[e] as you yourselves know. 23 This
man was handed over to you by God's set purpose and foreknowledge;[f] and you, with the help of wicked men,[b] put him to death by
nailing him to the cross.[g] 24 But God raised him from the dead,[h]
freeing him from the agony of death, because it was impossible for
death to keep its hold on him.[i] 25 David said about him:

" 'I saw the Lord always before me.
Because he is at my right hand,
I will not be shaken.
26 Therefore my heart is glad and my tongue rejoices;
my body also will live in hope,
27 because you will not abandon me to the grave,
nor will you let your Holy One see decay.[j]
28 You have made known to me the paths of life;
you will fill me with joy in your presence.'[c]

29 "Brothers, I can tell you confidently that the patriarch[k] David
died and was buried,[l] and his tomb is here[m] to this day. 30 But he
was a prophet and knew that God had promised him on oath that
he would place one of his descendants on his throne.[n] 31 Seeing
what was ahead, he spoke of the resurrection of the Christ,[d] that
he was not abandoned to the grave, nor did his body see decay.[o]
32 God has raised this Jesus to life,[p] and we are all witnesses[q] of the
fact. 33 Exalted[r] to the right hand of God,[s] he has received from
the Father[t] the promised Holy Spirit[u] and has poured out[v] what
you now see and hear. 34 For David did not ascend to heaven, and
yet he said,

2:18 [a] Ac 21:9-12
2:20 [b] Mt 24:29
2:21 [c] Ro 10:13
2:22 [d] Jn 4:48; Ac 10:38 [e] Jn 3:2
2:23 [f] Lk 22:22; Ac 3:18; 4:28 [g] Lk 24:20; Ac 3:13
2:24 [h] ver 32; 1Co 6:14; 2Co 4:14; Eph 1:20; Col 2:12; Heb 13:20; 1Pe 1:21 [i] Jn 20:9
2:27 [j] ver 31; Ac 13:35
2:29 [k] Ac 7:8,9 [l] Ac 13:36; 1Ki 2:10 [m] Ne 3:16
2:30 [n] 2Sa 7:12; Ps 132:11
2:31 [o] Ps 16:10
2:32 [p] ver 24 [q] Ac 1:8
2:33 [r] Php 2:9 [s] Mk 16:19 [t] Ac 1:4 [u] Jn 7:39; 14:26 [v] Ac 10:45

a *21* Joel 2:28-32 b *23* Or *of those not having the law* (that is, Gentiles) c *28* Psalm 16:8-11
d *31* Or *Messiah.* "The Christ" (Greek) and "the Messiah" (Hebrew) both mean "the Anointed One"; also in verse 36.

“‘The Lord said to my Lord:
“Sit at my right hand
35until I make your enemies
a footstool for your feet.”’[a][a]

36“Therefore let all Israel be assured of this: God has made this
Jesus, whom you crucified, both Lord and Christ.”[b]
37When the people heard this, they were cut to the heart and said
to Peter and the other apostles, “Brothers, what shall we do?”[c]
38Peter replied, “Repent and be baptized,[d] every one of you, in
the name of Jesus Christ for the forgiveness of your sins.[e] And
you will receive the gift of the Holy Spirit. 39The promise is for
you and your children[f] and for all who are far off[g]—for all whom
the Lord our God will call.”
40With many other words he warned them; and he pleaded
with them, “Save yourselves from this corrupt generation.”[h]
41Those who accepted his message were baptized, and about
three thousand were added to their number that day.
42They devoted themselves to the apostles’ teaching and to the
fellowship, to the breaking of bread and to prayer.[i] 43Everyone was
filled with awe, and many wonders and miraculous signs were
done by the apostles.[j] 44All the believers were together and had
everything in common.[k] 45Selling their possessions and goods,
they gave to anyone as he had need.[l] 46Every day they continued
to meet together in the temple courts.[m] They broke bread[n] in their
homes and ate together with glad and sincere hearts, 47praising
God and enjoying the favor of all the people.[o] And the Lord
added to their number[p] daily those who were being saved.

Chapter 3 Theme

3 One day Peter and John[q] were going up to the temple[r] at the
time of prayer—at three in the afternoon.[s] 2Now a man crippled from birth[t] was being carried to the temple gate[u] called
Beautiful, where he was put every day to beg[v] from those going
into the temple courts. 3When he saw Peter and John about to
enter, he asked them for money. 4Peter looked straight at him, as
did John. Then Peter said, “Look at us!” 5So the man gave them his
attention, expecting to get something from them.
6Then Peter said, “Silver or gold I do not have, but what I have I
give you. In the name of Jesus Christ of Nazareth,[w] walk.” 7Tak-
ing him by the right hand, he helped him up, and instantly the
man’s feet and ankles became strong. 8He jumped to his feet and
began to walk. Then he went with them into the temple courts,
walking and jumping,[x] and praising God. 9When all the people[y]

[a]35 Psalm 110:1

2:35 [a]Ps 110:1; Mt 22:44
2:36 [b]Lk 2:11
2:37 [c]Lk 3:10, 12,14
2:38 [d]Ac 8:12,16, 36,38; 22:16 [e]Lk 24:47; Ac 3:19
2:39 [f]Isa 44:3 [g]Ac 10:45; Eph 2:13
2:40 [h]Dt 32:5
2:42 [i]Ac 1:14
2:43 [j]Ac 5:12
2:44 [k]Ac 4:32
2:45 [l]Mt 19:21
2:46 [m]Lk 24:53; Ac 5:21,42 [n]Ac 20:7
2:47 [o]Ro 14:18 [p]ver 41; Ac 5:14
3:1 [q]Lk 22:8 [r]Ac 2:46 [s]Ps 55:17
3:2 [t]Ac 14:8 [u]Lk 16:20 [v]Jn 9:8
3:6 [w]ver 16; Ac 4:10
3:8 [x]Ac 14:10
3:9 [y]Ac 4:16,21

saw him walking and praising God, 10they recognized him as the
same man who used to sit begging at the temple gate called Beautiful,[a] and they were filled with wonder and amazement at what
had happened to him.
11While the beggar held on to Peter and John,[b] all the people
were astonished and came running to them in the place called
Solomon's Colonnade.[c] 12When Peter saw this, he said to them:
"Men of Israel, why does this surprise you? Why do you stare at us
as if by our own power or godliness we had made this man walk?
13The God of Abraham, Isaac and Jacob, the God of our fathers,[d]
has glorified his servant Jesus. You handed him over to be killed,
and you disowned him before Pilate,[e] though he had decided to let
him go.[f] 14You disowned the Holy[g] and Righteous One[h] and asked
that a murderer be released to you.[i] 15You killed the author of life,
but God raised him from the dead.[j] We are witnesses of this. 16By
faith in the name of Jesus, this man whom you see and know was
made strong. It is Jesus' name and the faith that comes through
him that has given this complete healing to him, as you can all see.
17"Now, brothers, I know that you acted in ignorance,[k] as did
your leaders.[l] 18But this is how God fulfilled what he had foretold[m]
through all the prophets,[n] saying that his Christ[a] would suffer.[o]
19Repent, then, and turn to God, so that your sins may be wiped
out,[p] that times of refreshing may come from the Lord, 20and that
he may send the Christ, who has been appointed for you—even
Jesus. 21He must remain in heaven[q] until the time comes for God
to restore everything,[r] as he promised long ago through his holy
prophets.[s] 22For Moses said, 'The Lord your God will raise up for
you a prophet like me from among your own people; you must
listen to everything he tells you.[t] 23Anyone who does not listen to
him will be completely cut off from among his people.'[b][u]
24"Indeed, all the prophets[v] from Samuel on, as many as have
spoken, have foretold these days. 25And you are heirs[w] of the
prophets and of the covenant[x] God made with your fathers. He
said to Abraham, 'Through your offspring all peoples on earth will
be blessed.'[c][y] 26When God raised up[z] his servant, he sent him first[a]
to you to bless you by turning each of you from your wicked ways."

Chapter 4 Theme ______________________

4

The priests and the captain of the temple guard[b] and the
Sadducees[c] came up to Peter and John while they were
speaking to the people. 2They were greatly disturbed because the
apostles were teaching the people and proclaiming in Jesus the
resurrection of the dead.[d] 3They seized Peter and John, and because

3:10 [a]ver 2
3:11 [b]Lk 22:8 [c]Jn 10:23; Ac 5:12
3:13 [d]Ac 5:30 [e]Mt 27:2 [f]Lk 23:4
3:14 [g]Mk 1:24; Ac 4:27 [h]Ac 7:52 [i]Mk 15:11; Lk 23:18-25
3:15 [j]Ac 2:24
3:17 [k]Lk 23:34 [l]Ac 13:27
3:18 [m]Ac 2:23 [n]Lk 24:27 [o]Ac 17:2,3; 26:22,23
3:19 [p]Ac 2:38
3:21 [q]Ac 1:11 [r]Mt 17:11 [s]Lk 1:70
3:22 [t]Dt 18:15,18; Ac 7:37
3:23 [u]Dt 18:19
3:24 [v]Lk 24:27
3:25 [w]Ac 2:39 [x]Ro 9:4,5 [y]Ge 12:3; 22:18; 26:4; 28:14
3:26 [z]ver 22; Ac 2:24 [a]Ac 13:46; Ro 1:16
4:1 [b]Lk 22:4 [c]Mt 3:7
4:2 [d]Ac 17:18

[a] *18* Or *Messiah;* also in verse 20 [b] *23* Deut. 18:15,18,19 [c] *25* Gen. 22:18; 26:4

it was evening, they put them in jail[a] until the next day. 4But many
who heard the message believed, and the number of men grew[b] to
about five thousand.
5The next day the rulers,[c] elders and teachers of the law met in
Jerusalem. 6Annas the high priest was there, and so were Caiaphas,[d] John, Alexander and the other men of the high priest's
family. 7They had Peter and John brought before them and began
to question them: "By what power or what name did you do this?"
8Then Peter, filled with the Holy Spirit, said to them: "Rulers and
elders of the people![e] 9If we are being called to account today for an
act of kindness shown to a cripple[f] and are asked how he was
healed, 10then know this, you and all the people of Israel: It is by
the name of Jesus Christ of Nazareth, whom you crucified but
whom God raised from the dead,[g] that this man stands before
you healed. 11He is

> " 'the stone you builders rejected,
> which has become the capstone.[a]'[b][h]

12Salvation is found in no one else, for there is no other name
under heaven given to men by which we must be saved."[i]
13When they saw the courage of Peter and John[j] and realized
that they were unschooled, ordinary men,[k] they were astonished
and they took note that these men had been with Jesus. 14But
since they could see the man who had been healed standing there
with them, there was nothing they could say. 15So they ordered
them to withdraw from the Sanhedrin[l] and then conferred
together. 16"What are we going to do with these men?"[m] they
asked. "Everybody living in Jerusalem knows they have done an
outstanding miracle,[n] and we cannot deny it. 17But to stop this
thing from spreading any further among the people, we must
warn these men to speak no longer to anyone in this name."
18Then they called them in again and commanded them not to
speak or teach at all in the name of Jesus.[o] 19But Peter and John
replied, "Judge for yourselves whether it is right in God's sight to
obey you rather than God.[p] 20For we cannot help speaking about
what we have seen and heard."
21After further threats they let them go. They could not decide
how to punish them, because all the people[q] were praising God[r]
for what had happened. 22For the man who was miraculously
healed was over forty years old.
23On their release, Peter and John went back to their own people
and reported all that the chief priests and elders had said to them.
24When they heard this, they raised their voices together in prayer

a *11* Or *cornerstone* b *11* Psalm 118:22

4:3 [a] Ac 5:18
4:4 [b] Ac 2:41
4:5 [c] Lk 23:13
4:6 [d] Mt 26:3; Lk 3:2
4:8 [e] ver 5; Lk 23:13
4:9 [f] Ac 3:6
4:10 [g] Ac 2:24
4:11 [h] Ps 118:22; Isa 28:16; Mt 21:42
4:12 [i] Mt 1:21; Ac 10:43; 1Ti 2:5
4:13 [j] Lk 22:8 [k] Mt 11:25
4:15 [l] Mt 5:22
4:16 [m] Jn 11:47 [n] Ac 3:6-10
4:18 [o] Ac 5:40
4:19 [p] Ac 5:29
4:21 [q] Ac 5:26 [r] Mt 9:8

to God. "Sovereign Lord," they said, "you made the heaven and the
earth and the sea, and everything in them. 25 You spoke by the Holy
Spirit through the mouth of your servant, our father David:[a]

> "'Why do the nations rage
> and the peoples plot in vain?
> 26 The kings of the earth take their stand
> and the rulers gather together
> against the Lord
> and against his Anointed One.[a]'[b][b]

27 Indeed Herod[c] and Pontius Pilate[d] met together with the Gentiles
and the people[c] of Israel in this city to conspire against your holy
servant Jesus,[e] whom you anointed. 28 They did what your power
and will had decided beforehand should happen.[f] 29 Now, Lord,
consider their threats and enable your servants to speak your word
with great boldness.[g] 30 Stretch out your hand to heal and perform
miraculous signs and wonders[h] through the name of your holy
servant Jesus."[i]

31 After they prayed, the place where they were meeting was
shaken.[j] And they were all filled with the Holy Spirit and spoke
the word of God boldly.[k]

32 All the believers were one in heart and mind. No one claimed
that any of his possessions was his own, but they shared everything they had.[l] 33 With great power the apostles continued to testify[m] to the resurrection[n] of the Lord Jesus, and much grace was
upon them all. 34 There were no needy persons among them. For
from time to time those who owned lands or houses sold them,[o]
brought the money from the sales 35 and put it at the apostles' feet,[p]
and it was distributed to anyone as he had need.[q]

36 Joseph, a Levite from Cyprus, whom the apostles called Barnabas[r] (which means Son of Encouragement), 37 sold a field he
owned and brought the money and put it at the apostles' feet.[s]

Chapter 5 Theme ______________________________

5 Now a man named Ananias, together with his wife Sapphira,
also sold a piece of property. 2 With his wife's full knowledge
he kept back part of the money for himself, but brought the rest
and put it at the apostles' feet.[t]

3 Then Peter said, "Ananias, how is it that Satan[u] has so filled
your heart[v] that you have lied to the Holy Spirit[w] and have kept
for yourself some of the money you received for the land? 4 Didn't
it belong to you before it was sold? And after it was sold, wasn't
the money at your disposal? What made you think of doing such
a thing? You have not lied to men but to God."

4:25 [a] Ac 1:16
4:26 [b] Ps 2:1,2; Da 9:25; Lk 4:18; Ac 10:38; Heb 1:9
4:27 [c] Mt 14:1 [d] Mt 27:2; Lk 23:12 [e] ver 30
4:28 [f] Ac 2:23
4:29 [g] ver 13,31; Ac 9:27; 14:3; Php 1:14
4:30 [h] Jn 4:48 [i] ver 27
4:31 [j] Ac 2:2 [k] ver 29
4:32 [l] Ac 2:44
4:33 [m] Lk 24:48 [n] Ac 1:22
4:34 [o] Mt 19:21; Ac 2:45
4:35 [p] ver 37; Ac 5:2 [q] Ac 2:45; 6:1
4:36 [r] Ac 9:27; 1Co 9:6
4:37 [s] ver 35; Ac 5:2
5:2 [t] Ac 4:35,37
5:3 [u] Mt 4:10 [v] Jn 13:2,27 [w] ver 9

a 26 That is, Christ or Messiah b 26 Psalm 2:1,2 c 27 The Greek is plural.

5 When Ananias heard this, he fell down and died.[a] And great
fear[b] seized all who heard what had happened. 6 Then the young
men came forward, wrapped up his body,[c] and carried him out
and buried him.

7 About three hours later his wife came in, not knowing what
had happened. 8 Peter asked her, "Tell me, is this the price you and
Ananias got for the land?"

"Yes," she said, "that is the price."[d]

9 Peter said to her, "How could you agree to test the Spirit of the
Lord?[e] Look! The feet of the men who buried your husband are at
the door, and they will carry you out also."

10 At that moment she fell down at his feet and died.[f] Then the
young men came in and, finding her dead, carried her out and
buried her beside her husband. 11 Great fear[g] seized the whole
church and all who heard about these events.

12 The apostles performed many miraculous signs and wonders[h]
among the people. And all the believers used to meet together[i] in
Solomon's Colonnade.[j] 13 No one else dared join them, even though
they were highly regarded by the people.[k] 14 Nevertheless, more
and more men and women believed in the Lord and were added to
their number. 15 As a result, people brought the sick into the streets
and laid them on beds and mats so that at least Peter's shadow
might fall on some of them as he passed by.[l] 16 Crowds gathered
also from the towns around Jerusalem, bringing their sick and
those tormented by evil[a] spirits, and all of them were healed.[m]

17 Then the high priest and all his associates, who were members
of the party[n] of the Sadducees,[o] were filled with jealousy. 18 They
arrested the apostles and put them in the public jail.[p] 19 But during
the night an angel[q] of the Lord opened the doors of the jail[r] and
brought them out. 20 "Go, stand in the temple courts," he said,
"and tell the people the full message of this new life."[s]

21 At daybreak they entered the temple courts, as they had been
told, and began to teach the people.

When the high priest and his associates[t] arrived, they called
together the Sanhedrin[u]—the full assembly of the elders of Israel—
and sent to the jail for the apostles. 22 But on arriving at the jail, the
officers did not find them there. So they went back and reported,
23 "We found the jail securely locked, with the guards standing at
the doors; but when we opened them, we found no one inside."
24 On hearing this report, the captain of the temple guard and the
chief priests[v] were puzzled, wondering what would come of this.

25 Then someone came and said, "Look! The men you put in jail
are standing in the temple courts teaching the people." 26 At that,

a *16* Greek *unclean*

5:5 [a] ver 10 [b] ver 11
5:6 [c] Jn 19:40
5:8 [d] ver 2
5:9 [e] ver 3
5:10 [f] ver 5
5:11 [g] ver 5; Ac 19:17
5:12 [h] Ac 2:43 [i] Ac 4:32 [j] Ac 3:11
5:13 [k] Ac 2:47; 4:21
5:15 [l] Ac 19:12
5:16 [m] Mk 16:17
5:17 [n] Ac 15:5 [o] Ac 4:1
5:18 [p] Ac 4:3
5:19 [q] Mt 1:20; Lk 1:11; Ac 8:26; 27:23 [r] Ac 16:26
5:20 [s] Jn 6:63,68
5:21 [t] Ac 4:5,6 [u] ver 27,34,41; Mt 5:22
5:24 [v] Ac 4:1

the captain went with his officers and brought the apostles. They
did not use force, because they feared that the people[a] would stone
them.
[27]Having brought the apostles, they made them appear before
the Sanhedrin[b] to be questioned by the high priest. [28]"We gave you
strict orders not to teach in this name,"[c] he said. "Yet you have
filled Jerusalem with your teaching and are determined to make
us guilty of this man's blood."[d]
[29]Peter and the other apostles replied: "We must obey God
rather than men![e] [30]The God of our fathers[f] raised Jesus from the
dead[g]—whom you had killed by hanging him on a tree.[h] [31]God
exalted him to his own right hand[i] as Prince and Savior[j] that he
might give repentance and forgiveness of sins to Israel.[k] [32]We are
witnesses of these things,[l] and so is the Holy Spirit,[m] whom God
has given to those who obey him."
[33]When they heard this, they were furious[n] and wanted to put
them to death. [34]But a Pharisee named Gamaliel,[o] a teacher of the
law,[p] who was honored by all the people, stood up in the Sanhedrin
and ordered that the men be put outside for a little while. [35]Then
he addressed them: "Men of Israel, consider carefully what you
intend to do to these men. [36]Some time ago Theudas appeared,
claiming to be somebody, and about four hundred men rallied to
him. He was killed, all his followers were dispersed, and it all came
to nothing. [37]After him, Judas the Galilean appeared in the days of
the census[q] and led a band of people in revolt. He too was killed,
and all his followers were scattered. [38]Therefore, in the present case
I advise you: Leave these men alone! Let them go! For if their purpose or activity is of human origin, it will fail.[r] [39]But if it is from
God, you will not be able to stop these men; you will only find
yourselves fighting against God."[s]
[40]His speech persuaded them. They called the apostles in and
had them flogged.[t] Then they ordered them not to speak in the
name of Jesus, and let them go.
[41]The apostles left the Sanhedrin, rejoicing[u] because they had
been counted worthy of suffering disgrace for the Name.[v] [42]Day
after day, in the temple courts[w] and from house to house, they
never stopped teaching and proclaiming the good news that
Jesus is the Christ.[a]

Chapter 6 Theme ________________________

6 In those days when the number of disciples was increasing,[x]
the Grecian Jews[y] among them complained against the
Hebraic Jews because their widows[z] were being overlooked in the

5:26 [a]Ac 4:21
5:27 [b]Mt 5:22
5:28 [c]Ac 4:18 [d]Mt 23:35; 27:25; Ac 2:23,36; 3:14,15; 7:52
5:29 [e]Ac 4:19
5:30 [f]Ac 3:13 [g]Ac 2:24 [h]Ac 10:39; 13:29; Gal 3:13; 1Pe 2:24
5:31 [i]Ac 2:33 [j]Lk 2:11 [k]Mt 1:21; Lk 24:47; Ac 2:38
5:32 [l]Lk 24:48 [m]Jn 15:26
5:33 [n]Ac 2:37; 7:54
5:34 [o]Ac 22:3 [p]Lk 2:46
5:37 [q]Lk 2:1,2
5:38 [r]Mt 15:13
5:39 [s]Pr 21:30; Ac 7:51; 11:17
5:40 [t]Mt 10:17
5:41 [u]Mt 5:12 [v]Jn 15:21
5:42 [w]Ac 2:46
6:1 [x]Ac 2:41 [y]Ac 9:29 [z]Ac 9:39,41

[a]42 Or *Messiah*

daily distribution of food.[a] 2So the Twelve gathered all the disciples together and said, "It would not be right for us to neglect the ministry of the word of God in order to wait on tables. 3Brothers,[b] choose seven men from among you who are known to be full of the Spirit and wisdom. We will turn this responsibility over to them 4and will give our attention to prayer[c] and the ministry of the word."

5This proposal pleased the whole group. They chose Stephen,[d] a man full of faith and of the Holy Spirit;[e] also Philip,[f] Procorus, Nicanor, Timon, Parmenas, and Nicolas from Antioch, a convert to Judaism. 6They presented these men to the apostles, who prayed[g] and laid their hands on them.[h]

7So the word of God spread.[i] The number of disciples in Jerusalem increased rapidly, and a large number of priests became obedient to the faith.

8Now Stephen, a man full of God's grace and power, did great wonders and miraculous signs[j] among the people. 9Opposition arose, however, from members of the Synagogue of the Freedmen (as it was called)—Jews of Cyrene[k] and Alexandria as well as the provinces of Cilicia[l] and Asia.[m] These men began to argue with Stephen, 10but they could not stand up against his wisdom or the Spirit by whom he spoke.[n]

11Then they secretly[o] persuaded some men to say, "We have heard Stephen speak words of blasphemy against Moses and against God."[p]

12So they stirred up the people and the elders and the teachers of the law. They seized Stephen and brought him before the Sanhedrin.[q] 13They produced false witnesses, who testified, "This fellow never stops speaking against this holy place[r] and against the law. 14For we have heard him say that this Jesus of Nazareth will destroy this place and change the customs Moses handed down to us."[s]

15All who were sitting in the Sanhedrin[t] looked intently at Stephen, and they saw that his face was like the face of an angel.

Chapter 7 Theme

7 Then the high priest asked him, "Are these charges true?"

2To this he replied: "Brothers and fathers,[u] listen to me! The God of glory[v] appeared to our father Abraham while he was still in Mesopotamia, before he lived in Haran.[w] 3'Leave your country and your people,' God said, 'and go to the land I will show you.'[a][x]

4"So he left the land of the Chaldeans and settled in Haran. After the death of his father, God sent him to this land where you

[a]3 Gen. 12:1

6:1 [a] Ac 4:35
6:3 [b] Ac 1:16
6:4 [c] Ac 1:14
6:5 [d] ver 8; Ac 11:19 [e] Ac 11:24 [f] Ac 8:5-40; 21:8
6:6 [g] Ac 1:24; 8:17; 13:3; 2Ti 1:6 [h] Nu 8:10; Ac 9:17; 1Ti 4:14
6:7 [i] Ac 12:24; 19:20
6:8 [j] Jn 4:48
6:9 [k] Mt 27:32 [l] Ac 15:23,41; 22:3; 23:34 [m] Ac 2:9
6:10 [n] Lk 21:15
6:11 [o] 1Ki 21:10 [p] Mt 26:59-61
6:12 [q] Mt 5:22
6:13 [r] Ac 21:28
6:14 [s] Ac 15:1; 21:21; 26:3; 28:17
6:15 [t] Mt 5:22
7:2 [u] Ac 22:1 [v] Ps 29:3 [w] Ge 11:31; 15:7
7:3 [x] Ge 12:1

are now living.[a] 5He gave him no inheritance here, not even a foot
of ground. But God promised him that he and his descendants
after him would possess the land,[b] even though at that time
Abraham had no child. 6God spoke to him in this way: 'Your
descendants will be strangers in a country not their own, and
they will be enslaved and mistreated four hundred years.[c] 7But I
will punish the nation they serve as slaves,' God said, 'and afterward they will come out of that country and worship me in this
place.'[a][d] 8Then he gave Abraham the covenant of circumcision.[e]
And Abraham became the father of Isaac and circumcised him
eight days after his birth.[f] Later Isaac became the father of Jacob,[g]
and Jacob became the father of the twelve patriarchs.[h]

9"Because the patriarchs were jealous of Joseph,[i] they sold him
as a slave into Egypt.[j] But God was with him[k] 10and rescued him
from all his troubles. He gave Joseph wisdom and enabled him to
gain the goodwill of Pharaoh king of Egypt; so he made him
ruler over Egypt and all his palace.[l]

11"Then a famine struck all Egypt and Canaan, bringing great
suffering, and our fathers could not find food.[m] 12When Jacob
heard that there was grain in Egypt, he sent our fathers on their
first visit.[n] 13On their second visit, Joseph told his brothers who
he was,[o] and Pharaoh learned about Joseph's family. 14After this,
Joseph sent for his father Jacob and his whole family,[p] seventy-five
in all.[q] 15Then Jacob went down to Egypt, where he and our fathers
died.[r] 16Their bodies were brought back to Shechem and placed
in the tomb that Abraham had bought from the sons of Hamor at
Shechem for a certain sum of money.[s]

17"As the time drew near for God to fulfill his promise to Abraham, the number of our people in Egypt greatly increased.[t] 18Then
another king, who knew nothing about Joseph, became ruler of
Egypt.[u] 19He dealt treacherously with our people and oppressed
our forefathers by forcing them to throw out their newborn
babies so that they would die.[v]

20"At that time Moses was born, and he was no ordinary child.[b]
For three months he was cared for in his father's house.[w] 21When
he was placed outside, Pharaoh's daughter took him and brought
him up as her own son.[x] 22Moses was educated in all the wisdom
of the Egyptians[y] and was powerful in speech and action.

23"When Moses was forty years old, he decided to visit his fellow
Israelites. 24He saw one of them being mistreated by an Egyptian,
so he went to his defense and avenged him by killing the Egyptian. 25Moses thought that his own people would realize that God
was using him to rescue them, but they did not. 26The next day

7:4 [a]Ge 12:5
7:5 [b]Ge 12:7; 17:8; 26:3
7:6 [c]Ex 12:40
7:7 [d]Ex 3:12
7:8 [e]Ge 17:9-14 [f]Ge 21:2-4 [g]Ge 25:26 [h]Ge 29:31-35; 30:5-13, 17-24; 35:16-18, 22-26
7:9 [i]Ge 37:4,11 [j]Ge 37:28; Ps 105:17 [k]Ge 39:2,21,23
7:10 [l]Ge 41:37-43
7:11 [m]Ge 41:54
7:12 [n]Ge 42:1,2
7:13 [o]Ge 45:1-4
7:14 [p]Ge 45:9,10 [q]Ge 46:26,27; Ex 1:5; Dt 10:22
7:15 [r]Ge 46:5-7; 49:33; Ex 1:6
7:16 [s]Ge 23:16-20; 33:18,19; 50:13; Jos 24:32
7:17 [t]Ex 1:7; Ps 105:24
7:18 [u]Ex 1:8
7:19 [v]Ex 1:10-22
7:20 [w]Ex 2:2; Heb 11:23
7:21 [x]Ex 2:3-10
7:22 [y]1Ki 4:30; Isa 19:11

[a]7 Gen. 15:13,14 [b]*20* Or *was fair in the sight of God*

Moses came upon two Israelites who were fighting. He tried to
reconcile them by saying, 'Men, you are brothers; why do you
want to hurt each other?'
27"But the man who was mistreating the other pushed Moses
aside and said, 'Who made you ruler and judge over us? 28Do you
want to kill me as you killed the Egyptian yesterday?'[a] 29When
Moses heard this, he fled to Midian, where he settled as a foreigner
and had two sons.[a]
30"After forty years had passed, an angel appeared to Moses in
the flames of a burning bush in the desert near Mount Sinai.
31When he saw this, he was amazed at the sight. As he went over
to look more closely, he heard the Lord's voice:[b] 32'I am the God
of your fathers, the God of Abraham, Isaac and Jacob.'[b] Moses
trembled with fear and did not dare to look.[c]
33"Then the Lord said to him, 'Take off your sandals; the place
where you are standing is holy ground.[d] 34I have indeed seen the
oppression of my people in Egypt. I have heard their groaning
and have come down to set them free. Now come, I will send you
back to Egypt.'[c][e]
35"This is the same Moses whom they had rejected with the
words, 'Who made you ruler and judge?'[f] He was sent to be their
ruler and deliverer by God himself, through the angel who
appeared to him in the bush. 36He led them out of Egypt[g] and did
wonders and miraculous signs in Egypt, at the Red Sea[d][h] and for
forty years in the desert.
37"This is that Moses who told the Israelites, 'God will send you
a prophet like me from your own people.'[e][i] 38He was in the
assembly in the desert, with the angel[j] who spoke to him on
Mount Sinai, and with our fathers;[k] and he received living words[l]
to pass on to us.[m]
39"But our fathers refused to obey him. Instead, they rejected
him and in their hearts turned back to Egypt.[n] 40They told Aaron,
'Make us gods who will go before us. As for this fellow Moses
who led us out of Egypt—we don't know what has happened to
him!'[f][o] 41That was the time they made an idol in the form of a
calf. They brought sacrifices to it and held a celebration in honor
of what their hands had made.[p] 42But God turned away[q] and gave
them over to the worship of the heavenly bodies.[r] This agrees
with what is written in the book of the prophets:

> "'Did you bring me sacrifices and offerings
> forty years in the desert, O house of Israel?

[a]28 Exodus 2:14 [b]32 Exodus 3:6 [c]34 Exodus 3:5,7,8,10 [d]36 That is, Sea of Reeds
[e]37 Deut. 18:15 [f]40 Exodus 32:1

7:29 *a* Ex 2:11-15
7:31 *b* Ex 3:1-4
7:32 *c* Ex 3:6
7:33 *d* Ex 3:5; Jos 5:15
7:34 *e* Ex 3:7-10
7:35 *f* ver 27
7:36 *g* Ex 12:41; 33:1 *h* Ex 14:21
7:37 *i* Dt 18:15,18; Ac 3:22
7:38 *j* ver 53 *k* Ex 19:17 *l* Dt 32:45-47; Heb 4:12 *m* Ro 3:2
7:39 *n* Nu 14:3,4
7:40 *o* Ex 32:1,23
7:41 *p* Ex 32:4-6; Ps 106:19,20; Rev 9:20
7:42 *q* Jos 24:20; Isa 63:10 *r* Jer 19:13

43 You have lifted up the shrine of Molech
 and the star of your god Rephan,
 the idols you made to worship.
Therefore I will send you into exile'[a] [a] beyond Babylon.

44 "Our forefathers had the tabernacle of the Testimony[b] with
them in the desert. It had been made as God directed Moses,
according to the pattern he had seen.[c] 45 Having received the
tabernacle, our fathers under Joshua brought it with them when
they took the land from the nations God drove out before them.[d]
It remained in the land until the time of David, 46 who enjoyed
God's favor and asked that he might provide a dwelling place for
the God of Jacob.[b] [e] 47 But it was Solomon who built the house for
him.

48 "However, the Most High does not live in houses made by
men.[f] As the prophet says:

49 " 'Heaven is my throne,
 and the earth is my footstool.[g]
What kind of house will you build for me?
 says the Lord.
 Or where will my resting place be?
50 Has not my hand made all these things?'[c] [h]

51 "You stiff-necked people,[i] with uncircumcised hearts[j] and
ears! You are just like your fathers: You always resist the Holy Spirit!
52 Was there ever a prophet your fathers did not persecute?[k] They
even killed those who predicted the coming of the Righteous One.
And now you have betrayed and murdered him[l]— 53 you who
have received the law that was put into effect through angels[m] but
have not obeyed it."

54 When they heard this, they were furious[n] and gnashed their
teeth at him. 55 But Stephen, full of the Holy Spirit, looked up to
heaven and saw the glory of God, and Jesus standing at the right
hand of God.[o] 56 "Look," he said, "I see heaven open[p] and the Son
of Man[q] standing at the right hand of God."

57 At this they covered their ears and, yelling at the top of their
voices, they all rushed at him, 58 dragged him out of the city[r] and
began to stone him.[s] Meanwhile, the witnesses laid their clothes[t] at
the feet of a young man named Saul.[u]

59 While they were stoning him, Stephen prayed, "Lord Jesus,
receive my spirit."[v] 60 Then he fell on his knees[w] and cried out,
"Lord, do not hold this sin against them."[x] When he had said this,
he fell asleep.

7:43 [a] Am 5:25-27
7:44 [b] Ex 38:21
[c] Ex 25:8,9,40
7:45 [d] Jos 3:14-17; 18:1; 23:9; 24:18; Ps 44:2
7:46 [e] 2Sa 7:8-16; Ps 132:1-5
7:48 [f] 1Ki 8:27; 2Ch 2:6
7:49 [g] Mt 5:34,35
7:50 [h] Isa 66:1,2
7:51 [i] Ex 32:9; 33:3,5
[j] Lev 26:41; Dt 10:16; Jer 4:4; 9:26
7:52 [k] 2Ch 36:16; Mt 5:12
[l] Ac 3:14; 1Th 2:15
7:53 [m] ver 38; Gal 3:19; Heb 2:2
7:54 [n] Ac 5:33
7:55 [o] Mk 16:19
7:56 [p] Mt 3:16
[q] Mt 8:20
7:58 [r] Lk 4:29
[s] Lev 24:14,16; Dt 13:9
[t] Ac 22:20
[u] Ac 8:1
7:59 [v] Ps 31:5; Lk 23:46
7:60 [w] Ac 9:40
[x] Mt 5:44

a *43* Amos 5:25-27 b *46* Some early manuscripts *the house of Jacob* c *50* Isaiah 66:1,2

Chapter 8 Theme ____

8 And Saul[a] was there, giving approval to his death.
On that day a great persecution broke out against the church
at Jerusalem, and all except the apostles were scattered[b] throughout
Judea and Samaria.[c] 2Godly men buried Stephen and mourned
deeply for him. 3But Saul[d] began to destroy the church.[e] Going
from house to house, he dragged off men and women and put
them in prison.

4Those who had been scattered[f] preached the word wherever
they went.[g] 5Philip[h] went down to a city in Samaria and proclaimed the Christ[a] there. 6When the crowds heard Philip and saw
the miraculous signs he did, they all paid close attention to what he
said. 7With shrieks, evil[b] spirits came out of many,[i] and many
paralytics and cripples were healed.[j] 8So there was great joy in
that city.

9Now for some time a man named Simon had practiced sorcery[k]
in the city and amazed all the people of Samaria. He boasted that
he was someone great,[l] 10and all the people, both high and low,
gave him their attention and exclaimed, "This man is the divine
power known as the Great Power."[m] 11They followed him because
he had amazed them for a long time with his magic. 12But when
they believed Philip as he preached the good news of the kingdom
of God[n] and the name of Jesus Christ, they were baptized,[o] both
men and women. 13Simon himself believed and was baptized. And
he followed Philip everywhere, astonished by the great signs and
miracles[p] he saw.

14When the apostles in Jerusalem heard that Samaria[q] had
accepted the word of God, they sent Peter and John[r] to them.
15When they arrived, they prayed for them that they might receive
the Holy Spirit,[s] 16because the Holy Spirit had not yet come upon
any of them;[t] they had simply been baptized into[c] the name of the
Lord Jesus.[u] 17Then Peter and John placed their hands on them,[v]
and they received the Holy Spirit.

18When Simon saw that the Spirit was given at the laying on of
the apostles' hands, he offered them money 19and said, "Give me
also this ability so that everyone on whom I lay my hands may
receive the Holy Spirit."

20Peter answered: "May your money perish with you, because
you thought you could buy the gift of God with money![w] 21You
have no part or share in this ministry, because your heart is
not right[x] before God. 22Repent of this wickedness and pray to
the Lord. Perhaps he will forgive you for having such a thought

[a]5 Or *Messiah* [b]7 Greek *unclean* [c]16 Or *in*

8:1 [a]Ac 7:58 [b]Ac 11:19 [c]Ac 9:31

8:3 [d]Ac 7:58 [e]Ac 22:4,19; 26:10,11; 1Co 15:9; Gal 1:13,23; Php 3:6; 1Ti 1:13

8:4 [f]ver 1 [g]Ac 15:35

8:5 [h]Ac 6:5

8:7 [i]Mk 16:17 [j]Mt 4:24

8:9 [k]Ac 13:6 [l]Ac 5:36

8:10 [m]Ac 14:11; 28:6

8:12 [n]Ac 1:3 [o]Ac 2:38

8:13 [p]ver 6; Ac 19:11

8:14 [q]ver 1 [r]Lk 22:8

8:15 [s]Ac 2:38

8:16 [t]Ac 19:2 [u]Mt 28:19; Ac 2:38

8:17 [v]Ac 6:6

8:20 [w]2Ki 5:16; Da 5:17; Mt 10:8; Ac 2:38

8:21 [x]Ps 78:37

in your heart. 23For I see that you are full of bitterness and captive to sin."

24Then Simon answered, "Pray to the Lord for me[a] so that nothing you have said may happen to me."

25When they had testified and proclaimed the word of the Lord, Peter and John returned to Jerusalem, preaching the gospel in many Samaritan villages.[b]

26Now an angel[c] of the Lord said to Philip, "Go south to the road—the desert road—that goes down from Jerusalem to Gaza."
27So he started out, and on his way he met an Ethiopian[a][d] eunuch,[e]
an important official in charge of all the treasury of Candace, queen of the Ethiopians. This man had gone to Jerusalem to worship,[f] 28and on his way home was sitting in his chariot reading the book of Isaiah the prophet. 29The Spirit told[g] Philip, "Go to that chariot and stay near it."

30Then Philip ran up to the chariot and heard the man reading Isaiah the prophet. "Do you understand what you are reading?" Philip asked.

31"How can I," he said, "unless someone explains it to me?" So he invited Philip to come up and sit with him.

32The eunuch was reading this passage of Scripture:

> "He was led like a sheep to the slaughter,
> and as a lamb before the shearer is silent,
> so he did not open his mouth.
> 33In his humiliation he was deprived of justice.
> Who can speak of his descendants?
> For his life was taken from the earth."[b][h]

34The eunuch asked Philip, "Tell me, please, who is the prophet talking about, himself or someone else?" 35Then Philip began[i] with that very passage of Scripture[j] and told him the good news about Jesus.

36As they traveled along the road, they came to some water and the eunuch said, "Look, here is water. Why shouldn't I be baptized?"[c][k] 38And he gave orders to stop the chariot. Then both Philip and the eunuch went down into the water and Philip baptized him. 39When they came up out of the water, the Spirit of the Lord suddenly took Philip away,[l] and the eunuch did not see him again, but went on his way rejoicing. 40Philip, however, appeared at Azotus and traveled about, preaching the gospel in all the towns[m] until he reached Caesarea.[n]

8:24 [a]Ex 8:8; Nu 21:7; 1Ki 13:6
8:25 [b]ver 40
8:26 [c]Ac 5:19
8:27 [d]Ps 68:31; 87:4; Zep 3:10 [e]Isa 56:3-5 [f]1Ki 8:41-43; Jn 12:20
8:29 [g]Ac 10:19; 11:12; 13:2; 20:23; 21:11
8:33 [h]Isa 53:7,8
8:35 [i]Mt 5:2 [j]Lk 24:27; Ac 17:2; 18:28; 28:23
8:36 [k]Ac 10:47
8:39 [l]1Ki 18:12; 2Ki 2:16; Eze 3:12,14; 8:3; 11:1,24; 43:5; 2Co 12:2
8:40 [m]ver 25 [n]Ac 10:1,24; 12:19; 21:8,16; 23:23,33; 25:1,4,6,13

See the "Insight" about the **Samaritans** on page 1824.

[a]*27* That is, from the upper Nile region [b]*33* Isaiah 53:7,8 [c]*36* Some late manuscripts *baptized?" 37Philip said, "If you believe with all your heart, you may." The eunuch answered, "I believe that Jesus Christ is the Son of God."*

Sequence of Events in Paul's Life after His Conversion*

**There are differing opinions on these dates. For continuity's sake this chart will be the basis for dates pertaining to Paul's life.*

Year A.D.	Event
33-34	Conversion, time in Damascus
35-47	Some silent years, except we know that Paul: 1. Spent time in Arabia and Damascus 2. Made first visit to Jerusalem 3. Went to Tarsus, Syria-Cilicia area 4. Was with Barnabas in Antioch 5. With Barnabas took relief to brethren in Judea—Paul's second visit to Jerusalem 6. Returned to Antioch; was sent out with Barnabas by church at Antioch
47-48	**First missionary journey:** *Galatians written(?)*
49	Apostolic Council at Jerusalem—Paul visits Jerusalem (compare Acts 15 with Galatians 2:1)
49-51	**Second missionary journey:** *1 and 2 Thessalonians written*
52-56	**Third missionary journey:** *1 and 2 Corinthians and Romans written*
56	Paul goes to Jerusalem and is arrested; held at Caesarea
57-59	Appearance before Felix and Drusilla; before Festus; before Agrippa
59-60	Appeals to Caesar, sent from Caesarea to Rome
60-62	First Roman imprisonment: *Ephesians, Philemon, Colossians, and Philippians written*
62	Paul's release; possible trip to Spain
62	Paul in Macedonia: *1 Timothy written*
62	Paul goes to Crete: *Titus written*
63-64	Paul taken to Rome and imprisoned: *2 Timothy written*
64	Paul is absent from the body and present with the Lord *(Others put Paul's conversion about A.D. 35, his death in A.D. 68.)*

Chapter 9 Theme ______________________

9 Meanwhile, Saul was still breathing out murderous threats
against the Lord's disciples.[a] He went to the high priest [2]and
asked him for letters to the synagogues in Damascus, so that if he
found any there who belonged to the Way,[b] whether men or
women, he might take them as prisoners to Jerusalem. [3]As he
neared Damascus on his journey, suddenly a light from heaven
flashed around him.[c] [4]He fell to the ground and heard a voice say
to him, "Saul, Saul, why do you persecute me?"

[5]"Who are you, Lord?" Saul asked.

"I am Jesus, whom you are persecuting," he replied. [6]"Now get
up and go into the city, and you will be told what you must do."[d]

[7]The men traveling with Saul stood there speechless; they heard
the sound[e] but did not see anyone.[f] [8]Saul got up from the ground,
but when he opened his eyes he could see nothing. So they led him
by the hand into Damascus. [9]For three days he was blind, and did
not eat or drink anything.

[10]In Damascus there was a disciple named Ananias. The Lord
called to him in a vision,[g] "Ananias!"

"Yes, Lord," he answered.

[11]The Lord told him, "Go to the house of Judas on Straight Street
and ask for a man from Tarsus[h] named Saul, for he is praying. [12]In
a vision he has seen a man named Ananias come and place his
hands on[i] him to restore his sight."

9:1 [a]Ac 8:3
9:2 [b]Ac 19:9,23; 22:4; 24:14,22
9:3 [c]1Co 15:8
9:6 [d]ver 16
9:7 [e]Jn 12:29 [f]Da 10:7; Ac 22:9
9:10 [g]Ac 10:3,17,19
9:11 [h]ver 30; Ac 21:39; 22:3
9:12 [i]Mk 5:23

13“Lord,” Ananias answered, “I have heard many reports about
this man and all the harm he has done to your saints[a] in Jerusalem.[b] 14And he has come here with authority from the chief
priests[c] to arrest all who call on your name.”
15But the Lord said to Ananias, “Go! This man is my chosen
instrument[d] to carry my name before the Gentiles[e] and their
kings[f] and before the people of Israel. 16I will show him how much
he must suffer for my name.”[g]
17Then Ananias went to the house and entered it. Placing his
hands on[h] Saul, he said, “Brother Saul, the Lord—Jesus, who
appeared to you on the road as you were coming here—has sent
me so that you may see again and be filled with the Holy Spirit.”
18Immediately, something like scales fell from Saul’s eyes, and he
could see again. He got up and was baptized, 19and after taking
some food, he regained his strength.
Saul spent several days with the disciples[i] in Damascus.[j] 20At
once he began to preach in the synagogues[k] that Jesus is the Son of
God.[l] 21All those who heard him were astonished and asked,
“Isn’t he the man who raised havoc in Jerusalem among those who
call on this name?[m] And hasn’t he come here to take them as
prisoners to the chief priests?”[n] 22Yet Saul grew more and more
powerful and baffled the Jews living in Damascus by proving that
Jesus is the Christ.[a][o]
23After many days had gone by, the Jews conspired to kill him,
24but Saul learned of their plan.[p] Day and night they kept close
watch on the city gates in order to kill him. 25But his followers
took him by night and lowered him in a basket through an opening in the wall.[q]
26When he came to Jerusalem,[r] he tried to join the disciples,
but they were all afraid of him, not believing that he really was a
disciple. 27But Barnabas[s] took him and brought him to the apostles. He told them how Saul on his journey had seen the Lord and
that the Lord had spoken to him,[t] and how in Damascus he had
preached fearlessly in the name of Jesus.[u] 28So Saul stayed with
them and moved about freely in Jerusalem, speaking boldly in the
name of the Lord. 29He talked and debated with the Grecian Jews,[v]
but they tried to kill him.[w] 30When the brothers[x] learned of this,
they took him down to Caesarea[y] and sent him off to Tarsus.[z]
31Then the church throughout Judea, Galilee and Samaria[a]
enjoyed a time of peace. It was strengthened; and encouraged by
the Holy Spirit, it grew in numbers, living in the fear of the Lord.
32As Peter traveled about the country, he went to visit the saints[b]
in Lydda. 33There he found a man named Aeneas, a paralytic who
had been bedridden for eight years. 34“Aeneas,” Peter said to him,

9:13 [a] ver 32; Ro 1:7; 16:2,15 [b] Ac 8:3
9:14 [c] ver 2,21
9:15 [d] Ac 13:2; Ro 1:1; Gal 1:15 [e] Ro 11:13; 15:15,16; Gal 2:7,8; Eph 3:7,8 [f] Ac 25:22,23; 26:1
9:16 [g] Ac 20:23; 21:11; 2Co 11:23-27
9:17 [h] Ac 6:6
9:19 [i] Ac 11:26 [j] Ac 26:20
9:20 [k] Ac 13:5,14 [l] Mt 4:3
9:21 [m] Ac 8:3 [n] Gal 1:13,23
9:22 [o] Ac 18:5,28
9:24 [p] Ac 20:3,19
9:25 [q] 1Sa 19:12; 2Co 11:32,33
9:26 [r] Ac 22:17; 26:20; Gal 1:17,18
9:27 [s] Ac 4:36 [t] ver 3-6 [u] ver 20,22
9:29 [v] Ac 6:1 [w] 2Co 11:26
9:30 [x] Ac 1:16 [y] Ac 8:40 [z] ver 11
9:31 [a] Ac 8:1
9:32 [b] ver 13

[a] *22* Or *Messiah*

"Jesus Christ heals you.[a] Get up and take care of your mat." Immediately Aeneas got up. 35All those who lived in Lydda and Sharon[b]
saw him and turned to the Lord.[c]
36In Joppa[d] there was a disciple named Tabitha (which, when
translated, is Dorcas[a]), who was always doing good[e] and helping
the poor. 37About that time she became sick and died, and her
body was washed and placed in an upstairs room.[f] 38Lydda was
near Joppa; so when the disciples[g] heard that Peter was in Lydda,
they sent two men to him and urged him, "Please come at once!"
39Peter went with them, and when he arrived he was taken
upstairs to the room. All the widows[h] stood around him, crying
and showing him the robes and other clothing that Dorcas had
made while she was still with them.
40Peter sent them all out of the room;[i] then he got down on his
knees[j] and prayed. Turning toward the dead woman, he said,
"Tabitha, get up." She opened her eyes, and seeing Peter she sat up.
41He took her by the hand and helped her to her feet. Then he
called the believers and the widows and presented her to them
alive. 42This became known all over Joppa, and many people
believed in the Lord. 43Peter stayed in Joppa for some time with a
tanner named Simon.[k]

Chapter 10 Theme ______________________

10 At Caesarea[l] there was a man named Cornelius, a centurion
in what was known as the Italian Regiment. 2He and all his
family were devout and God-fearing;[m] he gave generously to
those in need and prayed to God regularly. 3One day at about three
in the afternoon[n] he had a vision.[o] He distinctly saw an angel[p] of
God, who came to him and said, "Cornelius!"
4Cornelius stared at him in fear. "What is it, Lord?" he asked.
The angel answered, "Your prayers and gifts to the poor have
come up as a memorial offering[q] before God.[r] 5Now send men to
Joppa[s] to bring back a man named Simon who is called Peter. 6He
is staying with Simon the tanner,[t] whose house is by the sea."
7When the angel who spoke to him had gone, Cornelius called
two of his servants and a devout soldier who was one of his attendants. 8He told them everything that had happened and sent
them to Joppa.[u]
9About noon the following day as they were on their journey
and approaching the city, Peter went up on the roof[v] to pray. 10He
became hungry and wanted something to eat, and while the meal
was being prepared, he fell into a trance.[w] 11He saw heaven opened
and something like a large sheet being let down to earth by its four

a36 Both *Tabitha* (Aramaic) and *Dorcas* (Greek) mean *gazelle*.

9:34
[a] Ac 3:6,16; 4:10

9:35
[b] 1Ch 5:16; 27:29; Isa 33:9; 35:2; 65:10
[c] Ac 11:21

9:36
[d] Jos 19:46; 2Ch 2:16; Ezr 3:7; Jnh 1:3; Ac 10:5
[e] 1Ti 2:10; Tit 3:8

9:37
[f] Ac 1:13

9:38
[g] Ac 11:26

9:39
[h] Ac 6:1

9:40
[i] Mt 9:25
[j] Lk 22:41; Ac 7:60

9:43
[k] Ac 10:6

10:1
[l] Ac 8:40

10:2
[m] ver 22,35; Ac 13:16,26

10:3
[n] Ac 3:1
[o] Ac 9:10
[p] Ac 5:19

10:4
[q] Mt 26:13
[r] Rev 8:4

10:5
[s] Ac 9:36

10:6
[t] Ac 9:43

10:8
[u] Ac 9:36

10:9
[v] Mt 24:17

10:10
[w] Ac 22:17

corners. 12It contained all kinds of four-footed animals, as well as reptiles of the earth and birds of the air. 13Then a voice told him, "Get up, Peter. Kill and eat."

14"Surely not, Lord!"[a] Peter replied. "I have never eaten anything impure or unclean."[b]

15The voice spoke to him a second time, "Do not call anything impure that God has made clean."[c]

16This happened three times, and immediately the sheet was taken back to heaven.

17While Peter was wondering about the meaning of the vision, the men sent by Cornelius[d] found out where Simon's house was and stopped at the gate. 18They called out, asking if Simon who was known as Peter was staying there.

19While Peter was still thinking about the vision, the Spirit said[e] to him, "Simon, three[a] men are looking for you. 20So get up and go downstairs. Do not hesitate to go with them, for I have sent them."[f]

21Peter went down and said to the men, "I'm the one you're looking for. Why have you come?"

22The men replied, "We have come from Cornelius the centurion. He is a righteous and God-fearing man,[g] who is respected by all the Jewish people. A holy angel told him to have you come to his house so that he could hear what you have to say."[h] 23Then Peter invited the men into the house to be his guests.

The next day Peter started out with them, and some of the brothers[i] from Joppa went along.[j] 24The following day he arrived in Caesarea.[k] Cornelius was expecting them and had called together his relatives and close friends. 25As Peter entered the house, Cornelius met him and fell at his feet in reverence. 26But Peter made him get up. "Stand up," he said, "I am only a man myself."[l]

27Talking with him, Peter went inside and found a large gathering of people. 28He said to them: "You are well aware that it is against our law for a Jew to associate with a Gentile or visit him.[m] But God has shown me that I should not call any man impure or unclean.[n] 29So when I was sent for, I came without raising any objection. May I ask why you sent for me?"

30Cornelius answered: "Four days ago I was in my house praying at this hour, at three in the afternoon. Suddenly a man in shining clothes stood before me 31and said, 'Cornelius, God has heard your prayer and remembered your gifts to the poor. 32Send to Joppa for Simon who is called Peter. He is a guest in the home of Simon the tanner, who lives by the sea.' 33So I sent for you immediately, and it was good of you to come. Now we are all here in the presence of God to listen to everything the Lord has commanded you to tell us."

10:14 [a]Ac 9:5 [b]Lev 11:4-8, 13-20; 20:25; Dt 14:3-20; Eze 4:14

10:15 [c]Mt 15:11; Ro 14:14,17,20; 1Co 10:25; 1Ti 4:3,4; Tit 1:15

10:17 [d]ver 7,8

10:19 [e]Ac 8:29

10:20 [f]Ac 15:7-9

10:22 [g]ver 2 [h]Ac 11:14

10:23 [i]Ac 1:16 [j]ver 45; Ac 11:12

10:24 [k]Ac 8:40

10:26 [l]Ac 14:15; Rev 19:10

10:28 [m]Jn 4:9; 18:28; Ac 11:3 [n]Ac 15:8,9

a *19* One early manuscript *two*; other manuscripts do not have the number.

34 Then Peter began to speak: "I now realize how true it is that God does not show favoritism[a] 35 but accepts men from every nation who fear him and do what is right.[b] 36 You know the message God sent to the people of Israel, telling the good news[c] of peace[d] through Jesus Christ, who is Lord of all.[e] 37 You know what has happened throughout Judea, beginning in Galilee after the baptism that John preached— 38 how God anointed[f] Jesus of Nazareth with the Holy Spirit and power, and how he went around doing good and healing[g] all who were under the power of the devil, because God was with him.[h]

39 "We are witnesses[i] of everything he did in the country of the Jews and in Jerusalem. They killed him by hanging him on a tree,[j] 40 but God raised him from the dead[k] on the third day and caused him to be seen. 41 He was not seen by all the people,[l] but by witnesses whom God had already chosen—by us who ate[m] and drank with him after he rose from the dead. 42 He commanded us to preach to the people[n] and to testify that he is the one whom God appointed as judge of the living and the dead.[o] 43 All the prophets testify about him[p] that everyone[q] who believes in him receives forgiveness of sins through his name."

44 While Peter was still speaking these words, the Holy Spirit came on[r] all who heard the message. 45 The circumcised believers who had come with Peter[s] were astonished that the gift of the Holy Spirit had been poured out[t] even on the Gentiles.[u] 46 For they heard them speaking in tongues[a][v] and praising God.

Then Peter said, 47 "Can anyone keep these people from being baptized with water?[w] They have received the Holy Spirit just as we have."[x] 48 So he ordered that they be baptized in the name of Jesus Christ.[y] Then they asked Peter to stay with them for a few days.

Chapter 11 Theme ____________________

11 The apostles and the brothers[z] throughout Judea heard that the Gentiles also had received the word of God. 2 So when Peter went up to Jerusalem, the circumcised believers[a] criticized him 3 and said, "You went into the house of uncircumcised men and ate with them."[b]

4 Peter began and explained everything to them precisely as it had happened: 5 "I was in the city of Joppa praying, and in a trance I saw a vision.[c] I saw something like a large sheet being let down from heaven by its four corners, and it came down to where I was. 6 I looked into it and saw four-footed animals of the earth, wild beasts, reptiles, and birds of the air. 7 Then I heard a voice telling me, 'Get up, Peter. Kill and eat.'

a 46 Or *other languages*

10:34 [a] Dt 10:17; 2Ch 19:7; Job 34:19; Ro 2:11; Gal 2:6; Eph 6:9; Col 3:25; 1Pe 1:17
10:35 [b] Ac 15:9
10:36 [c] Ac 13:32 [d] Lk 2:14 [e] Mt 28:18; Ro 10:12
10:38 [f] Ac 4:26 [g] Mt 4:23 [h] Jn 3:2
10:39 [i] Lk 24:48 [j] Ac 5:30
10:40 [k] Ac 2:24
10:41 [l] Jn 14:17,22 [m] Lk 24:43; Jn 21:13
10:42 [n] Mt 28:19,20 [o] Jn 5:22; Ac 17:31; Ro 14:9; 2Co 5:10; 2Ti 4:1; 1Pe 4:5
10:43 [p] Isa 53:11 [q] Ac 15:9
10:44 [r] Ac 8:15,16; 11:15; 15:8
10:45 [s] ver 23 [t] Ac 2:33,38 [u] Ac 11:18
10:46 [v] Mk 16:17
10:47 [w] Ac 8:36 [x] Ac 11:17
10:48 [y] Ac 2:38; 8:16
11:1 [z] Ac 1:16
11:2 [a] Ac 10:45
11:3 [b] Ac 10:25,28; Gal 2:12
11:5 [c] Ac 10:9-32; 9:10

8"I replied, 'Surely not, Lord! Nothing impure or unclean has ever entered my mouth.'

9"The voice spoke from heaven a second time, 'Do not call anything impure that God has made clean.'[a] 10This happened three times, and then it was all pulled up to heaven again.

11"Right then three men who had been sent to me from Caesarea stopped at the house where I was staying. 12The Spirit told[b] me to have no hesitation about going with them.[c] These six brothers also went with me, and we entered the man's house. 13He told us how he had seen an angel appear in his house and say, 'Send to Joppa for Simon who is called Peter. 14He will bring you a message through which you and all your household[d] will be saved.'

15"As I began to speak, the Holy Spirit came on[e] them as he had come on us at the beginning.[f] 16Then I remembered what the Lord had said: 'John baptized with[a] water, but you will be baptized with the Holy Spirit.'[g] 17So if God gave them the same gift as he gave us,[h] who believed in the Lord Jesus Christ, who was I to think that I could oppose God?"

18When they heard this, they had no further objections and praised God, saying, "So then, God has granted even the Gentiles repentance unto life."[i]

19Now those who had been scattered by the persecution in connection with Stephen[j] traveled as far as Phoenicia, Cyprus and Antioch,[k] telling the message only to Jews. 20Some of them, however, men from Cyprus[l] and Cyrene,[m] went to Antioch and began to speak to Greeks also, telling them the good news about the Lord Jesus. 21The Lord's hand was with them,[n] and a great number of people believed and turned to the Lord.[o]

22News of this reached the ears of the church at Jerusalem, and they sent Barnabas[p] to Antioch. 23When he arrived and saw the evidence of the grace of God,[q] he was glad and encouraged them all to remain true to the Lord with all their hearts.[r] 24He was a good man, full of the Holy Spirit and faith, and a great number of people were brought to the Lord.[s]

25Then Barnabas went to Tarsus[t] to look for Saul, 26and when he found him, he brought him to Antioch. So for a whole year Barnabas and Saul met with the church and taught great numbers of people. The disciples[u] were called Christians first[v] at Antioch.

27During this time some prophets[w] came down from Jerusalem to Antioch. 28One of them, named Agabus,[x] stood up and through the Spirit predicted that a severe famine would spread over the entire Roman world.[y] (This happened during the reign of Claudius.)[z] 29The disciples,[a] each according to his ability, decided to

11:9 [a] Ac 10:15
11:12 [b] Ac 8:29 [c] Ac 15:9; Ro 3:22
11:14 [d] Jn 4:53; Ac 16:15,31-34; 1Co 1:11,16
11:15 [e] Ac 10:44 [f] Ac 2:4
11:16 [g] Mk 1:8; Ac 1:5
11:17 [h] Ac 10:45,47
11:18 [i] Ro 10:12,13; 2Co 7:10
11:19 [j] Ac 8:1,4 [k] ver 26,27; Ac 13:1; 18:22; Gal 2:11
11:20 [l] Ac 4:36 [m] Mt 27:32
11:21 [n] Lk 1:66 [o] Ac 2:47
11:22 [p] Ac 4:36
11:23 [q] Ac 13:43; 14:26; 20:24 11:23 [r] Ac 14:22
11:24 [s] ver 21; Ac 5:14
11:25 [t] Ac 9:11
11:26 [u] Ac 6:1,2; 13:52 [v] Ac 26:28; 1Pe 4:16
11:27 [w] Ac 13:1; 15:32; 1Co 12:28,29; Eph 4:11
11:28 [x] Ac 21:10 [y] Mt 24:14 [z] Ac 18:2
11:29 [a] ver 26

[a] *16* Or *in*

provide help[a] for the brothers[b] living in Judea. 30This they did, sending their gift to the elders[c] by Barnabas and Saul.[d]

Chapter 12 Theme ______________________

12 It was about this time that King Herod arrested some who belonged to the church, intending to persecute them. 2He had James, the brother of John,[e] put to death with the sword. 3When he saw that this pleased the Jews,[f] he proceeded to seize Peter also. This happened during the Feast of Unleavened Bread.[g] 4After arresting him, he put him in prison, handing him over to be guarded by four squads of four soldiers each. Herod intended to bring him out for public trial after the Passover.

5So Peter was kept in prison, but the church was earnestly praying to God for him.[h]

6The night before Herod was to bring him to trial, Peter was sleeping between two soldiers, bound with two chains,[i] and sentries stood guard at the entrance. 7Suddenly an angel[j] of the Lord appeared and a light shone in the cell. He struck Peter on the side and woke him up. "Quick, get up!" he said, and the chains fell off Peter's wrists.[k]

8Then the angel said to him, "Put on your clothes and sandals." And Peter did so. "Wrap your cloak around you and follow me," the angel told him. 9Peter followed him out of the prison, but he had no idea that what the angel was doing was really happening; he thought he was seeing a vision.[l] 10They passed the first and second guards and came to the iron gate leading to the city. It opened for them by itself,[m] and they went through it. When they had walked the length of one street, suddenly the angel left him.

11Then Peter came to himself[n] and said, "Now I know without a doubt that the Lord sent his angel and rescued me[o] from Herod's clutches and from everything the Jewish people were anticipating."

12When this had dawned on him, he went to the house of Mary the mother of John, also called Mark,[p] where many people had gathered and were praying.[q] 13Peter knocked at the outer entrance, and a servant girl named Rhoda came to answer the door.[r] 14When she recognized Peter's voice, she was so overjoyed[s] she ran back without opening it and exclaimed, "Peter is at the door!"

15"You're out of your mind," they told her. When she kept insisting that it was so, they said, "It must be his angel."[t]

16But Peter kept on knocking, and when they opened the door and saw him, they were astonished. 17Peter motioned with his hand[u] for them to be quiet and described how the Lord had brought him out of prison. "Tell James[v] and the brothers[w] about this," he said, and then he left for another place.

11:29 [a]Ro 15:26; 2Co 9:2 [b]Ac 1:16
11:30 [c]Ac 14:23 [d]Ac 12:25
12:2 [e]Mt 4:21
12:3 [f]Ac 24:27 [g]Ex 12:15; 23:15
12:5 [h]Eph 6:18
12:6 [i]Ac 21:33
12:7 [j]Ac 5:19 [k]Ac 16:26
12:9 [l]Ac 9:10
12:10 [m]Ac 5:19; 16:26
12:11 [n]Lk 15:17 [o]Ps 34:7; Da 3:28; 6:22; 2Co 1:10; 2Pe 2:9
12:12 [p]ver 25; Ac 15:37,39; Col 4:10; Phm 24; 1Pe 5:13 [q]ver 5
12:13 [r]Jn 18:16,17
12:14 [s]Lk 24:41
12:15 [t]Mt 18:10
12:17 [u]Ac 13:16; 19:33; 21:40 [v]Ac 15:13 [w]Ac 1:16

12:19 [a]Ac 16:27 [b]Ac 8:40
12:20 [c]Mt 11:21 [d]1Ki 5:9,11; Eze 27:17
12:23 [e]1Sa 25:38; 2Sa 24:16,17
12:24 [f]Ac 6:7; 19:20
12:25 [g]Ac 4:36 [h]Ac 11:30 [i]ver 12

18In the morning, there was no small commotion among the soldiers as to what had become of Peter. 19After Herod had a thorough
search made for him and did not find him, he cross-examined the
guards and ordered that they be executed.[a]
Then Herod went from Judea to Caesarea[b] and stayed there a
while. 20He had been quarreling with the people of Tyre and
Sidon;[c] they now joined together and sought an audience with
him. Having secured the support of Blastus, a trusted personal
servant of the king, they asked for peace, because they depended
on the king's country for their food supply.[d]
21On the appointed day Herod, wearing his royal robes, sat on
his throne and delivered a public address to the people. 22They
shouted, "This is the voice of a god, not of a man." 23Immediately,
because Herod did not give praise to God, an angel of the Lord
struck him down,[e] and he was eaten by worms and died.
24But the word of God continued to increase and spread.[f]
25When Barnabas[g] and Saul had finished their mission,[h] they
returned from[a] Jerusalem, taking with them John, also called
Mark.[i]

a 25 Some manuscripts *to*

Paul's First Missionary Journey (Acts 13–14)

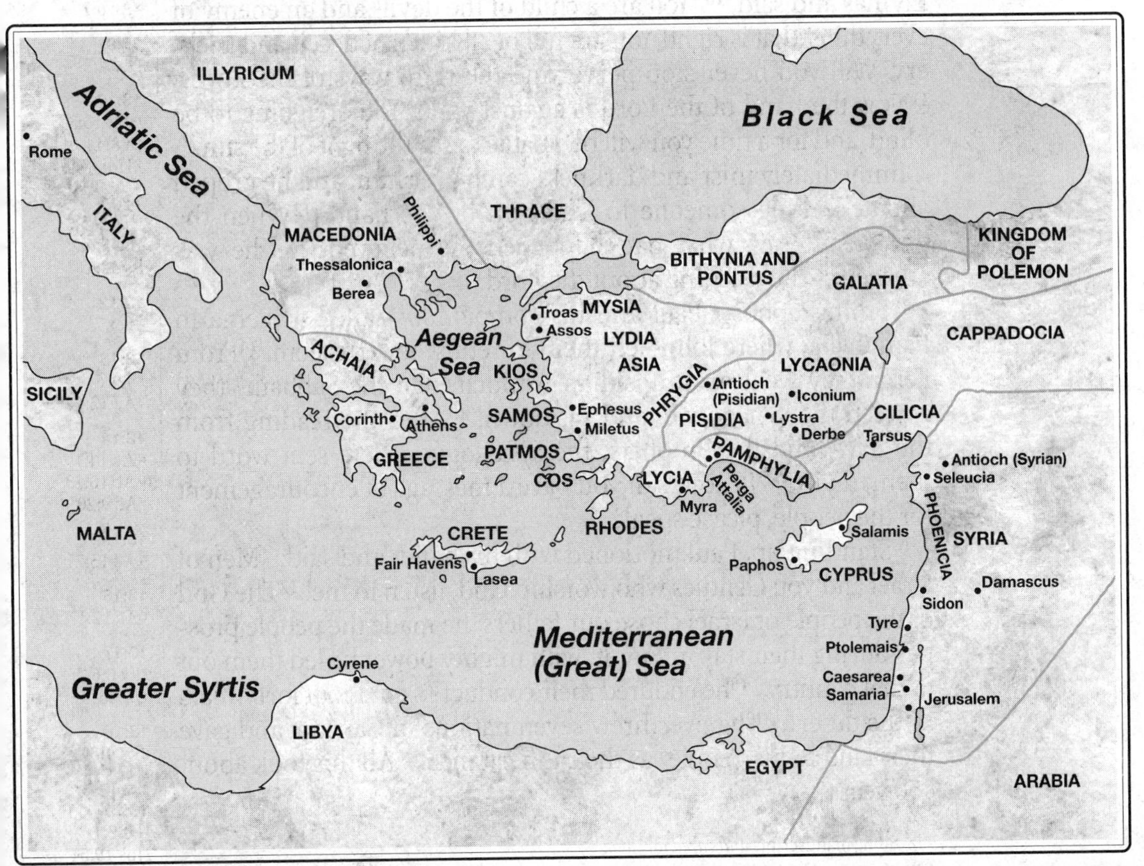

Chapter 13 Theme ________________

13 In the church at Antioch[a] there were prophets[b] and teachers:
Barnabas,[c] Simeon called Niger, Lucius of Cyrene, Manaen
(who had been brought up with Herod[d] the tetrarch) and Saul.
2While they were worshiping the Lord and fasting, the Holy Spirit
said,[e] "Set apart for me Barnabas and Saul for the work[f] to which
I have called them."[g] 3So after they had fasted and prayed, they
placed their hands on them[h] and sent them off.[i]
4The two of them, sent on their way by the Holy Spirit,[j] went
down to Seleucia and sailed from there to Cyprus.[k] 5When they
arrived at Salamis, they proclaimed the word of God in the Jewish
synagogues.[l] John[m] was with them as their helper.
6They traveled through the whole island until they came to
Paphos. There they met a Jewish sorcerer[n] and false prophet[o]
named Bar-Jesus, 7who was an attendant of the proconsul,[p] Sergius
Paulus. The proconsul, an intelligent man, sent for Barnabas and
Saul because he wanted to hear the word of God. 8But Elymas the
sorcerer[q] (for that is what his name means) opposed them and
tried to turn the proconsul[r] from the faith.[s] 9Then Saul, who was
also called Paul, filled with the Holy Spirit,[t] looked straight at
Elymas and said, 10"You are a child of the devil[u] and an enemy of
everything that is right! You are full of all kinds of deceit and trick-
ery. Will you never stop perverting the right ways of the Lord?[v]
11Now the hand of the Lord is against you.[w] You are going to be
blind, and for a time you will be unable to see the light of the sun."
Immediately mist and darkness came over him, and he groped
about, seeking someone to lead him by the hand. 12When the
proconsul[x] saw what had happened, he believed, for he was
amazed at the teaching about the Lord.
13From Paphos,[y] Paul and his companions sailed to Perga in
Pamphylia, where John[z] left them to return to Jerusalem. 14From
Perga they went on to Pisidian Antioch.[a] On the Sabbath[b] they
entered the synagogue[c] and sat down. 15After the reading from
the Law[d] and the Prophets, the synagogue rulers sent word to
them, saying, "Brothers, if you have a message of encouragement
for the people, please speak."
16Standing up, Paul motioned with his hand[e] and said: "Men of
Israel and you Gentiles who worship God, listen to me! 17The God
of the people of Israel chose our fathers; he made the people prosper during their stay in Egypt, with mighty power he led them out
of that country,[f] 18he endured their conduct[a][g] for about forty years
in the desert,[h] 19he overthrew seven nations in Canaan[i] and gave
their land to his people[j] as their inheritance. 20All this took about
450 years.

[a] 18 Some manuscripts *and cared for them*

13:1 [a] Ac 11:19 [b] Ac 11:27 [c] Ac 4:36; 11:22-26 [d] Mt 14:1
13:2 [e] Ac 8:29 [f] Ac 14:26 [g] Ac 22:21
13:3 [h] Ac 6:6 [i] Ac 14:26
13:4 [j] ver 2,3 [k] Ac 4:36
13:5 [l] Ac 9:20 [m] Ac 12:12
13:6 [n] Ac 8:9 [o] Mt 7:15
13:7 [p] ver 8,12; Ac 19:38
13:8 [q] Ac 8:9 [r] ver 7 [s] Ac 6:7
13:9 [t] Ac 4:8
13:10 [u] Mt 13:38; Jn 8:44 [v] Hos 14:9
13:11 [w] Ex 9:3; 1Sa 5:6,7; Ps 32:4
13:12 [x] ver 7
13:13 [y] ver 6 [z] Ac 12:12
13:14 [a] Ac 14:19,21 [b] Ac 16:13 [c] Ac 9:20
13:15 [d] Ac 15:21
13:16 [e] Ac 12:17
13:17 [f] Ex 6:6,7; Dt 7:6-8
13:18 [g] Dt 1:31 [h] Ac 7:36
13:19 [i] Dt 7:1 [j] Jos 19:51

"After this, God gave them judges[a] until the time of Samuel the prophet.[b] 21Then the people asked for a king,[c] and he gave them Saul[d] son of Kish, of the tribe of Benjamin,[e] who ruled forty years. 22After removing Saul,[f] he made David their king.[g] He testified concerning him: 'I have found David son of Jesse a man after my own heart;[h] he will do everything I want him to do.'

23"From this man's descendants[i] God has brought to Israel the Savior[j] Jesus,[k] as he promised.[l] 24Before the coming of Jesus, John preached repentance and baptism to all the people of Israel.[m] 25As John was completing his work,[n] he said: 'Who do you think I am? I am not that one.[o] No, but he is coming after me, whose sandals I am not worthy to untie.'[p]

26"Brothers, children of Abraham, and you God-fearing Gentiles, it is to us that this message of salvation[q] has been sent. 27The people of Jerusalem and their rulers did not recognize Jesus,[r] yet in condemning him they fulfilled the words of the prophets[s] that are read every Sabbath. 28Though they found no proper ground for a death sentence, they asked Pilate to have him executed.[t] 29When they had carried out all that was written about him,[u] they took him down from the tree[v] and laid him in a tomb.[w] 30But God raised him from the dead,[x] 31and for many days he was seen by those who had traveled with him from Galilee to Jerusalem.[y] They are now his witnesses[z] to our people.

32"We tell you the good news:[a] What God promised our fathers[b] 33he has fulfilled for us, their children, by raising up Jesus. As it is written in the second Psalm:

"'You are my Son;
today I have become your Father.[a]'[b][c]

34The fact that God raised him from the dead, never to decay, is stated in these words:

"'I will give you the holy and sure blessings promised
to David.'[c][d]

35So it is stated elsewhere:

"'You will not let your Holy One see decay.'[d][e]

36"For when David had served God's purpose in his own generation, he fell asleep; he was buried with his fathers[f] and his body decayed. 37But the one whom God raised from the dead did not see decay.

38"Therefore, my brothers, I want you to know that through Jesus the forgiveness of sins is proclaimed to you.[g] 39Through him

13:20 [a] Jdg 2:16 [b] 1Sa 3:19,20
13:21 [c] 1Sa 8:5,19 [d] 1Sa 10:1 [e] 1Sa 9:1,2
13:22 [f] 1Sa 15:23,26 [g] 1Sa 16:13; Ps 89:20 [h] 1Sa 13:14
13:23 [i] Mt 1:1 [j] Lk 2:11 [k] Mt 1:21 [l] ver 32
13:24 [m] Mk 1:4
13:25 [n] Ac 20:24 [o] Jn 1:20 [p] Mt 3:11; Jn 1:27
13:26 [q] Ac 4:12
13:27 [r] Ac 3:17 [s] Lk 24:27
13:28 [t] Mt 27:20-25; Ac 3:14
13:29 [u] Lk 18:31 [v] Ac 5:30 [w] Lk 23:53
13:30 [x] Mt 28:6; Ac 2:24
13:31 [y] Mt 28:16 [z] Lk 24:48
13:32 [a] Ac 5:42 [b] Ac 26:6; Ro 4:13
13:33 [c] Ps 2:7
13:34 [d] Isa 55:3
13:35 [e] Ps 16:10; Ac 2:27
13:36 [f] 1Ki 2:10; Ac 2:29
13:38 [g] Lk 24:47; Ac 2:38

[a] 33 Or *have begotten you* [b] 33 Psalm 2:7 [c] 34 Isaiah 55:3 [d] 35 Psalm 16:10

everyone who believes is justified from everything you could not
be justified from by the law of Moses.[a] 40Take care that what the
prophets have said does not happen to you:

> 41"'Look, you scoffers,
> wonder and perish,
> for I am going to do something in your days
> that you would never believe,
> even if someone told you.'[a]"[b]

42As Paul and Barnabas were leaving the synagogue,[c] the people
invited them to speak further about these things on the next Sabbath. 43When the congregation was dismissed, many of the Jews
and devout converts to Judaism followed Paul and Barnabas, who
talked with them and urged them to continue in the grace of God.[d]
44On the next Sabbath almost the whole city gathered to hear the
word of the Lord. 45When the Jews saw the crowds, they were filled
with jealousy and talked abusively[e] against what Paul was saying.[f]
46Then Paul and Barnabas answered them boldly: "We had to
speak the word of God to you first.[g] Since you reject it and do not
consider yourselves worthy of eternal life, we now turn to the
Gentiles.[h] 47For this is what the Lord has commanded us:

> "'I have made you[b] a light for the Gentiles,[i]
> that you[b] may bring salvation to the ends of
> the earth.'[c]"[j]

48When the Gentiles heard this, they were glad and honored the
word of the Lord; and all who were appointed for eternal life
believed.
49The word of the Lord spread through the whole region. 50But
the Jews incited the God-fearing women of high standing and the
leading men of the city. They stirred up persecution against Paul
and Barnabas, and expelled them from their region.[k] 51So they
shook the dust from their feet[l] in protest against them and went to
Iconium.[m] 52And the disciples were filled with joy and with the
Holy Spirit.

Chapter 14 Theme ______________________

14 At Iconium[n] Paul and Barnabas went as usual into the Jewish synagogue. There they spoke so effectively that a great
number of Jews and Gentiles believed. 2But the Jews who refused
to believe stirred up the Gentiles and poisoned their minds against
the brothers. 3So Paul and Barnabas spent considerable time there,
speaking boldly[o] for the Lord, who confirmed the message of his

13:39 [a] Ro 3:28
13:41 [b] Hab 1:5
13:42 [c] ver 14
13:43 [d] Ac 11:23; 14:22
13:45 [e] Ac 18:6; 1Pe 4:4; Jude 10 [f] 1Th 2:16
13:46 [g] ver 26; Ac 3:26 [h] Ac 18:6; 22:21; 28:28
13:47 [i] Lk 2:32 [j] Isa 49:6
13:50 [k] 1Th 2:16
13:51 [l] Mt 10:14; Ac 18:6 [m] Ac 14:1,19,21; 2Ti 3:11
14:1 [n] Ac 13:51
14:3 [o] Ac 4:29

[a] *41* Hab. 1:5 [b] *47* The Greek is singular. [c] *47* Isaiah 49:6

grace by enabling them to do miraculous signs and wonders.[a] 4The people of the city were divided; some sided with the Jews, others with the apostles.[b] 5There was a plot afoot among the Gentiles and Jews, together with their leaders, to mistreat them and stone them.[c] 6But they found out about it and fled[d] to the Lycaonian cities of Lystra and Derbe and to the surrounding country, 7where they continued to preach[e] the good news.[f]

8In Lystra there sat a man crippled in his feet, who was lame from birth[g] and had never walked. 9He listened to Paul as he was speaking. Paul looked directly at him, saw that he had faith to be healed[h] 10and called out, "Stand up on your feet!" At that, the man jumped up and began to walk.[i]

11When the crowd saw what Paul had done, they shouted in the Lycaonian language, "The gods have come down to us in human form!"[j] 12Barnabas they called Zeus, and Paul they called Hermes because he was the chief speaker. 13The priest of Zeus, whose temple was just outside the city, brought bulls and wreaths to the city gates because he and the crowd wanted to offer sacrifices to them.

14But when the apostles Barnabas and Paul heard of this, they tore their clothes[k] and rushed out into the crowd, shouting: 15"Men, why are you doing this? We too are only men,[l] human like you. We are bringing you good news,[m] telling you to turn from these worthless things[n] to the living God,[o] who made heaven and earth[p] and sea and everything in them.[q] 16In the past, he let[r] all nations go their own way.[s] 17Yet he has not left himself without testimony:[t] He has shown kindness by giving you rain from heaven and crops in their seasons;[u] he provides you with plenty of food and fills your hearts with joy." 18Even with these words, they had difficulty keeping the crowd from sacrificing to them.

19Then some Jews[v] came from Antioch and Iconium[w] and won the crowd over. They stoned Paul[x] and dragged him outside the city, thinking he was dead. 20But after the disciples[y] had gathered around him, he got up and went back into the city. The next day he and Barnabas left for Derbe.

21They preached the good news in that city and won a large number of disciples. Then they returned to Lystra, Iconium[z] and Antioch, 22strengthening the disciples and encouraging them to remain true to the faith.[a] "We must go through many hardships[b] to enter the kingdom of God," they said. 23Paul and Barnabas appointed elders[a][c] for them in each church and, with prayer and fasting,[d] committed them to the Lord,[e] in whom they had put their trust. 24After going through Pisidia, they came into Pamphylia,

14:3 [a] Jn 4:48; Heb 2:4
14:4 [b] Ac 17:4,5
14:5 [c] ver 19
14:6 [d] Mt 10:23
14:7 [e] Ac 16:10 [f] ver 15,21
14:8 [g] Ac 3:2
14:9 [h] Mt 9:28,29
14:10 [i] Ac 3:8
14:11 [j] Ac 8:10; 28:6
14:14 [k] Mk 14:63
14:15 [l] Ac 10:26; Jas 5:17 [m] ver 7,21; Ac 13:32 [n] 1Sa 12:21; 1Co 8:4; 1Th 1:9 [o] Mt 16:16 [p] Ge 1:1; Jer 14:22 [q] Ps 146:6; Rev 14:7
14:16 [r] Ac 17:30 [s] Ps 81:12; Mic 4:5
14:17 [t] Ac 17:27; Ro 1:20 [u] Dt 11:14; Job 5:10; Ps 65:10
14:19 [v] Ac 13:45 [w] Ac 13:51 [x] 2Co 11:25; 2Ti 3:11
14:20 [y] ver 22,28; Ac 11:26
14:21 [z] Ac 13:51
14:22 [a] Ac 11:23; 13:43 [b] Jn 16:33; 1Th 3:3; 2Ti 3:12
14:23 [c] Ac 11:30; Tit 1:5 [d] Ac 13:3 [e] Ac 20:32

[a] 23 Or *Barnabas ordained elders*; or *Barnabas had elders elected*

25 and when they had preached the word in Perga, they went down
to Attalia.
26 From Attalia they sailed back to Antioch,[a] where they had been
committed to the grace of God[b] for the work they had now completed.[c] 27 On arriving there, they gathered the church together
and reported all that God had done through them[d] and how he
had opened the door[e] of faith to the Gentiles. 28 And they stayed
there a long time with the disciples.

Chapter 15 Theme

15 Some men[f] came down from Judea to Antioch and were
teaching the brothers: "Unless you are circumcised,[g]
according to the custom taught by Moses,[h] you cannot be saved."
2 This brought Paul and Barnabas into sharp dispute and debate
with them. So Paul and Barnabas were appointed, along with some
other believers, to go up to Jerusalem[i] to see the apostles and
elders[j] about this question. 3 The church sent them on their way,
and as they traveled through Phoenicia and Samaria, they told
how the Gentiles had been converted.[k] This news made all the
brothers very glad. 4 When they came to Jerusalem, they were
welcomed by the church and the apostles and elders, to whom
they reported everything God had done through them.[l]
5 Then some of the believers who belonged to the party of the
Pharisees stood up and said, "The Gentiles must be circumcised
and required to obey the law of Moses."
6 The apostles and elders met to consider this question. 7 After
much discussion, Peter got up and addressed them: "Brothers, you
know that some time ago God made a choice among you that the
Gentiles might hear from my lips the message of the gospel and
believe. 8 God, who knows the heart,[m] showed that he accepted
them by giving the Holy Spirit to them,[n] just as he did to us. 9 He
made no distinction between us and them,[o] for he purified their
hearts by faith.[p] 10 Now then, why do you try to test God by
putting on the necks of the disciples a yoke[q] that neither we nor
our fathers have been able to bear? 11 No! We believe it is through
the grace[r] of our Lord Jesus that we are saved, just as they are."
12 The whole assembly became silent as they listened to Barnabas
and Paul telling about the miraculous signs and wonders[s] God had
done among the Gentiles through them.[t] 13 When they finished,
James[u] spoke up: "Brothers, listen to me. 14 Simon[a] has described
to us how God at first showed his concern by taking from the
Gentiles a people for himself. 15 The words of the prophets are in
agreement with this, as it is written:

14:26 [a] Ac 11:19 [b] Ac 15:40 [c] Ac 13:1,3
14:27 [d] Ac 15:4,12; 21:19 [e] 1Co 16:9; 2Co 2:12; Col 4:3; Rev 3:8
15:1 [f] ver 24; Gal 2:12 [g] ver 5; Gal 5:2,3 [h] Ac 6:14
15:2 [i] Gal 2:2 [j] Ac 11:30
15:3 [k] Ac 14:27
15:4 [l] ver 12; Ac 14:27
15:8 [m] Ac 1:24 [n] Ac 10:44,47
15:9 [o] Ac 10:28,34; 11:12 [p] Ac 10:43
15:10 [q] Mt 23:4; Gal 5:1
15:11 [r] Ro 3:24; Eph 2:5-8
15:12 [s] Jn 4:48 [t] Ac 14:27
15:13 [u] Ac 12:17

a *14* Greek *Simeon*, a variant of *Simon*; that is, Peter

16"'After this I will return
and rebuild David's fallen tent.
Its ruins I will rebuild,
and I will restore it,
17that the remnant of men may seek the Lord,
and all the Gentiles who bear my name,
says the Lord, who does these things'[a][a]
18 that have been known for ages.[b]

19"It is my judgment, therefore, that we should not make it difficult for the Gentiles who are turning to God. 20Instead we should
write to them, telling them to abstain from food polluted by idols,[b]
from sexual immorality,[c] from the meat of strangled animals and
from blood.[d] 21For Moses has been preached in every city from the
earliest times and is read in the synagogues on every Sabbath."[e]
22Then the apostles and elders, with the whole church, decided
to choose some of their own men and send them to Antioch with
Paul and Barnabas. They chose Judas (called Barsabbas) and
Silas,[f] two men who were leaders among the brothers. 23With
them they sent the following letter:

The apostles and elders, your brothers,

To the Gentile believers in Antioch,[g] Syria and Cilicia:[h]

Greetings.[i]

24We have heard that some went out from us without our
authorization and disturbed you, troubling your minds by
what they said.[j] 25So we all agreed to choose some men and
send them to you with our dear friends Barnabas and Paul—
26men who have risked their lives[k] for the name of our Lord
Jesus Christ. 27Therefore we are sending Judas and Silas to confirm by word of mouth what we are writing. 28It seemed good
to the Holy Spirit[l] and to us not to burden you with anything
beyond the following requirements: 29You are to abstain from
food sacrificed to idols, from blood, from the meat of strangled animals and from sexual immorality.[m] You will do well
to avoid these things.

Farewell.

30The men were sent off and went down to Antioch, where they
gathered the church together and delivered the letter. 31The people
read it and were glad for its encouraging message. 32Judas and
Silas, who themselves were prophets, said much to encourage and
strengthen the brothers. 33After spending some time there, they
were sent off by the brothers with the blessing of peace[n] to return

15:17 [a]Am 9:11,12
15:20 [b]1Co 8:7-13; 10:14-28; Rev 2:14,20 [c]1Co 10:7,8 [d]ver 29; Ge 9:4; Lev 3:17; Dt 12:16,23
15:21 [e]Ac 13:15; 2Co 3:14,15
15:22 [f]ver 27,32,40
15:23 [g]ver 1 [h]ver 41 [i]Ac 23:25,26; Jas 1:1
15:24 [j]ver 1; Gal 1:7; 5:10
15:26 [k]Ac 9:23-25; 14:19
15:28 [l]Ac 5:32
15:29 [m]ver 20; Ac 21:25
15:33 [n]Mk 5:34; Ac 16:36; 1Co 16:11

[a] *17* Amos 9:11,12 [b] *17,18* Some manuscripts *things'— / 18 known to the Lord for ages is his work*

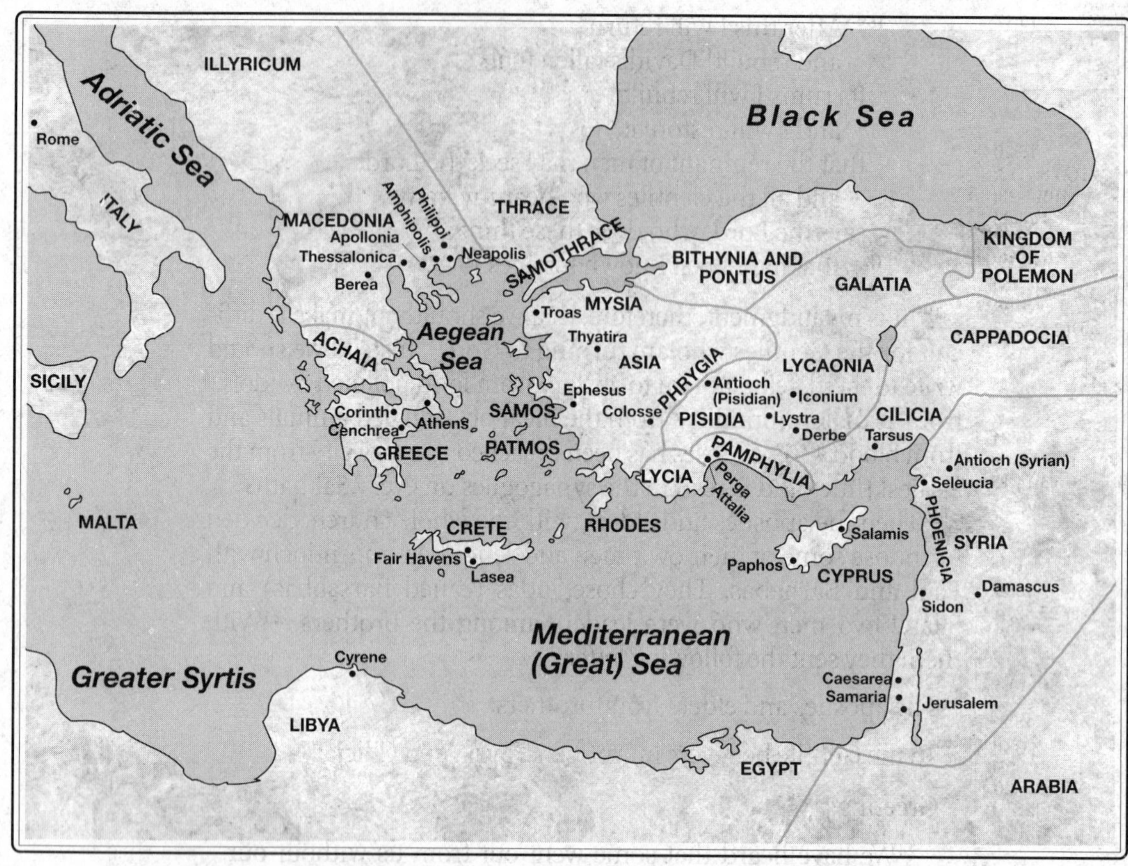

Paul's Second Missionary Journey (Acts 15:36–18:22)

to those who had sent them.[a] 35But Paul and Barnabas remained in
Antioch, where they and many others taught and preached[a] the
word of the Lord.
36Some time later Paul said to Barnabas, "Let us go back and
visit the brothers in all the towns[b] where we preached the word of
the Lord and see how they are doing." 37Barnabas wanted to take
John, also called Mark,[c] with them, 38but Paul did not think it wise
to take him, because he had deserted them[d] in Pamphylia and had
not continued with them in the work. 39They had such a sharp
disagreement that they parted company. Barnabas took Mark
and sailed for Cyprus, 40but Paul chose Silas[e] and left, commended
by the brothers to the grace of the Lord.[f] 41He went through Syria[g]
and Cilicia,[h] strengthening the churches.[i]

Chapter 16 Theme ______________________

16 He came to Derbe and then to Lystra,[j] where a disciple
named Timothy[k] lived, whose mother was a Jewess and a
believer, but whose father was a Greek. 2The brothers[l] at Lystra

a 33 Some manuscripts *them,* 34*but Silas decided to remain there*

15:35 [a] Ac 8:4
15:36 [b] Ac 13:4,13, 14,51; 14:1,6,24,25
15:37 [c] Ac 12:12
15:38 [d] Ac 13:13
15:40 [e] ver 22 [f] Ac 11:23
15:41 [g] ver 23 [h] Ac 6:9 [i] Ac 16:5
16:1 [j] Ac 14:6 [k] Ac 17:14; 18:5; 19:22; Ro 16:21; 1Co 4:17; 2Co 1:1,19; 1Th 3:2,6; 1Ti 1:2,18; 2Ti 1:2,5,6
16:2 [l] ver 40

and Iconium[a] spoke well of him. 3Paul wanted to take him along
on the journey, so he circumcised him because of the Jews who
lived in that area, for they all knew that his father was a Greek.[b]
4As they traveled from town to town, they delivered the decisions
reached by the apostles and elders[c] in Jerusalem[d] for the people to
obey.[e] 5So the churches were strengthened[f] in the faith and grew
daily in numbers.

6Paul and his companions traveled throughout the region of
Phrygia[g] and Galatia,[h] having been kept by the Holy Spirit from
preaching the word in the province of Asia.[i] 7When they came to
the border of Mysia, they tried to enter Bithynia, but the Spirit of
Jesus[j] would not allow them to. 8So they passed by Mysia and went
down to Troas.[k] 9During the night Paul had a vision[l] of a man of
Macedonia[m] standing and begging him, "Come over to Macedonia
and help us." 10After Paul had seen the vision, we[n] got ready at
once to leave for Macedonia, concluding that God had called us to
preach the gospel[o] to them.

11From Troas[p] we put out to sea and sailed straight for Samo-
thrace, and the next day on to Neapolis. 12From there we traveled
to Philippi,[q] a Roman colony and the leading city of that district
of Macedonia.[r] And we stayed there several days.

13On the Sabbath[s] we went outside the city gate to the river,
where we expected to find a place of prayer. We sat down and
began to speak to the women who had gathered there. 14One of
those listening was a woman named Lydia, a dealer in purple cloth
from the city of Thyatira,[t] who was a worshiper of God. The Lord
opened her heart[u] to respond to Paul's message. 15When she and
the members of her household[v] were baptized, she invited us to
her home. "If you consider me a believer in the Lord," she said,
"come and stay at my house." And she persuaded us.

16Once when we were going to the place of prayer,[w] we were met
by a slave girl who had a spirit[x] by which she predicted the future.
She earned a great deal of money for her owners by fortune-telling.
17This girl followed Paul and the rest of us, shouting, "These men
are servants of the Most High God,[y] who are telling you the way to
be saved." 18She kept this up for many days. Finally Paul became so
troubled that he turned around and said to the spirit, "In the name
of Jesus Christ I command you to come out of her!" At that
moment the spirit left her.[z]

19When the owners of the slave girl realized that their hope of
making money[a] was gone, they seized Paul and Silas[b] and
dragged[c] them into the marketplace to face the authorities. 20They
brought them before the magistrates and said, "These men are
Jews, and are throwing our city into an uproar[d] 21by advocating
customs unlawful for us Romans[e] to accept or practice."[f]

16:2 [a] Ac 13:51
16:3 [b] Gal 2:3
16:4 [c] Ac 11:30 [d] Ac 15:2 [e] Ac 15:28,29
16:5 [f] Ac 9:31; 15:41
16:6 [g] Ac 18:23 [h] Ac 18:23; Gal 1:2; 3:1 [i] Ac 2:9
16:7 [j] Ro 8:9; Gal 4:6
16:8 [k] ver 11; 2Co 2:12; 2Ti 4:13
16:9 [l] Ac 9:10 [m] Ac 20:1,3
16:10 [n] ver 10-17 [o] Ac 14:7
16:11 [p] ver 8
16:12 [q] Ac 20:6; Php 1:1; 1Th 2:2 [r] ver 9
16:13 [s] Ac 13:14
16:14 [t] Rev 1:11 [u] Lk 24:45
16:15 [v] Ac 11:14
16:16 [w] ver 13 [x] Dt 18:11; 1Sa 28:3,7
16:17 [y] Mk 5:7
16:18 [z] Mk 16:17
16:19 [a] ver 16; Ac 19:25,26 [b] Ac 15:22 [c] Ac 8:3; 17:6; 21:30; Jas 2:6
16:20 [d] Ac 17:6
16:21 [e] ver 12 [f] Est 3:8

22The crowd joined in the attack against Paul and Silas, and the
magistrates ordered them to be stripped and beaten.[a] 23After they
had been severely flogged, they were thrown into prison, and the
jailer[b] was commanded to guard them carefully. 24Upon receiving
such orders, he put them in the inner cell and fastened their feet in
the stocks.[c]

25About midnight Paul and Silas were praying and singing
hymns[d] to God, and the other prisoners were listening to them.
26Suddenly there was such a violent earthquake that the foundations of the prison were shaken.[e] At once all the prison doors flew
open,[f] and everybody's chains came loose.[g] 27The jailer woke up,
and when he saw the prison doors open, he drew his sword and
was about to kill himself because he thought the prisoners had
escaped.[h] 28But Paul shouted, "Don't harm yourself! We are all
here!"

29The jailer called for lights, rushed in and fell trembling before
Paul and Silas. 30He then brought them out and asked, "Sirs, what
must I do to be saved?"[i]

31They replied, "Believe in the Lord Jesus, and you will be
saved—you and your household."[j] 32Then they spoke the word of
the Lord to him and to all the others in his house. 33At that hour
of the night[k] the jailer took them and washed their wounds; then
immediately he and all his family were baptized. 34The jailer
brought them into his house and set a meal before them; he[l] was
filled with joy because he had come to believe in God—he and
his whole family.

35When it was daylight, the magistrates sent their officers to the
jailer with the order: "Release those men." 36The jailer[m] told Paul,
"The magistrates have ordered that you and Silas be released. Now
you can leave. Go in peace."[n]

37But Paul said to the officers: "They beat us publicly without a
trial, even though we are Roman citizens,[o] and threw us into
prison. And now do they want to get rid of us quietly? No! Let
them come themselves and escort us out."

38The officers reported this to the magistrates, and when they
heard that Paul and Silas were Roman citizens, they were alarmed.[p]
39They came to appease them and escorted them from the prison,
requesting them to leave the city.[q] 40After Paul and Silas came out
of the prison, they went to Lydia's house,[r] where they met with the
brothers[s] and encouraged them. Then they left.

Chapter 17 Theme

17 When they had passed through Amphipolis and Apollonia, they came to Thessalonica,[t] where there was a Jewish
synagogue. 2As his custom was, Paul went into the synagogue,[u]

16:22 [a] 2Co 11:25; 1Th 2:2
16:23 [b] ver 27,36
16:24 [c] Job 13:27; 33:11; Jer 20:2,3; 29:26
16:25 [d] Eph 5:19
16:26 [e] Ac 4:31 [f] Ac 12:10 [g] Ac 12:7
16:27 [h] Ac 12:19
16:30 [i] Ac 2:37
16:31 [j] Ac 11:14
16:33 [k] ver 25
16:34 [l] Ac 11:14
16:36 [m] ver 23,27 [n] Ac 15:33
16:37 [o] Ac 22:25-29
16:38 [p] Ac 22:29
16:39 [q] Mt 8:34
16:40 [r] ver 14 [s] ver 2; Ac 1:16
17:1 [t] ver 11,13; Php 4:16; 1Th 1:1; 2Th 1:1; 2Ti 4:10
17:2 [u] Ac 9:20

and on three Sabbath[a] days he reasoned with them from the Scriptures,[b] 3explaining and proving that the Christ[a] had to suffer[c] and
rise from the dead.[d] "This Jesus I am proclaiming to you is the
Christ,[a]"[e] he said. 4Some of the Jews were persuaded and joined
Paul and Silas,[f] as did a large number of God-fearing Greeks and
not a few prominent women.

5But the Jews were jealous; so they rounded up some bad characters from the marketplace, formed a mob and started a riot in the
city.[g] They rushed to Jason's[h] house in search of Paul and Silas in
order to bring them out to the crowd.[b] 6But when they did not find
them, they dragged[i] Jason and some other brothers before the
city officials, shouting: "These men who have caused trouble all
over the world[j] have now come here,[k] 7and Jason has welcomed
them into his house. They are all defying Caesar's decrees, saying
that there is another king, one called Jesus."[l] 8When they heard
this, the crowd and the city officials were thrown into turmoil.
9Then they made Jason[m] and the others post bond and let them go.

10As soon as it was night, the brothers sent Paul and Silas away to
Berea.[n] On arriving there, they went to the Jewish synagogue.
11Now the Bereans were of more noble character than the Thessalonians,[o] for they received the message with great eagerness and
examined the Scriptures[p] every day to see if what Paul said was
true. 12Many of the Jews believed, as did also a number of prominent Greek women and many Greek men.

13When the Jews in Thessalonica learned that Paul was preaching the word of God at Berea, they went there too, agitating the
crowds and stirring them up. 14The brothers immediately sent Paul
to the coast, but Silas[q] and Timothy[r] stayed at Berea. 15The men
who escorted Paul brought him to Athens[s] and then left with
instructions for Silas and Timothy to join him as soon as possible.[t]

16While Paul was waiting for them in Athens, he was greatly
distressed to see that the city was full of idols. 17So he reasoned in
the synagogue[u] with the Jews and the God-fearing Greeks, as well
as in the marketplace day by day with those who happened to be
there. 18A group of Epicurean and Stoic philosophers began to
dispute with him. Some of them asked, "What is this babbler trying to say?" Others remarked, "He seems to be advocating foreign
gods." They said this because Paul was preaching the good news
about Jesus and the resurrection.[v] 19Then they took him and
brought him to a meeting of the Areopagus,[w] where they said to
him, "May we know what this new teaching[x] is that you are presenting? 20You are bringing some strange ideas to our ears, and
we want to know what they mean." 21(All the Athenians and the

17:2 [a] Ac 13:14 [b] Ac 8:35
17:3 [c] Lk 24:26; Ac 3:18 [d] Lk 24:46 [e] Ac 9:22; 18:28
17:4 [f] Ac 15:22
17:5 [g] ver 13; 1Th 2:16 [h] Ro 16:21
17:6 [i] Ac 16:19 [j] Mt 24:14 [k] Ac 16:20
17:7 [l] Lk 23:2; Jn 19:12
17:9 [m] ver 5
17:10 [n] ver 13; Ac 20:4
17:11 [o] ver 1 [p] Lk 16:29; Jn 5:39
17:14 [q] Ac 15:22 [r] Ac 16:1
17:15 [s] ver 16,21,22; Ac 18:1; 1Th 3:1 [t] Ac 18:5
17:17 [u] Ac 9:20
17:18 [v] ver 31,32; Ac 4:2
17:19 [w] ver 22 [x] Mk 1:27

a3 Or *Messiah* b5 Or *the assembly of the people*

foreigners who lived there spent their time doing nothing but
talking about and listening to the latest ideas.)

22Paul then stood up in the meeting of the Areopagus and said:
"Men of Athens! I see that in every way you are very religious.
23For as I walked around and looked carefully at your objects of
worship, I even found an altar with this inscription: TO AN UNKNOWN
GOD. Now what you worship as something unknown[a] I am going to
proclaim to you.

24"The God who made the world and everything in it[b] is the
Lord of heaven and earth[c] and does not live in temples built by
hands.[d] 25And he is not served by human hands, as if he needed
anything, because he himself gives all men life and breath and
everything else.[e] 26From one man he made every nation of men,
that they should inhabit the whole earth; and he determined the
times set for them and the exact places where they should live.[f]
27God did this so that men would seek him and perhaps reach out
for him and find him, though he is not far from each one of us.[g]
28'For in him we live and move and have our being.'[h] As some of
your own poets have said, 'We are his offspring.'

29"Therefore since we are God's offspring, we should not think
that the divine being is like gold or silver or stone—an image
made by man's design and skill.[i] 30In the past God overlooked[j]
such ignorance,[k] but now he commands all people everywhere to
repent.[l] 31For he has set a day when he will judge[m] the world with
justice[n] by the man he has appointed.[o] He has given proof of this
to all men by raising him from the dead."[p]

32When they heard about the resurrection of the dead,[q] some of
them sneered, but others said, "We want to hear you again on this
subject." 33At that, Paul left the Council. 34A few men became followers of Paul and believed. Among them was Dionysius, a member of the Areopagus,[r] also a woman named Damaris, and a
number of others.

Chapter 18 Theme

18 After this, Paul left Athens[s] and went to Corinth.[t] 2There he
met a Jew named Aquila, a native of Pontus, who had
recently come from Italy with his wife Priscilla,[u] because Claudius[v]
had ordered all the Jews to leave Rome. Paul went to see them, 3and
because he was a tentmaker as they were, he stayed and worked
with them.[w] 4Every Sabbath[x] he reasoned in the synagogue, trying
to persuade Jews and Greeks.

5When Silas[y] and Timothy[z] came from Macedonia,[a] Paul devoted
himself exclusively to preaching, testifying to the Jews that Jesus
was the Christ.[a][b] 6But when the Jews opposed Paul and became

[a]5 Or *Messiah;* also in verse 28

17:23
[a] Jn 4:22
17:24
[b] Isa 42:5; Ac 14:15
[c] Dt 10:14; Mt 11:25
[d] Ac 7:48
17:25
[e] Ps 50:10-12; Isa 42:5
17:26
[f] Dt 32:8; Job 12:23
17:27
[g] Dt 4:7; Jer 23:23,24; Ac 14:17
17:28
[h] Job 12:10; Da 5:23
17:29
[i] Isa 40:18-20; Ro 1:23
17:30
[j] Ac 14:16; Ro 3:25
[k] ver 23; 1Pe 1:14
[l] Lk 24:47; Tit 2:11,12
17:31
[m] Mt 10:15
[n] Ps 9:8; 96:13; 98:9
[o] Ac 10:42
[p] Ac 2:24
17:32
[q] ver 18,31
17:34
[r] ver 19,22
18:1
[s] Ac 17:15
[t] Ac 19:1; 1Co 1:2; 2Co 1:1,23; 2Ti 4:20
18:2
[u] Ro 16:3; 1Co 16:19; 2Ti 4:19
[v] Ac 11:28
18:3
[w] Ac 20:34; 1Co 4:12; 1Th 2:9; 2Th 3:8
18:4
[x] Ac 13:14
18:5
[y] Ac 15:22
[z] Ac 16:1
[a] Ac 16:9; 17:14,15
[b] ver 28; Ac 17:3

abusive,[a] he shook out his clothes in protest and said to them,
"Your blood be on your own heads![b] I am clear of my responsibility.[c] From now on I will go to the Gentiles."[d]
7 Then Paul left the synagogue and went next door to the house
of Titius Justus, a worshiper of God.[e] 8 Crispus,[f] the synagogue
ruler,[g] and his entire household[h] believed in the Lord; and many
of the Corinthians who heard him believed and were baptized.
9 One night the Lord spoke to Paul in a vision: "Do not be afraid;
keep on speaking, do not be silent. 10 For I am with you,[i] and no
one is going to attack and harm you, because I have many people
in this city." 11 So Paul stayed for a year and a half, teaching them
the word of God.
12 While Gallio was proconsul of Achaia,[j] the Jews made a united
attack on Paul and brought him into court. 13 "This man," they
charged, "is persuading the people to worship God in ways contrary to the law."
14 Just as Paul was about to speak, Gallio said to the Jews, "If you
Jews were making a complaint about some misdemeanor or serious crime, it would be reasonable for me to listen to you. 15 But
since it involves questions about words and names and your own
law[k]—settle the matter yourselves. I will not be a judge of such
things." 16 So he had them ejected from the court. 17 Then they all
turned on Sosthenes[l] the synagogue ruler and beat him in front
of the court. But Gallio showed no concern whatever.
18 Paul stayed on in Corinth for some time. Then he left the
brothers[m] and sailed for Syria, accompanied by Priscilla and
Aquila. Before he sailed, he had his hair cut off at Cenchrea[n]
because of a vow he had taken.[o] 19 They arrived at Ephesus,[p] where
Paul left Priscilla and Aquila. He himself went into the synagogue
and reasoned with the Jews. 20 When they asked him to spend more
time with them, he declined. 21 But as he left, he promised, "I will
come back if it is God's will."[q] Then he set sail from Ephesus.
22 When he landed at Caesarea,[r] he went up and greeted the
church and then went down to Antioch.[s]
23 After spending some time in Antioch, Paul set out from there
and traveled from place to place throughout the region of Galatia[t]
and Phrygia, strengthening all the disciples.[u]
24 Meanwhile a Jew named Apollos,[v] a native of Alexandria, came
to Ephesus. He was a learned man, with a thorough knowledge of
the Scriptures. 25 He had been instructed in the way of the Lord,
and he spoke with great fervor[a][w] and taught about Jesus accurately,
though he knew only the baptism of John.[x] 26 He began to speak

a 25 Or *with fervor in the Spirit*

18:6 [a] Ac 13:45 [b] 2Sa 1:16; Eze 18:13; 33:4 [c] Ac 20:26 [d] Ac 13:46
18:7 [e] Ac 16:14
18:8 [f] 1Co 1:14 [g] Mk 5:22 [h] Ac 11:14
18:10 [i] Mt 28:20
18:12 [j] ver 27
18:15 [k] Ac 23:29; 25:11,19
18:17 [l] 1Co 1:1
18:18 [m] Ac 1:16 [n] Ro 16:1 [o] Nu 6:2,5,18; Ac 21:24
18:19 [p] ver 21,24; 1Co 15:32
18:21 [q] Ro 1:10; 1Co 4:19; Jas 4:15
18:22 [r] Ac 8:40 [s] Ac 11:19
18:23 [t] Ac 16:6 [u] Ac 14:22; 15:32,41
18:24 [v] Ac 19:1; 1Co 1:12; 3:5,6,22; 4:6; 16:12; Tit 3:13
18:25 [w] Ro 12:11 [x] Ac 19:3

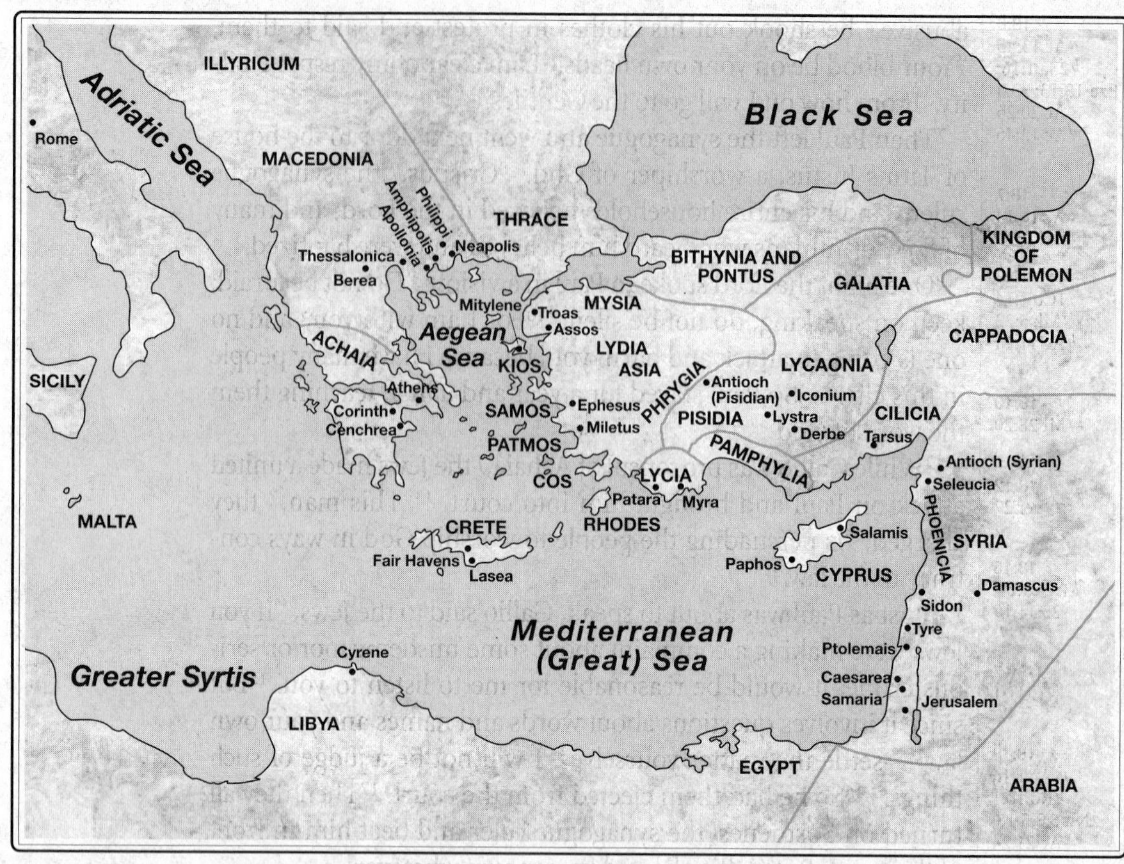

Paul's Third Missionary Journey (Acts 18:23–21:17)

boldly in the synagogue. When Priscilla and Aquila heard him,
they invited him to their home and explained to him the way of
God more adequately.
[27]When Apollos wanted to go to Achaia,[a] the brothers[b] encouraged him and wrote to the disciples there to welcome him. On
arriving, he was a great help to those who by grace had believed.
[28]For he vigorously refuted the Jews in public debate, proving
from the Scriptures[c] that Jesus was the Christ.[d]

Chapter 19 Theme __________________________

19 While Apollos was at Corinth,[e] Paul took the road through
the interior and arrived at Ephesus.[f] There he found some
disciples [2]and asked them, "Did you receive the Holy Spirit when[a]
you believed?"

They answered, "No, we have not even heard that there is a Holy
Spirit."

[3]So Paul asked, "Then what baptism did you receive?"

"John's baptism," they replied.

18:27 [a]ver 12 [b]ver 18

18:28 [c]Ac 17:2 [d]ver 5; Ac 9:22

19:1 [e]Ac 18:1 [f]Ac 18:19

[a]2 Or *after*

4Paul said, "John's baptism was a baptism of repentance. He told
the people to believe in the one coming after him, that is, in
Jesus."[a] 5On hearing this, they were baptized into[a] the name of the
Lord Jesus. 6When Paul placed his hands on them,[b] the Holy Spirit
came on them,[c] and they spoke in tongues[b][d] and prophesied.
7There were about twelve men in all.

8Paul entered the synagogue[e] and spoke boldly there for three
months, arguing persuasively about the kingdom of God.[f] 9But
some of them[g] became obstinate; they refused to believe and publicly maligned the Way.[h] So Paul left them. He took the disciples[i]
with him and had discussions daily in the lecture hall of Tyrannus.
10This went on for two years,[j] so that all the Jews and Greeks who
lived in the province of Asia[k] heard the word of the Lord.

11God did extraordinary miracles[l] through Paul, 12so that even
handkerchiefs and aprons that had touched him were taken to the
sick, and their illnesses were cured[m] and the evil spirits left them.
13Some Jews who went around driving out evil spirits[n] tried to
invoke the name of the Lord Jesus over those who were demon-
possessed. They would say, "In the name of Jesus,[o] whom Paul
preaches, I command you to come out." 14Seven sons of Sceva, a
Jewish chief priest, were doing this. 15⌊One day⌋ the evil spirit
answered them, "Jesus I know, and I know about Paul, but who are
you?" 16Then the man who had the evil spirit jumped on them and
overpowered them all. He gave them such a beating that they ran
out of the house naked and bleeding.

17When this became known to the Jews and Greeks living in
Ephesus,[p] they were all seized with fear,[q] and the name of the Lord
Jesus was held in high honor. 18Many of those who believed now
came and openly confessed their evil deeds. 19A number who had
practiced sorcery brought their scrolls together and burned them
publicly. When they calculated the value of the scrolls, the total
came to fifty thousand drachmas.[c] 20In this way the word of the
Lord spread widely and grew in power.[r]

21After all this had happened, Paul decided to go to Jerusalem,[s]
passing through Macedonia[t] and Achaia.[u] "After I have been
there," he said, "I must visit Rome also."[v] 22He sent two of his
helpers,[w] Timothy[x] and Erastus,[y] to Macedonia, while he stayed in
the province of Asia[z] a little longer.

23About that time there arose a great disturbance about the Way.[a]
24A silversmith named Demetrius, who made silver shrines of
Artemis, brought in no little business for the craftsmen. 25He
called them together, along with the workmen in related trades,
and said: "Men, you know we receive a good income from this

19:4 [a]Jn 1:7; Ac 13:24,25
19:6 [b]Ac 6:6; 8:17 [c]Ac 2:4 [d]Mk 16:17; Ac 10:46
19:8 [e]Ac 9:20 [f]Ac 1:3; 28:23
19:9 [g]Ac 14:4 [h]ver 23; Ac 9:2 [i]ver 30; Ac 11:26
19:10 [j]Ac 20:31 [k]ver 22,26,27
19:11 [l]Ac 8:13
19:12 [m]Ac 5:15
19:13 [n]Mt 12:27 [o]Mk 9:38
19:17 [p]Ac 18:19 [q]Ac 5:5,11
19:20 [r]Ac 6:7; 12:24
19:21 [s]Ac 20:16,22; Ro 15:25 [t]Ac 16:9 [u]Ac 18:12 [v]Ro 15:24,28
19:22 [w]Ac 13:5 [x]Ac 16:1 [y]Ro 16:23; 2Ti 4:20 [z]ver 10,26,27
19:23 [a]Ac 9:2

a5 Or *in* b6 Or *other languages* c19 A drachma was a silver coin worth about a day's wages.

business.[a] 26And you see and hear how this fellow Paul has convinced and led astray large numbers of people here in Ephesus[b] and in practically the whole province of Asia. He says that man-made gods are no gods at all.[c] 27There is danger not only that our trade will lose its good name, but also that the temple of the great goddess Artemis will be discredited, and the goddess herself, who is worshiped throughout the province of Asia and the world, will be robbed of her divine majesty."

28When they heard this, they were furious and began shouting: "Great is Artemis of the Ephesians!"[d] 29Soon the whole city was in an uproar. The people seized Gaius[e] and Aristarchus,[f] Paul's traveling companions from Macedonia,[g] and rushed as one man into the theater. 30Paul wanted to appear before the crowd, but the disciples would not let him. 31Even some of the officials of the province, friends of Paul, sent him a message begging him not to venture into the theater.

32The assembly was in confusion: Some were shouting one thing, some another.[h] Most of the people did not even know why they were there. 33The Jews pushed Alexander to the front, and some of the crowd shouted instructions to him. He motioned[i] for silence in order to make a defense before the people. 34But when they realized he was a Jew, they all shouted in unison for about two hours: "Great is Artemis of the Ephesians!"

35The city clerk quieted the crowd and said: "Men of Ephesus,[j] doesn't all the world know that the city of Ephesus is the guardian of the temple of the great Artemis and of her image, which fell from heaven? 36Therefore, since these facts are undeniable, you ought to be quiet and not do anything rash. 37You have brought these men here, though they have neither robbed temples[k] nor blasphemed our goddess. 38If, then, Demetrius and his fellow craftsmen have a grievance against anybody, the courts are open and there are proconsuls.[l] They can press charges. 39If there is anything further you want to bring up, it must be settled in a legal assembly. 40As it is, we are in danger of being charged with rioting because of today's events. In that case we would not be able to account for this commotion, since there is no reason for it." 41After he had said this, he dismissed the assembly.

Chapter 20 Theme ______________________

20 When the uproar had ended, Paul sent for the disciples[m] and, after encouraging them, said good-by and set out for Macedonia.[n] 2He traveled through that area, speaking many words of encouragement to the people, and finally arrived in Greece, 3where he stayed three months. Because the Jews made a plot against him[o] just as he was about to sail for Syria, he decided to go

19:25 [a] Ac 16:16, 19,20

19:26 [b] Ac 18:19 [c] Dt 4:28; Ps 115:4; Isa 44:10-20; Jer 10:3-5; Ac 17:29; 1Co 8:4; Rev 9:20

19:28 [d] Ac 18:19

19:29 [e] Ac 20:4; Ro 16:23; 1Co 1:14 [f] Ac 20:4; 27:2; Col 4:10; Phm 24 [g] Ac 16:9

19:32 [h] Ac 21:34

19:33 [i] Ac 12:17

19:35 [j] Ac 18:19

19:37 [k] Ro 2:22

19:38 [l] Ac 13:7,8,12

20:1 [m] Ac 11:26 [n] Ac 16:9

20:3 [o] ver 19; Ac 9:23,24; 23:12,15,30; 25:3; 2Co 11:26

back through Macedonia.[a] 4He was accompanied by Sopater son
of Pyrrhus from Berea, Aristarchus[b] and Secundus from Thessalonica,[c] Gaius[d] from Derbe, Timothy[e] also, and Tychicus[f] and
Trophimus[g] from the province of Asia. 5These men went on ahead
and waited for us[h] at Troas.[i] 6But we sailed from Philippi[j] after the
Feast of Unleavened Bread, and five days later joined the others at
Troas,[k] where we stayed seven days.

7On the first day of the week[l] we came together to break bread.
Paul spoke to the people and, because he intended to leave the next
day, kept on talking until midnight. 8There were many lamps in
the upstairs room[m] where we were meeting. 9Seated in a window
was a young man named Eutychus, who was sinking into a deep
sleep as Paul talked on and on. When he was sound asleep, he fell
to the ground from the third story and was picked up dead. 10Paul
went down, threw himself on the young man[n] and put his arms
around him. "Don't be alarmed," he said. "He's alive!"[o] 11Then he
went upstairs again and broke bread[p] and ate. After talking until
daylight, he left. 12The people took the young man home alive and
were greatly comforted.

13We went on ahead to the ship and sailed for Assos, where we
were going to take Paul aboard. He had made this arrangement
because he was going there on foot. 14When he met us at Assos, we
took him aboard and went on to Mitylene. 15The next day we set
sail from there and arrived off Kios. The day after that we crossed
over to Samos, and on the following day arrived at Miletus.[q] 16Paul
had decided to sail past Ephesus[r] to avoid spending time in the
province of Asia, for he was in a hurry to reach Jerusalem,[s] if possible, by the day of Pentecost.[t]

17From Miletus, Paul sent to Ephesus for the elders[u] of the
church. 18When they arrived, he said to them: "You know how I
lived the whole time I was with you,[v] from the first day I came into
the province of Asia. 19I served the Lord with great humility and
with tears, although I was severely tested by the plots of the
Jews.[w] 20You know that I have not hesitated to preach anything[x]
that would be helpful to you but have taught you publicly and
from house to house. 21I have declared to both Jews[y] and Greeks
that they must turn to God in repentance[z] and have faith in our
Lord Jesus.[a]

22"And now, compelled by the Spirit, I am going to Jerusalem,[b]
not knowing what will happen to me there. 23I only know that in
every city the Holy Spirit warns me[c] that prison and hardships are
facing me.[d] 24However, I consider my life worth nothing to me,[e] if
only I may finish the race and complete the task[f] the Lord Jesus
has given me[g]—the task of testifying to the gospel of God's grace.

20:3 [a] Ac 16:9
20:4 [b] Ac 19:29 [c] Ac 17:1 [d] Ac 19:29 [e] Ac 16:1 [f] Eph 6:21; Col 4:7; 2Ti 4:12; Tit 3:12 [g] Ac 21:29; 2Ti 4:20
20:5 [h] Ac 16:10 [i] Ac 16:8
20:6 [j] Ac 16:12 [k] Ac 16:8
20:7 [l] 1Co 16:2; Rev 1:10
20:8 [m] Ac 1:13
20:10 [n] 1Ki 17:21; 2Ki 4:34 [o] Mt 9:23,24
20:11 [p] ver 7
20:15 [q] ver 17; 2Ti 4:20
20:16 [r] Ac 18:19 [s] Ac 19:21 [t] Ac 2:1; 1Co 16:8
20:17 [u] Ac 11:30
20:18 [v] Ac 18:19-21; 19:1-41
20:19 [w] ver 3
20:20 [x] ver 27
20:21 [y] Ac 18:5 [z] Ac 2:38 [a] Ac 24:24; 26:18; Eph 1:15; Col 2:5; Phm 5
20:22 [b] ver 16
20:23 [c] Ac 21:4 [d] Ac 9:16
20:24 [e] Ac 21:13 [f] 2Co 4:1 [g] Gal 1:1; Tit 1:3

25 “Now I know that none of you among whom I have gone
about preaching the kingdom will ever see me again.[a] 26 Therefore,
I declare to you today that I am innocent of the blood of all men.[b]
27 For I have not hesitated to proclaim to you the whole will of
God.[c] 28 Keep watch over yourselves and all the flock of which the
Holy Spirit has made you overseers.[a][d] Be shepherds of the church
of God,[b] which he bought with his own blood. 29 I know that after
I leave, savage wolves[e] will come in among you and will not spare
the flock.[f] 30 Even from your own number men will arise and distort the truth in order to draw away disciples[g] after them. 31 So be
on your guard! Remember that for three years[h] I never stopped
warning each of you night and day with tears.[i]
32 “Now I commit you to God[j] and to the word of his grace,
which can build you up and give you an inheritance[k] among all
those who are sanctified.[l] 33 I have not coveted anyone’s silver or
gold or clothing.[m] 34 You yourselves know that these hands of mine
have supplied my own needs and the needs of my companions.[n]
35 In everything I did, I showed you that by this kind of hard work
we must help the weak, remembering the words the Lord Jesus
himself said: ‘It is more blessed to give than to receive.’ ”
36 When he had said this, he knelt down with all of them and
prayed.[o] 37 They all wept as they embraced him and kissed him.[p]
38 What grieved them most was his statement that they would never
see his face again.[q] Then they accompanied him to the ship.

Chapter 21 Theme ____________________

21 After we[r] had torn ourselves away from them, we put out
to sea and sailed straight to Cos. The next day we went to
Rhodes and from there to Patara. 2 We found a ship crossing over
to Phoenicia,[s] went on board and set sail. 3 After sighting Cyprus
and passing to the south of it, we sailed on to Syria. We landed at
Tyre, where our ship was to unload its cargo. 4 Finding the disciples[t] there, we stayed with them seven days. Through the Spirit[u]
they urged Paul not to go on to Jerusalem. 5 But when our time was
up, we left and continued on our way. All the disciples and their
wives and children accompanied us out of the city, and there on
the beach we knelt to pray.[v] 6 After saying good-by to each other,
we went aboard the ship, and they returned home.
7 We continued our voyage from Tyre[w] and landed at Ptolemais,
where we greeted the brothers[x] and stayed with them for a day.
8 Leaving the next day, we reached Caesarea[y] and stayed at the
house of Philip[z] the evangelist,[a] one of the Seven. 9 He had four
unmarried daughters who prophesied.[b]

[a] 28 Traditionally *bishops* [b] 28 Many manuscripts *of the Lord*

20:25 [a] ver 38
20:26 [b] Ac 18:6
20:27 [c] ver 20
20:28 [d] 1Pe 5:2
20:29 [e] Mt 7:15 [f] ver 28
20:30 [g] Ac 11:26
20:31 [h] Ac 19:10 [i] ver 19
20:32 [j] Ac 14:23 [k] Eph 1:14; Col 1:12; 3:24; Heb 9:15; 1Pe 1:4 [l] Ac 26:18
20:33 [m] 1Sa 12:3; 1Co 9:12; 2Co 7:2; 11:9; 12:14-17
20:34 [n] Ac 18:3
20:36 [o] Lk 22:41; Ac 21:5
20:37 [p] Lk 15:20
20:38 [q] ver 25
21:1 [r] Ac 16:10
21:2 [s] Ac 11:19
21:4 [t] Ac 11:26 [u] ver 11; Ac 20:23
21:5 [v] Ac 20:36
21:7 [w] Ac 12:20 [x] Ac 1:16
21:8 [y] Ac 8:40 [z] Ac 6:5; 8:5-40 [a] Eph 4:11; 2Ti 4:5
21:9 [b] Lk 2:36; Ac 2:17

[10]After we had been there a number of days, a prophet named Agabus[a] came down from Judea. [11]Coming over to us, he took Paul's belt, tied his own hands and feet with it and said, "The Holy Spirit says, 'In this way the Jews of Jerusalem will bind[b] the owner of this belt and will hand him over to the Gentiles.'"[c]

[12]When we heard this, we and the people there pleaded with Paul not to go up to Jerusalem. [13]Then Paul answered, "Why are you weeping and breaking my heart? I am ready not only to be bound, but also to die[d] in Jerusalem for the name of the Lord Jesus."[e] [14]When he would not be dissuaded, we gave up and said, "The Lord's will be done."

[15]After this, we got ready and went up to Jerusalem. [16]Some of the disciples from Caesarea[f] accompanied us and brought us to the home of Mnason, where we were to stay. He was a man from Cyprus[g] and one of the early disciples.

[17]When we arrived at Jerusalem, the brothers received us warmly.[h] [18]The next day Paul and the rest of us went to see James,[i] and all the elders[j] were present. [19]Paul greeted them and reported in detail what God had done among the Gentiles[k] through his ministry.[l]

[20]When they heard this, they praised God. Then they said to Paul: "You see, brother, how many thousands of Jews have believed, and all of them are zealous[m] for the law.[n] [21]They have been informed that you teach all the Jews who live among the Gentiles to turn away from Moses,[o] telling them not to circumcise their children[p] or live according to our customs.[q] [22]What shall we do? They will certainly hear that you have come, [23]so do what we tell you. There are four men with us who have made a vow.[r] [24]Take these men, join in their purification rites[s] and pay their expenses, so that they can have their heads shaved.[t] Then everybody will know there is no truth in these reports about you, but that you yourself are living in obedience to the law. [25]As for the Gentile believers, we have written to them our decision that they should abstain from food sacrificed to idols, from blood, from the meat of strangled animals and from sexual immorality."[u]

[26]The next day Paul took the men and purified himself along with them. Then he went to the temple to give notice of the date when the days of purification would end and the offering would be made for each of them.[v]

[27]When the seven days were nearly over, some Jews from the province of Asia saw Paul at the temple. They stirred up the whole crowd and seized him,[w] [28]shouting, "Men of Israel, help us! This is the man who teaches all men everywhere against our people and our law and this place. And besides, he has brought Greeks into the temple area and defiled this holy place."[x] [29](They had previously seen Trophimus[y] the Ephesian[z] in the city with Paul and assumed that Paul had brought him into the temple area.)

21:10 [a]Ac 11:28
21:11 [b]ver 33 [c]1Ki 22:11
21:13 [d]Ac 20:24 [e]Ac 9:16
21:16 [f]Ac 8:40 [g]ver 3,4
21:17 [h]Ac 15:4
21:18 [i]Ac 15:13 [j]Ac 11:30
21:19 [k]Ac 14:27 [l]Ac 1:17
21:20 [m]Ac 22:3; Ro 10:2; Gal 1:14 [n]Ac 15:1,5
21:21 [o]ver 28 [p]Ac 15:19-21; 1Co 7:18,19 [q]Ac 6:14
21:23 [r]Ac 18:18
21:24 [s]ver 26; Ac 24:18 [t]Ac 18:18
21:25 [u]Ac 15:20,29
21:26 [v]Nu 6:13-20; Ac 24:18
21:27 [w]Ac 24:18; 26:21
21:28 [x]Mt 24:15; Ac 24:5,6
21:29 [y]Ac 20:4 [z]Ac 18:19

30The whole city was aroused, and the people came running
from all directions. Seizing Paul,[a] they dragged him[b] from the
temple, and immediately the gates were shut. 31While they were
trying to kill him, news reached the commander of the Roman
troops that the whole city of Jerusalem was in an uproar. 32He at
once took some officers and soldiers and ran down to the crowd.
When the rioters saw the commander and his soldiers, they
stopped beating Paul.[c]

33The commander came up and arrested him and ordered him
to be bound[d] with two[e] chains.[f] Then he asked who he was and
what he had done. 34Some in the crowd shouted one thing and
some another,[g] and since the commander could not get at the
truth because of the uproar, he ordered that Paul be taken into the
barracks.[h] 35When Paul reached the steps,[i] the violence of the mob
was so great he had to be carried by the soldiers. 36The crowd that
followed kept shouting, "Away with him!"[j]

37As the soldiers were about to take Paul into the barracks,[k] he
asked the commander, "May I say something to you?"

"Do you speak Greek?" he replied. 38"Aren't you the Egyptian
who started a revolt and led four thousand terrorists out into the
desert[l] some time ago?"[m]

39Paul answered, "I am a Jew, from Tarsus[n] in Cilicia,[o] a citizen of
no ordinary city. Please let me speak to the people."

40Having received the commander's permission, Paul stood on
the steps and motioned[p] to the crowd. When they were all silent,
he said to them in Aramaic[a]:[q]

Chapter 22 Theme ______________________________

22 "Brothers and fathers,[r] listen now to my defense."
2When they heard him speak to them in Aramaic,[s] they
became very quiet.

Then Paul said: 3"I am a Jew,[t] born in Tarsus[u] of Cilicia, but
brought up in this city. Under[v] Gamaliel[w] I was thoroughly trained
in the law of our fathers[x] and was just as zealous[y] for God as any
of you are today. 4I persecuted[z] the followers of this Way to their
death, arresting both men and women and throwing them into
prison,[a] 5as also the high priest and all the Council[b] can testify. I
even obtained letters from them to their brothers[c] in Damascus,[d]
and went there to bring these people as prisoners to Jerusalem to
be punished.

6"About noon as I came near Damascus, suddenly a bright light
from heaven flashed around me.[e] 7I fell to the ground and heard a
voice say to me, 'Saul! Saul! Why do you persecute me?'

8"'Who are you, Lord?' I asked.

a *40* Or possibly *Hebrew*; also in 22:2

21:30 [a]Ac 26:21 [b]Ac 16:19
21:32 [c]Ac 23:27
21:33 [d]ver 11 [e]Ac 12:6 [f]Ac 20:23; Eph 6:20; 2Ti 2:9
21:34 [g]Ac 19:32 [h]ver 37; Ac 23:10, 16,32
21:35 [i]ver 40
21:36 [j]Lk 23:18; Jn 19:15; Ac 22:22
21:37 [k]ver 34
21:38 [l]Mt 24:26 [m]Ac 5:36
21:39 [n]Ac 9:11 [o]Ac 22:3
21:40 [p]Ac 12:17 [q]Jn 5:2
22:1 [r]Ac 7:2
22:2 [s]Ac 21:40
22:3 [t]Ac 21:39 [u]Ac 9:11 [v]Lk 10:39 [w]Ac 5:34 [x]Ac 26:5 [y]Ac 21:20
22:4 [z]Ac 8:3 [a]ver 19,20
22:5 [b]Lk 22:66 [c]Ac 13:26 [d]Ac 9:2
22:6 [e]Ac 9:3

"'I am Jesus of Nazareth, whom you are persecuting,' he replied.
9My companions saw the light,[a] but they did not understand the
voice[b] of him who was speaking to me.
10"'What shall I do, Lord?' I asked.
"'Get up,' the Lord said, 'and go into Damascus. There you will
be told all that you have been assigned to do.'[c] 11My companions
led me by the hand into Damascus, because the brilliance of the
light had blinded me.[d]
12"A man named Ananias came to see me.[e] He was a devout
observer of the law and highly respected by all the Jews living
there.[f] 13He stood beside me and said, 'Brother Saul, receive your
sight!' And at that very moment I was able to see him.
14"Then he said: 'The God of our fathers[g] has chosen you to
know his will and to see[h] the Righteous One[i] and to hear words
from his mouth. 15You will be his witness[j] to all men of what you
have seen and heard. 16And now what are you waiting for? Get up,
be baptized[k] and wash your sins away,[l] calling on his name.'[m]
17"When I returned to Jerusalem[n] and was praying at the temple,
I fell into a trance[o] 18and saw the Lord speaking. 'Quick!' he said to
me. 'Leave Jerusalem immediately, because they will not accept
your testimony about me.'
19"'Lord,' I replied, 'these men know that I went from one synagogue to another to imprison[p] and beat[q] those who believe in you.
20And when the blood of your martyr[a] Stephen was shed, I stood
there giving my approval and guarding the clothes of those who
were killing him.'[r]
21"Then the Lord said to me, 'Go; I will send you far away to the
Gentiles.'"[s]
22The crowd listened to Paul until he said this. Then they raised
their voices and shouted, "Rid the earth of him![t] He's not fit to
live!"[u]
23As they were shouting and throwing off their cloaks[v] and fling-
ing dust into the air,[w] 24the commander ordered Paul to be taken
into the barracks.[x] He directed[y] that he be flogged and questioned
in order to find out why the people were shouting at him like this.
25As they stretched him out to flog him, Paul said to the centurion
standing there, "Is it legal for you to flog a Roman citizen who
hasn't even been found guilty?"[z]
26When the centurion heard this, he went to the commander and
reported it. "What are you going to do?" he asked. "This man is a
Roman citizen."
27The commander went to Paul and asked, "Tell me, are you a
Roman citizen?"
"Yes, I am," he answered.

22:9 [a]Ac 26:13 [b]Ac 9:7
22:10 [c]Ac 16:30
22:11 [d]Ac 9:8
22:12 [e]Ac 9:17 [f]Ac 10:22
22:14 [g]Ac 3:13 [h]1Co 9:1; 15:8 [i]Ac 7:52
22:15 [j]Ac 23:11; 26:16
22:16 [k]Ac 2:38 [l]Heb 10:22 [m]Ro 10:13
22:17 [n]Ac 9:26 [o]Ac 10:10
22:19 [p]ver 4; Ac 8:3 [q]Mt 10:17
22:20 [r]Ac 7:57-60; 8:1
22:21 [s]Ac 9:15; 13:46
22:22 [t]Ac 21:36 [u]Ac 25:24
22:23 [v]Ac 7:58 [w]2Sa 16:13
22:24 [x]Ac 21:34 [y]ver 29
22:25 [z]Ac 16:37

[a] 20 Or *witness*

28Then the commander said, "I had to pay a big price for my
citizenship."
"But I was born a citizen," Paul replied.
29Those who were about to question him withdrew immediately.
The commander himself was alarmed when he realized that he
had put Paul, a Roman citizen,[a] in chains.
30The next day, since the commander wanted to find out exactly
why Paul was being accused by the Jews,[b] he released him[c] and
ordered the chief priests and all the Sanhedrin[d] to assemble. Then
he brought Paul and had him stand before them.

Chapter 23 Theme ______________________

23 Paul looked straight at the Sanhedrin[e] and said, "My brothers,[f] I have fulfilled my duty to God in all good conscience[g] to this day." 2At this the high priest Ananias[h] ordered
those standing near Paul to strike him on the mouth.[i] 3Then Paul
said to him, "God will strike you, you whitewashed wall![j] You sit
there to judge me according to the law, yet you yourself violate the
law by commanding that I be struck!"[k]
4Those who were standing near Paul said, "You dare to insult
God's high priest?"
5Paul replied, "Brothers, I did not realize that he was the high
priest; for it is written: 'Do not speak evil about the ruler of your
people.'[a]"[l]
6Then Paul, knowing that some of them were Sadducees and the
others Pharisees, called out in the Sanhedrin, "My brothers,[m] I am
a Pharisee,[n] the son of a Pharisee. I stand on trial because of my
hope in the resurrection of the dead."[o] 7When he said this, a dispute broke out between the Pharisees and the Sadducees, and the
assembly was divided. 8(The Sadducees say that there is no resurrection,[p] and that there are neither angels nor spirits, but the
Pharisees acknowledge them all.)
9There was a great uproar, and some of the teachers of the law
who were Pharisees[q] stood up and argued vigorously. "We find
nothing wrong with this man,"[r] they said. "What if a spirit or an
angel has spoken to him?"[s] 10The dispute became so violent that
the commander was afraid Paul would be torn to pieces by them.
He ordered the troops to go down and take him away from them
by force and bring him into the barracks.[t]
11The following night the Lord stood near Paul and said, "Take
courage![u] As you have testified about me in Jerusalem, so you
must also testify in Rome."[v]

a5 Exodus 22:28

22:29 [a] ver 24,25; Ac 16:38
22:30 [b] Ac 23:28 [c] Ac 21:33 [d] Mt 5:22
23:1 [e] Ac 22:30 [f] Ac 22:5 [g] Ac 24:16; 1Co 4:4; 2Co 1:12; 2Ti 1:3; Heb 13:18
23:2 [h] Ac 24:1 [i] Jn 18:22
23:3 [j] Mt 23:27 [k] Lev 19:15; Dt 25:1,2; Jn 7:51
23:5 [l] Ex 22:28
23:6 [m] Ac 22:5 [n] Ac 26:5; Php 3:5 [o] Ac 24:15,21; 26:8
23:8 [p] Mt 22:23
23:9 [q] Mk 2:16 [r] ver 29; Ac 25:25; 26:31 [s] Ac 22:7,17,18
23:10 [t] Ac 21:34
23:11 [u] Ac 18:9 [v] Ac 19:21; 28:23

12 The next morning the Jews formed a conspiracy and bound themselves with an oath not to eat or drink until they had killed Paul.[a] 13 More than forty men were involved in this plot. 14 They went to the chief priests and elders and said, "We have taken a solemn oath not to eat anything until we have killed Paul.[b] 15 Now then, you and the Sanhedrin[c] petition the commander to bring him before you on the pretext of wanting more accurate information about his case. We are ready to kill him before he gets here."

16 But when the son of Paul's sister heard of this plot, he went into the barracks[d] and told Paul.

17 Then Paul called one of the centurions and said, "Take this young man to the commander; he has something to tell him." 18 So he took him to the commander.

The centurion said, "Paul, the prisoner,[e] sent for me and asked me to bring this young man to you because he has something to tell you."

19 The commander took the young man by the hand, drew him aside and asked, "What is it you want to tell me?"

20 He said: "The Jews have agreed to ask you to bring Paul before the Sanhedrin[f] tomorrow on the pretext of wanting more accurate information about him.[g] 21 Don't give in to them, because more than forty[h] of them are waiting in ambush for him. They have taken an oath not to eat or drink until they have killed him.[i] They are ready now, waiting for your consent to their request."

22 The commander dismissed the young man and cautioned him, "Don't tell anyone that you have reported this to me."

23 Then he called two of his centurions and ordered them, "Get ready a detachment of two hundred soldiers, seventy horsemen and two hundred spearmen[a] to go to Caesarea[j] at nine tonight.[k] 24 Provide mounts for Paul so that he may be taken safely to Governor Felix."[l]

25 He wrote a letter as follows:

26 Claudius Lysias,

To His Excellency,[m] Governor Felix:

Greetings.[n]

27 This man was seized by the Jews and they were about to kill him,[o] but I came with my troops and rescued him,[p] for I had learned that he is a Roman citizen.[q] 28 I wanted to know why they were accusing him, so I brought him to their Sanhedrin.[r] 29 I found that the accusation had to do with questions about their law,[s] but there was no charge against him[t] that deserved death or imprisonment. 30 When I was informed[u] of a plot[v] to

23:12 [a] ver 14,21,30; Ac 25:3
23:14 [b] ver 12
23:15 [c] ver 1; Ac 22:30
23:16 [d] ver 10; Ac 21:34
23:18 [e] Eph 3:1
23:20 [f] ver 1 [g] ver 14,15
23:21 [h] ver 13 [i] ver 12,14
23:23 [j] Ac 8:40 [k] ver 33
23:24 [l] ver 26,33; Ac 24:1-3,10; 25:14
23:26 [m] Lk 1:3; Ac 24:3; 26:25 [n] Ac 15:23
23:27 [o] Ac 21:32 [p] Ac 21:33 [q] Ac 22:25-29
23:28 [r] Ac 22:30
23:29 [s] Ac 18:15; 25:19 [t] ver 9; Ac 26:31
23:30 [u] ver 20,21 [v] Ac 20:3

a *23* The meaning of the Greek for this word is uncertain.

be carried out against the man, I sent him to you at once. I also
ordered his accusers[a] to present to you their case against him.

31 So the soldiers, carrying out their orders, took Paul with them
during the night and brought him as far as Antipatris. 32 The next
day they let the cavalry[b] go on with him, while they returned to the
barracks.[c] 33 When the cavalry[d] arrived in Caesarea,[e] they delivered
the letter to the governor[f] and handed Paul over to him. 34 The
governor read the letter and asked what province he was from.
Learning that he was from Cilicia,[g] 35 he said, "I will hear your case
when your accusers[h] get here." Then he ordered that Paul be kept
under guard[i] in Herod's palace.

Chapter 24 Theme ________________________

24 Five days later the high priest Ananias[j] went down to Caesarea with some of the elders and a lawyer named Tertullus,
and they brought their charges[k] against Paul before the governor.[l]
2 When Paul was called in, Tertullus presented his case before Felix:
"We have enjoyed a long period of peace under you, and your fore-
sight has brought about reforms in this nation. 3 Everywhere and in
every way, most excellent[m] Felix, we acknowledge this with profound gratitude. 4 But in order not to weary you further, I would
request that you be kind enough to hear us briefly.
5 "We have found this man to be a troublemaker, stirring up
riots[n] among the Jews[o] all over the world. He is a ringleader of the
Nazarene[p] sect[q] 6 and even tried to desecrate the temple;[r] so we
seized him. 8 By [a] examining him yourself you will be able to learn
the truth about all these charges we are bringing against him."
9 The Jews joined in the accusation,[s] asserting that these things
were true.
10 When the governor[t] motioned for him to speak, Paul replied:
"I know that for a number of years you have been a judge over this
nation; so I gladly make my defense. 11 You can easily verify that no
more than twelve days[u] ago I went up to Jerusalem to worship.
12 My accusers did not find me arguing with anyone at the temple,[v]
or stirring up a crowd[w] in the synagogues or anywhere else in the
city. 13 And they cannot prove to you the charges they are now
making against me.[x] 14 However, I admit that I worship the God of
our fathers[y] as a follower of the Way,[z] which they call a sect.[a] I
believe everything that agrees with the Law and that is written in
the Prophets,[b] 15 and I have the same hope in God as these men,
that there will be a resurrection[c] of both the righteous and the

[a] 6-8 Some manuscripts *him and wanted to judge him according to our law.* 7 *But the commander, Lysias, came and with the use of much force snatched him from our hands* 8 *and ordered his accusers to come before you. By*

23:30 [a] ver 35; Ac 24:19; 25:16
23:32 [b] ver 23 [c] Ac 21:34
23:33 [d] ver 23,24 [e] Ac 8:40 [f] ver 26
23:34 [g] Ac 6:9; 21:39
23:35 [h] ver 30; Ac 24:19; 25:16 [i] Ac 24:27
24:1 [j] Ac 23:2 [k] Ac 23:30,35 [l] Ac 23:24
24:3 [m] Lk 1:3; Ac 23:26; 26:25
24:5 [n] Ac 16:20; 17:6 [o] Ac 21:28 [p] Mk 1:24 [q] ver 14; Ac 26:5; 28:22
24:6 [r] Ac 21:28
24:9 [s] 1Th 2:16
24:10 [t] Ac 23:24
24:11 [u] Ac 21:27; ver 1
24:12 [v] Ac 25:8; 28:17 [w] ver 18
24:13 [x] Ac 25:7
24:14 [y] Ac 3:13 [z] Ac 9:2 [a] ver 5 [b] Ac 26:6,22; 28:23
24:15 [c] Ac 23:6; 28:20

wicked.[a] 16So I strive always to keep my conscience clear[b] before
God and man.

17"After an absence of several years, I came to Jerusalem to bring
my people gifts for the poor[c] and to present offerings. 18I was ceremonially clean[d] when they found me in the temple courts doing
this. There was no crowd with me, nor was I involved in any disturbance.[e] 19But there are some Jews from the province of Asia,
who ought to be here before you and bring charges if they have
anything against me.[f] 20Or these who are here should state what
crime they found in me when I stood before the Sanhedrin—
21unless it was this one thing I shouted as I stood in their presence:
'It is concerning the resurrection of the dead that I am on trial
before you today.'"[g]

22Then Felix, who was well acquainted with the Way, adjourned
the proceedings. "When Lysias the commander comes," he said,
"I will decide your case." 23He ordered the centurion to keep Paul
under guard[h] but to give him some freedom[i] and permit his
friends to take care of his needs.[j]

24Several days later Felix came with his wife Drusilla, who was a
Jewess. He sent for Paul and listened to him as he spoke about
faith in Christ Jesus.[k] 25As Paul discoursed on righteousness, self-
control[l] and the judgment[m] to come, Felix was afraid and said,
"That's enough for now! You may leave. When I find it convenient,
I will send for you." 26At the same time he was hoping that Paul
would offer him a bribe, so he sent for him frequently and talked
with him.

27When two years had passed, Felix was succeeded by Porcius
Festus,[n] but because Felix wanted to grant a favor to the Jews,[o] he
left Paul in prison.[p]

Chapter 25 Theme ______________________

25 Three days after arriving in the province, Festus went up
from Caesarea[q] to Jerusalem, 2where the chief priests and
Jewish leaders appeared before him and presented the charges
against Paul.[r] 3They urgently requested Festus, as a favor to them,
to have Paul transferred to Jerusalem, for they were preparing an
ambush to kill him along the way. 4Festus answered, "Paul is being
held[s] at Caesarea, and I myself am going there soon. 5Let some of
your leaders come with me and press charges against the man
there, if he has done anything wrong."

6After spending eight or ten days with them, he went down to
Caesarea, and the next day he convened the court[t] and ordered
that Paul be brought before him. 7When Paul appeared, the Jews
who had come down from Jerusalem stood around him, bringing
many serious charges against him,[u] which they could not prove.[v]

24:15 [a]Da 12:2; Jn 5:28,29
24:16 [b]Ac 23:1
24:17 [c]Ac 11:29,30; Ro 15:25-28,31; 1Co 16:1-4,15; 2Co 8:1-4; Gal 2:10
24:18 [d]Ac 21:26 [e]ver 12
24:19 [f]Ac 23:30
24:21 [g]Ac 23:6
24:23 [h]Ac 23:35 [i]Ac 28:16 [j]Ac 23:16; 27:3
24:24 [k]Ac 20:21
24:25 [l]Gal 5:23; 2Pe 1:6 [m]Ac 10:42
24:27 [n]Ac 25:1,4, 9,14 [o]Ac 12:3; 25:9 [p]Ac 23:35; 25:14
25:1 [q]Ac 8:40
25:2 [r]ver 15; Ac 24:1
25:4 [s]Ac 24:23
25:6 [t]ver 17
25:7 [u]Mk 15:3; Lk 23:2,10; Ac 24:5,6 [v]Ac 24:13

8Then Paul made his defense: "I have done nothing wrong
against the law of the Jews or against the temple[a] or against Caesar."
9Festus, wishing to do the Jews a favor,[b] said to Paul, "Are you
willing to go up to Jerusalem and stand trial before me there on
these charges?"[c]
10Paul answered: "I am now standing before Caesar's court,
where I ought to be tried. I have not done any wrong to the Jews, as
you yourself know very well. 11If, however, I am guilty of doing
anything deserving death, I do not refuse to die. But if the charges
brought against me by these Jews are not true, no one has the right
to hand me over to them. I appeal to Caesar!"[d]
12After Festus had conferred with his council, he declared: "You
have appealed to Caesar. To Caesar you will go!"
13A few days later King Agrippa and Bernice arrived at Caesarea[e]
to pay their respects to Festus. 14Since they were spending many
days there, Festus discussed Paul's case with the king. He said:
"There is a man here whom Felix left as a prisoner.[f] 15When I went
to Jerusalem, the chief priests and elders of the Jews brought
charges against him[g] and asked that he be condemned.
16"I told them that it is not the Roman custom to hand over any
man before he has faced his accusers and has had an opportunity
to defend himself against their charges.[h] 17When they came here
with me, I did not delay the case, but convened the court the next
day and ordered the man to be brought in.[i] 18When his accusers
got up to speak, they did not charge him with any of the crimes I
had expected. 19Instead, they had some points of dispute[j] with him
about their own religion[k] and about a dead man named Jesus
who Paul claimed was alive. 20I was at a loss how to investigate such
matters; so I asked if he would be willing to go to Jerusalem and
stand trial there on these charges.[l] 21When Paul made his appeal to
be held over for the Emperor's decision, I ordered him held until
I could send him to Caesar."[m]
22Then Agrippa said to Festus, "I would like to hear this man
myself."
He replied, "Tomorrow you will hear him."[n]
23The next day Agrippa and Bernice[o] came with great pomp and
entered the audience room with the high ranking officers and the
leading men of the city. At the command of Festus, Paul was
brought in. 24Festus said: "King Agrippa, and all who are present
with us, you see this man! The whole Jewish community[p] has
petitioned me about him in Jerusalem and here in Caesarea,
shouting that he ought not to live any longer.[q] 25I found he had
done nothing deserving of death,[r] but because he made his appeal
to the Emperor[s] I decided to send him to Rome. 26But I have nothing definite to write to His Majesty about him. Therefore I have

25:8 [a] Ac 6:13; 24:12; 28:17
25:9 [b] Ac 24:27 [c] ver 20
25:11 [d] ver 21,25; Ac 26:32; 28:19
25:13 [e] Ac 8:40
25:14 [f] Ac 24:27
25:15 [g] ver 2; Ac 24:1
25:16 [h] ver 4,5; Ac 23:30
25:17 [i] ver 6,10
25:19 [j] Ac 18:15; 23:29 [k] Ac 17:22
25:20 [l] ver 9
25:21 [m] ver 11,12
25:22 [n] Ac 9:15
25:23 [o] ver 13; Ac 26:30
25:24 [p] ver 2,3,7 [q] Ac 22:22
25:25 [r] Ac 23:9 [s] ver 11

brought him before all of you, and especially before you, King
Agrippa, so that as a result of this investigation I may have something to write. 27For I think it is unreasonable to send on a prisoner
without specifying the charges against him."

Chapter 26 Theme

26 Then Agrippa said to Paul, "You have permission to speak
for yourself."[a]
So Paul motioned with his hand and began his defense: 2"King
Agrippa, I consider myself fortunate to stand before you today as I
make my defense against all the accusations of the Jews, 3and
especially so because you are well acquainted with all the Jewish
customs[b] and controversies.[c] Therefore, I beg you to listen to me
patiently.
4"The Jews all know the way I have lived ever since I was a child,[d]
from the beginning of my life in my own country, and also in
Jerusalem. 5They have known me for a long time[e] and can testify,
if they are willing, that according to the strictest sect of our religion, I lived as a Pharisee.[f] 6And now it is because of my hope[g] in
what God has promised our fathers[h] that I am on trial today.
7This is the promise our twelve tribes[i] are hoping to see fulfilled
as they earnestly serve God day and night.[j] O king, it is because of
this hope that the Jews are accusing me.[k] 8Why should any of you
consider it incredible that God raises the dead?[l]
9"I too was convinced[m] that I ought to do all that was possible to
oppose[n] the name of Jesus of Nazareth.[o] 10And that is just what I
did in Jerusalem. On the authority of the chief priests I put many
of the saints[p] in prison,[q] and when they were put to death, I cast
my vote against them.[r] 11Many a time I went from one synagogue
to another to have them punished,[s] and I tried to force them to
blaspheme. In my obsession against them, I even went to foreign
cities to persecute them.
12"On one of these journeys I was going to Damascus with the
authority and commission of the chief priests. 13About noon, O
king, as I was on the road, I saw a light from heaven, brighter than
the sun, blazing around me and my companions. 14We all fell to
the ground, and I heard a voice[t] saying to me in Aramaic,[a] 'Saul,
Saul, why do you persecute me? It is hard for you to kick against
the goads.'
15"Then I asked, 'Who are you, Lord?'
"'I am Jesus, whom you are persecuting,' the Lord replied.
16'Now get up and stand on your feet.[u] I have appeared to you to
appoint you as a servant and as a witness of what you have seen

26:1 [a] Ac 9:15; 25:22
26:3 [b] ver 7; Ac 6:14 [c] Ac 25:19
26:4 [d] Gal 1:13,14; Php 3:5
26:5 [e] Ac 22:3 [f] Ac 23:6; Php 3:5
26:6 [g] Ac 23:6; 24:15; 28:20 [h] Ac 13:32; Ro 15:8
26:7 [i] Jas 1:1 [j] 1Th 3:10; 1Ti 5:5 [k] ver 2
26:8 [l] Ac 23:6
26:9 [m] 1Ti 1:13 [n] Jn 16:2 [o] Jn 15:21
26:10 [p] Ac 9:13 [q] Ac 8:3; 9:2,14,21 [r] Ac 22:20
26:11 [s] Mt 10:17
26:14 [t] Ac 9:7
26:16 [u] Eze 2:1; Da 10:11

[a] *14* Or *Hebrew*

of me and what I will show you.[a] 17 I will rescue you[b] from your
own people and from the Gentiles.[c] I am sending you to them 18 to
open their eyes[d] and turn them from darkness to light,[e] and from
the power of Satan to God, so that they may receive forgiveness of
sins[f] and a place among those who are sanctified by faith in me.'[g]
19 "So then, King Agrippa, I was not disobedient to the vision
from heaven. 20 First to those in Damascus,[h] then to those in Jerusalem[i] and in all Judea, and to the Gentiles[j] also, I preached that
they should repent[k] and turn to God and prove their repentance by
their deeds.[l] 21 That is why the Jews seized me[m] in the temple courts
and tried to kill me.[n] 22 But I have had God's help to this very day,
and so I stand here and testify to small and great alike. I am saying
nothing beyond what the prophets and Moses said would happen[o]— 23 that the Christ[a] would suffer and, as the first to rise
from the dead,[p] would proclaim light to his own people and to the
Gentiles."[q]
24 At this point Festus interrupted Paul's defense. "You are out of
your mind,[r] Paul!" he shouted. "Your great learning[s] is driving you
insane."
25 "I am not insane, most excellent[t] Festus," Paul replied. "What I
am saying is true and reasonable. 26 The king is familiar with these
things,[u] and I can speak freely to him. I am convinced that none of
this has escaped his notice, because it was not done in a corner.
27 King Agrippa, do you believe the prophets? I know you do."
28 Then Agrippa said to Paul, "Do you think that in such a short
time you can persuade me to be a Christian?"[v]
29 Paul replied, "Short time or long—I pray God that not only
you but all who are listening to me today may become what I am,
except for these chains."[w]
30 The king rose, and with him the governor and Bernice[x] and
those sitting with them. 31 They left the room, and while talking
with one another, they said, "This man is not doing anything that
deserves death or imprisonment."[y]
32 Agrippa said to Festus, "This man could have been set free[z] if
he had not appealed to Caesar."[a]

Chapter 27 Theme ______________________

27

When it was decided that we[b] would sail for Italy,[c] Paul
and some other prisoners were handed over to a centurion
named Julius, who belonged to the Imperial Regiment.[d] 2 We
boarded a ship from Adramyttium about to sail for ports along the
coast of the province of Asia,[e] and we put out to sea. Aristarchus,[f]
a Macedonian[g] from Thessalonica,[h] was with us.

a 23 Or *Messiah*

26:16 [a] Ac 22:14,15
26:17 [b] Jer 1:8,19 [c] Ac 9:15
26:18 [d] Isa 35:5 [e] Isa 42:7,16; Eph 5:8; Col 1:13; 1Pe 2:9 [f] Lk 24:47; Ac 2:38 [g] Ac 20:21,32
26:20 [h] Ac 9:19-25 [i] Ac 9:26-29; 22:17-20 [j] Ac 9:15; 13:46 [k] Ac 3:19 [l] Mt 3:8; Lk 3:8
26:21 [m] Ac 21:27,30 [n] Ac 21:31
26:22 [o] Lk 24:27,44; Ac 10:43; 24:14
26:23 [p] 1Co 15:20,23; Col 1:18; Rev 1:5 [q] Lk 2:32
26:24 [r] Jn 10:20; 1Co 4:10 [s] Jn 7:15
26:25 [t] Ac 23:26
26:26 [u] ver 3
26:28 [v] Ac 11:26
26:29 [w] Ac 21:33
26:30 [x] Ac 25:23
26:31 [y] Ac 23:9
26:32 [z] Ac 28:18 [a] Ac 25:11
27:1 [b] Ac 16:10 [c] Ac 18:2; 25:12,25 [d] Ac 10:1
27:2 [e] Ac 2:9 [f] Ac 19:29 [g] Ac 16:9 [h] Ac 17:1

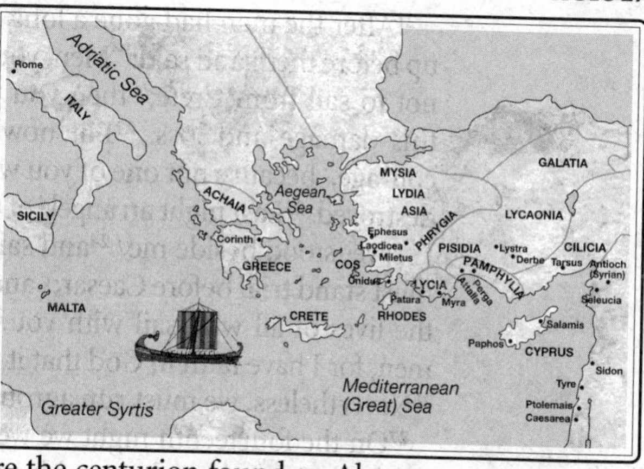

Paul Sails from Caesarea to Rome

3The next day we landed at Sidon;[a] and Julius, in kindness to Paul,[b] allowed him to go to his friends so they might provide for his needs.[c] 4From there we put out to sea again and passed to the lee of Cyprus because the winds were against us.[d] 5When we had sailed across the open sea off the coast of Cilicia[e] and Pamphylia, we landed at Myra in Lycia. 6There the centurion found an Alexandrian ship[f] sailing for Italy[g] and put us on board. 7We made slow headway for many days and had difficulty arriving off Cnidus. When the wind did not allow us to hold our course,[h] we sailed to the lee of Crete,[i] opposite Salmone. 8We moved along the coast with difficulty and came to a place called Fair Havens, near the town of Lasea.

9Much time had been lost, and sailing had already become dangerous because by now it was after the Fast.[a][j] So Paul warned them, 10"Men, I can see that our voyage is going to be disastrous and bring great loss to ship and cargo, and to our own lives also."[k] 11But the centurion, instead of listening to what Paul said, followed the advice of the pilot and of the owner of the ship. 12Since the harbor was unsuitable to winter in, the majority decided that we should sail on, hoping to reach Phoenix and winter there. This was a harbor in Crete, facing both southwest and northwest.

13When a gentle south wind began to blow, they thought they had obtained what they wanted; so they weighed anchor and sailed along the shore of Crete. 14Before very long, a wind of hurricane force,[l] called the "northeaster," swept down from the island. 15The ship was caught by the storm and could not head into the wind; so we gave way to it and were driven along. 16As we passed to the lee of a small island called Cauda, we were hardly able to make the lifeboat secure. 17When the men had hoisted it aboard, they passed ropes under the ship itself to hold it together. Fearing that they would run aground[m] on the sandbars of Syrtis, they lowered the sea anchor and let the ship be driven along. 18We took such a violent battering from the storm that the next day they began to throw the cargo overboard.[n] 19On the third day, they threw the ship's tackle overboard with their own hands. 20When neither sun nor stars appeared for many days and the storm continued raging, we finally gave up all hope of being saved.

27:3 [a]Mt 11:21 [b]ver 43 [c]Ac 24:23; 28:16
27:4 [d]ver 7
27:5 [e]Ac 6:9
27:6 [f]Ac 28:11 [g]ver 1
27:7 [h]ver 4 [i]ver 12,13,21
27:9 [j]Lev 16:29-31; 23:27-29; Nu 29:7
27:10 [k]ver 21
27:14 [l]Mk 4:37
27:17 [m]ver 26,39
27:18 [n]ver 19,38; Jnh 1:5

a9 That is, the Day of Atonement (Yom Kippur)

21After the men had gone a long time without food, Paul stood
up before them and said: "Men, you should have taken my advice[a]
not to sail from Crete;[b] then you would have spared yourselves
this damage and loss. 22But now I urge you to keep up your
courage,[c] because not one of you will be lost; only the ship will be
destroyed. 23Last night an angel[d] of the God whose I am and whom
I serve[e] stood beside me[f] 24and said, 'Do not be afraid, Paul. You
must stand trial before Caesar;[g] and God has graciously given you
the lives of all who sail with you.'[h] 25So keep up your courage,[i]
men, for I have faith in God that it will happen just as he told me.[j]
26Nevertheless, we must run aground[k] on some island."[l]

27On the fourteenth night we were still being driven across the
Adriatic[a] Sea, when about midnight the sailors sensed they were
approaching land. 28They took soundings and found that the water
was a hundred and twenty feet[b] deep. A short time later they took
soundings again and found it was ninety feet[c] deep. 29Fearing that
we would be dashed against the rocks, they dropped four anchors
from the stern and prayed for daylight. 30In an attempt to escape
from the ship, the sailors let the lifeboat[m] down into the sea, pre-
tending they were going to lower some anchors from the bow.
31Then Paul said to the centurion and the soldiers, "Unless these
men stay with the ship, you cannot be saved."[n] 32So the soldiers cut
the ropes that held the lifeboat and let it fall away.

33Just before dawn Paul urged them all to eat. "For the last fourteen days," he said, "you have been in constant suspense and have
gone without food—you haven't eaten anything. 34Now I urge
you to take some food. You need it to survive. Not one of you will
lose a single hair from his head."[o] 35After he said this, he took
some bread and gave thanks to God in front of them all. Then he
broke it[p] and began to eat. 36They were all encouraged[q] and ate
some food themselves. 37Altogether there were 276 of us on board.
38When they had eaten as much as they wanted, they lightened
the ship by throwing the grain into the sea.[r]

39When daylight came, they did not recognize the land, but they
saw a bay with a sandy beach,[s] where they decided to run the ship
aground if they could. 40Cutting loose the anchors,[t] they left them
in the sea and at the same time untied the ropes that held the rud-
ders. Then they hoisted the foresail to the wind and made for the
beach. 41But the ship struck a sandbar and ran aground. The bow
stuck fast and would not move, and the stern was broken to pieces
by the pounding of the surf.[u]

42The soldiers planned to kill the prisoners to prevent any of
them from swimming away and escaping. 43But the centurion

[a] *27* In ancient times the name referred to an area extending well south of Italy.
[b] *28* Greek *twenty orguias* (about 37 meters) [c] *28* Greek *fifteen orguias* (about 27 meters)

27:21 [a] ver 10 [b] ver 7
27:22 [c] ver 25,36
27:23 [d] Ac 5:19 [e] Ro 1:9 [f] Ac 18:9; 23:11; 2Ti 4:17
27:24 [g] Ac 23:11 [h] ver 44
27:25 [i] ver 22,36 [j] Ro 4:20,21
27:26 [k] ver 17,39 [l] Ac 28:1
27:30 [m] ver 16
27:31 [n] ver 24
27:34 [o] Mt 10:30
27:35 [p] Mt 14:19
27:36 [q] ver 22,25
27:38 [r] ver 18; Jnh 1:5
27:39 [s] Ac 28:1
27:40 [t] ver 29
27:41 [u] 2Co 11:25

27:43 [a] ver 3 wanted to spare Paul's life[a] and kept them from carrying out
their plan. He ordered those who could swim to jump overboard
27:44 first and get to land. 44The rest were to get there on planks or on
[b] ver 22,31 pieces of the ship. In this way everyone reached land in safety.[b]

Chapter 28 Theme

28:1 [c] Ac 16:10 **28** Once safely on shore, we[c] found out that the island[d] was
[d] Ac 27:26,39 called Malta. 2The islanders showed us unusual kindness.
28:4 They built a fire and welcomed us all because it was raining and
[e] Mk 16:18 cold. 3Paul gathered a pile of brushwood and, as he put it on the
[f] Lk 13:2,4 fire, a viper, driven out by the heat, fastened itself on his hand.
4When the islanders saw the snake hanging from his hand,[e] they
28:5 said to each other, "This man must be a murderer; for though he
[g] Lk 10:19 escaped from the sea, Justice has not allowed him to live."[f] 5But
Paul shook the snake off into the fire and suffered no ill effects.[g]
28:6 6The people expected him to swell up or suddenly fall dead, but
[h] Ac 14:11 after waiting a long time and seeing nothing unusual happen to
him, they changed their minds and said he was a god.[h]
28:8 7There was an estate nearby that belonged to Publius, the chief
[i] Jas 5:14,15 official of the island. He welcomed us to his home and for three
[j] Ac 9:40 days entertained us hospitably. 8His father was sick in bed, suffering from fever and dysentery. Paul went in to see him and, after
28:11 prayer,[i] placed his hands on him and healed him.[j] 9When this
[k] Ac 27:6 had happened, the rest of the sick on the island came and were
cured. 10They honored us in many ways and when we were ready
28:14 [l] Ac 1:16 to sail, they furnished us with the supplies we needed.
11After three months we put out to sea in a ship that had win-
tered in the island. It was an Alexandrian ship[k] with the figurehead
28:15 [m] Ac 1:16 of the twin gods Castor and Pollux. 12We put in at Syracuse and
stayed there three days. 13From there we set sail and arrived at
Rhegium. The next day the south wind came up, and on the fol-
28:16 lowing day we reached Puteoli. 14There we found some brothers[l]
[n] Ac 24:23; 27:3 who invited us to spend a week with them. And so we came to
Rome. 15The brothers[m] there had heard that we were coming, and
28:17 they traveled as far as the Forum of Appius and the Three Taverns
[o] Ac 25:2 to meet us. At the sight of these men Paul thanked God and was
[p] Ac 22:5 [q] Ac 25:8 encouraged. 16When we got to Rome, Paul was allowed to live by
[r] Ac 6:14 himself, with a soldier to guard him.[n]
17Three days later he called together the leaders of the Jews.[o]
28:18 When they had assembled, Paul said to them: "My brothers,[p]
[s] Ac 22:24 although I have done nothing against our people[q] or against the
[t] Ac 26:31,32 customs of our ancestors,[r] I was arrested in Jerusalem and handed
[u] Ac 23:9 over to the Romans. 18They examined me[s] and wanted to release
28:19 me,[t] because I was not guilty of any crime deserving death.[u] 19But
[v] Ac 25:11 when the Jews objected, I was compelled to appeal to Caesar[v]—

not that I had any charge to bring against my own people. 20For
this reason I have asked to see you and talk with you. It is because
of the hope of Israel[a] that I am bound with this chain."[b]
21They replied, "We have not received any letters from Judea
concerning you, and none of the brothers[c] who have come from
there has reported or said anything bad about you. 22But we want
to hear what your views are, for we know that people everywhere
are talking against this sect."[d]
23They arranged to meet Paul on a certain day, and came in even
larger numbers to the place where he was staying. From morning
till evening he explained and declared to them the kingdom of
God[e] and tried to convince them about Jesus[f] from the Law of
Moses and from the Prophets.[g] 24Some were convinced by what
he said, but others would not believe.[h] 25They disagreed among
themselves and began to leave after Paul had made this final
statement: "The Holy Spirit spoke the truth to your forefathers
when he said through Isaiah the prophet:

> 26" 'Go to this people and say,
> "You will be ever hearing but never understanding;
> you will be ever seeing but never perceiving."
> 27For this people's heart has become calloused;[i]
> they hardly hear with their ears,
> and they have closed their eyes.
> Otherwise they might see with their eyes,
> hear with their ears,
> understand with their hearts
> and turn, and I would heal them.'[a][j]

28"Therefore I want you to know that God's salvation[k] has been
sent to the Gentiles,[l] and they will listen!"[b]
30For two whole years Paul stayed there in his own rented house
and welcomed all who came to see him. 31Boldly and without
hindrance he preached the kingdom of God[m] and taught about
the Lord Jesus Christ.

a 27 Isaiah 6:9,10 b 28 Some manuscripts *listen!" 29After he said this, the Jews left, arguing vigorously among themselves.*

28:20 [a]Ac 26:6,7 [b]Ac 21:33
28:21 [c]Ac 22:5
28:22 [d]Ac 24:5,14
28:23 [e]Ac 19:8 [f]Ac 17:3 [g]Ac 8:35
28:24 [h]Ac 14:4
28:27 [i]Ps 119:70 [j]Isa 6:9,10
28:28 [k]Lk 2:30 [l]Ac 13:46
28:31 [m]ver 23; Mt 4:23

Acts at a Glance

Theme of Acts:

Author:

Date:

Purpose:

Key Words:

believe, have faith (believed, believers, put their trust)

baptized (baptism)

Spirit

witness, testify, confirmed, bore testimony, showed, martyr

word, preaching, message, statement (word of God, word of the Lord)

save, saved

church

Segment Divisions				Chapter Themes
				1
				2
				3
				4
				5
				6
				7
				8
				9
				10
				11
				12
				13
				14
				15
				16
				17
				18
				19
				20
				21
				22
				23
				24
				25
				26
				27
				28

ROMANS

The gospel Paul preached, justification by faith alone, was under siege. While many directly opposed this gospel, others twisted it to suit their own preferences. The Judaizers said salvation might be by grace but the believer is "kept" by the law. They insisted that circumcision was necessary for salvation. At the other extreme, the antinomians taught that you could be saved by grace and still live any way you wanted—even continue in sin.

Only a clear explanation of the gospel could refute such errors. Eager to prove the gospel's power to save and sanctify both Jew and Gentile, Paul, like a wise lawyer, calls the gospel to the witness stand and examines it from every angle. The result is the book of Romans, a theological masterpiece written around A.D. 56 or 57.

Things to Do

1. Romans is the constitution of the Christian faith. If you understand Romans you will have a plumb line for correctly interpreting any teaching on the gospel. It is a book you need to observe until you are so familiar with the text that its meaning is obvious.

   a. Read Romans in one sitting before you begin your study. If that is not possible, read it a chapter at a time. Every time you see the word *gospel*, mark it in a distinctive way so you can easily spot it in the text.

   b. Paul gives his reasons for writing Romans in the first and the last two chapters. Record these reasons in the appropriate place on the ROMANS OBSERVATIONS CHART on page 1949.

   c. Watch for references to the recipients of this letter and record on the OBSERVATIONS CHART what you learn about them. Note whether Paul is writing to Gentiles, Jews, or both. Also as you read, find out as much as you can about Paul. Record your insights on the chart.

2. The book of Romans can be divided into four segments, each building on the previous one: chapters 1 through 5, 6 through 8, 9 through 11, and 12 through 16. Instructions for each segment follow. As you complete each one, return to these general instructions so you can see what else you are to do in each segment.

Chapters 1-5

1. Read Romans 1 through 5 a chapter at a time, observing and marking the text. Complete instructions on how to observe the text are in the observation section in "How to Use The International Inductive Study Bible" on page IISB-15.

   a. Mark each of the following key words and their synonyms: *grace, faith (believe), law (law's, principle), justified (proved right, declared righteous, justify, just, deserved), righteous (righteousness, justice), wrath (punishment), judge (condemn, judgment), gospel, believe (faith), sin (sinning), Gentiles (nations), God, Jesus Christ,* and *Spirit* (when referring to the Holy Spirit).

   b. List these words on an index card to use as a bookmark when you study Romans. As you come to each new segment of Romans, add the next group of key words to your card. Mark or color code them on the card in the same way you plan to mark them in your Bible.

   c. Each chapter has key words or phrases which are unique to that chapter. Mark the following:

      1) In chapter 1 mark *exchanged (the)* and *God (he) gave them over*. Note the progression of events as you observe what the people did and how God responded.

      2) In chapter 4 mark and observe *credit* or *credited.*

3) In chapter 5 mark and observe *gift.*

4) Mark any other key words that are pertinent to a chapter or to the book.

2. List in the margin what you learn from the text about each key word. For example, *sin* is a key word. What do you learn from the text about *sin?* About *wrath (punishment)*? About *righteousness (justice)*? And so on.

3. From chapters 3 through 11 of Romans, Paul periodically asks an important question and then answers it. Mark each of Paul's questions. You might put a cloud like this ☁ around each question throughout the book. Carefully read each question and note how Paul answers it.

4. Watch for the words *therefore (then, this is why)* and see what they are "there for." Several chapters have these words in the first verse. When Paul uses *therefore, then,* or *this is why* he is making a point you will not want to miss.

5. When you finish observing each chapter, record the theme of that chapter in the text next to the chapter number and on the ROMANS AT A GLANCE chart on page 1950.

6. What do you see as the theme in this first segment of Romans? Write it (in pencil) on ROMANS AT A GLANCE in the first column under "Segment Divisions."

Chapters 6-8

1. Follow the same procedure as you did in the previous segment. Continue to mark the key words you marked in chapters 1 through 5, and in these chapters also mark the following words and their synonyms: *sinful nature (natural selves, unspiritual, sinful man, sinful, natural, human ancestry, race), dead (died, dying, death), life, reign, master (mastery), slaves (slavery),* and *freed from sin (set free from sin).*

2. If it is significant, list in the margin what you learn from marking the prominent key words in this segment of Romans.

3. Mark Paul's questions and in the margin list the main points of his answers.

4. Record the theme of each chapter and of this segment as you did before.

5. On the ROMANS OBSERVATIONS CHART on page 1949 is a place to record everything you learn from chapters 5 through 8 regarding our position in Adam (before we were saved) and our position in Christ (after we were saved). Do not read anything into the text, but simply record what you learn.

Chapters 9-11

1. Follow the same pattern you used in the first segment and mark the same key words you marked in chapters 1 through 8. Also mark the following key words in this segment of Romans: *foreknew,* predestined,* election (elect, chosen), Israel* (and its pronouns), *unbelief, saved* (*salvation*—go back and mark it in Romans 1:16), and *mercy.*

*These words are used in Romans 8:29, 30. Go back and mark them, and in the margin note what you learn from the text.

2. In this section it is critical that you follow Paul's reasoning by marking each question and then listing in the margin the main points of Paul's answers. Do not read into the text meanings that aren't there. Let God speak as you listen. Meditate on Romans 11:33-36.

3. Record chapter and segment themes as before.

Chapters 12-16

1. At this point Paul makes a transition and changes from explaining the doctrinal aspect of the gospel to describing how to live it out practically. As Paul turns from doctrine to duty, note the *therefore* and how it would relate to what has been written in the first eleven chapters of Romans. Think about what Paul is asking you to do. Is it reasonable? Why? What do you need to do?

2. Read Romans chapters 12 through 16 and identify the main topic or subject of each chapter. Mark

the following key words: *love, authority (rulers), brothers (brother), Lord, Gentiles (nations), minister (service, serving, servant, act of worship, serve, in the service of), judge (judgment, condemn, passing judgment on),* and *failings.*

3. Complete ROMANS AT A GLANCE. Fill in the chapter themes and segment divisions and then record the theme of Romans. (Do not forget to record your chapter themes in the text, too.)

Things to Think About

1. Suppose someone accused you of not being a Christian. What proof could you give of the fact that you are a true child of God?
2. Do you know how to share the gospel with someone? How?
3. From your study of Romans, how is a person saved?
4. How will your relationships to those in authority over you and to those who are your brothers and sisters in the faith change as you apply the truth of Romans to your life?
5. Are you ready to defend the gospel? Can you refute modern-day Judaizers and/or antinomians?

Chapter 1 Theme ____________________________

1 Paul, a servant of Christ Jesus, called to be an apostle[a] and set
apart[b] for the gospel of God[c]— 2the gospel he promised beforehand through his prophets in the Holy Scriptures[d] 3regarding his
Son, who as to his human nature[e] was a descendant of David, 4and
who through the Spirit[a] of holiness was declared with power to be
the Son of God[b] by his resurrection from the dead: Jesus Christ
our Lord. 5Through him and for his name's sake, we received
grace and apostleship to call people from among all the Gentiles[f]
to the obedience that comes from faith.[g] 6And you also are among
those who are called to belong to Jesus Christ.[h]

7To all in Rome who are loved by God[i] and called to be saints:

Grace and peace to you from God our Father and from the
Lord Jesus Christ.[j]

8First, I thank my God through Jesus Christ for all of you,[k]
because your faith is being reported all over the world.[l] 9God,
whom I serve[m] with my whole heart in preaching the gospel of his
Son, is my witness[n] how constantly I remember you 10in my prayers
at all times; and I pray that now at last by God's will the way may
be opened for me to come to you.[o]

11I long to see you[p] so that I may impart to you some spiritual
gift to make you strong— 12that is, that you and I may be mutu-
ally encouraged by each other's faith. 13I do not want you to be
unaware, brothers, that I planned many times to come to you
(but have been prevented from doing so until now)[q] in order that
I might have a harvest among you, just as I have had among the
other Gentiles.

1:1 [a] 1Co 1:1 [b] Ac 9:15 [c] 2Co 11:7
1:2 [d] Gal 3:8
1:3 [e] Jn 1:14
1:5 [f] Ac 9:15 [g] Ac 6:7
1:6 [h] Rev 17:14
1:7 [i] Ro 8:39 [j] 1Co 1:3
1:8 [k] 1Co 1:4 [l] Ro 16:19
1:9 [m] 2Ti 1:3 [n] Php 1:8
1:10 [o] Ro 15:32
1:11 [p] Ro 15:23
1:13 [q] Ro 15:22,23

[a] 4 *Or who as to his spirit* [b] 4 *Or was appointed to be the Son of God with power*

14 I am obligated[a] both to Greeks and non-Greeks, both to the
wise and the foolish. 15 That is why I am so eager to preach the
gospel also to you who are at Rome.[b]
16 I am not ashamed of the gospel,[c] because it is the power of God[d]
for the salvation of everyone who believes: first for the Jew,[e] then
for the Gentile.[f] 17 For in the gospel a righteousness from God is
revealed,[g] a righteousness that is by faith from first to last,[a] just as
it is written: "The righteous will live by faith."[b][h]
18 The wrath of God[i] is being revealed from heaven against all
the godlessness and wickedness of men who suppress the truth by
their wickedness, 19 since what may be known about God is plain
to them, because God has made it plain to them.[j] 20 For since the
creation of the world God's invisible qualities—his eternal power
and divine nature—have been clearly seen, being understood
from what has been made,[k] so that men are without excuse.
21 For although they knew God, they neither glorified him as
God nor gave thanks to him, but their thinking became futile
and their foolish hearts were darkened.[l] 22 Although they claimed
to be wise, they became fools[m] 23 and exchanged the glory of the
immortal God for images[n] made to look like mortal man and
birds and animals and reptiles.
24 Therefore God gave them over[o] in the sinful desires of their
hearts to sexual impurity for the degrading of their bodies with
one another.[p] 25 They exchanged the truth of God for a lie,[q] and
worshiped and served created things[r] rather than the Creator—
who is forever praised.[s] Amen.
26 Because of this, God gave them over[t] to shameful lusts.[u] Even
their women exchanged natural relations for unnatural ones.[v]
27 In the same way the men also abandoned natural relations with
women and were inflamed with lust for one another. Men committed indecent acts with other men, and received in themselves
the due penalty for their perversion.[w]
28 Furthermore, since they did not think it worthwhile to retain
the knowledge of God, he gave them over[x] to a depraved mind, to
do what ought not to be done. 29 They have become filled with every
kind of wickedness, evil, greed and depravity. They are full of envy,
murder, strife, deceit and malice. They are gossips,[y] 30 slanderers,
God-haters, insolent, arrogant and boastful; they invent ways of
doing evil; they disobey their parents;[z] 31 they are senseless, faithless, heartless,[a] ruthless. 32 Although they know God's righteous
decree that those who do such things deserve death,[b] they not
only continue to do these very things but also approve[c] of those
who practice them.

1:14 *a* 1Co 9:16
1:15 *b* Ro 15:20
1:16 *c* 2Ti 1:8 *d* 1Co 1:18 *e* Ac 3:26 *f* Ro 2:9,10
1:17 *g* Ro 3:21 *h* Hab 2:4; Gal 3:11; Heb 10:38
1:18 *i* Eph 5:6; Col 3:6
1:19 *j* Ac 14:17
1:20 *k* Ps 19:1-6
1:21 *l* Jer 2:5; Eph 4:17,18
1:22 *m* 1Co 1:20,27
1:23 *n* Ps 106:20; Jer 2:11; Ac 17:29
1:24 *o* Eph 4:19 *p* 1Pe 4:3
1:25 *q* Isa 44:20 *r* Jer 10:14 *s* Ro 9:5
1:26 *t* ver 24,28 *u* 1Th 4:5 *v* Lev 18:22,23
1:27 *w* Lev 18:22; 20:13
1:28 *x* ver 24,26
1:29 *y* 2Co 12:20
1:30 *z* 2Ti 3:2
1:31 *a* 2Ti 3:3
1:32 *b* Ro 6:23 *c* Ps 50:18; Lk 11:48; Ac 8:1; 22:20

[a] *17* Or *is from faith to faith* [b] *17* Hab. 2:4

Chapter 2 Theme ______________________

2 You, therefore, have no excuse,[a] you who pass judgment on
someone else, for at whatever point you judge the other, you
are condemning yourself, because you who pass judgment do the
same things.[b] 2Now we know that God's judgment against those
who do such things is based on truth. 3So when you, a mere man,
pass judgment on them and yet do the same things, do you think
you will escape God's judgment? 4Or do you show contempt for
the riches[c] of his kindness,[d] tolerance[e] and patience,[f] not realizing
that God's kindness leads you toward repentance?[g]

5But because of your stubbornness and your unrepentant heart,
you are storing up wrath against yourself for the day of God's
wrath, when his righteous judgment[h] will be revealed. 6God "will
give to each person according to what he has done."[a] [i] 7To those
who by persistence in doing good seek glory, honor[j] and immortality,[k] he will give eternal life. 8But for those who are self-seeking
and who reject the truth and follow evil,[l] there will be wrath and
anger. 9There will be trouble and distress for every human being
who does evil: first for the Jew, then for the Gentile;[m] 10but glory,
honor and peace for everyone who does good: first for the Jew,
then for the Gentile.[n] 11For God does not show favoritism.[o]

12All who sin apart from the law will also perish apart from the
law, and all who sin under the law[p] will be judged by the law.
13For it is not those who hear the law who are righteous in God's
sight, but it is those who obey[q] the law who will be declared
righteous. 14(Indeed, when Gentiles, who do not have the law, do
by nature things required by the law,[r] they are a law for themselves, even though they do not have the law, 15since they show
that the requirements of the law are written on their hearts, their
consciences also bearing witness, and their thoughts now accusing, now even defending them.) 16This will take place on the day
when God will judge men's secrets[s] through Jesus Christ,[t] as my
gospel[u] declares.

17Now you, if you call yourself a Jew; if you rely on the law and
brag about your relationship to God;[v] 18if you know his will and
approve of what is superior because you are instructed by the
law; 19if you are convinced that you are a guide for the blind, a
light for those who are in the dark, 20an instructor of the foolish,
a teacher of infants, because you have in the law the embodiment
of knowledge and truth— 21you, then, who teach others, do you
not teach yourself? You who preach against stealing, do you
steal?[w] 22You who say that people should not commit adultery, do
you commit adultery? You who abhor idols, do you rob temples?[x]

a6 Psalm 62:12; Prov. 24:12

2:1
a Ro 1:20
b 2Sa 12:5-7; Mt 7:1,2

2:4
c Ro 9:23; Eph 1:7,18; 2:7
d Ro 11:22
e Ro 3:25
f Ex 34:6
g 2Pe 3:9

2:5
h Jude 6

2:6
i Ps 62:12; Mt 16:27

2:7
j ver 10
k 1Co 15:53,54

2:8
l 2Th 2:12

2:9
m 1Pe 4:17

2:10
n ver 9

2:11
o Ac 10:34

2:12
p Ro 3:19; 1Co 9:20,21

2:13
q Jas 1:22,23,25

2:14
r Ac 10:35

2:16
s Ecc 12:14
t Ac 10:42
u Ro 16:25

2:17
v ver 23; Mic 3:11; Ro 9:4

2:21
w Mt 23:3,4

2:22
x Ac 19:37

23 You who brag about the law,[a] do you dishonor God by breaking
the law? 24 As it is written: "God's name is blasphemed among the
Gentiles because of you."[a] [b]

25 Circumcision has value if you observe the law,[c] but if you
break the law, you have become as though you had not been circumcised.[d] 26 If those who are not circumcised keep the law's
requirements,[e] will they not be regarded as though they were circumcised?[f] 27 The one who is not circumcised physically and yet
obeys the law will condemn you[g] who, even though you have the[b]
written code and circumcision, are a lawbreaker.

28 A man is not a Jew if he is only one outwardly,[h] nor is circumcision merely outward and physical.[i] 29 No, a man is a Jew if he is
one inwardly; and circumcision is circumcision of the heart, by
the Spirit,[j] not by the written code.[k] Such a man's praise is not
from men, but from God.[l]

Chapter 3 Theme

3 What advantage, then, is there in being a Jew, or what value
is there in circumcision? 2 Much in every way! First of all, they
have been entrusted with the very words of God.[m]

3 What if some did not have faith?[n] Will their lack of faith nullify
God's faithfulness?[o] 4 Not at all! Let God be true,[p] and every man
a liar.[q] As it is written:

> "So that you may be proved right when you speak
> and prevail when you judge."[c] [r]

5 But if our unrighteousness brings out God's righteousness more
clearly, what shall we say? That God is unjust in bringing his wrath
on us? (I am using a human argument.)[s] 6 Certainly not! If that
were so, how could God judge the world?[t] 7 Someone might argue,
"If my falsehood enhances God's truthfulness and so increases
his glory,[u] why am I still condemned as a sinner?" 8 Why not say—
as we are being slanderously reported as saying and as some claim
that we say—"Let us do evil that good may result"?[v] Their condemnation is deserved.

9 What shall we conclude then? Are we any better[d]? Not at all!
We have already made the charge that Jews and Gentiles alike are
all under sin.[w] 10 As it is written:

> "There is no one righteous, not even one;
> 11 there is no one who understands,
> no one who seeks God.
> 12 All have turned away,
> they have together become worthless;

2:23 [a] ver 17
2:24 [b] Isa 52:5; Eze 36:22
2:25 [c] Gal 5:3 [d] Jer 4:4
2:26 [e] Ro 8:4 [f] 1Co 7:19
2:27 [g] Mt 12:41,42
2:28 [h] Mt 3:9; Jn 8:39; Ro 9:6,7 [i] Gal 6:15
2:29 [j] Php 3:3; Col 2:1 [k] Ro 7:6 [l] Jn 5:44; 1Co 4:5; 2Co 10:18; 1Th 2:4; 1Pe 3:4
3:2 [m] Dt 4:8; Ps 147:19
3:3 [n] Heb 4:2 [o] 2Ti 2:13
3:4 [p] Jn 3:33 [q] Ps 116:11 [r] Ps 51:4
3:5 [s] Ro 6:19; Gal 3:15
3:6 [t] Ge 18:25
3:7 [u] ver 4
3:8 [v] Ro 6:1
3:9 [w] ver 19,23; Gal 3:22

[a] *24* Isaiah 52:5; Ezek. 36:22 [b] *27* Or *who, by means of a* [c] *4* Psalm 51:4 [d] *9* Or *worse*

there is no one who does good,
not even one."[a][a]
13"Their throats are open graves;
their tongues practice deceit."[b][b]
"The poison of vipers is on their lips."[c][c]
14 "Their mouths are full of cursing and bitterness."[d][d]
15"Their feet are swift to shed blood;
16 ruin and misery mark their ways,
17and the way of peace they do not know."[e]
18 "There is no fear of God before their eyes."[f][e]

19Now we know that whatever the law says,[f] it says to those who
are under the law,[g] so that every mouth may be silenced and the
whole world held accountable to God. 20Therefore no one will be
declared righteous in his sight by observing the law;[h] rather,
through the law we become conscious of sin.[i]

21But now a righteousness from God,[j] apart from law, has been
made known, to which the Law and the Prophets testify.[k] 22This
righteousness from God comes through faith[l] in Jesus Christ to
all who believe. There is no difference,[m] 23for all have sinned and
fall short of the glory of God, 24and are justified freely by his grace[n]
through the redemption[o] that came by Christ Jesus. 25God presented him as a sacrifice of atonement,[g][p] through faith in his blood.[q]
He did this to demonstrate his justice, because in his forbearance
he had left the sins committed beforehand unpunished[r]— 26he did
it to demonstrate his justice at the present time, so as to be just
and the one who justifies those who have faith in Jesus.

27Where, then, is boasting?[s] It is excluded. On what principle?
On that of observing the law? No, but on that of faith. 28For we
maintain that a man is justified by faith apart from observing the
law.[t] 29Is God the God of Jews only? Is he not the God of Gentiles
too? Yes, of Gentiles too,[u] 30since there is only one God, who will
justify the circumcised by faith and the uncircumcised through
that same faith.[v] 31Do we, then, nullify the law by this faith? Not
at all! Rather, we uphold the law.

Chapter 4 Theme ______________________________

4 What then shall we say that Abraham, our forefather, discovered in this matter? 2If, in fact, Abraham was justified by
works, he had something to boast about—but not before God.[w]
3What does the Scripture say? "Abraham believed God, and it
was credited to him as righteousness."[h][x]

[a] *12* Psalms 14:1-3; 53:1-3; Eccles. 7:20 [b] *13* Psalm 5:9 [c] *13* Psalm 140:3 [d] *14* Psalm 10:7
[e] *17* Isaiah 59:7,8 [f] *18* Psalm 36:1 [g] *25* Or *as the one who would turn aside his wrath, taking away sin* [h] *3* Gen. 15:6; also in verse 22

3:12 [a]Ps 14:1-3
3:13 [b]Ps 5:9 [c]Ps 140:3
3:14 [d]Ps 10:7
3:18 [e]Ps 36:1
3:19 [f]Jn 10:34 [g]Ro 2:12
3:20 [h]Ac 13:39; Gal 2:16 [i]Ro 7:7
3:21 [j]Ro 1:17; 9:30 [k]Ac 10:43
3:22 [l]Ro 9:30 [m]Ro 10:12; Gal 3:28; Col 3:11
3:24 [n]Ro 4:16; Eph 2:8 [o]Eph 1:7,14; Col 1:14; Heb 9:12
3:25 [p]1Jn 4:10 [q]Heb 9:12,14 [r]Ac 17:30
3:27 [s]Ro 2:17,23; 4:2; 1Co 1:29-31; Eph 2:9
3:28 [t]ver 20,21; Ac 13:39; Eph 2:9
3:29 [u]Ro 9:24
3:30 [v]Gal 3:8
4:2 [w]1Co 1:31
4:3 [x]ver 5,9,22; Ge 15:6; Gal 3:6; Jas 2:23

4 Now when a man works, his wages are not credited to him as a
gift,[a] but as an obligation. 5 However, to the man who does not
work but trusts God who justifies the wicked, his faith is credited
as righteousness. 6 David says the same thing when he speaks of
the blessedness of the man to whom God credits righteousness
apart from works:

> 7 "Blessed are they
> whose transgressions are forgiven,
> whose sins are covered.
> 8 Blessed is the man
> whose sin the Lord will never count against him."[a][b]

9 Is this blessedness only for the circumcised, or also for the
uncircumcised?[c] We have been saying that Abraham's faith was
credited to him as righteousness.[d] 10 Under what circumstances
was it credited? Was it after he was circumcised, or before? It was
not after, but before! 11 And he received the sign of circumcision,
a seal of the righteousness that he had by faith while he was still
uncircumcised.[e] So then, he is the father[f] of all who believe[g] but
have not been circumcised, in order that righteousness might be
credited to them. 12 And he is also the father of the circumcised who
not only are circumcised but who also walk in the footsteps of
the faith that our father Abraham had before he was circumcised.

13 It was not through law that Abraham and his offspring received
the promise[h] that he would be heir of the world,[i] but through the
righteousness that comes by faith. 14 For if those who live by law
are heirs, faith has no value and the promise is worthless,[j]
15 because law brings wrath.[k] And where there is no law there is
no transgression.[l]

16 Therefore, the promise comes by faith, so that it may be by
grace[m] and may be guaranteed[n] to all Abraham's offspring—not
only to those who are of the law but also to those who are of the
faith of Abraham. He is the father of us all. 17 As it is written: "I
have made you a father of many nations."[b][o] He is our father in
the sight of God, in whom he believed—the God who gives life[p]
to the dead and calls[q] things that are not[r] as though they were.

18 Against all hope, Abraham in hope believed and so became
the father of many nations,[s] just as it had been said to him, "So
shall your offspring be."[c][t] 19 Without weakening in his faith, he
faced the fact that his body was as good as dead[u]—since he was
about a hundred years old[v]—and that Sarah's womb was also
dead.[w] 20 Yet he did not waver through unbelief regarding the
promise of God, but was strengthened in his faith and gave glory
to God,[x] 21 being fully persuaded that God had power to do what

4:4 [a]Ro 11:6
4:8 [b]Ps 32:1,2; 2Co 5:19
4:9 [c]Ro 3:30 [d]ver 3
4:11 [e]Ge 17:10,11 [f]ver 16,17; Lk 19:9 [g]Ro 3:22
4:13 [h]Gal 3:16,29 [i]Ge 17:4-6
4:14 [j]Gal 3:18
4:15 [k]Ro 7:7-25; 1Co 15:56; 2Co 3:7; Gal 3:10; Ro 7:12 [l]Ro 3:20; 7:7
4:16 [m]Ro 3:24 [n]Ro 15:8
4:17 [o]Ge 17:5 [p]Jn 5:21 [q]Isa 48:13 [r]1Co 1:28
4:18 [s]ver 17 [t]Ge 15:5
4:19 [u]Heb 11:11,12 [v]Ge 17:17 [w]Ge 18:11
4:20 [x]Mt 9:8

[a] *8* Psalm 32:1,2 [b] *17* Gen. 17:5 [c] *18* Gen. 15:5

he had promised.[a] 22 This is why "it was credited to him as righteousness."[b] 23 The words "it was credited to him" were written
not for him alone, 24 but also for us,[c] to whom God will credit
righteousness—for us who believe in him[d] who raised Jesus our
Lord from the dead.[e] 25 He was delivered over to death for our
sins[f] and was raised to life for our justification.

Chapter 5 Theme ______________________________

5 Therefore, since we have been justified through faith,[g] we[a]
have peace with God through our Lord Jesus Christ, 2 through
whom we have gained access[h] by faith into this grace in which we
now stand.[i] And we[a] rejoice in the hope[j] of the glory of God. 3 Not
only so, but we[a] also rejoice in our sufferings,[k] because we know
that suffering produces perseverance;[l] 4 perseverance, character;
and character, hope. 5 And hope[m] does not disappoint us, because
God has poured out his love into our hearts by the Holy Spirit,[n]
whom he has given us.

6 You see, at just the right time,[o] when we were still powerless,
Christ died for the ungodly.[p] 7 Very rarely will anyone die for a
righteous man, though for a good man someone might possibly
dare to die. 8 But God demonstrates his own love for us in this:
While we were still sinners, Christ died for us.[q]

9 Since we have now been justified by his blood,[r] how much
more shall we be saved from God's wrath[s] through him! 10 For if,
when we were God's enemies,[t] we were reconciled[u] to him through
the death of his Son, how much more, having been reconciled,
shall we be saved through his life![v] 11 Not only is this so, but we
also rejoice in God through our Lord Jesus Christ, through whom
we have now received reconciliation.

12 Therefore, just as sin entered the world through one man,[w]
and death through sin,[x] and in this way death came to all men,
because all sinned— 13 for before the law was given, sin was in the
world. But sin is not taken into account when there is no law.[y]
14 Nevertheless, death reigned from the time of Adam to the time
of Moses, even over those who did not sin by breaking a command, as did Adam, who was a pattern of the one to come.[z]

15 But the gift is not like the trespass. For if the many died by the
trespass of the one man,[a] how much more did God's grace and
the gift that came by the grace of the one man, Jesus Christ,[b]
overflow to the many! 16 Again, the gift of God is not like the
result of the one man's sin: The judgment followed one sin and
brought condemnation, but the gift followed many trespasses
and brought justification. 17 For if, by the trespass of the one man,

a 1,2,3 Or *let us*

4:21 [a] Ge 18:14; Heb 11:19
4:22 [b] ver 3
4:24 [c] Ro 15:4; 1Co 9:10; 10:11 [d] Ro 10:9 [e] Ac 2:24
4:25 [f] Isa 53:5,6; Ro 5:6,8
5:1 [g] Ro 3:28
5:2 [h] Eph 2:18 [i] 1Co 15:1 [j] Heb 3:6
5:3 [k] Mt 5:12 [l] Jas 1:2,3
5:5 [m] Php 1:20 [n] Ac 2:33
5:6 [o] Gal 4:4 [p] Ro 4:25
5:8 [q] Jn 15:13; 1Pe 3:18
5:9 [r] Ro 3:25 [s] Ro 1:18
5:10 [t] Ro 11:28; Col 1:21 [u] 2Co 5:18,19; Col 1:20,22 [v] Ro 8:34
5:12 [w] ver 15,16,17; 1Co 15:21,22 [x] Ge 2:17; 3:19; Ro 6:23
5:13 [y] Ro 4:15
5:14 [z] 1Co 15:22,45
5:15 [a] ver 12,18,19 [b] Ac 15:11

death[a] reigned through that one man, how much more will those
who receive God's abundant provision of grace and of the gift of
righteousness reign in life through the one man, Jesus Christ.
18 Consequently, just as the result of one trespass was condemnation for all men,[b] so also the result of one act of righteousness
was justification[c] that brings life for all men. 19 For just as through
the disobedience of the one man[d] the many were made sinners,
so also through the obedience[e] of the one man the many will be
made righteous.
20 The law was added so that the trespass might increase.[f] But
where sin increased, grace increased all the more,[g] 21 so that, just
as sin reigned in death,[h] so also grace might reign through righteousness to bring eternal life through Jesus Christ our Lord.

Chapter 6 Theme ________________

6 What shall we say, then? Shall we go on sinning so that grace
may increase?[i] 2 By no means! We died to sin;[j] how can we
live in it any longer? 3 Or don't you know that all of us who were
baptized[k] into Christ Jesus were baptized into his death? 4 We
were therefore buried with him through baptism into death in
order that, just as Christ was raised from the dead[l] through the
glory of the Father, we too may live a new life.[m]
5 If we have been united with him like this in his death, we will
certainly also be united with him in his resurrection.[n] 6 For we know
that our old self[o] was crucified with him[p] so that the body of sin[q]
might be done away with,[a] that we should no longer be slaves to
sin— 7 because anyone who has died has been freed from sin.
8 Now if we died with Christ, we believe that we will also live
with him. 9 For we know that since Christ was raised from the
dead,[r] he cannot die again; death no longer has mastery over
him.[s] 10 The death he died, he died to sin[t] once for all; but the life
he lives, he lives to God.
11 In the same way, count yourselves dead to sin[u] but alive to
God in Christ Jesus. 12 Therefore do not let sin reign in your mortal
body so that you obey its evil desires. 13 Do not offer the parts of
your body to sin, as instruments of wickedness,[v] but rather offer
yourselves to God, as those who have been brought from death to
life; and offer the parts of your body to him as instruments of
righteousness.[w] 14 For sin shall not be your master, because you
are not under law,[x] but under grace.[y]
15 What then? Shall we sin because we are not under law but
under grace? By no means! 16 Don't you know that when you offer
yourselves to someone to obey him as slaves, you are slaves to the
one whom you obey—whether you are slaves to sin,[z] which leads

[a]6 Or *be rendered powerless*

5:17 [a]ver 12
5:18 [b]ver 12 [c]Ro 4:25
5:19 [d]ver 12 [e]Php 2:8
5:20 [f]Ro 7:7,8; Gal 3:19 [g]1Ti 1:13,14
5:21 [h]ver 12,14
6:1 [i]ver 15; Ro 3:5,8
6:2 [j]Col 3:3,5; 1Pe 2:24
6:3 [k]Mt 28:19
6:4 [l]Col 2:12 [m]Ro 7:6; Gal 6:15; Eph 4:22-24; Col 3:10
6:5 [n]2Co 4:10; Php 3:10,11
6:6 [o]Eph 4:22; Col 3:9 [p]Gal 2:20; Col 2:12,20 [q]Ro 7:24
6:9 [r]Ac 2:24 [s]Rev 1:18
6:10 [t]ver 2
6:11 [u]ver 2
6:13 [v]ver 16,19; Ro 7:5 [w]Ro 12:1; 1Pe 2:24
6:14 [x]Gal 5:18 [y]Ro 3:24
6:16 [z]Jn 8:34; 2Pe 2:19

to death,[a] or to obedience, which leads to righteousness? 17 But
thanks be to God[b] that, though you used to be slaves to sin, you
wholeheartedly obeyed the form of teaching[c] to which you were
entrusted. 18 You have been set free from sin[d] and have become
slaves to righteousness.
19 I put this in human terms[e] because you are weak in your natural selves. Just as you used to offer the parts of your body in slavery to impurity and to ever-increasing wickedness, so now offer
them in slavery to righteousness[f] leading to holiness. 20 When you
were slaves to sin,[g] you were free from the control of righteousness.
21 What benefit did you reap at that time from the things you are
now ashamed of? Those things result in death![h] 22 But now that
you have been set free from sin[i] and have become slaves to God,[j]
the benefit you reap leads to holiness, and the result is eternal
life. 23 For the wages of sin is death,[k] but the gift of God is eternal
life[l] in[a] Christ Jesus our Lord.

Chapter 7 Theme ________________________

7 Do you not know, brothers[m]—for I am speaking to men
who know the law—that the law has authority over a man
only as long as he lives? 2 For example, by law a married woman is
bound to her husband as long as he is alive, but if her husband
dies, she is released from the law of marriage.[n] 3 So then, if she
marries another man while her husband is still alive, she is called
an adulteress. But if her husband dies, she is released from that law
and is not an adulteress, even though she marries another man.
4 So, my brothers, you also died to the law[o] through the body of
Christ,[p] that you might belong to another, to him who was raised
from the dead, in order that we might bear fruit to God. 5 For
when we were controlled by the sinful nature,[b] the sinful passions
aroused by the law[q] were at work in our bodies,[r] so that we bore
fruit for death. 6 But now, by dying to what once bound us, we
have been released from the law so that we serve in the new way
of the Spirit, and not in the old way of the written code.[s]
7 What shall we say, then? Is the law sin? Certainly not! Indeed I
would not have known what sin was except through the law.[t] For
I would not have known what coveting really was if the law had not
said, "Do not covet."[c][u] 8 But sin, seizing the opportunity afforded
by the commandment,[v] produced in me every kind of covetous
desire. For apart from law, sin is dead.[w] 9 Once I was alive apart
from law; but when the commandment came, sin sprang to life
and I died. 10 I found that the very commandment that was
intended to bring life[x] actually brought death. 11 For sin, seizing the
opportunity afforded by the commandment, deceived me,[y] and

[a] 23 Or *through* [b] 5 Or *the flesh;* also in verse 25 [c] 7 Exodus 20:17; Deut. 5:21

6:16 [a] ver 23
6:17 [b] Ro 1:8; 2Co 2:14 [c] 2Ti 1:13
6:18 [d] ver 7,22; Ro 8:2
6:19 [e] Ro 3:5 [f] ver 13
6:20 [g] ver 16
6:21 [h] ver 23
6:22 [i] ver 18 [j] 1Co 7:22; 1Pe 2:16
6:23 [k] Ge 2:17; Ro 5:12; Gal 6:7,8; Jas 1:15 [l] Mt 25:46
7:1 [m] Ro 1:13
7:2 [n] 1Co 7:39
7:4 [o] Ro 8:2; Gal 2:19 [p] Col 1:22
7:5 [q] Ro 7:7-11 [r] Ro 6:13
7:6 [s] Ro 2:29; 2Co 3:6
7:7 [t] Ro 3:20; 4:15 [u] Ex 20:17; Dt 5:21
7:8 [v] ver 11 [w] Ro 4:15; 1Co 15:56
7:10 [x] Lev 18:5; Lk 10:26-28; Ro 10:5; Gal 3:12
7:11 [y] Ge 3:13

through the commandment put me to death. 12So then, the law is
holy, and the commandment is holy, righteous and good.[a]
13Did that which is good, then, become death to me? By no
means! But in order that sin might be recognized as sin, it produced death in me through what was good, so that through the
commandment sin might become utterly sinful.
14We know that the law is spiritual; but I am unspiritual,[b] sold[c]
as a slave to sin. 15I do not understand what I do. For what I want
to do I do not do, but what I hate I do.[d] 16And if I do what I do not
want to do, I agree that the law is good.[e] 17As it is, it is no longer I
myself who do it, but it is sin living in me.[f] 18I know that nothing
good lives in me, that is, in my sinful nature.[a][g] For I have the
desire to do what is good, but I cannot carry it out. 19For what I
do is not the good I want to do; no, the evil I do not want to do—
this I keep on doing.[h] 20Now if I do what I do not want to do, it is
no longer I who do it, but it is sin living in me that does it.[i]
21So I find this law at work:[j] When I want to do good, evil is right
there with me. 22For in my inner being[k] I delight in God's law;[l]
23but I see another law at work in the members of my body, waging war[m] against the law of my mind and making me a prisoner
of the law of sin at work within my members. 24What a wretched
man I am! Who will rescue me from this body of death?[n]
25Thanks be to God—through Jesus Christ our Lord!
So then, I myself in my mind am a slave to God's law, but in the
sinful nature a slave to the law of sin.

Chapter 8 Theme ______________________________

8 Therefore, there is now no condemnation[o] for those who are
in Christ Jesus,[b][p] 2because through Christ Jesus the law of the
Spirit of life[q] set me free[r] from the law of sin[s] and death. 3For what
the law was powerless[t] to do in that it was weakened by the sinful
nature,[c] God did by sending his own Son in the likeness of sinful
man[u] to be a sin offering.[d][v] And so he condemned sin in sinful man,[e]
4in order that the righteous requirements of the law might be fully
met in us, who do not live according to the sinful nature but according to the Spirit.[w]
5Those who live according to the sinful nature have their minds
set on what that nature desires;[x] but those who live in accordance
with the Spirit have their minds set on what the Spirit desires.[y]
6The mind of sinful man[f] is death, but the mind controlled by the
Spirit is life[z] and peace; 7the sinful mind[g] is hostile to God.[a] It
does not submit to God's law, nor can it do so. 8Those controlled
by the sinful nature cannot please God.

[a] *18* Or *my flesh* [b] *1* Some later manuscripts *Jesus, who do not live according to the sinful nature but according to the Spirit,* [c] *3* Or *the flesh*; also in verses 4, 5, 8, 9, 12 and 13 [d] *3* Or *man, for sin* [e] *3* Or *in the flesh* [f] *6* Or *mind set on the flesh* [g] *7* Or *the mind set on the flesh*

7:12 [a] 1Ti 1:8
7:14 [b] 1Co 3:1 [c] 1Ki 21:20,25; 2Ki 17:17
7:15 [d] ver 19; Gal 5:17
7:16 [e] ver 12
7:17 [f] ver 20
7:18 [g] ver 25
7:19 [h] ver 15
7:20 [i] ver 17
7:21 [j] ver 23,25
7:22 [k] Eph 3:16 [l] Ps 1:2
7:23 [m] Gal 5:17; Jas 4:1; 1Pe 2:11
7:24 [n] Ro 6:6; 8:2
8:1 [o] ver 34 [p] ver 39; Ro 16:3
8:2 [q] 1Co 15:45 [r] Ro 6:18 [s] Ro 7:4
8:3 [t] Ac 13:39; Heb 7:18 [u] Php 2:7 [v] Heb 2:14,17
8:4 [w] Gal 5:16
8:5 [x] Gal 5:19-21 [y] Gal 5:22-25
8:6 [z] Gal 6:8
8:7 [a] Jas 4:4

9You, however, are controlled not by the sinful nature but by the
Spirit, if the Spirit of God lives in you.[a] And if anyone does not
have the Spirit of Christ,[b] he does not belong to Christ. 10But if
Christ is in you,[c] your body is dead because of sin, yet your spirit
is alive because of righteousness. 11And if the Spirit of him who
raised Jesus from the dead[d] is living in you, he who raised Christ
from the dead will also give life to your mortal bodies[e] through
his Spirit, who lives in you.

12Therefore, brothers, we have an obligation—but it is not to
the sinful nature, to live according to it. 13For if you live according
to the sinful nature, you will die; but if by the Spirit you put to
death the misdeeds of the body, you will live,[f] 14because those
who are led by the Spirit of God[g] are sons of God.[h] 15For you did
not receive a spirit that makes you a slave again to fear,[i] but you
received the Spirit of sonship.[a] And by him we cry, "*Abba*,[b] Father."[j]
16The Spirit himself testifies with our spirit[k] that we are God's
children. 17Now if we are children, then we are heirs[l]—heirs of
God and co-heirs with Christ, if indeed we share in his sufferings
in order that we may also share in his glory.[m]

18I consider that our present sufferings are not worth comparing
with the glory that will be revealed in us.[n] 19The creation waits in
eager expectation for the sons of God to be revealed. 20For the
creation was subjected to frustration, not by its own choice, but
by the will of the one who subjected it,[o] in hope 21that[c] the creation
itself will be liberated from its bondage to decay[p] and brought
into the glorious freedom of the children of God.

22We know that the whole creation has been groaning[q] as in the
pains of childbirth right up to the present time. 23Not only so, but
we ourselves, who have the firstfruits of the Spirit,[r] groan[s] inwardly
as we wait eagerly[t] for our adoption as sons, the redemption of
our bodies. 24For in this hope we were saved.[u] But hope that is
seen is no hope at all. Who hopes for what he already has? 25But if
we hope for what we do not yet have, we wait for it patiently.

26In the same way, the Spirit helps us in our weakness. We do
not know what we ought to pray for, but the Spirit himself intercedes for us[v] with groans that words cannot express. 27And he
who searches our hearts[w] knows the mind of the Spirit, because
the Spirit intercedes for the saints in accordance with God's will.

28And we know that in all things God works for the good of those
who love him,[d] who[e] have been called[x] according to his purpose.
29For those God foreknew[y] he also predestined[z] to be conformed
to the likeness of his Son,[a] that he might be the firstborn among

8:9 [a] 1Co 6:19; Gal 4:6 [b] Jn 14:17; 1Jn 4:13
8:10 [c] Gal 2:20; Eph 3:17; Col 1:27
8:11 [d] Ac 2:24 [e] Jn 5:21
8:13 [f] Gal 6:8
8:14 [g] Gal 5:18 [h] Jn 1:12; Rev 21:7
8:15 [i] 2Ti 1:7; Heb 2:15 [j] Mk 14:36; Gal 4:5,6
8:16 [k] Eph 1:13
8:17 [l] Ac 20:32; Gal 4:7 [m] 1Pe 4:13
8:18 [n] 2Co 4:17; 1Pe 4:13
8:20 [o] Ge 3:17-19
8:21 [p] Ac 3:21; 2Pe 3:13; Rev 21:1
8:22 [q] Jer 12:4
8:23 [r] 2Co 5:5 [s] 2Co 5:2,4 [t] Gal 5:5
8:24 [u] 1Th 5:8
8:26 [v] Eph 6:18
8:27 [w] Rev 2:23
8:28 [x] 1Co 1:9; 2Ti 1:9
8:29 [y] Ro 11:2 [z] Eph 1:5,11 [a] 1Co 15:49; 2Co 3:18; Php 3:21; 1Jn 3:2

a *15* Or *adoption* b *15* Aramaic for *Father* c *20,21* Or *subjected it in hope.* [21]*For*
d *28* Some manuscripts *And we know that all things work together for good to those who love God*
e *28* Or *works together with those who love him to bring about what is good—with those who*

many brothers. [30]And those he predestined,[a] he also called; those
he called, he also justified;[b] those he justified, he also glorified.[c]
[31]What, then, shall we say in response to this?[d] If God is for us,
who can be against us?[e] [32]He who did not spare his own Son,[f] but
gave him up for us all—how will he not also, along with him, graciously give us all things? [33]Who will bring any charge[g] against
those whom God has chosen? It is God who justifies. [34]Who is he
that condemns? Christ Jesus, who died[h]—more than that, who
was raised to life—is at the right hand of God[i] and is also inter-
ceding for us.[j] [35]Who shall separate us from the love of Christ?
Shall trouble or hardship or persecution or famine or nakedness
or danger or sword?[k] [36]As it is written:

> "For your sake we face death all day long;
> we are considered as sheep to be slaughtered."[a][l]

[37]No, in all these things we are more than conquerors[m] through him
who loved us.[n] [38]For I am convinced that neither death nor life,
neither angels nor demons,[b] neither the present nor the future,
nor any powers,[o] [39]neither height nor depth, nor anything else in
all creation, will be able to separate us from the love of God[p] that
is in Christ Jesus our Lord.

Chapter 9 Theme ______________________________

9 I speak the truth in Christ—I am not lying,[q] my conscience
confirms[r] it in the Holy Spirit— [2]I have great sorrow and
unceasing anguish in my heart. [3]For I could wish that I myself[s]
were cursed[t] and cut off from Christ for the sake of my brothers,
those of my own race,[u] [4]the people of Israel. Theirs is the adoption as sons;[v] theirs the divine glory, the covenants,[w] the receiving
of the law,[x] the temple worship[y] and the promises.[z] [5]Theirs are
the patriarchs, and from them is traced the human ancestry of
Christ,[a] who is God over all,[b] forever praised![c][c] Amen.
[6]It is not as though God's word had failed. For not all who are
descended from Israel are Israel.[d] [7]Nor because they are his
descendants are they all Abraham's children. On the contrary, "It
is through Isaac that your offspring will be reckoned."[d][e] [8]In other
words, it is not the natural children who are God's children,[f] but
it is the children of the promise who are regarded as Abraham's
offspring. [9]For this was how the promise was stated: "At the
appointed time I will return, and Sarah will have a son."[e][g]
[10]Not only that, but Rebekah's children had one and the same
father, our father Isaac.[h] [11]Yet, before the twins were born or had
done anything good or bad—in order that God's purpose[i] in

[a]36 Psalm 44:22 [b]38 Or *nor heavenly rulers* [c]5 Or *Christ, who is over all. God be forever praised!* Or *Christ. God who is over all be forever praised!* [d]7 Gen. 21:12 [e]9 Gen. 18:10,14

8:30 [a]Eph 1:5,11 [b]1Co 6:11 [c]Ro 9:23
8:31 [d]Ro 4:1 [e]Ps 118:6
8:32 [f]Jn 3:16; Ro 4:25; 5:8
8:33 [g]Isa 50:8,9
8:34 [h]Ro 5:6-8 [i]Mk 16:19 [j]Heb 7:25; 9:24; 1Jn 2:1
8:35 [k]1Co 4:11
8:36 [l]Ps 44:22; 2Co 4:11
8:37 [m]1Co 15:57 [n]Gal 2:20; Rev 1:5; 3:9
8:38 [o]Eph 1:21; 1Pe 3:22
8:39 [p]Ro 5:8
9:1 [q]2Co 11:10; Gal 1:20; 1Ti 2:7 [r]Ro 1:9
9:3 [s]Ex 32:32 [t]1Co 12:3; 16:22 [u]Ro 11:14
9:4 [v]Ex 4:22 [w]Ge 17:2; Ac 3:25; Eph 2:12 [x]Ps 147:19 [y]Heb 9:1 [z]Ac 13:32
9:5 [a]Mt 1:1-16 [b]Jn 1:1 [c]Ro 1:25
9:6 [d]Ro 2:28,29; Gal 6:16
9:7 [e]Ge 21:12; Heb 11:18
9:8 [f]Ro 8:14
9:9 [g]Ge 18:10,14
9:10 [h]Ge 25:21
9:11 [i]Ro 8:28

election might stand: 12not by works but by him who calls—she
was told, "The older will serve the younger."[a a] 13Just as it is written:
"Jacob I loved, but Esau I hated."[b b]
14What then shall we say? Is God unjust? Not at all![c] 15For he
says to Moses,

> "I will have mercy on whom I have mercy,
> and I will have compassion on whom
> I have compassion."[c d]

16It does not, therefore, depend on man's desire or effort, but on
God's mercy.[e] 17For the Scripture says to Pharaoh: "I raised you
up for this very purpose, that I might display my power in you
and that my name might be proclaimed in all the earth."[d f]
18Therefore God has mercy on whom he wants to have mercy,
and he hardens whom he wants to harden.[g]
19One of you will say to me:[h] "Then why does God still blame
us? For who resists his will?"[i] 20But who are you, O man, to talk
back to God? "Shall what is formed say to him who formed it,[j]
'Why did you make me like this?' "[e k] 21Does not the potter have
the right to make out of the same lump of clay some pottery for
noble purposes and some for common use?[l]
22What if God, choosing to show his wrath and make his power
known, bore with great patience[m] the objects of his wrath—prepared for destruction? 23What if he did this to make the riches of
his glory[n] known to the objects of his mercy, whom he prepared
in advance for glory[o]— 24even us, whom he also called,[p] not only
from the Jews but also from the Gentiles?[q] 25As he says in Hosea:

> "I will call them 'my people' who are not my people;
> and I will call her 'my loved one' who is not
> my loved one,"[f r]

26and,

> "It will happen that in the very place where it was
> said to them,
> 'You are not my people,'
> they will be called 'sons of the living God.' "[g s]

27Isaiah cries out concerning Israel:

> "Though the number of the Israelites be like the
> sand by the sea,[t]
> only the remnant will be saved.[u]
> 28For the Lord will carry out
> his sentence on earth with speed and finality."[h v]

a *12* Gen. 25:23 b *13* Mal. 1:2,3 c *15* Exodus 33:19 d *17* Exodus 9:16 e *20* Isaiah 29:16; 45:9
f *25* Hosea 2:23 g *26* Hosea 1:10 h *28* Isaiah 10:22,23

9:12 *a* Ge 25:23
9:13 *b* Mal 1:2,3
9:14 *c* 2Ch 19:7
9:15 *d* Ex 33:19
9:16 *e* Eph 2:8
9:17 *f* Ex 9:16
9:18 *g* Ex 4:21
9:19 *h* Ro 11:19 *i* 2Ch 20:6; Da 4:35
9:20 *j* Isa 64:8 *k* Isa 29:16
9:21 *l* 2Ti 2:20
9:22 *m* Ro 2:4
9:23 *n* Ro 2:4 *o* Ro 8:30
9:24 *p* Ro 8:28 *q* Ro 3:29
9:25 *r* Hos 2:23; 1Pe 2:10
9:26 *s* Hos 1:10
9:27 *t* Ge 22:17; Hos 1:10 *u* Ro 11:5
9:28 *v* Isa 10:22,23

29 It is just as Isaiah said previously:

> "Unless the Lord Almighty[a]
> had left us descendants,
> we would have become like Sodom,
> we would have been like Gomorrah."[a][b]

30 What then shall we say? That the Gentiles, who did not pursue righteousness, have obtained it, a righteousness that is by faith;[c] 31 but Israel, who pursued a law of righteousness,[d] has not attained it.[e] 32 Why not? Because they pursued it not by faith but as if it were by works. They stumbled over the "stumbling stone."[f] 33 As it is written:

> "See, I lay in Zion a stone that causes men to stumble
> and a rock that makes them fall,
> and the one who trusts in him will never
> be put to shame."[b][g]

Chapter 10 Theme ______________________

10 Brothers, my heart's desire and prayer to God for the Israelites is that they may be saved. 2 For I can testify about them that they are zealous[h] for God, but their zeal is not based on knowledge. 3 Since they did not know the righteousness that comes from God and sought to establish their own, they did not submit to God's righteousness.[i] 4 Christ is the end of the law[j] so that there may be righteousness for everyone who believes.[k]

5 Moses describes in this way the righteousness that is by the law: "The man who does these things will live by them."[c][l] 6 But the righteousness that is by faith[m] says: "Do not say in your heart, 'Who will ascend into heaven?'[d]"[n] (that is, to bring Christ down) 7 "or 'Who will descend into the deep?'[e]" (that is, to bring Christ up from the dead). 8 But what does it say? "The word is near you; it is in your mouth and in your heart,"[f][o] that is, the word of faith we are proclaiming: 9 That if you confess[p] with your mouth, "Jesus is Lord," and believe in your heart that God raised him from the dead,[q] you will be saved. 10 For it is with your heart that you believe and are justified, and it is with your mouth that you confess and are saved. 11 As the Scripture says, "Anyone who trusts in him will never be put to shame."[g][r] 12 For there is no difference between Jew and Gentile[s]—the same Lord is Lord of all[t] and richly blesses all who call on him, 13 for, "Everyone who calls on the name of the Lord[u] will be saved."[h][v]

14 How, then, can they call on the one they have not believed in? And how can they believe in the one of whom they have not heard?

9:29 [a]Jas 5:4 [b]Isa 1:9; Dt 29:23; Isa 13:19; Jer 50:40
9:30 [c]Ro 1:17; 10:6; Gal 2:16; Php 3:9; Heb 11:7
9:31 [d]Isa 51:1; Ro 10:2,3 [e]Gal 5:4
9:32 [f]1Pe 2:8
9:33 [g]Isa 28:16; Ro 10:11
10:2 [h]Ac 21:20
10:3 [i]Ro 1:17
10:4 [j]Gal 3:24; Ro 7:1-4 [k]Ro 3:22
10:5 [l]Lev 18:5; Ne 9:29; Eze 20:11,13,21; Ro 7:10
10:6 [m]Ro 9:30 [n]Dt 30:12
10:8 [o]Dt 30:14
10:9 [p]Mt 10:32; Lk 12:8 [q]Ac 2:24
10:11 [r]Isa 28:16; Ro 9:33
10:12 [s]Ro 3:22,29 [t]Ac 10:36
10:13 [u]Ac 2:21 [v]Joel 2:32

[a] *29* Isaiah 1:9 [b] *33* Isaiah 8:14; 28:16 [c] *5* Lev. 18:5 [d] *6* Deut. 30:12 [e] *7* Deut. 30:13
[f] *8* Deut. 30:14 [g] *11* Isaiah 28:16 [h] *13* Joel 2:32

And how can they hear without someone preaching to them?
15And how can they preach unless they are sent? As it is written,
"How beautiful are the feet of those who bring good news!"[a][a]
16But not all the Israelites accepted the good news. For Isaiah
says, "Lord, who has believed our message?"[b][b] 17Consequently,
faith comes from hearing the message,[c] and the message is heard
through the word of Christ.[d] 18But I ask: Did they not hear? Of
course they did:

> "Their voice has gone out into all the earth,
> their words to the ends of the world."[c][e]

19Again I ask: Did Israel not understand? First, Moses says,

> "I will make you envious[f] by those who are not a nation;
> I will make you angry by a nation that
> has no understanding."[d][g]

20And Isaiah boldly says,

> "I was found by those who did not seek me;
> I revealed myself to those who did not ask for me."[e][h]

21But concerning Israel he says,

> "All day long I have held out my hands
> to a disobedient and obstinate people."[f][i]

Chapter 11 Theme ________________________

11 I ask then: Did God reject his people? By no means![j] I am an
Israelite myself, a descendant of Abraham,[k] from the tribe of
Benjamin.[l] 2God did not reject his people, whom he foreknew.[m]
Don't you know what the Scripture says in the passage about Elijah—how he appealed to God against Israel: 3"Lord, they have
killed your prophets and torn down your altars; I am the only
one left, and they are trying to kill me"[g]?[n] 4And what was God's
answer to him? "I have reserved for myself seven thousand who
have not bowed the knee to Baal."[h][o] 5So too, at the present time
there is a remnant[p] chosen by grace. 6And if by grace, then it is no
longer by works;[q] if it were, grace would no longer be grace.[i]
7What then? What Israel sought so earnestly it did not obtain,[r]
but the elect did. The others were hardened,[s] 8as it is written:

> "God gave them a spirit of stupor,
> eyes so that they could not see
> and ears so that they could not hear,[t]
> to this very day."[j][u]

[a] *15* Isaiah 52:7 [b] *16* Isaiah 53:1 [c] *18* Psalm 19:4 [d] *19* Deut. 32:21 [e] *20* Isaiah 65:1
[f] *21* Isaiah 65:2 [g] *3* 1Kings 19:10,14 [h] *4* 1Kings 19:18 [i] *6* Some manuscripts *by grace. But if by works, then it is no longer grace; if it were, work would no longer be work.*
[j] *8* Deut. 29:4; Isaiah 29:10

10:15 *a* Isa 52:7; Na 1:15
10:16 *b* Isa 53:1; Jn 12:38
10:17 *c* Gal 3:2,5 *d* Col 3:16
10:18 *e* Ps 19:4; Mt 24:14; Col 1:6,23; 1Th 1:8
10:19 *f* Ro 11:11,14 *g* Dt 32:21
10:20 *h* Isa 65:1; Ro 9:30
10:21 *i* Isa 65:2
11:1 *j* 1Sa 12:22; Jer 31:37 *k* 2Co 11:22 *l* Php 3:5
11:2 *m* Ro 8:29
11:3 *n* 1Ki 19:10,14
11:4 *o* 1Ki 19:18
11:5 *p* Ro 9:27
11:6 *q* Ro 4:4
11:7 *r* Ro 9:31 *s* ver 25; Ro 9:18
11:8 *t* Mt 13:13-15 *u* Dt 29:4; Isa 29:10

9And David says:

> "May their table become a snare and a trap,
> a stumbling block and a retribution for them.
> 10May their eyes be darkened so they cannot see,
> and their backs be bent forever."[a][a]

11Again I ask: Did they stumble so as to fall beyond recovery?
Not at all![b] Rather, because of their transgression, salvation has
come to the Gentiles[c] to make Israel envious.[d] 12But if their transgression means riches for the world, and their loss means riches
for the Gentiles,[e] how much greater riches will their fullness bring!

13I am talking to you Gentiles. Inasmuch as I am the apostle to
the Gentiles,[f] I make much of my ministry 14in the hope that I
may somehow arouse my own people to envy[g] and save[h] some of
them. 15For if their rejection is the reconciliation[i] of the world,
what will their acceptance be but life from the dead?[j] 16If the part
of the dough offered as firstfruits[k] is holy, then the whole batch is
holy; if the root is holy, so are the branches.

17If some of the branches have been broken off,[l] and you, though
a wild olive shoot, have been grafted in among the others[m] and now
share in the nourishing sap from the olive root, 18do not boast over
those branches. If you do, consider this: You do not support the
root, but the root supports you.[n] 19You will say then, "Branches were
broken off so that I could be grafted in." 20Granted. But they were
broken off because of unbelief, and you stand by faith.[o] Do not be
arrogant,[p] but be afraid.[q] 21For if God did not spare the natural
branches, he will not spare you either.

22Consider therefore the kindness[r] and sternness of God: sternness to those who fell, but kindness to you, provided that you
continue[s] in his kindness. Otherwise, you also will be cut off.[t]
23And if they do not persist in unbelief, they will be grafted in, for
God is able to graft them in again.[u] 24After all, if you were cut out
of an olive tree that is wild by nature, and contrary to nature were
grafted into a cultivated olive tree, how much more readily will
these, the natural branches, be grafted into their own olive tree!

25I do not want you to be ignorant[v] of this mystery,[w] brothers,
so that you may not be conceited:[x] Israel has experienced a hard-
ening[y] in part until the full number of the Gentiles has come in.[z]
26And so all Israel will be saved, as it is written:

> "The deliverer will come from Zion;
> he will turn godlessness away from Jacob.
> 27And this is[b] my covenant with them
> when I take away their sins."[c][a]

11:10 [a]Ps 69:22,23
11:11 [b]ver 1 [c]Ac 13:46 [d]Ro 10:19
11:12 [e]ver 25
11:13 [f]Ac 9:15
11:14 [g]ver 11; Ro 10:19 [h]1Co 1:21; 1Ti 2:4; Tit 3:5
11:15 [i]Ro 5:10 [j]Lk 15:24,32
11:16 [k]Lev 23:10,17; Nu 15:18-21
11:17 [l]Jer 11:16; Jn 15:2 [m]Ac 2:39; Eph 2:11-13
11:18 [n]Jn 4:22
11:20 [o]1Co 10:12; 2Co 1:24 [p]Ro 12:16; 1Ti 6:17 [q]1Pe 1:17
11:22 [r]Ro 2:4 [s]1Co 15:2; Heb 3:6 [t]Jn 15:2
11:23 [u]2Co 3:16
11:25 [v]Ro 1:13 [w]Ro 16:25 [x]Ro 12:16 [y]ver 7; Ro 9:18 [z]Lk 21:24
11:27 [a]Isa 27:9; Heb 8:10,12

[a] *10* Psalm 69:22,23 [b] *27* Or *will be* [c] *27* Isaiah 59:20,21; 27:9; Jer. 31:33,34

28As far as the gospel is concerned, they are enemies[a] on your
account; but as far as election is concerned, they are loved on
account of the patriarchs,[b] 29for God's gifts and his call[c] are irrevocable.[d] 30Just as you who were at one time disobedient[e] to God
have now received mercy as a result of their disobedience, 31so they
too have now become disobedient in order that they too may
now[a] receive mercy as a result of God's mercy to you. 32For God
has bound all men over to disobedience[f] so that he may have
mercy on them all.

33Oh, the depth of the riches[g] of the wisdom and[b]
knowledge of God![h]
How unsearchable his judgments,
and his paths beyond tracing out![i]
34"Who has known the mind of the Lord?
Or who has been his counselor?"[c][j]
35"Who has ever given to God,
that God should repay him?"[d][k]
36For from him and through him and to him are all things.[l]
To him be the glory forever! Amen.[m]

Chapter 12 Theme ________________

12 Therefore, I urge you,[n] brothers, in view of God's mercy,
to offer your bodies as living sacrifices,[o] holy and pleasing
to God—this is your spiritual[e] act of worship. 2Do not conform[p]
any longer to the pattern of this world,[q] but be transformed by
the renewing of your mind.[r] Then you will be able to test and
approve what God's will is[s]— his good, pleasing and perfect will.
3For by the grace given me[t] I say to every one of you: Do not
think of yourself more highly than you ought, but rather think of
yourself with sober judgment, in accordance with the measure of
faith God has given you. 4Just as each of us has one body with
many members, and these members do not all have the same
function,[u] 5so in Christ we who are many form one body,[v] and
each member belongs to all the others. 6We have different gifts,[w]
according to the grace given us. If a man's gift is prophesying, let
him use it in proportion to his[f] faith.[x] 7If it is serving, let him serve;
if it is teaching, let him teach;[y] 8if it is encouraging, let him
encourage;[z] if it is contributing to the needs of others, let him
give generously;[a] if it is leadership, let him govern diligently; if it
is showing mercy, let him do it cheerfully.
9Love must be sincere.[b] Hate what is evil; cling to what is good.
10Be devoted to one another in brotherly love.[c] Honor one another above yourselves.[d] 11Never be lacking in zeal, but keep your

a *31* Some manuscripts do not have *now.* b *33* Or *riches and the wisdom and the* c *34* Isaiah 40:13 d *35* Job 41:11 e *1* Or *reasonable* f *6* Or *in agreement with the*

11:28 *a* Ro 5:10 *b* Dt 7:8; 10:15; Ro 9:5
11:29 *c* Ro 8:28 *d* Heb 7:21
11:30 *e* Eph 2:2
11:32 *f* Ro 3:9
11:33 *g* Ro 2:4 *h* Ps 92:5 *i* Job 11:7
11:34 *j* Isa 40:13,14; Job 15:8; 36:22; 1Co 2:16
11:35 *k* Job 35:7
11:36 *l* 1Co 8:6; Col 1:16; Heb 2:10 *m* Ro 16:27
12:1 *n* Eph 4:1 *o* Ro 6:13,16,19; 1Pe 2:5
12:2 *p* 1Pe 1:14 *q* 1Jn 2:15 *r* Eph 4:23 *s* Eph 5:17
12:3 *t* Ro 15:15; Gal 2:9; Eph 4:7
12:4 *u* 1Co 12:12-14; Eph 4:16
12:5 *v* 1Co 10:17
12:6 *w* 1Co 7:7; 12:4,8-10 *x* 1Pe 4:10,11
12:7 *y* Eph 4:11
12:8 *z* Ac 15:32 *a* 2Co 9:5-13
12:9 *b* 1Ti 1:5
12:10 *c* Heb 13:1 *d* Php 2:3

spiritual fervor,[a] serving the Lord. [12]Be joyful in hope,[b] patient in
affliction,[c] faithful in prayer. [13]Share with God's people who are
in need. Practice hospitality.[d]

[14]Bless those who persecute you;[e] bless and do not curse. [15]Rejoice
with those who rejoice; mourn with those who mourn.[f] [16]Live in
harmony with one another.[g] Do not be proud, but be willing to
associate with people of low position.[a] Do not be conceited.[h]

[17]Do not repay anyone evil for evil.[i] Be careful to do what is right
in the eyes of everybody.[j] [18]If it is possible, as far as it depends on
you, live at peace with everyone.[k] [19]Do not take revenge,[l] my friends,
but leave room for God's wrath, for it is written: "It is mine to
avenge; I will repay,"[b][m] says the Lord. [20]On the contrary:

> "If your enemy is hungry, feed him;
> if he is thirsty, give him something to drink.
> In doing this, you will heap burning coals on his head."[c][n]

[21]Do not be overcome by evil, but overcome evil with good.

Chapter 13 Theme ____________________

13 Everyone must submit himself to the governing authorities,[o] for there is no authority except that which God has
established.[p] The authorities that exist have been established by
God. [2]Consequently, he who rebels against the authority is
rebelling against what God has instituted, and those who do so
will bring judgment on themselves. [3]For rulers hold no terror for
those who do right, but for those who do wrong. Do you want to
be free from fear of the one in authority? Then do what is right
and he will commend you.[q] [4]For he is God's servant to do you
good. But if you do wrong, be afraid, for he does not bear the
sword for nothing. He is God's servant, an agent of wrath to
bring punishment on the wrongdoer.[r] [5]Therefore, it is necessary
to submit to the authorities, not only because of possible punishment but also because of conscience.

[6]This is also why you pay taxes, for the authorities are God's
servants, who give their full time to governing. [7]Give everyone
what you owe him: If you owe taxes, pay taxes;[s] if revenue, then
revenue; if respect, then respect; if honor, then honor.

[8]Let no debt remain outstanding, except the continuing debt to
love one another, for he who loves his fellowman has fulfilled the
law.[t] [9]The commandments, "Do not commit adultery," "Do not
murder," "Do not steal," "Do not covet,"[d][u] and whatever other
commandment there may be, are summed up in this one rule:
"Love your neighbor as yourself."[e][v] [10]Love does no harm to its
neighbor. Therefore love is the fulfillment of the law.[w]

12:11 [a]Ac 18:25
12:12 [b]Ro 5:2 [c]Heb 10:32,36
12:13 [d]1Ti 3:2
12:14 [e]Mt 5:44
12:15 [f]Job 30:25
12:16 [g]Ro 15:5 [h]Jer 45:5; Ro 11:25
12:17 [i]Pr 20:22 [j]2Co 8:21
12:18 [k]Mk 9:50; Ro 14:19
12:19 [l]Lev 19:18; Pr 20:22; 24:29 [m]Dt 32:35
12:20 [n]Pr 25:21,22; Mt 5:44; Lk 6:27
13:1 [o]Tit 3:1; 1Pe 2:13,14 [p]Da 2:21; Jn 19:11
13:3 [q]1Pe 2:14
13:4 [r]1Th 4:6
13:7 [s]Mt 17:25; 22:17,21; Lk 23:2
13:8 [t]ver 10; Jn 13:34; Gal 5:14; Col 3:14
13:9 [u]Ex 20:13-15, 17; Dt 5:17-19,21 [v]Lev 19:18; Mt 19:19
13:10 [w]ver 8; Mt 22:39,40

[a] *16* Or *willing to do menial work* [b] *19* Deut. 32:35 [c] *20* Prov. 25:21,22 [d] *9* Exodus 20:13-15,17; Deut. 5:17-19,21 [e] *9* Lev. 19:18

11 And do this, understanding the present time. The hour has
come[a] for you to wake up from your slumber,[b] because our salvation is nearer now than when we first believed. 12 The night is
nearly over; the day is almost here.[c] So let us put aside the deeds
of darkness[d] and put on the armor[e] of light. 13 Let us behave
decently, as in the daytime, not in orgies and drunkenness, not in
sexual immorality and debauchery, not in dissension and jealousy.[f] 14 Rather, clothe yourselves with the Lord Jesus Christ,[g] and
do not think about how to gratify the desires of the sinful nature.[a]

Chapter 14 Theme

14 Accept him whose faith is weak,[h] without passing judgment on disputable matters. 2 One man's faith allows him
to eat everything, but another man, whose faith is weak, eats only
vegetables. 3 The man who eats everything must not look down
on[i] him who does not, and the man who does not eat everything
must not condemn[j] the man who does, for God has accepted
him. 4 Who are you to judge someone else's servant?[k] To his own
master he stands or falls. And he will stand, for the Lord is able to
make him stand.

5 One man considers one day more sacred than another;[l] another
man considers every day alike. Each one should be fully convinced
in his own mind. 6 He who regards one day as special, does so to the
Lord. He who eats meat, eats to the Lord, for he gives thanks to
God;[m] and he who abstains, does so to the Lord and gives thanks
to God. 7 For none of us lives to himself alone[n] and none of us dies to
himself alone. 8 If we live, we live to the Lord; and if we die, we die
to the Lord. So, whether we live or die, we belong to the Lord.[o]

9 For this very reason, Christ died and returned to life[p] so that
he might be the Lord of both the dead and the living.[q] 10 You,
then, why do you judge your brother? Or why do you look down
on your brother? For we will all stand before God's judgment
seat.[r] 11 It is written:

> "'As surely as I live,' says the Lord,
> 'every knee will bow before me;
> every tongue will confess to God.'"[b][s]

12 So then, each of us will give an account of himself to God.[t]

13 Therefore let us stop passing judgment[u] on one another.
Instead, make up your mind not to put any stumbling block or
obstacle in your brother's way. 14 As one who is in the Lord Jesus,
I am fully convinced that no food[c] is unclean in itself.[v] But if anyone regards something as unclean, then for him it is unclean.[w]
15 If your brother is distressed because of what you eat, you are no

[a] 14 Or *the flesh* [b] 11 Isaiah 45:23 [c] 14 Or *that nothing*

13:11 [a] 1Co 7:29-31; 10:11 [b] Eph 5:14; 1Th 5:5,6
13:12 [c] 1Jn 2:8 [d] Eph 5:11 [e] Eph 6:11,13
13:13 [f] Gal 5:20,21
13:14 [g] Gal 3:27; 5:16; Eph 4:24
14:1 [h] Ro 15:1; 1Co 8:9-12
14:3 [i] Lk 18:9 [j] Col 2:16
14:4 [k] Jas 4:12
14:5 [l] Gal 4:10
14:6 [m] Mt 14:19; 1Co 10:30,31; 1Ti 4:3,4
14:7 [n] 2Co 5:15; Gal 2:20
14:8 [o] Php 1:20
14:9 [p] Rev 1:18 [q] 2Co 5:15
14:10 [r] 2Co 5:10
14:11 [s] Isa 45:23; Php 2:10,11
14:12 [t] Mt 12:36; 1Pe 4:5
14:13 [u] Mt 7:1
14:14 [v] Ac 10:15 [w] 1Co 8:7

longer acting in love.[a] Do not by your eating destroy your brother for whom Christ died.[b] 16 Do not allow what you consider good to be spoken of as evil.[c] 17 For the kingdom of God is not a matter of eating and drinking,[d] but of righteousness, peace and joy in the Holy Spirit,[e] 18 because anyone who serves Christ in this way is pleasing to God and approved by men.[f]

19 Let us therefore make every effort to do what leads to peace[g] and to mutual edification.[h] 20 Do not destroy the work of God for the sake of food.[i] All food is clean, but it is wrong for a man to eat anything that causes someone else to stumble.[j] 21 It is better not to eat meat or drink wine or to do anything else that will cause your brother to fall.[k]

22 So whatever you believe about these things keep between yourself and God. Blessed is the man who does not condemn[l] himself by what he approves. 23 But the man who has doubts[m] is condemned if he eats, because his eating is not from faith; and everything that does not come from faith is sin.

Chapter 15 Theme ________________________

15 We who are strong ought to bear with the failings of the weak[n] and not to please ourselves. 2 Each of us should please his neighbor for his good,[o] to build him up.[p] 3 For even Christ did not please himself[q] but, as it is written: "The insults of those who insult you have fallen on me."[a][r] 4 For everything that was written in the past was written to teach us,[s] so that through endurance and the encouragement of the Scriptures we might have hope.

5 May the God who gives endurance and encouragement give you a spirit of unity[t] among yourselves as you follow Christ Jesus, 6 so that with one heart and mouth you may glorify the God and Father[u] of our Lord Jesus Christ.

7 Accept one another,[v] then, just as Christ accepted you, in order to bring praise to God. 8 For I tell you that Christ has become a servant of the Jews[b][w] on behalf of God's truth, to confirm the promises[x] made to the patriarchs 9 so that the Gentiles[y] may glorify God[z] for his mercy, as it is written:

> "Therefore I will praise you among the Gentiles;
> I will sing hymns to your name."[c][a]

10 Again, it says,

> "Rejoice, O Gentiles, with his people."[d][b]

11 And again,

> "Praise the Lord, all you Gentiles,
> and sing praises to him, all you peoples."[e][c]

[a] *3* Psalm 69:9 [b] *8* Greek *circumcision* [c] *9* 2 Samuel 22:50; Psalm 18:49 [d] *10* Deut. 32:43
[e] *11* Psalm 117:1

14:15 [a] Eph 5:2 [b] 1Co 8:11
14:16 [c] 1Co 10:30
14:17 [d] 1Co 8:8 [e] Ro 15:13
14:18 [f] 2Co 8:21
14:19 [g] Ps 34:14; Ro 12:18; Heb 12:14 [h] Ro 15:2; 2Co 12:19
14:20 [i] ver 15 [j] 1Co 8:9-12
14:21 [k] 1Co 8:13
14:22 [l] 1Jn 3:21
14:23 [m] ver 5
15:1 [n] Ro 14:1; Gal 6:1,2; 1Th 5:14
15:2 [o] 1Co 10:33 [p] Ro 14:19
15:3 [q] 2Co 8:9 [r] Ps 69:9
15:4 [s] Ro 4:23,24
15:5 [t] Ro 12:16; 1Co 1:10
15:6 [u] Rev 1:6
15:7 [v] Ro 14:1
15:8 [w] Mt 15:24; Ac 3:25,26 [x] 2Co 1:20
15:9 [y] Ro 3:29 [z] Mt 9:8 [a] 2Sa 22:50; Ps 18:49
15:10 [b] Dt 32:43
15:11 [c] Ps 117:1

12And again, Isaiah says,

"The Root of Jesse[a] will spring up,
one who will arise to rule over the nations;
the Gentiles will hope in him."[a][b]

13May the God of hope fill you with all joy and peace[c] as you
trust in him, so that you may overflow with hope by the power of
the Holy Spirit.[d]
14I myself am convinced, my brothers, that you yourselves are full
of goodness,[e] complete in knowledge[f] and competent to instruct
one another. 15I have written you quite boldly on some points, as if
to remind you of them again, because of the grace God gave me[g] 16to
be a minister of Christ Jesus to the Gentiles[h] with the priestly duty
of proclaiming the gospel of God,[i] so that the Gentiles might
become an offering[j] acceptable to God, sanctified by the Holy Spirit.
17Therefore I glory in Christ Jesus[k] in my service to God.[l] 18I
will not venture to speak of anything except what Christ has
accomplished through me in leading the Gentiles[m] to obey God[n]
by what I have said and done— 19by the power of signs and miracles,[o] through the power of the Spirit.[p] So from Jerusalem[q] all
the way around to Illyricum, I have fully proclaimed the gospel
of Christ. 20It has always been my ambition to preach the gospel
where Christ was not known, so that I would not be building on
someone else's foundation.[r] 21Rather, as it is written:

"Those who were not told about him will see,
and those who have not heard will understand."[b][s]

22This is why I have often been hindered from coming to you.[t]
23But now that there is no more place for me to work in these
regions, and since I have been longing for many years to see you,[u]
24I plan to do so when I go to Spain.[v] I hope to visit you while
passing through and to have you assist me on my journey there,
after I have enjoyed your company for a while. 25Now, however, I
am on my way to Jerusalem[w] in the service[x] of the saints there.
26For Macedonia[y] and Achaia[z] were pleased to make a contribution
for the poor among the saints in Jerusalem. 27They were pleased to
do it, and indeed they owe it to them. For if the Gentiles have shared
in the Jews' spiritual blessings, they owe it to the Jews to share with
them their material blessings.[a] 28So after I have completed this
task and have made sure that they have received this fruit, I will
go to Spain and visit you on the way. 29I know that when I come
to you,[b] I will come in the full measure of the blessing of Christ.
30I urge you, brothers, by our Lord Jesus Christ and by the love of
the Spirit,[c] to join me in my struggle by praying to God for me.[d]

a *12* Isaiah 11:10 b *21* Isaiah 52:15

15:12
[a] Rev 5:5
[b] Isa 11:10; Mt 12:21

15:13
[c] Ro 14:17
[d] ver 19; 1Co 2:4; 1Th 1:5

15:14
[e] Eph 5:9
[f] 2Pe 1:12

15:15
[g] Ro 12:3

15:16
[h] Ac 9:15; Ro 11:13
[i] Ro 1:1
[j] Isa 66:20

15:17
[k] Php 3:3
[l] Heb 2:17

15:18
[m] Ac 15:12; 21:19; Ro 1:5
[n] Ro 16:26

15:19
[o] Jn 4:48; Ac 19:11
[p] ver 13
[q] Ac 22:17-21

15:20
[r] 2Co 10:15,16

15:21
[s] Isa 52:15

15:22
[t] Ro 1:13

15:23
[u] Ac 19:21; Ro 1:10,11

15:24
[v] ver 28

15:25
[w] Ac 19:21
[x] Ac 24:17

15:26
[y] Ac 16:9; 2Co 8:1
[z] Ac 18:12

15:27
[a] 1Co 9:11

15:29
[b] Ro 1:10,11

15:30
[c] Gal 5:22
[d] 2Co 1:11; Col 4:12

31 Pray that I may be rescued[a] from the unbelievers in Judea and
that my service in Jerusalem may be acceptable to the saints there,
32 so that by God's will[b] I may come to you[c] with joy and together
with you be refreshed.[d] 33 The God of peace[e] be with you all. Amen.

Chapter 16 Theme ______________________

16 I commend[f] to you our sister Phoebe, a servant[a] of the
church in Cenchrea.[g] 2 I ask you to receive her in the Lord[h]
in a way worthy of the saints and to give her any help she may
need from you, for she has been a great help to many people,
including me.

3 Greet Priscilla[b] and Aquila,[i] my fellow workers in Christ Jesus.[j]
4 They risked their lives for me. Not only I but all the churches
of the Gentiles are grateful to them.
5 Greet also the church that meets at their house.[k]
Greet my dear friend Epenetus, who was the first convert[l] to
Christ in the province of Asia.
6 Greet Mary, who worked very hard for you.
7 Greet Andronicus and Junias, my relatives[m] who have been in
prison with me. They are outstanding among the apostles, and
they were in Christ before I was.
8 Greet Ampliatus, whom I love in the Lord.
9 Greet Urbanus, our fellow worker in Christ,[n] and my dear
friend Stachys.
10 Greet Apelles, tested and approved in Christ.
Greet those who belong to the household of Aristobulus.
11 Greet Herodion, my relative.[o]
Greet those in the household of Narcissus who are in the Lord.
12 Greet Tryphena and Tryphosa, those women who work hard in
the Lord.
Greet my dear friend Persis, another woman who has worked
very hard in the Lord.
13 Greet Rufus, chosen in the Lord, and his mother, who has been
a mother to me, too.
14 Greet Asyncritus, Phlegon, Hermes, Patrobas, Hermas and the
brothers with them.
15 Greet Philologus, Julia, Nereus and his sister, and Olympas and
all the saints[p] with them.[q]
16 Greet one another with a holy kiss.[r]
All the churches of Christ send greetings.

17 I urge you, brothers, to watch out for those who cause divisions
and put obstacles in your way that are contrary to the teaching you
have learned.[s] Keep away from them.[t] 18 For such people are not

15:31 [a] 2Th 3:2
15:32 [b] Ac 18:21 [c] Ro 1:10,13 [d] 1Co 16:18
15:33 [e] Ro 16:20; 2Co 13:11; Php 4:9; 1Th 5:23; Heb 13:20
16:1 [f] 2Co 3:1 [g] Ac 18:18
16:2 [h] Php 2:29
16:3 [i] Ac 18:2 [j] ver 7,9,10
16:5 [k] 1Co 16:19; Col 4:15; Phm 2 [l] 1Co 16:15
16:7 [m] ver 11,21
16:9 [n] ver 3
16:11 [o] ver 7,21
16:15 [p] ver 2 [q] ver 14
16:16 [r] 1Co 16:20; 2Co 13:12; 1Th 5:26
16:17 [s] Gal 1:8,9; 1Ti 1:3; 6:3 [t] 2Th 3:6,14; 2Jn 10

a *1* Or *deaconess* b *3* Greek *Prisca,* a variant of *Priscilla*

serving our Lord Christ, but their own appetites.[a] By smooth talk
and flattery they deceive[b] the minds of naive people. 19Everyone
has heard[c] about your obedience, so I am full of joy over you; but
I want you to be wise about what is good, and innocent about what
is evil.[d]

20The God of peace[e] will soon crush[f] Satan under your feet.

The grace of our Lord Jesus be with you.[g]

21Timothy,[h] my fellow worker, sends his greetings to you, as do
Lucius,[i] Jason[j] and Sosipater, my relatives.[k]

22I, Tertius, who wrote down this letter, greet you in the Lord.

23Gaius, whose hospitality I and the whole church here enjoy,
sends you his greetings.

Erastus,[l] who is the city's director of public works, and our
brother Quartus send you their greetings.[a]

25Now to him who is able[m] to establish you by my gospel[n] and
the proclamation of Jesus Christ, according to the revelation of the
mystery[o] hidden for long ages past, 26but now revealed and made
known through the prophetic writings by the command of the
eternal God, so that all nations might believe and obey him— 27to
the only wise God be glory forever through Jesus Christ! Amen.[p]

a 23 Some manuscripts *their greetings.* 24*May the grace of our Lord Jesus Christ be with all of you. Amen.*

16:18 a Php 3:19 b Col 2:4
16:19 c Ro 1:8 d Mt 10:16; 1Co 14:20
16:20 e Ro 15:33 f Ge 3:15 g 1Th 5:28
16:21 h Ac 16:1 i Ac 13:1 j Ac 17:5 k ver 7,11
16:23 l Ac 19:22
16:25 m Eph 3:20 n Ro 2:16 o Eph 1:9; Col 1:26,27
16:27 p Ro 11:36

Romans Observations Chart

About Paul

Why He Wrote

About the Recipients

In Adam (According to the sinful nature)	In Christ (According to the Spirit)

Theme of Romans:

SEGMENT DIVISIONS

			CHAPTER THEMES
			1
			2
			3
			4
			5
			6
			7
			8
			9
			10
			11
			12
			13
			14
			15
			16

Author:

Date:

Purpose:

Key Words:

1 CORINTHIANS

Sin abounded in the cosmopolitan city of Corinth, the chief city of Greece. Corinth overlooked the narrow isthmus that connected the Greek mainland with Peloponnesus and received ships in its two harbors. At one time it was home of at least twelve heathen temples. The Corinthians were intrigued by Greek philosophy and captivated by the disciplined training and athletic events held at the Isthmus. They desperately needed to hear the good news of Jesus Christ, the one crucified for sinners.

The worship ceremonies carried out by a thousand temple prostitutes connected with the temple of Aphrodite (the goddess of love) bred blatant immorality throughout Corinth—so much so that the Greek verb translated "to Corinthianize" meant to practice sexual immorality.

Prostitutes openly plied their wares and meat markets thrived on sales from the sacrifices offered in the temples. The Corinthians ate well, satisfied their sexual urges without condemnation, flirted with the wisdom of men, and did all they could to keep their bodies as beautiful as those of the Greek gods. They loved to listen to great orators. For the 250,000 citizens there were almost two slaves per person. What more did Corinth need? Freedom. Freedom from sin and death. God met that need by blocking Paul at every hand on his second missionary journey until he received the Macedonian call, "Come and help us."

After establishing the Corinthian church Paul eventually went to Ephesus, where he stayed for three years. From there he wrote his first epistle to the Corinthian believers, who so desperately needed help and correction. It was sometime between A.D. 52 and 56.

THINGS TO DO

Chapters 1-6

1. In chapter 1 note what Paul commends about the Corinthians. Make a list in the margin titled "Commendations."

2. Read chapters 1 through 6, one chapter at a time. As you read, keep in mind what you read in the introduction to this book. Do the following:

   a. Note the problems Paul deals with in the text (as he writes). You can see these problems several ways.

      1) As you read, ask the five W's and an H: Who? What? When? Where? Why? and How? Especially concentrate on the problems, subjects, or people mentioned. Ask questions such as: Why would Paul mention specific people by name in this chapter? Who is causing the problem? How did the Corinthians get this way? Why does Paul say what he does about himself or his ministry?

      2) Mark the key words in the text. Key words help you see the main topics in a chapter. In 1 Corinthians they indicate what the problems are and what the solution is.

      Write the following key words for this segment on an index card and use it as a bookmark while you study chapters 1 through 6. They are: *God, Jesus (Christ, Lord), Spirit, divisions (divided), spirit* (note whose spirit or what spirit), *power, mind, wise (expert, wisdom), preach, body (physically),* and *church.*

   b. As you read each of the first six chapters, note the problems Paul deals with in each chapter. In the margin make a list of these with the heading "Problems."

3. As you read, look for and note on the OBSERVATIONS CHART on page 1974 what you learn about the Corinthians, any commands directed to them, and the warnings Paul gives them.

4. As you finish each chapter, summarize the theme (subject) of that chapter and record it on 1 CORINTHIANS AT A GLANCE on page 1975 and in the text next to the chapter number.

5. Two things prompted Paul to write to the Corinthians, and it is these two things which cause a natural division in his epistle. Read 1 Corinthians 1:10, 11, where Paul states his reason for writing. Record this reason on the 1 CORINTHIANS AT A GLANCE chart in the space under "Major Segment Divisions."

Chapters 7-16

1. The second division of 1 Corinthians is noted by two phrases which are repeated throughout the last segment of this book: *now for* or *now about.* Read 7:1 and notice the transition. From this point on Paul deals with matters the Corinthians had questions on or issues that they needed to be instructed in.

2. Now look up the following verses and underline or mark in a distinctive way the phrases "now for" or "now about." As you mark these phrases, mark along with them the subject matter Paul is about to deal with. The verses are: 7:1; 7:25; 8:1; 12:1; 16:1. In the same way also mark in 15:1 the words *Now, brothers, I want to remind you of the gospel I preached to you.* Marking these wordings will give you the topical divisions of this second segment of 1 Corinthians.

3. As you read through this last segment of 1 Corinthians, mark the following key words: *God, Jesus (Christ, Lord), Spirit, body, unbelieving (not a believer, unbeliever, unbelievers), think (thinks, thinking, thought), church (churches, congregation), idol(s) (idolaters, idolatry), knowledge (knows), preach (preaching),* and *gospel.* Make a new list of key words to use as a bookmark in this segment. (*Divisions* and *differences* each are used one more time in chapter 11. This is significant, since Paul again deals with problems while giving further instruction to the church.)

4. As you deal with each topic, ask questions such as: Why does the church have this question or problem? How are they behaving? What is their thinking? What are Paul's instructions regarding this subject? Why are they to do this? What are the consequences if they don't?

5. As Paul moves through these final matters of concern, he intermittently explains his position and ministry. Watch for these explanations and note if and how he ties them in with his subject matter.

6. Note on the OBSERVATIONS CHART what you learn from this segment about the Corinthians and the commands and warnings Paul gives them.

7. Determine and record the theme of each chapter in the text next to the chapter number and on 1 CORINTHIANS AT A GLANCE.

8. Considering 7:1, give a title to the segment division for the second half of 1 Corinthians. Record your title on 1 CORINTHIANS AT A GLANCE.

9. Record the theme of 1 Corinthians and complete the 1 CORINTHIANS AT A GLANCE chart.

Things to Think About

1. Are you having any of the same problems in your own life or in your church that the Corinthians had? Do you think this letter has the answers for your problems or questions? How can you apply what you have learned?

2. According to the context of 1 Corinthians 3, what does it mean to be a carnal or fleshly Christian? Remember, context rules over all accurate interpretation.

3. Are you untaught—ignorant—concerning spiritual gifts? Do you know about one or two of them but not the others? Have you believed or even taught others in accord with what the whole counsel of God has to say on the subject, or have you merely gone by your experience or reasoning? Do you appreciate other people's gifts even though they may be different from yours?

4. On what do you base your beliefs about marriage, divorce, and remarriage? What did you learn from 1 Corinthians 7 about these topics? Did this change your belief?

5. Is the preaching of the cross foolishness to you, or is it a demonstration of the power of God?

Chapter 1 Theme ______________________________

1 Paul, called to be an apostle[a] of Christ Jesus by the will of God,[b]
and our brother Sosthenes,[c]

2To the church of God in Corinth,[d] to those sanctified in Christ
Jesus and called[e] to be holy, together with all those everywhere who
call on the name of our Lord Jesus Christ—their Lord and ours:

3Grace and peace to you from God our Father and the Lord Jesus
Christ.[f]

4I always thank God for you[g] because of his grace given you in
Christ Jesus. 5For in him you have been enriched[h] in every way—
in all your speaking and in all your knowledge[i]— 6because our
testimony[j] about Christ was confirmed in you. 7Therefore you do
not lack any spiritual gift as you eagerly wait for our Lord Jesus
Christ to be revealed.[k] 8He will keep you strong to the end, so that
you will be blameless[l] on the day of our Lord Jesus Christ. 9God,
who has called you into fellowship with his Son Jesus Christ our
Lord,[m] is faithful.[n]

10I appeal to you, brothers, in the name of our Lord Jesus Christ,
that all of you agree with one another so that there may be no divisions among you and that you may be perfectly united in mind
and thought. 11My brothers, some from Chloe's household have
informed me that there are quarrels among you. 12What I mean is
this: One of you says, "I follow Paul";[o] another, "I follow Apollos";[p]
another, "I follow Cephas[a]";[q] still another, "I follow Christ."

13Is Christ divided? Was Paul crucified for you? Were you baptized into[b] the name of Paul?[r] 14I am thankful that I did not baptize any of you except Crispus[s] and Gaius,[t] 15so no one can say
that you were baptized into my name. 16(Yes, I also baptized the
household of Stephanas;[u] beyond that, I don't remember if I baptized anyone else.) 17For Christ did not send me to baptize,[v] but
to preach the gospel—not with words of human wisdom,[w] lest
the cross of Christ be emptied of its power.

18For the message of the cross is foolishness to those who are
perishing,[x] but to us who are being saved it is the power of God.[y]
19For it is written:

> "I will destroy the wisdom of the wise;
> the intelligence of the intelligent I will frustrate."[c][z]

1:1 [a]Ro 1:1; Eph 1:1 [b]2Co 1:1 [c]Ac 18:17
1:2 [d]Ac 18:1 [e]Ro 1:7
1:3 [f]Ro 1:7
1:4 [g]Ro 1:8
1:5 [h]2Co 9:11 [i]2Co 8:7
1:6 [j]Rev 1:2
1:7 [k]Php 3:20; Tit 2:13; 2Pe 3:12
1:8 [l]1Th 3:13
1:9 [m]1Jn 1:3 [n]Isa 49:7; 1Th 5:24
1:12 [o]1Co 3:4,22 [p]Ac 18:24 [q]Jn 1:42
1:13 [r]Mt 28:19
1:14 [s]Ac 18:8; Ro 16:23 [t]Ac 19:29
1:16 [u]1Co 16:15
1:17 [v]Jn 4:2 [w]1Co 2:1,4,13
1:18 [x]2Co 2:15 [y]Ro 1:16
1:19 [z]Isa 29:14

[a]*12* That is, Peter [b]*13* Or *in*; also in verse 15 [c]*19* Isaiah 29:14

20Where is the wise man?[a] Where is the scholar? Where is the
philosopher of this age? Has not God made foolish[b] the wisdom
of the world? 21For since in the wisdom of God the world through
its wisdom did not know him, God was pleased through the foolishness of what was preached to save those who believe. 22Jews
demand miraculous signs[c] and Greeks look for wisdom, 23but we
preach Christ crucified: a stumbling block[d] to Jews and foolishness[e] to Gentiles, 24but to those whom God has called,[f] both Jews
and Greeks, Christ the power of God and the wisdom of God.[g]
25For the foolishness[h] of God is wiser than man's wisdom, and the
weakness[i] of God is stronger than man's strength.

26Brothers, think of what you were when you were called. Not
many of you were wise by human standards; not many were influ-
ential; not many were of noble birth. 27But God chose[j] the foolish[k]
things of the world to shame the wise; God chose the weak things
of the world to shame the strong. 28He chose the lowly things of this
world and the despised things—and the things that are not[l]—to
nullify the things that are, 29so that no one may boast before
him.[m] 30It is because of him that you are in Christ Jesus, who has
become for us wisdom from God—that is, our righteousness,[n]
holiness and redemption.[o] 31Therefore, as it is written: "Let him
who boasts boast in the Lord."[a][p]

Chapter 2 Theme ________________________________

2 When I came to you, brothers, I did not come with eloquence
or superior wisdom[q] as I proclaimed to you the testimony
about God.[b] 2For I resolved to know nothing while I was with you
except Jesus Christ and him crucified.[r] 3I came to you[s] in weakness
and fear, and with much trembling. 4My message and my preaching were not with wise and persuasive words, but with a demonstration of the Spirit's power,[t] 5so that your faith might not rest
on men's wisdom, but on God's power.[u]

6We do, however, speak a message of wisdom among the mature,[v]
but not the wisdom of this age[w] or of the rulers of this age, who are
coming to nothing. 7No, we speak of God's secret wisdom, a wisdom that has been hidden and that God destined for our glory
before time began. 8None of the rulers of this age understood it,
for if they had, they would not have crucified the Lord of glory.[x]
9However, as it is written:

> "No eye has seen,
>   no ear has heard,
> no mind has conceived
>   what God has prepared for those who love him"[c][y]—

[a] *31* Jer. 9:24 [b] *1* Some manuscripts *as I proclaimed to you God's mystery* [c] *9* Isaiah 64:4

1:20 [a] Isa 19:11,12 [b] Job 12:17; Ro 1:22
1:22 [c] Mt 12:38
1:23 [d] Lk 2:34; Gal 5:11 [e] 1Co 2:14
1:24 [f] Ro 8:28 [g] ver 30; Col 2:3
1:25 [h] ver 18 [i] 2Co 13:4
1:27 [j] Jas 2:5 [k] ver 20
1:28 [l] Ro 4:17
1:29 [m] Eph 2:9
1:30 [n] Jer 23:5,6; 2Co 5:21 [o] Ro 3:24; Eph 1:7,14
1:31 [p] Jer 9:23,24; 2Co 10:17
2:1 [q] 1Co 1:17
2:2 [r] Gal 6:14; 1Co 1:23
2:3 [s] Ac 18:1-18
2:4 [t] Ro 15:19
2:5 [u] 2Co 4:7; 6:7
2:6 [v] Eph 4:13; Php 3:15; Heb 5:14 [w] 1Co 1:20
2:8 [x] Ac 7:2; Jas 2:1
2:9 [y] Isa 64:4; 65:17

10but God has revealed[a] it to us by his Spirit.[b]
The Spirit searches all things, even the deep things of God. 11For
who among men knows the thoughts of a man[c] except the man's
spirit[d] within him? In the same way no one knows the thoughts
of God except the Spirit of God. 12We have not received the spirit[e]
of the world[f] but the Spirit who is from God, that we may understand what God has freely given us. 13This is what we speak, not
in words taught us by human wisdom[g] but in words taught by the
Spirit, expressing spiritual truths in spiritual words.[a] 14The man
without the Spirit does not accept the things that come from the
Spirit of God, for they are foolishness[h] to him, and he cannot
understand them, because they are spiritually discerned. 15The
spiritual man makes judgments about all things, but he himself is
not subject to any man's judgment:

> 16"For who has known the mind of the Lord
> that he may instruct him?"[b][i]

But we have the mind of Christ.[j]

Chapter 3 Theme ____________________________

3 Brothers, I could not address you as spiritual[k] but as worldly[l]—
mere infants[m] in Christ. 2I gave you milk, not solid food,[n] for
you were not yet ready for it.[o] Indeed, you are still not ready. 3You
are still worldly. For since there is jealousy and quarreling[p] among
you, are you not worldly? Are you not acting like mere men? 4For
when one says, "I follow Paul," and another, "I follow Apollos,"[q] are
you not mere men?
5What, after all, is Apollos? And what is Paul? Only servants,
through whom you came to believe—as the Lord has assigned to
each his task. 6I planted the seed,[r] Apollos watered it, but God made
it grow. 7So neither he who plants nor he who waters is anything,
but only God, who makes things grow. 8The man who plants and
the man who waters have one purpose, and each will be rewarded
according to his own labor.[s] 9For we are God's fellow workers;[t]
you are God's field,[u] God's building.[v]
10By the grace God has given me,[w] I laid a foundation[x] as an
expert builder, and someone else is building on it. But each one
should be careful how he builds. 11For no one can lay any foundation other than the one already laid, which is Jesus Christ.[y] 12If
any man builds on this foundation using gold, silver, costly stones,
wood, hay or straw, 13his work will be shown for what it is,[z] because
the Day[a] will bring it to light. It will be revealed with fire, and the
fire will test the quality of each man's work. 14If what he has built

a *13* Or *Spirit, interpreting spiritual truths to spiritual men* b *16* Isaiah 40:13

2:10 [a]Mt 13:11; Eph 3:3,5 [b]Jn 14:26
2:11 [c]Jer 17:9 [d]Pr 20:27
2:12 [e]Ro 8:15 [f]1Co 1:20,27
2:13 [g]1Co 1:17
2:14 [h]1Co 1:18
2:16 [i]Isa 40:13 [j]Jn 15:15
3:1 [k]1Co 2:15 [l]Ro 7:14; 1Co 2:14 [m]Heb 5:13
3:2 [n]Heb 5:12-14; 1Pe 2:2 [o]Jn 16:12
3:3 [p]1Co 1:11; Gal 5:20
3:4 [q]1Co 1:12
3:6 [r]Ac 18:4-11
3:8 [s]Ps 62:12
3:9 [t]2Co 6:1 [u]Isa 61:3 [v]Eph 2:20-22; 1Pe 2:5
3:10 [w]Ro 12:3 [x]Ro 15:20
3:11 [y]Isa 28:16; Eph 2:20
3:13 [z]1Co 4:5 [a]2Th 1:7-10

survives, he will receive his reward. 15 If it is burned up, he will suffer loss; he himself will be saved, but only as one escaping through
the flames.[a]
16 Don't you know that you yourselves are God's temple[b] and
that God's Spirit lives in you? 17 If anyone destroys God's temple,
God will destroy him; for God's temple is sacred, and you are that
temple.
18 Do not deceive yourselves. If any one of you thinks he is wise[c]
by the standards of this age, he should become a "fool" so that he
may become wise. 19 For the wisdom of this world is foolishness[d]
in God's sight. As it is written: "He catches the wise in their craftiness"[a];[e] 20 and again, "The Lord knows that the thoughts of the
wise are futile."[b][f] 21 So then, no more boasting about men![g] All
things are yours,[h] 22 whether Paul or Apollos or Cephas[c][i] or the
world or life or death or the present or the future[j]—all are yours,
23 and you are of Christ,[k] and Christ is of God.

Chapter 4 Theme ______________________

4 So then, men ought to regard us as servants of Christ and as
those entrusted[l] with the secret things[m] of God. 2 Now it is
required that those who have been given a trust must prove faithful. 3 I care very little if I am judged by you or by any human
court; indeed, I do not even judge myself. 4 My conscience is clear,
but that does not make me innocent.[n] It is the Lord who judges
me. 5 Therefore judge nothing[o] before the appointed time; wait till
the Lord comes. He will bring to light what is hidden in darkness
and will expose the motives of men's hearts. At that time each
will receive his praise from God.[p]
6 Now, brothers, I have applied these things to myself and Apollos for your benefit, so that you may learn from us the meaning
of the saying, "Do not go beyond what is written."[q] Then you will
not take pride in one man over against another.[r] 7 For who makes
you different from anyone else? What do you have that you did
not receive?[s] And if you did receive it, why do you boast as though
you did not?
8 Already you have all you want! Already you have become rich![t]
You have become kings—and that without us! How I wish that
you really had become kings so that we might be kings with you!
9 For it seems to me that God has put us apostles on display at the
end of the procession, like men condemned to die[u] in the arena.
We have been made a spectacle[v] to the whole universe, to angels
as well as to men. 10 We are fools for Christ,[w] but you are so wise
in Christ![x] We are weak, but you are strong![y] You are honored, we
are dishonored! 11 To this very hour we go hungry and thirsty, we

3:15 [a]Jude 23
3:16 [b]1Co 6:19; 2Co 6:16
3:18 [c]Isa 5:21; 1Co 8:2
3:19 [d]1Co 1:20,27 [e]Job 5:13
3:20 [f]Ps 94:11
3:21 [g]1Co 4:6 [h]Ro 8:32
3:22 [i]1Co 1:12 [j]Ro 8:38
3:23 [k]1Co 15:23; 2Co 10:7; Gal 3:29
4:1 [l]1Co 9:17; Tit 1:7 [m]Ro 16:25
4:4 [n]Ro 2:13
4:5 [o]Mt 7:1,2; Ro 2:1 [p]Ro 2:29
4:6 [q]1Co 1:19,31; 3:19,20 [r]1Co 1:12
4:7 [s]Jn 3:27; Ro 12:3,6
4:8 [t]Rev 3:17,18
4:9 [u]Ro 8:36 [v]Heb 10:33
4:10 [w]1Co 1:18; Ac 17:18 [x]1Co 3:18 [y]1Co 2:3

a *19* Job 5:13 b *20* Psalm 94:11 c *22* That is, Peter

are in rags, we are brutally treated, we are homeless.[a] 12We work hard with our own hands.[b] When we are cursed, we bless;[c] when we are persecuted, we endure it; 13when we are slandered, we answer kindly. Up to this moment we have become the scum of the earth, the refuse[d] of the world.

14I am not writing this to shame you, but to warn you, as my dear children.[e] 15Even though you have ten thousand guardians in Christ, you do not have many fathers, for in Christ Jesus I became your father through the gospel.[f] 16Therefore I urge you to imitate me.[g] 17For this reason I am sending to you Timothy, my son[h] whom I love, who is faithful in the Lord. He will remind you of my way of life in Christ Jesus, which agrees with what I teach everywhere in every church.[i]

18Some of you have become arrogant, as if I were not coming to you. 19But I will come to you very soon,[j] if the Lord is willing,[k] and then I will find out not only how these arrogant people are talking, but what power they have. 20For the kingdom of God is not a matter of talk but of power. 21What do you prefer? Shall I come to you with a whip,[l] or in love and with a gentle spirit?

Chapter 5 Theme

5 It is actually reported that there is sexual immorality among you, and of a kind that does not occur even among pagans: A man has his father's wife.[m] 2And you are proud! Shouldn't you rather have been filled with grief[n] and have put out of your fellowship the man who did this? 3Even though I am not physically present, I am with you in spirit.[o] And I have already passed judgment on the one who did this, just as if I were present. 4When you are assembled in the name of our Lord Jesus[p] and I am with you in spirit, and the power of our Lord Jesus is present, 5hand this man over[q] to Satan, so that the sinful nature[a] may be destroyed and his spirit saved on the day of the Lord.

6Your boasting is not good.[r] Don't you know that a little yeast[s] works through the whole batch of dough?[t] 7Get rid of the old yeast that you may be a new batch without yeast—as you really are. For Christ, our Passover lamb, has been sacrificed.[u] 8Therefore let us keep the Festival, not with the old yeast, the yeast of malice and wickedness, but with bread without yeast,[v] the bread of sincerity and truth.

9I have written you in my letter not to associate[w] with sexually immoral people— 10not at all meaning the people of this world[x] who are immoral, or the greedy and swindlers, or idolaters. In that case you would have to leave this world. 11But now I am writing you

a5 Or *that his body;* or *that the flesh*

4:11 [a] Ro 8:35; 2Co 11:23-27
4:12 [b] Ac 18:3 [c] 1Pe 3:9
4:13 [d] La 3:45
4:14 [e] 1Th 2:11
4:15 [f] 1Co 9:12,14, 18,23
4:16 [g] 1Co 11:1; Php 3:17; 1Th 1:6; 2Th 3:7,9
4:17 [h] 1Ti 1:2 [i] 1Co 7:17
4:19 [j] 2Co 1:15,16 [k] Ac 18:21
4:21 [l] 2Co 1:23; 13:2,10
5:1 [m] Lev 18:8; Dt 22:30
5:2 [n] 2Co 7:7-11
5:3 [o] Col 2:5
5:4 [p] 2Th 3:6
5:5 [q] 1Ti 1:20
5:6 [r] Jas 4:16 [s] Mt 16:6,12 [t] Gal 5:9
5:7 [u] Mk 14:12; 1Pe 1:19
5:8 [v] Ex 12:14,15; Dt 16:3
5:9 [w] Eph 5:11; 2Th 3:6,14
5:10 [x] 1Co 10:27

that you must not associate with anyone who calls himself a brother but is sexually immoral or greedy, an idolater[a] or a slanderer, a drunkard or a swindler. With such a man do not even eat.

12 What business is it of mine to judge those outside[b] the church? Are you not to judge those inside?[c] 13 God will judge those outside. "Expel the wicked man from among you."[a][d]

Chapter 6 Theme ______________________________

6 If any of you has a dispute with another, dare he take it before the ungodly for judgment instead of before the saints?[e] 2 Do you not know that the saints will judge the world?[f] And if you are to judge the world, are you not competent to judge trivial cases? 3 Do you not know that we will judge angels? How much more the things of this life! 4 Therefore, if you have disputes about such matters, appoint as judges even men of little account in the church![b] 5 I say this to shame you.[g] Is it possible that there is nobody among you wise enough to judge a dispute between believers?[h] 6 But instead, one brother goes to law against another—and this in front of unbelievers![i]

7 The very fact that you have lawsuits among you means you have been completely defeated already. Why not rather be wronged? Why not rather be cheated?[j] 8 Instead, you yourselves cheat and do wrong, and you do this to your brothers.[k]

9 Do you not know that the wicked will not inherit the kingdom of God?[l] Do not be deceived:[m] Neither the sexually immoral nor idolaters nor adulterers nor male prostitutes nor homosexual offenders 10 nor thieves nor the greedy nor drunkards nor slanderers nor swindlers will inherit the kingdom of God. 11 And that is what some of you were.[n] But you were washed,[o] you were sanctified,[p] you were justified in the name of the Lord Jesus Christ and by the Spirit of our God.

12 "Everything is permissible for me"—but not everything is beneficial.[q] "Everything is permissible for me"—but I will not be mastered by anything. 13 "Food for the stomach and the stomach for food"—but God will destroy them both.[r] The body is not meant for sexual immorality, but for the Lord, and the Lord for the body. 14 By his power God raised the Lord from the dead, and he will raise us also.[s] 15 Do you not know that your bodies are members of Christ himself?[t] Shall I then take the members of Christ and unite them with a prostitute? Never! 16 Do you not know that he who unites himself with a prostitute is one with her in body? For it is said, "The two will become one flesh."[c][u] 17 But he who unites himself with the Lord is one with him in spirit.[v]

[a] *13* Deut. 17:7; 19:19; 21:21; 22:21,24; 24:7 [b] *4* Or *matters, do you appoint as judges men of little account in the church?* [c] *16* Gen. 2:24

5:11 [a] 1Co 10:7,14
5:12 [b] Mk 4:11 [c] ver 3-5; 1Co 6:1-4
5:13 [d] Dt 13:5
6:1 [e] Mt 18:17
6:2 [f] Mt 19:28; Lk 22:30
6:5 [g] 1Co 4:14 [h] Ac 1:15
6:6 [i] 2Co 6:14,15
6:7 [j] Mt 5:39,40
6:8 [k] 1Th 4:6
6:9 [l] Gal 5:21 [m] 1Co 15:33; Jas 1:16
6:11 [n] Eph 2:2 [o] Ac 22:16 [p] 1Co 1:2
6:12 [q] 1Co 10:23
6:13 [r] Col 2:22
6:14 [s] Ro 6:5; Eph 1:19,20
6:15 [t] Ro 12:5
6:16 [u] Ge 2:24; Mt 19:5; Eph 5:31
6:17 [v] Jn 17:21-23; Gal 2:20

18 Flee from sexual immorality.[a] All other sins a man commits are outside his body, but he who sins sexually sins against his own body.[b] 19 Do you not know that your body is a temple[c] of the Holy Spirit, who is in you, whom you have received from God? You are not your own;[d] 20 you were bought at a price.[e] Therefore honor God with your body.

Chapter 7 Theme ________________________

7 Now for the matters you wrote about: It is good for a man not to marry.[a][f] 2 But since there is so much immorality, each man should have his own wife, and each woman her own husband. 3 The husband should fulfill his marital duty to his wife,[g] and likewise the wife to her husband. 4 The wife's body does not belong to her alone but also to her husband. In the same way, the husband's body does not belong to him alone but also to his wife. 5 Do not deprive each other except by mutual consent and for a time,[h] so that you may devote yourselves to prayer. Then come together again so that Satan[i] will not tempt you[j] because of your lack of self-control. 6 I say this as a concession, not as a command.[k] 7 I wish that all men were as I am.[l] But each man has his own gift from God; one has this gift, another has that.[m]

8 Now to the unmarried and the widows I say: It is good for them to stay unmarried, as I am.[n] 9 But if they cannot control themselves, they should marry,[o] for it is better to marry than to burn with passion.

10 To the married I give this command (not I, but the Lord): A wife must not separate from her husband.[p] 11 But if she does, she must remain unmarried or else be reconciled to her husband. And a husband must not divorce his wife.

12 To the rest I say this (I, not the Lord):[q] If any brother has a wife who is not a believer and she is willing to live with him, he must not divorce her. 13 And if a woman has a husband who is not a believer and he is willing to live with her, she must not divorce him. 14 For the unbelieving husband has been sanctified through his wife, and the unbelieving wife has been sanctified through her believing husband. Otherwise your children would be unclean, but as it is, they are holy.[r]

15 But if the unbeliever leaves, let him do so. A believing man or woman is not bound in such circumstances; God has called us to live in peace.[s] 16 How do you know, wife, whether you will save[t] your husband?[u] Or, how do you know, husband, whether you will save your wife?

17 Nevertheless, each one should retain the place in life that the

6:18 [a] 2Co 12:21; 1Th 4:3,4; Heb 13:4 [b] Ro 6:12
6:19 [c] Jn 2:21 [d] Ro 14:7,8
6:20 [e] Ac 20:28; 1Co 7:23; 1Pe 1:18,19; Rev 5:9
7:1 [f] ver 8,26
7:3 [g] Ex 21:10; 1Pe 3:7
7:5 [h] Ex 19:15; 1Sa 21:4,5 [i] Mt 4:10 [j] 1Th 3:5
7:6 [k] 2Co 8:8
7:7 [l] ver 8; 1Co 9:5 [m] Mt 19:11,12; Ro 12:6; 1Co 12:4,11
7:8 [n] ver 1,26
7:9 [o] 1Ti 5:14
7:10 [p] Mal 2:14-16; Mt 5:32; 19:3-9; Mk 10:11; Lk 16:18
7:12 [q] ver 6,10; 2Co 11:17
7:14 [r] Mal 2:15
7:15 [s] Ro 14:19; 1Co 14:33
7:16 [t] Ro 11:14 [u] 1Pe 3:1

a *1* Or *"It is good for a man not to have sexual relations with a woman."*

Lord assigned to him and to which God has called him.[a] This is
the rule I lay down in all the churches.[b] 18 Was a man already circumcised when he was called? He should not become uncircumcised. Was a man uncircumcised when he was called? He should
not be circumcised.[c] 19 Circumcision is nothing and uncircumcision is nothing.[d] Keeping God's commands is what counts. 20 Each
one should remain in the situation which he was in when God
called him.[e] 21 Were you a slave when you were called? Don't let it
trouble you—although if you can gain your freedom, do so. 22 For
he who was a slave when he was called by the Lord is the Lord's
freedman;[f] similarly, he who was a free man when he was called
is Christ's slave.[g] 23 You were bought at a price;[h] do not become
slaves of men. 24 Brothers, each man, as responsible to God, should
remain in the situation God called him to.[i]

25 Now about virgins: I have no command from the Lord,[j] but I
give a judgment as one who by the Lord's mercy[k] is trustworthy.
26 Because of the present crisis, I think that it is good for you to
remain as you are.[l] 27 Are you married? Do not seek a divorce. Are
you unmarried? Do not look for a wife. 28 But if you do marry, you
have not sinned; and if a virgin marries, she has not sinned. But
those who marry will face many troubles in this life, and I want to
spare you this.

29 What I mean, brothers, is that the time is short.[m] From now
on those who have wives should live as if they had none; 30 those
who mourn, as if they did not; those who are happy, as if they were
not; those who buy something, as if it were not theirs to keep;
31 those who use the things of the world, as if not engrossed in
them. For this world in its present form is passing away.[n]

32 I would like you to be free from concern. An unmarried man is
concerned about the Lord's affairs[o]—how he can please the Lord.
33 But a married man is concerned about the affairs of this
world—how he can please his wife— 34 and his interests are divided. An unmarried woman or virgin is concerned about the Lord's
affairs: Her aim is to be devoted to the Lord in both body and
spirit.[p] But a married woman is concerned about the affairs of
this world—how she can please her husband. 35 I am saying this
for your own good, not to restrict you, but that you may live in a
right way in undivided[q] devotion to the Lord.

36 If anyone thinks he is acting improperly toward the virgin he
is engaged to, and if she is getting along in years and he feels he
ought to marry, he should do as he wants. He is not sinning.[r] They
should get married. 37 But the man who has settled the matter in
his own mind, who is under no compulsion but has control over
his own will, and who has made up his mind not to marry the
virgin—this man also does the right thing. 38 So then, he who

7:17 [a] Ro 12:3 [b] 1Co 4:17; 14:33; 2Co 8:18; 11:28
7:18 [c] Ac 15:1,2
7:19 [d] Ro 2:25-27; Gal 5:6; 6:15; Col 3:11
7:20 [e] ver 24
7:22 [f] Jn 8:32,36; Phm 16 [g] Eph 6:6
7:23 [h] 1Co 6:20
7:24 [i] ver 20
7:25 [j] ver 6; 2Co 8:8 [k] 2Co 4:1; 1Ti 1:13,16
7:26 [l] ver 1,8
7:29 [m] ver 31; Ro 13:11,12
7:31 [n] 1Jn 2:17
7:32 [o] 1Ti 5:5
7:34 [p] Lk 2:37
7:35 [q] Ps 86:11
7:36 [r] ver 28

marries the virgin does right,[a] but he who does not marry her
does even better.[a]
39 A woman is bound to her husband as long as he lives.[b] But if
her husband dies, she is free to marry anyone she wishes, but he
must belong to the Lord.[c] 40 In my judgment,[d] she is happier if she
stays as she is—and I think that I too have the Spirit of God.

Chapter 8 Theme ____________________________

8 Now about food sacrificed to idols:[e] We know that we all
possess knowledge.[b][f] Knowledge puffs up, but love builds up.
2 The man who thinks he knows something[g] does not yet know as
he ought to know.[h] 3 But the man who loves God is known by God.[i]
4 So then, about eating food sacrificed to idols:[j] We know that
an idol is nothing at all in the world[k] and that there is no God but
one.[l] 5 For even if there are so-called gods,[m] whether in heaven or
on earth (as indeed there are many "gods" and many "lords"), 6 yet
for us there is but one God, the Father,[n] from whom all things came[o]
and for whom we live; and there is but one Lord,[p] Jesus Christ,
through whom all things came[q] and through whom we live.
7 But not everyone knows this. Some people are still so accustomed to idols that when they eat such food they think of it as
having been sacrificed to an idol, and since their conscience is
weak,[r] it is defiled. 8 But food does not bring us near to God;[s] we
are no worse if we do not eat, and no better if we do.
9 Be careful, however, that the exercise of your freedom does not
become a stumbling block[t] to the weak.[u] 10 For if anyone with a
weak conscience sees you who have this knowledge eating in an
idol's temple, won't he be emboldened to eat what has been sacrificed to idols? 11 So this weak brother, for whom Christ died, is
destroyed[v] by your knowledge. 12 When you sin against your
brothers[w] in this way and wound their weak conscience, you sin
against Christ. 13 Therefore, if what I eat causes my brother to fall
into sin, I will never eat meat again, so that I will not cause him to
fall.[x]

Chapter 9 Theme ____________________________

9 Am I not free? Am I not an apostle?[y] Have I not seen Jesus
our Lord?[z] Are you not the result of my work in the Lord?[a]
2 Even though I may not be an apostle to others, surely I am to
you! For you are the seal[b] of my apostleship in the Lord.

7:38 [a] Heb 13:4
7:39 [b] Ro 7:2,3 [c] 2Co 6:14
7:40 [d] ver 25
8:1 [e] Ac 15:20 [f] Ro 15:14
8:2 [g] 1Co 3:18 [h] 1Co 13:8,9,12; 1Ti 6:4
8:3 [i] Ro 8:29; Gal 4:9
8:4 [j] ver 1,7,10 [k] 1Co 10:19 [l] Dt 6:4; Eph 4:6
8:5 [m] 2Th 2:4
8:6 [n] Mal 2:10 [o] Ro 11:36 [p] Eph 4:5 [q] Jn 1:3
8:7 [r] Ro 14:14; 1Co 10:28
8:8 [s] Ro 14:17
8:9 [t] Gal 5:13 [u] Ro 14:1
8:11 [v] Ro 14:15,20
8:12 [w] Mt 18:6
8:13 [x] Ro 14:21
9:1 [y] 2Co 12:12 [z] 1Co 15:8 [a] 1Co 3:6; 4:15
9:2 [b] 2Co 3:2,3

[a] 36-38 Or *36 If anyone thinks he is not treating his daughter properly, and if she is getting along in years, and he feels she ought to marry, he should do as he wants. He is not sinning. He should let her get married. 37 But the man who has settled the matter in his own mind, who is under no compulsion but has control over his own will, and who has made up his mind to keep the virgin unmarried—this man also does the right thing. 38 So then, he who gives his virgin in marriage does right, but he who does not give her in marriage does even better.* [b] *1 Or "We all possess knowledge," as you say*

3 This is my defense to those who sit in judgment on me. 4 Don't we have the right to food and drink?[a] 5 Don't we have the right to take a believing wife[b] along with us, as do the other apostles and the Lord's brothers[c] and Cephas[a]? 6 Or is it only I and Barnabas[d] who must work for a living?

7 Who serves as a soldier at his own expense? Who plants a vineyard[e] and does not eat of its grapes? Who tends a flock and does not drink of the milk? 8 Do I say this merely from a human point of view? Doesn't the Law say the same thing? 9 For it is written in the Law of Moses: "Do not muzzle an ox while it is treading out the grain."[b][f] Is it about oxen that God is concerned?[g] 10 Surely he says this for us, doesn't he? Yes, this was written for us,[h] because when the plowman plows and the thresher threshes, they ought to do so in the hope of sharing in the harvest.[i] 11 If we have sown spiritual seed among you, is it too much if we reap a material harvest from you?[j] 12 If others have this right of support from you, shouldn't we have it all the more?

But we did not use this right.[k] On the contrary, we put up with anything rather than hinder[l] the gospel of Christ. 13 Don't you know that those who work in the temple get their food from the temple, and those who serve at the altar share in what is offered on the altar?[m] 14 In the same way, the Lord has commanded that those who preach the gospel should receive their living from the gospel.[n]

15 But I have not used any of these rights.[o] And I am not writing this in the hope that you will do such things for me. I would rather die than have anyone deprive me of this boast.[p] 16 Yet when I preach the gospel, I cannot boast, for I am compelled to preach.[q] Woe to me if I do not preach the gospel! 17 If I preach voluntarily, I have a reward;[r] if not voluntarily, I am simply discharging the trust committed to me.[s] 18 What then is my reward? Just this: that in preaching the gospel I may offer it free of charge,[t] and so not make use of my rights in preaching it.

19 Though I am free[u] and belong to no man, I make myself a slave to everyone,[v] to win as many as possible.[w] 20 To the Jews I became like a Jew, to win the Jews.[x] To those under the law I became like one under the law (though I myself am not under the law), so as to win those under the law. 21 To those not having the law I became like one not having the law[y] (though I am not free from God's law but am under Christ's law), so as to win those not having the law. 22 To the weak I became weak, to win the weak. I have become all things to all men[z] so that by all possible means I might save some.[a] 23 I do all this for the sake of the gospel, that I may share in its blessings.

[a]5 That is, Peter [b]9 Deut. 25:4

9:4 [a] 1Th 2:6
9:5 [b] 1Co 7:7,8 [c] Mt 12:46
9:6 [d] Ac 4:36
9:7 [e] Dt 20:6; Pr 27:18
9:9 [f] Dt 25:4; 1Ti 5:18 [g] Dt 22:1-4
9:10 [h] Ro 4:23,24 [i] 2Ti 2:6
9:11 [j] Ro 15:27
9:12 [k] Ac 18:3 [l] 2Co 11:7-12
9:13 [m] Lev 6:16,26; Dt 18:1
9:14 [n] Mt 10:10; 1Ti 5:18
9:15 [o] Ac 18:3 [p] 2Co 11:9,10
9:16 [q] Ro 1:14; Ac 9:15
9:17 [r] 1Co 3:8,14 [s] Gal 2:7; Col 1:25
9:18 [t] 2Co 11:7; 12:13
9:19 [u] ver 1 [v] Gal 5:13 [w] Mt 18:15; 1Pe 3:1
9:20 [x] Ac 16:3; 21:20-26; Ro 11:14
9:21 [y] Ro 2:12,14
9:22 [z] 1Co 10:33 [a] Ro 11:14

24Do you not know that in a race all the runners run, but only
one gets the prize? Run[a] in such a way as to get the prize. 25Every-
one who competes in the games goes into strict training. They do
it to get a crown that will not last; but we do it to get a crown that
will last forever.[b] 26Therefore I do not run like a man running
aimlessly; I do not fight like a man beating the air. 27No, I beat my
body[c] and make it my slave so that after I have preached to others, I myself will not be disqualified for the prize.

Chapter 10 Theme ____________________

10 For I do not want you to be ignorant of the fact, brothers,
that our forefathers were all under the cloud[d] and that they
all passed through the sea.[e] 2They were all baptized into Moses in
the cloud and in the sea. 3They all ate the same spiritual food 4and
drank the same spiritual drink; for they drank from the spiritual
rock[f] that accompanied them, and that rock was Christ. 5Never-
theless, God was not pleased with most of them; their bodies
were scattered over the desert.[g]

6Now these things occurred as examples[a] to keep us from setting our hearts on evil things as they did. 7Do not be idolaters,[h]
as some of them were; as it is written: "The people sat down to
eat and drink and got up to indulge in pagan revelry."[b][i] 8We should
not commit sexual immorality, as some of them did—and in one
day twenty-three thousand of them died.[j] 9We should not test the
Lord, as some of them did—and were killed by snakes.[k] 10And
do not grumble, as some of them did[l]—and were killed[m] by the
destroying angel.[n]

11These things happened to them as examples and were written
down as warnings for us, on whom the fulfillment of the ages has
come.[o] 12So, if you think you are standing firm,[p] be careful that you
don't fall! 13No temptation has seized you except what is common to man. And God is faithful;[q] he will not let you be tempted
beyond what you can bear.[r] But when you are tempted, he will
also provide a way out so that you can stand up under it.

14Therefore, my dear friends, flee from idolatry. 15I speak to
sensible people; judge for yourselves what I say. 16Is not the cup of
thanksgiving for which we give thanks a participation in the
blood of Christ? And is not the bread that we break a participation in the body of Christ?[s] 17Because there is one loaf, we, who
are many, are one body,[t] for we all partake of the one loaf.

18Consider the people of Israel: Do not those who eat the sacrifices[u] participate in the altar? 19Do I mean then that a sacrifice
offered to an idol is anything, or that an idol is anything?[v] 20No, but
the sacrifices of pagans are offered to demons,[w] not to God, and I

9:24 [a] Gal 2:2; 2Ti 4:7; Heb 12:1
9:25 [b] Jas 1:12; Rev 2:10
9:27 [c] Ro 8:13
10:1 [d] Ex 13:21 [e] Ex 14:22,29
10:4 [f] Ex 17:6; Nu 20:11; Ps 78:15
10:5 [g] Nu 14:29; Heb 3:17
10:7 [h] ver 14 [i] Ex 32:4,6,19
10:8 [j] Nu 25:1-9
10:9 [k] Nu 21:5,6
10:10 [l] Nu 16:41 [m] Nu 16:49 [n] Ex 12:23
10:11 [o] Ro 13:11
10:12 [p] Ro 11:20
10:13 [q] 1Co 1:9 [r] 2Pe 2:9
10:16 [s] Mt 26:26-28
10:17 [t] Ro 12:5; 1Co 12:27
10:18 [u] Lev 7:6,14,15
10:19 [v] 1Co 8:4
10:20 [w] Dt 32:17; Ps 106:37; Rev 9:20

[a] 6 Or *types*; also in verse 11 [b] 7 Exodus 32:6

do not want you to be participants with demons. 21You cannot
drink the cup of the Lord and the cup of demons too; you cannot
have a part in both the Lord's table and the table of demons.[a] 22Are
we trying to arouse the Lord's jealousy?[b] Are we stronger than he?[c]
23"Everything is permissible"—but not everything is beneficial.[d]
"Everything is permissible"—but not everything is constructive.
24Nobody should seek his own good, but the good of others.[e]
25Eat anything sold in the meat market without raising questions
of conscience,[f] 26for, "The earth is the Lord's, and everything in it."[a][g]
27If some unbeliever invites you to a meal and you want to go,
eat whatever is put before you[h] without raising questions of conscience. 28But if anyone says to you, "This has been offered in sacrifice," then do not eat it, both for the sake of the man who told
you and for conscience' sake[b][i]— 29the other man's conscience, I
mean, not yours. For why should my freedom[j] be judged by
another's conscience? 30If I take part in the meal with thankfulness, why am I denounced because of something I thank God
for?[k]
31So whether you eat or drink or whatever you do, do it all for
the glory of God.[l] 32Do not cause anyone to stumble,[m] whether
Jews, Greeks or the church of God[n]— 33even as I try to please
everybody in every way.[o] For I am not seeking my own good but
the good of many, so that they may be saved.[p]

Chapter 11 Theme ________________________

11 Follow my example,[q] as I follow the example of Christ.
2I praise you[r] for remembering me in everything[s] and for
holding to the teachings,[c] just as I passed them on to you.[t]
3Now I want you to realize that the head of every man is Christ,[u]
and the head of the woman is man,[v] and the head of Christ is
God.[w] 4Every man who prays or prophesies with his head covered dishonors his head. 5And every woman who prays or prophesies[x] with her head uncovered dishonors her head—it is just as
though her head were shaved.[y] 6If a woman does not cover her
head, she should have her hair cut off; and if it is a disgrace for a
woman to have her hair cut or shaved off, she should cover her
head. 7A man ought not to cover his head,[d] since he is the image[z]
and glory of God; but the woman is the glory of man. 8For man
did not come from woman, but woman from man;[a] 9neither was
man created for woman, but woman for man.[b] 10For this reason,

[a]26 Psalm 24:1 [b]28 Some manuscripts *conscience' sake, for "the earth is the Lord's and everything in it"* [c]2 Or *traditions* [d]4-7 Or *4Every man who prays or prophesies with long hair dishonors his head. 5And every woman who prays or prophesies with no covering ⌊of hair⌋ on her head dishonors her head—she is just like one of the "shorn women." 6If a woman has no covering, let her be for now with short hair, but since it is a disgrace for a woman to have her hair shorn or shaved, she should grow it again. 7A man ought not to have long hair*

10:21 [a]2Co 6:15,16
10:22 [b]Dt 32:16,21 [c]Ecc 6:10; Isa 45:9
10:23 [d]1Co 6:12
10:24 [e]ver 33; Ro 15:1,2; 1Co 13:5; Php 2:4,21
10:25 [f]Ac 10:15; 1Co 8:7
10:26 [g]Ps 24:1
10:27 [h]Lk 10:7
10:28 [i]1Co 8:7,10-12
10:29 [j]Ro 14:16; 1Co 9:1,19
10:30 [k]Ro 14:6
10:31 [l]Col 3:17; 1Pe 4:11
10:32 [m]Ac 24:16 [n]Ac 20:28
10:33 [o]Ro 15:2; 1Co 9:22 [p]Ro 11:14
11:1 [q]1Co 4:16
11:2 [r]ver 17,22 [s]1Co 4:17 [t]1Co 15:2,3; 2Th 2:15
11:3 [u]Eph 1:22 [v]Ge 3:16; Eph 5:23 [w]1Co 3:23
11:5 [x]Ac 21:9 [y]Dt 21:12
11:7 [z]Ge 1:26; Jas 3:9
11:8 [a]Ge 2:21-23; 1Ti 2:13
11:9 [b]Ge 2:18

and because of the angels, the woman ought to have a sign of
authority on her head.
11 In the Lord, however, woman is not independent of man, nor
is man independent of woman. 12 For as woman came from man,
so also man is born of woman. But everything comes from God.[a]
13 Judge for yourselves: Is it proper for a woman to pray to God
with her head uncovered? 14 Does not the very nature of things
teach you that if a man has long hair, it is a disgrace to him, 15 but
that if a woman has long hair, it is her glory? For long hair is giv-
en to her as a covering. 16 If anyone wants to be contentious about
this, we have no other practice—nor do the churches of God.[b]
17 In the following directives I have no praise for you,[c] for your
meetings do more harm than good. 18 In the first place, I hear that
when you come together as a church, there are divisions[d] among
you, and to some extent I believe it. 19 No doubt there have to be
differences among you to show which of you have God's approval.[e]
20 When you come together, it is not the Lord's Supper you eat, 21 for
as you eat, each of you goes ahead without waiting for anybody
else.[f] One remains hungry, another gets drunk. 22 Don't you have
homes to eat and drink in? Or do you despise the church of God[g]
and humiliate those who have nothing?[h] What shall I say to you?
Shall I praise you[i] for this? Certainly not!
23 For I received from the Lord[j] what I also passed on to you:[k]
The Lord Jesus, on the night he was betrayed, took bread, 24 and
when he had given thanks, he broke it and said, "This is my body,
which is for you; do this in remembrance of me." 25 In the same
way, after supper he took the cup, saying, "This cup is the new
covenant[l] in my blood;[m] do this, whenever you drink it, in remembrance of me." 26 For whenever you eat this bread and drink
this cup, you proclaim the Lord's death until he comes.
27 Therefore, whoever eats the bread or drinks the cup of the
Lord in an unworthy manner will be guilty of sinning against the
body and blood of the Lord.[n] 28 A man ought to examine himself[o]
before he eats of the bread and drinks of the cup. 29 For anyone
who eats and drinks without recognizing the body of the Lord eats
and drinks judgment on himself. 30 That is why many among you
are weak and sick, and a number of you have fallen asleep. 31 But
if we judged ourselves, we would not come under judgment.[p]
32 When we are judged by the Lord, we are being disciplined[q] so
that we will not be condemned with the world.
33 So then, my brothers, when you come together to eat, wait for
each other. 34 If anyone is hungry,[r] he should eat at home,[s] so that
when you meet together it may not result in judgment.
And when I come[t] I will give further directions.

11:12 [a] Ro 11:36
11:16 [b] 1Co 7:17
11:17 [c] ver 2,22
11:18 [d] 1Co 1:10-12; 3:3
11:19 [e] 1Jn 2:19
11:21 [f] 2Pe 2:13; Jude 12
11:22 [g] 1Co 10:32 [h] Jas 2:6 [i] ver 2,17
11:23 [j] Gal 1:12 [k] 1Co 15:3
11:25 [l] Lk 22:20 [m] 1Co 10:16
11:27 [n] Heb 10:29
11:28 [o] 2Co 13:5
11:31 [p] Ps 32:5; 1Jn 1:9
11:32 [q] Ps 94:12; Heb 12:7-10; Rev 3:19
11:34 [r] ver 21 [s] ver 22 [t] 1Co 4:19

Chapter 12 Theme ______________________________

12 Now about spiritual gifts,[a] brothers, I do not want you to
be ignorant. 2You know that when you were pagans,[b] somehow or other you were influenced and led astray to mute idols.[c]
3Therefore I tell you that no one who is speaking by the Spirit of
God says, "Jesus be cursed,"[d] and no one can say, "Jesus is Lord,"[e]
except by the Holy Spirit.[f]

4There are different kinds of gifts, but the same Spirit.[g] 5There
are different kinds of service, but the same Lord. 6There are different kinds of working, but the same God[h] works all of them in
all men.

7Now to each one the manifestation of the Spirit is given for the
common good.[i] 8To one there is given through the Spirit the message of wisdom,[j] to another the message of knowledge[k] by means
of the same Spirit, 9to another faith[l] by the same Spirit, to another gifts of healing[m] by that one Spirit, 10to another miraculous
powers,[n] to another prophecy, to another distinguishing between
spirits,[o] to another speaking in different kinds of tongues,[a][p] and
to still another the interpretation of tongues.[a] 11All these are the
work of one and the same Spirit,[q] and he gives them to each one,
just as he determines.

12The body is a unit, though it is made up of many parts; and
though all its parts are many, they form one body.[r] So it is with
Christ.[s] 13For we were all baptized by[b] one Spirit[t] into one body—
whether Jews or Greeks, slave or free[u]—and we were all given the
one Spirit to drink.[v]

14Now the body is not made up of one part but of many. 15If the
foot should say, "Because I am not a hand, I do not belong to the
body," it would not for that reason cease to be part of the body.
16And if the ear should say, "Because I am not an eye, I do not
belong to the body," it would not for that reason cease to be part
of the body. 17If the whole body were an eye, where would the
sense of hearing be? If the whole body were an ear, where would
the sense of smell be? 18But in fact God has arranged[w] the parts in
the body, every one of them, just as he wanted them to be.[x] 19If
they were all one part, where would the body be? 20As it is, there
are many parts, but one body.[y]

21The eye cannot say to the hand, "I don't need you!" And the
head cannot say to the feet, "I don't need you!" 22On the contrary, those parts of the body that seem to be weaker are indispensable, 23and the parts that we think are less honorable we
treat with special honor. And the parts that are unpresentable are
treated with special modesty, 24while our presentable parts need

a *10* Or *languages*; also in verse 28 b *13* Or *with*; or *in*

12:1 [a]Ro 1:11; 1Co 14:1,37

12:2 [b]Eph 2:11,12; 1Pe 4:3 [c]Ps 115:5; Jer 10:5; Hab 2:18,19; 1Th 1:9

12:3 [d]Ro 9:3 [e]Jn 13:13 [f]1Jn 4:2,3

12:4 [g]Ro 12:4-8; Eph 4:11; Heb 2:4

12:6 [h]Eph 4:6

12:7 [i]Eph 4:12

12:8 [j]1Co 2:6 [k]2Co 8:7

12:9 [l]Mt 17:19,20; 2Co 4:13 [m]ver 28,30

12:10 [n]Gal 3:5 [o]1Jn 4:1 [p]Mk 16:17

12:11 [q]ver 4

12:12 [r]Ro 12:5 [s]ver 27

12:13 [t]Eph 2:18 [u]Gal 3:28; Col 3:11 [v]Jn 7:37-39

12:18 [w]ver 28 [x]ver 11

12:20 [y]ver 12,14

no special treatment. But God has combined the members of the
body and has given greater honor to the parts that lacked it, 25so
that there should be no division in the body, but that its parts
should have equal concern for each other. 26If one part suffers,
every part suffers with it; if one part is honored, every part rejoices
with it.

27Now you are the body of Christ,[a] and each one of you is a part
of it.[b] 28And in the church[c] God has appointed first of all apostles,[d]
second prophets, third teachers, then workers of miracles, also
those having gifts of healing,[e] those able to help others, those
with gifts of administration,[f] and those speaking in different
kinds of tongues.[g] 29Are all apostles? Are all prophets? Are all
teachers? Do all work miracles? 30Do all have gifts of healing? Do
all speak in tongues[a]?[h] Do all interpret? 31But eagerly desire[b][i] the
greater gifts.

Chapter 13 Theme ____

And now I will show you the most excellent way.

13 If I speak in the tongues[c][j] of men and of angels, but have
not love, I am only a resounding gong or a clanging cymbal. 2If I have the gift of prophecy and can fathom all mysteries[k]
and all knowledge, and if I have a faith[l] that can move mountains,[m] but have not love, I am nothing. 3If I give all I possess to
the poor[n] and surrender my body to the flames,[d][o] but have not
love, I gain nothing.

4Love is patient,[p] love is kind. It does not envy, it does not boast,
it is not proud. 5It is not rude, it is not self-seeking,[q] it is not easily
angered, it keeps no record of wrongs. 6Love does not delight in
evil[r] but rejoices with the truth.[s] 7It always protects, always trusts,
always hopes, always perseveres.

8Love never fails. But where there are prophecies,[t] they will
cease; where there are tongues,[u] they will be stilled; where there
is knowledge, it will pass away. 9For we know in part[v] and we
prophesy in part, 10but when perfection comes,[w] the imperfect
disappears. 11When I was a child, I talked like a child, I thought
like a child, I reasoned like a child. When I became a man, I put
childish ways behind me. 12Now we see but a poor reflection as in
a mirror; then we shall see face to face.[x] Now I know in part; then
I shall know fully, even as I am fully known.[y]

13And now these three remain: faith, hope and love.[z] But the
greatest of these is love.[a]

12:27 [a]Eph 1:23; 4:12; Col 1:18,24 [b]Ro 12:5
12:28 [c]1Co 10:32 [d]Eph 4:11 [e]ver 9 [f]Ro 12:6-8 [g]ver 10
12:30 [h]ver 10
12:31 [i]1Co 14:1,39
13:1 [j]ver 8
13:2 [k]1Co 14:2 [l]1Co 12:9 [m]Mt 17:20; 21:21
13:3 [n]Mt 6:2 [o]Da 3:28
13:4 [p]1Th 5:14
13:5 [q]1Co 10:24
13:6 [r]2Th 2:12 [s]2Jn 4; 3Jn 3,4
13:8 [t]ver 2 [u]ver 1
13:9 [v]ver 12; 1Co 8:2
13:10 [w]Php 3:12
13:12 [x]Ge 32:30; 2Co 5:7; 1Jn 3:2 [y]1Co 8:3
13:13 [z]Gal 5:5,6 [a]1Co 16:14

[a]30 Or *other languages* [b]31 Or *But you are eagerly desiring* [c]1 Or *languages*
[d]3 Some early manuscripts *body that I may boast*

Chapter 14 Theme ______________________________

14 Follow the way of love[a] and eagerly desire[b] spiritual gifts,[c]
especially the gift of prophecy. 2For anyone who speaks in
a tongue[a][d] does not speak to men but to God. Indeed, no one
understands him; he utters mysteries[e] with his spirit.[b] 3But
everyone who prophesies speaks to men for their strengthening,[f]
encouragement and comfort. 4He who speaks in a tongue[g] edifies
himself, but he who prophesies[h] edifies the church. 5I would like
every one of you to speak in tongues,[c] but I would rather have
you prophesy.[i] He who prophesies is greater than one who speaks
in tongues,[c] unless he interprets, so that the church may be edified.

6Now, brothers, if I come to you and speak in tongues, what
good will I be to you, unless I bring you some revelation[j] or knowledge or prophecy or word of instruction?[k] 7Even in the case of
lifeless things that make sounds, such as the flute or harp, how
will anyone know what tune is being played unless there is a distinction in the notes? 8Again, if the trumpet does not sound a
clear call, who will get ready for battle?[l] 9So it is with you. Unless
you speak intelligible words with your tongue, how will anyone
know what you are saying? You will just be speaking into the air.
10Undoubtedly there are all sorts of languages in the world, yet
none of them is without meaning. 11If then I do not grasp the
meaning of what someone is saying, I am a foreigner to the speaker, and he is a foreigner to me. 12So it is with you. Since you are
eager to have spiritual gifts, try to excel in gifts that build up the
church.

13For this reason anyone who speaks in a tongue should pray
that he may interpret what he says. 14For if I pray in a tongue, my
spirit prays, but my mind is unfruitful. 15So what shall I do? I will
pray with my spirit, but I will also pray with my mind; I will sing[m]
with my spirit, but I will also sing with my mind. 16If you are praising God with your spirit, how can one who finds himself among
those who do not understand[d] say "Amen"[n] to your thanksgiving,[o]
since he does not know what you are saying? 17You may be giving
thanks well enough, but the other man is not edified.

18I thank God that I speak in tongues more than all of you.
19But in the church I would rather speak five intelligible words to
instruct others than ten thousand words in a tongue.

20Brothers, stop thinking like children.[p] In regard to evil be
infants,[q] but in your thinking be adults. 21In the Law[r] it is written:

[a]2 Or *another language;* also in verses 4, 13, 14, 19, 26 and 27 [b]2 Or *by the Spirit*
[c]5 Or *other languages;* also in verses 6, 18, 22, 23 and 39 [d]16 Or *among the inquirers*

14:1 [a]1Co 16:14 [b]ver 39; 1Co 12:31 [c]1Co 12:1

14:2 [d]Mk 16:17 [e]1Co 13:2

14:3 [f]ver 4,5,12,17, 26; Ro 14:19

14:4 [g]Mk 16:17 [h]1Co 13:2

14:5 [i]Nu 11:29

14:6 [j]ver 26; Eph 1:17 [k]Ro 6:17

14:8 [l]Nu 10:9; Jer 4:19

14:15 [m]Eph 5:19; Col 3:16

14:16 [n]Dt 27:15-26; 1Ch 16:36; Ne 8:6; Ps 106:48; Rev 5:14; 7:12 [o]1Co 11:24

14:20 [p]Eph 4:14; Heb 5:12,13; 1Pe 2:2 [q]Ro 16:19

14:21 [r]Jn 10:34

14:21 [a]Isa 28:11,12 “Through men of strange tongues
and through the lips of foreigners
I will speak to this people,
14:22 [b]ver 1 but even then they will not listen to me,”[a][a]
says the Lord.

22 Tongues, then, are a sign, not for believers but for unbeliev-
14:23 ers; prophecy,[b] however, is for believers, not for unbelievers. 23 So
[c]Ac 2:13 if the whole church comes together and everyone speaks in
tongues, and some who do not understand[b] or some unbelievers
come in, will they not say that you are out of your mind?[c] 24 But if
14:25 [d]Isa 45:14; an unbeliever or someone who does not understand[c] comes in
Zec 8:23 while everybody is prophesying, he will be convinced by all that
he is a sinner and will be judged by all, 25 and the secrets of his
heart will be laid bare. So he will fall down and worship God,
14:26 exclaiming, “God is really among you!”[d]
[e]1Co 12:7-10 [f]Eph 5:19 26 What then shall we say, brothers? When you come together,
[g]ver 6 [h]Ro 14:19 everyone[e] has a hymn,[f] or a word of instruction,[g] a revelation, a
tongue or an interpretation. All of these must be done for the
strengthening[h] of the church. 27 If anyone speaks in a tongue,
14:29 two—or at the most three—should speak, one at a time, and
[i]1Co 12:10 someone must interpret. 28 If there is no interpreter, the speaker
should keep quiet in the church and speak to himself and God.
29 Two or three prophets should speak, and the others should
14:32 [j]1Jn 4:1 weigh carefully what is said.[i] 30 And if a revelation comes to someone who is sitting down, the first speaker should stop. 31 For you
can all prophesy in turn so that everyone may be instructed and
14:33 [k]ver 40 encouraged. 32 The spirits of prophets are subject to the control of
[l]Ac 9:13 prophets.[j] 33 For God is not a God of disorder[k] but of peace.
As in all the congregations of the saints,[l] 34 women should
remain silent in the churches. They are not allowed to speak, but
14:34 [m]1Ti 2:11,12 must be in submission,[m] as the Law[n] says. 35 If they want to in-
[n]Ge 3:16 quire about something, they should ask their own husbands at
home; for it is disgraceful for a woman to speak in the church.
36 Did the word of God originate with you? Or are you the only
14:37 people it has reached? 37 If anybody thinks he is a prophet[o] or
[o]2Co 10:7 [p]1Jn 4:6 spiritually gifted, let him acknowledge that what I am writing to
you is the Lord’s command.[p] 38 If he ignores this, he himself will
be ignored.[d]
39 Therefore, my brothers, be eager[q] to prophesy, and do not
14:39 [q]1Co 12:31 forbid speaking in tongues. 40 But everything should be done in a
fitting and orderly[r] way.

14:40 [r]ver 33

[a] *21* Isaiah 28:11,12 [b] *23* Or *some inquirers* [c] *24* Or *or some inquirer* [d] *38* Some manuscripts *If he is ignorant of this, let him be ignorant*

Chapter 15 Theme ____________________

15 Now, brothers, I want to remind you of the gospel[a] I preached
to you, which you received and on which you have taken your
stand. 2By this gospel you are saved,[b] if you hold firmly[c] to the
word I preached to you. Otherwise, you have believed in vain.
3For what I received[d] I passed on to you[e] as of first importance[a]:
that Christ died for our sins[f] according to the Scriptures,[g] 4that
he was buried, that he was raised[h] on the third day[i] according to
the Scriptures,[j] 5and that he appeared to Peter,[b][k] and then to the
Twelve.[l] 6After that, he appeared to more than five hundred of the
brothers at the same time, most of whom are still living, though
some have fallen asleep. 7Then he appeared to James, then to all
the apostles,[m] 8and last of all he appeared to me also,[n] as to one
abnormally born.
9For I am the least of the apostles[o] and do not even deserve to
be called an apostle, because I persecuted[p] the church of God.
10But by the grace of God I am what I am, and his grace to me[q]
was not without effect. No, I worked harder than all of them[r]—yet
not I, but the grace of God that was with me.[s] 11Whether, then, it
was I or they, this is what we preach, and this is what you believed.
12But if it is preached that Christ has been raised from the dead,
how can some of you say that there is no resurrection of the dead?[t]
13If there is no resurrection of the dead, then not even Christ has
been raised. 14And if Christ has not been raised,[u] our preaching
is useless and so is your faith. 15More than that, we are then
found to be false witnesses about God, for we have testified about
God that he raised Christ from the dead.[v] But he did not raise
him if in fact the dead are not raised. 16For if the dead are not
raised, then Christ has not been raised either. 17And if Christ has
not been raised, your faith is futile; you are still in your sins.[w]
18Then those also who have fallen asleep in Christ are lost. 19If
only for this life we have hope in Christ, we are to be pitied more
than all men.[x]
20But Christ has indeed been raised from the dead,[y] the firstfruits[z] of those who have fallen asleep.[a] 21For since death came
through a man,[b] the resurrection of the dead comes also through
a man. 22For as in Adam all die, so in Christ all will be made alive.[c]
23But each in his own turn: Christ, the firstfruits;[d] then, when he
comes,[e] those who belong to him. 24Then the end will come,
when he hands over the kingdom[f] to God the Father after he has
destroyed all dominion, authority and power.[g] 25For he must
reign until he has put all his enemies under his feet.[h] 26The last
enemy to be destroyed is death.[i] 27For he "has put everything under

a3 Or *you at the first* b5 Greek *Cephas*

15:1 [a]Ro 2:16
15:2 [b]Ro 1:16 [c]Ro 11:22
15:3 [d]Gal 1:12 [e]1Co 11:23 [f]Isa 53:5; 1Pe 2:24 [g]Lk 24:27; Ac 26:22,23
15:4 [h]Ac 2:24 [i]Mt 16:21 [j]Ac 2:25,30,31
15:5 [k]Lk 24:34 [l]Mk 16:14
15:7 [m]Lk 24:33,36, 37; Ac 1:3,4
15:8 [n]Ac 9:3-6,17; 1Co 9:1
15:9 [o]Eph 3:8; 1Ti 1:15 [p]Ac 8:3
15:10 [q]Ro 12:3 [r]2Co 11:23 [s]Php 2:13
15:12 [t]Ac 17:32; 23:8; 2Ti 2:18
15:14 [u]1Th 4:14
15:15 [v]Ac 2:24
15:17 [w]Ro 4:25
15:19 [x]1Co 4:9
15:20 [y]1Pe 1:3 [z]ver 23; Ac 26:23; Rev 1:5 [a]ver 6,18
15:21 [b]Ro 5:12
15:22 [c]Ro 5:14-18
15:23 [d]ver 20 [e]ver 52
15:24 [f]Da 7:14,27 [g]Ro 8:38
15:25 [h]Ps 110:1; Mt 22:44
15:26 [i]2Ti 1:10; Rev 20:14; 21:4

his feet."[a][a] Now when it says that "everything" has been put
under him, it is clear that this does not include God himself, who
put everything under Christ.[b] 28When he has done this, then the
Son himself will be made subject to him who put everything
under him,[c] so that God may be all in all.[d]
29Now if there is no resurrection, what will those do who are
baptized for the dead? If the dead are not raised at all, why are
people baptized for them? 30And as for us, why do we endanger
ourselves every hour?[e] 31I die every day[f]—I mean that, brothers—just as surely as I glory over you in Christ Jesus our Lord.
32If I fought wild beasts[g] in Ephesus[h] for merely human reasons,
what have I gained? If the dead are not raised,

"Let us eat and drink,
for tomorrow we die."[b][i]

33Do not be misled: "Bad company corrupts good character."
34Come back to your senses as you ought, and stop sinning; for
there are some who are ignorant of God—I say this to your shame.
35But someone may ask,[j] "How are the dead raised? With what
kind of body will they come?"[k] 36How foolish![l] What you sow
does not come to life unless it dies.[m] 37When you sow, you do not
plant the body that will be, but just a seed, perhaps of wheat or of
something else. 38But God gives it a body as he has determined,
and to each kind of seed he gives its own body.[n] 39All flesh is not
the same: Men have one kind of flesh, animals have another,
birds another and fish another. 40There are also heavenly bodies
and there are earthly bodies; but the splendor of the heavenly
bodies is one kind, and the splendor of the earthly bodies is
another. 41The sun has one kind of splendor, the moon another
and the stars another; and star differs from star in splendor.
42So will it be[o] with the resurrection of the dead. The body that
is sown is perishable, it is raised imperishable; 43it is sown in dishonor, it is raised in glory;[p] it is sown in weakness, it is raised in
power; 44it is sown a natural body, it is raised a spiritual body.[q]
If there is a natural body, there is also a spiritual body. 45So it is
written: "The first man Adam became a living being"[c];[r] the last
Adam,[s] a life-giving spirit.[t] 46The spiritual did not come first, but
the natural, and after that the spiritual. 47The first man was of the
dust of the earth,[u] the second man from heaven.[v] 48As was the
earthly man, so are those who are of the earth; and as is the man
from heaven, so also are those who are of heaven.[w] 49And just as
we have borne the likeness of the earthly man,[x] so shall we[d] bear
the likeness of the man from heaven.[y]
50I declare to you, brothers, that flesh and blood[z] cannot inherit

15:27 [a]Ps 8:6 [b]Mt 28:18
15:28 [c]Php 3:21 [d]1Co 3:23
15:30 [e]2Co 11:26
15:31 [f]Ro 8:36
15:32 [g]2Co 1:8 [h]Ac 18:19 [i]Isa 22:13; Lk 12:19
15:35 [j]Ro 9:19 [k]Eze 37:3
15:36 [l]Lk 11:40 [m]Jn 12:24
15:38 [n]Ge 1:11
15:42 [o]Da 12:3; Mt 13:43
15:43 [p]Php 3:21; Col 3:4
15:44 [q]ver 50
15:45 [r]Ge 2:7 [s]Ro 5:14 [t]Jn 5:21; Ro 8:2
15:47 [u]Ge 2:7; 3:19 [v]Jn 3:13,31
15:48 [w]Php 3:20,21
15:49 [x]Ge 5:3 [y]Ro 8:29
15:50 [z]Jn 3:3,5

[a] *27* Psalm 8:6 [b] *32* Isaiah 22:13 [c] *45* Gen. 2:7 [d] *49* Some early manuscripts *so let us*

the kingdom of God, nor does the perishable inherit the imperishable. 51Listen, I tell you a mystery:[a] We will not all sleep, but we will all be changed[b]— 52in a flash, in the twinkling of an eye, at the last trumpet. For the trumpet will sound,[c] the dead[d] will be raised imperishable, and we will be changed. 53For the perishable must clothe itself with the imperishable,[e] and the mortal with immortality. 54When the perishable has been clothed with the imperishable, and the mortal with immortality, then the saying that is written will come true: "Death has been swallowed up in victory."[a][f]

55"Where, O death, is your victory?
Where, O death, is your sting?"[b][g]

56The sting of death is sin,[h] and the power of sin is the law.[i] 57But thanks be to God![j] He gives us the victory through our Lord Jesus Christ.[k]

58Therefore, my dear brothers, stand firm. Let nothing move you. Always give yourselves fully to the work of the Lord,[l] because you know that your labor in the Lord is not in vain.

Chapter 16 Theme ____

16 Now about the collection[m] for God's people:[n] Do what I told the Galatian[o] churches to do. 2On the first day of every week,[p] each one of you should set aside a sum of money in keeping with his income, saving it up, so that when I come no collections will have to be made.[q] 3Then, when I arrive, I will give letters of introduction to the men you approve[r] and send them with your gift to Jerusalem. 4If it seems advisable for me to go also, they will accompany me.

5After I go through Macedonia, I will come to you[s]—for I will be going through Macedonia.[t] 6Perhaps I will stay with you awhile, or even spend the winter, so that you can help me on my journey,[u] wherever I go. 7I do not want to see you now and make only a passing visit; I hope to spend some time with you, if the Lord permits.[v] 8But I will stay on at Ephesus[w] until Pentecost,[x] 9because a great door for effective work has opened to me,[y] and there are many who oppose me.

10If Timothy[z] comes, see to it that he has nothing to fear while he is with you, for he is carrying on the work of the Lord,[a] just as I am. 11No one, then, should refuse to accept him.[b] Send him on his way in peace[c] so that he may return to me. I am expecting him along with the brothers.

12Now about our brother Apollos:[d] I strongly urged him to go to you with the brothers. He was quite unwilling to go now, but he will go when he has the opportunity.

[a]54 Isaiah 25:8 [b]55 Hosea 13:14

15:51
[a] 1Co 13:2
[b] Php 3:21

15:52
[c] Mt 24:31
[d] Jn 5:25

15:53
[e] 2Co 5:2,4

15:54
[f] Isa 25:8; Rev 20:14

15:55
[g] Hos 13:14

15:56
[h] Ro 5:12
[i] Ro 4:15

15:57
[j] 2Co 2:14
[k] Ro 8:37

15:58
[l] 1Co 16:10

16:1
[m] Ac 24:17
[n] Ac 9:13
[o] Ac 16:6

16:2
[p] Ac 20:7
[q] 2Co 9:4,5

16:3
[r] 2Co 8:18,19

16:5
[s] 1Co 4:19
[t] Ac 19:21

16:6
[u] Ro 15:24

16:7
[v] Ac 18:21

16:8
[w] Ac 18:19
[x] Ac 2:1

16:9
[y] Ac 14:27

16:10
[z] Ac 16:1
[a] 1Co 15:58

16:11
[b] 1Ti 4:12
[c] Ac 15:33

16:12
[d] Ac 18:24; 1Co 1:12

eme of 1 Corinthians:

thor:

ate:

rpose:

y Words:

SEGMENT DIVISIONS

PROBLEMS OR TOPICS	MAJOR DIVISIONS	CHAPTER THEMES
		1
		2
		3
		4
		5
		6
		7
		8
		9
		10
		11
		12
		13
		14
		15
		16

2 CORINTHIANS

Paul, the apostle to the Gentiles, was taught and appointed by Jesus Christ. Strong in faith, confident, and greatly used by God, Paul was loved by multitudes and hated by thousands. Determined that the grace of God would not prove vain, he labored more than anyone.

However, Paul's labor was not without cost. He endured conflicts without and fears within. Yet he persevered. What were his conflicts, his fears, his sufferings? Are they similar to yours? And how did he endure? What held him? As Paul writes his second epistle to the Corinthians from Macedonia, probably in the winter of A.D. 55, he lets us see the answers to these questions.

Things to Do

General Instructions

1. Second Corinthians is different from Paul's other epistles. Watch the atmosphere or tone of this epistle. Paul is defending himself, which is unusual for Paul. As you read through the book, note the issues Paul addresses and what he says to the Corinthians, and you will understand what Paul is up against.

2. Study the OBSERVATIONS CHART on page 1991 and see what you'll need to observe as you study 2 Corinthians chapter by chapter. Make a duplicate of this chart so you can use it as a worksheet. When you have completed it, record the information on the chart in your Bible.

   a. As you read each chapter, list everything you learn about Paul. Be sure to note the afflictions he endured: What must he do in respect to the Corinthians? What has been done to him by the Corinthians? Ask God to show you Paul's character, his heart, his joys, and his sorrows.

   b. Note what you learn about the Corinthians. Remember to ask the five W's and an H: What are they like? What is their relationship with Paul like? What is going on in the Corinthian church at this time? What have they said about Paul? What problems has Paul had to deal with in respect to them?

   c. What is Paul's desire or goal for the Corinthians?

   d. Titus is mentioned several times in this letter. Record what you learn about him from 2 Corinthians.

3. As you read 2 Corinthians chapter by chapter, do the following:

   a. Mark in the text in a distinctive way the key words (and their synonyms and pronouns) listed on the 2 CORINTHIANS AT A GLANCE chart on page 1992. Write these on an index card that you can use as a bookmark while you study 2 Corinthians. (Hint: If you mark every reference to Satan with an appropriate symbol it will be easy to spot.)

   b. As you come to specific chapters you will notice other key words which are not listed on 2 CORINTHIANS AT A GLANCE. Mark these also.

   c. If there are several truths you learn from the use of a key word within a chapter, list in the margin what you learn from that word. For example, list all you learn about *affliction (trouble, hardships, distress, hard pressed, trial)* and *suffering*. Record the heading "Affliction/Suffering" in the margin of each chapter where you mark these key words. Mark the heading in a distinctive way so you can spot its recurrence throughout 2 Corinthians. Then under it list what you learn from that chapter.

4. Look for the theme (subject) of each chapter and record it next to the chapter number in the text and under "Chapter Themes" on 2 CORINTHIANS AT A GLANCE.

Chapters 1-7

1. In the midst of this very personal letter, Paul gives some important insights on several subjects. In the margin where they appear, list what you learn about each subject.

   a. Chapter 3 mentions the new covenant (which is grace) and the old covenant (which is law). These are described as ministries, and then the ministries are contrasted according to the result of each: condemnation or righteousness. List in the margin what you learn about each from the text.

   b. In chapter 5 Paul talks about what will happen to our earthly bodies when we die. He also discusses the judgment seat of Christ and our ministry of reconciliation. Identify how these relate to one another and what you learn about each from the text. Write your observations in the margins.

   c. In chapter 7 Paul deals with two kinds of sorrow and what they produce. Don't miss this. Take notes in the margin.

2. What is Paul writing about in chapters 1 through 7? Is there a theme which runs through these chapters? Remember that key words reveal the themes. What key words are repeated the most in this segment?

3. How does Paul begin and end this segment?

4. Record the theme for chapters 1 through 7 on 2 CORINTHIANS AT A GLANCE under "Segment Divisions."

Chapters 8, 9

1. What subject is Paul talking about in chapters 8 and 9? Note the use of the words *act of grace* and *service.* What service or act of grace is he referring to?

2. Record this subject as the theme of this segment in the appropriate space on 2 CORINTHIANS AT A GLANCE.

Chapters 10-13

1. Notice when the key word *boast* first appears in the text and what happens when it appears. Note what or whom the boasting is in and what you learn.

2. In the margin of chapter 11 list what you learn about Satan and spiritual warfare from these four chapters.

3. What does Paul seem to be doing in chapters 10 through 13? What opposition is there to Paul, and what is the opposition saying about him? What is his response to this opposition? Record the theme of this segment under "Segment Divisions" and complete the chart.

Things to Think About

1. What is the purpose of affliction? When you need to be comforted, do you turn to people or to God?

2. Is it always wrong to feel sorrow, to be hurt, or to have a broken heart? Is it always wrong to cause sorrow, to hurt, or to break another person's heart?

3. How do you deal with those who oppose you? How do you minister to those who are caught in the middle of a conflict and don't know who to believe?

4. Paul was human just like us; he had feelings just like we do. What can we learn from him about how we are to live and respond in spite of our feelings? When is the time to give a defense of one's self, of one's ministry?

5. Are you prepared to stand before the judgment seat of Christ?

6. What place does the ministry of giving play in your life?

7. If you were to examine yourself, would you find your Christianity genuine?

Chapter 1 Theme ______________________________

1 Paul, an apostle of Christ Jesus by the will of God,[a] and Timothy our brother,
To the church of God[b] in Corinth, together with all the saints
throughout Achaia:[c]
2Grace and peace to you from God our Father and the Lord
Jesus Christ.[d]
3Praise be to the God and Father of our Lord Jesus Christ,[e] the
Father of compassion and the God of all comfort, 4who comforts
us[f] in all our troubles, so that we can comfort those in any trouble
with the comfort we ourselves have received from God. 5For just as
the sufferings of Christ flow over into our lives,[g] so also through
Christ our comfort overflows. 6If we are distressed, it is for your
comfort and salvation;[h] if we are comforted, it is for your comfort,
which produces in you patient endurance of the same sufferings
we suffer. 7And our hope for you is firm, because we know that just
as you share in our sufferings,[i] so also you share in our comfort.
8We do not want you to be uninformed, brothers, about the
hardships we suffered[j] in the province of Asia. We were under
great pressure, far beyond our ability to endure, so that we de-
spaired even of life. 9Indeed, in our hearts we felt the sentence of
death. But this happened that we might not rely on ourselves but
on God,[k] who raises the dead. 10He has delivered us from such a
deadly peril,[l] and he will deliver us. On him we have set our hope
that he will continue to deliver us, 11as you help us by your
prayers.[m] Then many will give thanks[n] on our[a] behalf for the
gracious favor granted us in answer to the prayers of many.
12Now this is our boast: Our conscience[o] testifies that we have
conducted ourselves in the world, and especially in our relations
with you, in the holiness and sincerity[p] that are from God. We
have done so not according to worldly wisdom[q] but according to
God's grace. 13For we do not write you anything you cannot read
or understand. And I hope that, 14as you have understood us in
part, you will come to understand fully that you can boast of us
just as we will boast of you in the day of the Lord Jesus.[r]
15Because I was confident of this, I planned to visit you[s] first so
that you might benefit twice.[t] 16I planned to visit you on my way[u]
to Macedonia and to come back to you from Macedonia, and
then to have you send me on my way to Judea. 17When I planned
this, did I do it lightly? Or do I make my plans in a worldly manner[v] so that in the same breath I say, "Yes, yes" and "No, no"?
18But as surely as God is faithful,[w] our message to you is not "Yes"
and "No." 19For the Son of God, Jesus Christ, who was preached

[a] *11* Many manuscripts *your*

1:1 [a] 1Co 1:1; Eph 1:1; Col 1:1; 2Ti 1:1 [b] 1Co 10:32 [c] Ac 18:12
1:2 [d] Ro 1:7
1:3 [e] Eph 1:3; 1Pe 1:3
1:4 [f] 2Co 7:6,7,13
1:5 [g] 2Co 4:10; Col 1:24
1:6 [h] 2Co 4:15
1:7 [i] Ro 8:17
1:8 [j] 1Co 15:32
1:9 [k] Jer 17:5,7
1:10 [l] Ro 15:31
1:11 [m] Ro 15:30; Php 1:19 [n] 2Co 4:15
1:12 [o] Ac 23:1 [p] 2Co 2:17 [q] 1Co 2:1,4,13
1:14 [r] 1Co 1:8
1:15 [s] 1Co 4:19 [t] Ro 1:11,13; 15:29
1:16 [u] 1Co 16:5-7
1:17 [v] 2Co 10:2,3
1:18 [w] 1Co 1:9

among you by me and Silas[a] and Timothy, was not "Yes" and
"No," but in him it has always[a] been "Yes." 20For no matter how
many promises[b] God has made, they are "Yes" in Christ. And so
through him the "Amen"[c] is spoken by us to the glory of God.
21Now it is God who makes both us and you stand firm in Christ.
He anointed[d] us, 22set his seal of ownership on us, and put his Spirit in our hearts as a deposit, guaranteeing what is to come.[e]
23I call God as my witness[f] that it was in order to spare you[g] that
I did not return to Corinth. 24Not that we lord it over[h] your faith, but
we work with you for your joy, because it is by faith you stand firm.[i]

Chapter 2 Theme ____________________

2 So I made up my mind that I would not make another painful visit to you.[j] 2For if I grieve you,[k] who is left to make me
glad but you whom I have grieved? 3I wrote as I did[l] so that when
I came I should not be distressed[m] by those who ought to make
me rejoice. I had confidence[n] in all of you, that you would all
share my joy. 4For I wrote you[o] out of great distress and anguish
of heart and with many tears, not to grieve you but to let you
know the depth of my love for you.
5If anyone has caused grief,[p] he has not so much grieved me as
he has grieved all of you, to some extent—not to put it too severely. 6The punishment[q] inflicted on him by the majority is sufficient
for him. 7Now instead, you ought to forgive and comfort him,[r] so
that he will not be overwhelmed by excessive sorrow. 8I urge you,
therefore, to reaffirm your love for him. 9The reason I wrote you
was to see if you would stand the test and be obedient in everything.[s] 10If you forgive anyone, I also forgive him. And what I have
forgiven—if there was anything to forgive—I have forgiven in the
sight of Christ for your sake, 11in order that Satan[t] might not out-
wit us. For we are not unaware of his schemes.[u]
12Now when I went to Troas[v] to preach the gospel of Christ[w]
and found that the Lord had opened a door[x] for me, 13I still had
no peace of mind,[y] because I did not find my brother Titus[z]
there. So I said good-by to them and went on to Macedonia.
14But thanks be to God,[a] who always leads us in triumphal procession in Christ and through us spreads everywhere the fragrance[b] of the knowledge of him. 15For we are to God the aroma
of Christ among those who are being saved and those who are
perishing.[c] 16To the one we are the smell of death;[d] to the other,
the fragrance of life. And who is equal to such a task?[e] 17Unlike so
many, we do not peddle the word of God for profit.[f] On the contrary, in Christ we speak before God with sincerity,[g] like men
sent from God.[h]

a 19 Greek *Silvanus,* a variant of *Silas*

1:19 [a]Heb 13:8
1:20 [b]Ro 15:8
[c]1Co 14:16
1:21 [d]1Jn 2:20,27
1:22 [e]2Co 5:5
1:23 [f]Ro 1:9; Gal 1:20
[g]1Co 4:21; 2Co 2:1,3; 13:2,10
1:24 [h]1Pe 5:3
[i]Ro 11:20; 1Co 15:1
2:1 [j]2Co 1:23
2:2 [k]2Co 7:8
2:3 [l]2Co 7:8,12
[m]2Co 12:21
[n]2Co 8:22; Gal 5:10
2:4 [o]2Co 7:8,12
2:5 [p]1Co 5:1,2
2:6 [q]1Co 5:4,5
2:7 [r]Gal 6:1; Eph 4:32
2:9 [s]2Co 10:6
2:11 [t]Mt 4:10
[u]Lk 22:31; 2Co 4:4; 1Pe 5:8,9
2:12 [v]Ac 16:8
[w]Ro 1:1
[x]Ac 14:27
2:13 [y]2Co 7:5
[z]2Co 7:6,13; 12:18
2:14 [a]Ro 6:17
[b]Eph 5:2; Php 4:18
2:15 [c]1Co 1:18
2:16 [d]Lk 2:34
[e]2Co 3:5,6
2:17 [f]2Co 4:2
[g]1Co 5:8
[h]2Co 1:12

Chapter 3 Theme ______________________

3 Are we beginning to commend ourselves[a] again? Or do we
need, like some people, letters of recommendation[b] to you or
from you? 2You yourselves are our letter, written on our hearts,
known and read by everybody.[c] 3You show that you are a letter
from Christ, the result of our ministry, written not with ink but
with the Spirit of the living God, not on tablets of stone[d] but on
tablets of human hearts.[e]
4Such confidence[f] as this is ours through Christ before God.
5Not that we are competent in ourselves to claim anything for
ourselves, but our competence comes from God.[g] 6He has made
us competent as ministers of a new covenant[h]—not of the letter
but of the Spirit; for the letter kills, but the Spirit gives life.[i]
7Now if the ministry that brought death, which was engraved in
letters on stone, came with glory, so that the Israelites could not
look steadily at the face of Moses because of its glory,[j] fading
though it was, 8will not the ministry of the Spirit be even more
glorious? 9If the ministry that condemns men[k] is glorious, how
much more glorious is the ministry that brings righteousness![l]
10For what was glorious has no glory now in comparison with the
surpassing glory. 11And if what was fading away came with glory,
how much greater is the glory of that which lasts!
12Therefore, since we have such a hope, we are very bold.[m] 13We
are not like Moses, who would put a veil over his face[n] to keep the
Israelites from gazing at it while the radiance was fading away.
14But their minds were made dull,[o] for to this day the same veil remains when the old covenant[p] is read.[q] It has not been removed,
because only in Christ is it taken away. 15Even to this day when
Moses is read, a veil covers their hearts. 16But whenever anyone
turns to the Lord,[r] the veil is taken away.[s] 17Now the Lord is the
Spirit,[t] and where the Spirit of the Lord is, there is freedom.[u]
18And we, who with unveiled faces all reflect[a][v] the Lord's glory,[w]
are being transformed into his likeness[x] with ever-increasing glory, which comes from the Lord, who is the Spirit.

Chapter 4 Theme ______________________

4 Therefore, since through God's mercy[y] we have this ministry,
we do not lose heart. 2Rather, we have renounced secret and
shameful ways;[z] we do not use deception, nor do we distort the
word of God.[a] On the contrary, by setting forth the truth plainly
we commend ourselves to every man's conscience[b] in the sight of
God. 3And even if our gospel[c] is veiled,[d] it is veiled to those who
are perishing.[e] 4The god[f] of this age has blinded[g] the minds of

[a]18 Or *contemplate*

3:1 [a]2Co 5:12; 12:11 [b]Ac 18:27
3:2 [c]1Co 9:2
3:3 [d]Ex 24:12 [e]Pr 3:3; Jer 31:33; Eze 11:19
3:4 [f]Eph 3:12
3:5 [g]1Co 15:10
3:6 [h]Lk 22:20 [i]Jn 6:63
3:7 [j]Ex 34:29-35
3:9 [k]ver 7 [l]Ro 1:17; 3:21,22
3:12 [m]Eph 6:19
3:13 [n]ver 7; Ex 34:33
3:14 [o]Ro 11:7,8 [p]Ac 13:15 [q]ver 6
3:16 [r]Ro 11:23 [s]Ex 34:34
3:17 [t]Isa 61:1,2 [u]Jn 8:32
3:18 [v]1Co 13:12 [w]2Co 4:4,6 [x]Ro 8:29
4:1 [y]1Co 7:25
4:2 [z]1Co 4:5 [a]2Co 2:17 [b]2Co 5:11
4:3 [c]2Co 2:12 [d]2Co 3:14 [e]1Co 1:18
4:4 [f]Jn 12:31 [g]2Co 3:14

unbelievers, so that they cannot see the light of the gospel of the
glory of Christ, who is the image of God. 5 For we do not preach
ourselves,[a] but Jesus Christ as Lord, and ourselves as your
servants[b] for Jesus' sake. 6 For God, who said, "Let light shine out
of darkness,"[a][c] made his light shine in our hearts[d] to give us the
light of the knowledge of the glory of God in the face of Christ.
7 But we have this treasure in jars of clay[e] to show that this all-
surpassing power is from God[f] and not from us. 8 We are hard
pressed on every side,[g] but not crushed; perplexed, but not in
despair; 9 persecuted,[h] but not abandoned;[i] struck down, but not
destroyed.[j] 10 We always carry around in our body the death of
Jesus, so that the life of Jesus may also be revealed in our body.[k]
11 For we who are alive are always being given over to death for
Jesus' sake,[l] so that his life may be revealed in our mortal body.
12 So then, death is at work in us, but life is at work in you.[m]
13 It is written: "I believed; therefore I have spoken."[b][n] With that
same spirit of faith we also believe and therefore speak, 14 because
we know that the one who raised the Lord Jesus from the dead
will also raise us with Jesus[o] and present us with you in his presence.[p] 15 All this is for your benefit, so that the grace that is reaching more and more people may cause thanksgiving[q] to overflow to
the glory of God.
16 Therefore we do not lose heart. Though outwardly we are
wasting away, yet inwardly[r] we are being renewed[s] day by day.
17 For our light and momentary troubles are achieving for us an
eternal glory that far outweighs them all.[t] 18 So we fix our eyes not
on what is seen, but on what is unseen.[u] For what is seen is temporary, but what is unseen is eternal.

Chapter 5 Theme ______________________________

5 Now we know that if the earthly[v] tent[w] we live in is destroyed,
we have a building from God, an eternal house in heaven, not
built by human hands. 2 Meanwhile we groan,[x] longing to be clothed
with our heavenly dwelling,[y] 3 because when we are clothed, we
will not be found naked. 4 For while we are in this tent, we groan
and are burdened, because we do not wish to be unclothed but to
be clothed with our heavenly dwelling,[z] so that what is mortal
may be swallowed up by life. 5 Now it is God who has made us for
this very purpose and has given us the Spirit as a deposit, guaranteeing what is to come.[a]
6 Therefore we are always confident and know that as long as we
are at home in the body we are away from the Lord. 7 We live by
faith, not by sight.[b] 8 We are confident, I say, and would prefer to
be away from the body and at home with the Lord.[c] 9 So we make

4:5 [a] 1Co 1:13 [b] 1Co 9:19
4:6 [c] Ge 1:3 [d] 2Pe 1:19
4:7 [e] Job 4:19; 2Co 5:1 [f] 1Co 2:5
4:8 [g] 2Co 7:5
4:9 [h] Jn 15:20 [i] Heb 13:5 [j] Ps 37:24
4:10 [k] Ro 6:5
4:11 [l] Ro 8:36
4:12 [m] 2Co 13:9
4:13 [n] Ps 116:10
4:14 [o] 1Th 4:14 [p] Eph 5:27
4:15 [q] 2Co 1:11
4:16 [r] Ro 7:22 [s] Col 3:10
4:17 [t] Ro 8:18; 1Pe 1:6,7
4:18 [u] Ro 8:24; Heb 11:1
5:1 [v] 1Co 15:47 [w] 2Pe 1:13,14
5:2 [x] ver 4; Ro 8:23 [y] 1Co 15:53,54
5:4 [z] 1Co 15:53,54
5:5 [a] Ro 8:23; 2Co 1:22
5:7 [b] 1Co 13:12
5:8 [c] Php 1:23

[a] *6* Gen. 1:3 [b] *13* Psalm 116:10

it our goal to please him,[a] whether we are at home in the body or
away from it. 10For we must all appear before the judgment seat
of Christ, that each one may receive what is due him[b] for the
things done while in the body, whether good or bad.
11Since, then, we know what it is to fear the Lord,[c] we try to
persuade men. What we are is plain to God, and I hope it is also
plain to your conscience.[d] 12We are not trying to commend ourselves to you again,[e] but are giving you an opportunity to take
pride in us,[f] so that you can answer those who take pride in what
is seen rather than in what is in the heart. 13If we are out of our
mind,[g] it is for the sake of God; if we are in our right mind, it is
for you. 14For Christ's love compels us, because we are convinced
that one died for all, and therefore all died.[h] 15And he died for all,
that those who live should no longer live for themselves[i] but for
him who died for them and was raised again.
16So from now on we regard no one from a worldly[j] point of
view. Though we once regarded Christ in this way, we do so no
longer. 17Therefore, if anyone is in Christ, he is a new creation;[k]
the old has gone, the new has come![l] 18All this is from God, who
reconciled us to himself through Christ[m] and gave us the ministry
of reconciliation: 19that God was reconciling the world to himself
in Christ, not counting men's sins against them.[n] And he has
committed to us the message of reconciliation. 20We are therefore
Christ's ambassadors,[o] as though God were making his appeal
through us. We implore you on Christ's behalf: Be reconciled to
God. 21God made him who had no sin[p] to be sin[a] for us, so that in
him we might become the righteousness of God.[q]

Chapter 6 Theme ________________________

6 As God's fellow workers[r] we urge you not to receive God's
grace in vain. 2For he says,

> "In the time of my favor I heard you,
> and in the day of salvation I helped you."[b] [s]

I tell you, now is the time of God's favor, now is the day of salvation.
3We put no stumbling block in anyone's path,[t] so that our ministry will not be discredited. 4Rather, as servants of God we commend ourselves in every way: in great endurance; in troubles,
hardships and distresses; 5in beatings, imprisonments[u] and riots; in
hard work, sleepless nights and hunger;[v] 6in purity, understanding, patience and kindness; in the Holy Spirit[w] and in sincere love;
7in truthful speech[x] and in the power of God; with weapons of

a 21 Or *be a sin offering* b 2 Isaiah 49:8

5:9 [a]Ro 14:18
5:10 [b]Mt 16:27; Ro 14:10; Eph 6:8
5:11 [c]Heb 10:31; Jude 23 [d]2Co 4:2
5:12 [e]2Co 3:1 [f]2Co 1:14
5:13 [g]2Co 11:1, 16,17
5:14 [h]Gal 2:20
5:15 [i]Ro 14:7-9
5:16 [j]2Co 11:18
5:17 [k]Gal 6:15 [l]Isa 65:17; Rev 21:4,5
5:18 [m]Ro 5:10; Col 1:20
5:19 [n]Ro 4:8
5:20 [o]2Co 6:1; Eph 6:20
5:21 [p]Heb 4:15; 1Pe 2:22,24; 1Jn 3:5 [q]Ro 1:17
6:1 [r]1Co 3:9; 2Co 5:20
6:2 [s]Isa 49:8
6:3 [t]Ro 14:13,20; 1Co 9:12; 10:32
6:5 [u]2Co 11:23-25 [v]1Co 4:11
6:6 [w]1Th 1:5
6:7 [x]2Co 4:2

righteousness[a] in the right hand and in the left; 8through glory
and dishonor,[b] bad report and good report; genuine, yet regarded
as impostors;[c] 9known, yet regarded as unknown; dying,[d] and yet
we live on;[e] beaten, and yet not killed; 10sorrowful, yet always rejoicing;[f] poor, yet making many rich;[g] having nothing, and yet possessing everything.[h]

11We have spoken freely to you, Corinthians, and opened wide our
hearts to you.[i] 12We are not withholding our affection from you, but
you are withholding yours from us. 13As a fair exchange—I speak
as to my children[j]—open wide your hearts also.

14Do not be yoked together[k] with unbelievers. For what do righteousness and wickedness have in common? Or what fellowship
can light have with darkness?[l] 15What harmony is there between
Christ and Belial[a]? What does a believer[m] have in common with an
unbeliever? 16What agreement is there between the temple of God
and idols? For we are the temple[n] of the living God. As God has
said: "I will live with them and walk among them, and I will be
their God, and they will be my people."[b] [o]

17"Therefore come out from them[p]
and be separate,
says the Lord.
Touch no unclean thing,
and I will receive you."[c] [q]
18"I will be a Father to you,
and you will be my sons and daughters,[r]
says the Lord Almighty."[d]

Chapter 7 Theme ____

7 Since we have these promises,[s] dear friends, let us purify ourselves from everything that contaminates body and spirit, perfecting holiness out of reverence for God.

2Make room for us in your hearts.[t] We have wronged no one,
we have corrupted no one, we have exploited no one. 3I do not say
this to condemn you; I have said before that you have such a place
in our hearts[u] that we would live or die with you. 4I have great confidence in you; I take great pride in you. I am greatly encouraged;
in all our troubles my joy knows no bounds.[v]

5For when we came into Macedonia,[w] this body of ours had no
rest, but we were harassed at every turn[x]—conflicts on the outside, fears within.[y] 6But God, who comforts the downcast,[z] comforted us by the coming of Titus,[a] 7and not only by his coming
but also by the comfort you had given him. He told us about your

6:7 [a]2Co 10:4; Eph 6:10-18
6:8 [b]1Co 4:10 [c]Mt 27:63
6:9 [d]Ro 8:36 [e]2Co 1:8-10; 4:10,11
6:10 [f]2Co 7:4 [g]2Co 8:9 [h]Ro 8:32; 1Co 3:21
6:11 [i]2Co 7:3
6:13 [j]1Co 4:14
6:14 [k]1Co 5:9,10 [l]Eph 5:7,11; 1Jn 1:6
6:15 [m]Ac 5:14
6:16 [n]1Co 3:16 [o]Lev 26:12; Jer 32:38; Eze 37:27
6:17 [p]Rev 18:4 [q]Isa 52:11
6:18 [r]Isa 43:6
7:1 [s]2Co 6:17,18
7:2 [t]2Co 6:12,13
7:3 [u]2Co 6:11,12
7:4 [v]2Co 6:10
7:5 [w]2Co 2:13 [x]2Co 4:8 [y]Dt 32:25
7:6 [z]2Co 1:3,4 [a]ver 13; 2Co 2:13

a 15 Greek *Beliar*, a variant of *Belial* b 16 Lev. 26:12; Jer. 32:38; Ezek. 37:27 c 17 Isaiah 52:11; Ezek. 20:34,41 d 18 2 Samuel 7:14; 7:8

longing for me, your deep sorrow, your ardent concern for me, so
that my joy was greater than ever.
8Even if I caused you sorrow by my letter,[a] I do not regret it.
Though I did regret it—I see that my letter hurt you, but only for a
little while— 9yet now I am happy, not because you were made
sorry, but because your sorrow led you to repentance. For you
became sorrowful as God intended and so were not harmed in any
way by us. 10Godly sorrow brings repentance that leads to salvation[b]
and leaves no regret, but worldly sorrow brings death. 11See what
this godly sorrow has produced in you: what earnestness, what eagerness to clear yourselves, what indignation, what alarm, what longing, what concern,[c] what readiness to see justice done. At every
point you have proved yourselves to be innocent in this matter. 12So
even though I wrote to you,[d] it was not on account of the one who
did the wrong[e] or of the injured party, but rather that before God
you could see for yourselves how devoted to us you are. 13By all this
we are encouraged.

In addition to our own encouragement, we were especially delighted to see how happy Titus[f] was, because his spirit has been
refreshed by all of you. 14I had boasted to him about you,[g] and you
have not embarrassed me. But just as everything we said to you
was true, so our boasting about you to Titus[h] has proved to be true
as well. 15And his affection for you is all the greater when he
remembers that you were all obedient,[i] receiving him with fear and
trembling.[j] 16I am glad I can have complete confidence in you.[k]

Chapter 8 Theme ______________________________

8 And now, brothers, we want you to know about the grace that
God has given the Macedonian[l] churches. 2Out of the most
severe trial, their overflowing joy and their extreme poverty welled
up in rich generosity. 3For I testify that they gave as much as they
were able,[m] and even beyond their ability. Entirely on their own,
4they urgently pleaded with us for the privilege of sharing in this
service[n] to the saints.[o] 5And they did not do as we expected, but
they gave themselves first to the Lord and then to us in keeping
with God's will. 6So we urged[p] Titus,[q] since he had earlier made a
beginning, to bring also to completion[r] this act of grace on your
part. 7But just as you excel in everything[s]—in faith, in speech, in
knowledge,[t] in complete earnestness and in your love for us[a]—
see that you also excel in this grace of giving.
8I am not commanding you,[u] but I want to test the sincerity of
your love by comparing it with the earnestness of others. 9For you
know the grace of our Lord Jesus Christ,[v] that though he was rich,

[a]7 Some manuscripts *in our love for you*

7:8 [a]2Co 2:2,4
7:10 [b]Ac 11:18
7:11 [c]ver 7
7:12 [d]ver 8; 2Co 2:3,9 [e]1Co 5:1,2
7:13 [f]ver 6; 2Co 2:13
7:14 [g]ver 4 [h]ver 6
7:15 [i]2Co 2:9 [j]Php 2:12
7:16 [k]2Co 2:3
8:1 [l]Ac 16:9
8:3 [m]1Co 16:2
8:4 [n]Ac 24:17 [o]Ro 15:25; 2Co 9:1
8:6 [p]ver 17; 2Co 12:18 [q]ver 16,23 [r]ver 10,11
8:7 [s]2Co 9:8 [t]1Co 1:5
8:8 [u]1Co 7:6
8:9 [v]2Co 13:14

yet for your sakes he became poor,[a] so that you through his poverty
might become rich.
10And here is my advice[b] about what is best for you in this matter: Last year you were the first not only to give but also to have the
desire to do so.[c] 11Now finish the work, so that your eager willingness[d] to do it may be matched by your completion of it, according
to your means. 12For if the willingness is there, the gift is acceptable
according to what one has,[e] not according to what he does not have.
13Our desire is not that others might be relieved while you are
hard pressed, but that there might be equality. 14At the present
time your plenty will supply what they need,[f] so that in turn
their plenty will supply what you need. Then there will be equality, 15as it is written: "He who gathered much did not have too
much, and he who gathered little did not have too little."[a][g]
16I thank God,[h] who put into the heart[i] of Titus[j] the same concern I have for you. 17For Titus not only welcomed our appeal, but
he is coming to you with much enthusiasm and on his own initia-
tive.[k] 18And we are sending along with him the brother[l] who is
praised by all the churches[m] for his service to the gospel.[n] 19What
is more, he was chosen by the churches to accompany us[o] as we
carry the offering, which we administer in order to honor the
Lord himself and to show our eagerness to help.[p] 20We want to
avoid any criticism of the way we administer this liberal gift. 21For
we are taking pains to do what is right, not only in the eyes of the
Lord but also in the eyes of men.[q]
22In addition, we are sending with them our brother who has often
proved to us in many ways that he is zealous, and now even more so
because of his great confidence in you. 23As for Titus, he is my partner[r] and fellow worker[s] among you; as for our brothers,[t] they are
representatives of the churches and an honor to Christ. 24Therefore
show these men the proof of your love and the reason for our pride
in you,[u] so that the churches can see it.

Chapter 9 Theme

9 There is no need[v] for me to write to you about this service to
the saints.[w] 2For I know your eagerness to help, and I have been
boasting[x] about it to the Macedonians, telling them that since last
year[y] you in Achaia[z] were ready to give; and your enthusiasm has
stirred most of them to action. 3But I am sending the brothers in
order that our boasting about you in this matter should not prove
hollow, but that you may be ready, as I said you would be.[a] 4For if
any Macedonians[b] come with me and find you unprepared, we—
not to say anything about you—would be ashamed of having been

[a] *15* Exodus 16:18

8:9 [a] Mt 20:28; Php 2:6-8
8:10 [b] 1Co 7:25,40 [c] 1Co 16:2,3; 2Co 9:2
8:11 [d] 2Co 9:2
8:12 [e] Mk 12:43,44; Lk 21:3
8:14 [f] 2Co 9:12
8:15 [g] Ex 16:18
8:16 [h] 2Co 2:14 [i] Rev 17:17 [j] 2Co 2:13
8:17 [k] ver 6
8:18 [l] 2Co 12:18 [m] 1Co 7:17 [n] 2Co 2:12
8:19 [o] 1Co 16:3,4 [p] ver 11,12
8:21 [q] Ro 12:17; 14:18
8:23 [r] Phm 17 [s] Php 2:25 [t] ver 18,22
8:24 [u] 2Co 7:4,14; 9:2
9:1 [v] 1Th 4:9 [w] 2Co 8:4
9:2 [x] 2Co 7:4,14 [y] 2Co 8:10 [z] Ac 18:12
9:3 [a] 1Co 16:2
9:4 [b] Ro 15:26

so confident. 5So I thought it necessary to urge the brothers to visit
you in advance and finish the arrangements for the generous gift
you had promised. Then it will be ready as a generous gift,[a] not as
one grudgingly given.[b]
6Remember this: Whoever sows sparingly will also reap sparingly, and whoever sows generously will also reap generously.[c] 7Each
man should give what he has decided in his heart to give,[d] not
reluctantly or under compulsion,[e] for God loves a cheerful giver.[f]
8And God is able[g] to make all grace abound to you, so that in all
things at all times, having all that you need,[h] you will abound in
every good work. 9As it is written:

> "He has scattered abroad his gifts to the poor;
> his righteousness endures forever."[a][i]

10Now he who supplies seed to the sower and bread for food[j] will
also supply and increase your store of seed and will enlarge the
harvest of your righteousness.[k] 11You will be made rich[l] in every
way so that you can be generous on every occasion, and through
us your generosity will result in thanksgiving to God.[m]
12This service that you perform is not only supplying the needs[n]
of God's people but is also overflowing in many expressions of
thanks to God.[o] 13Because of the service[p] by which you have proved
yourselves, men will praise God[q] for the obedience that accompanies your confession of the gospel of Christ,[r] and for your generosity in sharing with them and with everyone else. 14And in
their prayers for you their hearts will go out to you, because of the
surpassing grace God has given you. 15Thanks be to God[s] for his
indescribable gift![t]

Chapter 10 Theme

10 By the meekness and gentleness[u] of Christ, I appeal to you—
I, Paul,[v] who am "timid" when face to face with you, but
"bold" when away! 2I beg you that when I come I may not have to
be as bold[w] as I expect to be toward some people who think that
we live by the standards of this world. 3For though we live in the
world, we do not wage war as the world does. 4The weapons we
fight with[x] are not the weapons of the world. On the contrary, they
have divine power[y] to demolish strongholds.[z] 5We demolish arguments and every pretension that sets itself up against the knowledge of God,[a] and we take captive every thought to make it
obedient[b] to Christ. 6And we will be ready to punish every act of
disobedience, once your obedience is complete.[c]

9:5 [a]Php 4:17 [b]2Co 12:17,18
9:6 [c]Pr 11:24,25; 22:9; Gal 6:7,9
9:7 [d]Ex 25:2; 2Co 8:12 [e]Dt 15:10 [f]Ro 12:8
9:8 [g]Eph 3:20 [h]Php 4:19
9:9 [i]Ps 112:9
9:10 [j]Isa 55:10 [k]Hos 10:12
9:11 [l]1Co 1:5 [m]2Co 1:11
9:12 [n]2Co 8:14 [o]2Co 1:11
9:13 [p]2Co 8:4 [q]Mt 9:8 [r]2Co 2:12
9:15 [s]2Co 2:14 [t]Ro 5:15,16
10:1 [u]Mt 11:29 [v]Gal 5:2
10:2 [w]1Co 4:21; 2Co 13:2,10
10:4 [x]2Co 6:7 [y]1Co 2:5 [z]Jer 1:10; 2Co 13:10
10:5 [a]Isa 2:11,12; 1Co 1:19 [b]2Co 9:13
10:6 [c]2Co 2:9; 7:15

[a]9 Psalm 112:9

7You are looking only on the surface of things.[a][a] If anyone is
confident that he belongs to Christ,[b] he should consider again that
we belong to Christ just as much as he.[c] 8For even if I boast some-
what freely about the authority the Lord gave us for building you
up rather than pulling you down,[d] I will not be ashamed of it. 9I
do not want to seem to be trying to frighten you with my letters.
10For some say, "His letters are weighty and forceful, but in person
he is unimpressive[e] and his speaking amounts to nothing."[f]
11Such people should realize that what we are in our letters when
we are absent, we will be in our actions when we are present.

12We do not dare to classify or compare ourselves with some who
commend themselves.[g] When they measure themselves by themselves and compare themselves with themselves, they are not wise.
13We, however, will not boast beyond proper limits, but will confine our boasting to the field God has assigned to us,[h] a field that
reaches even to you. 14We are not going too far in our boasting, as
would be the case if we had not come to you, for we did get as far as
you[i] with the gospel of Christ.[j] 15Neither do we go beyond our limits by boasting of work done by others.[b][k] Our hope is that, as your
faith continues to grow,[l] our area of activity among you will greatly
expand, 16so that we can preach the gospel in the regions beyond
you.[m] For we do not want to boast about work already done in
another man's territory. 17But, "Let him who boasts boast in the
Lord."[c][n] 18For it is not the one who commends himself[o] who is
approved, but the one whom the Lord commends.[p]

Chapter 11 Theme

11 I hope you will put up with[q] a little of my foolishness;[r] but
you are already doing that. 2I am jealous for you with a godly
jealousy. I promised you to one husband,[s] to Christ, so that I
might present you[t] as a pure virgin to him. 3But I am afraid that
just as Eve was deceived by the serpent's cunning,[u] your minds
may somehow be led astray from your sincere and pure devotion
to Christ. 4For if someone comes to you and preaches a Jesus other than the Jesus we preached,[v] or if you receive a different spirit[w]
from the one you received, or a different gospel[x] from the one you
accepted, you put up with it easily enough. 5But I do not think I
am in the least inferior to those "super-apostles."[y] 6I may not be a
trained speaker,[z] but I do have knowledge.[a] We have made this
perfectly clear to you in every way.

7Was it a sin[b] for me to lower myself in order to elevate you by

10:7 [a]Jn 7:24 [b]1Co 1:12; 3:23; 14:37 [c]2Co 11:23
10:8 [d]2Co 13:10
10:10 [e]1Co 2:3; Gal 4:13,14 [f]1Co 1:17
10:12 [g]2Co 3:1
10:13 [h]ver 15,16
10:14 [i]1Co 3:6 [j]2Co 2:12
10:15 [k]Ro 15:20 [l]2Th 1:3
10:16 [m]Ac 19:21
10:17 [n]Jer 9:24; 1Co 1:31
10:18 [o]ver 12 [p]Ro 2:29; 1Co 4:5
11:1 [q]ver 4,19,20; Mt 17:17 [r]ver 16,17,21; 2Co 5:13
11:2 [s]Hos 2:19; Eph 5:26,27 [t]2Co 4:14
11:3 [u]Ge 3:1-6,13; Jn 8:44; 1Ti 2:14; Rev 12:9
11:4 [v]1Co 3:11 [w]Ro 8:15 [x]Gal 1:6-9
11:5 [y]2Co 12:11; Gal 2:6
11:6 [z]1Co 1:17 [a]Eph 3:4
11:7 [b]2Co 12:13

a 7 Or *Look at the obvious facts* b 13-15 Or [13]*We, however, will not boast about things that cannot be measured, but we will boast according to the standard of measurement that the God of measure has assigned us—a measurement that relates even to you.* [14]. . . . [15]*Neither do we boast about things that cannot be measured in regard to the work done by others.* c 17 Jer. 9:24

preaching the gospel of God to you free of charge?[a] 8 I robbed other
churches by receiving support from them[b] so as to serve you. 9 And
when I was with you and needed something, I was not a burden to
anyone, for the brothers who came from Macedonia supplied
what I needed. I have kept myself from being a burden to you[c] in
any way, and will continue to do so. 10 As surely as the truth of
Christ is in me,[d] nobody in the regions of Achaia[e] will stop this
boasting[f] of mine. 11 Why? Because I do not love you? God knows
I do![g] 12 And I will keep on doing what I am doing in order to cut
the ground from under those who want an opportunity to be
considered equal with us in the things they boast about.

13 For such men are false apostles,[h] deceitful[i] workmen, masquerading as apostles of Christ.[j] 14 And no wonder, for Satan himself masquerades as an angel of light. 15 It is not surprising, then, if
his servants masquerade as servants of righteousness. Their end
will be what their actions deserve.[k]

16 I repeat: Let no one take me for a fool.[l] But if you do, then
receive me just as you would a fool, so that I may do a little boasting. 17 In this self-confident boasting I am not talking as the Lord
would,[m] but as a fool. 18 Since many are boasting in the way the
world does, I too will boast.[n] 19 You gladly put up with fools since
you are so wise![o] 20 In fact, you even put up with anyone who
enslaves you[p] or exploits you or takes advantage of you or pushes
himself forward or slaps you in the face. 21 To my shame I admit
that we were too weak[q] for that!

What anyone else dares to boast about—I am speaking as a
fool—I also dare to boast about.[r] 22 Are they Hebrews? So am I.[s]
Are they Israelites? So am I.[t] Are they Abraham's descendants?
So am I. 23 Are they servants of Christ? (I am out of my mind to
talk like this.) I am more. I have worked much harder,[u] been in
prison more frequently,[v] been flogged more severely, and been
exposed to death again and again. 24 Five times I received from
the Jews the forty lashes[w] minus one. 25 Three times I was beaten
with rods,[x] once I was stoned,[y] three times I was shipwrecked, I
spent a night and a day in the open sea, 26 I have been constantly
on the move. I have been in danger from rivers, in danger from
bandits, in danger from my own countrymen,[z] in danger from
Gentiles; in danger in the city,[a] in danger in the country, in danger at sea; and in danger from false brothers.[b] 27 I have labored
and toiled and have often gone without sleep; I have known
hunger and thirst and have often gone without food;[c] I have been
cold and naked. 28 Besides everything else, I face daily the pressure of my concern for all the churches. 29 Who is weak, and I do
not feel weak? Who is led into sin, and I do not inwardly burn?

30 If I must boast, I will boast of the things that show my weakness.[d] 31 The God and Father of the Lord Jesus, who is to be

11:7 [a] 1Co 9:18
11:8 [b] Php 4:15,18
11:9 [c] 2Co 12:13,14,16
11:10 [d] Ro 9:1 [e] Ac 18:12 [f] 1Co 9:15
11:11 [g] 2Co 12:15
11:13 [h] 2Pe 2:1 [i] Tit 1:10 [j] Rev 2:2
11:15 [k] Php 3:19
11:16 [l] ver 1
11:17 [m] 1Co 7:12,25
11:18 [n] Php 3:3,4
11:19 [o] 1Co 4:10
11:20 [p] Gal 2:4
11:21 [q] 2Co 10:1,10 [r] Php 3:4
11:22 [s] Php 3:5 [t] Ro 9:4
11:23 [u] 1Co 15:10 [v] Ac 16:23; 2Co 6:4,5
11:24 [w] Dt 25:3
11:25 [x] Ac 16:22 [y] Ac 14:19
11:26 [z] Ac 9:23; 14:5 [a] Ac 21:31 [b] Gal 2:4
11:27 [c] 1Co 4:11,12; 2Co 6:5
11:30 [d] 1Co 2:3

praised forever,[a] knows that I am not lying. 32In Damascus the
governor under King Aretas had the city of the Damascenes
guarded in order to arrest me.[b] 33But I was lowered in a basket
from a window in the wall and slipped through his hands.[c]

Chapter 12 Theme ______________________

12 I must go on boasting.[d] Although there is nothing to be
gained, I will go on to visions and revelations[e] from the
Lord. 2I know a man in Christ who fourteen years ago was caught
up[f] to the third heaven.[g] Whether it was in the body or out of the
body I do not know—God knows.[h] 3And I know that this man—
whether in the body or apart from the body I do not know, but
God knows— 4was caught up to paradise.[i] He heard inexpressible
things, things that man is not permitted to tell. 5I will boast about a
man like that, but I will not boast about myself, except about my
weaknesses. 6Even if I should choose to boast, I would not be a
fool,[j] because I would be speaking the truth. But I refrain, so no
one will think more of me than is warranted by what I do or say.
7To keep me from becoming conceited because of these surpass-
ingly great revelations, there was given me a thorn in my flesh,[k] a
messenger of Satan, to torment me. 8Three times I pleaded with
the Lord to take it away from me.[l] 9But he said to me, "My grace is
sufficient for you, for my power[m] is made perfect in weakness."
Therefore I will boast all the more gladly about my weaknesses, so
that Christ's power may rest on me. 10That is why, for Christ's sake,
I delight in weaknesses, in insults, in hardships,[n] in persecutions,[o]
in difficulties. For when I am weak, then I am strong.[p]
11I have made a fool of myself,[q] but you drove me to it. I ought to
have been commended by you, for I am not in the least inferior to
the "super-apostles,"[r] even though I am nothing.[s] 12The things
that mark an apostle—signs, wonders and miracles[t]—were done
among you with great perseverance. 13How were you inferior to
the other churches, except that I was never a burden to you?[u] Forgive me this wrong![v]
14Now I am ready to visit you for the third time,[w] and I will not
be a burden to you, because what I want is not your possessions
but you. After all, children should not have to save up for their parents,[x] but parents for their children.[y] 15So I will very gladly spend
for you everything I have and expend myself as well.[z] If I love you
more, will you love me less? 16Be that as it may, I have not been a
burden to you.[a] Yet, crafty fellow that I am, I caught you by trick-
ery! 17Did I exploit you through any of the men I sent you? 18I
urged[b] Titus to go to you and I sent our brother[c] with him. Titus
did not exploit you, did he? Did we not act in the same spirit and
follow the same course?

11:31 [a]Ro 9:5
11:32 [b]Ac 9:24
11:33 [c]Ac 9:25
12:1 [d]2Co 11:16,30 [e]ver 7
12:2 [f]Ac 8:39 [g]Eph 4:10 [h]2Co 11:11
12:4 [i]Lk 23:43; Rev 2:7
12:6 [j]2Co 11:16
12:7 [k]Nu 33:55
12:8 [l]Mt 26:39,44
12:9 [m]Php 4:13
12:10 [n]2Co 6:4 [o]Ro 5:3; 2Th 1:4 [p]2Co 13:4
12:11 [q]2Co 11:1 [r]2Co 11:5 [s]1Co 15:9,10
12:12 [t]Jn 4:48
12:13 [u]1Co 9:12,18 [v]2Co 11:7
12:14 [w]2Co 13:1 [x]1Co 4:14,15 [y]Pr 19:14
12:15 [z]Php 2:17; 1Th 2:8
12:16 [a]2Co 11:9
12:18 [b]2Co 8:6,16 [c]2Co 8:18

19Have you been thinking all along that we have been defending ourselves to you? We have been speaking in the sight of God[a]
as those in Christ; and everything we do, dear friends, is for your
strengthening.[b] 20For I am afraid that when I come[c] I may not
find you as I want you to be, and you may not find me as you
want me to be.[d] I fear that there may be quarreling,[e] jealousy, out-
bursts of anger, factions,[f] slander, gossip,[g] arrogance and disorder.[h] 21I am afraid that when I come again my God will humble
me before you, and I will be grieved[i] over many who have sinned
earlier[j] and have not repented of the impurity, sexual sin and
debauchery in which they have indulged.

Chapter 13 Theme ____

13 This will be my third visit to you.[k] "Every matter must be
established by the testimony of two or three witnesses."[a] [l] 2I
already gave you a warning when I was with you the second time.
I now repeat it while absent: On my return I will not spare[m] those
who sinned earlier[n] or any of the others, 3since you are demanding proof that Christ is speaking through me.[o] He is not weak in
dealing with you, but is powerful among you. 4For to be sure, he
was crucified in weakness,[p] yet he lives by God's power.[q] Likewise, we are weak[r] in him, yet by God's power we will live with
him to serve you.

5Examine yourselves[s] to see whether you are in the faith; test
yourselves.[t] Do you not realize that Christ Jesus is in you[u]—
unless, of course, you fail the test? 6And I trust that you will discover that we have not failed the test. 7Now we pray to God that you
will not do anything wrong. Not that people will see that we have
stood the test but that you will do what is right even though we
may seem to have failed. 8For we cannot do anything against the
truth, but only for the truth. 9We are glad whenever we are weak
but you are strong; and our prayer is for your perfection.[v] 10This is
why I write these things when I am absent, that when I come I may
not have to be harsh in my use of authority—the authority the
Lord gave me for building you up, not for tearing you down.[w]

11Finally, brothers,[x] good-by. Aim for perfection, listen to my
appeal, be of one mind, live in peace.[y] And the God of love and
peace[z] will be with you.

12Greet one another with a holy kiss.[a] 13All the saints send their
greetings.[b]

14May the grace of the Lord Jesus Christ,[c] and the love of God,[d]
and the fellowship of the Holy Spirit[e] be with you all.

[a] *1* Deut. 19:15

12:19
[a] Ro 9:1
[b] 2Co 10:8

12:20
[c] 2Co 2:1-4
[d] 1Co 4:21
[e] 1Co 1:11; 3:3
[f] Gal 5:20
[g] Ro 1:29
[h] 1Co 14:33

12:21
[i] 2Co 2:1,4
[j] 2Co 13:2

13:1
[k] 2Co 12:14
[l] Dt 19:15; Mt 18:16

13:2
[m] 2Co 1:23
[n] 2Co 12:21

13:3
[o] Mt 10:20; 1Co 5:4

13:4
[p] Php 2:7,8; 1Pe 3:18
[q] Ro 1:4; 6:4
[r] ver 9

13:5
[s] 1Co 11:28
[t] Jn 6:6
[u] Ro 8:10

13:9
[v] ver 11

13:10
[w] 2Co 10:8

13:11
[x] 1Th 4:1; 2Th 3:1
[y] Mk 9:50
[z] Ro 15:33; Eph 6:23

13:12
[a] Ro 16:16

13:13
[b] Php 4:22

13:14
[c] Ro 16:20; 2Co 8:9
[d] Ro 5:5; Jude 21
[e] Php 2:1

2 Corinthians Observations Chart

Paul

His character	His troubles	His conflict with the Corinthians

The Corinthians

Their strengths	Their weaknesses	Their problems with Paul

Paul's desire for the Corinthians	Insights on Titus

2 Corinthians at a Glance

Theme of 2 Corinthians:

Segment Divisions

		Chapter Themes
		1
		2
		3
		4
		5
		6
		7
		8
		9
		10
		11
		12
		13

Author:

Date:

Purpose:

Key Words:

comfort, have received, encouraged, encourageme had given hin (comforted, listen to my appeal)

hard pressed, harassed, distressed (trouble[s], hardships, dis tress, trial, su fer, sufferings not harmed)

sorrow(ful), painful, grieve(d), gri hurt, sorry

boast (boasti take pride)

confidence, confident, self-confident

commend

death (deadly

life

heart(s)

joy, happy (rejoice, glad, rejoicing, delighted)

ministry (service)

grace

Titus

mark referenc to the enemy (serpent, Sata as well as pronouns and synonyms)

GALATIANS

The gospel introduced the Jews to a new way of life—that of grace rather than law. The old covenant with all of its regulations was made obsolete by the new covenant (Hebrews 8:13). This transition was difficult for some Jewish believers to handle, and a group called the Judaizers sprang up. The Judaizers embraced Christianity but said that some of the old covenant rites, including circumcision, still must be observed.

As Paul, God's apostle to the Gentiles, went on his missionary journeys sharing the gospel of grace, many of these Judaizers followed him, teaching the necessity of keeping the law to one degree or another. They even went to Galatia. That is why Paul wrote what he did to the churches in Galatia.

There is some uncertainty about whether Galatians was written after Paul's first or second missionary journey, and so the exact date of his writing is not known. The debate centers on whether Paul was writing to the northern or southern churches of Galatia. If Paul wrote to the northern churches, the epistle would have been written sometime between A.D. 53 and 57, but if the letter was written to the southern churches, this would have been between A.D. 48 and 49.

However, the date does not affect the message of this critical letter. The truths in this epistle will liberate you to walk in that glorious freedom of a righteous life in the Spirit—truths you can glean through careful observation. Therefore, devote your energies to discovering these truths rather than to debating when Galatians was written.

The more you read and observe the text of this book, the more you will understand Paul's words: "I no longer live, but Christ lives in me. The life I live in the body, I live by faith in the Son of God, who loved me and gave himself for me" (Galatians 2:20).

THINGS TO DO

1. Read Acts 13 and 14 and then look at the map on page 1994 to acquaint yourself with the cities in this area. Also review the chart on page 1995 showing the sequence of events in Paul's life after his conversion.
2. As you read, mark in the text the key words (and their synonyms and pronouns) that are listed on the GALATIANS AT A GLANCE chart on page 2003. Mark any other key words you see as you read.
   a. The key words will help you see the theme of this epistle. The best way to see and absorb the book's message is to read through Galatians as many times as possible. Familiarity with the text and careful observation of what is being said is crucial when you study the Bible.
   b. After you mark the key words make a list of everything you learn from the text about the key words. This will give you great insights into Paul's message to the churches. You may want to record these lists in the margin for future reference.
   c. Jesus Christ is mentioned 38 times in Galatians. List everything you learn about him from this book.
3. Record the chapter themes on GALATIANS AT A GLANCE and in the text. Record the theme of the book and complete the chart.
4. As you read through the book, note Paul's emphasis in the first two chapters and then how the focus changes in chapter 3.
   a. Look for the questions Paul asks the recipients of this letter. Watch for words such as *brothers,*

you, and *foolish Galatians*. Make a list of these things on the chart PAUL'S CONCERN FOR THE CHURCHES AT GALATIA on pages 2002, 2003. (You may want to list these on separate paper before you write them in your Bible.)

b. Think about why Paul said all he did about himself in those first two chapters. What does this have to do with what follows in the rest of his epistle?

c. Notice the progression of events in Paul's life as presented in these chapters. (There is a chart of the chronology of these events on page 1995.)

d. Trace Paul's travels on the map below.

5. In chapter 3 mark *promise(d)*. Note what the promise is; the text will tell you.

6. Fill in the segment divisions on GALATIANS AT A GLANCE.

Things to Think About

1. Are you living under grace or under law? Have you accepted the grace of God for your salvation but still put yourself under the law for daily living?

2. According to Galatians 5:16-21, if you live under grace, under the control of the Spirit of God, you will not be able to live a life habitually controlled by the flesh, producing the works of the flesh. Evaluate your walk according to these verses.

3. What do you boast in?

4. As you look at Paul's life, what do you learn for your own life?

Chapter 1 Theme ______________________

Paul's Travels as a New Believer

1 Paul, an apostle—sent not from men nor by man, but by Jesus
Christ[a] and God the Father, who raised him from the dead[b]—
2and all the brothers with me,[c]

To the churches in Galatia:[d]

3Grace and peace to you from God our Father and the Lord Jesus
Christ,[e] 4who gave himself
for our sins[f] to rescue us
from the present evil age,
according to the will of our
God and Father,[g] 5to whom
be glory for ever and ever.
Amen.[h]

6I am astonished that you
are so quickly deserting the
one who called[i] you by the
grace of Christ and are turning to a different gospel[j]—
7which is really no gospel at all. Evidently some people are throwing you into confusion[k] and are trying to pervert the gospel of
Christ. 8But even if we or an angel from heaven should preach a
gospel other than the one we preached to you,[l] let him be eternally

1:1 [a]Ac 9:15 [b]Ac 2:24
1:2 [c]Php 4:21 [d]Ac 16:6; 1Co 16:1
1:3 [e]Ro 1:7
1:4 [f]Mt 20:28; Ro 4:25; Gal 2:20 [g]Php 4:20
1:5 [h]Ro 11:36
1:6 [i]Gal 5:8 [j]2Co 11:4
1:7 [k]Ac 15:24; Gal 5:10
1:8 [l]2Co 11:4

Sequence of Events in Paul's Life after His Conversion*

There are differing opinions on these dates. For continuity's sake this chart will be the basis for dates pertaining to Paul's life.

Year A.D.	Event
33-34	Conversion, time in Damascus
35-47	Some silent years, except we know that Paul:
	1. Spent time in Arabia and Damascus
	2. Made first visit to Jerusalem
	3. Went to Tarsus, Syria-Cilicia area
	4. Was with Barnabas in Antioch
	5. With Barnabas took relief to brethren in Judea—Paul's second visit to Jerusalem
	6. Returned to Antioch; was sent out with Barnabas by church at Antioch
47-48	**First missionary journey:** *Galatians written(?)*
49	Apostolic Council at Jerusalem—Paul visits Jerusalem (compare Acts 15 with Galatians 2:1)
49-51	**Second missionary journey:** *1 and 2 Thessalonians written*
52-56	**Third missionary journey:** *1 and 2 Corinthians and Romans written*
56	Paul goes to Jerusalem and is arrested; held at Caesarea
57-59	Appearance before Felix and Drusilla; before Festus; before Agrippa
59-60	Appeals to Caesar, sent from Caesarea to Rome
60-62	First Roman imprisonment: *Ephesians, Philemon, Colossians, and Philippians written*
62	Paul's release; possible trip to Spain
62	Paul in Macedonia: *1 Timothy written*
62	Paul goes to Crete: *Titus written*
63-64	Paul taken to Rome and imprisoned: *2 Timothy written*
64	Paul is absent from the body and present with the Lord
	(Others put Paul's conversion about A.D. 35, his death in A.D. 68.)

condemned![a] 9As we have already said, so now I say again: If anybody is preaching to you a gospel other than what you accepted,[b]
let him be eternally condemned!
10Am I now trying to win the approval of men, or of God? Or
am I trying to please men?[c] If I were still trying to please men, I
would not be a servant of Christ.
11I want you to know, brothers,[d] that the gospel I preached is
not something that man made up. 12I did not receive it from any
man,[e] nor was I taught it; rather, I received it by revelation[f] from
Jesus Christ.
13For you have heard of my previous way of life in Judaism,[g] how
intensely I persecuted the church of God and tried to destroy it.[h]
14I was advancing in Judaism beyond many Jews of my own age
and was extremely zealous for the traditions of my fathers.[i] 15But
when God, who set me apart from birth[a][j] and called me[k] by his
grace, was pleased 16to reveal his Son in me so that I might preach
him among the Gentiles,[l] I did not consult any man,[m] 17nor did I
go up to Jerusalem to see those who were apostles before I was, but
I went immediately into Arabia and later returned to Damascus.
18Then after three years,[n] I went up to Jerusalem[o] to get acquainted
with Peter[b] and stayed with him fifteen days. 19I saw none of the
other apostles—only James,[p] the Lord's brother. 20I assure you
before God that what I am writing you is no lie.[q] 21Later I went to

1:8 [a] Ro 9:3
1:9 [b] Ro 16:17
1:10 [c] Ro 2:29; 1Th 2:4
1:11 [d] 1Co 15:1
1:12 [e] ver 1 [f] ver 16
1:13 [g] Ac 26:4,5 [h] Ac 8:3
1:14 [i] Mt 15:2
1:15 [j] Isa 49:1,5; Jer 1:5 [k] Ac 9:15
1:16 [l] Gal 2:9 [m] Mt 16:17
1:18 [n] Ac 9:22,23 [o] Ac 9:26,27
1:19 [p] Mt 13:55
1:20 [q] Ro 9:1

[a] *15* Or *from my mother's womb* [b] *18* Greek *Cephas*

Syria and Cilicia.[a] 22I was personally unknown to the churches of
Judea[b] that are in Christ. 23They only heard the report: "The man
who formerly persecuted us is now preaching the faith[c] he once
tried to destroy." 24And they praised God[d] because of me.

Chapter 2 Theme ______________________

2 Fourteen years later I went up again to Jerusalem,[e] this time
with Barnabas. I took Titus along also. 2I went in response to
a revelation and set before them the gospel that I preach among the
Gentiles.[f] But I did this privately to those who seemed to be leaders, for fear that I was running or had run my race[g] in vain. 3Yet
not even Titus,[h] who was with me, was compelled to be circumcised, even though he was a Greek.[i] 4⌊This matter arose⌋ because
some false brothers[j] had infiltrated our ranks to spy on[k] the freedom[l] we have in Christ Jesus and to make us slaves. 5We did not
give in to them for a moment, so that the truth of the gospel[m] might
remain with you.

6As for those who seemed to be important[n]—whatever they were
makes no difference to me; God does not judge by external appearance[o]—those men added nothing to my message. 7On the contrary,
they saw that I had been entrusted with the task[p] of preaching the
gospel to the Gentiles,[a][q] just as Peter[r] had been to the Jews.[b] 8For
God, who was at work in the ministry of Peter as an apostle[s] to the
Jews, was also at work in my ministry as an apostle to the Gentiles.
9James, Peter[c][t] and John, those reputed to be pillars,[u] gave me and
Barnabas[v] the right hand of fellowship when they recognized the
grace given to me.[w] They agreed that we should go to the Gentiles,
and they to the Jews. 10All they asked was that we should continue
to remember the poor,[x] the very thing I was eager to do.

11When Peter[y] came to Antioch,[z] I opposed him to his face,
because he was clearly in the wrong. 12Before certain men came
from James, he used to eat with the Gentiles.[a] But when they
arrived, he began to draw back and separate himself from the Gentiles because he was afraid of those who belonged to the circumcision group.[b] 13The other Jews joined him in his hypocrisy, so that
by their hypocrisy even Barnabas[c] was led astray.

14When I saw that they were not acting in line with the truth of
the gospel,[d] I said to Peter[e] in front of them all, "You are a Jew, yet
you live like a Gentile and not like a Jew.[f] How is it, then, that you
force Gentiles to follow Jewish customs?

15"We who are Jews by birth[g] and not 'Gentile sinners'[h] 16know
that a man is not justified by observing the law, but by faith in Jesus

[a]7 Greek *uncircumcised* [b]7 Greek *circumcised*; also in verses 8 and 9 [c]9 Greek *Cephas*; also in verses 11 and 14

1:21 [a]Ac 6:9
1:22 [b]1Th 2:14
1:23 [c]Ac 6:7
1:24 [d]Mt 9:8
2:1 [e]Ac 15:2
2:2 [f]Ac 15:4,12 [g]1Co 9:24; Php 2:16
2:3 [h]2Co 2:13 [i]Ac 16:3; 1Co 9:21
2:4 [j]2Co 11:26 [k]Jude 4 [l]Ac 15:1; Gal 5:1,13
2:5 [m]ver 14
2:6 [n]Gal 6:3 [o]Ac 10:34
2:7 [p]1Th 2:4; 1Ti 1:11 [q]Ac 9:15 [r]ver 9,11,14
2:8 [s]Ac 1:25
2:9 [t]ver 7,11,14 [u]1Ti 3:15 [v]Ac 4:36 [w]Ro 12:3
2:10 [x]Ac 24:17
2:11 [y]ver 7,9,14 [z]Ac 11:19
2:12 [a]Ac 11:3 [b]Ac 11:2
2:13 [c]ver 1; Ac 4:36
2:14 [d]ver 5 [e]ver 7,9,11 [f]Ac 10:28
2:15 [g]Php 3:4,5 [h]1Sa 15:18

Christ.[a] So we, too, have put our faith in Christ Jesus that we may
be justified by faith in Christ and not by observing the law, because
by observing the law no one will be justified.
17"If, while we seek to be justified in Christ, it becomes evident
that we ourselves are sinners,[b] does that mean that Christ promotes
sin? Absolutely not![c] 18If I rebuild what I destroyed, I prove that I
am a lawbreaker. 19For through the law I died to the law[d] so that I
might live for God.[e] 20I have been crucified with Christ[f] and I no
longer live, but Christ lives in me.[g] The life I live in the body, I live
by faith in the Son of God,[h] who loved me[i] and gave himself for
me.[j] 21I do not set aside the grace of God, for if righteousness
could be gained through the law,[k] Christ died for nothing!"[a]

Chapter 3 Theme

3 You foolish Galatians! Who has bewitched you?[l] Before your
very eyes Jesus Christ was clearly portrayed as crucified.[m] 2I
would like to learn just one thing from you: Did you receive the
Spirit by observing the law, or by believing what you heard?[n] 3Are
you so foolish? After beginning with the Spirit, are you now trying to attain your goal by human effort? 4Have you suffered so
much for nothing—if it really was for nothing? 5Does God give you
his Spirit and work miracles[o] among you because you observe the
law, or because you believe what you heard?
6Consider Abraham: "He believed God, and it was credited to
him as righteousness."[b][p] 7Understand, then, that those who believe[q]
are children of Abraham. 8The Scripture foresaw that God would
justify the Gentiles by faith, and announced the gospel in advance
to Abraham: "All nations will be blessed through you."[c][r] 9So those
who have faith[s] are blessed along with Abraham, the man of faith.
10All who rely on observing the law are under a curse, for it is
written: "Cursed is everyone who does not continue to do everything written in the Book of the Law."[d][t] 11Clearly no one is justified before God by the law, because, "The righteous will live by
faith."[e][u] 12The law is not based on faith; on the contrary, "The man
who does these things will live by them."[f][v] 13Christ redeemed us
from the curse of the law[w] by becoming a curse for us, for it is written: "Cursed is everyone who is hung on a tree."[g][x] 14He redeemed
us in order that the blessing given to Abraham might come to the
Gentiles through Christ Jesus,[y] so that by faith we might receive
the promise of the Spirit.[z]
15Brothers, let me take an example from everyday life. Just as
no one can set aside or add to a human covenant that has been
duly established, so it is in this case. 16The promises were spoken

a *21* Some interpreters end the quotation after verse 14. b *6* Gen. 15:6 c *8* Gen. 12:3; 18:18; 22:18 d *10* Deut. 27:26 e *11* Hab. 2:4 f *12* Lev. 18:5 g *13* Deut. 21:23

2:16 a Ac 13:39; Ro 9:30
2:17 b ver 15; c Gal 3:21
2:19 d Ro 7:4; e Ro 6:10,11,14; 2Co 5:15
2:20 f Ro 6:6; g 1Pe 4:2; h Mt 4:3; i Ro 8:37; j Gal 1:4
2:21 k Gal 3:21
3:1 l Gal 5:7; m 1Co 1:23
3:2 n Ro 10:17
3:5 o 1Co 12:10
3:6 p Ge 15:6; Ro 4:3
3:7 q ver 9
3:8 r Ge 12:3; Ac 3:25
3:9 s ver 7; Ro 4:16
3:10 t Dt 27:26; Jer 11:3
3:11 u Hab 2:4; Gal 2:16; Heb 10:38
3:12 v Lev 18:5; Ro 10:5
3:13 w Gal 4:5; x Dt 21:23; Ac 5:30
3:14 y Ro 4:9,16; z ver 2; Joel 2:28; Ac 2:33

to Abraham and to his seed.[a] The Scripture does not say "and to
seeds," meaning many people, but "and to your seed,"[a] meaning
one person, who is Christ. 17What I mean is this: The law, introduced 430 years[b] later, does not set aside the covenant previously
established by God and thus do away with the promise. 18For if
the inheritance depends on the law, then it no longer depends on
a promise;[c] but God in his grace gave it to Abraham through a
promise.

19What, then, was the purpose of the law? It was added because
of transgressions[d] until the Seed[e] to whom the promise referred
had come. The law was put into effect through angels[f] by a mediator.[g] 20A mediator,[h] however, does not represent just one party;
but God is one.

21Is the law, therefore, opposed to the promises of God? Absolutely not![i] For if a law had been given that could impart life, then
righteousness would certainly have come by the law.[j] 22But the
Scripture declares that the whole world is a prisoner of sin,[k] so
that what was promised, being given through faith in Jesus Christ,
might be given to those who believe.

23Before this faith came, we were held prisoners[l] by the law,
locked up until faith should be revealed. 24So the law was put in
charge to lead us to Christ[b][m] that we might be justified by faith.[n]
25Now that faith has come, we are no longer under the supervision
of the law.

26You are all sons of God[o] through faith in Christ Jesus, 27for all
of you who were baptized into Christ[p] have clothed yourselves
with Christ.[q] 28There is neither Jew nor Greek, slave nor free,[r] male
nor female, for you are all one in Christ Jesus.[s] 29If you belong to
Christ,[t] then you are Abraham's seed, and heirs according to the
promise.[u]

Chapter 4 Theme ____________________

4 What I am saying is that as long as the heir is a child, he is no
different from a slave, although he owns the whole estate.
2He is subject to guardians and trustees until the time set by his
father. 3So also, when we were children, we were in slavery[v] under
the basic principles of the world.[w] 4But when the time had fully
come,[x] God sent his Son, born of a woman,[y] born under law,[z] 5to
redeem those under law, that we might receive the full rights[a] of
sons. 6Because you are sons, God sent the Spirit of his Son into
our hearts,[b] the Spirit who calls out, "*Abba*,[c] Father."[c] 7So you are
no longer a slave, but a son; and since you are a son, God has made
you also an heir.[d]

a *16* Gen. 12:7; 13:15; 24:7 b *24* Or *charge until Christ came* c *6* Aramaic for *Father*

3:16 [a] Lk 1:55; Ro 4:13,16
3:17 [b] Ge 15:13,14; Ex 12:40
3:18 [c] Ro 4:14
3:19 [d] Ro 5:20 [e] ver 16 [f] Ac 7:53 [g] Ex 20:19
3:20 [h] Heb 8:6; 9:15; 12:24
3:21 [i] Gal 2:17 [j] Gal 2:21
3:22 [k] Ro 3:9-19; 11:32
3:23 [l] Ro 11:32
3:24 [m] Ro 10:4 [n] Gal 2:16
3:26 [o] Ro 8:14
3:27 [p] Mt 28:19; Ro 6:3 [q] Ro 13:14
3:28 [r] Col 3:11 [s] Jn 10:16; 17:11; Eph 2:14,15
3:29 [t] 1Co 3:23 [u] ver 16
4:3 [v] Gal 2:4 [w] Col 2:8,20
4:4 [x] Mk 1:15; Eph 1:10 [y] Jn 1:14 [z] Lk 2:27
4:5 [a] Jn 1:12
4:6 [b] Ro 5:5 [c] Ro 8:15,16
4:7 [d] Ro 8:17

as I did before, that those who live like this will not inherit the
kingdom of God.
22But the fruit[a] of the Spirit is love,[b] joy, peace, patience, kindness,
goodness, faithfulness, 23gentleness and self-control.[c] Against such
things there is no law. 24Those who belong to Christ Jesus have
crucified the sinful nature[d] with its passions and desires.[e] 25Since
we live by the Spirit, let us keep in step with the Spirit. 26Let us
not become conceited,[f] provoking and envying each other.

Chapter 6 Theme ______________________________

6 Brothers, if someone is caught in a sin, you who are spiritual[g]
should restore him gently. But watch yourself, or you also may
be tempted. 2Carry each other's burdens, and in this way you will
fulfill the law of Christ.[h] 3If anyone thinks he is something[i] when he
is nothing, he deceives himself. 4Each one should test his own
actions. Then he can take pride in himself, without comparing himself to somebody else, 5for each one should carry his own load.
6Anyone who receives instruction in the word must share all good
things with his instructor.[j]
7Do not be deceived:[k] God cannot be mocked. A man reaps what
he sows.[l] 8The one who sows to please his sinful nature, from that
nature[a] will reap destruction;[m] the one who sows to please the
Spirit, from the Spirit will reap eternal life.[n] 9Let us not become
weary in doing good,[o] for at the proper time we will reap a harvest if we do not give up.[p] 10Therefore, as we have opportunity, let
us do good[q] to all people, especially to those who belong to the
family[r] of believers.
11See what large letters I use as I write to you with my own hand![s]
12Those who want to make a good impression outwardly are
trying to compel you to be circumcised.[t] The only reason they do
this is to avoid being persecuted[u] for the cross of Christ. 13Not
even those who are circumcised obey the law,[v] yet they want you
to be circumcised that they may boast about your flesh.[w] 14May I
never boast except in the cross of our Lord Jesus Christ, through
which[b] the world has been crucified to me, and I to the world.[x]
15Neither circumcision nor uncircumcision means anything;[y] what
counts is a new creation.[z] 16Peace and mercy to all who follow this
rule, even to the Israel of God.
17Finally, let no one cause me trouble, for I bear on my body the
marks[a] of Jesus.
18The grace of our Lord Jesus Christ[b] be with your spirit,[c] brothers. Amen.

a 8 Or *his flesh, from the flesh* b 14 Or *whom*

5:22 [a]Mt 7:16-20; Eph 5:9 [b]Col 3:12-15
5:23 [c]Ac 24:25
5:24 [d]Ro 6:6 [e]ver 16,17
5:26 [f]Php 2:3
6:1 [g]1Co 2:15
6:2 [h]Ro 15:1; Jas 2:8
6:3 [i]Ro 12:3; 1Co 8:2
6:6 [j]1Co 9:11,14
6:7 [k]1Co 6:9 [l]2Co 9:6
6:8 [m]Job 4:8; Hos 8:7 [n]Jas 3:18
6:9 [o]1Co 15:58 [p]Rev 2:10
6:10 [q]Pr 3:27 [r]Eph 2:19
6:11 [s]1Co 16:21
6:12 [t]Ac 15:1 [u]Gal 5:11
6:13 [v]Ro 2:25 [w]Php 3:3
6:14 [x]Ro 6:2,6
6:15 [y]1Co 7:19 [z]2Co 5:17
6:17 [a]Isa 44:5; 2Co 1:5
6:18 [b]Ro 16:20 [c]2Ti 4:22

(continue

Paul's Concern for the Churches at Galatia

Galatians at a Glance

heme of Galatians:

thor:

te:

rpose:

y Words:

- 'aul (and pronouns elating to him)
- ;ospel
- ;race
- aw
- pirit
- aith (believe, elieving, elievers)
- romise(d)
- :ovenant
- Christ (Jesus)
- ree (freedom)

Segment Divisions		Chapter Themes
		1
		2
		3
		4
		5
		6

ƐPHESIANS

Ɛphesus, the fourth-largest city in the Roman Empire, was the home of the temple of the goddess Artemis, sometimes referred to as Diana. Of all the deities in Asia, none was more sought after than Artemis.

But by the time of Paul, Ephesus's position as a center of trade was lost because the harbor became unnavigable. From that point on, the worship of Artemis became the city's means of economic survival. The tourist and pilgrim trade associated with Artemis made many people in Ephesus wealthy. Silversmiths made their living selling images of this goddess and her temple. Innkeepers and restaurant owners grew rich from the large influx of worshipers who traveled great distances to see the temple of Artemis, one of the seven wonders of the world. Even the temple treasury served as a bank, loaning large sums of money to many, including kings. And since Artemis was the patroness of sex, prostitutes sold their bodies without condemnation in the two-story brothel on Marble Road.

Although Artemis was the main attraction, all sorts of magic and sorcery were conjured up and then documented. This documentation would later be referred to as *Ephesia grammata.*

Then God sent Paul to live in Ephesus and called out for himself a church, a light to illumine the occultic darkness of this city.

This brief glimpse into the historical and cultural setting of Ephesians should help you understand why Paul wrote what he did to the church in Ephesus. The message of this epistle is needed as much today as it was in A.D. 60 to 62, when Paul wrote it as a prisoner in Rome.

Things to Do

General Instructions

1. Read Ephesians in one sitting before examining it chapter by chapter.

2. When you finish, read Acts 18:18-21 (Paul's first visit to Ephesus was on his second missionary journey). Then read Acts 19 for an account of Paul's second visit on his third missionary journey. This passage will help you understand why Ephesians deals with warfare and our position in Christ more extensively than any other epistle.

Chapters 1-3

Read Ephesians 1 through 3 one chapter at a time, doing the following:

1. Mark each reference to God, and in the margin list everything God does.

2. Mark distinctively each use of *in Christ* or *in him* so you can easily spot it in the text. Then on the OBSERVATIONS CHART on page 2012, under the heading "Our Wealth and Position in Christ," list what believers have *in Christ.* Pay particular attention to the phrase *in the heavenly realms,* which is key to warfare. Note the chapter and verse from which the information comes when you make your list (e.g., 1:13). (You may want to list this information on separate paper before you record it in your Bible.)

3. Mark each reference to the Spirit or Holy Spirit. On the OBSERVATIONS CHART, under the heading "Our Relationship with the Holy Spirit," list what is taught about the person and work of the Holy Spirit.

4. Mark distinctively each occurrence of *rich* or *riches.* Then in the margin list what you learn about these riches. Remember to ask the five W's and an H: Who is rich and in what? How are these riches described? What is done with the riches? And so on.

5. Mark each use of *formerly (used to, at one time, once).* Then on the OBSERVATIONS CHART under

the heading "Our Former Lifestyle," list what Ephesians says about how believers used to live before salvation.

6. Mark the other key words (with their synonyms and pronouns) listed on the EPHESIANS AT A GLANCE chart on page 2013. Put these on an index card and use it as a bookmark. Then in the margin list what is said about each key word. Just record the facts.

Chapters 4-6

1. Read Ephesians 4 through 6 chapter by chapter, doing the following:
   a. Mark each occurrence of *live.* Then on the OBSERVATIONS CHART, under the heading "The Way We Live in Christ," list what is taught about the lifestyle of a believer. Also go back to 2:2, 10 and mark and list what these verses teach about the believer's lifestyle. Then ask yourself: How am I to live? Why am I able to live this way?
   b. Continue to mark in the text the key words listed on your bookmark. Also list what you learn from the uses of *former* or *once* in this section of Ephesians. Note the contrast between our former lifestyle and our life in Christ.
   c. Mark the following: *Holy Spirit, in Christ,* and *in the Lord.* Then list what you learn and think about it. This will help you see how to live in him.

2. Record any other observations you have of the text as instructed in the observation section in "How to Use The International Inductive Study Bible" which is on page IISB-15.

3. On EPHESIANS AT A GLANCE:
   a. Record the theme of the book and of each chapter in the appropriate spaces. (Remember to go back and record each chapter's theme in the text next to the chapter number.)
   b. As you have seen, there is a change of emphasis between chapters 3 and 4. Write down under "Segment Divisions" what best summarizes the content of chapters 1 through 3 and then chapters 4 through 6.

Things to Think About

1. Stop and review all you observed and listed about your position as a child of God. Go through chapter 1 again and note everything God has done for you. Watch for the personal pronoun *he* (when referring to the Godhead). Also note the phrases *according to* and *in accordance with*, and the words *as* and *will.* Think about what God has done for you and why. Then thank him and tell him you want to live accordingly.

2. Ephesians 2:8-10 are extremely important verses. Think about what God is saying to you and ask God to show you whether you are trusting in his grace or in your works to get you to heaven. But don't stop there. Think about the relationship of good works to the life of a believer. How are you walking? Memorize these verses.

3. In your home do you live according to Ephesians 5:18 through 6:4?

4. Are you able to take a stand or are you defeated by the devil's schemes? Don't forget where you are seated. Think about the armor of God. Do you have it on and are you standing your ground in truth, righteousness, peace, salvation, and faith? Are you able to use the Word of God as your offensive weapon?

Chapter 1 Theme ______________________________

1 Paul, an apostle[a] of Christ Jesus by the will of God,[b]
To the saints in Ephesus,[a] the faithful[b][c] in Christ Jesus:

2 Grace and peace to you from God our Father and the Lord
Jesus Christ.[d]

3 Praise be to the God and Father of our Lord Jesus Christ,[e] who
has blessed us in the heavenly realms[f] with every spiritual blessing in Christ. 4 For he chose us in him before the creation of the
world to be holy and blameless[g] in his sight. In love[h] 5 he[c] predestined[i] us to be adopted as his sons through Jesus Christ, in accordance with his pleasure[j] and will— 6 to the praise of his glorious
grace, which he has freely given us in the One he loves.[k] 7 In him
we have redemption[l] through his blood, the forgiveness of sins,
in accordance with the riches of God's grace 8 that he lavished on
us with all wisdom and understanding. 9 And he[d] made known to
us the mystery[m] of his will according to his good pleasure, which
he purposed in Christ, 10 to be put into effect when the times will
have reached their fulfillment[n]—to bring all things in heaven
and on earth together under one head, even Christ.[o]
11 In him we were also chosen,[e] having been predestined according to the plan of him who works out everything in conformity
with the purpose[p] of his will, 12 in order that we, who were the first
to hope in Christ, might be for the praise of his glory.[q] 13 And you
also were included in Christ when you heard the word of truth,[r]
the gospel of your salvation. Having believed, you were marked in
him with a seal,[s] the promised Holy Spirit, 14 who is a deposit guaranteeing our inheritance[t] until the redemption of those who are
God's possession—to the praise of his glory.
15 For this reason, ever since I heard about your faith in the Lord
Jesus and your love for all the saints,[u] 16 I have not stopped giving
thanks for you,[v] remembering you in my prayers. 17 I keep asking
that the God of our Lord Jesus Christ, the glorious Father,[w] may
give you the Spirit[f] of wisdom[x] and revelation, so that you may
know him better. 18 I pray also that the eyes of your heart may be
enlightened[y] in order that you may know the hope to which he
has called you, the riches of his glorious inheritance in the saints,
19 and his incomparably great power for us who believe. That power[z]
is like the working of his mighty strength,[a] 20 which he exerted in
Christ when he raised him from the dead[b] and seated him at his
right hand in the heavenly realms, 21 far above all rule and authority,

a *1* Some early manuscripts do not have *in Ephesus.* b *1* Or *believers who are* c *4,5* Or *sight in love.* *5He* d *8,9* Or *us. With all wisdom and understanding,* *9he* e *11* Or *were made heirs* f *17* Or *a spirit*

1:1 *a* 1Co 1:1 *b* 2Co 1:1 *c* Col 1:2
1:2 *d* Ro 1:7
1:3 *e* 2Co 1:3 *f* Eph 2:6; 3:10; 6:12
1:4 *g* Eph 5:27; Col 1:22 *h* Eph 4:2,15,16
1:5 *i* Ro 8:29,30 *j* 1Co 1:21
1:6 *k* Mt 3:17
1:7 *l* Ro 3:24
1:9 *m* Ro 16:25
1:10 *n* Gal 4:4 *o* Col 1:20
1:11 *p* Eph 3:11; Heb 6:17
1:12 *q* ver 6,14
1:13 *r* Col 1:5 *s* Eph 4:30
1:14 *t* Ac 20:32
1:15 *u* Col 1:4
1:16 *v* Ro 1:8
1:17 *w* Jn 20:17 *x* Col 1:9
1:18 *y* Ac 26:18; 2Co 4:6
1:19 *z* Col 1:29 *a* Eph 6:10
1:20 *b* Ac 2:24

power and dominion, and every title[a] that can be given, not only in
the present age but also in the one to come. [22]And God placed all
things under his feet[b] and appointed him to be head[c] over everything for the church, [23]which is his body, the fullness of him who
fills everything in every way.

Chapter 2 Theme ______________________________

2 As for you, you were dead in your transgressions and sins,[d] [2]in
which you used to live[e] when you followed the ways of this
world and of the ruler of the kingdom of the air,[f] the spirit who is
now at work in those who are disobedient.[g] [3]All of us also lived
among them at one time, gratifying the cravings of our sinful
nature[a][h] and following its desires and thoughts. Like the rest, we
were by nature objects of wrath. [4]But because of his great love for
us, God, who is rich in mercy, [5]made us alive with Christ even when
we were dead in transgressions[i]—it is by grace you have been
saved.[j] [6]And God raised us up with Christ and seated us with him[k]
in the heavenly realms[l] in Christ Jesus, [7]in order that in the coming
ages he might show the incomparable riches of his grace, expressed
in his kindness[m] to us in Christ Jesus. [8]For it is by grace you have
been saved,[n] through faith—and this not from yourselves, it is the
gift of God— [9]not by works,[o] so that no one can boast.[p] [10]For we
are God's workmanship, created[q] in Christ Jesus to do good works,[r]
which God prepared in advance for us to do.

[11]Therefore, remember that formerly you who are Gentiles by
birth and called "uncircumcised" by those who call themselves "the
circumcision" (that done in the body by the hands of men)[s]—
[12]remember that at that time you were separate from Christ,
excluded from citizenship in Israel and foreigners to the covenants
of the promise,[t] without hope[u] and without God in the world.
[13]But now in Christ Jesus you who once were far away have been
brought near[v] through the blood of Christ.[w]

[14]For he himself is our peace, who has made the two one[x] and
has destroyed the barrier, the dividing wall of hostility, [15]by abolish-
ing in his flesh[y] the law with its commandments and regulations.[z]
His purpose was to create in himself one[a] new man out of the two,
thus making peace, [16]and in this one body to reconcile both of
them to God through the cross,[b] by which he put to death their hostility. [17]He came and preached peace to you who were far away
and peace to those who were near.[c] [18]For through him we both have
access[d] to the Father[e] by one Spirit.[f]

[19]Consequently, you are no longer foreigners and aliens,[g] but fellow citizens[h] with God's people and members of God's household,[i]
[20]built on the foundation[j] of the apostles and prophets, with Christ

1:21 [a]Php 2:9,10
1:22 [b]Mt 28:18 [c]Eph 4:15; 5:23
2:1 [d]ver 5; Col 2:13
2:2 [e]Col 3:7 [f]Jn 12:31; Eph 6:12 [g]Eph 5:6
2:3 [h]Gal 5:16
2:5 [i]ver 1 [j]ver 8; Ac 15:11
2:6 [k]Eph 1:20 [l]Eph 1:3
2:7 [m]Tit 3:4
2:8 [n]ver 5
2:9 [o]2Ti 1:9 [p]1Co 1:29
2:10 [q]Eph 4:24 [r]Tit 2:14
2:11 [s]Col 2:11
2:12 [t]Gal 3:17 [u]1Th 4:13
2:13 [v]ver 17; Ac 2:39 [w]Col 1:20
2:14 [x]1Co 12:13
2:15 [y]Col 1:21,22 [z]Col 2:14 [a]Gal 3:28
2:16 [b]Col 1:20,22
2:17 [c]Ps 148:14; Isa 57:19
2:18 [d]Eph 3:12 [e]Col 1:12 [f]1Co 12:13
2:19 [g]ver 12 [h]Php 3:20 [i]Gal 6:10
2:20 [j]Mt 16:18; Rev 21:14

[a]3 Or *our flesh*

Jesus himself as the chief cornerstone.[a] 21In him the whole building
is joined together and rises to become a holy temple[b] in the Lord.
22And in him you too are being built together to become a dwelling
in which God lives by his Spirit.

Chapter 3 Theme ______________________________

3 For this reason I, Paul, the prisoner[c] of Christ Jesus for the sake
of you Gentiles—
2Surely you have heard about the administration of God's grace
that was given to me[d] for you, 3that is, the mystery[e] made known to
me by revelation,[f] as I have already written briefly. 4In reading this,
then, you will be able to understand my insight[g] into the mystery of
Christ, 5which was not made known to men in other generations as
it has now been revealed by the Spirit to God's holy apostles and
prophets.[h] 6This mystery is that through the gospel the Gentiles
are heirs[i] together with Israel, members together of one body,[j] and
sharers together in the promise in Christ Jesus.
7I became a servant of this gospel[k] by the gift of God's grace given
me through the working of his power.[l] 8Although I am less than the
least of all God's people,[m] this grace was given me: to preach to
the Gentiles the unsearchable riches of Christ, 9and to make plain
to everyone the administration of this mystery,[n] which for ages past
was kept hidden in God, who created all things. 10His intent was
that now, through the church, the manifold wisdom of God[o] should
be made known[p] to the rulers and authorities[q] in the heavenly
realms, 11according to his eternal purpose which he accomplished
in Christ Jesus our Lord. 12In him and through faith in him we may
approach God[r] with freedom and confidence.[s] 13I ask you, therefore,
not to be discouraged because of my sufferings for you, which are
your glory.
14For this reason I kneel[t] before the Father, 15from whom his
whole family[a] in heaven and on earth derives its name. 16I pray
that out of his glorious riches he may strengthen you with power[u]
through his Spirit in your inner being,[v] 17so that Christ may dwell
in your hearts[w] through faith. And I pray that you, being rooted[x]
and established in love, 18may have power, together with all the
saints, to grasp how wide and long and high and deep[y] is the love
of Christ, 19and to know this love that surpasses knowledge—that
you may be filled[z] to the measure of all the fullness of God.[a]
20Now to him who is able[b] to do immeasurably more than all we
ask or imagine, according to his power that is at work within us,
21to him be glory in the church and in Christ Jesus throughout all
generations, for ever and ever! Amen.[c]

[a] *15* Or *whom all fatherhood*

2:20 [a] 1Pe 2:4-8
2:21 [b] 1Co 3:16,17
3:1 [c] Ac 23:18; Eph 4:1
3:2 [d] Col 1:25
3:3 [e] Ro 16:25 [f] 1Co 2:10
3:4 [g] 2Co 11:6
3:5 [h] Ro 16:26
3:6 [i] Gal 3:29 [j] Eph 2:15,16
3:7 [k] 1Co 3:5 [l] Eph 1:19
3:8 [m] 1Co 15:9
3:9 [n] Ro 16:25
3:10 [o] 1Co 2:7 [p] 1Pe 1:12 [q] Eph 1:21
3:12 [r] Eph 2:18 [s] Heb 4:16
3:14 [t] Php 2:10
3:16 [u] Col 1:11 [v] Ro 7:22
3:17 [w] Jn 14:23 [x] Col 1:23
3:18 [y] Job 11:8,9
3:19 [z] Col 2:10 [a] Eph 1:23
3:20 [b] Ro 16:25
3:21 [c] Ro 11:36

Chapter 4 Theme ______________________

4 As a prisoner[a] for the Lord, then, I urge you to live a life worthy[b] of the calling you have received. 2 Be completely humble
and gentle; be patient, bearing with one another[c] in love.[d] 3 Make
every effort to keep the unity[e] of the Spirit through the bond of
peace. 4 There is one body and one Spirit[f]—just as you were called
to one hope when you were called— 5 one Lord, one faith, one baptism; 6 one God and Father of all, who is over all and through all
and in all.[g]

7 But to each one of us[h] grace has been given[i] as Christ apportioned
it. 8 This is why it[a] says:

> "When he ascended on high,
> he led captives[j] in his train
> and gave gifts to men."[b][k]

9 (What does "he ascended" mean except that he also descended to
the lower, earthly regions[c]? 10 He who descended is the very one who
ascended higher than all the heavens, in order to fill the whole universe.) 11 It was he who gave some to be apostles,[l] some to be
prophets, some to be evangelists,[m] and some to be pastors and
teachers, 12 to prepare God's people for works of service, so that the
body of Christ[n] may be built up 13 until we all reach unity[o] in the faith
and in the knowledge of the Son of God and become mature,[p] attaining to the whole measure of the fullness of Christ.

14 Then we will no longer be infants,[q] tossed back and forth by
the waves,[r] and blown here and there by every wind of teaching
and by the cunning and craftiness of men in their deceitful scheming.[s] 15 Instead, speaking the truth in love, we will in all things grow
up into him who is the Head,[t] that is, Christ. 16 From him the whole
body, joined and held together by every supporting ligament,
grows[u] and builds itself up in love, as each part does its work.

17 So I tell you this, and insist on it in the Lord, that you must no
longer live as the Gentiles do, in the futility of their thinking.[v] 18 They
are darkened in their understanding[w] and separated from the life
of God[x] because of the ignorance that is in them due to the hard-
ening of their hearts.[y] 19 Having lost all sensitivity,[z] they have giv-
en themselves over[a] to sensuality[b] so as to indulge in every kind of
impurity, with a continual lust for more.

20 You, however, did not come to know Christ that way. 21 Surely
you heard of him and were taught in him in accordance with the
truth that is in Jesus. 22 You were taught, with regard to your former
way of life, to put off[c] your old self,[d] which is being corrupted by
its deceitful desires; 23 to be made new in the attitude of your minds;[e]

4:1 [a]Eph 3:1 [b]Php 1:27; Col 1:10
4:2 [c]Col 3:12,13 [d]Eph 1:4
4:3 [e]Col 3:14
4:4 [f]1Co 12:13
4:6 [g]Ro 11:36
4:7 [h]1Co 12:7,11 [i]Ro 12:3
4:8 [j]Col 2:15 [k]Ps 68:18
4:11 [l]1Co 12:28 [m]Ac 21:8
4:12 [n]1Co 12:27
4:13 [o]ver 3,5 [p]Col 1:28
4:14 [q]1Co 14:20 [r]Jas 1:6 [s]Eph 6:11
4:15 [t]Eph 1:22
4:16 [u]Col 2:19
4:17 [v]Ro 1:21
4:18 [w]Ro 1:21 [x]Eph 2:12 [y]2Co 3:14
4:19 [z]1Ti 4:2 [a]Ro 1:24 [b]Col 3:5
4:22 [c]1Pe 2:1 [d]Ro 6:6
4:23 [e]Col 3:10

[a]8 Or *God* [b]8 Psalm 68:18 [c]9 Or *the depths of the earth*

[24]and to put on the new self,[a] created to be like God in true righteousness and holiness.[b]
[25]Therefore each of you must put off falsehood and speak truth-
fully[c] to his neighbor, for we are all members of one body.[d] [26]"In
your anger do not sin"[a]: Do not let the sun go down while you are
still angry, [27]and do not give the devil a foothold. [28]He who has been
stealing must steal no longer, but must work,[e] doing something
useful with his own hands,[f] that he may have something to share
with those in need.[g]
[29]Do not let any unwholesome talk come out of your mouths,[h]
but only what is helpful for building others up according to their
needs, that it may benefit those who listen. [30]And do not grieve
the Holy Spirit of God,[i] with whom you were sealed for the day of
redemption.[j] [31]Get rid of all bitterness, rage and anger, brawling
and slander, along with every form of malice.[k] [32]Be kind and compassionate to one another, forgiving each other, just as in Christ
God forgave you.[l]

Chapter 5 Theme ______________________

5 Be imitators of God,[m] therefore, as dearly loved children [2]and
live a life of love, just as Christ loved us and gave himself up for
us[n] as a fragrant offering and sacrifice to God.[o]
[3]But among you there must not be even a hint of sexual immorality,
or of any kind of impurity, or of greed,[p] because these are improper
for God's holy people. [4]Nor should there be obscenity, foolish talk
or coarse joking, which are out of place, but rather thanksgiving.[q]
[5]For of this you can be sure: No immoral, impure or greedy person—
such a man is an idolater[r]—has any inheritance in the kingdom
of Christ and of God.[b][s] [6]Let no one deceive you with empty
words, for because of such things God's wrath[t] comes on those
who are disobedient. [7]Therefore do not be partners with them.
[8]For you were once[u] darkness, but now you are light in the
Lord. Live as children of light[v] [9](for the fruit[w] of the light consists
in all goodness, righteousness and truth) [10]and find out what
pleases the Lord. [11]Have nothing to do with the fruitless deeds of
darkness, but rather expose them. [12]For it is shameful even to mention what the disobedient do in secret. [13]But everything exposed by
the light[x] becomes visible, [14]for it is light that makes everything visible. This is why it is said:

> "Wake up, O sleeper,[y]
> rise from the dead,[z]
> and Christ will shine on you."[a]

a26 Psalm 4:4 b5 Or *kingdom of the Christ and God*

4:24 [a]Ro 6:4 [b]Eph 2:10
4:25 [c]Zec 8:16 [d]Ro 12:5
4:28 [e]Ac 20:35 [f]1Th 4:11 [g]Lk 3:11
4:29 [h]Col 3:8
4:30 [i]1Th 5:19 [j]Ro 8:23
4:31 [k]Col 3:8
4:32 [l]Mt 6:14,15
5:1 [m]Lk 6:36
5:2 [n]Gal 1:4 [o]2Co 2:15; Heb 7:27
5:3 [p]Col 3:5
5:4 [q]ver 20
5:5 [r]Col 3:5 [s]1Co 6:9
5:6 [t]Ro 1:18
5:8 [u]Eph 2:2 [v]Lk 16:8
5:9 [w]Gal 5:22
5:13 [x]Jn 3:20,21
5:14 [y]Ro 13:11 [z]Jn 5:25 [a]Isa 60:1

15Be very careful, then, how you live—not as unwise but as wise,
16making the most of every opportunity,[a] because the days are evil.[b]
17Therefore do not be foolish, but understand what the Lord's will
is.[c] 18Do not get drunk on wine,[d] which leads to debauchery. Instead,
be filled with the Spirit.[e] 19Speak to one another with psalms, hymns
and spiritual songs.[f] Sing and make music in your heart to the
Lord, 20always giving thanks[g] to God the Father for everything, in
the name of our Lord Jesus Christ.
21Submit to one another[h] out of reverence for Christ.
22Wives, submit to your husbands[i] as to the Lord.[j] 23For the husband is the head of the wife as Christ is the head of the church,[k] his
body, of which he is the Savior. 24Now as the church submits to Christ,
so also wives should submit to their husbands in everything.
25Husbands, love your wives,[l] just as Christ loved the church and
gave himself up for her[m] 26to make her holy, cleansing[a] her by the
washing[n] with water through the word, 27and to present her to himself as a radiant church, without stain or wrinkle or any other
blemish, but holy and blameless.[o] 28In this same way, husbands
ought to love their wives[p] as their own bodies. He who loves his wife
loves himself. 29After all, no one ever hated his own body, but he
feeds and cares for it, just as Christ does the church— 30for we are
members of his body.[q] 31"For this reason a man will leave his father
and mother and be united to his wife, and the two will become one
flesh."[b][r] 32This is a profound mystery—but I am talking about
Christ and the church. 33However, each one of you also must love his
wife[s] as he loves himself, and the wife must respect her husband.

Chapter 6 Theme ______________________________

6 Children, obey your parents in the Lord, for this is right.[t]
2"Honor your father and mother"—which is the first commandment with a promise— 3"that it may go well with you and
that you may enjoy long life on the earth."[c][u]
4Fathers, do not exasperate your children;[v] instead, bring them
up in the training and instruction of the Lord.[w]
5Slaves, obey your earthly masters with respect[x] and fear, and
with sincerity of heart,[y] just as you would obey Christ.[z] 6Obey
them not only to win their favor when their eye is on you, but like
slaves of Christ, doing the will of God from your heart. 7Serve wholeheartedly, as if you were serving the Lord, not men,[a] 8because you
know that the Lord will reward everyone for whatever good he
does,[b] whether he is slave or free.
9And masters, treat your slaves in the same way. Do not threaten
them, since you know that he who is both their Master and yours[c]
is in heaven, and there is no favoritism with him.

5:16 [a]Col 4:5 [b]Eph 6:13
5:17 [c]Ro 12:2; 1Th 4:3
5:18 [d]Pr 20:1 [e]Lk 1:15
5:19 [f]Ac 16:25; Col 3:16
5:20 [g]Ps 34:1
5:21 [h]Gal 5:13
5:22 [i]Ge 3:16; 1Pe 3:1,5,6 [j]Eph 6:5
5:23 [k]1Co 11:3; Eph 1:22
5:25 [l]Col 3:19 [m]ver 2
5:26 [n]Ac 22:16
5:27 [o]Eph 1:4; Col 1:22
5:28 [p]ver 25
5:30 [q]1Co 12:27
5:31 [r]Ge 2:24; Mt 19:5; 1Co 6:16
5:33 [s]ver 25
6:1 [t]Col 3:20
6:3 [u]Ex 20:12
6:4 [v]Col 3:21 [w]Ge 18:19; Dt 6:7
6:5 [x]1Ti 6:1 [y]Col 3:22 [z]Eph 5:22
6:7 [a]Col 3:23
6:8 [b]Col 3:24
6:9 [c]Job 31:13,14

[a]26 Or *having cleansed* [b]31 Gen. 2:24 [c]3 Deut. 5:16

[10]Finally, be strong in the Lord[a] and in his mighty power.[b] [11]Put on
the full armor of God[c] so that you can take your stand against the
devil's schemes. [12]For our struggle is not against flesh and blood, but
against the rulers, against the authorities,[d] against the powers[e] of this
dark world and against the spiritual forces of evil in the heavenly
realms.[f] [13]Therefore put on the full armor of God, so that when the
day of evil comes, you may be able to stand your ground, and after
you have done everything, to stand. [14]Stand firm then, with the belt
of truth buckled around your waist,[g] with the breastplate of righteousness in place,[h] [15]and with your feet fitted with the readiness that
comes from the gospel of peace.[i] [16]In addition to all this, take up the
shield of faith,[j] with which you can extinguish all the flaming arrows
of the evil one. [17]Take the helmet of salvation[k] and the sword of the
Spirit, which is the word of God.[l] [18]And pray in the Spirit on all occasions[m] with all kinds of prayers and requests.[n] With this in mind, be
alert and always keep on praying for all the saints.

[19]Pray also for me,[o] that whenever I open my mouth, words may
be given me so that I will fearlessly[p] make known the mystery of the
gospel, [20]for which I am an ambassador[q] in chains.[r] Pray that I may
declare it fearlessly, as I should.

[21]Tychicus,[s] the dear brother and faithful servant in the Lord, will
tell you everything, so that you also may know how I am and what
I am doing. [22]I am sending him to you for this very purpose, that
you may know how we are,[t] and that he may encourage you.

[23]Peace[u] to the brothers, and love with faith from God the Father
and the Lord Jesus Christ. [24]Grace to all who love our Lord Jesus
Christ with an undying love.

6:10 [a] 1Co 16:13 [b] Eph 1:19
6:11 [c] Ro 13:12
6:12 [d] Eph 1:21 [e] Ro 8:38 [f] Eph 1:3
6:14 [g] Isa 11:5 [h] Isa 59:17
6:15 [i] Isa 52:7
6:16 [j] 1Jn 5:4
6:17 [k] Isa 59:17 [l] Heb 4:12
6:18 [m] Lk 18:1 [n] Mt 26:41; Php 1:4
6:19 [o] 1Th 5:25 [p] Ac 4:29; 2Co 3:12
6:20 [q] 2Co 5:20 [r] Ac 21:33
6:21 [s] Ac 20:4
6:22 [t] Col 4:7-9
6:23 [u] Gal 6:16; 1Pe 5:14

EPHESIANS OBSERVATIONS CHART

OUR WEALTH AND POSITION IN CHRIST

(contin

EPHESIANS OBSERVATIONS CHART

OUR RELATIONSHIP WITH THE HOLY SPIRIT

OUR FORMER LIFESTYLE

THE WAY WE LIVE IN CHRIST

EPHESIANS AT A GLANCE

eme of Ephesians:

SEGMENT DIVISIONS

thor:

te:

rpose:

y Words:

every reference to God, in Christ (in him, in the Lord)

the (Holy) Spirit

rich(es)

in the heavenly realms

former (formerly, used to, at one time, once)

grace, benefit

power (strength)

body (church)

redemption

live (do)

mark every reference to the devil (including powers, rulers, authorities, etc.)

		CHAPTER THEMES
		1
		2
		3
		4
		5
		6

PHILIPPIANS

Blocked by the Spirit of God from going into Asia and Bithynia, Paul had a vision of a man from Macedonia asking him to come to Macedonia and help the churches there.

Confident that God had given him direction, Paul sailed with Timothy and Luke from Troas on a second missionary journey. Philippi, in Macedonia, basked in the fact that it was also a Roman colony which ensured its citizens all the benefits of Roman citizenship.

As was his custom, when Paul reached a city he sought out the Jews. While there were not enough Jews living in Philippi to form a synagogue, the Jews there met for prayer on the Sabbath. Little did Paul realize that he would end up in prison. God knew there was a Roman jailer and his family who needed Jesus.

The events of that day inaugurated the beginning of the church at Philippi, the church Paul addressed as he took pen in hand around the year A.D. 61 or 62.

Things to Do

1. Familiarize yourself with the message of Philippians by reading the entire book in one sitting. As you read, look for the verses in chapters 1 and 4 which tell where Paul is as he writes.

2. To understand the historical setting of Philippians, read Acts 15:35 through 17:1, which records Paul's first visit to Philippi. After his third missionary journey, Paul went to Jerusalem, where he was arrested. From there Paul was taken by a Roman guard to Caesarea, the Mediterranean seaport where the Roman consulate often went to escape the heat and confines of Jerusalem. After remaining a prisoner in Caesarea for over two years, Paul, who as a Roman citizen had appealed to Caesar, was sent to Rome, where he lived under house arrest. Read Acts 28:14-31 and note how long Paul remained a prisoner at Rome. How does this compare with where Paul was when he wrote Philippians?

3. As you read Philippians chapter by chapter, do the following.
   a. Under "Author" on your OBSERVATIONS CHART on page 2021 note where Paul is, why he is there, and what his attitude is in the midst of his difficult circumstances.
   b. In a distinctive way, mark in the text each key word (and its synonyms and pronouns) that is listed on the PHILIPPIANS AT A GLANCE chart on page 2023. This will help you discover the themes (main subjects) of each chapter and of the book itself. Watch for other key words which are not listed but which may be emphasized in a particular chapter of Philippians.
   c. In the margin list what you learn from the text about each of the key words in Philippians.
   d. Record any other observations as instructed and demonstrated in the observation section in "How to Use The International Inductive Study Bible" on page IISB-15.
   e. List each of the instructions Paul gives to the Philippian saints on the chart PAUL'S INSTRUCTIONS TO THE PHILIPPIANS on page 2022. As you list these instructions, evaluate your life in the light of each one.

4. On PHILIPPIANS AT A GLANCE:
   a. Fill in the theme for the book and for each chapter. (Be sure you also record the chapter theme in the text next to the chapter number.)
   b. Under "Segment Divisions" record what you see to be Paul's example in each chapter. Remember, in Philippians 3:17 Paul tells his readers to follow his example.
   c. In the next column under "Segment Divisions" write down what each chapter says about who or what Jesus Christ is in relation to the believer.

d. For another segment division, record a command to believers that correlates with the theme of each chapter.

Things to Think About

1. What have you learned from Philippians about your relationship to suffering as a Christian? How is it going to affect the way you respond to suffering?
2. Can you say with Paul, "For to me, to live is Christ and to die is gain"? If you can't, think about what has replaced Christ's rightful place in your life.
3. What have you learned from Jesus' example that you can apply to your own life? Do you have the attitude of Christ in respect to God and others? Do you regard others as more important than yourself?
4. Do you allow your circumstances to affect your peace? What is keeping you from his peace? After reading Philippians 4 do you see any way to handle life's anxieties?
5. What have you learned about your own needs and sharing with others in need?

Chapter 1 Theme ____________________

1 Paul and Timothy,[a] servants of Christ Jesus,
To all the saints[b] in Christ Jesus at Philippi,[c] together with the
overseers[a][d] and deacons:[e]

2 Grace and peace to you from God our Father and the Lord Jesus
Christ.[f]

3 I thank my God every time I remember you.[g] 4 In all my prayers
for all of you, I always pray[h] with joy 5 because of your partnership[i]
in the gospel from the first day[j] until now, 6 being confident of this,
that he who began a good work in you will carry it on to completion until the day of Christ Jesus.[k]

7 It is right[l] for me to feel this way about all of you, since I have you
in my heart;[m] for whether I am in chains[n] or defending[o] and confirming the gospel, all of you share in God's grace with me. 8 God can
testify[p] how I long for all of you with the affection of Christ Jesus.

9 And this is my prayer: that your love[q] may abound more and
more in knowledge and depth of insight, 10 so that you may be able
to discern what is best and may be pure and blameless until the
day of Christ,[r] 11 filled with the fruit of righteousness[s] that comes
through Jesus Christ—to the glory and praise of God.

12 Now I want you to know, brothers, that what has happened to
me has really served to advance the gospel. 13 As a result, it has
become clear throughout the whole palace guard[b] and to everyone else that I am in chains[t] for Christ. 14 Because of my chains,[u]
most of the brothers in the Lord have been encouraged to speak
the word of God more courageously and fearlessly.

1:1 [a] Ac 16:1; 2Co 1:1 [b] Ac 9:13 [c] Ac 16:12 [d] 1Ti 3:1 [e] 1Ti 3:8
1:2 [f] Ro 1:7
1:3 [g] Ro 1:8
1:4 [h] Ro 1:10
1:5 [i] Ac 2:42; Php 4:15 [j] Ac 16:12-40
1:6 [k] ver 10; 1Co 1:8
1:7 [l] 2Pe 1:13 [m] 2Co 7:3 [n] ver 13,14,17; Ac 21:33 [o] ver 16
1:8 [p] Ro 1:9
1:9 [q] 1Th 3:12
1:10 [r] ver 6; 1Co 1:8
1:11 [s] Jas 3:18
1:13 [t] ver 7,14,17
1:14 [u] ver 7,13,17

[a] 1 Traditionally *bishops* [b] 13 Or *whole palace*

15 It is true that some preach Christ out of envy and rivalry, but
others out of goodwill. 16 The latter do so in love, knowing that I am
put here for the defense of the gospel.[a] 17 The former preach Christ
out of selfish ambition,[b] not sincerely, supposing that they can stir
up trouble for me while I am in chains.[a][c] 18 But what does it matter?
The important thing is that in every way, whether from false motives
or true, Christ is preached. And because of this I rejoice.

Yes, and I will continue to rejoice, 19 for I know that through your
prayers[d] and the help given by the Spirit of Jesus Christ,[e] what has
happened to me will turn out for my deliverance.[b] 20 I eagerly expect[f]
and hope that I will in no way be ashamed, but will have sufficient
courage[g] so that now as always Christ will be exalted in my body,[h]
whether by life or by death.[i] 21 For to me, to live is Christ[j] and to die
is gain. 22 If I am to go on living in the body, this will mean fruitful
labor for me. Yet what shall I choose? I do not know! 23 I am torn
between the two: I desire to depart[k] and be with Christ,[l] which is
better by far; 24 but it is more necessary for you that I remain in the
body. 25 Convinced of this, I know that I will remain, and I will continue with all of you for your progress and joy in the faith, 26 so that
through my being with you again your joy in Christ Jesus will overflow on account of me.

27 Whatever happens, conduct yourselves in a manner worthy[m] of
the gospel of Christ. Then, whether I come and see you or only hear
about you in my absence, I will know that you stand firm[n] in one
spirit, contending[o] as one man for the faith of the gospel 28 without
being frightened in any way by those who oppose you. This is a sign
to them that they will be destroyed, but that you will be saved—and
that by God. 29 For it has been granted to you[p] on behalf of Christ not
only to believe on him, but also to suffer[q] for him, 30 since you are
going through the same struggle[r] you saw[s] I had, and now hear[t]
that I still have.

Chapter 2 Theme

2 If you have any encouragement from being united with Christ,
if any comfort from his love, if any fellowship with the Spirit,[u]
if any tenderness and compassion,[v] 2 then make my joy complete[w]
by being like-minded,[x] having the same love, being one[y] in spirit
and purpose. 3 Do nothing out of selfish ambition or vain conceit,[z]
but in humility consider others better than yourselves.[a] 4 Each of
you should look not only to your own interests, but also to the interests of others.

5 Your attitude should be the same as that of Christ Jesus:[b]

a *16,17* Some late manuscripts have verses 16 and 17 in reverse order. b *19* Or *salvation*

1:16 [a] ver 7,12
1:17 [b] Php 2:3 [c] ver 7,13,14
1:19 [d] 2Co 1:11 [e] Ac 16:7
1:20 [f] Ro 8:19 [g] ver 14 [h] 1Co 6:20 [i] Ro 14:8
1:21 [j] Gal 2:20
1:23 [k] 2Ti 4:6 [l] Jn 12:26; 2Co 5:8
1:27 [m] Eph 4:1 [n] 1Co 16:13 [o] Jude 3
1:29 [p] Mt 5:11,12 [q] Ac 14:22
1:30 [r] Col 2:1; 1Th 2:2 [s] Ac 16:19-40 [t] ver 13
2:1 [u] 2Co 13:14 [v] Col 3:12
2:2 [w] Jn 3:29 [x] Php 4:2 [y] Ro 12:16
2:3 [z] Gal 5:26 [a] Ro 12:10; 1Pe 5:5
2:5 [b] Mt 11:29

2:6 [a]Jn 1:1 [b]Jn 5:18
2:7 [c]Mt 20:28 [d]Jn 1:14; Heb 2:17
2:8 [e]Mt 26:39; Jn 10:18; Heb 5:8
2:9 [f]Ac 2:33; Heb 2:9 [g]Eph 1:20,21
2:10 [h]Ro 14:11 [i]Mt 28:18
2:11 [j]Jn 13:13
2:12 [k]2Co 7:15
2:13 [l]Ezr 1:5
2:14 [m]1Co 10:10; 1Pe 4:9
2:15 [n]Mt 5:45,48; Eph 5:1 [o]Ac 2:40
2:16 [p]1Th 2:19
2:17 [q]2Ti 4:6 [r]Ro 15:16
2:19 [s]ver 23
2:20 [t]1Co 16:10
2:21 [u]1Co 10:24; 13:5
2:22 [v]1Co 4:17; 1Ti 1:2
2:23 [w]ver 19
2:24 [x]Php 1:25
2:25 [y]Php 4:3 [z]Phm 2 [a]Php 4:18
2:26 [b]Php 1:8

6 Who, being in very nature[a] God,[a]
did not consider equality with God[b] something to
be grasped,
7 but made himself nothing,
taking the very nature[b] of a servant,[c]
being made in human likeness.[d]
8 And being found in appearance as a man,
he humbled himself
and became obedient to death[e]—
even death on a cross!
9 Therefore God exalted him[f] to the highest place
and gave him the name that is above every name,[g]
10 that at the name of Jesus every knee should bow,[h]
in heaven and on earth and under the earth,[i]
11 and every tongue confess that Jesus Christ is Lord,[j]
to the glory of God the Father.

12 Therefore, my dear friends, as you have always obeyed—not
only in my presence, but now much more in my absence—continue
to work out your salvation with fear and trembling,[k] 13 for it is God
who works in you[l] to will and to act according to his good purpose.
14 Do everything without complaining[m] or arguing, 15 so that you
may become blameless and pure, children of God[n] without fault in
a crooked and depraved generation,[o] in which you shine like stars
in the universe 16 as you hold out[c] the word of life—in order that I
may boast on the day of Christ that I did not run or labor for nothing.[p] 17 But even if I am being poured out like a drink offering[q] on the
sacrifice[r] and service coming from your faith, I am glad and rejoice
with all of you. 18 So you too should be glad and rejoice with me.
19 I hope in the Lord Jesus to send Timothy to you soon,[s] that I also
may be cheered when I receive news about you. 20 I have no one else
like him,[t] who takes a genuine interest in your welfare. 21 For everyone looks out for his own interests,[u] not those of Jesus Christ. 22 But
you know that Timothy has proved himself, because as a son with
his father[v] he has served with me in the work of the gospel. 23 I
hope, therefore, to send him as soon as I see how things go with
me.[w] 24 And I am confident[x] in the Lord that I myself will come soon.
25 But I think it is necessary to send back to you Epaphroditus, my
brother, fellow worker[y] and fellow soldier,[z] who is also your messenger, whom you sent to take care of my needs.[a] 26 For he longs for all
of you[b] and is distressed because you heard he was ill. 27 Indeed he
was ill, and almost died. But God had mercy on him, and not on
him only but also on me, to spare me sorrow upon sorrow. 28 Therefore I am all the more eager to send him, so that when you see him

[a] 6 Or *in the form of* [b] 7 Or *the form* [c] 16 Or *hold on to*

again you may be glad and I may have less anxiety. 29Welcome him
in the Lord with great joy, and honor men like him,[a] 30because he
almost died for the work of Christ, risking his life to make up for
the help you could not give me.[b]

Chapter 3 Theme ______________________

3 Finally, my brothers, rejoice in the Lord! It is no trouble for me
to write the same things to you again, and it is a safeguard for
you.

2Watch out for those dogs,[c] those men who do evil, those muti-
lators of the flesh. 3For it is we who are the circumcision,[d] we who
worship by the Spirit of God, who glory in Christ Jesus, and who
put no confidence in the flesh— 4though I myself have reasons for
such confidence.

If anyone else thinks he has reasons to put confidence in the flesh,
I have more: 5circumcised[e] on the eighth day, of the people of Israel,[f]
of the tribe of Benjamin,[g] a Hebrew of Hebrews; in regard to the
law, a Pharisee;[h] 6as for zeal, persecuting the church;[i] as for legalistic righteousness,[j] faultless.

7But whatever was to my profit I now consider loss[k] for the sake of
Christ. 8What is more, I consider everything a loss compared to the
surpassing greatness of knowing[l] Christ Jesus my Lord, for whose
sake I have lost all things. I consider them rubbish, that I may gain
Christ 9and be found in him, not having a righteousness of my
own that comes from the law,[m] but that which is through faith in
Christ—the righteousness that comes from God and is by faith.[n] 10I
want to know Christ and the power of his resurrection and the
fellowship of sharing in his sufferings,[o] becoming like him in his
death,[p] 11and so, somehow, to attain to the resurrection[q] from
the dead.

12Not that I have already obtained all this, or have already been
made perfect,[r] but I press on to take hold[s] of that for which Christ
Jesus took hold of me.[t] 13Brothers, I do not consider myself yet to
have taken hold of it. But one thing I do: Forgetting what is
behind[u] and straining toward what is ahead, 14I press on[v] toward
the goal to win the prize for which God has called[w] me heaven-
ward in Christ Jesus.

15All of us who are mature[x] should take such a view of things.[y]
And if on some point you think differently, that too God will make
clear to you. 16Only let us live up to what we have already attained.

17Join with others in following my example,[z] brothers, and take
note of those who live according to the pattern we gave you. 18For,
as I have often told you before and now say again even with tears,[a]
many live as enemies of the cross of Christ.[b] 19Their destiny is destruction, their god is their stomach,[c] and their glory is in their

2:29 [a] 1Co 16:18; 1Ti 5:17
2:30 [b] 1Co 16:17
3:2 [c] Ps 22:16,20
3:3 [d] Ro 2:28,29; Gal 6:15; Col 2:11
3:5 [e] Lk 1:59 [f] 2Co 11:22 [g] Ro 11:1 [h] Ac 23:6
3:6 [i] Ac 8:3 [j] Ro 10:5
3:7 [k] Mt 13:44; Lk 14:33
3:8 [l] Eph 4:13; 2Pe 1:2
3:9 [m] Ro 10:5 [n] Ro 9:30
3:10 [o] Ro 8:17 [p] Ro 6:3-5
3:11 [q] Rev 20:5,6
3:12 [r] 1Co 13:10 [s] 1Ti 6:12 [t] Ac 9:5,6
3:13 [u] Lk 9:62
3:14 [v] Heb 6:1 [w] Ro 8:28
3:15 [x] 1Co 2:6 [y] Gal 5:10
3:17 [z] 1Co 4:16; 1Pe 5:3
3:18 [a] Ac 20:31 [b] Gal 6:12
3:19 [c] Ro 16:18

shame.[a] Their mind is on earthly things.[b] 20 But our citizenship[c] is
in heaven.[d] And we eagerly await a Savior from there, the Lord Jesus
Christ,[e] 21 who, by the power[f] that enables him to bring everything under his control, will transform our lowly bodies[g] so that
they will be like his glorious body.[h]

Chapter 4 Theme ________________________

4 Therefore, my brothers, you whom I love and long for,[i] my joy
and crown, that is how you should stand firm[j] in the Lord,
dear friends!

2 I plead with Euodia and I plead with Syntyche to agree with
each other[k] in the Lord. 3 Yes, and I ask you, loyal yokefellow,[a] help
these women who have contended at my side in the cause of the
gospel, along with Clement and the rest of my fellow workers, whose
names are in the book of life.

4 Rejoice in the Lord always. I will say it again: Rejoice![l] 5 Let your
gentleness be evident to all. The Lord is near.[m] 6 Do not be anxious about anything,[n] but in everything, by prayer and petition,
with thanksgiving, present your requests to God.[o] 7 And the peace
of God,[p] which transcends all understanding, will guard your
hearts and your minds in Christ Jesus.

8 Finally, brothers, whatever is true, whatever is noble, whatever is
right, whatever is pure, whatever is lovely, whatever is admirable—
if anything is excellent or praiseworthy—think about such things.
9 Whatever you have learned or received or heard from me, or seen
in me—put it into practice.[q] And the God of peace[r] will be with you.

10 I rejoice greatly in the Lord that at last you have renewed your
concern for me.[s] Indeed, you have been concerned, but you had no
opportunity to show it. 11 I am not saying this because I am in need,
for I have learned to be content[t] whatever the circumstances. 12 I
know what it is to be in need, and I know what it is to have plenty.
I have learned the secret of being content in any and every situation,
whether well fed or hungry,[u] whether living in plenty or in want.[v] 13 I
can do everything through him who gives me strength.[w]

14 Yet it was good of you to share[x] in my troubles. 15 Moreover, as
you Philippians know, in the early days[y] of your acquaintance
with the gospel, when I set out from Macedonia, not one church
shared with me in the matter of giving and receiving, except you
only;[z] 16 for even when I was in Thessalonica,[a] you sent me aid again
and again when I was in need.[b] 17 Not that I am looking for a gift,
but I am looking for what may be credited to your account.[c] 18 I
have received full payment and even more; I am amply supplied,
now that I have received from Epaphroditus[d] the gifts you sent. They
are a fragrant[e] offering, an acceptable sacrifice, pleasing to God.

3:19 [a]Ro 6:21 [b]Ro 8:5,6
3:20 [c]Eph 2:19 [d]Col 3:1 [e]1Co 1:7
3:21 [f]Eph 1:19 [g]1Co 15:43-53 [h]Col 3:4
4:1 [i]Php 1:8 [j]1Co 16:13; Php 1:27
4:2 [k]Php 2:2
4:4 [l]Ro 12:12; Php 3:1
4:5 [m]Heb 10:37; Jas 5:8,9
4:6 [n]Mt 6:25-34 [o]Eph 6:18
4:7 [p]Isa 26:3; Jn 14:27; Col 3:15
4:9 [q]Php 3:17 [r]Ro 15:33
4:10 [s]2Co 11:9
4:11 [t]1Ti 6:6,8
4:12 [u]1Co 4:11 [v]2Co 11:9
4:13 [w]2Co 12:9
4:14 [x]Php 1:7
4:15 [y]Php 1:5 [z]2Co 11:8,9
4:16 [a]Ac 17:1 [b]1Th 2:9
4:17 [c]1Co 9:11,12
4:18 [d]Php 2:25 [e]2Co 2:14

[a]3 Or *loyal Syzygus*

[19]And my God will meet all your needs[a] according to his glorious
riches[b] in Christ Jesus.
[20]To our God and Father[c] be glory for ever and ever. Amen.[d]

[21]Greet all the saints in Christ Jesus. The brothers who are with
me[e] send greetings. [22]All the saints[f] send you greetings, especially
those who belong to Caesar's household.
[23]The grace of the Lord Jesus Christ[g] be with your spirit. Amen.[a]

[a] 23 Some manuscripts do not have *Amen.*

4:19 [a]Ps 23:1; 2Co 9:8 [b]Ro 2:4
4:20 [c]Gal 1:4 [d]Ro 11:36
4:21 [e]Gal 1:2
4:22 [f]Ac 9:13
4:23 [g]Ro 16:20

Philippians Observations Chart

ɪTHOR: *Look for both pronouns and direct references*

HE RECIPIENTS: *Look for* the saints, brothers, dear friends, you, *or any other ways Paul addresses those to whom he is writing.*
ɛemember to keep asking the five W's and an H: How does Paul describe the Philippians? What are their problems? What is his
ɪncern for them? Why is Paul writing to the Philippians?)

(continued)

Philippians Observations Chart

Paul's Instructions to the Philippians

(contin

Paul's Instructions to the Philippians

Philippians at a Glance

eme of Philippians:

hor:

te:

pose:

Words:

Christ Jesus

oy (rejoice, be lad)

ke-minded, hink(s) attitude, take uch a view of hings)

ospel

Segment Divisions

Command To:	Jesus Is:	Paul's Example		Chapter Themes
	1:21 My Life		1	
			2	
3:17 Follow Paul's Example			3	
		4:11 Learned to Be Content in His Circumstances	4	

COLOSSIANS

Colosse was located twelve miles from Laodicea and about a hundred miles east of Ephesus in the valley of the Lycus River in the southern part of ancient Phrygia, the adopted home of Oriental mysticism. Many Jews, Phrygians, and Greeks came to Colosse because it was on a main trade route. The mixture of backgrounds made the city an interesting cultural center where all sorts of new ideas and doctrines from the East were discussed and considered.

With all these ungodly influences, it is no wonder that the Christians at Colosse were on Paul's heart during his imprisonment in Rome. He may never have seen their faces, but they belonged to his Christ and he was one with them in spirit. Physically he might be bound by chains, but he could reach them by letter. This was one way he could protect them from the wolves who were out to devour God's flock.

Paul wrote sometime around A.D. 62. This letter to the faithful saints at Colosse was one whose message would be needed down through the ages. Maybe that is one of the reasons God didn't let Paul deliver this message in person.

~ THINGS TO DO

1. As you read Colossians chapter by chapter, learn all you can from the text about the author and the recipients and discover why the author writes what he does to this particular church. This will give you the key to understanding Colossians. Following this simple procedure will help:
   a. As you read, ask the five W's and an H: Who? What? Where? Why? When? and How? Ask questions such as: Who wrote this? To whom? Where were they? What were these people like? What were their situations? What were their problems? When was this written? What seemed to be going on? Why did the author say what he did?

      Asking questions like these—answered only from what the text says—gives insight into a book of the Bible and helps you to understand the context and purpose of the book and to keep its teachings and truths in their proper context.
   b. As you read, watch for every reference to the author(s) (including names and pronouns such as *I, my, we, us*). Keep asking the five W's and an H and record your insights on the OBSERVATIONS CHART on pages 2031, 2032.
   c. Look for pronouns such as *you* and note the relationship between the author and the recipients. Ask questions such as: How did the gospel get to the Colossians? Who preached the gospel to them? What was the author's main concern for the Colossians? The answers will help you understand why this letter was written. Record your insights on the OBSERVATIONS CHART.
2. Now read through Colossians again, a chapter at a time. As you read:
   a. Mark in the text the key words and phrases that are listed on the COLOSSIANS AT A GLANCE chart on page 2032. Be sure to mark the synonyms and pronouns for each key word, and also mark every reference to Jesus: *with him, by him, for him, through him,* and so on.
   b. In the margin, list what you learn from marking *in him,* and from marking other key words.
   c. Also record any other observations of the text as instructed in the observation section of "How to Use The International Inductive Study Bible" on page IISB-15.
3. When you get to chapter 2, note the warnings in this chapter by looking for the phrases *see to it* and *do not let anyone.*
   a. Record these warnings along with any instructions on the OBSERVATIONS CHART.

b. With these warnings in mind read the section called "Understanding Gnosticism" on page 2204.

4. Proceed through chapters 3 and 4, adding pertinent information to your OBSERVATIONS CHART.

5. Be sure to record the theme of the book and of each chapter on the COLOSSIANS AT A GLANCE chart. Remember to record the chapter theme in the text next to the chapter number. Also fill out the date the book was written, the name of the author, and his purpose for writing.

Things to Think About

1. What are you pursuing? Does it have eternal value? Is it drawing you closer to God or keeping you from time alone with God in prayer and in studying the Word? Are you seeking things above or earthly things?

2. Are you being deluded with any modern-day philosophies or traditions which contradict the Word or aren't in the Word? Any legalistic rules which are not clearly taught in the New Testament? Any mystical teachings or prophecies that can't be supported in the Word of God or that have a tendency to add something which isn't there or which seem to be only for an elite group of people?

3. Inductive Bible study is not easy. The enemy will do all he can to keep you from knowing God and his Word intimately, for it is your major defense and offense in spiritual warfare. Are you going to make it your goal to let the Word of Christ richly dwell within you and to walk in its precepts?

4. Are you proclaiming the Lord Jesus Christ and holding firmly to all he is and all that you have in him as he is presented in Colossians?

5. As you have studied Colossians, have you seen any areas in your life in which you are falling short or simply walking in disobedience to God's Word? What are you going to do about these?

1:1 [a]1Co 1:1 *Chapter 1 Theme* ______________________
[b]2Co 1:1 1 Paul, an apostle[a] of Christ Jesus by the will of God,[b] and Tim-
1:2 othy our brother,
[c]Col 4:18 [d]Ro 1:7 [2]To the holy and faithful[a] brothers in Christ at Colosse:
1:3 [e]Ro 1:8 Grace[c] and peace to you from God our Father.[b][d]
1:4 [3]We always thank God,[e] the Father of our Lord Jesus Christ,
[f]Gal 5:6 when we pray for you, [4]because we have heard of your faith in
[g]Eph 1:15 Christ Jesus and of the love[f] you have for all the saints[g]— [5]the
1:5 [h]1Th 5:8; faith and love that spring from the hope[h] that is stored up for you
Tit 1:2 [i]1Pe 1:4 in heaven[i] and that you have already heard about in the word of
truth, the gospel [6]that has come to you. All over the world[j] this
1:6 [j]Ro 10:18 gospel is bearing fruit[k] and growing, just as it has been doing
[k]Jn 15:16 among you since the day you heard it and understood God's
1:7 grace in all its truth. [7]You learned it from Epaphras,[l] our dear fel-
[l]Phm 23 low servant, who is a faithful minister[m] of Christ on our[c] behalf,
[m]Col 4:7 [8]and who also told us of your love in the Spirit.[n]
1:8 [n]Ro 15:30 [9]For this reason, since the day we heard about you,[o] we have

1:9 [o]Eph 1:15

[a]2 Or *believing* [b]2 Some manuscripts *Father and the Lord Jesus Christ* [c]7 Some manuscripts *your*

not stopped praying for you and asking God to fill you with the
knowledge of his will[a] through all spiritual wisdom and understanding.[b] 10 And we pray this in order that you may live a life worthy[c] of the Lord and may please him in every way: bearing fruit in
every good work, growing in the knowledge of God, 11 being
strengthened with all power[d]
according to his glorious
might so that you may have
great endurance and pa-
tience,[e] and joyfully 12 giving
thanks to the Father,[f] who
has qualified you[a] to share in
the inheritance[g] of the saints
in the kingdom of light.
13 For he has rescued us from
the dominion of darkness[h]
and brought us into the kingdom[i] of the Son he loves,[j]
14 in whom we have redemption,[b][k] the forgiveness of sins.[l]

Colosse

15 He is the image[m] of the invisible God,[n] the firstborn over all
creation. 16 For by him all things were created:[o] things in heaven
and on earth, visible and invisible, whether thrones or powers or
rulers or authorities;[p] all things were created by him and for him.[q]
17 He is before all things,[r] and in him all things hold together.
18 And he is the head[s] of the body, the church; he is the beginning
and the firstborn from among the dead,[t] so that in everything he
might have the supremacy. 19 For God was pleased[u] to have all his
fullness[v] dwell in him, 20 and through him to reconcile[w] to himself
all things, whether things on earth or things in heaven,[x] by making peace through his blood,[y] shed on the cross.

21 Once you were alienated from God and were enemies[z] in your
minds[a] because of[c] your evil behavior. 22 But now he has reconciled you by Christ's physical body[b] through death to present you
holy in his sight, without blemish and free from accusation[c]— 23 if
you continue in your faith, established[d] and firm, not moved from
the hope[e] held out in the gospel. This is the gospel that you heard
and that has been proclaimed to every creature under heaven,[f] and
of which I, Paul, have become a servant.[g]

24 Now I rejoice in what was suffered for you, and I fill up in my
flesh what is still lacking in regard to Christ's afflictions,[h] for the
sake of his body, which is the church. 25 I have become its servant[i]
by the commission God gave me[j] to present to you the word of
God in its fullness— 26 the mystery[k] that has been kept hidden for

1:9 [a] Eph 5:17 [b] Eph 1:17
1:10 [c] Eph 4:1
1:11 [d] Eph 3:16 [e] Eph 4:2
1:12 [f] Eph 5:20 [g] Ac 20:32
1:13 [h] Ac 26:18 [i] Eph 6:12; 2Pe 1:11 [j] Mt 3:17
1:14 [k] Ro 3:24 [l] Eph 1:7
1:15 [m] 2Co 4:4 [n] Jn 1:18
1:16 [o] Jn 1:3 [p] Eph 1:20,21 [q] Ro 11:36
1:17 [r] Jn 1:2
1:18 [s] Eph 1:22 [t] Ac 26:23; Rev 1:5
1:19 [u] Eph 1:5 [v] Jn 1:16
1:20 [w] 2Co 5:18 [x] Eph 1:10 [y] Eph 2:13
1:21 [z] Ro 5:10 [a] Eph 2:3
1:22 [b] Ro 7:4 [c] Eph 5:27
1:23 [d] Eph 3:17 [e] ver 5 [f] Ro 10:18 [g] ver 25; 1Co 3:5
1:24 [h] 2Co 1:5
1:25 [i] ver 23 [j] Eph 3:2
1:26 [k] Ro 16:25

[a] *12* Some manuscripts *us* [b] *14* A few late manuscripts *redemption through his blood*
[c] *21* Or *minds, as shown by*

ages and generations, but is now disclosed to the saints. 27 To them
God has chosen to make known[a] among the Gentiles the glorious
riches of this mystery, which is Christ in you, the hope of glory.
28 We proclaim him, admonishing[b] and teaching everyone with
all wisdom,[c] so that we may present everyone perfect[d] in Christ.
29 To this end I labor,[e] struggling[f] with all his energy, which so
powerfully works in me.[g]

Chapter 2 Theme Fullness of Christ who is the Head

2 I want you to know how much I am struggling[h] for you and
for those at Laodicea,[i] and for all who have not met me personally. 2 My purpose is that they may be encouraged in heart[j] and
united in love, so that they may have the full riches of complete
understanding, in order that they may know the mystery of God,
namely, Christ, 3 in whom are hidden all the treasures of wisdom
and knowledge.[k] 4 I tell you this so that no one may deceive you by
fine-sounding arguments.[l] 5 For though I am absent from you in
body, I am present with you in spirit[m] and delight to see how
orderly[n] you are and how firm[o] your faith in Christ is.
6 So then, just as you received Christ Jesus as Lord,[p] continue to
live in him, 7 rooted[q] and built up in him, strengthened in the
faith as you were taught, and overflowing with thankfulness.
8 See to it that no one takes you captive through hollow and
deceptive philosophy,[r] which depends on human tradition and
the basic principles of this world[s] rather than on Christ.
9 For in Christ all the fullness of the Deity lives in bodily form,
10 and you have been given fullness in Christ, who is the head[t]
over every power and authority. 11 In him you were also circumcised,[u] in the putting off of the sinful nature,[a][v] not with a circumcision done by the hands of men but with the circumcision
done by Christ, 12 having been buried with him in baptism and
raised with him[w] through your faith in the power of God, who
raised him from the dead.[x]
13 When you were dead in your sins[y] and in the uncircumcision
of your sinful nature,[b] God made you[c] alive with Christ. He forgave us all our sins, 14 having canceled the written code, with its
regulations,[z] that was against us and that stood opposed to us; he
took it away, nailing it to the cross.[a] 15 And having disarmed the
powers and authorities,[b] he made a public spectacle of them, triumphing over them[c] by the cross.[d]
16 Therefore do not let anyone judge you[d] by what you eat or
drink,[e] or with regard to a religious festival,[f] a New Moon celebration[g] or a Sabbath day.[h] 17 These are a shadow of the things

1:27 [a] Mt 13:11
1:28 [b] Col 3:16 [c] 1Co 2:6,7 [d] Eph 5:27
1:29 [e] 1Co 15:10 [f] Col 2:1 [g] Eph 1:19
2:1 [h] Col 1:29; 4:12 [i] Rev 1:11
2:2 [j] Col 4:8
2:3 [k] Ro 11:33; 1Co 1:24,30
2:4 [l] Ro 16:18
2:5 [m] 1Th 2:17 [n] 1Co 14:40 [o] 1Pe 5:9
2:6 [p] Col 1:10
2:7 [q] Eph 3:17
2:8 [r] 1Ti 6:20 [s] Gal 4:3
2:10 [t] Eph 1:22
2:11 [u] Ro 2:29; Php 3:3 [v] Gal 5:24
2:12 [w] Ro 6:5 [x] Ac 2:24
2:13 [y] Eph 2:1,5
2:14 [z] Eph 2:15 [a] 1Pe 2:24
2:15 [b] Eph 6:12 [c] Lk 10:18
2:16 [d] Ro 14:3,4 [e] Ro 14:17 [f] Ro 14:5 [g] 1Ch 23:31 [h] Gal 4:10

[a] 11 Or *the flesh* [b] 13 Or *your flesh* [c] 13 Some manuscripts *us* [d] 15 Or *them in him*

that were to come;[a] the reality, however, is found in Christ. 18Do
not let anyone who delights in false humility[b] and the worship of
angels disqualify you for the prize.[c] Such a person goes into great
detail about what he has seen, and his unspiritual mind puffs him
up with idle notions. 19He has lost connection with the Head,[d]
from whom the whole body, supported and held together by its
ligaments and sinews, grows as God causes it to grow.[e]

20Since you died with Christ to the basic principles of this
world,[f] why, as though you still belonged to it, do you submit to
its rules:[g] 21"Do not handle! Do not taste! Do not touch!"? 22These
are all destined to perish[h] with use, because they are based on
human commands and teachings.[i] 23Such regulations indeed have
an appearance of wisdom, with their self-imposed worship, their
false humility and their harsh treatment of the body, but they lack
any value in restraining sensual indulgence.

Chapter 3 Theme _________________________________

3 Since, then, you have been raised with Christ, set your hearts
on things above, where Christ is seated at the right hand of
God. 2Set your minds on things above, not on earthly things.[j] 3For
you died,[k] and your life is now hidden with Christ in God. 4When
Christ, who is your[a] life, appears,[l] then you also will appear with
him in glory.[m]

5Put to death, therefore, whatever belongs to your earthly
nature: sexual immorality, impurity, lust, evil desires and greed,[n]
which is idolatry.[o] 6Because of these, the wrath of God[p] is coming.[b] 7You used to walk in these ways, in the life you once lived.[q]
8But now you must rid yourselves[r] of all such things as these:
anger, rage, malice, slander,[s] and filthy language from your lips.[t]
9Do not lie to each other,[u] since you have taken off your old self
with its practices 10and have put on the new self, which is being
renewed[v] in knowledge in the image of its Creator.[w] 11Here there
is no Greek or Jew,[x] circumcised or uncircumcised,[y] barbarian,
Scythian, slave or free,[z] but Christ is all,[a] and is in all.

12Therefore, as God's chosen people, holy and dearly loved,
clothe yourselves with compassion, kindness, humility,[b] gentleness and patience.[c] 13Bear with each other[d] and forgive whatever
grievances you may have against one another. Forgive as the Lord
forgave you.[e] 14And over all these virtues put on love,[f] which
binds them all together in perfect unity.[g]

15Let the peace of Christ[h] rule in your hearts, since as members
of one body you were called to peace. And be thankful. 16Let the
word of Christ[i] dwell in you richly as you teach and admonish

[a]4 Some manuscripts *our* [b]6 Some early manuscripts *coming on those who are disobedient*

2:17 [a]Heb 8:5
2:18 [b]ver 23 [c]Php 3:14
2:19 [d]Eph 1:22 [e]Eph 4:16
2:20 [f]Gal 4:3,9 [g]ver 14,16
2:22 [h]1Co 6:13 [i]Isa 29:13; Mt 15:9; Tit 1:14
3:2 [j]Php 3:19,20
3:3 [k]Ro 6:2; 2Co 5:14
3:4 [l]1Co 1:7 [m]1Pe 1:13; 1Jn 3:2
3:5 [n]Eph 5:3 [o]Eph 5:5
3:6 [p]Ro 1:18
3:7 [q]Eph 2:2
3:8 [r]Eph 4:22 [s]Eph 4:31 [t]Eph 4:29
3:9 [u]Eph 4:22,25
3:10 [v]Ro 12:2; Eph 4:23 [w]Eph 2:10
3:11 [x]Ro 10:12 [y]1Co 7:19 [z]Gal 3:28 [a]Eph 1:23
3:12 [b]Php 2:3 [c]2Co 6:6; Gal 5:22,23
3:13 [d]Eph 4:2 [e]Eph 4:32
3:14 [f]1Co 13:1-13 [g]Eph 4:3
3:15 [h]Jn 14:27
3:16 [i]Ro 10:17

one another with all wisdom,[a] and as you sing psalms, hymns
and spiritual songs with gratitude in your hearts to God.[b] 17 And
whatever you do,[c] whether in word or deed, do it all in the name
of the Lord Jesus, giving thanks[d] to God the Father through him.
18 Wives, submit to your husbands,[e] as is fitting in the Lord.
19 Husbands, love your wives and do not be harsh with them.
20 Children, obey your parents in everything, for this pleases the
Lord.
21 Fathers, do not embitter your children, or they will become
discouraged.
22 Slaves, obey your earthly masters in everything; and do it, not
only when their eye is on you and to win their favor, but with sincerity of heart and reverence for the Lord. 23 Whatever you do,
work at it with all your heart, as working for the Lord, not for
men, 24 since you know that you will receive an inheritance[f] from
the Lord as a reward. It is the Lord Christ you are serving. 25 Anyone who does wrong will be repaid for his wrong, and there is no
favoritism.[g]

Chapter 4 Theme ______________________________

4 Masters, provide your slaves with what is right and fair,
because you know that you also have a Master in heaven.
2 Devote yourselves to prayer,[h] being watchful and thankful.
3 And pray for us, too, that God may open a door[i] for our message,
so that we may proclaim the mystery of Christ, for which I am in
chains.[j] 4 Pray that I may proclaim it clearly, as I should. 5 Be wise[k]
in the way you act toward outsiders;[l] make the most of every
opportunity.[m] 6 Let your conversation be always full of grace,[n] sea-
soned with salt,[o] so that you may know how to answer everyone.[p]
7 Tychicus[q] will tell you all the news about me. He is a dear brother, a faithful minister and fellow servant[r] in the Lord. 8 I am sending him to you for the express purpose that you may know about
our[a] circumstances and that he may encourage your hearts.[s] 9 He is
coming with Onesimus,[t] our faithful and dear brother, who is one
of you. They will tell you everything that is happening here.
10 My fellow prisoner Aristarchus[u] sends you his greetings, as
does Mark, the cousin of Barnabas.[v] (You have received instructions about him; if he comes to you, welcome him.) 11 Jesus, who
is called Justus, also sends greetings. These are the only Jews
among my fellow workers for the kingdom of God, and they have
proved a comfort to me. 12 Epaphras,[w] who is one of you and a
servant of Christ Jesus, sends greetings. He is always wrestling in
prayer for you,[x] that you may stand firm in all the will of God,

3:16 [a] Col 1:28 [b] Eph 5:19
3:17 [c] 1Co 10:31 [d] Eph 5:20
3:18 [e] Eph 5:22
3:24 [f] Ac 20:32
3:25 [g] Ac 10:34
4:2 [h] Lk 18:1
4:3 [i] Ac 14:27 [j] Eph 6:19,20
4:5 [k] Eph 5:15 [l] Mk 4:11 [m] Eph 5:16
4:6 [n] Eph 4:29 [o] Mk 9:50 [p] 1Pe 3:15
4:7 [q] Ac 20:4 [r] Eph 6:21,22
4:8 [s] Eph 6:21,22
4:9 [t] Phm 10
4:10 [u] Ac 19:29 [v] Ac 4:36
4:12 [w] Col 1:7; Phm 23 [x] Ro 15:30

[a] 8 Some manuscripts *that he may know about your*

mature[a] and fully assured. 13I vouch for him that he is working
hard for you and for those at Laodicea[b] and Hierapolis. 14Our
dear friend Luke,[c] the doctor, and Demas[d] send greetings. 15Give
my greetings to the brothers at Laodicea, and to Nympha and the
church in her house.[e]

16After this letter has been read to you, see that it is also read[f]
in the church of the Laodiceans and that you in turn read the letter from Laodicea.

17Tell Archippus:[g] "See to it that you complete the work you
have received in the Lord."[h]

18I, Paul, write this greeting in my own hand.[i] Remember[j] my
chains. Grace be with you.[k]

4:18 [i] 1Co 16:21 [j] Heb 13:3 [k] 1Ti 6:21; 2Ti 4:22; Tit 3:15; Heb 13:25

4:12 [a] 1Co 2:6
4:13 [b] Col 2:1
4:14 [c] 2Ti 4:11; Phm 24 [d] 2Ti 4:10
4:15 [e] Ro 16:5
4:16 [f] 2Th 3:14
4:17 [g] Phm 2 [h] 2Ti 4:5

Colossians Observations Chart

Author

Recipients

Warnings and Instructions

(continued)

COLOSSIANS OBSERVATIONS CHART

COLOSSIANS AT A GLANCE

Theme of Colossians:

SEGMENT DIVISIONS	CHAPTER THEMES
	1
	2
	3
	4

Author:

Date:

Purpose:

Key Words:

wisdom (wise)
know(ledge)
understanding
given fullness
all (every, grea
everything, ful
perfect, fullne
faith
mystery
in him, in Chr
(or in his sigh
through him,
etc.)

1 THESSALONIANS

Timothy joined Paul and Silas (Silvanus) while they were in Lystra on Paul's second missionary journey. Since his father was a Greek, Timothy hadn't been circumcised. There was no sense in causing any unnecessary conflicts with the Jews who were in those parts, so Paul had Timothy circumcised. Things went smoothly until Paul had his vision of a man from Macedonia appealing to him to come and help them.

Believing this call was of God, the three went to Philippi—and the persecution began. Paul and Silas were beaten with rods and thrown into prison. Undaunted and convinced of their heavenly commission, the trio traveled on through Amphipolis and Apollonia and came to Thessalonica. There they found a Jewish synagogue, where for three Sabbaths Paul reasoned with the Thessalonians from the Scriptures. Jews and Greeks, including a number of leading women, heard and believed. The other Jews became furious. Once again there was opposition, but this time the persecution was not directed only to the trio, but also to those who had believed.

Consequently, the Thessalonian believers sent Paul, Silas, and Timothy to Berea by night where again the gospel bore fruit. When the Jews of Thessalonica heard what happened in Berea, they couldn't bear it. They went to Berea to persecute the men who were upsetting the world.

From Berea Paul went to Athens, and from Athens to Corinth. But the church at Thessalonica was on his heart. How were they doing in the midst of such adamant opposition? Paul had to find out. So about A.D. 51, while in Corinth, Paul sat down to write his first epistle to the church at Thessalonica.

Things to Do

1. Read 1 Thessalonians chapter by chapter. Record the following information on the OBSERVATIONS CHART on page 2040. (Be sure to take your answers from the text.)

   a. List what you learn about the author(s). Look for the relationship of the author(s) to the recipients. In chapter 2, what comparisons are drawn to show how the author(s) feel about those to whom they are writing? Don't miss it.

   b. List everything you learn about the recipients. Who had they been serving? What happened when they heard and believed the gospel? What were they enduring?

   c. Note the different problems or concerns that are addressed in the letter.

2. Read through the book and mark in the text the key words (along with their synonyms and pronouns) listed on the 1 THESSALONIANS AT A GLANCE chart on page 2039. As you observe the key words, list in the margin everything you learn from the text about each word. List what you learn about *the coming of the Lord* in one place in the margin.

3. In chapters 4 and 5 are several truths about those "who have fallen asleep" and those "who are still alive and who are left." List what you observe from the text about each of these on the second page of the OBSERVATIONS CHART. As you do, note the progression of events in 1 Thessalonians 4:13-18. Ask the five W's and an H of the text: Who is involved? What will happen? Where will they meet the Lord? When? Why are they not to sorrow? How will all this happen?

4. Watch what you learn about "the day of the Lord" in chapter 5. Record this information on the chart THE DAY OF THE LORD beginning on page 2178.

5. On 1 THESSALONIANS AT A GLANCE, record the theme of the book. Then record the theme of each chapter on the chart and in the text next to the chapter number. Fill in any additional information under author, date, purpose, etc.

6. Often you will be able to note a turning point in the book because the subject being addressed will change. These topical changes divide the book into segments. Think through the following questions to see if you can determine a segment division in 1 Thessalonians.

   a. Where does the main subject of the book change?

   b. What is the topic in the first three chapters of the book?

   c. What does the subject become in the last two chapters?

   d. Title each segment of the book by thinking of the theme or subject discussed in the first three chapters and then in the last two. Record your segment divisions on 1 THESSALONIANS AT A GLANCE.

Things to Think About

1. In this book Paul pours his life into other men who could carry on the work of the gospel. Are you spending time imparting the things God has done in your life to another person who can in turn minister to others?

2. It is sometimes hard to give thanks in all things, yet that is the will of God. Go back over the last few days and think of the things that have happened in your life for which you have not given thanks. Determine in your heart to obey this command.

3. Are the circumstances in your life difficult? How are you responding? What will others say about your response? Can people imitate your walk with God?

4. Are you abstaining from sexual immorality? Are you defrauding others sexually in any way at all? Do you realize that if you are acting on your sexual passions in a way contrary to God's Word, God will act as the avenger against you?

5. Do you pray continually (5:17) for those in your life who don't know the Lord? Do you boldly approach the Lord for answers to your problems? Do you pray consistently for others?

Chapter 1 Theme ____________________________

1 Paul, Silas[a] and Timothy,[a]

To the church of the Thessalonians[b] in God the Father and the
Lord Jesus Christ:

Grace and peace to you.[bc]

2We always thank God for all of you,[d] mentioning you in our
prayers. 3We continually remember before our God and Father
your work produced by faith,[e] your labor prompted by love, and
your endurance inspired by hope in our Lord Jesus Christ.
4For we know, brothers loved by God, that he has chosen you,
5because our gospel[f] came to you not simply with words, but also
with power, with the Holy Spirit and with deep conviction. You
know how we lived among you for your sake. 6You became imitators of us[g] and of the Lord; in spite of severe suffering,[h] you welcomed the message with the joy given by the Holy Spirit.[i] 7And

1:1 [a]Ac 16:1; 2Th 1:1 [b]Ac 17:1 [c]Ro 1:7
1:2 [d]Ro 1:8
1:3 [e]2Th 1:11
1:5 [f]2Th 2:14
1:6 [g]1Co 4:16 [h]Ac 17:5-10 [i]Ac 13:52

a 1 Greek *Silvanus,* a variant of *Silas* b 1 Some early manuscripts *you from God our Father and the Lord Jesus Christ*

so you became a model to all the believers in Macedonia and
Achaia. 8 The Lord's message rang out from you not only in Macedonia and Achaia—your faith in God has become known everywhere.[a] Therefore we do not need to say anything about it,
9 for they themselves report what kind of reception you gave us.
They tell how you turned to God from idols[b] to serve the living
and true God, 10 and to wait for his Son from heaven, whom he
raised from the dead[c]—Jesus, who rescues us from the coming
wrath.[d]

Chapter 2 Theme ____________________

2 You know, brothers, that our visit to you[e] was not a failure.
2 We had previously suffered[f] and been insulted in Philippi,
as you know, but with the help of our God we dared to tell you his
gospel in spite of strong opposition. 3 For the appeal we make
does not spring from error or impure motives,[g] nor are we trying
to trick you. 4 On the contrary, we speak as men approved by God
to be entrusted with the gospel.[h] We are not trying to please men[i]
but God, who tests our hearts. 5 You know we never used flattery,
nor did we put on a mask to cover up greed[j]—God is our witness.[k] 6 We were not looking for praise from men, not from you or
anyone else.

As apostles[l] of Christ we could have been a burden to you, 7 but
we were gentle among you, like a mother caring for her little children.[m] 8 We loved you so much that we were delighted to share with
you not only the gospel of God but our lives as well,[n] because you
had become so dear to us. 9 Surely you remember, brothers, our toil
and hardship; we worked[o] night and day in order not to be a burden to anyone[p] while we preached the gospel of God to you.

10 You are witnesses,[q] and so is God, of how holy,[r] righteous and
blameless we were among you who believed. 11 For you know that
we dealt with each of you as a father deals with his own children,[s]
12 encouraging, comforting and urging you to live lives worthy[t] of
God, who calls you into his kingdom and glory.

13 And we also thank God continually[u] because, when you
received the word of God,[v] which you heard from us, you accepted it not as the word of men, but as it actually is, the word of God,
which is at work in you who believe. 14 For you, brothers, became
imitators of God's churches in Judea,[w] which are in Christ Jesus:
You suffered from your own countrymen[x] the same things those
churches suffered from the Jews, 15 who killed the Lord Jesus[y] and
the prophets[z] and also drove us out. They displease God and are
hostile to all men 16 in their effort to keep us from speaking to the
Gentiles[a] so that they may be saved. In this way they always heap

1:8 [a] Ro 1:8; 10:18
1:9 [b] 1Co 12:2; Gal 4:8
1:10 [c] Ac 2:24 [d] Ro 5:9
2:1 [e] 1Th 1:5,9
2:2 [f] Ac 16:22; Php 1:30
2:3 [g] 2Co 2:17
2:4 [h] Gal 2:7 [i] Gal 1:10
2:5 [j] Ac 20:33 [k] Ro 1:9
2:6 [l] 1Co 9:1,2
2:7 [m] ver 11
2:8 [n] 2Co 12:15; 1Jn 3:16
2:9 [o] Ac 18:3 [p] 2Th 3:8
2:10 [q] 1Th 1:5 [r] 2Co 1:12
2:11 [s] ver 7; 1Co 4:14
2:12 [t] Eph 4:1
2:13 [u] 1Th 1:2 [v] Heb 4:12
2:14 [w] Gal 1:22 [x] Ac 17:5; 2Th 1:4
2:15 [y] Ac 2:23 [z] Mt 5:12
2:16 [a] Ac 13:45,50

up their sins to the limit.[a] The wrath of God has come upon them
at last.[a]
17But, brothers, when we were torn away from you for a short
time (in person, not in thought),[b] out of our intense longing we
made every effort to see you.[c] 18For we wanted to come to you—
certainly I, Paul, did, again and again—but Satan[d] stopped us.[e]
19For what is our hope, our joy, or the crown[f] in which we will glory[g]
in the presence of our Lord Jesus when he comes?[h] Is it not you?
20Indeed, you are our glory[i] and joy.

Chapter 3 Theme ______________________

3 So when we could stand it no longer,[j] we thought it best to be
left by ourselves in Athens.[k] 2We sent Timothy, who is our
brother and God's fellow worker[b] in spreading the gospel of Christ,
to strengthen and encourage you in your faith, 3so that no one
would be unsettled by these trials. You know quite well that we
were destined for them.[l] 4In fact, when we were with you, we kept
telling you that we would be persecuted. And it turned out that
way, as you well know.[m] 5For this reason, when I could stand it no
longer,[n] I sent to find out about your faith. I was afraid that in some
way the tempter[o] might have tempted you and our efforts might
have been useless.[p]
6But Timothy has just now come to us from you[q] and has brought
good news about your faith and love.[r] He has told us that you
always have pleasant memories of us and that you long to see us,
just as we also long to see you. 7Therefore, brothers, in all our distress and persecution we were encouraged about you because of
your faith. 8For now we really live, since you are standing firm[s] in
the Lord. 9How can we thank God enough for you[t] in return for all
the joy we have in the presence of our God because of you? 10Night
and day we pray[u] most earnestly that we may see you again[v] and
supply what is lacking in your faith.
11Now may our God and Father himself and our Lord Jesus clear
the way for us to come to you. 12May the Lord make your love
increase and overflow for each other[w] and for everyone else, just as
ours does for you. 13May he strengthen your hearts so that you will
be blameless[x] and holy in the presence of our God and Father
when our Lord Jesus comes[y] with all his holy ones.

Chapter 4 Theme ______________________

4 Finally, brothers,[z] we instructed you how to live in order to
please God,[a] as in fact you are living. Now we ask you and

a 16 Or *them fully* b 2 Some manuscripts *brother and fellow worker*; other manuscripts *brother and God's servant*

2:16 [a] Mt 23:32
2:17 [b] 1Co 5:3; Col 2:5 [c] 1Th 3:10
2:18 [d] Mt 4:10 [e] Ro 1:13; 15:22
2:19 [f] Php 4:1 [g] 2Co 1:14 [h] Mt 16:27; 1Th 3:13
2:20 [i] 2Co 1:14
3:1 [j] ver 5 [k] Ac 17:15
3:3 [l] Ac 9:16; 14:22
3:4 [m] 1Th 2:14
3:5 [n] ver 1 [o] Mt 4:3 [p] Gal 2:2; Php 2:16
3:6 [q] Ac 18:5 [r] 1Th 1:3
3:8 [s] 1Co 16:13
3:9 [t] 1Th 1:2
3:10 [u] 2Ti 1:3 [v] 1Th 2:17
3:12 [w] 1Th 4:9,10
3:13 [x] 1Co 1:8 [y] 1Th 2:19
4:1 [z] 2Co 13:11 [a] 2Co 5:9

urge you in the Lord Jesus to do this more and more. 2For you
know what instructions we gave you by the authority of the Lord
Jesus.

3It is God's will that you should be sanctified: that you should
avoid sexual immorality;[a] 4that each of you should learn to control his own body[a][b] in a way that is holy and honorable, 5not in
passionate lust[c] like the heathen,[d] who do not know God; 6and
that in this matter no one should wrong his brother or take
advantage of him.[e] The Lord will punish men for all such sins,[f] as
we have already told you and warned you. 7For God did not call
us to be impure, but to live a holy life.[g] 8Therefore, he who rejects
this instruction does not reject man but God, who gives you his
Holy Spirit.[h]

9Now about brotherly love[i] we do not need to write to you,[j] for
you yourselves have been taught by God to love each other.[k] 10And
in fact, you do love all the brothers throughout Macedonia.[l] Yet
we urge you, brothers, to do so more and more.[m]

11Make it your ambition to lead a quiet life, to mind your own
business and to work with your hands,[n] just as we told you, 12so
that your daily life may win the respect of outsiders[o] and so that
you will not be dependent on anybody.

13Brothers, we do not want you to be ignorant about those who
fall asleep, or to grieve like the rest of men, who have no hope.[p]
14We believe that Jesus died and rose again and so we believe that
God will bring with Jesus those who have fallen asleep in him.[q]
15According to the Lord's own word, we tell you that we who are
still alive, who are left till the coming of the Lord, will certainly not
precede those who have fallen asleep.[r] 16For the Lord himself will
come down from heaven, with a loud command, with the voice of
the archangel and with the trumpet call of God,[s] and the dead in
Christ will rise first.[t] 17After that, we who are still alive and are left[u]
will be caught up together with them in the clouds[v] to meet the
Lord in the air. And so we will be with the Lord[w] forever. 18There-
fore encourage each other with these words.

Chapter 5 Theme ________________

5 Now, brothers, about times and dates[x] we do not need to write
to you,[y] 2for you know very well that the day of the Lord[z] will
come like a thief in the night.[a] 3While people are saying, "Peace
and safety," destruction will come on them suddenly, as labor pains
on a pregnant woman, and they will not escape.

4But you, brothers, are not in darkness[b] so that this day should
surprise you like a thief. 5You are all sons of the light and sons of

4:3 [a]1Co 6:18
4:4 [b]1Co 7:2,9
4:5 [c]Ro 1:26 [d]Eph 4:17
4:6 [e]1Co 6:8 [f]Heb 13:4
4:7 [g]Lev 11:44; 1Pe 1:15
4:8 [h]Ro 5:5; Gal 4:6
4:9 [i]Ro 12:10 [j]1Th 5:1 [k]Jn 13:34
4:10 [l]1Th 1:7 [m]1Th 3:12
4:11 [n]Eph 4:28; 2Th 3:10-12
4:12 [o]Mk 4:11
4:13 [p]Eph 2:12
4:14 [q]1Co 15:18
4:15 [r]1Co 15:52
4:16 [s]Mt 24:31 [t]1Co 15:23; 2Th 2:1
4:17 [u]1Co 15:52 [v]Ac 1:9; Rev 11:12 [w]Jn 12:26
5:1 [x]Ac 1:7 [y]1Th 4:9
5:2 [z]1Co 1:8 [a]2Pe 3:10
5:4 [b]Ac 26:18; 1Jn 2:8

[a]4 Or *learn to live with his own wife*; or *learn to acquire a wife*

the day. We do not belong to the night or to the darkness. 6So then,
let us not be like others, who are asleep,[a] but let us be alert and self-
controlled. 7For those who sleep, sleep at night, and those who get
drunk, get drunk at night.[b] 8But since we belong to the day, let us
be self-controlled, putting on faith and love as a breastplate,[c] and
the hope of salvation[d] as a helmet.[e] 9For God did not appoint us to
suffer wrath but to receive salvation through our Lord Jesus
Christ.[f] 10He died for us so that, whether we are awake or asleep,
we may live together with him.[g] 11Therefore encourage one another and build each other up, just as in fact you are doing.

12Now we ask you, brothers, to respect those who work hard
among you, who are over you in the Lord[h] and who admonish
you. 13Hold them in the highest regard in love because of their
work. Live in peace with each other.[i] 14And we urge you, brothers,
warn those who are idle,[j] encourage the timid, help the weak,[k] be
patient with everyone. 15Make sure that nobody pays back wrong
for wrong,[l] but always try to be kind to each other[m] and to everyone else.

16Be joyful always;[n] 17pray continually; 18give thanks in all circumstances, for this is God's will for you in Christ Jesus.

The Word Sounds Forth from Thessalonica

5:6 [a]Ro 13:11
5:7 [b]Ac 2:15; 2Pe 2:13
5:8 [c]Eph 6:14 [d]Ro 8:24 [e]Eph 6:17
5:9 [f]2Th 2:13,14
5:10 [g]2Co 5:15
5:12 [h]1Ti 5:17; Heb 13:17
5:13 [i]Mk 9:50
5:14 [j]2Th 3:6,7,11 [k]Ro 14:1
5:15 [l]1Pe 3:9 [m]Gal 6:10; Eph 4:32
5:16 [n]Php 4:4

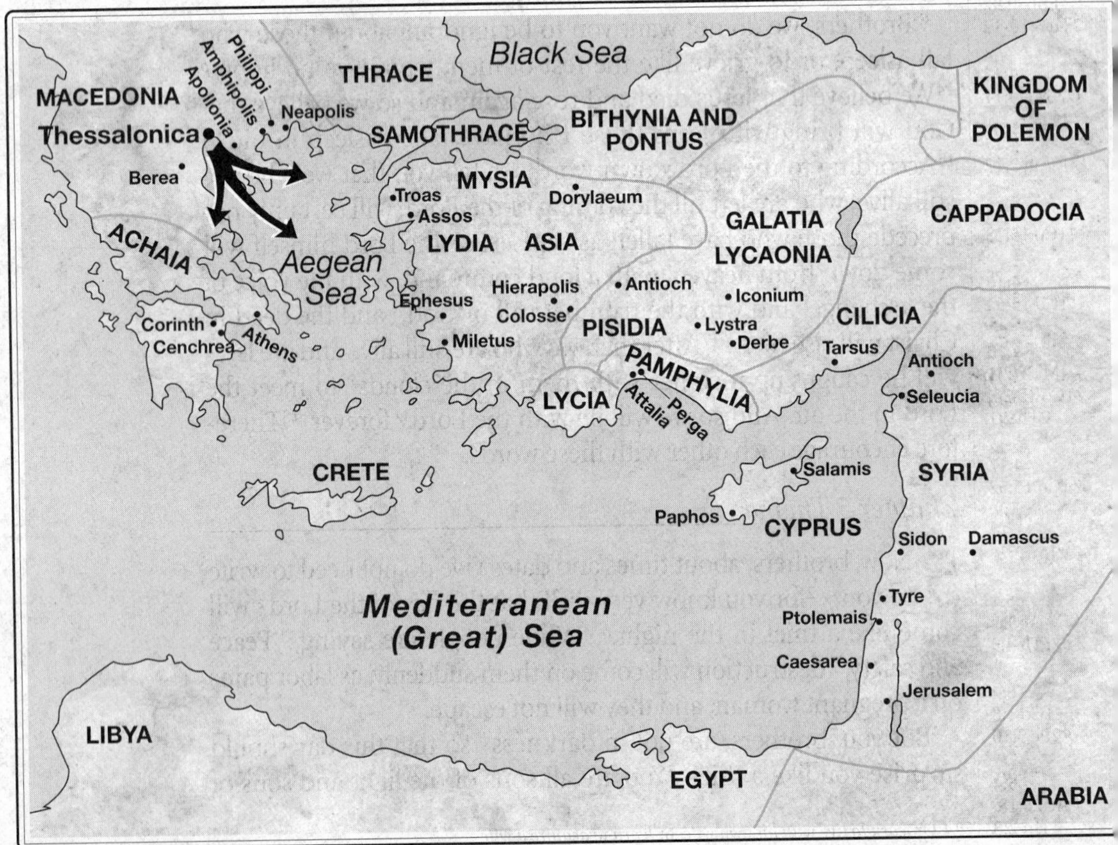

19 Do not put out the Spirit's fire;[a] 20 do not treat prophecies[b] with
contempt. 21 Test everything.[c] Hold on to the good. 22 Avoid every
kind of evil.
23 May God himself, the God of peace,[d] sanctify you through and
through. May your whole spirit, soul and body be kept blameless
at the coming of our Lord Jesus Christ. 24 The one who calls you is
faithful[e] and he will do it.

25 Brothers, pray for us.[f] 26 Greet all the brothers with a holy kiss.[g]
27 I charge you before the Lord to have this letter read to all the
brothers.[h]
28 The grace of our Lord Jesus Christ be with you.[i]

5:19 [a] Eph 4:30
5:20 [b] 1Co 14:1-40
5:21 [c] 1Co 14:29; 1Jn 4:1
5:23 [d] Ro 15:33
5:24 [e] 1Co 1:9
5:25 [f] Eph 6:19
5:26 [g] Ro 16:16
5:27 [h] Col 4:16 **5:28** [i] Ro 16:20

1 Thessalonians at a Glance

heme of 1 Thessalonians:

uthor:

ate:

rpose:

y Words:

gospel (word, words, message)
faith
ove
hope
ord Jesus Christ (any reference to Jesus)
God
Holy Spirit
e persecuted, ersecution suffering, uffered)
f the Lord
ay of the Lord

Segment Divisions	Chapter Themes
	1
	2
	3
	4
	5

1 Thessalonians Observations Chart

Author(s)

Who wrote 1 Thessalonians?

What relationship did these men have to one another?

Had they worked together before? If so, where? How? Why?

Describe the ministry these men had among the recipients.

Recipients

Who are they?

What was their relationship to the author(s)?

What was their condition when the author(s) first ministered to them? Who were they serving?

What conditions were they in when the letter was written?

How strongly did the author(s) feel about the recipients?

Did they think of them often? How do you know?

What comparisons show the kind of love the author(s) feel for them?

What had the recipients become?

Problems/Concerns/Struggles

(continu

1 Thessalonians 4:13-18

Those who have fallen asleep	Those who are alive and remain	Progression of events

2 THESSALONIANS

It had been four to six months since Paul wrote his first epistle in A.D. 51 to the church at Thessalonica. Their persecution had not subsided, but much to Paul's joy, his labor had not been in vain; they had withstood the attacks of the tempter.

However, Paul was concerned about some things in the church. Once again, during his second missionary journey he had to take time to write—and put his distinguishing mark on this letter. The church had to know without a doubt that it was from him.

THINGS TO DO

1. If you haven't studied 1 Thessalonians, you should do so before you begin 2 Thessalonians. However, if you have worked through 1 Thessalonians, then read it once again. Observe what Paul says about the coming of the Lord Jesus. Also give special attention to 1 Thessalonians 4:13 through 5:11.

2. Now read 2 Thessalonians. Watch how 1 Thessalonians ties in with 2 Thessalonians. Look for the following information and record it on the OBSERVATIONS CHART on page 2046.
   a. What do you learn about the author and the recipients of this letter? What are the circumstances of the recipients?
   b. Paul addresses several problems which need correction. List these in the margin and on the chart. This will help you see the author's purpose in writing. Then note the instructions or commands related to each problem addressed. List these on your OBSERVATIONS CHART.
   c. Paul also praises the Thessalonians and encourages them about the things they are doing well. List the exhortations he includes in his letter.
   d. Be certain you record what happens to those who do not obey the gospel.
   e. From what you have observed about the author and the recipients, why do you think Paul wrote this book? Record this on 2 THESSALONIANS AT A GLANCE on page 2047 under "Purpose."

3. Read through 2 Thessalonians again, a chapter at a time, and do the following:
   a. Mark in the text the key words (including their synonyms and pronouns) listed on 2 THESSALONIANS AT A GLANCE. Also watch for any words you feel are key but aren't listed.
   b. Now go back through the key words and in the margin make a list of what you have learned. Make one list for each word. In other words, you will have one list of everything these three chapters teach about *the coming of Christ*, one list for *trouble* and *suffering*, one list for *the day of the Lord*, and so on.

4. On the OBSERVATIONS CHART are two more headings: "When the Day of the Lord Comes" and "When the Man of Lawlessness Is Revealed."
   a. Carefully read 2 Thessalonians 2:1-12 and list everything the chapter says must happen before the day of the Lord can come.
   b. Do the same for the revelation of the man of lawlessness.
   c. Record your insights on the chart THE DAY OF THE LORD beginning on page 2178.

5. Think through each chapter and record its theme on 2 THESSALONIANS AT A GLANCE and in the appropriate place in the text. Also record the theme of the book, author, and date.

Things to Think About

1. How do you react to trials? How do you respond to persecution? Does your response glorify God? Do people see your faith? Is his love evident in your life?

2. Do you lead a disciplined life? Does your lifestyle encourage laziness in others? Or can you say, "Follow my example"? Are you doing your share for the furtherance of the kingdom, or are you just waiting for Jesus to come back?

3. When the good you do doesn't seem appreciated or even noticed, how do you feel? For whom are you doing it? Will you persevere?

4. Does what you believe about prophecy or any other doctrine come from a careful, personal study of God's Word, or is it from what others teach you? Are you holding fast to what you know of the Word of God, or are you easily persuaded by "faddish" teaching?

Chapter 1 Theme ______________________

1 Paul, Silas[a] and Timothy,[a]

To the church of the Thessalonians in God our Father and the
Lord Jesus Christ:

2 Grace and peace to you from God the Father and the Lord
Jesus Christ.[b]

3 We ought always to thank God for you, brothers, and rightly
so, because your faith is growing more and more, and the love
every one of you has for each other is increasing.[c] 4 Therefore,
among God's churches we boast[d] about your perseverance and
faith[e] in all the persecutions and trials you are enduring.[f]
5 All this is evidence[g] that God's judgment is right, and as a result
you will be counted worthy of the kingdom of God, for which you
are suffering. 6 God is just: He will pay back trouble to those who
trouble you[h] 7 and give relief to you who are troubled, and to us as
well. This will happen when the Lord Jesus is revealed from heav-
en in blazing fire with his powerful angels.[i] 8 He will punish those
who do not know God[j] and do not obey the gospel of our Lord
Jesus.[k] 9 They will be punished with everlasting destruction[l] and
shut out from the presence of the Lord and from the majesty of
his power[m] 10 on the day[n] he comes to be glorified[o] in his holy
people and to be marveled at among all those who have believed.
This includes you, because you believed our testimony to you.[p]
11 With this in mind, we constantly pray for you, that our God
may count you worthy[q] of his calling, and that by his power he
may fulfill every good purpose of yours and every act prompted
by your faith.[r] 12 We pray this so that the name of our Lord Jesus
may be glorified in you,[s] and you in him, according to the grace
of our God and the Lord Jesus Christ.[b]

1:1 [a] Ac 16:1; 1Th 1:1
1:2 [b] Ro 1:7
1:3 [c] 1Th 3:12
1:4 [d] 2Co 7:14 [e] 1Th 1:3 [f] 1Th 2:14
1:5 [g] Php 1:28
1:6 [h] Col 3:25; Rev 6:10
1:7 [i] 1Th 4:16; Jude 14
1:8 [j] Gal 4:8 [k] Ro 2:8
1:9 [l] Php 3:19; 2Pe 3:7 [m] 2Th 2:8
1:10 [n] 1Co 3:13 [o] Jn 17:10 [p] 1Co 1:6
1:11 [q] ver 5 [r] 1Th 1:3
1:12 [s] Php 2:9-11

[a] *1* Greek *Silvanus,* a variant of *Silas* [b] *12* Or *God and Lord, Jesus Christ*

Chapter 2 Theme ______________________________

2 Concerning the coming of our Lord Jesus Christ and our
being gathered to him,[a] we ask you, brothers, 2not to become
easily unsettled or alarmed by some prophecy, report or letter[b]
supposed to have come from us, saying that the day of the Lord[c]
has already come. 3Don't let anyone deceive you[d] in any way, for
⌊that day will not come⌋ until the rebellion occurs and the man of
lawlessness[a] is revealed,[e] the man doomed to destruction. 4He will
oppose and will exalt himself over everything that is called God[f]
or is worshiped, so that he sets himself up in God's temple, proclaiming himself to be God.[g]

5Don't you remember that when I was with you I used to tell
you these things? 6And now you know what is holding him back,
so that he may be revealed at the proper time. 7For the secret power
of lawlessness is already at work; but the one who now holds it
back will continue to do so till he is taken out of the way. 8And then
the lawless one will be revealed, whom the Lord Jesus will overthrow with the breath of his mouth[h] and destroy by the splendor
of his coming. 9The coming of the lawless one will be in accordance
with the work of Satan displayed in all kinds of counterfeit miracles, signs and wonders,[i] 10and in every sort of evil that deceives
those who are perishing.[j] They perish because they refused to
love the truth and so be saved. 11For this reason God sends them[k]
a powerful delusion so that they will believe the lie 12and so that
all will be condemned who have not believed the truth but have
delighted in wickedness.[l]

13But we ought always to thank God for you, brothers loved by
the Lord, because from the beginning God chose you[b][m] to be
saved[n] through the sanctifying work of the Spirit[o] and through
belief in the truth. 14He called you to this through our gospel, that
you might share in the glory of our Lord Jesus Christ. 15So then,
brothers, stand firm[p] and hold to the teachings[c] we passed on to
you,[q] whether by word of mouth or by letter.

16May our Lord Jesus Christ himself and God our Father, who
loved us[r] and by his grace gave us eternal encouragement and
good hope, 17encourage[s] your hearts and strengthen[t] you in
every good deed and word.

Chapter 3 Theme ______________________________

3 Finally, brothers,[u] pray for us[v] that the message of the Lord[w]
may spread rapidly and be honored, just as it was with you.
2And pray that we may be delivered from wicked and evil men,[x]

[a] 3 Some manuscripts *sin* [b] 13 Some manuscripts *because God chose you as his firstfruits*
[c] 15 Or *traditions*

2:1 [a] Mk 13:27; 1Th 4:15-17
2:2 [b] 2Th 3:17 [c] 1Co 1:8
2:3 [d] Eph 5:6-8 [e] Da 7:25; 8:25; 11:36; Rev 13:5,6
2:4 [f] 1Co 8:5 [g] Isa 14:13,14; Eze 28:2
2:8 [h] Isa 11:4; Rev 19:15
2:9 [i] Mt 24:24; Jn 4:48
2:10 [j] 1Co 1:18
2:11 [k] Ro 1:28
2:12 [l] Ro 1:32
2:13 [m] Eph 1:4 [n] 1Th 5:9 [o] 1Pe 1:2
2:15 [p] 1Co 16:13 [q] 1Co 11:2
2:16 [r] Jn 3:16
2:17 [s] 1Th 3:2 [t] 2Th 3:3
3:1 [u] 1Th 4:1 [v] 1Th 5:25 [w] 1Th 1:8
3:2 [x] Ro 15:31

for not everyone has faith. 3But the Lord is faithful,[a] and he will
strengthen and protect you from the evil one.[b] 4We have confidence[c] in the Lord that you are doing and will continue to do the
things we command. 5May the Lord direct your hearts[d] into God's
love and Christ's perseverance.

6In the name of the Lord Jesus Christ,[e] we command you,
brothers, to keep away from[f] every brother who is idle[g] and does
not live according to the teaching[a] you received from us.[h] 7For
you yourselves know how you ought to follow our example.[i] We
were not idle when we were with you, 8nor did we eat anyone's
food without paying for it. On the contrary, we worked[j] night
and day, laboring and toiling so that we would not be a burden to
any of you. 9We did this, not because we do not have the right to
such help,[k] but in order to make ourselves a model for you to follow.[l] 10For even when we were with you,[m] we gave you this rule:
"If a man will not work,[n] he shall not eat."

11We hear that some among you are idle. They are not busy;
they are busybodies.[o] 12Such people we command and urge in the
Lord Jesus Christ[p] to settle down and earn the bread they eat.[q]
13And as for you, brothers, never tire of doing what is right.[r]

14If anyone does not obey our instruction in this letter, take
special note of him. Do not associate with him,[s] in order that he
may feel ashamed. 15Yet do not regard him as an enemy, but warn
him as a brother.[t]

16Now may the Lord of peace[u] himself give you peace at all times
and in every way. The Lord be with all of you.[v]

17I, Paul, write this greeting in my own hand,[w] which is the distinguishing mark in all my letters. This is how I write.

18The grace of our Lord Jesus Christ be with you all.[x]

3:3 [a]1Co 1:9 [b]Mt 5:37
3:4 [c]2Co 2:3
3:5 [d]1Ch 29:18
3:6 [e]1Co 5:4 [f]Ro 16:17 [g]ver 7,11 [h]1Co 11:2
3:7 [i]1Co 4:16
3:8 [j]Ac 18:3; Eph 4:28
3:9 [k]1Co 9:4-14 [l]ver 7
3:10 [m]1Th 3:4 [n]1Th 4:11
3:11 [o]ver 6,7; 1Ti 5:13
3:12 [p]1Th 4:1 [q]1Th 4:11; Eph 4:28
3:13 [r]Gal 6:9
3:14 [s]ver 6
3:15 [t]Gal 6:1; 1Th 5:14
3:16 [u]Ro 15:33 [v]Ru 2:4
3:17 [w]1Co 16:21
3:18 [x]Ro 16:20

[a]6 Or *tradition*

2 Thessalonians Observations Chart

Author

Paul

Recipients

Those Who Do Not Obey the Gospel

Problems/Concerns

Instructions

Exhortations

When the Day of the Lord Comes

When the Man of Lawlessness Is Revealed

Theme of 2 Thessalonians:

Author: Paul

Date:

Purpose:

Key Words:

- trouble
- suffering (persecutions)
- coming of Jesus Christ (or synonymous references)
- God
- Spirit
- glory, majesty (glorified, honored)
- man of lawlessness
- idle
- day of the Lord (and pronouns)
- truth

SEGMENT DIVISIONS	CHAPTER THEMES
	1
	2
	3

1 TIMOTHY

Thirty years of labor for the gospel had taken its toll on Paul. His body bore the marks of a servant of Jesus Christ (see Galatians 6:17). However, the intensity of his sufferings was minor compared to the intensity of his love and concern for the churches etched upon his heart.

Undaunted by two years of house arrest in Rome, Paul pressed on toward the prize of the high calling in Christ Jesus. He intended to visit Asia, Macedonia, and possibly Spain. Spain had been on his heart before he became a prisoner of Rome.

He also was concerned about the church at Ephesus. Timothy, his faithful co-laborer, was pastoring that strategically important church. Possibly concerned that he might be delayed and that Timothy might need something in writing to set before others as an ever-present reminder, Paul took quill and ink, spread out the parchment, and wrote his first epistle to his beloved son in the faith, an epistle which would become a legacy for the church and a pillar and support of the truth. It was around A.D. 62.

Things to Do

1. Read 1 Timothy. Note 1:3 and 3:14, 15 to see why Paul wrote this epistle. Keep this in mind as you read the book. On the 1 TIMOTHY AT A GLANCE chart on page 2057, record Paul's purpose for writing.
2. Read 1 Timothy again, one chapter at a time. On your OBSERVATIONS CHART on pages 2055, 2056:
   a. Record how Paul describes himself. Note how he refers to himself, stating his position of authority which qualifies him to instruct Timothy in the matters described in this letter.
   b. Note how Paul describes Timothy, where Timothy is when the letter is written, and what his relationship is to Paul.
   c. Write down the commands and instructions Paul gives about specific groups of people or practices. Record what you learn about overseers (elders) and deacons. Also record what you see about general groups of believers in the church. There is a designated space for each of these groups on the OBSERVATIONS CHART.
   d. Record the specific charges Paul gives Timothy as his representative in Ephesus and as the one who is organizing and instructing the church there.
3. As you read, mark in the text the key words (and their synonyms and pronouns) that are listed on 1 TIMOTHY AT A GLANCE. These key words give clues about the most important and most often-mentioned instructions.
4. In the margin of the chapter, list everything you learn from the text about these key words. You can learn much about what was important to the health of the church.
5. What do you think is the theme of 1 Timothy? Are there any problems or concerns the author must address? How does the theme relate to these concerns? Record the theme of the book on 1 TIMOTHY AT A GLANCE and then list the theme of each chapter on the chart and also in the text. Finally, fill in any additional information under author, purpose, and so on.

Things to Think About

1. Do you operate in your own church according to these principles?
2. How do you esteem your local church leadership?
3. Do you pray on behalf of all men, including those in authority?

1:1 [a]Tit 1:3 [b]Col 1:27

Chapter 1 Theme ______________________________

1 Paul, an apostle of Christ Jesus by the command of God[a] our
Savior and of Christ Jesus our hope,[b]

1:2 [c]Ac 16:1 [d]2Ti 1:2; Tit 1:4

2 To Timothy[c] my true son[d] in the faith:

Grace, mercy and peace from God the Father and Christ Jesus
our Lord.

1:3 [e]Ac 18:19 [f]Gal 1:6,7

3 As I urged you when I went into Macedonia, stay there in Ephesus[e] so that you may com-
mand certain men not to
1:4 [g]1Ti 4:7; Tit 1:14 [h]1Ti 6:4
teach false doctrines[f] any
longer 4 nor to devote themselves to myths[g] and endless
genealogies. These promote
1:5 [i]2Ti 2:22 [j]2Ti 1:5
controversies[h] rather than
God's work—which is by
faith. 5 The goal of this com-
1:8 [k]Ro 7:12
mand is love, which comes
from a pure heart[i] and a
good conscience and a sin-
1:9 [l]Gal 3:19
cere faith.[j] 6 Some have wan-
dered away from these and turned to meaningless talk. 7 They
want to be teachers of the law, but they do not know what they
1:10 [m]2Ti 4:3; Tit 1:9
are talking about or what they so confidently affirm.
8 We know that the law is good[k] if one uses it properly. 9 We also
know that law[a] is made not for the righteous but for lawbreakers
1:11 [n]Gal 2:7
and rebels,[l] the ungodly and sinful, the unholy and irreligious; for
those who kill their fathers or mothers, for murderers, 10 for adulterers and perverts, for slave traders and liars and perjurers—and
1:12 [o]Php 4:13
for whatever else is contrary to the sound doctrine[m] 11 that con-
forms to the glorious gospel of the blessed God, which he entrusted
to me.[n]
1:13 [p]Ac 8:3 [q]Ac 26:9
12 I thank Christ Jesus our Lord, who has given me strength,[o] that
he considered me faithful, appointing me to his service. 13 Even
though I was once a blasphemer and a persecutor[p] and a violent
1:14 [r]Ro 5:20 [s]2Ti 1:13
man, I was shown mercy because I acted in ignorance and unbelief.[q] 14 The grace of our Lord was poured out on me abundantly,[r]
along with the faith and love that are in Christ Jesus.[s]
1:15 [t]1Ti 3:1; 2Ti 2:11; Tit 3:8
15 Here is a trustworthy saying[t] that deserves full acceptance:
Christ Jesus came into the world to save sinners—of whom I am
the worst. 16 But for that very reason I was shown mercy[u] so that in
me, the worst of sinners, Christ Jesus might display his unlimited
1:16 [u]ver 13
patience as an example for those who would believe on him and

To Timothy at Ephesus

[a]9 Or *that the law*

receive eternal life. 17Now to the King[a] eternal, immortal, invisible,[b] the only God, be honor and glory for ever and ever. Amen.[c]
18Timothy, my son, I give you this instruction in keeping with the
prophecies once made about you,[d] so that by following them you
may fight the good fight,[e] 19holding on to faith and a good conscience. Some have rejected these and so have shipwrecked their
faith.[f] 20Among them are Hymenaeus[g] and Alexander,[h] whom I
have handed over to Satan[i] to be taught not to blaspheme.

Chapter 2 Theme ______________________

2 I urge, then, first of all, that requests, prayers, intercession and
thanksgiving be made for everyone— 2for kings and all
those in authority,[j] that we may live peaceful and quiet lives in all
godliness and holiness. 3This is good, and pleases God our Savior,
4who wants[k] all men[l] to be saved and to come to a knowledge of
the truth.[m] 5For there is one God[n] and one mediator[o] between
God and men, the man Christ Jesus, 6who gave himself as a ransom for all men—the testimony[p] given in its proper time.[q] 7And
for this purpose I was appointed a herald and an apostle—I am
telling the truth, I am not lying—and a teacher[r] of the true faith
to the Gentiles.[s]
8I want men everywhere to lift up holy hands[t] in prayer, without anger or disputing.
9I also want women to dress modestly, with decency and propriety, not with braided hair or gold or pearls or expensive clothes,[u]
10but with good deeds, appropriate for women who profess to worship God.
11A woman should learn in quietness and full submission.[v] 12I do
not permit a woman to teach or to have authority over a man; she
must be silent. 13For Adam was formed first, then Eve.[w] 14And
Adam was not the one deceived; it was the woman who was
deceived and became a sinner.[x] 15But women[a] will be saved[b]
through childbearing—if they continue in faith, love[y] and holiness
with propriety.

Chapter 3 Theme ______________________

3 Here is a trustworthy saying:[z] If anyone sets his heart on being
an overseer,[c][a] he desires a noble task. 2Now the overseer must
be above reproach,[b] the husband of but one wife, temperate, self-
controlled, respectable, hospitable,[c] able to teach,[d] 3not given to
drunkenness, not violent but gentle, not quarrelsome,[e] not a
lover of money.[f] 4He must manage his own family well and see that
his children obey him with proper respect.[g] 5(If anyone does not

1:17 [a]Rev 15:3 [b]Col 1:15 [c]Ro 11:36
1:18 [d]1Ti 4:14 [e]2Ti 2:3
1:19 [f]1Ti 6:21
1:20 [g]2Ti 2:17 [h]2Ti 4:14 [i]1Co 5:5
2:2 [j]Ezr 6:10; Ro 13:1
2:4 [k]Eze 18:23,32 [l]Tit 2:11 [m]2Ti 2:25
2:5 [n]Ro 3:29,30 [o]Gal 3:20
2:6 [p]1Co 1:6 [q]1Ti 6:15
2:7 [r]2Ti 1:11 [s]Ac 9:15; Eph 3:7,8
2:8 [t]Ps 134:2; Lk 24:50
2:9 [u]1Pe 3:3
2:11 [v]1Co 14:34
2:13 [w]Ge 2:7,22; 1Co 11:8
2:14 [x]Ge 3:1-6,13; 2Co 11:3
2:15 [y]1Ti 1:14
3:1 [z]1Ti 1:15 [a]Ac 20:28
3:2 [b]Tit 1:6-8 [c]Ro 12:13 [d]2Ti 2:24
3:3 [e]2Ti 2:24 [f]Heb 13:5; 1Pe 5:2
3:4 [g]Tit 1:6

a *15* Greek *she* b *15* Or *restored* c *1* Traditionally *bishop*; also in verse 2

know how to manage his own family, how can he take care of
God's church?)[a] 6He must not be a recent convert, or he may
become conceited[b] and fall under the same judgment as the devil.
7He must also have a good reputation with outsiders, so that he
will not fall into disgrace and into the devil's trap.[c]

8Deacons,[d] likewise, are to be men worthy of respect, sincere, not
indulging in much wine,[e] and not pursuing dishonest gain. 9They
must keep hold of the deep truths of the faith with a clear conscience.[f] 10They must first be tested; and then if there is nothing
against them, let them serve as deacons.

11In the same way, their wives[a] are to be women worthy of
respect, not malicious talkers[g] but temperate and trustworthy in
everything.

12A deacon must be the husband of but one wife and must
manage his children and his household well.[h] 13Those who have
served well gain an excellent standing and great assurance in their
faith in Christ Jesus.

14Although I hope to come to you soon, I am writing you these
instructions so that, 15if I am delayed, you will know how people
ought to conduct themselves in God's household, which is the
church[i] of the living God, the pillar and foundation of the truth.
16Beyond all question, the mystery[j] of godliness is great:

He[b] appeared in a body,[c][k]
    was vindicated by the Spirit,
was seen by angels,
    was preached among the nations,[l]
was believed on in the world,
    was taken up in glory.[m]

Chapter 4 Theme

4 The Spirit[n] clearly says that in later times[o] some will abandon
the faith and follow deceiving spirits[p] and things taught by
demons. 2Such teachings come through hypocritical liars, whose
consciences have been seared as with a hot iron.[q] 3They forbid
people to marry[r] and order them to abstain from certain foods,[s]
which God created[t] to be received with thanksgiving[u] by those
who believe and who know the truth. 4For everything God created
is good,[v] and nothing is to be rejected if it is received with thanksgiving, 5because it is consecrated by the word of God and prayer.

6If you point these things out to the brothers, you will be a good
minister of Christ Jesus, brought up in the truths of the faith[w] and
of the good teaching that you have followed. 7Have nothing to do
with godless myths and old wives' tales;[x] rather, train yourself to

3:5 [a]1Co 10:32
3:6 [b]1Ti 6:4
3:7 [c]2Ti 2:26
3:8 [d]Php 1:1 [e]Tit 2:3
3:9 [f]1Ti 1:19
3:11 [g]2Ti 3:3; Tit 2:3
3:12 [h]ver 4
3:15 [i]ver 5; Eph 2:21
3:16 [j]Ro 16:25 [k]Jn 1:14 [l]Col 1:23 [m]Mk 16:19
4:1 [n]Jn 16:13 [o]2Ti 3:1 [p]2Th 2:3
4:2 [q]Eph 4:19
4:3 [r]Heb 13:4 [s]Col 2:16 [t]Ge 1:29 [u]Ro 14:6
4:4 [v]Ro 14:14-18
4:6 [w]1Ti 1:10
4:7 [x]2Ti 2:16

a *11* Or *way, deaconesses* b *16* Some manuscripts *God* c *16* Or *in the flesh*

be godly. 8For physical training is of some value, but godliness
has value for all things,[a] holding promise for both the present life[b]
and the life to come.
9This is a trustworthy saying[c] that deserves full acceptance
10(and for this we labor and strive), that we have put our hope in
the living God, who is the Savior of all men, and especially of
those who believe.
11Command and teach these things.[d] 12Don't let anyone look
down on you because you are young, but set an example[e] for the
believers in speech, in life, in love, in faith[f] and in purity. 13Until I
come, devote yourself to the public reading of Scripture, to
preaching and to teaching. 14Do not neglect your gift, which was
given you through a prophetic message[g] when the body of elders
laid their hands on you.[h]
15Be diligent in these matters; give yourself wholly to them, so
that everyone may see your progress. 16Watch your life and doctrine closely. Persevere in them, because if you do, you will save
both yourself and your hearers.

Chapter 5 Theme ____________________

5 Do not rebuke an older man[i] harshly,[j] but exhort him as if he
were your father. Treat younger men[k] as brothers, 2older
women as mothers, and younger women as sisters, with absolute
purity.
3Give proper recognition to those widows who are really in
need.[l] 4But if a widow has children or grandchildren, these
should learn first of all to put their religion into practice by caring
for their own family and so repaying their parents and grandpar-
ents,[m] for this is pleasing to God.[n] 5The widow who is really in
need[o] and left all alone puts her hope in God[p] and continues night
and day to pray[q] and to ask God for help. 6But the widow who lives
for pleasure is dead even while she lives.[r] 7Give the people these
instructions,[s] too, so that no one may be open to blame. 8If anyone
does not provide for his relatives, and especially for his immediate family, he has denied[t] the faith and is worse than an unbeliever.
9No widow may be put on the list of widows unless she is over
sixty, has been faithful to her husband,[a] 10and is well known for
her good deeds,[u] such as bringing up children, showing hospitality, washing the feet[v] of the saints, helping those in trouble[w] and
devoting herself to all kinds of good deeds.
11As for younger widows, do not put them on such a list. For
when their sensual desires overcome their dedication to Christ,
they want to marry. 12Thus they bring judgment on themselves,

4:8 [a]1Ti 6:6 [b]Ps 37:9,11; Mk 10:29,30
4:9 [c]1Ti 1:15
4:11 [d]1Ti 5:7; 6:2
4:12 [e]Tit 2:7; 1Pe 5:3 [f]1Ti 1:14
4:14 [g]1Ti 1:18 [h]Ac 6:6; 2Ti 1:6
5:1 [i]Tit 2:2 [j]Lev 19:32 [k]Tit 2:6
5:3 [l]ver 5,16
5:4 [m]Eph 6:1,2 [n]1Ti 2:3
5:5 [o]ver 3,16 [p]1Co 7:34; 1Pe 3:5 [q]Lk 2:37
5:6 [r]Lk 15:24
5:7 [s]1Ti 4:11
5:8 [t]2Pe 2:1; Jude 4; Tit 1:16
5:10 [u]Ac 9:36; 1Ti 6:18; 1Pe 2:12 [v]Lk 7:44 [w]ver 16

[a]9 Or *has had but one husband*

because they have broken their first pledge. 13Besides, they get into
the habit of being idle and going about from house to house. And
not only do they become idlers, but also gossips and busybodies,[a]
saying things they ought not to. 14So I counsel younger widows to
marry,[b] to have children, to manage their homes and to give the
enemy no opportunity for slander.[c] 15Some have in fact already
turned away to follow Satan.[d]

16If any woman who is a believer has widows in her family, she
should help them and not let the church be burdened with them,
so that the church can help those widows who are really in need.[e]

17The elders[f] who direct the affairs of the church well are worthy
of double honor,[g] especially those whose work is preaching and
teaching. 18For the Scripture says, "Do not muzzle the ox while it is
treading out the grain,"[a][h] and "The worker deserves his wages."[b][i]
19Do not entertain an accusation against an elder[j] unless it is
brought by two or three witnesses.[k] 20Those who sin are to be
rebuked[l] publicly, so that the others may take warning.[m]

21I charge you, in the sight of God and Christ Jesus[n] and the
elect angels, to keep these instructions without partiality, and to do
nothing out of favoritism.

22Do not be hasty in the laying on of hands,[o] and do not share in
the sins of others.[p] Keep yourself pure.

23Stop drinking only water, and use a little wine[q] because of your
stomach and your frequent illnesses.

24The sins of some men are obvious, reaching the place of
judgment ahead of them; the sins of others trail behind them. 25In
the same way, good deeds are obvious, and even those that are not
cannot be hidden.

Chapter 6 Theme ____________________________

6 All who are under the yoke of slavery should consider their
masters worthy of full respect,[r] so that God's name and our
teaching may not be slandered.[s] 2Those who have believing masters are not to show less respect for them because they are brothers.[t] Instead, they are to serve them even better, because those
who benefit from their service are believers, and dear to them.
These are the things you are to teach and urge on them.[u]

3If anyone teaches false doctrines[v] and does not agree to the
sound instruction[w] of our Lord Jesus Christ and to godly teaching,
4he is conceited and understands nothing. He has an unhealthy
interest in controversies and quarrels about words[x] that result in
envy, strife, malicious talk, evil suspicions 5and constant friction
between men of corrupt mind, who have been robbed of the truth[y]
and who think that godliness is a means to financial gain.

[a] *18* Deut. 25:4 [b] *18* Luke 10:7

5:13 [a]2Th 3:11
5:14 [b]1Co 7:9 [c]1Ti 6:1
5:15 [d]Mt 4:10
5:16 [e]ver 3-5
5:17 [f]Ac 11:30 [g]Php 2:29; 1Th 5:12
5:18 [h]Dt 25:4; 1Co 9:7-9 [i]Lk 10:7; Lev 19:13; Dt 24:14,15; Mt 10:10; 1Co 9:14
5:19 [j]Ac 11:30 [k]Mt 18:16
5:20 [l]2Ti 4:2; Tit 1:13 [m]Dt 13:11
5:21 [n]1Ti 6:13; 2Ti 4:1
5:22 [o]Ac 6:6 [p]Eph 5:11
5:23 [q]1Ti 3:8
6:1 [r]Eph 6:5; Tit 2:9; 1Pe 2:18 [s]Tit 2:5,8
6:2 [t]Phm 16 [u]1Ti 4:11
6:3 [v]1Ti 1:3 [w]1Ti 1:10
6:4 [x]2Ti 2:14
6:5 [y]Tit 1:15

[6]But godliness with contentment[a] is great gain.[b] [7]For we brought
nothing into the world, and we can take nothing out of it.[c] [8]But if
we have food and clothing, we will be content with that.[d] [9]People
who want to get rich[e] fall into temptation and a trap[f] and into
many foolish and harmful desires that plunge men into ruin and
destruction. [10]For the love of money[g] is a root of all kinds of evil.
Some people, eager for money, have wandered from the faith[h] and
pierced themselves with many griefs.

[11]But you, man of God,[i] flee from all this, and pursue righteousness, godliness, faith, love,[j] endurance and gentleness. [12]Fight the
good fight[k] of the faith. Take hold of[l] the eternal life to which you
were called when you made your good confession in the presence
of many witnesses. [13]In the sight of God, who gives life to everything, and of Christ Jesus, who while testifying before Pontius
Pilate[m] made the good confession, I charge you[n] [14]to keep this
command without spot or blame until the appearing of our Lord
Jesus Christ, [15]which God will bring about in his own time—God,
the blessed[o] and only Ruler,[p] the King of kings and Lord of
lords,[q] [16]who alone is immortal[r] and who lives in unapproachable light, whom no one has seen or can see.[s] To him be honor
and might forever. Amen.

[17]Command those who are rich in this present world not to be
arrogant nor to put their hope in wealth,[t] which is so uncertain,
but to put their hope in God,[u] who richly provides us with everything for our enjoyment.[v] [18]Command them to do good, to be rich
in good deeds,[w] and to be generous and willing to share.[x] [19]In this
way they will lay up treasure for themselves[y] as a firm foundation
for the coming age, so that they may take hold of the life that is
truly life.

[20]Timothy, guard what has been entrusted[z] to your care. Turn
away from godless chatter[a] and the opposing ideas of what is falsely called knowledge, [21]which some have professed and in so doing
have wandered from the faith.[b]

Grace be with you.[c]

6:6 [a]Php 4:11; Heb 13:5 [b]1Ti 4:8
6:7 [c]Job 1:21; Ecc 5:15
6:8 [d]Heb 13:5
6:9 [e]Pr 15:27 [f]1Ti 3:7
6:10 [g]1Ti 3:3 [h]Jas 5:19
6:11 [i]2Ti 3:17 [j]2Ti 2:22
6:12 [k]1Co 9:25,26; 1Ti 1:18 [l]Php 3:12
6:13 [m]Jn 18:33-37 [n]1Ti 5:21
6:15 [o]1Ti 1:11 [p]1Ti 1:17 [q]Rev 17:14; 19:16
6:16 [r]1Ti 1:17 [s]Jn 1:18
6:17 [t]Lk 12:20,21 [u]1Ti 4:10 [v]Ac 14:17
6:18 [w]1Ti 5:10 [x]Ro 12:8,13
6:19 [y]Mt 6:20
6:20 [z]2Ti 1:12,14 [a]2Ti 2:16
6:21 [b]2Ti 2:18 [c]Col 4:18

1 Timothy Observations Chart

Paul

Timothy

The Rich

Women

Overseers (Elders)

Deacons

Men

Slaves

Widows

(continued)

1 Timothy Observations Chart

Prayer	Charges and Instructions to Timothy

1 Timothy at a Glance

heme of 1 Timothy:

uthor:

ate:

urpose:

ey Words:

teach

faith

doctrines, teaching

godliness, godly

Segment Divisions	Chapter Themes
	1
	2
	3
	4
	5
	6

2 TIMOTHY

Paul now found himself in a new set of circumstances. It was about A.D. 64 (some say 67) and Timothy was heavy on his heart. Paul had to write one last letter to his disciple, reminding Timothy of crucial matters concerning the ministry and urging him to make every effort to come quickly—before winter.

THINGS TO DO

1. Read 2 Timothy. In chapters 1 and 2, and then in chapter 4, Paul refers to his circumstances: where he is and what is about to take place in his life. To help set the context of the letter, record on the OBSERVATIONS CHART on page 2063 what you learn about Paul's circumstances.

2. Read 2 Timothy again. Look for everything you learn about Timothy and record it on the OBSERVATIONS CHART.

3. As you read 2 Timothy you probably noticed the many commands and/or instructions Paul gave Timothy. These are easy to spot because the verb usually comes first in the sentence and the "you" is implied. An example of this is seen in 1:8: "So do not be ashamed to testify."

   a. List the instructions and/or commands Paul gives Timothy throughout the letter on the OBSERVATIONS CHART. (Be sure to note the chapter and verse in which you find each.)

   b. As you look for these instructions and/or commands, mark in the text the key words (and their synonyms and pronouns) that are listed on the 2 TIMOTHY AT A GLANCE chart on page 2064. Be sure to mark any reference to the gospel (*sound teaching, word, Scripture, Holy Scriptures,* etc.) and to suffering (*persecutions, hardship,* etc.).

4. Think back over the list of instructions and/or commands Paul gives Timothy and keep in mind the emphasis Paul places on the gospel. What do you think Paul's main message is to Timothy in this second epistle? Record this as the theme of the book on 2 TIMOTHY AT A GLANCE.

5. Look at the book one chapter at a time and summarize the main teaching or theme of each chapter and then record it on 2 TIMOTHY AT A GLANCE and in the text next to the chapter number. (Note: The theme of each chapter should relate to the general theme of the book.)

6. On 2 TIMOTHY AT A GLANCE you will see space to trace two themes, "Paul's Example" and "God's Provision," which run throughout the book. Doing this will give you additional insight into the practicality of 2 Timothy for your own life. Examine each chapter in the light of these two themes and record your insights on the appropriate space on the chart.

THINGS TO THINK ABOUT

1. What is your responsibility toward the gospel? To what lengths will you go in order to carry out this responsibility?

2. What are you doing to make sure you handle the Word of God accurately? Do you simply repeat what you have been taught or are you carefully studying the Word systematically?

3. Are you willing to suffer for the sake of those who would come to know the Lord Jesus Christ and receive salvation?

4. What kind of men and women do you need to beware of in these last days?

5. How are you living? Are you a coward or have you fought the good fight of faith?

6. Are you ready to die? How will you feel when you see Jesus Christ face-to-face?

Chapter 1 Theme ______________________

1

Paul, an apostle of Christ Jesus by the will of God,[a] according
to the promise of life that is in Christ Jesus,[b]

2To Timothy,[c] my dear son:[d]

Grace, mercy and peace from God the Father and Christ Jesus
our Lord.

3I thank God,[e] whom I serve, as my forefathers did, with a clear
conscience, as night and day I constantly remember you in my
prayers.[f] 4Recalling your tears,[g] I long to see you,[h] so that I may be
filled with joy. 5I have been reminded of your sincere faith,[i] which
first lived in your grandmother Lois and in your mother Eunice[j]
and, I am persuaded, now lives in you also. 6For this reason I remind
you to fan into flame the gift of God, which is in you through the
laying on of my hands.[k] 7For God did not give us a spirit of timidity,[l] but a spirit of power, of love and of self-discipline.
8So do not be ashamed[m] to testify about our Lord, or ashamed
of me his prisoner.[n] But join with me in suffering for the gospel,[o]
by the power of God, 9who has saved us and called[p] us to a holy
life—not because of anything we have done but because of his
own purpose and grace. This grace was given us in Christ Jesus
before the beginning of time, 10but it has now been revealed[q]
through the appearing of our Savior, Christ Jesus, who has destroyed death[r] and has brought life and immortality to light
through the gospel. 11And of this gospel I was appointed a herald
and an apostle and a teacher.[s] 12That is why I am suffering as I am.
Yet I am not ashamed, because I know whom I have believed, and
am convinced that he is able to guard[t] what I have entrusted to
him for that day.[u]
13What you heard from me, keep[v] as the pattern of sound teaching, with faith and love in Christ Jesus.[w] 14Guard the good deposit
that was entrusted to you—guard it with the help of the Holy
Spirit who lives in us.[x]
15You know that everyone in the province of Asia has deserted
me,[y] including Phygelus and Hermogenes.
16May the Lord show mercy to the household of Onesiphorus,[z]
because he often refreshed me and was not ashamed of my chains.
17On the contrary, when he was in Rome, he searched hard for
me until he found me. 18May the Lord grant that he will find
mercy from the Lord on that day! You know very well in how
many ways he helped me[a] in Ephesus.

Chapter 2 Theme ______________________

2

You then, my son, be strong[b] in the grace that is in Christ
Jesus. 2And the things you have heard me say[c] in the presence

1:1 [a]2Co 1:1 [b]Eph 3:6; 1Ti 6:19
1:2 [c]Ac 16:1 [d]1Ti 1:2
1:3 [e]Ro 1:8 [f]Ro 1:10
1:4 [g]Ac 20:37 [h]2Ti 4:9
1:5 [i]1Ti 1:5 [j]Ac 16:1
1:6 [k]1Ti 4:14
1:7 [l]Ro 8:15
1:8 [m]Mk 8:38; Ro 1:16 [n]Eph 3:1 [o]2Ti 2:3,9; 4:5
1:9 [p]Ro 8:28
1:10 [q]Eph 1:9 [r]1Co 15:26,54
1:11 [s]1Ti 2:7
1:12 [t]1Ti 6:20 [u]ver 18
1:13 [v]Tit 1:9 [w]1Ti 1:14
1:14 [x]Ro 8:9
1:15 [y]2Ti 4:10,11,16
1:16 [z]2Ti 4:19
1:18 [a]Heb 6:10
2:1 [b]Eph 6:10
2:2 [c]2Ti 1:13

of many witnesses[a] entrust to reliable men who will also be qualified to teach others. 3Endure hardship with us like a good soldier[b]
of Christ Jesus. 4No one serving as a soldier gets involved in civilian
affairs—he wants to please his commanding officer. 5Similarly, if
anyone competes as an athlete, he does not receive the victor's
crown[c] unless he competes according to the rules. 6The hardwork-
ing farmer should be the first to receive a share of the crops. 7Reflect
on what I am saying, for the Lord will give you insight into all this.
8Remember Jesus Christ, raised from the dead,[d] descended from
David.[e] This is my gospel,[f] 9for which I am suffering[g] even to the
point of being chained like a criminal. But God's word is not
chained. 10Therefore I endure everything[h] for the sake of the elect,
that they too may obtain the salvation that is in Christ Jesus, with
eternal glory.[i]
11Here is a trustworthy saying:

If we died with him,
we will also live with him;[j]
12if we endure,
we will also reign with him.[k]
If we disown him,
he will also disown us;[l]
13if we are faithless,
he will remain faithful,[m]
for he cannot disown himself.

14Keep reminding them of these things. Warn them before God
against quarreling about words;[n] it is of no value, and only ruins
those who listen. 15Do your best to present yourself to God as one
approved, a workman who does not need to be ashamed and
who correctly handles the word of truth.[o] 16Avoid godless chatter,[p]
because those who indulge in it will become more and more
ungodly. 17Their teaching will spread like gangrene. Among them
are Hymenaeus[q] and Philetus, 18who have wandered away from
the truth. They say that the resurrection has already taken place,
and they destroy the faith of some.[r] 19Nevertheless, God's solid
foundation stands firm,[s] sealed with this inscription: "The Lord
knows those who are his,"[a][t] and, "Everyone who confesses the
name of the Lord[u] must turn away from wickedness."
20In a large house there are articles not only of gold and silver,
but also of wood and clay; some are for noble purposes and some
for ignoble.[v] 21If a man cleanses himself from the latter, he will be
an instrument for noble purposes, made holy, useful to the Master and prepared to do any good work.[w]
22Flee the evil desires of youth, and pursue righteousness, faith,

a *19* Num. 16:5 (see Septuagint)

2:2 a 1Ti 6:12
2:3 b 1Ti 1:18
2:5 c 1Co 9:25
2:8 d Ac 2:24 e Mt 1:1 f Ro 2:16
2:9 g Ac 9:16
2:10 h Col 1:24 i 2Co 4:17
2:11 j Ro 6:2-11
2:12 k Ro 8:17; 1Pe 4:13 l Mt 10:33
2:13 m Nu 23:19; Ro 3:3
2:14 n 1Ti 6:4
2:15 o Eph 1:13; Jas 1:18
2:16 p Tit 3:9
2:17 q 1Ti 1:20
2:18 r 1Ti 1:19
2:19 s Isa 28:16 t Jn 10:14 u 1Co 1:2
2:20 v Ro 9:21
2:21 w 2Ti 3:17

love[a] and peace, along with those who call on the Lord out of a
pure heart.[b] 23Don't have anything to do with foolish and stupid
arguments, because you know they produce quarrels. 24And the
Lord's servant must not quarrel; instead, he must be kind to
everyone, able to teach, not resentful.[c] 25Those who oppose him
he must gently instruct, in the hope that God will grant them
repentance leading them to a knowledge of the truth,[d] 26and that
they will come to their senses and escape from the trap of the
devil,[e] who has taken them captive to do his will.

Chapter 3 Theme ____

3 But mark this: There will be terrible times in the last days.[f]
2People will be lovers of themselves, lovers of money,[g] boastful,
proud,[h] abusive, disobedient to their parents,[i] ungrateful, unholy,
3without love, unforgiving, slanderous, without self-control, brutal, not lovers of the good, 4treacherous, rash, conceited,[j] lovers
of pleasure rather than lovers of God— 5having a form of godliness but denying its power. Have nothing to do with them.

6They are the kind who worm their way[k] into homes and gain
control over weak-willed women, who are loaded down with sins
and are swayed by all kinds of evil desires, 7always learning but
never able to acknowledge the truth. 8Just as Jannes and Jambres
opposed Moses,[l] so also these men oppose[m] the truth—men of
depraved minds,[n] who, as far as the faith is concerned, are rejected.
9But they will not get very far because, as in the case of those
men,[o] their folly will be clear to everyone.

10You, however, know all about my teaching,[p] my way of life,
my purpose, faith, patience, love, endurance, 11persecutions, sufferings—what kinds of things happened to me in Antioch,[q] Iconium and Lystra, the persecutions I endured.[r] Yet the Lord
rescued me from all of them.[s] 12In fact, everyone who wants to
live a godly life in Christ Jesus will be persecuted,[t] 13while evil
men and impostors will go from bad to worse,[u] deceiving and
being deceived. 14But as for you, continue in what you have
learned and have become convinced of, because you know those
from whom you learned it,[v] 15and how from infancy[w] you have
known the holy Scriptures,[x] which are able to make you wise[y] for
salvation through faith in Christ Jesus. 16All Scripture is God-
breathed[z] and is useful for teaching,[a] rebuking, correcting and
training in righteousness, 17so that the man of God[b] may be thoroughly equipped for every good work.[c]

Chapter 4 Theme ____

4 In the presence of God and of Christ Jesus, who will judge the
living and the dead,[d] and in view of his appearing and his

2:22 [a]1Ti 1:14; 6:11 [b]1Ti 1:5
2:24 [c]1Ti 3:2,3
2:25 [d]1Ti 2:4
2:26 [e]1Ti 3:7
3:1 [f]1Ti 4:1
3:2 [g]1Ti 3:3 [h]Ro 1:30 [i]Ro 1:30
3:4 [j]1Ti 3:6
3:6 [k]Jude 4
3:8 [l]Ex 7:11 [m]Ac 13:8 [n]1Ti 6:5
3:9 [o]Ex 7:12
3:10 [p]1Ti 4:6
3:11 [q]Ac 13:14,50 [r]2Co 11:23-27 [s]Ps 34:19
3:12 [t]Ac 14:22
3:13 [u]2Ti 2:16
3:14 [v]2Ti 1:13
3:15 [w]2Ti 1:5 [x]Jn 5:39 [y]Ps 119:98,99
3:16 [z]2Pe 1:20,21 [a]Ro 4:23,24
3:17 [b]1Ti 6:11 [c]2Ti 2:21
4:1 [d]Ac 10:42

kingdom, I give you this charge:[a] 2Preach[b] the Word;[c] be prepared
in season and out of season; correct, rebuke[d] and encourage—
with great patience and careful instruction. 3For the time will
come when men will not put up with sound doctrine.[e] Instead, to
suit their own desires, they will gather around them a great number of teachers to say what their itching ears want to hear. 4They
will turn their ears away from the truth and turn aside to myths.[f]
5But you, keep your head in all situations, endure hardship,[g] do the
work of an evangelist,[h] discharge all the duties of your ministry.

6For I am already being poured out like a drink offering,[i] and
the time has come for my departure.[j] 7I have fought the good
fight,[k] I have finished the race,[l] I have kept the faith. 8Now there is
in store for me[m] the crown of righteousness, which the Lord, the
righteous Judge, will award to me on that day[n]—and not only to
me, but also to all who have longed for his appearing.

9Do your best to come to me quickly, 10for Demas,[o] because he
loved this world,[p] has deserted me and has gone to Thessalonica.
Crescens has gone to Galatia,[q] and Titus to Dalmatia. 11Only
Luke[r] is with me.[s] Get Mark[t] and bring him with you, because he
is helpful to me in my ministry. 12I sent Tychicus[u] to Ephesus.
13When you come, bring the cloak that I left with Carpus at Troas,
and my scrolls, especially the parchments.

14Alexander[v] the metalworker did me a great deal of harm. The
Lord will repay him for what he has done.[w] 15You too should be
on your guard against him, because he strongly opposed our
message.

16At my first defense, no one came to my support, but everyone
deserted me. May it not be held against them.[x] 17But the Lord stood
at my side[y] and gave me strength, so that through me the message
might be fully proclaimed and all the Gentiles might hear it.[z] And I
was delivered from the lion's mouth. 18The Lord will rescue me
from every evil attack[a] and will bring me safely to his heavenly
kingdom. To him be glory for ever and ever. Amen.[b]

19Greet Priscilla[a] and Aquila[c] and the household of Onesiphorus.
20Erastus[d] stayed in Corinth, and I left Trophimus[e] sick in Miletus.
21Do your best to get here before winter.[f] Eubulus greets you, and so
do Pudens, Linus, Claudia and all the brothers.

22The Lord be with your spirit.[g] Grace be with you.[h]

a 19 Greek *Prisca*, a variant of *Priscilla*

4:1 [a] 1Ti 5:21
4:2 [b] 1Ti 4:13 [c] Gal 6:6 [d] 1Ti 5:20; Tit 1:13; 2:15
4:3 [e] 1Ti 1:10
4:4 [f] 1Ti 1:4
4:5 [g] 2Ti 1:8 [h] Ac 21:8
4:6 [i] Php 2:17 [j] Php 1:23
4:7 [k] 1Ti 1:18 [l] 1Co 9:24
4:8 [m] Col 1:5 [n] 2Ti 1:12
4:10 [o] Col 4:14 [p] 1Jn 2:15 [q] Ac 16:6
4:11 [r] Col 4:14 [s] 2Ti 1:15 [t] Ac 12:12
4:12 [u] Ac 20:4
4:14 [v] Ac 19:33 [w] Ro 12:19
4:16 [x] Ac 7:60
4:17 [y] Ac 23:11 [z] Ac 9:15
4:18 [a] Ps 121:7 [b] Ro 11:36
4:19 [c] Ac 18:2
4:20 [d] Ac 19:22 [e] Ac 20:4
4:21 [f] ver 9
4:22 [g] Gal 6:18; Phm 25 [h] Col 4:18

2 Timothy Observations Chart

Paul	Timothy
Where is he?	How is he described?
Why is he there?	What is his relationship to Paul?
Who is with him?	What do you learn about him?
What is about to happen?	
How is he going to handle it?	

Paul's Instructions to Timothy

2 Timothy at a Glance

Theme of 2 Timothy:

Segment Divisions

God's Provision	Paul's Example	Chapter Themes
		1
		2
Delivered Paul Out of Persecutions	Endured Persecutions	3
		4

Author:

Date:

Purpose:

Key Words:

gospel

word

suffer (sufferings, persecution)

endure(d), put up with

faith

ashamed

2

TITUS

When Paul sailed past Crete on his way to Rome he was not the master of his own ship. He was Rome's prisoner. How wise the centurion guard would have been had he followed Paul's urging to put ashore in Crete! Despite the winds, they sailed on under much duress. As Paul had predicted, the ship was lost in Malta, the island 58 miles south of Sicily.

Paul's ship sank to the bottom of the sea; Crete had sunk to the depths of sin. Broken to pieces morally by the incessant pounding of a godless lifestyle, Crete needed the good news of the gospel. Unlike the ship, however, it was not beyond redemption.

Whether Crete was on Paul's heart before his two years' house arrest in Rome, we don't know. We only know that once Paul was free from Rome's chains he apparently went with Titus to Crete and left him there.

As Paul wrote Titus, it was about A.D. 62. He didn't know he would return to Rome for one final imprisonment.

Things to Do

1. Read through Titus without stopping so that you understand the general content and thrust of the letter.

2. Read Titus again, one chapter at a time. As you read each chapter:

   a. Look for the information about the author: who he is, how he describes himself, where he is, etc. Record your insights on the OBSERVATIONS CHART on page 2069. Note the chapter and verse in which you find your information; it helps when you want to find something later.

   b. Mark in the text the key words listed on the TITUS AT A GLANCE chart on page 2070. Be sure also to mark the synonyms and pronouns.

   c. In the margin of your Bible, list the truths you learn from the text about each key word.

3. The commands, warnings, and instructions Paul includes in his letter to Titus help define Paul's purpose for writing. Read Titus again chapter by chapter and note each command, warning, or instruction Paul gives Titus. List these on the OBSERVATIONS CHART under "Instructions to Titus."

4. Note on the OBSERVATIONS CHART what you learn about Titus and his relationship to Paul. In chapter 1 Paul clearly tells us where Titus is and why he is there.

5. In his letter Paul mentions various groups of people. List what you learn about each of these groups under the designated heading on your OBSERVATIONS CHART.

6. Listing Paul's commands, warnings, and instructions to Titus probably has helped you see the dominant subject of Titus. There are two verses, one in chapter 2 and one in chapter 3, which summarize the thrust of Paul's letter. These will help you determine the theme of the epistle. Record it on TITUS AT A GLANCE.

   a. Now summarize the theme or main message of each paragraph and then of each chapter and record these on TITUS AT A GLANCE. Also record the chapter theme in the text next to the chapter number.

   b. Fill in author, date, and purpose on the same chart.

Things to Think About

1. The world's lifestyle denies God. By your lifestyle and attitudes, do you deny ungodliness and worldly desires, or do you indulge the desires of your flesh?

2. It is difficult always to be considerate to everyone, isn't it? When did you last fail in this area? Have you determined afresh to be gentle and uncontentious even in the most difficult situation with the most difficult person? Your actions often will speak louder than your words ever can.

3. Your salvation was not based on performance but upon the mercy and grace of God. What has your heavenly Father saved you from? Think on his goodness that brought you from death into life and brought you out of the kingdom of darkness into the kingdom of his glorious light. Have you thanked him lately for his mercy and grace? Why not do it now? Pray for those close to you who have yet to experience the saving grace of God.

Chapter 1 Theme ________________________

To Titus at Crete

1 Paul, a servant of God[a] and an apostle of Jesus Christ for the
faith of God's elect and the knowledge of the truth[b] that leads
to godliness— 2a faith and knowledge resting on the hope of
eternal life,[c] which God, who does not lie, promised before the
beginning of time,[d] 3and at his appointed season[e] he brought his
word to light[f] through the preaching entrusted to me[g] by the
command of God our Savior,[h]

4To Titus,[i] my true son in our common faith:

Grace and peace from God the Father and Christ Jesus our Savior.

5The reason I left you in Crete[j] was that you might straighten out
what was left unfinished and appoint[a] elders[k] in every town, as I
directed you. 6An elder must
be blameless,[l] the husband of
but one wife, a man whose
children believe and are not
open to the charge of being
wild and disobedient. 7Since
an overseer[b][m] is entrusted
with God's work,[n] he must be
blameless—not overbearing,
not quick-tempered, not giv-
en to drunkenness, not violent, not pursuing dishonest
gain.[o] 8Rather he must be
hospitable,[p] one who loves what is good,[q] who is self-controlled,
upright, holy and disciplined. 9He must hold firmly[r] to the trustworthy message as it has been taught, so that he can encourage
others by sound doctrine[s] and refute those who oppose it.
10For there are many rebellious people, mere talkers[t] and
deceivers, especially those of the circumcision group.[u] 11They
must be silenced, because they are ruining whole households[v] by
teaching things they ought not to teach—and that for the sake of

a5 Or *ordain* b7 Traditionally *bishop*

1:1 [a]Ro 1:1 [b]1Ti 2:4
1:2 [c]2Ti 1:1 [d]2Ti 1:9
1:3 [e]1Ti 2:6 [f]2Ti 1:10 [g]1Ti 1:11 [h]Lk 1:47
1:4 [i]2Co 2:13
1:5 [j]Ac 27:7 [k]Ac 11:30
1:6 [l]1Ti 3:2
1:7 [m]1Ti 3:1 [n]1Co 4:1 [o]1Ti 3:3,8
1:8 [p]1Ti 3:2 [q]2Ti 3:3
1:9 [r]1Ti 1:19 [s]1Ti 1:10
1:10 [t]1Ti 1:6 [u]11:2
1:11 [v]2Ti 3:6

dishonest gain. 12 Even one of their own prophets[a] has said, "Cretans[b] are always liars, evil brutes, lazy gluttons." 13 This testimony
is true. Therefore, rebuke[c] them sharply, so that they will be sound
in the faith[d] 14 and will pay no attention to Jewish myths[e] or to the
commands[f] of those who reject the truth. 15 To the pure, all things
are pure, but to those who are corrupted and do not believe,
nothing is pure.[g] In fact, both their minds and consciences are
corrupted. 16 They claim to know God, but by their actions they
deny him.[h] They are detestable, disobedient and unfit for doing
anything good.

Chapter 2 Theme ____________________

2 You must teach what is in accord with sound doctrine.[i]
2 Teach the older men to be temperate, worthy of respect,
self-controlled, and sound in faith,[j] in love and in endurance.
3 Likewise, teach the older women to be reverent in the way they
live, not to be slanderers or addicted to much wine,[k] but to teach
what is good. 4 Then they can train the younger women to love
their husbands and children, 5 to be self-controlled and pure, to
be busy at home, to be kind, and to be subject to their husbands,[l]
so that no one will malign the word of God.[m]
6 Similarly, encourage the young men[n] to be self-controlled. 7 In
everything set them an example[o] by doing what is good. In your
teaching show integrity, seriousness 8 and soundness of speech
that cannot be condemned, so that those who oppose you may
be ashamed because they have nothing bad to say about us.[p]
9 Teach slaves to be subject to their masters in everything,[q] to try
to please them, not to talk back to them, 10 and not to steal from
them, but to show that they can be fully trusted, so that in every
way they will make the teaching about God our Savior attractive.[r]
11 For the grace of God that brings salvation has appeared to all
men.[s] 12 It teaches us to say "No" to ungodliness and worldly passions,[t] and to live self-controlled, upright and godly lives[u] in this
present age, 13 while we wait for the blessed hope—the glorious
appearing of our great God and Savior, Jesus Christ,[v] 14 who gave
himself for us to redeem us from all wickedness and to purify for
himself a people that are his very own,[w] eager to do what is good.[x]
15 These, then, are the things you should teach. Encourage and
rebuke with all authority. Do not let anyone despise you.

Chapter 3 Theme ____________________

3 Remind the people to be subject to rulers and authorities,[y] to
be obedient, to be ready to do whatever is good,[z] 2 to slander
no one,[a] to be peaceable and considerate, and to show true humility toward all men.

1:12 [a] Ac 17:28; [b] Ac 2:11
1:13 [c] 2Co 13:10; [d] Tit 2:2
1:14 [e] 1Ti 1:4; [f] Col 2:22
1:15 [g] Ro 14:14,23
1:16 [h] 1Jn 2:4
2:1 [i] 1Ti 1:10
2:2 [j] Tit 1:13
2:3 [k] 1Ti 3:8
2:5 [l] Eph 5:22; [m] 1Ti 6:1
2:6 [n] 1Ti 5:1
2:7 [o] 1Ti 4:12
2:8 [p] 1Pe 2:12
2:9 [q] Eph 6:5
2:10 [r] Mt 5:16
2:11 [s] 1Ti 2:4
2:12 [t] Tit 3:3; [u] 2Ti 3:12
2:13 [v] 2Pe 1:1
2:14 [w] Ex 19:5; [x] Eph 2:10
3:1 [y] Ro 13:1; [z] 2Ti 2:21
3:2 [a] Eph 4:31; 2Ti 2:24

3 At one time we too were foolish, disobedient, deceived and
enslaved by all kinds of passions and pleasures. We lived in malice and envy, being hated and hating one another. 4 But when the
kindness[a] and love of God our Savior appeared,[b] 5 he saved us,
not because of righteous things we had done,[c] but because of his
mercy. He saved us through the washing of rebirth and renewal[d]
by the Holy Spirit, 6 whom he poured out on us[e] generously through
Jesus Christ our Savior, 7 so that, having been justified by his grace,[f]
we might become heirs[g] having the hope[h] of eternal life.[i] 8 This is
a trustworthy saying.[j] And I want you to stress these things, so
that those who have trusted in God may be careful to devote
themselves to doing what is good.[k] These things are excellent and
profitable for everyone.

9 But avoid foolish controversies and genealogies and arguments
and quarrels[l] about the law, because these are unprofitable and
useless. 10 Warn a divisive person once, and then warn him a second time. After that, have nothing to do with him.[m] 11 You may be
sure that such a man is warped and sinful; he is self-condemned.

12 As soon as I send Artemas or Tychicus[n] to you, do your best to
come to me at Nicopolis, because I have decided to winter there.[o]
13 Do everything you can to help Zenas the lawyer and Apollos[p]
on their way and see that they have everything they need. 14 Our
people must learn to devote themselves to doing what is good,[q] in
order that they may provide for daily necessities and not live
unproductive lives.

15 Everyone with me sends you greetings. Greet those who love
us in the faith.[r]

Grace be with you all.[s]

3:4 [a] Eph 2:7 [b] Tit 2:11

3:5 [c] Eph 2:9 [d] Ro 12:2

3:6 [e] Ro 5:5

3:7 [f] Ro 3:24 [g] Ro 8:17 [h] Ro 8:24 [i] Tit 1:2

3:8 [j] 1Ti 1:15 [k] Tit 2:14

3:9 [l] 1Ti 1:4; 2Ti 2:14

3:10 [m] Ro 16:17

3:12 [n] Ac 20:4 [o] 2Ti 4:9,21

3:13 [p] Ac 18:24

3:14 [q] ver 8

3:15 [r] 1Ti 1:2 [s] Col 4:18

Titus Observations Chart

Paul	Titus	Instructions to Titus
Where is he?	Where is he? Why?	
How does he describe himself?	What is his relationship to Paul?	

Elders (Overseers)	Older Men	
	Cretans	Older Women
	Slaves	Younger Women
Young Men		

Titus at a Glance

Theme of Titus:

Segment Divisions	Paragraph Themes	Chapter Themes
	1:1-4	1
	1:5-9	
	1:10-16	
	2:1-15	2
	3:1-11	3
	3:12-15	

Author:

Date:

Purpose:

Key Words:

God

Jesus Christ

doctrine (teachings)

truth

grace

actions, righteous things we had done, do what is goo[d] doing what is good

*P*HILEMON

Slavery was a fact of life in Paul's day—a fact Paul couldn't change. But Paul could show slaves and masters how they were to behave toward one another as those redeemed by Jesus, who had become a bondservant on their behalf. In his epistles Paul shared these principles.

Now, however, something else had come up. Paul had to appeal to Philemon, a believer from Colosse, about a very personal matter: One of Philemon's slaves had run away, and according to Roman law he could be put to death by his master. So at about the same time he wrote Colossians, Paul wrote to Philemon from his rented quarters, where as a prisoner of Rome he also could be put to death. It was about A.D. 61 or 62.

Things to Do

1. Philemon is only one short chapter. Read it to gain an understanding of why this letter was written.
   a. When you finish reading, go back and note everything you learn about Paul on the OBSERVATIONS CHART on page 2073. Also watch for Paul's reason for writing and how he goes about achieving his purpose. Then record the reasons on the PHILEMON AT A GLANCE chart also on page 2073.
   b. Also note everything you learn about the recipients of Paul's letter and record this information in the appropriate section of the OBSERVATIONS CHART.
   c. Record on the OBSERVATIONS CHART everything you learn about Onesimus.
2. Carefully read the book again, marking in the text each of the key words (with their synonyms and pronouns) listed on the PHILEMON AT A GLANCE chart. Then in the margin list the truths you learn about each of these words from the text.
3. Record the theme of Philemon on PHILEMON AT A GLANCE and also in the text. Because Philemon is only one chapter, it is divided into paragraphs on the chart. Read the book paragraph by paragraph and record on the chart the theme of each paragraph. Then fill in the rest of the chart.

Things to Think About

1. Are you willing to appeal to someone on behalf of another person, to assume the role of an advocate?
2. What can you learn from Paul's example in the way he appealed to Philemon?
3. Is there someone you need to forgive and offer restoration?
4. Can someone appeal to you to do the right thing on the basis of your character, or does he have to force your hand through rules, regulations, or some sort of a "bribe"?

Chapter Theme ______________________

1:1 [a] ver 9,23; Eph 3:1 [b] 2Co 1:1 [c] Php 2:25

1Paul, a prisoner[a] of Christ Jesus, and Timothy our brother,[b]

To Philemon our dear friend and fellow worker,[c] 2to Apphia our
sister, to Archippus[d] our fellow soldier[e] and to the church that meets
in your home:[f]

1:2 [d] Col 4:17 [e] Php 2:25 [f] Ro 16:5

3Grace to you and peace from God our Father and the Lord
Jesus Christ.

1:4 [g] Ro 1:8

4I always thank my God[g] as I remember you in my prayers,
5because I hear about your faith in the Lord Jesus and your love

for all the saints.[a] 6I pray that you may be active in sharing your faith,
so that you will have a full understanding of every good thing we
have in Christ. 7Your love has given me great joy and encouragement,[b] because you, brother, have refreshed[c] the hearts of the saints.
8Therefore, although in Christ I could be bold and order you to
do what you ought to do, 9yet I appeal to you on the basis of love.
I then, as Paul—an old man and now also a prisoner[d] of Christ
Jesus— 10I appeal to you for my son[e] Onesimus,[a][f] who became
my son while I was in chains. 11Formerly he was useless to you,
but now he has become useful both to you and to me.
12I am sending him—who is my very heart—back to you. 13I
would have liked to keep him with me so that he could take your
place in helping me while I am in chains for the gospel. 14But I
did not want to do anything without your consent, so that any
favor you do will be spontaneous and not forced.[g] 15Perhaps the
reason he was separated from you for a little while was that you
might have him back for good— 16no longer as a slave, but better
than a slave, as a dear brother.[h] He is very dear to me but even
dearer to you, both as a man and as a brother in the Lord.
17So if you consider me a partner,[i] welcome him as you would
welcome me. 18If he has done you any wrong or owes you anything,
charge it to me. 19I, Paul, am writing this with my own hand. I will
pay it back—not to mention that you owe me your very self. 20I
do wish, brother, that I may have some benefit from you in the Lord;
refresh[j] my heart in Christ. 21Confident[k] of your obedience, I write
to you, knowing that you will do even more than I ask.
22And one thing more: Prepare a guest room for me, because I
hope to be[l] restored to you in answer to your prayers.[m]

23Epaphras,[n] my fellow prisoner in Christ Jesus, sends you greetings. 24And so do Mark,[o] Aristarchus,[p] Demas[q] and Luke, my fellow
workers.
25The grace of the Lord Jesus Christ be with your spirit.[r]

a 10 *Onesimus* means *useful.*

1:5 [a]Eph 1:15; Col 1:4
1:7 [b]2Co 7:4,13 [c]ver 20
1:9 [d]ver 1,23
1:10 [e]1Co 4:15 [f]Col 4:9
1:14 [g]2Co 9:7; 1Pe 5:2
1:16 [h]Mt 23:8; 1Ti 6:2
1:17 [i]2Co 8:23
1:20 [j]ver 7
1:21 [k]2Co 2:3
1:22 [l]Php 1:25; 2:24 [m]2Co 1:11
1:23 [n]Col 1:7
1:24 [o]Ac 12:12 [p]Ac 19:29 [q]Col 4:14
1:25 [r]2Ti 4:22

Philemon Observations Chart

The Author	The Recipients	Onesimus

Philemon at a Glance

me of Philemon:

or:

e:

pose:

Words:

ve

peal

ave

Segment Divisions	Paragraph Themes
	Verses 1-3
	Verses 4-7
	Verses 8-20
	Verses 21, 22
	Verses 23-25

HEBREWS

Persecution increased as the gospel spread. The persecution was especially intense for Jewish believers because they had turned their back on the world and its ways and had abandoned the ordinances of the law which Jews had embraced since the time of Moses. This left them in a no-man's land. Jews as well as Gentiles who did not believe in the Lord Jesus Christ could not understand them, nor would many tolerate their newfound faith without challenge or attack.

Imagine yourself in a similar situation. What if you were wrong about Jesus Christ? What if he were not really the Messiah? And what about the new covenant? What if it didn't replace the old covenant? What if you really did need a continuing blood sacrifice for your sins? *What if?*

So that we could be secure in our faith, God moved an unknown author to take up pen and parchment and write the book we call Hebrews. No other book in the New Testament gives us what Hebrews gives us—the assurance that we have a high priest who is touched with the feeling of our weaknesses, one who ever lives to make intercession for us.

Hebrews was probably written before A.D. 70, because the temple was still standing and the priests were still making religious sacrifices.

Things to Do

1. Before you begin your study of Hebrews, read Hebrews 13:22 to discover the author's purpose for writing. Record this on the HEBREWS AT A GLANCE chart on page 2095.

2. In order to grasp the truth of this book, you need to understand to whom the book is written. As you read Hebrews chapter by chapter:

   a. Learn all you can about the recipients of this letter. Look for and mark the words *we, you, dear friends,* and *brothers.* Then record what you learn about the recipients on the OBSERVATIONS CHART on page 2093 under "Recipients."

   b. Note on the OBSERVATIONS CHART what you learn from the text about the author.

   c. Keep in mind the author's purpose for writing. Throughout the book you will see him exhorting his readers. Most of his exhortations begin with "let us." Mark each *let us* and then list each exhortation on the OBSERVATIONS CHART.

   d. Observe how the author periodically warns his readers about certain things.

      1) Note each warning on the OBSERVATIONS CHART. An example of a warning is found in 2:1: "We must pay more careful attention, therefore, to what we have heard, so that we do not drift away."

      2) As you note the warning, watch for and record the consequences of not heeding the warning. Also remember to whom the book is addressed. Let the text speak for itself. Don't read into it—just let it say what it says.

3. As you study each chapter, do the following:

   a. Write the key words (including their synonyms and pronouns) listed on the HEBREWS AT A GLANCE chart on an index card and then mark them in a distinctive way in the text. (Beginning at chapter 7, mark every occurrence of the words *covenant* and *will.*) Use this card as a reminder of what you are looking for as you study the book of Hebrews.

   b. List in the margin what you learn from each key word.

c. As you finish reading a chapter, decide on the theme or subject of that chapter and record it next to the chapter number in the text and on HEBREWS AT A GLANCE.

4. To truly appreciate and understand the book of Hebrews, you need to do the following:

   a. Look back through your work and note all the times you marked *Jesus* and the pronouns referring to him. Also look for the phrase *superior to* or *better…than*. Then make a chart on THE SUPREMACY OF JESUS and list what you learn from Hebrews about our Lord. (Or record this information in the margin of your Bible.)

   b. There is much in Hebrews about the priesthood and about Jesus as our high priest. Make a chart entitled THE PRIESTHOOD AND JESUS and list your information in three columns: "Insights into Priests and the Priesthood," "Insights into Jesus, Our Great High Priest," and "How This Applies to Me." Record your insights in the proper columns. (Or list this information in the margin of your Bible.)

   c. Review what you learn from marking the words *covenant* and *will* and note what the text says on a chart you title A COMPARISON OF THE TWO COVENANTS: LAW AND GRACE AS TAUGHT IN HEBREWS. (Or in the margin next to chapters 8 through 10, list what you learn about the old covenant and law and the new covenant and grace.)

5. Complete HEBREWS AT A GLANCE by doing the following:

   a. Look at each of your chapter themes in order to determine the theme of Hebrews and record it on the chart.

   b. Fill in the section titled "Segment Divisions."

      1) Segment divisions indicate a change in the thrust or topic of the book. One change in emphasis occurs at Hebrews 10:19, where the author stops dealing with the doctrinal aspects of the truth he is sharing and begins to address the practical aspects. Record this segment division on the chart in the appropriate space.

      2) Look again at the chapter themes and see if there are any other divisions you can record. If so, record them on the chart. Completing this exercise will help you find where a specific truth is covered in Hebrews.

Things to Think About

1. Meditate on the truths you learned about Jesus. Do you see him as "superior to…"? How supreme is he in your life?

2. As you press on to Christian maturity, are you noticing a new sense of confidence in your God? Is your faith being strengthened? Are you drawing near to God? Do you think Jesus understands what you're going through? Can he really help?

3. Are you throwing off everything that hinders (every weighty thing that is slowing you down) and every sin, and running with perseverance the race marked out before you? If not, what is holding you back?

4. How are your morals? Do you live in the light of the fact that God will judge all who are sexually immoral and adulterers?

5. Are you continually offering up the sacrifice of praise? What are some things you can thank God for today?

Chapter 1 Theme ____________________

1 In the past God spoke[a] to our forefathers through the prophets[b]
at many times and in various ways,[c] 2but in these last days he
has spoken to us by his Son, whom he appointed heir[d] of all things,
and through whom[e] he made the universe. 3The Son is the radiance of God's glory[f] and the exact representation of his being,
sustaining all things[g] by his powerful word. After he had provided
purification for sins,[h] he sat down at the right hand of the Majesty
in heaven.[i] 4So he became as much superior to the angels as the
name he has inherited is superior to theirs.[j]

5For to which of the angels did God ever say,

> "You are my Son;
> today I have become your Father[a]"[b]?[k]

Or again,

> "I will be his Father,
> and he will be my Son"[c]?[l]

6And again, when God brings his firstborn into the world,[m] he says,

> "Let all God's angels worship him."[d][n]

7In speaking of the angels he says,

> "He makes his angels winds,
> his servants flames of fire."[e][o]

8But about the Son he says,

> "Your throne, O God, will last for ever and ever,
> and righteousness will be the scepter of your kingdom.
> 9You have loved righteousness and hated wickedness;
> therefore God, your God, has set you above
> your companions[p]
> by anointing you with the oil[q] of joy."[f]

10He also says,

> "In the beginning, O Lord, you laid the foundations of
> the earth,
> and the heavens are the work of your hands.
> 11They will perish, but you remain;
> they will all wear out like a garment.[r]
> 12You will roll them up like a robe;
> like a garment they will be changed.
> But you remain the same,[s]
> and your years will never end."[g][t]

a5 Or *have begotten you* b5 Psalm 2:7 c5 2 Samuel 7:14; 1 Chron. 17:13 d6 Deut. 32:43 (see Dead Sea Scrolls and Septuagint) e7 Psalm 104:4 f9 Psalm 45:6,7 g12 Psalm 102:25-27

1:1
a Jn 9:29; Heb 2:2,3
b Ac 2:30
c Nu 12:6,8

1:2
d Ps 2:8
e Jn 1:3

1:3
f Jn 1:14
g Col 1:17
h Heb 7:27
i Mk 16:19

1:4
j Eph 1:21; Php 2:9,10

1:5
k Ps 2:7
l 2Sa 7:14

1:6
m Heb 10:5
n Dt 32:43 (LXX and DSS) Ps 97:7

1:7
o Ps 104:4

1:9
p Php 2:9
q Isa 61:1,3

1:11
r Isa 34:4

1:12
s Heb 13:8
t Ps 102:25-27

13 To which of the angels did God ever say,

> "Sit at my right hand
> until I make your enemies
> a footstool[a] for your feet"[a]?[b]

14 Are not all angels ministering spirits[c] sent to serve those who will inherit salvation?[d]

Chapter 2 Theme ____________________

2

We must pay more careful attention, therefore, to what we have heard, so that we do not drift away. 2 For if the message spoken[e] by angels[f] was binding, and every violation and disobedience received its just punishment,[g] 3 how shall we escape if we ignore such a great salvation?[h] This salvation, which was first announced by the Lord,[i] was confirmed to us by those who heard him.[j] 4 God also testified to it by signs, wonders and various miracles,[k] and gifts of the Holy Spirit[l] distributed according to his will.[m]

5 It is not to angels that he has subjected the world to come, about which we are speaking. 6 But there is a place where someone has testified:

> "What is man that you are mindful of him,
> the son of man that you care for him?[n]
> 7 You made him a little[b] lower than the angels;
> you crowned him with glory and honor
> 8 and put everything under his feet."[c][o]

In putting everything under him, God left nothing that is not subject to him. Yet at present we do not see everything subject to him. 9 But we see Jesus, who was made a little lower than the angels, now crowned with glory and honor[p] because he suffered death,[q] so that by the grace of God he might taste death for everyone.[r]

10 In bringing many sons to glory, it was fitting that God, for whom and through whom everything exists,[s] should make the author of their salvation perfect through suffering.[t] 11 Both the one who makes men holy and those who are made holy[u] are of the same family. So Jesus is not ashamed to call them brothers.[v] 12 He says,

> "I will declare your name to my brothers;
> in the presence of the congregation I will sing
> your praises."[d][w]

13 And again,

> "I will put my trust in him."[e][x]

1:13 [a]Jos 10:24; Heb 10:13 [b]Ps 110:1
1:14 [c]Ps 103:20 [d]Heb 5:9
2:2 [e]Heb 1:1 [f]Dt 33:2; Ac 7:53 [g]Heb 10:28
2:3 [h]Heb 10:29 [i]Heb 1:2 [j]Lk 1:2
2:4 [k]Jn 4:48 [l]1Co 12:4 [m]Eph 1:5
2:6 [n]Job 7:17
2:8 [o]Ps 8:4-6; 1Co 15:25
2:9 [p]Ac 2:33; 3:13; Php 2:9 [q]Php 2:7-9 [r]Jn 3:16; 2Co 5:15
2:10 [s]Ro 11:36 [t]Lk 24:26; Heb 7:28
2:11 [u]Heb 10:10 [v]Mt 28:10; Jn 20:17
2:12 [w]Ps 22:22
2:13 [x]Isa 8:17

[a] *13* Psalm 110:1 [b] *7* Or *him for a little while*; also in verse 9 [c] *8* Psalm 8:4-6
[d] *12* Psalm 22:22 [e] *13* Isaiah 8:17

And again he says,

"Here am I, and the children God has given me."[a][a]

14 Since the children have flesh and blood, he too shared in their
humanity[b] so that by his death he might destroy[c] him who holds
the power of death—that is, the devil[d]— 15 and free those who all
their lives were held in slavery by their fear[e] of death. 16 For surely
it is not angels he helps, but Abraham's descendants. 17 For this reason he had to be made like his brothers[f] in every way, in order that
he might become a merciful[g] and faithful high priest[h] in service to
God,[i] and that he might make atonement for[b] the sins of the people. 18 Because he himself suffered when he was tempted, he is able
to help those who are being tempted.[j]

Chapter 3 Theme ______________________

3 Therefore, holy brothers,[k] who share in the heavenly calling,
fix your thoughts on Jesus, the apostle and high priest[l] whom
we confess.[m] 2 He was faithful to the one who appointed him, just
as Moses was faithful in all God's house.[n] 3 Jesus has been found
worthy of greater honor than Moses, just as the builder of a house
has greater honor than the house itself. 4 For every house is built by
someone, but God is the builder of everything. 5 Moses was faithful
as a servant[o] in all God's house,[p] testifying to what would be said
in the future. 6 But Christ is faithful as a son[q] over God's house.
And we are his house,[r] if we hold on[s] to our courage and the hope[t]
of which we boast.

7 So, as the Holy Spirit says:[u]

"Today, if you hear his voice,
8 do not harden your hearts
as you did in the rebellion,
during the time of testing in the desert,
9 where your fathers tested and tried me
and for forty years saw what I did.[v]
10 That is why I was angry with that generation,
and I said, 'Their hearts are always going astray,
and they have not known my ways.'
11 So I declared on oath in my anger,
'They shall never enter my rest.'[w]"[c][x]

12 See to it, brothers, that none of you has a sinful, unbelieving
heart that turns away from the living God. 13 But encourage one
another daily,[y] as long as it is called Today, so that none of you may

a *13* Isaiah 8:18 b *17* Or *and that he might turn aside God's wrath, taking away*
c *11* Psalm 95:7-11

2:13 [a]Isa 8:18; Jn 10:29
2:14 [b]Jn 1:14 [c]1Co 15:54-57; 2Ti 1:10 [d]1Jn 3:8
2:15 [e]2Ti 1:7
2:17 [f]Php 2:7 [g]Heb 5:2 [h]Heb 4:14,15; 7:26,28 [i]Heb 5:1
2:18 [j]Heb 4:15
3:1 [k]Heb 2:11 [l]Heb 2:17 [m]Heb 4:14
3:2 [n]Nu 12:7
3:5 [o]Ex 14:31 [p]ver 2; Nu 12:7
3:6 [q]Heb 1:2 [r]1Co 3:16 [s]Ro 11:22 [t]Ro 5:2
3:7 [u]Heb 9:8
3:9 [v]Ac 7:36
3:11 [w]Heb 4:3,5 [x]Ps 95:7-11
3:13 [y]Heb 10:24,25

be hardened by sin's deceitfulness.[a] 14We have come to share in
Christ if we hold firmly[b] till the end the confidence we had at first.
15As has just been said:

> "Today, if you hear his voice,
> do not harden your hearts
> as you did in the rebellion."[a][c]

16Who were they who heard and rebelled? Were they not all
those Moses led out of Egypt?[d] 17And with whom was he angry for
forty years? Was it not with those who sinned, whose bodies fell in
the desert?[e] 18And to whom did God swear that they would never
enter his rest[f] if not to those who disobeyed[b]?[g] 19So we see that
they were not able to enter, because of their unbelief.[h]

Chapter 4 Theme ____________________________

4 Therefore, since the promise of entering his rest still stands,
let us be careful that none of you be found to have fallen short
of it.[i] 2For we also have had the gospel preached to us, just as they
did; but the message they heard was of no value to them, because
those who heard did not combine it with faith.[c][j] 3Now we who
have believed enter that rest, just as God has said,

> "So I declared on oath in my anger,
> 'They shall never enter my rest.'"[d][k]

And yet his work has been finished since the creation of the world.
4For somewhere he has spoken about the seventh day in these
words: "And on the seventh day God rested from all his work."[e][l]
5And again in the passage above he says, "They shall never enter
my rest."[m]

6It still remains that some will enter that rest, and those who formerly had the gospel preached to them did not go in, because of
their disobedience.[n] 7Therefore God again set a certain day, calling
it Today, when a long time later he spoke through David, as was
said before:

> "Today, if you hear his voice,
> do not harden your hearts."[f][o]

8For if Joshua had given them rest,[p] God would not have spoken[q]
later about another day. 9There remains, then, a Sabbath-rest for
the people of God; 10for anyone who enters God's rest also rests
from his own work, just as God did from his.[r] 11Let us, therefore,
make every effort to enter that rest, so that no one will fall by following their example of disobedience.[s]

3:13 [a]Eph 4:22
3:14 [b]ver 6
3:15 [c]ver 7,8; Ps 95:7,8
3:16 [d]Nu 14:2
3:17 [e]Nu 14:29; Ps 106:26
3:18 [f]Nu 14:20-23 [g]Heb 4:6
3:19 [h]Jn 3:36
4:1 [i]Heb 12:15
4:2 [j]1Th 2:13
4:3 [k]Ps 95:11; Heb 3:11
4:4 [l]Ge 2:2,3; Ex 20:11
4:5 [m]Ps 95:11
4:6 [n]Heb 3:18
4:7 [o]Ps 95:7,8; Heb 3:7,8,15
4:8 [p]Jos 22:4 [q]Heb 1:1
4:10 [r]ver 4
4:11 [s]Heb 3:18

[a] *15* Psalm 95:7,8 [b] *18* Or *disbelieved* [c] *2* Many manuscripts *because they did not share in the faith of those who obeyed* [d] *3* Psalm 95:11; also in verse 5 [e] *4* Gen. 2:2 [f] *7* Psalm 95:7,8

12For the word of God[a] is living and active.[b] Sharper than any
double-edged sword,[c] it penetrates even to dividing soul and
spirit, joints and marrow; it judges the thoughts and attitudes of
the heart.[d] 13Nothing in all creation is hidden from God's sight.[e]
Everything is uncovered and laid bare before the eyes of him to
whom we must give account.

14Therefore, since we have a great high priest who has gone
through the heavens,[a][f] Jesus the Son of God, let us hold firmly to the
faith we profess.[g] 15For we do not have a high priest who is unable to
sympathize with our weaknesses, but we have one who has been
tempted in every way, just as we are[h]—yet was without sin.[i] 16Let us
then approach the throne of grace with confidence, so that we may
receive mercy and find grace to help us in our time of need.

Chapter 5 Theme ______________________

5 Every high priest is selected from among men and is appointed
to represent them in matters related to God, to offer gifts and
sacrifices[j] for sins.[k] 2He is able to deal gently with those who are
ignorant and are going astray,[l] since he himself is subject to weakness.[m] 3This is why he has to offer sacrifices for his own sins, as well
as for the sins of the people.[n]

4No one takes this honor upon himself; he must be called by
God, just as Aaron was.[o] 5So Christ also did not take upon himself
the glory[p] of becoming a high priest. But God said[q] to him,

> "You are my Son;
> today I have become your Father.[b]"[c][r]

6And he says in another place,

> "You are a priest forever,
> in the order of Melchizedek."[d][s]

7During the days of Jesus' life on earth, he offered up prayers and
petitions with loud cries and tears[t] to the one who could save him
from death, and he was heard because of his reverent submission.[u]
8Although he was a son, he learned obedience from what he suffered[v] 9and, once made perfect,[w] he became the source of eternal
salvation for all who obey him 10and was designated by God to be
high priest[x] in the order of Melchizedek.[y]

11We have much to say about this, but it is hard to explain
because you are slow to learn. 12In fact, though by this time you
ought to be teachers, you need someone to teach you the elementary truths[z] of God's word all over again. You need milk, not solid
food![a] 13Anyone who lives on milk, being still an infant,[b] is not
acquainted with the teaching about righteousness. 14But solid food
is for the mature,[c] who by constant use have trained themselves to
distinguish good from evil.[d]

a 14 Or *gone into heaven* b 5 Or *have begotten you* c 5 Psalm 2:7 d 6 Psalm 110:4

4:12 [a] 1Pe 1:23 [b] Jer 23:29 [c] Eph 6:17; Rev 1:16 [d] 1Co 14:24,25
4:13 [e] Ps 33:13-15
4:14 [f] Heb 6:20 [g] Heb 3:1
4:15 [h] Heb 2:18 [i] 2Co 5:21
5:1 [j] Heb 8:3 [k] Heb 7:27
5:2 [l] Heb 2:18 [m] Heb 7:28
5:3 [n] Heb 7:27; 9:7
5:4 [o] Ex 28:1
5:5 [p] Jn 8:54 [q] Heb 1:1 [r] Ps 2:7
5:6 [s] Ps 110:4; Heb 7:17,21
5:7 [t] Mt 27:46,50 [u] Mk 14:36
5:8 [v] Php 2:8
5:9 [w] Heb 2:10
5:10 [x] ver 5 [y] ver 6
5:12 [z] Heb 6:1 [a] 1Co 3:2; 1Pe 2:2
5:13 [b] 1Co 14:20
5:14 [c] 1Co 2:6 [d] Isa 7:15

Chapter 6 Theme ____________________

6 Therefore let us leave[a] the elementary teachings[b] about Christ
and go on to maturity, not laying again the foundation of
repentance from acts that lead to death,[a][c] and of faith in God,
2 instruction about baptisms,[d] the laying on of hands,[e] the resurrection of the dead,[f] and eternal judgment. 3 And God permit-
ting,[g] we will do so.
4 It is impossible for those who have once been enlightened,[h] who
have tasted the heavenly gift,[i] who have shared in the Holy Spirit,[j]
5 who have tasted the goodness of the word of God and the powers
of the coming age, 6 if they fall away, to be brought back to repentance,[k] because[b] to their loss they are crucifying the Son of God all
over again and subjecting him to public disgrace.
7 Land that drinks in the rain often falling on it and that produces
a crop useful to those for whom it is farmed receives the blessing of
God. 8 But land that produces thorns and thistles is worthless and
is in danger of being cursed.[l] In the end it will be burned.
9 Even though we speak like this, dear friends,[m] we are confident
of better things in your case—things that accompany salvation.
10 God is not unjust; he will not forget your work and the love you
have shown him as you have helped his people and continue to
help them.[n] 11 We want each of you to show this same diligence to
the very end, in order to make your hope[o] sure. 12 We do not want
you to become lazy, but to imitate[p] those who through faith and
patience[q] inherit what has been promised.[r]
13 When God made his promise to Abraham, since there was no
one greater for him to swear by, he swore by himself,[s] 14 saying, "I
will surely bless you and give you many descendants."[c][t] 15 And so
after waiting patiently, Abraham received what was promised.[u]
16 Men swear by someone greater than themselves, and the oath
confirms what is said and puts an end to all argument.[v] 17 Because
God wanted to make the unchanging[w] nature of his purpose very
clear to the heirs of what was promised,[x] he confirmed it with an
oath. 18 God did this so that, by two unchangeable things in which
it is impossible for God to lie,[y] we who have fled to take hold of the
hope[z] offered to us may be greatly encouraged. 19 We have this
hope as an anchor for the soul, firm and secure. It enters the inner
sanctuary behind the curtain,[a] 20 where Jesus, who went before us,
has entered on our behalf.[b] He has become a high priest[c] forever,
in the order of Melchizedek.[d]

Chapter 7 Theme ____________________

7 This Melchizedek was king of Salem and priest of God Most
High.[e] He met Abraham returning from the defeat of the kings

6:1 [a] Php 3:12-14; [b] Heb 5:12; [c] Heb 9:14
6:2 [d] Jn 3:25; [e] Ac 6:6; [f] Ac 17:18,32
6:3 [g] Ac 18:21
6:4 [h] Heb 10:32; [i] Eph 2:8; [j] Gal 3:2
6:6 [k] 2Pe 2:21; 1Jn 5:16
6:8 [l] Ge 3:17,18; Isa 5:6
6:9 [m] 1Co 10:14
6:10 [n] Mt 10:40,42; 25:40; 1Th 1:3
6:11 [o] Heb 3:6
6:12 [p] Heb 13:7; [q] 2Th 1:4; Jas 1:3; Rev 13:10; [r] Heb 10:36
6:13 [s] Ge 22:16; Lk 1:73
6:14 [t] Ge 22:17
6:15 [u] Ge 21:5
6:16 [v] Ex 22:11
6:17 [w] Ps 110:4; [x] Heb 11:9
6:18 [y] Nu 23:19; Tit 1:2; [z] Heb 3:6
6:19 [a] Lev 16:2; Heb 9:2,3,7
6:20 [b] Heb 4:14; [c] Heb 2:17; [d] Heb 5:6
7:1 [e] Mk 5:7

[a] 1 Or *from useless rituals* [b] 6 Or *repentance while* [c] 14 Gen. 22:17

and blessed him,[a] 2and Abraham gave him a tenth of everything.
First, his name means "king of righteousness"; then also, "king of
Salem" means "king of peace." 3Without father or mother, without
genealogy,[b] without beginning of days or end of life, like the Son of
God[c] he remains a priest forever.

4Just think how great he was: Even the patriarch[d] Abraham gave
him a tenth of the plunder![e] 5Now the law requires the descendants
of Levi who become priests to collect a tenth from the people[f]—
that is, their brothers—even though their brothers are descended
from Abraham. 6This man, however, did not trace his descent from
Levi, yet he collected a tenth from Abraham and blessed[g] him who
had the promises.[h] 7And without doubt the lesser person is blessed
by the greater. 8In the one case, the tenth is collected by men who
die; but in the other case, by him who is declared to be living.[i] 9One
might even say that Levi, who collects the tenth, paid the tenth
through Abraham, 10because when Melchizedek met Abraham,
Levi was still in the body of his ancestor.

11If perfection could have been attained through the Levitical
priesthood (for on the basis of it the law was given to the people),[j]
why was there still need for another priest to come[k]—one in the
order of Melchizedek,[l] not in the order of Aaron? 12For when there
is a change of the priesthood, there must also be a change of the
law. 13He of whom these things are said belonged to a different
tribe,[m] and no one from that tribe has ever served at the altar.[n]
14For it is clear that our Lord descended from Judah,[o] and in regard
to that tribe Moses said nothing about priests. 15And what we have
said is even more clear if another priest like Melchizedek appears,
16one who has become a priest not on the basis of a regulation as to
his ancestry but on the basis of the power of an indestructible life.
17For it is declared:

> "You are a priest forever,
> in the order of Melchizedek."[a][p]

18The former regulation is set aside because it was weak and useless[q] 19(for the law made nothing perfect),[r] and a better hope is
introduced, by which we draw near to God.[s]

20And it was not without an oath! Others became priests without
any oath, 21but he became a priest with an oath when God said to
him:

> "The Lord has sworn
> and will not change his mind:[t]
> 'You are a priest forever.'"[a][u]

22Because of this oath, Jesus has become the guarantee of a better
covenant.[v]

a 17,21 Psalm 110:4

7:1 a Ge 14:18-20
7:3 b ver 6; c Mt 4:3
7:4 d Ac 2:29; e Ge 14:20
7:5 f Nu 18:21,26
7:6 g Ge 14:19,20; h Ro 4:13
7:8 i Heb 5:6; 6:20
7:11 j ver 18,19; Heb 8:7; k Heb 10:1; l ver 17
7:13 m ver 11; n ver 14
7:14 o Isa 11:1; Mt 1:3; Lk 3:33
7:17 p Ps 110:4; ver 21; Heb 5:6
7:18 q Ro 8:3
7:19 r Ac 13:39; Ro 3:20; Heb 9:9; s Heb 4:16
7:21 t 1Sa 15:29; u Ps 110:4
7:22 v Heb 8:6

23 Now there have been many of those priests, since death prevented them from continuing in office; 24 but because Jesus lives forever, he has a permanent priesthood.[a] 25 Therefore he is able to save completely[a] those who come to God[b] through him, because he always lives to intercede for them.[c]

26 Such a high priest meets our need—one who is holy, blameless, pure, set apart from sinners,[d] exalted above the heavens.[e] 27 Unlike the other high priests, he does not need to offer sacrifices[f] day after day, first for his own sins,[g] and then for the sins of the people. He sacrificed for their sins once for all[h] when he offered himself.[i] 28 For the law appoints as high priests men who are weak;[j] but the oath, which came after the law, appointed the Son,[k] who has been made perfect[l] forever.

Chapter 8 Theme ______________________________

8 The point of what we are saying is this: We do have such a high priest,[m] who sat down at the right hand of the throne of the Majesty in heaven, 2 and who serves in the sanctuary, the true tabernacle[n] set up by the Lord, not by man.

3 Every high priest is appointed to offer both gifts and sacrifices,[o] and so it was necessary for this one also to have something to offer.[p] 4 If he were on earth, he would not be a priest, for there are already men who offer the gifts prescribed by the law.[q] 5 They serve at a sanctuary that is a copy[r] and shadow[s] of what is in heaven. This is why Moses was warned[t] when he was about to build the tabernacle: "See to it that you make everything according to the pattern shown you on the mountain."[b][u] 6 But the ministry Jesus has received is as superior to theirs as the covenant[v] of which he is mediator[w] is superior to the old one, and it is founded on better promises.

7 For if there had been nothing wrong with that first covenant, no place would have been sought for another.[x] 8 But God found fault with the people and said[c]:

"The time is coming, declares the Lord,
  when I will make a new covenant[y]
with the house of Israel
  and with the house of Judah.
9 It will not be like the covenant
  I made with their forefathers[z]
when I took them by the hand
  to lead them out of Egypt,
because they did not remain faithful to my covenant,
  and I turned away from them,
        declares the Lord.

7:24 [a] ver 28
7:25 [b] ver 19 [c] Ro 8:34
7:26 [d] 2Co 5:21 [e] Heb 4:14
7:27 [f] Heb 5:1 [g] Heb 5:3 [h] Heb 9:12, 26,28 [i] Eph 5:2; Heb 9:14,28
7:28 [j] Heb 5:2 [k] Heb 1:2 [l] Heb 2:10
8:1 [m] Heb 2:17
8:2 [n] Heb 9:11,24
8:3 [o] Heb 5:1 [p] Heb 9:14
8:4 [q] Heb 5:1
8:5 [r] Heb 9:23 [s] Col 2:17; Heb 10:1 [t] Heb 11:7; 12:25 [u] Ex 25:40
8:6 [v] Lk 22:20 [w] Heb 7:22
8:7 [x] Heb 7:11,18
8:8 [y] Jer 31:31
8:9 [z] Ex 19:5,6

[a] 25 Or *forever* [b] 5 Exodus 25:40 [c] 8 Some manuscripts may be translated *fault and said to the people.*

10 This is the covenant I will make with the house of Israel
after that time, declares the Lord.
I will put my laws in their minds
and write them on their hearts.[a]
I will be their God,
and they will be my people.[b]
11 No longer will a man teach his neighbor,
or a man his brother, saying, 'Know the Lord,'
because they will all know me,[c]
from the least of them to the greatest.
12 For I will forgive their wickedness
and will remember their sins no more.[d]"[a][e]

13 By calling this covenant "new," he has made the first one obsolete;[f] and what is obsolete and aging will soon disappear.

Chapter 9 Theme ______________________________

9 Now the first covenant had regulations for worship and also an
earthly sanctuary.[g] 2 A tabernacle[h] was set up. In its first room
were the lampstand,[i] the table[j] and the consecrated bread;[k] this was
called the Holy Place. 3 Behind the second curtain was a room called
the Most Holy Place,[l] 4 which had the golden altar of incense[m] and
the gold-covered ark of the covenant.[n] This ark contained the gold
jar of manna,[o] Aaron's staff that had budded,[p] and the stone tablets
of the covenant. 5 Above the ark were the cherubim of the Glory,[q]
overshadowing the atonement cover.[b] But we cannot discuss these
things in detail now.
6 When everything had been arranged like this, the priests entered
regularly[r] into the outer room to carry on their ministry. 7 But only
the high priest entered[s] the inner room, and that only once a year,[t]

a *12* Jer. 31:31-34 b *5* Traditionally *the mercy seat*

8:10 [a] 2Co 3:3; Heb 10:16 [b] Zec 8:8
8:11 [c] Isa 54:13; Jn 6:45
8:12 [d] Heb 10:17 [e] Jer 31:31-34
8:13 [f] 2Co 5:17
9:1 [g] Ex 25:8
9:2 [h] Ex 25:8,9 [i] Ex 25:31-39 [j] Ex 25:23-29 [k] Lev 24:5-8
9:3 [l] Ex 26:31-33
9:4 [m] Ex 30:1-5 [n] Ex 25:10-22 [o] Ex 16:32,33 [p] Nu 17:10
9:5 [q] Ex 25:17-19
9:6 [r] Nu 28:3
9:7 [s] Lev 16:11-19 [t] Lev 16:34

Inside the Tabernacle

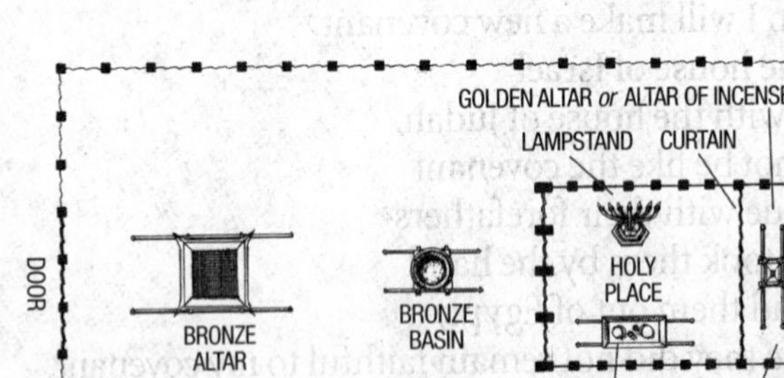

* The Old Testament places the Golden Altar or Altar of Incense outside the curtain (see Exodus 40:26).

and never without blood, which he offered for himself[a] and for the
sins the people had committed in ignorance. 8The Holy Spirit was
showing[b] by this that the way[c] into the Most Holy Place had not yet
been disclosed as long as the first tabernacle was still standing.
9This is an illustration for the present time, indicating that the gifts
and sacrifices being offered[d] were not able to clear the conscience
of the worshiper. 10They are only a matter of food[e] and drink[f] and
various ceremonial washings—external regulations[g] applying until
the time of the new order.

11When Christ came as high priest[h] of the good things that are
already here,[a][i] he went through the greater and more perfect
tabernacle[j] that is not man-made, that is to say, not a part of this
creation. 12He did not enter by means of the blood of goats and
calves;[k] but he entered the Most Holy Place[l] once for all[m] by his
own blood, having obtained eternal redemption. 13The blood of
goats and bulls and the ashes of a heifer[n] sprinkled on those who
are ceremonially unclean sanctify them so that they are outwardly
clean. 14How much more, then, will the blood of Christ, who
through the eternal Spirit[o] offered himself unblemished to God,
cleanse our consciences[p] from acts that lead to death,[b][q] so that we
may serve the living God!

15For this reason Christ is the mediator[r] of a new covenant, that
those who are called may receive the promised eternal inheritance—now that he has died as a ransom to set them free from the
sins committed under the first covenant.[s]

16In the case of a will,[c] it is necessary to prove the death of the
one who made it, 17because a will is in force only when somebody
has died; it never takes effect while the one who made it is living.
18This is why even the first covenant was not put into effect without blood.[t] 19When Moses had proclaimed every commandment
of the law to all the people, he took the blood of calves, together
with water, scarlet wool and branches of hyssop, and sprinkled
the scroll and all the people.[u] 20He said, "This is the blood of the
covenant, which God has commanded you to keep."[d][v] 21In the
same way, he sprinkled with the blood both the tabernacle and
everything used in its ceremonies. 22In fact, the law requires that
nearly everything be cleansed with blood,[w] and without the shedding of blood there is no forgiveness.[x]

23It was necessary, then, for the copies[y] of the heavenly things to
be purified with these sacrifices, but the heavenly things themselves
with better sacrifices than these. 24For Christ did not enter a man-made sanctuary that was only a copy of the true one;[z] he entered
heaven itself, now to appear for us in God's presence. 25Nor did he

9:7 [a]Heb 5:2,3
9:8 [b]Heb 3:7 [c]Jn 14:6; Heb 10:19,20
9:9 [d]Heb 5:1
9:10 [e]Lev 11:2-23 [f]Col 2:16 [g]Heb 7:16
9:11 [h]Heb 2:17 [i]Heb 10:1 [j]Heb 8:2
9:12 [k]Heb 10:4 [l]ver 24 [m]Heb 7:27
9:13 [n]Nu 19:9,17,18
9:14 [o]1Pe 3:18 [p]Tit 2:14; Heb 10:2,22 [q]Heb 6:1
9:15 [r]1Ti 2:5 [s]Heb 7:22
9:18 [t]Ex 24:6-8
9:19 [u]Ex 24:6-8
9:20 [v]Ex 24:8; Mt 26:28
9:22 [w]Lev 8:15 [x]Lev 17:11
9:23 [y]Heb 8:5
9:24 [z]Heb 8:2

[a] *11* Some early manuscripts *are to come* [b] *14* Or *from useless rituals* [c] *16* Same Greek word as *covenant*; also in verse 17 [d] *20* Exodus 24:8

enter heaven to offer himself again and again, the way the high
priest enters the Most Holy Place[a] every year with blood that is not
his own.[b] 26 Then Christ would have had to suffer many times since
the creation of the world.[c] But now he has appeared once for all[d] at
the end of the ages to do away with sin by the sacrifice of himself.
27 Just as man is destined to die once,[e] and after that to face judgment,[f] 28 so Christ was sacrificed once to take away the sins of many
people; and he will appear a second time,[g] not to bear sin,[h] but to
bring salvation to those who are waiting for him.[i]

Chapter 10 Theme ______________________________

10 The law is only a shadow[j] of the good things[k] that are coming—not the realities themselves.[l] For this reason it can
never, by the same sacrifices repeated endlessly year after year,
make perfect[m] those who draw near to worship. 2 If it could, would
they not have stopped being offered? For the worshipers would
have been cleansed once for all, and would no longer have felt
guilty for their sins. 3 But those sacrifices are an annual reminder
of sins,[n] 4 because it is impossible for the blood of bulls and goats[o]
to take away sins.

5 Therefore, when Christ came into the world,[p] he said:

> "Sacrifice and offering you did not desire,
> but a body you prepared for me;[q]
> 6 with burnt offerings and sin offerings
> you were not pleased.
> 7 Then I said, 'Here I am—it is written about me in
> the scroll[r]—
> I have come to do your will, O God.'"[a][s]

8 First he said, "Sacrifices and offerings, burnt offerings and sin
offerings you did not desire, nor were you pleased with them"[t]
(although the law required them to be made). 9 Then he said, "Here
I am, I have come to do your will."[u] He sets aside the first to
establish the second. 10 And by that will, we have been made holy[v]
through the sacrifice of the body[w] of Jesus Christ once for all.[x]
11 Day after day every priest stands and performs his religious
duties; again and again he offers the same sacrifices,[y] which can
never take away sins.[z] 12 But when this priest had offered for all
time one sacrifice for sins, he sat down at the right hand of God.
13 Since that time he waits for his enemies to be made his footstool,[a]
14 because by one sacrifice he has made perfect[b] forever those who
are being made holy.
15 The Holy Spirit also testifies[c] to us about this. First he says:

a 7 Psalm 40:6-8 (see Septuagint)

9:25 [a] Heb 10:19 [b] ver 7,8
9:26 [c] Heb 4:3 [d] Heb 7:27
9:27 [e] Ge 3:19 [f] 2Co 5:10
9:28 [g] Tit 2:13 [h] 1Pe 2:24 [i] 1Co 1:7
10:1 [j] Heb 8:5 [k] Heb 9:11 [l] Heb 9:23 [m] Heb 7:19
10:3 [n] Heb 9:7
10:4 [o] Heb 9:12,13
10:5 [p] Heb 1:6 [q] 1Pe 2:24
10:7 [r] Jer 36:2 [s] Ps 40:6-8
10:8 [t] ver 5,6; Mk 12:33
10:9 [u] ver 7
10:10 [v] Jn 17:19 [w] Heb 2:14; 1Pe 2:24 [x] Heb 7:27
10:11 [y] Heb 5:1 [z] ver 1,4
10:13 [a] Heb 1:13
10:14 [b] ver 1
10:15 [c] Heb 3:7

16“This is the covenant I will make with them
after that time, says the Lord.
I will put my laws in their hearts,
and I will write them on their minds.”[a][a]

17Then he adds:

“Their sins and lawless acts
I will remember no more.”[b][b]

18And where these have been forgiven, there is no longer any sacrifice for sin.

19Therefore, brothers, since we have confidence to enter the Most
Holy Place[c] by the blood of Jesus, 20by a new and living way[d]
opened for us through the curtain,[e] that is, his body, 21and since
we have a great priest[f] over the house of God, 22let us draw near
to God[g] with a sincere heart in full assurance of faith, having our
hearts sprinkled to cleanse us from a guilty conscience[h] and having our bodies washed with pure water. 23Let us hold unswervingly
to the hope[i] we profess, for he who promised is faithful.[j] 24And let
us consider how we may spur one another on toward love and
good deeds. 25Let us not give up meeting together,[k] as some are in
the habit of doing, but let us encourage one another[l]—and all the
more as you see the Day approaching.

26If we deliberately keep on sinning[m] after we have received the
knowledge of the truth, no sacrifice for sins is left, 27but only a fearful expectation of judgment and of raging fire[n] that will consume
the enemies of God. 28Anyone who rejected the law of Moses died
without mercy on the testimony of two or three witnesses.[o] 29How
much more severely do you think a man deserves to be punished
who has trampled the Son of God under foot,[p] who has treated as
an unholy thing the blood of the covenant[q] that sanctified him,
and who has insulted the Spirit[r] of grace?[s] 30For we know him who
said, “It is mine to avenge; I will repay,”[c][t] and again, “The Lord
will judge his people.”[d][u] 31It is a dreadful thing to fall into the
hands of the living God.[v]

32Remember those earlier days after you had received the light,[w]
when you stood your ground in a great contest in the face of suffering.[x] 33Sometimes you were publicly exposed to insult and persecution;[y] at other times you stood side by side with those who were
so treated.[z] 34You sympathized with those in prison[a] and joyfully
accepted the confiscation of your property, because you knew that
you yourselves had better and lasting possessions.[b]

35So do not throw away your confidence; it will be richly rewarded. 36You need to persevere[c] so that when you have done the will

10:16 [a]Jer 31:33; Heb 8:10
10:17 [b]Heb 8:12
10:19 [c]Eph 2:18; Heb 9:8,12,25
10:20 [d]Heb 9:8 [e]Heb 9:3
10:21 [f]Heb 2:17
10:22 [g]Heb 7:19 [h]Eze 36:25; Heb 9:14
10:23 [i]Heb 3:6 [j]1Co 1:9
10:25 [k]Ac 2:42 [l]Heb 3:13
10:26 [m]Nu 15:30; 2Pe 2:20
10:27 [n]Isa 26:11; 2Th 1:7; Heb 9:27
10:28 [o]Dt 17:6,7; Heb 2:2
10:29 [p]Heb 6:6 [q]Mt 26:28 [r]Eph 4:30; Heb 6:4 [s]Heb 2:3
10:30 [t]Dt 32:35; Ro 12:19 [u]Dt 32:36
10:31 [v]Mt 16:16
10:32 [w]Heb 6:4 [x]Php 1:29,30
10:33 [y]1Co 4:9 [z]Php 4:14; 1Th 2:14
10:34 [a]Heb 13:3 [b]Heb 11:16
10:36 [c]Lk 21:19; Heb 12:1

[a]*16* Jer. 31:33 [b]*17* Jer. 31:34 [c]*30* Deut. 32:35 [d]*30* Deut. 32:36; Psalm 135:14

of God, you will receive what he has promised. 37For in just a very little while,

> "He who is coming[a] will come and will not delay.[b]
> 38 But my righteous one[a] will live by faith.[c]
> And if he shrinks back,
> I will not be pleased with him."[b]

39But we are not of those who shrink back and are destroyed, but of those who believe and are saved.

Chapter 11 Theme ______________________________

11 Now faith is being sure of what we hope for and certain of what we do not see.[d] 2This is what the ancients were commended for.[e]

3By faith we understand that the universe was formed at God's command,[f] so that what is seen was not made out of what was visible.

4By faith Abel offered God a better sacrifice than Cain did. By faith he was commended as a righteous man, when God spoke well of his offerings.[g] And by faith he still speaks, even though he is dead.[h]

5By faith Enoch was taken from this life, so that he did not experience death; he could not be found, because God had taken him away.[i] For before he was taken, he was commended as one who pleased God. 6And without faith it is impossible to please God, because anyone who comes to him[j] must believe that he exists and that he rewards those who earnestly seek him.

7By faith Noah, when warned about things not yet seen, in holy fear built an ark[k] to save his family.[l] By his faith he condemned the world and became heir of the righteousness that comes by faith.

8By faith Abraham, when called to go to a place he would later receive as his inheritance,[m] obeyed and went,[n] even though he did not know where he was going. 9By faith he made his home in the promised land[o] like a stranger in a foreign country; he lived in tents,[p] as did Isaac and Jacob, who were heirs with him of the same promise.[q] 10For he was looking forward to the city[r] with foundations,[s] whose architect and builder is God.

11By faith Abraham, even though he was past age—and Sarah herself was barren[t]—was enabled to become a father[u] because he[c] considered him faithful who had made the promise. 12And so from this one man, and he as good as dead,[v] came descendants as numerous as the stars in the sky and as countless as the sand on the seashore.[w]

a 38 One early manuscript *But the righteous* b 38 Hab. 2:3,4 c 11 Or *By faith even Sarah, who was past age, was enabled to bear children because she*

10:37 [a]Mt 11:3 [b]Rev 22:20
10:38 [c]Ro 1:17; Gal 3:11
11:1 [d]Ro 8:24; 2Co 4:18
11:2 [e]ver 4,39
11:3 [f]Ge 1; Jn 1:3; 2Pe 3:5
11:4 [g]Ge 4:4; 1Jn 3:12 [h]Heb 12:24
11:5 [i]Ge 5:21-24
11:6 [j]Heb 7:19
11:7 [k]Ge 6:13-22 [l]1Pe 3:20
11:8 [m]Ge 12:7 [n]Ge 12:1-4; Ac 7:2-4
11:9 [o]Ac 7:5 [p]Ge 12:8; 18:1,9 [q]Heb 6:17
11:10 [r]Heb 12:22; 13:14 [s]Rev 21:2,14
11:11 [t]Ge 17:17-19; 18:11-14 [u]Ge 21:2
11:12 [v]Ro 4:19 [w]Ge 22:17

13 All these people were still living by faith when they died. They
did not receive the things promised;[a] they only saw them and welcomed them from a distance.[b] And they admitted that they were
aliens and strangers on earth.[c] 14 People who say such things show
that they are looking for a country of their own. 15 If they had been
thinking of the country they had left, they would have had opportunity to return.[d] 16 Instead, they were longing for a better country—a heavenly one.[e] Therefore God is not ashamed[f] to be called
their God,[g] for he has prepared a city[h] for them.
17 By faith Abraham, when God tested him, offered Isaac as a sacrifice.[i] He who had received the promises was about to sacrifice
his one and only son, 18 even though God had said to him, "It is
through Isaac that your offspring[a] will be reckoned."[b][j] 19 Abraham
reasoned that God could raise the dead,[k] and figuratively speaking,
he did receive Isaac back from death.
20 By faith Isaac blessed Jacob and Esau in regard to their future.[l]
21 By faith Jacob, when he was dying, blessed each of Joseph's
sons,[m] and worshiped as he leaned on the top of his staff.
22 By faith Joseph, when his end was near, spoke about the exodus
of the Israelites from Egypt and gave instructions about his bones.[n]
23 By faith Moses' parents hid him for three months after he was
born,[o] because they saw he was no ordinary child, and they were
not afraid of the king's edict.[p]
24 By faith Moses, when he had grown up, refused to be known as
the son of Pharaoh's daughter.[q] 25 He chose to be mistreated[r] along
with the people of God rather than to enjoy the pleasures of sin for
a short time. 26 He regarded disgrace[s] for the sake of Christ as of
greater value than the treasures of Egypt, because he was looking
ahead to his reward.[t] 27 By faith he left Egypt,[u] not fearing the king's
anger; he persevered because he saw him who is invisible. 28 By
faith he kept the Passover and the sprinkling of blood, so that the
destroyer of the firstborn would not touch the firstborn of Israel.[v]
29 By faith the people passed through the Red Sea[c] as on dry land;
but when the Egyptians tried to do so, they were drowned.[w]
30 By faith the walls of Jericho fell, after the people had marched
around them for seven days.[x]
31 By faith the prostitute Rahab, because she welcomed the spies,
was not killed with those who were disobedient.[d][y]
32 And what more shall I say? I do not have time to tell about
Gideon, Barak,[z] Samson, Jephthah, David,[a] Samuel[b] and the
prophets, 33 who through faith conquered kingdoms,[c] adminis-
tered justice, and gained what was promised; who shut the mouths
of lions,[d] 34 quenched the fury of the flames, and escaped the edge
of the sword; whose weakness was turned to strength;[e] and who

11:13 [a]ver 39 [b]Mt 13:17 [c]Ge 23:4; Ps 39:12; 1Pe 1:17
11:15 [d]Ge 24:6-8
11:16 [e]2Ti 4:18 [f]Mk 8:38 [g]Ex 3:6,15 [h]Heb 13:14
11:17 [i]Ge 22:1-10; Jas 2:21
11:18 [j]Ge 21:12; Ro 9:7
11:19 [k]Ro 4:21
11:20 [l]Ge 27:27-29, 39,40
11:21 [m]Ge 48:1,8-22
11:22 [n]Ge 50:24,25; Ex 13:19
11:23 [o]Ex 2:2 [p]Ex 1:16,22
11:24 [q]Ex 2:10,11
11:25 [r]ver 37
11:26 [s]Heb 13:13 [t]Heb 10:35
11:27 [u]Ex 12:50,51
11:28 [v]Ex 12:21-23
11:29 [w]Ex 14:21-31
11:30 [x]Jos 6:12-20
11:31 [y]Jos 2:1,9-14; 6:22-25; Jas 2:25
11:32 [z]Jdg 4–5 [a]1Sa 16:1,13 [b]1Sa 1:20
11:33 [c]2Sa 7:11; 8:1-3 [d]Da 6:22
11:34 [e]2Ki 20:7

[a] *18* Greek *seed* [b] *18* Gen. 21:12 [c] *29* That is, Sea of Reeds [d] *31* Or *unbelieving*

became powerful in battle and routed foreign armies.[a] 35Women
received back their dead, raised to life again.[b] Others were tortured
and refused to be released, so that they might gain a better resurrection. 36Some faced jeers and flogging,[c] while still others were
chained and put in prison.[d] 37They were stoned[a];[e] they were sawed
in two; they were put to death by the sword.[f] They went about in
sheepskins and goatskins,[g] destitute, persecuted and mistreated—
38the world was not worthy of them. They wandered in deserts and
mountains, and in caves[h] and holes in the ground.

39These were all commended[i] for their faith, yet none of them
received what had been promised.[j] 40God had planned something
better for us so that only together with us would they be made
perfect.

Chapter 12 Theme ______________________________

12 Therefore, since we are surrounded by such a great cloud of
witnesses, let us throw off everything that hinders and the
sin that so easily entangles, and let us run[k] with perseverance[l] the
race marked out for us. 2Let us fix our eyes on Jesus, the author
and perfecter of our faith, who for the joy set before him endured
the cross,[m] scorning its shame,[n] and sat down at the right hand of
the throne of God. 3Consider him who endured such opposition
from sinful men, so that you will not grow weary[o] and lose heart.

4In your struggle against sin, you have not yet resisted to the
point of shedding your blood.[p] 5And you have forgotten that word
of encouragement that addresses you as sons:

> "My son, do not make light of the Lord's discipline,
> and do not lose heart when he rebukes you,
> 6because the Lord disciplines those he loves,[q]
> and he punishes everyone he accepts as a son."[b][r]

7Endure hardship as discipline; God is treating you as sons.[s] For
what son is not disciplined by his father? 8If you are not disciplined
(and everyone undergoes discipline),[t] then you are illegitimate
children and not true sons. 9Moreover, we have all had human
fathers who disciplined us and we respected them for it. How
much more should we submit to the Father of our spirits[u] and
live![v] 10Our fathers disciplined us for a little while as they thought
best; but God disciplines us for our good, that we may share in his
holiness.[w] 11No discipline seems pleasant at the time, but painful.
Later on, however, it produces a harvest of righteousness and
peace[x] for those who have been trained by it.

12Therefore, strengthen your feeble arms and weak knees.[y]
13"Make level paths for your feet,"[c][z] so that the lame may not be
disabled, but rather healed.[a]

[a]*37* Some early manuscripts *stoned; they were put to the test;* [b]*6* Prov. 3:11,12 [c]*13* Prov. 4:26

11:34 [a]Jdg 15:8
11:35 [b]1Ki 17:22,23
11:36 [c]Jer 20:2 [d]Ge 39:20
11:37 [e]2Ch 24:21 [f]1Ki 19:10 [g]2Ki 1:8
11:38 [h]1Ki 18:4
11:39 [i]ver 2,4 [j]ver 13
12:1 [k]1Co 9:24 [l]Heb 10:36
12:2 [m]Php 2:8,9 [n]Heb 13:13
12:3 [o]Gal 6:9
12:4 [p]Heb 10:32-34
12:6 [q]Ps 94:12; Rev 3:19 [r]Pr 3:11,12
12:7 [s]Dt 8:5
12:8 [t]1Pe 5:9
12:9 [u]Nu 16:22 [v]Isa 38:16
12:10 [w]2Pe 1:4
12:11 [x]Isa 32:17; Jas 3:17,18
12:12 [y]Isa 35:3
12:13 [z]Pr 4:26 [a]Gal 6:1

14Make every effort to live in peace with all men[a] and to be holy;[b]
without holiness no one will see the Lord.[c] 15See to it that no one
misses the grace of God[d] and that no bitter root grows up to cause
trouble and defile many. 16See that no one is sexually immoral, or is
godless like Esau, who for a single meal sold his inheritance rights
as the oldest son.[e] 17Afterward, as you know, when he wanted to
inherit this blessing, he was rejected. He could bring about no
change of mind, though he sought the blessing with tears.[f]
18You have not come to a mountain that can be touched and that
is burning with fire; to darkness, gloom and storm;[g] 19to a trumpet
blast[h] or to such a voice speaking words that those who heard it
begged that no further word be spoken to them,[i] 20because they
could not bear what was commanded: "If even an animal touches
the mountain, it must be stoned."[a][j] 21The sight was so terrifying
that Moses said, "I am trembling with fear."[b]
22But you have come to Mount Zion, to the heavenly Jerusalem,[k]
the city[l] of the living God. You have come to thousands upon thousands of angels in joyful assembly, 23to the church of the firstborn,
whose names are written in heaven.[m] You have come to God, the
judge of all men,[n] to the spirits of righteous men made perfect,[o]
24to Jesus the mediator of a new covenant, and to the sprinkled
blood that speaks a better word than the blood of Abel.[p]
25See to it that you do not refuse him who speaks. If they did not
escape when they refused him who warned[q] them on earth, how
much less will we, if we turn away from him who warns us from
heaven?[r] 26At that time his voice shook the earth,[s] but now he has
promised, "Once more I will shake not only the earth but also the
heavens."[c][t] 27The words "once more" indicate the removing of
what can be shaken[u]—that is, created things—so that what cannot
be shaken may remain.
28Therefore, since we are receiving a kingdom that cannot be
shaken,[v] let us be thankful, and so worship God acceptably with
reverence and awe,[w] 29for our "God is a consuming fire."[d][x]

Chapter 13 Theme ____________________

13 Keep on loving each other as brothers.[y] 2Do not forget to
entertain strangers,[z] for by so doing some people have entertained angels without knowing it.[a] 3Remember those in prison[b] as
if you were their fellow prisoners, and those who are mistreated as
if you yourselves were suffering.
4Marriage should be honored by all, and the marriage bed kept
pure, for God will judge the adulterer and all the sexually immoral.[c]
5Keep your lives free from the love of money and be content with
what you have,[d] because God has said,

12:14 [a]Ro 14:19 [b]Ro 6:22 [c]Mt 5:8
12:15 [d]Gal 5:4; Heb 3:12
12:16 [e]Ge 25:29-34
12:17 [f]Ge 27:30-40
12:18 [g]Ex 19:12-22; Dt 4:11
12:19 [h]Ex 20:18 [i]Ex 20:19; Dt 5:5,25
12:20 [j]Ex 19:12,13
12:22 [k]Gal 4:26 [l]Heb 11:10
12:23 [m]Lk 10:20 [n]Ps 94:2 [o]Php 3:12
12:24 [p]Ge 4:10; Heb 11:4
12:25 [q]Heb 8:5; 11:7 [r]Heb 2:2,3
12:26 [s]Ex 19:18 [t]Hag 2:6
12:27 [u]1Co 7:31; 2Pe 3:10
12:28 [v]Da 2:44 [w]Heb 13:15
12:29 [x]Dt 4:24
13:1 [y]Ro 12:10; 1Pe 1:22
13:2 [z]Mt 25:35 [a]Ge 18:1-33
13:3 [b]Mt 25:36; Col 4:18
13:4 [c]1Co 6:9
13:5 [d]Php 4:11

[a] *20* Exodus 19:12,13 [b] *21* Deut. 9:19 [c] *26* Haggai 2:6 [d] *29* Deut. 4:24

"Never will I leave you;
never will I forsake you."[a][a]

[6]So we say with confidence,

"The Lord is my helper; I will not be afraid.
What can man do to me?"[b]

[7]Remember your leaders,[b] who spoke the word of God to you.
Consider the outcome of their way of life and imitate[c] their faith.
[8]Jesus Christ is the same yesterday and today and forever.[d]
[9]Do not be carried away by all kinds of strange teachings.[e] It is
good for our hearts to be strengthened[f] by grace, not by ceremonial foods,[g] which are of no value to those who eat them. [10]We
have an altar from which those who minister at the tabernacle
have no right to eat.[h]
[11]The high priest carries the blood of animals into the Most Holy
Place as a sin offering, but the bodies are burned outside the camp.[i]
[12]And so Jesus also suffered outside the city gate[j] to make the people holy through his own blood. [13]Let us, then, go to him outside
the camp, bearing the disgrace he bore.[k] [14]For here we do not have
an enduring city, but we are looking for the city that is to come.[l]
[15]Through Jesus, therefore, let us continually offer to God a sacrifice[m] of praise—the fruit of lips[n] that confess his name. [16]And
do not forget to do good and to share with others,[o] for with such
sacrifices[p] God is pleased.
[17]Obey your leaders and submit to their authority. They keep
watch over you[q] as men who must give an account. Obey them so
that their work will be a joy, not a burden, for that would be of no
advantage to you.
[18]Pray for us.[r] We are sure that we have a clear conscience[s] and
desire to live honorably in every way. [19]I particularly urge you to
pray so that I may be restored to you soon.[t]
[20]May the God of peace,[u] who through the blood of the eternal
covenant[v] brought back from the dead[w] our Lord Jesus, that great
Shepherd of the sheep,[x] [21]equip you with everything good for
doing his will, and may he work in us[y] what is pleasing to him,[z]
through Jesus Christ, to whom be glory for ever and ever. Amen.[a]

[22]Brothers, I urge you to bear with my word of exhortation, for I
have written you only a short letter.[b]
[23]I want you to know that our brother Timothy[c] has been released.
If he arrives soon, I will come with him to see you.
[24]Greet all your leaders[d] and all God's people. Those from Italy[e]
send you their greetings.
[25]Grace be with you all.[f]

[a]5 Deut. 31:6 [b]6 Psalm 118:6,7

13:5 [a]Dt 31:6,8; Jos 1:5
13:7 [b]ver 17,24 [c]Heb 6:12
13:8 [d]Heb 1:12
13:9 [e]Eph 4:14 [f]Col 2:7 [g]Col 2:16
13:10 [h]1Co 9:13; 10:18
13:11 [i]Ex 29:14; Lev 16:27
13:12 [j]Jn 19:17
13:13 [k]Heb 11:26
13:14 [l]Php 3:20; Heb 12:22
13:15 [m]1Pe 2:5 [n]Hos 14:2
13:16 [o]Ro 12:13 [p]Php 4:18
13:17 [q]Isa 62:6; Ac 20:28
13:18 [r]1Th 5:25 [s]Ac 23:1
13:19 [t]Phm 22
13:20 [u]Ro 15:33 [v]Isa 55:3; Eze 37:26; Zec 9:11 [w]Ac 2:24 [x]Jn 10:11
13:21 [y]Php 2:13 [z]1Jn 3:22 [a]Ro 11:36
13:22 [b]1Pe 5:12
13:23 [c]Ac 16:1
13:24 [d]ver 7,17 [e]Ac 18:2
13:25 [f]Col 4:18

Hebrews Observations Chart

Author

Recipients

Exhortations

(continued)

WARNINGS/CONSEQUENCES

HEBREWS AT A GLANCE

Theme of Hebrews:

Author:

unknown

Date:

Purpose:

Key Words:

- Jesus (son) (mark only when referring to Jesus as a son)
- God
- angels
- priest (priests, priesthood)
- therefore, for this reason, so, then, this (that) is why
- faith, believe (faithful)
- greater, many
- better, superior to (a better word than)
- let us
- perfect, clear
- mark the reference to the devil
- covenant, will

SEGMENT DIVISIONS		CHAPTER THEMES
		1
		2
		3
		4
		5
		6
		7
		8
		9
		10
		11
		12
		13

JAMES

What a turnaround from the day James told his half-brother what to do if he wanted to be known publicly! Full of unbelief and convinced that Jesus was nothing more than his eldest brother, James told Jesus to take his disciples and go up to the Feast of Booths and do his works there. Jesus might have found more disciples there, but James was not to be numbered as one of them—until Jesus rose from the dead (see 1 Corinthians 15:7).

Convinced from that point on that Jesus was the Christ, James would lay claim not to his physical relationship to Jesus but to his spiritual relationship as a bondservant of the Lord Jesus Christ.

James became a pillar of the church, a leader of the council of Jerusalem, and a friend of Peter and Paul. But most of all he was a friend of Jesus, a covenant friend for whom he would be martyred around A.D. 62.

Sometime before A.D. 50 or in the early 50s, James would write his one epistle to be included in the pages of Holy Scripture, an epistle that would show what the gospel is like when it is lived out in shoe leather.

THINGS TO DO

1. Read James in one sitting to familiarize yourself with the book as a whole. James structures his writing distinctively. Once you see the pattern he uses, you will better understand the flow of the book.
   a. First, James introduces a subject by making a statement or giving an instruction. For example, in James 1:2 he says to consider it pure joy whenever you face trials of many kinds.
   b. He then usually follows with more instructions concerning that particular subject, *or* he gives an illustration pertaining to the subject, *or* he gives an explanation of it.
2. As you read back through James, mark in the text the key words (and their synonyms and pronouns) listed on the JAMES AT A GLANCE chart on page 2104. (Key words help you see the subjects of the book.)
   a. Mark every use of *say (says, claims to)* and *deeds (actions* as well as *do, does,* and *did* since they refer to *actions)* in chapter 2.
   b. Don't miss marking *tongue* and its pronouns in chapter 3.
   c. You may find other key words which are not listed for you. Mark these and also mark *grace* and any reference to the devil (as you have done throughout your Bible).
3. Read James chapter by chapter:
   a. List the subjects introduced by the author on the JAMES SUBJECT BY SUBJECT chart on pages 2102-2104. Be sure to include the chapter and verse from which you took the information.
   b. Next, if the author gives instructions or illustrations regarding a particular subject, record that information in the appropriate column. See JAMES SUBJECT BY SUBJECT for an example of how to do this.
4. After you list the subjects in each chapter, determine the theme of each chapter and record these themes on JAMES AT A GLANCE and in the text by each chapter number.
5. Finally, look for the theme of James. From the information gathered, determine if one subject is more predominant than the others or if there is a common denominator among the subjects. The more dominant or common subject will be the theme of James and points to the author's reason for writing. Record the theme of James on JAMES AT A GLANCE and complete the chart.

THINGS TO THINK ABOUT

1. How are you handling the trials in your life?
2. Are you a doer of the Word or a hearer only?

3. Do you show favoritism in dealing with people? Are you a respecter of persons?
4. Is your faith seen by your works?
5. Are you a friend of the world?

Chapter 1 Theme

1 James,[a] a servant of God[b] and of the Lord Jesus Christ,
To the twelve tribes[c] scattered[d] among the nations:
Greetings.
2 Consider it pure joy, my brothers, whenever you face trials of
many kinds,[e] 3 because you know that the testing of your faith
develops perseverance. 4 Perseverance must finish its work so that
you may be mature and complete, not lacking anything. 5 If any of
you lacks wisdom, he should ask God,[f] who gives generously to all
without finding fault, and it will be given to him.[g] 6 But when he
asks, he must believe and not doubt,[h] because he who doubts is
like a wave of the sea, blown and tossed by the wind. 7 That man
should not think he will receive anything from the Lord; 8 he is a
double-minded man,[i] unstable in all he does.
9 The brother in humble circumstances ought to take pride in his
high position. 10 But the one who is rich should take pride in his
low position, because he will pass away like a wild flower.[j] 11 For
the sun rises with scorching heat and withers[k] the plant; its blossom falls and its beauty is destroyed.[l] In the same way, the rich
man will fade away even while he goes about his business.
12 Blessed is the man who perseveres under trial, because when
he has stood the test, he will receive the crown of life[m] that God has
promised to those who love him.[n]
13 When tempted, no one should say, "God is tempting me." For
God cannot be tempted by evil, nor does he tempt anyone; 14 but
each one is tempted when, by his own evil desire, he is dragged
away and enticed. 15 Then, after desire has conceived, it gives birth
to sin;[o] and sin, when it is full-grown, gives birth to death.[p]
16 Don't be deceived,[q] my dear brothers.[r] 17 Every good and perfect gift is from above,[s] coming down from the Father of the
heavenly lights, who does not change[t] like shifting shadows. 18 He
chose to give us birth[u] through the word of truth, that we might be
a kind of firstfruits[v] of all he created.
19 My dear brothers, take note of this: Everyone should be quick to
listen, slow to speak[w] and slow to become angry, 20 for man's anger
does not bring about the righteous life that God desires. 21 Therefore, get rid of[x] all moral filth and the evil that is so prevalent and
humbly accept the word planted in you,[y] which can save you.

1:1 [a] Ac 15:13 [b] Tit 1:1 [c] Ac 26:7 [d] Dt 32:26; Jn 7:35; 1Pe 1:1
1:2 [e] Mt 5:12; 1Pe 1:6
1:5 [f] 1Ki 3:9,10; Pr 2:3-6 [g] Mt 7:7
1:6 [h] Mk 11:24
1:8 [i] Jas 4:8
1:10 [j] 1Co 7:31; 1Pe 1:24
1:11 [k] Ps 102:4,11 [l] Isa 40:6-8
1:12 [m] 1Co 9:25 [n] Jas 2:5
1:15 [o] Job 15:35; Ps 7:14 [p] Ro 6:23
1:16 [q] 1Co 6:9 [r] ver 19
1:17 [s] Jn 3:27 [t] Nu 23:19; Mal 3:6
1:18 [u] Jn 1:13 [v] Eph 1:12; Rev 14:4
1:19 [w] Pr 10:19
1:21 [x] Eph 4:22 [y] Eph 1:13

22 Do not merely listen to the word, and so deceive yourselves. Do
what it says. 23 Anyone who listens to the word but does not do what
it says is like a man who looks at his face in a mirror 24 and, after
looking at himself, goes away and immediately forgets what he
looks like. 25 But the man who looks intently into the perfect law
that gives freedom,[a] and continues to do this, not forgetting what
he has heard, but doing it—he will be blessed in what he does.[b]

26 If anyone considers himself religious and yet does not keep a
tight rein on his tongue,[c] he deceives himself and his religion is
worthless. 27 Religion that God our Father accepts as pure and
faultless is this: to look after[d] orphans and widows[e] in their distress
and to keep oneself from being polluted by the world.[f]

Chapter 2 Theme ________________________

2 My brothers, as believers in our glorious[g] Lord Jesus Christ,
don't show favoritism.[h] 2 Suppose a man comes into your
meeting wearing a gold ring and fine clothes, and a poor man in
shabby clothes also comes in. 3 If you show special attention to the
man wearing fine clothes and say, "Here's a good seat for you,"
but say to the poor man, "You stand there" or "Sit on the floor by
my feet," 4 have you not discriminated among yourselves and
become judges[i] with evil thoughts?

5 Listen, my dear brothers:[j] Has not God chosen those who are
poor in the eyes of the world[k] to be rich in faith[l] and to inherit the
kingdom he promised those who love him?[m] 6 But you have insulted the poor.[n] Is it not the rich who are exploiting you? Are they not
the ones who are dragging you into court?[o] 7 Are they not the ones
who are slandering the noble name of him to whom you belong?

8 If you really keep the royal law found in Scripture, "Love your
neighbor as yourself,"[a][p] you are doing right. 9 But if you show
favoritism,[q] you sin and are convicted by the law as lawbreakers.[r]
10 For whoever keeps the whole law and yet stumbles at just one
point is guilty of breaking all of it.[s] 11 For he who said, "Do not
commit adultery,"[b][t] also said, "Do not murder."[c][u] If you do not
commit adultery but do commit murder, you have become a lawbreaker.

12 Speak and act as those who are going to be judged by the law
that gives freedom,[v] 13 because judgment without mercy will be
shown to anyone who has not been merciful.[w] Mercy triumphs
over judgment!

14 What good is it, my brothers, if a man claims to have faith but
has no deeds?[x] Can such faith save him? 15 Suppose a brother or sister is without clothes and daily food.[y] 16 If one of you says to him,

[a] *8* Lev. 19:18 [b] *11* Exodus 20:14; Deut. 5:18 [c] *11* Exodus 20:13; Deut. 5:17

1:25 [a] Jas 2:12 [b] Jn 13:17

1:26 [c] Ps 34:13; 1Pe 3:10

1:27 [d] Mt 25:36 [e] Isa 1:17,23 [f] Ro 12:2

2:1 [g] 1Co 2:8 [h] Lev 19:15

2:4 [i] Jn 7:24

2:5 [j] Jas 1:16,19 [k] 1Co 1:26-28 [l] Lk 12:21 [m] Jas 1:12

2:6 [n] 1Co 11:22 [o] Ac 8:3

2:8 [p] Lev 19:18

2:9 [q] ver 1 [r] Dt 1:17

2:10 [s] Mt 5:19; Gal 3:10

2:11 [t] Ex 20:14; Dt 5:18 [u] Ex 20:13; Dt 5:17

2:12 [v] Jas 1:25

2:13 [w] Mt 5:7; 18:32-35

2:14 [x] Mt 7:26; Jas 1:22-25

2:15 [y] Mt 25:35,36

"Go, I wish you well; keep warm and well fed," but does nothing about his physical needs, what good is it?[a] 17In the same way, faith by itself, if it is not accompanied by action, is dead.

18But someone will say, "You have faith; I have deeds."

Show me your faith without deeds,[b] and I will show you my faith by what I do.[c] 19You believe that there is one God.[d] Good! Even the demons believe that[e]—and shudder.

20You foolish man, do you want evidence that faith without deeds is useless[a]?[f] 21Was not our ancestor Abraham considered righteous for what he did when he offered his son Isaac on the altar?[g] 22You see that his faith and his actions were working together,[h] and his faith was made complete by what he did.[i] 23And the scripture was fulfilled that says, "Abraham believed God, and it was credited to him as righteousness,"[b][j] and he was called God's friend.[k] 24You see that a person is justified by what he does and not by faith alone.

25In the same way, was not even Rahab the prostitute considered righteous for what she did when she gave lodging to the spies and sent them off in a different direction?[l] 26As the body without the spirit is dead, so faith without deeds is dead.[m]

Chapter 3 Theme ______________________________

3

Not many of you should presume to be teachers, my brothers, because you know that we who teach will be judged more strictly. 2We all stumble[n] in many ways. If anyone is never at fault in what he says,[o] he is a perfect man,[p] able to keep his whole body in check.[q]

3When we put bits into the mouths of horses to make them obey us, we can turn the whole animal.[r] 4Or take ships as an example. Although they are so large and are driven by strong winds, they are steered by a very small rudder wherever the pilot wants to go. 5Likewise the tongue is a small part of the body, but it makes great boasts.[s] Consider what a great forest is set on fire by a small spark. 6The tongue also is a fire,[t] a world of evil among the parts of the body. It corrupts the whole person,[u] sets the whole course of his life on fire, and is itself set on fire by hell.

7All kinds of animals, birds, reptiles and creatures of the sea are being tamed and have been tamed by man, 8but no man can tame the tongue. It is a restless evil, full of deadly poison.[v]

9With the tongue we praise our Lord and Father, and with it we curse men, who have been made in God's likeness.[w] 10Out of the same mouth come praise and cursing. My brothers, this should not be. 11Can both fresh water and salt[c] water flow from the same

2:16 [a]1Jn 3:17,18
2:18 [b]Ro 3:28 [c]Jas 3:13
2:19 [d]Dt 6:4 [e]Mt 8:29; Lk 4:34
2:20 [f]ver 17,26
2:21 [g]Ge 22:9,12
2:22 [h]Heb 11:17 [i]1Th 1:3
2:23 [j]Ge 15:6; Ro 4:3 [k]2Ch 20:7; Isa 41:8
2:25 [l]Heb 11:31
2:26 [m]ver 17,20
3:2 [n]1Ki 8:46; Jas 2:10 [o]1Pe 3:10 [p]Mt 12:37 [q]Jas 1:26
3:3 [r]Ps 32:9
3:5 [s]Ps 12:3,4
3:6 [t]Pr 16:27 [u]Mt 15:11,18,19
3:8 [v]Ps 140:3; Ro 3:13
3:9 [w]Ge 1:26,27; 1Co 11:7

[a]*20* Some early manuscripts *dead* [b]*23* Gen. 15:6 [c]*11* Greek *bitter* (see also verse 14)

spring? 12My brothers, can a fig tree bear olives, or a grapevine
bear figs?[a] Neither can a salt spring produce fresh water.
13Who is wise and understanding among you? Let him show it[b]
by his good life, by deeds done in the humility that comes from
wisdom. 14But if you harbor bitter envy and selfish ambition[c] in
your hearts, do not boast about it or deny the truth.[d] 15Such "wisdom" does not come down from heaven[e] but is earthly, unspiritual,
of the devil.[f] 16For where you have envy and selfish ambition, there
you find disorder and every evil practice.
17But the wisdom that comes from heaven[g] is first of all pure;
then peace-loving, considerate, submissive, full of mercy[h] and good
fruit, impartial and sincere.[i] 18Peacemakers who sow in peace
raise a harvest of righteousness.[j]

Chapter 4 Theme ______________________________

4 What causes fights and quarrels[k] among you? Don't they
come from your desires that battle[l] within you? 2You want
something but don't get it. You kill and covet, but you cannot have
what you want. You quarrel and fight. You do not have, because
you do not ask God. 3When you ask, you do not receive,[m]
because you ask with wrong motives,[n] that you may spend what
you get on your pleasures.
4You adulterous people, don't you know that friendship with the
world[o] is hatred toward God?[p] Anyone who chooses to be a friend
of the world becomes an enemy of God.[q] 5Or do you think Scripture says without reason that the spirit he caused to live in us envies
intensely?[a] 6But he gives us more grace. That is why Scripture says:

> "God opposes the proud
> but gives grace to the humble."[b] [r]

7Submit yourselves, then, to God. Resist the devil,[s] and he will flee
from you. 8Come near to God and he will come near to you.[t] Wash
your hands,[u] you sinners, and purify your hearts, you double-
minded.[v] 9Grieve, mourn and wail. Change your laughter to
mourning and your joy to gloom.[w] 10Humble yourselves before the
Lord, and he will lift you up.
11Brothers, do not slander one another.[x] Anyone who speaks
against his brother or judges him[y] speaks against the law and
judges it. When you judge the law, you are not keeping it,[z] but sitting in judgment on it. 12There is only one Lawgiver and Judge, the
one who is able to save and destroy.[a] But you—who are you to
judge your neighbor?[b]
13Now listen, you who say, "Today or tomorrow we will go to this
or that city, spend a year there, carry on business and make money."[c]
14Why, you do not even know what will happen tomorrow. What is

[a]5 *Or that God jealously longs for the spirit that he made to live in us; or that the Spirit he caused to live in us longs jealously* [b]6 Prov. 3:34

3:12 [a]Mt 7:16
3:13 [b]Jas 2:18
3:14 [c]ver 16 [d]Jas 5:19
3:15 [e]Jas 1:17 [f]1Ti 4:1
3:17 [g]1Co 2:6 [h]Lk 6:36 [i]Ro 12:9
3:18 [j]Pr 11:18; Isa 32:17
4:1 [k]Tit 3:9 [l]Ro 7:23
4:3 [m]Ps 18:41 [n]1Jn 3:22; 5:14
4:4 [o]Jas 1:27 [p]1Jn 2:15 [q]Jn 15:19
4:6 [r]Ps 138:6; Pr 3:34; Mt 23:12
4:7 [s]Eph 4:27; 1Pe 5:6-9
4:8 [t]2Ch 15:2 [u]Isa 1:16 [v]Jas 1:8
4:9 [w]Lk 6:25
4:11 [x]1Pe 2:1 [y]Mt 7:1 [z]Jas 1:22
4:12 [a]Mt 10:28 [b]Ro 14:4
4:13 [c]Pr 27:1

your life? You are a mist that appears for a little while and then
vanishes.[a] 15 Instead, you ought to say, "If it is the Lord's will,[b] we
will live and do this or that." 16 As it is, you boast and brag. All
such boasting is evil.[c] 17 Anyone, then, who knows the good he
ought to do and doesn't do it, sins.[d]

Chapter 5 Theme ______________________________

5 Now listen, you rich people,[e] weep and wail because of the
misery that is coming upon you. 2 Your wealth has rotted, and
moths have eaten your clothes.[f] 3 Your gold and silver are corroded.
Their corrosion will testify against you and eat your flesh like fire.
You have hoarded wealth in the last days.[g] 4 Look! The wages you
failed to pay the workmen[h] who mowed your fields are crying out
against you. The cries[i] of the harvesters have reached the ears of
the Lord Almighty.[j] 5 You have lived on earth in luxury and self-
indulgence. You have fattened yourselves[k] in the day of slaughter.[a][l]
6 You have condemned and murdered innocent men,[m] who were
not opposing you.

7 Be patient, then, brothers, until the Lord's coming. See how the
farmer waits for the land to yield its valuable crop and how
patient he is for the autumn and spring rains.[n] 8 You too, be
patient and stand firm, because the Lord's coming is near.[o] 9 Don't
grumble against each other, brothers,[p] or you will be judged. The
Judge[q] is standing at the door![r]

10 Brothers, as an example of patience in the face of suffering, take
the prophets[s] who spoke in the name of the Lord. 11 As you know,
we consider blessed[t] those who have persevered. You have heard of
Job's perseverance[u] and have seen what the Lord finally brought
about.[v] The Lord is full of compassion and mercy.[w]

12 Above all, my brothers, do not swear—not by heaven or by
earth or by anything else. Let your "Yes" be yes, and your "No," no,
or you will be condemned.[x]

13 Is any one of you in trouble? He should pray.[y] Is anyone happy?
Let him sing songs of praise.[z] 14 Is any one of you sick? He should
call the elders of the church to pray over him and anoint him with
oil[a] in the name of the Lord. 15 And the prayer offered in faith will
make the sick person well; the Lord will raise him up. If he has
sinned, he will be forgiven. 16 Therefore confess your sins[b] to each
other and pray for each other so that you may be healed.[c] The
prayer of a righteous man is powerful and effective.[d]

17 Elijah was a man just like us.[e] He prayed earnestly that it would
not rain, and it did not rain on the land for three and a half years.[f]
18 Again he prayed, and the heavens gave rain, and the earth produced its crops.[g]

a5 Or *yourselves as in a day of feasting*

4:14 [a] Job 7:7; Ps 102:3
4:15 [b] Ac 18:21
4:16 [c] 1Co 5:6
4:17 [d] Lk 12:47; Jn 9:41
5:1 [e] Lk 6:24
5:2 [f] Job 13:28; Mt 6:19,20
5:3 [g] ver 7,8
5:4 [h] Lev 19:13 [i] Dt 24:15 [j] Ro 9:29
5:5 [k] Am 6:1 [l] Jer 12:3; 25:34
5:6 [m] Heb 10:38
5:7 [n] Dt 11:14; Jer 5:24
5:8 [o] Ro 13:11; 1Pe 4:7
5:9 [p] Jas 4:11 [q] 1Co 4:5; 1Pe 4:5 [r] Mt 24:33
5:10 [s] Mt 5:12
5:11 [t] Mt 5:10 [u] Job 1:21,22; 2:10 [v] Job 42:10,12-17 [w] Nu 14:18
5:12 [x] Mt 5:34-37
5:13 [y] Ps 50:15 [z] Col 3:16
5:14 [a] Mk 6:13
5:16 [b] Mt 3:6 [c] 1Pe 2:24 [d] Jn 9:31
5:17 [e] Ac 14:15 [f] 1Ki 17:1; Lk 4:25
5:18 [g] 1Ki 18:41-45

19My brothers, if one of you should wander from the truth[a] and
someone should bring him back,[b] 20remember this: Whoever
turns a sinner from the error of his way will save[c] him from death
and cover over a multitude of sins.[d]

5:19
[a] Jas 3:14
[b] Mt 18:15
5:20
[c] Ro 11:14
[d] 1 Pe 4:8

JAMES SUBJECT BY SUBJECT

SUBJECT	INSTRUCTION	ILLUSTRATION/EXPLANATION
Trials (1:2-8)	– consider it pure joy	
	– perseverance must finish its work	– when you persevere in trials you will be made more mature, complete, not lacking anything
	– ask God for wisdom	
	– believe when asking, not doubting	– doubter like a wave of the sea – doubter will not receive anything from the Lord

(continued)

James Subject by Subject

Subject	Instruction	Illustration/Explanation

(continued)

James Subject by Subject

Subject	Instruction	Illustration/Explanation

James at a Glance

Theme of James:

Segment Divisions	Chapter Themes
	1
	2
	3
	4
	5

Author:

Date:

Purpose:

Key Words:

brothers

faith (believe, believers)

mature, finish (made comple[te])

judge, sitting i[n] judgment (judges, judge[d], judgment, be condemned)

law

1 PETER

The hour had come for the Shepherd to be smitten and for the sheep to be scattered. Jesus chose to spend his final hours with his eleven, preparing them for the tribulation that would come.

Yet after Jesus' resurrection and ascension, the tribulation seemed to be relatively mild. The disgruntled Pharisees wanted to shut up the men who were turning Jerusalem upside down with their teaching and miracles, but nothing seemed life-threatening.

Then the first stone was thrown. Stephen, the first martyr, was brought to the ground. Saul watched him die. In hearty agreement with Stephen's death, Saul went to the high priest to gain permission to round up those of the Way who were spreading this gospel. Saul's purge was short-lived. Jesus saved Saul on the road to Damascus and changed his name to Paul. But the persecution of Christians continued. Herod the king became the adversary of believers, and Jews who had come to know Jesus as the Messiah were scattered abroad to other Roman provinces.

However, it wasn't until Nero that the persecution of Christians reached beyond the confines of Judah. Rumor had it that Nero had burned Rome so he could rebuild it as he wanted. Needing a scapegoat to divert attention from himself, Nero blamed the fire on the Christians and began the systematic persecution of God's children.

Jesus had prepared Peter for the world's tribulation; now Peter would prepare others. Peter wrote his first epistle on the eve of Nero's persecution, about A.D. 63 or 64.

Nero died in A.D. 68, but not before Rome put Peter to death.

THINGS TO DO

1. Read through 1 Peter and do the following:
   a. In the initial verses of the book Peter describes himself and states to whom he is writing, and in the last verses of the book, he tells why he wrote this epistle. Record your insights about the author and his purpose in writing on the 1 PETER AT A GLANCE chart on page 2113.
   b. Pay close attention to what you see about the recipients of 1 Peter. What is their condition? What is going on in their midst? Record what you learn about them on the OBSERVATIONS CHART on page 2112.
2. Read 1 Peter chapter by chapter, looking for and marking in a distinctive way the key words (and their synonyms and pronouns) that are listed on 1 PETER AT A GLANCE. Also remember to mark words such as *grace* and *gracious gift* and references to the devil which you are marking throughout your Bible. In the margin list the truths you learn from every mention of key words. This is imperative if you want to understand 1 Peter.
3. Peter gives the reader many commands or instructions about things to do. You notice these by the construction of the sentence. The verb usually comes first and the "you" is implied. An example is seen in 1:13: "Prepare your minds for action."
   a. Underline the instructions or commands that Peter gives throughout the book. Then list these under "General Instructions" on the OBSERVATIONS CHART.
   b. As you evaluate these instructions and commands you will see that 1 Peter was written not only for the recipients but also for you. Think about how these instructions apply to your own life.
4. Peter also gives instructions to specific groups of people such as slaves, wives, husbands, etc. List his instructions to each group under the proper heading on the OBSERVATIONS CHART.
5. From what you have read, why do you think the believers are to do these things? In other words, what future event is the motivation for living life in accordance with Peter's exhortations?

6. Finally, summarize the theme of each chapter and record these themes on 1 PETER AT A GLANCE and in the text next to the chapter number. Don't forget to record the overall theme of 1 Peter.

Things to Think About

1. What have you learned about the way you are to live? How are you to respond to others, even when they are not living properly or treating you properly? What is Jesus' example in 1 Peter 2:21-25? Will you follow it?
2. As you think about what those believers were suffering, should you be surprised if you undergo the same? What will suffering accomplish in your life?
3. Even if you don't have a Nero in your life, is your enemy the devil still prowling about like a lion, looking for someone to devour? What are you to do, according to 1 Peter?
4. When our Lord Jesus Christ returns, will you be found standing firm in the true grace that has been provided you? What must you do or change in order to be prepared to see him face-to-face?

Chapter 1 Theme ______________________

1 Peter, an apostle of Jesus Christ,[a]

To God's elect,[b] strangers in the world, scattered throughout
Pontus, Galatia, Cappadocia, Asia and Bithynia,[c] 2who have been
chosen according to the foreknowledge[d] of God the Father,
through the sanctifying work of the Spirit,[e] for obedience to Jesus
Christ and sprinkling by his blood:[f]

Grace and peace be yours in abundance.

3Praise be to the God and Father of our Lord Jesus Christ![g] In his
great mercy[h] he has given us new birth into a living hope through
the resurrection of Jesus Christ from the dead,[i] 4and into an
inheritance that can never perish, spoil or fade—kept in heaven
for you,[j] 5who through faith are shielded by God's power[k] until the
coming of the salvation that is ready to be revealed in the last time.
6In this you greatly rejoice,[l] though now for a little while[m] you may
have had to suffer grief in all kinds of trials.[n] 7These have come so
that your faith—of greater worth than gold, which perishes even
though refined by fire[o]—may be proved genuine[p] and may result
in praise, glory and honor when Jesus Christ is revealed.[q] 8Though
you have not seen him, you love him; and even though you do not
see him now, you believe in him[r] and are filled with an inexpressible and glorious joy, 9for you are receiving the goal of your faith,
the salvation of your souls.[s]

10Concerning this salvation, the prophets, who spoke[t] of the
grace that was to come to you, searched intently and with the
greatest care,[u] 11trying to find out the time and circumstances to
which the Spirit of Christ[v] in them was pointing when he predicted
the sufferings of Christ and the glories that would follow. 12It was

1:1 [a]2Pe 1:1 [b]Mt 24:22 [c]Ac 16:7
1:2 [d]Ro 8:29 [e]2Th 2:13 [f]Heb 10:22; 12:24
1:3 [g]2Co 1:3; Eph 1:3 [h]Tit 3:5; Jas 1:18 [i]1Co 15:20
1:4 [j]Col 1:5
1:5 [k]Jn 10:28
1:6 [l]Ro 5:2 [m]1Pe 5:10 [n]Jas 1:2
1:7 [o]Job 23:10; Ps 66:10; Pr 17:3 [p]Jas 1:3 [q]Ro 2:7
1:8 [r]Jn 20:29
1:9 [s]Ro 6:22
1:10 [t]Mt 26:24 [u]Mt 13:17
1:11 [v]2Pe 1:21

revealed to them that they were not serving themselves but you, when they spoke of the things that have now been told you by those who have preached the gospel to you[a] by the Holy Spirit sent from heaven. Even angels long to look into these things.

13 Therefore, prepare your minds for action; be self-controlled; set your hope fully on the grace to be given you when Jesus Christ is revealed. 14 As obedient children, do not conform[b] to the evil desires you had when you lived in ignorance.[c] 15 But just as he who called you is holy, so be holy in all you do;[d] 16 for it is written: "Be holy, because I am holy."[a][e]

17 Since you call on a Father who judges each man's work impartially,[f] live your lives as strangers here in reverent fear.[g] 18 For you know that it was not with perishable things such as silver or gold that you were redeemed[h] from the empty way of life handed down to you from your forefathers, 19 but with the precious blood of Christ, a lamb[i] without blemish or defect.[j] 20 He was chosen before the creation of the world[k] but was revealed in these last times[l] for your sake. 21 Through him you believe in God,[m] who raised him from the dead and glorified him, and so your faith and hope are in God.

22 Now that you have purified[n] yourselves by obeying the truth so that you have sincere love for your brothers, love one another deeply,[o] from the heart.[b] 23 For you have been born again,[p] not of perishable seed, but of imperishable, through the living and enduring word of God.[q] 24 For,

"All men are like grass,
and all their glory is like the flowers of the field;
the grass withers and the flowers fall,
25 but the word of the Lord stands forever."[c][r]

And this is the word that was preached to you.

Chapter 2 Theme ______________________________

2

Therefore, rid yourselves[s] of all malice and all deceit, hypocrisy, envy, and slander[t] of every kind. 2 Like newborn babies, crave pure spiritual milk,[u] so that by it you may grow up[v] in your salvation, 3 now that you have tasted that the Lord is good.[w]

4 As you come to him, the living Stone[x]—rejected by men but chosen by God and precious to him— 5 you also, like living stones, are being built[y] into a spiritual house[z] to be a holy priesthood,[a] offering spiritual sacrifices acceptable to God through Jesus Christ.[b] 6 For in Scripture it says:

1:12 *a* ver 25
1:14 *b* Ro 12:2; *c* Eph 4:18
1:15 *d* 2Co 7:1; 1Th 4:7
1:16 *e* Lev 11:44,45
1:17 *f* Ac 10:34; *g* Heb 12:28
1:18 *h* Mt 20:28; 1Co 6:20
1:19 *i* Jn 1:29; *j* Ex 12:5
1:20 *k* Eph 1:4; *l* Heb 9:26
1:21 *m* Ro 4:24
1:22 *n* Jas 4:8; *o* Jn 13:34; Heb 13:1
1:23 *p* Jn 1:13; *q* Heb 4:12
1:25 *r* Isa 40:6-8
2:1 *s* Eph 4:22; *t* Jas 4:11
2:2 *u* 1Co 3:2; *v* Eph 4:15,16
2:3 *w* Heb 6:5
2:4 *x* ver 7
2:5 *y* 1Co 3:9; *z* 1Ti 3:15; *a* Isa 61:6; *b* Php 4:18; Heb 13:15

a *16* Lev. 11:44,45; 19:2; 20:7 b *22* Some early manuscripts *from a pure heart*
c *25* Isaiah 40:6-8

"See, I lay a stone in Zion,
a chosen and precious cornerstone,[a]
and the one who trusts in him
will never be put to shame."[a][b]

7 Now to you who believe, this stone is precious. But to those who
do not believe,[c]

"The stone the builders rejected
has become the capstone,[b]"[c][d]

8 and,

"A stone that causes men to stumble
and a rock that makes them fall."[d][e]

They stumble because they disobey the message—which is also
what they were destined for.[f]
9 But you are a chosen people,[g] a royal priesthood, a holy nation,[h]
a people belonging to God, that you may declare the praises of him
who called you out of darkness into his wonderful light.[i] 10 Once
you were not a people, but now you are the people of God;[j] once
you had not received mercy, but now you have received mercy.
11 Dear friends, I urge you, as aliens and strangers in the world, to
abstain from sinful desires,[k] which war against your soul.[l] 12 Live
such good lives among the pagans that, though they accuse you of
doing wrong, they may see your good deeds[m] and glorify God[n]
on the day he visits us.
13 Submit yourselves for the Lord's sake to every authority[o] instituted among men: whether to the king, as the supreme authority,
14 or to governors, who are sent by him to punish those who do
wrong[p] and to commend those who do right.[q] 15 For it is God's
will[r] that by doing good you should silence the ignorant talk of
foolish men.[s] 16 Live as free men,[t] but do not use your freedom as a
cover-up for evil; live as servants of God.[u] 17 Show proper respect
to everyone: Love the brotherhood of believers,[v] fear God, honor
the king.[w]
18 Slaves, submit yourselves to your masters with all respect,[x] not
only to those who are good and considerate,[y] but also to those who
are harsh. 19 For it is commendable if a man bears up under the
pain of unjust suffering because he is conscious of God.[z] 20 But how
is it to your credit if you receive a beating for doing wrong and
endure it? But if you suffer for doing good and you endure it, this is
commendable before God.[a] 21 To this[b] you were called, because
Christ suffered for you, leaving you an example,[c] that you should
follow in his steps.

[a]6 Isaiah 28:16 [b]7 Or *cornerstone* [c]7 Psalm 118:22 [d]8 Isaiah 8:14

2:6 [a]Eph 2:20 [b]Isa 28:16
2:7 [c]2Co 2:16 [d]Ps 118:22
2:8 [e]Isa 8:14; 1Co 1:23 [f]Ro 9:22
2:9 [g]Dt 10:15 [h]Isa 62:12 [i]Ac 26:18
2:10 [j]Hos 1:9,10
2:11 [k]Gal 5:16 [l]Jas 4:1
2:12 [m]Php 2:15; 1Pe 3:16 [n]Mt 5:16; 9:8
2:13 [o]Ro 13:1
2:14 [p]Ro 13:4 [q]Ro 13:3
2:15 [r]1Pe 3:17 [s]ver 12
2:16 [t]Jn 8:32 [u]Ro 6:22
2:17 [v]Ro 12:10 [w]Ro 13:7
2:18 [x]Eph 6:5 [y]Jas 3:17
2:19 [z]1Pe 3:14,17
2:20 [a]1Pe 3:17
2:21 [b]Ac 14:22 [c]Mt 16:24

4:11 [a]Eph 6:10 serves, he should do it with the strength God provides,[a] so that in
[b]1Co 10:31 all things God may be praised[b] through Jesus Christ. To him be
the glory and the power for ever and ever. Amen.
4:12 [c]1Pe 1:6,7 12 Dear friends, do not be surprised at the painful trial you are
suffering,[c] as though something strange were happening to you.
4:13 13 But rejoice that you participate in the sufferings of Christ, so
[d]Ro 8:17 that you may be overjoyed when his glory is revealed.[d] 14 If you
4:14 are insulted because of the name of Christ, you are blessed,[e] for
[e]Mt 5:11 the Spirit of glory and of God rests on you. 15 If you suffer, it
should not be as a murderer or thief or any other kind of criminal,
4:16 [f]Ac 5:41 or even as a meddler. 16 However, if you suffer as a Christian, do not
be ashamed, but praise God that you bear that name.[f] 17 For it is
4:17 time for judgment to begin with the family of God;[g] and if it begins
[g]Jer 25:29 [h]2Th 1:8 with us, what will the outcome be for those who do not obey the
gospel of God?[h] 18 And,

4:18 [i]Pr 11:31; Lk 23:31

> "If it is hard for the righteous to be saved,
> what will become of the ungodly and the sinner?"[a][i]

5:1 [j]Ac 11:30 19 So then, those who suffer according to God's will should com-
[k]Lk 24:48 mit themselves to their faithful Creator and continue to do good.
[l]1Pe 1:5,7; Rev 1:9

Chapter 5 Theme ______________________________

5:2 [m]Jn 21:16 **5** To the elders among you, I appeal as a fellow elder,[j] a witness[k]
[n]1Ti 3:3 of Christ's sufferings and one who also will share in the glory
to be revealed:[l] 2 Be shepherds of God's flock[m] that is under your
5:3 [o]Eze 34:4 care, serving as overseers—not because you must, but because you
[p]Php 3:17 are willing, as God wants you to be; not greedy for money,[n] but
eager to serve; 3 not lording it over[o] those entrusted to you, but
5:4 [q]1Co 9:25 being examples[p] to the flock. 4 And when the Chief Shepherd
appears, you will receive the crown of glory[q] that will never fade
away.
5:5 [r]Eph 5:21 5 Young men, in the same way be submissive[r] to those who are
[s]Pr 3:34; Jas 4:6 older. All of you, clothe yourselves with humility toward one
another, because,

5:6 [t]Jas 4:10

> "God opposes the proud
> but gives grace to the humble."[b][s]

5:7 [u]Ps 37:5; Mt 6:25 6 Humble yourselves, therefore, under God's mighty hand, that he
[v]Heb 13:5 may lift you up in due time.[t] 7 Cast all your anxiety on him[u]
because he cares for you.[v]
5:8 [w]Job 1:7 8 Be self-controlled and alert. Your enemy the devil prowls
around[w] like a roaring lion looking for someone to devour. 9 Resist
5:9 him,[x] standing firm in the faith,[y] because you know that your
[x]Jas 4:7 [y]Col 2:5

[a] *18* Prov. 11:31 [b] *5* Prov. 3:34

brothers throughout the world are undergoing the same kind of
sufferings.[a]
10 And the God of all grace, who called you to his eternal glory[b] in
Christ, after you have suffered a little while, will himself restore you
and make you strong,[c] firm and steadfast. 11 To him be the power
for ever and ever. Amen.[d]

12 With the help of Silas,[a][e] whom I regard as a faithful brother, I
have written to you briefly,[f] encouraging you and testifying that
this is the true grace of God. Stand fast in it.
13 She who is in Babylon, chosen together with you, sends you
her greetings, and so does my son Mark.[g] 14 Greet one another
with a kiss of love.[h]
Peace[i] to all of you who are in Christ.

a 12 Greek *Silvanus*, a variant of *Silas*

5:9
[a] Ac 14:22

5:10
[b] 2Co 4:17
[c] 2Th 2:17

5:11
[d] Ro 11:36

5:12
[e] 2Co 1:19
[f] Heb 13:22

5:13
[g] Ac 12:12

5:14
[h] Ro 16:16
[i] Eph 6:23

1 Peter Observations Chart

Author

Recipients

General Instructions

(continu

1 Peter Observations Chart

Instructions to

Wives	Husbands	
Elders	Young men	Slaves

1 Peter at a Glance

heme of 1 Peter:

	Segment Divisions	Chapter Themes
uthor:		
ate:		1
urpose:		
y Words: suffering (and all its synonyms)		2
grace (gracious gift)		3
glory (glorious, glorified) salvation Jesus Christ		4
God Holy Spirit called chosen (elect) holy		5

2 PETER

A fisherman by trade, Peter had been captured and transformed by a Shepherd. Is it any wonder that even in Peter's darkest hour, the welfare of God's sheep was uppermost in his mind?

Ever since the day he stood with Jesus by a fire, the morning air full of the aroma of roasting fish, Peter had known the way he would die. But Peter would be faithful. His concern about his death and the way he would die would not override his concern for his Lord's sheep, the sheep Jesus had commissioned him to feed and shepherd. And so, sometime around A.D. 63 or 64, Peter writes "to those who . . . have received a faith as precious as ours."

In A.D. 64, according to tradition, Peter was crucified upside down for the Lord he once denied knowing. How Peter had grown in the grace and knowledge of his God!

Things to Do

1. To familiarize yourself with 2 Peter, read the book without stopping or taking notes. The message of this short book is easily seen in each of the paragraphs, so as you read, notice the content of each. You will see that Peter contrasts certain things. Based on this first reading, what major contrast is Peter making in this book?

2. Read 2 Peter again, looking for facts concerning the author (pronouns such as *I, we, us*) and the recipients (pronouns such as *you, your*). Mark these in a distinctive way in the text. Then on the OBSERVATIONS CHART on page 2119 record the answers to the following questions: What does the author say about himself? When in his life is he writing? Who are the recipients? How are they described?

3. In a distinctive way, mark in the text the key words (and their synonyms and pronouns) which are listed on the 2 PETER AT A GLANCE chart on page 2120. Then list in the margin the truths you learn by marking these key words. Be as thorough as possible because the lists will help you see the flow of the book.

4. Read through 2 Peter again and look for specific instructions that Peter gives the readers concerning their behavior and belief. Record these on the OBSERVATIONS CHART under "Instructions." Also look for and note any people or groups of people of which Peter warns them to beware.

5. In this book, Peter states specifically why he is writing. Look for and underline any verse in which Peter says, *"I have written . . . to . . . you."* Also, underline any other verses that indicate his purpose in writing. Record his purpose for writing on 2 PETER AT A GLANCE.

6. Summarize the message of each paragraph and record its theme on 2 PETER AT A GLANCE. Then determine the chapter themes and the book theme and record these in the appropriate places on the chart and in the text.

Things to Think About

1. What would it take to live your life so that you may be found spotless and blameless at Christ's coming?

2. Is there a danger today that false teachers will be among our brothers, as in Peter's day? What do you need to know to be able to detect them?

3. How can you keep from falling from your own secure position? Practically, what do you need to do in order to grow in the grace and knowledge of Jesus Christ?

Chapter 1 Theme __________________________________

1

Simon Peter, a servant[a] and apostle of Jesus Christ,[b]

To those who through the righteousness[c] of our God and Savior
Jesus Christ[d] have received a faith as precious as ours:

2Grace and peace be yours in abundance through the knowledge of God and of Jesus our Lord.[e]

3His divine power[f] has given us everything we need for life and
godliness through our knowledge of him who called us[g] by his
own glory and goodness. 4Through these he has given us his very
great and precious promises,[h] so that through them you may participate in the divine nature[i] and escape the corruption in the
world caused by evil desires.[j]

5For this very reason, make every effort to add to your faith
goodness; and to goodness, knowledge;[k] 6and to knowledge, self-
control;[l] and to self-control, perseverance; and to perseverance,
godliness;[m] 7and to godliness, brotherly kindness; and to brotherly kindness, love.[n] 8For if you possess these qualities in increasing
measure, they will keep you from being ineffective and unproductive[o] in your knowledge of our Lord Jesus Christ. 9But if anyone does not have them, he is nearsighted and blind,[p] and has
forgotten that he has been cleansed from his past sins.[q]

10Therefore, my brothers, be all the more eager to make your
calling and election sure. For if you do these things, you will never
fall,[r] 11and you will receive a rich welcome into the eternal kingdom of our Lord and Savior Jesus Christ.

12So I will always remind you of these things,[s] even though you
know them and are firmly established in the truth you now have.
13I think it is right to refresh your memory as long as I live in the
tent of this body,[t] 14because I know that I will soon put it aside,[u]
as our Lord Jesus Christ has made clear to me.[v] 15And I will make
every effort to see that after my departure[w] you will always be
able to remember these things.

16We did not follow cleverly invented stories when we told you
about the power and coming of our Lord Jesus Christ, but we
were eyewitnesses of his majesty.[x] 17For he received honor and
glory from God the Father when the voice came to him from the
Majestic Glory, saying, "This is my Son, whom I love; with him I
am well pleased."[a][y] 18We ourselves heard this voice that came
from heaven when we were with him on the sacred mountain.[z]

19And we have the word of the prophets made more certain,
and you will do well to pay attention to it, as to a light[a] shining in
a dark place, until the day dawns and the morning star[b] rises in

1:1 [a]Ro 1:1 [b]1Pe 1:1 [c]Ro 3:21-26 [d]Tit 2:13
1:2 [e]Php 3:8
1:3 [f]1Pe 1:5 [g]1Th 2:12
1:4 [h]2Co 7:1 [i]Eph 4:24; Heb 12:10; 1Jn 3:2 [j]2Pe 2:18-20
1:5 [k]Col 2:3
1:6 [l]Ac 24:25 [m]ver 3
1:7 [n]1Th 3:12
1:8 [o]Jn 15:2; Tit 3:14
1:9 [p]1Jn 2:11 [q]Eph 5:26
1:10 [r]2Pe 3:17
1:12 [s]Php 3:1; 1Jn 2:21
1:13 [t]2Co 5:1,4
1:14 [u]2Ti 4:6 [v]Jn 21:18,19
1:15 [w]Lk 9:31
1:16 [x]Mt 17:1-8
1:17 [y]Mt 3:17
1:18 [z]Mt 17:6
1:19 [a]Ps 119:105 [b]Rev 22:16

a *17* Matt. 17:5; Mark 9:7; Luke 9:35

your hearts. 20Above all, you must understand that no prophecy
of Scripture came about by the prophet's own interpretation. 21For
prophecy never had its origin in the will of man, but men spoke
from God[a] as they were carried along by the Holy Spirit.[b]

Chapter 2 Theme ____________________________

2 But there were also false prophets[c] among the people, just as
there will be false teachers among you.[d] They will secretly
introduce destructive heresies, even denying the sovereign Lord[e]
who bought them[f]—bringing swift destruction on themselves.
2Many will follow their shameful ways and will bring the way of
truth into disrepute. 3In their greed these teachers will exploit you[g]
with stories they have made up. Their condemnation has long been
hanging over them, and their destruction has not been sleeping.
4For if God did not spare angels when they sinned, but sent them
to hell,[a] putting them into gloomy dungeons[b] to be held for judgment;[h] 5if he did not spare the ancient world[i] when he brought the
flood on its ungodly people, but protected Noah, a preacher of
righteousness, and seven others;[j] 6if he condemned the cities of
Sodom and Gomorrah by burning them to ashes,[k] and made them
an example[l] of what is going to happen to the ungodly; 7and if he
rescued Lot,[m] a righteous man, who was distressed by the filthy
lives of lawless men[n] 8(for that righteous man, living among them
day after day, was tormented in his righteous soul by the lawless
deeds he saw and heard)— 9if this is so, then the Lord knows how
to rescue godly men from trials[o] and to hold the unrighteous for
the day of judgment, while continuing their punishment.[c] 10This
is especially true of those who follow the corrupt desire[p] of the
sinful nature[d] and despise authority.

Bold and arrogant, these men are not afraid to slander celestial
beings;[q] 11yet even angels, although they are stronger and more
powerful, do not bring slanderous accusations against such beings
in the presence of the Lord.[r] 12But these men blaspheme in matters they do not understand. They are like brute beasts, creatures
of instinct, born only to be caught and destroyed, and like beasts
they too will perish.[s]
13They will be paid back with harm for the harm they have done.
Their idea of pleasure is to carouse in broad daylight.[t] They are blots
and blemishes, reveling in their pleasures while they feast with you.[e][u]
14With eyes full of adultery, they never stop sinning; they seduce[v]
the unstable; they are experts in greed[w]—an accursed brood![x]
15They have left the straight way and wandered off to follow the

a 4 Greek *Tartarus* b 4 Some manuscripts *into chains of darkness* c 9 Or *unrighteous for punishment until the day of judgment* d 10 Or *the flesh* e 13 Some manuscripts *in their love feasts*

1:21 a 2Ti 3:16 b 2Sa 23:2; Ac 1:16; 1Pe 1:11
2:1 c Dt 13:1-3 d 1Ti 4:1 e Jude 4 f 1Co 6:20
2:3 g 2Co 2:17; 1Th 2:5
2:4 h Jude 6; Rev 20:1,2
2:5 i 2Pe 3:6 j Heb 11:7; 1Pe 3:20
2:6 k Ge 19:24,25 l Nu 26:10; Jude 7
2:7 m Ge 19:16 n 2Pe 3:17
2:9 o 1Co 10:13
2:10 p 2Pe 3:3 q Jude 8
2:11 r Jude 9
2:12 s Jude 10
2:13 t Ro 13:13 u 1Co 11:20,21; Jude 12
2:14 v ver 18 w ver 3 x Eph 2:3

way of Balaam[a] son of Beor, who loved the wages of wickedness.
16But he was rebuked for his wrongdoing by a donkey—a beast
without speech—who spoke with a man's voice and restrained
the prophet's madness.[b]
17These men are springs without water[c] and mists driven by a
storm. Blackest darkness is reserved for them.[d] 18For they mouth
empty, boastful words[e] and, by appealing to the lustful desires of
sinful human nature, they entice people who are just escaping
from those who live in error. 19They promise them freedom,
while they themselves are slaves of depravity—for a man is a
slave to whatever has mastered him.[f] 20If they have escaped the
corruption of the world by knowing[g] our Lord and Savior Jesus
Christ and are again entangled in it and overcome, they are worse
off at the end than they were at the beginning.[h] 21It would have
been better for them not to have known the way of righteousness,
than to have known it and then to turn their backs on the sacred
command that was passed on to them.[i] 22Of them the proverbs
are true: "A dog returns to its vomit,"[a][j] and, "A sow that is washed
goes back to her wallowing in the mud."

Chapter 3 Theme ______________________________

3 Dear friends, this is now my second letter to you. I have written both of them as reminders[k] to stimulate you to wholesome
thinking. 2I want you to recall the words spoken in the past by
the holy prophets and the command given by our Lord and Savior through your apostles.
3First of all, you must understand that in the last days[l] scoffers
will come, scoffing and following their own evil desires.[m] 4They
will say, "Where is this 'coming' he promised?[n] Ever since our
fathers died, everything goes on as it has since the beginning of
creation."[o] 5But they deliberately forget that long ago by God's
word[p] the heavens existed and the earth was formed out of water
and by water.[q] 6By these waters also the world of that time was
deluged and destroyed.[r] 7By the same word the present heavens
and earth are reserved for fire,[s] being kept for the day of judgment and destruction of ungodly men.
8But do not forget this one thing, dear friends: With the Lord a
day is like a thousand years, and a thousand years are like a day.[t]
9The Lord is not slow in keeping his promise,[u] as some understand slowness. He is patient[v] with you, not wanting anyone to
perish, but everyone to come to repentance.[w]
10But the day of the Lord will come like a thief.[x] The heavens
will disappear with a roar; the elements will be destroyed by fire,
and the earth and everything in it will be laid bare.[b][y]

2:15 [a]Nu 22:4-20; Jude 11
2:16 [b]Nu 22:21-30
2:17 [c]Jude 12 [d]Jude 13
2:18 [e]Jude 16
2:19 [f]Jn 8:34; Ro 6:16
2:20 [g]2Pe 1:2 [h]Mt 12:45
2:21 [i]Heb 6:4-6
2:22 [j]Pr 26:11
3:1 [k]2Pe 1:13
3:3 [l]1Ti 4:1 [m]2Pe 2:10; Jude 18
3:4 [n]Isa 5:19; Eze 12:22; Mt 24:48 [o]Mk 10:6
3:5 [p]Ge 1:6,9; Heb 11:3 [q]Ps 24:2
3:6 [r]Ge 7:21,22
3:7 [s]ver 10,12; 2Th 1:7
3:8 [t]Ps 90:4
3:9 [u]Hab 2:3; Heb 10:37 [v]Ro 2:4 [w]1Ti 2:4
3:10 [x]Lk 12:39; 1Th 5:2 [y]Mt 24:35; Rev 21:1

[a]*22* Prov. 26:11 [b]*10* Some manuscripts *be burned up*

[11]Since everything will be destroyed in this way, what kind of
people ought you to be? You ought to live holy and godly lives
[12]as you look forward[a] to the day of God and speed its coming.[a][b]
That day will bring about the destruction of the heavens by fire,
and the elements will melt in the heat.[c] [13]But in keeping with his
promise we are looking forward to a new heaven and a new
earth,[d] the home of righteousness.

[14]So then, dear friends, since you are looking forward to this,
make every effort to be found spotless, blameless[e] and at peace with
him. [15]Bear in mind that our Lord's patience[f] means salvation,[g]
just as our dear brother Paul also wrote you with the wisdom that
God gave him.[h] [16]He writes the same way in all his letters, speaking in them of these matters. His letters contain some things that
are hard to understand, which ignorant and unstable[i] people distort, as they do the other Scriptures,[j] to their own destruction.

[17]Therefore, dear friends, since you already know this, be on your
guard[k] so that you may not be carried away by the error[l] of lawless men and fall from your secure position.[m] [18]But grow in the
grace and knowledge of our Lord and Savior Jesus Christ.[n] To
him be glory both now and forever! Amen.

a *12* Or *as you wait eagerly for the day of God to come*

3:12
[a]1Co 1:7
[b]Ps 50:3
[c]ver 10

3:13
[d]Isa 65:17; 66:22; Rev 21:1

3:14
[e]1Th 3:13

3:15
[f]Ro 2:4
[g]ver 9
[h]Eph 3:3

3:16
[i]2Pe 2:14
[j]ver 2

3:17
[k]1Co 10:12
[l]2Pe 2:18
[m]Rev 2:5

3:18
[n]2Pe 1:11

2 Peter Observations Chart

Peter

Recipients

Instructions

Warnings

2 Peter at a Glance

Theme of 2 Peter:

Segment Divisions	Paragraph Themes	Chapter Themes
	1:1-4	1
	1:5-11	
	1:12-21	
	2:1-22	2
	3:1-7	3
	3:8-13	
	3:14-18	

Author:

Date:

Purpose:

Key Words:

prophecy (prophet[s], prophet's)

knowledge (know, unde stand, knowi known, told about)

remind (reminders, refresh your memory)

true (truth)

make every effort, eager

false, made u

destroyed, destruction

promise(d)

1 JOHN

As a boy, John thought of Jesus as just a cousin, one of the sons of Aunt Mary, his mother Salome's sister. Little did he realize that someday he would be chosen by God to be one of his twelve apostles.

He had been known as a "Son of Thunder" (Mark 3:17); but a transformation had taken place. Now he was called "the disciple whom Jesus loved."

Even though John's name is not mentioned in this epistle, there is much evidence that he is the author. John had been with Jesus. He had seen him, heard him, touched him, and been filled with his love. This is evident as you hear John's fatherly heart for those who belong to Jesus. He loves the fathers, the young men, the dear children. Yet as he writes about the antichrists and deceivers, you can hear the rumble of thunder in the background.

We don't know when John wrote this first epistle. It may have been between A.D. 85 and 95, when he was in Ephesus before being exiled to the Isle of Patmos. Love—and thunder—compelled him to write. He had to protect his children from a deception that could darken their understanding if they were not warned about the brewing storm of gnosticism—a teaching which could keep them from having fellowship with him (1 John 1:3).

Things to Do

1. If you want to handle a passage of Scripture accurately you must always interpret it in the light of its context. Context simply means that which goes "with" (*con*) the "text." Context must always rule when it comes to interpretation. Identifying the author's purpose for writing will help you discern the context of a passage. What the author says, he says in the light of his purpose for writing.

   In this particular letter the author tells us his purpose in seven different verses: 1:4; 2:1, 12-14, 21, and 26. Then in 1 John 5:13 he concludes by summarizing his purpose for writing. Read these verses and record his reasons for writing on the chart I WRITE THIS TO YOU on page 2128. Then read 1 John 5:13 and record on the 1 JOHN AT A GLANCE chart on page 2129 the author's purpose for writing.
2. One of the major heresies the church would face was gnosticism. Gnosticism wasn't in full bloom in John's time, but the seeds had been sown. Understanding gnosticism will help you better understand why John concentrated on the truths contained in his writing. Therefore, before you go any further, read the article "Understanding Gnosticism" on page 2204.
3. Now read 1 John chapter by chapter and observe the text, using the instructions outlined in the observation section in "How to Use The International Inductive Study Bible" on page IISB-15.
   a. Mark in the text in a distinctive way each of the key words (and their synonyms and pronouns) listed on 1 JOHN AT A GLANCE. When you finish marking these words, go to the chart 1 JOHN KEY WORDS on page 2128 and record the number of times each word is used in each chapter. Then add them up to see the number of times each word is used in 1 John. Doing this will help you see the main themes of 1 John.
   b. John uses a number of contrasts in order to make his point: light/darkness; children of God/children of the devil; etc. Watch for these contrasts, and in the margin next to where they are found list what you learn from them.
   c. When you finish your observations on each chapter:
      1) List in the margin the truths you learn from each of the key words.
      2) Remember, 1 John was written "so that you may know." When you finish reading all five

chapters, trace throughout 1 John the repeated use of the words *know, known,* and *recognize* and record what you learn from the text on the chart WHAT I CAN KNOW and HOW I CAN KNOW IT on pages 2128, 2129. As you make this list, watch the matters John deals with in respect to wrong behavior or wrong belief.

3) Keep a running list of everything you learn about God, Jesus Christ, and the Spirit from this book. Record it in the margin.

4. Record the theme of each chapter on 1 JOHN AT A GLANCE and in the text next to the chapter number. Fill in any remaining information called for on the chart.

THINGS TO THINK ABOUT

1. Based on the criteria given in this book, how can you know whether or not you have eternal life?
2. What have you learned about sin from 1 John? Do you live in sin or righteousness?
3. Do you love the things of the world? Are you caught up in boasting about what you have or do, or in desiring whatever your eyes see?
4. According to 1 John 3, what are you to do when your heart condemns you?
5. Does your belief about Jesus Christ match what 1 John teaches about him?

Chapter 1 Theme ______________________

1 That which was from the beginning,[a] which we have heard,
which we have seen with our eyes,[b] which we have looked at
and our hands have touched[c]—this we proclaim concerning the
Word of life. 2 The life appeared;[d] we have seen it and testify to it,
and we proclaim to you the eternal life, which was with the Father
and has appeared to us. 3 We proclaim to you what we have seen and
heard, so that you also may have fellowship with us. And our fellowship is with the Father and with his Son, Jesus Christ.[e] 4 We
write this[f] to make our[a] joy complete.[g]
5 This is the message we have heard[h] from him and declare to
you: God is light; in him there is no darkness at all. 6 If we claim to
have fellowship with him yet walk in the darkness,[i] we lie and do
not live by the truth.[j] 7 But if we walk in the light, as he is in the
light, we have fellowship with one another, and the blood of Jesus,
his Son, purifies us from all[b] sin.[k]
8 If we claim to be without sin,[l] we deceive ourselves and the
truth is not in us.[m] 9 If we confess our sins, he is faithful and just
and will forgive us our sins[n] and purify us from all unrighteousness. 10 If we claim we have not sinned, we make him out to be a
liar[o] and his word has no place in our lives.[p]

Chapter 2 Theme ______________________

2 My dear children,[q] I write this to you so that you will not sin.
But if anybody does sin, we have one who speaks to the

1:1 [a] Jn 1:2 [b] Jn 1:14; 2Pe 1:16 [c] Jn 20:27
1:2 [d] Jn 1:1-4; 1Ti 3:16
1:3 [e] 1Co 1:9
1:4 [f] 1Jn 2:1 [g] Jn 3:29
1:5 [h] 1Jn 3:11
1:6 [i] 2Co 6:14 [j] Jn 3:19-21
1:7 [k] Heb 9:14; Rev 1:5
1:8 [l] Pr 20:9; Jas 3:2 [m] 1Jn 2:4
1:9 [n] Ps 32:5; 51:2
1:10 [o] 1Jn 5:10 [p] 1Jn 2:14
2:1 [q] ver 12,13,28

[a] 4 Some manuscripts *your* [b] 7 Or *every*

Father in our defense[a]—Jesus Christ, the Righteous One. 2 He is the
atoning sacrifice for our sins,[b] and not only for ours but also for[a]
the sins of the whole world.

3 We know that we have come to know him if we obey his commands.[c] 4 The man who says, "I know him," but does not do what
he commands is a liar, and the truth is not in him.[d] 5 But if anyone
obeys his word,[e] God's love[b] is truly made complete in him.[f] This is
how we know we are in him: 6 Whoever claims to live in him must
walk as Jesus did.[g]

7 Dear friends, I am not writing you a new command but an old
one, which you have had since the beginning.[h] This old command
is the message you have heard. 8 Yet I am writing you a new command;[i] its truth is seen in him and you, because the darkness is
passing[j] and the true light[k] is already shining.[l]

9 Anyone who claims to be in the light but hates his brother is
still in the darkness. 10 Whoever loves his brother lives in the
light,[m] and there is nothing in him[c] to make him stumble. 11 But
whoever hates his brother is in the darkness and walks around in
the darkness; he does not know where he is going, because the
darkness has blinded him.[n]

12 I write to you, dear children,
because your sins have been forgiven on account
of his name.
13 I write to you, fathers,
because you have known him who is from
the beginning.
I write to you, young men,
because you have overcome the evil one.[o]
I write to you, dear children,
because you have known the Father.
14 I write to you, fathers,
because you have known him who is from
the beginning.
I write to you, young men,
because you are strong,[p]
and the word of God lives in you,[q]
and you have overcome the evil one.[r]

15 Do not love the world or anything in the world.[s] If anyone loves
the world, the love of the Father is not in him.[t] 16 For everything in
the world—the cravings of sinful man,[u] the lust of his eyes[v] and the
boasting of what he has and does—comes not from the Father but
from the world. 17 The world and its desires pass away,[w] but the
man who does the will of God lives forever.

[a] 2 Or *He is the one who turns aside God's wrath, taking away our sins, and not only ours but also*
[b] 5 Or *word, love for God* [c] 10 Or *it*

2:1 [a] Ro 8:34; Heb 7:25
2:2 [b] Ro 3:25
2:3 [c] Jn 14:15
2:4 [d] 1Jn 1:6,8
2:5 [e] Jn 14:21,23 [f] 1Jn 4:12
2:6 [g] Mt 11:29; 1Pe 2:21
2:7 [h] 1Jn 3:11,23; 2Jn 5,6
2:8 [i] Jn 13:34 [j] Ro 13:12 [k] Jn 1:9 [l] Eph 5:8; 1Th 5:5
2:10 [m] 1Jn 3:14
2:11 [n] Jn 12:35
2:13 [o] ver 14
2:14 [p] Eph 6:10 [q] Jn 5:38; 1Jn 1:10 [r] ver 13
2:15 [s] Ro 12:2 [t] Jas 4:4
2:16 [u] Ro 13:14 [v] Pr 27:20
2:17 [w] 1Co 7:31

18 Dear children, this is the last hour; and as you have heard that the antichrist is coming,[a] even now many antichrists have come.[b] This is how we know it is the last hour. 19 They went out from us,[c] but they did not really belong to us. For if they had belonged to us, they would have remained with us; but their going showed that none of them belonged to us.[d]

20 But you have an anointing[e] from the Holy One,[f] and all of you know the truth.[a][g] 21 I do not write to you because you do not know the truth, but because you do know it[h] and because no lie comes from the truth. 22 Who is the liar? It is the man who denies that Jesus is the Christ. Such a man is the antichrist—he denies the Father and the Son.[i] 23 No one who denies the Son has the Father; whoever acknowledges the Son has the Father also.[j]

24 See that what you have heard from the beginning remains in you. If it does, you also will remain in the Son and in the Father.[k] 25 And this is what he promised us—even eternal life.

26 I am writing these things to you about those who are trying to lead you astray.[l] 27 As for you, the anointing[m] you received from him remains in you, and you do not need anyone to teach you. But as his anointing teaches you about all things and as that anointing is real, not counterfeit—just as it has taught you, remain in him.

28 And now, dear children,[n] continue in him, so that when he appears[o] we may be confident[p] and unashamed before him at his coming.[q]

29 If you know that he is righteous,[r] you know that everyone who does what is right has been born of him.

Chapter 3 Theme ______________________

3 How great is the love[s] the Father has lavished on us, that we should be called children of God![t] And that is what we are! The reason the world does not know us is that it did not know him.[u] 2 Dear friends, now we are children of God, and what we will be has not yet been made known. But we know that when he appears,[b] we shall be like him,[v] for we shall see him as he is.[w] 3 Everyone who has this hope in him purifies himself,[x] just as he is pure.

4 Everyone who sins breaks the law; in fact, sin is lawlessness.[y] 5 But you know that he appeared so that he might take away our sins. And in him is no sin.[z] 6 No one who lives in him keeps on sinning.[a] No one who continues to sin has either seen him[b] or known him.[c]

7 Dear children,[d] do not let anyone lead you astray.[e] He who does what is right is righteous, just as he is righteous.[f] 8 He who

a 20 Some manuscripts *and you know all things* b 2 Or *when it is made known*

2:18 [a] ver 22; 1Jn 4:3; 2Jn 7 [b] 1Jn 4:1
2:19 [c] Ac 20:30 [d] 1Co 11:19
2:20 [e] 2Co 1:21 [f] Mk 1:24 [g] Jn 14:26
2:21 [h] 2Pe 1:12; Jude 5
2:22 [i] 2Jn 7
2:23 [j] Jn 8:19; 1Jn 4:15
2:24 [k] Jn 14:23
2:26 [l] 2Jn 7
2:27 [m] ver 20
2:28 [n] ver 1 [o] 1Jn 3:2 [p] 1Jn 4:17 [q] 1Th 2:19
2:29 [r] 1Jn 3:7
3:1 [s] Jn 3:16 [t] Jn 1:12 [u] Jn 16:3
3:2 [v] Ro 8:29; 2Pe 1:4 [w] 2Co 3:18
3:3 [x] 2Co 7:1; 2Pe 3:13,14
3:4 [y] 1Jn 5:17
3:5 [z] 2Co 5:21
3:6 [a] ver 9 [b] 3Jn 11 [c] 1Jn 2:4
3:7 [d] 1Jn 2:1 [e] 1Jn 2:26 [f] 1Jn 2:29

13Who is going to harm you if you are eager to do good?[a] 14But
even if you should suffer for what is right, you are blessed.[b] "Do
not fear what they fear[a]; do not be frightened."[b][c] 15But in your
hearts set apart Christ as Lord. Always be prepared to give an
answer[d] to everyone who asks you to give the reason for the hope
that you have. But do this with gentleness and respect, 16keeping
a clear conscience,[e] so that those who speak maliciously against
your good behavior in Christ may be ashamed of their slander.[f]
17It is better, if it is God's will,[g] to suffer for doing good[h] than for
doing evil. 18For Christ died for sins[i] once for all, the righteous
for the unrighteous, to bring you to God. He was put to death in
the body[j] but made alive by the Spirit,[k] 19through whom[c] also he
went and preached to the spirits in prison[l] 20who disobeyed long
ago when God waited patiently in the days of Noah while the ark
was being built.[m] In it only a few people, eight in all, were saved[n]
through water, 21and this water symbolizes baptism that now
saves you[o] also—not the removal of dirt from the body but the
pledge[d] of a good conscience toward God. It saves you by the resurrection of Jesus Christ,[p] 22who has gone into heaven and is at
God's right hand[q]—with angels, authorities and powers in submission to him.[r]

Chapter 4 Theme

4 Therefore, since Christ suffered in his body, arm yourselves
also with the same attitude, because he who has suffered in his
body is done with sin. 2As a result, he does not live the rest of his
earthly life for evil human desires,[s] but rather for the will of God.
3For you have spent enough time in the past[t] doing what pagans
choose to do—living in debauchery, lust, drunkenness, orgies,
carousing and detestable idolatry. 4They think it strange that you
do not plunge with them into the same flood of dissipation, and
they heap abuse on you.[u] 5But they will have to give account to him
who is ready to judge the living and the dead.[v] 6For this is the reason the gospel was preached even to those who are now dead,[w] so
that they might be judged according to men in regard to the
body, but live according to God in regard to the spirit.

7The end of all things is near.[x] Therefore be clear minded and
self-controlled so that you can pray. 8Above all, love each other
deeply,[y] because love covers over a multitude of sins.[z] 9Offer hospitality to one another without grumbling.[a] 10Each one should use
whatever gift he has received to serve others,[b] faithfully[c] administering God's grace in its various forms. 11If anyone speaks, he
should do it as one speaking the very words of God. If anyone

3:13 [a] Pr 16:7
3:14 [b] 1Pe 2:19,20; 4:15,16 [c] Isa 8:12,13
3:15 [d] Col 4:6
3:16 [e] Heb 13:18 [f] 1Pe 2:12,15
3:17 [g] 1Pe 2:15 [h] 1Pe 2:20
3:18 [i] 1Pe 2:21 [j] Col 1:22; 1Pe 4:1 [k] 1Pe 4:6
3:19 [l] 1Pe 4:6
3:20 [m] Ge 6:3,5, 13,14 [n] Heb 11:7
3:21 [o] Tit 3:5 [p] 1Pe 1:3
3:22 [q] Mk 16:19 [r] Ro 8:38
4:2 [s] Ro 6:2
4:3 [t] Eph 2:2
4:4 [u] 1Pe 3:16
4:5 [v] Ac 10:42; 2Ti 4:1
4:6 [w] 1Pe 3:19
4:7 [x] Ro 13:11
4:8 [y] 1Pe 1:22 [z] Pr 10:12
4:9 [a] Php 2:14
4:10 [b] Ro 12:6,7 [c] 1Co 4:2

[a] *14* Or *not fear their threats* [b] *14* Isaiah 8:12 [c] *18,19* Or *alive in the spirit,* [19] *through which*
[d] *21* Or *response*

22“He committed no sin,
and no deceit was found in his mouth.”[a][a]

23When they hurled their insults at him, he did not retaliate; when he suffered, he made no threats.[b] Instead, he entrusted himself[c] to him who judges justly. 24He himself bore our sins[d] in his body on the tree, so that we might die to sins[e] and live for righteousness; by his wounds you have been healed.[f] 25For you were like sheep going astray,[g] but now you have returned to the Shepherd[h] and Overseer of your souls.

Chapter 3 Theme ______________________________

3 Wives, in the same way be submissive[i] to your husbands[j] so that, if any of them do not believe the word, they may be won over[k] without words by the behavior of their wives, 2when they see the purity and reverence of your lives. 3Your beauty should not come from outward adornment, such as braided hair and the wearing of gold jewelry and fine clothes.[l] 4Instead, it should be that of your inner self,[m] the unfading beauty of a gentle and quiet spirit, which is of great worth in God’s sight. 5For this is the way the holy women of the past who put their hope in God[n] used to make themselves beautiful. They were submissive to their own husbands, 6like Sarah, who obeyed Abraham and called him her master.[o] You are her daughters if you do what is right and do not give way to fear.

7Husbands,[p] in the same way be considerate as you live with your wives, and treat them with respect as the weaker partner and as heirs with you of the gracious gift of life, so that nothing will hinder your prayers.

8Finally, all of you, live in harmony with one another; be sympathetic, love as brothers,[q] be compassionate and humble.[r] 9Do not repay evil with evil[s] or insult with insult,[t] but with blessing, because to this[u] you were called so that you may inherit a blessing.[v] 10For,

“Whoever would love life
and see good days
must keep his tongue from evil
and his lips from deceitful speech.
11He must turn from evil and do good;
he must seek peace and pursue it.
12For the eyes of the Lord are on the righteous
and his ears are attentive to their prayer,
but the face of the Lord is against those who do evil.”[b][w]

2:22 [a]Isa 53:9
2:23 [b]Isa 53:7 [c]Lk 23:46
2:24 [d]Heb 9:28 [e]Ro 6:2 [f]Isa 53:5; Heb 12:13; Jas 5:16
2:25 [g]Isa 53:6 [h]Jn 10:11
3:1 [i]1Pe 2:18 [j]Eph 5:22 [k]1Co 7:16; 9:19
3:3 [l]Isa 3:18-23; 1Ti 2:9
3:4 [m]Ro 7:22
3:5 [n]1Ti 5:5
3:6 [o]Ge 18:12
3:7 [p]Eph 5:25-33
3:8 [q]Ro 12:10 [r]1Pe 5:5
3:9 [s]Ro 12:17 [t]1Pe 2:23 [u]1Pe 2:21 [v]Heb 6:14
3:12 [w]Ps 34:12-16

[a]22 Isaiah 53:9 [b]12 Psalm 34:12-16

by the power of the Spirit.[a] It is the same now. 30 But what does the
Scripture say? "Get rid of the slave woman and her son, for the
slave woman's son will never share in the inheritance with the free
woman's son."[a b] 31 Therefore, brothers, we are not children of the
slave woman, but of the free woman.

Chapter 5 Theme ______________________________

5 It is for freedom that Christ has set us free.[c] Stand firm,[d] then,
and do not let yourselves be burdened again by a yoke of
slavery.[e]
2 Mark my words! I, Paul, tell you that if you let yourselves be
circumcised,[f] Christ will be of no value to you at all. 3 Again I
declare to every man who lets himself be circumcised that he is
obligated to obey the whole law.[g] 4 You who are trying to be justified by law have been alienated from Christ; you have fallen away
from grace.[h] 5 But by faith we eagerly await through the Spirit the
righteousness for which we hope.[i] 6 For in Christ Jesus neither circumcision nor uncircumcision has any value.[j] The only thing
that counts is faith expressing itself through love.[k]
7 You were running a good race.[l] Who cut in on you[m] and kept
you from obeying the truth? 8 That kind of persuasion does not
come from the one who calls you.[n] 9 "A little yeast works through
the whole batch of dough."[o] 10 I am confident[p] in the Lord that you
will take no other view.[q] The one who is throwing you into confusion[r] will pay the penalty, whoever he may be. 11 Brothers, if I am
still preaching circumcision, why am I still being persecuted?[s] In
that case the offense[t] of the cross has been abolished. 12 As for those
agitators,[u] I wish they would go the whole way and emasculate
themselves!
13 You, my brothers, were called to be free. But do not use your
freedom to indulge the sinful nature[b];[v] rather, serve one another[w]
in love. 14 The entire law is summed up in a single command: "Love
your neighbor as yourself."[c x] 15 If you keep on biting and devouring each other, watch out or you will be destroyed by each other.
16 So I say, live by the Spirit,[y] and you will not gratify the desires
of the sinful nature.[z] 17 For the sinful nature desires what is contrary to the Spirit, and the Spirit what is contrary to the sinful
nature.[a] They are in conflict with each other, so that you do not
do what you want.[b] 18 But if you are led by the Spirit, you are not
under law.[c] 19 The acts of the sinful nature are obvious: sexual
immorality,[d] impurity and debauchery; 20 idolatry and witchcraft;
hatred, discord, jealousy, fits of rage, selfish ambition, dissensions,
factions 21 and envy; drunkenness, orgies, and the like.[e] I warn you,

a *30* Gen. 21:10 b *13* Or *the flesh*; also in verses 16, 17, 19 and 24 c *14* Lev. 19:18

4:29 [a] Ge 21:9
4:30 [b] Ge 21:10
5:1 [c] Jn 8:32 [d] 1Co 16:13 [e] Ac 15:10; Gal 2:4
5:2 [f] Ac 15:1
5:3 [g] Gal 3:10
5:4 [h] Heb 12:15; 2Pe 3:17
5:5 [i] Ro 8:23,24
5:6 [j] 1Co 7:19 [k] 1Th 1:3
5:7 [l] 1Co 9:24 [m] Gal 3:1
5:8 [n] Ro 8:28; Gal 1:6
5:9 [o] 1Co 5:6
5:10 [p] 2Co 2:3 [q] Php 3:15 [r] Gal 1:7
5:11 [s] Gal 4:29; 6:12 [t] 1Co 1:23
5:12 [u] ver 10
5:13 [v] 1Co 8:9; 1Pe 2:16 [w] 1Co 9:19; Eph 5:21
5:14 [x] Lev 19:18; Mt 22:39
5:16 [y] Ro 8:2, 4-6,9,14 [z] ver 24
5:17 [a] Ro 8:5-8 [b] Ro 7:15-23
5:18 [c] Ro 6:14; 1Ti 1:9
5:19 [d] 1Co 6:18
5:21 [e] Ro 13:13

8Formerly, when you did not know God,[a] you were slaves to those
who by nature are not gods.[b] 9But now that you know God—or
rather are known by God[c]—how is it that you are turning back to
those weak and miserable principles? Do you wish to be enslaved[d]
by them all over again?[e] 10You are observing special days and months
and seasons and years![f] 11I fear for you, that somehow I have wasted
my efforts on you.[g]

12I plead with you, brothers,[h] become like me, for I became like
you. You have done me no wrong. 13As you know, it was because of
an illness[i] that I first preached the gospel to you. 14Even though my
illness was a trial to you, you did not treat me with contempt or
scorn. Instead, you welcomed me as if I were an angel of God, as if
I were Christ Jesus himself.[j] 15What has happened to all your joy? I
can testify that, if you could have done so, you would have torn
out your eyes and given them to me. 16Have I now become your
enemy by telling you the truth?[k]

17Those people are zealous to win you over, but for no good. What
they want is to alienate you ⌊from us⌋, so that you may be zealous
for them. 18It is fine to be zealous, provided the purpose is good,
and to be so always and not just when I am with you.[l] 19My dear
children,[m] for whom I am again in the pains of childbirth until
Christ is formed in you,[n] 20how I wish I could be with you now
and change my tone, because I am perplexed about you!

21Tell me, you who want to be under the law, are you not aware
of what the law says? 22For it is written that Abraham had two
sons, one by the slave woman[o] and the other by the free woman.[p]
23His son by the slave woman was born in the ordinary way;[q] but
his son by the free woman was born as the result of a promise.[r]

24These things may be taken figuratively, for the women represent two covenants. One covenant is from Mount Sinai and bears
children who are to be slaves: This is Hagar. 25Now Hagar stands
for Mount Sinai in Arabia and corresponds to the present city of
Jerusalem, because she is in slavery with her children. 26But the
Jerusalem that is above[s] is free, and she is our mother. 27For it is
written:

> "Be glad, O barren woman,
> who bears no children;
> break forth and cry aloud,
> you who have no labor pains;
> because more are the children of the desolate woman
> than of her who has a husband."[a][t]

28Now you, brothers, like Isaac, are children of promise. 29At that
time the son born in the ordinary way[u] persecuted the son born

4:8 [a]1Co 1:21; Eph 2:12; 1Th 4:5 [b]2Ch 13:9; Isa 37:19
4:9 [c]1Co 8:3 [d]ver 3 [e]Col 2:20
4:10 [f]Ro 14:5
4:11 [g]1Th 3:5
4:12 [h]Gal 6:18
4:13 [i]1Co 2:3
4:14 [j]Mt 10:40
4:16 [k]Am 5:10
4:18 [l]ver 13,14
4:19 [m]1Co 4:15 [n]Eph 4:13
4:22 [o]Ge 16:15 [p]Ge 21:2
4:23 [q]Ro 9:7,8 [r]Ge 18:10-14; Heb 11:11
4:26 [s]Heb 12:22; Rev 3:12
4:27 [t]Isa 54:1
4:29 [u]ver 23

a *27* Isaiah 54:1

does what is sinful is of the devil,[a] because the devil has been sinning from the beginning. The reason the Son of God appeared was
to destroy the devil's work. 9No one who is born of God[b] will continue to sin,[c] because God's seed[d] remains in him; he cannot go
on sinning, because he has been born of God. 10This is how we
know who the children of God are and who the children of the
devil are: Anyone who does not do what is right is not a child of
God; nor is anyone who does not love[e] his brother.

11This is the message you heard[f] from the beginning: We should
love one another.[g] 12Do not be like Cain, who belonged to the evil
one and murdered his brother.[h] And why did he murder him?
Because his own actions were evil and his brother's were righteous. 13Do not be surprised, my brothers, if the world hates you.[i]
14We know that we have passed from death to life,[j] because we
love our brothers. Anyone who does not love remains in death.[k]
15Anyone who hates his brother is a murderer,[l] and you know that
no murderer has eternal life in him.[m]

16This is how we know what love is: Jesus Christ laid down his life
for us. And we ought to lay down our lives for our brothers.[n] 17If
anyone has material possessions and sees his brother in need but
has no pity on him,[o] how can the love of God be in him?[p] 18Dear
children,[q] let us not love with words or tongue but with actions
and in truth.[r] 19This then is how we know that we belong to the
truth, and how we set our hearts at rest in his presence 20whenever
our hearts condemn us. For God is greater than our hearts, and he
knows everything.

21Dear friends, if our hearts do not condemn us, we have confidence before God[s] 22and receive from him anything we ask,[t] because we obey his commands and do what pleases him.[u] 23And
this is his command: to believe[v] in the name of his Son, Jesus
Christ, and to love one another as he commanded us.[w] 24Those
who obey his commands live in him,[x] and he in them. And this is
how we know that he lives in us: We know it by the Spirit he
gave us.[y]

Chapter 4 Theme ______________________

4 Dear friends, do not believe every spirit, but test the spirits
to see whether they are from God, because many false prophets have gone out into the world.[z] 2This is how you can recognize
the Spirit of God: Every spirit that acknowledges that Jesus Christ
has come in the flesh[a] is from God,[b] 3but every spirit that does
not acknowledge Jesus is not from God. This is the spirit of the
antichrist,[c] which you have heard is coming and even now is already in the world.

3:8 [a]Jn 8:44
3:9 [b]Jn 1:13 [c]1Jn 5:18 [d]1Pe 1:23
3:10 [e]1Jn 4:8
3:11 [f]1Jn 1:5 [g]Jn 13:34,35; 2Jn 5
3:12 [h]Ge 4:8
3:13 [i]Jn 15:18,19; 17:14
3:14 [j]Jn 5:24 [k]1Jn 2:9
3:15 [l]Mt 5:21,22; Jn 8:44 [m]Gal 5:20,21
3:16 [n]Jn 15:13
3:17 [o]Dt 15:7,8 [p]1Jn 4:20
3:18 [q]1Jn 2:1 [r]Eze 33:31; Ro 12:9
3:21 [s]1Jn 5:14
3:22 [t]Mt 7:7 [u]Jn 8:29
3:23 [v]Jn 6:29 [w]Jn 13:34
3:24 [x]1Jn 2:6 [y]1Jn 4:13
4:1 [z]2Pe 2:1; 1Jn 2:18
4:2 [a]Jn 1:14; 1Jn 2:23 [b]1Co 12:3
4:3 [c]1Jn 2:22; 2Jn 7

4You, dear children, are from God and have overcome them,
because the one who is in you[a] is greater than the one who is in the
world.[b] 5They are from the world[c] and therefore speak from the
viewpoint of the world, and the world listens to them. 6We are
from God, and whoever knows God listens to us; but whoever is
not from God does not listen to us.[d] This is how we recognize the
Spirit[a] of truth[e] and the spirit of falsehood.

7Dear friends, let us love one another,[f] for love comes from God.
Everyone who loves has been born of God and knows God.[g]
8Whoever does not love does not know God, because God is love.[h]
9This is how God showed his love among us: He sent his one and
only Son[b] into the world that we might live through him.[i] 10This is
love: not that we loved God, but that he loved us[j] and sent his Son
as an atoning sacrifice for[c] our sins.[k] 11Dear friends, since God so
loved us,[l] we also ought to love one another. 12No one has ever seen
God;[m] but if we love one another, God lives in us and his love is
made complete in us.[n]

13We know that we live in him and he in us, because he has given
us of his Spirit.[o] 14And we have seen and testify[p] that the Father has
sent his Son to be the Savior of the world.[q] 15If anyone acknowledges that Jesus is the Son of God,[r] God lives in him and he in God.
16And so we know and rely on the love God has for us.

God is love.[s] Whoever lives in love lives in God, and God in him.[t]
17In this way, love is made complete[u] among us so that we will have
confidence on the day of judgment, because in this world we are
like him. 18There is no fear in love. But perfect love drives out fear,[v]
because fear has to do with punishment. The one who fears is not
made perfect in love.

19We love because he first loved us.[w] 20If anyone says, "I love
God," yet hates his brother,[x] he is a liar.[y] For anyone who does not
love his brother, whom he has seen,[z] cannot love God, whom he
has not seen.[a] 21And he has given us this command: Whoever loves
God must also love his brother.[b]

Chapter 5 Theme ______________________________

5 Everyone who believes that Jesus is the Christ[c] is born of
God,[d] and everyone who loves the father loves his child as
well.[e] 2This is how we know that we love the children of God: by
loving God and carrying out his commands. 3This is love for God:
to obey his commands.[f] And his commands are not burdensome,[g]
4for everyone born of God overcomes[h] the world. This is the victory that has overcome the world, even our faith. 5Who is it that
overcomes the world? Only he who believes that Jesus is the Son
of God.

a6 Or *spirit* b9 Or *his only begotten Son* c10 Or *as the one who would turn aside his wrath, taking away*

4:4 a Ro 8:31; b Jn 12:31
4:5 c Jn 15:19
4:6 d Jn 8:47; e Jn 14:17
4:7 f 1Jn 3:11; g 1Jn 2:4
4:8 h ver 7,16
4:9 i Jn 3:16,17; 1Jn 5:11
4:10 j Ro 5:8,10; k 1Jn 2:2
4:11 l Jn 3:16
4:12 m Jn 1:18; 1Ti 6:16; n 1Jn 2:5
4:13 o 1Jn 3:24
4:14 p Jn 15:27; q Jn 3:17
4:15 r Ro 10:9
4:16 s ver 8; t 1Jn 3:24
4:17 u 1Jn 2:5
4:18 v Ro 8:15
4:19 w ver 10
4:20 x 1Jn 2:9; y 1Jn 2:4; z 1Jn 3:17; a ver 12
4:21 b Mt 5:43
5:1 c 1Jn 2:22; d Jn 1:13; 1Jn 2:23; e Jn 8:42
5:3 f Jn 14:15; 2Jn 6; g Mt 11:30
5:4 h Jn 16:33

6 This is the one who came by water and blood[a]—Jesus Christ.
He did not come by water only, but by water and blood. And it is
the Spirit who testifies, because the Spirit is the truth.[b] 7 For there
are three[c] that testify: 8 the[a] Spirit, the water and the blood; and the
three are in agreement. 9 We accept man's testimony,[d] but God's
testimony is greater because it is the testimony of God,[e] which he
has given about his Son. 10 Anyone who believes in the Son of
God has this testimony in his heart.[f] Anyone who does not believe
God has made him out to be a liar,[g] because he has not believed
the testimony God has given about his Son. 11 And this is the testimony: God has given us eternal life, and this life is in his Son.[h]
12 He who has the Son has life; he who does not have the Son of
God does not have life.[i]

13 I write these things to you who believe in the name of the Son
of God[j] so that you may know that you have eternal life.[k] 14 This is
the confidence[l] we have in approaching God: that if we ask anything according to his will, he hears us.[m] 15 And if we know that he
hears us—whatever we ask—we know[n] that we have what we
asked of him.

16 If anyone sees his brother commit a sin that does not lead to
death, he should pray and God will give him life.[o] I refer to those
whose sin does not lead to death. There is a sin that leads to death.[p]
I am not saying that he should pray about that.[q] 17 All wrongdoing
is sin,[r] and there is sin that does not lead to death.[s]

18 We know that anyone born of God does not continue to sin;
the one who was born of God keeps him safe, and the evil one
cannot harm him.[t] 19 We know that we are children of God,[u] and
that the whole world is under the control of the evil one.[v] 20 We
know also that the Son of God has come and has given us understanding,[w] so that we may know him who is true.[x] And we are in
him who is true—even in his Son Jesus Christ. He is the true God
and eternal life.[y]

21 Dear children, keep yourselves from idols.[z]

[a] 7,8 Late manuscripts of the Vulgate *testify in heaven: the Father, the Word and the Holy Spirit, and these three are one.* 8 *And there are three that testify on earth: the* (not found in any Greek manuscript before the sixteenth century)

5:6 [a] Jn 19:34 [b] Jn 14:17
5:7 [c] Mt 18:16
5:9 [d] Jn 5:34 [e] Mt 3:16,17; Jn 8:17,18
5:10 [f] Ro 8:16; Gal 4:6 [g] Jn 3:33
5:11 [h] Jn 1:4; 1Jn 2:25
5:12 [i] Jn 3:15,16,36
5:13 [j] 1Jn 3:23 [k] Jn 20:31; 1Jn 1:1,2
5:14 [l] 1Jn 3:21 [m] Mt 7:7
5:15 [n] ver 18,19,20
5:16 [o] Jas 5:15 [p] Heb 6:4-6; 10:26 [q] Jer 7:16
5:17 [r] 1Jn 3:4 [s] 1Jn 2:1
5:18 [t] Jn 14:30
5:19 [u] 1Jn 4:6 [v] Gal 1:4
5:20 [w] Lk 24:45 [x] Jn 17:3 [y] ver 11
5:21 [z] 1Co 10:14; 1Th 1:9

1 John Observations Charts

I Write This to You

1:4	
2:1	
2:12	
2:13	
2:14	
2:21	
2:26	
5:13	

1 John Key Words

Chapter	Fellowship	Remain (Continue)	Sin	Know (Recognize)	Love	Born of God	Write	Light	Trutl
1									
2									
3									
4									
5									
Total									

What I Can Know	How I Can Know It

(continue

1 John Observations Charts

What I Can Know	How I Can Know It

1 John at a Glance

heme of 1 John:

uthor:

ate:

urpose:

y Words:
ellowship
emain(s), continue, be in, ive in
in(s), sinning, what is sinful
now(n), ecognize
ove, loving
orn of God
ght
ruth (true, real)
rite (writing)
nark every eference to the evil (or evil one)

Segment Divisions	Chapter Themes
	1
	2
	3
	4
	5

2 JOHN

A caring father can't ignore something that threatens his children. So around A.D. 90 the paternal apostle John sat down to write yet another epistle. It is short, to the point, and needful—even today.

Things to Do

1. Read through 2 John as you would a letter you had just received. Then read it again and:
   a. Mark in the text the key words listed on the 2 JOHN AT A GLANCE chart on page 2131.
   b. List in the margin all you learn about the recipients of this letter. Note John's feelings toward them, his instructions (or commandments) to them, and his warnings. Note also the reason for his warnings.
2. Record the theme of 2 John in the appropriate space on 2 JOHN AT A GLANCE. Then record the theme of each paragraph and fill in any other pertinent information.

Things to Think About

1. What does this book say about someone who does not continue in the teaching of Christ? Do you know someone who could fit that description? What should you do?
2. You probably noted that verse 4 says "some" of the children are walking in truth. Are you careful to walk in all the truth you know? Do you realize that before God you are responsible to live out the truth that has been entrusted to you?
3. According to this little epistle, what does it mean to walk in love? Are you doing this?

Chapter Theme ______________________

1 The elder,[a]

To the chosen[b] lady and her children, whom I love in the truth—
and not I only, but also all who know the truth[c]— 2 because of the
truth,[d] which lives in us[e] and will be with us forever:

3 Grace, mercy and peace from God the Father and from Jesus
Christ,[f] the Father's Son, will be with us in truth and love.

4 It has given me great joy to find some of your children walking
in the truth,[g] just as the Father commanded us. 5 And now, dear
lady, I am not writing you a new command but one we have had
from the beginning.[h] I ask that we love one another. 6 And this is
love:[i] that we walk in obedience to his commands. As you have
heard from the beginning, his command is that you walk in love.

7 Many deceivers, who do not acknowledge Jesus Christ[j] as coming in the flesh, have gone out into the world.[k] Any such person is
the deceiver and the antichrist.[l] 8 Watch out that you do not lose
what you have worked for, but that you may be rewarded fully.[m]
9 Anyone who runs ahead and does not continue in the teaching of

1:1
a 3Jn 1
b Ro 16:13
c Jn 8:32

1:2
d 2Pe 1:12
e 1Jn 1:8

1:3
f Ro 1:7

1:4
g 3Jn 3,4

1:5
h 1Jn 2:7; 3:11

1:6
i 1Jn 2:5

1:7
j 1Jn 2:22; 4:2,3
k 1Jn 4:1
l 1Jn 2:18

1:8
m 1Co 3:8

1:9 [a] 1Jn 2:23 Christ does not have God; whoever continues in the teaching has
both the Father and the Son.[a] 10If anyone comes to you and does
1:10 [b] Ro 16:17 not bring this teaching, do not take him into your house or welcome him.[b] 11Anyone who welcomes him shares[c] in his wicked
1:11 [c] 1Ti 5:22 work.
12I have much to write to you, but I do not want to use paper and
1:12 [d] 3Jn 13,14 ink. Instead, I hope to visit you and talk with you face to face,[d] so
that our joy may be complete.

1:13 [e] ver 1 13The children of your chosen[e] sister send their greetings.

2 John at a Glance

heme of 2 John:

uthor:

ate:

urpose:

ey Words:
truth
love
command(ed)
(commands)
teaching
walk
continue(s)
(lives)
deceiver(s)

Segment Divisions	Paragraph Themes
	Verses 1-3
	Verses 4-11
	Verses 12, 13

3 JOHN

Love cares about the individual. Love encourages. Love rebukes. Love walks in truth. And so, in love, John wrote a third epistle before he was exiled to Patmos, where he wrote Revelation. It was around A.D. 90.

Things to Do

1. Read this short letter through once. Then read the book again, marking each of the key words listed on the 3 JOHN AT A GLANCE chart on page 2133. List in the margin what you learn from the key words.
2. To whom is the book written? List in the margin everything you learn about him from this letter.
3. Other names are mentioned. Who is named and what is said about each person? List this information in the margin of the text. What do you learn as you observe the contrast between these people?
4. Make a list of the instructions and warnings John gives in this short epistle.
5. Complete 3 JOHN AT A GLANCE.

Things to Think About

1. What is your testimony before others? Are you known for your love of others or for your love of yourself? Do you share what you have with others? Do you listen to others? Do you have to be first?
2. According to what John says in this epistle, what does the way you live have to do with your relationship to God?
3. Are you quick to love, to exhort, and to stand for truth? What do you need to do?

Chapter Theme ____________________

1The elder,[a]

To my dear friend Gaius, whom I love in the truth.

2Dear friend, I pray that you may enjoy good health and that all
may go well with you, even as your soul is getting along well. 3It
gave me great joy to have some brothers[b] come and tell about your
faithfulness to the truth and how you continue to walk in the
truth.[c] 4I have no greater joy than to hear that my children[d] are
walking in the truth.

5Dear friend, you are faithful in what you are doing for the
brothers, even though they are strangers to you.[e] 6They have told
the church about your love. You will do well to send them on their
way in a manner worthy of God. 7It was for the sake of the Name[f]
that they went out, receiving no help from the pagans.[g] 8We
ought therefore to show hospitality to such men so that we may
work together for the truth.

9I wrote to the church, but Diotrephes, who loves to be first, will
have nothing to do with us. 10So if I come,[h] I will call attention to

1:1 [a] 2Jn 1
1:3 [b] ver 5,10 [c] 2Jn 4
1:4 [d] 1Co 4:15; 1Jn 2:1
1:5 [e] Ro 12:13; Heb 13:2
1:7 [f] Jn 15:21 [g] Ac 20:33,35
1:10 [h] 2Jn 12

1:10 [a] ver 5 [b] Jn 9:22,34

what he is doing, gossiping maliciously about us. Not satisfied
with that, he refuses to welcome the brothers.[a] He also stops those
who want to do so and puts them out of the church.[b]

1:11 [c] Ps 37:27 [d] 1Jn 2:29 [e] 1Jn 3:6,9,10

11 Dear friend, do not imitate what is evil but what is good.[c]
Anyone who does what is good is from God.[d] Anyone who does
what is evil has not seen God.[e] 12 Demetrius is well spoken of by
everyone[f]—and even by the truth itself. We also speak well of him,
and you know that our testimony is true.[g]

1:12 [f] 1Ti 3:7 [g] Jn 21:24

13 I have much to write you, but I do not want to do so with pen
and ink. 14 I hope to see you soon, and we will talk face to face.[h]

1:14 [h] 2Jn 12 [i] Jn 10:3

Peace to you. The friends here send their greetings. Greet the
friends there by name.[i]

3 John at a Glance

heme of 3 John:

uthor:

ate:

urpose:

ey Words:

truth

good

evil

Segment Divisions	Paragraph Themes
	Verse 1
	Verses 2-4
	Verses 5-8
	Verses 9-12
	Verses 13, 14

JUDE

Jude had to speak up. Jude wasn't an apostle and wasn't a pillar in the church, like his brother James. Although he was the half-brother of the Lord Jesus Christ, Jude did not claim any relationship to Jesus Christ other than that of being his bondservant.

Initially Jude didn't believe in Jesus (John 7:5), but finally he saw Jesus as he was—the Son of God—and then he understood: Jude had grown up in the presence of the One who came to save his people from their sins (Matthew 1:21). No wonder Jude had to write what he did!

Things to Do

1. Though only one chapter in length, Jude is a pertinent book. Read it to familiarize yourself with the content.

2. Now read through Jude again. This time look for any place where Jude explains why he is writing. When you discover Jude's purpose for writing, put it on the JUDE AT A GLANCE chart on page 2138. If you do not see his purpose immediately, you will by the time you have finished Jude.

3. Now read through Jude again. This time find out what you can about the author and the recipients. Mark in a distinctive way every reference to the author and to the recipients and related pronouns.

4. Read through Jude again. List what you learn about Jude and the recipients on the OBSERVATIONS CHART on page 2137. Note *only* how Jude and the recipients are described. At this point *do not* list what the recipients are told to do; instead, list only how they are described.

5. Jude mentions other people in this letter. Recognizing who they are and what they are doing will help you to understand better the reason for the writing of this letter. Read through Jude again.
   a. This time mark every occurrence of *certain men, godless men, these men,* and *scoffers* in the same color or with the same symbol.
   b. Also mark in the same way the pronouns (*they, them, who, these,* etc.) which refer to *certain men, godless men, these men, these dreamers,* and *scoffers.*

6. Read Jude again. This time mark in the same way *condemnation, destroyed, judgment (judge), punishment,* and their synonyms. Be sure not to miss any contrasts and comparisons that Jude is making.

7. There is a pattern in this letter. First, Jude refers to "these godless men," then uses Old Testament examples or illustrations to make a point. Read through Jude again, and watch for this pattern. You may want to underline every Old Testament incident or reference that Jude uses. As you study, watch what the Old Testament people do and note how God deals with them. Be sure not to miss any contrasts and comparisons that Jude is making between these Old Testament people and "these godless men."

8. Now that you have marked every reference to "these godless men," and looked at the Old Testament illustrations Jude uses to make his point, fill in this portion of the OBSERVATIONS CHART.

9. On the OBSERVATIONS CHART, list Jude's instructions to the "dear friends" who were the recipients of this epistle by noting what they are to do. Also be sure to note what God will do for them.

10. Determine what you believe to be the theme of Jude and write it down on JUDE AT A GLANCE.

11. Finally, look at Jude paragraph by paragraph, determine what you believe to be the theme for each paragraph, and then record it in the designated place on JUDE AT A GLANCE. Fill in any other information requested.

12. If you want to study Jude further, look up the cross-references in the margin to the Old Testament characters and illustrations and see what you learn from each. This will deepen your insight into these godless men.

Things to Think About

1. Think about the promises to the "loved by God." Spend time in prayer, praising God for what he will do on your behalf. Then think of the responsibilities that are yours and talk with God about how you are to fulfill these.

2. Review the characteristics of the godless. Do you know of anyone who fits this description? How did God tell you to respond to these godless persons in verses 22 and 23? Are you willing to do so? Talk with God about it.

Chapter Theme ____________________

1 Jude,[a] a servant of Jesus Christ and a brother of James,

To those who have been called,[b] who are loved by God the
Father and kept by[a] Jesus Christ:[c]

2 Mercy, peace and love be yours in abundance.[d]

3 Dear friends, although I was very eager to write to you about
the salvation we share,[e] I felt I had to write and urge you to contend[f] for the faith that was once for all entrusted to the saints.
4 For certain men whose condemnation was written about[b] long
ago have secretly slipped in among you.[g] They are godless men,
who change the grace of our God into a license for immorality and
deny Jesus Christ our only Sovereign and Lord.[h]

5 Though you already know all this, I want to remind you that the
Lord[c] delivered his people out of Egypt, but later destroyed those
who did not believe.[i] 6 And the angels who did not keep their positions of authority but abandoned their own home—these he has
kept in darkness, bound with everlasting chains for judgment on
the great Day.[j] 7 In a similar way, Sodom and Gomorrah and the
surrounding towns[k] gave themselves up to sexual immorality and
perversion. They serve as an example of those who suffer the
punishment of eternal fire.[l]

8 In the very same way, these dreamers pollute their own bodies,
reject authority and slander celestial beings.[m] 9 But even the archangel Michael,[n] when he was disputing with the devil about the
body of Moses, did not dare to bring a slanderous accusation
against him, but said, "The Lord rebuke you!"[o] 10 Yet these men
speak abusively against whatever they do not understand; and
what things they do understand by instinct, like unreasoning animals—these are the very things that destroy them.[p]

11 Woe to them! They have taken the way of Cain;[q] they have

1:1 [a]Mt 13:55; Ac 1:13 [b]Ro 1:6,7 [c]Jn 17:12
1:2 [d]2Pe 1:2
1:3 [e]Tit 1:4 [f]1Ti 6:12
1:4 [g]Gal 2:4 [h]Tit 1:16; 2Pe 2:1
1:5 [i]Nu 14:29; Ps 106:26
1:6 [j]2Pe 2:4,9
1:7 [k]Dt 29:23 [l]2Pe 2:6
1:8 [m]2Pe 2:10
1:9 [n]Da 10:13,21 [o]Zec 3:2
1:10 [p]2Pe 2:12
1:11 [q]Ge 4:3-8; 1Jn 3:12

[a] *1* Or *for*; or *in* [b] *4* Or *men who were marked out for condemnation* [c] *5* Some early manuscripts *Jesus*

rushed for profit into Balaam's error;[a] they have been destroyed in
Korah's rebellion.[b]

12 These men are blemishes at your love feasts,[c] eating with you
without the slightest qualm—shepherds who feed only themselves. They are clouds without rain,[d] blown along by the wind;[e]
autumn trees, without fruit and uprooted[f]—twice dead. 13 They
are wild waves of the sea,[g] foaming up their shame;[h] wandering
stars, for whom blackest darkness has been reserved forever.[i]

14 Enoch,[j] the seventh from Adam, prophesied about these men:
"See, the Lord is coming with thousands upon thousands of his
holy ones[k] 15 to judge[l] everyone, and to convict all the ungodly of
all the ungodly acts they have done in the ungodly way, and of all
the harsh words ungodly sinners have spoken against him."[m]
16 These men are grumblers and faultfinders; they follow their
own evil desires; they boast[n] about themselves and flatter others
for their own advantage.

17 But, dear friends, remember what the apostles of our Lord
Jesus Christ foretold.[o] 18 They said to you, "In the last times[p] there
will be scoffers who will follow their own ungodly desires."[q] 19 These
are the men who divide you, who follow mere natural instincts
and do not have the Spirit.[r]

20 But you, dear friends, build yourselves up[s] in your most holy
faith and pray in the Holy Spirit.[t] 21 Keep yourselves in God's love
as you wait[u] for the mercy of our Lord Jesus Christ to bring you to
eternal life.

22 Be merciful to those who doubt; 23 snatch others from the fire
and save them;[v] to others show mercy, mixed with fear—hating
even the clothing stained by corrupted flesh.[w]

24 To him who is able[x] to keep you from falling and to present
you before his glorious presence[y] without fault[z] and with great
joy— 25 to the only God[a] our Savior be glory, majesty, power and
authority, through Jesus Christ our Lord, before all ages, now and
forevermore![b] Amen.[c]

1:11
[a] 2Pe 2:15
[b] Nu 16:1-3, 31-35
1:12
[c] 2Pe 2:13; 1Co 11:20-22
[d] Pr 25:14; 2Pe 2:17
[e] Eph 4:14
[f] Mt 15:13
1:13
[g] Isa 57:20
[h] Php 3:19
[i] 2Pe 2:17
1:14
[j] Ge 5:18,21-24
[k] Dt 33:2; Da 7:10
1:15
[l] 2Pe 2:6-9
[m] 1Ti 1:9
1:16
[n] 2Pe 2:18
1:17
[o] 2Pe 3:2
1:18
[p] 1Ti 4:1
[q] 2Pe 2:1
1:19
[r] 1Co 2:14,15
1:20
[s] Col 2:7
[t] Eph 6:18
1:21
[u] Tit 2:13; 2Pe 3:12
1:23
[v] Am 4:11; Zec 3:2-5
[w] Rev 3:4
1:24
[x] Ro 16:25
[y] 2Co 4:14
[z] Col 1:22
1:25
[a] Jn 5:44; 1Ti 1:17
[b] Heb 13:8
[c] Ro 11:36

Jude Observations Chart

Jude

The Recipients

Godless Men

(continued)

Jude Observations Chart

Jude's Instructions to Those Loved by God

Jude at a Glance

Theme of Jude:

Segment Divisions	Paragraph Themes
	Verse 1a
	Verse 1b
	Verse 2
	Verses 3, 4
	Verses 5–7
	Verses 8–10
	Verse 11
	Verses 12–13
	Verses 14–16
	Verses 17–19
	Verses 20–23
	Verses 24, 25

Author:

Date:

Purpose:

Key Words:

REVELATION

John, one of the sons of Zebedee, identifies himself throughout his Gospel not by his name, but as "the one whom Jesus loved." John walked in faith, taking Jesus at his word, and was secure in his love.

Therefore, when John was banished to the Isle of Patmos (and, according to tradition, submerged in a cauldron of hot oil), he remained steadfast in Jesus' love. He was faithful to his calling even in the midst of Nero's persecutions of Christians in A.D. 54 through 68 and then Domitian's in A.D. 81 through 96.

While John was on Patmos, God unveiled to him the coming of the Lord Jesus Christ and what soon would come to pass—a revelation unparalleled, the last to be given. It was about A.D. 95. With John's revelation the New Testament canon of Scripture would be complete. The church could be secure. Every prophecy would be fulfilled, just as God had said.

Things to Do

Chapters 1-3

1. To familiarize yourself with the first two segments of the book of Revelation, carefully read 1:1 through 4:1 in one sitting. (*Revelation* is a translation of the Greek word *apokalypsis,* which means "an uncovering.")

2. Mark the following key words (along with their synonyms and pronouns) in chapter 1, and then list in the margin everything you learn from the text about these words: *Jesus Christ, God (the Father), Spirit (seven spirits),* and *write.* Then transfer this information to the chart WHAT REVELATION TEACHES ABOUT GOD, JESUS, and THE HOLY SPIRIT on page 2173.

3. Revelation 1:19 gives an outline of the book of Revelation.
   a. List the three things John was to write:
      1) ______________________
      2) ______________________
      3) ______________________
   b. Now look at Revelation 4:1 and note how it relates to 1:19. Revelation 4 begins the third segment of Revelation. Chapter 1 describes what John saw, and chapters 2 and 3 are "what is now." What is the third segment that begins in 4:1?
   c. Using the terminology found in Revelation 1:19, record these three segments in the space for segment divisions on the REVELATION AT A GLANCE chart on page 2175. (The lines to divide the book into these sections are already drawn.)

4. Read Revelation 1 through 3 and do the following:
   a. Watch for key repeated phrases or words listed on REVELATION AT A GLANCE. Mark these in the text in a distinctive way so you can spot them immediately. In Jesus' messages to the churches, watch for a pattern as Jesus addresses each church.
   b. Now concentrate on Jesus' messages to the churches, one church at a time. Record what you learn about each church on the chart JESUS' MESSAGES TO THE CHURCHES beginning on page 2169. When you see what is said regarding those who overcome, note how John describes overcomers in 1 John 5:4, 5. Add what you learn to the chart.

5. Record the main theme of each chapter in the text next to the chapter number and on REVELATION AT A GLANCE.

REVELATION
Chapters 4-22

1. In the last nineteen chapters of Revelation, Jesus shows John "what will take place later." Read Revelation 4 through 22 one chapter at a time, and for each chapter do the following:

   a. As you read, ask the five W's and an H: Who? What? Why? When? Where? and How? For example, if it is an event, ask: What is happening? Who is involved? When will this happen and where? Why is this happening? How will it happen? If it is a person or a personage: Who is this? What is this person like? What does he do? When? Where? Why? What are the consequences? How will he accomplish it? These are very critical questions. If these are answered carefully after thoroughly observing the text and apart from preconceived ideas, you will learn much. Make a list of what you learn, and then if it is information you wish to keep, record the essence of your insights in the margin of the chapter.

   b. Mark key repeated words (along with their synonyms and pronouns—*he, she, it, we, they, us,* and *you*) in a distinctive way. Some key words are listed on REVELATION AT A GLANCE. Since it is a long list, write these on an index card, color code the words as you intend to mark them in the text, and use the card as a bookmark. When you finish marking these, list on a piece of paper what you learn from each one (unless you have been told to record that information on a chart). Then in the margins, record any information you learn from the key words that you want to have accessible in your Bible.

   c. As you go through Revelation chapter by chapter, let the text speak for itself. Remember, truth is revealed gradually, so don't become impatient. Simply observe what is being said without adding your own interpretation. Stay in an attitude of prayer, asking God to open the eyes of your understanding.

2. Mark in a distinctive way all references to time. Then note what happens during that time. In Jewish reckoning 42 months, 1260 days, and time, times and half a time all refer to a period of 3 1/2 years. When you finish studying this segment of Revelation, you might want to list in the margin what happens and when, and how these time periods and events relate to one another, if at all.

   Also watch *when* something begins and ends—for example, the great day of God's wrath, when the mystery of God is finished, when God begins to reign. Noting the timing of these will help you understand Revelation better.

3. Babylon intermittently plays an important role from Genesis to Revelation. As you mark every reference to Babylon, carefully note whether it is referring to "the woman" or to the city. Then discern whether they are one and the same or two separate but somehow related entities. In chapters 17 and 18, where Babylon is preeminent, list in the margin of the chapter what you learn from marking each reference to Babylon. Then compile your information on the chart WHAT THE BIBLE TEACHES ABOUT BABYLON beginning on page 2176.

4. As you observe what happens during each of the seals, trumpets, and bowls, record your insights on the chart on page 2174, THE SEVEN SEALS, TRUMPETS, AND BOWLS. Then consider whether the seals, trumpets, and bowls happen at the same time or follow one another.

5. As you study Revelation, you may want to consult any notes you have made on the chart THE DAY OF THE LORD beginning on page 2178 to see if there are any parallels between what you have observed in other books and what you see in Revelation.

6. There is much to learn about the Godhead in this book that you will want to remember and meditate on. Record what you learn on the chart WHAT REVELATION TEACHES ABOUT GOD, JESUS, and THE HOLY SPIRIT on page 2173.

7. When you finish going through Revelation, record the chapter themes in the text and on REVELATION AT A GLANCE, along with other pertinent information called for on the chart.

8. Finally, see how various chapters of the book group according to events, places, or persons. Use your chapter themes as a guide to see when these groupings occur. Record these groupings under "Segment Divisions" on REVELATION AT A GLANCE, placing them at the chapter numbers in which they occur.

Things to Think About

Chapters 1-3

1. As you look at the Lord's message to each church, do you think the message could be for the church today? Look back through Jesus' messages to the churches in chapters 2 and 3 and note what the Spirit is saying to him who has "an ear." To whom is the Spirit speaking? What does he want you to hear? To do?

2. Think about what you have learned about Jesus Christ from these three chapters and then spend some time worshiping him for who and what he is.

3. Are you an overcomer? How does it show? Is there anything you need to do that you are not presently doing so that when Jesus appears you won't be ashamed?

Chapters 4-22

1. Revelation gives insight into the judgment of God upon the wicked because of what they worship. It also gives a glimpse of the way the righteous worship. How would you compare your worship with the worship described in Revelation? You might want to go back through Revelation and look at the scenes where God is worshiped and use them as a pattern for worship.

2. Now that you have a better understanding of the wrath to come upon the unbeliever, what priority needs to be placed on sharing the gospel? Is witnessing a priority in your church? Is witnessing a priority in your personal life?

3. Are you sure that you are a child of God? If not, will you acknowledge the Lord Jesus Christ as God, receive his forgiveness for your sins, and let him take full control of your life? Surely you have seen that he is worthy—and trustworthy.

4. What have you learned about your God? In the light of this, are you living in anticipation of Jesus' coming?

1:1 [a]Rev 22:16 *Chapter 1 Theme* ______________________

1 The revelation of Jesus Christ, which God gave him to show
his servants what must soon take place. He made it known by
1:2 [b]1Co 1:6; Rev 12:17 sending his angel[a] to his servant John, 2who testifies to everything he saw—that is, the word of God and the testimony of
Jesus Christ.[b] 3Blessed is the one who reads the words of this
prophecy, and blessed are those who hear it and take to heart
1:3 [c]Lk 11:28 what is written in it,[c] because the time is near.

4John,

To the seven churches in the province of Asia:

1:4 [d]Rev 3:1; 4:5 Grace and peace to you from him who is, and who was, and who
is to come, and from the seven spirits[a][d] before his throne, 5and
from Jesus Christ, who is the faithful witness,[e] the firstborn from
1:5 [e]Rev 3:14 [f]Col 1:18 [g]Rev 17:14 the dead,[f] and the ruler of the kings of the earth.[g]

a4 Or *the sevenfold Spirit*

To him who loves us and has freed us from our sins by his blood,
6and has made us to be a kingdom and priests[a] to serve his God
and Father—to him be glory and power for ever and ever! Amen.[b]

7Look, he is coming with the clouds,[c]
and every eye will see him,
even those who pierced him;
and all the peoples of the earth will mourn[d]
because of him.
So shall it be! Amen.

8"I am the Alpha and the Omega,"[e] says the Lord God, "who is,
and who was, and who is to come, the Almighty."[f]

9I, John, your brother and companion in the suffering[g] and
kingdom and patient endurance[h] that are ours in Jesus, was on
the island of Patmos because of the word of God and the testimony
of Jesus. 10On the Lord's Day I was in the Spirit,[i] and I heard
behind me a loud voice like a trumpet,[j] 11which said: "Write on a
scroll what you see and send it to the seven churches:[k] to Ephesus,
Smyrna, Pergamum, Thyatira, Sardis,[l] Philadelphia and Laodicea."
12I turned around to see the voice that was speaking to me. And
when I turned I saw seven golden lampstands,[m] 13and among the
lampstands was someone "like a son of man,"[a][n] dressed in a robe
reaching down to his feet and
with a golden sash around
his chest.[o] 14His head and
hair were white like wool, as
white as snow, and his eyes
were like blazing fire.[p] 15His
feet were like bronze glowing
in a furnace,[q] and his voice
was like the sound of rushing waters.[r] 16In his right
hand he held seven stars,[s]
and out of his mouth came a
sharp double-edged sword.[t] His face was like the sun shining in
all its brilliance.
17When I saw him, I fell at his feet[u] as though dead. Then he
placed his right hand on me and said: "Do not be afraid. I am the
First and the Last.[v] 18I am the Living One; I was dead,[w] and behold
I am alive for ever and ever![x] And I hold the keys of death and
Hades.[y]
19"Write, therefore, what you have seen, what is now and what
will take place later. 20The mystery of the seven stars that you saw
in my right hand and of the seven golden lampstands[z] is this: The

The Seven Churches of Asia

[a] *13* Daniel 7:13

1:6 [a] 1Pe 2:5 [b] Ro 11:36
1:7 [c] Da 7:13 [d] Zec 12:10
1:8 [e] Rev 21:6 [f] Rev 4:8
1:9 [g] Php 4:14 [h] 2Ti 2:12
1:10 [i] Rev 4:2 [j] Rev 4:1
1:11 [k] ver 4,20 [l] Rev 3:1
1:12 [m] Ex 25:31-40; Zec 4:2
1:13 [n] Eze 1:26; Da 7:13; 10:16 [o] Da 10:5; Rev 15:6
1:14 [p] Da 7:9; 10:6; Rev 19:12
1:15 [q] Da 10:6 [r] Eze 43:2; Rev 14:2
1:16 [s] Rev 2:1; 3:1 [t] Isa 49:2; Heb 4:12; Rev 2:12,16
1:17 [u] Eze 1:28; Da 8:17,18 [v] Isa 41:4; 44:6; 48:12; Rev 22:13
1:18 [w] Ro 6:9 [x] Rev 4:9,10 [y] Rev 20:1
1:20 [z] Zec 4:2

seven stars are the angels[a] of the seven churches,[a] and the seven
lampstands are the seven churches.[b]

Chapter 2 Theme ______________________

2

"To the angel[b] of the church in Ephesus write:

These are the words of him who holds the seven stars in his
right hand[c] and walks among the seven golden lampstands:[d]
2I know your deeds,[e] your hard work and your perseverance.
I know that you cannot tolerate wicked men, that you have
tested[f] those who claim to be apostles but are not, and have
found them false.[g] 3You have persevered and have endured
hardships for my name,[h] and have not grown weary.
4Yet I hold this against you: You have forsaken your first
love.[i] 5Remember the height from which you have fallen!
Repent[j] and do the things you did at first. If you do not
repent, I will come to you and remove your lampstand[k] from
its place. 6But you have this in your favor: You hate the practices of the Nicolaitans,[l] which I also hate.
7He who has an ear, let him hear[m] what the Spirit says to the
churches. To him who overcomes, I will give the right to eat
from the tree of life,[n] which is in the paradise[o] of God.

8"To the angel of the church in Smyrna[p] write:

These are the words of him who is the First and the Last,[q]
who died and came to life again.[r] 9I know your afflictions and
your poverty—yet you are rich![s] I know the slander of those
who say they are Jews and are not,[t] but are a synagogue of
Satan.[u] 10Do not be afraid of what you are about to suffer. I tell
you, the devil will put some of you in prison to test you,[v] and
you will suffer persecution for ten days.[w] Be faithful,[x] even to
the point of death, and I will give you the crown of life.
11He who has an ear, let him hear what the Spirit says to the
churches. He who overcomes will not be hurt at all by the second death.[y]

12"To the angel of the church in Pergamum[z] write:

These are the words of him who has the sharp, double-edged
sword.[a] 13I know where you live—where Satan has his throne.
Yet you remain true to my name. You did not renounce your
faith in me,[b] even in the days of Antipas, my faithful witness,
who was put to death in your city—where Satan lives.[c]
14Nevertheless, I have a few things against you:[d] You have
people there who hold to the teaching of Balaam,[e] who taught

1:20 [a]ver 4,11 [b]Mt 5:14,15
2:1 [c]Rev 1:16 [d]Rev 1:12,13
2:2 [e]Rev 3:1,8,15 [f]1Jn 4:1 [g]2Co 11:13
2:3 [h]Jn 15:21
2:4 [i]Mt 24:12
2:5 [j]ver 16,22 [k]Rev 1:20
2:6 [l]ver 15
2:7 [m]Mt 11:15; Rev 3:6,13,22 [n]Ge 2:9; Rev 22:2,14,19 [o]Lk 23:43
2:8 [p]Rev 1:11 [q]Rev 1:17 [r]Rev 1:18
2:9 [s]Jas 2:5 [t]Rev 3:9 [u]Mt 4:10
2:10 [v]Rev 3:10 [w]Da 1:12,14 [x]ver 13
2:11 [y]Rev 20:6,14; 21:8
2:12 [z]Rev 1:11 [a]Rev 1:16
2:13 [b]Rev 14:12 [c]ver 9,24
2:14 [d]ver 20 [e]2Pe 2:15

a *20* Or *messengers* b *1* Or *messenger;* also in verses 8, 12 and 18

Balak to entice the Israelites to sin by eating food sacrificed to
idols and by committing sexual immorality.[a] 15Likewise you
also have those who hold to the teaching of the Nicolaitans.[b]
16Repent therefore! Otherwise, I will soon come to you and will
fight against them with the sword of my mouth.[c]
17He who has an ear, let him hear what the Spirit says to the
churches. To him who overcomes, I will give some of the hidden manna.[d] I will also give him a white stone with a new
name[e] written on it, known only to him who receives it.[f]

18"To the angel of the church in Thyatira[g] write:

These are the words of the Son of God, whose eyes are like
blazing fire and whose feet are like burnished bronze.[h] 19I
know your deeds,[i] your love and faith, your service and perseverance, and that you are now doing more than you did at first.
20Nevertheless, I have this against you: You tolerate that
woman Jezebel,[j] who calls herself a prophetess. By her teaching she misleads my servants into sexual immorality and the
eating of food sacrificed to idols. 21I have given her time[k] to
repent of her immorality, but she is unwilling.[l] 22So I will cast
her on a bed of suffering, and I will make those who commit
adultery[m] with her suffer intensely, unless they repent of her
ways. 23I will strike her children dead. Then all the churches
will know that I am he who searches hearts and minds,[n] and
I will repay each of you according to your deeds. 24Now I say
to the rest of you in Thyatira, to you who do not hold to her
teaching and have not learned Satan's so-called deep secrets
(I will not impose any other burden on you):[o] 25Only hold on
to what you have[p] until I come.
26To him who overcomes and does my will to the end, I will
give authority over the nations[q]—

> 27'He will rule them with an iron scepter;[r]
> he will dash them to pieces like pottery'[a][s]—

just as I have received authority from my Father. 28I will also
give him the morning star.[t] 29He who has an ear, let him hear[u]
what the Spirit says to the churches.

Chapter 3 Theme

3 "To the angel[b] of the church in Sardis write:

These are the words of him who holds the seven spirits[c][v] of
God and the seven stars.[w] I know your deeds;[x] you have a reputation of being alive, but you are dead.[y] 2Wake up! Strengthen

[a] *27* Psalm 2:9 [b] *1* Or *messenger;* also in verses 7 and 14 [c] *1* Or *the sevenfold Spirit*

2:14 [a] 1Co 6:13
2:15 [b] ver 6
2:16 [c] 2Th 2:8; Rev 1:16
2:17 [d] Jn 6:49,50 [e] Isa 62:2 [f] Rev 19:12
2:18 [g] Rev 1:11 [h] Rev 1:14,15
2:19 [i] ver 2
2:20 [j] 1Ki 16:31; 21:25; 2Ki 9:7
2:21 [k] Ro 2:4 [l] Rev 9:20
2:22 [m] Rev 17:2; 18:9
2:23 [n] 1Sa 16:7; Jer 11:20; Ac 1:24; Ro 8:27
2:24 [o] Ac 15:28
2:25 [p] Rev 3:11
2:26 [q] Ps 2:8; Rev 3:21
2:27 [r] Rev 12:5 [s] Isa 30:14; Jer 19:11
2:28 [t] Rev 22:16
2:29 [u] ver 7
3:1 [v] Rev 1:4 [w] Rev 1:16 [x] Rev 2:2 [y] 1Ti 5:6

what remains and is about to die, for I have not found your
deeds complete in the sight of my God. 3Remember, therefore,
what you have received and heard; obey it, and repent.[a] But if
you do not wake up, I will come like a thief,[b] and you will not
know at what time I will come to you.

4Yet you have a few people in Sardis who have not soiled
their clothes.[c] They will walk with me, dressed in white,[d] for
they are worthy. 5He who overcomes will, like them, be
dressed in white. I will never blot out his name from the book
of life,[e] but will acknowledge his name before my Father[f] and
his angels. 6He who has an ear, let him hear[g] what the Spirit
says to the churches.

7"To the angel of the church in Philadelphia[h] write:

These are the words of him who is holy and true,[i] who holds
the key of David.[j] What he opens no one can shut, and what
he shuts no one can open. 8I know your deeds. See, I have
placed before you an open door[k] that no one can shut. I know
that you have little strength, yet you have kept my word and
have not denied my name.[l] 9I will make those who are of the
synagogue of Satan,[m] who claim to be Jews though they are
not, but are liars—I will make them come and fall down at
your feet[n] and acknowledge that I have loved you.[o] 10Since
you have kept my command to endure patiently, I will also
keep you[p] from the hour of trial that is going to come upon
the whole world to test[q] those who live on the earth.[r]

11I am coming soon. Hold on to what you have,[s] so that no
one will take your crown.[t] 12Him who overcomes I will make
a pillar[u] in the temple of my God. Never again will he leave it. I
will write on him the name of my God[v] and the name of the
city of my God, the new Jerusalem,[w] which is coming down
out of heaven from my God; and I will also write on him my
new name. 13He who has an ear, let him hear what the Spirit
says to the churches.

14"To the angel of the church in Laodicea write:

These are the words of the Amen, the faithful and true witness, the ruler of God's creation.[x] 15I know your deeds, that
you are neither cold nor hot.[y] I wish you were either one or the
other! 16So, because you are lukewarm—neither hot nor
cold—I am about to spit you out of my mouth. 17You say, 'I am
rich; I have acquired wealth and do not need a thing.'[z] But you
do not realize that you are wretched, pitiful, poor, blind and
naked. 18I counsel you to buy from me gold refined in the fire,
so you can become rich; and white clothes to wear, so you can

3:3 [a]Rev 2:5 [b]2Pe 3:10
3:4 [c]Jude 23 [d]Rev 4:4; 6:11; 7:9,13,14
3:5 [e]Rev 20:12 [f]Mt 10:32
3:6 [g]Rev 2:7
3:7 [h]Rev 1:11 [i]1Jn 5:20 [j]Isa 22:22; Mt 16:19
3:8 [k]Ac 14:27 [l]Rev 2:13
3:9 [m]Rev 2:9 [n]Isa 49:23 [o]Isa 43:4
3:10 [p]2Pe 2:9 [q]Rev 2:10 [r]Rev 6:10; 17:8
3:11 [s]Rev 2:25 [t]Rev 2:10
3:12 [u]Gal 2:9 [v]Rev 14:1; 22:4 [w]Rev 21:2,10
3:14 [x]Col 1:16,18
3:15 [y]Ro 12:11
3:17 [z]Hos 12:8; 1Co 4:8

cover your shameful nakedness;[a] and salve to put on your eyes,
so you can see.
19Those whom I love I rebuke and discipline.[b] So be earnest,
and repent.[c] 20Here I am! I stand at the door[d] and knock. If
anyone hears my voice and opens the door,[e] I will come in[f]
and eat with him, and he with me.
21To him who overcomes, I will give the right to sit with me
on my throne,[g] just as I overcame[h] and sat down with my
Father on his throne. 22He who has an ear, let him hear[i] what
the Spirit says to the churches."

Chapter 4 Theme ______________________________

4 After this I looked, and there before me was a door standing
open in heaven. And the voice I had first heard speaking to
me like a trumpet[j] said, "Come up here,[k] and I will show you
what must take place after this."[l] 2At once I was in the Spirit,[m]
and there before me was a throne in heaven[n] with someone sitting
on it. 3And the one who sat there had the appearance of jasper and
carnelian. A rainbow,[o] resembling an emerald, encircled the
throne. 4Surrounding the throne were twenty-four other thrones,
and seated on them were twenty-four elders.[p] They were dressed
in white[q] and had crowns of gold on their heads. 5From the
throne came flashes of lightning, rumblings and peals of
thunder.[r] Before the throne, seven lamps[s] were blazing. These are
the seven spirits[a][t] of God. 6Also before the throne there was what
looked like a sea of glass,[u] clear as crystal.
In the center, around the throne, were four living creatures,[v]
and they were covered with eyes, in front and in back. 7The first
living creature was like a lion, the second was like an ox, the third
had a face like a man, the fourth was like a flying eagle.[w] 8Each of
the four living creatures had six wings[x] and was covered with
eyes all around, even under his wings. Day and night they never
stop saying:

> "Holy, holy, holy
> is the Lord God Almighty,[y]
> who was, and is, and is to come."[z]

9Whenever the living creatures give glory, honor and thanks to
him who sits on the throne[a] and who lives for ever and ever, 10the
twenty-four elders[b] fall down before him[c] who sits on the throne,[d]
and worship him who lives for ever and ever. They lay their crowns
before the throne and say:

[a] 5,6 Or *the sevenfold Spirit*

3:18 [a]Rev 16:15
3:19 [b]Pr 3:12; Heb 12:5,6 [c]Rev 2:5
3:20 [d]Mt 24:33 [e]Lk 12:36 [f]Jn 14:23
3:21 [g]Mt 19:28 [h]Rev 5:5
3:22 [i]Rev 2:7
4:1 [j]Rev 1:10 [k]Rev 11:12 [l]Rev 1:19
4:2 [m]Rev 1:10 [n]Isa 6:1; Eze 1:26-28; Da 7:9
4:3 [o]Eze 1:28
4:4 [p]Rev 11:16 [q]Rev 3:4,5
4:5 [r]Rev 8:5; 16:18 [s]Zec 4:2 [t]Rev 1:4
4:6 [u]Rev 15:2 [v]Eze 1:5
4:7 [w]Eze 1:10; 10:14
4:8 [x]Isa 6:2 [y]Isa 6:3; Rev 1:8 [z]Rev 1:4
4:9 [a]Ps 47:8
4:10 [b]ver 4 [c]Rev 5:8,14 [d]ver 2

11"You are worthy, our Lord and God,
to receive glory and honor and power,[a]
for you created all things,
and by your will they were created
and have their being."[b]

Chapter 5 Theme ______________________

5 Then I saw in the right hand of him who sat on the throne[c] a
scroll with writing on both sides[d] and sealed[e] with seven
seals. 2And I saw a mighty angel proclaiming in a loud voice,
"Who is worthy to break the seals and open the scroll?" 3But no
one in heaven or on earth or under the earth could open the
scroll or even look inside it. 4I wept and wept because no one was
found who was worthy to open the scroll or look inside. 5Then one
of the elders said to me, "Do not weep! See, the Lion[f] of the tribe of
Judah, the Root of David,[g] has triumphed. He is able to open the
scroll and its seven seals."
6Then I saw a Lamb,[h] looking as if it had been slain, standing in
the center of the throne, encircled by the four living creatures and
the elders. He had seven horns and seven eyes,[i] which are the seven
spirits[a] of God sent out into all the earth. 7He came and took the
scroll from the right hand of him who sat on the throne.[j] 8And
when he had taken it, the four living creatures and the twenty-
four elders fell down before the Lamb. Each one had a harp[k] and
they were holding golden bowls full of incense, which are the
prayers[l] of the saints. 9And they sang a new song:[m]

"You are worthy[n] to take the scroll
and to open its seals,
because you were slain,
and with your blood[o] you purchased[p] men for God
from every tribe and language and people and nation.
10You have made them to be a kingdom and priests[q] to
serve our God,
and they will reign on the earth."

11Then I looked and heard the voice of many angels, numbering thousands upon thousands, and ten thousand times ten
thousand.[r] They encircled the throne and the living creatures
and the elders. 12In a loud voice they sang:

"Worthy is the Lamb, who was slain,
to receive power and wealth and wisdom and strength
and honor and glory and praise!"[s]

4:11 [a]Rev 5:12 [b]Rev 10:6
5:1 [c]ver 7,13 [d]Eze 2:9,10 [e]Isa 29:11; Da 12:4
5:5 [f]Ge 49:9 [g]Isa 11:1,10; Ro 15:12; Rev 22:16
5:6 [h]Jn 1:29 [i]Zec 4:10
5:7 [j]ver 1
5:8 [k]Rev 14:2 [l]Ps 141:2
5:9 [m]Ps 40:3 [n]Rev 4:11 [o]Heb 9:12 [p]1Co 6:20
5:10 [q]1Pe 2:5
5:11 [r]Da 7:10; Heb 12:22
5:12 [s]Rev 4:11

[a]5,6 Or *the sevenfold Spirit*

13Then I heard every creature in heaven and on earth and under
the earth[a] and on the sea, and all that is in them, singing:

"To him who sits on the throne and to the Lamb[b]
be praise and honor and glory and power,
for ever and ever!"[c]

14The four living creatures said, "Amen,"[d] and the elders fell
down and worshiped.[e]

Chapter 6 Theme ____

6 I watched as the Lamb[f] opened the first of the seven seals.[g]
Then I heard one of the four living creatures[h] say in a voice
like thunder,[i] "Come!" 2I looked, and there before me was a white
horse![j] Its rider held a bow, and he was given a crown,[k] and he
rode out as a conqueror bent on conquest.[l]
3When the Lamb opened the second seal, I heard the second living
creature[m] say, "Come!" 4Then another horse came out, a fiery red
one.[n] Its rider was given power to take peace from the earth[o] and
to make men slay each other. To him was given a large sword.
5When the Lamb opened the third seal, I heard the third living
creature[p] say, "Come!" I looked, and there before me was a black
horse![q] Its rider was holding a pair of scales in his hand. 6Then I
heard what sounded like a voice among the four living creatures,[r]
saying, "A quart[a] of wheat for a day's wages,[b] and three quarts of
barley for a day's wages,[b] and do not damage[s] the oil and the
wine!"
7When the Lamb opened the fourth seal, I heard the voice of the
fourth living creature[t] say, "Come!" 8I looked, and there before me
was a pale horse![u] Its rider was named Death, and Hades[v] was
following close behind him. They were given power over a fourth
of the earth to kill by sword, famine and plague, and by the wild
beasts of the earth.[w]
9When he opened the fifth seal, I saw under the altar[x] the souls of
those who had been slain[y] because of the word of God and the
testimony they had maintained. 10They called out in a loud voice,
"How long,[z] Sovereign Lord, holy and true,[a] until you judge the
inhabitants of the earth and avenge our blood?"[b] 11Then each of
them was given a white robe,[c] and they were told to wait a little
longer, until the number of their fellow servants and brothers who
were to be killed as they had been was completed.[d]
12I watched as he opened the sixth seal. There was a great earthquake.[e] The sun turned black[f] like sackcloth made of goat hair, the
whole moon turned blood red, 13and the stars in the sky fell to

a6 Greek *a choinix* (probably about a liter) b6 Greek *a denarius*

5:13 [a]ver 3; Php 2:10 [b]Rev 6:16 [c]1Ch 29:11
5:14 [d]Rev 4:9 [e]Rev 4:10; 19:4
6:1 [f]Rev 5:6 [g]Rev 5:1 [h]Rev 4:6,7 [i]Rev 14:2; 19:6
6:2 [j]Zec 6:3; Rev 19:11 [k]Zec 6:11; Rev 14:14 [l]Ps 45:4
6:3 [m]Rev 4:7
6:4 [n]Zec 6:2 [o]Mt 10:34
6:5 [p]Rev 4:7 [q]Zec 6:2
6:6 [r]Rev 4:6,7 [s]Rev 9:4
6:7 [t]Rev 4:7
6:8 [u]Zec 6:3 [v]Hos 13:14 [w]Jer 15:2,3; Eze 5:12,17
6:9 [x]Rev 14:18; 16:7 [y]Rev 20:4
6:10 [z]Zec 1:12 [a]Rev 3:7 [b]Rev 19:2
6:11 [c]Rev 3:4 [d]Heb 11:40
6:12 [e]Rev 16:18 [f]Mt 24:29

earth,[a] as late figs drop from a fig tree[b] when shaken by a strong
wind. 14The sky receded like a scroll, rolling up, and every mountain and island was removed from its place.[c]
15Then the kings of the earth, the princes, the generals, the rich,
the mighty, and every slave and every free man hid in caves and
among the rocks of the mountains.[d] 16They called to the mountains and the rocks, "Fall on us[e] and hide us from the face of him
who sits on the throne and from the wrath of the Lamb! 17For the
great day[f] of their wrath has come, and who can stand?"[g]

Chapter 7 Theme ______________________

7 After this I saw four angels standing at the four corners of the
earth, holding back the four winds[h] of the earth to prevent
any wind from blowing on the land or on the sea or on any tree.
2Then I saw another angel coming up from the east, having the seal
of the living God. He called out in a loud voice to the four angels
who had been given power to harm the land and the sea: 3"Do not
harm[i] the land or the sea or the trees until we put a seal on the
foreheads[j] of the servants of our God." 4Then I heard the number[k]
of those who were sealed: 144,000[l] from all the tribes of Israel.

5From the tribe of Judah 12,000 were sealed,
from the tribe of Reuben 12,000,
from the tribe of Gad 12,000,
6from the tribe of Asher 12,000,
from the tribe of Naphtali 12,000,
from the tribe of Manasseh 12,000,
7from the tribe of Simeon 12,000,
from the tribe of Levi 12,000,
from the tribe of Issachar 12,000,
8from the tribe of Zebulun 12,000,
from the tribe of Joseph 12,000,
from the tribe of Benjamin 12,000.

9After this I looked and there before me was a great multitude
that no one could count, from every nation, tribe, people and
language,[m] standing before the throne[n] and in front of the Lamb.
They were wearing white robes and were holding palm branches
in their hands. 10And they cried out in a loud voice:

"Salvation belongs to our God,[o]
who sits on the throne,
and to the Lamb."

11All the angels were standing around the throne and around the
elders[p] and the four living creatures.[q] They fell down on their
faces[r] before the throne and worshiped God, 12saying:

6:13 [a]Mt 24:29; Rev 8:10; 9:1 [b]Isa 34:4
6:14 [c]Jer 4:24; Rev 16:20
6:15 [d]Isa 2:10,19,21
6:16 [e]Hos 10:8; Lk 23:30
6:17 [f]Zep 1:14,15; Rev 16:14 [g]Ps 76:7
7:1 [h]Da 7:2
7:3 [i]Rev 6:6 [j]Eze 9:4; Rev 22:4
7:4 [k]Rev 9:16 [l]Rev 14:1,3
7:9 [m]Rev 5:9 [n]ver 15
7:10 [o]Ps 3:8; Rev 12:10; 19:1
7:11 [p]Rev 4:4 [q]Rev 4:6 [r]Rev 4:10

"Amen!
Praise and glory
and wisdom and thanks and honor
and power and strength
be to our God for ever and ever.
Amen!"[a]

13Then one of the elders asked me, "These in white robes—who
are they, and where did they come from?"
14I answered, "Sir, you know."
And he said, "These are they who have come out of the great
tribulation; they have washed their robes[b] and made them white in
the blood of the Lamb.[c] 15Therefore,

"they are before the throne of God[d]
and serve him[e] day and night in his temple;[f]
and he who sits on the throne will spread his tent
over them.[g]
16Never again will they hunger;
never again will they thirst.
The sun will not beat upon them,
nor any scorching heat.[h]
17For the Lamb at the center of the throne will be
their shepherd;[i]
he will lead them to springs of living water.
And God will wipe away every tear from their eyes."[j]

Chapter 8 Theme ______________________

8 When he opened the seventh seal,[k] there was silence in heaven
for about half an hour.
2And I saw the seven angels[l] who stand before God, and to
them were given seven trumpets.
3Another angel,[m] who had a golden censer, came and stood at
the altar. He was given much incense to offer, with the prayers of
all the saints,[n] on the golden altar[o] before the throne. 4The smoke
of the incense, together with the prayers of the saints, went up
before God[p] from the angel's hand. 5Then the angel took the
censer, filled it with fire from the altar,[q] and hurled it on the
earth; and there came peals of thunder,[r] rumblings, flashes of
lightning and an earthquake.[s]
6Then the seven angels who had the seven trumpets[t] prepared to
sound them.
7The first angel sounded his trumpet, and there came hail and
fire[u] mixed with blood, and it was hurled down upon the earth.
A third[v] of the earth was burned up, a third of the trees were
burned up, and all the green grass was burned up.[w]

7:12
[a]Rev 5:12-14

7:14
[b]Rev 22:14
[c]Heb 9:14; 1Jn 1:7

7:15
[d]ver 9
[e]Rev 22:3
[f]Rev 11:19
[g]Isa 4:5,6; Rev 21:3

7:16
[h]Isa 49:10

7:17
[i]Ps 23:1; Jn 10:11
[j]Isa 25:8; Rev 21:4

8:1
[k]Rev 6:1

8:2
[l]ver 6-13; Rev 9:1,13; 11:15

8:3
[m]Rev 7:2
[n]Rev 5:8
[o]Ex 30:1-6; Heb 9:4; Rev 9:13

8:4
[p]Ps 141:2

8:5
[q]Lev 16:12,13
[r]Rev 4:5
[s]Rev 6:12

8:6
[t]ver 2

8:7
[u]Eze 38:22
[v]ver 7-12; Rev 9:15,18; 12:4
[w]Rev 9:4

8 The second angel sounded his trumpet, and something like a
huge mountain,[a] all ablaze, was thrown into the sea. A third[b] of
the sea turned into blood,[c] 9 a third[d] of the living creatures in the
sea died, and a third of the ships were destroyed.

10 The third angel sounded his trumpet, and a great star, blazing
like a torch, fell from the sky[e] on a third of the rivers and on the
springs of water[f]— 11 the name of the star is Wormwood.[a] A
third[g] of the waters turned bitter, and many people died from the
waters that had become bitter.[h]

12 The fourth angel sounded his trumpet, and a third of the sun
was struck, a third of the moon, and a third of the stars, so that a
third[i] of them turned dark.[j] A third of the day was without light,
and also a third of the night.

13 As I watched, I heard an eagle that was flying in midair[k] call
out in a loud voice: "Woe! Woe! Woe[l] to the inhabitants of the
earth, because of the trumpet blasts about to be sounded by the
other three angels!"

Chapter 9 Theme ________________________________

9 The fifth angel sounded his trumpet, and I saw a star that
had fallen from the sky to the earth.[m] The star was given the
key to the shaft of the Abyss.[n] 2 When he opened the Abyss,
smoke rose from it like the smoke from a gigantic furnace.[o] The
sun and sky were darkened[p] by the smoke from the Abyss. 3 And
out of the smoke locusts[q] came down upon the earth and were
given power like that of scorpions[r] of the earth. 4 They were told
not to harm[s] the grass of the earth or any plant or tree,[t] but only
those people who did not have the seal of God on their foreheads.[u]
5 They were not given power to kill them, but only to torture them
for five months.[v] And the agony they suffered was like that of the
sting of a scorpion[w] when it strikes a man. 6 During those days
men will seek death, but will not find it; they will long to die, but
death will elude them.[x]

7 The locusts looked like horses prepared for battle.[y] On their
heads they wore something like crowns of gold, and their faces
resembled human faces.[z] 8 Their hair was like women's hair, and
their teeth were like lions' teeth.[a] 9 They had breastplates like
breastplates of iron, and the sound of their wings was like the
thundering of many horses and chariots rushing into battle.[b]
10 They had tails and stings like scorpions, and in their tails they
had power to torment people for five months.[c] 11 They had as
king over them the angel of the Abyss,[d] whose name in Hebrew is
Abaddon, and in Greek, Apollyon.[b]

8:8 [a] Jer 51:25 [b] ver 7 [c] Rev 16:3
8:9 [d] ver 7
8:10 [e] Isa 14:12; Rev 6:13; 9:1 [f] Rev 14:7; 16:4
8:11 [g] ver 7 [h] Jer 9:15; 23:15
8:12 [i] ver 7 [j] Ex 10:21-23; Rev 6:12,13
8:13 [k] Rev 14:6; 19:17 [l] Rev 9:12; 11:14
9:1 [m] Rev 8:10 [n] ver 2,11; Lk 8:31
9:2 [o] Ge 19:28; Ex 19:18 [p] Joel 2:2,10
9:3 [q] Ex 10:12-15 [r] ver 5,10
9:4 [s] Rev 6:6 [t] Rev 8:7 [u] Rev 7:2,3
9:5 [v] ver 10 [w] ver 3
9:6 [x] Job 3:21; Jer 8:3; Rev 6:16
9:7 [y] Joel 2:4 [z] Da 7:8
9:8 [a] Joel 1:6
9:9 [b] Joel 2:5
9:10 [c] ver 3,5,19
9:11 [d] ver 1,2

[a] *11* That is, Bitterness [b] *11 Abaddon* and *Apollyon* mean *Destroyer.*

12 The first woe is past; two other woes are yet to come.[a]
13 The sixth angel sounded his trumpet, and I heard a voice
coming from the horns[a][b] of the golden altar that is before God.[c]
14 It said to the sixth angel who had the trumpet, "Release the four
angels who are bound at the great river Euphrates."[d] 15 And the
four angels who had been kept ready for this very hour and day
and month and year were released to kill a third of mankind.[e]
16 The number of the mounted troops was two hundred million. I
heard their number.[f]

17 The horses and riders I saw in my vision looked like this:
Their breastplates were fiery red, dark blue, and yellow as sulfur.
The heads of the horses resembled the heads of lions, and out of
their mouths[g] came fire, smoke and sulfur.[h] 18 A third of mankind
was killed[i] by the three plagues of fire, smoke and sulfur[j] that
came out of their mouths. 19 The power of the horses was in their
mouths and in their tails; for their tails were like snakes, having
heads with which they inflict injury.

20 The rest of mankind that were not killed by these plagues still
did not repent of the work of their hands;[k] they did not stop worshiping demons,[l] and idols of gold, silver, bronze, stone and
wood—idols that cannot see or hear or walk.[m] 21 Nor did they
repent[n] of their murders, their magic arts,[o] their sexual immorality[p] or their thefts.

Chapter 10 Theme ______________________________

10 Then I saw another mighty angel[q] coming down from
heaven. He was robed in a cloud, with a rainbow above his
head; his face was like the sun,[r] and his legs were like fiery pillars.[s]
2 He was holding a little scroll, which lay open in his hand. He
planted his right foot on the sea and his left foot on the land, 3 and
he gave a loud shout like the roar of a lion. When he shouted, the
voices of the seven thunders[t] spoke. 4 And when the seven thunders spoke, I was about to write; but I heard a voice from heaven
say, "Seal up what the seven thunders have said and do not write it
down."[u]

5 Then the angel I had seen standing on the sea and on the land
raised his right hand to heaven.[v] 6 And he swore by him who lives
for ever and ever, who created the heavens and all that is in them,
the earth and all that is in it, and the sea and all that is in it,[w] and
said, "There will be no more delay![x] 7 But in the days when the
seventh angel is about to sound his trumpet, the mystery[y] of God
will be accomplished, just as he announced to his servants the
prophets."

a 13 That is, projections

9:12 a Rev 8:13
9:13 b Ex 30:1-3; c Rev 8:3
9:14 d Rev 16:12
9:15 e ver 18
9:16 f Rev 5:11; 7:4
9:17 g Rev 11:5; h ver 18
9:18 i ver 15; j ver 17
9:20 k Dt 31:29; l 1Co 10:20; m Ps 115:4-7; 135:15-17; Da 5:23
9:21 n Rev 2:21; o Rev 18:23; p Rev 17:2,5
10:1 q Rev 5:2; r Mt 17:2; Rev 1:16; s Rev 1:15
10:3 t Rev 4:5
10:4 u Da 8:26; 12:4,9; Rev 22:10
10:5 v Da 12:7
10:6 w Rev 4:11; 14:7; x Rev 16:17
10:7 y Ro 16:25

8 Then the voice that I had heard from heaven[a] spoke to me once
more: "Go, take the scroll that lies open in the hand of the angel
who is standing on the sea and on the land."
9 So I went to the angel and asked him to give me the little scroll.
He said to me, "Take it and eat it. It will turn your stomach sour,
but in your mouth it will be as sweet as honey."[b] 10 I took the little
scroll from the angel's hand and ate it. It tasted as sweet as honey
in my mouth, but when I had eaten it, my stomach turned sour.
11 Then I was told, "You must prophesy[c] again about many peoples,
nations, languages and kings."

Chapter 11 Theme ______________________________

11 I was given a reed like a measuring rod[d] and was told, "Go
and measure the temple of God and the altar, and count the
worshipers there. 2 But exclude the outer court;[e] do not measure it,
because it has been given to the Gentiles.[f] They will trample on
the holy city[g] for 42 months.[h] 3 And I will give power to my two
witnesses,[i] and they will prophesy for 1,260 days, clothed in sackcloth."[j] 4 These are the two olive trees[k] and the two lampstands that
stand before the Lord of the earth.[l] 5 If anyone tries to harm them,
fire comes from their mouths and devours their enemies.[m] This
is how anyone who wants to harm them must die.[n] 6 These men
have power to shut up the sky so that it will not rain during the
time they are prophesying; and they have power to turn the
waters into blood[o] and to strike the earth with every kind of
plague as often as they want.
7 Now when they have finished their testimony, the beast[p] that
comes up from the Abyss will attack them,[q] and overpower and
kill them. 8 Their bodies will lie in the street of the great city, which
is figuratively called Sodom[r] and Egypt, where also their Lord
was crucified.[s] 9 For three and a half days men from every people,
tribe, language and nation will gaze on their bodies and refuse
them burial.[t] 10 The inhabitants of the earth[u] will gloat over them
and will celebrate by sending each other gifts,[v] because these two
prophets had tormented those who live on the earth.
11 But after the three and a half days a breath of life from God
entered them,[w] and they stood on their feet, and terror struck
those who saw them. 12 Then they heard a loud voice from heaven
saying to them, "Come up here."[x] And they went up to heaven in a
cloud,[y] while their enemies looked on.
13 At that very hour there was a severe earthquake[z] and a tenth of
the city collapsed. Seven thousand people were killed in the earthquake, and the survivors were terrified and gave glory[a] to the God
of heaven.[b]
14 The second woe has passed; the third woe is coming soon.[c]

10:8 [a] ver 4
10:9 [b] Jer 15:16; Eze 2:8–3:3
10:11 [c] Eze 37:4,9
11:1 [d] Eze 40:3; Rev 21:15
11:2 [e] Eze 40:17,20 [f] Lk 21:24 [g] Rev 21:2 [h] Da 7:25; Rev 13:5
11:3 [i] Rev 1:5 [j] Ge 37:34
11:4 [k] Ps 52:8; Jer 11:16; Zec 4:3,11 [l] Zec 4:14
11:5 [m] 2Ki 1:10; Jer 5:14 [n] Nu 16:29,35
11:6 [o] Ex 7:17,19
11:7 [p] Rev 13:1-4 [q] Da 7:21
11:8 [r] Isa 1:9 [s] Heb 13:12
11:9 [t] Ps 79:2,3
11:10 [u] Rev 3:10 [v] Est 9:19,22
11:11 [w] Eze 37:5,9, 10,14
11:12 [x] Rev 4:1 [y] 2Ki 2:11; Ac 1:9
11:13 [z] Rev 6:12 [a] Rev 14:7 [b] Rev 16:11
11:14 [c] Rev 8:13

15The seventh angel sounded his trumpet,[a] and there were loud
voices[b] in heaven, which said:

"The kingdom of the world has become the kingdom of
our Lord and of his Christ,[c]
and he will reign for ever and ever."[d]

16And the twenty-four elders,[e] who were seated on their thrones
before God, fell on their faces and worshiped God, 17saying:

"We give thanks to you, Lord God Almighty,[f]
the One who is and who was,
because you have taken your great power
and have begun to reign.[g]
18The nations were angry;[h]
and your wrath has come.
The time has come for judging the dead,
and for rewarding your servants the prophets[i]
and your saints and those who reverence your name,
both small and great[j]—
and for destroying those who destroy the earth."

19Then God's temple[k] in heaven was opened, and within his
temple was seen the ark of his covenant. And there came flashes of
lightning, rumblings, peals of thunder, an earthquake and a great
hailstorm.[l]

Chapter 12 Theme ____________________

12 A great and wondrous sign appeared in heaven: a woman
clothed with the sun, with the moon under her feet and a
crown of twelve stars on her head. 2She was pregnant and cried out
in pain[m] as she was about to give birth. 3Then another sign appeared in heaven: an enormous red dragon with seven heads and
ten horns[n] and seven crowns[o] on his heads. 4His tail swept a
third[p] of the stars out of the sky and flung them to the earth.[q]
The dragon stood in front of the woman who was about to give
birth, so that he might devour her child[r] the moment it was born.
5She gave birth to a son, a male child, who will rule all the nations
with an iron scepter.[s] And her child was snatched up to God and to
his throne. 6The woman fled into the desert to a place prepared for
her by God, where she might be taken care of for 1,260 days.[t]
7And there was war in heaven. Michael and his angels fought
against the dragon,[u] and the dragon and his angels fought back.
8But he was not strong enough, and they lost their place in heaven.
9The great dragon was hurled down—that ancient serpent[v]
called the devil,[w] or Satan, who leads the whole world astray.[x] He
was hurled to the earth,[y] and his angels with him.

11:15 [a]Rev 10:7 [b]Rev 16:17; 19:1 [c]Rev 12:10 [d]Da 2:44; 7:14,27
11:16 [e]Rev 4:4
11:17 [f]Rev 1:8 [g]Rev 19:6
11:18 [h]Ps 2:1 [i]Rev 10:7 [j]Rev 19:5
11:19 [k]Rev 15:5,8 [l]Rev 16:21
12:2 [m]Gal 4:19
12:3 [n]Da 7:7,20; Rev 13:1 [o]Rev 19:12
12:4 [p]Rev 8:7 [q]Da 8:10 [r]Mt 2:16
12:5 [s]Ps 2:9; Rev 2:27
12:6 [t]Rev 11:2
12:7 [u]ver 3
12:9 [v]Ge 3:1-7 [w]Mt 25:41 [x]Rev 20:3,8,10 [y]Lk 10:18; Jn 12:31

10 Then I heard a loud voice in heaven[a] say:
"Now have come the salvation and the power and the
kingdom of our God,
and the authority of his Christ.
For the accuser of our brothers,[b]
who accuses them before our God day and night,
has been hurled down.
11 They overcame him
by the blood of the Lamb[c]
and by the word of their testimony;[d]
they did not love their lives so much
as to shrink from death.[e]
12 Therefore rejoice, you heavens[f]
and you who dwell in them!
But woe[g] to the earth and the sea,[h]
because the devil has gone down to you!
He is filled with fury,
because he knows that his time is short."

13 When the dragon[i] saw that he had been hurled to the earth,
he pursued the woman who had given birth to the male child.[j]
14 The woman was given the two wings of a great eagle,[k] so that she
might fly to the place prepared for her in the desert, where she
would be taken care of for a time, times and half a time,[l] out of the
serpent's reach. 15 Then from his mouth the serpent spewed water
like a river, to overtake the woman and sweep her away with the
torrent. 16 But the earth helped the woman by opening its mouth
and swallowing the river that the dragon had spewed out of his
mouth. 17 Then the dragon was enraged at the woman and went
off to make war[m] against the rest of her offspring[n]—those who
obey God's commandments[o] and hold to the testimony of Jesus.[p]

Chapter 13 Theme

13 And the dragon[a] stood on the shore of the sea.
And I saw a beast coming out of the sea.[q] He had ten horns
and seven heads,[r] with ten crowns on his horns, and on each head a
blasphemous name.[s] 2 The beast I saw resembled a leopard,[t] but
had feet like those of a bear[u] and a mouth like that of a lion.[v] The
dragon gave the beast his power and his throne and great
authority.[w] 3 One of the heads of the beast seemed to have had a
fatal wound, but the fatal wound had been healed.[x] The whole
world was astonished[y] and followed the beast. 4 Men worshiped the
dragon because he had given authority to the beast, and they also
worshiped the beast and asked, "Who is like[z] the beast? Who can
make war against him?"

12:10 [a]Rev 11:15 [b]Job 1:9-11; Zec 3:1
12:11 [c]Rev 7:14 [d]Rev 6:9 [e]Lk 14:26
12:12 [f]Ps 96:11; Isa 49:13; Rev 18:20 [g]Rev 8:13 [h]Rev 10:6
12:13 [i]ver 3 [j]ver 5
12:14 [k]Ex 19:4 [l]Da 7:25
12:17 [m]Rev 11:7 [n]Ge 3:15 [o]Rev 14:12 [p]Rev 1:2
13:1 [q]Da 7:1-6; Rev 15:2 [r]Rev 12:3 [s]Da 11:36; Rev 17:3
13:2 [t]Da 7:6 [u]Da 7:5 [v]Da 7:4 [w]Rev 16:10
13:3 [x]ver 12,14 [y]Rev 17:8
13:4 [z]Ex 15:11

a *1* Some late manuscripts *And I*

5 The beast was given a mouth to utter proud words and blasphemies[a] and to exercise his authority for forty-two months.[b]
6 He opened his mouth to blaspheme God, and to slander his name
and his dwelling place and those who live in heaven.[c] 7 He was
given power to make war[d] against the saints and to conquer them.
And he was given authority over every tribe, people, language and
nation.[e] 8 All inhabitants of the earth[f] will worship the beast—all
whose names have not been written in the book of life[g] belonging to the Lamb that was slain from the creation of the world.[a][h]
9 He who has an ear, let him hear.[i]

> 10 If anyone is to go into captivity,
> into captivity he will go.
> If anyone is to be killed[b] with the sword,
> with the sword he will be killed.[j]

This calls for patient endurance and faithfulness[k] on the part of the
saints.[l]
11 Then I saw another beast, coming out of the earth. He had two
horns like a lamb, but he spoke like a dragon. 12 He exercised all the
authority[m] of the first beast on his behalf,[n] and made the earth and
its inhabitants worship the first beast,[o] whose fatal wound had
been healed.[p] 13 And he performed great and miraculous signs,[q]
even causing fire to come down from heaven[r] to earth in full view
of men. 14 Because of the signs[s] he was given power to do on behalf
of the first beast, he deceived[t] the inhabitants of the earth. He
ordered them to set up an image in honor of the beast who was
wounded by the sword and yet lived. 15 He was given power to
give breath to the image of the first beast, so that it could speak and
cause all who refused to worship the image to be killed.[u] 16 He
also forced everyone, small and great,[v] rich and poor, free and
slave, to receive a mark on his right hand or on his forehead,[w] 17 so
that no one could buy or sell unless he had the mark,[x] which is
the name of the beast or the number of his name.[y]
18 This calls for wisdom.[z] If anyone has insight, let him calculate
the number of the beast, for it is man's number.[a] His number is
666.

Chapter 14 Theme ____________________________

14 Then I looked, and there before me was the Lamb,[b] standing
on Mount Zion,[c] and with him 144,000[d] who had his name
and his Father's name[e] written on their foreheads. 2 And I heard a
sound from heaven like the roar of rushing waters[f] and like a

[a] 8 Or *written from the creation of the world in the book of life belonging to the Lamb that was slain* [b] 10 Some manuscripts *anyone kills*

13:5 [a] Da 7:8,11, 20,25; 11:36; 2Th 2:4 [b] Rev 11:2
13:6 [c] Rev 12:12
13:7 [d] Da 7:21; Rev 11:7 [e] Rev 5:9
13:8 [f] Rev 3:10 [g] Rev 3:5; 20:12 [h] Mt 25:34
13:9 [i] Rev 2:7
13:10 [j] Jer 15:2; 43:11 [k] Heb 6:12 [l] Rev 14:12
13:12 [m] ver 4 [n] ver 14 [o] Rev 14:9,11 [p] ver 3
13:13 [q] Mt 24:24 [r] 1Ki 18:38; Rev 20:9
13:14 [s] 2Th 2:9,10 [t] Rev 12:9
13:15 [u] Da 3:3-6
13:16 [v] Rev 19:5 [w] Rev 14:9
13:17 [x] Rev 14:9 [y] Rev 14:11; 15:2
13:18 [z] Rev 17:9 [a] Rev 15:2; 21:17
14:1 [b] Rev 5:6 [c] Ps 2:6 [d] Rev 7:4 [e] Rev 3:12
14:2 [f] Rev 1:15

loud peal of thunder. The sound I heard was like that of harpists
playing their harps.[a] 3And they sang a new song[b] before the throne
and before the four living creatures and the elders. No one could
learn the song except the 144,000[c] who had been redeemed from
the earth. 4These are those who did not defile themselves with
women, for they kept themselves pure.[d] They follow the Lamb
wherever he goes. They were purchased from among men[e] and
offered as firstfruits[f] to God and the Lamb. 5No lie was found in
their mouths;[g] they are blameless.[h]

6Then I saw another angel flying in midair,[i] and he had the
eternal gospel to proclaim to those who live on the earth[j]—to
every nation, tribe, language and people.[k] 7He said in a loud voice,
"Fear God[l] and give him glory,[m] because the hour of his judgment
has come. Worship him who made the heavens, the earth, the sea
and the springs of water."[n]

8A second angel followed and said, "Fallen! Fallen is Babylon the
Great,[o] which made all the nations drink the maddening wine of
her adulteries."[p]

9A third angel followed them and said in a loud voice: "If anyone
worships the beast and his image[q] and receives his mark on the
forehead or on the hand, 10he, too, will drink of the wine of God's
fury,[r] which has been poured full strength into the cup of his
wrath.[s] He will be tormented with burning sulfur in the presence
of the holy angels and of the Lamb. 11And the smoke of their torment rises for ever and ever.[t] There is no rest day or night for
those who worship the beast and his image, or for anyone who
receives the mark of his name." 12This calls for patient endurance
on the part of the saints[u] who obey God's commandments and
remain faithful to Jesus.

13Then I heard a voice from heaven say, "Write: Blessed are the
dead who die in the Lord[v] from now on."

"Yes," says the Spirit, "they will rest from their labor, for their
deeds will follow them."

14I looked, and there before me was a white cloud, and seated on
the cloud was one "like a son of man"[a][w] with a crown[x] of gold on
his head and a sharp sickle in his hand. 15Then another angel came
out of the temple and called in a loud voice to him who was sitting on the cloud, "Take your sickle[y] and reap, because the time to
reap has come, for the harvest[z] of the earth is ripe." 16So he who
was seated on the cloud swung his sickle over the earth, and the
earth was harvested.

17Another angel came out of the temple in heaven, and he too
had a sharp sickle. 18Still another angel, who had charge of the
fire, came from the altar and called in a loud voice to him who had

14:2 [a]Rev 5:8
14:3 [b]Rev 5:9 [c]ver 1
14:4 [d]2Co 11:2; Rev 3:4 [e]Rev 5:9 [f]Jas 1:18
14:5 [g]Ps 32:2; Zep 3:13 [h]Eph 5:27
14:6 [i]Rev 8:13 [j]Rev 3:10 [k]Rev 13:7
14:7 [l]Rev 15:4 [m]Rev 11:13 [n]Rev 8:10
14:8 [o]Isa 21:9; Jer 51:8 [p]Rev 17:2,4 18:3,9
14:9 [q]Rev 13:14
14:10 [r]Isa 51:17; Jer 25:15 [s]Rev 18:6
14:11 [t]Isa 34:10; Rev 19:3
14:12 [u]Rev 13:10
14:13 [v]1Co 15:18; 1Th 4:16
14:14 [w]Da 7:13; Rev 1:13 [x]Rev 6:2
14:15 [y]Joel 3:13 [z]Jer 51:33

a *14* Daniel 7:13

the sharp sickle, "Take your sharp sickle and gather the clusters of
grapes from the earth's vine, because its grapes are ripe." 19The
angel swung his sickle on the earth, gathered its grapes and threw
them into the great winepress of God's wrath.[a] 20They were trampled in the winepress[b] outside the city,[c] and blood flowed out of
the press, rising as high as the horses' bridles for a distance
of 1,600 stadia.[a]

Chapter 15 Theme ______________________

15 I saw in heaven another great and marvelous sign:[d] seven angels[e] with the seven last plagues[f]—last, because with them
God's wrath is completed. 2And I saw what looked like a sea of
glass[g] mixed with fire and, standing beside the sea, those who had
been victorious over the beast and his image[h] and over the number of his name. They held harps given them by God 3and sang the
song of Moses[i] the servant of God and the song of the Lamb:

"Great and marvelous are your deeds,[j]
  Lord God Almighty.
Just and true are your ways,[k]
  King of the ages.
4Who will not fear you, O Lord,[l]
  and bring glory to your name?
For you alone are holy.
All nations will come
  and worship before you,[m]
for your righteous acts have been revealed."

5After this I looked and in heaven the temple,[n] that is, the
tabernacle of the Testimony,[o] was opened. 6Out of the temple[p]
came the seven angels with the seven plagues.[q] They were dressed
in clean, shining linen and wore golden sashes around their
chests.[r] 7Then one of the four living creatures[s] gave to the seven
angels seven golden bowls filled with the wrath of God, who lives
for ever and ever. 8And the temple was filled with smoke[t] from
the glory of God and from his power, and no one could enter the
temple[u] until the seven plagues of the seven angels were completed.

Chapter 16 Theme ______________________

16 Then I heard a loud voice from the temple saying to the sev-
en angels,[v] "Go, pour out the seven bowls of God's wrath on
the earth."
2The first angel went and poured out his bowl on the land,[w] and
ugly and painful sores[x] broke out on the people who had the mark
of the beast and worshiped his image.[y]

a *20* That is, about 180 miles (about 300 kilometers)

14:19 *a* Rev 19:15
14:20 *b* Isa 63:3 *c* Heb 13:12; Rev 11:8
15:1 *d* Rev 12:1,3 *e* Rev 16:1 *f* Lev 26:21
15:2 *g* Rev 4:6 *h* Rev 13:14
15:3 *i* Ex 15:1; Dt 32:4 *j* Ps 111:2 *k* Ps 145:17
15:4 *l* Jer 10:7 *m* Isa 66:23
15:5 *n* Rev 11:19 *o* Nu 1:50
15:6 *p* Rev 14:15 *q* ver 1 *r* Rev 1:13
15:7 *s* Rev 4:6
15:8 *t* Isa 6:4 *u* Ex 40:34,35; 1Ki 8:10,11; 2Ch 5:13,14
16:1 *v* Rev 15:1
16:2 *w* Rev 8:7 *x* Ex 9:9-11 *y* Rev 13:15-17

3 The second angel poured out his bowl on the sea, and it turned
into blood like that of a dead man, and every living thing in the sea
died.[a]
4 The third angel poured out his bowl on the rivers and springs of
water,[b] and they became blood.[c] 5 Then I heard the angel in charge
of the waters say:

> "You are just in these judgments,[d]
> you who are and who were,[e] the Holy One,[f]
> because you have so judged;
> 6 for they have shed the blood of your saints and prophets,
> and you have given them blood to drink[g] as they
> deserve."

7 And I heard the altar[h] respond:

> "Yes, Lord God Almighty,
> true and just are your judgments."[i]

8 The fourth angel[j] poured out his bowl on the sun, and the sun
was given power to scorch people with fire.[k] 9 They were seared
by the intense heat and they cursed the name of God,[l] who had
control over these plagues, but they refused to repent[m] and glorify him.[n]
10 The fifth angel poured out his bowl on the throne of the beast,[o]
and his kingdom was plunged into darkness.[p] Men gnawed their
tongues in agony 11 and cursed[q] the God of heaven[r] because of
their pains and their sores,[s] but they refused to repent of what they
had done.[t]
12 The sixth angel poured out his bowl on the great river
Euphrates,[u] and its water was dried up to prepare the way for the
kings from the East.[v] 13 Then I saw three evil[a] spirits that looked
like frogs; they came out of the mouth of the dragon,[w] out of the
mouth of the beast[x] and out of the mouth of the false prophet.[y]
14 They are spirits of demons[z] performing miraculous signs, and
they go out to the kings of the whole world, to gather them for the
battle[a] on the great day of God Almighty.
15 "Behold, I come like a thief! Blessed is he who stays awake[b] and
keeps his clothes with him, so that he may not go naked and be
shamefully exposed."
16 Then they gathered the kings together to the place that in
Hebrew[c] is called Armageddon.[d]
17 The seventh angel poured out his bowl into the air,[e] and out
of the temple[f] came a loud voice[g] from the throne, saying, "It is
done!"[h] 18 Then there came flashes of lightning, rumblings, peals

a13 Greek *unclean*

16:3 [a] Ex 7:17-21; Rev 8:8,9
16:4 [b] Rev 8:10 [c] Ex 7:17-21
16:5 [d] Rev 15:3 [e] Rev 1:4 [f] Rev 15:4
16:6 [g] Isa 49:26; Rev 17:6
16:7 [h] Rev 6:9 [i] Rev 15:3; 19:2
16:8 [j] Rev 8:12 [k] Rev 14:18
16:9 [l] ver 11,21 [m] Rev 2:21 [n] Rev 11:13
16:10 [o] Rev 13:2 [p] Rev 9:2
16:11 [q] ver 9,21 [r] Rev 11:13 [s] ver 2 [t] Rev 2:21
16:12 [u] Rev 9:14 [v] Isa 41:2
16:13 [w] Rev 12:3 [x] Rev 13:1 [y] Rev 19:20
16:14 [z] 1Ti 4:1 [a] Rev 17:14
16:15 [b] Lk 12:37
16:16 [c] Rev 9:11 [d] 2Ki 23:29,30
16:17 [e] Eph 2:2 [f] Rev 14:15 [g] Rev 11:15 [h] Rev 21:6

of thunder[a] and a severe earthquake.[b] No earthquake like it has
ever occurred since man has been on earth,[c] so tremendous was
the quake. 19The great city[d] split into three parts, and the cities of
the nations collapsed. God remembered[e] Babylon the Great[f] and
gave her the cup filled with the wine of the fury of his wrath.[g]
20Every island fled away and the mountains could not be found.[h]
21From the sky huge hailstones[i] of about a hundred pounds each
fell upon men. And they cursed God on account of the plague of
hail,[j] because the plague was so terrible.

Chapter 17 Theme ________________________

17 One of the seven angels[k] who had the seven bowls[l] came
and said to me, "Come, I will show you the punishment[m] of
the great prostitute,[n] who sits on many waters.[o] 2With her the
kings of the earth committed adultery and the inhabitants of the
earth were intoxicated with the wine of her adulteries."[p]

3Then the angel carried me away in the Spirit into a desert.[q]
There I saw a woman sitting on a scarlet beast that was covered
with blasphemous names[r] and had seven heads and ten horns.[s]
4The woman was dressed in purple and scarlet, and was glittering
with gold, precious stones and pearls.[t] She held a golden cup[u] in
her hand, filled with abominable things and the filth of her adulteries. 5This title was written on her forehead:

MYSTERY
BABYLON THE GREAT[v]
THE MOTHER OF PROSTITUTES
AND OF THE ABOMINATIONS OF THE EARTH.

6I saw that the woman was drunk with the blood of the saints,[w]
the blood of those who bore testimony to Jesus.

When I saw her, I was greatly astonished. 7Then the angel said to
me: "Why are you astonished? I will explain to you the mystery[x] of
the woman and of the beast she rides, which has the seven heads
and ten horns.[y] 8The beast, which you saw, once was, now is not,
and will come up out of the Abyss and go to his destruction.[z] The
inhabitants of the earth[a] whose names have not been written in the
book of life[b] from the creation of the world will be astonished[c]
when they see the beast, because he once was, now is not, and yet
will come.

9"This calls for a mind with wisdom.[d] The seven heads are seven
hills on which the woman sits. 10They are also seven kings. Five
have fallen, one is, the other has not yet come; but when he does
come, he must remain for a little while. 11The beast who once was,
and now is not,[e] is an eighth king. He belongs to the seven and is
going to his destruction.

16:18 [a]Rev 4:5 [b]Rev 6:12 [c]Da 12:1
16:19 [d]Rev 17:18 [e]Rev 18:5 [f]Rev 14:8 [g]Rev 14:10
16:20 [h]Rev 6:14
16:21 [i]Rev 11:19 [j]Ex 9:23-25
17:1 [k]Rev 15:1 [l]Rev 21:9 [m]Rev 16:19 [n]Rev 19:2 [o]Jer 51:13
17:2 [p]Rev 14:8; 18:3
17:3 [q]Rev 12:6,14 [r]Rev 13:1 [s]Rev 12:3
17:4 [t]Rev 18:16 [u]Jer 51:7; Rev 18:6
17:5 [v]Rev 14:8
17:6 [w]Rev 18:24
17:7 [x]ver 5 [y]ver 3
17:8 [z]Rev 13:10 [a]Rev 3:10 [b]Rev 13:8 [c]Rev 13:3
17:9 [d]Rev 13:18
17:11 [e]ver 8

12"The ten horns[a] you saw are ten kings who have not yet
received a kingdom, but who for one hour[b] will receive authority
as kings along with the beast. 13They have one purpose and will
give their power and authority to the beast.[c] 14They will make war[d]
against the Lamb, but the Lamb will overcome them because he
is Lord of lords and King of kings[e]—and with him will be his
called, chosen[f] and faithful followers."

15Then the angel said to me, "The waters[g] you saw, where the
prostitute sits, are peoples, multitudes, nations and languages.[h]
16The beast and the ten horns you saw will hate the prostitute.
They will bring her to ruin[i] and leave her naked;[j] they will eat her
flesh[k] and burn her with fire.[l] 17For God has put it into their
hearts to accomplish his purpose by agreeing to give the beast
their power to rule, until God's words are fulfilled.[m] 18The woman
you saw is the great city[n] that rules over the kings of the earth."

Chapter 18 Theme

18 After this I saw another angel[o] coming down from heaven.[p]
He had great authority, and the earth was illuminated by
his splendor.[q] 2With a mighty voice he shouted:

"Fallen! Fallen is Babylon the Great![r]
She has become a home for demons
and a haunt for every evil[a] spirit,
a haunt for every unclean and detestable bird.[s]
3For all the nations have drunk
the maddening wine of her adulteries.[t]
The kings of the earth committed adultery with her,[u]
and the merchants of the earth grew rich[v] from her
excessive luxuries."[w]

4Then I heard another voice from heaven say:

"Come out of her, my people,[x]
so that you will not share in her sins,
so that you will not receive any of her plagues;
5for her sins are piled up to heaven,[y]
and God has remembered[z] her crimes.
6Give back to her as she has given;
pay her back[a] double for what she has done.
Mix her a double portion from her own cup.[b]
7Give her as much torture and grief
as the glory and luxury she gave herself.[c]
In her heart she boasts,
'I sit as queen; I am not a widow,
and I will never mourn.'[d]

17:12 [a]Rev 12:3 [b]Rev 18:10,17,19
17:13 [c]ver 17
17:14 [d]Rev 16:14 [e]1Ti 6:15; Rev 19:16 [f]Mt 22:14
17:15 [g]Isa 8:7 [h]Rev 13:7
17:16 [i]Rev 18:17,19 [j]Eze 16:37,39 [k]Rev 19:18 [l]Rev 18:8
17:17 [m]Rev 10:7
17:18 [n]Rev 16:19
18:1 [o]Rev 17:1 [p]Rev 10:1 [q]Eze 43:2
18:2 [r]Rev 14:8 [s]Isa 13:21,22; Jer 50:39
18:3 [t]Rev 14:8 [u]Rev 17:2 [v]Eze 27:9-25 [w]ver 7,9
18:4 [x]Isa 48:20; Jer 50:8; 2Co 6:17
18:5 [y]Jer 51:9 [z]Rev 16:19
18:6 [a]Ps 137:8; Jer 50:15,29 [b]Rev 14:10; 16:19
18:7 [c]Eze 28:2-8 [d]Isa 47:7,8; Zep 2:15

a 2 Greek *unclean*

[8]Therefore in one day[a] her plagues will overtake her:
death, mourning and famine.
She will be consumed by fire,[b]
for mighty is the Lord God who judges her.

[9]"When the kings of the earth who committed adultery with
her[c] and shared her luxury see the smoke of her burning,[d] they will
weep and mourn over her.[e] [10]Terrified at her torment, they will
stand far off[f] and cry:

"'Woe! Woe, O great city,[g]
O Babylon, city of power!
In one hour[h] your doom has come!'

[11]"The merchants[i] of the earth will weep and mourn over her
because no one buys their cargoes any more[j]— [12]cargoes of gold,
silver, precious stones and pearls; fine linen, purple, silk and
scarlet cloth; every sort of citron wood, and articles of every kind
made of ivory, costly wood, bronze, iron and marble;[k] [13]cargoes of
cinnamon and spice, of incense, myrrh and frankincense, of wine
and olive oil, of fine flour and wheat; cattle and sheep; horses and
carriages; and bodies and souls of men.[l]
[14]"They will say, 'The fruit you longed for is gone from you. All
your riches and splendor have vanished, never to be recovered.'
[15]The merchants who sold these things and gained their wealth
from her[m] will stand far off, terrified at her torment. They will
weep and mourn[n] [16]and cry out:

"'Woe! Woe, O great city,
dressed in fine linen, purple and scarlet,
and glittering with gold, precious stones and pearls![o]
[17]In one hour[p] such great wealth has been brought
to ruin!'[q]

"Every sea captain, and all who travel by ship, the sailors, and all
who earn their living from the sea,[r] will stand far off. [18]When they
see the smoke of her burning, they will exclaim, 'Was there ever a
city like this great city?'[s] [19]They will throw dust on their heads,[t]
and with weeping and mourning cry out:

"'Woe! Woe, O great city,
where all who had ships on the sea
became rich through her wealth!
In one hour she has been brought to ruin![u]
[20]Rejoice over her, O heaven![v]
Rejoice, saints and apostles and prophets!
God has judged her for the way she treated you.'"[w]

[21]Then a mighty angel[x] picked up a boulder the size of a large
millstone and threw it into the sea,[y] and said:

18:8 [a]ver 10; Isa 47:9; Jer 50:31,32 [b]Rev 17:16
18:9 [c]Rev 17:2,4 [d]ver 18; Rev 19:3 [e]Eze 26:17,18
18:10 [f]ver 15,17 [g]ver 16,19 [h]Rev 17:12
18:11 [i]Eze 27:27 [j]ver 3
18:12 [k]Rev 17:4
18:13 [l]Eze 27:13; 1Ti 1:10
18:15 [m]ver 3 [n]Eze 27:31
18:16 [o]Rev 17:4
18:17 [p]ver 10 [q]Rev 17:16 [r]Eze 27:28-30
18:18 [s]Eze 27:32; Rev 13:4
18:19 [t]Jos 7:6; Eze 27:30 [u]Rev 17:16
18:20 [v]Jer 51:48; Rev 12:12 [w]Rev 19:2
18:21 [x]Rev 5:2 [y]Jer 51:63

"With such violence
the great city of Babylon will be thrown down,
never to be found again.
22 The music of harpists and musicians, flute players
and trumpeters,
will never be heard in you again.[a]
No workman of any trade
will ever be found in you again.
The sound of a millstone
will never be heard in you again.[b]
23 The light of a lamp
will never shine in you again.
The voice of bridegroom and bride
will never be heard in you again.[c]
Your merchants were the world's great men.[d]
By your magic spell[e] all the nations were led astray.
24 In her was found the blood of prophets and of the saints,[f]
and of all who have been killed on the earth."[g]

Chapter 19 Theme

19 After this I heard what sounded like the roar of a great
multitude[h] in heaven shouting:

"Hallelujah!
Salvation[i] and glory and power[j] belong to our God,
2 for true and just are his judgments.
He has condemned the great prostitute
who corrupted the earth by her adulteries.
He has avenged on her the blood of his servants."[k]

3 And again they shouted:

"Hallelujah!
The smoke from her goes up for ever and ever."[l]

4 The twenty-four elders[m] and the four living creatures[n] fell down[o]
and worshiped God, who was seated on the throne. And they cried:

"Amen, Hallelujah!"

5 Then a voice came from the throne, saying:

"Praise our God,
all you his servants,[p]
you who fear him,
both small and great!"[q]

6 Then I heard what sounded like a great multitude,[r] like the
roar of rushing waters and like loud peals of thunder, shouting:

18:22 [a] Isa 24:8; Eze 26:13 [b] Jer 25:10
18:23 [c] Jer 7:34; 16:9; 25:10 [d] Isa 23:8 [e] Na 3:4
18:24 [f] Rev 16:6; 17:6 [g] Jer 51:49
19:1 [h] Rev 11:15 [i] Rev 7:10 [j] Rev 4:11
19:2 [k] Dt 32:43; Rev 6:10
19:3 [l] Isa 34:10; Rev 14:11
19:4 [m] Rev 4:4 [n] Rev 4:6 [o] Rev 5:14
19:5 [p] Ps 134:1 [q] Rev 11:18; 20:12
19:6 [r] Rev 11:15

"Hallelujah!
For our Lord God Almighty reigns.
7Let us rejoice and be glad
and give him glory!
For the wedding of the Lamb[a] has come,
and his bride[b] has made herself ready.
8Fine linen, bright and clean,
was given her to wear."
(Fine linen stands for the righteous acts[c] of the saints.)

9Then the angel said to me,[d] "Write:[e] 'Blessed are those who are
invited to the wedding supper of the Lamb!'"[f] And he added,
"These are the true words of God."[g]
10At this I fell at his feet to worship him.[h] But he said to me, "Do
not do it! I am a fellow servant with you and with your brothers
who hold to the testimony of Jesus. Worship God![i] For the testimony of Jesus[j] is the spirit of prophecy."
11I saw heaven standing open and there before me was a white
horse, whose rider[k] is called Faithful and True.[l] With justice he
judges and makes war.[m] 12His eyes are like blazing fire,[n] and on his
head are many crowns.[o] He has a name written on him that no one
knows but he himself.[p] 13He is dressed in a robe dipped in blood,[q]
and his name is the Word of God.[r] 14The armies of heaven were following him, riding on white horses and dressed in fine linen,[s] white
and clean. 15Out of his mouth comes a sharp sword[t] with which to
strike down[u] the nations. "He will rule them with an iron scepter."[a][v]
He treads the winepress[w] of the fury of the wrath of God Almighty.
16On his robe and on his thigh he has this name written:[x]

KING OF KINGS AND LORD OF LORDS.[y]

17And I saw an angel standing in the sun, who cried in a loud
voice to all the birds[z] flying in midair,[a] "Come,[b] gather together for
the great supper of God, 18so that you may eat the flesh of kings,
generals, and mighty men, of horses and their riders, and the flesh
of all people,[c] free and slave, small and great."
19Then I saw the beast and the kings of the earth[d] and their
armies gathered together to make war against the rider on the
horse and his army. 20But the beast was captured, and with him
the false prophet[e] who had performed the miraculous signs on his
behalf.[f] With these signs he had deluded those who had received
the mark of the beast and worshiped his image. The two of them
were thrown alive into the fiery lake[g] of burning sulfur.[h] 21The rest
of them were killed with the sword[i] that came out of the mouth of
the rider on the horse,[j] and all the birds[k] gorged themselves on
their flesh.

[a] 15 Psalm 2:9

19:7 [a]Mt 22:2; 25:10; Eph 5:32 [b]Rev 21:2,9
19:8 [c]Rev 15:4
19:9 [d]ver 10 [e]Rev 1:19 [f]Lk 14:15 [g]Rev 21:5; 22:6
19:10 [h]Rev 22:8 [i]Ac 10:25,26; Rev 22:9 [j]Rev 12:17
19:11 [k]Rev 6:2 [l]Rev 3:14 [m]Isa 11:4
19:12 [n]Rev 1:14 [o]Rev 6:2 [p]Rev 2:17
19:13 [q]Isa 63:2,3 [r]Jn 1:1
19:14 [s]ver 8
19:15 [t]Rev 1:16 [u]Isa 11:4; 2Th 2:8 [v]Ps 2:9; Rev 2:27 [w]Rev 14:20
19:16 [x]ver 12 [y]Rev 17:14
19:17 [z]ver 21 [a]Rev 8:13 [b]Eze 39:17
19:18 [c]Eze 39:18-20
19:19 [d]Rev 16:14,16
19:20 [e]Rev 16:13 [f]Rev 13:12 [g]Da 7:11; Rev 20:10, 14,15; 21:8 [h]Rev 14:10
19:21 [i]ver 15 [j]ver 11,19 [k]ver 17

Chapter 20 Theme ________________________

20 And I saw an angel coming down out of heaven,[a] having
the key[b] to the Abyss and holding in his hand a great chain.
2He seized the dragon, that ancient serpent, who is the devil, or
Satan,[c] and bound him for a thousand years.[d] 3He threw him into
the Abyss, and locked and sealed[e] it over him, to keep him from
deceiving the nations[f] anymore until the thousand years were
ended. After that, he must be set free for a short time.
4I saw thrones[g] on which were seated those who had been given
authority to judge. And I saw the souls of those who had been
beheaded[h] because of their testimony for Jesus and because of the
word of God. They had not worshiped the beast[i] or his image and
had not received his mark on their foreheads or their hands.[j] They
came to life and reigned with Christ a thousand years. 5(The rest of
the dead did not come to life until the thousand years were ended.)
This is the first resurrection.[k] 6Blessed[l] and holy are those who
have part in the first resurrection. The second death[m] has no power
over them, but they will be priests[n] of God and of Christ and will
reign with him[o] for a thousand years.
7When the thousand years are over,[p] Satan will be released from
his prison 8and will go out to deceive the nations[q] in the four corners of the earth—Gog and Magog[r]—to gather them for battle.[s]
In number they are like the sand on the seashore.[t] 9They marched
across the breadth of the earth and surrounded[u] the camp of God's
people, the city he loves. But fire came down from heaven[v] and
devoured them. 10And the devil, who deceived them,[w] was thrown
into the lake of burning sulfur, where the beast and the false
prophet had been thrown. They will be tormented day and night
for ever and ever.[x]
11Then I saw a great white throne[y] and him who was seated on it.
Earth and sky fled from his presence, and there was no place for
them. 12And I saw the dead, great and small, standing before the
throne, and books were opened.[z] Another book was opened, which
is the book of life.[a] The dead were judged according to what they
had done[b] as recorded in the books. 13The sea gave up the dead that
were in it, and death and Hades[c] gave up the dead[d] that were in
them, and each person was judged according to what he had done.
14Then death[e] and Hades were thrown into the lake of fire. The
lake of fire is the second death. 15If anyone's name was not found
written in the book of life,[f] he was thrown into the lake of fire.

Chapter 21 Theme ________________________

21 Then I saw a new heaven and a new earth,[g] for the first
heaven and the first earth had passed away, and there was
no longer any sea. 2I saw the Holy City, the new Jerusalem, coming

20:1 [a]Rev 10:1 [b]Rev 1:18
20:2 [c]Rev 12:9 [d]2Pe 2:4
20:3 [e]Da 6:17 [f]Rev 12:9
20:4 [g]Da 7:9 [h]Rev 6:9 [i]Rev 13:12 [j]Rev 13:16
20:5 [k]Lk 14:14; Php 3:11
20:6 [l]Rev 14:13 [m]Rev 2:11 [n]Rev 1:6 [o]ver 4
20:7 [p]ver 2
20:8 [q]ver 3,10 [r]Eze 38:2; 39:1 [s]Rev 16:14 [t]Heb 11:12
20:9 [u]Eze 38:9,16 [v]Eze 38:22; 39:6
20:10 [w]Rev 19:20 [x]Rev 14:10,11
20:11 [y]Rev 4:2
20:12 [z]Da 7:10 [a]Rev 3:5 [b]Jer 17:10; Mt 16:27; Rev 2:23
20:13 [c]Rev 6:8 [d]Isa 26:19
20:14 [e]1Co 15:26
20:15 [f]ver 12
21:1 [g]Isa 65:17; 2Pe 3:13

down out of heaven from God,[a] prepared as a bride beautifully
dressed for her husband. 3And I heard a loud voice from the throne
saying, "Now the dwelling of God is with men, and he will live with
them. They will be his people, and God himself will be with them
and be their God.[b] 4He will wipe every tear from their eyes.[c] There
will be no more death[d] or mourning or crying or pain,[e] for the old
order of things has passed away."
5He who was seated on the throne[f] said, "I am making everything new!" Then he said, "Write this down, for these words are
trustworthy and true."[g]
6He said to me: "It is done.[h] I am the Alpha and the Omega,[i] the
Beginning and the End. To him who is thirsty I will give to drink
without cost from the spring of the water of life.[j] 7He who overcomes will inherit all this, and I will be his God and he will be my
son. 8But the cowardly, the unbelieving, the vile, the murderers,
the sexually immoral, those who practice magic arts, the idolaters
and all liars[k]—their place will be in the fiery lake of burning sulfur.
This is the second death."[l]
9One of the seven angels who had the seven bowls full of the seven
last plagues[m] came and said to me, "Come, I will show you the
bride,[n] the wife of the Lamb." 10And he carried me away[o] in the
Spirit[p] to a mountain great and high, and showed me the Holy City,
Jerusalem, coming down out of heaven from God. 11It shone with
the glory of God,[q] and its brilliance was like that of a very precious
jewel, like a jasper, clear as crystal.[r] 12It had a great, high wall with
twelve gates, and with twelve angels at the gates. On the gates were
written the names of the twelve tribes of Israel.[s] 13There were three
gates on the east, three on the north, three on the south and three
on the west. 14The wall of the city had twelve foundations, and on
them were the names of the twelve apostles of the Lamb.
15The angel who talked with me had a measuring rod[t] of gold to
measure the city, its gates and its walls. 16The city was laid out like
a square, as long as it was wide. He measured the city with the rod
and found it to be 12,000 stadia[a] in length, and as wide and high
as it is long. 17He measured its wall and it was 144 cubits[b] thick,[c]
by man's measurement, which the angel was using. 18The wall was
made of jasper,[u] and the city of pure gold, as pure as glass.[v] 19The
foundations of the city walls were decorated with every kind of precious stone.[w] The first foundation was jasper, the second sapphire,
the third chalcedony, the fourth emerald, 20the fifth sardonyx, the
sixth carnelian,[x] the seventh chrysolite, the eighth beryl, the ninth
topaz, the tenth chrysoprase, the eleventh jacinth, and the twelfth
amethyst.[d] 21The twelve gates were twelve pearls, each gate made

[a] *16* That is, about 1,400 miles (about 2,200 kilometers) [b] *17* That is, about 200 feet (about 65 meters) [c] *17* Or *high* [d] *20* The precise identification of some of these precious stones is uncertain.

21:2
[a] Heb 11:10; 12:22; Rev 3:12

21:3
[b] 2Co 6:16

21:4
[c] Rev 7:17
[d] 1Co 15:26; Rev 20:14
[e] Isa 35:10; 65:19

21:5
[f] Rev 4:9; 20:11
[g] Rev 19:9

21:6
[h] Rev 16:17
[i] Rev 1:8; 22:13
[j] Jn 4:10

21:8
[k] 1Co 6:9
[l] Rev 2:11

21:9
[m] Rev 15:1,6,7
[n] Rev 19:7

21:10
[o] Rev 17:3
[p] Rev 1:10

21:11
[q] Rev 15:8; 22:5
[r] Rev 4:6

21:12
[s] Eze 48:30-34

21:15
[t] Rev 11:1

21:18
[u] ver 11
[v] ver 21

21:19
[w] Isa 54:11,12

21:20
[x] Rev 4:3

of a single pearl. The great street of the city was of pure gold, like
transparent glass.[a]
[22]I did not see a temple[b] in the city, because the Lord God
Almighty[c] and the Lamb[d] are its temple. [23]The city does not need
the sun or the moon to shine on it, for the glory of God gives it
light,[e] and the Lamb is its lamp. [24]The nations will walk by its
light, and the kings of the earth will bring their splendor into it.[f]
[25]On no day will its gates ever be shut,[g] for there will be no night
there.[h] [26]The glory and honor of the nations will be brought into
it. [27]Nothing impure will ever enter it, nor will anyone who does
what is shameful or deceitful,[i] but only those whose names are
written in the Lamb's book of life.

Chapter 22 Theme ______________________________

22

Then the angel showed me the river of the water of life, as
clear as crystal,[j] flowing[k] from the throne of God and of
the Lamb [2]down the middle of the great street of the city. On each
side of the river stood the tree of life,[l] bearing twelve crops of fruit,
yielding its fruit every month. And the leaves of the tree are for the
healing of the nations.[m] [3]No longer will there be any curse.[n] The
throne of God and of the Lamb will be in the city, and his servants
will serve him.[o] [4]They will see his face,[p] and his name will be on
their foreheads.[q] [5]There will be no more night.[r] They will not need
the light of a lamp or the light of the sun, for the Lord God will give
them light.[s] And they will reign for ever and ever.[t]
[6]The angel said to me,[u] "These words are trustworthy and true.[v]
The Lord, the God of the spirits of the prophets,[w] sent his angel[x] to
show his servants the things that must soon take place."
[7]"Behold, I am coming soon![y] Blessed[z] is he who keeps the words
of the prophecy in this book."

[8]I, John, am the one who heard and saw these things.[a] And when
I had heard and seen them, I fell down to worship at the feet[b] of the
angel who had been showing them to me. [9]But he said to me, "Do
not do it! I am a fellow servant with you and with your brothers
the prophets and of all who keep the words of this book.[c] Worship
God!"[d]
[10]Then he told me, "Do not seal up[e] the words of the prophecy
of this book, because the time is near.[f] [11]Let him who does wrong
continue to do wrong; let him who is vile continue to be vile; let
him who does right continue to do right; and let him who is holy
continue to be holy."[g]

[12]"Behold, I am coming soon![h] My reward is with me,[i] and I will
give to everyone according to what he has done. [13]I am the Alpha
and the Omega,[j] the First and the Last,[k] the Beginning and the
End.[l]

21:21 [a]ver 18
21:22 [b]Jn 4:21,23 [c]Rev 1:8 [d]Rev 5:6
21:23 [e]Isa 24:23; 60:19,20; Rev 22:5
21:24 [f]Isa 60:3,5
21:25 [g]Isa 60:11 [h]Zec 14:7; Rev 22:5
21:27 [i]Isa 52:1; Joel 3:17; Rev 22:14,15
22:1 [j]Rev 4:6 [k]Eze 47:1; Zec 14:8
22:2 [l]Rev 2:7 [m]Eze 47:12
22:3 [n]Zec 14:11 [o]Rev 7:15
22:4 [p]Mt 5:8 [q]Rev 14:1
22:5 [r]Rev 21:25 [s]Rev 21:23 [t]Da 7:27; Rev 20:4
22:6 [u]Rev 1:1 [v]Rev 19:9; 21:5 [w]Heb 12:9 [x]ver 16
22:7 [y]Rev 3:11 [z]Rev 1:3
22:8 [a]Rev 1:1 [b]Rev 19:10
22:9 [c]ver 10,18,19 [d]Rev 19:10
22:10 [e]Da 8:26; Rev 10:4 [f]Rev 1:3
22:11 [g]Eze 3:27; Da 12:10
22:12 [h]ver 7,20 [i]Isa 40:10
22:13 [j]Rev 1:8 [k]Rev 1:17 [l]Rev 21:6

14"Blessed are those who wash their robes, that they may have
the right to the tree of life[a] and may go through the gates[b] into the
city.[c] 15Outside[d] are the dogs,[e] those who practice magic arts, the
sexually immoral, the murderers, the idolaters and everyone who
loves and practices falsehood.

16"I, Jesus,[f] have sent my angel to give you[a] this testimony for
the churches.[g] I am the Root[h] and the Offspring of David, and the
bright Morning Star."[i]

17The Spirit[j] and the bride say, "Come!" And let him who hears
say, "Come!" Whoever is thirsty, let him come; and whoever wishes,
let him take the free gift of the water of life.

18I warn everyone who hears the words of the prophecy of this
book: If anyone adds anything to them,[k] God will add to him the
plagues described in this book.[l] 19And if anyone takes words away[m]
from this book of prophecy, God will take away from him his share
in the tree of life and in the holy city, which are described in this
book.

20He who testifies to these things[n] says, "Yes, I am coming soon."
Amen. Come, Lord Jesus.[o]

21The grace of the Lord Jesus be with God's people.[p] Amen.

a 16 The Greek is plural.

22:14
a Rev 2:7
b Rev 21:12
c Rev 21:27

22:15
d 1Co 6:9,10; Gal 5:19-21; Col 3:5,6
e Php 3:2

22:16
f Rev 1:1
g Rev 1:4
h Rev 5:5
i 2Pe 1:19; Rev 2:28

22:17
j Rev 2:7

22:18
k Dt 4:2; Pr 30:6
l Rev 15:6–16:21

22:19
m Dt 4:2

22:20
n Rev 1:2
o 1Co 16:22

22:21
p Ro 16:20

Jesus' Messages to the Churches

	Description of Jesus	Commendation to the Church	Reproof Given to the Church	Warnings and Instructions to the Church	Promise to the Overcomers
Ephesus					
Smyrna					

(continued)

Jesus' Messages to the Churches

	Description of Jesus	Commendation to the Church	Reproof Given to the Church	Warnings and Instructions to the Church	Promise to the Overcomers
Pergamum					
Thyatira					

(continue

Jesus' Messages to the Churches

	Description of Jesus	Commendation to the Church	Reproof Given to the Church	Warnings and Instructions to the Church	Promise to the Overcomers
Sardis					
Philadelphia					

(continued)

Jesus' Messages to the Churches

	Description of Jesus	Commendation to the Church	Reproof Given to the Church	Warnings and Instructions to the Church	Promise to the Overcomers
Laodicea					

What Revelation Teaches About

God	Jesus	The Holy Spirit

The Seven Seals, Trumpets, and Bowls

	Seals	Trumpets	Bowls
1st			
2nd			
3rd			
4th			
5th			
6th			
7th			

Revelation at a Glance

Theme of Revelation:

Author:

Date:

Purpose:

Key Words:

God
Jesus (Christ)
in the Spirit
church(es)
throne
mystery
repent
overcome, triumphed, overpower, conquer
mark every reference to Satan (demons, devil, dragon)
later, after this (that)
and I saw, I watched, then I saw, I saw (then I looked, I looked, [as] I watched)
angel(s)
seal(s)
nation(s), Gentiles, ages
trumpet(s)
bowl(s), plague(s)
wrath, fury
beast
Babylon (woman)
earthquake, quake, voices, thunder(s), lightning

Segment Divisions				Chapter Themes
				1
				2
				3
				4
				5
				6
				7
				8
				9
				10
				11
				12
				13
				14
				15
				16
				17
				18
				19
				20
				21
				22

What the Bible Teaches about Babylon

Its First Description in Scripture	Location of Babylon The City The Babylonian Empire *(see page 2310)*
Worship Connected with Babylon	**Warnings Given about Babylon**

What the Bible Teaches about Babylon

Prophecies Regarding Babylon

Destruction of Babylon

History of Babylon's Destruction

The City

The Babylonian Empire

Details Concerning Babylon's Final Destruction

The City

The Babylonian System

REFERENCE	HOW IS IT DESCRIBED

(For further notetaking, this two-page chart is duplicated on pages 2180, 2181.)

What Happens in Nature	Signs of Beginning or End

(continued)

REFERENCE	HOW IS IT DESCRIBED

What Happens in Nature	Signs of Beginning or End

BIBLE STUDY HELPS

ITSB

UNDERSTANDING THE VALUE OF GOD'S WORD

WHAT IS THE BIBLE?

The Bible is comprised of 66 separate writings or books. It was written over a period of approximately 1400 to 1800 years by more than 40 authors from various walks of life. While many of the authors are identified, some remain unknown.

The Bible is divided into the Old Testament, comprised of 39 books, and the New Testament, comprised of 27 books. The Old Testament, the Bible of the nation of Israel, was divided into three segments: the Law or Torah, the Prophets or Nebi'im, and the Writings or Kethubim.

Although the Old Testament was written in Hebrew and Aramaic, it was translated into Koine (common) Greek around 250-100 B.C. This translation is referred to as the Septuagint or the LXX. It contains the same books as the Hebrew Old Testament, but the order and breakdown of the books was changed to the form now used in the Old Testament.

While the Old Testament was originally written in two Semitic languages, Hebrew and Aramaic, the vast majority of it is in Hebrew. The New Testament was written in Koine Greek, the popular language used throughout most of the Mediterranean world in the time of the Lord Jesus Christ. However, a few Aramaic phrases are found in the New Testament because Aramaic was the vernacular of the people of Israel. Jesus and His disciples spoke Aramaic as well as Koine Greek. Much of the Old Testament was translated into Aramaic, and these works are referred to as the Targums.

HOW WAS THE BIBLE WRITTEN AND TRANSLATED?

The Bible itself tells us how it was written: "All Scripture is God-breathed" (2 Timothy 3:16). Men "spoke from God as they were carried along by the Holy Spirit" (2 Peter 1:21). The Holy Spirit carried men along, moving and guiding them as they wrote in their own words what God wanted them to say. Thus we have *verbal* inspiration, because the words of the original text were inspired by God. And because all Scripture was given by inspiration we have *plenary* inspiration, which means total or complete inspiration. Every part of the Bible is inspired. The Bible does not merely contain the words of God, but it actually is the Word of God. Thus the original writings, often called *autographs*, are infallible—without error. This concept is called the verbal, plenary inspiration of the autographs.

Autographs

In early history, writing was done on stone, clay tablets, leather (animal skins), and papyrus scrolls. The autographs were probably written on papyrus. Papyrus, made from the inner bark of a reed plant, was formed into a paper-like material which was glued together and rolled into a scroll. Normally the writing was done on only one side of the scroll, so that as it was read it was unrolled with one hand and rolled up with the other. The scrolls were kept in a cylindrical box called a *capsa*.

According to the Jewish Talmud, the Scriptures were to be copied only on the skins of what God deemed as clean animals, such as sheep, calves, and goats. Parchment (dried animal skin) was costly but more durable and permanent than papyrus.

The Accuracy of the Copies

Eventually the scrolls were replaced by the *codex*. The codex (plural *codices*) was made from folded sheets, *quires*, which were stitched together like a book. Copies of the Old Testament were transcribed by hand under the strictest measures. The men who copied the manuscripts were called *scribes*. If one error was found the entire copy was destroyed. Thus the accuracy of the Old Testament is phenomenal. This accuracy has been confirmed by the multiple number of copies, by the Septuagint, and by the Dead Sea Scrolls.

More than 5000 ancient Greek copies of all or portions of the New Testament have been found. Although there are minor variances in the copied manuscripts, none affect doctrinal issues.

The Canon

The same omnipotent Sovereign who inspired men to write the Word of God led other men to recognize that these were the books which would comprise the *canon* of Scripture. The canon is the group of books which are recognized to be inspired by God. This group comprises the Old and New Testaments. The Old Testament canon of 39 books was fairly widely accepted in the days of Jesus Christ. Jesus himself, who is one with the Father, always affirmed and never contradicted the Old Testament. Revelation, the last of the New Testament books to be written, was completed before the end of the first century A.D. By A.D. 367 Bishop Athanasius compiled the first known list of the current 27 books of the New Testament.

Translations

The Hebrew/Aramaic and Greek copies of the 66 books of the Bible are the basis of the translations made in the various languages of the world. A translator will study the original words of these copies, determine what those words mean, and then select the best way to faithfully transmit the meaning of the original words in their context into the language of their translation. This is called a *primary translation*.

A *secondary translation* occurs when a translation is made from a primary translation of another language, say English, into a third language. Thus a secondary translation is not made from a copy of the original language but from a second language translated from the original language (the primary translation).

HOW DO WE KNOW THE BIBLE IS WHAT IT CLAIMS TO BE—THE WORD OF GOD?

Believing the Bible is ultimately a matter of informed faith. You either believe what the Word of God says about itself or you don't. You either believe the testimony of Jesus Christ regarding the Word of God or you don't.

There are several areas of objective evidence that test and support the veracity of the verbal, plenary inspiration of the autographs.

First, there is *bibliographic evidence* for the Bible's authenticity. No other ancient writings have as much manuscript evidence as does the Bible. Aside from 643 copies of Homer's works, which were written about 850 B.C., the other classical works written between 450 B.C. and 10 B.C. have anywhere from 3 to 20 copies each, but the New Testament has about 14,000. And not only is there more than an ample *quantity* of copies of the Bible, but the *quality* of the biblical manuscripts surpasses that of other manuscripts as well.

The passage of time is also a factor. The Dead Sea Scrolls, which date from 200 B.C. to A.D. 68, greatly reduce the time span between the writing of the Old Testament books to our earliest existing copies of the Old Testament. The time span between the autographs of the New Testament and its oldest existing copies is between 100 and 400 years, a very low figure.

Second, there is *internal evidence* for the authenticity of the Bible. The Bible not only claims to be the Word of God, but it also states that not the smallest letter or stroke will pass away from the law (the Old Testament) until all is accomplished (Matthew 5:17, 18). Many of the writers claimed to be eyewitnesses who wrote what they saw, heard, or experienced. Although over 40 different authors wrote 66 separate books over a time span of almost two millennia, there are no contradictions in what they wrote. Also, what was written in the Old Testament, sealed and canonized, is often seen fulfilled in the New Testament. Thus there is the internal evidence of fulfilled prophecy, some of which is being fulfilled even in our time.

Finally, there is an abundance of *external evidence* that supports the Bible's infallibility. When the Bible speaks on matters of history or science, it speaks accurately. There were times when it was supposed that science or history contradicted the Bible; however, later it was discovered that all the facts had not yet been uncovered.

More recent archaeological evidence has affirmed the historicity of the Bible in a multitude of ways as it speaks regarding rulers, nations, languages, battles, customs, geographic locations, tragedies, and other events. Extrabiblical writings also affirm what the New Testament teaches about the historicity of Jesus Christ and other New Testament characters.

Have you accepted the Bible as the inerrant Word of God, profitable for teaching, rebuking, correcting, and training in righteousness, that you may be thoroughly equipped for every good work? (2 Timothy 3:16). As you study the Bible, you will discover that it is a supernatural book...the very words of life.

MAJOR EVENTS IN ISRAEL'S HISTORY

The Word of God takes on new life when a person understands the major events in Israel's history between the years of Abraham and the birth of Christ. Old and New Testament prophecies regarding Israel and her relationship to various world powers are seen in a new dimension.

Once you are acquainted with the religious, cultural, and political setting of Bible times, you will better understand God's plan for mankind and you will have a greater appreciation of the times in which our Lord lived and gave birth to his church.

FROM ADAM TO ABRAHAM
(The Beginning to About 2000 B.C.)

In the beginning there was no sin. Adam and Eve lived in unbroken fellowship with their Creator until they believed a lie and chose to disobey the explicit command of God. From that time on all mankind would be born in sin and bear its consequence: death.

Yet a merciful and loving God did not leave mankind in despair; he promised a Redeemer, born of a woman's seed. Over a thousand years passed, and with the passing of those years man's iniquity increased until every intent of his heart was only evil. God was grieved in his heart "that he had made man." And with that he determined to "wipe mankind…from the face of the earth." But Noah found favor in the eyes of the Lord, for he was a righteous man, blameless in his time.

When the flood came, only those in the ark were preserved: Noah and his family, eight people in all. However, the basic sin nature of those who survived had not changed, and it wasn't long before they too were in rebellion against God. And God knew that because they were one society and had the same language, nothing which they purposed to do would be impossible for them.

So once again God intervened, though not this time to destroy man from the face of the earth, for he had put a rainbow in the heavens and had made a covenant which he would not break. God intervened by confusing mankind's language and scattering them over the face of the whole earth.

Then around 2000 B.C. God called a man to leave Ur of the Chaldees and go to a land which he would show him. That man's name was Abram. From Abram God would not only make a great nation, but through him he would bless all the families of the earth. Thus God made a covenant with Abram and his descendants forever, and with that covenant he changed Abram's name to Abraham, "Father of Many." With that covenant also came the promise of the land of Canaan as the eternal possession of Abraham's descendants.

The Seed that God promised Adam and Eve, the one who would redeem mankind, would come not only through the seed of the woman, but also through the loins of Abraham and his descendants, Isaac and Jacob. To Isaac would be born Jacob, and to Jacob 12 sons. As God confirmed his covenant with Jacob, he changed Jacob's name to Israel, the one who fathered the heads of the 12 tribes of Israel. A covenant nation had been brought into existence by God. In the fullness of time the Redeemer, the messenger of the covenant, would come from the tribe of Judah.

But all was not well among Jacob's sons, for they were jealous of Joseph, Jacob's favorite, his firstborn by Rachel. As they plotted to take Joseph's life, Reuben and Judah intervened, and Joseph was sold into slavery and taken to Egypt. While Joseph's brothers meant to harm him, God meant it for good. Joseph went from being a slave in Potiphar's house to being a vice-regent in Pharaoh's palace via a prison. In his sovereignty God used Joseph's position in Egypt to deliver Israel's family from famine in Canaan. They lived in Egypt a total of 430 years, the majority of these as slaves. Then around 1525 B.C. a son by the name of Moses was born to two of these Hebrew slaves.

FROM THE EXODUS UNDER MOSES TO THE MONARCHY UNDER SAUL

(1445 B.C. to 1051 or 1043 B.C.)

It was about 80 years after the birth of Moses that the sons of Israel cried out to the God of Abraham, Isaac, and Jacob because of their great affliction. God heard their cry and appeared to Moses in a burning bush. The great I AM would deliver them from the house of bondage, from the land of Egypt, and take them to the land He promised to Abraham. Moses would serve as God's spokesman, as their human deliverer, and as the one to whom God would give the pattern for the tabernacle. In the tabernacle God would give the Israelites not only the means of worshiping him, but a picture of the Redeemer who was yet to come.

After the Israelites wandered in the wilderness for 40 years because of their unbelief, Joshua took them across the Jordan River into the promised land. The people served the Lord all the days of Joshua and the elders, and then there arose a generation who did not know Joshua, and the children of Israel served the gods of the people of Canaan and did evil in the sight of the Lord. So the Lord delivered them into the hands of their enemies. But when the people cried out to the Lord in their distress, God raised up judges from among the people. And God was with each judge all the days of his life. But when the judge died, the cycle of sin and slavery repeated itself. There was no visible king in Israel and everyone did what was right in his own eyes. It was to be a theocracy, with God as King, but the people did not obey their God.

Finally, in the days of Samuel, the prophet and judge, the people insisted on having a king over them like the other nations. Although this request grieved Samuel, God gave them what they wanted, for they had rejected him.

FROM UNITED KINGDOM TO DIVIDED KINGDOM

(1051 or 1043 B.C. to 931 B.C.)

Saul, Israel's first king, gave God sacrifice rather than obedience, and so God raised up a man after his own heart. David, the son of Jesse from the tribe of Judah, was anointed by God to become king.

David reigned from 1011 to 971 B.C. During that time his passion was to build a permanent dwelling for God in Jerusalem, the city of David. God saw the intent of David's heart, but because David had been a man of war, the building of the temple would be the task of David's son and successor, Solomon, born to Bathsheba.

On the day when the ark of the covenant was brought into the temple and the temple was dedicated to the Lord, Solomon fell on his face before God and reminded him of his covenant promises. Fire came from heaven and devoured the burnt offerings, and the glory of the Lord filled the temple.

But Solomon disobeyed God. He married foreign wives and set up their idols on high places in Jerusalem. When Solomon was old, his wives turned his heart away after other gods and his heart was not wholly devoted to serving God, as the heart of his father, David, had been.

After Solomon died, God tore the kingdom of Israel in two.

FROM 931 B.C. UNTIL THE BIRTH OF CHRIST

In 931 B.C. the tribes of Judah and Benjamin formed the southern kingdom of Judah, with Jerusalem as their capital. The remaining ten tribes formed the northern kingdom of Israel and eventually made Samaria their capital. The northern kingdom immediately began to worship idols, so in 722 B.C. God allowed the Assyrians to take them captive.

Although the southern kingdom was warned by the prophets of God that they too would go into captivity if they did not repent of their disobedience and idolatry, Judah did not listen. In 605 B.C., just before Nebuchadnezzar became king of Babylon, he attacked Jerusalem and took the king and some of his nobles captive to Babylon. Among them was Daniel (Daniel 1:1, 2). In 597 B.C. Nebuchadnezzar again attacked Judah, this time taking about 10,000 captives to Babylon, Ezekiel among them. Then in 586 B.C. Babylon, now the predominant world power, conquered Judah and destroyed not only the city of Jerusalem but the magnificent temple built by Solomon during his reign over Israel.

Separated from Jerusalem and their temple, the exiles established **synagogues** as a means of preserving their faith. The synagogues became centers of learning and worship where the Jews recited the **Shema** (Deuteronomy 6:4), read from the law and the prophets, prayed, and delivered messages.

Men trained in writing who recorded events and decisions were called **scribes**. They assumed the responsibility of copying, preserving, and even teaching the Word of God in the synagogues. By New Testament times the scribes were considered experts in interpreting and teaching the law and were referred to as lawyers.

Having experienced firsthand the cursings of disobedience as promised in the book of Deuteronomy, the exiled Jews seemed to gain a new respect and appreciation for the Word of God. They saw that God meant what he said and would not alter it even for his covenant people.

It was sometime after the kingdom divided and Judah went into captivity that the exiles became known as **men of Judah** or **Jews**.

The Persian Period
(539 to 331 B.C.)

When the Medes and the Persians conquered Babylon in 539 B.C., they became the predominant world power in Babylon's stead. Daniel 5 records this invasion.

Approximately 175 years before Cyrus (the king of Persia) was born, Isaiah prophesied that God would raise up Cyrus to accomplish all that he pleased (Isaiah 44:28). Second Chronicles 36:22, 23 records the fulfillment of God's plan: Cyrus issued a proclamation allowing the exiles of Judah to return to Jerusalem and rebuild their temple. Just as Jeremiah had prophesied (Jeremiah 29:10; Daniel 9:2), exactly 70 years from the time of Babylon's first attack on Jerusalem, the Israelites were allowed to return to their land.

The group which returned is referred to in Scripture as the **remnant**. ***Diaspora***, the Greek word for scattering, became the term used to describe the Jews who remained in exile among the nations.

The book of Ezra records the return of the remnant and the building of the **second temple** during the time of Haggai and Zechariah. The book of Nehemiah records the rebuilding of the walls of Jerusalem. Nehemiah and Ezra were contemporaries. Ezra is referred to as a **scribe**.

The book of Malachi records the last Old Testament prophecy given by God. After this prophecy God did not inspire canonical Scripture again for 400 years.

This 400 years of silence which followed the book of Malachi is called the **intertestament period**. Although God was silent in that he did not speak through his prophets during this time, the events of these 400 years testify to the fulfillment of much that was written by Daniel the prophet.

These years could be divided into three periods: the Greek, the Maccabean, and the beginning of the Roman period.

The Greek Period

(331 to 63 B.C.)

The Greek period encompasses four different rulerships over Jerusalem, which includes the Maccabean rule.

Under Alexander the Great
(331 to 323 B.C.)

As the Persian Empire grew and threatened the security of the city-states of Greece, Philip of Macedonia sought to consolidate Greece in an effort to resist attack from Persia.

In 336 B.C. Philip was murdered, and his son, Alexander, who was about 20 years old, became king over the Greek Empire. Within two years Alexander set out to conquer Persia, whose empire now extended westward as far as Asia Minor (modern-day Turkey).

Over the next two years Alexander conquered the territory from Asia Minor to Pakistan and to Egypt, which included the land of the Jews. Although the account is not universally accepted by other historians, Josephus, a Jewish historian who lived about A.D. 37-100, wrote that as Alexander marched into Jerusalem he was met by Jaddua and other Jewish priests dressed in their priestly garments and by the people of Jerusalem wearing white robes.

In a dream Jaddua had been told to put wreaths on the city walls in order to greet Alexander. Alexander also had a dream which coincided with this event. When Alexander was escorted into Jerusalem and shown the prophecy in Daniel 8 which described the destruction of the Medo-Persian Empire by a large horn on a goat (which represented Greece), Alexander felt the prophecy pertained to him and offered the Jews whatever they wanted. Alexander treated the Jews well and did not harm Jerusalem or their rebuilt temple.

When Alexander built the city of Alexandria in Egypt, he encouraged many Jews to settle there in order to help populate the city. Whenever Alexander conquered an area he established Greek cities and colonies, bringing in his Greek culture, ideas, and language. His goal was to consolidate his empire through a common way of life and thinking which became known as **Hellenization. Koine Greek** became the common language in the countries ruled by Greece and continued to be the primary language of civilization through the time of Christ. The New Testament was written in Koine Greek.

By 331 B.C. Alexander had conquered Persia. He and his war-weary army returned to Babylon in 323 B.C. When Alexander, one of the greatest military leaders in history, returned to Babylon, history tells us he sat down and wept because there were no more territories to conquer. He died in Babylon in 323 B.C. at the age of 33.

Because Alexander the Great died without an appointed heir, his kingdom fell into chaos. After 22 years of struggle among his generals, it was divided among four of them: Lysimachus, Cassander, Ptolemy I Soter, and Seleucus I Nicator. (See chart on next page.)

Under the Ptolemies of Egypt
(323 to 204 B.C.)

Ptolemy I Soter, who took Egypt, was given Jerusalem and Judea. The Jews fared well; they were allowed to govern themselves and practice their religion without interference. Under his leadership Jews were permitted to go to Egypt. Some Jews were invited to go to Alexandria and become scholars. The Ptolemies moved Egypt's capital from Memphis to Alexandria and made it the center of learning and commerce. There

The Division of Alexander the Great's Empire

Lysimachus took Thrace and Bithynia	**Cassander** took Macedonia	**Ptolemy I Soter** took Egypt	**Seleucus I Nicator** took Syria

Ptolemy I Soter and Seleucus I Nicator began a succession of competing dynasties for which the land of Israel became a pawn.

(see page 1524 for the chart showing these dynasties)

the Jews were encouraged to use the Greek library, at that time the most extensive and best in the world. As a result many were caught up in philosophy and logic and drank deeply from the cup of Hellenism.

It is believed that Ptolemy II Philadelphus commissioned the translation of the Pentateuch into the Koine Greek. The Greek translation of the entire Old Testament, eventually completed about 100 B.C., was referred to as the **Septuagint** (meaning 70), or abbreviated as the **LXX**. Many of the New Testament writers quoted from the Septuagint.

Other writings produced during this intertestament period are the **Apocrypha**, the **Pseudepigrapha**, and the **Qumran Scrolls** (also called the **Dead Sea Scrolls**). The **Apocrypha** are composed of a variety of writings, including apocalyptic, wisdom, and historical literature. It is from the apocryphal book of First Maccabees that historians gained insight into the period from the Maccabean revolt through the time of John Hyrcanus. The Apocrypha were included in the Septuagint, although they were not part of the Hebrew Scriptures.

The **Pseudepigrapha** are a collection of writings even more extensive than the Apocrypha, but scholars cannot entirely agree on which writings comprise this group. These writings are attributed to noted people such as Adam, Abraham, Enoch, Ezra, and Baruch—but scholars agree that these claims are not authentic.

The **Qumran** or **Dead Sea Scrolls** were manuscripts apparently written or copied between 200 B.C. and A.D. 70 by a Jewish religious sect called **Essenes**. The particular community of Essenes who lived close to the Dead Sea seem to have practiced celibacy and a strictly disciplined communal lifestyle, separating themselves from others. The Dead Sea Scrolls describe the lives and beliefs of this group which lived in the last two centuries before Christ; they also include the oldest known manuscripts of the Old Testament. The scrolls are so named because they were hidden and preserved in some caves near an archaeological excavation called Khirbet Qumran on the western side of the Dead Sea.

Under the Seleucid Kings of Syria (204 to 165 B.C.)

Those ruling Syria, referred to as the kings of the north in Daniel 11, wanted the beautiful land of Israel. When Antiochus III the Great conquered Ptolemy V Epiphanes of Egypt, Jerusalem and Judea were brought under Syrian dominance.

During this period the land of Israel was sectored into Judea, Samaria, Galilee, Perea, and Trachonitis (see map on next page).

After gaining dominance over the Jews, Antiochus was defeated by the Romans and ended up having to pay Rome a large sum of money for a period of years. To make sure he complied, Rome held his son, Antiochus IV, hostage in Rome.

Antiochus III the Great was succeeded by his son Seleucus IV Philopator, who ruled from 187-175 B.C. In 175 B.C. Antiochus IV Epiphanes (the son who had been held hostage in Rome) usurped the throne by killing his brother. He ruled until 163 B.C. He was called *Epiphanes*, which means "manifest" or "splendid."

Until this period in Israel's history, the priesthood had been a matter of birthright and the office was held for life. However, during his reign Antiochus IV Epiphanes sold the priesthood to Jason, the brother of the high priest. Jason also paid Antiochus a high price in order to build a Greek gymnasium near the temple. During this time many Jews were lured into a Hellenistic way of life. All this brought a great conflict among the orthodox Jews and the "Hellenistic" Jews.

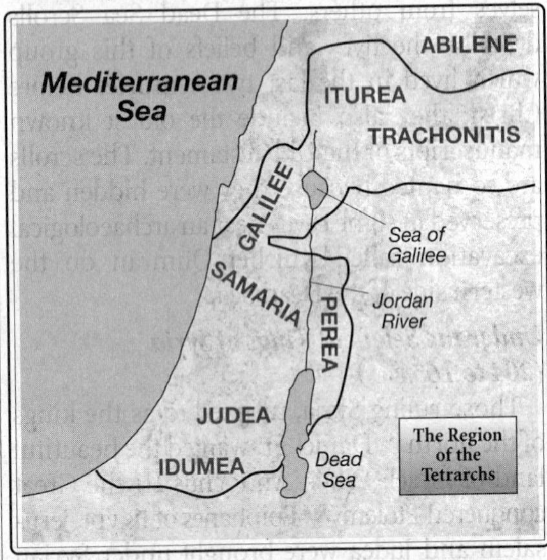

The conflict was heightened when Antiochus IV Epiphanes sought to take the throne of Egypt but was rebuffed by Rome. Because of that and because of what he surmised as a revolt in the priesthood, Antiochus unleashed his anger on those Jews who wouldn't curry his favor or fully adopt Hellenism. He was determined to destroy Judaism. Circumcision was forbidden; those who disobeyed were put to death. Copies of the law were desecrated with heathen symbols or burned, while anyone found with a copy of the law was to be put to death. The Jews were also forbidden to celebrate the Sabbath. Then Antiochus sacrificed a pig on the altar in the temple and erected a statue of Zeus, the abomination that causes desolation, in the holy place (Daniel 11:31).

Finally, Antiochus sent his officers throughout the land to compel Jews to make sacrifices to Zeus.

The Maccabean Period

(165 to 63 B.C.)

When Antiochus IV Epiphanes' officer arrived in the village of Modein (which lies halfway between Jerusalem and Joppa) and commanded the aged priest Mattathias to make a sacrifice to Zeus, the officer didn't know it was the last official duty he would perform in his life. As Mattathias refused, a younger Jew stepped forward to take his place. When he did, a furious Mattathias plunged his knife not only into the Jewish volunteer but also into the Syrian officer. Mattathias fled with his five sons to the hills…and the Maccabean revolt, led by Mattathias's third son, nicknamed Maccabeus (the Hammerer), began.

Three years after Antiochus IV Epiphanes defiled the temple, the Jews recaptured Jerusalem. They removed the statue of Zeus and refurbished the temple and reinstituted Jewish sacrifices. On December 25 the Jews celebrated with the Feast of Dedication (John 10:22), which from then on became the annual feast of lights or Hanukkah. (See Herod's Temple on page IISB-38.)

Thus began what is referred to as the **Hasmonean Dynasty** as the descendants of Mattathias ruled Israel until Rome conquered Jerusalem in 63 B.C.

When Simon, the last surviving son of Mattathias, was murdered, Simon's son, John Hyrcanus, named himself priest and king. He ruled from 134-104 B.C. He destroyed the Samaritan temple on Mount Gerizim, and from that time on the Jews had no dealings with the Samaritans. After that Hyrcanus moved southeast and conquered the land of the Idumeans, who came from the ancient kingdom of Edom. The peoples of this land were given the choice of emigrating or converting to Judaism. This was the land of Herod the Great, who would someday become Rome's appointed king of the Jews.

During the reign of John Hyrcanus, the **Pharisees**, a religious sect of the Jews, arose from the Hasidim. The **Hasidim**, a militant religious community dedicated to the obedience of the law and the worship of God, began around 168 B.C. and was active during the Maccabean revolt. The word *Pharisee* means "separated one" and was probably used to describe these men because they separated themselves from the strong influence of Hellenism. During New Testament times the majority of the scribes were Pharisees.

Doctrinally the Pharisees viewed the entire Old Testament as authoritative; however, they also accepted the oral tradition as equally authoritative. To the Pharisee, to study the law was true worship. They believed in life after death, the resurrection, and the existence of angels and demons. Although the Pharisees taught that the way to God was through keeping the law, they were more liberal in their interpretation of the law than were the Sadducees. The Pharisees represented the largest religious sect, but their numbers declined when they fell into John Hyrcanus' disfavor.

The **Sadducees**, a smaller religious sect comprised mostly of the upper classes, were often of the priestly line and were usually more wealthy than the Pharisees. For the most part the Pharisees were of the middle-class merchants and tradesmen. The Sadducees accepted only the **Torah** (the first five books of the Old Testament) as authoritative. While they were rigid in the observance of the law and held to its literal interpretation, they denied divine providence,

The Hasmonean Dynasty

Mattathias
Died 166/165 B.C.

John
Died 159 B.C.

Simon
Led revolt
141-135 B.C.

Judas Maccabeus
Died 160 B.C.
(*called Maccabeus–the Hammerer*)
First leader of revolt

Eleazar
Died 163 B.C.

Jonathan
Led revolt
160-141 B.C.

Judas
Died 134 B.C.

John Hyrcanus I
High priest and king, 134-104 B.C.

Mattathias
Died 134 B.C.

Judas Aristobulus I
Ruled 104-103 B.C.
married Salome Alexandra
murdered 103 B.C.

Alexander Jannaeus
High priest and king, 103-76 B.C.
married Salome Alexandra (Aristobulus' widow)
Salome ruled 76-67 B.C.

Antigonus

Hyrcanus II
High priest and governor, 63-40 B.C.,
died 30 B.C.

Aristobulus II
King 67-63 B.C.
died 49 B.C.
his granddaughter Miriam (Mariamne)
married Herod the Great

the resurrection, life after death, the existence of angels and demons, and any reward or punishment after death. They opposed the oral law as obligatory or binding and were materialistic.

The Sadducees controlled the temple and its services. However, because the Sadducees leaned toward Hellenism, they were unpopular with the majority of the Jewish populace.

Aristobulus I, who succeeded his father, John Hyrcanus, married Salome Alexandra. However, when Aristobulus died, Salome married his brother Alexander Jannaeus, who became high priest and king in 103 B.C. This marriage created many enemies for Alexander Jannaeus because the high priest was to marry only a virgin.

When he died in 76 B.C., his wife, Salome Alexandra, took the throne, but as a woman she could not hold the office of high priest, so her oldest son, Hyrcanus II, assumed that position.

Civil war broke out when Salome died, because her younger son, Aristobulus II, who was supported by the Sadducees, sought to take the throne from Hyrcanus II. He was willing to give up that position, but Antipater (an Idumean and the father of Herod the Great) befriended Hyrcanus and persuaded him to seek outside help in order to regain his position as the rightful heir. Hyrcanus' forces came against Aristobulus and defeated him. He had to flee and made the temple in Jerusalem his fortress, but he was besieged by Hyrcanus' forces.

Early in this period the Hasmoneans had made a treaty with Rome in order to keep Syria, their northern neighbors, in check. Now the Roman army under Scaurus was in Syria because Seleucid rule had collapsed. Scaurus heard about the civil war in Judea and went there. Both Aristobulus and Hyrcanus sought his help. Scaurus sided with Aristobulus and had the siege lifted from Jerusalem, but the fighting continued. An appeal was made to the Roman general Pompey, who said he would settle the dispute and urged them to keep peace until he arrived. However, Aristobulus went back to Jerusalem to prepare resistance, which caused Rome's support to turn to Hyrcanus. Pompey arrived and took Aristobulus and his family captive, besieging the city for three months.

The Period of Roman Rule

(63 B.C. to A.D. 70)

In 63 B.C. Pompey conquered Jerusalem and with some of his soldiers walked into the Most Holy Place. Although they didn't touch any of the furnishings, they alienated the Jews, who never forgave Pompey. About 12,000 Jews died during this Roman siege of Jerusalem, a supposed attempt to settle a civil war.

Rome broke up the Hasmonean dynasty and their territory. Judea was now reduced to smaller borders and its independence lost. It was now a territory of Rome. Hyrcanus II could be the rightful priest but not king. He was now under the governor of Syria, a Roman province. Scaurus was appointed governor. Aristobulus and many Jews were taken to Rome. Not much later Gabinius, a Roman governor of Syria, took control. He entrusted the temple to Hyrcanus and changed the government of Judea.

The Jewish state was divided into five districts governed by a council that remained under the jurisdiction of the governor of Syria; Hyrcanus, the high priest, was made ruler over Jerusalem. Antipater was his chief magistrate.

The high priest presided over the **Sanhedrin**, a 71-member council comprised of both Sadducees and Pharisees, which governed the Jews under the authority of Rome. Although the Sanhedrin seemed to have autonomy in the matters of the civil and criminal government of the Jews, apparently the Sanhedrin was not allowed to put people to death without the permission of the Roman procurator. The Sanhedrin is often referred to as "the council" in the Gospels and Acts.

In 55 B.C. three men—Pompey, Crassus (the governor of Syria), and Julius Caesar—controlled Rome. Crassus, considering himself another Alexander the Great, set out to conquer the world. However, just before this he stole the treasures from the temple in Jerusalem. Crassus and his army were later destroyed by the Parthians.

Parthia, southeast of the Caspian Sea and part of the Persian Empire, had been conquered by Alexander the Great. But Rome would not conquer them until A.D. 114.

After Crassus' death, Julius Caesar took Italy and then set out to destroy Pompey. Pompey fled to Egypt, where he was assassinated. During this time Antipater supported Caesar, so out of gratitude Caesar gave him the official title of Procurator of Judea.

Antipater made his son Phasael governor of Judea and his son Herod governor of Galilee. Hyrcanus II remained high priest, although Antipater and his two sons robbed him of his authority.

In 44 B.C. Caesar was murdered by Brutus and Cassius. Civil war broke out in Rome. Cassius took control of the east. Because of the instability of Rome, Hyrcanus' rivals made a bid for power.

Antipater was murdered in 43 B.C. Antigonus, Aristobulus' son (who was supported by the Parthians), invaded the country.

At that time Herod came to the aid of Hyrcanus, who out of gratitude gave Herod a beautiful woman named Miriam. They were not married until five years later.

After that Brutus and Cassius were defeated by Mark Antony and Caesar's nephew Octavian (who would later become Caesar Augustus). Mark Antony became ruler of the east. In 40 B.C., when the Parthians invaded Palestine, Herod fled to Rome.

That year, at the urging of Antony and Octavian, Herod was made king of the Jews. It took him three years to rid the area of the Parthians and establish his rule in Judea. Just before laying siege to Jerusalem, Herod married Miriam (also called Mariamne), hoping that his marriage into the Hasmonean family would make him more acceptable to the Jews.

In 20 B.C. Herod began rebuilding the temple. The one built by Zerubbabel after the Babylonian exile was so pitifully small in comparison to the first temple that Herod was determined to make it larger and more magnificent than Solomon's. Although the temple itself was completed in a year-and-a-half, the construction and decoration of its outer courts continued for years, so in A.D. 26 the Jews would say, "It has taken forty-six years to build this temple" (John 2:20).

Herod, whose people (the Idumeans) had been forced to convert to Judaism under John Hyrcanus, was only a Jew in practice when he lived in Judea. Although Rome gave Herod the title "King of the Jews," he was never accepted by those he ruled over.

Then "during the time of King Herod, Magi from the east came to Jerusalem and asked, 'Where is the one who has been born king of the Jews?'" (Matthew 2:1, 2).

The true King had come…the Ruler who would shepherd God's people Israel (Matthew 2:6).

Herod died in 4 B.C. But those living in Judea and Galilee saw a great light and heard with their own ears the voice of God, the King of kings.

The 400 years of silence had been broken.

FROM CHRIST TO MODERN TIMES

Many Jewish leaders were religious, but they did not know God. When Jesus came to explain the Father, they rejected Him. They rejected God's precious cornerstone. Consequently, once again they would be banished from their land. Jesus warned, "When you see Jerusalem surrounded by armies, you will know that its desolation is near. There will be great distress in the land and wrath against this people. They will fall by the sword and will be taken as prisoners to all the nations. Jerusalem will be trampled on by the Gentiles until the times of the Gentiles are fulfilled" (Luke 21:20, 23, 24). God had spoken. Had the people listened, they wouldn't have been caught unawares—but they refused to hear.

The Destruction of Jerusalem

(A.D. 70)

The conflict between the Jews and their Roman ruler intensified. Tacitus, the Roman historian, said the Jews put up with things until the procuratorship of Gessius Florus. When the Jews rose up against Florus' army, war became inevitable. Nero commanded T. Flavius Vespasian to subdue the Jews. Vespasian reduced northern Palestine and secured the rest of the country, except for Jerusalem, Masada, and two other fortresses.

During this time, Nero committed suicide and civil war broke out in Rome. Galba, Otho, and Vitellius succeeded one another as emperor. Then the eastern legions of Rome proclaimed Vespasian emperor, and Vitellius was murdered. Vespasian put his son Titus in charge of the war and sailed for Rome. In A.D. 70 Titus besieged Jerusalem. Over one million Jews died in five months. On August 6, Roman forces invaded the temple and, just as Jesus prophesied, not one stone was left upon the other. Jerusalem was burned. Titus went to Rome to celebrate his victory with his father.

Although some of the Jews fled to Masada, the Jewish state no longer existed. Sometime between A.D. 72-74 Masada fell to the Roman governor Flavius Silva.

Hadrian and Aelia Capitolina

In A.D. 132 the Emperor Hadrian banned circumcision and the observance of the Sabbath. He also made plans to build a temple to Zeus. These actions spurred Simon bar Kochba to lead another revolt. After Hadrian crushed the Bar Kochba revolt, Hadrian rebuilt Jerusalem in A.D. 136, named it Aelia Capitolina, and forbade the Jews entrance to the city on pain of death. That edict was enforced for about 500 years.

The Byzantine Period

(A.D. 324 to 638)

In A.D. 324 Constantine became sole emperor of Rome. In A.D. 330 the capital was moved from Rome to Byzantium, which was renamed Constantinople (present-day Istanbul, Turkey) in his honor. According to tradition, Constantine became a Christian after seeing a vision of a cross and hearing the words, "By this sign thou shalt conquer." He proclaimed Christianity as the official religion of the Roman Empire.

Constantine's mother, the empress Helena, began restoring the city of David (Jerusalem), locating Christian sites and building shrines over the places associated with Christianity. Helena and the city's bishop, Macarius, built the Church of the Holy Sepulchre on the site where they believed Jesus had been buried. Byzantine churches could be seen across the land. By the fifth century the Roman Empire divided and the eastern half became the Byzantine Empire, with its capital in Constantinople. Rome became the capital of the western Roman Empire.

In the fifth century the Jews were permitted to pray on the temple mount on Tisha B'Av, the anniversary of the destruction of the temple. By the middle of this century Jerusalem was recognized as a patriarchal territory equal in status to Constantinople, Alexandria, Rome, and Antioch.

In A.D. 614 the Persians conquered the land, massacred the people, and destroyed the churches. In A.D. 629 the Byzantine emperor Heraclius reconquered Jerusalem.

The Early Muslim Period
(A.D. 638 to 1099)

Nine years later the Muslims were ruling. During this time Christians and Jews were permitted to worship freely. Jews returned to Jerusalem. The Umayyad dynasty reigned from 660-750. The prophet Mohammed's journey from Mecca to Jerusalem on his winged horse Al-buraq was linked to the temple mount, thus making it a holy site for the Muslims. In the seventh century, Caliph Abd al-Malik commissioned the building of the mosque, the Dome of the Rock, on the temple mount. Thus Jerusalem became the third-holiest city for Islam. The Arabs built only one new city, Ramle, which Suleiman made his capital in the eighth century.

The Crusader Period
(A.D. 1099 to 1244)

In 1099, at Pope Urban II's appeal, the Crusaders crossed Europe to liberate the Christian holy places from the Muslims. The city was theirs after a five-week siege. Jerusalem became the capital of the Crusader kingdom of Jerusalem. European Christian noblemen and bourgeoisie came to settle in Jerusalem. Mosques were turned into churches, and new churches and monasteries were built. For the next 88 years, Jews and Muslims were not permitted to live in Jerusalem, but only visit it.

The Ayyubid Interlude
(A.D. 1187 to 1192)

In 1187 Saladin, the founder of the Ayyubid dynasty, took Jerusalem, destroyed the cross on top of the Dome of the Rock, and turned churches into mosques. The Jews were now allowed to return to Jerusalem. They came from North Africa, France, and England to settle alongside the Jews of Jerusalem.

Then in 1192 Richard the Lion Hearted and Phillipe Auguste of France restored the Crusader kingdom which had been conquered by Saladin. Jerusalem was divided. The temple mount and its mosques remained in Muslim hands while the other parts of the city came under Christian rule. In 1244 the Crusaders lost the city.

The Mamluk Period
(A.D. 1260 to 1517)

In 1260 Jerusalem was conquered by the Mamluks, military regiments from central Asia who were the new rulers of Egypt. The Mamluks established **madrasas** (institutes of religious instruction) and hostels for Muslim scholars and pilgrims.

The Ottoman Period
(A.D. 1517 to 1917)

The Ottoman Empire, comprised of Constantinople, Asia Minor, parts of Europe and the Balkans, Egypt, and Syria, added Palestine in 1517. Jerusalem was taken from the Mamluks by Ottoman Turks. Sultan Suleiman the Magnificent had the walls which still surround Jerusalem built at this time. After his death the Jewish community became more firmly entrenched as they built the Jewish quarter along the Zion Gate. Jewish scholastic centers were established in Jerusalem and Safed. The Christians split into various eastern communities.

In 1832 the Pasha of Egypt, Mohammed Ali, denuded the Holy Land of trees as he set out to build his ships. However, his approval of Christian missions and schools, foreign consulates, and archaeological expeditions opened up Jerusalem to Western influence. In the late 1800s a political movement called Zionism sprang up in Europe. Its goal was to create a homeland for Jewish people in Palestine. Jews fleeing eastern Europe and Russia and arriving in Abraham's land were quick to adopt Theodor Herzl's vision for a free state for Jews. In 1897, the first Zionist Congress was held.

The British Mandate
(A.D. 1917 to 1948)

Four hundred years of Ottoman rule came to an end on December 9, 1917. Two days later British Field Marshal Allenby entered the Citadel and Jerusalem was pronounced the capital of the country. The Balfour Declaration promised the establishment of a national home for the Jews. In 1920 and 1929 Jews and Arabs had violent clashes. The Arabs rebelled in 1936-1939, and open war erupted as Arabs and Jews fought for control over Jerusalem.

From 1939 to 1945 six million Jews were systematically murdered under the direction of Adolf Hitler. After World War II, world opinion strongly favored the establishment of a Jewish homeland. By November 1947 the tension between Jews and Arabs was so great the United Nations decided to intervene, end the Mandate, and make Jerusalem an international city. The United Nations voted 33 to 13 to partition Palestine west of the Jordan River into two parts—one for Arabs, one for Jews. The Jews agreed, but the Arabs rejected the plan.

The State of Israel
(May 14, 1948)

On May 14, 1948, when the British withdrew, the Jews proclaimed the independent State of Israel. The next day Israel was attacked by Iraq, Lebanon, Syria, Jordan, and Egypt. By December Israel won its independence. Jordanian soldiers, however, remained in the West Bank (biblical Judea and Samaria). Egypt held the Gaza Strip. When a cease-fire was declared in January 1949, the city was divided. Jordan held all the shrines encompassed by Suleiman's walls; the old city of Jerusalem was out-of-bounds for the Jews.

Israel prepared for the influx of more than 800,000 immigrants from 102 countries during the next seven years. Living conditions were austere, but the Jews were home! By 1957 the malarial swamps of the Hula Valley were drained and the waters of the Sea of Galilee flowed south through pipelines, bringing life to the arid Negev.

The Sinai Campaign
(1956)

In 1956 Israel executed a swift victory over Egypt in the Sinai Campaign. On the guarantee of freedom of navigation in the Straits of Tiran and the Gulf of Elath, Israel withdrew her troops from the Sinai. Then later, once again, Egyptian troops moved to Israel's borders.

The Six-Day War
(1967)

The Six-Day War broke out on June 5, 1967. During that war Israel occupied Judea, Samaria, and Gaza, took the Golan Heights, and reunited Jerusalem under Jewish sovereignty for the first time since the Bar Kochba revolt, more than 1800 years earlier. The Jews could finally weep at the holy wall of Jerusalem, the wall of the sacred temple mount.

The Yom Kippur War
(1973)

In 1973, on Yom Kippur, the highest of holy days, Israel was attacked on Syrian and Egyptian fronts. After three weeks the Israeli defense forces finally drove the attackers back. Disengagement agreements were signed between Israel and Egypt and between Israel and Syria.

The Peace Treaty Between Israel and Egypt
(1979)

In March of 1979 Israel and Egypt signed a historic peace treaty returning the Sinai to Egypt.

On June 6, 1982, Israel launched Operation Peace for Galilee in order to remove from Lebanese territory the Palestine Liberation Organization's threat to its northern settlements.

The Middle East Gulf War (1991)

In January 1991, when war broke out between Iraq and a coalition of nations headed by the United States of America, Iraq responded with missile attacks on Israel—although Israel was not part of the conflict and remained out of the conflict at the United States's urging. The Middle East Gulf Crisis came to an end approximately six weeks later.

The words of Zechariah the prophet remain unfulfilled, but because of all that is transpiring, they are read with new insight and great anticipation:

> *A day of the LORD is coming when your plunder will be divided among you. I will gather all the nations to Jerusalem to fight against it; the city will be captured, the houses ransacked, and the women raped. Half of the city will go into exile, but the rest of the people will not be taken from the city. Then the LORD will go out and fight against those nations, as he fights on the day of battle.*
>
> *On that day his feet will stand on the Mount of Olives, east of Jerusalem, and the Mount of Olives will be split in two from east to west, forming a great valley, with half of the mountain moving north and half moving south. . . .*
>
> *Then the LORD my God will come, and all the holy ones with him…*
>
> *The LORD will be king over the whole earth. On that day there will be one LORD, and his name the only name* (Zechariah 14:1-5, 9).
>
> *Amen. Come, Lord Jesus* (Revelation 22:20).

*H*ISTORICAL AND *G*RAMMATICAL *H*ELPS

The information in this section will provide you with additional tools for your inductive study of God's Word.

Take some time to familiarize yourself with the basic content of each part of this section so you will know what is at your fingertips when you need it.

THE ARK OF THE COVENANT

The one piece of furniture that is the most holy to the Jews is the ark of the covenant. The following information will help you understand why it is so important to them and why Orthodox Jews are still looking for it.

The ark, a box approximately 4 feet long by 2 1/2 feet wide by 2 1/2 feet high, was constructed of acacia wood and overlaid with gold inside and out. Because it symbolized God's presence, no one was allowed to touch it. Four gold rings were attached to the feet of the ark. Poles, made of acacia wood and overlaid with gold, were slipped through these rings so that the ark could be carried from place to place (Exodus 25:10-22). Only the Kohathites (a division of the Levites) were allowed to move the ark.

When the ark was in the tabernacle the cloud of God's presence hovered over the atonement cover (Leviticus 16:2; 1 Samuel 4:4). The atonement cover, made of pure gold with a gold cherub attached at each end, covered the ark of the covenant. On the Day of Atonement the high priest sprinkled the blood of sacrifice on the atonement cover as a covering for the sins of the people.

Inside the ark was the Testimony, the stone tablets bearing the ten commandments (Exodus 40:20; Deuteronomy 10:2). For a period of time the ark also contained Aaron's rod which budded (Numbers 17:10) and a gold jar of manna (Hebrews 9:4).

The tabernacle, where the ark resided in the Most Holy Place, and the furniture were made according to the pattern of God's throne in

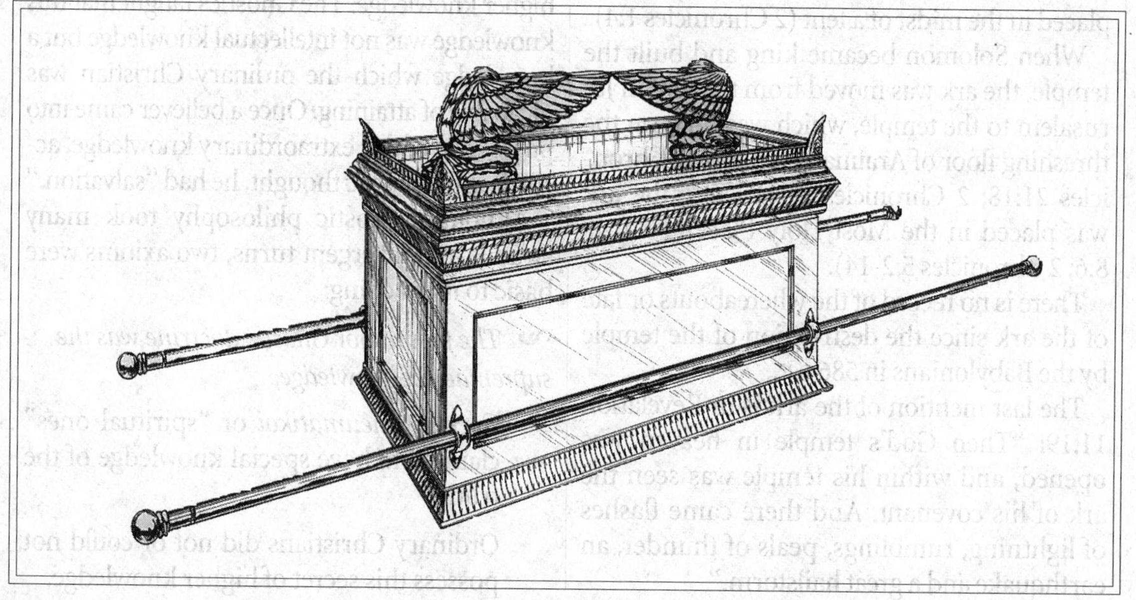

heaven. God gave Moses this pattern when he instructed him to build the tabernacle (Hebrews 8:1-5).

The ark journeyed before the children of Israel as they moved from Sinai to Canaan. It went before them as they crossed the Jordan River and conquered Jericho. It rested at Gilgal, Shechem, Bethel, and Shiloh. Then the Philistines at Ebenezer captured it and kept it for seven months. They took it to Aphek, Ashdod, Gath, and Ekron. From Ekron it went to Beth Shemesh. It was at Beth Shemesh that 50,070 people were killed because they looked into the ark. From there the ark was taken to Kiriath Jearim (Gibeath) and the house of Abinadab, where it remained for 20 years.

When David became king he wanted to move the ark to Jerusalem. The Israelites broke God's command by moving it on a cart rather than carrying it by the poles. When the ark started to fall off the cart, a man named Uzzah touched the ark and was killed by God. This incident occurred on the threshing floor of Nacon (also referred to as Kidon) (2 Samuel 6:6, 7; 1 Chronicles 13:9). The ark remained in the house of Obed-Edom the Gittite, a Philistine from Gath, for three months until David had the Kohathites move it to Jerusalem. There the ark was placed in the midst of a tent (2 Chronicles 1:4).

When Solomon became king and built the temple, the ark was moved from the tent in Jerusalem to the temple, which was built on the threshing floor of Araunah (Ornan) (1 Chronicles 21:18; 2 Chronicles 3:1). There the ark was placed in the Most Holy Place (1 Kings 8:6; 2 Chronicles 5:2-14).

There is no record of the whereabouts or fate of the ark since the destruction of the temple by the Babylonians in 586 B.C.

The last mention of the ark is in Revelation 11:19: "Then God's temple in heaven was opened, and within his temple was seen the ark of his covenant. And there came flashes of lightning, rumblings, peals of thunder, an earthquake and a great hailstorm."

UNDERSTANDING GNOSTICISM

Much like the church today, many members of the early church were significantly influenced by the prevailing philosophy of the day. While some of the New Testament was being written, the church in Asia was being threatened by gnosticism, a philosophy which became the major opponent of the gospel in the early apostolic church.

A familiarity with the teachings of gnosticism will give you a greater understanding of and appreciation for some of the warnings and teachings given in the epistles.

Many members of the early church were seeking enlightenment, and were easily deceived by Gnostic teachers and led astray from the simplicity and purity of devotion to Christ. Some had apparently left the church to form their own community, teaching a different gospel from what the apostles had preached. This movement away from the church caused those who remained to question what was true, and thus confusion crept in.

The term *gnosticism* comes from the Greek word *gnōsis*, meaning "knowledge." Gnosticism is a philosophy which centers on a search for higher knowledge. The Gnostics taught that this knowledge was not intellectual knowledge but a knowledge which the ordinary Christian was incapable of attaining. Once a believer came into possession of this extraordinary knowledge, according to Gnostic thought, he had "salvation."

Although Gnostic philosophy took many strange and divergent turns, two axioms were basic to its teaching:

❧ *The first major Gnostic doctrine was the supremacy of knowledge.*

Certain *pneumatikoi* or "spiritual ones" claimed to have special knowledge of the truth.

Ordinary Christians did not or could not possess this secret of higher knowledge.

The second major doctrine of gnosticism was the separation of spirit and matter.

All matter was considered to be evil and the source of evil.

The spirit was considered to be good and impervious to defilement by anything the body (matter) did.

Claiming a so-called higher knowledge beyond that revealed by God in Christ Jesus and through the prophets, gnosticism had its origins in the philosophies of the Greeks and the Romans, in the creeds of Plato and Philo, and in the religions of the East, especially those of Persia and India. As long as Christianity kept its Judaic roots, it was free from these heresies. However, when Christianity spread to Gentile territory, an attempt was made on the part of Eastern philosophical religion to form an alliance with it.

Many Gnostics allegorized the Old Testament and did not interpret its teachings literally. They strayed from the veracity of the Word, which would have exposed their erroneous teaching regarding creation, sin, and the restoration of all things. They failed to see how a supreme God, pure in spirit and essentially good, could create a universe of matter which they considered evil.

When the Gnostics embraced Christianity, they split into factions on the subject of Christ's deity. Two of the major factions taught as follows:

The Docetic Gnostics denied the humanity of Jesus. The word *docetic* comes from the Greek word *dokeō*, "to seem." According to the Docetists, it was impossible for God, who was spirit and good, to become flesh, which was matter and evil, in the person of Jesus Christ. They believed that Jesus was a phantom; He didn't possess a real flesh-and-blood body. He only seemed to have a body.

The Cerinthian Gnostics (followers of Cerinthus) separated the man Jesus from the *aeon*, the power of Christ. They believed that when the dove came on Jesus at his baptism, the power of Christ came and rested on the man Jesus. This power then departed before his death on the cross. So it was simply the "man" Jesus who died, not Jesus Christ, God in the flesh.

These Gnostic heresies denied that God became man and walked this earth in the person of Jesus Christ to bring redemption and salvation to mankind. Having eliminated Jesus Christ as the only way to God, the Gnostics believed they could make their own way to God through their inquiry and knowledge. Faith and one's deeds were viewed as having no significance in salvation or the life of a believer.

Understanding the basis of gnosticism and the forms of thought that it took in the early days of the Christian church will enable you to better understand the doctrinal heresy which some of the New Testament writers addressed.

GUIDELINES FOR INTERPRETING PREDICTIVE PROPHECY

From Genesis to Revelation the Bible is filled with prophecy. If you want to handle the prophecies in the Word of God accurately, the following guidelines will give you some important parameters.

The Greek word for prophecy, *prophēteía*, comes from two Greek words, *pró*, meaning "forth," and *phēmi*, meaning "to speak." It means to speak forth the mind and counsel of God. According to this definition, all Scripture is in a sense prophecy.

Predictive prophecy points to a future fulfillment and is of divine origin. In *Understanding and Applying the Bible*, Dr. Robertson McQuilkin says: "There are two purposes for predictive prophecy. The chief purpose is to affect the conduct of those who hear the prophecy. Another purpose is met only when the prophecy is fulfilled. That purpose is to build faith, to establish confidence in the God who miraculously foretold events (John 13:19; 14:29; 16:4)" (p. 215).

Some scholars divide predictive prophecy into two categories: forthtelling and foretelling. Forthtelling prophecies contain a message about the present or immediate time. (Often this is a call to godly living in the light of prophecy yet to be fulfilled.) Foretelling prophecies contain a message about what God will do in the future.

When a prophet spoke for God, the prophecy could refer to the following:

- a present or near fulfillment
- a future fulfillment
- a twofold fulfillment: a near fulfillment and then a later, future fulfillment

As you read the prophecies of the Bible, keep in mind the following guidelines and discern whether the prophecy refers to:

- the prophet's own time and/or a future time
- the captivity and/or restoration of Israel or Judah
- the first coming of Christ and any events connected with it
- the second coming of Christ
- the last days or end times

❧ *As you study prophecy, it is important to remember that the prophets did not always indicate intervals of time between events, nor did they always write their prophecies in chronological order.* For example, an Old Testament prophecy could include the first and second comings of Christ without any indication of the time span between the two comings. One such prophecy is found in Isaiah 65:17-25. In this prophecy, Isaiah first talks about the new heavens and the new earth (in which we know there is no death), and then in verses 18-25 he refers to a time when a youth dies at age 100 and the wolf and lamb feed together. Chronologically, verse 17 will be fulfilled *after* verses 18-25 become a reality.

❧ *Always approach a prophecy as literal (in its usual, ordinary meaning) unless one of the following occurs:*

- The grammatical context shows that it is figurative language by the use of similes, metaphors, parables, allegories, symbols, or types.
- A literal interpretation violates common sense, is contrary to what the author is saying, or is contrary to what the rest of Scripture teaches.

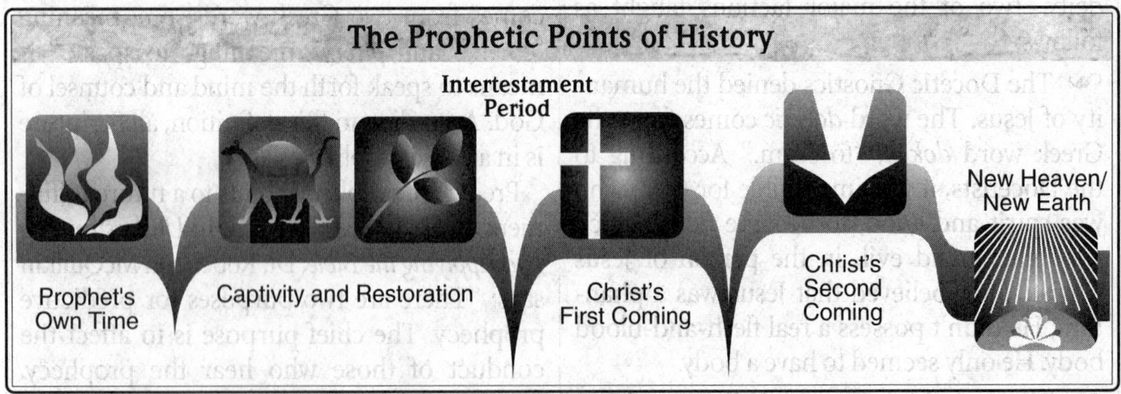

❧ *When a prophetic passage cannot be taken literally, look for what the author is trying to convey through his figurative or symbolic language.* To discern what the author is saying, look for answers in the following places:

- within the context of the book in which the passage appears
- in any other writings of that author
- in any other prophetic writings to which the author had access (for example, other prophetic books or passages in the Word of God)

❧ *Remember that often when a prophet refers to future events, he does not use the future tense.*

❧ *When you interpret Scripture, consider the historical context of that writing, remembering that God was delivering his prophecy to a particular people at a particular time.* Granted, it might have been a prophecy with a future fulfillment, but it would still be delivered in a way that was comprehensible to those receiving that prophecy—even though they might not understand the details, the symbolism, or the full implications of the prophecy.

Make a careful historical and cultural analysis of the text. Determine the identity of all historical events, proper names, and geographical locations before you attempt to interpret the text.

❧ *Remember that the meaning of a specific prophecy could not always be understood by the prophet or by the people who heard the message.* For example, Daniel could not understand what he had written, since it was to remain sealed until the time of the end (Daniel 12:8, 9).

However, many prophecies will come to light through the following:

a fulfillment as recorded in history

a fulfillment as recorded in the New Testament

an explanation given by an Old Testament or a New Testament writing (for example, Acts 4:24-28)

❧ *Remember that many New Testament prophecies include Old Testament quotations and allusions.* Scholars estimate that at least 350 Old Testament quotations or allusions appear in the book of Revelation alone. Revelation is replete with the language of Isaiah, Jeremiah, Ezekiel, Daniel, and the minor prophets. It is obvious that the author of Revelation was steeped in the Old Testament, for he talks in Old Testament phraseology. So to correctly interpret New Testament prophecy, check Old Testament cross-references.

❧ *When you study prophecy, watch for phrases which indicate periods of time.* For example, look for *in the last days, day of the Lord, day of wrath,* and *end of the age.* When you come across phrases such as these, carefully observe the things which occur during that particular time period. Then ask the following questions:

- Have these events ever occurred in history?
- Do these events coincide with any other particular period of time?
- Do these events parallel any events mentioned in another place in the Word of God?

FIGURES OF SPEECH

Although the Bible is to be interpreted literally, it is important to remember that, as with other writings, it contains figures of speech which must be interpreted for what they are and in the light of their intended purpose. As you seek to handle the Word of God accurately, you will find it helpful to understand the definitions of the different types of figures of speech.

A *figure of speech* is a word, a phrase, or an expression used in an imaginative rather than a literal sense.

Discerning the use of figures of speech is important in biblical interpretation. For example, there has been much controversy in the church over Jesus' statement regarding the bread at the Last Supper: "And he took bread, gave thanks and broke it, and gave it to them, saying, 'This is my body given for you'" (Luke 22:19). Some believe that the bread actually becomes his body (the doctrine of transubstantiation); others believe that Jesus was simply using a metaphor and that the bread is representative of his body.

Three principles for dealing with figurative language are:

- Identify the fact that the author is using figurative language.
- Identify the type of figurative language in use: simile, metaphor, hyperbole, and so on.
- Follow the guidelines for interpreting what the author meant by his use of that particular figure of speech.

You will be aided in your study of Scripture if you are able to identify when the author is using a figure of speech. The following are brief definitions of the types of figurative language used in the Bible.

❧ A *metaphor* is an implied comparison between two things which are different. In a metaphor the words of comparison—*like, as, as…so is,* and *such as*—are *not* used. An example is John 6:48, where Jesus says, "I am the bread of life."

❧ A *simile* is an expressed comparison of two different things or ideas that uses the words *like, as, as…so is,* and/or *such as.* An example is Revelation 1:14b, "his eyes were like blazing fire."

❧ *Hyperbole* is a deliberate exaggeration for effect or emphasis. Hyperboles are found in all languages, and they are frequently used among Semitic peoples. For example, "My soul is consumed with longing" (Psalm 119:20).

❧ *Metonymy* is used when the name of one object or concept is used for that of another to which it is related. This is a figure of association. An example of a metonymy is found in the statement, "The whole Judean countryside and all the people of Jerusalem went out to him." The metonymy is country, which refers to the people rather than the region itself. Note also the hyperbole, *all* the people of Jerusalem.

❧ *Synecdoche* is another figure of association where the whole can refer to the part or the part to the whole. This is often found in the use of the term *the law*, which can refer to the Pentateuch (the first five books of the Old Testament), the ten commandments, or the whole Old Testament.

A synecdoche can also be a singular for a plural or a plural for a singular. An example is in Jeremiah 25:29. God says He is going to call down "a sword upon all who live on the earth." The singular sword represents many swords.

❧ In *personification* an object is given characteristics or attributes that belong to people—for example, when the trees clap their hands and the mountains sing for joy (Isaiah 55:12).

❧ *Irony* is a statement which says the opposite of what is meant. Irony is used for emphasis or effect. When it is not easy to discern if a statement is ironic, then examine it first as a true statement. As such, does it make sense in its context? Second, examine it as figurative irony. If this makes sense and fits with the context, then accept it as irony. Otherwise, treat it as a truth.

Here are two examples of irony:

1. In 1 Kings 22:1-23, a true prophet tells the king what he wants to hear, but it is a lie. It's obvious he is using irony because the king tells him to stop prophesying falsely and to tell the truth.

2. In 1 Corinthians 4:8 Paul says to the Corinthians, "Already you have all you want! Already you have become rich! You have become kings—and that without us! How I wish that you really had become kings so that we might be kings with you." When you read this, it is

obvious the Corinthians are not kings, nor does Paul desire to reign with them.

Parables

A parable is a story which, although not usually factual, remains true to life and teaches a moral lesson or truth. Every detail of a parable will reinforce the main theme, but you shouldn't always attempt to ascribe a specific spiritual meaning and application to each point.

Jesus frequently used parables in his teaching for two reasons: to reveal truth to believers and to hide truth from those who had rejected it and/or hardened their hearts against it.

To correctly interpret a parable:

- *Determine the occasion of the parable.* Since parables clarify or emphasize a truth, discover why the parable was told. What prompted it?
- *Look for the intended meaning of the parable.* The meaning will sometimes be stated. If not, it can usually be determined by the application of the parable to the hearer.
- *Don't impose any meaning beyond what is clearly stated or applied to the hearers by the speaker of the parable.*
- *Identify the central or focal idea of the parable.* Every parable has one central theme or emphasis. No detail of the story is to be given any meaning that is independent of the main teaching of the parable.

Since a parable has one central point of emphasis, identify relevant details. To attach meaning that is not in the context of the occasion or relevant to its central emphasis is to go away from the meaning of the parable. A detail is relevant only if it reinforces the central theme of the parable.

How many sermons have you heard on the parable of the prodigal son? Many teachers violate the occasion and meaning of this parable, attaching all sorts of meanings to the details of this story. Jesus told this parable because he wanted the Pharisees to see what their hearts were like as they grumbled, "This man welcomes sinners and eats with them" (Luke 15:2). In order to make his point Jesus told three consecutive parables about three things which were lost: a sheep, a coin, and a son. In each of the parables Jesus uses the following words: *lost, found, sinner (sinned),*

Parable	Allegory
1. Has one central point.	1. Can have more than one central point.
2. Teaches one truth.	2. Can teach a number of truths.
3. Every relevant detail reinforces the central theme or point of emphasis.	3. The details of an allegory may be many and varied, relating to more than one theme.
4. Can have irrelevant details; all features of the parable do not have to be identified.	4. Can have irrelevant details; all the features of an allegory do not have to be identified.
5. Usually the story is separate from its interpretation and application.	5. Intertwines the story and the meaning.
6. Interpretation usually follows the parable.	6. Interpretation is found within the allegory.

and *rejoice (joyfully, rejoicing)*. When he gets to the story of the prodigal son, he shows them the kindness of the father's heart versus the hardness of the elder brother's, and in doing so, shows the Pharisees that their hearts are like the elder brother's, not the father's.

• *Interpret parables in the context of the culture of Bible times rather than the culture of today.* For example, in the parable of the wise and foolish virgins, the central emphasis of the parable is, "Therefore keep watch, because you do not know the day or the hour" (Matthew 25:13). Understanding Eastern wedding traditions would give insight into the parable and explain why some were ready and others were not.

• *Do not establish doctrine when parables are the primary or only source for that teaching.* Parables should amplify or affirm doctrine, not establish it.

Allegory

An *allegory* is a description of one thing using the image of another—a story with an underlying meaning different from the surface facts of the story itself. Some refer to an allegory as an extended metaphor, which is an implied comparison between two different things. An allegory is a realistic or nonrealistic story created to teach one or more truths which may or may not be related.

The chart below comparing parables and allegories will help you distinguish one from the other.

When interpreting an allegory, follow these guidelines:

• List the features of the allegory.

• Note any interpretation given within the text of the allegory.

• Study the allegory's features according to sound principles of biblical exegesis. Do not contradict the clear teaching of the Word of God by interpreting an unexplained detail in an allegory in a way contrary to other truths.

• Do not try to identify all the features of an allegory.

Types (Patterns)

A type or pattern is a prophetic symbol designated by God.

The word *type* (pattern) comes from the Greek word *tupos.* A *tupos* was a mark formed by a blow or an impression, creating a figure or an image on the object that was struck. Therefore, a type (pattern) prefigures something or someone to come. That which it prefigures is called an *antitype.*

A type (pattern) prefigures only one antitype, although it may parallel many points in the antitype. An illustration of this is the tabernacle, a type (pattern) of man's redemption. According to Hebrews 10:20, the curtain that separated the Holy Place from the Most Holy Place prefigured the body of Jesus Christ.

When determining types (patterns), although it may not be formally stated, there should be some evidence of divine affirmation of the corresponding type (pattern) and antitype. For example, in Romans 5:14 we read, "Nevertheless, death reigned from the time of Adam to the time of Moses, even over those who did not sin by breaking a command, as did Adam, who was a pattern of the one to come." The word translated *type* (pattern) is the Greek word *tupos.* Adam was a type (pattern) or figure of Christ, who was to come. In 1 Corinthians 15:45, Christ is referred to as "the last Adam." If the Word does not designate something as a type, then the Bible expositor should simply show the parallels without calling it a type.

Symbols

A symbol is a picture or an object that stands for or represents another thing. For example, the seven lampstands mentioned in Revelation 1:20 represent the seven churches described in Revelation 2 and 3.

When noting symbols it is important to remember the following:

• *The item used as a symbol can symbolize different things.* For example, water is used to symbolize the Word of God (Ephesians 5:26) and the Holy Spirit (John 7:37-39).

• *Although a symbol can represent many things, when it does symbolize something in a given passage, a single parallel is intended.* For instance, in John 7:37-39 water symbolizes the Holy Spirit, not the Word.

• *Interpret symbols in the light of a biblical setting and culture rather than the culture of the current interpreter.*

• *Symbols are timeless and can symbolize something past, present, or future.*

LAWS OF COMPOSITION

A literary composition is an arrangement of thoughts which conveys meaning to a reader. An understanding of the laws of composition will help you discern what the author is saying.

The following laws of composition can help you in your study of the Word of God.

1. **Comparison**—to compare in order to show similarities. A comparison is the association of like things.

2. **Contrast**—to compare in order to show differences. A contrast is the association of opposites.

3. **Repetition**—to use the same word or phrase a number of times.

4. **Progression**—to extend a specific theme throughout a portion of Scripture. Many times the author will amplify what he is saying as he progresses in his writing or adds to what he has said.

5. **Climax**—a high point built by a progression from the lesser to the greater. A climax is simply an extension of the law of progression until it reaches a peak of intensity.

6. **Pivotal point**—a changing or a turning so that the elements on each side of the point differ in some way. In the Gospel of John the pivotal point comes in 11:54, when Jesus turns from ministering mainly to the public to ministering to his disciples. (Read John 11:54.) In Genesis the pivotal point of the book comes in chapter 12, where Moses turns from recording major events to tell us of major characters.

7. **Radiation**—the central or single point from or to which other truths point. An illustration of this is 1 Corinthians 15, where the truths of that chapter all radiate to resurrection.

8. **Interchange**—to alternate, in sequence, at least two main thoughts, subjects, or characteristics. This is most apparent in the Gospel of Luke. Luke opens with the announcement of the birth of John the Baptist, then moves to the announcement of Jesus' birth. He then returns to John the Baptist's birth, then to the birth of Christ. This is alternation or interchange.

9. **General to particular (or vice versa)**—to move from the extensive or general to the specific or particular. This is beautifully seen in Genesis 1 and 2. Genesis 1 gives the general overview of creation, including the creation of man, male and female, on the sixth day. Genesis 2 moves from the general to the particular, giving more details of the creation of woman.

10. **Cause and effect (or vice versa)**—to move from the source to the consequence of it. An example of this is found in John 11. Verse 4 states that the cause of the death of Lazarus, the beloved friend of Christ, was to glorify the Son. The effect is seen in verse 45, where the people put their faith in Christ after seeing his power in raising Lazarus. The effect is also seen in John 12:17,18, where once again the Son is glorified.

11. **Explanation or analysis**—the presentation of an idea or event followed by its explanation. This is expertly done by our Lord in John 6, where he multiplies the loaves and the fishes and then brings forth his discourse stating that he is the bread who gives us life.

12. **Interrogation**—the presentation of a question, usually followed by its answer. Paul masterfully uses this technique in writing Romans. Paul anticipates his readers' questions or objections, states them usually in the form of a question, and then proceeds to answer the very questions he has raised. Romans 6 beautifully demonstrates this technique.

13. **Preparation or introduction**—the presentation of background information to prepare the reader for that which follows. The purpose of the Gospel of John is to prepare the reader to believe that Jesus is the Christ, the Son of God. In John 1:1-18 the writer thoroughly introduces his subject and prepares his readers for what is to come.

14. **Summarization**—to restate the main points, to sum up, or to briefly restate particular truths. Moses does this in chapters 1 to 4 of the book of Deuteronomy as he rehearses before the children of Israel those things that took place following the exodus from Egypt. Acts 7 provides a masterful summarization by Stephen of Israel's history.

TENSE, VOICE, AND MOOD OF GREEK VERBS

There are many excellent study tools which can help you examine the text more deeply through Greek word studies. If you would like to pursue Greek word studies further, a highly recommended book is *The Complete Word Study New Testament*, by Spiros Zodhiates.

The following explanation of the tense, voice, and mood of Greek verbs will help those who do not know Greek but want a better understanding of the implications of the kind of action indicated by the verbs.

Because verbs express action, they are often the most significant element in the expression of thought. Therefore, understanding the Greek verb is a key to correct interpretation and application of Scripture. (Context is the most important key to correct interpretation and application, since the Greek words get their meaning from the context.) The major features of Greek verbs are tense, voice, and mood.

Part of the beauty of the Greek language is that the construction of the verb clearly shows who does the action, whether the statement is a command or a suggestion, and whether the passage is speaking of reality or possibility.

By thinking through a simple, concise explanation of tense, voice, and mood, new vistas of insight will be opened to you. Keep in mind that the following is a simplified and nonexhaustive summarization of a complex subject. The purpose of this information is to give you an overview of terms that are frequently used in the more technical commentaries.

Tense

(Shows the Kind of Action)

Greek verb tenses differ from English verb tenses in that the kind of action portrayed is the most significant element, and time is a relatively minor consideration.

❧ Action as continuous

Present tense—continuous action. It is primarily progressive or linear; it shows action that is continuing.

Examples:

Jeff *is studying* the Bible.

John 15:4b—"No branch *can bear* fruit by itself; it *must remain* in the vine. Neither can you bear fruit unless you *remain* in me."

John 15:6—"If anyone *does not remain* in me."

Imperfect tense—continuous action, usually in the past.

Examples:

Jeff *was studying* the Bible.

John 15:19a—"If you belonged to the world, it *would love* you as its own." (Literally, "would have been loving" its own.)

❧ Action as completed

Perfect tense—punctiliar action in the past

with the results continuing into the present. (Punctiliar action is action that happens at a specific point in time.)

Examples:

Jeff is being transformed by *having studied* the Bible.

John 15:3—"You are already clean because of the word which I *have spoken* to you."

John 15:10b—"Just as I *have obeyed* my Father's commands and remain in his love."

Pluperfect tense—punctiliar action in the past with the results continuing in the past.

Examples:

Jeff was transformed because he *had studied* the Bible.

John 9:22—"For already the Jews *had decided.*"

❧ Action as occurring

Aorist tense—punctiliar action. The aorist tense states that an action occurs without regard to its duration; that is, it denotes the fact of an action without any reference to the length of that action. Compared to the present tense, the aorist tense expresses the action like a snapshot while the present tense action is like a moving picture, continuing on.

Examples:

Jeff *studied* the Bible.

John 15:4a—"*Remain* in me, and I will remain in you."

Future tense—indefinite action to occur in the future. Indicates continuing or punctiliar action in the future.

Examples:

Jeff *will be studying* his Bible.

John 15:7—"It *will be given* you."

John 15:8—"Showing yourselves to *be* my disciples."

Voice

(Shows How the Subject Is Related to the Action)

❧ **Active voice—indicates that the subject produces the action.**

Examples:

Jeff *hit* the ball.

John 15:2b—"...while every branch that does bear fruit he *trims* clean."

❧ **Passive voice—indicates that the subject is acted upon.**

Examples:

Jeff *was hit* by the ball.

John 15:6—"And *burned.*"

❧ **Middle voice—indicates that the subject initiates the action and also participates in the results of the action.** (This voice is unique to Greek construction.)

Examples:

Jeff *hit* himself with the ball.

John 15:26—"The Spirit of truth who *goes out* from the Father, he will testify about me."

One note of interest when looking up a verb in a Greek study tool: The middle and passive voices will have identical forms, but the context will show you if the subject is receiving the action (passive voice) or if the subject initiated the action and participated in it (middle voice).

Also, some verbs are *deponent verbs.* This means that their form in a Greek study tool may be listed as a passive or middle voice verb but their function or action is active. Usually your Greek study helps will list these as deponent verbs.

Mood

(Shows How the Action Is Related to Reality from the Speaker's Point of View)

❧ **Indicative mood—the declarative mood or mood of certainty.** It is a statement of fact which assumes reality from the speaker's point of view. This mood simply states a thing as being a fact.

Examples:

Bible study *has changed* Jeff's life.

John 15:6—"He is like a branch that is *thrown* away and *withers*; such branches are *picked* up, *thrown* into the fire and *burned*."

❧ **Imperative mood—usually a command or entreaty.** It is the mood of volition or will. The imperative mood in the Greek makes a demand on the will of the reader to obey the command; it is used to indicate prohibition and authority.

Examples:

Jeff, *study* your homework.

John 15:4—"*Remain* in me."

John 15:7—"*Ask* whatever you wish."

John 15:9—"*Remain* in my love."

John 15:20—"*Remember* the words I spoke to you."

One aspect which will help your study of God's Word is the understanding of the combination of the present tense and the imperative mood that is stating a negative command (a prohibition). The *present imperative prohibition* demands cessation of some act already in progress.

Example:

John 20:17—"Jesus said to her, '*Do not hold on* to me.' " In other words, Mary was already clinging to Jesus, and Jesus was telling her to stop clinging and to go on refusing to cling to him.

❧ **Subjunctive mood—the mood of probability.** It implies some doubt regarding the reality of the action from the speaker's point of view. It expresses an uncertainty or an action which may or should happen. This is the mood used for conditional clauses, strong suggestions, or "polite" commands.

Examples:

Jeff *may have done* his homework. Jeff, if you do not do your homework, you cannot participate in the class discussion.

John 15:2—"That it *will bear* more fruit."

John 15:4b—"No branch can bear fruit by itself; it *must remain* in the vine. Neither can you bear fruit unless you *remain* in me."

John 15:6—"If anyone *does not remain* in me."

John 15:7—"If you *remain* in me, and my words *remain* in you."

Something else which may help you in your study of God's Word is an understanding of the combination of the aorist tense and the subjunctive mood that is stating a negative command (a prohibition). The *aorist subjunctive prohibition* is a warning or an exhortation against doing a thing not yet begun.

Example:

John 13:8a—" 'No,' said Peter, 'you *shall never wash* my feet!' " In other words, Peter was telling Jesus that he was not to wash his feet and Jesus was not even to start washing his feet.

❧ **Optative mood—the mood of possibility.** This mood presents no definite anticipation of realization but merely presents the action as conceivable from the speaker's point of view. (Used less frequently than the other moods.)

Examples:

I *wish* my neighbor, Jeff, would take Precept Bible studies.

2 Thessalonians 3:5—"May the Lord *direct* your hearts."

TENSE, MOOD, AND VOICE OF GREEK VERBS

TENSE

The emphasis is on the *kind* of action, not the time of action.

Tense	Kind of Action	Example
Present	Continuous action	Jeff is studying the Bible.
Imperfect	Continuous action in the past	Jeff was studying the Bible.
Perfect	Punctiliar action in the past with the results continuing into the present	Jeff is being transformed by having studied the Bible.
Pluperfect	Punctiliar action in the past with the results continuing in the past	Jeff was transformed because he had studied the Bible.
Aorist	Punctiliar action (The time can be past, present, or future but is generally past.)	Jeff studied the Bible.
Future	Generally continuous action in the future, but on occasion it can be punctiliar.	Jeff will be studying his Bible.

Tense, Mood, and Voice of Greek Verbs

Mood

The mood expresses the relationship of the action to reality from the speaker's point of view.

Mood	Relation to Reality	Usage or Meaning	Example
Indicative	Mood of certainty (reality)	Used to declare a statement of fact as something which is true. Expresses that which is actual, factual, or real from the speaker's point of view.	Bible study has changed Jeff's life.
Imperative	Mood of volition or will (potential reality)	Usually used to express a command or entreaty. Denotes intention, authority, permission, or prohibition.	Jeff, study your homework.
Subjunctive	Mood of probability (probable reality)	Used to express an action which may or should happen but which is not necessarily true at the present, from the speaker's point of view. Expresses conditional or uncertain actions.	Jeff may have done his homework.
Optative	Mood of possibility (possible reality)	Merely presents an action as conceivable from the speaker's point of view, with no definite anticipation of realization.	I wish my neighbor, Jeff, would take Precept Bible studies.

Tense, Mood, and Voice of Greek Verbs

Voice

The voice expresses the relationship of the subject to the action.

Voice	How the Subject Is Related to the Action	Example
Active	Indicates that the subject produces the action	Jeff hit the ball.
Passive	Indicates that the subject is acted upon	Jeff was hit by the ball.
Middle	Indicates that the subject initiates the action and participates in the results of the action	Jeff hit himself with the ball.

Tense, Mood, and Voice of Greek Verbs

Prohibitions

This is when the speaker states a negative command.

Prohibition	Definition	Example
Present imperative (used with a negative)	This prohibition demands cessation of some act already in progress.	John 20:17
Aorist subjunctive (used with a negative)	This prohibition is a warning or exhortation against doing a thing not yet begun.	John 13:8

Historical Charts

Old Testament

New Testament

Topical Study Charts

Old Testament

New Testament

AT A GLANCE CHARTS

OLD TESTAMENT

NEW TESTAMENT

OBSERVATIONS CHARTS

MAPS

(All maps are approximate to scale.)

OLD TESTAMENT

NEW TESTAMENT

ILLUSTRATIONS

COLOR MAPS

CONCORDANCE

NEW INTERNATIONAL VERSION

THE NEW INTERNATIONAL VERSION
CONCORDANCE
TO THE OLD AND NEW TESTAMENTS

The NIV Concordance, created by Edward W. Goodrick and John R. Kohlenberger III, has been developed specifically for use with the New International Version. Like all concordances, it is a special index which contains an alphabetical listing of words used in the Bible text. By looking up key words, readers can find verses and passages for which they remember a word or two but not their location.

This concordance contains 2,000 word entries, with some 13,000 Scripture references. Each word entry is followed by the Scripture references in which that particular word is found, as well as by a brief excerpt from the surrounding context. The first letter of the entry word is italicized to conserve space and to allow for a longer context excerpt. Variant spellings due to number and tense and compound forms follow the entry in parentheses, and direct the reader to check other forms of that word in locating a passage.

This concordance contains a number of "block entries," which highlight some of the key events and characteristics in the lives of certain Bible figures. The descriptive phrases replace the brief context surrounding each occurrence of the name. In those instances where more than one Bible character has the same name, that name is placed under one block entry, and each person is given a number (1), (2), etc. Insignificant names are not included.

Word or block entries marked with an asterisk (*) list every verse in the Bible in which the word appears.

This concordance is a valuable tool for Bible study. While one of its key purposes is to help the reader find forgotten references to verses, it can also be used to do word studies and to locate and trace biblical themes. Be sure to use this concordance as more than just a verse finder. Whenever you look up a verse, aim to discover the intended meaning of the verse in context. Give special attention to the flow of thought from the beginning of the passage to the end.

ABBREVIATIONS FOR THE BOOKS OF THE BIBLE
As used in the NIV Concordance

Genesis	Ge	Job	Job	Habakkuk	Hab	1 Thessalonians	1Th
Exodus	Ex	Psalms	Ps	Zephaniah	Zep	2Thessalonians	2Th
Leviticus	Lev	Proverbs	Pr	Haggai	Hag	1 Timothy	1Ti
Numbers	Nu	Ecclesiastes	Ecc	Zechariah	Zec	2 Timothy	2Ti
Deuteronomy	Dt	Song of Songs	SS	Malachi	Mal	Titus	Tit
Joshua	Jos	Isaiah	Isa	Matthew	Mt	Philemon	Phm
Judges	Jdg	Jeremiah	Jer	Mark	Mk	Hebrews	Heb
Ruth	Ru	Lamentations	La	Luke	Lk	James	Jas
1 Samuel	1Sa	Ezekiel	Eze	John	Jn	1 Peter	1Pe
2 Samuel	2Sa	Daniel	Da	Acts	Ac	2 Peter	2Pe
1 Kings	1Ki	Hosea	Hos	Romans	Ro	1 John	1Jn
2 Kings	2Ki	Joel	Joel	1 Corinthians	1Co	2 John	2Jn
1 Chronicles	1Ch	Amos	Am	2 Corinthians	2Co	3 John	3Jn
2 Chronicles	2Ch	Obadiah	Ob	Galatians	Gal	Jude	Jude
Ezra	Ezr	Jonah	Jnh	Ephesians	Eph	Revelation	Rev
Nehemiah	Ne	Micah	Mic	Philippians	Php		
Esther	Est	Nahum	Na	Colossians	Col		

A

AARON

Priesthood of (Ex 28:1; Nu 17; Heb 5:1-4;7), garments (Ex 28; 39), consecration (Ex 29), ordination (Lev 8).

Spokesman for Moses (Ex 4:14-16, 27-31; 7:1-2). Supported Moses' hands in battle (Ex 17:8-13). Built golden calf (Ex 32; Dt 9:20). Talked against Moses (Nu 12). Priesthood opposed (Nu 16); staff budded (Nu 17). Forbidden to enter land (Nu 20:1-12). Death (Nu 20:22-29; 33:38-39).

ABANDON

Dt 4: 31 he will not *a* or destroy you
1Ti 4: 1 in later times some will *a* the faith

ABBA

Ro 8: 15 And by him we cry, "*A*, Father."
Gal 4: 6 the Spirit who calls out, "*A*, Father

ABEL

Second son of Adam (Ge 4:2). Offered proper sacrifice (Ge 4:4; Heb 11:4). Murdered by Cain (Ge 4:8; Mt 23:35; Lk 11:51; 1Jn 3:12).

ABHORS

Pr 11: 1 The LORD *a* dishonest scales,

ABIGAIL

Wife of Nabal (1Sa 25:30); pled for his life with David (1Sa 25:14-35). Became David's wife (1Sa 25:36-42).

ABIJAH

Son of Rehoboam; king of Judah (1Ki 14:31-15:8; 2Ch 12:16-14:1).

ABILITY (ABLE)

Ezr 2: 69 According to their *a* they gave
2Co 1: 8 far beyond our *a* to endure,
8: 3 were able, and even beyond their *a*.

ABIMELECH

1. King of Gerar who took Abraham's wife Sarah, believing her to be his sister (Ge 20). Later made a covenant with Abraham (Ge 21:22-33).

2. King of Gerar who took Isaac's wife Rebekah, believing her to be his sister (Ge 26:1-11). Later made a covenant with Isaac (Ge 26:12-31).

ABLE (ABILITY ENABLE ENABLED ENABLES)

Eze 7: 19 and gold will not be *a* to save them
Da 3: 17 the God we serve is *a* to save us
Ro 8: 39 will be *a* to separate us
14: 4 for the Lord is *a* to make him stand
16: 25 to him who is *a* to establish you
2Co 9: 8 God is *a* to make all grace abound
Eph 3: 20 him who is *a* to do immeasurably
2Ti 1: 12 and am convinced that he is *a*
3: 15 which are *a* to make you wise
Heb 7: 25 he is *a* to save completely
Jude 24 To him who is *a* to keep you
Rev 5: 5 He is *a* to open the scroll

ABOLISH

Mt 5: 17 that I have come to *a* the Law

ABOMINATION

Da 11: 31 set up the *a* that causes desolation.

ABOUND (ABOUNDING)

2Co 9: 8 able to make all grace *a* to you,
Php 1: 9 that your love may *a* more

ABOUNDING (ABOUND)

Ex 34: 6 slow to anger, *a* in love
Ps 86: 5 *a* in love to all who call to you.

ABRAHAM

Covenant relation with the LORD (Ge 12:1-3; 13:14-17; 15; 17; 22:15-18; Ex 2:24; Ne 9:8; Ps 105; Mic 7:20; Lk 1:68-75; Ro 4; Heb 6:13-15).

Called from Ur, via Haran, to Canaan (Ge 12:1; Ac 7:2-4; Heb 11:8-10). Moved to Egypt, nearly lost Sarah to Pharaoh (Ge 12:10-20). Divided the land with Lot (Ge 13). Saved Lot from four kings (Ge 14:1-16); blessed by Melchizedek (Ge 14:17-20; Heb 7:1-20). Declared righteous by faith (Ge 15:6; Ro 4:3; Gal 3:6-9). Fathered Ishmael by Hagar (Ge 16).

Name changed from Abram (Ge 17:5; Ne 9:7). Circumcised (Ge 17; Ro 4:9-12). Entertained three visitors (Ge 18); promised a son by Sarah (Ge 18:9-15; 17:16). Moved to Gerar; nearly lost Sarah to Abimelech (Ge 20). Fathered Isaac by Sarah (Ge 21:1-7; Ac 7:8; Heb 11:11-12); sent away Hagar and Ishmael (Ge 21:8-21; Gal 4:22-30). Tested by offering Isaac (Ge 22; Heb 11:17-19; Jas 2:21-24). Sarah died; bought field of Ephron for burial (Ge 23). Secured wife for Isaac (Ge 24). Death (Ge 25:7-11).

ABSALOM

Son of David by Maacah (2Sa 3:3; 1Ch 3:2). Killed Amnon for rape of his sister Tamar; banished by David (2Sa 13). Returned to Jerusalem; received by David (2Sa 14). Rebelled against David; seized kingdom (2Sa 15-17). Killed (2Sa 18).

ABSTAIN (ABSTAINS)

1Pe 2: 11 to *a* from sinful desires,

ABSTAINS* (ABSTAIN)

Ro 14: 6 thanks to God; and he who *a*,

ABUNDANCE (ABUNDANT)

Lk 12: 15 consist in the *a* of his possessions."
Jude : 2 peace and love be yours in *a*.

ABUNDANT (ABUNDANCE)

Dt 28: 11 will grant you *a* prosperity—
Ps 145: 7 will celebrate your *a* goodness
Pr 28: 19 works his land will have *a* food,
Ro 5: 17 who receive God's *a* provision

ACCEPT (ACCEPTED ACCEPTS)

Ex 23: 8 "Do not *a* a bribe,
Pr 10: 8 The wise in heart *a* commands,
19: 20 Listen to advice and *a* instruction,
Ro 15: 7 *A* one another, then, just
Jas 1: 21 humbly *a* the word planted in you,

ACCEPTED (ACCEPT)

Lk 4: 24 "no prophet is *a* in his hometown.

ACCEPTS (ACCEPT)

Ps 6: 9 the LORD *a* my prayer.
Jn 13: 20 whoever *a* anyone I send *a* me;

ACCOMPANY

Mk 16: 17 these signs will *a* those who believe
Heb 6: 9 your case—things that *a* salvation.

ACCOMPLISH

Isa 55: 11 but will *a* what I desire

ACCORD

Nu 24: 13 not do anything of my own *a*,
Jn 10: 18 but I lay it down of my own *a*.
12: 49 For I did not speak of my own *a*,

ACCOUNT (ACCOUNTABLE)

Mt 12: 36 to give *a* on the day of judgment
Ro 14: 12 each of us will give an *a* of himself
Heb 4: 13 of him to whom we must give *a*.

ACCOUNTABLE (ACCOUNT)

Eze 33: 6 but I will hold the watchman *a*
Ro 3: 19 and the whole world held *a* to God.

ACCUSATION (ACCUSE)

1Ti 5: 19 Do not entertain an *a*

ACCUSATIONS (ACCUSE)

2Pe 2: 11 do not bring slanderous *a*

ACCUSE (ACCUSATION ACCUSATIONS)

Pr 3: 30 Do not *a* a man for no reason—
Lk 3: 14 and don't *a* people falsely—

ACHAN*

Sin at Jericho caused defeat at Ai; stoned (Jos 7; 22:20; 1Ch 2:7).

ACHE*

Pr 14: 13 Even in laughter the heart may *a*,

ACKNOWLEDGE

Mt 10: 32 *a* him before my Father in heaven.
1Jn 4: 3 spirit that does not *a* Jesus is not

ACQUIT

Ex 23: 7 to death, for I will not *a* the guilty.

ACTION (ACTIONS ACTIVE ACTS)

Jas 2: 17 if it is not accompanied by *a*,
1Pe 1: 13 minds for *a*; be self-controlled;

ACTIONS (ACTION)

Mt 11: 19 wisdom is proved right by her *a*."
Gal 6: 4 Each one should test his own *a*.
Tit 1: 16 but by their *a* they deny him.

ACTIVE (ACTION)

Heb 4: 12 For the word of God is living and *a*

ACTS (ACTION)

Ps 145: 12 all men may know of your mighty *a*
150: 2 Praise him for his *a* of power;
Isa 64: 6 all our righteous *a* are like filthy
Mt 6: 1 not to do your '*a* of righteousness'

ADAM

First man (Ge 1:26-2:25; Ro 5:14; 1Ti 2:13). Sin of (Ge 3; Hos 6:7; Ro 5:12-21). Children of (Ge 4:1-5:5). Death of (Ge 5:5; Ro 5:12-21; 1Co 15:22).

ADD

Dt 12: 32 do not *a* to it or take away from it.
Pr 30: 6 Do not *a* to his words,
Lk 12: 25 by worrying can *a* a single hour
Rev 22: 18 God will *a* to him the plagues

ADMIRABLE*

Php 4: 8 whatever is lovely, whatever is *a*—

ADMONISH

Col 3: 16 and *a* one another with all wisdom,

ADOPTED (ADOPTION)

Eph 1: 5 In love he predestined us to be *a*

ADOPTION (ADOPTED)

Ro 8: 23 as we wait eagerly for our *a* as sons,

ADORE*

SS 1: 4 How right they are to *a* you!

ADORNMENT* (ADORNS)

1Pe 3: 3 should not come from outward *a*,

ADORNS (ADORNMENT)

Ps 93: 5 holiness *a* your house

ADULTERY

Ex 20: 14 "You shall not commit *a*.
Mt 5: 27 that it was said, 'Do not commit *a*.'
5: 28 lustfully has already committed *a*

5: 32 the divorced woman commits *a.*
15: 19 murder, *a,* sexual immorality, theft

ADULTS*
1Co 14: 20 but in your thinking be *a.*

ADVANCED
Job 32: 7 *a* years should teach wisdom.'

ADVANTAGE
Ex 22: 22 "Do not take *a* of a widow
Dt 24: 14 Do not take *a* of a hired man who is
1Th 4: 6 should wrong his brother or take *a*

ADVERSITY
Pr 17: 17 and a brother is born for *a.*

ADVICE
1Ki 12: 8 rejected the *a* the elders
12: 14 he followed the *a* of the young men
Pr 12: 5 but the *a* of the wicked is deceitful.
12: 15 but a wise man listens to *a.*
19: 20 Listen to *a* and accept instruction,
20: 18 Make plans by seeking *a;*

AFFLICTION
Ro 12: 12 patient in *a,* faithful in prayer.

AFRAID (FEAR)
Ge 26: 24 Do not be *a,* for I am with you;
Ex 3: 6 because he was *a* to look at God.
Ps 27: 1 of whom shall I be *a?*
56: 3 When I am *a,* / I will trust in you.
Pr 3: 24 lie down, you will not be *a;*
Jer 1: 8 Do not be *a* of them, for I am
Mt 8: 26 You of little faith, why are you so *a*
10: 28 be *a* of the One who can destroy
10: 31 So don't be *a;* you are worth more
Mk 5: 36 "Don't be *a;* just believe."
Jn 14: 27 hearts be troubled and do not be *a.*
Heb 13: 6 Lord is my helper; I will not be *a.*

AGED
Job 12: 12 Is not wisdom found among the *a?*
Pr 17: 6 children are a crown to the *a,*

AGREE
Mt 18: 19 on earth *a* about anything you ask
Ro 7: 16 want to do, I *a* that the law is good.
Php 4: 2 with Syntyche to *a* with each other

AHAB
Son of Omri; king of Israel (1Ki 16:28-22:40), husband of Jezebel (1Ki 16:31). Promoted Baal worship (1Ki 16:31-33); opposed by Elijah (1Ki 17:1; 18; 21), a prophet (1Ki 20:35-43), Micaiah (1Ki 22:1-28). Defeated Ben-Hadad (1Ki 20). Killed for failing to kill Ben-Hadad and for murder of Naboth (1Ki 20:35-21:40).

AHAZ
Son of Jotham; king of Judah, (2Ki 16; 2Ch 28; Isa 7).

AHAZIAH
1. Son of Ahab; king of Israel (1Ki 22:51-2Ki 1:18; 2Ch 20:35-37).
2. Son of Jehoram; king of Judah (2Ki 8:25-29; 9:14-29), also called Jehoahaz (2Ch 21:17-22:9; 25:23).

AIM
1Co 7: 34 Her *a* is to be devoted to the Lord
2Co 13: 11 *A* for perfection, listen

AIR
Mt 8: 20 and birds of the *a* have nests,
1Co 9: 26 not fight like a man beating the *a.*
Eph 2: 2 of the ruler of the kingdom of the *a,*
1Th 4: 17 clouds to meet the Lord in the *a.*

ALABASTER
Mt 26: 7 came to him with an *a* jar

ALERT
Jos 8: 4 All of you be on the *a.*
Mk 13: 33 Be *a!* You do not know
Eph 6: 18 be *a* and always keep on praying
1Th 5: 6 but let us be *a* and self-controlled.

ALIEN (ALIENATED)
Ex 22: 21 "Do not mistreat an *a*

ALIENATED (ALIEN)
Gal 5: 4 by law have been *a* from Christ;

ALIVE (LIVE)
Ac 1: 3 convincing proofs that he was *a.*
Ro 6: 11 but *a* to God in Christ Jesus.
1Co 15: 22 so in Christ all will be made *a.*

ALMIGHTY (MIGHT)
Ge 17: 1 "I am God *A;* walk before me
Job 11: 7 Can you probe the limits of the *A?*
33: 4 the breath of the *A* gives me life.
Ps 91: 1 will rest in the shadow of the *A.*
Isa 6: 3 "Holy, holy, holy is the LORD *A;*

ALTAR
Ge 22: 9 his son Isaac and laid him on the *a,*
Ex 27: 1 "Build an *a* of acacia wood,
1Ki 18: 30 and he repaired the *a* of the LORD
2Ch 4: 1 made a bronze *a* twenty cubits
4: 19 the golden *a;* the tables

ALWAYS
Ps 16: 8 I have set the LORD *a* before me.
51: 3 and my sin is *a* before me.
Mt 26: 11 The poor you will *a* have with you,
28: 20 And surely I will be with you *a,*
1Co 13: 7 *a* protects, *a* trusts, *a* hopes, *a*
Php 4: 4 Rejoice in the Lord *a.*
1Pe 3: 15 *A* be prepared to give an answer

AMAZIAH
Son of Joash; king of Judah (2Ki 14; 2Ch 25).

AMBASSADORS
2Co 5: 20 We are therefore Christ's *a,*

AMBITION
Ro 15: 20 It has always been my *a*
1Th 4: 11 Make it your *a* to lead a quiet life,

AMON
Son of Manasseh; king of Judah (2Ki 21:18-26; 1Ch 3:14; 2Ch 33:21-25).

ANANIAS
1. Husband of Sapphira; died for lying to God (Ac 5:1-11).
2. Disciple who baptized Saul (Ac 9:10-19).
3. High priest at Paul's arrest (Ac 22:30-24:1).

ANCHOR
Heb 6: 19 We have this hope as an *a*

ANCIENT
Da 7: 9 and the *A* of Days took his seat.

ANDREW*
Apostle; brother of Simon Peter (Mt 4:18; 10:2; Mk 1:16-18, 29; 3:18; 13:3; Lk 6:14; Jn 1:35-44; 6:8-9; 12:22; Ac 1:13).

ANGEL (ANGELS ARCHANGEL)
Ps 34: 7 The *a* of the LORD encamps
Ac 6: 15 his face was like the face of an *a.*
2Co 11: 14 Satan himself masquerades as an *a*
Gal 1: 8 or an *a* from heaven should preach

ANGELS (ANGEL)
Ps 91: 11 command his *a* concerning you
Mt 18: 10 For I tell you that their *a*
25: 41 prepared for the devil and his *a.*
Lk 20: 36 for they are like the *a.*
1Co 6: 3 you not know that we will judge *a?*
Heb 1: 4 as much superior to the *a*
1: 14 Are not all *a* ministering spirits
2: 7 made him a little lower than the *a;*
13: 2 some people have entertained *a*
1Pe 1: 12 Even *a* long to look
2Pe 2: 4 For if God did not spare *a*

ANGER (ANGERED ANGRY)
Ex 32: 10 alone so that my *a* may burn
34: 6 slow to *a,* abounding in love
Dt 29: 28 In furious *a* and in great wrath
2Ki 22: 13 Great is the LORD's *a* that burns
Ps 30: 5 For his *a* lasts only a moment,
Pr 15: 1 but a harsh word stirs up *a.*
29: 11 A fool gives full vent to his *a,*

ANGERED (ANGER)
Pr 22: 24 do not associate with one easily *a,*
1Co 13: 5 it is not easily *a,* it keeps no record

ANGRY (ANGER)
Ps 2: 12 Kiss the Son, lest he be *a*
Pr 29: 22 An *a* man stirs up dissension,
Jas 1: 19 slow to speak and slow to become *a*

ANGUISH
Ps 118: 5 In my *a* I cried to the LORD,

ANOINT
Ps 23: 5 You *a* my head with oil;
Jas 5: 14 and *a* him with oil in the name

ANT*
Pr 6: 6 Go to the *a,* you sluggard;

ANTICHRIST
1Jn 2: 18 have heard that the *a* is coming,
2Jn : 7 person is the deceiver and the *a.*

ANTIOCH
Ac 11: 26 were called Christians first at *A.*

ANXIETY (ANXIOUS)
1Pe 5: 7 Cast all your *a* on him

ANXIOUS (ANXIETY)
Pr 12: 25 An *a* heart weighs a man down,
Php 4: 6 Do not be *a* about anything,

APOLLOS*
Christian from Alexandria, learned in the Scriptures; instructed by Aquila and Priscilla (Ac 18:24-28). Ministered at Corinth (Ac 19:1; 1Co 1:12; 3; Tit 3:13).

APOSTLES

See also Andrew, Bartholomew, James, John, Judas, Matthew, Nathanael, Paul, Peter, Philip, Simon, Thaddaeus, Thomas.

Mk 3: 14 twelve—designating them *a*—
Ac 1: 26 so he was added to the eleven *a*.
2: 43 signs were done by the *a*.
1Co 12: 28 God has appointed first of all *a*,
15: 9 For I am the least of the *a*
2Co 11: 13 masquerading as *a* of Christ.
Eph 2: 20 built on the foundation of the *a*

APPEAR (APPEARANCE APPEARING)

Mk 13: 22 false prophets will *a* and perform
2Co 5: 10 we must all *a* before the judgment
Col 3: 4 also will *a* with him in glory.
Heb 9: 24 now to *a* for us in God's presence.
9: 28 and he will *a* a second time,

APPEARANCE (APPEAR)

1Sa 16: 7 Man looks at the outward *a*,
Gal 2: 6 God does not judge by external *a*—

APPEARING (APPEAR)

2Ti 4: 8 to all who have longed for his *a*.
Tit 2: 13 the glorious *a* of our great God

APPLY

Pr 22: 17 *a* your heart to what I teach,
23: 12 *A* your heart to instruction

APPROACH

Eph 3: 12 in him we may *a* God with freedom
Heb 4: 16 Let us then *a* the throne of grace

APPROVED

2Ti 2: 15 to present yourself to God as one *a*,

AQUILA*

Husband of Priscilla; co-worker with Paul, instructor of Apollos (Ac 18; Ro 16:3; 1Co 16:19; 2Ti 4:19).

ARARAT

Ge 8: 4 came to rest on the mountains of *A*.

ARCHANGEL* (ANGEL)

1Th 4: 16 with the voice of the *a*
Jude : 9 *a* Michael, when he was disputing

ARCHITECT*

Heb 11: 10 whose *a* and builder is God.

ARK

Ge 6: 14 So make yourself an *a*
Dt 10: 5 put the tablets in the *a* I had made,
2Ch 35: 3 "Put the sacred *a* in the temple that
Heb 9: 4 This *a* contained the gold jar

ARM (ARMY)

Nu 11: 23 "Is the LORD's *a* too short?
1Pe 4: 1 *a* yourselves also with the same

ARMAGEDDON*

Rev 16: 16 that in Hebrew is called *A*.

ARMOR (ARMY)

1Ki 20: 11 on his *a* should not boast like one
Eph 6: 11 Put on the full *a* of God
6: 13 Therefore put on the full *a* of God,

ARMS (ARMY)

Dt 33: 27 underneath are the everlasting *a*.
Ps 18: 32 It is God who *a* me with strength
Pr 31: 20 She opens her *a* to the poor
Isa 40: 11 He gathers the lambs in his *a*
Mk 10: 16 And he took the children in his *a*,

ARMY (ARM ARMOR ARMS)

Ps 33: 16 No king is saved by the size of his *a*
Rev 19: 19 the rider on the horse and his *a*.

AROMA

2Co 2: 15 For we are to God the *a* of Christ

ARRAYED*

Ps 110: 3 *A* in holy majesty,
Isa 61: 10 and *a* me in a robe of righteousness

ARROGANT

Ro 11: 20 Do not be *a*, but be afraid.

ARROWS

Eph 6: 16 you can extinguish all the flaming *a*

ASA

King of Judah (1Ki 15:8-24; 1Ch 3:10; 2Ch 14-16).

ASCENDED

Eph 4: 8 "When he *a* on high,

ASCRIBE

1Ch 16: 28 *a* to the LORD glory and strength,
Job 36: 3 I will *a* justice to my Maker.
Ps 29: 2 *A* to the LORD the glory due his

ASHAMED (SHAME)

Lk 9: 26 If anyone is *a* of me and my words,
Ro 1: 16 I am not *a* of the gospel,
2Ti 1: 8 So do not be *a* to testify about our
2: 15 who does not need to be *a*

ASSIGNED

Mk 13: 34 with his *a* task, and tells the one
1Co 3: 5 as the Lord has *a* to each his task.
7: 17 place in life that the Lord *a* to him

ASSOCIATE

Pr 22: 24 do not *a* with one easily angered,
Ro 12: 16 but be willing to *a* with people
1Co 5: 11 am writing you that you must not *a*
2Th 3: 14 Do not *a* with him,

ASSURANCE

Heb 10: 22 with a sincere heart in full *a* of faith

ASTRAY

Pr 10: 17 ignores correction leads others *a*.
Isa 53: 6 We all, like sheep, have gone *a*,
Jer 50: 6 their shepherds have led them *a*
Jn 16: 1 you so that you will not go *a*.
1Pe 2: 25 For you were like sheep going *a*,
1Jn 3: 7 do not let anyone lead you *a*.

ATHALIAH

Evil queen of Judah (2Ki 11; 2Ch 23).

ATHLETE*

2Ti 2: 5 if anyone competes as an *a*,

ATONEMENT

Ex 25: 17 "Make an *a* cover of pure gold—
30: 10 Once a year Aaron shall make *a*
Lev 17: 11 it is the blood that makes *a*
23: 27 this seventh month is the Day of *A*.
Nu 25: 13 and made *a* for the Israelites."
Ro 3: 25 presented him as a sacrifice of *a*,
Heb 2: 17 that he might make *a* for the sins

ATTENTION

Pr 4: 1 pay *a* and gain understanding.
5: 1 My son, pay *a* to my wisdom,
22: 17 Pay *a* and listen to the sayings
Tit 1: 14 and will pay no *a* to Jewish myths

ATTITUDE (ATTITUDES)

Eph 4: 23 new in the *a* of your minds;
Php 2: 5 Your *a* should be the same
1Pe 4: 1 yourselves also with the same *a*,

ATTITUDES (ATTITUDE)

Heb 4: 12 it judges the thoughts and *a*

ATTRACTIVE

Tit 2: 10 teaching about God our Savior *a*.

AUTHORITIES (AUTHORITY)

Ro 13: 5 it is necessary to submit to the *a*,
13: 6 for the *a* are God's servants,
Tit 3: 1 people to be subject to rulers and *a*,
1Pe 3: 22 *a* and powers in submission to him.

AUTHORITY (AUTHORITIES)

Mt 7: 29 because he taught as one who had *a*
9: 6 the Son of Man has *a* on earth
28: 18 "All *a* in heaven and on earth has
Ro 13: 1 for there is no *a* except that which
13: 2 rebels against the *a* is rebelling
1Co 11: 10 to have a sign of *a* on her head.
1Ti 2: 2 for kings and all those in *a*,
2: 12 to teach or to have *a* over a man;
Heb 13: 17 your leaders and submit to their *a*.

AVENGE (VENGEANCE)

Dt 32: 35 It is mine to *a*; I will repay.

AVOID

Pr 20: 3 It is to a man's honor to *a* strife,
20: 19 so *a* a man who talks too much.
1Th 4: 3 you should *a* sexual immorality;
5: 22 *A* every kind of evil.
2Ti 2: 16 *A* godless chatter, because those
Tit 3: 9 But *a* foolish controversies

AWAKE

Ps 17: 15 when I *a*, I will be satisfied

AWE (AWESOME)

Job 25: 2 "Dominion and *a* belong to God;
Ps 119:120 I stand in *a* of your laws.
Ecc 5: 7 Therefore stand in *a* of God.
Isa 29: 23 will stand in *a* of the God of Israel.
Jer 33: 9 they will be in *a* and will tremble
Hab 3: 2 I stand in *a* of your deeds,
Mal 2: 5 and stood in *a* of my name.
Mt 9: 8 they were filled with *a*;
Lk 7: 16 They were all filled with *a*
Ac 2: 43 Everyone was filled with *a*,
Heb 12: 28 acceptably with reverence and *a*,

AWESOME (AWE)

Ge 28: 17 and said, "How *a* is this place!
Ex 15: 11 *a* in glory,
Dt 7: 21 is among you, is a great and *a* God.
10: 17 the great God, mighty and *a*,
28: 58 revere this glorious and *a* name—

Jdg 13: 6 like an angel of God, very *a.*
Ne 1: 5 of heaven, the great and *a* God,
9: 32 the great, mighty and *a* God,
Job 10: 16 again display your *a* power
37: 22 God comes in *a* majesty.
Ps 45: 4 let your right hand display *a* deeds.
47: 2 How *a* is the LORD Most High,
66: 5 how *a* his works in man's behalf!
68: 35 You are *a,* O God,
89: 7 he is more *a* than all who surround
99: 3 praise your great and *a* name—
111: 9 holy and *a* is his name.
145: 6 of the power of your *a* works,
Da 9: 4 "O Lord, the great and *a* God,

B

BAAL
1Ki 18: 25 Elijah said to the prophets of *B,*

BAASHA
King of Israel (1Ki 15:16-16:7; 2Ch 16:1-6).

BABIES (BABY)
Lk 18: 15 also bringing *b* to Jesus
1Pe 2: 2 Like newborn *b,* crave pure

BABY (BABIES)
Isa 49: 15 "Can a mother forget the *b*
Lk 1: 44 the *b* in my womb leaped for joy.
2: 12 You will find a *b* wrapped in strips
Jn 16: 21 but when her *b* is born she forgets

BABYLON
Ps 137: 1 By the rivers of *B* we sat and wept

BACKSLIDING
Jer 3: 22 I will cure you of *b.*"
14: 7 For our *b* is great;
Eze 37: 23 them from all their sinful *b,*

BALAAM
Prophet who attempted to curse Israel (Nu 22-24; Dt 23:4-5; 2Pe 2:15; Jude 11). Killed (Nu 31:8; Jos 13:22).

BALM
Jer 8: 22 Is there no *b* in Gilead?

BANISH
Jer 25: 10 I will *b* from them the sounds of joy

BANQUET
SS 2: 4 He has taken me to the *b* hall,
Lk 14: 13 when you give a *b,* invite the poor,

BAPTIZE (BAPTIZED)
Mt 3: 11 He will *b* you with the Holy Spirit
Mk 1: 8 he will *b* you with the Holy Spirit."
1Co 1: 17 For Christ did not send me to *b,*

BAPTIZED (BAPTIZE)
Mt 3: 6 they were *b* by him in the Jordan
Mk 1: 9 and was *b* by John in the Jordan.
10: 38 or be *b* with the baptism I am
16: 16 believes and is *b* will be saved,
Jn 4: 2 in fact it was not Jesus who *b,*
Ac 1: 5 but in a few days you will be *b*

BARABBAS
Mt 27: 26 Then he released *B* to them.

BARBS*
Nu 33: 55 allow to remain will become *b*

BARE
Heb 4: 13 and laid *b* before the eyes of him

BARNABAS*
Disciple, originally Joseph (Ac 4:36), prophet (Ac 13:1), apostle (Ac 14:14). Brought Paul to apostles (Ac 9:27), Antioch (Ac 11:22-29; Gal 2:1-13), on the first missionary journey (Ac 13-14). Together at Jerusalem Council, they separated over John Mark (Ac 15). Later coworkers (1Co 9:6; Col 4:10).

BARREN
Ps 113: 9 He settles the *b* woman

BARTHOLOMEW*
Apostle (Mt 10:3; Mk 3:18; Lk 6:14; Ac 1:13). Possibly also known as Nathanael (Jn 1:45-49; 21:2).

BATH
Jn 13: 10 person who has had a *b* needs only

BATHSHEBA
Wife of Uriah who committed adultery with and became wife of David (2Sa 11), mother of Solomon (2Sa 12:24; 1Ki 1-2; 1Ch 3:5).

BATTLE
2Ch 20: 15 For the *b* is not yours, but God's.
Ps 24: 8 the LORD mighty in *b.*
Ecc 9: 11 or the *b* to the strong,

BEAR (BEARING BIRTH BIRTHRIGHT BORN FIRSTBORN NEWBORN)
Ge 4: 13 punishment is more than I can *b.*
Ps 38: 4 like a burden too heavy to *b.*
Isa 53: 11 and he will *b* their iniquities.
Da 7: 5 beast, which looked like a *b.*
Mt 7: 18 A good tree cannot *b* bad fruit,
Jn 15: 2 branch that does *b* fruit he prunes
15: 16 and appointed you to go and *b* fruit—
Ro 15: 1 ought to *b* with the failings
1Co 10: 13 tempted beyond what you can *b.*
Col 3: 13 *B* with each other and forgive

BEARING (BEAR)
Eph 4: 2 *b* with one another in love.
Col 1: 10 *b* fruit in every good work,

BEAST
Rev 13: 18 him calculate the number of the *b,*

BEAT (BEATING)
Isa 2: 4 They will *b* their swords
Joel 3: 10 *B* your plowshares into swords
1Co 9: 27 I *b* my body and make it my slave

BEATING (BEAT)
1Co 9: 26 I do not fight like a man *b* the air.
1Pe 2: 20 if you receive a *b* for doing wrong

BEAUTIFUL (BEAUTY)
Ge 6: 2 that the daughters of men were *b,*
12: 11 "I know what a *b* woman you are.
12: 14 saw that she was a very *b* woman.
24: 16 The girl was very *b,* a virgin;
26: 7 of Rebekah, because she is *b.*"
29: 17 Rachel was lovely in form, and *b.*
Job 38: 31 "Can you bind the *b* Pleiades?
Pr 11: 22 is a *b* woman who shows no
Ecc 3: 11 He has made everything *b*
Isa 4: 2 of the LORD will be *b*
52: 7 How *b* on the mountains
Eze 20: 6 and honey, the most *b* of all lands.
Zec 9: 17 How attractive and *b* they will be!
Mt 23: 27 which look *b* on the outside
26: 10 She has done a *b* thing to me.
Ro 10: 15 "How *b* are the feet
1Pe 3: 5 in God used to make themselves *b.*

BEAUTY (BEAUTIFUL)
Ps 27: 4 to gaze upon the *b* of the LORD
45: 11 The king is enthralled by your *b;*
Pr 31: 30 is deceptive, and *b* is fleeting;
Isa 33: 17 Your eyes will see the king in his *b*
53: 2 He had no *b* or majesty
61: 3 to bestow on them a crown of *b*
Eze 28: 12 full of wisdom and perfect in *b.*
1Pe 3: 4 the unfading *b* of a gentle

BED
Heb 13: 4 and the marriage *b* kept pure,

BEELZEBUB
Lk 11: 15 "By *B,* the prince of demons,

BEER
Pr 20: 1 Wine is a mocker and *b* a brawler;

BEERSHEBA
Jdg 20: 1 all the Israelites from Dan to *B*

BEGINNING
Ge 1: 1 In the *b* God created the heavens
Ps 102: 25 In the *b* you laid the foundations
111: 10 of the LORD is the *b* of wisdom;
Pr 1: 7 of the LORD is the *b* of knowledge
Jn 1: 1 In the *b* was the Word,
1Jn 1: 1 That which was from the *b,*
Rev 21: 6 and the Omega, the *B* and the End.

BEHAVE
Ro 13: 13 Let us *b* decently, as in the daytime

BELIEVE (BELIEVED BELIEVER BELIEVERS BELIEVES BELIEVING)
Mt 18: 6 one of these little ones who *b* in me
21: 22 If you *b,* you will receive whatever
Mk 1: 15 Repent and *b* the good news!"
9: 24 "I do *b;* help me overcome my
16: 17 signs will accompany those who *b:*
Lk 8: 50 just *b,* and she will be healed."
24: 25 to *b* all that the prophets have
Jn 1: 7 that through him all men might *b.*
3: 18 does not *b* stands condemned
6: 29 to *b* in the one he has sent."
10: 38 you do not *b* me, *b* the miracles,
11: 27 "I *b* that you are the Christ,
14: 11 *B* me when I say that I am
16: 30 This makes us *b* that you came
16: 31 "You *b* at last!" Jesus answered.
17: 21 that the world may *b* that you have
20: 27 Stop doubting and *b.*"
20: 31 written that you may *b* that Jesus is
Ac 16: 31 They replied, "*B* in the Lord Jesus,
24: 14 I *b* everything that agrees
Ro 3: 22 faith in Jesus Christ to all who *b.*
4: 11 he is the father of all who *b*
10: 9 *b* in your heart that God raised him
10: 14 And how can they *b* in the one
16: 26 so that all nations might *b*

1Th 4: 14 We *b* that Jesus died and rose again
2Th 2: 11 delusion so that they will *b* the lie
1Ti 4: 10 and especially of those who *b*.
Tit 1: 6 a man whose children *b*
Heb 11: 6 comes to him must *b* that he exists
Jas 2: 19 Even the demons *b* that—
1Jn 4: 1 Dear friends, do not *b* every spirit,

BELIEVED (BELIEVE)

Ge 15: 6 Abram *b* the LORD, and he
Jnh 3: 5 The Ninevites *b* God.
Jn 1: 12 to those who *b* in his name,
2: 22 Then they *b* the Scripture
3: 18 because he has not *b* in the name
20: 8 He saw and *b*.
20: 29 who have not seen and yet have *b*."
Ac 13: 48 were appointed for eternal life *b*.
Ro 4: 3 Scripture say? "Abraham *b* God,
10: 14 call on the one they have not *b* in?
1Co 15: 2 Otherwise, you have *b* in vain.
Gal 3: 6 Consider Abraham: "He *b* God,
2Ti 1: 12 because I know whom I have *b*,
Jas 2: 23 that says, "Abraham *b* God,

BELIEVER (BELIEVE)

1Co 7: 12 brother has a wife who is not a *b*
2Co 6: 15 What does a *b* have in common

BELIEVERS (BELIEVE)

Ac 4: 32 All the *b* were one in heart
5: 12 And all the *b* used to meet together
1Co 6: 5 to judge a dispute between *b*?
1Ti 4: 12 set an example for the *b* in speech,
1Pe 2: 17 Love the brotherhood of *b*,

BELIEVES (BELIEVE)

Pr 14: 15 A simple man *b* anything,
Mk 9: 23 is possible for him who *b*."
11: 23 *b* that what he says will happen,
16: 16 Whoever *b* and is baptized will be
Jn 3: 16 that whoever *b* in him shall not
3: 36 Whoever *b* in the Son has eternal
5: 24 *b* him who sent me has eternal life
6: 35 and he who *b* in me will never be
6: 40 and *b* in him shall have eternal life,
6: 47 he who *b* has everlasting life.
7: 38 Whoever *b* in me, as the Scripture
11: 26 and *b* in me will never die.
Ro 1: 16 for the salvation of everyone who *b*
10: 4 righteousness for everyone who *b*.
1Jn 5: 1 Everyone who *b* that Jesus is
5: 5 Only he who *b* that Jesus is the Son

BELIEVING (BELIEVE)

Jn 20: 31 and that by *b* you may have life

BELONG (BELONGS)

Dt 29: 29 The secret things *b*
Job 25: 2 "Dominion and awe *b* to God;
Ps 47: 9 for the kings of the earth *b* to God;
95: 4 and the mountain peaks *b* to him.
Jn 8: 44 You *b* to your father, the devil,
15: 19 As it is, you do not *b* to the world,
Ro 1: 6 called to *b* to Jesus Christ.
7: 4 that you might *b* to another,
14: 8 we live or die, we *b* to the Lord.
Gal 5: 24 Those who *b* to Christ Jesus have
1Th 5: 8 But since we *b* to the day, let us be

BELONGS (BELONG)

Job 41: 11 Everything under heaven *b* to me.
Ps 111: 10 To him *b* eternal praise.
Eze 18: 4 For every living soul *b* to me,
Jn 8: 47 He who *b* to God hears what God
Ro 12: 5 each member *b* to all the others.

BELOVED (LOVE)

Dt 33: 12 "Let the *b* of the LORD rest secure

BELT

Isa 11: 5 Righteousness will be his *b*
Eph 6: 14 with the *b* of truth buckled

BENEFIT (BENEFITS)

Ro 6: 22 the *b* you reap leads to holiness,
2Co 4: 15 All this is for your *b*,

BENEFITS (BENEFIT)

Ps 103: 2 and forget not all his *b*.
Jn 4: 38 you have reaped the *b* of their labor

BENJAMIN

Twelfth son of Jacob by Rachel (Ge 35:16-24; 46:19-21; 1Ch 2:2). Jacob refused to send him to Egypt, but relented (Ge 42-45).

BEREANS*

Ac 17: 11 the *B* were of more noble character

BESTOWS

Ps 84: 11 the LORD *b* favor and honor;

BETHLEHEM

Mt 2: 1 After Jesus was born in *B* in Judea,

BETRAY

Pr 25: 9 do not *b* another man's confidence,

BIND (BINDS)

Dt 6: 8 and *b* them on your foreheads.
Pr 6: 21 *B* them upon your heart forever;
Isa 61: 1 me to *b* up the brokenhearted,
Mt 16: 19 whatever you *b* on earth will be

BINDS (BIND)

Ps 147: 3 and *b* up their wounds.
Isa 30: 26 when the LORD *b* up the bruises

BIRDS

Mt 8: 20 and *b* of the air have nests,

BIRTH (BEAR)

Ps 58: 3 Even from *b* the wicked go astray;
Mt 1: 18 This is how the *b* of Jesus Christ
1Pe 1: 3 great mercy he has given us new *b*

BIRTHRIGHT (BEAR)

Ge 25: 34 So Esau despised his *b*.

BLAMELESS

Ge 17: 1 walk before me and be *b*.
Job 1: 1 This man was *b* and upright;
Ps 84: 11 from those whose walk is *b*.
119: 1 Blessed are they whose ways are *b*,
Pr 19: 1 Better a poor man whose walk is *b*
1Co 1: 8 so that you will be *b* on the day
Eph 5: 27 any other blemish, but holy and *b*.
Php 2: 15 so that you may become *b* and pure
1Th 3: 13 hearts so that you will be *b*
5: 23 and body be kept *b* at the coming
Tit 1: 6 An elder must be *b*, the husband of
Heb 7: 26 *b*, pure, set apart from sinners,
2Pe 3: 14 effort to be found spotless, *b*

BLASPHEMES

Mk 3: 29 whoever *b* against the Holy Spirit

BLEMISH

1Pe 1: 19 a lamb without *b* or defect.

BLESS (BLESSED BLESSING BLESSINGS)

Ge 12: 3 I will *b* those who *b* you,
Ro 12: 14 Bless those who persecute you; *b*

BLESSED (BLESS)

Ge 1: 22 God *b* them and said, "Be fruitful
2: 3 And God *b* the seventh day
22: 18 nations on earth will be *b*,
Ps 1: 1 *B* is the man
2: 12 *B* are all who take refuge in him.
33: 12 *B* is the nation whose God is
41: 1 *B* is he who has regard for the weak
84: 5 *B* are those whose strength is
106: 3 are they who maintain justice,
112: 1 *B* is the man who fears the LORD,
118: 26 *B* is he who comes in the name
Pr 29: 18 but *b* is he who keeps the law.
31: 28 Her children arise and call her *b*;
Mt 5: 3 saying: "*B* are the poor in spirit,
5: 4 *B* are those who mourn,
5: 5 *B* are the meek,
5: 6 *B* are those who hunger
5: 7 *B* are the merciful,
5: 8 *B* are the pure in heart,
5: 9 *B* are the peacemakers,
5: 10 *B* are those who are persecuted
5: 11 "*B* are you when people insult you,
Lk 1: 48 on all generations will call me *b*,
Jn 12: 13 "*B* is he who comes in the name
Ac 20: 35 'It is more *b* to give than to receive
Tit 2: 13 while we wait for the *b* hope—
Jas 1: 12 *B* is the man who perseveres
Rev 1: 3 *B* is the one who reads the words
22: 14 "*B* are those who wash their robes,

BLESSING (BLESS)

Eze 34: 26 there will be showers of *b*.

BLESSINGS (BLESS)

Pr 10: 6 *B* crown the head of the righteous,

BLIND

Mt 15: 14 a *b* man leads a *b* man, both will fall
23: 16 "Woe to you, *b* guides! You say,
Jn 9: 25 I was *b* but now I see!"

BLOOD

Ge 9: 6 "Whoever sheds the *b* of man,
Ex 12: 13 and when I see the *b*, I will pass
24: 8 "This is the *b* of the covenant that
Lev 17: 11 For the life of a creature is in the *b*,

Ps 72: 14 for precious is their *b* in his sight.
Pr 6: 17 hands that shed innocent *b,*
Mt 26: 28 This is my *b* of the covenant,
Ro 3: 25 of atonement, through faith in his *b*
5: 9 have now been justified by his *b,*
1Co 11: 25 cup is the new covenant in my *b;*
Eph 1: 7 we have redemption through his *b,*
2: 13 near through the *b* of Christ.
Col 1: 20 by making peace through his *b,*
Heb 9: 12 once for all by his own *b,*
9: 22 of *b* there is no forgiveness.
1Pe 1: 19 but with the precious *b* of Christ,
1Jn 1: 7 and the *b* of Jesus, his Son,
Rev 1: 5 has freed us from our sins by his *b,*
5: 9 with your *b* you purchased men
7: 14 white in the *b* of the Lamb.
12: 11 him by the *b* of the Lamb

BLOT (BLOTS)

Ex 32: 32 then *b* me out of the book you have
Ps 51: 1 *b* out my transgressions.
Rev 3: 5 I will never *b* out his name

BLOTS (BLOT)

Isa 43: 25 "I, even I, am he who *b* out

BLOWN

Eph 4: 14 and *b* here and there by every wind
Jas 1: 6 doubts is like a wave of the sea, *b*

BOAST

1Ki 20: 11 armor should not *b* like one who
Ps 34: 2 My soul will *b* in the LORD;
44: 8 In God we make our *b* all day long,
Pr 27: 1 Do not *b* about tomorrow,
1Co 1: 31 Let him who boasts *b* in the Lord."
Gal 6: 14 May I never *b* except in the cross
Eph 2: 9 not by works, so that no one can *b.*

BOAZ

Wealthy Bethlehemite who showed favor to Ruth (Ru 2), married her (Ru 4). Ancestor of David (Ru 4:18-22; 1Ch 2:12-15), Jesus (Mt 1:5-16; Lk 3:23-32).

BODIES (BODY)

Ro 12: 1 to offer your *b* as living sacrifices,
1Co 6: 15 not know that your *b* are members
Eph 5: 28 to love their wives as their own *b.*

BODY (BODIES)

Zec 13: 6 What are these wounds on your *b?*'
Mt 10: 28 afraid of those who kill the *b*
26: 26 saying, "Take and eat; this is my *b*
26: 41 spirit is willing, but the *b* is weak."
Jn 13: 10 wash his feet; his whole *b* is clean.
Ro 6: 13 Do not offer the parts of your *b*
12: 4 us has one *b* with many members,
1Co 6: 19 not know that your *b* is a temple
11: 24 "This is my *b,* which is for you;
12: 12 The *b* is a unit, though it is made up
Eph 5: 30 for we are members of his *b.*

BOLD (BOLDNESS)

Ps 138: 3 you made me *b* and stouthearted.
Pr 21: 29 A wicked man puts up a *b* front,
28: 1 but the righteous are as *b* as a lion.

BOLDNESS* (BOLD)

Ac 4: 29 to speak your word with great *b.*

BONDAGE

Ezr 9: 9 God has not deserted us in our *b.*

BOOK (BOOKS)

Jos 1: 8 Do not let this *B* of the Law depart
Ne 8: 8 They read from the *B* of the Law
Jn 20: 30 which are not recorded in this *b.*
Php 4: 3 whose names are in the *b* of life.
Rev 21: 27 written in the Lamb's *b* of life.

BOOKS (BOOK)

Ecc 12: 12 Of making many *b* there is no end,

BORN (BEAR)

Isa 9: 6 For to us a child is *b,*
Jn 3: 7 at my saying, 'You must be *b* again
1Pe 1: 23 For you have been *b* again,
1Jn 4: 7 Everyone who loves has been *b*
5: 1 believes that Jesus is the Christ is *b*

BORROWER

Pr 22: 7 and the *b* is servant to the lender.

BOUGHT

Ac 20: 28 which he *b* with his own blood.
1Co 6: 20 You are not your own; you were *b*
7: 23 You were *b* at a price; do not
2Pe 2: 1 the sovereign Lord who *b* them—

BOW

Ps 95: 6 Come, let us *b* down in worship,
Isa 45: 23 Before me every knee will *b;*
Ro 14: 11 'every knee will *b* before me;
Php 2: 10 name of Jesus every knee should *b,*

BRANCH (BRANCHES)

Isa 4: 2 In that day the *B* of the LORD will
Jer 33: 15 I will make a righteous *B* sprout

BRANCHES (BRANCH)

Jn 15: 5 "I am the vine; you are the *b.*

BRAVE

2Sa 2: 7 Now then, be strong and *b,*

BREAD

Dt 8: 3 that man does not live on *b* alone
Pr 30: 8 but give me only my daily *b.*
Ecc 11: 1 Cast your *b* upon the waters,
Isa 55: 2 Why spend money on what is not *b*
Mt 4: 4 'Man does not live on *b* alone,
6: 11 Give us today our daily *b.*
Jn 6: 35 Jesus declared, "I am the *b* of life.
21: 13 took the *b* and gave it to them,
1Co 11: 23 took *b,* and when he had given

BREAK (BREAKING BROKEN)

Nu 30: 2 he must not *b* his word
Jdg 2: 1 'I will never *b* my covenant
Isa 42: 3 A bruised reed he will not *b,*
Mt 12: 20 A bruised reed he will not *b,*

BREAKING (BREAK)

Jas 2: 10 at just one point is guilty of *b* all

BREASTPIECE (BREASTPLATE)

Ex 28: 15 Fashion a *b* for making decisions—

BREASTPLATE* (BREASTPIECE)

Isa 59: 17 He put on righteousness as his *b,*
Eph 6: 14 with the *b* of righteousness in place
1Th 5: 8 putting on faith and love as a *b,*

BREATHED (GOD-BREATHED)

Ge 2: 7 *b* into his nostrils the breath of life,
Jn 20: 22 And with that he *b* on them

BREEDS*

Pr 13: 10 Pride only *b* quarrels,

BRIBE

Ex 23: 8 "Do not accept a *b,*
Pr 6: 35 will refuse the *b,* however great it

BRIDE

Rev 19: 7 and his *b* has made herself ready,

BRIGHTER (BRIGHTNESS)

Pr 4: 18 shining ever *b* till the full light

BRIGHTNESS (BRIGHTER)

2Sa 22: 13 Out of the *b* of his presence
Da 12: 3 who are wise will shine like the *b*

BROAD

Mt 7: 13 and *b* is the road that leads

BROKEN (BREAK)

Ps 51: 17 The sacrifices of God are a *b* spirit;
Ecc 4: 12 of three strands is not quickly *b.*
Jn 10: 35 and the Scripture cannot be *b*—

BROKENHEARTED* (HEART)

Ps 34: 18 The LORD is close to the *b*
109: 16 and the needy and the *b.*
147: 3 He heals the *b*
Isa 61: 1 He has sent me to bind up the *b,*

BROTHER (BROTHER'S BROTHERS)

Pr 17: 17 and a *b* is born for adversity.
18: 24 a friend who sticks closer than a *b.*
27: 10 neighbor nearby than a *b* far away.
Mt 5: 24 and be reconciled to your *b;*
18: 15 "If your *b* sins against you,
Mk 3: 35 Whoever does God's will is my *b*
Lk 17: 3 "If your *b* sins, rebuke him,
1Co 8: 13 if what I eat causes my *b* to fall
1Jn 2: 10 Whoever loves his *b* lives
4: 21 loves God must also love his *b.*

BROTHER'S (BROTHER)

Ge 4: 9 "Am I my *b* keeper?" The LORD

BROTHERS (BROTHER)

Ps 133: 1 is when *b* live together in unity!
Pr 6: 19 who stirs up dissension among *b.*
Mt 25: 40 one of the least of these *b* of mine,
Mk 10: 29 or *b* or sisters or mother or father
Heb 13: 1 Keep on loving each other as *b.*
1Pe 3: 8 be sympathetic, love as *b,*
1Jn 3: 14 death to life, because we love our *b.*

BUILD (BUILDING BUILDS BUILT)

Mt 16: 18 and on this rock I will *b* my church,
Ac 20: 32 which can *b* you up and give you
1Co 14: 12 excel in gifts that *b* up the church.
1Th 5: 11 one another and *b* each other up,

BUILDING (BUILD)
1Co 3: 9 you are God's field, God's *b.*
2Co 10: 8 us for *b* you up rather
Eph 4: 29 helpful for *b* others up according

BUILDS (BUILD)
Ps 127: 1 Unless the LORD *b* the house,
1Co 3: 10 one should be careful how he *b.*
8: 1 Knowledge puffs up, but love *b* up.

BUILT (BUILD)
Mt 7: 24 is like a wise man who *b* his house
Eph 2: 20 *b* on the foundation of the apostles
4: 12 the body of Christ may be *b* up

BURDEN (BURDENED BURDENS)
Ps 38: 4 like a *b* too heavy to bear.
Mt 11: 30 my yoke is easy and my *b* is light."

BURDENED (BURDEN)
Gal 5: 1 do not let yourselves be *b* again

BURDENS (BURDEN)
Ps 68: 19 who daily bears our *b.*
Gal 6: 2 Carry each other's *b,*

BURIED
Ro 6: 4 *b* with him through baptism
1Co 15: 4 that he was *b,* that he was raised

BURNING
Lev 6: 9 the fire must be kept *b* on the altar.
Ro 12: 20 you will heap *b* coals on his head."

BUSINESS
Da 8: 27 and went about the king's *b.*
1Th 4: 11 to mind your own *b* and to work

BUSY
1Ki 20: 40 While your servant was *b* here
2Th 3: 11 They are not *b;* they are
Tit 2: 5 to be *b* at home, to be kind,

C

CAESAR
Mt 22: 21 "Give to *C* what is Caesar's,

CAIN
Firstborn of Adam (Ge 4:1), murdered brother Abel (Ge 4:1-16; 1Jn 3:12).

CALEB
Judahite who spied out Canaan (Nu 13:6); allowed to enter land because of faith (Nu 13:30-14:38; Dt 1:36). Possessed Hebron(Jos 14:6-15:19).

CALF
Ex 32: 4 into an idol cast in the shape of a *c,*
Lk 15: 23 Bring the fattened *c* and kill it.

CALL (CALLED CALLING CALLS)
Ps 105: 1 to the LORD, *c* on his name;
145: 18 near to all who *c* on him,
Pr 31: 28 children arise and *c* her blessed;
Isa 5: 20 Woe to those who *c* evil good
55: 6 *c* on him while he is near.
65: 24 Before they *c* I will answer;
Jer 33: 3 '*C* to me and I will answer you
Mt 9: 13 come to *c* the righteous,
Ro 10: 12 and richly blesses all who *c* on him,
11: 29 gifts and his *c* are irrevocable.
1Th 4: 7 For God did not *c* us to be impure,

CALLED (CALL)
1Sa 3: 5 and said, "Here I am; you *c* me."
2Ch 7: 14 if my people, who are *c*
Ps 34: 6 This poor man *c,* and the LORD
Mt 21: 13 "'My house will be *c* a house
Ro 8: 30 And those he predestined, he also *c*
1Co 7: 15 God has *c* us to live in peace.
Gal 5: 13 You, my brothers, were *c* to be free
1Pe 2: 9 of him who *c* you out of darkness

CALLING (CALL)
Jn 1: 23 I am the voice of one *c* in the desert
Ac 22: 16 wash your sins away, *c* on his name
Eph 4: 1 worthy of the *c* you have received.
2Pe 1: 10 all the more eager to make your *c*

CALLS (CALL)
Joel 2: 32 And everyone who *c*
Jn 10: 3 He *c* his own sheep by name
Ro 10: 13 "Everyone who *c* on the name

CAMEL
Mt 19: 24 it is easier for a *c* to go
23: 24 strain out a gnat but swallow a *c.*

CANAAN
1Ch 16: 18 "To you I will give the land of *C*

CANCELED
Lk 7: 42 so he *c* the debts of both.
Col 2: 14 having *c* the written code,

CAPITAL
Dt 21: 22 guilty of a *c* offense is put to death

CAPSTONE (STONE)
Ps 118: 22 has become the *c;*
1Pe 2: 7 has become the *c,*"

CARE (CAREFUL CARES CARING)
Ps 8: 4 the son of man that you *c* for him?
Pr 29: 7 The righteous *c* about justice
Lk 10: 34 him to an inn and took *c* of him.
Jn 21: 16 Jesus said, "Take *c* of my sheep."
Heb 2: 6 the son of man that you *c* for him?
1Pe 5: 2 of God's flock that is under your *c,*

CAREFUL (CARE)
Ex 23: 13 "Be *c* to do everything I have said
Dt 6: 3 be *c* to obey so that it may go well
Jos 23: 6 be *c* to obey all that is written
23: 11 be very *c* to love the LORD your
Pr 13: 24 he who loves him is *c*
Mt 6: 1 "Be *c* not to do your 'acts
Ro 12: 17 Be *c* to do what is right in the eyes
1Co 3: 10 each one should be *c* how he builds
8: 9 Be *c,* however, that the exercise
Eph 5: 15 Be very *c,* then, how you live

CARELESS
Mt 12: 36 for every *c* word they have spoken.

CARES (CARE)
Ps 55: 22 Cast your *c* on the LORD
Na 1: 7 He *c* for those who trust in him,
Eph 5: 29 but he feeds and *c* for it, just
1Pe 5: 7 on him because he *c* for you.

CARING* (CARE)
1Th 2: 7 like a mother *c* for her little
1Ti 5: 4 practice by *c* for their own family

CARRIED (CARRY)
Ex 19: 4 and how I *c* you on eagles' wings
Isa 53: 4 and *c* our sorrows,
Heb 13: 9 Do not be *c* away by all kinds
2Pe 1: 21 as they were *c* along by the Holy

CARRIES (CARRY)
Dt 32: 11 and *c* them on its pinions.
Isa 40: 11 and *c* them close to his heart;

CARRY (CARRIED CARRIES)
Lk 14: 27 anyone who does not *c* his cross
Gal 6: 2 *C* each other's burdens,
6: 5 for each one should *c* his own load.

CAST
Ps 22: 18 and *c* lots for my clothing.
55: 22 *C* your cares on the LORD
Ecc 11: 1 *C* your bread upon the waters,
Jn 19: 24 and *c* lots for my clothing."
1Pe 5: 7 *C* all your anxiety on him

CATCH (CAUGHT)
Lk 5: 10 from now on you will *c* men."

CATTLE
Ps 50: 10 and the *c* on a thousand hills.

CAUGHT (CATCH)
1Th 4: 17 and are left will be *c* up together

CAUSE (CAUSES)
Pr 24: 28 against your neighbor without *c,*
Ecc 8: 3 Do not stand up for a bad *c,*
Mt 18: 7 of the things that *c* people to sin!
Ro 14: 21 else that will *c* your brother
1Co 10: 32 Do not *c* anyone to stumble,

CAUSES (CAUSE)
Isa 8: 14 a stone that *c* men to stumble
Mt 18: 6 if anyone *c* one of these little ones

CAUTIOUS*
Pr 12: 26 A righteous man is *c* in friendship,

CEASE
Ps 46: 9 He makes wars *c* to the ends

CENSER
Lev 16: 12 is to take a *c* full of burning coals

CENTURION
Mt 8: 5 had entered Capernaum, a *c* came

CERTAIN (CERTAINTY)
2Pe 1: 19 word of the prophets made more *c,*

CERTAINTY* (CERTAIN)
Lk 1: 4 so that you may know the *c*
Jn 17: 8 They knew with *c* that I came

CHAFF
Ps 1: 4 They are like *c*

CHAINED
2Ti 2: 9 But God's word is not *c.*

CHAMPION
Ps 19: 5 like a *c* rejoicing to run his course.

CHANGE (CHANGED)
1Sa 15: 29 of Israel does not lie or *c* his mind;
Ps 110: 4 and will not *c* his mind:
Jer 7: 5 If you really *c* your ways
Mal 3: 6 "I the LORD do not *c.*
Mt 18: 3 unless you *c* and become like little
Heb 7: 21 and will not *c* his mind:
Jas 1: 17 who does not *c* like shifting

CHANGED (CHANGE)
1Co 15: 51 but we will all be *c*—in a flash,

CHARACTER
Ru 3: 11 that you are a woman of noble *c.*

Pr 31: 10 A wife of noble *c* who can find?
Ro 5: 4 perseverance, *c*; and *c*, hope.
1Co 15: 33 "Bad company corrupts good *c*."

CHARGE

Ro 8: 33 Who will bring any *c*
2Co 11: 7 the gospel of God to you free of *c*?
2Ti 4: 1 I give you this *c*: Preach the Word;

CHARIOTS

2Ki 6: 17 and *c* of fire all around Elisha.
Ps 20: 7 Some trust in *c* and some in horses,

CHARM

Pr 31: 30 *C* is deceptive, and beauty is

CHASES

Pr 12: 11 he who *c* fantasies lacks judgment.

CHATTER* (CHATTERING)

1Ti 6: 20 Turn away from godless *c*
2Ti 2: 16 Avoid godless *c*, because those

CHATTERING* (CHATTER)

Pr 10: 8 but a *c* fool comes to ruin.
10: 10 and a *c* fool comes to ruin.

CHEAT* (CHEATED)

Mal 1: 14 "Cursed is the *c* who has
1Co 6: 8 you yourselves *c* and do wrong,

CHEATED (CHEAT)

Lk 19: 8 if I have *c* anybody out of anything,
1Co 6: 7 Why not rather be *c*? Instead,

CHEEK

Mt 5: 39 someone strikes you on the right *c*,

CHEERFUL* (CHEERS)

Pr 15: 13 A happy heart makes the face *c*,
15: 15 but the *c* heart has a con tinual feast
15: 30 A *c* look brings joy to the heart,
17: 22 A *c* heart is good medicine,
2Co 9: 7 for God loves a *c* giver.

CHEERS (CHEERFUL)

Pr 12: 25 but a kind word *c* him up.

CHILD (CHILDISH CHILDREN)

Pr 20: 11 Even a *c* is known by his actions,
22: 6 Train a *c* in the way he should go,
22: 15 Folly is bound up in the heart of a *c*
23: 13 not withhold discipline from a *c*;
29: 15 *c* left to himself disgraces his mother.
Isa 7: 14 The virgin will be with *c*
9: 6 For to us a *c* is born,
11: 6 and a little *c* will lead them.
66: 13 As a mother comforts her *c*,
Mt 1: 23 "The virgin will be with *c*
18: 2 He called a little *c* and had him
Lk 1: 42 and blessed is the *c* you will bear!
1: 80 And the *c* grew and became strong
1Co 13: 11 When I was a *c*, I talked like a *c*,
1Jn 5: 1 who loves the father loves his *c*

CHILDISH* (CHILD)

1Co 13: 11 When I became a man, I put *c* ways

CHILDREN (CHILD)

Dt 4: 9 Teach them to your *c*
11: 19 them to your *c*, talking about them
Ps 8: 2 From the lips of *c* and infants
Pr 17: 6 Children's *c* are a crown
31: 28 Her *c* arise and call her blessed;
Mt 7: 11 how to give good gifts to your *c*,
11: 25 and revealed them to little *c*.
18: 3 you change and become like little *c*
19: 14 "Let the little *c* come to me,
21: 16 "'From the lips of *c* and infants
Mk 9: 37 one of these little *c* in my name
10: 14 "Let the little *c* come to me,
10: 16 And he took the *c* in his arms,
13: 12 *C* will rebel against their parents
Lk 10: 21 and revealed them to little *c*.
18: 16 "Let the little *c* come to me,
Ro 8: 16 with our spirit that we are God's *c*.
2Co 12: 14 parents, but parents for their *c*.
Eph 6: 1 *C*, obey your parents in the Lord,
6: 4 do not exasperate your *c*; instead,
Col 3: 20 *C*, obey your parents in everything,
3: 21 Fathers, do not embitter your *c*,
1Ti 3: 4 and see that his *c* obey him
3: 12 and must manage his *c* and his
5: 10 bringing up *c*, showing hospitality,
1Jn 3: 1 that we should be called *c* of God!

CHOOSE (CHOOSES CHOSE CHOSEN)

Dt 30: 19 Now *c* life, so that you
Jos 24: 15 then *c* for yourselves this day
Pr 8: 10 *C* my instruction instead of silver,
16: 16 to *c* understanding rather
Jn 15: 16 You did not *c* me, but I chose you

CHOOSES (CHOOSE)

Jn 7: 17 If anyone *c* to do God's will,

CHOSE (CHOOSE)

Ge 13: 11 So Lot *c* for himself the whole plain
Ps 33: 12 the people he *c* for his inheritance.
Jn 15: 16 but I *c* you and appointed you to go
1Co 1: 27 But God *c* the foolish things
Eph 1: 4 he *c* us in him before the creation
2Th 2: 13 from the beginning God *c* you

CHOSEN (CHOOSE)

Isa 41: 8 Jacob, whom I have *c*,
Mt 22: 14 For many are invited, but few are *c*
Lk 10: 42 Mary has *c* what is better,
23: 35 the Christ of God, the *C* One."
Jn 15: 19 but I have *c* you out of the world.
1Pe 1: 20 He was *c* before the creation
2: 9 But you are a *c* people, a royal

CHRIST (CHRIST'S CHRISTIAN CHRISTS)

Mt 1: 16 was born Jesus, who is called *C*.
16: 16 Peter answered, "You are the *C*,
22: 42 "What do you think about the *C*?
Jn 1: 41 found the Messiah" (that is, the *C*).
20: 31 you may believe that Jesus is the *C*,
Ac 2: 36 you crucified, both Lord and *C*."
5: 42 the good news that Jesus is the *C*.
9: 22 by proving that Jesus is the *C*.
17: 3 proving that the *C* had to suffer
18: 28 the Scriptures that Jesus was the *C*.
26: 23 that the *C* would suffer and,
Ro 3: 22 comes through faith in Jesus *C*
5: 6 we were still powerless, *C* died
5: 8 While we were still sinners, *C* died
5: 17 life through the one man, Jesus *C*.
6: 4 as *C* was raised from the dead
8: 1 for those who are in *C* Jesus,
8: 9 Spirit of *C*, he does not belong to *C*.
8: 35 us from the love of *C*?
10: 4 *C* is the end of the law
14: 9 *C* died and returned to life
15: 3 For even *C* did not please himself
1Co 1: 23 but we preach *C* crucified:
2: 2 except Jesus *C* and him crucified.
3: 11 one already laid, which is Jesus *C*.
5: 7 For *C*, our Passover lamb,
8: 6 and there is but one Lord, Jesus *C*,
10: 4 them, and that rock was *C*.
11: 1 as I follow the example of *C*.
11: 3 the head of every man is *C*,
12: 27 Now you are the body of *C*,
15: 3 that *C* died for our sins according
15: 14 And if *C* has not been raised,
15: 22 so in *C* all will be made alive.
15: 57 victory through our Lord Jesus *C*.
2Co 3: 3 show that you are a letter from *C*,
4: 5 not preach ourselves, but Jesus *C*
5: 10 before the judgment seat of *C*,
5: 17 Therefore, if anyone is in *C*,
11: 2 you to one husband, to *C*,
Gal 2: 20 I have been crucified with *C*
3: 13 *C* redeemed us from the curse
6: 14 in the cross of our Lord Jesus *C*,
Eph 1: 3 with every spiritual blessing in *C*.
3: 8 the unsearchable riches of *C*,
4: 13 measure of the fullness of *C*.
5: 2 as *C* loved us and gave himself up
5: 23 as *C* is the head of the church,
5: 25 just as *C* loved the church
Php 1: 21 to live is *C* and to die is gain.
1: 27 worthy of the gospel of *C*.
4: 19 to his glorious riches in *C* Jesus.
Col 1: 27 which is *C* in you, the hope of glory
1: 28 may present everyone perfect in *C*.
2: 6 as you received *C* Jesus as Lord,
2: 17 the reality, however, is found in *C*.
3: 15 Let the peace of *C* rule
2Th 2: 1 the coming of our Lord Jesus *C*
1Ti 1: 15 *C* Jesus came into the world
2: 5 the man *C* Jesus, who gave himself
2Ti 2: 3 us like a good soldier of *C* Jesus.
3: 15 salvation through faith in *C* Jesus.
Tit 2: 13 our great God and Savior, Jesus *C*,

Heb 3: 14 to share in *C* if we hold firmly
9: 14 more, then, will the blood of *C*,
9: 15 For this reason *C* is the mediator
9: 28 so *C* was sacrificed once
10: 10 of the body of Jesus *C* once for all.
13: 8 Jesus *C* is the same yesterday
1Pe 1: 19 but with the precious blood of *C*,
2: 21 because *C* suffered for you,
3: 18 For *C* died for sins once for all,
4: 14 insulted because of the name of *C*,
1Jn 2: 22 man who denies that Jesus is the *C*.
3: 16 Jesus *C* laid down his life for us.
5: 1 believes that Jesus is the *C* is born
Rev 20: 4 reigned with *C* a thousand years.

CHRIST'S (CHRIST)
2Co 5: 14 For *C* love compels us,
5: 20 We are therefore *C* ambassadors,
12: 9 so that *C* power may rest on me.

CHRISTIAN (CHRIST)
1Pe 4: 16 as a *C*, do not be ashamed,

CHRISTS (CHRIST)
Mt 24: 24 For false *C* and false prophets will

CHURCH
Mt 16: 18 and on this rock I will build my *c*,
18: 17 if he refuses to listen even to the *c*,
Ac 20: 28 Be shepherds of the *c* of God,
1Co 5: 12 of mine to judge those outside the *c*
14: 4 but he who prophesies edifies the *c*.
14: 12 to excel in gifts that build up the *c*.
14: 26 done for the strengthening of the *c*.
Eph 5: 23 as Christ is the head of the *c*,
Col 1: 24 the sake of his body, which is the *c*.

CIRCUMCISED
Ge 17: 10 Every male among you shall be *c*.

CIRCUMSTANCES
Php 4: 11 to be content whatever the *c*.
1Th 5: 18 continually; give thanks in all *c*,

CITIZENS (CITIZENSHIP)
Eph 2: 19 but fellow *c* with God's people

CITIZENSHIP (CITIZENS)
Php 3: 20 But our *c* is in heaven.

CITY
Mt 5: 14 A *c* on a hill cannot be hidden.
Heb 13: 14 here we do not have an enduring *c*,

CIVILIAN*
2Ti 2: 4 a soldier gets involved in *c* affairs—

CLAIM (CLAIMS)
Pr 25: 6 do not *c* a place among great men;
1Jn 1: 6 If we *c* to have fellowship
1: 8 If we *c* to be without sin, we
1: 10 If we *c* we have not sinned,

CLAIMS (CLAIM)
Jas 2: 14 if a man *c* to have faith
1Jn 2: 6 Whoever *c* to live in him must walk
2: 9 Anyone who *c* to be in the light

CLAP
Ps 47: 1 *C* your hands, all you nations;
Isa 55: 12 will *c* their hands.

CLAY
Isa 45: 9 Does the *c* say to the potter,
64: 8 We are the *c*, you are the potter;
Jer 18: 6 "Like *c* in the hand of the potter,
La 4: 2 are now considered as pots of *c*,
Da 2: 33 partly of iron and partly of baked *c*.
Ro 9: 21 of the same lump of *c* some pottery
2Co 4: 7 we have this treasure in jars of *c*
2Ti 2: 20 and *c*; some are for noble purposes

CLEAN
Lev 16: 30 you will be *c* from all your sins.
Ps 24: 4 He who has *c* hands and a pure
Mt 12: 44 the house unoccupied, swept *c*
23: 25 You *c* the outside of the cup
Mk 7: 19 Jesus declared all foods "*c*.")
Jn 13: 10 to wash his feet; his whole body is *c*
15: 3 are already *c* because of the word
Ac 10: 15 impure that God has made *c*."
Ro 14: 20 All food is *c*, but it is wrong

CLING (CLINGS)
Ro 12: 9 Hate what is evil; *c* to what is good.

CLINGS (CLING)
Ps 63: 8 My soul *c* to you;

CLOAK
2Ki 4: 29 "Tuck your *c* into your belt,

CLOSE (CLOSER)
Ps 34: 18 LORD is *c* to the brokenhearted
Isa 40: 11 and carries them *c* to his heart;
Jer 30: 21 himself to be *c* to me?'

CLOSER (CLOSE)
Ex 3: 5 "Do not come any *c*," God said.
Pr 18: 24 there is a friend who sticks *c*

CLOTHE (CLOTHED CLOTHES CLOTHING)
Ps 45: 3 *c* yourself with splendor
Isa 52: 1 *c* yourself with strength.
Ro 13: 14 *c* yourselves with the Lord Jesus
Col 3: 12 *c* yourselves with compassion,
1Pe 5: 5 *c* yourselves with humility

CLOTHED (CLOTHE)
Ps 30: 11 removed my sackcloth and *c* me
Pr 31: 25 She is *c* with strength and dignity;
Lk 24: 49 until you have been *c* with power

CLOTHES (CLOTHE)
Mt 6: 25 the body more important than *c*?
6: 28 "And why do you worry about *c*?
Jn 11: 44 Take off the grave *c* and let him go

CLOTHING (CLOTHE)
Dt 22: 5 A woman must not wear men's *c*,
Mt 7: 15 They come to you in sheep's *c*,

CLOUD (CLOUDS)
Ex 13: 21 them in a pillar of *c* to guide them
Isa 19: 1 See, the LORD rides on a swift *c*
Lk 21: 27 of Man coming in a *c* with power
Heb 12: 1 by such a great *c* of witnesses,

CLOUDS (CLOUD)
Ps 104: 3 He makes the *c* his chariot
Da 7: 13 coming with the *c* of heaven.
Mk 13: 26 coming in *c* with great power
1Th 4: 17 with them in the *c* to meet the Lord

CO-HEIRS* (INHERIT)
Ro 8: 17 heirs of God and *c* with Christ,

COALS
Pr 25: 22 you will heap burning *c* on his head
Ro 12: 20 you will heap burning *c* on his head

COLD
Pr 25: 25 Like *c* water to a weary soul
Mt 10: 42 if anyone gives even a cup of *c* water
24: 12 the love of most will grow *c*,

COMFORT (COMFORTED COMFORTS)
Ps 23: 4 rod and your staff, they *c* me.
119: 52 and I find *c* in them.
119: 76 May your unfailing love be my *c*,
Zec 1: 17 and the LORD will again *c* Zion
1Co 14: 3 encouragement and *c*.
2Co 1: 4 so that we can *c* those
2: 7 you ought to forgive and *c* him,

COMFORTED (COMFORT)
Mt 5: 4 for they will be *c*.

COMFORTS* (COMFORT)
Job 29: 25 I was like one who *c* mourners.
Isa 49: 13 For the LORD *c* his people
51: 12 "I, even I, am he who *c* you.
66: 13 As a mother *c* her child,
2Co 1: 4 who *c* us in all our troubles,
7: 6 But God, who *c* the downcast,

COMMAND (COMMANDED COMMANDING COMMANDMENT COMMANDMENTS COMMANDS)
Ex 7: 2 You are to say everything I *c* you,
Nu 24: 13 to go beyond the *c* of the LORD—
Dt 4: 2 Do not add to what I *c* you
30: 16 For I *c* you today to love
32: 46 so that you may *c* your children
Ps 91: 11 For he will *c* his angels concerning
Pr 13: 13 but he who respects a *c* is rewarded
Ecc 8: 2 Obey the king's *c*, I say,
Joel 2: 11 mighty are those who obey his *c*.
Jn 14: 15 love me, you will obey what I *c*.
15: 12 My *c* is this: Love each other
1Co 14: 37 writing to you is the Lord's *c*.
Gal 5: 14 law is summed up in a single *c*:
1Ti 1: 5 goal of this *c* is love, which comes
Heb 11: 3 universe was formed at God's *c*,
1Jn 3: 23 this is his *c*: to believe in the name
2Jn : 6 his *c* is that you walk in love.

COMMANDED (COMMAND)
Ps 33: 9 he *c*, and it stood firm.
148: 5 for he *c* and they were created.
Mt 28: 20 to obey everything I have *c* you.
1Co 9: 14 Lord has *c* that those who preach
1Jn 3: 23 and to love one another as he *c* us.

COMMANDING (COMMAND)
2Ti 2: 4 he wants to please his *c* officer.

COMMANDMENT (COMMAND)
Jos 22: 5 But be very careful to keep the *c*
Mt 22: 38 This is the first and greatest *c.*
Jn 13: 34 "A new *c* I give you: Love one
Ro 7: 12 and the *c* is holy, righteous
Eph 6: 2 which is the first *c* with a promise

COMMANDMENTS (COMMAND)
Ex 20: 6 who love me and keep my *c.*
34: 28 of the covenant—the Ten *C.*
Ecc 12: 13 Fear God and keep his *c,*
Mt 5: 19 one of the least of these *c*
22: 40 the Prophets hang on these two *c.*"

COMMANDS (COMMAND)
Dt 7: 9 those who love him and keep his *c.*
11: 27 the blessing if you obey the *c*
Ps 112: 1 who finds great delight in his *c.*
119: 47 for I delight in your *c*
119: 86 All your *c* are trustworthy;
119: 98 Your *c* make me wiser
119:127 Because I love your *c*
119:143 but your *c* are my delight.
119:172 for all your *c* are righteous.
Pr 3: 1 but keep my *c* in your heart,
6: 23 For these *c* are a lamp,
10: 8 The wise in heart accept *c,*
Da 9: 4 all who love him and obey his *c,*
Mt 5: 19 teaches these *c* will be called great
Jn 14: 21 Whoever has my *c* and obeys them,
Ac 17: 30 but now he *c* all people everywhere
1Co 7: 19 Keeping God's *c* is what counts.
1Jn 5: 3 And his *c* are not burdensome,
5: 3 This is love for God: to obey his *c.*

COMMEND (COMMENDED COMMENDS)
Ecc 8: 15 So I *c* the enjoyment of life,
Ro 13: 3 do what is right and he will *c* you.
1Pe 2: 14 and to *c* those who do right.

COMMENDED (COMMEND)
Heb 11: 39 These were all *c* for their faith,

COMMENDS (COMMEND)
2Co 10: 18 not the one who *c* himself who is

COMMIT (COMMITS COMMITTED)
Ex 20: 14 "You shall not *c* adultery.
Ps 37: 5 *C* your way to the LORD;
Mt 5: 27 that it was said, 'Do not *c* adultery.'
Lk 23: 46 into your hands I *c* my spirit."
Ac 20: 32 I *c* you to God and to the word
1Co 10: 8 We should not *c* sexual immorality,
1Pe 4: 19 to God's will should *c* themselves

COMMITS (COMMIT)
Pr 6: 32 man who *c* adultery lacks
29: 22 a hot-tempered one *c* many sins.
Mt 19: 9 marries another woman *c* adultery

COMMITTED (COMMIT)
Nu 5: 7 and must confess the sin he has *c.*
1Ki 8: 61 But your hearts must be fully *c*
2Ch 16: 9 those whose hearts are fully *c*
Mt 5: 28 lustfully has already *c* adultery
2Co 5: 19 And he has *c* to us the message
1Pe 2: 22 "He *c* no sin,

COMMON
Pr 22: 2 Rich and poor have this in *c:*
1Co 10: 13 has seized you except what is *c*
2Co 6: 14 and wickedness have in *c?*

COMPANION (COMPANIONS)
Pr 13: 20 but a *c* of fools suffers harm.
28: 7 a *c* of gluttons disgraces his father.
29: 3 *c* of prostitutes squanders his

COMPANIONS (COMPANION)
Pr 18: 24 A man of many *c* may come to ruin

COMPANY
Pr 24: 1 do not desire their *c;*
Jer 15: 17 I never sat in the *c* of revelers,
1Co 15: 33 "Bad *c* corrupts good character."

COMPARED (COMPARING)
Eze 31: 2 Who can be *c* with you in majesty?
Php 3: 8 I consider everything a loss *c*

COMPARING* (COMPARED)
Ro 8: 18 present sufferings are not worth *c*
2Co 8: 8 the sincerity of your love by *c* it
Gal 6: 4 without *c* himself to somebody else

COMPASSION (COMPASSIONATE COMPASSIONS)
Ex 33: 19 I will have *c* on whom I will have *c.*
Ne 9: 19 of your great *c* you did not
9: 28 in your *c* you delivered them time
Ps 51: 1 according to your great *c*
103: 4 and crowns you with love and *c.*
103: 13 As a father has *c* on his children,
145: 9 he has *c* on all he has made.
Isa 49: 13 and will have *c* on his afflicted ones
49: 15 and have no *c* on the child she has
Hos 2: 19 in love and *c.*
11: 8 all my *c* is aroused.
Jnh 3: 9 with *c* turn from his fierce anger
Mt 9: 36 When he saw the crowds, he had *c*
Mk 8: 2 "I have *c* for these people;
Ro 9: 15 and I will have *c* on whom I have *c*
Col 3: 12 clothe yourselves with *c,* kindness,
Jas 5: 11 The Lord is full of *c* and mercy.

COMPASSIONATE (COMPASSION)
Ne 9: 17 gracious and *c,* slow to anger
Ps 103: 8 The LORD is *c* and gracious,
112: 4 the gracious and *c* and righteous
Eph 4: 32 Be kind and *c* to one another,
1Pe 3: 8 love as brothers, be *c* and humble.

COMPASSIONS* (COMPASSION)
La 3: 22 for his *c* never fail.

COMPELLED (COMPELS)
Ac 20: 22 "And now, *c* by the Spirit,
1Co 9: 16 I cannot boast, for I am *c* to preach.

COMPELS (COMPELLED)
2Co 5: 14 For Christ's love *c* us, because we

COMPETENCE* (COMPETENT)
2Co 3: 5 but our *c* comes from God.

COMPETENT* (COMPETENCE)
Ro 15: 14 and *c* to instruct one another.
1Co 6: 2 are you not *c* to judge trivial cases?
2Co 3: 5 Not that we are *c* in ourselves
3: 6 He has made us *c* as ministers

COMPETES*
1Co 9: 25 Everyone who *c* in the games goes
2Ti 2: 5 Similarly, if anyone *c* as an athlete,
2: 5 unless he *c* according to the rules.

COMPLACENT
Am 6: 1 Woe to you who are *c* in Zion,

COMPLAINING*
Php 2: 14 Do everything without *c* or arguing

COMPLETE
Jn 15: 11 and that your joy may be *c.*
16: 24 will receive, and your joy will be *c.*
17: 23 May they be brought to *c* unity
Ac 20: 24 *c* the task the Lord Jesus has given
Php 2: 2 then make my joy *c*
Col 4: 17 to it that you *c* the work you have
Jas 1: 4 so that you may be mature and *c,*
2: 22 his faith was made *c* by what he did

CONCEAL (CONCEALED CONCEALS)
Ps 40: 10 I do not *c* your love and your truth
Pr 25: 2 It is the glory of God to *c* a matter;

CONCEALED (CONCEAL)
Jer 16: 17 nor is their sin *c* from my eyes.
Mt 10: 26 There is nothing *c* that will not be
Mk 4: 22 and whatever is *c* is meant

CONCEALS (CONCEAL)
Pr 28: 13 He who *c* his sins does not prosper,

CONCEITED
Ro 12: 16 Do not be *c.*
Gal 5: 26 Let us not become *c,* provoking
1Ti 6: 4 he is *c* and understands nothing.

CONCEIVED
Mt 1: 20 what is *c* in her is from the Holy
1Co 2: 9 no mind has *c*

CONCERN (CONCERNED)
Eze 36: 21 I had *c* for my holy name, which
1Co 7: 32 I would like you to be free from *c.*
12: 25 that its parts should have equal *c*
2Co 11: 28 of my *c* for all the churches.

CONCERNED (CONCERN)
Jnh 4: 10 "You have been *c* about this vine,
1Co 7: 32 An unmarried man is *c* about

CONDEMN (CONDEMNATION CONDEMNED CONDEMNING CONDEMNS)
Job 40: 8 Would you *c* me to justify yourself?
Isa 50: 9 Who is he that will *c* me?
Lk 6: 37 Do not *c,* and you will not be
Jn 3: 17 Son into the world to *c* the world,
12: 48 very word which I spoke will *c* him
Ro 2: 27 yet obeys the law will *c* you who,
1Jn 3: 20 presence whenever our hearts *c* us.

CONDEMNATION (CONDEMN)
Ro 5: 18 of one trespass was *c* for all men,
8: 1 there is now no *c* for those who are

CONDEMNED (CONDEMN)

Ps 34: 22 no one will be *c* who takes refuge
Mt 12: 37 and by your words you will be *c*."
23: 33 How will you escape being *c* to hell
Jn 3: 18 Whoever believes in him is not *c*,
5: 24 has eternal life and will not be *c*;
16: 11 prince of this world now stands *c*.
Ro 14: 23 But the man who has doubts is *c*
1Co 11: 32 disciplined so that we will not be *c*
Heb 11: 7 By his faith he *c* the world

CONDEMNING (CONDEMN)

Pr 17: 15 the guilty and *c* the innocent—
Ro 2: 1 judge the other, you are *c* yourself,

CONDEMNS (CONDEMN)

Ro 8: 34 Who is he that *c*? Christ Jesus,
2Co 3: 9 the ministry that *c* men is glorious,

CONDUCT

Pr 10: 23 A fool finds pleasure in evil *c*,
20: 11 by whether his *c* is pure and right.
21: 8 but the *c* of the innocent is upright.
Ecc 6: 8 how to *c* himself before others?
Jer 4: 18 "Your own *c* and actions
17: 10 to reward a man according to his *c*,
Eze 7: 3 I will judge you according to your *c*
Php 1: 27 *c* yourselves in a manner worthy
1Ti 3: 15 to *c* themselves in God's household

CONFESS (CONFESSION)

Lev 16: 21 and *c* over it all the wickedness
26: 40 "'But if they will *c* their sins
Nu 5: 7 must *c* the sin he has committed.
Ps 38: 18 I *c* my iniquity;
Ro 10: 9 That if you *c* with your mouth,
Php 2: 11 every tongue *c* that Jesus Christ is
Jas 5: 16 Therefore *c* your sins to each other
1Jn 1: 9 If we *c* our sins, he is faithful

CONFESSION (CONFESS)

Ezr 10: 11 Now make *c* to the LORD,
2Co 9: 13 obedience that accompanies your *c*

CONFIDENCE

Ps 71: 5 my *c* since my youth.
Pr 3: 26 for the LORD will be your *c*
11: 13 A gossip betrays a *c*,
25: 9 do not betray another man's *c*,
31: 11 Her husband has full *c* in her
Isa 32: 17 will be quietness and *c* forever.
Jer 17: 7 whose *c* is in him.
Php 3: 3 and who put no *c* in the flesh—
Heb 3: 14 till the end the *c* we had at first.
4: 16 the throne of grace with *c*,
10: 19 since we have *c* to enter the Most
10: 35 So do not throw away your *c*;
1Jn 5: 14 This is the *c* we have

CONFORM* (CONFORMED)

Ro 12: 2 Do not *c* any longer to the pattern
1Pe 1: 14 do not *c* to the evil desires you had

CONFORMED (CONFORM)

Ro 8: 29 predestined to be *c* to the likeness

CONQUERORS

Ro 8: 37 than *c* through him who loved us.

CONSCIENCE (CONSCIENCES)

Ro 13: 5 punishment but also because of *c*.
1Co 8: 7 since their *c* is weak, it is defiled.
8: 12 in this way and wound their weak *c*
10: 25 without raising questions of *c*,
10: 29 freedom be judged by another's *c*?
Heb 10: 22 to cleanse us from a guilty *c*
1Pe 3: 16 and respect, keeping a clear *c*,

CONSCIENCES* (CONSCIENCE)

Ro 2: 15 their *c* also bearing witness,
1Ti 4: 2 whose *c* have been seared
Tit 1: 15 their minds and *c* are corrupted.
Heb 9: 14 cleanse our *c* from acts that lead

CONSCIOUS*

Ro 3: 20 through the law we become *c* of sin
1Pe 2: 19 of unjust suffering because he is *c*

CONSECRATE (CONSECRATED)

Ex 13: 2 "*C* to me every firstborn male.
Lev 20: 7 "'*C* yourselves and be holy,

CONSECRATED (CONSECRATE)

Ex 29: 43 and the place will be *c* by my glory.
1Ti 4: 5 because it is *c* by the word of God

CONSIDER (CONSIDERATE CONSIDERED CONSIDERS)

1Sa 12: 24 *c* what great things he has done
Job 37: 14 stop and *c* God's wonders.
Ps 8: 3 When I *c* your heavens,
107: 43 and *c* the great love of the LORD.
143: 5 and *c* what your hands have done.
Lk 12: 24 *C* the ravens: They do not sow
12: 27 about the rest? "*C* how the lilies
Php 2: 3 but in humility *c* others better
3: 8 I *c* everything a loss compared
Heb 10: 24 And let us *c* how we may spur one
Jas 1: 2 *C* it pure joy, my brothers,

CONSIDERATE* (CONSIDER)

Tit 3: 2 to be peaceable and *c*,
Jas 3: 17 then peace-loving, *c*, submissive,
1Pe 2: 18 only to those who are good and *c*,
3: 7 in the same way be *c* as you live

CONSIDERED (CONSIDER)

Job 1: 8 "Have you *c* my servant Job?
2: 3 "Have you *c* my servant Job?
Ps 44: 22 we are *c* as sheep to be slaughtered.
Isa 53: 4 yet we *c* him stricken by God,
Ro 8: 36 we are *c* as sheep to be slaughtered

CONSIDERS (CONSIDER)

Pr 31: 16 She *c* a field and buys it;
Ro 14: 5 One man *c* one day more sacred
Jas 1: 26 If anyone *c* himself religious

CONSIST

Lk 12: 15 a man's life does not *c*

CONSOLATION

Ps 94: 19 your *c* brought joy to my soul.

CONSTRUCTIVE*

1Co 10: 23 but not everything is *c*.

CONSUME (CONSUMING)

Jn 2: 17 "Zeal for your house will *c* me."

CONSUMING (CONSUME)

Dt 4: 24 For the LORD your God is a *c* fire,
Heb 12: 29 and awe, for our "God is a *c* fire."

CONTAIN

1Ki 8: 27 the highest heaven, cannot *c* you.
2Pe 3: 16 His letters *c* some things that are

CONTAMINATES*

2Co 7: 1 from everything that *c* body

CONTEMPT

Pr 14: 31 He who oppresses the poor shows *c*
17: 5 He who mocks the poor shows *c*
18: 3 When wickedness comes, so does *c*
Da 12: 2 others to shame and everlasting *c*.
Ro 2: 4 Or do you show *c* for the riches
Gal 4: 14 you did not treat me with *c*
1Th 5: 20 do not treat prophecies with *c*.

CONTEND (CONTENDING)

Jude : 3 you to *c* for the faith that was once

CONTENDING* (CONTEND)

Php 1: 27 *c* as one man for the faith

CONTENT (CONTENTMENT)

Pr 13: 25 The righteous eat to their hearts' *c*,
Php 4: 11 to be *c* whatever the circumstances
4: 12 I have learned the secret of being *c*
1Ti 6: 8 and clothing, we will be *c* with that.
Heb 13: 5 and be *c* with what you have,

CONTENTMENT (CONTENT)

1Ti 6: 6 But godliness with *c* is great gain.

CONTINUAL (CONTINUE)

Pr 15: 15 but the cheerful heart has a *c* feast.

CONTINUE (CONTINUAL)

Php 2: 12 *c* to work out your salvation
2Ti 3: 14 *c* in what you have learned
1Jn 5: 18 born of God does not *c* to sin;
Rev 22: 11 and let him who is holy *c* to be holy
22: 11 let him who does right *c* to do right;

CONTRITE*

Ps 51: 17 a broken and *c* heart,
Isa 57: 15 also with him who is *c* and lowly
57: 15 and to revive the heart of the *c*.
66: 2 he who is humble and *c* in spirit,

CONTROL (CONTROLLED SELF-CONTROL SELF-CONTROLLED)

Pr 29: 11 a wise man keeps himself under *c*.
1Co 7: 9 But if they cannot *c* themselves,
7: 37 but has *c* over his own will,
1Th 4: 4 you should learn to *c* his own body

CONTROLLED (CONTROL)

Ps 32: 9 but must be *c* by bit and bridle

Ro 8: 6 but the mind *c* by the Spirit is life
8: 8 Those *c* by the sinful nature cannot

CONTROVERSIES
Tit 3: 9 But avoid foolish *c* and genealogies

CONVERSATION
Col 4: 6 Let your *c* be always full of grace,

CONVERT
1Ti 3: 6 He must not be a recent *c*,

CONVICT
Jn 16: 8 he will *c* the world of guilt in regard

CONVINCED (CONVINCING)
Ro 8: 38 For I am *c* that neither death
2Ti 1: 12 and am *c* that he is able
3: 14 have learned and have become *c*

CONVINCING* (CONVINCED)
Ac 1: 3 and gave many *c* proofs that he was

CORNELIUS*
Roman to whom Peter preached; first Gentile Christian (Ac 10).

CORNERSTONE (STONE)
Isa 28: 16 a precious *c* for a sure foundation;
Eph 2: 20 Christ Jesus himself as the chief *c*.
1Pe 2: 6 a chosen and precious *c*,

CORRECT (CORRECTING CORRECTION CORRECTS)
2Ti 4: 2 *c*, rebuke and encourage—

CORRECTING* (CORRECT)
2Ti 3: 16 *c* and training in righteousness,

CORRECTION (CORRECT)
Pr 10: 17 whoever ignores *c* leads others
12: 1 but he who hates *c* is stupid.
15: 5 whoever heeds *c* shows prudence.
15: 10 he who hates *c* will die.
29: 15 The rod of *c* imparts wisdom,

CORRECTS* (CORRECT)
Job 5: 17 "Blessed is the man whom God *c*;
Pr 9: 7 Whoever *c* a mocker invites insult;

CORRUPT (CORRUPTS)
Ge 6: 11 Now the earth was *c* in God's sight

CORRUPTS* (CORRUPT)
Ecc 7: 7 and a bribe *c* the heart.
1Co 15: 33 "Bad company *c* good character."
Jas 3: 6 It *c* the whole person, sets

COST
Pr 4: 7 Though it *c* all you have, get
Isa 55: 1 milk without money and without *c*.
Rev 21: 6 to drink without *c* from the spring

COUNSEL (COUNSELOR)
1Ki 22: 5 "First seek the *c* of the LORD."
Pr 15: 22 Plans fail for lack of *c*,
Rev 3: 18 I *c* you to buy from me gold refined

COUNSELOR (COUNSEL)
Isa 9: 6 Wonderful *C*, Mighty God,
Jn 14: 16 he will give you another *C* to be
14: 26 But the *C*, the Holy Spirit,

COUNT (COUNTING COUNTS)
Ro 4: 8 whose sin the Lord will never *c*
6: 11 *c* yourselves dead to sin

COUNTING (COUNT)
2Co 5: 19 not *c* men's sins against them.

COUNTRY
Jn 4: 44 prophet has no honor in his own *c*.)

COUNTS (COUNT)
Jn 6: 63 The Spirit gives life; the flesh *c*
1Co 7: 19 God's commands is what *c*.
Gal 5: 6 only thing that *c* is faith expressing

COURAGE (COURAGEOUS)
Ac 23: 11 "Take *c*! As you have testified
1Co 16: 13 stand firm in the faith; be men of *c*;

COURAGEOUS (COURAGE)
Dt 31: 6 Be strong and *c*.
Jos 1: 6 and *c*, because you will lead these

COURSE
Ps 19: 5 a champion rejoicing to run his *c*.
Pr 15: 21 of understanding keeps a straight *c*.

COURTS
Ps 84: 10 Better is one day in your *c*
100: 4 and his *c* with praise;

COVENANT (COVENANTS)
Ge 9: 9 "I now establish my *c* with you
Ex 19: 5 if you obey me fully and keep my *c*,
1Ch 16: 15 He remembers his *c* forever,
Job 31: 1 "I made a *c* with my eyes
Jer 31: 31 "when I will make a new *c*
1Co 11: 25 "This cup is the new *c* in my blood;
Gal 4: 24 One *c* is from Mount Sinai
Heb 9: 15 Christ is the mediator of a new *c*,

COVENANTS (COVENANT)
Ro 9: 4 theirs the divine glory, the *c*,
Gal 4: 24 for the women represent two *c*.

COVER (COVER-UP COVERED COVERS)
Ps 91: 4 He will *c* you with his feathers,
Jas 5: 20 and *c* over a multitude of sins.

COVER-UP (COVER)
1Pe 2: 16 but do not use your freedom as a *c*

COVERED (COVER)
Ps 32: 1 whose sins are *c*.
Isa 6: 2 With two wings they *c* their faces,
Ro 4: 7 whose sins are *c*.
1Co 11: 4 with his head *c* dishonors his head.

COVERS (COVER)
Pr 10: 12 but love *c* over all wrongs.
1Pe 4: 8 love *c* over a multitude of sins.

COVET
Ex 20: 17 You shall not *c* your neighbor's
Ro 13: 9 "Do not steal," "Do not *c*,"

COWARDLY*
Rev 21: 8 But the *c*, the unbelieving, the vile,

CRAFTINESS (CRAFTY)
1Co 3: 19 "He catches the wise in their *c*";

CRAFTY (CRAFTINESS)
Ge 3: 1 the serpent was more *c* than any
2Co 12: 16 *c* fellow that I am, I caught you

CRAVE
Pr 23: 3 Do not *c* his delicacies,
1Pe 2: 2 newborn babies, *c* pure spiritual

CREATE (CREATED CREATION CREATOR)
Ps 51: 10 *C* in me a pure heart, O God,
Isa 45: 18 he did not *c* it to be empty,

CREATED (CREATE)
Ge 1: 1 In the beginning God *c* the heavens
1: 21 God *c* the great creatures of the sea
1: 27 So God *c* man in his own image,
Ps 148: 5 for he commanded and they were *c*
Isa 42: 5 he who *c* the heavens and stretched
Ro 1: 25 and served *c* things rather
1Co 11: 9 neither was man *c* for woman,
Col 1: 16 For by him all things were *c*:
1Ti 4: 4 For everything God *c* is good,
Rev 10: 6 who *c* the heavens and all that is

CREATION (CREATE)
Mk 16: 15 and preach the good news to all *c*.
Jn 17: 24 me before the *c* of the world.
Ro 8: 19 The *c* waits in eager expectation
8: 39 depth, nor anything else in all *c*,
2Co 5: 17 he is a new *c*; the old has gone,
Col 1: 15 God, the firstborn over all *c*.
1Pe 1: 20 chosen before the *c* of the world,
Rev 13: 8 slain from the *c* of the world.

CREATOR (CREATE)
Ge 14: 22 God Most High, *C* of heaven
Ro 1: 25 created things rather than the *C*—

CREATURE (CREATURES)
Lev 17: 11 For the life of a *c* is in the blood,

CREATURES (CREATURE)
Ge 6: 19 bring into the ark two of all living *c*,
Ps 104: 24 the earth is full of your *c*.

CREDIT (CREDITED)
Ro 4: 24 to whom God will *c* righteousness
1Pe 2: 20 it to your *c* if you receive a beating

CREDITED (CREDIT)
Ge 15: 6 and he *c* it to him as righteousness.
Ro 4: 5 his faith is *c* as righteousness.
Gal 3: 6 and it was *c* to him as righteousness
Jas 2: 23 and it was *c* to him as righteousness

CRIED (CRY)
Ps 18: 6 I *c* to my God for help.

CRIMSON
Isa 1: 18 though they are red as *c*,

CRIPPLED
Mk 9: 45 better for you to enter life *c*

CRITICISM
2Co 8: 20 We want to avoid any *c*

CROOKED
Pr 10: 9 he who takes *c* paths will be found
Php 2: 15 children of God without fault in a *c*

CROSS
Mt 10: 38 and anyone who does not take his *c*
Lk 9: 23 take up his *c* daily and follow me.
Ac 2: 23 to death by nailing him to the *c*.
1Co 1: 17 lest the *c* of Christ be emptied
Gal 6: 14 in the *c* of our Lord Jesus Christ,
Php 2: 8 even death on a *c*!

Col 1: 20 through his blood, shed on the *c.*
2: 14 he took it away, nailing it to the *c.*
2: 15 triumphing over them by the *c.*
Heb 12: 2 set before him endured the *c,*

CROWD

Ex 23: 2 Do not follow the *c* in doing wrong.

CROWN (CROWNED CROWNS)

Pr 4: 9 present you with a *c* of splendor."
10: 6 Blessings *c* the head
12: 4 noble character is her husband's *c,*
17: 6 Children's children are a *c*
Isa 61: 3 to bestow on them a *c* of beauty
Zec 9: 16 like jewels in a *c.*
Mt 27: 29 then twisted together a *c* of thorns
1Co 9: 25 it to get a *c* that will last forever.
2Ti 4: 8 store for me the *c* of righteousness,
Rev 2: 10 and I will give you the *c* of life.

CROWNED (CROWN)

Ps 8: 5 and *c* him with glory and honor.
Pr 14: 18 the prudent are *c* with knowledge.
Heb 2: 7 you *c* him with glory and honor

CROWNS (CROWN)

Rev 4: 10 They lay their *c* before the throne
19: 12 and on his head are many *c.*

CRUCIFIED (CRUCIFY)

Mt 20: 19 to be mocked and flogged and *c.*
27: 38 Two robbers were *c* with him,
Lk 24: 7 be *c* and on the third day be raised
Jn 19: 18 Here they *c* him, and with him two
Ac 2: 36 whom you *c,* both Lord and Christ
Ro 6: 6 For we know that our old self was *c*
1Co 1: 23 but we preach Christ *c:* a stumbling
2: 2 except Jesus Christ and him *c.*
Gal 2: 20 I have been *c* with Christ
5: 24 Christ Jesus have *c* the sinful

CRUCIFY (CRUCIFIED CRUCIFYING)

Mt 27: 22 They all answered, "*C* him!" "Why
27: 31 Then they led him away to *c* him.

CRUCIFYING* (CRUCIFY)

Heb 6: 6 to their loss they are *c* the Son

CRUSH (CRUSHED)

Ge 3: 15 he will *c* your head,
Isa 53: 10 it was the LORD's will to *c* him
Ro 16: 20 The God of peace will soon *c* Satan

CRUSHED (CRUSH)

Ps 34: 18 and saves those who are *c* in spirit.
Isa 53: 5 he was *c* for our iniquities;
2Co 4: 8 not *c;* perplexed, but not in despair;

CRY (CRIED)

Ps 34: 15 and his ears are attentive to their *c;*
40: 1 he turned to me and heard my *c.*
130: 1 Out of the depths I *c* to you,

CUP

Ps 23: 5 my *c* overflows.
Mt 10: 42 if anyone gives even a *c* of cold water
23: 25 You clean the outside of the *c*
26: 39 may this *c* be taken from me.
1Co 11: 25 after supper he took the *c,* saying,

CURSE (CURSED)

Dt 11: 26 before you today a blessing and a *c*
21: 23 hung on a tree is under God's *c.*
Lk 6: 28 bless those who *c* you, pray
Gal 3: 13 of the law by becoming a *c* for us,
Rev 22: 3 No longer will there be any *c.*

CURSED (CURSE)

Ge 3: 17 "*C* is the ground because of you;
Dt 27: 15 "*C* is the man who carves an image
27: 16 "*C* is the man who dishonors his
27: 17 "*C* is the man who moves his
27: 18 "*C* is the man who leads the blind
27: 19 *C* is the man who withholds justice
27: 20 "*C* is the man who sleeps
27: 21 "*C* is the man who has sexual
27: 22 "*C* is the man who sleeps
27: 23 "*C* is the man who sleeps
27: 24 "*C* is the man who kills his
27: 25 "*C* is the man who accepts a bribe
27: 26 "*C* is the man who does not uphold
Ro 9: 3 I could wish that I myself were *c*
Gal 3: 10 "*C* is everyone who does not

CURTAIN

Ex 26: 33 The *c* will separate the Holy Place
Lk 23: 45 the *c* of the temple was torn in two.
Heb 10: 20 opened for us through the *c,*

CYMBAL*

1Co 13: 1 a resounding gong or a clanging *c.*

D

DANCE (DANCING)

Ecc 3: 4 a time to mourn and a time to *d,*
Mt 11: 17 and you did not *d;*

DANCING (DANCE)

Ps 30: 11 You turned my wailing into *d;*
149: 3 Let them praise his name with *d*

DANGER

Pr 27: 12 The prudent see *d* and take refuge,
Ro 8: 35 famine or nakedness or *d* or sword?

DANIEL

Hebrew exile to Babylon, name changed to Belteshazzar (Da 1:6-7). Refused to eat unclean food (Da 1:8-21). Interpreted Nebuchadnezzar's dreams (Da 2; 4), writing on the wall (Da 5). Thrown into lion's den (Da 6). Visions of (Da 7-12).

DARK (DARKNESS)

Job 34: 22 There is no *d* place, no deep
Pr 31: 15 She gets up while it is still *d;*
Ro 2: 19 a light for those who are in the *d,*
2Pe 1: 19 as to a light shining in a *d* place,

DARKNESS (DARK)

Ge 1: 4 he separated the light from the *d.*
2Sa 22: 29 the LORD turns my *d* into light.
Jn 3: 19 but men loved *d* instead of light
2Co 6: 14 fellowship can light have with *d?*
Eph 5: 8 For you were once *d,* but now you
1Pe 2: 9 out of *d* into his wonderful light.
1Jn 1: 5 in him there is no *d* at all.
2: 9 but hates his brother is still in the *d.*

DAUGHTERS

Joel 2: 28 sons and *d* will prophesy,

DAVID

Son of Jesse (Ru 4:17-22; 1Ch 2:13-15), ancestor of Jesus (Mt 1:1-17; Lk 3:31). Anointed king by Samuel (1Sa 16:1-13). Musician to Saul (1Sa 16:14-23; 18:10). Killed Goliath (1Sa 17). Relation with Jonathan (1Sa 18:1-4; 19-20; 23:16-18; 2Sa 1). Disfavor of Saul (1Sa 18:6-23:29). Spared Saul's life (1Sa 24; 26). Among Philistines (1Sa 21:10-14; 27-30). Lament for Saul and Jonathan (2Sa 1). Anointed king of Judah (2Sa 2:1-11); of Israel (2Sa 5:1-4; 1Ch 11:1-3). Promised eternal dynasty (2Sa 7; 1Ch 17; Ps 132). Adultery with Bathsheba (2Sa 11-12). Absalom's revolt (2Sa 14-18). Last words (2Sa 23:1-7). Death (1Ki 2:10-12; 1Ch 29:28).

DAWN

Ps 37: 6 your righteousness shine like the *d,*
Pr 4: 18 is like the first gleam of *d,*

DAY (DAYS)

Ge 1: 5 God called the light "*d,*"
Ex 20: 8 "Remember the Sabbath *d*
Lev 23: 28 because it is the *D* of Atonement,
Nu 14: 14 before them in a pillar of cloud by *d*
Jos 1: 8 meditate on it *d* and night,
Ps 84: 10 Better is one *d* in your courts
96: 2 proclaim his salvation *d* after *d.*
118: 24 This is the *d* the LORD has made;
Pr 27: 1 not know what a *d* may bring forth.
Joel 2: 31 and dreadful *d* of the LORD.
Ob : 15 The *d* of the LORD is near
Lk 11: 3 Give us each *d* our daily bread.
Ac 17: 11 examined the Scriptures every *d*
2Co 4: 16 we are being renewed *d* by *d.*
1Th 5: 2 for you know very well that the *d*
2Pe 3: 8 With the Lord a *d* is like

DAYS (DAY)

Dt 17: 19 he is to read it all the *d* of his life
Ps 23: 6 all the *d* of my life,
90: 10 The length of our *d* is seventy years
Ecc 12: 1 Creator in the *d* of your youth,
Joel 2: 29 I will pour out my Spirit in those *d.*
Mic 4: 1 In the last *d*
Heb 1: 2 in these last *d* he has spoken to us
2Pe 3: 3 that in the last *d* scoffers will come,

DEACONS

1Ti 3: 8 *D,* likewise, are to be men worthy

DEAD (DIE)

Dt 18: 11 or spiritist or who consults the *d.*
Mt 28: 7 'He has risen from the *d*
Ro 6: 11 count yourselves *d* to sin
Eph 2: 1 you were *d* in your transgressions
1Th 4: 16 and the *d* in Christ will rise first.
Jas 2: 17 is not accompanied by action, is *d.*
2: 26 so faith without deeds is *d.*

DEATH (DIE)
Nu 35: 16 the murderer shall be put to *d.*
Ps 23: 4 the valley of the shadow of *d,*
116: 15 is the *d* of his saints.
Pr 8: 36 all who hate me love *d.*"
14: 12 but in the end it leads to *d.*
Ecc 7: 2 for *d* is the destiny of every man;
Isa 25: 8 he will swallow up *d* forever.
53: 12 he poured out his life unto *d,*
Jn 5: 24 he has crossed over from *d* to life.
Ro 5: 12 and in this way *d* came to all men,
6: 23 For the wages of sin is *d,*
8: 13 put to *d* the misdeeds of the body,
1Co 15: 21 For since *d* came through a man,
15: 55 Where, O *d,* is your sting?"
Rev 1: 18 And I hold the keys of *d* and Hades
20: 6 The second *d* has no power
20: 14 The lake of fire is the second *d.*
21: 4 There will be no more *d*

DEBAUCHERY
Ro 13: 13 not in sexual immorality and *d,*
Eph 5: 18 drunk on wine, which leads to *d.*

DEBORAH
Prophetess who led Israel to victory over Canaanites (Jdg 4-5).

DEBT (DEBTORS DEBTS)
Ro 13: 8 Let no *d* remain outstanding,
13: 8 continuing *d* to love one another,

DEBTORS (DEBT)
Mt 6: 12 as we also have forgiven our *d.*

DEBTS (DEBT)
Dt 15: 1 seven years you must cancel *d.*
Mt 6: 12 Forgive us our *d,*

DECAY
Ps 16: 10 will you let your Holy One see *d.*
Ac 2: 27 will you let your Holy One see *d.*

DECEIT (DECEIVE)
Mk 7: 22 greed, malice, *d,* lewdness, envy,
1Pe 2: 1 yourselves of all malice and all *d,*
2: 22 and no *d* was found in his mouth."

DECEITFUL (DECEIVE)
Jer 17: 9 The heart is *d* above all things
2Co 11: 13 men are false apostles, *d* workmen,

DECEITFULNESS (DECEIVE)
Mk 4: 19 the *d* of wealth and the desires
Heb 3: 13 of you may be hardened by sin's *d.*

DECEIVE (DECEIT DECEITFUL DECEITFULNESS DECEIVED DECEIVES DECEPTIVE)
Lev 19: 11 "'Do not *d* one another.
Pr 14: 5 A truthful witness does not *d,*
Mt 24: 5 'I am the Christ,' and will *d* many.
Ro 16: 18 and flattery they *d* the minds
1Co 3: 18 Do not *d* yourselves.
Eph 5: 6 Let no one *d* you with empty words
Jas 1: 22 to the word, and so *d* yourselves.
1Jn 1: 8 we *d* ourselves and the truth is not

DECEIVED (DECEIVE)
Ge 3: 13 "The serpent *d* me, and I ate."
Gal 6: 7 Do not be *d:* God cannot be
1Ti 2: 14 And Adam was not the one *d;*
2Ti 3: 13 to worse, deceiving and being *d.*
Jas 1: 16 Don't be *d,* my dear brothers.

DECEIVES (DECEIVE)
Gal 6: 3 when he is nothing, he *d* himself.
Jas 1: 26 he *d* himself and his religion is

DECENCY*
1Ti 2: 9 women to dress modestly, with *d*

DECEPTIVE (DECEIVE)
Pr 31: 30 Charm is *d,* and beauty is fleeting;
Col 2: 8 through hollow and *d* philosophy,

DECLARE (DECLARED DECLARING)
1Ch 16: 24 *D* his glory among the nations,
Ps 19: 1 The heavens *d* the glory of God;
96: 3 *D* his glory among the nations,
Isa 42: 9 and new things I *d;*

DECLARED (DECLARE)
Mk 7: 19 Jesus *d* all foods "clean.")
Ro 2: 13 the law who will be *d* righteous.
3: 20 no one will be *d* righteous

DECLARING (DECLARE)
Ps 71: 8 *d* your splendor all day long.
Ac 2: 11 we hear them *d* the wonders

DECREED (DECREES)
La 3: 37 happen if the Lord has not *d* it?
Lk 22: 22 Son of Man will go as it has been *d,*

DECREES (DECREED)
Lev 10: 11 Israelites all the *d* the LORD has
Ps 119:112 My heart is set on keeping your *d*

DEDICATE (DEDICATION)
Nu 6: 12 He must *d* himself to the LORD
Pr 20: 25 for a man to *d* something rashly

DEDICATION (DEDICATE)
1Ti 5: 11 sensual desires overcome their *d*

DEED (DEEDS)
Col 3: 17 you do, whether in word or *d,*

DEEDS (DEED)
1Sa 2: 3 and by him *d* are weighed.
Ps 65: 5 with awesome *d* of righteousness,
66: 3 "How awesome are your *d!*
78: 4 the praiseworthy *d* of the LORD,
86: 10 you are great and do marvelous *d;*
92: 4 For you make me glad by your *d,*
111: 3 Glorious and majestic are his *d,*
Hab 3: 2 I stand in awe of your *d,* O LORD.
Mt 5: 16 that they may see your good *d*
Ac 26: 20 prove their repentance by their *d.*
Jas 2: 14 claims to have faith but has no *d?*
2: 20 faith without *d* is useless?
1Pe 2: 12 they may see your good *d*

DEEP (DEPTH)
1Co 2: 10 all things, even the *d* things
1Ti 3: 9 hold of the *d* truths of the faith

DEER
Ps 42: 1 As the *d* pants for streams of water,

DEFEND (DEFENSE)
Ps 74: 22 Rise up, O God, and *d* your cause;
Pr 31: 9 *d* the rights of the poor and needy
Jer 50: 34 He will vigorously *d* their cause

DEFENSE (DEFEND)
Ps 35: 23 Awake, and rise to my *d!*
Php 1: 16 here for the *d* of the gospel.
1Jn 2: 1 speaks to the Father in our *d* —

DEFERRED*
Pr 13: 12 Hope *d* makes the heart sick,

DEFILE (DEFILED)
Da 1: 8 Daniel resolved not to *d* himself

DEFILED (DEFILE)
Isa 24: 5 The earth is *d* by its people;

DEFRAUD
Lev 19: 13 Do not *d* your neighbor or rob him.

DEITY*
Col 2: 9 of the *D* lives in bodily form,

DELIGHT (DELIGHTS)
1Sa 15: 22 "Does the LORD *d*
Ps 1: 2 But his *d* is in the law of the LORD
16: 3 in whom is all my *d.*
35: 9 and *d* in his salvation.
37: 4 *D* yourself in the LORD
43: 4 to God, my joy and my *d.*
51: 16 You do not *d* in sacrifice,
119: 77 for your law is my *d.*
Pr 29: 17 he will bring *d* to your soul.
Isa 42: 1 my chosen one in whom I *d;*
55: 2 and your soul will *d* in the richest
61: 10 I *d* greatly in the LORD;
Jer 9: 24 for in these I *d,*"
15: 16 they were my joy and my heart's *d,*
Mic 7: 18 but *d* to show mercy.
Zep 3: 17 He will take great *d* in you,
Mt 12: 18 the one I love, in whom I *d;*
1Co 13: 6 Love does not *d* in evil
2Co 12: 10 for Christ's sake, I *d* in weaknesses,

DELIGHTS (DELIGHT)
Ps 22: 8 since he *d* in him."
35: 27 who *d* in the well-being
36: 8 from your river of *d.*
37: 23 if the LORD *d* in a man's way,
Pr 3: 12 as a father the son he *d* in.
12: 22 but he *d* in men who are truthful.
23: 24 he who has a wise son *d* in him.

DELILAH*
Woman who betrayed Samson (Jdg 16:4-22).

DELIVER (DELIVERANCE DELIVERED DELIVERER DELIVERS)
Ps 72: 12 For he will *d* the needy who cry out
79: 9 *d* us and forgive our sins
Mt 6: 13 but *d* us from the evil one.'
2Co 1: 10 hope that he will continue to *d* us,

DELIVERANCE (DELIVER)
Ps 3: 8 From the LORD comes *d.*
32: 7 and surround me with songs of *d.*
33: 17 A horse is a vain hope for *d;*

DELIVERED (DELIVER)
Ps 34: 4 he *d* me from all my fears.
Ro 4: 25 He was *d* over to death for our sins

DELIVERER (DELIVER)
Ps 18: 2 is my rock, my fortress and my *d;*
40: 17 You are my help and my *d;*
140: 7 O Sovereign LORD, my strong *d,*
144: 2 my stronghold and my *d,*

DISCERNMENT (DISCERN)
Pr 17: 10 A rebuke impresses a man of *d*
28: 11 a poor man who has *d* sees

DISCIPLE (DISCIPLES)
Mt 10: 42 these little ones because he is my *d,*
Lk 14: 27 and follow me cannot be my *d.*

DISCIPLES (DISCIPLE)
Mt 28: 19 Therefore go and make *d*
Jn 8: 31 to my teaching, you are really my *d*
13: 35 men will know that you are my *d*
Ac 11: 26 The *d* were called Christians first

DISCIPLINE (DISCIPLINED DISCIPLINES)
Ps 38: 1 or *d* me in your wrath.
39: 11 You rebuke and *d* men for their sin;
94: 12 Blessed is the man you *d,* O LORD
Pr 1: 7 but fools despise wisdom and *d.*
3: 11 do not despise the LORD's *d*
5: 12 You will say, "How I hated *d!*
5: 23 He will die for lack of *d,*
6: 23 and the corrections of *d*
10: 17 He who heeds *d* shows the way
12: 1 Whoever loves *d* loves knowledge,
13: 18 He who ignores *d* comes to poverty
13: 24 who loves him is careful to *d* him.
15: 5 A fool spurns his father's *d,*
15: 32 He who ignores *d* despises himself,
19: 18 *D* your son, for in that there is hope
22: 15 the rod of *d* will drive it far
23: 13 Do not withhold *d* from a child;
29: 17 *D* your son, and he will give you
Heb 12: 5 do not make light of the Lord's *d,*
12: 7 as *d;* God is treating you
12: 11 No *d* seems pleasant at the time,
Rev 3: 19 Those whom I love I rebuke and *d.*

DISCIPLINED (DISCIPLINE)
Pr 1: 3 for acquiring a *d* and prudent life,
Jer 31: 18 'You *d* me like an unruly calf,
1Co 11: 32 we are being *d* so that we will not
Tit 1: 8 upright, holy and *d.*
Heb 12: 7 For what son is not *d* by his father?

DISCIPLINES (DISCIPLINE)
Dt 8: 5 your heart that as a man *d* his son,
Pr 3: 12 the LORD *d* those he loves,
Heb 12: 6 because the Lord *d* those he loves,
12: 10 but God *d* us for our good,

DISCLOSED
Lk 8: 17 is nothing hidden that will not be *d,*

DISCOURAGED
Jos 1: 9 Do not be terrified; do not be *d,*
Jos 10: 25 "Do not be afraid; do not be *d.*
1Ch 28: 20 or *d,* for the LORD God,
Isa 42: 4 he will not falter or be *d*
Col 3: 21 children, or they will become *d.*

DISCREDITED
2Co 6: 3 so that our ministry will not be *d.*

DISCRETION*
1Ch 22: 12 May the LORD give you *d*
Pr 1: 4 knowledge and *d* to the young—
2: 11 *D* will protect you,
5: 2 that you may maintain *d*
8: 12 I possess knowledge and *d.*
11: 22 a beautiful woman who shows no *d.*

DISCRIMINATED*
Jas 2: 4 have you not *d* among yourselves

DISFIGURED
Isa 52: 14 his appearance was so *d*

DISGRACE (DISGRACEFUL DISGRACES)
Pr 11: 2 When pride comes, then comes *d,*
14: 34 but sin is a *d* to any people.
19: 26 is a son who brings shame and *d.*
Ac 5: 41 of suffering *d* for the Name.
Heb 13: 13 the camp, bearing the *d* he bore.

DISGRACEFUL (DISGRACE)
Pr 10: 5 during harvest is a *d* son.
17: 2 wise servant will rule over a *d* son,

DISGRACES (DISGRACE)
Pr 28: 7 of gluttons *d* his father.
29: 15 but a child left to itself *d* his mother

DISHONEST
Pr 11: 1 The LORD abhors *d* scales,
29: 27 The righteous detest the *d;*
Lk 16: 10 whoever is *d* with very little will
1Ti 3: 8 wine, and not pursuing *d* gain.

DISHONOR (DISHONORS)
Lev 18: 7 "'Do not *d* your father
Pr 30: 9 and so *d* the name of my God.
1Co 15: 43 it is sown in *d,* it is raised in glory;

DISHONORS (DISHONOR)
Dt 27: 16 Cursed is the man who *d* his father

DISMAYED
Isa 28: 16 the one who trusts will never be *d.*
41: 10 do not be *d,* for I am your God.

DISOBEDIENCE (DISOBEY)
Ro 5: 19 as through the *d* of the one man
11: 32 to *d* so that he may have mercy
Heb 2: 2 and *d* received its just punishment,
4: 6 go in, because of their *d.*
4: 11 fall by following their example of *d.*

DISOBEDIENT (DISOBEY)
2Ti 3: 2 proud, abusive, *d* to their parents,
Tit 1: 6 to the charge of being wild and *d.*
1: 16 *d* and unfit for doing any thing

DISOBEY (DISOBEDIENCE DISOBEDIENT)
Dt 11: 28 the curse if you *d* the commands
2Ch 24: 20 'Why do you *d* the LORD's
Ro 1: 30 they *d* their parents; they are

DISORDER
1Co 14: 33 For God is not a God of *d*
2Co 12: 20 slander, gossip, arrogance and *d.*
Jas 3: 16 there you find *d* and every evil

DISOWN
Pr 30: 9 I may have too much and *d* you
Mt 10: 33 I will *d* him before my Father
26: 35 to die with you, I will never *d* you."
2Ti 2: 12 If we *d* him,

DISPLAY (DISPLAYS)
Eze 39: 21 I will *d* my glory among the nations
1Ti 1: 16 Christ Jesus might *d* his unlimited

DISPLAYS (DISPLAY)
Isa 44: 23 he *d* his glory in Israel.

DISPUTE (DISPUTES)
Pr 17: 14 before a *d* breaks out.
1Co 6: 1 If any of you has a *d* with another,

DISPUTES (DISPUTE)
Pr 18: 18 Casting the lot settles *d*

DISQUALIFIED
1Co 9: 27 I myself will not be *d* for the prize.

DISREPUTE*
2Pe 2: 2 will bring the way of truth into *d.*

DISSENSION*
Pr 6: 14 he always stirs up *d.*
6: 19 and a man who stirs up *d*
10: 12 Hatred stirs up *d,*
15: 18 A hot-tempered man stirs up *d,*
16: 28 A perverse man stirs up *d,*
28: 25 A greedy man stirs up *d,*
29: 22 An angry man stirs up *d,*
Ro 13: 13 debauchery, not in *d* and jealousy.

DISSIPATION*
Lk 21: 34 will be weighed down with *d,*
1Pe 4: 4 with them into the same flood of *d,*

DISTINGUISH
1Ki 3: 9 and to *d* between right and wrong.
Heb 5: 14 themselves to *d* good from evil.

DISTORT
2Co 4: 2 nor do we *d* the word of God.
2Pe 3: 16 ignorant and unstable people *d,*

DISTRESS (DISTRESSED)
Ps 18: 6 In my *d* I called to the LORD;
Jnh 2: 2 "In my *d* I called to the LORD,
Jas 1: 27 after orphans and widows in their *d*

DISTRESSED (DISTRESS)
Ro 14: 15 If your brother is *d*

DIVIDED (DIVISION)
Mt 12: 25 household *d* against itself will not
Lk 23: 34 they *d* up his clothes by casting lots
1Co 1: 13 Is Christ *d?* Was Paul crucified

DIVINATION
Lev 19: 26 "'Do not practice *d* or sorcery.

DIVINE
Ro 1: 20 his eternal power and *d* nature—
2Co 10: 4 they have *d* power
2Pe 1: 4 you may participate in the *d* nature

DIVISION (DIVIDED DIVISIONS DIVISIVE)
Lk 12: 51 on earth? No, I tell you, but *d.*
1Co 12: 25 so that there should be no *d*

DIVISIONS (DIVISION)
Ro 16: 17 to watch out for those who cause *d*

1Co 1: 10 another so that there may be no *d*
11: 18 there are *d* among you,

DIVISIVE* (DIVISION)
Tit 3: 10 Warn a *d* person once,

DIVORCE
Mal 2: 16 "I hate *d*," says the LORD God
Mt 19: 3 for a man to *d* his wife for any
1Co 7: 11 And a husband must not *d* his wife.
7: 27 Are you married? Do not seek a *d*.

DOCTOR
Mt 9: 12 "It is not the healthy who need a *d*,

DOCTRINE
1Ti 4: 16 Watch your life and *d* closely.
Tit 2: 1 is in accord with sound *d*.

DOMINION
Ps 22: 28 for *d* belongs to the LORD

DOOR
Ps 141: 3 keep watch over the *d* of my lips.
Mt 6: 6 close the *d* and pray to your Father
7: 7 and the *d* will be opened to you.
Rev 3: 20 I stand at the *d* and knock.

DOORKEEPER
Ps 84: 10 I would rather be a *d* in the house

DOUBLE-EDGED
Heb 4: 12 Sharper than any *d* sword,
Rev 1: 16 of his mouth came a sharp *d* sword.
2: 12 of him who has the sharp, *d* sword.

DOUBLE-MINDED (MIND)
Ps 119:113 I hate *d* men,
Jas 1: 8 he is a *d* man, unstable

DOUBT
Mt 14: 31 he said, "why did you *d*?"
21: 21 if you have faith and do not *d*,
Mk 11: 23 and does not *d* in his heart
Jas 1: 6 he must believe and not *d*,
Jude : 22 Be merciful to those who *d*;

DOWNCAST
Ps 42: 5 Why are you *d*, O my soul?
2Co 7: 6 But God, who comforts the *d*,

DRAW (DRAWING DRAWS)
Mt 26: 52 "for all who *d* the sword will die
Jn 12: 32 up from the earth, will *d* all men
Heb 10: 22 let us *d* near to God

DRAWING (DRAW)
Lk 21: 28 because your redemption is *d* near

DRAWS (DRAW)
Jn 6: 44 the Father who sent me *d* him,

DREADFUL
Heb 10: 31 It is a *d* thing to fall into the hands

DRESS
1Ti 2: 9 I also want women to *d* modestly,

DRINK (DRUNK DRUNKARDS DRUNKENNESS)
Pr 5: 15 *D* water from your own cistern,
Lk 12: 19 Take life easy; eat, *d* and be merry
Jn 7: 37 let him come to me and *d*.
1Co 12: 13 were all given the one Spirit to *d*.
Rev 21: 6 to *d* without cost from the spring

DRIVES
1Jn 4: 18 But perfect love *d* out fear,

DROP
Pr 17: 14 so *d* the matter before a dispute
Isa 40: 15 Surely the nations are like a *d*

DRUNK (DRINK)
Eph 5: 18 Do not get *d* on wine, which leads

DRUNKARDS (DRINK)
Pr 23: 21 for *d* and gluttons become poor,
1Co 6: 10 nor the greedy nor *d* nor slanderers

DRUNKENNESS (DRINK)
Lk 21: 34 weighed down with dissipation, *d*
Ro 13: 13 and *d*, not in sexual immorality
Gal 5: 21 factions and envy; *d*, orgies,
1Pe 4: 3 living in debauchery, lust, *d*, orgies,

DRY
Isa 53: 2 and like a root out of *d* ground.
Eze 37: 4 '*D* bones, hear the word

DUST
Ge 2: 7 man from the *d* of the ground
Ps 103: 14 he remembers that we are *d*.
Ecc 3: 20 all come from *d*, and to *d* all return.

DUTY
Ecc 12: 13 for this is the whole *d* of man.
Ac 23: 1 I have fulfilled my *d* to God
1Co 7: 3 husband should fulfill his marital *d*

DWELL (DWELLING)
1Ki 8: 27 "But will God really *d* on earth?
Ps 23: 6 I will *d* in the house of the LORD
Isa 43: 18 do not *d* on the past.
Eph 3: 17 so that Christ may *d* in your hearts
Col 1: 19 to have all his fullness *d* in him,
3: 16 the word of Christ *d* in you richly

DWELLING (DWELL)
Eph 2: 22 to become a *d* in which God lives

E

EAGER
Pr 31: 13 and works with *e* hands.
1Pe 5: 2 greedy for money, but *e* to serve;

EAGLE'S (EAGLES)
Ps 103: 5 your youth is renewed like the *e*.

EAGLES (EAGLE'S)
Isa 40: 31 They will soar on wings like *e*;

EAR (EARS)
1Co 2: 9 no *e* has heard,
12: 16 if the *e* should say, "Because I am

EARNED
Pr 31: 31 Give her the reward she has *e*,

EARS (EAR)
Job 42: 5 My *e* had heard of you
Ps 34: 15 and his *e* are attentive to their cry;
Pr 21: 13 If a man shuts his *e* to the cry
2Ti 4: 3 to say what their itching *e* want

EARTH (EARTHLY)
Ge 1: 1 God created the heavens and the *e*.
Ps 24: 1 *e* is the LORD's, and everything
108: 5 and let your glory be over all the *e*.
Isa 6: 3 the whole *e* is full of his glory."
51: 6 the *e* will wear out like a garment
55: 9 the heavens are higher than the *e*,
66: 1 and the *e* is my footstool.
Jer 23: 24 "Do not I fill heaven and *e*?"
Hab 2: 20 let all the *e* be silent before him."
Mt 6: 10 done on *e* as it is in heaven.
16: 19 bind on *e* will be bound
24: 35 Heaven and *e* will pass away,
28: 18 and on *e* has been given to me.
Lk 2: 14 on *e* peace to men
1Co 10: 26 The *e* is the Lord's, and everything
Php 2: 10 in heaven and on *e* and under the *e*,
2Pe 3: 13 to a new heaven and a new *e*,

EARTHLY (EARTH)
Php 3: 19 Their mind is on *e* things.
Col 3: 2 on things above, not on *e* things.

EAST
Ps 103: 12 as far as the *e* is from the west,

EASY
Mt 11: 30 For my yoke is *e* and my burden is

EAT (EATING)
Ge 2: 17 but you must not *e* from the tree
Isa 55: 1 come, buy and *e*!
65: 25 and the lion will *e* straw like the ox,
Mt 26: 26 "Take and *e*; this is my body."
Ro 14: 2 faith allows him to *e* everything,
1Co 8: 13 if what I *e* causes my brother to fall
10: 31 So whether you *e* or drink
2Th 3: 10 man will not work, he shall not *e*."

EATING (EAT)
Ro 14: 17 kingdom of God is not a matter of *e*

EDICT
Heb 11: 23 they were not afraid of the king's *e*.

EDIFIES
1Co 14: 4 but he who prophesies *e* the church

EFFECT
Isa 32: 17 *e* of righteousness will be quietness
Heb 9: 18 put into *e* without blood.

EFFORT
Lk 13: 24 "Make every *e* to enter
Ro 9: 16 depend on man's desire or *e*,
14: 19 make every *e* to do what leads
Eph 4: 3 Make every *e* to keep the unity
Heb 4: 11 make every *e* to enter that rest,
12: 14 Make every *e* to live in peace
2Pe 1: 5 make every *e* to add
3: 14 make every *e* to be found spotless,

ELAH

Son of Baasha; king of Israel (1Ki 16:6-14).

ELDERLY* (ELDERS)
Lev 19: 32 show respect for the *e*

ELDERS (ELDERLY)
1Ti 5: 17 The *e* who direct the affairs

ELECTION
Ro 9: 11 God's purpose in *e* might stand:
2Pe 1: 10 to make your calling and *e* sure.

ELI

High priest in youth of Samuel (1Sa 1-4). Blessed Hannah (1Sa 1:12-18); raised Samuel (1Sa 2:11-26).

LIJAH

Prophet; predicted famine in Israel Ki 17:1; Jas 5:17). Fed by ravens (1Ki 7:2-6). Raised Sidonian widow's son Ki 17:7-24). Defeated prophets of Baal : Carmel (1Ki 18:16-46). Ran from zebel (1Ki 19:1-9). Prophesied death f Azariah (2Ki 1). Succeeded by Elishah Ki 19:19-21; 2Ki 2:1-18). Taken to eaven in whirlwind (2Ki 2:11-12). Return prophesied (Mal 4:5-6); equated ith John the Baptist (Mt 17:9-13; Mk 9-13; Lk 1:17). Appeared with Moses transfiguration of Jesus (Mt 17:1-8; lk 9:1-8).

LISHA

Prophet; successor of Elijah (1Ki 19:16-); inherited his cloak (2Ki 2:1-18). Iiracles of (2Ki 2-6).

LIZABETH*

Mother of John the Baptist, relative of Iary (Lk 1:5-58).

MBITTER*

Col 3: 21 Fathers, do not *e* your children,

MPTY

ph 5: 6 no one deceive you with *e* words,
Pe 1: 18 from the *e* way of life handed

NABLE (ABLE)

k 1: 74 to *e* us to serve him without fear
Ac 4: 29 *e* your servants to speak your word

NABLED (ABLE)

ev 26: 13 *e* you to walk with heads held high.
n 6: 65 unless the Father has *e* him."

NABLES (ABLE)

Php 3: 21 by the power that *e* him

NCAMPS*

Ps 34: 7 The angel of the LORD *e*

ENCOURAGE (ENCOURAGEMENT)

Ps 10: 17 you *e* them, and you listen
sa 1: 17 *e* the oppressed.
Ac 15: 32 to *e* and strengthen the brothers.
Ro 12: 8 if it is encouraging, let him *e*;
Th 4: 18 Therefore *e* each other
2Ti 4: 2 rebuke and *e*—with great patience
Tit 2: 6 *e* the young men to be
Heb 3: 13 But *e* one another daily, as long
10: 25 but let us *e* one another—

ENCOURAGEMENT (ENCOURAGE)

Ac 4: 36 Barnabas (which means Son of *E*),
Ro 15: 4 *e* of the Scriptures we might have
15: 5 and *e* give you a spirit of unity
1Co 14: 3 to men for their strengthening, *e*
Heb 12: 5 word of *e* that addresses you

END

Ps 119: 33 then I will keep them to the *e*.
Pr 14: 12 but in the *e* it leads to death.
19: 20 and in the *e* you will be wise.
23: 32 In the *e* it bites like a snake
Ecc 12: 12 making many books there is no *e*,
Mt 10: 22 firm to the *e* will be saved.
Lk 21: 9 but the *e* will not come right away
Ro 10: 4 Christ is the *e* of the law
1Co 15: 24 the *e* will come, when he hands

ENDURANCE (ENDURE)

Ro 15: 4 through *e* and the encouragement
15: 5 May the God who gives *e*
2Co 1: 6 which produces in you patient *e*
Col 1: 11 might so that you may have great *e*
1Ti 6: 11 faith, love, *e* and gentleness.
Tit 2: 2 and sound in faith, in love and in *e*.

ENDURE (ENDURANCE ENDURES)

Ps 72: 17 May his name *e* forever;
Pr 12: 19 Truthful lips *e* forever,
27: 24 for riches do not *e* forever,
Ecc 3: 14 everything God does will *e* forever;
Mal 3: 2 who can *e* the day of his coming?
2Ti 2: 3 *E* hardship with us like a good
2: 12 if we *e*, / we will also reign
Heb 12: 7 *E* hardship as discipline; God is
Rev 3: 10 kept my command to *e* patiently,

ENDURES (ENDURE)

Ps 112: 9 his righteousness *e* forever;
136: 1 *His love e forever.*
Da 9: 15 made for yourself a name that *e*

ENEMIES (ENEMY)

Ps 23: 5 in the presence of my *e*.
Mic 7: 6 a man's *e* are the members
Mt 5: 44 Love your *e* and pray
Lk 20: 43 hand until I make your *e*

ENEMY (ENEMIES ENMITY)

Pr 24: 17 Do not gloat when your *e* falls;
25: 21 If your *e* is hungry, give him food
27: 6 but an *e* multiplies kisses.
1Co 15: 26 The last *e* to be destroyed is death.
1Ti 5: 14 and to give the *e* no opportunity

ENJOY (JOY)

Dt 6: 2 and so that you may *e* long life.
Eph 6: 3 and that you may *e* long life
Heb 11: 25 rather than to *e* the pleasures of sin

ENJOYMENT (JOY)

Ecc 4: 8 and why am I depriving myself of *e*
1Ti 6: 17 us with everything for our *e*.

ENLIGHTENED* (LIGHT)

Eph 1: 18 that the eyes of your heart may be *e*
Heb 6: 4 for those who have once been *e*,

ENMITY* (ENEMY)

Ge 3: 15 And I will put *e*

ENOCH

Walked with God and taken by him (Ge 5:18-24; Heb 11:5). Prophet (Jude 14).

ENTANGLED (ENTANGLES)

2Pe 2: 20 and are again *e* in it and overcome,

ENTANGLES* (ENTANGLED)

Heb 12: 1 and the sin that so easily *e*,

ENTER (ENTERED ENTERS ENTRANCE)

Ps 100: 4 *E* his gates with thanksgiving
Mt 5: 20 will certainly not *e* the kingdom
7: 13 "*E* through the narrow gate.
18: 8 It is better for you to *e* life maimed
Mk 10: 15 like a little child will never *e* it."
10: 23 is for the rich to *e* the kingdom

ENTERED (ENTER)

Ro 5: 12 as sin *e* the world through one man,
Heb 9: 12 but he *e* the Most Holy Place once

ENTERS (ENTER)

Mk 7: 18 you see that nothing that *e* a man
Jn 10: 2 The man who *e* by the gate is

ENTERTAIN

1Ti 5: 19 Do not *e* an accusation
Heb 13: 2 Do not forget to *e* strangers,

ENTHRALLED*

Ps 45: 11 The king is *e* by your beauty;

ENTHRONED (THRONE)

1Sa 4: 4 who is *e* between the cherubim.
Ps 2: 4 The One *e* in heaven laughs;
102: 12 But you, O LORD, sit *e* forever;
Isa 40: 22 He sits *e* above the circle

ENTICE

Pr 1: 10 My son, if sinners *e* you,
2Pe 2: 18 they *e* people who are just escaping

ENTIRE

Gal 5: 14 The *e* law is summed up

ENTRUSTED (TRUST)

1Ti 6: 20 guard what has been *e* to your care.
2Ti 1: 12 able to guard what I have *e* to him
1: 14 Guard the good deposit that was *e*
Jude : 3 once for all *e* to the saints.

ENVY

Pr 3: 31 Do not *e* a violent man
14: 30 but *e* rots the bones.
1Co 13: 4 It does not *e*, it does not boast,

EPHRAIM

1. Second son of Joseph (Ge 41:52; 46:20). Blessed as firstborn by Jacob (Ge 48).
2. Synonymous with Northern Kingdom (Isa 7:17; Hos 5).

EQUAL

Isa 40: 25 who is my *e*?" says the Holy One.
Jn 5: 18 making himself *e* with God.
1Co 12: 25 that its parts should have *e* concern

EQUIP* (EQUIPPED)

Heb 13: 21 *e* you with everything good

EQUIPPED (EQUIP)

2Ti 3: 17 man of God may be thoroughly *e*

ERROR

Jas 5: 20 Whoever turns a sinner from the *e*

ESAU

Firstborn of Isaac, twin of Jacob (Ge 25:21-26). Also called Edom (Ge 25:30). Sold Jacob his birthright (Ge 25:29-34); lost blessing (Ge 27). Reconciled to Jacob (Gen 33).

ESCAPE (ESCAPING)

Ro 2: 3 think you will *e* God's judgment?
Heb 2: 3 how shall we *e* if we ignore such

ESCAPING (ESCAPE)

1Co 3: 15 only as one *e* through the flames.

ESTABLISH

Ge 6: 18 But I will *e* my covenant with you,
1Ch 28: 7 I will *e* his kingdom forever
Ro 10: 3 God and sought to *e* their own,

ESTEEMED

Pr 22: 1 to be *e* is better than silver or gold.
Isa 53: 3 he was despised, and we *e* him not.

ESTHER

Jewess who lived in Persia; cousin of Mordecai (Est 2:7). Chosen queen of Xerxes (Est 2:8-18). Foiled Haman's plan to exterminate the Jews (Est 3-4; 7-9).

ETERNAL (ETERNALLY ETERNITY)

Ps 16: 11 with *e* pleasures at your right hand.
111: 10 To him belongs *e* praise.
119: 89 Your word, O LORD, is *e*;
Isa 26: 4 LORD, the LORD, is the Rock *e*.
Mt 19: 16 good thing must I do to get *e* life?"
25: 41 into the *e* fire prepared for the devil
25: 46 they will go away to *e* punishment,
Jn 3: 15 believes in him may have *e* life.
3: 16 him shall not perish but have *e* life.
3: 36 believes in the Son has *e* life,
4: 14 spring of water welling up to *e* life."
5: 24 believes him who sent me has *e* life
6: 68 You have the words of *e* life.
10: 28 I give them *e* life, and they shall
17: 3 this is *e* life: that they may know
Ro 1: 20 his *e* power and divine nature—
6: 23 but the gift of God is *e* life
2Co 4: 17 for us an *e* glory that far outweighs
4: 18 temporary, but what is unseen is *e*.
1Ti 1: 16 believe on him and receive *e* life.
1: 17 Now to the King *e*, immortal,
Heb 9: 12 having obtained *e* redemption.
1Jn 5: 11 God has given us *e* life,
5: 13 you may know that you have *e* life.

ETERNALLY (ETERNAL)

Gal 1: 8 let him be *e* condemned! As we

ETERNITY (ETERNAL)

Ps 93: 2 you are from all *e*.
Ecc 3: 11 also set *e* in the hearts of men;

ETHIOPIAN

Jer 13: 23 Can the *E* change his skin

EUNUCHS

Mt 19: 12 For some are *e* because they were

EVANGELIST (EVANGELISTS)

2Ti 4: 5 hardship, do the work of an *e*,

EVANGELISTS* (EVANGELIST)

Eph 4: 11 some to be prophets, some to be *e*,

EVE

2Co 11: 3 as *E* was deceived by the serpent's
1Ti 2: 13 For Adam was formed first, then *E*

EVEN-TEMPERED*

Pr 17: 27 and a man of understanding is *e*.

EVER (EVERLASTING FOREVER)

Ex 15: 18 LORD will reign for *e* and *e*."
Dt 8: 19 If you *e* forget the LORD your
Ps 5: 11 let them *e* sing for joy.
10: 16 The LORD is King for *e* and *e*;
25: 3 will *e* be put to shame,
26: 3 for your love is *e* before me,
45: 6 O God, will last for *e* and *e*;
52: 8 God's unfailing love for *e* and *e*.
89: 33 nor will I *e* betray my faithfulness.
145: 1 I will praise your name for *e* and *e*.
Pr 4: 18 shining *e* brighter till the full light
5: 19 may you *e* be captivated
Isa 66: 8 Who has *e* heard of such a thing?
Jer 31: 36 the descendants of Israel *e* cease
Da 7: 18 it forever—yes, for *e* and *e*.'
12: 3 like the stars for *e* and *e*.
Mk 4: 12 *e* hearing but never understanding;
Jn 1: 18 No one has *e* seen God,
Rev 1: 18 and behold I am alive for *e* and *e*!
22: 5 And they will reign for *e* and *e*.

EVER-INCREASING* (INCREASE)

Ro 6: 19 to impurity and to *e* wickedness,
2Co 3: 18 into his likeness with *e* glory,

EVERLASTING (EVER)

Dt 33: 27 and underneath are the *e* arms.
Ne 9: 5 your God, who is from *e* to *e*."
Ps 90: 2 from *e* to *e* you are God.
139: 24 and lead me in the way *e*.
Isa 9: 6 *E* Father, Prince of Peace.
33: 14 Who of us can dwell with *e* burning
35: 10 *e* joy will crown their heads.
45: 17 the LORD with an *e* salvation;
54: 8 but with *e* kindness
55: 3 I will make an *e* covenant with you,
63: 12 to gain for himself *e* renown,
Jer 31: 3 "I have loved you with an *e* love;
Da 9: 24 to bring in *e* righteousness,
12: 2 some to *e* life, others to shame
Jn 6: 47 the truth, he who believes has *e* life.
2Th 1: 9 punished with *e* destruction
Jude : 6 bound with *e* chains for judgment

EVER-PRESENT*

Ps 46: 1 an *e* help in trouble

EVIDENCE (EVIDENT)

Jn 14: 11 on the *e* of the miracles themselves.

EVIDENT (EVIDENCE)

Php 4: 5 Let your gentleness be *e* to all.

EVIL

Ge 2: 9 of the knowledge of good and *e*.
Job 1: 1 he feared God and shunned *e*.
1: 8 a man who fears God and shuns *e*."
34: 10 Far be it from God to do *e*,
Ps 23: 4 I will fear no *e*,
34: 14 Turn from *e* and do good;
51: 4 and done what is *e* in your sight,
97: 10 those who love the LORD hate *e*,
101: 4 I will have nothing to do with *e*.
Pr 8: 13 To fear the LORD is to hate *e*;
10: 23 A fool finds pleasure in *e* conduct,
11: 27 *e* comes to him who searches for it.
24: 19 Do not fret because of *e* men
24: 20 for the *e* man has no future hope,
Isa 5: 20 Woe to those who call *e* good
13: 11 I will punish the world for its *e*,
55: 7 and the *e* man his thoughts.
Hab 1: 13 Your eyes are too pure to look on *e*;
Mt 5: 45 He causes his sun to rise on the *e*
6: 13 but deliver us from the *e* one.'
7: 11 If you, then, though you are *e*,
12: 35 and the *e* man brings *e* things out
Jn 17: 15 you protect them from the *e* one.
Ro 2: 9 for every human being who does *e*:
12: 9 Hate what is *e*; cling
12: 17 Do not repay anyone *e* for *e*.
16: 19 and innocent about what is *e*.
1Co 13: 6 Love does not delight in *e*
14: 20 In regard to *e* be infants,
Eph 6: 16 all the flaming arrows of the *e* one.
1Th 5: 22 Avoid every kind of *e*.
1Ti 6: 10 of money is a root of all kinds of *e*.
2Ti 2: 22 Flee the *e* desires of youth,
Jas 1: 13 For God cannot be tempted by *e*,
1Pe 2: 16 your freedom as a cover-up for *e*;
3: 9 Do not repay *e* with *e* or insult

EXACT

Heb 1: 3 the *e* representation of his being,

EXALT (EXALTED EXALTS)

Ps 30: 1 I will *e* you, O LORD,
34: 3 let us *e* his name together.
118: 28 you are my God, and I will *e* you.
Isa 24: 15 *e* the name of the LORD, the God

EXALTED (EXALT)

2Sa 22: 47 *E* be God, the Rock, my Savior!
1Ch 29: 11 you are *e* as head over all.
Ne 9: 5 and may it be *e* above all blessing
Ps 21: 13 Be *e*, O LORD, in your strength;
46: 10 I will be *e* among the nations,
57: 5 Be *e*, O God, above the heavens;
97: 9 you are *e* far above all gods.
99: 2 he is *e* over all the nations.
108: 5 Be *e*, O God, above the heavens,
148: 13 for his name alone is *e*;
Isa 6: 1 *e*, and the train of his robe filled
12: 4 and proclaim that his name is *e*.
33: 5 The LORD is *e*, for he dwells
Eze 21: 26 The lowly will be *e* and the *e* will be
Mt 23: 12 whoever humbles himself will be *e*.
Php 1: 20 always Christ will be *e* in my body,
2: 9 Therefore God *e* him

EXALTS (EXALT)

Ps 75: 7 He brings one down, he *e* another.
Pr 14: 34 Righteousness *e* a nation,
Mt 23: 12 For whoever *e* himself will be

EXAMINE (EXAMINED)

Ps 26: 2 *e* my heart and my mind;
Jer 17: 10 and *e* the mind,
La 3: 40 Let us *e* our ways and test them,
1Co 11: 28 A man ought to *e* himself
2Co 13: 5 *E* yourselves to see whether you

EXAMINED (EXAMINE)

Ac 17: 11 *e* the Scriptures every day to see

EXAMPLE (EXAMPLES)

Jn 13: 15 have set you an *e* that you should
1Co 11: 1 Follow my *e*, as I follow
1Ti 4: 12 set an *e* for the believers in speech,
Tit 2: 7 In everything set them an *e*
1Pe 2: 21 leaving you an *e*, that you should

EXAMPLES* (EXAMPLE)

1Co 10: 6 Now these things occurred as *e*
10: 11 as *e* and were written down
1Pe 5: 3 to you, but being *e* to the flock.

EXASPERATE*

Eph 6: 4 Fathers, do not *e* your children;

EXCEL (EXCELLENT)

1Co 14: 12 to *e* in gifts that build up the church
2Co 8: 7 But just as you *e* in everything—

EXCELLENT (EXCEL)

1Co 12: 31 now I will show you the most *e* way

hp 4: 8 if anything is *e* or praiseworthy—
Ti 3: 13 have served well gain an *e* standing
it 3: 8 These things are *e* and profitable

XCHANGED

o 1: 23 *e* the glory of the immortal God
1: 25 They *e* the truth of God for a lie,

XCUSE (EXCUSES)

n 15: 22 they have no *e* for their sin.
o 1: 20 so that men are without *e.*

XCUSES* (EXCUSE)

k 14: 18 "But they all alike began to make *e.*

XISTS

Ieb 2: 10 and through whom everything *e,*
11: 6 to him must believe that he *e*

XPECT (EXPECTATION)

Mt 24: 44 at an hour when you do not *e* him.

EXPECTATION (EXPECT)

Ro 8: 19 waits in eager *e* for the sons
Heb 10: 27 but only a fearful *e* of judgment

EXPEL*

1Co 5: 13 *E* the wicked man from among you

EXPENSIVE

1Ti 2: 9 or gold or pearls or *e* clothes,

EXPLOIT

Pr 22: 22 Do not *e* the poor because they are
2Co 12: 17 Did I *e* you through any

EXPOSE

1Co 4: 5 will *e* the motives of men's hearts.
Eph 5: 11 of darkness, but rather *e* them.

EXTENDS

Pr 31: 20 and *e* her hands to the needy.
Lk 1: 50 His mercy *e* to those who fear him,

EXTINGUISHED

2Sa 21: 17 the lamp of Israel will not be *e.*"

EXTOL*

Job 36: 24 Remember to *e* his work,
Ps 34: 1 I will *e* the LORD at all times;
68: 4 *e* him who rides on the clouds—
95: 2 and *e* him with music and song.
109: 30 mouth I will greatly *e* the LORD;
111: 1 I will *e* the LORD with all my heart
115: 18 it is we who *e* the LORD,
117: 1 *e* him, all you peoples.
145: 2 and *e* your name for ever and ever.
145: 10 your saints will *e* you.
147: 12 *E* the LORD, O Jerusalem;

EXTORT*

Lk 3: 14 "Don't *e* money and don't accuse

EYE (EYES)

Ex 21: 24 you are to take life for life, *e* for *e,*
Ps 94: 9 Does he who formed the *e* not see?
Mt 5: 29 If your right *e* causes you to sin,
5: 38 '*E* for *e,* and tooth for tooth.'
7: 3 of sawdust in your brother's *e*
1Co 2: 9 "No *e* has seen,
Col 3: 22 not only when their *e* is on you
Rev 1: 7 and every *e* will see him,

EYES (EYE)

Nu 33: 55 remain will become barbs in your *e*
Jos 23: 13 on your backs and thorns in your *e,*
2Ch 16: 9 For the *e* of the LORD range
Job 31: 1 "I made a covenant with my *e*
36: 7 He does not take his *e*
Ps 119: 18 Open my *e* that I may see
121: 1 I lift up my *e* to the hills—
141: 8 But my *e* are fixed on you,
Pr 3: 7 Do not be wise in your own *e;*
4: 25 Let your *e* look straight ahead,
15: 3 The *e* of the LORD are everywhere
Isa 6: 5 and my *e* have seen the King,
Hab 1: 13 Your *e* are too pure to look on evil;
Jn 4: 35 open your *e* and look at the fields!
2Co 4: 18 So we fix our *e* not on what is seen,
Heb 12: 2 Let us fix our *e* on Jesus, the author
Jas 2: 5 poor in the *e* of the world to be rich
1Pe 3: 12 For the *e* of the Lord are
Rev 7: 17 wipe away every tear from their *e.*"
21: 4 He will wipe every tear from their *e*

EZEKIEL

Priest called to be prophet to the exiles (Eze 1-3).

EZRA

Priest and teacher of the Law who led a return of exiles to Israel to reestablish temple and worship (Ezr 7-8). Corrected intermarriage of priests (Ezr 9-10). Read Law at celebration of Feast of Tabernacles (Neh 8).

F

FACE (FACES)

Ge 32: 30 "It is because I saw God *f* to *f,*
Ex 34: 29 was not aware that his *f* was radiant
Nu 6: 25 the LORD make his *f* shine
1Ch 16: 11 seek his *f* always.
2Ch 7: 14 and seek my *f* and turn
Ps 4: 6 Let the light of your *f* shine upon us
27: 8 Your *f,* LORD, I will seek.
31: 16 Let your *f* shine on your servant;
105: 4 seek his *f* always.
119: 135 Make your *f* shine
Isa 50: 7 Therefore have I set my *f* like flint,
Mt 17: 2 His *f* shone like the sun,
1Co 13: 12 mirror; then we shall see *f* to *f.*
2Co 4: 6 the glory of God in the *f* of Christ.
1Pe 3: 12 but the *f* of the Lord is
Rev 1: 16 His *f* was like the sun shining

FACES (FACE)

2Co 3: 18 who with unveiled *f* all reflect

FACTIONS

Gal 5: 20 selfish ambition, dissensions, *f*

FADE

1Pe 5: 4 of glory that will never *f* away.

FAIL (FAILING FAILINGS FAILS)

1Ch 28: 20 He will not *f* you or forsake you
2Ch 34: 33 they did not *f* to follow the LORD,
Ps 89: 28 my covenant with him will never *f.*
Pr 15: 22 Plans *f* for lack of counsel,
Isa 51: 6 my righteousness will never *f.*
La 3: 22 for his compassions never *f.*
2Co 13: 5 unless, of course, you *f* the test?

FAILING (FAIL)

1Sa 12: 23 sin against the LORD by *f* to pray

FAILINGS (FAIL)

Ro 15: 1 ought to bear with the *f* of the weak

FAILS (FAIL)

1Co 13: 8 Love never *f.*

FAINT

Isa 40: 31 they will walk and not be *f.*

FAIR

Pr 1: 3 doing what is right and just and *f;*
Col 4: 1 slaves with what is right and *f,*

FAITH (FAITHFUL FAITHFULLY FAITHFULNESS FAITHLESS)

2Ch 20: 20 Have *f* in the LORD your God
Hab 2: 4 but the righteous will live by his *f*—
Mt 9: 29 According to your *f* will it be done
17: 20 if you have *f* as small as a mustard
24: 10 many will turn away from the *f*
Mk 11: 22 "Have *f* in God," Jesus answered.
Lk 7: 9 I have not found such great *f*
12: 28 will he clothe you, O you of little *f!*
17: 5 "Increase our *f!*" He replied,
18: 8 will he find *f* on the earth?"
Ac 14: 9 saw that he had *f* to be healed
14: 27 the door of *f* to the Gentiles.
Ro 1: 12 encouraged by each other's *f.*
1: 17 is by *f* from first to last,
1: 17 "The righteous will live by *f.*"
3: 3 What if some did not have *f?*
3: 22 comes through *f* in Jesus Christ
3: 25 a sacrifice of atonement, through *f*
4: 5 his *f* is credited as righteousness.
5: 1 we have been justified through *f,*
10: 17 *f* comes from hearing the message,
14: 1 Accept him whose *f* is weak,
14: 23 that does not come from *f* is sin.
1Co 13: 2 and if I have a *f* that can move
13: 13 And now these three remain: *f,*
16: 13 stand firm in the *f;* be men
2Co 5: 7 We live by *f,* not by sight.
13: 5 to see whether you are in the *f;*
Gal 2: 16 Jesus that we may be justified by *f*
2: 20 I live by *f* in the Son of God,
3: 11 "The righteous will live by *f.*"
3: 24 that we might be justified by *f.*
Eph 2: 8 through *f*—and this not
4: 5 one Lord, one *f,* one baptism;
6: 16 to all this, take up the shield of *f,*
Col 1: 23 continue in your *f,* established
1Th 5: 8 on *f* and love as a breastplate,
1Ti 2: 15 if they continue in *f,* love
4: 1 later times some will abandon the *f*
5: 8 he has denied the *f* and is worse
6: 12 Fight the good fight of the *f.*
2Ti 3: 15 wise for salvation through *f*
4: 7 finished the race, I have kept the *f.*
Phm : 6 may be active in sharing your *f,*
Heb 10: 38 But my righteous one will live by *f.*
11: 1 *f* is being sure of what we hope for
11: 3 By *f* we understand that
11: 5 By *f* Enoch was taken from this life
11: 6 And without *f* it is impossible
11: 7 By *f* Noah, when warned about
11: 8 By *f* Abraham, when called to go

11: 17 By *f* Abraham, when God tested
11: 20 By *f* Isaac blessed Jacob
11: 21 By *f* Jacob, when he was dying,
11: 22 By *f* Joseph, when his end was near
11: 24 By *f* Moses, when he had grown up
11: 31 By *f* the prostitute Rahab,
12: 2 the author and perfecter of our *f*,
Jas 2: 14 if a man claims to have *f*
2: 17 In the same way, *f* by itself,
2: 26 so *f* without deeds is dead.
2Pe 1: 5 effort to add to your *f* goodness;
1Jn 5: 4 overcome the world, even our *f*.
Jude : 3 to contend for the *f* that was once

FAITHFUL (FAITH)
Nu 12: 7 he is *f* in all my house.
Dt 7: 9 your God is God; he is the *f* God,
32: 4 A *f* God who does no wrong,
2Sa 22: 26 "To the *f* you show yourself *f*,
Ps 25: 10 of the LORD are loving and *f*
31: 23 The LORD preserves the *f*,
33: 4 he is *f* in all he does.
37: 28 and will not forsake his *f* ones.
97: 10 for he guards the lives of his *f* ones
145: 13 The LORD is *f* to all his promises
146: 6 the LORD, who remains *f* forever.
Pr 31: 26 and *f* instruction is on her tongue.
Mt 25: 21 'Well done, good and *f* servant!
Ro 12: 12 patient in affliction, *f* in prayer.
1Co 4: 2 been given a trust must prove *f*.
10: 13 And God is *f*; he will not let you be
1Th 5: 24 The one who calls you is *f*
2Ti 2: 13 he will remain *f*,
Heb 3: 6 But Christ is *f* as a son
10: 23 for he who promised is *f*.
1Pe 4: 19 themselves to their *f* Creator
1Jn 1: 9 he is *f* and just and will forgive us
Rev 1: 5 who is the *f* witness, the firstborn
2: 10 Be *f*, even to the point of death,
19: 11 whose rider is called *F* and True.

FAITHFULLY (FAITH)
Dt 11: 13 if you *f* obey the commands I am
1Sa 12: 24 and serve him *f* with all your heart;
1Ki 2: 4 and if they walk *f* before me
1Pe 4: 10 *f* administering God's grace

FAITHFULNESS (FAITH)
Ps 57: 10 your *f* reaches to the skies.
85: 10 Love and *f* meet together;
86: 15 to anger, abounding in love and *f*.
89: 1 mouth I will make your *f* known
89: 14 love and *f* go before you.
91: 4 his *f* will be your shield
117: 2 the *f* of the LORD endures forever.
119: 75 and in *f* you have afflicted me.
Pr 3: 3 Let love and *f* never leave you;
Isa 11: 5 and *f* the sash around his waist.
La 3: 23 great is your *f*.
Ro 3: 3 lack of faith nullify God's *f*?
Gal 5: 22 patience, kindness, goodness, *f*,

FAITHLESS (FAITH)
Ps 119:158 I look on the *f* with loathing,
Jer 3: 22 "Return, *f* people;
Ro 1: 31 they are senseless, *f*, heartless,
2Ti 2: 13 if we are *f*,

FALL (FALLEN FALLING FALLS)
Ps 37: 24 though he stumble, he will not *f*,
55: 22 he will never let the righteous *f*.
69: 9 of those who insult you *f* on me.
Pr 11: 28 Whoever trusts in his riches will *f*,
Lk 11: 17 a house divided against itself will *f*.
Ro 3: 23 and *f* short of the glory of God,
Heb 6: 6 if they *f* away, to be brought back

FALLEN (FALL)
2Sa 1: 19 How the mighty have *f*!
Isa 14: 12 How you have *f* from heaven,
1Co 15: 20 of those who have *f* asleep.
Gal 5: 4 you have *f* away from grace.
1Th 4: 15 precede those who have *f* asleep.

FALLING (FALL)
Jude : 24 able to keep you from *f*

FALLS (FALL)
Pr 24: 17 Do not gloat when your enemy *f*;
Jn 12: 24 a kernel of wheat *f* to the ground
Ro 14: 4 To his own master he stands or *f*.

FALSE (FALSEHOOD FALSELY)
Ex 20: 16 "You shall not give *f* testimony
23: 1 "Do not spread *f* reports.
Pr 13: 5 The righteous hate what is *f*,
19: 5 A *f* witness will not go unpunished,
Mt 7: 15 "Watch out for *f* prophets.
19: 18 not steal, do not give *f* testimony,
24: 11 and many *f* prophets will appear
Php 1: 18 whether from *f* motives or true,
1Ti 1: 3 not to teach *f* doctrines any longer
2Pe 2: 1 there will be *f* teachers among you.

FALSEHOOD (FALSE)
Ps 119:163 I hate and abhor *f*
Pr 30: 8 Keep *f* and lies far from me;
Eph 4: 25 each of you must put off *f*

FALSELY (FALSE)
Lev 19: 12 "'Do not swear *f* by my name
Lk 3: 14 and don't accuse people *f*—
1Ti 6: 20 ideas of what is *f* called knowledge,

FALTER*
Pr 24: 10 If you *f* in times of trouble,
Isa 42: 4 he will not *f* or be discouraged

FAMILIES (FAMILY)
Ps 68: 6 God sets the lonely in *f*,

FAMILY (FAMILIES)
Pr 15: 27 greedy man brings trouble to his *f*,
31: 15 she provides food for her *f*
Lk 9: 61 go back and say good-by to my *f*."
12: 52 in one *f* divided against each other,
1Ti 3: 4 He must manage his own *f* well
3: 5 how to manage his own *f*,
5: 4 practice by caring for their own *f*
5: 8 and especially for his immediate *f*,

FAMINE
Ge 41: 30 seven years of *f* will follow them.
Am 8: 11 but a *f* of hearing the words
Ro 8: 35 or persecution or *f* or nakedness

FAN*
2Ti 1: 6 you to *f* into flame the gift of God,

FAST
Dt 13: 4 serve him and hold *f* to him.
Jos 22: 5 to hold *f* to him and to serve him
23: 8 to hold *f* to the LORD your God,
Ps 119: 31 I hold *f* to your statutes, O LORD;
139: 10 your right hand will hold me *f*.
Mt 6: 16 "When you *f*, do not look somber
1Pe 5: 12 Stand *f* in it.

FATHER (FATHER'S FATHERLESS FATHERS FOREFATHERS)
Ge 2: 24 this reason a man will leave his *f*
17: 4 You will be the *f* of many nations.
Ex 20: 12 "Honor your *f* and your mother,
21: 15 "Anyone who attacks his *f*
21: 17 "Anyone who curses his *f*
Lev 18: 7 "'Do not dishonor your *f*
19: 3 you must respect his mother and *f*,
Dt 5: 16 "Honor your *f* and your mother,
21: 18 son who does not obey his *f*
Ps 27: 10 Though my *f* and mother forsake
68: 5 A *f* to the fatherless, a defender
Pr 10: 1 A wise son brings joy to his *f*,
17: 21 there is no joy for the *f* of a fool.
23: 22 Listen to your *f*, who gave you life,
23: 24 *f* of a righteous man has great joy;
28: 7 of gluttons disgraces his *f*.
29: 3 loves wisdom brings joy to his *f*,
Isa 9: 6 Everlasting *F*, Prince of Peace.
Mt 6: 9 "'Our *F* in heaven,
10: 37 "Anyone who loves his *f*
15: 4 'Honor your *f* and mother'
19: 5 this reason a man will leave his *f*
Lk 12: 53 *f* against son and son against *f*,
23: 34 Jesus said, "*F*, forgive them,
Jn 6: 44 the *F* who sent me draws him,
6: 46 No one has seen the *F*
8: 44 You belong to your *f*, the devil,
10: 30 I and the *F* are one."
14: 6 No one comes to the *F*
14: 9 who has seen me has seen the *F*.
Ro 4: 11 he is the *f* of all who believe
2Co 6: 18 "I will be a *F* to you,
Eph 6: 2 "Honor your *f* and mother"—
Heb 12: 7 what son is not disciplined by his *f*?

FATHER'S (FATHER)
Pr 13: 1 A wise son heeds his *f* instruction,
15: 5 A fool spurns his *f* discipline,
19: 13 A foolish son is his *f* ruin,
Lk 2: 49 had to be in my *F* house?"
Jn 2: 16 How dare you turn my *F* house
10: 29 can snatch them out of my *F* hand.
14: 2 In my *F* house are many rooms;

FATHERLESS (FATHER)
Dt 10: 18 He defends the cause of the *f*
24: 17 Do not deprive the alien or the *f*
24: 19 Leave it for the alien, the *f*
Ps 68: 5 A father to the *f*, a defender
Pr 23: 10 or encroach on the fields of the *f*,

FATHERS (FATHER)
Ex 20: 5 for the sin of the *f* to the third
Lk 11: 11 "Which of you *f*, if your son asks
Eph 6: 4 *F*, do not exasperate your children;
Col 3: 21 *F*, do not embitter your children,

FATHOM*
Job 11: 7 "Can you *f* the mysteries of God?
Ps 145: 3 his greatness no one can *f*.
Ecc 3: 11 yet they cannot *f* what God has
Isa 40: 28 and his understanding no one can *f*
1Co 13: 2 and can *f* all mysteries and all

FAULT (FAULTS)
Mt 18: 15 and show him his *f*, just
Php 2: 15 of God without *f* in a crooked
Jas 1: 5 generously to all without finding *f*,
Jude : 24 his glorious presence without *f*

FAULTFINDERS*
Jude : 16 These men are grumblers and *f*;

FAULTS (FAULT)
Ps 19: 12 Forgive my hidden *f*.

FAVORITISM*
Ex 23: 3 and do not show *f* to a poor man
Lev 19: 15 to the poor or *f* to the great,
Ac 10: 34 true it is that God does not show *f*
Ro 2: 11 For God does not show *f*.
Eph 6: 9 and there is no *f* with him.
Col 3: 25 for his wrong, and there is no *f*.
1Ti 5: 21 and to do nothing out of *f*.
Jas 2: 1 Lord Jesus Christ, don't show *f*.
2: 9 But if you show *f*, you sin

FEAR (AFRAID FEARS)
Dt 6: 13 *F* the LORD your God, serve him
10: 12 but to *f* the LORD your God,
31: 12 and learn to *f* the LORD your God
Ps 19: 9 The *f* of the LORD is pure,
23: 4 I will *f* no evil,
27: 1 whom shall I *f*?
91: 5 You will not *f* the terror of night,
111: 10 *f* of the LORD is the beginning
Pr 8: 13 To *f* the LORD is to hate evil;
9: 10 *f* of the LORD is the beginning
10: 27 The *f* of the LORD adds length
14: 27 The *f* of the LORD is a fountain
15: 33 *f* of the LORD teaches a man
16: 6 through the *f* of the LORD a man
19: 23 The *f* of the LORD leads to life:
29: 25 *F* of man will prove to be a snare,
Isa 11: 3 delight in the *f* of the LORD.
41: 10 So do not *f*, for I am with you;
Lk 12: 5 I will show you whom you should *f*:
Php 2: 12 to work out your salvation with *f*
1Jn 4: 18 But perfect love drives out *f*,

FEARS (FEAR)
Job 1: 8 a man who *f* God and shuns evil."
Ps 34: 4 he delivered me from all my *f*.
Pr 31: 30 a woman who *f* the LORD is
1Jn 4: 18 The one who *f* is not made perfect

FEED
Jn 21: 15 Jesus said, "*F* my lambs."
21: 17 Jesus said, "*F* my sheep.
Ro 12: 20 "If your enemy is hungry, *f* him;
Jude : 12 shepherds who *f* only themselves.

FEET (FOOT)
Ps 8: 6 you put everything under his *f*:
22: 16 have pierced my hands and my *f*.
40: 2 he set my *f* on a rock
110: 1 a footstool for your *f*."
119:105 Your word is a lamp to my *f*
Ro 10: 15 "How beautiful are the *f*
1Co 12: 21 And the head cannot say to the *f*,
15: 25 has put all his enemies under his *f*.
Heb 12: 13 "Make level paths for your *f*,"

FELLOWSHIP
2Co 6: 14 what *f* can light have with darkness
13: 14 and the *f* of the Holy Spirit be
Php 3: 10 the *f* of sharing in his sufferings,
1Jn 1: 6 claim to have *f* with him yet walk
1: 7 we have *f* with one another,

FEMALE
Ge 1: 27 male and *f* he created them.
Gal 3: 28 *f*, for you are all one in Christ Jesus

FERVOR
Ro 12: 11 but keep your spiritual *f*, serving

FIELD (FIELDS)
Mt 6: 28 See how the lilies of the *f* grow.
13: 38 *f* is the world, and the good seed
1Co 3: 9 you are God's *f*, God's building.

FIELDS (FIELD)
Lk 2: 8 were shepherds living out in the *f*
Jn 4: 35 open your eyes and look at the *f*!

FIG (FIGS)
Ge 3: 7 so they sewed *f* leaves together

FIGHT (FOUGHT)
Ex 14: 14 The LORD will *f* for you; you need
Dt 1: 30 going before you, will *f* for you,
3: 22 the LORD your God himself will *f*
Ne 4: 20 Our God will *f* for us!"
Ps 35: 1 *f* against those who *f* against me.
Jn 18: 36 my servants would *f*
1Co 9: 26 I do not *f* like a man beating the air.
2Co 10: 4 The weapons we *f*
1Ti 1: 18 them you may *f* the good *f*,
6: 12 Fight the good *f* of the faith.
2Ti 4: 7 fought the good *f*, I have finished

FIGS (FIG)
Lk 6: 44 People do not pick *f*

FILL (FILLED FILLS FULL FULLNESS FULLY)
Ge 1: 28 and increase in number; *f* the earth
Ps 16: 11 you will *f* me with joy
81: 10 wide your mouth and I will *f* it.
Pr 28: 19 who chases fantasies will have his *f*
Hag 2: 7 and I will *f* this house with glory,'
Jn 6: 26 you ate the loaves and had your *f*.
Ac 2: 28 you will *f* me with joy
Ro 15: 13 the God of hope *f* you with all joy

FILLED (FILL)
Ps 72: 19 may the whole earth be *f*
119: 64 The earth is *f* with your love,
Eze 43: 5 the glory of the LORD *f* the temple
Hab 2: 14 For the earth will be *f*
Lk 1: 15 and he will be *f* with the Holy Spirit
1: 41 and Elizabeth was *f* with the Holy
Jn 12: 3 the house was *f* with the fragrance
Ac 2: 4 All of them were *f*
4: 8 Then Peter, *f* with the Holy Spirit,
9: 17 and be *f* with the Holy S
13: 9 called Paul, *f* with the Spirit,
Eph 5: 18 Instead, be *f* with
Php 1: 11 *f* with the fruit of righteousness

FILLS (FILL)
Nu 14: 21 of the LORD *f*
Ps 107: 9 and *f* the h things.
Eph 1: 23 fullness every

FILTHY
Isa 64: 6 all *f*

Col 3: 8 and *f* language from your lips.
2Pe 2: 7 by the *f* lives of lawless men

FIND (FINDS FOUND)
Nu 32: 23 be sure that your sin will *f* you out.
Dt 4: 29 you will *f* him if you look for him
1Sa 23: 16 and helped him *f* strength in God.
Ps 36: 7 *f* refuge in the shadow
91: 4 under his wings you will *f* refuge;
Pr 14: 22 those who plan what is good *f* love
31: 10 A wife of noble character who can *f*
Jer 6: 16 and you will *f* rest for your souls.
Mt 7: 7 seek and you will *f*; knock
11: 29 and you will *f* rest for your souls.
16: 25 loses his life for me will *f* it.
Lk 18: 8 will he *f* faith on the earth?"
Jn 10: 9 come in and go out, and *f* pasture.

FINDS (FIND)
Ps 62: 1 My soul finds rest in God alone;
112: 1 who *f* great delight
119:162 like one who *f* great spoil.
Pr 18: 22 He who *f* a wife *f* what is good
Mt 7: 8 he who seeks *f*; and to him who
10: 39 Whoever *f* his life will lose it,
Lk 12: 37 whose master *f* them watching
15: 4 go after the lost sheep until he

FINISH (FINISHED)
Jn 4: 34 who sent me and to *f* his work.
... that the Father has given me to *f*,
... only I may *f* the race
Ac ... Now *f* the work, so that
2Co ... your eager
... 4 Perseverance must *f* its work

FINISHED (FINISH)
... 2 seventh day God had *f* the work he
... 30 the drink, Jesus said, "It is *f*."
... 4: 7 I have *f* the race, I have kept

FIRE
... 13: 21 in a pillar of *f* to give them light,
Lev 6: 12 *f* on the altar must be kept burning;
Isa 30: 27 and his tongue is a consuming *f*.
Jer 23: 29 my word like *f*," declares
Mt 3: 11 you with the Holy Spirit and with *f*.
5: 22 will be in danger of the *f* of hell.
25: 41 into the eternal *f* prepared
Mk 9: 43 where the *f* never goes out.

Ac 2: 3 to be tongues of *f* that separated
1Co 3: 13 It will be revealed with *f*,
1Th 5: 19 Do not put out the Spirit's *f*;
Heb 12: 29 for our "God is a consuming *f*."
Jas 3: 5 set on *f* by a small spark.
2Pe 3: 10 the elements will be destroyed by *f*,
Jude : 23 snatch others from the *f*
Rev 20: 14 The lake of *f* is the second death.

FIRM
Ex 14: 13 Stand *f* and you will see
2Ch 20: 17 stand *f* and see the deliverance
Ps 33: 11 of the LORD stand *f* forever,
37: 23 he makes his steps *f*;
40: 2 and gave me a *f* place to stand.
89: 2 that your love stands *f* forever,
119: 89 it stands *f* in the heavens.
Pr 4: 26 and take only ways that are *f*.
Zec 8: 23 nations will take *f* hold of one Jew
Mk 13: 13 he who stands *f* to the end will be
1Co 16: 13 on your guard; stand *f* in the fa
2Co 1: 24 because is by faith you stand *f*.
Eph 6: 14 Stand *f* then, with the belt
Col 4: 12 that you may stand *f* in all the will
2Th 2: 15 stand *f* and hold to the teaching
2Ti 2: 19 God's sol undation stands *f*,
Heb 6: 19 an anchor soul, *f* and secure
1Pe 5: 9 Resist him, st in the faith,

FIRST
Isa 44: 6 I am the *f* and I am
48: 12 I am the *f* and I am t
Mt 5: 24 *F* go and be reconcile
6: 33 But seek *f* his kingdom
7: 5 *f* take the plank out
20: 27 wants to be *f* must be yo slave—
22: 38 This is the *f* and greatest
23: 26 *F* clean the inside of the cup
Mk 13: 10 And the gospel must *f* be preached
Ac 11: 26 disciples were called Christians *f*
Ro 1: 16 *f* for the Jew, then for the Gentile.
1Co 12: 28 in the church God has appointed *f*
2Co 8: 5 they gave themselves *f* to the Lord
1Ti 2: 13 For Adam was formed *f*, then Eve.
Jas 3: 17 comes from heaven is *f* of all pure;
1Jn 4: 19 We love because he *f* loved us.

3Jn : 9 but Diotrephes, who loves to be *f*,
Rev 1: 17 I am the *F* and the Last.
2: 4 You have forsaken your *f* love.

FIRSTBORN (BEAR)
Ex 11: 5 Every *f* son in Egypt will die,

FIRSTFRUITS
Ex 23: 19 "Bring the best of the *f* of your soil

FISHERS
Mk 1: 17 "and I will make you *f* of men."

FITTING*
Ps 33: 1 it is *f* for the upright to praise him.
147: 1 how pleasant and *f* to praise him!
Pr 10: 32 of the righteous know what is *f*,
19: 10 It is not *f* for a fool to live in luxury
26: 1 honor is not *f* for a fool.
1Co 14: 40 everything should be done in a *f*
Col 3: 18 to your husbands, as is *f* in the Lord
Heb 2: 10 sons to glory, it was *f* that God,

FIX
Dt 11: 18 *F* these words of mine
Pr 4: 25 *f* your gaze directly before you.
2Co 4: 18 we *f* our eyes not on what is seen,
Heb 3: 1 heavenly calling, *f* your thoughts
12: 2 Let us *f* our eyes on Jesus,

FLAME (FLAMES FLAMING)
2Ti 1: 6 you to fan into *f* the gift of God,

FLAMES (FLAME)
o 3: 15 only as one escaping through the *f*.
3: 3 and surrender my body to the *f*,

G (FLAME)
you can extinguish all the *f* rrows
1 in the twinkling of an
FLA
FLAT
Job 32 RING
Jude :
y man;
FLATTER r own
Ps 12: 2 d
12: 3 Ma
Pr 26: 28 and lips

FLATTERY (FLATTER)
Ro 16: 18 and *f* they deceive the minds
1Th 2: 5 You know we never used *f*,

FLAWLESS*
2Sa 22: 31 the word of the LORD is *f*.
Job 11: 4 You say to God, 'My beliefs are *f*
Ps 12: 6 And the words of the LORD are *f*,
18: 30 the word of the LORD is *f*.
Pr 30: 5 "Every word of God is *f*;
SS 5: 2 my dove, my *f* one.

FLEE
Ps 139: 7 Where can I *f* from your presence?
1Co 6: 18 *F* from sexual immorality.
10: 14 my dear friends, *f* from idolatry.
1Ti 6: 11 But you, man of God, *f* from all this
2Ti 2: 22 *F* the evil desires of youth,
Jas 4: 7 Resist the devil, and he will *f*

FLEETING
Ps 89: 47 Remember how *f* is my life.
Pr 31: 30 Charm is deceptive, and beauty is *f*

FLESH
Ge 2: 23 and *f* of my *f*;
2: 24 and they will become one *f*.
Job 19: 26 yet in my *f* I will see God;
Eze 11: 19 of stone and give them a heart of *f*.
36: 26 of stone and give you a heart of *f*.
Mk 10: 8 and the two will become one *f*.'
Jn 1: 14 The Word became *f* and made his
6: 51 This bread is my *f*, which I will give
1Co 6: 16 "The two will become one *f*."
Eph 5: 31 and the two will become one *f*."
6: 12 For our struggle is not against *f*

FLOCK (FLOCKS)
Isa 40: 11 He tends his *f* like a shepherd:
Eze 34: 2 not shepherds take care of the *f*?
Zec 11: 17 who deserts the *f*!
Mt 26: 31 the sheep of the *f* will be scattered.'
Ac 20: 28 all the *f* of which the Holy Spirit
1Pe 5: 2 Be shepherds of God's *f* that is

FLOCKS (FLOCK)
Lk 2: 8 keeping watch over their *f* at night.

FLOG
Ac 22: 25 to *f* a Roman citizen who hasn't

FLOODGATES
Mal 3: 10 see if I will not throw open the *f*

FLOURISHING
Ps 52: 8 *f* in the house of God;

FLOW (FLOWING)
Nu 13: 27 and it does *f* with milk and honey!
Jn 7: 38 streams of living water will *f*

FLOWERS
Isa 40: 7 The grass withers and the *f* fall,

FLOWING (FLOW)
Ex 3: 8 a land *f* with milk and honey—

FOLDING
Pr 6: 10 a little *f* of the hands to rest—

FOLLOW (FOLLOWING FOLLOWS)
Ex 23: 2 Do not *f* the crowd in doing wrong.
Lev 18: 4 and be careful to *f* my decrees.
Dt 5: 1 Learn them and be sure to *f* them.
Ps 23: 6 Surely goodness and love will *f* me
Mt 16: 24 and take up his cross and *f* me.
Jn 10: 4 his sheep *f* him because they know
1Co 14: 1 *F* the way of love and eagerly
Rev 14: 4 They *f* the Lamb wherever he goes.

FOLLOWING (FOLLOW)
1Ti 1: 18 by *f* them you may fight the good

FOLLOWS (FOLLOW)
Jn 8: 12 Whoever *f* me will never walk

FOOD (FOODS)
Pr 20: 13 you will have *f* to spare.
22: 9 for he shares his *f* with the poor.
25: 21 If your enemy is hungry, give him *f*
31: 15 she provides *f* for her family
Da 1: 8 to defile himself with the royal *f*
Jn 6: 27 Do not work for *f* that spoils,
Ro 14: 14 fully convinced that no *f* is unclean
1Co 8: 8 But *f* does not bring us near to God
1Ti 6: 8 But if we have *f* and clothing,
Jas 2: 15 sister is without clothes and daily *f*.

FOODS (FOOD)
Mk 7: 19 Jesus declared all *f* "clean.")

FOOL (FOOLISH FOOLISHNESS FOOLS)
Ps 14: 1 The *f* says in his heart,
Pr 15: 5 A *f* spurns his father's discipline,
17: 28 Even a *f* is thought wise

18: 2 A *f* finds no pleasure
26: 5 Answer a *f* according to his folly,
28: 26 He who trusts in himself is a *f*,
Mt 5: 22 But anyone who says, 'You *f*!'

FOOLISH (FOOL)

Pr 10: 1 but a *f* son grief to his mother.
17: 25 A *f* son brings grief to his father
Mt 7: 26 practice is like a *f* man who built
25: 2 of them were *f* and five were wise.
1Co 1: 27 God chose the *f* things of the world

FOOLISHNESS (FOOL)

1Co 1: 18 of the cross is *f* to those who are
1: 25 For the *f* of God is wiser
2: 14 for they are *f* to him, and he cannot
3: 19 of this world is *f* in God's sight.

FOOLS (FOOL)

Pr 14: 9 *F* mock at making amends for sin,
1Co 4: 10 We are *f* for Christ, but you are

FOOT (FEET FOOTHOLD)

Jos 1: 3 every place where you set your *f*,
Isa 1: 6 From the sole of your *f* to the top
1Co 12: 15 If the *f* should say, "Because I am

FOOTHOLD (FOOT)

Eph 4: 27 and do not give the devil a *f*.

FORBEARANCE*

Ro 3: 25 because in his *f* he had left the sins

FORBID

1Co 14: 39 and do not *f* speaking in tongues.

FOREFATHERS (FATHER)

Heb 1: 1 spoke to our *f* through the prophets

FOREKNEW* (KNOW)

Ro 8: 29 For those God *f* he
11: 2 not reject his people, whom he *f*.

FOREVER (EVER)

1Ch 16: 15 He remembers his covenant *f*,
16: 34 his love endures *f*.
Ps 9: 7 The LORD reigns *f*;
23: 6 dwell in the house of the LORD *f*.
33: 11 the plans of the LORD stand firm *f*
86: 12 I will glorify your name *f*.
92: 8 But you, O LORD, are exalted *f*.
110: 4 "You are a priest *f*,
119:111 Your statutes are my heritage *f*;
Jn 6: 51 eats of this bread, he will live *f*.
14: 16 Counselor to be with you *f* —
1Co 9: 25 it to get a crown that will last *f*.
1Th 4: 17 And so we will be with the Lord *f*.
Heb 13: 8 same yesterday and today and *f*.
1Pe 1: 25 but the word of the Lord stands *f*."
1Jn 2: 17 who does the will of God lives *f*.

FORFEIT

Lk 9: 25 and yet lose or *f* his very self?

FORGAVE (FORGIVE)

Ps 32: 5 and you *f*
Eph 4: 32 just as in Christ God *f* you.
Col 2: 13 He *f* us all our sins, having
3: 13 Forgive as the Lord *f* you.

FORGET (FORGETS FORGETTING)

Dt 6: 12 that you do not *f* the LORD,
Ps 103: 2 and *f* not all his benefits.
137: 5 may my right hand *f* ⌊its skill⌋.
Isa 49: 15 "Can a mother *f* the baby
Heb 6: 10 he will not *f* your work

FORGETS (FORGET)

Jn 16: 21 her baby is born she *f* the anguish
Jas 1: 24 immediately *f* what he looks like.

FORGETTING (FORGET)

Php 3: 13 *F* what is behind and straining

FORGIVE (FORGAVE FORGIVENESS FORGIVING)

2Ch 7: 14 will *f* their sin and will heal their
Ps 19: 12 *F* my hidden faults.
Mt 6: 12 *F* us our debts,
6: 14 For if you *f* men when they sin
18: 21 many times shall I *f* my brother
Mk 11: 25 in heaven may *f* you your sins."
Lk 11: 4 *F* us our sins,
23: 34 Jesus said, "Father, *f* them,
Col 3: 13 *F* as the Lord forgave you.
1Jn 1: 9 and just and will *f* us our sins

FORGIVENESS (FORGIVE)

Ps 130: 4 But with you there is *f*;
Ac 10: 43 believes in him receives *f* of sins
Eph 1: 7 through his blood, the *f* of sins,
Col 1: 14 in whom we have redemption, the *f*
Heb 9: 22 the shedding of blood there is no *f*.

FORGIVING (FORGIVE)

Ne 9: 17 But you are a *f* God, gracious
Eph 4: 32 to one another, *f* each other,

FORMED

Ge 2: 7 And the LORD God *f* man
Ps 103: 14 for he knows how we are *f*,
Isa 45: 18 but *f* it to be inhabited —
Ro 9: 20 "Shall what is *f* say to him who *f* it,
1Ti 2: 13 For Adam was *f* first, then Eve.
Heb 11: 3 understand that the universe was *f*

FORSAKE (FORSAKEN)

Jos 1: 5 I will never leave you nor *f* you.
24: 16 "Far be it from us to *f* the LORD
2Ch 15: 2 but if you *f* him, he will *f* you.
Ps 27: 10 Though my father and mother *f* me
Isa 55: 7 Let the wicked *f* his way
Heb 13: 5 never will I *f* you."

FORSAKEN (FORSAKE)

Ps 22: 1 my God, why have you *f* me?
37: 25 I have never seen the righteous *f*
Mt 27: 46 my God, why have you *f* me?"
Rev 2: 4 You have *f* your first love.

FORTRESS

Ps 18: 2 The LORD is my rock, my *f*
71: 3 for you are my rock and my *f*.

FOUGHT (FIGHT)

2Ti 4: 7 I have *f* the good fight, I have

FOUND (FIND)

1Ch 28: 9 If you seek him, he will be *f* by you;
Isa 55: 6 Seek the LORD while he may be *f*;
Da 5: 27 on the scales and *f* wanting.
Lk 15: 6 with me; I have *f* my lost sheep.'
15: 9 with me; I have *f* my lost coin.'
Ac 4: 12 Salvation is *f* in no one else,

FOUNDATION

Isa 28: 16 a precious cornerstone for a sure *f*;
1Co 3: 11 For no one can lay any *f* other
Eph 2: 20 built on the *f* of the apostles
2Ti 2: 19 God's solid *f* stands firm,

FOXES

Mt 8: 20 "*F* have holes and birds

FRAGRANCE

2Co 2: 16 of death; to the other, the *f* of life.

FREE (FREED FREEDOM FREELY)

Ps 146: 7 The LORD sets prisoners *f*,
Jn 8: 32 and the truth will set you *f*."
Ro 6: 18 You have been set *f* from sin
Gal 3: 28 slave nor *f*, male nor female,
1Pe 2: 16 *f* men, but do not use your freedom

FREED (FREE)

Rev 1: 5 has *f* us from our sins by his blood,

FREEDOM (FREE)

Ro 8: 21 into the glorious *f* of the children
2Co 3: 17 the Spirit of the Lord is, there is *f*.
Gal 5: 13 But do not use your *f* to indulge
1Pe 2: 16 but do not use your *f* as a cover-up

FREELY (FREE)

Isa 55: 7 and to our God, for he will *f* pardon
Mt 10: 8 Freely you have received, *f* give.
Ro 3: 24 and are justified *f* by his grace
Eph 1: 6 which he has *f* given us

FRIEND (FRIENDS)

Ex 33: 11 as a man speaks with his *f*.
Pr 17: 17 A *f* loves at all times,
18: 24 there is a *f* who sticks closer
27: 6 Wounds from a *f* can be trusted,
27: 10 Do not forsake your *f* and the *f*
Jas 4: 4 Anyone who chooses to be a *f*

FRIENDS (FRIEND)

Pr 16: 28 and a gossip separates close *f*.
Zec 13: 6 given at the house of my *f*.'
Jn 15: 13 that he lay down his life for his *f*.

FRUIT (FRUITFUL)

Ps 1: 3 which yields its *f* in season
Pr 11: 30 The *f* of the righteous is a tree
Mt 7: 16 By their *f* you will recognize them.
Jn 15: 2 branch in me that bears no *f*,
Gal 5: 22 But the *f* of the Spirit is love, joy,
Rev 22: 2 of *f*, yielding its *f* every month.

FRUITFUL (FRUIT)

Ge 1: 22 "Be *f* and increase in number
Ps 128: 3 Your wife will be like a *f* vine
Jn 15: 2 prunes so that it will be even more *f*.

FULFILL (FULFILLED FULFILLMENT)

Ps 116: 14 I will *f* my vows to the LORD
Mt 5: 17 come to abolish them but to *f* them.
1Co 7: 3 husband should *f* his marital duty

FULFILLED (FULFILL)

Pr 13: 19 A longing *f* is sweet to the soul,
Mk 14: 49 But the Scriptures must be *f*."
Ro 13: 8 loves his fellowman has *f* the law.

FULFILLMENT (FULFILL)

Ro 13: 10 Therefore love is the *f* of the law.

FULL (FILL)

Ps 127: 5 whose quiver is *f* of them.
Pr 31: 11 Her husband has *f* confidence

Isa 6: 3 the whole earth is *f* of his glory."
11: 9 for the earth will be *f*
Jn 10: 10 may have life, and have it to the *f*.
Ac 6: 3 known to be *f* of the Spirit

FULLNESS (FILL)
Col 1: 19 to have all his *f* dwell in him,
2: 9 in Christ all the *f* of the Deity lives

FULLY (FILL)
1Ki 8: 61 your hearts must be *f* committed
2Ch 16: 9 whose hearts are *f* committed
Ps 119: 4 that are to be *f* obeyed.
119:138 they are *f* trustworthy.
1Co 15: 58 Always give yourselves *f*

FUTURE
Ps 37: 37 there is a *f* for the man of peace.
Pr 23: 18 There is surely a *f* hope for you,
Ro 8: 38 neither the present nor the *f*,

G

GABRIEL*
Angel who interpreted Daniel's visions (Da 8:16-26; 9:20-27); announced births of John (Lk 1:11-20), Jesus (Lk 1:26-38).

GAIN (GAINED)
Ps 60: 12 With God we will *g* the victory,
Mk 8: 36 it for a man to *g* the whole world,
1Co 13: 3 but have not love, I *g* nothing.
Php 1: 21 to live is Christ and to die is *g*.
3: 8 that I may *g* Christ and be found
1Ti 6: 6 with contentment is great *g*.

GAINED (GAIN)
Ro 5: 2 through whom we have *g* access

GALILEE
Isa 9: 1 but in the future he will honor *G*

GALL
Mt 27: 34 mixed with *g*; but after tasting it,

GAP
Eze 22: 30 stand before me in the *g* on behalf

GARDENER
Jn 15: 1 true vine, and my Father is the *g*.

GARMENT (GARMENTS)
Ps 102: 26 they will all wear out like a *g*.
Mt 9: 16 of unshrunk cloth on an old *g*,
Jn 19: 23 This *g* was seamless, woven

GARMENTS (GARMENT)
Ge 3: 21 The LORD God made *g* of skin
Isa 61: 10 me with *g* of salvation
63: 1 with his *g* stained crimson?
Jn 19: 24 "They divided my *g* among them

GATE (GATES)
Mt 7: 13 For wide is the *g* and broad is
Jn 10: 9 I am the *g*; whoever enters

GATES (GATE)
Ps 100: 4 Enter his *g* with thanksgiving
Mt 16: 18 the *g* of Hades will not overcome it

GATHER (GATHERS)
Zec 14: 2 I will *g* all the nations to Jerusalem
Mt 12: 30 he who does not *g* with me scatters
23: 37 longed to *g* your children together,

GATHERS (GATHER)
Isa 40: 11 He *g* the lambs in his arms
Mt 23: 37 a hen *g* her chicks under her wings,

GAVE (GIVE)
Ezr 2: 69 According to their ability they *g*
Job 1: 21 LORD *g* and the LORD has taken
Jn 3: 16 so loved the world that he *g* his one
2Co 8: 5 they *g* themselves first to the Lord
Gal 2: 20 who loved me and *g* himself for me
1Ti 2: 6 who *g* himself as a ransom

GAZE
Ps 27: 4 to *g* upon the beauty of the LORD
Pr 4: 25 fix your *g* directly before you.

GENEALOGIES
1Ti 1: 4 themselves to myths and endless *g*.

GENERATIONS
Ps 22: 30 future *g* will be told about the Lord
102: 12 your renown endures through all *g*.
145: 13 dominion endures through all *g*.
Lk 1: 48 now on all *g* will call me blessed,
Eph 3: 5 not made known to men in other *g*

GENEROUS
Ps 112: 5 Good will come to him who is *g*
Pr 22: 9 A *g* man will himself be blessed,
2Co 9: 5 Then it will be ready as a *g* gift,
1Ti 6: 18 and to be *g* and willing to share.

GENTILE (GENTILES)
Ro 1: 16 first for the Jew, then for the *G*.
10: 12 difference between Jew and *G*—

GENTILES (GENTILE)
Isa 42: 6 and a light for the *G*,
Ro 3: 9 and *G* alike are all under sin.
11: 13 as I am the apostle to the *G*,
1Co 1: 23 block to Jews and foolishness to *G*,

GENTLE (GENTLENESS)
Pr 15: 1 A *g* answer turns away wrath,
Zec 9: 9 *g* and riding on a donkey,
Mt 11: 29 for I am *g* and humble in heart,
21: 5 *g* and riding on a donkey,
1Co 4: 21 or in love and with a *g* spirit?
1Pe 3: 4 the unfading beauty of a *g*

GENTLENESS* (GENTLE)
2Co 10: 1 By the meekness and *g* of Christ,
Gal 5: 23 faithfulness, *g* and self-control.
Php 4: 5 Let your *g* be evident to all.
Col 3: 12 kindness, humility, *g* and patience.
1Ti 6: 11 faith, love, endurance and *g*.
1Pe 3: 15 But do this with *g* and respect,

GETHSEMANE
Mt 26: 36 disciples to a place called *G*,

GIDEON*
Judge, also called Jerub-Baal; freed Israel from Midianites (Jdg 6-8; Heb 11:32). Given sign of fleece (Jdg 8:36-40).

GIFT (GIFTS)
Pr 21: 14 A *g* given in secret soothes anger,
Mt 5: 23 if you are offering your *g*
Ac 2: 38 And you will receive the *g*
Ro 6: 23 but the *g* of God is eternal life
1Co 7: 7 each man has his own *g* from God;
2Co 8: 12 the *g* is acceptable according
9: 15 be to God for his indescribable *g*!
Eph 2: 8 it is the *g* of God—not by works,
1Ti 4: 14 not neglect your *g*, which was
2Ti 1: 6 you to fan into flame the *g* of God,
Jas 1: 17 and perfect *g* is from above,
1Pe 4: 10 should use whatever *g* he has

GIFTS (GIFT)
Ro 11: 29 for God's *g* and his call are
12: 6 We have different *g*, according
1Co 12: 4 There are different kinds of *g*,
12: 31 But eagerly desire the greater *g*.
14: 1 and eagerly desire spiritual *g*,
14: 12 excel in *g* that build up the church.

GILEAD
Jer 8: 22 Is there no balm in *G*?

GIVE (GAVE GIVEN GIVER GIVES GIVING)
Nu 6: 26 and *g* you peace."'
1Sa 1: 11 then I will *g* him to the LORD
2Ch 15: 7 be strong and do not *g* up,
Pr 21: 26 but the righteous *g* without sparing
23: 26 My son, *g* me your heart
30: 8 but *g* me only my daily bread.
31: 31 *G* her the reward she has earned,
Isa 42: 8 I will not *g* my glory to another
Eze 36: 26 I will *g* you a new heart
Mt 6: 11 *G* us today our daily bread.
10: 8 Freely you have received, freely *g*.
22: 21 "*G* to Caesar what is Caesar's,
Mk 8: 37 Or what can a man *g* in exchange
Lk 6: 38 *G*, and it will be given to you.
11: 13 Father in heaven *g* the Holy Spirit
Jn 10: 28 I *g* them eternal life, and they shall
13: 34 "A new commandment I *g* you:
Ac 20: 35 blessed to *g* than to receive.'"
Ro 12: 8 let him *g* generously;
13: 7 *G* everyone what you owe him:
14: 12 each of us will *g* an account
2Co 9: 7 Each man should *g* what he has
Rev 14: 7 "Fear God and *g* him glory,

GIVEN (GIVE)
Nu 8: 16 are to be *g* wholly to me.
Ps 115: 16 but the earth he has *g* to man.
Isa 9: 6 to us a son is *g*,
Mt 6: 33 and all these things will be *g* to you
7: 7 "Ask and it will be *g* to you;
Lk 22: 19 saying, "This is my body *g* for you;
Jn 3: 27 man can receive only what is *g* him
Ro 5: 5 the Holy Spirit, whom he has *g* us.
1Co 4: 2 those who have been *g* a trust must
12: 13 we were all *g* the one Spirit to drink.
Eph 4: 7 to each one of us grace has been *g*

GIVER* (GIVE)
Pr 18: 16 A gift opens the way for the *g*
2Co 9: 7 for God loves a cheerful *g*.

GIVES (GIVE)
Ps 119:130 The unfolding of your words *g* light;
Pr 14: 30 A heart at peace *g* life to the body,
15: 30 good news *g* health to the bones.
28: 27 He who *g* to the poor will lack
Isa 40: 29 He *g* strength to the weary

Mt 10: 42 if anyone *g* even a cup of cold water
Jn 6: 63 The Spirit *g* life; the flesh counts
1Co 15: 57 He *g* us the victory
2Co 3: 6 the letter kills, but the Spirit *g* life.

GIVING (GIVE)

Ne 8: 8 *g* the meaning so that the people
Ps 19: 8 *g* joy to the heart.
Mt 6: 4 so that your *g* may be in secret.
2Co 8: 7 also excel in this grace of *g*.

GLAD (GLADNESS)

Ps 31: 7 I will be *g* and rejoice in your love,
46: 4 whose streams make *g* the city
97: 1 LORD reigns, let the earth be *g*;
118: 24 let us rejoice and be *g* in it.
Pr 23: 25 May your father and mother be *g*;
Zec 2: 10 and be *g*, O Daughter of Zion.
Mt 5: 12 be *g*, because great is your reward

GLADNESS (GLAD)

Ps 45: 15 They are led in with joy and *g*;
51: 8 Let me hear joy and *g*;
100: 2 Serve the LORD with *g*;
Jer 31: 13 I will turn their mourning into *g*;

GLORIFIED (GLORY)

Jn 13: 31 Son of Man *g* and God is *g* in him.
Ro 8: 30 those he justified, he also *g*.
2Th 1: 10 comes to be *g* in his holy people

GLORIFY (GLORY)

Ps 34: 3 *G* the LORD with me;
86: 12 I will *g* your name forever.
Jn 13: 32 God will *g* the Son in himself,
17: 1 *G* your Son, that your Son may

GLORIOUS (GLORY)

Ps 45: 13 All *g* is the princess
111: 3 *G* and majestic are his deeds,
145: 5 of the *g* splendor of your majesty,
sa 4: 2 the LORD will be beautiful and *g*,
12: 5 for he has done *g* things;
42: 21 to make his law great and *g*.
63: 15 from your lofty throne, holy and *g*.
Mt 19: 28 the Son of Man sits on his *g* throne,
Lk 9: 31 appeared in *g* splendor, talking
Ac 2: 20 of the great and *g* day of the Lord.
Co 3: 8 of the Spirit be even more *g*?
Php 3: 21 so that they will be like his *g* body.
4: 19 to his *g* riches in Christ Jesus.
Tit 2: 13 the *g* appearing of our great God

Jude : 24 before his *g* presence without fault

GLORY (GLORIFIED GLORIFY GLORIOUS)

Ex 15: 11 awesome in *g*,
33: 18 Moses said, "Now show me your *g*
1Sa 4: 21 "The *g* has departed from Israel"—
1Ch 16: 24 Declare his *g* among the nations,
16: 28 ascribe to the LORD *g*
29: 11 and the *g* and the majesty
Ps 8: 5 and crowned him with *g* and honor
19: 1 The heavens declare the *g* of God;
24: 7 that the King of *g* may come in.
29: 1 ascribe to the LORD *g*
72: 19 the whole earth be filled with his *g*.
96: 3 Declare his *g* among the nations,
Pr 19: 11 it is to his *g* to overlook an offense.
25: 2 It is the *g* of God to conceal
Isa 6: 3 the whole earth is full of his *g*."
48: 11 I will not yield my *g* to another.
Eze 43: 2 and the land was radiant with his *g*.
Mt 24: 30 of the sky, with power and great *g*.
25: 31 the Son of Man comes in his *g*,
Mk 8: 38 in his Father's *g* with the holy
13: 26 in clouds with great power and *g*.
Lk 2: 9 and the *g* of the Lord shone
2: 14 saying, "*G* to God in the highest,
Jn 1: 14 We have seen his *g*, the *g* of the One
17: 5 presence with the *g* I had with you
17: 24 to see my *g*, the *g* you have given
Ac 7: 2 The God of *g* appeared
Ro 1: 23 exchanged the *g* of the immortal
3: 23 and fall short of the *g* of God,
8: 18 with the *g* that will be revealed
9: 4 theirs the divine *g*, the covenants,
1Co 10: 31 whatever you do, do it all for the *g*
11: 7 but the woman is the *g* of man.
15: 43 it is raised in *g*; it is sown
2Co 3: 10 comparison with the surpassing *g*.
3: 18 faces all reflect the Lord's *g*,
4: 17 us an eternal *g* that far outweighs
Col 1: 27 Christ in you, the hope of *g*.
3: 4 also will appear with him in *g*.
1Ti 3: 16 was taken up in *g*.

Heb 1: 3 The Son is the radiance of God's *g*
2: 7 you crowned him with *g* and honor
1Pe 1: 24 and all their *g* is like the flowers
Rev 4: 11 to receive *g* and honor and power,
21: 23 for the *g* of God gives it light,

GLUTTONS

Tit 1: 12 always liars, evil brutes, lazy *g*."

GNASHING

Mt 8: 12 where there will be weeping and *g*

GNAT*

Mt 23: 24 You strain out a *g* but swallow

GOAL

2Co 5: 9 So we make it our *g* to please him,
Gal 3: 3 to attain your *g* by human effort?
Php 3: 14 on toward the *g* to win the prize

GOAT (GOATS SCAPEGOAT)

Isa 11: 6 the leopard will lie down with the *g*

GOATS (GOAT)

Nu 7: 17 five male *g* and five male lambs

GOD (GOD'S GODLINESS GODLY GODS)

Ge 1: 1 In the beginning *G* created
1: 2 and the Spirit of *G* was hovering
1: 26 Then *G* said, "Let us make man
1: 27 So *G* created man in his own image
1: 31 *G* saw all that he had made,
2: 3 And *G* blessed the seventh day
2: 22 Then the LORD *G* made a woman
3: 21 The LORD *G* made garments
3: 23 So the LORD *G* banished him
5: 22 Enoch walked with *G* 300 years
6: 2 sons of *G* saw that the daughters
9: 16 everlasting covenant between *G*
17: 1 "I am *G* Almighty; walk before me
21: 33 name of the LORD, the Eternal *G*.
22: 8 "*G* himself will provide the lamb
28: 12 and the angels of *G* were ascending
32: 28 because you have struggled with *G*
32: 30 "It is because I saw *G* face to face,
35: 10 *G* said to him, "Your name is Jacob

41: 51 *G* has made me forget all my
50: 20 but *G* intended it for good
Ex 2: 24 *G* heard their groaning
3: 6 because he was afraid to look at *G*.
6: 7 own people, and I will be your *G*.
8: 10 is no one like the LORD our *G*.
13: 18 So *G* led the people
15: 2 He is my *G*, and I will praise him,
17: 9 with the staff of *G* in my hands."
19: 3 Then Moses went up to *G*,
20: 2 the LORD your *G*, who brought
20: 5 the LORD your *G*, am a jealous *G*,
20: 19 But do not have *G* speak to us
22: 28 "Do not blaspheme *G*
31: 18 inscribed by the finger of *G*.
34: 6 the compassionate and gracious *G*,
34: 14 name is Jealous, is a jealous *G*.
Lev 18: 21 not profane the name of your *G*.
19: 2 the LORD your *G*, am holy.
26: 12 walk among you and be your *G*,
Nu 22: 38 I must speak only what *G* puts
23: 19 *G* is not a man, that he should lie,
Dt 1: 17 for judgment belongs to *G*.
3: 22 LORD your *G* himself will fight
3: 24 For what *g* is there in heaven
4: 24 is a consuming fire, a jealous *G*.
4: 31 the LORD your *G* is a merciful *G*;
4: 39 heart this day that the LORD is *G*
5: 11 the name of the LORD your *G*,
5: 14 a Sabbath to the LORD your *G*.
5: 26 of the living *G* speaking out of fire,
6: 4 LORD our *G*, the LORD is one.
6: 5 Love the LORD your *G*
6: 13 the LORD your *G*, serve him only
6: 16 Do not test the LORD your *G*
7: 9 your *G* is *G*; he is the faithful *G*,
7: 12 the LORD your *G* will keep his
7: 21 is a great and awesome *G*.
8: 5 the LORD your *G* disciplines you.
10: 12 but to fear the LORD your *G*,
10: 14 the LORD your *G* belong
10: 17 For the LORD your *G* is *G* of gods
11: 13 to love the LORD your *G*
13: 3 The LORD your *G* is testing you
13: 4 the LORD your *G* you must
15: 6 the LORD your *G* will bless you
19: 9 to love the LORD your *G*
25: 16 the LORD your *G* detests anyone
29: 29 belong to the LORD our *G*,

30: 2 return to the LORD your *G*
30: 16 today to love the LORD your *G*,
30: 20 you may love the LORD your *G*,
31: 6 for the LORD your *G* goes
32: 3 Oh, praise the greatness of our *G*!
32: 4 A faithful *G* who does no wrong,
33: 27 The eternal *G* is your refuge,
Jos 1: 9 for the LORD your *G* will be
14: 8 the LORD my *G* wholeheartedly.
22: 5 to love the LORD your *G*,
22: 34 Between Us that the LORD is *G*.
23: 11 careful to love the LORD your *G*.
23: 14 the LORD your *G* gave you has
Jdg 16: 28 O *G*, please strengthen me just
Ru 1: 16 be my people and your *G* my *G*.
1Sa 2: 2 there is no Rock like our *G*.
2: 3 for the LORD is a *G* who knows,
2: 25 another man, *G* may mediate
10: 26 men whose hearts *G* had touched.
12: 12 the LORD your *G* was your king.
17: 26 defy the armies of the living *G*?"
17: 46 world will know that there is a *G*
30: 6 strength in the LORD his *G*.
2Sa 14: 14 But *G* does not take away life;
22: 3 my *G* is my rock, in whom I take
22: 31 "As for *G*, his way is perfect;
1Ki 4: 29 *G* gave Solomon wisdom
8: 23 there is no *G* like you in heaven
8: 27 "But will *G* really dwell on earth?
8: 61 committed to the LORD our *G*,
18: 21 If the LORD is *G*, follow him;
18: 37 are *G*, and that you are turning
20: 28 a *g* of the hills and not a *g*
2Ki 19: 15 *G* of Israel, enthroned
1Ch 16: 35 Cry out, "Save us, O *G* our Savior;
28: 2 for the footstool of our *G*,
28: 9 acknowledge the *G* of your father,
29: 10 *G* of our father Israel,
29: 17 my *G*, that you test the heart
2Ch 2: 4 for the Name of the LORD my *G*
5: 14 of the LORD filled the temple of *G*
6: 18 "But will *G* really dwell on earth
18: 13 I can tell him only what my *G* says
20: 6 are you not the *G* who is in heaven?
25: 8 for *G* has the power to help
30: 9 for the LORD your *G* is gracious
33: 12 the favor of the LORD his *G*
Ezr 8: 22 "The good hand of our *G* is
9: 6 "O my *G*, I am too ashamed
9: 13 our *G*, you have punished us less
Ne 1: 5 the great and awesome *G*,
8: 8 from the Book of the Law of *G*,
9: 17 But you are a forgiving *G*,
9: 32 the great, mighty and awesome *G*,
Job 1: 1 he feared *G* and shunned evil.
2: 10 Shall we accept good from *G*,
4: 17 a mortal be more righteous than *G*?
5: 17 is the man whom *G* corrects;
11: 7 Can you fathom the mysteries of *G*
19: 26 yet in my flesh I will see *G*;
22: 13 Yet you say, 'What does *G* know?
25: 4 can a man be righteous before *G*?
33: 14 For *G* does speak—now one way,
34: 12 is unthinkable that *G* would do
36: 26 is *G*—beyond our understanding!
37: 22 *G* comes in awesome majesty.
Ps 18: 2 my *G* is my rock, in whom I take
18: 28 my *G* turns my darkness into light.
19: 1 The heavens declare the glory of *G*;
22: 1 *G*, my *G*, why have you forsaken
29: 3 the *G* of glory thunders,
31: 14 I say, "You are my *G*."
40: 3 a hymn of praise to our *G*.
40: 8 I desire to do your will, O my *G*;
42: 2 thirsts for *G*, for the living *G*.
42: 11 Put your hope in *G*,
45: 6 O *G*, will last for ever and ever;
46: 1 *G* is our refuge and strength,
46: 10 "Be still, and know that I am *G*;
47: 7 For *G* is the King of all the earth;
50: 3 Our *G* comes and will not be silent;
51: 1 Have mercy on me, O *G*,
51: 10 Create in me a pure heart, O *G*,
51: 17 O *G*, you will not despise.
62: 7 my honor depend on *G*;
65: 5 O *G* our Savior,
66: 1 Shout with joy to *G*, all the earth!
66: 16 listen, all you who fear *G*;
68: 6 *G* sets the lonely in families,
71: 17 my youth, O *G*, you have taught
71: 19 reaches to the skies, O *G*,
71: 22 harp for your faithfulness, O my *G*;
73: 26 but *G* is the strength of my heart
77: 13 What *g* is so great as our God?
78: 19 Can *G* spread a table in the desert?
81: 1 Sing for joy to *G* our strength;
84: 2 out for the living *G*.
84: 10 a doorkeeper in the house of my *G*
86: 12 O Lord my *G*, with all my heart;
89: 7 of the holy ones *G* is greatly feared;
90: 2 to everlasting you are *G*.
91: 2 my *G*, in whom I trust."
95: 7 for he is our *G*
100: 3 Know that the LORD is *G*.
108: 1 My heart is steadfast, O *G*;
113: 5 Who is like the LORD our *G*,
139: 23 Search me, O *G*, and know my
Pr 3: 4 in the sight of *G* and man.
25: 2 of *G* to conceal a matter;
30: 5 "Every word of *G* is flawless;
Ecc 3: 11 cannot fathom what *G* has done
11: 5 cannot understand the work of *G*,
12: 13 Fear *G* and keep his
Isa 9: 6 Wonderful Counselor, Mighty *G*,
37: 16 you alone are *G* over all
40: 3 a highway for our *G*.
40: 8 the word of our *G* stands forever."
40: 28 The LORD is the everlasting *G*,
41: 10 not be dismayed, for I am your *G*.
44: 6 apart from me there is no *G*.
52: 7 "Your *G* reigns!"
55: 7 to our *G*, for he will freely pardon.
57: 21 says my *G*, "for the wicked."
59: 2 you from your *G*;
61: 10 my soul rejoices in my *G*.
62: 5 so will your *G* rejoice over you.
Jer 23: 23 "Am I only a *G* nearby,"
31: 33 I will be their *G*,
32: 27 "I am the LORD, the *G*
Eze 28: 13 the garden of *G*;
Da 3: 17 the *G* we serve is able to save us
9: 4 O Lord, the great and awesome *G*,
Hos 12: 6 and wait for your *G* always.
Joel 2: 13 Return to the LORD your *G*,
Am 4: 12 prepare to meet your *G*, O Israel."
Mic 6: 8 and to walk humbly with your *G*.
Na 1: 2 LORD is a jealous and avenging *G*;
Zec 14: 5 Then the LORD my *G* will come,
Mal 3: 8 Will a man rob *G*? Yet you rob me.
Mt 1: 23 which means, "*G* with us."
5: 8 for they will see *G*.
6: 24 You cannot serve both *G*
19: 6 Therefore what *G* has joined
19: 26 but with *G* all things are possible."
22: 21 and to *G* what is God's."
22: 37 "'Love the Lord your *G*
27: 46 which means, "My *G*, my *G*,
Mk 12: 29 the Lord our *G*, the Lord is one.
16: 19 and he sat at the right hand of *G*.
Lk 1: 37 For nothing is impossible with *G*."
1: 47 my spirit rejoices in *G* my Savior,
10: 9 'The kingdom of *G* is near you.'
10: 27 "'Love the Lord your *G*
18: 19 "No one is good—except *G* alone.
Jn 1: 1 was with *G*, and the Word was *G*.
1: 18 seen *G*, but *G* the One and Only,
3: 16 "For *G* so loved the world that he
4: 24 *G* is spirit, and his worshipers must
14: 1 Trust in *G*; trust also in me.
20: 28 "My Lord and my *G*!"
Ac 2: 24 But *G* raised him from the dead,
5: 4 You have not lied to men but to *G*
5: 29 "We must obey *G* rather than men!
7: 55 to heaven and saw the glory of *G*,
17: 23 TO AN UNKNOWN *G*.
20: 27 to you the whole will of *G*.
20: 32 "Now I commit you to *G*
Ro 1: 17 a righteousness from *G* is revealed,
2: 11 For *G* does not show favoritism.
3: 4 Let *G* be true, and every man a liar.
3: 23 and fall short of the glory of *G*,
4: 24 to whom *G* will credit
5: 8 *G* demonstrates his own love for us
6: 23 but the gift of *G* is eternal life
8: 28 in all things *G* works for the good
11: 22 the kindness and sternness of *G*:
14: 12 give an account of himself to *G*.
1Co 1: 20 Has not *G* made foolish
2: 9 what *G* has prepared
3: 6 watered it, but *G* made it grow.
6: 20 Therefore honor *G* with your body.
7: 24 each man, as responsible to *G*,
8: 8 food does not bring us near to *G*;

10: 13 *G* is faithful; he will not let you be
10: 31 do it all for the glory of *G*.
14: 33 For *G* is not a *G* of disorder
15: 28 so that *G* may be all in all.
2Co 1: 9 rely on ourselves but on *G*,
2: 14 be to *G*, who always leads us
3: 5 but our competence comes from *G*.
4: 7 this all-surpassing power is from *G*
5: 19 that *G* was reconciling the world
5: 21 *G* made him who had no sin
6: 16 we are the temple of the living *G*.
9: 7 for *G* loves a cheerful giver.
2Co 9: 8 *G* is able to make all grace abound
Gal 2: 6 *G* does not judge by external
6: 7 not be deceived: *G* cannot be
Eph 2: 10 which *G* prepared in advance for us
4: 6 one baptism; one *G* and Father
5: 1 Be imitators of *G*, therefore,
Php 2: 6 Who, being in very nature *G*,
4: 19 And my *G* will meet all your needs
1Th 2: 4 trying to please men but *G*,
4: 7 For *G* did not call us to be impure,
4: 9 taught by *G* to love each other.
5: 9 For *G* did not appoint us
1Ti 2: 5 one mediator between *G* and men,
4: 4 For everything *G* created is good,
5: 4 for this is pleasing to *G*.
Tit 2: 13 glorious appearing of our great *G*
Heb 1: 1 In the past *G* spoke
4: 12 For the word of *G* is living
6: 10 *G* is not unjust; he will not forget
10: 31 to fall into the hands of the living *G*
11: 6 faith it is impossible to please *G*,
12: 10 but *G* disciplines us for our good,
12: 29 for our "*G* is a consuming fire."
13: 15 offer to *G* a sacrifice of praise—
Jas 1: 13 For *G* cannot be tempted by evil,
2: 19 You believe that there is one *G*.
2: 23 "Abraham believed *G*,
4: 4 the world becomes an enemy of *G*.
4: 8 Come near to *G* and he will come
1Pe 4: 11 it with the strength *G* provides,
2Pe 1: 21 but men spoke from *G*
1Jn 1: 5 *G* is light; in him there is no
3: 20 For *G* is greater than our hearts,
4: 7 for love comes from *G*.
4: 9 This is how *G* showed his love
4: 11 Dear friends, since *G* so loved us,
4: 12 No one has ever seen *G*;
4: 16 *G* is love.
Rev 4: 8 holy is the Lord *G* Almighty,
7: 17 *G* will wipe away every tear
19: 6 For our Lord *G* Almighty reigns.

GOD-BREATHED* (BREATHED)

2Ti 3: 16 All Scripture is *G* and is useful

GOD'S (GOD)

2Ch 20: 15 For the battle is not yours, but *G*.
Job 37: 14 stop and consider *G* wonders.
Ps 52: 8 I trust in *G* unfailing love
69: 30 I will praise *G* name in song
Mk 3: 35 Whoever does *G* will is my brother
Jn 7: 17 If anyone chooses to do *G* will,
10: 36 'I am *G* Son'? Do not believe me
Ro 2: 3 think you will escape *G* judgment?
2: 4 not realizing that *G* kindness leads
3: 3 lack of faith nullify *G* faithfulness?
7: 22 in my inner being I delight in *G* law
9: 16 or effort, but on *G* mercy.
11: 29 for *G* gifts and his call are
12: 2 and approve what *G* will is—
12: 13 Share with *G* people who are
13: 6 for the authorities are *G* servants,
1Co 7: 19 Keeping *G* commands is what
2Co 6: 2 now is the time of *G* favor,
Eph 1: 7 riches of *G* grace that he lavished
1Th 4: 3 It is *G* will that you should be
5: 18 for this is *G* will for you
1Ti 6: 1 so that *G* name and our teaching
2Ti 2: 19 *G* solid foundation stands firm,
Tit 1: 7 overseer is entrusted with *G* work,
Heb 1: 3 The Son is the radiance of *G* glory
9: 24 now to appear for us in *G* presence.
11: 3 was formed at *G* command,
1Pe 2: 15 For it is *G* will that
3: 4 which is of great worth in *G* sight.
1Jn 2: 5 *G* love is truly made complete

GODLINESS (GOD)

1Ti 2: 2 and quiet lives in all *g* and holiness.
4: 8 but *g* has value for all things,
6: 6 *g* with contentment is great gain.
6: 11 and pursue righteousness, *g*, faith,

GODLY (GOD)

Ps 4: 3 that the LORD has set apart the *g*
2Co 7: 10 *G* sorrow brings repentance that
11: 2 jealous for you with a *g* jealousy.
2Ti 3: 12 everyone who wants to live a *g* life
2Pe 3: 11 You ought to live holy and *g* lives

GODS (GOD)

Ex 20: 3 "You shall have no other *g*
Ac 19: 26 He says that man-made *g* are no *g*

GOLD

Job 23: 10 tested me, I will come forth as *g*.
Ps 19: 10 They are more precious than *g*,
119:127 more than *g*, more than pure *g*,
Pr 22: 1 esteemed is better than silver or *g*.

GOLGOTHA

Jn 19: 17 (which in Aramaic is called *G*).

GOLIATH

Philistine giant killed by David (1Sa17; 21:9).

GOOD

Ge 1: 4 God saw that the light was *g*,
1: 31 he had made, and it was very *g*.
2: 18 "It is not *g* for the man to be alone.
50: 20 but God intended it for *g*
Job 2: 10 Shall we accept *g* from God,
Ps 14: 1 there is no one who does *g*.
34: 8 Taste and see that the LORD is *g*;
37: 3 Trust in the LORD and do *g*;
84: 11 no *g* thing does he withhold
86: 5 You are forgiving and *g*, O Lord
103: 5 satisfies your desires with *g* things,
119: 68 You are *g*, and what you do is *g*;
133: 1 How *g* and pleasant it is
147: 1 How *g* it is to sing praises
Pr 3: 4 you will win favor and a *g* name
11: 27 He who seeks *g* finds *g* will,
17: 22 A cheerful heart is *g* medicine,
18: 22 He who finds a wife finds what is *g*
22: 1 A *g* name is more desirable
31: 12 She brings him *g*, not harm,
Isa 5: 20 Woe to those who call evil *g*
52: 7 the feet of those who bring *g* news,
Jer 6: 16 ask where the *g* way is,
32: 39 the *g* of their children after them.
Mic 6: 8 has showed you, O man, what is *g*.
Mt 5: 45 sun to rise on the evil and the *g*,
7: 17 Likewise every *g* tree bears *g* fruit,
12: 35 The *g* man brings *g* things out
19: 17 "There is only One who is *g*.
25: 21 'Well done, *g* and faithful servant!
Mk 3: 4 lawful on the Sabbath: to do *g*
8: 36 What *g* is it for a man
Lk 6: 27 do *g* to those who hate you,
Jn 10: 11 "I am the *g* shepherd.
Ro 8: 28 for the *g* of those who love him,
10: 15 feet of those who bring *g* news!"
12: 9 Hate what is evil; cling to what is *g*.
1Co 10: 24 should seek his own *g*, but the *g*
15: 33 Bad company corrupts *g* character
2Co 9: 8 you will abound in every *g* work.
Gal 6: 9 us not become weary in doing *g*,
6: 10 as we have opportunity, let us do *g*
Eph 2: 10 in Christ Jesus to do *g* works,
Php 1: 6 that he who began a *g* work
1Th 5: 21 Hold on to the *g*.
1Ti 3: 7 have a *g* reputation with outsiders,
4: 4 For everything God created is *g*,
6: 12 Fight the *g* fight of the faith.
6: 18 them to do *g*, to be rich in *g* deeds,
2Ti 3: 17 equipped for every *g* work.
4: 7 I have fought the *g* fight, I have
Heb 12: 10 but God disciplines us for our *g*,
1Pe 2: 3 you have tasted that the Lord is *g*.
2: 12 Live such *g* lives among the pagans

GOSPEL

Ro 1: 16 I am not ashamed of the *g*,
15: 16 duty of proclaiming the *g* of God,
1Co 1: 17 to preach the *g*—not with words
9: 16 Woe to me if I do not preach the *g*!
15: 1 you of the *g* I preached to you,
Gal 1: 7 a different *g*—which is really no *g*
Php 1: 27 in a manner worthy of the *g*

GOSSIP

Pr 11: 13 A *g* betrays a confidence,
16: 28 and a *g* separates close friends.
18: 8 of a *g* are like choice morsels;
26: 20 without *g* a quarrel dies down.

2Co 12: 20 slander, *g*, arrogance and disorder.

GRACE (GRACIOUS)

Ps 45: 2 lips have been anointed with *g*,
Jn 1: 17 *g* and truth came through Jesus
Ac 20: 32 to God and to the word of his *g*,
Ro 3: 24 and are justified freely by his *g*
5: 15 came by the *g* of the one man,
5: 17 God's abundant provision of *g*
5: 20 where sin increased, *g* increased all
6: 14 you are not under law, but under *g*.
11: 6 if by *g*, then it is no longer by works
2Co 6: 1 not to receive God's *g* in vain.
8: 9 For you know the *g*
9: 8 able to make all *g* abound to you,
12: 9 "My *g* is sufficient for you,
Gal 2: 21 I do not set aside the *g* of God,
5: 4 you have fallen away from *g*.
Eph 1: 7 riches of God's *g* that he lavished
2: 5 it is by *g* you have been saved.
2: 7 the incomparable riches of his *g*,
2: 8 For it is by *g* you have been saved,
Php 1: 7 all of you share in God's *g* with me.
Col 4: 6 conversation be always full of *g*,
2Th 2: 16 and by his *g* gave us eternal
2Ti 2: 1 be strong in the *g* that is
Tit 2: 11 For the *g* of God that brings
3: 7 having been justified by his *g*,
Heb 2: 9 that by the *g* of God he might taste
4: 16 find *g* to help us in our time of need
4: 16 the throne of *g* with confidence,
Jas 4: 6 but gives *g* to the humble."
2Pe 3: 18 But grow in the *g* and knowledge

GRACIOUS (GRACE)

Nu 6: 25 and be *g* to you;
Pr 22: 11 a pure heart and whose speech is *g*
Isa 30: 18 Yet the LORD longs to be *g* to you

GRAIN

1Co 9: 9 ox while it is treading out the *g*."

GRANTED

Php 1: 29 For it has been *g* to you on behalf

GRASS

Ps 103: 15 As for man, his days are like *g*,
1Pe 1: 24 "All men are like *g*,

GRAVE (GRAVES)

Pr 7: 27 Her house is a highway to the *g*,
Hos 13: 14 Where, O *g*, is your destruction?

GRAVES (GRAVE)

Jn 5: 28 are in their *g* will hear his voice
Ro 3: 13 "Their throats are open *g*;

GREAT (GREATER GREATEST GREATNESS)

Ge 12: 2 "I will make you into a *g* nation
Dt 10: 17 the *g* God, mighty and awesome,
2Sa 22: 36 you stoop down to make me *g*.
Ps 19: 11 in keeping them there is *g* reward.
89: 1 of the LORD's *g* love forever;
103: 11 so *g* is his love for those who fear
107: 43 consider the *g* love of the LORD.
108: 4 For *g* is your love, higher
119:165 *G* peace have they who love your
145: 3 *G* is the LORD and most worthy
Pr 23: 24 of a righteous man has *g* joy;
Isa 42: 21 to make his law *g* and glorious.
La 3: 23 *g* is your faithfulness.
Mk 10: 43 whoever wants to become *g*
Lk 21: 27 in a cloud with power and *g* glory.
1Ti 6: 6 with contentment is *g* gain.
Tit 2: 13 glorious appearing of our *g* God
Heb 2: 3 if we ignore such a *g* salvation?
1Jn 3: 1 How *g* is the love the Father has

GREATER (GREAT)

Mk 12: 31 There is no commandment *g*
Jn 1: 50 You shall see *g* things than that."
15: 13 *G* love has no one than this,
1Co 12: 31 But eagerly desire the *g* gifts.
Heb 11: 26 as of *g* value than the treasures
1Jn 3: 20 For God is *g* than our hearts,
4: 4 is in you is *g* than the one who is

GREATEST (GREAT)

Mt 22: 38 is the first and *g* commandment.
Lk 9: 48 least among you all—he is the *g*."
1Co 13: 13 But the *g* of these is love.

GREATNESS (GREAT)

Ps 145: 3 his *g* no one can fathom.
150: 2 praise him for his surpassing *g*.
Isa 63: 1 forward in the *g* of his strength?
Php 3: 8 compared to the surpassing *g*

GREED (GREEDY)

Lk 12: 15 on your guard against all kinds of *g*
Ro 1: 29 kind of wickedness, evil, *g*
Eph 5: 3 or of any kind of impurity, or of *g*,
Col 3: 5 evil desires and *g*, which is idolatry
2Pe 2: 14 experts in *g*—an accursed brood!

GREEDY (GREED)

Pr 15: 27 A *g* man brings trouble
1Co 6: 10 nor thieves nor the *g* nor drunkards
Eph 5: 5 No immoral, impure or *g* person—
1Pe 5: 2 not *g* for money, but eager to serve;

GREEN

Ps 23: 2 makes me lie down in *g* pastures,

GREW (GROW)

Lk 2: 52 And Jesus *g* in wisdom and stature,
Ac 16: 5 in the faith and *g* daily in numbers.

GRIEF (GRIEVE)

Ps 10: 14 O God, do see trouble and *g*;
Pr 14: 13 and joy may end in *g*.
La 3: 32 Though he brings *g*, he will show
Jn 16: 20 but your *g* will turn to joy.
1Pe 1: 6 had to suffer *g* in all kinds of trials.

GRIEVE (GRIEF)

Eph 4: 30 do not *g* the Holy Spirit of God,
1Th 4: 13 or to *g* like the rest of men,

GROUND

Ge 3: 17 "Cursed is the *g* because of you;
Ex 3: 5 where you are standing is holy *g*."
Eph 6: 13 you may be able to stand your *g*,

GROW (GREW)

Pr 13: 11 by little makes it *g*.
1Co 3: 6 watered it, but God made it *g*.
2Pe 3: 18 But *g* in the grace and knowledge

GRUMBLE (GRUMBLING)

1Co 10: 10 And do not *g*, as some of them did
Jas 5: 9 Don't *g* against each other,

GRUMBLING (GRUMBLE)

Jn 6: 43 "Stop *g* among yourselves,"
1Pe 4: 9 to one another without *g*.

GUARANTEE (GUARANTEEING)

Heb 7: 22 Jesus has become the *g*

GUARANTEEING (GUARANTEE)

2Co 1: 22 as a deposit, *g* what is to come.
Eph 1: 14 who is a deposit *g* our inheritance

GUARD (GUARDS)

Ps 141: 3 Set a *g* over my mouth, O LORD;
Pr 4: 23 Above all else, *g* your heart,
Isa 52: 12 the God of Israel will be your rear *g*
Mk 13: 33 Be on *g*! Be alert! You do not know
1Co 16: 13 Be on your *g*; stand firm in the faith
Php 4: 7 will *g* your hearts and your minds
1Ti 6: 20 *g* what has been entrusted

GUARDS (GUARD)

Pr 13: 3 He who *g* his lips *g* his life,
19: 16 who obeys instructions *g* his life,
21: 23 He who *g* his mouth and his tongue
22: 5 he who *g* his soul stays far

GUIDE

Ex 13: 21 of cloud to *g* them on their way
15: 13 In your strength you will *g* them
Ne 9: 19 cease to *g* them on their path,
Ps 25: 5 *g* me in your truth and teach me,
43: 3 let them *g* me;
48: 14 he will be our *g* even to the end.
67: 4 and *g* the nations of the earth.
73: 24 You *g* me with your counsel,
139: 10 even there your hand will *g* me,
Pr 4: 11 I *g* you in the way of wisdom
6: 22 When you walk, they will *g* you;
Isa 58: 11 The LORD will *g* you always;
Jn 16: 13 comes, he will *g* you into all truth.

GUILTY

Ex 34: 7 does not leave the *g* unpunished;
Jn 8: 46 Can any of you prove me *g* of sin?
Heb 10: 22 to cleanse us from a *g* conscience
Jas 2: 10 at just one point is *g* of breaking all

H

HADES

Mt 16: 18 the gates of *H* will not overcome it.

HAGAR

Servant of Sarah, wife of Abraham, mother of Ishmael (Ge 16:1-6; 25:12). Driven away by Sarah while pregnant (Ge 16:5-16); after birth of Isaac (Ge 21:9-21; Gal 4:21-31).

HAGGAI*

Post-exilic prophet who encouraged rebuilding of the temple (Ezr 5:1; 6:14; Hag 1-2).

HAIR (HAIRS)
Lk 21: 18 But not a *h* of your head will perish
1Co 11: 6 for a woman to have her *h* cut

HAIRS (HAIR)
Mt 10: 30 even the very *h* of your head are all

HALLELUJAH*
Rev 19: 1 3, 4, 6.

HALLOWED (HOLY)
Mt 6: 9 *h* be your name,

HAND (HANDS)
Ps 16: 8 Because he is at my right *h*,
37: 24 the LORD upholds him with his *h*.
139: 10 even there your *h* will guide me,
Ecc 9: 10 Whatever your *h* finds to do,
Mt 6: 3 know what your right *h* is doing,
Jn 10: 28 one can snatch them out of my *h*.
1Co 12: 15 I am not a *h*, I do not belong

HANDS (HAND)
Ps 22: 16 they have pierced my *h*
24: 4 He who has clean *h* and a pure
31: 5 Into your *h* I commit my spirit;
31: 15 My times are in your *h*;
Pr 10: 4 Lazy *h* make a man poor,
31: 20 and extends her *h* to the needy.
Isa 55: 12 will clap their *h*.
65: 2 All day long I have held out my *h*
Lk 23: 46 into your *h* I commit my spirit."
1Th 4: 11 and to work with your *h*,
1Ti 2: 8 to lift up holy *h* in prayer,
5: 22 hasty in the laying on of *h*,

HANNAH*
Wife of Elkanah, mother of Samuel (1Sa 1). Prayer at dedication of Samuel (1Sa 2:1-10). Blessed (1Sa 2:18-21).

HAPPY
Ps 68: 3 may they be *h* and joyful.
Pr 15: 13 A *h* heart makes the face cheerful,
Ecc 3: 12 better for men than to be *h*
Jas 5: 13 Is anyone *h*? Let him sing songs

HARD (HARDEN HARDSHIP)
Ge 18: 14 Is anything too *h* for the LORD?
Mt 19: 23 it is *h* for a rich man
1Co 4: 12 We work *h* with our own hands.
1Th 5: 12 to respect those who work *h*

HARDEN (HARD)
Ro 9: 18 he hardens whom he wants to *h*.
Heb 3: 8 do not *h* your hearts

HARDHEARTED* (HEART)
Dt 15: 7 do not be *h* or tightfisted

HARDSHIP (HARD)
Ro 8: 35 Shall trouble or *h* or persecution
2Ti 2: 3 Endure *h* with us like a good
4: 5 endure *h*, do the work
Heb 12: 7 Endure *h* as discipline; God is

HARM
Ps 121: 6 the sun will not *h* you by day,
Pr 3: 29 not plot *h* against your neighbor,
31: 12 She brings him good, not *h*,
Ro 13: 10 Love does no *h* to its neighbor.
1Jn 5: 18 and the evil one cannot *h* him.

HARMONY
Ro 12: 16 Live in *h* with one another.
2Co 6: 15 What *h* is there between Christ
1Pe 3: 8 live in *h* with one another;

HARVEST
Mt 9: 37 *h* is plentiful but the workers are
Jn 4: 35 at the fields! They are ripe for *h*.
Gal 6: 9 at the proper time we will reap a *h*
Heb 12: 11 it produces a *h* of righteousness

HASTE (HASTY)
Pr 21: 5 as surely as *h* leads to poverty.
29: 20 Do you see a man who speaks in *h*?

HASTY* (HASTE)
Pr 19: 2 nor to be *h* and miss the way.
Ecc 5: 2 do not be *h* in your heart
1Ti 5: 22 Do not be *h* in the laying

HATE (HATED HATES HATRED)
Lev 19: 17 "'Do not *h* your brother
Ps 5: 5 you *h* all who do wrong.
45: 7 righteousness and *h* wickedness;
97: 10 those who love the LORD *h* evil,
139: 21 Do I not *h* those who *h* you,
Pr 8: 13 To fear the LORD is to *h* evil;
Am 5: 15 *H* evil, love good;
Mal 2: 16 "I *h* divorce," says the LORD God
Mt 5: 43 your neighbor and *h* your enemy.'
10: 22 All men will *h* you because of me,
Lk 6: 27 do good to those who *h* you,
Ro 12: 9 *H* what is evil; cling to what is good

HATED (HATE)
Ro 9: 13 "Jacob I loved, but Esau I *h*."
Eph 5: 29 no one ever *h* his own body,
Heb 1: 9 righteousness and *h* wickedness;

HATES (HATE)
Pr 6: 16 There are six things the LORD *h*,
13: 24 He who spares the rod *h* his son,
Jn 3: 20 Everyone who does evil *h* the light,
1Jn 2: 9 *h* his brother is still in the darkness.

HATRED (HATE)
Pr 10: 12 *H* stirs up dissension,
Jas 4: 4 with the world is *h* toward God?

HAUGHTY
Pr 16: 18 a *h* spirit before a fall.

HAY
1Co 3: 12 costly stones, wood, *h* or straw,

HEAD (HEADS HOTHEADED)
Ge 3: 15 he will crush your *h*,
Ps 23: 5 You anoint my *h* with oil;
Pr 25: 22 will heap burning coals on his *h*,
Isa 59: 17 and the helmet of salvation on his *h*
Mt 8: 20 of Man has no place to lay his *h*."
Ro 12: 20 will heap burning coals on his *h*."
1Co 11: 3 and the *h* of Christ is God.
12: 21 And the *h* cannot say to the feet,
Eph 5: 23 For the husband is the *h* of the wife
2Ti 4: 5 keep your *h* in all situations,
Rev 19: 12 and on his *h* are many crowns.

HEADS (HEAD)
Lev 26: 13 you to walk with *h* held high.
Isa 35: 10 everlasting joy will crown their *h*.

HEAL (HEALED HEALING HEALS)
2Ch 7: 14 their sin and will *h* their land.
Ps 41: 4 *h* me, for I have sinned against you
Mt 10: 8 *H* the sick, raise the dead,
Lk 4: 23 to me: 'Physician, *h* yourself!
5: 17 present for him to *h* the sick.

HEALED (HEAL)
Isa 53: 5 and by his wounds we are *h*.
Mt 9: 22 he said, "your faith has *h* you."
14: 36 and all who touched him were *h*.
Ac 4: 10 this man stands before you *h*.
14: 9 saw that he had faith to be *h*
Jas 5: 16 for each other so that you may be *h*
1Pe 2: 24 by his wounds you have been *h*.

HEALING (HEAL)
Eze 47: 12 for food and their leaves for *h*."
Mal 4: 2 rise with *h* in its wings.
1Co 12: 9 to another gifts of *h*
12: 30 Do all have gifts of *h*? Do all speak
Rev 22: 2 are for the *h* of the nations.

HEALS (HEAL)
Ex 15: 26 for I am the LORD, who *h* you."
Ps 103: 3 and *h* all your diseases;
147: 3 He *h* the brokenhearted

HEALTH (HEALTHY)
Pr 3: 8 This will bring *h* to your body
15: 30 and good news gives *h* to the bones

HEALTHY (HEALTH)
Mk 2: 17 "It is not the *h* who need a doctor,

HEAR (HEARD HEARING HEARS)
Dt 6: 4 *H*, O Israel: The LORD our God,
31: 13 must *h* it and learn
2Ch 7: 14 then will I *h* from heaven
Ps 94: 9 he who implanted the ear not *h*?
Isa 29: 18 that day the deaf will *h* the words
65: 24 while they are still speaking I will *h*
Mt 11: 15 He who has ears, let him *h*.
Jn 8: 47 reason you do not *h* is that you do
2Ti 4: 3 what their itching ears want to *h*.

HEARD (HEAR)
Job 42: 5 My ears had *h* of you
Isa 66: 8 Who has ever *h* of such a thing?
Mt 5: 21 "You have *h* that it was said
5: 27 "You have *h* that it was said,
5: 33 you have *h* that it was said
5: 38 "You have *h* that it was said,
5: 43 "You have *h* that it was said,
1Co 2: 9 no ear has *h*,
1Th 2: 13 word of God, which you *h* from us,
2Ti 1: 13 What you *h* from me, keep
Jas 1: 25 not forgetting what he has *h*,

HEARING (HEAR)
Ro 10: 17 faith comes from *h* the message,

HEARS (HEAR)
Jn 5: 24 whoever *h* my word and believes
1Jn 5: 14 according to his will, he *h* us.
Rev 3: 20 If anyone *h* my voice and opens

HEART (BROKENHEARTED HARDHEARTED HEARTS WHOLEHEARTEDLY)
Ex 25: 2 each man whose *h* prompts him
Lev 19: 17 Do not hate your brother in your *h*.
Dt 4: 29 if you look for him with all your *h*
6: 5 LORD your God with all your *h*
10: 12 LORD your God with all your *h*
15: 10 and do so without a grudging *h*;
30: 6 you may love him with all your *h*
30: 10 LORD your God with all your *h*

Jos 22: 5 and to serve him with all your *h*
1Sa 13: 14 sought out a man after his own *h*
16: 7 but the LORD looks at the *h*."
2Ki 23: 3 with all his *h* and all his soul,
1Ch 28: 9 for the LORD searches every *h*
2Ch 7: 16 and my *h* will always be there.
Job 22: 22 and lay up his words in your *h*.
37: 1 "At this my *h* pounds
Ps 14: 1 The fool says in his *h*,
19: 14 and the meditation of my *h*
37: 4 will give you the desires of your *h*.
45: 1 My *h* is stirred by a noble theme
51: 10 Create in me a pure *h*, O God,
51: 17 a broken and contrite *h*,
66: 18 If I had cherished sin in my *h*,
86: 11 give me an undivided *h*,
119: 11 I have hidden your word in my *h*
119: 32 for you have set my *h* free.
139: 23 Search me, O God, and know my *h*
Pr 3: 5 Trust in the LORD with all your *h*
4: 21 keep them within your *h*;
4: 23 Above all else, guard your *h*,
7: 3 write them on the tablet of your *h*.
13: 12 Hope deferred makes the *h* sick,
14: 13 Even in laughter the *h* may ache,
15: 30 A cheerful look brings joy to the *h*,
17: 22 A cheerful *h* is good medicine,
24: 17 stumbles, do not let your *h* rejoice,
27: 19 so a man's *h* reflects the man.
Ecc 8: 5 wise *h* will know the proper time
SS 4: 9 You have stolen my *h*, my sister,
Isa 40: 11 and carries them close to his *h*;
57: 15 and to revive the *h* of the contrite.
Jer 17: 9 The *h* is deceitful above all things
29: 13 when you seek me with all your *h*.
Eze 36: 26 I will give you a new *h*
Mt 5: 8 Blessed are the pure in *h*,
6: 21 treasure is, there your *h* will be
12: 34 of the *h* the mouth speaks.
22: 37 the Lord your God with all your *h*
Lk 6: 45 overflow of his *h* his mouth speaks.
Ro 2: 29 is circumcision of the *h*,
10: 10 is with your *h* that you believe
1Co 14: 25 the secrets of his *h* will be laid bare.
Eph 5: 19 make music in your *h* to the Lord,
6: 6 doing the will of God from your *h*.
Col 3: 23 work at it with all your *h*,
1Pe 1: 22 one another deeply, from the *h*.

HEARTS (HEART)

Dt 11: 18 Fix these words of mine in your *h*
1Ki 8: 39 for you alone know the *h* of all men
8: 61 your *h* must be fully committed
Ps 62: 8 pour out your *h* to him,
Ecc 3: 11 also set eternity in the *h* of men;
Jer 31: 33 and write it on their *h*.
Lk 16: 15 of men, but God knows your *h*.
24: 32 "Were not our *h* burning within us
Jn 14: 1 "Do not let your *h* be troubled.
Ac 15: 9 for he purified their *h* by faith.
Ro 2: 15 of the law are written on their *h*,
2Co 3: 2 written on our *h*, known
3: 3 but on tablets of human *h*.
4: 6 shine in our *h* to give us the light
Eph 3: 17 dwell in your *h* through faith.
Col 3: 1 set your *h* on things above,
Heb 3: 8 do not harden your *h*
10: 16 I will put my laws in their *h*,
1Jn 3: 20 For God is greater than our *h*,

HEAT

2Pe 3: 12 and the elements will melt in the *h*.

HEAVEN (HEAVENLY HEAVENS)

Ge 14: 19 Creator of *h* and earth.
1Ki 8: 27 the highest *h*, cannot contain you.
2Ki 2: 1 up to *h* in a whirlwind,
2Ch 7: 14 then will I hear from *h*
Isa 14: 12 How you have fallen from *h*,
66: 1 "*H* is my throne,
Da 7: 13 coming with the clouds of *h*.
Mt 6: 9 "'Our Father in *h*,
6: 20 up for yourselves treasures in *h*,
16: 19 bind on earth will be bound in *h*,
19: 23 man to enter the kingdom of *h*.
24: 35 *H* and earth will pass away,
26: 64 and coming on the clouds of *h*."
28: 18 "All authority in *h*
Mk 16: 19 he was taken up into *h*
Lk 15: 7 in *h* over one sinner who repents
18: 22 and you will have treasure in *h*.
Ro 10: 6 'Who will ascend into *h*?'" (that is,
2Co 5: 1 an eternal house in *h*, not built
12: 2 ago was caught up to the third *h*.
Php 2: 10 *h* and on earth and under the earth,
3: 20 But our citizenship is in *h*.
1Th 1: 10 and to wait for his Son from *h*,
Heb 8: 5 and shadow of what is in *h*.
9: 24 he entered *h* itself, now to appear
2Pe 3: 13 we are looking forward to a new *h*
Rev 21: 1 Then I saw a new *h* and a new earth

HEAVENLY (HEAVEN)

Ps 8: 5 him a little lower than the *h* beings
2Co 5: 2 to be clothed with our *h* dwelling,
Eph 1: 3 in the *h* realms with every spiritual
1: 20 at his right hand in the *h* realms,
2Ti 4: 18 bring me safely to his *h* kingdom.
Heb 12: 22 to the *h* Jerusalem, the city

HEAVENS (HEAVEN)

Ge 1: 1 In the beginning God created the *h*
1Ki 8: 27 The *h*, even the highest heaven,
2Ch 2: 6 since the *h*, even the highest
Ps 8: 3 When I consider your *h*,
19: 1 The *h* declare the glory of God;
102: 25 the *h* are the work of your hands.
108: 4 is your love, higher than the *h*;
119: 89 it stands firm in the *h*.
139: 8 If I go up to the *h*, you are there;
Isa 51: 6 Lift up your eyes to the *h*,
55: 9 "As the *h* are higher than the earth,
65: 17 new *h* and a new earth.
Joel 2: 30 I will show wonders in the *h*
Eph 4: 10 who ascended higher than all the *h*,
2Pe 3: 10 The *h* will disappear with a roar;

HEBREW

Ge 14: 13 and reported this to Abram the *H*.

HEEDS

Pr 13: 1 wise son *h* his father's instruction,
13: 18 whoever *h* correction is honored.
15: 5 whoever *h* correction shows
15: 32 whoever *h* correction gains

HEEL

Ge 3: 15 and you will strike his *h*."

HEIRS (INHERIT)

Ro 8: 17 then we are *h*—*h* of God
Gal 3: 29 and *h* according to the promise.
Eph 3: 6 gospel the Gentiles are *h* together
1Pe 3: 7 as *h* with you of the gracious gift

HELL

Mt 5: 22 will be in danger of the fire of *h*.
Lk 16: 23 In *h*, where he was in torment,
2Pe 2: 4 but sent them to *h*, putting them

HELMET

Isa 59: 17 and the *h* of salvation on his head;
Eph 6: 17 Take the *h* of salvation
1Th 5: 8 and the hope of salvation as a *h*.

HELP (HELPED HELPER HELPING HELPS)

Ps 18: 6 I cried to my God for *h*.
30: 2 my God, I called to you for *h*
46: 1 an ever-present *h* in trouble.
79: 9 *H* us, O God our Savior,
121: 1 where does my *h* come from?
Isa 41: 10 I will strengthen you and *h* you;
Jnh 2: 2 depths of the grave I called for *h*,
Mk 9: 24 *h* me overcome my unbelief!"
Ac 16: 9 Come over to Macedonia and *h* us
1Co 12: 28 those able to *h* others, those

HELPED (HELP)

1Sa 7: 12 "Thus far has the LORD *h* us."

HELPER (HELP)

Ge 2: 18 I will make a *h* suitable for him."
Ps 10: 14 you are the *h* of the fatherless.
Heb 13: 6 Lord is my *h*; I will not be afraid.

HELPING (HELP)

Ac 9: 36 always doing good and *h* the poor.
1Ti 5: 10 *h* those in trouble and devoting

HELPS (HELP)

Ro 8: 26 the Spirit *h* us in our weakness.

HEN

Mt 23: 37 as a *h* gathers her chicks

HERITAGE (INHERIT)

Ps 127: 3 Sons are a *h* from the LORD,

HEROD

1. King of Judea who tried to kill Jesus (Mt 2; Lk 1:5).

2. Son of 1. Tetrarch of Galilee who arrested and beheaded John the Baptist (Mt 14:1-12; Mk 6:14-29; Lk 3:1, 19-20; 9:7-9); tried Jesus (Lk 23:6-15).

3. Grandson of 1. King of Judea who killed James (Ac 12:2); arrested Peter (Ac 12:3-19). Death (Ac 12:19-23).

HERODIAS

Wife of Herod the Tetrarch who persuaded her daughter to ask for John the Baptist's head (Mt 14:1-12; Mk 6:14-29).

HEZEKIAH

King of Judah. Restored the temple and worship (2Ch 29-31). Sought the LORD for help against Assyria (2Ki 18-19; 2Ch 32:1-23; Isa 36-37). Illness healed (2Ki 20:1-11; 2Ch 32:24-26; Isa 38). Judged for showing Babylonians his treasures (2Ki 20:12-21; 2Ch 32:31; Isa 39).

HID (HIDE)

Ge 3: 8 and they h from the LORD God
Ex 2: 2 she h him for three months.
Jos 6: 17 because she h the spies we sent.
Heb 11: 23 By faith Moses' parents h him

HIDDEN (HIDE)

Ps 19: 12 Forgive my h faults.
119: 11 I have h your word in my heart
Pr 2: 4 and search for it as for h treasure,
Isa 59: 2 your sins have h his face from you,
Mt 5: 14 A city on a hill cannot be h.
13: 44 of heaven is like treasure h
Col 1: 26 the mystery that has been kept h
2: 3 in whom are h all the treasures
3: 3 and your life is now h with Christ

HIDE (HID HIDDEN)

Ps 17: 8 h me in the shadow of your wings
143: 9 for I h myself in you.

HILL (HILLS)

Mt 5: 14 A city on a h cannot be hidden.

HILLS (HILL)

Ps 50: 10 and the cattle on a thousand h.
121: 1 I lift up my eyes to the h—

HINDER (HINDERS)

1Sa 14: 6 Nothing can h the LORD
Mt 19: 14 come to me, and do not h them,
1Co 9: 12 anything rather than h the gospel
1Pe 3: 7 so that nothing will h your prayers.

HINDERS (HINDER)

Heb 12: 1 let us throw off everything that h

HINT*

Eph 5: 3 even a h of sexual immorality,

HOLD

Ex 20: 7 LORD will not h anyone guiltless
Lev 19: 13 "'Do not h back the wages
Jos 22: 5 to h fast to him and to serve him
Ps 73: 23 you h me by my right hand.
Pr 4: 4 "Lay h of my words
Isa 54: 2 do not h back;
Mk 11: 25 if you h anything against anyone,
Php 2: 16 as you h out the word of life—
3: 12 but I press on to take h of that
Col 1: 17 and in him all things h together.
1Th 5: 21 H on to the good.
1Ti 6: 12 Take h of the eternal life
Heb 10: 23 Let us h unswervingly

HOLINESS (HOLY)

Ex 15: 11 majestic in h,
Ps 29: 2 in the splendor of his h.
96: 9 in the splendor of his h;
Ro 6: 19 to righteousness leading to h.
2Co 7: 1 perfecting h out of reverence
Eph 4: 24 God in true righteousness and h.
Heb 12: 10 that we may share in his h.
12: 14 without h no one will see the Lord.

HOLY (HALLOWED HOLINESS)

Ex 19: 6 kingdom of priests and a h nation.'
20: 8 the Sabbath day by keeping it h.
Lev 11: 44 and be h, because I am h.
20: 7 "'Consecrate yourselves and be h,
20: 26 You are to be h to me because I,
21: 8 Consider them h, because I
22: 32 Do not profane my h name.
Ps 16: 10 will you let your H One see decay.
24: 3 Who may stand in his h place?
77: 13 Your ways, O God, are h.
99: 3 he is h.
99: 5 he is h.
99: 9 for the LORD our God is h.
111: 9 h and awesome is his name.
Isa 5: 16 the h God will show himself h
6: 3 H, h, h is the LORD Almighty;
40: 25 who is my equal?" says the H One.
57: 15 who lives forever, whose name is h:
Eze 28: 25 I will show myself h among them
Da 9: 24 prophecy and to anoint the most h.
Hab 2: 20 But the LORD is in his h temple;
Ac 2: 27 will you let your H One see decay.
Ro 7: 12 and the commandment is h,
12: 1 as living sacrifices, h and pleasing
Eph 5: 3 improper for God's h people.
2Th 1: 10 to be glorified in his h people
2Ti 1: 9 saved us and called us to a h life—
3: 15 you have known the h Scriptures,
Tit 1: 8 upright, h and disciplined.
1Pe 1: 15 But just as he who called you is h,
1: 16 is written: "Be h, because I am h."
2: 9 a royal priesthood, a h nation,
2Pe 3: 11 You ought to live h and godly lives
Rev 4: 8 "H, h, h is the Lord God

HOME (HOMES)

Dt 6: 7 Talk about them when you sit at h
Ps 84: 3 Even the sparrow has found a h,
Pr 3: 33 but he blesses the h of the righteous
Mk 10: 29 "no one who has left h or brothers
Jn 14: 23 to him and make our h with him.
Tit 2: 5 to be busy at h, to be kind,

HOMES (HOME)

Ne 4: 14 daughters, your wives and your h."
1Ti 5: 14 to manage their h and to give

HOMOSEXUAL*

1Co 6: 9 male prostitutes nor h offenders

HONEST

Lev 19: 36 Use h scales and h weights,
Dt 25: 15 and h weights and measures,
Job 31: 6 let God weigh me in h scales
Pr 12: 17 truthful witness gives h testimony,

HONEY

Ex 3: 8 a land flowing with milk and h—
Ps 19: 10 than h from the comb.
119:103 sweeter than h to my mouth!

HONOR (HONORABLE HONORABLY HONORED HONORS)

Ex 20: 12 "H your father and your mother,
Nu 25: 13 he was zealous for the h of his God
Dt 5: 16 "H your father and your mother,
1Sa 2: 30 Those who h me I will h,
Ps 8: 5 and crowned him with glory and h.
Pr 3: 9 H the LORD with your wealth,
15: 33 and humility comes before h.
20: 3 It is to a man's h to avoid strife,
Mt 15: 4 'H your father and mother'
Ro 12: 10 H one another above yourselves.
1Co 6: 20 Therefore h God with your body.
Eph 6: 2 "H your father and mother"—
1Ti 5: 17 well are worthy of double h,
Heb 2: 7 you crowned him with glory and h
Rev 4: 9 h and thanks to him who sits

HONORABLE (HONOR)

1Th 4: 4 body in a way that is holy and h,

HONORABLY (HONOR)

Heb 13: 18 and desire to live h in every way.

HONORED (HONOR)

Ps 12: 8 when what is vile is h among men.
Pr 13: 18 but whoever heeds correction is h.
1Co 12: 26 if one part is h, every part rejoices
Heb 13: 4 Marriage should be h by all,

HONORS (HONOR)

Ps 15: 4 but h those who fear the LORD,
Pr 14: 31 to the needy h God.

HOOKS

Isa 2: 4 and their spears into pruning h.
Joel 3: 10 and your pruning h into spears.

HOPE (HOPES)

Job 13: 15 Though he slay me, yet will I h
Ps 42: 5 Put your h in God,
62: 5 my h comes from him.
119: 74 for I have put my h in your word.
130: 7 O Israel, put your h in the LORD,
147: 11 who put their h in his unfailing love
Pr 13: 12 H deferred makes the heart sick,
Isa 40: 31 but those who h in the LORD
Ro 5: 4 character; and character, h.
8: 24 But h that is seen is no h at all.
12: 12 Be joyful in h, patient in affliction,
15: 4 of the Scriptures we might have h.
1Co 13: 13 now these three remain: faith, h
15: 19 for this life we have h in Christ,
Col 1: 27 Christ in you, the h of glory.
1Th 5: 8 and the h of salvation as a helmet.
1Ti 6: 17 but to put their h in God,
Tit 2: 13 while we wait for the blessed h—
Heb 6: 19 We have this h as an anchor
11: 1 faith is being sure of what we h for
1Jn 3: 3 Everyone who has this h

HOPES (HOPE)

1Co 13: 7 always h, always perseveres.

HORSE

Ps 147: 10 not in the strength of the h,
Pr 26: 3 A whip for the h, a halter
Zec 1: 8 before me was a man riding a red h
Rev 6: 2 and there before me was a white h!
6: 4 Come!" Then another h came out,

6: 5 and there before me was a black *h!*
6: 8 and there before me was a pale *h!*
19: 11 and there before me was a white *h,*

HOSANNA

Mt 21: 9 "*H* in the highest!"

HOSHEA

Last king of Israel (2Ki 15:30; 17:1-6).

HOSPITABLE* (HOSPITALITY)

1Ti 3: 2 self-controlled, respectable, *h,*
Tit 1: 8 Rather he must be *h,* one who loves

HOSPITALITY (HOSPITABLE)

Ro 12: 13 Practice *h.*
1Ti 5: 10 as bringing up children, showing *h,*
1Pe 4: 9 Offer *h* to one another

HOSTILE

Ro 8: 7 the sinful mind is *h* to God.

HOT

1Ti 4: 2 have been seared as with a *h* iron.
Rev 3: 15 that you are neither cold nor *h.*

HOT-TEMPERED

Pr 15: 18 A *h* man stirs up dissension,
19: 19 A *h* man must pay the penalty;
22: 24 Do not make friends with a *h* man,
29: 22 and a *h* one commits many sins.

HOTHEADED (HEAD)

Pr 14: 16 but a fool is *h* and reckless.

HOUR

Ecc 9: 12 knows when his *h* will come:
Mt 6: 27 you by worrying can add a single *h*
Lk 12: 40 the Son of Man will come at an *h*
Jn 12: 23 The *h* has come for the Son of Man
12: 27 for this very reason I came to this *h*

HOUSE (HOUSEHOLD STOREHOUSE)

Ex 20: 17 shall not covet your neighbor's *h.*
Ps 23: 6 I will dwell in the *h* of the LORD
84: 10 a doorkeeper in the *h* of my God
122: 1 "Let us go to the *h* of the LORD."
127: 1 Unless the LORD builds the *h,*
Pr 7: 27 Her *h* is a highway to the grave,
21: 9 than share a *h* with a quarrelsome
Isa 56: 7 a *h* of prayer for all nations."
Zec 13: 6 given at the *h* of my friends.'
Mt 7: 24 is like a wise man who built his *h*
12: 29 can anyone enter a strong man's *h*
21: 13 My *h* will be called a *h* of prayer,'
Mk 3: 25 If a *h* is divided against itself,
Lk 11: 17 a *h* divided against itself will fall.
Jn 2: 16 How dare you turn my Father's *h*
12: 3 the *h* was filled with the fragrance
14: 2 In my Father's *h* are many rooms;
Heb 3: 3 the builder of a *h* has greater honor

HOUSEHOLD (HOUSE)

Jos 24: 15 my *h,* we will serve the LORD."
Mic 7: 6 are the members of his own *h.*
Mt 10: 36 will be the members of his own *h.'*
12: 25 or *h* divided against itself will not
1Ti 3: 12 manage his children and his *h* well.
3: 15 to conduct themselves in God's *h,*

HUMAN (HUMANITY)

Gal 3: 3 to attain your goal by *h* effort?

HUMANITY* (HUMAN)

Heb 2: 14 he too shared in their *h* so that

HUMBLE (HUMBLED HUMBLES HUMILIATE HUMILITY)

2Ch 7: 14 will *h* themselves and pray
Ps 25: 9 He guides the *h* in what is right
Pr 3: 34 but gives grace to the *h.*
Isa 66: 2 he who is *h* and contrite in spirit,
Mt 11: 29 for I am gentle and *h* in heart,
Eph 4: 2 Be completely *h* and gentle;
Jas 4: 10 *H* yourselves before the Lord,
1Pe 5: 6 *H* yourselves,

HUMBLED (HUMBLE)

Mt 23: 12 whoever exalts himself will be *h,*
Php 2: 8 he *h* himself

HUMBLES (HUMBLE)

Mt 18: 4 whoever *h* himself like this child is
23: 12 whoever *h* himself will be exalted.

HUMILIATE* (HUMBLE)

Pr 25: 7 than for him to *h* you
1Co 11: 22 and *h* those who have nothing?

HUMILITY (HUMBLE)

Pr 11: 2 but with *h* comes wisdom.
15: 33 and *h* comes before honor.
Php 2: 3 but in *h* consider others better
Tit 3: 2 and to show true *h* toward all men.
1Pe 5: 5 clothe yourselves with *h*

HUNGRY

Ps 107: 9 and fills the *h* with good things.
146: 7 and gives food to the *h.*
Pr 25: 21 If your enemy is *h,* give him food
Eze 18: 7 but gives his food to the *h*
Mt 25: 35 For I was *h* and you gave me
Lk 1: 53 He has filled the *h* with good things
Jn 6: 35 comes to me will never go *h,*
Ro 12: 20 "If your enemy is *h,* feed him;

HURT (HURTS)

Ecc 8: 9 it over others to his own *h.*
Mk 16: 18 deadly poison, it will not *h* them
Rev 2: 11 He who overcomes will not be *h*

HURTS* (HURT)

Ps 15: 4 even when it *h,*
Pr 26: 28 A lying tongue hates those it *h,*

HUSBAND (HUSBAND'S HUSBANDS)

1Co 7: 3 The *h* should fulfill his marital duty
7: 10 wife must not separate from her *h.*
7: 11 And a *h* must not divorce his wife.
7: 13 And if a woman has a *h* who is not
7: 39 A woman is bound to her *h* as long
2Co 11: 2 I promised you to one *h,* to Christ,
Eph 5: 23 For the *h* is the head of the wife
5: 33 and the wife must respect her *h.*
1Ti 3: 2 the *h* of but one wife, temperate,

HUSBAND'S (HUSBAND)

Pr 12: 4 of noble character is her *h* crown,
1Co 7: 4 the *h* body does not belong

HUSBANDS (HUSBAND)

Eph 5: 22 submit to your *h* as to the Lord.
5: 25 *H,* love your wives, just
Tit 2: 4 the younger women to love their *h*
1Pe 3: 1 same way be submissive to your *h*
3: 7 *H,* in the same way be considerate

HYMN

1Co 14: 26 everyone has a *h,* or a word

HYPOCRISY (HYPOCRITE HYPOCRITES)

Mt 23: 28 but on the inside you are full of *h*
1Pe 2: 1 *h,* envy, and slander of every kind.

HYPOCRITE (HYPOCRISY)

Mt 7: 5 You *h,* first take the plank out

HYPOCRITES (HYPOCRISY)

Ps 26: 4 nor do I consort with *h;*
Mt 6: 5 when you pray, do not be like the *h*

HYSSOP

Ps 51: 7 with *h,* and I will be clean;

I

IDLE (IDLENESS)

1Th 5: 14 those who are *i,* encourage
2Th 3: 6 away from every brother who is *i*
1Ti 5: 13 they get into the habit of being *i*

IDLENESS* (IDLE)

Pr 31: 27 and does not eat the bread of *i.*

IDOL (IDOLATRY IDOLS)

Isa 44: 17 From the rest he makes a god, his *i;*
1Co 8: 4 We know that an *i* is nothin at all

IDOLATRY (IDOL)

Col 3: 5 evil desires and greed, which is *i.*

IDOLS (IDOL)

1Co 8: 1 Now about food sacrificed to *i:*

IGNORANT (IGNORE)

1Co 15: 34 for there are some who are *i* of God
Heb 5: 2 to deal gently with those who are *i*
1Pe 2: 15 good you should silence the *i* talk
2Pe 3: 16 which *i* and unstable people distort

IGNORE (IGNORANT IGNORES)

Dt 22: 1 do not *i* it but be sure
Ps 9: 12 he does not *i* the cry of the afflicted
Heb 2: 3 if we *i* such a great salvation?

IGNORES (IGNORE)

Pr 10: 17 whoever *i* correction leads others
15: 32 He who *i* discipline despises

ILLUMINATED*

Rev 18: 1 and the earth was *i* by his splendor.

IMAGE

Ge 1: 26 "Let us make man in our *i,*
1: 27 So God created man in his own *i,*
1Co 11: 7 since he is the *i* and glory of God;

Col 1: 15 He is the *i* of the invisible God,
3: 10 in knowledge in the *i* of its Creator.

IMAGINE
Eph 3: 20 more than all we ask or *i*,

IMITATE (IMITATORS)
1Co 4: 16 Therefore I urge you to *i* me.
Heb 6: 12 but to *i* those who through faith
13: 7 of their way of life and *i* their faith.
3Jn : 11 do not *i* what is evil but what is

IMITATORS* (IMITATE)
Eph 5: 1 Be *i* of God, therefore,
1Th 1: 6 You became *i* of us and of the Lord
2: 14 became *i* of God's churches

IMMANUEL
Isa 7: 14 birth to a son, and will call him *I*.
Mt 1: 23 and they will call him *I*"—

IMMORAL* (IMMORALITY)
Pr 6: 24 keeping you from the *i* woman,
1Co 5: 9 to associate with sexually *i* people
5: 10 the people of this world who are *i*,
5: 11 but is sexually *i* or greedy,
6: 9 Neither the sexually *i* nor idolaters
Eph 5: 5 No *i*, impure or greedy person—
Heb 12: 16 See that no one is sexually *i*,
13: 4 the adulterer and all the sexually *i*.
Rev 21: 8 the murderers, the sexually *i*,
22: 15 the sexually *i*, the murderers,

IMMORALITY (IMMORAL)
1Co 6: 13 The body is not meant for sexual *i*,
6: 18 Flee from sexual *i*.
10: 8 We should not commit sexual *i*,
Gal 5: 19 sexual *i*, impurity and debauchery;
Eph 5: 3 must not be even a hint of sexual *i*,
1Th 4: 3 that you should avoid sexual *i*;
Jude : 4 grace of our God into a license for *i*

IMMORTAL* (IMMORTALITY)
Ro 1: 23 glory of the *i* God for images made
1Ti 1: 17 Now to the King eternal, *i*,
6: 16 who alone is *i* and who lives

IMMORTALITY (IMMORTAL)
Ro 2: 7 honor and *i*, he will give eternal life
1Co 15: 53 and the mortal with *i*.
2Ti 1: 10 and *i* to light through the gospel.

IMPERISHABLE
1Pe 1: 23 not of perishable seed, but of *i*,

IMPORTANCE* (IMPORTANT)
1Co 15: 3 passed on to you as of first *i*:

IMPORTANT (IMPORTANCE)
Mt 6: 25 Is not life more *i* than food,
23: 23 have neglected the more *i* matters
Mk 12: 29 "The most *i* one," answered Jesus,
12: 33 as yourself is more *i* than all burnt
Php 1: 18 The *i* thing is that in every way,

IMPOSSIBLE
Mt 17: 20 Nothing will be *i* for you."
Lk 1: 37 For nothing is *i* with God."
18: 27 "What is *i* with men is possible
Heb 6: 18 things in which it is *i* for God to lie,
11: 6 without faith it is *i* to please God,

IMPROPER*
Eph 5: 3 these are *i* for God's holy people.

IMPURE (IMPURITY)
Ac 10: 15 not call anything *i* that God has
Eph 5: 5 No immoral, *i* or greedy person—
1Th 4: 7 For God did not call us to be *i*,
Rev 21: 27 Nothing *i* will ever enter it,

IMPURITY (IMPURE)
Ro 1: 24 hearts to sexual *i* for the degrading
Eph 5: 3 or of any kind of *i*, or of greed,

INCENSE
Ex 40: 5 Place the gold altar of *i* in front
Ps 141: 2 my prayer be set before you like *i*;
Mt 2: 11 him with gifts of gold and of *i*

INCOME
Ecc 5: 10 wealth is never satisfied with his *i*.
1Co 16: 2 sum of money in keeping with his *i*,

INCOMPARABLE*
Eph 2: 7 ages he might show the *i* riches

INCREASE (EVER-INCREASING INCREASED INCREASES INCREASING)
Ge 1: 22 "Be fruitful and *i* in number
Ps 62: 10 though your riches *i*,
Isa 9: 7 Of the *i* of his government
Lk 17: 5 said to the Lord, "*I* our faith!"
1Th 3: 12 May the Lord make your love *i*

INCREASED (INCREASE)
Ac 6: 7 of disciples in Jerusalem *i* rapidly,
Ro 5: 20 But where sin *i*, grace *i* all the more

INCREASES (INCREASE)
Pr 24: 5 and a man of knowledge *i* strength;

INCREASING (INCREASE)
Ac 6: 1 when the number of disciples was *i*,
2Th 1: 3 one of you has for each other is *i*.
2Pe 1: 8 these qualities in *i* measure,

INDEPENDENT*
1Co 11: 11 however, woman is not *i* of man,
11: 11 of man, nor is man *i* of woman.

INDESCRIBABLE*
2Co 9: 15 Thanks be to God for his *i* gift!

INDISPENSABLE*
1Co 12: 22 seem to be weaker are *i*,

INEFFECTIVE*
2Pe 1: 8 they will keep you from being *i*

INEXPRESSIBLE*
2Co 12: 4 He heard *i* things, things that man
1Pe 1: 8 are filled with an *i* and glorious joy,

INFANTS
Mt 21: 16 " 'From the lips of children and *i*
1Co 14: 20 In regard to evil be *i*,

INFIRMITIES
Isa 53: 4 Surely he took up our *i*

INHERIT (CO-HEIRS HEIRS HERITAGE INHERITANCE)
Ps 37: 11 But the meek will *i* the land
37: 29 the righteous will *i* the land
Mt 5: 5 for they will *i* the earth.
Mk 10: 17 "what must I do to *i* eternal life?"
1Co 15: 50 blood cannot *i* the kingdom of God

INHERITANCE (INHERIT)
Dt 4: 20 to be the people of his *i*,
Pr 13: 22 A good man leaves an *i*
Eph 1: 14 who is a deposit guaranteeing our *i*
5: 5 has any *i* in the kingdom of Christ
Heb 9: 15 receive the promised eternal *i*—
1Pe 1: 4 and into an *i* that can never perish,

INIQUITIES (INIQUITY)
Ps 78: 38 he forgave their *i*
103: 10 or repay us according to our *i*.
Isa 59: 2 But your *i* have separated

Mic 7: 19 and hurl all our *i* into the depths

INIQUITY (INIQUITIES)
Ps 51: 2 Wash away all my *i*
Isa 53: 6 the *i* of us all.

INJUSTICE
2Ch 19: 7 the LORD our God there is no *i*

INNOCENT
Pr 17: 26 It is not good to punish an *i* man,
Mt 10: 16 shrewd as snakes and as *i* as doves.
27: 4 "for I have betrayed *i* blood."
1Co 4: 4 but that does not make me *i*.

INSCRIPTION
Mt 22: 20 And whose *i*?" "Caesar's,"

INSOLENT
Ro 1: 30 God-haters, *i*, arrogant

INSTITUTED
Ro 13: 2 rebelling against what God has *i*,
1Pe 2: 13 to every authority *i* among men:

INSTRUCT (INSTRUCTION)
Ps 32: 8 I will *i* you and teach you
Pr 9: 9 *I* a wise man and he will be wiser
Ro 15: 14 and competent to *i* one another.
2Ti 2: 25 who oppose him he must gently *i*,

INSTRUCTION (INSTRUCT)
Pr 1: 8 Listen, my son, to your father's *i*
4: 1 Listen, my sons, to a father's *i*;
4: 13 Hold on to *i*, do not let it go;
8: 10 Choose my *i* instead of silver,
8: 33 Listen to my *i* and be wise;
13: 1 A wise son heeds his father's *i*,
13: 13 He who scorns *i* will pay for it,
16: 20 Whoever gives heed to *i* prospers,
16: 21 and pleasant words promote *i*.
19: 20 Listen to advice and accept *i*,
23: 12 Apply your heart to *i*
1Co 14: 6 or prophecy or word of *i*?
14: 26 or a word of *i*, a revelation,
Eph 6: 4 up in the training and *i* of the Lord.
1Th 4: 8 he who rejects this *i* does not reject
2Th 3: 14 If anyone does not obey our *i*
1Ti 1: 18 I give you this *i* in keeping
6: 3 to the sound *i* of our Lord Jesus
2Ti 4: 2 with great patience and careful *i*.

INSULT
Pr 9: 7 corrects a mocker invites *i;*
12: 16 but a prudent man overlooks an *i.*
Mt 5: 11 Blessed are you when people *i* you,
Lk 6: 22 when they exclude you and *i* you
1Pe 3: 9 evil with evil or *i* with *i,*

INTEGRITY
1Ki 9: 4 if you walk before me in *i* of heart
Job 2: 3 And he still maintains his *i,*
27: 5 till I die, I will not deny my *i.*
Pr 10: 9 The man of *i* walks securely,
11: 3 The *i* of the upright guides them,
29: 10 Bloodthirsty men hate a man of *i*
Tit 2: 7 your teaching show *i,* seriousness

INTELLIGENCE
Isa 29: 14 the *i* of the intelligent will vanish."
1Co 1: 19 *i* of the intelligent I will frustrate."

INTELLIGIBLE
1Co 14: 19 I would rather speak five *i* words

INTERCEDE (INTERCEDES INTERCESSION)
Heb 7: 25 he always lives to *i* for them.

INTERCEDES (INTERCEDE)
Ro 8: 26 but the Spirit himself *i* for us

INTERCESSION* (INTERCEDE)
Isa 53: 12 and made *i* for the transgressors.
1Ti 2: 1 *i* and thanksgiving be made

INTERESTS
1Co 7: 34 his wife—and his *i* are divided.
Php 2: 4 only to your own *i,* but also to the *i*
2: 21 everyone looks out for his own *i,*

INTERMARRY (MARRY)
Dt 7: 3 Do not *i* with them.

INVENTED*
2Pe 1: 16 We did not follow cleverly *i* stories

INVESTIGATED
Lk 1: 3 I myself have carefully *i* everything

INVISIBLE
Ro 1: 20 of the world God's *i* qualities—
Col 1: 15 He is the image of the *i* God,
1Ti 1: 17 immortal, *i,* the only God,

INVITE (INVITED INVITES)
Lk 14: 13 you give a banquet, *i* the poor,

INVITED (INVITE)
Mt 22: 14 For many are *i,* but few are chosen
25: 35 I was a stranger and you *i* me in,

INVITES (INVITE)
1Co 10: 27 If some unbeliever *i* you to a meal

INVOLVED
2Ti 2: 4 a soldier gets *i* in civilian affairs—

IRON
1Ti 4: 2 have been seared as with a hot *i.*
Rev 2: 27 He will rule them with an *i* scepter;

IRREVOCABLE*
Ro 11: 29 for God's gifts and his call are *i.*

ISAAC
Son of Abraham by Sarah (Ge 17:19; 21:1-7; 1Ch 1:28). Offered up by Abraham (Ge 22; Heb 11:17-19). Rebekah taken as wife (Ge 24). Fathered Esau and Jacob (Ge 25:19-26; 1Ch 1:34). Tricked into blessing Jacob (Ge 27). Father of Israel (Ex 3:6; Dt 29:13; Ro 9:10).

ISAIAH
Prophet to Judah (Isa 1:1). Called by the LORD (Isa 6).

ISHMAEL
Son of Abraham by Hagar (Ge 16; 1Ch 1:28). Blessed, but not son of covenant (Ge 17:18-21; Gal 4:21-31). Sent away by Sarah (Ge 21:8-21).

ISRAEL (ISRAELITES)
1. Name given to Jacob (see JACOB).
2. Corporate name of Jacob's descendants; often specifically Northern Kingdom.
Dt 6: 4 Hear, O *I:* The LORD our God,
1Sa 4: 21 "The glory has departed from *I*"—
Isa 27: 6 *I* will bud and blossom
Jer 31: 10 'He who scattered *I* will gather
Eze 39: 23 of *I* went into exile for their sin,
Mk 12: 29 'Hear, O *I,* the Lord our God,
Lk 22: 30 judging the twelve tribes of *I.*
Ro 9: 6 all who are descended from *I* are *I.*
11: 26 And so all *I* will be saved,
Eph 3: 6 Gentiles are heirs together with *I,*

ISRAELITES (ISRAEL)
Ex 14: 22 and the *I* went through the sea
16: 35 The *I* ate manna forty years,
Hos 1: 10 "Yet the *I* will be like the sand
Ro 9: 27 the number of the *I* be like the sand

ITCHING*
2Ti 4: 3 to say what their *i* ears want to hear

J

JACOB
Second son of Isaac, twin of Esau (Ge 26:21-26; 1Ch 1:34). Bought Esau's birthright (Ge 26:29-34); tricked Isaac into blessing him (Ge 27:1-37). Abrahamic covenant perpetuated through (Ge 28:13-15; Mal 1:2). Vision at Bethel (Ge 28:10-22). Wives and children (Ge 29:1-30:24; 35:16-26; 1Ch 2-9). Wrestled with God; name changed to Israel (Ge 32:22-32). Sent sons to Egypt during famine (Ge 42-43). Settled in Egypt (Ge 46). Blessed Ephraim and Manasseh (Ge 48). Blessed sons (Ge 49:1-28; Heb 11:21). Death (Ge 49:29-33). Burial (Ge 50:1-14).

JAMES
1. Apostle; brother of John (Mt 4:21-22; 10:2; Mk 3:17; Lk 5:1-10). At transfiguration (Mt 17:1-13; Mk 9:1-13; Lk 9:28-36). Killed by Herod (Ac 12:2).
2. Apostle; son of Alphaeus (Mt 10:3; Mk 3:18; Lk 6:15).
3. Brother of Jesus (Mt 13:55; Mk 6:3; Lk 24:10; Gal 1:19) and Judas (Jude 1). With believers before Pentecost (Ac 1:13). Leader of church at Jerusalem (Ac 12:17; 15; 21:18; Gal 2:9, 12). Author of epistle (Jas 1:1).

JAPHETH
Son of Noah (Ge 5:32; 1Ch 1:4-5). Blessed (Ge 9:18-28).

JARS
2Co 4: 7 we have this treasure in *j* of clay

JEALOUS (JEALOUSY)
Ex 20: 5 the LORD your God, am a *j* God,
34: 14 whose name is Jealous, is a *j* God.
Dt 4: 24 God is a consuming fire, a *j* God.
Joel 2: 18 the LORD will be *j* for his land
Zec 1: 14 I am very *j* for Jerusalem and Zion,
2Co 11: 2 I am *j* for you with a godly jealousy

JEALOUSY (JEALOUS)
1Co 3: 3 For since there is *j* and quarreling
2Co 11: 2 I am jealous for you with a godly *j.*
Gal 5: 20 hatred, discord, *j,* fits of rage,

JEHOAHAZ
1. Son of Jehu; king of Israel (2Ki 13:1-9).
2. Son of Josiah; king of Judah (2Ki 23:31-34; 2Ch 36:1-4).

JEHOASH
Son of Jehoahaz; king of Israel (2Ki 13-14; 2Ch 25).

JEHOIACHIN
Son of Jehoiakim; king of Judah exiled by Nebuchadnezzar (2Ki 24:8-17; 2Ch 36:8-10; Jer 22:24-30; 24:1). Raised from prisoner status (2Ki 25:27-30; Jer 52:31-34).

JEHOIAKIM
Son of Josiah; king of Judah (2Ki 23:34-24:6; 2Ch 36:4-8; Jer 22:18-23; 36).

JEHORAM
Son of Jehoshaphat; king of Judah (2Ki 8:16-24).

JEHOSHAPHAT
Son of Asa; king of Judah (1Ki 22:41-50; 2Ki 3; 2Ch 17-20).

JEHU
King of Israel (1Ki 19:16-19; 2Ki 9-10).

JEPHTHAH
Judge from Gilead who delivered Israel from Ammon (Jdg 10:6-12:7). Made rash vow concerning his daughter (Jdg 11:30-40).

JEREMIAH
Prophet to Judah (Jer 1:1-3). Called by the LORD (Jer 1). Put in stocks (Jer 20:1-3). Threatened for prophesying (Jer 11:18-23; 26). Opposed by Hananiah (Jer 28). Scroll burned (Jer 36). Imprisoned (Jer 37). Thrown into cistern (Jer 38). Forced to Egypt with those fleeing Babylonians (Jer 43).

JEROBOAM
1. Official of Solomon; rebelled to become first king of Israel (1Ki 11:26-40; 12:1-20; 2Ch 10). Idolatry (1Ki 12:25-33); judgment for (1Ki 13-14; 2Ch 13).
2. Son of Jehoash; king of Israel (1Ki 14:23-29).

JERUSALEM
2Ki 23: 27 and I will reject *J,* the city I chose,
2Ch 6: 6 now I have chosen *J* for my Name
Ne 2: 17 Come, let us rebuild the wall of *J,*
Ps 122: 6 Pray for the peace of *J:*
125: 2 As the mountains surround *J,*
137: 5 If I forget you, O *J,*
Isa 40: 9 You who bring good tidings to *J,*
65: 18 for I will create *J* to be a delight
Joel 3: 17 *J* will be holy;
Zep 3: 16 On that day they will say to *J,*
Zec 2: 4 '*J* will be a city without walls
8: 8 I will bring them back to live in *J;*
14: 8 living water will flow out from *J,*
Mt 23: 37 "O *J, J,* you who kill the prophets
Lk 13: 34 die outside *J!* "O *J, J,*
21: 24 *J* will be trampled
Jn 4: 20 where we must worship is in *J.*"

Ac 1: 8 and you will be my witnesses in *J*,
Gal 4: 25 corresponds to the present city of *J*
Rev 21: 2 I saw the Holy City, the new *J*,

JESUS

LIFE: Genealogy (Mt 1:1-17; Lk 3:21-37). Birth announced (Mt 1:18-25; Lk 1:26-45). Birth (Mt 2:1-12; Lk 2:1-40). Escape to Egypt (Mt 2:13-23). As a boy in the temple (Lk 2:41-52). Baptism (Mt 3:13-17; Mk 1:9-11; Lk 3:21-22; Jn 1:32-34). Temptation (Mt 4:1-11; Mk 1:12-13; Lk 4:1-13). Ministry in Galilee (Mt 4:12-18:35; Mk 1:14-9:50; Lk 4:14-13:9; Jn 1:35-2:11; 4; 6), Transfiguration (Mt 17:1-8; Mk 9:2-8; Lk 9:28-36), on the way to Jerusalem (Mt 19-20; Mk 10; Lk 13:10-19:27), in Jerusalem (Mt 21-25; Mk 11-13; Lk 19:28-21:38; Jn 2:12-3:36; 5; 7-12). Last supper (Mt 26:17-35; Mk 14:12-31; Lk 22:1-38; Jn 13-17). Arrest and trial (Mt 26:36-27:31; Mk 14:43-15:20; Lk 22:39-23:25; Jn 18:1-19:16). Crucifixion (Mt 27:32-66; Mk 15:21-47; Lk 23:26-55; Jn 19:28-42). Resurrection and appearances (Mt 28; Mk 16; Lk 24; Jn 20-21; Ac 1:1-11; 7:56; 9:3-6; 1Co 15:1-8; Rev 1:1-20).

MIRACLES. Healings: official's son (Jn 4:43-54), demoniac in Capernaum (Mk 1:23-26; Lk 4:33-35), Peter's mother-in-law (Mt 8:14-17; Mk 1:29-31; Lk 4:38-39), leper (Mt 8:2-4; Mk 1:40-45; Lk 5:12-16), paralytic (Mt 9:1-8; Mk 2:1-12; Lk 5:17-26), cripple (Jn 5:1-9), shriveled hand (Mt 12:10-13; Mk 3:1-5; Lk 6:6-11), centurion's servant (Mt 8:5-13; Lk 7:1-10), widow's son raised (Lk 7:11-17), demoniac (Mt 12:22-23; Lk 11:14), Gadarene demoniacs (Mt 8:28-34; Mk 5:1-20; Lk 8:26-39), woman's bleeding and Jairus' daughter (Mt 9:18-26; Mk 5:21-43; Lk 8:40-56), blind man (Mt 9:27-31), mute man (Mt 9:32-33), Canaanite woman's daughter (Mt 15:21-28; Mk 7:24-30), deaf man (Mk 7:31-37), blind man (Mk 8:22-26), demoniac boy (Mt 17:14-18; Mk 9:14-29; Lk 9:37-43), ten lepers (Lk 17:11-19), man born blind (Jn 9:1-7), Lazarus raised (Jn 11), crippled woman (Lk 13:11-17), man with dropsy (Lk 14:1-6), two blind men (Mt 20:29-34; Mk 10:46-52; Lk 18:35-43), Malchus' ear (Lk 22:50-51). Other Miracles: water to wine (Jn 2:1-11), catch of fish (Lk 5:1-11), storm stilled (Mt 8:23-27; Mk 4:37-41; Lk 8:22-25), 5,000 fed (Mt 14:15-21; Mk 6:35-44; Lk 9:10-17; Jn 6:1-14), walking on water (Mt 14:25-33; Mk 6:48-52; Jn 6:15-21), 4,000 fed (Mt 15:32-39; Mk 8:1-9), money from fish (Mt 17:24-27), fig tree cursed (Mt 21:18-22; Mk 11:12-14), catch of fish (Jn 21:1-14).

MAJOR TEACHING: Sermon on the Mount (Mt 5-7; Lk 6:17-49), to Nicodemus (Jn 3), to Samaritan woman (Jn 4), Bread of Life (Jn 6:22-59), at Feast of Tabernacles (Jn 7-8), woes to Pharisees (Mt 23; Lk 11:37-54), Good Shepherd (Jn 10:1-18), Olivet Discourse (Mt 24-25; Mk 13; Lk 21:5-36), Upper Room Discourse (Jn 13-16).

PARABLES: Sower (Mt 13:3-23; Mk 4:3-25; Lk 8:5-18), seed's growth (Mk 4:26-29), wheat and weeds (Mt 13:24-30, 36-43), mustard seed (Mt 13:31-32; Mk 4:30-32), yeast (Mt 13:33-35; Mk 4:33-34), hidden treasure (Mt 13:44), valuable pearl (Mt 13:45-46), net (Mt 13:47-51), house owner (Mt 13:52), good Samaritan (Lk 10:25-37), unmerciful servant (Mt 18:15-35), lost sheep (Mt 18:10-14; Lk 15:4-7), lost coin (Lk 15:8-10), prodigal son (Lk 15:11-32), dishonest manager (Lk 16:1-13), rich man and Lazarus (Lk 16:19-31), persistent widow (Lk 18:1-8), Pharisee and tax collector (Lk 18:9-14), payment of workers (Mt 20:1-16), tenants and the vineyard (Mt 21:28-46; Mt 12:1-12; Lk 20:9-19), wedding banquet (Mt 22:1-14), faithful servant (Mt 24:45-51), ten virgins (Mt 25:1-13), talents (Mt 25:1-30; Lk 19:12-27).

DISCIPLES see APOSTLES. Call of (Jn 1:35-51; Mt 4:18-22; 9:9; Mk 1:16-20; 2:13-14; Lk 5:1-11, 27-28). Named Apostles (Mk 3:13-19; Lk 6:12-16). Twelve sent out (Mt 10; Mk 6:7-11; Lk 9:1-5). Seventy sent out (Lk 10:1-24). Defection of (Jn 6:60-71; Mt 26:56; Mk 14:50-52). Final commission (Mt 28:16-20; Jn 21:15-23; Ac 1:3-8).

Ac 2: 32 God has raised this *J* to life,
9: 5 "I am *J*, whom you are persecuting
15: 11 of our Lord *J* that we are saved,
16: 31 "Believe in the Lord *J*,
Ro 3: 24 redemption that came by Christ *J*.
5: 17 life through the one man, *J* Christ.
8: 1 for those who are in Christ *J*,
1Co 2: 2 except *J* Christ and him crucified.
8: 6 and there is but one Lord, *J* Christ,
12: 3 and no one can say, "*J* is Lord,"
2Co 4: 5 not preach ourselves, but *J* Christ
Gal 2: 16 but by faith in *J* Christ.
3: 28 for you are all one in Christ *J*.
5: 6 in Christ *J* neither circumcision
Eph 2: 10 created in Christ *J*
2: 20 with Christ *J* himself as the chief
Php 1: 6 until the day of Christ *J*.
2: 5 be the same as that of Christ *J*:
2: 10 name of *J* every knee should bow,
Col 3: 17 do it all in the name of the Lord *J*,
2Th 2: 1 the coming of our Lord *J* Christ
1Ti 1: 15 Christ *J* came into the world
2Ti 3: 12 life in Christ *J* will be persecuted,
Tit 2: 13 our great God and Savior, *J* Christ,
Heb 2: 9 But we see *J*, who was made a little
3: 1 fix your thoughts on *J*, the apostle
4: 14 through the heavens, *J* the Son
7: 22 *J* has become the guarantee
7: 24 but because *J* lives forever,
12: 2 Let us fix our eyes on *J*, the author
2Pe 1: 16 and coming of our Lord *J* Christ,
1Jn 1: 7 and the blood of *J*, his Son,
2: 1 *J* Christ, the Righteous One.
2: 6 to live in him must walk as *J* did.
4: 15 anyone acknowledges that *J* is
Rev 22: 20 Come, Lord *J*.

JEW (JEWS JUDAISM)

Zec 8: 23 of one *J* by the edge of his robe
Ro 1: 16 first for the *J*, then for the Gentile.
10: 12 there is no difference between *J*
1Co 9: 20 To the Jews I became like a *J*,
Gal 3: 28 There is neither *J* nor Greek,

JEWELRY (JEWELS)

1Pe 3: 3 wearing of gold *j* and fine clothes.

JEWELS (JEWELRY)

Isa 61: 10 as a bride adorns herself with her *j*.
Zec 9: 16 like *j* in a crown.

JEWS (JEW)

Mt 2: 2 who has been born king of the *J*?
27: 11 "Are you the king of the *J*?" "Yes,
Jn 4: 22 for salvation is from the *J*.
Ro 3: 29 Is God the God of *J* only?
1Co 1: 22 *J* demand miraculous signs
9: 20 To the *J* I became like a Jew,
12: 13 whether *J* or Greeks, slave or free
Gal 2: 8 of Peter as an apostle to the *J*,
Rev 3: 9 claim to be *J* though they are not,

JEZEBEL

Sidonian wife of Ahab (1Ki 16:31). Promoted Baal worship (1Ki 16:32-33). Killed prophets of the LORD (1Ki 18:4,13). Opposed Elijah (1Ki 19:1-2). Had Naboth killed (1Ki 21). Death prophesied (1Ki 21:17-24). Killed by Jehu (2Ki 9:30-37).

JOASH

Son of Ahaziah; king of Judah. Sheltered from Athaliah by Jehoiada (2Ki 11; 2Ch 22:10-23:21). Repaired temple (2Ki 12; 2Ch 24).

JOB

Wealthy man from Uz; feared God (Job 1:1-5). Righteousness tested by disaster (Job 1:6-22), personal affliction (Job 2). Maintained innocence in debate with three friends (Job 3-31), Elihu (Job 32-37). Rebuked by the LORD (Job 38-41). Vindicated and restored to greater stature by the LORD (Job 42). Example of righteousness (Eze 14:14, 20).

JOHN

1. Son of Zechariah and Elizabeth (Lk 1). Called the Baptist (Mt 3:1-12; Mk 1:2-8). Witness to Jesus (Mt 3:11-12; Mk 1:7-8; Lk 3:15-18; Jn 1:6-35; 3:27-30; 5:33-36). Doubts about Jesus (Mt 11:2-6; Lk 7:18-23). Arrest (Mt 4:12; Mk 1:14). Execution (Mt 14:1-12; Mk 6:14-29; Lk 9:7-9). Ministry compared to Elijah (Mt 11:7-19; Mk 9:11-13; Lk 7:24-35).

2. Apostle; brother of James (Mt 4:21-22; 10:2; Mk 3:17; Lk 5:1-10). At transfiguration (Mt 17:1-13; Mk 9:1-13; Lk 9:28-36). Desire to be greatest (Mk 10:35-45). Leader of church at Jerusalem (Ac 4:1-3; Gal 2:9). Elder who wrote epistles (2Jn 1; 3Jn 1). Prophet who wrote Revelation (Rev 1:1; 22:8).

3. Cousin of Barnabas, co-worker with Paul, (Ac 12:12-13:13; 15:37), see MARK.

JOIN (JOINED)

Pr 23: 20 Do not *j* those who drink too much
24: 21 and do not *j* with the rebellious,
Ro 15: 30 to *j* me in my struggle by praying
2Ti 1: 8 *j* with me in suffering for the gospel

JOINED (JOIN)

Mt 19: 6 Therefore what God has *j* together,
Mk 10: 9 Therefore what God has *j* together,
Eph 2: 21 him the whole building is *j* together
4: 16 *j* and held together

JOINTS

Heb 4: 12 even to dividing soul and spirit, *j*

JOKING

Eph 5: 4 or coarse *j*, which are out of place,

JONAH

Prophet in days of Jeroboam II (2Ki 14:25). Called to Nineveh; fled to Tarshish (Jnh 1:1-3). Cause of storm; thrown into sea (Jnh 1:4-16). Swallowed by fish (Jnh 1:17). Prayer (Jnh 2).

Preached to Nineveh (Jnh 3). Attitude reproved by the LORD (Jnh 4). Sign of (Mt 12:39-41; Lk 11:29-32).

JONATHAN

Son of Saul (1Sa 13:16; 1Ch 8:33). Valiant warrior (1Sa 13-14). Relation to David (1Sa 18:1-4;19-20; 23:16-18). Killed at Gilboa (1Sa 31). Mourned by David (2Sa 1).

JORAM

Son of Ahab; king of Israel (2Ki 3; 8-9; 2Ch 22).

JORDAN

Nu 34: 12 boundary will go down along the *J*
Jos 4: 22 Israel crossed the *J* on dry ground.'
Mt 3: 6 baptized by him in the *J* River.

JOSEPH

1. Son of Jacob by Rachel (Ge 30:24; 1Ch 2:2). Favored by Jacob, hated by brothers (Ge 37:3-4). Dreams (Ge 37:5-11). Sold by brothers (Ge 37:12-36). Served Potiphar; imprisoned by false accusation (Ge 39). Interpreted dreams of Pharaoh's servants (Ge 40), of Pharaoh (Ge 41:4-40). Made greatest in Egypt (Ge 41:41-57). Sold grain to brothers (Ge 42-45). Brought Jacob and sons to Egypt (Ge 46-47). Sons Ephraim and Manasseh blessed (Ge 48). Blessed (Ge 49:22-26; Dt 33:13-17). Death (Ge 50:22-26; Ex 13:19; Heb 11:22). 12,000 from (Rev 7:8).

2. Husband of Mary, mother of Jesus (Mt 1:16-24; 2:13-19; Lk 1:27; 2; Jn 1:45).

3. Disciple from Arimathea, who gave his tomb for Jesus' burial (Mt 27:57-61; Mk 15:43-47; Lk 24:50-52).

4. Original name of Barnabas (Ac 4:36).

JOSHUA

1. Son of Nun; name changed from Hoshea (Nu 13:8, 16; 1Ch 7:27). Fought Amalekites under Moses (Ex 17:9-14). Servant of Moses on Sinai (Ex 24:13; 32:17). Spied Canaan (Nu 13). With Caleb, allowed to enter land (Nu 14:6, 30). Succeeded Moses (Dt 1:38; 31:1-8; 34:9).

Charged Israel to conquer Canaan (Jos 1). Crossed Jordan (Jos 3-4). Circumcised sons of wilderness wanderings (Jos 5). Conquered Jericho (Jos 6), Ai (Jos 7-8), five kings at Gibeon (Jos 10:1-28), southern Canaan (Jos 10:29-43), northern Canaan (Jos 11-12). Defeated at Ai (Jos 7). Deceived by Gibeonites (Jos 9). Renewed covenant (Jos 8:30-35; 24:1-27). Divided land among tribes (Jos 13-22). Last words (Jos 23). Death (Jos 24:28-31).

2. High priest during rebuilding of temple (Hag 1-2; Zec 3:1-9; 6:11).

JOSIAH

Son of Amon; king of Judah (2Ki 22-23; 2Ch 34-35).

JOTHAM

Son of Azariah (Uzziah); king of Judah (2Ki 15:32-38; 2Ch 26:21-27:9).

JOY (ENJOY ENJOYMENT JOYFUL OVERJOYED REJOICE REJOICES REJOICING)

Dt 16: 15 and your *j* will be complete.
1Ch 16: 27 strength and *j* in his dwelling place.
Ne 8: 10 for the *j* of the LORD is your
Est 9: 22 their sorrow was turned into *j*
Job 38: 7 and all the angels shouted for *j*?
Ps 4: 7 have filled my heart with greater *j*
21: 6 with the *j* of your presence.
30: 11 sackcloth and clothed me with *j*,
43: 4 to God, my *j* and my delight.
51: 12 to me the *j* of your salvation
66: 1 Shout with *j* to God, all the earth!
96: 12 the trees of the forest will sing for *j*;
107: 22 and tell of his works with songs of *j*
119:111 they are the *j* of my heart.
Pr 10: 1 A wise son brings *j* to his father,
10: 28 The prospect of the righteous is *j*,
12: 20 but *j* for those who promote peace.
Isa 35: 10 everlasting *j* will crown their heads
51: 11 Gladness and *j* will overtake them,
55: 12 You will go out in *j*
Lk 1: 44 the baby in my womb leaped for *j*.
2: 10 news of great *j* that will be
Jn 15: 11 and that your *j* may be complete.
16: 20 but your grief will turn to *j*.
2Co 8: 2 their overflowing *j* and their
Php 2: 2 then make my *j* complete
4: 1 and long for, my *j* and crown,
1Th 2: 19 For what is our hope, our *j*,
Phm : 7 Your love has given me great *j*
Heb 12: 2 for the *j* set before him endured
Jas 1: 2 Consider it pure *j*, my brothers,
1Pe 1: 8 with an inexpressible and glorious *j*
2Jn : 4 It has given me great *j* to find some
3Jn : 4 I have no greater *j*

JOYFUL (JOY)

Ps 100: 2 come before him with *j* songs.
Hab 3: 18 I will be *j* in God my Savior.
1Th 5: 16 Be *j* always; pray continually;

JUDAH

1. Son of Jacob by Leah (Ge 29:35; 35:23; 1Ch 2:1). Tribe of blessed as ruling tribe (Ge 49:8-12; Dt 33:7).

2. Name used for people and land of Southern Kingdom.

Jer 13: 19 All *J* will be carried into exile,
Zec 10: 4 From *J* will come the cornerstone,
Heb 7: 14 that our Lord descended from *J*,

JUDAISM (JEW)

Gal 1: 13 of my previous way of life in *J*,

JUDAS

1. Apostle (Lk 6:16; Jn 14:22; Ac 1:13). Probably also called Thaddaeus (Mt 10:3; Mk 3:18).

2. Brother of James and Jesus (Mt 13:55; Mk 6:3), also called Jude (Jude 1).

3. Apostle, also called Iscariot, who betrayed Jesus (Mt 10:4; 26:14-56; Mk 3:19; 14:10-50; Lk 6:16; 22:3-53; Jn 6:71; 12:4; 13:2-30; 18:2-11). Suicide of (Mt 27:3-5; Ac 1:16-25).

JUDGE (JUDGED JUDGES JUDGING JUDGMENT)

Ge 18: 25 Will not the *J* of all the earth do
1Ch 16: 33 for he comes to *j* the earth.
Ps 9: 8 He will *j* the world in righteousness
Joel 3: 12 sit to *j* all the nations on every side.
Mt 7: 1 Do not *j*, or you too will be judged.
Jn 12: 47 For I did not come to *j* the world,
Ac 17: 31 a day when he will *j* the world
Ro 2: 16 day when God will *j* men's secrets
1Co 4: 3 indeed, I do not even *j* myself.
6: 2 that the saints will *j* the world?
Gal 2: 6 not *j* by external appearance—
2Ti 4: 1 who will *j* the living and the dead,
4: 8 which the Lord, the righteous *J*,
Jas 4: 12 There is only one Lawgiver and *J*,
4: 12 who are you to *j* your neighbor?
Rev 20: 4 who had been given authority to *j*.

JUDGED (JUDGE)

Mt 7: 1 "Do not judge, or you too will be *j*.
1Co 11: 31 But if we *j* ourselves, we would not
Jas 3: 1 who teach will be *j* more strictly.
Rev 20: 12 The dead were *j* according

JUDGES (JUDGE)

Jdg 2: 16 Then the LORD raised up *j*,
Ps 58: 11 there is a God who *j* the earth."
Heb 4: 12 it *j* the thoughts and attitudes
Rev 19: 11 With justice he *j* and makes war.

JUDGING (JUDGE)

Mt 19: 28 *j* the twelve tribes of Israel.
Jn 7: 24 Stop *j* by mere appearances,

JUDGMENT (JUDGE)

Dt 1: 17 of any man, for *j* belongs to God.
Ps 1: 5 the wicked will not stand in the *j*,
119: 66 Teach me knowledge and good *j*,
Pr 6: 32 man who commits adultery lacks *j*;
12: 11 but he who chases fantasies lacks *j*.
Ecc 12: 14 God will bring every deed into *j*,
Isa 66: 16 the LORD will execute *j*
Mt 5: 21 who murders will be subject to *j*.'
10: 15 on the day of *j* than for that town.
Mt 12: 36 have to give account on the day of *j*
Jn 5: 22 but has entrusted all *j* to the Son,
7: 24 appearances, and make a right *j*."
16: 8 to sin and righteousness and *j*:
Ro 14: 10 stand before God's *j* seat.
14: 13 Therefore let us stop passing *j*
1Co 11: 29 body of the Lord eats and drinks *j*
2Co 5: 10 appear before the *j* seat of Christ,
Heb 9: 27 to die once, and after that to face *j*,
10: 27 but only a fearful expectation of *j*
1Pe 4: 17 For it is time for *j* to begin
Jude : 6 bound with everlasting chains for *j*

JUST (JUSTICE JUSTIFICATION JUSTIFIED JUSTIFY JUSTLY)

Dt 32: 4 and all his ways are *j*.
Ps 37: 28 For the LORD loves the *j*
111: 7 of his hands are faithful and *j*;
Pr 1: 3 doing what is right and *j* and fair;
2: 8 for he guards the course of the *j*
Da 4: 37 does is right and all his ways are *j*.
Ro 3: 26 as to be *j* and the one who justifies
Heb 2: 2 received its *j* punishment,
1Jn 1: 9 and *j* and will forgive us our sins

Rev 16: 7 true and *j* are your judgments."

JUSTICE (JUST)

Ex 23: 2 do not pervert *j* by siding
23: 6 "Do not deny *j* to your poor people
Job 37: 23 in his *j* and great righteousness,
Ps 9: 8 he will govern the peoples with *j.*
9: 16 The LORD is known by his *j;*
11: 7 he loves *j;*
45: 6 a scepter of *j* will be the scepter
101: 1 I will sing of your love and *j;*
106: 3 Blessed are they who maintain *j,*
Pr 21: 15 When *j* is done, it brings joy
28: 5 Evil men do not understand *j,*
29: 4 By *j* a king gives a country stability
29: 26 from the LORD that man gets *j.*
Isa 9: 7 it with *j* and righteousness
28: 17 I will make *j* the measuring line
30: 18 For the LORD is a God of *j.*
42: 1 and he will bring *j* to the nations.
42: 4 till he establishes *j* on earth.
56: 1 "Maintain *j*
61: 8 "For I, the LORD, love *j;*
Jer 30: 11 I will discipline you but only with *j;*
Eze 34: 16 I will shepherd the flock with *j.*
Am 5: 15 maintain *j* in the courts.
5: 24 But let *j* roll on like a river,
Zec 7: 9 'Administer true *j;* show mercy
Lk 11: 42 you neglect *j* and the love of God.
Ro 3: 25 He did this to demonstrate his *j,*

JUSTIFICATION (JUST)

Ro 4: 25 and was raised to life for our *j.*
5: 18 of righteousness was *j* that brings

JUSTIFIED (JUST)

Ac 13: 39 him everyone who believes is *j*
Ro 3: 24 and are *j* freely by his grace
3: 28 For we maintain that a man is *j*
5: 1 since we have been *j* through faith,
5: 9 Since we have now been *j*
8: 30 those he called, he also *j;* those he *j,*
1Co 6: 11 you were *j* in the name
Gal 2: 16 observing the law no one will be *j.*
3: 11 Clearly no one is *j* before God
3: 24 to Christ that we might be *j* by faith
Jas 2: 24 You see that a person is *j*

JUSTIFY (JUST)

Gal 3: 8 that God would *j* the Gentiles

JUSTLY (JUST)

Mic 6: 8 To act *j* and to love mercy

K

KEEP (KEEPER KEEPING KEEPS KEPT)

Ge 31: 49 "May the LORD *k* watch
Ex 20: 6 and *k* my commandments.
Nu 6: 24 and *k* you;
Ps 18: 28 You, O LORD, *k* my lamp burning
19: 13 *K* your servant also from willful
119: 9 can a young man *k* his way pure?
121: 7 The LORD will *k* you
141: 3 *k* watch over the door of my lips.
Pr 4: 24 *k* corrupt talk far from your lips.
Isa 26: 3 You will *k* in perfect peace
Mt 10: 10 for the worker is worth his *k.*
Lk 12: 35 and *k* your lamps burning,
Gal 5: 25 let us *k* in step with the Spirit.
Eph 4: 3 Make every effort to *k* the unity
1Ti 5: 22 *K* yourself pure.
2Ti 4: 5 *k* your head in all situations,
Heb 13: 5 *K* your lives free from the love
Jas 1: 26 and yet does not *k* a tight rein
2: 8 If you really *k* the royal law found
Jude : 24 able to *k* you from falling

KEEPER (KEEP)

Ge 4: 9 I my brother's *k?"* The LORD

KEEPING (KEEP)

Ex 20: 8 the Sabbath day by *k* it holy.
Ps 19: 11 in *k* them there is great reward.
Mt 3: 8 Produce fruit in *k* with repentance.
Lk 2: 8 *k* watch over their flocks at night.
1Co 7: 19 *K* God's commands is what counts.
2Pe 3: 9 Lord is not slow in *k* his promise,

KEEPS (KEEP)

Pr 17: 28 a fool is thought wise if he *k* silent,
Am 5: 13 Therefore the prudent man *k* quiet
1Co 13: 5 is not easily angered, it *k* no record
Jas 2: 10 For whoever *k* the whole law

KEPT (KEEP)

Ps 130: 3 If you, O LORD, *k* a record of sins,
2Ti 4: 7 finished the race, I have *k* the faith.

1Pe 1: 4 spoil or fade—*k* in heaven for you,

KEYS

Mt 16: 19 I will give you the *k* of the kingdom

KILL (KILLS)

Mt 17: 23 They will *k* him, and on the third

KILLS (KILL)

Lev 24: 21 but whoever *k* a man must be put
2Co 3: 6 for the letter *k,* but the Spirit gives

KIND (KINDNESS KINDS)

Ge 1: 24 animals, each according to its *k."*
2Ch 10: 7 "If you will be *k* to these people
Pr 11: 17 A *k* man benefits himself,
12: 25 but a *k* word cheers him up.
14: 21 blessed is he who is *k* to the needy.
14: 31 whoever is *k* to the needy honors
19: 17 He who is *k* to the poor lends
Da 4: 27 by being *k* to the oppressed.
Lk 6: 35 because he is *k* to the ungrateful
1Co 13: 4 Love is patient, love is *k.*
15: 35 With what *k* of body will they
Eph 4: 32 Be *k* and compassionate
1Th 5: 15 but always try to be *k* to each other
2Ti 2: 24 instead, he must be *k* to everyone,
Tit 2: 5 to be busy at home, to be *k,*

KINDNESS (KIND)

Ac 14: 17 He has shown *k* by giving you rain
Ro 11: 22 Consider therefore the *k*
Gal 5: 22 peace, patience, *k,* goodness,
Eph 2: 7 expressed in his *k* to us
2Pe 1: 7 brotherly *k;* and to brotherly *k,*

KINDS (KIND)

1Co 12: 4 There are different *k* of gifts,
1Ti 6: 10 of money is a root of all *k* of evil.

KING (KINGDOM KINGS)

1. Kings of Judah and Israel: see Saul, David, Solomon.

2. Kings of Judah: see Rehoboam, Abijah, Asa, Jehoshaphat, Jehoram, Ahaziah, Athaliah (Queen), Joash, Amaziah, Uzziah, Jotham, Ahaz, Hezekiah, Manasseh, Amon, Josiah, Jehoahaz, Jehoiakim, Jehoiachin, Zedekiah.

3. Kings of Israel: see Jeroboam I, Nadab, Baasha, Elah, Zimri, Tibni, Omri, Ahab, Ahaziah, Joram, Jehu, Jehoahaz, Jehoash, Jeroboam II, Zechariah, Shallum, Menahem, Pekah, Pekahiah, Hoshea.

Jdg 17: 6 In those days Israel had no *k;*
1Sa 12: 12 the LORD your God was your *k.*
Ps 24: 7 that the *K* of glory may come in.
Isa 32: 1 See, a *k* will reign in righteousness
Zec 9: 9 See, your *k* comes to you,
1Ti 6: 15 the *K* of kings and Lord of lords,
1Pe 2: 17 of believers, fear God, honor the *k.*
Rev 19: 16 K OF KINGS AND LORD

KINGDOM (KING)

Ex 19: 6 you will be for me a *k* of priests
1Ch 29: 11 Yours, O LORD, is the *k;*
Ps 45: 6 justice will be the scepter of your *k.*
Da 4: 3 His *k* is an eternal *k;*
Mt 3: 2 Repent, for the *k* of heaven is near
5: 3 for theirs is the *k* of heaven.
6: 10 your *k* come,
6: 33 But seek first his *k* and his
7: 21 Lord,' will enter the *k* of heaven,
11: 11 least in the *k* of heaven is greater
13: 24 "The *k* of heaven is like a man who
13: 31 *k* of heaven is like a mustard seed,
13: 33 "The *k* of heaven is like yeast that
13: 44 *k* of heaven is like treasure hidden
13: 45 the *k* of heaven is like a merchant
13: 47 *k* of heaven is like a net that was let
16: 19 the keys of the *k* of heaven;
18: 23 the *k* of heaven is like a king who
19: 24 for a rich man to enter the *k* of God
24: 7 rise against nation, and *k* against *k.*
24: 14 gospel of the *k* will be preached
25: 34 the *k* prepared for you
Mk 9: 47 better for you to enter the *k* of God
10: 14 for the *k* of God belongs to such
10: 23 for the rich to enter the *k* of God!"
Lk 10: 9 'The *k* of God is near you.'
12: 31 seek his *k,* and these things will be
17: 21 because the *k* of God is within you
Jn 3: 5 no one can enter the *k* of God
18: 36 "My *k* is not of this world.
1Co 6: 9 the wicked will not inherit the *k*
15: 24 hands over the *k* to God the Father

Rev 1: 6 has made us to be a *k* and priests
11: 15 of the world has become the *k*

KINGS (KING)
Ps 2: 2 The *k* of the earth take their stand
72: 11 All *k* will bow down to him
Da 7: 24 ten horns are ten *k* who will come
1Ti 2: 2 for *k* and all those in authority,
Rev 1: 5 and the ruler of the *k* of the earth.

KINSMAN-REDEEMER (REDEEM)
Ru 3: 9 over me, since you are a *k*."

KISS
Ps 2: 12 *K* the Son, lest he be angry
Pr 24: 26 is like a *k* on the lips.
Lk 22: 48 the Son of Man with a *k*?"

KNEE (KNEES)
Isa 45: 23 Before me every *k* will bow;
Ro 14: 11 every *k* will bow before me;
Php 2: 10 name of Jesus every *k* should bow,

KNEES (KNEE)
Isa 35: 3 steady the *k* that give way;
Heb 12: 12 your feeble arms and weak *k*.

KNEW (KNOW)
Job 23: 3 If only I *k* where to find him;
Jnh 4: 2 I *k* that you are a gracious
Mt 7: 23 tell them plainly, 'I never *k* you.

KNOCK
Mt 7: 7 *k* and the door will be opened
Rev 3: 20 I am! I stand at the door and *k*.

KNOW (FOREKNEW KNEW KNOWING KNOWLEDGE KNOWN KNOWS)
Dt 18: 21 "How can we *k* when a message
Job 19: 25 I *k* that my Redeemer lives,
42: 3 things too wonderful for me to *k*.
Ps 46: 10 "Be still, and *k* that I am God;
139: 1 and you *k* me.
139: 23 Search me, O God, and *k* my heart;
Pr 27: 1 for you do not *k* what a day may
Jer 24: 7 I will give them a heart to *k* me,
31: 34 his brother, saying, '*K* the LORD,'
Mt 6: 3 let your left hand *k* what your right
24: 42 you do not *k* on what day your
Lk 1: 4 so that you may *k* the certainty
Jn 3: 11 we speak of what we *k*,
4: 22 we worship what we do *k*,
9: 25 One thing I do *k*.
10: 14 I *k* my sheep and my sheep *k* me—
17: 3 that they may *k* you, the only true
21: 24 We *k* that his testimony is true.
Ac 1: 7 "It is not for you to *k* the times
Ro 6: 6 For we *k* that our old self was
7: 18 I *k* that nothing good lives in me,
8: 28 we *k* that in all things God works
1Co 2: 2 For I resolved to *k* nothing
6: 15 Do you not *k* that your bodies are
6: 19 Do you not *k* that your body is
13: 12 Now I *k* in part; then I shall *k* fully,
15: 58 because you *k* that your labor
Php 3: 10 I want to *k* Christ and the power
2Ti 1: 12 because I *k* whom I have believed,
Jas 4: 14 *k* what will happen tomorrow.
1Jn 2: 4 The man who says, "I *k* him,"
3: 14 We *k* that we have passed
3: 16 This is how we *k* what love is:
5: 2 This is how we *k* that we love
5: 13 so that you may *k* that you have

KNOWING (KNOW)
Ge 3: 5 and you will be like God, *k* good
Php 3: 8 of *k* Christ Jesus my Lord,

KNOWLEDGE (KNOW)
Ge 2: 9 the tree of the *k* of good and evil.
Job 42: 3 obscures my counsel without *k*?'
Ps 19: 2 night after night they display *k*.
73: 11 Does the Most High have *k*?"
139: 6 Such *k* is too wonderful for me,
Pr 1: 7 of the LORD is the beginning of *k*,
10: 14 Wise men store up *k*,
12: 1 Whoever loves discipline loves *k*,
13: 16 Every prudent man acts out of *k*,
19: 2 to have zeal without *k*,
Isa 11: 9 full of the *k* of the LORD
Hab 2: 14 filled with the *k* of the glory
Ro 11: 33 riches of the wisdom and *k* of God!
1Co 8: 1 *K* puffs up, but love builds up.
8: 11 Christ died, is destroyed by your *k*.
13: 2 can fathom all mysteries and all *k*,
2Co 2: 14 everywhere the fragrance of the *k*
4: 6 light of the *k* of the glory of God
Eph 3: 19 to know this love that surpasses *k*
Col 2: 3 all the treasures of wisdom and *k*.
1Ti 6: 20 ideas of what is falsely called *k*,
2Pe 3: 18 grow in the grace and *k* of our Lord

KNOWN (KNOW)
Ps 16: 11 You have made *k* to me the path
105: 1 make *k* among the nations what he
Isa 46: 10 *k* the end from the beginning,
Mt 10: 26 or hidden that will not be made *k*.
Ro 1: 19 since what may be *k* about God is
11: 34 "Who has *k* the mind of the Lord?
15: 20 the gospel where Christ was not *k*,
2Co 3: 2 written on our hearts, *k*
2Pe 2: 21 than to have *k* it and then

KNOWS (KNOW)
1Sa 2: 3 for the LORD is a God who *k*,
Job 23: 10 But he *k* the way that I take;
Ps 44: 21 since he *k* the secrets of the heart?
94: 11 The LORD *k* the thoughts of man;
Ecc 8: 7 Since no man *k* the future,
Mt 6: 8 for your Father *k* what you need
24: 36 "No one *k* about that day or hour,
Ro 8: 27 who searches our hearts *k* the mind
1Co 8: 2 who thinks he *k* something does
2Ti 2: 19 The Lord *k* those who are his," and

L

LABAN
Brother of Rebekah (Ge 24:29-51), father of Rachel and Leah (Ge 29-31).

LABOR
Ex 20: 9 Six days you shall *l* and do all your
Isa 55: 2 and your *l* on what does not satisfy
Mt 6: 28 They do not *l* or spin.
1Co 3: 8 rewarded according to his own *l*.
15: 58 because you know that your *l*

LACK (LACKING LACKS)
Pr 15: 22 Plans fail for *l* of counsel,
Ro 3: 3 Will their *l* of faith nullify God's
Col 2: 23 *l* any value in restraining sensual

LACKING (LACK)
Ro 12: 11 Never be *l* in zeal, but keep your
Jas 1: 4 and complete, not *l* anything.

LACKS (LACK)
Pr 6: 32 who commits adultery *l* judgment;
12: 11 he who chases fantasies *l* judgment
Jas 1: 5 any of you *l* wisdom, he should ask

LAID (LAY)
Isa 53: 6 and the LORD has *l* on him
1Co 3: 11 other than the one already *l*,
1Jn 3: 16 Jesus Christ *l* down his life for us.

LAKE
Rev 19: 20 into the fiery *l* of burning sulfur.
20: 14 The *l* of fire is the second death.

LAMB (LAMB'S LAMBS)
Ge 22: 8 "God himself will provide the *l*
Ex 12: 21 and slaughter the Passover *l*.
Isa 11: 6 The wolf will live with the *l*,
53: 7 he was led like a *l* to the slaughter,
Jn 1: 29 *L* of God, who takes away the sin
1Co 5: 7 our Passover *l*, has been sacrificed.
1Pe 1: 19 a *l* without blemish or defect.
Rev 5: 6 Then I saw a *L*, looking
5: 12 "Worthy is the *L*, who was slain,
14: 4 They follow the *L* wherever he

LAMB'S (LAMB)
Rev 21: 27 written in the *L* book of life.

LAMBS (LAMB)
Lk 10: 3 I am sending you out like *l*
Jn 21: 15 Jesus said, "Feed my *l*."

LAMENT
2Sa 1: 17 took up this *l* concerning Saul

LAMP (LAMPS)
2Sa 22: 29 You are my *l*, O LORD;
Ps 18: 28 You, O LORD, keep my *l* burning;
119:105 Your word is a *l* to my feet
Pr 31: 18 and her *l* does not go out at night.
Lk 8: 16 "No one lights a *l* and hides it
Rev 21: 23 gives it light, and the Lamb is its *l*.

LAMPS (LAMP)
Mt 25: 1 be like ten virgins who took their *l*
Lk 12: 35 for service and keep your *l* burning,

LAND
Ge 1: 10 God called the dry ground "*l*,"

1: 11 "Let the *l* produce vegetation:
12: 7 To your offspring I will give this *l*."
Ex 3: 8 a *l* flowing with milk and honey—
Nu 35: 33 Do not pollute the *l* where you are.
Dt 34: 1 LORD showed him the whole *l*—
Jos 13: 2 "This is the *l* that remains:
14: 4 Levites received no share of the *l*
2Ch 7: 14 their sin and will heal their *l*.
7: 20 then I will uproot Israel from my *l*,
Eze 36: 24 and bring you back into your own *l*.

LANGUAGE

Ge 11: 1 Now the whole world had one *l*
Ps 19: 3 There is no speech or *l*
Jn 8: 44 When he lies, he speaks his native *l*
Ac 2: 6 heard them speaking in his own *l*.
Col 3: 8 slander, and filthy *l* from your lips.
Rev 5: 9 from every tribe and *l* and people

LAST (LASTING LASTS LATTER)

2Sa 23: 1 These are the *l* words of David:
Isa 44: 6 I am the first and I am the *l*;
Mt 19: 30 But many who are first will be *l*,
Mk 10: 31 are first will be *l*, and the *l* first."
Jn 15: 16 and bear fruit—fruit that will *l*.
Ro 1: 17 is by faith from first to *l*,
2Ti 3: 1 will be terrible times in the *l* days.
2Pe 3: 3 in the *l* days scoffers will come,
Rev 1: 17 I am the First and the *L*.
22: 13 the First and the *L*, the Beginning

LASTING (LAST)

Ex 12: 14 to the LORD—a *l* ordinance.
Lev 24: 8 of the Israelites, as a *l* covenant.
Nu 25: 13 have a covenant of a *l* priesthood,
Heb 10: 34 had better and *l* possessions.

LASTS (LAST)

Ps 30: 5 For his anger *l* only a moment,
2Co 3: 11 greater is the glory of that which *l*!

LATTER (LAST)

Job 42: 12 The LORD blessed the *l* part

LAUGH (LAUGHS)

Ecc 3: 4 a time to weep and a time to *l*,

LAUGHS (LAUGH)

Ps 2: 4 The One enthroned in heaven *l*;
37: 13 but the Lord *l* at the wicked,

LAVISHED

Eph 1: 8 of God's grace that he *l* on us
1Jn 3: 1 great is the love the Father has *l*

LAW (LAWS)

Dt 31: 11 you shall read this *l* before them
31: 26 "Take this Book of the *L*
Jos 1: 8 of the *L* depart from your mouth;
Ne 8: 8 from the Book of the *L* of God,
Ps 1: 2 and on his *l* he meditates day
19: 7 The *l* of the LORD is perfect,
119: 18 wonderful things in your *l*.
119: 72 *l* from your mouth is more precious
119: 97 Oh, how I love your *l*!
119:165 peace have they who love your *l*,
Isa 8: 20 To the *l* and to the testimony!
Jer 31: 33 "I will put my *l* in their minds
Mt 5: 17 that I have come to abolish the *L*
7: 12 sums up the *L* and the Prophets.
22: 40 All the *L* and the Prophets hang
Lk 16: 17 stroke of a pen to drop out of the *L*.
Jn 1: 17 For the *l* was given through Moses;
Ro 2: 12 All who sin apart from the *l* will
2: 15 of the *l* are written on their hearts,
5: 13 for before the *l* was given,
5: 20 *l* was added so that the trespass
6: 14 because you are not under *l*,
7: 6 released from the *l* so that we serve
7: 12 *l* is holy, and the commandment is
8: 3 For what the *l* was powerless to do
10: 4 Christ is the end of the *l*
13: 10 love is the fulfillment of the *l*.
Gal 3: 13 curse of the *l* by becoming a curse
3: 24 So the *l* was put in charge to lead us
5: 3 obligated to obey the whole *l*.
5: 4 justified by *l* have been alienated
5: 14 The entire *l* is summed up
Heb 7: 19 (for the *l* made nothing perfect),
10: 1 The *l* is only a shadow
Jas 1: 25 intently into the perfect *l* that gives
2: 10 For whoever keeps the whole *l*

LAWLESSNESS*

2Th 2: 3 and the man of *l* is revealed,
2: 7 power of *l* is already at work;
1Jn 3: 4 sins breaks the law; in fact, sin is *l*.

LAWS (LAW)

Lev 25: 18 and be careful to obey my *l*,
Ps 119: 30 I have set my heart on your *l*.
119:120 I stand in awe of your *l*.
Heb 8: 10 I will put my *l* in their minds
10: 16 I will put my *l* in their hearts,

LAY (LAID LAYING)

Job 22: 22 and *l* up his words in your heart.
Isa 28: 16 "See, I *l* a stone in Zion,
Mt 8: 20 of Man has no place to *l* his head."
Jn 10: 15 and I *l* down my life for the sheep.
15: 13 that he *l* down his life
1Co 3: 11 no one can *l* any foundation other
1Jn 3: 16 And we ought to *l* down our lives
Rev 4: 10 They *l* their crowns

LAYING (LAY)

1Ti 5: 22 Do not be hasty in the *l* on of hands
Heb 6: 1 not *l* again the foundation

LAZARUS

1. Poor man in Jesus' parable (Lk 16:19-31).
2. Brother of Mary and Martha whom Jesus raised from the dead (Jn 11:1-12:19).

LAZY

Pr 10: 4 *L* hands make a man poor,
Heb 6: 12 We do not want you to become *l*,

LEAD (LEADERS LEADERSHIP LEADS LED)

Ex 15: 13 "In your unfailing love you will *l*
Ps 27: 11 *l* me in a straight path
61: 2 *l* me to the rock that is higher
139: 24 and *l* me in the way everlasting.
143: 10 *l* me on level ground.
Ecc 5: 6 Do not let your mouth *l* you
Isa 11: 6 and a little child will *l* them.
Da 12: 3 those who *l* many to righteousness,
Mt 6: 13 And *l* us not into temptation,
1Jn 3: 7 do not let anyone *l* you astray.

LEADERS (LEAD)

Heb 13: 7 Remember your *l*, who spoke
13: 17 Obey your *l* and submit

LEADERSHIP (LEAD)

Ro 12: 8 if it is *l*, let him govern diligently;

LEADS (LEAD)

Ps 23: 2 he *l* me beside quiet waters,
Pr 19: 23 The fear of the LORD *l* to life:

Isa 40: 11 he gently *l* those that have young.
Mt 7: 13 and broad is the road that *l*
15: 14 If a blind man *l* a blind man,
Jn 10: 3 sheep by name and *l* them out.
Ro 14: 19 effort to do what *l* to peace
2Co 2: 14 always *l* us in triumphal procession

LEAH

Wife of Jacob (Ge 29:16-30); bore six sons and one daughter (Ge 29:31-30:21; 34:1; 35:23).

LEAN

Pr 3: 5 *l* not on your own understanding;

LEARN (LEARNED LEARNING)

Isa 1: 17 *l* to do right!
Mt 11: 29 yoke upon you and *l* from me,

LEARNED (LEARN)

Php 4: 11 for I have *l* to be content whatever
2Ti 3: 14 continue in what you have *l*

LEARNING (LEARN)

Pr 1: 5 let the wise listen and add to their *l*,
2Ti 3: 7 always *l* but never able

LED (LEAD)

Ps 68: 18 you *l* captives in your train;
Isa 53: 7 he was *l* like a lamb to the slaughter
Am 2: 10 and I *l* you forty years in the desert
Ro 8: 14 those who are *l* by the Spirit
Eph 4: 8 he *l* captives in his train

LEFT

Jos 1: 7 turn from it to the right or to the *l*,
Pr 4: 27 Do not swerve to the right or the *l*;
Mt 6: 3 do not let your *l* hand know what
25: 33 on his right and the goats on his *l*.

LEGION

Mk 5: 9 "My name is *L*," he replied,

LEND (LENDS)

Dt 15: 8 freely *l* him whatever he needs.
Ps 37: 26 are always generous and *l* freely;
Lk 6: 34 if you *l* to those from whom you

LENDS (LEND)

Pr 19: 17 to the poor *l* to the LORD,

LENGTH (LONG)

Ps 90: 10 The *l* of our days is seventy years—
Pr 10: 27 The fear of the LORD adds *l* to life

LEPROSY

2Ki 7: 3 men with *l* at the entrance

LETTER (LETTERS)
Mt 5: 18 not the smallest *l*, not the least
2Co 3: 2 You yourselves are our *l*, written
3: 6 for the *l* kills, but the Spirit gives
2Th 3: 14 not obey our instruction in this *l*,

LETTERS (LETTER)
2Co 3: 7 which was engraved in *l* on stone,
10: 10 "His *l* are weighty and forceful,
2Pe 3: 16 His *l* contain some things that are

LEVEL
Ps 143: 10 lead me on *l* ground.
Pr 4: 26 Make *l* paths for your feet
Isa 26: 7 The path of the righteous is *l*;
Heb 12: 13 "Make *l* paths for your feet,"

LEVI (LEVITES)
1. Son of Jacob by Leah (Ge 29:34; 46:11; 1Ch 2:1). Tribe of blessed (Ge 49:5-7; Dt 33:8-11), chosen as priests (Nu 3-4), numbered (Nu 3:39; 26:62), allotted cities, but not land (Nu 18; 35; Dt 10:9; Jos 13:14; 21), land (Eze 48:8-22), 12,000 from (Rev 7:7).
2. See MATTHEW.

LEVITES (LEVI)
Nu 1: 53 The *L* are to be responsible
8: 6 "Take the *L* from among the other
18: 21 I give to the *L* all the tithes in Israel

LEWDNESS
Mk 7: 22 malice, deceit, *l*, envy, slander,

LIAR (LIE)
Pr 19: 22 better to be poor than a *l*.
Jn 8: 44 for he is a *l* and the father of lies.
Ro 3: 4 Let God be true, and every man a *l*.

LIBERATED*
Ro 8: 21 that the creation itself will be *l*

LIE (LIAR LIED LIES LYING)
Lev 19: 11 "'Do not *l*.
Nu 23: 19 God is not a man, that he should *l*,
Dt 6: 7 when you *l* down and when you get
Ps 23: 2 me *l* down in green pastures,
Isa 11: 6 leopard will *l* down with the goat,
Eze 34: 14 they will *l* down in good grazing
Ro 1: 25 exchanged the truth of God for a *l*,
Col 3: 9 Do not *l* to each other,
Heb 6: 18 which it is impossible for God to *l*,

LIED (LIE)
Ac 5: 4 You have not *l* to men but to God."

LIES (LIE)
Ps 34: 13 and your lips from speaking *l*.
Jn 8: 44 for he is a liar and the father of *l*.

LIFE (LIVE)
Ge 2: 7 into his nostrils the breath of *l*,
2: 9 of the garden were the tree of *l*
9: 11 Never again will all *l* be cut
Ex 21: 23 you are to take *l* for *l*, eye for eye,
Lev 17: 14 the *l* of every creature is its blood.
24: 18 must make restitution—*l* for *l*.
Dt 30: 19 Now choose *l*, so that you
Ps 16: 11 known to me the path of *l*;
23: 6 all the days of my *l*,
34: 12 Whoever of you loves *l*
39: 4 let me know how fleeting is my *l*.
49: 7 No man can redeem the *l*
104: 33 I will sing to the LORD all my *l*;
Pr 1: 3 a disciplined and prudent *l*,
6: 23 are the way to *l*,
7: 23 little knowing it will cost him his *l*.
8: 35 For whoever finds me finds *l*
11: 30 of the righteous is a tree of *l*,
21: 21 finds *l*, prosperity and honor.
Jer 10: 23 that a man's *l* is not his own;
Eze 37: 5 enter you, and you will come to *l*.
Da 12: 2 some to everlasting *l*, others
Mt 6: 25 Is not *l* more important than food,
7: 14 and narrow the road that leads to *l*,
10: 39 Whoever finds his *l* will lose it,
16: 25 wants to save his *l* will lose it,
20: 28 to give his *l* as a ransom for many."
Mk 10: 45 to give his *l* as a ransom for many."
Lk 12: 15 a man's *l* does not consist
12: 22 do not worry about your *l*,
14: 26 even his own *l*—he cannot be my
Jn 1: 4 In him was *l*, and that *l* was
3: 15 believes in him may have eternal *l*.
3: 36 believes in the Son has eternal *l*,
4: 14 of water welling up to eternal *l*."
5: 24 him who sent me has eternal *l*
6: 35 Jesus declared, "I am the bread of *l*
6: 47 he who believes has everlasting *l*.
6: 68 You have the words of eternal *l*.
10: 10 I have come that they may have *l*,
10: 15 and I lay down my *l* for the sheep.
10: 28 I give them eternal *l*, and they shall
11: 25 "I am the resurrection and the *l*.
14: 6 am the way and the truth and the *l*.
15: 13 lay down his *l* for his friends.
20: 31 that by believing you may have *l*
Ac 13: 48 appointed for eternal *l* believed.
Ro 4: 25 was raised to *l* for our justification.
6: 13 have been brought from death to *l*;
6: 23 but the gift of God is eternal *l*
8: 38 convinced that neither death nor *l*,
1Co 15: 19 If only for this *l* we have hope
2Co 3: 6 letter kills, but the Spirit gives *l*.
Gal 2: 20 The *l* I live in the body, I live
Eph 4: 1 I urge you to live a *l* worthy
Php 2: 16 as you hold out the word of *l*—
Col 1: 10 order that you may live a *l* worthy
1Th 4: 12 so that your daily *l* may win
1Ti 4: 8 for both the present *l* and the *l*
4: 16 Watch your *l* and doctrine closely.
6: 19 hold of the *l* that is truly *l*.
2Ti 3: 12 to live a godly *l* in Christ Jesus will
Jas 1: 12 crown of *l* that God has promised
3: 13 Let him show it by his good *l*,
1Pe 3: 10 "Whoever would love *l*
2Pe 1: 3 given us everything we need for *l*
1Jn 3: 14 we have passed from death to *l*,
5: 11 has given us eternal *l*, and this *l* is
Rev 13: 8 written in the book of *l* belonging
20: 12 was opened, which is the book of *l*.
21: 27 written in the Lamb's book of *l*.
22: 2 side of the river stood the tree of *l*,

LIFT (LIFTED)
Ps 121: 1 I *l* up my eyes to the hills—
134: 2 *L* up your hands in the sanctuary
La 3: 41 Let us *l* up our hearts and our
1Ti 2: 8 everywhere to *l* up holy hands

LIFTED (LIFT)
Ps 40: 2 He *l* me out of the slimy pit,
Jn 3: 14 Moses *l* up the snake in the desert,
12: 32 when I am *l* up from the earth,

LIGHT (ENLIGHTENED)
Ge 1: 3 "Let there be *l*," and there was *l*.
2Sa 22: 29 LORD turns my darkness into *l*.
Job 38: 19 "What is the way to the abode of *l*?
Ps 4: 6 Let the *l* of your face shine upon us
19: 8 giving *l* to the eyes.
27: 1 LORD is my *l* and my salvation—
56: 13 God in the *l* of life.
76: 4 You are resplendent with *l*,
104: 2 He wraps himself in *l*
119:105 and a *l* for my path.
119:130 The unfolding of your words gives *l*;
Isa 2: 5 let us walk in the *l* of the LORD.
9: 2 have seen a great *l*;
49: 6 also make you a *l* for the Gentiles,
Mt 4: 16 have seen a great *l*;
5: 16 let your *l* shine before men,
11: 30 yoke is easy and my burden is *l*."
Jn 3: 19 but men loved darkness instead of *l*
8: 12 he said, "I am the *l* of the world.
2Co 4: 6 made his *l* shine in our hearts
6: 14 Or what fellowship can *l* have
11: 14 masquerades as an angel of *l*.
1Ti 6: 16 and who lives in unapproachable *l*,
1Pe 2: 9 of darkness into his wonderful *l*.
1Jn 1: 5 God is *l*; in him there is no
1: 7 But if we walk in the *l*,
Rev 21: 23 for the glory of God gives it *l*,

LIGHTNING
Da 10: 6 his face like *l*, his eyes like flaming
Mt 24: 27 For as the *l* that comes from the east
28: 3 His appearance was like *l*,

LIKENESS
Ge 1: 26 man in our image, in our *l*,
Ps 17: 15 I will be satisfied with seeing your *l*
Isa 52: 14 his form marred beyond human *l*—
Ro 8: 3 Son in the *l* of sinful man
8: 29 to be conformed to the *l* of his Son,
2Co 3: 18 his *l* with ever-increasing glory,
Php 2: 7 being made in human *l*.
Jas 3: 9 who have been made in God's *l*.

LILIES
Lk 12: 27 "Consider how the *l* grow.

LION
Isa 11: 7 and the *l* will eat straw like the ox.
1Pe 5: 8 around like a roaring *l* looking
Rev 5: 5 See, the *L* of the tribe of Judah,

LIPS
Ps 8: 2 From the *l* of children and infants
34: 1 his praise will always be on my *l*.
119:171 May my *l* overflow with praise,
Pr 13: 3 He who guards his *l* guards his life,
27: 2 someone else, and not your own *l*.
Isa 6: 5 For I am a man of unclean *l*,
Mt 21: 16 "'From the *l* of children
Col 3: 8 and filthy language from your *l*.

LISTEN (LISTENING LISTENS)
Dt 30: 20 *l* to his voice, and hold fast to him.
Pr 1: 5 let the wise *l* and add
Jn 10: 27 My sheep *l* to my voice; I know
Jas 1: 19 Everyone should be quick to *l*,
1: 22 Do not merely *l* to the word,

LISTENING (LISTEN)
1Sa 3: 9 Speak, LORD, for your servant is *l*
Pr 18: 13 He who answers before *l*—

LISTENS (LISTEN)
Pr 12: 15 but a wise man *l* to advice.

LIVE (ALIVE LIFE LIVES LIVING)
Ex 20: 12 so that you may *l* long
33: 20 for no one may see me and *l*."
Dt 8: 3 to teach you that man does not *l*
Job 14: 14 If a man dies, will he *l* again?
Ps 119:175 Let me *l* that I may praise you,
Isa 55: 3 hear me, that your soul may *l*.
Eze 37: 3 can these bones *l*?" I said,
Hab 2: 4 but the righteous will *l* by his faith
Mt 4: 4 'Man does not *l* on bread alone,
Ac 17: 24 does not *l* in temples built by hands
17: 28 'For in him we *l* and move
Ro 1: 17 "The righteous will *l* by faith."
2Co 5: 7 We *l* by faith, not by sight.
Gal 2: 20 The life I *l* in the body, I *l* by faith
5: 25 Since we *l* by the Spirit, let us keep
Php 1: 21 to *l* is Christ and to die is gain.
1Th 5: 13 *L* in peace with each other.
2Ti 3: 12 who wants to *l* a godly life
Heb 12: 14 Make every effort to *l* in peace
1Pe 1: 17 *l* your lives as strangers here

LIVES (LIVE)
Job 19: 25 I know that my Redeemer *l*,
Isa 57: 15 he who *l* forever, whose name is
Da 3: 28 to give up their *l* rather than serve
Jn 14: 17 for he *l* with you and will be in you.
Ro 7: 18 I know that nothing good *l* in me,
14: 7 For none of us *l* to himself alone
1Co 3: 16 and that God's Spirit *l* in you?
Gal 2: 20 I no longer live, but Christ *l* in me.
Heb 13: 5 Keep your *l* free from the love
2Pe 3: 11 You ought to live holy and godly *l*
1Jn 3: 16 to lay down our *l* for our brothers.
4: 16 Whoever *l* in love *l* in God,

LIVING (LIVE)
Ge 2: 7 and man became a *l* being.
Jer 2: 13 the spring of *l* water,
Mt 22: 32 the God of the dead but of the *l*."
Jn 7: 38 streams of *l* water will flow
Ro 12: 1 to offer your bodies as *l* sacrifices,
Heb 4: 12 For the word of God is *l* and active.
10: 31 to fall into the hands of the *l* God.
Rev 1: 18 I am the *L* One; I was dead,

LOAD
Gal 6: 5 for each one should carry his own *l*.

LOCUSTS
Mt 3: 4 His food was *l* and wild honey.

LOFTY
Ps 139: 6 too *l* for me to attain.
Isa 57: 15 is what the high and *l* One says—

LONELY
Ps 68: 6 God sets the *l* in families,

LONG (LENGTH LONGED LONGING LONGS)
1Ki 18: 21 "How *l* will you waver
Jn 9: 4 As *l* as it is day, we must do
Eph 3: 18 to grasp how wide and *l* and high
1Pe 1: 12 Even angels *l* to look

LONGED (LONG)
Mt 13: 17 righteous men *l* to see what you see
23: 37 how often I have *l*
2Ti 4: 8 to all who have *l* for his appearing.

LONGING (LONG)
Pr 13: 19 A *l* fulfilled is sweet to the soul,
2Co 5: 2 *l* to be clothed with our heavenly

LONGS (LONG)
Isa 30: 18 Yet the LORD *l* to be gracious

LOOK (LOOKING LOOKS)
Dt 4: 29 you will find him if you *l* for him
Job 31: 1 not to *l* lustfully at a girl.
Ps 34: 5 Those who *l* to him are radiant;
Pr 4: 25 Let your eyes *l* straight ahead,
Isa 60: 5 Then you will *l* and be radiant,
Hab 1: 13 Your eyes are too pure to *l* on evil;
Zec 12: 10 They will *l* on me, the one they
Mk 13: 21 '*L*, here is the Christ!' or, '*L*,
Lk 24: 39 *L* at my hands and my feet.
Jn 1: 36 he said, "*L*, the Lamb of God!"
4: 35 open your eyes and *l* at the fields!
19: 37 "They will *l* on the one they have
Jas 1: 27 to *l* after orphans and widows
1Pe 1: 12 long to *l* into these things.

LOOKING (LOOK)
2Co 10: 7 You are *l* only on the surface
Rev 5: 6 I saw a Lamb, *l* as if it had been

LOOKS (LOOK)
1Sa 16: 7 Man *l* at the outward appearance,
Lk 9: 62 and *l* back is fit for service
Php 2: 21 For everyone *l* out

LORD† (LORD'S† LORDING)
Ne 4: 14 Remember the *L*, who is great
Job 28: 28 'The fear of the *L*—that is wisdom,
Ps 54: 4 the *L* is the one who sustains me.
62: 12 and that you, O *L*, are loving.
86: 5 You are forgiving and good, O *L*,
110: 1 The LORD says to my *L*:
147: 5 Great is our *L* and mighty in power
Isa 6: 1 I saw the *L* seated on a throne,
Da 9: 4 "O *L*, the great and awe-some God,
Mt 3: 3 'Prepare the way for the *L*,
4: 7 'Do not put the *L* your God
7: 21 "Not everyone who says to me, '*L*,
22: 37 "'Love the *L* your God
22: 44 For he says, "'The *L* said to my *L*:
Mk 12: 11 the *L* has done this,
12: 29 the *L* our God, the *L* is one.
Lk 2: 9 glory of the *L* shone around them,
6: 46 "Why do you call me, '*L*, *L*,'
10: 27 "'Love the *L* your God
Ac 2: 21 on the name of the *L* will be saved.'
16: 31 replied, "Believe in the *L* Jesus,
Ro 10: 9 with your mouth, "Jesus is *L*,"
10: 13 on the name of the *L* will be saved
12: 11 your spiritual fervor, serving the *L*.
14: 8 we live to the *L*; and if we die,
1Co 1: 31 Let him who boasts boast in the *L*."
3: 5 the *L* has assigned to each his task.
7: 34 to be devoted to the *L* in both body
10: 9 We should not test the *L*,
11: 23 For I received from the *L* what I
12: 3 "Jesus is *L*," except by the Holy
15: 57 victory through our *L* Jesus Christ.
16: 22 If anyone does not love the *L*—
2Co 3: 17 Now the *L* is the Spirit,
8: 5 they gave themselves first to the *L*
10: 17 Let him who boasts boast in the *L*."
Gal 6: 14 in the cross of our *L* Jesus Christ,
Eph 4: 5 one *L*, one faith, one baptism;
5: 10 and find out what pleases the *L*.
5: 19 make music in your heart to the *L*,
Php 2: 11 confess that Jesus Christ is *L*,
3: 1 my brothers, rejoice in the *L*!
4: 4 Rejoice in the *L* always.
Col 2: 6 as you received Christ Jesus as *L*,
3: 17 do it all in the name of the *L* Jesus,
3: 23 as working for the *L*, not for men,
4: 17 work you have received in the *L*."
1Th 3: 12 May the *L* make your love increase
5: 2 day of the *L* will come like a thief
5: 23 at the coming of our *L* Jesus Christ.
2Th 2: 1 the coming of our *L* Jesus Christ
2Ti 2: 19 "The *L* knows those who are his,"
Heb 12: 14 holiness no one will see the *L*.
13: 6 *L* is my helper; I will not be afraid.
Jas 4: 10 Humble yourselves before the *L*,

1Pe 1: 25 the word of the *L* stands forever."
2: 3 you have tasted that the *L* is good.
3: 15 in your hearts set apart Christ as *L*.
2Pe 1: 16 and coming of our *L* Jesus Christ,
2: 1 the sovereign *L* who bought
3: 9 The *L* is not slow in keeping his
Jude : 14 the *L* is coming with thousands
Rev 4: 8 holy, holy is the *L* God Almighty,
4: 11 "You are worthy, our *L* and God,
17: 14 he is *L* of lords and King of kings—
22: 20 Come, *L* Jesus.

LORD'S† (LORD†)

Ac 21: 14 and said, "The *L* will be done."
1Co 10: 26 "The earth is the *L*, and everything
11: 26 you proclaim the *L* death
2Co 3: 18 faces all reflect the *L* glory,
2Ti 2: 24 And the *L* servant must not quarrel
Jas 4: 15 you ought to say, "If it is the *L* will,

LORDING* (LORD†)

1Pe 5: 3 not *l* it over those entrusted to you,

LORD‡ (LORD'S‡)

Ge 2: 4 When the *L* God made the earth
2: 7 the *L* God formed the man
3: 21 The *L* God made garments of skin
7: 16 Then the *L* shut him in.
15: 6 Abram believed the *L*,
18: 14 Is anything too hard for the *L*?
31: 49 "May the *L* keep watch
Ex 3: 2 the angel of the *L* appeared to him
9: 12 the *L* hardened Pharaoh's heart
14: 30 That day the *L* saved Israel
20: 2 "I am the *L* your God, who
33: 11 The *L* would speak to Moses face
40: 34 glory of the *L* filled the tabernacle.
Lev 19: 2 'Be holy because I, the *L* your God,
Nu 8: 5 *L* said to Moses: "Take the Levites
14: 21 glory of the *L* fills the whole earth,
Dt 2: 7 forty years the *L* your God has
5: 9 the *L* your God, am a jealous God,
6: 4 The *L* our God, the *L* is one.
6: 5 Love the *L* your God
6: 16 Do not test the *L* your God
10: 14 To the *L* your God belong
10: 17 For the *L* your God is God of gods
11: 1 Love the *L* your God and keep his
28: 1 If you fully obey the *L* your God
30: 16 today to love the *L* your God,
30: 20 For the *L* is your life, and he will
31: 6 for the *L* your God goes with you;
Jos 22: 5 to love the *L* your God, to walk
24: 15 my household, we will serve the *L*
1Sa 1: 28 So now I give him to the *L*.
2: 2 "There is no one holy like the *L*;
7: 12 "Thus far has the *L* helped us."
12: 22 his great name the *L* will not reject
15: 22 "Does the *L* delight
2Sa 22: 2 "The *L* is my rock, my fortress
1Ki 2: 3 and observe what the *L* your God
8: 11 the glory of the *L* filled his temple.
8: 61 fully committed to the *L* our God,
18: 21 If the *L* is God, follow him;
2Ki 13: 23 But the *L* was gracious to them
1Ch 16: 8 Give thanks to the *L*, call
16: 23 Sing to the *L*, all the earth;
28: 9 for the *L* searches every heart
29: 11 O *L*, is the greatness and the power
2Ch 5: 14 the glory of the *L* filled the temple
16: 9 of the *L* range throughout the earth
19: 6 judging for man but for the *L*,
30: 9 for the *L* your God is gracious
Ne 1: 5 Then I said: "O *L*, God of heaven,
Job 1: 21 *L* gave and the *L* has taken away;
38: 1 the *L* answered Job out
42: 9 and the *L* accepted Job's prayer.
Ps 1: 2 But his delight is in the law of the *L*
9: 9 The *L* is a refuge for the oppressed,
12: 6 And the words of the *L* are flawless
16: 8 I have set the *L* always before me.
18: 30 the word of the *L* is flawless.
19: 7 The law of the *L* is perfect,
19: 14 O *L*, my Rock and my Redeemer.
23: 1 The *L* is my shepherd, I shall not be
23: 6 I will dwell in the house of the *L*
27: 1 The *L* is my light and my salvation
27: 4 to gaze upon the beauty of the *L*
29: 1 Ascribe to the *L*, O mighty ones,
32: 2 whose sin the *L* does not count
33: 12 is the nation whose God is the *L*,
33: 18 But the eyes of the *L* are
34: 3 Glorify the *L* with me;
34: 7 The angel of the *L* encamps
34: 8 Taste and see that the *L* is good;
34: 18 The *L* is close to the broken-hearted
37: 4 Delight yourself in the *L*
40: 1 I waited patiently for the *L*;
47: 2 How awesome is the *L* Most High,
48: 1 Great is the *L*, and most worthy
55: 22 Cast your cares on the *L*
75: 8 In the hand of the *L* is a cup
84: 11 For the *L* God is a sun and shield;
86: 11 Teach me your way, O *L*,
89: 5 heavens praise your wonders, O *L*,
91: 2 I will say of the *L*, "He is my refuge
95: 1 Come, let us sing for joy to the *L*;
96: 1 Sing to the *L* a new song;
98: 4 Shout for joy to the *L*, all the earth,
100: 1 Shout for joy to the *L*, all the earth.
103: 1 Praise the *L*, O my soul;
103: 8 The *L* is compassionate
104: 1 O *L* my God, you are very great;
107: 8 to the *L* for his unfailing love
110: 1 The *L* says to my Lord:
113: 4 *L* is exalted over all the nations,
115: 1 Not to us, O *L*, not to us
116: 15 Precious in the sight of the *L*
118: 1 Give thanks to the *L*, for he is good
118: 24 This is the day the *L* has made;
121: 2 My help comes from the *L*,
121: 5 The *L* watches over you—
125: 2 so the *L* surrounds his people
127: 1 Unless the *L* builds the house,
127: 3 Sons are a heritage from the *L*,
130: 3 If you, O *L*, kept a record of sins,
135: 6 The *L* does whatever pleases him,
136: 1 Give thanks to the *L*, for he is good
139: 1 O *L*, you have searched me
144: 3 O *L*, what is man that you care
145: 3 Great is the *L* and most worthy
145: 18 The *L* is near to all who call on him
Pr 1: 7 The fear of the *L* is the beginning
3: 5 Trust in the *L* with all your heart
3: 9 Honor the *L* with your wealth,
3: 12 the *L* disciplines those he loves,
3: 19 By wisdom the *L* laid the earth's
5: 21 are in full view of the *L*,
6: 16 There are six things the *L* hates,
10: 27 The fear of the *L* adds length to life
11: 1 The *L* abhors dishonest scales,
12: 22 The *L* detests lying lips,
14: 26 He who fears the *L* has a secure
15: 3 The eyes of the *L* are everywhere,
16: 2 but motives are weighed by the *L*.
16: 4 The *L* works out everything
16: 9 but the *L* determines his steps.
16: 33 but its every decision is from the *L*.
18: 10 The name of the *L* is a strong tower
18: 22 and receives favor from the *L*.
19: 14 but a prudent wife is from the *L*.
19: 17 to the poor lends to the *L*,
21: 3 to the *L* than sacrifice.
21: 30 that can succeed against the *L*.
21: 31 but victory rests with the *L*.
22: 2 The *L* is the Maker of them all.
24: 18 or the *L* will see and disapprove
31: 30 a woman who fears the *L* is
Isa 6: 3 holy, holy is the *L* Almighty;
11: 2 The Spirit of the *L* will rest on him
11: 9 full of the knowledge of the *L*
12: 2 The *L*, the *L*, is my strength
24: 1 the *L* is going to lay waste the earth
25: 8 The Sovereign *L* will wipe away
29: 15 to hide their plans from the *L*,
33: 6 the fear of the *L* is the key
35: 10 the ransomed of the *L* will return.
40: 5 the glory of the *L* will be revealed,
40: 7 the breath of the *L* blows on them.

40: 10 the Sovereign *L* comes with power,
40: 28 The *L* is the everlasting God,
40: 31 but those who hope in the *L*
42: 8 "I am the *L;* that is my name!
43: 11 I, even I, am the *L,*
44: 24 I am the *L,*
45: 5 I am the *L,* and there is no other;
45: 21 Was it not I, the *L?*
51: 11 The ransomed of the *L* will return.
53: 6 and the *L* has laid on him
53: 10 and the will of the *L* will prosper
55: 6 Seek the *L* while he may be found;
58: 8 of the *L* will be your rear guard.
58: 11 The *L* will guide you always;
59: 1 the arm of the *L* is not too short
61: 3 a planting of the *L*
61: 10 I delight greatly in the *L;*
Jer 1: 9 Then the *L* reached out his hand
9: 24 I am the *L,* who exercises kindness,
16: 19 O *L,* my strength and my fortress,
17: 7 is the man who trusts in the *L,*
La 3: 40 and let us return to the *L.*
Eze 1: 28 of the likeness of the glory of the *L.*
Hos 1: 7 horsemen, but by the *L* their God."
3: 5 They will come trembling to the *L*
6: 1 "Come, let us return to the *L.*
Joel 2: 1 for the day of the *L* is coming.
2: 11 The day of the *L* is great;
3: 14 For the day of the *L* is near
Am 5: 18 long for the day of the *L?*
Jnh 1: 3 But Jonah ran away from the *L.*
Mic 4: 2 up to the mountain of the *L,*
6: 8 And what does the *L* require of you
Na 1: 2 The *L* takes vengeance on his foes
1: 3 The *L* is slow to anger
Hab 2: 14 knowledge of the glory of the *L,*
2: 20 But the *L* is in his holy temple;
Zep 3: 17 The *L* your God is with you,
Zec 1: 17 and the *L* will again comfort Zion
9: 16 The *L* their God will save them
14: 5 Then the *L* my God will come,
14: 9 The *L* will be king
Mal 4: 5 and dreadful day of the *L* comes.

LORD'S‡ (LORD‡)

Ex 34: 34 he entered the *L* presence
Nu 14: 41 you disobeying the *L* command?
Dt 6: 18 is right and good in the *L* sight,
32: 9 For the *L* portion is his people,
Jos 21: 45 Not one of all the *L* good promises
Ps 24: 1 The earth is the *L,* and everything
32: 10 but the *L* unfailing love
89: 1 of the *L* great love forever;
103: 17 *L* love is with those who fear him,
Pr 3: 11 do not despise the *L* discipline
Isa 24: 14 west they acclaim the *L* majesty.
62: 3 of splendor in the *L* hand,
Jer 48: 10 lax in doing the *L* work!
La 3: 22 of the *L* great love we are not
Mic 4: 1 of the *L* temple will be established

LOSE (LOSES LOSS LOST)

1Sa 17: 32 "Let no one *l* heart on account
Mt 10: 39 Whoever finds his life will *l* it,
Lk 9: 25 and yet *l* or forfeit his very self?
Jn 6: 39 that I shall *l* none of all that he has
Heb 12: 3 will not grow weary and *l* heart.
12: 5 do not *l* heart when he rebukes you

LOSES (LOSE)

Mt 5: 13 But if the salt *l* its saltiness,
Lk 15: 4 you has a hundred sheep and *l* one
15: 8 has ten silver coins and *l* one.

LOSS (LOSE)

Ro 11: 12 and their *l* means riches
1Co 3: 15 he will suffer *l;* he himself will be
Php 3: 8 I consider everything a *l* compared

LOST (LOSE)

Ps 73: 2 I had nearly *l* my foothold.
Jer 50: 6 "My people have been *l* sheep;
Eze 34: 4 the strays or searched for the *l.*
34: 16 for the *l* and bring back the strays.
Mt 18: 14 any of these little ones should be *l.*
Lk 15: 4 go after the *l* sheep until he finds it?
15: 6 with me; I have found my *l* sheep.'
15: 9 with me; I have found my *l* coin.'
15: 24 is alive again; he was *l* and is found
19: 10 to seek and to save what was *l.*"
Php 3: 8 for whose sake I have *l* all things.

LOT (LOTS)

Nephew of Abraham (Ge 11:27; 12:5). Chose to live in Sodom (Ge 13). Rescued from four kings (Ge 14). Rescued from Sodom (Ge 19:1-29; 2Pe 2:7). Fathered Moab and Ammon by his daughters (Ge 19:30-38).

Est 3: 7 the *l*) in the presence of Haman
9: 24 the *l*) for their ruin and destruction.
Pr 16: 33 The *l* is cast into the lap,
18: 18 Casting the *l* settles disputes
Ecc 3: 22 his work, because that is his *l.*
Ac 1: 26 Then they drew lots, and the *l* fell

LOTS (LOT)

Ps 22: 18 and cast *l* for my clothing.
Mt 27: 35 divided up his clothes by casting *l.*

LOVE (BELOVED LOVED LOVELY LOVER LOVERS LOVES LOVING)

Ge 22: 2 your only son, Isaac, whom you *l,*
Ex 15: 13 "In your unfailing *l* you will lead
20: 6 showing *l* to a thousand generations
20: 6 of those who *l* me
34: 6 abounding in *l* and faithfulness,
Lev 19: 18 but *l* your neighbor as yourself.
19: 34 *L* him as yourself,
Nu 14: 18 abounding in *l* and forgiving sin
Dt 5: 10 showing *l* to a thousand generations
5: 10 of those who *l* me
6: 5 *L* the LORD your God
7: 13 He will *l* you and bless you
10: 12 to walk in all his ways, to *l* him,
11: 13 to *l* the LORD your God
13: 6 wife you *l,* or your closest friend
30: 6 so that you may *l* him
Jos 22: 5 to *l* the LORD your God, to walk
1Ki 3: 3 Solomon showed his *l*
8: 23 you who keep your covenant of *l*
2Ch 5: 13 his *l* endures forever."
Ne 1: 5 covenant of *l* with those who *l* him
Ps 18: 1 I *l* you, O LORD, my strength.
23: 6 Surely goodness and *l* will follow
25: 6 O LORD, your great mercy and *l,*
31: 16 save me in your unfailing *l.*
32: 10 but the LORD's unfailing *l*
33: 5 the earth is full of his unfailing *l.*
33: 18 whose hope is in his unfailing *l,*
36: 5 Your *l,* O LORD, reaches
36: 7 How priceless is your unfailing *l!*
45: 7 You *l* righteousness and hate
51: 1 according to your unfailing *l;*
57: 10 For great is your *l,* reaching
63: 3 Because your *l* is better than life,
66: 20 or withheld his *l* from me!
70: 4 may those who *l* your salvation
77: 8 Has his unfailing *l* vanished forever
85: 7 Show us your unfailing *l,* O LORD
85: 10 *L* and faithfulness meet together;
86: 13 For great is your *l* toward me;
89: 1 of the LORD's great *l* forever;
89: 33 but I will not take my *l* from him,
92: 2 to proclaim your *l* in the morning
94: 18 your *l,* O LORD, supported me.
100: 5 is good and his *l* endures forever;
101: 1 I will sing of your *l* and justice;
103: 4 crowns you with *l* and compassion.
103: 8 slow to anger, abounding in *l.*
103: 11 so great is his *l* for those who fear
107: 8 to the LORD for his unfailing *l*
108: 4 For great is your *l,* higher
116: 1 I *l* the LORD, for he heard my
118: 1 his *l* endures forever.
119: 47 because I *l* them.
119: 64 The earth is filled with your *l,*
119: 76 May your unfailing *l* be my
119: 97 Oh, how I *l* your law!
119:119 therefore I *l* your statutes.
119:124 your servant according to your *l*
119:132 to those who *l* your name.
119:159 O LORD, according to your *l.*
119:163 but I *l* your law.
119:165 peace have they who *l* your law,
122: 6 "May those who *l* you be secure.
130: 7 for with the LORD is unfailing *l*
136: 1 -26 *His l endures forever.*
143: 8 of your unfailing *l,*
145: 8 slow to anger and rich in *l.*
145: 20 over all who *l* him,
147: 11 who put their hope in his unfailing *l*
Pr 3: 3 Let *l* and faithfulness never leave
4: 6 *l* her, and she will watch over you.
5: 19 you ever be captivated by her *l.*
8: 17 I *l* those who *l* me,
9: 8 rebuke a wise man and he will *l* you

10: 12 but *l* covers over all wrongs.
14: 22 those who plan what is good find *l*
15: 17 of vegetables where there is *l*
17: 9 over an offense promotes *l*,
19: 22 What a man desires is unfailing *l*;
20: 6 claims to have unfailing *l*,
20: 13 Do not *l* sleep or you will grow
20: 28 through *l* his throne is made secure
21: 21 who pursues righteousness and *l*
27: 5 rebuke than hidden *l*.
Ecc 9: 6 Their *l*, their hate
9: 9 life with your wife, whom you *l*,
SS 2: 4 and his banner over me is *l*.
8: 6 for *l* is as strong as death,
8: 7 Many waters cannot quench *l*;
8: 7 all the wealth of his house for *l*,
Isa 5: 1 I will sing for the one I *l*
16: 5 In *l* a throne will be established;
38: 17 In your *l* you kept me
54: 10 yet my unfailing *l* for you will not
55: 3 my faithful *l* promised to David.
61: 8 "For I, the LORD, *l* justice;
63: 9 In his *l* and mercy he redeemed
Jer 5: 31 and my people *l* it this way.
31: 3 you with an everlasting *l*;
32: 18 You show *l* to thousands
33: 11 his *l* endures forever."
La 3: 22 of the LORD's great *l* we are not
3: 32 so great is his unfailing *l*.
Eze 33: 32 more than one who sings *l* songs
Da 9: 4 covenant of *l* with all who *l* him
Hos 2: 19 in *l* and compassion.
3: 1 Go, show your *l* to your wife again,
11: 4 with ties of *l*;
12: 6 maintain *l* and justice,
Joel 2: 13 slow to anger and abounding in *l*,
Am 5: 15 Hate evil, *l* good;
Mic 3: 2 you who hate good and *l* evil;
6: 8 To act justly and to *l* mercy
Zep 3: 17 he will quiet you with his *l*,
Zec 8: 19 Therefore *l* truth and peace."
Mt 3: 17 "This is my Son, whom I *l*;
5: 44 *L* your enemies and pray
6: 24 he will hate the one and *l* the other,
17: 5 "This is my Son, whom I *l*;
19: 19 and *l* your neighbor as yourself.' "
22: 37 "'*L* the Lord your God
Lk 6: 32 Even 'sinners' *l* those who *l* them.
7: 42 which of them will *l* him more?"
20: 13 whom I *l*; perhaps they will respect
Jn 13: 34 I give you: *L* one another.
13: 35 disciples, if you *l* one another."
14: 15 "If you *l* me, you will obey what I
15: 13 Greater *l* has no one than this,
15: 17 This is my command: *L* each other.
21: 15 do you truly *l* me more than these
Ro 5: 5 because God has poured out his *l*
5: 8 God demonstrates his own *l* for us
8: 28 for the good of those who *l* him,
8: 35 us from the *l* of Christ?
8: 39 us from the *l* of God that is
12: 9 *L* must be sincere.
12: 10 to one another in brotherly *l*.
13: 8 continuing debt to *l* one another,
13: 9 "*L* your neighbor as yourself."
13: 10 Therefore *l* is the fulfillment
13: 10 *L* does no harm to its neighbor.
1Co 2: 9 prepared for those who *l* him"—
8: 1 Knowledge puffs up, but *l* builds up
13: 1 have not *l*, I am only a resounding
13: 2 but have not *l*, I am nothing.
13: 3 but have not *l*, I gain nothing.
13: 4 Love is patient, *l* is kind.
13: 4 *L* is patient, love is kind.
13: 6 *L* does not delight in evil
13: 8 *L* never fails.
13: 13 But the greatest of these is *l*.
13: 13 three remain: faith, hope and *l*.
14: 1 way of *l* and eagerly desire spiritual
16: 14 Do everything in *l*.
2Co 5: 14 For Christ's *l* compels us,
8: 8 sincerity of your *l* by comparing it
8: 24 show these men the proof of your *l*
Gal 5: 6 is faith expressing itself through *l*.
5: 13 rather, serve one another in *l*.
5: 22 But the fruit of the Spirit is *l*, joy,
Eph 1: 4 In *l* he predestined us
2: 4 But because of his great *l* for us,
3: 17 being rooted and established in *l*,
3: 18 and high and deep is the *l* of Christ,
3: 19 and to know this *l* that surpasses
4: 2 bearing with one another in *l*.
4: 15 Instead, speaking the truth in *l*,
5: 2 loved children and live a life of *l*,
5: 25 *l* your wives, just as Christ loved
5: 28 husbands ought to *l* their wives
5: 33 each one of you also must *l* his wife
Php 1: 9 that your *l* may abound more
2: 2 having the same *l*, being one
Col 1: 5 *l* that spring from the hope that is
2: 2 in heart and united in *l*,
3: 14 And over all these virtues put on *l*,
3: 19 *l* your wives and do not be harsh
1Th 1: 3 your labor prompted by *l*,
4: 9 taught by God to *l* each other.
5: 8 on faith and *l* as a breastplate,
2Th 3: 5 direct your hearts into God's *l*
1Ti 1: 5 The goal of this command is *l*,
2: 15 *l* and holiness with propriety.
4: 12 in life, in *l*, in faith and in purity.
6: 10 For the *l* of money is a root
6: 11 faith, *l*, endurance and gentleness.
2Ti 1: 7 of power, of *l* and of self-discipline.
2: 22 and pursue righteousness, faith, *l*
3: 10 faith, patience, *l*, endurance,
Tit 2: 4 women to *l* their husbands
Phm : 9 yet I appeal to you on the basis of *l*.
Heb 6: 10 and the *l* you have shown him
10: 24 may spur one another on toward *l*
13: 5 free from the *l* of money
Jas 1: 12 promised to those who *l* him.
2: 5 he promised those who *l* him?
2: 8 "*L* your neighbor as yourself,"
1Pe 1: 22 the truth so that you have sincere *l*
1: 22 *l* one another deeply,
2: 17 *L* the brotherhood of believers,
3: 8 be sympathetic, *l* as brothers,
3: 10 "Whoever would *l* life
4: 8 Above all, *l* each other deeply,
4: 8 *l* covers over a multitude of sins.
5: 14 Greet one another with a kiss of *l*.
2Pe 1: 7 and to brotherly kindness, *l*.
1: 17 "This is my Son, whom I *l*;
1Jn 2: 5 God's *l* is truly made complete
2: 15 Do not *l* the world or anything
3: 1 How great is the *l* the Father has
3: 10 anyone who does not *l* his brother.
3: 11 We should *l* one another.
3: 14 Anyone who does not *l* remains
3: 16 This is how we know what *l* is:
3: 18 let us not *l* with words or tongue
3: 23 to *l* one another as he commanded
4: 7 Dear friends, let us *l* one another,
4: 7 for *l* comes from God.
4: 8 Whoever does not *l* does not know
4: 9 This is how God showed his *l*
4: 10 This is *l*: not that we loved God,
4: 11 we also ought to *l* one another.
4: 12 and his *l* is made complete in us.
4: 16 God is *l*.
4: 16 Whoever lives in *l* lives in God,
4: 17 *l* is made complete among us
4: 18 But perfect *l* drives out fear,
4: 19 We *l* because he first loved us.
4: 20 If anyone says, "I *l* God,"
4: 21 loves God must also *l* his brother.
5: 2 we know that we *l* the children
5: 3 This is *l* for God: to obey his
2Jn : 5 I ask that we *l* one another.
: 6 his command is that you walk in *l*.
: 6 this is *l*: that we walk in obedience
Jude : 12 men are blemishes at your *l* feasts,
: 21 Keep yourselves in God's *l*
Rev 2: 4 You have forsaken your first *l*.
3: 19 Those whom I *l* I rebuke
12: 11 they did not *l* their lives so much

LOVED (LOVE)

Ge 24: 67 she became his wife, and he *l* her;
29: 30 and he *l* Rachel more than Leah.
37: 3 Now Israel *l* Joseph more than any
Dt 7: 8 But it was because the LORD *l* you
1Sa 1: 5 a double portion because he *l* her,
20: 17 because he *l* him as he *l* himself.
Ps 44: 3 light of your face, for you *l* them.
Jer 2: 2 how as a bride you *l* me
31: 3 "I have *l* you with an everlasting

os 2: 23 to the one I called 'Not my *l* one.'
3: 1 though she is *l* by another
9: 10 became as vile as the thing they *l*.
11: 1 "When Israel was a child, I *l* him,
al 1: 2 "But you ask, 'How have you *l* us?'
k 12: 6 left to send, a son, whom he *l*.
3: 16 so *l* the world that he gave his one
3: 19 but men *l* darkness instead of light
11: 5 Jesus *l* Martha and her sister
12: 43 for they *l* praise from men more
13: 1 Having *l* his own who were
13: 23 the disciple whom Jesus *l*,
13: 34 As I have *l* you, so you must love
14: 21 He who loves me will be *l*
15: 9 the Father has *l* me, so have I *l* you.
15: 12 Love each other as I have *l* you.
19: 26 the disciple whom he *l* standing
o 8: 37 conquerors through him who *l* us.
9: 13 "Jacob I *l*, but Esau I hated."
9: 25 her my '*l* one' who is not my *l* one,"
11: 28 they are *l* on account
al 2: 20 who *l* me and gave himself for me.
ph 5: 2 as Christ *l* us and gave himself up
5: 25 just as Christ *l* the church
Th 2: 16 who *l* us and by his grace gave us
Ti 4: 10 for Demas, because he *l* this world,
eb 1: 9 You have *l* righteousness
Jn 4: 10 This is love: not that we *l* God,
4: 11 Dear friends, since God so *l* us,
Jn 4: 19 We love because he first *l* us.

OVELY (LOVE)
s 84: 1 How *l* is your dwelling place,
S 2: 14 and your face is *l*.
5: 16 he is altogether *l*.
hp 4: 8 whatever is *l*, whatever is

OVER (LOVE)
S 2: 16 *Beloved* My *l* is mine and I am his;
7: 10 I belong to my *l*,
Ti 3: 3 not quarrelsome, not a *l* of money.

LOVERS (LOVE)
Ti 3: 2 People will be *l* of themselves,
3: 3 without self-control, brutal, not *l*
3: 4 *l* of pleasure rather than *l* of God—

LOVES (LOVE)
Ps 11: 7 he *l* justice;
33: 5 The LORD *l* righteousness
34: 12 Whoever of you *l* life
91: 14 Because he *l* me," says the LORD,
127: 2 for he grants sleep to those he *l*.
Pr 3: 12 the LORD disciplines those he *l*,
12: 1 Whoever *l* discipline *l* knowledge,
13: 24 he who *l* him is careful
17: 17 A friend *l* at all times,
17: 19 He who *l* a quarrel *l* sin;
22: 11 He who *l* a pure heart and whose
Ecc 5: 10 whoever *l* wealth is never satisfied
Mt 10: 37 anyone who *l* his son or daughter
Lk 7: 47 has been forgiven little *l* little."
Jn 3: 35 Father *l* the Son and has placed
10: 17 reason my Father *l* me is that I lay
12: 25 The man who *l* his life will lose it,
14: 21 obeys them, he is the one who *l* me.
14: 23 Jesus replied, "If anyone *l* me,
Ro 13: 8 for he who *l* his fellowman has
2Co 9: 7 for God *l* a cheerful giver.
Eph 5: 28 He who *l* his wife *l* himself.
5: 33 must love his wife as he *l* himself,
Heb 12: 6 the Lord disciplines those he *l*,
1Jn 2: 10 Whoever *l* his brother lives
2: 15 If anyone *l* the world, the love
4: 7 Everyone who *l* has been born
4: 21 Whoever *l* God must also love his
5: 1 who *l* the father *l* his child
3Jn : 9 but Diotrephes, who *l* to be first,
Rev 1: 5 To him who *l* us and has freed us

LOVING (LOVE)
Ps 25: 10 All the ways of the LORD are *l*
62: 12 and that you, O Lord, are *l*.
145: 17 and *l* toward all he has made.
Heb 13: 1 Keep on *l* each other as brothers.
1Jn 5: 2 by *l* God and carrying out his

LOWLY
Job 5: 11 The *l* he sets on high,
Pr 29: 23 but a man of *l* spirit gains honor.
Isa 57: 15 also with him who is contrite and *l*
Eze 21: 26 *l* will be exalted and the exalted

1Co 1: 28 He chose the *l* things of this world

LUKE*
Co-worker with Paul (Col 4:14; 2Ti 4:11; Phm 24).

LUKEWARM*
Rev 3: 16 So, because you are *l*—neither hot

LUST
Pr 6: 25 Do not *l* in your heart
Col 3: 5 sexual immorality, impurity, *l*,
1Th 4: 5 not in passionate *l* like the heathen,
1Jn 2: 16 the *l* of his eyes and the boasting

LYING (LIE)
Pr 6: 17 a *l* tongue,
26: 28 A *l* tongue hates those it hurts,

M

MACEDONIA
Ac 16: 9 "Come over to *M* and help us."

MADE (MAKE)
Ge 1: 16 He also *m* the stars.
1: 25 God *m* the wild animals according
2: 22 Then the LORD God *m* a woman
2Ki 19: 15 You have *m* heaven and earth.
Ps 95: 5 The sea is his, for he *m* it,
100: 3 It is he who *m* us, and we are his;
118: 24 This is the day the LORD has *m*;
139: 14 I am fearfully and wonderfully *m*;
Ecc 3: 11 He has *m* everything beautiful
Mk 2: 27 "The Sabbath was *m* for man,
Jn 1: 3 Through him all things were *m*;
Ac 17: 24 "The God who *m* the world
Heb 1: 2 through whom he *m* the universe.
Rev 14: 7 Worship him who *m* the heavens,

MAGI
Mt 2: 1 *M* from the east came to Jerusalem

MAGOG
Eze 38: 2 of the land of *M*, the chief prince
39: 6 I will send fire on *M*
Rev 20: 8 and *M*—to gather them for battle.

MAIDEN
Pr 30: 19 and the way of a man with a *m*.
Isa 62: 5 As a young man marries a *m*,
Jer 2: 32 Does a *m* forget her jewelry,

MAIMED
Mt 18: 8 It is better for you to enter life *m*

MAJESTIC (MAJESTY)
Ex 15: 6 was *m* in power.
15: 11 *m* in holiness,
Ps 8: 1 how *m* is your name in all the earth
29: 4 the voice of the LORD is *m*.
111: 3 Glorious and *m* are his deeds,
SS 6: 10 *m* as the stars in procession?
2Pe 1: 17 came to him from the *M* Glory,

MAJESTY (MAJESTIC)
Ex 15: 7 In the greatness of your *m*
Dt 33: 26 and on the clouds in his *m*.
1Ch 16: 27 Splendor and *m* are before him;
Est 1: 4 the splendor and glory of his *m*.
Job 37: 22 God comes in awesome *m*.
40: 10 and clothe yourself in honor and *m*
Ps 45: 4 In your *m* ride forth victoriously
93: 1 The LORD reigns, he is robed in *m*
110: 3 Arrayed in holy *m*,
145: 5 of the glorious splendor of your *m*,
Isa 53: 2 or *m* to attract us to him,
Eze 31: 2 can be compared with you in *m*?
2Pe 1: 16 but we were eyewitnesses of his *m*.
Jude : 25 only God our Savior be glory, *m*,

MAKE (MADE MAKER MAKES MAKING)
Ge 1: 26 "Let us *m* man in our image,
2: 18 I will *m* a helper suitable for him."
12: 2 "I will *m* you into a great nation
Ex 22: 3 thief must certainly *m* restitution,
Nu 6: 25 the LORD *m* his face shine
Ps 108: 1 *m* music with all my soul.
Isa 14: 14 I will *m* myself like the Most High
29: 16 "He did not *m* me"?
Jer 31: 31 "when I will *m* a new covenant
Mt 3: 3 *m* straight paths for him.' "
28: 19 and *m* disciples of all nations,
Mk 1: 17 "and I will *m* you fishers of men."
Lk 13: 24 "*M* every effort to enter
14: 23 country lanes and *m* them come in,
Ro 14: 19 *m* every effort to do what leads
2Co 5: 9 So we *m* it our goal to please him,
Eph 4: 3 *M* every effort to keep the unity

Col 4: 5 *m* the most of every opportunity.
1Th 4: 11 *M* it your ambition
Heb 4: 11 *m* every effort to enter that rest,
12: 14 *M* every effort to live in peace
2Pe 1: 5 *m* every effort to add
3: 14 *m* every effort to be found spotless,

MAKER (MAKE)

Job 4: 17 Can a man be more pure than his *M*
36: 3 I will ascribe justice to my *M.*
Ps 95: 6 kneel before the LORD our *M;*
Pr 22: 2 The LORD is the *M* of them all.
Isa 45: 9 to him who quarrels with his *M,*
54: 5 For your *M* is your husband—
Jer 10: 16 for he is the *M* of all things,

MAKES (MAKE)

1Co 3: 7 but only God, who *m* things grow.

MAKING (MAKE)

Ps 19: 7 *m* wise the simple.
Ecc 12: 12 Of *m* many books there is no end,
Jn 5: 18 *m* himself equal with God.
Eph 5: 16 *m* the most of every opportunity,

MALE

Ge 1: 27 *m* and female he created them.
Gal 3: 28 slave nor free, *m* nor female,

MALICE (MALICIOUS)

Ro 1: 29 murder, strife, deceit and *m.*
Col 3: 8 *m,* slander, and filthy language
1Pe 2: 1 rid yourselves of all *m*

MALICIOUS (MALICE)

Pr 26: 24 A *m* man disguises himself
1Ti 3: 11 not *m* talkers but temperate
6: 4 *m* talk, evil suspicions

MAN (MEN WOMAN WOMEN)

Ge 1: 26 "Let us make *m* in our image,
2: 7 God formed the *m* from the dust
2: 18 for the *m* to be alone
2: 23 she was taken out of *m.*
9: 6 Whoever sheds the blood of *m,*
Dt 8: 3 *m* does not live on bread
1Sa 13: 14 a *m* after his own heart
15: 29 he is not a *m* that he
Job 14: 1 *M* born of woman is of few
14: 14 If a *m* dies, will he live
Ps 1: 1 Blessed is the *m* who does
8: 4 what is *m* that you are
119: 9 can a young *m* keep his
127: 5 Blessed is the *m* whose quiver
Pr 14: 12 that seems right to a *m,*
30: 19 way of a *m* with a maiden.
Isa 53: 3 a *m* of sorrows,
Mt 19: 5 a *m* will leave his father
Mk 8: 36 What good is it for a *m*
Lk 4: 4 '*M* does not live on bread
Ro 5: 12 entered the world through one *m*
1Co 7: 2 each *m* should have his own
11: 3 head of every *m* is Christ,
11: 3 head of woman is *m*
13: 11 When I became a *m,*
Php 2: 8 found in appearance as a *m,*
1Ti 2: 5 the *m* Christ Jesus,
2: 11 have authority over a *m;*
Heb 9: 27 as *m* is destined to die

MANAGE

Jer 12: 5 how will you *m* in the thickets
1Ti 3: 4 He must *m* his own family well
3: 12 one wife and must *m* his children
5: 14 to *m* their homes and to give

MANASSEH

1. Firstborn of Joseph (Ge 41:51; 46:20). Blessed (Ge 48).

2. Son of Hezekiah; king of Judah (2Ki 21:1-18; 2Ch 33:1-20).

MANGER

Lk 2: 12 in strips of cloth and lying in a *m.*"

MANNA

Ex 16: 31 people of Israel called the bread *m.*
Dt 8: 16 He gave you *m* to eat in the desert,
Jn 6: 49 Your forefathers ate the *m*
Rev 2: 17 I will give some of the hidden *m.*

MANNER

1Co 11: 27 in an unworthy *m* will be guilty
Php 1: 27 conduct yourselves in a *m* worthy

MARITAL* (MARRY)

Ex 21: 10 of her food, clothing and *m* rights.
Mt 5: 32 except for *m* unfaithfulness,
19: 9 except for *m* unfaithfulness,
1Co 7: 3 husband should fulfill his *m* duty

MARK (MARKS)

Cousin of Barnabas (Col 4:10; 2Ti 4:11; Phm 24; 1Pe 5:13), see JOHN.

Ge 4: 15 Then the LORD put a *m* on Cain
Rev 13: 16 to receive a *m* on his right hand

MARKS (MARK)

Jn 20: 25 Unless I see the nail *m* in his hands
Gal 6: 17 bear on my body the *m* of Jesus.

MARRED

Isa 52: 14 his form *m* beyond human likeness

MARRIAGE (MARRY)

Mt 22: 30 neither marry nor be given in *m;*
24: 38 marrying and giving in *m,*
Ro 7: 2 she is released from the law of *m.*
Heb 13: 4 by all, and the *m* bed kept pure,

MARRIED (MARRY)

Ro 7: 2 by law a *m* woman is bound
1Co 7: 27 Are you *m?* Do not seek a divorce.
7: 33 But a *m* man is concerned about
7: 36 They should get *m.*

MARRIES (MARRY)

Mt 5: 32 and anyone who *m* the divorced
19: 9 and *m* another woman commits
Lk 16: 18 the man who *m* a divorced woman

MARRY (INTERMARRY MARITAL MARRIAGE MARRIED MARRIES)

Mt 22: 30 resurrection people will neither *m*
1Co 7: 1 It is good for a man not to *m.*
7: 9 control themselves, they should *m,*
1Ti 5: 14 So I counsel younger widows to *m,*

MARTHA*

Sister of Mary and Lazarus (Lk 10:38-42; Jn 11; 12:2).

MARVELED

Lk 2: 33 mother *m* at what was said about

MARY

1. Mother of Jesus (Mt 1:16-25; Lk 1:27-56; 2:1-40). With Jesus at temple (Lk 2:41-52), at the wedding in Cana (Jn 2:1-5), questioning his sanity (Mk 3:21), at the cross (Jn 19:25-27). Among disciples after Ascension (Ac 1:14).

2. Magdalene; former demoniac (Lk 8:2). Helped support Jesus' ministry (Lk 8:1-3). At the cross (Mt 27:56; Mk 15:40; Jn 19:25), burial (Mt 27:61; Mk 15:47). Saw angel after resurrection (Mt 28:1-10; Mk 16:1-9; Lk 24:1-12); also Jesus (Jn 20:1-18).

3. Sister of Martha and Lazarus (Jn 11). Washed Jesus' feet (Jn 12:1-8).

MASQUERADES*

2Co 11: 14 for Satan himself *m* as an angel

MASTER (MASTERED MASTERS)

Mt 10: 24 nor a servant above his *m.*
23: 8 for you have only one *M*
24: 46 that servant whose *m* finds him
25: 21 "His *m* replied, 'Well done,
Ro 6: 14 For sin shall not be your *m,*
14: 4 To his own *m* he stands or falls.
2Ti 2: 21 useful to the *M* and prepare

MASTERED* (MASTER)

1Co 6: 12 but I will not be *m* by any thing.
2Pe 2: 19 a slave to whatever has *m* him.

MASTERS (MASTER)

Mt 6: 24 "No one can serve two *m.*
Eph 6: 5 obey your earthly *m* with respect
6: 9 And *m,* treat your slaves
Tit 2: 9 subject to their *m* in everything,

MATTHEW*

Apostle; former tax collector (Mt 9:9-13; 10:3; Mk 3:18; Lk 6:15; Ac 1:13). Also called Levi (Mk 2:14-17; Lk 5:27-32).

MATURE (MATURITY)

Eph 4: 13 of the Son of God and become *m,*
Php 3: 15 of us who are *m* should take such
Heb 5: 14 But solid food is for the *m,*
Jas 1: 4 work so that you may be *m*

MATURITY* (MATURE)

Heb 6: 1 about Christ and go on to *m*

MEAL

Pr 15: 17 Better a *m* of vegetables where
1Co 10: 27 some unbeliever invites you to a *m*
Heb 12: 16 for a single *m* sold his inheritance

MEANING

Ne 8: 8 and giving the *m* so that the people

MEANS

1Co 9: 22 by all possible *m* I might save some

MEAT

Ro 14: 6 He who eats *m,* eats to the Lord,
14: 21 It is better not to eat *m*

MEDIATOR

1Ti 2: 5 and one *m* between God and men,
Heb 8: 6 of which he is *m* is superior
9: 15 For this reason Christ is the *m*
12: 24 to Jesus the *m* of a new covenant,

MEDICINE*

Pr 17: 22 A cheerful heart is good *m,*

MEDITATE (MEDITATES MEDITATION)

Jos 1: 8 from your mouth; *m* on it day
Ps 119: 15 I *m* on your precepts
119: 78 but I will *m* on your precepts.
119: 97 I *m* on it all day long.

145: 5 I will *m* on your wonderful works.

EDITATES* (MEDITATE)
1: 2 and on his law he *m* day and night.

EDITATION* (MEDITATE)
19: 14 of my mouth and the *m* of my heart
104: 34 May my *m* be pleasing to him,

EDIUM
ev 20: 27 "'A man or woman who is a *m*

EEK (MEEKNESS)
37: 11 But the *m* will inherit the land
It 5: 5 Blessed are the *m*,

EEKNESS* (MEEK)
Co 10: 1 By the *m* and gentleness of Christ,

EET (MEETING)
s 85: 10 Love and faithfulness *m* together;
m 4: 12 prepare to *m* your God, O Israel."
Th 4: 17 them in the clouds to *m* the Lord

EETING (MEET)
Ieb 10: 25 Let us not give up *m* together,

ELCHIZEDEK
ie 14: 18 *M* king of Salem brought out bread
's 110: 4 in the order of *M*."
Ieb 7: 11 in the order of *M*, not in the order

ELT
Pe 3: 12 and the elements will *m* in the heat.

MEMBERS
Mic 7: 6 a man's enemies are the *m*
Ro 7: 23 law at work in the *m* of my body,
12: 4 of us has one body with many *m*,
Co 6: 15 not know that your bodies are *m*
12: 24 But God has combined the *m*
Eph 4: 25 for we are all *m* of one body.
Col 3: 15 as *m* of one body you were called

MEN (MAN)
Mt 4: 19 will make you fishers of *m*
5: 16 your light shine before *m*
12: 36 *m* will have to give account
In 12: 32 will draw all *m* to myself
Ac 5: 29 obey God rather than *m*!
Ro 1: 27 indecent acts with other *m*,
5: 12 death came to all *m*,
1Co 9: 22 all things to all *m*
2Co 5: 11 we try to persuade *m*.
1Ti 2: 4 wants all *m* to be saved
2Ti 2: 2 entrust to reliable *m*
2Pe 1: 21 but *m* spoke from God

MENAHEM
King of Israel (2Ki 15:17-22).

MERCIFUL (MERCY)
Dt 4: 31 the LORD your God is a *m* God;
Ne 9: 31 for you are a gracious and *m* God.
Mt 5: 7 Blessed are the *m*,
Lk 6: 36 Be *m*, just as your Father is *m*.
Heb 2: 17 in order that he might become a *m*
Jude : 22 Be *m* to those who doubt; snatch

MERCY (MERCIFUL)
Ex 33: 19 *m* on whom I will have *m*,
Ps 25: 6 O LORD, your great *m* and love,
Isa 63: 9 and *m* he redeemed them;
Hos 6: 6 For I desire *m*, not sacrifice,
Mic 6: 8 To act justly and to love *m*
Hab 3: 2 in wrath remember *m*.
Mt 12: 7 I desire *m*, not sacrifice,'
you
23: 23 justice, *m* and faithfulness.
Ro 9: 15 "I will have *m* on whom I have *m*,
Eph 2: 4 who is rich in *m*, made us alive
Jas 2: 13 *M* triumphs over judgment!
1Pe 1: 3 In his great *m* he has given us new

MESSAGE
Isa 53: 1 Who has believed our *m*
Jn 12: 38 "Lord, who has believed our *m*
Ro 10: 17 faith comes from hearing the *m*,
1Co 1: 18 For the *m* of the cross is
2Co 5: 19 to us the *m* of reconciliation.

MESSIAH*
Jn 1: 41 "We have found the *M*" (that is,
4: 25 "I know that *M*" (called Christ) "is

METHUSELAH
Ge 5: 27 Altogether, *M* lived 969 years,

MICHAEL
Archangel (Jude 9); warrior in angelic realm, protector of Israel (Da 10:13, 21; 12:1; Rev 12:7).

MIDWIVES
Ex 1: 17 The *m*, however, feared God

MIGHT (ALMIGHTY MIGHTY)
Jdg 16: 30 Then he pushed with all his *m*,
2Sa 6: 14 before the LORD with all his *m*,
Ps 21: 13 we will sing and praise your *m*.
Zec 4: 6 'Not by *m* nor by power,
1Ti 6: 16 To him be honor and *m* forever.

MIGHTY (MIGHT)
Ex 6: 1 of my *m* hand he will drive them
Dt 7: 8 he brought you out with a *m* hand
2Sa 1: 19 How the *m* have fallen!
23: 8 the names of David's *m* men:
Ps 24: 8 The LORD strong and *m*,
50: 1 The *M* One, God, the LORD,
89: 8 You are *m*, O LORD,
136: 12 with a *m* hand and outstretched
147: 5 Great is our Lord and *m* in power;
Isa 9: 6 Wonderful Counselor, *M* God,
Zep 3: 17 he is *m* to save.
Eph 6: 10 in the Lord and in his *m* power.

MILE*
Mt 5: 41 If someone forces you to go one *m*,

MILK
Ex 3: 8 a land flowing with *m* and honey—
Isa 55: 1 Come, buy wine and *m*
1Co 3: 2 I gave you *m*, not solid food,
Heb 5: 12 You need *m*, not solid food!
1Pe 2: 2 babies, crave pure spiritual *m*,

MILLSTONE (STONE)
Lk 17: 2 sea with a *m* tied around his neck

MIND (DOUBLE-MINDED MINDFUL MINDS)
1Sa 15: 29 Israel does not lie or change his *m*;
1Ch 28: 9 devotion and with a willing *m*,
Ps 26: 2 examine my heart and my *m*;
Isa 26: 3 him whose *m* is steadfast,
Mt 22: 37 all your soul and with all your *m*.'
Ac 4: 32 believers were one in heart and *m*.
Ro 7: 25 I myself in my *m* am a slave
8: 7 the sinful *m* is hostile to God.
12: 2 by the renewing of your *m*.
1Co 2: 9 no *m* has conceived
14: 14 spirit prays, but my *m* is unfruitful.
2Co 13: 11 be of one *m*, live in peace.
Php 3: 19 Their *m* is on earthly things.
1Th 4: 11 to *m* your own business
Heb 7: 21 and will not change his *m*:

MINDFUL* (MIND)
Ps 8: 4 what is man that you are *m* of him,
Lk 1: 48 God my Savior, for he has been *m*
Heb 2: 6 What is man that you are *m* of him,

MINDS (MIND)
Ps 7: 9 who searches *m* and hearts,
Jer 31: 33 "I will put my law in their *m*
Eph 4: 23 new in the attitude of your *m*;
Col 3: 2 Set your *m* on things above,
Heb 8: 10 I will put my laws in their *m*
Rev 2: 23 I am he who searches hearts and *m*,

MINISTERING (MINISTRY)
Heb 1: 14 Are not all angels *m* spirits sent

MINISTRY (MINISTERING)
Ac 6: 4 to prayer and the *m* of the word."
2Co 5: 18 gave us the *m* of reconciliation:
2Ti 4: 5 discharge all the duties of your *m*.

MIRACLES (MIRACULOUS)
1Ch 16: 12 his *m*, and the judgments he
Ps 77: 14 You are the God who performs *m*;
Mt 11: 20 most of his *m* had been performed,
11: 21 If the *m* that were performed
24: 24 and perform great signs and *m*
Mk 6: 2 does *m*! Isn't this the carpenter?
Jn 10: 32 "I have shown you many great *m*
14: 11 the evidence of the *m* themselves.
Ac 2: 22 accredited by God to you by *m*,
19: 11 God did extraordinary *m*
1Co 12: 28 third teachers, then workers of *m*,
Heb 2: 4 it by signs, wonders and various *m*,

MIRACULOUS (MIRACLES)
Jn 3: 2 could perform the *m* signs you are
9: 16 "How can a sinner do such *m* signs
20: 30 Jesus did many other *m* signs
1Co 1: 22 Jews demand *m* signs and Greeks

MIRE
Ps 40: 2 out of the mud and *m*;
Isa 57: 20 whose waves cast up *m* and mud.

MIRIAM
Sister of Moses and Aaron (Nu 26:59). Led dancing at Red Sea (Ex 15:20-21). Struck with leprosy for criticizing Moses (Nu 12). Death (Nu 20:1).

MIRROR
Jas 1: 23 a man who looks at his face in a *m*

MISERY
Ex 3: 7 "I have indeed seen the *m*
Jdg 10: 16 he could bear Israel's *m* no longer.
Hos 5: 15 in their *m* they will earnestly seek
Ro 3: 16 ruin and *m* mark their ways,

Jas 5: 1 of the *m* that is coming upon you.

MISLED

1Co 15: 33 Do not be *m*: "Bad company

MISS

Pr 19: 2 nor to be hasty and *m* the way.

MIST

Hos 6: 4 Your love is like the morning *m*,
Jas 4: 14 You are a *m* that appears for a little

MISUSE*

Ex 20: 7 "You shall not *m* the name
Dt 5: 11 "You shall not *m* the name
Ps 139: 20 your adversaries *m* your name.

MOCK (MOCKED MOCKER MOCKERS MOCKING)

Ps 22: 7 All who see me *m* me;
Pr 14: 9 Fools *m* at making amends for sin,
Mk 10: 34 who will *m* him and spit on him,

MOCKED (MOCK)

Mt 27: 29 knelt in front of him and *m* him.
27: 41 of the law and the elders *m* him.
Gal 6: 7 not be deceived: God cannot be *m*.

MOCKER (MOCK)

Pr 9: 7 corrects a *m* invites insult;
9: 12 if you are a *m*, you alone will suffer
20: 1 Wine is a *m* and beer a brawler;
22: 10 Drive out the *m*, and out goes strife

MOCKERS (MOCK)

Ps 1: 1 or sit in the seat of *m*.

MOCKING (MOCK)

Isa 50: 6 face from *m* and spitting.

MODEL*

Eze 28: 12 "'You were the *m* of perfection,
1Th 1: 7 And so you became a *m*
2Th 3: 9 to make ourselves a *m* for you

MOMENT

Job 20: 5 the joy of the godless lasts but a *m*.
Ps 30: 5 For his anger lasts only a *m*,
Isa 66: 8 or a nation be brought forth in a *m*?
Gal 2: 5 We did not give in to them for a *m*,

MONEY

Ecc 5: 10 Whoever loves *m* never has *m*
Isa 55: 1 and you who have no *m*,
Mt 6: 24 You cannot serve both God and *M*.
Lk 9: 3 no bread, no *m*, no extra tunic.
1Co 16: 2 set aside a sum of *m* in keeping
1Ti 3: 3 not quarrelsome, not a lover of *m*.
6: 10 For the love of *m* is a root
2Ti 3: 2 lovers of *m*, boastful, proud,
Heb 13: 5 free from the love of *m*
1Pe 5: 2 not greedy for *m*, but eager to serve

MOON

Ps 121: 6 nor the *m* by night.
Joel 2: 31 and the *m* to blood
1Co 15: 41 *m* another and the stars another;

MORNING

Ge 1: 5 and there was *m*—the first day.
Dt 28: 67 In the *m* you will say, "If only it
Ps 5: 3 In the *m*, O LORD,
2Pe 1: 19 and the *m* star rises in your hearts.
Rev 22: 16 of David, and the bright *M* Star."

MORTAL

1Co 15: 53 and the *m* with immortality.

MOSES

Levite; brother of Aaron (Ex 6:20; 1Ch 6:3). Put in basket into Nile; discovered and raised by Pharaoh's daughter (Ex 2:1-10). Fled to Midian after killing Egyptian (Ex 2:11-15). Married to Zipporah, fathered Gershom (Ex 2:16-22).

Called by the LORD to deliver Israel (Ex 3-4). Pharaoh's resistance (Ex 5). Ten plagues (Ex 7-11). Passover and Exodus (Ex 12-13). Led Israel through Red Sea (Ex 14). Song of deliverance (Ex 15:1-21). Brought water from rock (Ex 17:1-7). Raised hands to defeat Amalekites (Ex 17:8-16). Delegated judges (Ex 18; Dt 1:9-18).

Received Law at Sinai (Ex 19-23; 25-31; Jn 1:17). Announced Law to Israel (Ex 19:7-8; 24; 35). Broke tablets because of golden calf (Ex 32; Dt 9). Saw glory of the LORD (Ex 33-34). Supervised building of tabernacle (Ex 36-40). Set apart Aaron and priests (Lev 8-9). Numbered tribes (Nu 1-4; 26). Opposed by Aaron and Miriam (Nu 12). Sent spies into Canaan (Nu 13). Announced forty years of wandering for failure to enter land (Nu 14). Opposed by Korah (Nu 16). Forbidden to enter land for striking rock (Nu 20:1-13; Dt 1:37). Lifted bronze snake for healing (Nu 21:4-9; Jn 3:14). Final address to Israel (Dt 1-33). Succeeded by Joshua (Nu 27:12-23; Dt 34). Death (Dt 34:5-12).

"Law of Moses" (1Ki 2:3; Ezr 3:2; Mk 12:26; Lk 24:44). "Book of Moses" (2Ch 25:12; Ne 13:1). "Song of Moses" (Ex 15:1-21; Rev 15:3). "Prayer of Moses" (Ps 90).

MOTH

Mt 6: 19 where *m* and rust destroy,

MOTHER (MOTHER'S)

Ge 2: 24 and *m* and be united to his wife,
3: 20 because she would become the *m*
Ex 20: 12 "Honor your father and your *m*,
Lev 20: 9 "'If anyone curses his father or *m*,
Dt 5: 16 "Honor your father and your *m*,
21: 18 who does not obey his father and *m*
27: 16 who dishonors his father or his *m*."
1Sa 2: 19 Each year his *m* made him a little
Ps 113: 9 as a happy *m* of children.
Pr 23: 25 May your father and *m* be glad;
29: 15 child left to himself disgraces his *m*.
31: 1 an oracle his *m* taught him:
Isa 49: 15 "Can a *m* forget the baby
66: 13 As a *m* comforts her child,
Mt 10: 37 or *m* more than me is not worthy
15: 4 'Honor your father and *m*'
19: 5 and *m* and be united to his wife,
Mk 7: 10 'Honor your father and your *m*,'
10: 19 honor your father and *m*.'"
Jn 19: 27 to the disciple, "Here is your *m*."

MOTHER'S (MOTHER)

Job 1: 21 "Naked I came from my *m* womb,
Pr 1: 8 and do not forsake your *m* teaching

MOTIVES*

Pr 16: 2 but *m* are weighed by the LORD.
1Co 4: 5 will expose the *m* of men's hearts.
Php 1: 18 whether from false *m* or true,
1Th 2: 3 spring from error or impure *m*,
Jas 4: 3 because you ask with wrong *m*,

MOUNTAIN (MOUNTAINS)

Mic 4: 2 let us go up to the *m* of the LORD,
Mt 17: 20 say to this *m*, 'Move from here

MOUNTAINS (MOUNTAIN)

Isa 52: 7 How beautiful on the *m*
55: 12 the *m* and hills
1Co 13: 2 if I have a faith that can move *m*,

MOURN (MOURNING)

Ecc 3: 4 a time to *m* and a time to dance,
Isa 61: 2 to comfort all who *m*,
Mt 5: 4 Blessed are those who *m*,
Ro 12: 15 *m* with those who *m*.

MOURNING (MOURN)

Jer 31: 13 I will turn their *m* into gladness;
Rev 21: 4 There will be no more deat[h] or *m*

MOUTH

Jos 1: 8 of the Law depart from your *m*;
Ps 19: 14 May the words of my *m*
40: 3 He put a new song in my *m*
119:103 sweeter than honey to my *m*
Pr 16: 23 A wise man's heart guides his *m*,
27: 2 praise you, and not your own *m*;
Isa 51: 16 I have put my words in your *m*
Mt 12: 34 overflow of the heart the *m* speaks.
15: 11 into a man's *m* does not make him
Ro 10: 9 That if you confess with your *m*,

MUD

Ps 40: 2 out of the *m* and mire;
Isa 57: 20 whose waves cast up mire and *m*.
2Pe 2: 22 back to her wallowing in the *m*."

MULTITUDE (MULTITUDES)

Isa 31: 1 who trust in the *m* of their chariots
1Pe 4: 8 love covers over a *m* of sins.
Rev 7: 9 me was a great *m* that no one could

MULTITUDES (MULTITUDE)

Joel 3: 14 *M*, *m* in the valley of decision!

MURDER (MURDERER MURDERERS)

Ex 20: 13 "You shall not *m*.
Mt 15: 19 *m*, adultery, sexual immorality,
Ro 13: 9 "Do not *m*," "Do not steal,"
Jas 2: 11 adultery," also said, "Do not *m*."

MURDERER (MURDER)

Nu 35: 16 he is a *m*; the *m* shall be put
Jn 8: 44 He was a *m* from the beginning,
1Jn 3: 15 who hates his brother is a *m*,

MURDERERS (MURDER)

1Ti 1: 9 for *m*, for adulterers and perverts,
Rev 21: 8 the *m*, the sexually immoral,

MUSIC

Jdg 5: 3 I will make *m* to the LORD,
Ps 27: 6 and make *m* to the LORD.

95: 2 and extol him with *m* and song.
98: 4 burst into jubilant song with *m;*
108: 1 make *m* with all my soul.
h 5: 19 make *m* in your heart to the Lord,

USTARD

t 13: 31 kingdom of heaven is like a *m* seed,
17: 20 you have faith as small as a *m* seed,

UZZLE

t 25: 4 Do not *m* an ox while it is treading
s 39: 1 I will put a *m* on my mouth
Co 9: 9 "Do not *m* an ox while it is

YRRH

t 2: 11 of gold and of incense and of *m*.
k 15: 23 offered him wine mixed with *m,*

YSTERY

o 16: 25 to the revelation of the *m* hidden
Co 15: 51 I tell you a *m*: We will not all sleep,
ph 5: 32 This is a profound *m*—
ol 1: 26 the *m* that has been kept hidden
Ti 3: 16 the *m* of godliness is great:

YTHS

Ti 4: 7 Have nothing to do with godless *m*

N

NADAB

Son of Jeroboam I; king of Israel (1Ki 15:25-32).

NAIL* (NAILING)

n 20: 25 "Unless I see the *n* marks

NAILING* (NAIL)

Ac 2: 23 him to death by *n* him to the cross.
Col 2: 14 he took it away, *n* it to the cross.

NAKED

Ge 2: 25 The man and his wife were both *n,*
Job 1: 21 *N* I came from my mother's womb,
Isa 58: 7 when you see the *n,* to clothe him,
2Co 5: 3 are clothed, we will not be found *n.*

NAME

Ex 3: 15 This is my *n* forever, the *n*
20: 7 "You shall not misuse the *n*
Dt 5: 11 "You shall not misuse the *n*
28: 58 this glorious and awesome *n*—
1Ki 5: 5 will build the temple for my *N.'*
2Ch 7: 14 my people, who are called by my *n,*
Ps 34: 3 let us exalt his *n* together.
103: 1 my inmost being, praise his holy *n.*
147: 4 and calls them each by *n.*
Pr 22: 1 A good *n* is more desirable
30: 4 What is his *n,* and the *n* of his son?
Isa 40: 26 and calls them each by *n.*
57: 15 who lives forever, whose *n* is holy:
Jer 14: 7 do something for the sake of your *n*
Da 12: 1 everyone whose *n* is found written
Joel 2: 32 on the *n* of the LORD will be saved
Zec 14: 9 one LORD, and his *n* the only *n.*
Mt 1: 21 and you are to give him the *n* Jesus,
6: 9 hallowed be your *n,*
18: 20 or three come together in my *n,*
Jn 10: 3 He calls his own sheep by *n*
16: 24 asked for anything in my *n.*
Ac 4: 12 for there is no other *n*
Ro 10: 13 "Everyone who calls on the *n*
Php 2: 9 him the *n* that is above every *n,*
Col 3: 17 do it all in the *n* of the Lord Jesus,
Heb 1: 4 as the *n* he has inherited is superior
Rev 20: 15 If anyone's *n* was not found written

NAOMI

Mother-in-law of Ruth (Ru 1). Advised Ruth to seek marriage with Boaz (Ru 2-4).

NARROW

Mt 7: 13 "Enter through the *n* gate.

NATHANAEL

Apostle (Jn 1:45-49; 21:2). Probably also called Bartholomew (Mt 10:3).

NATION (NATIONS)

Ge 12: 2 "I will make you into a great *n*
Ps 33: 12 Blessed is the *n* whose God is
Pr 14: 34 Righteousness exalts a *n,*
Isa 65: 1 To a *n* that did not call on my name
1Pe 2: 9 a royal priesthood, a holy *n,*
Rev 7: 9 from every *n,* tribe, people

NATIONS (NATION)

Ge 17: 4 You will be the father of many *n.*
18: 18 and all *n* on earth will be blessed
Ex 19: 5 of all *n* you will be my treasured
Ne 1: 8 I will scatter you among the *n,*
Ps 96: 3 Declare his glory among the *n,*
Isa 40: 15 Surely the *n* are like a drop
Eze 36: 23 *n* will know that I am the LORD,
Hag 2: 7 and the desired of all *n* will come,
Zec 8: 23 *n* will take firm hold of one Jew
14: 2 I will gather all the *n* to Jerusalem
Mt 28: 19 and make disciples of all *n,*
Rev 21: 24 The *n* will walk by its light,

NATURAL (NATURE)

Ro 6: 19 you are weak in your *n* selves.
1Co 15: 44 If there is a *n* body, there is

NATURE (NATURAL)

Ro 8: 4 do not live according to the sinful *n*
8: 8 by the sinful *n* cannot please God.
Gal 5: 19 The acts of the sinful *n* are obvious:
5: 24 Jesus have crucified the sinful *n*
Php 2: 6 Who, being in very *n* God,

NAZARENE

Mt 2: 23 prophets: "He will be called a *N.*"

NAZIRITE

Jdg 13: 7 because the boy will be a *N* of God

NECESSARY

Ro 13: 5 it is *n* to submit to the authorities,

NEED (NEEDS NEEDY)

Ps 116: 6 when I was in great *n,* he saved me.
Mt 6: 8 for your Father knows what you *n*
Ro 12: 13 with God's people who are in *n.*
1Co 12: 21 say to the hand, "I don't *n* you!"
1Jn 3: 17 sees his brother in *n* but has no pity

NEEDLE

Mt 19: 24 go through the eye of a *n*

NEEDS (NEED)

Isa 58: 11 he will satisfy your *n*
Php 4: 19 God will meet all your *n* according

NEEDY (NEED)

Pr 14: 21 blessed is he who is kind to the *n.*
14: 31 to the *n* honors God.
31: 20 and extends her hands to the *n.*
Mt 6: 2 "So when you give to the *n,*

NEGLECT (NEGLECTED)

Ne 10: 39 We will not *n* the house of our God
Ps 119: 16 I will not *n* your word.
Ac 6: 2 for us to *n* the ministry of the word
1Ti 4: 14 Do not *n* your gift, which was

NEGLECTED (NEGLECT)

Mt 23: 23 But you have *n* the more important

NEHEMIAH

Cupbearer of Artaxerxes (Ne 2:1); governor of Israel (Ne 8:9). Returned to Jerusalem to rebuild walls (Ne 2-6). With Ezra, reestablished worship (Ne 8). Prayer confessing nation's sin (Ne 9). Dedicated wall (Ne 12).

NEIGHBOR (NEIGHBOR'S)

Ex 20: 16 give false testimony against your *n.*
Lev 19: 13 Do not defraud your *n* or rob him.
19: 18 but love your *n* as yourself.
Pr 27: 10 better a *n* nearby than a brother far
Mt 19: 19 and 'love your *n* as yourself.' "
Lk 10: 29 who is my *n?*" In reply Jesus said:
Ro 13: 10 Love does no harm to its *n.*

NEIGHBOR'S (NEIGHBOR)

Ex 20: 17 You shall not covet your *n* wife,
Dt 5: 21 not set your desire on your *n* house
19: 14 not move your *n* boundary stone
Pr 25: 17 Seldom set foot in your *n* house—

NEW

Ps 40: 3 He put a *n* song in my mouth,
Ecc 1: 9 there is nothing *n* under the sun.
Isa 65: 17 *n* heavens and a *n* earth.
Jer 31: 31 "when I will make a *n* covenant
Eze 36: 26 give you a *n* heart and put a *n* spirit
Mt 9: 17 Neither do men pour *n* wine
Lk 22: 20 "This cup is the *n* covenant
2Co 5: 17 he is a *n* creation; the old has gone,
Eph 4: 24 and to put on the *n* self, created
2Pe 3: 13 to a *n* heaven and a *n* earth,
1Jn 2: 8 Yet I am writing you a *n* command;

NEWBORN (BEAR)

1Pe 2: 2 Like *n* babies, crave pure spiritual

NEWS

Isa 52: 7 the feet of those who bring good *n,*
Mk 1: 15 Repent and believe the good *n!*"
16: 15 preach the good *n* to all creation.
Lk 2: 10 I bring you good *n*
Ac 5: 42 proclaiming the good *n* that Jesus

17: 18 preaching the good *n* about Jesus
Ro 10: 15 feet of those who bring good *n!*"

NICODEMUS*

Pharisee who visted Jesus at night (Jn 3). Argued fair treatment of Jesus (Jn 7:50-52). With Joseph, prepared Jesus for burial (Jn 19:38-42).

NIGHT

Job 35: 10 who gives songs in the *n*,
Ps 1: 2 on his law he meditates day and *n*.
91: 5 You will not fear the terror of *n*,
Jn 3: 2 He came to Jesus at *n* and said,
1Th 5: 2 Lord will come like a thief in the *n*.
5: 5 We do not belong to the *n*
Rev 21: 25 for there will be no *n* there.

NOAH

Righteous man (Eze 14:14, 20) called to build ark (Ge 6-8; Heb 11:7; 1Pe 3:20; 2Pe 2:5). God's covenant with (Ge 9:1-17). Drunkenness of (Ge 9:18-23). Blessed sons, cursed Canaan (Ge 9:24-27).

NOBLE

Ru 3: 11 you are a woman of *n* character.
Ps 45: 1 My heart is stirred by a *n* theme
Pr 12: 4 of *n* character is her husband's
31: 10 A wife of *n* character who can find?
31: 29 "Many women do *n* things,
Isa 32: 8 But the *n* man makes *n* plans,
Lk 8: 15 good soil stands for those with a *n*
Ro 9: 21 of clay some pottery for *n* purposes
Php 4: 8 whatever is *n*, whatever is right,
2Ti 2: 20 some are for *n* purposes

NOTHING

Ne 9: 21 in the desert; they lacked *n*,
Jer 32: 17 *N* is too hard for you
Jn 15: 5 apart from me you can do *n*.

NULLIFY

Ro 3: 31 Do we, then, *n* the law by this faith

~ O

OATH

Dt 7: 8 and kept the *o* he swore

OBEDIENCE (OBEY)

2Ch 31: 21 in *o* to the law and the commands,
Pr 30: 17 that scorns *o* to a mother,
Ro 1: 5 to the *o* that comes from faith.
6: 16 to *o*, which leads to righteousness?
2Jn : 6 that we walk in *o* to his commands.

OBEDIENT (OBEY)

Lk 2: 51 with them and was *o* to them.
Php 2: 8 and became *o* to death—
1Pe 1: 14 As *o* children, do not conform

OBEY (OBEDIENCE OBEDIENT OBEYED)

Ex 12: 24 "*O* these instructions as a lasting
Dt 6: 3 careful to *o* so that it may go well
13: 4 Keep his commands and *o* him;
21: 18 son who does not *o* his father
30: 2 and *o* him with all your heart
32: 46 children to *o* carefully all the words
1Sa 15: 22 To *o* is better than sacrifice,
Ps 119: 34 and *o* it with all my heart.
Mt 28: 20 to *o* everything I have commanded
Jn 14: 23 loves me, he will *o* my teaching.
Ac 5: 29 "We must *o* God rather than men!
Ro 6: 16 slaves to the one whom you *o*—
Gal 5: 3 obligated to *o* the whole law.
Eph 6: 1 *o* your parents in the Lord,
6: 5 *o* your earthly masters with respect
Col 3: 20 *o* your parents in everything,
1Ti 3: 4 and see that his children *o* him
Heb 13: 17 *O* your leaders and submit
1Jn 5: 3 love for God: to *o* his commands.

OBEYED (OBEY)

Ps 119: 4 that are to be fully *o*.
Jnh 3: 3 Jonah *o* the word of the LORD
Jn 17: 6 and they have *o* your word.
Ro 6: 17 you wholeheartedly *o* the form
Heb 11: 8 *o* and went, even though he did not
1Pe 3: 6 who *o* Abraham and called him her

OBLIGATED

Ro 1: 14 I am *o* both to Greeks
Gal 5: 3 himself be circumcised that he is *o*

OBSCENITY

Eph 5: 4 Nor should there be *o*, foolish talk

OBSOLETE

Heb 8: 13 he has made the first one *o*;

OBTAINED

Ro 9: 30 not pursue righteousness, have *o* it,
Php 3: 12 Not that I have already *o* all this,
Heb 9: 12 having *o* eternal redemption.

OFFENDED (OFFENSE)

Pr 18: 19 An *o* brother is more unyielding

OFFENSE (OFFENDED OFFENSIVE)

Pr 17: 9 over an *o* promotes love,
19: 11 it is to his glory to overlook an *o*.

OFFENSIVE (OFFENSE)

Ps 139: 24 See if there is any *o* way in me,

OFFER (OFFERED OFFERING OFFERINGS)

Ro 12: 1 to *o* your bodies as living sacrifices,
Heb 13: 15 therefore, let us continually *o*

OFFERED (OFFER)

Heb 7: 27 once for all when he *o* himself.
11: 4 By faith Abel *o* God a better

OFFERING (OFFER)

Ge 22: 8 provide the lamb for the burnt *o*,
Ps 40: 6 Sacrifice and *o* you did not desire,
Isa 53: 10 the LORD makes his life a guilt *o*,
Mt 5: 23 if you are *o* your gift at the altar
Eph 5: 2 as a fragrant *o* and sacrifice to God.
Heb 10: 5 "Sacrifice and *o* you did not desire,

OFFERINGS (OFFER)

Mal 3: 8 do we rob you?' "In tithes and *o*.
Mk 12: 33 is more important than all burnt *o*

OFFICER

2Ti 2: 4 wants to please his commanding *o*.

OFFSPRING

Ge 3: 15 and between your *o* and hers;
12: 7 "To your *o* I will give this land."

OIL

Ps 23: 5 You anoint my head with *o*;
Isa 61: 3 the *o* of gladness
Heb 1: 9 by anointing you with the *o* of joy."

OLIVE (OLIVES)

Zec 4: 3 Also there are two *o* trees by it,
Ro 11: 17 and you, though a wild *o* shoot,
Rev 11: 4 These are the two *o* trees

OLIVES (OLIVE)

Jas 3: 12 a fig tree bear *o*, or a grapevine bear

OMEGA

Rev 1: 8 "I am the Alpha and the *O*,"

OMRI

King of Israel (1Ki 16:21-26).

OPINIONS*

1Ki 18: 21 will you waver between two *o*?
Pr 18: 2 but delights in airing his own *o*.

OPPORTUNITY

Ro 7: 11 seizing the *o* afforded
Gal 6: 10 as we have *o*, let us do goo
Eph 5: 16 making the most of every
Col 4: 5 make the most of every *o*.
1Ti 5: 14 to give the enemy no *o* for slander.

OPPOSES

Jas 4: 6 "God *o* the proud
1Pe 5: 5 because, "God *o* the proud

OPPRESS (OPPRESSED)

Ex 22: 21 "Do not mistreat an alien *o* him,
Zec 7: 10 Do not *o* the widow

OPPRESSED (OPPRESS)

Ps 9: 9 The LORD is a refuge for the
Isa 53: 7 He was *o* and afflicted,
Zec 10: 2 *o* for lack of a shepherd.

ORDAINED

Ps 8: 2 you have *o* praise

ORDERLY

1Co 14: 40 done in a fitting and *o* way.
Col 2: 5 and delight to see how *o* yo are

ORGIES*

Ro 13: 13 not in *o* and drunkenness,
Gal 5: 21 drunkenness, *o*, and the lik
1Pe 4: 3 *o*, carousing and detestable

ORIGIN

2Pe 1: 21 For prophecy never had its

ORPHANS

Jn 14: 18 will not leave you as *o*; I wil come
Jas 1: 27 to look after *o* and widows

OUTCOME

Heb 13: 7 Consider the *o* of their way of life
1Pe 4: 17 what will the *o* be for those who do

OUTSIDERS*

Col 4: 5 wise in the way you act toward *o*;
1Th 4: 12 daily life may win the respect of *o*
1Ti 3: 7 also have a good reputation with *o*,

OUTSTANDING

SS 5: 10 *o* among ten thousand.
Ro 13: 8 no debt remain *o*,

OUTSTRETCHED

Ex 6: 6 and will redeem you with an *o* arm
Jer 27: 5 and *o* arm I made the earth
Eze 20: 33 an *o* arm and with outpoured wrath

OUTWEIGHS

2Co 4: 17 an eternal glory that far *o* them all.

OVERCOME (OVERCOMES)
Mt 16: 18 and the gates of Hades will not *o* it.
Mk 9: 24 I do believe; help me *o* my unbelief
Jn 16: 33 But take heart! I have *o* the world."
Ro 12: 21 Do not be *o* by evil, but *o* evil
1Jn 5: 4 is the victory that has *o* the world,
Rev 17: 14 but the Lamb will *o* them

OVERCOMES* (OVERCOME)
1Jn 5: 4 born of God *o* the world.
5: 5 Who is it that *o* the world?
Rev 2: 7 To him who *o,* I will give the right
2: 11 He who *o* will not be hurt at all
2: 17 To him who *o,* I will give some
2: 26 To him who *o* and does my will
3: 5 He who *o* will, like them, be
3: 12 Him who *o* I will make a pillar
3: 21 To him who *o,* I will give the right
21: 7 He who *o* will inherit all this,

OVERFLOW (OVERFLOWS)
Ps 119:171 May my lips *o* with praise,
Lk 6: 45 out of the *o* of his heart his mouth
Ro 15: 13 so that you may *o* with hope
2Co 4: 15 to *o* to the glory of God.
1Th 3: 12 *o* for each other and for everyone

OVERFLOWS* (OVERFLOW)
Ps 23: 5 my cup *o.*
2Co 1: 5 also through Christ our comfort *o.*

OVERJOYED* (JOY)
Da 6: 23 The king was *o* and gave orders
Mt 2: 10 they saw the star, they were *o.*
Jn 20: 20 The disciples were *o*
Ac 12: 14 she was so *o* she ran back
1Pe 4: 13 so that you may be *o*

OVERSEER (OVERSEERS)
1Ti 3: 1 anyone sets his heart on being an *o,*
3: 2 Now the *o* must be above reproach,
Tit 1: 7 Since an *o* is entrusted

OVERSEERS* (OVERSEER)
Ac 20: 28 the Holy Spirit has made you *o.*
Php 1: 1 together with the *o* and deacons:
1Pe 5: 2 as *o*—not because you must,

OVERWHELMED
Ps 38: 4 My guilt has *o* me
65: 3 When we were *o* by sins,
Mt 26: 38 "My soul is *o* with sorrow
Mk 7: 37 People were *o* with amazement.

OWE
Ro 13: 7 If you *o* taxes, pay taxes; if revenue
Phm : 19 to mention that you *o* me your very

OX
Dt 25: 4 Do not muzzle an *o*
Isa 11: 7 and the lion will eat straw like the *o*
1Co 9: 9 "Do not muzzle an *o*

P

PAGANS
Mt 5: 47 Do not even *p* do that? Be perfect,
1Pe 2: 12 such good lives among the *p* that,

PAIN (PAINFUL)
Ge 3: 16 with *p* you will give birth
Job 33: 19 may be chastened on a bed of *p*
Jn 16: 21 woman giving birth to a child has *p*

PAINFUL (PAIN)
Ge 3: 17 through *p* toil you will eat of it
Heb 12: 11 seems pleasant at the time, but *p.*
1Pe 4: 12 at the *p* trial you are suffering,

PALMS
Isa 49: 16 you on the *p* of my hands;

PANTS
Ps 42: 1 As the deer *p* for streams of water,

PARADISE*
Lk 23: 43 today you will be with me in *p.*"
2Co 12: 4 God knows—was caught up to *p.*
Rev 2: 7 of life, which is in the *p* of God.

PARALYTIC
Mk 2: 3 bringing to him a *p,* carried by four

PARDON (PARDONS)
Isa 55: 7 and to our God, for he will freely *p.*

PARDONS* (PARDON)
Mic 7: 18 who *p* sin and forgives

PARENTS
Pr 17: 6 and *p* are the pride of their children
Lk 18: 29 left home or wife or brothers or *p*
21: 16 You will be betrayed even by *p,*
Ro 1: 30 they disobey their *p;* they are
2Co 12: 14 for their *p,* but *p* for their children.
Eph 6: 1 Children, obey your *p* in the Lord,
Col 3: 20 obey your *p* in everything,
2Ti 3: 2 disobedient to their *p,* ungrateful,

PARTIALITY
Dt 10: 17 who shows no *p* and accepts no
2Ch 19: 7 our God there is no injustice or *p*
Lk 20: 21 and that you do not show *p*

PARTICIPATION
1Co 10: 16 is not the bread that we break a *p*

PASS
Ex 12: 13 and when I see the blood, I will *p*
La 1: 12 to you, all you who *p* by?
Lk 21: 33 Heaven and earth will *p* away,
1Co 13: 8 there is knowledge, it will *p* away.

PASSION (PASSIONS)
1Co 7: 9 better to marry than to burn with *p.*

PASSIONS (PASSION)
Gal 5: 24 crucified the sinful nature with its *p*
Tit 2: 12 to ungodliness and worldly *p,*

PASSOVER
Ex 12: 11 Eat it in haste; it is the LORD's *P.*
Dt 16: 1 celebrate the *P* of the LORD your
1Co 5: 7 our *P* lamb, has been sacrificed.

PAST
Isa 43: 18 do not dwell on the *p.*
Ro 15: 4 in the *p* was written to teach us,
Heb 1: 1 In the *p* God spoke

PASTORS*
Eph 4: 11 and some to be *p* and teachers,

PASTURE (PASTURES)
Ps 37: 3 dwell in the land and enjoy safe *p.*
100: 3 we are his people, the sheep of his *p*
Jer 50: 7 against the LORD, their true *p,*
Eze 34: 13 I will *p* them on the mountains
Jn 10: 9 come in and go out, and find *p.*

PASTURES (PASTURE)
Ps 23: 2 He makes me lie down in green *p,*

PATCH
Mt 9: 16 No one sews a *p* of unshrunk cloth

PATH (PATHS)
Ps 27: 11 lead me in a straight *p*
119:105 and a light for my *p.*
Pr 15: 19 the *p* of the upright is a highway.
15: 24 The *p* of life leads upward
Isa 26: 7 The *p* of the righteous is level;
Lk 1: 79 to guide our feet into the *p* of peace
2Co 6: 3 no stumbling block in anyone's *p,*

PATHS (PATH)
Ps 23: 3 He guides me in *p* of righteousness
25: 4 teach me your *p;*
Pr 3: 6 and he will make your *p* straight.
Ro 11: 33 and his *p* beyond tracing out!
Heb 12: 13 "Make level *p* for your feet,"

PATIENCE (PATIENT)
Pr 19: 11 A man's wisdom gives him *p;*
2Co 6: 6 understanding, *p* and kindness;
Gal 5: 22 joy, peace, *p,* kindness, goodness,
Col 1: 11 may have great endurance and *p,*
3: 12 humility, gentleness and *p.*

PATIENT (PATIENCE PATIENTLY)
Pr 15: 18 but a *p* man calms a quarrel.
Ro 12: 12 Be joyful in hope, *p* in affliction,
1Co 13: 4 Love is *p,* love is kind.
Eph 4: 2 humble and gentle; be *p,*
1Th 5: 14 help the weak, be *p* with everyone.

PATIENTLY (PATIENT)
Ps 40: 1 I waited *p* for the LORD;
Ro 8: 25 we do not yet have, we wait for it *p.*

PATTERN
Ro 5: 14 who was a *p* of the one to come.
12: 2 longer to the *p* of this world,
2Ti 1: 13 keep as the *p* of sound teaching,

PAUL
Also called Saul (Ac 13:9). Pharisee from Tarsus (Ac 9:11; Php 3:5). Apostle (Gal 1). At stoning of Stephen (Ac 8:1). Persecuted Church (Ac 9:1-2; Gal 1:13). Vision of Jesus on road to Damascus (Ac 9:4-9; 26:12-18). In Arabia (Gal 1:17). Preached in Damascus; escaped death through the wall in a basket (Ac 9:19-25). In Jerusalem; sent back to Tarsus (Ac 9:26-30).

Brought to Antioch by Barnabas (Ac 11:22-26). First missionary journey to Cyprus and Galatia (Ac 13-14). Stoned at Lystra (Ac 14:19-20). At Jerusalem council (Ac 15). Split with Barnabas over Mark (Ac 15:36-41).

Second missionary journey with Silas (Ac 16-20). Called to Macedonia (Ac 16:6-10). Freed from prison in Philippi (Ac 16:16-40). In Thessalonica (Ac 17:1-9). Speech in Athens (Ac 17:16-33). In Corinth (Ac 18). In Ephesus (Ac 19). Return to Jerusalem (Ac 20). Farewell to Ephesian elders (Ac 20:13-38). Arrival in Jerusalem (Ac 21:1-26). Arrested (Ac

21:27-36). Addressed crowds (Ac 22), Sanhedrin (Ac 23:1-11). Transferred to Caesarea (Ac 23:12-35). Trial before Felix (Ac 24), Festus (Ac 25:1-12). Before Agrippa (Ac 25:13-26:32). Voyage to Rome; shipwreck (Ac 27). Arrival in Rome (Ac 28).

PAY (REPAID REPAY)

Lev 26: 43 They will *p* for their sins
Pr 22: 17 *P* attention and listen
Mt 22: 17 Is it right to *p* taxes to Caesar
Ro 13: 6 This is also why you *p* taxes,
2Pe 1: 19 you will do well to *p* attention to it,

PEACE (PEACEMAKERS)

Nu 6: 26 and give you *p*." '
Ps 34: 14 seek *p* and pursue it.
85: 10 righteousness and *p* kiss each other
119:165 Great *p* have they who love your
122: 6 Pray for the *p* of Jerusalem:
Pr 14: 30 A heart at *p* gives life to the body,
17: 1 Better a dry crust with *p* and quiet
Isa 9: 6 Everlasting Father, Prince of *P*.
26: 3 You will keep in perfect *p*
48: 22 "There is no *p*," says the LORD,
Zec 9: 10 He will proclaim *p* to the nations.
Mt 10: 34 I did not come to bring *p*,
Lk 2: 14 on earth *p* to men on whom his
Jn 14: 27 *P* I leave with you; my *p*
16: 33 so that in me you may have *p*.
Ro 5: 1 we have *p* with God
1Co 7: 15 God has called us to live in *p*.
14: 33 a God of disorder but of *p*.
Gal 5: 22 joy, *p*, patience, kindness,
Eph 2: 14 he himself is our *p*, who has made
Php 4: 7 the *p* of God, which transcends all
Col 1: 20 by making *p* through his blood,
3: 15 Let the *p* of Christ rule
1Th 5: 3 While people are saying, "*P*
2Th 3: 16 the Lord of *p* himself give you *p*
2Ti 2: 22 righteousness, faith, love and *p*,
1Pe 3: 11 he must seek *p* and pursue it.
Rev 6: 4 power to take *p* from the earth

PEACEMAKERS* (PEACE)

Mt 5: 9 Blessed are the *p*,
Jas 3: 18 *P* who sow in peace raise a harvest

PEARL* (PEARLS)

Rev 21: 21 each gate made of a single *p*.

PEARLS (PEARL)

Mt 7: 6 do not throw your *p* to pigs.
13: 45 like a merchant looking for fine *p*.
1Ti 2: 9 or gold or *p* or expensive clothes,
Rev 21: 21 The twelve gates were twelve *p*,

PEKAH

King of Israel (2Ki 15:25-31; Isa 7:1).

PEKAHIAH*

Son of Menahem; king of Israel (2Ki 15:22-26).

PEN

Mt 5: 18 letter, not the least stroke of a *p*,

PENTECOST

Ac 2: 1 of *P* came, they were all together

PEOPLE (PEOPLES)

Dt 32: 9 the LORD's portion is his *p*,
Ru 1: 16 Your *p* will be my *p*
2Ch 7: 14 if my *p*, who are called
Jer 24: 7 They will be my *p*,
Zec 2: 11 and will become my *p*.
Lk 2: 10 joy that will be for all the *p*.
Ac 15: 14 from the Gentiles a *p*.
2Co 6: 16 and they will be my *p*."
Tit 2: 14 a *p* that are his very own,
1Pe 2: 9 you are a chosen *p*,
Rev 21: 3 They will be his *p*,

PEOPLES (PEOPLE)

Da 7: 14 all *p*, nations and men
Mic 4: 1 and *p* will stream to it.

PERCEIVING

Isa 6: 9 be ever seeing, but never *p*.'

PERFECT (PERFECTER PERFECTION)

SS 6: 9 but my dove, my *p* one, is unique,
Isa 26: 3 You will keep in *p* peace
Mt 5: 48 as your heavenly Father is *p*.
Ro 12: 2 his good, pleasing and *p* will.
2Co 12: 9 for my power is made *p*
Col 1: 28 so that we may present everyone *p*
3: 14 binds them all together in *p* unity.
Heb 9: 11 and more *p* tabernacle that is not
10: 14 he has made *p* forever those who
Jas 1: 17 Every good and *p* gift is from above
1: 25 into the *p* law that gives freedom,
3: 2 he is a *p* man, able
1Jn 4: 18 But *p* love drives out fear,

PERFECTER* (PERFECT)

Heb 12: 2 the author and *p* of our faith,

PERFECTION (PERFECT)

Ps 119: 96 To all *p* I see a limit;
2Co 13: 11 Aim for *p*, listen to my appeal,
Heb 7: 11 If *p* could have been attained

PERFORMS

Ps 77: 14 You are the God who *p* miracles;

PERISH (PERISHABLE)

Ps 1: 6 but the way of the wicked will *p*.
102: 26 They will *p*, but you remain;
Lk 13: 3 unless you repent, you too will all *p*
Jn 10: 28 eternal life, and they shall never *p*;
Col 2: 22 These are all destined to *p* with use,
Heb 1: 11 They will *p*, but you remain;
2Pe 3: 9 not wanting anyone to *p*,

PERISHABLE (PERISH)

1Co 15: 42 The body that is sown is *p*,

PERJURERS

1Ti 1: 10 for slave traders and liars and *p*—

PERMISSIBLE (PERMIT)

1Co 10: 23 "Everything is *p*"—but not

PERMIT (PERMISSIBLE)

1Ti 2: 12 I do not *p* a woman to teach

PERSECUTE (PERSECUTED PERSECUTION)

Mt 5: 11 *p* you and falsely say all kinds
Jn 15: 20 they persecuted me, they will *p* you
Ac 9: 4 why do you *p* me?" "Who are you,
Ro 12: 14 Bless those who *p* you; bless

PERSECUTED (PERSECUTE)

1Co 4: 12 when we are *p*, we endure it;
2Ti 3: 12 life in Christ Jesus will be *p*,

PERSECUTION (PERSECUTE)

Ro 8: 35 or hardship or *p* or famine

PERSEVERANCE (PERSEVERE)

Ro 5: 3 we know that suffering produces *p*;
5: 4 *p*, character; and character, hope.
Heb 12: 1 run with *p* the race marked out
Jas 1: 3 the testing of your faith develops *p*.
2Pe 1: 6 *p*; and to *p*, godliness;

PERSEVERE* (PERSEVERANCE PERSEVERED PERSEVERES)

1Ti 4: 16 *P* in them, because if you do,
Heb 10: 36 You need to *p* so that

PERSEVERED* (PERSEVERE)

Heb 11: 27 he *p* because he saw him who is
Jas 5: 11 consider blessed those who have *p*.
Rev 2: 3 You have *p* and have endured

PERSEVERES* (PERSEVERE)

1Co 13: 7 trusts, always hopes, always *p*.
Jas 1: 12 Blessed is the man who *p*

PERSUADE

2Co 5: 11 is to fear the Lord, we try to *p* men.

PERVERSION (PERVERT)

Lev 18: 23 sexual relations with it; that is a *p*.
Jude : 7 up to sexual immorality and *p*.

PERVERT (PERVERSION PERVERTS)

Gal 1: 7 are trying to *p* the gospel of Christ.

PERVERTS* (PERVERT)

1Ti 1: 10 for murderers, for adulterers and *p*,

PESTILENCE

Ps 91: 6 nor the *p* that stalks in the darkness

PETER

Apostle, brother of Andrew, also called Simon (Mt 10:2; Mk 3:16; Lk 6:14; Ac 1:13), and Cephas (Jn 1:42). Confession of Christ (Mt 16:13-20; Mk 8:27-30; Lk 9:18-27). At transfiguration (Mt 17:1-8; Mk 9:2-8; Lk 9:28-36; 2Pe 1:16-18). Caught fish with coin (Mt 17:24-27). Denial of Jesus predicted (Mt 26:31-35; Mk 14:27-31; Lk 22:31-34; Jn 13:31-38). Denied Jesus (Mt 26:69-75; Mk 14:66-72; Lk 22:54-62; Jn 18:15-27). Commissioned by Jesus to shepherd his flock (Jn 21:15-23).

Speech at Pentecost (Ac 2). Healed beggar (Ac 3:1-10). Speech at temple (Ac 3:11-26), before Sanhedrin (Ac 4:1-22). In Samaria (Ac 8:14-25). Sent by vision to Cornelius (Ac 10). Announced salvation of Gentiles in Jerusalem (Ac 11;15). Freed from prison (Ac 12). Inconsistency at Antioch (Gal 2:11-21). At Jerusalem Council (Ac 15).

PHARISEES

Mt 5: 20 surpasses that of the *P*

PHILIP

1. Apostle (Mt 10:3; Mk 3:18; Lk 6:14; Jn 1:43-48; 14:8; Ac 1:13).

2. Deacon (Ac 6:1-7); evangelist in Samaria (Ac 8:4-25), to Ethiopian (Ac 8:26-40).

PHILOSOPHY*

Col 2: 8 through hollow and deceptive *p*,

PHYLACTERIES*

Mt 23: 5 They make their *p* wide

PHYSICAL

1Ti 4: 8 For *p* training is of some value,
Jas 2: 16 but does nothing about his *p* needs,

PIECES

Ge 15: 17 and passed between the *p*.
Jer 34: 18 and then walked between its *p*.

PIERCED

Ps 22: 16 they have *p* my hands and my feet.
Isa 53: 5 But he was *p* for our transgressions,
Zec 12: 10 look on me, the one they have *p*,
Jn 19: 37 look on the one they have *p*."

PIGS

Mt 7: 6 do not throw your pearls to *p*.

PILATE

Governor of Judea. Questioned Jesus (Mt 27:1-26; Mk 15:15; Lk 22:66-23:25; Jn 18:28-19:16); sent him to Herod (Lk 23:6-12); consented to his crucifixion when crowds chose Barabbas (Mt 27:15-26; Mk 15:6-15; Lk 23:13-25; Jn 19:1-10).

PILLAR

Ge 19: 26 and she became a *p* of salt.
Ex 13: 21 ahead of them in a *p* of cloud
1Ti 3: 15 the *p* and foundation of the truth.

PIT

Ps 40: 2 He lifted me out of the slimy *p*,
103: 4 who redeems your life from the *p*
Mt 15: 14 a blind man, both will fall into a *p*."

PITIED

1Co 15: 19 we are to be *p* more than all men.

PLAGUE

2Ch 6: 28 "When famine or *p* comes

PLAIN

Ro 1: 19 what may be known about God is *p*

PLAN (PLANNED PLANS)

Job 42: 2 no *p* of yours can be thwarted.
Pr 14: 22 those who *p* what is good find love
Eph 1: 11 predestined according to the *p*

PLANK

Mt 7: 3 attention to the *p* in your own eye?
Lk 6: 41 attention to the *p* in your own eye?

PLANNED (PLAN)

Ps 40: 5 The things you *p* for us
Isa 46: 11 what I have *p*, that will I do.
Heb 11: 40 God had *p* something better for us

PLANS (PLAN)

Ps 20: 4 and make all your *p* succeed.
33: 11 *p* of the LORD stand firm forever,
Pr 20: 18 Make *p* by seeking advice;
Isa 32: 8 But the noble man makes noble *p*,

PLANTED (PLANTS)

Ps 1: 3 He is like a tree *p* by streams
Mt 15: 13 Father has not *p* will be pulled
1Co 3: 6 I *p* the seed, Apollos watered it,

PLANTS (PLANTED)

1Co 3: 7 So neither he who *p* nor he who
9: 7 Who *p* a vineyard and does not eat

PLATTER

Mk 6: 25 head of John the Baptist on a *p*."

PLAYED

Lk 7: 32 " 'We *p* the flute for you,
1Co 14: 7 anyone know what tune is being *p*

PLEADED

2Co 12: 8 Three times I *p* with the Lord

PLEASANT (PLEASE)

Ps 16: 6 for me in *p* places;
133: 1 How good and *p* it is
147: 1 how *p* and fitting to praise him!
Heb 12: 11 No discipline seems *p* at the time,

PLEASE
(PLEASANT PLEASED PLEASES PLEASING PLEASURE PLEASURES)

Pr 20: 23 and dishonest scales do not *p* him.
Jer 6: 20 your sacrifices do not *p* me."
Jn 5: 30 for I seek not to *p* myself
Ro 8: 8 by the sinful nature cannot *p* God.
15: 2 Each of us should *p* his neighbor
1Co 7: 32 affairs—how he can *p* the Lord.
10: 33 I try to *p* everybody in every way.
2Co 5: 9 So we make it our goal to *p* him,
Gal 1: 10 or of God? Or am I trying to *p* men
1Th 4: 1 how to live in order to *p* God,
2Ti 2: 4 wants to *p* his commanding officer.
Heb 11: 6 faith it is impossible to *p* God,

PLEASED (PLEASE)

Mt 3: 17 whom I love; with him I am well *p*
1Co 1: 21 God was *p* through the foolishness
Col 1: 19 For God was *p* to have all his
Heb 11: 5 commended as one who *p* God.
2Pe 1: 17 whom I love; with him I am well *p*

PLEASES (PLEASE)

Ps 135: 6 The LORD does whatever *p* him,
Pr 15: 8 but the prayer of the upright *p* him.
Jn 3: 8 The wind blows wherever it *p*.
8: 29 for I always do what *p* him."
Col 3: 20 in everything, for this *p* the Lord.
1Ti 2: 3 This is good, and *p* God our Savior,
1Jn 3: 22 his commands and do what *p* him.

PLEASING (PLEASE)

Ps 104: 34 May my meditation be *p* to him,
Ro 12: 1 *p* to God—which is your spiritual
Php 4: 18 an acceptable sacrifice, *p* to God.
Heb 13: 21 may he work in us what is *p* to him,

PLEASURE (PLEASE)

Ps 5: 4 You are not a God who takes *p*
147: 10 His *p* is not in the strength
Pr 21: 17 He who loves *p* will become poor;
Eze 18: 32 For I take no *p* in the death
Eph 1: 5 in accordance with his *p* and will—
1: 9 of his will according to his good *p*,
2Ti 3: 4 lovers of *p* rather than lovers

PLEASURES (PLEASE)

Ps 16: 11 with eternal *p* at your right hand.
Heb 11: 25 rather than to enjoy the *p* of sin
2Pe 2: 13 reveling in their *p* while they feast

PLENTIFUL

Mt 9: 37 harvest is *p* but the workers are

PLOW (PLOWSHARES)

Lk 9: 62 "No one who puts his hand to the *p*

PLOWSHARES (PLOW)

Isa 2: 4 They will beat their swords into *p*
Joel 3: 10 Beat your *p* into swords

PLUNDER

Ex 3: 22 And so you will *p* the Egyptians."

POINT

Jas 2: 10 yet stumbles at just one *p* is guilty

POISON

Mk 16: 18 and when they drink deadly *p*,
Jas 3: 8 It is a restless evil, full of deadly *p*.

POLLUTE* (POLLUTED)

Nu 35: 33 " 'Do not *p* the land where you are.
Jude : 8 these dreamers *p* their own bodies,

POLLUTED* (POLLUTE)

Ezr 9: 11 entering to possess is a land *p*
Pr 25: 26 Like a muddied spring or a *p* well
Ac 15: 20 to abstain from food *p* by idols,
Jas 1: 27 oneself from being *p* by the world.

PONDER

Ps 64: 9 and *p* what he has done.
119: 95 but I will *p* your statutes.

POOR (POVERTY)

Dt 15: 4 there should be no *p* among you,
15: 11 There will always be *p* people
Ps 34: 6 This *p* man called, and the LORD
82: 3 maintain the rights of the *p*
112: 9 scattered abroad his gifts to the *p*,
Pr 10: 4 Lazy hands make a man *p*,
13: 7 to be *p*, yet has great wealth.
14: 31 oppresses the *p* shows contempt
19: 1 Better a *p* man whose walk is
19: 17 to the *p* lends to the LORD,
22: 2 Rich and *p* have this in common:
22: 9 for he shares his food with the *p*.
28: 6 Better a *p* man whose walk is
31: 20 She opens her arms to the *p*
Isa 61: 1 me to preach good news to the *p*.
Mt 5: 3 saying: "Blessed are the *p* in spirit,
11: 5 the good news is preached to the *p*.
19: 21 your possessions and give to the *p*,
26: 11 The *p* you will always have
Mk 12: 42 But a *p* widow came and put
Ac 10: 4 and gifts to the *p* have come up
1Co 13: 3 If I give all I possess to the *p*
2Co 8: 9 yet for your sakes he became *p*,
Jas 2: 2 and a *p* man in shabby clothes

PORTION

Dt 32: 9 For the LORD's *p* is his people,
2Ki 2: 9 "Let me inherit a double *p*

La 3: 24 to myself, "The LORD is my *p;*

POSSESS (POSSESSING POSSESSION POSSESSIONS)

Nu 33: 53 for I have given you the land to *p.*
Jn 5: 39 that by them you *p* eternal life.

POSSESSING* (POSSESS)

2Co 6: 10 nothing, and yet *p* everything.

POSSESSION (POSSESS)

Ge 15: 7 to give you this land to take *p* of it
Nu 13: 30 "We should go up and take *p*
Eph 1: 14 of those who are God's *p*—

POSSESSIONS (POSSESS)

Lk 12: 15 consist in the abundance of his *p.*"
2Co 12: 14 what I want is not your *p* but you.
1Jn 3: 17 If anyone has material *p*

POSSIBLE

Mt 19: 26 but with God all things are *p.*"
Mk 9: 23 "Everything is *p* for him who
10: 27 all things are *p* with God."
Ro 12: 18 If it is *p,* as far as it depends on you,
1Co 9: 22 by all *p* means I might save some.

POT (POTSHERD POTTER POTTERY)

2Ki 4: 40 there is death in the *p!*"
Jer 18: 4 But the *p* he was shaping

POTSHERD (POT)

Isa 45: 9 a *p* among the potsherds

POTTER (POT)

Isa 29: 16 Can the pot say of the *p,*
45: 9 Does the clay say to the *p,*
64: 8 We are the clay, you are the *p;*
Jer 18: 6 "Like clay in the hand of the *p,*
Ro 9: 21 Does not the *p* have the right

POTTERY (POT)

Ro 9: 21 of clay some *p* for noble purposes

POUR (POURED)

Ps 62: 8 *p* out your hearts to him,
Joel 2: 28 I will *p* out my Spirit on all people.
Mal 3: 10 *p* out so much blessing that you
Ac 2: 17 I will *p* out my Spirit on all people.

POURED (POUR)

Ac 10: 45 of the Holy Spirit had been *p* out
Ro 5: 5 because God has *p* out his love

POVERTY (POOR)

Pr 14: 23 but mere talk leads only to *p.*
21: 5 as surely as haste leads to *p.*
30: 8 give me neither *p* nor riches,
Mk 12: 44 out of her *p,* put in everything—
2Co 8: 2 and their extreme *p* welled up
8: 9 through his *p* might become rich.

POWER (POWERFUL POWERS)

1Ch 29: 11 LORD, is the greatness and the *p*
2Ch 32: 7 for there is a greater *p* with us
Job 36: 22 "God is exalted in his *p.*
Ps 63: 2 and beheld your *p* and your glory.
68: 34 Proclaim the *p* of God,
147: 5 Great is our Lord and mighty in *p;*
Pr 24: 5 A wise man has great *p,*
Isa 40: 10 the Sovereign LORD comes with *p*
Zec 4: 6 nor by *p,* but by my Spirit,'
Mt 22: 29 do not know the Scriptures or the *p*
24: 30 on the clouds of the sky, with *p*
Ac 1: 8 you will receive *p* when the Holy
4: 33 With great *p* the apostles
10: 38 with the Holy Spirit and *p,*
Ro 1: 16 it is the *p* of God for the salvation
1Co 1: 18 to us who are being saved it is the *p*
15: 56 of death is sin, and the *p*
2Co 12: 9 for my *p* is made perfect
Eph 1: 19 and his incomparably great *p*
Php 3: 10 and the *p* of his resurrection
Col 1: 11 strengthened with all *p* according
2Ti 1: 7 but a spirit of *p,* of love
Heb 7: 16 of the *p* of an indestructible life.
Rev 4: 11 to receive glory and honor and *p,*
19: 1 and glory and *p* belong to our God,
20: 6 The second death has no *p*

POWERFUL (POWER)

Ps 29: 4 The voice of the LORD is *p;*
Lk 24: 19 *p* in word and deed before God
2Th 1: 7 in blazing fire with his *p* angels.
Heb 1: 3 sustaining all things by his *p* word.
Jas 5: 16 The prayer of a righteous man is *p*

POWERLESS

Ro 5: 6 when we were still *p,* Christ died
8: 3 For what the law was *p* to do

POWERS (POWER)

Ro 8: 38 nor any *p,* neither height nor depth
1Co 12: 10 to another miraculous *p,*
Col 1: 16 whether thrones or *p* or rulers
2: 15 And having disarmed the *p*

PRACTICE

Lev 19: 26 "'Do not *p* divination or sorcery.
Mt 23: 3 for they do not *p* what they preach.
Lk 8: 21 hear God's word and put it into *p.*"
Ro 12: 13 *P* hospitality.
1Ti 5: 4 to put their religion into *p* by caring

PRAISE (PRAISED PRAISES PRAISING)

Ex 15: 2 He is my God, and I will *p* him,
Dt 32: 3 Oh, *p* the greatness of our God!
Ru 4: 14 said to Naomi: "*P* be to the LORD,
2Sa 22: 47 The LORD lives! *P* be to my Rock
1Ch 16: 25 is the LORD and most worthy of *p;*
2Ch 20: 21 and to *p* him for the splendor
Ps 8: 2 you have ordained *p*
33: 1 it is fitting for the upright to *p* him.
34: 1 his *p* will always be on my lips.
40: 3 a hymn of *p* to our God.
48: 1 the LORD, and most worthy of *p,*
68: 19 *P* be to the Lord, to God our Savior
89: 5 The heavens *p* your wonders,
100: 4 and his courts with *p;*
105: 2 Sing to him, sing *p* to him;
106: 1 *P* the LORD.
119:175 Let me live that I may *p* you,
139: 14 I *p* you because I am fearfully
145: 21 Let every creature *p* his holy name
146: 1 *P* the LORD, O my soul.
150: 2 *p* him for his surpassing greatness.
150: 6 that has breath *p* the LORD.
Pr 27: 2 Let another *p* you, and not your
27: 21 man is tested by the *p* he receives.
31: 31 let her works bring her *p*
Mt 5: 16 and *p* your Father in heaven.
21: 16 you have ordained *p* '?"
Jn 12: 43 for they loved *p* from men more
Eph 1: 6 to the *p* of his glorious grace,
1: 12 might be for the *p* of his glory.
1: 14 to the *p* of his glory.
Heb 13: 15 offer to God a sacrifice of *p*—
Jas 5: 13 happy? Let him sing songs of *p.*

PRAISED (PRAISE)

1Ch 29: 10 David *p* the LORD in the presence
Ne 8: 6 Ezra *p* the LORD, the great God;
Da 2: 19 Then Daniel *p* the God of heaven
Ro 9: 5 who is God over all, forever *p!*
1Pe 4: 11 that in all things God may be *p*

PRAISES (PRAISE)

2Sa 22: 50 I will sing *p* to your name.
Ps 47: 6 Sing *p* to God, sing *p;*
147: 1 How good it is to sing *p* to our God,
Pr 31: 28 her husband also, and he *p* her:

PRAISING (PRAISE)

Ac 10: 46 speaking in tongues and *p* God.
1Co 14: 16 If you are *p* God with your spirit,

PRAY (PRAYED PRAYER PRAYERS PRAYING)

Dt 4: 7 is near us whenever we *p* to him?
1Sa 12: 23 the LORD by failing to *p* for you.
2Ch 7: 14 will humble themselves and *p*
Job 42: 8 My servant Job will *p* for you,
Ps 122: 6 *P* for the peace of Jerusalem:
Mt 5: 44 and *p* for those who persecute you,
6: 5 "And when you *p,* do not be like
6: 9 "This, then, is how you should *p:*
26: 36 Sit here while I go over there and *p*
Lk 6: 28 *p* for those who mistreat you.
18: 1 them that they should always *p*
22: 40 "*P* that you will not fall
Ro 8: 26 do not know what we ought to *p,*
1Co 14: 13 in a tongue should *p* that he may
1Th 5: 17 Be joyful always; *p* continually;
Jas 5: 13 one of you in trouble? He should *p.*
5: 16 *p* for each other so that you may be

PRAYED (PRAY)

1Sa 1: 27 I *p* for this child, and the LORD
Jnh 2: 1 From inside the fish Jonah *p*
Mk 14: 35 *p* that if possible the hour might

PRAYER (PRAY)

2Ch 30: 27 for their *p* reached heaven,

zr 8: 23 about this, and he answered our *p*.
s 6: 9 the LORD accepts my *p*.
86: 6 Hear my *p*, O LORD;
r 15: 8 but the *p* of the upright pleases him
a 56: 7 a house of *p* for all nations."
t 21: 13 house will be called a house of *p*,'
k 11: 24 whatever you ask for in *p*,
n 17: 15 My *p* is not that you take them out
c 6: 4 and will give our attention to *p*
hp 4: 6 but in everything, by *p* and petition
as 5: 15 *p* offered in faith will make the sick
Pe 3: 12 and his ears are attentive to their *p*,

RAYERS (PRAY)

Ch 5: 20 He answered their *p*, because they
Mk 12: 40 and for a show make lengthy *p*.
Pe 3: 7 so that nothing will hinder your *p*.
Rev 5: 8 which are the *p* of the saints.

PRAYING (PRAY)

Mk 11: 25 And when you stand *p*,
n 17: 9 I am not *p* for the world,
Ac 16: 25 and Silas were *p* and singing hymns
Eph 6: 18 always keep on *p* for all the saints.

PREACH (PREACHED PREACHING)

Mt 23: 3 they do not practice what they *p*.
Mk 16: 15 and *p* the good news to all creation.
Ac 9: 20 At once he began to *p*
Ro 10: 15 how can they *p* unless they are sent
15: 20 to *p* the gospel where Christ was
1Co 1: 17 to *p* the gospel—not with words
1: 23 wisdom, but we *p* Christ crucified:
9: 14 that those who *p* the gospel should
9: 16 Woe to me if I do not *p* the gospel!
2Co 10: 16 so that we can *p* the gospel
Gal 1: 8 from heaven should *p* a gospel
2Ti 4: 2 I give you this charge: *P* the Word;

PREACHED (PREACH)

Mk 13: 10 And the gospel must first be *p*
Ac 8: 4 had been scattered *p* the word
1Co 9: 27 so that after I have *p* to others,
15: 1 you of the gospel I *p* to you,
2Co 11: 4 other than the Jesus we *p*,
Gal 1: 8 other than the one we *p* to you,
Php 1: 18 false motives or true, Christ is *p*.
1Ti 3: 16 was *p* among the nations,

PREACHING (PREACH)

Ro 10: 14 hear without someone *p* to them?
1Co 9: 18 in *p* the gospel I may offer it free
1Ti 4: 13 the public reading of Scripture, to *p*
5: 17 especially those whose work is *p*

PRECEPTS

Ps 19: 8 The *p* of the LORD are right,
111: 7 all his *p* are trustworthy.
111: 10 who follow his *p* have good
119: 40 How I long for your *p*!
119: 69 I keep your *p* with all my heart.
119:104 I gain understanding from your *p*;
119:159 See how I love your *p*;

PRECIOUS

Ps 19: 10 They are more *p* than gold,
116: 15 *P* in the sight of the LORD
Pr 8: 11 for wisdom is more *p* than rubies,
Isa 28: 16 a *p* cornerstone for a sure
1Pe 1: 19 but with the *p* blood of Christ,
2: 6 a chosen and *p* cornerstone,
2Pe 1: 4 us his very great and *p* promises,

PREDESTINED* (DESTINY)

Ro 8: 29 *p* to be conformed to the likeness
8: 30 And those he *p*, he also called;
Eph 1: 5 In love he *p* us to be adopted
1: 11 having been *p* according

PREDICTION*

Jer 28: 9 only if his *p* comes true."

PREPARE (PREPARED)

Ps 23: 5 You *p* a table before me
Am 4: 12 *p* to meet your God, O Israel."
Jn 14: 2 there to *p* a place for you.
Eph 4: 12 to *p* God's people for works

PREPARED (PREPARE)

Mt 25: 34 the kingdom *p* for you
1Co 2: 9 what God has *p* for those who love
Eph 2: 10 which God *p* in advance for us
2Ti 4: 2 be *p* in season and out of season;
1Pe 3: 15 Always be *p* to give an answer

PRESENCE (PRESENT)

Ex 25: 30 Put the bread of the *P* on this table
Ezr 9: 15 one of us can stand in your *p*."
Ps 31: 20 the shelter of your *p* you hide them
89: 15 who walk in the light of your *p*,
90: 8 our secret sins in the light of your *p*
139: 7 Where can I flee from your *p*?
Jer 5: 22 "Should you not tremble in my *p*?
Heb 9: 24 now to appear for us in God's *p*.
Jude : 24 before his glorious *p* without fault

PRESENT (PRESENCE)

2Co 11: 2 so that I might *p* you as a pure
Eph 5: 27 and to *p* her to himself
2Ti 2: 15 Do your best to *p* yourself to God

PRESERVES

Ps 119: 50 Your promise *p* my life.

PRESS (PRESSED PRESSURE)

Php 3: 14 I *p* on toward the goal

PRESSED (PRESS)

Lk 6: 38 *p* down, shaken together

PRESSURE (PRESS)

2Co 1: 8 We were under great *p*, far
11: 28 I face daily the *p* of my concern

PREVAILS

1Sa 2: 9 "It is not by strength that one *p*;

PRICE

Job 28: 18 the *p* of wisdom is beyond rubies.
1Co 6: 20 your own; you were bought at a *p*.
7: 23 bought at a *p*; do not become slaves

PRIDE (PROUD)

Pr 8: 13 I hate *p* and arrogance,
16: 18 *P* goes before destruction,
Da 4: 37 And those who walk in *p* he is able
Gal 6: 4 Then he can take *p* in himself,
Jas 1: 9 ought to take *p* in his high position.

PRIEST (PRIESTHOOD PRIESTS)

Heb 4: 14 have a great high *p* who has gone
4: 15 do not have a high *p* who is unable
7: 26 Such a high *p* meets our need—
8: 1 We do have such a high *p*,

PRIESTHOOD (PRIEST)

Heb 7: 24 lives forever, he has a permanent *p*.
1Pe 2: 5 into a spiritual house to be a holy *p*,
2: 9 you are a chosen people, a royal *p*,

PRIESTS (PRIEST)

Ex 19: 6 you will be for me a kingdom of *p*
Rev 5: 10 to be a kingdom and *p*

PRINCE

Isa 9: 6 Everlasting Father, *P* of Peace.
Jn 12: 31 now the *p* of this world will be
Ac 5: 31 as *P* and Savior that he might give

PRISON (PRISONER)

Isa 42: 7 to free captives from *p*
Mt 25: 36 I was in *p* and you came to visit me
1Pe 3: 19 spirits in *p* who disobeyed long ago
Rev 20: 7 Satan will be released from his *p*

PRISONER (PRISON)

Ro 7: 23 and making me a *p* of the law of sin
Gal 3: 22 declares that the whole world is a *p*
Eph 3: 1 the *p* of Christ Jesus for the sake

PRIVILEGE*

2Co 8: 4 pleaded with us for the *p* of sharing

PRIZE

1Co 9: 24 Run in such a way as to get the *p*.
Php 3: 14 on toward the goal to win the *p*

PROCLAIM (PROCLAIMED PROCLAIMING)

1Ch 16: 23 *p* his salvation day after day.
Ps 19: 1 the skies *p* the work of his hands.
50: 6 the heavens *p* his righteousness,
68: 34 *P* the power of God,
118: 17 will *p* what the LORD has done.
Zec 9: 10 He will *p* peace to the nations.
Ac 20: 27 hesitated to *p* to you the whole will
1Co 11: 26 you *p* the Lord's death

PROCLAIMED (PROCLAIM)

Ro 15: 19 I have fully *p* the gospel of Christ.
Col 1: 23 that has been *p* to every creature

PROCLAIMING (PROCLAIM)

Ro 10: 8 the word of faith we are *p*:

PRODUCE (PRODUCES)
Mt 3: 8 *P* fruit in keeping with repentance.
3: 10 tree that does not *p* good fruit will

PRODUCES (PRODUCE)
Pr 30: 33 so stirring up anger *p* strife."
Ro 5: 3 that suffering *p* perseverance;
Heb 12: 11 it *p* a harvest of righteousness

PROFANE
Lev 22: 32 Do not *p* my holy name.

PROFESS*
1Ti 2: 10 for women who *p* to worship God.
Heb 4: 14 let us hold firmly to the faith we *p*.
10: 23 unswervingly to the hope we *p*,

PROMISE (PROMISED PROMISES)
1Ki 8: 20 The LORD has kept the *p* he made
Ac 2: 39 The *p* is for you and your children
Gal 3: 14 that by faith we might receive the *p*
1Ti 4: 8 holding *p* for both the present life
2Pe 3: 9 Lord is not slow in keeping his *p*,

PROMISED (PROMISE)
Ex 3: 17 And I have *p* to bring you up out
Dt 26: 18 his treasured possession as he *p*,
Ps 119: 57 I have *p* to obey your words.
Ro 4: 21 power to do what he had *p*.
Heb 10: 23 for he who *p* is faithful.
2Pe 3: 4 "Where is this 'coming' he *p*?

PROMISES (PROMISE)
Jos 21: 45 one of all the LORD's good *p*
Ro 9: 4 the temple worship and the *p*.
2Pe 1: 4 us his very great and precious *p*,

PROMPTED
1Th 1: 3 your labor *p* by love, and your
2Th 1: 11 and every act *p* by your faith.

PROPHECIES (PROPHESY)
1Co 13: 8 where there are *p*, they will cease;
1Th 5: 20 do not treat *p* with contempt.

PROPHECY (PROPHESY)
1Co 14: 1 gifts, especially the gift of *p*.
2Pe 1: 20 you must understand that no *p*

PROPHESY (PROPHECIES PROPHECY PROPHESYING PROPHET PROPHETS)
Joel 2: 28 Your sons and daughters will *p*,
Mt 7: 22 Lord, did we not *p* in your name,
1Co 14: 39 my brothers, be eager to *p*,

PROPHESYING (PROPHESY)
Ro 12: 6 If a man's gift is *p*, let him use it

PROPHET (PROPHESY)
Dt 18: 18 up for them a *p* like you
Am 7: 14 "I was neither a *p* nor a prophet's
Mt 10: 41 Anyone who receives a *p*
Lk 4: 24 "no *p* is accepted in his hometown.

PROPHETS (PROPHESY)
Ps 105: 15 do my *p* no harm."
Mt 5: 17 come to abolish the Law or the *P*;
7: 12 for this sums up the Law and the *P*.
24: 24 false Christs and false *p* will appear
Lk 24: 25 believe all that the *p* have spoken!
Ac 10: 43 All the *p* testify about him that
1Co 12: 28 second *p*, third teachers, then
14: 32 The spirits of *p* are subject
Eph 2: 20 foundation of the apostles and *p*,
Heb 1: 1 through the *p* at many times
1Pe 1: 10 Concerning this salvation, the *p*,
2Pe 1: 19 word of the *p* made more certain,

PROSPER (PROSPERITY PROSPERS)
Pr 28: 25 he who trusts in the LORD will *p*.

PROSPERITY (PROSPER)
Ps 73: 3 when I saw the *p* of the wicked.
Pr 13: 21 but *p* is the reward of the righteous.

PROSPERS (PROSPER)
Ps 1: 3 Whatever he does *p*.

PROSTITUTE (PROSTITUTES)
1Co 6: 15 of Christ and unite them with a *p*?

PROSTITUTES (PROSTITUTE)
Lk 15: 30 property with *p* comes home,
1Co 6: 9 male *p* nor homosexual offenders

PROSTRATE
Dt 9: 18 again I fell *p* before the LORD

PROTECT (PROTECTS)
Ps 32: 7 you will *p* me from trouble
Pr 2: 11 Discretion will *p* you,
Jn 17: 11 *p* them by the power of your name

PROTECTS (PROTECT)
1Co 13: 7 It always *p*, always trusts,

PROUD (PRIDE)
Pr 16: 5 The LORD detests all the *p*
Ro 12: 16 Do not be *p*, but be willing
1Co 13: 4 it does not boast, it is not *p*.

PROVE
Ac 26: 20 *p* their repentance by their deeds.
1Co 4: 2 been given a trust must *p* faithful.

PROVIDE (PROVIDED PROVIDES)
Ge 22: 8 "God himself will *p* the lamb
Isa 43: 20 because I *p* water in the desert
1Ti 5: 8 If anyone does not *p*

PROVIDED (PROVIDE)
Jnh 1: 17 But the LORD *p* a great fish
4: 6 Then the LORD God *p* a vine
4: 7 dawn the next day God *p* a worm,
4: 8 God *p* a scorching east wind,

PROVIDES (PROVIDE)
1Ti 6: 17 who richly *p* us with everything
1Pe 4: 11 it with the strength God *p*,

PROVOKED
Ecc 7: 9 Do not be quickly *p* in your spirit,

PRUDENT
Pr 14: 15 a *p* man gives thought to his steps.
19: 14 but a *p* wife is from the LORD.
Am 5: 13 Therefore the *p* man keeps quiet

PRUNING
Isa 2: 4 and their spears into *p* hooks.
Joel 3: 10 and your *p* hooks into spears.

PSALMS
Eph 5: 19 Speak to one another with *p*,
Col 3: 16 and as you sing *p*, hymns

PUBLICLY
Ac 20: 20 have taught you *p* and from house
1Ti 5: 20 Those who sin are to be rebuked *p*,

PUFFS
1Co 8: 1 Knowledge *p* up, but love builds up

PULLING
2Co 10: 8 building you up rather than *p* you

PUNISH (PUNISHED PUNISHES)
Ex 32: 34 I will *p* them for their sin."
Pr 23: 13 if you *p* him with the rod, he will
Isa 13: 11 I will *p* the world for its evil,
1Pe 2: 14 by him to *p* those who do wrong

PUNISHED (PUNISH)
La 3: 39 complain when *p* for his sins?
2Th 1: 9 be *p* with everlasting destruction
Heb 10: 29 to be *p* who has trampled the Son

PUNISHES (PUNISH)
Heb 12: 6 and he *p* everyone he accepts

PURE (PURIFIES PURIFY PURITY)
2Sa 22: 27 to the *p* you show yourself *p*,
Ps 24: 4 who has clean hands and a *p* heart,
51: 10 Create in me a *p* heart, O God,
119: 9 can a young man keep his way *p*?
Pr 20: 9 can say, "I have kept my heart *p*;
Isa 52: 11 Come out from it and be *p*,
Hab 1: 13 Your eyes are too *p* to look on evil;
Mt 5: 8 Blessed are the *p* in heart,
2Co 11: 2 I might present you as a *p* virgin
Php 4: 8 whatever is *p*, whatever is lovely,
1Ti 5: 22 Keep yourself *p*.
Tit 1: 15 To the *p*, all things are *p*,
2: 5 to be self-controlled and *p*,
Heb 13: 4 and the marriage bed kept *p*,
1Jn 3: 3 him purifies himself, just as he is *p*.

PURGE
Pr 20: 30 and beatings *p* the inmost being.

PURIFIES* (PURE)
1Jn 1: 7 of Jesus, his Son, *p* us from all sin.
3: 3 who has this hope in him *p* himself,

PURIFY (PURE)
Tit 2: 14 to *p* for himself a people that are
1Jn 1: 9 and *p* us from all unrighteousness.

PURITY (PURE)
2Co 6: 6 in *p*, understanding, patience
1Ti 4: 12 in life, in love, in faith and in *p*.

PURPOSE
Pr 19: 21 but it is the LORD's *p* that prevails
Isa 55: 11 and achieve the *p* for which I sent it
Ro 8: 28 have been called according to his *p*.
Php 2: 2 love,being one in spirit and *p*.

PURSES
Lk 12: 33 Provide *p* for yourselves that will

PURSUE
Ps 34: 14 seek peace and *p* it.
2Ti 2: 22 and *p* righteousness, faith,
1Pe 3: 11 he must seek peace and *p* it.

Q

QUALITIES (QUALITY)
2Pe 1: 8 For if you possess these *q*

QUALITY (QUALITIES)
1Co 3: 13 and the fire will test the *q*

QUARREL (QUARRELSOME)
Pr 15: 18 but a patient man calms a *q*.
17: 14 Starting a *q* is like breaching a dam;
17: 19 He who loves a *q* loves sin;
2Ti 2: 24 And the Lord's servant must not *q*;

QUARRELSOME (QUARREL)
Pr 19: 13 a *q* wife is like a constant dripping.
1Ti 3: 3 not violent but gentle, not *q*,

QUICK-TEMPERED
Tit 1: 7 not *q*, not given to drunkenness,

QUIET (QUIETNESS)
Ps 23: 2 he leads me beside *q* waters,
Zep 3: 17 he will *q* you with his love,
Lk 19: 40 he replied, "if they keep *q*,
1Ti 2: 2 we may live peaceful and *q* lives
1Pe 3: 4 beauty of a gentle and *q* spirit,

QUIETNESS (QUIET)
Isa 30: 15 in *q* and trust is your strength,
32: 17 the effect of righteousness will be *q*
1Ti 2: 11 A woman should learn in *q*

QUIVER
Ps 127: 5 whose *q* is full of them.

R

RACE
Ecc 9: 11 The *r* is not to the swift
1Co 9: 24 that in a *r* all the runners run,
2Ti 4: 7 I have finished the *r*, I have kept
Heb 12: 1 perseverance the *r* marked out

RACHEL
Daughter of Laban (Ge 29:16); wife of Jacob (Ge 29:28); bore two sons (Ge 30:22-24; 35:16-24; 46:19).

RADIANCE (RADIANT)
Heb 1: 3 The Son is the *r* of God's glory

RADIANT (RADIANCE)
Ex 34: 29 he was not aware that his face was *r*
Ps 34: 5 Those who look to him are *r*;
SS 5: 10 *Beloved* My lover is *r* and ruddy,
Isa 60: 5 Then you will look and be *r*,
Eph 5: 27 her to himself as a *r* church,

RAIN (RAINBOW)
Mt 5: 45 and sends *r* on the righteous

RAINBOW (RAIN)
Ge 9: 13 I have set my *r* in the clouds,

RAISED (RISE)
Ro 4: 25 was *r* to life for our justification.
10: 9 in your heart that God *r* him
1Co 15: 4 that he was *r* on the third day

RAN (RUN)
Jnh 1: 3 But Jonah *r* away from the LORD

RANSOM
Mt 20: 28 and to give his life as a *r* for many."
Heb 9: 15 as a *r* to set them free

RAVENS
1Ki 17: 6 The *r* brought him bread
Lk 12: 24 Consider the *r*: They do not sow

READ (READS)
Jos 8: 34 Joshua *r* all the words of the law—
Ne 8: 8 They *r* from the Book of the Law
2Co 3: 2 known and *r* by everybody.

READS (READ)
Rev 1: 3 Blessed is the one who *r* the words

REAL (REALITY)
Jn 6: 55 is *r* food and my blood is *r* drink.

REALITY* (REAL)
Col 2: 17 the *r*, however, is found in Christ.

REAP (REAPS)
Job 4: 8 and those who sow trouble *r* it.
2Co 9: 6 generously will also *r* generously.

REAPS (REAP)
Gal 6: 7 A man *r* what he sows.

REASON
Isa 1: 18 "Come now, let us *r* together,"
1Pe 3: 15 to give the *r* for the hope that you

REBEKAH
Sister of Laban, secured as bride for Isaac (Ge 24). Mother of Esau and Jacob (Ge 25:19-26). Taken by Abimelech as sister of Isaac; returned (Ge 26:1-11). Encouraged Jacob to trick Isaac out of blessing (Ge 27:1-17).

REBEL
Mt 10: 21 children will *r* against their parents

REBUKE (REBUKED REBUKING)
Pr 9: 8 *r* a wise man and he will love you.
27: 5 Better is open *r*

Lk 17: 3 "If your brother sins, *r* him,
2Ti 4: 2 correct, *r* and encourage—
Rev 3: 19 Those whom I love I *r*

REBUKED (REBUKE)
1Ti 5: 20 Those who sin are to be *r* publicly,

REBUKING (REBUKE)
2Ti 3: 16 *r*, correcting and training

RECEIVE (RECEIVED RECEIVES)
Ac 1: 8 you will *r* power when the Holy
20: 35 'It is more blessed to give than to *r*
2Co 6: 17 and I will *r* you."
Rev 4: 11 to *r* glory and honor and power,

RECEIVED (RECEIVE)
Mt 6: 2 they have *r* their reward in full.
10: 8 Freely you have *r*, freely give.
1Co 11: 23 For I *r* from the Lord what I
Col 2: 6 just as you *r* Christ Jesus as Lord,
1Pe 4: 10 should use whatever gift he has *r*

RECEIVES (RECEIVE)
Mt 7: 8 everyone who asks *r*; he who seeks
10: 40 he who *r* me *r* the one who sent me.
Ac 10: 43 believes in him *r* forgiveness of sins

RECKONING
Isa 10: 3 What will you do on the day of *r*,

RECOGNIZE (RECOGNIZED)
Mt 7: 16 By their fruit you will *r* them.

RECOGNIZED (RECOGNIZE)
Mt 12: 33 for a tree is *r* by its fruit.
Ro 7: 13 in order that sin might be *r* as sin,

RECOMPENSE
Isa 40: 10 and his *r* accompanies him.

RECONCILE (RECONCILED RECONCILIATION)
Eph 2: 16 in this one body to *r* both of them

RECONCILED (RECONCILE)
Mt 5: 24 First go and be *r* to your brother;
Ro 5: 10 we were *r* to him through the death
2Co 5: 18 who *r* us to himself through Christ

RECONCILIATION* (RECONCILE)
Ro 5: 11 whom we have now received *r*.
11: 15 For if their rejection is the *r*
2Co 5: 18 and gave us the ministry of *r*:
5: 19 committed to us the message of *r*.

RECORD
Ps 130: 3 If you, O LORD, kept a *r* of sins,

RED
Isa 1: 18 though they are *r* as crimson,

REDEEM (KINSMAN-REDEEMER REDEEMED REDEEMER REDEMPTION)
2Sa 7: 23 on earth that God went out to *r*
Ps 49: 7 No man can *r* the life of another
Gal 4: 5 under law, to *r* those under law,

REDEEMED (REDEEM)
Gal 3: 13 Christ *r* us from the curse
1Pe 1: 18 or gold that you were *r*

REDEEMER (REDEEM)
Job 19: 25 I know that my *R* lives,

REDEMPTION (REDEEM)
Ps 130: 7 and with him is full *r*.
Lk 21: 28 because your *r* is drawing near."
Ro 8: 23 as sons, the *r* of our bodies.
Eph 1: 7 In him we have *r* through his blood
Col 1: 14 in whom we have *r*, the forgiveness
Heb 9: 12 having obtained eternal *r*.

REFLECT
2Co 3: 18 unveiled faces all *r* the Lord's

REFUGE
Nu 35: 11 towns to be your cities of *r*,
Dt 33: 27 The eternal God is your *r*,
Ru 2: 12 wings you have come to take *r*."
Ps 46: 1 God is our *r* and strength,
91: 2 "He is my *r* and my fortress,

REHOBOAM
Son of Solomon (1Ki 11:43; 1Ch 3:10). Harsh treatment of subjects caused divided kingdom (1Ki 12:1-24; 14:21-31; 2Ch 10-12).

REIGN
Ex 15: 18 The LORD will *r*
Ro 6: 12 Therefore do not let sin *r*
1Co 15: 25 For he must *r* until he has put all
2Ti 2: 12 we will also *r* with him.
Rev 20: 6 will *r* with him for a thousand years

REJECTED (REJECTS)
Ps 118: 22 The stone the builders *r*
Isa 53: 3 He was despised and *r* by men,
1Ti 4: 4 nothing is to be *r* if it is received
1Pe 2: 4 *r* by men but chosen by God
2: 7 "The stone the builders *r*

REJECTS (REJECTED)
Lk 10: 16 but he who *r* me *r* him who sent me

Jn 3: 36 whoever *r* the Son will not see life,

REJOICE (JOY)

Ps 2: 11 and *r* with trembling.
66: 6 come, let us *r* in him.
118: 24 let us *r* and be glad in it.
Pr 5: 18 may you *r* in the wife of your youth
Lk 10: 20 but *r* that your names are written
15: 6 '*R* with me; I have found my lost
Ro 12: 15 Rejoice with those who *r*; mourn
Php 4: 4 *R* in the Lord always.

REJOICES (JOY)

Isa 61: 10 my soul *r* in my God.
Lk 1: 47 and my spirit *r* in God my Savior,
1Co 12: 26 if one part is honored, every part *r*.
13: 6 delight in evil but *r* with the truth.

REJOICING (JOY)

Ps 30: 5 but *r* comes in the morning.
Lk 15: 7 in the same way there will be more *r*
Ac 5: 41 *r* because they had been counted

RELIABLE

2Ti 2: 2 witnesses entrust to *r* men who will

RELIGION

1Ti 5: 4 all to put their *r* into practice
Jas 1: 27 *R* that God our Father accepts

REMAIN (REMAINS)

Nu 33: 55 allow to *r* will become barbs
Jn 15: 7 If you *r* in me and my words
Ro 13: 8 Let no debt *r* outstanding,
1Co 13: 13 And now these three *r*: faith,
2Ti 2: 13 he will *r* faithful,

REMAINS (REMAIN)

Ps 146: 6 the LORD, who *r* faithful forever.
Heb 7: 3 Son of God he *r* a priest forever.

REMEMBER (REMEMBERS REMEMBRANCE)

Ex 20: 8 "*R* the Sabbath day
1Ch 16: 12 *R* the wonders he has done,
Ecc 12: 1 *R* your Creator
Jer 31: 34 and will *r* their sins no more."
Gal 2: 10 we should continue to *r* the poor,
Php 1: 3 I thank my God every time I *r* you.
Heb 8: 12 and will *r* their sins no more."

REMEMBERS (REMEMBER)

Ps 103: 14 he *r* that we are dust.
111: 5 he *r* his covenant forever.
Isa 43: 25 and *r* your sins no more.

REMEMBRANCE (REMEMBER)

1Co 11: 24 which is for you; do this in *r* of me

REMIND

Jn 14: 26 will *r* you of everything I have said

REMOVED

Ps 30: 11 you *r* my sackcloth and clothed me
103: 12 so far has he *r* our transgressions
Jn 20: 1 and saw that the stone had been *r*

RENEW (RENEWED RENEWING)

Ps 51: 10 and *r* a steadfast spirit within me.
Isa 40: 31 will *r* their strength.

RENEWED (RENEW)

Ps 103: 5 that your youth is *r* like the eagle's.
2Co 4: 16 yet inwardly we are being *r* day

RENEWING (RENEW)

Ro 12: 2 transformed by the *r* of your mind.

RENOUNCE (RENOUNCES)

Da 4: 27 *R* your sins by doing what is right,

RENOUNCES (RENOUNCE)

Pr 28: 13 confesses and *r* them finds

RENOWN

Isa 63: 12 to gain for himself everlasting *r*,
Jer 32: 20 have gained the *r* that is still yours.

REPAID (PAY)

Lk 14: 14 you will be *r* at the resurrection
Col 3: 25 Anyone who does wrong will be *r*

REPAY (PAY)

Dt 32: 35 It is mine to avenge; I will *r*.
Ru 2: 12 May the LORD *r* you
Ps 116: 12 How can I *r* the LORD
Ro 12: 19 "It is mine to avenge; I will *r*,"
1Pe 3: 9 Do not *r* evil with evil

REPENT (REPENTANCE REPENTS)

Job 42: 6 and *r* in dust and ashes."
Jer 15: 19 "If you *r*, I will restore you
Mt 4: 17 "*R*, for the kingdom of heaven is
Lk 13: 3 unless you *r*, you too will all perish.
Ac 2: 38 Peter replied, "*R* and be baptized,
17: 30 all people everywhere to *r*.

REPENTANCE (REPENT)

Lk 3: 8 Produce fruit in keeping with *r*.
5: 32 call the righteous, but sinners to *r*."

Ac 26: 20 and prove their *r* by their deeds.
2Co 7: 10 Godly sorrow brings *r* that leads

REPENTS (REPENT)

Lk 15: 10 of God over one sinner who *r*."
17: 3 rebuke him, and if he *r*, forgive him

REPROACH

1Ti 3: 2 Now the overseer must be above *r*,

REPUTATION

1Ti 3: 7 also have a good *r* with outsiders,

REQUESTS

Ps 20: 5 May the LORD grant all your *r*.
Php 4: 6 with thanksgiving, present your *r*

REQUIRE

Mic 6: 8 And what does the LORD *r* of you

RESCUE (RESCUES)

Da 6: 20 been able to *r* you from the lions?"
2Pe 2: 9 how to *r* godly men from trials

RESCUES (RESCUE)

1Th 1: 10 who *r* us from the coming wrath.

RESIST

Jas 4: 7 *R* the devil, and he will flee
1Pe 5: 9 *R* him, standing firm in the faith,

RESOLVED

Ps 17: 3 I have *r* that my mouth will not sin.
Da 1: 8 But Daniel *r* not to defile himself
1Co 2: 2 For I *r* to know nothing while I was

RESPECT (RESPECTABLE)

Lev 19: 3 " 'Each of you must *r* his mother
19: 32 show *r* for the elderly and revere
Pr 11: 16 A kindhearted woman gains *r*,
Mal 1: 6 where is the *r* due me?" says
1Th 4: 12 so that your daily life may win the *r*
5: 12 to *r* those who work hard
1Ti 3: 4 children obey him with proper *r*.
1Pe 2: 17 Show proper *r* to everyone:
3: 7 them with *r* as the weaker partner

RESPECTABLE* (RESPECT)

1Ti 3: 2 self-controlled, *r*, hospitable,

REST

Ex 31: 15 the seventh day is a Sabbath of *r*,

Ps 91: 1 will *r* in the shadow
Jer 6: 16 and you will find *r* for your souls.
Mt 11: 28 and burdened, and I will give you *r*.

RESTITUTION

Ex 22: 3 "A thief must certainly make *r*,
Lev 6: 5 He must make *r* in full, add a fifth

RESTORE (RESTORES)

Ps 51: 12 *R* to me the joy of your salvation
Gal 6: 1 are spiritual should *r* him gently.

RESTORES (RESTORE)

Ps 23: 3 he *r* my soul.

RESURRECTION

Mt 22: 30 At the *r* people will neither marry
Lk 14: 14 repaid at the *r* of the righteous."
Jn 11: 25 Jesus said to her, "I am the *r*
Ro 1: 4 Son of God by his *r* from the dead:
1Co 15: 12 some of you say that there is no *r*
Php 3: 10 power of his *r* and the fellowship
Rev 20: 5 This is the first *r*.

RETRIBUTION

Jer 51: 56 For the LORD is a God of *r*;

RETURN

2Ch 30: 9 If you *r* to the LORD, then your
Ne 1: 9 but if you *r* to me and obey my
Isa 55: 11 It will not *r* to me empty,
Hos 6: 1 "Come, let us *r* to the LORD.
Joel 2: 12 "*r* to me with all your heart,

REVEALED (REVELATION)

Dt 29: 29 but the things *r* belong to us
Isa 40: 5 the glory of the LORD will be *r*,
Mt 11: 25 and *r* them to little children.
Ro 1: 17 a righteousness from God is *r*,
8: 18 with the glory that will be *r* in us.

REVELATION (REVEALED)

Gal 1: 12 I received it by *r* from Jesus Christ.
Rev 1: 1 *r* of Jesus Christ, which God gave

REVENGE (VENGEANCE)

Lev 19: 18 " 'Do not seek *r* or bear a grudge
Ro 12: 19 Do not take *r*, my friends,

REVERE (REVERENCE)

Ps 33: 8 let all the people of the world *r* him

VERENCE (REVERE)
v 19: 30 and have *r* for my sanctuary.
5: 7 in *r* will I bow down
l 3: 22 of heart and *r* for the Lord.
e 3: 2 when they see the purity and *r*

VIVE (REVIVING)
85: 6 Will you not *r* us again,
a 57: 15 to *r* the spirit of the lowly

EVIVING (REVIVE)
19: 7 *r* the soul.

EWARD (REWARDED)
19: 11 in keeping them there is great *r*.
127: 3 children a *r* from him.
19: 17 he will *r* him for what he has done.
25: 22 and the LORD will *r* you.
31: 31 Give her the *r* she has earned,
r 17: 10 to *r* a man according to his conduct
t 5: 12 because great is your *r* in heaven,
6: 5 they have received their *r* in full.
16: 27 and then he will *r* each person
Co 3: 14 built survives, he will receive his *r*.
ev 22: 12 I am coming soon! My *r* is with me

EWARDED (REWARD)
u 2: 12 May you be richly *r* by the LORD,
s 18: 24 The LORD has *r* me according
r 14: 14 and the good man *r* for his.
Co 3: 8 and each will be *r* according

ICH (RICHES)
r 23: 4 Do not wear yourself out to get *r*;
er 9: 23 or the *r* man boast of his riches,
Mt 19: 23 it is hard for a *r* man
Co 6: 10 yet making many *r*; having nothing
8: 9 he was *r*, yet for your sakes he
Ti 6: 17 Command those who are *r*

RICHES (RICH)
Ps 119: 14 as one rejoices in great *r*.
Pr 30: 8 give me neither poverty nor *r*,
sa 10: 3 Where will you leave your *r*?
Ro 9: 23 to make the *r* of his glory known
11: 33 the depth of the *r* of the wisdom
Eph 2: 7 he might show the incomparable *r*
3: 8 to the Gentiles the unsearchable *r*
Col 1: 27 among the Gentiles the glorious *r*

RID
Ge 21: 10 "Get *r* of that slave woman
1Co 5: 7 Get *r* of the old yeast that you may
Gal 4: 30 "Get *r* of the slave woman

RIGHT (RIGHTS)
Ge 18: 25 the Judge of all the earth do *r*?"
Ex 15: 26 and do what is *r* in his eyes,
Dt 5: 32 do not turn aside to the *r*
Ps 16: 8 Because he is at my *r* hand,
19: 8 The precepts of the LORD are *r*,
63: 8 your *r* hand upholds me.
110: 1 "Sit at my *r* hand
Pr 4: 27 Do not swerve to the *r* or the left;
14: 12 There is a way that seems *r*
Isa 1: 17 learn to do *r*!
Jer 23: 5 and do what is just and *r* in the land
Hos 14: 9 The ways of the LORD are *r*;
Mt 6: 3 know what your *r* hand is doing,
Jn 1: 12 he gave the *r* to become children
Ro 9: 21 Does not the potter have the *r*
12: 17 careful to do what is *r* in the eyes
Eph 1: 20 and seated him at his *r* hand
Php 4: 8 whatever is *r*, whatever is pure,
2Th 3: 13 never tire of doing what is *r*.

RIGHTEOUS (RIGHTEOUSNESS)
Ps 34: 15 The eyes of the LORD are on the *r*
37: 25 yet I have never seen the *r* forsaken
119:137 *R* are you, O LORD,
143: 2 for no one living is *r* before you.
Pr 3: 33 but he blesses the home of the *r*.
11: 30 The fruit of the *r* is a tree of life,
18: 10 the *r* run to it and are safe.
Isa 64: 6 and all our *r* acts are like filthy rags
Hab 2: 4 but the *r* will live by his faith—
Mt 5: 45 rain on the *r* and the unrighteous.
9: 13 For I have not come to call the *r*,
13: 49 and separate the wicked from the *r*
25: 46 to eternal punishment, but the *r*
Ro 1: 17 as it is written: "The *r* will live
3: 10 "There is no one *r*, not even one;
1Ti 1: 9 that law is made not for the *r*
1Pe 3: 18 the *r* for the unrighteous,
1Jn 3: 7 does what is right is *r*, just as he is *r*.
Rev 19: 8 stands for the *r* acts of the saints.)

RIGHTEOUSNESS (RIGHTEOUS)
Ge 15: 6 and he credited it to him as *r*.
1Sa 26: 23 LORD rewards every man for his *r*
Ps 9: 8 He will judge the world in *r*;
23: 3 He guides me in paths of *r*
45: 7 You love *r* and hate wickedness;
85: 10 *r* and peace kiss each other.
89: 14 *R* and justice are the foundation
111: 3 and his *r* endures forever.
Pr 14: 34 *R* exalts a nation,
21: 21 He who pursues *r* and love
Isa 5: 16 will show himself holy by his *r*.
59: 17 He put on *r* as his breastplate,
Eze 18: 20 The *r* of the righteous man will be
Da 9: 24 to bring in everlasting *r*,
12: 3 and those who lead many to *r*,
Mal 4: 2 the sun of *r* will rise with healing
Mt 5: 6 those who hunger and thirst for *r*,
5: 20 unless your *r* surpasses that
6: 33 But seek first his kingdom and his *r*
Ro 4: 3 and it was credited to him as *r*."
4: 9 faith was credited to him as *r*.
6: 13 body to him as instruments of *r*.
2Co 5: 21 that in him we might become the *r*
Gal 2: 21 for if *r* could be gained
3: 6 and it was credited to him as *r*."
Eph 6: 14 with the breastplate of *r* in place,
Php 3: 9 not having a *r* of my own that
2Ti 3: 16 correcting and training in *r*,
4: 8 is in store for me the crown of *r*,
Heb 11: 7 became heir of the *r* that comes
2Pe 2: 21 not to have known the way of *r*,

RIGHTS (RIGHT)
La 3: 35 to deny a man his *r*
Gal 4: 5 that we might receive the full *r*

RISE (RAISED)
Isa 26: 19 their bodies will *r*.
Mt 27: 63 'After three days I will *r* again.'
Jn 5: 29 those who have done good will *r*
1Th 4: 16 and the dead in Christ will *r* first.

ROAD
Mt 7: 13 and broad is the *r* that leads

ROBBERS
Jer 7: 11 become a den of *r* to you?
Mk 15: 27 They crucified two *r* with him,
Lk 19: 46 but you have made it 'a den of *r*.' "
Jn 10: 8 came before me were thieves and *r*,

ROCK
Ps 18: 2 The LORD is my *r*, my fortress
40: 2 he set my feet on a *r*
Mt 7: 24 man who built his house on the *r*.
16: 18 and on this *r* I will build my church
Ro 9: 33 and a *r* that makes them fall,
1Co 10: 4 the spiritual *r* that accompanied

ROD
Ps 23: 4 your *r* and your staff,
Pr 13: 24 He who spares the *r* hates his son,
23: 13 if you punish him with the *r*,

ROOM (ROOMS)
Mt 6: 6 But when you pray, go into your *r*,
Lk 2: 7 there was no *r* for them in the inn.
Jn 21: 25 the whole world would not have *r*

ROOMS (ROOM)
Jn 14: 2 In my Father's house are many *r*;

ROOT
Isa 53: 2 and like a *r* out of dry ground.
1Ti 6: 10 of money is a *r* of all kinds of evil.

ROYAL
Jas 2: 8 If you really keep the *r* law found
1Pe 2: 9 a *r* priesthood, a holy nation,

RUBBISH*
Php 3: 8 I consider them *r*, that I may gain

RUDE*
1Co 13: 5 It is not *r*, it is not self-seeking,

RUIN (RUINS)
Pr 18: 24 many companions may come to *r*,
1Ti 6: 9 desires that plunge men into *r*

RUINS (RUIN)
Pr 19: 3 A man's own folly *r* his life,
2Ti 2: 14 and only *r* those who listen.

RULE (RULER RULERS RULES)
1Sa 12: 12 'No, we want a king to *r* over us'—

Ps 2: 9 You will *r* them with an iron
Ps 119:133 let no sin *r* over me.
Zec 9: 10 His *r* will extend from sea to sea
Col 3: 15 the peace of Christ *r* in your hearts,
Rev 2: 27 He will *r* them with an iron scepter;

RULER (RULE)

Ps 8: 6 You made him *r* over the works
Eph 2: 2 of the *r* of the kingdom of the air,
1Ti 6: 15 God, the blessed and only *R*,

RULERS (RULE)

Ps 2: 2 and the *r* gather together
Col 1: 16 or powers or *r* or authorities;

RULES (RULE)

Ps 103: 19 and his kingdom *r* over all.
Lk 22: 26 one who *r* like the one who serves.
2Ti 2: 5 he competes according to the *r*.

RUMORS

Mt 24: 6 You will hear of wars and *r* of wars,

RUN (RAN)

Isa 40: 31 they will *r* and not grow weary,
1Co 9: 24 *R* in such a way as to get the prize.
Heb 12: 1 let us *r* with perseverance the race

RUST

Mt 6: 19 where moth and *r* destroy,

RUTH*

Moabitess; widow who went to Bethlehem with mother-in-law Naomi (Ru 1). Gleaned in field of Boaz; shown favor (Ru 2). Proposed marriage to Boaz (Ru 3). Married (Ru 4:1-12); bore Obed, ancestor of David (Ru 4:13-22), Jesus (Mt 1:5).

S

SABBATH

Ex 20: 8 "Remember the *S* day
Dt 5: 12 "Observe the *S* day
Col 2: 16 a New Moon celebration or a *S* day

SACKCLOTH

Mt 11: 21 would have repented long ago in *s*

SACRED

Mt 7: 6 "Do not give dogs what is *s*;
1Co 3: 17 for God's temple is *s*, and you are

SACRIFICE
(SACRIFICED SACRIFICES)

Ge 22: 2 *S* him there as a burnt offering
Ex 12: 27 It is the Passover *s* to the LORD,
1Sa 15: 22 To obey is better than *s*,
Hos 6: 6 For I desire mercy, not *s*,
Mt 9: 13 this means: 'I desire mercy, not *s*.'
Heb 9: 26 away with sin by the *s* of himself.
13: 15 offer to God a *s* of praise—
1Jn 2: 2 He is the atoning *s* for our sins,

SACRIFICED (SACRIFICE)

1Co 5: 7 our Passover lamb, has been *s*.
8: 1 Now about food *s* to idols:
Heb 9: 28 so Christ was *s* once

SACRIFICES (SACRIFICE)

Ps 51: 17 The *s* of God are a broken spirit;
Ro 12: 1 to offer your bodies as living *s*,

SADDUCEES

Mk 12: 18 *S*, who say there is no resurrection,

SAFE (SAVE)

Ps 37: 3 in the land and enjoy *s* pasture.
Pr 18: 10 the righteous run to it and are *s*.

SAFETY (SAVE)

Ps 4: 8 make me dwell in *s*.
1Th 5: 3 people are saying, "Peace and *s*,"

SAINTS

Ps 116: 15 is the death of his *s*.
Ro 8: 27 intercedes for the *s* in accordance
Eph 1: 18 of his glorious inheritance in the *s*,
6: 18 always keep on praying for all the *s*
Rev 5: 8 which are the prayers of the *s*.
19: 8 for the righteous acts of the *s*.)

SAKE

Ps 44: 22 Yet for your *s* we face death all day
Php 3: 7 loss for the *s* of Christ.
Heb 11: 26 He regarded disgrace for the *s*

SALT

Ge 19: 26 and she became a pillar of *s*.
Mt 5: 13 "You are the *s* of the earth.

SALVATION (SAVE)

Ex 15: 2 he has become my *s*.
1Ch 16: 23 proclaim his *s* day after day.
Ps 27: 1 The LORD is my light and my *s*—
51: 12 Restore to me the joy of your *s*
62: 2 He alone is my rock and my *s*;
85: 9 Surely his *s* is near those who fear
96: 2 proclaim his *s* day after day.
Isa 25: 9 let us rejoice and be glad in his *s*."
45: 17 the LORD with an everlasting *s*;
51: 6 But my *s* will last forever,
59: 17 and the helmet of *s* on his head;
61: 10 me with garments of *s*
Jnh 2: 9 *S* comes from the LORD."
Zec 9: 9 righteous and having *s*,
Lk 2: 30 For my eyes have seen your *s*,
Jn 4: 22 for *s* is from the Jews.
Ac 4: 12 *S* is found in no one else,
13: 47 that you may bring *s* to the ends
Ro 11: 11 *s* has come to the Gentiles
2Co 7: 10 brings repentance that leads to *s*
Eph 6: 17 Take the helmet of *s* and the sword
Php 2: 12 to work out your *s* with fear
1Th 5: 8 and the hope of *s* as a helmet.
2Ti 3: 15 wise for *s* through faith
Heb 2: 3 escape if we ignore such a great *s*?
6: 9 case—things that accompany *s*.
1Pe 1: 10 Concerning this *s*, the prophets,
2: 2 by it you may grow up in your *s*,

SAMARITAN

Lk 10: 33 But a *S*, as he traveled, came where

SAMSON

Danite judge. Birth promised (Jdg 13). Married to Philistine (Jdg 14). Vengeance on Philistines (Jdg 15). Betrayed by Delilah (Jdg 16:1-22). Death (Jdg 16:23-31). Feats of strength: killed lion (Jdg 14:6), 30 Philistines (Jdg 14:19), 1,000 Philistines with jawbone (Jdg 15:13-17), carried off gates of Gaza (Jdg 16:3), pushed down temple of Dagon (Jdg 16:25-30).

SAMUEL

Ephraimite judge and prophet (Heb 11:32). Birth prayed for (1Sa 1:10-18). Dedicated to temple by Hannah (1Sa 1:21-28). Raised by Eli (1Sa 2:11,18-26). Called as prophet (1Sa 3). Led Israel to victory over Philistines (1Sa 7). Asked by Israel for a king (1Sa 8). Anointed Saul as king (1Sa 9-10). Farewell speech (1Sa 12). Rebuked Saul for sacrifice (1Sa 13). Announced rejection of Saul (1Sa 15). Anointed David as king (1Sa 16). Protected David from Saul (1Sa 19:18-24). Death (1Sa 25:1). Returned from dead to condemn Saul (1Sa 28).

SANCTIFIED (SANCTIFY)

Ac 20: 32 among all those who are *s*.
Ro 15: 16 to God, *s* by the Holy Spirit.
1Co 6: 11 But you were washed, you were *s*,
7: 14 and the unbelieving wife has been *s*
Heb 10: 29 blood of the covenant tha *s* him,

SANCTIFY
(SANCTIFIED SANCTIFYING)

1Th 5: 23 *s* you through and throug

SANCTIFYING (SANCTIFY)

2Th 2: 13 through the *s* work of the Spirit

SANCTUARY

Ex 25: 8 "Then have them make a for me,

SAND

Ge 22: 17 and as the *s* on the seashor
Mt 7: 26 man who built his house on *s*.

SANDALS

Ex 3: 5 off your *s*, for the place where you
Jos 5: 15 off your *s*, for the place where you

SANG (SING)

Job 38: 7 while the morning stars *s* together
Rev 5: 9 And they *s* a new song:

SARAH

Wife of Abraham, originally name Sarai; barren (Ge 11:29-31; 1Pe 3:6 Taken by Pharaoh as Abraham's siste returned (Ge 12:10-20). Gave Hagar Abraham; sent her away in pregnanc (Ge 16). Name changed; Isaac promise (Ge 17:15-21; 18:10-15; Heb 11:11 Taken by Abimelech as Abraham's si ter; returned (Ge 20). Isaac born; Hag and Ishmael sent away (Ge 21:1-21; G 4:21-31). Death (Ge 23).

SATAN

Job 1: 6 and *S* also came with them
Zec 3: 2 said to *S*, "The LORD rebuk you,
Mk 4: 15 *S* comes and takes away the word
2Co 11: 14 for *S* himself masquerades
12: 7 a messenger of *S*, to torment me.
Rev 12: 9 serpent called the devil, or *S*
20: 2 or *S*, and bound him for a thousand
20: 7 *S* will be released from his prison

SATISFIED (SATISFY)

Isa 53: 11 he will see the light ⌊of life⌋ and be *s*

SATISFIES (SATISFY)

Ps 103: 5 who *s* your desires with good things,

SATISFY (SATISFIED SATISFIES)

Isa 55: 2 and your labor on what does not *s*?

SAUL

1. Benjamite; anointed by Samuel as first king of Israel (1Sa 9-10). Defeate

Ammonites (1Sa 11). Rebuked for offering sacrifice (1Sa 13:1-15). Defeated Philistines (1Sa 14). Rejected as king for failing to annihilate Amalekites (1Sa 15). Soothed from evil spirit by David (1Sa 16:14-23). Sent David against Goliath (1Sa 17). Jealousy and attempted murder of David (1Sa 18:1-11). Gave David Michal as wife (1Sa 18:12-30). Second attempt to kill David (1Sa 19). Anger at Jonathan (1Sa 20:26-34). Pursued David: killed priests at Nob (1Sa 22), went to Keilah and Ziph (1Sa 23), life spared by David at En Gedi (1Sa 24) and in his tent (1Sa 26). Rebuked by Samuel's spirit for consulting witch at Endor (1Sa 28). Wounded by Philistines; took his own life (1Sa 31; 1Ch 10).

2. See PAUL

SAVE (SAFE SAFETY SALVATION SAVED SAVIOR)

Isa 63: 1 mighty to *s*."
Da 3: 17 the God we serve is able to *s* us
Zep 3: 17 he is mighty to *s*.
Mt 1: 21 he will *s* his people from their sins
16: 25 wants to *s* his life will lose it,
Lk 19: 10 to seek and to *s* what was lost."
Jn 3: 17 but to *s* the world through him.
1Ti 1: 15 came into the world to *s* sinners—
Jas 5: 20 of his way will *s* him from death

SAVED (SAVE)

Ps 34: 6 he *s* him out of all his troubles.
Isa 45: 22 "Turn to me and be *s*,
Joel 2: 32 on the name of the LORD will be *s*;
Mk 13: 13 firm to the end will be *s*.
16: 16 believes and is baptized will be *s*,
Jn 10: 9 enters through me will be *s*.
Ac 4: 12 to men by which we must be *s*."
16: 30 do to be *s*?" They replied,
Ro 9: 27 only the remnant will be *s*.
10: 9 him from the dead, you will be *s*.
1Co 3: 15 will suffer loss; he himself will be *s*,
15: 2 By this gospel you are *s*,
Eph 2: 5 it is by grace you have been *s*.
2: 8 For it is by grace you have been *s*,
1Ti 2: 4 who wants all men to be *s*

SAVIOR (SAVE)

Ps 89: 26 my God, the Rock my *S*.'
Isa 43: 11 and apart from me there is no *s*.
Hos 13: 4 no *S* except me.
Lk 1: 47 and my spirit rejoices in God my *S*,
2: 11 of David a *S* has been born to you;
Jn 4: 42 know that this man really is the *S*
Eph 5: 23 his body, of which he is the *S*.
1Ti 4: 10 who is the *S* of all men,
Tit 2: 10 about God our *S* attractive.
2: 13 appearing of our great God and *S*,
3: 4 and love of God our *S* appeared,
1Jn 4: 14 Son to be the *S* of the world.
Jude : 25 to the only God our *S* be glory,

SCALES

Lev 19: 36 Use honest *s* and honest weights,
Da 5: 27 You have been weighed on the *s*

SCAPEGOAT (GOAT)

Lev 16: 10 by sending it into the desert as a *s*.

SCARLET

Isa 1: 18 "Though your sins are like *s*,

SCATTERED

Jer 31: 10 'He who *s* Israel will gather them
Ac 8: 4 who had been *s* preached the word

SCEPTER

Rev 19: 15 "He will rule them with an iron *s*."

SCHEMES

2Co 2: 11 For we are not unaware of his *s*.
Eph 6: 11 stand against the devil's *s*.

SCOFFERS

2Pe 3: 3 that in the last days *s* will come,

SCORPION

Rev 9: 5 sting of a *s* when it strikes a man.

SCRIPTURE (SCRIPTURES)

Jn 10: 35 and the *S* cannot be broken—
1Ti 4: 13 yourself to the public reading of *S*,
2Ti 3: 16 All *S* is God-breathed
2Pe 1: 20 that no prophecy of *S* came about

SCRIPTURES (SCRIPTURE)

Lk 24: 27 said in all the *S* concerning himself.
Jn 5: 39 These are the *S* that testify about
Ac 17: 11 examined the *S* every day to see

SCROLL

Eze 3: 1 eat what is before you, eat this *s*;

SEA

Ex 14: 16 go through the *s* on dry ground.
Isa 57: 20 the wicked are like the tossing *s*,
Mic 7: 19 iniquities into the depths of the *s*.
Jas 1: 6 who doubts is like a wave of the *s*,
Rev 13: 1 I saw a beast coming out of the *s*.

SEAL (SEALS)

Jn 6: 27 God the Father has placed his *s*
2Co 1: 22 set his *s* of ownership on us,
Eph 1: 13 you were marked in him with a *s*,

SEALS (SEAL)

Rev 5: 2 "Who is worthy to break the *s*
6: 1 opened the first of the seven *s*.

SEARCH (SEARCHED SEARCHES SEARCHING)

Ps 4: 4 *s* your hearts and be silent.
139: 23 *S* me, O God, and know my heart;
Pr 2: 4 and *s* for it as for hidden treasure,
Jer 17: 10 "I the LORD *s* the heart
Eze 34: 16 I will *s* for the lost and bring back
Lk 15: 8 and *s* carefully until she finds it?

SEARCHED (SEARCH)

Ps 139: 1 O LORD, you have *s* me

SEARCHES (SEARCH)

Ro 8: 27 And he who *s* our hearts knows
1Co 2: 10 The Spirit *s* all things,

SEARCHING (SEARCH)

Am 8: 12 *s* for the word of the LORD,

SEARED

1Ti 4: 2 whose consciences have been *s*

SEASON

2Ti 4: 2 be prepared in *s* and out of *s*;

SEAT (SEATED SEATS)

Ps 1: 1 or sit in the *s* of mockers.
Da 7: 9 and the Ancient of Days took his *s*.
2Co 5: 10 before the judgment *s* of Christ,

SEATED (SEAT)

Ps 47: 8 God is *s* on his holy throne.
Isa 6: 1 I saw the Lord *s* on a throne,
Col 3: 1 where Christ is *s* at the right hand

SEATS (SEAT)

Lk 11: 43 you love the most important *s*

SECRET (SECRETS)

Dt 29: 29 The *s* things belong
Jdg 16: 6 Tell me the *s* of your great strength
Ps 90: 8 our *s* sins in the light
Pr 11: 13 but a trustworthy man keeps a *s*.
Mt 6: 4 so that your giving may be in *s*.
2Co 4: 2 we have renounced *s* and shameful
Php 4: 12 I have learned the *s*

SECRETS (SECRET)

Ps 44: 21 since he knows the *s* of the heart?
1Co 14: 25 the *s* of his heart will be laid bare.

SECURE (SECURITY)

Ps 112: 8 His heart is *s*, he will have no fear;
Heb 6: 19 an anchor for the soul, firm and *s*.

SECURITY (SECURE)

Job 31: 24 or said to pure gold, 'You are my *s*,'

SEED (SEEDS)

Lk 8: 11 of the parable: The *s* is the word
1Co 3: 6 I planted the *s*, Apollos watered it,
2Co 9: 10 he who supplies *s* to the sower
Gal 3: 29 then you are Abraham's *s*,
1Pe 1: 23 not of perishable *s*,

SEEDS (SEED)

Jn 12: 24 But if it dies, it produces many *s*.
Gal 3: 16 Scripture does not say "and to *s*,"

SEEK (SEEKS SELF-SEEKING)

Dt 4: 29 if from there you *s* the LORD your
1Ch 28: 9 If you *s* him, he will be found
2Ch 7: 14 themselves and pray and *s* my face
Ps 119: 10 I *s* you with all my heart;
Isa 55: 6 *S* the LORD while he may be
65: 1 found by those who did not *s* me.
Mt 6: 33 But *s* first his kingdom
Lk 19: 10 For the Son of Man came to *s*
Ro 10: 20 found by those who did not *s* me;
1Co 7: 27 you married? Do not *s* a divorce.

SEEKS (SEEK)

Jn 4: 23 the kind of worshipers the Father *s*.

SEER

1Sa 9: 9 of today used to be called a *s*.)

SELF-CONTROL (CONTROL)

1Co 7: 5 you because of your lack of *s*.

Gal 5: 23 faithfulness, gentleness and *s.*
2Pe 1: 6 and to knowledge, *s;* and to *s,*

SELF-CONTROLLED* (CONTROL)

1Th 5: 6 are asleep, but let us be alert and *s.*
5: 8 let us be *s,* putting on faith and love
1Ti 3: 2 *s,* respectable, hospitable,
Tit 1: 8 who is *s,* upright, holy
2: 2 worthy of respect, *s,* and sound
2: 5 to be *s* and pure, to be busy at home
2: 6 encourage the young men to be *s.*
2: 12 to live *s,* upright and godly lives
1Pe 1: 13 prepare your minds for action; be *s;*
4: 7 and *s* so that you can pray.
5: 8 Be *s* and alert.

SELF-INDULGENCE

Mt 23: 25 inside they are full of greed and *s.*

SELF-SEEKING (SEEK)

1Co 13: 5 it is not *s,* it is not easily angered,

SELFISH*

Ps 119: 36 and not toward *s* gain.
Pr 18: 1 An unfriendly man pursues *s* ends;
Gal 5: 20 fits of rage, *s* ambition, dissensions,
Php 1: 17 preach Christ out of *s* ambition,
2: 3 Do nothing out of *s* ambition
Jas 3: 14 and *s* ambition in your hearts,
3: 16 you have envy and *s* ambition,

SEND (SENDING SENT)

Isa 6: 8 *S* me!" He said, "Go and tell this
Mt 9: 38 to *s* out workers into his harvest
Jn 16: 7 but if I go, I will *s* him to you.

SENDING (SEND)

Jn 20: 21 Father has sent me, I am *s* you."

SENSES*

Lk 15: 17 "When he came to his *s,* he said,
1Co 15: 34 Come back to your *s* as you ought,
2Ti 2: 26 and that they will come to their *s*

SENSUAL

Col 2: 23 value in restraining *s* indulgence.

SENT (SEND)

Isa 55: 11 achieve the purpose for which I *s* it.
Mt 10: 40 me receives the one who *s* me.
Jn 4: 34 "is to do the will of him who *s* me
Ro 10: 15 can they preach unless they are *s?*
1Jn 4: 10 but that he loved us and *s* his Son

SEPARATE (SEPARATED SEPARATES)

Mt 19: 6 has joined together, let man not *s.*"
Ro 8: 35 Who shall *s* us from the love
1Co 7: 10 wife must not *s* from her husband.
2Co 6: 17 and be *s,* says the Lord.

SEPARATED (SEPARATE)

Isa 59: 2 But your iniquities have *s*

SEPARATES (SEPARATE)

Pr 16: 28 and a gossip *s* close friends.

SERPENT

Ge 3: 1 the *s* was more crafty than any
Rev 12: 9 that ancient *s* called the devil

SERVANT (SERVANTS)

1Sa 3: 10 "Speak, for your *s* is listening."
Mt 20: 26 great among you must be your *s,*
25: 21 'Well done, good and faithful *s!*
Lk 16: 13 "No *s* can serve two masters.
Php 2: 7 taking the very nature of a *s,*
2Ti 2: 24 And the Lord's *s* must not quarrel;

SERVANTS (SERVANT)

Lk 17: 10 should say, 'We are unworthy *s;*
Jn 15: 15 longer call you *s,* because a servant

SERVE (SERVICE SERVING)

Dt 10: 12 to *s* the LORD your God
Jos 22: 5 and to *s* him with all your heart
24: 15 this day whom you will *s,*
Mt 4: 10 Lord your God, and *s* him only.' "
6: 24 "No one can *s* two masters.
20: 28 but to *s,* and to give his life
Eph 6: 7 *S* wholeheartedly,

SERVICE (SERVE)

1Co 12: 5 There are different kinds of *s,*
Eph 4: 12 God's people for works of *s,*

SERVING (SERVE)

Ro 12: 11 your spiritual fervor, *s* the Lord.
Eph 6: 7 as if you were *s* the Lord, not men,

Col 3: 24 It is the Lord Christ you are *s.*
2Ti 2: 4 No one *s* as a soldier gets involved

SEVEN (SEVENTH)

Ge 7: 2 Take with you *s* of every kind
Jos 6: 4 march around the city *s* times,
1Ki 19: 18 Yet I reserve *s* thousand in Israel—
Pr 6: 16 *s* that are detestable to him:
24: 16 a righteous man falls *s* times,
Isa 4: 1 In that day *s* women
Da 9: 25 comes, there will be *s* 'sevens,'
Mt 18: 21 Up to *s* times?" Jesus answered,
Lk 11: 26 takes *s* other spirits more wicked
Ro 11: 4 for myself *s* thousand who have not
Rev 1: 4 To the *s* churches in the province
6: 1 opened the first of the *s* seals.
8: 2 and to them were given *s* trumpets.
10: 4 And when the *s* thunders spoke,
15: 7 to the *s* angels *s* golden bowls filled

SEVENTH (SEVEN)

Ge 2: 2 By the *s* day God had finished
Ex 23: 12 but on the *s* day do not work,

SEXUAL (SEXUALLY)

1Co 6: 13 body is not meant for *s* immorality,
6: 18 Flee from *s* immorality.
10: 8 should not commit *s* immorality,
Eph 5: 3 even a hint of *s* immorality,
1Th 4: 3 that you should avoid *s* immorality

SEXUALLY (SEXUAL)

1Co 5: 9 to associate with *s* immoral people
6: 18 he who sins *s* sins against his own

SHADOW

Ps 23: 4 through the valley of the *s* of death,
36: 7 find refuge in the *s* of your wings.
Heb 10: 1 The law is only a *s*

SHALLUM

King of Israel (2Ki 15:10-16).

SHAME (ASHAMED)

Ps 34: 5 their faces are never covered with *s.*
Pr 13: 18 discipline comes to poverty and *s,*

Heb 12: 2 endured the cross, scorning its *s,*

SHARE (SHARED)

Ge 21: 10 that slave woman's son will never *s*
Lk 3: 11 "The man with two tunics should *s*
Gal 4: 30 the slave woman's son will never *s*
6: 6 in the word must *s* all good things
Eph 4: 28 something to *s* with those in need.
1Ti 6: 18 and to be generous and willing to *s.*
Heb 12: 10 that we may *s* in his holiness.
13: 16 to do good and to *s* with others,

SHARED (SHARE)

Heb 2: 14 he too *s* in their humanity so that

SHARON

SS 2: 1 I am a rose of *S,*

SHARPER*

Heb 4: 12 *S* than any double-edged sword,

SHED (SHEDDING)

Ge 9: 6 by man shall his blood be *s;*
Col 1: 20 through his blood, *s* on the cross.

SHEDDING (SHED)

Heb 9: 22 without the *s* of blood there is no

SHEEP

Ps 100: 3 we are his people, the *s*
119:176 I have strayed like a lost *s.*
Isa 53: 6 We all, like *s,* have gone astray,
Jer 50: 6 "My people have been lost *s;*
Eze 34: 11 I myself will search for my *s*
Mt 9: 36 helpless, like *s* without a shepherd.
Jn 10: 3 He calls his own *s* by name
10: 15 and I lay down my life for the *s.*
10: 27 My *s* listen to my voice; I know
21: 17 Jesus said, "Feed my *s.*
1Pe 2: 25 For you were like *s* going astray,

SHELTER

Ps 61: 4 take refuge in the *s* of your wings.
91: 1 in the *s* of the Most High

SHEM

Son of Noah (Ge 5:32; 6:10). Blessed (Ge 9:26). Descendants (Ge 10:21-31; 11:10-32).

SHEPHERD (SHEPHERDS)

Ps 23: 1 LORD is my *s,* I shall not be in want.
Isa 40: 11 He tends his flock like a *s:*
Jer 31: 10 will watch over his flock like a *s.*'

Eze 34: 12 As a *s* looks after his scattered
Zec 11: 17 "Woe to the worthless *s*,
Mt 9: 36 and helpless, like sheep without a *s*.
Jn 10: 11 The good *s* lays down his life
10: 16 there shall be one flock and one *s*.
1Pe 5: 4 And when the Chief *S* appears,

SHEPHERDS (SHEPHERD)
Jer 23: 1 "Woe to the *s* who are destroying
Lk 2: 8 there were *s* living out in the fields
Ac 20: 28 Be *s* of the church of God,
1Pe 5: 2 Be *s* of God's flock that is

SHIELD
Ps 28: 7 LORD is my strength and my *s*;
Eph 6: 16 to all this, take up the *s* of faith,

SHINE (SHONE)
Ps 4: 6 Let the light of your face *s* upon us,
80: 1 between the cherubim, *s* forth
Isa 60: 1 "Arise, *s*, for your light has come,
Da 12: 3 are wise will *s* like the brightness
Mt 5: 16 let your light *s* before men,
13: 43 the righteous will *s* like the sun
2Co 4: 6 made his light *s* in our hearts
Eph 5: 14 and Christ will *s* on you."

SHIPWRECKED*
2Co 11: 25 I was stoned, three times I was *s*,
1Ti 1: 19 and so have *s* their faith.

SHONE (SHINE)
Mt 17: 2 His face *s* like the sun,
Lk 2: 9 glory of the Lord *s* around them,
Rev 21: 11 It *s* with the glory of God,

SHORT
Isa 59: 1 of the LORD is not too *s* to save,
Ro 3: 23 and fall *s* of the glory of God,

SHOULDERS
Isa 9: 6 and the government will be on his *s*
Lk 15: 5 he joyfully puts it on his *s*

SHOWED
1Jn 4: 9 This is how God *s* his love

SHREWD
Mt 10: 16 Therefore be as *s* as snakes and

SHUN*
Job 28: 28 and to *s* evil is understanding.' "
Pr 3: 7 fear the LORD and *s* evil.

SICK
Pr 13: 12 Hope deferred makes the heart *s*,
Mt 9: 12 who need a doctor, but the *s*.
25: 36 I was *s* and you looked after me,
Jas 5: 14 of you *s*? He should call the elders

SICKLE
Joel 3: 13 Swing the *s*,

SIDE
Ps 91: 7 A thousand may fall at your *s*,
124: 1 If the LORD had not been on our *s*
2Ti 4: 17 But the Lord stood at my *s*

SIGHT
Ps 90: 4 For a thousand years in your *s*
116: 15 Precious in the *s* of the LORD
2Co 5: 7 We live by faith, not by *s*.
1Pe 3: 4 which is of great worth in God's *s*.

SIGN (SIGNS)
Isa 7: 14 the Lord himself will give you a *s*:

SIGNS (SIGN)
Mk 16: 17 these *s* will accompany those who
Jn 20: 30 Jesus did many other miraculous *s*

SILENT
Pr 17: 28 a fool is thought wise if he keeps *s*,
Isa 53: 7 as a sheep before her shearers is *s*,
Hab 2: 20 let all the earth be *s* before him."
1Co 14: 34 women should remain *s*
1Ti 2: 12 over a man; she must be *s*.

SILVER
Pr 25: 11 is like apples of gold in settings of *s*.
Hag 2: 8 'The *s* is mine and the gold is mine,'
1Co 3: 12 *s*, costly stones, wood, hay or straw

SIMON
1. See PETER.
2. Apostle, called the Zealot (Mt 10:4; Mk 3:18; Lk 6:15; Ac 1:13).
3. Samaritan sorcerer (Ac 8:9-24).

SIN (SINFUL SINNED SINNER SINNERS SINNING SINS)
Nu 5: 7 and must confess the *s* he has
32: 23 be sure that your *s* will find you
Dt 24: 16 each is to die for his own *s*.
1Ki 8: 46 for there is no one who does not *s*
2Ch 7: 14 and will forgive their *s* and will heal
Ps 4: 4 In your anger do not *s*;
32: 2 whose *s* the LORD does not count
32: 5 Then I acknowledged my *s* to you
51: 2 and cleanse me from my *s*.
66: 18 If I had cherished *s* in my heart,
119: 11 that I might not *s* against you.
119:133 let no *s* rule over me.
Isa 6: 7 is taken away and your *s* atoned
Mic 7: 18 who pardons *s* and forgives
Mt 18: 6 little ones who believe in me to *s*,
Jn 1: 29 who takes away the *s* of the world!
8: 34 everyone who sins is a slave to *s*.
Ro 5: 12 as *s* entered the world
5: 20 where *s* increased, grace increased
6: 11 count yourselves dead to *s*
6: 23 For the wages of *s* is death,
14: 23 that does not come from faith is *s*.
2Co 5: 21 God made him who had no *s* to be *s*
Gal 6: 1 if someone is caught in a *s*,
Heb 9: 26 to do away with *s* by the sacrifice
11: 25 the pleasures of *s* for a short time.
12: 1 and the *s* that so easily entangles,
1Pe 2: 22 "He committed no *s*,
1Jn 1: 8 If we claim to be without *s*,
3: 4 in fact, *s* is lawlessness.
3: 5 And in him is no *s*.
3: 9 born of God will continue to *s*,
5: 18 born of God does not continue to *s*;

SINCERE
Ro 12: 9 Love must be *s*.
Heb 10: 22 near to God with a *s* heart

SINFUL (SIN)
Ps 51: 5 Surely I was *s* at birth
51: 5 *s* from the time my mother
Ro 7: 5 we were controlled by the *s* nature,
8: 4 not live according to the *s* nature
8: 9 are controlled not by the *s* nature
Gal 5: 19 The acts of the *s* nature are obvious
5: 24 Jesus have crucified the *s* nature
1Pe 2: 11 abstain from *s* desires, which war

SING (SANG SINGING SONG SONGS)
Ps 30: 4 *S* to the LORD, you saints of his;
47: 6 *S* praises to God, *s* praises;
59: 16 But I will *s* of your strength,
89: 1 I will *s* of the LORD's great love
101: 1 I will *s* of your love and justice;
Eph 5: 19 *S* and make music in your heart

SINGING (SING)
Ps 63: 5 with *s* lips my mouth will praise
Ac 16: 25 Silas were praying and *s* hymns

SINNED (SIN)
2Sa 12: 13 "I have *s* against the LORD."
Job 1: 5 "Perhaps my children have *s*
Ps 51: 4 Against you, you only, have I *s*
Da 9: 5 we have *s* and done wrong.
Mic 7: 9 Because I have *s* against him,
Lk 15: 18 I have *s* against heaven
Ro 3: 23 for all have *s* and fall short
1Jn 1: 10 claim we have not *s*, we make him

SINNER (SIN)
Ecc 9: 18 but one *s* destroys much good.
Lk 15: 7 in heaven over one *s* who repents
18: 13 'God, have mercy on me, a *s*.'
1Co 14: 24 convinced by all that he is a *s*
Jas 5: 20 Whoever turns a *s* from the error
1Pe 4: 18 become of the ungodly and the *s*?"

SINNERS (SIN)
Ps 1: 1 or stand in the way of *s*
Pr 23: 17 Do not let your heart envy *s*,
Mt 9: 13 come to call the righteous, but *s*."
Ro 5: 8 While we were still *s*, Christ died
1Ti 1: 15 came into the world to save *s*—

SINNING (SIN)
Ex 20: 20 be with you to keep you from *s*."
1Co 15: 34 stop *s*; for there are some who are
Heb 10: 26 If we deliberately keep on *s*
1Jn 3: 6 No one who lives in him keeps on *s*
3: 9 go on *s*, because he has been born

SINS (SIN)
2Ki 14: 6 each is to die for his own *s*."
Ezr 9: 6 our *s* are higher than our heads
Ps 19: 13 your servant also from willful *s*;
32: 1 whose *s* are covered.
103: 3 who forgives all your *s*
130: 3 O LORD, kept a record of *s*,
Pr 28: 13 who conceals his *s* does not
Isa 1: 18 "Though your *s* are like scarlet,

43: 25 and remembers your *s* no more.
59: 2 your *s* have hidden his face
Eze 18: 4 soul who *s* is the one who will die.
Mt 1: 21 he will save his people from their *s*
18: 15 "If your brother *s* against you,
Lk 11: 4 Forgive us our *s*,
17: 3 "If your brother *s*, rebuke him,
Ac 22: 16 be baptized and wash your *s* away,
1Co 15: 3 died for our *s* according
Eph 2: 1 dead in your transgressions and *s*,
Col 2: 13 us all our *s*, having canceled
Heb 1: 3 he had provided purification for *s*,
7: 27 He sacrificed for their *s* once for all
8: 12 and will remember their *s* no more
10: 12 for all time one sacrifice for *s*,
Jas 4: 17 ought to do and doesn't do it, *s*.
5: 16 Therefore confess your *s*
5: 20 and cover over a multitude of *s*.
1Pe 2: 24 He himself bore our *s* in his body
3: 18 For Christ died for *s* once for all,
1Jn 1: 9 If we confess our *s*, he is faithful
Rev 1: 5 has freed us from our *s* by his blood

SITS

Ps 99: 1 *s* enthroned between the cherubim,
Isa 40: 22 He *s* enthroned above the circle
Mt 19: 28 of Man *s* on his glorious throne,
Rev 4: 9 thanks to him who *s* on the throne

SKIN

Job 19: 20 with only the *s* of my teeth.
19: 26 And after my *s* has been destroyed,
Jer 13: 23 Can the Ethiopian change his *s*

SLAIN (SLAY)

Rev 5: 12 "Worthy is the Lamb, who was *s*,

SLANDER (SLANDERED SLANDERERS)

Lev 19: 16 "'Do not go about spreading *s*
1Ti 5: 14 the enemy no opportunity for *s*.
Tit 3: 2 to *s* no one, to be peaceable

SLANDERED (SLANDER)

1Co 4: 13 when we are *s*, we answer kindly.

SLANDERERS (SLANDER)

Ro 1: 30 They are gossips, *s*, God-haters,
1Co 6: 10 nor the greedy nor drunkards nor *s*
Tit 2: 3 not to be *s* or addicted

SLAUGHTER

Isa 53: 7 he was led like a lamb to the *s*,

SLAVE (SLAVERY SLAVES)

Ge 21: 10 "Get rid of that *s* woman
Mt 20: 27 wants to be first must be your *s*—
Jn 8: 34 everyone who sins is a *s* to sin.
1Co 12: 13 whether Jews or Greeks, *s* or free
Gal 3: 28 *s* nor free, male nor female,
4: 30 Get rid of the *s* woman and her son
2Pe 2: 19 a man is a *s* to whatever has

SLAVERY (SLAVE)

Ro 6: 19 parts of your body in *s* to impurity
Gal 4: 3 were in *s* under the basic principles

SLAVES (SLAVE)

Ro 6: 6 that we should no longer be *s* to sin
6: 22 and have become *s* to God,

SLAY (SLAIN)

Job 13: 15 Though he *s* me, yet will I hope

SLEEP (SLEEPING)

Ps 121: 4 will neither slumber nor *s*.
1Co 15: 51 We will not all *s*, but we will all be

SLEEPING (SLEEP)

Mk 13: 36 suddenly, do not let him find you *s*.

SLOW

Ex 34: 6 and gracious God, *s* to anger,
Jas 1: 19 *s* to speak and *s* to become angry,
2Pe 3: 9 The Lord is not *s* in keeping his

SLUGGARD

Pr 6: 6 Go to the ant, you *s*;
20: 4 A *s* does not plow in season;

SLUMBER

Ps 121: 3 he who watches over you will not *s*;
Pr 6: 10 A little sleep, a little *s*,
Ro 13: 11 for you to wake up from your *s*,

SNAKE (SNAKES)

Nu 21: 8 "Make a *s* and put it up on a pole;
Pr 23: 32 In the end it bites like a *s*
Jn 3: 14 Moses lifted up the *s* in the desert,

SNAKES (SNAKE)

Mt 10: 16 as shrewd as *s* and as innocent
Mk 16: 18 they will pick up *s* with their hands;

SNATCH

Jn 10: 28 no one can *s* them out of my hand.
Jude : 23 *s* others from the fire and save

SNOW

Ps 51: 7 and I will be whiter than *s*.

SOAR

Isa 40: 31 They will *s* on wings like eagles;

SODOM

Ge 19: 24 rained down burning sulfur on *S*
Ro 9: 29 we would have become like *S*,

SOIL

Ge 4: 2 kept flocks, and Cain worked the *s*.
Mt 13: 23 on good *s* is the man who hears

SOLDIER

1Co 9: 7 as a *s* at his own expense?
2Ti 2: 3 with us like a good *s* of Christ Jesus

SOLE

Dt 28: 65 place for the *s* of your foot.
Isa 1: 6 From the *s* of your foot to the top

SOLID

2Ti 2: 19 God's *s* foundation stands firm,
Heb 5: 12 You need milk, not *s* food!

SOLOMON

Son of David by Bathsheba; king of Judah (2Sa 12:24; 1Ch 3:5, 10). Appointed king by David (1Ki1); adversaries Adonijah, Joab, Shimei killed by Benaiah (1Ki 2). Asked for wisdom (1Ki 3; 2Ch1). Judged between two prostitutes (1Ki 3:16-28). Built temple (1Ki 5-7; 2Ch 2-5); prayer of dedication (1Ki 8; 2Ch 6). Visited by Queen of Sheba (1Ki 10; 2Ch 9). Wives turned his heart from God (1Ki11:1-13). Jeroboam rebelled against (1Ki 11:26-40). Death (1Ki 11:41-43; 2Ch9:29-31).

Proverbs of (1Ki 4:32; Pr1:1; 10:1; 25:1); psalms of (Ps 72; 127); song of (SS 1:1).

SON (SONS)

Ge 22: 2 "Take your *s*, your only *s*, Isaac,
Ex 11: 5 Every firstborn *s* in Egypt will die,
Dt 21: 18 rebellious *s* who does not obey his
Ps 2: 7 He said to me, "You are my *S*;
2: 12 Kiss the *S*, lest he be angry
Pr 10: 1 A wise *s* brings joy to his father,
13: 24 He who spares the rod hates his *s*,
29: 17 Discipline your *s*, and he will give
Isa 7: 14 with child and will give birth to a *s*,
Hos 11: 1 and out of Egypt I called my *s*.
Mt 2: 15 "Out of Egypt I called my *s*."
3: 17 "This is my *S*, whom I love;
11: 27 one knows the *S* except the Father,
16: 16 "You are the Christ, the *S*
17: 5 "This is my *S*, whom I love;
20: 18 and the *S* of Man will be betrayed
24: 30 They will see the *S* of Man coming
24: 44 the *S* of Man will come at an hour
27: 54 "Surely he was the *S* of God!"
28: 19 and of the *S* and of the Holy Spirit,
Mk 10: 45 even the *S* of Man did not come
14: 62 you will see the *S* of Man sitting
Lk 9: 58 but the *S* of Man has no place
18: 8 when the *S* of Man comes,
19: 10 For the *S* of Man came to seek
Jn 3: 14 so the *S* of Man must be lifted up,
3: 16 that he gave his one and only *S*,
17: 1 Glorify your *S*, that your *S* may
Ro 8: 29 conformed to the likeness of his *S*,
8: 32 He who did not spare his own *S*,
1Co 15: 28 then the *S* himself will be made
Gal 4: 30 rid of the slave woman and her *s*,
1Th 1: 10 and to wait for his *S* from heaven,
Heb 1: 2 days he has spoken to us by his *S*,
10: 29 punished who has trampled the *S*
1Jn 1: 7 his *S*, purifies us from all sin.
4: 9 only *S* into the world that we might
5: 5 he who believes that Jesus is the *S*
5: 11 eternal life, and this life is in his *S*.

SONG (SING)

Ps 40: 3 He put a new *s* in my mouth,
96: 1 Sing to the LORD a new *s*;
149: 1 Sing to the LORD a new *s*,
Isa 49: 13 burst into *s*, O mountains!
55: 12 will burst into *s* before you,
Rev 5: 9 And they sang a new *s*:

SPOTLESS
2Pe 3: 14 make every effort to be found *s,*

SPREAD (SPREADING)
Ac 12: 24 of God continued to increase and *s.*
19: 20 the word of the Lord *s* widely

SPREADING (SPREAD)
1Th 3: 2 God's fellow worker in *s* the gospel

SPRING
Jer 2: 13 the *s* of living water,
Jn 4: 14 in him a *s* of water welling up
Jas 3: 12 can a salt *s* produce fresh water.

SPUR*
Heb 10: 24 how we may *s* one another

SPURNS*
Pr 15: 5 A fool *s* his father's discipline,

STAFF
Ps 23: 4 your rod and your *s,*

STAKES
Isa 54: 2 strengthen your *s.*

STAND (STANDING STANDS)
Ex 14: 13 *S* firm and you will see
2Ch 20: 17 *s* firm and see the deliverance
Ps 1: 5 Therefore the wicked will not *s*
40: 2 and gave me a firm place to *s.*
119:120 I *s* in awe of your laws.
Eze 22: 30 *s* before me in the gap on behalf
Zec 14: 4 On that day his feet will *s*
Mt 12: 25 divided against itself will not *s.*
Ro 14: 10 we will all *s* before God's judgment
1Co 10: 13 out so that you can *s* up under it.
15: 58 Therefore, my dear brothers, *s* firm
Eph 6: 14 *S* firm then, with the belt
2Th 2: 15 *s* firm and hold to the teachings we
Jas 5: 8 You too, be patient and *s* firm,
Rev 3: 20 Here I am! I *s* at the door

STANDING (STAND)
Ex 3: 5 where you are *s* is holy ground."
Jos 5: 15 the place where you are *s* is holy."
1Pe 5: 9 Resist him, *s* firm in the faith,

STANDS (STAND)
Ps 89: 2 that your love *s* firm forever,
119: 89 it *s* firm in the heavens.
Mt 10: 22 but he who *s* firm to the end will be
2Ti 2: 19 God's solid foundation *s* firm,
1Pe 1: 25 but the word of the Lord *s* forever

STAR (STARS)
Nu 24: 17 A *s* will come out of Jacob;
Rev 22: 16 and the bright Morning *S.*"

STARS (STAR)
Da 12: 3 like the *s* for ever and ever.
Php 2: 15 in which you shine like *s*

STATURE
Lk 2: 52 And Jesus grew in wisdom and *s,*

STEADFAST
Ps 51: 10 and renew a *s* spirit within me.
Isa 26: 3 him whose mind is *s,*
1Pe 5: 10 and make you strong, firm and *s.*

STEAL
Ex 20: 15 "You shall not *s.*
Mt 19: 18 do not *s,* do not give false
Eph 4: 28 has been stealing must *s* no longer,

STEP (STEPS)
Gal 5: 25 let us keep in *s* with the Spirit.

STEPS (STEP)
Pr 16: 9 but the LORD determines his *s.*
Jer 10: 23 it is not for man to direct his *s.*
1Pe 2: 21 that you should follow in his *s.*

STICKS
Pr 18: 24 there is a friend who *s* closer

STIFF-NECKED
Ex 34: 9 Although this is a *s* people,

STILL
Ps 46: 10 "Be *s,* and know that I am God;
Zec 2: 13 Be *s* before the LORD, all mankind

STIRS
Pr 6: 19 and a man who *s* up dissension
10: 12 Hatred *s* up dissension,
15: 1 but a harsh word *s* up anger.
15: 18 hot-tempered man *s* up dissension,
16: 28 A perverse man *s* up dissension,
28: 25 A greedy man *s* up dissension,
29: 22 An angry man *s* up dissension,

STONE (CAPSTONE CORNERSTONE MILLSTONE)
1Sa 17: 50 the Philistine with a sling and a *s;*
Isa 8: 14 a *s* that causes men to stumble
Eze 11: 19 remove from them their heart of *s*
Mk 16: 3 "Who will roll the *s* away
Lk 4: 3 tell this *s* to become bread."
Jn 8: 7 the first to throw a *s* at her."
2Co 3: 3 not on tablets of *s* but on tablets

STOOP
2Sa 22: 36 you *s* down to make me great.

STORE
Pr 10: 14 Wise men *s* up knowledge,
Mt 6: 19 not *s* up for yourselves treasures

STOREHOUSE (HOUSE)
Mal 3: 10 Bring the whole tithe into the *s,*

STRAIGHT
Pr 3: 6 and he will make your paths *s.*
4: 25 Let your eyes look *s* ahead,
15: 21 of understanding keeps a *s* course.
Jn 1: 23 'Make *s* the way for the Lord.' "

STRAIN
Mt 23: 24 You *s* out a gnat but swallow

STRANGER (STRANGERS)
Mt 25: 35 I was a *s* and you invited me in,
Jn 10: 5 But they will never follow a *s;*

STRANGERS (STRANGER)
1Pe 2: 11 as aliens and *s* in the world,

STREAMS
Ps 1: 3 He is like a tree planted by *s*
46: 4 is a river whose *s* make glad
Ecc 1: 7 All *s* flow into the sea,
Jn 7: 38 *s* of living water will flow

STRENGTH (STRONG)
Ex 15: 2 The LORD is my *s* and my song;
Dt 6: 5 all your soul and with all your *s.*
2Sa 22: 33 It is God who arms me with *s*
Ne 8: 10 for the joy of the LORD is your *s.*"
Ps 28: 7 The LORD is my *s* and my shield;
46: 1 God is our refuge and *s,*
96: 7 ascribe to the LORD glory and *s.*
118: 14 The LORD is my *s* and my song;
147: 10 not in the *s* of the horse,
Isa 40: 31 will renew their *s.*
Mk 12: 30 all your mind and with all your *s.'*
1Co 1: 25 of God is stronger than man's *s.*
Php 4: 13 through him who gives me *s.*
1Pe 4: 11 it with the *s* God provides,

STRENGTHEN (STRONG)
2Ch 16: 9 to *s* those whose hearts are fully
Ps 119: 28 *s* me according to your word.
Isa 35: 3 *S* the feeble hands,
41: 10 I will *s* you and help you;
Eph 3: 16 of his glorious riches he may *s* you
2Th 2: 17 and *s* you in every good deed
Heb 12: 12 *s* your feeble arms and weak knees.

STRENGTHENING (STRONG)
1Co 14: 26 done for the *s* of the church.

STRIFE
Pr 20: 3 It is to a man's honor to avoid *s,*
22: 10 out the mocker, and out goes *s;*

STRIKE (STRIKES)
Ge 3: 15 and you will *s* his heel."
Zec 13: 7 "*S* the shepherd,
Mt 26: 31 "'I will *s* the shepherd,

STRIKES (STRIKE)
Mt 5: 39 If someone *s* you on the right

STRONG (STRENGTH STRENGTHEN STRENGTHENING)
Dt 31: 6 Be *s* and courageous.
1Ki 2: 2 "So be *s,* show yourself a man,
Pr 18: 10 The name of the LORD is a *s* tower
31: 17 her arms are *s* for her tasks.
SS 8: 6 for love is as *s* as death,
Lk 2: 40 And the child grew and became *s;*
Ro 15: 1 We who are *s* ought to bear
1Co 1: 27 things of the world to shame the *s.*
16: 13 in the faith; be men of courage; be *s*
2Co 12: 10 For when I am weak, then I am *s.*
Eph 6: 10 be *s* in the Lord and in his mighty

STRUGGLE
Ro 15: 30 me in my *s* by praying to God
Eph 6: 12 For our *s* is not against flesh
Heb 12: 4 In your *s* against sin, you have not

STUDY
Ezr 7: 10 Ezra had devoted himself to the *s*
Ecc 12: 12 and much *s* wearies the body.
Jn 5: 39 You diligently *s* the Scriptures

STUMBLE (STUMBLING)
Ps 37: 24 though he *s,* he will not fall,
119:165 and nothing can make them *s.*
Isa 8: 14 a stone that causes men to *s*

Jer 31: 9 a level path where they will not *s,*
Eze 7: 19 for it has made them *s* into sin.
1Co 10: 32 Do not cause anyone to *s,*
1Pe 2: 8 and, "A stone that causes men to *s*

STUMBLING (STUMBLE)
Ro 14: 13 up your mind not to put any *s* block
1Co 8: 9 freedom does not become a *s* block
2Co 6: 3 We put no *s* block in anyone's path,

SUBDUE
Ge 1: 28 in number; fill the earth and *s* it.

SUBJECT (SUBJECTED)
1Co 14: 32 of prophets are *s* to the control
15: 28 then the Son himself will be made *s*
Tit 2: 5 and to be *s* to their husbands,
2: 9 slaves to be *s* to their masters
3: 1 Remind the people to be *s* to rulers

SUBJECTED (SUBJECT)
Ro 8: 20 For the creation was *s*

SUBMISSION (SUBMIT)
1Co 14: 34 but must be in *s,* as the Law says.
1Ti 2: 11 learn in quietness and full *s.*

SUBMISSIVE (SUBMIT)
Jas 3: 17 then peace-loving, considerate, *s,*
1Pe 3: 1 in the same way be *s*
5: 5 in the same way be *s*

SUBMIT (SUBMISSION SUBMISSIVE SUBMITS)
Ro 13: 1 Everyone must *s* himself
13: 5 necessary to *s* to the authorities,
1Co 16: 16 to *s* to such as these
Eph 5: 21 *S* to one another out of reverence
Col 3: 18 Wives, *s* to your husbands,
Heb 12: 9 How much more should we *s*
13: 17 Obey your leaders and *s*
Jas 4: 7 *S* yourselves, then, to God.
1Pe 2: 18 *s* yourselves to your masters

SUBMITS* (SUBMIT)
Eph 5: 24 Now as the church *s* to Christ,

SUCCESSFUL
Jos 1: 7 that you may be *s* wherever you go.
2Ki 18: 7 he was *s* in whatever he undertook.
2Ch 20: 20 in his prophets and you will be *s.*"

SUFFER (SUFFERED SUFFERING SUFFERINGS SUFFERS)
Isa 53: 10 to crush him and cause him to *s,*
Mk 8: 31 the Son of Man must *s* many things
Lk 24: 26 the Christ have to *s* these things
24: 46 The Christ will *s* and rise
Php 1: 29 to *s* for him, since you are going
1Pe 4: 16 However, if you *s* as a Christian,

SUFFERED (SUFFER)
Heb 2: 9 and honor because he *s* death,
2: 18 Because he himself *s*
1Pe 2: 21 Christ *s* for you, leaving you

SUFFERING (SUFFER)
Isa 53: 3 of sorrows, and familiar with *s.*
Ac 5: 41 worthy of *s* disgrace for the Name.
2Ti 1: 8 But join with me in *s* for the gospel,
Heb 2: 10 of their salvation perfect through *s.*

SUFFERINGS (SUFFER)
Ro 8: 17 share in his *s* in order that we may
8: 18 that our present *s* are not worth
2Co 1: 5 as the *s* of Christ flow
Php 3: 10 the fellowship of sharing in his *s,*

SUFFERS (SUFFER)
Pr 13: 20 but a companion of fools *s* harm.
1Co 12: 26 If one part *s,* every part *s* with it;

SUFFICIENT
2Co 12: 9 said to me, "My grace is *s* for you,

SUITABLE
Ge 2: 18 I will make a helper *s* for him."

SUN
Ecc 1: 9 there is nothing new under the *s.*
Mal 4: 2 the *s* of righteousness will rise
Mt 5: 45 He causes his *s* to rise on the evil
17: 2 His face shone like the *s,*
Rev 1: 16 His face was like the *s* shining
21: 23 The city does not need the *s*

SUPERIOR
Heb 1: 4 he became as much *s* to the angels
8: 6 ministry Jesus has received is as *s*

SUPERVISION
Gal 3: 25 longer under the *s* of the law.

SUPREMACY* (SUPREME)
Col 1: 18 in everything he might have the *s.*

SUPREME (SUPREMACY)
Pr 4: 7 Wisdom is *s;* therefore get wisdom.

SURE
Nu 32: 23 you may be *s* that your sin will find
Dt 6: 17 Be *s* to keep the commands
14: 22 Be *s* to set aside a tenth
Isa 28: 16 cornerstone for a *s* foundation;
Heb 11: 1 faith is being *s* of what we hope for
2Pe 1: 10 to make your calling and election *s.*

SURPASS* (SURPASSES SURPASSING)
Pr 31: 29 but you *s* them all."

SURPASSES (SURPASS)
Mt 5: 20 unless your righteousness *s* that
Eph 3: 19 to know this love that *s* knowledge

SURPASSING* (SURPASS)
Ps 150: 2 praise him for his *s* greatness.
2Co 3: 10 in comparison with the *s* glory.
9: 14 of the *s* grace God has given you.
Php 3: 8 the *s* greatness of knowing Christ

SURROUNDED
Heb 12: 1 since we are *s* by such a great cloud

SUSPENDS*
Job 26: 7 he *s* the earth over nothing.

SUSTAINING* (SUSTAINS)
Heb 1: 3 *s* all things by his powerful word.

SUSTAINS (SUSTAINING)
Ps 18: 35 and your right hand *s* me;
146: 9 and *s* the fatherless and the widow,
147: 6 The LORD *s* the humble
Isa 50: 4 to know the word that *s* the weary.

SWALLOWED
1Co 15: 54 "Death has been *s* up in victory."
2Co 5: 4 so that what is mortal may be *s* up

SWEAR
Mt 5: 34 Do not *s* at all: either by heaven,

SWORD (SWORDS)
Ps 45: 3 Gird your *s* upon your side,
Pr 12: 18 Reckless words pierce like a *s,*
Mt 10: 34 come to bring peace, but a *s.*
26: 52 all who draw the *s* will die by the *s.*
Lk 2: 35 a *s* will pierce your own soul too."
Ro 13: 4 for he does not bear the *s*
Eph 6: 17 of salvation and the *s* of the Spirit,
Heb 4: 12 Sharper than any double-edged *s,*
Rev 1: 16 came a sharp double-edged *s.*

SWORDS (SWORD)
Isa 2: 4 They will beat their *s*
Joel 3: 10 Beat your plowshares into *s*

SYMPATHETIC*
1Pe 3: 8 in harmony with one another; be *s,*

SYNAGOGUE
Lk 4: 16 the Sabbath day he went into the *s,*
Ac 17: 2 custom was, Paul went into the *s,*

T

TABERNACLE
Ex 40: 34 the glory of the LORD filled the *t.*

TABLE (TABLES)
Ps 23: 5 You prepare a *t* before me

TABLES (TABLE)
Ac 6: 2 word of God in order to wait on *t.*

TABLET (TABLETS)
Pr 3: 3 write them on the *t* of your heart.
7: 3 write them on the *t* of your heart.

TABLETS (TABLET)
Ex 31: 18 he gave him the two *t*
Dt 10: 5 and put the *t* in the ark I had made,
2Co 3: 3 not on *t* of stone but on *t*

TAKE (TAKEN TAKES TAKING TOOK)
Dt 12: 32 do not add to it or *t* away from it.
31: 26 "*T* this Book of the Law
Job 23: 10 But he knows the way that I *t;*
Ps 49: 17 for he will *t* nothing with him
51: 11 or *t* your Holy Spirit from me.
Mt 10: 38 anyone who does not *t* his cross
11: 29 *T* my yoke upon you and learn
16: 24 deny himself and *t* up his cross

TAKEN (TAKE)
Lev 6: 4 must return what he has stolen or *t*
Isa 6: 7 your guilt is *t* away and your sin
Mt 24: 40 one will be *t* and the other left.

Mk 16: 19 he was *t* up into heaven
1Ti 3: 16 was *t* up in glory.

TAKES (TAKE)

1Ki 20: 11 should not boast like one who *t* it
Ps 5: 4 You are not a God who *t* pleasure
Jn 1: 29 who *t* away the sin of the world!
Rev 22: 19 And if anyone *t* words away

TAKING (TAKE)

Ac 15: 14 by *t* from the Gentiles a people
Php 2: 7 *t* the very nature of a servant,

TALENT

Mt 25: 15 to another one *t*, each according

TAME*

Jas 3: 8 but no man can *t* the tongue.

TASK

Mk 13: 34 each with his assigned *t*,
Ac 20: 24 complete the *t* the Lord Jesus has
1Co 3: 5 the Lord has assigned to each his *t*.
2Co 2: 16 And who is equal to such a *t*?

TASTE (TASTED)

Ps 34: 8 *T* and see that the LORD is good;
Col 2: 21 Do not *t*! Do not touch!"?
Heb 2: 9 the grace of God he might *t* death

TASTED (TASTE)

1Pe 2: 3 now that you have *t* that the Lord

TAUGHT (TEACH)

Mt 7: 29 he *t* as one who had authority,
1Co 2: 13 but in words *t* by the Spirit,
Gal 1: 12 nor was I *t* it; rather, I received it

TAXES

Mt 22: 17 Is it right to pay *t* to Caesar or not
Ro 13: 7 If you owe *t*, pay *t*; if revenue,

TEACH (TAUGHT TEACHER TEACHERS TEACHES TEACHING)

Ex 33: 13 *t* me your ways so I may know you
Dt 4: 9 *T* them to your children
8: 3 to *t* you that man does not live
11: 19 *T* them to your children, talking
1Sa 12: 23 I will *t* you the way that is good
Ps 32: 8 *t* you in the way you should go;
51: 13 I will *t* transgressors your ways,
90: 12 *T* us to number our days aright,
143: 10 *T* me to do your will,
Jer 31: 34 No longer will a man *t* his neighbor
Lk 11: 1 said to him, "Lord, *t* us to pray,
Jn 14: 26 will *t* you all things and will remind
1Ti 2: 12 I do not permit a woman to *t*
3: 2 respectable, hospitable, able to *t*,
Tit 2: 1 You must *t* what is in accord
Heb 8: 11 No longer will a man *t* his neighbor
Jas 3: 1 know that we who *t* will be judged
1Jn 2: 27 you do not need anyone to *t* you.

TEACHER (TEACH)

Mt 10: 24 "A student is not above his *t*,
Jn 13: 14 and *T*, have washed your feet,

TEACHERS (TEACH)

1Co 12: 28 third *t*, then workers of miracles,
Eph 4: 11 and some to be pastors and *t*,
Heb 5: 12 by this time you ought to be *t*,

TEACHES (TEACH)

1Ti 6: 3 If anyone *t* false doctrines

TEACHING (TEACH)

Pr 1: 8 and do not forsake your mother's *t*.
Mt 28: 20 *t* them to obey everything I have
Jn 7: 17 whether my *t* comes from God or
14: 23 loves me, he will obey my *t*.
1Ti 4: 13 of Scripture, to preaching and to *t*.
2Ti 3: 16 is God-breathed and is useful for *t*,
Tit 2: 7 In your *t* show integrity,

TEAR (TEARS)

Rev 7: 17 God will wipe away every *t*

TEARS (TEAR)

Ps 126: 5 Those who sow in *t*
Php 3: 18 and now say again even with *t*,

TEETH (TOOTH)

Mt 8: 12 will be weeping and gnashing of *t*."

TEMPERATE*

1Ti 3: 2 *t*, self-controlled, respectable,
3: 11 not malicious talkers but *t*
Tit 2: 2 Teach the older men to be *t*,

TEMPEST

Ps 55: 8 far from the *t* and storm."

TEMPLE (TEMPLES)

1Ki 8: 27 How much less this *t* I have built!
Hab 2: 20 But the LORD is in his holy *t*;
1Co 3: 16 that you yourselves are God's *t*
6: 19 you not know that your body is a *t*
2Co 6: 16 For we are the *t* of the living God.

TEMPLES (TEMPLE)

Ac 17: 24 does not live in *t* built by hands.

TEMPT (TEMPTATION TEMPTED)

1Co 7: 5 again so that Satan will not *t* you

TEMPTATION (TEMPT)

Mt 6: 13 And lead us not into *t*,
26: 41 pray so that you will not fall into *t*.
1Co 10: 13 No *t* has seized you except what is

TEMPTED (TEMPT)

Mt 4: 1 into the desert to be *t* by the devil.
1Co 10: 13 he will not let you be *t*
Heb 2: 18 he himself suffered when he was *t*,
4: 15 but we have one who has been *t*
Jas 1: 13 For God cannot be *t* by evil,

TEN (TENTH TITHE TITHES)

Ex 34: 28 covenant—the *T* Commandments.
Ps 91: 7 *t* thousand at your right hand,
Mt 25: 28 it to the one who has the *t* talents.
Lk 15: 8 suppose a woman has *t* silver coins

TENTH (TEN)

Dt 14: 22 Be sure to set aside a *t*

TERRIBLE (TERROR)

2Ti 3: 1 There will be *t* times

TERROR (TERRIBLE)

Ps 91: 5 You will not fear the *t* of night,
Lk 21: 26 Men will faint from *t*, apprehensive
Ro 13: 3 For rulers hold no *t*

TEST (TESTED TESTS)

Dt 6: 16 Do not *t* the LORD your God
Ps 139: 23 *t* me and know my anxious
Ro 12: 2 Then you will be able to *t*
1Co 3: 13 and the fire will *t* the quality
1Jn 4: 1 *t* the spirits to see whether they are

TESTED (TEST)

Ge 22: 1 Some time later God *t* Abraham.
Job 23: 10 when he has *t* me, I will come forth
Pr 27: 21 man is *t* by the praise he receives.
1Ti 3: 10 They must first be *t*; and then

TESTIFY (TESTIMONY)

Jn 5: 39 are the Scriptures that *t* about me,
2Ti 1: 8 ashamed to *t* about our Lord,

TESTIMONY (TESTIFY)

Isa 8: 20 and to the *t*! If they do not speak
Lk 18: 20 not give false *t*, honor your father

TESTS (TEST)

Pr 17: 3 but the LORD *t* the heart.
1Th 2: 4 but God, who *t* our hearts.

THADDAEUS

Apostle (Mt 10:3; Mk 3:18); probably also known as Judas son of James (Lk 6:16; Ac 1:13).

THANKFUL (THANKS)

Heb 12: 28 let us be *t*, and so worship God

THANKS (THANKFUL THANKSGIVING)

1Ch 16: 8 Give *t* to the LORD, call
Ne 12: 31 assigned two large choirs to give *t*.
Ps 100: 4 give *t* to him and praise his name.
1Co 15: 57 *t* be to God! He gives us the victory
2Co 2: 14 *t* be to God, who always leads us
9: 15 *T* be to God for his indescribable
1Th 5: 18 give *t* in all circumstances,

THANKSGIVING (THANKS)

Ps 95: 2 Let us come before him with *t*
100: 4 Enter his gates with *t*
Php 4: 6 by prayer and petition, with *t*,
1Ti 4: 3 created to be received with *t*

THIEF (THIEVES)

Ex 22: 3 A *t* must certainly make restitution
1Th 5: 2 day of the Lord will come like a *t*
Rev 16: 15 I come like a *t*! Blessed is he who

THIEVES (THIEF)

1Co 6: 10 nor homosexual offenders nor *t*

THINK (THOUGHT THOUGHTS)

Ro 12: 3 Do not *t* of yourself more highly
Php 4: 8 praiseworthy—*t* about such things

THIRST (THIRSTY)

Ps 69: 21 and gave me vinegar for my *t*.
Mt 5: 6 Blessed are those who hunger and *t*
Jn 4: 14 the water I give him will never *t*.

THIRSTY (THIRST)
Isa 55: 1 "Come, all you who are *t*,
Jn 7: 37 "If anyone is *t*, let him come to me
Rev 22: 17 Whoever is *t*, let him come;

THOMAS
Apostle (Mt 10:3; Mk 3:18; Lk 6:15; Jn 11:16; 14:5; 21:2; Ac 1:13). Doubted resurrection (Jn 20:24-28).

THONGS
Mk 1: 7 *t* of whose sandals I am not worthy

THORN (THORNS)
2Co 12: 7 there was given me a *t* in my flesh,

THORNS (THORN)
Nu 33: 55 in your eyes and *t* in your sides.
Mt 27: 29 then twisted together a crown of *t*
Heb 6: 8 But land that produces *t*

THOUGHT (THINK)
Pr 14: 15 a prudent man gives *t* to his steps.
1Co 13: 11 I talked like a child, I *t* like a child,

THOUGHTS (THINK)
Ps 94: 11 The LORD knows the *t* of man;
139: 23 test me and know my anxious *t*.
Isa 55: 8 "For my *t* are not your *t*,
Heb 4: 12 it judges the *t* and attitudes

THREE
Ecc 4: 12 of *t* strands is not quickly broken.
Mt 12: 40 *t* nights in the belly of a huge fish,
18: 20 or *t* come together in my name,
27: 63 'After *t* days I will rise again.'
1Co 13: 13 And now these *t* remain: faith,
14: 27 or at the most *t*—should speak,
2Co 13: 1 testimony of two or *t* witnesses."

THRESHING
2Sa 24: 18 an altar to the LORD on the *t* floor

THRONE (ENTHRONED)
2Sa 7: 16 your *t* will be established forever
Ps 45: 6 Your *t*, O God, will last for ever
47: 8 God is seated on his holy *t*.
Isa 6: 1 I saw the Lord seated on a *t*,
66: 1 "Heaven is my *t*
Heb 4: 16 Let us then approach the *t* of grace
12: 2 at the right hand of the *t* of God.
Rev 4: 10 They lay their crowns before the *t*
20: 11 Then I saw a great white *t*
22: 3 *t* of God and of the Lamb will be

THROW
Jn 8: 7 the first to *t* a stone at her."
Heb 10: 35 So do not *t* away your confidence;
12: 1 let us *t* off everything that hinders

THWART*
Isa 14: 27 has purposed, and who can *t* him?

TIBNI
King of Israel (1Ki 16:21-22).

TIME (TIMES)
Est 4: 14 come to royal position for such a *t*
Da 7: 25 to him for a *t*, times and half a *t*.
Hos 10: 12 for it is *t* to seek the LORD,
Ro 9: 9 "At the appointed *t* I will return,
Heb 9: 28 and he will appear a second *t*,
10: 12 for all *t* one sacrifice for sins,
1Pe 4: 17 For it is *t* for judgment to begin

TIMES (TIME)
Ps 9: 9 a stronghold in *t* of trouble.
31: 15 My *t* are in your hands;
62: 8 Trust in him at all *t*, O people;
Pr 17: 17 A friend loves at all *t*,
Am 5: 13 for the *t* are evil.
Mt 18: 21 how many *t* shall I forgive my
Ac 1: 7 "It is not for you to know the *t*
Rev 12: 14 *t* and half a time, out

TIMIDITY*
2Ti 1: 7 For God did not give us a spirit of *t*

TIMOTHY
Believer from Lystra (Ac 16:1). Joined Paul on second missionary journey (Ac 16-20). Sent to settle problems at Corinth (1Co 4:17; 16:10). Led church at Ephesus (1Ti 1:3). Co-writer with Paul (1Th 1:1; 2Th 1:1; Phm 1).

TIRE (TIRED)
2Th 3: 13 never *t* of doing what is right.

TIRED (TIRE)
Ex 17: 12 When Moses' hands grew *t*,
Isa 40: 28 He will not grow *t* or weary,

TITHE (TEN)
Lev 27: 30 "'A *t* of everything from the land,
Dt 12: 17 eat in your own towns the *t*
Mal 3: 10 the whole *t* into the storehouse,

TITHES (TEN)
Mal 3: 8 'How do we rob you?' "In *t*

TITUS
Gentile co-worker of Paul (Gal 2:1-3; 2Ti 4:10); sent to Corinth (2Co 2:13; 7-8; 12:18), Crete (Tit 1:4-5).

TODAY
Mt 6: 11 Give us *t* our daily bread.
Lk 23: 43 *t* you will be with me in paradise."
Heb 3: 13 daily, as long as it is called *T*,
13: 8 Christ is the same yesterday and *t*

TOIL
Ge 3: 17 through painful *t* you will eat of it

TOLERATE
Hab 1: 13 you cannot *t* wrong.
Rev 2: 2 that you cannot *t* wicked men,

TOMB
Mt 27: 65 make the *t* as secure as you know
Lk 24: 2 the stone rolled away from the *t*,

TOMORROW
Pr 27: 1 Do not boast about *t*,
Isa 22: 13 "for *t* we die!"
Mt 6: 34 Therefore do not worry about *t*,
Jas 4: 13 "Today or *t* we will go to this

TONGUE (TONGUES)
Ps 39: 1 and keep my *t* from sin;
Pr 12: 18 but the *t* of the wise brings healing.
1Co 14: 2 speaks in a *t* does not speak to men
14: 4 He who speaks in a *t* edifies himself
14: 13 in a *t* should pray that he may
14: 19 than ten thousand words in a *t*.
Php 2: 11 every *t* confess that Jesus Christ is
Jas 1: 26 does not keep a tight rein on his *t*,
3: 8 but no man can tame the *t*.

TONGUES (TONGUE)
Isa 28: 11 with foreign lips and strange *t*
66: 18 and gather all nations and *t*,
Mk 16: 17 in new *t*; they will pick up snakes
Ac 2: 4 and began to speak in other *t*
10: 46 For they heard them speaking in *t*
19: 6 and they spoke in *t* and prophesied
1Co 12: 30 Do all speak in *t*? Do all interpret?
14: 18 speak in *t* more than all of you.
14: 39 and do not forbid speaking in *t*.

TOOK (TAKE)
1Co 11: 23 the night he was betrayed, *t* bread,
Php 3: 12 for which Christ Jesus *t* hold of me.

TOOTH (TEETH)
Ex 21: 24 eye for eye, *t* for *t*, hand for hand,
Mt 5: 38 'Eye for eye, and *t* for *t*.'

TORMENTED
Rev 20: 10 They will be *t* day and night

TORN
Gal 4: 15 you would have *t* out your eyes
Php 1: 23 I do not know! I am *t*

TOUCH (TOUCHED)
Ps 105: 15 "Do not *t* my anointed ones;
Lk 24: 39 It is I myself! *T* me and see;
2Co 6: 17 *T* no unclean thing,
Col 2: 21 Do not taste! Do not *t*!"?

TOUCHED (TOUCH)
1Sa 10: 26 men whose hearts God had *t*.
Mt 14: 36 and all who *t* him were healed.

TOWER
Ge 11: 4 with a *t* that reaches to the heavens
Pr 18: 10 of the LORD is a strong *t*;

TOWNS
Nu 35: 2 to give the Levites *t* to live
35: 15 These six *t* will be a place of refuge

TRACING*
Ro 11: 33 and his paths beyond *t* out!

TRADITION
Mt 15: 6 word of God for the sake of your *t*.
Col 2: 8 which depends on human *t*

TRAIN (TRAINING)
Pr 22: 6 *T* a child in the way he should go,
Eph 4: 8 he led captives in his *t*

TRAINING (TRAIN)
1Co 9: 25 in the games goes into strict *t*.
2Ti 3: 16 correcting and *t* in righteousness,

TRAMPLED
Lk 21: 24 Jerusalem will be *t*
Heb 10: 29 to be punished who has *t* the Son

TRANCE
Ac 10: 10 was being prepared, he fell into a *t*.

TRANSCENDS*
Php 4: 7 which *t* all understanding,

TRANSFIGURED
Mt 17: 2 There he was *t* before them.

TRANSFORM* (TRANSFORMED)
Php 3: 21 will *t* our lowly bodies

TRANSFORMED (TRANSFORM)
Ro 12: 2 be *t* by the renewing of your mind.
2Co 3: 18 are being *t* into his likeness

TRANSGRESSION (TRANSGRESSIONS TRANSGRESSORS)
Isa 53: 8 for the *t* of my people he was
Ro 4: 15 where there is no law there is no *t*.

TRANSGRESSIONS (TRANSGRESSION)
Ps 32: 1 whose *t* are forgiven,
51: 1 blot out my *t*.
103: 12 so far has he removed our *t* from us
Isa 53: 5 But he was pierced for our *t*,
Eph 2: 1 you were dead in your *t* and sins,

TRANSGRESSORS (TRANSGRESSION)
Ps 51: 13 Then I will teach *t* your ways,
Isa 53: 12 and made intercession for the *t*.
53: 12 and was numbered with the *t*.

TREADING
Dt 25: 4 an ox while it is *t* out the grain.
1Co 9: 9 an ox while it is *t* out the grain."

TREASURE (TREASURED TREASURES)
Isa 33: 6 of the LORD is the key to this *t*.
Mt 6: 21 For where your *t* is, there your
2Co 4: 7 But we have this *t* in jars of clay

TREASURED (TREASURE)
Dt 7: 6 to be his people, his *t* possession.
Lk 2: 19 But Mary *t* up all these things

TREASURES (TREASURE)
Mt 6: 19 up for yourselves *t* on earth,
Col 2: 3 in whom are hidden all the *t*
Heb 11: 26 of greater value than the *t* of Egypt,

TREAT
Lev 22: 2 sons to *t* with respect the sacred
1Ti 5: 1 *T* younger men as brothers,
1Pe 3: 7 and *t* them with respect

TREATY
Dt 7: 2 Make no *t* with them, and show

TREE
Ge 2: 9 and the *t* of the knowledge of good
2: 9 of the garden were the *t* of life
Dt 21: 23 hung on a *t* is under God's curse.
Ps 1: 3 He is like a *t* planted by streams
Mt 3: 10 every *t* that does not produce good
12: 33 for a *t* is recognized by its fruit.
Gal 3: 13 is everyone who is hung on a *t*."
Rev 22: 14 they may have the right to the *t*

TREMBLE (TREMBLING)
1Ch 16: 30 *T* before him, all the earth!
Ps 114: 7 *T*, O earth, at the presence

TREMBLING (TREMBLE)
Ps 2: 11 and rejoice with *t*.
Php 2: 12 out your salvation with fear and *t*,

TRESPASS
Ro 5: 17 For if, by the *t* of the one man,

TRIALS
1Th 3: 3 one would be unsettled by these *t*.
Jas 1: 2 whenever you face *t* of many kinds,
2Pe 2: 9 how to rescue godly men from *t*

TRIBES
Ge 49: 28 All these are the twelve *t* of Israel,
Mt 19: 28 judging the twelve *t* of Israel.

TRIBULATION*
Rev 7: 14 who have come out of the great *t*;

TRIUMPHAL* (TRIUMPHING)
Isa 60: 11 their kings led in *t* procession.
2Co 2: 14 us in *t* procession in Christ

TRIUMPHING* (TRIUMPHAL)
Col 2: 15 of them, *t* over them by the cross.

TROUBLE (TROUBLED TROUBLES)
Job 14: 1 is of few days and full of *t*.
Ps 46: 1 an ever-present help in *t*.
107: 13 they cried to the LORD in their *t*,
Pr 11: 29 He who brings *t* on his family will
24: 10 If you falter in times of *t*,
Mt 6: 34 Each day has enough *t* of its own.
Jn 16: 33 In this world you will have *t*.
Ro 8: 35 Shall *t* or hardship or persecution

TROUBLED (TROUBLE)
Jn 14: 1 "Do not let your hearts be *t*.
14: 27 Do not let your hearts be *t*

TROUBLES (TROUBLE)
1Co 7: 28 those who marry will face many *t*
2Co 1: 4 who comforts us in all our *t*,
4: 17 and momentary *t* are achieving

TRUE (TRUTH)
Dt 18: 22 does not take place or come *t*,
1Sa 9: 6 and everything he says comes *t*.
Ps 119:160 All your words are *t*;
Jn 17: 3 the only *t* God, and Jesus Christ,
Ro 3: 4 Let God be *t*, and every man a liar.
Php 4: 8 whatever is *t*, whatever is noble,
Rev 22: 6 These words are trustworthy and *t*.

TRUMPET
1Co 14: 8 if the *t* does not sound a clear call,
15: 52 For the *t* will sound, the dead will

TRUST (ENTRUSTED TRUSTED TRUSTS TRUSTWORTHY)
Ps 20: 7 we *t* in the name of the LORD our
37: 3 *T* in the LORD and do good;
56: 4 in God I *t*; I will not be afraid.
119: 42 for I *t* in your word.
Pr 3: 5 *T* in the LORD with all your heart
Isa 30: 15 in quietness and *t* is your strength,
Jn 14: 1 *T* in God; *t* also in me.
1Co 4: 2 been given a *t* must prove faithful.

TRUSTED (TRUST)
Ps 26: 1 I have *t* in the LORD
Isa 25: 9 we *t* in him, and he saved us.
Da 3: 28 They *t* in him and defied the king's
Lk 16: 10 *t* with very little can also be *t*

TRUSTS (TRUST)
Ps 32: 10 surrounds the man who *t* in him.
Pr 11: 28 Whoever *t* in his riches will fall,
28: 26 He who *t* in himself is a fool,
Ro 9: 33 one who *t* in him will never be put

TRUSTWORTHY (TRUST)
Ps 119:138 they are fully *t*.
Pr 11: 13 but a *t* man keeps a secret.
Rev 22: 6 "These words are *t* and true.

TRUTH (TRUE TRUTHFUL TRUTHS)
Ps 51: 6 Surely you desire *t*
Isa 45: 19 I, the LORD, speak the *t*;
Zec 8: 16 are to do: Speak the *t* to each other,
Jn 4: 23 worship the Father in spirit and *t*,
8: 32 Then you will know the *t*,
8: 32 and the *t* will set you free."
14: 6 I am the way and the *t* and the life.
16: 13 comes, he will guide you into all *t*.
18: 38 "What is *t*?" Pilate asked.
Ro 1: 25 They exchanged the *t* of God
1Co 13: 6 in evil but rejoices with the *t*.
2Co 13: 8 against the *t*, but only for the *t*.
Eph 4: 15 Instead, speaking the *t* in love,
6: 14 with the belt of *t* buckled
2Th 2: 10 because they refused to love the *t*
1Ti 2: 4 to come to a knowledge of the *t*.
3: 15 the pillar and foundation of the *t*.
2Ti 2: 15 correctly handles the word of *t*.
3: 7 never able to acknowledge the *t*.
Heb 10: 26 received the knowledge of the *t*,
1Pe 1: 22 by obeying the *t* so that you have
2Pe 2: 2 the way of *t* into disrepute.
1Jn 1: 6 we lie and do not live by the *t*.
1: 8 deceive ourselves and the *t* is not

TRUTHFUL (TRUTH)
Pr 12: 22 but he delights in men who are *t*.
Jn 3: 33 it has certified that God is *t*.

TRUTHS (TRUTH)
1Co 2: 13 expressing spiritual *t*
1Ti 3: 9 hold of the deep *t* of the faith
Heb 5: 12 to teach you the elementary *t*

TRY (TRYING)
Ps 26: 2 Test me, O LORD, and *t* me,
Isa 7: 13 enough to *t* the patience of men?
1Co 14: 12 *t* to excel in gifts that build up
2Co 5: 11 is to fear the Lord, we *t*
1Th 5: 15 always *t* to be kind to each other

TRYING (TRY)
2Co 5: 12 We are not *t* to commend ourselves
1Th 2: 4 We are not *t* to please men but God

TUNIC
Lk 6: 29 do not stop him from taking your *t*.

TURN (TURNED TURNS)
Ex 32: 12 *T* from your fierce anger; relent
Dt 5: 32 do not *t* aside to the right
28: 14 Do not *t* aside from any
Jos 1: 7 do not *t* from it to the right
2Ch 7: 14 and *t* from their wicked ways,
30: 9 He will not *t* his face from you

Ps 78: 6 they in *t* would tell their children.
Pr 22: 6 when he is old he will not *t* from it.
Isa 29: 16 You *t* things upside down,
30: 21 Whether you *t* to the right
45: 22 "*T* to me and be saved,
55: 7 Let him *t* to the LORD,
Eze 33: 11 *T!* *T* from your evil ways!
Mal 4: 6 He will *t* the hearts of the fathers
Mt 5: 39 you on the right cheek, *t*
10: 35 For I have come to *t*
Jn 12: 40 nor *t*—and I would heal them."
Ac 3: 19 Repent, then, and *t* to God,
26: 18 and *t* them from darkness to light,
1Ti 6: 20 *T* away from godless chatter
1Pe 3: 11 He must *t* from evil and do good;

TURNED (TURN)
Ps 30: 11 You *t* my wailing into dancing;
40: 1 he *t* to me and heard my cry.
Isa 53: 6 each of us has *t* to his own way;
Hos 7: 8 Ephraim is a flat cake not *t* over.
Joel 2: 31 The sun will be *t* to darkness
Ro 3: 12 All have *t* away,

TURNS (TURN)
2Sa 22: 29 the LORD *t* my darkness into light
Pr 15: 1 A gentle answer *t* away wrath,
Isa 44: 25 and *t* it into nonsense,
Jas 5: 20 Whoever *t* a sinner from the error

TWELVE
Ge 49: 28 All these are the *t* tribes of Israel,
Mt 10: 1 He called his *t* disciples to him

TWINKLING*
1Co 15: 52 in a flash, in the *t* of an eye,

U

UNAPPROACHABLE*
1Ti 6: 16 immortal and who lives in *u* light,

UNBELIEF (UNBELIEVER UNBELIEVERS UNBELIEVING)
Mk 9: 24 help me overcome my *u!*"
Ro 11: 20 they were broken off because of *u*,
Heb 3: 19 able to enter, because of their *u*.

UNBELIEVER* (UNBELIEF)
1Co 7: 15 But if the *u* leaves, let him do so.
10: 27 If some *u* invites you to a meal
14: 24 if an *u* or someone who does not
2Co 6: 15 have in common with an *u?*
1Ti 5: 8 the faith and is worse than an *u*.

UNBELIEVERS (UNBELIEF)
1Co 6: 6 another—and this in front of *u!*
2Co 6: 14 Do not be yoked together with *u*.

UNBELIEVING (UNBELIEF)
1Co 7: 14 For the *u* husband has been
Rev 21: 8 But the cowardly, the *u*, the vile,

UNCERTAIN*
1Ti 6: 17 which is so *u*, but to put their hope

UNCHANGEABLE*
Heb 6: 18 by two *u* things in which it is

UNCIRCUMCISED
1Sa 17: 26 Who is this *u* Philistine that he
Col 3: 11 circumcised or *u*, barbarian,

UNCIRCUMCISION
1Co 7: 19 is nothing and *u* is nothing.
Gal 5: 6 neither circumcision nor *u* has any

UNCLEAN
Isa 6: 5 ruined! For I am a man of *u* lips,
Ro 14: 14 fully convinced that no food is *u*
2Co 6: 17 Touch no *u* thing,

UNCONCERNED*
Eze 16: 49 were arrogant, overfed and *u;*

UNCOVERED
Heb 4: 13 Everything is *u* and laid bare

UNDERSTAND (UNDERSTANDING UNDERSTANDS)
Job 42: 3 Surely I spoke of things I did not *u*,
Ps 73: 16 When I tried to *u* all this,
119:125 that I may *u* your statutes.
Lk 24: 45 so they could *u* the Scriptures.
Ac 8: 30 "Do you *u* what you are reading?"
Ro 7: 15 I do not *u* what I do.
1Co 2: 14 and he cannot *u* them,
Eph 5: 17 but *u* what the Lord's will is.
2Pe 3: 16 some things that are hard to *u*,

UNDERSTANDING (UNDERSTAND)
Ps 119:104 I gain *u* from your precepts;
147: 5 his *u* has no limit.
Pr 3: 5 and lean not on your own *u;*
4: 7 Though it cost all you have, get *u*.
10: 23 but a man of *u* delights in wisdom.
11: 12 but a man of *u* holds his tongue.
15: 21 a man of *u* keeps a straight course.
15: 32 whoever heeds correction gains *u*.
23: 23 get wisdom, discipline and *u*.
Isa 40: 28 and his *u* no one can fathom.
Da 5: 12 a keen mind and knowledge and *u*,
Mk 4: 12 and ever hearing but never *u;*
12: 33 with all your *u* and with all your
Php 4: 7 of God, which transcends all *u*,

UNDERSTANDS (UNDERSTAND)
1Ch 28: 9 and *u* every motive
1Ti 6: 4 he is conceited and *u* nothing.

UNDIVIDED*
1Ch 12: 33 to help David with *u* loyalty—
Ps 86: 11 give me an *u* heart,
Eze 11: 19 I will give them an *u* heart
1Co 7: 35 way in *u* devotion to the Lord.

UNDOING
Pr 18: 7 A fool's mouth is his *u*,

UNDYING*
Eph 6: 24 Lord Jesus Christ with an *u* love.

UNFADING*
1Pe 3: 4 the *u* beauty of a gentle

UNFAILING
Ps 33: 5 the earth is full of his *u* love.
119: 76 May your *u* love be my comfort,
143: 8 bring me word of your *u* love,
Pr 19: 22 What a man desires is *u* love;
La 3: 32 so great is his *u* love.

UNFAITHFUL (UNFAITHFULNESS)
Lev 6: 2 is *u* to the LORD by deceiving his
1Ch 10: 13 because he was *u* to the LORD;
Pr 13: 15 but the way of the *u* is hard.

UNFAITHFULNESS (UNFAITHFUL)
Mt 5: 32 except for marital *u*, causes her
19: 9 for marital *u*, and marries another

UNFOLDING
Ps 119:130 the *u* of your words gives light;

UNGODLINESS
Tit 2: 12 It teaches us to say "No" to *u*

UNIT
1Co 12: 12 body is a *u*, though it is made up

UNITED (UNITY)
Ro 6: 5 If we have been *u* with him
Php 2: 1 from being *u* with Christ,
Col 2: 2 encouraged in heart and *u* in love,

UNITY (UNITED)
Ps 133: 1 is when brothers live together in *u!*
Ro 15: 5 a spirit of *u* among yourselves
Eph 4: 3 effort to keep the *u* of the Spirit
4: 13 up until we all reach *u* in the faith
Col 3: 14 them all together in perfect *u*.

UNIVERSE
Php 2: 15 which you shine like stars in the *u*
Heb 1: 2 and through whom he made the *u*.

UNKNOWN
Ac 17: 23 TO AN *U* GOD.

UNLEAVENED
Ex 12: 17 "Celebrate the Feast of *U* Bread,

UNPROFITABLE
Tit 3: 9 because these are *u* and useless.

UNPUNISHED
Ex 34: 7 Yet he does not leave the guilty *u;*
Pr 19: 5 A false witness will not go *u*,

UNREPENTANT*
Ro 2: 5 stubbornness and your *u* heart,

UNRIGHTEOUS*
Zep 3: 5 yet the *u* know no shame.
Mt 5: 45 rain on the righteous and the *u*.
1Pe 3: 18 the righteous for the *u*, to bring you
2Pe 2: 9 and to hold the *u* for the day

UNSEARCHABLE
Ro 11: 33 How *u* his judgments,
Eph 3: 8 preach to the Gentiles the *u* riches

UNSEEN
2Co 4: 18 on what is seen, but on what is *u*.
4: 18 temporary, but what is *u* is eternal.

UNSTABLE*
Jas 1: 8 he is a double-minded man, *u*
2Pe 2: 14 they seduce the *u;* they are experts
3: 16 ignorant and *u* people distort,

UNTHINKABLE*
Job 34: 12 It is *u* that God would do wrong,

UNVEILED*
2Co 3: 18 with *u* faces all reflect the Lord's

UNWORTHY
Job 40: 4 "I am *u*—how can I reply to you?
Lk 17: 10 should say, 'We are *u* servants;

UPRIGHT
Job 1: 1 This man was blameless and *u;*
Pr 2: 7 He holds victory in store for the *u,*
15: 8 but the prayer of the *u* pleases him.
Tit 1: 8 who is self-controlled, *u,* holy
2: 12 *u* and godly lives in this present

UPROOTED
Jude : 12 without fruit and *u*—twice dead.

USEFUL
2Ti 2: 21 *u* to the Master and prepared
3: 16 Scripture is God-breathed and is *u*

USELESS
1Co 15: 14 our preaching is *u*
Jas 2: 20 faith without deeds is *u?*

USURY
Ne 5: 10 But let the exacting of *u* stop!

UTTER
Ps 78: 2 I will *u* hidden things, things from of

UZZIAH
Son of Amaziah; king of Judah also known as Azariah (2Ki 15:1-7; 1Ch 6:24; 2Ch 26).

V

VAIN
Ps 33: 17 A horse is a *v* hope for deliverance;
Isa 65: 23 They will not toil in *v*
1Co 15: 2 Otherwise, you have believed in *v.*
15: 58 labor in the Lord is not in *v.*
2Co 6: 1 not to receive God's grace in *v.*

VALLEY
Ps 23: 4 walk through the *v* of the shadow
Isa 40: 4 Every *v* shall be raised up,
Joel 3: 14 multitudes in the *v* of decision!

VALUABLE (VALUE)
Lk 12: 24 And how much more *v* you are

VALUE (VALUABLE)
Mt 13: 46 When he found one of great *v,*
1Ti 4: 8 For physical training is of some *v,*
Heb 11: 26 as of greater *v* than the treasures

VEIL
Ex 34: 33 to them, he put a *v* over his face.
2Co 3: 14 for to this day the same *v* remains

VENGEANCE (AVENGE REVENGE)
Isa 34: 8 For the LORD has a day of *v,*

VICTORIES (VICTORY)
Ps 18: 50 He gives his king great *v;*
21: 1 great is his joy in the *v* you give!

VICTORIOUSLY* (VICTORY)
Ps 45: 4 In your majesty ride forth *v*

VICTORY (VICTORIES VICTORIOUSLY)
Ps 60: 12 With God we will gain the *v,*
1Co 15: 54 "Death has been swallowed up in *v*
15: 57 He gives us the *v* through our Lord
1Jn 5: 4 This is the *v* that has overcome

VINDICATED
1Ti 3: 16 was *v* by the Spirit,

VINE
Jn 15: 1 "I am the true *v,* and my Father is

VINEGAR
Mk 15: 36 filled a sponge with wine *v,*

VIOLATION
Heb 2: 2 every *v* and disobedience received

VIOLENCE
Isa 60: 18 No longer will *v* be heard
Eze 45: 9 Give up your *v* and oppression

VIPERS
Ro 3: 13 "The poison of *v* is on their lips."

VIRGIN
Isa 7: 14 The *v* will be with child
Mt 1: 23 "The *v* will be with child
2Co 11: 2 that I might present you as a pure *v*

VIRTUES*
Col 3: 14 And over all these *v* put on love,

VISION
Ac 26: 19 disobedient to the *v* from heaven.

VOICE
Ps 95: 7 Today, if you hear his *v,*
Isa 30: 21 your ears will hear a *v* behind you,
Jn 5: 28 are in their graves will hear his *v*
10: 3 and the sheep listen to his *v.*
Heb 3: 7 "Today, if you hear his *v,*
Rev 3: 20 If anyone hears my *v* and opens

VOMIT
Pr 26: 11 As a dog returns to its *v,*
2Pe 2: 22 "A dog returns to its *v,*" and,

VOW
Nu 30: 2 When a man makes a *v*

W

WAGES
Lk 10: 7 for the worker deserves his *w.*
Ro 4: 4 his *w* are not credited to him
6: 23 For the *w* of sin is death,

WAILING
Ps 30: 11 You turned my *w* into dancing;

WAIST
2Ki 1: 8 with a leather belt around his *w.*"
Mt 3: 4 he had a leather belt around his *w.*

WAIT (WAITED WAITS)
Ps 27: 14 *W* for the LORD;
130: 5 I *w* for the LORD, my soul waits,
Isa 30: 18 Blessed are all who *w* for him!
Ac 1: 4 *w* for the gift my Father promised,
Ro 8: 23 as we *w* eagerly for our adoption
1Th 1: 10 and to *w* for his Son from heaven,
Tit 2: 13 while we *w* for the blessed hope—

WAITED (WAIT)
Ps 40: 1 I *w* patiently for the LORD;

WAITS (WAIT)
Ro 8: 19 creation *w* in eager expectation

WALK (WALKED WALKS)
Dt 11: 19 and when you *w* along the road,
Ps 1: 1 who does not *w* in the counsel
23: 4 Even though I *w*
89: 15 who *w* in the light of your presence
Isa 2: 5 let us *w* in the light of the LORD.
30: 21 saying, "This is the way; *w* in it."
40: 31 they will *w* and not be faint.
Jer 6: 16 ask where the good way is, and *w*
Da 4: 37 And those who *w* in pride he is able
Am 3: 3 Do two *w* together
Mic 6: 8 and to *w* humbly with your God.
Mk 2: 9 'Get up, take your mat and *w*'?
Jn 8: 12 Whoever follows me will never *w*
1Jn 1: 7 But if we *w* in the light,
2Jn : 6 his command is that you *w* in love.

WALKED (WALK)
Ge 5: 24 Enoch *w* with God; then he was no
Jos 14: 9 which your feet have *w* will be your
Mt 14: 29 *w* on the water and came toward

WALKS (WALK)
Pr 13: 20 He who *w* with the wise grows wise

WALL
Jos 6: 20 *w* collapsed; so every man charged
Ne 2: 17 let us rebuild the *w* of Jerusalem,
Rev 21: 12 It had a great, high *w*

WALLOWING
2Pe 2: 22 back to her *w* in the mud."

WANT (WANTED WANTING WANTS)
1Sa 8: 19 "We *w* a king over us.
Ps 23: 1 is my shepherd, I shall not be in *w.*
Lk 19: 14 'We don't *w* this man to be our king
Ro 7: 15 For what I *w* to do I do not do,
Php 3: 10 I *w* to know Christ and the power

WANTED (WANT)
1Co 12: 18 of them, just as he *w* them to be.

WANTING (WANT)
Da 5: 27 weighed on the scales and found *w.*
2Pe 3: 9 with you, not *w* anyone to perish,

WANTS (WANT)
Mt 20: 26 whoever *w* to become great
Mk 8: 35 For whoever *w* to save his life will
Ro 9: 18 he hardens whom he *w* to harden.
1Ti 2: 4 who *w* all men to be saved

WAR (WARS)
Isa 2: 4 nor will they train for *w* anymore.
Da 9: 26 *W* will continue until the end,
2Co 10: 3 we do not wage *w* as the world does
Rev 19: 11 With justice he judges and makes *w*

WARN (WARNED WARNINGS)
Eze 3: 19 But if you do *w* the wicked man

33: 9 if you do *w* the wicked man to turn

WARNED (WARN)
Ps 19: 11 By them is your servant *w;*

WARNINGS (WARN)
1Co 10: 11 and were written down as *w* for us,

WARS (WAR)
Ps 46: 9 He makes *w* cease to the ends
Mt 24: 6 You will hear of *w* and rumors of *w,*

WASH (WASHED WASHING)
Ps 51: 7 *w* me, and I will be whiter
Jn 13: 5 and began to *w* his disciples' feet,
Ac 22: 16 be baptized and *w* your sins away,
Rev 22: 14 Blessed are those who *w* their robes

WASHED (WASH)
1Co 6: 11 you were *w,* you were sanctified,
Rev 7: 14 they have *w* their robes

WASHING (WASH)
Eph 5: 26 cleansing her by the *w* with water
Tit 3: 5 us through the *w* of rebirth

WATCH (WATCHES WATCHING WATCHMAN)
Ge 31: 49 "May the LORD keep *w*
Jer 31: 10 will *w* over his flock like a shepherd
Mt 24: 42 "Therefore keep *w,* because you do
26: 41 *W* and pray so that you will not fall
Lk 2: 8 keeping *w* over their flocks at night
1Ti 4: 16 *W* your life and doctrine closely.

WATCHES (WATCH)
Ps 1: 6 For the LORD *w* over the way
121: 3 he who *w* over you will not slumber

WATCHING (WATCH)
Lk 12: 37 whose master finds them *w*

WATCHMAN (WATCH)
Eze 3: 17 I have made you a *w* for the house

WATER (WATERED WATERS)
Ps 1: 3 like a tree planted by streams of *w,*
22: 14 I am poured out like *w,*
Pr 25: 21 if he is thirsty, give him *w* to drink.
Isa 49: 10 and lead them beside springs of *w.*
Jer 2: 13 broken cisterns that cannot hold *w.*
Zec 14: 8 On that day living *w* will flow out
Mk 9: 41 anyone who gives you a cup of *w*
Jn 4: 10 he would have given you living *w.*"
7: 38 streams of living *w* will flow
Eph 5: 26 washing with *w* through the word,
1Pe 3: 21 this *w* symbolizes baptism that now
Rev 21: 6 cost from the spring of the *w* of life.

WATERED (WATER)
1Co 3: 6 I planted the seed, Apollos *w* it,

WATERS (WATER)
Ps 23: 2 he leads me beside quiet *w,*
Ecc 11: 1 Cast your bread upon the *w,*
Isa 58: 11 like a spring whose *w* never fail.
1Co 3: 7 plants nor he who *w* is anything,

WAVE (WAVES)
Jas 1: 6 he who doubts is like a *w* of the sea,

WAVES (WAVE)
Isa 57: 20 whose *w* cast up mire and mud.
Mt 8: 27 Even the winds and the *w* obey him
Eph 4: 14 tossed back and forth by the *w,*

WAY (WAYS)
Dt 1: 33 to show you the *w* you should go.
2Sa 22: 31 "As for God, his *w* is perfect;
Job 23: 10 But he knows the *w* that I take;
Ps 1: 1 or stand in the *w* of sinners
37: 5 Commit your *w* to the LORD;
119: 9 can a young man keep his *w* pure?
139: 24 See if there is any offensive *w* in me
Pr 14: 12 There is a *w* that seems right
16: 17 he who guards his *w* guards his life.
22: 6 Train a child in the *w* he should go,
Isa 30: 21 saying, "This is the *w;* walk in it."
53: 6 each of us has turned to his own *w;*
Isa 55: 7 Let the wicked forsake his *w*
Mt 3: 3 Prepare the *w* for the Lord,
Jn 14: 6 "I am the *w* and the truth
1Co 10: 13 also provide a *w* out so that you can
12: 31 will show you the most excellent *w.*
Heb 4: 15 who has been tempted in every *w,*
9: 8 was showing by this that the *w*
10: 20 and living *w* opened for us

WAYS (WAY)
Ex 33: 13 teach me your *w* so I may know
Ps 25: 10 All the *w* of the LORD are loving
51: 13 I will teach transgressors your *w,*
Pr 3: 6 in all your *w* acknowledge him,
Isa 55: 8 neither are your *w* my *w,*"
Jas 3: 2 We all stumble in many *w.*

WEAK (WEAKER WEAKNESS)
Mt 26: 41 spirit is willing, but the body is *w.*"
Ro 14: 1 Accept him whose faith is *w,*
1Co 1: 27 God chose the *w* things
8: 9 become a stumbling block to the *w.*
9: 22 To the *w* I became *w,* to win the *w.*
2Co 12: 10 For when I am *w,* then I am strong.
Heb 12: 12 your feeble arms and *w* knees.

WEAKER (WEAK)
1Co 12: 22 seem to be *w* are indispensable,
1Pe 3: 7 them with respect as the *w* partner

WEAKNESS (WEAK)
Ro 8: 26 the Spirit helps us in our *w.*
1Co 1: 25 and the *w* of God is stronger
2Co 12: 9 for my power is made perfect in *w*
Heb 5: 2 since he himself is subject to *w.*

WEALTH
Pr 3: 9 Honor the LORD with your *w,*
Mk 10: 22 away sad, because he had great *w.*
Lk 15: 13 and there squandered his *w*

WEAPONS
2Co 10: 4 The *w* we fight with are not

WEARIES (WEARY)
Ecc 12: 12 and much study *w* the body.

WEARY (WEARIES)
Isa 40: 31 they will run and not grow *w,*
Mt 11: 28 all you who are *w* and burdened,
Gal 6: 9 Let us not become *w* in doing good,

WEDDING
Mt 22: 11 who was not wearing *w* clothes.
Rev 19: 7 For the *w* of the Lamb has come,

WEEP (WEEPING WEPT)
Ecc 3: 4 a time to *w* and a time to laugh,
Lk 6: 21 Blessed are you who *w* now,

WEEPING (WEEP)
Ps 30: 5 *w* may remain for a night,
126: 6 He who goes out *w,*
Mt 8: 12 where there will be *w* and gnashing

WELCOMES
Mt 18: 5 whoever *w* a little child like this
2Jn : 11 Anyone who *w* him shares

WELL
Lk 17: 19 your faith has made you *w.*"
Jas 5: 15 in faith will make the sick person *w*

WEPT (WEEP)
Ps 137: 1 of Babylon we sat and *w*
Jn 11: 35 Jesus *w.*

WEST
Ps 103: 12 as far as the east is from the *w,*

WHIRLWIND (WIND)
2Ki 2: 1 to take Elijah up to heaven in a *w,*
Hos 8: 7 and reap the *w.*
Na 1: 3 His way is in the *w* and the storm,

WHITE (WHITER)
Isa 1: 18 they shall be as *w* as snow;
Da 7: 9 His clothing was as *w* as snow;
Rev 1: 14 hair were *w* like wool, as *w* as snow,
3: 4 dressed in *w,* for they are worthy.
20: 11 Then I saw a great *w* throne

WHITER (WHITE)
Ps 51: 7 and I will be *w* than snow.

WHOLE
Mt 16: 26 for a man if he gains the *w* world,
24: 14 will be preached in the *w* world
Jn 13: 10 to wash his feet; his *w* body is clean
21: 25 the *w* world would not have room
Ac 20: 27 proclaim to you the *w* will of God.
Ro 3: 19 and the *w* world held accountable
8: 22 know that the *w* creation has been
Gal 3: 22 declares that the *w* world is
5: 3 obligated to obey the *w* law.
Eph 4: 13 attaining to the *w* measure
Jas 2: 10 For whoever keeps the *w* law
1Jn 2: 2 but also for the sins of the *w* world.

WHOLEHEARTEDLY (HEART)
Dt 1: 36 because he followed the LORD *w*
Eph 6: 7 Serve *w,* as if you were serving

WICKED (WICKEDNESS)
Ps 1: 1 walk in the counsel of the *w*
1: 5 Therefore the *w* will not stand

73: 3 when I saw the prosperity of the *w*.
Pr 10: 20 the heart of the *w* is of little value.
11: 21 The *w* will not go unpunished,
Isa 53: 9 He was assigned a grave with the *w*
55: 7 Let the *w* forsake his way
57: 20 But the *w* are like the tossing sea,
Eze 3: 18 that *w* man will die for his sin,
18: 23 pleasure in the death of the *w*?
33: 14 to the *w* man, 'You will surely die,'

WICKEDNESS (WICKED)
Eze 28: 15 created till *w* was found in you.

WIDE
Isa 54: 2 stretch your tent curtains *w*,
Mt 7: 13 For *w* is the gate and broad is
Eph 3: 18 to grasp how *w* and long and high

WIDOW (WIDOWS)
Dt 10: 18 cause of the fatherless and the *w*,
Lk 21: 2 saw a poor *w* put in two very small

WIDOWS (WIDOW)
Jas 1: 27 look after orphans and *w*

WIFE (WIVES)
Ge 2: 24 and mother and be united to his *w*,
24: 67 she became his *w*, and he loved her;
Ex 20: 17 shall not covet your neighbor's *w*,
Dt 5: 21 shall not covet your neighbor's *w*.
Pr 5: 18 in the *w* of your youth.
12: 4 *w* of noble character is her
18: 22 He who finds a *w* finds what is
19: 13 quarrelsome *w* is like a constant
31: 10 *w* of noble character who can find?
Mt 19: 3 for a man to divorce his *w* for any
1Co 7: 2 each man should have his own *w*,
7: 33 how he can please his *w*—
Eph 5: 23 the husband is the head of the *w*
5: 33 must love his *w* as he loves himself,
1Ti 3: 2 husband of but one *w*, temperate,
Rev 21: 9 I will show you the bride, the *w*

WILD
Lk 15: 13 squandered his wealth in *w* living.

Ro 11: 17 and you, though a *w* olive shoot,

WILL (WILLING WILLINGNESS)
Ps 40: 8 I desire to do your *w*, O my God;
143: 10 Teach me to do your *w*,
Isa 53: 10 Yet it was the LORD's *w*
Mt 6: 10 your *w* be done
26: 39 Yet not as I *w*, but as you *w*."
Jn 7: 17 If anyone chooses to do God's *w*,
Ac 20: 27 to you the whole *w* of God.
Ro 12: 2 and approve what God's *w* is—
1Co 7: 37 but has control over his own *w*,
Eph 5: 17 understand what the Lord's *w* is.
Php 2: 13 for it is God who works in you to *w*
1Th 4: 3 God's *w* that you should be
5: 18 for this is God's *w* for you
Heb 9: 16 In the case of a *w*, it is necessary
10: 7 I have come to do your *w*, O God
Jas 4: 15 "If it is the Lord's *w*,
1Jn 5: 14 we ask anything according to his *w*,
Rev 4: 11 and by your *w* they were created

WILLING (WILL)
Ps 51: 12 grant me a *w* spirit, to sustain me.
Da 3: 28 were *w* to give up their lives rather
Mt 18: 14 Father in heaven is not *w* that any
23: 37 her wings, but you were not *w*.
26: 41 The spirit is *w*, but the body is weak

WILLINGNESS (WILL)
2Co 8: 12 For if the *w* is there, the gift is

WIN (WINS)
Php 3: 14 on toward the goal to *w* the prize
1Th 4: 12 your daily life may *w* the respect

WIND (WHIRLWIND)
Jas 1: 6 blown and tossed by the *w*.

WINE
Pr 20: 1 *W* is a mocker and beer a brawler;
Isa 55: 1 Come, buy *w* and milk
Mt 9: 17 Neither do men pour new *w*
Lk 23: 36 They offered him *w* vinegar
Ro 14: 21 not to eat meat or drink *w*
Eph 5: 18 on *w*, which leads to debauchery.

WINESKINS
Mt 9: 17 do men pour new wine into old *w*.

WINGS
Ru 2: 12 under whose *w* you have come
Ps 17: 8 hide me in the shadow of your *w*
Isa 40: 31 They will soar on *w* like eagles;
Mal 4: 2 rise with healing in its *w*.
Lk 13: 34 hen gathers her chicks under her *w*,

WINS (WIN)
Pr 11: 30 and he who *w* souls is wise.

WIPE
Rev 7: 17 God will *w* away every tear

WISDOM (WISE)
1Ki 4: 29 God gave Solomon *w* and very
Ps 111: 10 of the LORD is the beginning of *w*;
Pr 31: 26 She speaks with *w*,
Jer 10: 12 he founded the world by his *w*
Mt 11: 19 But *w* is proved right by her actions
Lk 2: 52 And Jesus grew in *w* and stature,
Ro 11: 33 the depth of the riches of the *w*
Col 2: 3 are hidden all the treasures of *w*
Jas 1: 5 of you lacks *w*, he should ask God,

WISE (WISDOM WISER)
1Ki 3: 12 give you a *w* and discerning heart,
Job 5: 13 He catches the *w* in their craftiness
Ps 19: 7 making *w* the simple.
Pr 3: 7 Do not be *w* in your own eyes;
9: 8 rebuke a *w* man and he will love
10: 1 A *w* son brings joy to his father,
11: 30 and he who wins souls is *w*.
13: 20 He who walks with the *w* grows *w*,
17: 28 Even a fool is thought *w*
Da 12: 3 Those who are *w* will shine like
Mt 11: 25 hidden these things from the *w*
1Co 1: 27 things of the world to shame the *w*;
2Ti 3: 15 able to make you *w* for salvation

WISER (WISE)
1Co 1: 25 of God is *w* than man's wisdom,

WITHER (WITHERS)
Ps 1: 3 and whose leaf does not *w*.

WITHERS (WITHER)
Isa 40: 7 The grass *w* and the flowers fall,

1Pe 1: 24 the grass *w* and the flowers fall,

WITHHOLD
Ps 84: 11 no good thing does he *w*
Pr 23: 13 Do not *w* discipline from a child;

WITNESS (WITNESSES)
Jn 1: 8 he came only as a *w* to the light.

WITNESSES (WITNESS)
Dt 19: 15 by the testimony of two or three *w*.
Ac 1: 8 and you will be my *w* in Jerusalem,

WIVES (WIFE)
Eph 5: 22 *W*, submit to your husbands
5: 25 love your *w*, just as Christ loved
1Pe 3: 1 words by the behavior of their *w*,

WOE
Isa 6: 5 "*W* to me!" I cried.

WOLF
Isa 65: 25 *w* and the lamb will feed together,

WOMAN (MAN)
Ge 2: 22 God made a *w* from
3: 15 between you and the *w*,
Lev 20: 13 as one lies with a *w*,
Dt 22: 5 *w* must not wear men's
Ru 3: 11 a *w* of noble character
Pr 31: 30 a *w* who fears the LORD
Mt 5: 28 looks at a *w* lustfully
Jn 8: 3 a *w* caught in adultery.
Ro 7: 2 a married *w* is bound to
1Co 11: 3 the head of the *w* is man,
11: 13 a *w* to pray to God with
1Ti 2: 11 A *w* should learn in

WOMEN (MAN)
Lk 1: 42 Blessed are you among *w*,
1Co 14: 34 *w* should remain silent in
1Ti 2: 9 want *w* to dress modestly
Tit 2: 3 teach the older *w* to be
1Pe 3: 5 the holy *w* of the past

WOMB
Job 1: 21 Naked I came from my mother's *w*,
Jer 1: 5 you in the *w* I knew you,
Lk 1: 44 the baby in my *w* leaped for joy.

WONDER (WONDERFUL WONDERS)
Ps 17: 7 Show the *w* of your great love,

WONDERFUL (WONDER)
Job 42: 3 things too *w* for me to know.
Ps 31: 21 for he showed his *w* love to me
119: 18 *w* things in your law.
119:129 Your statutes are *w*;
139: 6 Such knowledge is too *w* for me,

Isa 9: 6 *W* Counselor, Mighty God,
1Pe 2: 9 out of darkness into his *w* light.

WONDERS (WONDER)

Job 37: 14 stop and consider God's *w.*
Ps 119: 27 then I will meditate on your *w.*
Joel 2: 30 I will show *w* in the heavens
Ac 2: 19 I will show *w* in the heaven above

WOOD

Isa 44: 19 Shall I bow down to a block of *w?*"
1Co 3: 12 costly stones, *w,* hay or straw,

WORD (WORDS)

Dt 8: 3 but on every *w* that comes
2Sa 22: 31 the *w* of the LORD is flawless.
Ps 119: 9 By living according to your *w.*
119: 11 I have hidden your *w* in my heart
119:105 Your *w* is a lamp to my feet
Pr 12: 25 but a kind *w* cheers him up.
25: 11 A *w* aptly spoken
30: 5 "Every *w* of God is flawless;
Isa 55: 11 so is my *w* that goes out
Jn 1: 1 was the *W,* and the *W* was
1: 14 The *W* became flesh and made his
2Co 2: 17 we do not peddle the *w* of God
4: 2 nor do we distort the *w* of God.
Eph 6: 17 of the Spirit, which is the *w* of God.
Php 2: 16 as you hold out the *w* of life—
Col 3: 16 Let the *w* of Christ dwell
2Ti 2: 15 and who correctly handles the *w*
Heb 4: 12 For the *w* of God is living
Jas 1: 22 Do not merely listen to the *w,*
2Pe 1: 19 And we have the *w* of the prophets

WORDS (WORD)

Dt 11: 18 Fix these *w* of mine in your hearts
Ps 119:103 How sweet are your *w* to my taste
119:130 The unfolding of your *w* gives light;
119:160 All your *w* are true;
Pr 30: 6 Do not add to his *w,*
Jer 15: 16 When your *w* came, I ate them;
Mt 24: 35 but my *w* will never pass away.
Jn 6: 68 You have the *w* of eternal life.
15: 7 in me and my *w* remain in you,
1Co 14: 19 rather speak five intelligible *w*
Rev 22: 19 And if anyone takes *w* away

WORK (WORKER WORKERS WORKING WORKMAN WORKMANSHIP WORKS)

Ex 23: 12 "Six days do your *w,*
Nu 8: 11 ready to do the *w* of the LORD.
Dt 5: 14 On it you shall not do any *w,*
Ecc 5: 19 his lot and be happy in his *w*—
Jer 48: 10 lax in doing the LORD's *w!*
Jn 6: 27 Do not *w* for food that spoils,
9: 4 we must do the *w* of him who sent
1Co 3: 13 test the quality of each man's *w.*
Php 1: 6 that he who began a good *w*
2: 12 continue to *w* out your salvation
Col 3: 23 Whatever you do, *w* at it
1Th 5: 12 to respect those who *w* hard
2Th 3: 10 If a man will not *w,* he shall not eat
2Ti 3: 17 equipped for every good *w.*
Heb 6: 10 he will not forget your *w*

WORKER (WORK)

Lk 10: 7 for the *w* deserves his wages.
1Ti 5: 18 and "The *w* deserves his wages."

WORKERS (WORK)

Mt 9: 37 is plentiful but the *w* are few.
1Co 3: 9 For we are God's fellow *w;*

WORKING (WORK)

Col 3: 23 as *w* for the Lord, not for men,

WORKMAN (WORK)

2Ti 2: 15 a *w* who does not need

WORKMANSHIP* (WORK)

Eph 2: 10 For we are God's *w,* created

WORKS (WORK)

Pr 31: 31 let her *w* bring her praise
Ro 8: 28 in all things God *w* for the good
Eph 2: 9 not by *w,* so that no one can boast.
4: 12 to prepare God's people for *w*

WORLD (WORLDLY)

Ps 50: 12 for the *w* is mine, and all that is in it
Isa 13: 11 I will punish the *w* for its evil,
Mt 5: 14 "You are the light of the *w.*
16: 26 for a man if he gains the whole *w,*
Mk 16: 15 into all the *w* and preach the good
Jn 1: 29 who takes away the sin of the *w!*
3: 16 so loved the *w* that he gave his one
8: 12 he said, "I am the light of the *w.*
15: 19 As it is, you do not belong to the *w,*
16: 33 In this *w* you will have trouble.
18: 36 "My kingdom is not of this *w.*
Ro 3: 19 and the whole *w* held accountable
1Co 3: 19 the wisdom of this *w* is foolishness
2Co 5: 19 that God was reconciling the *w*
10: 3 For though we live in the *w,*
1Ti 6: 7 For we brought nothing into the *w,*
1Jn 2: 2 but also for the sins of the whole *w.*
2: 15 not love the *w* or anything in the *w.*
Rev 13: 8 slain from the creation of the *w.*

WORLDLY (WORLD)

Tit 2: 12 to ungodliness and *w* passions,

WORM

Mk 9: 48 "'their *w* does not die,

WORRY (WORRYING)

Mt 6: 25 I tell you, do not *w* about your life,
10: 19 do not *w* about what to say

WORRYING (WORRY)

Mt 6: 27 of you by *w* can add a single hour

WORSHIP

1Ch 16: 29 *w* the LORD in the splendor
Ps 95: 6 Come, let us bow down in *w,*
Mt 2: 2 and have come to *w* him."
Jn 4: 24 and his worshipers must *w* in spirit
Ro 12: 1 this is your spiritual act of *w.*

WORTH (WORTHY)

Job 28: 13 Man does not comprehend its *w;*
Pr 31: 10 She is *w* far more than rubies.
Mt 10: 31 are *w* more than many sparrows.
Ro 8: 18 sufferings are not *w* comparing
1Pe 1: 7 of greater *w* than gold,
3: 4 which is of great *w* in God's sight.

WORTHLESS

Pr 11: 4 Wealth is *w* in the day of wrath,
Jas 1: 26 himself and his religion is *w.*

WORTHY (WORTH)

1Ch 16: 25 For great is the LORD and most *w*
Eph 4: 1 to live a life *w* of the calling you
Php 1: 27 in a manner *w* of the gospel
3Jn : 6 on their way in a manner *w* of God.
Rev 5: 2 "Who is *w* to break the seals

WOUNDS

Pr 27: 6 *W* from a friend can be trusted,
Isa 53: 5 and by his *w* we are healed.
Zec 13: 6 'What are these *w* on your body?'
1Pe 2: 24 by his *w* you have been healed.

WRATH

2Ch 36: 16 scoffed at his prophets until the *w*
Ps 2: 5 and terrifies them in his *w,* saying,
76: 10 Surely your *w* against men brings
Pr 15: 1 A gentle answer turns away *w,*
Jer 25: 15 filled with the wine of my *w*
Ro 1: 18 The *w* of God is being revealed
5: 9 saved from God's *w* through him!
1Th 5: 9 God did not appoint us to suffer *w*
Rev 6: 16 and from the *w* of the Lamb!

WRESTLED

Ge 32: 24 and a man *w* with him till daybreak

WRITE (WRITING WRITTEN)

Dt 6: 9 *W* them on the doorframes
Pr 7: 3 *w* them on the tablet of your heart.
Heb 8: 10 and *w* them on their hearts.

WRITING (WRITE)

1Co 14: 37 him acknowledge that what I am *w*

WRITTEN (WRITE)

Jos 1: 8 careful to do everything *w* in it.
Da 12: 1 everyone whose name is found *w*
Lk 10: 20 but rejoice that your names are *w*
Jn 20: 31 these are *w* that you may believe
1Co 4: 6 "Do not go beyond what is *w.*"
2Co 3: 3 *w* not with ink but with the Spirit
Col 2: 14 having canceled the *w* code,
Heb 12: 23 whose names are *w* in heaven.

WRONG (WRONGDOING WRONGED WRONGS)

Ex 23: 2 Do not follow the crowd in doing *w*
Nu 5: 7 must make full restitution for his *w,*
Job 34: 12 unthinkable that God would do *w,*
1Th 5: 15 that nobody pays back *w* for *w,*

WRONGDOING (WRONG)

Job 1: 22 sin by charging God with *w.*

WRONGED (WRONG)

1Co 6: 7 not rather be *w?* Why not rather

WRONGS (WRONG)
Pr 10: 12 but love covers over all *w.*
1Co 13: 5 angered, it keeps no record of *w.*

Y

YEARS
Ps 90: 4 For a thousand *y* in your sight
90: 10 The length of our days is seventy *y*
2Pe 3: 8 the Lord a day is like a thousand *y,*
Rev 20: 2 and bound him for a thousand *y.*

YESTERDAY
Heb 13: 8 Jesus Christ is the same *y*

YOKE (YOKED)
Mt 11: 29 Take my *y* upon you and learn

YOKED (YOKE)
2Co 6: 14 Do not be *y* together

YOUNG (YOUTH)
Ps 119: 9 How can a *y* man keep his way
1Ti 4: 12 down on you because you are *y,*

YOUTH (YOUNG)
Ps 103: 5 so that your *y* is renewed like
Ecc 12: 1 Creator in the days of your *y,*
2Ti 2: 22 Flee the evil desires of *y,*

Z

ZEAL
Pr 19: 2 to have *z* without knowledge,
Ro 12: 11 Never be lacking in *z,*

ZECHARIAH
1. Son of Jeroboam II; king of Israel (2Ki 15:8-12).
2. Post-exilic prophet who encouraged rebuilding of temple (Ezr 5:1; 6:14; Zec 1:1).

ZEDEKIAH
Mattaniah, son of Josiah (1Ch 3:15), made king of Judah by Nebuchadnezzar (2Ki 24:17-25:7; 2Ch 36:10-14; Jer 37-39; 52:1-11).

ZERUBBABEL
Descendant of David (1Ch 3:19; Mt 1:3). Led return from exile (Ezr 2-3; Ne 7:7; Hag 1-2; Zec 4).

ZIMRI
King of Israel (1Ki 16:9-20).

ZION
Ps 137: 3 "Sing us one of the songs of *Z!*"
Jer 50: 5 They will ask the way to *Z*
Ro 9: 33 I lay in *Z* a stone that causes men
11: 26 "The deliverer will come from *Z;*

Modern Boundaries of Bible Lands

North America
Europe
Middle East
Asia
Africa
South America
Australia

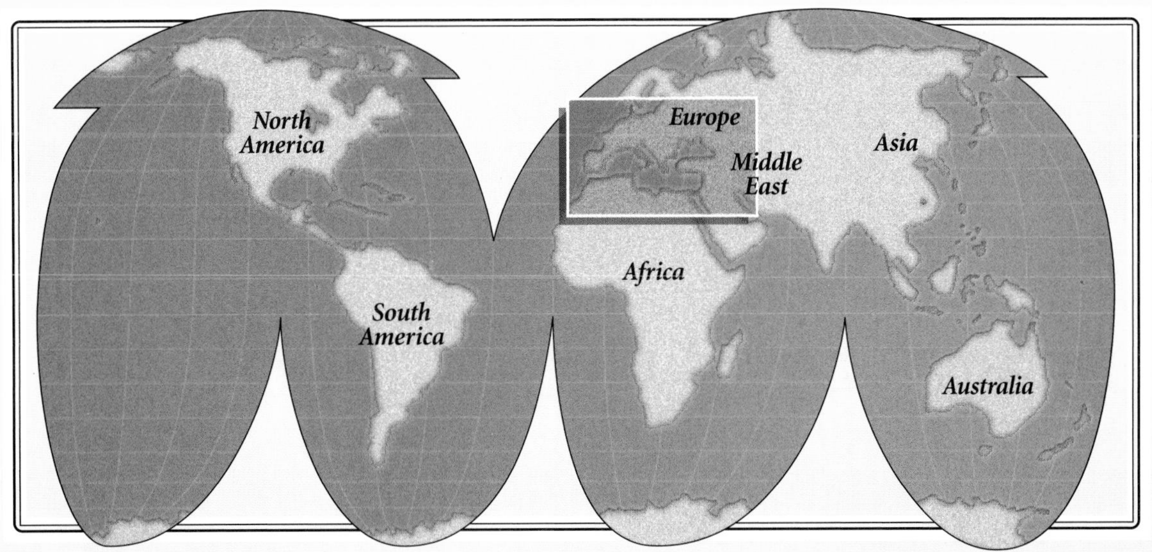

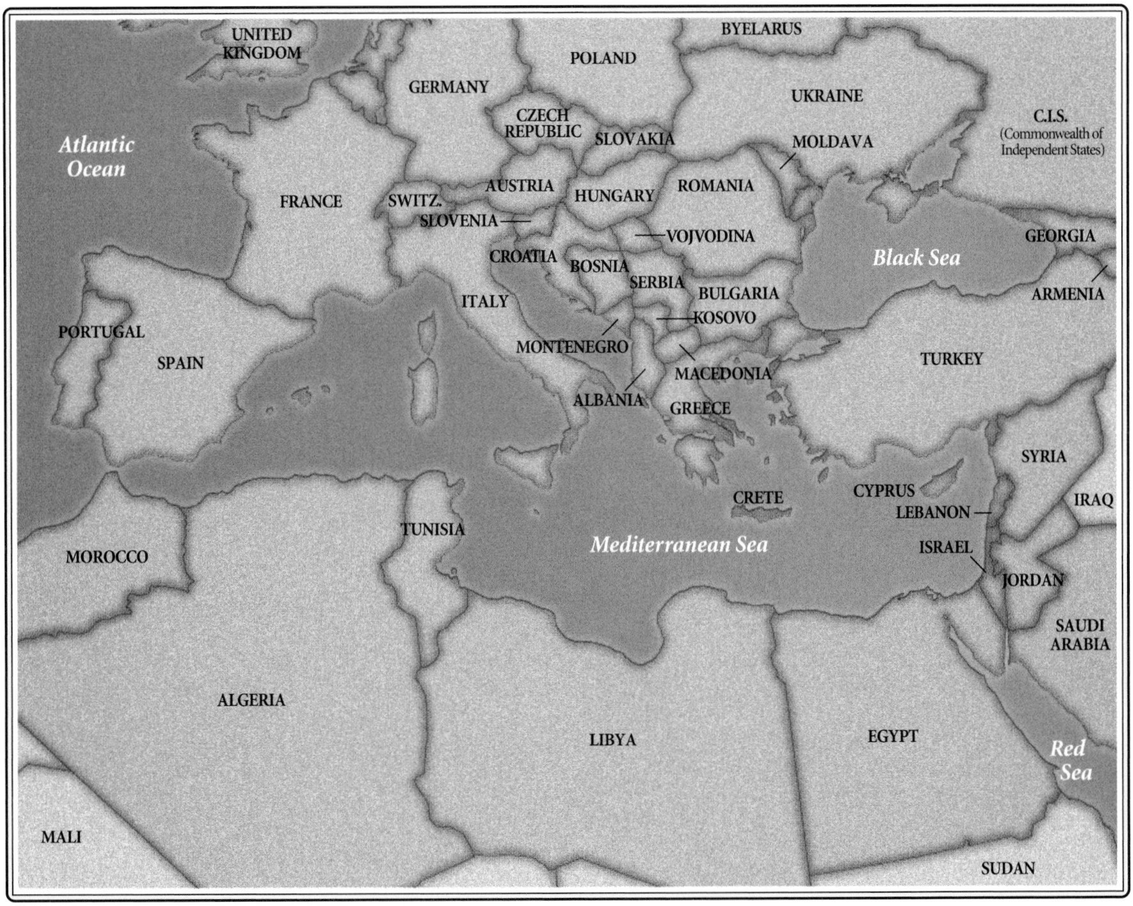

UNITED KINGDOM
BYELARUS
POLAND
GERMANY
UKRAINE
CZECH REPUBLIC
SLOVAKIA
MOLDAVA
C.I.S. (Commonwealth of Independent States)
Atlantic Ocean
AUSTRIA
HUNGARY
ROMANIA
FRANCE
SWITZ.
SLOVENIA
VOJVODINA
GEORGIA
Black Sea
CROATIA
BOSNIA
SERBIA
BULGARIA
ARMENIA
ITALY
KOSOVO
PORTUGAL
SPAIN
MONTENEGRO
TURKEY
MACEDONIA
ALBANIA
GREECE
SYRIA
CRETE
CYPRUS
LEBANON
IRAQ
TUNISIA
Mediterranean Sea
ISRAEL
MOROCCO
JORDAN
SAUDI ARABIA
ALGERIA
LIBYA
EGYPT
Red Sea
MALI
SUDAN

The Settlement of the Descendants of Shem, Ham, and Japheth

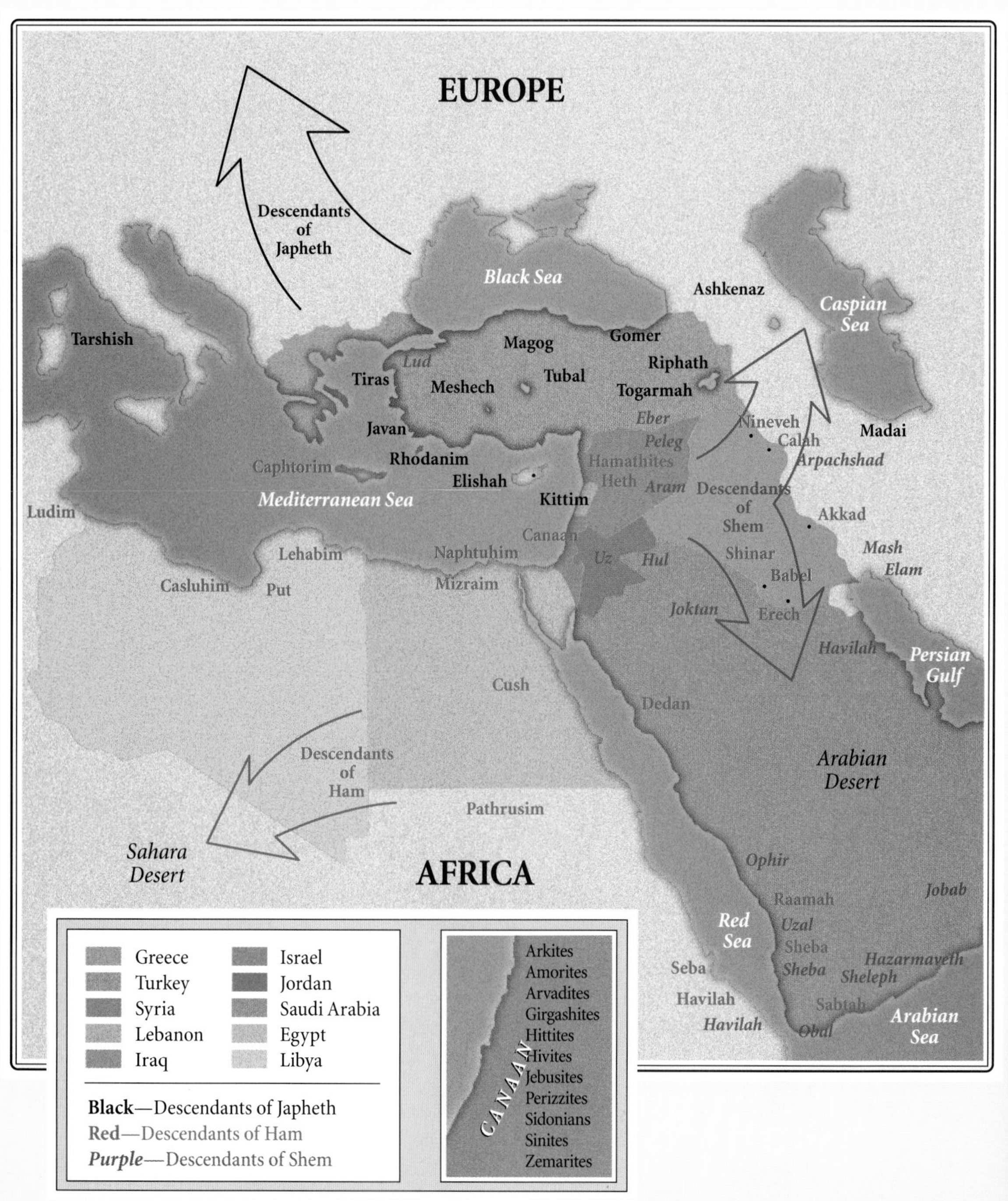
EUROPE
Descendants of Japheth
Black Sea
Ashkenaz
Caspian Sea
Tarshish
Magog
Gomer
Lud
Riphath
Tiras
Meshech
Tubal
Togarmah
Eber
Javan
Nineveh
Madai
Peleg
Calah
Rhodanim
Hamathites
Arpachshad
Caphtorim
Elishah
Heth
Aram
Descendants of Shem
Mediterranean Sea
Kittim
Ludim
Akkad
Canaan
Mash
Lehabim
Naphtuhim
Uz
Hul
Shinar
Elam
Casluhim
Put
Mizraim
Babel
Joktan
Erech
Havilah
Persian Gulf
Cush
Dedan
Descendants of Ham
Arabian Desert
Pathrusim
Sahara Desert
AFRICA
Ophir
Jobab
Raamah
Red Sea
Uzal
Sheba
Seba
Sheba
Hazarmaveth
Sheleph
Havilah
Sabtah
Havilah
Obal
Arabian Sea
Greece
Turkey
Syria
Lebanon
Iraq
Israel
Jordan
Saudi Arabia
Egypt
Libya
Black—Descendants of Japheth
Red—Descendants of Ham
Purple—Descendants of Shem
CANAAN
Arkites
Amorites
Arvadites
Girgashites
Hittites
Hivites
Jebusites
Perizzites
Sidonians
Sinites
Zemarites

The Ancient and Modern Sites of the Exodus

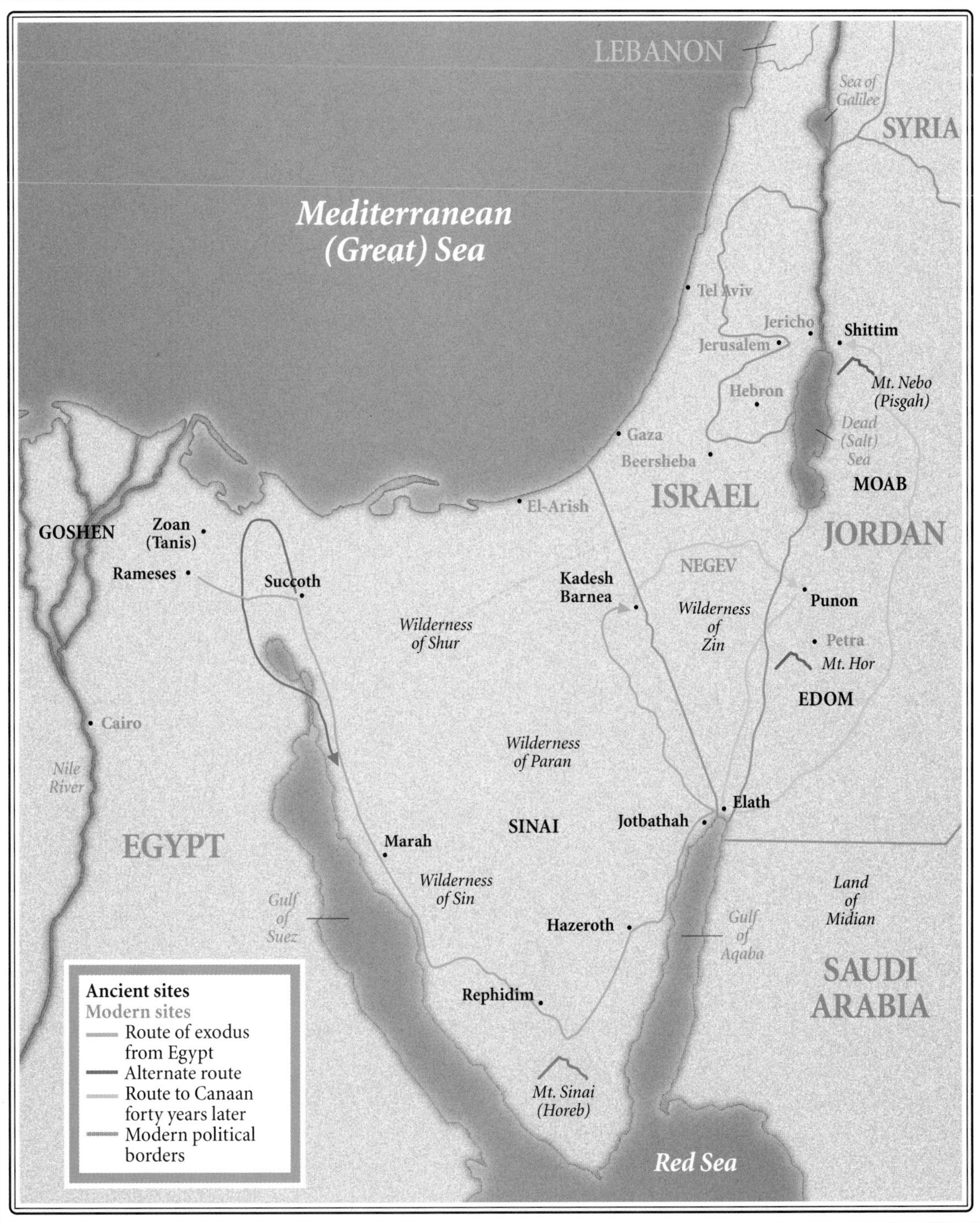

LEBANON
Sea of Galilee
SYRIA
Mediterranean (Great) Sea
Tel Aviv
Jericho
Shittim
Jerusalem
Mt. Nebo (Pisgah)
Hebron
Dead (Salt) Sea
Gaza
Beersheba
MOAB
ISRAEL
El-Arish
GOSHEN
Zoan (Tanis)
JORDAN
NEGEV
Rameses
Succoth
Kadesh Barnea
Punon
Wilderness of Zin
Wilderness of Shur
Petra
Mt. Hor
EDOM
Cairo
Wilderness of Paran
Nile River
Elath
Jotbathah
SINAI
Marah
EGYPT
Wilderness of Sin
Land of Midian
Gulf of Suez
Hazeroth
Gulf of Aqaba
SAUDI ARABIA
Rephidim
Ancient sites
Modern sites
Route of exodus from Egypt
Alternate route
Route to Canaan forty years later
Modern political borders
Mt. Sinai (Horeb)
Red Sea

EZEKIEL'S VISION OF THE PROMISED LAND

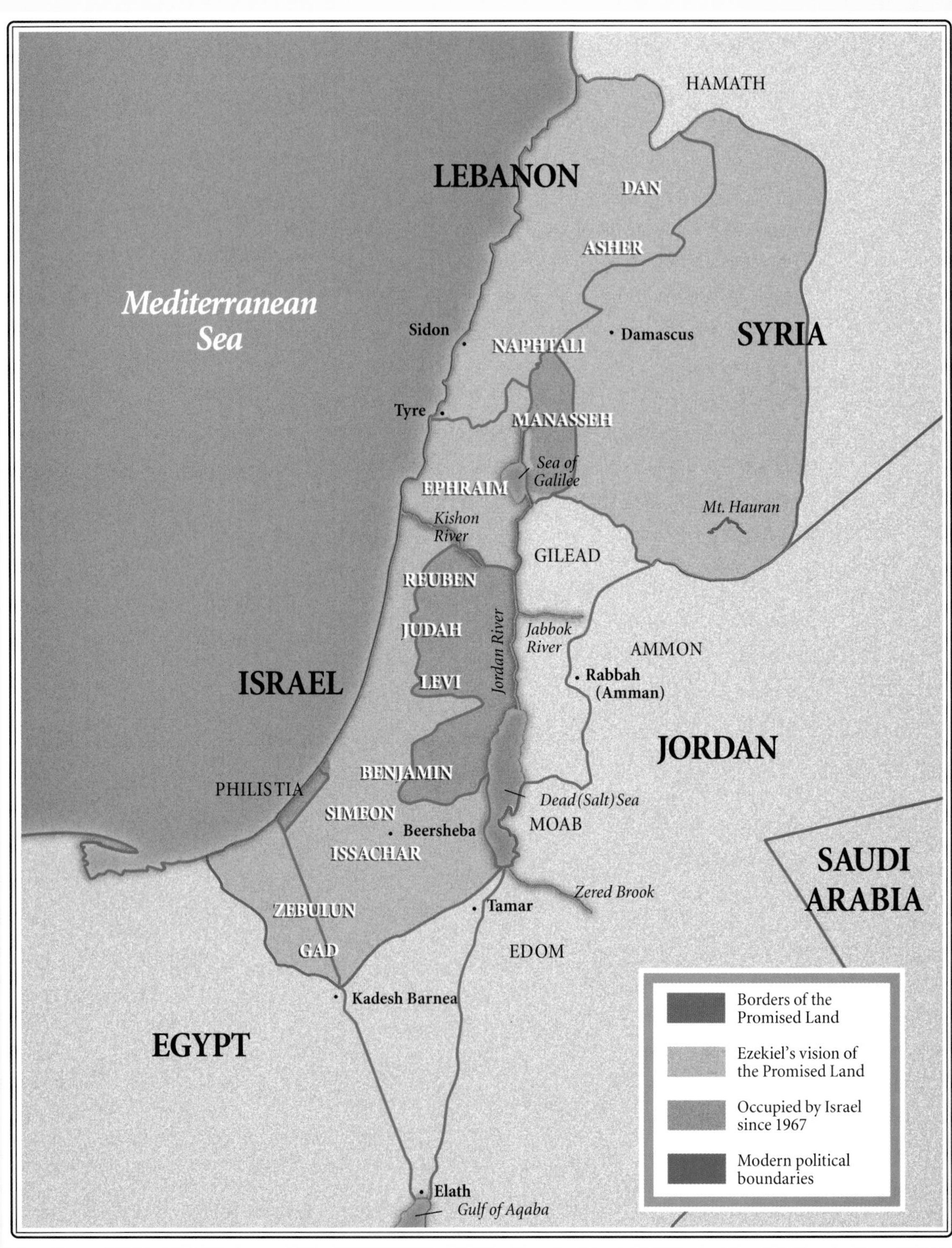

HAMATH
LEBANON
DAN
ASHER
Mediterranean Sea
Sidon
NAPHTALI
Damascus
SYRIA
Tyre
MANASSEH
Sea of Galilee
EPHRAIM
Mt. Hauran
Kishon River
GILEAD
REUBEN
JUDAH
Jordan River
Jabbok River
AMMON
ISRAEL
LEVI
Rabbah (Amman)
JORDAN
BENJAMIN
PHILISTIA
Dead (Salt) Sea
SIMEON
Beersheba
MOAB
ISSACHAR
SAUDI ARABIA
Zered Brook
ZEBULUN
Tamar
GAD
EDOM
Kadesh Barnea
EGYPT
Elath
Gulf of Aqaba
Borders of the Promised Land
Ezekiel's vision of the Promised Land
Occupied by Israel since 1967
Modern political boundaries

ISRAEL'S TERRITORIES: ANCIENT AND MODERN

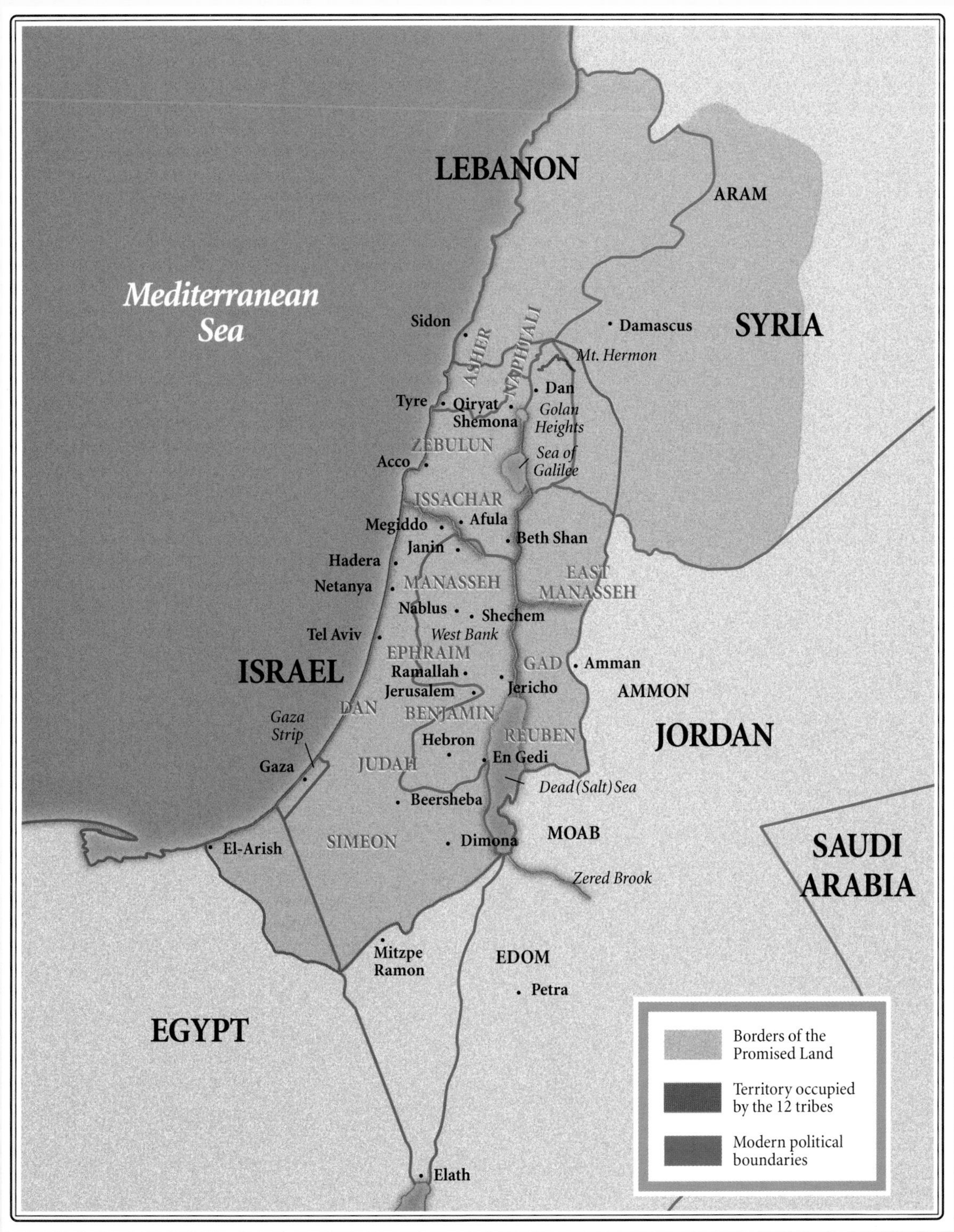

LEBANON
ARAM
Mediterranean Sea
Sidon
ASHER
NAPHTALI
Damascus
SYRIA
Mt. Hermon
Dan
Tyre
Qiryat Shemona
Golan Heights
ZEBULUN
Acco
Sea of Galilee
ISSACHAR
Megiddo
Afula
Janin
Beth Shan
Hadera
Netanya
MANASSEH
EAST MANASSEH
Nablus
Shechem
Tel Aviv
West Bank
EPHRAIM
ISRAEL
GAD
Amman
Ramallah
Jerusalem
Jericho
AMMON
DAN
BENJAMIN
Gaza Strip
REUBEN
JORDAN
Hebron
Gaza
JUDAH
En Gedi
Dead (Salt) Sea
Beersheba
SAUDI ARABIA
El-Arish
SIMEON
Dimona
MOAB
Zered Brook
Mitzpe Ramon
EDOM
Petra
EGYPT
Elath
Borders of the Promised Land
Territory occupied by the 12 tribes
Modern political boundaries

THE RELATIONSHIP OF ANCIENT

BABYLONIAN EMPIRE

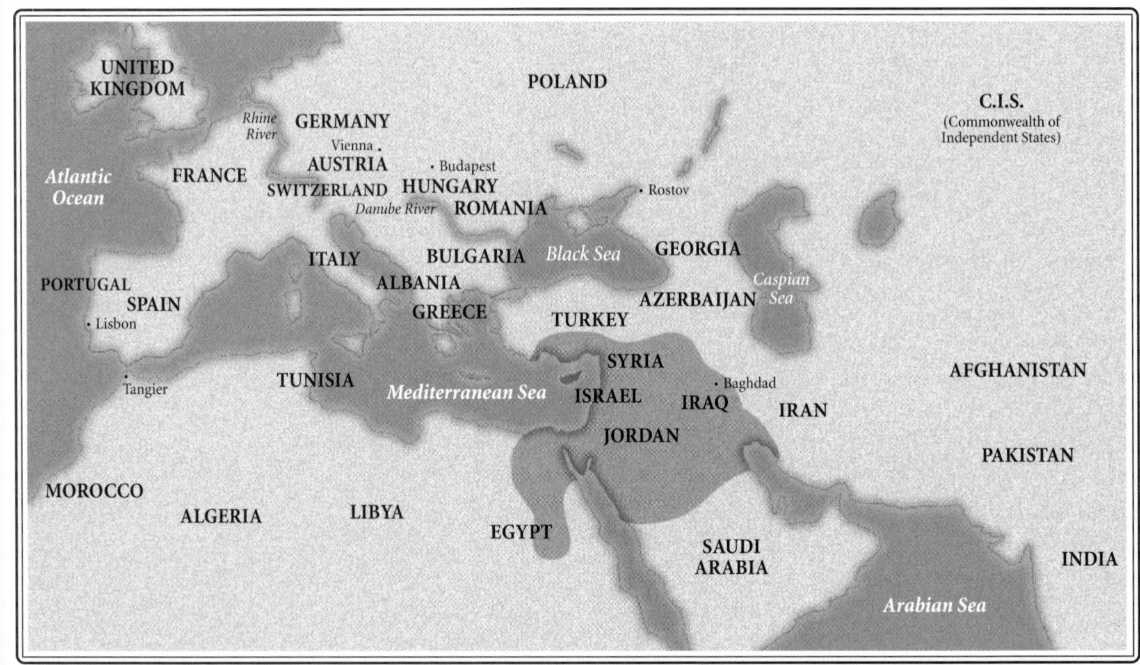

PERSIAN EMPIRE

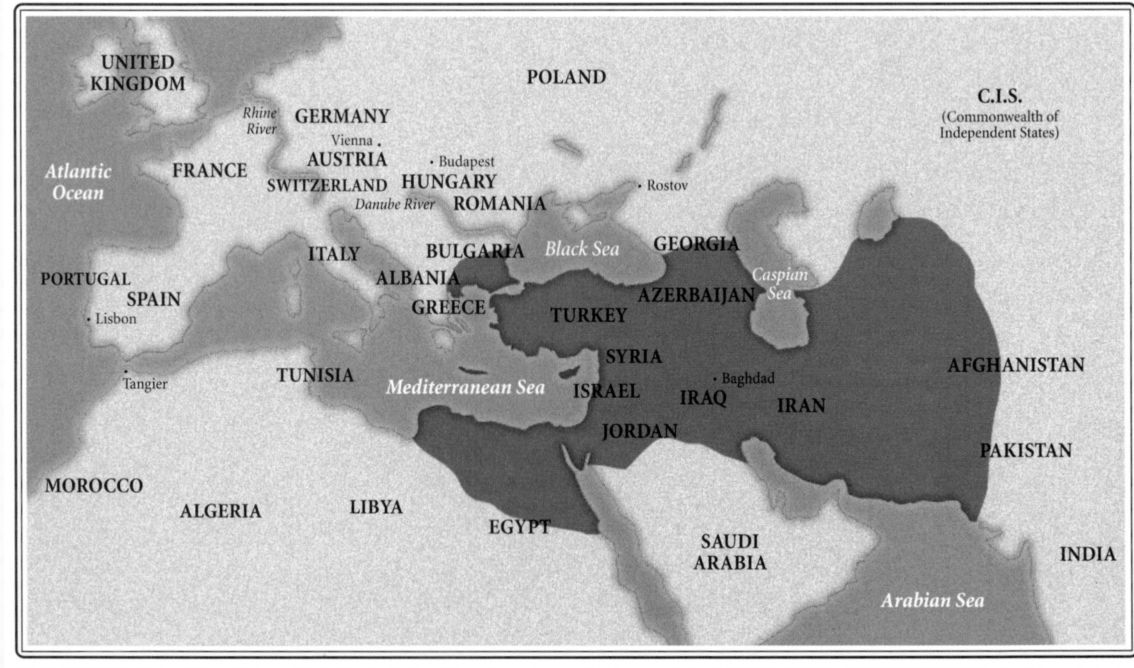

EMPIRES TO MODERN NATIONS

GREEK EMPIRE

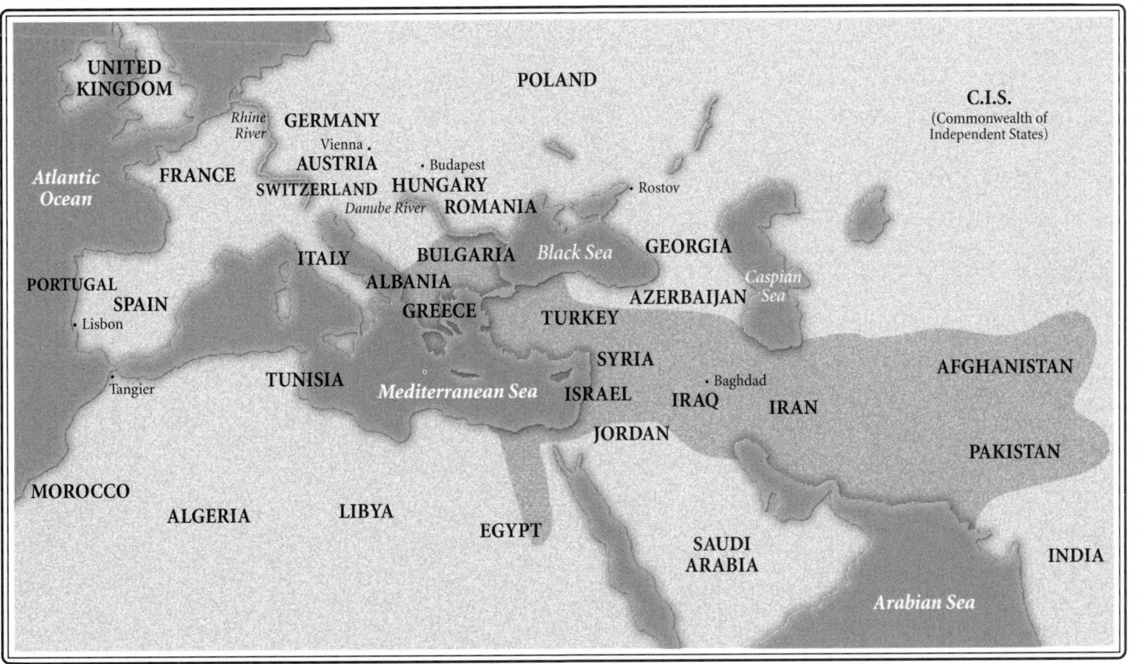

ROMAN EMPIRE

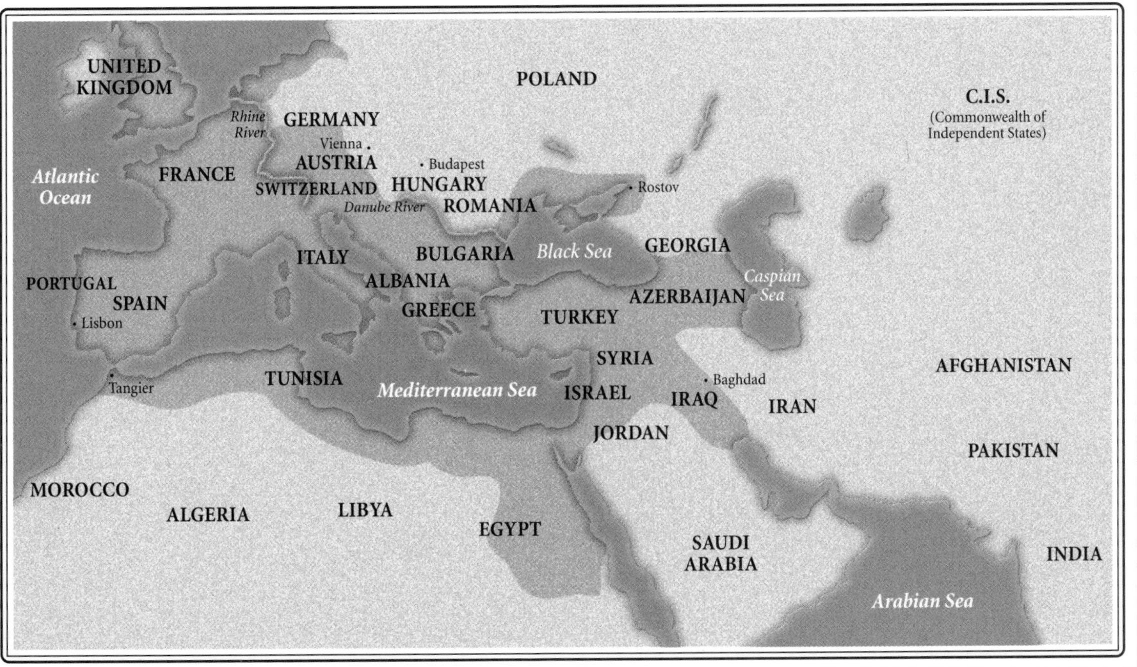

Development of Modern Israel

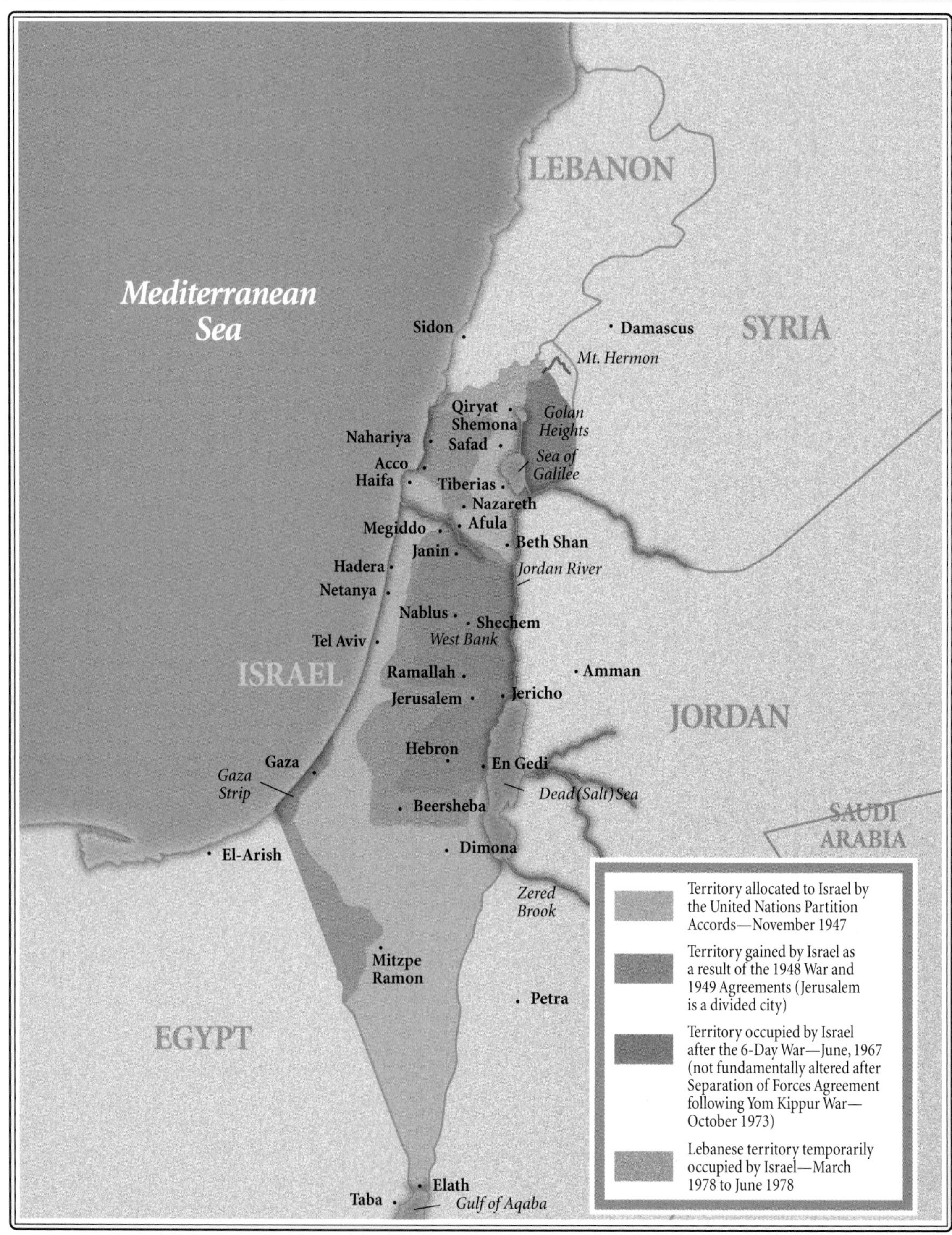
LEBANON
Mediterranean Sea
Sidon
Damascus
SYRIA
Mt. Hermon
Qiryat Shemona
Golan Heights
Nahariya
Safad
Sea of Galilee
Acco
Haifa
Tiberias
Nazareth
Megiddo
Afula
Beth Shan
Janin
Jordan River
Hadera
Netanya
Nablus
Shechem
West Bank
Tel Aviv
ISRAEL
Ramallah
Amman
Jerusalem
Jericho
JORDAN
Hebron
Gaza
En Gedi
Gaza Strip
Dead (Salt) Sea
Beersheba
SAUDI ARABIA
El-Arish
Dimona
Zered Brook
Mitzpe Ramon
Petra
EGYPT
Elath
Taba
Gulf of Aqaba
Territory allocated to Israel by the United Nations Partition Accords—November 1947
Territory gained by Israel as a result of the 1948 War and 1949 Agreements (Jerusalem is a divided city)
Territory occupied by Israel after the 6-Day War—June, 1967 (not fundamentally altered after Separation of Forces Agreement following Yom Kippur War—October 1973)
Lebanese territory temporarily occupied by Israel—March 1978 to June 1978